Racehorse Record

FLAT 1999

Raceform's A-Z Guide to horses which ran during the 1999 Flat Season

(November 8th 1998 - November 6th 1999)

Sponsored by:

Editor	Ashley Rumney
Production Editor	Steven Clarke
Comments by	Richard Lowther, David Bellingham, Andrew Ayres, Ashley Rumney
Production Assistants	Nicki Bowen, David Bellingham, Liz Addison, Duncan Roberts
Raceform Ratings	David Dickinson, Walter Glynn, Nicki Bowen
Design	Daniel Di Pol, Ashley Rumney, Mike Shaw
Photographs	Martin Lynch

Typeset and Published by Raceform Ltd,
Compton, Newbury, Berkshire, RG20 6NL
Tel: 01635 578080
Fax: 01635 578101
Web http://www.raceform.co.uk
EMail: raceform@raceform.co.uk
Printed by Polestar Wheatons Ltd, Exeter

© Raceform Ltd 1999

Copyright in all Raceform publications is strictly reserved by the publishers and no material therein may be stored or recorded in any storage and retrieval system, mechanical, electronic or photographic and no part of it may be transmitted or reproduced in any way without the written permission of the Publishers.

This book is sold subject to the condition that, when resold or otherwise supplied, it will appear in the same form in all respects exactly as supplied by the Publishers and that neither the cover nor the advertising matter therein or any other content of the publication may be altered, varied, added to or subtracted from without their prior consent in writing.

Whilst every effort is made to ensure the utmost accuracy, the Publishers accept no responsibility for any errors.

ISBN 1 901100 91 X

£22.00

SAVE £6.50

Usual Price £25.00
Purchasers of this book: £18.50

RACEFORM ANNUAL FOR 2000

(All the 1999 Returns)

- **COMPANION PUBLICATION TO RACEHORSE RECORD PRESENTED RACE-BY-RACE**
- **EACH RACE DETAILED IN MINUTE DETAIL - BEATEN DISTANCE, STARTING PRICES AND COMMENTS-IN RUNNING**
- **OFFICIAL BHB RATINGS, RACEFORM PERFORMANCE RATINGS**
- **FULL INDEX WITH EACH RACE NUMBER OF EVERY RACE PLUS RACEFORM MASTER RATINGS**
- **EXCLUSIVE NOTE-BOOK COMMENTS, BELOW EACH RACE WRITTEN BY RACEFORM'S ONCOURSE TEAM OF EXPERT RACE-READERS**

A superb and lasting record of the past season, designed to stand alone or beside Racehorse Record as a permanent and quality reference guide

- -

I wish to order *Raceform Flat Annual For 2000* and have already purchased Racehorse Record Flat. I enclose a cheque/p.o. @ £18.50 (normal price £25.00) made payable to Raceform Ltd. Or I wish to pay by Visa/Mastercard Switch/Delta. My card number is:

__________ __________ __________ __________ Exp date: __________

Name:..

Address:..

...Postcode.....................

Raceform Ltd, Freepost, Compton, Newbury, Berkshire, RG20 6NL

(NO STAMP REQUIRED)

Tel: 01635 578080 Fax: 01635 578101 Email: raceform@raceform.co.uk

CONTENTS

Full details of all Raceform services and publications are available from
Raceform, Compton, Newbury, Berkshire RG20 6NL.
Tel: 01635 578080 Fax: 01635 578101.
Web http://www.raceform.co.uk
Email: raceform@raceform.co.uk

Cover Photo: Martin Lynch
Right Wing (Richard Quinn) beats Captain Scott in the
William Hill Lincolnshire Handicap

INTRODUCTION

Racehorse Record is a companion publication to Raceform Annual for 2000, but is also incorporated as part of the Raceform Weekly Form Book subscription and we hope this will prove a popular addition to our subscribers' reference libraries. The book is designed not only as an historical reference, but also as a guide to the future.

As Flat racing becomes more global, it is also useful to have information on the top horses racing around the world and, to this end, we have included all horses trained abroad which appeared in Raceform, The Form Book and attained a rating of 90 or above.

The horses are listed in alphabetical order, together with their suffix. This is followed by the current Raceform Master Rating (RR) for the Flat (i.e. 74f), along with an All-Weather Master Rating if applicable (i.e. 65a). The figures after this are the Official BHB Ratings (Turf, and All-Weather where applicable) as at the end of the season (7th November), as long as the horse has been entered in a handicap during the season (otherwise a BHB Rating is not issued). It should be noted that BHB Handicappers officially rate no horse above 120 after September (100 for two-year-olds) in preparation for the International Classifications which assign a figure to all the best horses. These figures are released in January and appear in Raceform Update, and all other Trade publications.

The number to the far right is the number of the last race in the Form Book in which the horse competed, with finishing position. This allows the reader to refer quickly and easily to Racehorse Record's companion title, Raceform Flat Annual For 2000.

The second line displays the age, colour, sex and pedigree of the horse. The Sire's name and suffix is followed by the average winning distance of his progeny (excluding two-year-olds). This figure is the mean average winning distance of all wins by horses he has sired, displayed to the nearest tenth of a furlong. The number in BOLD type in parentheses which follows is the average highest winning rating of his progeny in the last 12 months. The same set of figures is given for the Grandsire (sire of dam), in his role as a Grandsire.

Full form figures are shown for the 1999 campaign, rather than just the last six runs, as trends often reveal themselves through the course of a season. For horses trained outside GB and Ireland, the figures relate only to races published in Raceform, The Official Form Book and Computer Raceform.

The win and total prizemoney is followed by the horse's win record, which displays the year, month, course, going, race type (H=Handicap, C=Claimer, S=Seller, L=listed, G1=Group One, G2=Group Two and G3=Group Three), distance to the nearest tenth of a furlong, BHB and Raceform Rating. Please note, the BHB Rating is the original mark of the horse at entry and NOT adjusted for such factors as overweight and penalties that may have been incurred. An Asterisk (*) at the start of the line indicates that the win was for the horse's current trainer, whilst an arrow at the end (<) indicates that it was the highest Raceform Rating gained thus far in its career.

The line directly above the narrative shows a breakdown of the runs in 1999 on Turf and All-Weather, listing the different distances and goings on which it raced, together with success rate.

The narrative itself produces an analysis of all the horse's runs and gives an assessment of physical attributes and ability. Distances at which the horse is effective, its optimum distance, going preferences, effectiveness in headgear, course preferences and best performance in the current season are all listed here. N.B. the going preferences shown are based on the Raceform going rather than the Official, as the latter is often called into question, whereas Raceform's is based on race times and takes into account other external influences. Where appropriate, the editorial also features an assessment of how the horse has run and views on its future prospects.

The final line details the trainer with wins-to-runs ratio in parentheses, followed by the owner's name. If the horse has been with more than one handler during its career, the previous trainer is shown, again with wins-to-runs ratio. N.B. National Hunt performances are included in the horse's total run figures for the trainer, for additional information.

ABBREVIATIONS AND THEIR MEANINGS

hvy	=	heavy	frm	=	firm
sft	=	soft	hrd	=	hard
g-s	=	good to soft	Equi	=	Equitrack All-Weather
gd	=	good	Fibr	=	Fibresand All-Weather
g-f	=	good to firm			

"acts on gd to frm, best on g-f" = horse is able to act effectively on any ground between good and firm, but is best when the ground is actually good to firm.
"Turf high" = this season's best performance rating
"AW high 68" = this season's performance rating if achieved on an All-Weather surface.
"(18 Aug Pont g-f RF 3637)" = the date, racecourse, going, and Raceform number in the Form Book where a horse achieved its highest rating.
"(1st run)" = indicates if a horse's rating was achieved on its first run on that surface.
"l.h. tracks" = courses with left-handed bends.
"r.h. tracks" = courses with right-handed bends.
"tight tracks" = courses with tight bends. (Raceform assess bend tightness, and these are not necessarily the tracks with the tightest circumference.

The tracks with the tightest bends are :-

Bath	Goodwood	Ripon
Catterick	Hamilton	Thirsk
Chester	Lingfield	Windsor
Epsom	Musselburgh	Wolverhampton
Folkestone	Redcar	Yarmouth

RACEFORM RATINGS

Raceform Ratings for each horse indicate the actual level of performance attained in that race. The figure shown after RR in the text represents the BEST public form that our Handicappers still believe each horse is capable of reproducing.

To use the ratings constructively in determining those horses best-in in future events, the following procedure should be followed:

(i) In races where all runners are the same age and are set to carry the same weight, no calculations are necessary. The horse with the highest rating is the horse best in.

(ii) In races where all runners are the same age but are set to carry different weights, add one point to the Raceform rating for every pound less than 10 stone to be carried, deduct one point for every pound more than 10 stone.

For example

Horse	Age & weight	Adjustment from 10 stone	RR base Rating	Adjusted Rating
Agincourt	3-10-1	-1	78	77
Brandywine Creek	3-9-13	+1	80	81
Culloden	3-9-7	+7	71	78
Goose Green	3-8-11	+17	60	77

Therefore Brandywine Creek is top-rated (best-in)

(iii) In races concerning horses of different ages the procedure in example (ii) should again be followed, but reference must also be made to the Official Scale of Weight-For-Age (see page facing).

For example

12 furlongs July 20th

Horse	Age & weight	Adjust fr 10 st	RPH Rating	Adjust Rating	W-F-A deduct	Final Rating
Mocha	5-10-0	0	90	90	Nil	90
Cappucino	4-9-9	+5	83	88	Nil	88
Cafe Latte	3-9-4	+10	85	95	-12	83
Espresso	4-8-7	+21	73	94	Nil	94

Therefore Espresso is top-rated (best-in)

(A 3-y.o is deemed 12lb less mature than a 4-y.o or older horse on 20th July over 12f. Therefore, the deduction of 12 points is necessary).

The following symbols are used in conjunction with the ratings:

++ almost certain to prove better
+ likely to prove better
d disappointing (has run well below best recently)
? form hard to evaluate - rating may prove unreliable
t tentative rating based on race time

Weight adjusted ratings for every race are published daily in Raceform Private Handicap. For subscription terms please contact the Subscription Department on 01635-578080.

The Official Scale of Weight, Age & Distance (Flat)

The following scale should only be used in conjunction with the Official ratings published in this book. Use of any other scale will introduce errors into calculations. The allowances are expressed as the number of pounds that is deemed the average horse in each group falls short of maturity at different dates and distances.

Dist		Jan		Feb		Mar		Apr		May		Jun		Jul		Aug		Sep		Oct		Nov		Dec	
(fur)	Age	1-15	16-31	1-14	15-28	1-15	16-31	1-15	16-30	1-15	16-31	1-15	16-30	1-15	16-31	1-15	16-31	1-15	16-30	1-15	16-31	1-15	16-30	1-15	16-31
5	2	-	-	-	-	-	47	44	41	38	36	34	32	30	28	26	24	22	20	19	18	17	17	16	16
	3	15	15	14	14	13	12	11	10	9	8	7	6	5	4	3	2	1	1	-	-	-	-	-	-
6	2	-	-	-	-	-	-	-	-	44	41	38	36	33	31	28	26	24	22	21	20	19	18	17	17
	3	16	16	15	15	14	13	12	11	10	9	8	7	6	5	4	3	2	2	1	1	-	-	-	-
7	2	-	-	-	-	-	-	-	-	-	-	-	-	38	35	32	30	27	25	23	22	21	20	19	19
	3	18	18	17	17	16	15	14	13	12	11	10	9	8	7	6	5	4	3	2	2	1	1	-	-
8	2	-	-	-	-	-	-	-	-	-	-	-	-	-	-	37	34	31	28	26	24	23	22	21	20
	3	20	20	19	19	18	17	15	14	13	12	11	10	9	8	7	6	5	4	3	3	2	2	1	1
9	3	22	22	21	21	20	19	17	15	14	13	12	11	10	9	8	7	6	5	4	4	3	3	2	2
	4	1	1	-	-	-	-	-	-	-	-	-	-	-	-	-	-	-	-	-	-	-	-	-	-
10	3	23	23	22	22	21	20	19	17	15	14	13	12	11	10	9	8	7	6	5	5	4	4	3	3
	4	2	2	1	1	-	-	-	-	-	-	-	-	-	-	-	-	-	-	-	-	-	-	-	-
11	3	24	24	23	23	22	21	20	19	17	15	14	13	12	11	10	9	8	7	6	6	5	5	4	4
	4	3	3	2	2	1	1	-	-	-	-	-	-	-	-	-	-	-	-	-	-	-	-	-	-
12	3	25	25	24	24	23	22	21	20	19	17	15	14	13	12	11	10	9	8	7	7	6	6	5	5
	4	4	4	3	3	2	2	1	1	-	-	-	-	-	-	-	-	-	-	-	-	-	-	-	-
13	3	26	26	25	25	24	23	22	21	20	19	17	15	14	13	12	11	10	9	8	8	7	7	6	6
	4	5	5	4	4	3	3	2	1	-	-	-	-	-	-	-	-	-	-	-	-	-	-	-	-
14	3	27	27	26	26	25	24	23	22	21	20	19	17	15	14	13	12	11	10	9	9	8	8	7	7
	4	6	6	5	5	4	4	3	2	1	-	-	-	-	-	-	-	-	-	-	-	-	-	-	-
15	3	28	28	27	27	26	25	24	23	22	21	20	19	17	15	14	13	12	11	10	9	8	8	7	7
	4	6	6	5	5	4	4	3	3	2	1	-	-	-	-	-	-	-	-	-	-	-	-	-	-
16	3	29	29	28	28	27	26	25	24	23	22	21	20	19	17	15	14	13	12	11	10	9	9	8	8
	4	7	7	6	6	5	5	4	4	3	2	1	-	-	-	-	-	-	-	-	-	-	-	-	-
18	3	31	31	30	30	29	28	27	26	25	24	23	22	21	20	18	16	14	13	12	11	10	10	9	9
	4	8	8	7	7	6	6	5	5	4	3	2	1	-	-	-	-	-	-	-	-	-	-	-	-
20	3	33	33	32	32	31	30	29	28	27	26	25	24	23	22	20	18	16	14	13	12	11	11	10	10
	4	9	9	8	8	7	7	6	6	5	4	3	2	1	-	-	-	-	-	-	-	-	-	-	-

RACEFORM TOP RATED THREE-YEAR-OLDS AND UPWARDS OF 1999

Daylami (IRE)	135
El Condor Pasa (USA)	135
Montjeu (IRE)	135
Royal Anthem	132
Stravinsky (USA)	128
Sendawar (IRE)	128
Croco Rouge (IRE)	127
Aljabr (USA)	127
Tiger Hill (IRE)	126
Mutafaweq (USA)	126
Air Jihad	125
Dark Moondancer (GB)	125
Gold Away (IRE)	125
Oath (IRE)	125
Fantastic Light (USA)	125
Docksider	125
Dansili	125
Grass Wonder (USA)	125
Cape Cross (IRE)	125
Dubai Millennium	124
Fruits of Love (USA)	123
Jim And Tonic (FR)	123
Nedawi	123

RACEFORM TOP RATED TWO-YEAR-OLDS OF 1999

Fasliyev (USA)	120
Auenklang	114
Distant Music (USA)	113
Rossini (USA)	111
Giant's Causeway (USA)	111
Manzor	110
Warm Heart (USA)	109
Primo Valentino (IRE)	108
Monashee Mountain (USA)	108
Lady Of Chad (IRE)	108
Aristotle (IRE)	108
Seazun (IRE)	107
Torgau (IRE)	107
Fath (USA)	107
Seven No Trumps	106
Halland Park Girl (IRE)	106
Race Leader (USA)	106
Invincible Spirit (IRE)	106
Lermontov (USA)	106
Dramatic Quest	105
Ekraar (USA)	105
French Fellow (IRE)	104
Mull Of Kintyre (USA)	104

AA-YOUKNOWNOTHING BHB 62f67a **RR 59f 67a** 2810[15]
3 b g Superpower 6.6f **(58)** - Bad Payer (Tanfirion) 7f **(61)**
Form - 320055080300
Record 1999 - 1st:0 2nd:1 3rd:2 Ran:12
Pre1999 - 1st:2 2nd:2 3rd:0 Ran:8
Win Prizemoney £6,079 *Total Prizemoney* £10,059
Wins 1998 May Thirsk (GD) 5f 68 <
1998 Apr Mussel (G-S) 5f 68 <
1999 Turf 0-8: (5f 6, 6f 2) (gd 2, g-f 3, frm 2, hrd) 1999 AW 0-4: (5f 4) (Equi, Fibr 3)
Workmanlike, above-average gelding, effective 5f, acts on g-f - acts on Fibr, has worn blinkers. Turf high 64. AW high 76 - 2nd of 6 giving 3lb to Trojan Girl (17 Feb Wolverhampton 5f Fibr RF 0306). Takes his name from a remark made to Raceform's esteemed race-reader Alan Amies during the infamous Top Cees libel case.
**Miss J F Craze [0-12] T Marshall (from M W Easterby [2-8] Aug 1998).*

ABAJANY BHB 77f **RR 76f** 5217[4]
5 b g Akarad (FR) 9.7f **(73)** -Miss Ivory Coast (USA) (Sir Ivor) 10.2f **(70)**
Form - 46480005603345833524
Record 1999 - 1st:0 2nd:1 3rd:4 Ran:20
Pre1999 - 1st:4 2nd:3 3rd:4 Ran:28
Win Prizemoney £18,444 *Total Prizemoney* £43,494
Wins * 1998 Aug Ayr (G-S) H 8f 78 85 <
* 1998 Jly Bath (GD) 10.2f 78
* 1997 Spt Sandow (G-F) H 8.1f 71 77
* 1997 Aug Leices (GD) H 8f 66 72
1999 Turf 0-20: (7f, 8f 14, 9f 4, 10f) (sft, g-s 2, gd 6, g-f 4, frm 7)
Above-average gelding, effective 8 to 10f, best at 8f, acts on g-s to frm, likes left handed tracks. Turf high 88 - 4th of 15 to Tertium (3 May Kempton 8f frm RF 0999). Consistent. Third in the Mail On Sunday mile final, he ran really well in the latter half of the season, often just finding one to good, or not enjoying the smoothest of passages. **M R Channon [4-54] John White and Partners.*

ABARIS (IRE) RR 2265[7]
2 ch c Kris 10f **(75)** - Amaranthus (Shirley Heights) 10.3f **(74)**
Form - 7
Record 1999 - 1st:0 2nd:0 3rd:0 Ran:1
1999 Turf 0-1: (7f) (frm)
Currently very poor colt. **T D Easterby [0-1] Mrs M Nowell.*

ABBAJABBA BHB 62f60a **RR 59f 60a** 5160[6]
3 b g Barrys Gamble 7f **(50)** - Bo' Babbity (Strong Gale) 5.6f **(66)**
Form - 00768666
Record 1999 - 1st:0 2nd:0 3rd:0 Ran:8
Pre1999 - 1st:0 2nd:1 3rd:0 Ran:5
Win Prizemoney £0 *Total Prizemoney* £1,261
1999 Turf 0-8: (5f 2, 6f 5, 7f) (gd 2, g-f, frm 5)
Workmanlike, fair gelding, effective 5 to 6f, acts on gd to g-f. Turf high 62. Consistent.
**C W Fairhurst [0-13] North Cheshire Trading & Storage Ltd.*

ABBEY THEATRE (IRE) BHB 17f **RR 29f** 2837[8]
5 b g Sadler's Wells (USA) 11.3f **(87)** - Altiyna (Troy) 10.4f **(68)**
Form - 3000008
Record 1999 - 1st:0 2nd:0 3rd:1 Ran:7
Pre1999 - 1st:0 2nd:0 3rd:0 Ran:4
Win Prizemoney £0 *Total Prizemoney* £653
1999 Turf 0-5: (12f 4, 13f) (g-f 3, frm, hrd) 1999 AW 0-2: (13f, 16f) (Equi, Fibr)
Little account gelding, has worn blinkers. Turf high 29.
**M Salaman [0-13] M J Lewin.*

ABBYANN BHB 42f **RR 46f** 4156[14]
3 b f Nalchik (USA) 12.6f **(44)** - Zoomar (Legend of France (USA)) 9.5f **(61)**
Form - 3400
Record 1999 - 1st:0 2nd:0 3rd:1 Ran:4
Win Prizemoney £0 *Total Prizemoney* £272
1999 Turf 0-4: (8f 4) (gd, g-f, frm 2)
Scopey, moderate filly. Turf high 46 (began Jly).
**B Palling [0-4] J Hamilton-Jones.*

ABCO BOY (IRE) RR 4341[15]
2 b c Full Extent (USA) 5.2f **(50)** - Double Stitch (Wolver Hollow) 8f **(56)**
Form - 0
Record 1999 - 1st:0 2nd:0 3rd:0 Ran:1
1999 Turf 0-1: (8f) (gd)
Currently very poor colt. **Martyn Wane [0-1] E Sidebottom.*

ABDERIAN (IRE) BHB 99f **RR 83f** 4952[2]
2 b c Machiavellian (USA) 9.8f **(83)** - Aminata (Glenstal (USA)) 10.1f **(64)**
Form - 142
Record 1999 - 1st:1 2nd:1 3rd:0 Ran:3
Win Prizemoney £3,707 *Total Prizemoney* £5,200
Wins * **1999** Aug Ripon (GD) 6f 77 <
1999 Turf 1-3: (6f 1-1, 7f 2) (gd, g-f 1-2)
Currently decent colt. Turf high 83 (began Aug) - 2nd of 7 to Catchy Word (19 Oct Yarmouth 7f g-f RF 4952) - also 1st of 21 from Corridor Creeper (21 Aug Ripon RF 3818). Beat a big field of maidens on his Ripon debut over six furlongs, but was found wanting for pace over a furlong further at Ayr next time. Ran well on his final start and should do well at three.
**J Noseda [1-3] Hesmonds Stud.*

ABERFELDY BHB 38f **RR 32f** 4090[8]
3 b f Petong 7.6f **(58)** - Klewraye (Lord Gayle (USA)) 8.8f **(62)**
Form - 805588
Record 1999 - 1st:0 2nd:0 3rd:0 Ran:6
Pre1999 - 1st:0 2nd:0 3rd:1 Ran:3
Win Prizemoney £0 *Total Prizemoney* £487
1999 Turf 0-6: (5f 3, 6f, 7f 2) (gd 2, g-f 2, frm 2)
Scopey, very moderate filly, effective 6f, acts on g-f. Turf high 37.
**J Berry [0-9] Miss Gill Campion.*

ABERKEEN BHB 59f54a **RR 62f 54a** 4536[10]
4 ch g Keen 11.1f **(58)** - Miss Aboyne (Lochnager) 6f **(59)**
Form - 336177452060
Record 1999 - 1st:1 2nd:1 3rd:2 Ran:12
Pre1999 - 1st:1 2nd:2 3rd:1 Ran:14
Win Prizemoney £5,495 *Total Prizemoney* £10,743
Wins * **1999** May Doncas (G-F) H 7f 56 60 <
* 1997 Jun Pontef (G-F) 6f 57
1999 Turf 1-10: (7f 1-9, 8f) (g-s, gd 3, g-f 2, frm 1-4) 1999 AW 0-2: (6f, 7f) (Fibr 2)
Workmanlike, average gelding, effective 7f, acts on gd to frm, best on frm, has worn blinkers. Turf high 62 - 2nd of 22 giving 11lb to Melodian (29 Jly Doncaster 7f frm RF 3218) - also 1st of 21 getting 14lb from Bintang Timor (29 May Doncaster RF 1566). AW high 55 (began Jly). Scored at Doncaster in May, but has a modest strike rate. Seven furlongs and fast ground seem to suit.
**M Dods [2-26] N A Riddell.*

ABISSINIA BHB 42f46a **RR 47f 46a** 2261[13]
3 b f Puissance 7.1f **(60)** - Amathus Glory (Mummy's Pet) 7.7f **(60)**
Form - 60500700
Record 1999 - 1st:0 2nd:0 3rd:0 Ran:4
Pre1999 - 1st:0 2nd:1 3rd:1 Ran:9
Win Prizemoney £0 *Total Prizemoney* £845
1999 Turf 0-4: (5f 3, 6f) (gd, g-f, frm, hrd)
Moderate filly, effective 5f, - acts on Fibr. Turf high 47. Inconsistent. **N Tinkler [0-13] Mrs Christine Cawley.*

ABLE AYR BHB 76f **RR 79f** 3673[12]
2 ch c Formidable (USA) 7.8f **(60)** - Ayr Classic (Local Suitor (USA)) 8.4f **(67)**
Form - 34410450
Record 1999 - 1st:1 2nd:0 3rd:1 Ran:8
Win Prizemoney £2,771 *Total Prizemoney* £3,694
Wins * **1999** Jun Carlis (GD) 5f 74 <
1999 Turf 1-8: (5f 1-5, 6f 3) (g-s, gd, g-f 1-4, frm 2)
Above-average colt, effective 5f, acts on g-f. Turf high 79 - also 1st of 10 from Corunna (10 Jun Carlisle RF 1880).
**J S Goldie [1-8] Frank Brady.*

ABLE LASS (IRE) BHB 35f30a **RR 32f 30a** 59[12]
5 ch m Classic Music (USA) 7.2f **(57)** - Miami Life (Miami Springs) 9.9f **(59)**
Form - 0
Record 1999 - 1st:0 2nd:0 3rd:0 Ran:1
Pre1999 - 1st:0 2nd:0 3rd:0 Ran:4

1999 AW 0-1: (10f) (Equi)
Very moderate filly. **R W Armstrong [0-5] Dr Cornel Li.*

ABLE MILLENIUM (IRE) RR 5147[3]
3 ch g Be My Guest (USA) 10.2f **(66)** - Miami Life (Miami Springs) 9.9f **(59)**
Form - 33
Record 1999 - 1st:0 2nd:0 3rd:2 Ran:2
Win Prizemoney £0 *Total Prizemoney* £816
1999 AW 0-2: (7f, 8f) (Fibr 2)
Unfurnished, currently average gelding. AW high 60.
**R W Armstrong [0-2] Dr Cornel Li.*

ABLE NATIVE (IRE) BHB 70f **RR 75f** 5100[5]
2 b f Thatching 7.8f **(69)** - Native Joy (IRE) (Be My Native (USA)) 10.2f **(71)**
Form - 725
Record 1999 - 1st:0 2nd:1 3rd:0 Ran:3
Win Prizemoney £0 *Total Prizemoney* £930
1999 Turf 0-3: (7f 2, 8f) (g-s 2, gd)
Currently above-average filly. Turf high 75 (began Aug) - 2nd of 9 to So Precious (20 Spt Kempton 7f g-s RF 4428).
**R W Armstrong [0-3] Dr Cornel Li.*

ABLE PETE BHB 44f48a **RR 51f 48a** 1382[12]
3 b c Formidable (USA) 7.8f **(60)** - An Empress (USA) (Affirmed (USA)) 9.3f **(79)**
Form - 08000
Record 1999 - 1st:0 2nd:0 3rd:0 Ran:5
Pre1999 - 1st:0 2nd:0 3rd:0 Ran:2
1999 Turf 0-3: (8f 2, 10f) (sft, gd, g-f) 1999 AW 0-2: (6f, 8f) (Fibr 2)
Workmanlike, fair colt, effective 6f, acts on frm. Turf high 51. AW high 30.
**D J S Cosgrove [0-5] Alex Gorrie (from J L Dunlop [0-2] Oct 1998).*

ABLE PLAYER (USA) BHB 35f **RR 34f** 1495[6]
12 b or br g Solford (USA) - Grecian Snow (CAN) (Snow Knight) 10.3f **(88)**
Form - 6
Record 1999 - 1st:0 2nd:0 3rd:0 Ran:1
Pre1999 - 1st:2 2nd:3 3rd:3 Ran:23
Win Prizemoney £8,684 *Total Prizemoney* £11,876
1999 Turf 0-1: (12f) (gd)
Very moderate gelding, has worn blinkers. Inconsistent.
**K J Drewry [1-18] K J Drewry (from C W Thornton [4-21] Spt 1992).*

A BOB LIGHT (IRE) BHB 62f **RR 63f** 4722[9]
2 br f Bob's Return (IRE) - Light Hand (Star Appeal) 9.6f **(65)**
Form - 642450
Record 1999 - 1st:0 2nd:1 3rd:0 Ran:6
Win Prizemoney £0 *Total Prizemoney* £1,688
1999 Turf 0-6: (6f, 7f 4, 8f) (gd 3, g-f, frm 2)
Average filly, effective 7f, acts on frm. Turf high 63.
**M H Tompkins [0-6] Robert Levitt.*

ABOO HOM BHB 55f **RR 72f** 4800[12]
5 b h Sadler's Wells (USA) 11.3f **(87)** - Maria Waleska (Filiberto (USA)) 9.5f **(66)**
Form - 0
Record 1999 - 1st:0 2nd:0 3rd:0 Ran:1
Pre1999 - 1st:0 2nd:0 3rd:1 Ran:6
Win Prizemoney £0 *Total Prizemoney* £816
1999 Turf 0-1: (14f) (gd)
Above-average colt.
**S Dow [0-1] Byerley Bloodstock (from A C Stewart [0-6] Oct 1997).*

ABOVE BOARD BHB 39a **RR 28f** 4691[10]
4 b g Night Shift (USA) 8.1f **(73)** - Bundled Up (USA) (Sharpen Up) 8.3f **(67)**
Form - 085480600
Record 1999 - 1st:0 2nd:0 3rd:0 Ran:9
Pre1999 - 1st:0 2nd:0 3rd:1 Ran:7
Win Prizemoney £0 *Total Prizemoney* £705
1999 Turf 0-2: (5f, 6f) (g-f, hrd) 1999 AW 0-7: (6f 6, 7f) (Fibr 7)
Scopey, very moderate gelding, effective 6f, - acts on Fibr, has worn blinkers, likes left handed tracks. Turf high 28. AW high 53 - 5th of 10 to Rock Island Line (8 Feb Southwell 6f Fibr RF 0253).
Consistent.
**R F Marvin [0-9] R A B Saville (from J Hanson [0-5] Spt 1998).*

ABRAKA RR 41f 2944[12]
2 gr f Petong 7.6f **(58)** - Lady Lucy Linnet **(21f 25a)** (Zalazl (USA))
Form - 6060
Record 1999 - 1st:0 2nd:0 3rd:0 Ran:4
1999 Turf 0-4: (5f 2, 6f 2) (gd 2, g-f, frm)
Moderate filly, often wears blinkers. Turf high 41.
**J S Wainwright [0-4] J S Wainwright.*

A BREEZE BHB 42f35a **RR 38f 35a** 298[12]
5 br g Precocious 7.2f **(54)** - Wasimah (Caerleon (USA)) 8.6f **(71)**
Form - 70
Record 1999 - 1st:0 2nd:0 3rd:0 Ran:1
Pre1999 - 1st:1 2nd:0 3rd:0 Ran:23
Win Prizemoney £4,162 *Total Prizemoney* £4,890
Wins * 1996 Aug Pontef (G-F) 5f 82 <
1999 AW 0-1: (8f) (Equi)
Very moderate gelding, has worn blinkers. Inconsistent.
**D Morris [1-24] The A Breeze Fan Club.*

ABREEZE (USA) BHB 104f **RR 106df** 557a[3]
4 b c Danzig (USA) 8.1f **(88)** - Priceless Pearl (USA) (Alydar (USA)) 9.1f **(76)**
Form - 3
1999 AW 0-1: (10f) (Dirt)
Well made, Pattern-class colt, has worn blinkers. (1st run) - 3rd of 9 giving 1lb to Ramp And Rave (28 Mar Nad Al Sheba 10f Dirt RF 0557a). **S bin Suroor [2-7] Godolphin .*

ABSALOM'S LAD BHB 60f60a **RR 50f 60a** 907[18]
4 ch c Absalom 7.1f **(56)** - Rose Bouquet (General Assembly (USA)) 10f **(68)**
Form - 1800
Record 1999 - 1st:0 2nd:0 3rd:0 Ran:2
Pre1999 - 1st:1 2nd:0 3rd:2 Ran:7
Win Prizemoney £2,123 *Total Prizemoney* £3,590
Wins * 1998 *Nov Wolver (STD) 8.5f 54* <
1999 Turf 0-1: (10f) (gd) 1999 AW 0-1: (9f) (Fibr)
Workmanlike, fair colt, effective 8f, acts on g-f - acts on Fibr, prefers left handed tracks. **P W Harris [1-9] The Absolute Twelve.*

ABSCOND (USA) RR 93f 3936[2]
2 b f Unbridled (USA) - Lemhi Go (USA) (Lemhi Gold (USA))
Form - 22
Record 1999 - 1st:0 2nd:2 3rd:0 Ran:2
Win Prizemoney £0 *Total Prizemoney* £4,355
1999 Turf 0-2: (7f 2) (frm 2)
Currently useful filly. Turf high 93 (began Jly) - 2nd of 9 to My Hansel (27 Aug Newmarket 7f frm RF 3936). She made an encouraging start to her career at Goodwood, but was beaten by a useful sort when 2/9 at Newmarket. She will improve with time.
**Sir Michael Stoute [0-2] Cheveley Park Stud.*

ABSENTEE BHB 26f **RR 28f** 4287[5]
4 br f Slip Anchor 12.7f **(75)** -Meliora (Crowned Prince (USA)) 10.1f **(67)**
Form - 0700005
Record 1999 - 1st:0 2nd:0 3rd:0 Ran:7
Pre1999 - 1st:1 2nd:0 3rd:0 Ran:8
Win Prizemoney £3,132 *Total Prizemoney* £3,342
Wins * 1998 Aug Nottin (G-F) H 14.1f 56 59 <
1999 Turf 0-7: (12f, 14f 4, 16f 2) (sft 2, gd 2, g-f 2, frm)
Leggy, fair filly, effective 14 to 16f, acts on gd to g-f, likes left handed tracks, favours tight tracks. Turf high 50.
**J L Harris [1-12] J H Henderson (from W Jarvis [0-3] Jun 1998).*

ABSENT FRIENDS RR 78?f 5045[12]
2 b c Rock City 8.8f **(62)** - Green Supreme (Primo Dominie) 6.2f **(80)**
Form - 0300
Record 1999 - 1st:0 2nd:0 3rd:1 Ran:4
Win Prizemoney £0 *Total Prizemoney* £492
1999 Turf 0-4: (5f 2, 6f 2) (sft, g-s, g-f, frm)
Above-average colt. Turf high 78. **J Cullinan [0-4] Miss L Vollaro.*

ABSINTHER BHB 64f **RR 66f** 5076[11]
2 b c Presidium 7.5f **(56)** - Heavenly Queen (Scottish Reel) 7f **(61)**

Form - 0370
Record 1999 - 1st:0 2nd:0 3rd:1 Ran:4
Win Prizemoney £0 *Total Prizemoney* £522
1999 Turf 0-4: (6f 2, 7f 2) (g-s, gd, frm 2)
Average colt. Turf high 66 (began Spt). **E J Alston [0-4] J E Abbey.*

ABSOLUTE FANTASY BHB 35f **RR 32f** 5193[13]

3 b f Beveled (USA) 6.9f **(64)** - Sharp Venita (Sharp Edge) 10f **(56)**
Form - 000
Record 1999 - 1st:0 2nd:0 3rd:0 Ran:3
1999 Turf 0-3: (6f, 8f 2) (gd 2, g-f)
Currently very moderate filly. Turf high 32 (began Oct).
**E A Wheeler [0-3] The Red Square Partnership.*

ABSOLUTELY ABSTONE BHB 28f **RR 29f** 2163[10]

5 gr m Petong 7.6f **(58)** - Odilese (Mummy's Pet) 7.7f **(60)**
Form - 000000
Record 1999 - 1st:0 2nd:0 3rd:0 Ran:6
Pre1999 - 1st:0 2nd:0 3rd:1 Ran:5
Win Prizemoney £0 *Total Prizemoney* £741
1999 Turf 0-4: (5f, 6f, 7f 2) (gd 3, frm) 1999 AW 0-2: (5f 2) (Fibr 2)
Little account filly, often wears blinkers. Turf high 29. AW high 13.
**W M Brisbourne [0-6] J E Abbey (from P D Evans [0-5] Nov 1997).*

ABSOLUTE MAJORITY BHB 49f60a **RR 35f 60a** 1228[3]

4 ch g Absalom 7.1f **(56)** - Shall We Run (Hotfoot) 10.5f **(59)**
Form - 75150003
Record 1999 - 1st:1 2nd:0 3rd:1 Ran:8
Win Prizemoney £2,814 *Total Prizemoney* £3,046
Wins 1999 *Feb Wolver (STD) 9.4f 66+* <
1999 Turf 0-2: (8f, 10f) (gd, frm) 1999 AW 1-6: (7f, 8f, 9f 1-2, 10f, 12f) (Equi, Fibr 1-5)
Fair gelding, effective 9f, - acts on Fibr, likes left handed tracks. Turf high 35. AW high 66 - 1st of 10 from My Little Man (17 Feb Wolverhampton RF 0303). He landed a bit of a gamble when winning a maiden on the Wolverhampton Fibresand in February, though it looked a very poor race.
**P Howling [0-5] Richard Berenson (from B J Curley [1-3] Feb 1999).*

ABSOLUTE UTOPIA (USA) BHB 68f **RR 68f** 4788[8]

6 b g Mr Prospector (USA) 8.6f **(88)** - Magic Gleam (USA) (Danzig (USA)) 8.4f **(76)**
Form - 032428
Record 1999 - 1st:0 2nd:2 3rd:1 Ran:6
Pre1999 - 1st:3 2nd:2 3rd:0 Ran:23
Win Prizemoney £10,619 *Total Prizemoney* £21,828
Wins * 1998 Aug Kempto (G-F) H 12f 63 67 <
* 1997 Oct Salisb (GD) H 10f 55 62
* 1997 Aug Bath (GD) H 8f 53 60
1999 Turf 0-6: (10f, 11f, 12f 4) (g-s, gd, g-f 2, frm 2)
Average gelding, effective 9 to 12f, best at 12f, acts on gd to frm, prefers right handed tracks, excels at Goodwood and Kempton. Turf high 68 - 2nd of 15 getting 6lb from Canta Ke Brave (29 Aug Goodwood 12f g-f RF 3993).
**N E Berry [3-25] M T Lawrance (from E A L Dunlop [0-4] May 1996).*

ABSTRACT (IRE) BHB 36a **RR 19f** 2756[6]

3 b f Perugino (USA) - Kalapa (FR) (Mouktar)
Form - 0564704006
Record 1999 - 1st:0 2nd:0 3rd:0 Ran:10
Pre1999 - 1st:0 2nd:0 3rd:0 Ran:5
Win Prizemoney £0 *Total Prizemoney* £209
1999 Turf 0-5: (5f 2, 7f 2, 10f) (g-f 3, frm 2) 1999 AW 0-5: (6f, 7f 3, 8f) (Equi 3, Fibr 2)
Small, very moderate filly, has worn blinkers. Turf high 35. AW high 37.
**J S Wainwright [0-10] J S Wainwright (from D J S Cosgrove [0-5] Spt 1998).*

ABTAAL BHB 57f59a **RR 52f 59a** 4864[12]

9 b g Green Desert (USA) 7.8f **(78)** - Stufida (Bustino) 10.4f **(64)**
Form - 03070514103243176500
Record 1999 - 1st:3 2nd:1 3rd:2 Ran:17
Pre1999 - 1st:5 2nd:3 3rd:4 Ran:41
Win Prizemoney £18,236 *Total Prizemoney* £26,160
Wins * 1999 *May Wolver (STD) H 7f 59 63*
*** 1999** *Mar Wolver (STD) C 7f 58*
*** 1999** *Feb Southw (STD) S 7f 50*
* 1998 *Aug Southw (STD) C 7f 59+*
* 1998 Aug Bright (FRM) 7f 64
1998 Jly Bright (G-F) C 7f 50
1997 Jun Lingfi (G-F) SH 7f 49 48
1999 Turf 0-2: (7f 2) (g-f, hrd) 1999 AW 3-15: (6f 2, 7f 3-13) (Equi 2, Fibr 3-13)
Average gelding, effective 7f, acts on g-f - acts on AW, best on Fibr, often wears blinkers (extremely effectively), prefers left handed tracks, prefers tight tracks, does well at Brighton and likes Southwell. Turf high 52. AW high 64 - 2nd of 10 getting 2lb from Seven (22 Mar Southwell 7f Fibr RF 0458) - also 1st of 12 giving 4lb to Tayovullin (22 May Wolverhampton RF 1417). A bit of a quirky customer, he is an effective sort in modest company on turf and Fibresand, but needs to do it on the bridle.
**Mrs N Macauley [5-26] Andy Peake (from R J Hodges [2-25] Jly 1998).*

ABU CAMP BHB 45f **RR 41f** 3218[19]

4 b g Indian Ridge 7.6f **(74)** - Artistic Licence (High Top) 10.2f **(67)**
Form - 00860
Record 1999 - 1st:0 2nd:0 3rd:0 Ran:5
Pre1999 - 1st:0 2nd:0 3rd:1 Ran:7
Win Prizemoney £0 *Total Prizemoney* £474
1999 Turf 0-5: (7f 2, 8f 3) (gd 2, frm 3)
Workmanlike, moderate gelding, has worn blinkers. Turf high 50. Consistent. **M J Heaton-Ellis [0-12] John Manser.*

ABULJJOOD (IRE) BHB 58f63a **RR 70f 63a** 2663[3]

4 b g Marju (IRE) 9.2f **(76)** -Midway Lady (USA)(Alleged (USA))10f **(76)**
Form - 2162003
Record 1999 - 1st:1 2nd:2 3rd:1 Ran:7
Pre1999 - 1st:0 2nd:0 3rd:1 Ran:6
Win Prizemoney £2,088 *Total Prizemoney* £4,429
Wins 1999 *Jan Wolver (STD) C 12f 78* <
1999 Turf 0-1: (12f) (frm) 1999 AW 1-6: (12f 1-5, 16f) (Equi, Fibr 1-5)
Above-average gelding, effective 12f, - acts on Fibr, mostly wears blinkers (effectively). AW high 78 - 1st of 9 giving 14lb to Monaco Gold (20 Jan Wolverhampton RF 0128). He has shown better form since being tried on sand, getting off the mark in a Wolverhampton claimer in January.
**Ian Williams [0-1] P B R Abrasives (W'ton) Ltd (from M Waring [0-2] Mar 1999).*

ABUSAMRAH (USA) BHB 50f40a **RR 57f 40a** 1670[9]

4 b g Riverman (USA) 9.7f **(78)** - Azayim (Be My Guest (USA)) 9.3f **(67)**
Form - 005000
Record 1999 - 1st:0 2nd:0 3rd:0 Ran:3
Pre1999 - 1st:0 2nd:0 3rd:1 Ran:8
Win Prizemoney £0 *Total Prizemoney* £556
1999 Turf 0-1: (10f) (g-s) 1999 AW 0-2: (8f, 16f) (Equi, Fibr)
Workmanlike, fair gelding, effective 7f, acts on g-f, has worn blinkers. AW high 11. Becoming disappointing.
**A T Murphy [0-8] E H Jones (Paints) Ltd (from R W Armstrong [0-5] Jun 1998).*

ABUZAID (USA) BHB 87f **RR 79f** 4981[1]

2 br c Nureyev (USA) 8.4f **(84)** - Elle Seule (USA) (Exclusive Native (USA)) 9.1f **(81)**
Form - 571
Record 1999 - 1st:1 2nd:0 3rd:0 Ran:3
Win Prizemoney £3,631 *Total Prizemoney* £3,631
Wins * 1999 Oct Newcas (G-S) 6f 79 <
1999 Turf 1-3: (6f 1-3) (g-f 1-2, frm)
Currently above-average colt. Turf high 79 (began Jly) - 1st of 12 from Boanerges (20 Oct Newcastle RF 4981).
**J L Dunlop [1-3] Hamdan Al Maktoum.*

ABYAAN (IRE) BHB 102f **RR 108?f** 5221[11]

4 b f Ela-Mana-Mou 12.7f **(72)** - Anna Comnena (IRE) (Shareef Dancer (USA)) 9.9f **(73)**
Form - 32653830
Record 1999 - 1st:0 2nd:1 3rd:3 Ran:8
Pre1999 - 1st:1 2nd:0 3rd:0 Ran:2
Win Prizemoney £3,095 *Total Prizemoney* £22,052
Wins * 1998 Apr Bath (SFT) 10.2f 85 <
1999 Turf 0-8: (10f 3, 12f 3, 13f, 15f) (hvy, sft 2, g-s, gd 2, g-f, frm)
Scopey, Pattern-class filly, effective 13f, acts on hvy, has worn blinkers. Turf high 108 - 3rd of 11 giving 1lb to Fairy Queen (2 Oct

Longchamp 13f hvy RF 4769a). Lightly raced at three, she ran some fine races in handicap and Pattern company last season without quite being able to win, her best effort probably coming when third in the Prix Royallieu. She is suited by give in the ground. **J H M Gosden [1-10] Sheikh Ahmed Al Maktoum.*

ACAMBARO (GER) RR 120f 2660a[2]

3 b c Goofalik (USA) 15.4f **(66)** - Astica (GER) (Surumu (GER)) 10f **(83)**
Form - 12
1999 Turf 1-2: (10f 1-1, 12f) (sft 1-1, gd)
Currently very high-class colt. Turf high 120 - 2nd of 18 to Belenus (4 Jly Hamburg 12f gd RF 2660a). A decent German-trained colt, winner of a Group Two at Munich before finishing runner-up in the German Derby. **P Rau in GER [1-2].*

ACCENTO RR 113f 2859a[6]

6 b h Midyan (USA) 9.9f **(64)** - Daleside Ladybird (Tolomeo) 5.6f **(60)**
Form - 26
1999 Turf 0-2: (8f 2) (gd 2)
Group-class horse. Turf high 105 (1st run) - 2nd of 8 to Stanott (6 Jun San Siro 8f gd RF 1906b). Consistent.
**R Suerland in GER [1-9] (from F Gang in GER [0-1] Jly 1998).*

ACCEPTING RR 82f 4537[2]

2 b c Mtoto 11.5f **(71)** - D'Azy (Persian Bold) 9.3f **(66)**
Form - 82
Record 1999 - 1st:0 2nd:1 3rd:0 Ran:2
Win Prizemoney £0 *Total Prizemoney* £933
1999 Turf 0-2: (8f, 9f) (gd, frm)
Currently decent colt. Turf high 82 (began Spt) - 2nd of 10 giving 5lb to Miletrian (24 Spt Redcar 9f frm RF 4537). A moderate first effort was followed by a good second over nine furlongs at Redcar. Running green that day and inclined to hang under pressure, staying certainly looks to be where his future lies.
**J H M Gosden [0-2] George Strawbridge.*

ACCESS ALL AREAS (IRE) RR 112f 2421a[3]

3 b c Approach The Bench (IRE) - Adjalisa (IRE) (Darshaan) 9.9f **(84)**
Form - 263
1999 Turf 0-3: (8f 2, 9f) (gd 2, g-f)
Group-class colt, effective 6 to 9f, acts on gd to frm, best on gd. Turf high 112 (1st run) - 2nd of 8 getting 17lb from Burden Of Proof (9 May Leopardstown 8f gd RF 1172a). A useful juvenile, he ran creditably on all his starts in 1999 but lacks the pace necessary to win Group races. **J E Mulhern in IRE [2-9] J E Mulhern.*

ACCYSTAN BHB 50f69a RR 33f 69a 3316[10]

4 ch g Efisio 7.7f **(69)** - Amia (CAN) (Nijinsky (CAN)) 10.3f **(77)**
Form - 010
Record 1999 - 1st:1 2nd:0 3rd:0 Ran:3
Pre1999 - 1st:2 2nd:0 3rd:4 Ran:12
Win Prizemoney £5,975 *Total Prizemoney* £7,824
Wins * **1999** *Jly Southw (STD) S 12f 63*
1998 *Feb Southw (STD) H 11f 60 67+* <
1998 *Jan Wolver (STD) C 9.4f 66*
1999 Turf 0-2: (8f, 14f) (frm 2) 1999 AW 1-1: (12f 1-1) (Fibr 1-1)
Strong, average gelding, effective 9 to 12f, acts on gd - acts on Fibr. Turf high 33 (began Jly). (1st run) - 1st of 8 getting 5lb from Waiting Knight (24 Jly Southwell RF 3114).
**M D Hammond [2-10] Middleham Racing Bureau/G Heap (from P C Haslam [2-12] Jly 1998).*

ACEBO LYONS (IRE) BHB 56f49a RR 56f 49a 5133[13]

4 b f Waajib 8.9f **(67)** - Etage (Ile de Bourbon (USA)) 10.1f **(67)**
Form - 0603726040
Record 1999 - 1st:0 2nd:1 3rd:1 Ran:10
Pre1999 - 1st:1 2nd:1 3rd:1 Ran:10
Win Prizemoney £2,810 *Total Prizemoney* £5,959
Wins * 1998 Aug Haydoc (GD) 10.5f 70 <
1999 Turf 0-9: (10f 3, 11f 3, 12f 2, 14f) (g-s, gd, g-f 5, frm 2) 1999 AW 0-1: (12f) (Fibr)
Leggy, fair filly, effective 10 to 11f, acts on gd to g-f, has worn blinkers, likes tight tracks. Turf high 56.
**A P Jarvis [1-20] Terence Lyons II.*

ACE OF PARKES BHB 85f RR 90f 4588[6]

3 b g Teenoso (USA) 10.5f **(62)** - Summerhill Spruce (Windjammer (USA)) 7f **(59)**
Form - 665506
Record 1999 - 1st:0 2nd:0 3rd:0 Ran:6
Pre1999 - 1st:3 2nd:0 3rd:1 Ran:7
Win Prizemoney £16,831 *Total Prizemoney* £23,349
Wins * 1998 Aug Cheste (G-S) 6.1f 98 <
* 1998 Jly Cheste (G-F) 6.1f 98 <
* 1998 Jly Hamilt (FRM) 5f 91+
1999 Turf 0-6: (5f 2, 6f 4) (gd 3, g-f, frm 2)
Scopey, useful gelding, effective 5 to 6f, best at 6f, acts on gd to frm, best on gd. Turf high 92. Comes from a family of prolific sprinting winners and completed a hat-trick in 1998. Highly tried on his first two outings last term, he ran his best races at Chester, a track he is particularly suited by. He is gradually slipping to a realistic mark, and can is one to watch, particularly at the Roodeye. **J Berry [3-13] Joseph Heler.*

ACE OF TRUMPS BHB 50f43a RR 49f 43a 5145[9]

3 ch g First Trump - Elle Reef (Shareef Dancer (USA)) 9.9f **(73)**
Form - 7110700353350
Record 1999 - 1st:2 2nd:0 3rd:3 Ran:13
Pre1999 - 1st:1 2nd:3 3rd:0 Ran:11
Win Prizemoney £8,208 *Total Prizemoney* £12,157
Wins **1999** May Warwic (SFT) C 10.5f 59
1999 May Nottin (FRM) SH 8.2f 55 59
1998 Aug Newmar (FRM) S 7f 68 <
1999 Turf 2-12: (7f, 8f 1-2, 9f 3, 10f 2, 11f 1-3, 12f) (sft 1-3, gd 3, g-f 1-4, frm, hrd) 1999 AW 0-1: (12f) (Fibr)
Neat, moderate gelding, effective 6 to 11f, best at 7f, acts on sft to frm, best on g-f, has worn blinkers. Turf high 59 - 1st of 5 getting 2lb from Challenges (29 May Warwick RF 1588) - also 1st of 18 giving 2lb to Prince Consort (21 May Nottingham RF 1382).
**J Hetherton [0-10] C D Barber-Lomax (from W J Haggas [3-14] May 1999).*

A CHEF TOO FAR BHB 51f RR 65f 4791[4]

6 b g Be My Chief (USA) 10.2f **(62)** -Epithet (Mill Reef (USA)) 10.5f **(78)**
Form - 04
Record 1999 - 1st:0 2nd:0 3rd:0 Ran:2
Pre1999 - 1st:1 2nd:0 3rd:0 Ran:6
Win Prizemoney £5,407 *Total Prizemoney* £5,968
Wins 1996 May Newbur (SFT) 7.3f 70+ <
1999 Turf 0-2: (9f, 12f) (g-s, gd)
Average gelding. Turf high 46 (began Spt).
**R G Frost [0-2] Hon Mervyn Greenway (from R Rowe [1-6] Oct 1996).*

Achilles showed no weakness at York

ACHILLES BHB 92f RR 103f 4391[3]

4 ch g Deploy 11.4f **(67)** - Vatersay (USA) (Far North (CAN)) 9.7f **(75)**
Form - 62101223
Record 1999 - 1st:2 2nd:3 3rd:1 Ran:8
Pre1999 - 1st:1 2nd:3 3rd:2 Ran:11
Win Prizemoney £82,588 *Total Prizemoney* £113,726
Wins * **1999** Jly York (G-F) H 10.4f 90 103 <
* **1999** Jun York (G-S) 11.9f 91
1998 Mar Doncas (GD) 10.3f 97

1999 Turf 2-8: (10f 1-6, 11f, 12f 1-1) (g-s 1-1, gd 3, g-f 1-2, frm 2)
Unfurnished, very useful gelding, effective 10 to 12f, best at 10f, acts on sft to frm, best on gd, has worn blinkers, prefers left handed tracks, excels at York. Turf high 103 - 1st of 16 giving 2lb to Siege (10 Jly York RF 2733). Consistent. A real street fighter of a horse, he recorded two game wins at York in the summer, notably when fending off Siege in the John Smith's Cup. Well worth another try over a mile and a half, he sweats freely in the preliminaries and responds well to enterprising tactics.
**K R Burke [2-12] Achilles International (from N P Littmoden [1-3] May 1998).*

ACHILLES SKY BHB 71f **RR 71f** 4126[6]

3 b c Hadeer 8.9f **(58)** - Diva Madonna (Chief Singer) 8.9f **(66)**
Form - 016
Record 1999 - 1st:1 2nd:0 3rd:0 Ran:3
Pre1999 - 1st:0 2nd:0 3rd:0 Ran:3
Win Prizemoney £4,757 *Total Prizemoney* £5,014
Wins * 1999 Jly Nottin (GD) H 10f 68 71 <
1999 Turf 1-3: (9f, 10f 1-1, 12f) (g-f 1-2, frm)
Scopey, above-average colt, effective 10f, acts on g-f. Turf high 71 - 1st of 16 giving 6lb to Game Tufty (3 Jly Nottingham RF 2540). He had not shown much since a promising debut, but the step up to ten furlongs at Nottingham in July worked the oracle. He still has scope for improvement over middle distances.
**K R Burke [1-6] Achilles International.*

ACHILLES STAR BHB 99f84a **RR 99f 84a** 4894[8]

3 ch g Deploy 11.4f **(67)** - Norbella (Nordico (USA)) 6.5f **(62)**
Form - 247511052018
Record 1999 - 1st:3 2nd:1 3rd:0 Ran:10
Pre1999 - 1st:2 2nd:2 3rd:0 Ran:10
Win Prizemoney £54,624 *Total Prizemoney* £61,399
Wins * 1999 Spt Newbur (G-F) H 8f 92 99 <
*** 1999** Jun Epsom (G-S) H 7f 86 88
*** 1999** Apr Newmar (GD) H 7f 79 84
* 1998 Oct York (GD) H 6f 76 80
1998 May Kempto (GD) 5f 80+
1999 Turf 3-10: (6f, 7f 2-6, 8f 1-2, 9f) (g-s, gd 1-4, g-f, frm 2-4)
Workmanlike, very useful gelding, effective 7 to 8f, acts on gd to frm, excels at Newbury. Turf high 99 - 1st of 13 giving 8lb to Tarawan (18 Spt Newbury RF 4406). He had a tremendous season, winning three valuable handicaps and earning promotion to listed events by the autumn. Proven up to a mile, he handles most types of ground and is game.
**K R Burke [4-18] Achilles International (from N P Littmoden [1-2] May 1998).*

ACICULA (IRE) BHB 85f **RR 91f** 4984[6]

3 b f Night Shift (USA) 8.1f **(73)** - Crystal City (Kris) 9.5f **(73)**
Form - 4025856
Record 1999 - 1st:0 2nd:1 3rd:0 Ran:7
Pre1999 - 1st:2 2nd:3 3rd:0 Ran:7
Win Prizemoney £10,707 *Total Prizemoney* £20,443
Wins * 1998 Oct Newmar (GD) H 6f 89 90 <
* 1998 Spt Mussel (GD) 5f 85
1999 Turf 0-6: (6f 4, 7f 2) (gd, g-f 4, frm) 1999 AW 0-1: (8f) (Dirt)
Scopey, useful filly, effective 5 to 7f, best at 6f, acts on g-f to frm, best on g-f. Turf high 91. Becoming disappointing.
**M Johnston [2-14] P D Savill.*

ACID TEST BHB 68f65a **RR 64f 65a** 4805[17]

4 ch g Sharpo 7.5f **(68)** - Clunk Click (Star Appeal) 9.6f **(65)**
Form - 008103181272461107400
Record 1999 - 1st:4 2nd:2 3rd:1 Ran:16
Pre1999 - 1st:4 2nd:3 3rd:0 Ran:27
Win Prizemoney £32,180 *Total Prizemoney* £38,649
Wins * 1999 Jun Cheste (SFT) H 7f 70 78 <
*** 1999** May Catter (FRM) H 7f 67 72
*** 1999** *Jan Lingfi (STD) H 6f 62 67*
*** 1999** *Jan Lingfi (STD) H 6f 58 64*
* 1998 *Dec Lingfi (STD) H 6f 52 60*
1998 Jun Lingfi (GD) 7f 72
1997 Aug Newmar (G-F) H 7f 65 69
1997 Jly Lingfi (G-F) S 6f 63
1999 Turf 2-7: (6f 2, 7f 2-5) (g-s 1-1, gd 3, frm 1-2, hrd) 1999 AW 2-9: (6f 2-6, 7f 3) (Equi 2-9)
Unfurnished, average gelding, effective 7 to 8f, best at 7f, acts on g-s to frm, best on frm, likes left handed tracks, likes tight tracks, likes Lingfield. Turf high 78 - 1st of 8 getting 12lb from Silca Blanka (2 Jun Chester RF 1668) - also 1st of 14 getting 12lb from Mount Holly (22 May Catterick RF 1388). AW high 68. Changed stables in '98, and showed pretty good form in sprint handicap company on Equitrack before scoring twice on turf last term at Catterick and Chester. Out of form afterwards.
**M A Buckley [5-21] Fair Price Racing (from W R Muir [3-22] Oct 1998).*

ACQUITTAL (IRE) BHB 35f34a **RR 37f 34a** 4488[8]

7 b g Danehill (USA) 9.1f **(79)** - Perfect Alibi (Law Society (USA)) 9.9f **(70)**
Form - 3243U008
Record 1999 - 1st:0 2nd:1 3rd:2 Ran:8
Pre1999 - 1st:1 2nd:4 3rd:4 Ran:31
Win Prizemoney £2,668 *Total Prizemoney* £9,669
Wins 1995 Jun Mussel (G-F) H 11.1f 59 61 <
1999 Turf 0-8: (10f 6, 11f, 12f) (g-s, g-f 3, frm 4)
Moderate gelding, effective 10 to 11f, best at 10f, acts on gd to frm, often wears blinkers (effectively). Turf high 43 - 2nd of 13 getting 2lb from Gold Blade (6 Jly Pontefract 10f frm RF 2580). Becoming disappointing.
**A Streeter [0-28] In The Clear Racing (from J Mackie [0-3] Jan 1996).*

ACROBATIC **RR 85f** 5029[6]

2 br c Warning 8.1f **(77)** - Ayodhya (IRE) (Astronef)
Form - 16
Record 1999 - 1st:1 2nd:0 3rd:0 Ran:2
Win Prizemoney £4,792 *Total Prizemoney* £4,792
Wins * 1999 Spt Newbur (G-F) 6f 85 <
1999 Turf 1-2: (6f 1-1, 7f) (g-s, frm 1-1)
Currently useful colt. Turf high 85 (1st run) (began Spt) - 1st of 15 from Hilltop Warning (18 Spt Newbury RF 4408). Got off the mark by the minimum margin at Newbury in September. Ran respectably in a Group Three next time, and is probably capable of a deal of improvement. **J R Fanshawe [1-2] Dr Catherine Wills.*

ACTION JACKSON BHB 33f50a **RR 31f 50a** 2536[4]

7 ch g Hadeer 8.9f **(58)** - Water Woo (USA) (Tom Rolfe) 9.4f **(75)**
Form - 0204604
Record 1999 - 1st:0 2nd:1 3rd:0 Ran:7
Pre1999 - 1st:2 2nd:9 3rd:2 Ran:44
Win Prizemoney £4,854 *Total Prizemoney* £13,234
Wins * 1996 Spt Pontef (GD) S 10f 45
* 1996 Jly Nottin (G-F) S 10f 55 <
1999 Turf 0-4: (9f, 10f, 14f 2) (gd, g-f 2, frm) 1999 AW 0-3: (11f, 14f, 16f) (Fibr 3)
Very moderate gelding, effective 10 to 14f, best at 14f, acts on g-s to frm, excels at Yarmouth, likes Nottingham. Turf high 41. AW high 37. **B J McMath [2-45] O Pointing (from G Rimmer [0-6] Jly 1995).*

ACTUALLY (IRE) BHB 40f **RR 48f** 5138[17]

2 b f Namaqualand (USA) - Extra Time **(75f 51a)** (Shadeed (USA)) 8.2f **(70)**
Form - 0050
Record 1999 - 1st:0 2nd:0 3rd:0 Ran:4
1999 Turf 0-4: (5f, 6f, 7f, 8f) (sft, gd, g-f, frm)
Moderate filly. Turf high 48. **Andrew Reid [0-4] A S Reid.*

ADAIR (USA) **RR 122f** 4266[3]

3 ch c Theatrical 11.5f **(78)** - Amore Cielo (USA) (Conquistador Cielo (USA)) 8.8f **(69)**
Form - 03
Record 1999 - 1st:0 2nd:0 3rd:1 Ran:2
Pre1999 - 1st:1 2nd:0 3rd:0 Ran:1
Win Prizemoney £14,268 *Total Prizemoney* £53,318
Wins 1998 Oct Belmon (FRM) 9f 105++ <
1999 Turf 0-2: (12f, 15f) (gd, frm)
Currently very high-class colt. Turf high 122 - 3rd of 9 to Mutafaweq (11 Spt Doncaster 15f frm RF 4266). A runaway winner of his only outing at two, he was subsequently bought by Godolphin, but managed only two outings in 1999. He took his chance in the Derby following positive home reports, only to finish down the field. Given a long break subsequently, he returned to run third to Stable companion Mutafaweq in the St Leger. An

imposing sort, he obviously has ability, and can make up for lost time in 2000.
**S bin Suroor [0-2] Godolphin (from W Mott in USA [1-1] Oct 1998).*

ADAMAS (IRE) RR 80f 4542[2]
2 b f Fairy King (USA) 7.7f **(75)** - Corynida (USA) (Alleged (USA)) 10f **(76)**
Form - 2
Record 1999 - 1st:0 2nd:1 3rd:0 Ran:1
Win Prizemoney £0 *Total Prizemoney* £982
1999 Turf 0-1: (6f) (frm)
Currently decent filly. (1st run) - 2nd of 13 to Melanzana (24 Spt Redcar 6f frm RF 4542). **Andrew Turnell [0-1] Mrs Claire Hollowood.*

A DAY ON THE DUB BHB 50f47a **RR 54f 47a** 5156[2]
6 b g Presidium 7.5f **(56)** - Border Mouse (Border Chief)
Form - 1464072112
Record 1999 - 1st:3 2nd:2 3rd:0 Ran:10
Pre1999 - 1st:0 2nd:0 3rd:0 Ran:1
Win Prizemoney £7,137 *Total Prizemoney* £9,464
Wins * **1999** Oct Redcar (SFT) C 11f 50 <
* **1999** Oct Newcas (G-S) CH 8f 36 40
* **1999** *Jan Southw (STD) 12f 49*
1999 Turf 2-9: (7f, 8f 1-3, 9f, 10f 2, 11f 1-1, 12f) (g-s, gd 2-4, g-f, frm 3)
1999 AW 1-1: (12f 1-1) (Fibr 1-1)
Fair gelding, effective 8 to 12f, acts on gd - acts on Fibr, prefers left handed tracks. Turf high 54 - 2nd of 17 giving 4lb to Davis Rock (1 Nov Nottingham 8f gd RF 5156) - also 1st of 17 giving 4lb to Bolt From The Blue (26 Oct Redcar RF 5071). (1st run) - 1st of 8 giving 4lb to Le Sauvage (11 Jan Southwell RF 0074).
**D Eddy [3-13] Revblayd.*

ADDICKS ADDICTS RR 5194[5]
2 b c King's Signet (USA) 7f **(51)** - Alzamina (Alzao (USA)) 7.1f **(68)**
Form - W
Record 1999 - 1st:0 2nd:0 3rd:0 Ran:1
1999 Turf 0-1: (gd)
Withdrawn on only appearance. **M R Channon [0-1] Mrs C Roper.*

ADDITION BHB 58f **RR 40f** 5068[15]
3 b f Dilum (USA) 7.1f **(56)** - Cedar Lady (Telsmoss)
Form - 6002310060
Record 1999 - 1st:1 2nd:1 3rd:1 Ran:10
Pre1999 - 1st:0 2nd:0 3rd:1 Ran:5
Win Prizemoney £4,199 *Total Prizemoney* £6,524
Wins * **1999** Jly Warwic (G-F) H 6.8f 52 60 <
1999 Turf 1-10: (6f 5, 7f 1-4, 8f) (sft, g-s, gd 2, g-f 1-1, frm 4, hrd)
Neat, moderate filly, effective 7f, acts on g-f, likes left handed tracks. Turf high 60 - 1st of 12 getting 25lb from Nice One Clare (10 Jly Warwick RF 2728). **R J Hodges [1-15] J W Mursell.*

ADELPHI BOY (IRE) BHB 72f90a **RR 73f 90a** 5166[4]
3 ch g Ballad Rock 7.2f **(63)** - Toda (Absalom) 7.2f **(58)**
Form - 21112343740003705024
Record 1999 - 1st:0 2nd:2 3rd:3 Ran:16
Pre1999 - 1st:3 2nd:1 3rd:0 Ran:8
Win Prizemoney £8,368 *Total Prizemoney* £17,570
Wins * 1998 *Dec Lingfi (STD) H 5f 85 82*
* 1998 *Dec Southw (STD) H 5f 79 84* <
* 1998 *Dec Southw (STD) 5f 71*
1999 Turf 0-13: (6f 4, 7f 3, 8f 4, 10f 2) (g-s 2, gd 4, g-f 4, frm 2, hrd)
1999 AW 0-3: (6f, 7f 2) (Fibr 3)
Workmanlike, useful gelding, effective 7 to 8f, acts on gd - acts on Fibr. Turf high 101 (1st run) - 3rd of 7 giving 7lb to Kuwait Dawn (27 Mar Doncaster 8f gd RF 0484). AW high 92 - 3rd of 11 getting 15lb from Italian Symphony (17 Feb Wolverhampton 7f Fibr RF 0305). He deteriorated during a busy turf campaign, dropping 20lb in the ratings and chancing his arm over a variety of trips. A better horse on the All-Weather, he can return to the winner's enclosure this winter. **M C Chapman [3-24] Barry Brown.*

ADILABAD (USA) RR 91+f 4897[1]
2 b c Gulch (USA) 9.6f **(79)** - Adaiyka (IRE) **(103f)** (Doyoun) 9f **(69)**
Form - 11
Record 1999 - 1st:2 2nd:0 3rd:0 Ran:2
Win Prizemoney £11,977 *Total Prizemoney* £11,977
Wins * **1999** Oct Newmar (GD) 7f 82+
* **1999** Spt Sandow (GD) 7.1f 91+ <
1999 Turf 2-2: (7f 2-2) (gd 2-2)
Currently useful colt. Turf high 91 (1st run) (began Spt) - 1st of 5 getting 11lb from Nicobar (15 Spt Sandown RF 4330) - also 1st of 4 giving 3lb to Camberley (15 Oct Newmarket RF 4897). Made a winning debut at Sandown, and had two subsequent winners behind. Followed up with a fluent victory in the Houghton Stakes, and could be useful. **Sir Michael Stoute [2-2] H H Aga Khan.*

ADILOV BHB 31f18a **RR 25f 18a** 269[10]
7 b g Soviet Star (USA) 8.6f **(74)** - Volida (Posse (USA)) 8.9f **(61)**
Form - 50
Record 1999 - 1st:0 2nd:0 3rd:0 Ran:2
Pre1999 - 1st:0 2nd:0 3rd:1 Ran:18
Win Prizemoney £0 *Total Prizemoney* £656
1999 AW 0-2: (13f, 16f) (Equi 2)
Little account gelding, has worn blinkers. AW high 12. Becoming disappointing.
**J J Bridger [2-39] T Mitchell & Mrs H Veal (from K O Cunningham-Brown [0-5] Spt 1996).*

ADIRPOUR (IRE) BHB 46f37a **RR 42f 37a** 5156[13]
5 gr g Nishapour (FR) 11.1f **(58)** - Adira (IRE) (Ballad Rock) 7.8f **(63)**
Form - 52504040681108644040040070
Record 1999 - 1st:2 2nd:0 3rd:0 Ran:23
Pre1999 - 1st:0 2nd:2 3rd:3 Ran:11
Win Prizemoney £4,168 *Total Prizemoney* £6,556
Wins * **1999** May Newcas (G-F) C 7f 60 <
* **1999** Apr Leices (G-S) S 7f 53
1999 Turf 2-15: (6f, 7f 2-8, 8f 6) (g-s, gd 1-7, g-f 4, frm 1-3) 1999 AW 0-8: (5f, 7f, 8f 5, 9f) (Fibr 8)
Moderate gelding, effective 6 to 8f, acts on gd to frm, has worn blinkers. Turf high 60 - 1st of 11 getting 1lb from Birchwood Sun (3 May Newcastle RF 1006) - also 1st of 18 from Bettron (1 Apr Leicester RF 0537). AW high 45. A winner twice early in the season over seven furlongs at Newcastle and Leicester, she was out of sorts afterwards.
**R Hollinshead [2-24] Ed Weetman (from Noel Chance [0-2] Dec 1998).*

ADJUTANT BHB 92f **RR 97f** 5155[3]
4 b g Batshoof 9.5f **(66)** - Indian Love Song (Be My Guest (USA)) 9.3f **(67)**
Form - 84002313
Record 1999 - 1st:1 2nd:1 3rd:2 Ran:8
Pre1999 - 1st:2 2nd:2 3rd:2 Ran:11
Win Prizemoney £19,581 *Total Prizemoney* £31,107
Wins * **1999** Oct Leices (SFT) 7f 97 <
* 1998 Spt Haydoc (G-F) H 7.1f 86 88
* 1998 May Goodwo (G-F) H 7f 83 88
1999 Turf 1-8: (7f 1-6, 8f 2) (gd 1-4, g-f 3, frm)
Workmanlike, very useful gelding, effective 7f, acts on gd to frm, best on gd, excels at Haydock. Turf high 97 - 1st of 10 from Premier Baron (25 Oct Leicester RF 5055). Ran creditably on most starts in '98, but did not fire early on this season. Ran much better at Newbury in September after a three-month break and followed that up with a sound effort at Newmarket behind Family Man. Gained a deserved victory when winning at Leicester in October.
**B J Meehan [3-19] J R Good.*

ADMIRALS FLAME (IRE) BHB 56f60a **RR 62f 60a** 4814[14]
8 b g Doulab (USA) 7.4f **(61)** - Fan The Flame (Grundy) 10.3f **(65)**
Form - 01400
Record 1999 - 1st:1 2nd:0 3rd:0 Ran:5
Pre1999 - 1st:5 2nd:3 3rd:4 Ran:46
Win Prizemoney £21,756 *Total Prizemoney* £30,190
Wins * **1999** Jun Leices (G-S) H 8f 55 62
* 1998 Jun Windso (SFT) H 8.3f 55 60+
* 1996 Aug Windso (G-F) H 8.3f 74 80 <
* 1995 Jly Kempto (G-F) H 8f 66 72+
* 1995 Jun Windso (GD) H 8.3f 60 64+
1999 Turf 1-5: (7f, 8f 1-4) (gd 1-2, g-f, frm 2)
Average gelding, effective 8f, acts on gd to g-f, best on gd. Turf high 62 - 1st of 20 giving 2lb to Internal Affair (12 Jun Leicester RF 1946). **C F Wall [6-51] Mrs C A Wall.*

ADMIRAL'S GUEST (IRE) BHB 35f **RR** 2536[16]
7 ch g Be My Guest (USA) 10.2f **(66)** - Watership (USA) (Foolish Pleasure (USA)) 8.9f **(72)**

Form - 0
Record 1999 - 1st:0 2nd:0 3rd:0 Ran:1
Pre1999 - 1st:0 2nd:0 3rd:0 Ran:7
1999 Turf 0-1: (14f) (g-f)
Very poor gelding, has worn blinkers.
**W Clay [0-31] J R Jardine (from G Harwood [0-7] Spt 1995).*

ADMIRALS PLACE (IRE) BHB 64f58a **RR 67f 58a** 4930[8]

3 ch c Perugino (USA) - Royal Daughter (High Top) 10.2f **(67)**
Form - 331226128
Record 1999 - 1st:2 2nd:3 3rd:2 Ran:9
Pre1999 - 1st:0 2nd:0 3rd:0 Ran:2
Win Prizemoney £5,064 *Total Prizemoney* £9,195
Wins * 1999 Spt Beverl (SFT) H 9.9f 55 60 <
*** 1999** *Jun Lingfi (STD) H 8f 54 58*
1999 Turf 1-4: (10f 1-4) (g-s 1-2, g-f 2) 1999 AW 1-5: (6f, 7f, 8f 1-1, 9f, 12f) (Equi 1-3, Fibr 2)
Neat, average colt, effective 8 to 10f, best at 10f, acts on g-s - acts on AW, likes left handed tracks, prefers tight tracks. Turf high 67 (began Aug) - 2nd of 17 getting 7lb from Eyeballs Out (5 Oct Nottingham 10f g-s RF 4733) - also 1st of 18 giving 2lb to Silent Sound (21 Spt Beverley RF 4448). AW high 58 - 2nd of 11 getting 5lb from The Shadow (23 Jly Wolverhampton 9f Fibr RF 3079) - also 1st of 8 giving 10lb to Tick N Pick (19 Jun Lingfield RF 2151).
**R W Armstrong [2-11] C G Donovan.*

ADMIRALS SECRET (USA) BHB 50f40a **RR 51f 40a** 2162[7]

10 ch g Secreto (USA) 9.9f **(72)** - Noble Mistress (USA) (Vaguely Noble) 10.1f **(72)**
Form - 70067
Record 1999 - 1st:0 2nd:0 3rd:0 Ran:5
Pre1999 - 1st:9 2nd:7 3rd:4 Ran:62
Win Prizemoney £26,202 *Total Prizemoney* £35,812
Wins * 1998 Jun Lingfi (GD) H 11.5f 64 68
* 1998 Jun Lingfi (GD) H 11.5f 62 61
* 1998 Apr Bright (GD) H 11.9f 47 57
* 1997 Jly Windso (G-F) H 11.6f 50 53
* 1995 Aug Catter (G-F) H 13.8f 67 72 <
* 1995 Jun Catter (GD) H 12f 62 65
* 1995 May Pontef (GD) H 12f 55 57
1999 Turf 0-4: (12f 4) (g-f 3, frm) 1999 AW 0-1: (12f) (Fibr)
Fair gelding, effective 11 to 12f, best at 11f, acts on frm, prefers left handed tracks, favours tight tracks. Turf high 53.
**C F Wall [9-69] Mrs C A Wall.*

ADNAAN (IRE) BHB 105f **RR 113f** 4523[2]

3 ch c Nashwan (USA) 10.3f **(79)** - Whakilyric (USA) (Miswaki (USA)) 9f **(81)**
Form - 851332
Record 1999 - 1st:1 2nd:1 3rd:2 Ran:6
Pre1999 - 1st:2 2nd:2 3rd:1 Ran:5
Win Prizemoney £20,307 *Total Prizemoney* £33,743
Wins * 1999 Jly Newmar (G-F) 12f 109 <
* 1998 Oct Newmar (SFT) L 10f 93
* 1998 Oct Leices (G-S) 10f 86+
1999 Turf 1-6: (10f 2, 12f 1-2, 14f 2) (gd 3, frm 1-3)
Scopey, Group-class colt, effective 12 to 14f, best at 12f, acts on gd to frm, best on frm, has worn blinkers, prefers right handed tracks. Turf high 113 - 3rd of 6 to Compton Ace (27 Jly Goodwood 12f frm RF 3168) - also 1st of 6 getting 9lb from Memorise (16 Jly Newmarket RF 2882). Something of an equine Adonis, he beat an out of form field at Newmarket in July and ran his best race when finishing a close third in the Goodwood Sport on 5 March Stakes. Blinkered at Haydock in September, he may not be one to trust implicitly. **J L Dunlop [3-11] Hamdan Al Maktoum.*

ADOBE BHB 49f47a **RR 43f 47a** 5191[10]

4 b g Green Desert (USA) 7.8f **(78)** - Shamshir (Kris) 9.5f **(73)**
Form - 30308021821848053300
Record 1999 - 1st:2 2nd:2 3rd:4 Ran:20
Pre1999 - 1st:0 2nd:0 3rd:0 Ran:4
Win Prizemoney £6,320 *Total Prizemoney* £10,210
Wins * 1999 Jly Nottin (G-F) H 8.2f 51 55 <
*** 1999** Jun Bath (GD) H 8f 45 54
1999 Turf 2-19: (7f 2, 8f 2-15, 9f, 10f) (hvy, sft 2, g-s, gd 5, g-f 3, frm 2-7) 1999 AW 0-1: (8f) (Fibr)
Moderate gelding, effective 8f, acts on g-f to frm, best on frm, prefers left handed tracks, likes tight tracks. Turf high 55 - 4th of 17 to Noble Cyrano (6 Aug Haydock 8f g-f RF 3417) - also 1st of 16 giving 14lb to Dark Age (23 Jly Nottingham RF 3068).
**W M Brisbourne [2-20] P R Kirk (from J H M Gosden [0-4] Aug 1998).*

ADORA'S DREAM (IRE) BHB 42f **RR 36f** 597[8]

3 b c Mujtahid (USA) 7.4f **(69)** - Shady Bank (USA) **(42f)** (Alleged (USA)) 10f **(76)**
Form - 08
Record 1999 - 1st:0 2nd:0 3rd:0 Ran:2
Pre1999 - 1st:0 2nd:0 3rd:0 Ran:2
1999 Turf 0-1: (13f) (gd) 1999 AW 0-1: (8f) (Fibr)
Lengthy, very moderate colt, has worn blinkers.
**J W Hills [0-4] George Tong.*

ADORNMENT BHB 60f55a **RR 66?f 55a** 4938[12]

3 b f Magic Ring (IRE) 6.5f **(64)** -Miss Loving (Northfields (USA)) 9f **(72)**
Form - 06040000
Record 1999 - 1st:0 2nd:0 3rd:0 Ran:8
Win Prizemoney £0 *Total Prizemoney* £187
1999 Turf 0-7: (6f 4, 7f 2, 8f) (hvy, g-s, gd 2, g-f 3) 1999 AW 0-1: (6f) (Fibr)
Average filly, effective 7f, acts on gd. Turf high 66. Becoming disappointing.
**K McAuliffe [0-1] K W J McAuliffe (from J C Harley in IRE [0-7] Spt 1999).*

ADRENALIN BHB 49f41a **RR 54df 41a** 163[14]

4 ch g Risk Me (FR) 8f **(53)** -High Cairn (FR) (Ela-Mana-Mou) 10.1f **(70)**
Form - 00
Record 1999 - 1st:0 2nd:0 3rd:0 Ran:1
Pre1999 - 1st:1 2nd:0 3rd:1 Ran:12
Win Prizemoney £2,085 *Total Prizemoney* £2,538
Wins * 1998 *Feb Southw (STD) 6f 59* <
1999 AW 0-1: (6f) (Fibr)
Scopey, fair gelding, has broken blood-vessels, effective 6f, - acts on Fibr, has worn blinkers, favours left handed tracks, favours tight tracks.
**T T Clement [1-8] C Holcroft (from Mrs J R Ramsden [0-5] Jly 1997).*

ADULATION (USA) BHB 66f75a **RR 60f 75a** 4729[5]

5 ch g Sheikh Albadou 9.2f **(75)** - Pedestal (High Line) 10.3f **(70)**
Form - 2804005
Record 1999 - 1st:0 2nd:1 3rd:0 Ran:7
Pre1999 - 1st:0 2nd:2 3rd:2 Ran:4
Win Prizemoney £0 *Total Prizemoney* £4,725
1999 Turf 0-6: (7f 2, 8f 4) (g-s, gd 2, g-f 2, frm) 1999 AW 0-1: (8f) (Fibr)
Above-average gelding, effective 8f, acts on g-f to frm - acts on Fibr, likes tight tracks. Turf high 75 - 4th of 12 giving 5lb to Night Chorus (23 Jun Warwick 8f g-f RF 2257). (1st run) - 2nd of 12 giving 20lb to Tipsy (10 Apr Wolverhampton 8f Fibr RF 0641). Becoming disappointing.
**P W Chapple-Hyam [0-11] Chapple Hyam,Bloomsb Collins.*

AEGEAN BHB 31f26a **RR 36f 26a** 2264[9]

5 b g Rock Hopper 10.6f **(54)** - Sayulita (Habitat) 9.4f **(70)**
Form - 0
Record 1999 - 1st:0 2nd:0 3rd:0 Ran:1
Pre1999 - 1st:0 2nd:0 3rd:0 Ran:5
1999 Turf 0-1: (8f) (hrd)
Very moderate gelding, has worn blinkers.
**Mrs S J Smith [0-1] R Mellish, Mrs A Skene & W S Skene (from K T Ivory [0-2] Aug 1997).*

AEGEAN DREAM (IRE) BHB 78f **RR 81f** 4823[5]

3 b f Royal Academy (USA) 7.8f **(77)** - L'Ideale (USA) (Alysheba (USA)) 9f **(84)**
Form - 82225105
Record 1999 - 1st:1 2nd:3 3rd:0 Ran:8
Win Prizemoney £3,777 *Total Prizemoney* £7,342
Wins * 1999 Spt Epsom (GD) 8.5f 81 <
1999 Turf 1-8: (8f, 9f 1-1, 10f 6) (gd, g-f 1-3, frm 4)
Lengthy, decent filly, effective 9 to 10f, best at 10f, acts on g-f to frm, best on g-f, likes tight tracks. Turf high 81 - 1st of 9 getting 5lb from Alfath (3 Spt Epsom RF 4120). **R Hannon [1-8] Theobalds Stud.*

AEGEAN FLAME BHB 70f **RR 61f** 4329[10]

3 ch f Anshan 8.2f **(63)** - Dizzydaisy **(38f 52a)** (Sharpo) 7.7f **(59)**
Form - 040000

Record 1999 - 1st:0 2nd:0 3rd:0 Ran:6
Pre1999 - 1st:2 2nd:2 3rd:2 Ran:8
Win Prizemoney £9,309 *Total Prizemoney* £13,166
Wins 1998 Jly Newbur (GD) 5.2f 78 <
1998 Jly Ripon (GD) 5f 77
1999 Turf 0-6: (5f, 6f 3, 7f, 8f) (g-s, gd, g-f 3, frm)
Leggy, average filly, effective 5f, acts on g-s to g-f. Turf high 80 - 4th of 9 getting 9lb from Damalis (24 Apr Sandown 5f g-s RF 0842). Becoming disappointing.
**B J Meehan [0-6] Theobalds Stud (from K T Ivory [2-8] Jly 1998).*

AEGEAN GLORY BHB 47f46a **RR 49f 46a** 4079[20]
3 b f Shareef Dancer (USA) 10.1f **(67)** - Sayulita (Habitat) 9.4f **(70)**
Form - 0502033340
Record 1999 - 1st:0 2nd:1 3rd:3 Ran:10
Pre1999 - 1st:0 2nd:0 3rd:0 Ran:1
Win Prizemoney £0 *Total Prizemoney* £2,099
1999 Turf 0-8: (7f 3, 8f, 9f 2, 10f 2) (gd 2, g-f 2, frm 4) 1999 AW 0-2: (10f 2) (Equi 2)
Workmanlike, moderate filly, effective 8f, acts on gd. Turf high 62 - 2nd of 9 getting 5lb from Mytton's Moment (5 Jun Newmarket 8f gd RF 1771). AW high 46 (began Jly).
**J G M O'Shea [0-3] Gary Roberts (from R M Flower [0-3] Jly 1999).*

AEGEAN WIND RR 20f 5207[14]
2 b c Dolphin Street (FR) - Perdicula (IRE) (Persian Heights)
Form - 0
Record 1999 - 1st:0 2nd:0 3rd:0 Ran:1
1999 Turf 0-1: (7f) (g-s)
Currently little account colt. **J L Dunlop [0-1] Theobalds Stud.*

AESOPS (USA) BHB 93f **RR 81f** 4754[12]
3 ch c Diesis 9f **(80)** -Affirmative Fable (USA) (Affirmed (USA)) 9.3f **(79)**
Form - 4160
Record 1999 - 1st:1 2nd:0 3rd:0 Ran:4
Pre1999 - 1st:0 2nd:1 3rd:1 Ran:2
Win Prizemoney £4,854 *Total Prizemoney* £7,380
Wins * **1999** Aug Yarmou (GD) 10.1f 80++ <
1999 Turf 1-4: (8f, 10f 1-3) (gd 1-2, g-f 2)
Scopey, decent colt, effective 8 to 10f, best at 10f, acts on gd to g-f, best on g-f. Turf high 81 (1st run) - 4th of 15 to Mirjan (13 Apr Newmarket 10f g-f RF 0668) - also 1st of 7 giving 5lb to Sanariya (19 Aug Yarmouth RF 3763). Looked useful at Yarmouth, but tends to pull too hard. **J H M Gosden [1-6] Sheikh Mohammed.*

AFAAN (IRE) BHB 95f80a **RR 98f 80a** 4873[9]
6 ch h Cadeaux Genereux 7.9f **(76)** - Rawaabe (USA) (Nureyev (USA)) 8.7f **(78)**
Form - 688057550
Record 1999 - 1st:0 2nd:0 3rd:0 Ran:9
Pre1999 - 1st:6 2nd:8 3rd:3 Ran:29
Win Prizemoney £21,548 *Total Prizemoney* £38,739
Wins * 1998 Jly Newmar (GD) H 5f 76 91+ <
* 1998 Jly Catter (FRM) H 5f 73 79
* 1997 *Dec Southw (STD) H 5f 65 72+*
* 1997 Nov Redcar (GD) 5f 79
* 1997 Oct Pontef (G-S) H 5f 62 67
* 1997 May Redcar (G-F) H 6f 56 64
1999 Turf 0-9: (5f 8, 6f) (g-s, gd 5, g-f, frm 2)
Very useful horse, effective 5f, acts on gd to frm, best on gd, often wears blinkers (extremely effectively). Turf high 101. Exceptionally speedy, he is best at the minimum trip but difficult to place. Perhaps a couple of outings in claimers would help to boost his confidence. **R F Marvin [6-38] Afaan Partnership.*

AFARKA (IRE) BHB 57f **RR 78f** 3084[8]
6 b m Kahyasi 12.9f **(74)** - Afasara 00
Form - 8
Record 1999 - 1st:0 2nd:0 3rd:0 Ran:1
Pre1999 - 1st:2 2nd:4 3rd:0 Ran:16
Win Prizemoney £9,932 *Total Prizemoney* £14,825
Wins 1996 Spt Fairyh (G-F) H 12f 78 63 <
1996 Aug Tralee (G-Y) 12f 62
1999 AW 0-1: (16f) (Fibr)
Above-average mare, has worn blinkers.
**B Palling [0-3] Brennan Accountants (from S J Treacy in IRE [4-28] Aug 1998).*

AFFIDAVIT RR 60f 2497[3]
3 b f Slip Anchor 12.7f **(75)** -Lady Barrister(Law Society(USA)) 9.9f **(70)**
Form - 042333
Record 1999 - 1st:0 2nd:1 3rd:3 Ran:6
Pre1999 - 1st:0 2nd:0 3rd:0 Ran:2
Win Prizemoney £0 *Total Prizemoney* £3,380
1999 Turf 0-6: (10f, 12f 2, 13f, 14f 2) (gd 3, g-f, frm 2)
Small, average filly, effective 12 to 14f, acts on gd to frm, best on gd, prefers tight tracks. Turf high 63 - 2nd of 11 giving 8lb to Bustling Rio (18 May Pontefract 12f gd RF 1303). Consistent.
**M L W Bell [0-8] Cheveley Park Stud.*

AFFIRMED SUCCESS (USA) RR 5227a[12]
5 b g Affirmed (USA) 10.3f **(75)** - Towering Success (USA) (Irish Tower (USA))
Form - 0
1999 AW 0-1: (6f) (Dirt)
Currently useful gelding, unplaced in the last two Breeders' Cup Sprints. **R Schosberg in USA [0-2].*

AFICIONADO (IRE) BHB 41f41a **RR 40f 41a** 134[9]
5 b g Marju (IRE) 9.2f **(76)** - Haneena (Habitat) 9.4f **(70)**
Form - 0
Record 1999 - 1st:0 2nd:0 3rd:0 Ran:1
Pre1999 - 1st:1 2nd:3 3rd:3 Ran:24
Win Prizemoney £4,077 *Total Prizemoney* £7,950
Wins 1996 Nov Newmar (GD) S 8f 71 <
1999 AW 0-1: (10f) (Equi)
Moderate gelding, effective 8f, acts on gd to g-f, has worn blinkers. Inconsistent.
**R J Hodges [0-26] Mrs C J Cole (from R F JohnsonHoughton [1-9] Nov 1996).*

AFREET RR 53f 4180[7]
3 ch c Kris 10f **(75)** - Cambara (Dancing Brave (USA)) 8.4f **(76)**
Form - 7
Record 1999 - 1st:0 2nd:0 3rd:0 Ran:1
1999 Turf 0-1: (7f) (frm)
Scopey, currently fair colt.
**A C Stewart [0-1] Sheikh Ahmed Al Maktoum.*

AFRICA (IRE) RR 62f 5158[15]
2 b f Namaqualand (USA) - Tannerrun (IRE) **(70df)** (Runnett) 7f **(59)**
Form - 0U0514267330
Record 1999 - 1st:1 2nd:1 3rd:2 Ran:12
Win Prizemoney £2,038 *Total Prizemoney* £4,147
Wins * **1999** Jly Catter (GD) S 7f 57 <
1999 Turf 1-12: (5f 3, 6f, 7f 1-7, 8f) (gd 4, g-f 1-2, frm 5, hrd)
Average filly, effective 7f, acts on gd to hrd, best on frm, has worn blinkers. Turf high 62 - 4th of 12 getting 1lb from It's Allowed (30 Jly Thirsk 7f frm RF 3256) - also 1st of 18 from Dakisi Royale (21 Jly Catterick RF 3003). Consistent.
**T D Barron [1-12] Laurence O'Kane.*

AFRICAN PETE BHB 66f **RR 78f** 5063[6]
2 b c Lugana Beach 7f **(63)** - Highland Bonnie (Dreams to Reality (USA)) 6.4f **(73)**
Form - 036
Record 1999 - 1st:0 2nd:0 3rd:1 Ran:3
Win Prizemoney £0 *Total Prizemoney* £265
1999 Turf 0-3: (6f 2, 8f) (gd, g-f 2)
Currently above-average colt. Turf high 78.
**G G Margarson [0-3] Dr Neil Dorward.*

AFRICAN SUN (IRE) BHB 33f29a **RR 55?f 29a** 5165[8]
6 b g Mtoto 11.5f **(71)** - Nuit D'Ete (USA) (Super Concorde (USA)) 10.9f **(66)**
Form - 00658
Record 1999 - 1st:0 2nd:0 3rd:0 Ran:5
Pre1999 - 1st:0 2nd:1 3rd:0 Ran:33
Win Prizemoney £0 *Total Prizemoney* £1,281
1999 Turf 0-5: (8f, 10f 2, 12f, 14f) (g-s 2, gd, g-f, frm)
Fair gelding, has worn blinkers. Turf high 55.
**M C Chapman [2-57] Noel Fletcher (from B Hanbury [0-7] Jun 1996).*

AFRIETINO BHB 34f38a **RR 23f 38a** 3295^{14}
5 b m Tina's Pet 7.4f **(56)** - African Lass (Skyliner) 7.3f **(53)**
Form - 0560060
Record 1999 - 1st:0 2nd:0 3rd:0 Ran:7
1999 Turf 0-5: (5f 2, 6f 2, 8f) (gd 2, g-f, frm 2) 1999 AW 0-2: (5f, 7f) (Fibr 2)
Very moderate filly, had worn blinkers. Turf high 36. AW high 37. (DEAD) **Mrs N Macauley [0-7] Aubrey Ellis.*

AFTER EIGHT BHB 37f46a **RR 37f 46a** 4293^{16}
4 b g Presidium 7.5f **(56)** - Vickenda (Giacometti) 11.2f **(56)**
Form - 00060500670
Record 1999 - 1st:0 2nd:0 3rd:0 Ran:9
Pre1999 - 1st:1 2nd:1 3rd:1 Ran:15
Win Prizemoney £1,838 *Total Prizemoney* £2,938
Wins * 1998 *Feb Lingfi (STD) S 6f 63* <
1999 Turf 0-7: (5f, 6f 2, 7f 3, 8f) (gd, g-f 2, frm 4) 1999 AW 0-2: (6f 2) (Equi 2)
Small, moderate gelding, effective 6f, - acts on Equi, often wears blinkers, likes tight tracks. Turf high 39. AW high 40. Inconsistent. **M S Saunders [1-18] M S Saunders (from R W Armstrong [0-6] Jan 1998).*

AFTERJACKO (IRE) BHB 83f **RR 84f** 4817^{3}
3 ch c Seattle Dancer (USA) 10.1f **(74)** - Shilka (Soviet Star (USA))
Form - 77153
Record 1999 - 1st:1 2nd:0 3rd:1 Ran:5
Win Prizemoney £3,974 *Total Prizemoney* £5,089
Wins * **1999** Spt Bath (FRM) 11.7f 84 <
1999 Turf 1-5: (8f, 9f, 10f, 12f 1-2) (gd 2, g-f, frm 1-2)
Scopey, decent colt. Turf high 89 (began Aug) - 3rd of 8 giving 3lb to High Tatra (11 Oct Leicester 12f gd RF 4817) - also 1st of 9 from Anamore (6 Spt Bath RF 4158). Seemed to appreciate the step up in distance when winning a Bath maiden on his third start, though it was not the greatest of races. May be an interesting prospect over hurdles. **D R C Elsworth [1-5] D R C Elsworth.*

AFTER THE BLUE (IRE) **RR 75f** 5102^{6}
2 b c Last Tycoon 9.4f **(73)** - Sudden Interest (FR) (Highest Honor (FR))
Form - 6
Record 1999 - 1st:0 2nd:0 3rd:0 Ran:1
1999 Turf 0-1: (8f) (gd)
Currently above-average colt.
**M R Channon [0-1] Timberhill Racing Partnership.*

AGAINST THE BILL (IRE) BHB 42f **RR 37f** 2362^{5}
3 b g Petorius 8f **(66)** - Galka (Deep Diver) 6.6f **(62)**
Form - 86805075
Record 1999 - 1st:0 2nd:0 3rd:0 Ran:8
1999 Turf 0-8: (5f 3, 6f 4, 7f) (gd 3, g-f 4, frm)
Strong, very moderate gelding, often wore blinkers. Turf high 40. Consistent. (DEAD) **T D Easterby [0-8] I Bray.*

AGANON BHB 49f **RR 25f** 3435^{15}
4 b g Aragon 7.7f **(58)** - Plain Tree (Wolver Hollow) 8f **(56)**
Form - 000
Record 1999 - 1st:0 2nd:0 3rd:0 Ran:3
Pre1999 - 1st:0 2nd:0 3rd:0 Ran:4
1999 Turf 0-3: (6f, 7f, 8f) (frm 3)
Scopey, little account gelding, has worn blinkers. Turf high 25 (began Jly). **M R Channon [0-7] Kingsdown Racing.*

AGENT LE BLANC (IRE) BHB 70f **RR 71f** 3666^{7}
4 b g Kahyasi 12.9f **(74)** - White Witch (USA) (Nureyev (USA)) 8.7f **(78)**
Form - 5287
Record 1999 - 1st:0 2nd:1 3rd:0 Ran:4
Pre1999 - 1st:0 2nd:1 3rd:0 Ran:3
Win Prizemoney £0 *Total Prizemoney* £1,944
1999 Turf 0-4: (10f, 12f, 15f, 16f) (gd, g-f, frm 2)
Workmanlike, above-average gelding, effective 10 to 16f, acts on g-f to frm, best on frm. Turf high 71 - 8th of 17 giving 21lb to Northern Motto (10 Jly Chester 16f frm RF 2709).
**T J Etherington [0-7] E Oliver.*

AGENT MULDER BHB 75f58a **RR 76f 58a** 5033^{10}
5 b g Kylian (USA) 8.1f **(66)** - Precious Caroline (IRE) **(26a)** (The Noble Player (USA)) 6.5f **(67)**
Form - 51461700
Record 1999 - 1st:2 2nd:0 3rd:0 Ran:8
Pre1999 - 1st:3 2nd:2 3rd:1 Ran:15
Win Prizemoney £19,466 *Total Prizemoney* £22,843
Wins * **1999** Jun Salisb (GD) H 6f 70 77 <
* **1999** Apr Nottin (SFT) H 6.1f 64 70
* 1998 Oct Nottin (SFT) 6.1f 58
* 1998 Oct Nottin (SFT) 6.1f 62
* 1997 Jun Windso (G-F) H 8.3f 55 61
1999 Turf 2-7: (6f 2-5, 7f 2) (sft, g-s, gd 1-4, g-f 1-1) 1999 AW 0-1: (7f) (Fibr)
Above-average gelding, effective 6f, acts on gd to g-f, best on gd, often wears blinkers (extremely effectively). Turf high 77 - 1st of 19 giving 6lb to Frederick James (8 Jun Salisbury RF 1815) - also 1st of 20 giving 4lb to Rum Lad (19 Apr Nottingham RF 0748). A winner twice last season, he has a fine winning record at Nottingham. Six furlongs and cut in the ground seem to suit.
**P D Cundell [5-23] P D Cundell.*

AGIOTAGE BHB 73f **RR 76f** 3791^{8}
3 br c Zafonic (USA) 9f **(83)** - Rakli **(85+f)** (Warning)
Form - 06048
Record 1999 - 1st:0 2nd:0 3rd:0 Ran:5
Pre1999 - 1st:1 2nd:0 3rd:0 Ran:3
Win Prizemoney £3,525 *Total Prizemoney* £4,234
Wins * 1998 Nov Redcar (G-S) 7f 84+ <
1999 Turf 0-5: (9f 2, 10f 3) (gd 2, g-f 3)
Scopey, above-average colt, effective 7f, acts on gd, has worn blinkers. Turf high 78. **H R A Cecil [1-8] K Abdulla.*

AGITANDO (IRE) BHB 90f **RR 92f** 4571^{6}
3 b g Tenby 10.4f **(76)** - Crown Rose (Dara Monarch) 8.8f **(59)**
Form - 8610226
Record 1999 - 1st:1 2nd:2 3rd:0 Ran:7
Win Prizemoney £3,926 *Total Prizemoney* £9,300
Wins * **1999** Jun Goodwo (G-F) 9.9f 81+ <
1999 Turf 1-7: (8f, 10f 1-3, 12f 3) (sft, g-s, gd, g-f 2, frm 1-2)
Neat, useful gelding, effective 12f, acts on sft to frm. Turf high 92 - 2nd of 7 getting 8lb from Serpentine (2 Spt York 12f frm RF 4102). Unraced at two, he got off the mark in a Goodwood maiden over ten furlongs on in June, but was down the field in a competitive handicap at the same track next time. Better efforts in decent handicaps subsequently. **R Charlton [1-7] K Abdulla.*

AGNES WORLD (USA) **RR 120f** $4777a^{1}$
4 c Danzig (USA) 8.1f **(88)** - Mysteries (USA) (Seattle Slew (USA)) 9.4f **(76)**
Form - 1
1999 Turf 1-1: (5f 1-1) (sft 1-1)
Currently very high-class colt. (1st run) - 1st of 14 giving 3lb to Imperial Beauty (3 Oct Longchamp RF 4777a). Beat Europe's top sprinters in the Prix de L'Abbaye, a fine feat of training.
**H Mori in JPN [1-1] T Watanabe.*

AGOL LACK (USA) **RR 109f** $4659a^{2}$
3 ch c Gulch (USA) 9.6f **(79)** - Garvin's Gal (USA) (Seattle Slew (USA)) 9.4f **(76)**
Form - 2
1999 Turf 0-1: (10f) (g-s)
Currently Pattern-class colt. (1st run) - 2nd of 8 to Chelsea Manor (22 Spt Maisons-Laffitte 10f g-s RF 4659a). **A Fabre in FR [0-1].*

AGRIPPINA BHB 100f **RR 95f** 4680^{1}
2 b f Timeless Times (USA) 6.1f **(56)** - Boadicea's Chariot (Commanche Run) 8.5f **(58)**
Form - 211
Record 1999 - 1st:2 2nd:1 3rd:0 Ran:3
Win Prizemoney £15,951 *Total Prizemoney* £17,101
Wins * **1999** Oct Newmar (SFT) L 7f 95 <
* **1999** Spt Ayr (G-S) 7f 77
1999 Turf 2-3: (5f, 7f 2-2) (gd 2-2, g-f)
Currently very useful filly. Turf high 95 (began Spt) - 1st of 12 from High Walden (2 Oct Newmarket RF 4680). She made all at Ayr in September and underlined her adaptability when pouncing late to win a Listed event at Newmarket the following month. Held in high regard by her shrewd connections, she is bred to stay beyond a mile and is an interesting prospect.
**A Bailey [2-3] Mrs W & Ms M Wright & Mrs F S Williams.*

AGUA CABALLO (IRE) BHB 64f **RR 82f** 5164[6]
2 b g Petorius 8f **(66)** - Beauty Appeal (USA) (Shadeed (USA)) 8.2f **(70)**
Form - 31641070656
Record 1999 - 1st:2 2nd:0 3rd:1 Ran:11
Win Prizemoney £5,246 *Total Prizemoney* £6,264
Wins * 1999 Jly Beverl (G-F) C 5f 82 <
*** 1999** Jun Carlis (GD) 5f 80
1999 Turf 2-11: (5f 2-5, 6f 4, 7f 2) (g-s 2, gd 1-4, g-f 1-3, frm, hrd)
Decent gelding, effective 5f, acts on gd to g-f. Turf high 82 - 1st of 14 giving 10lb to Blackpool Mamma's (19 Jly Beverley RF 2944) - also 1st of 11 from Pretending (10 Jun Carlisle RF 1874).
**S E Kettlewell [2-11] Middleham Park Racing XII.*

AHDAAB (USA) BHB 64f **RR 64f** 4445[8]
3 ch f Rahy (USA) 9.1f **(80)** - Dish Dash (Bustino) 10.4f **(64)**
Form - 358
Record 1999 - 1st:0 2nd:0 3rd:1 Ran:3
Pre1999 - 1st:0 2nd:0 3rd:0 Ran:1
Win Prizemoney £0 *Total Prizemoney* £696
1999 Turf 0-3: (7f, 10f 2) (g-s, gd, frm)
Light-framed, average filly. Turf high 64 (began Aug).
**R W Armstrong [0-4] Hamdan Al Maktoum.*

AHOUOD BHB 50f **RR 48f** 2936[6]
3 b f Merdon Melody 6.8f **(56)** - Balidilemma (Balidar) 7.9f **(63)**
Form - 67036
Record 1999 - 1st:0 2nd:0 3rd:1 Ran:4
Pre1999 - 1st:0 2nd:0 3rd:0 Ran:1
Win Prizemoney £0 *Total Prizemoney* £408
1999 Turf 0-4: (6f 2, 8f, 10f) (g-f, frm 3)
Workmanlike, moderate filly. Turf high 48 - 3rd of 18 getting 12lb from Diamond Geezer (5 Jly Windsor 6f frm RF 2571).
**K Mahdi [0-5] Solaiman Alsaiary.*

AIMA (IRE) BHB 96f **RR 81f** 3692[4]
2 b br c Brief Truce (USA) 9.1f **(73)** - Palmyra (GER) (Arratos (FR)) 12.2f **(60)**
Form - 7224
Record 1999 - 1st:0 2nd:2 3rd:0 Ran:4
Win Prizemoney £0 *Total Prizemoney* £4,199
1999 Turf 0-4: (6f, 7f 3) (g-f, frm 3)
Decent colt. Turf high 81 - 4th of 5 getting 3lb from King's Best (17 Aug York 7f g-f RF 3692). Showed promising form in 1999, and should pay his way at three.
**G C H Chung [0-4] The Happy Valley Leisure Club.*

AIRA FORCE (USA) BHB 81f **RR 81f** 4444[8]
2 ch g Dehere (USA) - Cinnamon Splendor (USA) (Trempolino (USA)) 12f **(71)**
Form - 83318
Record 1999 - 1st:1 2nd:0 3rd:2 Ran:5
Win Prizemoney £3,805 *Total Prizemoney* £4,667
Wins * 1999 Spt Haydoc (G-F) 5f 81 <
1999 Turf 1-5: (5f 1-5) (g-s, g-f 1-2, frm 2)
Decent gelding. Turf high 81 - 1st of 13 giving 5lb to Agrippina (3 Spt Haydock RF 4123). **J Noseda [1-5] Mrs H Raw.*

AIR ATTACHE (USA) BHB 56f **RR 59f** 4999[2]
4 b g Sky Classic (CAN) 10f **(83)** - Diplomatic Cover (USA) (Roberto (USA)) 10f **(76)**
Form - 0626440322
Record 1999 - 1st:0 2nd:3 3rd:1 Ran:10
Pre1999 - 1st:0 2nd:2 3rd:2 Ran:10
Win Prizemoney £0 *Total Prizemoney* £7,851
1999 Turf 0-8: (10f 2, 11f, 12f 4, 14f) (gd 5, g-f, frm 2) 1999 AW 0-2: (12f 2) (Equi, Fibr)
Workmanlike, average gelding, effective 12 to 14f, best at 12f, acts on gd to frm, has worn blinkers, likes tight tracks. Turf high 62. AW high 62 (began Oct). Consistent.
**D Sasse [0-10] Christopher Ranson (from G Lewis [0-10] Oct 1998).*

AIR DEFENCE RR 78f 4840[2]
2 br c Warning 8.1f **(77)** - Cruising Height (Shirley Heights) 10.3f **(74)**
Form - 2
Record 1999 - 1st:0 2nd:1 3rd:0 Ran:1
Win Prizemoney £0 *Total Prizemoney* £1,100
1999 Turf 0-1: (7f) (gd)
Currently above-average colt. (1st run) - 2nd of 15 to Ferzao (12 Oct Leicester 7f gd RF 4840). He will come into his own over middle distances at three. **B W Hills [0-1] K Abdulla.*

AIR JIHAD (JPN) RR 125f 2101a[1]
4 c Sakura Yutaka O (JPN) -Icy Goggle (JPN)(Royal Ski (USA)) 5f **(79)**
Form - 121
1999 Turf 1-2: (7f, 8f 1-1) (frm)
Currently top-class colt. Turf high 125 - 1st of 14 from Grass Wonder (13 Jun Fuchu RF 2101a). This very useful Japanese-trained colt ran a good second to Grass Wonder in the Keio Hai Spring Cup, before reversing the form on worse terms in the Yasuda Kinen. Won the Mile Championship at Kyoto in November.
**M Ito in JPN [2-3] Licky Field Co.*

AIR MARSHALL (IRE) BHB 100f **RR 91+f** 5037[4]
2 ch c In The Wings 11.2f **(77)** - Troyanna (Troy) 10.4f **(68)**
Form - 214
Record 1999 - 1st:1 2nd:1 3rd:0 Ran:3
Win Prizemoney £4,410 *Total Prizemoney* £14,190
Wins * 1999 Spt Goodwo (G-F) 8f 91+ <
1999 Turf 1-3: (7f, 8f 1-2) (g-s, g-f 1-1, frm)
Currently useful colt. Turf high 91 (began Aug) - also 1st of 7 from Halhoo Lammtarra (11 Spt Goodwood RF 4274). Touched off by Jalad on his Leicester debut, he made all to win his second start convincingly at Goodwood in September. A respectable fourth in the Racing Post Trophy, he is a useful middle-distance prospect.
**Sir Michael Stoute [1-3] Lord Weinstock.*

AIR OF ESTEEM BHB 69f69a **RR 65f 69a** 4802[16]
3 b g Forzando 7.2f **(63)** - Shadow Bird (Martinmas) 7.6f **(59)**
Form - 21281300260
Record 1999 - 1st:2 2nd:3 3rd:1 Ran:11
Pre1999 - 1st:0 2nd:0 3rd:0 Ran:1
Win Prizemoney £6,576 *Total Prizemoney* £10,278
Wins * 1999 Jun Haydoc (SFT) H 8.1f 69 80 <
*** 1999** *Jan Lingfi (STD) 8f 60*
1999 Turf 1-8: (8f 1-5, 9f 2, 10f) (gd 1-4, g-f, frm 3) 1999 AW 1-3: (8f 1-3) (Equi 1-1, Fibr 2)
Scopey, average gelding, effective 8f, acts on gd, prefers tight tracks. Turf high 80 - 1st of 16 from Col-Woody (4 Jun Haydock RF 1740). AW high 69. A winner on Equitrack at the start of the year, he got off the mark on turf at Haydock in June, but has been a little in-and-out since. He needs soft ground on turf.
**P C Haslam [2-12] Middleham Park Racing XV.*

AISLE BHB 61f61a **RR 58f 61a** 5150[1]
2 b c Arazi (USA) 9.2f **(74)** - Chancel (USA) **(47f 50a)** (Al Nasr (FR)) 9.3f **(68)**
Form - 0638711
Record 1999 - 1st:2 2nd:0 3rd:1 Ran:7
Win Prizemoney £6,077 *Total Prizemoney* £6,382
Wins * 1999 Nov Nottin (SFT) H 6.1f 55 58
*** 1999** *Oct Southw (STD) H 6f 53 61* <
1999 Turf 1-5: (5f 2, 6f 1-2, 7f) (g-s 1-1, gd 3, frm) 1999 AW 1-2: (6f 1-2) (Fibr 1-2)
Average colt, effective 6f, acts on g-s - acts on Fibr. Turf high 61 - also 1st of 13 getting 10lb from Frampant (1 Nov Nottingham RF 5150). AW high 61 (began Jly) - 1st of 15 getting 13lb from Janiceland (18 Oct Southwell RF 4937). He did not look anything special in his early starts, but showed improved form at the back-end.
**S R Bowring [2-4] Roland Wheatley (from I A Balding [0-3] Jly 1999).*

AIWAI (IRE) BHB 86f **RR 77f** 4942[14]
2 b c Thatching 7.8f **(69)** - Peach Melba (So Blessed) 8.7f **(67)**
Form - 820
Record 1999 - 1st:0 2nd:1 3rd:0 Ran:3
Win Prizemoney £0 *Total Prizemoney* £1,198
1999 Turf 0-3: (6f 2, 7f) (g-s, gd, frm)
Currently above-average colt. Turf high 77 (began Spt) - 2nd of 22 giving 4lb to Avezzano (16 Spt Ayr 6f g-s RF 4342).
**G C H Chung [0-3] The Happy Valley Leisure Club.*

AIX EN PROVENCE (USA) BHB 58f53a **RR 51f 53a** 4334[9]
4 b g Geiger Counter (USA) 7.8f **(85)** - Low Hill (Rousillon (USA)) 8.2f **(74)**
Form - 7800071050
Record 1999 - 1st:1 2nd:0 3rd:0 Ran:10

Pre1999 - 1st:2 2nd:0 3rd:1 Ran:7
Win Prizemoney £8,595 *Total Prizemoney* £10,953
Wins * 1999 Aug Yarmou (FRM) SH 8f 55 62
1997 Aug Ripon (G-F) 6f 84+
1997 Jun Ayr (GD) 6f 85+ <
1999 Turf 1-9: (7f 3, 8f 1-3, 10f 3) (sft, g-s, gd 3, g-f 1-4) 1999 AW 0-1: (8f) (Fibr)
Scopey, fair gelding, has broken blood-vessels. Turf high 71. Inconsistent.
**C A Dwyer [1-4] Cedar Lodge Syndicate (from M Johnston [2-13] Jun 1999).*

AJDAR BHB 34f44a **RR 24f 44a** 612[9]
8 b g Slip Anchor 12.7f **(75)** - Loucoum (FR) (Iron Duke (FR)) 8.8f **(60)**
Form - 74470
Record 1999 - 1st:0 2nd:0 3rd:0 Ran:5
Pre1999 - 1st:2 2nd:3 3rd:1 Ran:31
Win Prizemoney £3,957 *Total Prizemoney* £6,935
Wins * 1998 *Jan Southw (STD) H 12f 44 46+* <
1996 *Jan Southw (STD) H 11f 42 44*
1999 Turf 0-1: (12f) (g-f) 1999 AW 0-4: (11f, 12f 3) (Equi, Fibr 3)
Moderate gelding, effective 11 to 14f, best at 11f, - acts on Fibr, has worn blinkers, likes left handed tracks, favours tight tracks. AW high 46.
**Mrs S Lamyman [1-28] P Lamyman (from Miss Gay Kelleway [1-11] Jly 1996).*

AJHIBA (IRE) BHB 104f **RR 107+f** 4209[10]
3 ch f Barathea (IRE) - Welsh Love (Ela-Mana-Mou) 10.1f **(70)**
Form - 110
Record 1999 - 1st:2 2nd:0 3rd:0 Ran:3
Win Prizemoney £21,326 *Total Prizemoney* £21,326
Wins * 1999 Aug Salisb (G-S) L 9.9f 107 <
*** 1999** May Newmar (G-F) 8f 93
1999 Turf 2-3: (8f 1-1, 10f 1-1, 15f) (gd 1-2, frm 1-1)
Scopey, currently Pattern-class filly. Turf high 107 - 1st of 9 from Choirgirl (11 Aug Salisbury RF 3554). Beat some nice types in a Newmarket maiden on her debut, and followed up at Salisbury in Listed company. Tailed off in the Park Hill Stakes on her final start, however. **S bin Suroor [2-3] Godolphin.*

AJIG DANCER BHB 75f62a **RR 74f 62a** 4538[6]
4 b f Niniski (USA) 13.2f **(67)** - Gloire (Thatching) 8f **(66)**
Form - 854423203170826121476
Record 1999 - 1st:3 2nd:3 3rd:2 Ran:16
Pre1999 - 1st:1 2nd:2 3rd:1 Ran:19
Win Prizemoney £14,478 *Total Prizemoney* £23,087
Wins * 1999 Aug Yarmou (GD) H 7f 70 74
*** 1999** Aug Bright (G-F) 7f 68
*** 1999** Mar Warwic (G-S) H 7f 64 71
* 1997 Spt Bath (GD) 5.1f 82+ <
1999 Turf 3-12: (6f 3, 7f 3-8, 8f) (sft, g-s 1-2, gd 1-2, g-f 1-3, frm 4)
1999 AW 0-4: (7f 4) (Equi 4)
Strong, above-average filly, effective 6 to 7f, best at 7f, acts on g-s to g-f, best on gd. Turf high 74 - 1st of 9 giving 12lb to La Isla Bonita (29 Aug Yarmouth RF 4002) - also 1st of 14 giving 13lb to Strat's Quest (27 Mar Warwick RF 0491). AW high 62. She was given a fine ride by John Reid to win at Warwick on her first start back on turf last term and, after disappointing subsequently, she returned to winning ways at Brighton over seven furlongs on fast ground in August. Added to her tally with a win at Yarmouth.
**M R Channon [4-35] Timberhill Racing Partnership.*

AJJAE (IRE) BHB 41f **RR 48f** 5190[13]
3 b g High Estate 10.5f **(66)** - Lake Ormond (Kings Lake (USA)) 10.8f **(67)**
Form - 70251260
Record 1999 - 1st:1 2nd:2 3rd:0 Ran:8
Pre1999 - 1st:0 2nd:0 3rd:0 Ran:4
Win Prizemoney £2,402 *Total Prizemoney* £3,928
Wins * 1999 Aug Beverl (GD) C 7.5f 46 <
1999 Turf 1-8: (7f 1-3, 8f 3, 9f, 12f) (gd 2, g-f 2, frm 1-4)
Strong, moderate gelding, effective 7 to 9f, acts on frm, mostly wears blinkers (effectively), likes right handed tracks. Turf high 48 - 2nd of 13 getting 1lb from Murphy's Gold (6 Spt Hamilton 9f frm RF 4163) - also 1st of 10 getting 7lb from Future Coup (29 Aug Beverley RF 3991). **I Semple [1-12] Andy Dickie.*

AJNAD (IRE) BHB 57f74a **RR 57f 74a** 1100[13]
5 b g Efisio 7.7f **(69)** - Lotte Lenta (Gorytus (USA)) 7.8f **(60)**
Form - 2312630
Record 1999 - 1st:1 2nd:1 3rd:1 Ran:5
Pre1999 - 1st:0 2nd:3 3rd:3 Ran:18
Win Prizemoney £3,582 *Total Prizemoney* £8,767
Wins * 1999 *Jan Lingfi (STD) 6f 67* <
1999 Turf 0-2: (5f, 6f) (gd, hrd) 1999 AW 1-3: (6f 1-3) (Equi 1-2, Fibr)
Above-average gelding, effective 6f, - acts on AW, best on Equi, often wears blinkers, likes left handed tracks, likes tight tracks. Turf high 56. AW high 76 - 2nd of 14 giving 3lb to Mukarrab (14 Jan Lingfield 6f Equi RF 0095) - also 1st of 10 giving 16lb to Wild Thing (7 Jan Lingfield RF 0046). He has ability, but took a while to get his head in front. He did so in no uncertain terms on the Lingfield Equitrack and was unlucky not to follow up. He can win a decent handicap on sand, but does not look so good on turf.
**R F Marvin [1-22] J Shine (from C J Benstead [0-1] Aug 1996).*

AKALIM BHB 68f55a **RR 69f 55a** 5166[9]
6 b g Petong 7.6f **(58)** - Tiszta Sharok (Song) 7.2f **(61)**
Form - 05280210
Record 1999 - 1st:1 2nd:2 3rd:0 Ran:8
Pre1999 - 1st:3 2nd:3 3rd:3 Ran:27
Win Prizemoney £14,164 *Total Prizemoney* £19,712
Wins * 1999 Oct Newbur (SFT) H 7f 62 69
* 1998 Spt Chepst (G-S) H 7.1f 56 60
1995 Oct Nottin (G-F) H 6.1f 76 78 <
1995 Jly Newmar (GD) 6f 77
1999 Turf 1-8: (7f 1-8) (sft, g-s 1-4, gd 3)
Average gelding, effective 6 to 7f, best at 7f, acts on g-s to g-f, best on g-s, has worn blinkers, likes left handed tracks, excels at Brighton and Chepstow. Turf high 69 - 1st of 25 getting 4lb from Ca'd'oro (22 Oct Newbury RF 5033). Inconsistent.
**L G Cottrell [2-25] Mrs Lucy Halloran (from D Morley [2-10] Jly 1996).*

AKBAR (IRE) BHB 99f **RR 106f** 5221[7]
3 bb c Doyoun 10.7f **(69)** - Akishka (Nishapour (FR)) 9.1f **(61)**
Form - 52203237
Record 1999 - 1st:0 2nd:3 3rd:2 Ran:8
Pre1999 - 1st:1 2nd:0 3rd:1 Ran:2
Win Prizemoney £3,781 *Total Prizemoney* £22,229
Wins 1998 Oct Tipper (HVY) 7f 57 <
1999 Turf 0-8: (8f, 10f, 12f 5, 14f) (hvy, sft, g-s 2, gd 2, g-f 2)
Pattern-class colt, effective 10 to 14f, acts on gd to g-f. Turf high 106 - 3rd of 7 to Yeoman's Point (17 Jly Leopardstown 14f g-f RF 2995a). Ex-Irish, he ran a good race for Johnston at Ascot in October but lacks a turn of foot.
**M Johnston [0-2] Markus Graff (from FR [0-1] Spt 1999).*

AKEED (USA) RR 90f 5263a[4]
2 ch c Affirmed (USA) 10.3f **(75)** - Victorious Lil (CAN) (Vice Regent (CAN)) 8.7f **(74)**
Form - 144
Record 1999 - 1st:1 2nd:0 3rd:0 Ran:3
Win Prizemoney £6,758 *Total Prizemoney* £10,790
Wins * 1999 Spt York (G-F) 7f 85++ <
1999 Turf 1-3: (7f 1-3) (g-s, g-f, frm 1-1)
Currently useful colt. Turf high 90 (began Spt) - 4th of 8 to Touch Of The Blues (5 Nov Maisons-Laffitte 7f g-s RF 5263a) - also 1st of 10 from Peteuresque (1 Spt York RF 4083). Bolted up over seven furlongs on his York debut and the winning margin flatters the opposition. Failed to progress from that when most disappointing next time out at Leicester over the same trip. Sent off at 1/4 in the Midlands, he ran a decent race in a French Group two on his final start, but is not living up to his reputation. **P F I Cole [1-3].*

AKHIRA RR 87f 4982[5]
2 b f Emperor Jones (USA) -Fakhira (IRE) **(29f)**(Jareer (USA)) 5.9f **(75)**
Form - 45
Record 1999 - 1st:0 2nd:0 3rd:0 Ran:2
Win Prizemoney £0 *Total Prizemoney* £13,985
1999 Turf 0-2: (7f 2) (g-f 2)
Currently useful filly. Turf high 87 (1st run) (began Spt) - 4th of 17 getting 5lb from Inchlonaig (28 Spt Newmarket 7f g-f RF 4595). Sure to win a race or two judged on her juvenile form.
**S P C Woods [0-2] Dennis Yardy.*

ALAAMA (IRE) BHB 64f **RR 71f** 4446[12]
3 ch f Elmaamul (USA) 8.1f **(70)** - Rahik (Wassl) 9.7f **(62)**
Form - 24770
Record 1999 - 1st:0 2nd:1 3rd:0 Ran:5
Pre1999 - 1st:0 2nd:0 3rd:0 Ran:1
Win Prizemoney £0 *Total Prizemoney* £1,707
1999 Turf 0-5: (7f, 8f 3, 10f) (g-s, gd 2, g-f, hrd)
Workmanlike, above-average filly, effective 7 to 8f, acts on frm to hrd. Turf high 71 - 4th of 9 getting 5lb from Eaglesham (16 Jun Ripon 8f hrd RF 2062). **R W Armstrong [0-6] Hamdan Al Maktoum.*

ALABAMA JACKS (IRE) RR 105f 1906b[7]
3 ch c Magical Wonder (USA) 7.2f **(60)** - Oh Jemima
Form - 17
1999 Turf 1-2: (8f 1-2) (sft 1-1, gd)
Pattern-class colt, effective 8f, acts on sft. Turf high 104 (1st run) - 1st of 11 from Timboroa (25 Apr Capannelle RF 0930a). Trained by Kevin Prendergast as a juvenile, he did his new connections proud, making all to win the Italian 2,000 Guineas.
**R Feligioni in ITY [1-4] (from K Prendergast in IRE [1-4] Jly 1998).*

ALABAMA WURLEY BHB 65f64a **RR 70f 64a** 4358[3]
2 b f Environment Friend 7.5f **(67)** - Logarithm (King of Spain) 7.8f **(52)**
Form - 306242183
Record 1999 - 1st:1 2nd:2 3rd:2 Ran:9
Win Prizemoney £3,785 *Total Prizemoney* £5,638
Wins * 1999 Aug Newmar (GD) S 7f 70 <
1999 Turf 1-8: (5f 2, 6f, 7f 1-4, 8f) (sft, g-s, gd, g-f 1-2, frm 3) 1999 AW 0-1: (7f) (Fibr)
Above-average filly, effective 7 to 8f, best at 7f, acts on g-s to frm - acts on Fibr, best on g-f. Turf high 70 - 1st of 11 getting 5lb from Bandler Ching (6 Aug Newmarket RF 3425). (1st run) - 2nd of 11 to Sally Gardens (23 Jly Wolverhampton 7f Fibr RF 3083). **D Morris [1-9] Wacky Racing.*

Alabaq was useful in filles' Pattern events

ALABAQ (USA) BHB 106f **RR 107f** 5017a[1]
3 b br f Riverman (USA) 9.7f **(78)** - Salsabil (Sadler's Wells (USA)) 10f **(76)**
Form - 2136241
Record 1999 - 1st:2 2nd:2 3rd:1 Ran:7
Pre1999 - 1st:1 2nd:1 3rd:0 Ran:3
Win Prizemoney £35,661 *Total Prizemoney* £73,091
Wins * 1999 Oct San Si (G-F) G2 8f 105+ <
*** 1999** May Newmar (G-F) L 10f 97
*** 1998** Spt Lingfi (G-S) 7f 84+
1999 Turf 2-7: (8f 1-2, 10f 1-4, 12f) (g-f 1-5, frm 1-2)
Workmanlike, Pattern-class filly, effective 8 to 12f, best at 10f, acts on g-f to frm, best on g-f. Turf high 107 - 2nd of 8 getting 3lb from Zindabad (28 Aug Windsor 10f frm RF 3983) - also 1st of 15 from Euryanthe (17 Oct San Siro RF 5017a). Consistent. This daughter of Salsabil was runner-up in a Kempton Listed race on her seasonal debut before winning the Pretty Polly with something in hand. Bypassed the Oaks to wait for faster ground in the Ribblesdale in which she finished third, not quite seeing out the trip, and has since landed an Italian Group Two. To be frank, however, she has not achieved what seemed likely at the start of the season.
**J L Dunlop [3-10] Hamdan Al Maktoum.*

ALAKDAR (CAN) BHB 41f46a **RR 30f 46a** 2064[2]
5 ch g Green Dancer (USA) 11.9f **(77)** - Population (General Assembly (USA)) 10f **(68)**
Form - 002
Record 1999 - 1st:0 2nd:1 3rd:0 Ran:3
Pre1999 - 1st:1 2nd:0 3rd:2 Ran:10
Win Prizemoney £2,784 *Total Prizemoney* £4,344
Wins 1997 Oct Catter (SFT) 12f 73 <
1999 Turf 0-2: (12f 2) (gd, frm) 1999 AW 0-1: (16f) (Fibr)
Fair gelding. Turf high 25. Inconsistent.
**B J Meehan [0-3] Mrs Judith Mendonca (from R Champion [0-5] Jly 1998).*

ALAMEIN (USA) BHB 55f71a **RR 44f 71a** 3015[10]
6 ch g Roi Danzig (USA) 10.5f **(62)** - Pollination (Pentotal) 7f **(53)**
Form - 3114602440
Record 1999 - 1st:2 2nd:1 3rd:1 Ran:10
Pre1999 - 1st:3 2nd:2 3rd:6 Ran:24
Win Prizemoney £13,315 *Total Prizemoney* £22,429
Wins * 1999 *Feb Lingfi (STD) H* 7f 65 66+
*** 1999** *Feb Lingfi (STD) C* 7f 57
* 1998 *Mar Southw (STD) C* 7f 72+
1996 Jun Thirsk (FRM) 7f 78 <
1996 Jun Catter (GD) 7f 73
1999 Turf 0-5: (7f 2, 8f 3) (gd 2, frm 3) 1999 AW 2-5: (7f 2-3, 8f 2) (Equi 2-4, Fibr)
Average gelding, effective 7 to 8f, best at 7f, acts on frm - acts on AW, often wears blinkers, prefers left handed tracks, likes tight tracks. Turf high 44. AW high 66 - 1st of 15 giving 3lb to Kings Harmony (13 Feb Lingfield RF 0284). A fair handicapper for Willie Haggas, he has shown good form on sand for Dandy Nicholls. There are more successes to come on that surface.
**D Nicholls [3-19] R J H Ltd (from W J Haggas [2-11] Aug 1997).*

ALANA'S CAVALIER (IRE) BHB 33f41a **RR 45f 41a** 4988[12]
3 b c Forest Wind (USA) - Annais Nin (Dominion) 8.5f **(63)**
Form - 44487170764647053303234080
Record 1999 - 1st:1 2nd:1 3rd:4 Ran:22
Pre1999 - 1st:0 2nd:0 3rd:2 Ran:10
Win Prizemoney £1,872 *Total Prizemoney* £4,245
Wins * 1999 *Jan Southw (STD) S* 8f 60 <
1999 Turf 0-14: (10f 7, 11f 2, 12f 2, 13f, 14f 2) (gd 4, g-f 7, frm 3) 1999 AW 1-8: (7f, 8f 1-3, 11f 2, 12f 2) (Fibr 1-8)
Light-framed, fair colt, effective 8 to 10f, best at 8f, acts on gd - acts on Fibr, has worn blinkers (effectively). Turf high 48. AW high 60 - 1st of 6 from Golden Syrup (11 Jan Southwell RF 0076). Inconsistent. **R Hollinshead [1-33] The Three R's.*

ALARMING MOTOWN RR 57f 82[9]
4 b f Warning 8.1f **(77)** - Sweet Soul Dream (USA) (Conquistador Cielo (USA)) 8.8f **(69)**
Form - 0
Record 1999 - 1st:0 2nd:0 3rd:0 Ran:1
Pre1999 - 1st:0 2nd:0 3rd:0 Ran:1
1999 AW 0-1: (8f) (Equi)
Light-framed, currently fair filly.
**M R Channon [0-1] Tim Corby (from I A Balding [0-1] Oct 1997).*

ALASAN (IRE) RR 72+f 3427[3]
2 b c Zilzal (USA) 8.5f **(79)** - Alasana (IRE) (Darshaan) 9.9f **(84)**
Form - 3
Record 1999 - 1st:0 2nd:0 3rd:1 Ran:1
Win Prizemoney £0 *Total Prizemoney* £636
1999 Turf 0-1: (7f) (g-f)
Currently above-average colt. Shaped with promise in a good maiden on his debut. **L M Cumani [0-1] H H Aga Khan.*

ALASTAIR SMELLIE BHB 89f **RR 96f** 5222[4]
3 ch g Sabrehill (USA) 8.5f **(64)** - Reel Foyle (USA) (Irish River (FR)) 8.6f **(78)**
Form - 354004
Record 1999 - 1st:0 2nd:0 3rd:1 Ran:6
Pre1999 - 1st:1 2nd:0 3rd:2 Ran:7
Win Prizemoney £5,394 *Total Prizemoney* £10,700
Wins * 1998 Spt Ayr (G-S) H 6f 75 79 <
1999 Turf 0-6: (6f 4, 7f 2) (g-s, gd 3, g-f 2)
Workmanlike, very useful gelding. Turf high 96. Useful handicapper at six or seven furlongs, but a tricky customer who tends to find trouble in running. **B W Hills [1-13] W J Gredley.*

AL ATAYA (USA) RR 65f 5021[7]
2 b g Dayjur (USA) 6.8f **(79)** - Sajjaya (USA) (Blushing Groom (FR)) 10.3f **(76)**
Form - 57
Record 1999 - 1st:0 2nd:0 3rd:0 Ran:2
1999 Turf 0-2: (7f 2) (gd 2)
Currently average gelding. Turf high 65 (began Oct).
**J L Dunlop [0-2] Hamdan Al Maktoum.*

ALAWAR BHB 72f **RR 77f** 4942[8]
2 ch c Wolfhound (USA) 7.3f **(71)** - Ghassanah (Pas de Seul) 9.1f **(67)**
Form - 038
Record 1999 - 1st:0 2nd:0 3rd:1 Ran:3
Win Prizemoney £0 *Total Prizemoney* £695
1999 Turf 0-3: (5f, 6f 2) (gd, g-f, frm)
Currently above-average colt. Turf high 77 (began Spt).
**C G Cox [0-3] Sheikh Amin Dahlawi.*

ALA WASHAK RR 67f 5113[5]
3 b g Green Desert (USA) 7.8f **(78)** - Shadha (USA) (Devil's Bag (USA)) 12.4f **(78)**
Form - 45
Record 1999 - 1st:0 2nd:0 3rd:0 Ran:2
Win Prizemoney £0 *Total Prizemoney* £224
1999 Turf 0-2: (6f 2) (gd, frm)
Rangy, currently average gelding. Turf high 67 (began Oct).
**Mrs L Stubbs [0-2] Doug Kirk and Darren Kirk.*

ALAZAN BHB 40f **RR 36f** 3573[P]
4 ch c Risk Me (FR) 8f **(53)** - Gunnard (Gunner B) 11.2f **(58)**
Form - 00P
Record 1999 - 1st:0 2nd:0 3rd:0 Ran:3
Pre1999 - 1st:0 2nd:0 3rd:0 Ran:4
Win Prizemoney £0 *Total Prizemoney* £740
1999 Turf 0-3: (8f, 10f, 12f) (g-f, frm 2)
Scopey, very moderate colt. Turf high 36 (began Jly).
**W de Best-Turner [0-3] The Spanish Connection (from D M Hyde [0-4] May 1998).*

AL AZHAR BHB 94f **RR 94f** 4876[11]
5 b g Alzao (USA) 9.8f **(73)** - Upend (Main Reef) 9.6f **(57)**
Form - 265430
Record 1999 - 1st:0 2nd:1 3rd:1 Ran:6
Pre1999 - 1st:3 2nd:2 3rd:1 Ran:10
Win Prizemoney £34,856 *Total Prizemoney* £48,235
Wins * 1997 Oct Doncas (GD) H 12f 91 96
* 1996 Spt Doncas (G-F) H 8f 85 98+ <
* 1996 Aug Chepst (GD) 8.1f 86+
1999 Turf 0-6: (8f, 10f 2, 12f 3) (g-s 2, gd 2, g-f, frm)
Useful gelding, effective 8 to 12f, best at 12f, acts on g-s to frm, best on g-s. Turf high 97 (1st run) - 2nd of 9 giving 3lb to Silk St John (23 Apr Sandown 8f g-s RF 0821). Consistent. He needs time between his races and was a shade disappointing in the second half of the campaign. Effective from a mile to a mile and a half, he appears to be one-paced. Sold for 21,000 gns in October.
**I A Balding [3-16] Nagy Azar.*

ALBAADRI RR 39f 4824[12]
4 b c Cadeaux Genereux 7.9f **(76)** - Actraphane (Shareef Dancer (USA)) 9.9f **(73)**
Form - 0
Record 1999 - 1st:0 2nd:0 3rd:0 Ran:1
1999 Turf 0-1: (8f) (g-f)
Currently very moderate colt.
**J H M Gosden [0-1] Sheikh Ahmed Al Maktoum.*

ALBARAHIN (USA) BHB 107f **RR 108+f** 5140[2]
4 b c Silver Hawk (USA) 11.2f **(85)** - My Dear Lady (USA) (Mr Prospector (USA)) 8.8f **(78)**
Form - 11612
Record 1999 - 1st:3 2nd:1 3rd:0 Ran:5
Pre1999 - 1st:0 2nd:2 3rd:1 Ran:4
Win Prizemoney £24,149 *Total Prizemoney* £35,685
Wins * **1999** Oct Newbur (HVY) H 9f 96 108+ <
* **1999** Aug Sandow (GD) H 10f 88 93++
* **1999** Aug Leices (GD) H 10f 80 90
1999 Turf 3-5: (8f, 9f 1-1, 10f 2-3) (sft 1-1, gd 2, g-f 1-1, frm 1-1)
Well made, Pattern-class colt, effective 8 to 9f, acts on sft to gd. Turf high 108 (began Aug) - 2nd of 8 to Bomb Alaska (30 Oct Newmarket 8f gd RF 5140) - also 1st of 15 giving 1lb to Island House (23 Oct Newbury RF 5042). He had his problems and was restricted to two outings in the autumn of 1998. However, last season this former Godolphin inmate was in fine form, bolting home in a Leicester handicap and following up in a competitive event at Sandown. Suited by ten furlongs, he ran well in the Cambridgeshire considering things did not go his way, and gained compensation in bottomless ground at Newbury on his next start, before running well in listed company at the back-end.
**M P Tregoning [3-5] Hamdan Al Maktoum (from S bin Suroor [0-4] Oct 1998).*

ALBARAN (GER) RR 107f 4778a[12]
6 b h Sure Blade (USA) 10.6f **(66)** - Araqueen (GER) (Konigsstuhl (GER)) 11.2f **(76)**
Form - 1310
1999 Turf 2-4: (9f, 12f 2-3) (sft, gd 1-2, frm 1-1)
Pattern-class horse, effective 12f, acts on sft to frm. Turf high 107 (1st run) (began Aug) - 1st of 13 from Yavana's Pace (1 Aug Klampenborg RF 3410a) - also 1st of 9 from Inchrory (12 Spt Taby RF 4374a). He is a useful performer over middle distances in Scandinavia, and gained a short-head victory over Yavana's Pace at Klampenborg in August. Outclassed in the Arc under his veteran Hungarian rider Janos Tandari.
**Catherine Erichsen in NOR [3-6] Stall Albaran.*

ALBARDEN RR 62f 2754[12]
2 ch c Mujtahid (USA) 7.4f **(69)** - Aljood (Kris) 9.5f **(73)**
Form - 40
Record 1999 - 1st:0 2nd:0 3rd:0 Ran:2
Win Prizemoney £0 *Total Prizemoney* £243
1999 Turf 0-2: (6f, 7f) (frm 2)
Currently average colt. Turf high 62.
**T D Easterby [0-2] C H Newton Jnr Ltd.*

ALBATA RR 23f 4220[11]
2 b g Alhijaz 7.7f **(57)** - Basenite (Mansingh (USA)) 7.4f **(55)**
Form - 00
Record 1999 - 1st:0 2nd:0 3rd:0 Ran:2
1999 Turf 0-1: (7f) (frm) 1999 AW 0-1: (8f) (Fibr)
Currently little account gelding. **M A Jarvis [0-2] T G Warner.*

ALBEMINE (USA) BHB 40f40a **RR 23f 40a** 1374[8]
10 b g Al Nasr (FR) 9.9f **(72)** - Lady Be Mine (USA) (Sir Ivor) 10.2f **(70)**
Form - 532858
Record 1999 - 1st:0 2nd:1 3rd:1 Ran:6
Pre1999 - 1st:1 2nd:0 3rd:2 Ran:10
Win Prizemoney £2,511 *Total Prizemoney* £5,269
1999 Turf 0-1: (14f) (frm) 1999 AW 0-5: (14f, 15f 2, 16f 2) (Equi, Fibr 4)
Very moderate gelding. AW high 47. Inconsistent.
**A G Juckes [0-16] A C W Price (from R T Juckes [1-6] Feb 1998).*

ALBERGO (IRE) RR 35f 4994[9]
2 b g Deploy 11.4f **(67)** - River Dove (USA) (Riverman (USA)) 9.1f **(76)**
Form - 00
Record 1999 - 1st:0 2nd:0 3rd:0 Ran:2
1999 Turf 0-2: (7f, 8f) (g-s, gd)
Currently very moderate gelding. Turf high 35 (began Spt).
**M Blanshard [0-2] Goldring Hotels Ltd.*

ALBERICH (IRE) BHB 95f **RR 92f** 4403[1]
4 b g Night Shift (USA) 8.1f **(73)** - Tetradonna (IRE) (Teenoso (USA))

9.9f **(72)**
Form - 0520731
Record 1999 - 1st:1 2nd:1 3rd:1 Ran:7
Pre1999 - 1st:2 2nd:0 3rd:1 Ran:5
Win Prizemoney £35,644 *Total Prizemoney* £42,068
Wins * **1999** Spt Newbur (G-F) H 13.3f 90 92 <
* 1998 Spt York (GD) H 11.9f 86 89
* 1997 Aug Beverl (GD) 8.5f 80+
1999 Turf 1-7: (10f, 12f 3, 13f 1-1, 14f 2) (sft, g-s, gd, frm 1-4)
Strong, useful gelding, effective 12 to 13f, best at 12f, acts on g-f to frm, best on frm. Turf high 92 - 1st of 13 getting 2lb from Bold Gait (18 Spt Newbury RF 4403). Consistent. Useful at three, his form last season was somewhat hit and miss, but he was a very game winner of the Newbury Autumn Cup, making all.
**M Johnston [3-12] David Abell.*

ALBERKINNIE BHB 31f36a **RR 30f 36a** 4949[2]

4 b f Ron's Victory (USA) 9.2f **(52)** - Trojan Desert (Troy) 10.4f **(68)**
Form - 7070758264402
Record 1999 - 1st:0 2nd:2 3rd:0 Ran:12
Pre1999 - 1st:0 2nd:0 3rd:0 Ran:10
Win Prizemoney £0 *Total Prizemoney* £2,116
1999 Turf 0-12: (8f 5, 9f, 10f 3, 11f 2, 12f) (gd 3, g-f 4, frm 5)
Workmanlike, very moderate filly, effective 7 to 9f, acts on gd to g-f, likes left handed tracks, likes tight tracks. Turf high 40 - 7th of 15 getting 12lb from Ollie's Chuckle (29 Apr Redcar 9f gd RF 0917). Consistent. **J L Harris [0-22] Paddy Barrett.*

ALBERTINA JANE BHB 43f **RR 48f** 2772[4]

2 b f Beveled (USA) 6.9f **(64)** - Austral Jane (Dominion) 8.5f **(63)**
Form - 074
Record 1999 - 1st:0 2nd:0 3rd:0 Ran:3
1999 Turf 0-3: (5f 2, 7f) (g-f, frm, hrd)
Currently moderate filly. Turf high 48.
**M D I Usher [0-3] Mrs M J Wilson.*

ALBERT THE BEAR BHB 62f80a **RR 60f 80a** 5160[10]

6 b g Puissance 7.1f **(60)** - Florentynna Bay (Aragon) 8.1f **(60)**
Form - 80541123704600
Record 1999 - 1st:2 2nd:1 3rd:1 Ran:14
Pre1999 - 1st:6 2nd:5 3rd:3 Ran:39
Win Prizemoney £41,272 *Total Prizemoney* £55,057
Wins * **1999** Jly Pontef (G-S) H 6f 62 64
* **1999** Jun Carlis (G-F) S 5.9f 52
* 1997 Jun Cheste (G-F) H 7f 84 87 <
* 1997 May Cheste (HVY) H 7.6f 78 87 <
* 1996 Jun Cheste (G-F) H 7f 77 77
* 1995 Aug Catter (G-F) H 6f 61 65
* 1995 Aug Bath (HRD) H 5.7f 61 65
* 1995 Jun Carlis (FRM) S 5f 60
1999 Turf 2-14: (6f 2-9, 7f 4, 8f) (g-s, g-f 3, frm 2-10)
Average gelding, effective 7f, acts on frm, has worn blinkers. Turf high 65. Consistent. He was finding it hard to win, but he dropped right down the handicap as a result and that, together with being fitted with a visor, enabled him to show some decent form, including winning a Carlisle seller and a Pontefract handicap.
**J Berry [8-56] Chris & Antonia Deuters.*

ALBOOSTAN BHB 98f **RR 102f** 4393[5]

4 b c Sabrehill (USA) 8.5f **(64)** - Russian Countess (USA) (Nureyev (USA)) 8.7f **(78)**
Form - 0244385
Record 1999 - 1st:0 2nd:1 3rd:1 Ran:7
Pre1999 - 1st:2 2nd:2 3rd:1 Ran:7
Win Prizemoney £17,029 *Total Prizemoney* £59,847
Wins 1997 Spt Goodwo (GD) L 8f 101 <
1997 Jly Beverl (GD) 7.5f 86+
1999 Turf 0-7: (8f 3, 9f, 10f 3) (gd 5, g-f, frm)
Very useful colt, effective 9 to 10f, best at 10f, acts on gd to frm, best on gd, has worn blinkers. Turf high 102. Consistent. A one-time Derby contender, he has not looked the same horse since being troubled by a stifle injury. Suited by easy ground, he lacks a finishing kick and is probably best ridden forcefully over a mile and a quarter.
**B W Hills [0-10] Hamdan Al Maktoum (from D Morley [2-4] Oct 1997).*

ALBORADA BHB 121f **RR 122f** 4919[1]

4 gr f Alzao (USA) 9.8f **(73)** - Alouette (Darshaan) 9.9f **(84)**
Form - 51
Record 1999 - 1st:1 2nd:0 3rd:0 Ran:2
Pre1999 - 1st:5 2nd:1 3rd:2 Ran:8
Win Prizemoney £557,824 *Total Prizemoney* £599,976
Wins * **1999** Oct Newmar (GD) G1 10f 119
* 1998 Oct Newmar (GD) G1 10f 122 <
* 1998 Aug Goodwo (GD) G2 9.9f 116
* 1998 Jun Currag (SFT) G2 10f 104
* 1997 Oct Currag (G-S) G3 7f 101
* 1997 Spt Beverl (G-F) 7.5f 77+
1999 Turf 1-2: (10f 1-2) (gd 1-1, g-f)
Light-framed, very high-class filly, effective 10f, acts on gd. Turf high 119 (began Jly) - 1st of 13 from Shiva (16 Oct Newmarket RF 4919). Took some time to get going at two, but landed the Pretty Polly at the Curragh in tidy style on her return in 1998. A brave win in the Nassau Stakes was then followed by a second to Swain in the Irish Champion before she took the British version. She missed her intended reappearance in the Eclipse this year because of a dirty throat, before running reasonably well in the Nassau. She then returned to Newmarket to become the first horse since the mighty Triptych to win successive Champion Stakes. A particularly game and consistent mare, and superbly handled by her trainer, she is due to end her career in the Japan Cup.
**Sir Mark Prescott [6-10] Miss K Rausing.*

ALCONLEIGH BHB 43f81a **RR 31f 81a** 5156[10]

4 ch g Pursuit of Love 9.5f **(69)** - Serotina (IRE) (Mtoto)
Form - 00350535250070000
Record 1999 - 1st:0 2nd:1 3rd:2 Ran:17
Pre1999 - 1st:2 2nd:4 3rd:1 Ran:12
Win Prizemoney £8,600 *Total Prizemoney* £21,720
Wins 1997 Jly Thirsk (GD) 7f 90 <
1997 May Ripon (G-S) 6f 77
1999 Turf 0-16: (7f 2, 8f 6, 10f 8) (gd 4, g-f 5, frm 7) 1999 AW 0-1: (8f) (Fibr)
Scopey, average gelding, effective 8 to 10f, best at 8f, acts on g-f to frm, best on g-f, has worn blinkers. Turf high 84 - 5th of 11 getting 5lb from Free Option (16 May Kempton 8f frm RF 1257).
**B Ellison [0-8] Alconleigh Partnership (from M Johnston [2-21] Jly 1999).*

ALDBURGH **RR 44f** 760[D]

3 ch f Bluebird (USA) 7.9f **(71)** - Eastern Shore (Sun Prince) 12.4f **(52)**
Form - D
Record 1999 - 1st:0 2nd:0 3rd:0 Ran:1
1999 Turf 0-1: (8f) (frm)
Workmanlike, currently moderate filly.
**J H M Gosden [0-1] Sheikh Mohammed.*

AL DESIMA BHB 92f **RR 89f** 4920[10]

2 b f Emperor Jones (USA) - Miss Up N Go (Gorytus (USA)) 7.8f **(60)**
Form - 314340
Record 1999 - 1st:1 2nd:0 3rd:2 Ran:6
Win Prizemoney £2,476 *Total Prizemoney* £4,983
Wins * **1999** Jly Folkes (G-F) 7f 79 <
1999 Turf 1-6: (7f 1-5, 8f) (gd 2, g-f, frm 1-3)
Useful filly, effective 7f, acts on gd to frm, best on frm. Turf high 89 - 4th of 12 to Agrippina (2 Oct Newmarket 7f gd RF 4680). Showed some promise on her Kempton debut before comfortably winning a Folkestone maiden auction event. Outclassed in Listed company after that and showed signs of temperament on her fourth and fifth starts, but nevertheless ran well on the latter occasion. **K McAuliffe [1-6] Aidan Ryan.*

ALDWYCH ARROW (IRE) BHB 60f50a **RR 58df 50a** 5168[11]

4 ch g Rainbows For Life (CAN) 9.3f **(64)** - Shygate (Shy Groom (USA)) 10f **(66)**
Form - 45042823120000
Record 1999 - 1st:1 2nd:3 3rd:1 Ran:13
Pre1999 - 1st:2 2nd:5 3rd:3 Ran:21
Win Prizemoney £11,474 *Total Prizemoney* £21,674
Wins * **1999** Apr Catter (SFT) H 12f 60 66
1998 Jun Mussel (SFT) H 14f 63 66
1998 Jun Ayr (GD) H 13.1f 60 67 <
1999 Turf 1-8: (12f 1-3, 14f 5) (g-s, gd 1-3, g-f 3, frm) 1999 AW 0-5: (11f 3, 12f, 16f) (Fibr 5)
Fair gelding, effective 11 to 16f, acts on g-s to g-f - acts on Fibr, has worn blinkers, prefers tight tracks, does well at Catterick. Turf

high 66 - 1st of 12 getting 3lb from Aspirant Dancer (21 Apr Catterick RF 0793). AW high 49. Becoming disappointing.
**M A Buckley [1-15] M A Buckley (from M L W Bell [2-19] Spt 1998).*

ALEANBH (IRE) BHB 35f **RR 42?f** 5050[18]
4 ch g Classic Secret (USA) 8.8f **(56)** - Highdrive (Ballymore) 7.3f **(64)**
Form - 0
Record 1999 - 1st:0 2nd:0 3rd:0 Ran:1
Pre1999 - 1st:0 2nd:0 3rd:0 Ran:1
1999 Turf 0-1: (8f) (gd)
Rangy, currently moderate gelding.
**R A Fahey [0-1] Tommy Staunton (from Miss Gay Kelleway [0-1] Mar 1998).*

ALEGRIA RR 85f 4803[9]
3 b f Night Shift (USA) 8.1f **(73)** - High Habit (Slip Anchor) 9.8f **(73)**
Form - 20364530
Record 1999 - 1st:0 2nd:1 3rd:2 Ran:8
Pre1999 - 1st:1 2nd:0 3rd:0 Ran:2
Win Prizemoney £3,436 *Total Prizemoney* £10,118
Wins * 1998 Jly Windso (GD) 6f 84 <
1999 Turf 0-8: (5f 2, 6f 6) (gd 5, g-f, frm 2)
Scopey, useful filly, effective 5 to 6f, best at 6f, acts on gd to frm. Turf high 87 (1st run) - 2nd of 9 getting 7lb from Magic Rainbow (29 May Kempton 6f frm RF 1579). **J M P Eustace [1-10] J C Smith.*

ALEKTRA (GER) RR 94f 4243a[6]
3 f
Form - 6
1999 Turf 0-1: (6f) (gd)
Currently useful filly. **E Groschel in GER [0-1].*

AL EURO (FR) BHB 62f **RR 55f** 4872[14]
2 ch f Mujtahid (USA) 7.4f **(69)** - Ibtisamm (USA) (Caucasus (USA)) 8.2f **(74)**
Form - 0430
Record 1999 - 1st:0 2nd:0 3rd:1 Ran:4
Win Prizemoney £0 *Total Prizemoney* £749
1999 Turf 0-4: (6f 4) (g-s, gd 2, g-f)
Fair filly. Turf high 55. **C E Brittain [0-4] Mohamed Obaida.*

ALEXANDER BHB 50f45a **RR 61f 45a** 2529[4]
3 b g Be My Chief (USA) 10.2f **(62)** - Arminda (Blakeney) 10.5f **(64)**
Form - 454
Record 1999 - 1st:0 2nd:0 3rd:0 Ran:3
Pre1999 - 1st:0 2nd:0 3rd:0 Ran:3
Win Prizemoney £0 *Total Prizemoney* £199
1999 Turf 0-2: (13f, 18f) (frm 2) 1999 AW 0-1: (12f) (Fibr)
Workmanlike, average gelding. Turf high 48.
**B P J Baugh [0-2] Mrs Joan Chrimes (from C W Thornton [0-4] Feb 1999).*

ALEXANDRINE (IRE) BHB 52f **RR 54f** 5109[10]
2 b f Nashwan (USA) 10.3f **(79)** - Alruccaba (Crystal Palace (FR)) 12.5f **(76)**
Form - 060
Record 1999 - 1st:0 2nd:0 3rd:0 Ran:3
1999 Turf 0-3: (7f 2, 8f) (gd 2, g-f)
Currently fair filly. Turf high 54 (began Oct).
**Sir Mark Prescott [0-3] Miss K Rausing.*

ALEXIS (IRE) BHB 101f **RR 95f** 1358a[9]
3 b f Alzao (USA) 9.8f **(73)** - Sister Golden Hair (IRE) (Glint of Gold) 9.3f **(66)**
Form - 310
Record 1999 - 1st:1 2nd:0 3rd:1 Ran:3
Pre1999 - 1st:1 2nd:0 3rd:2 Ran:5
Win Prizemoney £19,195 *Total Prizemoney* £25,246
Wins * 1999 Apr Chanti (SFT) L 8f 95 <
1998 Jly Galway (G-S) 7f 74
1999 Turf 1-3: (8f 1-3) (sft 1-1, gd, g-f)
Very useful filly, effective 8f, acts on sft to g-f. Turf high 95 - also 1st of 5 from Ares Vallis (28 Apr Chantilly RF 1067a). Improving. She did her job when winning a Listed race at Chantilly in April. Predictably outclassed in the French 1,000 Guineas, she missed the second half of the campaign but should stay beyond a mile if called back into duty.
**J Noseda [1-3] (from D K Weld in IRE [1-5] Oct 1998).*

ALFAHAAL (IRE) BHB 46f56a **RR 44f 56a** 5156[8]
6 b g Green Desert (USA) 7.8f **(78)** - Fair of the Furze (Ela-Mana-Mou) 10.1f **(70)**
Form - 0705215766067848
Record 1999 - 1st:1 2nd:1 3rd:0 Ran:16
Pre1999 - 1st:2 2nd:1 3rd:2 Ran:21
Win Prizemoney £10,405 *Total Prizemoney* £14,300
Wins * 1999 May Yarmou (FRM) H 7f 51 52
1997 Oct Leices (SFT) 8f 63 <
1997 Jly Doncas (GD) H 8f 52 56
1999 Turf 1-16: (6f 2, 7f 1-6, 8f 7, 10f) (sft, g-s 2, gd 4, g-f 1-5, frm 4)
Fair gelding, effective 7f, acts on g-f. Turf high 52 - 1st of 13 giving 14lb to Italian Symphony (26 May Yarmouth RF 1510).
**C A Dwyer [1-23] M M Foulger (from R F JohnsonHoughton [2-11] Oct 1997).*

AL FAHDA BHB 88f **RR 90f** 3554[9]
3 b f Be My Chief (USA) 10.2f **(62)** - Fleetwood Fancy (Taufan (USA)) 7f **(57)**
Form - 75310
Record 1999 - 1st:1 2nd:0 3rd:1 Ran:5
Pre1999 - 1st:2 2nd:1 3rd:2 Ran:7
Win Prizemoney £13,748 *Total Prizemoney* £23,433
Wins * 1999 Aug Salisb (GD) 8f 90 <
* 1998 Jun Warwic (G-S) 7f 84
* 1998 May Leices (GD) 6f 73
1999 Turf 1-5: (8f 1-3, 10f 2) (g-s 2, gd 2, frm 1-1)
Leggy, useful filly, effective 6 to 8f, best at 7f, acts on gd to frm, best on g-f, excels at Warwick. Turf high 90 - also 1st of 8 getting 9lb from King Midas (6 Aug Salisbury RF 3432). Consistent. Although unable to make an impression in Listed company last term she did score in a classified stakes race at Salisbury on decent ground over a mile in August, beating some useful sorts like King Midas and Tom Dougal. **R Hannon [3-12] Hassan Ahmadi.*

ALFAILAK BHB 100f **RR 93f** 4793[7]
2 b c Green Desert (USA) 7.8f **(78)** - Great Inquest **(79f)** (Shernazar) 10.2f **(73)**
Form - 1443287
Record 1999 - 1st:1 2nd:1 3rd:1 Ran:7
Win Prizemoney £4,467 *Total Prizemoney* £15,505
Wins * 1999 Apr Newmar (GD) 5f 85 <
1999 Turf 1-7: (5f 1-6, 6f) (gd 3, g-f 1-2, frm 2)
Useful colt, effective 5f, acts on gd to g-f, best on g-f. Turf high 93 - 3rd of 10 giving 5lb to Misty Miss (30 Jly Goodwood 5f g-f RF 3236) - also 1st of 10 from Sheer Sabo (15 Apr Newmarket RF 0704). A speedy juvenile, he made a winning debut at Newmarket, and has run well in decent events since, including when a good third in the Molecomb and when just touched off in a Listed race at York. Never got in a blow in the Flying Childers.
**M R Channon [1-7] Sheikh Mohammed Obaid Al Maktoum.*

ALFATH (USA) BHB 76f **RR 79f** 4541[4]
3 ch c Diesis 9f **(80)** - Lady Express (IRE) (Soviet Star (USA))
Form - 525224
Record 1999 - 1st:0 2nd:3 3rd:0 Ran:6
Win Prizemoney £0 *Total Prizemoney* £3,906
1999 Turf 0-6: (5f, 6f 2, 7f 2, 9f) (gd, g-f 3, frm, hrd)
Well made, above-average colt, effective 6 to 9f, acts on g-f. Turf high 87 - 2nd of 18 to Heroic Blue (12 Jun Lingfield 6f g-f RF 1955).
**A C Stewart [0-6] Hamdan Al Maktoum.*

ALFIE BOY (IRE) BHB 100f **RR 106f** 3259[4]
3 b g Forest Wind (USA) - Ballinlee (IRE) (Skyliner) 7.3f **(53)**
Form - 134
Record 1999 - 1st:1 2nd:0 3rd:1 Ran:3
Win Prizemoney £3,835 *Total Prizemoney* £7,405
Wins * 1999 Jun Goodwo (G-S) 7f 87 <
1999 Turf 1-3: (7f 1-1, 8f 2) (g-s 1-1, gd, g-f)
Scopey, currently Pattern-class gelding. Turf high 106 - 3rd of 7 getting 15lb from Ramooz (27 Jun Goodwood 8f gd RF 2358). Unraced at two, he won a Goodwood maiden auction event on his debut, but stepped up considerably on that when a close third to the smart Ramooz at the same track next time. Not seen since

reaching the frame in another Goodwood listed race, he may still have improvement in him if all is well.
**A P Jarvis [1-3] Mrs Ann Jarvis.*

ALFIE LEE (IRE) BHB 93f **RR 82f** 2070[9]
2 ch c Case Law 6f **(64)** - Nordic Living (IRE) (Nordico (USA)) 6.5f **(62)**
Form - 54170
Record 1999 - 1st:1 2nd:0 3rd:0 Ran:5
Win Prizemoney £4,123 *Total Prizemoney* £4,852
Wins * 1999 May Goodwo (GD) 5f 74 <
1999 Turf 1-5: (5f 1-5) (gd 1-1, g-f 4)
Decent colt. Turf high 82 - also 1st of 8 from Keep Tapping (18 May Goodwood RF 1296). Beat two subsequent winners when scoring at Goodwood, but held since in better company.
**C N Allen [1-5] J T B Racing.*

ALFINI RR 95+f 4875[1]
2 ch c Selkirk (USA) 7.9f **(76)** - Vivre En Paix (Nureyev (USA)) 8.7f **(78)**
Form - 21
Record 1999 - 1st:1 2nd:1 3rd:0 Ran:2
Win Prizemoney £5,708 *Total Prizemoney* £10,316
Wins * 1999 Oct Newmar (GD) 6f 95+ <
1999 Turf 1-2: (6f 1-1, 7f) (sft, gd 1-1)
Currently very useful colt. Turf high 95 (began Spt) - 1st of 14 from Free Rider (14 Oct Newmarket RF 4875). A tank of a horse, he caught the eye on his two starts, winning very impressively at Newmarket in October. That form is nothing special, but he is held in high regard, has bags of scope and could develop into a lively outsider for the 2000 Guineas.
**D R C Elsworth [1-2] A Heaney & A Tuckerman.*

AL GHABRAA RR 81+f 4907[1]
2 ch f Pursuit of Love 9.5f **(69)** - Tenderetta (Tender King) 6.8f **(54)**
Form - 1
Record 1999 - 1st:1 2nd:0 3rd:0 Ran:1
Win Prizemoney £3,414 *Total Prizemoney* £3,414
Wins * 1999 Oct Redcar (GD) 8f 81+ <
1999 Turf 1-1: (8f 1-1) (frm 1-1)
Currently decent filly. (1st run) - 1st of 14 getting 5lb from Riddlesdown (15 Oct Redcar RF 4907). Ran green on her debut, but showed a nice turn of foot. **J W Hills [1-1] Hassan Ahmadi.*

ALGUNNAAS BHB 105f **RR 106f** 4253[2]
4 b c Red Ransom (USA) 8.6f **(83)** -Swame (USA) (Jade Hunter (USA))
Form - 214531112
Record 1999 - 1st:4 2nd:2 3rd:1 Ran:9
Win Prizemoney £35,498 *Total Prizemoney* £50,859
Wins * 1999 Spt Haydoc (G-F) H 11.9f 100 102 <
*** 1999** Aug York (GD) H 10.4f 96 102 <
*** 1999** Aug Newmar (GD) 10f 95
*** 1999** Apr Leices (GD) 10f 81+
1999 Turf 4-9: (8f, 10f 3-6, 12f 1-2) (sft, gd 2-3, g-f 1-3, frm 1-2)
Pattern-class colt, effective 10 to 12f, best at 12f, acts on gd to frm, often wears blinkers (extremely effectively). Turf high 106 - 2nd of 5 giving 9lb to Azouz Pasha (10 Spt Doncaster 12f g-f RF 4253) - also 1st of 4 giving 8lb to Glenmead (4 Spt Haydock RF 4136). Improving. Unraced as a three-year-old, he ran a fine third to Moutahddee in the Hong Kong Jockey Cup Trophy at Sandown when visored for the first time, and regained winning form in the headgear at Newmarket. Followed up with a last-gasp victory in a rated stakes at the Ebor meeting before taking a similar event at Haydock. A most likeable sort, he was sold in October to race in the Middle East. **J H M Gosden [4-9] Sheikh Ahmed Al Maktoum.*

ALHASAD (USA) BHB 89f **RR 87f** 4562[2]
3 b c Sheikh Albadou 9.2f **(75)** - Valley Prospector (USA) (Northern Prospect (USA)) 9.5f **(71)**
Form - 1282
Record 1999 - 1st:1 2nd:2 3rd:0 Ran:4
Pre1999 - 1st:0 2nd:1 3rd:1 Ran:4
Win Prizemoney £4,110 *Total Prizemoney* £14,028
Wins * 1999 Jun Nottin (GD) 8.2f 81 <
1999 Turf 1-4: (8f 1-1, 10f 3) (gd, g-f 1-2, frm)
Strong, useful colt, effective 8 to 10f, best at 10f, acts on gd to frm. Turf high 87 - 2nd of 13 getting 13lb from Zindabad (7 Jly Newmarket 10f frm RF 2630) - also 1st of 8 from Sapphire Trio (21 Jun Nottingham RF 2172). After winning a mile maiden at Nottingham in June, he showed great improvement to finish narrowly beaten in the Duke of Cambridge at Newmarket.
**A C Stewart [1-8] Hamdan Al Maktoum.*

ALHAWA (USA) BHB 79f **RR 81f** 4917[6]
6 ch g Mt Livermore (USA) 7.7f **(90)** - Petrava (NZ) (Imposing (AUS)) 7.7f **(74)**
Form - 504331111886
Record 1999 - 1st:4 2nd:0 3rd:2 Ran:12
Pre1999 - 1st:2 2nd:0 3rd:2 Ran:22
Win Prizemoney £27,674 *Total Prizemoney* £34,010
Wins * 1999 Aug Newmar (G-F) H 16.1f 76 81 <
*** 1999** Jly Newmar (G-F) H 14.8f 70 72
*** 1999** Jly Newmar (G-F) H 14.8f 61 68
*** 1999** Jly Doncas (G-F) H 12f 61 67
1996 May Lingfi (G-F) 7.6f 81 <
1995 Oct Lingfi (GD) 7f 78
1999 Turf 4-12: (11f, 12f 1-4, 13f 2, 15f 2-3, 16f 1-1, 17f) (gd 2, g-f 2-4, frm 2-5, hrd)
Decent gelding, effective 8 to 17f, acts on gd to frm, has worn blinkers, likes right handed tracks, excels at Newmarket. Turf high 81 - 6th of 32 getting 14lb from Top Cees (16 Oct Newmarket 17f gd RF 4917) - also 1st of 6 giving 2lb to Fnan (6 Aug Newmarket RF 3424). Consistent. He had been on a long losing run, but was in brilliant form in the summer, completing a fine fast-ground four-timer at Doncaster and Newmarket three times. Stays well.
**N P Littmoden [4-12] DGH Partnership (from Mrs J R Ramsden [0-10] Nov 1998).*

ALHESN (USA) BHB 45f65a **RR 42f 65a** 4940[5]
4 b br g Woodman (USA) 9.7f **(77)** - Deceit Princess (CAN) (Vice Regent (CAN)) 8.7f **(74)**
Form - 000116016125
Record 1999 - 1st:4 2nd:1 3rd:0 Ran:12
Pre1999 - 1st:0 2nd:1 3rd:1 Ran:6
Win Prizemoney £12,131 *Total Prizemoney* £14,677
Wins * 1999 *Spt Wolver (STD) H 16.2f 57 63* <
*** 1999** *Aug Lingfi (STD) H 16f 45 52*
*** 1999** Jly Yarmou (FRM) H 16f 33 41
*** 1999** Jly Yarmou (FRM) H 14.1f 40 43
1999 Turf 2-8: (11f, 12f 3, 14f 1-2, 16f 1-2) (gd 2, g-f 1-2, frm 1-2, hrd 2)
1999 AW 2-4: (14f, 15f, 16f 2-2) (Equi 1-1, Fibr 1-3)
Average gelding, effective 14 to 16f, acts on g-f - acts on Fibr, prefers left handed tracks, prefers tight tracks, and excels at Wolverhampton. Turf high 43. AW high 68 (began Aug) - 2nd of 8 giving 17lb to Cindesti (18 Spt Wolverhampton 15f Fibr RF 4413) - also 1st of 11 getting 7lb from Pipe Music (8 Spt Wolverhampton RF 4225). Won a couple of modest fast-ground staying events at Yarmouth in the summer, and showed himself to be well suited by Equitrack and the Wolverhampton in the autumn, winning well on each. Very disappointing when tried at Southwell. Ideally needs two miles and a truly-run race. **C N Allen [4-18] J T B Racing.*

ALHEYRAH BHB 59f **RR 60f** 4529[8]
3 b f Ezzoud (IRE) - Hamama (USA) (Majestic Light (USA)) 10.6f **(75)**
Form - 52208
Record 1999 - 1st:0 2nd:2 3rd:0 Ran:5
Win Prizemoney £0 *Total Prizemoney* £2,093
1999 Turf 0-5: (8f, 10f 2, 11f, 12f) (g-s, gd 2, g-f, frm)
Leggy, average filly. Turf high 62.
**B Hanbury [0-5] Hamdan Al Maktoum.*

ALHUFOOF (USA) RR 91+f 3171[1]
2 b f Dayjur (USA) 6.8f **(79)** - Cheval Volant (USA) (Kris S (USA)) 7.9f **(71)**
Form - 31
Record 1999 - 1st:1 2nd:0 3rd:1 Ran:2
Win Prizemoney £6,905 *Total Prizemoney* £7,761
Wins * 1999 Jly Goodwo (G-F) 6f 91+ <
1999 Turf 1-2: (6f 1-2) (frm 1-2)
Currently useful filly. Turf high 91 (began Jly) - 1st of 6 from Terra Nova (27 Jly Goodwood RF 3171). Ran green on her Newmarket debut, but showed plenty of promise for the future and bolted up in a Goodwood maiden next time. It was not the strongest race of its type, but she looks useful.
**M P Tregoning [1-2] Hamdan Al Maktoum.*

ALHUWBILL BHB 33f **RR 42f** 4789[8]
4 b g Full Extent (USA) 5.2f **(50)** - Hale Lane (Comedy Star (USA)) 7.5f

(50)
Form - 87000507088
Record 1999 - 1st:0 2nd:0 3rd:0 Ran:11
1999 Turf 0-9: (6f 2, 7f 3, 8f, 9f, 10f 2) (g-s, gd, g-f 4, frm 3) 1999 AW 0-2: (7f, 10f) (Equi 2)
Workmanlike, moderate gelding. Turf high 49. Inconsistent.
**J J Bridger [0-11] W R Shere.*

ALIABAD (IRE) BHB 65f **RR 64f** 4581[17]
4 b br g Doyoun 10.7f **(69)** - Alannya (FR) (Relko) 9.9f **(59)**
Form - 0
Record 1999 - 1st:0 2nd:0 3rd:0 Ran:1
Pre1999 - 1st:0 2nd:2 3rd:0 Ran:5
Win Prizemoney £0 *Total Prizemoney* £2,320
1999 Turf 0-1: (17f) (gd)
Scopey, average gelding, effective 11 to 12f, acts on g-f to frm, has worn blinkers.
**P G Murphy [0-11] Jack Brown (Bookmaker) Ltd (from Sir Michael Stoute [0-5] Spt 1998).*

ALIGN BHB 53f57a **RR 42f 57a** 5056[13]
3 gr f Petong 7.6f **(58)** - Affirmation (Tina's Pet) 6.8f **(59)**
Form - 1600000
Record 1999 - 1st:1 2nd:0 3rd:0 Ran:7
Pre1999 - 1st:0 2nd:0 3rd:0 Ran:1
Win Prizemoney £2,123 *Total Prizemoney* £2,123
Wins * 1999 *Apr Southw (STD) 8f 72* <
1999 Turf 0-4: (8f, 10f 3) (gd, g-f 2, frm) 1999 AW 1-3: (8f 1-2, 10f) (Equi, Fibr 1-2)
Neat, moderate filly, effective 8f, - acts on Fibr. Turf high 65. AW high 72 (1st run) - 1st of 12 from Face The Class (26 Apr Southwell RF 0854). Becoming disappointing. **J W Hills [1-8] Wyck Hall Stud.*

ALI YA YA RR 7f 4440[19]
3 b f Puissance 7.1f **(60)** -Manor Adventure**(26f 47a)**(Smackover)6f **(52)**
Form - 00
Record 1999 - 1st:0 2nd:0 3rd:0 Ran:2
1999 Turf 0-2: (6f, 7f) (g-f 2)
Scopey, currently very poor filly. Turf high 7 (began Aug).
**B Smart [0-2] Mrs Julie Martin.*

ALIZEE (IRE) BHB 62f **RR 69f** 2241[11]
3 b f College Chapel - Richly Deserved (IRE) (Kings Lake (USA)) 10.8f **(67)**
Form - 000
Record 1999 - 1st:0 2nd:0 3rd:0 Ran:3
1999 Turf 0-3: (8f 2, 10f) (g-f 2, frm)
Scopey, currently average filly. Turf high 69.
**P W Chapple-Hyam [0-3] Mrs C Cordle & Mrs B V Sangster.*

Aljabr was an impressive winner of the Sussex Stakes

ALJABR (USA) BHB 123f **RR 127f** 4246a[4]
3 gr c Storm Cat (USA) 7f **(86)** - Sierra Madre (FR) **(111+f)** (Baillamont (USA)) 7f **(78)**
Form - 214
Record 1999 - 1st:1 2nd:1 3rd:0 Ran:3
Pre1999 - 1st:3 2nd:0 3rd:0 Ran:3
Win Prizemoney £212,828 *Total Prizemoney* £279,726

Wins						
* 1999	Jly	Goodwo (G-F)	G1	8f	127	<
* 1998	Spt	Longch (SFT)	G1	7f	116	
* 1998	Jly	Goodwo (GD)	G3	7f	117+	
* 1998	Jly	Sandow (GD)		7.1f	90+	

1999 Turf 1-3: (8f 1-3) (gd, g-f 1-2)
Scopey, top-class colt, effective 7 to 8f, best at 8f, acts on gd to g-f, best on g-f. Turf high 127 - 1st of 8 getting 8lb from Docksider (28 Jly Goodwood RF 3209). He looked a class act from day one and was never headed in three outings at two, the last of which was a decisive half-length victory from the subsequently demoted Stravinsky in the Salamandre. It was intended that he make his return in the Kentucky Derby, but he missed that event after being found to be lame on the eve of the race. He eventually made his comeback in the St James's Palace Stakes at Royal Ascot, in which he finished a fine runner-up to Sendawar, with the rest well beaten. He franked that form with a decisive win in the Sussex Stakes, but once again found Sendawar too good when fourth in the Prix du Moulin in September. There was no disgrace in either defeat as Sendawar was the best miler in Europe in 1999. He is genuine Group One material and, if he stays in training, there are more top races to be won. **S bin Suroor [4-6].*

ALJA LAD RR 66f 4178[10]
2 br g Forzando 7.2f **(63)** - Cactus Road (FR) (Iron Duke (FR)) 8.8f **(60)**
Form - 50
Record 1999 - 1st:0 2nd:0 3rd:0 Ran:2
1999 Turf 0-2: (5f, 6f) (gd, frm)
Currently average gelding. Turf high 66 (began Aug).
**B Palling [0-2] Mrs P K Chick.*

ALJAWF (USA) RR 90+f 4284[1]
2 gr ro c Dehere (USA) - Careless Kitten (USA) (Caro)
Form - 51
Record 1999 - 1st:1 2nd:0 3rd:0 Ran:2
Win Prizemoney £4,142 *Total Prizemoney* £4,142
Wins * 1999 Spt Nottin (G-F) 6.1f 90+ <
1999 Turf 1-2: (6f 1-2) (gd, frm 1-1)
Currently useful colt. Turf high 90 (began Aug) - 1st of 12 giving 5lb to Nuts In May (13 Spt Nottingham RF 4284). Won a Nottingham maiden over six furlongs on his second start. Showed plenty of pace that day. **E A L Dunlop [1-2] Hamdan Al Maktoum.*

ALJAZ BHB 53f62a **RR 17f 62a** 4607[2]
9 b g Al Nasr (FR) 9.9f **(72)** - Santa Linda (USA) (Sir Ivor) 10.2f **(70)**
Form - 0836870438100202
Record 1999 - 1st:1 2nd:2 3rd:2 Ran:16
Pre1999 - 1st:6 2nd:12 3rd:6 Ran:55
Win Prizemoney £19,919 *Total Prizemoney* £34,935

Wins								
* 1999	*May*	*Southw*	*(STD)*	*H*	*6f*	*57*	*61*	
1998	*Jun*	*Wolver*	*(STD)*	*H*	*6f*	*62*	*67*	<
* 1998	*Jan*	*Wolver*	*(STD)*	*C*	*5f*		*52*	
* 1998	*Jan*	*Wolver*	*(STD)*	*H*	*5f*	*52*	*52*	
* 1996	*Aug*	*Wolver*	*(STD)*	*H*	*5f*	*42*	*43*	
1995	Mar	Hamilt	(HVY)	H	6f	60	62	

1999 AW 1-16: (5f 5, 6f 1-9, 7f, 8f) (Equi 4, Fibr 1-12)
Above-average gelding, effective 5 to 6f, best at 6f, - acts on Fibr, has worn blinkers, prefers left handed tracks, prefers tight tracks, and excels at Wolverhampton. AW high 61 - 1st of 16 giving 6lb to Kosevo (17 May Southwell RF 1284). Inconsistent.
**Miss Gay Kelleway [5-44] Dorchester Racing Club (from Mrs N Macauley [1-10] Jly 1998).*

ALJAZIR BHB 59f **RR 56f** 4809[4]
2 b c Alhijaz 7.7f **(57)** - Duxyana (IRE) (Cyrano de Bergerac) 6f **(68)**
Form - 3067854
Record 1999 - 1st:0 2nd:0 3rd:1 Ran:7
Win Prizemoney £0 *Total Prizemoney* £909
1999 Turf 0-7: (5f 4, 6f 3) (sft, g-s, gd, g-f 3, frm)
Fair colt, effective 5f, acts on g-s, has worn blinkers. Turf high 71 (1st run) - 3rd of 6 to Watching (2 Jun Chester 5f g-s RF 1667).
**E J Alston [0-7] Liam & Tony Ferguson.*

ALLEGRESSE (IRE) RR 74f 4176[6]
2 b f Alzao (USA) 9.8f **(73)** - Millie Musique (Miller's Mate) 7f **(63)**
Form - 36
Record 1999 - 1st:0 2nd:0 3rd:1 Ran:2
Win Prizemoney £0 *Total Prizemoney* £537
1999 Turf 0-2: (7f 2) (g-s, frm)
Currently above-average filly. Turf high 74 (1st run) (began Aug) - 3rd of 13 to Naval Affair (18 Aug Kempton 7f g-s RF 3740).
**J L Dunlop [0-2] R J McAulay.*

ALLEZ CYRANO (IRE) BHB 55f35a **RR 46?f 35a** 41[6]
8 b g Alzao (USA) 9.8f **(73)** - Miss Bergerac (Bold Lad (IRE)) 8.4f **(68)**
Form - 66
Record 1999 - 1st:0 2nd:0 3rd:0 Ran:1
Pre1999 - 1st:3 2nd:3 3rd:1 Ran:25
Win Prizemoney £15,256 *Total Prizemoney* £20,532
Wins 1996 *Feb Wolver (STD) C 7f 59*
1999 AW 0-1: (9f) (Fibr)
Moderate gelding, has worn blinkers.
**D Burchell [0-3] P Riddick (from O O'Neill [0-3] Feb 1997).*

ALL GLORY RR 110f 2098a[6]
3 b f Alzao (USA) 9.8f **(73)** - Dazzling Heights (Shirley Heights) 10.3f **(74)**
Form - 306
1999 Turf 0-3: (9f, 10f, 11f) (g-s 2, gd)
Currently Group-class filly. Turf high 110 - 6th of 14 to Daryaba (13 Jun Chantilly 11f g-s RF 2098a). **J E Pease in FR [0-3].*

ALL GOOD THINGS (IRE) RR 62f 5021[8]
2 b c Marju (IRE) 9.2f **(76)** - Garah (Ajdal (USA)) 9.2f **(89)**
Form - 08
Record 1999 - 1st:0 2nd:0 3rd:0 Ran:2
1999 Turf 0-2: (7f 2) (gd 2)
Currently average colt. Turf high 62 (began Oct).
**J L Dunlop [0-2] Prince A A Faisal.*

ALLIED IMPERIAL RR 4f 4529[9]
3 b f Morpeth - Super Sarena (IRE) (Taufan (USA)) 7f **(57)**
Form - 0
Record 1999 - 1st:0 2nd:0 3rd:0 Ran:1
1999 Turf 0-1: (10f) (g-s)
Workmanlike, currently very poor filly.
**R J O'Sullivan [0-1] Allied Manufacturing Company.*

ALLINSON'S MATE (IRE) BHB 38f43a **RR 38f 43a** 1978[7]
11 b g Fayruz 6.6f **(63)** - Piney Pass (Persian Bold) 9.3f **(66)**
Form - 40407
Record 1999 - 1st:0 2nd:0 3rd:0 Ran:5
Pre1999 - 1st:18 2nd:14 3rd:11 Ran:136
Win Prizemoney £63,044 *Total Prizemoney* £93,842

Wins							
* 1998	Jly	Doncas	(G-F)	H	7f	44	47
* 1997	May	Doncas	(GD)	H	7f	58	64
* 1997	May	Carlis	(G-S)	C	6.9f		59
* 1996	Oct	Catter	(GD)	H	7f	56	61
* 1996	Jly	Mussel	(GD)	H	7.1f	55	57
* 1995	Jly	York	(G-F)	H	7f	71	73
* 1995	Jun	Doncas	(GD)	H	7f	68	71
* 1995	Apr	Carlis	(GD)	C	6.9f		69

1999 Turf 0-5: (7f 5) (gd, g-f, frm 3)
Fair gelding, effective 7f, acts on gd to g-f - acts on Fibr, often wears blinkers, likes left handed tracks. Turf high 38.
**T D Barron [18-141] Harrowgate Bloodstock Ltd.*

ALLITERATION RR 102f 4109a[5]
4 b c Polish Precedent (USA) 9f **(73)** - African Peace (USA) (Roberto (USA)) 10f **(76)**
Form - 25
1999 Turf 0-2: (8f 2) (sft, g-s)
Currently very useful colt. Turf high 102 (1st run) - 2nd of 6 giving 3lb to Field of Hope (10 Jun Chantilly 8f sft RF 2091a). He is a useful miler, but lacks a turn-of-foot and could be worth trying over middle-distances. **A Fabre in FR [0-3].*

ALLMAITES BHB 63f63a **RR 29f 63a** 657[R]
4 b g Komaite (USA) 6.9f **(61)** - Darling Miss Daisy (Tina's Pet) 6.8f **(59)**
Form - R
Record 1999 - 1st:0 2nd:0 3rd:0 Ran:1
Pre1999 - 1st:0 2nd:2 3rd:3 Ran:15
Win Prizemoney £0 *Total Prizemoney* £4,468
1999 Turf 0-1: (5f) (g-s)
Scopey, average gelding, effective 5f, acts on g-f - acts on Fibr, has worn blinkers. Becoming disappointing.
**A J McNae [0-1] R J H Ltd (from S R Bowring [0-1] Oct 1998).*

ALL NIGHT LONG (IRE) RR 59f 5005[14]
2 b f Night Shift (USA) 8.1f **(73)** - Shakey (IRE) (Caerleon (USA)) 8.6f **(71)**
Form - 6636320040
Record 1999 - 1st:0 2nd:1 3rd:2 Ran:10
Win Prizemoney £0 *Total Prizemoney* £2,417
1999 Turf 0-10: (5f 7, 6f 3) (g-s, gd 4, g-f, frm 4)
Fair filly, effective 5f, acts on gd. Turf high 67 - 2nd of 13 giving 2lb to Frampant (16 Aug Windsor 5f gd RF 3684). Becoming disappointing. **R Guest [0-10] Cosmic Greyhound Racing Partnership III.*

ALLOTROPE (IRE) BHB 60f **RR 58df** 4081[9]
4 b g Nashwan (USA) 10.3f **(79)** - Graphite (USA) (Mr Prospector (USA)) 8.8f **(78)**
Form - 0460
Record 1999 - 1st:0 2nd:0 3rd:0 Ran:4
Pre1999 - 1st:1 2nd:1 3rd:0 Ran:4
Win Prizemoney £3,437 *Total Prizemoney* £4,344
Wins 1998 Aug Tralee (GD) 14f 78 <
1999 Turf 0-4: (14f, 16f 3) (gd, frm 3)
Fair gelding, effective 9 to 14f, acts on hvy to gd, has worn blinkers, favours left handed tracks. Turf high 58. Becoming disappointing.
**Mrs M Reveley [0-4] Mrs Stephanie Smith (from J Oxx in IRE [1-4] Oct 1998).*

ALL OUR HOPE (USA) BHB 94f **RR 95f** 4794[9]
3 b f Gulch (USA) 9.6f **(79)** -Knoosh (USA)(Storm Bird (CAN))10.3f **(74)**
Form - 8130
Record 1999 - 1st:1 2nd:0 3rd:1 Ran:4
Pre1999 - 1st:0 2nd:0 3rd:1 Ran:1
Win Prizemoney £2,880 *Total Prizemoney* £9,622
Wins * 1999 *Spt Wolver (STD) 8.5f 80+* <
1999 Turf 0-3: (10f, 11f, 12f) (gd 2, g-f) 1999 AW 1-1: (8f 1-1) (Fibr 1-1)
Well made, very useful filly. Turf high 95. (1st run). She ran away with a Wolverhampton maiden before grabbing some black type in the Sun Chariot Stakes. She should stay a mile and a half, but may be difficult to place. **Sir Michael Stoute [1-5] Maktoum Al Maktoum.*

ALLRIGHTHEN BHB 33f45a **RR 33f 45a** 2379[12]
3 b g Sizzling Melody 6.3f **(49)** - Luckifosome (Smackover) 6f **(52)**
Form - 000600
Record 1999 - 1st:0 2nd:0 3rd:0 Ran:6
Pre1999 - 1st:0 2nd:0 3rd:0 Ran:6
1999 Turf 0-4: (7f 2, 8f 2) (gd 3, g-f) 1999 AW 0-2: (6f, 7f) (Fibr 2)
Light-framed, very moderate gelding. Turf high 33. Inconsistent.
**T Wall [0-12] L R Perry.*

ALL ROSES (IRE) BHB 61f54a **RR 63f 54a** 4414[10]
2 b f River Falls 8.2f **(56)** - All Laughter (Vision (USA)) 9f **(64)**
Form - 7200
Record 1999 - 1st:0 2nd:1 3rd:0 Ran:4
Win Prizemoney £0 *Total Prizemoney* £735
1999 Turf 0-3: (6f, 7f 2) (gd, frm 2) 1999 AW 0-1: (7f) (Fibr)
Average filly. Turf high 63 (began Aug) - 2nd of 16 getting 5lb from Shaman (26 Aug Folkestone 7f gd RF 3911).
**Noel Chance [0-4] Mrs M Chance.*

ALLSPICE BHB 60f **RR 43f** 4358[15]
2 b f Alzao (USA) 9.8f **(73)** - Allegra (Niniski (USA)) 10.6f **(65)**
Form - 7830
Record 1999 - 1st:0 2nd:0 3rd:1 Ran:4
Win Prizemoney £0 *Total Prizemoney* £439
1999 Turf 0-4: (7f 3, 8f) (g-s, gd, frm 2)
Moderate filly. Turf high 43 (began Jly).
**Sir Mark Prescott [0-4] Miss K Rausing.*

ALLSTARS DANCER BHB 34f29a **RR 38f 29a** 2434[11]
6 b m Primo Dominie 7.2f **(67)** - Danzig Harbour (USA) (Private Account (USA)) 8.5f **(74)**

Form - 66080
Record 1999 - 1st:0 2nd:0 3rd:0 Ran:5
Pre1999 - 1st:1 2nd:3 3rd:2 Ran:25
Win Prizemoney £2,999 *Total Prizemoney* £6,180
Wins * 1998 Aug Mussel (G-F) H 5f 24 38 <
1999 Turf 0-2: (5f, 6f) (gd, g-f) 1999 AW 0-3: (6f 3) (Equi 2, Fibr)
Very moderate mare, effective 5 to 7f, acts on gd - acts on Equi, has worn blinkers (extremely effectively). Turf high 17. AW high 19. **T J Naughton [1-30] T J Naughton.*

ALL THE GEARS (USA) BHB 85f **RR 84f** 5157[3]

2 b c Gone West (USA) 7.8f **(82)** - Buckeye Gal (USA) (Good Counsel (USA)) 6.9f **(69)**
Form - 023
Record 1999 - 1st:0 2nd:1 3rd:1 Ran:3
Win Prizemoney £0 *Total Prizemoney* £1,711
1999 Turf 0-3: (7f 3) (gd 2, frm)
Currently decent colt. Turf high 84 (began Spt) - 2nd of 22 giving 5lb to Fame At Last (22 Oct Doncaster 7f gd RF 5021). Cost $450,000, and showed ability in maidens.
**Sir Michael Stoute [0-3] The Thoroughbred Corporation.*

ALL THE WAY (IRE) BHB 115f **RR 119+f** 4266[4]

3 b c Shirley Heights 12.1f **(76)** - Future Past (USA) (Super Concorde (USA)) 10.9f **(66)**
Form - 2154
Record 1999 - 1st:1 2nd:1 3rd:0 Ran:4
Pre1999 - 1st:0 2nd:0 3rd:1 Ran:1
Win Prizemoney £6,184 *Total Prizemoney* £45,263
Wins * **1999** May Newmar (G-F) 12f 91 <
1999 Turf 1-4: (12f 1-3, 15f) (gd, g-f, frm 1-2)
Neat, high-class colt. Turf high 119 - 5th of 16 to Oath (5 Jun Epsom 12f gd RF 1760). Chased home Ramruma at Newmarket on his seasonal reappearance before winning a minor event at the same track. Ran a fine fifth in the Derby after making the running, and was then off the track for five months before the St Leger in which he played an active role until tiring in the last half-mile. Now with Godolphin.
**T G Mills [1-5] John Humphreys (Turf Accountants) Ltd.*

ALL TO EASY **RR 91?f** 4612a[3]

3 b f Alzao (USA) 9.8f **(73)** - Easy to Copy (USA) (Affirmed (USA)) 9.3f **(79)**
Form - 5283
1999 Turf 0-4: (7f, 8f 3) (sft, gd, g-f 2)
Useful filly, effective 8f, acts on gd, often wears blinkers (very effectively). Turf high 91 (1st run) - 5th of 7 to Carambola (9 May Leopardstown 8f gd RF 1170a).
**D K Weld in IRE [0-7] Moyglare Stud Farm.*

ALLURING (IRE) **RR 94f** 5178a[4]

2 b f Lure (USA) - Shelbiana (USA) (Chieftain II) 10.4f **(75)**
Form - 2224524
1999 Turf 0-7: (5f, 6f, 7f 4, 8f) (hvy, sft 3, g-s 3)
Useful filly, effective 7f, acts on sft to g-s, best on sft, often wears blinkers. Turf high 96 (1st run) (began Aug) - 2nd of 16 to Mandama (19 Aug Tipperary 7f g-s RF 3883a). She was expensive for backers to follow and does not appear to have a trip. A free-runner that wears blinkers, she is one to treat with caution.
**A P O'Brien in IRE [0-7] Mrs John Magnier.*

ALLZI (USA) BHB 77f **RR 76f** 2875[4]

3 ch f Zilzal (USA) 8.5f **(79)** - All For Hope (USA) (Sensitive Prince (USA)) 9.1f **(60)**
Form - 0734
Record 1999 - 1st:0 2nd:0 3rd:1 Ran:4
Win Prizemoney £0 *Total Prizemoney* £874
1999 Turf 0-4: (8f 3, 10f) (gd, g-f, frm 2)
Scopey, above-average filly. Turf high 76 - 4th of 13 giving 20lb to Flossy (16 Jly Newbury 10f frm RF 2875).
**Lady Herries [0-4] Hesmonds Stud.*

AL MABROOK (IRE) BHB 58f66a **RR 49f 66a** 4947[14]

4 b c Rainbows For Life (CAN) 9.3f **(64)** - Sky Lover (Ela-Mana-Mou) 10.1f **(70)**
Form - 164050
Record 1999 - 1st:0 2nd:0 3rd:0 Ran:4
Pre1999 - 1st:1 2nd:1 3rd:1 Ran:12
Win Prizemoney £2,741 *Total Prizemoney* £4,243
Wins * 1998 *Nov Lingfi (STD) 6f 66* <
1999 Turf 0-3: (6f 2, 7f) (g-s, gd, hrd) 1999 AW 0-1: (7f) (Equi)
Unfurnished, average colt, effective 6f, - acts on Equi, likes tight tracks. Turf high 49. **K Mahdi [1-16] Hamad Al-Mutawa.*

ALMAMZAR (USA) BHB 23f **RR 32f** 4717[8]

9 b g Theatrical 11.5f **(78)** - Promising Risk (USA) (Exclusive Native (USA)) 9.1f **(81)**
Form - 8586478
Record 1999 - 1st:0 2nd:0 3rd:0 Ran:7
Pre1999 - 1st:1 2nd:1 3rd:2 Ran:11
Win Prizemoney £2,898 *Total Prizemoney* £7,698
1999 Turf 0-7: (12f 2, 14f, 16f 2, 17f 2) (g-s, gd 3, g-f, frm 2)
Very moderate gelding. Turf high 32.
**Don Enrico Incisa [0-6] Don Enrico Incisa (from N Tinkler [0-14] Jun 1999).*

ALMASHROUK (IRE) BHB 75f **RR 68f** 5209[8]

2 b c Common Grounds 8.1f **(66)** - Red Note (Rusticaro (FR)) 8.2f **(65)**
Form - 748
Record 1999 - 1st:0 2nd:0 3rd:0 Ran:3
Win Prizemoney £0 *Total Prizemoney* £315
1999 Turf 0-3: (6f 2, 7f) (g-s, gd 2)
Currently average colt. Turf high 68 (began Oct).
**K Mahdi [0-3] Greenfield Stud.*

ALMASI (IRE) BHB 74f **RR 75f** 4805[15]

7 b m Petorius 8f **(66)** - Best Niece (Vaigly Great) 7f **(58)**
Form - 00137206830
Record 1999 - 1st:1 2nd:1 3rd:2 Ran:11
Pre1999 - 1st:7 2nd:6 3rd:6 Ran:46
Win Prizemoney £29,677 *Total Prizemoney* £48,435
Wins * **1999** Jun Doncas (GD) H 6f 74 76
* 1997 Spt Haydoc (G-S) 6f 88 <
* 1997 Aug Newbur (G-F) H 6f 77 82
* 1997 Jun Salisb (SFT) H 6f 68 72
* 1997 Jun Doncas (GD) H 6f 62 67
* 1996 Jun Doncas (GD) H 6f 62 64
* 1996 Apr Nottin (G-F) H 6.1f 54 56
1999 Turf 1-11: (6f 1-11) (gd 2, g-f 1-4, frm 4, hrd)
Above-average mare, effective 6f, acts on gd to frm, best on g-f. Turf high 76 - 1st of 15 giving 14lb to Bolshaya (5 Jun Doncaster RF 1755). Showed little in 1998, but generally performed better last season, including winning a competitive Doncaster handicap over six furlongs in June. She likes to come from off a strong pace.
**C F Wall [8-57] The Equema Partnership.*

ALMATY (IRE) BHB 101f **RR 106f** 4873[3]

6 b h Dancing Dissident (USA) 6.8f **(65)** - Almaaseh (IRE) (Dancing Brave (USA)) 8.4f **(76)**
Form - 42064673
Record 1999 - 1st:0 2nd:1 3rd:1 Ran:8
Pre1999 - 1st:5 2nd:4 3rd:3 Ran:23
Win Prizemoney £60,802 *Total Prizemoney* £98,105
Wins * 1998 Oct Newmar (GD) H 5f 105 107
* 1998 Spt Beverl (G-F) 5f 97
1997 May Kempto (G-F) L 5f 108+
1995 Jly Goodwo (GD) G3 5f 111 <
1995 Jly Currag (SFT) G3 5f 100
1999 Turf 0-8: (5f 8) (gd 3, g-f 3, frm 2)
Pattern-class horse, effective 5f, acts on gd to frm, best on frm, has worn blinkers, and excels at Beverley. Turf high 109 - 2nd of 9 to Proud Native (22 May Kempton 5f frm RF 1395). Consistent. This speed merchant failed to add to his score in '99 and became a little inconsistent. He fetched 40,000 gns as a stallion prospect at Tattersalls in October.
**W R Muir [2-18] J Bernstein (from J H M Gosden [1-7] Spt 1997).*

ALMAZHAR (IRE) BHB 49f64a **RR 45f 64a** 4865[6]

4 b g Last Tycoon 9.4f **(73)** -Mosaique Bleue(Shirley Heights) 10.3f **(74)**
Form - 500220465611100026
Record 1999 - 1st:3 2nd:3 3rd:0 Ran:18
Pre1999 - 1st:0 2nd:0 3rd:0 Ran:4
Win Prizemoney £8,555 *Total Prizemoney* £10,437
Wins * **1999** *Jly Southw (STD) H 7f 57 62* <

* **1999** *Jun Southw (STD) H 8f 53 56*
* **1999** Jun Redcar (FRM) H 8f 48 49

1999 Turf 1-8: (7f 2, 8f 1-4, 9f, 10f) (g-s, gd, g-f 3, frm 1-3) 1999 AW 2-10: (6f, 7f 1-3, 8f 1-6) (Fibr 2-10)

Scopey, average gelding, effective 6 to 8f, - acts on Fibr, has worn blinkers, likes left handed tracks, likes tight tracks, excels at Southwell. Turf high 49. AW high 62 - 1st of 13 getting 10lb from Guilsborough (10 Jly Southwell RF 2720) - also 1st of 16 giving 6lb to Girlie Set (28 Jun Southwell RF 2374). He took his time in getting off the mark, but when he did, he went on to complete a hat-trick with wins at Redcar and Southwell twice. Suited by Fibresand and fast ground on turf.

**J L Eyre [3-18] Sunpak Potatoes 2 (from E A L Dunlop [0-4] Jly 1998).*

ALMERINA (IRE) BHB 66f **RR 81f** 4752[11]

4 b f Erins Isle 8.3f **(76)** - Pennine Music (IRE) (Pennine Walk) 8.5f **(61)**

Form - 05240060

Record 1999 - 1st:0 2nd:1 3rd:0 Ran:8
Pre1999 - 1st:2 2nd:0 3rd:0 Ran:7

Win Prizemoney £8,250 *Total Prizemoney* £10,425

Wins 1998 Oct Cork (G-S) H 8f 77 80 <
1998 Oct Punche (SFT) 7.5f 66

1999 Turf 0-8: (7f, 8f 3, 9f, 10f 2, 11f) (sft, g-s, gd 3, g-f 2, frm)

Decent filly, effective 8 to 9f, best at 8f, acts on g-s to g-f. Turf high 81 - 4th of 7 giving 14lb to She's Our Mare (12 Jun Navan 8f g-f RF 2034a).

**J Mackie [0-3] Ms Caroline Breay (from J S Bolger in IRE [2-12] Jun 1999).*

ALMINSTAR BHB 37f **RR 43f** 3690[9]

3 b f Minshaanshu Amad (USA) 11.3f **(53)** - Joytime (John de Coombe) 7.9f **(40)**

Form - 0687550

Record 1999 - 1st:0 2nd:0 3rd:0 Ran:7
Pre1999 - 1st:0 2nd:0 3rd:0 Ran:1

1999 Turf 0-6: (8f, 10f 3, 12f, 16f) (gd 2, g-f, frm 3) 1999 AW 0-1: (15f) (Fibr)

Light-framed, moderate filly. Turf high 49.

**C A Cyzer [0-8] Mrs G M Gooderham.*

ALMOHAD BHB 46f31a **RR 49f 31a** 4647[8]

4 ch g Belmez (USA) 11.4f **(65)** - Anna Paola (GER) (Prince Ippi (GER)) 10.4f **(68)**

Form - 700038168

Record 1999 - 1st:1 2nd:0 3rd:1 Ran:8
Pre1999 - 1st:0 2nd:0 3rd:0 Ran:5

Win Prizemoney £2,878 *Total Prizemoney* £3,589

Wins * **1999** Aug Windso (HVY) H 11.6f 40 49 <

1999 Turf 1-5: (10f, 11f 2, 12f 1-2) (g-s 2, gd 1-1, g-f 2) 1999 AW 0-3: (11f, 14f, 16f) (Equi, Fibr 2)

Workmanlike, moderate gelding, effective 11 to 12f, acts on g-s to gd, has worn blinkers, likes tight tracks. Turf high 49 - 1st of 13 getting 1lb from Slims Lady (9 Aug Windsor RF 3487). AW high 11. Inconsistent. **Dr J D Scargill [1-13] Mrs Janet Mudd.*

ALMOST AMBER (USA) BHB 85f **RR 55f** 3972[R]

3 ch f Mt Livermore (USA) 7.7f **(90)** - Kelly Amber (USA) (Highland Park (USA))

Form - 0R

Record 1999 - 1st:0 2nd:0 3rd:0 Ran:2
Pre1999 - 1st:1 2nd:1 3rd:0 Ran:4

Win Prizemoney £3,538 *Total Prizemoney* £5,204

Wins * 1998 Jun Salisb (G-F) 5f 76+ <

1999 Turf 0-2: (6f 2) (g-f 2)

Strong, fair filly, effective 5f, acts on g-f to frm. Turf high 55.

**J H M Gosden [1-6] Sheikh Mohammed.*

ALMOST GOT IT BHB 28f **RR 39f** 3110[17]

4 ch f St Ninian - Star Leader (Kafu) 6f **(47)**

Form - 000

Record 1999 - 1st:0 2nd:0 3rd:0 Ran:3
Pre1999 - 1st:0 2nd:1 3rd:0 Ran:2

Win Prizemoney £0 *Total Prizemoney* £675

1999 Turf 0-1: (10f) (gd) 1999 AW 0-2: (11f, 12f) (Fibr 2)

Unfurnished, very moderate filly, has worn blinkers.

**J Parkes [0-5] C W Moore.*

AL MUALLIM (USA) BHB 97f **RR 98f** 2105[8]

5 b h Theatrical 11.5f **(78)** - Gerri N Jo Go (USA) (Top Command (USA)) 10f **(77)**

Form - 5028

Record 1999 - 1st:0 2nd:1 3rd:0 Ran:4
Pre1999 - 1st:3 2nd:3 3rd:2 Ran:11

Win Prizemoney £15,261 *Total Prizemoney* £33,935

Wins * 1997 Oct Newmar (G-F) H 7f 88 94 <
* 1997 Aug Lingfi (G-F) H 6f 80 87
* 1996 Oct Catter (GD) 6f 78

1999 Turf 0-4: (6f, 7f 3) (gd, g-f 2, frm)

Very useful colt, effective 7f, acts on g-s to frm. Turf high 98 - 2nd of 6 to Fa-Eq (16 May Kempton 7f frm RF 1255). He is quite lightly raced and usually attracts plenty of support in valuable handicaps. Despite that confidence, he is on a long losing streak and may not be a straightforward ride. **J W Payne [3-15] Al Muallim Partnership.*

ALMUSHTARAK (IRE) BHB 118f **RR 115f** 4919[12]

6 b h Fairy King (USA) 7.7f **(75)** - Exciting (Mill Reef (USA)) 10.5f **(78)**

Form - 333334320

Record 1999 - 1st:0 2nd:1 3rd:5 Ran:8
Pre1999 - 1st:5 2nd:5 3rd:4 Ran:31

Win Prizemoney £78,369 *Total Prizemoney* £369,844

Wins * 1998 Apr Sandow (SFT) G2 8.1f 116 <
* 1997 Spt Doncas (G-F) G3 8f 114
1996 Jly Lingfi (G-F) LH 7.6f 105 107
1996 Jun Kempto (G-F) H 7f 85 90
1995 Spt Bright (GD) 6f 86?

1999 Turf 0-8: (8f 6, 10f 2) (sft, g-s, gd 3, g-f 3)

High-class horse, effective 8 to 10f, best at 8f, acts on sft to g-f, best on gd, likes tight tracks, excels at Sandown and Goodwood. Turf high 118 - 3rd of 6 to Fly To The Stars (15 May Newbury 8f gd RF 1235). Consistent. Regularly in the frame in the last couple of seasons, but rarely gets his head in front. He again gave a good account in some of the top mile events, but he does find genuine Group One company a bit too much for him. Effective on most types of ground, he does not seem to quite get ten furlongs.

**K Mahdi [2-30] Hamad Al-Mutawa (from Miss Gay Kelleway [3-9] Jly 1996).*

ALMUTAWAKEL BHB 118f124a **RR 120f 124a** 5231a[5]

4 b c Machiavellian (USA) 9.8f **(83)** - Elfaslah (IRE) (Green Desert (USA)) 8.6f **(78)**

Form - 17235

Record 1999 - 1st:1 2nd:1 3rd:1 Ran:5
Pre1999 - 1st:3 2nd:2 3rd:0 Ran:8

Win Prizemoney £1,857,643 *Total Prizemoney* £2,084,781

Wins **1999** *Mar Nad Al (FST) G1 10f 126* <
1998 May Chanti (GD) G1 9f 117
* 1997 Aug Newmar (GD) 7f 101+
* 1997 Jly Sandow (G-S) 7.1f 85+

1999 Turf 0-1: (10f) (g-f) 1999 AW 1-4: (9f, 10f 1-3) (Dirt 1-4)

Scopey, top-class colt, effective 9 to 10f, best at 10f, acts on gd - acts on Dirt, excels at Belmont Park. AW high 126 (1st run) - 1st of 8 from Malek (28 Mar Nad Al Sheba RF 0556a). An emotional 'home' winner of the world's richest race, the Dubai World Cup, his season was geared to a tilt at the Breeders' Cup Classic. He made his European reappearance in very different conditions in the Juddmonte International, finishing seventh, but was then switched to America. He twice found ex-British All-Weather winner River Keen too good, in the Woodward and Jockey Club Gold Cup, but ran with credit nevertheless. He produced a similar effort at Gulfstream Park, being beaten less than four lengths after failing to accelerate in the straight. Another crack at the Dubai World Cup in March 2000 looks on the cards.

**S bin Suroor [3-12] (from S bin Suroor in UAE [1-1] Mar 1999).*

AL NABA (USA) BHB 98f **RR 99f** 4675[15]

3 ch c Mr Prospector (USA) 8.6f **(88)** - Forest Flower (USA) (Green Forest (USA)) 9.9f **(68)**

Form - 5210

Record 1999 - 1st:1 2nd:1 3rd:0 Ran:4
Pre1999 - 1st:1 2nd:1 3rd:0 Ran:2

Win Prizemoney £12,572 *Total Prizemoney* £15,261

Wins * **1999** Spt Goodwo (G-F) 7f 99 <
* 1998 Oct Newmar (GD) 6f 88+

1999 Turf 1-4: (6f, 7f 1-3) (gd 2, g-f 1-1, frm)

Scopey, very useful colt, effective 7f, acts on g-f to frm. Turf high

99 - 1st of 5 from Mutamayyaz (10 Spt Goodwood RF 4259). He is less durable than his Classic-winning dam, but put up a brave effort when winning a conditions race at Goodwood in September. Likely to stay a mile, he may yet make a mark in Listed events.
E A L Dunlop [2-6] Hamdan Al Maktoum.

ALNAJASHEE BHB 55f **RR 61f** 3860[6]
3 b c Generous (IRE) 11.5f **(82)** - Tahdid (Mtoto)
Form - 2556
Record 1999 - 1st:0 2nd:1 3rd:0 Ran:4
Pre1999 - 1st:0 2nd:0 3rd:0 Ran:2
Win Prizemoney £0 *Total Prizemoney* £1,080
1999 Turf 0-4: (12f 2, 14f, 16f) (g-f, frm 2, hrd)
Scopey, average colt, effective 12f, acts on hrd. Turf high 73 (1st run) - 2nd of 4 giving 5lb to Caerless (26 Jun Bath 12f hrd RF 2320). *P T Walwyn [0-6] Hamdan Al Maktoum.*

AL NAKHLAH (USA) BHB 60f **RR 65f** 4488[13]
3 b f Sheikh Albadou 9.2f **(75)** - Magic Slipper (Habitat) 9.4f **(70)**
Form - 5250
Record 1999 - 1st:0 2nd:1 3rd:0 Ran:4
Pre1999 - 1st:0 2nd:0 3rd:0 Ran:1
Win Prizemoney £0 *Total Prizemoney* £666
1999 Turf 0-4: (7f, 10f 2, 12f) (g-s, g-f 2, frm)
Average filly. Turf high 65 (began Jly).
P T Walwyn [0-5] Hamdan Al Maktoum.

ALONSA (IRE) BHB 56f **RR 56f** 4630[6]
3 b f Trempolino (USA) 11.9f **(77)** - Alimana (Akarad (FR)) 9f **(76)**
Form - 5750406
Record 1999 - 1st:0 2nd:0 3rd:0 Ran:7
Pre1999 - 1st:0 2nd:0 3rd:0 Ran:2
Win Prizemoney £0 *Total Prizemoney* £497
1999 Turf 0-7: (9f, 10f, 11f, 12f 4) (g-s, gd 3, frm 3)
Light-framed, fair filly. Turf high 68. Inconsistent.
C E Brittain [0-9] Saeed Manana.

Pre1999 - 1st:0 2nd:0 3rd:0 Ran:1
Win Prizemoney £0 *Total Prizemoney* £555
1999 Turf 0-1: (9f) (g-f)
Scopey, currently fair filly. *J H M Gosden [0-2] Sheikh Mohammed.*

ALPATHAR (IRE) BHB 58f **RR 72?f** 4722[5]
2 ch f Simply Great (FR) 11.9f **(61)** - Royal Language (USA) (Conquistador Cielo (USA)) 8.8f **(69)**
Form - 5564825
Record 1999 - 1st:0 2nd:1 3rd:0 Ran:7
Win Prizemoney £0 *Total Prizemoney* £509
1999 Turf 0-6: (5f 2, 6f, 7f 3) (gd 3, g-f 2, hrd) 1999 AW 0-1: (6f) (Fibr)
Above-average filly, effective 7f, acts on gd. Turf high 72 - 2nd of 11 getting 8lb from Romantic Affair (29 Spt Newcastle 7f gd RF 4633). *M Dods [0-7] Harry Whitton.*

ALPENGLOW BHB 100f **RR 100f** 5140[3]
3 b f Ezzoud (IRE) - Aquaglow (Caerleon (USA)) 8.6f **(71)**
Form - 1613
Record 1999 - 1st:2 2nd:0 3rd:1 Ran:4
Win Prizemoney £10,394 *Total Prizemoney* £13,020
Wins * **1999** Oct Leices (GD) 8f 99 <
* **1999** Apr Newmar (GD) 7f 82
1999 Turf 2-4: (7f 1-2, 8f 1-2) (gd 1-3, frm 1-1)
Very useful filly. Turf high 100 - 3rd of 8 getting 8lb from Bomb Alaska (30 Oct Newmarket 8f gd RF 5140) - also 1st of 7 giving 4lb to Jig (12 Oct Leicester RF 4838). She found her feet at the back-end, running a super race behind Bomb Alaska and Albarahin at Newmarket in October. Open to greater improvement than that pair, she will stay beyond a mile and should win a Listed race at least in 2000. *J H M Gosden [2-4] Sheikh Mohammed.*

ALPEN WOLF (IRE) BHB 77f **RR 79f** 4161[5]
4 ch g Wolfhound (USA) 7.3f **(71)** - Oatfield (Great Nephew) 9.9f **(64)**
Form - 0136327105
Record 1999 - 1st:2 2nd:1 3rd:2 Ran:10

Almutawakel, surprise winner of the Dubai World Cup, became a top class dirt performer

ALOYSIA (USA) RR 52?f 3367[3]
3 ch f Diesis 9f **(80)** - Alyanaabi (USA) (Roberto (USA)) 10f **(76)**
Form - 3
Record 1999 - 1st:0 2nd:0 3rd:1 Ran:1

Pre1999 - 1st:4 2nd:0 3rd:2 Ran:20
Win Prizemoney £20,977 *Total Prizemoney* £26,326
Wins * **1999** Aug Bath (GD) H 5.7f 76 79 <
* **1999** Apr Bright (G-F) H 6f 70 69

* 1998 Spt Bright (FRM) 7f 68
* 1998 Aug Folkes (G-F) 6f 68
* 1998 Aug Bright (G-F) H 6f 56 64
* 1998 Aug Bright (FRM) S 6f 41

1999 Turf 2-10: (6f 2-8, 7f 2) (gd 2, g-f 3, frm 2-5)

Above-average gelding, effective 6 to 7f, best at 6f, acts on gd to frm, best on frm, has worn blinkers, likes left handed tracks, likes tight tracks, does well at Brighton and Folkestone. Turf high 79 - 1st of 14 getting 10lb from Cauda Equina (22 Aug Bath RF 3833). Consistent. Completed a fine four-timer within the space of three weeks during the autumn of 1998. Three of those wins came at Brighton, and he regained winning form back at that track on his second start of last season. Ran well in competitive sprints before scoring at Bath in August. **W R Muir [6-30] R Haim.*

ALPHA RR 49f 2225[12]

3 b g Primo Dominie 7.2f **(67)** - Preening (Persian Bold) 9.3f **(66)**

Form - 0

Record 1999 - 1st:0 2nd:0 3rd:0 Ran:1
Pre1999 - 1st:1 2nd:0 3rd:0 Ran:5

Win Prizemoney £3,523 *Total Prizemoney* £3,746

Wins * 1998 Jly Beverl (GD) 5f 77+ <

1999 Turf 0-1: (6f) (frm)

Scopey, moderate gelding, effective 5f, acts on g-f to frm. **C W Thornton [1-6] Guy Reed and Mrs Ailsa Daniels.*

ALPHA BLUES RR 3933a[4]

4 ch c Acatenango (GER) - Alpha Belle (GER) **00**

Form - 4

1999 Turf 0-1: (15f) (gd)

Currently very poor colt. **A Wohler in GER [0-1].*

ALPHA HEIGHTS (IRE) BHB 73f RR 70f 4103[13]

2 b f Namaqualand (USA) - Mnaafa (IRE) **(64f)** (Darshaan) 9.9f **(84)**

Form - 37500

Record 1999 - 1st:0 2nd:0 3rd:1 Ran:5

Win Prizemoney £0 *Total Prizemoney* £490

1999 Turf 0-5: (5f 2, 6f, 7f, 8f) (g-f, frm 4)

Above-average filly. Turf high 83 - 5th of 16 getting 5lb from Bally Pride (25 Jun Curragh 6f frm RF 2404a). **Mrs P N Dutfield [0-5] Alpha Dorset Plumber Merchants.*

ALPHA ROSE RR 59f 4428[6]

2 ch f Inchinor 8.9f **(64)** - Philgwyn (Milford) 9f **(61)**

Form - 6

Record 1999 - 1st:0 2nd:0 3rd:0 Ran:1

1999 Turf 0-1: (7f) (g-s)

Currently fair filly. **R J R Williams [0-1] Richard Morris Jr.*

ALPHILDA BHB 83f RR 81f 4599[19]

2 gr f Ezzoud (IRE) - Desert Delight (IRE) (Green Desert (USA)) 8.6f **(78)**

Form - 3424102220

Record 1999 - 1st:1 2nd:4 3rd:1 Ran:10

Win Prizemoney £2,916 *Total Prizemoney* £9,136

Wins * **1999** Jly Ayr (GD) H 6f 77 <

1999 Turf 1-10: (5f 2, 6f 1-7, 7f) (gd 1-3, g-f 4, frm 3)

Decent filly, effective 6f, acts on gd to frm, best on gd. Turf high 81 - 2nd of 14 giving 16lb to Top of The Class (17 Spt Ayr 6f gd RF 4375) - also 1st of 5 giving 8lb to Bettyjoe (17 Jly Ayr RF 2895). Ran with great consistency in some well contested events, and has been more unlucky than ungenuine. Six furlongs and good or softer ground seem to suit. **B W Hills [1-10] S W Transport (Swindon) Ltd.*

ALPINE FUGUE (IRE) RR 66f 2715[5]

5 b g Classic Music (USA) 7.2f **(57)** - Val Gardena (Ahonoora) 8.1f **(73)**

Form - 5

Record 1999 - 1st:0 2nd:0 3rd:0 Ran:1

1999 Turf 0-1: (14f) (frm)

Average gelding. **J W Mullins [0-5] P C & Mrs S I Fry & D Shine.*

ALPINE HIDEAWAY (IRE) BHB 50f60a RR 51f 60a 4040[3]

6 b g Tirol 8.1f **(64)** - Arbour (USA) (Graustark) 10.1f **(70)**

Form - 60080163

Record 1999 - 1st:1 2nd:0 3rd:1 Ran:8
Pre1999 - 1st:3 2nd:6 3rd:5 Ran:32

Win Prizemoney £10,273 *Total Prizemoney* £19,708

Wins * **1999** Aug Beverl (GD) C 8.5f 51
1997 Aug Ripon (G-F) C 8f 61
1997 *Jly Southw (STD) C 7f 66*
1996 Oct Leices (G-F) 7f 71 <

1999 Turf 1-8: (7f 2, 8f 1-6) (sft, g-s, g-f 1-4, frm, hrd)

Average gelding, effective 8f, acts on gd, has worn blinkers. Turf high 67.

**M W Easterby [4-34] Easterby Trailers (from B Hanbury [3-23] Aug 1997).*

ALPINE PARK (IRE) BHB 92f RR 83f 3656[7]

2 ch f Barathea (IRE) - Park Charger **(96f)** (Tirol)

Form - 12167

Record 1999 - 1st:2 2nd:1 3rd:0 Ran:5

Win Prizemoney £6,744 *Total Prizemoney* £7,915

Wins * **1999** Jun Pontef (SFT) 6f 81+
* **1999** May Kempto (GD) 6f 83 <

1999 Turf 2-5: (6f 2-4, 7f) (gd 1-2, g-f 2, frm 1-1)

Decent filly. Turf high 83 - 2nd of 4 giving 7lb to Camp Fire (28 May Nottingham 6f g-f RF 1551) - also 1st of 15 from Eurolink Raindance (16 May Kempton RF 1254). A winner of two of her first three starts, she disappointed when upped in class on her fourth run, although the race may have come too soon after her Pontefract victory. **J Noseda [2-5] Mrs Seamus Burns.*

ALPINE RED BHB 52f RR 50f 834[8]

3 b g Tirol 8.1f **(64)** - Rohita (IRE) **(83df)** (Waajib)

Form - 008

Record 1999 - 1st:0 2nd:0 3rd:0 Ran:3

1999 Turf 0-3: (8f 2, 10f) (sft, gd 2)

Workmanlike, fair gelding. Turf high 50. (DEAD) **M L W Bell [0-3] Terry Neill.*

ALQAWAASER (USA) RR 53f 4875[12]

2 b br c Dayjur (USA) 6.8f **(79)** - Alghuzaylah (Habitat) 9.4f **(70)**

Form - 30

Record 1999 - 1st:0 2nd:0 3rd:1 Ran:2

Win Prizemoney £0 *Total Prizemoney* £535

1999 Turf 0-2: (6f, 7f) (g-s, gd)

Currently fair colt. Turf high 53 (began Spt). **E A L Dunlop [0-2] Hamdan Al Maktoum.*

ALRABYAH (IRE) BHB 35f RR 33df 2057[20]

4 br g Brief Truce (USA) 9.1f **(73)** - Bean Siamsa (Solinus) 9f **(71)**

Form - 000

Record 1999 - 1st:0 2nd:0 3rd:0 Ran:3
Pre1999 - 1st:0 2nd:0 3rd:0 Ran:7

1999 Turf 0-3: (8f 3) (gd, g-f, hrd)

Tall, very moderate gelding, has worn blinkers. Becoming disappointing. **K A Morgan [0-6] J A Outwin (from P T Walwyn [0-5] Jly 1998).*

ALRASSAAM BHB 108f RR 112f 3778a[2]

3 b c Zafonic (USA) 9f **(83)** - Lady Blackfoot (Prince Tenderfoot (USA)) 9f **(61)**

Form - 101612

Record 1999 - 1st:3 2nd:1 3rd:0 Ran:6
Pre1999 - 1st:0 2nd:0 3rd:0 Ran:1

Win Prizemoney £34,475 *Total Prizemoney* £49,252

Wins * **1999** Jly Chanti (GD) G3 9f 107
* **1999** May Haydoc (GD) 8.1f 112 <
* **1999** Apr Newbur (G-F) 8f 97+

1999 Turf 3-6: (8f 2-4, 9f 1-1, 10f) (gd 2-3, g-f 1-2, frm)

Light-framed, Group-class colt, effective 8 to 10f, acts on gd. Turf high 112 - 2nd of 5 to Val Royal (14 Aug Deauville 10f gd RF 3778a) - also 1st of 7 getting 9lb from Teapot Row (28 May Haydock RF 1542). He exposed Killer Instinct's feet of clay in a Newbury maiden during the spring and improved throughout the campaign, winning the Group Three Prix Daphnis at Chantilly in July. From a family that progress with age, he will make a smart four-year-old. **M A Jarvis [3-7].*

ALSAHIB (USA) BHB 40f73a RR 41f 73a 3973[4]

6 b g Slew O' Gold (USA) 10.2f **(73)** - Khwlah (USA) (Best Turn (USA)) 10.2f **(78)**

Form - 42431315534354

Record 1999 - 1st:2 2nd:1 3rd:4 Ran:14
Pre1999 - 1st:3 2nd:2 3rd:2 Ran:29
Win Prizemoney £15,951 *Total Prizemoney* £23,915
Wins *** 1999** *Apr Southw (STD) C 12f 73*
*** 1999** *Feb Southw (STD) C 12f 70*
* 1998 *Oct Wolver (STD) C 12f 81* <
* 1998 *Jan Southw (STD) H 11f 76 80*
* 1997 *Jun Wolver (STD) H 9.4f 64 76*
1999 Turf 0-7: (12f 6, 14f) (gd, g-f 3, frm 3) 1999 AW 2-7: (11f, 12f 2-6) (Equi, Fibr 2-6)
Above-average gelding, effective 11 to 12f, best at 12f, - acts on AW, best on Fibr, has worn blinkers, prefers left handed tracks, favours tight tracks, excels at Lingfield and Southwell, likes Wolverhampton. Turf high 56. AW high 73 - 1st of 11 giving 9lb to Count de Money (26 Apr Southwell RF 0853).
**W R Muir [5-40] S Channing-Williams (from H ThomsonJones [0-4] Jun 1996).*

AL SAQIYA (USA) BHB 67f RR 54f 1189[10]

3 b f Woodman (USA) 9.7f **(77)** - Augusta Springs (USA) (Nijinsky (CAN)) 10.3f **(77)**
Form - 00
Record 1999 - 1st:0 2nd:0 3rd:0 Ran:2
Pre1999 - 1st:0 2nd:0 3rd:0 Ran:3
Win Prizemoney £0 *Total Prizemoney* £262
1999 Turf 0-2: (8f 2) (frm 2)
Rangy, fair filly, has worn blinkers. Turf high 47.
**J L Dunlop [0-5] Hamdan Al Maktoum.*

AL'S FELLA (IRE) BHB 61f66a RR 64+f 66a 3484[1]

4 br g Alzao (USA) 9.8f **(73)** - Crystal Cross (USA) **(73f)** (Roberto (USA)) 10f **(76)**
Form - 6574141
Record 1999 - 1st:2 2nd:0 3rd:0 Ran:7
Pre1999 - 1st:1 2nd:3 3rd:2 Ran:15
Win Prizemoney £7,900 *Total Prizemoney* £12,245
Wins *** 1999** Aug Windso (HVY) S 11.6f 64+
*** 1999** Jly Leices (G-F) C 11.8f 63
* 1998 Nov Redcar (G-S) H 11f 65 69+
1999 Turf 2-7: (12f 2-4, 14f 3) (g-s, gd 1-1, g-f 1-4, frm)
Neat, average gelding, effective 8 to 14f, best at 12f, acts on gd to frm - acts on Fibr, best on gd, has worn blinkers, favours tight tracks. Turf high 67 - 5th of 12 giving 6lb to Mono Lady (6 May Chester 12f g-f RF 1054) - also 1st of 9 giving 15lb to Verposen (9 Aug Windsor RF 3484). Consistent.
**P F I Cole [3-22] Mrs Christopher Hanbury.*

ALSHAKR RR 73f 4731[4]

2 b f Bahri (USA) - Give Thanks (Relko) 9.9f **(59)**
Form - 64
Record 1999 - 1st:0 2nd:0 3rd:0 Ran:2
Win Prizemoney £0 *Total Prizemoney* £371
1999 Turf 0-2: (6f, 7f) (gd, frm)
Currently above-average filly. Turf high 73 (began Spt) - 4th of 15 to Resounding (5 Oct Nottingham 6f gd RF 4731).
**P T Walwyn [0-2] Hamdan Al Maktoum.*

ALTAY BHB 63f RR 60f 4423[6]

2 b c Erins Isle 8.3f **(76)** - Aliuska (IRE) (Fijar Tango (FR))
Form - 506
Record 1999 - 1st:0 2nd:0 3rd:0 Ran:3
1999 Turf 0-3: (5f, 6f, 7f) (frm 2, hrd)
Currently average colt. Turf high 60 (began Aug).
**R A Fahey [0-3] John Robson.*

ALTIBR (USA) RR 112f 2421a[2]

4 ch c Diesis 9f **(80)** - Love's Reward (Nonoalco (USA)) 8.5f **(66)**
Form - 142
Record 1999 - 1st:1 2nd:1 3rd:0 Ran:3
Pre1999 - 1st:1 2nd:0 3rd:0 Ran:2
Win Prizemoney £154,384 *Total Prizemoney* £172,207
Wins 1999 *Mar Nad Al (FST) G3 10f 124* <
* 1997 Oct Leices (GD) 7f 101++
1999 Turf 0-2: (9f 2) (gd 2) 1999 AW 1-1: (10f 1-1) (Dirt 1-1)
Very high-class colt. Turf high 112. (1st run) - 1st of 9 from Spindrift (28 Mar Nad Al Sheba RF 0555a). Impressive winner of the Dubai Duty Free, but was a very disappointing favourite in the Diomed, and was comfortably beaten by Great Dane in an ordinary Group Two at the Curragh. Although turf-bred, he may benefit from a try on dirt, where his apparent lack of acceleration will be less exposed.
**S bin Suroor [1-4] Godolphin (from S bin Suroor in UAE [1-1] Mar 1999).*

ALTICHIERO BHB 80f85a RR 75++f 85a 4704[1]

3 b g Polish Precedent (USA) 9f **(73)** - Anna Matrushka (Mill Reef (USA)) 10.5f **(78)**
Form - 21
Record 1999 - 1st:1 2nd:1 3rd:0 Ran:2
Pre1999 - 1st:0 2nd:0 3rd:0 Ran:2
Win Prizemoney £3,876 *Total Prizemoney* £5,130
Wins *** 1999** *Oct Wolver (STD) H 12f 77 94+* <
1999 Turf 0-1: (10f) (g-f) 1999 AW 1-1: (12f 1-1) (Fibr 1-1)
Well made, useful gelding. (1st run) - 1st of 6 getting 3lb from High Tatra (2 Oct Wolverhampton RF 4704). Ran well to finish runner-up in a maiden at Goodwood on his belated reappearance, and bolted up in a handicap on the Wolverhampton Fibresand next time. He looks to be improving and can win again, especially if tried again on sand. **Sir Michael Stoute [1-4] Sheikh Mohammed.*

ALTIZAF RR 67f 4084[7]

3 b f Zafonic (USA) 9f **(83)** - Altiyna (Troy) 10.4f **(68)**
Form - 57
Record 1999 - 1st:0 2nd:0 3rd:0 Ran:2
1999 Turf 0-2: (10f 2) (frm 2)
Scopey, currently average filly. Turf high 67 (began Jly).
**W R Muir [0-2] D J Deer.*

AL TOWD (USA) BHB 94f RR 90f 5130[3]

2 b c Kingmambo (USA) 10.9f **(85)** - Toujours Elle (USA) (Lyphard (USA)) 9.9f **(72)**
Form - 3123
Record 1999 - 1st:1 2nd:1 3rd:2 Ran:4
Win Prizemoney £3,761 *Total Prizemoney* £8,129
Wins *** 1999** Spt Newcas (G-F) 7f 75+ <
1999 Turf 1-4: (7f 1-3, 8f) (gd 2, frm 1-2)
Useful colt. Turf high 90 (began Aug) - 3rd of 6 to Autonomy (29 Oct Newmarket 8f gd RF 5130). Got off the mark in a Newmarket maiden on his second start, and showed useful form in two minor races on softish ground. **J L Dunlop [1-4] Hamdan Al Maktoum.*

ALUSTAR BHB 66f RR 78f 4857[11]

2 b f Emarati (USA) 6.6f **(63)** - Chiming Melody (Cure The Blues (USA)) 9.5f **(63)**
Form - 83312800
Record 1999 - 1st:1 2nd:1 3rd:2 Ran:8
Win Prizemoney £2,379 *Total Prizemoney* £3,837
Wins *** 1999** Jun Pontef (G-S) 5f 64 <
1999 Turf 1-7: (5f 1-6, 6f) (g-s, gd 1-4, g-f 2) 1999 AW 0-1: (5f) (Fibr)
Above-average filly, effective 5f, acts on g-f. Turf high 78 - 2nd of 6 getting 7lb from Singsong (16 Jun Ripon 5f g-f RF 2058).
**M W Easterby [1-8] T R Beston.*

ALVA GLEN (USA) RR 88f 5001[1]

2 b c Gulch (USA) 9.6f **(79)** -Domludge (USA)(Lyphard (USA)) 9.9f **(72)**
Form - 421
Record 1999 - 1st:1 2nd:1 3rd:0 Ran:3
Win Prizemoney £3,687 *Total Prizemoney* £5,071
Wins *** 1999** Oct Nottin (GD) 8.2f 88 <
1999 Turf 1-3: (6f, 7f, 8f 1-1) (g-s, gd 1-1, frm)
Currently useful colt. Turf high 88 - 1st of 11 from Hidden Brave (21 Oct Nottingham RF 5001). Hung badly when winning his maiden. **Sir Michael Stoute [1-3] Sheikh Mohammed.*

AL WAFFI BHB 100f RR 97f 4110a[2]

3 b c Fairy King (USA) 7.7f **(75)** - Darrery **(98f)** (Darshaan) 9.9f **(84)**
Form - 422
Record 1999 - 1st:0 2nd:2 3rd:0 Ran:3
Pre1999 - 1st:2 2nd:1 3rd:1 Ran:5
Win Prizemoney £7,070 *Total Prizemoney* £46,207
Wins 1998 Spt Leices (G-F) 7f 94 <
1998 Aug Salisb (G-F) 7f 77
1999 Turf 0-3: (8f 2, 11f) (gd 2, g-f)
Leggy, very useful colt, effective 7 to 8f, best at 8f, acts on sft to frm. Turf high 97 - 2nd of 7 giving 6lb to Miami Blues (29 Aug

Baden-Baden 8f gd RF 4110a). Improving. He falls short of Group class and has not always looked entirely genuine. Possibly suited by a strong pace, he is worth another chance beyond a mile.
**S bin Suroor [0-3] (from D R Loder [2-5] Oct 1998).*

ALWAYS ALIGHT BHB 90f **RR 90f** 4588[3]
5 ch g Never so Bold 7.1f **(62)** - Fire Sprite (Mummy's Game) 8.2f **(60)**
Form - 3600740363
Record **1999** - 1st:0 2nd:0 3rd:3 Ran:10
Pre1999 - 1st:6 2nd:3 3rd:6 Ran:35
Win Prizemoney £77,012 *Total Prizemoney* £92,874
Wins * 1998 Spt Ayr (G-S) H 6f 89 97 <
* 1998 Aug Ayr (G-S) 6f 87
* 1998 Mar Doncas (GD) H 6f 81 86
* 1997 Oct Newcas (G-F) H 6f 75 78
* 1997 Jun Goodwo (G-S) H 6f 72 74
* 1997 May Newbur (G-F) H 6f 62 69
1999 Turf 0-10: (6f 10) (g-s, gd 4, g-f 3, frm 2)
Useful gelding, effective 6f, acts on sft to g-f, has worn blinkers. Turf high 95. Consistent. Successful in the 1998 Ayr Gold Cup, he is a smart sprint handicapper. That said, he needs a strong pilot nowadays and has become a touch frustrating. Usually reluctant to post, he has worn blinkers and a visor.
**K R Burke [6-45] M Nelmes-Crocker.*

ALWENA BHB 23a **RR 3f 23a** 92[15]
4 ch f Henbit (USA) 10.2f **(46)** - Brenig (Horage) 10.3f **(61)**
Form - 07550
Record **1999** - 1st:0 2nd:0 3rd:0 Ran:2
Pre1999 - 1st:0 2nd:0 3rd:0 Ran:4
1999 AW 0-2: (11f, 12f) (Equi, Fibr)
Lengthy, very moderate filly, has worn blinkers. AW high 7.
**S C Williams [0-6] Edgar Lloyd.*

ALYPORTENT BHB 40f **RR 14f** 3104[8]
5 b g Warning 8.1f **(77)** - Alilisa (USA) **(14f)** (Alydar (USA)) 9.1f **(76)**
Form - 00808
Record **1999** - 1st:0 2nd:0 3rd:0 Ran:5
Pre1999 - 1st:0 2nd:0 3rd:0 Ran:2
1999 Turf 0-5: (6f 3, 7f, 8f) (gd, frm 4)
Poor gelding, has worn blinkers. Turf high 42.
**Mrs J Jordan [0-5] J E Hulme (from W J Haggas [0-2] Oct 1996).*

ALYSKA (IRE) RR 22f 2127[8]
2 b f Owington - Simouna (Ela-Mana-Mou) 10.1f **(70)**
Form - 8
Record **1999** - 1st:0 2nd:0 3rd:0 Ran:1
1999 Turf 0-1: (5f) (frm)
Currently little account filly. **J Berry [0-1] J E M Hawkins Ltd.*

ALZAO STORM (IRE) RR 7f 2817[10]
2 ch f Mukaddamah (USA) 7.6f **(74)** - Brockley Hill Lass (IRE) (Alzao (USA)) 7.1f **(68)**
Form - 00
Record **1999** - 1st:0 2nd:0 3rd:0 Ran:2
1999 Turf 0-2: (6f, 7f) (g-f, frm)
Currently very poor filly. Turf high 7 (began Jly).
**J W Payne [0-2] Sean Gollogly.*

ALZITA (IRE) RR 57f 4433[9]
2 b f Alzao (USA) 9.8f **(73)** - Tiavanita (USA)(J O Tobin (USA)) 9.4f **(67)**
Form - 0
Record **1999** - 1st:0 2nd:0 3rd:0 Ran:1
1999 Turf 0-1: (7f) (g-s)
Currently fair filly. **J A R Toller [0-1] A Ilsley.*

ALZOLA (IRE) RR 56f 3616[11]
2 b f Alzao (USA) 9.8f **(73)** - Polistatic (Free State) 8.7f **(61)**
Form - 0
Record **1999** - 1st:0 2nd:0 3rd:0 Ran:1
1999 Turf 0-1: (6f) (g-f)
Currently fair filly. **C A Horgan [0-1] Mrs B Sumner.*

ALZOOMO (IRE) BHB 54f63a **RR 34f 63a** 463[13]
7 b g Alzao (USA) 9.8f **(73)** - Fandangerina (USA) (Grey Dawn II) 11.1f **(72)**
Form - 0
Record **1999** - 1st:0 2nd:0 3rd:0 Ran:1
Pre1999 - 1st:0 2nd:1 3rd:3 Ran:9
Win Prizemoney £0 *Total Prizemoney* £2,952
1999 Turf 0-1: (12f) (g-f)
Fair gelding, has worn blinkers.
**J A Glover [3-17] L A Jackson (from H R A Cecil [0-1] Apr 1995).*

AMADOUR (IRE) BHB 58f75a **RR 51?f 75a** 998[16]
6 b g Contract Law (USA) 8.9f **(54)** - Truly Flattering (Hard Fought) 8.8f **(62)**
Form - 0
Record **1999** - 1st:0 2nd:0 3rd:0 Ran:1
Pre1999 - 1st:3 2nd:3 3rd:1 Ran:15
Win Prizemoney £9,047 *Total Prizemoney* £12,182
Wins * 1998 *Jan Lingfi (STD) H 12f 70 73* <
* 1997 *Feb Lingfi (STD) H 12f 65 66*
* 1996 Oct Bright (GD) H 11.9f 63 66
1999 Turf 0-1: (12f) (frm)
Above-average gelding. Inconsistent.
**P Mitchell [3-16] Lovine Partnership.*

AMAD'S PRINCESS BHB 43f **RR 36f** 1175[8]
3 b f Minshaanshu Amad (USA) 11.3f **(53)** - Cleeveland Lady (Turn Back The Time (USA))
Form - 68
Record **1999** - 1st:0 2nd:0 3rd:0 Ran:2
Pre1999 - 1st:0 2nd:0 3rd:0 Ran:3
1999 Turf 0-2: (12f 2) (hvy, g-f)
Very moderate filly. Turf high 34.
**W G M Turner [0-2] Mrs Philomena Reich (from G M O'Neill in IRE [0-3] Oct 1998).*

AMALIA (IRE) BHB 99f **RR 96f** 4871[10]
3 b f Danehill (USA) 9.1f **(79)** - Cheviot Amble (IRE) **(97f)** (Pennine Walk) 8.5f **(61)**
Form - 21321410
Record **1999** - 1st:3 2nd:2 3rd:1 Ran:8
Pre1999 - 1st:0 2nd:0 3rd:1 Ran:2
Win Prizemoney £36,281 *Total Prizemoney* £42,613
Wins * **1999** Spt Doncas (G-F) H 10.3f 93 96 <
* **1999** Aug Cheste (G-S) H 7.6f 89 91
* **1999** Jun Redcar (FRM) 8f 82
1999 Turf 3-8: (8f 2-5, 9f, 10f 1-2) (gd 1-3, g-f, frm 2-4)
Light-framed, very useful filly, effective 8 to 10f, best at 8f, acts on gd to frm, best on frm. Turf high 96 - 1st of 17 getting 2lb from Robin Lane (11 Spt Doncaster RF 4267) - also 1st of 9 giving 28lb to Only For Gold (21 Aug Chester RF 3814). Tough and progressive, she proven suited by a step-up in distance during the autumn and stays a mile and a quarter. Effective on any ground, she can win another handicap before returning to Listed company.
**P W Harris [3-10] Mrs P W Harris.*

AMAL JUMAIRAH BHB 62f **RR 67df** 2822[7]
3 b c Barathea (IRE) - Fair Shirley (IRE) (Shirley Heights) 10.3f **(74)**
Form - 64437
Record **1999** - 1st:0 2nd:0 3rd:1 Ran:5
Pre1999 - 1st:0 2nd:0 3rd:0 Ran:2
Win Prizemoney £0 *Total Prizemoney* £689
1999 Turf 0-5: (8f, 10f 4) (gd 2, g-f, frm 2)
Scopey, average colt, effective 8 to 10f, acts on g-f to frm, prefers tight tracks. Turf high 70.
**M A Jarvis [0-7] Sheikh Ahmed Al Maktoum.*

AMARANTH (IRE) BHB 80f **RR 80f** 4427[6]
3 b g Mujadil (USA) 7.7f **(70)** - Zoes Delight (IRE) (Hatim (USA))
Form - 88231067716
Record **1999** - 1st:2 2nd:1 3rd:1 Ran:11
Pre1999 - 1st:1 2nd:1 3rd:0 Ran:2
Win Prizemoney £9,754 *Total Prizemoney* £13,318
Wins * **1999** Aug Newmar (G-F) H 5f 77 80
* **1999** Jun Newcas (G-F) H 6f 77 83 <
* 1998 Oct Redcar (SFT) 5f 79
1999 Turf 2-11: (5f 1-7, 6f 1-3, 7f) (gd 6, g-f, frm 2-4)
Scopey, decent gelding, effective 5 to 6f, best at 5f, acts on gd to frm, best on frm. Turf high 83 - 1st of 13 getting 6lb from Pepperdine (2 Jun Newcastle RF 1691) - also 1st of 14 giving 9lb to Caution (28 Aug Newmarket RF 3962). **J L Eyre [3-13] M Gleason.*

AMARETTO FLAME (IRE) BHB 60f **RR 58f** 3254[3]
3 ch f First Trump - Vestal Flame (Habitat) 9.4f **(70)**
Form - 020313
Record 1999 - 1st:1 2nd:1 3rd:2 Ran:6
Pre1999 - 1st:0 2nd:0 3rd:0 Ran:1
Win Prizemoney £1,926 *Total Prizemoney* £3,779
Wins * **1999** Jly Windso (G-F) S 11.6f 52 <
1999 Turf 1-6: (10f 2, 12f 1-3, 16f) (sft, g-f 2, frm 1-3)
Lengthy, fair filly, effective 10f, acts on sft. Turf high 70 - 2nd of 9 getting 22lb from Drakensberg (24 Apr Leicester 10f sft RF 0833).
**B J Meehan [1-7] The Second Harlequin Partnership.*

AMARICE BHB 78f **RR 82f** 3287[3]
3 b f Suave Dancer (USA) 10.7f **(68)** - Almitra (Targowice (USA)) 11.4f **(70)**
Form - 02253
Record 1999 - 1st:0 2nd:2 3rd:1 Ran:5
Pre1999 - 1st:1 2nd:0 3rd:1 Ran:4
Win Prizemoney £3,496 *Total Prizemoney* £7,315
Wins * 1998 Oct Ayr (G-S) 7f 81 <
1999 Turf 0-5: (8f 2, 9f, 10f 2) (g-f 3, frm 2)
Tall, decent filly, effective 6 to 10f, acts on sft to frm, best on g-f, prefers tight tracks. Turf high 82 - 2nd of 10 giving 3lb to Mcgillycuddy Reeks (22 Jun Beverley 10f g-f RF 2192).
**M Johnston [1-9] Mrs S W O'Brien.*

AMARO BHB 45f **RR 44f** 4986[7]
3 b f Emarati (USA) 6.6f **(63)** - Redcross Miss (Tower Walk) 10f **(62)**
Form - 545220477
Record 1999 - 1st:0 2nd:2 3rd:0 Ran:9
Win Prizemoney £0 *Total Prizemoney* £1,640
1999 Turf 0-7: (5f 6, 7f) (sft, g-s, gd, g-f 2, frm 2) 1999 AW 0-2: (5f, 6f) (Fibr 2)
Scopey, moderate filly, effective 5f, acts on g-f to frm, best on frm. Turf high 46 - 2nd of 17 getting 12lb from Bodfari Komaite (28 Jly Doncaster 5f frm RF 3200). AW high 40. **J Wharton [0-9] J Rose.*

AMAZED RR 59+f 5070[6]
2 ch f Clantime 6.6f **(57)** - Indigo (Primo Dominie) 6.2f **(80)**
Form - 6
Record 1999 - 1st:0 2nd:0 3rd:0 Ran:1
1999 Turf 0-1: (5f) (gd)
Currently fair filly. **I A Balding [0-1] D R Brotherton.*

AMAZING DREAM (IRE) BHB 86f **RR 83f** 4173[6]
3 b f Thatching 7.8f **(69)** - Aunty Eileen (Ahonoora) 8.1f **(73)**
Form - 0780076
Record 1999 - 1st:0 2nd:0 3rd:0 Ran:7
Pre1999 - 1st:3 2nd:1 3rd:0 Ran:7
Win Prizemoney £86,603 *Total Prizemoney* £96,429
Wins * 1998 Aug Currag (GD) 6f 95 <
* 1998 Aug Newbur (GD) L 5.2f 94
* 1998 Jly Windso (GD) 5f 84
1999 Turf 0-7: (5f 3, 6f 2, 7f 2) (g-f 4, frm 3)
Scopey, decent filly, effective 5 to 6f, best at 5f, acts on gd. Turf high 88. Consistent. Useful at two, she rather struggled last season. **R Hannon [3-14] Jubert Family.*

AMAZING FACT (USA) BHB 32f **RR 18f** 4985[10]
4 b g Known Fact (USA) 8.3f **(72)** - Itsamazing (USA) (The Minstrel (CAN)) 10f **(72)**
Form - 0000
Record 1999 - 1st:0 2nd:0 3rd:0 Ran:4
Pre1999 - 1st:0 2nd:0 3rd:1 Ran:6
Win Prizemoney £0 *Total Prizemoney* £455
1999 Turf 0-3: (6f, 8f 2) (gd, g-f 2) 1999 AW 0-1: (7f) (Fibr)
Scopey, little account gelding. Turf high 18 (began Aug). Becoming disappointing.
**J M Bradley [0-4] Robert Bailey (from Lady Herries [0-6] Oct 1998).*

AMBER BAY BHB 44f **RR 47f** 3911[13]
2 b c Petong 7.6f **(58)** - Dependable (Formidable (USA)) 9.2f **(63)**
Form - 080
Record 1999 - 1st:0 2nd:0 3rd:0 Ran:3
1999 Turf 0-3: (7f 3) (gd, g-f 2)
Currently moderate colt. Turf high 47.
**C A Dwyer [0-3] Wessex House Racing.*

AMBER BROWN BHB 58f **RR 60f** 2503[9]
3 b f Thowra (FR) 11.2f **(47)** - High Velocity (Frimley Park) 6.5f **(67)**
Form - 6066850
Record 1999 - 1st:0 2nd:0 3rd:0 Ran:7
1999 Turf 0-7: (5f 4, 6f 3) (g-s, gd 2, g-f 3, frm)
Lengthy, average filly, effective 6f, acts on gd. Turf high 60.
**K T Ivory [0-7] Mrs P A Brown.*

AMBER FORT BHB 72f70a **RR 73f 70a** 4804[17]
6 gr g Indian Ridge 7.6f **(74)** - Lammastide (Martinmas) 7.6f **(59)**
Form - 05533040832080
Record 1999 - 1st:0 2nd:1 3rd:3 Ran:14
Pre1999 - 1st:5 2nd:4 3rd:6 Ran:39
Win Prizemoney £17,848 *Total Prizemoney* £34,319
Wins 1998 Jly Kempto (G-S) H 7f 75 82 <
1998 Jun Goodwo (G-F) H 7f 75 81
1997 Jun Goodwo (G-S) H 7f 74 77
1996 Oct Newbur (SFT) H 7f 69 74
1996 *Jun Lingfi (STD) C 7f 60*
1999 Turf 0-14: (7f 13, 8f) (g-s, gd 6, g-f 2, frm 5)
Above-average gelding, effective 7 to 8f, best at 7f, acts on gd to frm, best on gd, mostly wears blinkers (effectively), prefers right handed tracks, likes tight tracks. Turf high 79.
**J M Bradley [0-14] I'm Out Of Here Racing (from D R C Elsworth [4-27] Oct 1998).*

AMBER GO GO BHB 42f **RR 44f** 4504[16]
2 ch f Rudimentary (USA) 8.2f **(66)** - Plaything (High Top) 10.2f **(67)**
Form - 0007300
Record 1999 - 1st:0 2nd:0 3rd:1 Ran:7
Win Prizemoney £0 *Total Prizemoney* £517
1999 Turf 0-7: (5f 6, 8f) (gd 2, g-f 4, frm)
Moderate filly. Turf high 44. **K W Hogg [0-7] K W Hogg.*

AMBER JASMINE (IRE) BHB 58f **RR 70f** 601[3]
3 b g Petardia 8.2f **(58)** - Hollyberry (IRE) (Runnett) 7f **(59)**
Form - 253
Record 1999 - 1st:0 2nd:1 3rd:1 Ran:3
Pre1999 - 1st:0 2nd:0 3rd:1 Ran:4
Win Prizemoney £0 *Total Prizemoney* £1,589
1999 AW 0-3: (5f 2, 6f) (Fibr 3)
Workmanlike, above-average gelding. AW high 61.
**P C Haslam [0-7] Mrs E Chung.*

AMBER MUSIC RR 1283[3]
2 ch f Interrex (CAN) 7.7f **(51)** - Silly Sally (Music Boy) 6.8f **(57)**
Form - 3
Record 1999 - 1st:0 2nd:0 3rd:1 Ran:1
Win Prizemoney £0 *Total Prizemoney* £247
1999 AW 0-1: (6f) (Fibr)
Very moderate filly. (DEAD) **W G M Turner [0-1] T Jarvis.*

AMBER REGENT BHB 50f35a **RR 25f 35a** 416[14]
4 ch g King's Signet (USA) 7f **(51)** - Silly Sally (Music Boy) 6.8f **(57)**
Form - 0600
Record 1999 - 1st:0 2nd:0 3rd:0 Ran:3
Pre1999 - 1st:1 2nd:2 3rd:1 Ran:18
Win Prizemoney £3,436 *Total Prizemoney* £6,011
Wins 1998 *Feb Wolver (STD) H 7f 57 65* <
1999 AW 0-3: (7f, 8f, 9f) (Fibr 3)
Scopey, very moderate gelding, effective 7f, - acts on AW, has worn blinkers, favours left handed tracks. AW high 33. Inconsistent.
**Miss S J Wilton [0-7] John Pointon and Sons (from P C Haslam [1-15] Jly 1998).*

AMBIDEXTROUS (IRE) BHB 47f35a **RR 44f 35a** 5190[8]
7 b h Shareef Dancer (USA) 10.1f **(67)** - Amber Fizz (USA) (Effervescing (USA)) 8.1f **(79)**
Form - 0536028500352771155628
Record 1999 - 1st:2 2nd:3 3rd:2 Ran:21
Pre1999 - 1st:4 2nd:5 3rd:11 Ran:58
Win Prizemoney £20,370 *Total Prizemoney* £35,965
Wins * **1999** Aug Carlis (G-F) C 12f 50
* **1999** Aug Cheste (G-S) H 12.3f 43 47
* 1997 Jly Cheste (G-F) H 10.3f 58 58 <
* 1997 Jun Mussel (GD) H 12f 45 53

* 1996	Jun	Mussel (G-F)	H	11.1f	43	48
* 1996	Jun	Mussel (FRM)	H	11.1f	43	48

1999 Turf 2-17: (10f 5, 12f 2-11, 14f) (g-s, gd 1-3, g-f 6, frm 1-6, hrd)
1999 AW 0-4: (11f 2, 12f 2) (Fibr 4)

Moderate horse, effective 10 to 12f, best at 10f, acts on gd to frm, best on g-f, has worn blinkers, likes right handed tracks, favours tight tracks, excels at Carlisle and Musselburgh, does well at Chester. Turf high 50 - 1st of 13 giving 4lb to Wellcome Inn (25 Aug Carlisle RF 3898) - also 1st of 6 getting 32lb from Rutland Chantry (20 Aug Chester RF 3786). AW high 39.

**E J Alston [8-94] Mrs Carol McPhail (from C E Brittain [0-4] Jly 1995).*

AMBITIOUS BHB 78f62a RR 76f 62a 5110[12]

4 b f Ardkinglass 5f **(64)** - Ayodhya (IRE) (Astronef)
Form - 2462155282818021306611 20

Record	**1999 -**	1st:5	2nd:5	3rd:1	Ran:22
	Pre1999 -	1st:0	2nd:2	3rd:0	Ran:6

Win Prizemoney £20,650 *Total Prizemoney* £28,435

Wins	*** 1999**	Oct	York (G-S)	H	5f	66	76 <
	*** 1999**	Oct	Redcar (GD)		5f		69
	*** 1999**	Aug	Sandow (G-S)	H	5f	63	65
	*** 1999**	Jun	Sandow (GD)	C	5f		57
	1999	*Feb*	*Southw (STD)*	*H*	*6f*	*57*	*65*

1999 Turf 4-18: (5f 4-11, 6f 6, 7f) (gd 2-9, g-f 1-4, frm 1-4, hrd) 1999 AW 1-4: (6f 1-3, 7f) (Equi, Fibr 1-3)

Unfurnished, above-average filly, effective 5f, acts on gd to g-f, best on g-f, has worn blinkers, does well at Sandown. Turf high 76 - 2nd of 18 getting 1lb from Azizzi (18 Oct Pontefract 5f g-f RF 4933) - also 1st of 23 getting 5lb from Ivory's Joy (6 Oct York RF 4755). AW high 65. A fair sprint handicapper, she won on Fibresand at the start of the year, but has shown herself to be at least as equally effective on turf with four victories last season.

**K T Ivory [4-14] Dean Ivory (from J R Fanshawe [1-14] May 1999).*

AMEENA (USA) BHB 50f50a RR 38f 50a 4789[7]

4 b f Irish River (FR) 9f **(77)** - London Pride (USA) (Lear Fan (USA)) 8.5f **(73)**
Form - 320078807

Record	**1999 -**	1st:0	2nd:1	3rd:1	Ran:9
	Pre1999 -	1st:0	2nd:0	3rd:1	Ran:7

Win Prizemoney £0 *Total Prizemoney* £2,148

1999 Turf 0-7: (6f 4, 7f 2, 9f) (g-s, gd 4, g-f, frm) 1999 AW 0-2: (7f 2) (Fibr 2)

Neat, very moderate filly, effective 6f, acts on gd to g-f. Turf high 65 - 2nd of 13 giving 9lb to Oriel Girl (27 Apr Nottingham 6f gd RF 0866). AW high 33 (began Jly). Consistent.

**R A Fahey [0-15] R Meredith (from P F I Cole [0-1] Spt 1997).*

AMELIA JESS (IRE) BHB 44f RR 45f 4877[14]

2 ch f Mac's Imp (USA) 5.6f **(54)** - Vieux Carre (Pas de Seul) 9.1f **(67)**
Form - 0000

Record	**1999 -**	1st:0	2nd:0	3rd:0	Ran:4

1999 Turf 0-4: (5f, 6f 3) (gd 2, g-f, frm)

Moderate filly. Turf high 45 (began Aug).

**B S Rothwell [0-4] Michael Saunders.*

AMERCIUS BHB 31f RR 30f 2391[8]

7 ch g Old Vic 12.8f **(72)** - Elarrih (USA) (Sharpen Up) 8.3f **(67)**
Form - 8

Record	**1999 -**	1st:0	2nd:0	3rd:0	Ran:1
	Pre1999 -	1st:0	2nd:0	3rd:1	Ran:9

Win Prizemoney £0 *Total Prizemoney* £714

1999 Turf 0-1: (18f) (g-f)

Very moderate gelding, has worn blinkers.

**R Simpson [1-7] R Clarke (from J L Harris [0-2] Apr 1996).*

AMERICAN COUSIN BHB 59f69a RR 60f 69a 4755[21]

4 b g Distant Relative 7f **(69)** - Zelda (USA) (Sharpen Up) 8.3f **(67)**
Form - 0000214215240

Record	**1999 -**	1st:2	2nd:3	3rd:0	Ran:13
	Pre1999 -	1st:0	2nd:1	3rd:3	Ran:11

Win Prizemoney £5,292 *Total Prizemoney* £11,322

Wins	*** 1999**	Jly	Doncas (G-F)	H	5f	51	58 <
	*** 1999**	Jun	Doncas (G-F)	H	6f	44	48

1999 Turf 2-13: (5f 1-8, 6f 1-5) (g-s, gd 3, g-f 1-3, frm 1-6)

Scopey, average gelding, effective 5 to 6f, best at 5f, acts on g-f to frm, best on g-f, has worn blinkers. Turf high 60 - 2nd of 16 giving 12lb to Encounter (11 Aug Hamilton 6f g-f RF 3542) - also 1st of 18 getting 11lb from Eastern Prophets (14 Jly Doncaster RF 2810).

**D Nicholls [2-13] Middleham Park Racing XIV (from R F JohnsonHoughton [0-6] Aug 1998).*

AMERICAN TABLOID (IRE) RR 90f 2994a[5]

3 bb c Turtle Island (IRE) - Run Bonnie (Runnett) 7f **(59)**
Form - 2427045

1999 Turf 0-7: (6f 5, 7f 2) (sft, g-s 2, gd 2, g-f 2)

Useful colt, effective 5 to 6f, best at 6f, acts on hvy to frm, has worn blinkers. Turf high 92 - 2nd of 7 getting 9lb from Tarry Flynn (9 May Leopardstown 6f gd RF 1168a). Consistent.

**E Lynam in IRE [1-12] Gerard Purcell.*

AMETHYST (IRE) RR 101f 5036[3]

2 b f Sadler's Wells (USA) 11.3f **(87)** - Zummerudd (Habitat) 9.4f **(70)**
Form - 1243

1999 Turf 1-4: (6f 1-2, 7f 2) (g-s, gd 1-1, g-f 2)

Very useful filly. Turf high 101 - 3rd of 8 getting 3lb from Halland Park Girl (23 Oct Doncaster 6f g-s RF 5036). Landed the odds very easily over six furlongs on her Naas debut, but then had a rear view of Preseli both in a Leopardstown Listed event and in the Group One Moyglare Stud Stakes. Should stay a mile.

**A P O'Brien in IRE [1-4] Mrs John Magnier & John T L Jones Jr.*

AMEZOLA BHB 81f RR 88df 5028[6]

3 gr c Northern Park (USA) 10f **(57)** - Yamamah (Siberian Express (USA)) 8.8f **(65)**
Form - 43206

Record	**1999 -**	1st:0	2nd:1	3rd:1	Ran:5
	Pre1999 -	1st:1	2nd:0	3rd:0	Ran:2

Win Prizemoney £2,479 *Total Prizemoney* £5,274

Wins	* 1998	Oct	Bath (HVY)		8f		74 <

1999 Turf 0-5: (10f, 12f, 14f, 15f, 16f) (g-s, gd 3, g-f)

Scopey, useful colt, effective 10 to 14f, acts on gd. Turf high 88 - 2nd of 12 giving 2lb to Copernicus (15 Spt Sandown 14f gd RF 4331). He had no trouble with the heavy ground when scoring over a mile on his second and final start at two, and ran pretty well in two handicaps in June. Given a three-month break, he ran very well to finish runner-up in a 14-furlong handicap on soft ground at Sandown. **Mrs A J Perrett [1-7] Bernard Keay.*

AMIARGE BHB 25f38a RR 37f 38a 3582[13]

9 b g Reference Point 12f **(66)** - Scotia Rose (Tap On Wood) 10.3f **(65)**
Form - 78080

Record	**1999 -**	1st:0	2nd:0	3rd:0	Ran:5
	Pre1999 -	1st:4	2nd:4	3rd:4	Ran:54

Win Prizemoney £12,852 *Total Prizemoney* £20,645

Wins	* 1997	Aug	Ripon (G-F)	H	16f	44	50
	* 1997	Jun	Doncas (G-S)	H	14.6f	45	52 <
	* 1996	Oct	Nottin (GD)	H	17.9f	44	49
	* 1995	Aug	Nottin (G-F)	H	16f	31	37

1999 Turf 0-5: (14f, 16f 4) (gd 2, g-f 2, frm)

Very moderate gelding, effective 16f, acts on gd, has worn blinkers (effectively). Turf high 37. Inconsistent.

**M Brittain [4-59] Miss Debi Woods.*

AMICO D'ORO BHB 35f RR 31f 4923[12]

2 b c Mistertopogigo (IRE) - Don't Jump (IRE) **(66df 61a)** (Entitled)
Form - 800

Record	**1999 -**	1st:0	2nd:0	3rd:0	Ran:3

1999 Turf 0-2: (5f, 6f) (g-s, frm) 1999 AW 0-1: (6f) (Fibr)

Currently very moderate colt. Turf high 31 (began Jly).

**J Berry [0-3] Chris Deuters.*

AMILYNX (FR) RR 118f 5121a[1]

3 gr c Linamix (FR) 8.2f **(64)** - Amen (USA) (Alydar (USA)) 9.1f **(76)**
Form - 2311

1999 Turf 2-4: (15f 1-3, 16f 1-1) (hvy 2-2, g-s, gd)

High-class colt. Turf high 118 (began Aug) - 1st of 7 getting 9lb from Tajoun (24 Oct Longchamp RF 5121a) - also 1st of 6 from Northerntown (2 Oct Longchamp RF 4771a). He coped well with atrocious conditions when winning a Group 2 at Longchamp in October, and confirmed himself Europe's top young stayer when beating Tajoun and Leggera in the Prix Royal-Oak later that month. Brave in a desperate finish there, he goes particularly well on easy ground and will be a major player next year's Ascot Gold Cup if we have a wet summer. **A Fabre in FR [2-4] J-L Lagadere.*

AMINGTON GIRL BHB 38f36a **RR 41f 36a** 1586[18]
4 b f Tragic Role (USA) 9.4f **(63)** - Millfields House (Record Token) 6.3f **(53)**
Form - 704388735534080
Record 1999 - 1st:0 2nd:0 3rd:3 Ran:14
Pre1999 - 1st:1 2nd:2 3rd:3 Ran:17
Win Prizemoney £2,637 *Total Prizemoney* £6,696
Wins * 1998 Jly Nottin (G-F) C 8.2f 45 <
1999 Turf 0-2:(8f 2)(sft, gd) 1999AW0-12:(6f, 7f 6, 8f 5)(Equi 2, Fibr 10)
Leggy, moderate filly, effective 6 to 8f, best at 8f, acts on gd to g-f - acts on Fibr, best on g-f, often wears blinkers. Turf high 39 (1st run) - 4th of 20 getting 10lb from Antarctic Storm (16 May Ripon 8f gd RF 1260). AW high 42 - 3rd of 8 getting 11lb from Abtaal (3 Mar Wolverhampton 7f Fibr RF 0397). **P D Evans [1-31] P D Evans.*

AMIRANTES BHB 30f **RR 22f** 3375[8]
3 b c Elmaamul (USA) 8.1f **(70)** - Angel Drummer (Dance In Time (CAN)) 8.9f **(59)**
Form - 6000008
Record 1999 - 1st:0 2nd:0 3rd:0 Ran:7
1999 Turf 0-5: (5f 3, 6f, 8f) (gd 2, g-f, frm 2) 1999 AW 0-2: (7f 2) (Fibr 2)
Workmanlike, little account colt, had worn blinkers. Turf high 41. (DEAD) **M J Polglase [0-7] M J Polglase.*

AMONG ISLANDS BHB 32f **RR 37?f** 356[6]
8 b m Jupiter Island 10.4f **(57)** -Queen of The Nile(Hittite Glory)8.7f **(50)**
Form - 6
Record 1999 - 1st:0 2nd:0 3rd:0 Ran:1
Pre1999 - 1st:0 2nd:0 3rd:0 Ran:3
1999 AW 0-1: (12f) (Equi)
Very moderate mare.
**G F H Charles-Jones [0-2] R A Hughes (from R Lee [0-1] Oct 1997).*

AMORAS (IRE) BHB 74f **RR 74f** 5048[4]
2 b f Hamas (IRE) 8f **(72)** - Red Lory (Bay Express) 7.1f **(60)**
Form - 06253154
Record 1999 - 1st:1 2nd:1 3rd:1 Ran:8
Win Prizemoney £7,197 *Total Prizemoney* £8,657
Wins * **1999** Spt Bath (FRM) H 8f 68 74 <
1999 Turf 1-8: (5f 2, 6f 3, 7f, 8f 1-2) (hvy, gd 2, g-f, frm 1-4)
Above-average filly, effective 6 to 8f, best at 6f, acts on gd to frm, best on frm. Turf high 74 - 1st of 8 getting 9lb from Seeking Utopia (6 Spt Bath RF 4157). **J W Hills [1-8] Espresso Racing.*

AMRAK AJEEB (IRE) BHB 67f **RR 72df** 5031[11]
7 b h Danehill (USA) 9.1f **(79)** - Noble Dust (USA) (Dust Commander (USA)) 10.3f **(77)**
Form - 6004070
Record 1999 - 1st:0 2nd:0 3rd:0 Ran:7
Pre1999 - 1st:5 2nd:4 3rd:2 Ran:34
Win Prizemoney £58,982 *Total Prizemoney* £82,218
Wins 1996 Spt Ascot (GD) H 8f 99 105 <
1996 Aug York (GD) H 10.4f 92 98
1996 May Newbur (SFT) H 8f 85 95
1995 Aug Haydoc (G-F) H 10.5f 79 85
1995 Jun Kempto (GD) 7f 79
1999 Turf 0-7: (8f, 9f, 10f 3, 12f, 13f) (g-s 2, g-f, frm 4)
Above-average horse. Turf high 76 (began Aug). A former smart handicapper, he has returned from a spell in Dubai but has not recaptured his sparkle. Has joined Rodney Baker's yard.
**M R Channon [0-7] A Merza (from B Hanbury [5-34] Spt 1997).*

AMRON BHB 50f **RR 57f** 4808[10]
12 b g Bold Owl 9.7f **(47)** - Sweet Minuet (Setay) 5.7f **(103)**
Form - 451007068120000
Record 1999 - 1st:2 2nd:1 3rd:0 Ran:15
Pre1999 - 1st:13 2nd:8 3rd:7 Ran:104
Win Prizemoney £75,919 *Total Prizemoney* £96,160
Wins * **1999** Aug Ayr (G-F) H 10f 50 53
* **1999** May Redcar (SFT) H 8f 49 59
* 1998 Oct Redcar (SFT) H 8f 45 48
* 1997 Mar Newcas (GD) H 5f 57 63
1999 Turf 2-15: (8f 1-9, 9f 2, 10f 1-3, 11f) (sft, gd 1-5, g-f 4, frm 1-5)
Fair gelding, effective 8 to 10f, acts on gd to frm. Turf high 59 - 1st of 30 giving 2lb to Sand Hawk (10 May Redcar RF 1125) - also 1st of 8 getting 9lb from Bowcliffe (10 Aug Ayr RF 3496). **J Berry [15-119] Roy Peebles.*

AMSARA (IRE) BHB 31f39a **RR 32f 39a** 4600[10]
3 b f Taufan (USA) 8.3f **(65)** - Legend of Spain (USA) (Alleged (USA)) 10f **(76)**
Form - 618040525700
Record 1999 - 1st:1 2nd:1 3rd:0 Ran:12
Pre1999 - 1st:0 2nd:0 3rd:0 Ran:2
Win Prizemoney £2,301 *Total Prizemoney* £2,976
Wins 1999 Apr Pontef (G-S) S 12f 52 <
1999 Turf 1-6: (12f 1-2, 13f, 14f, 16f 2) (gd 1-4, g-f, frm) 1999 AW 0-6: (12f 4, 14f, 15f) (Fibr 6)
Rangy, moderate filly, effective 12f, acts on gd, likes left handed tracks. Turf high 52 - 1st of 9 getting 5lb from Diamond Lad (28 Apr Pontefract RF 0903). AW high 41.
**D W Chapman [0-10] David Chapman (from M R Channon [1-4] Apr 1999).*

ANAAM RR 75+f 4992[1]
3 b f Caerleon (USA) 10.9f **(79)** - Narwala (Darshaan) 9.9f **(84)**
Form - 1
Record 1999 - 1st:1 2nd:0 3rd:0 Ran:1
Win Prizemoney £4,500 *Total Prizemoney* £4,500
Wins * **1999** Oct Nottin (FRM) 10f 75 <
1999 Turf 1-1: (10f 1-1) (frm 1-1)
Light-framed, currently above-average filly. (1st run) - 1st of 15 getting 5lb from Wood Pound (20 Oct Nottingham RF 4992). It will be significant if he is kept in training at four.
**S bin Suroor [1-1] Godolphin.*

ANAK-KU BHB 53f64a **RR 54f 64a** 4948[6]
6 ch g Efisio 7.7f **(69)** - City Link Lass (Double Jump) 9.4f **(58)**
Form - 0500070376
Record 1999 - 1st:0 2nd:0 3rd:1 Ran:10
Pre1999 - 1st:6 2nd:6 3rd:3 Ran:24
Win Prizemoney £22,277 *Total Prizemoney* £30,325
Wins * 1998 Jun Salisb (G-S) 9.9f 86 <
* 1997 Jly Windso (G-F) H 10f 75 79
* 1997 Jun Ripon (GD) 10f 75
* 1997 Jun Chepst (G-F) H 10.2f 65 72
* 1997 *Apr Lingfi (STD) H 10f 69 74*
* 1996 Jly Mussel (G-S) 8.1f 68
1999 Turf 0-8: (10f 6, 11f 2) (g-s 2, g-f 3, frm 2, hrd) 1999 AW 0-2: (10f, 12f) (Equi 2)
Average gelding, effective 10f, acts on gd, has worn blinkers. Turf high 60. AW high 65. He was most consistent in 1997, notching four victories, but since putting up a decent performance to win on his 1998 reappearance at Salisbury, has struggled to produce his best. He is very much suited by forcing tactics.
**Miss Gay Kelleway [6-34] H R H Sultan Ahmad Shah.*

ANALYTICAL BHB 75f **RR 76f** 5143[14]
3 b g Pursuit of Love 9.5f **(69)** - Risha Flower (Kris) 9.5f **(73)**
Form - 31300
Record 1999 - 1st:1 2nd:0 3rd:2 Ran:5
Win Prizemoney £3,260 *Total Prizemoney* £4,715
Wins * **1999** Jly Nottin (G-F) 8.2f 67+ <
1999 Turf 1-5: (7f, 8f 1-4) (gd 2, g-f, frm 1-2)
Scopey, above-average gelding. Turf high 79 (1st run) (began Jly) - 3rd of 7 giving 5lb to Be Thankfull (10 Jly Ascot 8f g-f RF 2704).
**R Charlton [1-5] Mountgrange Stud.*

ANAMORE RR 86f 4697[1]
3 b br g Sanglamore (USA) 12.9f **(67)** - Ancara **(104f)** (Dancing Brave (USA)) 8.4f **(76)**
Form - 21
Record 1999 - 1st:1 2nd:1 3rd:0 Ran:2
Win Prizemoney £4,086 *Total Prizemoney* £5,288
Wins * **1999** Oct Sandow (SFT) 10f 86 <
1999 Turf 1-2: (10f 1-1, 12f) (g-s 1-1, frm)
Strong, currently useful gelding. Turf high 86 (began Spt) - 1st of 13 giving 5lb to Variety Shop (2 Oct Sandown RF 4697). Got off the mark in a soft-ground Sandown maiden, and should do well at four. **R Charlton [1-2] K Abdulla.*

ANBARI BHB 77f **RR 81f** 4762[10]
2 b c Muhtarram (USA) - Mashair (USA) (Diesis) 9.3f **(69)**
Form - 13570
Record 1999 - 1st:1 2nd:0 3rd:1 Ran:5

Win Prizemoney £2,314 *Total Prizemoney* £3,336
Wins * **1999** Jly Lingfi (G-F) 7f 81 <
1999 Turf 1-5: (7f 1-2, 8f 3) (gd 2, frm 1-3)
Decent colt. Turf high 81 (1st run) (began Jly) - 1st of 18 from Resplendent Star (8 Jly Lingfield RF 2635). Gained a hard-fought success on his Lingfield debut in July, but has not shown very much since. **J L Dunlop [1-5] Hamdan Al Maktoum.*

ANCHOR VENTURE BHB 29f38a **RR 24f 38a** 183[P]
6 b g Slip Anchor 12.7f **(75)** - Ski Michaela (USA) (Devil's Bag (USA)) 12.4f **(78)**
Form - 0678P
Record 1999 - 1st:0 2nd:0 3rd:0 Ran:1
Pre1999 - 1st:1 2nd:1 3rd:4 Ran:28
Win Prizemoney £2,406 *Total Prizemoney* £5,197
Wins 1997 Jun Pontef (G-F) S 10f 45 <
1999 AW 0-1: (10f) (Equi)
Little account gelding, effective 8f, - acts on Equi.
**D W Chapman [0-10] David Chapman (from S P C Woods [1-19] May 1998).*

ANCIENT CITY (USA) RR 74f 3415[4]
2 b g Dehere (USA) -Lilian Bayliss(IRE)(Sadler's Wells(USA)) 10f **(76)**
Form - 5564
Record 1999 - 1st:0 2nd:0 3rd:0 Ran:4
Win Prizemoney £0 *Total Prizemoney* £432
1999 Turf 0-4: (5f 2, 6f 2) (gd, g-f 3)
Above-average gelding. Turf high 74 (1st run) - 5th of 8 to Desert Fury (5 May Chester 5f g-f RF 1043).
**P W Chapple-Hyam [0-4] A K Collins & R E Sangster.*

ANDAMAN BHB 47f55a **RR 59df 55a** 1604[13]
5 b g Riverman (USA) 9.7f **(78)** -Balleta (USA)(Lyphard (USA)) 9.9f **(72)**
Form - 764700
Record 1999 - 1st:0 2nd:0 3rd:0 Ran:6
Pre1999 - 1st:0 2nd:3 3rd:0 Ran:10
Win Prizemoney £0 *Total Prizemoney* £3,728
1999 Turf 0-3: (12f, 13f, 14f) (sft, g-s, g-f) 1999 AW 0-3: (12f 2, 16f) (Fibr 3)
Fair gelding, effective 12 to 13f, best at 13f, acts on g-s to gd - acts on Fibr, has worn blinkers, likes left handed tracks. Turf high 59. AW high 54. Inconsistent.
**D J G MurraySmith [0-16] Mrs Susan Nash.*

ANDREYEV (IRE) BHB 107f **RR 103f** 5222[19]
5 ch h Presidium 7.5f **(56)** - Missish (Mummy's Pet) 7.7f **(60)**
Form - 403025002440
Record 1999 - 1st:0 2nd:2 3rd:1 Ran:12
Pre1999 - 1st:7 2nd:0 3rd:2 Ran:21
Win Prizemoney £65,780 *Total Prizemoney* £115,737
Wins * 1998 Aug Deauvi (GD) G3 6f 119 <
* 1998 Jun Newcas (SFT) L 6f 117
* 1998 Apr Kempto (SFT) 6f 107+
* 1997 May Newmar (GD) L 7f 100
* 1996 Oct Ascot (GD) 7f 102+
* 1996 Aug Cheste (G-S) 6.1f 104+
* 1996 Jun Windso (G-F) 5f 88
1999 Turf 0-12: (5f 4, 6f 7, 7f) (g-s, gd 7, g-f 3, frm)
Very useful colt, effective 6f, acts on sft to gd, has worn blinkers. Turf high 110 - 2nd of 11 to Keos (13 Jly Deauville 6f gd RF 3036a). Inconsistent. He had a long and arduous season, returning to form during the autumn without managing to win when blinkers helped rekindle his enthusiasm. Best on easy ground, he has won when fresh in the past and could be one to catch early next term. **R Hannon [7-33] J Palmer-Brown.*

ANDROMEDES (USA) RR 79+f 5208[3]
2 b c Sadler's Wells (USA) 11.3f **(87)** - Utr (USA) **(56tf)** (Mr Prospector (USA)) 8.8f **(78)**
Form - 3
Record 1999 - 1st:0 2nd:0 3rd:1 Ran:1
Win Prizemoney £0 *Total Prizemoney* £492
1999 Turf 0-1: (7f) (g-s)
Currently above-average colt. (1st run) - 3rd of 20 to Golovin (5 Nov Doncaster 7f g-s RF 5208).
**H R A Cecil [0-1] Mrs John Magnier & M Tabor.*

ANDY'S ELECTIVE BHB 66f **RR 56f** 4670[4]
2 b c Democratic (USA) - English Mint (Jalmood (USA)) 10.1f **(52)**
Form - 054
Record 1999 - 1st:0 2nd:0 3rd:0 Ran:3
Win Prizemoney £0 *Total Prizemoney* £220
1999 Turf 0-3: (5f, 6f 2) (g-s, frm 2)
Currently fair colt. Turf high 56 (began Jly).
**J R Jenkins [0-3] Mrs Stella Peirce.*

ANEED (USA) RR 67f 1814[4]
3 ch c Woodman (USA) 9.7f **(77)** - Crockadore (USA) (Nijinsky (CAN)) 10.3f **(77)**
Form - 4
Record 1999 - 1st:0 2nd:0 3rd:0 Ran:1
Win Prizemoney £0 *Total Prizemoney* £260
1999 Turf 0-1: (7f) (g-f)
Currently average colt.
**J H M Gosden [0-1] Prince Abdul Aziz Bin Saud.*

ANEES (USA) RR 5229a[1]
2 c Unbridled (USA) - Ivory Idol (USA) (Alydar (USA)) 9.1f **(76)**
Form - 1
1999 AW 1-1: (9f 1-1) (Dirt 1-1)
Currently Group-class. (1st run) - 1st of 14 from Chief Seattle (6 Nov Gulfstream Park RF 5229a). Very promising winner of the Breeders' Cup Juvenile.
**A Hassinger jr in USA [1-1] The Thoroughbred Corporation.*

ANEMOS (IRE) BHB 71f **RR 75f** 5162[15]
4 ch g Be My Guest (USA) 10.2f **(66)** - Frendly Persuasion (General Assembly (USA)) 10f **(68)**
Form - 0030107620
Record 1999 - 1st:1 2nd:1 3rd:1 Ran:10
Pre1999 - 1st:0 2nd:1 3rd:4 Ran:7
Win Prizemoney £2,937 *Total Prizemoney* £9,323
Wins * **1999** Aug Nottin (G-F) 10f 75 <
1999 Turf 1-10: (8f, 9f 2, 10f 1-7) (gd 1-3, g-f 3, frm 4)
Scopey, above-average gelding, effective 10f, acts on gd, often wears blinkers (very effectively), likes tight tracks. Turf high 75 - 1st of 6 giving 6lb to Luz Bay (13 Aug Nottingham RF 3627). Finally got off the mark at Nottingham in August, but basically disappointed afterwards.
**M A Jarvis [1-16] Andreas Michael (from M H Tompkins [0-1] Spt 1997).*

AN EXECUTIVE DO BHB 66f64a **RR 65f 64a** 367[3]
3 ch g Executive Man 8.9f **(52)** - Annacando (Derrylin) 8.8f **(54)**
Form - 52313
Record 1999 - 1st:1 2nd:1 3rd:2 Ran:5
Pre1999 - 1st:1 2nd:0 3rd:0 Ran:2
Win Prizemoney £4,749 *Total Prizemoney* £6,129
Wins * **1999** *Feb Lingfi (STD) C 10f 64*
* 1998 Jly Thirsk (GD) C 7f 65 <
1999 AW 1-5: (8f, 10f 1-3, 12f) (Equi 1-4, Fibr)
Scopey, average gelding, effective 7 to 10f, best at 10f, acts on g-f - acts on Equi, prefers left handed tracks, prefers tight tracks. AW high 66 - 2nd of 11 giving 3lb to Tragic Dancer (26 Jan Lingfield 10f Equi RF 0169) - also 1st of 8 giving 2lb to King Flyer (9 Feb Lingfield RF 0256). **P C Haslam [2-7] Terry Rowley.*

ANGE D'HONOR (FR) BHB 58f **RR 71df** 4763[20]
4 b g Hero's Honor (USA) 9.2f **(76)** - Surfing Angel (FR) (Monseigneur (USA)) 7.7f **(63)**
Form - 5300
Record 1999 - 1st:0 2nd:0 3rd:1 Ran:4
Pre1999 - 1st:0 2nd:1 3rd:0 Ran:1
Win Prizemoney £0 *Total Prizemoney* £1,589
1999 Turf 0-4: (12f 2, 14f 2) (gd, g-f 2, frm)
Workmanlike, above-average gelding. Turf high 76 (began Jly).
**S E H Sherwood [0-7] Wood Hall Stud Ltd.*

ANGELA'S PET (IRE) BHB 48f **RR 45f** 4784[13]
2 ch f Ridgewood Ben - Centenary Year (Malinowski (USA)) 10f **(56)**
Form - 0060000
Record 1999 - 1st:0 2nd:0 3rd:0 Ran:7
1999 Turf 0-7: (5f 2, 6f 2, 7f 3) (g-s 2, gd, g-f 2, frm 2)
Moderate filly. Turf high 45. **J C Fox [0-7] Christy Kissane.*

ANGEL BORNE (USA) BHB 57f **RR 74f** 4883[14]
3 b f Exbourne (USA) - Secret Angel (Halo (USA)) 10.6f **(75)**
Form - 460
Record 1999 - 1st:0 2nd:0 3rd:0 Ran:3
Pre1999 - 1st:0 2nd:0 3rd:0 Ran:1
Win Prizemoney £0 *Total Prizemoney* £247
1999 Turf 0-3: (10f 3) (g-s, gd, frm)
Unfurnished, above-average filly. Turf high 60.
**B W Hills [0-4] K Abdulla.*

ANGEL HILL BHB 67f **RR 64f** 5160[17]
4 ch f King's Signet (USA) 7f **(51)** - Tawny (Grey Ghost) 9.9f **(60)**
Form - 033701604070
Record 1999 - 1st:1 2nd:0 3rd:2 Ran:12
Pre1999 - 1st:1 2nd:2 3rd:3 Ran:13
Win Prizemoney £6,377 *Total Prizemoney* £16,513
Wins * **1999** Jly Newcas (G-F) H 6f 74 76 <
1997 May Newcas (GD) 5f 63+
1999 Turf 1-12: (5f 4, 6f 1-8) (g-s, gd 4, g-f 2, frm 1-4, hrd)
Scopey, average filly, effective 5 to 6f, best at 6f, acts on gd to hrd, best on frm, has worn blinkers. Turf high 76 - 1st of 4 giving 20lb to Wishbone Alley (12 Jly Newcastle RF 2759). She has made the frame on several occasions in the last couple of seasons, but did not get her head in front since her two-year-old days until landing a four-runner handicap at Newcastle in July when blinkered for the first time.
**R A Fahey [1-17] Keith Taylor (from T D Barron [1-8] Oct 1997).*

ANGEL LANE BHB 53f **RR 50f** 5196[7]
2 b f Merdon Melody 6.8f **(56)** - Young Whip (Bold Owl) 8.5f **(45)**
Form - 00007
Record 1999 - 1st:0 2nd:0 3rd:0 Ran:5
1999 Turf 0-5: (6f 4, 8f) (g-s, gd 2, frm 2)
Fair filly. Turf high 50 (began Aug).
**A W Carroll [0-5] Aramis Racing Syndicate.*

ANGELLO RR 5208[20]
2 ch c Selkirk (USA) 7.9f **(76)** - Pomorie (IRE) **(66f)** (Be My Guest (USA)) 9.3f **(67)**
Form - 00
Record 1999 - 1st:0 2nd:0 3rd:0 Ran:2
1999 Turf 0-2: (7f, 8f) (g-s, gd)
Currently very poor colt. (began Oct) - 20th of 20 to Golovin (5 Nov Doncaster 7f g-s RF 5208). **M L W Bell [0-2] Mrs Anne Yearley.*

ANGELS VENTURE BHB 82f **RR 84f** 4999[1]
3 ch c Unfuwain (USA) 11.4f **(74)** - City of Angels (Woodman (USA)) 9f **(74)**
Form - 334333120321
Record 1999 - 1st:2 2nd:2 3rd:6 Ran:12
Pre1999 - 1st:0 2nd:0 3rd:0 Ran:1
Win Prizemoney £6,711 *Total Prizemoney* £14,221
Wins * **1999** Oct Bright (GD) H 11.9f 80 84 <
* **1999** Jly Yarmou (FRM) 11.5f 79
1999 Turf 2-12: (8f 3, 10f 2, 11f 1-2, 12f 1-5) (g-s, gd 1-4, g-f 1-5, frm, hrd)
Well made, decent colt, effective 8 to 12f, best at 12f, acts on g-s to hrd, best on gd, prefers left handed tracks, likes tight tracks. Turf high 84 - 1st of 7 giving 18lb to Air Attache (21 Oct Brighton RF 4999) - also 1st of 7 from Peajay (20 Jly Yarmouth RF 2961). Consistent. He was sold for 44,000gns in the autumn.
**S P C Woods [2-13] Dr Frank Chao.*

ANGHARAD LYN BHB 45f **RR 58f** 4816[15]
3 b f Perpendicular - Champers Galore (Governor General)
Form - 4807600
Record 1999 - 1st:0 2nd:0 3rd:0 Ran:7
Win Prizemoney £0 *Total Prizemoney* £273
1999 Turf 0-7: (7f, 8f 2, 10f 3, 12f) (g-s, gd 2, g-f, frm 3)
Unfurnished, fair filly. Turf high 65. **D Burchell [0-7] Lyn Phillips.*

ANGIE BABY BHB 71f **RR 71f** 5065[15]
3 b f Puissance 7.1f **(60)** - Hyde Princess (Touch Paper) 6.8f **(57)**
Form - 105667822520600
Record 1999 - 1st:1 2nd:3 3rd:0 Ran:15
Pre1999 - 1st:4 2nd:1 3rd:0 Ran:7
Win Prizemoney £15,930 *Total Prizemoney* £26,898
Wins 1999 Apr Ripon (G-S) C 5f 75
1998 Aug Lingfi (FRM) 5f 87 <
1998 Jly Hamilt (FRM) 5f 86+
1998 May Nottin (G-F) 5.1f 87 <
1998 Apr Redcar (SFT) 5f 60
1999 Turf 1-15: (5f 1-13, 6f 2) (g-s, gd 1-6, g-f 4, frm 4)
Above-average filly, effective 5f, acts on g-f to frm, best on frm. Turf high 75 (1st run). A winner four times at two, she won first time out last season over five furlongs at Ripon, but then went off the boil. However, she showed a bit of her old dash during the late summer, having received a little bit of leniency from the Handicapper.
**R Ingram [0-8] The Barracuda Boys (from J Berry [5-14] Jly 1999).*

ANGIE MARINIE BHB 64f42a **RR 67f 42a** 2672[5]
3 b f Sabrehill (USA) 8.5f **(64)** - Lambast (Relkino) 8.9f **(65)**
Form - 780132375
Record 1999 - 1st:1 2nd:1 3rd:2 Ran:9
Pre1999 - 1st:0 2nd:0 3rd:0 Ran:1
Win Prizemoney £2,110 *Total Prizemoney* £5,322
Wins 1999 Apr Nottin (SFT) S 8.2f 53 <
1999 Turf 1-5: (8f 1-2, 10f 2, 11f) (sft, g-s 1-2, g-f, frm) 1999 AW 0-4: (6f, 7f, 8f, 9f) (Fibr 4)
Unfurnished, average filly, effective 8 to 11f, acts on sft to frm. Turf high 67 - 2nd of 19 getting 17lb from Procedure (24 May Leicester 10f frm RF 1432). AW high 37. Inconsistent.
**M C Pipe [0-5] C R Fleet (from R A Fahey [1-5] Apr 1999).*

ANGIES QUEST BHB 82f **RR 73f** 4208[16]
2 b f Inchinor 8.9f **(64)** - Chanson D'Avril **(39f)** (Chief Singer) 8.9f **(66)**
Form - 630
Record 1999 - 1st:0 2nd:0 3rd:1 Ran:3
Win Prizemoney £0 *Total Prizemoney* £580
1999 Turf 0-3: (6f, 7f, 8f) (gd 2, frm)
Currently above-average filly. Turf high 73 (began Jly) - 3rd of 9 to Starlyte Girl (13 Aug Warwick 8f gd RF 3629). Failed to get in a blow in the valuable St Leger Yearling Sales race at Doncaster, but had shown enough previously to suggest she can win a race
. **K R Burke [0-3] High Havens Stables.*

ANGLESEY SEA VIEW BHB 46f40a **RR 47f 40a** 4726[9]
10 gr m Seymour Hicks (FR) 9.6f **(51)** -Lexham View(Abwah) 11.5f **(52)**
Form - 720
Record 1999 - 1st:0 2nd:1 3rd:0 Ran:3
Pre1999 - 1st:1 2nd:1 3rd:1 Ran:17
Win Prizemoney £4,152 *Total Prizemoney* £9,209
Wins 1995 Jun Newmar (GD) 16.1f 67 <
1999 Turf 0-3: (16f 3) (g-s, gd, g-f)
Moderate mare, has worn blinkers. Turf high 47.
**Mrs M Reveley [1-6] Mrs P Hewitt (from A Bailey [3-23] Jan 1997).*

ANGUILLA RR 103f 5228a[13]
4 b g Rudimentary (USA) 8.2f **(66)** - More Wise (Ballymore) 7.3f **(64)**
Form - 0
1999 Turf 0-1: (11f) (frm)
Currently very useful gelding. **T Skiffington in USA [0-1].*

ANGUS-G BHB 83f **RR 79f** 3374[5]
7 br g Chief Singer 8.6f **(62)** - Horton Line (High Line) 10.3f **(70)**
Form - 02375
Record 1999 - 1st:0 2nd:1 3rd:1 Ran:5
Pre1999 - 1st:4 2nd:2 3rd:3 Ran:14
Win Prizemoney £24,544 *Total Prizemoney* £48,598
Wins * 1997 May York (GD) H 11.9f 88 93 <
* 1997 Apr Newmar (GD) H 12f 82 87
* 1996 Aug Newmar (G-F) H 10f 73 78
* 1996 Jly Newmar (G-F) H 10f 71 74
1999 Turf 0-5: (10f, 12f 4) (gd 2, frm 3)
Above-average gelding, effective 10f, acts on gd. Turf high 87 - 2nd of 10 giving 9lb to Rapier (21 May Ayr 10f gd RF 1364). Consistent. A horse who has had injury problems which kept him off the track for much of 1998, he ran creditably three times last season without fully convincing one that he retains his former ability. **Mrs M Reveley [4-19] W Ginzel.*

ANGUS THE BOLD BHB 45f **RR 44df** 2163[11]
3 b g Puissance 7.1f **(60)** - Floral Spark **(61f 72a)** (Forzando) 7.6f **(59)**
Form - 00

Record 1999 - 1st:0 2nd:0 3rd:0 Ran:2
Pre1999 - 1st:0 2nd:1 3rd:0 Ran:1
Win Prizemoney £0 *Total Prizemoney* £642
1999 Turf 0-1: (6f) (g-f) 1999 AW 0-1: (5f) (Fibr)
Light-framed, currently moderate gelding.
**J L Eyre [0-2] Diamond Racing Ltd (from J Berry [0-1] Mar 1998).*

ANITA AT DAWN (IRE) BHB 56f60a **RR 51f 60a** 2690^{7}

4 br f Anita's Prince 6f **(62)** - Dawn is Breaking (Import) 6.6f **(68)**
Form - 08607
Record 1999 - 1st:0 2nd:0 3rd:0 Ran:5
Pre1999 - 1st:2 2nd:1 3rd:1 Ran:10
Win Prizemoney £7,067 *Total Prizemoney* £9,512
Wins * 1998 *Spt Southw (STD) H 7f 64 53*
* 1997 Jun Nottin (SFT) 6.1f 72 <
1999 Turf 0-1: (8f) (g-f) 1999 AW 0-4: (7f 3, 9f) (Equi, Fibr 3)
Light-framed, fair filly, effective 6f, - acts on Fibr, likes left handed tracks, likes tight tracks. AW high 53. Consistent.
**B Palling [2-15] D Brennan.*

AN JOLIEN BHB 60f **RR 65f** 5111^{8}

2 b f Aragon 7.7f **(58)** - Joli's Girl (Mansingh (USA)) 7.4f **(55)**
Form - 0758
Record 1999 - 1st:0 2nd:0 3rd:0 Ran:4
1999 Turf 0-4: (5f 2, 6f 2) (gd 2, frm 2)
Average filly, has worn blinkers. Turf high 65.
**M J Ryan [0-4] & Mrs W J Foley.*

ANNADAWI BHB 32f **RR 36f** 4905^{14}

4 b g Sadler's Wells (USA) 11.3f **(87)** - Prayers'n Promises (USA) (Foolish Pleasure (USA)) 8.9f **(72)**
Form - 7670
Record 1999 - 1st:0 2nd:0 3rd:0 Ran:4
1999 Turf 0-4: (6f, 8f, 12f 2) (g-f, frm 3)
Very moderate gelding. Turf high 36 (began Jly).
**C N Kellett [0-4] Sean Taylor.*

ANNANDALE (IRE) BHB 41f43a **RR 39f 43a** 2485^{5}

3 ch f Balla Cove - Gruinard Bay (Doyoun) 9f **(69)**
Form - 006005
Record 1999 - 1st:0 2nd:0 3rd:0 Ran:6
Pre1999 - 1st:0 2nd:0 3rd:1 Ran:4
Win Prizemoney £0 *Total Prizemoney* £402
1999 Turf 0-5: (8f 3, 9f, 10f) (sft, gd, g-f, frm, hrd) 1999 AW 0-1: (8f) (Fibr)
Leggy, very moderate filly, has worn blinkers. Turf high 39. Consistent.
**K A Ryan [0-6] C H McGhie (from R A Fahey [0-4] Spt 1998).*

ANNAPURNA (IRE) RR 94f $3931a^{9}$

3 b f Brief Truce (USA) 9.1f **(73)** - National Ballet (Shareef Dancer (USA)) 9.9f **(73)**
Form - 220
Record 1999 - 1st:0 2nd:2 3rd:0 Ran:3
Pre1999 - 1st:1 2nd:1 3rd:0 Ran:4
Win Prizemoney £4,413 *Total Prizemoney* £10,777
Wins * 1998 Spt Kempto (SFT) 7f 89 <
1999 Turf 0-3: (8f, 10f 2) (gd 2, g-f)
Useful filly, effective 7 to 10f, acts on gd to g-f. Turf high 94 (began Jly) - 2nd of 10 giving 1lb to Ipledgeallegiance (13 Aug Newbury 10f g-f RF 3618). **B J Meehan [1-7].*

ANNELIINA BHB 60f **RR 55f** 4712^{11}

3 b f Cadeaux Genereux 7.9f **(76)** - Blasted Heath (Thatching) 8f **(66)**
Form - 00250
Record 1999 - 1st:0 2nd:1 3rd:0 Ran:5
Pre1999 - 1st:0 2nd:0 3rd:0 Ran:4
Win Prizemoney £0 *Total Prizemoney* £1,780
1999 Turf 0-5: (6f 2, 7f 2, 8f) (gd 2, g-f, frm 2)
Neat, fair filly. Turf high 55 (began Aug). Inconsistent. Ran her best race of the season when runner-up in a Yarmouth maiden in September. **C N Allen [0-9] Mrs K A Hyytiainen.*

ANNESPRIDE RR 4542^{13}

2 b f Komaite (USA) 6.9f **(61)** - Lindrake's Pride (Mandrake Major) 7.6f **(53)**
Form - 0

Record 1999 - 1st:0 2nd:0 3rd:0 Ran:1
1999 Turf 0-1: (6f) (frm)
Currently very poor filly. **Mrs M Reveley [0-1] Mrs Muriel Ward.*

ANNIE APPLE (IRE) BHB 53f54a **RR 54f 54a** 5068^{11}

3 ch f Petardia 8.2f **(58)** - Art Duo (Artaius (USA)) 9f **(69)**
Form - 70314400004224230
Record 1999 - 1st:1 2nd:3 3rd:2 Ran:16
Pre1999 - 1st:1 2nd:0 3rd:0 Ran:5
Win Prizemoney £3,534 *Total Prizemoney* £7,717
Wins 1999 *Jan Lingfi (STD) S 8f 60* <
1998 Aug Folkes (G-F) S 7f 60 <
1999 Turf 0-11: (6f 2, 7f 4, 8f 4, 10f) (g-s 2, gd 2, g-f 2, frm 5) 1999 AW 1-5: (7f 2, 8f 1-2, 10f) (Equi 1-4, Fibr)
Leggy, fair filly, effective 7 to 8f, best at 7f, acts on gd to frm - acts on Equi, has worn blinkers. Turf high 54 - 3rd of 30 getting 11lb from Intricate Web (15 Oct Redcar 7f frm RF 4906). AW high 60 - 1st of 7 from Golden Syrup (19 Jan Lingfield RF 0122).
**N Hamilton [0-4] City Industrial Supplies Ltd (from G Lewis [0-4] Jly 1999).*

ANNIJAZ BHB 68f **RR 75f** 4870^{2}

2 b f Alhijaz 7.7f **(57)** - Figment (Posse (USA)) 8.9f **(61)**
Form - 4232
Record 1999 - 1st:0 2nd:2 3rd:1 Ran:4
Win Prizemoney £0 *Total Prizemoney* £3,352
1999 Turf 0-4: (6f 2, 7f 2) (gd 2, g-f, frm)
Above-average filly. Turf high 75 - 2nd of 20 getting 5lb from Castle Sempill (14 Oct Newmarket 7f gd RF 4870).
**A P Jarvis [0-4] Christopher Shankland.*

ANNIVERSARY DAY BHB 50f **RR 54f** 4906^{26}

3 ch g Lion Cavern (USA) 7.5f **(74)** - Doyce **(72f)** (Formidable (USA)) 9.2f **(63)**
Form - 7660
Record 1999 - 1st:0 2nd:0 3rd:0 Ran:4
Pre1999 - 1st:0 2nd:1 3rd:0 Ran:3
Win Prizemoney £0 *Total Prizemoney* £1,050
1999 Turf 0-4: (7f, 8f, 9f 2) (gd 3, frm)
Lengthy, fair gelding, effective 6f, acts on g-s, has worn blinkers. Turf high 54. **W S Cunningham [0-7] Mrs Ann Bell.*

ANN'S MILL BHB 60f **RR 64f** 5139^{10}

2 b f Pelder (IRE) - Honey Mill (Milford) 9f **(61)**
Form - 08100
Record 1999 - 1st:1 2nd:0 3rd:0 Ran:5
Win Prizemoney £2,810 *Total Prizemoney* £2,810
Wins 1999 Aug Thirsk (G-F) S 7f 64 <
1999 Turf 1-5: (6f 2, 7f 1-2, 10f) (gd, g-f, frm 2, hrd 1-1)
Average filly. Turf high 64 - 1st of 14 from Wilemmgeo (27 Aug Thirsk RF 3944).
**Derrick Morris [0-1] Mrs A Anidjah (from M Blanshard [1-4] Spt 1999).*

ANNUS MIRABILIS (FR) BHB 113f117a **RR 115f 117a** 1108^{10}

7 b h Warning 8.1f **(77)** - Anna Petrovna (FR) (Wassl) 9.7f **(62)**
Form - 0
Record 1999 - 1st:0 2nd:0 3rd:0 Ran:1
Pre1999 - 1st:9 2nd:5 3rd:6 Ran:27
Win Prizemoney £647,426 *Total Prizemoney* £995,813
Wins * 1998 Aug Windso (G-F) G3 10f 115
1998 *Mar Nad Al (FST) 10f 126* <
* 1997 Aug Windso (GD) G3 10f 122
* 1997 Aug Newmar (G-F) 10f 107+
* 1996 Oct Fuchu (FRM) G2 9f 114
* 1996 Aug Windso (G-F) G3 10f 114
1995 Spt Ayr (GD) L 10.9f 89++
1999 Turf 0-1: (10f) (gd)
Top-class horse, effective 10f, acts on hvy - acts on Dirt, has worn blinkers (extremely effectively). Inconsistent. A real flag-bearer for Godolphin, he sadly died on the eve of a stud career.
**S bin Suroor [6-18] Godolphin.*

ANOKATO BHB 48f64a **RR 49f 64a** 3691^{2}

5 b g Tina's Pet 7.4f **(56)** - High Velocity (Frimley Park) 6.5f **(67)**
Form - 41221266461540783715 2
Record 1999 - 1st:3 2nd:4 3rd:1 Ran:19
Pre1999 - 1st:6 2nd:1 3rd:9 Ran:45

Win Prizemoney £23,581 *Total Prizemoney* £34,266
Wins **1999** *Jly Lingfi (STD) S 10f 59*
1999 *Mar Lingfi (STD) C 7f 68*
1999 *Jan Lingfi (STD) C 6f 71* <
1998 *Dec Lingfi (STD) H 5f 58 65*
1998 *Jan Lingfi (STD) C 5f 64*
1998 *Jan Lingfi (STD) C 5f 67*
1997 *Nov Lingfi (STD) H 5f 61 65*
1997 May Bright (FRM) H 5.3f 59 60
1996 Spt Folkes (G-F) 5f 71 <
1999 Turf 0-6: (6f 3, 7f, 10f 2) (gd 2, frm 3, hrd) 1999 AW 3-13: (5f, 6f 1-7, 7f 1-3, 8f, 10f 1-1) (Equi 3-9, Fibr 4)
Fair gelding, effective 5 to 7f, best at 6f, acts on frm - acts on Equi, mostly wears blinkers (effectively), prefers left handed tracks, prefers tight tracks, excels at Lingfield. Turf high 54. AW high 73 - 2nd of 8 getting 2lb from Aoife (2 Feb Lingfield 6f Equi RF 0212) - also 1st of 6 from Polar Mist (16 Jan Lingfield RF 0107).
**R J Hodges [0-2] P Slade (from Mrs N Macauley [2-14] Jly 1999).*

ANONYM (IRE) BHB 45f51a **RR 43f 51a** 1654[14]
7 b g Nashamaa 8.1f **(58)** - Bonny Bertha (Capistrano) 9.4f **(64)**
Form - 0002153250
Record **1999** - 1st:1 2nd:2 3rd:1 Ran:7
Pre1999 - 1st:8 2nd:4 3rd:7 Ran:58
Win Prizemoney £24,642 *Total Prizemoney* £35,771
Wins *** 1999** *Feb Southw (STD) H 8f 44 49*
1998 *Jan Wolver (STD) S 8.5f 62*
1998 *Jan Wolver (STD) S 9.4f 59+*
1997 *May Wolver (STD) H 8.5f 68 74* <
1997 *Jan Wolver (STD) H 8.5f 63 68*
1997 *Jan Southw (STD) C 7f 71*
1996 Jly Mussel (GD) C 7.1f 55
1995 Aug Leices (G-F) H 8f 68 70
1995 Jly Doncas (FRM) H 7f 63 65
1999 Turf 0-3: (8f, 9f 2) (g-f, frm 2) 1999 AW 1-4: (8f 1-4) (Fibr 1-4)
Fair gelding, effective 8 to 9f, best at 8f, - acts on AW, best on Fibr, often wears blinkers (very effectively), prefers left handed tracks, favours tight tracks. Turf high 43. AW high 59 - 3rd of 13 to Kingchip Boy (19 Mar Southwell 8f Fibr RF 0451).
**G M Moore [1-7] G A Arthur (from C N Allen [0-11] Dec 1998).*

ANOTHER ARTHUR BHB 24a **RR 24a** 228[10]
3 b c Puissance 7.1f **(60)** - Traumatic Laura (Pragmatic)
Form - 070
Record **1999** - 1st:0 2nd:0 3rd:0 Ran:2
Pre1999 - 1st:0 2nd:0 3rd:0 Ran:1
1999 AW 0-2: (11f 2) (Fibr 2)
Leggy, currently poor colt. AW high 11.
**W McKeown [0-3] Miss Susan Blain.*

ANOTHERBAMBO (IRE) BHB 37f **RR 44f** 3642[12]
4 b g Conquering Hero (USA) 10.6f **(50)** - Twilight In Paris (Kampala) 8.5f **(56)**
Form - 403500
Record **1999** - 1st:0 2nd:0 3rd:1 Ran:6
Win Prizemoney £0 *Total Prizemoney* £300
1999 Turf 0-6: (8f 2, 10f 2, 12f 2) (g-f 3, frm 3)
Workmanlike, moderate gelding, has worn blinkers. Turf high 59.
**R J Baker [0-9] Mrs Maureen Shenkin.*

ANOTHER CENTURY RR 281[12]
4 gr g Belfort (FR) 6.7f **(53)** - Miss Cuddles (Mummy's Game) 8.2f **(60)**
Form - 0
Record **1999** - 1st:0 2nd:0 3rd:0 Ran:1
1999 AW 0-1: (7f) (Fibr)
Leggy, currently poor gelding. **D Nicholls [0-1] B Franks.*

ANOTHER LAURA BHB 48f **RR 45f** 1363[4]
4 b f Puissance 7.1f **(60)** - Traumatic Laura (Pragmatic)
Form - 84
Record **1999** - 1st:0 2nd:0 3rd:0 Ran:2
Pre1999 - 1st:0 2nd:0 3rd:0 Ran:1
Win Prizemoney £0 *Total Prizemoney* £244
1999 Turf 0-2: (10f 2) (gd, g-f)
Workmanlike, currently moderate filly. Turf high 45.
**W McKeown [0-3] Miss Susan Blain.*

ANOTHER LOVER BHB 32f32a **RR 26f 32a** 762[15]
3 ch f Then Again 7.4f **(52)** - Love Street (Mummy's Pet) 7.7f **(60)**
Form - 60
Record **1999** - 1st:0 2nd:0 3rd:0 Ran:2
Pre1999 - 1st:0 2nd:0 3rd:0 Ran:2
1999 Turf 0-1: (6f) (sft) 1999 AW 0-1: (5f) (Equi)
Lengthy, little account filly. **S G Knight [0-4] Mrs Ginny Withers.*

ANOTHER MONK (IRE) BHB 43f49a **RR 43f 49a** 5057[3]
8 br g Supreme Leader 10.9f **(66)** - Royal Demon (Tarboosh (USA)) 10f **(55)**
Form - 2033
Record **1999** - 1st:0 2nd:1 3rd:2 Ran:4
Pre1999 - 1st:2 2nd:1 3rd:0 Ran:5
Win Prizemoney £4,551 *Total Prizemoney* £7,027
Wins 1997 *Nov Lingfi (STD) H 12f 27 48* <
1997 *Nov Lingfi (STD) H 16f 27 37*
1999 Turf 0-2: (11f, 14f) (gd, g-f) 1999 AW 0-2: (12f, 16f) (Equi, Fibr)
Fair gelding. Turf high 43 (began Spt). AW high 56 - 3rd of 11 giving 11lb to Virgin Soldier (25 Oct Lingfield 12f Equi RF 5057).
**B R Johnson [0-4] D G Wheatley (from R Ingram [2-3] Nov 1997).*

ANOTHER NIGHT (IRE) BHB 60f **RR 51f** 1329[6]
5 ch h Waajib 8.9f **(67)** - Little Me (Connaught) 7.7f **(63)**
Form - 6
Record **1999** - 1st:0 2nd:0 3rd:0 Ran:1
Pre1999 - 1st:1 2nd:2 3rd:1 Ran:15
Win Prizemoney £3,647 *Total Prizemoney* £6,378
Wins 1997 Jun Haydoc (G-F) 8.1f 75+ <
1999 Turf 0-1: (18f) (gd)
Fair colt. Becoming disappointing.
**P G Murphy [2-24] Sunset Partnership (from R Hannon [1-10] Spt 1997).*

ANOTHER NIGHTMARE (IRE) BHB 49f48a **RR 46f 48a** 4344[18]
7 b m Treasure Kay 6.5f **(53)** - Carange (Known Fact (USA)) 7.4f **(67)**
Form - 83881187821766 0120
Record **1999** - 1st:4 2nd:2 3rd:0 Ran:14
Pre1999 - 1st:6 2nd:4 3rd:6 Ran:81
Win Prizemoney £24,904 *Total Prizemoney* £34,144
Wins *** 1999** Aug Hamilt (G-F) H 5f 40 45
*** 1999** May Hamilt (G-F) H 5f 37 48
*** 1999** *Jan Lingfi (STD) H 6f 44 49*
*** 1999** *Jan Wolver (STD) H 6f 37 46*
1997 Aug Thirsk (GD) SH 6f 44 50
1997 Jly Hamilt (SFT) H 5f 41 46
1997 *Mar Wolver (STD) H 6f 41 42*
1996 Aug Ripon (SFT) H 6f 47 53 <
1996 Aug Hamilt (G-F) H 6f 39 48
1999 Turf 2-10: (5f 2-9, 6f) (g-s, gd 2, g-f 1-2, frm 1-5) 1999 AW 2-4: (5f, 6f 2-3) (Equi 1-2, Fibr 1-2)
Moderate mare, effective 5 to 6f, best at 5f, acts on gd to frm - acts on AW, has worn blinkers, likes left handed tracks, likes tight tracks, likes Hamilton. Turf high 48 - 1st of 18 getting 14lb from Silk Cottage (6 May Hamilton RF 1060) - also 1st of 16 giving 3lb to Petite Danseuse (24 Aug Hamilton RF 3868). AW high 49 - 1st of 9 giving 7lb to Tachycardia (19 Jan Lingfield RF 0120) - also 1st of 9 getting 26lb from Takhlid (6 Jan Wolverhampton RF 0035). She was on a long losing run before winning twice on sand at the start of the year. Both victories came when the surface could be described as sloppy, which suited her front-running style.
**D W Barker [4-20] GM Engineering (from R M McKellar [5-64] Aug 1998).*

ANOTHER PEARL RR 77f 5047[1]
2 br f Ezzoud (IRE) - Pearly River **(72f 54a)** (Elegant Air) 13.2f **(61)**
Form - 1
Record **1999** - 1st:1 2nd:0 3rd:0 Ran:1
Win Prizemoney £4,792 *Total Prizemoney* £4,792
Wins *** 1999** Oct Newbur (HVY) 6f 77 <
1999 Turf 1-1: (6f 1-1) (hvy 1-1)
Currently above-average filly. (1st run) - 1st of 15 from Star Princess (23 Oct Newbury RF 5047).
**L G Cottrell [1-1] Manor Farm Packers Ltd.*

ANOTHER QUESTION (USA) **RR 42f** 4583[6]
3 b c Quest for Fame 12.8f **(75)** - Another Notch (USA) (Cox's Ridge (USA)) 8f **(68)**
Form - 6
Record 1999 - 1st:0 2nd:0 3rd:0 Ran:1
1999 Turf 0-1: (10f) (gd)
Well made, currently moderate colt. He has joined Andrew Turnell to go hurdling. **R Charlton [0-1] K Abdulla.*

ANOTHER RAINBOW (IRE) BHB 63f **RR 70f** 4182[2]
3 br f Rainbows For Life (CAN) 9.3f **(64)** - Phylella (Persian Bold) 9.3f **(66)**
Form - 57245362
Record 1999 - 1st:0 2nd:2 3rd:1 Ran:8
Pre1999 - 1st:0 2nd:1 3rd:0 Ran:3
Win Prizemoney £0 *Total Prizemoney* £3,837
1999 Turf 0-8: (8f, 9f, 10f 2, 11f, 12f 3) (gd 2, frm 6)
Workmanlike, above-average filly, effective 6 to 10f, acts on gd to g-f, prefers left handed tracks, likes tight tracks. Turf high 72 - 2nd of 8 to Azula (29 May Lingfield 10f gd RF 1583). Consistent.
**Miss Gay Kelleway [0-11] Pot Of Gold Racing.*

ANOTHER TIME BHB 83f84a **RR 79f 84a** 4954[7]
7 ch g Clantime 6.6f **(57)** - Another Move (Farm Walk) 11.6f **(55)**
Form - 5536884712777
Record 1999 - 1st:1 2nd:1 3rd:1 Ran:13
Pre1999 - 1st:9 2nd:3 3rd:2 Ran:46
Win Prizemoney £56,086 *Total Prizemoney* £85,737

Wins								
	* **1999**	Aug	Leices	(G-F)	H	10f	81	82
	* 1998	Aug	Lingfi	(G-F)		10f		93 <
	* 1998	Jun	Ascot	(G-S)	H	10f	87	90
	* 1997	Jly	Newbur	(G-F)	H	9f	84	89
	* 1997	Apr	Pontef	(G-F)	H	8f	80	84
	* 1996	Aug	Lingfi	(G-F)	H	10f	70	77
	* 1996	Jun	Ripon	(G-F)		10f		73
	* 1995	Oct	Redcar	(FRM)		10f		72
	* 1995	Spt	Bright	(GD)		8f		68
	* 1995	Spt	Thirsk	(G-F)	S	8f		58+

1999 Turf 1-12:(10f 1-12)(g-s, gd, g-f 5, frm 1-5)1999 AW 0-1: (8f) (Fibr)
Above-average gelding, effective 10f, acts on gd to frm, excels at Folkestone and likes Ascot and Epsom. Turf high 87 - 2nd of 4 to Shadoof (3 Spt Epsom 10f g-f RF 4118). Consistent. A rather in-and-out handicapper, is suited by coming off a fast pace, though he is not very consistent, and needs things to go his way in a race.
**S P C Woods [10-55] W J P Jackson (from Miss S E Hall [0-5] May 1995).*

ANSARI (IRE) BHB 85f **RR 81f** 5124[1]
2 b c Selkirk (USA) 7.9f **(76)** - Anaza (Darshaan) 9.9f **(84)**
Form - 5521
Record 1999 - 1st:1 2nd:1 3rd:0 Ran:4
Win Prizemoney £3,582 *Total Prizemoney* £4,702
Wins * **1999** Oct Bright (G-S) H 8f 78 81 <
1999 Turf 1-4: (7f 3, 8f 1-1) (g-s 2, gd 1-2)
Decent colt. Turf high 81 (began Jly) - 1st of 11 getting 7lb from Kookaburra (29 Oct Brighton RF 5124). **L M Cumani [1-4] H H Aga Khan.*

ANSCHLUSS BHB 86f **RR 81f** 3234[11]
3 gr c Alzao (USA) 9.8f **(73)** - Avice Caro (USA) (Caro)
Form - 66337410
Record 1999 - 1st:1 2nd:0 3rd:2 Ran:8
Pre1999 - 1st:0 2nd:0 3rd:1 Ran:1
Win Prizemoney £3,745 *Total Prizemoney* £7,106
Wins * **1999** Jly Newcas (FRM) 10.1f 81 <
1999 Turf 1-8: (8f 2, 10f 1-6) (gd, g-f 4, frm 1-3)
Scopey, decent colt, has worn blinkers. Turf high 92. Consistent. He has faced some stiff tasks in his races to date, but did not get off the mark until landing a Newcastle maiden on very fast ground in July. **C E Brittain [1-9] H E Sheikh Rashid Al Maktoum.*

ANSELLAD (IRE) BHB 90f **RR 88f** 4208[18]
2 b c Dancing Dissident (USA) 6.8f **(65)** - Dutch Queen (Ahonoora) 8.1f **(73)**
Form - 3120330
Record 1999 - 1st:1 2nd:1 3rd:3 Ran:7
Win Prizemoney £3,533 *Total Prizemoney* £6,716
Wins * **1999** Jun Bath (GD) 5.1f 84 <
1999 Turf 1-7: (5f 1-4, 6f 3) (gd 2, g-f 1-4, frm)
Useful colt, effective 5 to 6f, best at 5f, acts on g-f to frm, best on g-f. Turf high 88 - also 1st of 8 from Deep Blue (12 Jun Bath RF 1940). **J Berry [1-7] Ansells of Watford.*

ANSELLMAN BHB 66f78a **RR 64f 78a** 5212[7]
9 gr g Absalom 7.1f **(56)** - Grace Poole (Sallust) 8.4f **(63)**
Form - 0400044788010000377
Record 1999 - 1st:1 2nd:0 3rd:1 Ran:19
Pre1999 - 1st:9 2nd:15 3rd:9 Ran:86
Win Prizemoney £38,569 *Total Prizemoney* £94,341

Wins								
	* **1999**	Aug	Bath	(HRD)	H	5.1f	69	72
	* 1998	May	Redcar	(GD)	C	6f		84
	* 1997	Spt	Leices	(G-F)	H	5f	78	80
	* 1997	Apr	Ripon	(G-F)	C	5f		77
	* 1996	Jly	Chepst	(G-F)	H	5.1f	75	77
	* 1996	Apr	Bath	(GD)	H	5.1f	70	78
	* 1995	Aug	Catter	(G-F)	C	5f		74

1999 Turf 1-19: (5f 1-12, 6f 7) (sft, g-s 2, gd 5, g-f 5, frm 1-6)
Above-average gelding, effective 5 to 6f, best at 5f, acts on gd to g-f, best on gd, often wears blinkers (effectively), excels at Haydock. Turf high 73.
**J Berry [8-88] Ansells of Watford (from B Smart [0-3] Nov 1993).*

AN SMEARDUBH (IRE) BHB 49f **RR 47f** 2055[11]
3 b f Dolphin Street (FR) - Forest Berries (IRE) (Thatching) 8f **(66)**
Form - 80000
Record 1999 - 1st:0 2nd:0 3rd:0 Ran:5
1999 Turf 0-5: (8f 4, 10f) (gd, g-f 2, frm 2)
Leggy, moderate filly. Turf high 48. **M J Ryan [0-5] & Mrs W J Foley.*

ANSOMAR BHB 30f **RR 17f** 4724[13]
3 b f Never so Bold 7.1f **(62)** - Lorlanne (Bustino) 10.4f **(64)**
Form - 6000
Record 1999 - 1st:0 2nd:0 3rd:0 Ran:4
1999 Turf 0-4: (10f 2, 12f 2) (g-s, gd, frm 2)
Leggy, poor filly. Turf high 31 (began Jly).
**D Moffatt [0-4] David Doughty.*

ANSTAND BHB 66f **RR 66f** 2317[7]
4 b g Anshan 8.2f **(63)** - Pussy Foot (Red Sunset) 8.2f **(63)**
Form - 00587
Record 1999 - 1st:0 2nd:0 3rd:0 Ran:5
Pre1999 - 1st:2 2nd:0 3rd:1 Ran:14
Win Prizemoney £10,209 *Total Prizemoney* £11,429
Wins 1998 Oct York (GD) 6f 76
1998 May Ripon (GD) H 6f 66 86 <
1999 Turf 0-5: (5f 2, 6f 3) (g-s, gd 2, g-f, hrd)
Light-framed, average gelding, effective 6f, acts on gd to g-f, best on gd, has worn blinkers. Turf high 66.
**M S Saunders [0-5] Earl Toups (from Mrs J R Ramsden [2-14] Oct 1998).*

ANSTAR BHB 72f **RR 70f** 3996[6]
2 ch c Anshan 8.2f **(63)** - Star Arrangement (Star Appeal) 9.6f **(65)**
Form - 250156
Record 1999 - 1st:1 2nd:1 3rd:0 Ran:6
Win Prizemoney £3,752 *Total Prizemoney* £4,536
Wins * **1999** Jly Leices (G-F) H 6f 65 <
1999 Turf 1-6: (5f 2, 6f 1-2, 7f 2) (g-f 1-3, frm 2, hrd)
Above-average colt, effective 6 to 7f, acts on g-f, often wears blinkers. Turf high 70 - 6th of 9 getting 4lb from Common Place (29 Aug Goodwood 7f g-f RF 3996) - also 1st of 7 getting 7lb from Gain Time (15 Jly Leicester RF 2851). Got off the mark by the narrowest margin on his nursery debut at Leicester, but had a very hard race there. **I A Balding [1-6] Park House Partnership.*

ANTARCTIC STORM BHB 55f57a **RR 59f 57a** 4638[16]
6 b g Emarati (USA) 6.6f **(63)** - Katie Scarlett (Lochnager) 6f **(59)**
Form - 45801212004230
Record 1999 - 1st:2 2nd:3 3rd:1 Ran:11
Pre1999 - 1st:4 2nd:1 3rd:3 Ran:29
Win Prizemoney £24,164 *Total Prizemoney* £34,640

Wins								
	* **1999**	May	Ripon	(G-S)	S	8f		57
	* **1999**	May	Newcas	(G-F)	C	7f		51
	* 1997	Nov	Mussel	(G-S)	H	8f	69	73 <

* 1997 Spt Hamilt (GD) H 8.3f 61 66
* 1997 Aug Ayr (G-F) H 8f 56 59
1996 Jun Windso (G-F) H 8.3f 60 62

1999 Turf 2-10: (7f 1-3, 8f 1-7) (gd 1-4, g-f 3, frm 1-2, hrd) 1999 AW 0-1: (8f) (Fibr)

Fair gelding, effective 6 to 8f, best at 8f, acts on gd to frm - acts on Fibr, has worn blinkers, likes right handed tracks, likes tight tracks, excels at Hamilton. Turf high 59 - 2nd of 12 getting 27lb from The Prince (6 Spt Hamilton 8f frm RF 4165). Inconsistent. Has been sold to race in Kuwait.

**R A Fahey [5-36] Northumbria Leisure Ltd (from E A L Dunlop [1-5] Jun 1996).*

ANTARCTIQUE (IRE) RR 105f 4768a[5]

5 h Sadler's Wells (USA) 11.3f **(87)** - Arctique Royale (Royal And Regal (USA)) 9.5f **(60)**

Form - 5

1999 Turf 0-1: (20f) (hvy)

Currently Pattern-class colt, has worn blinkers. **R Collet in FR [0-3].*

ANTHEM BHB 90f RR 80f 1146[5]

3 b c Saddlers' Hall (IRE) 10.5f **(65)** - Full Orchestra (Shirley Heights) 10.3f **(74)**

Form - 315

Record 1999 - 1st:1 2nd:0 3rd:1 Ran:3
Pre1999 - 1st:0 2nd:0 3rd:0 Ran:2

Win Prizemoney £4,289 *Total Prizemoney* £5,611

Wins * 1999 May Thirsk (G-F) 12f 80+ <

1999 Turf 1-3: (12f 1-2, 14f) (gd 2, g-f 1-1)

Workmanlike, decent colt. Turf high 80 - 1st of 10 from Upon A Wish (1 May Thirsk RF 0963). Absolutely bolted up in a Thirsk maiden in May, but disappointed at York later the same month and was not seen again. **M A Jarvis [1-5] Mohammed Bin Hendi.*

ANTHEM FLIGHT (USA) RR 49f 1925[16]

3 b f Fly So Free (USA) - Anthem (USA) (Deputy Minister (CAN)) 7.4f **(80)**

Form - 8P0

Record 1999 - 1st:0 2nd:0 3rd:0 Ran:3

1999 Turf 0-3: (8f, 10f 2) (g-f, frm 2)

Light-framed, currently moderate filly. Turf high 49.

**P W Harris [0-3] The Pendley Chorus.*

ANTHEMION (IRE) BHB 70f RR 60f 3281[8]

2 ch c Night Shift (USA) 8.1f **(73)** - New Sensitive (Wattlefield) 5.8f **(71)**

Form - 8308

Record 1999 - 1st:0 2nd:0 3rd:1 Ran:4

Win Prizemoney £0 *Total Prizemoney* £461

1999 Turf 0-4: (5f 2, 6f 2) (g-f 2, frm 2)

Average colt. Turf high 60. Ran well enough when third in a Ripon maiden on his second start but faced a big ask when thrown in the Coventry. A drop in class should ensure success.

**P C Haslam [0-4] Lord Scarsdale.*

ANTHEM OF LOVE (USA) RR 95f 4069a[10]

3 ch f Silver Hawk (USA) 11.2f **(85)** - Missing Love 00

Form - 10

1999 Turf 1-2: (7f 1-1, 10f) (gd 1-2)

Very useful filly, often wears blinkers. Turf high 95 (1st run) (began Aug) - 1st of 4 from Lady Belzoni (9 Aug Cork RF 3701a). She has proved disappointing and did not get home when tried over a mile and a quarter at the Curragh in August.

**D K Weld in IRE [2-4] Moyglare Stud Farm.*

ANTHONY MON AMOUR (USA) BHB 62f66a RR 59f 66a 5032[27]

4 b g Nicholas (USA) 6.1f **(63)** - Reine de La Ciel (USA) (Conquistador Cielo (USA)) 8.8f **(69)**

Form - 2237040

Record 1999 - 1st:0 2nd:2 3rd:1 Ran:7
Pre1999 - 1st:2 2nd:0 3rd:2 Ran:8

Win Prizemoney £5,382 *Total Prizemoney* £9,504

Wins * 1998 *Jly Southw (STD) 6f 69*
* 1998 Jly Chepst (GD) H 6.1f 56 74 <

1999 Turf 0-5: (5f 2, 6f 3) (g-s 3, g-f, frm) 1999 AW 0-2: (6f 2) (Fibr 2)

Rangy, average gelding, effective 6f, acts on g-s to gd - acts on Fibr, likes left handed tracks, likes tight tracks. Turf high 66 (1st run) - 2nd of 10 giving 12lb to Mister Westsound (21 May Ayr 6f g-s RF 1362). AW high 66 (1st run) - 2nd of 10 getting 6lb from Mallia (14 May Wolverhampton 6f Fibr RF 1229). Has been bought by David Nicholls, possibly to race at Mijas in Spain.

**W J Haggas [2-15] The Winning Line.*

ANTIGONEL (IRE) RR 51f 5209[12]

2 b f Fairy King (USA) 7.7f **(75)** - Euromill (Shirley Heights) 10.3f **(74)**

Form - 00

Record 1999 - 1st:0 2nd:0 3rd:0 Ran:2

1999 Turf 0-2: (6f, 7f) (g-s 2)

Currently fair filly. Turf high 51 (began Oct).

**R Hannon [0-2] Stonethorn Stud Farms Ltd.*

ANTINNAZ (IRE) RR 113f 4777a[5]

3 ch f Thatching 7.8f **(69)** - Tootling (IRE) (Pennine Walk) 8.5f **(61)**

Form - 31535

1999 Turf 1-5: (5f 2, 6f 1-3) (sft 2, gd 1-2, frm)

Group-class filly, effective 5f, acts on sft to gd. Turf high 113 - 5th of 14 to Agnes World (3 Oct Longchamp 5f sft RF 4777a). Useful sprinter, winner of a listed race at Haydock and a most commendable close-up fifth in the Prix de l'Abbaye. She likes cut in the ground. **T Stack in IRE [2-9] Mrs T Stack.*

ANTINOUS (FR) RR 91f 2659a[2]

3 b f Double Bed (FR) 13.9f **(54)** -Arjona (GER)(Caracol (FR))14.3f **(75)**

Form - 2

1999 Turf 0-1: (10f) (gd)

Currently useful filly. (1st run) - 2nd of 8 to Passinetti (3 Jly Le Lion D'angers 10f gd RF 2659a). **F Doumen in FR [1-2].*

ANTONIA'S DOUBLE BHB 76f69a RR 74f 69a 4013[13]

4 ch f Primo Dominie 7.2f **(67)** - Mainly Sunset (Red Sunset) 8.2f **(63)**

Form - 20201212210

Record 1999 - 1st:3 2nd:5 3rd:0 Ran:11
Pre1999 - 1st:1 2nd:0 3rd:1 Ran:8

Win Prizemoney £21,197 *Total Prizemoney* £30,108

Wins * 1999 Jly Newcas (G-F) H 5f 74 74 <
*** 1999** Jun Salisb (FRM) H 5f 66 69
*** 1999** Jun Redcar (FRM) H 5f 59 61
* 1998 Jly Newcas (G-F) 5f 61

1999 Turf 3-8: (5f 3-8) (gd 2, g-f 1-2, frm 2-4) 1999 AW 0-3: (5f 3) (Equi, Fibr 2)

Scopey, above-average filly, effective 5f, acts on g-f to frm - acts on Fibr, best on frm, excels at Newcastle and Wolverhampton. Turf high 74 - 1st of 12 getting 7lb from Double Oscar (24 Jly Newcastle RF 3101) - also 1st of 11 getting 6lb from Faute de Mieux (24 Jun Salisbury RF 2273). AW high 67 - 2nd of 13 giving 22lb to Heavenly Miss (24 Apr Wolverhampton 5f Fibr RF 0846). Consistent. A winner three times last term over the minimum trip, each victory coming on a fast surface. **J Berry [4-19] Chris & Antonia Deuters.*

ANTONIA'S DREAM BHB 65f RR 62f 4277[4]

2 ch f Clantime 6.6f **(57)** - Militia Girl (Rarity) 10.1f **(60)**

Form - 6346454

Record 1999 - 1st:0 2nd:0 3rd:1 Ran:7

Win Prizemoney £0 *Total Prizemoney* £1,430

1999 Turf 0-7: (5f 7) (g-s, g-f 2, frm 4)

Average filly, has worn blinkers. Turf high 62.

**J Berry [0-7] Chris & Antonia Deuters.*

ANTONIO CANOVA BHB 74f RR 76f 4805[3]

3 ch c Komaite (USA) 6.9f **(61)** - Joan's Venture (Beldale Flutter (USA)) 9.7f **(71)**

Form - 6223

Record 1999 - 1st:0 2nd:2 3rd:1 Ran:4

Win Prizemoney £0 *Total Prizemoney* £3,782

1999 Turf 0-4: (5f, 6f 3) (gd 2, g-f 2)

Workmanlike, above-average colt. Turf high 76 - 2nd of 11 giving 5lb to Stridhana (24 Aug Lingfield 6f g-f RF 3873).

**Bob Jones [0-4] The Antonio Canova Partnership.*

ANTONIOCASTIGLIONE (IRE) RR 99f 1719a[4]

3 ch c Pursuit of Love 9.5f **(69)** - Blue Wedding (USA) (Irish River (FR)) 8.6f **(78)**

Form - 24

1999 Turf 0-2: (10f, 12f) (g-f 2)

Currently very useful colt. Turf high 99 - 4th of 13 to Mukhalif (30 May Capannelle 12f g-f RF 1719a).
**M Guarnieri in ITY [0-1] (from M Guarneri in ITY [0-1] May 1999).*

ANUSHKA (IRE) BHB 66f RR 53f 3660[5]

3 ch f Indian Ridge 7.6f **(74)** - Shaping Up (USA) (Storm Bird (CAN)) 10.3f **(74)**
Form - 045
Record 1999 - 1st:0 2nd:0 3rd:0 Ran:3
Win Prizemoney £0 *Total Prizemoney* £293
1999 Turf 0-3: (6f, 7f, 8f) (g-f, frm 2)
Unfurnished, currently fair filly. Turf high 53 (began Jly).
**H R A Cecil [0-3] Clark Industrial Services Partnership.*

ANYHOW (IRE) RR 3670[3]

2 b f Distant Relative 7f **(69)** - Fast Chick (Henbit (USA)) 9f **(61)**
Form - 3
Record 1999 - 1st:0 2nd:0 3rd:1 Ran:1
Win Prizemoney £0 *Total Prizemoney* £539
1999 AW 0-1: (7f) (Fibr)
Currently average filly. **Andrew Reid [0-1] A S Reid.*

ANZARI (IRE) RR 90f 3715a[2]

2 b c Nicolotte - Anazara (USA) 0**0**
Form - 4112
1999 Turf 2-4: (6f, 7f 2-3) (gd 1-1, g-f 1-2, frm)
Useful colt. Turf high 90 - 1st of 9 giving 15lb to Rainbow Melody (31 Jly Galway RF 3341a). **J Oxx in IRE [2-4] H H Aga Khan.*

ANZIO (IRE) BHB 109f95a RR 105f 95a 2855a[2]

8 b g Hatim (USA) 7.8f **(56)** - Highdrive (Ballymore) 7.3f **(64)**
Form - 2
1999 Turf 0-1: (7f) (sft)
Pattern-class gelding, often wears blinkers.
**A Lund in NOR [0-2] (from Miss Gay Kelleway [5-10] Dec 1996).*

AOIFE (IRE) BHB 69f78a RR 65f 78a 212[1]

4 ch f Thatching 7.8f **(69)** - Aunt Hester (IRE) (Caerleon (USA)) 8.6f **(71)**
Form - 141

Record	**1999** -	1st:1	2nd:0	3rd:0	Ran:1			
	Pre1999 -	1st:1	2nd:2	3rd:0	Ran:5			

Win Prizemoney £6,312 *Total Prizemoney* £9,337

Wins	*** 1999**	*Feb Lingfi*	*(STD)*	*H*	*6f*	*74*	*76*	<
	* 1998	*Nov Lingfi*	*(STD)*		*6f*		*67*	

1999 AW 1-1: (6f 1-1) (Equi 1-1)
Workmanlike, above-average filly, effective 6f, - acts on Equi. (1st run) - 1st of 8 giving 2lb to Anokato (2 Feb Lingfield RF 0212).
**G Wragg [2-6] Kaniz Bloodstock Investments Ltd.*

API SA (IRE) RR 99f 4661a[6]

3 f
Form - 6
1999 Turf 0-1: (10f) (gd)
Currently very useful filly. **A Wohler in GER [0-1].*

APLOY BHB 71f RR 75f 4784[7]

2 b f Deploy 11.4f **(67)** - Amidst **(74f)** (Midyan (USA)) 6f **(60)**
Form - 2537
Record 1999 - 1st:0 2nd:1 3rd:1 Ran:4
Win Prizemoney £0 *Total Prizemoney* £1,579
1999 Turf 0-4: (6f 3, 7f) (g-s, g-f, frm 2)
Above-average filly. Turf high 75 (began Aug).
**R F JohnsonHoughton [0-4] Mrs P Robeson.*

APOLLO RED BHB 52f79a RR 54f 79a 5127[2]

10 ch g Dominion 8.9f **(65)** - Woolpack (Golden Fleece (USA)) 7.9f **(74)**
Form - 400050432302

Record	**1999** -	1st:0	2nd:2	3rd:2	Ran:10			
	Pre1999 -	1st:12	2nd:7	3rd:17	Ran:86			

Win Prizemoney £36,248 *Total Prizemoney* £54,293

Wins	* 1998	Jly	Bright	(GD)	H	7f	68	72	
	* 1997	*Dec*	*Lingfi*	*(STD)*	*H*	*6f*	*85*	*87*	<
	* 1997	*Nov*	*Lingfi*	*(STD)*	*H*	*6f*	*80*	*83*	
	* 1997	May	Bright	(G-F)	H	7f	68	76	
	* 1997	*Apr*	*Lingfi*	*(STD)*	*H*	*6f*	*72*	*79*	•
	* 1997	*Feb*	*Lingfi*	*(STD)*	*H*	*6f*	*60*	*65*	
	1996	*Dec*	*Lingfi*	*(STD)*	*H*	*7f*	*58*	*62*	
	1996	*Nov*	*Lingfi*	*(STD)*	*C*	*7f*		*59*	
	1996	May	Lingfi	(G-F)	H	7f	54	57	
	1996	Apr	Bright	(FRM)	H	5.3f	51	53	

1999 Turf 0-10: (5f, 6f 2, 7f 3, 8f 4) (g-s, gd 4, g-f, frm 4)
Useful gelding, effective 7f, acts on gd, has worn blinkers. Turf high 69. **G L Moore [6-43] A Moore (from A Moore [6-42] Jan 1997).*

APOLLO VICTORIA (FR) RR 98f 5170a[1]

2 b c Sadler's Wells (USA) 11.3f **(87)** - Dame Solitaire (CAN) (Halo (USA)) 10.6f **(75)**
Form - 1
1999 Turf 1-1: (7f 1-1) (sft 1-1)
Currently very useful colt. (1st run) - 1st of 17 from Legal Jousting (25 Oct Leopardstown RF 5170a).
**A P O'Brien in IRE [1-1] Mrs John Magnier.*

APOLLO WELLS RR 109f 1715a[2]

4 b c Sagal Wells - Sharrara (CAN) (Blushing Groom (FR)) 10.3f **(76)**
Form - 72
1999 Turf 0-2: (10f, 12f) (gd, frm)
Pattern-class colt. Turf high 109 - 2nd of 10 to Ivan Luis (29 May Capannelle 12f frm RF 1715a). **R Brogi in ITY [0-4] Scuderia Itaca.*

APPALACHIA (IRE) RR 90f 2416a[3]

2 b f Imperial Frontier (USA) 7f **(65)** - Hawksbill Special (IRE) (Taufan (USA)) 7f **(57)**
Form - 1333
1999 Turf 1-4: (5f 1-2, 6f 2) (gd 1-3, g-f)
Useful filly. Turf high 90 - 3rd of 5 giving 1lb to Monashee Mountain (7 Jun Leopardstown 6f gd RF 2010a).
**J C Harley in IRE [1-4] S and L Racing Syndicate.*

APPARATCHIK RR 103f 2411a[7]

3 b f Selkirk (USA) 7.9f **(76)** - Last Exit (Dominion) 8.5f **(63)**
Form - 2217
1999 Turf 1-4: (7f, 8f, 10f 1-2) (gd, g-f 1-3)
Very useful filly, effective 7 to 10f, acts on gd to g-f, best on g-f, often wears blinkers (extremely effectively). Turf high 103 (1st run) - 2nd of 7 getting 5lb from Show Me The Money (18 Apr Leopardstown 7f g-f RF 0784a) - also 1st of 5 getting 3lb from Castle Quest (23 May Curragh RF 1486a). Inconsistent. She has drifted under pressure, but did nothing wrong when winning a Listed race over 10 furlongs at The Curragh in May. Disappointing over the same course and distance the following month, she missed the second half of the campaign and may have a problem.
**J Oxx in IRE [2-8] Mrs Adam Gurney.*

APPLE GREEN BHB 64f RR 65f 3572[6]

2 b f Superlative 8.8f **(57)** - Green Divot **(37f)** (Green Desert (USA)) 8.6f **(78)**
Form - 636
Record 1999 - 1st:0 2nd:0 3rd:1 Ran:3
Win Prizemoney £0 *Total Prizemoney* £329
1999 Turf 0-3: (6f, 7f 2) (g-f, frm, hrd)
Currently average filly. Turf high 65.
**R Charlton [0-3] Miss J Frankham.*

APPLE OF KENT (USA) BHB 93f RR 85?f 4290[6]

3 b br f Kris S (USA) 9.3f **(76)** - Proflare (USA) (Mr Prospector (USA)) 8.8f **(78)**
Form - 2106
Record 1999 - 1st:1 2nd:1 3rd:0 Ran:4
Win Prizemoney £4,854 *Total Prizemoney* £6,264

Wins	*** 1999**	May Newmar	(GD)	8f		85	<

1999 Turf 1-4: (7f, 8f 1-1, 10f, 11f) (g-s, g-f 1-2, frm)
Leggy, useful filly. Turf high 85 - 1st of 9 from Palm Tree (15 May Newmarket RF 1242). Well beaten in Pattern company after winning her maiden. **J H M Gosden [1-4] K Abdulla.*

APPLE PEELER (IRE) BHB 54f RR 68f 4320[5]

2 ch f Rainbows For Life (CAN) 9.3f **(64)** - Golden Pleasure (Glint of Gold) 9.3f **(66)**
Form - 081072670385
Record 1999 - 1st:1 2nd:1 3rd:1 Ran:12
Win Prizemoney £2,916 *Total Prizemoney* £3,785

Wins	*** 1999**	May Thirsk	(G-S)	C	5f		65	<

1999 Turf 1-11: (5f 1-6, 6f 4, 7f) (gd 1-3, g-f 4, frm 4) 1999 AW 0-1: (5f) (Fibr)

Average filly, effective 5f, acts on gd to g-f, mostly wears blinkers (very effectively). Turf high 65 - 2nd of 15 giving 5lb to Printsmith (1 Jly Catterick 5f g-f RF 2454) - also 1st of 14 getting 4lb from Diamond Promise (15 May Thirsk RF 1247).

**K A Ryan [1-12] Clayton Bigley Partnership Ltd.*

APPLES AND PEARS (IRE) BHB 51f **RR 48f** 5065[9]

3 b f High Estate 10.5f **(66)** - Tiempo (King of Spain) 7.8f **(52)**

Form - 745204360

Record	**1999** -	1st:0	2nd:1	3rd:1	Ran:9
	Pre1999 -	1st:0	2nd:0	3rd:0	Ran:3

Win Prizemoney £0 *Total Prizemoney* £1,048

1999 Turf 0-8: (5f 7, 6f) (g-s 2, gd 4, g-f, frm) 1999 AW 0-1: (5f) (Fibr)

Unfurnished, moderate filly, effective 5f, acts on gd to frm - acts on Fibr. Turf high 49 - 4th of 19 getting 2lb from Three Leaders (22 Jun Beverley 5f g-f RF 2194). (1st run) - 4th of 8 getting 5lb from Legal Venture (8 May Wolverhampton 5f Fibr RF 1121). Consistent.

**M H Tompkins [0-12] www raceworld co uk.*

APPLE SAUCE BHB 49f **RR 53f** 4094[12]

4 b f Prince Sabo 6.6f **(64)** - Mrs Bacon (Balliol) 5f **(43)**

Form - 00460

Record	**1999** -	1st:0	2nd:0	3rd:0	Ran:5
	Pre1999 -	1st:1	2nd:2	3rd:0	Ran:12

Win Prizemoney £3,582 *Total Prizemoney* £6,042

Wins	* 1998	Aug	Bath	(GD)	H	5.1f	55	58 <

1999 Turf 0-5: (5f 2, 6f 2, 8f) (gd, g-f, frm 3)

Scopey, fair filly, effective 5 to 6f, best at 5f, acts on gd to g-f, best on gd. Turf high 53. Inconsistent.

**L G Cottrell [1-12] Mrs B Skinner (from J R Arnold [0-5] Spt 1997).*

APPROACHABLE (USA) BHB 50f61a **RR 47f 61a** 4706[6]

4 b br c Known Fact (USA) 8.3f **(72)** - Western Approach (USA) (Gone West (USA)) 6.5f **(75)**

Form - 3518031166

Record	**1999** -	1st:3	2nd:0	3rd:2	Ran:10
	Pre1999 -	1st:0	2nd:0	3rd:0	Ran:3

Win Prizemoney £6,419 *Total Prizemoney* £7,222

Wins	**1999**	*Jly*	*Wolver*	*(STD)*	*C*	*8.5f*		*65* <
	1999	*Jly*	*Wolver*	*(STD)*	*C*	*9.4f*		*61+*
	1999	*Mar*	*Wolver*	*(STD)*	*H*	*7f*	*49*	*57*

1999 Turf 0-1: (8f) (frm) 1999 AW 3-9: (7f 1-2, 8f 1-3, 9f 1-2, 10f 2) (Equi 2, Fibr 3-7)

Scopey, average colt, effective 7 to 9f, - acts on Fibr, has worn blinkers, prefers left handed tracks, likes tight tracks. AW high 66 - also 1st of 11 giving 10lb to Doberman (23 Jly Wolverhampton RF 3080). His best form so far has been on the Wolverhampton Fibresand.

**Miss S J Wilton [0-2] John Pointon and Sons (from K A Morgan [2-3] Jly 1999).*

APPROBATION (USA) BHB 72f **RR 73f** 5207[17]

2 ch c With Approval (CAN) 8.7f **(80)** - Exotic Beauty (USA) (Java Gold (USA))

Form - 040

Record	**1999** -	1st:0	2nd:0	3rd:0	Ran:3

Win Prizemoney £0 *Total Prizemoney* £229

1999 Turf 0-3: (7f 3) (g-s, gd, frm)

Currently above-average colt. Turf high 73.

**P W Harris [0-3] Atkinson, Rodway and Mrs P W Harris.*

APPROVED QUALITY (IRE) BHB 40f **RR 52f** 498[9]

6 b m Persian Heights 10.5f **(61)** - Greatest Pleasure (Be My Guest (USA)) 9.3f **(67)**

Form - 20

Record	**1999** -	1st:0	2nd:1	3rd:0	Ran:2
	Pre1999 -	1st:0	2nd:0	3rd:2	Ran:12

Win Prizemoney £0 *Total Prizemoney* £1,174

1999 AW 0-2: (12f 2) (Fibr 2)

Fair mare, effective 12f, acts on g-f, has worn blinkers. AW high 41. Inconsistent.

**F Murphy [0-2] Ben Collins (from J G Coogan in IRE [0-15] Aug 1998).*

APPYABO BHB 28f35a **RR 26f 35a** 3348[6]

4 ch g Never so Bold 7.1f **(62)** - Cardinal Palace (Royal Palace) 9f **(56)**

Form - 3064006

Record	**1999** -	1st:0	2nd:0	3rd:1	Ran:7
	Pre1999 -	1st:0	2nd:4	3rd:2	Ran:17

Win Prizemoney £0 *Total Prizemoney* £4,458

1999 Turf 0-2: (12f 2) (g-f, frm) 1999 AW 0-5: (12f 3, 14f, 16f) (Equi, Fibr 4)

Leggy, moderate gelding, effective 10f, - acts on Equi, has worn blinkers. Turf high 26. AW high 44.

**M Quinn [0-20] M Quinn (from M R Channon [0-5] Aug 1997).*

APRIL ACE BHB 57f73a **RR 57f 73a** 4133[3]

3 ch g First Trump - Champ d'Avril (Northfields (USA)) 9f **(72)**

Form - 06500362317214323

Record	**1999** -	1st:2	2nd:3	3rd:4	Ran:17
	Pre1999 -	1st:1	2nd:0	3rd:0	Ran:9

Win Prizemoney £12,593 *Total Prizemoney* £18,064

Wins	*** 1999**	Aug	Bright	(G-F)	H	8f	54	56
	*** 1999**	Jly	Nottin	(FRM)	H	8.2f	52	49
	* 1998	Jun	Bath	(G-S)		5.7f		70 <

1999 Turf 2-16: (6f 2, 7f 5, 8f 2-6, 9f 3) (gd 5, g-f 1-7, frm 1-4) 1999 AW 0-1: (6f) (Fibr)

Unfurnished, average gelding, effective 6 to 7f, acts on gd to frm, has worn blinkers, prefers left handed tracks, likes tight tracks. Turf high 59. Consistent. A modest performer, he gained a couple of battling victories in small-field handicaps last season. A mile looks as far as he wants. **M Quinn [3-26] John Breslin.*

APRIL'S COMAIT BHB 45f45a **RR 52f 45a** 5187[9]

2 br f Komaite (USA) 6.9f **(61)** - Sweet Caroline **(29f 35a)** (Squill (USA))

Form - 0448000

Record	**1999** -	1st:0	2nd:0	3rd:0	Ran:7

1999 Turf 0-5: (5f 4, 6f) (gd 2, g-f 2, frm) 1999 AW 0-2: (5f 2) (Fibr 2)

Fair filly. Turf high 52. AW high 42.

**Miss J F Craze [0-7] K Briggs And Holgate Four.*

APRIL SPIRIT BHB 20f **RR 45f** 246[6]

4 b f Nomination 7.3f **(57)** - Seraphim (FR) (Lashkari) 9.8f **(67)**

Form - 0666

Record	**1999** -	1st:0	2nd:0	3rd:0	Ran:2
	Pre1999 -	1st:0	2nd:0	3rd:0	Ran:4

1999 AW 0-2: (16f 2) (Fibr 2)

Scopey, moderate filly. AW high 14.

**R Hollinshead [0-6] Mrs B Ramsden.*

APRIL STOCK BHB 73f **RR 74f** 5133[9]

4 ch f Beveled (USA) 6.9f **(64)** - Stockline (Capricorn Line) 14.6f **(62)**

Form - 108410

Record	**1999** -	1st:2	2nd:0	3rd:0	Ran:6
	Pre1999 -	1st:0	2nd:3	3rd:2	Ran:6

Win Prizemoney £7,846 *Total Prizemoney* £12,881

Wins	*** 1999**	Oct	Windso	(G-S)		11.6f		74 <
	1999	Apr	Folkes	(HVY)		12f		68

1999 Turf 2-6: (12f 2-4, 14f, 18f) (hvy 1-1, gd 2, g-f 1-2, frm)

Workmanlike, above-average filly, effective 12 to 17f, acts on hvy to g-f, best on gd, excels at Newbury. Turf high 74 - 1st of 14 giving 4lb to Grosvenor Flyer (11 Oct Windsor RF 4822) - also 1st of 11 giving 20lb to Pacaera (13 Apr Folkestone RF 0660).

**G A Butler [1-2] Stock Hill Racing (from Miss Gay Kelleway [1-10] Jun 1999).*

APRIL TREASURE BHB 36f **RR 57f** 4413[8]

4 b f Stani (USA) - Eleri (Rolfe (USA)) 12.1f **(65)**

Form - 8

Record	**1999** -	1st:0	2nd:0	3rd:0	Ran:1
	Pre1999 -	1st:0	2nd:0	3rd:0	Ran:5

1999 AW 0-1: (15f) (Fibr)

Light-framed, fair filly, has worn blinkers.

**Mrs P Ford [0-1] W E Donohue (from J L Spearing [0-5] Spt 1998).*

A PROPER CHARLIE BHB 31f **RR 31f** 4601[12]

3 b g Cashwyn - Kate's Girl (Lighter)

Form - 6000

Record	**1999** -	1st:0	2nd:0	3rd:0	Ran:4

1999 Turf 0-3: (8f, 10f, 12f) (frm 3) 1999 AW 0-1: (11f) (Fibr)

Light-framed, very moderate gelding, has worn blinkers. Turf high 31. **J L Spearing [0-4] R J Lewis.*

AQRABA RR 77f 1299^{4}
3 b f Polish Precedent (USA) 9f **(73)** - Aquaba (USA) (Damascus (USA)) 8.9f **(71)**
Form - 24
Record 1999 - 1st:0 2nd:1 3rd:0 Ran:2
Win Prizemoney £0 *Total Prizemoney* £1,209
1999 Turf 0-2: (8f, 10f) (gd, frm)
Well made, currently above-average filly. Turf high 77 (1st run) - 2nd of 14 to Greenstone (3 May Warwick 8f frm RF 1017).
**L M Cumani [0-2] Sheikh Mohammed.*

AQUARIUM (IRE) BHB 94f **RR 91f** 3258^{2}
2 b c Dolphin Street (FR) - Mo Pheata (Petorius) 7.3f **(61)**
Form - 8132
Record 1999 - 1st:1 2nd:1 3rd:1 Ran:4
Win Prizemoney £3,485 *Total Prizemoney* £7,300
Wins * **1999** Jun Windso (G-F) 6f 76 <
1999 Turf 1-4: (6f 1-3, 7f) (gd, g-f 2, frm 1-1)
Useful colt. Turf high 91 - 2nd of 13 giving 6lb to Carousing (31 Jly Goodwood 7f g-f RF 3258). Got off the mark in a Windsor maiden before running with credit in nurseries. Seven furlongs and some cut in the ground may be in order.
**J L Dunlop [1-4] Anglia Bloodstock Syndicate 1998.*

AQUATIC KING (IRE) BHB 49f42a **RR 48f 42a** 4949^{9}
4 b g In The Wings 11.2f **(77)** - Sea Ballad (USA) (Bering) 7.4f **(61)**
Form - 73570860
Record 1999 - 1st:0 2nd:0 3rd:1 Ran:8
Win Prizemoney £0 *Total Prizemoney* £511
1999 Turf 0-7: (8f, 10f 2, 11f, 12f, 13f, 14f) (sft 2, g-s, gd 3, g-f) 1999 AW 0-1: (15f) (Fibr)
Moderate gelding. Turf high 54. **K R Burke [0-8] Leydens Farm Stud.*

ARABELLA GIRL RR 48f 3002^{8}
2 ch f Aragon 7.7f **(58)** - Bella Helena (Balidar) 7.9f **(63)**
Form - 088
Record 1999 - 1st:0 2nd:0 3rd:0 Ran:3
1999 Turf 0-3: (5f, 6f 2) (g-f, frm 2)
Currently moderate filly. Turf high 48.
**P D Evans [0-3] Mrs F A Veasey.*

ARABESQUE RR 86f 5136^{2}
2 b f Zafonic (USA) 9f **(83)** - Prophecy (IRE) **(99f)** (Warning)
Form - 32
Record 1999 - 1st:0 2nd:1 3rd:1 Ran:2
Win Prizemoney £0 *Total Prizemoney* £2,106
1999 Turf 0-2: (6f, 7f) (gd 2)
Currently useful filly. Turf high 86 (began Oct) - 2nd of 16 to Premier Prize (30 Oct Newmarket 7f gd RF 5136).
**H R A Cecil [0-2] K Abdulla.*

ARAB GOLD BHB 37f34a **RR 32f 34a** 2622^{9}
4 b g Presidium 7.5f **(56)** - Parklands Belle (Stanford) 7.9f **(56)**
Form - 70836050
Record 1999 - 1st:0 2nd:0 3rd:1 Ran:8
Pre1999 - 1st:0 2nd:0 3rd:0 Ran:5
Win Prizemoney £0 *Total Prizemoney* £522
1999 Turf 0-2: (7f, 10f) (g-f, frm) 1999 AW 0-6: (6f 2, 7f 2, 8f, 10f) (Equi 3, Fibr 3)
Leggy, very moderate gelding. Turf high 32. AW high 40.
**M Quinn [0-8] W Trezise (from Miss S E Hall [0-5] Jly 1998).*

ARABIAN HEIGHTS BHB 40f52a **RR 52a** 1226^{7}
6 ch g Persian Heights 10.5f **(61)** - Arabian Rose (USA) (Lyphard (USA)) 9.9f **(72)**
Form - 7
Record 1999 - 1st:0 2nd:0 3rd:0 Ran:1
Pre1999 - 1st:1 2nd:0 3rd:1 Ran:12
Win Prizemoney £3,631 *Total Prizemoney* £4,322
Wins 1996 Jun Doncas (G-F) H 10.3f 49 52 <
1999 AW 0-1: (9f) (Fibr)
Very poor gelding.
**J Mackie [0-8] Fools Who Dream (from Mrs J R Ramsden [1-12] Aug 1996).*

ARABIAN MOON (IRE) BHB 87f **RR 87f** 4571^{12}
3 ch c Barathea (IRE) - Excellent Alibi (USA)(Exceller (USA)) 12.5f **(74)**
Form - 0884211300
Record 1999 - 1st:2 2nd:1 3rd:1 Ran:10
Pre1999 - 1st:0 2nd:0 3rd:0 Ran:2
Win Prizemoney £8,503 *Total Prizemoney* £12,892
Wins * **1999** Jly Windso (G-F) H 11.6f 78 84 <
* **1999** Jun Ripon (G-F) H 12.3f 68 80
1999 Turf 2-10: (7f 2, 8f, 10f 2, 12f 2-3, 14f, 16f) (sft, gd 5, g-f, frm 1-2, hrd 1-1)
Scopey, useful colt, effective 12 to 16f, best at 12f, acts on gd to hrd, likes right handed tracks. Turf high 87 - 3rd of 7 to First Ballot (7 Aug Ascot 16f gd RF 3443) - also 1st of 12 giving 3lb to Ledham (12 Jly Windsor RF 2762). Second to the progressive Mary Stuart at Goodwood, he then won twice over trips around twelve furlongs at Ripon and Windsor, and though only third when stepped up to two miles at Ascot, he seemed to stay well enough. Disappointing in warm handicaps subsequently. **C E Brittain [2-12] Salem Suhail.*

ARABIS BHB 80f **RR 81f** 4759^{4}
3 ch f Arazi (USA) 9.2f **(74)** -Mill on the Floss (Mill Reef (USA)) 0.5f **(78)**
Form - 1374
Record 1999 - 1st:1 2nd:0 3rd:1 Ran:4
Win Prizemoney £4,662 *Total Prizemoney* £6,631
Wins * **1999** Jun Newmar (GD) 10f 79 <
1999 Turf 1-4: (10f 1-2, 12f, 13f) (gd 1-2, frm 2)
Leggy, decent filly. Turf high 81 - 3rd of 4 getting 13lb from Vicious Circle (25 Jun Newcastle 10f frm RF 2302) - also 1st of 13 from Petal (5 Jun Newmarket RF 1775). **H R A Cecil [1-4] Cliveden Stud.*

ARAGANT (FR) BHB 75f **RR 76f** 4718^{18}
3 b br g Aragon 7.7f **(58)** - Soolaimon (IRE) **(68f)** (Shareef Dancer (USA)) 9.9f **(73)**
Form - 445330
Record 1999 - 1st:0 2nd:0 3rd:2 Ran:6
Win Prizemoney £0 *Total Prizemoney* £2,126
1999 Turf 0-6: (7f, 8f 2, 10f 3) (gd 2, g-f 3, frm)
Unfurnished, above-average gelding, effective 8 to 10f, acts on g-f. Turf high 77.
**R J Hodges [0-1] Mrs S Y Thomas (from P W Chapple-Hyam [0-5] Aug 1999).*

ARAGROVE BHB 39f29a **RR 24f 29a** 181^{12}
9 b g Aragon 7.7f **(58)** - Grovehurst (Homing) 7.8f **(59)**
Form - 050
Record 1999 - 1st:0 2nd:0 3rd:0 Ran:3
Pre1999 - 1st:8 2nd:4 3rd:4 Ran:51
Win Prizemoney £32,136 *Total Prizemoney* £40,696
Wins 1995 Jly Goodwo (G-F) H 5f 77 80 <
1995 Jun Bright (G-F) H 6f 71 73
1995 Jun Folkes (GD) H 6f 67 66
1995 May Lingfi (G-F) H 5f 60 65
1995 Apr Bright (G-F) H 5.3f 52 53
1999 AW 0-3: (6f 2, 8f) (Equi 3)
Little account gelding, effective 5f, acts on frm, has worn blinkers. AW high 13. Becoming disappointing.
**M D I Usher [0-13] Bryan Fry (from J W Payne [5-22] Aug 1995).*

ARAMIL RR 47f 3668^{10}
2 ch f First Trump - Ever So Artful (Never so Bold) 6.3f **(66)**
Form - 00
Record 1999 - 1st:0 2nd:0 3rd:0 Ran:2
1999 Turf 0-1: (6f) (frm) 1999 AW 0-1: (6f) (Fibr)
Currently moderate filly. **D W P Arbuthnot [0-2] Miss Samantha Dare.*

ARANA BHB 37f **RR 55f** 5193^{10}
4 b f Noble Patriarch 12.2f **(43)** - Pod's Daughter (IRE) (Tender King) 6.8f **(54)**
Form - 708000
Record 1999 - 1st:0 2nd:0 3rd:0 Ran:6
Pre1999 - 1st:0 2nd:0 3rd:0 Ran:2
1999 Turf 0-6: (7f, 8f 5) (gd 3, g-f 2, frm)
Fair filly. Turf high 55 (began Jly). Inconsistent.
**W de Best-Turner [0-6] The Spanish Connection (from D M Hyde [0-2] Dec 1997).*

ARANYI (USA) BHB 84f **RR 81f** 5000^{4}
2 gr c El Gran Senor (USA) 8.9f **(85)** - Heather's It (USA) (Believe It (USA)) 9.4f **(70)**

Form - 644
Record 1999 - 1st:0 2nd:0 3rd:0 Ran:3
Win Prizemoney £0 *Total Prizemoney* £562
1999 Turf 0-3: (7f 2, 8f) (gd 2, frm)
Currently decent colt. Turf high 81 (began Spt).
**J L Dunlop [0-3] Benny Andersson.*

ARAWAK PRINCE (IRE) BHB 83f **RR 84f** 4434[6]
3 ch g College Chapel - Alpine Symphony (Northern Dancer) 9.6f **(80)**
Form - 516
Record 1999 - 1st:1 2nd:0 3rd:0 Ran:3
Win Prizemoney £2,866 *Total Prizemoney* £3,037
Wins *** 1999** Aug Windso (GD) 10f 70 <
1999 Turf 1-3: (7f, 10f 1-1, 12f) (g-s, gd 1-2)
Strong, currently decent gelding. Turf high 84 (began Jly). Could possibly have found 12 furlongs on heavy ground too much last time, although the fact he downed tools once asked for an effort would worry potential backers that he is not entirely genuine.
**J Noseda [1-3] Lucayan Stud.*

ARBENIG (IRE) BHB 48f50a **RR 46f 50a** 4398[12]
4 b f Anita's Prince 6f **(62)** - Out On Her Own (Superlative) 7.2f **(56)**
Form - 3036238826600
Record 1999 - 1st:0 2nd:2 3rd:2 Ran:11
Pre1999 - 1st:2 2nd:1 3rd:4 Ran:22
Win Prizemoney £4,617 *Total Prizemoney* £9,301
Wins * 1998 May Salisb (FRM) C 7f 60+
* 1997 *Oct Wolver (STD) 6f 77* <
1999 Turf 0-11: (7f 5, 8f 6) (g-s, gd 2, frm 8)
Fair filly, effective 7 to 8f, best at 7f, acts on gd to frm - acts on Fibr, best on frm, has worn blinkers, does well at Chepstow. Turf high 57 - 2nd of 17 getting 3lb from Moon At Night (23 Jly Chepstow 7f frm RF 3056). Consistent.
**B Palling [2-33] Andrew Smallwood.*

ARBOR EALIS (IRE) BHB 39f46a **RR 38f 46a** 4075[4]
3 b f Woods of Windsor (USA) - North Lady (Northfields (USA)) 9f **(72)**
Form - 00500064
Record 1999 - 1st:0 2nd:0 3rd:0 Ran:8
Pre1999 - 1st:1 2nd:0 3rd:2 Ran:9
Win Prizemoney £1,725 *Total Prizemoney* £3,254
Wins 1998 *Jun Wolver (STD) S 5f 66* <
1999 Turf 0-6: (5f, 6f, 8f 2, 10f, 12f) (gd, g-f 2, frm 3) 1999 AW 0-2: (6f, 8f) (Fibr 2)
Moderate filly, effective 5f, - acts on Fibr, has worn blinkers, likes left handed tracks, likes tight tracks. Turf high 53. AW high 17.
**R J Baker [0-8] Dr Ian Shenkin (from H S Howe [1-9] Spt 1998).*

ARC (IRE) BHB 64a **RR 62f** 2919[10]
5 b g Archway (IRE) 8.5f **(60)** - Columbian Sand (IRE) (Salmon Leap (USA)) 11f **(61)**
Form - 20321784072262210
Record 1999 - 1st:2 2nd:5 3rd:1 Ran:16
Pre1999 - 1st:0 2nd:2 3rd:2 Ran:17
Win Prizemoney £4,966 *Total Prizemoney* £11,442
Wins *** 1999** Jly Carlis (GD) 8f 61
*** 1999** *Feb Wolver (STD) H 7f 62 65* <
1999 Turf 1-7: (8f 1-3, 9f, 10f 3) (g-f 4, frm 1-1, hrd 2) 1999 AW 1-9: (7f 1-3, 8f 4, 9f 2) (Fibr 1-9)
Average gelding, effective 7 to 10f, acts on g-f to hrd - acts on Fibr, has worn blinkers, favours tight tracks, and excels at Carlisle. Turf high 62 - 2nd of 13 giving 10lb to Time To Wyn (24 Jun Carlisle 8f hrd RF 2264) - also 1st of 9 giving 6lb to Time To Wyn (3 Jly Carlisle RF 2523). AW high 65 - 1st of 11 giving 22lb to Scintilating Sound (3 Feb Wolverhampton RF 0214).
**F Jordan [2-22] Mrs A Roddis (from Mrs A Swinbank [0-4] Spt 1998).*

ARCADIAN CHIEF BHB 44f **RR 52f** 3094[4]
2 b g Be My Chief (USA) 10.2f **(62)** - May Hinton (Main Reef) 9.6f **(57)**
Form - 06474
Record 1999 - 1st:0 2nd:0 3rd:0 Ran:5
1999 Turf 0-5: (5f 3, 6f 2) (gd, g-f 2, frm 2)
Fair gelding. Turf high 52. **K T Ivory [0-5] M Z Tarlowski.*

ARCANE STAR (IRE) BHB 36f40a **RR 24f 40a** 4607[10]
4 b g Arcane (USA) 11.6f **(66)** - Chatsworth Bay (IRE) (Fairy King (USA)) 7.7f **(59)**

Form - 0000
Record 1999 - 1st:0 2nd:0 3rd:0 Ran:4
Pre1999 - 1st:0 2nd:2 3rd:2 Ran:18
Win Prizemoney £0 *Total Prizemoney* £1,913
1999 Turf 0-2: (6f, 8f) (sft, frm) 1999 AW 0-2: (6f 2) (Fibr 2)
Scopey, little account gelding, effective 6f, acts on g-s to gd - acts on Fibr, has worn blinkers (extremely effectively), favours left handed tracks, favours tight tracks. AW high 19. Inconsistent.
**B P J Baugh [0-4] The Buckers (from A P Jarvis [0-18] Oct 1998).*

ARCETTA (USA) BHB 54f **RR 34f** 1894[14]
3 b f Woodman (USA) 9.7f **(77)** - Dawn Deal (USA) (Grey Dawn II) 11.1f **(72)**
Form - 4000
Record 1999 - 1st:0 2nd:0 3rd:0 Ran:4
Pre1999 - 1st:0 2nd:0 3rd:0 Ran:2
Win Prizemoney £0 *Total Prizemoney* £229
1999 Turf 0-4: (8f 2, 10f, 14f) (g-f 2, frm 2)
Very moderate filly. Turf high 56. (DEAD)
**C E Brittain [0-6] R A Pledger.*

ARCHELLO (IRE) BHB 43f **RR 46f** 4880[28]
5 b m Archway (IRE) 8.5f **(60)** - Golden Room (African Sky) 7.9f **(63)**
Form - 07070070400
Record 1999 - 1st:0 2nd:0 3rd:0 Ran:11
Pre1999 - 1st:1 2nd:4 3rd:4 Ran:21
Win Prizemoney £3,452 *Total Prizemoney* £9,740
Wins 1997 Aug Ripon (G-F) 5f 46+ <
1999 Turf 0-11: (6f 3, 7f 6, 8f 2) (gd 2, g-f 5, frm 4)
Moderate filly, effective 7 to 8f, best at 7f, acts on gd to frm, best on frm, has worn blinkers. Turf high 46.
**M Brittain [0-11] Robert Cook (from G R Oldroyd [1-21] Spt 1998).*

ARCHIE BABE (IRE) BHB 67f **RR 66f** 5159[1]
3 ch g Archway (IRE) 8.5f **(60)** - Frensham Manor (Le Johnstan) 7.4f **(55)**
Form - 051132542531
Record 1999 - 1st:3 2nd:2 3rd:2 Ran:12
Pre1999 - 1st:1 2nd:0 3rd:1 Ran:8
Win Prizemoney £17,892 *Total Prizemoney* £22,185
Wins *** 1999** Nov Redcar (G-S) H 11f 65 66
*** 1999** May Pontef (GD) H 10f 56 61
*** 1999** May Redcar (SFT) H 10f 56 63
* 1998 Spt Thirsk (GD) 7f 75 <
1999 Turf 3-12: (8f 2, 10f 2-4, 11f 1-1, 12f 5) (sft, g-s 1-2, gd 1-4, g-f 1-2, frm 2, hrd)
Light-framed, average gelding, effective 7 to 12f, acts on g-s to frm, prefers tight tracks, excels at Redcar. Turf high 67 - also 1st of 7 giving 3lb to Santa Lucia (1 Nov Redcar RF 5159). Consistent.
**J J Quinn [4-20] Mrs K Mapp.*

ARCHITECT (IRE) **RR 98f** 4571[8]
3 b c Grand Lodge (USA) - Olean (Sadler's Wells (USA)) 10f **(76)**
Form - 128
Record 1999 - 1st:1 2nd:1 3rd:0 Ran:3
Pre1999 - 1st:0 2nd:0 3rd:1 Ran:2
Win Prizemoney £4,149 *Total Prizemoney* £11,463
Wins *** 1999** Aug Haydoc (GD) 10.5f 88+ <
1999 Turf 1-3: (11f 1-1, 12f 2) (sft, gd 1-1, g-f)
Scopey, very useful colt. Turf high 98 (began Aug) - 2nd of 18 giving 3lb to Dee Pee Tee Cee (17 Aug York 12f g-f RF 3696). An imposing individual, he should have won at York in August and attracted plenty of support before Ascot's Ritz Club Handicap the following month. Below par on heavy ground there, he remains an interesting prospect over middle-distances and is a likely type for the Duke Of Edinburgh Handicap at Royal Ascot, a race his stable has won for the past two years.
**Sir Michael Stoute [1-5] Highclere Thoroughbred Racing Ltd.*

ARCHIVE FOOTAGE BHB 98f **RR 103f** 1465a[4]
7 b g Sadler's Wells (USA) 11.3f **(87)** - Trusted Partner (USA) (Affirmed (USA)) 9.3f **(79)**
Form - 634
1999 Turf 0-2: (12f, 14f) (hvy, gd)
Very useful gelding, has broken blood-vessels, effective 14f, acts on sft to g-s, mostly wears blinkers (extremely effectively). Turf high 103. He remains capable of useful form on the Flat, but is better employed over hurdles. **D K Weld in IRE [6-22] Michael Smurfit.*

ARCH RIVAL (IRE) RR 32f 3256[10]
2 ch g Archway (IRE) 8.5f **(60)** -Abbessingh (Mansingh (USA)) 7.4f **(55)**
Form - 000
Record 1999 - 1st:0 2nd:0 3rd:0 Ran:3
1999 Turf 0-3: (5f, 6f, 7f) (frm 3)
Currently very moderate gelding. Turf high 32.
**J R Turner [0-3] Robin Ellerbeck.*

ARC ROYAL (GER) RR 102f 4244a[2]
2 ch c Big Shuffle (USA) - Alepha (GER) (Celestial Storm (USA))
Form - 2
1999 Turf 0-1: (6f) (gd)
Currently very useful colt. Second to top-rated German two-year-old Auenklang over six furlongs at Baden-Baden in September.
**C Sprengel in GER [0-1].*

ARCTIC (FR) RR 100f 4768a[6]
4 c Arctic Tern (USA) 12.2f **(71)** - Fiasco Argento (USA) (Silver Hawk (USA)) 8.6f **(70)**
Form - P176
1999 Turf 1-4: (16f, 17f 1-2, 20f) (hvy, sft, gd)
Very useful colt, often wears blinkers. Turf high 100 - also 1st of 6 getting 2lb from River Lake (7 Aug Vichy RF 7094a).
**F Chappet in FR [1-4].*

ARCTIC CHAR BHB 98f **RR 101f** 5114a[2]
3 br f Polar Falcon (USA) 9f **(74)** - Breadcrumb (Final Straw) 7.9f **(64)**
Form - 1123052
Record 1999 - 1st:2 2nd:2 3rd:1 Ran:7
Win Prizemoney £9,944 *Total Prizemoney* £23,994

Wins * **1999**	May	Kempto	(GD)	6f	96	<
* **1999**	Apr	Leices	(G-S)	7f	80	

1999 Turf 2-7: (6f 1-2, 7f 1-5) (gd 1-5, g-f, frm 1-1)
Light-framed, very useful filly, effective 6 to 7f, best at 7f, acts on gd to frm, best on gd. Turf high 101 - 2nd of 5 to Fragrant Oasis (15 May Newmarket 7f g-f RF 1243) - also 1st of 7 from Dominant Dancer (3 May Kempton RF 1000). Unraced at two, she won her first two starts and only failed by a short-head when tried in Listed company at Newmarket in May. A shade disappointing thereafter, she seems better over seven furlongs than six and may stay a mile. **B J Meehan [2-7].*

ARCTIC FANCY (USA) BHB 76f **RR 75f** 2750[2]
6 ch g Arctic Tern (USA) 12.2f **(71)** - Fit And Fancy (USA) (Vaguely Noble) 10.1f **(72)**
Form - 622
Record 1999 - 1st:0 2nd:2 3rd:0 Ran:3
Pre1999 - 1st:3 2nd:4 3rd:7 Ran:26
Win Prizemoney £8,849 *Total Prizemoney* £22,878

Wins * 1998	Oct	Bright	(G-S)	H	11.9f	73	75	<
* 1998	Spt	Newbur	(gd)	H	12f	69	70	
1996	Jun	Haydoc	(GD)		14f		73	

1999 Turf 0-3: (12f 3) (gd, frm, hrd)
Above-average gelding, effective 12 to 14f, best at 12f, acts on sft to hrd, prefers left handed tracks, likes tight tracks, likes Brighton. Turf high 75 - 2nd of 8 to Hibernate (12 Jly Brighton 12f hrd RF 2750). Consistent.
**J G Smyth-Osbourne [4-17] The Cool Customers (from P W Harris [1-17] Spt 1997).*

ARCTIC OWL BHB 118f **RR 123f** 5121a[6]
5 b g Most Welcome 8.6f **(66)** - Short Rations (Lorenzaccio) 10f **(64)**
Form - 312226
Record 1999 - 1st:1 2nd:3 3rd:1 Ran:6
Pre1999 - 1st:6 2nd:1 3rd:2 Ran:11
Win Prizemoney £114,877 *Total Prizemoney* £180,554

Wins * **1999**	May	Sandow	(GD)	G3	16.4f		123	<
* 1998	Oct	Newmar	()	G3	16f		120	
* 1998	Aug	Deauvi	(SFT)	G2	15f		115	
* 1998	Jun	York	(G-S)	H	13.9f	100	114	
* 1998	May	Newmar	(GD)	H	12f	95	99	
* 1997	Spt	York	(SFT)	H	11.9f	88	95	
* 1997	Jun	Windso	(G-F)		10f		78	

1999 Turf 1-6: (12f, 14f, 16f 1-4) (hvy, gd 2, g-f, frm 1-2)
Very high-class gelding, effective 12 to 16f, best at 16f, acts on sft to frm, likes right handed tracks, does well at Newmarket and York. Turf high 123 - 2nd of 3 giving 5lb to Rainbow High (2 Oct Newmarket 16f gd RF 4684) - also 1st of 11 giving 7lb to Rainbow High (31 May Sandown RF 1612). Consistent. A progressive stayer, he showed he was a Group horse with an emphatic victory in the Jockey Club Cup in 1998, and started off last season with a close third in the Yorkshire Cup. He landed Sandown's Henry II Stakes by a whisker, and ran a fine race to chase home Craigsteel over a trip short of his best in the Princess Of Wales's Stakes. Lost little in defeat when second in the Lonsdale Stakes and the Jockey Club Cup, but a hard race in the latter event may have taken its toll when he put up a lack-lustre effort in the Prix Royal-Oak on his final start. As a gelding, he is likely to be around for a few seasons yet, and will continue to be a force to be reckoned with in the top staying events. **J R Fanshawe [7-17].*

Arctic Owl (right), finishes well to touch off Rainbow High at Sandown

ARCTIC PATCH BHB 56f **RR 63f** 4870[10]
2 ch c Inchinor 8.9f **(64)** - Arctic Poppy (USA) **(55f 39a)** (Arctic Tern (USA)) 8.9f **(69)**
Form - 00030
Record 1999 - 1st:0 2nd:0 3rd:1 Ran:5
Win Prizemoney £0 *Total Prizemoney* £370
1999 Turf 0-5: (5f, 7f 3, 8f) (gd 2, g-f, frm 2)
Average colt, has worn blinkers. Turf high 63 - 3rd of 11 getting 6lb from Just Bremner (30 Aug Newcastle 8f g-f RF 4022).
**I A Balding [0-5] Robert Hitchins.*

ARCTIC STAR BHB 48f59a **RR 40f 59a** 548[12]
4 b g Polar Falcon (USA) 9f **(74)** - Three Stars (Star Appeal) 9.6f **(65)**
Form - 00
Record 1999 - 1st:0 2nd:0 3rd:0 Ran:2
Pre1999 - 1st:0 2nd:0 3rd:2 Ran:14
Win Prizemoney £0 *Total Prizemoney* £1,511
1999 Turf 0-1: (9f) (g-f) 1999 AW 0-1: (12f) (Fibr)
Leggy, moderate gelding. Becoming disappointing.
**V Thompson [0-7] Mrs V Thompson (from M R Channon [0-11] Apr 1998).*

ARCTIC THUNDER (USA) BHB 63f64a **RR 69f 64a** 90[6]
8 b g Far North (CAN) 10.3f **(76)** - Flying Cloud (USA) (Roberto (USA)) 10f **(76)**
Form - 016
Record 1999 - 1st:0 2nd:0 3rd:0 Ran:1

Pre1999 - 1st:4 2nd:3 3rd:2 Ran:30
Win Prizemoney £25,539 *Total Prizemoney* £40,494
Wins * 1998 *Dec Wolver (STD) H 14.8f 62 67*
1995 May York (G-F) H 11.9f 89 95 <
1999 AW 0-1: (15f) (Fibr)
Average gelding, effective 12 to 15f, - acts on Fibr, likes left handed tracks, favours tight tracks.
**B Palling [1-16] Merthyr Motor Auctions (from Lady Herries [3-17] Jun 1996).*

ARDENT BHB 49f50a **RR 49f 50a** 5033[15]
5 b g Aragon 7.7f **(58)** - Forest of Arden (Tap On Wood) 10.3f **(65)**
Form - 221001376620
Record 1999 - 1st:2 2nd:2 3rd:1 Ran:11
Pre1999 - 1st:1 2nd:3 3rd:1 Ran:21
Win Prizemoney £9,584 *Total Prizemoney* £14,994
Wins * **1999** Jun Windso (G-F) H 8.3f 46 49
* **1999** May Kempto (G-F) H 9f 46 50
1998 Apr Bright (GD) H 8f 47 54 <
1999 Turf 2-11: (7f, 8f 1-6, 9f 1-3, 10f) (g-s, gd 2, g-f, frm 2-7)
Fair gelding, effective 8 to 9f, best at 8f, acts on g-s to frm - acts on Equi, best on frm, has worn blinkers, favours tight tracks, does well at Brighton. Turf high 50 - 1st of 12 getting 21lb from Harmony Hall (22 May Kempton RF 1392) - also 1st of 16 getting 12lb from Byzantium (28 Jun Windsor RF 2380).
**Miss B Sanders [2-11] R Lamb (from C J Benstead [1-21] Nov 1998).*

ARDLEIGH CHARMER BHB 65f **RR 63f** 3139[4]
4 ch g Theatrical Charmer 10.9f **(63)** -Miss Adventure(Adonijah)10f **(61)**
Form - 2183404
Record 1999 - 1st:1 2nd:1 3rd:1 Ran:7
Pre1999 - 1st:4 2nd:1 3rd:0 Ran:16
Win Prizemoney £22,327 *Total Prizemoney* £25,128
Wins * **1999** Apr Hamilt (HVY) H 13f 67 70 <
* 1998 Jun Ripon (SFT) H 12.3f 58 68
* 1998 Jun Sandow (G-S) H 11.4f 58 64
* 1998 May Redcar (GD) H 10f 52 61
* 1998 Apr Redcar (SFT) H 9f 46 52
1999 Turf 1-7: (12f 3, 13f 1-3, 14f) (hvy 1-1, g-s, gd 2, g-f 2, frm)
Workmanlike, average gelding, effective 10 to 14f, best at 12f, acts on hvy to g-f, has worn blinkers, likes right handed tracks, prefers tight tracks, excels at Hamilton and Redcar. Turf high 70 - 1st of 17 getting 9lb from The Butterwick Kid (10 Apr Hamilton RF 0638).
**C A Dwyer [5-23] Roalco Ltd.*

ARDUINE RR 63f 5021[6]
2 ch f Diesis 9f **(80)** - Ardisia (USA) (Affirmed (USA)) 9.3f **(79)**
Form - 6
Record 1999 - 1st:0 2nd:0 3rd:0 Ran:1
1999 Turf 0-1: (7f) (gd)
Currently average filly. **J H M Gosden [0-1] Sheikh Mohammed.*

AREEN ALASAD BHB 60f **RR 61f** 3849[8]
3 b c Cadeaux Genereux 7.9f **(76)** - Pass the Peace (Alzao (USA)) 7.1f **(68)**
Form - 40448
Record 1999 - 1st:0 2nd:0 3rd:0 Ran:5
Win Prizemoney £0 *Total Prizemoney* £795
1999 Turf 0-5: (6f, 7f 3, 8f) (gd, g-f 2, frm 2)
Workmanlike, average colt. Turf high 64.
**M A Jarvis [0-5] Sheikh Ahmed Al Maktoum.*

AREION (GER) RR 108f 4243a[4]
4 b c Big Shuffle (USA) - Aerleona (GER) (Caerleon (USA)) 8.6f **(71)**
Form - 34
1999 Turf 0-2: (6f, 7f) (gd 2)
Pattern-class colt. Turf high 106 (began Jly) - 4th of 8 to Keos (1 Spt Baden-Baden 6f gd RF 4243a). **A Wohler in GER [2-4].*

AREISH (IRE) BHB 33f51a **RR 30f 51a** 4415[9]
6 b m Keen 11.1f **(58)** - Cool Combination (Indian King (USA)) 7.4f **(64)**
Form - 212213230
Record 1999 - 1st:2 2nd:4 3rd:2 Ran:9
Pre1999 - 1st:2 2nd:0 3rd:2 Ran:21
Win Prizemoney £8,749 *Total Prizemoney* £13,329
Wins * **1999** *Feb Southw (STD) H 8f 48 52* <
* **1999** *Jan Wolver (STD) S 9.4f 51*
1998 *Spt Wolver (STD) SH 12f 39 41*
1998 *Jan Southw (STD) H 11f 38 43*
1999 AW 2-9: (8f 1-2, 9f 1-5, 11f, 12f) (Fibr 2-9)
Fair mare, effective 8 to 9f, best at 8f, - acts on Fibr, has worn blinkers, and excels at Wolverhampton. AW high 57 - 2nd of 12 getting 13lb from Prodigal Son (27 Mar Wolverhampton 8f Fibr RF 0493) - also 1st of 14 getting 14lb from Rouge (15 Feb Southwell RF 0294). Consistent.
**J Balding [2-12] Mrs J Coghlan-Everitt (from M C Pipe [1-1] Spt 1998).*

ARES VALLIS (IRE) RR 105f 4369a[10]
3 b f Caerleon (USA) 10.9f **(79)** - Hoedown Honey (CAN) (Country Light (USA))
Form - 230
1999 Turf 0-3: (8f, 10f, 12f) (hvy, sft, gd)
Currently Pattern-class filly. Turf high 105.
**A Fabre in FR [0-3] E Puerari.*

ARETHA (IRE) RR 94f 5142[5]
2 ch f Indian Ridge 7.6f **(74)** - Smaoineamh (Tap On Wood) 10.3f **(65)**
Form - 483135
1999 Turf 1-6: (6f 1-1, 7f 4, 8f) (sft 1-3, gd 2, g-f)
Useful filly, effective 6 to 8f, best at 7f, acts on sft to gd, best on sft. Turf high 94 (began Aug) - 3rd of 7 to Theoretically (2 Oct Curragh 7f sft RF 4740a) - also 1st of 22 from Regal Ash (10 Oct Naas RF 4853a). Supposedly appreciated the drop back to six from seven when chalking up her first win at Naas. Cast confusion over her preferred distance however when running third at Newbury over seven furlongs in bottomless ground in October; hard to assess. **J S Bolger in IRE [1-6] D H W Dobson.*

ARETINO (IRE) BHB 92f **RR 83+f** 4952[3]
2 ch c Common Grounds 8.1f **(66)** - Inonder (Belfort (FR)) 6.8f **(63)**
Form - 12283
Record 1999 - 1st:1 2nd:2 3rd:1 Ran:5
Win Prizemoney £3,321 *Total Prizemoney* £7,749
Wins * **1999** Jly Pontef (G-F) 6f 83+ <
1999 Turf 1-5: (6f 1-2, 7f 3) (sft, g-s, g-f, frm 1-2)
Decent colt. Turf high 83 (1st run) (began Jly) - 1st of 10 from Ocean Rain (16 Jly Pontefract RF 2887).
**P W Harris [1-5] Mrs A M Palmer.*

AREYDHA BHB 97f **RR 87+f** 2575[9]
2 b f Cadeaux Genereux 7.9f **(76)** - Elaine's Honor (USA) (Chief's Crown (USA)) 9.8f **(72)**
Form - 170
Record 1999 - 1st:1 2nd:0 3rd:0 Ran:3
Win Prizemoney £7,115 *Total Prizemoney* £7,115
Wins * **1999** May York (G-S) 5f 87+ <
1999 Turf 1-3: (5f 1-1, 6f 2) (gd 1-1, g-f, frm)
Currently useful filly. Turf high 87 (1st run) - 1st of 7 from Total Love (11 May York RF 1147). She was reportedly useful before she made her York debut, and she did not disappoint. She found taking on the colts in the Coventry a little too much on her second start and was bumped around, but was not disgraced in the Cherry Hinton Stakes.
**M R Channon [1-3] Sheikh Ahmed Al Maktoum.*

ARGENTAN (USA) RR 83f 5099[3]
2 b c Gulch (USA) 9.6f **(79)** - Honfleur (IRE) **(97f)** (Sadler's Wells (USA)) 10f **(76)**
Form - 33
Record 1999 - 1st:0 2nd:0 3rd:2 Ran:2
Win Prizemoney £0 *Total Prizemoney* £1,184
1999 Turf 0-2: (7f 2) (gd 2)
Currently decent colt. Turf high 83 (began Spt) - 3rd of 12 to Fast Track (27 Oct Yarmouth 7f gd RF 5099).
**A G Foster [0-1] R E Sangster & A K Collins (from P W Chapple-Hyam [0-1] Spt 1999).*

ARGENT FACILE (IRE) BHB 82f **RR 87f** 3804[7]
2 b c Midhish - Rosinish (IRE) (Lomond (USA)) 8.8f **(65)**
Form - 56620417
Record 1999 - 1st:1 2nd:1 3rd:0 Ran:8
Win Prizemoney £2,882 *Total Prizemoney* £3,803
Wins * **1999** Jly Leices (G-F) H 5f 87 <
1999 Turf 1-8: (5f 1-8) (gd 3, g-f 2, frm 1-3)

Useful colt, effective 5f, acts on frm. Turf high 87 - 1st of 7 giving 13lb to Siana Springs (21 Jly Leicester RF 3010).
**D J S Cosgrove [1-8] Winning Circle Racing Club Ltd.*

ARIAS (IRE) RR 16f 3818[20]
2 b g Dancing Dissident (USA) 6.8f **(65)** - Nollia (IRE) (Belmez (USA))
Form - 0
Record 1999 - 1st:0 2nd:0 3rd:0 Ran:1
1999 Turf 0-1: (6f) (g-f)
Currently poor gelding. **P Calver [0-1] Mrs Janis MacPherson.*

ARIF (IRE) BHB 28f34a **RR 35f 34a** 2767[5]
7 bb g Try My Best (USA) 7.8f **(68)** - Sable Royale (USA) (Real Value (USA)) 13f **(41)**
Form - 6465
Record 1999 - 1st:0 2nd:0 3rd:0 Ran:4
Pre1999 - 1st:2 2nd:1 3rd:0 Ran:14
Win Prizemoney £5,116 *Total Prizemoney* £5,994
Wins 1997 Jly Nottin (SFT) SH 14.1f 35 41 <
1997 Jun Folkes (SFT) H 12f 35 40
1999 Turf 0-4: (16f 3, 18f) (gd, g-f 2, frm)
Very moderate gelding, has worn blinkers (extremely effectively). Turf high 35 - 4th of 14 getting 20lb from Mazzelmo (29 Jun Chepstow 18f g-f RF 2391).
**Mrs H L Walton [0-15] A E Walton (from John Harris [0-3] Oct 1997).*

ARISTOCRAT RR 68f 4834[3]
2 b c Bin Ajwaad (IRE) - Bereeka (Main Reef) 9.6f **(57)**
Form - 73
Record 1999 - 1st:0 2nd:0 3rd:1 Ran:2
Win Prizemoney £0 *Total Prizemoney* £525
1999 Turf 0-2: (6f, 7f) (gd, frm)
Currently average colt. Turf high 68 (began Spt).
**R Hannon [0-2] Noodles Racing.*

ARISTOTLE (IRE) RR 108f 5037[1]
2 b c Sadler's Wells (USA) 11.3f **(87)** - Flamenco Wave (USA) (Desert Wine (USA)) 9.7f **(80)**
Form - 11
1999 Turf 2-2: (7f 1-1, 8f 1-1) (g-s 1-1, gd 1-1)
Currently Pattern-class colt. Turf high 108 (began Jly) - 1st of 9 from Lermontov (23 Oct Doncaster RF 5037). Won a seven-furlong maiden at Galway in July in fine style, before beating stablemate Lermontov in the Racing Post Trophy. He looks a high-clas staying prospect, although recent winners of the Doncaster event have a poor record at three. **A P O'Brien in IRE [2-2] Mrs John Magnier.*

ARIUS RR 5043[10]
3 ch c Royal Academy (USA) 7.8f **(77)** - Ville Eternelle (USA) (Slew O' Gold (USA)) 8f **(75)**
Form - 0
Record 1999 - 1st:0 2nd:0 3rd:0 Ran:1
1999 Turf 0-1: (12f) (sft)
Currently very poor colt. **P J Hobbs [0-1] E M Thornton.*

ARIZONA LADY BHB 58f **RR 66f** 5158[12]
2 ch f Lion Cavern (USA) 7.5f **(74)** - Unfuwaanah **(67f)** (Unfuwain (USA))
Form - 43040
Record 1999 - 1st:0 2nd:0 3rd:1 Ran:5
Win Prizemoney £0 *Total Prizemoney* £691
1999 Turf 0-5: (6f, 7f 3, 8f) (gd, frm 3, hrd)
Average filly. Turf high 66 (began Aug) - 4th of 23 giving 4lb to Bescaby Blue (15 Oct Redcar 7f frm RF 4901).
**I Semple [0-5] Ian Crawford.*

ARKADIAN HERO (USA) BHB 118f **RR 116+f** 4777a[8]
4 ch c Trempolino (USA) 11.9f **(77)** - Careless Kitten (USA) (Caro)
Form - 641138
Record 1999 - 1st:2 2nd:0 3rd:1 Ran:6
Pre1999 - 1st:3 2nd:1 3rd:0 Ran:11
Win Prizemoney £82,640 *Total Prizemoney* £119,226
Wins * **1999** Aug Newmar (G-F) L 6f 114+
* **1999** Jly Newbur (G-F) L 6f 116+ <
* 1997 Spt Newbur (G-S) G2 6f 99
* 1997 Aug Ripon (G-F) L 6f 104+
* 1997 Jly Goodwo (G-F) 6f 102
1999 Turf 2-6: (5f, 6f 2-5) (sft, g-f 1-2, frm 1-3)
High-class colt, effective 6f, acts on g-f to frm, best on frm. Turf high 116 - 1st of 10 from Night Shot (17 Jly Newbury RF 2900) - also 1st of 10 giving 4lb to Ho Leng (27 Aug Newmarket RF 3939). Consistent. Winner of the Mill Reef Stakes in soft ground at two, he ran his best race of '98 when fourth in the July Cup, and filled the same position in last term's renewal. Since then he has won a couple of Listed races with the utmost ease, but just seems to miss out in the very highest class, as was again the case when he finished third to Diktat at Haydock. Best suited by six furlongs and fast ground. **L M Cumani [5-17] M Tabor.*

ARMEN (FR) RR 43f 4839[16]
2 b c Kaldoun (FR) 9.9f **(84)** - Anna Edes (FR) (Fabulous Dancer (USA)) 9.4f **(70)**
Form - 0
Record 1999 - 1st:0 2nd:0 3rd:0 Ran:1
1999 Turf 0-1: (8f) (gd)
Currently moderate colt. **M C Pipe [0-1] T M Hely-Hutchinson.*

ARMENIA (IRE) RR 68f 5060[3]
2 ch f Arazi (USA) 9.2f **(74)** - Atlantic Flyer (USA) (Storm Bird (CAN)) 10.3f **(74)**
Form - 5403
Record 1999 - 1st:0 2nd:0 3rd:1 Ran:4
Win Prizemoney £0 *Total Prizemoney* £1,000
1999 Turf 0-4: (7f 3, 8f) (sft, g-s 2, gd)
Average filly. Turf high 68 (began Aug).
**R Hannon [0-3] Barouche Stud Ltd (from N Meade in IRE [0-1] Aug 1999).*

ARMILINA (FR) RR 91f 4856a[11]
4 gr f Linamix (FR) 8.2f **(64)** - Armarama (Persian Bold) 9.3f **(66)**
Form - 35605560
1999 Turf 0-8: (7f 2, 8f 3, 9f, 10f 2) (hvy, sft, g-s 4, gd, g-f)
Useful filly, effective 7f, acts on g-s, has worn blinkers. Turf high 105 (1st run) - 3rd of 7 getting 6lb from Two-Twenty-Two (11 Apr Curragh 7f g-s RF 0680a). Inconsistent.
**M Halford in IRE [0-8] Shane Ryan (from S Wattel in FR [0-1] Oct 1998).*

ARNAQUEUR (USA) RR 108f 1069a[2]
4 b c Miswaki (USA) 8.1f **(81)** - All Along (FR) (Targowice (USA)) 11.4f **(70)**
Form - 2
1999 Turf 0-1: (12f) (sft)
Currently Pattern-class colt. (1st run) - 2nd of 6 to Persian Ruler (29 Apr Longchamp 12f sft RF 1069a).
**A Fabre in FR [0-3] D Wildenstein.*

AROB PETE RR 2f 3739[15]
2 b c Robellino (USA) 9.5f **(68)** - An Empress (USA) (Affirmed (USA)) 9.3f **(79)**
Form - 0
Record 1999 - 1st:0 2nd:0 3rd:0 Ran:1
1999 Turf 0-1: (6f) (g-s)
Currently very poor colt. **A J McNae [0-1] Paul Locke.*

AROGANT PRINCE BHB 56f **RR 65f** 3644[10]
2 ch c Aragon 7.7f **(58)** - Versaillesprincess (Legend of France (USA)) 9.5f **(61)**
Form - 37460
Record 1999 - 1st:0 2nd:0 3rd:1 Ran:5
Win Prizemoney £0 *Total Prizemoney* £565
1999 Turf 0-5: (5f 5) (g-s, g-f, frm 2, hrd)
Average colt. Turf high 65. **J J Bridger [0-5] Miss Julie Self.*

AROUND THE WORLD (IRE) BHB 52f **RR 40f** 5135[15]
3 b f Thatching 7.8f **(69)** - Wild Applause (IRE) (Sadler's Wells (USA)) 10f **(76)**
Form - 14506080700
Record 1999 - 1st:1 2nd:0 3rd:0 Ran:11
Pre1999 - 1st:0 2nd:0 3rd:0 Ran:3
Win Prizemoney £4,565 *Total Prizemoney* £5,283
Wins * **1999** May Pontef (G-F) H 8f 72 75 <
1999 Turf 1-11: (7f, 8f 1-7, 9f, 10f, 12f) (gd 4, g-f 1-2, frm 5)
Tall, moderate filly, effective 8f, acts on g-f to frm, has worn blink-

ers, prefers left handed tracks, likes tight tracks. Turf high 75 (1st run) - 1st of 13 getting 7lb from The Whistling Teal (28 May Pontefract RF 1557). Becoming disappointing. Won a competitive Pontefract handicap in May over a mile on fast ground, but has lost her way since. **M Johnston [1-14] The Walter S Partnership.*

ARPEGGIO BHB 75f **RR 69f** 4380[13]
4 b c Polar Falcon (USA) 9f **(74)** - Hilly (Town Crier) 10.2f **(55)**
Form - 1800
Record 1999 - 1st:1 2nd:0 3rd:0 Ran:4
Pre1999 - 1st:0 2nd:2 3rd:1 Ran:8
Win Prizemoney £3,535 *Total Prizemoney* £7,514
Wins * 1999 May Thirsk (Sft) 6f 72 <
1999 Turf 1-4: (6f 1-2, 7f 2) (gd 1-2, g-f, frm)
Scopey, average colt. Turf high 72 (1st run). Consistent.
**D Nicholls [1-6] Lhendup Dorji (from R Hannon [0-6] May 1998).*

ARROGANT BHB 37f **RR 48f** 4995[10]
2 b g Aragon 7.7f **(58)** - Miss Ark Royal (Broadsword (USA))
Form - 000400
Record 1999 - 1st:0 2nd:0 3rd:0 Ran:6
Win Prizemoney £0 *Total Prizemoney* £193
1999 Turf 0-6: (5f, 6f, 7f 4) (g-s, gd 2, frm 3)
Moderate gelding. Turf high 48. **R M Flower [0-6] The Secret Circle II.*

ARRY MARTIN BHB 47f **RR 43f** 4355[7]
4 b g Aragon 7.7f **(58)** - Bells of St Martin (Martinmas) 7.6f **(59)**
Form - 08640217
Record 1999 - 1st:1 2nd:1 3rd:0 Ran:8
Pre1999 - 1st:0 2nd:0 3rd:3 Ran:12
Win Prizemoney £2,215 *Total Prizemoney* £4,518
Wins * 1999 Aug Lingfi (G-F) SH 6f 44 43 <
1999 Turf 1-8: (6f 1-6, 7f 2) (g-s, g-f 1-5, frm 2)
Workmanlike, moderate gelding, effective 6 to 7f, best at 6f, acts on gd to g-f, best on g-f, has worn blinkers. Turf high 43.
**W R Muir [1-20] Mrs Marion Wickham.*

ARTAN (IRE) RR 119f 4519a[8]
7 b h Be My Native (USA) 11.2f **(62)** - Cambridge Lodge (Tower Walk) 10f **(62)**
Form - 8
1999 Turf 0-1: (10f) (gd)
High-class horse. Consistent.
**M Rolke in GER [3-13] (from H-A Pantall in FR [1-1] Oct 1996).*

ARTAX (USA) RR 5227a[1]
4 b or br f Marquetry (USA) 10f **(88)** - Raging Apalachee (USA) (Apalachee (USA)) 9.4f **(71)**
Form - 1
1999 AW 1-1: (6f 1-1) (Dirt 1-1)
Currently top-class. (1st run) - 1st of 14 from Kona Gold (6 Nov Gulfstream Park RF 5227a). Equalled the track record when winning the Breeders' Cup Sprint.
**L Albertrani in USA [1-1] Paraneck Stable.*

ARTERXERXES BHB 75f79a **RR 77f 79a** 4874[13]
6 b g Anshan 8.2f **(63)** - Hanglands (Bustino) 10.4f **(64)**
Form - 67471720
Record 1999 - 1st:1 2nd:1 3rd:0 Ran:8
Pre1999 - 1st:3 2nd:5 3rd:1 Ran:24
Win Prizemoney £13,585 *Total Prizemoney* £24,435
Wins 1999 Jly Kempto (G-F) H 8f 72 76
1998 Aug Folkes (G-F) H 6.9f 73 76
1997 Aug Yarmou (G-F) H 7f 75 81 <
1996 Apr Folkes (FRM) 6.9f 71
1999 Turf 1-8: (7f 3, 8f 1-5) (gd 2, g-f 2, frm 1-4)
Above-average gelding, effective 7 to 8f, best at 8f, acts on g-f to frm - acts on Equi, best on frm, has worn blinkers. Turf high 77 - 2nd of 24 getting 3lb from Pension Fund (1 Spt York 8f frm RF 4085) - also 1st of 13 giving 8lb to Grand Slam (14 Jly Kempton RF 2828). A front-runner, he used those tactics to fine effect when winning at Kempton in July and was only just beaten in a big field at York in September.
**C G Cox [0-2] S P Tindall & Partners (from M J Heaton-Ellis [4-30] Aug 1999).*

ARTFUL DANE (IRE) BHB 43f70a **RR 43f 70a** 4260[4]
7 b g Danehill (USA) 9.1f **(79)** - Art Age (Artaius (USA)) 9f **(69)**
Form - 540028704
Record 1999 - 1st:0 2nd:1 3rd:0 Ran:9
Pre1999 - 1st:4 2nd:3 3rd:3 Ran:41
Win Prizemoney £42,193 *Total Prizemoney* £56,163
Wins 1997 Mar Doncas (G-F) H 8f 72 79 <
1996 Spt Newbur (G-F) H 8f 64 72
1996 Aug Bath (G-F) H 8f 62 66
1995 Jly Windso (G-F) 8.3f 74
1999 Turf 0-9: (8f 8, 9f) (gd, g-f 3, frm 5)
Moderate gelding, often wears blinkers. Turf high 53.
**C G Cox [0-1] S P Lansdown Racing (from M J Heaton-Ellis [4-49] Aug 1999).*

ARTHURS KINGDOM (IRE) BHB 63f63a **RR 61f 63a** 2563[6]
3 b g Roi Danzig (USA) 10.5f **(62)** - Merrie Moment (IRE) (Taufan (USA)) 7f **(57)**
Form - 203786
Record 1999 - 1st:0 2nd:1 3rd:1 Ran:6
Pre1999 - 1st:0 2nd:0 3rd:1 Ran:4
Win Prizemoney £0 *Total Prizemoney* £1,989
1999 Turf 0-4: (10f, 12f 3)(gd, g-f 2, frm)1999 AW 0-2: (11f, 12f) (Fibr 2)
Workmanlike, average gelding, effective 7 to 12f, acts on gd to frm - acts on Fibr, best on g-f, has worn blinkers, likes tight tracks. Turf high 67 (1st run) - 3rd of 19 getting 11lb from Procedure (24 May Leicester 10f frm RF 1432). AW high 61 (1st run) - 2nd of 14 getting 21lb from Zaha (5 Feb Southwell 11f Fibr RF 0228). Consistent. **A P Jarvis [0-10] Mrs Ann Jarvis.*

ARTIC BAY BHB 55f **RR 58df** 4709[6]
7 b g Arctic Lord 11.7f **(37)** - Galley Bay (Welsh Saint) 7.6f **(64)**
Form - 456
Record 1999 - 1st:0 2nd:0 3rd:0 Ran:3
Pre1999 - 1st:2 2nd:0 3rd:0 Ran:9
Win Prizemoney £5,333 *Total Prizemoney* £6,267
Wins 1996 Oct Lingfi (GD) 11.5f 72 <
1996 Jly Salisb (G-F) H 12f 63 66
1999 Turf 0-3: (12f 3) (g-s, gd, frm)
Fair gelding. Turf high 58 (began Spt).
**C L Popham [0-1] C L Popham (from Denys Smith [0-2] Spt 1999).*

ARTIC COURIER BHB 45f69a **RR 36f 69a** 4014[12]
8 gr g Siberian Express (USA) 9f **(58)** - La Reine de France (Queen's Hussar) 11.6f **(58)**
Form - 33325022730
Record 1999 - 1st:0 2nd:3 3rd:4 Ran:11
Pre1999 - 1st:3 2nd:12 3rd:8 Ran:53
Win Prizemoney £13,240 *Total Prizemoney* £48,117
Wins * 1996 Jly Epsom (G-F) H 12f 80 85 <
* 1996 May Kempto (G-F) H 12f 76 80
* 1995 Jun Ripon (FRM) 12.3f 68
1999 Turf 0-5: (12f 5) (g-f 4, frm) 1999 AW 0-6: (12f 2, 13f 2, 16f 2) (Equi 4, Fibr 2)
Moderate gelding, effective 12 to 14f, best at 12f, acts on gd to g-f, best on g-f, has worn blinkers, prefers right handed tracks. Turf high 48. AW high 54. **D J S Cosgrove [3-64] D J S Cosgrove.*

ARTISTIC BLUE (USA) RR 104f 4971a[4]
3 b f Diesis 9f **(80)** - Tapolite (Tap On Wood) 10.3f **(65)**
Form - 35254
1999 Turf 0-5: (6f 2, 7f 3) (sft, g-s 2, gd, g-f)
Very useful filly, effective 7f, acts on g-f. Turf high 104 (1st run) - 3rd of 7 getting 2lb from Show Me The Money (18 Apr Leopardstown 7f g-f RF 0784a). She beat Mus-If comfortably as a juvenile, but was slightly disappointing in 1999. However, she spent most of the campaign running on a soft surface and is worth another try on faster ground. **J S Bolger in IRE [1-8] Mrs J M Ryan.*

ARTISTIQUE (FR) RR 94f 3405a[1]
3 gr f Linamix (FR) 8.2f **(64)** - Armarama (Persian Bold) 9.3f **(66)**
Form - 1
1999 Turf 1-1: (15f 1-1) (gd 1-1)
Currently useful filly. (1st run) - 1st of 7 getting 3lb from Lord Brex (30 Jly Chantilly RF 3405a). **A Fabre in FR [1-1] J-L Lagadere.*

ART SOCIETY (IRE) BHB 33f **RR 34f** 1745[6]
3 ch c Perugino (USA) - Nisha Society (IRE) (Law Society (USA)) 9.9f **(70)**
Form - 06
Record 1999 - 1st:0 2nd:0 3rd:0 Ran:2
Pre1999 - 1st:0 2nd:0 3rd:0 Ran:3
1999 AW 0-2: (8f, 12f) (Fibr 2)
Workmanlike, very moderate colt. AW high 18.
**J J Sheehan [0-5] P J Sheehan.*

ARTS PROJECT (IRE) BHB 50f **RR 39f** 5053[15]
5 b m Project Manager 7.2f **(47)** - Amparo 00
Form - 5041362680
Record 1999 - 1st:1 2nd:1 3rd:1 Ran:10
Pre1999 - 1st:1 2nd:2 3rd:0 Ran:15
Win Prizemoney £6,187 *Total Prizemoney* £9,243
Wins 1999 Jly Dundal (FRM) H 12f 45 52 <
1998 Aug Tramor (G-F) H 12f 38 52 <
1999 Turf 1-10: (8f 2, 12f 1-7, 13f) (g-s, gd 3, g-f 5, frm 1-1)
Very moderate filly, effective 12f, acts on g-s to frm, likes right handed tracks. Turf high 52 - 1st of 15 giving 12lb to Spring To Mind (12 Jly Dundalk RF 2969a). Consistent.
**P D Evans [0-2] Brian McAtavey (from C Roche in IRE [3-20] Aug 1999).*

ARZILLO BHB 55f **RR 59f** 3872[13]
3 b g Forzando 7.2f **(63)** - Titania's Dance (IRE) **(49a)** (Fairy King (USA)) 7.7f **(59)**
Form - 047030
Record 1999 - 1st:0 2nd:0 3rd:1 Ran:6
Pre1999 - 1st:0 2nd:0 3rd:0 Ran:3
Win Prizemoney £0 *Total Prizemoney* £738
1999 Turf 0-6: (6f 3, 7f, 8f 2) (g-f 2, frm 3, hrd)
Neat, fair gelding, effective 8f, acts on frm. Turf high 62. Inconsistent. **S Dow [0-9] Brian Solomon and Miss Jo-Ann Wood.*

ASAAL BHB 98f **RR 93f** 5029[9]
2 b c Machiavellian (USA) 9.8f **(83)** - Rawaabe (USA) (Nureyev (USA)) 8.7f **(78)**
Form - 3110
Record 1999 - 1st:2 2nd:0 3rd:1 Ran:4
Win Prizemoney £9,883 *Total Prizemoney* £10,918
Wins * 1999 Spt Salisb (HVY) 6f 93+ <
* **1999** Aug Pontef (G-F) 6f 76+
1999 Turf 2-4: (6f 2-3, 7f) (g-s 1-2, gd, frm 1-1)
Useful colt. Turf high 93 (began Jly) - 1st of 7 from Launfal (29 Spt Salisbury RF 4643). Showed ability in a newcomers' race at Ascot in July and had little trouble landing long odds-on at Pontefract in early August. Demonstrated an ability to handle heavy ground at Salisbury next time, showing a nice turn of foot in such testing conditions. Finished last in a Group Three on his final start.
**B W Hills [2-4] Hamdan Al Maktoum.*

ASAALA (USA) BHB 53f **RR 58f** 4632[18]
3 ch f Slew O' Gold (USA) 10.2f **(73)** - Alghuzaylah (Habitat) 9.4f **(70)**
Form - 0340
Record 1999 - 1st:0 2nd:0 3rd:1 Ran:4
Pre1999 - 1st:0 2nd:0 3rd:1 Ran:2
Win Prizemoney £0 *Total Prizemoney* £815
1999 Turf 0-4: (8f, 10f 2, 11f) (g-s, gd 2, frm)
Scopey, fair filly, effective 7f, acts on gd. Turf high 58.
**M P Tregoning [0-6] Hamdan Al Maktoum.*

ASANOVO (USA) RR 96f 2070[3]
2 ch c Nureyev (USA) 8.4f **(84)** - Golden Darling (USA) (Slew O' Gold (USA)) 8f **(75)**
Form - 13
1999 Turf 1-2: (5f 1-2) (g-s 1-1, g-f)
Currently very useful colt. Turf high 96 - 3rd of 13 to Warm Heart (17 Jun Ascot 5f g-f RF 2070). He was beaten by lack of pace in the Norfolk Stakes and should be suited by seven furlongs or beyond.
**A P O'Brien in IRE [1-2] M Tabor & Mrs John Magnier.*

ASCARI BHB 62f56a **RR 62f 56a** 5007[1]
3 br g Presidium 7.5f **(56)** - Ping Pong (Petong) 6.6f **(58)**
Form - 48005228631
Record 1999 - 1st:1 2nd:2 3rd:1 Ran:9
Pre1999 - 1st:0 2nd:0 3rd:0 Ran:7
Win Prizemoney £3,330 *Total Prizemoney* £6,561
Wins * 1999 Oct Nottin (GD) H 10f 55 62 <
1999 Turf 1-9: (7f, 8f 2, 10f 1-6) (g-s, gd 1-1, g-f 3, frm 4)
Light-framed, average gelding, effective 10f, acts on gd to frm, has worn blinkers, likes left handed tracks, likes tight tracks. Turf high 62 - 1st of 16 getting 3lb from Tiger Grass (21 Oct Nottingham RF 5007). **P W Harris [1-16] Bernstein, Shaw, Williams & Willis.*

ASCOT MASCOT (USA) BHB 84f **RR 82f** 5038[5]
3 b br c Storm Bird (CAN) 8.5f **(82)** - Croquetallie (USA) (Alydar (USA)) 9.1f **(76)**
Form - 4165
Record 1999 - 1st:1 2nd:0 3rd:0 Ran:4
Win Prizemoney £3,956 *Total Prizemoney* £4,281
Wins * 1999 May Newcas (G-F) 10.1f 78 <
1999 Turf 1-4: (10f 1-2, 12f 2) (sft, g-s, gd, g-f 1-1)
Leggy, decent colt. Turf high 82 - also 1st of 11 getting 15lb from Rainshack (3 May Newcastle RF 1008). Won his maiden in May over ten furlongs at Newcastle, and after a long lay-off he returned in October and was well beaten in two starts.
**J L Dunlop [1-4] Wafic Said.*

ASEF ALHIND BHB 84f **RR 83f** 3463[7]
5 ch g Indian Ridge 7.6f **(74)** - Willowbed (Wollow) 8.2f **(61)**
Form - 243127
Record 1999 - 1st:1 2nd:2 3rd:1 Ran:6
Pre1999 - 1st:1 2nd:1 3rd:2 Ran:11
Win Prizemoney £6,375 *Total Prizemoney* £16,383
Wins 1999 Jun Sandow (GD) C 8.1f 74
1997 Jun Beverl (G-F) 8.5f 77 <
1999 Turf 1-6: (7f 2, 8f 1-4) (gd 2, g-f 2, frm 1-2)
Decent gelding, has broken blood-vessels, effective 7 to 8f, best at 8f, acts on gd to frm, prefers tight tracks. Turf high 83 - 3rd of 7 to Tom Dougal (20 May Ayr 8f gd RF 1339) - also 1st of 14 from No Extras (1 Jun Sandown RF 1655). Consistent.
**G A Butler [0-2] Mrs H F Prendergast (from B Hanbury [2-15] Jun 1999).*

ASH BOLD (IRE) RR 60f 5207[16]
2 ch g Persian Bold 10f **(69)** - Pasadena Lady (Captain James) 5f **(59)**
Form - 00
Record 1999 - 1st:0 2nd:0 3rd:0 Ran:2
1999 Turf 0-2: (7f 2) (g-s, gd)
Currently average gelding. Turf high 60 (began Oct).
**R M Whitaker [0-2] Harvey Ashworth.*

ASHBOURNE PAT BHB 85f **RR 77f** 1110[7]
3 b f Mtoto 11.5f **(71)** - Actraphane (Shareef Dancer (USA)) 9.9f **(73)**
Form - 7
Record 1999 - 1st:0 2nd:0 3rd:0 Ran:1
Pre1999 - 1st:1 2nd:0 3rd:0 Ran:2
Win Prizemoney £3,947 *Total Prizemoney* £4,285
Wins * 1998 Spt Leices (G-S) 8f 77 <
1999 Turf 0-1: (11f) (gd)
Light-framed, currently above-average filly.
**J Pearce [1-3] Hon Robert Acton.*

ASHBRITTLE LADY BHB 53f42a **RR 60f 42a** 331[4]
3 ch f King's Signet (USA) 7f **(51)** - Lady Longmead (Crimson Beau) 9.8f **(52)**
Form - 744
Record 1999 - 1st:0 2nd:0 3rd:0 Ran:2
Pre1999 - 1st:0 2nd:0 3rd:0 Ran:4
1999 AW 0-2: (7f, 8f) (Equi, Fibr)
Workmanlike, average filly. AW high 43.
**L G Cottrell [0-6] Mrs Jenny Hopkins.*

ASHGAR (USA) BHB 107f **RR 108f** 4360a[9]
3 ch c Bien Bien (USA) - Ardisia (USA) (Affirmed (USA)) 9.3f **(79)**
Form - 421340
Record 1999 - 1st:1 2nd:1 3rd:1 Ran:6
Win Prizemoney £3,057 *Total Prizemoney* £9,180
Wins * 1999 Jun Redcar (FRM) 14.1f 86 <
1999 Turf 1-6: (10f, 12f, 14f 1-1, 15f 2, 16f) (sft, gd, g-f, frm 1-3)
Leggy, Pattern-class colt, effective 16f, acts on g-f. Turf high 108 - 4th of 8 getting 17lb from Celeric (17 Aug York 16f g-f RF 3693). He

put in a couple of useful efforts, notably when a very creditable fourth in York's Lonsdale Stakes over two miles, before getting bogged down in the Longchamp mud on his final start. He looks as if he will develop into an out-and-out stayer. **C E Brittain [1-6].*

ASHJAAN (USA) BHB 84f **RR 86f** 5142[10]
2 gr f Silver Hawk (USA) 11.2f **(85)** - Shadayid (USA) (Shadeed (USA)) 8.2f **(70)**
Form - 222210
Record 1999 - 1st:1 2nd:4 3rd:0 Ran:6
Win Prizemoney £3,810 *Total Prizemoney* £8,534
Wins * 1999 Oct Newcas (G-S) 7f 86 <
1999 Turf 1-6: (7f 1-5, 8f) (gd 3, g-f 1-1, frm 2)
Useful filly, effective 7f, acts on gd to g-f. Turf high 86 (began Jly) - 2nd of 11 to Scottish Spice (26 Aug Folkestone 7f gd RF 3912) - also 1st of 10 from Peacock Alley (20 Oct Newcastle RF 4982). A bit of a madam, she had been a runner-up four times before winning over seven at Newcastle in October. She is a little quirky - she hung both ways in front - but is obviously talented and consistent. **J L Dunlop [1-6] Hamdan Al Maktoum.*

ASHLEIGH BAKER (IRE) BHB 51f49a **RR 53f 49a** 5190[3]
4 b br f Don't Forget Me 9.5f **(66)** - Gayla Orchestra (Lord Gayle (USA)) 8.8f **(62)**
Form - 340053
Record 1999 - 1st:0 2nd:0 3rd:2 Ran:6
Pre1999 - 1st:1 2nd:0 3rd:0 Ran:12
Win Prizemoney £2,851 *Total Prizemoney* £4,045
Wins 1998 Jly Ayr (SFT) H 10.9f 60 66 <
1999 Turf 0-5: (8f, 9f, 10f 2, 12f) (gd, g-f 2, frm 2) 1999 AW 0-1: (9f) (Fibr)
Light-framed, fair filly, effective 10 to 11f, acts on gd, has worn blinkers, likes left handed tracks, favours tight tracks. Turf high 53 (began Aug).
**M Johnston [0-6] The David James Partnership (from A Bailey [1-12] Nov 1998).*

ASH MILLSHAW (IRE) BHB 40f49a **RR 45f 49a** 2379[11]
3 gr g Archway (IRE) 8.5f **(60)** - Yalciyna (Nishapour (FR)) 9.1f **(61)**
Form - 544006000
Record 1999 - 1st:0 2nd:0 3rd:0 Ran:7
Pre1999 - 1st:1 2nd:0 3rd:0 Ran:7
Win Prizemoney £2,066 *Total Prizemoney* £2,066
Wins * 1998 Oct Bath (SFT) S 5.7f 63 <
1999 Turf 0-5: (6f 2, 7f, 8f 2) (g-s, gd 3, g-f)1999 AW 0-2: (6f, 7f)(Fibr 2)
Light-framed, moderate gelding, effective 6f, acts on sft, has worn blinkers. Turf high 45. AW high 39. Becoming disappointing.
**R Hollinshead [1-14] Clayton Bigley Partnership Ltd.*

ASHOVER AMBER BHB 73f68a **RR 67f 68a** 3031[3]
3 b f Green Desert (USA) 7.8f **(78)** - Zafaaf **(98df)** (Kris) 9.5f **(73)**
Form - 1276661313
Record 1999 - 1st:3 2nd:1 3rd:2 Ran:10
Pre1999 - 1st:0 2nd:0 3rd:2 Ran:3
Win Prizemoney £9,109 *Total Prizemoney* £12,145
Wins * 1999 Jly Carlis (FRM) 5f 67
*** 1999** Jun Carlis (G-F) H 5f 61 64
*** 1999** *Feb Southw (STD)* *6f* *69* <
1999 Turf 2-6: (5f 2-5, 6f) (sft, gd, frm 1-2, hrd 1-2) 1999 AW 1-4: (6f 1-4) (Fibr 1-4)
Strong, average filly, effective 5 to 6f, best at 6f, acts on frm to hrd - acts on Fibr. Turf high 67 - also 1st of 6 giving 3lb to Ring of Love (16 Jly Carlisle RF 2861). AW high 69 (1st run) - 1st of 6 getting 20lb from Bahamian Pirate (22 Feb Southwell RF 0339). Improving. **T D Barron [3-13] Timothy Cox.*

ASILANA (IRE) BHB 38f43a **RR 35f 43a** 1006[8]
3 b g College Chapel - Uninvited Guest (Be My Guest (USA)) 9.3f **(67)**
Form - 4688
Record 1999 - 1st:0 2nd:0 3rd:0 Ran:4
Pre1999 - 1st:0 2nd:0 3rd:0 Ran:1
1999 Turf 0-1: (7f) (frm) 1999 AW 0-3: (7f 2, 8f) (Fibr 3)
Workmanlike, moderate gelding. AW high 44. (DEAD)
**T D Easterby [0-5] C H Newton Jnr Ltd.*

AS-IS BHB 62f38a **RR 64f 38a** 309[5]
5 b g Lomond (USA) 9.9f **(74)** - Capriati (USA) (Diesis) 9.3f **(69)**
Form - 5
Record 1999 - 1st:0 2nd:0 3rd:0 Ran:1
Pre1999 - 1st:4 2nd:4 3rd:0 Ran:22
Win Prizemoney £10,387 *Total Prizemoney* £13,766
Wins 1997 Apr Mussel (G-F) H 12f 60 62
1997 *Feb Lingfi (STD) C* *12f* *63* <
1997 *Feb Lingfi (STD) C* *10f* *51*
1997 *Jan Lingfi (STD) S* *8f* *58*
1999 AW 0-1: (12f) (Equi)
Average gelding. Inconsistent.
**J J Bridger [0-1] K J Walls (from K Bell [0-1] Jly 1998).*

ASPEN LEAVES (USA) RR 91f 4203a[6]
3 ch f Woodman (USA) 9.7f **(77)** -Fall Aspen (USA) (Pretense) 6.3f **(88)**
Form - 16
1999 Turf 1-2: (7f 1-1, 8f) (g-s 1-1, g-f)
Currently useful filly. Turf high 91 (1st run) - 1st from Institutrice (2 May Gowran Park RF 1040a).
**A P O'Brien in IRE [1-3] Mrs John Magnier.*

ASPIRANT DANCER BHB 71f70a **RR 71f 70a** 4710[6]
4 b g Marju (IRE) 9.2f **(76)** - Fairy Ballerina (Fairy King (USA)) 7.7f **(59)**
Form - 042133213816
Record 1999 - 1st:3 2nd:2 3rd:3 Ran:12
Pre1999 - 1st:3 2nd:2 3rd:0 Ran:12
Win Prizemoney £30,189 *Total Prizemoney* £37,023
Wins * 1999 Spt Pontef (GD) 10f 71+ <
*** 1999** Jly Pontef (G-S) 10f 71+ <
*** 1999** Apr Pontef (G-S) H 10f 63 69+
* 1998 May Haydoc (GD) H 10.5f 65 69
* 1998 Apr Folkes (SFT) H 9.7f 57 63
* 1998 *Apr Southw (STD) H* *11f* *49* *63*
1999 Turf 3-10: (10f 3-5, 11f, 12f 4) (gd 1-5, g-f 1-2, frm 1-3) 1999 AW 0-2: (10f, 12f) (Equi, Fibr)
Above-average gelding, effective 10 to 12f, best at 10f, acts on sft to frm - acts on Fibr, excels at Southwell, does well at Pontefract, likes Haydock. Turf high 72 - 3rd of 9 giving 3lb to Farmost (11 Jun Chepstow 10f gd RF 1910) - also 1st of 10 giving 2lb to Space Race (23 Spt Pontefract RF 4508). AW high 70 - 2nd of 8 giving 8lb to Quintrell Downs (28 Jun Southwell 12f Fibr RF 2376). Consistent.
**M L W Bell [6-24] Peter Coe.*

ASPRILLA (IRE) BHB 32f **RR 41df** 4987[13]
4 b g Sharp Victor (USA) 10f **(56)** - Aspire (Nebbiolo) 8.1f **(75)**
Form - 0
Record 1999 - 1st:0 2nd:0 3rd:0 Ran:1
Pre1999 - 1st:0 2nd:0 3rd:0 Ran:4
1999 Turf 0-1: (8f) (gd)
Neat, moderate gelding. **B Ellison [0-9] Mrs C L Bell.*

ASSURED GAMBLE BHB 70f **RR 67?f** 2174[7]
5 b g Rock Hopper 10.6f **(54)** - Willowbank (Gay Fandango (USA)) 8.5f **(59)**
Form - 37
Record 1999 - 1st:0 2nd:0 3rd:1 Ran:2
Pre1999 - 1st:2 2nd:0 3rd:2 Ran:14
Win Prizemoney £11,882 *Total Prizemoney* £13,921
Wins 1998 Apr Epsom (SFT) H 12f 77 80
1997 May Newmar (GD) 12f 82 <
1999 Turf 0-2: (10f, 16f) (g-f 2)
Average gelding, effective 10 to 12f, best at 12f, acts on sft to g-f. Turf high 64.
**R J Hodges [0-2] P Slade (from C E Brittain [2-14] Spt 1998).*

ASSURED MOVEMENTS (USA) BHB 54f **RR 54f** 4930[7]
3 b c Northern Flagship (USA) 12.2f **(72)** - Love At Dawn (USA) (Grey Dawn II) 11.1f **(72)**
Form - 527070547
Record 1999 - 1st:0 2nd:1 3rd:0 Ran:9
Pre1999 - 1st:0 2nd:0 3rd:0 Ran:3
Win Prizemoney £0 *Total Prizemoney* £1,121
1999 Turf 0-9: (9f, 10f 5, 11f, 12f 2) (gd 2, g-f 3, frm 4)
Scopey, fair colt, effective 10f, acts on g-f, likes tight tracks. Turf high 72 - 2nd of 17 giving 5lb to Comic (10 May Windsor 10f g-f RF 1141). A maiden, he is struggling to make his mark in handicaps.
**C E Brittain [0-12] Peter Head Racing Ltd.*

ASSURED PHYSIQUE BHB 73f **RR 77f** 5124[9]
2 b c Salse (USA) 10.9f **(71)** - Metaphysique (FR) (Law Society (USA)) 9.9f **(70)**
Form - 8670
Record 1999 - 1st:0 2nd:0 3rd:0 Ran:4
1999 Turf 0-4: (8f 3, 9f) (g-s, gd 2, frm)
Above-average colt. Turf high 77 (began Spt).
**C E Brittain [0-4] Peter Head Racing Ltd.*

ASTON EYRE BHB 35f45a **RR 25f 45a** 4945[12]
3 ch f Pharly (FR) 11.5f **(64)** - Lady Keyser (Le Johnstan) 7.4f **(55)**
Form - 500000
Record 1999 - 1st:0 2nd:0 3rd:0 Ran:6
Pre1999 - 1st:0 2nd:0 3rd:0 Ran:3
1999 Turf 0-5: (5f 2, 6f 2, 7f) (gd 4, frm) 1999 AW 0-1: (6f) (Fibr)
Unfurnished, little account filly, has worn blinkers. Turf high 58. Inconsistent.
**J Pearce [0-3] Paul Sandy (from A G Juckes [0-6] Jly 1999).*

ASTONISHED BHB 95f **RR 110f** 4392[13]
3 ch g Weldnaas (USA) 8.4f **(55)** - Indigo (Primo Dominie) 6.2f **(80)**
Form - 10
1999 Turf 1-2: (6f 1-2) (gd 1-2)
Scopey, Group-class gelding, effective 6f, acts on gd. Turf high 110 (1st run) (began Spt) - 1st of 21 getting 3lb from Cretan Gift (8 Spt Doncaster RF 4207). Trained by Lynda Ramsden as a juvenile, he has thrived since joining the excellent John Hammond and turned Doncaster's Portland Handicap into a procession. Disappointing in the Ayr Gold Cup (he has run badly on both his visits to that track), he remains unexposed and is a Group class sprinter in the making.
**J E Hammond in FR [1-2] D R Brotherton (from Mrs J R Ramsden [2-5] Oct 1998).*

Record 1999 - 1st:1 2nd:0 3rd:2 Ran:16
Pre1999 - 1st:10 2nd:2 3rd:6 Ran:54
Win Prizemoney £104,070 *Total Prizemoney* £119,256

Wins								
*** 1999**	Oct	Catter	(SFT)		6f		83	
1998	Spt	Hamilt	(SFT)		6f		95	
1998	May	Ayr	(GD)	H	6f	85	93	
1996	Nov	Evry	(SFT)	L	6f		113	<
1996	Nov	Doncas	(SFT)	L	6f		111	
1996	Oct	Nottin	(SFT)		6.1f		92+	
1995	Jun	Ascot	(FRM)	H	6f	89	96	

1999 Turf 1-15: (5f 3, 6f 1-9, 7f 2, 8f) (sft, gd 1-6, g-f 5, frm 3) 1999 AW 0-1: (7f) (Fibr)
Useful gelding, effective 5 to 6f, best at 6f, acts on g-s to g-f, has worn blinkers. Turf high 83. An admirable veteran sprint handicapper, he scored his first victory since last September when winning at Catterick. A fair sixth in a big York sprint next time, he is especially effective in soft ground.
**A J McNae [1-11] Clive Titcomb (from D Nicholls [2-14] May 1999).*

ASTRAL INVADER (IRE) BHB 37f36a **RR 36f 36a** 97[9]
7 ch g Astronef 7.9f **(59)** - Numidia (Sallust) 8.4f **(63)**
Form - 060
Record 1999 - 1st:0 2nd:0 3rd:0 Ran:2
Pre1999 - 1st:3 2nd:5 3rd:6 Ran:54
Win Prizemoney £7,253 *Total Prizemoney* £16,071
Wins * 1997 Mar Leices (G-F) S 7f 55 <
1999 AW 0-2: (6f, 7f) (Equi, Fibr)
Very moderate gelding, effective 7f, - acts on Equi, has worn blinkers (extremely effectively). AW high 32. Consistent.
**M S Saunders [3-58] M S Saunders.*

ASTRAL RHYTHM BHB 45f **RR 53f** 3967[14]
4 b c Scorpio (FR) - Suzannah's Song (Song) 7.2f **(61)**

Astonished's performance in the Portland Handicap came as no surprise to his supporters

Form - 070
Record 1999 - 1st:0 2nd:0 3rd:0 Ran:3
1999 Turf 0-3: (8f, 10f 2) (gd, frm 2)
Lengthy, currently fair colt. Turf high 53 (began Aug).
**G G Margarson [0-3] Four Jays Racing Partnership.*

ASTON MARA BHB 86f **RR 75+f** 4858[4]
2 b c Bering 9.6f **(80)** - Coigach **(97f)** (Niniski (USA)) 10.6f **(65)**
Form - 154
Record 1999 - 1st:1 2nd:0 3rd:0 Ran:3
Win Prizemoney £3,468 *Total Prizemoney* £3,878
Wins * **1999** Jun Newcas (GD) 7f 75+ <
1999 Turf 1-3: (7f 1-1, 8f 2) (sft, g-f, frm 1-1)
Currently above-average colt. Turf high 75 (1st run) - 1st of 7 from Bold Ewar (24 Jun Newcastle RF 2265).
**M Johnston [1-3] Mrs D J Buckley.*

ASTRAC (IRE) BHB 84f84a **RR 81f 84a** 5141[16]
8 b g Nordico (USA) 8.2f **(59)** - Shirleen(Daring Display (USA)) 6.9f **(69)**
Form - 0700653008316400

ASTROLFELL (IRE) BHB 24f **RR 26f** 4075[7]
4 ch f River Falls 8.2f **(56)** - Indian Starlight (Kafu) 6f **(47)**
Form - 00087
Record 1999 - 1st:0 2nd:0 3rd:0 Ran:5
Pre1999 - 1st:0 2nd:0 3rd:1 Ran:2
Win Prizemoney £0 *Total Prizemoney* £288
1999 Turf 0-5: (7f 2, 8f 2, 10f) (gd, g-f, frm 3)
Light-framed, little account filly. **J S Moore [0-7] Mrs P M Ratcliffe.*

ASTRONOMER RR 73f 4998[3]
3 br g Ardkinglass 5f **(64)** - Ayodhya (IRE) (Astronef)
Form - 4310603
Record 1999 - 1st:1 2nd:0 3rd:2 Ran:7
Pre1999 - 1st:0 2nd:0 3rd:1 Ran:3
Win Prizemoney £3,832 *Total Prizemoney* £5,417
Wins * 1999 Jun Beverl (SFT) 7.5f 87 <
1999 Turf 1-7: (7f 1-5, 8f 2) (g-s 1-2, gd, g-f, frm 3)
Light-framed, above-average gelding, effective 7f, acts on g-s. Turf high 87 - 1st of 12 from Smart Predator (9 Jun Beverley RF 1853). Consistent. He got off the mark over seven and a half furlongs at Beverley before being upped into smart handicap company. Likes cut in the ground. **J R Fanshawe [1-10] Dr Catherine Wills.*

ASTURIAN LADY (IRE) BHB 95f **RR 88f** 4389[5]
2 b f Zieten (USA) - Thubut (USA) (Tank's Prospect (USA))
Form - 5155
Record 1999 - 1st:1 2nd:0 3rd:0 Ran:4
Win Prizemoney £3,063 *Total Prizemoney* £4,875
Wins * 1999 Aug Nottin (G-F) 6.1f 88 <
1999 Turf 1-4: (5f, 6f 1-3) (gd 2, g-f 1-2)
Useful filly. Turf high 88 (began Jly) - also 1st of 5 getting 2lb from Safranine (9 Aug Nottingham RF 3474). She stayed on really well to win over six at Nottingham, and was by no means disgraced when fifth in the Lowther. Rather disappointing in a listed race at Ayr. **A P Jarvis [1-4] Ambrose Turnbull.*

ASYAAD (USA) BHB 56f52a **RR 57f 52a** 983[14]
4 b g Zilzal (USA) 8.5f **(79)** - Shihama (USA) (Shadeed (USA)) 8.2f **(70)**
Form - 750
Record 1999 - 1st:0 2nd:0 3rd:0 Ran:2
Pre1999 - 1st:0 2nd:0 3rd:1 Ran:8
Win Prizemoney £0 *Total Prizemoney* £1,069
1999 Turf 0-1: (6f) (frm) 1999 AW 0-1: (6f) (Equi)
Light-framed, fair gelding.
**Mrs L Stubbs [0-5] A P Griffin (from B W Hills [0-5] May 1998).*

ATALYA RR 65f 5000[6]
2 ch g Afzal - Sandy Looks (Music Boy) 6.8f **(57)**
Form - 6
Record 1999 - 1st:0 2nd:0 3rd:0 Ran:1
1999 Turf 0-1: (8f) (gd)
Currently average gelding. **F Jordan [0-1] W E Catstrey.*

ATAVUS BHB 80f **RR 90f** 4943[1]
2 b c Distant Relative 7f **(69)** - Elysian (Northfields (USA)) 9f **(72)**
Form - 531
Record 1999 - 1st:1 2nd:0 3rd:1 Ran:3
Win Prizemoney £3,509 *Total Prizemoney* £12,509
Wins * 1999 Oct Lingfi (G-F) 7f 75+ <
1999 Turf 1-3: (6f, 7f 1-2) (sft, gd 1-2)
Currently useful colt. Turf high 90 (began Spt) - 3rd of 20 getting 1lb from Magic of Love (15 Oct Newmarket 6f gd RF 4895). Got off the mark at Lingfield in fine style, and could make up into a decent handicapper. **W R Muir [1-3] Stableside Racing Partnership II.*

ATHENIAN HEIGHTS BHB 25a **RR 25a** 232[14]
4 b f Timeless Times (USA) 6.1f **(56)** - Woodbegood (Athens Wood) 19.6f **(38)**
Form - 0680
Record 1999 - 1st:0 2nd:0 3rd:0 Ran:2
Pre1999 - 1st:0 2nd:0 3rd:0 Ran:2
1999 AW 0-2: (7f, 11f) (Fibr 2)
Small, poor filly. AW high 17.
**M Waring [0-4] R A M Racecourses Ltd.*

ATHENRY BHB 79f **RR 84f** 2909[6]
6 b h Siberian Express (USA) 9f **(58)** - Heresheis (Free State) 8.7f **(61)**
Form - 684006
Record 1999 - 1st:0 2nd:0 3rd:0 Ran:6
Pre1999 - 1st:2 2nd:2 3rd:0 Ran:6
Win Prizemoney £9,060 *Total Prizemoney* £25,696
Wins * 1996 May York (G-F) 13.9f 90 <
* 1996 Apr Newcas (GD) 12.4f 89+
1999 Turf 0-6: (14f 2, 15f, 16f, 18f, 20f) (g-s, gd 2, g-f, frm 2)
Decent horse. Turf high 86. He looked an out-and-out stayer as a three-year-old. Unfortunately, injury halted his career and, since he has been back in action, he has been rather highly-tried and has not looked up to it. **J Pearce [2-12] A J Thompson.*

ATIENZA (USA) BHB 27f48a **RR 10f 48a** 5101[12]
6 ch m Chief's Crown (USA) 10.2f **(75)** - Hattab Voladora (USA) (Dewan (USA)) 7.4f **(65)**
Form - 00
Record 1999 - 1st:0 2nd:0 3rd:0 Ran:2
Pre1999 - 1st:0 2nd:1 3rd:2 Ran:12
Win Prizemoney £0 *Total Prizemoney* £1,757
1999 Turf 0-1: (14f) (g-s) 1999 AW 0-1: (15f) (Fibr)
Little account mare. Becoming disappointing.
**Dr J D Scargill [0-2] W J de Ruiter (from S C Williams [0-12] Apr 1997).*

ATLANTA BHB 45f49a **RR 4f 49a** 3800[20]
4 b f Rock City 8.8f **(62)** - Olympic Run (Salse (USA)) 7.5f **(66)**
Form - 000
Record 1999 - 1st:0 2nd:0 3rd:0 Ran:2
Pre1999 - 1st:0 2nd:1 3rd:1 Ran:13
Win Prizemoney £0 *Total Prizemoney* £1,442
1999 Turf 0-1: (6f) (g-f) 1999 AW 0-1: (6f) (Fibr)
Scopey, little account filly, has worn blinkers. Becoming disappointing.
**G Woodward [0-12] J Pownall (from J L Dunlop [0-3] Oct 1997).*

ATLANTIC ACE RR 60f 3870[7]
2 b c First Trump - Risalah **(37f)** (Marju (IRE))
Form - 7
Record 1999 - 1st:0 2nd:0 3rd:0 Ran:1
1999 Turf 0-1: (5f) (g-f)
Currently average colt. **B Smart [0-1] Richard Page.*

ATLANTIC CHARTER (USA) BHB 70f65a **RR 72f 65a** 4836[17]
3 b c Gone West (USA) 7.8f **(82)** - Silk Slippers (USA) (Nureyev (USA)) 8.7f **(78)**
Form - 06038710
Record 1999 - 1st:1 2nd:0 3rd:1 Ran:8
Win Prizemoney £6,157 *Total Prizemoney* £6,740
Wins 1999 Oct Redcar (GD) H 10f 66 72 <
1999 Turf 1-7: (7f 3, 8f, 10f 1-3) (gd 2, g-f 1-3, frm 2) 1999 AW 0-1: (8f) (Fibr)
Scopey, above-average colt, effective 7 to 10f, best at 10f, acts on g-f to frm, best on frm, prefers tight tracks. Turf high 72 - 1st of 16 getting 17lb from Radar (2 Oct Redcar RF 4692).
**A G Foster [0-1] A K Collins (from P W Chapple-Hyam [1-7] Oct 1999).*

ATLANTIC DESTINY (IRE) BHB 100f **RR 103f** 2700[6]
3 b f Royal Academy (USA) 7.8f **(77)** - Respectfully (USA) (The Minstrel (CAN)) 10f **(72)**
Form - 504056
Record 1999 - 1st:0 2nd:0 3rd:0 Ran:6
Pre1999 - 1st:2 2nd:1 3rd:1 Ran:7
Win Prizemoney £16,463 *Total Prizemoney* £29,896
Wins * 1998 Spt Kempto (G-S) L 6f 93+ <
* 1998 May York (GD) 6f 87+
1999 Turf 0-6: (6f 3, 7f, 8f 2) (gd, g-f 3, frm 2)
Light-framed, very useful filly, effective 6 to 7f, best at 6f, acts on gd to frm, best on frm. Turf high 103 - 5th of 9 getting 8lb from Halmahera (26 Jun Newcastle 6f frm RF 2339). Consistent. Talented but headstrong, she is a difficult ride and failed to progress. **M Johnston [2-13] Atlantic Racing Ltd.*

ATLANTIC PRINCE (IRE) BHB 70f **RR 80df** 4579[14]
3 b g Fairy King (USA) 7.7f **(75)** - Idle Chat (USA) (Assert) 10.6f **(85)**
Form - 1047000
Record 1999 - 1st:1 2nd:0 3rd:0 Ran:7
Win Prizemoney £3,556 *Total Prizemoney* £4,174
Wins * 1999 Jun Beverl (GD) 7.5f 81+ <
1999 Turf 1-7: (6f, 7f 1-3, 8f 2, 10f) (gd 1-3, g-f 2, frm 2)
Scopey, decent gelding, effective 7f, acts on gd. Turf high 81 (1st run) - 1st of 8 from Liberty Lines (2 Jun Beverley RF 1666). Unraced at two, he made a winning debut at Beverley in June, but has been well held since. **M Johnston [1-7] Atlantic Racing Ltd.*

ATLANTIC RHAPSODY (FR) BHB 88f **RR 89f** 5049[2]
2 b c Machiavellian (USA) 9.8f **(83)** - First Waltz (FR) (Green Dancer (USA)) 10.3f **(74)**

Form - 2232
Record 1999 - 1st:0 2nd:3 3rd:1 Ran:4
Win Prizemoney £0 *Total Prizemoney* £4,151
1999 Turf 0-4: (6f 2, 7f, 8f) (gd 2, g-f, frm)
Useful colt. Turf high 89 - 2nd of 19 to Delius (25 Oct Leicester 8f gd RF 5049). Beaten under a length on each of his starts, he deserves to pick up a race. **M Johnston [0-4] Atlantic Racing Ltd.*

ATLANTIC VIKING (IRE) BHB 88f **RR 86f** 3298[1]
4 b g Danehill (USA) 9.1f **(79)** - Hi Bettina (Henbit (USA)) 9f **(61)**
Form - 202060141
Record 1999 - 1st:2 2nd:2 3rd:0 Ran:9
Pre1999 - 1st:1 2nd:1 3rd:2 Ran:14
Win Prizemoney £16,747 *Total Prizemoney* £25,067
Wins * **1999** Aug Ripon (G-F) H 6f 85 86
* **1999** Jly Pontef (G-F) H 5f 80 82
1997 Jun Newcas (FRM) 5f 97+ <
1999 Turf 2-9: (5f 1-6, 6f 1-3) (gd 2, g-f 2, frm 2-5)
Scopey, useful gelding, effective 5 to 7f, acts on g-f to frm, best on frm, has worn blinkers. Turf high 86 - 1st of 6 giving 9lb to Almasi (2 Aug Ripon RF 3298) - also 1st of 8 giving 9lb to Antonia's Double (16 Jly Pontefract RF 2889). Found his form in the summer, including a victory in the first-time blinkers.
**D Nicholls [2-9] David Faulkner (from M Johnston [1-14] Oct 1998).*

AT LARGE (IRE) BHB 71f **RR 70f** 4431[13]
5 b g Night Shift (USA) 8.1f **(73)** - Lady Donna (Dominion) 8.5f **(63)**
Form - 48074200
Record 1999 - 1st:0 2nd:1 3rd:0 Ran:8
Pre1999 - 1st:1 2nd:3 3rd:3 Ran:10
Win Prizemoney £5,995 *Total Prizemoney* £14,123
Wins 1997 Oct Nottin (G-F) H 6.1f 74 77 <
1999 Turf 0-8: (5f 3, 6f 5) (g-s, gd 2, g-f, frm 4)
Above-average gelding, effective 5 to 6f, best at 5f, acts on gd to frm, best on frm, has worn blinkers. Turf high 74. He looked quite a promising sprint handicapper in 1997, but was lightly raced the following year and has not really fulfilled his potential. There still lurks the feeling that he can win a decent handicap, and he ran well when second to Ambitious at Sandown.
**J A R Toller [0-10] The Half Moon Club (from J R Fanshawe [1-8] Oct 1997).*

AT LIBERTY (IRE) BHB 29f64a **RR 29f 64a** 3389[15]
7 b g Danehill (USA) 9.1f **(79)** - Music of The Night (USA) (Blushing Groom (FR)) 10.3f **(76)**
Form - 700
Record 1999 - 1st:0 2nd:0 3rd:0 Ran:3
Pre1999 - 1st:4 2nd:4 3rd:5 Ran:42
Win Prizemoney £19,399 *Total Prizemoney* £35,226
Wins 1997 *Mar Lingfi (STD) C 12f* 75
1996 Aug Goodwo (G-F) C 8f 76
1995 Jun Lingfi (GD) H 10f 82 80 <
1999 Turf 0-3: (8f, 12f 2) (frm 3)
Moderate gelding, has worn blinkers. Turf high 29 (began Jly). Becoming disappointing.
**J C Tuck [0-9] James Tuck (from R Hannon [4-44] Nov 1997).*

AT MY COMMAND (IRE) BHB 41f **RR 38f** 3954[9]
3 ch f Barathea (IRE) - Fly Dont Run (USA) **(53f)** (Lear Fan (USA)) 8.5f **(73)**
Form - 0000050
Record 1999 - 1st:0 2nd:0 3rd:0 Ran:7
Pre1999 - 1st:0 2nd:0 3rd:1 Ran:3
Win Prizemoney £0 *Total Prizemoney* £455
1999 Turf 0-7: (5f, 6f 3, 7f, 8f, 10f) (gd, frm 6)
Unfurnished, very moderate filly, has worn blinkers. Turf high 43. Consistent.
**M W Easterby [0-7] K P Seow (from W Jarvis [0-3] Oct 1998).*

A TOUCH OF FROST BHB 81f **RR 84f** 4915[8]
4 gr f Distant Relative 7f **(69)** - Pharland (FR) (Bellypha) 9.8f **(73)**
Form - 001217158
Record 1999 - 1st:3 2nd:1 3rd:0 Ran:9
Pre1999 - 1st:1 2nd:0 3rd:0 Ran:4
Win Prizemoney £27,693 *Total Prizemoney* £28,887
Wins * **1999** Spt Salisb (G-F) H 7f 73 79 <
* **1999** Jly York (G-F) H 7f 71 74
* **1999** Jun Salisb (GD) CH 7f 58 64
* 1998 Aug Salisb (G-F) 8f 68
1999 Turf 3-9: (7f 3-5, 8f 3, 10f) (gd 5, g-f 2-2, frm 1-2)
Decent filly, effective 7f, acts on gd to frm, often wears blinkers (extremely effectively). Turf high 84 - 5th of 15 getting 6lb from Family Man (1 Oct Newmarket 7f gd RF 4675) - also 1st of 12 getting 7lb from Gracious Gift (2 Spt Salisbury RF 4095).
**G G Margarson [4-13] Mrs Patricia Williams.*

ATTARIKH (IRE) BHB 34f **RR 46df** 84[P]
6 b g Mujtahid (USA) 7.4f **(69)** - Silly Tune (IRE) (Coquelin (USA)) 8.4f **(58)**
Form - 5P
Record 1999 - 1st:0 2nd:0 3rd:0 Ran:2
Pre1999 - 1st:0 2nd:0 3rd:2 Ran:21
Win Prizemoney £0 *Total Prizemoney* £1,235
1999 AW 0-2: (8f 2) (Equi, Fibr)
Moderate gelding, has worn blinkers. AW high 24.
**Mrs A L M King [0-19] T P Hilliam (from J H M Gosden [0-5] Jly 1996).*

ATWAAR (USA) BHB 89f **RR 86f** 4818[2]
2 ch c Woodman (USA) 9.7f **(77)** - Haniya (IRE) **(86f)** (Caerleon (USA)) 8.6f **(71)**
Form - 2132
Record 1999 - 1st:1 2nd:2 3rd:1 Ran:4
Win Prizemoney £2,921 *Total Prizemoney* £7,585
Wins * **1999** Jly Redcar (FRM) 7f 86+ <
1999 Turf 1-4: (7f 1-2, 8f, 10f) (gd, g-f, frm, hrd 1-1)
Useful colt. Turf high 86 - 2nd of 8 giving 2lb to Bow Strada (11 Oct Leicester 10f gd RF 4818) - also 1st of 5 giving 5lb to Pix Me Up (17 Jly Redcar RF 2920). Has ability but also a hint of temperament.
**J L Dunlop [1-4] Hamdan Al Maktoum.*

ATYLAN BOY (IRE) BHB 70f **RR 69f** 4672[15]
2 b c Efisio 7.7f **(69)** - Gold Flair (Tap On Wood) 10.3f **(65)**
Form - 8650
Record 1999 - 1st:0 2nd:0 3rd:0 Ran:4
1999 Turf 0-4: (5f 2, 6f, 7f) (g-s 2, gd, frm)
Average colt. Turf high 69. **B J Meehan [0-4] Mrs Sheila Tucker.*

AUBERGADE (FR) RR 102f 4889a[3]
3 gr f Kaldoun (FR) 9.9f **(84)** - Anna Edes (FR) (Fabulous Dancer (USA)) 9.4f **(70)**
Form - 23
1999 Turf 0-2: (11f, 12f) (hvy, g-s)
Currently very useful filly. Turf high 102 (1st run) - 2nd of 8 to La Sylphide (14 Apr Saint-Cloud 11f g-s RF 0809a). She acts well on soft ground and may benefit from enterprising tactics.
**Mme M Bollack-Badel in FR [0-2].*

AUBRIETA (USA) BHB 50f56a **RR 46f 56a** 5032[8]
3 b f Dayjur (USA) 6.8f **(79)** - Fennel (Slew O' Gold (USA)) 8f **(75)**
Form - 0068387068
Record 1999 - 1st:0 2nd:0 3rd:1 Ran:10
Pre1999 - 1st:0 2nd:0 3rd:3 Ran:7
Win Prizemoney £0 *Total Prizemoney* £3,974
1999 Turf 0-10: (5f, 6f 5, 7f 3, 8f) (g-s, gd 3, g-f 3, frm 3)
Leggy, fair filly, has worn blinkers. Turf high 65.
**D HaydnJones [0-6] Hugh O'Donnell (from C E Brittain [0-11] Jly 1999).*

AUCHONVILLERS RR 63f 4751[6]
2 b c Deploy 11.4f **(67)** - Forbearance (Bairn (USA)) 7.7f **(59)**
Form - 6
Record 1999 - 1st:0 2nd:0 3rd:0 Ran:1
1999 Turf 0-1: (8f) (gd)
Currently average colt. **B A McMahon [0-1] Major W R Paton-Smith.*

AUCTION HOUSE (USA) BHB 102f **RR 102f** 4916[7]
3 b c Exbourne (USA) - Fast Flow (USA) (Riverman (USA)) 9.1f **(76)**
Form - 0487
Record 1999 - 1st:0 2nd:0 3rd:0 Ran:4
Pre1999 - 1st:3 2nd:1 3rd:0 Ran:5
Win Prizemoney £78,641 *Total Prizemoney* £131,164
Wins * 1998 Spt Doncas (GD) G2 7f 114 <
* 1998 Aug York (G-F) L 7f 101
* 1998 Jly Doncas (G-F) 7f 86+
1999 Turf 0-4: (7f 2, 8f 2) (gd, g-f 2, frm)

Neat, very useful colt, effective 7f, acts on gd to g-f. Turf high 102. Consistent. A top-class juvenile, he had not come to himself when disappointing in the 2,000 Guineas and was rested for three months during the summer. Below par when returned to action.
**B W Hills [3-9] K Abdulla.*

AUDACITY BHB 31f **RR 31f** 4667[7]
3 b g Minshaanshu Amad (USA) 11.3f **(53)** - Glory Isle (Hittite Glory) 8.7f **(50)**
Form - 00507
Record 1999 - 1st:0 2nd:0 3rd:0 Ran:5
Pre1999 - 1st:0 2nd:0 3rd:0 Ran:3
1999 Turf 0-3: (8f 2, 10f) (frm 3) 1999 AW 0-2: (12f, 13f) (Equi, Fibr)
Strong, very moderate gelding. Turf high 53 (began Jly). AW high 36 (began Aug).
**N Hamilton [0-5] City Industrial Supplies Ltd (from G Lewis [0-3] Aug 1998).*

AUDIOSTREETDOTCOM BHB 52f **RR 51f** 5048[9]
2 ch g Risk Me (FR) 8f **(53)** - Ballagarrow Girl (North Stoke) 10.4f **(55)**
Form - 00000
Record 1999 - 1st:0 2nd:0 3rd:0 Ran:5
1999 Turf 0-5: (5f 2, 6f 2, 7f) (hvy, g-s 2, gd, frm)
Fair gelding, often wears blinkers. Turf high 51 (began Aug).
**G B Balding [0-5] The Infront Partnership.*

AUDITION **RR 74f** 4710[8]
3 b f Machiavellian (USA) 9.8f **(83)** - Dance to the Top **(93f)** (Sadler's Wells (USA)) 10f **(76)**
Form - 2323718
Record 1999 - 1st:1 2nd:2 3rd:2 Ran:7
Win Prizemoney £3,815 *Total Prizemoney* £7,394
Wins * 1999 Spt Lingfi (HVY) 10f 74+ <
1999 Turf 1-7: (7f, 8f 3, 9f, 10f 1-2) (g-s 1-1, gd, g-f, frm 4)
Workmanlike, above-average filly, effective 7 to 10f, best at 8f, acts on g-s to frm, best on frm. Turf high 74 - 3rd of 7 to Bassinello (4 Aug Pontefract 8f frm RF 3371) - also 1st of 11 from Paperweight (24 Spt Lingfield RF 4529).
**Sir Michael Stoute [1-7] Cheveley Park Stud.*

AUENADLER (GER) **RR 108f** 1897a[1]
7 b h Big Shuffle (USA) - Auenmaid (Luciano) 11.2f **(65)**
Form - 31
1999 Turf 1-2: (5f, 6f 1-1) (sft 1-1, gd)
Pattern-class horse. Turf high 102 - 1st of 8 from Dyhim Diamond (4 Jun Baden-Baden RF 1897a). Consistent. He holds his form remarkably well and put up an excellent effort when beating Dyhim Diamond and Gorse at Baden-Baden in June. Best over six furlongs, he goes particularly well on a soft surface.
**U Ostmann in GER [3-8] Gestut Auenquelle.*

AUENKLANG (GER) **RR 114+f** 4244a[1]
2 b c Big Shuffle (USA) - Auenglocke (GER) (Surumu (GER)) 10f **(83)**
Form - 21
1999 Turf 1-2: (6f 1-2) (gd 1-2)
Currently Group-class colt, always wears blinkers. Turf high 114 (began Jly) - 1st of 5 from Arc Royal (3 Spt Baden-Baden RF 4244a). A smart German-trained colt, he looked pedestrian behind Rossini in the Prix Robert Papin but made all to win easily at Baden-Baden in September. Snapped up by Godolphin, he may stay a mile and can make a nice three-year-old.
**H Hiller in GER [1-2] Stall Dario.*

AUGUSTAN BHB 42f53a **RR 44f 53a** 1770[23]
8 b g Shareef Dancer (USA) 10.1f **(67)** - Krishnagar (Kris) 9.5f **(73)**
Form - 00
Record 1999 - 1st:0 2nd:0 3rd:0 Ran:2
Pre1999 - 1st:5 2nd:8 3rd:13 Ran:78
Win Prizemoney £17,523 *Total Prizemoney* £34,489
Wins * 1997 Aug Pontef (G-F) H 10f 55 60
* 1997 May Doncas (GD) H 12f 53 59
* 1996 Jly Chepst (G-F) H 12.1f 51 57
* 1995 Jun York (G-F) H 11.9f 60 65 <
1999 Turf 0-2: (11f, 12f) (g-f, frm)
Fair gelding, effective 10 to 12f, best at 12f, acts on gd to frm, best on g-f, has worn blinkers, prefers right handed tracks, prefers tight tracks. Turf high 5.

**S Gollings [4-69] Robert Jones (from John Harris [1-8] Nov 1994).*

AUNT DORIS BHB 65f **RR 66f** 4164[7]
2 b f Distant Relative 7f **(69)** - Nevis (Connaught) 7.7f **(63)**
Form - 0137
Record 1999 - 1st:1 2nd:0 3rd:1 Ran:4
Win Prizemoney £2,094 *Total Prizemoney* £2,611
Wins * 1999 Aug Leices (GD) S 5f 66 <
1999 Turf 1-4: (5f 1-1, 6f 3) (g-f 1-2, frm 2)
Average filly. Turf high 66 (began Jly) - 1st of 16 getting 5lb from Baytown Melody (18 Aug Leicester RF 3745). Hacked up at Leicester over six furlongs on decent ground, before running well when third over the same trip at Ripon. **J Berry [1-4] Mrs Joy Hobby.*

AUNT FLO (IRE) BHB 93f **RR 94f** 4678[11]
3 b f Royal Academy (USA) 7.8f **(77)** - Quinsigimond (Formidable (USA)) 9.2f **(63)**
Form - 25430170
Record 1999 - 1st:1 2nd:1 3rd:1 Ran:8
Pre1999 - 1st:1 2nd:2 3rd:0 Ran:6
Win Prizemoney £9,617 *Total Prizemoney* £22,778
Wins * 1999 Jly Newmar (G-F) 6f 91 <
* 1998 Jly Nottin (G-F) 5.1f 88+
1999 Turf 1-8: (6f 1-7, 7f) (gd 2, g-f 2, frm 1-4)
Scopey, useful filly, effective 6f, acts on gd to frm, best on g-f. Turf high 99 (1st run) - 2nd of 8 getting 14lb from Nanoushka (15 May Newmarket 6f g-f RF 1245) - also 1st of 5 from Ellway Star (30 Jly Newmarket RF 3243). Consistent. She is a useful sprinter, but falls below Group class and is difficult to place. Probably indifferent to the state of the ground, she is unlikely to improve.
**M L W Bell [2-14] Stamford Bridge Partnership.*

AUNTY ROSE (IRE) BHB 100f **RR 91f** 4920[7]
2 b f Caerleon (USA) 10.9f **(79)** - Come on Rosi (Valiyar) 8.5f **(73)**
Form - 137
Record 1999 - 1st:1 2nd:0 3rd:1 Ran:3
Win Prizemoney £5,061 *Total Prizemoney* £8,786
Wins * 1999 Jly Newmar (G-F) 7f 78+ <
1999 Turf 1-3: (7f 1-2, 8f) (gd, g-f, frm 1-1)
Currently useful filly. Turf high 91 (began Jly). A half-sister to Bin Rosie, she scored nicely on her Newmarket debut and ran well to finish third in the May Hill. However, she showed temperament on her final run. **J L Dunlop [1-3] Wafic Said.*

AURAMINE (IRE) BHB 50f **RR 37f** 4350[16]
4 ch g Rainbows For Life (CAN) 9.3f **(64)** - Les Saintes (Kris) 9.5f **(73)**
Form - 80355060
Record 1999 - 1st:0 2nd:0 3rd:1 Ran:8
Win Prizemoney £0 *Total Prizemoney* £562
1999 Turf 0-8: (7f 2, 8f 3, 10f 2, 11f) (gd 2, g-f, frm 4, hrd)
Workmanlike, very moderate gelding, effective 8f, acts on frm. Turf high 62. Becoming disappointing. **J L Eyre [0-8] M Gleason.*

AURA OF GRACE (USA) **RR 56f** 1680[7]
2 b br f Southern Halo (USA) - Avarice (USA) (Manila (USA)) 9.3f **(71)**
Form - 7
Record 1999 - 1st:0 2nd:0 3rd:0 Ran:1
1999 Turf 0-1: (6f) (g-f)
Currently fair filly. **R W Armstrong [0-1] R N Bracher.*

AURIGNY BHB 83f **RR 91f** 4795[21]
4 b f Timeless Times (USA) 6.1f **(56)** -Dear Glenda(Gold Song)5.5f **(61)**
Form - 08456351000
Record 1999 - 1st:1 2nd:0 3rd:1 Ran:11
Pre1999 - 1st:2 2nd:1 3rd:4 Ran:15
Win Prizemoney £21,620 *Total Prizemoney* £46,962
Wins * 1999 Jly Goodwo (G-F) 5f 62+
* 1997 Aug Newbur (G-F) L 5.2f 91 <
* 1997 May Bright (G-F) 5.3f 80+
1999 Turf 1-11: (5f 1-11) (gd 4, g-f 1-3, frm 4)
Workmanlike, useful filly, effective 5f, acts on gd to frm. Turf high 91 - 4th of 11 getting 12lb from To the Roof (5 Jun Epsom 5f gd RF 1758). A very useful sprinting juvenile in 1997, she has been difficult to place since and has found Pattern company beyond her. A decent effort at Epsom in June when fourth behind To The Roof was followed by a number of good placed efforts, and she finally got off the mark for the season in a three-runner classified event

at Goodwood in July. **S Dow [3-26] J & S Kelly.*

AUSPICIOUS BHB 93f **RR 94f** 5219[4]
3 b f Shirley Heights 12.1f **(76)** - Blessed Event (Kings Lake (USA)) 10.8f **(67)**
Form - 1444
Record **1999** - 1st:1 2nd:0 3rd:0 Ran:4
Pre1999 - 1st:0 2nd:1 3rd:0 Ran:2
Win Prizemoney £3,772 *Total Prizemoney* £8,184
Wins *** 1999** May Bath (GD) 10.2f 71 <
1999 Turf 1-4: (10f 1-2, 12f 2) (sft, gd 2, g-f 1-1)
Scopey, useful filly, effective 10 to 12f, acts on gd. Turf high 94 - 4th of 13 to Khibrah (14 Oct Newmarket 10f gd RF 4871). A staying type, she won her maiden at Bath in May, but was off the track for three months afterwards and has looked out of her depth in Listed company after returning.
**Sir Michael Stoute [1-6] Cheveley Park Stud.*

AUSTIN POWERS (IRE) RR 28f 2641[6]
3 b c Sadler's Wells (USA) 11.3f **(87)** - Guess Again (GER) (Stradavinsky) 12.5f **(64)**
Form - 6
Record **1999** - 1st:0 2nd:0 3rd:0 Ran:1
1999 Turf 0-1: (10f) (frm)
Well made, currently little account colt. **J Noseda [0-1] Ecurie Pharos.*

AUTOMATIC BHB 71f70a **RR 69f 70a** 4925[1]
3 b g Clantime 6.6f **(57)** - Gentle Gypsy (Junius (USA)) 7.7f **(65)**
Form - 33832232221
Record **1999** - 1st:1 2nd:5 3rd:4 Ran:11
Pre1999 - 1st:0 2nd:0 3rd:0 Ran:1
Win Prizemoney £2,360 *Total Prizemoney* £11,205
Wins *** 1999** *Oct Wolver (STD) 7f 58* <
1999 Turf 0-8: (7f 5, 8f 2, 9f) (gd 2, g-f 2, frm 4) 1999 AW 1-3: (7f 1-1, 8f, 9f) (Fibr 1-3)
Scopey, average gelding, effective 7 to 9f, best at 8f, acts on gd to frm, best on gd, has worn blinkers, likes tight tracks. Turf high 69 - 2nd of 14 giving 1lb to Perfect Peach (26 Spt Musselburgh 7f gd RF 4579). AW high 67. Consistent. He was rapidly becoming a frustrating sort before finally losing his maiden tag on the Wolverhampton Fibresand in October, though even then he did not look happy about being in front. **M L W Bell [1-12] Billy Maguire.*

AUTONOMY (IRE) BHB 100f **RR 95f** 5130[1]
2 b c Doyoun 10.7f **(69)** - Debbie's Next (USA) (Arctic Tern (USA)) 8.9f **(69)**
Form - 151
Record **1999** - 1st:2 2nd:0 3rd:0 Ran:3
Win Prizemoney £9,392 *Total Prizemoney* £9,392
Wins *** 1999** Oct Newmar (G-S) 8f 95 <
*** 1999** Aug Sandow (G-S) 7.1f 74+
1999 Turf 2-3: (7f 1-2, 8f 1-1) (gd 1-1, g-f 1-2)
Currently very useful colt. Turf high 95 (began Aug) - 1st of 6 giving 2lb to Francesco Guardi (29 Oct Newmarket RF 5130). Found out in Group Three company inbetween victories in a Sandown maiden, and a Newmarket Conditions event
**M L W Bell [2-3] Deln Ltd.*

AUTUMN COVER BHB 69f60a **RR 73f 60a** 1291[12]
7 gr g Nomination 7.3f **(57)** - Respray (Rusticaro (FR)) 8.2f **(65)**
Form - 030
Record **1999** - 1st:0 2nd:0 3rd:1 Ran:2
Pre1999 - 1st:7 2nd:1 3rd:2 Ran:37
Win Prizemoney £56,269 *Total Prizemoney* £63,350
Wins * 1998 Apr Bright (GD) 8f 78
* 1997 May Kempto (GD) H 8f 75 79 <
* 1996 Spt Goodwo (G-F) H 9f 70 74
* 1996 Jly Goodwo (G-F) H 8f 64 70
* 1996 Jun Sandow (FRM) H 8.1f 55 58
1996 Apr Bright (FRM) H 8f 50 54
1996 Apr Bright (FRM) H 8f 43 51
1999 Turf 0-2: (8f 2) (gd, g-f)
Above-average gelding, effective 8f, acts on gd to g-f, has worn blinkers. Turf high 73 (1st run) - 3rd of 29 getting 1lb from Scene (28 Apr Ascot 8f g-f RF 0901).
**P R Hedger [5-27] G A Alexander (from R M Flower [2-15] May 1996).*

AUTUMN LEAVES RR 38f 5198[13]
3 b f Warning 8.1f **(77)** - Misty Goddess (IRE) **(51df 37a)** (Godswalk (USA)) 7.3f **(58)**
Form - 00
Record **1999** - 1st:0 2nd:0 3rd:0 Ran:2
1999 Turf 0-2: (8f 2) (gd 2)
Neat, currently very moderate filly. Turf high 29 (began Oct).
**N P Littmoden [0-2] J R Good.*

AUTUMN RAIN (USA) RR 67f 4551[5]
2 br c Dynaformer (USA) 12f **(82)** - Edda (USA) (Ogygian (USA))
Form - 55
Record **1999** - 1st:0 2nd:0 3rd:0 Ran:2
1999 Turf 0-2: (7f 2) (g-s, frm)
Currently average colt. Turf high 67 (began Spt) - 5th of 11 to Jathaab (25 Spt Haydock 7f g-s RF 4551).
**E A L Dunlop [0-2] Khalifa Sultan.*

AUTUM ROUGE (IRE) RR 4228[19]
5 ch m Phardante (FR) 12.8f **(46)** - Red Leaf (Carry Off)
Form - 0
Record **1999** - 1st:0 2nd:0 3rd:0 Ran:1
1999 Turf 0-1: (8f) (frm)
Formerly very poor filly. **Mrs P Ford [0-4] J T Jones.*

AVANTI BHB 72f **RR 73f** 3872[7]
3 gr c Reprimand 8.2f **(63)** - Dolly Bevan (Another Realm) 6.6f **(55)**
Form - 84127
Record **1999** - 1st:1 2nd:1 3rd:0 Ran:5
Pre1999 - 1st:0 2nd:0 3rd:0 Ran:1
Win Prizemoney £4,474 *Total Prizemoney* £5,664
Wins *** 1999** May Sandow (GD) H 7.1f 70 72 <
1999 Turf 1-5: (7f 1-1, 8f 4) (gd, g-f, frm 1-3)
Scopey, above-average colt, effective 7 to 8f, acts on frm. Turf high 73 - 2nd of 6 getting 1lb from Lafite (9 Jly Chepstow 8f frm RF 2668) - also 1st of 14 giving 6lb to Tous Les Jours (31 May Sandown RF 1616). He made a successful handicap debut at Sandown in May, responding well to a positive ride.
**P J Makin [1-6] Mrs P J Makin.*

AVARITIOUS RR 865[14]
3 br f Avarice - Captain Bonnie (Captain James) 5f **(59)**
Form - 0
Record **1999** - 1st:0 2nd:0 3rd:0 Ran:1
1999 Turf 0-1: (6f) (gd)
Light-framed, currently very poor filly.
**Miss J F Craze [0-1] Rex Holdsworth.*

AVEIRO (IRE) BHB 50f **RR 49f** 4350[13]
3 b c Darshaan 11.9f **(81)** - Avila (Ajdal (USA)) 9.2f **(89)**
Form - 85300
Record **1999** - 1st:0 2nd:0 3rd:1 Ran:5
Win Prizemoney £0 *Total Prizemoney* £642
1999 Turf 0-5: (8f 2, 10f, 11f, 12f) (gd 2, g-f, frm 2)
Workmanlike, moderate colt, has worn blinkers. Turf high 63.
**C E Brittain [0-5] Saeed Manana.*

AVENGING ANGEL (IRE) BHB 60f70a **RR 43f 70a** 87[1]
3 b f College Chapel - Dromacomer Lady (IRE) (Taufan (USA)) 7f **(57)**
Form - 021
Record **1999** - 1st:1 2nd:0 3rd:0 Ran:1
Pre1999 - 1st:0 2nd:1 3rd:0 Ran:4
Win Prizemoney £2,879 *Total Prizemoney* £3,743
Wins *** 1999** *Jan Wolver (STD) 6f 75+* <
1999 AW 1-1: (6f 1-1) (Fibr 1-1)
Leggy, above-average filly. (1st run) - 1st of 12 from Muddy Water (13 Jan Wolverhampton RF 0087).
**N P Littmoden [1-5] Plyvine, Guy, Howles & Slater.*

AVERHAM STAR BHB 20f32a **RR 37?f 32a** 4128[10]
4 ch g Absalom 7.1f **(56)** - Upper Sister (Upper Case (USA)) 8.2f **(55)**
Form - 60060680050
Record **1999** - 1st:0 2nd:0 3rd:0 Ran:11
Pre1999 - 1st:0 2nd:0 3rd:1 Ran:14
Win Prizemoney £0 *Total Prizemoney* £619
1999 Turf 0-5: (5f, 8f, 10f, 11f, 12f) (gd, g-f 2, frm, hrd) 1999 AW 0-6: (6f, 7f 2, 8f, 12f 2) (Equi, Fibr 5)

Strong, very moderate gelding, effective 8f, - acts on Fibr, has worn blinkers (effectively). Turf high 37. AW high 10.
**W Clay [0-8] Lee Heath (from B D Leavy [0-4] Jly 1999).*

AVERTI (IRE) BHB 114f **RR 113?f** 4777a10
8 b h Warning 8.1f **(77)** - Imperial Jade (Lochnager) 6f **(59)**
Form - 700
Record 1999 - 1st:0 2nd:0 3rd:0 Ran:3
Pre1999 - 1st:5 2nd:2 3rd:6 Ran:38
Win Prizemoney £47,269 *Total Prizemoney* £130,611
Wins * 1997 Jly Goodwo (G-F) G3 5f 107 <
* 1997 Apr Bath (G-F) 5.1f 106
* 1996 Jly Haydoc (GD) 6f 102
1999 Turf 0-3: (5f 3) (sft, gd, frm)
Group-class horse, effective 5 to 6f, best at 5f, acts on sft to frm. Turf high 98 (began Jly). A smart sprinter at his best, he was below par last term after a spell at stud in the spring.
**W R Muir [5-41] D J Deer.*

AVEZZANO BHB 100f **RR 98+f** 50341
2 b g Most Welcome 8.6f **(66)** - Moushka (Song) 7.2f **(61)**
Form - 66111
Record 1999 - 1st:3 2nd:0 3rd:0 Ran:5
Win Prizemoney £17,469 *Total Prizemoney* £17,469
Wins * **1999** Oct Doncas (SFT) H 7f 92 98+ <
* **1999** Oct York (G-S) H 6f 86 91
* **1999** Spt Ayr (G-S) 6f 78
1999 Turf 3-5: (5f 2, 6f 2-2, 7f 1-1) (g-s 2-2, gd 1-1, g-f 2)
Very useful gelding. Turf high 98 (began Aug) - 1st of 13 from Eastways (23 Oct Doncaster RF 5034) - also 1st of 15 getting 16lb from Seven No Trumps (6 Oct York RF 4757). Won a maiden at Ayr with cut in the ground most authoritatively, and went on to complete the hat-trick. Travels well in his races.
**W McKeown [3-5] Mrs L E McKeown.*

AVONDALE GIRL (IRE) BHB 70f66a **RR 68f 66a** 226110
3 ch f Case Law 6f **(64)** - Battle Queen (Kind of Hush) 10.1f **(62)**
Form - 66432130610
Record 1999 - 1st:2 2nd:1 3rd:2 Ran:10
Pre1999 - 1st:1 2nd:0 3rd:2 Ran:4
Win Prizemoney £6,583 *Total Prizemoney* £10,176
Wins * **1999** Jun Thirsk (G-F) H 6f 66 68
1999 *Mar Wolver (STD) S 5f 60*
1998 Jun Yarmou (GD) S 5.2f 79+ <
1999 Turf 1-5: (5f 3, 6f 1-2) (gd 2, frm 1-2, hrd) 1999 AW 1-5: (5f 1-3, 6f 2) (Equi 2, Fibr 1-3)
Light-framed, average filly, effective 5f, acts on gd, has worn blinkers. Turf high 68. AW high 67.
**M Dods [1-3] C A Lynch (from C A Dwyer [2-11] May 1999).*

AVRO ANSON BHB 53f **RR 44f** 109917
11 b g Ardross 12.4f **(67)** - Tremellick (Mummy's Pet) 7.7f **(60)**
Form - 60
Record 1999 - 1st:0 2nd:0 3rd:0 Ran:2
Pre1999 - 1st:3 2nd:1 3rd:0 Ran:12
Win Prizemoney £9,224 *Total Prizemoney* £11,050
1999 Turf 0-2: (16f, 18f) (g-s, gd)
Moderate gelding. Turf high 44. Consistent. A useful staying chaser, he makes infrequent appearances on the level.
**Miss J A Camacho [0-6] Axom (from M J Camacho [8-24] Oct 1994).*

AWAKE BHB 90f **RR 91+f** 50451
2 ch c First Trump - Pluvial (Habat) 7.6f **(61)**
Form - 211
Record 1999 - 1st:2 2nd:1 3rd:0 Ran:3
Win Prizemoney £9,707 *Total Prizemoney* £10,957
Wins * **1999** Oct Newbur (HVY) H 6f 81 91+ <
* **1999** Aug Epsom (GD) 6f 73
1999 Turf 2-3: (5f, 6f 2-2) (sft 1-1, g-f 1-2)
Currently useful colt. Turf high 91 (began Aug) - 1st of 17 getting 9lb from First Blood (23 Oct Newbury RF 5045). Showed promise on his Leicester debut, but was not particularly impressive when winning at long odds-on at Epsom next time. Authoritative winner of a nursey on his final start. **M Johnston [2-3] Lord Hartington.*

AWARD ACADEMY (IRE) RR 95f 5204a2
3 b c Royal Academy (USA) 7.8f **(77)** - Onesixnine (IRE) (Trojan Fen) 8.1f **(62)**
Form - 2
1999 Turf 0-1: (12f) (g-s)
Currently very useful colt. (1st run) - 2nd of 6 getting 3lb from Endless Hall (31 Oct San Siro 12f g-s RF 5204a).
**F Turner in ITY [0-1].*

AWESOME VENTURE BHB 30f35a **RR 23f 35a** 46025
9 b g Formidable (USA) 7.8f **(60)** - Pine Ridge (High Top) 10.2f **(67)**
Form - 755450453463245500006070085
Record 1999 - 1st:0 2nd:1 3rd:2 Ran:26
Pre1999 - 1st:4 2nd:15 3rd:9 Ran:97
Win Prizemoney £10,287 *Total Prizemoney* £28,590
Wins * 1996 *May Southw (STD) C 7f 73* <
* 1996 *Apr Southw (STD) C 8f 69*
* 1996 *Apr Southw (STD) H 8f 62 63*
1999 Turf 0-4: (7f, 8f 3) (gd 2, g-f, frm) 1999 AW 0-22: (6f 5, 7f 7, 8f 8, 11f 2) (Fibr 22)
Moderate gelding, effective 6 to 8f, best at 7f, - acts on Fibr, has worn blinkers, favours left handed tracks, favours tight tracks, favours Southwell. Turf high 23. AW high 56.
**M C Chapman [3-120] Market Rasen Racing Club (from J A R Toller [1-9] Oct 1994).*

AWTAAN (USA) RR 73f 50013
2 b f Arazi (USA) 9.2f **(74)** - Bashayer (USA) (Mr Prospector (USA)) 8.8f **(78)**
Form - 43
Record 1999 - 1st:0 2nd:0 3rd:1 Ran:2
Win Prizemoney £0 *Total Prizemoney* £768
1999 Turf 0-2: (8f 2) (gd 2)
Currently above-average filly. Turf high 73 (began Spt).
**M P Tregoning [0-2] Hamdan Al Maktoum.*

AWWALIYA BHB 62f **RR 63df** 47232
3 b f Distant Relative 7f **(69)** - El Rabab (USA) (Roberto (USA)) 10f **(76)**
Form - 707572
Record 1999 - 1st:0 2nd:1 3rd:0 Ran:6
Pre1999 - 1st:0 2nd:1 3rd:0 Ran:2
Win Prizemoney £0 *Total Prizemoney* £1,858
1999 Turf 0-6: (6f, 7f 4, 9f) (g-s, gd, g-f 2, frm 2)
Scopey, average filly, effective 6 to 7f, acts on gd to g-f, has worn blinkers. Turf high 64. Consistent.
**P T Walwyn [0-8] Hamdan Al Maktoum.*

AYEM (IRE) BHB 62f59a **RR 66f 59a** 32744
4 ch c Sharp Victor (USA) 10f **(56)** - Morning Crown (USA) (Chief's Crown (USA)) 9.8f **(72)**
Form - 044
Record 1999 - 1st:0 2nd:0 3rd:0 Ran:3
Pre1999 - 1st:0 2nd:0 3rd:0 Ran:3
Win Prizemoney £0 *Total Prizemoney* £712
1999 Turf 0-2: (16f, 20f) (g-f, frm) 1999 AW 0-1: (16f) (Equi)
Average colt. Turf high 66. He has shown very little on the Flat since arriving from Ireland, though he has been placed over hurdles.
**C Weedon [1-12] Mrs M A Peet (from L Browne in IRE [0-3] Jun 1998).*

AYE READY BHB 16f **RR** 106018
6 ch g Music Boy 6.5f **(56)** - Cindy's Princess (Electric) 10.1f **(61)**
Form - 00
Record 1999 - 1st:0 2nd:0 3rd:0 Ran:2
Pre1999 - 1st:0 2nd:0 3rd:0 Ran:13
Win Prizemoney £0 *Total Prizemoney* £207
1999 Turf 0-2: (5f, 8f) (g-f 2)
Very poor gelding, often wears blinkers.
**D A Nolan [0-5] Mrs J McFadyen-Murray (from Miss L A Perratt [0-10] Aug 1996).*

AYIDA (IRE) RR 23f 51077
3 b f Shernazar 11.8f **(71)** - Flower Dell (Wolver Hollow) 8f **(56)**
Form - 07
Record 1999 - 1st:0 2nd:0 3rd:0 Ran:2
1999 Turf 0-2: (10f, 11f) (gd, frm)
Unfurnished, currently little account filly. Turf high 23 (began Spt).
**G L Moore [0-2] Royal Palm Racing.*

AZIHAAM (USA) BHB 60f65a **RR 61f 65a** 4823[17]
3 ch f Cozzene (USA) 10.1f **(87)** - Tatwij (USA) (Topsider (USA)) 8.3f **(71)**
Form - 5601125520
Record 1999 - 1st:2 2nd:2 3rd:0 Ran:8
Pre1999 - 1st:0 2nd:0 3rd:0 Ran:4
Win Prizemoney £5,191 *Total Prizemoney* £6,993
Wins * **1999** *Feb Lingfi (STD) H 10f 55 66* <
* **1999** *Feb Lingfi (STD) H 10f 49 60*
1999 Turf 0-5: (9f, 10f 3, 11f) (gd 3, g-f, frm) 1999 AW 2-3: (10f 2-3) (Equi 2-3)
Scopey, average filly, effective 10 to 11f, best at 10f, acts on gd to frm - acts on Equi, often wears blinkers (extremely effectively), favours left handed tracks, favours tight tracks. Turf high 67 (1st run) - 2nd of 11 giving 11lb to Harp Player (5 Apr Warwick 11f gd RF 0595). AW high 66 - 1st of 8 getting 1lb from Lucky Nemo (27 Feb Lingfield RF 0377) - also 1st of 8 getting 23lb from Hormuz (6 Feb Lingfield RF 0238). She gradually improved on Equitrack at the start of the year, winning at Lingfield in February, losing the race in the Stewards' Room, but being reinstated on appeal. There was no such problem with her easy follow-up win over the same ten-furlong trip, and she has shown ability on turf since.
**N A Graham [2-10] Flying Colours Racing (from M P Tregoning [0-2] Spt 1998).*

AZIMAH BHB 68f **RR 68?f** 5197[19]
3 b f Unfuwain (USA) 11.4f **(74)** - Rafif (USA) (Riverman (USA)) 9.1f **(76)**
Form - 023240
Record 1999 - 1st:0 2nd:2 3rd:1 Ran:6
Win Prizemoney £0 *Total Prizemoney* £3,522
1999 Turf 0-6: (10f 4, 11f, 12f) (sft, gd 3, g-f, frm)
Workmanlike, average filly, effective 10 to 12f, acts on gd to frm. Turf high 68 - 2nd of 8 to Tariyfa (24 Spt Haydock 11f gd RF 4525).
**A C Stewart [0-6] Hamdan Al Maktoum.*

AZIRA **RR 38f** 5123[5]
2 ch f Arazi (USA) 9.2f **(74)** - Free City (USA) (Danzig (USA)) 8.4f **(76)**
Form - 5
Record 1999 - 1st:0 2nd:0 3rd:0 Ran:1
1999 Turf 0-1: (6f) (gd)
Currently moderate filly. **P R Chamings [0-1] Mrs Ann Jenkins.*

AZIZZI BHB 93f **RR 98f** 5110[1]
7 ch g Indian Ridge 7.6f **(74)** - Princess Silca Key (Grundy) 10.3f **(65)**
Form - 1453131
Record 1999 - 1st:3 2nd:0 3rd:2 Ran:7
Pre1999 - 1st:1 2nd:3 3rd:0 Ran:10
Win Prizemoney £22,232 *Total Prizemoney* £43,103
Wins * **1999** Oct Windso (SFT) H 5f 79 89+
* **1999** Oct Pontef (GD) H 5f 79 82
* **1999** Aug Newmar (GD) C 7f 69+
* **1996** Apr Kempto (G-F) 7f 91 <
1999 Turf 3-7: (5f 2-4, 6f, 7f 1-2) (g-s 2, gd 1-2, g-f 2-3)
Very useful gelding, effective 5f, acts on g-s to g-f. Turf high 89 (began Aug) - 1st of 19 giving 4lb to Classy Cleo (28 Oct Windsor RF 5110) - also 1st of 18 giving 1lb to Ambitious (18 Oct Pontefract RF 4933). This lightly-raced sort was runner-up in a Leopardstown Group Three in 1997, and also ran well in that year's Ayr Gold Cup, but showed nothing in just two starts the following year. He was having his first race for 11 months when outclassing the opposition in a seven-furlong Newmarket claimer in August, and ended the season in fine form with further victories in sprint handicaps at Pontefract and Windsor. **C R Egerton [4-17] Chris Brasher.*

AZOUZ PASHA (USA) BHB 110f **RR 109f** 4253[1]
3 b c Lyphard (USA) 10.6f **(75)** - Empress Club (ARG)(Farnesio (ARG))
Form - 14121
Record 1999 - 1st:3 2nd:1 3rd:0 Ran:5
Pre1999 - 1st:0 2nd:0 3rd:0 Ran:1
Win Prizemoney £56,216 *Total Prizemoney* £58,985
Wins * **1999** Spt Doncas (G-F) L 12f 109 <
* **1999** Jly Goodwo (FRM) H 9.9f 96 100
* **1999** Jun Lingfi (GD) 10f 87+
1999 Turf 3-5: (8f, 10f 2-2, 12f 1-2) (g-f 2-3, frm 1-2)
Scopey, Pattern-class colt, effective 10 to 12f, best at 12f, acts on g-f to frm, best on g-f, has worn blinkers. Turf high 109 - 1st of 5 getting 9lb from Algunnaas (10 Spt Doncaster RF 4253) - also 1st of 17 giving 13lb to West Escape (30 Jly Goodwood RF 3234). Made no mistake in a weak ten-furlong maiden at Lingfield on his reappearance, but found the likes of Rhythm Band and Sunstreak too good at Doncaster when dropped back to a mile. Back up to ten furlongs, he landed the competitive Globetrotter Handicap at Glorious Goodwood, but was just touched off after a thrilling battle with stable-companion New Abbey at Windsor. Ended his campaign with a fluent victory in a listed race at the St Leger meeting, when sporting a visor. **H R A Cecil [3-6] Wafic Said.*

AZULA BHB 72f **RR 77f** 5197[8]
3 b f Bluebird (USA) 7.9f **(71)** - Dimant Rose (USA) (Tromos) 11.3f **(72)**
Form - 71408
Record 1999 - 1st:1 2nd:0 3rd:0 Ran:5
Win Prizemoney £3,799 *Total Prizemoney* £4,287
Wins 1999 May Lingfi (G-F) 10f 76 <
1999 Turf 1-5: (8f, 10f 1-4) (g-s, gd 1-2, g-f, frm)
Leggy, above-average filly. Turf high 77 - 4th of 6 getting 7lb from Night Venture (26 Jun Newcastle 10f frm RF 2338) - also 1st of 8 from Another Rainbow (29 May Lingfield RF 1583).
**H Morrison [0-2] & Mrs John Wilson (from P W Chapple-Hyam [1-3] Jun 1999).*

AZUR (IRE) BHB 83f **RR 82+f** 4944[1]
2 b f Brief Truce (USA) 9.1f **(73)** - Bayadere (USA) (Green Dancer (USA)) 10.3f **(74)**
Form - 81
Record 1999 - 1st:1 2nd:0 3rd:0 Ran:2
Win Prizemoney £3,509 *Total Prizemoney* £3,509
Wins * **1999** Oct Lingfi (G-F) 7f 82+ <
1999 Turf 1-2: (7f 1-2) (gd 1-1, g-f)
Currently decent filly. Turf high 82 (began Oct) - 1st of 16 getting 3lb from Cracow (19 Oct Lingfield RF 4944).
**J R Fanshawe [1-2] B M Guerin.*

AZZAN (USA) BHB 65f **RR 67df** 4094[18]
3 b br c Gulch (USA) 9.6f **(79)** - Dixieland Dream (USA) (Dixieland Band (USA)) 7f **(74)**
Form - 40480
Record 1999 - 1st:0 2nd:0 3rd:0 Ran:5
Pre1999 - 1st:0 2nd:0 3rd:0 Ran:3
Win Prizemoney £0 *Total Prizemoney* £845
1999 Turf 0-5: (8f 5) (gd, frm 4)
Workmanlike, average colt, effective 6 to 8f, best at 8f, acts on gd to frm, best on gd, has worn blinkers. Turf high 74 (1st run) - 4th of 13 giving 4lb to Prairie Wolf (15 Apr Ripon 8f gd RF 0708).
**J L Dunlop [0-8] Hamdan Al Maktoum.*

BAAJIL BHB 56f62a **RR 44f 62a** 1553[9]
4 b g Marju (IRE) 9.2f **(76)** - Arctic River (FR) (Arctic Tern (USA)) 8.9f **(69)**
Form - 422400
Record 1999 - 1st:0 2nd:2 3rd:0 Ran:5
Pre1999 - 1st:0 2nd:1 3rd:1 Ran:4
Win Prizemoney £0 *Total Prizemoney* £4,385
1999 Turf 0-2: (8f, 10f) (sft, g-f) 1999 AW 0-3: (10f 3) (Equi 3)
Neat, average gelding. Turf high 22. AW high 66.
**D J S Cosgrove [0-8] Crown Pkg & Mailing Svs Ltd (from L M Cumani [0-1] Oct 1997).*

BAALBEK BHB 71f **RR 75f** 5197[6]
3 b f Barathea (IRE) - Temple Row (Ardross) 10.6f **(68)**
Form - 5054201336
Record 1999 - 1st:1 2nd:1 3rd:2 Ran:10
Win Prizemoney £4,162 *Total Prizemoney* £7,248
Wins * **1999** Aug Bright (SFT) 8f 75 <
1999 Turf 1-10: (7f, 8f 1-7, 10f, 11f) (g-s 1-1, gd 3, g-f 2, frm 3, hrd)
Above-average filly, effective 8 to 10f, best at 8f, acts on g-s to gd, best on gd, prefers tight tracks. Turf high 75 - 1st of 6 getting 5lb from Global Concept (18 Aug Brighton RF 3734). Consistent. She got off the mark by the narrowest of margins at Brighton when racing on soft ground for the first time, and ran well at a mile throughout the final quarter of the season. A mile on soft ground suits her. **L M Cumani [1-10] Lord Hartington.*

BABY BARRY BHB 84f **RR 77f** 5023[2]
2 b c Komaite (USA) 6.9f **(61)** - Malcesine (IRE) **(38f 31a)** (Auction Ring

(USA)) 8.6f **(65)**
Form - 022362334012
Record 1999 - 1st:1 2nd:4 3rd:3 Ran:12
Win Prizemoney £2,547 *Total Prizemoney* £13,294
Wins * 1999 Oct Redcar (GD) 5f 77 <
1999 Turf 1-10: (5f 1-7, 6f 3) (g-s 2, gd 3, g-f 2, frm 1-3) 1999 AW 0-2: (5f 2) (Fibr 2)
Above-average colt, effective 5 to 6f, best at 5f, acts on gd to frm - acts on Fibr, has worn blinkers (extremely effectively). Turf high 77 - 1st of 22 giving 2lb to Footprints (14 Oct Redcar RF 4877). AW high 79 (1st run) - 2nd of 10 giving 3lb to Bescaby Blue (6 May Southwell 5f Fibr RF 1064). **Mrs G S Rees [1-12] John Barry.*

BABY ROCKET (IRE) BHB 33f RR 23f 4943^{15}

2 ch f Imperial Frontier (USA) 7f **(65)** - Boherbawn (IRE) **(50f)** (Shernazar) 10.2f **(73)**
Form - 000
Record 1999 - 1st:0 2nd:0 3rd:0 Ran:3
1999 Turf 0-3: (6f 2, 7f) (g-s, gd, frm)
Currently little account filly. Turf high 23 (began Aug).
**R Hannon [0-3] Mrs H F Prendergast.*

BABY SPICE BHB 36f44a RR 37df 44a 4228^{4}

4 ch f Then Again 7.4f **(52)** - Starawak (Star Appeal) 9.6f **(65)**
Form - 07053770404
Record 1999 - 1st:0 2nd:0 3rd:1 Ran:9
Pre1999 - 1st:1 2nd:0 3rd:0 Ran:12
Win Prizemoney £2,553 *Total Prizemoney* £2,874
Wins * 1998 *Oct Wolver (STD) 7f 47* <
1999 Turf 0-8: (8f 6, 9f, 10f) (gd 3, g-f 2, frm 3) 1999 AW 0-1: (8f) (Fibr)
Leggy, very moderate filly, effective 7 to 8f, acts on g-f - acts on Fibr, has worn blinkers, likes tight tracks. Turf high 51 - 3rd of 18 getting 13lb from Tumbleweed Hero (10 May Windsor 8f g-f RF 1136). Inconsistent.
**R F JohnsonHoughton [1-12] W H Ponsonby (from M R Channon [0-9] Jly 1998).*

BACCHUS RR 63f 4880^{5}

5 b g Prince Sabo 6.6f **(64)** - Bonica (Rousillon (USA)) 8.2f **(74)**
Form - 0015015
Record 1999 - 1st:2 2nd:0 3rd:0 Ran:7
Pre1999 - 1st:1 2nd:0 3rd:0 Ran:8
Win Prizemoney £11,597 *Total Prizemoney* £11,888
Wins * 1999 Aug Beverl (GD) H 7.5f 58 63
*** 1999** Jly Beverl (G-F) SH 7.5f 54 58
1997 Jly Newmar (G-S) 6f 80 <
1999 Turf 2-7: (7f 2-5, 8f 2) (g-s, gd, g-f 2, frm 2-3)
Average gelding, effective 7f, acts on frm. Turf high 63 - 1st of 15 giving 5lb to Bachelors Pad (28 Aug Beverley RF 3952) - also 1st of 15 giving 5lb to Fancy A Fortune (2 Jly Beverley RF 2480). Popped up at double carpet in a Beverley seller in July, and was heavily backed to follow up at the same track next time, but could not deliver. He still had a chance of winning at Haydock in August until hampered by a loosening bandage, and he gained compensation for that misfortune when taking a Beverley handicap next time.
**Miss J A Camacho [2-9] L A Bolingbroke (from A C Stewart [1-6] Oct 1997).*

BACH (IRE) RR 92f 2073^{1}

2 b c Caerleon (USA) 10.9f **(79)** - Producer (USA) (Nashua) 10.3f **(67)**
Form - 11
1999 Turf 2-2: (7f 2-2) (gd 1-1, g-f 1-1)
Currently useful colt. Turf high 92 - 1st of 7 giving 5lb to Hastenby (17 Jun Ascot RF 2073). Bred to be something special, he easily won his maiden but had to work to follow up in the Chesham Stakes at Royal Ascot. It is difficult to work out where he figures among the O'Brien juveniles.
**A P O'Brien in IRE [2-2] Satish K Sanan & Mrs John Magnier.*

BACHELOR BHB 67f RR 62+f 4648^{1}

3 b c In The Wings 11.2f **(77)** - So Romantic (IRE) (Teenoso (USA)) 9.9f **(72)**
Form - 76321
Record 1999 - 1st:1 2nd:1 3rd:1 Ran:5
Win Prizemoney £3,126 *Total Prizemoney* £4,525
Wins * 1999 Spt Salisb (HVY) H 14.1f 60 62+ <
1999 Turf 1-5: (10f 2, 14f 1-3) (g-s 1-1, gd, g-f, frm 2)
Lengthy, average colt. Turf high 62 (began Jly) - 1st of 15 getting 2lb from Tommy Carson (29 Spt Salisbury RF 4648).
**M A Jarvis [1-5] Saif Ali.*

BACHELORS PAD BHB 54f RR 60f 4758^{11}

5 b g Pursuit of Love 9.5f **(69)** - Note Book (Mummy's Pet) 7.7f **(60)**
Form - 06324070572520
Record 1999 - 1st:0 2nd:3 3rd:1 Ran:14
Pre1999 - 1st:1 2nd:2 3rd:2 Ran:18
Win Prizemoney £4,413 *Total Prizemoney* £16,818
Wins 1996 Spt Goodwo (G-F) 6f 96+ <
1999 Turf 0-14: (7f 2, 8f 6, 9f 2, 10f 4) (gd 7, g-f, frm 5, hrd)
Average gelding, effective 7 to 8f, acts on g-f to hrd, has worn blinkers. Turf high 62. Generally ran well last term, but he has not won since his two-year-old days. Suited by forcing tactics.
**D Nicholls [0-14] David Waters (from W Jarvis [1-18] Spt 1998).*

BACHIR (IRE) RR 103f $4514a^{3}$

2 b c Desert Style (IRE) - Morning Welcome (IRE) (Be My Guest (USA)) 9.3f **(67)**
Form - 1133
Record 1999 - 1st:2 2nd:0 3rd:2 Ran:4
Win Prizemoney £27,359 *Total Prizemoney* £53,193
Wins * 1999 Jly Goodwo (G-F) G2 6f 103+ <
*** 1999** Jly Chepst (G-F) 6.1f 84++
1999 Turf 2-4: (6f 2-3, 7f) (sft, gd, frm 2-2)
Very useful colt. Turf high 103 (began Jly) - also 1st of 7 from Hunting Lion (28 Jly Goodwood RF 3208). He won a relatively weak renewal of the Richmond Stakes and was put in his place behind Fasliyev and Giant's Causeway later in the season. Bred for speed, he ran freely when tried over seven furlongs in the Prix de la Salamandre and is unlikely to stay beyond that trip. He has reportedly joined Godolphin.
**J H M Gosden [2-4] Sheikh Maktoum Al Maktoum.*

BACKCLOTH (IRE) BHB 97f RR 97f 4798^{2}

3 b g Scenic 10.6f **(66)** - Traumerei (GER) (Surumu (GER)) 10f **(83)**
Form - 3132112
Record 1999 - 1st:3 2nd:2 3rd:2 Ran:7
Pre1999 - 1st:0 2nd:0 3rd:1 Ran:2
Win Prizemoney £20,923 *Total Prizemoney* £28,346
Wins * 1999 Spt Pontef (GD) H 10f 87 94 <
*** 1999** Aug Sandow (G-S) H 10f 82 83++
*** 1999** Apr Leices (HVY) H 11.8f 73 88+
1999 Turf 3-7: (10f 2-5, 12f 1-2) (sft 1-1, gd 2, g-f 2-4)
Light-framed, very useful gelding, effective 10 to 12f, best at 10f, acts on sft to g-f, likes tight tracks. Turf high 97 - 2nd of 13 getting 15lb from Monsajem (9 Oct Ascot 10f gd RF 4798) - also 1st of 11 getting 6lb from Weet-A-Minute (23 Spt Pontefract RF 4505). He went from strength-to-strength once waiting tactics were employed and has developed into a smart middle-distance handicapper. Sold for 110,000 guineas at Newmarket in October to continue his career in Saudi Arabia.
**J L Dunlop [3-9] The Hon Sir David Sieff.*

BACKEND CHARLIE RR 39f 1721^{5}

5 b g Sylvan Express 9.6f **(45)** - Red Eska (Smackover) 6f **(52)**
Form - 65
Record 1999 - 1st:0 2nd:0 3rd:0 Ran:2
1999 Turf 0-2: (12f, 14f) (g-f, frm)
Very moderate gelding. Turf high 39. **B W Murray [0-6] G Bulmer.*

BACKHANDER (IRE) BHB 26f34a RR 39tf 34a 127^{8}

7 b g Cadeaux Genereux 7.9f **(76)** - Chevrefeuille (Ile de Bourbon (USA)) 10.1f **(67)**
Form - 748
Record 1999 - 1st:0 2nd:0 3rd:0 Ran:3
Pre1999 - 1st:0 2nd:6 3rd:1 Ran:41
Win Prizemoney £0 *Total Prizemoney* £5,030
1999 AW 0-3: (6f 2, 8f) (Fibr 3)
Very moderate gelding, has worn blinkers. AW high 32.
**M Waring [0-19] Lester Metcalf (from R T Phillips [0-10] Spt 1997).*

BACKSCRATCHER BHB 26f RR 35f 4912^{8}

5 b g Backchat (USA) 11.8f **(53)** - Tiernee Quintana (Artaius (USA)) 9f **(69)**
Form - 568

Record 1999 - 1st:0 2nd:0 3rd:0 Ran:3
Pre1999 - 1st:0 2nd:0 3rd:0 Ran:1
1999 Turf 0-3: (12f 2, 16f) (g-s, gd, frm)
Very moderate gelding. Turf high 35 (began Aug).
**S Gollings [0-7] G D Dalrymple.*

BADAAYER (USA) BHB 96f **RR 100f** 5219[2]
3 b br f Silver Hawk (USA) 11.2f **(85)** - Katiba (USA) (Gulch (USA)) 8f **(81)**
Form - 14132
Record 1999 - 1st:2 2nd:1 3rd:1 Ran:5
Win Prizemoney £10,991 *Total Prizemoney* £18,283
Wins * **1999** Spt Nottin (GD) 10f 88 <
* **1999** Aug Salisb (GD) 8f 84
1999 Turf 2-5: (8f 1-1, 10f 1-3, 12f) (sft, gd 1-2, frm 1-2)
Scopey, very useful filly. Turf high 100 (began Aug) - 2nd of 7 getting 11lb from Maylane (6 Nov Doncaster 12f sft RF 5219). She did not live up to her Classic entry, but developed into a useful and enthusiastic filly. Effective up to a mile and a half, she has plenty of physical scope and should win a Listed race in 2000.
**J L Dunlop [2-5] Hamdan Al Maktoum.*

BADAGARA BHB 89f **RR 87f** 3050[8]
3 b g Warning 8.1f **(77)** - Badawi (USA) (Diesis) 9.3f **(69)**
Form - 138
Record 1999 - 1st:1 2nd:0 3rd:1 Ran:3
Pre1999 - 1st:0 2nd:1 3rd:1 Ran:3
Win Prizemoney £9,296 *Total Prizemoney* £12,488
Wins * **1999** Apr Newbur (G-F) H 8f 85 87 <
1999 Turf 1-3: (8f 1-2, 10f) (g-s, gd, frm 1-1)
Light-framed, useful gelding, effective 7 to 8f, best at 8f, acts on g-s to frm. Turf high 87 - 3rd of 5 giving 6lb to Tiger Talk (24 Apr Sandown 8f g-s RF 0845) - also 1st of 12 giving 2lb to Mayaro Bay (16 Apr Newbury RF 0718).
**C E Brittain [1-6] Sheikh Marwan Al Maktoum.*

BADGE (USA) RR 1351a[3]
3 ch c Air Forbes Won (USA) - Revenge Time (USA) (Raja's Revenge (USA))
Form - 3
1999 AW 0-1: (10f) (Dirt)
Currently high-class colt. (1st run) - 3rd of 13 to Charismatic (15 May Pimlico 10f Dirt RF 1351a). High-class American-trained colt who finished third behind Charismatic in the Preakness Stakes.
**J Aquilino in USA [0-1] Southbelle Stable.*

BADRINATH (IRE) BHB 58f45a **RR 59f 45a** 5162[5]
5 b g Imperial Frontier (USA) 7f **(65)** - Badedra (Kings Lake (USA)) 10.8f **(67)**
Form - 000842035
Record 1999 - 1st:0 2nd:1 3rd:1 Ran:8
Pre1999 - 1st:3 2nd:3 3rd:2 Ran:19
Win Prizemoney £9,566 *Total Prizemoney* £13,905
Wins * 1998 Spt Redcar (G-F) SH 10f 47 53
* 1998 Jun Newmar (GD) H 8f 40 48
* 1998 *Jan Lingfi (STD) 10f 55* <
1999 Turf 0-6: (10f 5, 12f) (gd 2, g-f 3, frm) 1999 AW 0-2: (10f, 12f) (Equi 2)
Fair gelding, effective 8 to 11f, best at 10f, acts on g-f to frm - acts on AW, likes tight tracks, and excels at Redcar. Turf high 59 (began Jly) - 3rd of 18 getting 1lb from Imprevue (20 Oct Nottingham 10f frm RF 4993). AW high 18. Inconsistent.
**H J Collingridge [3-24] The Headquarters Partnership IV (from J Pearce [0-3] Jan 1999).*

BADR RAINBOW BHB 82f **RR 86f** 5024[2]
2 b c Rainbow Quest (USA) 11.2f **(81)** - Baaderah (IRE) **(102df)** (Cadeaux Genereux)
Form - 0042
Record 1999 - 1st:0 2nd:1 3rd:0 Ran:4
Win Prizemoney £0 *Total Prizemoney* £1,616
1999 Turf 0-4: (7f 3, 8f) (g-s, gd, frm 2)
Useful colt. Turf high 80 (began Jly) - 4th of 18 to Frontier (8 Oct Lingfield 7f g-s RF 4784).
**M A Jarvis [0-4] Sheikh Ahmed Al Maktoum.*

BAFFIN BAY BHB 79f **RR 78f** 4594[10]
4 b c Bustino 11f **(64)** - Surf Bird (Shareef Dancer (USA)) 9.9f **(73)**
Form - 000020
Record 1999 - 1st:0 2nd:1 3rd:0 Ran:6
Pre1999 - 1st:2 2nd:0 3rd:0 Ran:8
Win Prizemoney £8,651 *Total Prizemoney* £11,243
Wins * 1998 May Haydoc (GD) H 14f 85 91+ <
* 1997 Oct Leices (GD) 8f 76
1999 Turf 0-6: (10f, 12f 4, 16f) (gd 2, g-f 2, frm, hrd)
Well made, above-average colt, effective 12 to 14f, acts on gd, has worn blinkers. Turf high 78. **H R A Cecil [2-14] L B Holliday.*

BAGNI DI PETRIOLO (ITY) RR 100f 1719a[10]
3 b c Nordance (USA) 7.4f **(69)** - Tanah Lot (ITY) (Scouting Miller)
Form - 410
1999 Turf 1-2: (10f 1-1, 12f) (g-f 1-2)
Currently very useful colt. Turf high 100 (1st run) - 1st of 6 from Antoniocastiglione (2 May San Siro RF 1075a). A Listed race winner in Italy, he goes particularly well over ten furlongs on good to firm ground, but was unable to make his mark in Group company.
**F Camici in ITY [1-3].*

BAHAMAS (IRE) BHB 58f **RR 47f** 4995[13]
2 b c Barathea (IRE) - Rum Cay (USA) (Our Native (USA)) 11.2f **(63)**
Form - 0000
Record 1999 - 1st:0 2nd:0 3rd:0 Ran:4
1999 Turf 0-4: (6f, 7f 3) (g-s 2, gd, frm)
Moderate colt. Turf high 47 (began Spt).
**Sir Mark Prescott [0-4] Eclipse Thoro'breds House III.*

BAHAMIAN BANDIT BHB 109f **RR 110f** 3983[7]
3 b c First Trump - Sound of the Sea (Windjammer (USA)) 7f **(59)**
Form - 16827
Record 1999 - 1st:1 2nd:1 3rd:0 Ran:5
Pre1999 - 1st:1 2nd:0 3rd:0 Ran:2
Win Prizemoney £8,473 *Total Prizemoney* £16,651
Wins * **1999** Apr Newmar (GD) 7f 97+ <
* 1998 Spt Lingfi (G-S) 6f 95+
1999 Turf 1-5: (7f 1-1, 8f 3, 10f) (gd, g-f 1-2, frm 2)
Scopey, Group-class colt, effective 8f, acts on g-f to frm. Turf high 110 - 6th of 16 to Island Sands (1 May Newmarket 8f frm RF 0958). Highly regarded, he suffered from stomach ulcers after chancing his arm in the English and German 2,000 Guineas. A creditable second behind Slip Stream at Goodwood in July, he failed to stay an extended 10 furlongs at Windsor the following month and is worth another chance over slightly shorter trips. He has reportedly come under the Godolphin umbrella. **R Hannon [2-7] Lucayan Stud.*

BAHAMIAN PIRATE (USA) BHB 65f58a **RR 68f 58a** 3661[1]
4 ch g Housebuster (USA) 7f **(81)** - Shining Through (USA) (Deputy Minister (CAN)) 7.4f **(80)**
Form - 4321
Record 1999 - 1st:1 2nd:1 3rd:1 Ran:4
Pre1999 - 1st:0 2nd:1 3rd:0 Ran:5
Win Prizemoney £3,485 *Total Prizemoney* £6,339
Wins * **1999** Aug Ripon (GD) 5f 68 <
1999 Turf 1-1: (5f 1-1) (gd 1-1) 1999 AW 0-3: (6f 2, 7f) (Fibr 3)
Average gelding. (1st run). AW high 61.
**D Nicholls [1-7] Lhendup Dorji (from C Collins in IRE [0-2] May 1998).*

BAHAMIAN PRINCE (IRE) RR 17f 3577[13]
2 b c Night Shift (USA) 8.1f **(73)** - Fairy Water **(82f)** (Warning)
Form - 0
Record 1999 - 1st:0 2nd:0 3rd:0 Ran:1
1999 Turf 0-1: (7f) (g-f)
Currently poor colt. **H R A Cecil [0-1] Lucayan Stud.*

BAHIA BLANCA SUN (IRE) BHB 52f **RR 54f** 419[3]
4 b g Tirol 8.1f **(64)** - Wild Applause (IRE) (Sadler's Wells (USA)) 10f **(76)**
Form - 3
Record 1999 - 1st:0 2nd:0 3rd:1 Ran:1
Pre1999 - 1st:0 2nd:0 3rd:0 Ran:3
Win Prizemoney £0 *Total Prizemoney* £506
1999 AW 0-1: (14f) (Fibr)
Leggy, fair gelding. (1st run) - 3rd of 11 giving 17lb to Mrs Pickles (10 Mar Southwell 14f Fibr RF 0419). **J L Eyre [0-4] Sunpak Potatoes.*

BAHRAIN (IRE) RR 67f 1393[10]
3 ch c Lahib (USA) 8f **(69)** - Twin Island (IRE) (Standaan (FR)) 7f **(55)**
Form - 50
Record 1999 - 1st:0 2nd:0 3rd:0 Ran:2
Pre1999 - 1st:0 2nd:0 3rd:0 Ran:1
1999 Turf 0-2: (7f, 8f) (gd, frm)
Scopey, currently average colt. Turf high 67.
**A P Jarvis [0-2] Ms Julie Greenacre (from Sir Mark Prescott [0-1] Oct 1998).*

BAILEYS BLACK TIE BHB 62f **RR 62f** 4105[14]
3 b g Suave Dancer (USA) 10.7f **(68)** - Three Stars (Star Appeal) 9.6f **(65)**
Form - 6010710
Record 1999 - 1st:2 2nd:0 3rd:0 Ran:7
Win Prizemoney £4,917 *Total Prizemoney* £4,917
Wins * **1999** Aug Ripon (GD) SH 10f 57 62 <
* **1999** Jly Ripon (GD) S 10f 55
1999 Turf 2-7: (10f 2-5, 11f, 13f) (g-s, gd 1-2, g-f 1-2, frm 2)
Unfurnished, average gelding, effective 10f, acts on gd to g-f, prefers tight tracks. Turf high 62 - 1st of 16 giving 19lb to Miss Arch (21 Aug Ripon RF 3817) - also 1st of 17 getting 11lb from Raed (5 Jly Ripon RF 2561).
**M Johnston [2-7] G R Bailey Ltd (Baileys Horse Feeds).*

BAILEYS FIRECAT RR 66f 1434[3]
2 b f Catrail (USA) - Dazzling Fire (IRE) (Bluebird (USA)) 7.5f **(69)**
Form - 83
Record 1999 - 1st:0 2nd:0 3rd:1 Ran:2
Win Prizemoney £0 *Total Prizemoney* £504
1999 Turf 0-2: (5f 2) (frm 2)
Currently average filly. Turf high 66.
**M Johnston [0-2] G R Bailey Ltd (Baileys Horse Feeds).*

BAILEYS PRIZE (USA) RR 73f 4910[5]
2 ch c Mister Baileys - Mar Mar (USA) (Forever Casting (USA))
Form - 45
Record 1999 - 1st:0 2nd:0 3rd:0 Ran:2
Win Prizemoney £0 *Total Prizemoney* £430
1999 Turf 0-2: (6f, 7f) (gd 2)
Currently above-average colt. Turf high 73 (began Oct).
**M Johnston [0-2] Mrs Val Armstrong.*

BAILEY'S WHIRLWIND (USA) BHB 99f **RR 90f** 4596[12]
2 b f Mister Baileys - Tornado Cat (USA) (Storm Cat (USA))
Form - 0110
Record 1999 - 1st:2 2nd:0 3rd:0 Ran:4
Win Prizemoney £9,324 *Total Prizemoney* £9,324
Wins * **1999** Spt Yarmou (SFT) 6f 90+ <
* **1999** Aug Windso (GD) 6f 90+ <
1999 Turf 2-4: (6f 2-4) (g-s 1-1, g-f 2, frm 1-1)
Useful filly. Turf high 90 - 1st of 4 getting 7lb from Distinctly East (16 Spt Yarmouth RF 4354) - also 1st of 16 from Out of Africa (28 Aug Windsor RF 3981). Left her debut effort well behind when easily winning a Windsor novice event in August, and followed up at Yarmouth. Outclassed on her final start.
**M L W Bell [2-4] W J P Jackson.*

BAILIWICK FRONTIER (IRE) BHB 56f57a **RR 9f 57a** 5162[16]
8 b g Imperial Frontier (USA) 7f **(65)** - Twilight In Paris (Kampala) 8.5f **(56)**
Form - 4706600
Record 1999 - 1st:0 2nd:0 3rd:0 Ran:7
Pre1999 - 1st:4 2nd:2 3rd:7 Ran:26
Win Prizemoney £15,755 *Total Prizemoney* £20,841
Wins 1997 Oct Leopar (G-S) H 10f 71 68
1997 Spt Leopar (GD) H 10f 66 71+ <
1997 Jly Leopar (GD) H 7f 60 52+
1996 Aug Fairyh (GD) H 8f 58 58
1999 Turf 0-6: (8f 3, 9f, 10f 2) (sft, g-f 4, frm) 1999 AW 0-1: (8f) (Fibr)
Very poor gelding, effective 8f, acts on g-f, likes left handed tracks. Turf high 63 (1st run) (began Jly) - 4th of 15 getting 6lb from Markskeepingfaith (21 Jly Naas 8f g-f RF 3183a). Inconsistent.
**D Carroll [0-2] John Geoghegan (from John Geoghegan in IRE [3-17] Spt 1999).*

BAISSE D'ARGENT (IRE) BHB 52f **RR 38f** 3854[11]
3 b g Common Grounds 8.1f **(66)** - Fabulous Pet (Somethingfabulous (USA)) 9.5f **(75)**
Form - 87600
Record 1999 - 1st:0 2nd:0 3rd:0 Ran:5
Pre1999 - 1st:1 2nd:0 3rd:0 Ran:3
Win Prizemoney £3,184 *Total Prizemoney* £3,447
Wins * 1998 Spt Mussel (GD) 8f 74 <
1999 Turf 0-5: (10f 2, 12f 2, 14f) (sft, g-f 3, frm)
Workmanlike, very moderate gelding, effective 8f, acts on frm, has worn blinkers. Turf high 60.
**D J S Cosgrove [1-8] Winning Circle Racing Club Ltd.*

BAJAN BELLE (IRE) BHB 78f **RR 71+f** 2862[1]
2 b f Efisio 7.7f **(69)** - With Love (Be My Guest (USA)) 9.3f **(67)**
Form - 31
Record 1999 - 1st:1 2nd:0 3rd:1 Ran:2
Win Prizemoney £2,697 *Total Prizemoney* £3,097
Wins * **1999** Jly Carlis (FRM) 5f 71+ <
1999 Turf 1-2: (5f 1-2) (frm 1-2)
Currently above-average filly. Turf high 71 (began Jly) - 1st of 6 from Shalarise (16 Jly Carlisle RF 2862).
**M Johnston [1-2] R H A Smith.*

BAJAN BROKER (IRE) RR 65f 4943[3]
2 br f Turtle Island (IRE) - Foxrock (Ribero) 9.3f **(56)**
Form - 43
Record 1999 - 1st:0 2nd:0 3rd:1 Ran:2
Win Prizemoney £0 *Total Prizemoney* £506
1999 Turf 0-2: (7f 2) (sft, gd)
Currently average filly. Turf high 65 (began Spt) - 3rd of 15 getting 3lb from Atavus (19 Oct Lingfield 7f gd RF 4943).
**J E Banks [0-2] P D Burnett.*

BAJAN SUNSET (IRE) RR 53f 4898[12]
2 ch c Mujtahid (USA) 7.4f **(69)** - Dubai Lady (Kris) 9.5f **(73)**
Form - 0
Record 1999 - 1st:0 2nd:0 3rd:0 Ran:1
1999 Turf 0-1: (8f) (gd)
Currently fair colt. **J D Bethell [0-1] Mrs John Lee.*

BAKKAR (IRE) BHB 79f **RR 78f** 2336[15]
5 b g Darshaan 11.9f **(81)** - Bayyasa (IRE) (Caerleon (USA)) 8.6f **(71)**
Form - 70
Record 1999 - 1st:0 2nd:0 3rd:0 Ran:2
Pre1999 - 1st:2 2nd:1 3rd:0 Ran:3
Win Prizemoney £4,966 *Total Prizemoney* £5,896
Wins 1997 Oct Cork (GD) 12f 87+ <
1997 Spt Dundal (SFT) 12f 80
1999 Turf 0-2: (16f, 19f) (g-f, frm)
Above-average gelding. Turf high 78. Better known as a hurdler these days.
**T D Easterby [1-9] Burke's 5th Family Settlement (from J Oxx in IRE [2-3] Oct 1997).*

BALA BHB 35f **RR 24f** 2275[20]
4 ch f Casteddu 7.4f **(54)** - Baladee (Mummy's Pet) 7.7f **(60)**
Form - 000
Record 1999 - 1st:0 2nd:0 3rd:0 Ran:3
Pre1999 - 1st:0 2nd:0 3rd:1 Ran:7
Win Prizemoney £0 *Total Prizemoney* £760
1999 Turf 0-3: (5f, 6f 2) (gd, frm 2)
Scopey, little account filly. Turf high 24.
**N E Berry [0-3] M T Lawrance (from H Morrison [0-7] Oct 1998).*

BALA HASAD BHB 71f **RR 62f** 5059[7]
2 b c Elmaamul (USA) 8.1f **(70)** - Astern (USA) (Polish Navy (USA)) 8f **(67)**
Form - 407
Record 1999 - 1st:0 2nd:0 3rd:0 Ran:3
Win Prizemoney £0 *Total Prizemoney* £218
1999 Turf 0-3: (7f, 8f 2) (g-s 2, gd)
Currently average colt. Turf high 62 (began Spt).
**M P Tregoning [0-3] Khalid Khalifa Al Nabooda.*

BALANAK (USA) BHB 59f **RR 61f** 4581[14]
8 b g Shahrastani (USA) 11.5f **(69)** - Banque Privee (USA) (Private Account (USA)) 8.5f **(74)**
Form - 4230
Record 1999 - 1st:0 2nd:1 3rd:1 Ran:4
Win Prizemoney £0 *Total Prizemoney* £2,336
1999 Turf 0-4: (16f 2, 17f, 18f) (g-s, gd, g-f 2)
Average gelding, often wears blinkers. Turf high 61 (1st run) (began Aug) - 4th of 13 giving 4lb to Galapino (12 Aug Sandown 16f g-f RF 3582).
**D R Gandolfo [5-37] M A Dore.*

BALANITA (IRE) BHB 72f56a **RR 72f 56a** 4240[19]
4 b g Anita's Prince 6f **(62)** - Ballybannon (Ballymore) 7.3f **(64)**
Form - 46200
Record 1999 - 1st:0 2nd:1 3rd:0 Ran:3
Pre1999 - 1st:2 2nd:0 3rd:0 Ran:13
Win Prizemoney £6,353 *Total Prizemoney* £8,007
Wins * 1998 Jly Windso (GD) H 6f 67 76 <
* 1997 Oct Bright (G-F) H 7f 60 67
1999 Turf 0-3: (7f 3) (gd, g-f, frm)
Neat, above-average gelding, effective 6 to 7f, acts on g-f to frm. Turf high 72 (1st run) (began Aug) - 2nd of 15 giving 4lb to Point of Dispute (13 Aug Lingfield 7f frm RF 3612).
**B Palling [2-16] Philip Reynolds & Mrs Anita Quinn.*

BALENO (GER) RR 110f 932a[1]
5 b h Heraldiste (USA) 8.9f **(54)** - Blumme (GER) (Jadar (GER))
Form - 1
1999 Turf 1-1: (8f 1-1) (sft 1-1)
Group-class colt. (1st run) - 1st of 11 getting 2lb from Desert Track (25 Apr Dielsdorf RF 0932a).
**U Suter in SWI [1-1] Stall Weissenstein (from B Schutz in GER [0-4] Nov 1997).*

BALFOUR (IRE) BHB 57f **RR 64f** 4627[10]
2 b c Green Desert (USA) 7.8f **(78)** - Badawi (USA) (Diesis) 9.3f **(69)**
Form - 670
Record 1999 - 1st:0 2nd:0 3rd:0 Ran:3
1999 Turf 0-3: (6f, 7f 2) (g-s, gd, frm)
Currently average colt. Turf high 64 (began Aug).
**C E Brittain [0-3] Sheikh Marwan Al Maktoum.*

BALI BATIK (IRE) RR 44f 3212[12]
2 b g Barathea (IRE) - Miss Garuda (Persian Bold) 9.3f **(66)**
Form - 0
Record 1999 - 1st:0 2nd:0 3rd:0 Ran:1
1999 Turf 0-1: (6f) (frm)
Currently moderate gelding. **G Wragg [0-1] J L C Pearce.*

BALI DANCE BHB 36f53a **RR 27f 53a** 5153[7]
4 br f Rambo Dancer (CAN) 8.4f **(59)** - Baliana **(47df)** (Midyan (USA)) 6f **(60)**
Form - 07707
Record 1999 - 1st:0 2nd:0 3rd:0 Ran:5
Pre1999 - 1st:2 2nd:0 3rd:5 Ran:22
Win Prizemoney £4,710 *Total Prizemoney* £8,273
Wins * 1998 Jun Carlis (G-S) 8f 60
* 1997 *Dec Lingfi (STD) 7f 65* <
1999 Turf 0-5: (7f, 8f 3, 10f) (gd 3, g-f 2)
Neat, average filly, effective 8f, acts on gd to g-f, best on g-f, has worn blinkers, likes left handed tracks, likes tight tracks. Turf high 38 (began Spt). Becoming disappointing.
**C B B Booth [2-27] J A Porteous.*

BALIDARE RR 51f 4531[16]
2 b f King's Signet (USA) 7f **(51)** - Baligay (Balidar) 7.9f **(63)**
Form - 00
Record 1999 - 1st:0 2nd:0 3rd:0 Ran:2
1999 Turf 0-2: (5f, 6f) (g-s, frm)
Currently fair filly. Turf high 51 (began Spt).
**M J Weeden [0-2] E W Carnell.*

BALISADA BHB 116f **RR 114df** 4566[4]
3 ch f Kris 10f **(75)** - Balnaha (Lomond (USA)) 8.8f **(65)**
Form - 21244
Record 1999 - 1st:1 2nd:2 3rd:0 Ran:5
Pre1999 - 1st:1 2nd:1 3rd:1 Ran:3
Win Prizemoney £137,862 *Total Prizemoney* £180,125
Wins * 1999 Jun Ascot (G-F) G1 8f 113 <
* 1998 Oct Lingfi (HVY) 7f 84
1999 Turf 1-5: (8f 1-5) (sft, gd, g-f 1-2, frm)
Workmanlike, Group-class filly, effective 8f, acts on g-f to frm. Turf high 114 - 2nd of 8 giving 6lb to Ronda (7 Jly Newmarket 8f frm RF 2631) - also 1st of 9 from Golden Silca (16 Jun Ascot RF 2041). Inconsistent. She was heavily supported at long odds before producing an excellent turn-of-foot to win the Group 1 Coronation Stakes at Royal Ascot. A shade disappointing thereafter, she got in a tizz before her races toward the end of the season. She is likely to have one race in Dubai in the spring before retiring to stud.
**G Wragg [2-8] A E Oppenheimer.*

Balisada produced a good turn of foot to take the Coronation Stakes

BALI-STAR BHB 50f **RR 48f** 1955[11]
4 b g Alnasr Alwasheek 9.4f **(62)** - Baligay (Balidar) 7.9f **(63)**
Form - 800
Record 1999 - 1st:0 2nd:0 3rd:0 Ran:3
1999 Turf 0-3: (6f 2, 7f) (g-s, g-f, frm)
Workmanlike, currently moderate gelding. Turf high 48.
**M J Weeden [0-3] E W Carnell.*

BALLA D'AIRE (IRE) BHB 30f **RR 59f** 1582[9]
4 b br g Balla Cove - Silius (Junius (USA)) 7.7f **(65)**
Form - 0440
Record 1999 - 1st:0 2nd:0 3rd:0 Ran:2
Pre1999 - 1st:0 2nd:0 3rd:0 Ran:11
Win Prizemoney £0 *Total Prizemoney* £242
1999 AW 0-2: (16f 2) (Equi 2)
Workmanlike, fair gelding, has worn blinkers.
**B R Johnson [0-8] Miss Julie Reeves (from M L W Bell [0-6] Spt 1998).*

BALLADONIA BHB 94f **RR 94f** 4876[4]
3 b f Primo Dominie 7.2f **(67)** - Susquehanna Days (USA) (Chief's Crown (USA)) 9.8f **(72)**
Form - 21434824
Record 1999 - 1st:1 2nd:2 3rd:1 Ran:8
Pre1999 - 1st:0 2nd:2 3rd:0 Ran:2
Win Prizemoney £4,381 *Total Prizemoney* £16,455
Wins * 1999 May Goodwo (GD) 9f 82 <
1999 Turf 1-8: (8f, 9f 1-1, 10f 4, 12f 2) (g-s, gd 1-4, frm 3)
Scopey, useful filly, effective 10 to 12f, best at 10f, acts on g-s to frm, best on gd. Turf high 98 - 4th of 6 to Fairy Godmother (10 Jun Newbury 10f gd RF 1884). Consistent. She is genuine, but lacks the basic speed to win Listed races. From the family of Silver Patriarch, she is worth a try over extended distances.
**Lady Herries [1-10] D K R & Mrs J B C Oliver.*

BALLASILLA BHB 37f39a **RR 13f 39a** 863[17]
4 b f Puissance 7.1f **(60)** - Darussalam (Tina's Pet) 6.8f **(59)**
Form - 50848500
Record 1999 - 1st:0 2nd:0 3rd:0 Ran:3
Pre1999 - 1st:0 2nd:0 3rd:0 Ran:13
1999 Turf 0-1: (5f) (g-s) 1999 AW 0-2: (5f 2) (Fibr 2)
Workmanlike, very moderate filly, has worn blinkers. AW high 39. Consistent. **B Palling [0-16] Merthyr Motor Auctions.*

BALLET HIGH (IRE) BHB 70f **RR 72f** 723[3]
6 b g Sadler's Wells (USA) 11.3f **(87)** - Marie D'Argonne (FR) (Jefferson) 7.9f **(89)**
Form - 3
Record 1999 - 1st:0 2nd:0 3rd:1 Ran:1
Pre1999 - 1st:0 2nd:1 3rd:2 Ran:4
Win Prizemoney £0 *Total Prizemoney* £3,813
1999 Turf 0-1: (16f) (frm)
Above-average gelding. A half-brother to Polar Falcon, he ran quite well in a two-mile handicap at Newbury in April having been in action over hurdles during the winter.
**R Dickin [1-4] Wholebuild Ltd (from I A Balding [0-4] Spt 1996).*

BALLET-K BHB 76f **RR 76f** 2336[12]
5 ch m Gunner B 11.2f **(45)** - Nicolene (Nice Music)
Form - 83410
Record 1999 - 1st:1 2nd:0 3rd:1 Ran:5
Win Prizemoney £3,772 *Total Prizemoney* £4,616
Wins * 1999 Jun Bath (GD) H 17.2f 74 76 <
1999 Turf 1-5: (10f 3, 16f, 17f 1-1) (gd, g-f 1-1, frm 3)
Above-average filly. Turf high 76 - 1st of 10 giving 17lb to Legend of Love (12 Jun Bath RF 1941). A very useful bumper performer, she won on her handicap debut at Bath after three runs over too short a trip. **J Neville [4-9] Gallagher Enterprises Ltd.*

BALLET MASTER (USA) RR 83++f 820[4]
3 ch c Kingmambo (USA) 10.9f **(85)** - Danse Royale (IRE) (Caerleon (USA)) 8.6f **(71)**
Form - 4
Record 1999 - 1st:0 2nd:0 3rd:0 Ran:1
Pre1999 - 1st:1 2nd:0 3rd:0 Ran:1
Win Prizemoney £3,157 *Total Prizemoney* £3,582
Wins * 1998 Oct Yarmou (SFT) 7f 78++ <
1999 Turf 0-1: (8f) (g-s)
Tall, currently decent colt. Lived up to his lofty home reputation when winning a back-end maiden in 1998 by seven lengths. Out of a Group-winning half-sister to Salsabil and Marju, he looked an exciting prospect but had just the one outing at Sandown in the spring. **H R A Cecil [1-2] M Tabor Mrs Magnier & Niarchos Family.*

BALLETS RUSSES (IRE) BHB 50f **RR 58f** 5109[11]
2 b f Marju (IRE) 9.2f **(76)** - Elminya (IRE)(Sure Blade (USA)) 11.3f **(67)**
Form - 580
Record 1999 - 1st:0 2nd:0 3rd:0 Ran:3
1999 Turf 0-3: (6f, 7f, 8f) (g-s, gd 2)
Currently fair filly. Turf high 58 (began Spt).
**H J Collingridge [0-3] G B Amy.*

BALLINA LAD (IRE) BHB 58f **RR 67df** 4878[15]
3 b g Mac's Imp (USA) 5.6f **(54)** - Nationalartgallery (IRE) (Tate Gallery (USA)) 7.4f **(67)**
Form - 130000
Record 1999 - 1st:1 2nd:0 3rd:1 Ran:6
Pre1999 - 1st:1 2nd:0 3rd:0 Ran:7
Win Prizemoney £5,344 *Total Prizemoney* £6,151
Wins * 1999 May Ripon (G-F) H 6f 58 60
* 1998 May Newcas (G-S) 5f 81+ <
1999 Turf 1-6: (5f, 6f 1-4, 7f) (g-f 2, frm 1-4)
Neat, average gelding, effective 5f, acts on gd, has worn blinkers. Turf high 67. Becoming disappointing.
**J G FitzGerald [2-13] Mike Browne.*

BALLISTIC BOY BHB 65f **RR 61f** 4797[7]
2 ch c First Trump - Be Discreet (Junius (USA)) 7.7f **(65)**
Form - 007
Record 1999 - 1st:0 2nd:0 3rd:0 Ran:3
1999 Turf 0-3: (7f 3) (gd, frm 2)
Currently average colt. Turf high 61. **A T Murphy [0-3] A J Oliver.*

BALLSBRIDGE (IRE) RR 44f 4641[7]
2 b c Sadler's Wells (USA) 11.3f **(87)** - Future Treasure (Habitat) 9.4f **(70)**
Form - 7
Record 1999 - 1st:0 2nd:0 3rd:0 Ran:1
1999 Turf 0-1: (8f) (g-s)
Currently moderate colt.
**Sir Michael Stoute [0-1] M Tabor & Mrs John Magnier.*

BALLY CYRANO BHB 57f **RR 70df** 3396[10]
2 b c Cyrano de Bergerac 7.3f **(58)** - Iolite (Forzando) 7.6f **(59)**
Form - 3000
Record 1999 - 1st:0 2nd:0 3rd:1 Ran:4
Win Prizemoney £0 *Total Prizemoney* £376
1999 Turf 0-4: (5f 3, 6f) (g-f 3, frm)
Above-average colt. Turf high 70. **B A McMahon [0-4] C G Conway.*

BALLYKISSANGEL BHB 9f16a **RR 19df 16a** 3564[15]
6 ro g Hadeer 8.9f **(58)** - April Wind (Windjammer (USA)) 7f **(59)**
Form - 000
Record 1999 - 1st:0 2nd:0 3rd:0 Ran:3
Pre1999 - 1st:0 2nd:0 3rd:1 Ran:17
Win Prizemoney £0 *Total Prizemoney* £360
1999 Turf 0-2: (14f, 16f) (g-f, frm) 1999 AW 0-1: (14f) (Fibr)
Poor gelding, has worn blinkers. (began Aug).
**N Bycroft [0-29] G J Allison.*

BALLYMORRIS BOY (IRE) BHB 47f40a **RR 47f 40a** 5056[10]
3 b c Dolphin Street (FR) - Solas Abu (IRE) (Red Sunset) 8.2f **(63)**
Form - 430700382607700
Record 1999 - 1st:0 2nd:1 3rd:1 Ran:11
Pre1999 - 1st:0 2nd:0 3rd:1 Ran:5
Win Prizemoney £0 *Total Prizemoney* £2,021
1999 Turf 0-10: (6f 2, 7f 4, 8f 3, 10f) (g-s 2, gd, frm 6, hrd) 1999 AW 0-1: (10f) (Equi)
Leggy, moderate colt. Turf high 53. Inconsistent.
**J Pearce [0-15] Saracen Racing (from W R Muir [0-1] Oct 1998).*

BALLY PRIDE (IRE) BHB 100f **RR 100f** 4801[2]
2 ch c Pips Pride 6.7f **(70)** - Ballysnip (Ballymore) 7.3f **(64)**
Form - 352153762
Record 1999 - 1st:1 2nd:2 3rd:2 Ran:9
Win Prizemoney £59,000 *Total Prizemoney* £81,635
Wins * 1999 Jun Currag (G-F) 6.3f 93 <
1999 Turf 1-9: (5f, 6f 1-8) (gd 3, g-f 3, frm 1-3)
Very useful colt, effective 6f, acts on gd to frm, has worn blinkers. Turf high 100 - 2nd of 6 giving 8lb to Out of Africa (9 Oct York 6f gd RF 4801) - also 1st of 16 giving 5lb to Yara (25 Jun Curragh RF 2404a). He had shown promise before causing a surprise when winning a valuable sales race at the Curragh. A good third in the Gimcrack, he was only just touched off in a Listed race at York in October. Worth a try over seven furlongs.
**T D Easterby [1-9] Mrs Jennifer Pallister.*

BALSOX BHB 79f **RR 85f** 4553[16]
3 b g Alzao (USA) 9.8f **(73)** - Bobbysoxer (Valiyar) 8.5f **(73)**
Form - 1276540
Record 1999 - 1st:1 2nd:1 3rd:0 Ran:7
Pre1999 - 1st:0 2nd:0 3rd:0 Ran:2
Win Prizemoney £3,419 *Total Prizemoney* £7,256
Wins * 1999 Mar Nottin (G-S) 8.2f 76+ <
1999 Turf 1-7: (8f 1-2, 9f, 10f 2, 12f, 14f) (sft 1-1, g-s 2, gd 2, g-f, frm)
Workmanlike, useful gelding, effective 8f, acts on g-s, has worn blinkers, prefers tight tracks. Turf high 91 - 2nd of 5 giving 5lb to Tiger Talk (24 Apr Sandown 8f g-s RF 0845). He has shown his best form when there has been give in the ground, including when landing the odds on his reappearance, but has also not looked too keen when faced with a battle and may be one to treat with caution. **J L Dunlop [1-9] Hesmonds Stud.*

BAMBOO GARDEN (USA) BHB 59f58a **RR 52f 58a** 406[8]
3 b g Desert Secret (IRE) - Miss Mischievous (USA) (Brazen Brother (USA))
Form - 61358
Record 1999 - 1st:1 2nd:0 3rd:1 Ran:5
Pre1999 - 1st:0 2nd:0 3rd:0 Ran:3
Win Prizemoney £1,872 *Total Prizemoney* £2,341

Wins * **1999** *Feb Southw (STD) SH 8f 55 59* **<**
1999 AW 1-5: (8f 1-4, 10f) (Equi, Fibr 1-4)
Well made, fair gelding, effective 8f, - acts on Fibr, often wears blinkers (very effectively), favours left handed tracks, likes tight tracks. AW high 59 - 1st of 14 giving 20lb to Fourth Time Lucky (1 Feb Southwell RF 0205). Very moderate, his Southwell Fibresand victory came in a seller. **G C H Chung [1-8] J Tse.*

BANAFSAJYH (IRE) BHB 81f **RR 77f** 4542[3]
2 b f Lion Cavern (USA) 7.5f **(74)** -Arylh(USA)(Lyphard (USA)) 9.9f **(72)**
Form - 623
Record 1999 - 1st:0 2nd:1 3rd:1 Ran:3
Win Prizemoney £0 *Total Prizemoney* £1,733
1999 Turf 0-3: (6f 3) (g-f, frm 2)
Currently above-average filly. Turf high 77 (began Jly) - 3rd of 13 to Melanzana (24 Spt Redcar 6f frm RF 4542).
**A C Stewart [0-3] Hamdan Al Maktoum.*

BANBURY (USA) BHB 94f92a **RR 96f 92a** 2732[2]
5 b g Silver Hawk (USA) 11.2f **(85)** - Sugar Hollow (USA) (Val de L'Orne (FR)) 12f **(75)**
Form - 21011243222
Record 1999 - 1st:3 2nd:5 3rd:1 Ran:11
Pre1999 - 1st:1 2nd:0 3rd:2 Ran:7
Win Prizemoney £11,992 *Total Prizemoney* £36,674
Wins * **1999** *Mar Lingfi (STD) 12f 79*
* **1999** *Feb Lingfi (STD) H 12f 72 74*
* **1999** *Jan Lingfi (STD) C 12f 65+*
1997 May Redcar (GD) 10f 94 **<**
1999 Turf 0-5: (12f 4, 14f) (g-s, gd, g-f 2, frm) 1999 AW 3-6: (10f, 12f 3-4, 16f) (Equi 3-6)
Very useful gelding, effective 12 to 14f, acts on g-f, has worn blinkers (very effectively). Turf high 96 - 2nd of 8 getting 5lb from Rainbow Ways (10 Jly York 14f g-f RF 2732). AW high 82. A tough and useful middle-distance handicapper, he had a Listed race in the bag at York in July, but went lame close home and had to surrender the advantage. Off the track since then, he will win a decent prize granted a full recovery.
**C A Dwyer [3-11] Cedar Lodge Syndicate (from M Johnston [0-2] Jly 1998).*

BANCO SUIVI (IRE) RR 83f 5136[5]
2 b f Nashwan (USA) 10.3f **(79)** - Pay the Bank (High Top) 10.2f **(67)**
Form - 5
Record 1999 - 1st:0 2nd:0 3rd:0 Ran:1
1999 Turf 0-1: (7f) (gd)
Currently decent filly. (1st run) - 5th of 16 to Premier Prize (30 Oct Newmarket 7f gd RF 5136). **B W Hills [0-1] Wafic Said.*

BANDANNA BHB 94f **RR 82f** 5023[7]
2 gr f Bandmaster (USA) - Gratclo (Belfort (FR)) 6.8f **(63)**
Form - 142357
Record 1999 - 1st:1 2nd:1 3rd:1 Ran:6
Win Prizemoney £2,276 *Total Prizemoney* £10,869
Wins * **1999** May Chepst (GD) S 6.1f 68+ **<**
1999 Turf 1-6: (5f, 6f 1-5) (g-s, gd 1-3, g-f 2)
Decent filly, effective 5 to 6f, acts on gd to g-f. Turf high 82 - 2nd of 10 to Vita Spericolata (2 Jly Sandown 5f g-f RF 2499). Won a Chepstow seller on her debut, but has not been disgraced in much better company since, including when a fine third in the Princess Margaret. Suited by six furlongs. **R J Hodges [1-6] Miss R Dobson.*

BANDAR PERAK BHB 23f48a **RR 48a** 2767[10]
8 b g Aragon 7.7f **(58)** - Noire Small (USA) (Elocutionist (USA)) 8f **(77)**
Form - 800
Record 1999 - 1st:0 2nd:0 3rd:0 Ran:3
Pre1999 - 1st:2 2nd:0 3rd:3 Ran:17
Win Prizemoney £7,654 *Total Prizemoney* £8,117
1999 Turf 0-2: (14f, 16f) (gd, frm) 1999 AW 0-1: (14f) (Fibr)
Very poor gelding, has worn blinkers.
**R C Spicer [0-3] Miss Lara-May Benson (from M J Haynes [0-3] Spt 1995).*

BANDBOX (IRE) BHB 65f **RR 64df** 4699[11]
4 ch g Imperial Frontier (USA) 7f **(65)** - Dublah (USA) (Private Account (USA)) 8.5f **(74)**
Form - 70760323318300
Record 1999 - 1st:1 2nd:1 3rd:4 Ran:14
Pre1999 - 1st:1 2nd:7 3rd:2 Ran:23
Win Prizemoney £5,778 *Total Prizemoney* £15,552
Wins * **1999** Aug Leices (GD) 6f 66
1997 Oct Leices (GD) 6f 78 **<**
1999 Turf 1-14: (5f 5, 6f 1-9) (sft, gd 3, g-f 1-4, frm 6)
Workmanlike, average gelding, effective 5 to 6f, best at 6f, acts on gd to frm, best on frm, has worn blinkers. Turf high 66 - 1st of 8 from Fairy Prince (11 Aug Leicester RF 3551).
**M Salaman [1-26] Salaman, Brookes, Else (from S Mellor [1-11] Oct 1997).*

BANDLER CHING (IRE) BHB 71f **RR 75f** 4820[3]
2 b c Sri Pekan (USA) - Stanerra's Wish (IRE) (Caerleon (USA)) 8.6f **(71)**
Form - 32533
Record 1999 - 1st:0 2nd:1 3rd:3 Ran:5
Win Prizemoney £0 *Total Prizemoney* £4,089
1999 Turf 0-5: (7f 2, 8f 3) (g-f 2, frm 3)
Above-average colt. Turf high 75 (began Jly) - 2nd of 11 giving 5lb to Alabama Wurley (6 Aug Newmarket 7f g-f RF 3425).
**Pat Mitchell [0-3] Newmarket Connections Ltd (from C N Allen [0-2] Aug 1999).*

BANDOLERA BOY BHB 37f **RR 48f** 5002[10]
2 b c Casteddu 7.4f **(54)** - Explosiva (USA) (Explodent (USA)) 9.4f **(87)**
Form - 50070
Record 1999 - 1st:0 2nd:0 3rd:0 Ran:5
1999 Turf 0-5: (5f 2, 6f, 7f, 8f) (gd, frm 4)
Moderate colt. Turf high 48. **T J Naughton [0-5] T J Naughton.*

BANGALORE BHB 81f **RR 82f** 4677[6]
3 ch c Sanglamore (USA) 12.9f **(67)** - Ajuga (USA) (The Minstrel (CAN)) 10f **(72)**
Form - 1258336
Record 1999 - 1st:1 2nd:1 3rd:2 Ran:7
Pre1999 - 1st:0 2nd:0 3rd:0 Ran:2
Win Prizemoney £2,624 *Total Prizemoney* £7,626
Wins * **1999** Apr Pontef (SFT) 10f 85 **<**
1999 Turf 1-7: (10f 1-3, 12f 3, 15f) (sft 1-1, gd 4, g-f, frm)
Scopey, decent colt, effective 10 to 12f, best at 12f, acts on sft to frm, excels at Newmarket. Turf high 85 - 2nd of 10 giving 17lb to Enfilade (5 May Chester 12f g-f RF 1047) - also 1st of 9 from Truant (20 Apr Pontefract RF 0771). Consistent. Has joined Amanda Perrett. **B W Hills [1-9] K Abdulla.*

BAN GARDAI (IRE) BHB 48f35a **RR 52df 35a** 4091[12]
4 b f Mukaddamah (USA) 7.6f **(74)** - Femme Gendarme (USA) (Policeman (FR)) 9.8f **(80)**
Form - 768300040
Record 1999 - 1st:0 2nd:0 3rd:1 Ran:9
Win Prizemoney £0 *Total Prizemoney* £395
1999 Turf 0-6: (6f 2, 7f 2, 8f 2) (frm 5, hrd) 1999 AW 0-3: (7f, 8f, 9f) (Fibr 3)
Fair filly, effective 6 to 7f, acts on frm to hrd. Turf high 60 (1st run) - 3rd of 9 giving 2lb to Square Dancer (24 Jun Carlisle 6f hrd RF 2259). AW high 16. **E J Alston [0-9] Edges Farm Racing Stables Ltd.*

BANGLED BHB 63f **RR 67f** 4286[18]
2 ch c Beveled (USA) 6.9f **(64)** - Bangles **(62f 61a)** (Chilibang)
Form - 38450
Record 1999 - 1st:0 2nd:0 3rd:1 Ran:5
Win Prizemoney £0 *Total Prizemoney* £777
1999 Turf 0-5: (5f 2, 6f 3) (gd 2, g-f, frm 2)
Average colt. Turf high 67. **D J Coakley [0-5] J Rose.*

BANIYAR (IRE) RR 62f 4655[12]
2 ch c Alzao (USA) 9.8f **(73)** - Banaja (IRE) (Sadler's Wells (USA)) 10f **(76)**
Form - 0
Record 1999 - 1st:0 2nd:0 3rd:0 Ran:1
1999 Turf 0-1: (7f) (gd)
Currently average colt. **Sir Michael Stoute [0-1] H H Aga Khan.*

BANK HOUSE (IRE) BHB 53f37a **RR 51+f 37a** 2928[1]
4 ch g Zafonic (USA) 9f **(83)** - Shebasis (USA) (General Holme (USA)) 5.7f **(63)**

Form - 0U1
Record 1999 - 1st:1 2nd:0 3rd:0 Ran:2
Pre1999 - 1st:0 2nd:0 3rd:1 Ran:5
Win Prizemoney £3,215 *Total Prizemoney* £3,753
Wins * **1999** Jly Ripon (G-F) H 6f 42 51+ <
1999 Turf 1-2: (5f, 6f 1-1) (g-f, frm 1-1)
Workmanlike, fair gelding, effective 6f, acts on frm. Turf high 51 (began Jly) - 1st of 17 getting 24lb from Bedevilled (17 Jly Ripon RF 2928). **G P Kelly [1-7] G P Kelly.*

BANK ON HER (USA) BHB 76f RR 76+f 4880[18]

3 ch f Rahy (USA) 9.1f **(80)** - Bank On Love (USA) (Gallant Romeo (USA)) 8.4f **(64)**
Form - 10
Record 1999 - 1st:1 2nd:0 3rd:0 Ran:2
Pre1999 - 1st:0 2nd:0 3rd:1 Ran:1
Win Prizemoney £5,052 *Total Prizemoney* £5,545
Wins * **1999** May Goodwo (GD) 7f 76 <
1999 Turf 1-2: (7f 1-2) (gd 1-1, frm)
Leggy, currently above-average filly. Turf high 76 (1st run) - 1st of 9 from Mirbeck (19 May Goodwood RF 1333).
**J H M Gosden [1-3] Mrs Shirley Taylor.*

BANK ON HIM BHB 48f75a RR 43f 75a 2147[4]

4 b g Elmaamul (USA) 8.1f **(70)** - Feather Flower (Relkino) 8.9f **(65)**
Form - 253117404
Record 1999 - 1st:2 2nd:0 3rd:0 Ran:6
Pre1999 - 1st:1 2nd:4 3rd:3 Ran:14
Win Prizemoney £12,535 *Total Prizemoney* £17,061
Wins * **1999** *Feb Lingfi (STD) H 10f* 74 75 <
* **1999** *Jan Lingfi (STD) H 10f* 67 75 <
* 1998 *Spt Wolver (STD) H 8.5f* 56 63
1999 Turf 0-2: (9f 2) (gd, hrd) 1999 AW 2-4: (10f 2-4) (Equi 2-4)
Light-framed, above-average gelding, effective 10f, - acts on Equi, favours left handed tracks, excels at Lingfield. Turf high 43. AW high 75 - 1st of 10 giving 1lb to Thekryaati (16 Feb Lingfield RF 0300) - also 1st of 8 giving 12lb to Roi de Danse (19 Jan Lingfield RF 0124). **G L Moore [3-20] Allen House Partnership.*

BANK ON MEE BHB 41f RR 58f 1854[16]

3 b f Weldnaas (USA) 8.4f **(55)** - Heemee (On Your Mark) 7.7f **(58)**
Form - 8000
Record 1999 - 1st:0 2nd:0 3rd:0 Ran:4
Pre1999 - 1st:0 2nd:1 3rd:0 Ran:2
Win Prizemoney £0 *Total Prizemoney* £580
1999 Turf 0-4: (5f, 6f 2, 7f) (gd 2, frm 2)
Neat, fair filly, effective 5f, acts on g-f, has worn blinkers. Turf high 20. **J J Quinn [0-6] B S Adamson.*

BANNERET (USA) BHB 44f62a RR 19f 62a 5145[3]

6 b g Imperial Falcon (CAN) 9.2f **(72)** - Dashing Partner (Formidable (USA)) 9.2f **(63)**
Form - 5201153
Record 1999 - 1st:2 2nd:1 3rd:1 Ran:6
Pre1999 - 1st:3 2nd:1 3rd:1 Ran:15
Win Prizemoney £10,463 *Total Prizemoney* £12,082
Wins * **1999** *Oct Wolver (STD) H 12f* 56 63
* **1999** *Spt Southw (STD) C 11f* 60+
* 1998 *Jly Southw (STD) S 12f* 64
1998 *Jly Wolver (STD) S 12f* 64
1998 *Mar Wolver (STD) 9.4f* 72+ <
1999 Turf 0-1: (10f) (frm) 1999 AW 2-5: (11f 1-1, 12f 1-4) (Fibr 2-5)
Average gelding, effective 9 to 12f, best at 12f, - acts on Fibr, has worn blinkers, favours tight tracks, and excels at Southwell. AW high 63 - 1st of 12 giving 16lb to Premiere Foulee (13 Oct Wolverhampton RF 4869). Consistent.
**Miss S J Wilton [3-9] John Pointon and Sons (from G Woodward [2-5] Jly 1998).*

BANNINGHAM BELLE BHB 30f30a RR 30df 30a 3744[16]

4 gr f Touch of Grey 8.1f **(47)** - Fire Gold (Never so Bold) 6.3f **(66)**
Form - 06760070
Record 1999 - 1st:0 2nd:0 3rd:0 Ran:8
1999 Turf 0-6: (5f 3, 6f 3) (gd 3, g-f 2, frm) 1999 AW 0-2: (6f, 7f) (Fibr 2)
Very moderate filly, effective 5f, acts on g-f, has worn blinkers. Turf high 36. AW high 23. **D Shaw [0-8] Crown Select.*

BANNINGHAM BREEZE BHB 42f49a RR 41f 49a 4349[15]

3 br g Cyrano de Bergerac 7.3f **(58)** - Strapped **(55f)** (Reprimand)
Form - 8660508080
Record 1999 - 1st:0 2nd:0 3rd:0 Ran:10
Pre1999 - 1st:1 2nd:1 3rd:1 Ran:16
Win Prizemoney £3,468 *Total Prizemoney* £6,073
Wins 1998 Aug Goodwo (G-F) S 6f 66 <
1999 Turf 0-7: (5f, 6f 4, 7f, 8f) (g-s, g-f 2, frm 3, hrd) 1999 AW 0-3: (6f 3) (Equi, Fibr 2)
Scopey, fair gelding, effective 6f, acts on g-f, has worn blinkers. Turf high 47. AW high 48.
**D Nicholls [0-10] Rick Heap (from K T Ivory [1-16] Oct 1998).*

BANSHEE BREEZE (USA) RR 5224a[2]

4 b f Unbridled (USA) - Banshee Winds (USA) (Known Fact (USA)) 7.4f **(67)**
Form - 2
1999 AW 0-1: (9f) (Dirt)
Currently high-class filly. (1st run) - 2nd of 8 to Beautiful Pleasure (6 Nov Gulfstream Park 9f Dirt RF 5224a). **C Nafzger in USA [0-2].*

BANYUMANIK (IRE) RR 112f 2660a[13]

3 c
Form - 440
1999 Turf 0-3: (8f, 11f, 12f) (gd 3)
Currently Group-class. Turf high 112 - 4th of 9 to Silvano (13 Jun Cologne 11f gd RF 2100a). Hampered when fourth in the German 2,000 Guineas, he continued to take on the best without making any real impression. **M Hofer in GER [0-3].*

BAPSFORD BHB 41f40a RR 39f 40a 1930[7]

5 b g Shalford (IRE) 7.8f **(63)** - Bap's Miracle (Track Spare) 8.8f **(62)**
Form - 637216250567
Record 1999 - 1st:1 2nd:1 3rd:0 Ran:8
Pre1999 - 1st:2 2nd:4 3rd:3 Ran:28
Win Prizemoney £5,109 *Total Prizemoney* £9,179
Wins * **1999** *Jan Wolver (STD) S 12f* 60 <
1997 *Spt Wolver (STD) C 8.5f* 60 <
1997 *Aug Lingfi (STD) SH 10f* 45 49
1999 AW 1-8: (9f, 11f 2, 12f 1-5) (Equi, Fibr 1-7)
Moderate gelding, effective 8 to 12f, - acts on AW, best on Equi, has worn blinkers, favours left handed tracks. AW high 60 (1st run) - 1st of 8 from Banneret (9 Jan Wolverhampton RF 0068).
**M Waring [1-22] Dunstall Park Select Racing (from G L Moore [2-14] Spt 1997).*

BAPTISMAL ROCK (IRE) BHB 51f53a RR 51f 53a 5149[8]

5 ch g Ballad Rock 7.2f **(63)** - Flower From Heaven (Baptism) 10f **(59)**
Form - 21113462352322636638
Record 1999 - 1st:3 2nd:5 3rd:5 Ran:20
Pre1999 - 1st:0 2nd:1 3rd:0 Ran:16
Win Prizemoney £10,212 *Total Prizemoney* £20,807
Wins * **1999** *Jan Southw (STD) H 6f* 44 57 <
* **1999** *Jan Lingfi (STD) H 6f* 44 54
* **1999** *Jan Wolver (STD) H 6f* 37 37
1999 Turf 0-11: (5f 10, 6f) (g-s 2, gd, frm 6, hrd 2) 1999 AW 3-9: (5f 2, 6f 3-7) (Equi 1-3, Fibr 2-6)
Fair gelding, effective 5 to 6f, best at 6f, acts on gd to frm - acts on AW, best on Fibr, likes left handed tracks, likes tight tracks, and excels at Southwell. Turf high 51 - 2nd of 12 getting 16lb from Brutal Fantasy (8 Aug Ascot 5f gd RF 3460). AW high 57 - 1st of 16 getting 21lb from Ocker (25 Jan Southwell RF 0162) - also 1st of 8 getting 9lb from Half Tone (19 Jan Lingfield RF 0125). Consistent. He had shown virtually nothing for a couple of seasons, but was in fine form in sprints on sand at the start of the year, completing a hat-trick on all three All-Weather tracks. Followed that with a string of solid efforts in competitive sprint handicaps on turf without quite managing to win. There are more races on sand to be won with him.
**A G Newcombe [3-20] M Patel (from B J Curley [0-9] Aug 1998).*

BARABASCHI BHB 72f RR 73f 5026[2]

3 b c Elmaamul (USA) 8.1f **(70)** - Hills' Presidium (Presidium)
Form - 28240322
Record 1999 - 1st:0 2nd:4 3rd:1 Ran:8
Pre1999 - 1st:0 2nd:0 3rd:1 Ran:2
Win Prizemoney £0 *Total Prizemoney* £3,858

1999 Turf 0-8: (6f 2, 7f 5, 8f) (sft 2, gd 2, g-f, frm 2, hrd)
Leggy, above-average colt, effective 7f, acts on gd to frm, has worn blinkers. Turf high 78.
**A G Foster [0-2] Dr Ornella Carlini Cozzi (from P W Chapple-Hyam [0-8] Aug 1999).*

BARAFAMY (IRE) BHB 100f **RR 94f** 4682[6]
3 gr f Barathea (IRE) - Infamy (Shirley Heights) 10.3f **(74)**
Form - 3456
Record 1999 - 1st:0 2nd:0 3rd:1 Ran:4
Pre1999 - 1st:2 2nd:2 3rd:1 Ran:5
Win Prizemoney £26,025 *Total Prizemoney* £51,307
Wins * 1998 Oct San Si (HLD) G3 8f 92 <
* 1998 Aug Newcas (GD) 7f 84
1999 Turf 0-4: (8f, 10f 2, 11f) (gd 3, frm)
Workmanlike, useful filly, effective 8 to 11f, best at 8f, acts on g-s to gd, best on gd. Turf high 95. Consistent. She failed to grow over the winter and found life tough in Group races.
**J L Dunlop [2-9] & Mrs Gary Pinchen.*

BARAKULA RR 83f 4565[5]
2 b f Barathea (IRE) - Bright Generation (IRE) (Rainbow Quest (USA)) 10.4f **(75)**
Form - 15
Record 1999 - 1st:1 2nd:0 3rd:0 Ran:2
Win Prizemoney £4,981 *Total Prizemoney* £8,456
Wins * **1999** Jun Windso (G-F) 6f 75+ <
1999 Turf 1-2: (6f 1-1, 8f) (sft, frm 1-1)
Currently decent filly. Turf high 83 - also 1st of 6 getting 3lb from Embezl (28 Jun Windsor RF 2382). She had previous winners behind when making a successful debut at Windsor in June. The six-furlong trip looked barely adequate there but she failed to handle heavy conditions in the Fillies' Mile.
**P F I Cole [1-2] H R H Prince Fahd Salman.*

BARANN BHB 35f30a **RR 35f 30a** 5147[8]
3 ch g Henbit (USA) 10.2f **(46)** - Opalkino (Relkino) 8.9f **(65)**
Form - 08
Record 1999 - 1st:0 2nd:0 3rd:0 Ran:2
1999 Turf 0-1: (10f) (frm) 1999 AW 0-1: (8f) (Fibr)
Unfurnished, currently very moderate gelding.
**J M Bradley [0-2] Mrs Ann Tomlinson.*

BARATHEA GUEST BHB 100f **RR 90f** 4888a[2]
2 b c Barathea (IRE) - Western Heights (Shirley Heights) 10.3f **(74)**
Form - 10112
Record 1999 - 1st:3 2nd:1 3rd:0 Ran:5
Win Prizemoney £51,150 *Total Prizemoney* £94,207
Wins * **1999** Aug Deauvi (HVY) L 8f 90 <
* **1999** Aug Salisb (G-S) 7f 85
* **1999** Jun Yarmou (G-F) 6f 82
1999 Turf 3-5: (6f 1-2, 7f 1-1, 8f 1-2) (hvy, gd 3-3, g-f)
Useful colt. Turf high 90 - 2nd of 3 to Ciro (10 Oct Longchamp 8f hvy RF 4888a) - also 1st of 7 from Anshaam (21 Aug Deauville RF 3929a). Enjoyed a fine season, and was rather unfortunate to be demoted after finishing first in the three-runner Grand Criterium. Will stay ten furlongs. **G G Margarson [3-5].*

BARBADOS BHB 56f **RR 67f** 5002[7]
2 b c Muhtarram (USA) - Brisighella (IRE) (Al Hareb (USA))
Form - 058522087
Record 1999 - 1st:0 2nd:2 3rd:0 Ran:9
Win Prizemoney £0 *Total Prizemoney* £1,623
1999 Turf 0-9: (5f 2, 6f 2, 7f 2, 8f 3) (gd 5, g-f 2, frm 2)
Average colt, effective 7f, acts on frm. Turf high 67 - 2nd of 16 giving 4lb to Inch Pincher (21 Aug Sandown 7f frm RF 3823).
**M H Tompkins [0-9] P H Betts.*

BARBASON BHB 66f68a **RR 73f 68a** 5126[8]
7 ch g Polish Precedent (USA) 9f **(73)** - Barada (USA) (Damascus (USA)) 8.9f **(71)**
Form - 32236180160141068
Record 1999 - 1st:4 2nd:0 3rd:1 Ran:14
Pre1999 - 1st:9 2nd:6 3rd:10 Ran:46
Win Prizemoney £39,812 *Total Prizemoney* £52,510
Wins * **1999** Spt Bright (G-F) C 8f 64
* **1999** Jly Sandow (G-F) C 8.1f 67
* **1999** Jun Newbur (GD) H 10f 68 71
* **1999** *Feb Lingfi (STD) C 8f 71*
* 1998 Jun Bright (FRM) H 8f 66 71
* 1998 *Jan Lingfi (STD) H 8f 69 72* <
* 1997 Jly Bright (FRM) H 7f 64 68
* 1997 Apr Bright (FRM) H 7f 59 67
* 1997 Apr Lingfi (FRM) H 7f 50 62
* 1997 *Mar Lingfi (STD) H 8f 57 68*
* 1997 *Mar Lingfi (STD) 7f 60*
* 1997 *Feb Lingfi (STD) H 7f 53 56*
1996 *Feb Lingfi (STD) 7f 52+*
1999 Turf 3-10: (8f 2-6, 9f 2, 10f 1-2) (g-s, gd 1-3, g-f, frm 2-5) 1999 AW 1-4: (8f 1-3, 10f) (Equi 1-4)
Above-average gelding, effective 7 to 10f, best at 8f, acts on gd to frm - acts on Equi, has worn blinkers (extremely effectively), likes right handed tracks, and excels at Kempton. Turf high 73 - also 1st of 11 giving 10lb to Boater (10 Jun Newbury RF 1881). AW high 72 (1st run) - 3rd of 8 giving 19lb to Critical Air (16 Jan Lingfield 8f Equi RF 0111) - also 1st of 6 giving 8lb to Soaking (20 Feb Lingfield RF 0326).
**G L Moore [12-47] A Moore (from A Moore [1-11] Jan 1997).*

BARBOLA (USA) RR 119f 4770a[4]
4 ch c Diesis 9f **(80)** - Barboukh (Night Shift (USA)) 7.2f **(69)**
Form - 12334
1999 Turf 1-5: (10f 1-5) (hvy 2, g-s 1-2, gd)
High-class colt, effective 10f, acts on hvy to gd, best on hvy. Turf high 119 (1st run) - 1st of 12 giving 3lb to Borgia (13 Mar Saint-Cloud RF 0448a). He improved from three to four, and was in good form in the spring of 1999. After taking a couple of notable scalps in the Prix Exbury, he chased home Dark Moondancer in the Prix d'Harcourt and ran a creditable third behind Central Park in an Italian Group One. **J deRoualle in FR [1-6].*

BARCELONA BHB 68f **RR 80f** 5102[3]
2 b c Barathea (IRE) - Pipitina (Bustino) 10.4f **(64)**
Form - 703
Record 1999 - 1st:0 2nd:0 3rd:1 Ran:3
Win Prizemoney £0 *Total Prizemoney* £465
1999 Turf 0-3: (8f 3) (gd 2, g-f)
Currently decent colt. Turf high 80 (began Spt).
**J Noseda [0-3] K Y Lim.*

BARDEN LADY RR 24f 5207[11]
2 b f Presidium 7.5f **(56)** - Pugilistic (Hard Fought) 8.8f **(62)**
Form - 00
Record 1999 - 1st:0 2nd:0 3rd:0 Ran:2
1999 Turf 0-2: (6f, 7f) (g-s, gd)
Currently little account filly. Turf high 24 (began Oct).
**B C Morgan [0-2] D G Blagden.*

BARDONECCHIA (IRE) RR 108f 4780a[8]
4 ch f Indian Ridge 7.6f **(74)** - Rosa de Caerleon (Caerleon (USA)) 8.6f **(71)**
Form - 5438
1999 Turf 0-3: (8f, 9f, 10f) (sft, gd 2)
Pattern-class filly, effective 9 to 10f, best at 10f, acts on sft to gd, best on gd. Turf high 107 (began Aug) - 3rd of 8 to Zomaradah (25 Spt Capannelle 10f gd RF 4661a). Consistent.
**L Camici in ITY [1-11].*

BARITONE BHB 42f **RR 25f** 4866[12]
5 b g Midyan (USA) 9.9f **(64)** - Zinzi (Song) 7.2f **(61)**
Form - 002410500500
Record 1999 - 1st:1 2nd:1 3rd:0 Ran:12
Pre1999 - 1st:0 2nd:2 3rd:7 Ran:27
Win Prizemoney £3,081 *Total Prizemoney* £8,875
Wins * **1999** *Feb Southw (STD) H 6f 47 57* <
1999 Turf 0-2: (5f, 6f) (g-f 2) 1999 AW 1-10: (5f, 6f 1-7, 7f 2) (Equi 4, Fibr 1-6)
Fair gelding, effective 6 to 8f, best at 6f, acts on gd to frm - acts on AW, has worn blinkers, likes left handed tracks, favours tight tracks, and likes Lingfield. Turf high 25 (began Aug). AW high 57 - 1st of 11 giving 3lb to Little Ibnr (1 Feb Southwell RF 0203). A half-brother to Ayr Gold Cup winner Sarcita, it took him 32 races to get off the mark, which about says it all.
**S E Kettlewell [1-28] Hollinbridge Racing (from J W Watts [0-11] Jly 1997).*

BARLEY MEADOW (IRE) BHB 41f **RR 53f** 4456^{7}

7 ch g Phardante (FR) 12.8f **(46)** - Foredefine (Bonne Noel) 10.7f **(71)**

Form - 3787

Record 1999 - 1st:0 2nd:0 3rd:1 Ran:4
Pre1999 - 1st:0 2nd:0 3rd:0 Ran:2

Win Prizemoney £0 *Total Prizemoney* £412

1999 Turf 0-4: (12f 2, 16f 2) (sft, g-f, frm 2)

Fair gelding. Turf high 53 (1st run) (began Jly) - 3rd of 5 giving 4lb to Brodessa (5 Jly Musselburgh 16f frm RF 2559).

**R Ford [4-25] Bodies, Bills & Beer (from T G McCourt in IRE [0-10] Aug 1997).*

BARNABY RR 8f 2635^{17}

2 b g Theatrical Charmer 10.9f **(63)** - Fruitful Affair (IRE) **(35df 30a)** (Taufan (USA)) 7f **(57)**

Form - 0

Record 1999 - 1st:0 2nd:0 3rd:0 Ran:1

1999 Turf 0-1: (7f) (frm)

Currently very poor gelding.

**J R Arnold [0-1] Barnes, George, Else Partnership.*

BARNACLA (IRE) BHB 79f **RR 76f** 2564^{6}

3 ch f Bluebird (USA) 7.9f **(71)** - Reticent Bride (IRE) (Shy Groom (USA)) 10f **(66)**

Form - 02176

Record 1999 - 1st:1 2nd:1 3rd:0 Ran:5
Pre1999 - 1st:0 2nd:0 3rd:0 Ran:1

Win Prizemoney £2,878 *Total Prizemoney* £3,938

Wins * 1999 Jun Windso (SFT) H 6f 75 76+ <

1999 Turf 1-5: (6f 1-5) (gd 1-3, frm 2)

Neat, above-average filly, effective 6f, acts on gd. Turf high 76 - 6th of 13 giving 19lb to Piggy Bank (5 Jly Ripon 6f gd RF 2564) - also 1st of 17 giving 4lb to Lively Lady (7 Jun Windsor RF 1801).

**C F Wall [1-6] Zubieta Ltd.*

BARNEY KNOWS (IRE) RR 63f 1381^{8}

4 b g In The Wings 11.2f **(77)** - Afeefa (Lyphard (USA)) 9.9f **(72)**

Form - 8

Record 1999 - 1st:0 2nd:0 3rd:0 Ran:1

1999 Turf 0-1: (14f) (g-f)

Average gelding. **M A Peill [2-5] C N Barnes.*

BARNIE RUBBLE RR 4878^{23}

3 ch c Pharly (FR) 11.5f **(64)** - Sharp Fairy (Sharpo) 7.7f **(59)**

Form - 0

Record 1999 - 1st:0 2nd:0 3rd:0 Ran:1

1999 Turf 0-1: (6f) (frm)

Lengthy, currently very poor colt. **A Bailey [0-1] A H Bennett.*

BARN OWL BHB 26f **RR 33f** 4442^{9}

3 ch f Sabrehill (USA) 8.5f **(64)** - Ever Welcome (Be My Guest (USA)) 9.3f **(67)**

Form - 00

Record 1999 - 1st:0 2nd:0 3rd:0 Ran:2
Pre1999 - 1st:0 2nd:0 3rd:0 Ran:3

1999 Turf 0-2: (12f, 14f) (g-s, frm)

Scopey, very moderate filly. (began Spt).

**K W Hogg [0-2] K W Hogg (from J L Dunlop [0-3] Oct 1998).*

BARON DE PICHON (IRE) BHB 67f83a **RR 64f 83a** 3439^{6}

3 b c Perugino (USA) - Ariadne (Bustino) 10.4f **(64)**

Form - 0221111217046206

Record 1999 - 1st:5 2nd:3 3rd:0 Ran:14
Pre1999 - 1st:0 2nd:1 3rd:0 Ran:5

Win Prizemoney £20,023 *Total Prizemoney* £24,085

Wins * 1999 *Feb Lingfi (STD) H 8f 75 84* <
*** 1999** *Jan Southw (STD) H 7f 62 70*
*** 1999** *Jan Wolver (STD) H 8.5f 62 74*
*** 1999** *Jan Wolver (STD) H 7f 60 66*
*** 1999** *Jan Wolver (STD) H 8.5f 54 67*

1999 Turf 0-3: (7f, 8f 2) (gd, g-f, frm) 1999 AW 5-11: (7f 2-3, 8f 3-7, 9f) (Equi 1-2, Fibr 4-9)

Scopey, decent colt, effective 8f, - acts on AW, best on Fibr, has worn blinkers, prefers left handed tracks, prefers tight tracks, excels at Wolverhampton. Turf high 64. AW high 84 - 2nd of 7 giving 3lb to Hever Golf Glory (20 Feb Wolverhampton 8f Fibr RF 0332) - also 1st of 6 giving 8lb to Lincoln Dean (23 Feb Lingfield RF 0347). Inconsistent. Started off this year in sparkling form on Fibresand, looking a most progressive sort. He has continued to run good races on sand, but has done little on turf.

**N P Littmoden [5-17] DGH Partnership (from Miss Gay Kelleway [0-2] Spt 1998).*

BARON FERDINAND BHB 85f **RR 95?f** 1576^{11}

9 ch g Ferdinand (USA) 9.6f **(82)** -In Perpetuity(Great Nephew)9.9f **(64)**

Form - 0

Record 1999 - 1st:0 2nd:0 3rd:0 Ran:1
Pre1999 - 1st:5 2nd:6 3rd:3 Ran:19

Win Prizemoney £76,736 *Total Prizemoney* £115,154

Wins * 1995 Jly Ayr (GD) G3 10f 115
* 1995 May Goodwo (FRM) L 10f 117 <
* 1995 May Newmar (GD) 10f 106+

1999 Turf 0-1: (10f) (frm)

Very useful gelding. Consistent. **R Charlton [5-21] Lady Rothschild.*

BARR BEACON BHB 63f59a **RR 54f 59a** 432^{8}

3 br c Puissance 7.1f **(60)** - Lominda (IRE) (Lomond (USA)) 8.8f **(65)**

Form - 6258

Record 1999 - 1st:0 2nd:0 3rd:0 Ran:2
Pre1999 - 1st:0 2nd:1 3rd:0 Ran:3

Win Prizemoney £0 *Total Prizemoney* £585

1999 AW 0-2: (5f 2) (Equi, Fibr)

Light-framed, above-average colt, has worn blinkers. AW high 51.

**T G Mills [0-5] Thorpe Vernon.*

BARREN LANDS BHB 57f **RR 49f** 901^{15}

4 b g Green Desert (USA) 7.8f **(78)** - Current Raiser (Filiberto (USA)) 9.5f **(66)**

Form - 0

Record 1999 - 1st:0 2nd:0 3rd:0 Ran:1
Pre1999 - 1st:1 2nd:1 3rd:0 Ran:10

Win Prizemoney £3,376 *Total Prizemoney* £4,024

Wins 1998 Jun Redcar (G-S) 6f 73 <

1999 Turf 0-1: (8f) (g-f)

Strong, moderate gelding, effective 5 to 6f, best at 6f, acts on gd, has worn blinkers. Becoming disappointing.

**K Bishop [0-1] Mrs E K Ellis (from R Guest [1-10] Oct 1998).*

BARRETTSTOWN BHB 65f48a **RR 70f 48a** 2688^{4}

4 ch g Cadeaux Genereux 7.9f **(76)** - Sagar (Habitat) 9.4f **(70)**

Form - 3204

Record 1999 - 1st:0 2nd:1 3rd:1 Ran:4

Win Prizemoney £0 *Total Prizemoney* £1,072

1999 Turf 0-2: (10f, 12f) (gd, g-f) 1999 AW 0-2: (11f, 12f) (Fibr 2)

Lengthy, above-average gelding. Turf high 70 - 2nd of 16 giving 8lb to Zidac (12 Jun Bath 10f g-f RF 1939). AW high 40.

**M C Pipe [0-6] D A Johnson.*

BARRIER REEF (IRE) RR 100f $4974a^{2}$

2 b c Perugino (USA) - Singing Millie (Millfontaine)

Form - 104152

1999 Turf 2-6: (5f, 6f 1-3, 8f 1-2) (hvy 1-1, sft, g-s, gd, g-f 1-2)

Very useful colt, effective 6 to 8f, best at 8f, acts on hvy to gd. Turf high 100 - 2nd of 6 to Lermontov (16 Oct Curragh 8f g-s RF 4974a) - also 1st of 13 giving 9lb to Hill Style (8 Spt Galway RF 4305a). A winner twice so far in contrasting ground, he looks a Nationwide League performer by Ballydoyle standards, although his form with Lermontov reads well. **A P O'Brien in IRE [2-6] Mrs E M Stockwell.*

BARRIER RIDGE BHB 49f43a **RR 52f 43a** 4997^{4}

5 ch g Lycius (USA) 8.8f **(71)** - Star Ridge (USA) (Storm Bird (CAN)) 10.3f **(74)**

Form - 370102084

Record 1999 - 1st:1 2nd:1 3rd:0 Ran:6
Pre1999 - 1st:1 2nd:1 3rd:2 Ran:16

Win Prizemoney £5,675 *Total Prizemoney* £8,411

Wins * 1999 May Bright (FRM) S 10f 54
1997 Jun Thirsk (FRM) 8f 59++ <

1999 Turf 1-5: (8f, 10f 1-3, 11f) (sft, gd, g-f, frm, hrd 1-1) 1999 AW 0-1: (8f) (Equi)

Fair gelding, effective 10f, acts on hrd, has worn blinkers. Turf high 54 (1st run) - 1st of 15 giving 15lb to Gold Honor (4 May Brighton RF 1020). Inconsistent.

**G L Moore [1-21] Miss C A Hockridge (from H Cecil [1-3] Jun 1997).*

BARRINGER (IRE) BHB 91f **RR 89f** 5045[8]
2 b c Nicolotte - Prosaic Star (IRE) (Common Grounds)
Form - 212161078
Record 1999 - 1st:3 2nd:2 3rd:0 Ran:9
Win Prizemoney £13,191 *Total Prizemoney* £16,140
Wins * **1999** May Windso (GD) 5f 89 <
* **1999** Apr Nottin (HVY) 5.1f 86++
* **1999** Apr Hamilt (HVY) 5f 89+
1999 Turf 3-9: (5f 3-7, 6f 2) (hvy 1-1, sft, g-s, gd 2-3, g-f 3)
Useful colt, effective 5f, acts on hvy to g-f. Turf high 89 - 1st of 5 giving 6lb to Primo Valentino (17 May Windsor RF 1288) - also 1st of 5 giving 5lb to Cautionary (10 Apr Hamilton RF 0636). Consistent. A tough early-season juvenile who won three times in the spring, he was given a break after finishing down the field in the Norfolk at Royal Ascot, but did not show much on his return. Needs soft ground. **M R Channon [3-9] Kingsdown Racing.*

BARRISTER (IRE) BHB 97f **RR 98f** 2543[5]
3 ch g Barathea (IRE) - Silver Hut (USA) **(73f)** (Silver Hawk (USA)) 8.6f **(70)**
Form - 315155
Record 1999 - 1st:2 2nd:0 3rd:1 Ran:6
Win Prizemoney £10,494 *Total Prizemoney* £11,419
Wins * **1999** Jun Haydoc (GD-) H 8.1f 87 95+ <
* **1999** Apr Windso (G-S) 8.3f 80
1999 Turf 2-6: (8f 2-5, 10f) (sft, gd 2-3, g-f, frm)
Workmanlike, very useful gelding, effective 8f, acts on gd to g-f. Turf high 98 - 5th of 32 giving 3lb to Pythios (15 Jun Ascot 8f g-f RF 1999) - also 1st of 7 getting 2lb from Northern Spring (5 Jun Haydock RF 1769). He enjoys easy ground, but ran creditably on a fast surface at Royal Ascot. Probably best when ridden close to the pace, he is open to plenty of improvement.
**R Charlton [2-6] Highclere Thoroughbred Racing Ltd.*

BARROW (SWI) BHB 70f **RR 67f** 4449[4]
2 br c Caerleon (USA) 10.9f **(79)** - Bestow (Shirley Heights) 10.3f **(74)**
Form - 034
Record 1999 - 1st:0 2nd:0 3rd:1 Ran:3
Win Prizemoney £0 *Total Prizemoney* £832
1999 Turf 0-3: (7f, 8f 2) (sft, g-f 2)
Currently average colt. Turf high 67 (began Aug).
**J L Dunlop [0-3] Mrs S Egloff.*

BARRYS DOUBLE BHB 60f63a **RR 53f 63a** 5187[11]
2 br c Barrys Gamble 7f **(50)** - Pennine Star (IRE) (Pennine Walk) 8.5f **(61)**
Form - 40730
Record 1999 - 1st:0 2nd:0 3rd:1 Ran:5
Win Prizemoney £0 *Total Prizemoney* £658
1999 Turf 0-4: (5f 4) (gd, frm 3) 1999 AW 0-1: (6f) (Fibr)
Average colt. Turf high 53 (began Jly).
**C W Fairhurst [0-5] North Cheshire Trading & Storage Ltd.*

BARTHOLOMEW (IRE) BHB 96f91a **RR 94f 91a** 1967[13]
3 b c Second Set (IRE) 9.2f **(67)** - Why Not Glow (IRE) (Glow (USA)) 6.7f **(71)**
Form - 111114300
Record 1999 - 1st:4 2nd:0 3rd:1 Ran:9
Pre1999 - 1st:1 2nd:2 3rd:0 Ran:5
Win Prizemoney £23,601 *Total Prizemoney* £31,480
Wins * **1999** Mar Saint- (HVY) 6f 87
* **1999** *Feb Lingfi (STD) H 6f 79 91* <
* **1999** *Feb Lingfi (STD) H 7f 79 84*
* **1999** *Jan Lingfi (STD) H 6f 75 79*
* 1998 *Nov Lingfi (STD) H 6f 68 72*
1999 Turf 1-6: (6f 1-5, 8f) (hvy 1-2, gd 2, g-f, frm) 1999 AW 3-3: (6f 2-2, 7f 1-1) (Equi 3-3)
Leggy, useful colt, effective 6 to 7f, best at 6f, acted on hvy to g-f - acted on Equi, liked left handed tracks, liked tight tracks, excelled at Lingfield. Turf high 94 - 3rd of 20 giving 15lb to Midhish Two (8 May Lingfield 6f g-f RF 1113) - also 1st of 3 giving 5lb to Emerald Park (18 Mar Saint-Cloud RF 0559b). AW high 91 - 1st of 6 giving 6lb to Polly Mills (20 Feb Lingfield RF 0329). (DEAD)
**T J Naughton [5-14] E J Fenaroli.*

BARTON MISS RR 26f 5108[13]
2 ch f Whittingham (IRE) - Miss Derby (USA) (Master Derby (USA)) 9.5f **(69)**
Form - 00
Record 1999 - 1st:0 2nd:0 3rd:0 Ran:2
1999 Turf 0-2: (5f, 8f) (gd 2)
Currently little account filly. Turf high 26 (began Oct).
**G L Moore [0-2] Stanley Clarke.*

BASHER JACK BHB 40f47a **RR 43f 47a** 3904[4]
3 b c Suave Dancer (USA) 10.7f **(68)** - Possessive Lady (Dara Monarch) 8.8f **(59)**
Form - 00554164
Record 1999 - 1st:1 2nd:0 3rd:0 Ran:8
Pre1999 - 1st:0 2nd:0 3rd:0 Ran:1
Win Prizemoney £1,815 *Total Prizemoney* £2,018
Wins * **1999** *Aug Wolver (STD) H 12f 44 46* <
1999 Turf 0-5: (10f 3, 11f, 12f) (g-s 2, gd 2, frm) 1999 AW 1-3: (12f 1-1, 15f, 16f) (Equi, Fibr 1-2)
Neat, moderate colt, effective 12f, - acts on Fibr, likes left handed tracks, favours tight tracks. Turf high 55. AW high 46. He looks one-paced, so was very much suited by the twelve furlongs on the Wolverhampton Fibresand in August. It was a poor race though.
**C N Allen [1-9] J T B Racing.*

BASHFUL BRAVE BHB 30f33a **RR 27f 33a** 3924[13]
8 ch g Indian Ridge 7.6f **(74)** - Shy Dolly (Cajun) 5.2f **(54)**
Form - 003000500
Record 1999 - 1st:0 2nd:0 3rd:1 Ran:9
Pre1999 - 1st:6 2nd:6 3rd:4 Ran:53
Win Prizemoney £19,767 *Total Prizemoney* £28,423
Wins 1997 Aug Ripon (G-F) SH 5f 48 51
1996 Apr Bright (FRM) H 6f 70 71 <
1995 Jly Warwic (FRM) H 5f 61 66
1995 Jun Folkes (FRM) H 5f 61 65
1995 May Folkes (G-F) H 5f 60 56
1995 Apr Folkes (G-F) 5f 54
1999 Turf 0-7: (5f 7) (gd 2, g-f, frm 4) 1999 AW 0-2: (6f 2) (Fibr 2)
Little account gelding, effective 6f, acts on frm, has worn blinkers, likes left handed tracks, likes tight tracks. Turf high 33. AW high 6.
**J L Eyre [0-9] W P Burnell (from B P J Baugh [1-27] Spt 1998).*

BASHKIR (USA) RR 100f 5171a[2]
2 b c Nureyev (USA) 8.4f **(84)** - Palestrina (USA)
Form - 182
1999 Turf 1-3: (7f 1-2, 8f) (sft, g-f 1-2)
Currently very useful colt, has worn blinkers. Turf high 100 (began Aug) - 2nd of 5 to Monashee Mountain (25 Oct Leopardstown 7f sft RF 5171a). Won his maiden at Naas over seven furlongs on firm ground in August, just holding on by a head from the second close home, and chased home a useful stablemate on his third run. **A P O'Brien in IRE [1-3] Mrs John Magnier.*

BASIC INSTINCT BHB 53f **RR 50f** 4605[5]
2 ch f Prince Sabo 6.6f **(64)** - Constant Delight (Never so Bold) 6.3f **(66)**
Form - 035
Record 1999 - 1st:0 2nd:0 3rd:1 Ran:3
Win Prizemoney £0 *Total Prizemoney* £278
1999 Turf 0-1: (6f) (g-f) 1999 AW 0-2: (7f 2) (Fibr 2)
Currently fair filly. AW high 52 (began Spt).
**M H Tompkins [0-3] Old Suffolk Stud.*

BASMAN (IRE) BHB 88f **RR 93df** 5051[5]
5 b h Persian Heights 10.5f **(61)** - Gepares (IRE) (Mashhor Dancer (USA)) 10f **(65)**
Form - 5
Record 1999 - 1st:0 2nd:0 3rd:0 Ran:1
Pre1999 - 1st:1 2nd:2 3rd:1 Ran:11
Win Prizemoney £3,993 *Total Prizemoney* £12,401
Wins * 1997 Oct Nottin (SFT) 10f 101 <
1999 Turf 0-1: (12f) (gd)
Useful colt. Inconsistent. Showed useful form in '97, but has had his training problems since.
**B Smart [2-16] Nelson, Edmondson And Partners.*

BASSINELLO (USA) BHB 76f **RR 75f** 4838[6]
3 ch f Nureyev (USA) 8.4f **(84)** - Feminine Wiles (IRE) (Ahonoora) 8.1f **(73)**
Form - 186

Record 1999 - 1st:1 2nd:0 3rd:0 Ran:3
Pre1999 - 1st:0 2nd:0 3rd:0 Ran:1
Win Prizemoney £3,550 *Total Prizemoney* £3,872
Wins 1999 Aug Pontef (G-F) 8f 75 <
1999 Turf 1-3: (8f 1-2, 10f) (gd 2, frm 1-1)
Scopey, above-average filly. Turf high 75 (began Aug) - also 1st of 7 getting 5lb from Smart Predator (4 Aug Pontefract RF 3371).
**A G Foster [0-1] R E Sangster (from P W Chapple-Hyam [1-3] Aug 1999).*

BATALEUR BHB 52f35a RR 49f 35a 5167[1]

6 b g Midyan (USA) 9.9f **(64)** - Tinkerbird (Music Boy) 6.8f **(57)**
Form - 00800721
Record 1999 - 1st:1 2nd:1 3rd:0 Ran:5
Pre1999 - 1st:2 2nd:0 3rd:2 Ran:23
Win Prizemoney £8,157 *Total Prizemoney* £10,029
Wins * 1999 Nov Catter (SFT) C 5f 49
* 1998 Oct Newcas (SFT) H 6f 45 49
1996 Spt Hamilt (G-S) H 6f 55 56 <
1999 Turf 1-5: (5f 1-1, 6f 4) (g-s 1-1, gd, frm 3)
Moderate gelding, effective 5 to 6f, best at 6f, acts on sft to frm, has worn blinkers. Turf high 49 (began Aug) - 1st of 14 giving 2lb to Torrent (2 Nov Catterick RF 5167). Improving.
**G Woodward [2-20] Michael Worth (from Miss J Bower [1-8] May 1997).*

BATANTA RR 53+f 1141[10]

3 br f Bob's Return (IRE) - Atlantic Air (Air Trooper) 9.1f **(63)**
Form - 0
Record 1999 - 1st:0 2nd:0 3rd:0 Ran:1
1999 Turf 0-1: (10f) (g-f)
Leggy, fair filly. (DEAD) **K R Burke [0-1] Mrs Alison Ruggles.*

BATCHWORTH BELLE BHB 93f82a RR 92f 82a 4795[2]

4 b f Interrex (CAN) 7.7f **(51)** - Treasurebound (Beldale Flutter (USA)) 9.7f **(71)**
Form - 13586333138032
Record 1999 - 1st:2 2nd:1 3rd:6 Ran:14
Pre1999 - 1st:3 2nd:4 3rd:5 Ran:21
Win Prizemoney £25,477 *Total Prizemoney* £51,258
Wins * 1999 Jly Newmar (G-F) H 5f 88 92 <
* **1999** *Apr Lingfi (STD) H 5f 75 76*
* 1998 Spt Epsom (SFT) H 5f 77 80
* 1998 Aug Bright (G-F) H 5.3f 73 76
* 1997 *Dec Lingfi (G-S) 6f 66*
1999 Turf 1-13: (5f 1-12, 6f) (g-s, gd 2, g-f 4, frm 1-6) 1999 AW 1-1: (5f 1-1) (Equi 1-1)
Leggy, useful filly, effective 5f, acts on gd to frm, best on frm, has worn blinkers, excels at Epsom and Newmarket. Turf high 92 - 2nd of 21 getting 12lb from Superior Premium (9 Oct Ascot 5f gd RF 4795) - also 1st of 9 getting 3lb from Emma Peel (17 Jly Newmarket RF 2911). (1st run). A winner twice last season one of which was on Equitrack, she is a very speedy handicapper who is very difficult to catch when able to dominate, but she has tended to dwell in the stalls on occasions which has scuppered her chances. Fast ground and a sharp five furlongs suit her best.
**E A Wheeler [5-35] Mrs Diana Price.*

BATHWICK (IRE) BHB 96f81a RR 106f 81a 3832[1]

3 b c Midyan (USA) 9.9f **(64)** - Dancing Heights (IRE) **(80f)** (High Estate)
Form - 51710601
Record 1999 - 1st:3 2nd:0 3rd:0 Ran:8
Pre1999 - 1st:3 2nd:2 3rd:0 Ran:9
Win Prizemoney £61,815 *Total Prizemoney* £64,069
Wins * 1999 Aug Bath (GD) 8f 106 <
* **1999** May Goodwo (GD) H 9f 92 94
* **1999** Apr Windso (GD) 8.3f 93
* 1998 Spt Sandow (GD) 8.1f 88
* 1998 Spt Bath (GD) H 8f 83 85
* 1998 Jly Warwic (GD) 7f 83
1999 Turf 3-8: (8f 2-4, 9f 1-1, 10f 3) (g-s, gd 1-1, g-f 3, frm 2-3)
Small, Pattern-class colt, effective 8f, acts on frm, has worn blinkers, likes right handed tracks, prefers tight tracks, excels at Bath. Turf high 106 - 1st of 5 giving 5lb to Sir Effendi (22 Aug Bath RF 3832). Small but tough, he put some disappointing efforts in hot handicaps behind him when winning at Bath.
**B Smart [6-17] W Clifford.*

BATHWICK BABE (IRE) RR 56f 5109[9]

2 b f Sri Pekan (USA) - Olean (Sadler's Wells (USA)) 10f **(76)**
Form - 00
Record 1999 - 1st:0 2nd:0 3rd:0 Ran:2
1999 Turf 0-2: (8f 2) (gd 2)
Currently fair filly. Turf high 56 (began Spt).
**B Smart [0-2] W Clifford.*

BATOUTOFTHEBLUE BHB 42f65a RR 44f 65a 3844[3]

6 br g Batshoof 9.5f **(66)** - Action Belle (Auction Ring (USA)) 8.6f **(65)**
Form - 010244443
Record 1999 - 1st:1 2nd:1 3rd:1 Ran:9
Pre1999 - 1st:3 2nd:2 3rd:2 Ran:25
Win Prizemoney £11,616 *Total Prizemoney* £17,243
Wins * 1999 Apr Mussel (GD) H 16f 43 47
1998 Aug Pontef (G-F) H 17.1f 39 43
* 1996 *Spt Wolver (STD) 14.8f 67* <
* 1996 *Spt Southw (STD) H 14f 58 62*
1999 Turf 1-9: (14f, 16f 1-6, 17f, 18f) (gd 2, g-f 1-4, frm 3)
Average gelding, effective 14 to 15f, - acts on Fibr, has worn blinkers, likes left handed tracks, likes tight tracks. Turf high 48.
**W W Haigh [3-26] Mrs I Gibson (from J M Jefferson [0-1] Oct 1998).*

BATSMAN BHB 39f49a RR 42f 49a 4349[19]

5 b g Batshoof 9.5f **(66)** - Lady Bequick (Sharpen Up) 8.3f **(67)**
Form - 370730342070666450
Record 1999 - 1st:0 2nd:1 3rd:3 Ran:18
Pre1999 - 1st:1 2nd:4 3rd:0 Ran:23
Win Prizemoney £2,398 *Total Prizemoney* £7,575
Wins 1998 *Feb Wolver (STD) H 7f 48 50* <
1999 Turf 0-14: (7f 7, 8f 6, 10f) (gd 4, g-f 3, frm 5, hrd 2) 1999 AW 0-4: (7f 2, 8f, 12f) (Fibr 4)
Moderate gelding, effective 7f, - acts on Fibr, has worn blinkers, likes left handed tracks. Turf high 53. AW high 67 (1st run) - 3rd of 12 giving 1lb to Elite Hope (15 Feb Southwell 7f Fibr RF 0292). Consistent.
**M Dods [0-18] N A Riddell (from W J Musson [1-23] Oct 1998).*

BATSWING BHB 68f RR 70f 4262[6]

4 b g Batshoof 9.5f **(66)** - Magic Milly (Simply Great (FR)) 8.2f **(65)**
Form - 730476
Record 1999 - 1st:0 2nd:0 3rd:1 Ran:6
Pre1999 - 1st:1 2nd:2 3rd:0 Ran:13
Win Prizemoney £3,315 *Total Prizemoney* £8,367
Wins 1997 Jun Lingfi (SFT) 5f 66+ <
1999 Turf 0-6: (12f 4, 13f, 14f) (g-s 2, g-f 3, frm)
Neat, above-average gelding, effective 13f, acts on g-f, has worn blinkers. Turf high 71 - 3rd of 14 giving 14lb to Compton Ace (26 May Newbury 13f g-f RF 1501).
**B R Millman [1-11] Richard Withers (from M Meade [1-10] Oct 1997).*

BATTLE GLEN (FR) BHB 42f49a RR 37?f 49a 3380[14]

4 ch g Green Forest (USA) 7.4f **(73)** - Battle Quest (FR) (Noblequest (FR))
Form - 300
Record 1999 - 1st:0 2nd:0 3rd:0 Ran:2
Pre1999 - 1st:0 2nd:0 3rd:1 Ran:2
Win Prizemoney £0 *Total Prizemoney* £356
1999 Turf 0-1: (8f) (g-f) 1999 AW 0-1: (7f) (Fibr)
Moderate gelding, had worn blinkers. (DEAD)
**A Bailey [0-4] Bodfari Stud Ltd.*

BATTLE GREEN RR 108f 1532a[6]

6 b g Old Vic 12.8f **(72)** - Sword Lily (UAE) (Mr Prospector (USA)) 8.8f **(78)**
Form - 6
1999 Turf 0-1: (16f) (g-s)
Currently Pattern-class gelding. (1st run) - 6th of 9 getting 7lb from Kayf Tara (23 May Longchamp 16f g-s RF 1532a).
**P Demercastel in FR [0-1] (from K P McLaughlin in USA [0-1] Apr 1997).*

BATTLE WARNING BHB 57f RR 61df 4733[12]

4 b g Warning 8.1f **(77)** - Royal Ballet (IRE) (Sadler's Wells (USA)) 10f **(76)**
Form - 0500
Record 1999 - 1st:0 2nd:0 3rd:0 Ran:4

Pre1999 - 1st:0 2nd:0 3rd:0 Ran:2
1999 Turf 0-4: (10f 3, 12f) (g-s, frm 2, hrd)
Light-framed, average gelding. Turf high 61 - 5th of 10 giving 9lb to Il Destino (5 Jly Bath 10f hrd RF 2551).
**H Candy [0-5] Mrs C M Poland (from H R A Cecil [0-1] Oct 1997).*

BAUGET JOUETTE BHB 38f **RR 31f** 5192[11]

2 gr f Son Pardo - Petite Louie (Chilibang)
Form - 0553508000
Record 1999 - 1st:0 2nd:0 3rd:1 Ran:10
Win Prizemoney £0 *Total Prizemoney* £500
1999 Turf 0-10: (5f 2, 6f 5, 7f, 8f 2) (g-s 2, gd 2, g-f, frm 3, hrd 2)
Very moderate filly, effective 6f, acts on g-s, has worn blinkers. Turf high 59 - 3rd of 7 to Olivias Choice (2 Jun Goodwood 6f g-s RF 1673). **J R Poulton [0-10] Mrs J Druce.*

BAVARIO (USA) BHB 53f **RR 23f** 752[11]

6 ch g Theatrical 11.5f **(78)** - Hawaiian Miss (USA) (Hawaii) 9.4f **(66)**
Form - 0
Record 1999 - 1st:0 2nd:0 3rd:0 Ran:1
Pre1999 - 1st:1 2nd:0 3rd:2 Ran:11
Win Prizemoney £4,110 *Total Prizemoney* £4,872
Wins 1996 Spt Leopar (GD) H 10f 73 61 <
1999 Turf 0-1: (10f) (g-s)
Little account gelding, often wears blinkers. Becoming disappointing.
**D L Williams [0-6] Miss B W Palmer (from D K Weld in IRE [1-11] Aug 1997).*

BAWSIAN BHB 87f86a **RR 95f 86a** 3085[B]

4 b g Persian Bold 10f **(69)** - Bawaeth (USA) (Blushing Groom (FR)) 10.3f **(76)**
Form - 24404384B
Record 1999 - 1st:0 2nd:1 3rd:1 Ran:9
Pre1999 - 1st:5 2nd:2 3rd:1 Ran:19
Win Prizemoney £30,734 *Total Prizemoney* £46,582

Wins								
* 1998	May	York	(GD)	H	10.4f	90	96	<
* 1998	Mar	Doncas	(GD)	H	10.3f	81	90	
* 1998	*Jan*	*Wolver*	*(STD)*	*H*	*8.5f*	*80*	*82*	
* 1998	*Jan*	*Wolver*	*(STD)*	*H*	*8.5f*	*75*	*77*	
* 1997	Nov	Redcar	(GD)	H	8f	65	72	

1999 Turf 0-8: (10f 6, 12f 2) (sft, gd 4, g-f, frm 2) 1999 AW 0-1: (12f) (Fibr)
Very useful gelding, effective 10 to 12f, best at 10f, acts on sft to frm - acts on Fibr, prefers left handed tracks, prefers tight tracks, and excels at Wolverhampton. Turf high 95 - 4th of 16 getting 3lb from Achilles (10 Jly York 10f g-f RF 2733). (1st run) - 2nd of 7 getting 13lb from China Castle (22 Mar Southwell 12f Fibr RF 0460). A poor mover, he had an in-and-out campaign, running his best race when finishing fourth under a poor ride in the John Smith's Cup. Off the track after being brought down at Ascot in late July, he stays a mile and a half and appreciates easy ground.
**J L Eyre [5-28] David Scott.*

BAYANIYA (IRE) BHB 74f **RR 84+f** 5198[2]

3 b f Barathea (IRE) - Bayrika (IRE) **(107f)** (Kahyasi)
Form - 242
Record 1999 - 1st:0 2nd:2 3rd:0 Ran:3
Win Prizemoney £0 *Total Prizemoney* £2,442
1999 Turf 0-3: (8f 3) (gd, g-f 2)
Workmanlike, currently decent filly. Turf high 74 (began Jly).
**L M Cumani [0-3] H H Aga Khan.*

BAYARD LADY BHB 40f **RR 42f** 5135[5]

3 b f Robellino (USA) 9.5f **(68)** - Lurking (Formidable (USA)) 9.2f **(63)**
Form - 4044040055
Record 1999 - 1st:0 2nd:0 3rd:0 Ran:10
Pre1999 - 1st:1 2nd:0 3rd:2 Ran:8
Win Prizemoney £3,074 *Total Prizemoney* £4,079
Wins 1998 May Hamilt (GD) 5f 67 <
1999 Turf 0-10: (7f, 8f 6, 10f, 12f 2) (hvy, gd 4, g-f 2, frm 3)
Unfurnished, moderate filly, effective 5f, acts on gd. Turf high 42.
**L R Lloyd-James [0-2] Bay Horse Racing Syndicate (from D Moffatt [1-16] Aug 1999).*

BAYCHESTER BHB 35f **RR 6f** 5215[18]

2 ch g Chaddleworth (IRE) - Runabay (Run The Gantlet (USA)) 12.1f **(59)**
Form - 000
Record 1999 - 1st:0 2nd:0 3rd:0 Ran:3
1999 Turf 0-3: (7f, 8f 2) (g-s, gd 2)
Currently very poor gelding. Turf high 6 (began Oct).
**G Woodward [0-3] Mrs Helen Godfrey.*

BAYFORD GREEN (IRE) BHB 52f **RR 45f** 2362[4]

3 b f Distinctly North (USA) 7.4f **(63)** - Paddys Cocktail (IRE) (Tremblant)
Form - 04
Record 1999 - 1st:0 2nd:0 3rd:0 Ran:2
Pre1999 - 1st:0 2nd:1 3rd:0 Ran:4
Win Prizemoney £0 *Total Prizemoney* £860
1999 Turf 0-2: (5f, 6f) (gd, frm)
Workmanlike, moderate filly, effective 5f, acts on frm, has worn blinkers. Turf high 45. **J Berry [0-6] Mrs Jean Turner.*

BAY OF BENGAL (IRE) BHB 47f **RR 31f** 4396[8]

3 ch f Persian Bold 10f **(69)** - Adjamiya (USA) (Shahrastani (USA)) 8.8f **(72)**
Form - 11748
Record 1999 - 1st:2 2nd:0 3rd:0 Ran:5
Pre1999 - 1st:0 2nd:0 3rd:1 Ran:5
Win Prizemoney £4,778 *Total Prizemoney* £5,459

Wins								
*** 1999**	Jun	Pontef	(GD)	SH	12f	47	50	<
*** 1999**	May	Nottin	(FRM)	SH	10f	43	44	

1999 Turf 2-5: (10f 1-2, 11f, 12f 1-1, 14f) (g-f 1-1, frm 1-4)
Scopey, very moderate filly, effective 10 to 12f, acts on g-f to frm, likes tight tracks. Turf high 50 - 1st of 11 getting 2lb from Melody Lady (28 Jun Pontefract RF 2368) - also 1st of 16 giving 3lb to Walter Plinge (28 May Nottingham RF 1548).
**J S Wainwright [2-5] Rosaly Racing (from H Alexander [0-5] Spt 1998).*

BAY OF ISLANDS BHB 94f **RR 90f** 2336[3]

7 b g Jupiter Island 10.4f **(57)** - Lawyer's Wave (USA) (Advocator) 10.9f **(80)**
Form - 0123
Record 1999 - 1st:1 2nd:1 3rd:1 Ran:4
Pre1999 - 1st:3 2nd:1 3rd:3 Ran:18
Win Prizemoney £19,861 *Total Prizemoney* £49,026

Wins								
*** 1999**	May	Nottin	(FRM)	H	14.1f	80	82	
* 1998	Jun	Doncas	(GD)	H	12f	78	84	<
* 1997	Jun	Cheste	(G-F)	H	10.3f	75	81	
1995	Aug	York	(G-F)		10.4f		74	

1999 Turf 1-4: (12f, 14f 1-1, 16f 2) (gd, g-f 1-1, frm 2)
Useful gelding, effective 12 to 16f, acts on gd to frm, best on frm, has worn blinkers (very effectively), prefers left handed tracks, excels at Haydock. Turf high 90 - 3rd of 20 getting 2lb from Far Cry (26 Jun Newcastle 16f frm RF 2336) - also 1st of 9 giving 5lb to Domappel (22 May Nottingham RF 1416). He put in some decent efforts last term, notably when third in the Northumberland Plate. Needs distances beyond twelve furlongs nowadays.
**D Morris [3-19] Bloomsbury Stud (from C E Brittain [1-3] Aug 1995).*

BAYONET BHB 56f50a **RR 62f 50a** 4606[16]

3 b f Then Again 7.4f **(52)** - Lambay (Lorenzaccio) 10f **(64)**
Form - 80804080
Record 1999 - 1st:0 2nd:0 3rd:0 Ran:8
Pre1999 - 1st:0 2nd:2 3rd:0 Ran:3
Win Prizemoney £0 *Total Prizemoney* £2,005
1999 Turf 0-7: (6f 4, 7f 2, 8f) (frm 7) 1999 AW 0-1: (6f) (Fibr)
Light-framed, average filly, effective 5f, acts on gd to frm, has worn blinkers. Turf high 62. Inconsistent.
**Jane Southcombe [0-3] Mark Savill (from R F JohnsonHoughton [0-8] Jly 1999).*

BAY PRINCE (IRE) BHB 75f **RR 47f** 4644[18]

4 b c Mujadil (USA) 7.7f **(70)** - Kingston Rose (Tudor Music) 6.8f **(59)**
Form - 00
Record 1999 - 1st:0 2nd:0 3rd:0 Ran:2
Pre1999 - 1st:2 2nd:0 3rd:0 Ran:8
Win Prizemoney £16,245 *Total Prizemoney* £20,033

Wins							
1997	Aug	York	(GD)	L	5f	95	<
1997	Aug	Pontef	(G-F)		5f	95	<

1999 Turf 0-2: (5f, 6f) (g-s, frm)
Workmanlike, moderate colt, has worn blinkers. Becoming disappointing.

**Miss Gay Kelleway [0-1] A P Griffin (from Mrs L Stubbs [0-1] Apr 1999).*

BAYT ALASAD (IRE) BHB 73f73a **RR 72f 73a** 5147[1]
3 b f Lion Cavern (USA) 7.5f **(74)** - Safa (Shirley Heights) 10.3f **(74)**
Form - 323731
Record 1999 - 1st:1 2nd:1 3rd:3 Ran:6
Win Prizemoney £3,054 *Total Prizemoney* £5,930
Wins * 1999 *Oct Wolver (STD) 8.5f 66* <
1999 Turf 0-5: (10f 4, 12f) (frm 4, hrd) 1999 AW 1-1: (8f 1-1) (Fibr 1-1)
Neat, above-average filly, effective 8 to 10f, best at 10f, acts on frm to hrd - acts on Fibr, best on frm. Turf high 72 (began Jly) - 3rd of 15 to Anaam (20 Oct Nottingham 10f frm RF 4992). (1st run) - 1st of 13 from Trafford (30 Oct Wolverhampton RF 5147).
**M P Tregoning [1-6] Sheikh Ahmed Al Maktoum.*

BAYTOWN HARMONY RR 53f 1889[8]
2 ch f Muhtarram (USA) - Merryhill Maid (IRE) (M Double M (USA)) 14.1f **(52)**
Form - 8558
Record 1999 - 1st:0 2nd:0 3rd:0 Ran:4
1999 Turf 0-3: (5f 2, 7f) (sft, gd, g-f) 1999 AW 0-1: (6f) (Fibr)
Fair filly. Turf high 53. **P S McEntee [0-4] Mrs B A McEntee.*

BAYTOWN MELODY BHB 55f55a **RR 58f 55a** 4626[8]
2 b f Alhijaz 7.7f **(57)** - Wendy's Way **(44f 41a)** (Merdon Melody)
Form - 5404212342258
Record 1999 - 1st:1 2nd:4 3rd:1 Ran:13
Win Prizemoney £2,022 *Total Prizemoney* £4,653
Wins * 1999 Jly Yarmou (GD) S 6f 68 <
1999 Turf 1-11: (5f 6, 6f 1-5) (sft, g-s, gd 1-2, g-f 4, frm 3) 1999 AW 0-2: (5f, 6f) (Fibr 2)
Fair filly, effective 6f, acts on gd, has worn blinkers. Turf high 68 - 1st of 7 getting 5lb from Lord Yasmin (1 Jly Yarmouth RF 2466). AW high 44. Consistent. **P S McEntee [1-13] Mrs B A McEntee.*

BAYTOWN RHAPSODY BHB 49f **RR 60f** 4627[8]
2 b f Emperor Jones (USA) - Sing a Rainbow (IRE) (Rainbow Quest (USA)) 10.4f **(75)**
Form - 265578
Record 1999 - 1st:0 2nd:1 3rd:0 Ran:6
Win Prizemoney £0 *Total Prizemoney* £1,075
1999 Turf 0-6: (6f, 7f 5) (g-s, gd, g-f 2, frm 2)
Average filly. Turf high 60. **P S McEntee [0-6] Mrs B A McEntee.*

BAY VIEW RR 71f 4629[2]
4 b f Slip Anchor 12.7f **(75)** - Carmita (Caerleon (USA)) 8.6f **(71)**
Form - 72
Record 1999 - 1st:0 2nd:1 3rd:0 Ran:1
Pre1999 - 1st:0 2nd:0 3rd:0 Ran:1
Win Prizemoney £0 *Total Prizemoney* £1,020
1999 Turf 0-1: (8f) (g-s)
Leggy, currently above-average filly. (1st run) - 2nd of 8 giving 4lb to Flame Cutter (29 Spt Brighton 8f g-s RF 4629).
**K Mahdi [0-2] Greenfield Stud.*

BEACON SILVER BHB 45f **RR 61?f** 4219[13]
5 b m Belmez (USA) 11.4f **(65)** - Nettle (Kris) 9.5f **(73)**
Form - 000
Record 1999 - 1st:0 2nd:0 3rd:0 Ran:3
Pre1999 - 1st:0 2nd:1 3rd:1 Ran:4
Win Prizemoney £0 *Total Prizemoney* £1,895
1999 Turf 0-2: (10f, 12f) (sft, g-f) 1999 AW 0-1: (9f) (Fibr)
Average filly.
**Ian Williams [0-3] R L Croft (from Lord Huntingdon [0-4] Spt 1997).*

BEACON VALE (IRE) BHB 35f **RR 57df** 2083[16]
3 ch g Forest Wind (USA) - Pam Story (Sallust) 8.4f **(63)**
Form - 300
Record 1999 - 1st:0 2nd:0 3rd:1 Ran:3
Win Prizemoney £0 *Total Prizemoney* £402
1999 Turf 0-2: (11f, 12f) (hvy, gd) 1999 AW 0-1: (11f) (Fibr)
Unfurnished, currently fair gelding. Turf high 57.
**M G Meagher [0-3] B Collier.*

BEADING RR 40f 4815[19]
2 b f Polish Precedent (USA) 9f **(73)** - Silver Braid (USA) (Miswaki (USA)) 9f **(81)**
Form - 0
Record 1999 - 1st:0 2nd:0 3rd:0 Ran:1
1999 Turf 0-1: (7f) (gd)
Currently moderate filly. **J W Hills [0-1] Wyck Hall Stud.*

BE ADMONISHED RR 4322[15]
2 b f Warning 8.1f **(77)** - La Sorrela (IRE) (Cadeaux Genereux)
Form - 00
Record 1999 - 1st:0 2nd:0 3rd:0 Ran:2
1999 Turf 0-2: (5f, 7f) (gd 2)
Currently very poor filly. (began Aug).
**Mrs P N Dutfield [0-2] The Bobbin And Weavin Partnership.*

BEAT ALL (USA) BHB 117f **RR 121f** 2419a[4]
3 b br c Dynaformer (USA) 12f **(82)** - Spirited Missus (USA) (Distinctive (USA)) 10.7f **(70)**
Form - 134
Record 1999 - 1st:1 2nd:0 3rd:1 Ran:3
Pre1999 - 1st:1 2nd:1 3rd:0 Ran:2
Win Prizemoney £15,855 *Total Prizemoney* £154,142
Wins * 1999 Apr Newmar (GD) L 10f 107 <
* 1998 Spt Chepst (G-S) 7.1f 93
1999 Turf 1-3: (10f 1-1, 12f 2) (gd 2, frm 1-1)
Unfurnished, very high-class colt. Turf high 121 - 3rd of 16 to Oath (5 Jun Epsom 12f gd RF 1760). Was unlucky enough to run into Auction House on his two-year-old debut in 1998, but got off the mark as expected next time. He made a big impression when winning the Newmarket Stakes on his reappearance in 1999, and was a good third in the Derby following an interrupted preparation. The ground turned against him in the Budweiser Irish Derby, and he was absent afterwards. Suited by fast ground, he is with the right trainer for handling older colts, and looks to have a big race in him, providing he has not suffered any long-term damage.
**Sir Michael Stoute [2-5] Saeed Suhail.*

Beat All developed into a Derby colt, but missed the second half of the season

BEAT HOLLOW RR 93++f 4357[1]
2 b c Sadler's Wells (USA) 11.3f **(87)** - Wemyss Bight (Dancing Brave (USA)) 8.4f **(76)**
Form - 1
Record 1999 - 1st:1 2nd:0 3rd:0 Ran:1
Win Prizemoney £4,092 *Total Prizemoney* £4,092
Wins * 1999 Spt Yarmou (SFT) 8f 93++ <
1999 Turf 1-1: (8f 1-1) (g-s 1-1)
Currently useful colt. (1st run) - 1st of 12 from Peacock Jewel (16 Spt Yarmouth RF 4357). Out of an Irish Oaks winner, he should make up into a very useful middle-distance colt.
**H R A Cecil [1-1] K Abdulla.*

BEAUCHAMP KING BHB 96f **RR 100df** 950^{9}

6 gr h Nishapour (FR) 11.1f **(58)** - Afariya (FR) (Silver Shark) 7.9f **(81)**

Form - 00

Record **1999** - 1st:0 2nd:0 3rd:0 Ran:2
Pre1999 - 1st:7 2nd:0 3rd:2 Ran:21

Win Prizemoney £146,988 *Total Prizemoney* £180,729

Wins * 1998 May Haydoc (G-S) LH 7.1f 104 108
1997 Jly Doncas (GD) 8f 96
1996 Apr Newmar (G-F) G3 8f 116
1995 Oct Doncas (G-F) G1 8f 116
1995 Oct Ascot (SFT) L 8f 117 <
1995 Spt Haydoc (GD) 8.1f 109+
1995 Aug Ayr (G-F) 7f 74+

1999 Turf 0-2: (7f, 8f) (gd, g-f)

Very useful horse, effective 7f, acts on gd. Turf high 78. Becoming disappointing.
**G A Butler [1-7] E Penser (from J L Dunlop [6-16] Aug 1997).*

BEAUCHAMP MAGIC BHB 40f **RR 44df** 5006^{13}

4 b g Northern Park (USA) 10f **(57)** - Beauchamp Buzz (High Top) 10.2f **(67)**

Form - 068000

Record **1999** - 1st:0 2nd:0 3rd:0 Ran:6
Pre1999 - 1st:0 2nd:1 3rd:1 Ran:9

Win Prizemoney £0 *Total Prizemoney* £1,240

1999 Turf 0-6: (12f 2, 15f, 16f 3) (hvy, g-s, gd, frm 2, hrd)

Scopey, moderate gelding, effective 12 to 16f, acts on gd to frm, best on frm, has worn blinkers, prefers tight tracks. Turf high 54. Becoming disappointing.
**M D I Usher [0-3] M D I Usher (from G A Butler [0-9] Jun 1999).*

BEAUCHAMP NOBLE BHB 70f **RR 75f** 2181^{6}

3 b g Northern Park (USA) 10f **(57)** - Beauchamp Cactus (Niniski (USA)) 10.6f **(65)**

Form - 454446

Record **1999** - 1st:0 2nd:0 3rd:0 Ran:6
Pre1999 - 1st:0 2nd:0 3rd:0 Ran:2

Win Prizemoney £0 *Total Prizemoney* £894

1999 Turf 0-6: (10f, 11f, 12f 2, 14f, 15f) (g-s 2, gd, g-f, frm, hrd)

Workmanlike, above-average gelding, effective 14f, acts on g-f, likes left handed tracks, likes tight tracks. Turf high 77.
**G A Butler [0-8] E Penser.*

BEAUCHAMP NYX BHB 37f **RR 30f** 4861^{14}

3 b f Northern Park (USA) 10f **(57)** - Beauchamp Image (Midyan (USA)) 6f **(60)**

Form - 00

Record **1999** - 1st:0 2nd:0 3rd:0 Ran:2
Pre1999 - 1st:0 2nd:0 3rd:0 Ran:1

1999 Turf 0-2: (10f, 12f) (sft, g-s)

Scopey, currently very moderate filly. Turf high 30 (began Oct).
**G A Butler [0-3] E Penser.*

BEAU CHEVALIER BHB 52f **RR 39f** 4810^{15}

3 b g Up and At 'em - Exceptional Beauty (Sallust) 8.4f **(63)**

Form - 50000

Record **1999** - 1st:0 2nd:0 3rd:0 Ran:5

1999 Turf 0-5: (5f 2, 6f 2, 7f) (sft, g-s, gd 2, frm)

Scopey, very moderate gelding. Turf high 65 (1st run) - 5th of 16 to Francport (8 May Beverley 5f gd RF 1102).
**J L Eyre [0-5] Mark Ford & Nick Tritton.*

BEAUMONT (IRE) BHB 61f55a **RR 65df 55a** 4917^{30}

9 br g Be My Native (USA) 11.2f **(62)** - Say Yes(Junius (USA)) 7.7f **(65)**

Form - 604400

Record **1999** - 1st:0 2nd:0 3rd:0 Ran:6
Pre1999 - 1st:9 2nd:3 3rd:3 Ran:44

Win Prizemoney £38,396 *Total Prizemoney* £46,050

Wins * 1997 Jly Newmar (GD) H 14.8f 67 72
* 1996 Oct York (GD) H 13.9f 61 69+
* 1996 Spt Cheste (GD) H 15.9f 59 66
* 1996 *Jan Wolver (STD) H 12f 56 66*
* 1995 *Dec Southw (STD) H 11f 52 54*

1999 Turf 0-6: (12f, 14f 2, 15f, 16f, 17f) (g-s, gd 2, g-f, frm 2)

Average gelding, has worn blinkers. Turf high 65.
**J E Banks [6-38] P Cunningham (from J Pearce [4-23] Jun 1995).*

BEAU REGARDE RR 4422^{11}

8 b m Clantime 6.6f **(57)** - Noor Jehan (Taj Dewan)

Form - 0

Record **1999** - 1st:0 2nd:0 3rd:0 Ran:1

1999 Turf 0-1: (8f) (frm)

Currently very poor mare. **J S Wainwright [0-1] J S Wainwright.*

BEAU ROBERTO BHB 54f43a **RR 55f 43a** 5190^{2}

5 b g Robellino (USA) 9.5f **(68)** - Night Jar (Night Shift (USA)) 7.2f **(69)**

Form - 04832600144313424052

Record **1999** - 1st:2 2nd:3 3rd:3 Ran:20
Pre1999 - 1st:2 2nd:1 3rd:8 Ran:33

Win Prizemoney £11,539 *Total Prizemoney* £24,122

Wins * **1999** Aug Hamilt (G-F) H 13f 47 49 <
* **1999** Jly Hamilt (FRM) H 13f 44 45
* 1998 Aug Hamilt (SFT) H 11.1f 39 46+
* 1998 Jly Hamilt (FRM) H 11.1f 31 40

1999 Turf 2-20: (9f, 10f, 11f 2, 12f 9, 13f 2-4, 14f 2, 16f) (hvy, sft 2, gd, g-f 1-8, frm 1-7, hrd)

Fair gelding, effective 12 to 13f, best at 12f, acts on gd to frm, has worn blinkers, prefers right handed tracks, favours tight tracks, does well at Hamilton, likes Musselburgh. Turf high 61 - 4th of 11 getting 28lb from Montecristo (27 Spt Hamilton 13f gd RF 4590). Consistent.
**J S Goldie [4-46] J W Armstrong (from M Johnston [0-7] Jun 1997).*

BEAUTIFUL PLEASURE (USA) RR $5224a^{1}$

4 b f General Meeting - Beautiful Bid (USA) (Baldski (USA))

Form - 1

1999 AW 1-1: (9f 1-1) (Dirt 1-1)

Currently high-class filly. (1st run) - 1st of 8 from Banshee Breeze (6 Nov Gulfstream Park RF 5224a). An inpressive all-the-way winner of the Breeders' Cup Distaff. **J Ward Jnr in USA [1-2] J Oxley.*

BEAU VIENNA BHB 28f28a **RR 16f 28a** 501^{7}

4 b f Superpower 6.6f **(58)** - Waltz on Air (Doc Marten)

Form - 007

Record **1999** - 1st:0 2nd:0 3rd:0 Ran:2
Pre1999 - 1st:0 2nd:0 3rd:0 Ran:9

Win Prizemoney £0 *Total Prizemoney* £211

1999 Turf 0-1: (9f) (hvy) 1999 AW 0-1: (7f) (Fibr)

Neat, very moderate filly, has worn blinkers. Becoming disappointing. **A R Dicken [0-14] The Forth Partnership.*

BEBE COSMONAUT BHB 33f46a **RR 23f 46a** 4632^{19}

3 ch f Cosmonaut - Bebe Altesse (GER)(Alpenkonig (GER)) 10.8f **(76)**

Form - 438500000

Record **1999** - 1st:0 2nd:0 3rd:1 Ran:8
Pre1999 - 1st:0 2nd:0 3rd:0 Ran:3

Win Prizemoney £0 *Total Prizemoney* £481

1999 Turf 0-4: (7f, 8f 2, 10f) (g-s, g-f, frm 2) 1999 AW 0-4: (7f, 8f 2, 10f) (Equi 2, Fibr 2)

Scopey, very moderate filly. Turf high 23 (began Jly). AW high 48. Inconsistent. **A G Newcombe [0-11] D Bass.*

BEBE DE CHAM BHB 74f **RR 78f** 4690^{23}

2 b f Tragic Role (USA) 9.4f **(63)** - Champenoise (Forzando) 7.6f **(59)**

Form - 71085026100

Record **1999** - 1st:2 2nd:1 3rd:0 Ran:11

Win Prizemoney £8,344 *Total Prizemoney* £9,904

Wins * **1999** Aug Thirsk (G-F) H 6f 68 78 <
* **1999** Apr Thirsk (GD) 5f 67

1999 Turf 2-10: (5f 1-3, 6f 1-3, 7f 4) (gd 1-3, g-f 3, frm 2, hrd 1-2) 1999 AW 0-1: (5f) (Fibr)

Above-average filly, effective 6 to 7f, acts on frm to hrd, has worn blinkers. Turf high 78 - 1st of 9 from Night Shifter (27 Aug Thirsk RF 3947). **J L Eyre [2-11] Lovely Bubbly Racing.*

BE BRAVE BHB 40f45a **RR 45a** 57^{8}

9 b g Never so Bold 7.1f **(62)** - Boo (Bustino) 10.4f **(64)**

Form - 8

Record **1999** - 1st:0 2nd:0 3rd:0 Ran:1
Pre1999 - 1st:0 2nd:0 3rd:0 Ran:4

1999 AW 0-1: (16f) (Fibr)

Moderate gelding, has worn blinkers.
**T J Etherington [1-32] Mrs Stephanie Parsons.*

BECKMANN (ITY) RR 93f 3227a[1]
3 b c Robellino (USA) 9.5f **(68)** - Karvis (USA) (Be My Guest (USA)) 9.3f **(67)**
Form - 821
1999 Turf 1-2: (8f 1-2) (g-f 1-2)
Currently useful colt. Turf high 93 - 1st of 9 from Onice Nero (21 Jly San Siro RF 3227a). **A Peraino in ITY [1-3] Razza Del Sila.*

BECKON BHB 43f **RR 55f** 5058[8]
3 ch f Beveled (USA) 6.9f **(64)** - Carolynchristensen (Sweet Revenge) 7.2f **(54)**
Form - 4563808
Record 1999 - 1st:0 2nd:0 3rd:1 Ran:7
Pre1999 - 1st:0 2nd:0 3rd:0 Ran:3
Win Prizemoney £0 *Total Prizemoney* £552
1999 Turf 0-4: (7f 2, 8f, 9f) (gd, g-f 3) 1999 AW 0-3: (7f 2, 8f) (Equi, Fibr 2)
Leggy, fair filly. Turf high 55. AW high 43.
**B R Johnson [0-4] B A Whittaker (from T D Barron [0-6] Jun 1999).*

BECKON THE KING (USA) RR 100f 4070a[1]
3 b g Ghazi (USA) - Our Locket (USA) 00
Form - 21241
1999 Turf 2-5: (6f 1-4, 7f 1-1) (gd 2-3, g-f 2)
Very useful gelding, effective 6 to 7f, best at 6f, acts on gd to g-f, best on gd, mostly wears blinkers (extremely effectively). Turf high 100 - 1st of 12 giving 20lb to Mighty Pip (29 Aug Curragh RF 4070a). Improving. He ran away with a maiden in May and defied a welter-weight at The Curragh three months later. Raced solely over six and seven furlongs up to that point, he was taken to America to win a valuable three-year-old event at Gulfstream Park the day after the Breeders' Cup.
**D K Weld in IRE [2-9] Kenneth Ramsey.*

BEDARA RR 94f 5142[2]
2 b f Barathea (IRE) - Cutting Reef (IRE) (Kris) 9.5f **(73)**
Form - 02
Record 1999 - 1st:0 2nd:1 3rd:0 Ran:2
Win Prizemoney £0 *Total Prizemoney* £4,019
1999 Turf 0-2: (7f, 8f) (gd 2)
Currently useful filly. Turf high 94 (began Oct) - 2nd of 10 to Silver Colours (30 Oct Newmarket 8f gd RF 5142). Stepped up on her debut to finish second in a listed race.
**B W Hills [0-2] John Poynton.*

BEDAZZLE BHB 20f35a **RR 22f 35a** 232[12]
8 b g Formidable (USA) 7.8f **(60)** - Wasimah (Caerleon (USA)) 8.6f **(71)**
Form - 00
Record 1999 - 1st:0 2nd:0 3rd:0 Ran:1
Pre1999 - 1st:1 2nd:8 3rd:4 Ran:54
Win Prizemoney £2,326 *Total Prizemoney* £10,671
Wins * 1996 Apr Mussel (GD) SH 8.1f 34 38 <
1999 AW 0-1: (11f) (Fibr)
Little account gelding, has worn blinkers.
**M Brittain [1-55] Northgate Lodge Racing Club.*

BEDAZZLING (IRE) BHB 98f **RR 92f** 5041[9]
2 gr f Darshaan 11.9f **(81)** - Dazzlingly Radiant (Try My Best (USA)) 7.6f **(67)**
Form - 73120
Record 1999 - 1st:1 2nd:1 3rd:1 Ran:5
Win Prizemoney £3,062 *Total Prizemoney* £85,527
Wins * **1999** Spt Kempto (HVY) 7f 90+ <
1999 Turf 1-5: (6f, 7f 1-4) (sft, g-s 1-1, gd, g-f, frm)
Useful filly. Turf high 92 (began Aug) - 2nd of 17 getting 5lb from Inchlonaig (28 Spt Newmarket 7f g-f RF 4595) - also 1st of 10 from Welsh Ploy (20 Spt Kempton RF 4433). Relished the heavy ground when winning at Kempton on her third start, and finished second in a hot race next time. **J R Fanshawe [1-5] B McAllister.*

BEDEVILLED BHB 67f **RR 68f** 4154[12]
4 ch c Beveled (USA) 6.9f **(64)** - Putout (Dowsing (USA))
Form - 00626810
Record 1999 - 1st:1 2nd:1 3rd:0 Ran:8
Pre1999 - 1st:0 2nd:1 3rd:1 Ran:6
Win Prizemoney £3,764 *Total Prizemoney* £6,964
Wins * **1999** Aug Beverl (GD) 5f 68 <
1999 Turf 1-7: (5f 1-2, 6f 5) (sft, gd, g-f, frm 1-4)1999 AW 0-1: (6f) (Fibr)
Neat, average colt, has broken blood-vessels, effective 5 to 6f, acts on gd to frm, has worn blinkers. Turf high 68 - 1st of 12 giving 2lb to Blackfoot (28 Aug Beverley RF 3949). Inconsistent.
**T D Barron [1-5] Mrs J Hazell (from M J Heaton-Ellis [0-9] Jun 1999).*

BEDFORD FORREST (GER) RR 107f 3591a[4]
3 c
Form - 84
1999 Turf 0-2: (12f 2) (gd 2)
Currently Pattern-class colt. Turf high 107.
**H Steinmetz in GER [0-2].*

BEDOUIN QUEEN BHB 70f66a **RR 72?f 66a** 4990[3]
2 ch f Aragon 7.7f **(58)** - Petra's Star **(55f)** (Rock City)
Form - 803
Record 1999 - 1st:0 2nd:0 3rd:1 Ran:3
Win Prizemoney £0 *Total Prizemoney* £366
1999 Turf 0-3: (5f, 6f 2) (g-f, frm 2)
Currently above-average filly. Turf high 72.
**R F JohnsonHoughton [0-3] Zara Campbell-Harris & Partners.*

BEECHCROFT BAY RR 35f 2715[7]
5 b g Teamster 11.4f **(22)** - Galley Bay (Welsh Saint) 7.6f **(64)**
Form - 7
Record 1999 - 1st:0 2nd:0 3rd:0 Ran:1
1999 Turf 0-1: (14f) (frm)
Very moderate gelding. **Mrs P N Dutfield [0-5] W A Harrison-Allan.*

BEE EIGHT BHB 100f **RR 101f** 3208[4]
2 b c Mujtahid (USA) 7.4f **(69)** - Creme de Menthe (IRE) (Green Desert (USA)) 8.6f **(78)**
Form - 72328344
Record 1999 - 1st:0 2nd:2 3rd:2 Ran:8
Win Prizemoney £0 *Total Prizemoney* £15,747
1999 Turf 0-8: (5f 3, 6f 5) (g-s, gd, g-f 4, frm 2)
Very useful colt, effective 5f, acts on g-f. Turf high 101 - 4th of 25 giving 6lb to Don Puccini (17 Jly Newbury 5f g-f RF 2901). Still a maiden, he has run some super races in defeat, notably when finishing fourth in the Weatherbys Super Sprint and Richmond Stakes. Likely to stay seven furlongs, he is set to continue his career in America after realising 85,000 guineas at Newmarket in October. **D R C Elsworth [0-8] J Wotherspoon.*

BEE GEE BHB 44f **RR 48f** 4439[10]
2 b f Beveled (USA) 6.9f **(64)** - Bunny Gee **(54f)** (Last Tycoon) 8.5f **(62)**
Form - 0800
Record 1999 - 1st:0 2nd:0 3rd:0 Ran:4
1999 Turf 0-4: (6f, 7f 2, 8f) (gd, g-f 2, frm)
Moderate filly. Turf high 48 (began Jly).
**M Blanshard [0-4] Mara Racing.*

BEE HEALTH BOY BHB 46f59a **RR 45f 59a** 4127[16]
6 b g Superpower 6.6f **(58)** - Rekindle (Relkino) 8.9f **(65)**
Form - 00600320
Record 1999 - 1st:0 2nd:1 3rd:1 Ran:8
Pre1999 - 1st:5 2nd:6 3rd:4 Ran:52
Win Prizemoney £22,420 *Total Prizemoney* £33,674
Wins 1998 Jun Redcar (G-S) H 6f 65 69 <
1996 Aug Newmar (G-F) H 6f 66 68
1996 Aug Doncas (G-F) H 6f 62 65
1996 Jly Catter (G-S) H 6f 57 60
1995 Spt Haydoc (SFT) SH 6f 59 64
1999 Turf 0-8: (6f 7, 7f) (gd 2, g-f, frm 5)
Moderate gelding, effective 5 to 6f, best at 6f, acts on sft to frm, best on gd, mostly wears blinkers (effectively). Turf high 49. Consistent.
**G Holmes [0-8] Chantquote Ltd (from M W Easterby [5-52] Oct 1998).*

BEGGARS BELIEF (IRE) BHB 77f **RR 76f** 5197[17]
3 b f Common Grounds 8.1f **(66)** - Perfect Alibi (Law Society (USA)) 9.9f **(70)**
Form - 033300110
Record 1999 - 1st:2 2nd:0 3rd:3 Ran:9
Win Prizemoney £5,988 *Total Prizemoney* £8,095
Wins * **1999** Oct Leices (G-S) H 8f 70 76+ <
* **1999** Spt Warwic (SFT) 7.7f 68

1999 Turf 2-9: (7f, 8f 2-4, 9f, 10f 3) (sft 1-1, gd 1-4, g-f 2, frm 2)
Workmanlike, above-average filly, effective 8 to 10f, best at 8f, acts on sft to frm, best on gd. Turf high 76 - 3rd of 7 giving 15lb to Quedex (4 Jun Goodwood 10f gd RF 1738) - also 1st of 19 giving 9lb to Signs And Wonders (11 Oct Leicester RF 4813). Inconsistent. Unraced at two, it took her some time to get the hang of things, but her two wins over a distances of around a mile on soft ground have shown her to best effect.
**J L Dunlop [2-9] C A Washbourn.*

BE GONE BHB 85f RR 79f 3770[20]

4 ch g Be My Chief (USA) 10.2f **(62)** - Hence (USA) (Mr Prospector (USA)) 8.8f **(78)**
Form - 330050
Record 1999 - 1st:0 2nd:0 3rd:2 Ran:6
Pre1999 - 1st:1 2nd:0 3rd:0 Ran:2
Win Prizemoney £3,452 *Total Prizemoney* £6,148
Wins * 1998 Aug Newcas (GD) 9f 89 <
1999 Turf 0-6: (8f 2, 10f, 12f 3) (gd 3, g-f 2, frm)
Workmanlike, above-average gelding, effective 9 to 12f, acts on gd to g-f, has worn blinkers. Turf high 97. Becoming disappointing. He broke his pelvis after winning as a three-year-old and struggled last term. Sold for 10,000 guineas at Newmarket in October, he has dropped to a fair mark and could pay his way in run-of-the-mill handicaps around 10 furlongs.
**H R A Cecil [1-8] Exors of the late P E Burrell.*

BEGORRAT (IRE) BHB 60f RR 61f 2155[10]

5 ch g Ballad Rock 7.2f **(63)** - Hada Rani (Jaazeiro (USA)) 9.2f **(54)**
Form - 708270
Record 1999 - 1st:0 2nd:1 3rd:0 Ran:6
Pre1999 - 1st:3 2nd:1 3rd:1 Ran:24
Win Prizemoney £8,948 *Total Prizemoney* £15,680
Wins * 1998 Oct Ayr (G-S) H 10f 58 65
1997 Oct Ayr (SFT) C 10.9f 69 <
1997 Aug Haydoc (G-F) S 8.1f 68
1999 Turf 0-6: (9f, 10f 2, 11f 2, 12f) (hvy, gd 3, frm 2)
Average gelding, effective 10 to 12f, best at 10f, acts on sft to frm, has worn blinkers, likes left handed tracks. Turf high 61 - 2nd of 6 giving 5lb to Bold Amusement (2 Jun Newcastle 10f frm RF 1689).
**J S Goldie [2-15] Mike Flynn (from D Moffatt [1-12] Aug 1998).*

BEGUILE BHB 49f44a RR 44a 355[10]

5 b g Most Welcome 8.6f **(66)** - Captivate (Mansingh (USA)) 7.4f **(55)**
Form - 80533460
Record 1999 - 1st:0 2nd:0 3rd:0 Ran:3
Pre1999 - 1st:0 2nd:0 3rd:2 Ran:6
Win Prizemoney £0 *Total Prizemoney* £881
1999 AW 0-3: (6f, 8f, 10f) (Equi 3)
Moderate gelding, effective 7 to 8f, - acts on Equi. AW high 44.
**B R Johnson [0-3] D G Wheatley (from R Ingram [0-6] Dec 1998).*

BEHARI (IRE) RR 38f 4861[11]

5 b g Kahyasi 12.9f **(74)** - Berhala (IRE) (Doyoun) 9f **(69)**
Form - 0
Record 1999 - 1st:0 2nd:0 3rd:0 Ran:1
1999 Turf 0-1: (12f) (sft)
Very moderate gelding. **R Hollinshead [0-1] John Marriott.*

BEHIND THE SCENES BHB 54f54a RR 52f 54a 2427[4]

5 ch g Kris 10f **(75)** - Free Guest (Be My Guest (USA)) 9.3f **(67)**
Form - 302144
Record 1999 - 1st:1 2nd:1 3rd:1 Ran:6
Pre1999 - 1st:1 2nd:1 3rd:2 Ran:18
Win Prizemoney £5,952 *Total Prizemoney* £8,950
Wins * **1999** *May Lingfi (STD) C 16f 52*
* 1997 May Goodwo (GD) 9f 65 <
1999 Turf 0-1: (17f) (frm) 1999 AW 1-5: (16f 1-5) (Equi 1-4, Fibr)
Fair gelding, effective 16f, - acts on Fibr, has worn blinkers, favours left handed tracks. AW high 52. Inconsistent. His only win in the last couple of seasons came in a two-mile claimer on the Lingfield Equitrack. That looks as good as he is.
**C A Cyzer [2-24] R M Cyzer.*

BEHRENS (USA) RR 5231a[7]

5 Pleasant Colony (USA) 12.4f **(88)** - Hot Novel (USA) (Mari's Book (USA))
Form - 127
1999 AW 1-3: (9f 1-1, 10f 2) (Dirt 1-3)
Top-class, has worn blinkers. AW high 125 (1st run) - 1st of 6 giving 5lb to Running Stag (29 May Suffolk Downs RF 1716a). Outclassed behind such as Skip Away and Silver Charm in the past, following their retirements he rose to the top of the pile in America in 1999, winning four and being second four times from nine starts. After beating our own Running Stag at Suffolk Downs, he found the improving River Keen too good in the Jockey Club Gold Cup before his only disappointing effort in the Breeders' Cup Classic. **H J Bond in USA [1-5] .*

BELA-M (IRE) RR 99f 5117a[1]

3 b f Ela-Mana-Mou 12.7f **(72)** -Bay Empress(Empery (USA)) 11.2f **(69)**
Form - 621
1999 Turf 1-3: (10f 1-1, 11f 2) (sft 1-2, gd)
Currently very useful filly. Turf high 99 - 1st of 11 from Intuition (23 Oct Gelsenkirchen-horst RF 5117a).
**P Schiergen in GER [1-3] Hyperion Breeding.*

BELEAGUER BHB 87f RR 94f 5198[1]

4 ch f Rainbow Quest (USA) 11.2f **(81)** - Armeria (USA) (Northern Dancer) 9.6f **(80)**
Form - 351
Record 1999 - 1st:1 2nd:0 3rd:1 Ran:3
Win Prizemoney £2,528 *Total Prizemoney* £3,117
Wins * **1999** Nov Windso (G-S) 8.3f 84 <
1999 Turf 1-3: (8f 1-1, 10f, 11f) (gd 1-2, frm)
Currently useful filly. Turf high 84 (began Jly) - 1st of 17 giving 2lb to Bayaniya (4 Nov Windsor RF 5198).
**H R A Cecil [1-3] K Abdulla.*

BELENUS (GER) RR 121f 4663a[1]

3 ch c Lomitas - Beaute (GER) (Lord Udo)
Form - 31131
1999 Turf 3-5: (9f, 12f 3-4) (sft 1-2, gd 2-3)
Very high-class colt. Turf high 121 - 1st of 18 from Acambaro (4 Jly Hamburg RF 2660a) - also 1st of 5 from Ituango (8 Aug Hoppegarten RF 3591a). Broke the track record when winning the Deutsches Derby, and won two more major Group Ones in Germany, the BMW Eurochampionat and the Europa-Preis. A game sort, his limitations were exposed by the older Tiger Hill and his contemporary Flamingo Road in the Grosser Preis von Baden. Both of those took their chance in the Arc and, if he remains in training, it may be worth racing him outside Germany in 2000.
**A Wohler in GER [3-5] Turf Syndicate 99.*

BELIEVING BHB 78f74a RR 77f 74a 4786[11]

2 b f Belmez (USA) 11.4f **(65)** - Australia Fair (AUS) (Without Fear (FR)) 5.9f **(55)**
Form - 4150
Record 1999 - 1st:1 2nd:0 3rd:0 Ran:4
Win Prizemoney £2,529 *Total Prizemoney* £2,774
Wins * **1999** Jly Bright (FRM) 5.3f 71+ <
1999 Turf 1-3: (5f 1-2, 6f) (frm 2, hrd 1-1) 1999 AW 0-1: (6f) (Equi)
Above-average filly. Turf high 77 - also 1st of 6 from Dawn's Dancer (12 Jly Brighton RF 2748). She had little to beat when making all to win on very fast ground at Brighton on her second start.
**R Hannon [1-4] The Queen.*

BELISARIO (IRE) RR 74[6]

5 b br g Distinctly North (USA) 7.4f **(63)** - Bold Kate (Bold Lad (IRE)) 8.4f **(68)**
Form - 6
Record 1999 - 1st:0 2nd:0 3rd:0 Ran:1
1999 AW 0-1: (12f) (Fibr)
Poor gelding. **N A Graham [1-5] Paul Jacobs.*

BELLA BHB 35f35a RR 13f 35a 196[5]

3 ch f Inchinor 8.9f **(64)** - Indian Jubilee (Indian King (USA)) 7.4f **(64)**
Form - 05
Record 1999 - 1st:0 2nd:0 3rd:0 Ran:2
Pre1999 - 1st:0 2nd:0 3rd:0 Ran:1
1999 AW 0-2: (7f, 8f) (Equi 2)
Light-framed, currently little account filly, has worn blinkers. AW high 23. **I A Balding [0-3] Lord Lloyd-Webber.*

BELLA BELLISIMO (IRE) BHB 86f **RR 83f** 4760[5]
2 b f Alzao (USA) 9.8f **(73)** - Bella Vitessa (IRE) **(60df)** (Thatching) 8f **(66)**
Form - 125535
Record 1999 - 1st:1 2nd:1 3rd:1 Ran:6
Win Prizemoney £5,498 *Total Prizemoney* £9,281
Wins * **1999** Jun York (G-S) 6f 78 <
1999 Turf 1-6: (6f 1-1, 7f 3, 8f 2) (gd 1-4, g-f, frm)
Decent filly, effective 6 to 8f, acts on gd to g-f, best on gd, has worn blinkers. Turf high 83 - also 1st of 6 getting 5lb from Il Capitano (12 Jun York RF 1965). Knew her job first time up when scoring at York on soft ground, and ran well to finish runner-up to Kingsclere next time. Held in better company.
**T D Easterby [1-6] M P Burke.*

BELLA PUPA RR 3836[18]
3 ch f Theatrical Charmer 10.9f **(63)** - Louisa Anne (Mummy's Pet) 7.7f **(60)**
Form - 00
Record 1999 - 1st:0 2nd:0 3rd:0 Ran:2
1999 Turf 0-1: (7f) (frm) 1999 AW 0-1: (9f) (Fibr)
Unfurnished, currently very poor filly, always wears blinkers.
**Mrs N Macauley [0-2] A Saccomando.*

BELLAS GATE BOY BHB 59f48a **RR 63?f 48a** 4711[14]
7 b g Doulab (USA) 7.4f **(61)** - Celestial Air (Rheingold) 10.4f **(62)**
Form - 6110
Record 1999 - 1st:2 2nd:0 3rd:0 Ran:4
Pre1999 - 1st:2 2nd:6 3rd:1 Ran:38
Win Prizemoney £10,307 *Total Prizemoney* £18,171
Wins * **1999** *Jun Wolver (STD) H 8.5f 40 42*
* **1999** May Warwic (SFT) H 7.7f 49 63? <
* 1998 May Lingfi (GD) H 7f 46 52
* 1997 May Lingfi (G-F) H 7f 46 51
1999 Turf 1-3: (7f, 8f 1-2) (sft 1-1, gd, frm) 1999 AW 1-1: (8f 1-1) (Fibr 1-1)
Average gelding, effective 8f, acts on sft, has worn blinkers. Turf high 63 - 1st of 20 getting 6lb from Noblely (29 May Warwick RF 1586). (1st run). He is not inconvenienced by carrying big weights, and goes well for an amateur.
**J Pearce [4-30] Miss Ann Pauline Meadows (from G Lewis [0-3] Jly 1995).*

BELLE DE JOUR RR 67f 5002[4]
2 b f Exit To Nowhere (USA) 8.7f **(77)** - Nikiya (IRE) (Lead on Time (USA)) 8f **(65)**
Form - 664
Record 1999 - 1st:0 2nd:0 3rd:0 Ran:3
1999 Turf 0-3: (7f 2, 8f) (sft, gd 2)
Currently average filly. Turf high 67 (began Spt).
**D R C Elsworth [0-3] Mrs P T Fenwick.*

BELLEFONTE (IRE) BHB 78f **RR 83df** 3052[5]
3 b c Scenic 10.6f **(66)** - La Bella Fontana (Lafontaine (USA)) 8.7f **(49)**
Form - 5225
Record 1999 - 1st:0 2nd:2 3rd:0 Ran:4
Win Prizemoney £0 *Total Prizemoney* £2,328
1999 Turf 0-4: (9f, 10f 2, 12f) (gd, g-f, frm 2)
Leggy, decent colt. Turf high 83 - 2nd of 12 to Minuit Noir (6 Jly Pontefract 10f frm RF 2582). **C E Brittain [0-4] Saeed Manana.*

BELLEME (IRE) RR 36f 948[15]
3 b f Fairy King (USA) 7.7f **(75)** - Belle Passe (Be My Guest (USA)) 9.3f **(67)**
Form - 0
Record 1999 - 1st:0 2nd:0 3rd:0 Ran:1
1999 Turf 0-1: (7f) (frm)
Workmanlike, currently very moderate filly.
**J H M Gosden [0-1] Sheikh Mohammed.*

BELLE OF HEARTS BHB 39f46a **RR 30f 46a** 4879[20]
3 gr f Belfort (FR) 6.7f **(53)** - Three of Hearts **(56f 50a)** (Governor General)
Form - 00000
Record 1999 - 1st:0 2nd:0 3rd:0 Ran:5
Pre1999 - 1st:0 2nd:1 3rd:3 Ran:9
Win Prizemoney £0 *Total Prizemoney* £2,041
1999 Turf 0-4: (5f, 6f 3) (gd, frm 3) 1999 AW 0-1: (6f) (Fibr)
Light-framed, very moderate filly, effective 6f, acts on gd. Turf high 18. Inconsistent.
**C B B Booth [0-3] Mrs Valerie Dixon (from A B Mulholland [0-3] Jun 1999).*

BELLE REGARD RR 6f 4116[11]
2 ch f Alhijaz 7.7f **(57)** - Imagery (Vision (USA)) 9f **(64)**
Form - 80
Record 1999 - 1st:0 2nd:0 3rd:0 Ran:2
1999 Turf 0-2: (6f, 7f) (g-f, frm)
Very poor filly. Turf high 6 (began Aug). (DEAD)
**T M Jones [0-2] A F Merritt.*

BELLES RIVES BHB 62f **RR 71f** 5138[10]
2 ch f Alflora (IRE) - Dorazine **(53f 59a)** (Kalaglow) 9.8f **(67)**
Form - 040
Record 1999 - 1st:0 2nd:0 3rd:0 Ran:3
Win Prizemoney £0 *Total Prizemoney* £447
1999 Turf 0-3: (5f, 7f, 8f) (g-s, gd 2)
Currently above-average filly. Turf high 71 (began Spt) - 4th of 20 getting 5lb from Castle Sempill (14 Oct Newmarket 7f gd RF 4870).
**M R Channon [0-3] Robin Olley.*

BELMARITA (IRE) BHB 55f **RR 63f** 152[6]
6 ch m Belmez (USA) 11.4f **(65)** - Congress Lady (General Assembly (USA)) 10f **(68)**
Form - 6
Record 1999 - 1st:0 2nd:0 3rd:0 Ran:1
Pre1999 - 1st:0 2nd:3 3rd:2 Ran:15
Win Prizemoney £0 *Total Prizemoney* £5,183
1999 AW 0-1: (12f) (Equi)
Average mare. Inconsistent. A one-paced staying maiden on the Flat, her attitude is open to question.
**G A Hubbard [4-20] G A Hubbard (from M H Tompkins [0-11] Oct 1996).*

BELONG IN LOVE (AUS) BHB 59f **RR 58f** 4625[R]
2 ch f Marscay (AUS) - I'm Alert (AUS) (Red Alert) 7.6f **(66)**
Form - 556R
Record 1999 - 1st:0 2nd:0 3rd:0 Ran:4
Win Prizemoney £0 *Total Prizemoney* £524
1999 Turf 0-4: (5f, 6f 3) (g-s, frm 3)
Fair filly. Turf high 58. **J A R Toller [0-4] J E Baxter.*

BELTESHAZZAR (IRE) BHB 25f29a **RR 33f 29a** 2622[12]
4 b g Un Desperado (FR) 9.3f **(42)** - Annalena (IRE) (Ela-Mana-Mou) 10.1f **(70)**
Form - 7080
Record 1999 - 1st:0 2nd:0 3rd:0 Ran:3
Pre1999 - 1st:0 2nd:0 3rd:0 Ran:3
1999 Turf 0-1: (12f) (frm) 1999 AW 0-2: (8f, 10f) (Equi, Fibr)
Neat, very moderate gelding.
**Mrs L C Jewell [0-3] John Jess (from B R Johnson [0-3] Nov 1998).*

BELVEDERE BHB 49f **RR 60f** 4926[9]
2 ch f Dilum (USA) 7.1f **(56)** - Belle's A Singer (Chief Singer) 8.9f **(66)**
Form - 00400
Record 1999 - 1st:0 2nd:0 3rd:0 Ran:5
1999 Turf 0-4: (6f 2, 8f 2) (g-f 3, hrd) 1999 AW 0-1: (8f) (Fibr)
Average filly, has worn blinkers. Turf high 60 (began Jly) - 4th of 11 getting 5lb from Just Bremner (30 Aug Newcastle 8f g-f RF 4022). **T J Etherington [0-5] J C Smith.*

BE MY PAL RR 46f 4681[11]
2 b f Be My Chief (USA) 10.2f **(62)** - White Domino (Sharpen Up) 8.3f **(67)**
Form - 0
Record 1999 - 1st:0 2nd:0 3rd:0 Ran:1
1999 Turf 0-1: (6f) (gd)
Currently moderate filly. **W Jarvis [0-1] Miss E G Macgregor.*

BE MY WISH BHB 52f70a **RR 53f 70a** 1952[10]
4 b f Be My Chief (USA) 10.2f **(62)** - Spinner (Blue Cashmere) 6.4f **(54)**
Form - 823680400
Record 1999 - 1st:0 2nd:0 3rd:0 Ran:5
Pre1999 - 1st:1 2nd:1 3rd:3 Ran:15

Win Prizemoney £5,368 *Total Prizemoney* £8,855
Wins 1998 Aug Ascot (G-F) 7f 77 <
1999 Turf 0-5: (8f, 10f 3, 11f) (gd, g-f 3, frm)
Well made, above-average filly, effective 7f, acts on gd to g-f - acts on Equi, best on g-f, has worn blinkers. Turf high 53.
**S P C Woods [0-6] T Tran (from Miss Gay Kelleway [1-14] Nov 1998).*

BENATOM (USA) BHB 96f **RR 95f** 4096[5]
6 gr g Hawkster (USA) 12.4f **(71)** - Dance Til Two (USA) (Sovereign Dancer (USA)) 11.2f **(68)**
Form - 65424612845
Record 1999 - 1st:1 2nd:2 3rd:0 Ran:11
Pre1999 - 1st:4 2nd:1 3rd:2 Ran:18
Win Prizemoney £39,065 *Total Prizemoney* £59,474
Wins * **1999** Jly Newmar (GD) H 16.1f 90 95
1997 Jly York (GD) LH 13.9f 90 97 <
1996 Aug Goodwo (G-F) H 14f 90 95
1996 Jly Newmar (GD) H 16.1f 85 90
1996 Apr Thirsk (G-F) 12f 76
1999 Turf 1-11: (14f 4, 16f 1-6, 20f) (gd 2, g-f 2, frm 1-7)
Very useful gelding, effective 14 to 20f, best at 16f, acts on gd to frm, best on frm, has worn blinkers, likes right handed tracks, and excels at Kempton. Turf high 95 - 1st of 6 giving 5lb to Eminence Grise (7 Jly Newmarket RF 2634). Consistent. He ran well in most of our top staying handicaps and seems to need two miles these days. Unlikely to improve, he has run his best races on a sound surface but is quite high in the handicap at present.
**D R C Elsworth [2-22] Lordship Stud (from H R A Cecil [4-15] Jly 1997).*

BENBYAS BHB 60f **RR 73f** 4575[9]
2 b g Rambo Dancer (CAN) 8.4f **(59)** - Light the Way (Nicholas Bill) 10.1f **(56)**
Form - 00400
Record 1999 - 1st:0 2nd:0 3rd:0 Ran:5
Win Prizemoney £0 *Total Prizemoney* £252
1999 Turf 0-5: (6f 2, 8f 3) (gd 2, g-f, frm, hrd)
Above-average gelding. Turf high 73 (began Aug).
**J L Eyre [0-5] C H Stephenson & Partners.*

BEN EWAR RR 110f 3231a[4]
5 b h Old Vic 12.8f **(72)** - Sunset Reef (Mill Reef (USA)) 10.5f **(78)**
Form - 44
1999 Turf 0-2: (12f, 13f) (gd 2)
Currently Group-class. Turf high 110 - 4th of 6 to Lucky Dream (24 Jly Maisons-Laffitte 13f gd RF 3231a). **F Doumen in FR [1-3].*

BEN GUNN BHB 69f62a **RR 72f 62a** 4711[7]
7 b g Faustus (USA) 9.1f **(54)** - Pirate Maid (Auction Ring (USA)) 8.6f **(65)**
Form - 755476107
Record 1999 - 1st:1 2nd:0 3rd:0 Ran:9
Pre1999 - 1st:7 2nd:4 3rd:6 Ran:41
Win Prizemoney £31,992 *Total Prizemoney* £46,611
Wins * **1999** Aug Chepst (G-F) H 8.1f 68 72
* 1998 Jun Salisb (G-F) H 8f 73 78
* 1998 May Newmar (G-F) H 8f 70 75
* 1997 Jly Newmar (GD) H 8f 65 73
* 1997 May Salisb (G-F) H 7f 60 66
* 1995 Jly Windso (G-F) H 6f 67 68
1999 Turf 1-8: (8f 1-8) (gd 2, g-f 3, frm 1-3) 1999 AW 0-1: (8f) (Equi)
Above-average gelding, effective 8f, acts on gd to frm, best on g-f, has worn blinkers. Turf high 72 - 1st of 17 giving 16lb to Doberman (5 Aug Chepstow RF 3389). Consistent. Suited by a fast-run mile.
**P T Walwyn [8-50] Michael White.*

BENHABEEBI (IRE) BHB 62f **RR 71f** 4169[8]
2 b g Bin Ajwaad (IRE) - Alfaaselah (GER) **(70f)** (Dancing Brave (USA)) 8.4f **(76)**
Form - 43338
Record 1999 - 1st:0 2nd:0 3rd:3 Ran:5
Win Prizemoney £0 *Total Prizemoney* £1,867
1999 Turf 0-5: (6f, 7f 3, 8f) (gd, g-f 2, frm 2)
Above-average gelding. Turf high 71 - 3rd of 11 giving 5lb to Alabama Wurley (6 Aug Newmarket 7f g-f RF 3425).
**B Hanbury [0-5] A Merza.*

BENNOCHY BHB 54f **RR 61f** 5187[7]
2 ch g Factual (USA) - Agreloui (Tower Walk) 10f **(62)**
Form - 866007
Record 1999 - 1st:0 2nd:0 3rd:0 Ran:6
1999 Turf 0-6: (5f 5, 6f) (gd 2, g-f 2, frm 2)
Average gelding. Turf high 61. **J Berry [0-6] Mrs Norma Peebles.*

BENOUI SPRINGS (IRE) RR 70f 4655[8]
2 br c Caerleon (USA) 10.9f **(79)** - Afrique Bleu Azur (USA) (Sagace (FR)) 8f **(124)**
Form - 8
Record 1999 - 1st:0 2nd:0 3rd:0 Ran:1
1999 Turf 0-1: (7f) (gd)
Currently above-average colt.
**P W Chapple-Hyam [0-1] R E Sangster & A K Collins.*

BEN SAMSON RR 15f 2891[6]
3 ch g Bold Arrangement 8.7f **(57)** - Mr Chris Cakemaker (Hotfoot) 10.5f **(59)**
Form - 66
Record 1999 - 1st:0 2nd:0 3rd:0 Ran:2
1999 Turf 0-2: (10f, 13f) (frm 2)
Currently poor gelding. Turf high 15.
**E J Alston [0-2] Philip Davies & Peter J Davies.*

BENS GIFT BHB 57f **RR 57f** 4011[14]
4 ch f Keen 11.1f **(58)** - Monstrosa (Monsanto (FR)) 6.5f **(59)**
Form - 71200
Record 1999 - 1st:1 2nd:1 3rd:0 Ran:5
Pre1999 - 1st:0 2nd:0 3rd:1 Ran:5
Win Prizemoney £2,962 *Total Prizemoney* £4,271
Wins * **1999** Jly Windso (G-F) H 10f 50 52 <
1999 Turf 1-5: (9f, 10f 1-4) (gd, g-f, frm 1-3)
Workmanlike, fair filly, effective 10f, acts on frm, favours tight tracks. Turf high 57 (began Jly) - 2nd of 15 giving 9lb to Little Tumbler (4 Aug Brighton 10f frm RF 3349) - also 1st of 17 getting 5lb from Sea Danzig (26 Jly Windsor RF 3147). Inconsistent.
**Mrs Merrita Jones [1-5] The Gift Horse Partnership (from C F Wall [0-5] Spt 1998).*

BENTYHEATH LANE RR 51f 5216[10]
2 b g Puissance 7.1f **(60)** - Eye Sight (Roscoe Blake) 11f **(66)**
Form - 00
Record 1999 - 1st:0 2nd:0 3rd:0 Ran:2
1999 Turf 0-2: (7f, 8f) (g-s, gd)
Currently fair gelding. Turf high 51 (began Oct).
**M Mullineaux [0-2] Lord Leverhulme.*

BENZOE (IRE) BHB 57f **RR 45f** 4878[13]
9 b g Taufan (USA) 8.3f **(65)** - Saintly Guest (What A Guest) 7f **(62)**
Form - 00068001000770
Record 1999 - 1st:1 2nd:0 3rd:0 Ran:14
Pre1999 - 1st:9 2nd:9 3rd:10 Ran:89
Win Prizemoney £51,180 *Total Prizemoney* £81,757
Wins * **1999** Jly Leices (G-F) H 6f 62 61
1998 Spt Redcar (G-F) H 6f 70 74
1998 May Thirsk (G-F) H 6f 68 73
1997 Jly Thirsk (GD) H 6f 73 77
1997 Jun Thirsk (G-F) H 5f 64 65
1996 Aug Thirsk (G-F) H 6f 77 81
1996 May Thirsk (G-F) H 6f 69 72
1995 May Thirsk (G-F) H 6f 66 71+
1999 Turf 1-14: (5f, 6f 1-11, 7f 2) (sft, gd 4, g-f 1-2, frm 7)
Moderate gelding, has broken blood-vessels, effective 5 to 6f, best at 6f, acts on gd to frm, best on frm, has worn blinkers, likes Thirsk. Turf high 61. Consistent. Formerly with Lynda Ramsden, he is a useful performer if everything goes his way, although he is often slowly away. He excels at Thirsk, though he can win elsewhere.
**Andrew Turnell [1-14] Tony Fawcett (from Mrs J R Ramsden [7-64] Nov 1998).*

BERBERIS BHB 45f **RR 50f** 4951[12]
3 b c Green Desert (USA) 7.8f **(78)** - Babita (Habitat) 9.4f **(70)**
Form - 800
Record 1999 - 1st:0 2nd:0 3rd:0 Ran:3
1999 Turf 0-3: (7f 2, 8f) (g-s, g-f, frm)

Workmanlike, currently fair colt. Turf high 50.
**C E Brittain [0-3] Saeed Manana.*

BERGAMO BHB 74f **RR 73f** 4273[5]
3 b c Robellino (USA) 9.5f **(68)** - Pretty Thing (Star Appeal) 9.6f **(65)**
Form - 06015661344435
Record 1999 - 1st:2 2nd:0 3rd:2 Ran:14
Pre1999 - 1st:1 2nd:0 3rd:1 Ran:6
Win Prizemoney £9,653 *Total Prizemoney* £14,036
Wins * 1999 Jun Yarmou (GD) H 14.1f 74 79 <
*** 1999** May Beverl (GD) H 12f 70 73
*** 1998** Spt Bath (G-S) 10.2f 78
1999 Turf 2-14: (10f 2, 12f 1-5, 13f, 14f 1-4, 16f 2) (gd 2-4, g-f 5, frm 4, hrd)
Workmanlike, above-average colt, effective 8 to 16f, best at 14f, acts on gd to hrd, best on g-f, often wears blinkers (extremely effectively), likes left handed tracks, prefers tight tracks, excels at Chepstow, likes Kempton. Turf high 79 - 1st of 11 getting 2lb from Cheek To Cheek (30 Jun Yarmouth RF 2453) - also 1st of 15 giving 12lb to Burma Baby (25 May Beverley RF 1449). Consistent. A winner twice last season, he showed he stayed fourteen furlongs when winning at Yarmouth, but seemed to find two miles too far subsequently. A tricky ride, he has reportedly joined Brian Ellison.
**J Noseda [3-20] Mrs M Conti-Dack.*

BERGEN (IRE) BHB 74f **RR 75f** 5004[11]
4 b c Ballad Rock 7.2f **(63)** - Local Custom (IRE) (Be My Native (USA)) 10.2f **(71)**
Form - 760720
Record 1999 - 1st:0 2nd:1 3rd:0 Ran:6
Pre1999 - 1st:1 2nd:1 3rd:1 Ran:7
Win Prizemoney £3,485 *Total Prizemoney* £8,028
Wins 1997 Jly Pontef (G-F) 6f 86+ <
1999 Turf 0-6: (8f 5, 9f) (gd 2, g-f 2, frm 2)
Light-framed, above-average colt, effective 8 to 9f, best at 8f, acts on g-s to frm, best on frm, prefers left handed tracks. Turf high 75. Inconsistent.
**B W Hills [0-6] J Hanson (from J Hanson [1-7] Spt 1998).*

BERING GIFTS (IRE) BHB 70f **RR 70f** 4489[8]
4 b g Bering 9.6f **(80)** - Bobbysoxer (Valiyar) 8.5f **(73)**
Form - 00152858
Record 1999 - 1st:1 2nd:1 3rd:0 Ran:8
Pre1999 - 1st:2 2nd:2 3rd:2 Ran:11
Win Prizemoney £18,715 *Total Prizemoney* £25,585
Wins * 1999 May Folkes (G-F) H 9.7f 78 78
* 1998 Aug Folkes (G-F) H 9.7f 78 83 <
* 1998 Aug Warwic (G-F) 8f 67
1999 Turf 1-8: (8f, 9f 3, 10f 1-2, 12f 2) (g-s, gd 1-3, g-f, frm 3)
Well made, above-average gelding, effective 10 to 12f, best at 10f, acts on gd to frm, has worn blinkers, likes right handed tracks, prefers tight tracks. Turf high 78 - 1st of 7 giving 3lb to Praetorian Gold (26 May Folkestone RF 1493). Consistent. Has joined Charlie Mann as a jumper.
**P F I Cole [3-19] GG Partnership.*

BERKELEY DIDO (IRE) BHB 54f **RR 52f** 3488[6]
2 b f Foxhound (USA) - Dignified Air (FR) (Wolver Hollow) 8f **(56)**
Form - 70306
Record 1999 - 1st:0 2nd:0 3rd:1 Ran:5
Win Prizemoney £0 *Total Prizemoney* £497
1999 Turf 0-5: (5f 2, 6f 2, 7f) (g-s, gd 2, g-f, frm)
Fair filly. Turf high 52. **M L W Bell [0-5] Capt B W Bell.*

BERKELEY HALL BHB 60f **RR 55f** 4928[3]
2 b f Saddlers' Hall (IRE) 10.5f **(65)** - Serious Affair (Valiyar) 8.5f **(73)**
Form - 703
Record 1999 - 1st:0 2nd:0 3rd:1 Ran:3
Win Prizemoney £0 *Total Prizemoney* £266
1999 Turf 0-3: (6f 2, 8f) (gd, g-f, frm)
Currently fair filly. Turf high 55 (began Aug).
**B Palling [0-3] D Brennan.*

BERKOUTCHI (FR) RR 104f 1357a[14]
3 c Take Risks (FR) - Valley Road (FR) 00
Form - 10
1999 Turf 1-2: (7f 1-1, 8f) (g-s 1-1, gd)
Currently very useful colt. Turf high 104 (1st run) - 1st of 7 from Restless War (9 Apr Maisons-Laffitte RF 0714a). He needs to be ridden with exaggerated waiting tactics, but was out of his depth when beating just one home in the French 2,000 Guineas.
**H-A Pantall in FR [1-3].*

BERLIOZ BHB 105f **RR 102f** 2358[7]
3 b c Dolphin Street (FR) - Biraya (Valiyar) 8.5f **(73)**
Form - 67
Record 1999 - 1st:0 2nd:0 3rd:0 Ran:2
Pre1999 - 1st:1 2nd:1 3rd:0 Ran:2
Win Prizemoney £11,576 *Total Prizemoney* £16,854
Wins 1998 Spt Newbur (GD) 7f 87++ <
1999 Turf 0-2: (8f 2) (gd 2)
Scopey, very useful colt. Turf high 102 (1st run) - 6th of 11 to Sumitas (16 May Cologne 8f gd RF 1355a). He looked promising as a juvenile, but proved disappointing in 1999. Reported to have swollen up around the girth when finishing last at Goodwood in June, he has plenty to prove.
**S bin Suroor [0-2] Godolphin (from D R Loder [1-2] Oct 1998).*

BERL'S GIFT BHB 36f **RR 63f** 4539[14]
4 b f Prince Sabo 6.6f **(64)** - Primitive Gift (Primitive Rising (USA))
Form - 0
Record 1999 - 1st:0 2nd:0 3rd:0 Ran:1
Pre1999 - 1st:0 2nd:0 3rd:2 Ran:5
Win Prizemoney £0 *Total Prizemoney* £741
1999 Turf 0-1: (10f) (frm)
Unfurnished, average filly, effective 7f, acts on sft.
**Mrs M Reveley [0-6] Minster Commercials.*

BERMUDA TRIANGLE (IRE) BHB 36f46a **RR 31f 46a** 2760[7]
4 b f Conquering Hero (USA) 10.6f **(50)** - Bermuda Princess (Lord Gayle (USA)) 8.8f **(62)**
Form - 7
Record 1999 - 1st:0 2nd:0 3rd:0 Ran:1
Pre1999 - 1st:1 2nd:2 3rd:0 Ran:15
Win Prizemoney £2,337 *Total Prizemoney* £4,122
Wins * 1997 Aug Lingfi (G-F) S 6f 50 <
1999 Turf 0-1: (12f) (frm)
Leggy, moderate filly. **M J Haynes [1-21] M J Haynes.*

BERNARDO BELLOTTO (IRE) BHB 57f76a **RR 59f 76a** 2269[14]
4 b g High Estate 10.5f **(66)** - Naivity (IRE) (Auction Ring (USA)) 8.6f **(65)**
Form - 73007110
Record 1999 - 1st:2 2nd:0 3rd:1 Ran:8
Pre1999 - 1st:1 2nd:5 3rd:1 Ran:14
Win Prizemoney £8,274 *Total Prizemoney* £14,461
Wins * 1999 Jun Mussel (GD) C 7.1f 59
*** 1999** May Redcar (FRM) S 7f 56
1997 Aug Epsom (GD) 6f 78 <
1999 Turf 2-8: (6f 3, 7f 2-5) (gd 2, g-f 1-1, frm 1-5)
Above-average gelding, effective 7f, acts on g-f to frm, has worn blinkers. Turf high 59 - 1st of 14 giving 6lb to Detroit City (14 Jun Musselburgh RF 1978) - also 1st of 16 from Batsman (31 May Redcar RF 1606).
**D Nicholls [2-8] Mrs E G Faulkner (from M L W Bell [1-14] Oct 1998).*

BERNIE'S STAR (IRE) BHB 21f **RR 9f** 504[5]
5 b br g Arcane (USA) 11.6f **(66)** - Abaca(USA)(Manila (USA)) 9.3f **(71)**
Form - 05
Record 1999 - 1st:0 2nd:0 3rd:0 Ran:2
Pre1999 - 1st:0 2nd:0 3rd:0 Ran:7
1999 Turf 0-1: (12f) (hvy) 1999 AW 0-1: (16f) (Fibr)
Very poor gelding, has worn blinkers. Becoming disappointing.
**N Bycroft [0-15] Bernard Rayner.*

BERNSTEIN (USA) RR 107f 4478a[5]
2 b c Storm Cat (USA) 7f **(86)** - La Affirmed (USA) 00
Form - 115
1999 Turf 2-3: (6f 2-2, 8f) (g-s, gd 1-1, g-f 1-1)
Currently Pattern-class colt. Turf high 107 - 1st of 4 giving 6lb to Desert Sky (27 Jun Curragh RF 2416a). One of the most precocious of the Aidan O'Brien juveniles, he made an impressive debut at the Curragh in May before landing a Group Three over the same course and distance in June. He looked sure to follow up in the

National Stakes over a mile, only to fold like a deck of cards when his stamina ran dry inside the last. He was found to have a 'respiratory abnormality' after the race, and might still stay a mile on a sounder surface. He remains a high-class prospect.

**A P O'Brien in IRE [2-3] Michael Tabor.*

BERSAGLIO BHB 59f RR 47f 4356[5]

4 ch c Rainbow Quest (USA) 11.2f **(81)** - Escrime (USA) (Sharpen Up) 8.3f **(67)**

Form - 02005

Record 1999 - 1st:0 2nd:1 3rd:0 Ran:5
Pre1999 - 1st:0 2nd:0 3rd:2 Ran:8

Win Prizemoney £0 *Total Prizemoney* £2,692

1999 Turf 0-5: (14f 4, 18f) (g-s, gd, g-f, frm 2)

Scopey, moderate colt, effective 12 to 14f, best at 14f, acts on g-f to frm, best on frm. Turf high 67. Inconsistent.

**K A Morgan [0-1] J A Outwin (from W Jarvis [0-12] Jun 1999).*

BERTOLINI (USA) BHB 120f RR 119f 4777a[12]

3 b c Danzig (USA) 8.1f **(88)** - Aquilegia (USA) (Alydar (USA)) 9.1f **(76)**

Form - 1033320

Record 1999 - 1st:1 2nd:1 3rd:3 Ran:7
Pre1999 - 1st:1 2nd:3 3rd:0 Ran:7

Win Prizemoney £35,410 *Total Prizemoney* £144,774

Wins * 1999 Apr Newmar (GD) LH 7f 113 113 <
* 1998 Jly Newmar (G-F) G3 6f 106+

1999 Turf 1-7: (5f, 6f 2, 7f 1-3, 8f) (hvy, sft, gd 1-3, frm 2)

Scopey, high-class colt, effective 6 to 7f, best at 7f, acts on hvy to frm, has worn blinkers (effectively). Turf high 119 - 2nd of 16 getting 2lb from Diktat (4 Spt Haydock 6f frm RF 4138) - also 1st of 6 giving 1lb to Indiana Legend (14 Apr Newmarket RF 0694). He showed he had trained on when winning the Free Handicap in good style on his return. Well beaten in the French Guineas on his first attempt at a mile, he was then brought back in trip, finishing third in the Jersey Stakes, July Cup, and Prix Maurice de Gheest. The heavy ground just seemed to find him out at Deauville, and he demonstrated his liking for a better surface when second to Diktat at Haydock in the Stanley Leisure Sprint Cup. Ended the season by running poorly in the Prix de l'Abbaye, when the heavy ground and minimum trip looked totally unsuitable. Has joined Godolphin.

**J H M Gosden [2-14] Sheikh Mohammed.*

BERTY BOY BHB 42f RR 48f 4724[15]

3 ch g Alhijaz 7.7f **(57)** - Bridge Player (The Noble Player (USA)) 6.5f **(67)**

Form - 0640

Record 1999 - 1st:0 2nd:0 3rd:0 Ran:4

1999 Turf 0-4: (8f, 10f, 11f, 12f) (gd 2, g-f, hrd)

Scopey, moderate gelding. Turf high 48.

**Mrs G S Rees [0-4] Miss Marjorie Thompson.*

BERYL BHB 70f RR 77f 4553[14]

3 ch f Bering 9.6f **(80)** - Fayrooz (USA) **(81df)** (Gulch (USA)) 8f **(81)**

Form - 2103500

Record 1999 - 1st:1 2nd:1 3rd:1 Ran:7
Pre1999 - 1st:0 2nd:2 3rd:0 Ran:4

Win Prizemoney £4,003 *Total Prizemoney* £8,382

Wins * 1999 Apr Thirsk (GD) 12f 71 <

1999 Turf 1-7: (10f, 11f, 12f 1-2, 14f 2, 15f) (g-s, gd 1-3, frm 3)

Workmanlike, above-average filly, effective 10 to 12f, acts on gd to frm, best on gd, prefers left handed tracks, prefers tight tracks. Turf high 77 - 3rd of 7 giving 13lb to Common Cause (22 Jun Lingfield 11f frm RF 2200) - also 1st of 7 getting 5lb from Gold Lodge (16 Apr Thirsk RF 0727). Winner of a 12-furlong maiden at Thirsk in April. She has failed to make her mark in handicap company since and did not appear to stay when tried at a mile and three-quarters. **J L Dunlop [1-11] Capt J Macdonald-Buchanan.*

BERYL THE PERIL BHB 32f RR 322[7]

3 b f Presidium 7.5f **(56)** - Vague Reply (Vaigly Great) 7f **(58)**

Form - 7

Record 1999 - 1st:0 2nd:0 3rd:0 Ran:1
Pre1999 - 1st:0 2nd:0 3rd:0 Ran:2

1999 AW 0-1: (7f) (Fibr)

Light-framed, currently very poor filly. **N Bycroft [0-3] C Lawson.*

BESCABY BLUE (IRE) BHB 61f65a RR 64f 65a 5218[6]

2 b f Blues Traveller (IRE) - Nurse Tyra (USA) (Dr Blum (USA)) 9.8f **(70)**

Form - 12558176

Record 1999 - 1st:2 2nd:1 3rd:0 Ran:8

Win Prizemoney £5,070 *Total Prizemoney* £5,894

Wins * 1999 Oct Redcar (GD) C 7f 64
*** 1999** *May Southw (STD) 5f 76* <

1999 Turf 1-6: (5f 2, 6f, 7f 1-3) (g-s, gd 3, frm 1-2) 1999 AW 1-2: (5f 1-1, 6f) (Fibr 1-2)

Above-average filly, effective 5f, acts on gd - acts on Fibr. Turf high 73 (1st run) - 2nd of 3 giving 1lb to Paris Star (24 May Hamilton 5f gd RF 1424). AW high 76 (1st run) - 1st of 10 getting 3lb from Baby Barry (6 May Southwell RF 1064). **J Wharton [2-8] John Wharton.*

BESEECHING (IRE) BHB 49f RR 45f 3251[7]

4 b br f Hamas (IRE) 8f **(72)** - Na-Ammah (IRE) **(84f)** (Ela-Mana-Mou) 10.1f **(70)**

Form - 087

Record 1999 - 1st:0 2nd:0 3rd:0 Ran:3
Pre1999 - 1st:0 2nd:0 3rd:0 Ran:3

Win Prizemoney £0 *Total Prizemoney* £255

1999 Turf 0-3: (8f, 10f, 14f) (gd, frm 2)

Workmanlike, moderate filly. Turf high 45.

**J A R Toller [0-6] P C J Dalby.*

BEST BOND BHB 68f RR 71f 4449[5]

2 ch c Cadeaux Genereux 7.9f **(76)** - My Darlingdaughter **(18f)** (Night Shift (USA)) 7.2f **(69)**

Form - 855

Record 1999 - 1st:0 2nd:0 3rd:0 Ran:3

1999 Turf 0-3: (6f, 7f, 8f) (sft, gd, frm)

Currently above-average colt. Turf high 71 (began Jly).

**J L Dunlop [0-3] Wafic Said.*

BEST EVER RR 70f 5052[15]

2 ch c Rock City 8.8f **(62)** - Better Still (IRE) (Glenstal (USA)) 10.1f **(64)**

Form - 0003252070

Record 1999 - 1st:0 2nd:2 3rd:1 Ran:10

Win Prizemoney £0 *Total Prizemoney* £4,238

1999 Turf 0-10: (5f 3, 7f 6, 8f) (gd 4, g-f, frm 4, hrd)

Above-average colt, effective 7 to 8f, best at 7f, acts on g-f to hrd, best on frm. Turf high 70 - 2nd of 14 getting 17lb from The Wife (2 Spt York 8f frm RF 4103). **M W Easterby [0-10] Mrs Jean Turpin.*

BEST GREY RR 107f 5016a[5]

3 gr c Ezzoud (IRE) - Best Girl Friend (Sharrood (USA)) 10.5f **(72)**

Form - 35

1999 Turf 0-2: (12f 2) (g-f 2)

Currently Pattern-class colt. Turf high 107 - 5th of 6 to Sumati (17 Oct San Siro 12f g-f RF 5016a). He was hampered when finishing fourth (promoted to third) in the Italian Derby and is capable of winning Group races over a mile and a half.

**V Caruso in ITY [0-2].*

BEST KEPT SECRET BHB 16f32a RR 19f 32a 4588[8]

8 b g Petong 7.6f **(58)** - Glenfield Portion (Mummy's Pet) 7.7f **(60)**

Form - 05087000008

Record 1999 - 1st:0 2nd:0 3rd:0 Ran:11
Pre1999 - 1st:6 2nd:9 3rd:13 Ran:69

Win Prizemoney £17,921 *Total Prizemoney* £33,410

1999 Turf 0-11: (5f 3, 6f 4, 7f, 8f, 9f, 12f) (hvy, gd 4, g-f 3, frm 3)

Very moderate gelding, has worn blinkers. Turf high 33.

**D A Nolan [0-17] Mrs J McFadyen-Murray (from L J Barratt [0-7] Aug 1997).*

BEST MUSIC METROFM RR 580[3]

2 b c Governor General 6.8f **(45)** - Dancing May (Tina's Pet) 6.8f **(59)**

Form - 3

Record 1999 - 1st:0 2nd:0 3rd:1 Ran:1

Win Prizemoney £0 *Total Prizemoney* £452

1999 Turf 0-1: (5f) (gd)

Currently very poor colt. **D Eddy [0-1] Charles Castle.*

BEST OF ALL (IRE) BHB 72f70a RR 74f 70a 5217[F]

7 b m Try My Best (USA) 7.8f **(68)** -Skisette(Malinowski (USA)) 10f **(56)**

Form - 440582617F

Record 1999 - 1st:1 2nd:1 3rd:0 Ran:10
Pre1999 - 1st:8 2nd:4 3rd:4 Ran:46
Win Prizemoney £37,303 *Total Prizemoney* £46,675
Wins * **1999** Spt Mussel (G-S) 8f **74**
* 1998 Aug Ripon (G-F) H 10f 75 77 <
* 1998 Jly Goodwo (G-S) H 9f 68 72
* 1998 Jly Mussel (GD) H 9f 60 68
* 1997 Jun Mussel (GD) H 8f 62 74
* 1997 Jun Redcar (FRM) H 8f 62 67
* 1996 *Nov Southw (STD) C 8f 61*
* 1995 Nov Mussel (SFT) H 8.1f 67 72
1999 Turf 1-10: (8f 1-5, 9f, 10f 4) (g-s, gd 1-5, g-f 2, frm, hrd)
Above-average mare, effective 8 to 10f, best at 10f, acts on gd to hrd, best on frm, often wears blinkers (effectively), likes right handed tracks, likes tight tracks, excels at Thirsk and Musselburgh. Turf high 76 (1st run) - 4th of 13 giving 6lb to Ratatuia (15 Jun Thirsk 8f frm RF 2006) - also 1st of 8 giving 4lb to Isle Au Haut (26 Spt Musselburgh RF 4578).
**J Berry [12-66] Robert Aird.*

BEST OF THE BESTS (IRE) BHB 100f **RR 100f** 4570[2]

2 ch c Machiavellian (USA) 9.8f **(83)** - Sueboog (IRE) (Darshaan) 9.9f **(84)**
Form - 312
Record 1999 - 1st:1 2nd:1 3rd:1 Ran:3
Win Prizemoney £16,075 *Total Prizemoney* £43,470
Wins * **1999** Aug Sandow (GD) G3 7.1f 98+ <
1999 Turf 1-3: (7f 1-2, 8f) (sft, g-f 1-1, frm)
Currently very useful colt. Turf high 100 (began Jly) - 2nd of 6 giving 3lb to Royal Kingdom (26 Spt Ascot 8f sft RF 4570) - also 1st of 7 from Sarafan (20 Aug Sandown RF 3807). He sprang a 20-1 surprise when winning the Solario Stakes at Sandown in August, and showed that was no fluke when finishing half a length second to Royal Kingdom (received three pounds) in the Royal Lodge Stakes the following month. Easily the pick of the paddock that day, he is out of a mare that finished fourth in the Oaks and should stay at least a mile and a quarter. An imposing individual with bags of scope, he is an interesting prospect.
**C E Brittain [1-3] Mohamed Obaida.*

BEST PORT (IRE) BHB 22f **RR 41f** 4988[6]

3 b g Be My Guest (USA) 10.2f **(66)** - Portree (Slip Anchor) 9.8f **(73)**
Form - 8006076
Record 1999 - 1st:0 2nd:0 3rd:0 Ran:7
Pre1999 - 1st:0 2nd:0 3rd:0 Ran:2
1999 Turf 0-6: (8f, 10f 3, 14f 2) (gd, g-f, frm 3, hrd) 1999 AW 0-1: (11f) (Fibr)
Neat, moderate gelding. Turf high 41 (began Aug).
**J Parkes [0-7] W A Sellers (from M A Jarvis [0-2] Nov 1998).*

BEST QUEST BHB 59f64a **RR 60f 64a** 442[3]

4 b c Salse (USA) 10.9f **(71)** - Quest for the Best (Rainbow Quest (USA)) 10.4f **(75)**
Form - 536184000473
Record 1999 - 1st:0 2nd:0 3rd:1 Ran:8
Pre1999 - 1st:2 2nd:2 3rd:2 Ran:14
Win Prizemoney £7,231 *Total Prizemoney* £10,736
Wins * 1998 *Dec Lingfi (STD) H 7f 68 70* <
1998 Oct Doncas (SFT) C 7f 55
1999 AW 0-8: (6f 4, 7f 4) (Equi 3, Fibr 5)
Workmanlike, average colt, effective 6 to 8f, - acts on AW, best on Equi, has worn blinkers, likes left handed tracks, does well at Lingfield. AW high 71 - 4th of 13 giving 12lb to Tom Tun (8 Jan Southwell 6f Fibr RF 0054).
**K R Burke [1-12] Nigel Shields (from J H M Gosden [1-10] Oct 1998).*

BE THANKFULL (IRE) BHB 85f **RR 86f** 4677[1]

3 gr f Linamix (FR) 8.2f **(64)** - Thank One's Stars(Alzao (USA)) 7.1f **(68)**
Form - 1621
Record 1999 - 1st:2 2nd:1 3rd:0 Ran:4
Pre1999 - 1st:0 2nd:0 3rd:0 Ran:1
Win Prizemoney £13,354 *Total Prizemoney* £17,834
Wins * **1999** Oct Newmar (G-S) H 10f 81 85 <
* **1999** Jly Ascot (G-F) 8f 76
1999 Turf 2-4: (8f 1-2, 9f, 10f 1-1) (gd 1-2, g-f 1-2)
Unfurnished, useful filly. Turf high 86 (began Jly) - 2nd of 15 getting 4lb from Dashiba (29 Aug Goodwood 9f g-f RF 3994) - also 1st of 12 getting 2lb from Lamerie (1 Oct Newmarket RF 4677). Kept on very determinedly in her first start for over 11 months when winning on her seasonal reappearance at Ascot. Well beaten in a Listed race after that, but ran better when runner-up in a Goodwood handicap next time, before winning gamely at Headquarters. **Major D N Chappell [2-5] Mrs G C Maxwell.*

BE THE CHIEF BHB 80f **RR 64f** 3941[5]

3 ch c Be My Chief (USA) 10.2f **(62)** - Blink Naskra (USA) (Naskra (USA)) 8.8f **(69)**
Form - 075
Record 1999 - 1st:0 2nd:0 3rd:0 Ran:3
Pre1999 - 1st:1 2nd:1 3rd:0 Ran:2
Win Prizemoney £3,494 *Total Prizemoney* £14,769
Wins * 1998 May Doncas (GD) 6f 97+ <
1999 Turf 0-3: (7f 2, 8f) (g-f 2, frm)
Workmanlike, average colt. Turf high 64. He looked a colt of some potential when runner-up behind Red Sea in the 1998 Coventry Stakes, but missed the rest of the season after injuring a pastern, and showed very little on his return.
**T G Mills [1-5] Mrs Stephanie Merrydew.*

BETHESDA BHB 94f **RR 90f** 4801[5]

2 gr f Distant Relative 7f **(69)** - Anneli Rose (Superlative) 7.2f **(56)**
Form - 265
Record 1999 - 1st:0 2nd:1 3rd:0 Ran:3
Win Prizemoney £0 *Total Prizemoney* £1,856
1999 Turf 0-3: (6f 3) (g-s, gd, g-f)
Currently useful filly. Turf high 90 (began Spt).
**J M P Eustace [0-3] K J Mercer.*

BETTINA BLUE (IRE) BHB 68f63a **RR 69f 63a** 5061[6]

2 b f Paris House 5.9f **(64)** - Born to Fly (IRE) (Last Tycoon) 8.5f **(62)**
Form - 576
Record 1999 - 1st:0 2nd:0 3rd:0 Ran:3
1999 Turf 0-3: (5f 3) (g-s 2, frm)
Currently average filly. Turf high 69 (began Oct).
**R Ingram [0-3] Epsom Sporting Proposals Ltd.*

BETTRON BHB 65f **RR 47?f** 1129[11]

4 b g Alnasr Alwasheek 9.4f **(62)** - Aigua Blava (USA) (Solford (USA)) 13f **(71)**
Form - 20
Record 1999 - 1st:0 2nd:1 3rd:0 Ran:2
Pre1999 - 1st:2 2nd:1 3rd:2 Ran:12
Win Prizemoney £5,065 *Total Prizemoney* £9,503
Wins 1998 Jun Sandow (G-S) C 10f 69+
1997 Jly Bright (FRM) C 7f 71+ <
1999 Turf 0-1: (7f) (gd) 1999 AW 0-1: (7f) (Fibr)
Unfurnished, above-average gelding, effective 7 to 9f, acts on g-s to g-f - acts on Fibr, prefers tight tracks. Becoming disappointing.
**D J Wintle [0-1] D J Wintle (from R Hannon [2-13] Apr 1999).*

BETTY BATHWICK (IRE) BHB 56f **RR 57f** 3419[2]

2 b f Common Grounds 8.1f **(66)** - Tynaghmile (IRE) (Lyphard's Special (USA)) 10.3f **(72)**
Form - 0002
Record 1999 - 1st:0 2nd:1 3rd:0 Ran:4
Win Prizemoney £0 *Total Prizemoney* £615
1999 Turf 0-4: (5f, 6f 2, 7f) (gd, g-f, frm 2)
Fair filly. Turf high 57. **B Smart [0-4] The Parrot Club.*

BETTYJOE BHB 55f **RR 66f** 5218[14]

2 ch f Inchinor 8.9f **(64)** - Jay Gee Ell (Vaigly Great) 7f **(58)**
Form - 36523080
Record 1999 - 1st:0 2nd:1 3rd:2 Ran:8
Win Prizemoney £0 *Total Prizemoney* £1,868
1999 Turf 0-8: (5f 2, 6f 5, 7f) (sft, g-s, gd 2, g-f, frm 2, hrd)
Average filly, effective 6f, acts on gd. Turf high 66. Becoming disappointing. **J S Goldie [0-8] Martin Delaney.*

BE VALIANT BHB 40f42a **RR 31f 42a** 1599[16]

5 gr g Petong 7.6f **(58)** - Fetlar (Pharly (FR)) 9.8f **(68)**
Form - 0440
Record 1999 - 1st:0 2nd:0 3rd:0 Ran:3
Pre1999 - 1st:1 2nd:1 3rd:0 Ran:10
Win Prizemoney £2,295 *Total Prizemoney* £2,963
Wins 1998 Jly Ripon (GD) S 10f 50 <

1999 Turf 0-1: (10f) (g-f) 1999 AW 0-2: (8f, 10f) (Equi, Fibr)
Moderate gelding, effective 10f, acts on gd to g-f, best on g-f, has worn blinkers, prefers tight tracks. AW high 41. Inconsistent.
**Mrs N Macauley [0-7] G Wiltshire (from J R Fanshawe [1-7] Spt 1998).*

BEVELED CRYSTAL BHB 30f **RR 31f** 4699[6]

5 ro m Beveled (USA) 6.9f **(64)** - Countess Mariga (Amboise)
Form - 0086
Record 1999 - 1st:0 2nd:0 3rd:0 Ran:4
Pre1999 - 1st:0 2nd:0 3rd:0 Ran:7
1999 Turf 0-4: (5f, 7f, 8f, 10f) (sft, gd, frm 2)
Very moderate filly. Turf high 31 (began Aug). Inconsistent.
**M Madgwick [0-4] Mrs J E M Powell (from C James [0-7] Oct 1997).*

BEVELED HAWTHORN BHB 32f **RR 28f** 4148[1]

4 b f Beveled (USA) 6.9f **(64)** - Sideloader Special (Song) 7.2f **(61)**
Form - 61
Record 1999 - 1st:1 2nd:0 3rd:0 Ran:2
Pre1999 - 1st:0 2nd:0 3rd:0 Ran:2
Win Prizemoney £3,013 *Total Prizemoney* £3,013
Wins * 1999 Spt Thirsk (FRM) H 5f 25 28 <
1999 Turf 1-2: (5f 1-1, 7f) (g-f, hrd 1-1)
Leggy, little account filly. Turf high 28 (began Aug) - 1st of 18 getting 27lb from Colonel Sam (4 Spt Thirsk RF 4148).
**D Nicholls [1-2] Mrs Margaret Dunning (from M P Bielby [0-2] Jun 1998).*

BEVELENA BHB 77f **RR 77f** 3762[20]

3 ch f Beveled (USA) 6.9f **(64)** - Bella Helena (Balidar) 7.9f **(63)**
Form - 31500
Record 1999 - 1st:1 2nd:0 3rd:1 Ran:5
Pre1999 - 1st:1 2nd:3 3rd:0 Ran:5
Win Prizemoney £6,134 *Total Prizemoney* £9,809
Wins * 1999 Apr Catter (SFT) H 5f 74 79 <
* 1998 Aug Haydoc (G-S) H 5f 62 76
1999 Turf 1-5: (5f 1-4, 6f) (gd 1-3, g-f, frm)
Unfurnished, above-average filly, effective 5 to 6f, best at 5f, acts on gd to frm, best on g-f. Turf high 79 - 1st of 16 giving 8lb to Rose's Treasure (21 Apr Catterick RF 0796).
**P D Evans [2-10] Mrs F A Veasey.*

BEVERLEY MONKEY (IRE) BHB 41f55a **RR 40f 55a** 4440[5]

3 b f Fayruz 6.6f **(63)** - Godly Light (FR) (Vayrann) 9.7f **(74)**
Form - 0003U755
Record 1999 - 1st:0 2nd:0 3rd:1 Ran:8
Pre1999 - 1st:3 2nd:2 3rd:1 Ran:12
Win Prizemoney £6,898 *Total Prizemoney* £9,560
Wins * 1998 Aug Lingfi (FRM) C 6f 66
* 1998 Jun Hamilt (GD) C 5f 47+
* 1998 May Newcas (G-F) C 6f 83+ <
1999 Turf 0-7: (6f 5, 7f, 8f) (sft, g-f, frm 5) 1999 AW 0-1: (6f) (Fibr)
Scopey, moderate filly, effective 6f, acts on frm, has worn blinkers. Turf high 40. Inconsistent. **J Berry [3-20] The Monkey Partnership.*

BEVIER BHB 50f **RR 51f** 1599[15]

5 b g Nashwan (USA) 10.3f **(79)** - Bevel (USA) (Mr Prospector (USA)) 8.8f **(78)**
Form - 630
Record 1999 - 1st:0 2nd:0 3rd:1 Ran:3
Pre1999 - 1st:1 2nd:0 3rd:0 Ran:8
Win Prizemoney £3,613 *Total Prizemoney* £3,978
Wins 1997 Jun Yarmou (FRM) 8f 69 <
1999 Turf 0-3: (8f, 10f 2) (g-f 3)
Fair gelding, has worn blinkers. Turf high 51.
**W Jarvis [0-3] Mrs J Cecil (from Mrs J Cecil [0-2] May 1998).*

BEWARE **RR 69f** 5072[11]

4 br g Warning 8.1f **(77)** - Dancing Spirit (IRE) (Ahonoora) 8.1f **(73)**
Form - 3508200
Record 1999 - 1st:0 2nd:1 3rd:1 Ran:7
Pre1999 - 1st:1 2nd:2 3rd:3 Ran:14
Win Prizemoney £5,345 *Total Prizemoney* £12,477
Wins 1997 Oct Newbur (G-S) H 6f 81 84 <
1999 Turf 0-7: (5f 3, 6f 3, 7f) (gd 5, g-f, hrd)
Scopey, average gelding, effective 5 to 6f, best at 5f, acts on gd to g-f, best on gd. Turf high 74 (1st run) - 3rd of 13 giving 6lb to Ivory's Joy (14 May Thirsk 5f gd RF 1225).

**D Nicholls [0-9] A A Bloodstock Ltd (from R W Armstrong [1-12] Aug 1998).*

BE WARNED BHB 57f78a **RR 58f 78a** 5145[1]

8 b g Warning 8.1f **(77)** - Sagar (Habitat) 9.4f **(70)**
Form - 42233478230577041
Record 1999 - 1st:1 2nd:1 3rd:3 Ran:14
Pre1999 - 1st:10 2nd:12 3rd:8 Ran:79
Win Prizemoney £42,719 *Total Prizemoney* £72,079
Wins * 1999 *Oct Wolver (STD) C 12f 68+*
* 1998 Oct Newbur (HVY) H 7f 56 66
* 1998 *Mar Southw (STD) H 8f 73 79* <
* 1998 *Mar Wolver (STD) H 9.4f 69 73*
* 1998 *Feb Wolver (STD) H 9.4f 62 69*
* 1998 *Jan Southw (STD) H 7f 55 55+*
* 1997 Spt Yarmou (FRM) H 6f 44 49
1995 *Nov Southw (STD) H 7f 75 76*
1995 Spt Yarmou (GD) H 6f 70 72
1999 Turf 0-6: (7f 3, 8f 2, 9f) (sft, gd 3, g-f, frm) 1999 AW 1-8: (8f, 9f 2, 11f, 12f 1-4) (Equi, Fibr 1-7)
Above-average gelding, effective 8 to 12f, best at 12f, - acts on AW, best on Fibr, mostly wears blinkers (effectively), prefers left handed tracks, prefers tight tracks, excels at Wolverhampton, likes Southwell. Turf high 66. AW high 86 - 3rd of 10 giving 2lb to Pas de Memoires (13 Jan Wolverhampton 9f Fibr RF 0088).
**J Pearce [7-42] Mrs Linda Leech (from M Dods [0-13] Aug 1997).*

BEWILDERED (IRE) **RR 62f** 2330[4]

2 br f Prince Sabo 6.6f **(64)** - Collage (Ela-Mana-Mou) 10.1f **(70)**
Form - 064
Record 1999 - 1st:0 2nd:0 3rd:0 Ran:3
Win Prizemoney £0 *Total Prizemoney* £230
1999 Turf 0-3: (5f 2, 6f) (gd, g-f, frm)
Currently average filly. Turf high 62. **G Lewis [0-3] John Manley.*

BEYOND CALCULATION (USA) BHB 65f **RR 71f** 4826[13]

5 ch g Geiger Counter (USA) 7.8f **(85)** - Placer Queen(Habitat) 9.4f **(70)**
Form - 005056213211104000
Record 1999 - 1st:4 2nd:2 3rd:1 Ran:18
Pre1999 - 1st:1 2nd:1 3rd:2 Ran:18
Win Prizemoney £22,178 *Total Prizemoney* £28,554
Wins * 1999 Aug Bright (FRM) H 6f 62 73
*** 1999** Jly Thirsk (FRM) H 6f 57 64
*** 1999** Jly Bath (FRM) H 5.7f 54 60
*** 1999** Jun Windso (G-F) H 6f 47 52
1997 Oct Redcar (G-F) 6f 74 <
1999 Turf 4-18: (5f 3, 6f 4-15) (sft, g-s, gd 2, g-f 4, frm 4-10)
Above-average gelding, effective 6f, acts on gd to frm, best on frm, prefers left handed tracks, excels at Bath. Turf high 73 - 1st of 5 from Dancing Mystery (4 Aug Brighton RF 3350) - also 1st of 10 giving 3lb to Kosevo (30 Jly Thirsk RF 3252). Went from strength to strength last term, winning four times. Six furlongs on fast ground are ideal, and he likes to go from the front.
**J M Bradley [4-28] E A Hayward (from P W Harris [1-8] Oct 1997).*

BEYOND THE CLOUDS (IRE) BHB 54f **RR 52f** 3200[5]

3 b g Midhish - Tongabezi (IRE) (Shernazar) 10.2f **(73)**
Form - 76073065
Record 1999 - 1st:0 2nd:0 3rd:1 Ran:8
Win Prizemoney £0 *Total Prizemoney* £575
1999 Turf 0-7: (5f, 6f 5, 8f) (sft, gd, g-f 2, frm 3) 1999 AW 0-1: (8f) (Fibr)
Fair gelding, effective 5 to 6f, acts on frm, has worn blinkers. Turf high 52 - 3rd of 19 getting 8lb from Venika Vitesse (23 Jun Carlisle 6f frm RF 2225). **J S Wainwright [0-8] The Camelot Members.*

B GRADE THE SECOND BHB 27f35a **RR 30f 35a** 3817[14]

3 b f Lugana Beach 7f **(63)** - B Grade (Lucky Wednesday) 8f **(50)**
Form - 006080
Record 1999 - 1st:0 2nd:0 3rd:0 Ran:4
Pre1999 - 1st:0 2nd:0 3rd:0 Ran:2
1999 Turf 0-3: (6f, 8f, 10f) (g-f, frm 2) 1999 AW 0-1: (6f) (Fibr)
Light-framed, very moderate filly. Turf high 30.
**Miss J F Craze [0-6] Mrs O Tunstall.*

BHAVNAGAR (IRE) BHB 25f **RR 10?f** 4913[9]

8 gr g Darshaan 11.9f **(81)** - Banana Peel (Green Dancer (USA)) 10.3f

(74)
Form - 00
Record 1999 - 1st:0 2nd:0 3rd:0 Ran:2
Pre1999 - 1st:0 2nd:0 3rd:0 Ran:2
1999 Turf 0-2: (14f, 17f) (gd 2)
Poor gelding. Turf high 6 (began Oct). **B Ellison [2-13] E J Berry.*

BHUTAN (IRE) RR 65f
5188[4]
4 b g Polish Patriot (USA) 7.8f **(70)** - Bustinetta (Bustino) 10.4f **(64)**
Form - 33133307144
Record 1999 - 1st:2 2nd:0 3rd:5 Ran:11
Pre1999 - 1st:3 2nd:0 3rd:1 Ran:13
Win Prizemoney £21,240 *Total Prizemoney* £24,944
Wins * **1999** Oct Catter (GD,) 13.8f 59+
* **1999** Jly Newcas (FRM) H 12.4f 64 67
1998 Oct Currag (SFT) H 8f 66 71 <
1998 Jly Killar (GD) H 11f 56 71+
1998 Jun Cork (G-S) H 9f 53 71 <
1999 Turf 2-11: (9f, 10f 3, 11f, 12f 1-4, 14f 1-1, 16f) (gd 1-3, g-f 4, frm 1-4)
Average gelding, effective 8 to 16f, acts on g-s to frm, best on gd, prefers right handed tracks, likes tight tracks, excels at Beverley. Turf high 71 - 3rd of 7 getting 2lb from Over To You (17 Jly Ripon 12f frm RF 2926) - also 1st of 12 giving 2lb to Bold Amusement (12 Jly Newcastle RF 2758). Consistent.
**Mrs M Reveley [3-18] P D Savill (from C Collins in IRE [3-13] Oct 1998).*

BHUTAN PRINCE BHB 83f RR 82f
4910[2]
2 b c Robellino (USA) 9.5f **(68)** - Seal Indigo (IRE) (Glenstal (USA)) 10.1f **(64)**
Form - 42225322
Record 1999 - 1st:0 2nd:5 3rd:1 Ran:8
Win Prizemoney £0 *Total Prizemoney* £6,234
1999 Turf 0-8: (7f 5, 8f 3) (sft, g-s, gd 2, g-f, frm 3)
Decent colt, effective 7 to 8f, best at 8f, acts on sft to frm, prefers tight tracks. Turf high 82 - 2nd of 12 to Francesco Guardi (16 Oct Catterick 7f gd RF 4910). Improving. **J Noseda [0-8] Lucayan Stud.*

BIANCONI (USA) RR 109f
3589a[8]
4 b c Danzig (USA) 8.1f **(88)** - Fall Aspen (USA) (Pretense) 6.3f **(88)**
Form - 4008
1999 Turf 0-4: (6f 3, 7f) (hvy, g-f 2, frm)
Pattern-class colt, effective 6f, acts on gd to frm, best on g-f, has worn blinkers. Turf high 112 (1st run) - 4th of 10 giving 7lb to Eastern Purple (22 May Curragh 6f g-f RF 1476a). Consistent. He looked a potential star sprinter at the end of his three-year-old season, but failed to fire in 1999. It would seem that, like his brother Hamas, this colt can be labelled talented but unreliable. He has been retired to stud in Kentucky. **A P O'Brien in IRE [3-12].*

BICTON PARK BHB 34f35a RR 41f 35a
5193[17]
5 b g Distant Relative 7f **(69)** - Merton Mill (Dominion) 8.5f **(63)**
Form - 7002070060
Record 1999 - 1st:0 2nd:1 3rd:0 Ran:8
Pre1999 - 1st:0 2nd:0 3rd:0 Ran:16
Win Prizemoney £0 *Total Prizemoney* £858
1999 Turf 0-2: (7f, 8f) (gd, frm) 1999 AW 0-6: (5f, 6f, 7f 3, 8f) (Fibr 6)
Moderate gelding, effective 7f, - acts on Fibr, has worn blinkers, likes tight tracks. Turf high 41. AW high 47 - 2nd of 12 to Far-So-La (15 Jan Southwell 7f Fibr RF 0103).
**K C Comerford [0-20] The Old Style Partnership (from D Morley [0-4] Nov 1996).*

BID ME WELCOME BHB 81f RR 81f
4893[1]
3 b g Alzao (USA) 9.8f **(73)** - Blushing Barada (USA) (Blushing Groom (FR)) 10.3f **(76)**
Form - 6815540332151
Record 1999 - 1st:3 2nd:1 3rd:2 Ran:13
Pre1999 - 1st:0 2nd:0 3rd:0 Ran:1
Win Prizemoney £19,560 *Total Prizemoney* £21,995
Wins * **1999** Oct Newmar (GD) H 14.8f 77 81 <
* **1999** Aug Nottin (G-F) H 14.1f 69 75
* **1999** May Warwic (GD) H 12.5f 67 73
1999 Turf 3-13: (8f, 10f, 11f, 12f 4, 13f 1-1, 14f 1-4, 15f 1-1) (g-s, gd 1-6, g-f 3, frm 2-3)
Workmanlike, decent gelding, effective 13 to 15f, acts on gd to frm, best on frm, likes left handed tracks. Turf high 81 - 1st of 16 getting 5lb from Trellis Bay (15 Oct Newmarket RF 4893) - also 1st of 12 giving 2lb to King Flyer (23 Aug Nottingham RF 3860). Consistent. Enjoyed an uncontested lead when bolting up in a Nottingham handicap in August, but did not enjoy that luxury at Yarmouth next time. Finished the season with a vey game victory at Newmarket.
**H J Collingridge [3-13] P Burban (from M Johnston [0-1] Jly 1998).*

BIENAMADO (USA) BHB 119f RR 119f
5019a[5]
3 ch c Bien Bien (USA) - Nakterjal (Vitiges (FR)) 8.2f **(59)**
Form - 5225
Record 1999 - 1st:0 2nd:2 3rd:0 Ran:4
Pre1999 - 1st:2 2nd:1 3rd:0 Ran:3
Win Prizemoney £27,131 *Total Prizemoney* £82,390
Wins 1998 Oct Longch (SFT) G3 9f 102+ <
1998 Spt Haydoc (GD) 8.1f 82+
1999 Turf 0-4: (12f 4) (gd 2, g-f, frm)
Rangy, high-class colt, effective 12f, acts on gd to g-f. Turf high 119 (began Jly) - 2nd of 4 to Montjeu (12 Spt Longchamp 12f gd RF 4370a). He made a disappointing return to the track when easily dismissed behind Craigsteel at Newmarket but ran a lot better when runner-up in the Great Voltigeur at York. Flattered when only beaten a head by Montjeu in the Prix Niel, he went on to finish fifth in the Canadian International before moving on to be trained in California. **A G Foster [0-1] (from P W Chapple-Hyam [2-6] Spt 1999).*

BIENCARN (USA) RR 55f
2389[6]
3 ch f Bien Bien (USA) - Newdaydawning (USA) (Gone West (USA)) 6.5f **(75)**
Form - 76
Record 1999 - 1st:0 2nd:0 3rd:0 Ran:2
1999 Turf 0-2: (8f, 10f) (g-f, hrd)
Lengthy, currently fair filly. Turf high 55.
**P W Chapple-Hyam [0-2] J Toffan & T McCaffery.*

BIENNALE (IRE) BHB 96f RR 98f
2074[3]
3 b c Caerleon (USA) 10.9f **(79)** - Malvern Beauty (Shirley Heights) 10.3f **(74)**
Form - 13
Record 1999 - 1st:1 2nd:0 3rd:1 Ran:2
Pre1999 - 1st:0 2nd:3 3rd:0 Ran:3
Win Prizemoney £3,566 *Total Prizemoney* £14,498
Wins * **1999** May Hamilt (GD) 11.1f 73 <
1999 Turf 1-2: (11f 1-1, 12f) (g-f 1-2)
Scopey, very useful colt. Turf high 98 - 3rd of 19 giving 4lb to Elmutabaki (17 Jun Ascot 12f g-f RF 2074). He injured himself in the stalls when making a winning reappearance, but came back with all guns blazing to finish third in the King George V Handicap at Royal Ascot. More a galloper than a quickener, he will stay beyond a mile and a half.
**Sir Michael Stoute [1-5] M Tabor & Mrs John Magnier.*

BIFF-EM (IRE) BHB 40f RR 27f
4832[22]
5 ch g Durgam (USA) 12.3f **(53)** - Flash The Gold (Ahonoora) 8.1f **(73)**
Form - 432283000
Record 1999 - 1st:0 2nd:2 3rd:2 Ran:9
Pre1999 - 1st:2 2nd:0 3rd:5 Ran:28
Win Prizemoney £6,707 *Total Prizemoney* £12,629
Wins * 1998 Jly Hamilt (FRM) H 6f 37 45
* 1996 Jun Hamilt (GD) 5f 61 <
1999 Turf 0-9: (5f 4, 6f 5) (sft, gd 2, g-f 3, frm 3)
Little account gelding, effective 5 to 7f, best at 6f, acts on sft to frm, does well at Hamilton. Turf high 45 - 3rd of 8 getting 19lb from Windy Gulch (16 Jly Hamilton 6f frm RF 2871). Becoming disappointing. **Miss L A Perratt [2-37] Cree Lodge Racing Club.*

BIG AL (IRE) BHB 49f RR 47f
5159[7]
3 b g Shalford (IRE) 7.8f **(63)** - Our Pet (Mummy's Pet) 7.7f **(60)**
Form - 6086077
Record 1999 - 1st:0 2nd:0 3rd:0 Ran:7
Pre1999 - 1st:1 2nd:0 3rd:0 Ran:3
Win Prizemoney £2,304 *Total Prizemoney* £2,304
Wins 1998 Jly Haydoc (G-S) S 6f 72 <
1999 Turf 0-7: (7f, 8f 4, 10f, 11f) (gd 2, g-f, frm 4)
Moderate gelding, effective 6f, acts on frm. Turf high 63. Inconsistent.
**R A Fahey [0-8] Mrs A C Brown (from R Hannon [1-2] Jly 1998).*

BIG BEN BHB 68a **RR 49f** 4121[11]
5 ch h Timeless Times (USA) 6.1f **(56)** - Belltina (Belfort (FR)) 6.8f **(63)**
Form - 156330535600
Record 1999 - 1st:0 2nd:0 3rd:3 Ran:9
Pre1999 - 1st:7 2nd:1 3rd:5 Ran:35
Win Prizemoney £24,067 *Total Prizemoney* £31,426
Wins * 1998 *Nov Lingfi (STD) H* 7f *64 67*
* 1998 May Newmar (G-F) 7f 77
* 1998 Apr Folkes (GD) H 6.9f 64 69
* 1997 *Jun Lingfi (STD) C* 7f *61*
* 1997 Jun Goodwo (G-F) C 7f 71+
* 1996 Aug Lingfi (G-F) 5f 93+ <
* 1996 Jly Sandow (G-F) 5f 80
1999 Turf 0-8: (6f, 7f 5, 8f 2) (gd 2, g-f 4, frm 2) 1999 AW 0-1: (7f) (Equi)
Average colt, effective 6 to 7f, best at 7f, acts on gd to frm - acts on Equi, best on gd, likes right handed tracks. Turf high 68 (1st run) - 3rd of 20 giving 2lb to Broughtons Turmoil (17 May Windsor 6f gd RF 1285). **R Hannon [7-44] Lady Davis.*

BIG CHIEF RR 33f 4031[18]
3 ch g Be My Chief (USA) 10.2f **(62)** - Grove Daffodil (IRE) (Salt Dome (USA))
Form - 085056880
Record 1999 - 1st:0 2nd:0 3rd:0 Ran:9
Pre1999 - 1st:0 2nd:0 3rd:0 Ran:3
1999 Turf 0-9: (7f 4, 8f 2, 10f 2, 12f) (gd 4, g-f 3, frm 2)
Workmanlike, very moderate gelding, has worn blinkers. Turf high 45. Consistent.
**M E Sowersby [0-1] The Three County Partnership (from M H Tompkins [0-11] Aug 1999).*

BIG ISSUE BHB 60f **RR 50f** 5218[22]
2 b c First Trump - Hollow Heart (Wolver Hollow) 8f **(56)**
Form - 0710
Record 1999 - 1st:1 2nd:0 3rd:0 Ran:4
Win Prizemoney £2,164 *Total Prizemoney* £2,164
Wins * 1999 Oct Bath (SFT) S 5.7f
1999 Turf 1-4: (6f 1-2, 7f 2) (g-s, gd 1-2, frm)
Fair colt. Turf high 50 (began Jly).
**B Smart [1-3] Willie McKay (from K McAuliffe [0-1] Jly 1999).*

BIG JAG (USA) RR 5227a[3]
6 g Kleven (USA) - In Hopes (USA) (Affirmed (USA)) 9.3f **(79)**
Form - 3
1999 AW 0-1: (6f) (Dirt)
Currently high-class gelding, ran a fast finishing third in the Breeders' Cup Sprint. **T Pinfield in USA [0-1].*

BIG MOVIE STAR BHB 65f **RR 75f** 4708[5]
2 ch f Risk Me (FR) 8f **(53)** - Bocas Rose (Jalmood (USA)) 10.1f **(52)**
Form - 63685
Record 1999 - 1st:0 2nd:0 3rd:1 Ran:5
Win Prizemoney £0 *Total Prizemoney* £1,317
1999 Turf 0-5: (5f 3, 6f 2) (g-s 2, gd, g-f 2)
Above-average filly, has worn blinkers. Turf high 75.
**B J Meehan [0-5] Roldvale Ltd.*

BIG TARGET (IRE) BHB 43f **RR 49f** 3545[4]
5 b g Suave Dancer (USA) 10.7f **(68)** - Prima Domina (FR) (Dominion) 8.5f **(63)**
Form - 6204
Record 1999 - 1st:0 2nd:1 3rd:0 Ran:4
Pre1999 - 1st:0 2nd:0 3rd:0 Ran:6
Win Prizemoney £0 *Total Prizemoney* £978
1999 Turf 0-4: (8f, 9f, 11f 2) (g-f 2, frm 2)
Moderate gelding, has broken blood-vessels, has worn blinkers. Turf high 49. Inconsistent.
**R Allan [0-14] Ian Dalgleish (from Sir Michael Stoute [0-4] Oct 1997).*

BIG WHEEL BHB 58f **RR 57f** 5153[1]
4 ch g Mujtahid (USA) 7.4f **(69)** - Numuthej (USA) (Nureyev (USA)) 8.7f **(78)**
Form - 01
Record 1999 - 1st:1 2nd:0 3rd:0 Ran:2
Pre1999 - 1st:0 2nd:1 3rd:1 Ran:4
Win Prizemoney £2,320 *Total Prizemoney* £3,820
Wins * 1999 Nov Nottin (SFT) S 10f 51 <
1999 Turf 1-2: (10f 1-2) (gd 1-2)
Light-framed, fair gelding, effective 9 to 10f, acts on gd to frm, often wears blinkers. Turf high 51 (began Oct).
**M C Pipe [1-8] Jim Ennis.*

BIGWIG (IRE) BHB 46f46a **RR 22f 46a** 419[4]
6 ch g Thatching 7.8f **(69)** - Sabaah (USA) (Nureyev (USA)) 8.7f **(78)**
Form - 46114
Record 1999 - 1st:2 2nd:0 3rd:0 Ran:5
Pre1999 - 1st:0 2nd:0 3rd:0 Ran:4
Win Prizemoney £5,418 *Total Prizemoney* £5,418
Wins * **1999** *Mar Lingfi (STD) H 13f 40 45* <
* **1999** *Feb Lingfi (STD) H 13f 25 43*
1999 AW 2-5: (12f, 13f 2-2, 14f, 16f) (Equi 2-4, Fibr)
Moderate gelding, has broken blood-vessels, often wears blinkers. AW high 45 - 4th of 11 giving 15lb to Mrs Pickles (10 Mar Southwell 14f Fibr RF 0419) - also 1st of 12 giving 2lb to Catchment (2 Mar Lingfield RF 0386).
**G L Moore [4-22] Mrs Elizabeth Kiernan (from A Moore [0-4] Dec 1996).*

BIJA BHB 25f **RR 31f** 3851[4]
4 b g Librate 10.4f **(37)** - Guilty Sparkle (Roc Imp)
Form - 70074684
Record 1999 - 1st:0 2nd:0 3rd:0 Ran:8
1999 Turf 0-6: (7f, 8f, 9f, 10f 3) (gd, g-f 2, frm 2, hrd) 1999 AW 0-2: (8f 2) (Fibr 2)
Very moderate gelding, effective 9f, acts on g-f, favours tight tracks. Turf high 35. AW high 27. Inconsistent.
**J M Bradley [0-8] Martyn James.*

BILKO BHB 63f74a **RR 64df 74a** 4141[13]
5 gr g Risk Me (FR) 8f **(53)** - Princess Tara (Prince Sabo) 7.2f **(62)**
Form - 8000332600
Record 1999 - 1st:0 2nd:1 3rd:2 Ran:10
Pre1999 - 1st:3 2nd:3 3rd:2 Ran:14
Win Prizemoney £10,590 *Total Prizemoney* £17,402
Wins 1998 Spt Ayr (G-S) H 5f 63 73 <
1998 Aug Catter (G-F) C 5f 59
1996 Apr Lingfi (G-S) 5f 64
1999 Turf 0-9: (5f 7, 6f 2) (g-s, gd 3, g-f 2, frm 3) 1999 AW 0-1: (5f) (Fibr)
Average gelding, has broken blood-vessels, effective 5f, acts on g-s to frm, excels at Catterick. Turf high 65 - 3rd of 13 giving 13lb to Sweet Magic (30 Jun Catterick 5f frm RF 2437). Inconsistent.
**E J Alston [0-5] Steve Barker (from D Nicholls [2-14] Jun 1999).*

BILLADDIE BHB 68f58a **RR 66f 58a** 3741[10]
6 b g Touch of Grey 8.1f **(47)** -Young Lady(Young Generation) 7.7f **(63)**
Form - 780
Record 1999 - 1st:0 2nd:0 3rd:0 Ran:3
Pre1999 - 1st:5 2nd:4 3rd:8 Ran:30
Win Prizemoney £20,975 *Total Prizemoney* £31,978
Wins * 1998 Oct Newbur (HVY) H 10f 66 70 <
* 1998 Spt Kempto (G-S) H 12f 58 61
* 1998 Jun Newmar (GD) H 12f 52 58
* 1998 *Jan Lingfi (STD) H 10f 51 61*
1996 *Jan Lingfi (STD) 8f 53*
1999 Turf 0-3: (12f 3) (g-s 2, frm)
Average gelding, effective 10 to 12f, best at 12f, acts on sft to frm - acts on Equi, likes right handed tracks. Turf high 66. Consistent.
**R M Flower [4-25] Richard Gurr (from R Boss [1-8] Mar 1997).*

BILLICHANG BHB 45f50a **RR 51f 50a** 3671[3]
3 b c Chilibang 7f **(55)** - Swing O'The Kilt (Hotfoot) 10.5f **(59)**
Form - 445282475303
Record 1999 - 1st:0 2nd:2 3rd:2 Ran:12
Pre1999 - 1st:0 2nd:0 3rd:0 Ran:4
Win Prizemoney £0 *Total Prizemoney* £2,465
1999 Turf 0-4: (8f 3, 10f) (sft, g-f 2, frm) 1999 AW 0-8: (7f, 8f 2, 9f 3, 10f 2) (Equi 4, Fibr 4)
Workmanlike, fair colt, effective 9f, - acts on Fibr, has worn blinkers. Turf high 51. AW high 57.
**P Howling [0-16] Paul Howling Racing Syndicate.*

BILLY BATHWICK (IRE) BHB 70f **RR 70f** 5216[6]
2 ch c Fayruz 6.6f **(63)** - Cut it Fine (USA) (Big Spruce (USA)) 11f **(71)**
Form - 440406
Record 1999 - 1st:0 2nd:0 3rd:0 Ran:6
Win Prizemoney £0 *Total Prizemoney* £296
1999 Turf 0-6: (6f 3, 7f, 8f 2) (g-s 2, g-f, frm 2, hrd)
Above-average colt. Turf high 70 (began Jly).
**B Smart [0-6] W Clifford.*

BILLY BOX BHB 45f45a **RR 48f 45a** 436[10]
7 gr g Lord Bud 8.2f **(52)** - Counter Coup (Busted) 10.2f **(61)**
Form - 200
Record 1999 - 1st:0 2nd:1 3rd:0 Ran:3
Pre1999 - 1st:0 2nd:0 3rd:0 Ran:4
Win Prizemoney £0 *Total Prizemoney* £428
1999 AW 0-3: (12f, 14f, 16f) (Fibr 3)
Moderate gelding, effective 12f, - acts on Fibr, often wears blinkers. AW high 47 (1st run) - 2nd of 13 getting 14lb from Copper Shell (29 Jan Southwell 12f Fibr RF 0185).
**I A Balding [0-3] Alec Tuckerman (from G M McCourt [2-11] Jly 1998).*

BILLY BUSHWACKER BHB 69f **RR 69?f** 4758[7]
8 b g Most Welcome 8.6f **(66)** - Secret Valentine (Wollow) 8.2f **(61)**
Form - 7
Record 1999 - 1st:0 2nd:0 3rd:0 Ran:1
Pre1999 - 1st:3 2nd:8 3rd:4 Ran:34
Win Prizemoney £13,136 *Total Prizemoney* £45,506
Wins * 1995 May Doncas (G-F) H 8f 82 85+ <
1999 Turf 0-1: (10f) (gd)
Average gelding, has worn blinkers. Becoming disappointing.
**Mrs M Reveley [3-37] T S Child.*

BILLY MCCAW BHB 90f **RR 90f** 1999[21]
3 b c Efisio 7.7f **(69)** - Thakhayr (Sadler's Wells (USA)) 10f **(76)**
Form - 15300
Record 1999 - 1st:1 2nd:0 3rd:1 Ran:5
Pre1999 - 1st:1 2nd:0 3rd:2 Ran:4
Win Prizemoney £11,169 *Total Prizemoney* £14,003
Wins * 1999 Apr Newmar (GD) H 7f 84 90 <
* 1998 Aug Epsom (G-F) 6f 85
1999 Turf 1-5: (6f, 7f 1-1, 8f 3) (gd, g-f 1-3, frm)
Useful colt, effective 6 to 8f, acts on gd to g-f, best on gd. Turf high 90 (1st run) - 1st of 20 giving 6lb to Black Silk (13 Apr Newmarket RF 0665). Scored over seven on his return, and ran better than his final position would suggest when unplaced at Haydock in May. A mile has looked beyond him when he has been tried over it. Well beaten in the Britannia. He fetched 22,000gns in the autumn. **P F I Cole [2-9] Lord Lloyd-Webber.*

BILLY MOONSHINE BHB 45f53a **RR 42f 53a** 3835[11]
7 ch g Nicholas Bill 9.8f **(56)** - Indian Moonshine (Warpath) 12.3f **(52)**
Form - 3860
Record 1999 - 1st:0 2nd:0 3rd:0 Ran:2
Pre1999 - 1st:0 2nd:0 3rd:1 Ran:6
Win Prizemoney £0 *Total Prizemoney* £344
1999 Turf 0-1: (17f) (frm) 1999 AW 0-1: (16f) (Equi)
Fair gelding, effective 13f, - acts on Equi, favours left handed tracks.**P Bowen [0-3] Graham Haupt (from G L Moore [0-7] Jan 1999).*

BIMBOLA (FR) RR 117f 4769a[5]
5 br m Bikala 12f **(79)** - Agnes Lily (USA) (Raise A Cup (USA)) 7.6f **(74)**
Form - 1125
1999 Turf 2-4: (12f 1-1, 13f 2, 14f 1-1) (hvy, gd 1-2, g-f 1-1)
High-class filly, effective 13 to 14f, best at 13f, acts on hvy to gd, and does well at Deauville. Turf high 117 - 2nd of 6 to Courteous (29 Aug Deauville 13f gd RF 4113a) - also 1st of 11 from Innuendo (1 Aug Deauville RF 3408a). She has progressed to become a genuine Group performer, winning a couple of Group races including the Prix de Pomone, and just losing out in the Grand Prix de Deauville. Not disgraced when fifth behind Fairy Queen in the Prix de Royallieu. **J BertranDeBalanda in FR [3-7].*

BIN ALMOOJID RR 5067[14]
3 b g Almoojid 7f **(36)** - Stella Royale (Astronef)
Form - 0
Record 1999 - 1st:0 2nd:0 3rd:0 Ran:1
Pre1999 - 1st:0 2nd:0 3rd:0 Ran:1
1999 Turf 0-1: (12f) (gd)
Scopey, currently very poor gelding.
**A D Smith [0-1] Duckhaven Stud (from Miss Kate Whitehouse [0-1] Apr 1998).*

BINT ALJOOD BHB 58f **RR 62f** 5150[5]
2 b f Bin Ajwaad (IRE) - Shareehan (Dancing Brave (USA)) 8.4f **(76)**
Form - 807545
Record 1999 - 1st:0 2nd:0 3rd:0 Ran:6
Win Prizemoney £0 *Total Prizemoney* £276
1999 Turf 0-5: (5f, 6f 4) (g-s, gd, g-f 2, frm) 1999 AW 0-1: (7f) (Fibr)
Average filly, effective 6f, acts on gd to frm. Turf high 62 (began Aug). **B A McMahon [0-6] Khalifa Dasmal.*

BINTANG TIMOR (USA) BHB 70f **RR 69f** 5143[3]
5 ch g Mt Livermore (USA) 7.7f **(90)** - Frisky Kitten (USA) (Isopach (USA)) 6f **(84)**
Form - 310223030000013
Record 1999 - 1st:2 2nd:2 3rd:4 Ran:15
Pre1999 - 1st:1 2nd:4 3rd:0 Ran:20
Win Prizemoney £14,146 *Total Prizemoney* £26,984
Wins * 1999 Oct Yarmou (G-S) H 7f 62 65
* 1999 May Newmar (G-F) H 7f 64 68
* 1998 Jly Leices (GD) H 6f 67 70 <
1999 Turf 2-15: (6f 2, 7f 2-13) (gd 1-5, g-f 2, frm 1-8)
Average gelding, effective 6 to 7f, best at 7f, acts on gd to frm, best on frm, excels at Doncaster, likes Newmarket. Turf high 72 - 2nd of 15 giving 3lb to Teofilio (18 Jun Newmarket 7f frm RF 2124) - also 1st of 20 getting 7lb from Sky Dome (1 May Newmarket RF 0962).
**W J Musson [3-30] Goodey & Broughton (from P F I Cole [0-5] May 1997).*

BINT HABIBI BHB 63f **RR 66f** 4820[10]
2 b f Bin Ajwaad (IRE) - High Stepping (IRE) (Taufan (USA)) 7f **(57)**
Form - 4200
Record 1999 - 1st:0 2nd:1 3rd:0 Ran:4
Win Prizemoney £0 *Total Prizemoney* £860
1999 Turf 0-4: (7f 3, 8f) (g-f 2, frm 2)
Average filly. Turf high 66 (began Jly). **M R Channon [0-4] A Merza.*

BINT ST JAMES BHB 54f44a **RR 54f 44a** 317[8]
4 b f Shareef Dancer (USA) 10.1f **(67)** - St James's Antigua (IRE) (Law Society (USA)) 9.9f **(70)**
Form - 3048
Record 1999 - 1st:0 2nd:0 3rd:0 Ran:2
Pre1999 - 1st:0 2nd:0 3rd:3 Ran:11
Win Prizemoney £0 *Total Prizemoney* £2,353
1999 AW 0-2: (12f, 16f) (Fibr 2)
Lengthy, fair filly, effective 12 to 15f, best at 12f, acts on gd - acts on Fibr, prefers tight tracks. AW high 46. Inconsistent.
**W Clay [0-1] Dave Dutton (from J D Bethell [0-12] Jan 1999).*

BIRCH GROVE (IRE) BHB 25f **RR 20f** 2368[8]
3 b f Forest Wind (USA) - Volkova **(60f)**(Green Desert (USA)) 8.6f **(78)**
Form - 0008
Record 1999 - 1st:0 2nd:0 3rd:0 Ran:4
1999 Turf 0-4: (7f, 8f 2, 12f) (sft, g-s, g-f, frm)
Strong, little account filly. Turf high 20.
**W J Musson [0-4] Mrs Rita Brown.*

BIRCHWOOD SUN BHB 49f54a **RR 40f 54a** 2678[3]
9 b g Bluebird (USA) 7.9f **(71)** - Shapely Test (USA) (Elocutionist (USA)) 8f **(77)**
Form - 01320083
Record 1999 - 1st:1 2nd:1 3rd:2 Ran:8
Pre1999 - 1st:12 2nd:10 3rd:8 Ran:94
Win Prizemoney £38,888 *Total Prizemoney* £53,339
Wins * 1999 Apr Pontef (SFT) S 6f 61
* 1998 Jun Carlis (G-S) S 5.9f 58
* 1998 May Newcas (G-S) C 7f 61
* 1998 Apr Redcar (SFT) S 7f 62
* 1998 Apr Carlis (G-S) H 5.9f 48 52
* 1997 May Carlis (G-S) H 5.9f 49 59
* 1995 Spt Newcas (GD) H 7f 61 69
* 1995 Jun Carlis (FRM) H 5.9f 54 60
* 1995 Jun Hamilt (FRM) H 6f 54 58

1999 Turf 1-8: (6f 1-5, 7f 3) (sft 1-1, gd 2, g-f, frm 4)
Moderate gelding, effective 6 to 7f, best at 7f, acts on sft to frm, best on sft, mostly wears blinkers, and excels at Newcastle and Pontefract. Turf high 61 - 1st of 18 from Dandy Regent (20 Apr Pontefract RF 0770). Becoming disappointing. A stiff six furlongs suits him best, though he has won over seven. He needs holding up until the last possible moment, and is not an ideal investment for anyone with a weak heart.
**M Dods [10-86] A G Watson (from R Hollinshead [3-16] May 1993).*

BIRD OF PREY (IRE) BHB 50f54a RR 50f 54a 4528[14]

4 b f Last Tycoon 9.4f **(73)** - Red Partridge (Solinus) 9f **(71)**
Form - 54201868400
Record 1999 - 1st:1 2nd:1 3rd:0 Ran:11
Pre1999 - 1st:0 2nd:0 3rd:1 Ran:6
Win Prizemoney £2,346 *Total Prizemoney* £4,511
Wins * 1999 May Hamilt (SFT) 8.3f 57 <
1999 Turf 1-8: (8f 1-5, 9f 2, 10f) (gd 1-5, g-f 2, frm) 1999 AW 0-3: (8f, 9f, 10f) (Equi, Fibr 2)
Average filly, likes right handed tracks, likes tight tracks. Turf high 57. AW high 60. Her only win to date came in soft ground at Hamilton and she looks best suited by those conditions.
**A G Newcombe [1-11] Cann, Bedford, Harley & Patel (from T Stack in IRE [0-6] Oct 1998).*

BIRDSAND RR 51f 3943[13]

2 ch f Bluebird (USA) 7.9f **(71)** - Nottash (IRE) **(72f)** (Royal Academy (USA))
Form - 0
Record 1999 - 1st:0 2nd:0 3rd:0 Ran:1
1999 Turf 0-1: (6f) (hrd)
Currently fair filly. **J R Fanshawe [0-1] Lord Vestey.*

BIRTHDAY VENTURE BHB 54f59a RR 53f 59a 2063[3]

4 b f Soviet Star (USA) 8.6f **(74)** - Maestrale (Top Ville) 11.7f **(68)**
Form - 14021133
Record 1999 - 1st:2 2nd:1 3rd:2 Ran:7
Pre1999 - 1st:1 2nd:0 3rd:1 Ran:2
Win Prizemoney £7,849 *Total Prizemoney* £10,124
Wins * 1999 *May Lingfi (STD)* *10f* *62* <
*** 1999** *May Southw (STD) H* *8f* *55* *61*
*** 1998** *Nov Southw (STD)* *7f* *57*
1999 Turf 0-1: (8f) (gd) 1999 AW 2-6: (7f, 8f 1-2, 9f, 10f 1-1, 12f) (Equi 1-1, Fibr 1-5)
Neat, average filly, effective 7 to 12f, best at 8f, - acts on AW, best on Fibr, favours left handed tracks, favours tight tracks, excels at Southwell, does well at Wolverhampton. AW high 62 - 1st of 11 getting 1lb from Hawksbill Henry (29 May Lingfield RF 1585) - also 1st of 11 giving 15lb to Stravsea (17 May Southwell RF 1279). Consistent. She has been rather more successful on sand than on turf so far, winning three to date. She has proved headstrong in some of her races, and looks as if ten furlongs is right on the limit of her stamina. **S P C Woods [3-9] Dr Frank Chao.*

BIRTH OF THE BLUES BHB 67f RR 64f 4126[12]

3 ch c Efisio 7.7f **(69)** - Great Steps **(70f)** (Vaigly Great) 7f **(58)**
Form - 81870
Record 1999 - 1st:1 2nd:0 3rd:0 Ran:5
Pre1999 - 1st:0 2nd:0 3rd:0 Ran:3
Win Prizemoney £3,574 *Total Prizemoney* £3,574
Wins 1999 Apr Leices (HVY) H 8f 65 73 <
1999 Turf 1-5: (8f 1-3, 10f, 12f) (sft 1-1, gd 3, g-f)
Average colt, effective 8f, acts on sft. Turf high 73 - 1st of 12 giving 2lb to Pebble Moon (24 Apr Leicester RF 0831). Consistent.
**N P Littmoden [0-2] Supreme Racing Ltd (from J L Dunlop [1-6] May 1999).*

BIRTHPLACE (IRE) BHB 40f49a RR 56df 49a 283[15]

9 b or br g Top Ville 11f **(71)** - Birthday Party (FR) (Windwurf (GER)) 12.7f **(72)**
Form - 0
Record 1999 - 1st:0 2nd:0 3rd:0 Ran:1
Pre1999 - 1st:0 2nd:0 3rd:0 Ran:6
1999 AW 0-1: (16f) (Fibr)
Fair gelding.
**J L Eyre [0-1] J L Eyre (from John Harris [0-4] Nov 1994).*

BISHOPSTONE MAN BHB 68f RR 59f 4821[15]

2 b c Piccolo - Auntie Gladys (Great Nephew) 9.9f **(64)**
Form - 07030
Record 1999 - 1st:0 2nd:0 3rd:1 Ran:5
Win Prizemoney £0 *Total Prizemoney* £495
1999 Turf 0-5: (6f 2, 7f 3) (sft, g-s, gd, g-f, frm)
Fair colt. Turf high 59 (began Aug).
**S Mellor [0-5] The Bishopstone Ducks.*

BISHOPSTONE POND (IRE) BHB 34f30a RR 33f 30a 2485[10]

3 b f Persian Bold 10f **(69)** - Swift And Early (IRE) (Alzao (USA)) 7.1f **(68)**
Form - 030750
Record 1999 - 1st:0 2nd:0 3rd:1 Ran:6
Pre1999 - 1st:0 2nd:0 3rd:0 Ran:4
Win Prizemoney £0 *Total Prizemoney* £331
1999 Turf 0-5: (10f 3, 11f, 12f) (hvy, g-s, gd, g-f, frm) 1999 AW 0-1: (12f) (Fibr)
Unfurnished, very moderate filly. Turf high 35. Inconsistent.
**S Mellor [0-10] The Bishopstone Ducks.*

BISQUET-DE-BOUCHE BHB 31f RR 35?f 5006[9]

5 ch m Most Welcome 8.6f **(66)** - Larive (Blakeney) 10.5f **(64)**
Form - 70
Record 1999 - 1st:0 2nd:0 3rd:0 Ran:2
Pre1999 - 1st:0 2nd:0 3rd:1 Ran:7
Win Prizemoney £0 *Total Prizemoney* £732
1999 Turf 0-2: (14f, 16f) (gd 2)
Very moderate filly. Turf high 28 (began Spt).
**A W Carroll [0-2] Martin Brook (from R Dickin [0-7] Jly 1997).*

BITTER SWEET RR 62f 4946[7]

3 gr f Deploy 11.4f **(67)** - Julia Flyte (Drone) 10.3f **(74)**
Form - 77027
Record 1999 - 1st:0 2nd:1 3rd:0 Ran:5
Pre1999 - 1st:0 2nd:0 3rd:1 Ran:7
Win Prizemoney £0 *Total Prizemoney* £1,634
1999 Turf 0-5: (9f, 10f 3, 13f) (sft, g-s, g-f 2, frm)
Unfurnished, average filly, effective 8f, acts on g-f. Turf high 62.
**D R C Elsworth [0-12] J McGarry.*

BITTY MARY BHB 55f RR 52f 4504[9]

2 ch f Be My Chief (USA) 10.2f **(62)** - Souadah (USA) (General Holme (USA)) 5.7f **(63)**
Form - 0050
Record 1999 - 1st:0 2nd:0 3rd:0 Ran:4
1999 Turf 0-4: (6f 2, 7f, 8f) (g-f 2, frm 2)
Fair filly. Turf high 52. **J D Bethell [0-4] M W Territt.*

BLACK AMBER (IRE) RR 101f 4896[19]

3 b c College Chapel - Flying Diva (Chief Singer) 8.9f **(66)**
Form - 8506020
Record 1999 - 1st:0 2nd:1 3rd:0 Ran:7
Pre1999 - 1st:2 2nd:0 3rd:1 Ran:4
Win Prizemoney £39,701 *Total Prizemoney* £50,438
Wins * 1998 Jly Maison (GD) G2 5.5f 99 <
***** 1998 Jun Newmar (GD) 6f 82+
1999 Turf 0-7: (5f, 6f 5, 7f) (sft, gd 3, g-f 3)
Scopey, very useful colt, effective 6 to 7f, best at 6f, acts on gd to frm, has worn blinkers. Turf high 101 - 6th of 10 giving 4lb to Cretan Gift (29 Aug Yarmouth 6f gd RF 4001). He beat Bertolini in the Prix Robert Papin as a juvenile, but failed to make the grade last term, dropping 21lbs in the official ratings. As that suggests, he will be well treated if able to rediscover his form. David Nicholls has obviously taken note, as he shelled out 45,000gns for the colt in October. **N A Callaghan [2-11] M Tabor & Mrs John Magnier.*

BLACK ARMY BHB 70f74a RR 66f 74a 5110[18]

4 b g Aragon 7.7f **(58)** - Morgannwg (IRE) (Simply Great (FR)) 8.2f **(65)**
Form - 40108530
Record 1999 - 1st:1 2nd:0 3rd:1 Ran:8
Pre1999 - 1st:0 2nd:0 3rd:0 Ran:3
Win Prizemoney £4,744 *Total Prizemoney* £5,349
Wins * 1999 May Beverl (GD) H 5f 69 72 <
1999 Turf 1-7: (5f 1-4, 6f 3) (sft, gd 1-4, g-f, frm)1999 AW 0-1: (5f) (Fibr)
Above-average gelding, effective 5 to 6f, best at 5f, acts on sft to gd - acts on Fibr, has worn blinkers. Turf high 72 - 1st of 19 from

Legs Be Frendly (8 May Beverley RF 1100). (1st run) - 3rd of 15 giving 13lb to Samwar (24 Jly Southwell 5f Fibr RF 3115).
**J M P Eustace [1-11] K J Mercer.*

BLACK EMPEROR RR 5216[18]

2 br c Emperor Jones (USA) - Hush Baby (IRE) (Ballacashtal (CAN)) 5.3f **(50)**
Form - 0
Record 1999 - 1st:0 2nd:0 3rd:0 Ran:1
1999 Turf 0-1: (8f) (g-s)
Currently very poor colt.
**P L Gilligan [0-1] The Three Tuns Turf Team.*

BLACKEYED BOY (IRE) BHB 27f RR 6f 3817[13]

3 ch g Forest Wind (USA) - Blackeye (Busted) 10.2f **(61)**
Form - 00P00
Record 1999 - 1st:0 2nd:0 3rd:0 Ran:5
Pre1999 - 1st:0 2nd:0 3rd:0 Ran:4
1999 Turf 0-2: (10f, 14f) (g-f, frm) 1999 AW 0-3: (12f 2, 15f) (Fibr 3)
Unfurnished, very poor gelding, has worn blinkers.
**A Bailey [0-9] WWW Mark-Kilner-Raci (15).*

BLACKFOOT (IRE) BHB 59f65a RR 58df 65a 4326[12]

3 br g River Falls 8.2f **(56)** - Northern Amber (Shack (USA)) 5.8f **(53)**
Form - 2720
Record 1999 - 1st:0 2nd:2 3rd:0 Ran:4
Win Prizemoney £0 *Total Prizemoney* £1,746
1999 Turf 0-3: (5f 3) (gd, frm 2) 1999 AW 0-1: (5f) (Fibr)
Scopey, average gelding, always wears blinkers. Turf high 58 (began Jly). (1st run) - 2nd of 6 giving 5lb to La Piazza (25 Jun Wolverhampton 5f Fibr RF 2311). **J Balding [0-4] John Balding.*

BLACKHEATH (IRE) RR 95f 4561[17]

3 ch c Common Grounds 8.1f **(66)** - Queen Caroline (USA) (Chief's Crown (USA)) 9.8f **(72)**
Form - 23180330
Record 1999 - 1st:1 2nd:1 3rd:3 Ran:8
Win Prizemoney £3,786 *Total Prizemoney* £11,105
Wins * 1999 Jun Lingfi (GD) 6f 79 <
1999 Turf 1-8: (6f 1-7, 7f) (gd 3, g-f 1-1, frm 4)
Scopey, very useful colt, effective 6f, acts on gd to frm, best on frm. Turf high 98. He was unlucky in some decent sprint handicaps, meeting interference on one occasion and suffering a slipping saddle on another. A scopey sort, he will improve over the winter and should pick up a decent prize next term.
**J A R Toller [1-8] G H Toller.*

BLACK ICE BOY (IRE) BHB 44f31a RR 48f 31a 4932[9]

8 b g Law Society (USA) 11.6f **(71)** - Hogan's Sister (USA) (Speak John) 10.7f **(72)**
Form - 67010
Record 1999 - 1st:1 2nd:0 3rd:0 Ran:5
Pre1999 - 1st:3 2nd:0 3rd:3 Ran:21
Win Prizemoney £12,971 *Total Prizemoney* £14,387

Wins * 1999	Oct	Pontef	(SFT)	H	17.1f	39	48	<
* 1998	Apr	Pontef	(G-S)	H	21.6f	36	42	
* 1997	Jly	Beverl	(HVY)	H	16.2f	32	37	
* 1997	Jun	Carlis	(G-F)	H	17.2f	28	31	

1999 Turf 1-3: (16f, 17f 1-1, 18f) (gd 1-2, g-f) 1999 AW 0-2: (14f, 16f) (Fibr 2)
Moderate gelding, effective 17 to 22f, best at 18f, acts on g-s to gd, best on gd, often wears blinkers (very effectively), favours left handed tracks, likes tight tracks. Turf high 48 - 1st of 16 getting 25lb from Fisherman's Cove (4 Oct Pontefract RF 4717). AW high 10. Inconsistent. Requires a real test of stamina.
**R Bastiman [4-35] Mrs Judith Marshall.*

BLACK JACK GIRL (IRE) RR 1648[12]

2 br f Ridgewood Ben - Shiyra (Darshaan) 9.9f **(84)**
Form - 0
Record 1999 - 1st:0 2nd:0 3rd:0 Ran:1
1999 Turf 0-1: (6f) (frm)
Currently very poor filly. **J S Wainwright [0-1] Adrian Goodings.*

BLACK MAGIC RR 2083[14]

5 b m Cigar 6.3f **(43)** - Mossage (Ballymoss) 8.5f **(55)**
Form - 0
Record 1999 - 1st:0 2nd:0 3rd:0 Ran:1
1999 AW 0-1: (11f) (Fibr)
Currently very poor filly. **P Howling [0-3] Mark Hollingsworth.*

BLACK ORPHEUS (IRE) BHB 47f RR 46f 1649[2]

4 b g Astronef 7.9f **(59)** - Cri Basque (Gay Fandango (USA)) 8.5f **(59)**
Form - 002
Record 1999 - 1st:0 2nd:1 3rd:0 Ran:3
Pre1999 - 1st:0 2nd:0 3rd:0 Ran:9
Win Prizemoney £0 *Total Prizemoney* £835
1999 Turf 0-3: (5f, 6f 2) (gd, g-f, frm)
Moderate gelding. Turf high 46.
**P S Felgate [0-6] J M Flynn (from E J O'Grady in IRE [0-6] Jun 1998).*

BLACKPOOL MAMMA'S BHB 63f68a RR 72f 68a 3268[4]

2 b f Merdon Melody 6.8f **(56)** - Woodland Steps (Bold Owl) 8.5f **(45)**
Form - 15213315224
Record 1999 - 1st:3 2nd:3 3rd:2 Ran:11
Win Prizemoney £7,214 *Total Prizemoney* £10,735

Wins * 1999	Jun	Chepst	(G-F)	C	6.1f	71	<
*** 1999**	May	Newcas	(G-F)	C	6f	67	
*** 1999**	Apr	Mussel	(GD)		5f	68	

1999 Turf 3-10: (5f 1-5, 6f 2-5) (gd 1-3, g-f 1-4, frm 2, hrd 1-1) 1999 AW 0-1: (6f) (Fibr)
Above-average filly, effective 5 to 6f, best at 5f, acts on gd to frm - acts on Fibr, excels at Newcastle. Turf high 81 - 2nd of 12 giving 2lb to Palmstead Belle (21 May Nottingham 5f g-f RF 1379). (1st run) - 2nd of 7 getting 5lb from Water Hunter (24 Jly Southwell 6f Fibr RF 3111). Consistent. **J Berry [3-11] G Tiribocchi.*

BLACK ROCK DESERT (USA) RR 112f 4777a[14]

3 b c Danzig (USA) 8.1f **(88)** - City Dance (USA)
Form - 6160
1999 Turf 1-4: (5f 1-3, 7f) (sft, g-s, gd 1-2)
Group-class colt. Turf high 112 - 1st of 8 getting 3lb from Imperfect World (16 May Longchamp RF 1360a). He was found to have a respiratory problem after flopping on his reappearance, but did nothing wrong when winning a Group 3 at Longchamp in May. There are valid excuses for his two subsequent defeats, a pulled muscle at Leopardstown and heavy ground at Longchamp, and he deserves another chance against top class sprinters.
**A P O'Brien in IRE [2-5] M Tabor.*

BLACK ROCKET (IRE) BHB 53f48a RR 52f 48a 4951[6]

3 br f Perugino (USA) - Betelgeuse (Kalaglow) 9.8f **(67)**
Form - 876
Record 1999 - 1st:0 2nd:0 3rd:0 Ran:3
Pre1999 - 1st:0 2nd:0 3rd:0 Ran:5
1999 Turf 0-2: (6f, 7f) (g-f, frm) 1999 AW 0-1: (8f) (Equi)
Fair filly. Turf high 52. **K Mahdi [0-8] Hamad Al-Mutawa.*

BLACK SILK BHB 85f RR 87f 4874[3]

3 b c Zafonic (USA) 9f **(83)** - Mademoiselle Chloe (Night Shift (USA)) 7.2f **(69)**
Form - 2221538503
Record 1999 - 1st:1 2nd:3 3rd:2 Ran:10
Pre1999 - 1st:0 2nd:1 3rd:1 Ran:4
Win Prizemoney £5,057 *Total Prizemoney* £15,324
Wins * 1999 Jly Warwic (G-F) 7.7f 75+ <
1999 Turf 1-10: (7f 6, 8f 1-4) (gd 2, g-f 1-2, frm 6)
Useful colt, effective 7 to 8f, best at 7f, acts on gd to frm, best on frm. Turf high 87 - 3rd of 10 giving 4lb to Nice One Clare (4 Aug Kempton 7f frm RF 3355). Consistent. Broke his duck when scoring on fast ground over the extended seven furlongs at Warwick in July. Has since run well in competitive handicaps, but he is not an easy ride and has not looked too keen on occasions.
**C F Wall [1-14] S Fustok.*

BLACKWATCH (IRE) BHB 57f52a RR 63f 52a 4939[8]

2 b c Night Shift (USA) 8.1f **(73)** - Hollybank Lady (USA) (Sir Ivor) 10.2f **(70)**
Form - 745008
Record 1999 - 1st:0 2nd:0 3rd:0 Ran:6
Win Prizemoney £0 *Total Prizemoney* £237
1999 Turf 0-5: (5f 3, 6f, 7f) (gd 2, g-f, frm 2) 1999 AW 0-1: (7f) (Fibr)
Average colt. Turf high 63. **N A Callaghan [0-6] Paul & Jenny Green.*

BLACK WEASEL (IRE) BHB 40f **RR 35f** 3296[7]
4 b c Lahib (USA) 8f **(69)** - Glowlamp (IRE) (Glow (USA)) 6.7f **(71)**
Form - 00007
Record 1999 - 1st:0 2nd:0 3rd:0 Ran:5
Pre1999 - 1st:1 2nd:0 3rd:1 Ran:9
Win Prizemoney £2,736 *Total Prizemoney* £5,297
Wins 1998 Jly Pontef (G-F) 10f 61 <
1999 Turf 0-2: (8f, 12f) (sft, frm) 1999 AW 0-3: (6f, 8f, 11f) (Fibr 3)
Very moderate colt, effective 10f, acts on frm, has worn blinkers (very effectively), likes left handed tracks. Turf high 26. AW high 24. **A Bailey [0-1] S A Pritchard (from Miss J F Craze [0-9] Jun 1999).*

BLAIR (IRE) RR 44f 5163[9]
2 b g Persian Bold 10f **(69)** - Zara's Birthday (IRE) (Waajib)
Form - 0
Record 1999 - 1st:0 2nd:0 3rd:0 Ran:1
1999 Turf 0-1: (7f) (g-s)
Currently moderate gelding. **W W Haigh [0-1] Miss M Swinbank.*

BLAKENMOR BHB 33f **RR 22f** 3145[8]
6 b g No Evil - Kinz (Great Nephew) 9.9f **(64)**
Form - 7068
Record 1999 - 1st:0 2nd:0 3rd:0 Ran:4
Pre1999 - 1st:0 2nd:0 3rd:0 Ran:2
1999 Turf 0-3: (10f, 12f, 14f) (gd 2, g-f) 1999 AW 0-1: (16f) (Fibr)
Little account gelding. Turf high 35.
**J R Best [0-4] Mrs S Forgan (from J Neville [0-1] Spt 1996).*

BLAKESET BHB 74f **RR 75f** 5033[11]
4 ch c Midyan (USA) 9.9f **(64)** - Penset (Red Sunset) 8.2f **(63)**
Form - 020500260
Record 1999 - 1st:0 2nd:2 3rd:0 Ran:9
Pre1999 - 1st:1 2nd:3 3rd:2 Ran:12
Win Prizemoney £4,347 *Total Prizemoney* £17,777
Wins * 1997 Apr Newmar (G-F) 5f 76 <
1999 Turf 0-9: (6f, 7f 5, 8f 3) (g-s, gd 3, g-f 2, frm 3)
Scopey, above-average colt, effective 7 to 8f, best at 7f, acts on gd to frm, best on g-f, has worn blinkers, does well at Newbury and Lingfield. Turf high 84 - 2nd of 7 to The Prince (7 May Lingfield 8f g-f RF 1085). **R Hannon [1-21] Mrs Caroline Parker.*

BLAKEY (IRE) BHB 60a **RR 46f** 4282[8]
3 b g Maledetto (IRE) - Villars (Home Guard (USA)) 9.3f **(66)**
Form - 2325508748
Record 1999 - 1st:0 2nd:2 3rd:1 Ran:10
Pre1999 - 1st:0 2nd:0 3rd:0 Ran:3
Win Prizemoney £0 *Total Prizemoney* £2,177
1999 Turf 0-9: (5f 4, 6f 3, 7f 2) (g-s, g-f, frm 4, hrd 3) 1999 AW 0-1: (5f) (Fibr)
Moderate gelding, effective 5f, acts on g-f. Turf high 61 - 2nd of 9 to Regal Song (16 Jun Hamilton 5f g-f RF 2048). Consistent.
**J Berry [0-13] J Berry.*

BLANKENBERGE (IRE) BHB 72f68a **RR 75f 68a** 4824[4]
3 ch g Pips Pride 6.7f **(70)** - Renata's Ring (IRE) (Auction Ring (USA)) 8.6f **(65)**
Form - 622454
Record 1999 - 1st:0 2nd:2 3rd:0 Ran:6
Win Prizemoney £0 *Total Prizemoney* £1,632
1999 Turf 0-5: (8f 4, 10f) (sft, gd, g-f 2, frm) 1999 AW 0-1: (9f) (Fibr)
Leggy, above-average gelding, effective 8 to 10f, best at 8f, acts on gd to frm. Turf high 83.
**A G Foster [0-1] R E Sangster (from P W Chapple-Hyam [0-5] Spt 1999).*

BLAST OF STORM (IRE) RR 101f 1486a[5]
3 b c Perugino (USA) - Key Partner (Law Society (USA)) 9.9f **(70)**
Form - 135
1999 Turf 1-3: (7f 1-1, 8f, 10f) (hvy 1-1, g-f 2)
Currently very useful colt. Turf high 101 - 3rd of 7 to Saffron Walden (18 Apr Leopardstown 8f g-f RF 0786a) - also 1st of 9 from Lucky Legend (5 Apr Cork RF 0670a). He won a decent maiden at Cork in April and ran a blinder behind Saffron Walden and Mus-If in a Listed event at Leopardstown later that month. Sidelined through the second half of the season, he remains open to improvement and should stay beyond a mile.
**W M Roper in IRE [1-3] B Demuyser.*

BLAYNEY DANCER RR 29f 5123[6]
2 b c Contract Law (USA) 8.9f **(54)** - Lady Poly **(12?f 18a)** (Dunbeath (USA)) 7.8f **(70)**
Form - 06
Record 1999 - 1st:0 2nd:0 3rd:0 Ran:2
1999 Turf 0-2: (6f 2) (g-s, gd)
Currently little account colt. Turf high 29 (began Spt).
**J R Poulton [0-2] Mrs M Liston.*

BLAZER'S BABY BHB 16f18a **RR 26f 18a** 4442[13]
5 ch m Norton Challenger 10f **(41)** - Qualitair Blazer (Blazing Saddles (AUS)) 6.7f **(46)**
Form - 500
Record 1999 - 1st:0 2nd:0 3rd:0 Ran:3
Pre1999 - 1st:1 2nd:0 3rd:0 Ran:13
Win Prizemoney £1,984 *Total Prizemoney* £1,984
Wins 1997 Jly Nottin (G-F) S 10f 49 <
1999 Turf 0-2: (11f, 12f) (g-s, gd) 1999 AW 0-1: (14f) (Fibr)
Little account filly. Turf high 26 (began Aug).
**K S Bridgwater [0-8] Mrs Linda Donovan (from Mrs N Macauley [0-11] Aug 1998).*

BLAZING BILLY BHB 33f **RR 27f** 3744[11]
4 ch g Anshan 8.2f **(63)** - Worthy Venture (Northfields (USA)) 9f **(72)**
Form - 0000
Record 1999 - 1st:0 2nd:0 3rd:0 Ran:4
Pre1999 - 1st:0 2nd:0 3rd:0 Ran:7
1999 Turf 0-4: (5f, 6f 2, 8f) (gd, g-f 2, frm)
Leggy, little account gelding, has worn blinkers. Turf high 27.
**C A Dwyer [0-12] R West.*

BLAZING FLAME BHB 25a **RR 22f** 3671[7]
3 br g Chaddleworth (IRE) - Blazing Sunset (Blazing Saddles (AUS)) 6.7f **(46)**
Form - 007
Record 1999 - 1st:0 2nd:0 3rd:0 Ran:3
Pre1999 - 1st:0 2nd:0 3rd:0 Ran:6
1999 Turf 0-2: (6f, 7f) (g-f, frm) 1999 AW 0-1: (9f) (Fibr)
Light-framed, moderate gelding. Turf high 8.
**Mrs N Macauley [0-1] A Saccomando (from Miss Kate Milligan [0-2] Jun 1999).*

BLAZING IMP (USA) BHB 32f **RR 30f** 4167[7]
6 ch g Imp Society (USA) 7.1f **(63)** - Marital (USA) (Marine Patrol (USA)) 5f **(52)**
Form - 0000707
Record 1999 - 1st:0 2nd:0 3rd:0 Ran:7
Pre1999 - 1st:2 2nd:0 3rd:1 Ran:22
Win Prizemoney £6,034 *Total Prizemoney* £6,618
Wins * 1998 Jly Hamilt (FRM) S 5f 49
* 1997 Jun Mussel (G-S) 5f 52 <
1999 Turf 0-7: (5f 6, 6f) (gd, g-f, frm 5)
Very moderate gelding, effective 5f, acts on gd to frm. Turf high 30.
**Mrs J Jordan [2-25] Forties Joint Venture (from W S Cunningham [0-4] Aug 1996).*

BLAZING PEBBLES BHB 30f **RR 26f** 5138[18]
2 ch f Pebble Powder - Wrightway Blues (Majority Blue)
Form - 000
Record 1999 - 1st:0 2nd:0 3rd:0 Ran:3
1999 Turf 0-3: (6f 2, 8f) (gd 2, frm)
Currently little account filly. Turf high 26.
**P S McEntee [0-3] Mrs S van der Meulen.*

BLEND OF PACE (IRE) RR 98f 4614a[4]
3 b f Sadler's Wells (USA) 11.3f **(87)** - Trusted Partner (USA) (Affirmed (USA)) 9.3f **(79)**
Form - 415334
1999 Turf 1-6: (10f, 12f 1-5) (sft, g-s 1-2, gd, g-f 2)
Very useful filly, effective 12f, acts on g-s to g-f, often wears blinkers. Turf high 98. She stays well and is worth a try beyond middle-distances. **D K Weld in IRE [1-6] Moyglare Stud Farm.*

BLESS BHB 54f **RR 67df** 3850[6]
2 ch f Beveled (USA) 6.9f **(64)** -Ballystate (Ballacashtal (CAN)) 5.3f **(50)**
Form - 47086

Record 1999 - 1st:0 2nd:0 3rd:0 Ran:5
1999 Turf 0-5: (5f, 6f 3, 7f) (sft, gd 2, frm 2)
Average filly, has worn blinkers. Turf high 67.
**M Madgwick [0-5] Gail Gaisford And Friends.*

BLESSINGINDISGUISE BHB 77f RR 76f 4911[9]

6 b g Kala Shikari 6f **(48)** - Blowing Bubbles (Native Admiral (USA)) 5f **(80)**
Form - 07078400010
Record 1999 - 1st:1 2nd:0 3rd:0 Ran:11
Pre1999 - 1st:8 2nd:5 3rd:3 Ran:38
Win Prizemoney £64,958 *Total Prizemoney* £84,309
Wins * **1999** Spt Newcas (G-F) H 5f 73 76
* 1998 Jly Ascot (G-F) H 5f 97 100 <
* 1998 Jly York (G-F) H 5f 92 97
* 1997 Jly Ascot (GD) H 5f 76 94
* 1997 Jly Ayr (G-F) H 5f 76 80+
* 1997 Jly Haydoc (GD) H 5f 70 71+
* 1997 Jun Ripon (GD) H 5f 64 67
* 1997 May Redcar (G-F) H 5f 58 61
* 1995 May Newcas (GD) 5f 58t
1999 Turf 1-11: (5f 1-9, 6f 2) (gd 4, g-f 2, frm 1-5)
Above-average gelding, effective 5f, acts on gd to frm, often wears blinkers. Turf high 81. Consistent. He did not show a great deal last term until he struck gold in a decent sprint handicap, and is still well handicapped on his best form. Sometimes has given trouble at the stalls. **M W Easterby [9-49] A G Black.*

BLESS THE BRIDE (IRE) BHB 72f RR 77f 5109[6]

2 b f Darshaan 11.9f **(81)** - Feather Bride (IRE) (Groom Dancer (USA))
Form - 466
Record 1999 - 1st:0 2nd:0 3rd:0 Ran:3
Win Prizemoney £0 *Total Prizemoney* £218
1999 Turf 0-3: (7f, 8f 2) (g-s 2, gd)
Currently above-average filly. Turf high 77 (began Spt).
**J L Dunlop [0-3] Mrs Dan Abbott (Susan Ab Racing) II.*

BLINDING MISSION (IRE) RR 69f 4898[8]

2 b f Marju (IRE) 9.2f **(76)** - Blinding (IRE) (High Top) 10.2f **(67)**
Form - 58
Record 1999 - 1st:0 2nd:0 3rd:0 Ran:2
1999 Turf 0-2: (7f, 8f) (gd, frm)
Currently average filly. Turf high 69 (began Spt).
**J Noseda [0-2] Exors of the late Mrs James McAllister.*

BLIND TRUST (IRE) RR 75f 982[F]

3 b c Mtoto 11.5f **(71)** - Ancestry (Persepolis (FR)) 6.4f **(67)**
Form - F
Record 1999 - 1st:0 2nd:0 3rd:0 Ran:1
Pre1999 - 1st:0 2nd:0 3rd:0 Ran:1
1999 Turf 0-1: (8f) (frm)
Neat, above-average colt. (DEAD) **C F Wall [0-2] N Ahamad.*

BLISS (IRE) BHB 47f RR 41f 3148[10]

4 b f Statoblest 6.4f **(63)** - Moira My Girl (Henbit (USA)) 9f **(61)**
Form - 0740
Record 1999 - 1st:0 2nd:0 3rd:0 Ran:4
Pre1999 - 1st:3 2nd:1 3rd:0 Ran:19
Win Prizemoney £13,901 *Total Prizemoney* £15,203
Wins * 1997 Oct Newmar (GD) H 5f 71 74 <
* 1997 Spt Sandow (GD) H 5f 63 70
* 1997 Spt Bright (G-F) H 5.3f 56 60
1999 Turf 0-4: (5f 3, 6f) (g-f, frm, hrd 2)
Neat, moderate filly, effective 6f, acts on frm. Turf high 41. Consistent. **Mrs P N Dutfield [3-23] W A Harrison-Allan.*

BLIZZARD RR 42f 1136[17]

3 gr f Petong 7.6f **(58)** - Tempesta Rossa (IRE) (Persian Heights)
Form - 800
Record 1999 - 1st:0 2nd:0 3rd:0 Ran:1
Pre1999 - 1st:0 2nd:0 3rd:0 Ran:3
1999 Turf 0-1: (8f) (g-f)
Workmanlike, moderate filly. **B Smart [0-4] The Dyball Partnership.*

BLOCKADE (USA) BHB 37f RR 41f 3968[8]

10 b g Imperial Falcon (CAN) 9.2f **(72)** - Stolen Date (USA) (Sadair) 9.1f **(68)**
Form - 3100808
Record 1999 - 1st:1 2nd:0 3rd:1 Ran:7
Pre1999 - 1st:17 2nd:6 3rd:7 Ran:70
Win Prizemoney £66,114 *Total Prizemoney* £80,760
Wins * **1999** Jun Yarmou (G-F) H 10.1f 45 45
* 1997 Jun Nottin (G-F) 10f 55+
* 1997 May Yarmou (G-F) H 10.1f 55 57
* 1996 Jly Bright (FRM) C 7f 61
* 1996 Jly Yarmou (G-F) C 8f 61
* 1995 Aug Bright (FRM) C 8f 74
* 1995 Jly Yarmou (G-F) C 8f 74
* 1995 Jun Goodwo (FRM) C 9f 81 <
* 1995 May Newmar (GD) 7f 72
1999 Turf 1-7: (10f 1-6, 11f) (gd 1-2, g-f 3, frm 2)
Moderate gelding. Turf high 46. Consistent. He is still capable of winning in the right company, and is an ideal mount for an inexperienced rider. **M L W Bell [18-77] A M Warrender.*

BLOOD ORANGE BHB 50a RR 30f 1240[17]

5 ch h Ron's Victory (USA) 9.2f **(52)** - Little Bittern (USA) (Riva Ridge (USA)) 8.2f **(68)**
Form - 0
Record 1999 - 1st:0 2nd:0 3rd:0 Ran:1
Pre1999 - 1st:0 2nd:0 3rd:0 Ran:10
1999 Turf 0-1: (8f) (g-f)
Fair colt. **G G Margarson [0-11] G G Margarson.*

BLOODY MARY (IRE) BHB 68f RR 65f 4820[4]

2 ch f Prince of Birds (USA) - Royaltess (Royal And Regal (USA)) 9.5f **(60)**
Form - 0230234
Record 1999 - 1st:0 2nd:2 3rd:2 Ran:7
Win Prizemoney £0 *Total Prizemoney* £2,667
1999 Turf 0-7: (5f, 6f 2, 7f 3, 8f) (gd 2, g-f 3, frm 2)
Average filly, effective 6f, acts on g-f. Turf high 76 - 2nd of 13 giving 3lb to Flyover (8 Jun Salisbury 6f g-f RF 1812).
**R Hannon [0-7] Gamahada Partners.*

BLOOMING AMAZING BHB 70f54a RR 72f 54a 4578[5]

5 b g Mazilier (USA) 8.5f **(56)** - Cornflower Blue (Tyrnavos) 10.1f **(55)**
Form - 5803020705
Record 1999 - 1st:0 2nd:1 3rd:1 Ran:10
Pre1999 - 1st:4 2nd:5 3rd:3 Ran:29
Win Prizemoney £16,396 *Total Prizemoney* £24,142
Wins * 1998 Aug Pontef (G-F) H 8f 78 85 <
* 1998 Aug Beverl (G-F) H 7.5f 78 76
* 1998 May Beverl (GD) H 7.5f 70 77
* 1997 Apr Beverl (G-F) H 8.5f 72 76
1999 Turf 0-8: (7f, 8f 7) (gd 2, g-f 3, frm 3) 1999 AW 0-2:(8f, 11f)(Fibr 2)
Above-average gelding, effective 7 to 8f, best at 8f, acts on gd to frm, best on frm, has worn blinkers, prefers right handed tracks, likes tight tracks, excels at Beverley. Turf high 78 (began Jly) - 2nd of 12 giving 32lb to Clarinch Claymore (12 Aug Beverley 8f g-f RF 3565). AW high 47. **J L Eyre [4-39] Billy Parker.*

BLOT BHB 72f RR 82f 4874[20]

5 b g Warning 8.1f **(77)** - Rattle Along (Tap On Wood) 10.3f **(65)**
Form - 0
Record 1999 - 1st:0 2nd:0 3rd:0 Ran:1
Pre1999 - 1st:1 2nd:0 3rd:2 Ran:4
Win Prizemoney £3,601 *Total Prizemoney* £4,705
Wins 1997 Aug Thirsk (GD) 8f 82 <
1999 Turf 0-1: (8f) (gd)
Decent gelding.
**C R Egerton [0-1] Bernard Gover Bloodstock Trading Ltd (from Mrs J Cecil [1-4] Aug 1997).*

BLOWING AWAY (IRE) BHB 40f RR 44f 4600[7]

5 b br m Last Tycoon 9.4f **(73)** -Taken By Force(Persian Bold) 9.3f **(66)**
Form - 87
Record 1999 - 1st:0 2nd:0 3rd:0 Ran:2
Pre1999 - 1st:1 2nd:2 3rd:6 Ran:22
Win Prizemoney £2,868 *Total Prizemoney* £6,661
Wins 1997 Oct Leices (GD) C 8f 54 <
1999 Turf 0-1: (10f) (frm) 1999 AW 0-1: (14f) (Fibr)
Moderate filly, effective 8 to 12f, best at 10f, acts on gd to frm, best on frm, has worn blinkers, likes Yarmouth and Pontefract.
**J Pearce [0-2] Jeff Pearce (from M H Tompkins [2-25] Oct 1998).*

BLOW ME A KISS BHB 55f52a **RR 63df 52a** 3978[12]
4 ch f Kris 10f **(75)** - Lassoo (Caerleon (USA)) 8.6f **(71)**
Form - 880
Record 1999 - 1st:0 2nd:0 3rd:0 Ran:2
Pre1999 - 1st:0 2nd:4 3rd:2 Ran:9
Win Prizemoney £0 *Total Prizemoney* £5,618
1999 Turf 0-1: (11f) (frm) 1999 AW 0-1: (12f) (Fibr)
Tall, average filly, effective 8 to 10f, best at 10f, acts on gd. Becoming disappointing. **C W Thornton [0-11] Guy Reed.*

BLU AIR FORCE (IRE) RR 91f 5263a[2]
2 b c Sri Pekan (USA) - Carillon Miss (USA) (The Minstrel (CAN)) 10f **(72)**
Form - 2
1999 Turf 0-1: (7f) (g-s)
Currently useful colt. (1st run) - 2nd of 8 to Touch Of The Blues (5 Nov Maisons-laffitte 7f g-s RF 5263a). **B Grizzetti in ITY [0-1].*

BLU CARILLON (IRE) RR 107f 1354a[2]
4 ch c Love the Groom (USA) - Carillon Miss (USA) (The Minstrel (CAN)) 10f **(72)**
Form - 12
1999 Turf 0-1: (6f) (gd)
Pattern-class colt. (1st run) - 2nd of 12 giving 9lb to Su Tirolesu (16 May Capannelle 6f gd RF 1354a). He ran well in Group 3 company and acts on easy ground. **O Pessi in ITY [2-7] O Pessi.*

BLUE ANCHOR BHB 39f35a **RR 43f 35a** 29[14]
4 b g Robellino (USA) 9.5f **(68)** - Fair Seas (General Assembly (USA)) 10f **(68)**
Form - 060
Record 1999 - 1st:0 2nd:0 3rd:0 Ran:1
Pre1999 - 1st:1 2nd:0 3rd:1 Ran:13
Win Prizemoney £1,735 *Total Prizemoney* £2,264
Wins 1998 *Feb Southw (STD) H 11f 40 35* <
1999 AW 0-1: (13f) (Equi)
Moderate gelding, effective 11 to 14f, acts on gd - acts on Fibr.
**A W Carroll [0-5] D R Wellicome (from Mrs M Reveley [1-10] May 1998).*

BLUEBELLE BHB 75f **RR 51f** 3815[11]
4 b f Generous (IRE) 11.5f **(82)** - Hi Lass (Shirley Heights) 10.3f **(74)**
Form - 0P0
Record 1999 - 1st:0 2nd:0 3rd:0 Ran:3
Pre1999 - 1st:1 2nd:0 3rd:1 Ran:3
Win Prizemoney £4,224 *Total Prizemoney* £5,004
Wins * 1998 Aug Cheste (G-S) 12.3f 72 <
1999 Turf 0-3: (14f 2, 16f) (gd 2, frm)
Scopey, fair filly, effective 10 to 12f, acts on gd. Turf high 51 (began Jly). **Sir Mark Prescott [1-6] Faisal Salman & C M Budgett.*

BLUEBELL WOOD (IRE) RR 38f 4785[8]
2 ch f Bluebird (USA) 7.9f **(71)** - Jungle Jezebel (Thatching) 8f **(66)**
Form - 8
Record 1999 - 1st:0 2nd:0 3rd:0 Ran:1
1999 Turf 0-1: (7f) (g-s)
Currently very moderate filly. **A J McNae [0-1] The Iona Stud.*

BLUE BOLIVAR (IRE) BHB 100f **RR 95f** 4570[5]
2 b c Blues Traveller (IRE) -Cappuchino (IRE)**(59a)**(Roi Danzig (USA))
Form - 125
Record 1999 - 1st:1 2nd:1 3rd:0 Ran:3
Win Prizemoney £4,299 *Total Prizemoney* £64,779
Wins * 1999 Jun Sandow (GD) 7.1f 86 <
1999 Turf 1-3: (6f, 7f 1-1, 8f) (sft, gd, frm 1-1)
Currently very useful colt. Turf high 95 - 2nd of 21 to Sheer Hamas (8 Spt Doncaster 6f gd RF 4208) - also 1st of 11 giving 5lb to Wadenhoe (11 Jun Sandown RF 1920). He was absent for three months after a winning debut, but returned in fine form to finish second in the £200,000 St Leger Yearling Stakes. A fast finisher there, he failed to improve when stepped-up to a mile in the Royal Lodge Stakes and may fall short of Group class. **R Hannon [1-3] Hippodrome Racing.*

BLUE CLOUD (IRE) RR 104f 715a[1]
3 ch f Nashwan (USA) 10.3f **(79)** - Batave (Posse (USA)) 8.9f **(61)**
Form - 1
1999 Turf 1-1: (7f 1-1) (g-s 1-1)
Currently very useful filly. (1st run) - 1st of 6 from Ronda (9 Apr Maisons-Laffitte RF 0715a). She did not make her date in the 1000 Guineas, but is clearly a smart miler. **A Fabre in FR [1-2] Daniel Wildenstein.*

BLUE DAWN (IRE) BHB 50f37a **RR 69f 37a** 43[9]
4 ch f Bluebird (USA) 7.9f **(71)** - Spring Carnival (USA) (Riverman (USA)) 9.1f **(76)**
Form - 55050
Record 1999 - 1st:0 2nd:0 3rd:0 Ran:2
Pre1999 - 1st:0 2nd:0 3rd:0 Ran:10
Win Prizemoney £0 *Total Prizemoney* £211
1999 AW 0-2: (7f, 10f) (Equi 2)
Light-framed, average filly, effective 8f, acts on gd, has worn blinkers, likes tight tracks. AW high 31.
**B R Johnson [0-5] B Scott (from E A L Dunlop [0-7] Oct 1998).*

BLUE DIAMOND BHB 38f **RR 19f** 1548[12]
3 b f First Trump - Lammastide (Martinmas) 7.6f **(59)**
Form - 00
Record 1999 - 1st:0 2nd:0 3rd:0 Ran:2
Pre1999 - 1st:0 2nd:0 3rd:0 Ran:2
1999 Turf 0-2: (10f 2) (g-f, frm)
Workmanlike, poor filly, has worn blinkers. Turf high 17.
**J S Moore [0-2] R Danvers (from M L W Bell [0-2] Oct 1998).*

BLUE DOVE (IRE) RR 45f 4407[12]
2 b f Bluebird (USA) 7.9f **(71)** - Paradise Forum (Prince Sabo) 7.2f **(62)**
Form - 0
Record 1999 - 1st:0 2nd:0 3rd:0 Ran:1
1999 Turf 0-1: (6f) (frm)
Currently moderate filly. **C A Horgan [0-1] Mrs B Sumner.*

BLUE GLASS BHB 56f **RR 30f** 406[4]
3 b f Ardkinglass 5f **(64)** - Kajetana (FR) (Caro)
Form - 4
Record 1999 - 1st:0 2nd:0 3rd:0 Ran:1
Pre1999 - 1st:1 2nd:0 3rd:0 Ran:3
Win Prizemoney £2,180 *Total Prizemoney* £2,389
Wins * 1998 *Oct Wolver (STD) S 8.5f 65* <
1999 AW 0-1: (8f) (Fibr)
Scopey, average filly. **N P Littmoden [1-4] T Clarke.*

BLUE GOLD BHB 93f **RR 83f** 4833[3]
2 b c Rainbow Quest (USA) 11.2f **(81)** - Relatively Special **(105f)** (Alzao (USA)) 7.1f **(68)**
Form - 5133
Record 1999 - 1st:1 2nd:0 3rd:2 Ran:4
Win Prizemoney £3,761 *Total Prizemoney* £6,111
Wins * 1999 Jly Sandow (G-F) 7.1f 83+ <
1999 Turf 1-4: (6f, 7f 1-2, 8f) (gd, frm 1-3)
Decent colt. Turf high 83 (began Jly) - 3rd of 8 giving 5lb to Sun Charm (12 Oct Leicester 7f gd RF 4833) - also 1st of 14 from Sanguine (21 Jly Sandown RF 3016). Got off the mark on his second start when landing a seven-furlong Sandown maiden, despite wandering about in the final two furlongs. Not disgraced subsequently. **R Hannon [1-4] Mohamed Suhail.*

BLUEGRASS MOUNTAIN BHB 71f **RR 54f** 1541[10]
2 b c Primo Dominie 7.2f **(67)** - Florentynna Bay (Aragon) 8.1f **(60)**
Form - 360
Record 1999 - 1st:0 2nd:0 3rd:1 Ran:3
Win Prizemoney £0 *Total Prizemoney* £408
1999 Turf 0-3: (5f 2, 6f) (gd 2, g-f)
Currently fair colt. Turf high 66.
**T D Easterby [0-3] T G & Mrs M E Holdcroft.*

BLUE HAWAII (IRE) BHB 54f **RR 75f** 5158[25]
2 ch c Up and At 'em - Astral Way (Hotfoot) 10.5f **(59)**
Form - 36000
Record 1999 - 1st:0 2nd:0 3rd:1 Ran:5
Win Prizemoney £0 *Total Prizemoney* £545
1999 Turf 0-5: (6f 2, 7f 2, 8f) (gd, g-f, frm 3)
Above-average colt. Turf high 75 (1st run) (began Jly) - 3rd of 10 to Nicholas Dudley (26 Jly Ayr 6f gd RF 3134).
**B S Rothwell [0-5] Norman Jackson.*

BLUE HAWK (IRE) BHB 67f **RR 63f** 4910[9]
2 ch c Prince of Birds (USA) - Classic Queen (IRE) (Classic Secret (USA))
Form - 050380
Record 1999 - 1st:0 2nd:0 3rd:1 Ran:6
Win Prizemoney £0 *Total Prizemoney* £557
1999 Turf 0-6: (6f, 7f 4, 10f) (g-s, gd 2, g-f, frm 2)
Average colt. Turf high 63. **R Hollinshead [0-6] Mrs Dianne Edwards.*

BLUE HOLLY (IRE) BHB 76f **RR 76+f** 5214[3]
2 b f Blues Traveller (IRE) - Holly Bird (Runnett) 7f **(59)**
Form - 800223123
Record 1999 - 1st:1 2nd:3 3rd:2 Ran:9
Win Prizemoney £2,594 *Total Prizemoney* £7,115
Wins * **1999** Oct Lingfi (G-F) 5f 87 <
1999 Turf 1-9: (5f 1-9) (sft, g-s 3, gd 1-3, frm 2)
Above-average filly, effective 5f, acts on gd. Turf high 87 - 1st of 16 from Queensmead (19 Oct Lingfield RF 4941).
**J S Moore [1-9] Tony Usher.*

BLUE HOPPER BHB 30f32a **RR 35f 32a** 114[6]
5 b m Rock Hopper 10.6f **(54)** - Kimble Blue (Blue Refrain)
Form - 236
Record 1999 - 1st:0 2nd:1 3rd:1 Ran:3
Pre1999 - 1st:0 2nd:2 3rd:3 Ran:25
Win Prizemoney £0 *Total Prizemoney* £4,429
1999 AW 0-3: (11f, 12f 2) (Fibr 3)
Moderate filly, effective 8 to 12f, acts on frm - acts on Fibr, has worn blinkers, favours tight tracks. AW high 41 - 3rd of 8 getting 5lb from A Day On The Dub (11 Jan Southwell 12f Fibr RF 0074).
**M Quinn [0-23] M Quinn (from M R Channon [0-7] Jun 1997).*

BLUE KITE BHB 50f66a **RR 39f 66a** 5146[3]
4 ch g Silver Kite (USA) 10.2f **(51)** - Gold And Blue (IRE) (Bluebird (USA)) 7.5f **(69)**
Form - 8058574204800501223
Record 1999 - 1st:1 2nd:3 3rd:1 Ran:15
Pre1999 - 1st:1 2nd:6 3rd:0 Ran:24
Win Prizemoney £5,209 *Total Prizemoney* £21,015
Wins * **1999** *Spt Wolver (STD) H 6f 59 66*
* 1997 *Spt Wolver (STD) 5f 72* <
1999 Turf 0-8: (5f 2, 6f 4, 7f 2) (g-s 2, gd, g-f 3, frm 2) 1999 AW 1-7: (5f, 6f 1-4, 7f 2) (Fibr 1-7)
Average gelding, effective 6 to 7f, acts on g-f - acts on Fibr, has worn blinkers. Turf high 62. AW high 66. Inconsistent. He showed a useful level of form on both Fibresand and turf as a juvenile, but went on a long losing run after that. He finally came good in a handicap at Wolverhampton in September having slipped considerably in the weights, but tends to get outpaced in his races these days and seems to find trouble before finishing well.
**N P Littmoden [2-33] T Clarke (from P D Evans [0-6] Jun 1999).*

BLUE LASER (IRE) BHB 48f **RR 34f** 1671[14]
3 b g Mujtahid (USA) 7.4f **(69)** - Dazzling Fire (IRE) (Bluebird (USA)) 7.5f **(69)**
Form - 0000
Record 1999 - 1st:0 2nd:0 3rd:0 Ran:4
Pre1999 - 1st:0 2nd:0 3rd:0 Ran:2
1999 Turf 0-4: (6f, 8f 2, 9f) (g-s 2, frm 2)
Scopey, very moderate gelding, has worn blinkers. Turf high 34.
**B J Meehan [0-6] Miss J Semple.*

BLUE LEGEND (IRE) BHB 48f56a **RR 65f 56a** 5002[9]
2 b f Blues Traveller (IRE) - Swoon Along (Dunphy) 9.4f **(57)**
Form - 07216000
Record 1999 - 1st:1 2nd:1 3rd:0 Ran:8
Win Prizemoney £2,571 *Total Prizemoney* £3,231
Wins * **1999** Jly Bright (FRM) C 7f 65 <
1999 Turf 1-7: (6f 2, 7f 1-4, 8f) (gd 3, g-f, frm 1-2, hrd) 1999 AW 0-1: (7f) (Fibr)
Average filly, effective 7f, acts on gd to frm. Turf high 65 - 1st of 9 getting 11lb from Inch Pincher (13 Jly Brighton RF 2772).
**J S Moore [1-8] D L Cunliffe.*

BLUE LINE ANGEL BHB 48f **RR 48f** 4906[13]
3 b g Cyrano de Bergerac 7.3f **(58)** - Northern Line (Camden Town) 9.3f **(53)**
Form - 73448400
Record 1999 - 1st:0 2nd:0 3rd:1 Ran:8
Pre1999 - 1st:0 2nd:0 3rd:0 Ran:3
Win Prizemoney £0 *Total Prizemoney* £1,074
1999 Turf 0-8: (7f 3, 8f 4, 9f) (g-s, g-f 4, frm 2, hrd)
Leggy, moderate gelding, effective 7 to 9f, best at 8f, acts on g-f to frm, best on g-f. Turf high 50 - 4th of 14 giving 2lb to Border Glen (21 Jun Musselburgh 8f g-f RF 2170). Consistent.
**R A Fahey [0-11] Peter Tingey.*

BLUE LINE LADY (IRE) BHB 60f **RR 74+f** 5218[21]
2 b f Common Grounds 8.1f **(66)** - Best Academy (USA) (Roberto (USA)) 10f **(76)**
Form - 27206000
Record 1999 - 1st:0 2nd:2 3rd:0 Ran:8
Win Prizemoney £0 *Total Prizemoney* £2,872
1999 Turf 0-8: (5f 2, 6f 4, 7f 2) (g-s, gd, g-f 3, frm 3)
Above-average filly, effective 5 to 6f, acts on g-f to frm. Turf high 74 - 2nd of 14 getting 5lb from Follow Suit (10 Jly York 6f g-f RF 2729). Becoming disappointing. **R A Fahey [0-8] Peter Tingey.*

BLUE MELODY (USA) BHB 92f **RR 92f** 5222[17]
3 b br f Dayjur (USA) 6.8f **(79)** - Blue Note (FR) (Habitat) 9.4f **(70)**
Form - 0020
Record 1999 - 1st:0 2nd:1 3rd:0 Ran:4
Pre1999 - 1st:1 2nd:3 3rd:0 Ran:6
Win Prizemoney £3,600 *Total Prizemoney* £14,720
Wins 1998 Jun Leices (GD) 5f 85++ <
1999 Turf 0-4: (5f, 6f 3) (g-s, gd 2, g-f)
Scopey, useful filly, effective 7f, acts on gd. Turf high 92. Consistent. Closely related to top-class sprinters Zieten and Blue Duster, she is not as good as her superb pedigree suggests, and has been well beaten in her forays into Listed and Group company.
**J H M Gosden [0-3] Sheikh Mohammed (from S bin Suroor [0-1] May 1999).*

BLUE MONK (IRE) BHB 31f42a **RR 39f 42a** 2913[13]
4 ch g Bluebird (USA) 7.9f **(71)** - High Habit (Slip Anchor) 9.8f **(73)**
Form - 7000670
Record 1999 - 1st:0 2nd:0 3rd:0 Ran:7
Pre1999 - 1st:0 2nd:0 3rd:0 Ran:3
1999 Turf 0-4: (8f, 10f, 14f 2) (g-f 2, frm 2) 1999 AW 0-3: (11f, 12f 2) (Fibr 3)
Workmanlike, very moderate gelding. Turf high 39. AW high 37. Inconsistent.
**A G Newcombe [0-7] Chris Bradbury (from I A Balding [0-3] Oct 1997).*

BLUE MOON (FR) RR 93f 5115a[2]
2 ch f Lomitas -To The Rainbow(FR)(Rainbow Quest (USA))10.4f **(75)**
Form - 2
1999 Turf 0-1: (8f) (gd)
Currently useful filly. (1st run) - 2nd of 7 to Volvoreta (19 Oct Deauville 8f gd RF 5115a). **X Nakkachdji in FR [0-1].*

BLUE MOUNTAIN RR 80f 4100[5]
2 ch c Elmaamul (USA) 8.1f **(70)** -Glenfinlass (Lomond (USA)) 8.8f **(65)**
Form - 235
Record 1999 - 1st:0 2nd:1 3rd:1 Ran:3
Win Prizemoney £0 *Total Prizemoney* £1,974
1999 Turf 0-3: (5f, 6f 2) (frm 3)
Currently decent colt. Turf high 80 (began Jly) - 3rd of 13 to Invincible Spirit (28 Jly Goodwood 6f frm RF 3212).
**R F JohnsonHoughton [0-3] Mrs Hue Williams.*

BLUE MUSIC (IRE) RR 61?f 4217[17]
4 ch g Keen 11.1f **(58)** - Coast Wind (USA) (Chief's Crown (USA)) 9.8f **(72)**
Form - 0
Record 1999 - 1st:0 2nd:0 3rd:0 Ran:1
Pre1999 - 1st:1 2nd:0 3rd:0 Ran:8
Win Prizemoney £2,226 *Total Prizemoney* £2,226
Wins 1998 May Clonme (G-F) H 10f 51 61 <
1999 Turf 0-1: (12f) (frm)
Average gelding, effective 10 to 12f, acts on sft to g-f, prefers right handed tracks.
**P J Hobbs [3-11] Jack Joseph (from D Gillespie in IRE [2-7] Oct 1998).*

BLUE OF THE NIGHT RR 36f 2886[11]
3 b f Runnett 6.7f **(56)** - Upping The Tempo (Dunbeath (USA)) 7.8f **(70)**
Form - 60
Record 1999 - 1st:0 2nd:0 3rd:0 Ran:2
1999 Turf 0-2: (6f 2) (frm 2)
Workmanlike, currently very moderate filly. Turf high 36.
**C F Wall [0-2] M Edwards.*

BLUE PERU (IRE) BHB 40f40a **RR 54f 40a** 1022[16]
3 b f Perugino (USA) - Blue Czarina (Sandhurst Prince) 7.9f **(63)**
Form - 700
Record 1999 - 1st:0 2nd:0 3rd:0 Ran:1
Pre1999 - 1st:0 2nd:0 3rd:0 Ran:5
1999 Turf 0-1: (7f) (hrd)
Neat, fair filly, effective 7f, acts on gd.
**B Smart [0-6] The Dyball Partnership.*

BLUEPRINT (IRE) BHB 113f89a **RR 116?f 89a** 4132[2]
4 b c Generous (IRE) 11.5f **(82)** - Highbrow (Shirley Heights) 10.3f **(74)**
Form - 11142
Record 1999 - 1st:3 2nd:1 3rd:0 Ran:5
Pre1999 - 1st:3 2nd:1 3rd:2 Ran:11
Win Prizemoney £81,266 *Total Prizemoney* £102,275
Wins * **1999** Jun Newmar (G-F) L 12f 116+ <
* **1999** Jun Ascot (G-F) H 12f 99 104
* **1999** May Newmar (G-F) H 12f 92 94
1998 Aug York (G-F) H 13.9f 89 93
1998 *May Lingfi (STD) H 12f 65 78+*
1998 *May Southw (STD) H 12f 65 69+*
1999 Turf 3-5: (12f 3-4, 13f) (gd, g-f 2-2, frm 1-2)
Scopey, high-class colt, effective 12 to 13f, best at 12f, acts on gd to frm, has worn blinkers, likes left handed tracks, likes Newmarket. Turf high 116 - 1st of 4 getting 3lb from Yavana's Pace (26 Jun Newmarket RF 2343). An improved performer for Her Majesty at the start of the season, he made a winning reappearance at Newmarket and ran out an appropriate winner of the Duke of Edinburgh Handicap at the Royal Meeting. Had no problems handling a step up to Listed company when scoring nicely at Newmarket, but could only manage last of four in a messy renewal of the Group Two Geoffrey Freer Stakes, before coming off worst in a scrap with Yavana's Pace in the September Stakes.
**Sir Michael Stoute [3-5] The Queen (from Lord Huntingdon [3-11] Oct 1998).*

BLUE ROCK LADY BHB 41f **RR 50f** 2341[7]
3 br f Rock City 8.8f **(62)** - Blues Player (Jaazeiro (USA)) 9.2f **(54)**
Form - 07
Record 1999 - 1st:0 2nd:0 3rd:0 Ran:2
Pre1999 - 1st:0 2nd:0 3rd:0 Ran:2
1999 Turf 0-2: (8f 2) (gd, g-f)
Light-framed, fair filly. Turf high 50.
**C F Wall [0-4] Framlingham Racing Partners.*

BLUE SAPPHIRE (IRE) BHB 39f **RR 48f** 4877[12]
2 b f Blues Traveller (IRE) - Era (Dalsaan) 9.8f **(64)**
Form - 80360000
Record 1999 - 1st:0 2nd:0 3rd:1 Ran:8
Win Prizemoney £0 *Total Prizemoney* £300
1999 Turf 0-7: (5f 5, 6f, 7f) (g-s, gd 2, g-f 2, frm 2) 1999 AW 0-1: (5f) (Fibr)
Moderate filly. Turf high 48. **D W Barker [0-8] D W Barker.*

BLUE SNAKE (USA) BHB 95f **RR 89f** 2846[1]
3 br c Gone West (USA) 7.8f **(82)** - Dabaweyaa (Shareef Dancer (USA)) 9.9f **(73)**
Form - 1
Record 1999 - 1st:1 2nd:0 3rd:0 Ran:1
Pre1999 - 1st:0 2nd:0 3rd:1 Ran:3
Win Prizemoney £4,260 *Total Prizemoney* £5,554
Wins * **1999** Jly Doncas (G-F) 8f 86+ <
1999 Turf 1-1: (8f 1-1) (g-f 1-1)
Scopey, useful colt. (1st run) - 1st of 9 giving 5lb to Bayaniya (15 Jly Doncaster RF 2846). Out of a very useful mare, he won a Doncaster maiden in good style and should have more improvement to come. **S bin Suroor [1-4] Godolphin.*

BLUES OF THE NIGHT BHB 28f **RR 35f** 4031[17]
3 gr f Petong 7.6f **(58)** - Candane **(77f)** (Danehill (USA)) 10f **(72)**
Form - 74350
Record 1999 - 1st:0 2nd:0 3rd:1 Ran:5
Pre1999 - 1st:0 2nd:0 3rd:0 Ran:2
Win Prizemoney £0 *Total Prizemoney* £254
1999 Turf 0-5: (7f, 10f 2, 12f 2) (g-f 3, frm 2)
Workmanlike, very moderate filly, effective 12f, acts on g-f. Turf high 35 (began Jly) - 3rd of 7 getting 16lb from Mithraic (4 Aug Newcastle 12f g-f RF 3366). **N Tinkler [0-7] Mrs D E Sharp.*

BLUE STAR BHB 66f84a **RR 66f 84a** 4213[15]
3 b c Whittingham (IRE) - Gold And Blue (IRE) (Bluebird (USA)) 7.5f **(69)**
Form - 000774343050
Record 1999 - 1st:0 2nd:0 3rd:2 Ran:12
Pre1999 - 1st:1 2nd:2 3rd:1 Ran:6
Win Prizemoney £18,990 *Total Prizemoney* £23,170
Wins * 1998 *Aug Wolver (STD) 6f 87* <
1999 Turf 0-12: (6f 8, 7f 3, 8f) (gd 2, g-f 4, frm 6)
Rangy, useful colt, effective 6f, - acts on Fibr, has worn blinkers, prefers left handed tracks, prefers tight tracks. Turf high 69. Difficult to know what his future may be as he has yet to show an aptitude for turf, and a transatlantic purchase may be his best chance in the long term. **N P Littmoden [1-18] T Clarke.*

BLUE SUGAR (USA) RR 93+f 3905[1]
2 ch c Shuailaan (USA) - Chelsea My Love (USA) **(23f)** (Opening Verse (USA))
Form - 1
Record 1999 - 1st:1 2nd:0 3rd:0 Ran:1
Win Prizemoney £2,165 *Total Prizemoney* £2,165
Wins * **1999** Aug Lingfi (G-F) 7.6f 88+ <
1999 Turf 1-1: (8f 1-1) (g-f 1-1)
Currently useful colt. (1st run) - 1st of 16 from First Manassas (25 Aug Lingfield RF 3905). **J R Fanshawe [1-1] G Algranti.*

BLUES WHISPERER (IRE) RR 41f 3837[11]
2 b c Blues Traveller (IRE) - Princess Roxanne (Prince Tenderfoot (USA)) 9f **(61)**
Form - 0
Record 1999 - 1st:0 2nd:0 3rd:0 Ran:1
1999 Turf 0-1: (7f) (frm)
Currently moderate colt.
**B R Millman [0-1] The Blues Whisperer Partnership.*

BLUE VELVET BHB 86f **RR 91f** 5045[4]
2 gr f Formidable (USA) 7.8f **(60)** - Sweet Whisper **(14f 46a)** (Petong) 6.6f **(58)**
Form - 442342120061724
Record 1999 - 1st:2 2nd:4 3rd:1 Ran:15
Win Prizemoney £10,278 *Total Prizemoney* £33,548
Wins * **1999** Spt Newmar (G-S) H 5f 78 81 <
* **1999** *Jun Southw (STD) 5f 79*
1999 Turf 1-13: (5f 1-10, 6f 3) (sft, gd 1-3, g-f 6, frm 3) 1999 AW 1-2: (5f 1-2) (Equi, Fibr 1-1)
Useful filly, effective 5 to 6f, acts on gd. Turf high 91 - 2nd of 20 getting 2lb from Magic of Love (15 Oct Newmarket 6f gd RF 4895). AW high 79. Possesses bags of early speed, an asset which enabled her to make all in a modest maiden on the Southwell Fibresand in June. Regained winning form in a decent Newmarket nursery and was a most creditable seventh in the Redcar Two-Year-Old Trophy. **K T Ivory [2-15] K T Ivory.*

BLUEWAIN LADY BHB 64f **RR 65f** 2453[5]
4 b f Unfuwain (USA) 11.4f **(74)** - Blue Guitar (Cure The Blues (USA)) 9.5f **(63)**
Form - 58255
Record 1999 - 1st:0 2nd:1 3rd:0 Ran:5
Pre1999 - 1st:1 2nd:0 3rd:2 Ran:8
Win Prizemoney £2,941 *Total Prizemoney* £6,196
Wins * 1998 Nov Bright (SFT) 11.9f 52 <
1999 Turf 0-5: (14f 4, 16f) (sft, gd 2, g-f, frm)
Scopey, average filly, effective 14f, acts on frm, has worn blinkers, likes left handed tracks, favours tight tracks. Turf high 65 - 2nd of 12 giving 19lb to Kintavi (22 May Catterick 14f frm RF 1391). Consistent. **P W Harris [1-13] The Blue Notes.*

BLUEWATER BAY BHB 52f62a **RR 52f 62a** 4091[13]
3 b f Lugana Beach 7f **(63)** - Dominion Blue (Dominion) 8.5f **(63)**
Form - 334472140
Record 1999 - 1st:1 2nd:1 3rd:1 Ran:8
Pre1999 - 1st:0 2nd:0 3rd:1 Ran:1
Win Prizemoney £2,018 *Total Prizemoney* £3,599
Wins 1999 *Aug Wolver (STD) S 9.4f 64* <
1999 Turf 0-4: (8f 2, 10f 2) (g-f 3, frm) 1999 AW 1-4: (6f, 7f, 8f, 9f 1-1) (Equi, Fibr 1-3)
Workmanlike, average filly, effective 6 to 9f, acts on g-f - acts on Fibr. Turf high 57 (1st run) - 4th of 15 getting 12lb from Picture Puzzle (26 May Yarmouth 8f g-f RF 1509). AW high 64 - 1st of 11 getting 5lb from Heathyards Jake (14 Aug Wolverhampton RF 3671). Inconsistent. She showed some ability on sand before easily winning a seller at Wolverhampton in August. Bought at the subsequent auction, she is worth watching out for if embarked on an All-Weather campaign during the winter.
**Andrew Reid [0-2] A S Reid (from J M P Eustace [1-7] Aug 1999).*

BLUNDELL LANE (IRE) BHB 67f67a **RR 67f 67a** 4154[7]
4 ch g Shalford (IRE) 7.8f **(63)** - Rathbawn Realm (Doulab (USA)) 9.8f **(65)**
Form - 87410360007
Record 1999 - 1st:1 2nd:0 3rd:1 Ran:11
Pre1999 - 1st:2 2nd:1 3rd:1 Ran:14
Win Prizemoney £17,089 *Total Prizemoney* £21,537
Wins * 1999 May Warwic (Gd) 6f 74
***** 1998 May Cheste (GD) H 6.1f 75 86+ <
***** 1997 Oct Redcar (G-F) H 6f 69 76
1999 Turf 1-9: (5f 2, 6f 1-7) (g-s, gd, g-f 4, frm 1-3) 1999 AW 0-2: (5f, 6f) (Fibr 2)
Workmanlike, average gelding, effective 6f, acts on g-f, has worn blinkers, likes left handed tracks, likes tight tracks. Turf high 74. AW high 68. Consistent. A pacey front runner.
**A P Jarvis [3-25] Nick Coverdale.*

BLURRED (IRE) BHB 55f **RR 45f** 2774[8]
6 ch g Al Hareb (USA) 9.4f **(53)** - I'll Take Paris (USA) (Vaguely Noble) 10.1f **(72)**
Form - 0008
Record 1999 - 1st:0 2nd:0 3rd:0 Ran:4
Pre1999 - 1st:1 2nd:1 3rd:3 Ran:12
Win Prizemoney £4,727 *Total Prizemoney* £7,620
Wins * 1996 Oct Doncas (GD) H 10.3f 70 74 <
1999 Turf 0-4: (10f, 11f, 12f 2) (gd 2, frm 2)
Moderate gelding. Turf high 57.
**M H Tompkins [1-26] Mrs Patricia Kalman.*

BLURRED IMAGE (IRE) BHB 34f54a **RR 42f 54a** 3968[13]
8 ch g Exactly Sharp (USA) 8.4f **(66)** - Bear's Affair (Gay Fandango (USA)) 8.5f **(59)**
Form - 070
Record 1999 - 1st:0 2nd:0 3rd:0 Ran:3
Pre1999 - 1st:3 2nd:3 3rd:3 Ran:24
Win Prizemoney £9,912 *Total Prizemoney* £16,307
1999 Turf 0-3: (7f, 10f 2) (g-f 2, frm)
Fair gelding. Turf high 37 (began Aug). Becoming disappointing.
**J C Poulton [0-13] Gerald West (from Miss Gay Kelleway [0-11] Spt 1995).*

BLUSHING GRENADIER (IRE) BHB 57f51a **RR 57f 51a** 5149[7]
7 ch g Salt Dome (USA) 6.5f **(59)** - La Duse (Junius (USA)) 7.7f **(65)**
Form - 7047062140123507
Record 1999 - 1st:2 2nd:2 3rd:1 Ran:14
Pre1999 - 1st:6 2nd:4 3rd:6 Ran:54
Win Prizemoney £25,204 *Total Prizemoney* £32,176
Wins * 1999 Jun Carlis (GD) C 5.9f 57
*** 1999** May Redcar (SFT) C 6f 65 <
***** 1998 Oct Newcas (SFT) H 6f 56 62
***** 1998 Spt Haydoc (GD) SH 6f 50 55
1998 Jun Warwic (GD) C 6f 47
1998 *Mar Wolver (STD) S 6f 56*
1996 Jly Windso (GD) H 6f 46 57?
1995 Jly Doncas (GD) H 6f 50 52
1999 Turf 2-8: (5f, 6f 2-7) (sft, gd 1-3, g-f 1-4) 1999 AW 0-6: (5f, 6f 2, 7f 3) (Fibr 6)
Fair gelding, effective 5 to 6f, best at 6f, acts on g-s to frm - acts on Fibr, best on gd, mostly wears blinkers (effectively), excels at Catterick. Turf high 65 - 1st of 13 getting 8lb from Marengo (10 May Redcar RF 1124) - also 1st of 19 giving 5lb to Most Respectful (10 Jun Carlisle RF 1875). AW high 53. Consistent. An effective sprinter on turf and Fibresand, six furlongs is his trip. Needs soft ground.
**S R Bowring [4-27] S R Bowring (from M J Fetherston-Godley [4-40] Jun 1998).*

BLUSHING RISK (FR) RR 116f 2662a[8]
4 gr c Take Risks (FR) - Sea Goddess (Slip Anchor) 9.8f **(73)**
Form - 8
1999 Turf 0-1: (12f) (gd)
High-class colt, mostly wears blinkers. **H-A Pantall in FR [1-4].*

BLUSHING VICTORIA BHB 45f50a **RR 48f 50a** 1950[16]
4 b f Weldnaas (USA) 8.4f **(55)** - Bollin Victoria (Jalmood (USA)) 10.1f **(52)**
Form - 0000
Record 1999 - 1st:0 2nd:0 3rd:0 Ran:4
Pre1999 - 1st:1 2nd:0 3rd:0 Ran:6
Win Prizemoney £3,203 *Total Prizemoney* £3,203
Wins 1997 Apr Nottin (G-F) 5.1f 74 <
1999 Turf 0-3: (6f 3) (gd 3) 1999 AW 0-1: (7f) (Fibr)
Scopey, moderate filly, has worn blinkers. Turf high 48. Inconsistent.
**J A Glover [0-4] Paul Dixon (from M Meade [1-6] Aug 1997).*

BLUSIENKA (IRE) RR 91f 5215[1]
2 b f Blues Traveller (IRE) - Pudgy Poppet (Danehill (USA)) 10f **(72)**
Form - 1
Record 1999 - 1st:1 2nd:0 3rd:0 Ran:1
Win Prizemoney £3,225 *Total Prizemoney* £3,225
Wins * 1999 Nov Doncas (SFT) 8f 91 <
1999 Turf 1-1: (8f 1-1) (g-s 1-1)
Currently useful filly. (1st run) - 1st of 18 getting 5lb from Grand Oro (6 Nov Doncaster RF 5215). Made a winning debut on the last day of the turf season. **G A Butler [1-1] Gary Tanaka.*

BOADICEA THE RED (IRE) BHB 71f **RR 64f** 5218[7]
2 gr f Inchinor 8.9f **(64)** - Kanika (Be My Chief (USA))
Form - 25627
Record 1999 - 1st:0 2nd:2 3rd:0 Ran:5
Win Prizemoney £0 *Total Prizemoney* £1,744
1999 Turf 0-5: (5f, 6f 3, 7f) (g-s 2, gd, g-f 2)
Average filly. Turf high 64 (began Aug).
**B S Rothwell [0-5] Mrs D E Sharp.*

BOANERGES (IRE) BHB 82f **RR 74f** 4981[2]
2 br c Caerleon (USA) 10.9f **(79)** - Sea Siren (Slip Anchor) 9.8f **(73)**
Form - 432
Record 1999 - 1st:0 2nd:1 3rd:1 Ran:3
Win Prizemoney £0 *Total Prizemoney* £1,892
1999 Turf 0-3: (6f 2, 7f) (g-s, gd, g-f)
Currently above-average colt, has worn blinkers. Turf high 74 (began Spt) - 2nd of 12 to Abuzaid (20 Oct Newcastle 6f g-f RF 4981). Sold for 17,500gns in the autumn to join Rae Guest.
**J Noseda [0-3] M Tabor.*

BOAST BHB 100f **RR 91f** 4920[6]
2 ch f Most Welcome 8.6f **(66)** - Bay Bay (Bay Express) 7.1f **(60)**
Form - 162416
Record 1999 - 1st:2 2nd:1 3rd:0 Ran:6
Win Prizemoney £7,652 *Total Prizemoney* £10,006
Wins * 1999 Jly Newmar (GD) 6f 87 <
*** 1999** May Nottin (GD) 5.1f 69+
1999 Turf 2-6: (5f 1-2, 6f 1-3, 7f) (gd 3, g-f, frm 2-2)
Useful filly, effective 6f, acts on g-f to frm. Turf high 91 - also 1st of 8 giving 1lb to Mastermind (7 Jly Newmarket RF 2632). Finished fourth in a six-furlong maiden event at Newmarket behind Hoh Dear before winning over the same course and distance next time out at the July meeting. **R F JohnsonHoughton [2-6] Lady Rothschild.*

BOATER BHB 60f73a **RR 61f 73a** 4791[16]
5 b g Batshoof 9.5f **(66)** - Velvet Beret (IRE) (Dominion) 8.5f **(63)**
Form - 0420
Record 1999 - 1st:0 2nd:1 3rd:0 Ran:3

Pre1999 - 1st:1 2nd:2 3rd:4 Ran:17
Win Prizemoney £3,044 *Total Prizemoney* £10,350
Wins 1997 Apr Bright (FRM) H 8f 69 71 <
1999 Turf 0-3: (10f 2, 12f) (gd 2, g-f)
Above-average gelding, effective 9 to 10f, acts on gd, has worn blinkers, likes tight tracks. Turf high 61. Capable of winning more races, although he carries his head high and is not very resolute.
**A T Murphy [3-15] Childcraft (from R G Frost [0-3] Aug 1998).*

BOATING SONG (IRE) RR 80df 5045[10]

2 b f College Chapel - Flower From Heaven (Baptism) 10f **(59)**
Form - 3351000
Record 1999 - 1st:1 2nd:0 3rd:2 Ran:7
Win Prizemoney £3,550 *Total Prizemoney* £4,768
Wins * **1999** Aug Windso (HVY) H 6f 77 80 <
1999 Turf 1-7: (5f 2, 6f 1-4, 7f) (sft, gd 1-4, g-f, frm)
Decent filly, effective 6f, acts on gd. Turf high 80 - 1st of 10 giving 17lb to Bombellina (9 Aug Windsor RF 3488).
**R Hannon [1-7] Lord Carnarvon.*

BOATMAN (USA) BHB 90f RR 91f 5031[6]

3 ch c Irish River (FR) 9f **(77)** - Peplum (USA) (Nijinsky (CAN)) 10.3f **(77)**
Form - 43756
Record 1999 - 1st:0 2nd:0 3rd:1 Ran:5
Pre1999 - 1st:1 2nd:1 3rd:0 Ran:2
Win Prizemoney £9,223 *Total Prizemoney* £15,860
Wins * 1998 Spt Newbur (gd) 8f 86+ <
1999 Turf 0-5: (10f 5) (g-s, gd 2, frm 2)
Scopey, useful colt, effective 8 to 10f, best at 10f, acts on g-s to frm, often wears blinkers (extremely effectively). Turf high 93 (began Aug) - 3rd of 13 giving 11lb to Fantazia (28 Aug Newmarket 10f frm RF 3964). After winning his maiden as a juvenile he ran second to Daliapour in a Listed race at Ascot. He ran mostly in handicap company last term, performing creditably if not setting the world alight. **R Charlton [1-7] K Abdulla.*

BOB-BOY RR 3317[7]

7 ch g Executive Man 8.9f **(52)** - Quay Seat (Quayside) 12f **(43)**
Form - 7
Record 1999 - 1st:0 2nd:0 3rd:0 Ran:1
1999 Turf 0-1: (12f) (frm)
Currently very poor gelding. **P D Evans [0-1] P D Evans.*

BOBBYDAZZLE BHB 58f RR 45f 5053[9]

4 ch f Rock Hopper 10.6f **(54)** - Billie Blue (Ballad Rock) 7.8f **(63)**
Form - 5530000
Record 1999 - 1st:0 2nd:0 3rd:1 Ran:7
Pre1999 - 1st:2 2nd:1 3rd:0 Ran:13
Win Prizemoney £33,943 *Total Prizemoney* £36,323
Wins * 1998 Jun Newcas (SFT) H 8f 76 79+ <
* 1997 Aug Newcas (GD) H 8f 74 78
1999 Turf 0-7: (8f 6, 9f) (gd 5, frm 2)
Light-framed, moderate filly, effective 8f, acts on gd, has worn blinkers. Turf high 82. Becoming disappointing. Seems to have lost her way since winning a very valuable nursery at Newcastle in '97 and disappointed last term in the face of some stiff tasks.
**Dr J D Scargill [2-20] Ms Bobby Cohen.*

BOBONA BHB 25f29a RR 29f 29a 4988[11]

3 b c Interrex (CAN) 7.7f **(51)** - Puella Bona **(48df)** (Handsome Sailor)
Form - 000500340
Record 1999 - 1st:0 2nd:0 3rd:1 Ran:9
Win Prizemoney £0 *Total Prizemoney* £425
1999 Turf 0-5: (6f, 7f, 10f, 12f, 14f) (g-s, gd, g-f, frm 2) 1999 AW 0-4: (5f, 7f 2, 12f) (Fibr 4)
Scopey, little account colt, has worn blinkers. Turf high 42. AW high 28.
**M D I Usher [0-9] Mrs J Black.*

BOB'S BUSTER BHB 52f48a RR 53f 48a 2717[5]

3 b g Bob's Return (IRE) - Saltina (Bustino) 10.4f **(64)**
Form - 403705
Record 1999 - 1st:0 2nd:0 3rd:1 Ran:6
Pre1999 - 1st:0 2nd:1 3rd:0 Ran:5
Win Prizemoney £0 *Total Prizemoney* £1,253
1999 Turf 0-5: (8f 4, 11f) (sft, g-s, gd, g-f 2) 1999 AW 0-1: (8f) (Fibr)
Leggy, fair gelding, effective 5f, acts on sft. Turf high 53.
**J Wharton [0-6] Eric Atkinson (from J L Harris [0-5] Spt 1998).*

BOB'S PRINCESS BHB 52f RR 51f 5069[16]

3 b f Bob's Return (IRE) - Princess Rosananti (IRE) (Shareef Dancer (USA)) 9.9f **(73)**
Form - 004040
Record 1999 - 1st:0 2nd:0 3rd:0 Ran:6
Pre1999 - 1st:1 2nd:0 3rd:1 Ran:2
Win Prizemoney £2,224 *Total Prizemoney* £3,286
Wins * 1998 Aug Warwic (G-F) 7f 64 <
1999 Turf 0-6: (8f, 9f, 10f 2, 11f, 12f) (gd, g-f 2, frm 3)
Leggy, fair filly, effective 7f, acts on frm, has worn blinkers. Turf high 60. Consistent.
**P R Chamings [1-8] Mrs J E L Wright.*

BOCA CHICA BHB 35f RR 34f 4341[14]

2 gr f Environment Friend 7.5f **(67)** - Scoffera **(49f 30a)** (Scottish Reel) 7f **(61)**
Form - 8080
Record 1999 - 1st:0 2nd:0 3rd:0 Ran:4
1999 Turf 0-4: (6f, 7f 2, 8f) (gd 2, g-f, hrd)
Very moderate filly. Turf high 34. **N Tinkler [0-4] D Callaghan.*

BODFARI ANNA BHB 46f43a RR 48f 43a 4906[20]

3 br f Casteddu 7.4f **(54)** - Lowrianna(IRE) (Cyrano de Bergerac) 6f **(68)**
Form - 0700043542417800
Record 1999 - 1st:1 2nd:1 3rd:1 Ran:15
Pre1999 - 1st:1 2nd:4 3rd:0 Ran:15
Win Prizemoney £4,568 *Total Prizemoney* £9,812
Wins * **1999** Spt Haydoc (G-F) SH 6f 45 46
1998 Aug Nottin (G-F) S 6.1f 64 <
1999 Turf 1-13: (6f 1-11, 7f 2) (sft, gd, g-f 1-3, frm 8) 1999 AW 0-2: (5f, 6f) (Fibr 2)
Light-framed, moderate filly, effective 6f, acts on gd to frm, mostly wears blinkers (very effectively). Turf high 48. AW high 37.
**J L Eyre [1-16] The Haydock Badgeholders (from M W Easterby [1-14] Oct 1998).*

BODFARI JET (IRE) BHB 54f RR 62f 4981[10]

2 b f Grand Lodge (USA) - River Jet (USA) (Lear Fan (USA)) 8.5f **(73)**
Form - 400
Record 1999 - 1st:0 2nd:0 3rd:0 Ran:3
Win Prizemoney £0 *Total Prizemoney* £279
1999 Turf 0-3: (5f, 6f 2) (gd, g-f, frm)
Currently average filly. Turf high 57 (1st run) (began Spt) - 4th of 17 getting 5lb from Royal Romeo (15 Spt Beverley 5f gd RF 4325).
**M W Easterby [0-3] Bodfari Stud Ltd.*

BODFARI KOMAITE BHB 61f RR 56f 4636[6]

3 b g Komaite (USA) 6.9f **(61)** - Gypsy's Barn Rat (Balliol) 5f **(43)**
Form - 0601414066
Record 1999 - 1st:2 2nd:0 3rd:0 Ran:10
Pre1999 - 1st:1 2nd:0 3rd:1 Ran:8
Win Prizemoney £8,999 *Total Prizemoney* £9,988
Wins * **1999** Jly Doncas (G-F) H 5f 59 61
* **1999** Jun Mussel (GD) H 5f 56 58
* 1998 Spt Redcar (G-F) H 5f 62 68 <
1999 Turf 2-10: (5f 2-7, 6f, 7f 2) (gd 5, g-f 1-3, frm 1-2)
Scopey, fair gelding, effective 5f, acts on g-f to frm, best on frm. Turf high 61 - 1st of 17 giving 3lb to Danny Power (28 Jly Doncaster RF 3200). Consistent.
**M W Easterby [3-18] Bodfari Stud Ltd.*

BODFARI QUARRY BHB 64f75a RR 68f 75a 5069[7]

3 b f Efisio 7.7f **(69)** - Last Quarry **(44f)** (Handsome Sailor)
Form - 604173508107
Record 1999 - 1st:2 2nd:0 3rd:1 Ran:12
Pre1999 - 1st:1 2nd:0 3rd:2 Ran:4
Win Prizemoney £10,424 *Total Prizemoney* £12,287
Wins * **1999** *Oct Wolver (STD) H 9.4f 68 77* <
* **1999** Jun Ayr (GD) H 9.1f 73 76
1998 Aug Beverl (G-F) 5f 72+
1999 Turf 1-11: (7f, 8f 3, 9f 1-2, 10f 5) (gd 5, g-f 1-4, frm 2) 1999 AW 1-1: (9f 1-1) (Fibr 1-1)
Strong, above-average filly, effective 5 to 10f, best at 9f, acts on gd to frm - acts on Fibr, has worn blinkers, likes left handed tracks.

Turf high 76 - 1st of 7 getting 7lb from Amarice (18 Jun Ayr RF 2112). (1st run) - 1st of 13 giving 13lb to Kafil (2 Oct Wolverhampton RF 4706). A winner at Ayr in June, her turf form has been rather in and out, but she appeared to appreciate Fibresand when winning in fine style at Wolverhampton in October. She can win again on that surface.
**B W Hills [2-12] Bodfari Stud Ltd (from Mrs J R Ramsden [1-4] Nov 1998).*

BODFARI SIGNET BHB 54f49a **RR 54f 49a** 3160[5]

3 ch g King's Signet (USA) 7f **(51)** - Darakah **(37f 46a)** (Doulab (USA)) 9.8f **(65)**
Form - 00080155
Record 1999 - 1st:1 2nd:0 3rd:0 Ran:8
Pre1999 - 1st:0 2nd:2 3rd:0 Ran:12
Win Prizemoney £3,712 *Total Prizemoney* £5,446
Wins * 1999 Jun Hamilt (GD) H 8.3f 52 54 <
1999 Turf 1-7: (8f 1-2, 9f, 10f 4) (sft, gd, g-f 2, frm 1-3) 1999 AW 0-1: (8f) (Fibr)
Scopey, fair gelding, effective 7f, acts on g-s to frm, often wears blinkers (very effectively), likes left handed tracks, likes tight tracks. Turf high 54. **M W Easterby [1-20] Bodfari Stud Ltd.*

BODFARI TIMES BHB 55f61a **RR 64f 61a** 4810[14]

3 ch f Clantime 6.6f **(57)** - Tendency (Ballad Rock) 7.8f **(63)**
Form - 080
Record 1999 - 1st:0 2nd:0 3rd:0 Ran:2
Pre1999 - 1st:0 2nd:1 3rd:0 Ran:7
Win Prizemoney £0 *Total Prizemoney* £2,041
1999 Turf 0-2: (5f 2) (sft, gd)
Light-framed, average filly, effective 5f, acts on g-f. Turf high 24 (began Spt). Becoming disappointing. Sure to win a sprint maiden.
**L J Barratt [0-2] L J Barratt (from A Bailey [0-7] Nov 1998).*

BODFARI VISTA BHB 44f **RR 36f** 3398[9]

3 b f Scenic 10.6f **(66)** - Tomard (Thatching) 8f **(66)**
Form - 0670
Record 1999 - 1st:0 2nd:0 3rd:0 Ran:4
1999 Turf 0-4: (7f 2, 8f 2) (g-s, gd, g-f 2)
Scopey, very moderate filly. Turf high 47.
**B W Hills [0-4] Bodfari Stud Ltd.*

BOFFY (IRE) BHB 33f29a **RR 23f 29a** 253[9]

6 ch h Mac's Imp (USA) 5.6f **(54)** - No Dowry (Shy Groom (USA)) 10f **(66)**
Form - 07705070
Record 1999 - 1st:0 2nd:0 3rd:0 Ran:3
Pre1999 - 1st:4 2nd:4 3rd:3 Ran:63
Win Prizemoney £11,507 *Total Prizemoney* £16,706
Wins * 1996 *Feb Southw (STD) S* *5f* *52*
* 1996 *Jan Wolver (STD) S* *5f* *73*
* 1995 Spt Haydoc (GD) C 6f 74 <
* 1995 Aug Leices (GD) S 5f 70
1999 AW 0-3: (5f, 6f 2) (Fibr 3)
Little account horse, has worn blinkers. AW high 25.
**B P J Baugh [4-66] Mrs J Gill.*

BOGUS DREAMS (IRE) BHB 100f **RR 98f** 4931[3]

2 ch c Lahib (USA) 8f **(69)** - Dreams Are Free (IRE) (Caerleon (USA)) 8.6f **(71)**
Form - 113
Record 1999 - 1st:2 2nd:0 3rd:1 Ran:3
Win Prizemoney £15,728 *Total Prizemoney* £18,058
Wins * 1999 Spt Ascot (HVY) 7f 98 <
*** 1999** Spt Thirsk (FRM) 7f 84+
1999 Turf 2-3: (7f 2-2, 8f) (sft 1-1, g-f, hrd 1-1)
Currently very useful colt. Turf high 98 (began Spt) - 1st of 5 giving 3lb to Alfini (26 Spt Ascot RF 4567). Successful on firm and heavy ground, he looked one-paced when tried in Listed company. A mile might prove the limit of his stamina.
**S P C Woods [2-3] Dwayne Woods.*

BOHEMIA BHB 63f **RR 66f** 2586[4]

3 b f Polish Precedent (USA) 9f **(73)** - Horseshoe Reef (Mill Reef (USA)) 10.5f **(78)**
Form - 604
Record 1999 - 1st:0 2nd:0 3rd:0 Ran:3
Pre1999 - 1st:0 2nd:0 3rd:0 Ran:3
Win Prizemoney £0 *Total Prizemoney* £516
1999 Turf 0-3: (8f, 10f 2) (gd, g-f, frm)
Neat, average filly. Turf high 66. **J R Fanshawe [0-6] Lord Halifax.*

BOLD AMUSEMENT BHB 65f74a **RR 65f 74a** 4802[7]

9 ch g Never so Bold 7.1f **(62)** - Hysterical (High Top) 10.2f **(67)**
Form - 55112257
Record 1999 - 1st:2 2nd:2 3rd:0 Ran:8
Pre1999 - 1st:4 2nd:5 3rd:1 Ran:33
Win Prizemoney £21,801 *Total Prizemoney* £31,989
Wins * 1999 Jun Newcas (GD) H 10.1f 58 60
*** 1999** Jun Newcas (G-F) H 10.1f 55 58
* 1998 Nov Redcar (G-S) H 10f 55 60
* 1995 Jly Beverl (G-F) H 8.5f 78 84
1999 Turf 2-8: (8f, 9f, 10f 2-4, 11f, 12f) (gd 3, g-f, frm 2-4)
Average gelding, effective 10 to 12f, best at 10f, acts on gd to frm, best on frm, has worn blinkers, favours left handed tracks, excels at Newcastle. Turf high 65 - 2nd of 5 getting 20lb from St Helensfield (24 Jly Newcastle 10f g-f RF 3103) - also 1st of 11 getting 17lb from Rutland Chantry (25 Jun Newcastle RF 2297). Consistent. He is not getting any younger, but he was running well in the summer, scoring twice at Newcastle and placed on several other occasions. Ten furlongs is his trip.
**W S Cunningham [4-34] Mrs Ann Bell (from Mrs M Reveley [2-12] Spt 1994).*

BOLD ARISTOCRAT (IRE) BHB 43f60a **RR 41f 60a** 424[3]

8 b g Bold Arrangement 8.7f **(57)** - Wyn Mipet (Welsh Saint) 7.6f **(64)**
Form - 80547622113
Record 1999 - 1st:2 2nd:2 3rd:1 Ran:8
Pre1999 - 1st:9 2nd:8 3rd:16 Ran:95
Win Prizemoney £23,619 *Total Prizemoney* £36,529
Wins * 1999 *Feb Southw (STD) S* *6f* *65*
*** 1999** *Feb Southw (STD) C* *6f* *64*
* 1998 *Mar Southw (STD) S* *6f* *61*
* 1998 *Feb Southw (STD) S* *6f* *60*
* 1998 *Feb Southw (STD) S* *6f* *56*
* 1997 *Jun Southw (STD)* *6f* *68*
* 1997 *Feb Southw (STD) SH* *6f* *60 60*
* 1996 *Feb Southw (STD) SH* *6f* *50 46*
* 1996 *Jan Southw (STD) C* *6f* *48*
* 1995 *Jly Southw (STD) H* *6f* *45 47*
1999 AW 2-8: (6f 2-7, 7f) (Fibr 2-8)
Average gelding, effective 6 to 7f, best at 6f, - acts on Fibr. AW high 65 - 1st of 8 giving 5lb to Little Ibnr (22 Feb Southwell RF 0340) - also 1st of 12 getting 4lb from Maiteamia (19 Feb Southwell RF 0319). He did seem to run almost every week, but was given a break in the second half of 1998. He pops up in modest company on Fibresand from time to time, though all of his recent victories have been over six furlongs at Southwell.
**R Hollinshead [11-103] Mrs J Hughes.*

BOLD BAHAMIAN (IRE) BHB 70f **RR 72f** 5100[8]

2 b c Persian Bold 10f **(69)** - Nordic Pride (Horage) 10.3f **(61)**
Form - 548
Record 1999 - 1st:0 2nd:0 3rd:0 Ran:3
Win Prizemoney £0 *Total Prizemoney* £252
1999 Turf 0-3: (8f 3) (gd 2, g-f)
Currently above-average colt. Turf high 72 (began Spt).
**J Noseda [0-3] Lucayan Stud.*

BOLD BECKY BHB 47a **RR 60?f 47a** 278[10]

5 b m Never so Bold 7.1f **(62)** - Princess Silca Key (Grundy) 10.3f **(65)**
Form - 45600
Record 1999 - 1st:0 2nd:0 3rd:0 Ran:3
Pre1999 - 1st:0 2nd:0 3rd:1 Ran:3
Win Prizemoney £0 *Total Prizemoney* £777
1999 AW 0-3: (8f, 10f, 13f) (Equi 2, Fibr)
Average filly. AW high 43. **A P Jones [0-6] A P Jones.*

BOLDBIRD **RR 51f** 4821[19]

2 b c Puissance 7.1f **(60)** - Plum Bold (Be My Guest (USA)) 9.3f **(67)**
Form - 0
Record 1999 - 1st:0 2nd:0 3rd:0 Ran:1
1999 Turf 0-1: (6f) (g-f)
Currently fair colt. **D J Coakley [0-1] Mrs George Ward.*

BOLD BLUE (IRE) RR 43f 4282[12]
3 b g Bluebird (USA) 7.9f **(71)** - Evangola (Persian Bold) 9.3f **(66)**
Form - 786700
Record 1999 - 1st:0 2nd:0 3rd:0 Ran:6
1999 Turf 0-6: (6f, 7f 2, 8f 3) (gd, frm 4, hrd)
Light-framed, moderate gelding, often wears blinkers. Turf high 59. **M Johnston [0-6] Mrs Caroline Parker.*

BOLD BOUNTY RR 25f 1545[8]
2 ch f Absalom 7.1f **(56)** - Daring Gift **(25f)** (Never so Bold) 6.3f **(66)**
Form - 008
Record 1999 - 1st:0 2nd:0 3rd:0 Ran:3
1999 Turf 0-3: (5f 3) (sft, g-s, g-f)
Currently little account filly. Turf high 25.
**M Brittain [0-3] Northgate Lodge Racing Club.*

BOLD BUSTER BHB 62f RR 65f 4387[13]
6 b g Bustino 11f **(64)** - Truly Bold (Bold Lad (IRE)) 8.4f **(68)**
Form - 340
Record 1999 - 1st:0 2nd:0 3rd:1 Ran:3
Pre1999 - 1st:1 2nd:1 3rd:1 Ran:9
Win Prizemoney £3,836 *Total Prizemoney* £6,841
Wins * 1997 Aug Lingfi (G-S) H 11.5f 64 67 <
1999 Turf 0-3: (12f 3) (g-f 2, frm)
Average gelding. Turf high 65 (1st run) - 3rd of 18 giving 3lb to Water Flower (8 Jun Salisbury 12f g-f RF 1816).
**I A Balding [1-16] Mrs I A Balding.*

BOLD CARDOWAN (IRE) BHB 48f RR 45f 5188[9]
3 br g Persian Bold 10f **(69)** - Moving Trend (IRE) (Be My Guest (USA)) 9.3f **(67)**
Form - 060331460
Record 1999 - 1st:1 2nd:0 3rd:2 Ran:9
Pre1999 - 1st:0 2nd:0 3rd:0 Ran:2
Win Prizemoney £3,038 *Total Prizemoney* £4,576
Wins * **1999** Spt Lingfi (HVY) H 16f 40 53 <
1999 Turf 1-9: (7f, 9f, 11f, 12f, 14f, 16f 1-3, 18f) (g-s 1-3, g-f 3, frm 3)
Workmanlike, moderate gelding, effective 11 to 16f, acts on g-s, likes left handed tracks, favours tight tracks. Turf high 53 - 1st of 8 getting 21lb from Pipa (24 Spt Lingfield RF 4533). Consistent.
**John Berry [1-11] J McCarthy.*

BOLD CONQUEROR BHB 24f RR 26f 2386[11]
3 br f Anshan 8.2f **(63)** - Freudenau (Wassl) 9.7f **(62)**
Form - 000
Record 1999 - 1st:0 2nd:0 3rd:0 Ran:3
Pre1999 - 1st:0 2nd:0 3rd:0 Ran:3
1999 Turf 0-3: (6f, 7f, 8f) (sft, g-f, hrd)
Leggy, little account filly. **J M Bradley [0-6] E A Hayward.*

BOLD EDGE BHB 119f RR 118f 4568[1]
4 ch c Beveled (USA) 6.9f **(64)** - Daring Ditty (Daring March) 7.1f **(61)**
Form - 1012041
Record 1999 - 1st:3 2nd:1 3rd:0 Ran:7
Pre1999 - 1st:4 2nd:3 3rd:2 Ran:15
Win Prizemoney £168,367 *Total Prizemoney* £234,472

Wins
* **1999** Spt Ascot (HVY) G2 6f 118
* **1999** Jun Ascot (G-F) G2 6f 119 <
* **1999** Apr Newmar (GD) L 6f 108+
* 1998 Oct Newmar (GD) L 6f 108
* 1998 May Newbur (GD) 6f 107
* 1998 Apr Leices (SFT) 6f 100
* 1997 May Newbur (SFT) 6f 94+

1999 Turf 3-7: (5f, 6f 3-6) (sft 1-1, gd, g-f 2-2, frm 3)
Scopey, high-class colt, effective 6f, acts on sft to frm, and excels at Newbury. Turf high 119 - 1st of 19 from Russian Revival (17 Jun Ascot RF 2072) - also 1st of 11 giving 6lb to Munjiz (26 Spt Ascot RF 4568). He had a very productive 1999, landing the Abernant, Cork And Orrery and Diadem. On each occasion he was able to dominate his field and is especially effective when able to do that. He just finds Group One company a bit too much, but ran very well in both starts at that level, and without Stravinsky would have been a game winner of the July Cup. He has won on soft ground, but is reported by his trainer to be better suited by a sound surface. **R Hannon [7-22] Lady Whent and Friends.*

Bold Edge, whose front-running tactics brought rich reward in 1999.

BOLD EFFORT (FR) BHB 81f95a RR 83f 95a 4644[17]
7 b g Bold Arrangement 8.7f **(57)** - Malham Tarn (Riverman (USA)) 9.1f **(76)**
Form - 00145806400
Record 1999 - 1st:1 2nd:0 3rd:0 Ran:9
Pre1999 - 1st:10 2nd:9 3rd:5 Ran:70
Win Prizemoney £116,711 *Total Prizemoney* £146,550

Wins
* **1999** *Feb Lingfi (STD) H 6f 86 97* <
* 1998 Jly Sandow (G-S) H 5f 92 95
* 1998 May Kempto (G-F) H 6f 89 91
* 1997 *May Wolver (STD) H 6f 90 94*
* 1996 *Dec Lingfi (STD) H 6f 82 89*
* 1996 Spt Maison (SFT) H 6f 80
* 1996 Aug Claire (SFT) 8f 78
* 1995 Jun York (G-F) H 6f 87 94
* 1995 May Salisb (G-F) H 6f 74 82
* 1995 *Feb Lingfi (STD) H 6f 72 74*
* 1995 *Jan Lingfi (STD) 6f 64*

1999 Turf 0-6: (5f, 6f 5) (g-s, gd, g-f 2, frm 2) 1999 AW 1-3: (6f 1-2, 7f) (Equi 1-1, Fibr 2)
Very useful gelding, effective 5 to 6f, best at 6f, acts on gd to frm - acts on Equi, often wears blinkers. Turf high 83. AW high 97 (1st run) - 1st of 9 giving 10lb to Mukarrab (16 Feb Lingfield RF 0301).
**K O Cunningham-Brown [11-79] A J Richards.*

BOLDER ALEXANDER (IRE) BHB 52f RR 62f 5192[9]
2 b c Persian Bold 10f **(69)** - Be Yourself (USA) (Noalcoholic (FR)) 7.3f **(62)**
Form - 806162307370
Record 1999 - 1st:1 2nd:1 3rd:2 Ran:12
Win Prizemoney £1,850 *Total Prizemoney* £3,074
Wins 1999 Jun Bright (GD) S 7f 62 <
1999 Turf 1-11: (5f, 6f 2, 7f 1-7, 8f) (gd 1-5, g-f 2, frm 4) 1999 AW 0-1: (6f) (Fibr)
Average colt, effective 5 to 7f, acts on gd to g-f, has worn blinkers (effectively). Turf high 62 - 2nd of 4 getting 3lb from Magical Millie (26 Jly Folkestone 5f g-f RF 3140) - also 1st of 9 from College Rock (30 Jun Brighton RF 2432).
**G L Moore [0-8] C F Sparrowhawk (from P F I Cole [1-4] Jun 1999).*

BOLD EWAR (IRE) BHB 75f70a RR 80f 70a 4996[8]
2 ch c Persian Bold 10f **(69)** - Hot Curry (USA) (Sharpen Up) 8.3f **(67)**
Form - 8275308

Record 1999 - 1st:0 2nd:1 3rd:1 Ran:7
Win Prizemoney £0 *Total Prizemoney* £2,760
1999 Turf 0-7: (7f 5, 8f 2) (gd 3, g-f 2, frm 2)
Decent colt, effective 7f, acts on g-f to frm, often wears blinkers. Turf high 80 - 3rd of 17 getting 9lb from French Fellow (17 Aug York 7f g-f RF 3698). Ran a cracker in first-time blinkers when third to French Fellow at York. **C E Brittain [0-7] A J Richards.*

BOLD FACT (USA) BHB 113f **RR 115f** 2643[15]

4 b c Known Fact (USA) 8.3f **(72)** - Sookera (USA) (Roberto (USA)) 10f **(76)**
Form - 8100
Record 1999 - 1st:1 2nd:0 3rd:0 Ran:4
Pre1999 - 1st:4 2nd:1 3rd:2 Ran:9
Win Prizemoney £62,257 *Total Prizemoney* £97,941

Wins							
* **1999**	May	Lingfi	(G-F)	L	6f	115	<
* 1998	Aug	York	(FRM)	L	7f	111	
* 1998	May	Newmar	(G-F)	L	7f	115+	
* 1997	Jly	Newmar	(GD)	G3	6f	102	
* 1997	Jun	Goodwo	(G-F)		6f	73+	

1999 Turf 1-4: (6f 1-4) (g-f 2, frm 1-2)
Unfurnished, high-class colt, effective 6 to 7f, best at 7f, acts on frm. Turf high 115 - 1st of 6 from Tipsy Creek (22 May Lingfield RF 1402). Inconsistent. Back to form when winning a Listed race at Lingfield this year, he was well beaten in top sprint company afterwards. **H R A Cecil [5-13] K Abdulla.*

BOLD FELICITER BHB 34f **RR 28f** 2397[5]

3 ch f Bold Arrangement 8.7f **(57)** -Jersey Maid(On Your Mark) 7.7f **(58)**
Form - 64005
Record 1999 - 1st:0 2nd:0 3rd:0 Ran:5
Pre1999 - 1st:0 2nd:0 3rd:0 Ran:8
1999 Turf 0-5: (12f 4, 14f) (gd, g-f 2, frm 2)
Leggy, little account filly, effective 12f, acts on gd to frm, likes tight tracks. Turf high 46 (1st run) - 6th of 12 getting 1lb from Hi-Jenny (14 Apr Beverley 12f frm RF 0689). Becoming disappointing. **D Moffatt [0-13] Mrs Jennie Moffatt.*

BOLD FRONTIER BHB 51f66a **RR 52f 66a** 216[7]

7 gr g Chief Singer 8.6f **(62)** - Mumtaz Flyer (USA) (Al Hattab (USA)) 9.3f **(74)**
Form - 17
Record 1999 - 1st:1 2nd:0 3rd:0 Ran:2
Pre1999 - 1st:6 2nd:4 3rd:3 Ran:30
Win Prizemoney £17,270 *Total Prizemoney* £23,392

Wins								
* **1999**	*Jan*	*Wolver*	*(STD)*	*C*	*5f*		*63*	
* 1998	Aug	Lingfi	(G-F)	SH	5f	47	52	
* 1998	*Jly*	*Lingfi*	*(STD)*	*C*	*5f*		*57*	
* 1997	*Mar*	*Wolver*	*(STD)*	*H*	*5f*	*67*	*73*	*<*
* 1995	*Apr*	*Wolver*	*(STD)*	*H*	*5f*	*62*	*70*	

1999 AW 1-2: (5f 1-2) (Fibr 1-2)
Average gelding, effective 5f, - acts on Fibr, mostly wears blinkers (effectively). AW high 63 (1st run) - 1st of 11 getting 8lb from Pride of Brixton (23 Jan Wolverhampton RF 0154). He was a very smart Fibresand sprinter a few years back, but his best form these days is in plating class. **K T Ivory [7-32] K T Ivory.*

BOLD GAIT BHB 97f **RR 93f** 4403[2]

8 ch g Persian Bold 10f **(69)** - Miller's Gait (Mill Reef (USA)) 10.5f **(78)**
Form - 102
Record 1999 - 1st:1 2nd:1 3rd:0 Ran:3
Pre1999 - 1st:5 2nd:2 3rd:1 Ran:16
Win Prizemoney £95,231 *Total Prizemoney* £109,830

Wins								
* **1999**	Aug	Newbur	(GD)	H	13.3f	90	91	
* 1995	Jly	Newcas	(FRM)	H	16.1f	105	115	<
* 1995	Apr	Newbur	(G-F)	H	16f	95	102	

1999 Turf 1-3: (13f 1-2, 15f) (g-f 1-2, frm)
Useful gelding. Turf high 93 (began Aug). Consistent.
**J R Fanshawe [8-27] Mrs I Phillips.*

BOLD HUNTER BHB 47f **RR 31f** 2931[10]

5 b g Polish Precedent (USA) 9f **(73)** - Pumpona (USA) (Sharpen Up) 8.3f **(67)**
Form - 000
Record 1999 - 1st:0 2nd:0 3rd:0 Ran:3
Pre1999 - 1st:1 2nd:3 3rd:2 Ran:20
Win Prizemoney £2,740 *Total Prizemoney* £7,515

Wins							
1997	Jun	Sligo	(FRM)		6.5f	77	<

1999 Turf 0-3: (6f, 7f, 9f) (gd, g-f, frm)
Very moderate gelding, effective 6 to 9f, acts on gd to g-f, best on g-f, mostly wears blinkers (effectively). Turf high 30. Becoming disappointing.
**Mrs P N Dutfield [0-16] The Carpetbaggers (from J S Bolger in IRE [1-9] Oct 1997).*

BOLD KING BHB 86f83a **RR 89f 83a** 4921[4]

4 br g Anshan 8.2f **(63)** - Spanish Heart (King of Spain) 7.8f **(52)**
Form - 23281524
Record 1999 - 1st:1 2nd:3 3rd:1 Ran:8
Pre1999 - 1st:1 2nd:3 3rd:1 Ran:11
Win Prizemoney £15,806 *Total Prizemoney* £30,136

Wins								
* **1999**	Aug	Newbur	(GD)	H	7f	81	87	<
* 1998	*Apr*	*Southw*	*(STD)*		*8f*		*72+*	

1999 Turf 1-8: (7f 1-6, 8f 2) (gd 1-7, frm)
Workmanlike, useful gelding, effective 7f, acts on gd. Turf high 89 - 2nd of 6 giving 4lb to Jo Mell (29 Spt Newcastle 7f gd RF 4637) - also 1st of 18 getting 2lb from Achilles Star (14 Aug Newbury RF 3647). Consistent. A seven-furlong specialist, he enjoyed a fine season. Should continue to pay his way.
**J W Hills [2-19] Avon Industries Ltd.*

BOLDLY GOES BHB 95f **RR 98?f** 2710[3]

3 b c Bold Arrangement 8.7f **(57)** - Reine de Thebes (FR) (Darshaan) 9.9f **(84)**
Form - 63
Record 1999 - 1st:0 2nd:0 3rd:1 Ran:2
Pre1999 - 1st:4 2nd:0 3rd:0 Ran:5
Win Prizemoney £24,947 *Total Prizemoney* £26,808

Wins							
* 1998	Aug	Ripon	(G-F)	L	6f	98+	<
* 1998	Jly	Thirsk	(FRM)		7f	88	
* 1998	*Jun*	*Wolver*	*(STD)*		*6f*	*87*	
* 1998	Apr	Pontef	(G-S)		5f	62	

1999 Turf 0-2: (7f, 8f) (gd, frm)
Workmanlike, very useful colt, effective 6 to 7f, acts on gd to frm. Turf high 94. A useful two-year-old, he failed to recapture his best at three. **C W Fairhurst [4-7] G H & S Leggott.*

BOLD ORIENTAL (IRE) BHB 74f70a **RR 73f 70a** 3959[2]

5 b g Tirol 8.1f **(64)** - Miss Java (Persian Bold) 9.3f **(66)**
Form - 173D014102
Record 1999 - 1st:2 2nd:1 3rd:1 Ran:9
Pre1999 - 1st:3 2nd:2 3rd:2 Ran:22
Win Prizemoney £15,089 *Total Prizemoney* £20,936

Wins								
* **1999**	Jly	Nottin	(G-F)	H	10f	70	66	
* **1999**	Jun	Salisb	(G-F)	C	8f		76	
* 1998	*Dec*	*Lingfi*	*(STD)*	*H*	*8f*	*70*	*71*	
1997	Apr	Bath	(G-F)	H	10.2f	79	81+	
1996	Spt	Goodwo	(G-F)	H	8f	72	83	<

1999 Turf 2-7: (8f 1-4, 9f 2, 10f 1-1) (gd, g-f 1-1, frm 1-5) 1999 AW 0-2: (10f 2) (Equi 2)
Above-average gelding, effective 8 to 10f, best at 8f, acts on gd to frm - acts on Equi, has worn blinkers. Turf high 76 - 1st of 10 giving 8lb to Fuegian (23 Jun Salisbury RF 2246). AW high 66. Winner of a claimer over a mile at Salisbury in June, he added to that taking an Amateurs riders race over ten furlongs at Nottingham, before coming second in a similar event at Goodwood. Likes a decent surface, and has also won on sand.
**J W Hills [3-10] Uplands Bloodstock (from S Sherwood [0-3] Spt 1998).*

BOLD PRECEDENT **RR 54f** 5100[10]

2 b c Polish Precedent (USA) 9f **(73)** - Shining Water (USA) (Riverman (USA)) 9.1f **(76)**
Form - 0
Record 1999 - 1st:0 2nd:0 3rd:0 Ran:1
1999 Turf 0-1: (8f) (gd)
Currently fair colt. **P W Harris [0-1] The Shining Examples.*

BOLD RAIDER **RR 61f** 4627[7]

2 b c Rudimentary (USA) 8.2f **(66)** - Spanish Heart (King of Spain) 7.8f **(52)**
Form - 807
Record 1999 - 1st:0 2nd:0 3rd:0 Ran:3
1999 Turf 0-3: (7f 3) (g-s, gd, frm)
Currently average colt. Turf high 61.
**I A Balding [0-3] Avon Industries Ltd.*

BOLD SABOTEUR BHB 55f **RR 51f** 5044[12]
2 b c Prince Sabo 6.6f **(64)** - Latest Flame (IRE) (Last Tycoon) 8.5f **(62)**
Form - 000
Record 1999 - 1st:0 2nd:0 3rd:0 Ran:3
1999 Turf 0-3: (6f, 7f 2) (sft, g-s, gd)
Currently fair colt. Turf high 51 (began Spt).
**D R C Elsworth [0-3] Woodhaven Racing Syndicate.*

BOLD SARAH BHB 22f **RR 49f** 118[7]
5 ch m Bold Arrangement 8.7f **(57)** - Miss Sarajane (Skyliner) 7.3f **(53)**
Form - U07
Record 1999 - 1st:0 2nd:0 3rd:0 Ran:2
Pre1999 - 1st:0 2nd:0 3rd:0 Ran:8
1999 AW 0-2: (11f, 12f) (Fibr 2)
Moderate filly. Becoming disappointing.
**R Hollinshead [0-11] J Smyth.*

BOLD STATE BHB 75f **RR 80f** 4899[11]
2 b c Never so Bold 7.1f **(62)** - Multi-Sofft **(42f)** (Northern State (USA))
Form - 2536252100
Record 1999 - 1st:1 2nd:3 3rd:1 Ran:10
Win Prizemoney £7,278 *Total Prizemoney* £10,096
Wins * **1999** Spt York (G-F) 7.9f 80 <
1999 Turf 1-10: (5f, 6f 2, 7f 4, 8f 1-3) (sft, gd 2, g-f 5, frm 1-2)
Decent colt, effective 5 to 8f, best at 7f, acts on gd to frm, best on g-f, has worn blinkers. Turf high 80 - 2nd of 8 giving 7lb to Seeking Utopia (18 Aug Musselburgh 7f g-f RF 3750) - also 1st of 20 from Service Star (1 Spt York RF 4080). He had made the frame several times before getting off the mark at York in September on his first attempt at a mile. **M H Tompkins [1-10] The Toy Boy Partnership.*

BOLD WILLY RR 50f 2517[8]
2 b c Never so Bold 7.1f **(62)** - Indian Star (Indian King (USA)) 7.4f **(64)**
Form - 068
Record 1999 - 1st:0 2nd:0 3rd:0 Ran:3
1999 Turf 0-3: (6f 2, 7f) (gd 2, hrd)
Currently fair colt. Turf high 50. **C W Fairhurst [0-3] William Hill.*

BOLEYN CASTLE (USA) BHB 100f **RR 92f** 2671[5]
2 ch c River Special (USA) - Dance Skirt (CAN) (Caucasus (USA)) 8.2f **(74)**
Form - 165
Record 1999 - 1st:1 2nd:0 3rd:0 Ran:3
Win Prizemoney £3,485 *Total Prizemoney* £3,800
Wins * **1999** Apr Windso (G-S) 5f 78 <
1999 Turf 1-3: (5f 1-3) (gd 1-1, g-f 2)
Currently useful colt. Turf high 92. Ran green when making a winning debut on softish ground at Windsor, and failed to get a clear run in the Norfolk at Ascot. **T G Mills [1-3] Shipman Racing Ltd.*

BOLLIN ANN BHB 60f **RR 60f** 4755[17]
4 b f Anshan 8.2f **(63)** - Bollin Zola (Alzao (USA)) 7.1f **(68)**
Form - 6470418300240
Record 1999 - 1st:1 2nd:1 3rd:1 Ran:13
Pre1999 - 1st:1 2nd:2 3rd:1 Ran:14
Win Prizemoney £6,552 *Total Prizemoney* £11,086
Wins * **1999** Jly Beverl (G-F) H 5f 51 55
* 1998 Aug Ripon (G-F) 5f 64 <
1999 Turf 1-13: (5f 1-10, 6f 3) (gd 3, g-f 2, frm 1-8)
Light-framed, average filly, effective 5 to 6f, best at 6f, acts on gd to frm, excels at Beverley and Nottingham, does well at Ripon. Turf high 60 - 2nd of 20 giving 2lb to Carambo (13 Spt Nottingham 6f frm RF 4285) - also 1st of 20 from American Cousin (13 Jly Beverley RF 2771). **T D Easterby [2-27] Lady Westbrook.*

BOLLIN ETHOS BHB 54f56a **RR 55f 56a** 4732[12]
4 b g Precocious 7.2f **(54)** - Bollin Harriet (Lochnager) 6f **(59)**
Form - 00336026200
Record 1999 - 1st:0 2nd:2 3rd:2 Ran:11
Pre1999 - 1st:1 2nd:1 3rd:0 Ran:10
Win Prizemoney £3,886 *Total Prizemoney* £8,153
Wins * 1998 Jly Catter (GD) H 7f 56 60 <
1999 Turf 0-9: (6f 3, 7f 6) (g-s, gd 4, g-f, frm 2, hrd) 1999 AW 0-2: (6f, 7f) (Fibr 2)
Workmanlike, fair gelding, effective 6 to 7f, best at 7f, acts on gd to frm - acts on Fibr, best on gd, prefers left handed tracks, prefers tight tracks, excels at Catterick. Turf high 55 - 3rd of 15 getting 7lb from Tipperary Sunset (2 Jun Beverley 7f gd RF 1661). AW high 55 (1st run) (began Jly) - 2nd of 15 getting 7lb from Rock Island Line (24 Jly Southwell 7f Fibr RF 3113).
**T D Easterby [1-21] Sir Neil Westbrook.*

BOLLIN FRANK BHB 63f **RR 63f** 4528[4]
7 b g Rambo Dancer (CAN) 8.4f **(59)** - Bollin Emily (Lochnager) 6f **(59)**
Form - 030020264444
Record 1999 - 1st:0 2nd:2 3rd:1 Ran:12
Pre1999 - 1st:4 2nd:9 3rd:3 Ran:45
Win Prizemoney £18,320 *Total Prizemoney* £44,156
Wins * 1998 May Nottin (FRM) 8.2f 62
* 1996 Jun Haydoc (G-S) H 8.1f 66 68 <
* 1996 May Haydoc (G-S) H 8.1f 62 64
1995 Jly Haydoc (G-F) H 8.1f 53 58
1999 Turf 0-12: (7f, 8f 11) (gd 3, g-f 6, frm 3)
Average gelding, effective 8f, acts on gd to frm, has worn blinkers, prefers right handed tracks, favours tight tracks, and excels at Ripon and Beverley. Turf high 64 - 2nd of 13 getting 6lb from Kass Alhawa (27 Jly Beverley 8f frm RF 3162). Consistent. Did not enjoy much luck last term, and is more than due a win.
**T D Easterby [3-44] Sir Neil Westbrook (from M H Easterby [1-16] Oct 1995).*

BOLLIN NELLIE BHB 63f **RR 70f** 4504[4]
2 ch f Rock Hopper 10.6f **(54)** - Bollin Magdalene (Teenoso (USA)) 9.9f **(72)**
Form - 4354
Record 1999 - 1st:0 2nd:0 3rd:1 Ran:4
Win Prizemoney £0 *Total Prizemoney* £876
1999 Turf 0-4: (7f 3, 8f) (g-f, frm 2, hrd)
Above-average filly. Turf high 70.
**T D Easterby [0-4] Lady Westbrook.*

BOLLIN RITA BHB 72f **RR 73f** 4805[14]
3 b f Rambo Dancer (CAN) 8.4f **(59)** - Bollin Harriet (Lochnager) 6f **(59)**
Form - 142866300
Record 1999 - 1st:1 2nd:1 3rd:1 Ran:9
Pre1999 - 1st:0 2nd:3 3rd:1 Ran:6
Win Prizemoney £3,548 *Total Prizemoney* £11,571
Wins * **1999** Apr Thirsk (GD) 6f 72 <
1999 Turf 1-9: (5f 2, 6f 1-7) (gd 1-3, g-f 3, frm 3)
Leggy, above-average filly, effective 5 to 6f, best at 6f, acts on gd to hrd, best on g-f, has worn blinkers, excels at Ripon, likes Haydock. Turf high 77 - 2nd of 11 giving 8lb to Don Bosco (16 Jun Ripon 6f g-f RF 2060) - also 1st of 13 getting 5lb from Rocklands Lane (16 Apr Thirsk RF 0730). **T D Easterby [1-15] Lady Westbrook.*

BOLLIN ROBERTA BHB 60f **RR 64f** 4879[12]
3 b f Bob's Return (IRE) - Bollin Emily (Lochnager) 6f **(59)**
Form - 503542247100
Record 1999 - 1st:1 2nd:2 3rd:1 Ran:12
Pre1999 - 1st:0 2nd:2 3rd:1 Ran:6
Win Prizemoney £2,248 *Total Prizemoney* £7,672
Wins * **1999** Spt Mussel (G-F) 7.1f 46 <
1999 Turf 1-12: (5f, 6f 2, 7f 1-8, 8f) (g-s, gd 4, g-f, frm 1-6)
Scopey, average filly, effective 6 to 7f, best at 7f, acts on gd to frm, excels at Nottingham. Turf high 66 - 3rd of 9 getting 5lb from Gemini Guest (1 May Thirsk 7f g-f RF 0965). Took an age in getting off the mark, but managed it at the sixteenth attempt when landing a seven-furlong Musselburgh maiden in September.
**T D Easterby [1-18] Lady Westbrook.*

BOLLIN ROLAND BHB 47f **RR 39f** 1740[16]
3 b c Reprimand 8.2f **(63)** - Bollin Zola (Alzao (USA)) 7.1f **(68)**
Form - 08000
Record 1999 - 1st:0 2nd:0 3rd:0 Ran:5
1999 Turf 0-5: (6f 2, 7f, 8f 2) (gd 4, hrd)
Strong, very moderate colt. Turf high 50.
**T D Easterby [0-5] Sir Neil Westbrook.*

BOLLIN TERRY BHB 76f **RR 66f** 3820[10]
5 b h Terimon 8.7f **(58)** - Bollin Zola (Alzao (USA)) 7.1f **(68)**
Form - 00
Record 1999 - 1st:0 2nd:0 3rd:0 Ran:2
Pre1999 - 1st:2 2nd:2 3rd:4 Ran:18
Win Prizemoney £11,647 *Total Prizemoney* £26,967

Wins * 1998 Jly Newcas (G-F) H 8f 76 83 <
* 1997 Jun Newcas (FRM) H 8f 72 79
1999 Turf 0-2: (8f, 9f) (sft, g-f)
Average colt, effective 7 to 8f, best at 8f, acts on gd to frm, likes left handed tracks. Turf high 66. Becoming disappointing.
**T D Easterby [2-20] Sir Neil Westbrook.*

BOLSHAYA BHB 64f **RR 62f** 4986[10]

4 gr f Cadeaux Genereux 7.9f **(76)** - Mainly Dry(The Brianstan) 5.9f **(55)**
Form - 002414653320
Record **1999** - 1st:1 2nd:2 3rd:2 Ran:12
Pre1999 - 1st:2 2nd:0 3rd:0 Ran:9
Win Prizemoney £9,467 *Total Prizemoney* £13,487
Wins * **1999** Jun Salisb (FRM) H 6f 61 63
* 1998 Jly Pontef (G-F) 6f 75 <
* 1998 Jun Newcas (GD) 6f 66
1999 Turf 1-12: (5f 3, 6f 1-8, 7f) (gd, g-f 7, frm 1-4)
Rangy, average filly, effective 6f, acts on gd to frm. Turf high 63. Consistent. Consistent sprinter best suited by six furlongs and fast ground, she won under those conditions at Salisbury in June and has been running well since. **J Berry [3-21] Chris Deuters.*

BOLT FROM THE BLUE **RR 52f** 5159[4]

3 b g Grand Lodge (USA) - Lightning Legacy (USA) (Super Concorde (USA)) 10.9f **(66)**
Form - 0030658224
Record **1999** - 1st:0 2nd:2 3rd:1 Ran:10
Pre1999 - 1st:0 2nd:0 3rd:0 Ran:4
Win Prizemoney £0 *Total Prizemoney* £2,141
1999 Turf 0-10: (6f, 7f, 8f, 10f 2, 11f 3, 14f, 16f) (sft 2, gd 4, g-f 2, frm, hrd)
Light-framed, fair gelding, effective 11f, acts on sft to gd, has worn blinkers, likes left handed tracks, likes tight tracks. Turf high 52 - 2nd of 17 getting 4lb from A Day On The Dub (26 Oct Redcar 11f gd RF 5071).
**Don Enrico Incisa [0-6] Don Enrico Incisa (from N Tinkler [0-8] May 1999).*

BOMB ALASKA BHB 109f **RR 110+f** 5140[1]

4 br g Polar Falcon (USA) 9f **(74)** - So True (So Blessed) 8.7f **(67)**
Form - 1131221
Record **1999** - 1st:4 2nd:2 3rd:1 Ran:7
Pre1999 - 1st:1 2nd:3 3rd:0 Ran:11
Win Prizemoney £57,325 *Total Prizemoney* £94,980
Wins * **1999** Oct Newmar (SFT) L 8f 109 <
* **1999** May Goodwo (GD) H 8f 85 95
* **1999** Apr Newbur (G-F) H 8f 77 85+
* **1999** Mar Doncas (G-S) H 8f 73 79
* 1998 Spt Newbur (gd) 8f 81
1999 Turf 4-7: (8f 4-6, 10f) (g-s 1-1, gd 2-4, g-f 1-1, frm)
Lengthy, Group-class gelding, effective 8 to 10f, best at 8f, acts on gd, excels at Newmarket, does well at Newbury. Turf high 110 - 2nd of 33 giving 17lb to She's Our Mare (2 Oct Newmarket 10f gd RF 4683) - also 1st of 8 from Albarahin (30 Oct Newmarket RF 5140). Inconsistent. He enjoyed a fantastic season, winning three valuable handicaps and a Listed event at Newmarket in October. A gallant second in the Cambridgeshire between those victories, he is proven on everything bar firm ground and is likely to improve again in 2000. Tough and genuine, he is a credit to his connections. **G B Balding [5-18] Miss B Swire.*

BOMBARD (USA) **RR 103df** 4015[4]

3 ch c Lord At War (ARG) 6.6f **(67)** - Mama Hawk (USA) (Silver Hawk (USA)) 8.6f **(70)**
Form - 4304
Record **1999** - 1st:0 2nd:0 3rd:1 Ran:4
Pre1999 - 1st:1 2nd:1 3rd:0 Ran:2
Win Prizemoney £4,386 *Total Prizemoney* £13,262
Wins * 1998 Jun Goodwo (G-F) 7f 81+ <
1999 Turf 0-4: (10f 3, 12f) (g-s, g-f 3)
Leggy, very useful colt, effective 10f, acts on g-s, has worn blinkers. Turf high 103 (1st run) - 4th of 7 to Fantastic Light (24 Apr Sandown 10f g-s RF 0843). He ran a fair race behind Oath in the Dee Stakes at Chester, but showed little on his two subsequent starts. A hard puller, he is one to treat with caution.
**P F I Cole [1-6] H R H Prince Fahd Salman.*

BOMBAY MIX (IRE) BHB 48f **RR 47f** 4646[16]

4 b g Shalford (IRE) 7.8f **(63)** - Some Spice (Horage) 10.3f **(61)**
Form - 000
Record **1999** - 1st:0 2nd:0 3rd:0 Ran:3
Pre1999 - 1st:3 2nd:0 3rd:2 Ran:15
Win Prizemoney £9,247 *Total Prizemoney* £10,622
Wins 1998 Apr Listow (G-S) H 8f 66 82 <
1997 Spt Sligo (SFT) 6.5f 79
1997 Jun Sligo (SFT) 6.5f 75
1999 Turf 0-2: (8f, 10f) (g-s, frm) 1999 AW 0-1: (8f) (Fibr)
Moderate gelding, effective 8f, acts on g-s, mostly wears blinkers. Turf high 33. Becoming disappointing.
**J G Portman [0-5] Madhatter Racing (from D Wachman in IRE [3-15] Jun 1998).*

BOMBELLINA (IRE) BHB 55f **RR 61f** 4524[9]

2 b f Robellino (USA) 9.5f **(68)** - Beetwentysix (USA) (Buckaroo (USA))
Form - 8022560
Record **1999** - 1st:0 2nd:2 3rd:0 Ran:7
Win Prizemoney £0 *Total Prizemoney* £1,935
1999 Turf 0-7: (5f 2, 6f 4, 7f) (gd 2, g-f, frm 4)
Average filly, effective 6f, acts on gd to frm. Turf high 61 - 2nd of 10 getting 17lb from Boating Song (9 Aug Windsor 6f gd RF 3488).
**J M P Eustace [0-7] Park Lane Racing.*

BONAGUIL (USA) **RR 65f** 4834[4]

2 b c Septieme Ciel (USA) - Chateaubrook (USA) (Alleged (USA)) 10f **(76)**
Form - 84
Record **1999** - 1st:0 2nd:0 3rd:0 Ran:2
Win Prizemoney £0 *Total Prizemoney* £237
1999 Turf 0-2: (7f 2) (gd, g-f)
Currently average colt. Turf high 65 (began Aug).
**C F Wall [0-2] Mrs R M S Neave.*

BON AMI (IRE) BHB 98f **RR 99f** 4392[9]

3 b c Paris House 5.9f **(64)** - Felin Special (Lyphard's Special (USA)) 10.3f **(72)**
Form - 48880324220
Record **1999** - 1st:0 2nd:3 3rd:1 Ran:11
Pre1999 - 1st:3 2nd:5 3rd:2 Ran:12
Win Prizemoney £10,612 *Total Prizemoney* £35,930
Wins * 1998 Aug Ripon (G-F) 6f 88
* 1998 Aug Newcas (GD) H 6f 100? <
* 1998 Apr Leices (SFT) 5f 77
1999 Turf 0-11: (5f, 6f 9, 7f) (gd 4, g-f 4, frm 3)
Leggy, very useful colt, effective 5 to 7f, best at 6f, acts on gd to frm, best on frm, excels at Ripon and Leicester. Turf high 99 - 2nd of 10 giving 11lb to Champagne Rider (22 Aug Leicester 6f frm RF 3839). Consistent. A top-notch sprint handicapper, he was short-headed in the Great St Wilfrid at Ripon in August. A horse who has to be dropped in front on the line, he handles any ground and stays an easy seven furlongs. **J Berry [3-23] K T Ivory.*

BONAPARTISTE (FR) **RR 122f** 5230a[6]

5 b h Kendor - Fab's Melody (FR) (Devil's Bag (USA)) 12.4f **(78)**
Form - 36
1999 Turf 0-2: (10f, 12f) (frm 2)
Very high-class colt. Turf high 122 (began Oct). Showed some useful form in '97, when racing in France. Moved to race in America and enjoyed a very successful campaign before finishing down the field in the Breeders' Cup Turf.
**R McNally in USA [0-1] (from R McAnally in USA [0-2] Oct 1999).*

BOND BOY BHB 86f **RR 86f** 4531[2]

2 b c Piccolo - Arabellajill (Aragon) 8.1f **(60)**
Form - 4362
Record **1999** - 1st:0 2nd:1 3rd:1 Ran:4
Win Prizemoney £0 *Total Prizemoney* £7,532
1999 Turf 0-4: (5f, 6f 3) (g-s, gd, g-f, frm)
Useful colt. Turf high 86 (began Aug) - 2nd of 17 giving 5lb to Inventive (24 Spt Lingfield 5f g-s RF 4531). **B Smart [0-4] R C Bond.*

BOND DIAMOND BHB 63f **RR 64f** 4145[4]

2 gr g Prince Sabo 6.6f **(64)** - Alsiba (Northfields (USA)) 9f **(72)**
Form - 0754
Record **1999** - 1st:0 2nd:0 3rd:0 Ran:4

Win Prizemoney £0 *Total Prizemoney* £263
1999 Turf 0-4: (6f 3, 8f) (gd 2, frm, hrd)
Average gelding. Turf high 64. **B Smart [0-4] R C Bond.*

BOND GIRL BHB 45f **RR 46f** 4410[8]
3 b f Magic Ring (IRE) 6.5f **(64)** - Whirling Words (Sparkler) 8.4f **(55)**
Form - 0708
Record 1999 - 1st:0 2nd:0 3rd:0 Ran:4
Pre1999 - 1st:0 2nd:0 3rd:0 Ran:1
1999 Turf 0-3: (7f 2, 8f) (g-f, frm 2) 1999 AW 0-1: (8f) (Fibr)
Strong, moderate filly. Turf high 46. **B Smart [0-5] R C Bond.*

BONDI BAY (IRE) BHB 55f **RR 53f** 4942[9]
2 b f Catrail (USA) - Sodium's Niece (Northfields (USA)) 9f **(72)**
Form - 500070
Record 1999 - 1st:0 2nd:0 3rd:0 Ran:6
1999 Turf 0-5: (5f 3, 6f 2) (gd 2, g-f 2, frm) 1999 AW 0-1: (7f) (Fibr)
Fair filly, has worn blinkers. Turf high 53.
**A T Murphy [0-6] A J Oliver.*

BONDOSAN RR 71f 1246[5]
3 b c Barathea (IRE) - Fern (Shirley Heights) 10.3f **(74)**
Form - 55
Record 1999 - 1st:0 2nd:0 3rd:0 Ran:2
1999 Turf 0-2: (11f, 12f) (g-f, frm)
Scopey, currently above-average colt. Turf high 71.
**H R A Cecil [0-2] Wafic Said.*

BONDS GULLY (IRE) BHB 60f **RR 71f** 4453[8]
3 b c Pips Pride 6.7f **(70)** - Classic Ring (IRE) (Auction Ring (USA)) 8.6f **(65)**
Form - 04708
Record 1999 - 1st:0 2nd:0 3rd:0 Ran:5
Win Prizemoney £0 *Total Prizemoney* £300
1999 Turf 0-5: (7f, 8f 4) (sft, gd, g-f, frm 2)
Scopey, above-average colt. Turf high 71 - 4th of 9 to Lover's Leap (10 Jun Newbury 7f gd RF 1886).
**R W Armstrong [0-5] Mrs L Alexander.*

BONELLI BHB 46f **RR 51f** 5069[18]
3 ch c Casteddu 7.4f **(54)** - Tawnais (Artaius (USA)) 9f **(69)**
Form - 7460
Record 1999 - 1st:0 2nd:0 3rd:0 Ran:4
Pre1999 - 1st:0 2nd:0 3rd:0 Ran:2
Win Prizemoney £0 *Total Prizemoney* £238
1999 Turf 0-4: (7f, 8f 2, 10f) (sft 2, gd, frm)
Workmanlike, fair colt. Turf high 51.
**J R Arnold [0-6] Lofal Partnership.*

BONNES NOUVELLES BHB 76f **RR 77f** 5133[14]
3 b f Shirley Heights 12.1f **(76)** - La Belle Creole (Rainbow Quest (USA)) 10.4f **(75)**
Form - 30
Record 1999 - 1st:0 2nd:0 3rd:1 Ran:2
Pre1999 - 1st:0 2nd:0 3rd:0 Ran:2
Win Prizemoney £0 *Total Prizemoney* £622
1999 Turf 0-2: (12f 2) (sft, gd)
Light-framed, above-average filly. Turf high 76 (1st run) (began Oct) - 3rd of 14 getting 12lb from Roman King (13 Oct Haydock 12f sft RF 4861). **J L Dunlop [0-4] Miss K Rausing.*

BONNE VILLE BHB 28f36a **RR 22f 36a** 2536[15]
5 gr m Good Times (ITY) 8.7f **(53)** - Ville Air (Town Crier) 10.2f **(55)**
Form - 15366550
Record 1999 - 1st:0 2nd:0 3rd:1 Ran:7
Pre1999 - 1st:2 2nd:5 3rd:2 Ran:24
Win Prizemoney £4,328 *Total Prizemoney* £8,031
Wins 1998 *Dec Wolver (STD) S 12f 52*
1996 *Oct Wolver (STD) S 8.5f 71* <
1999 Turf 0-1: (14f) (g-f) 1999 AW 0-6: (9f, 11f 2, 12f, 15f, 16f) (Fibr 6)
Little account filly, effective 12 to 15f, best at 12f, - acts on Fibr, has worn blinkers. AW high 44. Becoming disappointing.
**Miss S J Wilton [0-7] John Pointon and Sons (from B Palling [2-25] Dec 1998).*

BONNIE DUNDEE RR 47f 5068[8]
3 b f Rock City 8.8f **(62)** - Shy Dolly (Cajun) 5.2f **(54)**
Form - 1057056268
Record 1999 - 1st:1 2nd:1 3rd:0 Ran:10
Pre1999 - 1st:0 2nd:0 3rd:0 Ran:4
Win Prizemoney £2,458 *Total Prizemoney* £3,310
Wins * 1999 May Salisb (G-F) C 7f 60 <
1999 Turf 1-10: (7f 1-5, 8f 5) (gd 5, g-f, frm 1-4)
Neat, moderate filly, effective 5 to 7f, acts on gd to frm, has worn blinkers. Turf high 60 (1st run) - 1st of 16 getting 8lb from Ivor's Investment (13 May Salisbury RF 1192).
**M Kettle [1-14] Graham Racing.*

BONNIE FLORA RR 62f 1872[7]
3 b f Then Again 7.4f **(52)** -My Minnie **(46f 62a)**(Kind of Hush)10.1f **(62)**
Form - 77
Record 1999 - 1st:0 2nd:0 3rd:0 Ran:2
1999 Turf 0-2: (8f, 10f) (g-f, frm)
Well made, currently average filly. Turf high 62.
**D R C Elsworth [0-2] Mrs W Protheroe-Beynon.*

BOOGY WOOGY BHB 62f **RR 63f** 4904[3]
3 ch g Rock Hopper 10.6f **(54)** - Primulette (Mummy's Pet) 7.7f **(60)**
Form - 7703213437333
Record 1999 - 1st:1 2nd:1 3rd:6 Ran:13
Pre1999 - 1st:2 2nd:0 3rd:0 Ran:9
Win Prizemoney £12,772 *Total Prizemoney* £19,736
Wins * 1999 Jly Thirsk (FRM) H 12f 66 70 <
* 1998 Oct Doncas (HVY) H 7f 64 68
* 1998 Oct Redcar (g-s) C 7f 66
1999 Turf 1-13: (8f 2, 9f, 10f, 11f 2, 12f 1-5, 14f 2) (gd 2, g-f 4, frm 1-7)
Scopey, average gelding, effective 6 to 14f, acts on g-s to frm, best on frm, mostly wears blinkers (very effectively), likes tight tracks, excels at Redcar, does well at Ripon. Turf high 70 - 1st of 5 getting 7lb from Rahayeb (23 Jly Thirsk RF 3074). Consistent. **T D Easterby [3-22] Mrs P D Croft.*

BOOMERANG BLADE BHB 90f **RR 93f** 5030[10]
3 b f Sure Blade (USA) 10.6f **(66)** - Opuntia (Rousillon (USA)) 8.2f **(74)**
Form - 4006535200
Record 1999 - 1st:0 2nd:1 3rd:1 Ran:10
Pre1999 - 1st:2 2nd:1 3rd:1 Ran:5
Win Prizemoney £182,161 *Total Prizemoney* £189,863
Wins * 1998 Spt Doncas (GD) 6f 97 <
* 1998 Jly Folkes (GD) 6f 73
1999 Turf 0-10: (6f 5, 7f 2, 8f 2, 10f) (g-s, gd 5, frm 4)
Scopey, useful filly, effective 6 to 7f, acts on gd to frm. Turf high 106 (1st run) - 4th of 11 to Wince (16 Apr Newbury 7f frm RF 0719). Consistent. Earned a huge payday when winning Doncaster's St Leger Yearling Stakes as a two-year-old, and ran respectably against the top fillies in the Fred Darling and 1000 Guineas on her first two starts of '99. Below-par afterwards, apart from a fair effort when second to Tajasur at Hamilton in September.
**B Smart [2-15] John Ford.*

BOOMSHADOW RR 57f 5157[13]
2 ch g Imperial Frontier (USA) 7f **(65)** - Marie de Sologne (Lashkari) 9.8f **(67)**
Form - 00
Record 1999 - 1st:0 2nd:0 3rd:0 Ran:2
1999 Turf 0-2: (7f 2) (gd, frm)
Currently fair gelding. Turf high 57 (began Oct).
**J L Eyre [0-2] The Claire King Partnership 2.*

BORANI BHB 77f **RR 77f** 4386[3]
4 b g Shirley Heights 12.1f **(76)** - Ower (IRE) (Lomond (USA)) 8.8f **(65)**
Form - 0026313
Record 1999 - 1st:1 2nd:1 3rd:2 Ran:7
Pre1999 - 1st:0 2nd:1 3rd:1 Ran:7
Win Prizemoney £5,083 *Total Prizemoney* £10,764
Wins * 1999 Spt Goodwo (G-F) H 8f 69 77 <
1999 Turf 1-7: (7f, 8f 1-5, 10f) (gd, g-f 1-3, frm 3)
Lengthy, above-average gelding, effective 7 to 10f, best at 8f, acts on gd to frm, best on g-f. Turf high 77 - 1st of 22 giving 3lb to Grand Slam (10 Spt Goodwood RF 4260). Consistent. Had been running really well before gaining a well-deserved victory at Goodwood over a mile on decent ground in a 0-70. Good effort next time. **I A Balding [1-14] Dr J A E Hobby.*

BORDER ARROW BHB 118f **RR 119f** 1108[3]
4 ch c Selkirk (USA) 7.9f **(76)** - Nibbs Point (IRE) (Sure Blade (USA)) 11.3f **(67)**
Form - 3
Record 1999 - 1st:0 2nd:0 3rd:1 Ran:1
Pre1999 - 1st:2 2nd:0 3rd:3 Ran:5
Win Prizemoney £19,503 *Total Prizemoney* £182,583
Wins * 1998 Apr Newmar (SFT) L 9f 104+ <
* 1997 Oct Newmar (G-S) 8f 95++
1999 Turf 0-1: (10f) (gd)
Neat, high-class colt. (1st run) - 3rd of 10 to Handsome Ridge (8 May Goodwood 10f gd RF 1108). Created a very favourable impression when scoring at Newmarket as a two-year-old, and showed that he had trained on with a game victory in the Feilden Stakes on his first run at three. He then finished third in the Guineas, Dante, and the Derby, giving the impression each time that he needs a galloping track to be seen at his best. He was not seen out again that season and, having been pin-fired in the interim, appeared just once last term when a running-on third behind Handsome Ridge at Goodwood in May.
**I A Balding [2-6] R P B Michaelson & Wafic Said.*

BORDER GLEN BHB 53f61a **RR 54f 61a** 5068[4]
3 b g Selkirk (USA) 7.9f **(76)** - Sulitelma (USA) (The Minstrel (CAN)) 10f **(72)**
Form - 001100054
Record 1999 - 1st:2 2nd:0 3rd:0 Ran:9
Pre1999 - 1st:0 2nd:0 3rd:0 Ran:5
Win Prizemoney £5,350 *Total Prizemoney* £5,350
Wins 1999 Jun Mussel (G-F) H 8f 51 55
1999 *Jun Southw (STD) H 8f 51 56* <
1999 Turf 1-8: (6f, 8f 1-7) (gd 3, g-f 1-1, frm 3, hrd) 1999 AW 1-1: (8f 1-1) (Fibr 1-1)
Scopey, fair gelding, effective 8f, acts on gd to g-f - acts on Fibr, has worn blinkers (extremely effectively), prefers tight tracks. Turf high 55 - 1st of 14 giving 1lb to Love Diamonds (21 Jun Musselburgh RF 2170). (1st run) - 1st of 16 giving 5lb to Broke Road (4 Jun Southwell RF 1745). A winner twice last term, once on the All-Weather, and once at Musselburgh, he has disappointed since and appeared wired to the moon when wearing blinkers for the second time at Carlisle in June.
**D HaydnJones [0-4] Hugh O'Donnell (from Sir Mark Prescott [2-10] Jun 1999).*

BORDER PRINCE BHB 80f **RR 83f** 2726[2]
3 ch c Selkirk (USA) 7.9f **(76)** - Princess Oberon (IRE) **(85f)** (Fairy King (USA)) 7.7f **(59)**
Form - 22032
Record 1999 - 1st:0 2nd:3 3rd:1 Ran:5
Pre1999 - 1st:0 2nd:0 3rd:0 Ran:2
Win Prizemoney £0 *Total Prizemoney* £4,160
1999 Turf 0-5: (6f, 7f 2, 8f, 9f) (g-s, g-f 3, frm)
Scopey, decent colt, effective 6 to 9f, acts on g-s to g-f, best on g-f. Turf high 83 - 2nd of 7 giving 5lb to Goes A Treat (10 Jly Warwick 7f g-f RF 2726). He has made the frame in maidens, but does not seem to be progressing. **I A Balding [0-7] R P B Michaelson.*

BORDER RUN BHB 68f **RR 63f** 4598[6]
2 b g Missed Flight - Edraianthus (Windjammer (USA)) 7f **(59)**
Form - 056
Record 1999 - 1st:0 2nd:0 3rd:0 Ran:3
1999 Turf 0-3: (7f, 8f, 9f) (gd, g-f, frm)
Currently average gelding. Turf high 63 (began Aug).
**B J Meehan [0-3] N B Attenborough.*

BORDERS BHB 104f **RR 91f** 4773a[2]
3 b g Selkirk (USA) 7.9f **(76)** - Pretty Poppy (Song) 7.2f **(61)**
Form - 2314212
Record 1999 - 1st:2 2nd:3 3rd:1 Ran:7
Pre1999 - 1st:0 2nd:0 3rd:0 Ran:2
Win Prizemoney £10,256 *Total Prizemoney* £24,369
Wins * 1999 Spt Beverl (SFT) 5f 91 <
*** 1999** Jun Doncas (GD) 5f 85
1999 Turf 2-7: (5f 2-5, 6f 2) (sft, g-s 1-1, gd 2, g-f 1-2, frm)
Scopey, useful gelding, effective 5f, acts on g-s to g-f. Turf high 91 - 1st of 10 giving 2lb to First Maite (21 Spt Beverley RF 4443) - also 1st of 10 giving 5lb to Bridge Pool (5 Jun Doncaster RF 1756). Consistent. Started his career over six furlongs, but it was only when he was dropped to the minimum that he got off the mark, bolting home at Doncaster. Continued to run well including winning at Beverley, and can make his mark in listed company. **H Candy [2-9].*

BORDER STARLETTE (IRE) BHB 26f **RR 19f** 2540[10]
4 b f Ela-Mana-Mou 12.7f **(72)** - Fillette Lalo (FR) (Huntercombe) 7.3f **(56)**
Form - 00
Record 1999 - 1st:0 2nd:0 3rd:0 Ran:2
Pre1999 - 1st:0 2nd:0 3rd:0 Ran:6
1999 Turf 0-2: (10f, 12f) (g-f 2)
Neat, poor filly. Turf high 19. **Mrs M Reveley [0-9] D Young.*

BORDER TRADER (IRE) BHB 44f **RR 57f** 1[12]
4 ch g Sharp Victor (USA) 10f **(56)** - Hi Dad (USA) (Verbatim (USA)) 8.5f **(64)**
Form - 0
Record 1999 - 1st:0 2nd:0 3rd:0 Ran:1
Pre1999 - 1st:0 2nd:0 3rd:0 Ran:6
Win Prizemoney £0 *Total Prizemoney* £253
1999 AW 0-1: (12f) (Equi)
Workmanlike, fair gelding.
**J S Moore [0-8] J Mulholland and Danny Hughes.*

BOREHILL JOKER BHB 39f43a **RR 39f 43a** 3394[7]
3 ch g Pure Melody (USA) - Queen Matilda (Castle Keep) 8.3f **(57)**
Form - 77
Record 1999 - 1st:0 2nd:0 3rd:0 Ran:2
Pre1999 - 1st:0 2nd:1 3rd:0 Ran:5
Win Prizemoney £0 *Total Prizemoney* £515
1999 Turf 0-1: (7f) (frm) 1999 AW 0-1: (9f) (Fibr)
Lengthy, moderate gelding, often wears blinkers.
**W G M Turner [0-7] O J Stokes.*

BORGIA RR 83f 5132[6]
4 ch f Machiavellian (USA) 9.8f **(83)** - Cut Ahead (Kalaglow) 9.8f **(67)**
Form - 25323104156
Record 1999 - 1st:2 2nd:2 3rd:2 Ran:11
Pre1999 - 1st:1 2nd:0 3rd:1 Ran:5
Win Prizemoney £24,410 *Total Prizemoney* £30,987
Wins * 1999 Spt York (G-F) H 13.9f 76 78 <
*** 1999** Jly Newbur (G-F) H 13.3f 74 73
* 1998 Oct Leices (G-S) H 11.8f 66 71
1999 Turf 2-11: (12f 4, 13f 1-2, 14f 1-4, 16f) (g-s, gd 2, g-f 1-2, frm 1-6)
Scopey, decent filly, effective 13 to 16f, acts on gd to frm, best on frm, often wears blinkers (extremely effectively), likes left handed tracks, excels at Newbury. Turf high 83 - 6th of 12 giving 10lb to Eilean Shona (29 Oct Newmarket 16f gd RF 5132) - also 1st of 9 giving 6lb to Follow That Dream (1 Spt York RF 4081). Consistent. She is an extremely difficult ride, as she needs to be produced on the bridle as late as possible. Richard Hughes rode her to perfection in her victories at Newbury and York.
**R Charlton [3-16] Lady Rothschild.*

BORGIA (GER) RR 121f 5228a[5]
5 b m Acatenango (GER) - Britannia (GER) (Tarim)
Form - 2455275
1999 Turf 0-7: (10f, 11f, 12f 5) (sft, g-s, gd 3, frm 2)
Very high-class filly, effective 10 to 12f, best at 12f, acts on g-s to frm, best on gd. Turf high 121 - 2nd of 3 getting 4lb from El Condor Pasa (12 Spt Longchamp 12f gd RF 4368a). Consistent. A fine third in the Arc and close second in the Breeders' Cup Turf in 1997 when trained in Germany, she has been trained in France for the past two seasons and, despite some first-class efforts, has failed to win. She struggled a little in 1999, but was a fine second to El Condor Pasa in the Prix Foy with Fallon believing she was back to her best. She was well beaten in the Arc, but again ran well when an unlucky fifth at the Breeders' Cup meeting. A tough, top-class mare, it is likely that she may now retire to the paddocks.
**A Fabre in FR [0-8] (from A Schutz in GER [0-1] Mar 1998).*

BORN A LADY BHB 27f36a **RR 27f 36a** 331[7]
6 ch m Komaite (USA) 6.9f **(61)** - Lucky Candy (Lucky Wednesday) 8f **(50)**
Form - 00767
Record 1999 - 1st:0 2nd:0 3rd:0 Ran:5

Pre1999 - 1st:1 2nd:2 3rd:6 Ran:40
Win Prizemoney £2,519 *Total Prizemoney* £7,873
Wins * 1995 *May Southw (STD) 5f 49 <*
1999 AW 0-5: (7f, 8f 4) (Fibr 5)
Little account mare, effective 5f, acts on frm, often wears blinkers. AW high 27.
**N P Littmoden [1-19] Paul Dixon (from Mrs V A Aconley [0-10] Aug 1997).*

BORN FREE RR 73f 5197[3]

3 ch f Caerleon (USA) 10.9f **(79)** - Culture Vulture (USA) (Timeless Moment (USA)) 6f **(72)**
Form - 023
Record 1999 - 1st:0 2nd:1 3rd:1 Ran:3
Pre1999 - 1st:0 2nd:1 3rd:0 Ran:2
Win Prizemoney £0 *Total Prizemoney* £2,971
1999 Turf 0-3: (8f, 10f 2) (gd, g-f, frm)
Leggy, above-average filly. Turf high 73 - 2nd of 13 giving 20lb to Karakul (21 Jun Windsor 10f frm RF 2177).
**P F I Cole [0-5] H R H Prince Fahd Salman.*

BORN TO RULE BHB 70f RR 66f 4261[4]

2 ch c Mujtahid (USA) 7.4f **(69)** - Born To Glamour (Ajdal (USA)) 9.2f **(89)**
Form - 844
Record 1999 - 1st:0 2nd:0 3rd:0 Ran:3
Win Prizemoney £0 *Total Prizemoney* £535
1999 Turf 0-3: (5f 2, 6f) (gd, g-f 2)
Currently average colt. Turf high 66 (began Aug).
**M S Saunders [0-3] Naylor,B McFadzean,M Mulchrone.*

BOSSCAT BHB 65f RR 67f 3905[7]

2 b c Presidium 7.5f **(56)** - Belltina (Belfort (FR)) 6.8f **(63)**
Form - 0607
Record 1999 - 1st:0 2nd:0 3rd:0 Ran:4
1999 Turf 0-4: (5f 2, 6f, 8f) (g-s, g-f 2, frm)
Average colt. Turf high 62. **K McAuliffe [0-4] Boss Racing.*

BOSS TWEED (IRE) BHB 54f52a RR 58f 52a 4867[5]

2 b g Persian Bold 10f **(69)** - Betty Kenwood **(43f 35a)** (Dominion) 8.5f **(63)**
Form - 765
Record 1999 - 1st:0 2nd:0 3rd:0 Ran:3
1999 Turf 0-2: (5f, 6f) (gd, frm) 1999 AW 0-1: (6f) (Fibr)
Currently fair gelding. Turf high 58 (began Aug).
**G C Bravery [0-3] G C Bravery.*

BOSSY SPICE BHB 37f RR 37f 5002[12]

2 br f Emperor Jones (USA) - Million Heiress (Auction Ring (USA)) 8.6f **(65)**
Form - 6070
Record 1999 - 1st:0 2nd:0 3rd:0 Ran:4
1999 Turf 0-3: (5f 2, 8f) (g-s 2, gd) 1999 AW 0-1: (8f) (Fibr)
Very moderate filly, has worn blinkers. Turf high 37.
**N M Babbage [0-2] David James (from M R Channon [0-2] Apr 1999).*

BOTTELINO JOE (IRE) BHB 63f RR 68f 4669[5]

2 b br c Bluebird (USA) 7.9f **(71)** - My-O-My (IRE) **(84f)** (Waajib)
Form - 8045
Record 1999 - 1st:0 2nd:0 3rd:0 Ran:4
Win Prizemoney £0 *Total Prizemoney* £267
1999 Turf 0-4: (5f, 6f 2, 7f) (g-s, gd, g-f, frm)
Average colt. Turf high 56. **M S Saunders [0-4] Il Bottelino.*

BOULEVARD ROUGE (USA) BHB 43f56a RR 23f 56a 1654[11]

4 b f Red Ransom (USA) 8.6f **(83)** - Beetwentysix (USA) (Buckaroo (USA))
Form - 000
Record 1999 - 1st:0 2nd:0 3rd:0 Ran:3
Pre1999 - 1st:0 2nd:3 3rd:4 Ran:15
Win Prizemoney £0 *Total Prizemoney* £4,810
1999 Turf 0-3: (7f, 8f, 9f) (gd 2, frm)
Scopey, average filly, effective 8 to 11f, acts on frm - acts on Equi, favours left handed tracks, prefers tight tracks. Turf high 23. Becoming disappointing.
**M W Easterby [0-5] K Hodgson & Mrs J Hodgson (from M Johnston [0-13] Spt 1998).*

BOUNDARY EXPRESS BHB 41f50a RR 27f 50a 2767[P]

7 b g Sylvan Express 9.6f **(45)** - Addison's Jubilee (Sparkler) 8.4f **(55)**
Form - 8P
Record 1999 - 1st:0 2nd:0 3rd:0 Ran:2
Pre1999 - 1st:2 2nd:3 3rd:1 Ran:23
Win Prizemoney £5,758 *Total Prizemoney* £10,644
Wins 1995 Spt Haydoc (GD) H 11.9f 47 57 <
1995 Aug Pontef (G-F) S 12f 52
1999 Turf 0-2: (14f, 16f) (g-f, frm)
Moderate gelding, had worn blinkers. Turf high 27 (began Jly). (DEAD)
**S Gollings [0-2] Mrs Stella Barclay (from E J Alston [2-10] May 1996).*

BOUND FOR PLEASURE (IRE) BHB 75f RR 75f 1732[13]

3 gr c Barathea (IRE) - Dazzlingly Radiant (Try My Best (USA)) 7.6f **(67)**
Form - 0600
Record 1999 - 1st:0 2nd:0 3rd:0 Ran:4
Pre1999 - 1st:1 2nd:1 3rd:0 Ran:3
Win Prizemoney £3,525 *Total Prizemoney* £5,801
Wins * 1998 Oct Lingfi (HVY) 7f 82 <
1999 Turf 0-4: (7f 2, 9f, 10f) (gd 3, frm)
Scopey, above-average colt, effective 7f, acts on sft, has worn blinkers. Turf high 75. **G L Moore [1-7] Action Bloodstock.*

BOUND TO PLEASE BHB 48f70a RR 56f 70a 4606[8]

4 b g Warrshan (USA) 9.7f **(59)** - Hong Kong Girl (Petong) 6.6f **(58)**
Form - 60058
Record 1999 - 1st:0 2nd:0 3rd:0 Ran:5
Pre1999 - 1st:0 2nd:1 3rd:0 Ran:7
Win Prizemoney £0 *Total Prizemoney* £1,180
1999 Turf 0-4: (6f 3, 7f) (g-s, g-f 2, frm) 1999 AW 0-1: (6f) (Fibr)
Scopey, above-average gelding. Turf high 56. Inconsistent.
**P J Makin [0-12] D A Poole.*

BOUNTIFUL LADY (USA) BHB 98f RR 95f 1144[4]

3 ch f Irish River (FR) 9f **(77)** - Bounding Away (CAN) (Vice Regent (CAN)) 8.7f **(74)**
Form - 04
Record 1999 - 1st:0 2nd:0 3rd:0 Ran:2
Pre1999 - 1st:1 2nd:0 3rd:0 Ran:1
Win Prizemoney £3,338 *Total Prizemoney* £5,188
Wins * 1998 Oct Newcas (SFT) 7f 80+ <
1999 Turf 0-2: (8f, 10f) (gd, frm)
Workmanlike, currently very useful filly. Turf high 95. She did well physically over the winter, but that improvement was not mirrored on the racecourse. **Sir Michael Stoute [1-3] Nasser Abdullah.*

BOWCLIFFE BHB 57f73a RR 53f 73a 5004[10]

8 b g Petoski 10.4f **(56)** - Gwiffina (Welsh Saint) 7.6f **(64)**
Form - 01880002220600
Record 1999 - 1st:1 2nd:3 3rd:0 Ran:14
Pre1999 - 1st:6 2nd:4 3rd:5 Ran:48
Win Prizemoney £37,714 *Total Prizemoney* £60,611
Wins * **1999** Apr Mussel (G-F) 8f 66
* 1998 Spt Doncas (GD) H 8f 62 68 <
* 1998 *Jan Wolver (STD) H 9.4f 63 62+*
* 1997 Jly Carlis (GD) H 8f 51 62
* 1997 Jun Pontef (G-F) H 8f 46 54
1996 May Mussel (G-S) H 8.1f 44 50
1999 Turf 1-13: (8f 1-9, 10f 4) (gd 3, g-f 1-4, frm 6) 1999 AW 0-1: (9f) (Fibr)
Above-average gelding, effective 8 to 9f, best at 8f, acts on g-f - acts on Fibr, has worn blinkers, likes left handed tracks. Turf high 66 (1st run) - 1st of 6 from Ryefield (30 Apr Musselburgh RF 0937). Inconsistent. Suited by a strongly-run mile.
**E J Alston [5-45] Philip Davies (from Mrs A M Naughton [1-9] Nov 1996).*

BOWCLIFFE GRANGE (IRE) BHB 39f43a RR 36f 43a 4167[1]

7 b g Dominion Royale 7.8f **(63)** - Cala-Vadella (Mummy's Pet) 7.7f **(60)**
Form - 661060374001
Record 1999 - 1st:2 2nd:0 3rd:1 Ran:12
Pre1999 - 1st:4 2nd:3 3rd:6 Ran:43
Win Prizemoney £16,494 *Total Prizemoney* £22,889
Wins * **1999** Spt Hamilt (G-F) H 5f 35 36
* ***1999*** *Mar Lingfi (STD) H 5f 37 40*

* 1996 Jly Doncas (G-F) H 5f 44 50 <
* 1996 Jly Windso (G-F) H 5f 44 50 <
* 1996 Jun Lingfi (FRM) H 5f 34 39
* 1996 Jun Beverl (G-F) H 5f 23 25

1999 Turf 1-8: (5f 1-8) (gd, g-f, frm 1-6) 1999 AW 1-4: (5f 1-4) (Equi 1-2, Fibr 2)

Moderate gelding, effective 5f, acts on gd - acts on AW, has worn blinkers. Turf high 36. AW high 40 - 1st of 7 getting 24lb from Half Tone (2 Mar Lingfield RF 0387). Has tremendous early pace.

**D W Chapman [6-54] David Chapman (from J Hanson [0-1] Oct 1994).*

BOWLERS BOY BHB 50f66a **RR 49f 66a** 5065^{5}

6 ch g Risk Me (FR) 8f **(53)** - Snow Wonder (Music Boy) 6.8f **(57)**

Form - 0005500000035

Record 1999 - 1st:0 2nd:0 3rd:1 Ran:13
Pre1999 - 1st:7 2nd:8 3rd:4 Ran:48

Win Prizemoney £27,437 *Total Prizemoney* £39,555

Wins * 1998 Nov Redcar (G-S) 5f 65
* 1998 Oct Pontef (SFT) H 5f 68 74 <
* 1998 Jun Pontef (SFT) H 6f 68 70
* 1997 Aug Ripon (GD) H 6f 67 71
* 1997 Jly Beverl (HVY) H 5f 66 68
* 1996 Spt Pontef (G-F) H 5f 68 69
* 1996 Jly Pontef (G-F) 6f 64

1999 Turf 0-13: (5f 6, 6f 7) (sft, gd 6, g-f 4, frm 2)

Moderate gelding, effective 5 to 6f, best at 5f, acts on sft to gd, best on gd, has worn blinkers, and excels at Redcar. Turf high 62.

**J J Quinn [7-61] Bowlers Racing.*

BOW PEEP (IRE) BHB 46f62a **RR 47f 62a** 3953^{8}

4 b br f Shalford (IRE) 7.8f **(63)** - Gale Force Seven (Strong Gale) 5.6f **(66)**

Form - 007008

Record 1999 - 1st:0 2nd:0 3rd:0 Ran:6
Pre1999 - 1st:2 2nd:0 3rd:0 Ran:11

Win Prizemoney £6,854 *Total Prizemoney* £7,100

Wins * 1998 Jly Nottin (G-F) 5.1f 63 <
* 1998 Jly Ripon (GD) H 6f 60 63 <

1999 Turf 0-6: (5f 4, 6f 2) (gd, g-f 2, frm 3)

Moderate filly, effective 5 to 6f, best at 6f, acts on gd to frm, has worn blinkers. Turf high 47. Looks to need six furlongs.

**M W Easterby [2-17] Mrs Anne Jarvis.*

BOW STRADA **RR 86f** 4818^{1}

2 ch c Rainbow Quest (USA) 11.2f **(81)** - La Strada (Niniski (USA)) 10.6f **(65)**

Form - 11

Record 1999 - 1st:2 2nd:0 3rd:0 Ran:2

Win Prizemoney £8,774 *Total Prizemoney* £8,774

Wins * **1999** Oct Leices (G-S) 10f 86 <
* **1999** Aug Yarmou (GD) 8f 79+

1999 Turf 2-2: (8f 1-1, 10f 1-1) (gd 2-2)

Currently useful colt. Turf high 86 (began Aug) - 1st of 8 getting 2lb from Atwaar (11 Oct Leicester RF 4818) - also 1st of 12 giving 9lb to Titian Angel (29 Aug Yarmouth RF 4003).

**P W Harris [2-2] Doolan, Haygarth, Rice & Strachan.*

BOXBERRY BHB 41f **RR 49f** 4707^{8}

2 b f Owington - Chatterberry (Aragon) 8.1f **(60)**

Form - 87008

Record 1999 - 1st:0 2nd:0 3rd:0 Ran:5

1999 Turf 0-5: (5f 4, 6f) (gd 2, frm 3)

Moderate filly, has worn blinkers. Turf high 49.

**N A Callaghan [0-5] Peter Bickmore.*

BOX CAR (IRE) BHB 56f **RR 56f** 5196^{6}

2 b c Blues Traveller (IRE) - Racey Naskra (USA) (Star de Naskra (USA)) 9.7f **(65)**

Form - 0006

Record 1999 - 1st:0 2nd:0 3rd:0 Ran:4

1999 Turf 0-4: (7f 2, 8f 2) (gd, g-f, frm 2)

Fair colt. Turf high 56. **G L Moore [0-4] R Kiernan.*

BRAHMS (USA) **RR 104f** $5229a^{7}$

2 br c Danzig (USA) 8.1f **(88)** - Queena (USA) (Mr Prospector (USA)) 8.8f **(78)**

Form - 212327

1999 Turf 1-5: (6f 1-3, 7f 2) (gd 1-4, frm) 1999 AW 0-1: (9f) (Dirt)

Very useful colt, effective 6 to 7f, acts on gd, mostly wears blinkers (extremely effectively). Turf high 104 (began Jly) - 2nd of 5 to Distant Music (16 Oct Newmarket 7f gd RF 4918). One maiden race win from six starts does not begin to do this colt justice. Still green when finishing second to Giant's Causeway in a Group 3 at The Curragh in August, he was beaten for speed when chasing Primo Valentino and Fath home in the Middle Park Stakes at Newmarket the following month. Stepped-up to seven furlongs for the Dewhurst Stakes back at Headquarters in October, he was given a poor tactical ride by Olivier Peslier, who allowed Distant Music to kick clear before giving chase. Pulling the winner back up the final climb, he was only a length down at the wire and should stay a mile as a three-year-old, but was well beaten over that trip in the Breeders' Cup Juvenile. While not the most straightforward colt - he has worn blinkers or a visor since his second start - he has stacks of ability and should make his presence felt in the top-class in 2000. **A P O'Brien in IRE [1-6].*

BRAMBLE BEAR BHB 52f **RR 53f** 5065^{3}

5 b m Beveled (USA) 6.9f **(64)** - Supreme Rose (Frimley Park) 6.5f **(67)**

Form - 0304373535653

Record 1999 - 1st:0 2nd:0 3rd:5 Ran:13
Pre1999 - 1st:4 2nd:3 3rd:3 Ran:30

Win Prizemoney £13,478 *Total Prizemoney* £22,858

Wins * 1998 May Lingfi (GD) H 5f 65 72 <
* 1997 May Catter (G-F) H 5f 62 67
* 1997 May Windso (SFT) H 5f 62 64
* 1996 Jly Bath (FRM) 5.1f 67

1999 Turf 0-13: (5f 12, 6f) (g-s 3, gd 3, g-f, frm 6)

Fair filly, effective 5f, acts on g-f to frm, best on frm. Turf high 60. Consistent. She often makes the frame, but is on a long losing run. **M Blanshard [4-43] Mrs Michael Hill & Mrs Heather Chakko.*

BRAMBLES WAY BHB 34f44a **RR 42f 44a** 1930^{13}

10 ch g Clantime 6.6f **(57)** - Streets Ahead (Ovid) 10f **(32)**

Form - 0

Record 1999 - 1st:0 2nd:0 3rd:0 Ran:1
Pre1999 - 1st:3 2nd:4 3rd:4 Ran:46

Win Prizemoney £8,439 *Total Prizemoney* £12,888

Wins 1997 Oct Newcas (G-F) H 10.1f 45 53
1997 Apr Beverl (G-F) H 9.9f 50 54 <
1996 Spt Redcar (FRM) SH 10f 41 49

1999 AW 0-1: (11f) (Fibr)

Moderate gelding, has worn blinkers.

**F Jordan [1-8] Birmingham Bloodstock (from Mrs M Reveley [9-39] Oct 1998).*

BRANCASTER (USA) BHB 112f **RR 113f** $2476a^{8}$

3 br c Riverman (USA) 9.7f **(78)** - Aseltine's Angels (USA) (Fappiano (USA)) 8.7f **(77)**

Form - 2408

Record 1999 - 1st:0 2nd:1 3rd:0 Ran:4
Pre1999 - 1st:2 2nd:0 3rd:0 Ran:2

Win Prizemoney £23,793 *Total Prizemoney* £43,993

Wins * 1998 Oct Newbur (HVY) G3 7.3f 104 <
* 1998 Spt Haydoc (G-F) 7.1f 94++

1999 Turf 0-4: (8f 2, 10f, 12f) (gd 2, g-f, frm)

Leggy, Group-class colt, effective 7 to 8f, best at 8f, acts on sft to frm, has worn blinkers. Turf high 113 - 4th of 16 to Island Sands (1 May Newmarket 8f frm RF 0958). He made a bright start to the season, finishing fourth in the 2,000 Guineas. However, he failed to progress thereafter, flopping when tried in a visor at Longchamp. Time may show that he had one tough race too many as a youngster. **P W Chapple-Hyam [2-6].*

BRANDON COURT (IRE) BHB 58f **RR 59f** 4347^{1}

8 b g Law Society (USA) 11.6f **(71)** - Dance Date (IRE) (Sadler's Wells (USA)) 10f **(76)**

Form - 4006201

Record 1999 - 1st:1 2nd:1 3rd:0 Ran:7
Pre1999 - 1st:2 2nd:3 3rd:2 Ran:15

Win Prizemoney £12,292 *Total Prizemoney* £25,838

Wins * **1999** Spt Ayr (G-S) H 10.9f 57 59

1999 Turf 1-7: (9f, 10f, 11f 1-1, 12f 2, 13f, 14f) (hvy, sft, gd 1-2, g-f, frm 2)

Fair gelding, likes tight tracks. Turf high 69. Consistent.

**I A Balding [3-25] Tunnel Vision.*

BRANDON MAGIC BHB 79f65a **RR 84f 65a** 227[1]
6 ch g Primo Dominie 7.2f **(67)** - Silk Stocking (Pardao) 8.6f **(60)**
Form - 01
Record 1999 - 1st:1 2nd:0 3rd:0 Ran:2
Pre1999 - 1st:3 2nd:4 3rd:3 Ran:23
Win Prizemoney £17,803 *Total Prizemoney* £36,089
Wins * 1999 *Feb Southw (STD) C 8f 37*
1995 Oct Ascot (SFT) 7f 98 <
1995 Spt Salisb (G-S) 6f 92+
1995 Spt Pontef (GD) 6f 80
1999 AW 1-2: (7f, 8f 1-1) (Fibr 1-2)
Decent gelding, has worn blinkers. AW high 37. Inconsistent.
**D Nicholls [1-2] V Greaves (from I A Balding [3-26] Aug 1997).*

BRANDON ROCK BHB 78f **RR 82f** 4872[15]
2 b c Robellino (USA) 9.5f **(68)** - The Kings Daughter (Indian King (USA)) 7.4f **(64)**
Form - 0170
Record 1999 - 1st:1 2nd:0 3rd:0 Ran:4
Win Prizemoney £3,777 *Total Prizemoney* £3,777
Wins * 1999 Spt Sandow (G-F) 5f 82 <
1999 Turf 1-4: (5f 1-2, 6f, 7f) (sft, gd 1-2, frm)
Decent colt. Turf high 82 (began Aug) - 1st of 11 giving 6lb to Strand of Gold (15 Spt Sandown RF 4327). Successfully reverted back to five at Sandown on his second start after his debut at Kempton over seven, but had no luck in running at the same track next time. **I A Balding [1-4] R P B Michaelson.*

BRANDONVILLE BHB 51f44a **RR 60f 44a** 4935[12]
6 b g Never so Bold 7.1f **(62)** - Enduring (Sadler's Wells (USA)) 10f **(76)**
Form - 0
Record 1999 - 1st:0 2nd:0 3rd:0 Ran:1
Pre1999 - 1st:2 2nd:0 3rd:0 Ran:15
Win Prizemoney £6,113 *Total Prizemoney* £6,848
Wins * 1997 Jly Haydoc (G-S) H 7.1f 56 60 <
* 1997 May Ayr (SFT) H 7f 52 56
1999 AW 0-1: (8f) (Fibr)
Average gelding. Inconsistent.
**N Tinkler [2-13] Philip Grundy (from I A Balding [0-3] Oct 1995).*

BRANDY N PORT (IRE) **RR** 5192[17]
2 ch g Forest Wind (USA) - Achtung Lady (IRE) (Warning)
Form - 0
Record 1999 - 1st:0 2nd:0 3rd:0 Ran:1
1999 Turf 0-1: (8f) (gd)
Currently very poor gelding. **John Harris [0-1] James Gough.*

BRANSTON BERRY (IRE) BHB 67f80a **RR 68f 80a** 866[7]
4 ch f Mukaddamah (USA) 7.6f **(74)** -Food of Love(Music Boy) 6.8f **(57)**
Form - 007
Record 1999 - 1st:0 2nd:0 3rd:0 Ran:3
Pre1999 - 1st:3 2nd:5 3rd:2 Ran:19
Win Prizemoney £25,263 *Total Prizemoney* £31,504
Wins * 1998 Oct Catter (SFT) H 5f 66 73
* 1997 Spt Doncas (G-F) H 6.5f 74 72
* 1997 May Beverl (HVY) 5f 79 <
1999 Turf 0-2: (6f 2) (gd 2) 1999 AW 0-1: (6f) (Fibr)
Workmanlike, above-average filly, effective 5 to 6f, acts on g-s - acts on Fibr. Turf high 50.
**J L Eyre [3-21] Diamond Racing Ltd (from M Johnston [0-1] Apr 1997).*

BRANSTON FIZZ BHB 82f77a **RR 73f 77a** 5054[2]
2 b f Efisio 7.7f **(69)** - Tuxford Hideaway (Cawston's Clown) 8f **(60)**
Form - 22
Record 1999 - 1st:0 2nd:2 3rd:0 Ran:2
Win Prizemoney £0 *Total Prizemoney* £1,538
1999 Turf 0-2: (6f 2) (gd 2)
Currently above-average filly. Turf high 73 (began Oct) - 2nd of 13 to Picot (25 Oct Leicester 6f gd RF 5054).
**M Johnston [0-2] David Abell.*

BRANSTON LUCY BHB 61f **RR 62f** 4543[1]
2 b f Prince Sabo 6.6f **(64)** - Softly Spoken (Mummy's Pet) 7.7f **(60)**
Form - 48531
Record 1999 - 1st:1 2nd:0 3rd:1 Ran:5
Win Prizemoney £3,183 *Total Prizemoney* £3,813
Wins * 1999 Spt Redcar (G-F) H 5f 56 62 <
1999 Turf 1-4: (5f 1-4) (g-f, frm 1-3) 1999 AW 0-1: (5f) (Fibr)
Average filly. Turf high 62 - 1st of 21 getting 1lb from Tick Tock (24 Spt Redcar RF 4543). **T J Etherington [1-5] David Abell.*

BRANSTON PICKLE BHB 77f **RR 80f** 5214[10]
2 ch c Piccolo - Indefinite Article (IRE) (Indian Ridge)
Form - 660361410
Record 1999 - 1st:2 2nd:0 3rd:1 Ran:9
Win Prizemoney £5,788 *Total Prizemoney* £6,397
Wins * 1999 Nov Catter (SFT) H 6f 69 80 <
*** 1999** *Oct Wolver (STD) S 5f 69*
1999 Turf 1-7: (5f 4, 6f 1-3) (g-s 1-2, gd 3, frm 2) 1999 AW 1-2: (5f 1-2) (Fibr 1-2)
Decent colt, effective 6f, acts on g-s. Turf high 80 (began Aug) - 1st of 8 getting 15lb from It's Allowed (2 Nov Catterick RF 5164). AW high 69 (began Spt). **T J Etherington [2-9] David Abell.*

BRATBY (IRE) BHB 33f47a **RR 38f 47a** 4945[8]
3 b g Distinctly North (USA) 7.4f **(63)** - Aridje (Mummy's Pet) 7.7f **(60)**
Form - 156054008
Record 1999 - 1st:1 2nd:0 3rd:0 Ran:9
Pre1999 - 1st:0 2nd:0 3rd:0 Ran:3
Win Prizemoney £1,891 *Total Prizemoney* £1,891
Wins * 1999 *Jan Lingfi (STD) H 8f 42 44 <*
1999 Turf 0-6: (7f 2, 8f 2, 10f 2) (gd 2, g-f 2, frm 2) 1999 AW 1-3: (7f, 8f 1-2) (Equi 1-3)
Light-framed, moderate gelding, effective 8f, - acts on Equi, likes left handed tracks, likes tight tracks. Turf high 38. AW high 44 (1st run) - 1st of 9 getting 14lb from Compton Akka (30 Jan Lingfield RF 0193). Inconsistent.
**D R C Elsworth [0-4] Del & Jake Partnership (from M L W Bell [1-9] Jun 1999).*

BRAVACCIO (IRE) BHB 65f60a **RR 62f 60a** 367[6]
3 b c Petorius 8f **(66)** - So Stylish (Great Nephew) 9.9f **(64)**
Form - 06
Record 1999 - 1st:0 2nd:0 3rd:0 Ran:2
Pre1999 - 1st:0 2nd:0 3rd:0 Ran:3
Win Prizemoney £0 *Total Prizemoney* £261
1999 AW 0-2: (8f, 12f) (Equi, Fibr)
Workmanlike, average colt, has worn blinkers. AW high 25.
**P S McEntee [0-5] R B Collier.*

BRAVE ACT BHB 100f **RR 116f** 5226a[6]
5 b h Persian Bold 10f **(69)** - Circus Act (Shirley Heights) 10.3f **(74)**
Form - 6
1999 Turf 0-1: (8f) (frm)
High-class colt - 6th of 14 to Silic (6 Nov Gulfstream Park 8f frm RF 5226a).
**R McAnally in USA [0-1] (from Sir Mark Prescott [3-4] Aug 1996).*

BRAVE BURT (IRE) BHB 97f **RR 92f** 2499[9]
2 ch c Pips Pride 6.7f **(70)** - Friendly Song (Song) 7.2f **(61)**
Form - 1130
Record 1999 - 1st:2 2nd:0 3rd:1 Ran:4
Win Prizemoney £6,600 *Total Prizemoney* £10,300
Wins * 1999 May Bath (GD) 5.1f 92 <
*** 1999** May Carlis (FRM) 5f 81+
1999 Turf 2-4: (5f 2-4) (g-f 1-3, frm 1-1)
Useful colt. Turf high 92 - 1st of 10 giving 7lb to Cookie (17 May Bath RF 1267). Sprint-bred, he won two ordinary events before being found out in better company. **J Berry [2-4] Lucayan Stud.*

BRAVE EDGE BHB 91f **RR 92f** 5160[8]
8 b g Beveled (USA) 6.9f **(64)** - Daring Ditty (Daring March) 7.1f **(61)**
Form - 200360206870448
Record 1999 - 1st:0 2nd:2 3rd:1 Ran:15
Pre1999 - 1st:7 2nd:9 3rd:8 Ran:65
Win Prizemoney £58,267 *Total Prizemoney* £145,093
Wins * 1998 Jly Newbur (GD) H 6f 98 100
* 1997 Spt Hamilt (GD) 6f 90
* 1996 Jun Kempto (G-F) L 5f 107 <
* 1995 May York (GD) H 5f 90 92+
* 1995 Apr Sandow (GD) H 5f 86 83
1999 Turf 0-15: (5f, 6f 14) (g-s 3, gd 3, g-f 4, frm 5)
Useful gelding, effective 5 to 6f, best at 6f, acts on gd to frm, best on gd, likes York and Newbury. Turf high 95 (1st run) - 2nd of 9 to

Hill Magic (5 Apr Kempton 6f g-f RF 0574). Consistent. He is a useful sprint handicapper, but on a long losing run and difficult to win with. Effective on any ground, he has often gone well for Pat Eddery. **R Hannon [7-80] Horris Vale Racing Partnership.*

BRAVE ENVOY BHB 49f **RR 48f** 4902[15]
5 b g High Estate 10.5f **(66)** - Restless Anna (Thatching) 8f **(66)**
Form - 70345500
Record 1999 - 1st:0 2nd:0 3rd:1 Ran:8
Pre1999 - 1st:3 2nd:2 3rd:1 Ran:19
Win Prizemoney £9,659 *Total Prizemoney* £12,410
Wins 1998 Oct Nottin (SFT) H 8.2f 58 61
1997 Oct Nottin (GD) H 8.2f 56 65 <
1997 Apr Leices (FRM) S 6f 56
1999 Turf 0-8: (8f 2, 9f, 10f 4, 11f) (sft, gd 2, g-f 2, frm 3)
Moderate gelding, effective 8 to 10f, best at 8f, acts on g-s to frm, best on gd, has worn blinkers, likes left handed tracks, likes tight tracks, does well at Nottingham. Turf high 55.
**C G Cox [0-4] Tom Burge (from M J Heaton-Ellis [3-26] Jun 1999).*

BRAVE KNIGHT RR 45f 4751[16]
2 b c Presidium 7.5f **(56)** - Agnes Jane (Sweet Monday) 8.3f **(25)**
Form - 0
Record 1999 - 1st:0 2nd:0 3rd:0 Ran:1
1999 Turf 0-1: (8f) (gd)
Currently moderate colt. **N Bycroft [0-1] P Casimir-Mrowczynski.*

BRAVE REWARD (USA) BHB 105f **RR 105f** 3756[7]
4 b c Lear Fan (USA) 10.4f **(80)** - A Tad Better (USA) (Northern Prospect (USA)) 9.5f **(71)**
Form - 2037
Record 1999 - 1st:0 2nd:1 3rd:1 Ran:4
Pre1999 - 1st:2 2nd:0 3rd:2 Ran:8
Win Prizemoney £8,951 *Total Prizemoney* £30,789
Wins * 1998 Aug Cheste (GD) H 10.3f 92 98 <
* 1997 Oct Leices (G-S) 7f 79+
1999 Turf 0-4: (10f 4) (gd 2, g-f, frm)
Light-framed, Pattern-class colt, effective 8 to 10f, best at 10f, acts on gd to frm, best on gd, likes tight tracks. Turf high 105 - 3rd of 8 giving 13lb to Ormelie (27 Jly Goodwood 10f frm RF 3165). Consistent. Threatened to land a good handicap, but a promising reappearance at Epsom behind Monsajem was followed by a disappointing performance in the Hong Kong Jockey Club Trophy at Sandown, when Gary Stevens did not cover himself in glory. The colt put in a better effort when a close-up third at Glorious Goodwood handicap but made no show on his final start at York. Sold for 125,000gns to go to Saudi Arabia.
**Sir Michael Stoute [2-12] Saeed Suhail.*

BRAVE VISION BHB 41f40a **RR 46f 40a** 5156[7]
3 b g Clantime 6.6f **(57)** - Kinlet Vision (IRE) (Vision (USA)) 9f **(64)**
Form - 43048057
Record 1999 - 1st:0 2nd:0 3rd:1 Ran:8
Pre1999 - 1st:0 2nd:0 3rd:0 Ran:3
Win Prizemoney £0 *Total Prizemoney* £380
1999 Turf 0-8: (8f, 10f 5, 11f, 12f) (hvy, sft, g-s, gd 2, g-f, frm 2)
Workmanlike, moderate gelding, effective 10f, acts on sft, has worn blinkers, likes tight tracks. Turf high 57 - 3rd of 12 getting 12lb from Rada's Daughter (27 Apr Bath 10f sft RF 0864). Consistent. **J R Arnold [0-11] J K Gale.*

BRAVO TWO ZERO (IRE) RR 593[8]
2 b f Desert Style (IRE) - Nozet (Nishapour (FR)) 9.1f **(61)**
Form - 8
Record 1999 - 1st:0 2nd:0 3rd:0 Ran:1
1999 Turf 0-1: (5f) (gd)
Very poor filly. (DEAD) **M L W Bell [0-1] The Fitzrovians.*

BRAZILIAN MOOD (IRE) RR 71f 5193[2]
3 b c Doyoun 10.7f **(69)** - Sea Mistress (Habitat) 9.4f **(70)**
Form - 02
Record 1999 - 1st:0 2nd:1 3rd:0 Ran:2
Win Prizemoney £0 *Total Prizemoney* £768
1999 Turf 0-2: (8f 2) (gd 2)
Lengthy, currently above-average colt. Turf high 71 (began Oct).
**C E Brittain [0-2] C E Brittain.*

BREAD WINNER BHB 56f **RR 58f** 4586[5]
3 b c Reprimand 8.2f **(63)** - Khubza (Green Desert (USA)) 8.6f **(78)**
Form - 432573224405
Record 1999 - 1st:0 2nd:3 3rd:2 Ran:12
Pre1999 - 1st:0 2nd:0 3rd:0 Ran:2
Win Prizemoney £0 *Total Prizemoney* £3,498
1999 Turf 0-12: (6f 2, 7f 5, 8f 2, 9f, 10f, 13f) (sft, gd 2, g-f 4, frm 5)
Fair colt, has worn blinkers. Turf high 61. Consistent.
**I A Balding [0-14] Anthony Hogarth.*

BREAKIN EVEN BHB 37f42a **RR 24f 42a** 3004[11]
4 ch g Chilibang 7f **(55)** -Bee Dee Dancer (Ballacashtal (CAN)) 5.3f **(50)**
Form - 010000000
Record 1999 - 1st:1 2nd:0 3rd:0 Ran:8
Pre1999 - 1st:1 2nd:0 3rd:0 Ran:10
Win Prizemoney £5,768 *Total Prizemoney* £5,768
Wins * **1999** *Mar Southw (STD) H 6f 38 43*
* 1998 May Haydoc (GD) H 6f 51 56 <
1999 Turf 0-6: (6f 3, 7f 3) (gd, g-f, frm 3, hrd) 1999 AW 1-2: (6f 1-1, 7f) (Fibr 1-2)
Workmanlike, moderate gelding, effective 6f, acts on gd, mostly wears blinkers (effectively). Turf high 27. AW high 43 (1st run).
**J L Eyre [2-18] Mrs Frank Campbell.*

BREAK THE CODE (USA) BHB 81f **RR 82f** 4686[6]
2 b c Red Ransom (USA) 8.6f **(83)** - Kissogram Girl (USA) (Danzig (USA)) 8.4f **(76)**
Form - 721856
Record 1999 - 1st:1 2nd:1 3rd:0 Ran:6
Win Prizemoney £3,434 *Total Prizemoney* £5,664
Wins * **1999** Aug Hamilt (G-F) 6f 78 <
1999 Turf 1-6: (5f, 6f 1-3, 7f, 8f) (g-s, gd, g-f, frm 1-2, hrd)
Decent colt, effective 6f, acts on frm, has worn blinkers. Turf high 82 - also 1st of 6 giving 1lb to Sabre Lady (24 Aug Hamilton RF 3865). Got off the mark in a six-furlong maiden at Hamilton on his third start, but had a very hard race in the process and has not run anything like up to that form since.
**M Johnston [1-6] Maktoum Al Maktoum.*

BREAK THE GLASS (USA) RR 57f 3969[4]
2 b br c Dynaformer (USA) 12f **(82)** - Greek Wedding (USA) (Blushing Groom (FR)) 10.3f **(76)**
Form - 44
Record 1999 - 1st:0 2nd:0 3rd:0 Ran:2
Win Prizemoney £0 *Total Prizemoney* £530
1999 Turf 0-2: (7f, 8f) (g-f, frm)
Currently fair colt. Turf high 57 (began Jly).
**E A L Dunlop [0-2] Maktoum Al Maktoum.*

BREAK THE RULES BHB 66f59a **RR 53?f 59a** 4032[8]
7 b g Dominion 8.9f **(65)** - Surf Bird (Shareef Dancer (USA)) 9.9f **(73)**
Form - 8
Record 1999 - 1st:0 2nd:0 3rd:0 Ran:1
Pre1999 - 1st:8 2nd:5 3rd:6 Ran:45
Win Prizemoney £46,538 *Total Prizemoney* £57,166
Wins 1998 May Cheste (GD) H 10.3f 66 71+
1997 Jun Cheste (SFT) C 10.3f 70
1997 May Cheste (SFT) H 10.3f 79 83 <
1997 Mar Doncas (G-F) H 10.3f 73 82
1996 Oct Doncas (GD) C 10.3f 79
1996 Jly Cheste (G-F) 12.3f 68+
1995 Aug Redcar (G-F) H 8f 71 75
1999 Turf 0-1: (11f) (gd)
Average gelding, effective 10f, acts on g-s to g-f, has worn blinkers, prefers left handed tracks, favours tight tracks.
**A G Juckes [0-1] Nick Shutts (from D Nicholls [1-22] Jun 1998).*

BREAKWATER (USA) RR 80f 5136[7]
2 b f Boundary (USA) - Flippers (USA) (Coastal (USA)) 11.5f **(72)**
Form - 47
Record 1999 - 1st:0 2nd:0 3rd:0 Ran:2
Win Prizemoney £0 *Total Prizemoney* £221
1999 Turf 0-2: (7f 2) (gd, g-f)
Currently decent filly. Turf high 80 (began Oct) - 7th of 16 to Premier Prize (30 Oct Newmarket 7f gd RF 5136).
**L M Cumani [0-2] Flippers Partnership.*

BREATHLESS DREAMS (IRE) RR 75f 2271[1]
2 ch c College Chapel - Foston Bridge (Relkino) 8.9f **(65)**
Form - 21
Record 1999 - 1st:1 2nd:1 3rd:0 Ran:2
Win Prizemoney £2,495 *Total Prizemoney* £3,363
Wins * 1999 Jun Salisb (FRM) 7f 75 <
1999 Turf 1-2: (6f, 7f 1-1) (gd, frm 1-1)
Currently above-average colt. Turf high 75 - 1st of 16 from Clonmany (24 Jun Salisbury RF 2271).
**M L W Bell [1-2] Cable Media Consultancy Ltd.*

BRECONGILL LAD BHB 74f **RR 74f** 4755[3]
7 b g Clantime 6.6f **(57)** - Chikala (Pitskelly) 8.5f **(53)**
Form - 6060601112133
Record 1999 - 1st:4 2nd:1 3rd:2 Ran:13
Pre1999 - 1st:3 2nd:6 3rd:9 Ran:48
Win Prizemoney £42,023 *Total Prizemoney* £61,608
Wins * 1999 Spt Goodwo (G-F) H 6f 68 74
*** 1999** Aug Yarmou (GD) H 5.2f 62 65+
*** 1999** Aug Pontef (GD) H 5f 56 59+
*** 1999** Aug Catter (FRM) H 5f 50 53+
1996 Aug Beverl (GD) H 5f 65 67
1995 Aug Thirsk (G-F) H 5f 74 78 <
1995 Jun Newmar (GD) H 6f 65 69
1999 Turf 4-13: (5f 3-9, 6f 1-4) (gd 1-3, g-f 1-3, frm 2-7)
Above-average gelding, effective 5 to 6f, best at 5f, acts on gd to frm, has worn blinkers. Turf high 74 - 1st of 15 getting 16lb from Easy Dollar (11 Spt Goodwood RF 4272) - also 1st of 8 getting 6lb from Brutal Fantasy (29 Aug Yarmouth RF 4004). Yet another performer to be sprinkled with the Dandy Nicholls magic dust, he was on a very modest handicap mark from which to take advantage once his new trainer had found the key to him.
**D Nicholls [4-7] P Davidson-Brown (from M D Hammond [0-16] Jun 1999).*

BREEDS HILL BHB 39f **RR 36f** 4398[13]
3 b f Chaddleworth (IRE) -Breed Reference(Reference Point) 6.8f **(70)**
Form - 00700
Record 1999 - 1st:0 2nd:0 3rd:0 Ran:5
Pre1999 - 1st:0 2nd:0 3rd:0 Ran:3
1999 Turf 0-5: (6f 2, 7f 3) (g-f, frm 4)
Light-framed, very moderate filly. Turf high 43. Inconsistent.
**C F Wall [0-8] The Boadicea Partners.*

BREEZED WELL BHB 36f29a **RR 36f 29a** 3389[7]
13 b g Wolverlife 8.8f **(67)** - Precious Baby (African Sky) 7.9f **(63)**
Form - 80050377
Record 1999 - 1st:0 2nd:0 3rd:1 Ran:8
Pre1999 - 1st:2 2nd:3 3rd:11 Ran:98
Win Prizemoney £5,580 *Total Prizemoney* £23,131
Wins 1997 Jly Beverl (HVY) H 9.9f 43 51 <
1999 Turf 0-6: (7f 2, 8f, 10f 2, 11f) (gd 2, frm 4) 1999 AW 0-2: (6f, 8f) (Fibr 2)
Very moderate gelding. Turf high 36. AW high 30.
**B R Cambidge [1-50] Mrs H Noonan (from K G Wingrove [1-16] Aug 1998).*

BREEZY LOUISE BHB 60f63a **RR 69+f 63a** 3911[9]
2 b f Dilum (USA) 7.1f **(56)** - Louise Moillon (Mansingh (USA)) 7.4f **(55)**
Form - 044U16250
Record 1999 - 1st:1 2nd:1 3rd:0 Ran:9
Win Prizemoney £1,968 *Total Prizemoney* £4,246
Wins * 1999 Jun Windso (G-F) S 5f 69+ <
1999 Turf 1-7: (5f 1-6, 7f) (gd, g-f 2, frm 1-3, hrd) 1999 AW 0-2: (6f 2) (Fibr 2)
Average filly, effective 5f, acts on frm. Turf high 69 - 1st of 11 getting 5lb from Risky Gem (14 Jun Windsor RF 1989). AW high 53 (began Jly). **R J Hodges [1-9] R J Hodges.*

BREEZY MELODY BHB 25f33a **RR 3f 33a** 3295[22]
3 b f Sizzling Melody 6.3f **(49)** - Breezy Day (Day Is Done) 6.3f **(67)**
Form - 0006000
Record 1999 - 1st:0 2nd:0 3rd:0 Ran:6
Pre1999 - 1st:0 2nd:0 3rd:0 Ran:1
1999 Turf 0-3: (5f, 6f, 7f) (g-s, gd, frm) 1999 AW 0-3: (6f 3) (Fibr 3)
Scopey, very moderate filly. Turf high 3. AW high 22.
**J G Given [0-3] G D Kendrick (from B A McMahon [0-4] Feb 1999).*

BREEZY TIME BHB 60f **RR 54f** 2687[3]
3 ch c Timeless Times (USA) 6.1f **(56)** - Miss Merlin (Manacle) 7.8f **(56)**
Form - 003
Record 1999 - 1st:0 2nd:0 3rd:1 Ran:3
Win Prizemoney £0 *Total Prizemoney* £368
1999 Turf 0-2: (5f, 6f) (gd, frm) 1999 AW 0-1: (6f) (Fibr)
Workmanlike, currently average colt. Turf high 54.
**V Soane [0-3] Force Ten.*

BREMRIDGE (IRE) BHB 77f **RR 79f** 4820[2]
2 ch g Ridgewood Ben - Eimkar (Junius (USA)) 7.7f **(65)**
Form - 05882
Record 1999 - 1st:0 2nd:1 3rd:0 Ran:5
Win Prizemoney £0 *Total Prizemoney* £856
1999 Turf 0-5: (6f 2, 7f, 8f 2) (gd, g-f 3, frm)
Above-average gelding. Turf high 79 - 2nd of 16 giving 8lb to Polar Red (11 Oct Windsor 8f g-f RF 4820).
**A G Foster [0-1] Anglia Bloodstock Syndicate 1998 (from P W Chapple-Hyam [0-4] Aug 1999).*

BRENDA DEE (IRE) BHB 60f52a **RR 61f 52a** 4149[4]
3 br f Perugino (USA) - Children's Hour (Mummy's Pet) 7.7f **(60)**
Form - 33743004
Record 1999 - 1st:0 2nd:0 3rd:3 Ran:8
Pre1999 - 1st:0 2nd:2 3rd:0 Ran:5
Win Prizemoney £0 *Total Prizemoney* £4,397
1999 Turf 0-3: (8f 3) (gd, g-f, frm) 1999 AW 0-5: (8f 2, 10f, 11f 2) (Equi 2, Fibr 3)
Leggy, average filly, effective 6 to 8f, acts on gd to frm. Turf high 61. AW high 58. **A P Jarvis [0-13] Mrs Ann Jarvis.*

BRENNER'S PARK (IRE) BHB 48f62a **RR 60f 62a** 4575[11]
2 b g Night Shift (USA) 8.1f **(73)** - Brentwood (IRE) **(53f)** (Waajib)
Form - 6530870
Record 1999 - 1st:0 2nd:0 3rd:1 Ran:7
Win Prizemoney £0 *Total Prizemoney* £422
1999 Turf 0-6: (5f, 7f 3, 8f 2) (gd 2, g-f 2, frm, hrd) 1999 AW 0-1: (7f) (Fibr)
Above-average gelding, has worn blinkers. Turf high 60.
**M Johnston [0-7] P D Savill.*

BRETECHE (FR) RR 604[3]
4 b f Fijar Tango (FR) - Foinery (Reference Point) 6.8f **(70)**
Form - 3
Record 1999 - 1st:0 2nd:0 3rd:1 Ran:1
Win Prizemoney £0 *Total Prizemoney* £251
1999 AW 0-1: (12f) (Fibr)
Very moderate filly. **M C Pipe [1-11] Gerry Scanlon & Miss J Kirk.*

BREVITY BHB 61f **RR 62f** 4984[10]
4 b c Tenby 10.4f **(76)** - Rive (USA) (Riverman (USA)) 9.1f **(76)**
Form - 70000541225760
Record 1999 - 1st:1 2nd:2 3rd:0 Ran:14
Pre1999 - 1st:0 2nd:1 3rd:0 Ran:2
Win Prizemoney £3,727 *Total Prizemoney* £7,137
Wins * 1999 Aug Newbur (GD) H 6f 49 57 <
1999 Turf 1-11: (5f, 6f 1-4, 7f, 8f 2, 10f 2, 12f) (sft, gd, g-f 1-6, frm 3)
1999 AW 0-3: (6f 2, 7f) (Fibr 3)
Scopey, average colt, effective 6 to 10f, best at 6f, acts on g-s to frm. Turf high 62 - 2nd of 18 getting 5lb from Kilmeena Lad (27 Aug Newmarket 6f frm RF 3938). AW high 57 (began Jly).
**D Sasse [1-14] Christopher Ranson (from J H M Gosden [0-2] Jun 1998).*

BREW BHB 60f **RR 57f** 4493[12]
3 b c Primo Dominie 7.2f **(67)** - Boozy (Absalom) 7.2f **(58)**
Form - 200760
Record 1999 - 1st:0 2nd:1 3rd:0 Ran:6
Pre1999 - 1st:0 2nd:1 3rd:0 Ran:3
Win Prizemoney £0 *Total Prizemoney* £1,902
1999 Turf 0-6: (5f 4, 6f 2) (sft, g-f 5)
Workmanlike, fair colt, effective 5f, acts on g-f. Turf high 76 (1st run) - 2nd of 7 giving 18lb to Gochinos (12 May Brighton 5f g-f RF 1177). Inconsistent. **R Hannon [0-9] Mrs Robert Heathcote.*

BREYDON BHB 28f44a **RR 31f 44a** 4166[12]
6 ch g Be My Guest (USA) 10.2f **(66)** - Palmella (USA) (Grundy) 10.3f

(65)
Form - 6866500
Record 1999 - 1st:0 2nd:0 3rd:0 Ran:7
Pre1999 - 1st:1 2nd:4 3rd:6 Ran:25
Win Prizemoney £2,346 *Total Prizemoney* £7,459
Wins * 1998 May Hamilt (SFT) SH 12.1f 26 32 <
1999 Turf 0-7: (11f 5, 12f, 16f) (g-s, g-f 3, frm 3)
Moderate gelding, effective 11 to 12f, acts on gd to g-f. Turf high 40.
**P Monteith [4-35] The Dregs Of Humanity (from M H Tompkins [0-8] Aug 1996).*

BRIAN'S BLUE (IRE) BHB 30f RR 5f 1124[13]
4 ch c Statoblest 6.4f **(63)** - Lamya (Hittite Glory) 8.7f **(50)**
Form - 000
Record 1999 - 1st:0 2nd:0 3rd:0 Ran:3
Pre1999 - 1st:0 2nd:0 3rd:0 Ran:2
1999 Turf 0-2: (6f 2) (gd 2) 1999 AW 0-1: (6f) (Fibr)
Light-framed, poor colt. Turf high 5.
**B P J Baugh [0-3] D E Simpson (from P Eccles [0-2] Feb 1998).*

BRIDAL WHITE BHB 43f57a RR 31f 57a 5162[17]
3 b f Robellino (USA) 9.5f **(68)** - Alwatar (USA) (Caerleon (USA)) 8.6f **(71)**
Form - 05000000
Record 1999 - 1st:0 2nd:0 3rd:0 Ran:8
Pre1999 - 1st:0 2nd:0 3rd:2 Ran:5
Win Prizemoney £0 *Total Prizemoney* £1,265
1999 Turf 0-6: (6f, 7f 2, 8f 2, 10f) (gd 2, g-f 2, frm 2) 1999 AW 0-2: (7f, 8f) (Fibr 2)
Workmanlike, very moderate filly, effective 6f, acts on g-f to frm. Turf high 63. AW high 20.
**M J Ryan [0-8] Peter Scott (from K G Wingrove [0-5] Spt 1998).*

BRIDE'S ANSWER BHB 40f RR 26f 5075[11]
4 ch f Anshan 8.2f **(63)** - Ivory Bride (Domynsky) 8f **(82)**
Form - 800000
Record 1999 - 1st:0 2nd:0 3rd:0 Ran:6
Pre1999 - 1st:1 2nd:0 3rd:3 Ran:5
Win Prizemoney £3,793 *Total Prizemoney* £6,510
Wins 1998 May Kempto (GD) 8f 80 <
1999 Turf 0-6: (8f, 10f 4, 12f) (gd 3, g-f 2, frm)
Little account filly, effective 8f, acts on gd to g-f, has worn blinkers. Turf high 38 (began Jly).
**C Grant [0-8] Mrs Jean Keegan (from M R Channon [1-5] Oct 1998).*

BRIDGEND BLUE (IRE) BHB 43f50a RR 38f 50a 2755[9]
3 b g Up and At 'em - Sperrin Mist (Camden Town) 9.3f **(53)**
Form - 6000380
Record 1999 - 1st:0 2nd:0 3rd:1 Ran:5
Pre1999 - 1st:0 2nd:0 3rd:0 Ran:6
Win Prizemoney £0 *Total Prizemoney* £262
1999 Turf 0-5: (5f, 6f, 7f 2, 10f) (g-f, frm 4)
Light-framed, fair gelding, has worn blinkers. Turf high 38.
**M L W Bell [0-11] Ceredig, Dalton, Daw Mercer.*

BRIDGE POOL BHB 50f RR 52f 5103[17]
3 ch f First Trump - Treble Hook (IRE) (Ballad Rock) 7.8f **(63)**
Form - 2221383700
Record 1999 - 1st:1 2nd:3 3rd:2 Ran:10
Pre1999 - 1st:0 2nd:0 3rd:1 Ran:4
Win Prizemoney £2,280 *Total Prizemoney* £6,682
Wins * **1999** Jly Leices (G-F) 5f 48+ <
1999 Turf 1-10: (5f 1-4, 6f 4, 7f 2) (g-s, gd 4, g-f, frm 1-4)
Fair filly, effective 5 to 6f, acts on frm, has worn blinkers. Turf high 76 - 2nd of 8 getting 5lb from Trinity (29 May Doncaster 5f frm RF 1561). Got off the mark in a maiden at Leicester over five furlongs in July on fast ground, but has shown very little in tougher company since.
**Dr J D Scargill [1-7] A C Edwards (from J Noseda [0-3] Jun 1999).*

BRIDIE'S PRIDE BHB 68f45a RR 69df 45a 2000[29]
8 b g Alleging (USA) 8.8f **(57)** - Miss Monte Carlo (Reform) 8.9f **(62)**
Form - 3200
Record 1999 - 1st:0 2nd:1 3rd:1 Ran:4
Pre1999 - 1st:2 2nd:4 3rd:2 Ran:22
Win Prizemoney £8,575 *Total Prizemoney* £19,337
Wins * 1998 Jun Ascot (G-S) H 16.2f 50 57 <
* 1997 Jly Chepst (G-S) H 18f 46 50
1999 Turf 0-4: (16f 2, 18f, 20f) (g-s, gd, g-f 2)
Average gelding, effective 16f, acts on g-s to g-f, prefers right handed tracks. Turf high 69 - 2nd of 10 getting 2lb from Wave of Optimism (23 Apr Sandown 16f g-s RF 0823). This doughty stayer finished lame at Royal Ascot. **G A Ham [2-33] K C White.*

BRIEF CALL (IRE) BHB 54f RR 54f 5144[5]
2 ch f Case Law 6f **(64)** - Collected (IRE) (Taufan (USA)) 7f **(57)**
Form - 300557035
Record 1999 - 1st:0 2nd:0 3rd:2 Ran:9
Win Prizemoney £0 *Total Prizemoney* £598
1999 Turf 0-7: (5f 5, 6f 2) (g-f 3, frm 3, hrd) 1999 AW 0-2:(5f, 6f) (Fibr 2)
Fair filly, has worn blinkers. Turf high 57. AW high 54 (began Oct). Consistent. **B Palling [0-9] The Lanebrook Partners.*

BRIEF ENCOUNTA (FR) BHB 50f RR 46f 3934a[1]
3 ch g Brief Truce (USA) 9.1f **(73)** -Villa Blanca(SPA)(Rheffissimo (FR))
Form - 8401
Record 1999 - 1st:1 2nd:0 3rd:0 Ran:4
Pre1999 - 1st:1 2nd:0 3rd:0 Ran:5
Win Prizemoney £15,616 *Total Prizemoney* £20,262
Wins * **1999** Aug Deauvi (HVY) C 10f 46
* 1998 Jun Chanti (SFT) 6f 80? <
1999 Turf 1-4: (7f, 8f, 9f, 10f 1-1) (gd 1-1, g-f, frm 2)
Workmanlike, moderate gelding, effective 6f, acts on sft, has worn blinkers. Turf high 46. Inconsistent.
**B J Meehan [2-9] Abbott Racing Ltd.*

BRIERY MEC BHB 43f RR 41f 5154[3]
4 b g Ron's Victory (USA) 9.2f **(52)** - Briery Fille (Sayyaf)
Form - 777233
Record 1999 - 1st:0 2nd:1 3rd:2 Ran:6
Pre1999 - 1st:0 2nd:0 3rd:0 Ran:5
Win Prizemoney £0 *Total Prizemoney* £2,167
1999 Turf 0-6: (8f, 10f 4, 11f) (gd 3, g-f 2, frm)
Unfurnished, moderate gelding, effective 10 to 11f, best at 10f, acts on gd to g-f, best on gd. Turf high 41 - 3rd of 17 getting 28lb from Scene (1 Nov Nottingham 10f gd RF 5154). Consistent.
**H J Collingridge [0-11] N H Gardner.*

BRIGHSTONE BHB 38f RR 36df 4454[20]
6 ch h Cadeaux Genereux 7.9f **(76)** - High Fountain (High Line) 10.3f **(70)**
Form - 00
Record 1999 - 1st:0 2nd:0 3rd:0 Ran:2
Pre1999 - 1st:6 2nd:3 3rd:0 Ran:20
Win Prizemoney £21,369 *Total Prizemoney* £23,138
Wins 1997 Oct Nottin (SFT) C 8.2f 60
1997 Spt York (SFT) C 8.9f 52+
1997 Aug Windso (G-F) S 11.6f 60
1997 Jun Bath (G-F) C 10.2f 72
1995 Nov Doncas (G-F) 8f 99+ <
1995 Oct Yarmou (FRM) 7f 72+
1999 Turf 0-2: (10f, 11f) (sft, frm)
Very moderate horse, effective 10 to 11f, acts on gd to g-f, prefers left handed tracks, favours tight tracks. Turf high 9 (began Spt). Becoming disappointing.
**Mrs A L M King [0-2] Mrs Ann Leonard (from M C Pipe [5-20] Aug 1998).*

BRIGHT BLADE RR 43f 5198[14]
3 b c Sure Blade (USA) 10.6f **(66)** - Gay Gem (Sparkler) 8.4f **(55)**
Form - 00
Record 1999 - 1st:0 2nd:0 3rd:0 Ran:2
1999 Turf 0-2: (8f 2) (gd 2)
Unfurnished, currently moderate colt. Turf high 38 (began Oct).
**P Mitchell [0-2] Mrs Sara Sorby.*

BRIGHTER (USA) BHB 65f RR 68f 4126[10]
3 ch f Gone West (USA) 7.8f **(82)** - Top Trestle (USA) (Nijinsky (CAN)) 10.3f **(77)**
Form - 750
Record 1999 - 1st:0 2nd:0 3rd:0 Ran:3
Pre1999 - 1st:0 2nd:0 3rd:0 Ran:1
Win Prizemoney £0 *Total Prizemoney* £291

1999 Turf 0-3: (10f, 12f 2) (gd, g-f, frm)
Leggy, average filly, has worn blinkers. Turf high 68 (began Aug).
**H R A Cecil [0-4] H R H Prince Fahd Salman.*

BRIGHTEST STAR BHB 73f RR 74f 2961[3]

3 b f Unfuwain (USA) 11.4f **(74)** - Shirley Superstar (Shirley Heights) 10.3f **(74)**
Form - 323
Record 1999 - 1st:0 2nd:1 3rd:2 Ran:3
Win Prizemoney £0 *Total Prizemoney* £1,966
1999 Turf 0-3: (10f, 11f, 12f) (gd, g-f, frm)
Currently above-average filly. Turf high 74 (1st run) - 3rd of 13 to Arabis (5 Jun Newmarket 10f gd RF 1775).
**H R A Cecil [0-3] Helena Springfield Ltd.*

BRIGHT HOPE (IRE) BHB 83f RR 82+f 4353[1]

3 b f Danehill (USA) 9.1f **(79)** - Crystal Cross (USA) **(73f)** (Roberto (USA)) 10f **(76)**
Form - 31
Record 1999 - 1st:1 2nd:0 3rd:1 Ran:2
Pre1999 - 1st:0 2nd:0 3rd:0 Ran:1
Win Prizemoney £3,875 *Total Prizemoney* £4,553
Wins * **1999** Spt Pontef (G-F) 10f 82+ <
1999 Turf 1-2: (10f 1-2) (frm 1-2)
Tall, currently decent filly. Turf high 82 - 1st of 11 from Zariliya (16 Spt Pontefract RF 4353). **P W Harris [1-3] Mrs P W Harris.*

BRIGHT QUESTION RR 77f 4385[7]

2 ch c Nashwan (USA) 10.3f **(79)** - Ozone Friendly (USA) (Green Forest (USA)) 9.9f **(68)**
Form - 57
Record 1999 - 1st:0 2nd:0 3rd:0 Ran:2
1999 Turf 0-2: (7f, 8f) (g-f, frm)
Currently above-average colt. Turf high 77 (began Aug).
**B W Hills [0-2] Maktoum Al Maktoum.*

BRIG O'TURK RR 75f 5063[8]

2 ch c Inchinor 8.9f **(64)** - Sharmood (USA) (Sharpen Up) 8.3f **(67)**
Form - 8
Record 1999 - 1st:0 2nd:0 3rd:0 Ran:1
1999 Turf 0-1: (8f) (gd)
Currently above-average colt. **Mrs A J Perrett [0-1] Mrs G Harwood.*

BRILLIANCE DAWNS RR 856[8]

2 ch f Chilibang 7f **(55)** - Mrs Dawson (Sharrood (USA)) 10.5f **(72)**
Form - 08
Record 1999 - 1st:0 2nd:0 3rd:0 Ran:2
1999 Turf 0-1: (5f) (gd) 1999 AW 0-1: (5f) (Fibr)
Currently very poor filly. **D Nicholls [0-2] The Higham Partnership.*

BRILLIANT RED BHB 102f97a RR 107f 97a 5141[2]

6 b g Royal Academy (USA) 7.8f **(77)** - Red Comes Up (USA) (Blushing Groom (FR)) 10.3f **(76)**
Form - 821137072
Record 1999 - 1st:2 2nd:2 3rd:1 Ran:9
Pre1999 - 1st:5 2nd:3 3rd:6 Ran:27
Win Prizemoney £97,532 *Total Prizemoney* £130,953

Wins								
* **1999**	Jly	Sandow	(G-F)	H	8.1f	97	99	<
* **1999**	Jun	Ascot	(G-F)	H	10f	95	98	
1998	Spt	Newbur	(GD)	H	10f	92	95	
1998	*Feb*	*Lingfi*	*(SLW)*	*H*	*10f*	*85*	*92*	
1998	*Feb*	*Lingfi*	*(SLW)*	*H*	*10f*	*78*	*81*	
1997	Jly	Lingfi	(G-F)		7.6f		83	
1995	Aug	Kempto	(G-F)		7f		90+	

1999 Turf 2-9: (8f 1-5, 10f 1-4) (gd 5, g-f 1-1, frm 1-3)
Pattern-class gelding, effective 8 to 10f, best at 8f, acts on gd to frm, best on frm, prefers left handed tracks, and excels at Newbury. Turf high 107 - 2nd of 19 giving 18lb to Tayseer (30 Oct Newmarket 8f gd RF 5141) - also 1st of 10 getting 3lb from Lonesome Dude (3 Jly Sandown RF 2543). Consistent. He did well for his new connections and is a hard horse to pass once in command. Best when ridden enterprisingly, he is effective from a mile to ten furlongs and handles any ground.
**Mrs L Richards [2-9] Mrs M J George (from P R Hedger [4-21] Oct 1998).*

BRIMSTONE (IRE) BHB 68f RR 53f 5212[20]

4 ch g Ballad Rock 7.2f **(63)** -Blazing Glory (IRE) (Glow (USA)) 6.7f **(71)**
Form - 00
Record 1999 - 1st:0 2nd:0 3rd:0 Ran:2
Pre1999 - 1st:1 2nd:2 3rd:0 Ran:7
Win Prizemoney £3,485 *Total Prizemoney* £6,276
Wins 1997 Jly Sandow (G-F) 5f 78 <
1999 Turf 0-2: (5f 2) (g-s, g-f)
Well made, fair gelding. Turf high 18 (began Oct). Becoming disappointing.
**H J Collingridge [0-2] Miss Linsey Knocker (from R McGhin [0-3] Jly 1998).*

BRING SWEETS BHB 92f RR 91f 1292[16]

3 b g Sabrehill (USA) 8.5f **(64)** - Che Gambe (USA) (Lyphard (USA)) 9.9f **(72)**
Form - 2330
Record 1999 - 1st:0 2nd:0 3rd:2 Ran:3
Pre1999 - 1st:2 2nd:1 3rd:0 Ran:5
Win Prizemoney £8,217 *Total Prizemoney* £14,950
Wins * 1998 Nov Doncas (SFT) 8f 87 <
* 1998 Oct Redcar (HVY) 8f 79
1999 Turf 0-3: (9f 2, 10f) (sft, gd, g-f)
Scopey, useful gelding, effective 8 to 10f, best at 8f, acts on hvy to gd, has worn blinkers. Turf high 91 - 3rd of 5 giving 2lb to Deal Fair (27 Apr Bath 10f sft RF 0859). **B W Hills [2-8] W J Gredley.*

BRISBANE ROAD (IRE) RR 47f 5062[8]

2 b c Blues Traveller (IRE) - Eva Fay (IRE) (Fayruz)
Form - 08
Record 1999 - 1st:0 2nd:0 3rd:0 Ran:2
1999 Turf 0-2: (8f 2) (gd 2)
Currently moderate colt. Turf high 47 (began Oct).
**I A Balding [0-2] Lord Lloyd-Webber.*

BRISTOL BEAUFORT RR 29f 5157[15]

2 b g Forzando 7.2f **(63)** - Fairey Firefly **(48f 50a)** (Hallgate)
Form - 0
Record 1999 - 1st:0 2nd:0 3rd:0 Ran:1
1999 Turf 0-1: (7f) (frm)
Currently little account gelding.
**Miss J A Camacho [0-1] B P Skirton.*

BRITANNIA (USA) RR 95?f 4565[2]

2 b f Sea Hero (USA) - Brave And True (USA) (Fappiano (USA)) 8.7f **(77)**
Form - 3322
Record 1999 - 1st:0 2nd:2 3rd:2 Ran:4
Win Prizemoney £0 *Total Prizemoney* £44,794
1999 Turf 0-4: (7f, 8f 3) (sft, gd 2, frm)
Very useful filly. Turf high 95 (began Jly) - 2nd of 6 to Teggiano (26 Spt Ascot 8f sft RF 4565). She looked unlucky when touched off in a maiden at Sandown and was only beaten narrowly in the Group One Fillies' Mile at Ascot on her final start. Forcing tactics suited her well there and, granted a similarly direct approach, she should develop into a smart middle-distance performer.
**I A Balding [0-4] Mrs Paul Mellon.*

BROADSTAIRS BEAUTY (IRE) BHB 80f82a RR 67f 82a 614[22]

9 ch g Dominion Royale 7.8f **(63)** - Holy Water (Monseigneur (USA)) 7.7f **(63)**
Form - 00
Record 1999 - 1st:0 2nd:0 3rd:0 Ran:2
Pre1999 - 1st:12 2nd:13 3rd:7 Ran:69
Win Prizemoney £54,089 *Total Prizemoney* £73,327

Wins								
* 1998	Jun	Doncas	(GD)	H	5f	84	87	<
* 1998	Jun	Windso	(GD)		5f		77	
* 1998	Jun	Thirsk	(GD)	H	5f	68	71	
* 1998	*Jan*	*Southw*	*(STD)*	*H*	*6f*	*74*	*76*	
1995	*Nov*	*Southw*	*(STD)*	*H*	*5f*	*75*	*77*	
1995	Jly	Newmar	(G-F)	H	5f	75	75	
1995	May	Ripon	(GD)	H	5f	70	71	

1999 Turf 0-2: (6f 2) (g-s, g-f)
Above-average gelding, effective 5f, acts on g-f, often wears blinkers. Turf high 55.
**D Shaw [4-33] Mrs Judy Hunt (from P Howling [0-2] Jly 1996).*

BROADWAY LEGEND (IRE) RR 73f 4920[11]
2 b f Caerleon (USA) 10.9f **(79)** - Tetradonna (IRE) (Teenoso (USA)) 9.9f **(72)**
Form - 30
Record 1999 - 1st:0 2nd:0 3rd:1 Ran:2
Win Prizemoney £0 *Total Prizemoney* £450
1999 Turf 0-2: (7f 2) (g-s, gd)
Currently above-average filly. Turf high 73 (began Spt). A 100,000 guineas half-sister to Alberich.
**J W Hills [0-2] Freddy Bienstock,Mar Hills.*

BROCATELLE RR 62f 3829[7]
3 b f Green Desert (USA) 7.8f **(78)** - Brocade (Habitat) 9.4f **(70)**
Form - 37
Record 1999 - 1st:0 2nd:0 3rd:1 Ran:2
Win Prizemoney £0 *Total Prizemoney* £636
1999 Turf 0-2: (7f, 8f) (frm 2)
Well made, currently average filly. Turf high 62 (1st run) (began Jly) - 3rd of 10 getting 5lb from Halberd (17 Jly Newmarket 7f frm RF 2912). **L M Cumani [0-2] Gerald Leigh.*

BROCTUNE GOLD BHB 42f56a **RR 41f 56a** 3479[7]
8 b g Superpower 6.6f **(58)** - Golden Sunlight (Ile de Bourbon (USA)) 10.1f **(67)**
Form - 008767
Record 1999 - 1st:0 2nd:0 3rd:0 Ran:6
Pre1999 - 1st:12 2nd:10 3rd:6 Ran:62
Win Prizemoney £32,883 *Total Prizemoney* £47,964

Wins								
* 1998	Aug	Catter	(GD)	H	7f	58	59	
* 1998	Jun	Mussel	(SFT)	H	8f	54	57	
* 1997	Jly	Mussel	(GD)	C	7.1f		62	
* 1997	Jun	Mussel	(GD)	C	7.1f		56+	
* 1996	Aug	Beverl	(GD)	C	8.5f		64	
* 1996	Jly	Mussel	(G-F)	H	8.1f	60	68	
* 1996	Jun	Mussel	(FRM)	C	7.1f		61	
* 1996	May	Thirsk	(G-F)	S	7f		55	
* 1995	May	Redcar	(FRM)	C	6f		60+	
* 1995	May	Newcas	(GD)	C	7f		58	

1999 Turf 0-6: (7f 3, 8f 3) (gd 2, g-f 2, frm 2)
Moderate gelding, effective 7 to 8f, best at 8f, acts on gd, favours tight tracks. Turf high 41.
**Mrs M Reveley [12-67] Mrs M B Thwaites (from B W Hills [0-1] Aug 1997).*

BROCTUNE LINE BHB 36f50a **RR 38f 50a** 1280[5]
5 ch g Safawan 6.6f **(60)** - Ra Ra (Lord Gayle (USA)) 8.8f **(62)**
Form - 033705
Record 1999 - 1st:0 2nd:0 3rd:2 Ran:6
Pre1999 - 1st:2 2nd:2 3rd:1 Ran:20
Win Prizemoney £5,208 *Total Prizemoney* £7,861

Wins								
* 1997	*Apr*	*Southw*	*(STD)*	*H*	*11f*	*55*	*58*	<
* 1997	*Jan*	*Southw*	*(STD)*	*H*	*8f*	*45*	*46*	

1999 Turf 0-1: (9f) (g-f) 1999 AW 0-5: (8f 3, 11f 2) (Fibr 5)
Moderate gelding, effective 11f, - acts on Fibr, has worn blinkers, likes left handed tracks, likes tight tracks. AW high 57 - 3rd of 16 to Pickens (5 Feb Southwell 11f Fibr RF 0232).
**Mrs M Reveley [2-33] Gerry Slater, Allen Evans & John Snaith.*

BRODESSA BHB 56f54a **RR 53f 54a** 3976[2]
13 gr g Scallywag 15.1f **(43)** - Jeanne du Barry (Dubassoff (USA)) 14.2f **(55)**
Form - 112112
Record 1999 - 1st:4 2nd:2 3rd:0 Ran:6
Pre1999 - 1st:16 2nd:15 3rd:7 Ran:60
Win Prizemoney £50,839 *Total Prizemoney* £66,805

Wins								
* **1999**	Aug	Redcar	(FRM)	C	14.1f		43	
* **1999**	Jly	Mussel	(G-S)	C	16f		53	
* **1999**	Jun	Catter	(GD)	C	13.8f		54	
* **1999**	May	Catter	(G-F)	S	13.8f		56	
* 1998	Spt	Mussel	(GD)	H	16f	55	58	
* 1998	Aug	Redcar	(G-F)	S	14.1f		56	
* 1998	Aug	Beverl	(G-F)	SH	16.2f	48	55	
* 1998	Jly	Catter	(FRM)	C	12f		49	
* 1998	Jly	Mussel	(GD)	C	16f		38	
* 1997	*Nov*	*Wolver*	*(STD)*	*C*	*14.8f*		*47*	
* 1997	Jun	Nottin	(SFT)	C	16f		48	
* 1996	Aug	Beverl	(FRM)	SH	16.2f	57	58	
* 1996	Jun	Nottin	(G-F)	C	16f		57	
* 1995	Aug	Redcar	(G-F)	S	14.1f		53+	
* 1995	Aug	Beverl	(G-F)	SH	16.2f	57	61	
* 1995	Jun	Redcar	(FRM)	C	14.1f		50+	
* 1995	Jun	Redcar	(G-F)	C	16f		51+	

1999 Turf 4-6: (14f 3-4, 16f 1-2) (g-f, frm 4-5)
Fair gelding, effective 12 to 16f, best at 14f, acts on gd to frm, best on frm, favours tight tracks, and does well at Musselburgh. Turf high 56 (1st run) - 1st of 10 from Oversman (21 May Catterick RF 1374) - also 1st of 7 getting 14lb from Hullbank (4 Jun Catterick RF 1721). Consistent. This popular old veteran just keeps on mopping up northern claimers like a sponge.
**Mrs M Reveley [23-73] The Mary Reveley Racing Club.*

BROKENBOROUGH RR 62f 2635[8]
2 ch c Beveled (USA) 6.9f **(64)** - Swilly Express (Ballacashtal (CAN)) 5.3f **(50)**
Form - 8068
Record 1999 - 1st:0 2nd:0 3rd:0 Ran:4
1999 Turf 0-4: (5f, 6f, 7f 2) (gd, g-f, frm 2)
Average colt. Turf high 62. **M Blanshard [0-4] Brig Parker Bowles.*

BROKE ROAD (IRE) BHB 48f48a **RR 42f 48a** 4724[4]
3 b g Deploy 11.4f **(67)** - Shamaka **(57df 41a)** (Kris) 9.5f **(73)**
Form - 8042034333614
Record 1999 - 1st:1 2nd:1 3rd:4 Ran:12
Pre1999 - 1st:0 2nd:0 3rd:0 Ran:1
Win Prizemoney £2,944 *Total Prizemoney* £5,923

Wins								
* **1999**	Spt	Hamilt	(SFT)	H	8.3f	40	42+	<

1999 Turf 1-9: (7f, 8f 1-2, 9f, 10f 4, 12f) (g-s, gd 1-2, g-f 3, frm 3) 1999 AW 0-3: (7f 2, 8f) (Fibr 3)
Unfurnished, moderate gelding, effective 7 to 12f, best at 8f, acts on gd to frm - acts on Fibr, has worn blinkers (extremely effectively), likes right handed tracks, likes Beverley. Turf high 42 - 3rd of 18 getting 16lb from Swing Bar (28 Aug Beverley 10f frm RF 3954) - also 1st of 16 getting 9lb from Shontaine (27 Spt Hamilton RF 4593). AW high 43 - 2nd of 16 getting 5lb from Border Glen (4 Jun Southwell 8f Fibr RF 1745). Consistent. Has joined Val Ward.
**T D Barron [1-13] Harrowgate Bloodstock Ltd.*

BROMPTON BARRAGE BHB 76f **RR 71f** 4452[12]
2 b c Rudimentary (USA) 8.2f **(66)** -Song of Hope(Chief Singer)8.9f **(66)**
Form - 0640
Record 1999 - 1st:0 2nd:0 3rd:0 Ran:4
Win Prizemoney £0 *Total Prizemoney* £281
1999 Turf 0-4: (6f 2, 7f, 8f) (sft, g-s, gd, frm)
Above-average colt. Turf high 71.
**R Hannon [0-4] Thurloe Thoroughbreds.*

BRON HILDA (IRE) BHB 50f **RR 50f** 4995[9]
2 b f Namaqualand (USA) - Maura's Guest (IRE) (Be My Guest (USA)) 9.3f **(67)**
Form - 3234400
Record 1999 - 1st:0 2nd:1 3rd:2 Ran:7
Win Prizemoney £0 *Total Prizemoney* £1,582
1999 Turf 0-7: (5f 2, 6f 2, 7f 3) (gd, g-f 4, frm 2)
Fair filly, effective 5 to 6f, acts on g-f. Turf high 55 (1st run) - 3rd of 11 to Kigema (14 Jun Brighton 6f g-f RF 1971).
**R C Spicer [0-4] John Purcell (from R Guest [0-3] Jly 1999).*

BRONZE LASS RR 14f 3541[9]
2 b f Formidable (USA) 7.8f **(60)** - Bronzess (Magic Mirror)
Form - 40
Record 1999 - 1st:0 2nd:0 3rd:0 Ran:2
Win Prizemoney £0 *Total Prizemoney* £246
1999 Turf 0-2: (5f 2) (g-f, frm)
Currently poor filly. Turf high 14 (began Jly).
**W T Kemp [0-2] W T Kemp.*

BRONZINO BHB 54f **RR 51f** 5154[13]
4 ch g Midyan (USA) 9.9f **(64)** - Indubitable (Sharpo) 7.7f **(59)**
Form - 530701400
Record 1999 - 1st:1 2nd:0 3rd:1 Ran:9
Pre1999 - 1st:0 2nd:0 3rd:2 Ran:11
Win Prizemoney £3,127 *Total Prizemoney* £4,638

Wins								
* **1999**	Aug	Salisb	(G-S)	H	9.9f	52	56	<

1999 Turf 1-9: (10f 1-6, 11f, 12f 2) (sft, g-s, gd 1-5, frm 2)
Light-framed, fair gelding, effective 10 to 11f, best at 10f, acts on

gd, has worn blinkers, prefers tight tracks. Turf high 60 - 3rd of 19 to Statajack (27 Apr Windsor 10f gd RF 0877) - also 1st of 13 giving 2lb to Wings Awarded (11 Aug Salisbury RF 3555). Consistent.
**G B Balding [1-21] Miss B Swire.*

BROOKFURLONG RR 11f 4291[7]

3 br f Rock City 8.8f **(62)** - Call of the Night (IRE) **(68f)** (Night Shift (USA)) 7.2f **(69)**

Form - 87

Record **1999** - 1st:0 2nd:0 3rd:0 Ran:2

1999 Turf 0-2: (5f, 6f) (gd, g-f)

Workmanlike, currently poor filly. Turf high 11 (began Aug).
**J R Fanshawe [0-2] Raymond Tooth.*

BROOKHOUSE LADY (IRE) BHB 40f46a RR 34f 46a 5050[11]

4 b f Polish Patriot (USA) 7.8f **(70)** - Honagh Lee (Main Reef) 9.6f **(57)**

Form - 0000

Record **1999** - 1st:0 2nd:0 3rd:0 Ran:4
Pre1999 - 1st:1 2nd:1 3rd:0 Ran:17

Win Prizemoney £3,095 *Total Prizemoney* £4,520

Wins * 1998 Spt Leices (G-S) H 10f 50 56 <

1999 Turf 0-4: (8f 2, 10f 2) (g-s, gd 3)

Light-framed, very moderate filly, effective 8 to 11f, best at 11f, acts on sft to frm, has worn blinkers, prefers tight tracks. Turf high 34 (began Oct). Consistent.
**Ian Williams [1-13] & Mrs D J Smart (from R Hollinshead [0-8] Nov 1997).*

BROOKSEES DREAM BHB 22f RR 2841[13]

5 ch m Glacial Storm (USA) - Good Holidays (Good Times (ITY)) 6.6f **(54)**

Form - 0000

Record **1999** - 1st:0 2nd:0 3rd:0 Ran:4
Pre1999 - 1st:0 2nd:0 3rd:0 Ran:1

1999 Turf 0-4: (7f, 10f 3) (gd, g-f, frm 2)

Formerly very poor filly, has worn blinkers.
**B J Llewellyn [0-4] Caleb Davies (from B Palling [0-1] Dec 1997).*

BROTHER BEACON BHB 40f36a RR 54df 36a 91[8]

8 ch g High Line - Flaming Peace (Queen's Hussar) 11.6f **(58)**

Form - 8

Record **1999** - 1st:0 2nd:0 3rd:0 Ran:1
Pre1999 - 1st:0 2nd:0 3rd:0 Ran:5

1999 AW 0-1: (16f) (Equi)

Fair gelding.
**P R Chamings [0-5] Mrs J E L Wright (from H Candy [0-5] Nov 1994).*

BROTHER TOM BHB 33f RR 41f 3307[9]

2 b c Prince Sabo 6.6f **(64)** - Danseuse Davis (FR) **(46f 42a)** (Glow (USA)) 6.7f **(71)**

Form - 78740

Record **1999** - 1st:0 2nd:0 3rd:0 Ran:5

1999 Turf 0-5: (5f 4, 6f) (gd 2, g-f 2, frm)

Moderate colt. Turf high 40. **P D Evans [0-5] Mrs H Raw.*

BROUGHTON BELLE BHB 24f RR 9f 4650[15]

3 b f Chaddleworth (IRE) - Broughtons Pet (IRE) (Cyrano de Bergerac) 6f **(68)**

Form - 00

Record **1999** - 1st:0 2nd:0 3rd:0 Ran:2
Pre1999 - 1st:0 2nd:0 3rd:0 Ran:1

1999 Turf 0-2: (7f, 12f) (gd, frm)

Currently very poor filly. (began Aug) - 15th of 15 getting 15lb from Suez Tornado (30 Spt Newmarket 12f gd RF 4650).
**W J Musson [0-3] Broughton Thermal Insulation.*

BROUGHTONS ERROR BHB 66f59a RR 65f 59a 3280[1]

5 ch g Most Welcome 8.6f **(66)** - Eloquent Charm (USA) (Private Account (USA)) 8.5f **(74)**

Form - 04180121

Record **1999** - 1st:3 2nd:1 3rd:0 Ran:8
Pre1999 - 1st:1 2nd:0 3rd:0 Ran:10

Win Prizemoney £22,694 *Total Prizemoney* £25,787

Wins * **1999** Jly Newmar (G-F) H 10f 62 65
* **1999** Jly Windso (GD) H 10f 55 58
* **1999** Apr Newmar (GD) H 10f 53 56
* 1996 Oct Doncas (GD) H 7f 66 68 <

1999 Turf 3-6: (8f, 10f 3-5) (g-f, frm 3-5) 1999 AW 0-2: (8f, 10f) (Equi 2)

Average gelding, effective 10f, acts on frm. Turf high 65 - 1st of 8 giving 4lb to Bowcliffe (31 Jly Newmarket RF 3280) - also 1st of 20 giving 8lb to Dizzy Tilly (5 Jly Windsor RF 2567). AW high 47.
**W J Musson [4-18] M W Goodey.*

BROUGHTON SIREN BHB 25f28a RR 33f 28a 1582[7]

4 b f Most Welcome 8.6f **(66)** - Royal Form(Formidable (USA)) 9.2f **(63)**

Form - 03037

Record **1999** - 1st:0 2nd:0 3rd:2 Ran:5
Pre1999 - 1st:0 2nd:0 3rd:0 Ran:3

Win Prizemoney £0 *Total Prizemoney* £635

1999 Turf 0-1: (12f) (g-f) 1999 AW 0-4: (8f, 11f 2, 16f) (Equi, Fibr 3)

Strong, very moderate filly, effective 11f, - acts on Fibr. AW high 33 - 3rd of 11 getting 9lb from Golden Lyric (10 Mar Southwell 11f Fibr RF 0422). Inconsistent.
**W J Musson [0-8] Broughton Thermal Insulation.*

BROUGHTONS LURE (IRE) BHB 43f38a RR 34f 38a 5133[8]

5 ch m Archway (IRE) 8.5f **(60)** - Vaal Salmon (IRE) (Salmon Leap (USA)) 11f **(61)**

Form - 008

Record **1999** - 1st:0 2nd:0 3rd:0 Ran:3
Pre1999 - 1st:0 2nd:2 3rd:0 Ran:10

Win Prizemoney £0 *Total Prizemoney* £2,922

1999 Turf 0-3: (10f, 12f 2) (gd 2, g-f)

Moderate filly, effective 11 to 13f, acts on g-f to frm, best on frm. Turf high 34 (began Spt). **W J Musson [0-13] Broughton Bloodstock.*

BROUGHTONS MILL BHB 39f44a RR 41f 44a 4983[3]

4 ch g Ron's Victory (USA) 9.2f **(52)** - Sandra's Desire (Grey Desire) 8.7f **(50)**

Form - 5003

Record **1999** - 1st:0 2nd:0 3rd:1 Ran:4
Pre1999 - 1st:0 2nd:0 3rd:0 Ran:1

Win Prizemoney £0 *Total Prizemoney* £330

1999 Turf 0-2: (10f 2) (g-s, gd) 1999 AW 0-2: (7f 2) (Equi, Fibr)

Leggy, moderate gelding. Turf high 41 (began Spt). AW high 40.
**W J Musson [0-5] Windmill Racing.*

BROUGHTONS TURMOIL BHB 57f68a RR 47f 68a 3659[14]

10 b g Petorius 8f **(66)** - Rustic Stile (Rusticaro (FR)) 8.2f **(65)**

Form - 001450680

Record **1999** - 1st:1 2nd:0 3rd:0 Ran:9
Pre1999 - 1st:7 2nd:7 3rd:8 Ran:56

Win Prizemoney £29,528 *Total Prizemoney* £53,891

Wins * **1999** May Windso (GD) C 6f 69
* 1998 *Jun Southw (STD) H 8f 67 72*
* 1997 Apr Ascot (G-F) H 8f 70 77 <
1996 Aug Kempto (GD) H 7f 66 70
1995 Aug Sandow (G-F) H 7.1f 60 66
1995 Jly Newmar (G-F) H 7f 52 63
1995 *Feb Lingfi (STD) SH 8f 55 54*
1995 *Jan Southw (STD) H 8f 49 62*

1999 Turf 1-9: (5f, 6f 1-4, 7f 3, 8f) (gd 1-2, g-f 2, frm 5)

Above-average gelding, effective 6 to 8f, acts on gd to frm - acts on Fibr, best on g-f, excels at Goodwood. Turf high 69 - 1st of 20 giving 12lb to Ambitious (17 May Windsor RF 1285).
**B R Millman [3-31] R Marlow (from W J Musson [5-34] Mar 1997).*

BROWNING BHB 57f64a RR 61f 64a 2548[13]

4 b g Warrshan (USA) 9.7f **(59)** - Mossy Rose (King of Spain) 7.8f **(52)**

Form - 4002200

Record **1999** - 1st:0 2nd:2 3rd:0 Ran:6
Pre1999 - 1st:1 2nd:3 3rd:0 Ran:12

Win Prizemoney £3,013 *Total Prizemoney* £8,394

Wins 1998 Aug Windso (G-F) H 11.6f 54 60 <

1999 Turf 0-6: (11f, 12f 4, 14f) (gd, g-f, frm 4)

Scopey, average gelding, effective 8 to 12f, acts on frm to hrd - acts on AW, favours tight tracks, excels at Lingfield. Turf high 61 - 2nd of 11 getting 8lb from Prince Alex (22 May Kempton 12f frm RF 1397).
**D J Coakley [0-6] Stanley Sharp (from Lord Huntingdon [1-12] Dec 1998).*

BROWNS DELIGHT BHB 63f RR 62f 4786[2]

2 b f Runnett 6.7f **(56)** - Fearless Princess (Tyrnavos) 10.1f **(55)**

Form - 7072
Record 1999 - 1st:0 2nd:1 3rd:0 Ran:4
Win Prizemoney £0 *Total Prizemoney* £1,160
1999 Turf 0-3: (6f 3) (gd, g-f, frm) 1999 AW 0-1: (6f) (Equi)
Average filly. Turf high 62 (began Jly). (1st run) - 2nd of 14 giving 5lb to Illusive (8 Oct Lingfield 6f Equi RF 4786).
**S Dow [0-4] Cecil Brown.*

BROWN'S FLIGHT BHB 48f52a RR 43f 52a 4002[9]

3 b f Jupiter Island 10.4f **(57)** - Fearless Princess (Tyrnavos) 10.1f **(55)**
Form - 0506670740
Record 1999 - 1st:0 2nd:0 3rd:0 Ran:10
Pre1999 - 1st:0 2nd:1 3rd:1 Ran:6
Win Prizemoney £0 *Total Prizemoney* £1,792
1999 Turf 0-9: (6f 2, 7f 2, 9f, 10f 4) (gd 4, g-f, frm 4) 1999 AW 0-1: (12f) (Equi)
Light-framed, moderate filly, effective 6 to 7f, best at 6f, acts on gd to g-f, best on gd, has worn blinkers, likes left handed tracks. Turf high 59. Inconsistent. **S Dow [0-16] Cecil Brown.*

BRUFF STREAM (IRE) BHB 52a RR 52a 271[6]

5 b g Accordion 11.3f **(75)** - Littlepace (Indian King (USA)) 7.4f **(64)**
Form - 3306
Record 1999 - 1st:0 2nd:0 3rd:2 Ran:4
Win Prizemoney £0 *Total Prizemoney* £834
1999 AW 0-4: (8f 2, 10f, 12f) (Equi 2, Fibr 2)
Fair gelding. AW high 57 - 3rd of 9 to Magical Shot (20 Jan Wolverhampton 8f Fibr RF 0127). **M Johnston [0-4] John Keaney.*

BRUMON (IRE) BHB 40f RR 45?f 4717[15]

8 b g Sadler's Wells (USA) 11.3f **(87)** - Loveliest (USA) (Tibaldo)
Form - 0
Record 1999 - 1st:0 2nd:0 3rd:0 Ran:1
Pre1999 - 1st:2 2nd:0 3rd:1 Ran:17
Win Prizemoney £6,766 *Total Prizemoney* £7,752
Wins 1995 Aug Warwic (FRM) H 16.1f 56 66
1999 Turf 0-1: (17f) (gd)
Moderate gelding, often wears blinkers. Consistent.
**M Mullineaux [0-4] P T Hollins (from D Moffatt [1-5] Apr 1997).*

BRUTAL FANTASY (IRE) BHB 66f68a RR 70f 68a 4755[19]

5 b g Distinctly North (USA) 7.4f **(63)** - Flash Donna (USA) (Well Decorated (USA)) 7.6f **(64)**
Form - 0271075001626000
Record 1999 - 1st:2 2nd:2 3rd:0 Ran:16
Pre1999 - 1st:5 2nd:3 3rd:2 Ran:29
Win Prizemoney £27,208 *Total Prizemoney* £36,601

Wins	* **1999**	Aug Ascot	(SFT)	H	5f	65	67	
	1999	May Lingfi	(G-F)	H	5f	68	70	
	1997	Apr Catter	(GD)	H	5f	78	83	<
	1997	Mar Doncas	(G-F)	H	5f	72	78	
	1997	*Feb Wolver*	*(STD)*	*H*	*5f*	*72*	*72*	
	1997	*Jan Southw*	*(STD)*	*H*	*6f*	*65*	*74*	
	1996	May Mussel	(G-S)	S	5f		65+	

1999 Turf 2-16: (5f 2-15, 6f) (sft, g-s, gd 2-4, g-f 6, frm 4)
Above-average gelding, effective 5f, acts on gd, has worn blinkers. Turf high 70 - 2nd of 8 giving 6lb to Brecongill Lad (29 Aug Yarmouth 5f gd RF 4004) - also 1st of 18 from That Man Again (29 May Lingfield RF 1581).
**P Howling [1-9] C Hammond (from P G Murphy [1-7] Jun 1999).*

BRYNKIR BHB 39f49a RR 45f 49a 3835[3]

5 b g Batshoof 9.5f **(66)** - Felinwen (White Mill) 16.2f **(66)**
Form - 73
Record 1999 - 1st:0 2nd:0 3rd:1 Ran:2
Pre1999 - 1st:1 2nd:0 3rd:0 Ran:14
Win Prizemoney £2,085 *Total Prizemoney* £2,642
Wins *1998 Feb Wolver (STD) H 16.2f 44 53* <
1999 Turf 0-2: (12f, 17f) (frm 2)
Fair gelding, effective 16 to 17f, acts on frm - acts on Fibr. Turf high 45 (began Jly) - 3rd of 13 getting 17lb from Monte Calvo (22 Aug Bath 17f frm RF 3835).
**B J Llewellyn [0-3] Miss Emily Jane Jones (from D J G MurraySmith [1-14] Oct 1998).*

BRYONY BRIND (IRE) BHB 98f RR 98f 5132[5]

4 ch f Kris 10f **(75)** - Bayadere (USA) (Green Dancer (USA)) 10.3f **(74)**
Form - 538235
Record 1999 - 1st:0 2nd:1 3rd:2 Ran:6
Pre1999 - 1st:3 2nd:1 3rd:1 Ran:8
Win Prizemoney £25,318 *Total Prizemoney* £36,168

Wins	* 1998	Aug Deauvi	(GD)	L	12.5f		105	<
	* 1998	Jly Haydoc	(G-F)	H	11.9f	86	87	
	* 1998	May Nottin	(G-F)		8.2f		76	

1999 Turf 0-6: (12f 2, 13f, 14f 2, 16f) (gd 2, g-f 2, frm 2)
Workmanlike, very useful filly, effective 12 to 14f, best at 13f, acts on gd to frm, likes tight tracks, likes Newmarket. Turf high 100 (1st run) - 5th of 7 getting 6lb from Sadian (6 May Chester 13f g-f RF 1050). Consistent. She is genuine, but lacks the turn of foot required to win Group races.
**J R Fanshawe [3-14] Mrs Denis Haynes.*

BUCENTAURE BHB 25f RR 23f 4983[19]

4 ch f Ron's Victory (USA) 9.2f **(52)** - Gecko Rouge (Rousillon (USA)) 8.2f **(74)**
Form - 70000
Record 1999 - 1st:0 2nd:0 3rd:0 Ran:5
Pre1999 - 1st:0 2nd:0 3rd:0 Ran:2
1999 Turf 0-5: (8f, 9f, 10f 2, 11f) (gd 2, g-f 2, frm)
Unfurnished, little account filly. Turf high 23.
**Martyn Wane [0-7] J A Kavanagh.*

BUCKLE (IRE) BHB 72f RR 75f 2006[12]

3 b f Common Grounds 8.1f **(66)** - Maratona (Be My Guest (USA)) 9.3f **(67)**
Form - 10
Record 1999 - 1st:1 2nd:0 3rd:0 Ran:2
Pre1999 - 1st:0 2nd:0 3rd:1 Ran:2
Win Prizemoney £3,858 *Total Prizemoney* £4,479
Wins * 1999 Jun Goodwo (G-S) 8f 75 <
1999 Turf 1-2: (8f 1-2) (gd 1-1, frm)
Lengthy, above-average filly. Turf high 75 (1st run) - 1st of 5 getting 5lb from Mustafhel (4 Jun Goodwood RF 1737).
**W Jarvis [1-4] Anthony Foster.*

BUCKMINSTER (USA) RR 67f 5207[4]

2 br c Silver Hawk (USA) 11.2f **(85)** -Buckarina(USA) (Buckaroo (USA))
Form - 4
Record 1999 - 1st:0 2nd:0 3rd:0 Ran:1
Win Prizemoney £0 *Total Prizemoney* £233
1999 Turf 0-1: (7f) (g-s)
Currently average colt. **J H M Gosden [0-1] Sheikh Mohammed.*

BUCK'S BOY (USA) RR 129f 5230a[3]

6 b g Bucksplasher (USA) - Molly's Colleen (USA) (Verbatim (USA)) 8.5f **(64)**
Form - 3
1999 Turf 0-1: (12f) (frm)
Top-class gelding. (1st run) - 3rd of 14 to Daylami (6 Nov Gulfstream Park 12f frm RF 5230a). All-the-way winner of the Breeders' Cup Turf in 1998, he put up a fine performance in finishing third in the same race in 1999. **N Hickey in USA [1-4].*

BUCKSTONES ROAD (IRE) BHB 39f45a RR 29f 45a 3547[13]

2 ch c Shalford (IRE) 7.8f **(63)** - Grave Error (Northern Treat (USA)) 6f **(50)**
Form - 7350
Record 1999 - 1st:0 2nd:0 3rd:1 Ran:4
Win Prizemoney £0 *Total Prizemoney* £253
1999 Turf 0-2: (5f, 6f) (gd, g-f) 1999 AW 0-2: (5f, 6f) (Fibr 2)
Moderate colt. Turf high 29. AW high 42 (began Jly).
**N Tinkler [0-4] Clayton Bigley Partnership Ltd.*

BUDELLI (IRE) RR 71f 5194[5]

2 b c Elbio 9f **(62)** - Eves Temptation (IRE) (Glenstal (USA)) 10.1f **(64)**
Form - 5
Record 1999 - 1st:0 2nd:0 3rd:0 Ran:1
1999 Turf 0-1: (6f) (gd)
Currently above-average colt. **M R Channon [0-1] Mrs C Roper.*

BUDROYALE (USA) RR 5231a[2]

6 b g Cee's Tizzy (USA) - Cee's Song (USA) (Seattle Slew (USA)) 9.4f **(76)**
Form - 2

1999 AW 0-1: (10f) (Dirt)
Currently top-class gelding. (1st run) - 2nd of 14 giving 4lb to Cat Thief (6 Nov Gulfstream Park 10f Dirt RF 5231a). He was a tremendously game second in the Breeders' Cup Classic.
**T West in USA [0-1].*

BUGGY RIDE (IRE) BHB 67f **RR 73f** 4820[14]
2 b c Blues Traveller (IRE) - Tambora (Darshaan) 9.9f **(84)**
Form - 03580
Record 1999 - 1st:0 2nd:0 3rd:1 Ran:5
Win Prizemoney £0 *Total Prizemoney* £469
1999 Turf 0-5: (6f, 7f 3, 8f) (gd, g-f 2, frm 2)
Above-average colt, has worn blinkers. Turf high 73 (began Jly).
**R Charlton [0-5] Michael Pescod.*

BULAWAYO RR 34f 5209[14]
2 b c Prince Sabo 6.6f **(64)** - Ra Ra Girl (Shack (USA)) 5.8f **(53)**
Form - 0
Record 1999 - 1st:0 2nd:0 3rd:0 Ran:1
1999 Turf 0-1: (6f) (g-s)
Currently moderate colt. **B A McMahon [0-1] D J Allen.*

BULLET BHB 73f64a **RR 73f 64a** 4081[8]
4 b g Alhijaz 7.7f **(57)** - Beacon (High Top) 10.2f **(67)**
Form - 245612128
Record 1999 - 1st:2 2nd:3 3rd:0 Ran:9
Pre1999 - 1st:0 2nd:1 3rd:2 Ran:3
Win Prizemoney £5,387 *Total Prizemoney* £11,978
Wins * 1999 Jly Carlis (FRM) 12f 72 <
1999 Jun Beverl (G-F) C 12f 65
1999 Turf 2-8: (11f, 12f 2-5, 14f 2) (hvy, g-f 1-1, frm 1-6) 1999 AW 0-1: (15f) (Fibr)
Tall, above-average gelding, effective 10 to 12f, acts on hvy to frm, likes right handed tracks, favours tight tracks. Turf high 73 - 2nd of 5 getting 10lb from Glenmead (4 Aug Pontefract 12f frm RF 3374) - also 1st of 3 giving 10lb to L S Lowry (16 Jly Carlisle RF 2866).
**Martin Todhunter [1-4] Mrs Rita Butler & Mrs Gabrielle McNeela (from W J Haggas [1-8] Jun 1999).*

BULLETIN BHB 74f **RR 76+f** 4651[13]
2 b f Prince Sabo 6.6f **(64)** - Storm Warning (Tumble Wind (USA)) 7.5f **(57)**
Form - 3100
Record 1999 - 1st:1 2nd:0 3rd:1 Ran:4
Win Prizemoney £2,438 *Total Prizemoney* £2,900
Wins * 1999 Aug Bright (G-F) 6f 76+ <
1999 Turf 1-4: (5f 2, 6f 1-2) (gd 3, frm 1-1)
Above-average filly. Turf high 76 (began Aug) - 1st of 8 from Inventive (23 Aug Brighton RF 3850). Showed a bit of ability on soft ground at Thirsk on her debut, and went on to score quite comfortably on much faster ground at Brighton next time, although was disappointing subsequently.
**M L W Bell [1-4] Cheveley Park Stud.*

BUMBLE BE BHB 32f **RR 14f** 2115[12]
4 b g Precocious 7.2f **(54)** - Lingering (Kind of Hush) 10.1f **(62)**
Form - 00
Record 1999 - 1st:0 2nd:0 3rd:0 Ran:2
Pre1999 - 1st:0 2nd:0 3rd:0 Ran:4
1999 Turf 0-2: (5f, 6f) (gd, g-f)
Strong, poor gelding. Turf high 14. **S Dow [0-6] J A Redmond.*

BUN ALLEY BHB 73f **RR 68f** 4905[6]
3 b g Be My Guest (USA) 10.2f **(66)** - Neptunalia **(66f)** (Slip Anchor) 9.8f **(73)**
Form - 3202446
Record 1999 - 1st:0 2nd:2 3rd:1 Ran:7
Pre1999 - 1st:0 2nd:0 3rd:0 Ran:2
Win Prizemoney £0 *Total Prizemoney* £4,492
1999 Turf 0-7: (6f, 7f 5, 8f) (g-s, gd, g-f, frm 3, hrd)
Workmanlike, average gelding, effective 7f, acts on frm to hrd, best on frm. Turf high 78 - 2nd of 6 getting 7lb from Tayif (21 Jly Sandown 7f frm RF 3017). Consistent.
**J A R Toller [0-9] Lady Sophia Morrison.*

BUNDY BHB 56f67a **RR 49f 67a** 3922[11]
3 b g Ezzoud (IRE) - Sanctuary Cove (Habitat) 9.4f **(70)**
Form - 8343644700
Record 1999 - 1st:0 2nd:0 3rd:2 Ran:9
Pre1999 - 1st:2 2nd:0 3rd:2 Ran:11
Win Prizemoney £5,483 *Total Prizemoney* £8,030
Wins * 1998 Aug Warwic (G-F) H 6f 69 71 <
1998 Jly Newcas (G-F) S 6f 68
1999 Turf 0-9: (6f 5, 7f 3, 8f) (sft 2, gd, g-f 2, frm 4)
Light-framed, moderate gelding, effective 5 to 6f, best at 6f, acts on sft to frm, best on frm, has worn blinkers. Turf high 69 (1st run) - 3rd of 18 giving 4lb to Lively Lady (29 Mar Nottingham 6f sft RF 0508). Consistent.
**M Dods [1-14] A J Henderson (from M R Channon [1-6] Jly 1998).*

BUNNIES OWN BHB 38f36a **RR 35f 36a** 2890[13]
4 b f Flockton's Own 7f **(42)** - Walsham Witch (Music Maestro) 7.7f **(66)**
Form - 6063375328600
Record 1999 - 1st:0 2nd:1 3rd:3 Ran:10
Pre1999 - 1st:1 2nd:1 3rd:1 Ran:15
Win Prizemoney £1,738 *Total Prizemoney* £4,259
Wins * 1998 *Feb Southw (STD) S 7f 54* <
1999 Turf 0-5: (8f 2, 10f 3) (gd 2, g-f, frm 2) 1999 AW 0-5: (8f 2, 11f 2, 12f) (Fibr 5)
Unfurnished, very moderate filly, effective 7 to 8f, best at 7f, - acts on Fibr, favours left handed tracks, favours tight tracks. Turf high 43. AW high 41. Becoming disappointing.
**J L Harris [1-25] J Starbuck.*

BUNTY BHB 48f38a **RR 50f 38a** 5151[1]
3 b f Presidium 7.5f **(56)** - Shirlstar Investor (Some Hand) 9f **(50)**
Form - 87706702416001
Record 1999 - 1st:2 2nd:1 3rd:0 Ran:14
Pre1999 - 1st:0 2nd:0 3rd:1 Ran:10
Win Prizemoney £6,795 *Total Prizemoney* £8,275
Wins * 1999 Nov Nottin (SFT) H 8.2f 46 50 <
*** 1999** Jly Epsom (G-F) H 8.5f 42 47
1999 Turf 2-11: (6f 2, 7f, 8f 1-6, 9f 1-1, 10f) (gd 1-5, g-f, frm 1-5) 1999 AW 0-3: (7f 3) (Equi, Fibr 2)
Small, fair filly, effective 5 to 8f, best at 5f, acts on gd to hrd, likes left handed tracks, likes tight tracks, excels at Epsom. Turf high 50. AW high 34.
**C A Dwyer [2-21] John Purcell (from Mrs S Lamyman [0-3] Feb 1999).*

BUONA SERA BHB 64f77a **RR 66f 77a** 4179[11]
3 b c Marju (IRE) 9.2f **(76)** - Blueberry Walk (Green Desert (USA)) 8.6f **(78)**
Form - 21504000
Record 1999 - 1st:0 2nd:0 3rd:0 Ran:5
Pre1999 - 1st:1 2nd:1 3rd:1 Ran:6
Win Prizemoney £2,938 *Total Prizemoney* £4,548
Wins * 1998 *Nov Lingfi (STD) H 7f 73 74* <
1999 Turf 0-5: (6f, 7f 4) (g-f 3, frm 2)
Leggy, above-average colt, effective 6 to 7f, best at 7f, acts on g-f - acts on Equi. Turf high 66.
**W R Muir [1-11] Fayzad Thoroughbred Ltd.*

BURCOT GIRL (IRE) BHB 30f **RR 24f** 5163[12]
2 b f Petardia 8.2f **(58)** - Phoenix Forli (USA) (Forli (ARG)) 9.6f **(67)**
Form - 000
Record 1999 - 1st:0 2nd:0 3rd:0 Ran:3
1999 Turf 0-3: (6f, 7f, 8f) (g-s, gd 2)
Currently little account filly. Turf high 24 (began Spt).
**J L Spearing [0-3] Colin Ross.*

BURDEN OF PROOF (IRE) RR 116f 4472a[8]
7 b h Fairy King (USA) 7.7f **(75)** - Belle Passe (Be My Guest (USA)) 9.3f **(67)**
Form - 168
1999 Turf 1-3: (7f, 8f 1-2) (g-s, gd 1-1, g-f)
High-class horse, effective 6 to 8f, best at 8f, acts on sft to hrd, best on gd, and likes Leopardstown. Turf high 116 (1st run) - 1st of 8 giving 17lb to Access All Areas (9 May Leopardstown RF 1172a). He had a very successful 1998, winning four times in Pattern company at distances from six furlongs to a mile, but after making a winning reappearance in a Leopardstown Listed event last season, did not show much in two subsequent starts. He is especially

effective in soft ground.
**A P O'Brien in IRE [2-4] Michael Tabor (from C O'Brien in IRE [7-25] Aug 1998).*

BURES (IRE) BHB 47f55a **RR 48f 55a** 3478[16]
8 b g Bold Arrangement 8.7f **(57)** - Grid (FR) (Grundy) 10.3f **(65)**
Form - 830
Record 1999 - 1st:0 2nd:0 3rd:1 Ran:3
Pre1999 - 1st:1 2nd:3 3rd:2 Ran:20
Win Prizemoney £2,745 *Total Prizemoney* £7,426
1999 Turf 0-3: (14f, 16f 2) (gd, g-f, frm)
Fair gelding, often wears blinkers. Turf high 48 (began Jly) - 3rd of 12 giving 5lb to Stolen Music (3 Aug Catterick 14f frm RF 3316).
**Mrs J Brown [3-24] J H Hewitt (from M H Tompkins [3-27] Jun 1995).*

BURGUNDIAN RED (USA) BHB 80f **RR 76f** 5099[4]
2 b c Red Ransom (USA) 8.6f **(83)** - Chesa Plana (Niniski (USA)) 10.6f **(65)**
Form - 504
Record 1999 - 1st:0 2nd:0 3rd:0 Ran:3
Win Prizemoney £0 *Total Prizemoney* £210
1999 Turf 0-3: (6f, 7f 2) (gd 3)
Currently above-average colt. Turf high 76 (began Spt).
**R W Armstrong [0-3] Dr G W W Tsoi.*

BURMA BABY (USA) BHB 62f **RR 65f** 3987[6]
3 ch c Woodman (USA) 9.7f **(77)** -Rangoon Ruby**(99f)**(Sallust) 8.4f **(63)**
Form - 0251326
Record 1999 - 1st:1 2nd:2 3rd:1 Ran:7
Pre1999 - 1st:0 2nd:0 3rd:0 Ran:2
Win Prizemoney £3,288 *Total Prizemoney* £5,302
Wins * **1999** Jly Warwic (G-F) H 14.6f 61 64 <
1999 Turf 1-7: (8f, 12f 2, 15f 1-1, 16f 3) (gd, g-f 1-3, frm 3)
Scopey, average colt, effective 12 to 16f, best at 16f, acts on gd to frm, best on g-f, prefers tight tracks. Turf high 65 - 2nd of 6 giving 18lb to Rigadoon (23 Jly Nottingham 16f frm RF 3070) - also 1st of 9 giving 2lb to Reaganesque (2 Jly Warwick RF 2509).
**B W Hills [1-9] Maktoum Al Maktoum.*

BURNING (USA) BHB 53f **RR 51f** 3655[8]
7 b g Bering 9.6f **(80)** - Larnica (USA) (Alydar (USA)) 9.1f **(76)**
Form - 1521547588103278
Record 1999 - 1st:2 2nd:2 3rd:1 Ran:14
Pre1999 - 1st:3 2nd:2 3rd:2 Ran:30
Win Prizemoney £14,530 *Total Prizemoney* £22,039
Wins 1999 Jun Doncas (G-F) H 10.3f 53 55
1999 *Jan Wolver (STD) S 8.5f 51+*
1998 *Dec Wolver (STD) S 8.5f 55*
1998 Aug Bright (G-F) C 10f 63
1995 Apr Newmar (G-F) 10f 85 <
1999 Turf 1-7: (10f 1-6, 11f) (gd, g-f 1-3, frm 2, hrd) 1999 AW 1-7: (8f 1-5, 9f, 10f) (Equi, Fibr 1-6)
Fair gelding, effective 8 to 10f, best at 10f, acts on g-f to frm - acts on Fibr, best on frm, has worn blinkers, favours left handed tracks, and excels at Doncaster and Brighton. Turf high 55 - 1st of 10 giving 15lb to Seconds Away (27 Jun Doncaster RF 2348). AW high 55 (1st run) - 2nd of 8 giving 11lb to Areish (6 Jan Wolverhampton 9f Fibr RF 0041).
**C N Kellett [0-5] P Royle (from N P Littmoden [4-21] Jun 1999).*

BURNING LOVE BHB 26f **RR 20df** 4829[14]
4 b f Forzando 7.2f **(63)** - Latest Flame (IRE) (Last Tycoon) 8.5f **(62)**
Form - 0000
Record 1999 - 1st:0 2nd:0 3rd:0 Ran:4
Pre1999 - 1st:0 2nd:0 3rd:0 Ran:7
1999 Turf 0-4: (5f 2, 6f, 9f) (sft, frm, hrd 2)
Lengthy, little account filly, has worn blinkers. (began Aug).
**B W Murray [0-4] Peter Barratt-Atkin (from N Tinkler [0-4] Jun 1998).*

BURNING SUNSET **RR 75f** 4687[3]
2 ch f Caerleon (USA) 10.9f **(79)** - Lingerie (Shirley Heights) 10.3f **(74)**
Form - 63
Record 1999 - 1st:0 2nd:0 3rd:1 Ran:2
Win Prizemoney £0 *Total Prizemoney* £643
1999 Turf 0-2: (7f 2) (g-f, frm)
Currently above-average filly. Turf high 75 (began Spt) - 3rd of 16 to Lahan (2 Oct Redcar 7f g-f RF 4687). A half-sister to Shiva, she has not lived up to her home reputation.
**H R A Cecil [0-2] Niarchos Family.*

BURNING TRUTH (USA) BHB 63f63a **RR 66f 63a** 5075[4]
5 ch g Known Fact (USA) 8.3f**(72)** -Galega(Sure Blade (USA))11.3f **(67)**
Form - 033044
Record 1999 - 1st:0 2nd:0 3rd:2 Ran:6
Pre1999 - 1st:0 2nd:5 3rd:3 Ran:14
Win Prizemoney £0 *Total Prizemoney* £11,403
1999 Turf 0-5: (8f 3, 9f, 10f) (hvy, gd 2, g-f, frm) 1999 AW 0-1: (8f) (Fibr)
Average gelding, effective 8 to 10f, best at 8f, acts on gd to frm, best on frm. Turf high 66 - 3rd of 11 getting 5lb from Far Removed (28 Aug Redcar 8f frm RF 3975).
**Mrs A Swinbank [0-14] Middleham Park Racing IV (from R Charlton [0-7] Spt 1997).*

BURN PARK BHB 57f **RR 62f** 4672[16]
2 ch f Fraam - Dewberry (Bay Express) 7.1f **(60)**
Form - 1670
Record 1999 - 1st:1 2nd:0 3rd:0 Ran:4
Win Prizemoney £1,884 *Total Prizemoney* £1,973
Wins * **1999** Apr Nottin (G-S) S 5.1f 56 <
1999 Turf 1-4: (5f 1-2, 6f, 7f) (sft 1-1, g-s, frm 2)
Average filly. Turf high 62 - also 1st of 9 from Paradise Yangshuo (5 Apr Nottingham RF 0586). **B R Millman [1-4] Seasons Holidays.*

BURTONS FOLLY BHB 37f **RR 46f** 345[6]
3 b g Casteddu 7.4f **(54)** - Nelliellamay (Super Splash (USA)) 7.3f **(54)**
Form - 36356
Record 1999 - 1st:0 2nd:0 3rd:1 Ran:4
Pre1999 - 1st:0 2nd:0 3rd:1 Ran:4
Win Prizemoney £0 *Total Prizemoney* £575
1999 AW 0-4: (8f, 10f, 12f 2) (Equi 3, Fibr)
Strong, moderate gelding, has worn blinkers. AW high 47.
**R Ingram [0-8] Christopher Burton & Roger Ingram.*

BURUNDI (IRE) BHB 65f75a **RR 66f 75a** 4791[3]
5 b g Danehill (USA) 9.1f **(79)** - Sofala (Home Guard (USA)) 9.3f **(66)**
Form - 43
Record 1999 - 1st:0 2nd:0 3rd:1 Ran:2
Pre1999 - 1st:1 2nd:4 3rd:0 Ran:14
Win Prizemoney £1,998 *Total Prizemoney* £8,127
Wins * 1997 *Nov Southw (STD) S 11f 64* <
1999 Turf 0-2: (12f 2) (gd 2)
Average gelding, effective 10 to 16f, best at 14f, acts on g-s to frm, best on frm, has worn blinkers, prefers tight tracks, likes Sandown. Turf high 60 (1st run) (began Spt) - 4th of 8 getting 17lb from Minivet (24 Spt Haydock 12f gd RF 4526). Consistent.
**A W Carroll [3-14] Gary Roberts (from P W Chapple-Hyam [0-6] Jly 1997).*

BUSHWHACKER BHB 50f **RR 46f** 1604[10]
5 b g Green Desert (USA) 7.8f **(78)** - Missed Again(High Top) 10.2f **(67)**
Form - 0000
Record 1999 - 1st:0 2nd:0 3rd:0 Ran:4
Pre1999 - 1st:0 2nd:1 3rd:0 Ran:3
Win Prizemoney £0 *Total Prizemoney* £1,432
1999 Turf 0-4: (7f, 8f, 10f, 12f) (sft 2, g-f 2)
Moderate gelding, effective 7f, acts on hvy, has worn blinkers. Turf high 46. **C R Egerton [0-7] The Bushwhacker Partnership.*

BUSINESS WOMAN BHB 38f **RR 27f** 796[14]
3 b f Primo Dominie 7.2f **(67)** - Golden Cay (Habitat) 9.4f **(70)**
Form - 60
Record 1999 - 1st:0 2nd:0 3rd:0 Ran:2
Pre1999 - 1st:0 2nd:0 3rd:0 Ran:3
1999 Turf 0-1: (5f) (gd) 1999 AW 0-1: (5f) (Fibr)
Scopey, very moderate filly. **M W Easterby [0-5] Stephen Curtis.*

BUSTLING RIO (IRE) BHB 58f58a **RR 56f 58a** 4223[4]
3 b g Up and At 'em - Une Venitienne (FR) (Green Dancer (USA)) 10.3f **(74)**
Form - 043141434
Record 1999 - 1st:2 2nd:0 3rd:2 Ran:8
Pre1999 - 1st:0 2nd:0 3rd:0 Ran:3
Win Prizemoney £6,808 *Total Prizemoney* £8,353

Wins * **1999** May Pontef (GD) H 12f 55 56 <
* **1999** *Feb Southw (STD) H 11f 47 55*

1999 Turf 1-2: (12f 1-1, 14f) (gd 1-1, g-f) 1999 AW 1-6: (8f 2, 11f 1-2, 12f, 15f) (Fibr 1-6)

Average gelding, effective 11 to 15f, acts on gd - acts on Fibr, prefers left handed tracks, prefers tight tracks. Turf high 56 (1st run) - 1st of 11 getting 8lb from Affidavit (18 May Pontefract RF 1303). AW high 55 - 3rd of 8 giving 13lb to Netherhall (5 Jun Wolverhampton 15f Fibr RF 1781) - also 1st of 13 getting 9lb from Minty (19 Feb Southwell RF 0318).

**P C Haslam [2-11] Rio Stainless Engineering Ltd/R Tutton.*

BUSTOPHER JONES BHB 49f49a RR 47f 49a 3576[3]

5 b g Robellino (USA) 9.5f **(68)** - Catkin (USA) (Sir Ivor) 10.2f **(70)**

Form - 3

Record 1999 - 1st:0 2nd:0 3rd:1 Ran:1
Pre1999 - 1st:1 2nd:0 3rd:0 Ran:4

Win Prizemoney £2,463 *Total Prizemoney* £2,900

Wins * 1998 *Mar Southw (STD) H 11f 45 46* <

1999 Turf 0-1: (14f) (g-f)

Moderate gelding. (1st run) - 3rd of 12 getting 14lb from Male-Ana-Mou (12 Aug Salisbury 14f g-f RF 3576).

**C R Egerton [1-5] Chris Brasher.*

BUSY BUSY BEE BHB 68f RR 33f 3670[2]

2 gr f Batshoof 9.5f **(66)** - Rectitude (Runnymede) 9.3f **(50)**

Form - 802

Record 1999 - 1st:0 2nd:1 3rd:0 Ran:3

Win Prizemoney £0 *Total Prizemoney* £1,108

1999 Turf 0-2: (7f 2) (g-f, frm) 1999 AW 0-1: (7f) (Fibr)

Currently average filly. Turf high 33 (began Jly). (1st run) - 2nd of 9 getting 5lb from Dance In Tune (14 Aug Wolverhampton 7f Fibr RF 3670). **N P Littmoden [0-3] Nick Littmoden.*

BUSY GUNNER RR 28f 4125[14]

2 ch f Gunner B 11.2f **(45)** - Bustle'em (IRE) **(54df 40a)** (Burslem) 8.8f **(53)**

Form - 60

Record 1999 - 1st:0 2nd:0 3rd:0 Ran:2

1999 Turf 0-2: (6f, 7f) (gd, g-f)

Currently little account filly. Turf high 28 (began Aug).

**D McCain [0-2] D A Malam.*

BUSY JACQ (IRE) RR 5f 1889[14]

2 b f Petardia 8.2f **(58)** - Saga's Humour (Bustino) 10.4f **(64)**

Form - 70

Record 1999 - 1st:0 2nd:0 3rd:0 Ran:2

1999 Turf 0-1: (7f) (g-f) 1999 AW 0-1: (6f) (Fibr)

Currently very poor filly. **C N Allen [0-2] J T B Racing.*

BUSY LIZZIE (IRE) RR 55f 5020[15]

2 b f Sadler's Wells (USA) 11.3f **(87)** - Impatiente (USA) (Vaguely Noble) 10.1f **(72)**

Form - 00

Record 1999 - 1st:0 2nd:0 3rd:0 Ran:2

1999 Turf 0-2: (7f, 8f) (gd 2)

Currently fair filly. Turf high 55 (began Oct).

**J L Dunlop [0-2] Nigel Clark (Susan A Racing).*

BUTRINTO BHB 46f68a RR 39f 68a 5103[11]

5 ch g Anshan 8.2f **(63)** - Bay Bay (Bay Express) 7.1f **(60)**

Form - 251007250080000

Record 1999 - 1st:0 2nd:1 3rd:0 Ran:11
Pre1999 - 1st:3 2nd:1 3rd:1 Ran:21

Win Prizemoney £9,819 *Total Prizemoney* £12,636

Wins * 1998 *Dec Lingfi (STD) H 7f 70 70*
* 1998 May Newbur (GD) H 6f 71 74 <
1997 Aug Salisb (G-F) 6f 69

1999 Turf 0-6: (6f 4, 7f, 8f) (g-s, gd 3, g-f 2) 1999 AW 0-5: (7f 3, 8f 2) (Equi 2, Fibr 3)

Fair gelding, effective 6 to 8f, best at 6f, acts on sft to frm - acts on AW, has worn blinkers. Turf high 39. AW high 70 - 2nd of 9 getting 4lb from Sharp Scotch (8 Feb Southwell 8f Fibr RF 0251). Inconsistent.

**J Pearce [2-25] Mrs Jennifer Marsh & Bob Beard (from Major W R Hern [1-7] Spt 1997).*

BUTTERSCOTCH BHB 49f RR 53f 4347[9]

3 b g Aragon 7.7f **(58)** - Gwiffina (Welsh Saint) 7.6f **(64)**

Form - 044043360200

Record 1999 - 1st:0 2nd:1 3rd:2 Ran:12
Pre1999 - 1st:0 2nd:0 3rd:1 Ran:5

Win Prizemoney £0 *Total Prizemoney* £3,063

1999 Turf 0-12: (7f, 8f 2, 10f 6, 11f 2, 12f) (gd 3, g-f 3, frm 6)

Fair gelding, effective 7 to 10f, acts on gd to frm, likes right handed tracks, likes tight tracks. Turf high 65 - 4th of 15 getting 12lb from Nathan's Boy (22 Apr Beverley 10f gd RF 0805).

**J L Eyre [0-17] Sunpak Potatoes.*

BUXTED'S FIRST RR 38f 5195[8]

2 gr f Mystiko (USA) 7.7f **(59)** - Sea Fairy (Wollow) 8.2f **(61)**

Form - 08

Record 1999 - 1st:0 2nd:0 3rd:0 Ran:2

1999 Turf 0-2: (6f 2) (gd 2)

Currently very moderate filly. Turf high 38 (began Oct).

**G L Moore [0-2] Buxted Partnership.*

BUYERS DREAM (IRE) RR 16tf 3006[4]

9 b g Adonijah 11.2f **(56)** - Twist and Shout (Cure The Blues (USA)) 9.5f **(63)**

Form - 64

Record 1999 - 1st:0 2nd:0 3rd:0 Ran:2

Win Prizemoney £0 *Total Prizemoney* £194

1999 Turf 0-2: (10f, 14f) (g-f, frm)

Poor gelding. Turf high 16 (began Jly). **B Ellison [3-19] R Wagner.*

BUYING A DREAM (IRE) BHB 77f RR 78f 3073[4]

2 ch c Prince of Birds (USA) - Cartagena Lady (IRE) (Prince Rupert (FR))

Form - 7124

Record 1999 - 1st:1 2nd:1 3rd:0 Ran:4

Win Prizemoney £2,526 *Total Prizemoney* £4,881

Wins * **1999** Jun Thirsk (G-F) 7f 56+ <

1999 Turf 1-4: (5f, 6f, 7f 1-2) (frm 1-4)

Above-average colt. Turf high 78.

**Andrew Turnell [1-4] Mrs Claire Hollowood.*

BUY OR SELL (IRE) BHB 100f RR 92f 4268[6]

2 b c Brief Truce (USA) 9.1f **(73)** -Repetitious(Northfields (USA)) 9f **(72)**

Form - 2122116

Record 1999 - 1st:3 2nd:3 3rd:0 Ran:7

Win Prizemoney £27,077 *Total Prizemoney* £34,832

Wins * **1999** Aug York (GD) L 5f 92 <
* **1999** Aug Ripon (GD) 6f 92 <
* **1999** Jun Pontef (GD) 5f 79

1999 Turf 3-7: (5f 2-3, 6f 1-3, 7f) (gd 2-2, g-f, frm 1-4)

Useful colt, effective 5 to 6f, best at 5f, acts on gd to frm, best on gd. Turf high 92 - 6th of 14 giving 5lb to Mrs P (11 Spt Doncaster 5f frm RF 4268) - also 1st of 7 from Alfailak (18 Aug York RF 3760). Although he is bred to need much further, the minimum trip proved no problem for him when he scored at Pontefract on his debut. He has continued to run well since and regained winning form with a battling victory in a four-runner event at Ripon. Followed up with a last-gasp win in the listed Roses Stakes at York, and is a tough and likeable sort.

**T D Easterby [3-7] Sporting Index Racing Club.*

BUZZ BHB 74f RR 81f 4752[19]

4 b g Anshan 8.2f **(63)** - Ryewater Dream (Touching Wood (USA)) 8.2f **(55)**

Form - 00

Record 1999 - 1st:0 2nd:0 3rd:0 Ran:2
Pre1999 - 1st:2 2nd:3 3rd:1 Ran:17

Win Prizemoney £8,235 *Total Prizemoney* £16,103

Wins 1998 Aug Ripon (GD) H 9f 79 87 <
1997 Jun Mussel (G-S) 7.1f 77+

1999 Turf 0-2: (8f, 10f) (gd 2)

Workmanlike, decent gelding, effective 6 to 12f, best at 12f, acts on g-s to frm, and excels at Hamilton. Turf high 45 (began Spt). Inconsistent.

**J J O'Neill [0-2] Mrs Ian Bellamy (from C W Thornton [2-17] Oct 1998).*

BUZZING (IRE) BHB 54f RR 33f 909[8]

4 ch g Ballad Rock 7.2f **(63)** - Buzzing Around (Prince Bee) 12f **(46)**

Form - 08
Record 1999 - 1st:0 2nd:0 3rd:0 Ran:2
Pre1999 - 1st:0 2nd:0 3rd:0 Ran:5
Win Prizemoney £0 *Total Prizemoney* £242
1999 Turf 0-2: (5f, 6f) (g-f, frm)
Workmanlike, very moderate gelding. Turf high 33.
**R Hannon [0-7] Mrs P Jubert.*

BUZZ THE AGENT BHB 36f **RR 35f** 4448[3]

4 b g Prince Sabo 6.6f **(64)** - Chess Mistress (USA) (Run The Gantlet (USA)) 12.1f **(59)**
Form - 05648453
Record 1999 - 1st:0 2nd:0 3rd:1 Ran:8
Pre1999 - 1st:1 2nd:2 3rd:1 Ran:16
Win Prizemoney £3,036 *Total Prizemoney* £5,639
Wins * 1998 Spt Beverl (G-F) H 12f 51 56 <
1999 Turf 0-8: (10f 2, 11f, 12f 5) (g-s, frm 6, hrd)
Workmanlike, very moderate gelding, effective 8 to 12f, best at 12f, acts on g-f to frm, best on frm, often wears blinkers (very effectively), prefers right handed tracks, likes tight tracks. Turf high 40. Consistent. **M W Easterby [1-24] Alan Black & Co.*

B W LEADER **RR 60f** 872[10]

2 b c Owington - Showery **(73+f)** (Rainbow Quest (USA)) 10.4f **(75)**
Form - 0
Record 1999 - 1st:0 2nd:0 3rd:0 Ran:1
1999 Turf 0-1: (5f) (gd)
Currently average colt.
**P F I Cole [0-1] Richard Green (Fine Paintings).*

BY THE GLASS BHB 30f **RR 32f** 4719[15]

3 b g Ardkinglass 5f **(64)** - Mia Fillia (Formidable (USA)) 9.2f **(63)**
Form - 000076000600
Record 1999 - 1st:0 2nd:0 3rd:0 Ran:12
Pre1999 - 1st:1 2nd:0 3rd:1 Ran:8
Win Prizemoney £2,721 *Total Prizemoney* £3,222
Wins 1998 May Leices (GD) 5f 73 <
1999 Turf 0-12: (6f 2, 7f 4, 8f 5, 10f) (sft, gd 5, g-f, frm 5)
Average gelding, effective 5 to 7f, acts on g-f, has worn blinkers (effectively). Turf high 39. Inconsistent.
**Don Enrico Incisa [0-5] Don Enrico Incisa (from N Tinkler [0-7] Jly 1999).*

BYZANTIUM BHB 71a **RR 70f** 5004[7]

5 b g Shirley Heights 12.1f **(76)** - Dulceata (IRE) (Rousillon (USA)) 8.2f **(74)**
Form - 3112340532412357
Record 1999 - 1st:1 2nd:2 3rd:3 Ran:12
Pre1999 - 1st:3 2nd:1 3rd:1 Ran:13
Win Prizemoney £11,560 *Total Prizemoney* £18,530
Wins * **1999** Aug Windso (G-F) H 8.3f 59 63
1998 *Dec Lingfi (STD) H 10f 64 67*
1998 *Nov Lingfi (STD) H 10f 57 61*
1997 May Kempto (GD) 8f 78 <
1999 Turf 1-11: (8f 1-7, 9f, 10f 2, 11f) (g-s 2, gd, g-f 3, frm 1-5) 1999 AW 0-1: (10f) (Equi)
Above-average gelding, effective 8 to 10f, acts on g-f to frm - acts on AW, has worn blinkers, does well at Lingfield. Turf high 70 - 3rd of 24 getting 10lb from Pension Fund (1 Spt York 8f frm RF 4085) - also 1st of 17 giving 3lb to Fuegian (2 Aug Windsor RF 3302).
**M J Fetherston-Godley [1-12] R Van Gelder (from Lord Huntingdon [3-13] Dec 1998).*

CABALLE (USA) **RR 87+f** 5020[2]

2 ch f Opening Verse (USA) 11.8f **(70)** - Attirance (FR) (Crowned Prince (USA)) 10.1f **(67)**
Form - 2
Record 1999 - 1st:0 2nd:1 3rd:0 Ran:1
Win Prizemoney £0 *Total Prizemoney* £1,170
1999 Turf 0-1: (8f) (gd)
Currently useful filly. (1st run) - 2nd of 18 to Interlude (22 Oct Doncaster 8f gd RF 5020).
**S P C Woods [0-1] B Allen/R Hine/R Dawson/A Duke.*

CABALLERO **RR 104f** 4416[7]

3 b c Cadeaux Genereux 7.9f **(76)** -On Tiptoes (Shareef Dancer (USA)) 9.9f **(73)**
Form - 6830212027
Record 1999 - 1st:1 2nd:3 3rd:1 Ran:10
Pre1999 - 1st:1 2nd:1 3rd:0 Ran:6
Win Prizemoney £10,576 *Total Prizemoney* £34,361
Wins * **1999** Jly Yarmou (GD) 7f 105 <
* 1998 Aug Windso (G-F) 6f 87+
1999 Turf 1-10: (5f, 6f 2, 7f 1-7) (gd 1-7, frm 3)
Workmanlike, very useful colt, effective 7f, acts on gd to frm, best on gd. Turf high 113 - 2nd of 6 giving 5lb to Cybinka (5 Jun Epsom 7f gd RF 1762) - also 1st of 7 getting 8lb from Kumait (1 Jly Yarmouth RF 2467). Consistent. Vigorously campaigned, he held his form well but became increasingly difficult to place at home. It would be no surprise if he clocked-up a few air miles in the millennium. **C E Brittain [2-16] Sheikh Marwan Al Maktoum.*

CABARET QUEST BHB 64f **RR 67f** 1991[6]

3 ch g Pursuit of Love 9.5f **(69)** - Cabaret Artiste (Shareef Dancer (USA)) 9.9f **(73)**
Form - 00136
Record 1999 - 1st:1 2nd:0 3rd:1 Ran:5
Pre1999 - 1st:0 2nd:0 3rd:0 Ran:3
Win Prizemoney £2,742 *Total Prizemoney* £3,174
Wins * **1999** May Leices (G-F) C 8f 57 <
1999 Turf 1-5: (8f 1-3, 10f 2) (sft, frm 1-4)
Scopey, average gelding, effective 8f, acts on frm. Turf high 67 - 3rd of 14 getting 15lb from Asef Alhind (1 Jun Sandown 8f frm RF 1655). **R Hannon [1-8] Thurloe Thoroughbreds III.*

CABBAGE CRUSADER BHB 32f **RR 27f** 765[8]

3 b f Mon Tresor 7.9f **(60)** - Edith Piaf (Thatch (USA)) 9.8f **(62)**
Form - 8
Record 1999 - 1st:0 2nd:0 3rd:0 Ran:1
Pre1999 - 1st:0 2nd:0 3rd:0 Ran:2
1999 Turf 0-1: (7f) (sft)
Workmanlike, currently little account filly.
**P L Gilligan [0-3] The Great Leap Forward Partnership.*

CABCHARGE BLUE BHB 37f30a **RR 39f 30a** 4648[11]

7 b m Midyan (USA) 9.9f **(64)** - Mashobra (Vision (USA)) 9f **(64)**
Form - 045152P84070
Record 1999 - 1st:1 2nd:1 3rd:0 Ran:11
Pre1999 - 1st:7 2nd:5 3rd:5 Ran:50
Win Prizemoney £20,136 *Total Prizemoney* £29,052
Wins * **1999** May Bright (FRM) H 11.9f 43 45
* 1997 Oct Bright (G-F) SH 10f 36 48
* 1996 *Jan Southw (STD) H 8f 48 52*
1999 Turf 1-11: (10f 3, 12f 1-5, 14f 3) (hvy, sft, g-s, g-f 1-4, frm 4)
Very moderate mare, effective 8 to 12f, best at 8f, acts on g-s to frm, likes right handed tracks. Turf high 45 - 1st of 11 getting 23lb from Tallulah Belle (12 May Brighton RF 1175). Inconsistent. He does not win very often, but goes on any ground. 12 furlongs looks his trip now.
**T J Naughton [4-52] Four Counties Partnership (from M H Tompkins [4-10] Spt 1994).*

CABCHARGE GLORY BHB 32f23a **RR 28f 23a** 236[6]

5 ch m Executive Man 8.9f **(52)** - Clipsall (Petitioner)
Form - 56
Record 1999 - 1st:0 2nd:0 3rd:0 Ran:2
Pre1999 - 1st:0 2nd:0 3rd:1 Ran:10
Win Prizemoney £0 *Total Prizemoney* £725
1999 AW 0-2: (12f, 13f) (Equi, Fibr)
Little account filly, effective 13f, - acts on Equi, has worn blinkers. AW high 21.
**T T Clement [0-7] Glyn Lewis (from G G Margarson [0-5] Jly 1997).*

CABLE MEDIA GIRL (IRE) BHB 37f **RR 54f** 377[8]

3 b f River Falls 8.2f **(56)** - Brass Button (IRE) (Fools Holme (USA))
Form - 8
Record 1999 - 1st:0 2nd:0 3rd:0 Ran:1
Pre1999 - 1st:0 2nd:0 3rd:0 Ran:3
1999 AW 0-1: (10f) (Equi)
Unfurnished, fair filly.
**S E Kettlewell [0-4] Cable Media Consultancy Ltd.*

CABRIAC **RR 85f** 4595[9]

2 b br c Machiavellian (USA) 9.8f **(83)** - Chief Bee **(89f)** (Chief's Crown

(USA)) 9.8f **(72)**
Form - 20
Record 1999 - 1st:0 2nd:1 3rd:0 Ran:2
Win Prizemoney £0 *Total Prizemoney* £1,170
1999 Turf 0-2: (7f 2) (g-f, frm)
Currently useful colt. Turf high 85 (1st run) (began Aug) - 2nd of 16 to Merry Merlin (27 Aug Newmarket 7f frm RF 3937). Just touched off on his debut, he looks sure to win races.
**J L Dunlop [0-2] Benny Andersson.*

CACHUCHA (USA) RR 73f 2582[3]
3 ch f Diesis 9f **(80)** -Baffling Ballerina(USA)(Northern Dancer) 9.6f **(80)**
Form - 5843
Record 1999 - 1st:0 2nd:0 3rd:1 Ran:4
Win Prizemoney £0 *Total Prizemoney* £803
1999 Turf 0-4: (10f 4) (frm 4)
Scopey, above-average filly. Turf high 73 - 3rd of 12 getting 5lb from Minuit Noir (6 Jly Pontefract 10f frm RF 2582).
**P W Harris [0-4] Mrs A M Palmer.*

CACOPHONY BHB 50f **RR 55f** 2849[10]
2 b c Son Pardo - Ansellady **(62f 60a)** (Absalom) 7.2f **(58)**
Form - 008460
Record 1999 - 1st:0 2nd:0 3rd:0 Ran:6
1999 Turf 0-5: (5f 3, 6f 2) (g-f 2, frm 2, hrd) 1999 AW 0-1: (6f) (Fibr)
Fair colt, effective 6f, acts on hrd, has worn blinkers. Turf high 55.
**S Dow [0-6] Gatecrasher Partnership.*

CADEAUX CHER BHB 76f **RR 75f** 5160[9]
5 ch g Cadeaux Genereux 7.9f **(76)** - Home Truth (Known Fact (USA)) 7.4f **(67)**
Form - 00670000840
Record 1999 - 1st:0 2nd:0 3rd:0 Ran:11
Pre1999 - 1st:5 2nd:2 3rd:0 Ran:26
Win Prizemoney £57,456 *Total Prizemoney* £61,986
Wins * 1998 Spt Doncas (GD) H 5.6f 89 93 <
* 1998 Aug Ripon (G-F) H 6f 79 86
* 1998 Aug Leices (GD) 6f 76
* 1998 Jly Doncas (G-F) 6f 78?
* 1997 Mar Doncas (G-F) 6f 76
1999 Turf 0-11: (6f 11) (g-s, gd 5, g-f 2, frm 3)
Above-average gelding, effective 6f, acts on gd to g-f, has worn blinkers. Turf high 90. Consistent. A promising sixth in the Wokingham, he failed to show in the major sprint handicaps afterwards, and became frustrating. **B W Hills [5-37] N N Browne.*

CADIE RR 4816[18]
3 b f St Ninian - Lucky Lena (Leander)
Form - 0
Record 1999 - 1st:0 2nd:0 3rd:0 Ran:1
1999 Turf 0-1: (10f) (gd)
Scopey, currently very poor filly. **B D Leavy [0-1] Mrs C G Heath.*

CADILLA BHB 63f **RR 62f** 5052[11]
2 ch f Cadeaux Genereux 7.9f **(76)** - Tahilla (Moorestyle) 6.9f **(64)**
Form - 0600
Record 1999 - 1st:0 2nd:0 3rd:0 Ran:4
1999 Turf 0-4: (6f, 7f 3) (gd 2, g-f 2)
Average filly. Turf high 62 (began Aug).
**E A L Dunlop [0-4] The Serendipity Partnership.*

CADMAX (IRE) BHB 41f **RR 39f** 1514[11]
4 b g Second Set (IRE) 9.2f **(67)** - Stella Ann (Ahonoora) 8.1f **(73)**
Form - 00
Record 1999 - 1st:0 2nd:0 3rd:0 Ran:2
Pre1999 - 1st:0 2nd:1 3rd:2 Ran:8
Win Prizemoney £0 *Total Prizemoney* £1,664
1999 Turf 0-2: (10f, 12f) (gd, frm)
Leggy, very moderate gelding, effective 12f, acts on gd, likes tight tracks. Turf high 21. Inconsistent. **K R Burke [0-10] A J Allright.*

CADMUS (IRE) BHB 23f31a **RR 12f 31a** 3817[15]
3 ch g Shalford (IRE) 7.8f **(63)** - Candle Hill (Sallust) 8.4f **(63)**
Form - 08060000000
Record 1999 - 1st:0 2nd:0 3rd:0 Ran:11
1999 Turf 0-7: (6f 4, 8f 2, 10f) (sft, gd, g-f 2, frm 3) 1999 AW 0-4: (6f 3, 7f) (Fibr 4)
Workmanlike, little account gelding. Turf high 24. AW high 27.
**D W Chapman [0-11] Miss N F Thesiger.*

CA'D'ORO BHB 66f **RR 65f** 5217[9]
6 ch g Cadeaux Genereux 7.9f **(76)** - Palace Street (USA) (Secreto (USA)) 8.7f **(72)**
Form - 20001067280
Record 1999 - 1st:1 2nd:2 3rd:0 Ran:11
Pre1999 - 1st:5 2nd:4 3rd:5 Ran:38
Win Prizemoney £26,483 *Total Prizemoney* £36,699
Wins * **1999** Aug Kempto (SFT) H 7f 64 69 <
* 1998 Oct Nottin () H 8.2f 59 63
* 1997 Oct Nottin (G-S) H 8.2f 58 64
* 1997 Jun Goodwo (G-S) H 8f 53 59
* 1997 Jun Newbur (GD) H 8f 53 57
* 1996 Aug Bath (GD) H 8f 56 60
1999 Turf 1-11: (6f, 7f 1-6, 8f 4) (sft, g-s 1-5, gd 3, g-f 2)
Average gelding, effective 7 to 8f, best at 8f, acts on sft to g-f, likes tight tracks. Turf high 69 - 1st of 16 giving 20lb to Daynabee (18 Aug Kempton RF 3743). Inconsistent. He is best at distances of seven furlongs plus, and goes particularly well with some give in the ground. **G B Balding [6-49] Miss B Swire.*

CADW (IRE) BHB 63f **RR 63f** 2056[14]
4 b c Cadeaux Genereux 7.9f **(76)** -Night Jar(Night Shift(USA)) 7.2f **(69)**
Form - 7030
Record 1999 - 1st:0 2nd:0 3rd:1 Ran:4
Pre1999 - 1st:0 2nd:0 3rd:0 Ran:4
Win Prizemoney £0 *Total Prizemoney* £1,362
1999 Turf 0-4: (7f 3, 8f) (sft, g-f 2, frm)
Scopey, average colt. Turf high 63. Inconsistent.
**I A Balding [0-4] J T Thomas (from Lord Huntingdon [0-4] Nov 1998).*

CAERAU BHB 90f **RR 83f** 5106[1]
3 ch f Nashwan (USA) 10.3f **(79)** - Charming Life (Habitat) 9.4f **(70)**
Form - 511
Record 1999 - 1st:2 2nd:0 3rd:0 Ran:3
Win Prizemoney £12,657 *Total Prizemoney* £12,657
Wins * **1999** Oct Yarmou (G-S) 10.1f 83 <
* **1999** Oct York (G-S) 10.4f 76
1999 Turf 2-3: (10f 2-3) (g-s 1-1, gd 1-1, hrd)
Currently decent filly. Turf high 83 (began Jly) - 1st of 7 getting 2lb from Evander (27 Oct Yarmouth RF 5106) - also 1st of 5 from Rahcak (6 Oct York RF 4756). Unraced at two, she gained victories over ten furlongs at York and Yarmouth in October with cut in the ground. **H R A Cecil [2-3] Derek D & Mrs Jean P Clee.*

CAERDYDD FACH BHB 30f35a **RR 20f 35a** 3764[8]
3 b f Bluebird (USA) 7.9f **(71)** - Waitingformargaret (Kris) 9.5f **(73)**
Form - 056705044658
Record 1999 - 1st:0 2nd:0 3rd:0 Ran:11
Pre1999 - 1st:0 2nd:0 3rd:1 Ran:8
Win Prizemoney £0 *Total Prizemoney* £245
1999 Turf 0-8: (8f 5, 10f 2, 11f) (gd 5, g-f 2, frm) 1999 AW 0-3: (9f, 10f, 11f) (Equi, Fibr 2)
Light-framed, very moderate filly, effective 6f, acts on g-f. Turf high 47. AW high 38. Becoming disappointing.
**J A Gilbert [0-8] Terry Connors (from P L Gilligan [0-3] Feb 1999).*

CAERLESS (IRE) BHB 70f **RR 78f** 5133[4]
3 b f Caerleon (USA) 10.9f **(79)** - Barger (USA) (Riverman (USA)) 9.1f **(76)**
Form - 551544
Record 1999 - 1st:1 2nd:0 3rd:0 Ran:6
Win Prizemoney £3,577 *Total Prizemoney* £4,622
Wins * **1999** Jun Bath (FRM) 11.7f 72+ <
1999 Turf 1-6: (10f 2, 12f 1-4) (gd 5, hrd 1-1)
Workmanlike, above-average filly, effective 12f, acts on gd to hrd, best on gd. Turf high 78 - 4th of 8 getting 5lb from High Tatra (11 Oct Leicester 12f gd RF 4817) - also 1st of 4 getting 5lb from Alnajashee (26 Jun Bath RF 2320).
**L M Cumani [1-6] Sheikh Mohammed.*

CAERNARFON BAY (IRE) BHB 47f50a **RR 52f 50a** 2444[6]
4 ch g Royal Academy (USA) 7.8f **(77)** -Bay Shade (USA)(Sharpen Up) 8.3f **(67)**
Form - 4135312026

Record 1999 - 1st:2 2nd:2 3rd:2 Ran:10
Pre1999 - 1st:0 2nd:1 3rd:1 Ran:9
Win Prizemoney £4,936 *Total Prizemoney* £8,866
Wins * 1999 Apr Bright (G-F) H 11.9f 46 49
** 1999 Jan Lingfi (STD) H 10f 48 53 <*
1999 Turf 1-5: (10f, 11f, 12f 1-3) (g-f 3, frm 1-1, hrd) 1999 AW 1-5: (10f 1-2, 12f 3) (Equi 1-4, Fibr)
Workmanlike, fair gelding, effective 9 to 12f, best at 12f, acts on gd - acts on AW, has worn blinkers, prefers left handed tracks, prefers tight tracks. Turf high 52. AW high 54 - 3rd of 8 getting 1lb from Law Dancer (25 Feb Lingfield 12f Equi RF 0356) - also 1st of 13 giving 4lb to Clonoe (28 Jan Lingfield RF 0183). A fair handicapper in modest company, he was successful on Equitrack and on turf at Brighton last season. Goes well for an amateur rider.
**G L Moore [2-10] J B R Leisure Ltd (from P F I Cole [0-9] Oct 1998).*

CAEROSA BHB 60f40a RR 59f 40a

5190[5]
4 b f Caerleon (USA) 10.9f **(79)** - Famosa (Dancing Brave (USA)) 8.4f **(76)**
Form - 505227523034313625 1215
Record 1999 - 1st:3 2nd:5 3rd:4 Ran:22
Pre1999 - 1st:0 2nd:0 3rd:0 Ran:7
Win Prizemoney £14,812 *Total Prizemoney* £22,550
Wins * 1999 Oct Bath (SFT) H 11.7f 55 59+ <
*** 1999** Oct York (G-S) H 11.9f 51 54
*** 1999** Aug Hamilt (G-F) H 11.1f 44 45
1999 Turf 3-20: (10f 6, 11f 1-4, 12f 2-8, 13f, 14f) (sft, g-s, gd 2-4, g-f 1-9, frm 5) 1999 AW 0-2: (10f, 12f) (Equi 2)
Scopey, fair filly, effective 7 to 12f, best at 12f, acts on gd to frm, often wears blinkers (effectively), likes right handed tracks. Turf high 59 - 1st of 17 getting 4lb from Corvino (26 Oct Bath RF 5066) - also 1st of 20 giving 8lb to Joli Flyers (7 Oct York RF 4763). AW high 26.
**M Johnston [3-22] & Mrs G Middlebrook (from J G FitzGerald [0-7] Oct 1998).*

CAFE OPERA (USA) RR 71f

4098[2]
2 b f Sadler's Wells (USA) 11.3f **(87)** - Takreem (USA) **(51f)** (Mr Prospector (USA)) 8.8f **(78)**
Form - 42
Record 1999 - 1st:0 2nd:1 3rd:0 Ran:2
Win Prizemoney £0 *Total Prizemoney* £1,828
1999 Turf 0-2: (7f 2) (g-s, frm)
Currently above-average filly. Turf high 71 (began Aug) - 2nd of 10 to Dancing Mirage (2 Spt Salisbury 7f frm RF 4098). Came up against a decent sort on her second start at Salisbury and should find a race. **J W Hills [0-2] Christopher Wright.*

CAFFE LATTE (USA) RR 123f

5228a[4]
3 b f Seattle Dancer (USA) 10.1f **(74)** - Debbie's Next (USA) (Arctic Tern (USA)) 8.9f **(69)**
Form - 4
1999 Turf 0-1: (11f) (frm)
Neat, currently very high-class. (1st run) - 4th of 14 to Soaring Softly (6 Nov Gulfstream Park 11f frm RF 5228a). Looked unlucky when a close fourth in the Breeders' Cup Filly and Mare Turf.
**J Canani in USA [0-1].*

CAIRN DHU BHB 36f38a RR 29f 38a

1124[9]
5 ch g Presidium 7.5f **(56)** - My Precious Daisy (Sharpo) 7.7f **(59)**
Form - 0
Record 1999 - 1st:0 2nd:0 3rd:0 Ran:1
Pre1999 - 1st:1 2nd:0 3rd:0 Ran:17
Win Prizemoney £1,634 *Total Prizemoney* £2,092
Wins 1997 Apr Nottin (G-F) S 6.1f 62+ <
1999 Turf 0-1: (6f) (gd)
Little account gelding, has worn blinkers.
**D W Barker [0-11] Mrs S J Barker (from Mrs J R Ramsden [1-8] May 1997).*

CAIR PARAVEL (IRE) BHB 85f RR 78+f

2353[1]
2 b br c Dolphin Street (FR) - Queen's Ransom (IRE) **(66f)** (Last Tycoon) 8.5f **(62)**
Form - 11
Record 1999 - 1st:2 2nd:0 3rd:0 Ran:2
Win Prizemoney £6,933 *Total Prizemoney* £6,933
Wins * 1999 Jun Doncas (G-S) 6f 71+
*** 1999** Jun Leices (GD) 5f 78+ <
1999 Turf 2-2: (5f 1-1, 6f 1-1) (gd 1-1, g-f 1-1)
Currently above-average colt. Turf high 78 (1st run) - 1st of 16 from Commonwood (1 Jun Leicester RF 1645) - also 1st of 2 from Cautionary (27 Jun Doncaster RF 2353). Made all on his Leicester debut and followed up in a Doncaster match. Not seen afterwards, it is difficult to gauge his potential.
**R Hannon [2-2] Mrs Caroline Parker.*

CAITANO RR 125f

2474a[1]
5 b h Niniski (USA) 13.2f **(67)** - Eversince (USA) (Foolish Pleasure (USA)) 8.9f **(72)**
Form - 04311
1999 Turf 2-3: (11f 2-2, 12f) (sft 1-1, gd 1-1, g-f)
Top-class colt, effective 8 to 12f, best at 12f, acts on sft to gd, best on sft, has worn blinkers. Turf high 121 - 1st of 5 getting 6lb from Tiger Hill (6 Jun Baden-Baden RF 1902a). A high-class German-trained colt, successful twice at the top level in 1997, he has competed in most of the top races around the world since, his best efforts being a fifth in the 1998 Arc, a fourth in the Hong Kong International Vase, and a third at the Dubai World Cup meeting. He appeared to need soft ground to show his best, and on his return to Germany in 1999 he won successive Group Twos, on one occasion beating the top-class Tiger Hill. Remarkably durable, he will make a valuable addition to the German stallion register, especially now the great Surumu has passed on.
**A Schutz in GER [2-10] Gary Tanaka (from B Schutz in GER [3-7] Nov 1997).*

CAJOLE (IRE) BHB 58f RR 74f

4181[2]
3 ch f Barathea (IRE) - Frendly Persuasion (General Assembly (USA)) 10f **(68)**
Form - 600072
Record 1999 - 1st:0 2nd:1 3rd:0 Ran:6
Win Prizemoney £0 *Total Prizemoney* £1,103
1999 Turf 0-6: (7f, 8f 3, 10f 2) (gd, frm 5)
Workmanlike, above-average filly, effective 7f, acts on frm. Turf high 74 - 2nd of 11 to Snowy Range (7 Spt Lingfield 7f frm RF 4181). **R F JohnsonHoughton [0-6] Mrs Hue Williams.*

CAKEBREAD CELLAR RR 40f

4407[14]
2 b g Piccolo - Little Bittern (USA) (Riva Ridge (USA)) 8.2f **(68)**
Form - 0
Record 1999 - 1st:0 2nd:0 3rd:0 Ran:1
1999 Turf 0-1: (6f) (frm)
Currently moderate gelding. **J M P Eustace [0-1] R Carstairs.*

CALAMA (IRE) BHB 52f RR 56f

5064[4]
2 b f Desert Style (IRE) - Popcorn **(50df)** (Pharly (FR)) 9.8f **(68)**
Form - 004
Record 1999 - 1st:0 2nd:0 3rd:0 Ran:3
1999 Turf 0-3: (6f 3) (gd 2, g-f)
Currently fair filly. Turf high 56 (began Spt).
**P G Murphy [0-3] Mrs Louise Murphy.*

CALANDO (USA) BHB 110f RR 111f

4661a[2]
3 b f Storm Cat (USA) 7f **(86)** - Diminuendo (USA) (Diesis) 9.3f **(69)**
Form - 38302
Record 1999 - 1st:0 2nd:1 3rd:2 Ran:5
Pre1999 - 1st:2 2nd:1 3rd:0 Ran:4
Win Prizemoney £22,087 *Total Prizemoney* £103,440
Wins 1998 Spt Doncas (GD) G3 8f 103+ <
1998 Jly Folkes (G-F) 7f 81++
1999 Turf 0-5: (8f, 10f 2, 11f, 12f) (g-s, gd 3, g-f)
Workmanlike, Group-class filly, effective 8 to 10f, best at 8f, acts on gd to g-f, best on gd. Turf high 111 (1st run) - 3rd of 14 to Valentine Waltz (16 May Longchamp 8f gd RF 1358a). Consistent. She lacks scope, as did her outstandingly game dam Diminuendo, and failed to improve on her juvenile form. Still, she did manage to make the frame in the French 1,000 Guineas and, as a Group winning juvenile, will be a valuable addition to Sheikh Mohammed's broodmare band. **S bin Suroor [0-5] (from D R Loder [2-4] Spt 1998).*

CALANDRELLA BHB 40f26a RR 39f 26a

4285[10]
6 b m Sizzling Melody 6.3f **(49)** - Maravilla (Mandrake Major) 7.6f **(53)**
Form - 73247201500
Record 1999 - 1st:1 2nd:2 3rd:1 Ran:11
Pre1999 - 1st:0 2nd:0 3rd:1 Ran:22

Win Prizemoney £2,736 *Total Prizemoney* £5,272
Wins * **1999** Aug Mussel (G-S) H 5f 38 38 <
1999 Turf 1-10: (5f 1-7, 6f 2, 7f) (gd, g-f 1-3, frm 6) 1999 AW 0-1: (6f) (Fibr)
Very moderate mare, effective 5 to 6f, best at 5f, acts on sft to frm. Turf high 39 - also 1st of 10 getting 11lb from Record Time (18 Aug Musselburgh RF 3753).
**A G Newcombe [1-11] M B Clemence (from G B Balding [0-23] Jly 1998).*

CALCAVELLA BHB 64f **RR 61f** 5033[24]

3 b f Pursuit of Love 9.5f **(69)** - Brightside (IRE) **(84f)** (Last Tycoon) 8.5f **(62)**
Form - 000
Record 1999 - 1st:0 2nd:0 3rd:0 Ran:3
Pre1999 - 1st:0 2nd:2 3rd:1 Ran:4
Win Prizemoney £0 *Total Prizemoney* £3,936
1999 Turf 0-3: (6f 2, 7f) (g-s, gd, frm)
Workmanlike, average filly, effective 5 to 6f, acts on gd. Turf high 61 (began Oct). **M Kettle [0-7] Graham Racing.*

CALCI (USA) **RR 107f** 1715a[5]

4 c
Form - 5
1999 Turf 0-1: (12f) (frm)
Pattern-class colt, has worn blinkers. (1st run) - 5th of 10 to Ivan Luis (29 May Capannelle 12f frm RF 1715a). **O Pessi in ITY [0-4].*

CALCUTTA BHB 100f **RR 98f** 5141[6]

3 b c Indian Ridge 7.6f **(74)** - Echoing (Formidable (USA)) 9.2f **(63)**
Form - 3470122106
Record 1999 - 1st:2 2nd:2 3rd:1 Ran:10
Pre1999 - 1st:1 2nd:0 3rd:2 Ran:3
Win Prizemoney £26,160 *Total Prizemoney* £48,177
Wins * **1999** Spt Doncas (G-F) H 8f 93 98+ <
* **1999** Jly Newmar (G-F) H 8f 83 86
* 1998 Jly Ayr (GD) 6f 80
1999 Turf 2-10: (7f 3, 8f 2-6, 10f) (gd 5, g-f 2, frm 2-3)
Well made, very useful colt, effective 8f, acts on gd to frm, best on frm. Turf high 98 - 1st of 10 getting 9lb from Indian Lodge (11 Spt Doncaster RF 4265). He put up a superb performance when sprinting clear to win a hot handicap at Doncaster in September and seemed unsuited by soft ground on his two subsequent starts. Best over a mile on a sound surface, he would be an interesting runner in the Royal Hunt Cup.
**B W Hills [3-13] The Hon Mrs J M Corbett & C Wright.*

CALCUTTA KING BHB 25f **RR 15f** 3295[21]

3 ch c Democratic (USA) -Calcutta Queen (Night Shift (USA)) 7.2f **(69)**
Form - 0000
Record 1999 - 1st:0 2nd:0 3rd:0 Ran:4
Pre1999 - 1st:0 2nd:0 3rd:0 Ran:3
1999 Turf 0-4: (5f, 6f, 7f 2) (frm 4)
Unfurnished, poor colt, has worn blinkers. Turf high 15 (began Jly). **W Storey [0-4] W Storey (from R Simpson [0-3] Oct 1998).*

CALDEY ISLAND (IRE) BHB 69f64a **RR 73f 64a** 4937[13]

2 b c Turtle Island (IRE) - Lady Taufan (IRE) (Taufan (USA)) 7f **(57)**
Form - 0463835600
Record 1999 - 1st:0 2nd:0 3rd:2 Ran:10
Win Prizemoney £0 *Total Prizemoney* £1,868
1999 Turf 0-9: (5f, 6f 6, 7f 2) (sft, gd, g-f 2, frm 5) 1999 AW 0-1: (6f) (Fibr)
Above-average colt, effective 6 to 7f, acts on g-f, has worn blinkers. Turf high 73. **D W P Arbuthnot [0-10] Derrick Broomfield.*

CALEB'S BOY **RR 50f** 4751[23]

2 b c Son Pardo - Lon Isa **(39f 47a)** (Grey Desire) 8.7f **(50)**
Form - 00
Record 1999 - 1st:0 2nd:0 3rd:0 Ran:2
1999 Turf 0-2: (8f 2) (sft, gd)
Currently fair colt. Turf high 50 (began Spt).
**B Palling [0-2] H Weeks.*

CALEDONIAN EXPRESS BHB 53f **RR 58df** 5154[17]

4 b f Northern Park (USA) 10f **(57)** - New Edition (Great Nephew) 9.9f **(64)**
Form - 60
Record 1999 - 1st:0 2nd:0 3rd:0 Ran:2
Pre1999 - 1st:0 2nd:0 3rd:1 Ran:6
Win Prizemoney £0 *Total Prizemoney* £434
1999 Turf 0-1: (10f) (gd) 1999 AW 0-1: (12f) (Equi)
Scopey, fair filly.
**J R Best [0-6] B T W Bones (from J L Dunlop [0-6] Jly 1998).*

CALICO BHB 68f **RR 64f** 4504[8]

2 b f Barathea (IRE) - Craigmill **(78f)** (Slip Anchor) 9.8f **(73)**
Form - 0558
Record 1999 - 1st:0 2nd:0 3rd:0 Ran:4
1999 Turf 0-4: (7f 2, 8f 2) (gd, g-f, frm 2)
Average filly. Turf high 64.
**J G Smyth-Osbourne [0-4] J H Henderson.*

CALICO LADY BHB 30f **RR 71f** 5176a[6]

3 ch f First Trump - Cottonwood (Teenoso (USA)) 9.9f **(72)**
Form - 3068086
Record 1999 - 1st:0 2nd:0 3rd:1 Ran:7
Pre1999 - 1st:0 2nd:1 3rd:0 Ran:10
Win Prizemoney £0 *Total Prizemoney* £1,911
1999 Turf 0-7: (7f, 8f 2, 9f 2, 12f, 13f) (g-s 2, gd 2, g-f 2, frm)
Light-framed, above-average filly, has worn blinkers. Turf high 71. Inconsistent.
**M Hourigan in IRE [0-4] Shattered Racegoers Syndicate (from W T Kemp [0-16] Jly 1999).*

CALIFORNIA SON (IRE) BHB 36f **RR 44f** 4816[16]

3 ch g Lycius (USA) 8.8f **(71)** - Madame Nureyev (USA) (Nureyev (USA)) 8.7f **(78)**
Form - 0520
Record 1999 - 1st:0 2nd:1 3rd:0 Ran:4
Win Prizemoney £0 *Total Prizemoney* £808
1999 Turf 0-4: (8f, 10f 3) (gd, g-f 2, frm)
Workmanlike, moderate gelding. Turf high 44.
**M Quinn [0-3] W Trezise (from P F I Cole [0-1] Jun 1999).*

CALIWAG (IRE) BHB 77f **RR 72f** 1814[12]

3 b c Lahib (USA) 8f **(69)** -Mitsubishi Style(Try My Best (USA)) 7.6f **(67)**
Form - 4650
Record 1999 - 1st:0 2nd:0 3rd:0 Ran:4
Win Prizemoney £0 *Total Prizemoney* £223
1999 Turf 0-4: (6f, 7f 2, 8f) (g-f, frm 3)
Rangy, above-average colt. Turf high 72.
**D R C Elsworth [0-4] The Caledonian Racing Society.*

CALKO BHB 59f **RR 56f** 5187[3]

2 ch g Timeless Times (USA)6.1f **(56)**-Jeethgaya(USA)(Critique (USA))
Form - 030063
Record 1999 - 1st:0 2nd:0 3rd:2 Ran:6
Win Prizemoney £0 *Total Prizemoney* £814
1999 Turf 0-6: (5f 3, 6f 3) (gd 3, g-f 3)
Fair gelding, effective 5f, acts on gd, has worn blinkers. Turf high 65 (began Aug). **T D Barron [0-6] T Calver.*

CALLAS **RR 71f** 4996[4]

2 b f Mtoto 11.5f **(71)** - Ower (IRE) (Lomond (USA)) 8.8f **(65)**
Form - 84
Record 1999 - 1st:0 2nd:0 3rd:0 Ran:2
Win Prizemoney £0 *Total Prizemoney* £276
1999 Turf 0-2: (7f, 8f) (gd 2)
Currently above-average filly. Turf high 71 (began Spt). Should come into her own over middle distances at three.
**R F JohnsonHoughton [0-2] Dr J A E Hobby.*

CALLDAT SEVENTEEN BHB 77f72a **RR 78f 72a** 5197[4]

3 b g Komaite (USA) 6.9f **(61)** - Westminster Waltz (Dance In Time (CAN)) 8.9f **(59)**
Form - 1710737816304
Record 1999 - 1st:3 2nd:0 3rd:2 Ran:13
Pre1999 - 1st:0 2nd:0 3rd:0 Ran:1
Win Prizemoney £9,870 *Total Prizemoney* £12,206
Wins * **1999** Aug Epsom (GD) H 8.5f 75 80 <
* **1999** Apr Epsom (SFT) 8.5f 79
* **1999** *Feb Lingfi (STD) 8f 70*
1999 Turf 2-12: (7f 3, 8f, 9f 2-5, 10f 3) (g-s 1-1, gd 4, g-f 1-5, frm 2)

1999 AW 1-1: (8f 1-1) (Equi 1-1)
Scopey, above-average gelding, effective 7 to 10f, best at 9f, acts on g-s to frm - acts on Equi, likes left handed tracks, likes tight tracks, excels at Epsom. Turf high 80 - 1st of 7 giving 13lb to Royal Fusilier (13 Aug Epsom RF 3605) - also 1st of 12 getting 10lb from Peaceful Sarah (21 Apr Epsom RF 0802). (1st run). A winner on Equitrack earlier in the year, he scored nicely in soft ground at Epsom in April over a mile, and repeated the dose at the same track on slightly better ground in August.
**P W D'Arcy [3-14] Keith Harrison & Terry Miller.*

CALLING THE SHOTS BHB 53f **RR 47f** 4881[12]
2 b c Democratic (USA) - Two Shots (Dom Racine (FR)) 9.2f **(62)**
Form - 070
Record 1999 - 1st:0 2nd:0 3rd:0 Ran:3
1999 Turf 0-3: (6f 2, 7f) (gd, frm 2)
Currently moderate colt. Turf high 47 (began Spt).
**W Storey [0-3] Gremlin Racing.*

CALLITWHATYOUWANT BHB 65f52a **RR 71f 52a** 79[11]
3 b g Weldnaas (USA) 8.4f **(55)** - Alcassa (FR) (Satingo) 8.9f **(69)**
Form - 60
Record 1999 - 1st:0 2nd:0 3rd:0 Ran:1
Pre1999 - 1st:0 2nd:2 3rd:0 Ran:6
Win Prizemoney £0 *Total Prizemoney* £1,315
1999 AW 0-1: (7f) (Equi)
Lengthy, above-average gelding, effective 5f, acts on gd, has worn blinkers.
**J R Poulton [0-2] Come Racing Ltd (from J J O'Neill [0-5] Jly 1998).*

CALL ME LUCKY BHB 49f **RR 48f** 4879[16]
3 b f Magic Ring (IRE) 6.5f **(64)** - Lucky Message (USA) **(59f)** (Phone Trick (USA))
Form - 05400
Record 1999 - 1st:0 2nd:0 3rd:0 Ran:5
Pre1999 - 1st:1 2nd:1 3rd:1 Ran:10
Win Prizemoney £6,408 *Total Prizemoney* £7,950
Wins *1998 Jly York (FRM) 6f 71 <
1999 Turf 0-5: (6f 5) (sft, gd, g-f, frm 2)
Unfurnished, moderate filly, effective 5 to 6f, acts on frm. Turf high 48. **M Brittain [1-15] Northgate Bronze.*

CALL MY GUEST (IRE) BHB 27f26a **RR 24f 26a** 3412[6]
9 b g Be My Guest (USA) 10.2f **(66)** - Overcall (Bustino) 10.4f **(64)**
Form - 046
Record 1999 - 1st:0 2nd:0 3rd:0 Ran:3
Pre1999 - 1st:0 2nd:0 3rd:0 Ran:9
1999 Turf 0-1: (12f) (frm) 1999 AW 0-2: (12f 2) (Equi, Fibr)
Little account gelding. AW high 23.
**R E Peacock [2-38] Derek D & Mrs Jean P Clee (from J G FitzGerald [0-6] Oct 1994).*

CALYS HALO **RR 30f** 801[7]
4 ch g Cigar 6.3f **(43)** - My-Ninon (Grand Conde (FR))
Form - 57
Record 1999 - 1st:0 2nd:0 3rd:0 Ran:2
1999 Turf 0-1: (9f) (g-s) 1999 AW 0-1: (8f) (Equi)
Currently very moderate gelding.
**J G Smyth-Osbourne [0-2] T E Short.*

CAMAIR CRUSADER (IRE) BHB 34f **RR 22f** 4980[18]
5 br g Jolly Jake (NZ) - Sigrid's Dream (USA) (Triple Bend (USA))
Form - 380000
Record 1999 - 1st:0 2nd:0 3rd:1 Ran:6
Win Prizemoney £0 *Total Prizemoney* £527
1999 Turf 0-6: (8f, 10f 2, 11f, 12f 2) (g-s, gd, g-f, frm 3)
Little account gelding. Turf high 53.
**W McKeown [0-8] Colin German.*

CAMANOE (USA) **RR 64df** 3032[10]
3 br f Gone West (USA) 7.8f **(82)** -Prodigious(FR)(Pharly (FR)) 9.8f **(68)**
Form - 60
Record 1999 - 1st:0 2nd:0 3rd:0 Ran:2
1999 Turf 0-2: (8f 2) (frm 2)
Scopey, currently average filly. Turf high 64 (began Jly).
**H R A Cecil [0-2] K Abdulla.*

CAMARADERIE BHB 48f **RR 47f** 4980[4]
3 b g Most Welcome 8.6f **(66)** - Secret Valentine (Wollow) 8.2f **(61)**
Form - 66570034
Record 1999 - 1st:0 2nd:0 3rd:1 Ran:8
Win Prizemoney £0 *Total Prizemoney* £712
1999 Turf 0-7: (7f 2, 8f 2, 10f 2, 12f) (gd 3, g-f, frm 3) 1999 AW 0-1: (6f) (Fibr)
Light-framed, moderate gelding. Turf high 60 (began Jly).
**Mrs M Reveley [0-8] The Mary Reveley Racing Club.*

CAMBERLEY (IRE) **RR 72f** 4897[2]
2 b c Sri Pekan (USA) - Nsx **(56df)** (Roi Danzig (USA))
Form - 62
Record 1999 - 1st:0 2nd:1 3rd:0 Ran:2
Win Prizemoney £0 *Total Prizemoney* £2,848
1999 Turf 0-2: (7f 2) (gd 2)
Currently above-average colt. Turf high 72 (began Spt) - 2nd of 4 getting 3lb from Adilabad (15 Oct Newmarket 7f gd RF 4897).
**Miss Gay Kelleway [0-2] H R H Sultan Ahmad Shah.*

CAMBRAI (IRE) BHB 68f **RR 66f** 4140[11]
3 b g Indian Ridge 7.6f **(74)** - Cambrel (IRE) **(78f)** (Soviet Star (USA))
Form - 780
Record 1999 - 1st:0 2nd:0 3rd:0 Ran:3
Pre1999 - 1st:0 2nd:0 3rd:0 Ran:1
1999 Turf 0-3: (7f, 8f 2) (gd, frm 2)
Average gelding. Turf high 66 (began Jly).
**M P Tregoning [0-4] Sheikh Mohammed.*

CAMEO (IRE) BHB 47f50a **RR 42df 50a** 655[16]
4 b g Statoblest 6.4f **(63)** - Centella (IRE) (Thatching) 8f **(66)**
Form - 75574810600
Record 1999 - 1st:1 2nd:0 3rd:0 Ran:10
Pre1999 - 1st:0 2nd:1 3rd:0 Ran:12
Win Prizemoney £1,872 *Total Prizemoney* £2,706
Wins * **1999** *Mar Wolver (SLW) S 5f 51* **<**
1999 Turf 0-2: (5f, 6f) (g-s, gd) 1999 AW 1-8: (5f 1-4, 6f 4) (Equi 4, Fibr 1-4)
Workmanlike, fair gelding, effective 5 to 6f, acts on gd - acts on Fibr, has worn blinkers. Turf high 14. AW high 51. Inconsistent.
**M R Channon [1-22] Park Farm Racing.*

CAMERON JACK BHB 40f **RR 39f** 3457[5]
4 b g Elmaamul (USA) 8.1f **(70)** - Ile de Reine (Ile de Bourbon (USA)) 10.1f **(67)**
Form - 2300055
Record 1999 - 1st:0 2nd:1 3rd:1 Ran:7
Pre1999 - 1st:0 2nd:0 3rd:1 Ran:7
Win Prizemoney £0 *Total Prizemoney* £2,139
1999 Turf 0-7: (10f 2, 12f 5) (g-f 2, frm 4, hrd)
Light-framed, very moderate gelding, effective 12f, acts on g-f to frm, best on g-f, has worn blinkers. Turf high 52 (1st run) - 2nd of 19 giving 2lb to Linea-G (3 May Newcastle 12f g-f RF 1010).
**J D Bethell [0-14] M W Territt.*

CAMEROSA BHB 20f **RR** 5050[16]
3 b c Risk Me (FR) 8f **(53)** - High Heather (Shirley Heights) 10.3f **(74)**
Form - 00
Record 1999 - 1st:0 2nd:0 3rd:0 Ran:2
1999 Turf 0-2: (8f 2) (gd 2)
Leggy, currently very poor colt. (began Oct).
**A G Newcombe [0-2] Advanced Marketing Services Ltd.*

CAMPAIGN BHB 52f75a **RR 44f 75a** 904[5]
8 b g Sure Blade (USA) 10.6f **(66)** - Just Cause (Law Society (USA)) 9.9f **(70)**
Form - 65
Record 1999 - 1st:0 2nd:0 3rd:0 Ran:2
Pre1999 - 1st:1 2nd:0 3rd:0 Ran:5
Win Prizemoney £3,367 *Total Prizemoney* £3,507
1999 Turf 0-2: (16f, 22f) (gd 2)
Moderate gelding. Turf high 44.
**M D Hammond [3-18] Spectrum (from Major W R Hern [1-2] Aug 1994).*

CAMPARI (IRE) BHB 32f42a **RR 10f 42a** 804[17]
4 b f Distinctly North (USA) 7.4f **(63)** - Foolish Flight (IRE) (Fools Holme

(USA))
Form - 00080
Record 1999 - 1st:0 2nd:0 3rd:0 Ran:3
Pre1999 - 1st:0 2nd:0 3rd:2 Ran:10
Win Prizemoney £0 *Total Prizemoney* £1,561
1999 Turf 0-3: (9f 2, 10f) (hvy, gd, g-f)
Unfurnished, poor filly, had worn blinkers. Turf high 10. (DEAD)
**Mrs A M Naughton [0-5] M F Hyman (from J Pearce [0-3] Dec 1998).*

CAMP FIRE (IRE) RR 79f
2253[3]
2 ch f Lahib (USA) 8f **(69)** -Smouldering (IRE)(Caerleon(USA)) 8.6f **(71)**
Form - 13
Record 1999 - 1st:1 2nd:0 3rd:1 Ran:2
Win Prizemoney £3,590 *Total Prizemoney* £3,985
Wins * 1999 May Nottin (FRM) 6.1f 77+ <
1999 Turf 1-2: (6f 1-1, 7f) (g-f 1-2)
Currently above-average filly. Turf high 79 - 3rd of 9 giving 9lb to Flowington (23 Jun Warwick 7f g-f RF 2253) - also 1st of 4 getting 7lb from Alpine Park (28 May Nottingham RF 1551).
**R Charlton [1-2] Lady Vestey.*

CAMPIONE (IRE) BHB 34f32a RR 31f 32a
3022[9]
4 b g Common Grounds 8.1f **(66)** - Kyrenia (Zino) 12.9f **(54)**
Form - 006080
Record 1999 - 1st:0 2nd:0 3rd:0 Ran:5
Pre1999 - 1st:0 2nd:0 3rd:0 Ran:10
1999 Turf 0-2: (5f, 7f) (frm 2) 1999 AW 0-3: (5f, 6f, 7f) (Equi 2, Fibr)
Leggy, very moderate gelding, has worn blinkers. Turf high 31. AW high 27. **M H Tompkins [0-17] Mrs Patricia Kalman.*

CAMPO CATINO (IRE) RR 106f
3718a[9]
4 br c Woodman (USA) 9.7f **(77)** - Karri Valley (USA) (Storm Bird (CAN)) 10.3f **(74)**
Form - 140
1999 Turf 1-3: (10f 1-2, 14f) (hvy 1-1, g-f, frm)
Pattern-class colt, effective 12f, acts on sft. Turf high 105 (1st run). Won a poor listed race on his seasonal debut, but did little of note afterwards. **C O'Brien in IRE [3-10] Dr M V O'Brien.*

CANADIAN APPROVAL (USA) BHB 72f RR 71df
3766[9]
3 ch f With Approval (CAN) 8.7f **(80)** - A Taste For Lace (USA) (Laomedonte (USA))
Form - 737440
Record 1999 - 1st:0 2nd:0 3rd:1 Ran:6
Pre1999 - 1st:1 2nd:0 3rd:2 Ran:4
Win Prizemoney £2,098 *Total Prizemoney* £5,447
Wins * 1998 Aug Lingfi (FRM) 7.6f 82 <
1999 Turf 0-6: (7f, 8f 5) (gd 2, g-f 2, frm 2)
Light-framed, above-average filly, effective 7 to 8f, best at 8f, acts on gd to g-f, best on gd. Turf high 78 - 3rd of 21 getting 1lb from Renown (19 May Goodwood 8f gd RF 1334). Consistent.
**P W Harris [1-10] Ayton, Cordero, Rodway & Harris.*

CANALETTO RR 90f
3498a[5]
3 b c Royal Academy (USA) 7.8f **(77)** - Diavolina (USA) (Lear Fan (USA)) 8.5f **(73)**
Form - 15
1999 Turf 1-2: (8f 1-1, 9f) (gd, frm 1-1)
Currently useful colt. Turf high 90 (1st run) (began Jly) - 1st of 9 from McCracken (7 Jly Leopardstown RF 2783a).
**C O'Brien in IRE [1-3] Mrs John Magnier.*

CANDELLINO BHB 42f RR 41f
1548[11]
3 b f Robellino (USA) 9.5f **(68)** - By Candlelight (IRE) **(80f)** (Roi Danzig (USA))
Form - 68070
Record 1999 - 1st:0 2nd:0 3rd:0 Ran:5
Pre1999 - 1st:0 2nd:0 3rd:0 Ran:4
1999 Turf 0-5: (6f, 7f, 8f 2, 10f) (g-s, gd, g-f 2, frm)
Light-framed, moderate filly, has worn blinkers. Turf high 44.
**T R Watson [0-9] G H Dodsworth.*

CANDLERIGGS (IRE) BHB 84f RR 85f
2743[5]
3 ch c Indian Ridge 7.6f **(74)** - Ridge Pool (IRE) (Bluebird (USA)) 7.5f **(69)**
Form - 16205
Record 1999 - 1st:1 2nd:1 3rd:0 Ran:5
Pre1999 - 1st:0 2nd:1 3rd:0 Ran:3
Win Prizemoney £4,318 *Total Prizemoney* £7,707
Wins * 1999 Apr Kempto (GD) H 6f 79 81 <
1999 Turf 1-5: (6f 1-5) (gd 2, g-f 1-2, frm)
Workmanlike, useful colt, effective 6f, acts on gd to g-f. Turf high 85 - 2nd of 13 giving 4lb to Roseum (15 May Newbury 6f gd RF 1239) - also 1st of 14 giving 4lb to Ranaan (3 Apr Kempton RF 0568). Consistent. He made a winning reappearance in a six-furlongs Kempton handicap. Despite some stiff tasks afterwards, he was far from disgraced. **E A L Dunlop [1-8] The Right Angle Club.*

CANDLE SMILE (USA) BHB 85f RR 86f
1044[9]
7 b g Pleasant Colony (USA) 12.4f **(88)** - Silent Turn (USA) (Silent Cal (USA)) 14.5f **(91)**
Form - 20
Record 1999 - 1st:0 2nd:1 3rd:0 Ran:2
Pre1999 - 1st:2 2nd:3 3rd:2 Ran:14
Win Prizemoney £11,746 *Total Prizemoney* £25,908
Wins 1996 Spt Goodwo (G-F) H 16f 90 97 <
1996 May Ayr (GD) 13.1f 76
1999 Turf 0-2: (16f, 19f) (g-f, frm)
Useful gelding. Turf high 86. Ran a fine second to Rainbow High on his reappearance but stopped very quickly behind the same horse in the Chester Cup.
**G Barnett [0-4] J C Bradbury (from Sir Michael Stoute [2-12] Oct 1996).*

CANFORD (IRE) RR 81f
5104[4]
2 b c Caerleon (USA) 10.9f **(79)** - Veronica (Persian Bold) 9.3f **(66)**
Form - 4
Record 1999 - 1st:0 2nd:0 3rd:0 Ran:1
Win Prizemoney £0 *Total Prizemoney* £207
1999 Turf 0-1: (7f) (gd)
Currently decent colt. (1st run) - 4th of 11 to Shaibani (27 Oct Yarmouth 7f gd RF 5104). **W Jarvis [0-1] Woodcote Stud Ltd.*

CANNY BHB 46f RR 50f
4625[9]
2 b f Piccolo - Shady Deed (USA) **(66f 57a)** (Shadeed (USA)) 8.2f **(70)**
Form - 070080
Record 1999 - 1st:0 2nd:0 3rd:0 Ran:6
1999 Turf 0-6: (6f 3, 7f 3) (g-s, g-f 4, frm)
Fair filly, has worn blinkers. Turf high 58.
**C E Brittain [0-6] C E Brittain.*

CANNY CHIFTANE BHB 56f62a RR 66f 62a
4553[12]
3 b g Be My Chief (USA) 10.2f **(62)** - Prudence (Grundy) 10.3f **(65)**
Form - 4666310
Record 1999 - 1st:1 2nd:0 3rd:1 Ran:7
Win Prizemoney £2,297 *Total Prizemoney* £2,853
Wins * 1999 *Spt Wolver (STD) H 12f 50 50+* <
1999 Turf 0-4: (10f, 11f, 14f 2) (g-s, gd, frm 2) 1999 AW 1-3: (9f, 12f 1-2) (Fibr 1-3)
Unfurnished, average gelding. Turf high 66. AW high 50 (began Aug). He has improved since being tried on Fibresand, and bolted up in a 12-furlong handicap at Wolverhampton in September.
**M A Jarvis [1-7] & Mrs Raymond Anderson Green.*

CANNY HILL RR 53f
5186[6]
2 ch g Bold Arrangement 8.7f **(57)** -Jersey Maid(On Your Mark)7.7f **(58)**
Form - 06
Record 1999 - 1st:0 2nd:0 3rd:0 Ran:2
1999 Turf 0-2: (5f, 7f) (gd, g-f)
Currently fair gelding. Turf high 53 (began Oct).
**D Moffatt [0-2] The Sheroot Partnership.*

CANON CAN (USA) BHB 103f RR 100f
3693[6]
6 ch g Green Dancer (USA) 11.9f **(77)** - Lady Argyle (USA) (Don B (USA)) 18f **(116)**
Form - 36356
Record 1999 - 1st:0 2nd:0 3rd:2 Ran:5
Pre1999 - 1st:5 2nd:2 3rd:3 Ran:20
Win Prizemoney £54,695 *Total Prizemoney* £101,878
Wins * 1997 Spt Doncas (G-F) G3 18f 114 <
* 1997 Jun Ascot (SFT) 22.2f 100
* 1997 Apr Newbur (G-F) H 16f 92 100
* 1996 Spt Pontef (GD) 18f 109
* 1996 Aug Newmar (G-F) H 16.1f 81 85

1999 Turf 0-5: (16f 4, 22f) (g-f 3, frm 2)

Very useful gelding, effective 16 to 20f, best at 16f, acts on g-s to g-f, best on gd, has worn blinkers. Turf high 108 (1st run) - 3rd of 9 to Celeric (28 Apr Ascot 16f g-f RF 0897). Consistent. Suited by a severe teat of stamina, he was third in the Queen Alexandra at Ascot, a race he won in 1997. He does not do anything very quickly and has been rather found out by the top stayers. He is now likely to go hurdling, having been sold in the autumn for 34,000 gns to a patron of Noel Meade's yard.

**H R A Cecil [5-25] Canon (Anglia) O A Ltd.*

CANOVAS HEART BHB 82f70a **RR 84f 70a** 4804[1]

10 b g Balidar 6.5f **(58)** - Worthy Venture (Northfields (USA)) 9f **(72)**

Form - 476571

Record					
1999 -	1st:1	2nd:0	3rd:0	Ran:6
Pre1999 -	1st:10	2nd:2	3rd:3	Ran:38

Win Prizemoney £67,336 *Total Prizemoney* £71,912

Wins								
* **1999**	Oct	York	(SFT)	H	7f	79	81	
* 1998	Spt	Nottin	(G-F)	H	6.1f	82	86	<
* 1997	Oct	York	(GD)	H	5f	79	86	<
* 1997	May	Ripon	(G-S)	H	5f	78	84	
* 1996	Spt	Yarmou	(GD)	H	5.2f	72	73	
* 1996	Jun	York	(GD)	H	5f	70	71	
* 1996	May	Folkes	(GD)	H	5f	65	68	
* 1996	Apr	Warwic	(GD)	H	5f	60	66	
* 1995	*Jun*	*Southw*	*(STD)*	*H*	*5f*	*49*	*53*	
* 1995	Apr	Warwic	(G-S)	H	5f	53	54	

1999 Turf 1-6: (6f 5, 7f 1-1) (gd 1-3, g-f, frm 2)

Decent gelding, effective 5 to 7f, best at 6f, acts on gd to frm, excels at York. Turf high 84 - 6th of 13 giving 9lb to Royal Result (10 Jly York 6f g-f RF 2734) - also 1st of 24 giving 2lb to Premier Baron (9 Oct York RF 4804). A veteran handicapper, he scored on his final start of the season at York in October, where the step up to seven furlongs appeared to suit.

**Bob Jones [11-47] D S Blake And M J Osborne.*

CANTABELLA RR 1014[15]

4 b f Tragic Role (USA) 9.4f **(63)** - Bella Travaille (Workboy) 7.3f **(46)**

Form - 70

Record 1999 - 1st:0 2nd:0 3rd:0 Ran:2

1999 Turf 0-1: (8f) (frm) 1999 AW 0-1: (7f) (Fibr)

Currently very poor filly. **H J Collingridge [0-2] N H Gardner.*

CANTA KE BRAVE (USA) BHB 93f93a **RR 92f 93a** 4876[12]

3 ch c River Special (USA) - Stubborn Star (USA) (Star Choice (USA))

Form - 5600013120

Record				
1999 -	1st:2	2nd:1	3rd:1	Ran:10
Pre1999 -	1st:1	2nd:1	3rd:0	Ran:3

Win Prizemoney £25,404 *Total Prizemoney* £31,557

Wins								
* **1999**	Aug	Goodwo	(GD)	H	12f	84	89	<
* **1999**	Aug	Ripon	(G-F)	H	9f	80	86	
* 1998	Spt	Goodwo	(G-F)		8f		77	

1999 Turf 2-9: (8f 2, 9f 1-3, 10f, 12f 1-3) (gd 2, g-f 1-5, frm 1-2) 1999 AW 0-1: (9f) (Fibr)

Workmanlike, useful colt, effective 9 to 12f, best at 12f, acts on g-f to frm - acts on Fibr, best on g-f, prefers right handed tracks, prefers tight tracks. Turf high 92 - 2nd of 10 giving 2lb to Rada's Daughter (28 Spt Newmarket 12f g-f RF 4594) - also 1st of 15 giving 6lb to Absolute Utopia (29 Aug Goodwood RF 3993). (1st run) - 3rd of 8 to Over To You (14 Aug Wolverhampton 9f Fibr RF 3669). Inconsistent. He ran far too freely in his early starts last term, but returned to winning ways at Ripon in August. Beaten by a couple of decent performers on his Fibresand debut at Wolverhampton before an all-the-way win at Goodwood over 12 furlongs. Suited by fast ground. Sold for 100,000 gns at Tattersalls to go hurdling with Jim Old. **S P C Woods [3-13] Dwayne Woods.*

CANTGETYOURBREATH (IRE) BHB 49f52a **RR 35f 52a** 4701[11]

3 ch g College Chapel - Cathy Garcia (IRE) (Be My Guest (USA)) 9.3f **(67)**

Form - 31462403480000000

Record				
1999 -	1st:0	2nd:0	3rd:1	Ran:12
Pre1999 -	1st:1	2nd:2	3rd:2	Ran:9

Win Prizemoney £1,966 *Total Prizemoney* £4,967

Wins							
1998	*Nov*	*Southw*	*(STD)*	*S*	*6f*	*69*	<

1999 Turf 0-4: (6f, 7f 3) (gd, frm 3)1999 AW 0-8:(6f 7, 7f)(Equi 3, Fibr 5)

Unfurnished, very moderate gelding, effective 6f, acts on g-s - acts on AW, mostly wears blinkers, likes left handed tracks, likes tight tracks. Turf high 35. AW high 69. His only victory to date came when he bolted home in a seller on the Southwell Fibresand at the end of last year, but looks very moderate now.

**Mrs N Macauley [0-11] Mrs Anna Sanders (from B J Meehan [1-10] Jan 1999).*

CANTINA BHB 66f **RR 66f** 4140[13]

5 b m Tina's Pet 7.4f **(56)** - Real Claire (Dreams to Reality (USA)) 6.4f **(73)**

Form - 67056130450

Record				
1999 -	1st:1	2nd:0	3rd:1	Ran:11
Pre1999 -	1st:3	2nd:0	3rd:3	Ran:14

Win Prizemoney £15,985 *Total Prizemoney* £20,303

Wins								
* **1999**	Jly	Redcar	(FRM)		7f		68	
* 1998	Aug	Lingfi	(G-F)	H	7.6f	73	77	<
* 1998	Jly	Cheste	(G-F)	H	7.6f	69	72	
* 1997	Spt	Catter	(G-F)		7f		62	

1999 Turf 1-11: (6f, 7f 1-7, 8f 3) (g-s, gd 2, g-f 3, frm 1-5)

Average filly, effective 7 to 8f, best at 8f, acts on gd to frm, best on frm. Turf high 71 - also 1st of 10 giving 4lb to Perigeux (24 Jly Redcar RF 3104). Seven furlongs and fast ground suit her admirably, and she is hard to peg back when on song.

**A Bailey [4-25] R Kinsey,Mrs M Kinsey & Miss B Roberts.*

CANTON VENTURE BHB 48f41a **RR 43f 41a** 4666[10]

7 ch g Arctic Tern (USA) 12.2f **(71)** - Ski Michaela (USA) (Devil's Bag (USA)) 12.4f **(78)**

Form - 687740

Record				
1999 -	1st:0	2nd:0	3rd:0	Ran:6
Pre1999 -	1st:10	2nd:5	3rd:2	Ran:33

Win Prizemoney £34,926 *Total Prizemoney* £41,179

Wins								
* 1997	*May*	*Lingfi*	*(STD)*	*H*	*12f*	*74*	*79+*	<
* 1996	Aug	Bright	(FRM)	H	11.9f	70	73	
* 1996	Jly	Bright	(FRM)	H	11.9f	64	67	
* 1996	Jun	Newcas	(FRM)	H	12.4f	60	63	
* 1996	Jun	Thirsk	(FRM)	H	12f	51	61	
* 1996	Jun	Warwic	(FRM)	H	12.5f	51	54	
* 1996	May	Folkes	(GD)		12f		55	
* 1996	*May*	*Southw*	*(STD)*	*H*	*11f*	*64*	*70*	
* 1995	*Spt*	*Wolver*	*(STD)*	*H*	*12f*	*60*	*67*	
* 1995	*Jly*	*Wolver*	*(STD)*	*H*	*12f*	*59*	*65+*	

1999 Turf 0-3: (14f 2, 16f) (gd, frm 2) 1999 AW 0-3: (12f, 15f, 16f) (Equi 2, Fibr)

Moderate gelding, effective 12f, - acts on Fibr, has worn blinkers. Turf high 43. AW high 45. Consistent.

**S P C Woods [15-61] Dr Frank Chao.*

CANYOUHEARME BHB 48f43a **RR 58f 43a** 2[8]

3 b f Sabrehill (USA) 8.5f **(64)** - Fiveofive (IRE) (Fairy King (USA)) 7.7f **(59)**

Form - 68

Record				
1999 -	1st:0	2nd:0	3rd:0	Ran:1
Pre1999 -	1st:0	2nd:0	3rd:0	Ran:6

1999 AW 0-1: (8f) (Equi)

Workmanlike, fair filly, effective 6 to 8f, acts on g-f.

**N A Callaghan [0-7] Mrs T A Foreman.*

CAPA RR 81f 4598[2]

2 b c Salse (USA) 10.9f **(71)** - Pippas Song (Reference Point) 6.8f **(70)**

Form - 22

Record 1999 - 1st:0 2nd:2 3rd:0 Ran:2

Win Prizemoney £0 *Total Prizemoney* £2,898

1999 Turf 0-2: (8f 2) (gd, g-f)

Currently decent colt. Turf high 81 (began Spt) - 2nd of 8 to Peacock Jewel (28 Spt Newmarket 8f g-f RF 4598).

**B W Hills [0-2] R J McCreery.*

CAPACOOSTIC RR 53f 4542[12]

2 ch f Savahra Sound 7.8f **(55)** - Cocked Hat Girl (Ballacashtal (CAN)) 5.3f **(50)**

Form - 00

Record 1999 - 1st:0 2nd:0 3rd:0 Ran:2

1999 Turf 0-2: (5f, 6f) (gd, frm)

Currently fair filly. Turf high 51 (began Spt).

**S R Bowring [0-2] J E Reed & P M Sedgwick.*

CAPE CLEAR BHB 65f **RR 67?f** 3006^{2}
3 b f Slip Anchor 12.7f **(75)** - Wise Speculation (USA) (Mr Prospector (USA)) 8.8f **(78)**
Form - 742
Record 1999 - 1st:0 2nd:1 3rd:0 Ran:3
Win Prizemoney £0 *Total Prizemoney* £866
1999 Turf 0-3: (12f 2, 14f) (g-f, frm, hrd)
Scopey, currently average filly. Turf high 67 - 4th of 5 to Sedrah (30 Jun Catterick 12f frm RF 2440). **R A Fahey [0-3] Nick O'Toole.*

CAPE COAST (IRE) RR 71f 4178^{6}
2 b c Common Grounds 8.1f **(66)** - Strike It Rich (FR) (Rheingold) 10.4f **(62)**
Form - 26
Record 1999 - 1st:0 2nd:1 3rd:0 Ran:2
Win Prizemoney £0 *Total Prizemoney* £1,080
1999 Turf 0-2: (6f 2) (frm 2)
Currently above-average colt. Turf high 71 (began Aug). **D Marks [0-2] Godiva.*

Cape Cross proved difficult to catch in Group Two company last season

CAPE CROSS (IRE) BHB 123f **RR 125f** $4657a^{6}$
5 b h Green Desert (USA) 7.8f **(78)** - Park Appeal (Ahonoora) 8.1f **(73)**
Form - 3116
Record 1999 - 1st:2 2nd:0 3rd:1 Ran:4
Pre1999 - 1st:3 2nd:2 3rd:2 Ran:13
Win Prizemoney £206,121 *Total Prizemoney* £257,322
Wins * **1999** Aug Goodwo (GD) G2 8f 125 <
* **1999** Jun Ascot (G-F) G2 8f 121
* 1998 May Newbur (G-F) G1 8f 121
1997 Aug Goodwo (G-F) 8f 107
1996 Spt Doncas (G-F) 8f 95+
1999 Turf 2-3: (8f 2-3) (gd 1-1, g-f 1-1, frm) 1999 AW 0-1: (8f) (Dirt)
Top-class colt, effective 8f, acts on gd to frm. Turf high 125 - 1st of 5 giving 12lb to Josr Algarhoud (28 Aug Goodwood RF 3957) - also 1st of 8 giving 5lb to Docksider (15 Jun Ascot RF 1995). Winner of the 1998 Lockinge, where he was an intended pacemaker for Kahal, he was well beaten in Dubai at the World Cup meeting this year, but returned to his best when putting up a battling front-running display in the Queen Anne at Royal Ascot when again the lesser fancied of the Godolphin runners. Disposing of Fa-Eq that day, he then repeated the dose when taking care of the relatively inexperienced Josr Algarhoud at Goodwood in the Celebration Mile. Well beaten in Woodbine's Atto Mile, he is due to have one more race, at Sha Tin in December, before retiring to stud in Ireland. **S bin Suroor [3-9] Godolphin.*

CAPE GRACE (IRE) BHB 99f **RR 95f** 738^{4}
3 b f Priolo (USA) 10.9f **(71)** - Saffron (FR) (Fabulous Dancer (USA)) 9.4f **(70)**
Form - 44
Record 1999 - 1st:0 2nd:0 3rd:0 Ran:2
Pre1999 - 1st:1 2nd:1 3rd:0 Ran:3
Win Prizemoney £6,840 *Total Prizemoney* £11,016
Wins * 1998 Jly Ascot (G-F) 6f 86t <
1999 Turf 0-2: (8f, 10f) (g-f 2)
Scopey, very useful filly. Turf high 95 - 4th of 8 getting 5lb from Lucido (17 Apr Newbury 10f g-f RF 0738). She seems to stay a mile and a quarter, but lacks a turn-of-foot against decent opposition. **R Hannon [1-5] George Strawbridge.*

CAPE HOPE BHB 48f38a **RR 28f 38a** 642^{8}
4 b c Risk Me (FR) 8f **(53)** - Bernstein Bette **(35f 44a)** (Petong) 6.6f **(58)**
Form - 0008
Record 1999 - 1st:0 2nd:0 3rd:0 Ran:2
Pre1999 - 1st:1 2nd:0 3rd:1 Ran:17
Win Prizemoney £2,490 *Total Prizemoney* £2,950
Wins 1998 Apr Leices (SFT) S 6f 68 <
1999 Turf 0-1: (6f) (sft) 1999 AW 0-1: (5f) (Fibr)
Workmanlike, little account colt, effective 6f, acts on sft, has worn blinkers. Becoming disappointing.
**S R Bowring [0-4] Ace Employment (from J Akehurst [1-7] Jly 1998).*

CAPERCAILLIE BHB 49a **RR 35f** 1710^{2}
4 ch g Deploy 11.4f **(67)** - Tee Gee Jay **(36f 36a)** (Northern Tempest (USA))
Form - 64022
Record 1999 - 1st:0 2nd:2 3rd:0 Ran:3
Pre1999 - 1st:0 2nd:0 3rd:3 Ran:15
Win Prizemoney £0 *Total Prizemoney* £2,384
1999 Turf 0-3: (10f 2, 12f) (gd, frm, hrd)
Workmanlike, moderate gelding, effective 8f, - acts on Fibr, has worn blinkers, favours left handed tracks, favours tight tracks. Turf high 35.
**J E Banks [0-3] Future Electrical Services Ltd (from D Morris [0-15] Nov 1998).*

CAPE TOWN (IRE) RR 93+f 5029^{2}
2 gr c Desert Style (IRE) - Rossaldene (Mummy's Pet) 7.7f **(60)**
Form - 12
Record 1999 - 1st:1 2nd:1 3rd:0 Ran:2
Win Prizemoney £3,752 *Total Prizemoney* £11,694
Wins * **1999** Oct Lingfi (G-S) 7f 85+ <
1999 Turf 1-2: (7f 1-2) (g-s 1-2)
Currently useful colt. Turf high 93 (began Oct) - 2nd of 9 to Umistim (22 Oct Newbury 7f g-s RF 5029) - also 1st of 18 from Alva Glen (8 Oct Lingfield RF 4785). Well backed before winning a Lingfield maiden in impressive fashion on his debut, he did not get the best of runs when beaten by stable-companion Umistim in the Horris Hill, and remains a very interesting prospect. **R Hannon [1-2] S A Six.*

CAPE VERDI (IRE) BHB 115f **RR 112f** 3260^{8}
4 b f Caerleon (USA) 10.9f **(79)** - Afrique Bleu Azur (USA) (Sagace (FR)) 8f **(124)**
Form - 38
Record 1999 - 1st:0 2nd:0 3rd:1 Ran:2
Pre1999 - 1st:3 2nd:1 3rd:0 Ran:6
Win Prizemoney £177,919 *Total Prizemoney* £196,485
Wins * 1998 May Newmar (GD) G1 8f 124+ <
1997 Aug York (GD) G2 6f 106
1997 May Newmar (G-F) 6f 94++
1999 Turf 0-2: (8f, 10f) (g-f, frm)
Well made, Group-class filly. Turf high 112 (began Jly). Outstanding when winning the 1998 1,000 Guineas, her failure to recapture top form after sustaining a hairline fracture of a hind pastern was one of the season's disappointments. She should not be remembered for faltering efforts in the Falmouth or Nassau Stakes, but rather that five-length demolition of Shahtoush (herself later successful in the Oaks) on the Rowley Mile at Newmarket.
**S bin Suroor [1-4] Godolphin (from P W Chapple-Hyam [2-4] Spt 1997).*

CAPILANO PRINCESS BHB 81f71a **RR 84f 71a** 2570^{3}
6 b m Tragic Role (USA) 9.4f **(63)** - Lady Capilano (Nebbiolo) 8.1f **(75)**
Form - 683

Record 1999 - 1st:0 2nd:0 3rd:1 Ran:3
Pre1999 - 1st:6 2nd:1 3rd:2 Ran:21
Win Prizemoney £24,833 *Total Prizemoney* £29,187
Wins * 1997 Spt Ayr (G-S) H 10f 86 89 <
* 1997 Jly Doncas (GD) H 10.3f 81 84
* 1997 Jly Chepst (G-S) H 10.2f 78 81
* 1997 May Nottin (GD) 10f 80
* 1996 May Newbur (SFT) H 7.3f 72 78
* 1995 Nov Doncas (G-F) H 7f 66 76
1999 Turf 0-3: (10f 2, 12f) (g-f, frm 2)
Decent mare. Turf high 84 (1st run) - 6th of 13 giving 9lb to King Darius (4 May Chester 10f g-f RF 1028). Consistent.
**D HaydnJones [6-24] H G Collis.*

CAPISTRANO DAY (USA) BHB 108f RR 105f 5114a[1]

3 b f Diesis 9f **(80)** - Alcando (Alzao (USA)) 7.1f **(68)**
Form - 3405D31
Record 1999 - 1st:1 2nd:0 3rd:2 Ran:7
Pre1999 - 1st:1 2nd:0 3rd:0 Ran:2
Win Prizemoney £18,634 *Total Prizemoney* £33,834
Wins * **1999** Oct Deauvi (GD) L 7f 105 <
* 1998 Oct Redcar (HVY) 7f 84
1999 Turf 1-7: (7f 1-4, 8f 3) (gd 1-1, g-f 2, frm 4)
Scopey, Pattern-class filly, effective 7 to 8f, best at 7f, acts on gd to frm, best on frm. Turf high 109 - 4th of 22 to Wince (2 May Newmarket 8f frm RF 0979) - also 1st of 14 giving 5lb to Arctic Char (18 Oct Deauville RF 5114a). Consistent. Unlucky in running behind Wince in the Fred Darling on her reappearance, she appeared to have no excuses when behind the same filly in the 1000 Guineas, and was well beaten in the Irish version. Well held until putting in a better effort at Doncaster, she ended her European career with a victory in a Deauville listed event, before racing in America. **J H M Gosden [2-9] Anthony Speelman.*

CAPITALIST BHB 48f45a RR 29f 45a 4758[15]

3 br g Bigstone (IRE) - Pinkie Rose (FR) (Kenmare (FR)) 6.5f **(72)**
Form - 066688000
Record 1999 - 1st:0 2nd:0 3rd:0 Ran:9
Pre1999 - 1st:0 2nd:0 3rd:1 Ran:8
Win Prizemoney £0 *Total Prizemoney* £1,099
1999 Turf 0-8: (8f 2, 9f 2, 10f 2, 11f, 12f) (g-s, gd 3, frm 4) 1999 AW 0-1: (8f) (Fibr)
Scopey, very moderate gelding, effective 7 to 8f, best at 7f, acts on frm, has worn blinkers. Turf high 63. Becoming disappointing.
**R M Whitaker [0-9] GRP Group (from Mrs J R Ramsden [0-8] Oct 1998).*

CAPLAW SKEEN BHB 34f RR 46?f 2226[14]

4 b g Sure Blade (USA) 10.6f **(66)** - Mary From Dunlow (Nicholas Bill) 10.1f **(56)**
Form - 0
Record 1999 - 1st:0 2nd:0 3rd:0 Ran:1
Pre1999 - 1st:0 2nd:1 3rd:0 Ran:3
Win Prizemoney £0 *Total Prizemoney* £695
1999 Turf 0-1: (17f) (frm)
Scopey, moderate gelding. (DEAD)
**J J O'Neill [0-2] J J Wright (from J L Eyre [0-2] Nov 1997).*

CAPPELLA (IRE) BHB 63f RR 63f 4440[9]

3 br f College Chapel - Mavahra (Mummy's Pet) 7.7f **(60)**
Form - 680308840
Record 1999 - 1st:0 2nd:0 3rd:1 Ran:9
Pre1999 - 1st:2 2nd:1 3rd:1 Ran:8
Win Prizemoney £6,789 *Total Prizemoney* £9,325
Wins * 1998 Aug Sandow (G-F) H 5f 74 73 <
* 1998 Jun Salisb (G-S) 5f 73 <
1999 Turf 0-9: (5f 2, 6f 7) (gd 2, g-f 5, frm 2)
Leggy, average filly, effective 5 to 6f, best at 5f, acts on gd to g-f, best on gd, has worn blinkers. Turf high 65 - 3rd of 17 getting 7lb from Barnacla (7 Jun Windsor 6f gd RF 1801).
**R Hannon [2-17] Thurloe Thoroughbreds III.*

CAPPELLINA (IRE) RR 56f 3570[13]

2 b f College Chapel - Santa Ana Wind (Busted) 10.2f **(61)**
Form - 70
Record 1999 - 1st:0 2nd:0 3rd:0 Ran:2
1999 Turf 0-2: (7f 2) (g-f 2)
Currently fair filly. Turf high 56.
**P G Murphy [0-2] Mrs John Spielman.*

CAPPUCINO LADY BHB 40f RR 60f 3960[6]

2 b f Prince Sabo 6.6f **(64)** - Cubist (IRE) (Tate Gallery (USA)) 7.4f **(67)**
Form - 0U306
Record 1999 - 1st:0 2nd:0 3rd:1 Ran:5
Win Prizemoney £0 *Total Prizemoney* £299
1999 Turf 0-5: (5f, 6f 3, 7f) (gd, g-f 2, frm 2)
Average filly. Turf high 60. **J J Bridger [0-5] J J Bridger.*

CAPRI BHB 114f RR 117f 2576[7]

4 ch c Generous (IRE) 11.5f **(82)** - Island Jamboree (USA) (Explodent (USA)) 9.4f **(87)**
Form - 717
Record 1999 - 1st:1 2nd:0 3rd:0 Ran:3
Pre1999 - 1st:3 2nd:3 3rd:1 Ran:7
Win Prizemoney £79,374 *Total Prizemoney* £95,193
Wins * **1999** Jun Chanti (G-S) G2 12f 117 <
* 1998 Spt Ascot (G-F) G3 12f 113
* 1998 May Newmar (G-S) 12f 99+
* 1998 Apr Newmar (G-S) 12f 93+
1999 Turf 1-3: (12f 1-3) (g-s 1-1, g-f, frm)
Scopey, high-class colt, effective 12f, acts on g-s to g-f. Turf high 117 - 1st of 4 getting 5lb from Epistolaire (13 Jun Chantilly RF 2097a). He won three times in 1998, but ran just three times in total last season. He had the easy ground he likes when making all to win the Grand Prix de Chantilly on his second run, but was not seen out again after running poorly behind stable-companion Craigsteel at Newmarket in July.
**H R A Cecil [4-10] H R H Prince Fahd Salman.*

CAPRICE RR 15f 5192[16]

2 gr f Mystiko (USA) 7.7f **(59)** - Tebre (USA) (Sir Ivor) 10.2f **(70)**
Form - 0
Record 1999 - 1st:0 2nd:0 3rd:0 Ran:1
1999 Turf 0-1: (8f) (gd)
Currently poor filly. **S C Williams [0-1] Bruce Wyatt.*

CAPRIOLO (IRE) BHB 71f RR 72f 4836[1]

3 ch g Priolo (USA) 10.9f **(71)** - Carroll's Canyon (IRE) (Hatim (USA))
Form - 002312062001
Record 1999 - 1st:2 2nd:3 3rd:1 Ran:12
Pre1999 - 1st:0 2nd:0 3rd:2 Ran:4
Win Prizemoney £10,692 *Total Prizemoney* £16,705
Wins * **1999** Oct Leices (GD) H 10f 69 72 <
* **1999** Jun Salisb (FRM) H 9.9f 62 67
1999 Turf 2-12: (9f, 10f 2-4, 11f, 12f 6) (g-s, gd 1-3, g-f 2, frm 1-6)
Above-average gelding, effective 6f, acts on g-f, often wears blinkers. Turf high 72. A tough sort, he has run some of his best races at Salisbury. **R Hannon [2-16] John Homer Racing.*

CAPTAIN BLIGH RR 68tf 1002[14]

3 b c Green Desert (USA) 7.8f **(78)** - Hyabella (Shirley Heights) 10.3f **(74)**
Form - 40
Record 1999 - 1st:0 2nd:0 3rd:0 Ran:2
Win Prizemoney £0 *Total Prizemoney* £305
1999 Turf 0-2: (8f 2) (gd, frm)
Well made, currently average colt. Turf high 68.
**Sir Michael Stoute [0-2] M Tabor & Mrs John Magnier.*

CAPTAIN BRADY (IRE) BHB 51f RR 55f 4930[13]

4 ch g Soviet Lad (USA) 9.4f **(63)** - Eight Mile Rock (Dominion) 8.5f **(63)**
Form - 3815230210030
Record 1999 - 1st:2 2nd:2 3rd:3 Ran:13
Pre1999 - 1st:0 2nd:0 3rd:1 Ran:6
Win Prizemoney £11,381 *Total Prizemoney* £15,669
Wins * **1999** Aug Ripon (GD) H 9f 50 55 <
* **1999** May Hamilt (Sft) H 8.3f 44 52
1999 Turf 2-13: (8f 1-4, 9f 1-5, 10f 3, 11f) (hvy, sft, g-s 1-1, gd 3, g-f 1-5, frm 2)
Unfurnished, fair gelding, effective 8 to 10f, best at 9f, acts on g-s to frm, best on g-f, has worn blinkers, prefers right handed tracks. Turf high 55 - 1st of 13 getting 3lb from Amron (21 Aug Ripon RF 3820) - also 1st of 10 giving 6lb to Napoleon's Return (14 May

Hamilton RF 1208). Inconsistent.
**J S Goldie [3-18] Frank Brady (from W G M Turner [0-6] Oct 1997).*

CAPTAIN CARAT BHB 29f35a RR 7f 35a 4167[10]
8 gr g Handsome Sailor 6.6f **(53)** - Gem of Gold (Jellaby) 6.4f **(58)**
Form - 00540000
Record 1999 - 1st:0 2nd:0 3rd:0 Ran:7
Pre1999 - 1st:6 2nd:9 3rd:11 Ran:92
Win Prizemoney £22,411 *Total Prizemoney* £40,556
Wins 1997 May Catter (G-F) C 5f 57
1996 May Newcas (GD) H 5f 62 65 <
1996 Apr Pontef (GD) H 5f 60 61
1995 May Doncas (G-F) H 6f 59 60
1999 Turf 0-7: (5f 3, 6f 3, 7f) (gd, g-f 3, frm 3)
Very moderate gelding, effective 6f, acts on frm, has worn blinkers (extremely effectively). Turf high 30. Becoming disappointing.
**D W Chapman [0-19] David Chapman (from Ronald Thompson [0-1] Nov 1997).*

CAPTAIN FLINT BHB 32f42a RR 50f 42a 2653[15]
5 b br g Bedford (USA) - Sun Yat Chen (Chou Chin Chow)
Form - 00
Record 1999 - 1st:0 2nd:0 3rd:0 Ran:2
Pre1999 - 1st:1 2nd:0 3rd:0 Ran:8
Win Prizemoney £2,574 *Total Prizemoney* £2,574
Wins * 1997 Jun Pontef (SFT) SH 12f 40 50 <
1999 AW 0-2: (11f, 14f) (Fibr 2)
Fair gelding. Inconsistent. **A Smith [1-10] Mrs G Wood.*

CAPTAIN LOGAN (IRE) BHB 65f RR 56f 5035[13]
4 b c Fairy King (USA) 7.7f **(75)** - Heaven High (High Line) 10.3f **(70)**
Form - 000
Record 1999 - 1st:0 2nd:0 3rd:0 Ran:3
Pre1999 - 1st:1 2nd:2 3rd:0 Ran:6
Win Prizemoney £3,548 *Total Prizemoney* £6,594
Wins 1998 Jun Ayr (GD) 7f 91 <
1999 Turf 0-3: (7f, 8f 2) (g-s, gd 2)
Scopey, fair colt, effective 7 to 8f, best at 7f, acts on gd, has worn blinkers. Turf high 56 (began Spt). Becoming disappointing.
**J Noseda [0-3] Lucayan Stud (from D R Loder [1-6] Spt 1998).*

CAPTAIN MARMALADE BHB 37f23a RR 37f 23a 269[8]
10 ch g Myjinski (USA) - Lady Seville (Orange Bay)
Form - 88
Record 1999 - 1st:0 2nd:0 3rd:0 Ran:1
Pre1999 - 1st:4 2nd:10 3rd:10 Ran:96
Win Prizemoney £9,653 *Total Prizemoney* £22,729
Wins * 1996 *Mar Lingfi (STD) C 16f 48*
* 1995 Apr Nottin (GD) H 10f 40 46
1999 AW 0-1: (16f) (Equi)
Very moderate gelding, has broken blood-vessels, has worn blinkers. **D T Thom [5-111] Mrs Alison Thom.*

CAPTAIN MCCLOY (USA) BHB 44f44a RR 46f 44a 4700[12]
4 ch g Lively One (USA) - Fly Me First (USA) (Herbager) 13f **(65)**
Form - 0344416326400
Record 1999 - 1st:1 2nd:1 3rd:2 Ran:13
Pre1999 - 1st:0 2nd:0 3rd:2 Ran:14
Win Prizemoney £2,267 *Total Prizemoney* £4,905
Wins * **1999** Jly Warwic (G-F) SH 10.5f 33 38 <
1999 Turf 1-13: (10f 9, 11f 1-3, 12f) (sft 2, g-s, gd 2, g-f 1-6, frm 2)
Scopey, moderate gelding, effective 10f, acts on gd to g-f - acts on Equi, has worn blinkers. Turf high 52.
**N E Berry [1-20] D W Smith (from Mrs J R Ramsden [0-7] Oct 1997).*

CAPTAIN MILLER BHB 67f RR 70f 1921[9]
3 b g Batshoof 9.5f **(66)** - Miller's Gait (Mill Reef (USA)) 10.5f **(78)**
Form - 110210
Record 1999 - 1st:3 2nd:1 3rd:0 Ran:6
Pre1999 - 1st:1 2nd:1 3rd:0 Ran:12
Win Prizemoney £14,334 *Total Prizemoney* £16,079
Wins * **1999** May Ripon (G-F) C 8f 70
* **1999** Apr Hamilt (HVY) 8.3f 69++
* **1999** Apr Leices (G-S) H 7f 62 70
* 1998 Jun Lingfi (G-S) 7f 82+ <
1999 Turf 3-6: (7f 1-1, 8f 2-5) (hvy 1-1, gd 1-1, g-f, frm 1-3)
Light-framed, above-average gelding, effective 6 to 7f, acts on gd to frm, likes tight tracks. Turf high 70. In fine form in the spring, winning three times on varying ground, he is now with Nicky Henderson. **M R Channon [4-18] John Carey.*

CAPTAIN SCOTT (IRE) BHB 90f92a RR 92f 92a 2733[14]
5 b g Polar Falcon (USA) 9f **(74)** - Camera Girl (Kalaglow) 9.8f **(67)**
Form - 12400
Record 1999 - 1st:1 2nd:1 3rd:0 Ran:5
Pre1999 - 1st:2 2nd:1 3rd:3 Ran:10
Win Prizemoney £39,245 *Total Prizemoney* £59,437
Wins * **1999** *Mar Wolver (STD) H 8.5f 85 94* <
* 1997 Jly Ayr (G-F) 10f 84
* 1997 *Mar Southw (STD) 8f 70+*
1999 Turf 0-4: (8f 2, 10f 2) (gd 2, g-f, frm)1999 AW 1-1:(8f 1-1)(Fibr 1-1)
Useful gelding, effective 8 to 10f, best at 8f, acts on gd to frm - acts on Fibr, likes tight tracks. Turf high 96 (1st run) - 2nd of 24 getting 10lb from Right Wing (27 Mar Doncaster 8f gd RF 0485). (1st run) - 1st of 13 getting 6lb from Welville (13 Mar Wolverhampton RF 0431). He disappointed after being touched-off in the Lincoln, running poorly in the John Smith's Cup on his final start. Effective up to a mile and a quarter, he goes well on a sound surface and has shown his best form when ridden patiently in a fast-run race. **J A Glover [3-15] The Write State Partnership.*

CAPTAIN'S LOG BHB 72f RR 77f 5053[8]
4 b g Slip Anchor 12.7f **(75)** - Cradle of Love (USA) (Roberto (USA)) 10f **(76)**
Form - 45248668
Record 1999 - 1st:0 2nd:1 3rd:0 Ran:8
Pre1999 - 1st:2 2nd:1 3rd:0 Ran:12
Win Prizemoney £10,787 *Total Prizemoney* £19,892
Wins * 1998 Jun Newcas (GD) H 9f 73 76 <
* 1998 May Warwic (GD) 8f 74
1999 Turf 0-8: (8f, 10f 5, 11f, 12f) (gd 2, g-f 5, frm)
Light-framed, above-average gelding, effective 8 to 12f, best at 10f, acts on g-s to frm, best on g-f, prefers left handed tracks, excels at Newcastle. Turf high 80 (1st run) - 4th of 20 getting 16lb from Carry The Flag (5 Apr Kempton 10f g-f RF 0576). Consistent. His come-from-behind style means he often finds trouble in running, and wins are hard to come by. **M L W Bell [2-20] Christopher Wright.*

CARABINE (USA) BHB 55f RR 56f 3294[8]
3 gr f Dehere (USA) - Caracciola (FR) (Zeddaan) 9f **(76)**
Form - 8
Record 1999 - 1st:0 2nd:0 3rd:0 Ran:1
Pre1999 - 1st:0 2nd:0 3rd:0 Ran:3
1999 Turf 0-1: (7f) (frm)
Neat, fair filly. **Sir Mark Prescott [0-4] Miss K Rausing.*

CARADOC BHB 42f52a RR 53?f 52a 4387[21]
4 ch g Bustino 11f **(64)** - Hathaway (Connaught) 7.7f **(63)**
Form - 0
Record 1999 - 1st:0 2nd:0 3rd:0 Ran:1
Pre1999 - 1st:0 2nd:0 3rd:0 Ran:6
1999 Turf 0-1: (12f) (frm)
Leggy, fair gelding.
**Mrs L C Jewell [0-1] John Hurd (from S C Williams [0-6] Jun 1998).*

CARAMBO BHB 60f75a RR 60f 75a 5073[10]
4 b f Rambo Dancer (CAN) 8.4f **(59)** - Light the Way (Nicholas Bill) 10.1f **(56)**
Form - 5708003637513040
Record 1999 - 1st:1 2nd:0 3rd:3 Ran:14
Pre1999 - 1st:2 2nd:5 3rd:1 Ran:21
Win Prizemoney £9,861 *Total Prizemoney* £18,552
Wins **1999** Spt Nottin (G-F) H 6.1f 56 61
1997 *Oct Wolver (STD) H 7f 82 86* <
1997 *Jly Wolver (STD) H 6f 77*
1999 Turf 1-14: (6f 1-2, 7f 9, 8f 3) (gd 4, g-f, frm 1-9)
Workmanlike, decent filly, effective 7 to 8f, best at 7f, acts on gd, has worn blinkers (effectively). Turf high 64. A fair performer at Wolverhampton on the Fibresand, she had not scored on turf until taking a competitive Nottingham sprint in September. Seems to want a fast surface on turf.
**T D Barron [0-1] Nigel Shields (from J L Eyre [3-34] Oct 1999).*

CARAMBOLA (IRE) RR 100f 4315a[7]
3 b f Danehill (USA) 9.1f **(79)** - Purchasepaperchase (Young Generation) 7.7f **(63)**
Form - 1416027
1999 Turf 2-7: (7f, 8f 2-4, 10f, 12f) (sft 1-1, gd 1-2, g-f 4)
Very useful filly, effective 7 to 8f, acts on gd to g-f. Turf high 100 - 4th of 7 getting 5lb from Show Me The Money (18 Apr Leopardstown 7f g-f RF 0784a) - also 1st of 7 from Apparatchik (9 May Leopardstown RF 1170a). Inconsistent. Tough and genuine, she progressed well, running her best race when finishing sixth in the Irish 1,000 Guineas. Disappointing when tried over middle-distances, she may not stay beyond a mile.
**A P O'Brien in IRE [2-8] Michael Tabor.*

CARBON BHB 39f **RR 44f** 3910[16]
4 b g Batshoof 9.5f **(66)** - Reyah (Young Generation) 7.7f **(63)**
Form - 00000
Record 1999 - 1st:0 2nd:0 3rd:0 Ran:5
Pre1999 - 1st:1 2nd:0 3rd:1 Ran:11
Win Prizemoney £4,260 *Total Prizemoney* £5,313
Wins 1997 Jun York (G-S) 6f 75+ <
1999 Turf 0-4: (7f 3, 10f) (gd 2, frm 2) 1999 AW 0-1: (7f) (Equi)
Scopey, moderate gelding, has worn blinkers. Turf high 44. Becoming disappointing.
**Lady Herries [0-12] I R Corke (from D Morley [1-4] Aug 1997).*

CARD GAMES BHB 88f **RR 85f** 4686[13]
2 b f First Trump - Pericardia **(60df)** (Petong) 6.6f **(58)**
Form - 340131420
Record 1999 - 1st:2 2nd:1 3rd:2 Ran:9
Win Prizemoney £6,219 *Total Prizemoney* £11,240
Wins * 1999 Aug Pontef (GD) H 6f 78 85 <
*** 1999** Jly Salisb (G-F) 6f 76
1999 Turf 2-9: (5f 3, 6f 2-4, 7f 2) (g-s, gd 2, g-f 2, frm 2-4)
Useful filly, effective 5 to 7f, best at 7f, acts on g-s to frm, has worn blinkers, does well at Salisbury. Turf high 85 - 1st of 12 giving 3lb to Alphilda (16 Aug Pontefract RF 3673) - also 1st of 12 getting 5lb from Heritage Park (10 Jly Salisbury RF 2712). A game winner in a Salisbury maiden before a sound effort at Kempton, she gained another victory in a Pontefract nursery.
**I A Balding [2-9] Park House Partnership.*

CARDIFF ARMS (NZ) RR 88f 4674[9]
5 b g Lowell (USA) - Shuzohra (NZ) (Tom's Shu (USA))
Form - 0
Record 1999 - 1st:0 2nd:0 3rd:0 Ran:1
1999 Turf 0-1: (12f) (gd)
Currently useful gelding. **M Johnston [0-1] The Winning Line.*

CARDINAL FAIR (IRE) RR 5193[9]
2 b f Namaqualand (USA) - Irish Affaire (IRE) (Fairy King (USA)) 7.7f **(59)**
Form -
Record 1999 - 1st:0 2nd:0 3rd:0 Ran:3
1999 Turf 0-3: (hvy, g-s, gd)
Leggy, currently fair filly. Turf high 57 (began Oct).
**J G Portman [0-3] Mrs Heather Murat.*

CAREFREE CHEETAH (USA) BHB 65f **RR 63f** 1925[9]
3 gr f Trempolino (USA) 11.9f **(77)** - Careless Kitten (USA) (Caro)
Form - 260
Record 1999 - 1st:0 2nd:1 3rd:0 Ran:3
Win Prizemoney £0 *Total Prizemoney* £840
1999 Turf 0-3: (10f 3) (g-s, gd, frm)
Workmanlike, currently average filly. Turf high 63.
**J Noseda [0-3] G J Beck.*

CARELESS BHB 57f **RR 63f** 4451[8]
2 b f Robellino (USA) 9.5f **(68)** - Life's Too Short (IRE) **(51f)** (Astronef)
Form - 408
Record 1999 - 1st:0 2nd:0 3rd:0 Ran:3
1999 Turf 0-3: (6f, 7f 2) (sft, g-f, frm)
Currently average filly. Turf high 63 (began Jly).
**J E Banks [0-3] Giles Pritchard-Gordon.*

CARENS HERO (IRE) RR 59f 5216[8]
2 ch c Petardia 8.2f **(58)** - Clear Glade (Vitiges (FR)) 8.2f **(59)**
Form - 8
Record 1999 - 1st:0 2nd:0 3rd:0 Ran:1
1999 Turf 0-1: (8f) (g-s)
Currently fair colt. **Mrs A J Perrett [0-1] Mrs R Doel.*

CAREQUICK BHB 45f **RR 34f** 1671[7]
3 ch f Risk Me (FR) 8f **(53)** - Miss Serlby (Runnett) 7f **(59)**
Form - 0007
Record 1999 - 1st:0 2nd:0 3rd:0 Ran:4
Pre1999 - 1st:0 2nd:0 3rd:0 Ran:5
1999 Turf 0-3: (5f, 6f, 7f) (g-s, g-f 2) 1999 AW 0-1: (7f) (Fibr)
Light-framed, very moderate filly, has worn blinkers. Turf high 34. Consistent. **A Bailey [0-9] Carequick Ltd-Conser Units.*

CARHUE GOLD (IRE) RR 69f 5185a[4]
3 ch f Bob Back (USA) 11.5f **(71)** - Return Journey (IRE) (Pennine Walk) 8.5f **(61)**
Form - 26644
1999 Turf 0-5: (8f 4, 10f) (sft 4, g-s)
Average filly, effective 8f, acts on sft. Turf high 90 (1st run) - 2nd of 26 getting 5lb from Saffron Walden (28 Mar Curragh 8f sft RF 0521a). **P O'Leary in IRE [0-6] P O'Leary.*

CARHUE LASS (IRE) RR 104f 4654[14]
5 b m Common Grounds 8.1f **(66)** - Return Journey (IRE) (Pennine Walk) 8.5f **(61)**
Form - 51280
1999 Turf 1-5: (5f 1-5) (sft, g-s 1-1, gd 3)
Very useful filly, effective 5f, acts on sft to gd. Turf high 104 - 2nd of 7 getting 3lb from Proud Native (7 Jun Leopardstown 5f gd RF 2011a). She has plenty of early pace and appreciated the soft ground when landing a Bath listed event.
**P O'Leary in IRE [2-20] P O'Leary.*

CARIBBEAN MONARCH (IRE) BHB 93f **RR 93?f** 5222[11]
4 b c Fairy King (USA) 7.7f **(75)** - Whos The Blonde (Cure The Blues (USA)) 9.5f **(63)**
Form - 040
Record 1999 - 1st:0 2nd:0 3rd:0 Ran:3
Pre1999 - 1st:2 2nd:0 3rd:0 Ran:4
Win Prizemoney £9,981 *Total Prizemoney* £12,537
Wins * 1998 Jun Windso (G-F) 6f 93 <
* 1998 Apr Newmar (G-S) 6f 83
1999 Turf 0-3: (6f, 7f 2) (g-s, gd 2)
Scopey, useful colt, effective 6 to 8f, acts on gd to g-f. Turf high 84 (began Oct). He was off the track for 16 months before reappearing in October, but showed little.
**Sir Michael Stoute [2-7] Pierpont Scott & C H Scott.*

CARIBBEAN SURFER (USA) BHB 31f **RR 45f** 1582[12]
10 b g Summing (USA) -Caribbean Surfing (USA) (Northjet) 10.3f **(74)**
Form - 0
Record 1999 - 1st:0 2nd:0 3rd:0 Ran:1
Pre1999 - 1st:0 2nd:0 3rd:0 Ran:4
1999 AW 0-1: (16f) (Equi)
Moderate gelding.
**P Eccles [0-7] Plough Twenty (Ashto Keynes) (from J S Goldie [1-7] Nov 1995).*

CARINTHIA (IRE) BHB 65f **RR 66f** 4508[7]
4 br f Tirol 8.1f **(64)** - Hot Lavender (CAN) (Shadeed (USA)) 8.2f **(70)**
Form - 4007
Record 1999 - 1st:0 2nd:0 3rd:0 Ran:3
Pre1999 - 1st:1 2nd:1 3rd:2 Ran:8
Win Prizemoney £2,981 *Total Prizemoney* £8,393
Wins * 1998 Aug Salisb (G-F) H 6f 68 70 <
1999 Turf 0-3: (7f, 8f, 10f) (gd, g-f, frm)
Light-framed, average filly, effective 8f, acts on hvy. Turf high 64 (began Jly). Inconsistent.
**C F Wall [1-11] Hintlesham Thoroughbreds.*

CARISBROOKE BHB 85f **RR 97?f** 823[10]
5 b h Kahyasi 12.9f **(74)** - Dayanata (Shirley Heights) 10.3f **(74)**
Form - 0
Record 1999 - 1st:0 2nd:0 3rd:0 Ran:1
Pre1999 - 1st:1 2nd:1 3rd:0 Ran:3
Win Prizemoney £3,485 *Total Prizemoney* £4,892

Wins 1997 Spt Kempto (G-F) 12f 80 <
1999 Turf 0-1: (16f) (g-s)
Very useful colt.
**D R C Elsworth [0-1] Michael Poland (from H R A Cecil [1-3] Nov 1997).*

CARLISLE BAY (IRE) BHB 52f RR 72df 3138[12]
5 b g Darshaan 11.9f **(81)** - My Potters (USA)(Irish River (FR)) 8.6f **(78)**
Form - 00
Record 1999 - 1st:0 2nd:0 3rd:0 Ran:2
Pre1999 - 1st:1 2nd:0 3rd:1 Ran:6
Win Prizemoney £6,850 *Total Prizemoney* £9,100
Wins 1996 Spt Currag (GD) 6f 85 <
1999 Turf 0-2: (7f, 11f) (g-s, g-f)
Above-average gelding. Turf high 1 (began Jly).
**J S Goldie [0-2] Martin Delaney (from J Oxx in IRE [1-6] Jun 1998).*

CARL'S BOY BHB 45f RR 40f 2172[8]
3 ch g Itsu (USA) - Adelbaran (FR) (No Pass No Sale) 11.9f **(85)**
Form - 408
Record 1999 - 1st:0 2nd:0 3rd:0 Ran:3
Win Prizemoney £0 *Total Prizemoney* £249
1999 Turf 0-3: (8f, 12f 2) (gd, g-f 2)
Unfurnished, moderate gelding. Turf high 40.
**D Burchell [0-3] F H Williams.*

CARLTON (IRE) BHB 52a RR 75f 5199[1]
5 ch g Thatching 7.8f **(69)** - Hooray Lady (Ahonoora) 8.1f **(73)**
Form - 00035133831231
Record 1999 - 1st:3 2nd:1 3rd:5 Ran:14
Pre1999 - 1st:3 2nd:4 3rd:3 Ran:25
Win Prizemoney £21,239 *Total Prizemoney* £34,842

Wins								
*	**1999**	Nov	Windso	(G-S)	H	6f	70	72 <
*	**1999**	Oct	Windso	(G-S)	H	6f	60	65
	1999	Jly	Epsom	(G-F)	H	6f	57	59
	1998	Jly	Newbur	(G-F)	H	7f	60	62
	1998	Jun	Windso	(GD)	H	6f	55	58
	1997	May	Beverl	(GD)	H	7.5f	53	60

1999 Turf 3-14: (6f 3-9, 7f 4, 8f) (g-s 2, gd 1-3, g-f 1-4, frm 1-4, hrd)
Above-average gelding, effective 6 to 7f, best at 6f, acts on g-s to g-f, best on gd, often wears blinkers (effectively), likes right handed tracks, excels at Windsor. Turf high 75 - 3rd of 21 giving 2lb to Susan's Pride (23 Oct Doncaster 7f g-s RF 5035) - also 1st of 25 giving 14lb to Prix Star (4 Nov Windsor RF 5199). A busy handicapper who wins his share, he was first past the post four times last season, but was disqualified at Doncaster. Effective over six and seven furlongs.
**D R C Elsworth [2-4] City Slickers (from G Lewis [4-35] Aug 1999).*

CARLYS QUEST BHB 82f80a RR 83f 80a 5221[2]
5 ch g Primo Dominie 7.2f **(67)** - Tuppy (USA) (Sharpen Up) 8.3f **(67)**
Form - 40033302
Record 1999 - 1st:0 2nd:1 3rd:3 Ran:8
Pre1999 - 1st:2 2nd:4 3rd:4 Ran:21
Win Prizemoney £10,673 *Total Prizemoney* £41,809

Wins								
*	1998	May	Warwic	(G-F)	H	10.8f	70	79 <
*	1998	May	Newmar	(G-S)	H	10f	64	70

1999 Turf 0-8: (10f, 12f 6, 16f) (sft, g-s, gd 4, frm 2)
Decent gelding, effective 11 to 12f, best at 12f, acts on sft to frm, best on gd, often wears blinkers, excels at Ascot and Doncaster. Turf high 83 - 2nd of 16 giving 2lb to Flossy (6 Nov Doncaster 12f sft RF 5221). Ended the season by finishing runner-up in the November Handicap for the second successive year, but his style of racing makes it difficult for him to win as he lacks early pace, and often finds himself caught for a turn of foot when staying on towards the finish. **J Neville [2-35] J Powell-Tuck.*

CARMARTHEN (IRE) BHB 52a RR 51f 4787[7]
3 ch g Hamas (IRE) 8f **(72)** - Solar Attraction (IRE) (Salt Dome (USA))
Form - 70303277837
Record 1999 - 1st:0 2nd:1 3rd:3 Ran:11
Pre1999 - 1st:0 2nd:1 3rd:0 Ran:4
Win Prizemoney £0 *Total Prizemoney* £2,742
1999 Turf 0-10: (5f 8, 6f 2) (g-s, gd 5, g-f, frm, hrd 2) 1999 AW 0-1: (6f) (Equi)
Neat, fair gelding. Turf high 54.
**K R Burke [0-4] Robert Merrigan (from D L Williams [0-2] Jly 1999).*

CARMARTHEN BAY BHB 25f82a RR 47f 82a 92[14]
6 ch h Prionsaa 8f **(48)** - Pattie's Grey (Valiyar) 8.5f **(73)**
Form - 00
Record 1999 - 1st:0 2nd:0 3rd:0 Ran:1
Pre1999 - 1st:2 2nd:2 3rd:1 Ran:21
Win Prizemoney £6,856 *Total Prizemoney* £10,086

Wins							
1996	*Feb*	*Lingfi*	*(STD)*	*H*	*8f*	*77*	*74*
1995	*Dec*	*Lingfi*	*(STD)*		*6f*	*81*	<

1999 AW 0-1: (12f) (Equi)
Moderate horse, has worn blinkers. Becoming disappointing.
**B J Llewellyn [0-11] D R W Jones (from G L Moore [2-13] Oct 1996).*

CARMENTA (IRE) RR 4879[19]
3 b f Unfuwain (USA) 11.4f **(74)** - Armorique
Form -
Record 1999 - 1st:0 2nd:1 3rd:0 Ran:6
Pre1999 - 1st:0 2nd:0 3rd:0 Ran:1
Win Prizemoney £0 *Total Prizemoney* £806
1999 Turf 0-6: (g-f 2, frm 3, hrd)
Workmanlike, average colt. Turf high 62.
**Dr J D Scargill [0-3] A C Edwards (from J H M Gosden [0-4] Jly 1999).*

CARNAGE (IRE) BHB 52f RR 55f 4582[9]
2 b c Catrail (USA) - Caranina (USA) (Caro)
Form - 700
Record 1999 - 1st:0 2nd:0 3rd:0 Ran:3
1999 Turf 0-3: (6f 2, 10f) (gd, frm 2)
Currently fair colt. Turf high 55.
**Mrs P N Dutfield [0-3] The Wheelwright Wanderers.*

CAROL AGAIN BHB 25f26a RR 27f 26a 1930[10]
7 b m Kind of Hush 9.6f **(50)** - Lady Carol (Lord Gayle (USA)) 8.8f **(62)**
Form - 60000
Record 1999 - 1st:0 2nd:0 3rd:0 Ran:5
Pre1999 - 1st:5 2nd:5 3rd:2 Ran:43
Win Prizemoney £11,802 *Total Prizemoney* £16,707

Wins								
*	1998	*Mar*	*Southw*	*(STD)*	*H*	*14f*	*40*	*46*
*	1998	*Feb*	*Southw*	*(STD)*	*H*	*11f*	*35*	*38*
*	1997	*Feb*	*Southw*	*(STD)*	*H*	*11f*	*39*	*43*
*	1996	*Apr*	*Southw*	*(STD)*	*H*	*12f*	*40*	*48+* <
*	1996	*Apr*	*Southw*	*(STD)*	*H*	*11f*	*33*	*39*

1999 AW 0-5: (11f, 12f 2, 14f, 16f) (Fibr 5)
Little account mare, effective 11 to 14f, - acts on Fibr, has worn blinkers. AW high 27. Inconsistent. **N Bycroft [5-56] J G Lumsden.*

CAROLE'S DOVE RR 16f 492[10]
3 b f Manhal - Nimble Dove (Starch Reduced) 11.5f **(52)**
Form - 0
Record 1999 - 1st:0 2nd:0 3rd:0 Ran:1
1999 Turf 0-1: (5f) (g-s)
Neat, currently poor filly. **C J Price [0-1] Mrs C A Crawford.*

CAROLINE'S PET (IRE) BHB 42f37a RR 46f 37a 206[15]
4 b f Contract Law (USA) 8.9f **(54)** - Princess Roxanne (Prince Tenderfoot (USA)) 9f **(61)**
Form - 80
Record 1999 - 1st:0 2nd:0 3rd:0 Ran:2
Pre1999 - 1st:0 2nd:0 3rd:0 Ran:7
Win Prizemoney £0 *Total Prizemoney* £236
1999 AW 0-2: (8f, 9f) (Fibr 2)
Light-framed, moderate filly, has worn blinkers. AW high 5.
**P D Evans [0-2] G J White (from A Bailey [0-7] Aug 1998).*

CAROLS CHOICE BHB 68f RR 59f 2381[6]
2 ch f Emarati (USA) 6.6f **(63)** - Lucky Song (Lucky Wednesday) 8f **(50)**
Form - 07536
Record 1999 - 1st:0 2nd:0 3rd:1 Ran:5
Win Prizemoney £0 *Total Prizemoney* £420
1999 Turf 0-5: (5f 4, 6f) (gd, g-f, frm 3)
Fair filly. Turf high 59.
**D HaydnJones [0-5] Monolithic Refractories Ltd.*

CAROL'S DREAM (USA) BHB 50f55a RR 50f 55a 106[7]
7 ch g Risen Star (USA) - Merle Halton (USA) (Rattle Dancer)
Form - 7
Record 1999 - 1st:0 2nd:0 3rd:0 Ran:1
Pre1999 - 1st:1 2nd:3 3rd:2 Ran:17

Win Prizemoney £3,794 *Total Prizemoney* £8,194
Wins 1996 *Mar Lingfi (STD) 10f 74+* <
1999 AW 0-1: (12f) (Equi)
Fair gelding.
**M Pitman [0-8] The Fountains Partnership (from J W Hills [1-16] Jun 1997).*

CAROUSAL (IRE) BHB 39f **RR 52f** 1129[7]
3 b f Distinctly North (USA) 7.4f **(63)** - Mountain Hop (IRE) (Tirol)
Form - 7
Record 1999 - 1st:0 2nd:0 3rd:0 Ran:1
Pre1999 - 1st:0 2nd:0 3rd:0 Ran:5
1999 AW 0-1: (7f) (Fibr)
Unfurnished, fair filly.
**J P Leigh [0-1] J W Rowles (from R Hannon [0-5] Spt 1998).*

CAROUSING BHB 90f **RR 86+f** 3258[1]
2 b c Selkirk (USA) 7.9f **(76)** - Moon Carnival **(96f)** (Be My Guest (USA)) 9.3f **(67)**
Form - 611
Record 1999 - 1st:2 2nd:0 3rd:0 Ran:3
Win Prizemoney £13,387 *Total Prizemoney* £13,387
Wins * **1999** Jly Goodwo (FRM) H 7f 86+ <
* **1999** Jun Lingfi (GD) 7f 79+
1999 Turf 2-3: (5f, 7f 2-2) (g-f 2-2, frm)
Currently useful colt. Turf high 86 - 1st of 13 getting 6lb from Aquarium (31 Jly Goodwood RF 3258) - also 1st of 16 giving 1lb to Timaru (12 Jun Lingfield RF 1954). He showed promise on his debut over five, but was stepped up to seven for his next run and that paid dividends with a fluent victory at Lingfield. Showed he was on the upgrade when landing a warm nursery at Goodwood.
**M Johnston [2-3] P D Savill.*

CARPETSMADEINDEVON BHB 36f **RR 34f** 5153[17]
3 ch g Elmaamul (USA) 8.1f **(70)** - Hollow Heart (Wolver Hollow) 8f **(56)**
Form - 0080
Record 1999 - 1st:0 2nd:0 3rd:0 Ran:4
1999 Turf 0-4: (6f, 7f 2, 10f) (gd, g-f 3)
Workmanlike, very moderate gelding. Turf high 34.
**Mrs P N Dutfield [0-4] Axminster Carpets Ltd.*

CARRIE POOTER BHB 70f69a **RR 69f 69a** 4151[5]
3 b f Tragic Role (USA) 9.4f **(63)** - Ginny Binny (Ahonoora) 8.1f **(73)**
Form - 432212332200017245
Record 1999 - 1st:2 2nd:6 3rd:3 Ran:18
Pre1999 - 1st:1 2nd:0 3rd:0 Ran:5
Win Prizemoney £12,289 *Total Prizemoney* £21,378
Wins * **1999** Jly Hamilt (G-F) H 6f 63 65
* **1999** *Mar Southw (SLW) H 7f 59 62+*
* 1998 May Redcar (G-F) 6f 73 <
1999 Turf 1-10: (6f 1-6, 7f 4) (sft, gd 3, g-f 1-3, frm 3) 1999 AW 1-8: (6f 2, 7f 1-5, 8f) (Fibr 1-8)
Tall, above-average filly, effective 6 to 7f, best at 6f, acts on sft to g-f - acts on Fibr, often wears blinkers (extremely effectively), and excels at Hamilton and Redcar. Turf high 70 - 3rd of 24 giving 13lb to Heavenly Miss (16 Apr Thirsk 6f gd RF 0731) - also 1st of 8 giving 8lb to Piccolo Cativo (31 Jly Hamilton RF 3269). AW high 70 - 2nd of 16 getting 1lb from Keen Hands (26 Apr Southwell 6f Fibr RF 0855). Failed to better her win at Hamilton in July over six furlongs on fast ground, although she does have some form on the All-Weather. **T D Barron [3-23] Stephen Woodall.*

CARROLLS MARC (IRE) BHB 27f28a **RR 17f 28a** 853[11]
11 b g Horage 11.4f **(58)** - Rare Find (Rarity) 10.1f **(60)**
Form - 00
Record 1999 - 1st:0 2nd:0 3rd:0 Ran:2
Pre1999 - 1st:14 2nd:7 3rd:13 Ran:80
Win Prizemoney £33,929 *Total Prizemoney* £44,023
Wins * 1998 *Mar Wolver (STD) 16.2f 42*
1997 May Lingfi (STD) SH 16f 40 42
1997 Apr Southw (STD) C 12f 48
1996 Jan Lingfi (STD) 12f 55
1996 Jan Lingfi (STD) SH 12f 40 45
1999 AW 0-2: (12f, 14f) (Fibr 2)
Little account gelding, effective 11 to 16f, best at 16f, - acts on AW, best on Fibr, has worn blinkers, favours left handed tracks. Becoming disappointing.
**Pat Mitchell [1-14] Mrs G Dunlop (from C Murray [4-17] Jun 1997).*

CARRY THE FLAG BHB 104f **RR 105f** 4391[2]
4 b c Tenby 10.4f **(76)** - Tamassos (Dance In Time (CAN)) 8.9f **(59)**
Form - 11442
Record 1999 - 1st:2 2nd:1 3rd:0 Ran:5
Pre1999 - 1st:2 2nd:1 3rd:1 Ran:8
Win Prizemoney £53,053 *Total Prizemoney* £76,200
Wins * **1999** May Goodwo (GD) H 12f 94 97
* **1999** Apr Kempto (G-F) H 10f 94 100 <
* 1997 Oct Warwic (G-F) H 8f 84 91
* 1997 Jun Thirsk (GD) 7f 62+
1999 Turf 2-5: (10f 1-1, 11f, 12f 1-3) (gd 1-3, g-f 1-2)
Neat, Pattern-class colt, effective 10 to 12f, best at 12f, acts on gd to g-f, best on gd. Turf high 105 - 2nd of 7 giving 5lb to Leggera (18 Spt Ayr 11f gd RF 4391) - also 1st of 20 getting 8lb from Rokeby Bowl (5 Apr Kempton RF 0576). Consistent. He enjoyed a fine season, winning two valuable handicaps including the Rosebery at Kempton. Creditable efforts afterwards, including when runner-up to Leggera in an Ayr Listed event, before landing a huge prize in Singapore in October for his new trainer.
**P F I Cole [4-13] Luciano Gaucci.*

CARTESIAN BHB 73f **RR 70f** 5067[3]
3 b f Shirley Heights 12.1f **(76)** -Danilova(USA)(Lyphard(USA)) 9.9f **(72)**
Form - 043
Record 1999 - 1st:0 2nd:0 3rd:1 Ran:3
Win Prizemoney £0 *Total Prizemoney* £841
1999 Turf 0-3: (9f, 12f 2) (g-s, gd 2)
Currently above-average filly. Turf high 70 (began Aug) - 3rd of 15 to Ski Run (26 Oct Bath 12f gd RF 5067). **R Charlton [0-3] K Abdulla.*

CARTMEL PARK BHB 80f **RR 79?f** 4911[1]
3 ch g Skyliner 6.8f **(51)** - Oh My Oh My (Ballacashtal (CAN)) 5.3f **(50)**
Form - 000321605081
Record 1999 - 1st:2 2nd:1 3rd:1 Ran:12
Pre1999 - 1st:2 2nd:4 3rd:1 Ran:9
Win Prizemoney £15,603 *Total Prizemoney* £22,051
Wins * **1999** Oct Catter (GD,) H 5f 73 79? <
* **1999** Jly Sandow (GD) H 5f 74 77
* 1998 Spt Newcas (GD) 5f 60+
* 1998 Jly Mussel (GD) 5f 69
1999 Turf 2-11: (5f 2-11) (g-s 2, gd 1-5, g-f 1-2, frm, hrd) 1999 AW 0-1: (5f) (Fibr)
Leggy, above-average gelding, effective 5f, acts on gd to hrd, has worn blinkers. Turf high 79 - 1st of 15 getting 2lb from Goretski (16 Oct Catterick RF 4911) - also 1st of 12 giving 2lb to Sir Sandrovitch (2 Jly Sandown RF 2503). He has plenty of early pace, and used that effectively to win at Sandown and Catterick. Sometimes tends to hang right. **J Berry [4-21] P G Airey & R R Whitton.*

CASAMASA (IRE) RR 96f 3926a[3]
3 b c Sadler's Wells (USA) 11.3f **(87)** - Millieme (Mill Reef (USA)) 10.5f **(78)**
Form - 333
1999 Turf 0-3: (13f, 15f 2) (g-s, gd 2)
Currently very useful colt, has worn blinkers. Turf high 96 - 3rd of 5 giving 4lb to Colour Scheme (18 Aug Deauville 15f g-s RF 3926a). He stays well and, being from a late-maturing family, is open to further improvement. **E Lellouche in FR [0-3].*

CASATI (IRE) BHB 28a **RR 64f 28a** 232[16]
4 b f Silver Kite (USA) 10.2f **(51)** - Inishmot (IRE) (Glenstal (USA)) 10.1f **(64)**
Form - 0830
Record 1999 - 1st:0 2nd:0 3rd:1 Ran:4
Pre1999 - 1st:0 2nd:2 3rd:0 Ran:13
Win Prizemoney £0 *Total Prizemoney* £1,789
1999 AW 0-4: (6f 2, 8f, 11f) (Fibr 4)
Average filly. AW high 19. Becoming disappointing.
**P S Felgate [0-4] P S Felgate (from T G McCourt in IRE [0-13] Spt 1998).*

CASHAPLENTY BHB 45f45a **RR 14f 45a** 98[6]
6 ch g Ballacashtal (CAN) 7.9f **(51)** - Storm of Plenty (Billion (USA)) 12f **(43)**
Form - 626
Record 1999 - 1st:0 2nd:0 3rd:0 Ran:1
Pre1999 - 1st:1 2nd:1 3rd:0 Ran:8

Win Prizemoney £2,713 *Total Prizemoney* £3,234
Wins * 1997 *Feb Wolver (STD) 12f 44+* <
1999 AW 0-1: (11f) (Fibr)
Moderate gelding. **N P Littmoden [4-18] J R Salter.*

CASHIKI (IRE) BHB 46f42a **RR 49f 42a** 5154[11]
3 ch f Case Law 6f **(64)** - Nishiki (USA) (Brogan (USA))
Form - 00400874280
Record 1999 - 1st:0 2nd:1 3rd:0 Ran:11
Pre1999 - 1st:3 2nd:3 3rd:1 Ran:12
Win Prizemoney £7,395 *Total Prizemoney* £10,960
Wins * 1998 Aug Pontef (G-F) H 6f 70 73 <
* 1998 Jun Chepst (G-S) C 6.1f 61
* 1998 Jun Lingfi (GD) S 6f 58
1999 Turf 0-10: (6f, 7f 2, 8f 4, 10f 3) (gd 3, g-f 2, frm 5) 1999 AW 0-1: (7f) (Fibr)
Light-framed, moderate filly, effective 6f, acts on gd to frm, best on frm. Turf high 63. Consistent.
**B Palling [3-23] The Valley Commandos.*

CASHMERE LADY BHB 56f77a **RR 52f 77a** 5073[6]
7 b m Hubbly Bubbly (USA) 9.5f **(43)** - Choir (High Top) 10.2f **(67)**
Form - 448743610006
Record 1999 - 1st:1 2nd:0 3rd:1 Ran:10
Pre1999 - 1st:8 2nd:7 3rd:2 Ran:51
Win Prizemoney £33,522 *Total Prizemoney* £51,516
Wins * **1999** Spt Haydoc (G-F) H 10.5f 60 63
* 1998 Apr Thirsk (G-S) H 8f 73 78
* 1998 *Mar Southw (STD) H 12f 87 89* <
* 1997 Aug Redcar (FRM) H 8f 72 78
* 1997 *Jun Wolver (STD) H 8.5f 76 89* <
* 1997 Jun Thirsk (GD) H 8f 65 70
* 1996 *Mar Wolver (STD) H 8.5f 72 77+*
* 1995 *Dec Wolver (STD) H 7f 65 66*
* 1995 *Nov Wolver (STD) 8.5f 64*
1999 Turf 1-10: (8f 2, 9f, 10f 4, 11f 1-1, 12f 2) (gd 3, g-f 1-2, frm 5)
Useful mare, effective 9 to 12f, - acts on Fibr, likes left handed tracks, likes tight tracks. Turf high 64. Inconsistent, she was ending a very long losing run when gaining a narrow victory in a Haydock amateurs' event in September.
**J L Eyre [9-63] Mrs Sybil Howe.*

CASH RUN (USA) RR 5225a[1]
2 b f Seeking the Gold (USA) 7.4f **(80)** - Shared Interest (USA) (Pleasant Colony (USA)) 7f **(70)**
Form - 1
1999 AW 1-1: (9f 1-1) (Dirt 1-1)
Currently very useful, always wears blinkers. (1st run) - 1st of 9 from Chilukki (6 Nov Gulfstream Park RF 5225a). She was a surprise winner of the Breeders' Cup Juvenile Fillies, having made all the running. **D W Lukas in USA [1-1] Padua Stables.*

CASIMIR (IRE) BHB 93f **RR 91f** 4569[19]
3 b c Roi Danzig (USA) 10.5f **(62)** - Have A Cut (IRE) (Al Hareb (USA))
Form - 841120
Record 1999 - 1st:2 2nd:1 3rd:0 Ran:6
Pre1999 - 1st:1 2nd:1 3rd:0 Ran:5
Win Prizemoney £15,034 *Total Prizemoney* £20,214
Wins * **1999** Jly Ascot (FRM) H 8f 83 87 <
* **1999** Jly Chepst (G-F) H 8.1f 78 82+
* 1998 Jly Beverl (G-F) 5f 81+
1999 Turf 2-6: (7f, 8f 2-5) (sft, g-f 1-2, frm 1-3)
Unfurnished, useful colt, effective 5 to 8f, best at 8f, acts on g-f to frm, best on frm. Turf high 91 - 2nd of 20 giving 7lb to Naviasky (22 Aug Leicester 8f frm RF 3838) - also 1st of 5 giving 7lb to Westender (25 Jly Ascot RF 3119). Ran creditably without troubling the judge before winning at Chepstow in July. Showing his liking for decent ground that day, he saw out the mile really well and added to his tally at Ascot next time.
**A C Stewart [3-11] P McGuinness & S J Hammond.*

CASINO ROYALE (IRE) BHB 77f **RR 78f** 5046[3]
3 b c Royal Academy (USA) 7.8f **(77)** - Sharata (IRE) (Darshaan) 9.9f **(84)**
Form - 3435633
Record 1999 - 1st:0 2nd:0 3rd:4 Ran:7
Pre1999 - 1st:0 2nd:0 3rd:1 Ran:1
Win Prizemoney £0 *Total Prizemoney* £3,894
1999 Turf 0-7: (8f 2, 10f 5) (hvy, g-s 2, gd, g-f 2, frm)
Tall, above-average colt, effective 8 to 10f, best at 10f, acts on g-s to g-f, best on g-s. Turf high 82 (1st run) - 3rd of 5 getting 4lb from Little Rock (23 Apr Sandown 8f g-s RF 0820). Consistent. Fully exposed and basically disappointing last term, he found no benefit from being stepped up to ten from eight furlongs.
**J W Hills [0-8] C Wright & Partners.*

CASSANDRA RR 44f 4359[11]
3 b f Catrail (USA) - Circo (High Top) 10.2f **(67)**
Form - 647570
Record 1999 - 1st:0 2nd:0 3rd:0 Ran:6
Win Prizemoney £0 *Total Prizemoney* £256
1999 Turf 0-6: (6f, 7f, 8f 2, 10f 2) (g-s, gd, g-f, frm 3)
Tall, moderate filly. Turf high 70. **M Brittain [0-6] Mel Brittain.*

CASSANDRA GO (IRE) BHB 98f **RR 97f** 4896[8]
3 gr f Indian Ridge 7.6f **(74)** - Rahaam (USA) (Secreto (USA)) 8.7f **(72)**
Form - 1301468
Record 1999 - 1st:2 2nd:0 3rd:1 Ran:7
Pre1999 - 1st:0 2nd:0 3rd:0 Ran:1
Win Prizemoney £10,243 *Total Prizemoney* £13,349
Wins * **1999** Jun Newmar (G-F) 6f 94 <
* **1999** Apr Newmar (GD) 7f 89
1999 Turf 2-7: (6f 1-4, 7f 1-1, 8f 2) (g-s, gd 1-2, g-f 1-3, frm)
Light-framed, very useful filly, effective 6 to 8f, best at 6f, acts on gd to frm. Turf high 97 - 4th of 7 to Imperial Beauty (9 Jly York 6f frm RF 2695) - also 1st of 5 from Greensand (25 Jun Newmarket RF 2308). She won twice, but was found lacking in Group and Listed events. A free-runner, she is bred to stay a mile but must relax to do so. She has run well with and without a tongue-strap.
**G Wragg [2-8] Trevor Stewart.*

CASSINI (IRE) RR 46f 3448[14]
3 b c Exit To Nowhere (USA) 8.7f **(77)** - Venerate (IRE) (Ahonoora) 8.1f **(73)**
Form - 00
Record 1999 - 1st:0 2nd:0 3rd:0 Ran:2
1999 Turf 0-2: (10f, 12f) (gd, frm)
Lengthy, currently moderate colt. Turf high 46.
**M Brittain [0-2] Miss Debi Woods.*

CASTANEA SATIVA (IRE) BHB 62f **RR 63f** 4762[17]
2 b f In The Wings 11.2f **(77)** - Chesnut Tree (USA) (Shadeed (USA)) 8.2f **(70)**
Form - 6420
Record 1999 - 1st:0 2nd:1 3rd:0 Ran:4
Win Prizemoney £0 *Total Prizemoney* £1,313
1999 Turf 0-4: (7f 2, 8f 2) (g-s, gd, frm 2)
Average filly. Turf high 63 (began Aug).
**T D Easterby [0-4] Chris & Antonia Deuters.*

CASTARA BEACH (IRE) BHB 63f **RR 61f** 4120[5]
3 b f Danehill (USA) 9.1f **(79)** - Sea Harrier (Grundy) 10.3f **(65)**
Form - 05
Record 1999 - 1st:0 2nd:0 3rd:0 Ran:2
Pre1999 - 1st:0 2nd:0 3rd:0 Ran:3
Win Prizemoney £0 *Total Prizemoney* £217
1999 Turf 0-2: (8f, 9f) (g-f 2)
Scopey, average filly. Turf high 59 (began Aug).
**N A Callaghan [0-5] M Tabor & Mrs John Magnier.*

CASTAWAY PRINCESS BHB 29f **RR 15f** 1987[11]
3 b f Casteddu 7.4f **(54)** - Princess Dina (Huntercombe) 7.3f **(56)**
Form - 00
Record 1999 - 1st:0 2nd:0 3rd:0 Ran:2
Pre1999 - 1st:0 2nd:0 3rd:0 Ran:4
1999 Turf 0-2: (8f, 12f) (gd, g-f)
Small, poor filly. Turf high 15. **D W Barker [0-6] D W Barker.*

CASTEL ROSSELO BHB 48f72a **RR 36f 72a** 3489[13]
9 br h Rousillon (USA) 10.4f **(69)** - On The House (FR) (Be My Guest (USA)) 9.3f **(67)**
Form - 00
Record 1999 - 1st:0 2nd:0 3rd:0 Ran:2
Pre1999 - 1st:4 2nd:4 3rd:5 Ran:35
Win Prizemoney £16,220 *Total Prizemoney* £29,644

Wins 1997 Jun Thirsk (GD) H 7f 57 65
1999 Turf 0-2: (8f 2) (gd, frm)
Moderate horse, has worn blinkers. Turf high 36 (began Aug). Consistent.
**D HaydnJones [0-2] R J Dawson (from I Campbell [1-4] Jly 1997).*

CASTIYA (IRE) RR 95f 3777a[1]

2 gr f Bluebird (USA) 7.9f **(71)** - Comme D'Habitude (USA) (Caro)
Form - 1
1999 Turf 1-1: (7f 1-1) (gd 1-1)
Currently very useful filly. (1st run) - 1st of 7 getting 3lb from Lord Flasheart (13 Aug Vichy RF 3777a).
**C Laffon-Parias in FR [1-1] Mme M de Chambure.*

CASTLE ASHBY JACK BHB 38f36a RR 42f 36a 1777[9]

5 gr g Chilibang 7f **(55)** - Carly-B (IRE) (Commanche Run) 8.5f **(58)**
Form - 0733775025700
Record 1999 - 1st:0 2nd:1 3rd:0 Ran:9
Pre1999 - 1st:1 2nd:11 3rd:10 Ran:48
Win Prizemoney £3,403 *Total Prizemoney* £16,576
Wins * 1998 *Jan Lingfi (STD) 7f 59* <
1999 AW 0-9: (7f 3, 8f 4, 10f, 11f) (Equi 7, Fibr 2)
Moderate gelding, effective 7f, - acts on Equi, has worn blinkers. AW high 50. **P Howling [1-57] Mrs J Lewis.*

CASTLE BELLE RR 33f 3873[10]

3 ch f King's Signet (USA) 7f **(51)** - Castle Maid **(28f)** (Castle Keep) 8.3f **(57)**
Form - 000
Record 1999 - 1st:0 2nd:0 3rd:0 Ran:3
1999 Turf 0-3: (5f, 6f, 7f) (g-f 2, frm)
Leggy, currently very moderate filly. Turf high 33 (began Jly).
**R J Hodges [0-3] R T Sercombe.*

CASTLE QUEST (IRE) RR 101f 4742a[5]

3 b f Grand Lodge (USA) - In Unison (Bellypha) 9.8f **(73)**
Form - 4142451235
1999 Turf 2-10: (7f 2, 8f 2-3, 9f, 10f 3, 12f) (hvy, sft 2, g-s 1-2, gd, g-f 2, frm 1-2)
Very useful filly, effective 7 to 10f, best at 8f, acts on sft to frm, has worn blinkers, excels at Curragh. Turf high 101 - 1st of 6 from Pink Coral (11 Apr Curragh RF 0683a) - also 1st of 10 giving 6lb to Crystal Downs (7 Jly Leopardstown RF 2784a). Consistent. She thrived on a busy campaign and gained just reward for some game efforts when winning a Listed race at Leopardstown in July. Probably best over a mile, she has run well on all types of ground and is a likeable individual.
**J S Bolger in IRE [3-11] Dermot McAuliffe.*

CASTLES BURNING (USA) BHB 55f67a RR 59f 67a 3910[4]

5 b br g Minshaanshu Amad (USA) 11.3f **(53)** - Major Overhaul (Known Fact (USA)) 7.4f **(67)**
Form - 5311413522314254
Record 1999 - 1st:2 2nd:3 3rd:2 Ran:12
Pre1999 - 1st:6 2nd:3 3rd:5 Ran:37
Win Prizemoney £21,361 *Total Prizemoney* £30,675

Wins * **1999**	*Jun Lingfi*	*(STD)*	*8f*		*71*	
* **1999**	*Mar Lingfi*	*(STD)*	*8f*		*67*	
* 1998	*Dec Lingfi*	*(STD)*	*10f*		*65*	
* 1998	*Dec Lingfi*	*(STD) H*	*10f*	*59*	*65*	
* 1998	Aug Bright	(FRM) H	10f	50	56	
* 1997	*Oct Lingfi*	*(STD) H*	*10f*	*65*	*67*	
* 1997	Aug Bright	(FRM) H	11.9f	50	54	
* 1997	*Mar Lingfi*	*(STD) H*	*8f*	*69*	*78*	<

1999 Turf 0-1: (12f) (gd) 1999 AW 2-11: (7f, 8f 2-4, 9f, 10f 4, 16f) (Equi 2-9, Fibr 2)
Average gelding, effective 8 to 10f, best at 8f, - acts on AW, best on Equi, has worn blinkers (very effectively), favours left handed tracks. AW high 71 - 1st of 7 getting 2lb from Nautical Warning (22 Jun Lingfield RF 2199) - also 1st of 7 giving 4lb to Mister Tricky (2 Mar Lingfield RF 0391). Consistent. He is probably a better horse on Equitrack, but has also shown a liking for the turf at Brighton. Obviously suited by a sharp left-handed track.
**C A Cyzer [8-49] R M Cyzer.*

CASTLE SECRET BHB 35f48a RR 42?f 48a 4413[7]

13 b g Castle Keep 10.5f **(58)** - Baffle (Petingo) 11f **(72)**
Form - 7
Record 1999 - 1st:0 2nd:0 3rd:0 Ran:1
Pre1999 - 1st:2 2nd:6 3rd:1 Ran:30
Win Prizemoney £12,226 *Total Prizemoney* £17,915
Wins * 1997 *May Wolver (STD) H 16.2f 47 52* <
1999 AW 0-1: (15f) (Fibr)
Moderate gelding, has worn blinkers. Becoming disappointing.
**D Burchell [9-65] Mrs Ruth Burchell (from J L Dunlop [1-5] Aug 1990).*

CASTLE SEMPILL BHB 69f RR 81f 5218[13]

2 b c Presidium 7.5f **(56)** - La Suquet **(60f 60a)** (Puissance)
Form - 243743310
Record 1999 - 1st:1 2nd:1 3rd:3 Ran:9
Win Prizemoney £6,417 *Total Prizemoney* £9,276
Wins 1999 Oct Newmar (GD) S 7f 81 <
1999 Turf 1-9: (5f 4, 6f, 7f 1-3, 8f) (sft 2, g-s, gd 1-2, g-f 2, frm 2)
Decent colt, effective 5 to 7f, acts on gd to g-f. Turf high 81 - 1st of 20 giving 5lb to Annijaz (14 Oct Newmarket RF 4870).
**R M H Cowell [0-1] Mrs J M Penney (from J R Fanshawe [1-8] Oct 1999).*

CATALONIA (IRE) RR 74f 5021[5]

2 ch f Catrail (USA) - Shakanda (IRE) (Shernazar) 10.2f **(73)**
Form - 65
Record 1999 - 1st:0 2nd:0 3rd:0 Ran:2
1999 Turf 0-2: (7f 2) (gd 2)
Currently above-average filly. Turf high 74 (began Spt) - 5th of 22 to Fame At Last (22 Oct Doncaster 7f gd RF 5021).
**J A Glover [0-2] B H Farr.*

CATAMARAN RR 75f 4584[9]

4 ch c Rainbow Quest (USA) 11.2f **(81)** - Cattermole (USA) (Roberto (USA)) 10f **(76)**
Form - 30
Record 1999 - 1st:0 2nd:0 3rd:1 Ran:2
Win Prizemoney £0 *Total Prizemoney* £575
1999 Turf 0-2: (10f 2) (gd, frm)
Currently above-average colt. Turf high 75 (began Spt).
**J H M Gosden [0-2] K Abdulla.*

CATAPULT (IRE) BHB 42f RR 55?f 4906[21]

3 ch g Catrail (USA) - Flimmering (Dancing Brave (USA)) 8.4f **(76)**
Form - 460673066550
Record 1999 - 1st:0 2nd:0 3rd:1 Ran:12
Pre1999 - 1st:0 2nd:0 3rd:0 Ran:1
Win Prizemoney £0 *Total Prizemoney* £538
1999 Turf 0-12: (5f 2, 6f 2, 7f 6, 8f, 9f) (gd, g-f 6, frm 4, hrd)
Scopey, fair gelding, effective 7f, acts on frm, has worn blinkers, likes right handed tracks, likes tight tracks. Turf high 55.
**I Semple [0-12] The T B Consortium (from J Noseda [0-1] Spt 1998).*

CATCH BALL BHB 48f RR 59f 1447[10]

3 ch f Prince Sabo 6.6f **(64)** - Canoodle (Warpath) 12.3f **(52)**
Form - 060
Record 1999 - 1st:0 2nd:0 3rd:0 Ran:3
Pre1999 - 1st:0 2nd:0 3rd:0 Ran:3
1999 Turf 0-3: (10f 2, 12f) (hvy, frm 2)
Lengthy, fair filly. Turf high 59. **T R Watson [0-6] Newitt and Co Ltd.*

CATCH ME BHB 63f RR 57f 2006[10]

3 b f Rudimentary (USA) 8.2f **(66)** - Fast Chick (Henbit (USA)) 9f **(61)**
Form - 050
Record 1999 - 1st:0 2nd:0 3rd:0 Ran:3
Pre1999 - 1st:2 2nd:1 3rd:0 Ran:7
Win Prizemoney £5,972 *Total Prizemoney* £6,980
Wins * 1998 Jly Cheste (G-F) H 7f 65
* 1998 Jun Beverl (GD) 7.5f 67 <
1999 Turf 0-3: (8f 3) (gd, g-f, frm)
Workmanlike, fair filly, effective 7f, acts on gd to g-f, prefers tight tracks. Turf high 57. Consistent.
**T D Easterby [2-10] Mrs J B Mountifield.*

CATCHMENT BHB 31f37a RR 38f 37a 414[7]

5 ch g Persian Bold 10f **(69)** - Cachou (USA) (Roberto (USA)) 10f **(76)**
Form - 8284027
Record 1999 - 1st:0 2nd:1 3rd:0 Ran:3
Pre1999 - 1st:0 2nd:1 3rd:0 Ran:11

Win Prizemoney £0 *Total Prizemoney* £1,302
1999 AW 0-3: (13f, 16f 2) (Equi 2, Fibr)
Very moderate gelding, effective 13 to 16f, - acts on AW, best on Equi, prefers left handed tracks. AW high 39 - 2nd of 12 getting 2lb from Bigwig (2 Mar Lingfield 13f Equi RF 0386).
**Mrs A J Perrett [0-14] Miss G Harwood.*

CATCHTHEBATCH BHB 54f65a **RR 50f 65a** 5032[11]

3 b g Beveled (USA) 6.9f **(64)** - Batchworth Dancer (Ballacashtal (CAN)) 5.3f **(50)**
Form - 04415650030
Record 1999 - 1st:1 2nd:0 3rd:1 Ran:9
Pre1999 - 1st:0 2nd:0 3rd:0 Ran:3
Win Prizemoney £2,583 *Total Prizemoney* £3,151
Wins * 1999 *Jan Lingfi (STD) 6f 77 <*
1999 Turf 0-6: (5f 4, 6f 2) (g-s, gd, g-f, frm 3) 1999 AW 1-3: (5f, 6f 1-2) (Equi 1-2, Fibr)
Workmanlike, above-average gelding, effective 6f, - acts on Equi, likes left handed tracks, likes tight tracks. Turf high 56. AW high 77 - 1st of 6 from Pisces Lad (16 Jan Lingfield RF 0108).
**E A Wheeler [1-12] The Over The Bridge Partnership.*

CATCH THE DRAGON (IRE) RR 100+f 1465a[5]

4 b c Sharp Victor (USA) 10f **(56)** - Roblanna (Roberto (USA)) 10f **(76)**
Form - 15
1999 Turf 0-1: (14f) (gd)
Very useful colt. **L Browne in IRE [2-8] Mrs P K Cooper.*

CATCHY WORD BHB 100f **RR 89f** 4952[1]

2 ch c Cadeaux Genereux 7.9f **(76)** - Lora's Guest (Be My Guest (USA)) 9.3f **(67)**
Form - 1361
Record 1999 - 1st:2 2nd:0 3rd:1 Ran:4
Win Prizemoney £7,058 *Total Prizemoney* £10,264
Wins * 1999 Oct Yarmou (G-F) 7f 89 <
*** 1999** Jun Haydoc (SFT) 6f 78+
1999 Turf 2-4: (6f 1-1, 7f 1-3) (gd 1-2, g-f 1-2)
Useful colt. Turf high 89 - 1st of 7 from Abderian (19 Oct Yarmouth RF 4952). A half-brother to Centre Stalls, he won at Haydock first time but was a shade disappointing in his next two starts. Ended the season with a victory in a Yarmouth novices' stakes.
**E A L Dunlop [2-4] Abdullah Ali.*

CATELLA (GER) RR 112f 4519a[1]

3 ch f Generous (IRE) 11.5f **(82)** - Crystal Ring (IRE) (Kris) 9.5f **(73)**
Form - 111
1999 Turf 3-3: (10f 2-2, 11f 1-1) (gd 3-3)
Currently Group-class filly. Turf high 112 - 1st of 10 getting 13lb from Icemoon (18 Jly Frankfurt RF 3041a) - also 1st of 12 getting 2lb from Maestoso (19 Spt Frankfurt RF 4519a). Probably the best middle-distance filly of her generation in Germany, this strong galloper slaughtered her opponents in a Group 2 at Frankfurt in September and deserves to take her chance against top-class opposition. Still improving, she will make a smart four-year-old and is a name to note.
**P Schiergen in GER [3-3] Gestut Schlenderhan.*

CATERINA SFORZA RR 68f 1181[6]

4 ch f Machiavellian (USA) 9.8f **(83)** - Symeterie (USA) (Seattle Song (USA)) 9f **(77)**
Form - 6
Record 1999 - 1st:0 2nd:0 3rd:0 Ran:1
Pre1999 - 1st:0 2nd:0 3rd:0 Ran:2
Win Prizemoney £0 *Total Prizemoney* £127
1999 Turf 0-1: (10f) (g-s)
Currently average filly, has worn blinkers.
**J L Dunlop [0-1] Grundy Bloodstock Ltd (from G Botti in ITY [0-2] Spt 1998).*

CATHERINA (IRE) RR 100f 5174a[3]

3 b f Sadler's Wells (USA) 11.3f **(87)** - Katie McLain (USA)
Form - 124023
1999 Turf 1-6: (9f 1-2, 10f, 12f 2, 14f) (sft 2, g-s, gd 1-2, g-f)
Very useful filly, effective 9 to 14f, acts on sft to g-f. Turf high 100 - 4th of 7 getting 3lb from Yeoman's Point (17 Jly Leopardstown 14f g-f RF 2995a) - also 1st of 6 from Aspiration (3 May Gowran Park RF 1148a). She was stepped straight into Listed races after winning a maiden and ran with credit. A mile and a half may prove her optimum in 2000. **D K Weld in IRE [1-6] Mrs C L Weld.*

CATIENUS (USA) BHB 110f **RR 111df** 5231a[13]

5 b br h Storm Cat (USA) 7f **(86)** - Diamond City (USA) (Mr Prospector (USA)) 8.8f **(78)**
Form - 20
1999 AW 0-2: (10f 2) (Dirt 2)
Group-class colt. AW high 111 (1st run) (began Aug) - 2nd of 8 getting 7lb from Running Stag (29 Aug Saratoga 10f Dirt RF 4115a). Good enough to beat Intikhab when trained by Sir Michael Stoute as a three-year-old, he had no answer to the globe-trotting Running Stag at Saratoga in August.
**R Schosberg in USA [0-2] (from Sir Michael Stoute [3-8] Spt 1997).*

CATOKI (USA) RR 104f 4887a[2]

6 b h Storm Cat (USA) 7f **(86)** -Matoki(USA)(Hail To Reason) 10.1f **(82)**
Form - 32
1999 Turf 0-2: (8f, 9f) (sft 2)
Very useful horse. Turf high 103 (1st run) (began Spt) - 3rd of 7 to El Divino (25 Spt Cologne 8f sft RF 4662a). He remains capable of smart form over seven furlongs or a mile, but lacks the pace to beat genuine Group horses.
**P Lautner in GER [0-2] (from H Steguweit in GER [0-1] Aug 1997).*

CATRIONA RR 71f 3384[5]

3 b f Bustino 11f **(64)** - Nadia Nerina (CAN) (Northern Dancer) 9.6f **(80)**
Form - 38323715
Record 1999 - 1st:1 2nd:1 3rd:3 Ran:8
Pre1999 - 1st:0 2nd:0 3rd:0 Ran:1
Win Prizemoney £2,157 *Total Prizemoney* £4,699
Wins * 1999 Jly Catter (FRM) 7f 71+ <
1999 Turf 1-8: (7f 1-3, 8f 5) (g-s, gd 3, g-f, frm 1-2, hrd)
Workmanlike, above-average filly, effective 7 to 8f, best at 8f, acts on gd to hrd, best on gd, has worn blinkers, prefers left handed tracks. Turf high 74 - 3rd of 15 getting 5lb from Regal Philosopher (17 May Bath 8f gd RF 1266) - also 1st of 6 from Cladantom (14 Jly Catterick RF 2808). **J Noseda [1-9] B E Nielsen.*

CAT THIEF (USA) RR 117f 5231a[1]

3 ch c Storm Cat (USA) 7f **(86)** - Train Robbery (USA) (Alydar (USA)) 9.1f **(76)**
Form - 31
1999 Turf 0-1: (10f) (frm) 1999 AW 1-1: (10f 1-1) (Dirt 1-1)
Currently top-class colt, often wears blinkers. (1st run) - 1st of 14 getting 4lb from Budroyale (6 Nov Gulfstream Park RF 5231a). He seemed to be one of those horses who was always there or thereabouts in the top American races, his third to Charismatic in the Kentucky Derby being a case in point. However, he got it right to land the monster pot in the Breeders' Cup Classic, showing real grit and determination in the closing stages to beat a top-class field. **D W Lukas in USA [1-3] Overbrook Farm et al.*

CATULLUS BHB 55a **RR 66f** 4693[11]

3 b g Prince Sabo 6.6f **(64)** - Rive-Jumelle (IRE) (M Double M (USA)) 14.1f **(52)**
Form - 24144334100
Record 1999 - 1st:2 2nd:1 3rd:2 Ran:11
Pre1999 - 1st:0 2nd:0 3rd:0 Ran:5
Win Prizemoney £6,682 *Total Prizemoney* £10,298
Wins * 1999 Aug Nottin (G-F) H 14.1f 66 66 <
*** 1999** May Nottin (FRM) H 10f 65 65
1999 Turf 2-9: (10f 1-3, 11f, 12f 2, 14f 1-3) (gd, g-f 2-5, frm 3) 1999 AW 0-2: (9f, 13f) (Equi, Fibr)
Light-framed, average gelding, effective 7 to 14f, acts on g-f to frm, best on g-f. Turf high 66 - 1st of 13 giving 11lb to Whistling Dixie (9 Aug Nottingham RF 3476) - also 1st of 12 getting 11lb from Ursa Major (28 May Nottingham RF 1549). AW high 48. A winner twice at Nottingham on fast ground, he ran well otherwise. Has joined Martin Pipe. **M L W Bell [2-16] M D F Racing Partnership.*

CAUDA EQUINA BHB 81f **RR 78f** 5040[13]

5 gr g Statoblest 6.4f **(63)** - Sea Fret (Habat) 7.6f **(61)**
Form - 6530120640100431200838O
Record 1999 - 1st:3 2nd:2 3rd:3 Ran:23
Pre1999 - 1st:6 2nd:5 3rd:5 Ran:39
Win Prizemoney £30,031 *Total Prizemoney* £50,349

Wins * **1999** Aug Lingfi (GD) 5f 79
* **1999** Jun Bath (GD) 5.1f 81 <
* **1999** May Bath (GD) 5.1f 79
* 1998 Spt Bath (GD) H 5.7f 64 76
* 1998 Spt Salisb (GD) H 5f 62 67
* 1998 Aug Bath (GD) C 5.7f 64
* 1997 Jly Ripon (GD) H 6f 75 76
* 1997 May Bath (G-S) 5.1f 71
* 1997 Apr Bath (G-F) S 5.1f 63

1999 Turf 3-23: (5f 3-9, 6f 14) (g-s 2, gd 1-11, g-f 1-3, frm 1-7)

Above-average gelding, effective 5 to 6f, best at 6f, acts on g-s to frm, best on frm, has worn blinkers, likes left handed tracks, excels at Bath. Turf high 89 - 2nd of 14 giving 10lb to Alpen Wolf (22 Aug Bath 6f frm RF 3833) - also 1st of 6 from Mungo Park (30 Jun Bath RF 2428). Consistent. A genuine sprinter who is kept very busy, he paid his way again last year. He appears to go on all types of ground with two victories over five furlongs at Bath in the early summer proved his liking for that track.

**M R Channon [9-62] Michael Foy.*

CAUDILLO (IRE) BHB 53f55a RR 54f 55a 71[12]

6 b m Nordico (USA) 8.2f **(59)** - Over Swing (FR) (Saint Cyrien (FR)) 8.4f **(80)**

Form - 0

Record 1999 - 1st:0 2nd:0 3rd:0 Ran:1
Pre1999 - 1st:2 2nd:7 3rd:3 Ran:30

Win Prizemoney £7,424 *Total Prizemoney* £14,832

Wins 1997 *Nov Wolver (STD) H 7f 53 57*
1996 Aug Leopar (G-S) 8f 70 <

1999 AW 0-1: (8f) (Fibr)

Fair mare, effective 7 to 8f, best at 7f, acts on gd - acts on Fibr. Consistent.

**Miss Gay Kelleway [0-4] Stable Investments Ltd (from Mrs P N Dutfield [1-22] Jun 1998).*

CAUNTON BHB 65f RR 62f 4728[10]

2 b f Suave Dancer (USA) 10.7f **(68)** - Arminda (Blakeney) 10.5f **(64)**

Form - 740

Record 1999 - 1st:0 2nd:0 3rd:0 Ran:3

Win Prizemoney £0 *Total Prizemoney* £270

1999 Turf 0-3: (7f, 8f 2) (g-s, frm 2)

Currently average filly. Turf high 62 (began Aug).

**M L W Bell [0-3] B H Farr.*

CAUSED CONFUSION (USA) RR 59f 4584[5]

4 ch g Miswaki (USA) 8.1f **(81)** - Reassert (USA) (Assert) 10.6f **(85)**

Form - 65

Record 1999 - 1st:0 2nd:0 3rd:0 Ran:2

1999 Turf 0-2: (10f, 12f) (gd 2)

Lengthy, currently fair gelding. Turf high 59.

**G Barnett [0-2] J C Bradbury.*

CAUTION BHB 67f RR 67f 4933[5]

5 b m Warning 8.1f **(77)** - Fairy Flax (IRE) (Dancing Brave (USA)) 8.4f **(76)**

Form - 8202385

Record 1999 - 1st:0 2nd:2 3rd:1 Ran:7
Pre1999 - 1st:4 2nd:4 3rd:3 Ran:27

Win Prizemoney £13,910 *Total Prizemoney* £24,212

Wins * 1998 Oct Redcar (HVY) 5f 65
1997 Jly Beverl (G-F) C 7.5f 61+
1997 Jun Cheste (G-F) C 6.1f 70
1996 Spt Ayr (G-F) 6f 79 <

1999 Turf 0-7: (5f 5, 6f 2) (g-s, gd, g-f 2, frm 3)

Average filly, effective 5 to 6f, best at 6f, acts on sft to frm, best on frm, has worn blinkers, prefers left handed tracks, prefers tight tracks, excels at Pontefract, likes Newmarket. Turf high 67 (began Aug) - 2nd of 13 giving 8lb to Inchalong (16 Spt Pontefract 6f frm RF 4352). Can go in any ground, and is equally at home over five or six furlongs. Good placed efforts in fair handicap company last season.

**S Gollings [1-28] Ian & Mrs Irene Thomas (from Mrs J R Ramsden [3-6] Jly 1997).*

CAUTIONARY (IRE) BHB 81f RR 77f 3135[8]

2 b f Warning 8.1f **(77)** - Iltimas (USA) **(90f)** (Dayjur (USA))

Form - 21228

Record 1999 - 1st:1 2nd:3 3rd:0 Ran:5

Win Prizemoney £3,403 *Total Prizemoney* £6,377

Wins * **1999** May Hamilt (GD) 5f 70+ <

1999 Turf 1-5: (5f 1-2, 6f 2, 7f) (hvy, gd 2, g-f 1-2)

Above-average filly. Turf high 77 - also 1st of 6 getting 5lb from Gain Time (2 May Hamilton RF 0970). **J Berry [1-5] Mrs J M Berry.*

CAUTIOUS JOE BHB 78f RR 64f 1662[8]

2 b f First Trump - Jomel Amou (IRE) (Ela-Mana-Mou) 10.1f **(70)**

Form - 18

Record 1999 - 1st:1 2nd:0 3rd:0 Ran:2

Win Prizemoney £2,379 *Total Prizemoney* £2,379

Wins * **1999** May Newcas (G-F) 5f 64+ <

1999 Turf 1-2: (5f 1-2) (gd, frm 1-1)

Currently average filly. Turf high 64 (1st run) - 1st of 19 giving 4lb to Magic Grand (3 May Newcastle RF 1004).

**R A Fahey [1-2] Tommy Staunton.*

CAVALIER BHB 82f RR 83f 4860[1]

2 b c Bigstone (IRE) - Belle Arrivee (Bustino) 10.4f **(64)**

Form - 651

Record 1999 - 1st:1 2nd:0 3rd:0 Ran:3

Win Prizemoney £3,842 *Total Prizemoney* £3,842

Wins * **1999** Oct Haydoc (HVY) 7.1f 83 <

1999 Turf 1-3: (7f 1-2, 8f) (g-s 1-2, g-f)

Currently decent colt. Turf high 83 (began Aug) - 1st of 9 from Nooshman (13 Oct Haydock RF 4860). The sort to improve with experience, he got off the mark with a narrow victory in heavy ground at Haydock.

**W J Haggas [1-3] Highclere Thoroughbred Racing Ltd.*

CAVALLINA (USA) BHB 60a RR 90f 294[14]

4 b f Theatrical 11.5f **(78)** - Sedulous (Tap On Wood) 10.3f **(65)**

Form - 00

Record 1999 - 1st:0 2nd:0 3rd:0 Ran:2
Pre1999 - 1st:0 2nd:0 3rd:2 Ran:5

Win Prizemoney £0 *Total Prizemoney* £948

1999 AW 0-2: (8f 2) (Equi, Fibr)

Useful filly, has worn blinkers. AW high 22.

**K R Burke [0-2] Mrs Elaine Burke (from D K Weld in IRE [0-5] Nov 1998).*

CAVERNISTA BHB 78f RR 72f 2328[4]

3 b f Lion Cavern (USA) 7.5f **(74)** - Princess Genista (Ile de Bourbon (USA)) 10.1f **(67)**

Form - 44

Record 1999 - 1st:0 2nd:0 3rd:0 Ran:2
Pre1999 - 1st:0 2nd:0 3rd:0 Ran:2

Win Prizemoney £0 *Total Prizemoney* £109

1999 Turf 0-2: (8f, 9f) (g-f, frm)

Light-framed, above-average filly. Turf high 72.

**J L Dunlop [0-4] I H Stewart-Brown.*

CAVERSFIELD BHB 53f56a RR 46f 56a 4094[8]

4 ch c Tina's Pet 7.4f **(56)** - Canoodle (Warpath) 12.3f **(52)**

Form - 3662443533078

Record 1999 - 1st:0 2nd:1 3rd:3 Ran:11
Pre1999 - 1st:2 2nd:2 3rd:4 Ran:21

Win Prizemoney £6,643 *Total Prizemoney* £13,231

Wins * 1997 Oct Leices (GD) H 7f 75 76 <
* 1997 Aug Windso (G-F) H 6f 72 76 <

1999 Turf 0-10: (7f 4, 8f 6) (gd, g-f, frm 7, hrd) 1999 AW 0-1: (8f) (Equi)

Leggy, fair colt, effective 7 to 8f, best at 7f, acts on g-s to frm, best on g-s, has worn blinkers. Turf high 61 (1st run) - 2nd of 18 giving 10lb to Mysticism (12 May Brighton 7f g-f RF 1179). Consistent. He won two back-end nurseries in 1997 but is currently on a massive losing run dating back to that year. **R Hannon [2-32] William Kelly.*

CAXTON LAD BHB 78f RR 78+f 5105[6]

2 b c Cyrano de Bergerac 7.3f **(58)** - Urania **(54f)** (Most Welcome)

Form - 36816

Record 1999 - 1st:1 2nd:0 3rd:1 Ran:5

Win Prizemoney £3,663 *Total Prizemoney* £4,188

Wins * **1999** Oct Haydoc (HVY) H 5f 65 78+ <

1999 Turf 1-5: (5f 1-3, 6f 2) (g-s 1-2, gd 2, g-f)

Above-average colt. Turf high 78 - 1st of 13 giving 5lb to Judiam (13 Oct Haydock RF 4857). **P J Makin [1-5] Four Seasons Racing Ltd.*

CD FLYER (IRE) BHB 80f **RR 80f** 5048[5]
2 ch g Grand Lodge (USA) -Pretext(Polish Precedent(USA)) 10.2f **(60)**
Form - 6341347185
Record 1999 - 1st:2 2nd:0 3rd:2 Ran:10
Win Prizemoney £10,592 *Total Prizemoney* £13,408
Wins * **1999** Oct Newmar (SFT) H 6f 75 80 <
* **1999** May Thirsk (G-S) 5f 77
1999 Turf 2-10: (5f 1-6, 6f 1-2, 7f 2) (hvy, gd 2-5, frm 4)
Decent gelding, effective 5 to 6f, best at 5f, acts on gd to frm, best on gd. Turf high 80 - 1st of 16 getting 16lb from Nothing Daunted (2 Oct Newmarket RF 4686) - also 1st of 7 getting 2lb from Nifty Major (15 May Thirsk RF 1252). Consistent. Successful in a Thirsk maiden and a Newmarket nursery, he seems well suited by six furlongs and cut in the ground.
**M R Channon [2-10] Circular Distributors Ltd.*

CEDAR CHIEF BHB 40f **RR 47f** 4582[12]
2 b c Saddlers' Hall (IRE) 10.5f **(65)** -Dame Ashfield (Grundy) 10.3f **(65)**
Form - 0000
Record 1999 - 1st:0 2nd:0 3rd:0 Ran:4
1999 Turf 0-4: (7f 2, 8f, 10f) (gd, g-f 2, frm)
Moderate colt. Turf high 42.
**R J O'Sullivan [0-4] The Mayfair Partnership.*

CEDAR GUV'NOR (IRE) BHB 55f57a **RR 54f 57a** 4786[6]
2 b g Perugino (USA) - Start Again (IRE) (Cyrano de Bergerac) 6f **(68)**
Form - 04036006
Record 1999 - 1st:0 2nd:0 3rd:1 Ran:8
Win Prizemoney £0 *Total Prizemoney* £780
1999 Turf 0-7: (5f 4, 6f 3) (g-s, g-f 3, frm 2, hrd) 1999 AW 0-1: (6f) (Equi)
Fair gelding, effective 5f, acts on frm. Turf high 54 - 3rd of 7 getting 21lb from Russian Fox (7 Jly Lingfield 5f frm RF 2623).
**R J O'Sullivan [0-8] Mrs R J Doorgachurn.*

CEDAR LIGHT (IRE) RR 44f 872[13]
2 b c Dolphin Street (FR) - Maxencia (FR) (Tennyson (FR)) 12.1f **(50)**
Form - 0
Record 1999 - 1st:0 2nd:0 3rd:0 Ran:1
1999 Turf 0-1: (5f) (gd)
Currently moderate colt. **R J O'Sullivan [0-1] M J Marchant.*

CEDAR LORD RR 5f 1398[12]
2 b c Emperor Jones (USA) - Bint Damascus (USA) (Damascus (USA)) 8.9f **(71)**
Form - 0
Record 1999 - 1st:0 2nd:0 3rd:0 Ran:1
1999 Turf 0-1: (5f) (frm)
Currently very poor colt. **R J O'Sullivan [0-1] M J Marchant.*

CEDAR MASTER (IRE) BHB 92f **RR 90df** 5027[4]
2 b c Soviet Lad (USA) 9.4f **(63)** - Samriah (IRE) (Wassl) 9.7f **(62)**
Form - 5310333724
Record 1999 - 1st:1 2nd:1 3rd:4 Ran:10
Win Prizemoney £2,864 *Total Prizemoney* £19,862
Wins * **1999** May Chepst (GD) 6.1f 83 <
1999 Turf 1-10: (5f 3, 6f 1-5, 7f, 8f) (g-s, gd 1-2, g-f 4, frm 3)
Useful colt, effective 5 to 7f, acts on g-f, has worn blinkers (extremely effectively). Turf high 95 - 3rd of 25 getting 1lb from Don Puccini (17 Jly Newbury 5f g-f RF 2901). He stood up well to an arduous campaign, running his best race to finish third in the Weatherbys Super Sprint Stakes. He appears to stay seven furlongs, but will be difficult to place against less exposed rivals in 2000. **R J O'Sullivan [1-10] Robert Allen.*

CEDAR PRINCE (IRE) BHB 81f **RR 81f** 4491[9]
2 b c Namaqualand (USA) - Supreme Crown (USA) (Chief's Crown (USA)) 9.8f **(72)**
Form - 82073120
Record 1999 - 1st:1 2nd:2 3rd:1 Ran:8
Win Prizemoney £5,875 *Total Prizemoney* £8,881
Wins * **1999** Aug Ascot (GD) H 7f 69 77 <
1999 Turf 1-8: (6f 4, 7f 1-4) (sft, gd 1-3, g-f, frm 3)
Decent colt, effective 7f, acts on gd to g-f, has worn blinkers. Turf high 81 - 2nd of 9 giving 2lb to Common Place (29 Aug Goodwood 7f g-f RF 3996) - also 1st of 7 getting 9lb from Clever Girl (7 Aug Ascot RF 3446). **R J O'Sullivan [1-8] B S Chatwal.*

CEDAR WELLS (USA) BHB 57f61a **RR 61f 61a** 4260[21]
3 b g Desert Secret (IRE) - Sans Sorrow (USA) (Barachois (CAN)) 8.3f **(63)**
Form - 3105052280
Record 1999 - 1st:0 2nd:2 3rd:0 Ran:8
Pre1999 - 1st:1 2nd:0 3rd:1 Ran:6
Win Prizemoney £2,778 *Total Prizemoney* £5,824
Wins * 1998 *Dec Lingfi (STD) H 7f 55 64* <
1999 Turf 0-8: (6f, 7f, 8f 5, 9f) (g-f 2, frm 5, hrd)
Scopey, average gelding, has broken blood-vessels, effective 7f, - acts on Equi, likes left handed tracks, likes tight tracks. Turf high 61. Inconsistent. Showed improved form when switched to Equitrack at the end of 1998, and got off the mark in a small nursery on that surface. **G Lewis [1-14] & Mrs Kantis.*

CEEDEBEE RR 5113[20]
3 b f Cyrano de Bergerac 7.3f **(58)** -Bonita Bee (King of Spain) 7.8f **(52)**
Form - 0
Record 1999 - 1st:0 2nd:0 3rd:0 Ran:1
1999 Turf 0-1: (6f) (gd)
Unfurnished, currently very poor filly.
**J C McConnochie [0-1] Mrs R E Stocks.*

CEE-N-K (IRE) BHB 24f44a **RR 26f 44a** 3978[11]
5 b g Thatching 7.8f **(69)** - Valois (Lyphard (USA)) 9.9f **(72)**
Form - 0707800
Record 1999 - 1st:0 2nd:0 3rd:0 Ran:7
Pre1999 - 1st:2 2nd:4 3rd:1 Ran:32
Win Prizemoney £8,746 *Total Prizemoney* £13,529
Wins 1997 Jly Beverl (G-F) H 7.5f 69 75
1996 *Dec Lingfi (STD) H 8f 73 76* <
1999 Turf 0-7: (8f 3, 10f, 11f 2, 12f) (gd 2, g-f, frm 3, hrd)
Moderate gelding, effective 9 to 10f, acts on gd - acts on Fibr, has worn blinkers (effectively), likes left handed tracks. Turf high 26.
**Mrs G S Rees [0-3] North West Racing Club - Owners Group (from D Nicholls [0-4] Jly 1999).*

CELANDINE BHB 46f65a **RR 48f 65a** 4445[9]
6 b m Warning 8.1f **(77)** - Silly Bold (Rousillon (USA)) 8.2f **(74)**
Form - 40508600080
Record 1999 - 1st:0 2nd:0 3rd:0 Ran:11
Pre1999 - 1st:3 2nd:2 3rd:4 Ran:25
Win Prizemoney £9,709 *Total Prizemoney* £14,226
Wins * 1998 Spt Catter (G-F) H 7f 56 61
* 1998 Jly Warwic (G-F) H 7f 51 57
1995 Spt Bath (G-F) 5.7f 83 <
1999 Turf 0-11: (7f 11) (g-s, gd 2, g-f, frm 7)
Average mare, effective 7f, acts on gd to frm, has worn blinkers, prefers left handed tracks, likes tight tracks. Turf high 61 (1st run) - 4th of 15 getting 4lb from Rambo Waltzer (16 Apr Thirsk 7f gd RF 0729).
**Andrew Turnell [2-28] Mrs Claire Hollowood (from J L Eyre [0-4] Jun 1996).*

CELEBES BHB 77f **RR 72f** 2616[4]
2 b c Weldnaas (USA) 8.4f **(55)** - Shift Over (USA) (Night Shift (USA)) 7.2f **(69)**
Form - 564
Record 1999 - 1st:0 2nd:0 3rd:0 Ran:3
Win Prizemoney £0 *Total Prizemoney* £238
1999 Turf 0-3: (6f 2, 7f) (gd 2, frm)
Currently above-average colt. Turf high 72.
**I A Balding [0-3] Robert Hitchins.*

CELEBRATE (IRE) BHB 69a **RR 70f** 4410[9]
3 ch f Generous (IRE) 11.5f **(82)** - Bright Generation (IRE) (Rainbow Quest (USA)) 10.4f **(75)**
Form - 3753730
Record 1999 - 1st:0 2nd:0 3rd:3 Ran:7
Pre1999 - 1st:0 2nd:0 3rd:0 Ran:1
Win Prizemoney £0 *Total Prizemoney* £2,022
1999 Turf 0-6: (8f 4, 10f 2) (gd, g-f, frm 3, hrd) 1999 AW 0-1: (8f) (Fibr)
Light-framed, above-average filly, effective 8f, acts on frm to hrd. Turf high 70 - 3rd of 8 getting 5lb from Minetta (19 Jly Windsor 8f frm RF 2951).
**S P C Woods [0-7] Northmore Stud (from P F I Cole [0-1] May 1998).*

CELEBRATION CAKE (IRE) BHB 23f **RR 28f** 4163[12]
7 b g Mister Majestic 9.9f **(56)** - My Louise (Manado) 9.6f **(63)**
Form - 00086030

Record	**1999** -	1st:0	2nd:0	3rd:1	Ran:8
	Pre1999 -	1st:5	2nd:2	3rd:4	Ran:38

Win Prizemoney £22,756 *Total Prizemoney* £27,546

Wins								
* 1998	Aug	Hamilt	(SFT)	C	9.2f		46	
* 1996	Spt	Ayr	(G-F)	H	7f	70	76	<
* 1996	Aug	Haydoc	(G-F)	H	8.1f	58	73	
* 1996	Aug	Hamilt	(G-F)	H	8.3f	58	67	
* 1995	Jun	Ayr	(G-F)	H	8f	56	55	

1999 Turf 0-8: (8f, 9f 5, 11f, 12f) (g-f 4, frm 4)
Little account gelding, effective 9f, acts on g-s to gd, has worn blinkers, likes right handed tracks, favours tight tracks. Turf high 28. **Miss L A Perratt [5-49] T P Finch.*

CELEBRATION TOWN (IRE) BHB 67f **RR 48f** 3899[5]
2 b br g Case Law 6f **(64)** - Battle Queen (Kind of Hush) 10.1f **(62)**
Form - 505

Record	**1999** -	1st:0	2nd:0	3rd:0	Ran:3

1999 Turf 0-3: (5f 3) (gd, frm 2)
Currently moderate gelding. Turf high 57.
**J J O'Neill [0-3] Meadowcrest Ltd.*

Evergreen Celeric returned to winning form

CELERIC BHB 116f **RR 115?f** 4684[3]
7 b g Mtoto 11.5f **(71)** - Hot Spice (Hotfoot) 10.5f **(59)**
Form - 1546133

Record	**1999** -	1st:2	2nd:0	3rd:2	Ran:7
	Pre1999 -	1st:11	2nd:7	3rd:2	Ran:32

Win Prizemoney £365,847 *Total Prizemoney* £460,322

Wins								
* **1999**	Aug	York	(GD)	G3	15.9f		115	
* **1999**	Apr	Ascot	(GD)	G3	16.2f		111	
1997	Jun	Ascot	(GD)	G1	20f		121	<
1997	May	York	(GD)	G2	13.9f		115	
1996	Oct	Newmar	(G-F)	G3	16f		112	
1996	Aug	York	(GD)	L	15.9f		113+	
1996	Jly	York	(GD)	LH	13.9f	102	104	
1996	Jun	Newcas	(FRM)	H	16.1f	96	100	
1996	May	York	(G-F)	H	13.9f	90	94+	
1995	Aug	York	(G-F)	H	13.9f	87	93	
1995	Jly	Newbur	(GD)	H	13.3f	83	91	
1995	May	Nottin	(GD)	H	14.1f	79	81	
1995	May	Warwic	(FRM)	H	12.5f	75	81	

1999 Turf 2-7: (16f 2-5, 18f, 20f) (gd, g-f 2-4, frm 2)
High-class gelding, effective 16 to 20f, best at 16f, acts on gd to g-f, best on g-f, does well at York and Ascot. Turf high 115 - 4th of 17 giving 2lb to Enzeli (17 Jun Ascot 20f g-f RF 2071) - also 1st of 8 getting 3lb from Arctic Owl (17 Aug York RF 3693). This most likeable of racehorses, winner of the 1997 Gold Cup, finished fourth in this last season's renewal and proved he is still a force in the top staying events when landing the Sagaro Stakes on his reappearance and York's Lonsdale Stakes. However, these days he very much needs things to go his own way.
**J L Dunlop [2-13] Christopher Spence (from D Morley [11-26] Oct 1997).*

CELESTIAL BAY (IRE) BHB 54f45a **RR 55f 45a** 2275[14]
4 b f Star de Naskra (USA) 8.8f **(63)** - Kandara (FR) (Dalsaan) 9.8f **(64)**
Form - 5420200

Record	**1999** -	1st:0	2nd:2	3rd:0	Ran:7
	Pre1999 -	1st:0	2nd:0	3rd:3	Ran:13

Win Prizemoney £0 *Total Prizemoney* £4,573
1999 Turf 0-7: (6f 5, 7f, 8f) (g-s, gd, g-f, frm 2, hrd 2)
Leggy, fair filly, effective 6f, acts on frm. Turf high 55.
**E A Wheeler [0-16] You're Having A Laugh Racing Club (from A G Foster [0-4] Aug 1997).*

CELESTIAL CHOIR BHB 75f87a **RR 68f 87a** 2005[9]
9 b m Celestial Storm (USA) 11.8f **(58)** - Choir (High Top) 10.2f **(67)**
Form - 0

Record	**1999** -	1st:0	2nd:0	3rd:0	Ran:1
	Pre1999 -	1st:12	2nd:11	3rd:6	Ran:77

Win Prizemoney £84,126 *Total Prizemoney* £114,678

Wins								
* 1997	Oct	York	(SFT)		11.9f		90	
* 1997	Aug	Pontef	(G-F)	H	12f	83	91	
* 1996	Aug	York	(GD)	H	11.9f	86	93	<
* 1996	Jly	Doncas	(G-F)	H	10.3f	83	85	
* 1996	*Jan*	*Southw*	*(STD)*		*12f*		*83*	
* 1996	*Jan*	*Lingfi*	*(STD)*	*H*	*10f*	*75*	*83*	
* 1995	Aug	Pontef	(G-F)	H	8f	78	84	

1999 Turf 0-1: (12f) (frm)
Useful mare, has worn blinkers. **J L Eyre [18-94] Mrs Carole Sykes.*

CELESTIAL KEY (USA) BHB 85f76a **RR 89f 76a** 932a[3]
9 br g Star de Naskra (USA) 8.8f **(63)** - Casa Key (USA) (Cormorant (USA)) 8.2f **(104)**
Form - 7803

Record	**1999** -	1st:0	2nd:0	3rd:1	Ran:2
	Pre1999 -	1st:11	2nd:7	3rd:7	Ran:77

Win Prizemoney £72,444 *Total Prizemoney* £109,304

Wins								
* 1998	Aug	Dielsd	(GD)		9f		89	
* 1997	Spt	Dielsd	(GD)		8f		96	
* 1997	Aug	Dielsd	(GD)		8f		89	
* 1995	Oct	Newmar	(G-F)	L	8f		105	<
* 1995	Jun	Newbur	(G-F)	H	7f	93	99	
* 1995	Jun	Haydoc	(GD)	H	8.1f	93	97	
* 1995	May	Thirsk	(FRM)	H	7f	90	95	

1999 Turf 0-1: (8f) (sft) 1999 AW 0-1: (8f) (Fibr)
Useful gelding, effective 8 to 9f, best at 8f, acts on g-s to g-f, has worn blinkers. A versatile performer, he showed he retains plenty of ability when narrowly beaten at Newcastle in June 1998, but looks a bit high in the weights in this country, and his wins in recent seasons have been at Dielsdorf in Switzerland.
**M Johnston [7-54] (from S G Norton [4-28] Spt 1994).*

CELESTIAL WELCOME BHB 85f **RR 78f** 5038[6]
4 b f Most Welcome 8.6f **(66)** - Choral Sundown (Night Shift (USA)) 7.2f **(69)**
Form - 12210166076

Record	**1999** -	1st:3	2nd:2	3rd:0	Ran:11
	Pre1999 -	1st:4	2nd:0	3rd:0	Ran:11

Win Prizemoney £61,180 *Total Prizemoney* £63,804

Wins								
* **1999**	Jly	Haydoc	(G-S)	H	11.9f	85	92	<
* **1999**	Jun	Haydoc	(G-S)	H	10.5f	80	86	
* **1999**	Apr	Newcas	(GD)	H	8f	71	76	
* 1998	May	Redcar	(GD)	H	7f	62	74	
* 1998	May	Newcas	(G-S)	H	8f	62	65	
* 1998	Apr	Carlis	(G-S)	H	9.3f	54	56	
* 1998	Apr	Hamilt	(HVY)		8.3f		52	

1999 Turf 3-11: (8f 1-1, 9f, 10f 3, 11f 1-1, 12f 1-5) (sft 2, g-s, gd 3-5, g-f, frm 2)
Scopey, above-average filly, effective 10 to 12f, best at 12f, acts on gd to frm, best on gd, likes tight tracks, excels at Haydock and

Newcastle. Turf high 92 - 1st of 15 giving 12lb to Hill Farm Blues (3 Jly Haydock RF 2532) - also 1st of 9 giving 2lb to Captain's Log (3 Jun Haydock RF 1701). Consistent. Was successful three times, including the Old Newton Cup, and was not disgraced afterwards. Stays 12 furlongs, but does not want fast ground.

**Mrs M Reveley [7-22] The Welcome Alliance.*

CELESTRIA RR 59f — 1708[4]

3 b f Cosmonaut - Celestial Air (Rheingold) 10.4f **(62)**
Form - 74
Record 1999 - 1st:0 2nd:0 3rd:0 Ran:2
Win Prizemoney £0 *Total Prizemoney* £255
1999 Turf 0-2: (7f 2) (gd, frm)
Leggy, currently fair filly. Turf high 59.
**W Jarvis [0-2] Mrs J H Weller-Poley & Partners.*

CELTIC CROSS BHB 99f RR 92f — 2268[2]

4 b f Selkirk (USA) 7.9f **(76)** - Abbey Strand (USA) (Shadeed (USA)) 8.2f **(70)**
Form - 12
Record 1999 - 1st:1 2nd:1 3rd:0 Ran:2
Pre1999 - 1st:0 2nd:1 3rd:0 Ran:2
Win Prizemoney £3,850 *Total Prizemoney* £11,324
Wins * **1999** May Haydoc (GD) 7.1f 81 <
1999 Turf 1-2: (7f 1-1, 8f) (g-f 1-1, frm)
Scopey, useful filly. Turf high 92 - 2nd of 5 giving 3lb to Risque Lady (24 Jun Newcastle 8f frm RF 2268). Having missed her three-year-old season, she returned at four with an impressive victory in a Haydock maiden in May, before losing to Risque Lady over a mile in a Newcastle conditions race. Given she is lightly-raced, improvement can be expected.
**Sir Michael Stoute [1-2] The Queen (from Lord Huntingdon [0-2] Spt 1997).*

CELTIC FLING BHB 77f RR 76f — 5193[1]

3 b f Lion Cavern (USA) 7.5f **(74)** -Celtic Ring (Welsh Pageant) 10f **(65)**
Form - 21
Record 1999 - 1st:1 2nd:1 3rd:0 Ran:2
Win Prizemoney £2,541 *Total Prizemoney* £3,809
Wins * **1999** Nov Windso (G-S) 8.3f 76 <
1999 Turf 1-2: (7f, 8f 1-1) (gd 1-2)
Light-framed, currently above-average filly. Turf high 76 (began Jly) - 1st of 17 getting 5lb from Brazilian Mood (4 Nov Windsor RF 5193). Lightly-raced, she bolted up in a Windsor maiden in November, and looks an interesting prospect at four.
**Lady Herries [1-2] Angmering Park Stud.*

CELTIC SEAL BHB 56f54a RR 59f 54a — 4606[14]

3 br f Lugana Beach 7f **(63)** - Celtic Bird (Celtic Cone) 9.8f **(43)**
Form - 17470
Record 1999 - 1st:0 2nd:0 3rd:0 Ran:3
Pre1999 - 1st:1 2nd:0 3rd:0 Ran:5
Win Prizemoney £2,295 *Total Prizemoney* £2,554
Wins * 1998 *Nov Southw (STD) 5f 67* <
1999 Turf 0-1: (5f) (gd) 1999 AW 0-2: (5f, 6f) (Fibr 2)
Scopey, average filly, effective 5f, - acts on Fibr. AW high 55. Inconsistent. **J Balding [1-8] Mrs Paula Haigh.*

CELTIC VENTURE BHB 55f RR 47f — 2150[11]

4 ch g Risk Me (FR) 8f **(53)** - Celtic River (IRE) (Caerleon (USA)) 8.6f **(71)**
Form - 100
Record 1999 - 1st:1 2nd:0 3rd:0 Ran:3
Pre1999 - 1st:0 2nd:1 3rd:0 Ran:3
Win Prizemoney £2,232 *Total Prizemoney* £2,972
Wins * **1999** Apr Bright (GD) C 5.3f 47 <
1999 Turf 1-3: (5f 1-3) (gd, frm 1-1, hrd)
Workmanlike, moderate gelding. Turf high 47 (1st run).
**J C Poulton [1-3] Gerald West (from M R Channon [0-3] Aug 1997).*

CENSOR BHB 48f RR 48f — 2837[3]

6 b g Kris 10f **(75)** - Mixed Applause (USA) (Nijinsky (CAN)) 10.3f **(77)**
Form - 0043
Record 1999 - 1st:0 2nd:0 3rd:1 Ran:4
Pre1999 - 1st:1 2nd:0 3rd:1 Ran:17
Win Prizemoney £3,492 *Total Prizemoney* £6,022
Wins 1995 Oct Nottin (G-F) 8.2f 83 <
1999 Turf 0-4: (10f 3, 12f) (frm 4)
Moderate gelding, effective 10 to 12f, best at 10f, acts on frm, has worn blinkers. Turf high 48 - 3rd of 9 to Silver Prey (15 Jly Bath 12f frm RF 2837).
**B J Llewellyn [1-10] Thomas Leonard (from D Nicholls [0-13] Oct 1998).*

CENTAUR SPIRIT RR 38f — 5138[9]

2 b c Distant Relative 7f **(69)** - Winnie Reckless (Local Suitor (USA)) 8.4f **(67)**
Form - 0
Record 1999 - 1st:0 2nd:0 3rd:0 Ran:1
1999 Turf 0-1: (8f) (gd)
Currently very moderate colt. **A Streeter [0-1] Centaur Racing Ltd.*

CENTER STAGE (IRE) RR 71f — 5208[6]

2 ch c In The Wings 11.2f **(77)** - Secret Feeling (USA) (Riverman (USA)) 9.1f **(76)**
Form - 46
Record 1999 - 1st:0 2nd:0 3rd:0 Ran:2
Win Prizemoney £0 *Total Prizemoney* £320
1999 Turf 0-2: (7f 2) (g-s 2)
Currently above-average colt. Turf high 71 (began Oct).
**R Hannon [0-2] Mrs Derek Strauss.*

CENTRAL COAST (IRE) BHB 84f RR 84f — 3697[19]

3 b c Hamas (IRE) 8f **(72)** - Clairification (IRE) **(56f 58a)** (Shernazar) 10.2f **(73)**
Form - 80544120
Record 1999 - 1st:1 2nd:1 3rd:0 Ran:8
Pre1999 - 1st:1 2nd:1 3rd:0 Ran:3
Win Prizemoney £10,866 *Total Prizemoney* £16,004
Wins * **1999** Jly Newbur (G-F) H 6f 77 79
* 1998 Aug Nottin (G-F) 6.1f 82 <
1999 Turf 1-8: (5f, 6f 1-5, 7f, 8f) (g-f 4, frm 1-4)
Strong, decent colt, effective 6f, acts on g-f to frm, best on g-f. Turf high 84 - 2nd of 13 getting 19lb from Cretan Gift (25 Jly Ascot 6f g-f RF 3117) - also 1st of 12 getting 22lb from Brave Edge (16 Jly Newbury RF 2879). He looked a progressive young sprinter last season, winning a fair race at Newbury and running well to finish second to Cretan Gift in a competitive event at Ascot. Looks better suited by six furlongs than five. **J M P Eustace [2-11] R Carstairs.*

CENTRAL PARK (IRE) BHB 120f RR 122f — 5223a[2]

4 ch c In The Wings 11.2f **(77)** - Park Special (Relkino) 8.9f **(65)**
Form - 41702
Record 1999 - 1st:1 2nd:1 3rd:0 Ran:5
Pre1999 - 1st:5 2nd:0 3rd:1 Ran:11
Win Prizemoney £309,072 *Total Prizemoney* £669,515
Wins * **1999** May Capann (GD) G1 10f 118 <
* 1998 Aug Hoppeg (GD) G2 12f 112
* 1998 May Capann (G-F) G1 12f 111
1997 Jly Goodwo (G-F) G3 7f 111+
1997 Jun Ascot (GD) L 7f 103
1997 Jun Haydoc (G-F) 6f 92+
1999 Turf 1-4: (10f 1-2, 12f, 16f) (gd 1-3, g-f) 1999 AW 0-1: (10f) (Dirt)
Scopey, very high-class colt, effective 10 to 16f, best at 10f, acts on gd - acts on Dirt, likes right handed tracks. Turf high 122 - 2nd of 24 giving 17lb to Rogan Josh (2 Nov Flemington 16f gd RF 5223a) - also 1st of 8 giving 3lb to Elle Danzig (16 May Capannelle RF 1353a). (1st run) - 4th of 8 to Almutawakel (28 Mar Nad Al Sheba 10f Dirt RF 0556a). He has spent much of the last two seasons acting as pacemaker for his stable companions. He won the Derby Italiano and a German Group Two in 1998, and was successful in Group One company in Italy again last term, but he seemed to struggle against the very best middle-distance horses. Possibly his finest hour came when, as a last-minute substitute for the injured Kayf Tara, he ran a terrific race to be just touched off in the Melbourne Cup. He will be very interesting if he is campaigned at around two miles in 2000.
**S bin Suroor [3-10] Godolphin (from S bin Suroor in UAE [0-1] Mar 1999).*

CEPHALONIA BHB 75f RR 82f — 5109[4]

2 b f Slip Anchor 12.7f **(75)** - Cephira (FR) (Abdos) 10f **(77)**
Form - 804
Record 1999 - 1st:0 2nd:0 3rd:0 Ran:3
Win Prizemoney £0 *Total Prizemoney* £213

1999 Turf 0-3: (7f, 8f 2) (g-s 2, gd)
Currently decent filly. Turf high 82 (began Spt).
**J L Dunlop [0-3] Exors of the late Lord Howard de Walden.*

CERIAD RR 47f 3836[16]
3 b f Merdon Melody 6.8f **(56)** - Teanarco (IRE) **(53df)** (Kafu) 6f **(47)**
Form - 80
Record 1999 - 1st:0 2nd:0 3rd:0 Ran:2
1999 Turf 0-2: (7f 2) (frm 2)
Unfurnished, currently moderate filly. Turf high 47 (began Aug).
**J Neville [0-2] Brian Symonds.*

CERULEAN SKY (IRE) RR 114f 5018a[2]
3 b f Darshaan 11.9f **(81)** - Solo De Lune (FR) (Law Society (USA)) 9.9f **(70)**
Form - 167382
1999 Turf 1-6: (10f 1-2, 11f, 12f 3) (sft, g-s 1-2, gd 3)
Group-class filly, effective 10 to 12f, best at 10f, acts on g-s to gd, best on gd. Turf high 114 - 2nd of 7 getting 5lb from Insight (17 Oct Woodbine 10f gd RF 5018a) - also 1st of 10 from Juvenia (23 May Longchamp RF 1530a). She contested a string of Group 1 events, winning the Prix Saint-Alary at Longchamp in May. Often made to look a shade one-paced thereafter, she might benefit from more aggressive tactics. **R Collet in FR [1-7].*

CHABROL (CAN) BHB 35f58a **RR 41f 58a** 4650[13]
6 b g El Gran Senor (USA) 8.9f **(85)** - Off The Record (USA) (Chas Conerly (USA)) 10.1f **(76)**
Form - 3550050
Record 1999 - 1st:0 2nd:0 3rd:1 Ran:7
Pre1999 - 1st:1 2nd:3 3rd:2 Ran:23
Win Prizemoney £2,945 *Total Prizemoney* £7,505
Wins 1996 Aug Yarmou (G-F) C 10.1f 61 <
1999 Turf 0-3: (12f 2, 16f) (gd, g-f 2) 1999 AW 0-4: (12f, 15f, 16f 2) (Equi 2, Fibr 2)
Average gelding, effective 15 to 16f, best at 16f, - acts on Fibr, prefers left handed tracks, prefers tight tracks. Turf high 37. AW high 65 - 5th of 6 getting 8lb from Sudest (13 Jan Wolverhampton 15f Fibr RF 0090). Becoming disappointing.
**J A Gilbert [0-4] The Chabrol Partnership (from P L Gilligan [0-4] Feb 1999).*

CHAKA ZULU BHB 40f **RR 28f** 5194[17]
2 b g Muhtarram (USA) - African Dance (USA) (El Gran Senor (USA)) 9.6f **(76)**
Form - 000
Record 1999 - 1st:0 2nd:0 3rd:0 Ran:3
1999 Turf 0-3: (6f 3) (gd 3)
Currently little account gelding. Turf high 28 (began Oct).
**W J Haggas [0-3] J D Ashenheim.*

CHAKRA BHB 41f **RR 44f** 4233[13]
5 gr g Mystiko (USA) 7.7f **(59)** - Maracuja (USA) (Riverman (USA)) 9.1f **(76)**
Form - 0084238786403040
Record 1999 - 1st:0 2nd:1 3rd:2 Ran:16
Pre1999 - 1st:3 2nd:0 3rd:2 Ran:22
Win Prizemoney £8,213 *Total Prizemoney* £11,167
Wins * 1998 Aug Warwic (G-F) H 5f 47 52 <
* 1998 Jly Warwic (G-F) H 5f 42 46
1997 Jly Bright (FRM) H 5.3f 45 48
1999 Turf 0-16: (5f 15, 6f) (gd 4, g-f 4, frm 8)
Moderate gelding, effective 5f, acts on g-f to hrd, best on frm, likes left handed tracks, excels at Warwick and Brighton. Turf high 46 - 2nd of 14 getting 15lb from Sealed By Fate (10 Jun Carlisle 5f g-f RF 1879). **J M Bradley [2-29] Clifton Hunt (from S Dow [1-9] Spt 1997).*

CHALCEDONY BHB 56f66a **RR 61df 66a** 2236[10]
3 ch g Highest Honor (FR) 10.9f **(72)** - Sweet Holland (USA) (Alydar (USA)) 9.1f **(76)**
Form - 3411350
Record 1999 - 1st:2 2nd:0 3rd:1 Ran:5
Pre1999 - 1st:0 2nd:0 3rd:1 Ran:5
Win Prizemoney £4,861 *Total Prizemoney* £6,047
Wins * **1999** *Apr Southw (STD) H 11f 60 63* <
* **1999** *Jan Lingfi (STD) H 10f 55 59*
1999 Turf 0-3: (12f, 14f, 15f) (g-f, frm, hrd) 1999 AW 2-2: (10f 1-1, 11f 1-1) (Equi 1-1, Fibr 1-1)
Leggy, average gelding, effective 10 to 15f, acts on hrd - acts on AW, has worn blinkers, prefers left handed tracks. Turf high 61 (1st run) - 3rd of 9 getting 12lb from Fnan (3 May Doncaster 15f hrd RF 0994). AW high 63 - 1st of 9 giving 3lb to The Last Word (6 Apr Southwell RF 0605) - also 1st of 10 getting 5lb from Rolling Rio (5 Jan Lingfield RF 0034). He showed ability on sand at the start of the year, winning twice, but also showed a bit of a quirk. He has not shown much on turf. **T D Barron [2-10] J Baggott.*

CHALIAPIN BHB 51f **RR 49f** 623[10]
4 b g Tragic Role (USA) 9.4f **(63)** - Last Note (Welsh Pageant) 10f **(65)**
Form - 420
Record 1999 - 1st:0 2nd:1 3rd:0 Ran:3
Win Prizemoney £0 *Total Prizemoney* £571
1999 Turf 0-1: (12f) (gd) 1999 AW 0-2: (11f, 12f) (Fibr 2)
Fair gelding. AW high 55 - 2nd of 6 giving 3lb to Linea-G (1 Mar Southwell 12f Fibr RF 0383).
**Bob Jones [0-4] The Chaliapin Partnership.*

CHALLENGES (FR) BHB 60f **RR 58f** 1702[10]
3 b c Zieten (USA) - La Toscanella (FR) (Riverton (FR))
Form - 3007320
Record 1999 - 1st:0 2nd:1 3rd:2 Ran:7
Pre1999 - 1st:0 2nd:1 3rd:3 Ran:5
Win Prizemoney £0 *Total Prizemoney* £9,049
1999 Turf 0-7: (10f 2, 11f 2, 12f 3) (sft, g-s, gd, g-f 4)
Leggy, fair colt, effective 6 to 8f, acts on gd, has worn blinkers. Turf high 71. **B J Meehan [0-12] J S Gutkin.*

CHALOUPE BHB 51f **RR 53f** 5113[11]
3 b f College Chapel - Shallop **(44f 53a)** (Salse (USA)) 7.5f **(66)**
Form - 0567200
Record 1999 - 1st:0 2nd:1 3rd:0 Ran:7
Pre1999 - 1st:0 2nd:0 3rd:0 Ran:3
Win Prizemoney £0 *Total Prizemoney* £768
1999 Turf 0-7: (6f 5, 7f 2) (g-s, gd, g-f, frm 4)
Unfurnished, fair filly, effective 6f, acts on g-f. Turf high 53.
**H Candy [0-10] W M Lidsey.*

CHALUZ BHB 37f50a **RR 31f 50a** 4864[2]
5 b g Night Shift (USA) 8.1f **(73)** - Laluche (USA) (Alleged (USA)) 10f **(76)**
Form - 5881324056452
Record 1999 - 1st:1 2nd:2 3rd:1 Ran:13
Pre1999 - 1st:3 2nd:2 3rd:2 Ran:25
Win Prizemoney £7,791 *Total Prizemoney* £11,636
Wins **1999** *Feb Wolver (STD) C 6f 50*
1998 *Jan Southw (STD) H 7f 53 59* <
1998 *Jan Southw (STD) H 8f 53 55*
1997 *Nov Southw (STD) H 7f 48 53*
1999 AW 1-13: (5f, 6f 1-7, 7f 3, 8f 2) (Equi, Fibr 1-12)
Fair gelding, effective 5 to 8f, best at 8f, - acts on Fibr. AW high 51 - 2nd of 12 giving 6lb to Cameo (6 Mar Wolverhampton 5f Fibr RF 0409) - also 1st of 8 giving 1lb to Strat's Quest (10 Feb Wolverhampton RF 0264). Consistent. A modest performer overall, he does win from time to time on Fibresand.
**N P Littmoden [0-9] Supreme Racing Ltd (from K R Burke [4-25] Feb 1999).*

CHAMBOLLE MUSIGNY (USA) BHB 44f **RR 54df** 4438[7]
3 b f Majestic Light (USA) 9.5f **(78)** - Bridal Up (USA) (Sharpen Up) 8.3f **(67)**
Form - 0704577
Record 1999 - 1st:0 2nd:0 3rd:0 Ran:7
1999 Turf 0-7: (7f, 8f, 10f 3, 11f, 12f) (gd, g-f 2, frm 4)
Unfurnished, fair filly, effective 11f, acts on frm, has worn blinkers, likes tight tracks. Turf high 55. **P F I Cole [0-7] Christopher Wright.*

CHAMBRE SEPAREE (USA) BHB 80f **RR 81f** 4335[8]
3 ro f Cozzene (USA) 10.1f **(87)** - Ice House (Northfields (USA)) 9f **(72)**
Form - 853021078
Record 1999 - 1st:1 2nd:1 3rd:1 Ran:9
Pre1999 - 1st:0 2nd:0 3rd:0 Ran:2
Win Prizemoney £5,524 *Total Prizemoney* £7,672
Wins * **1999** Jly Ascot (FRM) 8f 81 <
1999 Turf 1-9: (7f 2, 8f 1-5, 9f, 10f) (hvy, sft, g-s, gd, g-f 1-2, frm 3)

Rangy, decent filly, effective 7 to 9f, best at 8f, acts on gd to frm. Turf high 81 - 1st of 6 from Pleasing Prospect (25 Jly Ascot RF 3120). **G Wragg [1-11] Miss K Rausing.*

CHAMELI BHB 44f55a RR 51df 55a 2005[10]

4 b f Nordico (USA) 8.2f **(59)** - Try Vickers (USA) (Fuzzbuster (USA)) 6.3f **(63)**

Form - 00

Record 1999 - 1st:0 2nd:0 3rd:0 Ran:1
Pre1999 - 1st:0 2nd:0 3rd:2 Ran:9

Win Prizemoney £0 *Total Prizemoney* £1,097

1999 Turf 0-1: (12f) (frm)

Lengthy, fair filly, effective 8f, - acts on Equi, has worn blinkers, likes left handed tracks. Becoming disappointing.

**C N Kellett [0-1] P Royle (from J L Eyre [0-3] Nov 1998).*

CHAMPAGNE RR 65f 4088[8]

3 b g Efisio 7.7f **(69)** - Success Story **(47f 55a)** (Sharrood (USA)) 10.5f **(72)**

Form - 8418

Record 1999 - 1st:1 2nd:0 3rd:0 Ran:4

Win Prizemoney £2,637 *Total Prizemoney* £2,924

Wins 1999 Aug Leices (GD) C 10f 65 <

1999 Turf 1-4: (7f, 10f 1-2, 12f) (gd 1-1, g-f, frm, hrd)

Workmanlike, average gelding. Turf high 65 - 1st of 15 giving 13lb to Jane Ann (18 Aug Leicester RF 3748).

**Andrew Reid [0-1] A S Reid (from R Charlton [1-3] Aug 1999).*

CHAMPAGNE LADY (IRE) BHB 69f RR 68f 4944[8]

2 b f Turtle Island (IRE) - Lucky Fountain (IRE) (Lafontaine (USA)) 8.7f **(49)**

Form - 604368

Record 1999 - 1st:0 2nd:0 3rd:1 Ran:6

Win Prizemoney £0 *Total Prizemoney* £896

1999 Turf 0-6: (5f 2, 7f 4) (gd 2, g-f 2, frm 2)

Average filly, effective 7f, acts on frm. Turf high 68.

**R Hannon [0-6] N A Woodcock.*

CHAMPAGNE N DREAMS BHB 56f50a RR 55f 50a 4689[9]

7 b m Rambo Dancer (CAN) 8.4f **(59)** -Pink Sensation(Sagaro) 9.7f **(55)**

Form - 3470410

Record 1999 - 1st:1 2nd:0 3rd:1 Ran:7
Pre1999 - 1st:2 2nd:2 3rd:5 Ran:33

Win Prizemoney £8,497 *Total Prizemoney* £13,837

Wins * 1999 Spt Catter (G-F) H 7f 51 55
1998 Aug Chepst (G-F) H 8.1f 48 54
1995 May Mussel (GD) H 8.1f 53 58 <

1999 Turf 1-7: (5f, 7f 1-2, 8f 2, 9f, 10f) (g-f 2, frm 1-5)

Fair mare, effective 7 to 10f, acts on g-f to frm, best on frm, has worn blinkers, prefers left handed tracks, prefers tight tracks, excels at Catterick. Turf high 55 - 1st of 14 getting 1lb from Young Rosein (18 Spt Catterick RF 4398). Consistent.

**W W Haigh [1-7] P D R Construction Ltd (from D Nicholls [2-36] Spt 1998).*

CHAMPAGNE RIDER BHB 88f RR 89f 4561[18]

3 b c Presidium 7.5f **(56)** - Petitesse (Petong) 6.6f **(58)**

Form - 04758330500100

Record 1999 - 1st:1 2nd:0 3rd:2 Ran:14
Pre1999 - 1st:2 2nd:0 3rd:1 Ran:7

Win Prizemoney £17,465 *Total Prizemoney* £29,437

Wins * 1999 Aug Leices (G-F) H 6f 86 89 <
* 1998 May Kempto (GD) 6f 83
* 1998 Apr Kempto (HVY) 5f 74

1999 Turf 1-14: (6f 1-10, 7f 3, 8f) (gd 4, g-f 7, frm 1-3)

Leggy, useful colt, effective 5 to 6f, best at 6f, acts on gd to frm, best on frm, excels at Kempton. Turf high 89 - 1st of 10 getting 11lb from Bon Ami (22 Aug Leicester RF 3839). Won two of his first three starts at two, but was then found out when taking on some decent company. He was busy last term, generally running well, and after some fair efforts in hot handicap company his forcing tactics came good at Leicester in August.

**K McAuliffe [3-21] Highgrove Developments Ltd.*

CHAMPFIS RR 63f 4721[3]

2 b c Efisio 7.7f **(69)** - Champ d'Avril (Northfields (USA)) 9f **(72)**

Form - 03

Record 1999 - 1st:0 2nd:0 3rd:1 Ran:2

Win Prizemoney £0 *Total Prizemoney* £502

1999 Turf 0-2: (5f, 6f) (gd 2)

Currently average colt. Turf high 63 (began Spt) - 3rd of 14 giving 5lb to Poppy's Song (5 Oct Catterick 5f gd RF 4721).

**M Johnston [0-2] Henderson (Co Durham).*

CHAPEL ROYALE (IRE) BHB 85f RR 69f 4640[1]

2 gr c College Chapel - Merci Royale (Fairy King (USA)) 7.7f **(59)**

Form - 701

Record 1999 - 1st:1 2nd:0 3rd:0 Ran:3

Win Prizemoney £1,819 *Total Prizemoney* £1,819

Wins * 1999 Spt Newcas (SFT) 7f 69+ <

1999 Turf 1-3: (6f 2, 7f 1-1) (g-s, gd 1-2)

Currently average colt. Turf high 69 (began Aug) - 1st of 11 giving 6lb to Infotec (29 Spt Newcastle RF 4640).

**Andrew Turnell [1-3] Prospect Estates Ltd.*

CHARALAMBOUS (USA) RR 46f 4339[4]

2 b c Hermitage (USA) 8.6f **(84)** - Hula Lei (USA) (State Dinner (USA)) 9.4f **(74)**

Form - 4

Record 1999 - 1st:0 2nd:0 3rd:0 Ran:1

Win Prizemoney £0 *Total Prizemoney* £242

1999 Turf 0-1: (7f) (g-s)

Currently moderate colt. **W J Haggas [0-1] A A Goodman.*

CHARGE BHB 69f RR 72f 4160[4]

3 gr c Petong 7.6f **(58)** - Madam Petoski (Petoski) 5.7f **(62)**

Form - 0434

Record 1999 - 1st:0 2nd:0 3rd:1 Ran:4
Pre1999 - 1st:0 2nd:0 3rd:2 Ran:3

Win Prizemoney £0 *Total Prizemoney* £2,120

1999 Turf 0-4: (5f, 6f 3) (sft, gd, g-f, frm)

Light-framed, above-average colt, effective 6f, acts on gd. Turf high 72. **B Smart [0-7] Lacey, Buckham.*

CHARISMATIC (USA) RR 119f 1899a[3]

3 ch c Summer Squall (USA) 7f **(80)** -Bali Babe(USA)(Drone) 10.3f **(74)**

Form - 113

1999 Turf 1-1: (10f 1-1) (frm 1-1) 1999 AW 1-2: (10f 1-1, 12f) (Dirt 1-2)

Currently very high-class colt. (1st run) - 1st of 19 from Menifee (1 May Churchill Downs RF 1070a). AW high 122 (1st run) - 1st of 13 from Menifee (15 May Pimlico RF 1351a). He was a surprise winner of the Kentucky Derby, but proved the performance was no fluke when following up in the Preakness. He looked on course to be the first American Triple Crown winner since Affirmed, and appeared to have every chance when faltering approaching the final furlong and pulling up very lame in third. It transpired that he had fractured his off fore and, although his career was finished, happily he was saved for stud duties. **D W Lukas in USA [2-3].*

CHARITY CRUSADER BHB 47f RR 39f 4089[12]

8 b g Rousillon (USA) 10.4f **(69)** - Height of Folly (Shirley Heights) 10.3f **(74)**

Form - 2672480

Record 1999 - 1st:0 2nd:2 3rd:0 Ran:7
Pre1999 - 1st:4 2nd:5 3rd:2 Ran:28

Win Prizemoney £16,535 *Total Prizemoney* £27,202

Wins * 1998 Aug Mussel (G-F) H 16f 48 51
* 1997 Aug Redcar (G-F) C 14.1f 41

1999 Turf 0-7: (12f 2, 14f 4, 16f) (gd, frm 6)

Very moderate gelding, effective 12 to 16f, acts on g-s to frm, best on frm, often wears blinkers (very effectively), likes left handed tracks, favours tight tracks, excels at Redcar. Turf high 55 - 2nd of 7 getting 12lb from Copernicus (3 Aug Catterick 12f frm RF 3317). Consistent.

**Mrs M Reveley [5-40] The Mary Reveley Racing Club (from P W Chapple-Hyam [2-10] Jun 1995).*

CHARLEIGH KEARY BHB 51f RR 56f 5064[9]

2 b f Sulaafah (USA) 8.6f **(44)** - Woolcana (Some Hand) 9f **(50)**

Form - 1470

Record 1999 - 1st:1 2nd:0 3rd:0 Ran:4

Win Prizemoney £2,143 *Total Prizemoney* £2,143

Wins * 1999 Apr Folkes (SFT) C 5f 60 <

1999 Turf 1-3: (5f 1-2, 6f) (sft 1-1, g-s, gd) 1999 AW 0-1: (6f) (Fibr)

Fair filly. Turf high 60 (1st run) - 1st of 7 getting 4lb from Flyover (20 Apr Folkestone RF 0761). **J S Moore [1-4] G A Bosley.*

CHARLEM RR 38f 5207[13]
2 br f Petardia 8.2f **(58)** - La Neva (FR) (Arctic Tern (USA)) 8.9f **(69)**
Form - 00
Record 1999 - 1st:0 2nd:0 3rd:0 Ran:2
1999 Turf 0-2: (7f 2) (g-s, gd)
Currently very moderate filly. Turf high 38 (began Oct). **D Shaw [0-2] R A B Saville.*

CHARLENE LACY (IRE) BHB 72f68a **RR 55f 68a** 3762[11]
3 ch f Pips Pride 6.7f **(70)** - Friendly Song (Song) 7.2f **(61)**
Form - 0000
Record 1999 - 1st:0 2nd:0 3rd:0 Ran:4
Pre1999 - 1st:1 2nd:0 3rd:0 Ran:4
Win Prizemoney £5,598 *Total Prizemoney* £5,819
Wins * 1998 Mar Doncas (GD) 5f 72 <
1999 Turf 0-3: (5f, 6f 2) (gd, g-f 2) 1999 AW 0-1: (6f) (Fibr)
Light-framed, fair filly, effective 5f, acts on gd to frm. Turf high 55. Consistent. **A P Jarvis [1-8] Mrs Ann Jarvis.*

CHARLIE CHANG (IRE) BHB 36f35a **RR 34f 35a** 4648[10]
6 b g Don't Forget Me 9.5f **(66)** - East River (FR) (Arctic Tern (USA)) 8.9f **(69)**
Form - 050
Record 1999 - 1st:0 2nd:0 3rd:0 Ran:3
Pre1999 - 1st:1 2nd:2 3rd:1 Ran:19
Win Prizemoney £3,095 *Total Prizemoney* £6,439
Wins 1995 *Nov Lingfi (STD) 8f 73* <
1999 Turf 0-2: (14f, 16f) (sft, g-s) 1999 AW 0-1: (9f) (Fibr)
Very moderate gelding, has worn blinkers. Turf high 34 (began Spt). Inconsistent.
**B J Llewellyn [2-19] Lodge Cross Partnership (from D W Barker [0-3] Spt 1997).*

CHARLIE GIRL BHB 69f **RR 64f** 2437[10]
3 b f Puissance 7.1f **(60)** - Charolles (Ajdal (USA)) 9.2f **(89)**
Form - 607080
Record 1999 - 1st:0 2nd:0 3rd:0 Ran:6
Pre1999 - 1st:1 2nd:2 3rd:4 Ran:9
Win Prizemoney £2,757 *Total Prizemoney* £7,146
Wins * 1998 May Mussel (G-F) 5f 69 <
1999 Turf 0-6: (5f 6) (gd 2, g-f, frm, hrd 2)
Light-framed, average filly, effective 5f, acts on gd to hrd, best on frm, excels at Musselburgh. Turf high 64 - 7th of 19 giving 5lb to Premium Princess (27 May Newcastle 5f hrd RF 1525).
**J Berry [1-15] T G & Mrs M E Holdcroft.*

CHARLIE K (IRE) RR 10f 1424[3]
2 ch c River Falls 8.2f **(56)** - So Ladylike (Malinowski (USA)) 10f **(56)**
Form - 3
Record 1999 - 1st:0 2nd:0 3rd:1 Ran:1
Win Prizemoney £0 *Total Prizemoney* £402
1999 Turf 0-1: (5f) (gd)
Currently poor colt. **J G Given [0-1] A Clarke.*

CHARLIES BRIDE (IRE) BHB 59f **RR 51f** 2585[8]
4 b br f Rich Charlie 5.9f **(50)** - Nordic Bride (IRE) (Nordico (USA)) 6.5f **(62)**
Form - 73088
Record 1999 - 1st:0 2nd:0 3rd:1 Ran:5
Pre1999 - 1st:2 2nd:1 3rd:0 Ran:10
Win Prizemoney £5,158 *Total Prizemoney* £6,462
Wins * 1998 Aug Carlis (G-S) 6.9f 73 <
* 1998 Apr Pontef (G-S) S 6f 52
1999 Turf 0-5: (7f 2, 8f 3) (gd 3, g-f, frm)
Fair filly, effective 7f, acts on gd, often wears blinkers, likes tight tracks. Turf high 58. Consistent.
**J J O'Neill [2-15] Pointerfarm Racing Partnership.*

CHARLIE'S DESTINY (HUN) RR 45f 1734[8]
3 ch c Try Star - Masolat (HUN) (Andor (HUN))
Form - 08
Record 1999 - 1st:0 2nd:0 3rd:0 Ran:2
1999 Turf 0-2: (10f, 12f) (gd 2)
Leggy, currently moderate colt. Turf high 45. **G P Enright [0-2] E McMullen.*

CHARLIE'S GOLD BHB 40f47a **RR 36f 47a** 5190[5]
4 b g Shalford (IRE) 7.8f **(63)** - Ballet (Sharrood (USA)) 10.5f **(72)**
Form - 003225005
Record 1999 - 1st:0 2nd:2 3rd:1 Ran:9
Pre1999 - 1st:1 2nd:0 3rd:0 Ran:7
Win Prizemoney £1,966 *Total Prizemoney* £3,808
Wins 1998 *Aug Wolver (STD) H 14.8f 46 51* <
1999 Turf 0-8: (12f 4, 14f 3, 16f) (gd 2, g-f 3, frm 3) 1999 AW 0-1: (16f) (Equi)
Light-framed, very moderate gelding, effective 15f, - acts on Fibr, often wears blinkers, likes left handed tracks. Turf high 41.
**A Bailey [2-17] Classic Gold (from A Kelleway [2-7] Aug 1998).*

CHARLIE SILLETT BHB 65f70a **RR 34f 70a** 3821[21]
7 ch g Handsome Sailor 6.6f **(53)** -Bystrouska (Gorytus (USA)) 7.8f **(60)**
Form - 8000
Record 1999 - 1st:0 2nd:0 3rd:0 Ran:4
Pre1999 - 1st:5 2nd:0 3rd:1 Ran:25
Win Prizemoney £28,436 *Total Prizemoney* £29,095
Wins * 1997 Jun Cheste (SFT) H 6.1f 80 88 <
* 1996 Oct Chepst (SFT) H 6.1f 80 82
* 1995 Nov Doncas (G-F) H 7f 76 84
* 1995 Oct Haydoc (SFT) H 6f 68 74
1999 Turf 0-4: (6f 4) (sft, g-f 2, hrd)
Moderate gelding. Turf high 72. Becoming disappointing. **B W Hills [5-29] John Sillett.*

CHARLIE'S QUEST BHB 51f **RR 56f** 5046[6]
3 b g Kylian (USA) 8.1f **(66)** - Pleasure Quest (Efisio)
Form - 806
Record 1999 - 1st:0 2nd:0 3rd:0 Ran:3
1999 Turf 0-3: (8f 2, 10f) (hvy, g-f, frm)
Leggy, currently fair gelding. Turf high 56 (began Aug). **D W P Arbuthnot [0-3] Miss P E Decker.*

CHARLOTTE RUSSE RR 36f 4812[19]
2 b f Rudimentary (USA) 8.2f **(66)** - Do Run Run (Commanche Run) 8.5f **(58)**
Form - 00
Record 1999 - 1st:0 2nd:0 3rd:0 Ran:2
1999 Turf 0-2: (6f, 7f) (gd, frm)
Currently very moderate filly. Turf high 36 (began Spt). **Mrs N Macauley [0-2] Appleby Racing.*

CHARLOTTE'S CHOICE RR 856[5]
2 b f Noble Patriarch 12.2f **(43)** - Covent Garden Girl **(38f 55a)** (Sizzling Melody)
Form - 075
Record 1999 - 1st:0 2nd:0 3rd:0 Ran:3
1999 Turf 0-2: (5f 2) (gd, g-f) 1999 AW 0-1: (5f) (Fibr)
Currently very poor filly. Turf high 37. **M W Easterby [0-3] M W Easterby.*

CHARLOTTEVALENTINA (IRE) BHB 83f **RR 77f** 3787[6]
2 ch f Perugino (USA) - The Top Diesis (USA) (Diesis) 9.3f **(69)**
Form - 460106
Record 1999 - 1st:1 2nd:0 3rd:0 Ran:6
Win Prizemoney £2,770 *Total Prizemoney* £3,312
Wins * 1999 Jun Catter (G-F) 6f 77 <
1999 Turf 1-6: (5f 3, 6f 1-3) (gd 3, frm 1-3)
Above-average filly, effective 6f, acts on frm, has worn blinkers. Turf high 77 - also 1st of 6 from Zagaleta (30 Jun Catterick RF 2438). **P D Evans [1-6] Ron Monte-Colombo.*

CHARMANOVA BHB 50f **RR 55f** 3360[6]
3 ch f Theatrical Charmer 10.9f **(63)** - Mazurkanova (Song) 7.2f **(61)**
Form - 80606
Record 1999 - 1st:0 2nd:0 3rd:0 Ran:5
1999 Turf 0-5: (7f, 8f 3, 10f) (gd 2, g-f, frm 2)
Light-framed, fair filly. Turf high 55. **B R Millman [0-5] J W P Clark.*

CHARMING ADMIRAL (IRE) BHB 48f46a **RR 50f 46a** 1986[5]
6 b g Shareef Dancer (USA) 10.1f **(67)** -Lilac Charm (Bustino)10.4f **(64)**
Form - 00423345

Record 1999 - 1st:0 2nd:1 3rd:2 Ran:6
Pre1999 - 1st:0 2nd:3 3rd:2 Ran:14
Win Prizemoney £0 *Total Prizemoney* £6,915
1999 Turf 0-5: (13f, 16f, 18f 2, 22f) (g-s 2, gd 2, g-f) 1999 AW 0-1: (16f) (Fibr)
Fair gelding, effective 14 to 18f, acts on gd - acts on Fibr, has worn blinkers, likes left handed tracks. Turf high 50 - 3rd of 8 to Jamaican Flight (18 May Pontefract 18f gd RF 1300).
**Mrs A Swinbank [3-24] The Old Spice Girls (from C F Wall [0-9] Jly 1997).*

CHARMING LOTTE BHB 76f RR 76f 5045[5]
2 b f Nicolotte - Courtisane (Persepolis (FR)) 6.4f **(67)**
Form - 32807315
Record 1999 - 1st:1 2nd:1 3rd:2 Ran:8
Win Prizemoney £3,730 *Total Prizemoney* £5,641
Wins * 1999 Oct Ayr (SFT) H 6f 66 76 <
1999 Turf 1-8: (5f 3, 6f 1-3, 7f 2) (sft 1-2, g-s 2, gd 2, g-f, frm)
Above-average filly, effective 5 to 6f, acts on sft to gd, has worn blinkers. Turf high 76 - 1st of 15 getting 2lb from Slick Willie (11 Oct Ayr RF 4809). **P Shakespeare [1-8] Midas Touch.*

C-HARRY (IRE) BHB 59f62a RR 57f 62a 5146[5]
5 ch h Imperial Frontier (USA) 7f **(65)** - Desert Gale (Taufan (USA)) 7f **(57)**
Form - 111215423081124021675
Record 1999 - 1st:5 2nd:4 3rd:1 Ran:19
Pre1999 - 1st:7 2nd:8 3rd:9 Ran:49
Win Prizemoney £28,247 *Total Prizemoney* £43,784
Wins * **1999** *Spt Wolver (STD) C 7f 71* <
* **1999** *Jun Wolver (STD) H 6f 58 64*
* **1999** May Leices (G-F) SH 6f 52 56
* **1999** *Jan Wolver (STD) C 7f 67*
* **1999** *Jan Southw (STD) C 7f 62*
* 1998 *Dec Wolver (SLW) H 7f 56 59*
* 1998 *Nov Wolver (STD) S 7f 57*
* 1997 Jly Ayr (G-F) H 7f 60 64
* 1997 *Mar Wolver (STD) H 6f 68 67*
* 1997 *Feb Wolver (STD) H 7f 64 64*
* 1996 May Haydoc (G-S) S 5f 51
* 1996 *May Wolver (STD) S 6f 51*
1999 Turf 1-4: (6f 1-2, 7f 2) (gd, g-f, frm 1-2) 1999 AW 4-15: (6f 1-1, 7f 3-13, 8f) (Fibr 4-15)
Fair colt, effective 6 to 7f, best at 7f, - acts on Fibr, has worn blinkers, and does well at Southwell. Turf high 57. AW high 71 - 1st of 12 from Circuiteer (4 Spt Wolverhampton RF 4150) - also 1st of 12 giving 10lb to Faym (27 Jan Wolverhampton RF 0173). A useful performer over seven furlongs on the Wolverhampton Fibresand, he also has the speed to win over six on both the All-Weather and on turf. A winner at Leicester in May over six, he bettered that effort when second of 22 in a competitive York handicap in September. He needs a decent surface on turf.
**R Hollinshead [12-68] D Coppenhall.*

CHARTER FLIGHT BHB 61a RR 44f 4149[1]
3 b g Cosmonaut - Irene's Charter (Persian Bold) 9.3f **(66)**
Form - 2301
Record 1999 - 1st:1 2nd:0 3rd:1 Ran:3
Pre1999 - 1st:0 2nd:1 3rd:0 Ran:2
Win Prizemoney £2,409 *Total Prizemoney* £3,381
Wins * 1999 *Spt Wolver (STD) H 8.5f 61 63* <
1999 Turf 0-1: (8f) (frm) 1999 AW 1-2: (8f 1-2) (Fibr 1-2)
Average gelding. AW high 63 - 1st of 13 giving 2lb to Smoke Signal (4 Spt Wolverhampton RF 4149). He had shown some ability on Fibresand before getting off the mark in a maiden handicap at Wolverhampton in September. **A G Newcombe [1-5] D Bass.*

CHASE THE PENNANT (USA) RR 72f 1767[2]
2 ch c Miswaki (USA) 8.1f **(81)** - Ruth Pitcher (USA) (Ack Ack (USA)) 12.7f **(82)**
Form - 652
Record 1999 - 1st:0 2nd:1 3rd:0 Ran:3
Win Prizemoney £0 *Total Prizemoney* £995
1999 Turf 0-3: (5f 3) (gd 2, frm)
Currently above-average colt. Turf high 72. (DEAD)
**B W Hills [0-3] Maktoum Al Maktoum.*

CHASETOWN CAILIN BHB 36f RR 34f 5073[9]
4 b f Suave Dancer (USA) 10.7f **(68)** - Kilvarnet (Furry Glen) 8.9f **(63)**
Form - 0074872500030
Record 1999 - 1st:0 2nd:1 3rd:1 Ran:13
Pre1999 - 1st:0 2nd:0 3rd:0 Ran:6
Win Prizemoney £0 *Total Prizemoney* £1,497
1999 Turf 0-12: (6f, 8f 7, 9f, 10f 3) (gd 4, g-f 2, frm 5, hrd) 1999 AW 0-1: (8f) (Fibr)
Light-framed, very moderate filly. Turf high 42. Consistent.
**Don Enrico Incisa [0-13] Don Enrico Incisa (from R Hollinshead [0-6] Aug 1998).*

CHASKA BHB 38f40a RR 40f 40a 5188[11]
4 b f Reprimand 8.2f **(63)** - Royal Passion (Ahonoora) 8.1f **(73)**
Form - 0050530
Record 1999 - 1st:0 2nd:0 3rd:1 Ran:7
Pre1999 - 1st:1 2nd:0 3rd:0 Ran:9
Win Prizemoney £2,598 *Total Prizemoney* £3,116
Wins 1997 Aug Hamilt (G-F) C 6f 68 <
1999 Turf 0-5: (7f, 8f, 9f, 11f, 16f) (sft, gd 2, g-f 2) 1999 AW 0-2: (6f, 8f) (Fibr 2)
Lengthy, moderate filly, effective 7 to 11f, acts on gd to g-f, has worn blinkers, prefers left handed tracks. Turf high 42 (1st run) (began Jly) - 5th of 17 giving 10lb to Zibak (17 Jly Ayr 7f gd RF 2894). AW high 30. Inconsistent.
**A Bailey [0-12] J B Wilcox (from M Johnston [1-4] Aug 1997).*

CHATER FLAIR RR 55f 3011[12]
2 b c Efisio 7.7f **(69)** - Native Flair (Be My Native (USA)) 10.2f **(71)**
Form - 70
Record 1999 - 1st:0 2nd:0 3rd:0 Ran:2
1999 Turf 0-2: (7f 2) (frm 2)
Currently fair colt. Turf high 55 (began Jly).
**A P Jarvis [0-2] Hong Kong Cricket Club.*

CHATER JADE (USA) BHB 85f RR 79f 2542[2]
2 ch c Miswaki (USA) 8.1f **(81)** - Hispanolia (FR) (Kris) 9.5f **(73)**
Form - 7632
Record 1999 - 1st:0 2nd:1 3rd:1 Ran:4
Win Prizemoney £0 *Total Prizemoney* £1,890
1999 Turf 0-4: (6f 2, 7f 2) (gd, g-f, frm 2)
Above-average colt. Turf high 79 - 2nd of 8 to Dare Hunter (3 Jly Sandown 7f frm RF 2542). **A P Jarvis [0-4] Hong Kong Cricket Club.*

CHATTING (USA) BHB 100f RR 98?f 4254[5]
3 b c Exbourne (USA) - Non Stop Talker (USA) (Arctic Tern (USA)) 8.9f **(69)**
Form - 35
Record 1999 - 1st:0 2nd:0 3rd:1 Ran:2
Pre1999 - 1st:2 2nd:0 3rd:0 Ran:3
Win Prizemoney £7,741 *Total Prizemoney* £8,923
Wins * 1998 Oct Haydoc (SFT) 8.1f 92+ <
* 1998 Spt Chepst (G-S) 7.1f 81
1999 Turf 0-2: (8f, 10f) (gd, g-f)
Well made, very useful colt. Turf high 98. He ran poorly on both his starts and may not be entirely genuine.
**Sir Michael Stoute [2-5] The Thoroughbred Corporation.*

CHAYANEE'S ARENA (IRE) BHB 28f RR 10f 4647[15]
4 b f High Estate 10.5f **(66)** - Arena (Sallust) 8.4f **(63)**
Form - 00
Record 1999 - 1st:0 2nd:0 3rd:0 Ran:2
Pre1999 - 1st:0 2nd:0 3rd:0 Ran:6
1999 Turf 0-2: (10f 2) (g-s, frm)
Light-framed, poor filly. Turf high 10 (began Aug). Becoming disappointing. **A G Newcombe [0-8] A G Newcombe.*

CHECKERS SPEECH (USA) RR 90f 4767a[4]
2 c Arazi (USA) 9.2f **(74)** - Cascassi (USA) (Nijinsky (CAN)) 10.3f **(77)**
Form - 24
1999 Turf 0-2: (8f, 9f) (hvy, sft)
Currently useful colt. Turf high 90 (began Aug). **A Fabre in FR [0-2].*

CHEEK TO CHEEK BHB 65f48a RR 64f 48a 3793[5]
5 b m Shavian 7.7f **(67)** - Intoxication (Great Nephew) 9.9f **(64)**
Form - 54662325
Record 1999 - 1st:0 2nd:2 3rd:1 Ran:8

Pre1999 - 1st:3 2nd:2 3rd:1 Ran:15
Win Prizemoney £14,150 *Total Prizemoney* £18,948
Wins * 1998 Jly Yarmou (GD) H 14.1f 60 63 <
* 1998 May Bath (FRM) H 13.1f 59 63 <
* 1998 *Apr Wolver (STD)* *12f* *63* <
1999 Turf 0-5: (12f, 13f, 14f, 15f, 16f) (gd 2, g-f, frm 2) 1999 AW 0-3: (12f, 15f, 16f) (Equi, Fibr 2)
Average filly, effective 12 to 16f, acts on gd to frm - acts on Fibr, best on frm, likes left handed tracks, excels at Yarmouth. Turf high 64 - 2nd of 9 giving 26lb to Alhesn (26 Jly Yarmouth 16f frm RF 3152). AW high 52. **C A Cyzer [3-23] R M Cyzer.*

CHEEKY MONKEY (USA) BHB 57a RR 56f 4666[11]

3 ch f Beau Genius (CAN) - Crystal Lake (IRE) **(88+f)** (Shirley Heights) 10.3f **(74)**
Form - 002120
Record 1999 - 1st:1 2nd:2 3rd:0 Ran:6
Pre1999 - 1st:0 2nd:0 3rd:0 Ran:4
Win Prizemoney £2,040 *Total Prizemoney* £3,295
Wins * 1999 Jun Warwic (G-F) S 10.5f 39 <
1999 Turf 1-5: (10f 2, 11f 1-1, 12f 2) (g-f 1-4, frm) 1999 AW 0-1: (12f) (Equi)
Leggy, fair filly, effective 10 to 12f, acts on g-f to frm, prefers tight tracks. Turf high 56 - 2nd of 17 giving 12lb to Purple Dawn (16 Jun Nottingham 10f g-f RF 2054). Inconsistent.
**R T Phillips [1-6] North and South (from J Noseda [0-4] Oct 1998).*

CHEERFUL GROOM (IRE) BHB 33f33a RR 35f 33a 4174[17]

8 ch g Shy Groom (USA) 8.2f **(59)** - Carange (Known Fact (USA)) 7.4f **(67)**
Form - 0000075066700
Record 1999 - 1st:0 2nd:0 3rd:0 Ran:13
Pre1999 - 1st:5 2nd:7 3rd:10 Ran:74
Win Prizemoney £14,961 *Total Prizemoney* £23,787
Wins * 1998 *Jly Wolver (STD) H* *8.5f* *56* *59* <
* 1998 *Jun Wolver (STD) H* *8.5f* *51* *52*
* 1998 *May Wolver (STD) H* *8.5f* *41* *50*
1996 May Doncas (G-F) H 7f 36 42
1999 Turf 0-4: (7f 3, 10f) (gd, g-f 3) 1999 AW 0-9: (7f, 8f 7, 9f) (Equi, Fibr 8)
Moderate gelding, effective 8f, - acts on Fibr, has worn blinkers, likes left handed tracks, likes tight tracks. Turf high 35. AW high 40. He has enjoyed a fair amount of success at around a mile on Fibresand, especially over Wolverhampton's extended mile, but the signs are that time is catching up with him.
**D Shaw [3-43] Bill Cahill (from S R Bowring [1-9] Jly 1996).*

CHELONIA (IRE) RR 64f 2885[3]

2 gr f Turtle Island (IRE) - Whirl (Bellypha) 9.8f **(73)**
Form - 3
Record 1999 - 1st:0 2nd:0 3rd:1 Ran:1
Win Prizemoney £0 *Total Prizemoney* £618
1999 Turf 0-1: (7f) (frm)
Currently average filly. (1st run) - 3rd of 8 to Solaia (16 Jly Newmarket 7f frm RF 2885). **B W Hills [0-1] A N Foster.*

CHELSEA BARRACKS BHB 88f RR 89f 4876[D]

3 b g Deploy 11.4f **(67)** - Hymne D'Amour (USA) (Dixieland Band (USA)) 7f **(74)**
Form - 68210D
Record 1999 - 1st:1 2nd:1 3rd:0 Ran:6
Pre1999 - 1st:1 2nd:1 3rd:0 Ran:3
Win Prizemoney £10,657 *Total Prizemoney* £15,637
Wins * 1999 Aug Ripon (GD) H 12.3f 86 89 <
* 1998 Nov Doncas (SFT) 8f 77
1999 Turf 1-6: (8f, 10f 2, 12f 1-3) (sft, gd 1-4, frm)
Scopey, useful gelding, effective 8 to 12f, acts on gd to frm, best on gd. Turf high 89 - 1st of 10 giving 20lb to Flossy (14 Aug Ripon RF 3666). He built on the promise of his juvenile season when defeated a neck by the smart Fiori over ten furlongs at York, and went on to dead-heat with the in-form Flossy over two furlongs further at Ripon, though he eventually got the race outright in the Stewards' Room. Sold for 45,000 gns in October.
**J L Dunlop [2-9] The Earl Cadogan.*

CHELSEA MANOR RR 111f 4659a[1]

3 b c Grand Lodge (USA) - Docklands (Theatrical)
Form - 1
1999 Turf 1-1: (10f 1-1) (g-s 1-1)
Currently Group-class colt. (1st run) - 1st of 8 from Agol Lack (22 Spt Maisons-Laffitte RF 4659a). Relatively lightly raced, he found conditions ideal when quickening smartly on rain-softened ground to win La Coupe de Maisons-Laffitte in September. Connections are keen to keep him in training and further success should follow. **P Bary in FR [1-1] K Abdulla.*

CHEMCAST BHB 42f45a RR 37f 45a 4087[10]

6 ch g Chilibang 7f **(55)** - Golden October (Young Generation) 7.7f **(63)**
Form - 705800720
Record 1999 - 1st:0 2nd:1 3rd:0 Ran:7
Pre1999 - 1st:7 2nd:4 3rd:6 Ran:59
Win Prizemoney £22,129 *Total Prizemoney* £30,292
Wins * 1997 Mar Mussel (SFT) H 5f 68 68? <
* 1996 *Nov Lingfi (STD) H* *5f* *63* *64*
1996 Jun Mussel (FRM) H 5f 65 66
1996 *Jan Lingfi (STD) C* *5f* *65*
1996 *Jan Lingfi (STD) H* *5f* *55* *62*
1995 Spt Folkes (G-F) H 5f 66 68
1995 Aug Goodwo (G-F) CH 5f 63 61
1999 Turf 0-7: (5f 7) (gd, g-f 2, frm 4)
Fair gelding, often wears blinkers. Turf high 39.
**J L Eyre [2-41] Neil Midgley (from D Nicholls [3-14] Aug 1996).*

CHEMIN-DE-FER RR 3641[11]

7 b g Darshaan 11.9f **(81)** - Whitehaven (Top Ville) 11.7f **(68)**
Form - 0
Record 1999 - 1st:0 2nd:0 3rd:0 Ran:1
1999 Turf 0-1: (14f) (g-f)
Formerly very poor gelding. **B A Pearce [0-2] Richard Gray.*

CHEM'S TRUCE (IRE) BHB 90f RR 82+f 5163[1]

2 b c Brief Truce (USA) 9.1f **(73)** - In the Rigging (USA) (Topsider (USA)) 8.3f **(71)**
Form - 521
Record 1999 - 1st:1 2nd:1 3rd:0 Ran:3
Win Prizemoney £2,882 *Total Prizemoney* £4,380
Wins * 1999 Nov Catter (SFT) 7f 82+ <
1999 Turf 1-3: (5f, 6f, 7f 1-1) (g-s 1-1, g-f 2)
Currently decent colt. Turf high 82 - 1st of 14 from Sea Squirt (2 Nov Catterick RF 5163). He had no problem with the soft ground when overcoming a five-month break to win at Catterick. Should make his mark at three. **W R Muir [1-3] The Parkside Partnership.*

CHENNELL'S HILL BHB 35f RR 16f 4105[19]

4 ch f Hubbly Bubbly (USA) 9.5f **(43)** - Oakhurst (Mandrake Major) 7.6f **(53)**
Form - 00
Record 1999 - 1st:0 2nd:0 3rd:0 Ran:2
Pre1999 - 1st:0 2nd:0 3rd:0 Ran:2
Win Prizemoney £0 *Total Prizemoney* £241
1999 Turf 0-2: (10f, 12f) (frm, hrd)
Workmanlike, poor filly. Turf high 16.
**J Norton [0-1] Chennell's Syndicate (from A Bailey [0-3] Jun 1999).*

CHERISH ME BHB 70f RR 66f 5103[8]

3 b f Polar Falcon (USA) 9f **(74)** - Princess Zepoli (Persepolis (FR)) 6.4f **(67)**
Form - 5238
Record 1999 - 1st:0 2nd:1 3rd:1 Ran:4
Win Prizemoney £0 *Total Prizemoney* £1,824
1999 Turf 0-4: (6f 2, 7f 2) (gd 2, frm 2)
Scopey, average filly. Turf high 66 (began Spt).
**J G Given [0-4] J R Good.*

CHEROKEE CHARLIE BHB 22f42a RR 30f 42a 4448[17]

4 ch g Interrex (CAN) 7.7f **(51)** - Valentine Song (Pas de Seul) 9.1f **(67)**
Form - 00
Record 1999 - 1st:0 2nd:0 3rd:0 Ran:2
Pre1999 - 1st:0 2nd:0 3rd:0 Ran:7
1999 Turf 0-2: (10f, 16f) (g-s, frm)
Very moderate gelding. Turf high 12 (began Spt).
**R Craggs [0-9] Ray Craggs.*

CHEROKEE FLIGHT BHB 54f50a RR 54f 50a 4415[7]

5 b g Green Desert (USA) 7.8f **(78)** - Totham (Shernazar) 10.2f **(73)**

Form - 07040737

Record	**1999** -	1st:0	2nd:0	3rd:1	Ran:8
	Pre1999 -	1st:4	2nd:2	3rd:2	Ran:27

Win Prizemoney £12,703 *Total Prizemoney* £17,298

Wins								
* 1998	Aug	Chepst	(G-F)	H	10.2f	59	63	
* 1997	*Aug*	*Wolver*	*(STD)*	*H*	*9.4f*	*61*	*64*	<
* 1997	*Jly*	*Wolver*	*(STD)*	*H*	*9.4f*	*55*	*60*	
1996	Jly	Nottin	(G-F)		5.1f		63	

1999 Turf 0-7: (10f 7) (gd, g-f 3, frm 3) 1999 AW 0-1: (12f) (Fibr)

Fair gelding, effective 10f, acts on gd to frm, best on frm, has worn blinkers, prefers tight tracks. Turf high 55. Inconsistent.

**S Mellor [3-31] Silver Knight Exhibitions Ltd (from Mrs J R Ramsden [1-6] Spt 1996).*

CHERRY PICKINGS (USA) BHB 61f **RR 65f** 4575[10]

2 b c Miner's Mark (USA) - Cherry D'Or (USA) (Cassaleria (USA))

Form - 607430

Record	**1999** -	1st:0	2nd:0	3rd:1	Ran:6

Win Prizemoney £0 *Total Prizemoney* £1,359

1999 Turf 0-6: (6f 4, 8f 2) (gd 3, frm 3)

Average colt, effective 8f, acts on frm, has worn blinkers. Turf high 65. **J H M Gosden [0-6] Sheikh Mohammed.*

CHESHIRE CAT (IRE) BHB 74f **RR 66f** 2939[1]

3 b f Ezzoud (IRE) - Riyda (Be My Guest (USA)) 9.3f **(67)**

Form - 0621

Record	**1999** -	1st:1	2nd:1	3rd:0	Ran:4
	Pre1999 -	1st:0	2nd:1	3rd:1	Ran:3

Win Prizemoney £3,532 *Total Prizemoney* £6,506

Wins							
*** 1999**	Jly	Ayr	(SFT)	10f		66	<

1999 Turf 1-4: (10f 1-4) (g-s 1-1, gd, frm, hrd)

Lengthy, average filly, effective 7f, acts on gd, has worn blinkers. Turf high 66. **B W Hills [1-7] C Wright & The Hon Mrs J M Corbett.*

Chester House may find richer pickings in America in 2000

CHESTER HOUSE (USA) BHB 119f **RR 118f** 5231a[4]

4 b c Mr Prospector (USA) 8.6f **(88)** - Toussaud (USA) (El Gran Senor (USA)) 9.6f **(76)**

Form - 114434

1999 Turf 2-5: (10f 2-5) (g-f 1-3, frm 1-2) 1999 AW 0-1: (10f) (Dirt)

Scopey, very high-class colt, effective 10f, acts on gd to frm - acts on Dirt, likes left handed tracks, does well at Sandown and Ascot. Turf high 118 - 4th of 8 giving 11lb to Compton Admiral (3 Jly Sandown 10f frm RF 2545) - also 1st of 6 getting 3lb from Generous Rosi (1 Jun Sandown RF 1658). (1st run) - 4th of 14 giving 4lb to Cat Thief (6 Nov Gulfstream Park 10f Dirt RF 5231a). He seemed to be the type of horse that promise more than they deliver, but the 1999 season started off well as he recorded victories in a Chester Listed event and in the Group Three Brigadier Gerard Stakes. However, it then became the familiar story of 'nearly but not quite', and he was subsequently carted off to be trained in the US after finishing third to Royal Anthem in the Juddmonte International. He made his Stateside debut in the Breeders' Cup Classic and ran an astonishing race. Down on his nose at the start and virtually tailed off after two furlongs, he made up an enormous amount of ground to finish fourth. Perhaps he will finally start to make up for lost time on the American dirt tracks.

**R Frankel in USA [0-1] (from H R A Cecil [5-14] Aug 1999).*

CHEWIT BHB 85f100a **RR 79f 100a** 5141[13]

7 gr g Beveled (USA) 6.9f **(64)** - Sylvan Song (Song) 7.2f **(61)**

Form - 70

Record	**1999** -	1st:0	2nd:0	3rd:0	Ran:2
	Pre1999 -	1st:9	2nd:8	3rd:4	Ran:46

Win Prizemoney £48,433 *Total Prizemoney* £70,761

Wins								
* 1998	May	Goodwo	(G-F)	H	7f	84	90	
* 1998	*Mar*	*Wolver*	*(STD)*		*7f*		*89*	
* 1997	*Dec*	*Wolver*	*(STD)*	*H*	*7f*	*99*	*102*	<
* 1997	Aug	Ascot	(GD)	H	7f	82	83	
1996	Spt	Lingfi	(FRM)		7.6f		79+	
1996	Spt	Lingfi	(G-F)	H	7f	77	75	
1996	*Feb*	*Lingfi*	*(STD)*	*H*	*6f*	*90*	*88*	
1996	*Jan*	*Lingfi*	*(STD)*	*H*	*6f*	*80*	*88+*	
1995	*Mar*	*Lingfi*	*(STD)*	*H*	*6f*	*73*	*74*	

1999 Turf 0-2: (8f 2) (gd 2)

Very useful gelding, effective 6 to 7f, best at 7f, acts on gd to frm - acts on Fibr, has worn blinkers, excels at Ascot. Turf high 79. Not the force he was a few years ago, he ran disappointingly on his return and bolted to the stalls on his next intended start in April. Not seen until the autumn, connections may be preparing for an All-Weather campaign as he did well on that surface a few years ago.

**G L Moore [4-24] Ballard (1834) Ltd (from A Moore [5-24] Dec 1996).*

CHEZ CHERIE **RR 97f** 4776a[5]

2 ch f Wolfhound (USA) 7.3f **(71)** - Gerante (USA) (Private Account (USA)) 8.5f **(74)**

Form - 145

Record	**1999** -	1st:1	2nd:0	3rd:0	Ran:3

Win Prizemoney £10,650 *Total Prizemoney* £12,462

Wins						
*** 1999**	Jly	Goodwo	(G-F)	7f	95+	<

1999 Turf 1-3: (7f 1-2, 8f) (sft, g-f, frm 1-1)

Currently very useful filly. Turf high 97 (began Jly) - also 1st of 11 from Abscond (29 Jly Goodwood RF 3224). She sprang a surprise on her debut and went on to run a couple of sound races in Group company. She should stay at least a mile and a quarter next term, but lacks the basic speed to beat top-notchers.

**P W Chapple-Hyam [1-3] Ivan Allan.*

CHICADEE (FR) BHB 67f **RR 65f** 4651[14]

2 ch f In A Tiff (IRE) - Cos I Do (IRE) (Double Schwartz) 7.9f **(55)**

Form - 6060

Record	**1999** -	1st:0	2nd:0	3rd:0	Ran:4

1999 Turf 0-4: (5f 2, 6f 2) (gd, g-f 3)

Average filly. Turf high 65 (began Aug).

**D Sasse [0-4] Christopher Ranson.*

CHICAGO BEAR (IRE) BHB 54f **RR 30f** 4733[16]

3 ch g Night Shift (USA) 8.1f **(73)** - Last Drama (IRE) (Last Tycoon) 8.5f **(62)**

Form - 81000

Record	**1999** -	1st:1	2nd:0	3rd:0	Ran:5
	Pre1999 -	1st:0	2nd:0	3rd:0	Ran:3

Win Prizemoney £2,788 *Total Prizemoney* £2,788
Wins 1999 Jun Sandow (GD) C 10f 63 <
1999 Turf 1-5: (10f 1-3, 11f, 12f) (g-s, g-f 1-2, frm 2)
Scopey, very moderate gelding, effective 10f, acts on g-f, often wears blinkers (very effectively). Turf high 63 - 1st of 8 giving 4lb to Jade Tiger (12 Jun Sandown RF 1958). Becoming disappointing. Much improved performance at Sandown in June, benefiting fully from his first time blinkers, dictating from the front, but showed little else.
**J Mackie [0-2] The Festival Dream Partnership (from P F I Cole [1-6] Jun 1999).*

CHICAGO BLUES (IRE) BHB 50f46a **RR 50f 46a** 5148[4]

2 b f Blues Traveller (IRE) - Flight of Pleasure (USA) (Roberto (USA)) 10f **(76)**
Form - 070075064
Record 1999 - 1st:0 2nd:0 3rd:0 Ran:9
1999 Turf 0-8: (5f 2, 6f 3, 7f 2, 8f) (g-s, gd 3, g-f 2, frm 2) 1999 AW 0-1: (8f) (Fibr)
Fair filly. Turf high 52. **A G Newcombe [0-9] Chris Bradbury.*

CHICODOVE BHB 82f **RR 81+f** 4893[14]

3 b f In The Wings 11.2f **(77)** - Chicobin (USA) (J O Tobin (USA)) 9.4f **(67)**
Form - 212352110
Record 1999 - 1st:3 2nd:3 3rd:1 Ran:9
Pre1999 - 1st:0 2nd:0 3rd:1 Ran:3
Win Prizemoney £13,096 *Total Prizemoney* £17,491
Wins * 1999 Spt Catter (G-F) H 12f 80 81 <
*** 1999** Spt Goodwo (G-F) H 12f 76 78
*** 1999** May Redcar (FRM) H 11f 73 71
1999 Turf 3-9:(9f, 11f 1-1, 12f 2-3, 14f 2, 15f, 16f)(gd 3, g-f 1-3, frm 2-3)
Scopey, decent filly, effective 11 to 14f, best at 12f, acts on g-f to frm, best on g-f, prefers tight tracks. Turf high 81 - 1st of 5 giving 20lb to Sing And Dance (18 Spt Catterick RF 4397) - also 1st of 7 giving 28lb to Famous (10 Spt Goodwood RF 4262). Very consistent, she won three times last season and looked a real trier. Suited by 12 furlongs and fast ground.
**Sir Mark Prescott [3-12] Hesmonds Stud.*

CHIEF ABBA BHB 45f **RR 45f** 2504[17]

3 ch c Be My Chief (USA) 10.2f **(62)** - Themeda (Sure Blade (USA)) 11.3f **(67)**
Form - 640
Record 1999 - 1st:0 2nd:0 3rd:0 Ran:3
Pre1999 - 1st:0 2nd:0 3rd:0 Ran:4
1999 Turf 0-3: (10f 2, 11f) (g-f 2, hrd)
Workmanlike, moderate colt. Turf high 45. (DEAD)
**G Woodward [0-1] Mrs Jo Hardy (from R Hannon [0-6] May 1999).*

CHIEF CASHIER BHB 81f **RR 83f** 1757[8]

4 b g Persian Bold 10f **(69)** - Kentfield (Busted) 10.2f **(61)**
Form - 2148
Record 1999 - 1st:1 2nd:1 3rd:0 Ran:4
Pre1999 - 1st:2 2nd:1 3rd:1 Ran:13
Win Prizemoney £16,921 *Total Prizemoney* £21,461
Wins * 1999 Apr Epsom (SFT) H 10.1f 75 83+ <
* 1998 Spt Epsom (SFT) H 10.1f 71 75
* 1998 Jly Epsom (G-F) H 10.1f 69 72
1999 Turf 1-4: (10f 1-3, 13f) (g-s 1-2, gd, g-f)
Workmanlike, decent gelding, effective 8 to 13f, best at 10f, acts on g-s to frm, prefers left handed tracks, excels at Epsom. Turf high 83 - 1st of 12 getting 27lb from Royal Amaretto (21 Apr Epsom RF 0800). Consistent. A useful handicapper on his day, he landed the City And Suburban Handicap on his second start of this season. He has a fine record at Epsom but disappointed there on Derby Day. **G B Balding [3-20] Surgical Spirits.*

CHIEF JUSTICE **RR 35f** 1335[10]

2 b c Be My Chief (USA) 10.2f **(62)** - Supreme Kingdom (Take A Reef) 7.5f **(59)**
Form - 0
Record 1999 - 1st:0 2nd:0 3rd:0 Ran:1
1999 Turf 0-1: (6f) (gd)
Currently very moderate colt. **N P Littmoden [0-1] J R Good.*

CHIEF MONARCH BHB 70f **RR 86df** 4880[22]

5 b g Be My Chief (USA) 10.2f **(62)** - American Beauty (Mill Reef (USA)) 10.5f **(78)**
Form - 00
Record 1999 - 1st:0 2nd:0 3rd:0 Ran:2
Pre1999 - 1st:1 2nd:1 3rd:1 Ran:12
Win Prizemoney £3,517 *Total Prizemoney* £6,285
Wins 1997 Jly Sandow (G-F) 8.1f 75 <
1999 Turf 0-2: (7f, 8f) (g-f, frm)
Useful gelding, effective 9f, acts on gd. Turf high 54 (began Oct). Becoming disappointing.
**R A Fahey [0-6] Tommy Staunton (from B Smart [1-8] Spt 1997).*

CHIEF MOUSE BHB 42f60a **RR 39f 60a** 4456[10]

6 b g Be My Chief (USA) 10.2f **(62)** - Top Mouse (High Top) 10.2f **(67)**
Form - 0
Record 1999 - 1st:0 2nd:0 3rd:0 Ran:1
Pre1999 - 1st:1 2nd:0 3rd:0 Ran:7
Win Prizemoney £3,582 *Total Prizemoney* £3,582
Wins 1996 *Mar Wolver (STD) 8.5f 71* <
1999 Turf 0-1: (16f) (sft)
Above-average gelding, has worn blinkers. Becoming disappointing. **Ian Williams [0-1] Bill Gavan (from F Jordan [2-7] Aug 1997).*

CHIEF OF JUSTICE BHB 58f **RR 46f** 4840[14]

2 b c Be My Chief (USA) 10.2f **(62)** -Clare Court (Glint of Gold) 9.3f **(66)**
Form - 700
Record 1999 - 1st:0 2nd:0 3rd:0 Ran:3
1999 Turf 0-3: (7f 3) (g-s, gd, frm)
Currently moderate colt. Turf high 46 (began Spt).
**D Shaw [0-3] J C Fretwell.*

CHIEF PREDATOR (USA) BHB 36f60a **RR 40?f 60a** 3835[8]

5 ch g Chief's Crown (USA) 10.2f **(75)** - Tsavorite (USA) (Halo (USA)) 10.6f **(75)**
Form - 8
Record 1999 - 1st:0 2nd:0 3rd:0 Ran:1
Pre1999 - 1st:0 2nd:2 3rd:3 Ran:15
Win Prizemoney £0 *Total Prizemoney* £3,095
1999 Turf 0-1: (17f) (frm)
Average gelding, has worn blinkers.
**D L Williams [2-22] No Win No Feed Syndicate (from Miss K M George [0-1] Spt 1997).*

CHIEF REBEL (USA) BHB 87f **RR 96f** 4679[2]

3 b c Chief's Crown (USA) 10.2f **(75)** - Robellino Miss (USA) (Robellino (USA)) 7.6f **(80)**
Form - 33072
Record 1999 - 1st:0 2nd:1 3rd:2 Ran:5
Pre1999 - 1st:1 2nd:1 3rd:0 Ran:3
Win Prizemoney £4,230 *Total Prizemoney* £10,591
Wins * 1998 Aug Newmar (G-F) 6f 79 <
1999 Turf 0-5: (7f 2, 8f 3) (gd 3, g-f, hrd)
Neat, very useful colt, effective 8f, acts on gd. Turf high 96. He stays a mile and is capable of useful form. However, while the ability is there, a degree of application is lacking.
**G Wragg [1-8] The Eclipse Partnership.*

CHIEF RESPONSE BHB 85f **RR 80f** 4792[8]

2 b c Be My Chief (USA) 10.2f **(62)** - Red Rosein (Red Sunset) 8.2f **(63)**
Form - 22415208
Record 1999 - 1st:1 2nd:3 3rd:0 Ran:8
Win Prizemoney £3,168 *Total Prizemoney* £7,243
Wins * 1999 Aug Thirsk (SFT) 5f 79 <
1999 Turf 1-8: (5f 1-4, 6f 3, 8f) (gd 1-4, g-f 2, frm 2)
Decent colt, effective 5f, acts on gd to frm. Turf high 80 - also 1st of 8 giving 5lb to Medina de Rioseco (9 Aug Thirsk RF 3482). Landed a soft-ground Thirsk maiden on his fourth start, but is nothing out of the ordinary. **Miss Gay Kelleway [1-8] A P Griffin.*

CHIEF SEATTLE (USA) RR 5229a[2]

2 c Seattle Slew (USA) 7.8f **(64)** - Skatingonthinice (USA) (Icecapade (USA)) 11f **(62)**
Form - 2
1999 AW 0-1: (9f) (Dirt)
Currently Pattern-class. (1st run) - 2nd of 14 to Anees (6 Nov Gulfstream Park 9f Dirt RF 5229a). **J Kimmel in USA [0-1].*

CHIEF'S SONG BHB 32f **RR 33f** 3808[8]
9 b g Chief Singer 8.6f **(62)** - Tizzy (Formidable (USA)) 9.2f **(63)**
Form - 8
Record 1999 - 1st:0 2nd:0 3rd:0 Ran:1
Pre1999 - 1st:0 2nd:2 3rd:1 Ran:20
Win Prizemoney £0 *Total Prizemoney* £3,069
1999 Turf 0-1: (16f) (g-f)
Very moderate gelding, has worn blinkers.
**S Dow [10-57] Mrs Anne Devine (from B W Hills [0-5] Oct 1993).*

CHIEF WALLAH RR 55f 4992[6]
3 b c Be My Chief (USA) 10.2f **(62)** - Arusha (IRE) (Dance of Life (USA)) 7f **(66)**
Form - 6
Record 1999 - 1st:0 2nd:0 3rd:0 Ran:1
1999 Turf 0-1: (10f) (frm)
Currently fair colt. **D R C Elsworth [0-1] Raymond Tooth.*

CHIKAL BHB 46f45a **RR 53f 45a** 643[9]
4 b g Nalchik (USA) 12.6f **(44)** - Ty-With-Belle (Pamroy) 12.5f **(55)**
Form - 0
Record 1999 - 1st:0 2nd:0 3rd:0 Ran:1
Pre1999 - 1st:0 2nd:0 3rd:1 Ran:9
Win Prizemoney £0 *Total Prizemoney* £297
1999 AW 0-1: (16f) (Fibr)
Unfurnished, fair gelding. (DEAD) **B Palling [0-11] Mrs M M Palling.*

CHIKO BHB 65f59a **RR 62f 59a** 5218[19]
2 b g Afif - Walsham Witch (Music Maestro) 7.7f **(66)**
Form - 10808540
Record 1999 - 1st:1 2nd:0 3rd:0 Ran:8
Win Prizemoney £2,221 *Total Prizemoney* £3,044
Wins * 1999 Mar Doncas (G-S) S 5f 62 <
1999 Turf 1-7: (5f 1-3, 6f 3, 7f) (g-s 1-3, gd 3, frm) 1999 AW 0-1: (7f) (Fibr)
Average gelding, effective 5 to 6f, acts on g-s, has worn blinkers. Turf high 71 - also 1st of 11 giving 5lb to Foxkey (26 Mar Doncaster RF 0476). Inconsistent. **J L Harris [1-8] J Starbuck.*

CHILDREN'S CHOICE (IRE) BHB 42f38a **RR 46f 38a** 5006[8]
8 b m Taufan (USA) 8.3f **(65)** -Alice Brackloon (USA)(Melyno)10.4f **(55)**
Form - 06046032321381358
Record 1999 - 1st:2 2nd:2 3rd:4 Ran:17
Pre1999 - 1st:7 2nd:6 3rd:2 Ran:50
Win Prizemoney £32,900 *Total Prizemoney* £44,196
Wins * 1999 Aug Redcar (G-F) S 14.1f 39
*** 1999** Aug Bright (G-F) SH 11.9f 41 42
1998 Oct Newmar (G-S) H 12f 50 54
1997 Oct Nottin (G-F) H 14.1f 50 57
1997 Jly Yarmou (G-F) H 16f 49 51
1996 Aug Yarmou (G-F) H 14.1f 52 56
1995 Mar Doncas (GD) H 10.3f 53 60 <
1999 Turf 2-14: (12f 1-2, 13f, 14f 1-3, 15f, 16f 5, 17f 2) (hvy, gd 4, g-f 1-4, frm 1-4, hrd) 1999 AW 0-3: (11f, 16f 2) (Equi, Fibr 2)
Moderate mare, effective 12 to 16f, acts on g-f to frm, best on g-f, has worn blinkers, and excels at Redcar and Newmarket. Turf high 46 - 3rd of 16 getting 8lb from Rosa Canina (13 Spt Nottingham 16f frm RF 4287). AW high 40. Consistent.
**J Pearce [2-15] & Mrs S Fernandes (from D Morris [1-11] Jan 1999).*

CHI-LIN BHB 37f35a **RR 29f 35a** 5128[16]
4 b f Precocious 7.2f **(54)** - Cool Combination (Indian King (USA)) 7.4f **(64)**
Form - 8000
Record 1999 - 1st:0 2nd:0 3rd:0 Ran:2
Pre1999 - 1st:0 2nd:1 3rd:1 Ran:11
Win Prizemoney £0 *Total Prizemoney* £1,067
1999 Turf 0-1: (6f) (gd) 1999 AW 0-1: (6f) (Fibr)
Workmanlike, very moderate filly, effective 6f, acts on sft. Becoming disappointing.
**P Butler [0-10] Mrs Janet Coleman (from J Ffitch-Heyes [0-3] Nov 1997).*

CHILI PEPPER BHB 58f **RR 67f** 4320[13]
2 b f Chilibang 7f **(55)** - Game Germaine (Mummy's Game) 8.2f **(60)**
Form - 2744450
Record 1999 - 1st:0 2nd:1 3rd:0 Ran:7
Win Prizemoney £0 *Total Prizemoney* £635
1999 Turf 0-7: (5f 3, 6f 2, 7f 2) (gd 6, frm)
Average filly, effective 5f, acts on gd, often wears blinkers. Turf high 67. **A Smith [0-7] Mrs R Auchterlounie.*

CHILLI BHB 54f **RR 57f** 4934[18]
2 br c Most Welcome 8.6f **(66)** - So Saucy **(35f 41a)** (Teenoso (USA)) 9.9f **(72)**
Form - 0040
Record 1999 - 1st:0 2nd:0 3rd:0 Ran:4
Win Prizemoney £0 *Total Prizemoney* £243
1999 Turf 0-4: (6f, 7f 2, 8f) (g-f 4)
Fair colt. Turf high 57. **C E Brittain [0-4] C E Brittain.*

CHILLIAN BHB 34f **RR 19f** 2755[18]
3 b g Chilibang 7f **(55)** - Five Islands (Bairn (USA)) 7.7f **(59)**
Form - 000
Record 1999 - 1st:0 2nd:0 3rd:0 Ran:3
Pre1999 - 1st:0 2nd:0 3rd:0 Ran:5
1999 Turf 0-3: (5f 2, 7f) (g-f, frm 2)
Scopey, poor gelding. Turf high 19. Becoming disappointing.
**M Brittain [0-8] Mel Brittain.*

CHILUKKI (USA) RR 5225a[2]
2 f Cherokee Run (USA) - Song of Syria (USA) (Damascus (USA)) 8.9f **(71)**
Form - 2
1999 AW 0-1: (9f) (Dirt)
Currently very useful. (1st run) - 2nd of 9 to Cash Run (6 Nov Gulfstream Park 9f Dirt RF 5225a). Appeared to not quite get the trip and weakened in the closing stages when favourite for the Breeders' Cup Juvenile Fillies. **B Baffert in USA [0-1].*

CHILWORTH (IRE) BHB 71f **RR 72f** 1954[4]
2 ch c Shalford (IRE) 7.8f **(63)** - Close the Till (Formidable (USA)) 9.2f **(63)**
Form - 064
Record 1999 - 1st:0 2nd:0 3rd:0 Ran:3
1999 Turf 0-3: (5f, 6f, 7f) (gd, g-f, frm)
Currently above-average colt. Turf high 72 - 4th of 16 getting 2lb from Carousing (12 Jun Lingfield 7f g-f RF 1954).
**T M Jones [0-3] John Crouch.*

CHIMES OF PEACE BHB 36f **RR 32f** 3544[4]
4 b f Magic Ring (IRE) 6.5f **(64)** - Leprechaun Lady (Royal Blend) 11.9f **(58)**
Form - 0783584
Record 1999 - 1st:0 2nd:0 3rd:1 Ran:7
Pre1999 - 1st:1 2nd:1 3rd:1 Ran:13
Win Prizemoney £2,965 *Total Prizemoney* £5,311
Wins * 1998 May Mussel (GD) 8f 55 <
1999 Turf 0-7: (9f 2, 10f 4, 12f) (sft, gd 2, g-f 2, frm 2)
Leggy, very moderate filly, effective 8 to 12f, best at 10f, acts on g-s to frm, best on g-f, likes right handed tracks, and excels at Beverley. Turf high 45. Consistent.
**J L Eyre [1-20] The Secret Seven Partnership.*

CHIMNEY DUST BHB 84f **RR 83f** 5218[4]
2 b c Pelder (IRE) - Evening Falls **(45f 60a)** (Beveled (USA)) 9f **(59)**
Form - 01204
Record 1999 - 1st:1 2nd:1 3rd:0 Ran:5
Win Prizemoney £2,048 *Total Prizemoney* £3,725
Wins * 1999 Aug Warwic (GD) 6.8f 82 <
1999 Turf 1-5: (6f, 7f 1-4) (sft, g-s, gd 1-1, g-f, frm)
Decent colt. Turf high 83 (began Aug) - 2nd of 17 giving 4lb to Father Juninho (11 Spt Doncaster 7f frm RF 4269) - also 1st of 16 getting 4lb from Groesfaen Lad (30 Aug Warwick RF 4033). Got off the mark at Warwick and ran with credit afterwards. Best on fast ground. **G C H Chung [1-5] Osvaldo Pedroni.*

CHINABERRY BHB 44f44a **RR 43f 44a** 4398[4]
5 b m Soviet Star (USA) 8.6f **(74)** - Crimson Conquest (USA) (Diesis) 9.3f **(69)**
Form - 34100033848272064
Record 1999 - 1st:1 2nd:2 3rd:2 Ran:15
Pre1999 - 1st:0 2nd:1 3rd:1 Ran:15
Win Prizemoney £2,788 *Total Prizemoney* £7,886

Wins * **1999** *Jan Southw (STD) H* *8f* *48* *56* <
1999 Turf 0-7: (7f, 8f 4, 9f 2) (gd 2, g-f 2, frm 3) 1999 AW 1-8: (7f, 8f 1-7) (Fibr 1-8)
Moderate filly, effective 8f, - acts on Fibr. Turf high 44. AW high 56 (1st run) - 1st of 13 giving 14lb to Oxbane (25 Jan Southwell RF 0161).
**M Brittain [1-26] Northgate Lodge Racing Club (from C E Brittain [0-4] Jly 1997).*

CHINA CASTLE BHB 51f100a RR 51f 100a 3265[9]

6 b g Sayf El Arab (USA) 8.2f **(57)** -oney Plum (Kind of Hush) 10.1f **(62)**
Form - 811113113180501O

Record	**1999** -	1st:8	2nd:0	3rd:2	Ran:15
	Pre1999 -	1st:10	2nd:3	3rd:5	Ran:45

Win Prizemoney £80,267 *Total Prizemoney* £88,571

Wins								
	* **1999**	Jly Hamilt	(FRM)	H	11.1f	48	51	
	* **1999**	*Mar Southw*	*(STD)*	*H*	*12f*	*101*	*103*	<
	* **1999**	*Feb Wolver*	*(STD)*	*H*	*12f*	*94*	*96*	
	* **1999**	*Feb Wolver*	*(STD)*	*H*	*12f*	*90*	*94*	
	* **1999**	*Jan Wolver*	*(STD)*	*H*	*12f*	*73*	*86*	
	* **1999**	*Jan Southw*	*(STD)*	*H*	*11f*	*73*	*93*	
	* **1999**	*Jan Southw*	*(STD)*		*12f*		*76*	
	* **1999**	*Jan Southw*	*(STD)*	*H*	*11f*	*73*	*73*	
	* 1998	*Jan Wolver*	*(STD)*	*H*	*12f*	*71*	*75*	
	* 1998	*Jan Southw*	*(STD)*		*12f*		*75*	
	* 1997	*Jan Southw*	*(STD)*	*H*	*12f*	*67*	*82+*	
	* 1997	*Jan Southw*	*(STD)*	*H*	*11f*	*67*	*87*	
	* 1997	*Jan Southw*	*(STD)*	*H*	*11f*	*67*	*77*	
	* 1996	*Feb Southw*	*(STD)*	*C*	*11f*		*67+*	
	* 1996	*Jan Wolver*	*(STD)*	*H*	*8.5f*	*68*	*72*	
	* 1996	*Jan Lingfi*	*(STD)*	*H*	*10f*	*54*	*64*	
	* 1996	*Jan Southw*	*(STD)*	*H*	*7f*	*54*	*72*	
	* 1995	*Aug Southw*	*(STD)*	*S*	*6f*		*64+*	

1999 Turf 1-6: (11f 1-3, 12f, 13f, 14f) (hvy, g-s, gd, g-f, frm 1-2) 1999 AW 7-9: (9f 2, 11f 2-2, 12f 5-5) (Fibr 7-9)
Very useful gelding, effective 9 to 12f, best at 12f, - acts on Fibr, favours left handed tracks, and excels at Southwell. Turf high 51. AW high 103 - 1st of 7 giving 13lb to Bawsian (22 Mar Southwell RF 0460) - also 1st of 6 giving 29lb to Green Bopper (24 Feb Wolverhampton RF 0350). Inconsistent. Modest on the turf, he is a very smart handicapper on the All-Weather, being particularly effective on Fibresand. Best over a mile and a half these days, he needs to be produced late.
**P C Haslam [18-63] J M Davis & Middleham Park Racing I.*

CHINAIDER (IRE) BHB 52f58a RR 44f 58a 4144[5]

4 b f Mujadil (USA) 7.7f **(70)** - We Two (Glenstal (USA)) 10.1f **(64)**
Form - 57805

Record	**1999** -	1st:0	2nd:0	3rd:0	Ran:5
	Pre1999 -	1st:3	2nd:2	3rd:2	Ran:17

Win Prizemoney £16,086 *Total Prizemoney* £18,583

Wins							
	1997	Aug York	(GD)	S	6f	73	<
	1997	Aug Redcar	(G-F)	S	6f	69	
	1997	*Jun Southw*	*(STD)*	*S*	*5f*	*65+*	

1999 Turf 0-3: (6f, 7f, 8f) (gd, frm, hrd) 1999 AW 0-2: (6f, 8f) (Fibr 2)
Scopey, fair filly, effective 6f, acts on gd to frm, has worn blinkers. Turf high 44 (began Aug). AW high 57.
**D Nicholls [0-17] A A Bloodstock Ltd (from M C Pipe [1-2] Spt 1997).*

CHINA MAIL (IRE) BHB 30f20a RR 35f 20a 269[11]

7 b g Slip Anchor 12.7f **(75)** - Fenney Mill (Levmoss) 11.4f **(66)**
Form - 070

Record	**1999** -	1st:0	2nd:0	3rd:0	Ran:3
	Pre1999 -	1st:0	2nd:0	3rd:0	Ran:12

1999 AW 0-3: (16f 3) (Equi 2, Fibr)
Very moderate gelding. Becoming disappointing.
**M Quinn [0-3] The Merlin Syndicate (from J A Bennett [0-7] Jly 1997).*

CHINA RED (USA) BHB 86f98a RR 84f 98a 2357[8]

5 br g Red Ransom (USA) 8.6f **(83)** -Akamare(FR)(Akarad (FR)) 9f **(76)**
Form - 013108

Record	**1999** -	1st:2	2nd:0	3rd:1	Ran:6
	Pre1999 -	1st:3	2nd:3	3rd:0	Ran:15

Win Prizemoney £35,449 *Total Prizemoney* £43,872

Wins								
	* **1999**	*May Lingfi*	*(STD)*	*H*	*8f*	*90*	*95*	<
	* **1999**	*May Lingfi*	*(STD)*	*H*	*8f*	*78*	*89*	
	* 1998	Jly Goodwo	(GD)	H	8f	82	85	
	* 1998	May Goodwo	(G-F)	H	8f	78	82	
	* 1997	Apr Nottin	(G-F)		8.2f		85	

1999 Turf 0-4: (8f 4) (gd 4) 1999 AW 2-2: (8f 2-2) (Equi 2-2)
Very useful gelding, effective 8f, acts on gd to g-f - acts on Equi. Turf high 84. AW high 95 - 1st of 11 giving 19lb to Prodigal Son (25 May Lingfield RF 1458) - also 1st of 7 getting 6lb from Silca Blanka (7 May Lingfield RF 1086). He is a game front-runner and goes particularly well on turning tracks, such as Goodwood and the Lingfield Equitrack. **J W Hills [5-21] N N Browne And Partners.*

CHINATOWN (IRE) RR 92f 4570[4]

2 br c Marju (IRE) 9.2f **(76)** - Sunley Saint (Artaius (USA)) 9f **(69)**
Form - 314

Record	**1999** -	1st:1	2nd:0	3rd:1	Ran:3

Win Prizemoney £3,452 *Total Prizemoney* £9,899

Wins						
	* **1999**	Aug Newcas (GD)	7f	90	<	

1999 Turf 1-3: (7f 1-2, 8f) (sft, gd 1-1, g-f)
Currently useful colt. Turf high 92 (began Aug) - 4th of 6 to Royal Kingdom (26 Spt Ascot 8f sft RF 4570) - also 1st of 6 from Nooshman (30 Aug Newcastle RF 4021). Third to the useful Nicobar over seven furlongs at Haydock in early August, he then got off the mark when winning a maiden at Newcastle later in the month despite running a little green. Creditable effort to finish fourth in the Royal Lodge, but may not have appreciated the very soft ground. **P W Chapple-Hyam [1-3] Ivan Allan & Sir Alex Ferguson.*

CHIN UP (IRE) RR 62f 3146[5]

2 b f Port Lucaya - Tiempo (King of Spain) 7.8f **(52)**
Form - 075

Record	**1999** -	1st:0	2nd:0	3rd:0	Ran:3

1999 Turf 0-3: (5f, 6f 2) (g-f 2, frm)
Currently average filly. Turf high 62.
**M H Tompkins [0-3] www raceworld co uk.*

CHIPS (IRE) BHB 64f RR 61f 4035[2]

4 ch g Common Grounds 8.1f **(66)** - Inonder (Belfort (FR)) 6.8f **(63)**
Form - 705032

Record	**1999** -	1st:0	2nd:1	3rd:1	Ran:6
	Pre1999 -	1st:3	2nd:1	3rd:2	Ran:12

Win Prizemoney £19,880 *Total Prizemoney* £24,660

Wins						
	* 1997	Aug Baden- (GD)	L	7.5f	90+	
	* 1997	May Kempto (GD)		6f	83+	
	* 1997	May Salisb (G-F)		5f	93	<

1999 Turf 0-6: (5f, 6f 3, 7f, 8f) (gd, g-f 2, frm 3)
Scopey, average gelding, has worn blinkers. Turf high 72. Sold for just 10,600 gns at Ascot, to race abroad.
**D R C Elsworth [3-18] Mrs Anne Coughlan.*

CHIQUITA (IRE) BHB 80f80a RR 75f 80a 4694[1]

2 ch f College Chapel - Council Rock (General Assembly (USA)) 10f **(68)**
Form - 53211

Record	**1999** -	1st:2	2nd:1	3rd:1	Ran:5

Win Prizemoney £7,148 *Total Prizemoney* £8,343

Wins								
	* **1999**	Oct Sandow	(HVY)	H	5f	75	75	<
	* **1999**	*Spt Wolver*	*(STD)*	*H*	*5f*	*73*	*74*	

1999 Turf 1-4: (5f 1-3, 6f) (sft 1-1, gd, frm, hrd) 1999 AW 1-1: (5f 1-1) (Fibr 1-1)
Above-average filly. Turf high 75 (began Jly) - 1st of 8 giving 15lb to Blue Holly (2 Oct Sandown RF 4694). (1st run) - 1st of 12 giving 13lb to Cost Auditing (8 Spt Wolverhampton RF 4221). Showed ability in turf maidens, but got off the mark in a nursery on the Wolverhampton Fibresand in September. Maintained the improvement by following up in a similar event on heavy ground at Sandown. Her wins have been over five furlongs, but she does stay six. **W J Haggas [2-5] Tony Hirschfeld.*

CHIST (USA) BHB 106f RR 108f 1196[6]

4 b br c Lear Fan (USA) 10.4f **(80)** - Morna (Blakeney) 10.5f **(64)**
Form - 56

Record	**1999** -	1st:0	2nd:0	3rd:0	Ran:2
	Pre1999 -	1st:1	2nd:1	3rd:1	Ran:4

Win Prizemoney £3,655 *Total Prizemoney* £8,992

Wins						
	* 1998	Apr Leices	(SFT)	10f	86+	<

1999 Turf 0-2: (12f, 14f) (gd, frm)
Leggy, Pattern-class colt. Turf high 108 (1st run) - 5th of 11 getting 5lb from Silver Patriarch (30 Apr Newmarket 12f frm RF 0945). He was not beaten far in the Jockey Club Stakes and the Yorkshire Cup, but has been absent since and has presumably been difficult

to train. **M H Tompkins [1-6] Mrs Jane Bailey.*

CHIT CHAT (IRE) RR 3437[10]
3 b g Mujadil (USA) 7.7f **(70)** - Rhoman Ruby (IRE) (Rhoman Rule (USA))
Form - 0
Record 1999 - 1st:0 2nd:0 3rd:0 Ran:1
1999 AW 0-1: (9f) (Fibr)
Light-framed, currently poor gelding.
**D Burchell [0-1] Brian Henderson.*

CHLOANNA (IRE) BHB 35f **RR 48f** 4938[14]
3 bb f Up and At 'em - Exclusive Lass (IRE) (Doulab (USA)) 9.8f **(65)**
Form - 8000
Record 1999 - 1st:0 2nd:0 3rd:0 Ran:4
Pre1999 - 1st:0 2nd:0 3rd:0 Ran:3
1999 Turf 0-3: (5f, 6f, 7f) (gd, g-f 2) 1999 AW 0-1: (6f) (Fibr)
Moderate filly. Turf high 48.
**D Carroll [0-1] Sam Murphy (from J G Coogan in IRE [0-6] Jun 1999).*

CHOICE SPIRIT (USA) RR 93f 3584a[1]
3 f b Danzig (USA) 8.1f **(88)** - Zaizafon (USA) (The Minstrel (CAN)) 10f **(72)**
Form - 121
1999 Turf 2-3: (8f 2-3) (hvy 2-2, sft)
Currently useful. Turf high 93 - 1st of 10 from First Night (5 Aug Deauville RF 3584a). **A Fabre in FR [2-3] K Abdulla.*

CHOIRGIRL BHB 105f **RR 104df** 4290[4]
3 b f Unfuwain (USA) 11.4f **(74)** - Choir Mistress (Chief Singer) 8.9f **(66)**
Form - 0246824
Record 1999 - 1st:0 2nd:2 3rd:0 Ran:7
Pre1999 - 1st:1 2nd:1 3rd:0 Ran:5
Win Prizemoney £3,392 *Total Prizemoney* £30,688
Wins * 1998 Aug Redcar (G-F) 7f 87 <
1999 Turf 0-7: (7f, 8f 4, 10f 2) (gd 3, g-f 2, frm 2)
Very useful filly, effective 8 to 10f, best at 8f, acts on gd to g-f, best on gd, prefers right handed tracks. Turf high 107 - 6th of 9 to Balisada (16 Jun Ascot 8f g-f RF 2041). Proved beatable in decent fillies' races, giving the impression she was keeping something back for herself. **J H M Gosden [1-12] Cheveley Park Stud.*

CHOK-DI BHB 38f **RR 28f** 4148[7]
3 b g Beveled (USA) 6.9f **(64)** - Pendona (Blue Cashmere) 6.4f **(54)**
Form - 085007
Record 1999 - 1st:0 2nd:0 3rd:0 Ran:6
Pre1999 - 1st:0 2nd:0 3rd:0 Ran:5
1999 Turf 0-6: (5f 3, 6f 3) (sft, gd, frm 3, hrd)
Leggy, little account gelding, effective 6f, acts on frm. Turf high 46 - 5th of 14 getting 21lb from Lady Melbourne (31 Jly Thirsk 6f frm RF 3285). **Mrs M Reveley [0-11] The Desert Rats Racing Club.*

CHORUS BHB 75f **RR 72+f** 5214[4]
2 b f Bandmaster (USA) - Name That Tune **(43f 36a)** (Fayruz)
Form - 86244552544
Record 1999 - 1st:0 2nd:2 3rd:0 Ran:11
Win Prizemoney £0 *Total Prizemoney* £3,708
1999 Turf 0-11: (5f 9, 6f 2) (g-s 2, gd 4, g-f 3, frm 2)
Above-average filly, effective 5f, acts on g-s to frm. Turf high 72 - 4th of 12 giving 2lb to Indian Music (5 Nov Doncaster 5f g-s RF 5214). Consistent. **B R Millman [0-11] B R Millman.*

CHORUS OF APPROVAL BHB 37f **RR 28f** 3136[17]
3 b g Clantime 6.6f **(57)** - Fyas (Sayf El Arab (USA)) 7.1f **(54)**
Form - 007300
Record 1999 - 1st:0 2nd:0 3rd:1 Ran:6
Pre1999 - 1st:0 2nd:0 3rd:0 Ran:5
Win Prizemoney £0 *Total Prizemoney* £467
1999 Turf 0-6: (5f 2, 6f 2, 7f 2) (gd, g-f 3, frm 2)
Scopey, little account gelding. Turf high 28.
**Miss L A Perratt [0-11] Gordon Cowan.*

CHRISMAS CAROL (IRE) BHB 44f **RR 42f** 4906[16]
3 b f Common Grounds 8.1f **(66)** - Stockrose (Horage) 10.3f **(61)**
Form - 870080
Record 1999 - 1st:0 2nd:0 3rd:0 Ran:6
Pre1999 - 1st:0 2nd:0 3rd:1 Ran:2
Win Prizemoney £0 *Total Prizemoney* £680
1999 Turf 0-6: (6f 2, 7f 4) (gd, g-f 2, frm 3)
Light-framed, moderate filly, has worn blinkers. Turf high 48. Inconsistent. **P W Harris [0-8] Resplendent Racing Ltd.*

CHRIS'S LITTLE LAD (IRE) BHB 66f **RR 69f** 4178[13]
2 ch c Hamas (IRE) 8f **(72)** - Jeema (Thatch (USA)) 9.8f **(62)**
Form - 040
Record 1999 - 1st:0 2nd:0 3rd:0 Ran:3
1999 Turf 0-3: (6f, 7f, 8f) (g-f, frm 2)
Currently average colt. Turf high 64 (began Jly).
**W R Muir [0-3] Hugh Smith.*

CHRISTIANSTED (IRE) BHB 78f **RR 75f** 3320a[2]
4 ch g Soviet Lad (USA) 9.4f **(63)** - How True (Known Fact (USA)) 7.4f **(67)**
Form - 14152
Record 1999 - 1st:2 2nd:1 3rd:0 Ran:5
Pre1999 - 1st:1 2nd:0 3rd:2 Ran:5
Win Prizemoney £9,103 *Total Prizemoney* £17,001
Wins * 1999 Jun Nottin (GD) H 14.1f 68 75
*** 1999** Apr Ripon (G-F) H 12.3f 63 69
1998 May Killar (SFT) C 12f 90 <
1999 Turf 2-5: (12f 1-1, 14f 1-2, 16f 2) (gd, g-f 2-2, frm 2)
Above-average gelding, effective 9 to 12f, acts on sft. Turf high 75. Consistent. He had won three times over hurdles before winning over a mile and a half at Ripon in April, but pulled too hard at Kempton next time. More patient tactics were used at Nottingham and that did the trick. Ran very well from out of the handicap in the Northumberland Plate.
**F Murphy [5-8] John Duddy (from Ms J Morgan in IRE [0-1] Spt 1998).*

CHRISTOPHENE (USA) RR 106f 3783a[2]
3 b c Kingmambo (USA) 10.9f **(85)** - Miss Summer (Luthier) 9.8f **(71)**
Form - 2
1999 Turf 0-1: (10f) (hvy)
Currently Pattern-class colt. (1st run) - 2nd of 8 to Espionage (15 Aug Deauville 10f hvy RF 3783a). **P Bary in FR [0-1].*

CHRISTOPHERSSISTER BHB 67f62a **RR 68f 62a** 4542[5]
2 br f Timeless Times (USA) 6.1f **(56)** - Petite Elite (Anfield) 8.5f **(59)**
Form - 6645
Record 1999 - 1st:0 2nd:0 3rd:0 Ran:4
1999 Turf 0-4: (5f 3, 6f) (gd, frm 3)
Average filly. Turf high 68 (began Jly).
**N Bycroft [0-4] Mike Smallman.*

CHRYSOLITE (IRE) BHB 58f60a **RR 59f 60a** 5162[13]
4 ch g Kris 10f **(75)** - Alamiya (IRE) (Doyoun) 9f **(69)**
Form - 65000
Record 1999 - 1st:0 2nd:0 3rd:0 Ran:5
Pre1999 - 1st:1 2nd:0 3rd:1 Ran:8
Win Prizemoney £5,711 *Total Prizemoney* £6,865
Wins * 1998 May Lingfi (GD) H 9f 74 78 <
1999 Turf 0-4: (8f, 10f 3) (gd, g-f 3) 1999 AW 0-1: (8f) (Fibr)
Workmanlike, fair gelding, effective 9f, acts on g-f, likes left handed tracks, likes tight tracks. Turf high 63. Becoming disappointing.
**B W Hills [1-13] Mrs B W Hills.*

CHURCH FARM FLYER (IRE) BHB 44f **RR 50f** 5138[6]
2 b f College Chapel - Young Isabel (IRE) (Last Tycoon) 8.5f **(62)**
Form - 086
Record 1999 - 1st:0 2nd:0 3rd:0 Ran:3
1999 Turf 0-3: (7f 2, 8f) (gd, g-f, frm)
Currently fair filly. Turf high 49. **C N Allen [0-3] Felix Snell.*

CHURCHILL'S SHADOW (IRE) BHB 52f49a **RR 51f 49a** 3612[5]
5 b h Polish Precedent (USA) 9f **(73)** - Shy Princess (USA) (Irish River (FR)) 8.6f **(78)**
Form - 507054801245
Record 1999 - 1st:1 2nd:1 3rd:0 Ran:8
Pre1999 - 1st:3 2nd:2 3rd:0 Ran:16
Win Prizemoney £10,104 *Total Prizemoney* £13,463
Wins * 1999 Jly Chepst (G-F) SH 8.1f 45 47
* 1998 May Doncas (GD) H 7f 45 49
* 1997 *Nov Lingfi (STD) H 7f 44 53* <

* 1997 *Nov Lingfi (STD) H 7f 44 46*
1999 Turf 1-8: (7f 5, 8f 1-3) (g-f 4, frm 1-4)
Fair colt, effective 7 to 8f, best at 7f, acts on g-f to frm, best on g-f. Turf high 51 - 2nd of 6 getting 15lb from Redswan (15 Jly Leicester 7f g-f RF 2850) - also 1st of 19 from Shontaine (9 Jly Chepstow RF 2667). **B A Pearce [4-24] Richard Gray.*

CHURCHSTANTON (IRE) RR 2108[10]
7 b g Celio Rufo - Bailieboro (Bonne Noel) 10.7f **(71)**
Form - 0
Record 1999 - 1st:0 2nd:0 3rd:0 Ran:1
1999 Turf 0-1: (22f) (g-f)
Formerly very poor gelding. **Paddy Farrell [1-4] Michael Lowe.*

CHURLISH CHARM BHB 112f **RR 115f** 2071[11]
4 b c Niniski (USA) 13.2f **(67)** - Blushing Storm (USA) (Blushing Groom (FR)) 10.3f **(76)**
Form - 310
Record 1999 - 1st:1 2nd:0 3rd:1 Ran:3
Pre1999 - 1st:3 2nd:1 3rd:0 Ran:7
Win Prizemoney £97,963 *Total Prizemoney* £104,028
Wins * **1999** May York (SFT) G2 13.9f 115 <
* 1998 Spt Newbur (GD) H 16f 99 104
* 1998 Jun Goodwo (GD) 12f 95
* 1998 May Newmar (G-F) 12f 81
1999 Turf 1-3: (12f, 14f 1-1, 20f) (gd 1-2, g-f)
High-class colt, effective 14f, acts on gd. Turf high 115 - 1st of 9 getting 1lb from Largesse (13 May York RF 1196). This strapping individual won three times in 1998 and, after running well on his reappearance at Goodwood, improved on that when a surprise winner of the Yorkshire Cup, having no difficulty with the soft ground. He finished down the field in the Ascot Gold Cup on his next start and was not seen out again.
**R Hannon [4-10] Mohamed Suhail.*

Churlish Charm (Richard Hughes) caused an upset in the Yorkshire Cup

CIBENZE BHB 66f **RR 68f** 5105[3]
2 b f Owington - Maria Cappuccini (Siberian Express (USA)) 8.8f **(65)**
Form - 52653
Record 1999 - 1st:0 2nd:1 3rd:1 Ran:5
Win Prizemoney £0 *Total Prizemoney* £1,460
1999 Turf 0-5: (5f 4, 6f) (sft, gd, g-f, frm 2)
Average filly. Turf high 68 (began Aug).
**M R Channon [0-5] Miletrian Plc.*

CICERONE BHB 37f39a **RR 19f 39a** 972[7]
9 br g Tina's Pet 7.4f **(56)** - Emma Royale (Royal And Regal (USA)) 9.5f **(60)**
Form - 7
Record 1999 - 1st:0 2nd:0 3rd:0 Ran:1
Pre1999 - 1st:6 2nd:4 3rd:1 Ran:40
Win Prizemoney £15,700 *Total Prizemoney* £19,931
Wins 1996 May Ripon (GD) S 8f 66 <
1996 Apr Leices (GD) S 7f 56
1995 Oct Leices (FRM) CH 8f 42 47
1999 Turf 0-1: (9f) (g-f)
Moderate gelding, has worn blinkers. Consistent.
**Miss Lucinda Russell [0-7] Peter Russell (from J L Harris [4-15] May 1996).*

CIEL DE REVE (USA) BHB 50f55a **RR 45f 55a** 1095[16]
5 b g Septieme Ciel (USA) - Reve de Reine (USA) (Lyphard (USA)) 9.9f **(72)**
Form - 86868070
Record 1999 - 1st:0 2nd:0 3rd:0 Ran:4
Pre1999 - 1st:0 2nd:0 3rd:0 Ran:4
1999 Turf 0-3: (8f, 10f, 14f) (sft, g-f, frm) 1999 AW 0-1: (16f) (Fibr)
Moderate gelding. Turf high 45. **K C Comerford [0-8] Alan Brackley.*

CILANTRO BHB 43f **RR 51f** 4923[11]
2 b c Minshaanshu Amad (USA) 11.3f **(53)** - Laquette **(33f)** (Bairn (USA)) 7.7f **(59)**
Form - 50000
Record 1999 - 1st:0 2nd:0 3rd:0 Ran:5
1999 Turf 0-4: (5f, 6f, 7f 2) (sft, gd, g-f, frm) 1999 AW 0-1: (6f) (Fibr)
Fair colt. Turf high 51. **Miss A Stokell [0-5] Ms Caron Stokell.*

CINDER HILLS BHB 60f60a **RR 46f 60a** 5168[12]
4 ch f Deploy 11.4f **(67)** - Dame du Moulin (Shiny Tenth) 9.2f **(56)**
Form - 00
Record 1999 - 1st:0 2nd:0 3rd:0 Ran:2
Pre1999 - 1st:2 2nd:2 3rd:1 Ran:12
Win Prizemoney £6,610 *Total Prizemoney* £9,865
Wins * 1998 Apr Ripon (SFT) H 12.3f 53 64 <
* 1998 Apr Ripon (SFT) H 10f 53 60
1999 Turf 0-2: (14f, 16f) (g-s, gd)
Leggy, fair filly, effective 10 to 14f, best at 12f, acts on sft to frm, favours tight tracks. Turf high 41. Becoming disappointing.
**M W Easterby [2-17] Winton Bloodstock Ltd.*

CINDESTI (IRE) BHB 56f66a **RR 58f 66a** 4413[1]
3 b c Barathea (IRE) - Niamh Cinn Oir (IRE) (King of Clubs) 7.1f **(57)**
Form - 40011
Record 1999 - 1st:2 2nd:0 3rd:0 Ran:5
Pre1999 - 1st:0 2nd:0 3rd:0 Ran:2
Win Prizemoney £4,496 *Total Prizemoney* £4,793
Wins * **1999** *Spt Wolver (STD) 14.8f 64* <
* **1999** *Spt Wolver (STD) H 12f 56 58*
1999 Turf 0-3: (10f 2, 12f) (gd, g-f 2) 1999 AW 2-2: (12f 1-1, 15f 1-1) (Fibr 2-2)
Scopey, average colt, effective 12 to 15f, - acts on Fibr. Turf high 58. AW high 64 (began Spt) - 1st of 8 getting 17lb from Alhesn (18 Spt Wolverhampton RF 4413) - also 1st of 12 getting 6lb from Western Command (8 Spt Wolverhampton RF 4223). Showed much-improved form when tried on Fibresand, winning twice at Wolverhampton in September. He seemed to get the extended 14 furlongs well on the second occasion and still has plenty of scope on sand.
**B A McMahon [2-5] Merit Racing (from L M Cumani [0-2] Oct 1998).*

CINEMA POINT (IRE) BHB 42f **RR 34f** 5216[17]
2 b g Doyoun 10.7f **(69)** - Airport (Warpath) 12.3f **(52)**
Form - 000
Record 1999 - 1st:0 2nd:0 3rd:0 Ran:3
1999 Turf 0-3: (7f, 8f 2) (g-s, gd 2)
Currently very moderate gelding. Turf high 33 (began Spt).
**M H Tompkins [0-3] www raceworld co uk.*

CINNAMON COURT (IRE) RR 57f 4944[13]
2 b f College Chapel - Henrietta Street (IRE) **(53f)** (Royal Academy (USA))
Form - 70

Record 1999 - 1st:0 2nd:0 3rd:0 Ran:2
1999 Turf 0-2: (6f, 7f) (gd 2)
Currently fair filly. Turf high 57 (began Oct).
**J R Arnold [0-2] Prof Green.*

CINNAMON LADY BHB 69f65a RR 74f 65a 4718[11]

3 ch f Emarati (USA) 6.6f **(63)** - Nice Lady (Connaught) 7.7f **(63)**
Form - 2310300
Record 1999 - 1st:1 2nd:1 3rd:2 Ran:7
Pre1999 - 1st:0 2nd:1 3rd:0 Ran:4
Win Prizemoney £4,438 *Total Prizemoney* £7,367
Wins * 1999 May Newbur (SFT) H 7f 68 74 <
1999 Turf 1-6: (7f 1-5, 8f) (sft, gd 1-5) 1999 AW 0-1: (7f) (Fibr)
Leggy, above-average filly, effective 7f, acts on g-s to gd. Turf high 74 - 1st of 24 getting 8lb from Sari (15 May Newbury RF 1238).
**D Morris [1-11] Mason Racing Ltd.*

CINNAMON STICK (IRE) BHB 18f36a RR 13f 36a 4225[7]

6 ch g Don't Forget Me 9.5f **(66)** - Gothic Lady (Godswalk (USA)) 7.3f **(58)**
Form - 0877
Record 1999 - 1st:0 2nd:0 3rd:0 Ran:4
Pre1999 - 1st:0 2nd:0 3rd:0 Ran:11
1999 Turf 0-3: (12f, 16f, 17f) (g-f 2, frm) 1999 AW 0-1: (16f) (Fibr)
Poor gelding, has worn blinkers. Turf high 13.
**Mrs S Lamyman [0-5] Michael Robson (from M E Sowersby [1-3] May 1998).*

CINOLOGIST (IRE) RR 94f 3777a[3]

2 b c Sri Pekan (USA) - Wasmette (IRE) (Wassl) 9.7f **(62)**
Form - 3
1999 Turf 0-1: (7f) (gd)
Currently useful colt. (1st run) - 3rd of 7 giving 3lb to Castiya (13 Aug Vichy 7f gd RF 3777a). **D R Loder in FR [0-1].*

CIRCLE OF GOLD (IRE) BHB 107f RR 101f 979[14]

3 ch f Royal Academy (USA) 7.8f **(77)** - Never so Fair (Never so Bold) 6.3f **(66)**
Form - 30
Record 1999 - 1st:0 2nd:0 3rd:1 Ran:2
Pre1999 - 1st:2 2nd:1 3rd:0 Ran:4
Win Prizemoney £25,915 *Total Prizemoney* £32,950
Wins * 1998 Aug Goodwo (G-F) G3 7f 89
* 1998 Aug Newbur (G-F) 6f 90 <
1999 Turf 0-2: (7f, 8f) (g-f, frm)
Scopey, very useful filly, effective 6f, acts on frm, has worn blinkers. Turf high 101. A smart if slightly quirky juvenile, she shaped promisingly on her reappearance but cut no ice in the 1,000 Guineas. Not seen again.
**P W Chapple-Hyam [2-6] R E Sangster & Mrs B V Sangster.*

CIRCLE OF LIGHT RR 85+f 4236[8]

2 b f Anshan 8.2f **(63)** - Cockatoo Island (High Top) 10.2f **(67)**
Form - 18
Record 1999 - 1st:1 2nd:0 3rd:0 Ran:2
Win Prizemoney £2,165 *Total Prizemoney* £2,165
Wins * 1999 Aug Lingfi (G-F) 7.6f 85+ <
1999 Turf 1-2: (8f 1-2) (g-f 1-2)
Currently useful filly. Turf high 85 (1st run) (began Aug) - 1st of 16 getting 5lb from Water Jump (25 Aug Lingfield RF 3906). Absolutely bolted up in modest maiden at Lingfield on her debut, but ran too free in the May Hill and paid the penalty.
**P W D'Arcy [1-2] Lord Derby.*

CIRCUITEER (IRE) BHB 42f67a RR 43f 67a 4349[8]

4 ch g Pips Pride 6.7f **(70)** - Day Dress (Ashmore (FR)) 8.5f **(65)**
Form - 00400836728
Record 1999 - 1st:0 2nd:1 3rd:1 Ran:11
Pre1999 - 1st:3 2nd:2 3rd:3 Ran:16
Win Prizemoney £10,235 *Total Prizemoney* £14,260
Wins * 1998 *Jun Wolver (STD) H* *7f* *72* *75*
* 1998 May Pontef (G-F) H 8f 78 81
* 1998 May Mussel (GD) 7.1f 85 <
1999 Turf 0-9: (7f, 8f 8) (sft, gd, g-f 3, frm 4) 1999 AW 0-2: (7f, 8f) (Fibr 2)
Leggy, above-average gelding, effective 7 to 8f, best at 7f, acts on gd to frm - acts on Fibr, best on gd, has worn blinkers, likes right handed tracks, likes tight tracks. Turf high 43. AW high 70.
**J Berry [3-27] David Fish.*

CIRO (USA) RR 95f 4888a[1]

2 ch c Woodman (USA) 9.7f **(77)** - Gioconda (ARG) (Good Manners (USA))
Form - 211
1999 Turf 2-3: (7f, 8f 2-2) (hvy 1-1, sft 1-1, gd)
Currently very useful colt. Turf high 95 - 1st of 12 from Mythical Nature (7 Spt Galway RF 4300a) - also 1st of 3 from Barathea Guest (10 Oct Longchamp RF 4888a). He ran away with an ordinary maiden before being awarded a weak renewal of the Group One Grand Criterium on the controversial disqualification of Barathea Guest. Very much a staying type, he will stay middle-distances but could fall short of the top-class.
**A P O'Brien in IRE [2-3] M Tabor.*

CIRO'S PEARL (IRE) BHB 36f RR 37f 4922[7]

5 b m Petorius 8f **(66)** - Cut it Fine (USA) (Big Spruce (USA)) 11f **(71)**
Form - 80807
Record 1999 - 1st:0 2nd:0 3rd:0 Ran:5
Pre1999 - 1st:2 2nd:1 3rd:3 Ran:20
Win Prizemoney £8,067 *Total Prizemoney* £15,469
Wins 1997 Jun Goodwo (GD) H 12f 77 79 <
1997 May Lingfi (G-F) H 10f 74 78
1999 Turf 0-4: (12f 3, 16f) (gd 2, g-f, frm) 1999 AW 0-1: (12f) (Fibr)
Very moderate filly, effective 12f, acts on hrd, has worn blinkers. Turf high 37.
**A W Carroll [0-5] Mrs J Lewis (from M H Tompkins [2-20] Nov 1998).*

CITIZEN KANE (IRE) BHB 65f RR 66f 2716[14]

5 b g Sadler's Wells (USA) 11.3f **(87)** - Princess Tiara (Crowned Prince (USA)) 10.1f **(67)**
Form - 50
Record 1999 - 1st:0 2nd:0 3rd:0 Ran:2
Pre1999 - 1st:2 2nd:2 3rd:0 Ran:6
Win Prizemoney £7,535 *Total Prizemoney* £9,085
Wins 1997 Aug Leopar (G-S) H 10f 80 82 <
1997 Jly Killar (G-S) 11f 74
1999 Turf 0-2: (12f 2) (gd, frm)
Average gelding, has worn blinkers. Turf high 66.
**O Sherwood [1-12] Kenneth Kornfeld (from A P O'Brien in IRE [2-6] Aug 1997).*

CITY FLYER BHB 63f RR 74f 4934[4]

2 br c Night Shift (USA) 8.1f **(73)** - Al Guswa (Shernazar) 10.2f **(73)**
Form - 84584
Record 1999 - 1st:0 2nd:0 3rd:0 Ran:5
Win Prizemoney £0 *Total Prizemoney* £519
1999 Turf 0-5: (6f 3, 8f 2) (gd 2, g-f, frm 2)
Above-average colt. Turf high 74 - 4th of 16 giving 5lb to Zestril (23 Jun Carlisle 6f frm RF 2221). **J D Bethell [0-5] N D Fisher.*

CITY GAMBLER BHB 50f62a RR 51f 62a 4488[7]

5 b m Rock City 8.8f **(62)** - Sun Street (Ile de Bourbon (USA)) 10.1f **(67)**
Form - 00357580547
Record 1999 - 1st:0 2nd:0 3rd:1 Ran:11
Pre1999 - 1st:3 2nd:3 3rd:5 Ran:28
Win Prizemoney £9,463 *Total Prizemoney* £18,917
Wins * 1998 Aug Leices (GD) H 10f 57 62
* 1997 Aug Leices (GD) H 8f 67 73 <
* 1997 Aug Lingfi (G-F) 7.6f 57
1999 Turf 0-11: (8f 2, 10f 5, 11f, 12f 3) (g-s, gd 2, g-f 4, frm 4)
Fair filly, effective 10 to 12f, acts on gd to frm, best on frm, likes right handed tracks, prefers tight tracks, excels at Leicester, does well at Yarmouth. Turf high 60. Consistent.
**G C Bravery [3-39] J J May.*

CITY GOLF BAR (IRE) BHB 62f RR 60f 4820[16]

2 b c Namaqualand (USA) -Zalamera**(44f 39a)**(Rambo Dancer (CAN))
Form - 00600
Record 1999 - 1st:0 2nd:0 3rd:0 Ran:5
1999 Turf 0-5: (5f, 7f 3, 8f) (g-f 2, frm 3)
Average colt. Turf high 59. **W Jarvis [0-5] David Murrell.*

CITY GUILD BHB 56f RR 60f 1924[12]

3 b g Saddlers' Hall (IRE) 10.5f **(65)** - Indubitable (Sharpo) 7.7f **(59)**

Form - 0

Record	**1999** -	1st:0	2nd:0	3rd:0	Ran:1
	Pre1999 -	1st:0	2nd:0	3rd:0	Ran:3

Win Prizemoney £0 *Total Prizemoney* £353

1999 Turf 0-1: (11f) (frm)

Scopey, average gelding. **G B Balding [0-4] Miss B Swire.*

CITY OF GOLD (IRE) BHB 82f RR 76f 4771a[6]

3 b f Sadler's Wells (USA) 11.3f **(87)** - Northern Script (USA) (Arts And Letters (USA)) 12.7f **(68)**

Form - 16

Record	**1999** -	1st:1	2nd:0	3rd:0	Ran:2
	Pre1999 -	1st:1	2nd:0	3rd:0	Ran:1

Win Prizemoney £7,702 *Total Prizemoney* £7,702

Wins	* **1999**	Aug	Beverl	(GD)	12f	74	
	1998	Oct	Lingfi	(HVY)	7f	76	<

1999 Turf 1-2: (12f 1-1, 15f) (hvy, frm 1-1)

Scopey, currently above-average filly. Turf high 74 (1st run) (began Aug) - 1st of 5 getting 13lb from Minivet (28 Aug Beverley RF 3950). Winner of her only race as a juvenile, she came back from a ten-month absence to scrape home at Beverley in August. Tailed off in heavy ground in a Longchamp Group Two.

**J H M Gosden [1-2] (from D R Loder [1-1] Oct 1998).*

CITY ON A HILL (USA) RR 105+f 3932a[7]

2 ch c Rahy (USA) 9.1f **(80)** - Ville D'Amore (USA) (Irish River (FR)) 8.6f **(78)**

Form - 117

1999 Turf 2-3: (6f 2-3) (sft 1-1, gd, frm 1-1)

Currently Pattern-class colt. Turf high 105 - 1st of 7 giving 3lb to Mull Of Kintyre (7 Jly Newmarket RF 2629). He thrashed a classy field in the July Stakes, including Ballydoyle raider Mull Of Kintyre and Coventry runner-up Sir Nicholas. Having gone to post with a lovely relaxed attitude, he came back showing bags of speed. He failed to handle the heavy ground in the Prix Morny, but remains a colt of considerable potential, although Godolphin almost certainly had several better than him under wraps at their Evry base.

**D R Loder in FR [2-3] Godolphin.*

CITY PRINCESS BHB 68f61a RR 73f 61a 4923[6]

2 b f Rock City 8.8f **(62)** - Nordico Princess **(52f 67a)** (Nordico (USA)) 6.5f **(62)**

Form - 64011030206

Record	**1999** -	1st:2	2nd:1	3rd:1	Ran:11

Win Prizemoney £4,867 *Total Prizemoney* £6,656

Wins	* **1999**	Aug	Hamilt	(G-F)	S	5f	73	<
	* **1999**	Aug	Redcar	(FRM)	S	6f	58	

1999 Turf 2-10: (5f 1-5, 6f 1-4, 7f) (g-s, gd 3, g-f 1-4, frm 1-2) 1999 AW 0-1: (6f) (Fibr)

Above-average filly, effective 5 to 6f, acts on g-f to frm. Turf high 73 - 1st of 10 giving 6lb to Landfall Lil (11 Aug Hamilton RF 3541). Inconsistent. Has given trouble in the stalls, but has ability and won a couple of moderate events on fast ground during August. Good efforts since, she looks to need six furlongs now.

**M Dods [2-11] A G Watson.*

CITY PURSUIT BHB 56f RR 60f 624[11]

3 b c Pursuit of Love 9.5f **(69)** - Diabaig **(70f)** (Precocious) 8.6f **(62)**

Form - 0

Record	**1999** -	1st:0	2nd:0	3rd:0	Ran:1
	Pre1999 -	1st:0	2nd:0	3rd:0	Ran:2

Win Prizemoney £0 *Total Prizemoney* £256

1999 Turf 0-1: (10f) (gd)

Lengthy, currently average colt.

**J Pearce [0-3] Harvey White Partnership II.*

CITY REACH BHB 63f55a RR 71f 55a 4938[5]

3 b g Petong 7.6f **(58)** - Azola (IRE) (Alzao (USA)) 7.1f **(68)**

Form - 7065

Record	**1999** -	1st:0	2nd:0	3rd:0	Ran:4
	Pre1999 -	1st:0	2nd:1	3rd:0	Ran:1

Win Prizemoney £0 *Total Prizemoney* £1,288

1999 Turf 0-3: (8f 3) (sft, gd, frm) 1999 AW 0-1: (6f) (Fibr)

Scopey, above-average gelding. Turf high 61.

**P J Makin [0-5] T W Wellard Partnership.*

City On A Hill was an early success for the new Godolphin operation at Evry

CITY STANDARD (IRE) BHB 74f **RR 71f** 4331[9]
3 b c Rainbow Quest (USA) 11.2f **(81)** - City Fortress (Troy) 10.4f **(68)**
Form - 43370
Record 1999 - 1st:0 2nd:0 3rd:2 Ran:5
Win Prizemoney £0 *Total Prizemoney* £1,319
1999 Turf 0-5: (10f, 11f, 12f 2, 14f) (gd 3, frm 2)
Workmanlike, above-average colt, has worn blinkers. Turf high 71.
**Sir Michael Stoute [0-5] Lord Weinstock.*

CIVIL LIBERTY BHB 56f65a **RR 55f 65a** 4983[6]
6 b g Warning 8.1f **(77)** - Libertine (Hello Gorgeous (USA)) 9.7f **(63)**
Form - 676201246
Record 1999 - 1st:1 2nd:2 3rd:0 Ran:9
Pre1999 - 1st:2 2nd:4 3rd:0 Ran:20
Win Prizemoney £9,166 *Total Prizemoney* £16,997
Wins * 1999 *Spt Wolver (STD) H 9.4f 56 73*
1997 Spt Nottin (G-F) H 10f 60 64
1996 Aug Windso (G-F) 8.3f 79 <
1999 Turf 0-7: (8f, 9f 2, 10f 4) (g-s, gd, g-f 3, frm 2) 1999 AW 1-2: (9f 1-2) (Fibr 1-2)
Above-average gelding, effective 9f, - acts on Fibr, has worn blinkers, likes left handed tracks, likes tight tracks. Turf high 55. AW high 73 (1st run) (began Spt) - 1st of 13 getting 4lb from Haydn James (8 Spt Wolverhampton RF 4219). A fair sort in handicap company on turf, he was very impressive when making a successful Fibresand debut at Wolverhampton in September. He was not given the best of rides when only fourth at the same track the following month, and is still one to keep in mind when racing again on that surface.
**D Sasse [1-9] Christopher Ranson (from G Lewis [2-20] Oct 1997).*

CLADANTOM (IRE) BHB 60f **RR 68df** 4380[16]
3 b f High Estate 10.5f **(66)** - Riflebird (IRE) (Runnett) 7f **(59)**
Form - 72100
Record 1999 - 1st:1 2nd:1 3rd:0 Ran:5
Pre1999 - 1st:0 2nd:0 3rd:0 Ran:2
Win Prizemoney £4,238 *Total Prizemoney* £5,045
Wins * 1999 Jly Thirsk (FRM) 7f 68 <
1999 Turf 1-5: (7f 1-5) (gd 2, g-f, frm 1-2)
Leggy, average filly, effective 7f, acts on frm. Turf high 68 - 1st of 11 getting 5lb from Plutocrat (23 Jly Thirsk RF 3072). Gradually improving, she got off the mark in a Thirsk maiden in July under a hard ride, but suffered from a slipping saddle next time. Acts on fast ground.
**D W Barker [1-4] L H Gilmurray & T J Docherty (2) (from W Jarvis [0-1] May 1999).*

CLAIM GEBAL CLAIM BHB 38f51a **RR 39f 51a** 3817[6]
3 b g Ardkinglass 5f **(64)** - Infra Blue (IRE) **(35f)** (Bluebird (USA)) 7.5f **(69)**
Form - 25787546
Record 1999 - 1st:0 2nd:1 3rd:0 Ran:8
Pre1999 - 1st:0 2nd:0 3rd:3 Ran:8
Win Prizemoney £0 *Total Prizemoney* £1,919
1999 Turf 0-8: (5f, 6f 3, 7f 3, 10f) (sft, gd, g-f 2, frm 3, hrd)
Neat, very moderate gelding, effective 5 to 6f, acts on gd to g-f, has worn blinkers. Turf high 55. Consistent.
**Mrs A Swinbank [0-16] Stan Moffat.*

CLAIRESWAN (IRE) BHB 42f48a **RR 40?f 48a** 904[11]
7 ch g Rhoman Rule (USA) 15.1f **(64)** - Choclate Baby (Kashiwa)
Form - 50
Record 1999 - 1st:0 2nd:0 3rd:0 Ran:2
Pre1999 - 1st:4 2nd:1 3rd:0 Ran:14
Win Prizemoney £11,070 *Total Prizemoney* £11,777
Wins 1995 *Aug Lingfi (STD) H 16f 54 64* <
1995 Aug Ayr (G-F) H 15f 55 63
1995 *Jly Wolver (STD) H 16.2f 49 60*
1995 Jly Hamilt (FRM) H 13f 49 56
1999 Turf 0-1: (22f) (gd) 1999 AW 0-1: (16f) (Fibr)
Moderate gelding, has worn blinkers. Becoming disappointing.
**Mrs N Macauley [0-2] G Wiltshire (from M H Tompkins [2-14] Oct 1997).*

CLANBLUE CHICK BHB 40f **RR 7f** 2175[20]
4 b f Clantime 6.6f **(57)** - Lavenham Blue (Streetfighter) 6f **(56)**
Form - 0
Record 1999 - 1st:0 2nd:0 3rd:0 Ran:1
Pre1999 - 1st:0 2nd:0 3rd:0 Ran:5
1999 Turf 0-1: (6f) (frm)
Light-framed, moderate filly.
**P D Evans [0-1] Aled Griffiths (from J Berry [0-5] May 1998).*

CLANDESTINE RR 91f 4209[9]
3 b f Saddlers' Hall (IRE) 10.5f **(65)** - Fleeting Affair (Hotfoot) 10.5f **(59)**
Form - 4160
Record 1999 - 1st:1 2nd:0 3rd:0 Ran:4
Win Prizemoney £3,915 *Total Prizemoney* £4,169
Wins * 1999 Aug Haydoc (SFT) 11.9f 85 <
1999 Turf 1-4: (12f 1-3, 15f) (gd 1-4)
Well made, useful filly. Turf high 91 - 6th of 8 getting 10lb from Innuendo (19 Aug York 12f gd RF 3771) - also 1st of 14 getting 5lb from Dark Trojan (7 Aug Haydock RF 3448). Won a maiden at Haydock over 12 furlongs in soft ground on her second start, but was well held in Pattern company.
**J H M Gosden [1-4] Cheveley Park Stud.*

CLANSMAN BHB 65f **RR 62f** 4072[5]
2 ch g Clantime 6.6f **(57)** - Chili Lass **(8f)** (Chilibang)
Form - 5045
Record 1999 - 1st:0 2nd:0 3rd:0 Ran:4
Win Prizemoney £0 *Total Prizemoney* £275
1999 Turf 0-4: (5f 3, 6f) (g-f 2, frm 2)
Average gelding. Turf high 62 (began Jly). **T R Watson [0-4] J Rose.*

CLANTYRE BHB 40f **RR 34f** 1878[14]
3 b c Clantime 6.6f **(57)** - Tyrian Belle (Enchantment) 5.4f **(52)**
Form - 4070
Record 1999 - 1st:0 2nd:0 3rd:0 Ran:4
Pre1999 - 1st:0 2nd:0 3rd:0 Ran:3
Win Prizemoney £0 *Total Prizemoney* £198
1999 Turf 0-4: (5f 2, 6f 2) (sft, gd, g-f 2)
Scopey, very moderate colt, has worn blinkers. Turf high 38.
**Miss J F Craze [0-1] The Mathieson Partnership (from M Johnston [0-6] May 1999).*

CLARA BLUE BHB 42f **RR 25f** 5032[22]
3 gr f Alhijaz 7.7f **(57)** - Hazy Kay (IRE) (Treasure Kay)
Form - 00U0000
Record 1999 - 1st:0 2nd:0 3rd:0 Ran:7
Pre1999 - 1st:1 2nd:0 3rd:0 Ran:7
Win Prizemoney £2,070 *Total Prizemoney* £2,070
Wins 1998 Oct Folkes (G-S) 5f 76 <
1999 Turf 0-7: (5f 6, 6f) (sft, g-s, gd 2, g-f 2, frm)
Neat, little account filly, effective 5f, acts on g-s. Turf high 41.
**R Ingram [0-5] Epsom Sporting Proposals Ltd (from T D McCarthy [1-9] May 1999).*

CLARANET RR 74f 5108[4]
2 ch f Arazi (USA) 9.2f **(74)** - Carmita (Caerleon (USA)) 8.6f **(71)**
Form - 34
Record 1999 - 1st:0 2nd:0 3rd:1 Ran:2
Win Prizemoney £0 *Total Prizemoney* £796
1999 Turf 0-2: (8f 2) (gd 2)
Currently above-average filly. Turf high 74 (began Oct).
**K Mahdi [0-2] Greenfield Stud.*

CLARANNA BHB 51f **RR 51f** 865[7]
3 b f Local Suitor (USA) 9.7f **(58)** - Zolica (Beveled (USA)) 9f **(59)**
Form - 507
Record 1999 - 1st:0 2nd:0 3rd:0 Ran:3
Pre1999 - 1st:1 2nd:2 3rd:1 Ran:6
Win Prizemoney £4,992 *Total Prizemoney* £6,381
Wins * 1998 Jun Newcas (G-S) S 6f 65 <
1999 Turf 0-3: (6f 3) (sft, gd 2)
Unfurnished, fair filly, effective 5 to 6f, best at 6f, acts on g-s to gd, best on gd. Turf high 51. Inconsistent.
**R A Fahey [1-9] Miss M J Barber.*

CLARENDON (IRE) BHB 77f **RR 76f** 5031[9]
3 ch c Forest Wind (USA) - Sparkish (IRE) (Persian Bold) 9.3f **(66)**
Form - 411300
Record 1999 - 1st:2 2nd:0 3rd:1 Ran:6
Pre1999 - 1st:0 2nd:0 3rd:0 Ran:8

Win Prizemoney £12,234 *Total Prizemoney* £14,296
Wins *** 1999** Jly Ascot (G-F) H 10f 69 73 <
*** 1999** Jun Chepst (G-F) H 10.2f 62 65+
1999 Turf 2-6: (9f, 10f 2-5) (g-s, gd 1-1, g-f 1-3, frm)
Well made, above-average colt, effective 10f, acts on gd to g-f, has worn blinkers, likes tight tracks. Turf high 76 - 3rd of 13 getting 6lb from Backcloth (12 Aug Sandown 10f g-f RF 3580) - also 1st of 10 getting 15lb from Penang Pearl (23 Jly Ascot RF 3050). Progressive sort, winner of competitive handicaps at Chester and Ascot in the summer, before his form tailed off. Needs fast ground.
**V Soane [2-6] Mrs Jane Gillett (from J D Bethell [0-8] Nov 1998).*

CLARINCH CLAYMORE BHB 52f **RR 55f** 4347[2]
3 b g Sabrehill (USA) 8.5f **(64)** - Salu **(58f)** (Ardross) 10.6f **(68)**
Form - 00034142
Record **1999** - 1st:1 2nd:1 3rd:1 Ran:8
Pre1999 - 1st:0 2nd:0 3rd:0 Ran:4
Win Prizemoney £2,979 *Total Prizemoney* £4,300
Wins *** 1999** Aug Beverl (GD) H 8.5f 47 55 <
1999 Turf 1-8: (8f 1-2, 9f 2, 10f, 11f 2, 12f) (g-s, gd, g-f 1-3, frm 3)
Scopey, fair gelding, effective 8 to 11f, best at 11f, acts on gd to g-f, best on g-f, prefers tight tracks. Turf high 55 - 1st of 12 getting 32lb from Blooming Amazing (12 Aug Beverley RF 3565).
**J M Jefferson [1-12] John Donald.*

CLASSIC COLOURS (USA) BHB 36f34a **RR 35f 34a** 5151[13]
6 ch g Blushing John (USA) 8.9f **(75)** - All Agleam (USA) (Gleaming (USA)) 11.5f **(75)**
Form - 046238000
Record **1999** - 1st:0 2nd:1 3rd:1 Ran:8
Pre1999 - 1st:0 2nd:2 3rd:2 Ran:19
Win Prizemoney £0 *Total Prizemoney* £5,371
1999 Turf 0-6: (8f, 10f 2, 11f 3) (sft, gd 2, g-f 2, frm) 1999 AW 0-2: (9f, 12f) (Fibr 2)
Very moderate gelding, effective 8 to 11f, acts on gd to frm, has worn blinkers, favours left handed tracks. Turf high 59 (1st run) - 2nd of 19 getting 17lb from Swift (5 Apr Warwick 11f gd RF 0596). AW high 32. Becoming disappointing.
**G H Yardley [0-21] Philip Jones (from R Harris [0-5] Spt 1996).*

CLASSIC CONKERS (IRE) BHB 34f **RR 46f** 5101[14]
5 b g Conquering Hero (USA) 10.6f **(50)** - Erck (Sun Prince) 12.4f **(52)**
Form - 00486075460
Record **1999** - 1st:0 2nd:0 3rd:0 Ran:11
Pre1999 - 1st:1 2nd:1 3rd:0 Ran:10
Win Prizemoney £2,005 *Total Prizemoney* £2,771
Wins * 1998 Oct Yarmou (G-S) SH 11.5f 45 49 <
1999 Turf 0-11: (10f 2, 11f, 12f 3, 14f 4, 16f) (g-s, gd 4, g-f 2, frm 4)
Moderate gelding, effective 11 to 14f, acts on g-s to g-f, likes left handed tracks, likes tight tracks. Turf high 46.
**Pat Mitchell [1-21] Classic Bloodstock Plc.*

CLASSIC EAGLE BHB 56f **RR 46f** 5125[4]
6 b g Unfuwain (USA) 11.4f **(74)** - La Lutine (My Swallow) 9.2f **(71)**
Form - 704
Record **1999** - 1st:0 2nd:0 3rd:0 Ran:3
Pre1999 - 1st:1 2nd:0 3rd:0 Ran:10
Win Prizemoney £3,855 *Total Prizemoney* £4,501
Wins 1995 Oct Chepst (SFT) 8.1f 91? <
1999 Turf 0-3: (8f, 10f, 12f) (gd 3)
Moderate gelding. Turf high 46 (began Oct).
**Pat Mitchell [0-3] Classic Bloodstock Plc (from I Campbell [0-2] Oct 1997).*

CLASSIC FIGHTER (IRE) BHB 29f **RR 13f** 2276[10]
3 ch g Up and At 'em - Classic Choice (Patch) 11.5f **(51)**
Form - 60700
Record **1999** - 1st:0 2nd:0 3rd:0 Ran:5
Pre1999 - 1st:0 2nd:0 3rd:0 Ran:2
1999 Turf 0-3: (7f, 8f, 10f) (gd, g-f, frm) 1999 AW 0-2: (8f 2) (Fibr 2)
Scopey, very moderate gelding. Turf high 13. AW high 32.
**J J Sheehan [0-7] P J Sheehan.*

CLASSIC IMPACT (IRE) BHB 76f **RR 79?f** 5028[16]
4 ch g Generous (IRE) 11.5f **(82)** - Vaison la Romaine (Arctic Tern (USA)) 8.9f **(69)**
Form - 0
Record **1999** - 1st:0 2nd:0 3rd:0 Ran:1
Pre1999 - 1st:1 2nd:2 3rd:0 Ran:9
Win Prizemoney £3,571 *Total Prizemoney* £6,951
Wins 1998 Jun Newbur (HVY) H 12f 70 72 <
1999 Turf 0-1: (16f) (g-s)
Scopey, above-average gelding, effective 11 to 12f, best at 12f, acts on g-s to frm, best on gd.
**P G Murphy [0-4] J M Brown & M J Blackburn (from P W Chapple-Hyam [1-9] Oct 1998).*

CLASSIC LORD BHB 59f **RR 63f** 4828[7]
2 b c Wolfhound (USA) 7.3f **(71)** - Janaat (Kris) 9.5f **(73)**
Form - 25507
Record **1999** - 1st:0 2nd:1 3rd:0 Ran:5
Win Prizemoney £0 *Total Prizemoney* £1,056
1999 Turf 0-5: (7f 3, 8f 2) (sft, gd 2, g-f, frm)
Average colt, has worn blinkers. Turf high 77.
**M Johnston [0-5] Maktoum Al Maktoum.*

CLASSIC MANOEUVRE (USA) BHB 65f68a **RR 60f 68a** 1816[7]
4 ch g Sky Classic (CAN) 10f **(83)** - Maid of Honor (USA) (Blushing Groom (FR)) 10.3f **(76)**
Form - 7
Record **1999** - 1st:0 2nd:0 3rd:0 Ran:1
Pre1999 - 1st:0 2nd:2 3rd:4 Ran:12
Win Prizemoney £0 *Total Prizemoney* £7,317
1999 Turf 0-1: (12f) (g-f)
Neat, average gelding, effective 10 to 11f, best at 10f, acts on gd, has worn blinkers. Consistent.
**M C Pipe [0-1] Paul & Jenny Green (from R Hannon [0-12] Oct 1998).*

CLASSIC MASQUERADE (CAN) BHB 47f **RR 50f** 1193[16]
4 b g Regal Classic (CAN) - Muskoka Command (USA) (Top Command (USA)) 10f **(77)**
Form - 0
Record **1999** - 1st:0 2nd:0 3rd:0 Ran:1
Pre1999 - 1st:0 2nd:0 3rd:0 Ran:6
Win Prizemoney £0 *Total Prizemoney* £696
1999 Turf 0-1: (12f) (frm)
Scopey, fair gelding.
**M C Pipe [0-4] Paul & Jenny Green (from R Hannon [0-6] Aug 1998).*

CLASSIC REFERENDUM (IRE) BHB 57f **RR 28f** 5168[14]
5 ch g Classic Music (USA) 7.2f **(57)** - My Alanna (Dalsaan) 9.8f **(64)**
Form - 112278000
Record **1999** - 1st:2 2nd:2 3rd:0 Ran:9
Pre1999 - 1st:0 2nd:3 3rd:3 Ran:10
Win Prizemoney £6,359 *Total Prizemoney* £12,241
Wins **1999** Jun Wexfor (G-F) H 13f 63 74+
1999 Jun Leopar (G-S) 14f 78 <
1999 Turf 2-9: (12f 2, 13f 1-1, 14f 1-6) (g-s 2, gd 1-4, g-f 1-2, frm)
Little account gelding, effective 12 to 14f, best at 14f, acts on gd to g-f, best on gd, has worn blinkers. Turf high 85 - 2nd of 11 giving 15lb to Halcyon (11 Jly Curragh 12f g-f RF 2797a) - also 1st of 14 from Beneficent (7 Jun Leopardstown RF 2015a). Becoming disappointing. Formerly trained in Ireland and won twice over there in June. Now with Barney Curley, he has not shown much since arriving here, but is still one to watch.
**B J Curley [0-5] Mrs B J Curley (from L Browne in IRE [2-4] Jly 1999).*

CLASS WAN BHB 72f **RR 57f** 731[18]
3 ch f Safawan 6.6f **(60)** - Ayr Classic (Local Suitor (USA)) 8.4f **(67)**
Form - 00
Record **1999** - 1st:0 2nd:0 3rd:0 Ran:2
Pre1999 - 1st:2 2nd:0 3rd:0 Ran:9
Win Prizemoney £6,638 *Total Prizemoney* £6,830
Wins * 1998 Oct Ayr (G-S) H 6f 67 76 <
* 1998 Aug Mussel (G-F) H 5f 66 71
1999 Turf 0-2: (6f, 7f) (gd 2)
Light-framed, fair filly, effective 5 to 6f, acts on sft to gd. Turf high 53. Consistent. **J S Goldie [2-11] The Jersey Syndicate.*

CLASSY CLEO (IRE) BHB 86f93a **RR 83f 93a** 5160[1]
4 b f Mujadil (USA) 7.7f **(70)** - Sybaris(Crowned Prince (USA))10.1f **(67)**
Form - 345667050203437883275875552321

Record 1999 - 1st:1 2nd:5 3rd:5 Ran:32
Pre1999 - 1st:9 2nd:9 3rd:5 Ran:41
Win Prizemoney £48,136 *Total Prizemoney* £82,382
Wins * **1999** Nov Redcar (G-S) H 6f 82 83
* 1998 Nov Redcar (G-S) H 6f 90 93
* 1998 Jly Cheste (G-F) H 5.1f 85 88
* 1998 May Cheste (GD) H 5.1f 85 87
* *1997 Nov Lingfi (STD) H 5f 87 105* <
* *1997 Nov Southw (STD) H 6f 87 86*
* 1997 Oct Yarmou (FRM) H 5.2f 79 86
1997 Spt Haydoc (G-S) C 6f 68
1997 Apr Pontef (GD) 5f 79
1997 Apr Beverl (G-F) 5f 79
1999 Turf 1-25: (5f 10, 6f 1-14, 7f) (g-s 2, gd 8, g-f 6, frm 1-9) 1999 AW 0-7: (5f 2, 6f 2, 7f 3) (Equi 2, Fibr 5)
Unfurnished, very useful filly, effective 5 to 7f, best at 7f, acts on sft to frm - acts on AW, best on Equi, likes left handed tracks, likes tight tracks, excels at Lingfield and Redcar and likes Wolverhampton. Turf high 87. AW high 95 - 4th of 11 giving 7lb to Italian Symphony (17 Feb Wolverhampton 7f Fibr RF 0305). Vigorously campaigned - as are most of her stablemates - she is a tough sprint handicapper who acts on any ground, including the All-Weather. A suitable mount for inexperienced riders, she will win again.
**P D Evans [7-63] J E Abbey (from R Hannon [3-10] Spt 1997).*

CLAUDIUS BHB 43f **RR 30f** 3459[18]
3 b g Clantime 6.6f **(57)** - Pokey's Pet (Uncle Pokey) 10.1f **(49)**
Form - 000
Record 1999 - 1st:0 2nd:0 3rd:0 Ran:3
Pre1999 - 1st:0 2nd:0 3rd:0 Ran:4
Win Prizemoney £0 *Total Prizemoney* £241
1999 Turf 0-3: (6f 2, 8f) (frm 3)
Strong, very moderate gelding. Turf high 30.
**K A Ryan [0-3] Mrs Rosie Richer (from R A Fahey [0-4] Spt 1998).*

CLAUDIUS TERTIUS BHB 49f **RR 62f** 5158[24]
2 b g Rudimentary (USA) 8.2f **(66)** - Sanctuary Cove (Habitat) 9.4f **(70)**
Form - 87080
Record 1999 - 1st:0 2nd:0 3rd:0 Ran:5
1999 Turf 0-5: (7f 3, 8f 2) (sft, gd, g-f 2, frm)
Average gelding. Turf high 62. **M A Jarvis [0-5] R L Capon.*

CLAXON BHB 108f **RR 106+f** 1729[5]
3 b f Caerleon (USA) 10.9f **(79)** - Bulaxie **(103f)** (Bustino) 10.4f **(64)**
Form - 115
Record 1999 - 1st:2 2nd:0 3rd:0 Ran:3
Pre1999 - 1st:1 2nd:1 3rd:1 Ran:3
Win Prizemoney £36,359 *Total Prizemoney* £41,049
Wins * **1999** May Goodwo (GD) L 9.9f 106 <
* **1999** Apr Kempto (GD) L 8f 101
* 1998 Oct Ayr (SFT) 8f 82
1999 Turf 2-3: (8f 1-1, 10f 1-1, 12f) (gd 1-2, g-f 1-1)
Scopey, Pattern-class filly, effective 8 to 10f, acts on gd to g-f. Turf high 106 - 1st of 8 giving 3lb to Musical Treat (19 May Goodwood RF 1331) - also 1st of 8 from Alabaq (3 Apr Kempton RF 0569). The first foal of a very useful racemare, she made all for clear-cut victories in listed races at Kempton (Masaka) and Goodwood (Lupe) on her first two starts. She had looked likely to stay the mile and a half of the Oaks, but appeared to run out of stamina, and was not seen again. **J L Dunlop [3-6] Hesmonds Stud.*

CLEAR CRYSTAL BHB 65f **RR 75f** 3912[8]
2 b f Zilzal (USA) 8.5f **(79)** - Shoot Clear (Bay Express) 7.1f **(60)**
Form - 568
Record 1999 - 1st:0 2nd:0 3rd:0 Ran:3
1999 Turf 0-3: (7f 3) (gd 2, g-f)
Currently above-average filly. Turf high 75 (began Jly).
**R M H Cowell [0-3] J B Robinson.*

CLEAR MOON (IRE) BHB 58f **RR 56f** 5164[3]
2 b c Lake Coniston (IRE) - Tenea (Reform) 8.9f **(62)**
Form - 00063
Record 1999 - 1st:0 2nd:0 3rd:1 Ran:5
Win Prizemoney £0 *Total Prizemoney* £550
1999 Turf 0-5: (5f 2, 6f 3) (g-s, gd 2, frm 2)
Fair colt. Turf high 56 (began Aug).
**Miss L A Perratt [0-5] C D Barber-Lomax.*

CLEAR NIGHT BHB 55f48a **RR 50f 48a** 3738[9]
3 b c Night Shift (USA) 8.1f **(73)** - Clarista (USA) (Riva Ridge (USA)) 8.2f **(68)**
Form - 000071060
Record 1999 - 1st:1 2nd:0 3rd:0 Ran:9
Pre1999 - 1st:0 2nd:0 3rd:1 Ran:4
Win Prizemoney £2,346 *Total Prizemoney* £3,176
Wins 1999 Jun Chepst (G-F) S 8.1f 63 <
1999 Turf 1-9: (6f 2, 7f 4, 8f 1-2, 9f) (g-s 2, gd, g-f 1-5, frm)
Workmanlike, fair colt, effective 6f, acts on g-f, has worn blinkers. Turf high 63. Inconsistent. Appreciated the step up in trip to a mile when winning a modest affair at Chepstow on good to firm ground.
**J J Sheehan [0-3] Mrs Eileen Sheehan (from R Hannon [1-10] Jun 1999).*

CLEAR PROSPECT (USA) BHB 84f **RR 82f** 4818[3]
2 b c Virginia Rapids (USA) - Cameo Performance (USA) (Be My Guest (USA)) 9.3f **(67)**
Form - 643
Record 1999 - 1st:0 2nd:0 3rd:1 Ran:3
Win Prizemoney £0 *Total Prizemoney* £1,241
1999 Turf 0-3: (7f, 8f, 10f) (gd, g-f, frm)
Currently decent colt. Turf high 82 (began Jly) - 3rd of 8 getting 2lb from Bow Strada (11 Oct Leicester 10f gd RF 4818). Sold for 40,000 gns at Tattersalls in October.
**A G Foster [0-1] R E Sangster & H Lester (from P W Chapple-Hyam [0-2] Spt 1999).*

CLEF OF SILVER BHB 87f **RR 84f** 797[12]
4 b c Indian Ridge 7.6f **(74)** - Susquehanna Days (USA) (Chief's Crown (USA)) 9.8f **(72)**
Form - 0
Record 1999 - 1st:0 2nd:0 3rd:0 Ran:1
Pre1999 - 1st:2 2nd:4 3rd:0 Ran:9
Win Prizemoney £5,266 *Total Prizemoney* £13,476
Wins * 1998 Oct Catter (gd,) 6f 74
* 1997 Aug Catter (G-F) H 6f 80 85 <
1999 Turf 0-1: (6f) (g-s)
Workmanlike, decent colt. Consistent.
**W Jarvis [2-10] Silver Clef Racing Venture.*

CLEVER CITATION (USA) **RR 80f** 4952[5]
2 b c Chief's Crown (USA) 10.2f **(75)** - Besha (USA) (Turkoman (USA))
Form - 35
Record 1999 - 1st:0 2nd:0 3rd:1 Ran:2
Win Prizemoney £0 *Total Prizemoney* £565
1999 Turf 0-2: (6f, 7f) (gd, g-f)
Currently decent colt. Turf high 80 (1st run) (began Spt) - 3rd of 12 giving 5lb to Shannon Dore (25 Spt Nottingham 6f gd RF 4560).
**Sir Michael Stoute [0-2] Ivan Allan.*

CLEVER GIRL (IRE) BHB 90f **RR 90f** 5213[5]
2 b f College Chapel - Damezao (Alzao (USA)) 7.1f **(68)**
Form - 653161215
Record 1999 - 1st:3 2nd:1 3rd:1 Ran:9
Win Prizemoney £11,260 *Total Prizemoney* £13,784
Wins * **1999** Oct Ayr (SFT) H 8f 82 90 <
* **1999** Jly Ayr (GD) H 7f 77
* **1999** Jun Pontef (G-S) 6f 65
1999 Turf 3-9: (5f 2, 6f 1-2, 7f 1-3, 8f 1-2) (sft 1-1, g-s, gd, g-f 2-3, frm 3)
Useful filly, effective 8f, acts on sft. Turf high 90 - 1st of 11 giving 13lb to Papi Special (12 Oct Ayr RF 4828). Winner of a Pontefract median auction event and two Ayr nurseries so far, she looks best on easy ground. **T D Easterby [3-9] Peter Bourke.*

CLIPPER **RR 76f** 4827[1]
2 b f Salse (USA) 10.9f **(71)** - Yawl **(93f)** (Rainbow Quest (USA)) 10.4f **(75)**
Form - 71
Record 1999 - 1st:1 2nd:0 3rd:0 Ran:2
Win Prizemoney £3,574 *Total Prizemoney* £3,574
Wins * **1999** Oct Ayr (SFT) 8f 76 <
1999 Turf 1-2: (7f, 8f 1-1) (sft 1-1, gd)
Currently above-average filly. Turf high 76 (began Spt) - 1st of 6 from Sabreon (12 Oct Ayr RF 4827). From a staying family, she

looks suited by soft ground and will get middle distances at three.
**B W Hills [1-2] R D Hollingsworth.*

CLOAK OF DARKNESS (IRE) BHB 85f **RR 88f** 3696[14]
4 b g Thatching 7.8f **(69)** - Madame Nureyev (USA) (Nureyev (USA)) 8.7f **(78)**
Form - 0614420
Record 1999 - 1st:1 2nd:1 3rd:0 Ran:7
Pre1999 - 1st:1 2nd:0 3rd:2 Ran:9
Win Prizemoney £7,792 *Total Prizemoney* £12,844
Wins * 1999 Jun Windso (SFT) H 10f 81 83 <
* 1998 Jun Windso (G-F) 10f 83 <
1999 Turf 1-7: (10f 1-5, 12f 2) (gd 1-1, g-f 4, frm 2)
Workmanlike, useful gelding, effective 10 to 12f, best at 10f, acts on gd to frm, best on frm, excels at Newmarket and Kempton and Windsor. Turf high 88 - 2nd of 8 giving 9lb to Forest Fire (16 Jly Newmarket 10f frm RF 2884) - also 1st of 8 giving 19lb to Gypsy Hill (7 Jun Windsor RF 1802). Consistent. Made all to score on soft ground at Windsor in June, but was less effective when ridden more patiently on his next two starts. Performed well at Newmarket when ridden up with the pace, tactics which seem to compensate for a lack of toe. Has joined David Nicholls.
**R Hannon [2-16] Mohamed Suhail.*

CLODION (IRE) RR 99f 1293[3]
3 b c Nikos - Didia Clara (FR) (Sea Break)
Form - 3
Record 1999 - 1st:0 2nd:0 3rd:1 Ran:1
Win Prizemoney £0 *Total Prizemoney* £3,000
1999 Turf 0-1: (10f) (gd)
Scopey, currently very useful colt. He should stay beyond a mile and a quarter, but missed the second half of the campaign and may have a problem. **S bin Suroor [0-1] Godolphin.*

CLOG DANCE RR 99f 4920[2]
2 b f Pursuit of Love 9.5f **(69)** - Discomatic (USA) (Roberto (USA)) 10f **(76)**
Form - 32
Record 1999 - 1st:0 2nd:1 3rd:1 Ran:2
Win Prizemoney £0 *Total Prizemoney* £8,962
1999 Turf 0-2: (7f, 8f) (gd 2)
Currently very useful filly. Turf high 99 (began Spt) - 2nd of 12 to Lahan (16 Oct Newmarket 7f gd RF 4920). A big, scopey filly, she finished strongly when narrowly thwarted in the Group 2 Rockfel Stakes at Newmarket in October. A half-sister to the Ebor winner Tuning, she has a bright future and could develop into an Oaks contender. **B W Hills [0-2] K Abdulla.*

CLOHAMON BHB 37f43a **RR 18f 43a** 2678[8]
4 b g Aragon 7.7f **(58)** - Almadaniyah (Dunbeath (USA)) 7.8f **(70)**
Form - 0000008
Record 1999 - 1st:0 2nd:0 3rd:0 Ran:4
Pre1999 - 1st:0 2nd:0 3rd:0 Ran:7
Win Prizemoney £0 *Total Prizemoney* £204
1999 Turf 0-4: (5f 2, 6f 2) (gd, frm 3)
Leggy, poor gelding, has worn blinkers. Turf high 18.
**M A Peill [0-3] C N Barnes (from S E Kettlewell [0-8] Apr 1999).*

CLONMANY (IRE) BHB 91f **RR 86f** 4760[4]
2 ch c Petardia 8.2f **(58)** - Romangoddess (IRE) (Rhoman Rule (USA))
Form - 8221434
Record 1999 - 1st:1 2nd:2 3rd:1 Ran:7
Win Prizemoney £7,475 *Total Prizemoney* £12,353
Wins * 1999 Jly Goodwo (FRM) 7f 86+ <
1999 Turf 1-7: (5f, 7f 1-5, 8f) (gd, g-f 1-5, frm)
Useful colt, effective 7f, acts on gd to g-f. Turf high 86 - 4th of 6 to Zoning (7 Oct York 7f gd RF 4760) - also 1st of 3 from Compton Bolter (31 Jly Goodwood RF 3263). Sold to continue his career in America. **R Hannon [1-7] The South-Western Partnership.*

CLONOE BHB 43f36a **RR 31f 36a** 5035[21]
5 b g Syrtos 8.1f **(57)** - Anytime Anywhere (Daring March) 7.1f **(61)**
Form - 0271250038000017060
Record 1999 - 1st:2 2nd:2 3rd:1 Ran:18
Pre1999 - 1st:2 2nd:3 3rd:5 Ran:27
Win Prizemoney £9,983 *Total Prizemoney* £16,323
Wins * 1999 Jly Folkes (G-F) H 7f 39 48 <
*** 1999** *Jan Lingfi (STD) H 10f 37 43*
* 1998 Aug Kempto (G-F) H 8f 43 46
* 1998 Apr Folkes (SFT) H 6f 36 47?
1999 Turf 1-11: (6f, 7f 1-6, 8f 4) (g-s, g-f 1-4, frm 5, hrd) 1999 AW 1-7: (7f, 8f 4, 10f 1-2) (Equi 1-7)
Moderate gelding, effective 6 to 10f, acts on sft to frm - acts on AW, has worn blinkers, and excels at Folkestone. Turf high 48 - 1st of 14 getting 6lb from Muddy Water (26 Jly Folkestone RF 3142). AW high 43 - 1st of 11 getting 3lb from Mendoza (21 Jan Lingfield RF 0133). **R Ingram [4-45] P McKernan.*

CLOSER NOW (USA) RR 51f 4430[10]
2 b c Distant View (USA) - Stageira (CAN) (Halo (USA)) 10.6f **(75)**
Form - 00
Record 1999 - 1st:0 2nd:0 3rd:0 Ran:2
1999 Turf 0-2: (7f, 8f) (g-s, g-f)
Currently fair colt. Turf high 51 (began Aug).
**P W Chapple-Hyam [0-2] R Barnett.*

CLOTH OF GOLD RR 48f 5208[15]
2 b c Barathea (IRE) - Bustinetta (Bustino) 10.4f **(64)**
Form - 0
Record 1999 - 1st:0 2nd:0 3rd:0 Ran:1
1999 Turf 0-1: (7f) (g-s)
Currently moderate colt. **Lady Herries [0-1] Mrs H A Cameron-Rose.*

CLOTTED CREAM (USA) RR 80f 4531[3]
2 gr f Eagle Eyed (USA) - Seattle Victory (USA) (Seattle Song (USA)) 9f **(77)**
Form - 03
Record 1999 - 1st:0 2nd:0 3rd:1 Ran:2
Win Prizemoney £0 *Total Prizemoney* £437
1999 Turf 0-2: (5f, 6f) (g-s, g-f)
Currently decent filly. Turf high 80 (began Aug) - 3rd of 17 to Inventive (24 Spt Lingfield 5f g-s RF 4531).
**P J Makin [0-2] Dr Carlos Stelling.*

CLOUD INSPECTOR (IRE) BHB 30f40a **RR 49df 40a** 4932[5]
8 b g Persian Bold 10f **(69)** - Timbale d'Argent (Petingo) 11f **(72)**
Form - 0060005
Record 1999 - 1st:0 2nd:0 3rd:0 Ran:7
Pre1999 - 1st:2 2nd:5 3rd:1 Ran:14
Win Prizemoney £20,936 *Total Prizemoney* £36,388
Wins * 1997 Aug Dielsd (GD) 15f 89+ <
* 1997 Jly Goodwo (G-F) H 20f 75 82
1999 Turf 0-6: (14f 3, 16f 2, 18f) (g-f 4, frm 2) 1999 AW 0-1: (14f) (Fibr)
Moderate gelding, effective 14 to 16f, acts on sft to g-f, has worn blinkers. Turf high 59. **M Johnston [2-21] Markus Graff.*

CLOUDS OF GLORY BHB 30f40a **RR 14f 40a** 2132[18]
4 b f Lycius (USA) 8.8f **(71)** - Dance a Jig (Dance In Time (CAN)) 8.9f **(59)**
Form - 000000
Record 1999 - 1st:0 2nd:0 3rd:0 Ran:6
Pre1999 - 1st:0 2nd:0 3rd:0 Ran:8
1999 Turf 0-3: (8f 2, 12f) (gd, frm, hrd) 1999 AW 0-3: (7f, 8f, 11f)(Fibr 3)
Moderate filly, effective 8f, acts on frm, has worn blinkers, likes left handed tracks, likes tight tracks. Turf high 14. AW high 26. Inconsistent. **J Norton [0-6] J Norton (from R Charlton [0-8] Jly 1998).*

CLOUDY SKY (IRE) BHB 99f **RR 102f** 4674[7]
3 b c Sadler's Wells (USA) 11.3f **(87)** - Dancing Shadow (Dancers Image (USA)) 9.3f **(71)**
Form - 2147
Record 1999 - 1st:1 2nd:1 3rd:0 Ran:4
Win Prizemoney £4,455 *Total Prizemoney* £6,490
Wins * 1999 Jun Sandow (GD) 10f 93 <
1999 Turf 1-4: (8f, 10f 1-2, 12f) (gd 2, g-f, frm 1-1)
Scopey, very useful colt. Turf high 102 - also 1st of 16 from Marnor (1 Jun Sandown RF 1660). He had a hard race when winning a maiden at Sandown in May and was promptly given a three-and-a-half-month holiday. Slightly disappointing when pitted against decent opposition in the autumn, he has plenty of scope and should win a race or two in 2000.
**Sir Michael Stoute [1-4] Lord Weinstock.*

CLOVERWAY MAGIC (IRE) BHB 25f **RR 25f** 5107[12]
3 ch g Magical Strike (USA) 5.5f **(61)** - A New Rose (IRE) (Saher)
Form - 0500080
Record 1999 - 1st:0 2nd:0 3rd:0 Ran:7
1999 Turf 0-7: (7f, 8f, 10f 5) (gd 2, g-f 3, frm 2)
Scopey, little account gelding, has worn blinkers. Turf high 36.
**R P C Hoad [0-11] Foray Racing.*

CLUED UP BHB 51f48a **RR 41f 48a** 5154[8]
6 b m Beveled (USA) 6.9f **(64)** - Scharade (Lombard (GER)) 10.5f **(66)**
Form - 6208106008
Record 1999 - 1st:1 2nd:1 3rd:0 Ran:10
Pre1999 - 1st:5 2nd:2 3rd:2 Ran:40
Win Prizemoney £18,789 *Total Prizemoney* £23,027
Wins * **1999** Apr Nottin (HVY) H 10f 50 56
* 1998 Jly Haydoc (G-S) H 11.9f 52 61 <
* 1998 Jun Cheste (G-S) H 12.3f 52 55
* 1997 Jly Chepst (G-S) H 8.1f 50 57
* 1997 May Hamilt (SFT) H 8.3f 46 50
* 1996 Aug Redcar (G-F) C 10f 43
1999 Turf 1-10: (10f 1-4, 12f 4, 13f 2) (hvy 2, sft 1-1, g-s 2, gd 3, g-f 2)
Moderate mare, effective 10 to 16f, best at 12f, acts on hvy to frm, best on frm, mostly wears blinkers (effectively), favours tight tracks, excels at Chester. Turf high 56 - 1st of 5 getting 27lb from Celestial Welcome (27 Apr Nottingham RF 0870).
**P D Evans [6-47] Mrs E J Williams (from M H Easterby [0-3] Spt 1995).*

CLUNIE BHB 80f **RR 78f** 2964[8]
3 ch f Inchinor 8.9f **(64)** - Bonita **(60f)** (Primo Dominie) 6.2f **(80)**
Form - 41738
Record 1999 - 1st:1 2nd:0 3rd:1 Ran:5
Pre1999 - 1st:3 2nd:0 3rd:0 Ran:6
Win Prizemoney £13,531 *Total Prizemoney* £14,566
Wins * **1999** Jun Goodwo (G-F) H 6f 73 77 <
* 1998 Spt Haydoc (G-F) H 6f 58 71
* 1998 Spt Nottin (GD) H 6.1f 58 67
* 1998 Aug Windso (G-F) S 6f 59
1999 Turf 1-5: (5f 2, 6f 1-3) (gd 1-2, g-f 3)
Unfurnished, above-average filly, effective 5 to 6f, best at 6f, acts on gd to frm. Turf high 78 - 3rd of 12 giving 6lb to Cartmel Park (2 Jly Sandown 5f g-f RF 2503) - also 1st of 10 getting 1lb from Seren Teg (11 Jun Goodwood RF 1918). She looks a real six-furlong specialist, winning three times over that trip at two and again at Goodwood on her second start of last season.
**W J Haggas [4-11] Tony Hirschfeld.*

CLYTHA HILL LAD BHB 36f **RR 41f** 4454[15]
8 b g Domitor (USA) 7.6f **(56)** - Quae Supra (On Your Mark) 7.7f **(58)**
Form - 0082083373850
Record 1999 - 1st:0 2nd:1 3rd:3 Ran:13
Pre1999 - 1st:4 2nd:2 3rd:1 Ran:20
Win Prizemoney £11,045 *Total Prizemoney* £14,666
Wins * 1997 Aug Haydoc (G-F) H 8.1f 45 56 <
* 1997 Aug Redcar (FRM) H 7f 45 49
* 1997 Jly Chepst (G-F) H 7.1f 31 43
* 1997 Jly Redcar (G-F) H 8f 31 35
1999 Turf 0-13: (7f 3, 8f 6, 9f, 10f 2, 11f) (sft, gd 2, g-f 3, frm 6, hrd)
Moderate gelding, effective 8 to 10f, best at 8f, acts on g-f to frm, best on g-f, has worn blinkers (effectively). Turf high 46 - 3rd of 17 getting 24lb from Ben Gunn (5 Aug Chepstow 8f frm RF 3389). Consistent. **J M Bradley [4-35] Mrs Marion Morgan.*

COACH (FR) RR 95f 5008a[3]
4 ch c Bering 9.6f **(80)** - Charara (USA) (Top Command (USA)) 10f **(77)**
Form - 263
1999 Turf 0-2: (10f, 14f) (gd 2)
Currently very useful colt. Turf high 94 - 3rd of 12 to Kadance Ville (11 Oct Parc-borely 10f gd RF 5008a). **Francois Rohaut in FR [0-3].*

COASTAL BLUFF BHB 79f **RR 69f** 5110[15]
7 gr g Standaan (FR) 5.4f **(46)** - Combattente (Reform) 8.9f **(62)**
Form - 086000000
Record 1999 - 1st:0 2nd:0 3rd:0 Ran:9
Pre1999 - 1st:7 2nd:2 3rd:1 Ran:19
Win Prizemoney £185,821 *Total Prizemoney* £203,212
Wins 1997 Aug York (GD) G1 5f 115 <
1997 Jly Newmar (G-F) 5f 108+
1996 Spt Ayr (G-F) H 6f 104 115+
1996 Aug Goodwo (G-F) H 6f 88 101+
1996 Jly York (GD) H 5f 88 91+
1995 Oct Ascot (SFT) H 5f 84 88
1995 Apr Nottin (G-F) 5.1f 79+
1999 Turf 0-9: (5f 3, 6f 6) (gd 4, g-f 3, frm 2)
Average gelding, has worn blinkers. Turf high 91. Consistent. This fine stamp of a gelding dead-heated with Ya Malak in a sensational Nunthorpe in 1997, with rider Kevin Darley performing miracles after the bit broke early on. He did not fire at all in 1998, but it was sad to see this old warrior go through the sales ring at Newmarket in October that year. He is now with Nick Littmoden, but the change of yard has not made much difference so far.
**N P Littmoden [0-9] Paul Dixon (from T D Barron [7-19] Jun 1998).*

COASTGUARDS HERO BHB 15f20a **RR 17f 20a** 3145[6]
6 ch g Chilibang 7f **(55)** - Aldwick Colonnade **(43f 41a)** (Kind of Hush) 10.1f **(62)**
Form - 08567806686
Record 1999 - 1st:0 2nd:0 3rd:0 Ran:10
Pre1999 - 1st:4 2nd:3 3rd:4 Ran:40
Win Prizemoney £8,279 *Total Prizemoney* £12,441
Wins * *1998 Jun Lingfi (STD) SH 13f 30 36*
1998 Feb Lingfi (SLW) SH 16f 35 36
1998 Jan Lingfi (STD) H 13f 30 35
1996 Feb Southw (STD) 6f 45 <
1999 Turf 0-3: (12f 3) (g-f, hrd 2) 1999 AW 0-7: (10f, 12f, 13f 4, 16f) (Equi 7)
Poor gelding, effective 13 to 16f, best at 16f, - acts on Equi, favours left handed tracks, excels at Lingfield. Turf high 17. AW high 24.
**B A Pearce [1-27] D Newman (from M D I Usher [3-29] Feb 1998).*

COBOURG LODGE (IRE) RR 85f 5175a[3]
3 b c Unblest - Rachel Pringle (IRE) 00
Form - 57550673573
1999 Turf 0-11: (6f 4, 7f 2, 8f 5) (hvy 2, sft 2, g-s 2, gd, g-f 3, frm)
Useful colt, effective 6f, acts on g-s, has worn blinkers. Turf high 92. Consistent. **J T Gorman in IRE [2-19] Andrews Syndicate.*

COCHISE BHB 40f **RR 18?f** 4913[10]
3 ch g Cosmonaut - Paircullis (Tower Walk) 10f **(62)**
Form - 00
Record 1999 - 1st:0 2nd:0 3rd:0 Ran:2
Pre1999 - 1st:0 2nd:0 3rd:0 Ran:3
1999 Turf 0-2: (10f, 14f) (g-s, gd)
Neat, poor gelding. (began Spt).
**J Cullinan [0-2] Rainbow Racing UK Ltd (from Miss Gay Kelleway [0-3] Jly 1998).*

COCHITI BHB 19f18a **RR 27f 18a** 3023[8]
5 b m Kris 10f **(75)** - Sweet Jaffa (Never so Bold) 6.3f **(66)**
Form - 0568
Record 1999 - 1st:0 2nd:0 3rd:0 Ran:4
Pre1999 - 1st:0 2nd:0 3rd:1 Ran:11
Win Prizemoney £0 *Total Prizemoney* £342
1999 Turf 0-3: (12f 3) (g-f 2, frm) 1999 AW 0-1: (12f) (Fibr)
Little account filly, often wears blinkers. Turf high 27.
**P W Hiatt [0-26] The Equus Club (from C W Thornton [0-9] Spt 1997).*

COCKATRICE BHB 57f **RR 64df** 1302[10]
3 b f Petong 7.6f **(58)** - Noble Peregrine (Lomond)
Form - 00
Record 1999 - 1st:0 2nd:0 3rd:0 Ran:2
Pre1999 - 1st:0 2nd:0 3rd:0 Ran:5
1999 Turf 0-2: (6f, 8f) (sft, gd)
Scopey, average filly, effective 7f, acts on g-s, has worn blinkers. Turf high 33. **D Morris [0-7] Mrs David Sieff.*

COCO (USA) RR 55f 5060[7]
2 ch f Storm Bird (CAN) 8.5f **(82)** - Fond Romance (USA) (Fappiano (USA)) 8.7f **(77)**
Form - 7
Record 1999 - 1st:0 2nd:0 3rd:0 Ran:1
1999 Turf 0-1: (7f) (g-s)
Currently fair filly. **Sir Michael Stoute [0-1] Philip Newton.*

COCOBAY BHB 29f **RR** 2840[18]
3 b f Runnett 6.7f **(56)** - Romantic Melody (Battle Hymn)
Form - 0000
Record 1999 - 1st:0 2nd:0 3rd:0 Ran:4
Pre1999 - 1st:0 2nd:0 3rd:0 Ran:1
1999 Turf 0-4: (5f 2, 7f, 10f) (g-s, gd, g-f 2)
Light-framed, formerly very poor filly, has worn blinkers.
**G M McCourt [0-5] Mercaston Consultants Ltd.*

COCO DE MER RR 92f 4343[10]
2 ch c Prince Sabo 6.6f **(64)** - Musica **(78df)** (Primo Dominie) 6.2f **(80)**
Form - 245210220
Record 1999 - 1st:1 2nd:4 3rd:0 Ran:9
Win Prizemoney £4,120 *Total Prizemoney* £11,186
Wins * 1999 Jly Cheste (G-F) 5.1f 70 <
1999 Turf 1-9: (5f 1-9) (g-s, g-f 6, frm 1-2)
Useful colt, effective 5f, acts on g-f. Turf high 92 - 2nd of 9 to Digital Image (4 May Chester 5f g-f RF 1025). He deserved to get off the mark, and duly did so at Chester in July after an two-month break. **A P Jarvis [1-9] Ms Julie Greenacre.*

COCO GIRL BHB 42f **RR 50f** 4863[7]
3 ch f Mystiko (USA) 7.7f **(59)** - Cantico (Green Dancer (USA)) 10.3f **(74)**
Form - 407467
Record 1999 - 1st:0 2nd:0 3rd:0 Ran:6
Pre1999 - 1st:0 2nd:0 3rd:0 Ran:2
Win Prizemoney £0 *Total Prizemoney* £267
1999 Turf 0-4: (8f, 9f, 10f, 11f) (g-f 2, frm 2) 1999 AW 0-2: (12f, 15f) (Equi, Fibr)
Unfurnished, fair filly, effective 7f, acts on frm, favours tight tracks. Turf high 61. AW high 37 (began Oct). Becoming disappointing.
**Mrs A E Johnson [0-3] Chasers IV (from I A Balding [0-5] May 1999).*

COCO LOCO RR 42f 5099[10]
2 b f Bin Ajwaad (IRE) - Mainly Me **(17f)** (Huntingdale)
Form - 0
Record 1999 - 1st:0 2nd:0 3rd:0 Ran:1
1999 Turf 0-1: (7f) (gd)
Currently moderate filly. **J Pearce [0-1] & Mrs J Matthews.*

COCONUT BHB 40f **RR 15f** 2448[6]
3 b g Shirley Heights 12.1f **(76)** - Magical Retreat (USA) **(112f)** (Sir Ivor) 10.2f **(70)**
Form - 406
Record 1999 - 1st:0 2nd:0 3rd:0 Ran:3
Win Prizemoney £0 *Total Prizemoney* £257
1999 Turf 0-3: (7f, 10f, 11f) (gd, frm 2)
Scopey, currently poor gelding. Turf high 15.
**C A Cyzer [0-3] R M Cyzer.*

CODICIL BHB 52f **RR 56f** 2938[5]
3 ch f Then Again 7.4f **(52)** - Own Free Will (Nicholas Bill) 10.1f **(56)**
Form - 0035
Record 1999 - 1st:0 2nd:0 3rd:1 Ran:4
Pre1999 - 1st:1 2nd:0 3rd:1 Ran:9
Win Prizemoney £2,388 *Total Prizemoney* £4,075
Wins 1998 Jly Redcar (G-S) 5f 72+ <
1999 Turf 0-4: (8f 2, 10f, 11f) (g-s, gd 2, g-f)
Scopey, fair filly, effective 5f, acts on gd. Turf high 56. Consistent.
**M Dods [0-4] Harry Whitton (from Mrs J R Ramsden [1-9] Oct 1998).*

COEUR DE LA MER (IRE) RR 84+f 5108[1]
2 b f Caerleon (USA) 10.9f **(79)** - Cochineal (USA) (Vaguely Noble) 10.1f **(72)**
Form - 31
Record 1999 - 1st:1 2nd:0 3rd:1 Ran:2
Win Prizemoney £3,078 *Total Prizemoney* £3,594
Wins * 1999 Oct Windso (SFT) 8.3f 84+ <
1999 Turf 1-2: (8f 1-2) (sft, gd 1-1)
Currently decent filly. Turf high 84 (began Oct) - 1st of 13 from Original Spin (28 Oct Windsor RF 5108).
**A G Foster [1-2] R E Sangster.*

COEUR DU LION BHB 35f **RR 19f** 4148[12]
3 b f Whittingham (IRE) - The Fernhill Flyer (IRE) **(21f 65a)** (Red Sunset) 8.2f **(63)**
Form - 000
Record 1999 - 1st:0 2nd:0 3rd:0 Ran:3
Pre1999 - 1st:0 2nd:0 3rd:0 Ran:3
1999 Turf 0-2: (5f, 7f) (frm, hrd) 1999 AW 0-1: (7f) (Fibr)
Workmanlike, poor filly, has worn blinkers. Turf high 19 (began Jly). **D Nicholls [0-6] J M G Promotions Ltd.*

COFFEE CREAM BHB 78f **RR 79f** 3965[12]
3 b f Common Grounds 8.1f **(66)** - Sugar Town (IRE) **(57f)** (Tate Gallery (USA)) 7.4f **(67)**
Form - 3821050
Record 1999 - 1st:1 2nd:1 3rd:1 Ran:7
Pre1999 - 1st:1 2nd:0 3rd:0 Ran:3
Win Prizemoney £5,550 *Total Prizemoney* £10,012
Wins * 1999 Jly Windso (G-F) H 8.3f 80 81 <
* 1998 Spt Kempto (GD) 7f 79
1999 Turf 1-7: (7f 4, 8f 1-2, 9f) (gd 2, g-f 2, frm 1-3)
Unfurnished, above-average filly, effective 7 to 8f, best at 8f, acts on g-f to frm, best on frm. Turf high 81 - 1st of 6 getting 7lb from Gaily Mill (12 Jly Windsor RF 2763). Winner at Windsor over a mile on fast ground in July, she has ability, but has faced tough tasks in hot races since.
**B J Meehan [2-10] Penelope, Viscountess Portman.*

COHAN RR 58f 1327[9]
2 b c Petong 7.6f **(58)** - Katie Jo (Taufan (USA)) 7f **(57)**
Form - 7740
Record 1999 - 1st:0 2nd:0 3rd:0 Ran:4
Win Prizemoney £0 *Total Prizemoney* £198
1999 Turf 0-4: (5f 3, 6f) (sft, gd, g-f, frm)
Fair colt. Turf high 58. (DEAD) **B Palling [0-4] B A Evans.*

COHIBA BHB 42f43a **RR 48?f 43a** 4010[6]
6 b g Old Vic 12.8f **(72)** - Circus Ring (High Top) 10.2f **(67)**
Form - 216
Record 1999 - 1st:1 2nd:1 3rd:0 Ran:3
Pre1999 - 1st:2 2nd:1 3rd:0 Ran:22
Win Prizemoney £7,144 *Total Prizemoney* £9,199
Wins 1999 Jly Nottin (FRM) SH 14.1f 37 41
1998 May Bright (G-F) H 11.9f 38 44 <
1997 Jly Nottin (G-F) SH 14.1f 34 42
1999 Turf 1-3: (10f, 12f, 14f 1-1) (g-f 2, frm 1-1)
Moderate gelding, effective 12f, acts on sft. Turf high 48.
**A G Juckes [0-1] D W Thorne (from B J Curley [3-18] Jly 1999).*

COIS CUAIN (IRE) RR 92f 5178a[1]
2 b f Night Shift (USA) 8.1f **(73)** - Pitmarie (Pitskelly) 8.5f **(53)**
Form - 01
1999 Turf 1-2: (6f 1-2) (sft 1-1, gd)
Currently useful filly. Turf high 92 (began Oct) - 1st of 29 from Still As Sweet (29 Oct Curragh RF 5178a). **J Oxx in IRE [1-2] E Keena.*

COLD CLIMATE BHB 60f **RR 62df** 4431[15]
4 b g Pursuit of Love 9.5f **(69)** - Sharpthorne (USA) (Sharpen Up) 8.3f **(67)**
Form - 06205024831300
Record 1999 - 1st:1 2nd:2 3rd:2 Ran:14
Pre1999 - 1st:0 2nd:0 3rd:1 Ran:6
Win Prizemoney £4,503 *Total Prizemoney* £9,336
Wins * 1999 Aug Newmar (GD) H 6f 55 56 <
1999 Turf 1-14: (5f 6, 6f 1-7, 7f) (sft, g-s, gd 4, g-f 1-4, frm 3, hrd)
Workmanlike, average gelding, effective 6f, acts on gd, has worn blinkers. Turf high 62. Inconsistent.
**Bob Jones [1-17] Sandbaggers Club (from R Charlton [0-3] May 1998).*

COLD FRONT BHB 40f52a **RR 51f 52a** 3667[5]
4 br c Polar Falcon (USA) 9f **(74)** - Chandni (IRE) (Ahonoora) 8.1f **(73)**
Form - 2005
Record 1999 - 1st:0 2nd:0 3rd:0 Ran:3
Pre1999 - 1st:0 2nd:1 3rd:0 Ran:7
Win Prizemoney £0 *Total Prizemoney* £545
1999 Turf 0-2: (8f 2) (frm 2) 1999 AW 0-1: (12f) (Fibr)
Scopey, fair colt, effective 8f, - acts on Fibr, likes tight tracks. Turf high 20 (began Jly).
**N P Littmoden [0-4] Miss Vanessa Church (from J W Hills [0-6] Aug 1998).*

COLDHARBOUR LASS RR 8f 5193[16]
3 ch f Aragon 7.7f **(58)** - Don't Loiter (Town And Country) 8.1f **(68)**
Form - 0
Record 1999 - 1st:0 2nd:0 3rd:0 Ran:1
1999 Turf 0-1: (8f) (gd)
Currently very poor filly. **E L James [0-1] & Mrs David Sowry.*

COLERIDGE BHB 28f46a **RR 35f 46a** 3582[11]
11 gr g Bellypha 11.9f **(66)** - Quay Line (High Line) 10.3f **(70)**
Form - 7551247133742600
Record 1999 - 1st:1 2nd:2 3rd:2 Ran:12
Pre1999 - 1st:10 2nd:12 3rd:7 Ran:84
Win Prizemoney £31,377 *Total Prizemoney* £52,313
Wins * **1999** *Feb Southw (STD) H 16f 47 53*
* 1998 *Dec Lingfi (STD) H 16f 45 50*
* 1997 *Feb Lingfi (STD) H 16f 51 55*
* 1996 May Bath (G-F) H 17.2f 47 56
* 1995 *Nov Lingfi (STD) H 16f 41 51*
* 1995 Oct Warwic (G-S) H 16.1f 39 49
1999 Turf 0-3: (16f 2, 18f) (g-s, g-f 2) 1999 AW 1-9: (16f 1-9) (Equi 2, Fibr 1-7)
Moderate gelding, effective 16f, - acts on AW, best on Fibr, mostly wears blinkers, favours left handed tracks, favours tight tracks. Turf high 35. AW high 53 - 3rd of 11 giving 2lb to Quezon City (8 Mar Southwell 16f Fibr RF 0414) - also 1st of 10 giving 25lb to Tillyboy (19 Feb Southwell RF 0317).
**J J Sheehan [6-76] P J Sheehan (from D Shaw [4-17] Feb 1993).*

COLETTE (IRE) RR 70f 5108[9]
2 b f Nicolotte - Ascensiontide (Ela-Mana-Mou) 10.1f **(70)**
Form - 0
Record 1999 - 1st:0 2nd:0 3rd:0 Ran:1
1999 Turf 0-1: (8f) (gd)
Currently above-average filly.
**Major D N Chappell [0-1] Super Sprinters.*

COLEY RR 40f 5192[10]
2 ch f Pursuit of Love 9.5f **(69)** - Cole Slaw (Absalom) 7.2f **(58)**
Form - 8100
Record 1999 - 1st:1 2nd:0 3rd:0 Ran:4
Win Prizemoney £1,708 *Total Prizemoney* £1,708
Wins 1999 Spt Lingfi (HVY) C 6f 63 <
1999 Turf 1-4: (6f 1-2, 7f, 8f) (g-s 1-1, gd 2, g-f)
Moderate filly. Turf high 63 - 1st of 19 getting 4lb from Diamond Promise (24 Spt Lingfield RF 4530).
**L MontagueHall [0-2] J Daniels,M C Lane & K Ovenden (from H Candy [1-2] Spt 1999).*

COLINS CHOICE BHB 44f37a **RR 46f 37a** 98[11]
5 ch m Risk Me (FR) 8f **(53)** -Give Me a Day(Lucky Wednesday) 8f **(50)**
Form - 40
Record 1999 - 1st:0 2nd:0 3rd:0 Ran:1
Pre1999 - 1st:3 2nd:1 3rd:3 Ran:21
Win Prizemoney £5,878 *Total Prizemoney* £8,426
Wins * 1997 *Dec Wolver (STD) H 9.4f 49 53* <
* 1997 *Spt Wolver (STD) C 8.5f 49*
* 1997 *Jly Wolver (STD) C 8.5f 51*
1999 AW 0-1: (11f) (Fibr)
Moderate filly, effective 10 to 12f, acts on sft to g-s.
**J L Spearing [3-22] Colin Ross.*

COLISEUM (IRE) RR 98f 606a[1]
3 b c Sadler's Wells (USA) 11.3f **(87)** - Gravieres (FR) (Saint Estephe (FR)) 16.4f **(79)**
Form - 1
1999 Turf 1-1: (9f 1-1) (sft 1-1)
Very useful colt. (1st run) - 1st of 9 from Piranesi (3 Apr Cork RF 0606a). A well regarded juvenile, he went missing after winning a maiden in April. **A P O'Brien in IRE [1-5] Michael Tabor.*

COLLEGE BLUE (IRE) BHB 75f73a **RR 71f 73a** 289[2]
3 b f College Chapel - Mitsubishi Centre (IRE) (Thatching) 8f **(66)**
Form - 5032
Record 1999 - 1st:0 2nd:1 3rd:0 Ran:1
Pre1999 - 1st:0 2nd:2 3rd:1 Ran:6
Win Prizemoney £0 *Total Prizemoney* £4,103
1999 AW 0-1: (5f) (Equi)
Workmanlike, above-average filly, effective 5f, acts on g-f to frm - acts on Equi, often wears blinkers. **T G Mills [0-7] M J Legg.*

COLLEGE CHOIR (IRE) RR 11f 747[13]
3 b g College Chapel - Lyphard's Special (USA)) 10.3f **(72)**
Form - 80
Record 1999 - 1st:0 2nd:0 3rd:0 Ran:2
1999 Turf 0-1: (8f) (g-s) 1999 AW 0-1: (6f) (Equi)
Scopey, currently poor gelding. **G L Moore [0-2] C J & B V Pennick.*

COLLEGE DEAN (IRE) BHB 38f **RR 43f** 3991[7]
3 ch g College Chapel - Phyllode **(53f)** (Pharly (FR)) 9.8f **(68)**
Form - 5000000007
Record 1999 - 1st:0 2nd:0 3rd:0 Ran:10
Pre1999 - 1st:1 2nd:0 3rd:1 Ran:7
Win Prizemoney £3,192 *Total Prizemoney* £3,918
Wins * 1998 Aug Hamilt (SFT) H 6f 70 <
1999 Turf 0-9: (6f 3, 7f 4, 8f, 9f) (g-s, gd 3, g-f 2, frm 3) 1999 AW 0-1: (6f) (Fibr)
Scopey, moderate gelding, effective 6f, acts on gd, has worn blinkers. Turf high 61. **J J O'Neill [1-17] Clayton Bigley Partnership Ltd.*

COLLEGE GALLERY BHB 50f **RR 59f** 3665[9]
2 b c College Chapel - Gallarus (IRE) (Standaan (FR)) 7f **(55)**
Form - 00
Record 1999 - 1st:0 2nd:0 3rd:0 Ran:2
1999 Turf 0-2: (6f 2) (gd, frm)
Currently fair colt. Turf high 59 (began Jly).
**C G Cox [0-1] E R Arkwright (from M J Heaton-Ellis [0-1] Jly 1999).*

COLLEGE KING (IRE) BHB 63f **RR 57f** 1666[5]
3 b c College Chapel - Genetta (Green Desert (USA)) 8.6f **(78)**
Form - 745
Record 1999 - 1st:0 2nd:0 3rd:0 Ran:3
Win Prizemoney £0 *Total Prizemoney* £261
1999 Turf 0-3: (7f 2, 8f) (gd, g-f 2)
Workmanlike, currently fair colt. Turf high 57.
**M Brittain [0-3] Mel Brittain.*

COLLEGE MAID (IRE) RR 57f 5214[6]
2 b f College Chapel - Maid of Mourne (Fairy King (USA)) 7.7f **(59)**
Form - 74221234348056
Record 1999 - 1st:1 2nd:3 3rd:2 Ran:14
Win Prizemoney £2,654 *Total Prizemoney* £7,237
Wins * **1999** May Mussel (G-F) 5f 61 <
1999 Turf 1-14: (5f 1-10, 6f 4) (hvy, g-s, gd 8, g-f 2, frm 1-2)
Fair filly, effective 5 to 6f, best at 5f, acts on gd to frm, best on gd. Turf high 66 - 3rd of 6 getting 1lb from Maron (31 Jly Hamilton 5f g-f RF 3267) - also 1st of 9 getting 5lb from Scafell (17 May Musselburgh RF 1273). Consistent.
**J S Goldie [1-14] Bruce Partnership.*

COLLEGE MUSIC (IRE) BHB 47f47a **RR 38f 47a** 3624[14]
3 b br f College Chapel - Lute and Lyre (IRE) (The Noble Player (USA)) 6.5f **(67)**
Form - 850800500
Record 1999 - 1st:0 2nd:0 3rd:0 Ran:9
Pre1999 - 1st:1 2nd:2 3rd:1 Ran:10
Win Prizemoney £1,934 *Total Prizemoney* £5,171
Wins * 1998 May Newcas (G-S) 5f 74 <
1999 Turf 0-8: (5f, 6f 6, 7f) (sft, gd 4, frm 2, hrd) 1999 AW 0-1: (6f) (Fibr)
Leggy, moderate filly, effective 5 to 6f, best at 5f, acts on sft to hrd. Turf high 53. **M Brittain [1-19] Mel Brittain.*

COLLEGE PRINCESS BHB 36f52a **RR 35f 52a** 3284[12]
5 b m Anshan 8.2f **(63)** - Tinkers Fairy (Myjinski (USA)) 9.5f **(54)**
Form - 47540
Record 1999 - 1st:0 2nd:0 3rd:0 Ran:5
Pre1999 - 1st:1 2nd:1 3rd:4 Ran:19
Win Prizemoney £2,337 *Total Prizemoney* £4,878
Wins * 1997 Jly Redcar (G-F) SH 5f 47 46 <
1999 Turf 0-5: (5f 4, 6f) (gd, g-f 3, frm)
Moderate filly, effective 5f, acts on frm. Turf high 35.
**S C Williams [1-18] Mrs Christine Dunnett (from C A Dwyer [0-6] Apr 1997).*

COLLEGE ROCK BHB 61f **RR 62f** 4900[3]
2 ch c Rock Hopper 10.6f **(54)** - Sea Aura (Roi Soleil) 8.7f **(57)**
Form - 70220033
Record 1999 - 1st:0 2nd:2 3rd:2 Ran:8
Win Prizemoney £0 *Total Prizemoney* £1,457
1999 Turf 0-8: (5f, 6f 2, 7f 5) (sft, g-s, gd 3, g-f, frm, hrd)
Average colt, effective 6 to 7f, acts on gd to hrd, has worn blinkers. Turf high 62. Inconsistent.
**Mrs A E Johnson [0-1] Mrs S N J Embiricos (from S C Williams [0-7] Oct 1999).*

COLLEGE ROSE BHB 26f **RR 16f** 3753[9]
4 b f Prince Sabo 6.6f **(64)** - Tinkers Fairy (Myjinski (USA)) 9.5f **(54)**
Form - 000
Record 1999 - 1st:0 2nd:0 3rd:0 Ran:3
Pre1999 - 1st:0 2nd:0 3rd:0 Ran:4
Win Prizemoney £0 *Total Prizemoney* £271
1999 Turf 0-3: (5f 2, 6f) (g-f, frm 2)
Light-framed, poor filly, has worn blinkers. Turf high 16 (began Jly). **S C Williams [0-7] Mrs Christine Dunnett.*

COLLISION TIME BHB 62f **RR 70f** 2735[9]
2 b f Timeless Times (USA) 6.1f **(56)** - Kaleidophone (Kalaglow) 9.8f **(67)**
Form - 334430
Record 1999 - 1st:0 2nd:0 3rd:3 Ran:6
Win Prizemoney £0 *Total Prizemoney* £1,260
1999 Turf 0-6: (5f 5, 6f) (gd 2, g-f 3, hrd)
Above-average filly, effective 5f, acts on g-f, has worn blinkers. Turf high 70 - 4th of 10 to Lady-Love (14 Jun Musselburgh 5f g-f RF 1977). **P D Evans [0-6] D Maloney.*

COLNE VALLEY AMY BHB 50f **RR 59f** 5215[16]
2 b f Mizoram (USA) - Panchellita (USA)**(34f 44a)**(Pancho Villa (USA))
Form - 080
Record 1999 - 1st:0 2nd:0 3rd:0 Ran:3
1999 Turf 0-3: (5f, 6f, 8f) (g-s, gd, frm)
Currently fair filly. Turf high 59 (began Spt).
**G L Moore [0-3] Colne Valley Golf (Deluxeward Ltd).*

COLOMBE D'OR BHB 59f **RR 56f** 3400[8]
2 gr g Petong 7.6f **(58)** - Deep Divide **(74f)** (Nashwan (USA))
Form - 778
Record 1999 - 1st:0 2nd:0 3rd:0 Ran:3
1999 Turf 0-3: (5f, 6f, 7f) (gd 2, g-f)
Currently fair gelding. Turf high 56.
**P C Haslam [0-3] S A B Dinsmore.*

COLONEL CUSTER BHB 57f58a **RR 56f 58a** 5154[9]
4 ch g Komaite (USA) 6.9f **(61)** - Mohican (Great Nephew) 9.9f **(64)**
Form - 0501560
Record 1999 - 1st:1 2nd:0 3rd:0 Ran:6
Pre1999 - 1st:1 2nd:1 3rd:1 Ran:8
Win Prizemoney £4,708 *Total Prizemoney* £6,312
Wins * 1999 *Feb Southw (STD) H 11f 57 60*
1997 *Jly Southw (STD) 6f 61* <
1999 Turf 0-1: (10f) (gd) 1999 AW 1-5:(8f, 11f 1-2, 12f 2)(Equi, Fibr 1-4)
Scopey, average gelding, effective 7 to 11f, - acts on Fibr. AW high 60 - 1st of 14 giving 9lb to Aldwych Arrow (22 Feb Southwell RF 0341). **J Pearce [1-6] D Leech (from C W Thornton [1-8] Nov 1998).*

COLONEL MUSTARD BHB 73f **RR 75f** 2762[11]
3 ch c Keen 11.1f **(58)** - Juliet Bravo (Glow (USA)) 6.7f **(71)**
Form - 086100
Record 1999 - 1st:1 2nd:0 3rd:0 Ran:6
Pre1999 - 1st:1 2nd:0 3rd:0 Ran:4
Win Prizemoney £5,966 *Total Prizemoney* £5,966
Wins * 1999 Jun Windso (G-F) H 10f 71 75
* 1998 Aug Lingfi (FRM) 7.6f 83+ <
1999 Turf 1-6: (7f, 9f 2, 10f 1-2, 12f) (g-f, frm 1-5)
Lengthy, above-average colt, effective 8 to 10f, acts on g-f to frm. Turf high 75 - 1st of 11 getting 5lb from Philatelic Lady (14 Jun Windsor RF 1991). Inconsistent.
**J R Fanshawe [2-10] Mrs Jan Hopper.*

COLONEL NORTH (IRE) BHB 73f70a **RR 73f 70a** 2513[6]
3 b g Distinctly North (USA) 7.4f **(63)** - Tricky (Song) 7.2f **(61)**
Form - 600116
Record 1999 - 1st:2 2nd:0 3rd:0 Ran:6
Pre1999 - 1st:0 2nd:0 3rd:0 Ran:1
Win Prizemoney £7,692 *Total Prizemoney* £7,692
Wins * 1999 Jun Carlis (G-F) H 8f 64 73 <
1999 Jun Newmar (G-F) C 8f 67
1999 Turf 2-6: (8f 2-4, 10f, 11f) (gd, g-f, frm 1-3, hrd 1-1)
Leggy, above-average gelding, effective 8f, acts on frm to hrd. Turf high 73 - 1st of 14 giving 25lb to Trois Elles (24 Jun Carlisle RF 2262) - also 1st of 14 giving 6lb to September Harvest (18 Jun Newmarket RF 2125). He won a couple of fast-ground handicaps in June and seems to require those conditions.
**Andrew Reid [1-2] A S Reid (from W R Muir [1-5] Jun 1999).*

COLONEL SAM BHB 52f54a **RR 52f 54a** 4656[14]
3 b g Puissance 7.1f **(60)** -Indian Summer (Young Generation) 7.7f **(63)**
Form - 576066002700
Record 1999 - 1st:0 2nd:1 3rd:0 Ran:12
Pre1999 - 1st:0 2nd:0 3rd:1 Ran:4
Win Prizemoney £0 *Total Prizemoney* £1,290
1999 Turf 0-9: (5f 5, 6f 2, 7f, 8f) (gd 4, g-f, frm 3, hrd) 1999 AW 0-3: (5f, 6f 2) (Fibr 3)
Fair gelding, effective 5f, acts on g-f, has worn blinkers. Turf high 53. AW high 55. **J A Glover [0-16] W I Derry.*

COLONIAL RULE (USA) BHB 94f **RR 87f** 4996[1]
2 b c Pleasant Colony (USA) 12.4f **(88)** - Musicale (USA) (The Minstrel (CAN)) 10f **(72)**
Form - 7231
Record 1999 - 1st:1 2nd:1 3rd:1 Ran:4
Win Prizemoney £3,954 *Total Prizemoney* £5,711
Wins * 1999 Oct Bright (GD) 8f 87+ <
1999 Turf 1-4: (7f 2, 8f 1-2) (gd 1-3, frm)
Useful colt. Turf high 87 (began Jly) - 1st of 11 from Makasseb (21 Oct Brighton RF 4996). Bolted up in a Brighton maiden on his final start.
**A G Foster [1-1] R E Sangster (from P W Chapple-Hyam [0-3] Spt 1999).*

COLONIAL STATE (USA) BHB 68f **RR 57f** 5022[8]
3 b c Pleasant Colony (USA) 12.4f **(88)** - Star Pastures (Northfields (USA)) 9f **(72)**
Form - 538088
Record 1999 - 1st:0 2nd:0 3rd:1 Ran:6
Win Prizemoney £0 *Total Prizemoney* £537
1999 Turf 0-6: (10f 2, 11f, 12f 3) (gd 4, g-f 2)
Light-framed, fair colt, effective 10 to 12f, acts on gd, has worn blinkers. Turf high 77.
**A G Foster [0-1] R E Sangster (from P W Chapple-Hyam [0-5] Aug 1999).*

COLORFUL AMBITION BHB 36f63a **RR 36f 63a** 3898[6]
9 b g Slip Anchor 12.7f **(75)** - Reprocolor (Jimmy Reppin) 8.8f **(64)**
Form - 06
Record 1999 - 1st:0 2nd:0 3rd:0 Ran:2
Pre1999 - 1st:3 2nd:4 3rd:3 Ran:22
Win Prizemoney £9,315 *Total Prizemoney* £15,440
Wins 1995 May Redcar (FRM) H 9f 62 64 <
1995 May Newcas (GD) 9f 64
1999 Turf 0-2: (12f, 16f) (g-f, frm)
Very moderate gelding. Turf high 36 (began Aug).
**W W Haigh [0-3] Alan Swinbank (from Mrs A Swinbank [5-27] Spt 1996).*

COLOUR SCHEME (FR) RR 93f 3926a[1]
3 b f Perrault - Perfect Rainbow (Rainbow Quest (USA)) 10.4f **(75)**
Form - 31
1999 Turf 1-2: (11f, 15f 1-1) (g-s 1-1, gd)
Currently useful. Turf high 93 - 1st of 5 getting 4lb from Amilynx (18 Aug Deauville RF 3926a).
**D Smaga in FR [1-2] Baron T de Zuylen de Nyevelt.*

COLOURS TO GOLD (IRE) BHB 41f **RR 33f** 918[11]
4 ch f Rainbows For Life (CAN) 9.3f **(64)** - Brave Ivy (Decoy Boy) 6.7f **(56)**
Form - 00
Record 1999 - 1st:0 2nd:0 3rd:0 Ran:2

Pre1999 - 1st:0 2nd:0 3rd:1 Ran:9
Win Prizemoney £0 *Total Prizemoney* £345
1999 Turf 0-2: (7f, 9f) (hvy, gd)
Scopey, very moderate filly, effective 8f, acts on frm, has worn blinkers, likes tight tracks. Turf high 27. Consistent.
**J L Eyre [0-2] J E Wilson (from R A Fahey [0-9] Aug 1998).*

COLUMNA BHB 40f RR 56f 4949[7]
3 gr f Deploy 11.4f **(67)** - Copper Trader (Faustus (USA)) 10f **(58)**
Form - 0767
Record 1999 - 1st:0 2nd:0 3rd:0 Ran:4
Pre1999 - 1st:0 2nd:0 3rd:0 Ran:1
1999 Turf 0-4: (10f, 11f, 12f, 16f) (g-s, gd 2, g-f)
Unfurnished, fair filly, has worn blinkers. Turf high 56.
**M D I Usher [0-2] The Ridgeway Partnership (from H Candy [0-3] Jun 1999).*

COLWAY RITZ BHB 75f RR 76f 5072[16]
5 b g Rudimentary (USA) 8.2f **(66)** -Million Heiress(Auction Ring (USA)) 8.6f **(65)**
Form - 00301181345736500
Record 1999 - 1st:3 2nd:0 3rd:3 Ran:17
Pre1999 - 1st:2 2nd:3 3rd:5 Ran:25
Win Prizemoney £33,944 *Total Prizemoney* £48,275

Wins									
	* 1999	Jun	Redcar	(FRM)	H	10f	78	82	<
	* 1999	May	Redcar	(FRM)	H	10f	74	78	
	* 1999	May	Ripon	(G-S)	H	10f	69	75	
	* 1998	Jly	Beverl	(GD)	H	8.5f	68	70	
	1997	Oct	Doncas	(GD)	H	7f	65	69	

1999 Turf 3-17: (7f 2, 8f 3, 9f 2, 10f 3-6, 12f 4) (gd 1-6, g-f 3, frm 2-8)
Above-average gelding, effective 8 to 12f, acts on gd to frm, best on frm, has worn blinkers, prefers right handed tracks, likes tight tracks, excels at Beverley, does well at Ripon, likes Redcar. Turf high 84 - 4th of 7 getting 8lb from Mardani (9 Jly York 12f frm RF 2696) - also 1st of 12 giving 8lb to Pinchincha (19 Jun Redcar RF 2155). A winner three times this year, including the Zetland Gold Cup but lost his way latterly, but a useful performer in a fast-run race over ten furlongs. Likes fast ground.
**W Storey [4-33] R Coleman (from J W Watts [1-12] Oct 1997).*

COL-WOODY BHB 60f56a RR 68df 56a 3976[6]
3 ch g Safawan 6.6f **(60)** - Sky Fighter (Hard Fought) 8.8f **(62)**
Form - 020273206
Record 1999 - 1st:0 2nd:3 3rd:1 Ran:8
Pre1999 - 1st:0 2nd:0 3rd:0 Ran:6
Win Prizemoney £0 *Total Prizemoney* £3,902
1999 Turf 0-8: (8f 4, 10f, 12f, 14f 2) (gd 2, g-f 4, frm 2)
Workmanlike, average gelding, effective 8 to 12f, best at 8f, acts on g-f to frm, best on g-f, has worn blinkers. Turf high 71 (1st run) - 2nd of 14 giving 7lb to Fallachan (1 Apr Musselburgh 8f g-f RF 0553). **A P Jarvis [0-14] Mrs Ann Jarvis.*

COMANCHE QUEEN BHB 52f RR 50f 4506[13]
2 ch f Totem (USA) 5f **(38)** - Chess Mistress (USA) (Run The Gantlet (USA)) 12.1f **(59)**
Form - 0700
Record 1999 - 1st:0 2nd:0 3rd:0 Ran:4
1999 Turf 0-4: (6f 2, 7f, 8f) (gd, g-f 2, frm)
Fair filly. Turf high 50. **K W Hogg [0-4] Hurn Racing Club.*

COMBINED VENTURE (IRE) BHB 33f RR 39f 4334[6]
3 b c Dolphin Street (FR) - Centinela **(47f)** (Caerleon (USA)) 8.6f **(71)**
Form - 0005477366
Record 1999 - 1st:0 2nd:0 3rd:1 Ran:10
Pre1999 - 1st:0 2nd:1 3rd:2 Ran:6
Win Prizemoney £0 *Total Prizemoney* £2,470
1999 Turf 0-10: (7f 2, 8f 2, 10f 5, 11f) (g-s, gd, g-f 2, frm 6)
Very moderate colt. Turf high 39.
**K A Morgan [0-3] R E Gray (from E Weymes [0-13] Aug 1999).*

COME FLY WITH ME RR 46f 4982[7]
2 b f Bluebird (USA) 7.9f **(71)** - Waffle on **(87f)** (Chief Singer) 8.9f **(66)**
Form - 7
Record 1999 - 1st:0 2nd:0 3rd:0 Ran:1
1999 Turf 0-1: (7f) (g-f)
Currently moderate filly. **J H M Gosden [0-1] Cheveley Park Stud.*

COME ON GEORGE (IRE) BHB 69f RR 73f 4861[7]
3 b c Barathea (IRE) - Lacovia (USA) (Majestic Light (USA)) 10.6f **(75)**
Form - 847
Record 1999 - 1st:0 2nd:0 3rd:0 Ran:3
Win Prizemoney £0 *Total Prizemoney* £275
1999 Turf 0-3: (10f 2, 12f) (sft, frm 2)
Well made, currently above-average colt. Turf high 73 (began Spt).
**J L Dunlop [0-3] Wafic Said.*

COME ON MURGY BHB 45f RR 42f 5187[10]
2 b f Weldnaas (USA) 8.4f **(55)** - Forest Song (Forzando) 7.6f **(59)**
Form - 06700060
Record 1999 - 1st:0 2nd:0 3rd:0 Ran:8
1999 Turf 0-7: (5f 5, 6f 2) (gd 4, g-f 2, frm) 1999 AW 0-1: (5f) (Fibr)
Moderate filly, has worn blinkers. Turf high 42.
**A Bailey [0-8] K W Weale.*

COMEOUTOFTHEFOG (IRE) BHB 44f57a RR 45f 57a 3910[8]
4 b g Mujadil (USA) 7.7f **(70)** - Local Belle (Ballymore) 7.3f **(64)**
Form - 633450476461738
Record 1999 - 1st:1 2nd:0 3rd:1 Ran:11
Pre1999 - 1st:2 2nd:4 3rd:4 Ran:26
Win Prizemoney £7,133 *Total Prizemoney* £12,135

Wins									
	* 1999	*Jun*	*Lingfi*	*(STD)*	*SH*	*7f*	*52*	*59*	
	1998	*Feb*	*Lingfi*	*(SLW)*	*C*	*8f*		*68*	<
	1998	*Feb*	*Lingfi*	*(SLW)*	*C*	*7f*		*61+*	

1999 Turf 0-5: (7f 2, 8f 3) (gd, frm 4) 1999 AW 1-6: (6f, 7f 1-4, 8f) (Equi 1-6)
Fair gelding, effective 7 to 8f, best at 8f, - acts on Equi, has worn blinkers, likes left handed tracks, likes tight tracks, excels at Lingfield. Turf high 45. AW high 59 - 1st of 15 giving 11lb to Dark Menace (12 Jun Lingfield RF 1951). He does not win that often, but when he does it is on the Lingfield Equitrack.
**A J McNae [1-19] Raging Rhinos (from Mrs A L M King [1-7] Aug 1998).*

COMET DUST RR 5109[13]
2 b f Ezzoud (IRE) - Galaxie Dust (USA) (Blushing Groom (FR)) 10.3f **(76)**
Form - 00
Record 1999 - 1st:0 2nd:0 3rd:0 Ran:2
1999 Turf 0-2: (7f, 8f) (g-s, gd)
Currently very poor filly. (began Oct).
**T D McCarthy [0-2] Hesmonds Stud.*

COMEX FLYER (IRE) BHB 63f RR 63f 4322[6]
2 ch g Prince of Birds (USA) - Smashing Pet (Mummy's Pet) 7.7f **(60)**
Form - 0646
Record 1999 - 1st:0 2nd:0 3rd:0 Ran:4
Win Prizemoney £0 *Total Prizemoney* £258
1999 Turf 0-4: (5f, 6f, 7f 2) (gd, g-f 2, frm)
Average gelding. Turf high 63. **J Berry [0-4] Neil Smith.*

COMIC (IRE) BHB 82f RR 80f 3747[5]
3 b f Be My Chief (USA) 10.2f **(62)** - Circus Act (Shirley Heights) 10.3f **(74)**
Form - 1105
Record 1999 - 1st:2 2nd:0 3rd:0 Ran:4
Pre1999 - 1st:0 2nd:0 3rd:0 Ran:2
Win Prizemoney £7,244 *Total Prizemoney* £7,502

Wins									
	* 1999	Jun	Yarmou	(G-F)	H	11.5f	76	80	<
	* 1999	May	Windso	(GD)		10f		69	

1999 Turf 2-4: (10f 1-1, 11f 1-1, 12f 2) (gd 1-2, g-f 1-2)
Scopey, decent filly, effective 11f, acts on gd. Turf high 80 - 1st of 7 giving 12lb to Moon Shot (3 Jun Yarmouth RF 1705). After two promising efforts as a juvenile, she won her first two races last term. Well beaten subsequently.
**J H M Gosden [2-6] Lord Hartington & The Duke of Roxburghe.*

COMILLAS (FR) RR 107+f 1358a[14]
3 gr f Kaldoun (FR) 9.9f **(84)** - Rive Du Sud (USA) 00
Form - 40
1999 Turf 0-2: (8f 2) (g-s, gd)
Currently Pattern-class filly. Turf high 91. **J deRoualle in FR [1-3].*

COMING UP ROSES RR 45f 2123[10]
2 b f Sabrehill (USA) 8.5f **(64)** - Peaches Polly **(87?f 58a)** (Slip Anchor)

9.8f **(73)**
Form - 0
Record 1999 - 1st:0 2nd:0 3rd:0 Ran:1
1999 Turf 0-1: (6f) (frm)
Currently moderate filly. **B W Hills [0-1] W J Gredley.*

COMMANCHE RIDGE RR 51f 4818[7]

2 b c Bonny Scot (IRE) -Cleeveland Lady(Turn Back The Time (USA))
Form - 77
Record 1999 - 1st:0 2nd:0 3rd:0 Ran:2
1999 Turf 0-2: (10f 2) (gd 2)
Currently fair colt. Turf high 51 (began Spt). **W G M Turner [0-2] Mrs Philomena Reich.*

COMMANDER RR 66f 5003[5]

3 b c Puissance 7.1f **(60)** - Tarkhana (IRE) (Dancing Brave (USA)) 8.4f **(76)**
Form - 85
Record 1999 - 1st:0 2nd:0 3rd:0 Ran:2
1999 Turf 0-2: (8f 2) (gd, frm)
Scopey, currently average colt. Turf high 66. **H R A Cecil [0-2] H R H Prince Fahd Salman.*

COMMANDER COLLINS (IRE) BHB 115f RR 114f 3778a[4]

3 b c Sadler's Wells (USA) 11.3f **(87)** - Kanmary (FR) (Kenmare (FR)) 6.5f **(72)**
Form - 04
Record 1999 - 1st:0 2nd:0 3rd:0 Ran:2
Pre1999 - 1st:2 2nd:1 3rd:0 Ran:3
Win Prizemoney £107,407 *Total Prizemoney* £131,644
Wins * 1998 Oct Doncas (HVY) G1 8f 112 <
* 1998 Jly Newmar (FRM) L 7f 102+
1999 Turf 0-2: (8f, 10f) (gd, frm)
Well made, Group-class colt. Turf high 104. He won a weak renewal of the Racing Post Trophy as a juvenile and was probably overrated at the end of that season. Given a poor tactical ride when unplaced in the 2,000 Guineas, he ran moderately at Deauville in August. **P W Chapple-Hyam [2-5].*

COMMENDATORE BHB 36f28a RR 42f 28a 1927[6]

4 b g Magic Ring (IRE) 6.5f **(64)** - Miss Hocroft (Dominion) 8.5f **(63)**
Form - 6066
Record 1999 - 1st:0 2nd:0 3rd:0 Ran:2
Pre1999 - 1st:0 2nd:0 3rd:0 Ran:3
1999 Turf 0-1: (7f) (sft) 1999 AW 0-1: (14f) (Fibr)
Moderate gelding.
**Miss A Stokell [0-1] Ms Caron Stokell (from D R C Elsworth [0-1] Apr 1999).*

COMMONBIRD BHB 40f RR 63f 4073[7]

2 b f Common Grounds 8.1f **(66)** - Queenbird **(63f 52a)** (Warning)
Form - 87357577587
Record 1999 - 1st:0 2nd:0 3rd:1 Ran:11
Win Prizemoney £0 *Total Prizemoney* £504
1999 Turf 0-10: (5f 5, 6f 3, 7f 2) (sft 2, g-s, gd, g-f 4, frm 2) 1999 AW 0-1: (7f) (Fibr)
Average filly, effective 6f, acts on g-f, has worn blinkers. Turf high 59. **Andrew Reid [0-11] A S Reid.*

COMMON CAUSE BHB 77f RR 74f 4126[11]

3 b f Polish Patriot (USA) 7.8f **(70)** - Alongside (Slip Anchor) 9.8f **(73)**
Form - 08312310
Record 1999 - 1st:2 2nd:1 3rd:2 Ran:8
Win Prizemoney £11,002 *Total Prizemoney* £12,668
Wins * **1999** Aug Leices (GD) H 11.8f 72 74+ <
* **1999** Jun Lingfi (GD) H 11.5f 65 67
1999 Turf 2-8: (8f, 10f, 11f 1-2, 12f 1-4) (g-s, gd 1-2, g-f 2, frm 1-3)
Light-framed, above-average filly, effective 11 to 12f, best at 12f, acts on gd to frm, favours tight tracks. Turf high 74 - 1st of 8 getting 18lb from Key Academy (18 Aug Leicester RF 3747) - also 1st of 7 giving 3lb to Common Consent (22 Jun Lingfield RF 2200). Unraced at two, she has gradually improved and got off the mark by winning a Lingfield handicap in June. Added a Leicester handicap in August, winning more easily than the winning margin would suggest. **C F Wall [2-8] T Taniguchi.*

COMMON CONSENT (IRE) BHB 54f RR 60f 5125[3]

3 b f Common Grounds 8.1f **(66)** - Santella Bell (Ballad Rock) 7.8f **(63)**
Form - 72470303
Record 1999 - 1st:0 2nd:1 3rd:2 Ran:8
Pre1999 - 1st:0 2nd:0 3rd:0 Ran:2
Win Prizemoney £0 *Total Prizemoney* £2,339
1999 Turf 0-8: (10f 2, 11f 3, 12f 2, 16f) (gd 3, g-f 2, frm 3)
Scopey, average filly, effective 11f, acts on frm, prefers left handed tracks, likes tight tracks. Turf high 62.
**S Woodman [0-10] Mrs Fiona Gordon & Mrs Jenny Carter.*

COMMON PLACE BHB 79f RR 79f 4899[18]

2 b c Common Grounds 8.1f **(66)** - One Wild Oat **(53f 43a)** (Shareef Dancer (USA)) 9.9f **(73)**
Form - 4447100
Record 1999 - 1st:1 2nd:0 3rd:0 Ran:7
Win Prizemoney £4,279 *Total Prizemoney* £4,732
Wins * 1999 Aug Goodwo (GD) H 7f 77 79 <
1999 Turf 1-7: (6f 3, 7f 1-3, 8f) (gd 2, g-f 1-2, frm 2, hrd)
Above-average colt, effective 6 to 7f, acts on g-f. Turf high 79 - 1st of 9 getting 2lb from Cedar Prince (29 Aug Goodwood RF 3996).
**C F Wall [1-7] N Ahamad.*

COMMONWEALTH (IRE) BHB 75f RR 76f 4880[17]

3 b c Common Grounds 8.1f **(66)** - Silver Slipper **(62f)** (Indian Ridge)
Form - 210380
Record 1999 - 1st:1 2nd:1 3rd:1 Ran:6
Pre1999 - 1st:0 2nd:0 3rd:0 Ran:2
Win Prizemoney £4,071 *Total Prizemoney* £6,861
Wins 1999 Jly Windso (G-F) 8.3f 76 <
1999 Turf 1-6: (7f 2, 8f 1-3, 10f) (g-f 3, frm 1-3)
Scopey, above-average colt, effective 7 to 8f, best at 8f, acts on g-f to frm, best on g-f. Turf high 80 (1st run) (began Jly) - 2nd of 7 giving 5lb to Be Thankfull (10 Jly Ascot 8f g-f RF 2704) - also 1st of 12 giving 5lb to Flight Sequence (26 Jly Windsor RF 3151). Consistent.
**M L W Bell [0-3] Highclere Thoroughbred Racing Ltd (from G Lewis [1-5] Aug 1999).*

COMMONWOOD BHB 63f RR 63f 5052[6]

2 b g Rudimentary (USA) 8.2f **(66)** - Mira Lady (Henbit (USA)) 9f **(61)**
Form - 30204406
Record 1999 - 1st:0 2nd:1 3rd:1 Ran:8
Win Prizemoney £0 *Total Prizemoney* £1,557
1999 Turf 0-8: (5f 4, 6f 3, 7f) (gd 2, g-f 4, frm 2)
Average gelding, effective 5f, acts on g-f. Turf high 76 - 2nd of 16 to Cair Paravel (1 Jun Leicester 5f g-f RF 1645).
**J G Smyth-Osbourne [0-8] Highfields Partnership I.*

COMPATIBLE (IRE) RR 71+f 2570[P]

3 b c Ela-Mana-Mou 12.7f **(72)** - Good Enough (IRE) (Simply Great (FR)) 8.2f **(65)**
Form - 1P
Record 1999 - 1st:1 2nd:0 3rd:0 Ran:2
Win Prizemoney £3,761 *Total Prizemoney* £3,761
Wins * **1999** May Windso (G-F) 10f 71+ <
1999 Turf 1-2: (10f 1-1, 12f) (frm 1-2)
Scopey, above-average colt. Turf high 71 (1st run) - 1st of 13 from Corvino (24 May Windsor RF 1447). (DEAD)
**J H M Gosden [1-2] Sheikh Mohammed.*

COMPATRIOT (IRE) RR 60f 4951[4]

3 b g Bigstone (IRE) - Campestral (USA) (Alleged (USA)) 10f **(76)**
Form - 230344374
Record 1999 - 1st:0 2nd:1 3rd:3 Ran:9
Pre1999 - 1st:0 2nd:1 3rd:0 Ran:4
Win Prizemoney £0 *Total Prizemoney* £5,760
1999 Turf 0-9: (5f 3, 6f 2, 7f 3, 8f) (gd 5, g-f 2, frm 2)
Well made, average gelding, effective 6f, acts on frm, has worn blinkers. Turf high 82. Consistent. **N A Callaghan [0-13] M Tabor.*

COMPENSATION (IRE) RR 65df 5026[12]

3 gr g Turtle Island (IRE) - Fontenoy (USA) (Lyphard's Wish (FR)) 9f **(74)**
Form - 263424730
Record 1999 - 1st:0 2nd:2 3rd:2 Ran:9
Pre1999 - 1st:0 2nd:1 3rd:0 Ran:5

Win Prizemoney £0 *Total Prizemoney* £5,465
1999 Turf 0-9: (7f 7, 8f 2) (sft, gd 3, g-f 3, frm 2)
Unfurnished, average gelding, effective 6 to 8f, acts on g-s to frm, has worn blinkers. Turf high 69. Consistent.
**M A Jarvis [0-14] Mrs G R Smith.*

COMPLIMENTARY BHB 54f48a RR 57f 48a 2429[1]

3 b g Superpower 6.6f **(58)** - Syke Lane (Clantime)
Form - 42245611
Record 1999 - 1st:2 2nd:2 3rd:0 Ran:7
Pre1999 - 1st:0 2nd:0 3rd:0 Ran:4
Win Prizemoney £5,077 *Total Prizemoney* £6,300
Wins * 1999 Jun Bath (GD) H 10.2f 44 57 <
*** 1999** Jun Nottin (GD) SH 8.2f 45 49
1999 Turf 2-3: (7f, 8f 1-1, 10f 1-1) (g-f 1-2, frm 1-1) 1999 AW 0-4: (6f 2, 7f 2) (Equi, Fibr 3)
Workmanlike, fair gelding, effective 6 to 10f, acts on g-f to frm - acts on Equi, has worn blinkers, favours left handed tracks, favours tight tracks. Turf high 57 - 1st of 9 giving 6lb to Kingfishers Bonnet (30 Jun Bath RF 2429) - also 1st of 18 giving 2lb to Who Goes There (21 Jun Nottingham RF 2171). AW high 51.
**W J Haggas [2-11] W J Haggas.*

COMPLIMENTARY PASS RR 74f 4592[4]

3 b f Danehill (USA) 9.1f **(79)** - Capo Di Monte (Final Straw) 7.9f **(64)**
Form - 24
Record 1999 - 1st:0 2nd:1 3rd:0 Ran:2
Win Prizemoney £0 *Total Prizemoney* £1,625
1999 Turf 0-2: (8f, 9f) (gd, frm)
Strong, currently above-average filly. Turf high 74 (1st run) (began Aug) - 2nd of 14 to Katy Nowaitee (28 Aug Newmarket 8f frm RF 3967). **G C Bravery [0-2] The Complimentary Partnership.*

COMPRADORE BHB 62f RR 63f 5033[19]

4 b f Mujtahid (USA) 7.4f **(69)** - Keswa (Kings Lake (USA)) 10.8f **(67)**
Form - 74355802645730
Record 1999 - 1st:0 2nd:1 3rd:2 Ran:14
Pre1999 - 1st:2 2nd:1 3rd:0 Ran:15
Win Prizemoney £6,819 *Total Prizemoney* £12,161
Wins * 1998 Oct Folkes (G-S) 6f 69
***** 1997 May Newbur (G-F) 5.2f 82 <
1999 Turf 0-14: (6f 4, 7f 5, 8f 5) (sft, g-s 2, gd, g-f 4, frm 6)
Unfurnished, average filly, effective 6 to 7f, best at 6f, acts on g-s to frm, best on frm. Turf high 69 - 3rd of 20 giving 5lb to Samara Song (13 May Salisbury 7f frm RF 1191).
**M Blanshard [2-29] C McKenna.*

COMPREHENSION (USA) BHB 85f RR 77f 3462[R]

3 b f Diesis 9f **(80)** - Je Comprend (USA) (Caerleon (USA)) 8.6f **(71)**
Form - 13R
Record 1999 - 1st:1 2nd:0 3rd:1 Ran:3
Pre1999 - 1st:0 2nd:0 3rd:0 Ran:1
Win Prizemoney £3,968 *Total Prizemoney* £5,073
Wins * 1999 Jun Yarmou (G-F) 8f 77 <
1999 Turf 1-3: (7f, 8f 1-2) (gd 2, frm 1-1)
Scopey, above-average filly. Turf high 77 (1st run) - 1st of 6 from Musical Tones (21 Jun Yarmouth RF 2187). Got off the mark against a subsequent winner on her reappearance, but was very disappointing next time, and refused to race at Ascot.
**C E Brittain [1-4] Saeed Manana.*

COMPTON ACE BHB 112f90a RR 118f 90a 3168[1]

3 ch c Pharly (FR) 11.5f **(64)** - Mountain Lodge (Blakeney) 10.5f **(64)**
Form - 22131
Record 1999 - 1st:2 2nd:2 3rd:1 Ran:5
Pre1999 - 1st:0 2nd:0 3rd:0 Ran:3
Win Prizemoney £32,546 *Total Prizemoney* £43,749
Wins * 1999 Jly Goodwo (G-F) G3 12f 118 <
*** 1999** May Newbur (G-F) H 13.3f 80 83+
1999 Turf 2-5: (12f 1-2, 13f 1-1, 14f, 16f) (gd 2, g-f 1-2, frm 1-1)
Workmanlike, high-class colt, effective 12f, acts on frm. Turf high 118 - 1st of 6 from Time Zone (27 Jly Goodwood RF 3168). Improving. He started off the season looking a much-improved performer. Got off the mark in a Newbury handicap in May and, after finishing a fine third in the Queen's Vase, enjoyed his finest moment by winning the Gordon Stakes at Glorious Goodwood. Unfortunately, he sustained a fractured knee in the process and that was him finished for the season. **G A Butler [2-8] E Penser.*

COMPTON ADMIRAL BHB 122f RR 122f 3694[5]

3 b c Suave Dancer (USA) 10.7f **(68)** - Sumoto (Mtoto)
Form - 10815
Record 1999 - 1st:2 2nd:0 3rd:0 Ran:5
Pre1999 - 1st:1 2nd:3 3rd:0 Ran:4
Win Prizemoney £201,472 *Total Prizemoney* £221,691
Wins * 1999 Jly Sandow (G-F) G1 10f 122 <
*** 1999** Apr Newmar (GD) G3 8f 110
***** 1998 Jly Ascot (G-F) 7f 96
1999 Turf 2-5: (8f 1-2, 10f 1-2, 12f) (gd, g-f 1-2, frm 1-2)
Strong, very high-class colt, effective 10f, acts on frm. Turf high 122 - 1st of 8 getting 11lb from Xaar (3 Jly Sandown RF 2545). A useful performer at two, Gerard Butler's stable star made a fine 1999 reappearance with a clear-cut victory in the Craven, but was well beaten in the Guineas. He redeemed his reputation somewhat when a respectable eighth in the Derby. The slowish pace and drop back to ten furlongs suited him admirably in the Eclipse, when he pounced fast and late to win despite rider Darryll Holland briefly losing his reins. A respectable fifth in the York International, he picked up a knee injury there and will be out for a year. **G A Butler [3-9] E Penser.*

Compton Admiral sails home in the Craven

COMPTON AJAX (IRE) RR 47f 710[10]

3 gr g Paris House 5.9f **(64)** - Fear Naught (Connaught) 7.7f **(63)**
Form - 0
Record 1999 - 1st:0 2nd:0 3rd:0 Ran:1
Pre1999 - 1st:0 2nd:0 3rd:0 Ran:1
1999 Turf 0-1: (8f) (gd)
Scopey, moderate gelding. (DEAD) **G A Butler [0-2] E Penser.*

COMPTON AKKA (IRE) BHB 53f64a RR 53f 64a 3871[F]

3 b f Balla Cove - Adjanada (Nishapour (FR)) 9.1f **(61)**
Form - 6221152080F
Record 1999 - 1st:2 2nd:3 3rd:0 Ran:10
Pre1999 - 1st:0 2nd:1 3rd:1 Ran:7
Win Prizemoney £3,998 *Total Prizemoney* £7,405
Wins * 1999 *Feb Lingfi (STD) 7f 64* <
*** 1999** *Feb Lingfi (STD) 7f 62*
1999 Turf 0-3: (6f 3) (g-f, frm 2) 1999 AW 2-7: (7f 2-4, 8f 3) (Equi 2-6, Fibr)
Workmanlike, average filly, effective 6 to 8f, best at 7f, acted on g-f - acted on Equi, had worn blinkers, liked left handed tracks, liked tight tracks. Turf high 23. AW high 64 - 1st of 6 getting 20lb from

Village Native (20 Feb Lingfield RF 0325) - also 1st of 6 from Golconda (11 Feb Lingfield RF 0272). (DEAD)
**G A Butler [2-17] E Penser.*

COMPTON AMBER BHB 58f47a **RR 66f 47a** 4938[7]

3 b f Puissance 7.1f **(60)** - Amber Mill (Doulab (USA)) 9.8f **(65)**
Form - 37760R677
Record 1999 - 1st:0 2nd:0 3rd:1 Ran:9
Pre1999 - 1st:0 2nd:1 3rd:1 Ran:8
Win Prizemoney £0 *Total Prizemoney* £9,191
1999 Turf 0-4: (5f, 8f 3) (sft, g-f 2, frm) 1999 AW 0-5: (6f 3, 8f, 10f) (Equi 2, Fibr 3)
Unfurnished, average filly, has worn blinkers. Turf high 66. AW high 42. Inconsistent. **G A Butler [0-19] E Penser.*

COMPTON AMICA (IRE) BHB 78f **RR 77f** 4345[4]

3 gr f High Estate 10.5f **(66)** - Nephrite (Godswalk (USA)) 7.3f **(58)**
Form - 131104384
Record 1999 - 1st:3 2nd:0 3rd:2 Ran:9
Pre1999 - 1st:0 2nd:0 3rd:0 Ran:4
Win Prizemoney £9,757 *Total Prizemoney* £12,068
Wins * 1999 Jun Sandow (GD) H 11.4f 78 81 <
*** 1999** May Windso (GD) H 11.6f 70 74
*** 1999** Mar Folkes (SFT) H 9.7f 64 68
1999 Turf 3-9: (10f 1-1, 11f 1-2, 12f 1-5, 15f) (hvy 1-1, gd 2, g-f 1-4, frm 1-2)
Well made, above-average filly, effective 11 to 12f, best at 12f, acts on g-f to frm, best on frm, prefers right handed tracks, prefers tight tracks. Turf high 81 - 4th of 8 giving 2lb to Rada's Daughter (25 Jly Ascot 12f g-f RF 3116) - also 1st of 10 getting 1lb from Theseus (1 Jun Sandown RF 1656). Consistent. She seems to have improved from two to three, and appeared to relish the step up in trip when winning nicely over the extended nine furlongs at Folkestone on her reappearance. Two further wins over an extended 11 furlongs followed, but she was well held afterwards.
**G A Butler [3-13] E Penser.*

COMPTON ANGEL (IRE) BHB 61f70a **RR 64f 70a** 5056[1]

3 b f Fairy King (USA) 7.7f **(75)** - Embla (Dominion) 8.5f **(63)**
Form - 064824461
Record 1999 - 1st:1 2nd:1 3rd:0 Ran:9
Pre1999 - 1st:0 2nd:0 3rd:0 Ran:2
Win Prizemoney £2,952 *Total Prizemoney* £4,633
Wins * 1999 *Oct Lingfi (STD) H 10f 64 67* <
1999 Turf 0-7: (7f 2, 8f, 10f 3, 11f) (sft, g-s, gd 3, g-f, frm) 1999 AW 1-2: (10f 1-2) (Equi 1-2)
Scopey, average filly, effective 10f, acts on gd - acts on Equi, prefers left handed tracks, prefers tight tracks. Turf high 64 - 4th of 14 giving 3lb to Orbital Star (29 May Lingfield 10f gd RF 1584). AW high 67 (began Jly) - 1st of 14 giving 16lb to Rookie (25 Oct Lingfield RF 5056).
**G A Butler [1-11] E Penser.*

COMPTON ARROW (IRE) BHB 97f **RR 100f** 3770[19]

3 b c Petardia 8.2f **(58)** - Impressive Lady (Mr Fluorocarbon) 6f **(55)**
Form - 3670330
Record 1999 - 1st:0 2nd:0 3rd:3 Ran:7
Pre1999 - 1st:2 2nd:0 3rd:1 Ran:6
Win Prizemoney £10,452 *Total Prizemoney* £16,197
Wins * 1998 Oct Ascot (SFT) 6f 95 <
***** 1998 Aug Haydoc (G-S) 6f 86+
1999 Turf 0-7: (7f 3, 8f 4) (gd 2, g-f 4, frm)
Scopey, very useful colt, effective 6 to 8f, acts on g-s to frm. Turf high 100 (1st run) - 3rd of 11 to Dehoush (3 Apr Kempton 8f g-f RF 0570). Consistent. Sharp enough to beat Mitcham as a juvenile, he fell short of Group class in 1999. **G A Butler [2-13] E Penser.*

COMPTON AVIATOR BHB 80f **RR 80f** 3998[3]

3 ch c First Trump - Rifada (Ela-Mana-Mou) 10.1f **(70)**
Form - 433
Record 1999 - 1st:0 2nd:0 3rd:2 Ran:3
Win Prizemoney £0 *Total Prizemoney* £1,630
1999 Turf 0-3: (7f, 10f 2) (gd, g-f, frm)
Scopey, currently decent colt. Turf high 80 (began Jly) - 3rd of 14 giving 5lb to Houdini's Honey (2 Aug Windsor 10f frm RF 3304).
**G A Butler [0-3] E Penser.*

COMPTON BANKER (IRE) BHB 83f **RR 76f** 5195[5]

2 br c Distinctly North (USA) 7.4f **(63)** - Mary Hinge **(96f)** (Dowsing (USA))
Form - 675
Record 1999 - 1st:0 2nd:0 3rd:0 Ran:3
1999 Turf 0-3: (6f 3) (gd 2, frm)
Currently above-average colt. Turf high 76 (began Jly). Lost his chance on his debut with a slow start, and was pitched in to Group Two company next time, never landing a blow. Obviously well thought of, and should win races. **G A Butler [0-3] E Penser.*

COMPTON BOLTER (IRE) BHB 100f **RR 91f** 5263a[3]

2 b c Red Sunset 9f **(57)** - Milk And Honey (So Blessed) 8.7f **(67)**
Form - 32123
Record 1999 - 1st:1 2nd:2 3rd:2 Ran:5
Win Prizemoney £2,808 *Total Prizemoney* £17,797
Wins * 1999 Spt Chepst (GD) 8.1f 85 <
1999 Turf 1-5: (7f 4, 8f 1-1) (g-s, gd, g-f 2, frm 1-1)
Useful colt. Turf high 91 (began Jly) - 3rd of 8 to Touch Of The Blues (5 Nov Maisons-Laffitte 7f g-s RF 5263a) - also 1st of 12 from Water Jump (9 Spt Chepstow RF 4227). Improving steadily, and got off the mark with a battling short-head victory in a Chepstow maiden on his third start. Ran well to finish runner-up in Ascot's Hyperion Stakes next time and looks likely to make up into a nice middle-distance handicapper at three. **G A Butler [1-5].*

CONCER ARALL BHB 30a **RR 30a** 43[11]

5 ch g Ron's Victory (USA) 9.2f **(52)** - Drudwen (Sayf El Arab (USA)) 7.1f **(54)**
Form - 0000
Record 1999 - 1st:0 2nd:0 3rd:0 Ran:2
Pre1999 - 1st:0 2nd:2 3rd:1 Ran:10
Win Prizemoney £0 *Total Prizemoney* £1,589
1999 AW 0-2: (7f, 8f) (Equi 2)
Little account gelding, has worn blinkers. AW high 29. Inconsistent.
**P D Evans [0-4] Edgar Lloyd (from S C Williams [0-8] Feb 1998).*

CONCER UN BHB 74f82a **RR 78f 82a** 4802[10]

7 ch g Lord Bud 8.2f **(52)** - Drudwen (Sayf El Arab (USA)) 7.1f **(54)**
Form - 7065540
Record 1999 - 1st:0 2nd:0 3rd:0 Ran:7
Pre1999 - 1st:10 2nd:6 3rd:5 Ran:44
Win Prizemoney £95,472 *Total Prizemoney* £109,875
Wins * 1997 Aug York (GD) H 7.9f 86 92
* 1996 Aug Cheste (GD) H 7f 90 98 <
* 1996 Aug York (GD) H 7.9f 90 97
* 1996 Jly Sandow (G-S) H 8.1f 87 89
* 1996 Jun Bath (FRM) H 8f 81 83+
* 1996 Jun Bath (G-F) H 8f 78 82
* 1995 Spt Kempto (GD) H 8f 72 78
* 1995 Aug Thirsk (G-F) H 8f 61 70
* 1995 Aug Bath (HRD) H 8f 61 65
* 1995 Mar Hamilt (HVY) 8.3f 56
1999 Turf 0-7: (7f 2, 8f 3, 9f 2) (g-s, gd 4, g-f, frm)
Above-average gelding, effective 8f, acts on frm. Turf high 78 (began Jly) - 5th of 24 getting 1lb from Pension Fund (1 Spt York 8f frm RF 4085). Consistent. A smart handicapper a few seasons back, he does not look the same horse he once was, although he ran from an unfavourable draw more than once last season following a year's absence. **S C Williams [10-51] Stuart Williams.*

CONCINO (FR) BHB 42f **RR 40f** 4627[11]

2 b c Zafonic (USA) 9f **(83)** - Petronella (USA)(Nureyev (USA)) 8.7f **(78)**
Form - 000
Record 1999 - 1st:0 2nd:0 3rd:0 Ran:3
1999 Turf 0-3: (6f 2, 7f) (g-s, g-f, frm)
Currently moderate colt. Turf high 40 (began Aug).
**P W Harris [0-3] Mrs P W Harris.*

CONCLUSION BHB 63f **RR 65f** 4923[8]

2 ch c Prince Sabo 6.6f **(64)** - High Finish (High Line) 10.3f **(70)**
Form - 037617038
Record 1999 - 1st:1 2nd:0 3rd:2 Ran:9
Win Prizemoney £2,038 *Total Prizemoney* £2,865
Wins * 1999 Aug Leices (GD) SH 6f 59 65 <
1999 Turf 1-7: (6f 1-7) (g-s, gd, g-f 1-2, frm, hrd 2) 1999 AW 0-2: (6f 2)

(Equi, Fibr)
Average colt, effective 6f, acts on g-f. Turf high 65 - 1st of 14 giving 7lb to Little Christian (11 Aug Leicester RF 3547). AW high 62 (began Oct). **M Blanshard [1-9] J A Oliver.*

CONFIDENTIAL RR 52f

2354[4]
3 ch f Generous (IRE) 11.5f **(82)** - Just You Wait (Nonoalco (USA)) 8.5f **(66)**
Form - 64
Record 1999 - 1st:0 2nd:0 3rd:0 Ran:2
Win Prizemoney £0 *Total Prizemoney* £285
1999 Turf 0-2: (12f 2) (gd, g-f)
Scopey, currently fair filly. Turf high 52.
**H R A Cecil [0-2] H R H Prince Fahd Salman.*

CONFLICT (FR) BHB 98f RR 97f

3756[6]
3 b c Warning 8.1f **(77)** - La Dama Bonita (USA) (El Gran Senor (USA)) 9.6f **(76)**
Form - 6645616
Record 1999 - 1st:1 2nd:0 3rd:0 Ran:7
Pre1999 - 1st:1 2nd:0 3rd:0 Ran:2
Win Prizemoney £11,941 *Total Prizemoney* £14,057
Wins * 1999 Aug Haydoc (G-S) H 10.5f 94 97 <
* 1998 Oct Leices (G-S) 7f 90
1999 Turf 1-7: (6f, 10f 4, 11f 1-1, 12f) (g-s, gd 1-5, g-f)
Leggy, very useful colt, effective 7 to 11f, acts on gd. Turf high 97 - 1st of 9 giving 12lb to Ex Gratia (5 Aug Haydock RF 3399). Consistent. Best on easy ground, he spent most of the season chasing shadows and appreciated the drop in class when winning a handicap at Haydock in August. Suited by forcing the pace over a mile and a quarter, he is game.
**C E Brittain [2-9] Sheikh Marwan Al Maktoum.*

CONFRONTER BHB 44f60a RR 39f 60a

1733[8]
10 ch g Bluebird (USA) 7.9f **(71)** - Grace Darling (USA) (Vaguely Noble) 10.1f **(72)**
Form - 23210541558
Record 1999 - 1st:2 2nd:1 3rd:0 Ran:9
Pre1999 - 1st:10 2nd:19 3rd:11 Ran:111
Win Prizemoney £40,036 *Total Prizemoney* £75,876
Wins * 1999 *Apr Lingfi (STD) H 10f 58 61*
*** 1999** *Jan Lingfi (STD) H 10f 55 60*
* 1997 *Nov Lingfi (STD) H 10f 52 54*
* 1997 Jun Bath (G-F) H 8f 53 57
* 1995 Spt Bright (GD) H 8f 70 86 <
* 1995 Spt Yarmou (GD) H 8f 70 77
* 1995 Apr Bright (GD) H 8f 63 72
* 1995 Jan Cagnes (G-S) 8f
1999 Turf 0-5: (8f 2, 9f, 10f 2) (sft, gd 2, g-f, frm) 1999 AW 2-4: (10f 2-4) (Equi 2-4)
Average gelding, effective 8 to 10f, best at 10f, acts on sft to g-s - acts on Equi, has worn blinkers, prefers tight tracks, excels at Lingfield. Turf high 39. AW high 63 (1st run) - 2nd of 8 giving 2lb to Kings Arrow (1 Jan Lingfield 10f Equi RF 0004) - also 1st of 13 getting 8lb from Il Destino (9 Apr Lingfield RF 0633). Becoming disappointing. Still capable over ten furlongs on Equitrack.
**S Dow [9-103] Hatfield Ltd (from P F I Cole [3-17] Spt 1992).*

CONNECT RR 88f

4793[6]
2 b c Petong 7.6f **(58)** - Natchez Trace (Commanche Run) 8.5f **(58)**
Form - 2136
Record 1999 - 1st:1 2nd:1 3rd:1 Ran:4
Win Prizemoney £2,944 *Total Prizemoney* £5,033
Wins * 1999 Spt Pontef (G-F) 5f 79 <
1999 Turf 1-4: (5f 1-4) (gd 3, frm 1-1)
Useful colt. Turf high 88 - 3rd of 16 giving 7lb to Blue Velvet (30 Spt Newmarket 5f gd RF 4651) - also 1st of 12 from Firepower (16 Spt Pontefract RF 4348). Second to the progressive Hammer And Sickle in April, he was off the track for five months before landing a Pontefract maiden in September. Followed that with a fine third in a competitive Newmarket nursery and can win more races.
**M H Tompkins [1-4] www raceworld co uk.*

CONORA (NZ) RR 15f

5155[7]
6 b g Conquistarose (USA) - Soundora (NZ) (Sound Reason (CAN))
Form - 7
Record 1999 - 1st:0 2nd:0 3rd:0 Ran:1
1999 Turf 0-1: (8f) (gd)
Poor gelding. **O O'Neill [0-4] J Russell.*

CONORMARA (USA) RR 98f

4737a[2]
2 bb c Carr de Naskra (USA) 10.4f **(76)** - Teeming Shore (USA) (L'Emigrant (USA)) 10.5f **(62)**
Form - 72
1999 Turf 0-2: (6f, 7f) (sft, g-s)
Currently very useful colt. Turf high 98 (began Spt) - 2nd of 6 giving 3lb to Poco A Poco (2 Oct Curragh 6f sft RF 4737a). He kept on well when finishing second in a Listed race at The Curragh in October and should stay a mile. A maiden race is there for the taking. **D Hanley in IRE [0-2] Timothy Rooney.*

CONSIDERATION (IRE) BHB 53f45a RR 57f 45a

2721[4]
2 ch f Perugino (USA) - Reflection Time (IRE) (Fayruz)
Form - 6244
Record 1999 - 1st:0 2nd:1 3rd:0 Ran:4
Win Prizemoney £0 *Total Prizemoney* £660
1999 Turf 0-2: (5f 2) (gd, g-f) 1999 AW 0-2: (6f, 7f) (Fibr 2)
Fair filly. Turf high 57. AW high 31.
**J Berry [0-4] Clayton Bigley Partnership Ltd.*

CONSORT BHB 75f RR 74f

5217[11]
6 b h Groom Dancer (USA) 9.5f **(75)** - Darnelle (Shirley Heights) 10.3f **(74)**
Form - 00060446080
Record 1999 - 1st:0 2nd:0 3rd:0 Ran:11
Pre1999 - 1st:2 2nd:5 3rd:2 Ran:21
Win Prizemoney £27,496 *Total Prizemoney* £70,226
Wins * 1997 Nov Newmar (G-F) H 8f 84 89 <
1996 Aug Salisb (G-F) 7f 74
1999 Turf 0-11: (7f 3, 8f 6, 9f, 10f) (g-s, gd 4, g-f 4, frm 2)
Above-average horse, effective 7 to 9f, acts on g-f to hrd. Turf high 83 - 4th of 16 getting 7lb from Cruinn A Bhord (14 Aug Newmarket 7f g-f RF 3657). He did not show much last season, and failed to build on his fourth in a hot Newmarket handicap in August. Wants a straight track, and strongly run race at about a mile.
**Mrs A J Perrett [1-26] Mrs S L Whitehead (from G Harwood [1-6] Oct 1996).*

CONSPICUOUS (IRE) BHB 82f86a RR 81f 86a

4791[1]
9 b g Alzao (USA) 9.8f **(73)** - Mystery Lady (USA) (Vaguely Noble) 10.1f **(72)**
Form - 66668011
Record 1999 - 1st:2 2nd:0 3rd:0 Ran:8
Pre1999 - 1st:7 2nd:12 3rd:7 Ran:59
Win Prizemoney £55,143 *Total Prizemoney* £102,035
Wins * 1999 Oct Ascot (G-S) H 12f 78 81
*** 1999** Spt Kempto (HVY) H 9f 73 75+
* 1998 Nov Bright (SFT) H 10f 83 89
* 1997 Oct Newbur (GD) H 10f 86 91 <
* 1997 Aug Salisb (G-F) H 8f 82 89
* 1996 Aug Goodwo (GD) 9f 84
* 1995 Spt Goodwo (GD) H 9f 69 75
* 1995 Aug Kempto (G-F) H 10f 59 65
1999 Turf 2-8: (9f 1-2, 10f 5, 12f 1-1) (g-s 1-1, gd 1-4, g-f, frm 2)
Decent gelding, effective 8 to 10f, best at 8f, acts on g-s to frm, has worn blinkers, likes right handed tracks, and likes Ascot. Turf high 82. Consistent. A decent handicapper, but he can be a little frustrating as he likes to come from behind off a strong pace and these tactics often get him into trouble. Had the ground in his favour when winning two amateur events at the end of the season.
**L G Cottrell [8-54] Mrs Jenny Hopkins (from P F I Cole [1-13] Jly 1993).*

CONSTANT BHB 74f RR 77f

4839[5]
2 b c Deploy 11.4f **(67)** - Avowal (Kris) 9.5f **(73)**
Form - 085
Record 1999 - 1st:0 2nd:0 3rd:0 Ran:3
1999 Turf 0-3: (7f, 8f 2) (gd, g-f, frm)
Currently above-average colt. Turf high 77 (began Jly) - 5th of 19 to Imperial Rocket (12 Oct Leicester 8f gd RF 4839).
**B W Hills [0-3] K Abdulla.*

CONSULTANT BHB 54f60a RR 53f 60a

5146[7]
3 b g Man of May - Avenita Lady (Free State) 8.7f **(61)**
Form - 662406007

Record 1999 - 1st:0 2nd:1 3rd:0 Ran:9
Pre1999 - 1st:2 2nd:1 3rd:1 Ran:8
Win Prizemoney £5,188 *Total Prizemoney* £10,223
Wins * 1998 *Spt Wolver (STD) 6f 82* <
* 1998 *Apr Wolver (STD) S 5f 60+*
1999 Turf 0-3: (5f 2, 6f) (gd, frm, hrd) 1999 AW 0-6: (5f 4, 6f, 7f) (Equi 2, Fibr 4)
Leggy, above-average gelding, effective 5 to 6f, best at 6f, - acts on Fibr, prefers left handed tracks, prefers tight tracks. Turf high 46. AW high 73 - 2nd of 13 getting 29lb from Dil (29 Apr Wolverhampton 5f Fibr RF 0926). Becoming disappointing.
**N P Littmoden [2-17] J W C Coxon.*

CONTENTMENT (IRE) BHB 47a RR 45f 4837[8]
5 b h Fairy King (USA) 7.7f **(75)** - Quality Of Life (Auction Ring (USA)) 8.6f **(65)**
Form - 67700877048
Record 1999 - 1st:0 2nd:0 3rd:0 Ran:8
Pre1999 - 1st:1 2nd:2 3rd:1 Ran:22
Win Prizemoney £3,662 *Total Prizemoney* £6,709
Wins 1997 Jun Windso (G-F) H 10f 69 77 <
1999 Turf 0-7: (8f, 10f 4, 11f, 12f) (sft, g-s, gd 2, frm 3) 1999 AW 0-1: (8f) (Equi)
Moderate colt, effective 7 to 10f, acts on g-f to frm, has worn blinkers, favours tight tracks. Turf high 56. Consistent.
**B R Millman [0-4] The Oberons Partnership (from Miss Gay Kelleway [0-11] Jly 1999).*

CONTINUOUS TIME (USA) BHB 42f RR 36f 4835[18]
3 b f Shadeed (USA) 7.7f **(72)** - Trattoria (USA) (Alphabatim (USA))
Form - 0000
Record 1999 - 1st:0 2nd:0 3rd:0 Ran:4
Pre1999 - 1st:0 2nd:0 3rd:0 Ran:3
1999 Turf 0-4: (7f 3, 8f) (gd 2, g-f, frm)
Workmanlike, very moderate filly, has worn blinkers. Turf high 36.
**J R Jenkins [0-7] Khalifa Dasmal.*

CONTRACT GIRL (IRE) RR 334[7]
5 b m Contract Law (USA) 8.9f **(54)** - Paradise Regained (North Stoke) 10.4f **(55)**
Form - 67
Record 1999 - 1st:0 2nd:0 3rd:0 Ran:2
1999 AW 0-2: (9f, 12f) (Fibr 2)
Very poor filly. AW high 9.
**B D Leavy [0-1] Paul Hollinshead (from P J Bevan [0-5] Jan 1999).*

CONTRARIE BHB 29f32a RR 49?f 32a 4454[17]
6 b m Floose 16f **(5)** - Chanita (Averof) 8.2f **(62)**
Form - 00
Record 1999 - 1st:0 2nd:0 3rd:0 Ran:2
Pre1999 - 1st:1 2nd:2 3rd:1 Ran:16
Win Prizemoney £3,362 *Total Prizemoney* £6,095
Wins * 1997 Oct Nottin (SFT) H 16f 37 44 <
1999 Turf 0-2: (11f, 16f) (sft, g-f)
Moderate mare. Turf high 5 (began Aug). (DEAD)
**M J Ryan [1-18] M J Ryan.*

CONTRARY MARY BHB 59f68a RR 58f 68a 5199[5]
4 b f Mujadil (USA) 7.7f **(70)** - Love Street (Mummy's Pet) 7.7f **(60)**
Form - 0178440345
Record 1999 - 1st:1 2nd:0 3rd:1 Ran:10
Pre1999 - 1st:2 2nd:2 3rd:2 Ran:18
Win Prizemoney £9,772 *Total Prizemoney* £14,381
Wins * **1999** Apr Folkes (SFT) 7f 66
* 1998 Aug Lingfi (G-F) H 7f 65 71
1997 May Lingfi (G-F) 5f 82+ <
1999 Turf 1-10: (6f 7, 7f 1-3) (sft 1-1, gd 2, g-f, frm 6)
Tall, fair filly, effective 6 to 7f, best at 7f, acts on sft to g-f. Turf high 66 - 1st of 12 getting 5lb from Indian Blaze (20 Apr Folkestone RF 0764). Consistent. Not particularly consistent, she scored in soft ground at Folkestone on her second start last season, but was well beaten otherwise. Seven furlongs is her trip.
**J Akehurst [2-19] Flisher Foods (from S P C Woods [0-3] May 1998).*

COOGAN (ITY) RR 77f 578[5]
3 ch c Caerleon (USA) 10.9f **(79)** - Tapage Nocturne (USA) (Irish River (FR)) 8.6f **(78)**
Form - 5
Record 1999 - 1st:0 2nd:0 3rd:0 Ran:1
1999 Turf 0-1: (11f) (g-f)
Workmanlike, currently above-average colt.
**P F I Cole [0-1] Luciano Gaucci.*

COOGEE BAY BHB 41f RR 42f 4925[7]
3 br f Petong 7.6f **(58)** - Dark Eyed Lady (IRE) **(42f 58a)** (Exhibitioner) 8.7f **(61)**
Form - 00807
Record 1999 - 1st:0 2nd:0 3rd:0 Ran:5
1999 Turf 0-3: (6f 2, 7f) (gd 2, frm) 1999 AW 0-2: (7f 2) (Fibr 2)
Unfurnished, moderate filly, has worn blinkers. Turf high 42 (began Aug). AW high 32 (began Oct).
**D W P Arbuthnot [0-5] Mrs M Gutkin.*

COOKIE BHB 87f RR 84f 1419[1]
2 ch c Then Again 7.4f **(52)** - Baking (King of Spain) 7.8f **(52)**
Form - 021
Record 1999 - 1st:1 2nd:1 3rd:0 Ran:3
Win Prizemoney £2,192 *Total Prizemoney* £3,167
Wins * **1999** *May Wolver (STD) 5f 84+* <
1999 Turf 0-2: (5f 2) (g-s, g-f) 1999 AW 1-1: (5f 1-1) (Fibr 1-1)
Currently decent colt. Turf high 84 - 2nd of 10 getting 7lb from Brave Burt (17 May Bath 5f g-f RF 1267). (1st run) - 1st of 5 getting 2lb from Plas Ucha (22 May Wolverhampton RF 1419).
**R Hannon [1-3] Mrs B Burchett.*

COOL AFFAIR (IRE) BHB 50f RR 53f 2156[14]
4 ch g Statoblest 6.4f **(63)** - Ukraine's Affair (USA) (The Minstrel (CAN)) 10f **(72)**
Form - 70
Record 1999 - 1st:0 2nd:0 3rd:0 Ran:2
Pre1999 - 1st:0 2nd:0 3rd:0 Ran:2
1999 Turf 0-2: (6f, 10f) (frm 2)
Scopey, fair gelding. Turf high 53.
**K W Hogg [0-2] S J Crawford (from A B Mulholland [0-2] Oct 1997).*

COOL EDGE (IRE) BHB 85f RR 85f 5155[5]
8 ch g Nashamaa 8.1f **(58)** - Mochara (Last Fandango) 7.8f **(61)**
Form - 150067085
Record 1999 - 1st:1 2nd:0 3rd:0 Ran:9
Pre1999 - 1st:6 2nd:7 3rd:8 Ran:39
Win Prizemoney £67,501 *Total Prizemoney* £113,890
Wins * **1999** Jun Leices (GD) 7f 104
* 1997 Apr Currag (GD) G3 7f 106 <
* 1996 Aug Newbur (GD) H 7.3f 96 99
* 1996 May Haydoc (G-S) LH 7.1f 91 95
* 1996 Mar Doncas (G-S) H 8f 80 86
* 1995 May Hamilt (G-F) 5f 61
1999 Turf 1-9: (7f 1-7, 8f 2) (gd 6, g-f 1-3)
Useful gelding, effective 7 to 9f, acts on gd to g-f, best on gd, has worn blinkers, likes left handed tracks. Turf high 104 (1st run). Consistent. Best when forcing the pace, he goes well when fresh and put up a typically game performance to make a winning reappearance at Leicester in June. The rest of his campaign was an anti-climax and, at eight, he seems to be on the downgrade.
**M H Tompkins [7-49] Henry Chan.*

COOLING CASTLE (FR) BHB 49f RR 52f 4632[11]
3 ch g Sanglamore (USA) 12.9f **(67)** - Syphaly (USA) (Lyphard (USA)) 9.9f **(72)**
Form - 01856500
Record 1999 - 1st:1 2nd:0 3rd:0 Ran:8
Pre1999 - 1st:0 2nd:0 3rd:1 Ran:3
Win Prizemoney £2,364 *Total Prizemoney* £2,838
Wins **1999** Apr Beverl (GD) C 9.9f 59 <
1999 Turf 1-8: (9f, 10f 1-3, 12f 3, 15f) (g-s 2, gd 1-1, g-f 2, frm 2, hrd)
Workmanlike, fair gelding, effective 10f, acts on gd, likes tight tracks. Turf high 59 - 1st of 11 giving 9lb to Tikotino (22 Apr Beverley RF 0803).
**Ronald Thompson [0-6] B Bruce (from B J Meehan [1-5] Apr 1999).*

COOL INVESTMENT (IRE) RR 48+f 4278[1]
2 b c Prince of Birds (USA) - Superb Investment (IRE) (Hatim (USA))
Form - 1
Record 1999 - 1st:1 2nd:0 3rd:0 Ran:1

Win Prizemoney £3,436 *Total Prizemoney* £3,436
Wins * **1999** Spt Mussel (G-F) 8f 48+ <
1999 Turf 1-1: (8f 1-1) (frm 1-1)
Currently moderate colt. (1st run) - 1st of 5 getting 2lb from Principle (13 Spt Musselburgh RF 4278).
**M Johnston [1-1] Markus Graff.*

COOL JUDGE (IRE) BHB 50f **RR 65f** 3598[8]
2 b g Superpower 6.6f **(58)** - Carlton Glory (Blakeney) 10.5f **(64)**
Form - 00623078
Record 1999 - 1st:0 2nd:1 3rd:1 Ran:8
Win Prizemoney £0 *Total Prizemoney* £997
1999 Turf 0-8: (5f 3, 6f 3, 7f 2) (gd 2, g-f 2, frm 3, hrd)
Average gelding, effective 6f, acts on frm to hrd. Turf high 65 - 2nd of 10 getting 1lb from Blackpool Mamma's (27 May Newcastle 6f hrd RF 1522). **W W Haigh [0-8] P D R Construction Ltd.*

COOL KATIE BHB 25f51a **RR 21f 51a** 4148[17]
3 b f Komaite (USA) 6.9f **(61)** - Pomade (Luthier) 9.8f **(71)**
Form - 040800000
Record 1999 - 1st:0 2nd:0 3rd:0 Ran:9
Pre1999 - 1st:0 2nd:2 3rd:0 Ran:6
Win Prizemoney £0 *Total Prizemoney* £1,863
1999 Turf 0-8: (5f 5, 6f 2, 7f) (gd, g-f 2, frm 2, hrd 3) 1999 AW 0-1: (6f) (Fibr)
Little account filly, has worn blinkers. Turf high 51. Becoming disappointing. **K A Ryan [0-15] Roses Racing Club.*

COOL LOCATION BHB 30f **RR 34f** 5002[13]
2 b f Pelder (IRE) - Hello Lady (Wolverlife) 9.3f **(54)**
Form - 000
Record 1999 - 1st:0 2nd:0 3rd:0 Ran:3
1999 Turf 0-2: (6f, 8f) (gd 2) 1999 AW 0-1: (7f) (Fibr)
Currently very moderate filly. Turf high 34. **M Quinn [0-3] V K Cox.*

COOL PROSPECT BHB 47f58a **RR 38f 58a** 4701[9]
4 b g Mon Tresor 7.9f **(60)** - I Ran Lovely (Persian Bold) 9.3f **(66)**
Form - 370006874100000
Record 1999 - 1st:1 2nd:0 3rd:1 Ran:15
Pre1999 - 1st:0 2nd:4 3rd:2 Ran:14
Win Prizemoney £2,360 *Total Prizemoney* £8,160
Wins * **1999** Jun Redcar (FRM) H 6f 44 49 <
1999 Turf 1-11: (6f 1-2, 7f 3, 8f 2, 9f 2, 12f 2) (gd 4, g-f 3, frm 1-3, hrd)
1999 AW 0-4: (6f 2, 7f, 8f) (Fibr 4)
Leggy, average gelding, effective 6f, acts on gd to g-f - acts on Fibr, has worn blinkers, excels at Redcar and Wolverhampton. Turf high 50. AW high 64 (1st run) - 3rd of 8 giving 13lb to Nifty Norman (12 Feb Southwell 6f Fibr RF 0280).
**K A Ryan [1-23] Mrs Candice Reilly (from A B Mulholland [0-6] Apr 1998).*

COOL SECRET BHB 75f **RR 60f** 3170[14]
4 gr g Petong 7.6f **(58)** - Cool Run (Deep Run) 18f **(46)**
Form - 106121061250
Record 1999 - 1st:4 2nd:2 3rd:0 Ran:12
Pre1999 - 1st:1 2nd:0 3rd:1 Ran:15
Win Prizemoney £19,637 *Total Prizemoney* £26,029
Wins * **1999** *Jun Wolver (STD) H 8.5f 85 88* <
* **1999** *Mar Southw (STD) H 7f 75 82*
* **1999** *Feb Southw (STD) H 6f 70 76*
1999 *Feb Southw (STD) C 6f 67*
1997 Aug Redcar (FRM) H 6f 70 80
1999 Turf 0-4: (6f, 8f 2, 9f) (gd 2, frm 2) 1999 AW 4-8: (6f 2-2, 7f 1-3, 8f 1-3) (Equi 2, Fibr 4-6)
Light-framed, useful gelding, effective 7 to 8f, - acts on Fibr, prefers left handed tracks, likes tight tracks. Turf high 60. AW high 88 - 1st of 12 giving 13lb to Baron de Pichon (19 Jun Wolverhampton RF 2161) - also 1st of 9 giving 12lb to Live Project (19 Mar Southwell RF 0453). Becoming disappointing. He won a Redcar nursery at two, but has looked better suited by Fibresand since and showed some decent form on that surface last year, winning four. He started off winning over six furlongs, but got the extended mile at Wolverhampton very well when gaining his fourth win. His handicap mark is getting dangerously high and he may need to go abroad to find further opportunities.
**K R Burke [3-11] Nigel Shields (from K A Ryan [1-7] Feb 1999).*

COOL TEMPER BHB 80f **RR 80f** 2886[2]
3 b g Magic Ring (IRE) 6.5f **(64)** - Ovideo **(58f)** (Domynsky) 8f **(82)**
Form - 222222
Record 1999 - 1st:0 2nd:6 3rd:0 Ran:6
Win Prizemoney £0 *Total Prizemoney* £6,505
1999 Turf 0-6: (6f 5, 7f) (sft, g-f 2, frm 3)
Workmanlike, decent gelding, effective 6 to 7f, best at 6f, acts on g-f to frm, best on frm. Turf high 80 - 2nd of 11 giving 5lb to Talaria (16 Jly Newmarket 6f frm RF 2886). **J E Banks [0-6] The Academy.*

COOL VIBES BHB 70f **RR 76f** 2430[5]
4 br g Rock City 8.8f **(62)** - Meet Again (Lomond (USA)) 8.8f **(65)**
Form - 805
Record 1999 - 1st:0 2nd:0 3rd:0 Ran:3
Pre1999 - 1st:1 2nd:0 3rd:1 Ran:3
Win Prizemoney £4,737 *Total Prizemoney* £5,581
Wins * 1998 Aug Newmar (G-F) 8f 83 <
1999 Turf 0-3: (10f 3) (gd, frm 2)
Well made, above-average gelding, effective 8 to 10f, acts on frm. Turf high 76 (1st run) - 8th of 20 giving 21lb to Gypsy Hill (24 May Windsor 10f frm RF 1442). **J Pearce [1-6] James Furlong.*

COOL WATERS BHB 25f **RR 18f** 1136[18]
4 b f Puissance 7.1f **(60)** -Keep Cool (FR)(Northern Treat (USA)) 6f **(50)**
Form - 0
Record 1999 - 1st:0 2nd:0 3rd:0 Ran:1
Pre1999 - 1st:0 2nd:0 3rd:0 Ran:5
1999 Turf 0-1: (8f) (g-f)
Leggy, poor filly.
**R Dickin [0-1] Mrs Susan Keable (from L P Grassick [0-2] Aug 1998).*

COOPER ISLAND BHB 60f **RR 63f** 3860[11]
3 ch c Generous (IRE) 11.5f **(82)** - Colza (USA) **(74f)** (Alleged (USA)) 10f **(76)**
Form - 043330
Record 1999 - 1st:0 2nd:0 3rd:3 Ran:6
Pre1999 - 1st:0 2nd:0 3rd:0 Ran:2
Win Prizemoney £0 *Total Prizemoney* £2,244
1999 Turf 0-6: (8f, 12f 3, 14f 2) (gd 2, frm 3, hrd)
Scopey, average colt, effective 12f, acts on gd to frm. Turf high 66.
**B W Hills [0-8] K Abdulla.*

COPELAND **RR 111+f** 1532a[7]
4 b c Generous (IRE) 11.5f **(82)** - Whitehaven (Top Ville) 11.7f **(68)**
Form - 237
1999 Turf 0-2: (16f 2) (g-s, gd)
Group-class colt, effective 12 to 16f, best at 12f, acts on hvy to g-f, has worn blinkers. Turf high 111 (1st run) - 3rd of 8 to Katun (2 May Longchamp 16f gd RF 1074a). He falls a fraction short of the top-class and was put firmly in his place by Kayf Tara and Tajoun at Longchamp in May. Has now joined Martin Pipe.
**H-A Pantall in FR [2-6].*

COPERNICUS BHB 80a **RR 76f** 4912[1]
4 b g Polish Precedent (USA) 9f **(73)** - Oxslip (Owen Dudley) 8.3f **(61)**
Form - 5325621171
Record 1999 - 1st:3 2nd:2 3rd:1 Ran:10
Pre1999 - 1st:0 2nd:2 3rd:0 Ran:3
Win Prizemoney £8,576 *Total Prizemoney* £13,471
Wins * **1999** Oct Catter (GD) C 12f 63+
* **1999** Spt Sandow (G-S) H 14f 67 76 <
* **1999** Aug Catter (FRM) C 12f 67
1999 Turf 3-9: (10f 2, 12f 2-2, 14f 1-4, 16f) (g-s, gd 2-4, g-f, frm 1-3)
1999 AW 0-1: (12f) (Fibr)
Scopey, above-average gelding, effective 10 to 16f, best at 10f, acts on gd to frm, best on gd, often wears blinkers (very effectively), does well at Catterick and Sandown. Turf high 80 (1st run) - 3rd of 12 giving 15lb to Hoh No (7 May Nottingham 10f g-f RF 1093) - also 1st of 12 getting 2lb from Amezola (15 Spt Sandown RF 4331). Consistent. Seems to have got his act together, having been upped in trip this term. After a number of fair efforts, he ended the season with three victories, two at Catterick. Has joined Pat Hughes. **P F I Cole [3-13] Christopher Wright.*

COPPER COOKIE BHB 30f23a **RR 44f 23a** 4729[6]
4 ch f Selkirk (USA) 7.9f **(76)** - Festival Fanfare (Ile de Bourbon (USA)) 10.1f **(67)**

Form - 03000004070886
Record 1999 - 1st:0 2nd:0 3rd:0 Ran:12
Pre1999 - 1st:0 2nd:0 3rd:1 Ran:8
Win Prizemoney £0 *Total Prizemoney* £717
1999 Turf 0-5: (7f, 8f 2, 10f 2) (g-s, gd, g-f 2, frm) 1999 AW 0-7: (8f, 12f 5, 16f) (Fibr 7)
Light-framed, moderate filly. Turf high 44. AW high 7. Inconsistent.
**M J Polglase [0-20] M J Polglase.*

COPPER SHELL BHB 59f69a **RR 44?f 69a** 1193[15]
5 ch g Beveled (USA) 6.9f **(64)** - Luly My Love (Hello Gorgeous (USA)) 9.7f **(63)**
Form - 15112120
Record 1999 - 1st:4 2nd:2 3rd:0 Ran:8
Pre1999 - 1st:0 2nd:0 3rd:0 Ran:7
Win Prizemoney £8,074 *Total Prizemoney* £9,899
Wins * 1999 *Feb Wolver (STD) H* *12f* *65* *66* <
*** 1999** *Jan Southw (STD) H* *12f* *59* *66* <
*** 1999** *Jan Southw (STD) H* *11f* *55* *60*
*** 1999** *Jan Southw (STD) H* *12f* *50* *58*
1999 Turf 0-1: (12f) (frm) 1999 AW 4-7: (11f 1-2, 12f 3-4, 16f) (Fibr 4-7)
Average gelding, effective 11 to 12f, best at 12f, - acts on Fibr, favours left handed tracks, excels at Wolverhampton and Southwell. AW high 68 - 2nd of 11 giving 5lb to Isabella Gonzaga (20 Feb Wolverhampton 12f Fibr RF 0335) - also 1st of 13 giving 14lb to Billy Box (29 Jan Southwell RF 0185). He is a fair middle-distance handicapper on Fibresand.
**Mrs L C Jewell [4-17] Gallagher Equine Ltd (from A P Jones [0-6] Oct 1997).*

COPPLESTONE (IRE) BHB 76f **RR 78f** 1493[4]
3 b g Second Set (IRE) 9.2f **(67)** - Queen of the Brush (Averof) 8.2f **(62)**
Form - 4
Record 1999 - 1st:0 2nd:0 3rd:0 Ran:1
Pre1999 - 1st:0 2nd:0 3rd:3 Ran:6
Win Prizemoney £0 *Total Prizemoney* £5,552
1999 Turf 0-1: (10f) (gd)
Leggy, above-average gelding, effective 7 to 10f, best at 8f, acts on gd to hrd - acts on Fibr, best on g-f, has worn blinkers. (1st run) - 4th of 7 getting 13lb from Bering Gifts (26 May Folkestone 10f gd RF 1493). **P W Harris [0-7] Mrs P W Harris.*

COPYFORCE BOY BHB 49f **RR 47f** 1259[14]
3 ch g Mystiko (USA) 7.7f **(59)** - Surpassing (Superlative) 7.2f **(56)**
Form - 0
Record 1999 - 1st:0 2nd:0 3rd:0 Ran:1
Pre1999 - 1st:0 2nd:0 3rd:0 Ran:3
1999 Turf 0-1: (7f) (frm)
Workmanlike, moderate gelding.
**Miss B Sanders [0-4] Copyforce Ltd.*

COPYFORCE GIRL BHB 58f55a **RR 65f 55a** 5197[10]
3 b f Elmaamul (USA) 8.1f **(70)** - Sabaya (USA) (Seattle Dancer (USA))
Form - 66027840
Record 1999 - 1st:0 2nd:1 3rd:0 Ran:7
Pre1999 - 1st:0 2nd:0 3rd:1 Ran:4
Win Prizemoney £0 *Total Prizemoney* £1,423
1999 Turf 0-6: (10f 2, 11f 2, 12f, 16f) (gd 3, frm 3) 1999 AW 0-1: (13f) (Equi)
Unfurnished, average filly, has broken blood-vessels, effective 7f, acts on frm. Turf high 65. **Miss B Sanders [0-11] Copy Xpress Ltd.*

COQUELLES (FR) RR 50tf 4096[7]
3 b f In The Wings 11.2f **(77)** - La Toja (FR) (Gift Card (FR)) 8.6f **(61)**
Form - 77
Record 1999 - 1st:0 2nd:0 3rd:0 Ran:2
1999 Turf 0-2: (12f, 14f) (frm 2)
Workmanlike, currently fair filly. Turf high 50 (began Aug).
**P Eccles [0-2] A P Holland.*

CORAL BEACH RR 15f 1955[17]
3 gr f Lugana Beach 7f **(63)** - Thames Glow (Kalaglow) 9.8f **(67)**
Form - 0
Record 1999 - 1st:0 2nd:0 3rd:0 Ran:1
1999 Turf 0-1: (6f) (g-f)
Leggy, currently poor filly. **M J Haynes [0-1] J P Saunders.*

CORAL ISLAND BHB 42f **RR 43f** 2190[7]
5 b g Charmer 9f **(59)** - Misowni (Niniski (USA)) 10.6f **(65)**
Form - 7
Record 1999 - 1st:0 2nd:0 3rd:0 Ran:1
Pre1999 - 1st:1 2nd:0 3rd:0 Ran:9
Win Prizemoney £2,908 *Total Prizemoney* £2,908
Wins * 1997 May Carlis (FRM) H 8f 55 55 <
1999 Turf 0-1: (12f) (g-f)
Moderate gelding, has worn blinkers. Inconsistent.
**J G FitzGerald [3-20] F Patten.*

CORAL REEF (IRE) BHB 55a **RR 53f** 689[5]
3 ch f Karinga Bay - Mamara Reef **(57df)** (Salse (USA)) 7.5f **(66)**
Form - 5635
Record 1999 - 1st:0 2nd:0 3rd:1 Ran:4
Pre1999 - 1st:0 2nd:1 3rd:1 Ran:5
Win Prizemoney £0 *Total Prizemoney* £1,344
1999 Turf 0-2: (12f, 13f) (gd, frm) 1999 AW 0-2: (8f, 10f) (Equi, Fibr)
Fair filly, effective 7 to 13f, acts on gd to frm - acts on Fibr, best on gd, mostly wears blinkers (extremely effectively), likes left handed tracks, favours tight tracks. Turf high 53 - 5th of 12 giving 5lb to Hi-Jenny (14 Apr Beverley 12f frm RF 0689). AW high 44. Consistent. **W G M Turner [0-9] K B Racing.*

CORAL REEF (ITY) RR 112f 1715a[7]
6 b h Big Reef - All the Crown (Chief's Crown (USA)) 9.8f **(72)**
Form - 7
1999 Turf 0-1: (12f) (frm)
Group-class horse. **G Colleo in ITY [2-7].*

CORAL SHELLS BHB 57f **RR 57f** 4934[5]
2 b f Formidable (USA) 7.8f **(60)** - Elle Reef (Shareef Dancer (USA)) 9.9f **(73)**
Form - 06725
Record 1999 - 1st:0 2nd:1 3rd:0 Ran:5
Win Prizemoney £0 *Total Prizemoney* £1,416
1999 Turf 0-5: (6f, 7f 3, 8f) (sft, gd, g-f, frm 2)
Fair filly. Turf high 57 (began Jly). **P T Walwyn [0-5] Eric Perry.*

CORAL WATERS (IRE) BHB 42f40a **RR 37f 40a** 3276[10]
3 b f College Chapel -Premier Leap(IRE)(Salmon Leap (USA))11f **(61)**
Form - 00064300
Record 1999 - 1st:0 2nd:0 3rd:1 Ran:8
Pre1999 - 1st:0 2nd:0 3rd:0 Ran:3
Win Prizemoney £0 *Total Prizemoney* £280
1999 Turf 0-5: (7f 2, 8f 2, 12f) (gd, g-f 2, frm 2) 1999 AW 0-3: (7f, 8f, 10f) (Equi 3)
Scopey, moderate filly. Turf high 37. AW high 42. Inconsistent.
**R Curtis [0-2] Mrs R A Smith (from C A Cyzer [0-9] Jun 1999).*

CORBLETS BHB 68f **RR 74f** 4941[9]
2 b f Timeless Times (USA) 6.1f **(56)** -Dear Glenda(Gold Song)5.5f **(61)**
Form - 4250
Record 1999 - 1st:0 2nd:1 3rd:0 Ran:4
Win Prizemoney £0 *Total Prizemoney* £1,197
1999 Turf 0-4: (5f 3, 6f) (gd, g-f, frm 2)
Above-average filly. Turf high 74 (began Aug) - 2nd of 8 getting 5lb from Nantucket (24 Aug Lingfield 5f g-f RF 3870).
**S Dow [0-4] J & S Kelly.*

CORDIAL KNIGHT (USA) BHB 50f **RR 43f** 3389[11]
6 b g Night Shift (USA) 8.1f **(73)** - Temperence Cordial (USA) (Temperence Hill (USA)) 11f **(58)**
Form - 0
Record 1999 - 1st:0 2nd:0 3rd:0 Ran:1
Pre1999 - 1st:0 2nd:1 3rd:1 Ran:14
Win Prizemoney £0 *Total Prizemoney* £925
1999 Turf 0-1: (8f) (frm)
Moderate gelding, often wears blinkers. Consistent.
**C P Morlock [0-14] C P H Morlock (from D K Weld in IRE [0-13] May 1997).*

CORETTA (IRE) BHB 96f **RR 118f** 5228a[2]
5 b m Caerleon (USA) 10.9f **(79)** - Free At Last (Shirley Heights) 10.3f **(74)**
Form - 2
1999 Turf 0-1: (11f) (frm)

High-class filly. (1st run) - 2nd of 14 to Soaring Softly (6 Nov Gulfstream Park 11f frm RF 5228a).
**N Clement in FR [0-1] (from L M Cumani [1-6] Spt 1997).*

CORINIUM (IRE) BHB 100f **RR 100+f** 5041[1]
2 br f Turtle Island (IRE) - Searching Star (Rainbow Quest (USA)) 10.4f **(75)**
Form - 311
Record 1999 - 1st:2 2nd:0 3rd:1 Ran:3
Win Prizemoney £16,555 *Total Prizemoney* £17,086
Wins * **1999** Oct Newbur (HVY) L 7.3f 100+ <
* **1999** Spt Warwic (SFT) 7.7f 88+
1999 Turf 2-3: (7f 1-2, 8f 1-1) (sft 2-2, frm)
Currently very useful filly. Turf high 100 (began Aug) - 1st of 12 from Iftiraas (23 Oct Newbury RF 5041). Bolted up in a soft-ground Warwick maiden on her second start, and followed up with a narrow victory in a Newbury listed event. She loves soft ground.
**H R A Cecil [2-3] Derek D & Mrs Jean P Clee.*

CORK HARBOUR (FR) RR 66f 4831[3]
3 ch g Grand Lodge (USA) - Irish Sea (Irish River (FR)) 8.6f **(78)**
Form - 63
Record 1999 - 1st:0 2nd:0 3rd:1 Ran:2
Win Prizemoney £0 *Total Prizemoney* £546
1999 Turf 0-2: (10f 2) (sft, gd)
Scopey, currently average gelding. Turf high 66 (began Spt).
**B W Hills [0-2] Sheikh Mohammed.*

CORNDAVON (USA) BHB 68f **RR 71f** 4696[11]
3 b f Sheikh Albadou 9.2f **(75)** - Ferber's Follies (USA) (Saratoga Six (USA)) 7f **(73)**
Form - 58163770
Record 1999 - 1st:1 2nd:0 3rd:1 Ran:8
Pre1999 - 1st:0 2nd:2 3rd:1 Ran:6
Win Prizemoney £4,449 *Total Prizemoney* £8,380
Wins * **1999** Jly Warwic (G-F) 6f 76 <
1999 Turf 1-8: (5f 2, 6f 1-4, 7f 2) (g-s, gd 2, g-f 1-3, frm 2)
Leggy, above-average filly, effective 5 to 7f, best at 6f, acts on g-f to frm, best on g-f. Turf high 76 - 1st of 5 getting 5lb from Cool Temper (2 Jly Warwick RF 2508). Her one win to date came in a weak event at Warwick on firm ground in July. Well held since.
**M J Fetherston-Godley [1-14] Mrs Julia Scott.*

CORN DOLLY (IRE) BHB 50f **RR 55f** 5193[11]
3 ch f Thatching 7.8f **(69)** - Keepers Lock (USA) (Sunny's Halo (CAN)) 6.7f **(70)**
Form - 080
Record 1999 - 1st:0 2nd:0 3rd:0 Ran:3
1999 Turf 0-3: (6f 2, 8f) (gd 2, frm)
Currently fair filly. Turf high 55 (began Spt).
**R F JohnsonHoughton [0-3] Bob Lanigan.*

CORNELIUS BHB 100f **RR 91f** 5037[6]
2 b c Barathea (IRE) - Rainbow Mountain **(75f)** (Rainbow Quest (USA)) 10.4f **(75)**
Form - 136
Record 1999 - 1st:1 2nd:0 3rd:1 Ran:3
Win Prizemoney £7,700 *Total Prizemoney* £14,330
Wins * **1999** May York (SFT) 6f 81+ <
1999 Turf 1-3: (6f 1-2, 8f) (g-s, gd 1-1, g-f)
Currently useful colt. Turf high 91. He seemed to need every yard of the six furlongs when winning on his York debut, and therefore the same trip on fast ground in the Coventry was inadequate. He was off the track for four months afterwards, and showed little in the Racing Post Trophy on his return.
**P F I Cole [1-3] Sir George Meyrick.*

CORNISH ECLIPSE BHB 35f **RR 4f** 5195[17]
2 b c Formidable (USA) 7.8f **(60)** - Julie's Star (IRE) (Thatching) 8f **(66)**
Form - 000
Record 1999 - 1st:0 2nd:0 3rd:0 Ran:3
1999 Turf 0-3: (5f, 6f 2) (hvy, gd, frm)
Currently very poor colt. Turf high 4 (began Jly).
**M D I Usher [0-3] Kinsmen Racing.*

CORRIDOR CREEPER (FR) BHB 90f **RR 76f** 5123[1]
2 ch c Polish Precedent (USA) 9f **(73)** - Sonia Rose (USA) (Superbity (USA))
Form - 7221
Record 1999 - 1st:1 2nd:2 3rd:0 Ran:4
Win Prizemoney £3,598 *Total Prizemoney* £6,158
Wins * **1999** Oct Bright (G-S) 6f 74+ <
1999 Turf 1-4: (6f 1-3, 7f) (gd 1-1, g-f, frm 2)
Above-average colt. Turf high 84 (began Jly).
**P W Harris [1-4] T Rattee & Mrs P W Harris.*

CORTACHY CASTLE (IRE) BHB 110f **RR 114df** 4418[13]
4 ch g Pips Pride 6.7f **(70)** - Maricica (Ahonoora) 8.1f **(73)**
Form - 2336710380
Record 1999 - 1st:1 2nd:1 3rd:3 Ran:10
Pre1999 - 1st:3 2nd:3 3rd:1 Ran:13
Win Prizemoney £29,851 *Total Prizemoney* £64,493
Wins * **1999** Jly Sandow (GD) L 5f 114 <
* 1998 Aug Sandow (G-F) H 5f 100 104
* 1998 Jun Sandow (SFT) 5f 93
* 1997 Jun Nottin (G-F) 5.1f 66+
1999 Turf 1-10: (5f 1-9, 6f) (gd 3, g-f 3, frm 1-4)
Leggy, Group-class gelding, effective 5f, acts on gd to frm, best on frm. Turf high 114 - 1st of 9 giving 10lb to Flanders (3 Jly Sandown RF 2544). Becoming disappointing. Tough and speedy, this five-furlong specialist enjoyed another creditable season, gaining his third course and distance win when beating Flanders at Sandown in July. Not quite up to the job when tried in Group races, he is game but cannot be particularly easy to place.
**B J Meehan [4-23] Mrs E A Lerpiniere.*

CORUNNA BHB 73f **RR 75f** 4444[6]
2 b c Puissance 7.1f **(60)** - Kind of Shy (Kind of Hush) 10.1f **(62)**
Form - 0222362486
Record 1999 - 1st:0 2nd:4 3rd:1 Ran:10
Win Prizemoney £0 *Total Prizemoney* £4,323
1999 Turf 0-10: (5f 6, 6f 4) (g-s, g-f 2, frm 5, hrd 2)
Above-average colt, effective 5 to 6f, best at 5f, acts on g-f to hrd, best on hrd. Turf high 75. Consistent.
**J Berry [0-10] Chris & Antonia Deuters.*

CORUSCATING BHB 68f **RR 76+f** 5102[5]
2 gr c Highest Honor (FR) 10.9f **(72)** - Mytilene (IRE) **(94f)** (Soviet Star (USA))
Form - 005
Record 1999 - 1st:0 2nd:0 3rd:0 Ran:3
1999 Turf 0-3: (7f, 8f 2) (g-s, gd 2)
Currently above-average colt. Turf high 76 (began Oct).
**Sir Mark Prescott [0-3] Mrs F R Watts.*

CORVINO BHB 66f **RR 67f** 5188[2]
3 b c Tragic Role (USA) 9.4f **(63)** - Clare Island (Connaught) 7.7f **(63)**
Form - 562022
Record 1999 - 1st:0 2nd:3 3rd:0 Ran:6
Win Prizemoney £0 *Total Prizemoney* £4,555
1999 Turf 0-6: (10f 3, 11f, 12f, 16f) (gd, g-f 2, frm 3)
Workmanlike, average colt, effective 10 to 16f, acts on gd to frm. Turf high 67 - 2nd of 16 giving 14lb to Virgin Soldier (3 Nov Musselburgh 16f g-f RF 5188).
**M Kettle [0-6] J Ainsworth & Pillar To Post Racing(III).*

COSCOROBA (IRE) BHB 30f **RR 34f** 4829[11]
5 ch m Shalford (IRE) 7.8f **(63)** - Tameeza (USA) (Shahrastani (USA)) 8.8f **(72)**
Form - 357260
Record 1999 - 1st:0 2nd:1 3rd:1 Ran:6
Pre1999 - 1st:1 2nd:2 3rd:3 Ran:9
Win Prizemoney £3,566 *Total Prizemoney* £6,808
Wins * 1998 Jun Hamilt (SFT) S 9.2f 43 <
1999 Turf 0-6: (9f 2, 10f, 11f 2, 12f) (sft, gd, g-f, frm 3)
Very moderate filly, effective 8f, acts on gd, favours tight tracks. Turf high 34.
**P Monteith [1-16] M G Davidson (from J Berry [0-3] May 1997).*

COSMENA BHB 63f **RR 65f** 3919[2]
2 b f Cosmonaut - Royal Deed (USA) (Shadeed (USA)) 8.2f **(70)**
Form - 24434402
Record 1999 - 1st:0 2nd:2 3rd:1 Ran:8
Win Prizemoney £0 *Total Prizemoney* £3,073

1999 Turf 0-8: (5f 7, 6f) (sft, gd 4, g-f, frm 2)
Average filly, effective 5f, acts on sft to gd. Turf high 65. Consistent. **R M Whitaker [0-8] D Bass.*

COSMIC ALTITUDE BHB 42f30a RR 44f 30a 461[11]

3 b c Cosmonaut - Elaine Ann (Garda's Revenge (USA)) 8.3f **(51)**
Form - 00
Record 1999 - 1st:0 2nd:0 3rd:0 Ran:2
Pre1999 - 1st:0 2nd:0 3rd:0 Ran:3
1999 AW 0-2: (5f 2) (Fibr 2)
Light-framed, moderate colt. AW high 1.
**A G Newcombe [0-5] M Patel.*

COSMIC BUZZ BHB 68f70a RR 73df 70a 5196[12]

2 ch g Cosmonaut - G'Ime a Buzz (Electric) 10.1f **(61)**
Form - 07015500
Record 1999 - 1st:1 2nd:0 3rd:0 Ran:8
Win Prizemoney £2,318 *Total Prizemoney* £2,318
Wins * **1999** Aug Salisb (G-S) C 7f 78? <
1999 Turf 1-6: (5f, 7f 1-2, 8f 3) (gd 1-4, frm 2) 1999 AW 0-2: (6f, 8f) (Fibr 2)
Above-average gelding, effective 7f, acts on gd. Turf high 78 - 1st of 13 giving 12lb to Barbados (11 Aug Salisbury RF 3553). AW high 41. Inconsistent. **A T Murphy [1-8] Exmoor Racing Partnership.*

COSMIC CASE BHB 39f RR 41f 4279[9]

4 b f Casteddu 7.4f **(54)** - La Fontainova (IRE) (Lafontaine (USA)) 8.7f **(49)**
Form - 075000
Record 1999 - 1st:0 2nd:0 3rd:0 Ran:6
Pre1999 - 1st:1 2nd:0 3rd:5 Ran:21
Win Prizemoney £2,981 *Total Prizemoney* £6,064
Wins * 1998 May Mussel (G-F) H 8f 57 64 <
1999 Turf 0-6: (7f, 9f, 10f, 11f, 12f 2) (g-f 2, frm 4)
Scopey, moderate filly, effective 8f, acts on g-f, has worn blinkers, likes right handed tracks, likes tight tracks. Turf high 44.
**J S Goldie [1-27] Strathayr Publishing Ltd.*

COSMIC SONG RR 37f 5209[13]

2 b f Cosmonaut - Hotaria **(52df)** (Sizzling Melody)
Form 00
Record 1999 - 1st:0 2nd:0 3rd:0 Ran:2
1999 Turf 0-2: (5f, 6f) (g-s, gd)
Currently very moderate filly. Turf high 37 (began Jly).
**R M Whitaker [0-2] Mrs Julia Richmond.*

COSMOGRAPHE (FR) RR 94f 5201a[3]

2 b c Lomitas - Volcania (FR) (Neustrien (FR))
Form - 3
1999 Turf 0-1: (10f) (hvy)
Currently useful colt. (1st run) - 3rd of 7 giving 4lb to Goldamix (31 Oct Saint-Cloud 10f hvy RF 5201a). **J M Beguigne in FR [0-1].*

COSMO JACK (IRE) BHB 50f RR 47f 4228[1]

3 b g Balla Cove - Foolish Law (IRE) (Law Society (USA)) 9.9f **(70)**
Form - 06714501
Record 1999 - 1st:2 2nd:0 3rd:0 Ran:8
Pre1999 - 1st:2 2nd:1 3rd:2 Ran:10
Win Prizemoney £9,644 *Total Prizemoney* £10,972
Wins * **1999** Spt Chepst (GD) S 8.1f 46
* **1999** Aug Haydoc (GD) S 8.1f 55
* 1998 Aug Sandow (G-F) SH 7.1f 68 68 <
1998 Jly Bath (GD) S 5.1f 68 <
1999 Turf 2-8: (7f, 8f 2-2, 9f, 10f 2, 12f 2) (gd 1-3, g-f, frm 1-2, hrd 2)
Lengthy, moderate gelding, effective 5 to 7f, best at 7f, acts on gd to g-f, best on g-f, has worn blinkers, does well at Bath. Turf high 61. He is only a plater, but won two such races last term.
**M C Pipe [3-12] Kammac Plc (from B J Meehan [1-6] Jly 1998).*

COSSACK COUNT BHB 69f82a RR 60f 82a 1498[20]

6 ch h Nashwan (USA) 10.3f **(79)** - Russian Countess (USA) (Nureyev (USA)) 8.7f **(78)**
Form - 00
Record 1999 - 1st:0 2nd:0 3rd:0 Ran:2
Pre1999 - 1st:3 2nd:0 3rd:0 Ran:10
Win Prizemoney £11,826 *Total Prizemoney* £11,826
Wins * 1997 *Dec Lingfi (STD) H 7f 68 79+* <
1996 May Leopar (GD) H 6f 78
1996 Mar Naas (SFT) 6f 76
1999 Turf 0-2: (6f 2) (g-f, frm)
Useful horse. Turf high 60. Inconsistent.
**S Dow [1-7] Normandy Developments (London) (from M Kauntze in IRE [2-5] Jun 1996).*

COST AUDITING BHB 57f65a RR 59f 65a 4937[14]

2 ch f Bluebird (USA) 7.9f **(71)** - Elabella (Ela-Mana-Mou) 10.1f **(70)**
Form - 6442000
Record 1999 - 1st:0 2nd:1 3rd:0 Ran:7
Win Prizemoney £0 *Total Prizemoney* £1,237
1999 Turf 0-5: (5f 5) (gd, g-f, frm 3) 1999 AW 0-2: (5f, 6f) (Fibr 2)
Fair filly, effective 5f, - acts on Fibr. Turf high 59 (began Jly). AW high 59 (1st run) (began Spt) - 2nd of 12 getting 13lb from Chiquita (8 Spt Wolverhampton 5f Fibr RF 4221).
**Sir Mark Prescott [0-7] A S Reid.*

COTE SOLEIL BHB 90f RR 87f 4137[4]

2 ch c Inchinor 8.9f **(64)** - Sunshine Coast (Posse (USA)) 8.9f **(61)**
Form - 12046404
Record 1999 - 1st:1 2nd:1 3rd:0 Ran:8
Win Prizemoney £2,723 *Total Prizemoney* £6,819
Wins * **1999** Apr Nottin (G-S) 5.1f 66 <
1999 Turf 1-8: (5f 1-1, 6f 4, 7f 2, 8f) (sft 1-1, gd, g-f 3, frm 3)
Useful colt, effective 6 to 8f, acts on g-f to frm, best on frm, has worn blinkers. Turf high 87 - 2nd of 7 giving 4lb to Dramatic Quest (28 May Pontefract 6f g-f RF 1556). Got off the mark on his debut over the minimum at Nottingham in April and was only just touched off over an extra furlong at Pontefract next time. Comfortably held since however, and is unlikely to improve.
**M R Channon [1-8] Mrs Evelyn Hankinson.*

COTTAGE MAID BHB 32f RR 46f 2429[5]

3 ch f Inchinor 8.9f **(64)** - Mossy Rose (King of Spain) 7.8f **(52)**
Form - 0085
Record 1999 - 1st:0 2nd:0 3rd:0 Ran:3
Pre1999 - 1st:0 2nd:0 3rd:0 Ran:2
1999 Turf 0-2: (8f, 10f) (gd, frm) 1999 AW 0-1: (12f) (Fibr)
Light-framed, moderate filly. Turf high 46.
**D J Coakley [0-3] Stanley Sharp (from Lord Huntingdon [0-2] Nov 1998).*

COTTAGE PRINCE (IRE) BHB 35f RR 38f 3316[5]

6 b g Classic Secret (USA) 8.8f **(56)** - Susan's Blues (Cure The Blues (USA)) 9.5f **(63)**
Form - 06385
Record 1999 - 1st:0 2nd:0 3rd:1 Ran:5
Pre1999 - 1st:2 2nd:1 3rd:3 Ran:20
Win Prizemoney £5,679 *Total Prizemoney* £8,318
Wins * 1997 Jun Catter (GD) H 12f 46 49 <
* 1997 May Redcar (FRM) H 11f 41 47
1999 Turf 0-5: (11f, 12f 3, 14f) (gd, g-f, frm 2, hrd)
Very moderate gelding, effective 11 to 14f, best at 12f, acts on g-f to hrd, best on g-f, has worn blinkers. Turf high 38 - 3rd of 14 getting 19lb from Mr Fortywinks (17 Jun Ripon 12f hrd RF 2079).
**J J Quinn [6-39] Mrs Kay Thomas.*

COTTAM LILLY RR 10f 4877[22]

2 b f Sabrehill (USA) 8.5f **(64)** - Karminski (Pitskelly) 8.5f **(53)**
Form - 0
Record 1999 - 1st:0 2nd:0 3rd:0 Ran:1
1999 Turf 0-1: (5f) (frm)
Currently poor filly. **M W Easterby [0-1] Peter Easterby.*

COTTEIR CHIEF (IRE) BHB 75f95a RR 101?f 95a 4429[15]

8 b g Chief Singer 8.6f **(62)** - Hasty Key (USA) (Key To The Mint (USA)) 9.4f **(75)**
Form - 0
Record 1999 - 1st:0 2nd:0 3rd:0 Ran:1
Pre1999 - 1st:6 2nd:3 3rd:3 Ran:20
Win Prizemoney £25,163 *Total Prizemoney* £41,746
1999 Turf 0-1: (9f) (g-s)
Very useful gelding.
**J Neville [0-5] J Neville (from M C Pipe [6-18] Jun 1995).*

COTTON HOUSE (IRE) BHB 87f **RR 84f** 1662[4]
2 b f Mujadil (USA) 7.7f **(70)** - Romanovna (Mummy's Pet) 7.7f **(60)**
Form - 124
Record 1999 - 1st:1 2nd:1 3rd:0 Ran:3
Win Prizemoney £2,880 *Total Prizemoney* £5,559
Wins * **1999** Apr Warwic (GD) 5f 88+ <
1999 Turf 1-3: (5f 1-3) (gd 1-2, frm)
Currently decent filly. Turf high 88 (1st run) - 1st of 10 from Kilbrannan Sound (5 Apr Warwick RF 0593).
**M R Channon [1-3] Michael Foy.*

COUCHANT (IRE) BHB 39f **RR 37f** 4456[2]
8 b g Petoski 10.4f **(56)** - Be Easy (Be Friendly) 9.3f **(53)**
Form - 2
Record 1999 - 1st:0 2nd:1 3rd:0 Ran:1
Pre1999 - 1st:0 2nd:0 3rd:2 Ran:10
Win Prizemoney £0 *Total Prizemoney* £1,793
1999 Turf 0-1: (16f) (sft)
Very moderate gelding, has worn blinkers. Becoming disappointing.
**P J Hobbs [0-1] Aramis Racing Syndicate (from J White [2-12] May 1997).*

COUGHLAN'S GIFT BHB 61f **RR 63f** 5151[2]
3 ch f Alnasr Alwasheek 9.4f **(62)** - Superfrost (Tickled Pink) 6.5f **(59)**
Form - 000275208812
Record 1999 - 1st:1 2nd:3 3rd:0 Ran:12
Pre1999 - 1st:0 2nd:0 3rd:1 Ran:3
Win Prizemoney £2,640 *Total Prizemoney* £5,656
Wins * **1999** Oct Bath (SFT) H 8f 55 58 <
1999 Turf 1-12: (6f 2, 7f 7, 8f 1-3) (g-s 2, gd 1-4, g-f 3, frm 3)
Light-framed, average filly, effective 6 to 8f, best at 8f, acts on g-s to g-f, best on gd, likes tight tracks. Turf high 63 - 2nd of 18 giving 15lb to Bunty (1 Nov Nottingham 8f gd RF 5151) - also 1st of 15 giving 5lb to Grannys Reluctance (26 Oct Bath RF 5068).
**J C Fox [1-15] Mrs J A Cleary.*

COUL BANK BHB 36f **RR 43f** 4441[17]
3 b g Robellino (USA) 9.5f **(68)** - Future Options **(56f)** (Lomond (USA)) 8.8f **(65)**
Form - 0
Record 1999 - 1st:0 2nd:0 3rd:0 Ran:1
Pre1999 - 1st:0 2nd:0 3rd:0 Ran:3
1999 Turf 0-1: (8f) (g-f)
Moderate gelding.
**J G Smyth-Osbourne [0-1] Mrs Robert Bingley (from P T Walwyn [0-3] Oct 1998).*

COULD BE EXPENSIVE BHB 47f **RR 46f** 5207[19]
2 b c Pursuit of Love 9.5f **(69)** - High Typha **(53f)** (Dowsing (USA))
Form - 000
Record 1999 - 1st:0 2nd:0 3rd:0 Ran:3
1999 Turf 0-3: (7f 2, 8f) (g-s, gd 2)
Currently moderate colt. Turf high 46 (began Oct).
**M H Tompkins [0-3] Bernard Hathaway.*

COULTHARD (IRE) BHB 86f **RR 89f** 4876[7]
6 ch g Glenstal (USA) 10f **(59)** - Royal Aunt (Martinmas) 7.6f **(59)**
Form - 1707
Record 1999 - 1st:1 2nd:0 3rd:0 Ran:4
Pre1999 - 1st:1 2nd:1 3rd:0 Ran:7
Win Prizemoney £11,022 *Total Prizemoney* £12,504
Wins * **1999** Apr Haydoc (SFT) H 11.9f 85 89 <
* 1998 Jun Windso (SFT) 10f 84
1999 Turf 1-4: (12f 1-4) (gd 1-3, g-f)
Useful gelding, effective 10 to 12f, best at 10f, acts on gd to g-f, best on gd, has worn blinkers. Turf high 89 (1st run) - 1st of 9 getting 8lb from Elhayq (3 Apr Haydock RF 0561). Better known as a hurdler, he won a Haydock handicap first time out. Ideally suited by soft ground.
**Mrs P Sly [5-16] R Brazier (from A Leahy in IRE [0-8] Aug 1997).*

COUNSEL BHB 40a **RR 18f** 1410[15]
4 ch g Most Welcome 8.6f **(66)** - My Polished Corner (IRE) (Tate Gallery (USA)) 7.4f **(67)**
Form - 00880
Record 1999 - 1st:0 2nd:0 3rd:0 Ran:4
Pre1999 - 1st:0 2nd:3 3rd:0 Ran:21
Win Prizemoney £0 *Total Prizemoney* £2,558
1999 Turf 0-1: (9f) (g-f) 1999 AW 0-3: (8f, 9f, 11f) (Fibr 3)
Neat, very moderate gelding, effective 10f, - acts on Equi, has worn blinkers, likes left handed tracks. AW high 32. Becoming disappointing.
**D W Chapman [0-13] Miss N F Thesiger (from K R Burke [0-6] Aug 1998).*

COUNT BASIE BHB 74f **RR 82f** 117[8]
6 b g Batshoof 9.5f **(66)** - Quiet Harbour (Mill Reef (USA)) 10.5f **(78)**
Form - 8
Record 1999 - 1st:0 2nd:0 3rd:0 Ran:1
Pre1999 - 1st:1 2nd:1 3rd:1 Ran:5
Win Prizemoney £3,176 *Total Prizemoney* £4,628
Wins 1996 Jun Windso (G-F) 10f 82 <
1999 AW 0-1: (11f) (Fibr)
Decent gelding.
**J L Eyre [0-1] Sunpak Potatoes (from H R A Cecil [1-5] Jly 1996).*

COUNT DE MONEY (IRE) BHB 35f54a **RR 37f 54a** 5145[2]
4 b g Last Tycoon 9.4f **(73)** - Menominee (Soviet Star (USA))
Form - 1331502150110254512
Record 1999 - 1st:5 2nd:3 3rd:1 Ran:17
Pre1999 - 1st:1 2nd:0 3rd:3 Ran:10
Win Prizemoney £12,572 *Total Prizemoney* £16,521
Wins * **1999** *Oct Southw (STD) 12f 64+*
* **1999** *Jun Southw (STD) C 11f 59*
* **1999** *Jun Southw (STD) C 11f 50*
* **1999** *May Wolver (STD) C 12f 65* <
* **1999** *Feb Southw (STD) H 12f 53 57*
* 1998 *Nov Southw (STD) H 12f 44 53*
1999 Turf 0-7: (10f 4, 12f 3) (gd, g-f 4, frm 2) 1999 AW 5-10: (11f 2-3, 12f 3-7) (Equi, Fibr 5-9)
Scopey, average gelding, effective 11 to 12f, best at 12f, - acts on Fibr, prefers left handed tracks, favours tight tracks, excels at Wolverhampton and Southwell. Turf high 37. AW high 65 - 1st of 10 giving 4lb to Key To The City (8 May Wolverhampton RF 1118) - also 1st of 11 from Air Attache (18 Oct Southwell RF 4936). Inconsistent. He is a very effective middle-distance handicapper on Fibresand, and has a string of victories to his name under those conditions since the autumn of 1998. There will be more to come.
**S R Bowring [6-19] Roland Wheatley (from A P Jarvis [0-8] Oct 1998).*

COUNTERFEIT (IRE) RR 53f 771[4]
3 b c In The Wings 11.2f **(77)** -Bogus John(CAN)(Blushing John (USA))
Form - 4
Record 1999 - 1st:0 2nd:0 3rd:0 Ran:1
1999 Turf 0-1: (10f) (sft)
Currently fair colt. **M Johnston [0-1] Sheikh Mohammed.*

COUNTESS PARKER BHB 72f **RR 85df** 4631[4]
3 ch f First Trump - Hoist (IRE) **(72df 63a)** (Bluebird (USA)) 7.5f **(69)**
Form - 204
Record 1999 - 1st:0 2nd:1 3rd:0 Ran:3
Win Prizemoney £0 *Total Prizemoney* £1,407
1999 Turf 0-3: (8f 3) (g-s, gd, frm)
Leggy, currently useful filly. Turf high 85 (1st run) - 2nd of 11 getting 5lb from Fair Warning (3 Jun Yarmouth 8f gd RF 1706).
**H R A Cecil [0-3] Angus Dundee Plc.*

COUNT FREDERICK RR 47f 5069[14]
3 b g Anshan 8.2f **(63)** - Minteen (Teenoso (USA)) 9.9f **(72)**
Form - 8304368220
Record 1999 - 1st:0 2nd:2 3rd:2 Ran:10
Pre1999 - 1st:0 2nd:0 3rd:0 Ran:1
Win Prizemoney £0 *Total Prizemoney* £2,859
1999 Turf 0-10: (7f 2, 8f 3, 9f, 10f 3, 12f) (sft 2, g-s 2, gd, g-f, frm 4)
Moderate gelding, effective 10f, acts on frm, likes tight tracks. Turf high 52. **J R Jenkins [0-11] Mrs Stella Peirce.*

COUNT ON THUNDER (USA) BHB 62f **RR 60f** 5049[10]
2 ch c Thunder Gulch (USA) - Count On A Change (USA) (Time For A Change (USA))
Form - 070
Record 1999 - 1st:0 2nd:0 3rd:0 Ran:3

1999 Turf 0-3: (7f 2, 8f) (gd 3)
Currently average colt. Turf high 60 (began Spt).
**E A L Dunlop [0-3] Maktoum Al Maktoum.*

COUNTRY BUMPKIN RR 21f 3306[8]

3 ch g Village Star (FR) 5.7f **(61)** - Malham Tarn (Riverman (USA)) 9.1f **(76)**
Form - 08
Record 1999 - 1st:0 2nd:0 3rd:0 Ran:2
1999 Turf 0-2: (8f, 10f) (frm, hrd)
Unfurnished, currently little account gelding. Turf high 21 (began Jly). **K O Cunningham-Brown [0-2] A J Richards.*

COUNTRY CLUB RR 112f 3591a[3]

3 ch c Suave Dancer (USA) 10.7f **(68)** - Cut No Ice (Great Nephew) 9.9f **(64)**
Form - 3
1999 Turf 0-1: (12f) (gd)
Currently Group-class colt. (1st run) - 3rd of 5 to Belenus (8 Aug Hoppegarten 12f gd RF 3591a). The Polish Derby winner, he acquitted himself with great credit when finishing third in a Group One at Hoppegarten in August. **S Walotek in GER [0-1].*

COUNTRY ORCHID BHB 58f RR 56f 2888[1]

8 b m Town And Country 8.5f **(47)** - Star Flower (Star Appeal) 9.6f **(65)**
Form - 341
Record 1999 - 1st:1 2nd:0 3rd:1 Ran:3
Pre1999 - 1st:0 2nd:0 3rd:0 Ran:2
Win Prizemoney £3,535 *Total Prizemoney* £4,043
Wins * 1999 Jly Pontef (G-F) H 12f 52 56 <
1999 Turf 1-2: (12f 1-2) (frm 1-2) 1999 AW 0-1: (12f) (Fibr)
Fair mare. Turf high 56 (began Jly) - 1st of 12 getting 11lb from Macca Luna (16 Jly Pontefract RF 2888). (1st run) - 3rd of 10 getting 5lb from Robellita (8 Mar Southwell 12f Fibr RF 0413).
**Mrs M Reveley [7-27] Mrs J V Kehoe.*

COUNT TIROL (IRE) BHB 63f RR 65f 2836[3]

2 b c Tirol 8.1f **(64)** - Bid High (IRE) (High Estate)
Form - 003
Record 1999 - 1st:0 2nd:0 3rd:1 Ran:3
Win Prizemoney £0 *Total Prizemoney* £336
1999 Turf 0-3: (5f, 6f 2) (g-f 3)
Currently average colt. Turf high 65.
**M J Heaton-Ellis [0-3] M Heaton-Ellis.*

COUPLED BHB 45f RR 44f 4091[14]

4 ch f Wolfhound (USA) 7.3f **(71)** - Twice A Fool (USA) (Foolish Pleasure (USA)) 8.9f **(72)**
Form - 007680
Record 1999 - 1st:0 2nd:0 3rd:0 Ran:6
Pre1999 - 1st:0 2nd:1 3rd:0 Ran:5
Win Prizemoney £0 *Total Prizemoney* £1,195
1999 Turf 0-6: (7f 5, 8f) (sft, g-f, frm 4)
Scopey, moderate filly, effective 7f, acts on gd, has worn blinkers. Turf high 52. Inconsistent. **S C Williams [0-11] Mrs Celia Miller.*

COURAGE UNDER FIRE BHB 51f49a RR 55f 49a 4869[5]

4 b g Risk Me (FR) 8f **(53)** - Dreamtime Quest (Blakeney) 10.5f **(64)**
Form - 45
Record 1999 - 1st:0 2nd:0 3rd:0 Ran:2
Pre1999 - 1st:1 2nd:2 3rd:2 Ran:11
Win Prizemoney £2,206 *Total Prizemoney* £4,747
Wins * 1998 *Jun Southw (STD) H 12f 44 45* <
1999 Turf 0-1: (10f) (g-s) 1999 AW 0-1: (12f) (Fibr)
Workmanlike, fair gelding, effective 10 to 12f, best at 10f, acts on gd to frm - acts on Fibr, best on frm, likes left handed tracks, favours tight tracks. **D W P Arbuthnot [1-14] Mrs Adrian Ireland.*

COURTEOUS BHB 114f RR 121f 5230a[7]

4 b c Generous (IRE) 11.5f **(82)** - Dayanata (Shirley Heights) 10.3f **(74)**
Form - 137
Record 1999 - 1st:1 2nd:0 3rd:1 Ran:3
Pre1999 - 1st:2 2nd:1 3rd:0 Ran:7
Win Prizemoney £98,508 *Total Prizemoney* £166,528
Wins * 1999 Aug Deauvi (GD) G2 12.5f 117 <
* 1998 Apr Sandow (SFT) G3 10f 107
* 1997 Oct Salisb (GD) 8f 84
1999 Turf 1-3: (12f 2, 13f 1-1) (gd 1-2, frm)
Scopey, very high-class colt, effective 12 to 13f, best at 12f, acts on gd to g-f, best on gd. Turf high 121 (began Aug) - also 1st of 6 from Bimbola (29 Aug Deauville RF 4113a). He showed how well he went after a layoff when winning first time out in 1998, and repeated the feat last season by winning the Grand Prix de Deauville after a ten-month break. His two subsequent starts were in North America, finishing runner-up in the Canadian International before running seventh to Daylami in the Breeders' Cup Turf. **P F I Cole [3-10] F Salman.*

COURT EXPRESS BHB 52a RR 74f 4689[7]

5 b g Then Again 7.4f **(52)** - Moon Risk (Risk Me (FR)) 5.9f **(53)**
Form - 001213111507
Record 1999 - 1st:5 2nd:1 3rd:1 Ran:12
Pre1999 - 1st:2 2nd:1 3rd:1 Ran:21
Win Prizemoney £33,709 *Total Prizemoney* £38,691
Wins * 1999 Aug Redcar (FRM) H 8f 72 74 <
*** 1999** Jly Beverl (G-F) H 9.9f 68 69
*** 1999** Jly Hamilt (FRM) H 9.2f 62 66
*** 1999** Jun Carlis (GD) H 8f 57 59
*** 1999** May Hamilt (FRM) H 8.3f 50 51
1997 Jun Carlis (G-F) H 5.9f 63 68
1997 Jun Carlis (FRM) 5.9f 61
1999 Turf 5-11: (8f 3-8, 9f 1-2, 10f 1-1) (gd, g-f 3-5, frm 2-5) 1999 AW 0-1: (8f) (Fibr)
Above-average gelding, effective 8 to 10f, acts on g-f to frm, best on frm, has worn blinkers, prefers right handed tracks, likes tight tracks, excels at Hamilton. Turf high 74 - 1st of 7 getting 13lb from Yeast (7 Aug Redcar RF 3456) - also 1st of 6 getting 1lb from Mcgillycuddy Reeks (19 Jly Beverley RF 2947). Consistent. Has found his forte at distances between eight and ten furlongs last term, and notched up a hat-trick in the summer to add to two early season successes. The Handicapper has noticed however, and life is now that much harder. Very much suited by fast ground.
**W W Haigh [5-12] Tim Hawkins (from J M Jefferson [0-3] Oct 1998).*

COURT FLIRT RR 29f 4901[17]

2 b f Charmer 9f **(59)** -Willow Court(USA)(Little Current (USA)) 9.6f **(75)**
Form - 0
Record 1999 - 1st:0 2nd:0 3rd:0 Ran:1
1999 Turf 0-1: (7f) (frm)
Currently little account filly. **C W Fairhurst [0-1] David Hawes.*

COURT HOUSE BHB 32f30a RR 30f 30a 3614[5]

5 b g Reprimand 8.2f **(63)** - Chalet Girl (Double Form) 7.3f **(58)**
Form - 65
Record 1999 - 1st:0 2nd:0 3rd:0 Ran:2
Pre1999 - 1st:1 2nd:0 3rd:0 Ran:19
Win Prizemoney £2,448 *Total Prizemoney* £2,448
Wins 1997 Jun Pontef (GD) S 8f 60 <
1999 Turf 0-1: (7f) (g-f) 1999 AW 0-1: (12f) (Equi)
Very moderate gelding, has broken blood-vessels.
**B R Johnson [0-2] K Tork (from M C Chapman [0-17] Oct 1998).*

COURTING RR 90+f 4236[7]

2 gr f Pursuit of Love 9.5f **(69)** - Doctor's Glory (USA) **(90f)** (Elmaamul (USA))
Form - 111107
Record 1999 - 1st:4 2nd:0 3rd:0 Ran:6
Win Prizemoney £17,815 *Total Prizemoney* £17,815
Wins * 1999 Jly Newmar (G-F) 7f 87+
*** 1999** Jly Thirsk (FRM) 7f 90+ <
*** 1999** Jly Catter (FRM) 7f 77+
*** 1999** Jun Catter (G-F) 7f 77+
1999 Turf 4-6: (7f 4-5, 8f) (g-f 2, frm 4-4)
Useful filly, effective 7f, acts on frm. Turf high 90 - 1st of 4 getting 5lb from Buy Or Sell (23 Jly Thirsk RF 3073) - also 1st of 3 getting 3lb from Minkash (31 Jly Newmarket RF 3277). Unbeaten in her first four starts, all over seven furlongs on fast ground, some of those races were not particularly competitive, and she was well and truly found out when well beaten in a Newmarket Listed event in August. Ran a better race on her final start.
**Sir Mark Prescott [4-6] Cheveley Park Stud.*

COURTLEDGE BHB 42f RR 51f 3602[8]

4 b g Unfuwain (USA) 11.4f **(74)** - Tremellick (Mummy's Pet) 7.7f **(60)**
Form - 4008

Record 1999 - 1st:0 2nd:0 3rd:0 Ran:4
Pre1999 - 1st:0 2nd:0 3rd:0 Ran:4
1999 Turf 0-4: (12f, 16f 3) (gd 2, g-f, frm)
Strong, fair gelding, effective 12f, acts on g-f. Turf high 51 (1st run) - 4th of 19 giving 1lb to Linea-G (3 May Newcastle 12f g-f RF 1010). Becoming disappointing. **Miss J A Camacho [0-8] B P Skirton.*

COURTNEY GYM (IRE) BHB 34f RR 24f 3687[15]

4 ch g Shalford (IRE) 7.8f **(63)** - Fair Or Foul (Patch) 11.5f **(51)**
Form - 006000752700
Record 1999 - 1st:0 2nd:1 3rd:0 Ran:12
Pre1999 - 1st:0 2nd:2 3rd:0 Ran:14
Win Prizemoney £0 *Total Prizemoney* £2,026
1999 Turf 0-8: (5f 2, 6f 4, 7f, 8f) (gd 3, g-f 2, frm 2, hrd) 1999 AW 0-4: (7f 2, 8f 2) (Equi 3, Fibr)
Very moderate gelding, effective 6f, acts on gd to hrd, has worn blinkers (very effectively), likes left handed tracks, likes tight tracks. Turf high 34 - 5th of 11 getting 28lb from Ivory Dawn (30 Jun Brighton 6f gd RF 2434). AW high 34.
**P Burgoyne [0-21] Philip Saunders (from M R Channon [0-5] Oct 1997).*

COURT OF APPEAL RR 72f 5100[9]

2 ch c Bering 9.6f **(80)** - Hiawatha's Song (USA) (Chief's Crown (USA)) 9.8f **(72)**
Form - 0
Record 1999 - 1st:0 2nd:0 3rd:0 Ran:1
1999 Turf 0-1: (8f) (gd)
Currently above-average colt. **J R Fanshawe [0-1] Mrs Susan Davis.*

COURT OF JUSTICE (USA) RR 62f 662[8]

3 b c Alleged (USA) 11.8f **(81)** - Captive Island (Northfields (USA)) 9f **(72)**
Form - 8
Record 1999 - 1st:0 2nd:0 3rd:0 Ran:1
1999 Turf 0-1: (12f) (g-f)
Scopey, currently average colt.
**P W Chapple-Hyam [0-1] R E Sangster.*

COURT SHAREEF BHB 54f RR 57f 5066[5]

4 b g Shareef Dancer (USA) 10.1f **(67)** - Fairfields Cone (Celtic Cone) 9.8f **(43)**
Form - 4574405
Record 1999 - 1st:0 2nd:0 3rd:0 Ran:7
Pre1999 - 1st:2 2nd:0 3rd:2 Ran:9
Win Prizemoney £6,110 *Total Prizemoney* £8,356
Wins * 1998 May Leices (GD) H 11.8f 66 75 <
* 1998 May Windso (G-F) H 11.6f 58 62
1999 Turf 0-7: (12f 2, 13f, 14f 2, 15f, 16f) (g-s, gd 2, g-f 2, frm 2)
Neat, fair gelding, effective 12f, acts on gd to g-f, best on g-f, likes right handed tracks, prefers tight tracks. Turf high 62 (began Aug). Consistent. **R Dickin [2-16] Derek & Cheryl Holder.*

COVER UP (IRE) RR 77f 4858[2]

2 b c Machiavellian (USA) 9.8f **(83)** - Sought Out (IRE) (Rainbow Quest (USA)) 10.4f **(75)**
Form - 32
Record 1999 - 1st:0 2nd:1 3rd:1 Ran:2
Win Prizemoney £0 *Total Prizemoney* £2,695
1999 Turf 0-2: (8f 2) (sft, g-f)
Currently above-average colt. Turf high 77 (began Spt).
**Sir Michael Stoute [0-2] Lord Weinstock.*

COWBOYS AND ANGELS BHB 73f RR 75f 908[9]

2 b c Bin Ajwaad (IRE) - Halimah (Be My Guest (USA)) 9.3f **(67)**
Form - 320
Record 1999 - 1st:0 2nd:1 3rd:1 Ran:3
Win Prizemoney £0 *Total Prizemoney* £956
1999 Turf 0-3: (5f 3) (sft, frm 2)
Currently above-average colt. Turf high 75 - 2nd of 13 giving 8lb to Sweet Haven (14 Apr Beverley 5f frm RF 0688).
**W G M Turner [0-3] Mascalls Stud.*

COY DEBUTANTE (IRE) BHB 49f RR 51f 4128[3]

5 ch m Archway (IRE) 8.5f **(60)** - Presentable (Sharpen Up) 8.3f **(67)**
Form - 0000853
Record 1999 - 1st:0 2nd:0 3rd:1 Ran:7
Win Prizemoney £0 *Total Prizemoney* £390
1999 Turf 0-7: (8f 3, 9f, 10f 2, 11f) (sft, g-f 3, frm 3)
Fair filly, effective 10 to 11f, acts on g-f to frm, prefers tight tracks. Turf high 51 - 3rd of 12 getting 10lb from Cashmere Lady (3 Spt Haydock 11f g-f RF 4128).
**W J Musson [0-7] The Flying Temple Partnership.*

CRACK DANCER (IRE) BHB 57f52a RR 67f 52a 5150[8]

2 b f Dancing Dissident (USA) 6.8f **(65)** - Polish Crack (IRE) (Polish Patriot (USA))
Form - 080888068
Record 1999 - 1st:0 2nd:0 3rd:0 Ran:9
1999 Turf 0-8: (5f, 6f 6, 7f) (g-s 2, gd 2, g-f, frm 3) 1999 AW 0-1: (5f) (Fibr)
Average filly. Turf high 72. **Mrs P N Dutfield [0-9] Three Devon Legs.*

CRACKER BHB 33f35a RR 34df 35a 2082[12]

5 br g Lugana Beach 7f **(63)** - Greta's Song (Faraway Times (USA)) 7.4f **(52)**
Form - 00
Record 1999 - 1st:0 2nd:0 3rd:0 Ran:2
Pre1999 - 1st:0 2nd:0 3rd:0 Ran:4
1999 AW 0-2: (6f 2) (Fibr 2)
Very moderate gelding, has worn blinkers. AW high 3.
**A Senior [0-5] A Senior (from G Fierro [0-1] Nov 1997).*

CRACKLE BHB 77f RR 77f 5159[3]

3 gr f Anshan 8.2f **(63)** - Crackling **(31f 35a)** (Electric) 10.1f **(61)**
Form - 5143833
Record 1999 - 1st:1 2nd:0 3rd:3 Ran:7
Pre1999 - 1st:2 2nd:2 3rd:1 Ran:9
Win Prizemoney £10,487 *Total Prizemoney* £17,406
Wins * 1999 May Beverl (GD) H 9.9f 77 84 <
* 1998 Oct Doncas (SFT) H 8f 72 77
* 1998 Jly Bath (GD) 5.7f 75
1999 Turf 1-7: (10f 1-5, 11f, 14f) (gd 1-2, g-f 5)
Unfurnished, above-average filly, effective 6 to 11f, acts on gd to frm, likes left handed tracks. Turf high 84 - 1st of 15 getting 1lb from Nathan's Boy (25 May Beverley RF 1452).
**B W Hills [3-16] S P Tindall.*

CRACK SHOT BHB 63f RR 60f 1962[11]

5 ch m Gunner B 11.2f **(45)** - Lucky Angel (Lucky Wednesday) 8f **(50)**
Form - 7050
Record 1999 - 1st:0 2nd:0 3rd:0 Ran:4
1999 Turf 0-3: (8f, 10f, 14f) (gd 2, g-f) 1999 AW 0-1: (12f) (Fibr)
Average filly. Turf high 60. **J Neville [2-8] Mrs P A Barratt.*

CRACOW (IRE) BHB 82f RR 79f 4944[2]

2 b c Polish Precedent (USA) 9f **(73)** - Height of Secrecy (Shirley Heights) 10.3f **(74)**
Form - 052
Record 1999 - 1st:0 2nd:1 3rd:0 Ran:3
Win Prizemoney £0 *Total Prizemoney* £1,052
1999 Turf 0-3: (7f 3) (gd 2, g-f)
Currently above-average colt. Turf high 79 (began Aug) - 2nd of 16 giving 3lb to Azur (19 Oct Lingfield 7f gd RF 4944).
**J W Hills [0-3] N N Browne.*

CRAGGY MOUNTAIN BHB 68f RR 61f 1259[13]

3 ch c Cadeaux Genereux 7.9f **(76)** - Jet Ski Lady (USA) (Vaguely Noble) 10.1f **(72)**
Form - 870
Record 1999 - 1st:0 2nd:0 3rd:0 Ran:3
1999 Turf 0-3: (6f, 7f, 8f) (gd, g-f, frm)
Strong, currently average colt. Turf high 61. **B W Hills [0-3] Gainsborough Stud.*

CRAIGARY BHB 28f RR 29f 3863[6]

8 b g Dunbeath (USA) 9.9f **(53)** - Velvet Pearl (Record Token) 6.3f **(53)**
Form - 0056
Record 1999 - 1st:0 2nd:0 3rd:0 Ran:3
Pre1999 - 1st:1 2nd:1 3rd:3 Ran:15
Win Prizemoney £2,444 *Total Prizemoney* £4,371
Wins * 1997 Spt Hamilt (GD) SH 12.1f 37 41 <
1999 Turf 0-3: (11f, 12f, 13f) (g-f 2, frm)
Little account gelding, has worn blinkers. Turf high 29 (began Jly).

**Mrs A Swinbank [3-28] James Cringan (from T Kinane in IRE [0-8] Aug 1996).*

CRAIGSTEEL BHB 117f RR 118?f 5043[7]

4 b c Suave Dancer (USA) 10.7f **(68)** - Applecross (Glint of Gold) 9.3f **(66)**

Form - 127

Record **1999** - 1st:1 2nd:1 3rd:0 Ran:3
Pre1999 - 1st:3 2nd:1 3rd:0 Ran:7

Win Prizemoney £54,782 *Total Prizemoney* £78,855

Wins * **1999** Jly Newmar (GD) G2 12f 117 <
* 1998 Nov Doncas (SFT) 14.6f 115
* 1998 Spt Doncas (GD) L 12f 111
* 1997 Jly Newmar (GD) 7f 96

1999 Turf 1-3: (12f 1-2, 13f) (sft, gd, frm 1-1)

Leggy, high-class colt, effective 12 to 16f, acts on gd to frm, best on gd. Turf high 118 (began Jly) - 2nd of 4 getting 3lb from Silver Patriarch (14 Aug Newbury 13f gd RF 3649) - also 1st of 8 getting 3lb from Arctic Owl (6 Jly Newmarket RF 2576). As was the case the previous year, he made a belated reappearance last season, but put up his best performance to date in winning the Group Two Princess Of Wales's Stakes at Newmarket. Outgunned in the Geoffrey Freer by Silver Patriarch, he was very disappointing when tailed off in the St Simon Stakes on his final start.
**H R A Cecil [4-10] Sir David Wills.*

CRASH CALL LADY BHB 33f36a RR 23f 36a 1512[5]

3 b f Batshoof 9.5f **(66)** - Petite Louie (Chilibang)

Form - 3774512670725

Record **1999** - 1st:1 2nd:2 3rd:0 Ran:10
Pre1999 - 1st:0 2nd:0 3rd:2 Ran:12

Win Prizemoney £2,211 *Total Prizemoney* £4,021

Wins * **1999** *Feb Wolver (STD) 12f 64* <

1999 Turf 0-2: (12f, 16f) (hvy, frm) 1999 AW 1-8: (11f 3, 12f 1-4, 15f) (Fibr 1-8)

Scopey, fair filly, effective 12f, - acts on Fibr, often wears blinkers. Turf high 15. AW high 64 - 1st of 7 getting 24lb from Order In Court (10 Feb Wolverhampton RF 0261). Inconsistent.
**C N Allen [1-22] Crash Call Ltd.*

CREAM TEASE BHB 93f RR 87f 5041[12]

2 b f Pursuit of Love 9.5f **(69)** - Contralto (Busted) 10.2f **(61)**

Form - 41600

Record **1999** - 1st:1 2nd:0 3rd:0 Ran:5

Win Prizemoney £3,746 *Total Prizemoney* £4,150

Wins * **1999** Aug Salisb (GD) 7f 80 <

1999 Turf 1-5: (7f 1-4, 8f) (sft, g-f 2, frm 1-2)

Useful filly. Turf high 87 (began Jly) - also 1st of 14 from Ghuffran (6 Aug Salisbury RF 3433). Narrow winner of a Salisbury maiden on her second start, she has been totally outclassed in Group company since then. **D J S ffrenchDavis [1-5] Badgers Holt.*

CREDENZA BHB 39f39a RR 49f 39a 2452[13]

3 ch f Superlative 8.8f **(57)** - Carousel Music **(36f)** (On Your Mark) 7.7f **(58)**

Form - 050800

Record **1999** - 1st:0 2nd:0 3rd:0 Ran:6
Pre1999 - 1st:0 2nd:1 3rd:1 Ran:8

Win Prizemoney £0 *Total Prizemoney* £781

1999 Turf 0-2: (5f, 6f) (g-s, gd) 1999 AW 0-4: (5f, 6f 2, 7f) (Equi 3, Fibr)

Small, moderate filly, effective 5f, acts on frm. Turf high 1. AW high 40. Becoming disappointing.
**R C Spicer [0-6] Mrs J A Nichols (from R Hannon [0-8] Aug 1998).*

CREDIT-A-PLENTY BHB 106f RR 109f 4794[7]

3 ch f Generous (IRE) 11.5f **(82)** - On Credit (FR) (No Pass No Sale) 11.9f **(85)**

Form - 20227

Record **1999** - 1st:0 2nd:3 3rd:0 Ran:5
Pre1999 - 1st:1 2nd:0 3rd:0 Ran:1

Win Prizemoney £3,111 *Total Prizemoney* £21,206

Wins * 1998 Oct Haydoc (SFT) 7.1f 81+ <

1999 Turf 0-5: (11f, 12f 3, 15f) (gd 4, g-f)

Workmanlike, Pattern-class filly, has broken blood-vessels, effective 11 to 15f, acts on gd. Turf high 109 - 2nd of 10 to Mistle Song (8 Spt Doncaster 15f gd RF 4209). Undoubtedly a high-class filly, she gave Ramruma a fight in the Lingfield Oaks Trial on her first outing and was narrowly beaten in the Galtres at York and the Park Hill at Doncaster. However she twice broke blood vessels on the track, and has been retired. **J L Dunlop [1-6] Hesmonds Stud.*

CREME CARAMEL (USA) RR 85f 4329[6]

3 b f Septieme Ciel (USA) - Vexation (USA) (Vice Regent (CAN)) 8.7f **(74)**

Form - 036

Record **1999** - 1st:0 2nd:0 3rd:1 Ran:3
Pre1999 - 1st:1 2nd:1 3rd:0 Ran:4

Win Prizemoney £3,452 *Total Prizemoney* £6,277

Wins * 1998 Spt Yarmou (G-S) H 7f 85 86 <

1999 Turf 0-3: (8f 3) (gd, g-f, frm)

Scopey, useful filly, effective 7 to 8f, best at 7f, acts on gd to frm, best on gd. Turf high 85 - 6th of 11 to Khibrah (15 Spt Sandown 8f gd RF 4329). **P W Chapple-Hyam [1-7] Mrs C A Waters.*

CREME DE CASSIS BHB 39f RR 40f 4988[3]

3 ch f Alhijaz 7.7f **(57)** - Lucky Flinders (Free State) 8.7f **(61)**

Form - 87000R083

Record **1999** - 1st:0 2nd:0 3rd:1 Ran:8
Pre1999 - 1st:0 2nd:0 3rd:0 Ran:2

Win Prizemoney £0 *Total Prizemoney* £275

1999 Turf 0-8: (7f, 8f 2, 9f, 10f 3, 14f) (g-s 2, g-f 2, frm 4)

Neat, moderate filly. Turf high 51. Inconsistent.
**P J Makin [0-10] Mrs Pauline Smith & Four Seasons Racing.*

CRESSET RR 59f 1574[10]

3 ch c Arazi (USA) 9.2f **(74)** - Mixed Applause (USA) (Nijinsky (CAN)) 10.3f **(77)**

Form - 070

Record **1999** - 1st:0 2nd:0 3rd:0 Ran:3

1999 Turf 0-3: (8f 3) (g-f 2, frm)

Tall, currently fair colt. Turf high 59.
**W Jarvis [0-3] Rams Racing Club.*

CRESTED KNIGHT (IRE) BHB 41f RR 40f 3357[5]

7 gr g Night Shift (USA) 8.1f **(73)** - Casual (USA) (Caro)

Form - 05

Record **1999** - 1st:0 2nd:0 3rd:0 Ran:2
Pre1999 - 1st:1 2nd:1 3rd:0 Ran:16

Win Prizemoney £4,467 *Total Prizemoney* £6,900

Wins * 1996 Spt Goodwo (G-F) CH 8f 47 53 <

1999 Turf 0-2: (7f, 8f) (frm 2)

Moderate gelding. Turf high 40. Consistent.
**C A Horgan [1-18] Mrs B Sumner.*

CRETAN GIFT BHB 99f105a RR 99f 105a 5222[8]

8 ch g Cadeaux Genereux 7.9f **(76)** - Caro's Niece (USA) (Caro)

Form - 54208227618851204038

Record **1999** - 1st:2 2nd:4 3rd:1 Ran:20
Pre1999 - 1st:12 2nd:16 3rd:5 Ran:82

Win Prizemoney £96,816 *Total Prizemoney* £166,355

Wins * **1999** Aug Yarmou (GD) 6f 100
* **1999** Jly Ascot (FRM) H 6f 95 102
* 1998 *Mar Wolver (STD) H 5f 98 103* <
* 1997 Aug Leopar (G-S) G3 6f 102
* 1997 Jun Newcas (HVY) H 6f 93 96
* 1997 *Feb Southw (STD) H 6f 90 97*
* 1996 Nov Redcar (G-F) H 6f 73 81
* 1996 Spt Ayr (G-F) H 6f 68 70
* 1996 Spt Nottin (FRM) H 5.1f 66 69
* 1996 *Jun Wolver (STD) H 6f 85 86*
* 1996 *Apr Wolver (STD) C 5f 82*
* 1995 *Oct Wolver (STD) H 6f 66 70*
* 1995 *Spt Wolver (STD) H 6f 59 64*
* 1995 *Apr Southw (STD) H 6f 54 56*

1999 Turf 2-20: (6f 2-15, 7f 5) (g-s 2, gd 1-11, g-f 1-5, frm 2)

Very useful gelding, effective 5 to 6f, best at 6f, acts on g-s to gd, best on gd, mostly wears blinkers (effectively), and does well at Ascot. Turf high 104. He is as hard as nails and stood up well to another vigorous campaign. Invariably fitted with blinkers or a visor, he stays seven furlongs, acts on any ground and is best when finishing late from behind a fast pace.
**N P Littmoden [14-95] T Clarke (from John Harris [0-4] Jun 1994).*

CRICKET'S SONG (IRE) BHB 37f RR 26f 3753[6]

3 b f College Chapel - The Multiyorker (IRE) **(68f)** (Digamist (USA))

Form - 006
Record 1999 - 1st:0 2nd:0 3rd:0 Ran:3
Pre1999 - 1st:0 2nd:0 3rd:0 Ran:4
1999 Turf 0-3: (5f 3) (gd, g-f, frm)
Light-framed, little account filly, often wore blinkers. Turf high 26 (began Jly). (DEAD)
Miss Gay Kelleway [0-3] Dr Felicity Simpson (from B J Meehan [0-4] Aug 1998).

CRIMPLENE (IRE) BHB 100f RR 100f 4596[3]

2 ch f Lion Cavern (USA) 7.5f **(74)** - Crimson Conquest (USA) (Diesis) 9.3f **(69)**
Form - 213713
Record 1999 - 1st:2 2nd:1 3rd:2 Ran:6
Win Prizemoney £12,073 *Total Prizemoney* £29,256
Wins * 1999 Spt Salisb (G-F) 6f 88 <
*** 1999** Jun Redcar (FRM) 6f 87+
1999 Turf 2-6: (6f 2-6) (gd 2, g-f 2, frm 2-2)
Very useful filly, effective 6f, acts on g-f. Turf high 100 - 3rd of 15 to Seazun (28 Spt Newmarket 6f g-f RF 4596). She enjoyed a fruitful campaign, her only disappointing effort coming in the Lowther Stakes, where she pulled hard and failed to get home. Seen in a better light when finishing third in the Cheveley Park Stakes, she is out of a mare that stayed middle-distances and should get at least a mile in 2000. There will be worse long-shots in the 1,000 Guineas. *C E Brittain [2-6] Sheikh Marwan Al Maktoum.

CRIMSON GLORY RR 68f 4230[16]

3 ch f Lycius (USA) 8.8f **(71)** -Crimson Conquest(USA)(Diesis) 9.3f **(69)**
Form - 723540
Record 1999 - 1st:0 2nd:1 3rd:1 Ran:6
Pre1999 - 1st:0 2nd:0 3rd:0 Ran:2
Win Prizemoney £0 *Total Prizemoney* £2,441
1999 Turf 0-6: (7f 2, 8f 3, 10f) (gd, g-f 2, frm 3)
Neat, average filly, effective 7 to 8f, best at 8f, acts on g-f to frm, best on frm. Turf high 70 - 2nd of 11 giving 5lb to Khibrah (14 Jun Brighton 8f g-f RF 1974). Inconsistent.
C E Brittain [0-8] Sheikh Marwan Al Maktoum.

CRISIS (IRE) RR 66f 1370[7]

3 b g Second Set (IRE) 9.2f **(67)** - Special Offer (IRE) (Shy Groom (USA)) 10f **(66)**
Form - 077
Record 1999 - 1st:0 2nd:0 3rd:0 Ran:3
1999 Turf 0-3: (7f, 8f, 10f) (g-f 2, frm)
Well made, average gelding. Turf high 66.
L M Cumani [0-3] Mrs Angie Silver.

CRISOS IL MONACO (IRE) RR 107f 4892a[4]

4 b c Common Grounds 8.1f **(66)** - Gayshuka (Lord Gayle (USA)) 8.8f **(62)**
Form - 264
1999 Turf 0-2: (8f, 10f) (gd 2)
Pattern-class colt. Turf high 107. *L Camici in ITY [1-5].*

CRISS CROSS (IRE) RR 73f 3552[6]

2 b c Lahib (USA) 8f **(69)** - La Belle Katherine (USA) (Lyphard (USA)) 9.9f **(72)**
Form - 6
Record 1999 - 1st:0 2nd:0 3rd:0 Ran:1
1999 Turf 0-1: (6f) (gd)
Currently above-average colt. *R Hannon [0-1] Michael Pescod.*

CRITICAL AIR BHB 52f56a RR 52f 56a 5033[3]

4 b g Reprimand 8.2f **(63)** - Area Girl (Jareer (USA)) 5.9f **(75)**
Form - 74341740023743753
Record 1999 - 1st:1 2nd:1 3rd:3 Ran:14
Pre1999 - 1st:1 2nd:1 3rd:4 Ran:17
Win Prizemoney £6,218 *Total Prizemoney* £11,939
Wins * 1999 *Jan Lingfi (STD) H 8f 54 58* <
1998 Aug Mussel (GD) H 7.1f 51 55
1999 Turf 0-9: (7f, 8f 5, 9f 2, 10f) (g-s, gd 2, g-f 2, frm 3, hrd) 1999 AW 1-5: (7f, 8f 1-3, 10f) (Equi 1-4, Fibr)
Scopey, fair gelding, effective 7 to 10f, acts on gd to frm - acts on Equi, has worn blinkers, excels at Windsor, likes Lingfield. Turf high 52 - 3rd of 13 getting 21lb from Arterxerxes (14 Jly Kempton 8f frm RF 2828). AW high 58 - 1st of 8 getting 21lb from Hugwity (16 Jan Lingfield RF 0111). Consistent. A fair sort on Equitrack, he has made the frame over ten furlongs, but his wins have been at around a mile.
A J McNae [1-17] A J McNae (from Sir Mark Prescott [1-14] Oct 1998).

CROAGH PATRICK BHB 38f30a RR 35f 30a 1813[18]

7 b g Faustus (USA) 9.1f **(54)** - Pink Pumpkin (Tickled Pink) 6.5f **(59)**
Form - 0
Record 1999 - 1st:0 2nd:0 3rd:0 Ran:1
Pre1999 - 1st:0 2nd:0 3rd:0 Ran:7
1999 Turf 0-1: (7f) (g-f)
Very moderate gelding. Inconsistent. *J C Fox [0-20] Mrs J A Cleary.*

CROCO ROUGE (IRE) RR 127f 4778a[3]

4 b c Rainbow Quest (USA) 11.2f **(81)** - Alligatrix (USA) (Alleged (USA)) 10f **(76)**
Form - 31733
1999 Turf 1-5: (9f 1-1, 10f, 11f, 12f 2) (sft, g-s 1-1, gd 2, frm)
Top-class colt, effective 9 to 12f, best at 12f, acts on hvy to gd, excels at Longchamp. Turf high 127 - also 1st of 8 from El Condor Pasa (23 May Longchamp RF 1531a). Consistent. A top-class performer, he regained winning form in the Prix d'Ispahan on his second start of last season, beating El Condor Pasa, but was a big disappointment on fast ground in the Eclipse, though he apparently did not travel well. After a break he never landed a blow when last of three in the Prix Foy and, although beaten further by his old rival El Condor Pasa in the Arc, still ran a creditable third. He has reportedly retired to the Irish National Stud.
P Bary in FR [3-12] Wafic Said.

CROESO ADREF BHB 42f RR 18f 5138[14]

2 ch f Most Welcome 8.6f **(66)** - Grugiar (Red Sunset) 8.2f **(63)**
Form - 080
Record 1999 - 1st:0 2nd:0 3rd:0 Ran:3
1999 Turf 0-1: (8f) (gd) 1999 AW 0-2: (5f 2) (Fibr 2)
Currently moderate filly. AW high 41 (began Oct).
S C Williams [0-3] Edgar Lloyd.

CROESO CARIAD BHB 100f RR 98f 4595[7]

2 b f Most Welcome 8.6f **(66)** - Colorsnap (Shirley Heights) 10.3f **(74)**
Form - 515217
Record 1999 - 1st:2 2nd:1 3rd:0 Ran:6
Win Prizemoney £19,230 *Total Prizemoney* £27,966
Wins * 1999 Spt San Si (GD) L 7f 97+ <
*** 1999** Aug Chepst (G-F) 5.1f 86+
1999 Turf 2-6: (5f 1-1, 6f, 7f 1-4) (gd 1-1, g-f 4, frm 1-1)
Very useful filly, effective 7f, acts on gd to g-f. Turf high 98 - 2nd of 9 to Icicle (29 Aug Goodwood 7f g-f RF 3995) - also 1st of 9 from Xua (12 Spt San Siro RF 4371a). She improved with experience, running her only poor race on easy ground at Newmarket in September. From the family of Stagecraft and Bella Colora, she should stay a mile and a quarter and can win a Group race on the continent. *M L W Bell [2-6] K J Mercer & Mrs S Mercer.*

CROFTERS EDGE BHB 40f45a RR 30f 45a 1094[7]

4 ch g Beveled (USA) 6.9f **(64)** - Zamindara (Crofter (USA)) 8.4f **(56)**
Form - 638607
Record 1999 - 1st:0 2nd:0 3rd:1 Ran:6
Pre1999 - 1st:0 2nd:2 3rd:2 Ran:13
Win Prizemoney £0 *Total Prizemoney* £2,134
1999 Turf 0-3: (8f, 9f, 10f) (g-f 2, frm) 1999 AW 0-3: (8f, 9f, 10f) (Equi, Fibr 2)
Scopey, fair gelding, effective 8 to 9f, acts on frm - acts on Fibr, has worn blinkers, likes left handed tracks, likes tight tracks. Turf high 30. AW high 50 - 3rd of 13 giving 5lb to The Wild Widow (20 Feb Wolverhampton 9f Fibr RF 0334). Becoming disappointing.
A P Jarvis [0-19] Crofter's Edge.

CROMABOO COUNTESS BHB 30f RR 11f 4605[15]

2 b f Makbul - La Belle Epoque (Tachypous) 8.6f **(55)**
Form - 000
Record 1999 - 1st:0 2nd:0 3rd:0 Ran:3
1999 Turf 0-2: (5f, 6f) (g-f 2) 1999 AW 0-1: (7f) (Fibr)
Currently poor filly. Turf high 11 (began Aug).
B D Leavy [0-3] John Wardle.

CROMER PIER BHB 26f38a **RR 28f 38a** 1374[9]
4 b g Reprimand 8.2f **(63)** - Fleur du Val (Valiyar) 8.5f **(73)**
Form - 00070
Record 1999 - 1st:0 2nd:0 3rd:0 Ran:5
Pre1999 - 1st:0 2nd:1 3rd:2 Ran:11
Win Prizemoney £0 *Total Prizemoney* £1,496
1999 Turf 0-5: (10f, 12f 2, 14f 2) (sft, gd 3, frm)
Workmanlike, little account gelding, effective 12f, acts on gd to g-f, often wears blinkers, favours tight tracks. Turf high 50. Becoming disappointing.
**G Fierro [0-5] M D Benniston (from M H Tompkins [0-11] Oct 1998).*

CROOKFORD WATER BHB 60f **RR 63f** 4910[11]
2 b g Rock City 8.8f **(62)** -Blue Nile(IRE) **(69f)** (Bluebird (USA)) 7.5f **(69)**
Form - 800
Record 1999 - 1st:0 2nd:0 3rd:0 Ran:3
1999 Turf 0-3: (6f, 7f, 8f) (gd, frm 2)
Currently average gelding. Turf high 63 (began Aug).
**J A Glover [0-3] Vic Atherton.*

CROSBY DONJOHN BHB 63f **RR 68f** 5158[21]
2 ch c Magic Ring (IRE) 6.5f **(64)** - Ovideo **(58f)** (Domynsky) 8f **(82)**
Form - 545050
Record 1999 - 1st:0 2nd:0 3rd:0 Ran:6
Win Prizemoney £0 *Total Prizemoney* £200
1999 Turf 0-6: (6f, 7f 4, 8f) (g-f 2, frm 3, hrd)
Average colt. Turf high 68. **E Weymes [0-6] Don Raper.*

CROSS DALL (IRE) BHB 58f **RR 70f** 5109[8]
2 b f Blues Traveller (IRE) - Faapette (Runnett) 7f **(59)**
Form - 008
Record 1999 - 1st:0 2nd:0 3rd:0 Ran:3
1999 Turf 0-3: (7f 2, 8f) (gd 3)
Currently above-average filly, has worn blinkers. Turf high 70 (began Oct). **R Ingram [0-3] Brian McAtavey & Peter Mooney.*

CROSS TALK (IRE) BHB 40f44a **RR 33f 44a** 3487[13]
7 b g Darshaan 11.9f **(81)** - Liaison (USA) (Blushing Groom (FR)) 10.3f **(76)**
Form - 27000
Record 1999 - 1st:0 2nd:1 3rd:0 Ran:5
Pre1999 - 1st:3 2nd:3 3rd:0 Ran:31
Win Prizemoney £9,267 *Total Prizemoney* £13,787

Wins	1996	Oct	Yarmou	(GD)	C	14.1f		51	
	1996	Mar	Catter	(G-S)	H	13.8f	65	71	<
	1995	Jly	Catter	(G-F)		13.8f		68	

1999 Turf 0-5: (10f, 11f, 12f 2, 14f) (sft, gd, g-f 2, frm)
Very moderate gelding. Turf high 46. Becoming disappointing.
**E A Wheeler [0-5] Diamant Precision Engineering Ltd (from R M Stronge [0-3] Feb 1997).*

CROWDED AVENUE BHB 85f **RR 90?f** 4873[4]
7 b g Sizzling Melody 6.3f **(49)** - Lady Bequick (Sharpen Up) 8.3f **(67)**
Form - 204
Record 1999 - 1st:0 2nd:1 3rd:0 Ran:3
Pre1999 - 1st:6 2nd:4 3rd:5 Ran:36
Win Prizemoney £39,805 *Total Prizemoney* £66,514

Wins	* 1996	Aug	Sandow	(GD)	H	5f	95	93	<
	* 1995	Spt	Epsom	(G-F)	H	5f	82	92	
	* 1995	Aug	Epsom	(G-F)	H	5f	82	83	
	* 1995	Jly	Goodwo	(GD)	H	5f	67	75	
	* 1995	Jun	Mussel	(G-F)	H	5f	56	57+	
	* 1995	Jun	Ayr	(G-F)	H	5f	48	49	

1999 Turf 0-3: (5f 3) (gd, g-f 2)
Useful gelding, effective 5f, acts on frm. Turf high 83 (began Jly). His belated reappearance saw him finish second to Aurigny in a three-horse race at Goodwood, but he failed to build on that. **P J Makin [6-39] T W Wellard.*

CROWN MINT (USA) RR 45f 5129[17]
2 gr c Chief's Crown (USA) 10.2f **(75)** - Add Mint (USA) (Vigors (USA)) 10f **(72)**
Form - 00
Record 1999 - 1st:0 2nd:0 3rd:0 Ran:2
1999 Turf 0-2: (6f, 7f) (gd 2)
Currently moderate colt. Turf high 45 (began Oct).
**R T Phillips [0-2] Wilwyn Racing.*

CROWN SECRET BHB 62f **RR 65f** 1975[11]
3 b g Zafonic (USA) 9f **(83)** - Free City (USA) (Danzig (USA)) 8.4f **(76)**
Form - 00
Record 1999 - 1st:0 2nd:0 3rd:0 Ran:2
Pre1999 - 1st:0 2nd:0 3rd:0 Ran:4
Win Prizemoney £0 *Total Prizemoney* £236
1999 Turf 0-2: (7f, 8f) (gd, g-f)
Scopey, average gelding. Turf high 45.
**P W Harris [0-6] Lawrence, Merchack, Williams.*

CRUINN A BHORD BHB 94f **RR 98df** 5140[7]
4 b f Inchinor 8.9f **(64)** - Selection Board (Welsh Pageant) 10f **(65)**
Form - 0211007
Record 1999 - 1st:2 2nd:1 3rd:0 Ran:7
Pre1999 - 1st:1 2nd:2 3rd:0 Ran:4
Win Prizemoney £39,071 *Total Prizemoney* £44,105

Wins	* **1999**	Aug	Newmar	(GD)	H	7f	89	98	<
	* **1999**	Jly	Newmar	(G-F)	H	7f	86	88	
	* 1998	Jly	Catter	(G-F)		7f		60+	

1999 Turf 2-7: (7f 2-3, 8f 4) (gd 2, g-f 1-2, frm 1-3)
Scopey, very useful filly, effective 7f, acts on g-f to frm. Turf high 98 - 1st of 16 giving 2lb to Family Man (14 Aug Newmarket RF 3657). She has twice been found out in Listed races, but is a useful performer in handicap company. She has scored all her successes over seven furlongs and connections believe she will enjoy easy ground. **A C Stewart [3-11] Lord Derby.*

CRUISE AHEAD BHB 48f **RR 42f** 4359[9]
3 b g Arazi (USA) 9.2f **(74)** - Cut Clear (Kris) 9.5f **(73)**
Form - 0050
Record 1999 - 1st:0 2nd:0 3rd:0 Ran:4
1999 Turf 0-4: (8f 2, 10f, 11f) (g-s, g-f, frm 2)
Workmanlike, moderate gelding, has worn blinkers. Turf high 62.
**R M H Cowell [0-4] Bottisham Heath Stud.*

CRUISING BHB 61f72a **RR 21f 72a** 3673[11]
2 ch g Superpower 6.6f **(58)** - Petitesse (Petong) 6.6f **(58)**
Form - 004270
Record 1999 - 1st:0 2nd:1 3rd:0 Ran:6
Win Prizemoney £0 *Total Prizemoney* £833
1999 Turf 0-3: (5f, 6f 2) (gd, frm 2) 1999 AW 0-3: (6f 2, 7f) (Fibr 3)
Above-average gelding, effective 6f, - acts on Fibr, often wears blinkers (very effectively). Turf high 36. AW high 73.
**K McAuliffe [0-6] Alex Fraser.*

CRUMPTON HILL (IRE) BHB 76f **RR 71f** 4179[14]
7 b g Thatching 7.8f **(69)** - Senane (Vitiges (FR)) 8.2f **(59)**
Form - 070
Record 1999 - 1st:0 2nd:0 3rd:0 Ran:3
Pre1999 - 1st:4 2nd:1 3rd:7 Ran:29
Win Prizemoney £39,388 *Total Prizemoney* £89,266

Wins	* 1998	May	Kempto	(G-F)		7f		95	<
	* 1996	Jly	Newmar	(GD)	H	7f	86	93	
	* 1995	Apr	Newbur	(G-F)	H	8f	75	75+	

1999 Turf 0-3: (7f 2, 8f) (frm 2, hrd)
Above-average gelding, effective 7 to 8f, best at 8f, acts on gd to frm, has worn blinkers. Turf high 71 (began Jly). Becoming disappointing. Has reportedly been retired.
**N A Graham [4-32] T H Chadney.*

CRUSTY LILY BHB 43f **RR 42f** 4787[10]
3 gr f Whittingham (IRE) - Miss Crusty **(35df)** (Belfort (FR)) 6.8f **(63)**
Form - 60725170
Record 1999 - 1st:1 2nd:1 3rd:0 Ran:8
Pre1999 - 1st:0 2nd:0 3rd:0 Ran:1
Win Prizemoney £3,132 *Total Prizemoney* £3,750

Wins	* **1999**	Aug	Yarmou	(GD)	H	6f	39	42	<

1999 Turf 1-6: (6f 1-3, 7f 2, 8f) (gd 1-1, g-f 2, frm 3) 1999 AW 0-2: (6f, 7f) (Equi, Fibr)
Light-framed, moderate filly, effective 6 to 7f, acts on gd to g-f. Turf high 42 - 1st of 16 getting 28lb from Night Life (19 Aug Yarmouth RF 3768). AW high 24.
**N P Littmoden [1-8] Three Of A Kind Racing (from L P Grassick [0-1] Spt 1998).*

CRUZ SANTA BHB 26f27a **RR 27f 27a** 3478[4]
6 b m Lord Bud 8.2f **(52)** - Linpac Mapleleaf (Dominion) 8.5f **(63)**

Form - 0P4
Record 1999 - 1st:0 2nd:0 3rd:0 Ran:3
Pre1999 - 1st:1 2nd:1 3rd:1 Ran:23
Win Prizemoney £2,085 *Total Prizemoney* £3,581
Wins 1998 *Jan Southw (STD) 11f 40* <
1999 Turf 0-3: (16f 3) (gd, g-f, frm)
Moderate mare, effective 7 to 11f, acts on gd - acts on Fibr, likes left handed tracks, likes tight tracks. Turf high 27 (began Jly).
**Mrs M Reveley [0-3] Mrs M Reveley (from M C Chapman [1-16] Aug 1998).*

CRY FOR FREEDOM BHB 53f41a **RR 53f 41a** 269[1]
4 b f Komaite (USA) 6.9f **(61)** - Heresheis (Free State) 8.7f **(61)**
Form - 50441
Record 1999 - 1st:1 2nd:0 3rd:0 Ran:3
Pre1999 - 1st:1 2nd:1 3rd:0 Ran:10
Win Prizemoney £3,985 *Total Prizemoney* £5,155
Wins * 1999 *Feb Lingfi (STD) SH 16f 40 45*
* 1998 Oct Bright (G-S) SH 10f 44 53 <
1999 AW 1-3: (13f 2, 16f 1-1) (Equi 1-3)
Scopey, fair filly, effective 8 to 16f, acts on g-s to hrd - acts on Equi. AW high 45 - 1st of 14 giving 7lb to Keepsake (11 Feb Lingfield RF 0269). **J Pearce [2-13] Michael Whatley.*

Cryhavoc was in tremendous form in 1999, in common with many of the Nicholls team

CRYHAVOC BHB 88f **RR 91f** 4392[11]
5 b g Polar Falcon (USA) 9f **(74)** - Sarabah (IRE) (Ela-Mana-Mou) 10.1f **(70)**
Form - 001114311225650
Record 1999 - 1st:5 2nd:2 3rd:1 Ran:15
Pre1999 - 1st:2 2nd:1 3rd:1 Ran:16
Win Prizemoney £31,742 *Total Prizemoney* £42,619
Wins * 1999 Jly Beverl (SFT) H 5f 73 88+
*** 1999** Jun Catter (G-F) H 7f 71 83
*** 1999** Jun Windso (G-F) H 6f 63 75+
*** 1999** Jun Goodwo (G-F) H 6f 58 68
*** 1999** Jun Yarmou (GD) H 6f 58 61
1996 Oct Newmar (G-F) H 6f 86 96 <
1996 Spt Epsom (G-F) 6f 83
1999 Turf 5-15: (5f 1-4, 6f 3-8, 7f 1-3) (gd 1-4, g-f 2-6, frm 2-5)
Useful gelding, effective 5 to 7f, best at 7f, acts on gd to frm, has worn blinkers. Turf high 91 - 2nd of 14 giving 18lb to A Touch of Frost (10 Jly York 7f g-f RF 2731) - also 1st of 13 giving 21lb to Dominelle (3 Jly Beverley RF 2515). Consistent. He suddenly hit an extraordinary vein of form in the summer, winning five times and running well in defeat. His victories have been gained over trips ranging from five to seven furlongs, and on ground ranging from soft to good to firm. Yet another testament to his trainer's skill, but the Handicapper has not surprisingly got stuck in and he has been forced to take on rather better company than was previously the case.
**D Nicholls [5-15] John Gilbertson (from J R Arnold [2-16] Oct 1998).*

CRYSTAL CANYON RR 62f 3971[12]
2 ch f Efisio 7.7f **(69)** - Manor Adventure **(26f 47a)** (Smackover) 6f **(52)**
Form - 60
Record 1999 - 1st:0 2nd:0 3rd:0 Ran:2
1999 Turf 0-2: (6f 2) (g-f 2)
Currently average filly. Turf high 61 (began Aug).
**B Smart [0-2] Mrs Julie Martin.*

CRYSTAL CRAZE BHB 39f34a **RR 32f 34a** 457[10]
4 b f Warrshan (USA) 9.7f **(59)** - Single Gal (Mansingh (USA)) 7.4f **(55)**
Form - 00
Record 1999 - 1st:0 2nd:0 3rd:0 Ran:2
Pre1999 - 1st:0 2nd:1 3rd:0 Ran:6
Win Prizemoney £0 *Total Prizemoney* £570
1999 AW 0-2: (8f 2) (Equi, Fibr)
Light-framed, very moderate filly.
**P Bowen [0-4] W R Connell (from C A Cyzer [0-6] Spt 1998).*

CRYSTAL CREEK (IRE) BHB 86f **RR 90f** 4406[8]
3 b g River Falls 8.2f **(56)** - Dazzling Maid (IRE) (Tate Gallery (USA)) 7.4f **(67)**
Form - 107133258
Record 1999 - 1st:2 2nd:1 3rd:2 Ran:9
Pre1999 - 1st:0 2nd:0 3rd:0 Ran:2
Win Prizemoney £10,126 *Total Prizemoney* £14,386
Wins * 1999 Jun Bath (FRM) H 8f 84 85 <
*** 1999** May Kempto (G-F) 8f 80
1999 Turf 2-9: (7f 2, 8f 2-5, 9f, 10f) (gd 3, g-f 2, frm 1-3, hrd 1-1)
Scopey, useful gelding, effective 8 to 10f, best at 8f, acts on gd to hrd. Turf high 90 - also 1st of 7 giving 1lb to Whitewater Boy (26 Jun Bath RF 2318). Winner of a Kempton maiden in May and a Bath handicap in June, he continued to run with credit afterwards.
**Mrs A J Perrett [2-11] Fred Cotton & Mrs Gaynor Scruton.*

CRYSTAL D'ASS (FR) RR 100f 5201a[4]
2 f Northern Crystal - Asslana (FR) (Al Nasr (FR)) 9.3f **(68)**
Form - 6P124
1999 Turf 1-5: (6f 2, 7f 1-1, 9f, 10f) (hvy 2, sft 1-2, gd)
Very useful. Turf high 100 - 2nd of 6 to Lord Flasheart (2 Oct Longchamp 9f hvy RF 4767a).
**T Clout in FR [0-2] (from F Chappet in FR [1-3] Aug 1999).*

CRYSTAL DOWNS (USA) RR 104f 4856a[2]
3 b f Alleged (USA) 11.8f **(81)** -Gazayil (USA)(Irish River (FR)) 8.6f **(78)**
Form - 24822
1999 Turf 0-5: (7f, 8f 3, 12f) (hvy, sft, gd, g-f, frm)
Very useful filly, effective 7 to 8f, best at 8f, acts on sft to g-f. Turf high 104 - 4th of 17 to Hula Angel (23 May Curragh 8f g-f RF 1485a). Becoming disappointing. Group One-placed as a juvenile, she finished fourth in the Irish 1,000 Guineas but was consistently beaten by her lack of finishing pace. Likely to stay beyond a mile, she ought to win a listed race. **A P O'Brien in IRE [1-9] Mrs T Hyde.*

CRYSTAL FALLS (IRE) BHB 72f **RR 70f** 793[3]
6 b g Alzao (USA) 9.8f **(73)** - Honourable Sheba (USA) (Roberto (USA)) 10f **(76)**
Form - 3
Record 1999 - 1st:0 2nd:0 3rd:1 Ran:1
Pre1999 - 1st:2 2nd:7 3rd:4 Ran:25
Win Prizemoney £10,004 *Total Prizemoney* £25,261
Wins * 1998 Jly Ripon (G-F) H 12.3f 74 77
1995 Oct Doncas (G-F) H 8f 77 79 <
1999 Turf 0-1: (12f) (gd)
Above-average gelding, effective 10 to 14f, best at 12f, acts on g-s to frm, best on g-f, has worn blinkers, likes tight tracks, and excels

at Thirsk. Consistent.
**T D Easterby [1-16] C H Stevens (from J J O'Neill [1-10] Jun 1997).*

CRYSTAL FLITE (IRE) BHB 72f RR 79f 5048^{3}

2 b f Darshaan 11.9f **(81)** - Crystal City (Kris) 9.5f **(73)**

Form - 75763

Record 1999 - 1st:0 2nd:0 3rd:1 Ran:5

Win Prizemoney £0 *Total Prizemoney* £590

1999 Turf 0-5: (7f 5) (hvy, gd, g-f, frm 2)

Above-average filly. Turf high 79 (began Jly).
**W R Muir [0-5] The Wheet Partnership.*

CRYSTAL LASS BHB 52f69a RR 34f 69a 5026^{16}

3 b f Ardkinglass 5f **(64)** - That's Rich (Hot Spark) 7.6f **(62)**

Form - 42501040

Record 1999 - 1st:1 2nd:1 3rd:0 Ran:7
Pre1999 - 1st:0 2nd:1 3rd:2 Ran:9

Win Prizemoney £2,814 *Total Prizemoney* £5,382

Wins * 1999 *Jun Southw (STD) H 8f 63 73+* <

1999 Turf 0-2: (7f, 8f) (gd, hrd) 1999 AW 1-5: (7f 3, 8f 1-2) (Fibr 1-5)

Rangy, average filly, effective 8f, - acts on Fibr, often wears blinkers, likes left handed tracks, likes tight tracks. Turf high 34. AW high 73 - 1st of 13 giving 9lb to Stravsea (4 Jun Southwell RF 1747). She had shown ability on Fibresand, but took an awfully long time getting off the mark. It was not until she was stepped up to a mile that she did so, winning a very bad maiden handicap at Southwell, but she was well beaten when taking on much better company afterwards. **J Balding [1-16] White House Racing Club.*

CRYSTAL LOUGH (IRE) BHB 35f RR 23f 991^{10}

4 b f Maelstrom Lake 8.8f **(53)** - Holy Water (Monseigneur (USA)) 7.7f **(63)**

Form - 00

Record 1999 - 1st:0 2nd:0 3rd:0 Ran:2
Pre1999 - 1st:0 2nd:0 3rd:0 Ran:5

1999 Turf 0-1: (6f) (hrd) 1999 AW 0-1: (5f) (Fibr)

Scopey, little account filly.
**N Tinkler [0-2] W F Burton (from G R Oldroyd [0-5] May 1998).*

CRYSTAL ROSIE BHB 42f42a RR 13f 42a 2057^{19}

3 gr f Ardkinglass 5f **(64)** - Indian Crystal **(45f 42a)** (Petong) 6.6f **(58)**

Form - 00

Record 1999 - 1st:0 2nd:0 3rd:0 Ran:2
Pre1999 - 1st:0 2nd:0 3rd:1 Ran:3

Win Prizemoney £0 *Total Prizemoney* £325

1999 Turf 0-2: (7f, 8f) (frm, hrd)

Light-framed, poor filly. Turf high 13.
**Mrs A Swinbank [0-5] Starnotes Racing.*

CUBISM (USA) BHB 107f RR 107f 4234^{4}

3 b c Miswaki (USA) 8.1f **(81)** - Seattle Kat (USA) (Seattle Song (USA)) 9f **(77)**

Form - 012166064

Record 1999 - 1st:2 2nd:1 3rd:0 Ran:9
Pre1999 - 1st:2 2nd:0 3rd:0 Ran:5

Win Prizemoney £32,173 *Total Prizemoney* £44,840

Wins * 1999 May Haydoc (GD) LH 6f 96 98 <
*** 1999** May Salisb (G-F) H 6f 87 91
* 1998 Aug Windso (G-F) H 6f 85 89
* 1998 Jly Yarmou (GD) 6f 77+

1999 Turf 2-9: (5f, 6f 2-7, 7f) (gd 2, g-f 3, frm 2-4)

Small, Pattern-class colt, effective 5 to 6f, best at 6f, acts on g-f to frm, best on frm. Turf high 108 - 6th of 9 getting 3lb from Halmahera (26 Jun Newcastle 6f frm RF 2339). Twice a winner over six furlongs last term, his most impressive success was at Haydock in a Listed race in May. Since then this progressive sort has been highly tried, and although a little disappointing mid-season, he came back well over an inadequate five furlongs at Doncaster when fourth in the Scarbrough Stakes.
**J W Hills [4-14] K Y Lim.*

CUGINA BHB 90f RR 91f 1936^{3}

5 b m Distant Relative 7f **(69)** - Indubitable (Sharpo) 7.7f **(59)**

Form - 3133

Record 1999 - 1st:1 2nd:0 3rd:3 Ran:4
Pre1999 - 1st:3 2nd:3 3rd:0 Ran:15

Win Prizemoney £22,427 *Total Prizemoney* £34,512

Wins * 1999 Apr Pontef (SFT) 10f 90
* 1998 Jun Sandow (G-S) H 10f 89 95 <
* 1997 Aug Sandow (SFT) H 10f 78 84
* 1997 Jly Chepst (G-S) H 10.2f 73 75

1999 Turf 1-4: (10f 1-2, 12f 2) (sft 1-1, g-s, gd 2)

Useful filly, effective 10 to 12f, best at 12f, acts on sft to gd, best on gd, likes left handed tracks, likes York. Turf high 91 - 3rd of 3 giving 1lb to Achilles (11 Jun York 12f g-s RF 1936) - also 1st of 8 getting 5lb from Somayda (20 Apr Pontefract RF 0772). Had the ground to suit when winning a Pontefract classified stakes on her second start of last season. She is suited by plenty of give underfoot. **G B Balding [4-19] Miss B Swire.*

CULTURED PEARL (IRE) RR 74+f 5108^{5}

2 ch f Lammtarra (USA) - Culture Vulture (USA) (Timeless Moment (USA)) 6f **(72)**

Form - 5

Record 1999 - 1st:0 2nd:0 3rd:0 Ran:1

1999 Turf 0-1: (8f) (gd)

Currently above-average filly. The result of a mating between two Classic winners, she could well show considerable improvement as a three-year-old. **P F I Cole [0-1] Christopher Wright.*

CULZEAN (IRE) BHB 85f RR 88f 4562^{3}

3 b g Machiavellian (USA) 9.8f **(83)** - Eileen Jenny (IRE) (Kris) 9.5f **(73)**

Form - 2700455373

Record 1999 - 1st:0 2nd:1 3rd:2 Ran:10
Pre1999 - 1st:1 2nd:0 3rd:0 Ran:2

Win Prizemoney £3,427 *Total Prizemoney* £8,309

Wins * 1998 Spt Leices (G-S) 7f 80+ <

1999 Turf 0-10: (10f 6, 11f, 12f 3) (sft, gd 4, g-f 3, frm 2)

Leggy, useful gelding, effective 7 to 11f, best at 10f, acts on sft to frm, likes left handed tracks. Turf high 90 (1st run) - 2nd of 5 to Deal Fair (27 Apr Bath 10f sft RF 0859).
**R Hannon [1-12] Stonethorn Stud Farms Ltd.*

CUMBRIAN BLUE BHB 67f70a RR 69f 70a 3136^{16}

3 b g Weldnaas (USA) 8.4f **(55)** - Baroness Gymcrak (Pharly (FR)) 9.8f **(68)**

Form - 00158400

Record 1999 - 1st:1 2nd:0 3rd:0 Ran:8

Win Prizemoney £2,263 *Total Prizemoney* £2,669

Wins * 1999 *Apr Southw (STD) 7f 71* <

1999 Turf 0-5: (6f, 7f 2, 8f 2) (gd 2, g-f, frm 2) 1999 AW 1-3: (7f 1-2, 8f) (Fibr 1-3)

Unfurnished, above-average gelding, effective 7 to 8f, acts on frm - acts on Fibr. Turf high 73 - 5th of 18 giving 15lb to Time Temptress (3 May Newcastle 8f frm RF 1007). AW high 71 - 1st of 10 giving 5lb to Tess (6 Apr Southwell RF 0600). Inconsistent. He has shown a little bit on turf, but his only win to date came in a modest maiden on the Southwell Fibresand.
**T D Easterby [1-8] Cumbrian Industrials Ltd.*

CUMBRIAN CARUSO BHB 49f RR 48f 1875^{6}

4 b g Primo Dominie 7.2f **(67)** - Conquista (Aragon) 8.1f **(60)**

Form - 000036

Record 1999 - 1st:0 2nd:0 3rd:1 Ran:6
Pre1999 - 1st:1 2nd:2 3rd:2 Ran:15

Win Prizemoney £3,338 *Total Prizemoney* £8,342

Wins * 1997 Jun Redcar (FRM) 6f 68 <

1999 Turf 0-6: (6f, 7f 3, 8f 2) (gd 3, g-f 2, frm)

Workmanlike, moderate gelding, effective 5f, acts on gd, has worn blinkers. Turf high 48. Consistent.
**T D Easterby [1-21] Cumbrian Industrials Ltd.*

CUMBRIAN CONCERTO RR 48f 3818^{19}

2 br f Petong 7.6f **(58)** - Peperonata (IRE) **(71df)** (Cyrano de Bergerac) 6f **(68)**

Form - 0050

Record 1999 - 1st:0 2nd:0 3rd:0 Ran:4

1999 Turf 0-4: (5f, 6f 3) (gd, g-f 2, frm)

Moderate filly, has worn blinkers. Turf high 48 (began Jly).
**T D Easterby [0-4] Cumbrian Industrials Ltd.*

CUMBRIAN PRINCESS BHB 61f RR 60f 5111^{10}

2 gr f Mtoto 11.5f **(71)** - Cumbrian Melody (Petong) 6.6f **(58)**

Form - 60810

Record 1999 - 1st:1 2nd:0 3rd:0 Ran:5
Win Prizemoney £3,366 *Total Prizemoney* £3,366
Wins * **1999** Oct Pontef (SFT) H 6f 57 60 <
1999 Turf 1-5: (6f 1-3, 7f 2) (g-s, gd 1-2, g-f, frm)
Average filly. Turf high 60 - 1st of 18 getting 11lb from Slick Willie (4 Oct Pontefract RF 4716). **M Blanshard [1-5] David Sykes.*

CUPBOARD LOVER BHB 64f60a **RR 60f 60a** 4904[11]
3 ch g Risk Me (FR) 8f **(53)** - Galejade **(50df 37a)** (Sharrood (USA)) 10.5f **(72)**
Form - 050103010
Record 1999 - 1st:2 2nd:0 3rd:1 Ran:8
Pre1999 - 1st:0 2nd:0 3rd:0 Ran:4
Win Prizemoney £6,592 *Total Prizemoney* £7,707
Wins * **1999** Spt Nottin (GD) H 14.1f 58 60 <
* **1999** Jun Hamilt (GD) H 12.1f 59 60 <
1999 Turf 2-8: (10f, 12f 1-4, 14f 1-3) (gd 1-1, g-f 2, frm 1-5)
Average gelding, effective 12 to 14f, acts on gd to frm, has worn blinkers, favours tight tracks. Turf high 60 - 1st of 18 getting 2lb from Bachelor (25 Spt Nottingham RF 4563) - also 1st of 18 giving 23lb to Danny Deever (23 Jun Hamilton RF 2236).
**D HaydnJones [2-12] Mrs Judy Mihalop.*

CUPID (IRE) **RR 93+f** 788a[1]
3 ch c Generous (IRE) 11.5f **(82)** - Idyllic (USA) (Foolish Pleasure (USA)) 8.9f **(72)**
Form - 1
1999 Turf 1-1: (10f 1-1) (g-f 1-1)
Useful colt. (1st run) - 1st of 7 from Royal Rebel (18 Apr Leopardstown RF 0788a). Made a winning reappearance in the Ballysax Stakes thanks to a fine tactical ride by Mick Kinane, but was not seen again. **A P O'Brien in IRE [2-4] Michael Tabor.*

CUPIDS CHARM **RR 76f** 4542[4]
2 b f Cadeaux Genereux 7.9f **(76)** - Chapka (IRE) (Green Desert (USA)) 8.6f **(78)**
Form - 4
Record 1999 - 1st:0 2nd:0 3rd:0 Ran:1
Win Prizemoney £0 *Total Prizemoney* £219
1999 Turf 0-1: (6f) (frm)
Currently above-average filly.
**P W Chapple-Hyam [0-1] I Allan, Ming Yi Chen & Hung Chao-Hong.*

CUPID'S DART BHB 76a **RR 76f** 5138[12]
2 ch g Pursuit of Love 9.5f **(69)** - Tisza (Kris) 9.5f **(73)**
Form - U43206630
Record 1999 - 1st:0 2nd:1 3rd:2 Ran:9
Win Prizemoney £0 *Total Prizemoney* £2,467
1999 Turf 0-8: (6f 4, 7f 3, 8f) (gd 3, g-f 2, frm 3) 1999 AW 0-1: (6f) (Fibr)
Above-average gelding, effective 6 to 7f, acts on gd to frm, has worn blinkers. Turf high 76. Fair form in maiden company.
**B J Meehan [0-9] Lindy Regis & Geoff Howard-Spink.*

CUSIN BHB 74f **RR 74f** 4954[8]
3 ch c Arazi (USA) 9.2f **(74)** - Fairy Tern (Mill Reef (USA)) 10.5f **(78)**
Form - 0400108
Record 1999 - 1st:1 2nd:0 3rd:0 Ran:7
Pre1999 - 1st:0 2nd:2 3rd:0 Ran:3
Win Prizemoney £3,956 *Total Prizemoney* £6,418
Wins * **1999** Spt Salisb (G-F) H 8f 70 74 <
1999 Turf 1-7: (7f 2, 8f 1-4, 10f) (g-s, gd, g-f 3, frm 1-2)
Neat, above-average colt, effective 6 to 8f, best at 6f, acts on frm. Turf high 74 - 1st of 18 giving 3lb to Mr Bergerac (2 Spt Salisbury RF 4094). Got off the mark in a mile handicap at Salisbury in September, showing a nice turn-of-foot.
**J R Fanshawe [1-7] Mrs M Slater (from Mrs J Cecil [0-3] Spt 1998).*

CUTE CAROLINE BHB 52f **RR 55df** 4321[16]
3 ch f First Trump - Hissma (Midyan (USA)) 6f **(60)**
Form - 8370
Record 1999 - 1st:0 2nd:0 3rd:1 Ran:4
Pre1999 - 1st:0 2nd:0 3rd:0 Ran:1
Win Prizemoney £0 *Total Prizemoney* £517
1999 Turf 0-4: (7f 3, 8f) (gd 2, g-f, frm)
Neat, fair filly. Turf high 55.
**C W Thornton [0-4] Murray Grubb (from G Holmes [0-1] Spt 1998).*

CUT THE SPICE BHB 73f **RR 74f** 5159[5]
3 b g Suave Dancer (USA) 10.7f **(68)** - No Chili (Glint of Gold) 9.3f **(66)**
Form - 7635115125
Record 1999 - 1st:3 2nd:1 3rd:1 Ran:10
Pre1999 - 1st:0 2nd:0 3rd:0 Ran:2
Win Prizemoney £12,985 *Total Prizemoney* £14,785
Wins * **1999** Oct Catter (SFT) H 12f 63 65+ <
* **1999** Jly Catter (FRM) H 12f 60 63+
* **1999** Jly Beverl (G-F) H 12f 54 56
1999 Turf 3-10: (8f, 10f, 11f, 12f 3-4, 13f, 14f 2) (gd 1-4, g-f 2, frm 2-4)
Above-average gelding, effective 10 to 12f, acts on gd. Turf high 74 - 2nd of 12 getting 4lb from Intensity (22 Oct Doncaster 10f gd RF 5022) - also 1st of 16 getting 7lb from Salestria (5 Oct Catterick RF 4724). **T D Easterby [3-12] April Fools.*

CUTTING ANSHAKE BHB 42f60a **RR 43f 60a** 2455[10]
4 gr g Anshan 8.2f **(63)** - Golden Scissors (Kalaglow) 9.8f **(67)**
Form - 40
Record 1999 - 1st:0 2nd:0 3rd:0 Ran:2
Pre1999 - 1st:1 2nd:0 3rd:1 Ran:10
Win Prizemoney £1,998 *Total Prizemoney* £2,687
Wins 1997 *Dec Southw (STD) S 8f 60 <*
1999 Turf 0-2: (14f, 16f) (g-f 2)
Lengthy, average gelding, effective 8f, acts on hrd. Turf high 43.
**Martin Todhunter [3-13] UGM Racing Club (from M R Channon [1-7] Jun 1998).*

CYBER BABE (IRE) BHB 60f45a **RR 69f 45a** 5148[7]
2 b f Persian Bold 10f **(69)** - Ervedya (IRE) (Doyoun) 9f **(69)**
Form - 5642200D07
Record 1999 - 1st:0 2nd:2 3rd:0 Ran:10
Win Prizemoney £0 *Total Prizemoney* £1,099
1999 Turf 0-6: (6f 2, 7f 3, 8f) (gd 3, g-f 2, frm) 1999 AW 0-4: (5f 2, 7f, 8f) (Fibr 4)
Average filly, often wears blinkers. Turf high 69. AW high 52. Inconsistent. She was a little unlucky not to have won a seller before the end of the season.
**Andrew Reid [0-5] A S Reid (from M H Tompkins [0-5] Jun 1999).*

CYBERTECHNOLOGY BHB 64f **RR 60f** 5073[12]
5 b g Environment Friend 7.5f **(67)** - Verchinina (Star Appeal) 9.6f **(65)**
Form - 077632105080
Record 1999 - 1st:1 2nd:1 3rd:1 Ran:12
Pre1999 - 1st:3 2nd:4 3rd:0 Ran:23
Win Prizemoney £20,591 *Total Prizemoney* £30,356
Wins * **1999** Jly Doncas (G-F) H 8f 65 68
1998 Jly Redcar (G-S) H 7f 80 82
1997 Aug Newmar (G-F) H 7f 77 80
1996 Oct York (GD) 7.9f 84 <
1999 Turf 1-12: (7f, 8f 1-11) (sft, gd 2, g-f 1-3, frm 6)
Average gelding, effective 7 to 8f, best at 7f, acts on gd to g-f, best on gd, has worn blinkers. Turf high 69. Consistent. Difficult to win with, but ended a pretty long losing run when winning in good style at Doncaster in July.
**M Dods [1-12] Mrs H M Carr (from Mrs J Cecil [1-13] Oct 1998).*

CYBINKA BHB 97f **RR 111df** 4678[12]
3 ch f Selkirk (USA) 7.9f **(76)** - Sarmatia (USA) (Danzig (USA)) 8.4f **(76)**
Form - 801700
Record 1999 - 1st:1 2nd:0 3rd:0 Ran:6
Pre1999 - 1st:1 2nd:0 3rd:0 Ran:3
Win Prizemoney £26,188 *Total Prizemoney* £26,188
Wins * **1999** Jun Epsom (GD,) L 7f 111 <
* **1998** Spt Salisb (GD) 7f 78
1999 Turf 1-6: (6f 3, 7f 1-2, 8f) (gd 1-2, g-f 2, frm 2)
Light-framed, Group-class filly, effective 7f, acts on gd. Turf high 111 - 1st of 6 getting 5lb from Caballero (5 Jun Epsom RF 1762). She sprang a 33-1 surprise when winning a Listed event at Epsom in June, but showed little on her remaining starts. Best over a sharp seven furlongs, she will be difficult to place.
**R Hannon [2-9] Lady Howard de Walden.*

CYCLONE FLYER BHB 65f **RR 60f** 3200[12]
3 br f College Chapel - Mainly Dry (The Brianstan) 5.9f **(55)**
Form - 2342210
Record 1999 - 1st:1 2nd:3 3rd:1 Ran:7
Pre1999 - 1st:0 2nd:0 3rd:1 Ran:3

Win Prizemoney £3,712 *Total Prizemoney* £7,695
Wins * **1999** Jly Newcas (G-F) 5f 47 <
1999 Turf 1-7: (5f 1-6, 6f) (gd 3, g-f, frm 1-3)
Leggy, average filly, effective 5f, acts on gd to g-f. Turf high 75 (1st run) - 2nd of 12 getting 5lb from Paradise Lane (19 Apr Nottingham 5f gd RF 0749). Consistent. **J Berry [1-10] R Leah.*

CYMBAL MELODY BHB 19f **RR 31f** 5145[8]
3 b f Merdon Melody 6.8f **(56)** - Cymbal (Ribero) 9.3f **(56)**
Form - 0087878
Record 1999 - 1st:0 2nd:0 3rd:0 Ran:7
Pre1999 - 1st:0 2nd:0 3rd:0 Ran:4
1999 Turf 0-5: (10f, 12f 3, 14f) (hvy, gd, g-f 3) 1999 AW 0-2: (11f, 12f) (Fibr 2)
Workmanlike, very moderate filly. Turf high 31. AW high 16 (began Spt).
**R Hollinshead [0-3] Norman Hill (from J R Jenkins [0-8] Jun 1999).*

CYPRESS CREEK (IRE) BHB 56f **RR 59f** 4943[8]
2 b f College Chapel - Akayid **(73f)** (Old Vic)
Form - 0088
Record 1999 - 1st:0 2nd:0 3rd:0 Ran:4
1999 Turf 0-4: (7f 3, 8f) (gd 2, g-f, frm)
Fair filly. Turf high 59. **J S Moore [0-4] Geoffrey Morgan.*

CYRAN PARK BHB 64f52a **RR 68df 52a** 2719[8]
3 b c Cyrano de Bergerac 7.3f **(58)** - Kimberley Park (Try My Best (USA)) 7.6f **(67)**
Form - 8868
Record 1999 - 1st:0 2nd:0 3rd:0 Ran:4
Pre1999 - 1st:0 2nd:0 3rd:0 Ran:3
1999 Turf 0-2: (5f, 6f) (gd, g-f) 1999 AW 0-2: (6f, 7f) (Equi, Fibr)
Workmanlike, average colt, effective 6f, acts on frm. Turf high 58. AW high 37. **W Jarvis [0-7] J K Racing.*

CYRO BHB 53f57a **RR 46f 57a** 792[13]
3 b g Cyrano de Bergerac 7.3f **(58)** - Odile (Green Dancer (USA)) 10.3f **(74)**
Form - 8313000
Record 1999 - 1st:1 2nd:0 3rd:2 Ran:6
Pre1999 - 1st:1 2nd:0 3rd:0 Ran:9
Win Prizemoney £4,867 *Total Prizemoney* £5,406
Wins * **1999** *Jan Southw (STD) S 7f 64*
1998 Jun Nottin (GD) 5.1f 72 <
1999 Turf 0-2: (6f, 7f) (sft, gd) 1999 AW 1-4:(7f 1-1, 8f 3)(Equi, Fibr 1-3)
Workmanlike, average gelding, effective 5 to 8f, best at 7f, acts on gd to frm - acts on Fibr, likes left handed tracks, likes tight tracks. Turf high 26. AW high 64 - 1st of 6 giving 10lb to Stutton Gal (8 Jan Southwell RF 0056). Becoming disappointing.
**D Nicholls [1-7] W G Swiers (from M A Jarvis [1-8] Oct 1998).*

CZARINA'S SISTER BHB 39f **RR 47f** 5046[10]
3 b f Soviet Lad (USA) 9.4f **(63)** - Tallow Hill (Dunphy) 9.4f **(57)**
Form - 00000
Record 1999 - 1st:0 2nd:0 3rd:0 Ran:5
1999 Turf 0-5: (7f 2, 8f, 10f 2) (hvy, gd, g-f, frm 2)
Workmanlike, moderate filly. Turf high 49.
**V Soane [0-5] The Red Brigade.*

CZAR WARS BHB 40f42a **RR 42f 42a** 5167[3]
4 b g Warrshan (USA) 9.7f **(59)** - Dutch Czarina (Prince Sabo) 7.2f **(62)**
Form - 805455800000073
Record 1999 - 1st:0 2nd:0 3rd:1 Ran:14
Pre1999 - 1st:1 2nd:2 3rd:0 Ran:17
Win Prizemoney £2,319 *Total Prizemoney* £5,916
Wins * 1997 Aug Warwic (G-S) 7f 70 <
1999 Turf 0-8: (5f, 6f, 7f, 8f 4, 11f) (g-s, gd 3, g-f 3, frm) 1999 AW 0-6: (8f 3, 9f, 11f, 12f) (Fibr 6)
Neat, moderate gelding, effective 6 to 8f, acts on gd, has worn blinkers. Turf high 42. AW high 46.
**P T Dalton [1-31] Mrs Julie Martin.*

DAAWE (USA) BHB 63f70a **RR 59f 70a** 5212[17]
8 b h Danzig (USA) 8.1f **(88)** - Capo Di Monte (Final Straw) 7.9f **(64)**
Form - 565045060000871167 60
Record 1999 - 1st:2 2nd:0 3rd:0 Ran:19
Pre1999 - 1st:11 2nd:5 3rd:6 Ran:62
Win Prizemoney £53,104 *Total Prizemoney* £66,064

Wins * **1999**	Spt	Newcas	(SFT)	H	5f	54	59	
* **1999**	Spt	Pontef	(GD)	H	5f	54	57	
1998	May	Doncas	(GD)		6f		84	<
1998	Apr	Thirsk	(G-S)		5f		77	
1997	Jun	Redcar	(GD)	H	6f	75	78	
1997	*Apr*	*Southw*	*(STD)*	*H*	*5f*	*70*	*75*	
1996	Jun	York	(GD)	H	6f	63	66	
1996	*May*	*Southw*	*(STD)*	*H*	*5f*	*65*	*72*	
1996	May	Doncas	(G-F)	H	6f	56	63	
1996	*Mar*	*Southw*	*(STD)*	*H*	*6f*	*58*	*57*	
1996	*Jan*	*Southw*	*(STD)*	*H*	*6f*	*52*	*57*	

1999 Turf 2-16: (5f 2-6, 6f 7, 7f 3) (g-s 2, gd 1-5, g-f 1-4, frm 4, hrd)
1999 AW 0-3: (5f 2, 6f) (Fibr 3)
Average horse, effective 5 to 6f, best at 6f, acts on g-s to frm, often wears blinkers (extremely effectively). Turf high 71. AW high 69. The move from Jeremy Glover to Dandy Nicholls brought out the best in him as, on his first run for his new trainer, he won at Pontefract. He followed that up with another win, again over five, at Newcastle.
**D Nicholls [2-6] Mrs Andrea Mallinson (from J A Glover [2-27] Aug 1999).*

DABUS BHB 92f **RR 74?f** 5155[6]
4 b g Kris 10f **(75)** - Licorne (Sadler's Wells (USA)) 10f **(76)**
Form - 36
Record 1999 - 1st:0 2nd:0 3rd:1 Ran:2
Pre1999 - 1st:1 2nd:0 3rd:2 Ran:3
Win Prizemoney £3,598 *Total Prizemoney* £6,436
Wins 1998 Jly Sandow (G-F) 10f 84+ <
1999 Turf 0-2: (8f, 10f) (gd, g-f)
Well made, above-average gelding. Turf high 74.
**M C Chapman [0-1] Alan Mann (from H R A Cecil [1-4] Jun 1999).*

D'ACCORD RR 75f 4941[3]
2 ch c Beveled (USA) 6.9f **(64)** - National Time (USA) (Lord Avie (USA)) 5.3f **(61)**
Form - 0443
Record 1999 - 1st:0 2nd:0 3rd:1 Ran:4
Win Prizemoney £0 *Total Prizemoney* £616
1999 Turf 0-4: (5f 3, 6f) (g-s 2, gd, frm)
Above-average colt. Turf high 75 (began Aug).
**E A Wheeler [0-4] R P Group.*

DACOIT (USA) BHB 62f **RR 54f** 3103[5]
5 b h Red Ransom (USA) 8.6f **(83)** - Krishka (CAN) (Drone) 10.3f **(74)**
Form - 555
Record 1999 - 1st:0 2nd:0 3rd:0 Ran:3
Pre1999 - 1st:1 2nd:1 3rd:0 Ran:2
Win Prizemoney £3,476 *Total Prizemoney* £6,357
Wins 1996 Oct Salisb (G-S) 7f 90+ <
1999 Turf 0-3: (10f 3) (gd 2, g-f)
Fair colt. Turf high 54.
**A R Dicken [0-2] D & M Cased Hole (from K A Morgan [1-5] Jun 1999).*

DADDY'S POLLY (IRE) BHB 27f16a **RR 16a** 269[7]
5 b m Waajib 8.9f **(67)** - Pollys Glow (IRE) (Glow (USA)) 6.7f **(71)**
Form - 67
Record 1999 - 1st:0 2nd:0 3rd:0 Ran:2
Pre1999 - 1st:0 2nd:0 3rd:0 Ran:7
Win Prizemoney £0 *Total Prizemoney* £113
1999 AW 0-2: (16f 2) (Equi 2)
Very poor filly. AW high 8.
**B J Llewellyn [0-4] Mackworth Snooker Club PT (from S J Treacy in IRE [1-11] Jly 1998).*

DAFA BHB 37f **RR 50f** 2087[5]
3 b g Deploy 11.4f **(67)** - Linpac North Moor (Moorestyle) 6.9f **(64)**
Form - 80005
Record 1999 - 1st:0 2nd:0 3rd:0 Ran:5
1999 Turf 0-3: (8f, 10f, 12f) (gd, frm 2) 1999 AW 0-2: (9f, 12f) (Fibr 2)
Workmanlike, fair gelding. Turf high 50. AW high 36.
**B J Curley [0-5] Mrs B J Curley.*

DAHIYAH (USA) BHB 34f37a **RR 33f 37a** 3301[7]
8 b g Ogygian (USA) 6.6f **(65)** - Sticky Prospect (USA) (Mr Prospector (USA)) 8.8f **(78)**

Form - 0487
Record 1999 - 1st:0 2nd:0 3rd:0 Ran:4
Pre1999 - 1st:4 2nd:2 3rd:4 Ran:33
Win Prizemoney £12,418 *Total Prizemoney* £15,548
Wins 1997 *Jan Southw (STD) C 7f 52*
1996 Jun Goodwo (G-F) SH 6f 60 64 <
1996 *Jan Lingfi (STD) H 6f 54 58*
1995 May Bright (FRM) H 6f 53 61
1999 Turf 0-4: (8f, 12f 2, 15f) (g-f, frm 3)
Moderate gelding, often wears blinkers. Turf high 33 (began Jly).
**D L Williams [1-17] P F Moore (from B Smart [1-7] Jan 1998).*

DAHLIDYA BHB 34f45a **RR 24f 45a** 3078[11]
4 b f Midyan (USA) 9.9f **(64)** -Dahlawise(IRE)(Caerleon (USA)) 8.6f **(71)**
Form - 413443640200070
Record 1999 - 1st:0 2nd:1 3rd:2 Ran:13
Pre1999 - 1st:2 2nd:0 3rd:1 Ran:17
Win Prizemoney £6,286 *Total Prizemoney* £9,130
Wins * 1998 *Dec Southw (STD) H 6f 43 56* <
* 1998 *Feb Wolver (STD) H 5f 39 52*
1999 Turf 0-2: (6f, 7f) (g-f, frm) 1999 AW 0-11: (6f 5, 7f 5, 8f) (Fibr 11)
Tall, very moderate filly, effective 5 to 7f, best at 6f, - acts on Fibr, has worn blinkers, likes left handed tracks, likes tight tracks. Turf high 24. AW high 53 (1st run) - 3rd of 15 giving 1lb to Intiaash (4 Jan Southwell 6f Fibr RF 0024).
**M J Polglase [2-30] Gen Sir Geoffrey Howlett.*

DAHSHAH BHB 70f **RR 78f** 4718[14]
3 ch f Mujtahid (USA) 7.4f **(69)** - Rawaabe (USA) (Nureyev (USA)) 8.7f **(78)**
Form - 41550
Record 1999 - 1st:1 2nd:0 3rd:0 Ran:5
Pre1999 - 1st:0 2nd:1 3rd:1 Ran:3
Win Prizemoney £7,197 *Total Prizemoney* £9,546
Wins * 1999 May Bath (GD) 8f 78 <
1999 Turf 1-5: (7f, 8f 1-4) (gd 2, g-f 1-2, frm)
Scopey, above-average filly, effective 6 to 8f, acts on g-f to frm, best on g-f. Turf high 78 - 1st of 14 from Ermine (21 May Bath RF 1371). After some fair efforts, she got off the mark in a Bath maiden, but may have been fortunate to do so and she has not run up to that form since. **B W Hills [1-8] Hamdan Al Maktoum.*

DAINTREE (IRE) BHB 54f40a **RR 55f 40a** 4813[7]
5 b m Tirol 8.1f **(64)** - Aunty Eileen (Ahonoora) 8.1f **(73)**
Form - 06322350377
Record 1999 - 1st:0 2nd:2 3rd:3 Ran:10
Pre1999 - 1st:1 2nd:5 3rd:6 Ran:29
Win Prizemoney £3,062 *Total Prizemoney* £16,165
Wins * 1998 Aug Windso (G-F) H 8.3f 49 47 <
1999 Turf 0-10: (7f 2, 8f 7, 9f) (g-s, gd 4, g-f, frm 4)
Fair filly, effective 7 to 8f, best at 8f, acts on g-f to hrd, best on frm, has worn blinkers, prefers right handed tracks, prefers tight tracks, excels at Windsor. Turf high 60 - 3rd of 6 getting 19lb from Gaily Mill (12 Jly Windsor 8f frm RF 2763). Consistent.
**H J Collingridge [1-39] G B Amy.*

DAINTY DISH (IRE) BHB 36f **RR 33f** 5035[16]
3 ch f Nucleon (USA) - Thornhaven (IRE) (Doulab (USA)) 9.8f **(65)**
Form - 000330
Record 1999 - 1st:0 2nd:0 3rd:2 Ran:5
Pre1999 - 1st:0 2nd:0 3rd:0 Ran:6
Win Prizemoney £0 *Total Prizemoney* £768
1999 Turf 0-5: (5f 3, 7f 2) (g-s, gd, g-f, frm 2)
Very moderate filly, has worn blinkers. Turf high 33 (began Jly).
**K A Ryan [0-1] M Sawers (from M A Peill [0-4] Aug 1999).*

DAJAN BOY RR 12f 4928[9]
2 b g Mistertopogigo (IRE) - Joseno **(47f 40a)** (Siberian Express (USA)) 8.8f **(65)**
Form - 0
Record 1999 - 1st:0 2nd:0 3rd:0 Ran:1
1999 Turf 0-1: (6f) (g-f)
Currently poor gelding. **S R Bowring [0-1] David Garner.*

DAKISI ROYALE BHB 49f44a **RR 57f 44a** 4929[6]
2 ch f King's Signet (USA) 7f **(51)** - Marcroft (Crofthall) 6.3f **(59)**
Form - 7882030006
Record 1999 - 1st:0 2nd:1 3rd:1 Ran:10
Win Prizemoney £0 *Total Prizemoney* £948
1999 Turf 0-10: (5f 3, 6f, 7f 5, 8f) (gd 3, g-f 2, frm 2, hrd 3)
Fair filly, effective 7f, acts on g-f to hrd, has worn blinkers, prefers left handed tracks, prefers tight tracks. Turf high 57 - 2nd of 18 to Africa (21 Jly Catterick 7f g-f RF 3003). Becoming disappointing.
**R M Whitaker [0-10] Mrs M A Clayton.*

DAKOTA SIOUX (IRE) RR 69+f 4277[3]
2 ch f College Chapel - Batilde (IRE) (Victory Piper (USA))
Form - 3
Record 1999 - 1st:0 2nd:0 3rd:1 Ran:1
Win Prizemoney £0 *Total Prizemoney* £404
1999 Turf 0-1: (5f) (frm)
Currently average filly. (1st run) - 3rd of 7 to Desert Safari (13 Spt Musselburgh 5f frm RF 4277). **R A Fahey [0-1] Mrs Una Towell.*

DALAAUNA BHB 59f55a **RR 51f 55a** 4410[6]
3 ch f Cadeaux Genereux 7.9f **(76)** - Gunner's Belle (Gunner B) 11.2f **(58)**
Form - 66606
Record 1999 - 1st:0 2nd:0 3rd:0 Ran:5
Pre1999 - 1st:0 2nd:0 3rd:0 Ran:1
1999 Turf 0-4: (5f, 6f 3) (sft, g-f 2, frm) 1999 AW 0-1: (8f) (Fibr)
Unfurnished, fair filly. Turf high 61.
**J H M Gosden [0-6] Nabil Mourad.*

DALBY OF YORK BHB 57f51a **RR 58f 51a** 5197[11]
3 ch g Polar Falcon (USA) 9f **(74)** - Miller's Creek (USA) (Star de Naskra (USA)) 9.7f **(65)**
Form - 131523880
Record 1999 - 1st:2 2nd:1 3rd:2 Ran:9
Pre1999 - 1st:0 2nd:0 3rd:0 Ran:5
Win Prizemoney £5,350 *Total Prizemoney* £7,357
Wins * 1999 May Mussel (FRM) 14f 70? <
*** 1999** Apr Windso (G-F) H 11.6f 55 60+
1999 Turf 2-8: (10f, 12f 1-2, 14f 1-3, 15f, 17f) (g-s, gd 2, g-f 2, frm 2-3)
1999 AW 0-1: (12f) (Fibr)
Scopey, fair gelding, effective 12 to 15f, acts on g-f to frm, best on frm, has worn blinkers, likes tight tracks. Turf high 70 - 1st of 4 giving 6lb to Lady Coldunell (17 May Musselburgh RF 1277). Consistent. **P F I Cole [2-14] Richard Green (Fine Paintings).*

DALI BHB 58f **RR 64f** 658[10]
4 b g Rock City 8.8f **(62)** - Supreme Kingdom (Take A Reef) 7.5f **(59)**
Form - 0
Record 1999 - 1st:0 2nd:0 3rd:0 Ran:1
Pre1999 - 1st:0 2nd:0 3rd:1 Ran:2
Win Prizemoney £0 *Total Prizemoney* £905
1999 Turf 0-1: (7f) (g-s)
Workmanlike, currently average gelding.
**B J Meehan [0-3] J R Good.*

DALIAPOUR (IRE) BHB 119f **RR 123f** 3088[8]
3 b c Sadler's Wells (USA) 11.3f **(87)** - Dalara (IRE) **(113f)** (Doyoun) 9f **(69)**
Form - 12228
Record 1999 - 1st:1 2nd:3 3rd:0 Ran:5
Pre1999 - 1st:2 2nd:0 3rd:1 Ran:4
Win Prizemoney £24,810 *Total Prizemoney* £416,539
Wins * 1999 Apr Epsom (SFT) 10.1f 111+ <
* 1998 Oct Ascot (SFT) L 8f 98+
* 1998 Aug Chepst (G-F) 8.1f 78
1999 Turf 1-5: (10f 1-1, 11f, 12f 3) (g-s 1-1, gd 4)
Neat, very high-class colt, effective 11 to 12f, best at 12f, acts on gd, excels at Epsom. Turf high 123 - 2nd of 10 to Montjeu (27 Jun Curragh 12f gd RF 2419a). Inconsistent. Twice a winner at two, he showed that he had trained on by winning the Blue Riband Trial at Epsom on his 1999 reappearance, but appeared to have no excuses when beaten by Lucido in the Lingfield Derby Trial. He ran a blinder in the Derby, only finding Oath too strong but, like all the others, was swept aside by Montjeu in the Irish version. He suffered a bad cut to his near-fore when last in the King George and missed the remainder of the season. However, he reportedly stays in training. **L M Cumani [3-9] H H Aga Khan.*

Daliapour, a top-level prospect for 2000

DALLACHIO (IRE) BHB 44f **RR 7f** 5066[14]
8 ch g Shernazar 11.8f **(71)** - Mafiosa (Miami Springs) 9.9f **(59)**
Form - 0
Record 1999 - 1st:0 2nd:0 3rd:0 Ran:1
Pre1999 - 1st:0 2nd:0 3rd:0 Ran:1
1999 Turf 0-1: (12f) (gd)
Very poor gelding.
**A G Newcombe [0-1] C T Brinson (from P J Hobbs [0-1] Apr 1995).*

DALLIMORE BANKES BHB 26f **RR 5f** 3440[13]
3 b g Keen 11.1f **(58)** - Run for Love (Runnett) 7f **(59)**
Form - 00
Record 1999 - 1st:0 2nd:0 3rd:0 Ran:2
Pre1999 - 1st:0 2nd:0 3rd:0 Ran:3
1999 Turf 0-1: (5f) (hrd) 1999 AW 0-1: (6f) (Fibr)
Scopey, very moderate gelding, has worn blinkers.
**W G M Turner [0-5] T Lightbowne.*

DALLY BOY BHB 44f45a **RR 43f 45a** 3844[15]
7 b g Efisio 7.7f **(69)** - Gay Hostess (FR) (Direct Flight) 13.1f **(51)**
Form - 20
Record 1999 - 1st:0 2nd:1 3rd:0 Ran:2
Pre1999 - 1st:2 2nd:3 3rd:0 Ran:25
Win Prizemoney £5,295 *Total Prizemoney* £9,466
Wins * 1998 Jun Mussel (SFT) H 14f 40 45 <
* 1998 May Mussel (GD) H 16f 35 39
1999 Turf 0-2: (12f, 17f) (frm 2)
Moderate gelding, effective 12 to 16f, best at 14f, acts on gd to frm - acts on Fibr, has worn blinkers, and excels at Southwell. Turf high 43 (1st run) (began Aug) - 2nd of 12 getting 18lb from Noukari (13 Aug Catterick 12f frm RF 3597).
**T D Easterby [3-32] T H Bennett (from M H Easterby [0-14] Nov 1995).*

DALWHINNIE BHB 39f35a **RR 42f 35a** 3973[8]
6 b m Persian Bold 10f **(69)** - Land Line (High Line) 10.3f **(70)**
Form - 0000058
Record 1999 - 1st:0 2nd:0 3rd:0 Ran:5
Pre1999 - 1st:2 2nd:3 3rd:2 Ran:25
Win Prizemoney £4,155 *Total Prizemoney* £9,587
Wins 1998 Oct Yarmou (SFT) C 14.1f 47
1998 *Jan Southw (STD) 12f 51+* <
1999 Turf 0-4: (13f, 14f 3) (sft, gd, g-f 2) 1999 AW 0-1: (16f) (Fibr)
Moderate mare, effective 12 to 14f, best at 12f, acts on g-s to g-f - acts on Fibr, has worn blinkers. Turf high 42. Inconsistent.
**J G Given [0-1] The Highly Sociable Syndicate (from J Wharton [2-19] Jun 1999).*

DALYAN (IRE) BHB 70f **RR 75f** 4322[5]
2 b c Turtle Island (IRE) - Salette (Sallust) 8.4f **(63)**
Form - 8445
Record 1999 - 1st:0 2nd:0 3rd:0 Ran:4
Win Prizemoney £0 *Total Prizemoney* £675
1999 Turf 0-4: (7f 3, 8f) (gd, g-f 2, frm)
Above-average colt. Turf high 75 (began Aug) - 4th of 20 to Bold State (1 Spt York 8f frm RF 4080).
**T D Easterby [0-4] Mrs J B Mountifield.*

DAMALIS (IRE) BHB 89f **RR 92f** 4678[9]
3 b f Mukaddamah (USA) 7.6f **(74)** - Art Age (Artaius (USA)) 9f **(69)**
Form - 314646440
Record 1999 - 1st:1 2nd:0 3rd:1 Ran:9
Pre1999 - 1st:2 2nd:1 3rd:2 Ran:9
Win Prizemoney £19,051 *Total Prizemoney* £30,913
Wins *** 1999** Apr Sandow (SFT) H 5f 93 93 <
* 1998 Spt Ripon (SFT) 5f 86
* 1998 May Cheste (G-F) 5.1f 86
1999 Turf 1-9: (5f 1-7, 6f 2) (sft, g-s 1-2, gd 3, g-f 2, frm)
Strong, useful filly, effective 5f, acts on sft to g-f. Turf high 93 - also 1st of 9 getting 7lb from Light The Rocket (24 Apr Sandown RF 0842). A winner twice at two, she scored at Sandown second time out last term, and ran respectably on most of her starts.
**E J Alston [3-18] Liam & Tony Ferguson.*

DAMASQUINER BHB 52f **RR 57f** 4707[6]
2 b f Casteddu 7.4f **(54)** - Hymn Book (IRE) (Darshaan) 9.9f **(84)**
Form - 07006
Record 1999 - 1st:0 2nd:0 3rd:0 Ran:5
1999 Turf 0-5: (5f 4, 6f) (gd 2, g-f, frm 2)
Fair filly. Turf high 57. **T E Powell [0-5] Miss P I Westbrook.*

DAME FONTEYN BHB 59f **RR 64f** 5108[10]
2 b f Suave Dancer (USA) 10.7f **(68)** - Her Honour (Teenoso (USA)) 9.9f **(72)**
Form - 800
Record 1999 - 1st:0 2nd:0 3rd:0 Ran:3
1999 Turf 0-3: (8f 3) (g-s, gd 2)
Currently average filly. Turf high 64 (began Oct).
**M L W Bell [0-3] Frank Farrant.*

DAME JUDE BHB 57f **RR 50f** 4293[12]
3 ch f Dilum (USA) 7.1f **(56)** - Three Lucky (IRE) (Final Straw) 7.9f **(64)**
Form - 066304800
Record 1999 - 1st:0 2nd:0 3rd:1 Ran:9
Pre1999 - 1st:2 2nd:0 3rd:0 Ran:10
Win Prizemoney £5,724 *Total Prizemoney* £7,853
Wins * 1998 Aug Sandow (G-F) 5f 78 <
* 1998 Apr Bright (GD) 5.3f 67
1999 Turf 0-9: (6f 5, 7f 4) (g-f 5, frm 4)
Light-framed, fair filly, effective 5f, acts on g-f. Turf high 66.
**W R Muir [2-19] Stableside Racing Partnership.*

DAMIEN'S LAW RR 3572[16]
2 b g Contract Law (USA) 8.9f **(54)** - Cinderella Derek (Hittite Glory) 8.7f **(50)**
Form - 0
Record 1999 - 1st:0 2nd:0 3rd:0 Ran:1
1999 Turf 0-1: (7f) (g-f)
Currently very poor gelding. **A D Smith [0-1] Duckhaven Stud.*

DANAKIL BHB 63f69a **RR 64f 69a** 2569[6]
4 b g Warning 8.1f **(77)** - Danilova (USA) (Lyphard (USA)) 9.9f **(72)**
Form - 5710036
Record 1999 - 1st:1 2nd:0 3rd:1 Ran:7
Pre1999 - 1st:0 2nd:0 3rd:1 Ran:1
Win Prizemoney £2,736 *Total Prizemoney* £3,146
Wins *** 1999** *Mar Wolver (STD) 9.4f 68* <
1999 Turf 0-4: (8f 3, 10f) (gd, frm 3) 1999 AW 1-3: (6f 2, 9f 1-1) (Equi,

Fibr 1-2)
Average gelding, effective 8 to 9f, acts on frm - acts on Fibr, prefers tight tracks. Turf high 64 - 3rd of 16 giving 16lb to Ardent (28 Jun Windsor 8f frm RF 2380). AW high 68 - 1st of 9 from Star Fantasy (27 Mar Wolverhampton RF 0495). Won a Wolverhampton maiden in March, but it did not look much of a race.
**J E Banks [1-7] The Danakilists (from FR [0-1] Oct 1997).*

DANAKIM BHB 78f **RR 78f** 4249[12]
2 b g Emarati (USA) 6.6f **(63)** - Kangra Valley **(41f 54a)** (Indian Ridge)
Form - 642740
Record 1999 - 1st:0 2nd:1 3rd:0 Ran:6
Win Prizemoney £0 *Total Prizemoney* £1,730
1999 Turf 0-6: (5f 3, 6f 3) (gd, g-f 2, frm 3)
Above-average gelding, effective 5 to 6f, best at 5f, acts on g-f to frm, best on g-f. Turf high 78 - 2nd of 12 to Travesty of Law (13 May Salisbury 5f frm RF 1188).
**E Weymes [0-3] Mrs Kim Fritz (from R Hannon [0-3] May 1999).*

DANAMALA BHB 70f **RR 68f** 2383[8]
3 b f Danehill (USA) 9.1f **(79)** - Carmelized (CAN) (Key To The Mint (USA)) 9.4f **(75)**
Form - 8338
Record 1999 - 1st:0 2nd:0 3rd:2 Ran:4
Win Prizemoney £0 *Total Prizemoney* £1,118
1999 Turf 0-4: (6f, 7f 3) (g-f 2, frm 2)
Scopey, average filly. Turf high 68.
**R Hannon [0-4] Ananda Krishnan.*

DANANEYEV (FR) RR 95f 1717a[3]
3 br c Goldeneyev (USA) - Danagroom (USA) (Groom Dancer (USA))
Form - 3
1999 Turf 0-1: (6f) (g-s)
Currently very useful colt. (1st run) - 3rd of 12 giving 7lb to Emma Peel (30 May Baden-Baden 6f g-s RF 1717a).
**C Laffon-Parias in FR [0-2].*

DANA POINT (IRE) BHB 56f **RR 65?f** 525[6]
7 br g Phardante (FR) 12.8f **(46)** - Wallpark Princess (Balidar) 7.9f **(63)**
Form - 6
Record 1999 - 1st:0 2nd:0 3rd:0 Ran:1
Pre1999 - 1st:2 2nd:0 3rd:0 Ran:10
Win Prizemoney £5,683 *Total Prizemoney* £5,958
Wins 1996 Oct Catter (GD) C 12f 65 <
1995 Aug Redcar (G-F) H 8f 60 64
1999 Turf 0-1: (14f) (gd)
Average gelding.
**Mrs S J Smith [3-14] Mrs S Smith (from T D Barron [2-10] Oct 1996).*

DANARI (IRE) BHB 37f **RR 54f** 4439[15]
2 b f Petorius 8f **(66)** - Base Camp (Derring-Do) 11.1f **(64)**
Form - 800880
Record 1999 - 1st:0 2nd:0 3rd:0 Ran:6
1999 Turf 0-5: (5f, 6f 3, 7f) (gd, g-f 3, hrd) 1999 AW 0-1: (5f) (Fibr)
Fair filly. Turf high 54 (began Jly).
**N P Littmoden [0-6] The Lohcin Racing Partnership.*

DANCE IN TUNE BHB 85f **RR 90f** 4833[8]
2 ch c Mujtahid (USA) 7.4f **(69)** - Dancing Prize (IRE) (Sadler's Wells (USA)) 10f **(76)**
Form - 3211438
Record 1999 - 1st:2 2nd:1 3rd:2 Ran:7
Win Prizemoney £7,137 *Total Prizemoney* £10,127
Wins * 1999 Aug Mussel (G-F) H 7.1f 83 90 <
*** 1999** *Aug Wolver (STD) 7f 79+*
1999 Turf 1-6: (7f 1-4, 8f 2) (g-s, gd, g-f 1-1, frm 3) 1999 AW 1-1: (7f 1-1) (Fibr 1-1)
Useful colt, effective 7 to 8f, acts on g-f to frm. Turf high 90 (began Jly) - 1st of 10 giving 24lb to Yenaled (26 Aug Musselburgh RF 3923). (1st run). Placed in turf maidens before getting off the mark on the Wolverhampton Fibresand on his third start. Followed up at Musselburgh, but disappointed on easier ground afterwards.
**Sir Mark Prescott [2-7] Cheveley Park Stud.*

DANCE LADY RR 1609[6]
3 b f Cosmonaut - Lady Lustre (On Your Mark) 7.7f **(58)**
Form - 6
Record 1999 - 1st:0 2nd:0 3rd:0 Ran:1
1999 Turf 0-1: (6f) (frm)
Currently very poor filly.
**J A Gilbert [0-1] The Dance Lady Partnership.*

DANCE LITTLE LADY (IRE) BHB 57f **RR 57f** 5214[7]
2 b f Common Grounds 8.1f **(66)** - Kentucky Tears (USA) (Cougar (CHI)) 12.6f **(64)**
Form - 07677
Record 1999 - 1st:0 2nd:0 3rd:0 Ran:5
1999 Turf 0-5: (5f 4, 6f) (g-s, gd 2, frm 2)
Fair filly. Turf high 53 (began Jly) - 7th of 14 to Poppy's Song (5 Oct Catterick 5f gd RF 4721). **J Berry [0-5] G B Stuart.*

DANCEMMA BHB 74f **RR 77f** 4731[2]
2 ch f Emarati (USA) 6.6f **(63)** - Hanglands (Bustino) 10.4f **(64)**
Form - 47732602
Record 1999 - 1st:0 2nd:2 3rd:1 Ran:8
Win Prizemoney £0 *Total Prizemoney* £3,109
1999 Turf 0-8: (5f 5, 6f 3) (gd 3, g-f 2, frm 3)
Above-average filly, effective 5 to 6f, best at 6f, acts on gd. Turf high 77 - 2nd of 15 to Resounding (5 Oct Nottingham 6f gd RF 4731). **M Blanshard [0-8] M Blanshard.*

DANCE SO SUITE BHB 96f80a **RR 95f 80a** 2978a[6]
7 b g Shareef Dancer (USA) 10.1f **(67)** - Three Piece (Jaazeiro (USA)) 9.2f **(54)**
Form - 2246
1999 Turf 0-4: (8f, 12f 3) (sft, g-s, gd, g-f)
Very useful gelding, effective 12f, acts on gd. Turf high 95 - 4th of 15 giving 10lb to Try For Ever (27 Jun Curragh 12f gd RF 2422a). Consistent.
**E J O'Grady in IRE [4-14] J S Gutkin (from P F I Cole [5-29] Oct 1997).*

DANCE TO THE BEAT BHB 37f45a **RR 39f 45a** 3840[10]
4 b f Batshoof 9.5f **(66)** - Woodleys (Tyrnavos) 10.1f **(55)**
Form - 8086540
Record 1999 - 1st:0 2nd:0 3rd:0 Ran:7
Pre1999 - 1st:1 2nd:2 3rd:0 Ran:14
Win Prizemoney £1,998 *Total Prizemoney* £3,382
Wins 1997 *Dec Wolver (STD) S 6f 60* <
1999 Turf 0-5: (8f 3, 10f, 12f) (gd 2, g-f, frm 2) 1999 AW 0-2: (12f 2) (Equi, Fibr)
Workmanlike, moderate filly, effective 12f, - acts on AW, often wears blinkers (very effectively), prefers left handed tracks, likes tight tracks. Turf high 39. AW high 45 (1st run) (began Jly) - 5th of 17 giving 20lb to Nubile (24 Jly Southwell 12f Fibr RF 3110).
**P Shakespeare [0-7] The Country Life Partnership (from M Meade [1-14] Jly 1998).*

DANCE TRIBUNE (USA) BHB 70f **RR 70f** 2528[9]
3 ch f Nureyev (USA) 8.4f **(84)** - Sam's Diary (USA) (Private Account (USA)) 8.5f **(74)**
Form - 080
Record 1999 - 1st:0 2nd:0 3rd:0 Ran:3
1999 Turf 0-3: (7f, 8f, 10f) (g-f, frm 2)
Scopey, currently above-average filly. Turf high 70.
**P W Chapple-Hyam [0-3] R E Sangster.*

DANCIN' DOLL BHB 38f **RR 23f** 4281[6]
3 ch f Grand Lodge (USA) - Tisza (Kris) 9.5f **(73)**
Form - 00006
Record 1999 - 1st:0 2nd:0 3rd:0 Ran:5
Pre1999 - 1st:0 2nd:0 3rd:0 Ran:3
1999 Turf 0-5: (10f, 12f 3, 16f) (gd 2, g-f, frm 2)
Workmanlike, little account filly. Turf high 33. Becoming disappointing. **J J O'Neill [0-8] Clayton Bigley Partnership Ltd.*

DANCING-ALONE BHB 37f48a **RR 48a** 139[7]
7 ch g Adbass (USA) 12.2f **(45)** - Lady Alone (Mr Fluorocarbon) 6f **(55)**
Form - 0167
Record 1999 - 1st:0 2nd:0 3rd:0 Ran:2
Pre1999 - 1st:1 2nd:1 3rd:1 Ran:7
Win Prizemoney £1,945 *Total Prizemoney* £2,855
Wins * 1998 *Dec Southw (STD) H 11f 37 55+* <
1999 AW 0-2: (10f, 12f) (Equi 2)
Fair gelding. AW high 43. He has had his problems, but has shown

ability over middle distances on Fibresand, including a runaway success at Southwell.
**D Morris [1-5] Miss June Frankham (from R J R Williams [0-1] Feb 1997).*

DANCING BAY RR 71+f 4910[7]

2 b c Suave Dancer (USA) 10.7f **(68)** - Kabayil **(74f)** (Dancing Brave (USA)) 8.4f **(76)**
Form - 57
Record 1999 - 1st:0 2nd:0 3rd:0 Ran:2
1999 Turf 0-2: (7f 2) (gd, frm)
Currently above-average colt. Turf high 71 (began Spt).
**Miss J A Camacho [0-2] Elite Racing Club.*

DANCING DERVISH BHB 73f RR 59f 1240[10]

4 b g Shareef Dancer (USA) 10.1f **(67)** - Taj Victory (Final Straw) 7.9f **(64)**
Form - 00
Record 1999 - 1st:0 2nd:0 3rd:0 Ran:2
Pre1999 - 1st:1 2nd:2 3rd:1 Ran:12
Win Prizemoney £2,913 *Total Prizemoney* £5,122
Wins 1998 Aug Bright (G-F) H 8f 55 59 <
1999 Turf 0-2: (8f, 11f) (g-f, frm)
Workmanlike, fair gelding, effective 7f, acts on gd, has worn blinkers. Turf high 35. Becoming disappointing. **S Mellor [0-7] The Felix Bowness Partnership (from I A Balding [1-12] Spt 1998).*

DANCING EM BHB 48f43a RR 49f 43a 4398[11]

4 b f Rambo Dancer (CAN) 8.4f **(59)** - Militia Girl (Rarity) 10.1f **(60)**
Form - 073133032300
Record 1999 - 1st:1 2nd:1 3rd:5 Ran:12
Pre1999 - 1st:2 2nd:2 3rd:2 Ran:19
Win Prizemoney £8,100 *Total Prizemoney* £14,672
Wins * 1999 Jun Mussel (SFT) H 8f 46 48
* 1998 Aug Carlis (G-S) 6.9f 50 <
* 1998 Jly Thirsk (FRM) SH 8f 42 47
1999 Turf 1-12: (7f 6, 8f 1-5, 9f) (gd 1-2, g-f, frm 9)
Leggy, moderate filly, effective 7 to 8f, best at 8f, acts on gd to frm, best on frm, has worn blinkers, likes right handed tracks, prefers tight tracks, excels at Thirsk and Carlisle. Turf high 49 - 3rd of 17 giving 6lb to Gymcrak Flyer (25 Aug Carlisle 8f frm RF 3902) - also 1st of 13 giving 14lb to Formidable Spirit (28 Jun Musselburgh RF 2366). **T D Easterby [3-31] D B Lamplough.*

DANCING EMPRESS BHB 74f RR 77f 4895[17]

2 b f Emperor Jones (USA) - Music Khan (Music Boy) 6.8f **(57)**
Form - 7023230
Record 1999 - 1st:0 2nd:2 3rd:2 Ran:7
Win Prizemoney £0 *Total Prizemoney* £3,452
1999 Turf 0-7: (5f 5, 6f 2) (gd 2, g-f, frm 4)
Above-average filly, effective 5 to 6f, best at 5f, acts on gd to frm, best on frm. Turf high 77 - 3rd of 10 to Boating Song (9 Aug Windsor 6f gd RF 3488). Fair efforts in maiden and nursery company, but normally finds one or two to beat her.
**M A Jarvis [0-7] The C H F Partnership.*

DANCING GISELLE (IRE) BHB 25f RR 21f 3380[8]

3 b f Dancing Dissident (USA) 6.8f **(65)** - Lady Bidder (Auction Ring (USA)) 8.6f **(65)**
Form - 8008
Record 1999 - 1st:0 2nd:0 3rd:0 Ran:4
Pre1999 - 1st:0 2nd:0 3rd:0 Ran:4
1999 Turf 0-4: (6f, 8f 3) (gd, g-f, frm 2)
Workmanlike, moderate filly. Turf high 21. Becoming disappointing. **P Howling [0-4] J J Amass (from M Blanshard [0-4] Aug 1998).*

DANCING JACK BHB 36f38a RR 41f 38a 4713[7]

6 ch g Clantime 6.6f **(57)** - Sun Follower (Relkino) 8.9f **(65)**
Form - 72666256550004007037
Record 1999 - 1st:0 2nd:1 3rd:1 Ran:18
Pre1999 - 1st:1 2nd:4 3rd:3 Ran:42
Win Prizemoney £2,211 *Total Prizemoney* £8,947
Wins * 1995 *Nov Lingfi (STD) H 5f 49 53* <
1999 Turf 0-9: (5f 5, 6f 3, 7f) (sft, g-s, gd 2, g-f 3, frm 2) 1999 AW 0-9: (5f 5, 6f 4) (Equi 9)
Moderate gelding, effective 5f, acts on hrd, has worn blinkers. Turf high 41. AW high 42. Inconsistent. **J J Bridger [1-60] Mrs J M Stamp.*

DANCING KING (IRE) RR 52f 995[14]

3 b c Fairy King (USA) 7.7f **(75)** - Zariysha (IRE) (Darshaan) 9.9f **(84)**
Form - 0
Record 1999 - 1st:0 2nd:0 3rd:0 Ran:1
Pre1999 - 1st:0 2nd:0 3rd:0 Ran:1
1999 Turf 0-1: (7f) (hrd)
Light-framed, currently fair colt. **L M Cumani [0-2] M J Dawson.*

DANCING KRIS RR 99f 4492[8]

6 b g Kris 10f **(75)** - Liska's Dance (USA) (Riverman (USA)) 9.1f **(76)**
Form - 2318
Record 1999 - 1st:1 2nd:1 3rd:1 Ran:4
Pre1999 - 1st:0 2nd:0 3rd:0 Ran:1
Win Prizemoney £18,299 *Total Prizemoney* £30,223
Wins * 1999 Aug Deauvi (HVY) H 8f 97+ <
1999 Turf 1-4: (8f 1-2, 10f 2) (hvy 1-2, sft, g-f)
Very useful gelding. Turf high 99 (began Aug) - 3rd of 20 giving 9lb to Orso (15 Aug Deauville 8f hvy RF 3781a) - also 1st of 18 giving 10lb to Takamatsu (24 Aug Deauville RF 4106a). Bought to go jumping, he hacked-up under top-weight in a valuable handicap at Deauville in August. He fractured a splint-bone when unplaced at Goodwood the following month but remains an interesting dual-purpose prospect.
**Ian Williams [1-4] & Mrs John Poynton (from Mme C Head in FR [0-1] May 1998).*

DANCING LAWYER BHB 39f43a RR 30f 43a 4985[12]

8 b g Thowra (FR) 11.2f **(47)** - Miss Lawsuit (Neltino) 7.6f **(54)**
Form - 3640240800
Record 1999 - 1st:0 2nd:1 3rd:1 Ran:10
Pre1999 - 1st:7 2nd:6 3rd:9 Ran:68
Win Prizemoney £19,446 *Total Prizemoney* £36,469
Wins 1998 May Warwic (GD) H 8f 44 56
1998 Apr Bright (GD) H 8f 44 52
1996 *Jan Lingfi (STD) C 8f 81* <
1995 *Nov Lingfi (STD) H 8f 73 78*
1999 Turf 0-10: (8f 5, 9f 2, 10f 2, 11f) (g-s, gd 4, g-f 2, frm 3)
Moderate gelding, effective 7 to 8f, best at 8f, acts on gd to g-f, best on gd, has worn blinkers, likes right handed tracks, likes tight tracks. Turf high 49.
**B Ellison [0-12] Brian Ellison Racing Club (from K R Burke [2-14] Spt 1998).*

DANCING LILY BHB 49f RR 55f 4327[8]

2 ch f Clantime 6.6f **(57)** - Sun Follower (Relkino) 8.9f **(65)**
Form - 0005008
Record 1999 - 1st:0 2nd:0 3rd:0 Ran:7
1999 Turf 0-7: (5f 4, 6f 3) (g-s, gd, g-f 2, frm 3)
Fair filly. Turf high 55. **J J Bridger [0-7] Mrs J M Stamp.*

DANCING MARY BHB 68f RR 65f 5001[7]

2 gr f Sri Pekan (USA) - Fontenoy (USA) (Lyphard's Wish (FR)) 9f **(74)**
Form - 5557
Record 1999 - 1st:0 2nd:0 3rd:0 Ran:4
1999 Turf 0-4: (7f 2, 8f 2) (gd, g-f 2, frm)
Average filly. Turf high 65 (began Aug). **B Smart [0-4] R Bond.*

DANCING MIRAGE (IRE) BHB 88f RR 77f 4595[13]

2 ch f Machiavellian (USA) 9.8f **(83)** - Kraemer (USA) (Lyphard (USA)) 9.9f **(72)**
Form - 822310
Record 1999 - 1st:1 2nd:2 3rd:1 Ran:6
Win Prizemoney £5,199 *Total Prizemoney* £9,304
Wins * 1999 Spt Salisb (G-F) 7f 77+ <
1999 Turf 1-6: (5f, 6f 2, 7f 1-3) (g-f 3, frm 1-3)
Above-average filly, effective 6 to 7f, best at 7f, acts on frm. Turf high 77 - 1st of 10 from Cafe Opera (2 Spt Salisbury RF 4098). She made the frame behind some decent sorts in maiden company before getting off the mark at Salisbury in September. Appreciated the step back up to seven furlongs there.
**R Hannon [1-6] Mohamed Suhail.*

DANCING MYSTERY BHB 75f80a RR 73f 80a 5161[1]

5 b g Beveled (USA) 6.9f **(64)** - Batchworth Dancer (Ballacashtal (CAN)) 5.3f **(50)**
Form - 631231051354224771
Record 1999 - 1st:4 2nd:3 3rd:3 Ran:18

Pre1999 - 1st:4 2nd:4 3rd:3 Ran:30
Win Prizemoney £24,548 *Total Prizemoney* £40,029
Wins *** 1999** Nov Redcar (G-S) 5f 68+
*** 1999** Jly Warwic (G-F) H 5f 63 67
*** 1999** *Jun Southw (STD) H 5f 73 78* <
*** 1999** May Lingfi (G-F) H 5f 57 59
* 1998 Spt Goodwo (G-F) H 5f 51 56
* 1998 Jly Windso (GD) H 5f 48 50
* 1997 *Nov Lingfi (STD) H 5f 65 67*
* 1997 *Oct Southw (STD) 6f 63*
1999 Turf 3-17: (5f 3-15, 6f 2) (g-s, gd 4, g-f 2-5, frm 1-6, hrd) 1999 AW 1-1: (5f 1-1) (Fibr 1-1)
Above-average gelding, effective 5 to 6f, best at 6f, acts on g-f to frm - acts on Fibr, has worn blinkers, likes left handed tracks, prefers tight tracks, and excels at Wolverhampton. Turf high 73 - 2nd of 5 to Beyond Calculation (4 Aug Brighton 6f frm RF 3350). (1st run) - 1st of 11 giving 15lb to Polar Mist (11 Jun Southwell RF 1928). A consistent come-from-behind sprinter who won four times last season. Equally effective on turf and Fibresand, he is very well suited by the minimum trip.
**E A Wheeler [8-48] Austin Stroud & Co Ltd.*

DANCING PHANTOM BHB 98f RR 97f 5038[1]

4 b g Darshaan 11.9f **(81)** - Dancing Prize (IRE) (Sadler's Wells (USA)) 10f **(76)**
Form - 004002081
Record 1999 - 1st:1 2nd:1 3rd:0 Ran:9
Pre1999 - 1st:1 2nd:2 3rd:0 Ran:4
Win Prizemoney £14,687 *Total Prizemoney* £20,519
Wins *** 1999** Oct Doncas (SFT) H 12f 89 97 <
1998 May Sandow (G-S) 10f 91+
1999 Turf 1-9: (8f 2, 10f 5, 12f 1-2) (g-s 1-2, gd 4, g-f 2, frm)
Workmanlike, very useful gelding, effective 8 to 12f, acts on g-s to g-f, prefers tight tracks. Turf high 97 - 1st of 13 giving 21lb to Legal Lunch (23 Oct Doncaster RF 5038). An in-and-out performer, he was given a fine tactical ride by Ray Cochrane when winning on soft ground at Doncaster in October. Best over middle-distances, he is not one to rely on.
**M W Easterby [1-9] Bernard Bargh & John Walsh (from Sir Michael Stoute [1-4] Jun 1998).*

DANCING RIDGE (IRE) BHB 54f RR 56f 4857[13]

2 b c Ridgewood Ben - May We Dance (IRE) **(14f)** (Dance of Life (USA)) 7f **(66)**
Form - 662060
Record 1999 - 1st:0 2nd:1 3rd:0 Ran:6
Win Prizemoney £0 *Total Prizemoney* £651
1999 Turf 0-6: (5f 3, 6f 2, 7f) (sft, g-s, gd 2, g-f, frm)
Fair colt. Turf high 56 (began Aug).
**P D Evans [0-3] Michael Duffy (from G Lewis [0-2] Spt 1999).*

DANCING RIO (IRE) BHB 72f76a RR 69f 76a 3819[7]

4 ch g Roi Danzig (USA) 10.5f **(62)** -Tameen (FR)(Pharly (FR))9.8f **(68)**
Form - 5133524400657
Record 1999 - 1st:1 2nd:1 3rd:2 Ran:12
Pre1999 - 1st:6 2nd:3 3rd:0 Ran:22
Win Prizemoney £24,435 *Total Prizemoney* £29,844
Wins *** 1999** *Jan Lingfi (STD) H 12f 74 77*
* 1998 May Ripon (G-F) H 12.3f 74 78 <
* 1998 Apr Beverl (SFT) C 9.9f 72
* 1998 *Feb Southw (STD) C 12f 77*
* 1998 *Feb Lingfi (SLW) C 10f 71*
* 1998 *Feb Southw (STD) H 8f 68 73*
* 1998 *Jan Southw (STD) H 8f 61 69*
1999 Turf 0-6: (12f, 13f, 16f 3, 20f) (gd, g-f 2, frm 3) 1999 AW 1-6: (11f 2, 12f 1-4) (Equi 1-3, Fibr 3)
Above-average gelding, effective 8 to 20f, best at 12f, acted on gd to frm - acted on Equi to Fibr, preferred right handed tracks, favoured tight tracks, excelled at Lingfield and did well at Ripon. Turf high 77 - 9th of 29 getting 7lb from High And Mighty (15 Jun Ascot 20f g-f RF 2000). AW high 78 - 3rd of 6 giving 2lb to Space Race (28 Jan Lingfield 12f Equi RF 0182) - also 1st of 12 getting 20lb from Swan Hunter (2 Jan Lingfield RF 0011). (DEAD)
**P C Haslam [7-35] Rio Stainless Engineering Ltd.*

DANDANNA (IRE) RR 85+f 3464[1]

2 br f Linamix (FR) 8.2f **(64)** - Dayanata (Shirley Heights) 10.3f **(74)**
Form - 1
Record 1999 - 1st:1 2nd:0 3rd:0 Ran:1
Win Prizemoney £5,550 *Total Prizemoney* £5,550
Wins *** 1999** Aug Ascot (SFT) 6f 85+ <
1999 Turf 1-1: (6f 1-1) (gd 1-1)
Currently useful filly. (1st run) - 1st of 4 from Garota do Leblon (8 Aug Ascot RF 3464). She was badly in need of her debut, but still managed to win, and is sure to benefit from the experience.
**P F I Cole [1-1] H R H Prince Fahd Salman.*

DANDE'S RAMBO RR 50f 5215[17]

2 gr g Rambo Dancer (CAN) 8.4f **(59)** - Kajetana (FR) (Caro)
Form - 80
Record 1999 - 1st:0 2nd:0 3rd:0 Ran:2
1999 Turf 0-2: (8f 2) (g-s, frm)
Currently fair gelding. Turf high 50 (began Oct).
**D W P Arbuthnot [0-2] Dandelion Distribution Ltd.*

DANDE TIMES BHB 43f46a RR 44f 46a 1581[16]

4 ch g Timeless Times (USA) 6.1f **(56)** - Miss Merlin (Manacle) 7.8f **(56)**
Form - 60063330733466550
Record 1999 - 1st:0 2nd:0 3rd:5 Ran:13
Pre1999 - 1st:1 2nd:3 3rd:2 Ran:19
Win Prizemoney £1,813 *Total Prizemoney* £6,852
Wins * 1998 *Mar Southw (STD) S 5f 58* <
1999 Turf 0-4: (5f 4) (gd 3, g-f) 1999 AW 0-9: (5f 9) (Equi 7, Fibr 2)
Light-framed, moderate gelding, effective 5f, - acts on AW, best on Fibr, mostly wears blinkers (effectively). Turf high 48. AW high 46.
**K T Ivory [1-29] Crown Select (from D W P Arbuthnot [0-3] Jly 1997).*

DANDILUM BHB 88f RR 86f 4990[2]

2 b c Dilum (USA) 7.1f **(56)** - Renira (Relkino) 8.9f **(65)**
Form - 23722
Record 1999 - 1st:0 2nd:3 3rd:1 Ran:5
Win Prizemoney £0 *Total Prizemoney* £2,965
1999 Turf 0-5: (5f 2, 6f 3) (gd, g-f 3, frm)
Useful colt. Turf high 86 - 2nd of 6 getting 12lb from Heathyardsblessing (20 Oct Nottingham 6f frm RF 4990).
**V Soane [0-5] The Dandy Cavaliers.*

DANDY NIGHT BHB 100f RR 89f 2484[2]

2 b f Lion Cavern (USA) 7.5f **(74)** - Desert Venus (Green Desert (USA)) 8.6f **(78)**
Form - 1472
Record 1999 - 1st:1 2nd:1 3rd:0 Ran:4
Win Prizemoney £5,150 *Total Prizemoney* £6,455
Wins *** 1999** May Newmar (G-F) 5f 89 <
1999 Turf 1-4: (5f 1-4) (gd 2, frm 1-2)
Useful filly. Turf high 89 - 2nd of 6 getting 5lb from Far Mount (2 Jly Beverley 5f frm RF 2484) - also 1st of 10 getting 5lb from Victory Day (1 May Newmarket RF 0956). She looked smart when winning on her Newmarket debut, but disappointed in soft ground at Newbury. Fair efforts at Royal Ascot and Beverley, and she looks best suited by being held up. **B Hanbury [1-4] Abdullah Ali.*

DANDY REGENT BHB 46f26a RR 49f 26a 2505[11]

5 b g Green Desert (USA) 7.8f **(78)** - Tahilla (Moorestyle) 6.9f **(64)**
Form - D056080254450
Record 1999 - 1st:0 2nd:1 3rd:0 Ran:10
Pre1999 - 1st:1 2nd:2 3rd:1 Ran:17
Win Prizemoney £3,582 *Total Prizemoney* £6,690
Wins 1998 Apr Bright (GD) H 7f 65 73 <
1999 Turf 0-6: (6f 4, 7f, 8f) (sft, gd 2, g-f, frm 2) 1999 AW 0-4: (6f, 7f, 8f 2) (Equi 2, Fibr 2)
Moderate gelding, effective 7 to 8f, acts on g-s to gd, likes left handed tracks, likes tight tracks. Turf high 52. AW high 30.
**J L Harris [0-13] J L Harris (from C A Cyzer [1-14] Aug 1998).*

DANE BHB 89f RR 95f 4573[8]

3 b f Doyoun 10.7f **(69)** - Iviza (IRE) (Sadler's Wells (USA)) 10f **(76)**
Form - 148
Record 1999 - 1st:1 2nd:0 3rd:0 Ran:3
Win Prizemoney £5,117 *Total Prizemoney* £5,687
Wins *** 1999** Jly Newmar (G-F) 10f 87+ <
1999 Turf 1-3: (10f 1-2, 12f) (sft, g-f, frm 1-1)
Well made, currently very useful filly. Turf high 95 (began Jly) - 4th of 5 to Sheba Spring (25 Jly Ascot 10f g-f RF 3121) - also 1st of 6 getting 5lb from El Mobasherr (8 Jly Newmarket RF 2641). She

flashes her tail, runs in snatches and is one to have reservations about. **A C Stewart [1-3] Sheikh Ahmed Al Maktoum.*

DANE FRIENDLY RR 45f 1116[8]

3 b c Danehill (USA) 9.1f **(79)** - Always Friendly (High Line) 10.3f **(70)**
Form - 08
Record 1999 - 1st:0 2nd:0 3rd:0 Ran:2
1999 Turf 0-2: (7f, 10f) (gd, g-f)
Scopey, currently moderate colt. Turf high 45.
**P W Chapple-Hyam [0-2] Luciano Gaucci.*

DANEGOLD (IRE) BHB 63f68a RR 72?f 68a 5188[8]

7 b g Danehill (USA) 9.1f **(79)** - Cistus (Sun Prince) 12.4f **(52)**
Form - 106305132760008
Record 1999 - 1st:2 2nd:1 3rd:2 Ran:15
Pre1999 - 1st:8 2nd:4 3rd:7 Ran:52
Win Prizemoney £52,072 *Total Prizemoney* £69,439

Wins								
*** 1999**	Jly	Ascot	(G-F)	H	16.2f	64	66	
*** 1999**	Mar	Doncas	(G-S)	H	18f	65	68	
* 1998	Oct	Ascot	(SFT)	H	16.2f	58	65+	
* 1998	Oct	Catter	(GD)	H	15.8f	58	58	
* 1998	Spt	Goodwo	(G-F)	H	16f	52	58	
* 1998	Jly	Yarmou	(G-F)	H	16f	50	52	
* 1995	Spt	Sandow	(G-S)	H	8.1f	78	81+	<
* 1995	Jun	Goodwo	(G-F)	H	10f	73	81+	<
* 1995	Jun	Bath	(GD)	H	8f	67	66+	
* 1995	Apr	Ripon	(G-F)		8f		64	

1999 Turf 2-15: (14f 2, 15f, 16f 1-7, 17f, 18f 1-2, 20f, 22f) (g-s 1-2, gd 1-5, g-f 6, frm 2)
Above-average gelding, effective 14 to 22f, acts on g-s to frm, best on g-f, often wears blinkers (extremely effectively), likes tight tracks, excels at Ascot and Goodwood and Doncaster. Turf high 72 - also 1st of 8 giving 7lb to Yes Keemo Sabee (26 Mar Doncaster RF 0478). He bounced back to form when winning at Doncaster on his reappearance, and ran some fine races after, including a spectacular last-to-first success at Ascot. Likes to come late, but his style of racing means that he occasionally finds trouble when trying to get a run.
**M R Channon [16-85] Circular Distributors Ltd (from J W Hills [0-5] Oct 1994).*

DANEHILL FLAME (IRE) BHB 53f RR 52f 4586[15]

4 b f Danehill (USA) 9.1f **(79)** - Hillbrow (Swing Easy (USA)) 6.5f **(55)**
Form - 700000
Record 1999 - 1st:0 2nd:0 3rd:0 Ran:6
1999 Turf 0-6: (7f 2, 8f 3, 10f) (gd, g-f 5)
Workmanlike, fair filly. Turf high 64.
**P W Harris [0-6] The Buckaneers.*

DANE RIVER (IRE) RR 105f 3886a[11]

4 b c Danehill (USA) 9.1f **(79)** - Allegheny River (USA) (Lear Fan (USA)) 8.5f **(73)**
Form - 22230
1999 Turf 0-5: (5f, 6f, 7f 2, 8f) (gd 3, g-f 2)
Pattern-class colt, effective 5 to 7f, acts on gd, has worn blinkers. Turf high 105 - 2nd of 9 getting 4lb from Tumbleweed Ridge (9 Jun Leopardstown 7f gd RF 2023a). **J S Bolger in IRE [1-9] T F Brennan.*

DANESTAR BHB 42f RR 39f 4347[20]

4 b f Danehill (USA) 9.1f **(79)** - Ministra (USA) (Deputy Minister (CAN)) 7.4f **(80)**
Form - 500
Record 1999 - 1st:0 2nd:0 3rd:0 Ran:3
Pre1999 - 1st:0 2nd:0 3rd:0 Ran:3
1999 Turf 0-3: (10f 2, 11f) (gd, g-f 2)
Very moderate filly. Turf high 39 (began Aug).
**K R Burke [0-3] Metropolitan Properties Ltd (from D P Kelly in IRE [0-3] Oct 1998).*

DANGER BABY BHB 51f RR 51f 4932[4]

9 ch g Bairn (USA) 9.4f **(55)** - Swordlestown Miss (USA) (Apalachee (USA)) 9.4f **(71)**
Form - 314
Record 1999 - 1st:1 2nd:0 3rd:1 Ran:3
Pre1999 - 1st:1 2nd:1 3rd:1 Ran:8
Win Prizemoney £6,737 *Total Prizemoney* £8,264
Wins * 1999 Spt Bath (G-S) H 17.2f 37 51 <
1999 Turf 1-3: (16f, 17f 1-1, 18f) (gd 1-1, g-f, frm)
Fair gelding, has worn blinkers. Turf high 51 (began Spt) - 1st of 17 getting 20lb from Royal Expression (27 Spt Bath RF 4581). A rogue over fences, he nonetheless has ability on the level and won a stayers' event at Bath in September.
**P Bowen [8-28] Shark Racing (from Bob Jones [1-8] Aug 1993).*

DANGEROUS DANCER BHB 65f66a RR 43f 66a 4213[19]

3 b f Warning 8.1f **(77)** - Silabteni (USA) (Nureyev (USA)) 8.7f **(78)**
Form - 843310
Record 1999 - 1st:1 2nd:0 3rd:2 Ran:6
Pre1999 - 1st:0 2nd:3 3rd:0 Ran:4
Win Prizemoney £2,050 *Total Prizemoney* £5,979
Wins * 1999 *Aug Wolver (STD) S 6f 60 <*
1999 Turf 0-5: (5f 4, 8f) (gd, g-f 2, frm 2) 1999 AW 1-1: (6f 1-1)(Fibr 1-1)
Neat, average filly, effective 5f, acted on frm to hrd, best on frm. Turf high 68. (1st run). (DEAD) **B W Hills [1-10] Stephen Crown.*

DANGEROUS FORTUNE (USA) BHB 81f78a RR 81f 78a 5004[5]

3 b c Barathea (IRE) - Miss Demure (Shy Groom (USA)) 10f **(66)**
Form - 523215
Record 1999 - 1st:1 2nd:2 3rd:1 Ran:6
Win Prizemoney £3,179 *Total Prizemoney* £6,308
Wins * 1999 Spt Redcar (G-F) 7f 81 <
1999 Turf 1-5: (7f 1-3, 8f 2) (gd 2, frm 1-3) 1999 AW 0-1: (8f) (Fibr)
Workmanlike, decent colt, effective 7 to 8f, best at 8f, acts on gd to frm, best on frm. Turf high 81 - 1st of 10 giving 5lb to Vanille (24 Spt Redcar RF 4541). Well bred, he finally got off the mark at Redcar in September, and could well improve at four.
**J W Hills [1-6] Sara Warren, Amanda Hills.*

DANGEROUS LADY RR 5195[17]

2 ch f Rock Hopper 10.6f **(54)** - Society Arch (CAN) (Legal Bid (USA))
Form -
Record 1999 - 1st:0 2nd:0 3rd:0 Ran:3
1999 Turf 0-3: (hvy, gd, frm)
Currently very poor colt. Turf high 4 (began Jly).
**M D I Usher [0-3] Kinsmen Racing.*

DANIEL DERONDA BHB 58f55a RR 57f 55a 2915[1]

5 b h Danehill (USA) 9.1f **(79)** - Kilvarnet (Furry Glen) 8.9f **(63)**
Form - 0005621
Record 1999 - 1st:1 2nd:1 3rd:0 Ran:6
Pre1999 - 1st:0 2nd:2 3rd:0 Ran:7
Win Prizemoney £4,354 *Total Prizemoney* £6,902
Wins * 1999 Jly Nottin (FRM) H 10f 54 57 <
1999 Turf 1-6: (10f 1-3, 11f, 12f, 14f) (sft, g-s, gd, g-f, frm 1-2)
Fair colt, effective 11f, acts on g-f, likes left handed tracks, favours tight tracks. Turf high 57. Inconsistent.
**J Cullinan [1-7] Rainbow Racing UK Ltd (from P W Harris [0-6] Aug 1998).*

DANIELLA RIDGE (IRE) BHB 70f RR 71f 4421[11]

3 b f Indian Ridge 7.6f **(74)** - Daniella Drive (USA) (Shelter Half (USA)) 7.9f **(79)**
Form - 36330
Record 1999 - 1st:0 2nd:0 3rd:3 Ran:5
Pre1999 - 1st:0 2nd:0 3rd:1 Ran:2
Win Prizemoney £0 *Total Prizemoney* £2,571
1999 Turf 0-5: (8f 3, 10f 2) (gd, g-f 2, frm 2)
Scopey, above-average filly, effective 6 to 10f, acts on g-f to frm, best on g-f. Turf high 71 (1st run) - 3rd of 11 getting 5lb from Debbie's Warning (29 May Kempton 8f frm RF 1574).
**R Hannon [0-7] A F Harrington.*

DANIELLE'S LAD BHB 88f85a RR 86f 85a 5222[15]

3 b g Emarati (USA) 6.6f **(63)** - Cactus Road (FR) (Iron Duke (FR)) 8.8f **(60)**
Form - 00203607250
Record 1999 - 1st:0 2nd:2 3rd:1 Ran:10
Pre1999 - 1st:2 2nd:0 3rd:2 Ran:7
Win Prizemoney £7,216 *Total Prizemoney* £14,375

Wins								
* 1998	Nov	Doncas	(SFT)	H	5f	81	84	<
* 1998	Aug	Goodwo	(G-F)		5f		77	

1999 Turf 0-10: (5f 4, 6f 6) (g-s 2, gd 3, g-f 5)
Strong, useful gelding, effective 5 to 6f, best at 6f, acts on g-s to g-

f, best on g-f. Turf high 89 - 2nd of 12 giving 14lb to Lively Lady (9 Jun Kempton 6f g-f RF 1865). **B Palling [2-17] Mrs P K Chick.*

DANISH RHAPSODY (IRE) BHB 115f **RR 114f** 3235[1]

6 b g Danehill (USA) 9.1f **(79)** - Ardmelody(Law Society(USA)) 9.9f **(70)**
Form - 55311

Record	**1999** -	1st:2	2nd:0	3rd:1	Ran:5
	Pre1999 -	1st:7	2nd:3	3rd:2	Ran:21

Win Prizemoney £145,755 *Total Prizemoney* £171,511

Wins							
* **1999**	Jly	Goodwo (FRM)	LH	12f	110	114	<
* **1999**	Jly	Newbur (G-F)		10f		109	
* 1998	Spt	Goodwo (G-F)	L	9.9f		101	
* 1998	May	Haydoc (GD)	L	10.5f		110	
* 1997	Spt	Goodwo (G-F)	L	10f		105	
* 1997	Spt	Goodwo (GD)	H	9f	95	100	
* 1997	Jly	Goodwo (G-F)	H	10f	90	95	
* 1997	Jly	Lingfi (G-F)		10f		96	
* 1997	May	Folkes (G-F)	H	9.7f	80	85	

1999 Turf 2-5: (10f 1-4, 12f 1-1) (gd 2, g-f 1-1, frm 1-2)
Group-class gelding, effective 7 to 12f, acts on gd to frm, best on g-f, likes right handed tracks, prefers tight tracks, does well at Newbury and Goodwood. Turf high 114 - 1st of 8 giving 14lb to Mardani (30 Jly Goodwood RF 3235) - also 1st of 4 giving 3lb to Redbridge (11 Jly Newbury RF 2746). Consistent. A free-runner, he continued his love affair with Goodwood when defying top-weight in a Listed event there in July. Effective up to a mile and a half, he falls short of Group class in this country, but might be able to score at that level on the continent.
**Lady Herries [9-26] Chris Hardy & Friends.*

DANIYSHA (IRE) RR 71+f 5054[4]

2 b f Doyoun 10.7f **(69)** - Danishara (IRE) (Slew O' Gold (USA)) 8f **(75)**
Form - 4

Record	**1999** -	1st:0	2nd:0	3rd:0	Ran:1

1999 Turf 0-1: (6f) (gd)
Currently above-average filly. (1st run) - 4th of 13 to Picot (25 Oct Leicester 6f gd RF 5054). **Sir Michael Stoute [0-1] H H Aga Khan.*

DANKA BHB 32f44a **RR 33f 44a** 5006[4]

5 gr g Petong 7.6f **(58)** -Angel Drummer(Dance In Time(CAN)) 8.9f **(59)**
Form - 030108074

Record	**1999** -	1st:1	2nd:0	3rd:0	Ran:7
	Pre1999 -	1st:0	2nd:0	3rd:2	Ran:14

Win Prizemoney £1,813 *Total Prizemoney* £3,036
Wins * **1999** *Mar Southw (STD) S 11f 47 <*
1999 Turf 0-2: (16f 2) (gd 2) 1999 AW 1-5: (8f 2, 9f, 11f 1-1, 12f) (Fibr 1-5)
Moderate gelding, effective 11f, - acts on Fibr, often wears blinkers. Turf high 33 (began Oct). AW high 47 - 1st of 5 getting 4lb from State Approval (16 Mar Southwell RF 0439).
**K C Comerford [1-13] S J V Construction (from P T Walwyn [0-8] Dec 1997).*

DANNY DEEVER BHB 32f **RR 36f** 4988[13]

3 b g Deploy 11.4f **(67)** - Yes (Blakeney) 10.5f **(64)**
Form - 00586257470

Record	**1999** -	1st:0	2nd:1	3rd:0	Ran:11
	Pre1999 -	1st:0	2nd:0	3rd:0	Ran:5

Win Prizemoney £0 *Total Prizemoney* £1,366
1999 Turf 0-9: (10f 2, 11f, 12f 4, 14f 2) (gd, g-f, frm 7) 1999 AW 0-2: (12f, 16f) (Equi, Fibr)
Strong, very moderate gelding, effective 8f, acts on frm, has worn blinkers (very effectively). Turf high 37. AW high 39.
**D T Thom [0-18] D T Thom.*

DANNY POWER (IRE) BHB 54f **RR 45f** 4087[6]

3 gr g Priolo (USA) 10.9f **(71)** - Fillette Lalo(FR)(Huntercombe) 7.3f **(56)**
Form - 604305102776

Record	**1999** -	1st:1	2nd:1	3rd:1	Ran:12
	Pre1999 -	1st:0	2nd:0	3rd:0	Ran:3

Win Prizemoney £2,458 *Total Prizemoney* £3,536
Wins * **1999** Jly Mussel (G-S) H 5f 52 54 <
1999 Turf 1-11: (5f 1-8, 6f 3) (gd 3, g-f 3, frm 1-5) 1999 AW 0-1: (6f) (Equi)
Moderate gelding, effective 5f, acts on frm, has worn blinkers (effectively). Turf high 55 - 2nd of 17 getting 3lb from Bodfari Komaite (28 Jly Doncaster 5f frm RF 3200) - also 1st of 14 getting 2lb from Skyers Flyer (5 Jly Musselburgh RF 2558). Consistent. Finally got off the mark with a last-gasp victory over the minimum trip at Musselburgh in July, and is obviously better suited by that sort of trip than the longer distances over which he started his career in Ireland.
**T D Barron [1-12] M A Ryan (from T M Walsh in IRE [0-3] Spt 1998).*

DANSE CLASSIQUE (IRE) RR 92f 4856a[8]

3 ch f Night Shift (USA) 8.1f **(73)** - Ballet Shoes (IRE) (Ela-Mana-Mou) 10.1f **(70)**
Form - 31208
1999 Turf 1-5: (7f 1-3, 8f 2) (hvy, sft, g-s 2, gd 1-1)
Useful filly. Turf high 92 - 2nd of 13 getting 16lb from Free To Speak (27 Aug Tralee 8f g-s RF 4058a).
**J Oxx in IRE [1-5] Mrs Chryss O'Reilly.*

DANSEUSE ARGENTINE (FR) BHB 32f **RR 24f** 2227[9]

4 b f Fijar Tango (FR) - Danseuse Etoile (FR) (Green Dancer (USA)) 10.3f **(74)**
Form - 700

Record	**1999** -	1st:0	2nd:0	3rd:0	Ran:3

1999 Turf 0-2: (10f, 14f) (frm 2) 1999 AW 0-1: (11f) (Fibr)
Little account filly. Turf high 24.
**F Jordan [0-7] The French Connection.*

DANSILI (FR) RR 125f 4246a[3]

3 b c Danehill (USA) 9.1f **(79)** - Hasili (IRE) (Kahyasi))
Form - 124133
1999 Turf 2-6: (8f 2-5, 9f) (hvy, sft 1-1, gd 1-4)
Top-class colt, effective 8f, acts on hvy to gd, best on gd, does well at Longchamp and Deauville. Turf high 125 - 3rd of 9 to Sendawar (5 Spt Longchamp 8f gd RF 4246a) - also 1st of 8 getting 9lb from Kabool (10 Jly Deauville RF 2856a). Ran really well for an inexperienced colt when second to Sendawar in the Poule d'Essai des Poulains, but failed to build on that when fourth in the Prix Jean Prat. Had a nice confidence booster when taking a Group Three next time, and showed his true ability when third in both the Jacques Le Marois and the Moulin. He is lightly raced and, providing he remains in training, will prove a major challenger to old rival Sendawar in the mile division in 2000. **A Fabre in FR [3-7].*

DANSKER (IRE) BHB 74f71a **RR 75f 71a** 4808[11]

3 b c Darshaan 11.9f **(81)** -Nassma (IRE)(Sadler's Wells(USA)) 10f **(76)**
Form - 218020

Record	**1999** -	1st:1	2nd:2	3rd:0	Ran:6
	Pre1999 -	1st:0	2nd:1	3rd:0	Ran:4

Win Prizemoney £3,242 *Total Prizemoney* £8,410
Wins * **1999** Jun Mussel (SFT) 9f 75+ <
1999 Turf 1-6: (9f 1-1, 10f 4, 13f) (sft, gd 1-3, g-f, frm)
Tall, above-average colt, effective 7 to 10f, acts on gd to frm - acts on Fibr, best on gd, likes left handed tracks, favours tight tracks. Turf high 75 - 2nd of 10 getting 6lb from Lafite (4 Oct Brighton 10f gd RF 4710) - also 1st of 3 from Floorso'theforest (28 Jun Musselburgh RF 2364). Only beaten a head on his belated reappearance at Pontefract, he had little to beat when strolling home from two modest opponents at Musselburgh next time. Basically inconsistent afterwards.
**Sir Mark Prescott [1-10] Sheikh Ahmed bin Saeed Al Maktoum.*

DANZAS BHB 40f **RR 38f** 4866[5]

5 b g Polish Precedent (USA) 9f **(73)** - Dancing Rocks (Green Dancer (USA)) 10.3f **(74)**
Form - 0047126208004025

Record	**1999** -	1st:1	2nd:3	3rd:0	Ran:17
	Pre1999 -	1st:0	2nd:0	3rd:3	Ran:13

Win Prizemoney £1,971 *Total Prizemoney* £5,927
Wins * **1999** May Nottin (FRM) H 8.2f 40 44 <
1999 Turf 1-16: (7f 3, 8f 1-10, 9f 2, 10f) (g-s, gd 3, g-f 1-4, frm 7, hrd)
1999 AW 0-1: (7f) (Fibr)
Very moderate gelding, has worn blinkers. Turf high 44. Consistent.
**J M Bradley [1-30] Martyn James & Pete Smith (from R Charlton [0-6] Oct 1997).*

DANZIGAWAY (USA) RR 114f 5264a[1]

3 b f Danehill (USA) 9.1f **(79)** - Blushing Away (FR) (Blushing Groom (FR)) 10.3f **(76)**
Form - 141

1999 Turf 2-3: (7f, 8f 2-2) (hvy 1-1, g-s 1-1)
Group-class filly. Turf high 114 (began Spt) - 1st of 8 getting 3lb from Sossus Vlei (6 Nov Saint-Cloud RF 5264a).
**Mme C Head in FR [2-5] Wertheimer Brothers.*

DANZIGEUSE (IRE) BHB 64f **RR 59f** 4407[9]
2 b f Zieten (USA) - Baliana **(47df)** (Midyan (USA)) 6f **(60)**
Form - 570
Record 1999 - 1st:0 2nd:0 3rd:0 Ran:3
1999 Turf 0-3: (5f 2, 6f) (g-f, frm 2)
Currently fair filly. Turf high 59.
**R Charlton [0-3] Mrs H J Heinz.*

DANZIG FLYER (IRE) BHB 25f55a **RR 6f 55a** 4334[8]
4 b c Roi Danzig (USA) 10.5f **(62)** - Fenland Express (IRE) (Reasonable (FR))
Form - 807008
Record 1999 - 1st:0 2nd:0 3rd:0 Ran:5
Pre1999 - 1st:0 2nd:1 3rd:1 Ran:14
Win Prizemoney £0 *Total Prizemoney* £1,365
1999 Turf 0-3: (7f, 10f 2) (g-s, g-f, frm) 1999 AW 0-2: (11f, 12f) (Fibr 2)
Workmanlike, moderate colt, has worn blinkers. Turf high 6.
**B P J Baugh [0-12] Mrs Renee Farrington-Kirkham (from P W Harris [0-13] Oct 1998).*

DAPHNE'S DOLL (IRE) BHB 49f **RR 55f** 5151[11]
4 b f Polish Patriot (USA) 7.8f **(70)** - Helietta (Tyrnavos) 10.1f **(55)**
Form - 4100403200
Record 1999 - 1st:0 2nd:1 3rd:1 Ran:8
Pre1999 - 1st:1 2nd:0 3rd:1 Ran:6
Win Prizemoney £2,697 *Total Prizemoney* £5,322
Wins * 1998 *Dec Lingfi (STD) 7f 65* <
1999 Turf 0-7: (5f, 6f, 7f 2, 8f 3) (gd 2, g-f 2, frm 3) 1999 AW 0-1: (7f) (Equi)
Scopey, average filly, effective 7 to 8f, acts on gd - acts on Equi, prefers left handed tracks, likes tight tracks. Turf high 55. She has made the frame a few times on turf, but her only win to date came on Equitrack, though even then she probably would not have won had the favourite not broken down.
**Miss Gay Kelleway [1-14] Mrs Alan Gordon.*

DARA DANCER BHB 40f **RR 40f** 4180[9]
3 b f Batshoof 9.5f **(66)** - Dara Dee (Dara Monarch) 8.8f **(59)**
Form - 05480
Record 1999 - 1st:0 2nd:0 3rd:0 Ran:5
1999 Turf 0-4: (7f 2, 8f 2) (g-f 2, frm 2) 1999 AW 0-1: (8f) (Fibr)
Scopey, moderate filly. Turf high 57.
**P Howling [0-5] King Size Racing.*

DARAJAT (IRE) BHB 25f **RR 42f** 70[14]
4 b g Imperial Frontier (USA) 7f **(65)** - Fantasy To Reality (IRE) (Jester)
Form - 0
Record 1999 - 1st:0 2nd:0 3rd:0 Ran:1
Pre1999 - 1st:0 2nd:0 3rd:0 Ran:5
1999 AW 0-1: (8f) (Fibr)
Neat, moderate gelding.
**J G Portman [0-6] Mrs J Portman.*

DARAK (IRE) **RR 68f** 1862[5]
3 b c Doyoun 10.7f **(69)** - Dararita (IRE) (Halo (USA)) 10.6f **(75)**
Form - 05
Record 1999 - 1st:0 2nd:0 3rd:0 Ran:2
1999 Turf 0-2: (10f, 12f) (g-f, frm)
Workmanlike, currently average colt. Turf high 68.
**Sir Michael Stoute [0-2] H H Aga Khan.*

DARAKIYLA (IRE) **RR 92f** 4776a[6]
2 b f Last Tycoon 9.4f **(73)** - Daralinsha (USA) (Empery (USA)) 11.2f **(69)**
Form - 16
1999 Turf 1-2: (8f 1-2) (sft, gd 1-1)
Currently useful filly. Turf high 92 (began Spt).
**A deRoyerDupre in FR [1-2] Aga Khan.*

DARAYDAN (IRE) BHB 84f **RR 79?f** 2000[28]
7 b g Kahyasi 12.9f **(74)** - Delsy (FR) (Abdos) 10f **(77)**
Form - 0
Record 1999 - 1st:0 2nd:0 3rd:0 Ran:1
Pre1999 - 1st:1 2nd:2 3rd:1 Ran:12
Win Prizemoney £11,053 *Total Prizemoney* £34,396
Wins 1995 Oct Newmar (G-F) LH 16f 96 106 <
1999 Turf 0-1: (20f) (g-f)
Above-average gelding. Becoming disappointing. **M C Pipe [9-29] D A Johnson (from Lady Herries [1-9] Aug 1996).*

DARCY DANCER BHB 64f **RR 68f** 4537[10]
2 b c Be My Chief (USA) 10.2f **(62)** - Little White Star (Mill Reef (USA)) 10.5f **(78)**
Form - 350
Record 1999 - 1st:0 2nd:0 3rd:1 Ran:3
Win Prizemoney £0 *Total Prizemoney* £542
1999 Turf 0-3: (7f, 8f, 9f) (g-f 2, frm)
Currently average colt. Turf high 68 (began Jly).
**Martyn Wane [0-3] J P Racing.*

DARE BHB 57f **RR 55+f** 5069[5]
4 b g Beveled (USA) 6.9f **(64)** - Run Amber Run (Run The Gantlet (USA)) 12.1f **(59)**
Form - 700011115
Record 1999 - 1st:4 2nd:0 3rd:0 Ran:9
Pre1999 - 1st:0 2nd:0 3rd:0 Ran:7
Win Prizemoney £16,057 *Total Prizemoney* £16,305
Wins * **1999** Oct Leices (SFT) H 8f 47 55 <
* **1999** *Oct Southw (STD) H 8f 47 51*
* **1999** Spt Salisb (HVY) H 9.9f 35 46+
* **1999** Spt Hamilt (SFT) H 8.3f 35 44+
1999 Turf 3-8: (8f 2-5, 10f 1-3) (g-s 1-1, gd 2-3, g-f 2, frm, hrd) 1999 AW 1-1: (8f 1-1) (Fibr 1-1)
Leggy, fair gelding, effective 8f, acts on gd, has worn blinkers. Turf high 55 - 1st of 18 getting 14lb from Tipperary Sunset (25 Oct Leicester RF 5053). (1st run). He did not show very much for Ed James but has been a revelation since joining David Evans. He won two soft-ground handicaps in the space of three days in September, and was very impressive when making a successful debut on Fibresand at Southwell in October. There are more races to be won with him.
**P D Evans [4-5] J E Potter (from E L James [0-12] Jun 1999).*

DARE HUNTER (USA) BHB 88f **RR 85f** 4760[6]
2 ch c Gulch (USA) 9.6f **(79)** - Dabaweyaa (Shareef Dancer (USA)) 9.9f **(73)**
Form - 156
Record 1999 - 1st:1 2nd:0 3rd:0 Ran:3
Win Prizemoney £4,143 *Total Prizemoney* £4,597
Wins * **1999** Jly Sandow (G-F) 7.1f 85+ <
1999 Turf 1-3: (7f 1-3) (gd, g-f, frm 1-1)
Currently useful colt. Turf high 85 (began Jly) - also 1st of 8 from Chater Jade (3 Jly Sandown RF 2542). Made a winning debut in a Sandown maiden but failed to build on that.
**B W Hills [1-3] Mohamed Obaida.*

DARGO BHB 65f61a **RR 47f 61a** 433[3]
5 b g Formidable (USA) 7.8f **(60)** - Mountain Memory (High Top) 10.2f **(67)**
Form - 213
Record 1999 - 1st:1 2nd:0 3rd:1 Ran:2
Pre1999 - 1st:0 2nd:4 3rd:1 Ran:15
Win Prizemoney £2,284 *Total Prizemoney* £6,223
Wins * **1999** *Feb Wolver (STD) H 16.2f 43 77+* <
1999 AW 1-2: (16f 1-2) (Fibr 1-2)
Above-average gelding, effective 16f, - acts on Fibr, likes left handed tracks, favours tight tracks. AW high 77 - 3rd of 8 getting 17lb from Far Cry (13 Mar Wolverhampton 16f Fibr RF 0433) - also 1st of 8 giving 3lb to Harvey White (20 Feb Wolverhampton RF 0333). Managed to win a two-mile handicap at Wolverhampton by a distance, though the opposition was modest, and he was unable to cope with a better field at the same track next time.
**D G Bridgwater [1-2] The Rule Racing Syndicate (from C W Thornton [0-13] Nov 1998).*

DARIALANN (IRE) **RR 91f** 4621a[1]
4 b c Kahyasi 12.9f **(74)** - Delsy (FR) (Abdos) 10f **(77)**
Form - 135131
1999 Turf 3-6: (12f 1-1, 14f 2-3, 16f, 17f) (hvy 1-1, g-s 1-2, g-f, frm 1-2)
Useful colt, effective 12 to 17f, best at 14f, acts on hvy to g-f, often

wears blinkers. Turf high 91 (began Jly) - 1st of 9 giving 3lb to Take Five (24 Spt Listowel RF 4621a) - also 1st of 3 giving 22lb to Rose Of Tara (16 Aug Roscommon RF 3878a).
**D K Weld in IRE [3-6] Michael Watt.*

DARING MISS RR 107f 4769a[2]
3 b f Sadler's Wells (USA) 11.3f **(87)** - Bourbon Girl (Ile de Bourbon (USA)) 10.1f **(67)**
Form - 112
1999 Turf 2-3: (12f 1-1, 13f, 15f 1-1) (hvy 1-2)
Currently Pattern-class filly. Turf high 107 (began Jly) - 2nd of 11 getting 7lb from Fairy Queen (2 Oct Longchamp 13f hvy RF 4769a).
**A Fabre in FR [2-3].*

DARING NEWS BHB 36f30a RR 40f 30a 334[10]
4 b g Risk Me (FR) 8f **(53)** - Hot Sunday Sport (Star Appeal) 9.6f **(65)**
Form - 8080
Record 1999 - 1st:0 2nd:0 3rd:0 Ran:4
Pre1999 - 1st:0 2nd:0 3rd:0 Ran:9
Win Prizemoney £0 *Total Prizemoney* £352
1999 AW 0-4: (7f, 8f, 9f, 12f) (Equi, Fibr 3)
Scopey, moderate gelding, has worn blinkers. AW high 19. Becoming disappointing.
**O O'Neill [0-9] Frank Clarke (from R Hannon [0-5] Oct 1997).*

DARK AGE (IRE) BHB 38f70a RR 39f 70a 3201[1]
6 b g Darshaan 11.9f **(81)** - Sarela (USA) (Danzig (USA)) 8.4f **(76)**
Form - 0521
Record 1999 - 1st:1 2nd:1 3rd:0 Ran:4
Pre1999 - 1st:0 2nd:0 3rd:0 Ran:13
Win Prizemoney £2,780 *Total Prizemoney* £4,067
Wins * 1999 Jly Epsom (G-F) H 10.1f 31 39 <
1999 Turf 1-4: (8f 3, 10f 1-1) (frm 1-3, hrd)
Moderate gelding, effective 7 to 10f, acts on gd to frm, best on frm, favours left handed tracks, favours tight tracks. Turf high 39 - 2nd of 16 getting 14lb from Adobe (23 Jly Nottingham 8f frm RF 3068) - also 1st of 13 getting 28lb from Homestead (28 Jly Epsom RF 3201). **J Akehurst [1-8] A D Spence (from R Akehurst [0-10] Nov 1997).*

DARK ALBATROSS (USA) BHB 76f RR 78f 5126[2]
3 b f Sheikh Albadou 9.2f **(75)** - Rossard (DEN) (Glacial (DEN))
Form - 0230654362
Record 1999 - 1st:0 2nd:2 3rd:2 Ran:10
Pre1999 - 1st:1 2nd:1 3rd:2 Ran:7
Win Prizemoney £3,663 *Total Prizemoney* £13,525
Wins * 1998 May Kempto (G-F) 6f 63+ <
1999 Turf 0-10: (8f, 9f, 10f 7, 12f) (gd 5, g-f, frm 4)
Leggy, above-average filly, effective 7 to 10f, acts on gd to frm, best on frm, has worn blinkers, prefers left handed tracks, prefers tight tracks, excels at Brighton, likes Newbury. Turf high 82 - 2nd of 7 giving 11lb to Golconda (22 May Lingfield 10f frm RF 1401). Consistent. **J L Dunlop [1-17] Thorpe (Susan Abbot Racing).*

DARK MENACE BHB 49f49a RR 51f 49a 4864[3]
7 br g Beveled (USA) 6.9f **(64)** - Sweet and Sure (Known Fact (USA)) 7.4f **(67)**
Form - 356352143522724236023
Record 1999 - 1st:1 2nd:6 3rd:5 Ran:21
Pre1999 - 1st:3 2nd:2 3rd:3 Ran:43
Win Prizemoney £10,337 *Total Prizemoney* £18,518
Wins * 1999 May Bright (FRM) H 7f 42 47
* 1998 *Jun Southw (STD) SH 7f 32 37*
* 1997 Jun Bright (FRM) H 7f 47 52 <
* 1996 Jly Bright (FRM) H 6f 45 47
1999 Turf 1-8: (5f, 7f 1-5, 8f 2) (g-f 3, frm 3, hrd 1-2) 1999 AW 0-13: (6f, 7f 8, 8f 4) (Equi 9, Fibr 4)
Fair gelding, effective 7 to 8f, best at 8f, acts on g-f to hrd - acts on AW, best on frm, mostly wears blinkers (very effectively), likes tight tracks, and does well at Brighton. Turf high 55 - 2nd of 9 giving 5lb to Tigrello (12 Jly Brighton 8f hrd RF 2749) - also 1st of 14 getting 24lb from Mutabassir (4 May Brighton RF 1021). AW high 49 - 2nd of 12 giving 5lb to Feel No Fear (8 Oct Lingfield 8f Equi RF 4783). Consistent. He has a poor strike-rate, but he does go well at Brighton and he can act on sand.
**E A Wheeler [4-52] M V Kirby (from S Mellor [0-12] Spt 1995).*

DARK MOONDANCER BHB 112f RR 125f 5230a[9]
4 b c Anshan 8.2f **(63)** - Oh So Well (IRE) (Sadler's Wells (USA)) 10f **(76)**
Form - 1110
1999 Turf 3-4: (10f 1-1, 11f 1-1, 12f 1-2) (hvy 1-1, gd 1-1, g-f 1-1, frm)
Scopey, top-class colt, effective 11 to 12f, acts on gd to g-f, prefers right handed tracks, excels at Longchamp. Turf high 125 - 1st of 5 from Dream Well (2 May Longchamp RF 1072a). A winner three times in 1998 for Peter Chapple-Hyam, his only poor performance came in the St Leger, when he moved poorly and probably found the ground a shade fast. Trained in France in 1999, he did well last season, winning the Prix d'Harcourt and a competitive Prix Ganay at Longchamp plus a Group One at San Siro. He then left France and, after a break, made his first start for Ron McNally in America when well beaten in the Breeders' Cup Turf. He acts on fast ground, but is especially suited by soft, and looks the type to do well in American turf races in 2000.
**R McNally in USA [0-1] (from A deRoyerDupre in FR [3-3] Jun 1999).*

DARK SHELL (IRE) BHB 115f RR 117f 3232a[3]
4 b c Darshaan 11.9f **(81)** - Grecian Urn (Ela-Mana-Mou) 10.1f **(70)**
Form - 313
Record 1999 - 1st:1 2nd:0 3rd:2 Ran:3
Pre1999 - 1st:1 2nd:1 3rd:0 Ran:5
Win Prizemoney £17,587 *Total Prizemoney* £42,698
Wins * 1999 May Newbur (SFT) L 13.3f 115+ <
* 1998 Jun Sandow (G-S) 10f 92
1999 Turf 1-3: (10f, 12f, 13f 1-1) (g-s, gd 1-2)
Scopey, high-class colt, effective 10 to 13f, acts on g-s to g-f, best on gd. Turf high 117 - 3rd of 5 to Ungaro (25 Jly Dusseldorf 12f gd RF 3232a) - also 1st of 6 giving 5lb to Kadaka (15 May Newbury RF 1234). Needs time in between his races, yet confirmed his promise when taking a soft-ground Listed event at Newbury on his second start last season. Stepped up to Group One company at Dusseldorf in July, he plugged on well for third place given the ground and track were against him. That proved to be his final start of the season. **Sir Michael Stoute [2-8].*

DARK TROJAN (IRE) BHB 85f RR 85f 4861[5]
3 b c Darshaan 11.9f **(81)** - Trojan Miss (Troy) 10.4f **(68)**
Form - 223225
Record 1999 - 1st:0 2nd:4 3rd:1 Ran:6
Win Prizemoney £0 *Total Prizemoney* £7,395
1999 Turf 0-6: (10f, 12f 5) (sft, g-s, gd 2, g-f, frm)
Scopey, useful colt, effective 10 to 12f, best at 12f, acts on g-s to frm, best on gd. Turf high 85 (began Aug). Sold for 65,000 gns in October to join Pat Hughes in Ireland.
**Sir Michael Stoute [0-6] Lord Weinstock.*

DARLING COREY BHB 72f RR 73f 4584[4]
3 b f Caerleon (USA) 10.9f **(79)** - Tass (Soviet Star (USA))
Form - 624
Record 1999 - 1st:0 2nd:1 3rd:0 Ran:3
Win Prizemoney £0 *Total Prizemoney* £1,628
1999 Turf 0-3: (8f, 10f 2) (gd 2, g-f)
Scopey, currently above-average filly. Turf high 73 - 2nd of 10 to Ranelle (7 Spt Leicester 10f g-f RF 4170).
**R Charlton [0-3] Lindy Regis & Geoff Howard-Spink.*

DARRAS SKY BHB 52f RR 47f 3678[15]
3 ch g Clantime 6.6f **(57)** - Sky Music **(82f)** (Absalom) 7.2f **(58)**
Form - 00
Record 1999 - 1st:0 2nd:0 3rd:0 Ran:2
Pre1999 - 1st:0 2nd:0 3rd:1 Ran:4
Win Prizemoney £0 *Total Prizemoney* £263
1999 Turf 0-2: (6f, 7f) (frm 2)
Leggy, moderate gelding, has worn blinkers. Turf high 47 (began Jly). **Miss S E Hall [0-6] Mrs Joan Hodgson.*

DARU (USA) BHB 80f37a RR 77f 37a 419[11]
10 gr g Caro - Frau Daruma (ARG) (Frari (ARG)) 11.6f **(74)**
Form - 0
Record 1999 - 1st:0 2nd:0 3rd:0 Ran:1
Pre1999 - 1st:6 2nd:1 3rd:1 Ran:18
Win Prizemoney £39,113 *Total Prizemoney* £50,208
1999 AW 0-1: (14f) (Fibr)
Above-average gelding, mostly wears blinkers. Becoming disap-

pointing.
R Hollinshead [1-11] Mrs J Hughes (from G Fierro [0-2] Nov 1994).

DARVAN BHB 54f **RR 57f** 4909[15]
2 b g Efisio 7.7f **(69)** - Do You Miss Me (CAN) (El Gran Senor (USA)) 9.6f **(76)**
Form - 45060
Record 1999 - 1st:0 2nd:0 3rd:0 Ran:5
Win Prizemoney £0 *Total Prizemoney* £197
1999 Turf 0-5: (5f, 6f, 7f 2, 8f) (gd 2, g-f, frm, hrd)
Fair gelding. Turf high 74 (began Jly).
M W Easterby [0-5] Guy Reed.

DARWELL'S FOLLY (USA) BHB 60f83a **RR 56f 83a** 5103[19]
4 ch g Blushing John (USA) 8.9f **(75)** - Hispanolia (FR) (Kris) 9.5f **(73)**
Form - 01020010
Record 1999 - 1st:2 2nd:1 3rd:0 Ran:8
Pre1999 - 1st:3 2nd:0 3rd:0 Ran:8
Win Prizemoney £15,985 *Total Prizemoney* £17,064
Wins * **1999** *Oct Wolver (STD) C* *7f* *56*
* **1999** Spt Leices (FRM) H 7f 62 66
* 1998 *Mar Wolver (STD) H* *7f* *83* *87* <
* 1998 *Feb Wolver (STD) H* *6f* *77* *82*
* 1997 Jly Newcas (GD) 6f 79
1999 Turf 1-7: (7f 1-5, 8f, 9f) (g-s, gd 3, g-f 2, frm 1-1) 1999 AW 1-1: (7f 1-1) (Fibr 1-1)
Strong, useful gelding, effective 6 to 7f, - acts on Fibr, likes left handed tracks. Turf high 66 (began Aug). (1st run). Inconsistent. He was suited by being blinkered for the first time when winning on very fast ground at Leicester on his second start of the season, but is a bit inconsistent on turf. He has been much more successful on Fibresand, winning three times at Wolverhampton. Not the most straightforward of rides. *M Johnston [5-16] S & P Darwell Ltd.*

DARYABA (IRE) RR 117f 4778a[13]
3 b f Night Shift (USA) 8.1f **(73)** - Darata (IRE) (Vayrann) 9.7f **(74)**
Form - 21110
1999 Turf 3-5: (10f 1-2, 11f 1-1, 12f 1-2) (sft 2, g-s 1-1, gd 2-2)
High-class filly. Turf high 117 - 1st of 11 from Etizaaz (12 Spt Longchamp RF 4369a) - also 1st of 14 from Star Of Akkar (13 Jun Chantilly RF 2098a). Another top-class Aga Khan home-bred, she proved to be a top-class filly last season, landing the Prix de Diane on only her third start. Given a summer break, she warmed up for the Arc with a fluent victory in the Prix Vermeille, but failed to cope with the heavy ground in the big race itself. Reportedly retired, she had a turn of foot and stayed twelve furlongs well.
A deRoyerDupre in FR [3-5] Aga Khan.

DARYABAD (IRE) BHB 49f69a **RR 36f 69a** 5058[1]
7 b g Thatching 7.8f **(69)** - Dayanata (Shirley Heights) 10.3f **(74)**
Form - 420001
Record 1999 - 1st:1 2nd:0 3rd:0 Ran:4
Pre1999 - 1st:2 2nd:2 3rd:1 Ran:23
Win Prizemoney £9,017 *Total Prizemoney* £11,701
Wins * **1999** *Oct Lingfi (STD)* *7f* *59*
* 1998 Jly Catter (GD) 7f 64
1996 Aug Redcar (G-F) H 7f 72 73 <
1999 Turf 0-3: (7f, 8f 2) (g-s, gd, g-f) 1999 AW 1-1: (7f 1-1) (Equi 1-1)
Average gelding, effective 7 to 8f, best at 7f, acts on g-f to frm - acts on Equi, best on frm, has worn blinkers (extremely effectively). Turf high 31 (began Aug). (1st run) - 1st of 13 getting 2lb from Mawkab (25 Oct Lingfield RF 5058).
R McGhin [2-15] The Three Amigos (from T J Naughton [1-12] Feb 1997).

DASHARAN (IRE) BHB 59f **RR 50f** 1573[11]
6 b g Shahrastani (USA) 11.5f **(69)** - Delsy (FR) (Abdos) 10f **(77)**
Form - 0
Record 1999 - 1st:0 2nd:0 3rd:0 Ran:1
Pre1999 - 1st:1 2nd:1 3rd:2 Ran:9
Win Prizemoney £2,100 *Total Prizemoney* £3,565
Wins 1996 Aug Currag (G-Y) 10f 69 <
1999 Turf 0-1: (14f) (g-f)
Fair gelding. Consistent.
Ian Williams [0-5] & Mrs John Poynton (from J Oxx in IRE [1-9] Oct 1997).

DASHIBA BHB 91f **RR 96+f** 4682[7]
3 gr f Dashing Blade 7.9f **(80)** - Alsiba (Northfields (USA)) 9f **(72)**
Form - 32237117
Record 1999 - 1st:2 2nd:2 3rd:2 Ran:8
Pre1999 - 1st:0 2nd:1 3rd:4 Ran:7
Win Prizemoney £18,725 *Total Prizemoney* £29,149
Wins * **1999** Aug Goodwo (GD) H 9f 83 96 <
* **1999** Aug Sandow (GD) 10f 80
1999 Turf 2-8: (6f, 7f 2, 8f, 9f 1-1, 10f 1-3) (gd, g-f 2-5, frm 2)
Scopey, very useful filly, effective 9f, acts on g-f, likes right handed tracks, prefers tight tracks. Turf high 96 - 1st of 15 giving 4lb to Be Thankfull (29 Aug Goodwood RF 3994). She ended a long losing run under Kieren Fallon's urgings and looked useful when winning a handicap at Goodwood in August. Out of her depth in the Sun Chariot Stakes, she is best around ten furlongs and open to further improvement.
D R C Elsworth [2-15] J C Smith.

DASHING BHB 42f50a **RR 45f 50a** 2552[9]
3 b g Suave Dancer (USA) 10.7f **(68)** - Pearly River **(72f 54a)** (Elegant Air) 13.2f **(61)**
Form - 00470
Record 1999 - 1st:0 2nd:0 3rd:0 Ran:4
Pre1999 - 1st:0 2nd:0 3rd:0 Ran:1
1999 Turf 0-3: (10f 3) (sft, g-f, hrd) 1999 AW 0-1: (9f) (Fibr)
Workmanlike, moderate gelding. Turf high 45. (DEAD)
L G Cottrell [0-5] Manor Farm Packers Ltd.

DASHING BLUE BHB 107f **RR 109f** 4795[19]
6 ch g Dashing Blade 7.9f **(80)** - Blubella (Balidar) 7.9f **(63)**
Form - 72134353680
Record 1999 - 1st:1 2nd:1 3rd:3 Ran:11
Pre1999 - 1st:6 2nd:6 3rd:8 Ran:36
Win Prizemoney £61,056 *Total Prizemoney* £151,603
Wins * **1999** Jun Sandow (GD) 5f 103
* 1997 Oct Newmar (GD) L 5f 108
* 1997 Spt Doncas (G-F) H 5.6f 105 111 <
* 1997 Jly York (GD) H 5f 99 103
* 1996 Apr Sandow (GD) H 5f 93 94
* 1995 Oct York (GD) H 6f 86 91
* 1995 Aug Ripon (G-F) 6f 85
1999 Turf 1-11: (5f 1-10, 6f) (gd 1-6, g-f 2, frm 3)
Pattern-class gelding, effective 5f, acts on gd to frm, excels at Doncaster. Turf high 109 - also 1st of 5 giving 3lb to Rocco Tower (12 Jun Sandown RF 1960). He remains in good form, but does not win that often these days despite giving his all on every occasion. Ran a cracker on his second start of this season and landed a minor race at Sandown next time, but just finds winning in Group company a bit too much for him.
I A Balding [7-47] Mrs Duncan Allen.

DASHING CHIEF (IRE) BHB 74f **RR 67f** 3490[5]
4 b g Darshaan 11.9f **(81)** - Calaloo Sioux (USA) (Our Native (USA)) 11.2f **(63)**
Form - 0365
Record 1999 - 1st:0 2nd:0 3rd:1 Ran:4
Pre1999 - 1st:1 2nd:0 3rd:2 Ran:10
Win Prizemoney £3,915 *Total Prizemoney* £11,932
Wins 1997 Oct Pontef (G-F) 10f 87 <
1999 Turf 0-4: (8f, 9f, 10f 2) (gd, g-f, frm 2)
Average gelding, effective 11f, acts on g-f, favours tight tracks. Turf high 77. Becoming disappointing.
W J Musson [0-4] Magnificent Seven (from M A Jarvis [1-10] Aug 1998).

DASHING DENISE RR 8f 741[10]
2 b f Noble Patriarch 12.2f **(43)** - Maid O'Cannie **(56f 68a)** (Efisio)
Form - 50
Record 1999 - 1st:0 2nd:0 3rd:0 Ran:2
1999 Turf 0-2: (5f 2) (sft, gd)
Currently very poor filly. Turf high 8.
M W Easterby [0-2] Winton Bloodstock Ltd.

DASHING DUKE (IRE) RR 79+f 4100[1]
2 b c Mujadil (USA) 7.7f **(70)** - Alzeam (IRE) **(51f)** (Alzao (USA)) 7.1f **(68)**
Form - 1

Record 1999 - 1st:1 2nd:0 3rd:0 Ran:1
Win Prizemoney £6,498 *Total Prizemoney* £6,498
Wins * 1999 Spt York (G-F) 6f 79+ <
1999 Turf 1-1: (6f 1-1) (frm 1-1)
Currently above-average colt. (1st run) - 1st of 5 getting 8lb from Aretino (2 Spt York RF 4100).
**J Noseda [1-1] Lucayan Stud.*

DASHING INVADER (USA) BHB 32f39a **RR 34f 39a** 386[12]
6 ch g Pirate Army (USA) - Cherie's Hope (USA) (Flying Paster (USA))
Form - 0
Record 1999 - 1st:0 2nd:0 3rd:0 Ran:1
Pre1999 - 1st:1 2nd:1 3rd:2 Ran:20
Win Prizemoney £2,277 *Total Prizemoney* £4,119
Wins 1997 *Jly Southw (STD) H 14f 35 44+* <
1999 AW 0-1: (13f) (Equi)
Very moderate gelding, had worn blinkers. Consistent. (DEAD)
**D L Williams [0-3] D L Williams (from P W Harris [1-20] Spt 1997).*

DATE RR 102f 1569[1]
3 b c Cadeaux Genereux 7.9f **(76)** - Faribole (IRE) (Esprit du Nord (USA))
Form - 121
Record 1999 - 1st:2 2nd:1 3rd:0 Ran:3
Pre1999 - 1st:0 2nd:0 3rd:1 Ran:1
Win Prizemoney £48,887 *Total Prizemoney* £52,843
Wins * 1999 May Haydoc (GD) H 8.1f 97 102 <
*** 1999** Apr Newmar (GD) 7f 81
1999 Turf 2-3: (7f 1-1, 8f 1-2) (gd, g-f 2-2)
Well made, very useful colt. Turf high 102 - 1st of 18 giving 10lb to Riverblue (29 May Haydock RF 1569). Beaten by inexperience when short-headed at Thirsk in mid-May, he showed that lesson had not been wasted when winning a valuable handicap later in the month. Missing for the remainder of the campaign - he was entered during the autumn - he remains an interesting prospect and should stay beyond a mile. **E A L Dunlop [2-4] Abdullah Ali.*

DATURA RR 80f 5218[17]
2 b f Darshaan 11.9f **(81)** - Realize **(77f)** (Al Nasr (FR)) 9.3f **(68)**
Form - 73240
Record 1999 - 1st:0 2nd:1 3rd:1 Ran:5
Win Prizemoney £0 *Total Prizemoney* £1,596
1999 Turf 0-5: (6f 2, 7f 3) (g-s, gd 2, g-f, frm)
Decent filly. Turf high 80 - 2nd of 8 to Via Camp (28 Aug Beverley 7f frm RF 3951). **J H M Gosden [0-5] Lord Hartington.*

DAUNTED (IRE) BHB 58f80a **RR 60f 80a** 5197[15]
3 b g Priolo (USA) 10.9f **(71)** - Dauntess (Formidable (USA)) 9.2f **(63)**
Form - 1321122357383450640
Record 1999 - 1st:1 2nd:2 3rd:3 Ran:15
Pre1999 - 1st:2 2nd:2 3rd:1 Ran:9
Win Prizemoney £8,580 *Total Prizemoney* £16,021
Wins * 1999 *Jan Lingfi (STD) C 8f 83+*
* 1998 *Dec Lingfi (STD) 8f 84* <
* 1998 *Nov Lingfi (STD) 8f 80*
1999 Turf 0-8: (8f 3, 9f 2, 10f 3) (g-s, gd 3, g-f 2, frm 2) 1999 AW 1-7: (7f 2, 8f 1-3, 10f, 12f) (Equi 1-3, Fibr 4)
Scopey, decent gelding, effective 7 to 12f, - acts on AW, best on Equi, mostly wears blinkers (extremely effectively), prefers left handed tracks, prefers tight tracks, excels at Lingfield, does well at Wolverhampton. Turf high 71. AW high 86 - 2nd of 6 giving 10lb to Scraggys Dream (13 Feb Lingfield 10f Equi RF 0288) - also 1st of 9 giving 10lb to Paddock Inspection (1 Jan Lingfield RF 0002). Very much suited by a mile on Equitrack, his turf form has been a bit disappointing. **G L Moore [3-24] Allen & Associates.*

DAUNTING (IRE) BHB 45f **RR 54f** 2627[9]
4 br f Formidable (USA) 7.8f **(60)** - Durun (Run The Gantlet (USA)) 12.1f **(59)**
Form - 0
Record 1999 - 1st:0 2nd:0 3rd:0 Ran:1
Pre1999 - 1st:0 2nd:0 3rd:0 Ran:5
1999 AW 0-1: (12f) (Equi)
Scopey, fair filly.
**G L Moore [0-1] Antony Sofroniou (from Lady Herries [0-5] Oct 1998).*

DAUNTING LADY (IRE) BHB 95f **RR 93f** 4373a[2]
4 b f Mujadil (USA) 7.7f **(70)** - Dauntess (Formidable (USA)) 9.2f **(63)**
Form - 63032
1999 Turf 0-4: (7f 4) (sft, gd 2, frm) 1999 AW 0-1: (8f) (Dirt)
Unfurnished, useful filly, effective 7 to 8f, acts on sft to gd, has worn blinkers. Turf high 93. **W Neuroth in NOR [0-2] (from R Hannon [3-17] May 1999).*

DAUPHIN (IRE) BHB 26f44a **RR 41f 44a** 19[11]
6 b br g Astronef 7.9f **(59)** - Va Toujours (Alzao (USA)) 7.1f **(68)**
Form - 0
Record 1999 - 1st:0 2nd:0 3rd:0 Ran:1
Pre1999 - 1st:3 2nd:2 3rd:2 Ran:33
Win Prizemoney £10,961 *Total Prizemoney* £14,213
Wins 1997 Oct Ascot (HVY) H 12f 42 52 <
1997 May Warwic (FRM) H 10.8f 41 44
1996 Spt Haydoc (GD) H 11.9f 34 43
1999 AW 0-1: (11f) (Fibr)
Moderate gelding. Inconsistent.
**H S Howe [0-2] Mrs J Di Marte (from W J Musson [3-33] Oct 1998).*

DAVID BHB 56f50a **RR 72f 50a** 396[7]
3 ch g Risk Me (FR) 8f **(53)** - Capriati (USA) (Diesis) 9.3f **(69)**
Form - 02757
Record 1999 - 1st:0 2nd:0 3rd:0 Ran:3
Pre1999 - 1st:1 2nd:1 3rd:1 Ran:8
Win Prizemoney £1,819 *Total Prizemoney* £2,861
Wins * 1998 Jun Bright (GD) S 6f 72+ <
1999 AW 0-3: (5f, 7f, 8f) (Equi 2, Fibr)
Neat, above-average gelding, effective 6f, acts on gd, likes left handed tracks, likes tight tracks. AW high 46.
**Miss Gay Kelleway [1-11] A Bit On The Side Partnership.*

DAVIS ROCK BHB 47f55a **RR 55f 55a** 5156[1]
5 ch m Rock City 8.8f **(62)** - Sunny Davis (USA) (Alydar (USA)) 9.1f **(76)**
Form - 1802627351
Record 1999 - 1st:1 2nd:2 3rd:1 Ran:8
Pre1999 - 1st:4 2nd:10 3rd:5 Ran:34
Win Prizemoney £12,944 *Total Prizemoney* £25,912
Wins * 1999 Nov Nottin (SFT) H 8.2f 45 51
* 1998 *Nov Wolver (STD) S 7f 64*
* 1998 *Jan Lingfi (STD) H 7f 64 67*
* 1997 Oct Folkes (GD) S 6.9f 52
1996 *Oct Wolver (STD) 6f 69* <
1999 Turf 1-6: (6f, 7f 4, 8f 1-1) (g-s, gd 1-1, g-f, frm 3) 1999 AW 0-2: (7f 2) (Equi, Fibr)
Fair filly, effective 7f, acts on g-s - acts on AW, best on Fibr, prefers left handed tracks, prefers tight tracks, does well at Wolverhampton. Turf high 55. AW high 50. She is a consistent sort over seven furlongs on turf or sand, but seemed to get the mile well when winning at Nottingham.
**W R Muir [4-33] Gordon Cunningham (from R M McKellar [0-5] Aug 1998).*

DAWN BHB 70f **RR 67f** 2438[4]
2 b f Owington - Realisatrice (USA) (Raja Baba (USA)) 10f **(64)**
Form - 634
Record 1999 - 1st:0 2nd:0 3rd:1 Ran:3
Win Prizemoney £0 *Total Prizemoney* £702
1999 Turf 0-3: (5f 2, 6f) (gd, g-f, frm)
Currently average filly. Turf high 67.
**N A Graham [0-3] Anthony Leftwich.*

DAWN ALARM BHB 56f **RR 54f** 4815[10]
2 b f Warning 8.1f **(77)** - Throw Away Line (USA) (Assert) 10.6f **(85)**
Form - 070
Record 1999 - 1st:0 2nd:0 3rd:0 Ran:3
1999 Turf 0-3: (5f, 7f 2) (gd, g-f, frm)
Currently fair filly, has worn blinkers. Turf high 54.
**A G Foster [0-1] Lady Bamford (from P W Chapple-Hyam [0-2] Spt 1999).*

DAWN PATROL BHB 50f **RR 38f** 919[10]
4 ch f Weldnaas (USA) 8.4f **(55)** - Silverdale Rose (Nomination) 7f **(60)**
Form - U0
Record 1999 - 1st:0 2nd:0 3rd:0 Ran:2

Pre1999 - 1st:1 2nd:1 3rd:0 Ran:14
Win Prizemoney £2,940 *Total Prizemoney* £4,229
Wins * 1998 Jun Mussel (SFT) H 5f 49 54 <
1999 Turf 0-2: (5f, 6f) (gd 2)
Lengthy, very moderate filly, effective 5 to 6f, best at 5f, acts on gd to frm, best on gd. Turf high 15. Inconsistent.
**K W Hogg [1-16] Auldyn Stud Ltd.*

DAWN'S DANCER (IRE) BHB 69f **RR 65f** 2748[2]

2 b f Petardia 8.2f **(58)** - Cree's Figurine (Creetown) 6.9f **(50)**
Form - 342
Record 1999 - 1st:0 2nd:1 3rd:1 Ran:3
Win Prizemoney £0 *Total Prizemoney* £1,386
1999 Turf 0-3: (5f 3) (frm 2, hrd)
Currently average filly. Turf high 65 - 2nd of 6 to Believing (12 Jly Brighton 5f hrd RF 2748).
**G C H Chung [0-3] Mrs D J Murphy.*

DAWN TREADER (USA) BHB 38f26a **RR 26f 26a** 176[9]

4 gr g El Prado (IRE) 8f **(74)** - Marie de La Ferte (Amber Rama (USA)) 10.2f **(45)**
Form - 560
Record 1999 - 1st:0 2nd:0 3rd:0 Ran:3
Pre1999 - 1st:0 2nd:1 3rd:0 Ran:11
Win Prizemoney £0 *Total Prizemoney* £624
1999 AW 0-3: (12f, 13f, 15f) (Equi 2, Fibr)
Workmanlike, little account gelding, has worn blinkers. AW high 13. **J S Moore [0-6] Alljays Racing (from R Hannon [0-11] Oct 1998).*

DAY-BOY BHB 69f **RR 70f** 4380[7]

3 b g Prince Sabo 6.6f **(64)** - Lady Day (FR) (Lightning (FR)) 7.9f **(74)**
Form - 047437
Record 1999 - 1st:0 2nd:0 3rd:1 Ran:6
Pre1999 - 1st:1 2nd:0 3rd:0 Ran:3
Win Prizemoney £2,804 *Total Prizemoney* £4,353
Wins * 1998 May Ayr (GD) 6f 70 <
1999 Turf 0-6: (7f 4, 8f 2) (gd 3, g-f 2, frm)
Scopey, above-average gelding, effective 6 to 7f, acts on gd to g-f. Turf high 71. Consistent. **Denys Smith [1-9] Duke of Sutherland.*

DAY JOURNEY (USA) BHB 100f **RR 93f** 3759[4]

2 b c Dayjur (USA) 6.8f **(79)** - Dayflower (USA) (Majestic Light (USA)) 10.6f **(75)**
Form - 20114
Record 1999 - 1st:2 2nd:1 3rd:0 Ran:5
Win Prizemoney £9,972 *Total Prizemoney* £16,417
Wins * **1999** Aug Haydoc (G-S) 6f 87 <
* **1999** Jly Newmar (G-F) 6f 81+
1999 Turf 2-5: (6f 2-5) (gd, g-f 1-2, frm 1-2)
Useful colt. Turf high 93 - also 1st of 5 giving 5lb to Icicle (6 Aug Haydock RF 3415). Got off the mark with an easy win in a four-runner Newmarket novice event, but only just scrambled home at Haydock on rather softer ground. A fair fourth in the Gimcrack, staying on well. **E A L Dunlop [2-5] Maktoum Al Maktoum.*

DAYLAMI (IRE) BHB 135f **RR 135f** 5230a[1]

5 gr h Doyoun 10.7f **(69)** - Daltawa (IRE) (Miswaki (USA)) 9f **(81)**
Form - 5211101
Record 1999 - 1st:4 2nd:1 3rd:0 Ran:7
Pre1999 - 1st:5 2nd:2 3rd:4 Ran:12
Win Prizemoney £1,967,521 *Total Prizemoney* £2,267,674

Wins	* **1999**	Nov	Gulfst	(GD)	G1	12f	135 <
	* **1999**	Spt	Leopar	(SFT)	G1	10f	133+
	* **1999**	Jly	Ascot	(G-F)	G1	12f	130
	* **1999**	Jun	Epsom	(G-S)	G1	12f	125
	* 1998	Spt	Belmon	(FRM)		11f	123
	* 1998	Jly	Sandow	(GD)	G1	10f	123
	* 1998	May	Currag	(G-F)	G2	10f	119+
	1997	May	Longch	(SFT)	G1	8f	118
	1997	Apr	Longch	(GD)	G3	8f	109

1999 Turf 4-6: (10f 1-1, 11f, 12f 3-4) (sft, gd 3-3, g-f, frm 1-1) 1999 AW 0-1: (10f) (Dirt)
Exceptional colt, effective 10 to 12f, best at 12f, acts on gd to frm, best on gd. Turf high 135 - 1st of 14 from Royal Anthem (6 Nov Gulfstream Park RF 5230a) - also 1st of 7 giving 10lb to Dazzling Park (11 Spt Leopardstown RF 4316a). One of the leading three-year-old milers of 1997, winner of the French Guineas, he was

Daylami proved himself a true World Champion racehorse on turf in 1999

leased by the Godolphin team in 1998, and did them proud in a busy campaign, landing the Eclipse and the Man O'War Stakes, and running well in almost all his starts. A little below his best on his first two runs of 1999, he bounced back to land the Coronation Cup, having no problems with the 12 furlongs, thanks to the steady gallop set by his pacemaker. He proved conclusively that he stayed the trip when a runaway winner of the King George at Ascot, and was arguably even more impressive when landing the Irish Champion Stakes by nine lengths. A sporting tilt at the Arc provided his only really below par performance of the season, but the desperate ground was probably to blame, and he was not given a hard time. He was still well enough to take his chance in the Breeders' Cup Turf, and wrapped up the first Emirates World Series title with another impressive victory. A most admirable racehorse, he will now retire to the Aga Khan's Gilltown Stud in Ireland. **S bin Suroor [7-13] Godolphin.*

DAYLIGHT IN DUBAI (USA) BHB 92f **RR 89f** 3958[10]

5 ch h Twilight Agenda (USA) - Lady Godolphin (USA) (Son Ange (USA)) 6f **(86)**

Form - 075016000

Record **1999** - 1st:1 2nd:0 3rd:0 Ran:9
Pre1999 - 1st:2 2nd:1 3rd:1 Ran:6

Win Prizemoney £26,248 *Total Prizemoney* £39,312

Wins * **1999** Jun Yarmou (G-F) 6f 95
1996 Jun Currag (GD) G3 6f 104 <
1996 Apr Newbur (GD) 5.2f 90+

1999 Turf 1-9: (5f, 6f 1-3, 7f 5) (gd 4, g-f 2, frm 1-3)

Useful colt, effective 6 to 7f, acts on frm, has worn blinkers. Turf high 103 - also 1st of 7 giving 10lb to Ellway Star (21 Jun Yarmouth RF 2186). He ran creditably in mixed company, winning a fair contest over six furlongs at Yarmouth in June. Despite that success, his connections probably got the better end of the deal when he made 28,000 Guineas at Newmarket in October.

**D Nicholls [1-9] Phil Lake (from P W Chapple-Hyam [2-6] Oct 1996).*

DAYMARTI (IRE) **RR 113f** 3411a[6]

4 b c Caerleon (USA) 10.9f **(79)** - Daltawa (IRE) (Miswaki (USA)) 9f **(81)**

Form - 6

1999 Turf 0-1: (10f) (gd)

Group-class colt, has worn blinkers. **A deRoyerDupre in FR [0-6].*

DAYNABEE BHB 41f44a **RR 29f 44a** 5032[10]

4 b f Common Grounds 8.1f **(66)** - Don't Wary (FR) (Lomond (USA)) 8.8f **(65)**

Form - 65300063820080

Record **1999** - 1st:0 2nd:1 3rd:1 Ran:11
Pre1999 - 1st:4 2nd:4 3rd:3 Ran:27

Win Prizemoney £10,621 *Total Prizemoney* £16,554

Wins * 1998 Jly Windso (G-F) H 6f 52 56
1997 Aug Nottin (G-F) C 5.1f 64 <
1997 Jly Newcas (GD) S 6f 61
1997 Jly Leices (GD) S 5f 59

1999 Turf 0-10: (5f 2, 6f 6, 7f 2) (g-s 2, gd, g-f 3, frm 4) 1999 AW 0-1: (7f) (Fibr)

Unfurnished, moderate filly, effective 6f, acts on g-f to frm, best on frm, likes right handed tracks. Turf high 46.

**A J McNae [1-21] T L Beecroft (from N Tinkler [3-17] May 1998).*

DAYRAVEN BHB 35f **RR 24f** 2751[6]

3 ch g Midyan (USA) 9.9f **(64)** - Aunt Judy (Great Nephew) 9.9f **(64)**

Form - 07006

Record **1999** - 1st:0 2nd:0 3rd:0 Ran:5
Pre1999 - 1st:0 2nd:0 3rd:0 Ran:3

1999 Turf 0-5: (10f 3, 12f 2) (gd, g-f 2, frm, hrd)

Scopey, little account gelding, often wears blinkers. Turf high 44. Becoming disappointing. **I A Balding [0-8] T M Mason.*

DAYS OF GRACE BHB 52f61a **RR 53f 61a** 5149[1]

4 gr f Wolfhound (USA) 7.3f **(71)** - Inshirah (USA) (Caro)

Form - 30834034131

Record **1999** - 1st:2 2nd:0 3rd:4 Ran:11
Pre1999 - 1st:1 2nd:0 3rd:2 Ran:13

Win Prizemoney £7,475 *Total Prizemoney* £12,748

Wins * **1999** *Oct Wolver (STD) H 6f 57 60*
* **1999** *Spt Southw (STD) H 6f 50 52*
1997 May Redcar (FRM) 5f 69 <

1999 Turf 0-9: (5f 5, 6f 4) (g-s 2, gd, g-f 2, frm 3, hrd) 1999 AW 2-2: (6f 2-2) (Fibr 2-2)

Average filly, effective 5 to 6f, best at 6f, acts on g-s to frm - acts on Fibr. Turf high 55 (1st run) - 3rd of 9 getting 9lb from Polar Mist (13 Apr Folkestone 5f g-s RF 0657). AW high 60 (began Spt) - 1st of 13 from Trojan Hero (30 Oct Wolverhampton RF 5149) - also 1st of 16 getting 10lb from Almazhar (28 Spt Southwell RF 4606). She ended a long losing run when gaining a narrow victory in a handicap at Southwell in September, but showed her liking for Fibresand by winning again at Wolverhampton.

**L MontagueHall [2-11] Stephen & Michelle Bayless (from M Meade [1-13] Jly 1998).*

DAYS OF THUNDER BHB 30f40a **RR 31f 40a** 4032[11]

11 ch g Vaigly Great - Silent Prayer (Queen's Hussar) 11.6f **(58)**

Form - 0

Record **1999** - 1st:0 2nd:0 3rd:0 Ran:1
Pre1999 - 1st:0 2nd:0 3rd:0 Ran:10

Win Prizemoney £0 *Total Prizemoney* £235

1999 Turf 0-1: (11f) (gd)

Very moderate gelding.

**Mrs P Ford [0-4] David Lee (from J White [4-23] Mar 1995).*

DAY STAR BHB 67f **RR 65f** 5199[18]

3 b f Dayjur (USA) 6.8f **(79)** - Krisalya (Kris) 9.5f **(73)**

Form - 04010

Record **1999** - 1st:1 2nd:0 3rd:0 Ran:5
Pre1999 - 1st:0 2nd:0 3rd:0 Ran:1

Win Prizemoney £4,670 *Total Prizemoney* £4,948

Wins * **1999** Oct Redcar (GD) H 6f 62 65 <

1999 Turf 1-5: (5f, 6f 1-4) (gd 3, g-f, frm 1-1)

Unfurnished, average filly, effective 6f, acts on frm. Turf high 65 - 1st of 22 giving 5lb to Frilly Front (14 Oct Redcar RF 4879). She did not show a great deal in maiden company, but made a successful debut in handicap company at Redcar in October.

**C F Wall [1-6] A E Oppenheimer.*

DAYTIME BHB 83f **RR 83+f** 3233[9]

3 b c Danehill (USA) 9.1f **(79)** - Zenith (Shirley Heights) 10.3f **(74)**

Form - 22210

Record **1999** - 1st:1 2nd:3 3rd:0 Ran:5
Pre1999 - 1st:0 2nd:0 3rd:0 Ran:1

Win Prizemoney £7,425 *Total Prizemoney* £11,084

Wins * **1999** Jly Sandow (GD) H 7.1f 76 83+ <

1999 Turf 1-5: (7f 1-3, 8f 2) (gd 2, g-f 1-2, frm)

Leggy, decent colt, effective 7 to 8f, best at 7f, acts on gd to frm. Turf high 83 - 1st of 16 getting 4lb from Lover's Leap (2 Jly Sandown RF 2498). Has run with credit at both a mile and seven furlongs, but looks more effective at the latter trip.

**R Hannon [1-5] The Queen (from Lord Huntingdon [0-1] Aug 1998).*

DAZILYN LADY (USA) BHB 92f **RR 97f** 4921[13]

4 ch f Zilzal (USA) 8.5f **(79)** - Jetbeeah (IRE) (Lomond (USA)) 8.8f **(65)**

Form - 054040

Record **1999** - 1st:0 2nd:0 3rd:0 Ran:6
Pre1999 - 1st:2 2nd:5 3rd:1 Ran:15

Win Prizemoney £10,365 *Total Prizemoney* £36,581

Wins * 1997 Spt Pontef (G-S) 6f 96 <
* 1997 Jly Nottin (G-F) 6.1f 79

1999 Turf 0-6: (7f 4, 8f 2) (gd 3, g-f, frm 2)

Scopey, very useful filly, effective 7 to 8f, best at 8f, acts on hvy to g-f, best on gd, excels at Doncaster. Turf high 97 - 4th of 15 giving 3lb to Family Man (1 Oct Newmarket 7f gd RF 4675). Like most of Zilzal's stock, she is a fidget. That is no reflection on her generosity, however, and she ran a series of fine races in Listed events last term without getting her head in front. Little show this season, she does not look an obvious improver.

**P W Harris [2-21] M Parker G Knight & Mrs G Godfrey.*

DAZZLING PARK (IRE) **RR 117f** 4780a[6]

3 br f Warning 8.1f **(77)** - Park Express (Ahonoora) 8.1f **(73)**

Form - 4331126

1999 Turf 2-7: (8f 1-3, 9f 1-2, 10f 2) (sft, g-s, gd 1-3, g-f 1-2)

High-class filly, effective 8f, acts on g-f. Turf high 117 - also 1st of 6 from Carambola (5 Spt Curragh RF 4203a). Tough and genuine, as was her dam, this filly stood up well to a hectic campaign, setting a personal best when chasing Daylami home in the Esat Digital Irish Champion Stakes at Leopardstown in September.

Effective up to a mile and a quarter, she probably acts on any ground and is thoroughly reliable. **J S Bolger in IRE [3-10].*

DAZZLING QUINTET BHB 46f **RR 43f** 5032[13]

3 ch f Superlative 8.8f **(57)** - Miss Display (Touch Paper) 6.8f **(57)**
Form - 0000020
Record 1999 - 1st:0 2nd:1 3rd:0 Ran:7
Pre1999 - 1st:1 2nd:0 3rd:2 Ran:9
Win Prizemoney £2,477 *Total Prizemoney* £4,299
Wins * 1998 Jly Beverl (GD) 5f 78 <
1999 Turf 0-7: (5f 4, 6f 3) (g-s, gd, g-f 2, frm 3)
Moderate filly, effective 5 to 6f, best at 5f, acts on gd to g-f, best on gd. Turf high 43. **C Smith [1-16] Roman Bath V.*

DAZZLING STONE BHB 41f40a **RR 45f 40a** 2864[5]

5 b g Mujtahid (USA) 7.4f **(69)** - Lady In Green (Shareef Dancer (USA)) 9.9f **(73)**
Form - 30085
Record 1999 - 1st:0 2nd:0 3rd:1 Ran:5
Pre1999 - 1st:0 2nd:2 3rd:1 Ran:12
Win Prizemoney £0 *Total Prizemoney* £3,238
1999 Turf 0-3: (6f, 7f 2) (gd, g-f, frm) 1999 AW 0-2: (6f, 7f) (Fibr 2)
Moderate gelding, effective 6f, acts on g-f, has worn blinkers. Turf high 45. AW high 37.
**C W Fairhurst [0-12] David Bartlett (from Lady Herries [0-6] Oct 1997).*

DEAD AIM (IRE) BHB 60f **RR 75f** 2483[10]

5 b g Sadler's Wells (USA) 11.3f **(87)** -Dead Certain (Absalom) 7.2f **(58)**
Form - 0
Record 1999 - 1st:0 2nd:0 3rd:0 Ran:1
Pre1999 - 1st:1 2nd:2 3rd:4 Ran:16
Win Prizemoney £3,467 *Total Prizemoney* £7,889
Wins 1997 Aug Windso (G-F) H 11.6f 75 78 <
1999 Turf 0-1: (12f) (frm)
Above-average gelding, effective 12 to 13f, acts on g-f to frm, has worn blinkers. Becoming disappointing.
**Mrs J Brown [0-8] Mrs Karan Ridley (from I A Balding [1-12] May 1998).*

DEADLY NIGHTSHADE (IRE) RR 102?f 4896[7]

3 b f Night Shift (USA) 8.1f **(73)** - Dead Certain (Absalom) 7.2f **(58)**
Form - 07
Record 1999 - 1st:0 2nd:0 3rd:0 Ran:2
Pre1999 - 1st:2 2nd:1 3rd:0 Ran:3
Win Prizemoney £7,146 *Total Prizemoney* £16,171
Wins * 1998 Spt Goodwo (G-F) 6f 88+ <
* 1998 Aug Bath (FRM) 5.1f 74+
1999 Turf 0-2: (5f, 6f) (gd, g-f)
Scopey, very useful filly. Turf high 98. She failed to fulfil her juvenile promise. **D R C Elsworth [2-5] M Tabor & Mrs John Magnier.*

DEAL FAIR BHB 97f **RR 100f** 2074[18]

3 b c Grand Lodge (USA) - Darshay (FR) (Darshaan) 9.9f **(84)**
Form - 1330
Record 1999 - 1st:1 2nd:0 3rd:2 Ran:4
Pre1999 - 1st:1 2nd:0 3rd:1 Ran:2
Win Prizemoney £7,658 *Total Prizemoney* £12,694
Wins *** 1999** Apr Bath (SFT) 10.2f 92 <
* 1998 Spt Salisb (HVY) 8f 86
1999 Turf 1-4: (10f 1-3, 12f) (sft 1-1, gd 2, g-f)
Lengthy, very useful colt, effective 10f, acts on sft to gd. Turf high 100 - also 1st of 5 from Culzean (27 Apr Bath RF 0859). Tough but lazy, he is a typical twilight horse, stuck between handicaps and Listed company. A good sort physically, he would make a decent hurdler. **H R A Cecil [2-6] Baron G Von Ullmann.*

DEAR PRUDENCE BHB 43f **RR 57f** 5193[9]

3 b f Puissance 7.1f **(60)** - Coir 'a' Ghaill (Jalmood (USA)) 10.1f **(52)**
Form - 770
Record 1999 - 1st:0 2nd:0 3rd:0 Ran:3
1999 Turf 0-3: (8f, 10f 2) (hvy, g-s, gd)
Leggy, currently fair filly. Turf high 57 (began Oct).
**J G Portman [0-3] Mrs Heather Murat.*

DE BALLIOL BHB 75f **RR 78f** 3448[5]

3 b c Sadler's Wells (USA) 11.3f **(87)** - Khalafiya (Darshaan) 9.9f **(84)**
Form - 65235
Record 1999 - 1st:0 2nd:1 3rd:1 Ran:5
Pre1999 - 1st:0 2nd:0 3rd:0 Ran:2
Win Prizemoney £0 *Total Prizemoney* £1,874
1999 Turf 0-5: (10f 4, 12f) (sft, gd, g-f, frm 2)
Strong, above-average colt, effective 10f, acts on g-f, has worn blinkers. Turf high 78 - 2nd of 6 to Goombayland (30 Jun Epsom 10f g-f RF 2443). **B W Hills [0-7] Sheikh Mohammed.*

DEBBIE'S HOPE BHB 52f53a **RR 56df 53a** 5026[20]

3 ch f Be My Chief (USA) 10.2f **(62)** - Appleton Heights (Shirley Heights) 10.3f **(74)**
Form - 532373330700
Record 1999 - 1st:0 2nd:1 3rd:4 Ran:10
Pre1999 - 1st:0 2nd:0 3rd:1 Ran:3
Win Prizemoney £0 *Total Prizemoney* £2,855
1999 Turf 0-10: (6f, 7f 4, 8f 5) (sft, g-s, gd, g-f 3, frm 3, hrd)
Strong, fair filly, effective 6 to 7f, acts on g-f to frm. Turf high 65 (1st run) - 2nd of 17 getting 5lb from Losada (22 May Catterick 7f frm RF 1390). **K Mahdi [0-13] Greenfield Stud.*

DEBBIE'S WARNING BHB 100f **RR 91f** 4416[8]

3 b c Warning 8.1f **(77)** - Lomond Blossom (Lomond (USA)) 8.8f **(65)**
Form - 237150538
Record 1999 - 1st:1 2nd:1 3rd:2 Ran:9
Win Prizemoney £3,907 *Total Prizemoney* £11,860
Wins *** 1999** May Kempto (G-F) 8f 80 <
1999 Turf 1-9: (7f 3, 8f 1-6) (g-s, gd 3, g-f 3, frm 1-2)
Tall, useful colt, effective 8f, acts on g-f to frm. Turf high 110 - 7th of 16 to Island Sands (1 May Newmarket 8f frm RF 0958). Becoming disappointing. Unraced at two, he looked a Group-class horse in the spring but lost his way after being set a series of impossible tasks. Connections will be well advised to lower their sights. **K Mahdi [1-9] Greenfield Stud.*

DEB'S DELIGHT BHB 38f **RR 27f** 3754[6]

4 ch f Most Welcome 8.6f **(66)** - Adana (FR) (Green Dancer (USA)) 10.3f **(74)**
Form - 08506
Record 1999 - 1st:0 2nd:0 3rd:0 Ran:5
Pre1999 - 1st:0 2nd:0 3rd:0 Ran:4
1999 Turf 0-5: (8f 2, 9f, 10f, 12f) (gd, g-f, frm 3)
Leggy, little account filly. Turf high 27.
**D A Nolan [0-5] Trevor Grice (from C W Thornton [0-4] Oct 1998).*

DEB'S SON BHB 62f **RR 53f** 4715[4]

2 b g Minster Son 10.9f **(56)** - Deb's Ball **(43f)** (Glenstal (USA)) 10.1f **(64)**
Form - 454
Record 1999 - 1st:0 2nd:0 3rd:0 Ran:3
Win Prizemoney £0 *Total Prizemoney* £269
1999 Turf 0-3: (8f 2, 10f) (gd, g-f, frm)
Currently fair gelding. Turf high 53 (began Aug).
**D Moffatt [0-3] & Mrs A G Milligan.*

DECARCHY (USA) RR 76++f 4339[1]

2 b c Distant View (USA) - Toussaud (USA) (El Gran Senor (USA)) 9.6f **(76)**
Form - 1
Record 1999 - 1st:1 2nd:0 3rd:0 Ran:1
Win Prizemoney £3,752 *Total Prizemoney* £3,752
Wins *** 1999** Spt Yarmou (G-S) 7f 76++ <
1999 Turf 1-1: (7f 1-1) (g-s 1-1)
Currently above-average colt. (1st run) - 1st of 9 from Infotec (15 Spt Yarmouth RF 4339). A three-parts brother to Chester House, he was most impressive on his debut and is very much one to keep on the right side of. **H R A Cecil [1-1] K Abdulla.*

DECISION MAID (USA) BHB 85f **RR 81+f** 5060[1]

2 b f Diesis 9f **(80)** - Robellino Miss (USA) (Robellino (USA)) 7.6f **(80)**
Form - 51
Record 1999 - 1st:1 2nd:0 3rd:0 Ran:2
Win Prizemoney £4,987 *Total Prizemoney* £4,987
Wins *** 1999** Oct Lingfi (HVY) 7f 81+ <
1999 Turf 1-2: (6f, 7f 1-1) (g-s 1-1, gd)
Currently decent filly. Turf high 81 (began Oct) - 1st of 11 from Eljariha (25 Oct Lingfield RF 5060).
**G Wragg [1-2] The Eclipse Partnership - 2.*

DECISIVE ACTION (USA) BHB 70f67a **RR 70f 67a** 4739a[9]

4 br g Alleged (USA) 11.8f **(81)** - Maria Balastiere (USA) (Majestic Light (USA)) 10.6f **(75)**

Form - 2015820

Record 1999 - 1st:1 2nd:2 3rd:0 Ran:7
Pre1999 - 1st:1 2nd:0 3rd:0 Ran:2

Win Prizemoney £6,342 *Total Prizemoney* £7,622

Wins 1999 Jun Windso (SFT) C 11.6f 58+
1997 Oct Nottin (SFT) 8.2f 91+ <

1999 Turf 1-5: (10f, 11f, 12f 1-1, 16f 2) (sft 2, g-s, gd 1-1, frm) 1999 AW 0-2: (9f, 12f) (Fibr 2)

Strong, above-average gelding. Turf high 70. AW high 73. Seems to appreciate soft ground.
**A Slattery in IRE [0-3] John Bernard O'Connor (from P F I Cole [2-6] Jun 1999).*

DECODED BHB 45f **RR 54f** 4639[7]

3 ch c Deploy 11.4f **(67)** - Golden Panda (Music Boy) 6.8f **(57)**

Form - 7

Record 1999 - 1st:0 2nd:0 3rd:0 Ran:1
Pre1999 - 1st:0 2nd:0 3rd:0 Ran:7

Win Prizemoney £0 *Total Prizemoney* £236

1999 Turf 0-1: (16f) (gd)

Fair colt, has worn blinkers. Becoming disappointing.
**G M Moore [0-1] A G Watson (from J L Eyre [0-7] Nov 1998).*

DEECEEBEE BHB 41f **RR 33f** 1566[20]

4 b g Rudimentary (USA) 8.2f **(66)** - Do Run Run (Commanche Run) 8.5f **(58)**

Form - 00

Record 1999 - 1st:0 2nd:0 3rd:0 Ran:2
Pre1999 - 1st:1 2nd:0 3rd:1 Ran:13

Win Prizemoney £3,615 *Total Prizemoney* £4,105

Wins 1997 Jun Newcas (HVY) 6f 74 <

1999 Turf 0-2: (7f, 10f) (gd, frm)

Workmanlike, very moderate gelding, has worn blinkers. Turf high 26. **J L Eyre [0-6] D C Batey (from W Storey [1-9] Nov 1997).*

DEE DIAMOND (USA) **RR 68f** 4554[7]

2 b f Eagle Eyed (USA) - Noumea (USA) (Plugged Nickle (USA)) 7.8f **(68)**

Form - 47

Record 1999 - 1st:0 2nd:0 3rd:0 Ran:2

Win Prizemoney £0 *Total Prizemoney* £248

1999 Turf 0-2: (7f, 8f) (g-s, frm)

Currently average filly. Turf high 68 (began Aug).
**Andrew Turnell [0-2] Mrs Claire Hollowood.*

DEEP BLUE **RR 80f** 4325[8]

2 b c Lake Coniston (IRE) - Billie Blue (Ballad Rock) 7.8f **(63)**

Form - 53228

Record 1999 - 1st:0 2nd:2 3rd:1 Ran:5

Win Prizemoney £0 *Total Prizemoney* £2,990

1999 Turf 0-5: (5f 5) (g-s, gd, g-f 2, frm)

Decent colt. Turf high 80 - 2nd of 8 to Ansellad (12 Jun Bath 5f g-f RF 1940). In the frame in maidens over the minimum trip, he looks short of a turn of foot and should be suited by further.
**Dr J D Scargill [0-5] Ms Bobby Cohen.*

DEE PEE TEE CEE (IRE) BHB 86f **RR 86df** 4683[30]

5 b g Tidaro (USA) 8.2f **(75)** - Silver Glimpse (Petingo) 11f **(72)**

Form - 611116100

Record 1999 - 1st:5 2nd:0 3rd:0 Ran:9
Pre1999 - 1st:6 2nd:0 3rd:1 Ran:22

Win Prizemoney £66,263 *Total Prizemoney* £67,602

Wins									
*	**1999**	Aug	York	(GD)	H	11.9f	82	86	<
*	**1999**	Jun	Hamilt	(GD)	H	9.2f	70	82	
*	**1999**	Jun	York	(G-S)	H	8.9f	70	78	
*	**1999**	Jun	Pontef	(SFT)	H	10f	63	74+	
*	**1999**	Jun	Cheste	(SFT)	H	10.3f	63	66	
*	1997	Jly	Mussel	(GD)	H	8f	62	74+	
*	1997	Jly	Beverl	(HVY)	H	8.5f	62	74	
*	1997	Jun	Carlis	(GD)		8f		65	
*	1997	Jun	Redcar	(GD)	H	9f	54	58	
*	1997	Jun	Beverl	(SFT)	H	7.5f	46	54	
*	1996	Jun	Redcar	(G-F)	S	7f		59+	

1999 Turf 5-9: (8f, 9f 2-2, 10f 2-4, 12f 1-2) (sft, g-s 1-1, gd 2-4, g-f 2-3)

Useful gelding, effective 9 to 12f, best at 9f, acts on gd to g-f, best on g-f, prefers left handed tracks. Turf high 86 - 1st of 18 getting 3lb from Architect (17 Aug York RF 3696) - also 1st of 8 giving 25lb to Captain Brady (16 Jun Hamilton RF 2046). A credit to connections, he won four races in June 1999, all at around ten furlongs with cut in the ground. He took a big step up in class, and a rise in the handicap, when beaten on fast ground in the John Smith's Cup next time, but bounced back over twelve furlongs to take the Knavesmire Handicap at the Ebor meeting.
**M W Easterby [11-35] Mrs M E Curtis.*

DEEP SPACE (IRE) BHB 107f **RR 109f** 4896[15]

4 br g Green Desert (USA) 7.8f **(78)** - Dream Season (USA) (Mr Prospector (USA)) 8.8f **(78)**

Form - 0162100120

Record 1999 - 1st:3 2nd:2 3rd:0 Ran:10
Pre1999 - 1st:2 2nd:1 3rd:0 Ran:11

Win Prizemoney £82,633 *Total Prizemoney* £89,014

Wins									
*	**1999**	Aug	Nottin	(G-F)		6.1f		106	<
*	**1999**	Jun	Ascot	(G-F)	H	6f	88	97	
*	**1999**	May	Lingfi	(G-F)	H	7f	82	88	
*	1998	Aug	Newmar	(FRM)	H	6f	79	85	
*	1998	Jly	Sandow	(GD)	H	5f	73	79	

1999 Turf 3-10: (6f 2-6, 7f 1-4) (gd 1-4, g-f 2-4, frm 2)

Scopey, Pattern-class gelding, effective 6f, acts on gd. Turf high 109 - 2nd of 10 giving 10lb to Cretan Gift (29 Aug Yarmouth 6f gd RF 4001) - also 1st of 10 from Harmonic Way (13 Aug Nottingham RF 3625). A narrow winner of the Wokingham at the Royal meeting, he continued to run well all term and looked equally adept at either six or seven furlongs. His come from behind style means he finds more than his share of trouble in running.
**E A L Dunlop [5-21] Maktoum Al Maktoum.*

Deep Space was in fine form in sprints through the summer

DEFIANCE BHB 35f **RR 35f** 4233[15]

4 b g Warning 8.1f **(77)** - Princess Athena (Ahonoora) 8.1f **(73)**

Form - 0000750

Record 1999 - 1st:0 2nd:0 3rd:0 Ran:7
Pre1999 - 1st:0 2nd:0 3rd:2 Ran:4

Win Prizemoney £0 *Total Prizemoney* £1,032

1999 Turf 0-7: (5f 2, 6f, 8f 4) (sft 2, g-f 3, frm, hrd)

Lengthy, very moderate gelding, has worn blinkers. Turf high 35.
**A P James [0-7] Anne & Mahendra Ramkaran (from B W Hills [0-4] May 1998).*

DEHOUSH (USA) BHB 109f **RR 108f** 2940[4]

3 ch c Diesis 9f **(80)** - Dream Play (USA) (Blushing Groom (FR)) 10.3f

(76)
Form - 1284
Record 1999 - 1st:1 2nd:1 3rd:0 Ran:4
Pre1999 - 1st:1 2nd:0 3rd:1 Ran:3
Win Prizemoney £18,391 *Total Prizemoney* £36,538
Wins * 1999 Apr Kempto (GD) L 8f 104 <
* 1998 Jun Newmar (GD) 6f 76+
1999 Turf 1-4: (8f 1-1, 10f 2, 12f) (g-s 2, g-f 1-2)
Scopey, Pattern-class colt, effective 7 to 10f, acts on g-s to frm. Turf high 108 - 2nd of 7 to Fantastic Light (24 Apr Sandown 10f g-s RF 0843) - also 1st of 11 from Wallace (3 Apr Kempton RF 0570). Began the season with victory in the Easter Stakes at Kempton, showing a useful turn of foot in the process, and put up a terrific effort when short-headed by Fantastic Light in the Sandown Classic Trial. That was as good as it got, however.
**A C Stewart [2-7] Sheikh Ahmed Al Maktoum.*

DEKELSMARY BHB 45f44a RR 43f 44a 4732[11]
4 b f Komaite (USA) 6.9f **(61)** - Final Call (Town Crier) 10.2f **(55)**
Form - 316062506334001800
Record 1999 - 1st:1 2nd:1 3rd:2 Ran:15
Pre1999 - 1st:1 2nd:1 3rd:3 Ran:18
Win Prizemoney £5,934 *Total Prizemoney* £10,214
Wins * 1999 Aug Thirsk (G-F) H 5f 41 43
* 1998 *Nov Southw (STD) H 7f 45 48* <
1999 Turf 1-8: (5f 1-6, 6f 2) (gd 2, g-f 3, frm 2, hrd 1-1) 1999 AW 0-7: (5f 2, 6f, 7f 3, 8f) (Fibr 7)
Workmanlike, moderate filly, effective 5 to 8f, best at 7f, acts on hrd - acts on Fibr, has worn blinkers, likes left handed tracks, likes tight tracks. Turf high 43 - 1st of 16 getting 3lb from Time To Fly (27 Aug Thirsk RF 3948). AW high 48 - 2nd of 16 getting 7lb from Sure To Dream (6 May Southwell 7f Fibr RF 1063).
**J Balding [2-33] Derrick Moss.*

DELAMERE (USA) RR 65f 4821[8]
2 b f Brocco (USA) - Shelia Dacre (USA) (Nureyev (USA)) 8.7f **(78)**
Form - 8
Record 1999 - 1st:0 2nd:0 3rd:0 Ran:1
1999 Turf 0-1: (6f) (g-f)
Currently average filly.
**A G Foster [0-1] R E Sangster, H Lester & R Clifton.*

DELAY OF GAME (USA) RR 116f 5226a[8]
6 br h Summer Squall (USA) 7f **(80)** - Wimbledon (USA) (Blushing Groom (FR)) 10.3f **(76)**
Form - 8
1999 Turf 0-1: (8f) (frm)
Currently high-class. (1st run) - 8th of 14 to Silic (6 Nov Gulfstream Park 8f frm RF 5226a). **G R Arnold II in USA [0-1].*

DELCIANA (IRE) BHB 29f32a RR 37f 32a 4949[4]
4 b f Danehill (USA) 9.1f **(79)** - Delvecchia (Glint of Gold) 9.3f **(66)**
Form - 0000780324
Record 1999 - 1st:0 2nd:1 3rd:1 Ran:10
Pre1999 - 1st:0 2nd:0 3rd:3 Ran:13
Win Prizemoney £0 *Total Prizemoney* £2,407
1999 Turf 0-9: (6f 2, 7f 2, 8f 2, 10f 2, 11f) (g-s 2, g-f 4, frm, hrd 2) 1999 AW 0-1: (11f) (Fibr)
Neat, moderate filly, effective 7f, acts on frm, has worn blinkers, likes left handed tracks, likes tight tracks. Turf high 37.
**G G Margarson [0-10] The Del Boys (from P W Harris [0-13] Spt 1998).*

DELEGATE BHB 100f RR 103f 5030[12]
6 ch g Polish Precedent (USA) 9f **(73)** - Dangora (USA) (Sovereign Dancer (USA)) 11.2f **(68)**
Form - 43630
Record 1999 - 1st:0 2nd:0 3rd:2 Ran:5
Pre1999 - 1st:0 2nd:1 3rd:0 Ran:2
Win Prizemoney £0 *Total Prizemoney* £11,082
1999 Turf 0-5: (5f 2, 6f 3) (g-s 3, gd, frm)
Very useful gelding, effective 6f, acts on gd. Turf high 103 (began Jly) - 3rd of 20 to Gaelic Storm (15 Oct Newmarket 6f gd RF 4896). Runner-up in the Prix Djebel at Evry as a three-year-old for Andre Fabre, has obviously had his training problems and was bought for 14,000 guineas. He seemed to find the trip inadequate at Leicester on his only start last term, and although there are not many miles on the clock his performances this term have not really inspired hopes of him achieving much, though he ran above himself when third in a Newmarket Listed event in October.
**J E Banks [0-6] Mrs P Reditt (from A Fabre in FR [0-1] Apr 1996).*

DELIGHT OF DAWN BHB 45f45a RR 42f 45a 5033[6]
7 b m Never so Bold 7.1f **(62)** - Vogos Angel (Song) 7.2f **(61)**
Form - 831057541707706746
Record 1999 - 1st:2 2nd:0 3rd:0 Ran:16
Pre1999 - 1st:9 2nd:8 3rd:4 Ran:71
Win Prizemoney £36,575 *Total Prizemoney* £48,101
Wins * 1999 Apr Windso (GD) H 8.3f 53 55
* **1999** *Jan Lingfi (STD) H 8f 40 50*
* 1998 Oct Leices (G-S) H 8f 49 53
* 1998 Mar Warwic (G-S) H 7f 48 54
1996 May Windso (G-F) C 8.3f 57
1995 Aug Newmar (G-F) C 7f 67
1995 Aug Leices (G-F) C 7f 70
1995 Jly Newmar (G-F) C 7f 70
1999 Turf 1-11: (7f 4, 8f 1-6, 9f) (g-s 2, g-f 2, frm 1-6, hrd) 1999 AW 1-5: (7f 2, 8f 1-3) (Equi 1-4, Fibr)
Moderate mare, effective 7 to 8f, best at 8f, acts on g-s to frm - acts on Equi, often wears blinkers (effectively), likes right handed tracks, excels at Goodwood. Turf high 55 - 1st of 18 giving 3lb to Homestead (12 Apr Windsor RF 0652). AW high 50 (1st run) - 1st of 12 from Homestead (5 Jan Lingfield RF 0028). Consistent.
**E A Wheeler [4-49] Diamant Precision Engineering Ltd (from R M Stronge [0-10] Oct 1996).*

DELIUS (USA) RR 90+f 5049[1]
2 b br c A P Indy (USA) - Hot Novel (USA) (Mari's Book (USA))
Form - 1
Record 1999 - 1st:1 2nd:0 3rd:0 Ran:1
Win Prizemoney £4,630 *Total Prizemoney* £4,630
Wins * 1999 Oct Leices (SFT) 8f 90+ <
1999 Turf 1-1: (8f 1-1) (gd 1-1)
Currently useful colt. (1st run) - 1st of 19 from Atlantic Rhapsody (25 Oct Leicester RF 5049). Showed a good attitude when winning his maiden and looks useful.
**Sir Michael Stoute [1-1] M Tabor & Mrs John Magnier.*

DELLUA (IRE) BHB 60f55a RR 56f 55a 4262[7]
5 b m Suave Dancer (USA) 10.7f **(68)** - Joma Kaanem (Double Form) 7.3f **(58)**
Form - 3216817557
Record 1999 - 1st:2 2nd:1 3rd:1 Ran:10
Pre1999 - 1st:1 2nd:1 3rd:0 Ran:13
Win Prizemoney £10,066 *Total Prizemoney* £12,232
Wins * 1999 Jun Newcas (G-F) 12.4f 59
* **1999** Apr Windso (GD) H 11.6f 53 58
1997 Spt Folkes (FRM) 9.7f 62+ <
1999 Turf 2-7: (12f 2-7) (g-f 3, frm 2-4) 1999 AW 0-3: (10f, 12f 2) (Equi 3)
Average filly, effective 10 to 12f, best at 12f, acts on frm - acts on Equi, likes left handed tracks. Turf high 59 - 1st of 5 getting 1lb from Righty Ho (2 Jun Newcastle RF 1690) - also 1st of 12 getting 11lb from Mono Lady (12 Apr Windsor RF 0651). AW high 67 - 2nd of 6 getting 11lb from Opera Buff (18 Feb Lingfield 12f Equi RF 0309). **J W Hills [2-16] Khalid Affara (from R Guest [1-7] Oct 1997).*

DELMO BHB 30a RR 38f 30a 176[7]
4 ch g Democratic (USA) - Charlotte Piaf (Morston (FR)) 9.4f **(55)**
Form - U7
Record 1999 - 1st:0 2nd:0 3rd:0 Ran:2
Pre1999 - 1st:0 2nd:0 3rd:0 Ran:2
1999 AW 0-2: (12f, 15f) (Equi, Fibr)
Workmanlike, very moderate gelding. AW high 18.
**R Simpson [0-6] D J Christopher.*

DELPHINI (IRE) BHB 60f64a RR 28f 64a 4445[15]
3 b f Seattle Dancer (USA) 10.1f **(74)** - Breyani (Commanche Run) 8.5f **(58)**
Form - 021130
Record 1999 - 1st:2 2nd:1 3rd:1 Ran:6
Win Prizemoney £5,653 *Total Prizemoney* £6,692
Wins * 1999 *Jly Lingfi (STD) 8f 69* <
* **1999** *Jly Southw (STD) 8f 60*
1999 Turf 0-2: (7f, 10f) (g-s, frm) 1999 AW 2-4: (8f 2-3, 10f) (Equi 1-2, Fibr 1-2)

Scopey, average filly, effective 8 to 10f, best at 8f, - acts on AW, best on Equi. Turf high 28. AW high 69 - 1st of 10 getting 3lb from Survival Venture (24 Jly Lingfield RF 3097) - also 1st of 8 getting 5lb from Mr Perry (10 Jly Southwell RF 2717). She came into her own over a mile on sand during the summer, winning at Southwell and Lingfield, but she is a very hard ride who does no more than is absolutely necessary. She has to be ridden vigorously to go about her business, which has got a couple of her riders into trouble over their use of the whip.

**J Noseda [2-6] Mrs Charlotte Musgrave.*

DELPHINIUS (IRE) RR 94f 3664[2]

2 br c Dolphin Street (FR) - Stellar Empress (USA) (Star de Naskra (USA)) 9.7f **(65)**
Form - 12
Record 1999 - 1st:1 2nd:1 3rd:0 Ran:2
Win Prizemoney £3,883 *Total Prizemoney* £5,936
Wins * 1999 Jly Windso (G-F) 6f 78+ <
1999 Turf 1-2: (6f 1-2) (gd, g-f 1-1)
Useful colt. Turf high 94 (began Jly) - 2nd of 4 giving 2lb to Buy Or Sell (14 Aug Ripon 6f gd RF 3664). Looked a useful prospect, but met with a fatal injury on the gallops. (DEAD)
**G Wragg [1-2] Mollers Racing.*

DELTA GEORGIA BHB 47f RR 49f 2386[2]

3 ch f Tina's Pet 7.4f **(56)** - Bacolet (Dominion) 8.5f **(63)**
Form - 5502
Record 1999 - 1st:0 2nd:1 3rd:0 Ran:4
Win Prizemoney £0 *Total Prizemoney* £656
1999 Turf 0-2: (7f, 8f) (g-f 2) 1999 AW 0-2: (6f, 7f) (Fibr 2)
Moderate filly. Turf high 49. AW high 31.
**A Bailey [0-4] David English.*

DELTA SOLEIL (USA) BHB 68f70a RR 68df 70a 4989[15]

7 b h Riverman (USA) 9.7f **(78)** - Sunny Roberta (USA) (Robellino (USA)) 7.6f **(80)**
Form - 00100038000
Record 1999 - 1st:1 2nd:0 3rd:1 Ran:11
Pre1999 - 1st:3 2nd:3 3rd:1 Ran:35
Win Prizemoney £27,054 *Total Prizemoney* £39,424
Wins * 1999 May Kempto (GD) H 6f 71 76
* 1998 Jly Newbur (G-F) H 6f 71 75
* 1998 Jun Salisb (G-S) H 6f 65 71
1995 Aug York (G-F) 7.9f 86 <
1999 Turf 1-11: (5f, 6f 1-10) (g-s, g-f 5, frm 1-5)
Average horse, effective 6f, acts on gd to frm. Turf high 76 - 1st of 19 giving 16lb to Rainbow Rain (16 May Kempton RF 1258). Becoming disappointing. He is basically inconsistent, but wins in his turn. Enjoys forcing tactics and is suited by six furlongs.
**V Soane [3-24] American Quartet (from P W Harris [1-22] Nov 1997).*

DEMERARA RR 2008[12]

2 br f Dilum (USA) 7.1f **(56)** - Springtime Sugar (USA) (Halo (USA)) 10.6f **(75)**
Form - 0
Record 1999 - 1st:0 2nd:0 3rd:0 Ran:1
1999 Turf 0-1: (7f) (frm)
Currently very poor filly. **C E Brittain [0-1] C E Brittain.*

DEMETER (USA) RR 88f 5109[3]

2 b f Diesis 9f **(80)** - Nicer (IRE) (Pennine Walk) 8.5f **(61)**
Form - 3
Record 1999 - 1st:0 2nd:0 3rd:1 Ran:1
Win Prizemoney £0 *Total Prizemoney* £452
1999 Turf 0-1: (8f) (gd)
Currently useful filly. Daughter of an Irish 1000 Guineas winner, she should make her mark as a three-year-old.
**H R A Cecil [0-1] Lord Lloyd-Webber.*

DEMI-MONDAINE RR 42f 2962[9]

2 b f Democratic (USA) - Alo Ez (Alzao (USA)) 7.1f **(68)**
Form - 60
Record 1999 - 1st:0 2nd:0 3rd:0 Ran:2
1999 Turf 0-2: (6f, 7f) (gd, g-f)
Currently moderate filly. Turf high 42 (began Jly).
**J G Smyth-Osbourne [0-2] T H Rossiter.*

DEMOCRACY (IRE) BHB 78f RR 81f 4160[1]

3 ch c Common Grounds 8.1f **(66)** - Inonder (Belfort (FR)) 6.8f **(63)**
Form - 63632334221
Record 1999 - 1st:1 2nd:3 3rd:4 Ran:11
Pre1999 - 1st:0 2nd:0 3rd:1 Ran:1
Win Prizemoney £3,779 *Total Prizemoney* £9,727
Wins * 1999 Spt Bath (FRM) 5.7f 78 <
1999 Turf 1-11: (6f 1-2, 7f 4, 8f 4, 9f) (sft, g-s, gd, g-f 4, frm 1-4)
Lengthy, decent colt, effective 6 to 9f, acts on gd to frm, best on frm, often wears blinkers (extremely effectively), excels at Brighton. Turf high 81 - 2nd of 9 to Quiet Millfit (26 Jun Lingfield 9f frm RF 2328) - also 1st of 8 giving 5lb to Galanty Show (6 Spt Bath RF 4160). Consistent.
**R Hannon [1-12] Highclere Thoroughbred Racing Ltd.*

DEMOLITION JO BHB 74f65a RR 71f 65a 5212[2]

4 gr f Petong 7.6f **(58)** - Fire Sprite (Mummy's Game) 8.2f **(60)**
Form - 06786002005530000332
Record 1999 - 1st:0 2nd:2 3rd:3 Ran:20
Pre1999 - 1st:3 2nd:11 3rd:1 Ran:37
Win Prizemoney £13,160 *Total Prizemoney* £44,083
Wins * 1998 Jun Cheste (G-S) H 7f 69 71
* 1997 Oct Newmar (G-S) H 6f 77 81 <
* 1997 Aug Mussel (G-F) 7.1f 73
1999 Turf 0-18: (5f 9, 6f 8, 8f) (hvy, g-s 5, gd 7, g-f 2, frm 3) 1999 AW 0-2: (5f, 6f) (Fibr 2)
Light-framed, above-average filly, effective 5 to 6f, best at 5f, acts on gd to g-f, best on gd, mostly wears blinkers. Turf high 84 (1st run) - 7th of 17 getting 20lb from Night Shot (25 Mar Doncaster 5f gd RF 0466). **P D Evans [3-57] John Pugh.*

DENA RR 69+f 5208[5]

2 b f Deploy 11.4f **(67)** - Isabena (Star Appeal) 9.6f **(65)**
Form - 5
Record 1999 - 1st:0 2nd:0 3rd:0 Ran:1
1999 Turf 0-1: (7f) (g-s)
Currently average filly. **W Jarvis [0-1] Cuadra Africa.*

DENBRAE (IRE) BHB 51f51a RR 53f 51a 5199[13]

7 b g Sure Blade (USA) 10.6f **(66)** - Fencing (Viking (USA)) 6.7f **(65)**
Form - 312012D380
Record 1999 - 1st:2 2nd:2 3rd:2 Ran:10
Pre1999 - 1st:4 2nd:3 3rd:7 Ran:49
Win Prizemoney £17,201 *Total Prizemoney* £29,339
Wins * 1999 May Hamilt (SFT) H 6f 47 51
*** 1999** *Mar Southw (STD) H 7f 46 49*
1997 Aug Leices (GD) 7f 68
1996 Jun Chepst (G-F) H 6.1f 68 69 <
1995 Apr Nottin (GD) H 6.1f 66 64
1995 *Feb Southw (STD) 6f 57*
1999 Turf 1-5: (5f 2, 6f 1-3) (gd 1-2, g-f, frm 2) 1999 AW 1-5: (7f 1-2, 8f 3) (Equi 2, Fibr 1-3)
Fair gelding, effective 6 to 7f, best at 7f, acts on gd to g-f, best on gd. Turf high 53 - also 1st of 16 getting 10lb from Sun Dancing (24 May Hamilton RF 1428). AW high 51. Broke a long losing run when winning on the All-Weather at Southwell in March, and added a six-furlong event in the soft at Hamilton in May.
**J Pearce [2-10] Jeff Pearce (from D J G MurraySmith [4-49] Oct 1998).*

DENNIS BERGKAMP (IRE) BHB 48f RR 58df 5052[20]

2 b g Night Shift (USA) 8.1f **(73)** - Indian Express **(59f)** (Indian Ridge)
Form - 008300
Record 1999 - 1st:0 2nd:0 3rd:1 Ran:6
Win Prizemoney £0 *Total Prizemoney* £290
1999 Turf 0-6: (5f 3, 6f, 7f 2) (gd 2, g-f 3, frm)
Fair gelding, has worn blinkers. Turf high 58.
**W Clay [0-1] Dave Dutton (from M R Channon [0-5] Aug 1999).*

DENOUEMENT RR 6f 3286[7]

3 b br f Lapierre - Star Attention (Northfields (USA)) 9f **(72)**
Form - 7
Record 1999 - 1st:0 2nd:0 3rd:0 Ran:1
1999 Turf 0-1: (7f) (frm)
Small, currently very poor filly. **C W Fairhurst [0-1] Mrs J Smethurst.*

DEN'S-JOY RR 59f 4951[3]

3 b f Archway (IRE) 8.5f **(60)** - Bonvin (Taufan (USA)) 7f **(57)**

Form - 3
Record 1999 - 1st:0 2nd:0 3rd:1 Ran:1
Win Prizemoney £0 *Total Prizemoney* £616
1999 Turf 0-1: (7f) (g-f)
Workmanlike, currently fair filly. (1st run) - 3rd of 14 getting 5lb from Hyperactive (19 Oct Yarmouth 7f g-f RF 4951).
**H J Collingridge [0-1] P Burban.*

DENTARDIA (IRE) BHB 26f41a **RR 22f 41a** 2174[8]
4 br g Petardia 8.2f **(58)** - Modena (Sassafras (FR)) 9.6f **(69)**
Form - 608608
Record 1999 - 1st:0 2nd:0 3rd:0 Ran:6
Pre1999 - 1st:0 2nd:1 3rd:2 Ran:12
Win Prizemoney £0 *Total Prizemoney* £2,292
1999 Turf 0-3: (11f, 12f, 16f) (g-f 2, frm) 1999 AW 0-3: (10f, 13f 2) (Equi 3)
Moderate gelding, effective 12 to 14f, acts on g-f - acts on Fibr, likes tight tracks. Turf high 22. AW high 44.
**J M P Eustace [0-20] Charles Curtis.*

DENTON LADY BHB 46f **RR 61f** 4722[10]
2 br f Inchinor 8.9f **(64)** - Lammastide (Martinmas) 7.6f **(59)**
Form - 047550450
Record 1999 - 1st:0 2nd:0 3rd:0 Ran:9
Win Prizemoney £0 *Total Prizemoney* £692
1999 Turf 0-9: (5f, 6f 3, 7f 3, 8f 2) (g-s, gd 3, g-f 3, frm, hrd)
Average filly, has worn blinkers. Turf high 61. Inconsistent.
**W T Kemp [0-9] Mrs M Irwin.*

DEPLOY VENTURE BHB 93f **RR 97f** 4830[3]
3 ch g Deploy 11.4f **(67)** -Tasseled (USA) (Tate Gallery (USA)) 7.4f **(67)**
Form - 25125015403
Record 1999 - 1st:2 2nd:2 3rd:1 Ran:11
Pre1999 - 1st:1 2nd:2 3rd:2 Ran:6
Win Prizemoney £17,862 *Total Prizemoney* £27,220
Wins * 1999 Jly Ascot (G-F) H 12f 92 97 <
*** 1999** May Newbur (GD) H 12f 83 88+
* 1998 *Spt Wolver (STD) 8.5f* 77
1999 Turf 2-11: (9f, 10f, 12f 2-7,13f, 14f)(sft 2,g-s 1-2, gd 1-4, g-f 2, frm)
Scopey, very useful gelding, effective 12f, acts on g-s to gd, best on g-s. Turf high 98 - 2nd of 5 giving 14lb to Ligne Gagnante (2 Jun Goodwood 12f g-s RF 1674) - also 1st of 9 giving 5lb to Livius (24 Jly Ascot RF 3091). He is a useful middle-distance handicapper and suited by a sound surface. Although game in a finish, he travels strongly and does not find much off the bridle. He made 92,000 guineas at Newmarket in October and is likely to continue his career in America. **S P C Woods [3-17] Dr Frank Chao.*

DEPUTISE (IRE) BHB 78f **RR 80f** 4831[2]
3 b c Caerleon (USA) 10.9f **(79)** - Depaze (USA) (Deputy Minister (CAN)) 7.4f **(80)**
Form - 52
Record 1999 - 1st:0 2nd:1 3rd:0 Ran:2
Pre1999 - 1st:0 2nd:0 3rd:0 Ran:1
Win Prizemoney £0 *Total Prizemoney* £1,132
1999 Turf 0-2: (10f, 11f) (sft, g-f)
Scopey, currently decent colt. Turf high 80.
**J H M Gosden [0-3] Sheikh Mohammed.*

DEPUTY DIAMOND (USA) RR 2096a[2]
4 b c Deputy Minister (CAN) 9.2f **(71)** - Rose Diamond (USA) (Diamond Shoal) 9.1f **(66)**
Form - 2
1999 AW 0-1: (9f) (Dirt)
Currently very useful colt. **F Schulhofer in USA [0-1].*

DERBY AFFAIR BHB 43f **RR 35f** 3748[7]
3 b f Teenoso (USA) 10.5f **(62)** - Formal Affair **(56f)** (Rousillon (USA)) 8.2f **(74)**
Form - 54087
Record 1999 - 1st:0 2nd:0 3rd:0 Ran:5
1999 Turf 0-5: (10f 4, 12f) (gd, g-f, frm 2, hrd)
Light-framed, very moderate filly. Turf high 60.
**D Nicholson [0-5] Mrs Claire Smith.*

DERRYQUIN BHB 52f **RR 50f** 5199[10]
4 b g Lion Cavern (USA) 7.5f **(74)** - Top Berry (High Top) 10.2f **(67)**
Form - 056400
Record 1999 - 1st:0 2nd:0 3rd:0 Ran:6
Pre1999 - 1st:2 2nd:0 3rd:0 Ran:9
Win Prizemoney £7,571 *Total Prizemoney* £7,961
Wins 1997 Nov Doncas (GD) 8f 95 <
1997 Oct Lingfi (GD) 7f 81
1999 Turf 0-6: (6f 3, 7f, 8f, 10f) (gd 4, g-f, frm)
Light-framed, fair gelding, has worn blinkers. Turf high 53.
**P L Gilligan [0-6] Lady Bland (from R Charlton [2-9] Oct 1998).*

DESARU (USA) BHB 108f **RR 108f** 2039[11]
3 br c Chief's Crown (USA) 10.2f **(75)** - Team Colors (USA) (Mr Prospector (USA)) 8.8f **(78)**
Form - 00
Record 1999 - 1st:0 2nd:0 3rd:0 Ran:2
Pre1999 - 1st:1 2nd:1 3rd:1 Ran:3
Win Prizemoney £5,552 *Total Prizemoney* £19,882
Wins * 1998 Spt Doncas (GD) 7f 99+ <
1999 Turf 0-2: (7f, 8f) (gd, frm)
Scopey, Pattern-class colt. Turf high 108. Decent as a two-year-old, he was beaten under six lengths in the 2000 Guineas when appearing to be racing on the wrong side. He faded after showing speed in the Jersey at Ascot next time, and was not seen again.
**J Noseda [1-5] K Y Lim.*

DESCANT (IRE) RR 58f 1886[8]
3 b f Bluebird (USA) 7.9f **(71)** - Dubai Lady (Kris) 9.5f **(73)**
Form - 8
Record 1999 - 1st:0 2nd:0 3rd:0 Ran:1
Pre1999 - 1st:0 2nd:0 3rd:0 Ran:1
Win Prizemoney £0 *Total Prizemoney* £354
1999 Turf 0-1: (7f) (gd)
Workmanlike, currently fair filly.
**R Hannon [0-2] The Royal Ascot Racing Club.*

DESDEMONA (IRE) BHB 85f **RR 85f** 3469[2]
3 b f Lahib (USA) 8f **(69)** - Tragic Point (IRE) **(88f)** (Tragic Role (USA))
Form - 0216722
Record 1999 - 1st:1 2nd:3 3rd:0 Ran:7
Pre1999 - 1st:0 2nd:1 3rd:0 Ran:2
Win Prizemoney £3,984 *Total Prizemoney* £12,940
Wins * 1999 Jun Yarmou (G-F) 7f 82 <
1999 Turf 1-7: (7f 1-4, 8f, 9f, 11f) (gd 1-2, g-f 3, frm 2)
Rangy, useful filly, effective 6 to 11f, acts on gd to frm, best on frm, has worn blinkers. Turf high 85 - 2nd of 5 giving 7lb to Fantazia (8 Aug Redcar 11f frm RF 3469) - also 1st of 5 from Tebyaan (3 Jun Yarmouth RF 1708). It took a while for the penny to drop, but she got it right at Yarmouth in June.
**G Wragg [1-9] Cheveley Park Stud.*

DESERT CAT (IRE) BHB 39f **RR 31f** 4985[11]
6 b g Green Desert (USA) 7.8f **(78)** - Mahabba (USA) (Elocutionist (USA)) 8f **(77)**
Form - 074010000
Record 1999 - 1st:1 2nd:0 3rd:0 Ran:9
Pre1999 - 1st:1 2nd:0 3rd:4 Ran:24
Win Prizemoney £4,827 *Total Prizemoney* £6,862
Wins * 1999 Jly Mussel (G-S) SH 8f 42 44
* 1998 Spt Mussel (GD) H 7.1f 46 48 <
1999 Turf 1-9: (7f 3, 8f 1-6) (gd 3, g-f, frm 1-4, hrd)
Very moderate gelding, effective 7 to 8f, best at 8f, acts on g-s to frm, best on frm, has worn blinkers, likes right handed tracks, likes tight tracks, excels at Carlisle and Musselburgh. Turf high 44 - 1st of 14 getting 11lb from Tornado Prince (5 Jly Musselburgh RF 2556). Becoming disappointing. He goes well at Musselburgh and regained winning form there in July.
**Martyn Wane [2-30] Mrs Linda Miller (from H ThomsonJones [0-5] Jun 1996).*

DESERT CHARM BHB 42f **RR 40f** 4687[13]
2 b f Desert Style (IRE) - Autumn Fall (USA) (Sanglamore (USA))
Form - 000
Record 1999 - 1st:0 2nd:0 3rd:0 Ran:3
1999 Turf 0-3: (7f, 8f 2) (gd 2, g-f)
Currently moderate filly. Turf high 40 (began Spt).
**N Tinkler [0-3] & Mrs G Middlebrook.*

DESERT DARLING BHB 60f57a **RR 55f 57a** 2692[5]
3 b f Green Desert (USA) 7.8f **(78)** - Habibti (Habitat) 9.4f **(70)**
Form - 8045
Record 1999 - 1st:0 2nd:0 3rd:0 Ran:4
Pre1999 - 1st:0 2nd:0 3rd:1 Ran:3
Win Prizemoney £0 *Total Prizemoney* £453
1999 Turf 0-3: (5f 2, 6f) (gd, frm 2) 1999 AW 0-1: (5f) (Fibr)
Workmanlike, fair filly, effective 5f, acts on frm, has worn blinkers. Turf high 55. **J Berry [0-7] The Sussex Stud Ltd.*

DESERT DUKE BHB 83f **RR 82f** 1026[3]
3 b c Green Desert (USA) 7.8f **(78)** - Guilty Secret (IRE) (Kris) 9.5f **(73)**
Form - 83
Record 1999 - 1st:0 2nd:0 3rd:1 Ran:2
Pre1999 - 1st:0 2nd:0 3rd:2 Ran:2
Win Prizemoney £0 *Total Prizemoney* £4,566
1999 Turf 0-2: (7f, 8f) (g-s, g-f)
Scopey, decent colt. Turf high 82 - 3rd of 15 getting 14lb from Sporting Lad (4 May Chester 8f g-f RF 1026).
**Sir Michael Stoute [0-4] Abdulla Al Khalifa.*

DESERT FIGHTER BHB 64f **RR 65f** 4146[4]
8 b g Green Desert (USA) 7.8f **(78)** - Jungle Rose (Shirley Heights) 10.3f **(74)**
Form - 311114
Record 1999 - 1st:4 2nd:0 3rd:1 Ran:6
Pre1999 - 1st:5 2nd:3 3rd:5 Ran:28
Win Prizemoney £29,473 *Total Prizemoney* £36,340

Wins							
* **1999**	Jly	Catter	(FRM)	C	12f		65
* **1999**	Jly	Hamilt	(FRM)	C	11.1f		55
* **1999**	Jly	Haydoc	(G-S)	C	11.9f		68
* **1999**	May	Thirsk	(G-S)	C	12f		50
* 1997	May	Newcas	(G-F)	H	12.4f	68	75
* 1997	Apr	Thirsk	(G-F)		12f		76

1999 Turf 4-6: (11f 1-1, 12f 3-5) (gd 1-2, g-f 1-1, frm 2-2, hrd)
Above-average gelding, effective 10 to 12f, best at 12f, acts on g-s to hrd, excels at Thirsk. Turf high 68 (1st run) - 3rd of 4 giving 16lb to High Tatra (17 Apr Thirsk 12f gd RF 0740) - also 1st of 6 giving 13lb to Col-Woody (2 Jly Haydock RF 2486). He is a fair middle-distance performer, but all his victories last season were in claimers. Not nearly so effective in handicaps.
**Mrs M Reveley [10-48] A Frame (from D Nicholson [0-5] May 1995).*

DESERT FURY RR 95+f 4263[3]
2 b c Warning 8.1f **(77)** - Number One Spot (Reference Point) 6.8f **(70)**
Form - 13
Record 1999 - 1st:1 2nd:0 3rd:1 Ran:2
Win Prizemoney £7,067 *Total Prizemoney* £8,097
Wins * **1999** May Cheste (G-F) 5.1f 82+ <
1999 Turf 1-2: (5f 1-1, 6f) (g-f 1-1, frm)
Currently very useful colt. Turf high 95 - 3rd of 7 giving 5lb to Tabheej (11 Spt Doncaster 6f frm RF 4263). He lacks scope, but showed above-average ability when returning from a four-month break to finish third in a hot conditions race at Doncaster in September. Likely to stay a mile, he may not be easy to place at home. **B Hanbury [1-2] Abdullah Ali.*

DESERT INVADER (IRE) BHB 35f43a **RR 24f 43a** 2086[3]
8 br g Lead on Time (USA) 7.5f **(69)** - Aljood (Kris) 9.5f **(73)**
Form - 65766020053
Record 1999 - 1st:0 2nd:1 3rd:1 Ran:11
Pre1999 - 1st:9 2nd:12 3rd:12 Ran:93
Win Prizemoney £23,046 *Total Prizemoney* £38,610

Wins								
* 1998	*Jun*	*Wolver*	*(STD)*	*H*	*6f*	*60*	*63*	
* 1998	*Jun*	*Southw*	*(STD)*	*H*	*7f*	*55*	*60*	
* 1997	*Jun*	*Wolver*	*(STD)*	*H*	*6f*	*63*	*70*	<
* 1997	*May*	*Southw*	*(STD)*	*C*	*7f*		*63*	
* 1997	*May*	*Wolver*	*(STD)*	*C*	*6f*		*56+*	
* 1996	*Feb*	*Southw*	*(STD)*	*H*	*7f*	*57*	*61*	
* 1995	*Spt*	*Wolver*	*(STD)*	*H*	*6f*	*62*	*61*	
* 1995	*Feb*	*Southw*	*(STD)*	*H*	*8f*	*60*	*62*	

1999 AW 0-11: (6f 4, 7f 5, 8f 2) (Equi, Fibr 10)
Moderate gelding, effective 6 to 7f, best at 6f, - acts on Fibr, has worn blinkers, favours left handed tracks, favours tight tracks. AW high 49. Consistent. He must be one of the busiest horses in training, though he races almost exclusively on Fibresand these days. His strike rate is not brilliant overall though he is perfectly capable of winning races over six or seven furlongs. Not seen out after June.
**D W Chapman [8-100] David Chapman (from A A Scott [1-4] Jly 1994).*

DESERT ISLAND DISC BHB 69f **RR 67f** 5216[7]
2 b f Turtle Island (IRE) - Distant Music (Darshaan) 9.9f **(84)**
Form - 757
Record 1999 - 1st:0 2nd:0 3rd:0 Ran:3
1999 Turf 0-3: (7f 2, 8f) (g-s 3)
Currently average filly. Turf high 67 (began Oct).
**N A Graham [0-3] Flying Colours Racing.*

DESERT KNIGHT RR 97f 4254[2]
3 b c Green Desert (USA) 7.8f **(78)** - Green Leaf (USA) (Alydar (USA)) 9.1f **(76)**
Form - 12
Record 1999 - 1st:1 2nd:1 3rd:0 Ran:2
Win Prizemoney £4,513 *Total Prizemoney* £6,318
Wins * **1999** Aug Pontef (GD) 8f 92+ <
1999 Turf 1-2: (8f 1-2) (g-f, frm 1-1)
Rangy, currently very useful colt. Turf high 97 (began Aug) - 2nd of 5 giving 3lb to Swallow Flight (10 Spt Doncaster 8f g-f RF 4254) - also 1st of 11 from Tarawan (22 Aug Pontefract RF 3849). He created a favourable impression on his debut and may have found the ground too firm when a creditable second on his only subsequent start. Likely to be best around a mile, he can win a listed race in 2000 and is one to look out for in the first half of the season.
**J Noseda [1-2] Sheikh Khaled Duaij Al Sabah.*

DESERT LORE BHB 30f35a **RR 33f 35a** 2678[9]
8 b g Green Desert (USA) 7.8f **(78)** - Chinese Justice (USA) (Diesis) 9.3f **(69)**
Form - 00
Record 1999 - 1st:0 2nd:0 3rd:0 Ran:2
Pre1999 - 1st:1 2nd:1 3rd:2 Ran:18
Win Prizemoney £3,699 *Total Prizemoney* £7,753
1999 Turf 0-2: (5f, 6f) (g-f, frm)
Very moderate gelding. Turf high 7. Inconsistent.
**D A Nolan [0-5] A S McPherson (from R M McKellar [0-2] Jan 1997).*

DESERT RECRUIT BHB 46f **RR 44f** 3540[4]
3 b g Marju (IRE) 9.2f **(76)** - Storm Gayle (IRE) (Sadler's Wells (USA)) 10f **(76)**
Form - 64078514
Record 1999 - 1st:1 2nd:0 3rd:0 Ran:8
Pre1999 - 1st:0 2nd:0 3rd:0 Ran:1
Win Prizemoney £2,780 *Total Prizemoney* £3,352
Wins * **1999** Jly Hamilt (G-F) H 11.1f 42 42 <
1999 Turf 1-8: (6f, 7f, 8f 2, 9f 2, 11f 1-2) (gd 2, g-f 1-5, frm)
Workmanlike, moderate gelding, likes right handed tracks, favours tight tracks. Turf high 55. **I Semple [1-9] David McKenzie.*

DESERT ROSE RR 4982[10]
2 b f Green Desert (USA) 7.8f **(78)** - Splice **(101f)** (Sharpo) 7.7f **(59)**
Form - 0
Record 1999 - 1st:0 2nd:0 3rd:0 Ran:1
1999 Turf 0-1: (7f) (g-f)
Currently very poor filly. **Sir Michael Stoute [0-1] Cheveley Park Stud.*

DESERT SAFARI (IRE) BHB 74f71a **RR 72f 71a** 4277[1]
2 b f Desert Style (IRE) - Dublah (USA) (Private Account (USA)) 8.5f **(74)**
Form - 03374254041
Record 1999 - 1st:1 2nd:1 3rd:2 Ran:11
Win Prizemoney £2,736 *Total Prizemoney* £4,499
Wins * **1999** Spt Mussel (G-F) 5f 72 <
1999 Turf 1-10: (5f 1-7, 6f 3) (gd 4, g-f 2, frm 1-4) 1999 AW 0-1: (5f) (Fibr)
Above-average filly, effective 5f, acts on frm, has worn blinkers. Turf high 72 - 1st of 7 from Its Another Gift (13 Spt Musselburgh RF 4277). **E J Alston [1-11] The Burlington Partnership.*

DESERT SAND BHB 43f **RR 44f** 4949[5]
4 b f Tragic Role (USA) 9.4f **(63)** - Miss Suntan (Bruni) 8.2f **(50)**
Form - 68605
Record 1999 - 1st:0 2nd:0 3rd:0 Ran:5
Pre1999 - 1st:2 2nd:0 3rd:0 Ran:7
Win Prizemoney £7,769 *Total Prizemoney* £7,769

Wins 1998 Spt Ayr (G-S) C 9.1f 69+
1997 Spt Ayr (G-S) 6f 76 <
1999 Turf 0-5: (9f, 10f 2, 11f, 12f) (g-s, g-f 3, frm)
Scopey, moderate filly, effective 8 to 9f, acts on sft to frm, favours left handed tracks. Turf high 44. Consistent.
**K A Morgan [0-5] Peter Davis (from J Hanson [1-4] Spt 1998).*

DESERT SKY (IRE) RR 95f 4849a[1]
2 b f Green Desert (USA) 7.8f **(78)** - Badrah (USA) (Private Account (USA)) 8.5f **(74)**
Form - 2212211
1999 Turf 3-7: (5f 3, 6f 2-3, 7f 1-1) (hvy, sft 1-1, gd 1-2, g-f 1-3)
Very useful filly, effective 5 to 7f, best at 6f, acts on sft to g-f, best on g-f. Turf high 95 - 2nd of 7 getting 3lb from Fasliyev (22 May Curragh 5f g-f RF 1475a) - also 1st of 8 from Buffalo Berry (17 Jly Leopardstown RF 2993a). She was a tough and reliable juvenile and thoroughly deserved her listed win at Leopardstown in July. A mile may prove the limit of her stamina.
**J S Bolger in IRE [3-7] Mrs J M Ryan.*

DESERT SONG BHB 42f RR 36f 4293[13]
4 ch f Desert Dirham (USA) - Affaire de Coeur (Imperial Fling (USA)) 7.1f **(58)**
Form - 80
Record 1999 - 1st:0 2nd:0 3rd:0 Ran:2
Pre1999 - 1st:0 2nd:0 3rd:3 Ran:5
Win Prizemoney £0 *Total Prizemoney* £1,208
1999 Turf 0-2: (7f, 8f) (g-f, frm)
Workmanlike, very moderate filly, effective 7f, acts on frm, likes tight tracks. Turf high 36 (began Spt).
**R G Frost [0-4] Mrs B M Blake (from S Dow [0-5] Oct 1998).*

DESERT TRACK BHB 94f RR 103f 932a[2]
5 b h Green Desert (USA) 7.8f **(78)** - Mill Path (Mill Reef (USA)) 10.5f **(78)**
Form - 2
1999 Turf 0-1: (8f) (sft)
Very useful colt. (1st run) - 2nd of 11 giving 2lb to Baleno (25 Apr Dielsdorf 8f sft RF 0932a).
**M Weiss in SWI [1-2] (from J H M Gosden [2-5] Nov 1997).*

DESERT VALENTINE BHB 45f RR 45f 5069[10]
4 b g Midyan (USA) 9.9f **(64)** - Mo Ceri (Kampala) 8.5f **(56)**
Form - 0050
Record 1999 - 1st:0 2nd:0 3rd:0 Ran:4
Pre1999 - 1st:1 2nd:0 3rd:0 Ran:8
Win Prizemoney £3,465 *Total Prizemoney* £3,465
Wins * 1998 Spt Goodwo (G-S) H 8f 55 60 <
1999 Turf 0-4: (8f 2, 10f 2) (g-s, gd, frm 2)
Leggy, moderate gelding, effective 8f, acts on gd. Turf high 45 (began Jly). Consistent. **L G Cottrell [1-12] Mrs Lucy Halloran.*

DESERT WARRIOR (IRE) BHB 50f RR 48f 1517[15]
5 b h Fairy King (USA) 7.7f **(75)** - Highland Girl (USA) (Sir Ivor) 10.2f **(70)**
Form - 2200
Record 1999 - 1st:0 2nd:2 3rd:0 Ran:4
Pre1999 - 1st:0 2nd:0 3rd:0 Ran:7
Win Prizemoney £0 *Total Prizemoney* £1,783
1999 Turf 0-4: (7f 2, 8f 2) (g-f, frm 2, hrd)
Moderate colt, effective 7f, acts on g-f. Turf high 67 (1st run) - 2nd of 13 giving 19lb to Quite Incredible (5 Apr Kempton 7f g-f RF 0573).
**K Mahdi [0-10] Hamad Al-Mutawa (from Miss Gay Kelleway [0-1] Spt 1996).*

DESILU RR 51f 4395[5]
2 b f Skyliner 6.8f **(51)** - Munequita (Marching On) 6f **(60)**
Form - 05
Record 1999 - 1st:0 2nd:0 3rd:0 Ran:2
1999 Turf 0-2: (6f 2) (frm, hrd)
Currently fair filly. Turf high 51 (began Aug).
**W W Haigh [0-2] Coal Trade Partnership.*

DESIRE'S GOLD BHB 35f RR 42f 4912[5]
4 br g Grey Desire 9.3f **(49)** - Glory Gold (Hittite Glory) 8.7f **(50)**
Form - 0805
Record 1999 - 1st:0 2nd:0 3rd:0 Ran:4
Pre1999 - 1st:0 2nd:0 3rd:0 Ran:7
1999 Turf 0-4: (10f 2, 12f 2) (sft 2, gd, g-f)
Leggy, moderate gelding. Turf high 42. **M Brittain [0-11] Mel Brittain.*

DESRAYA (IRE) BHB 67f RR 69f 4378[15]
2 b g Desert Style (IRE) - Madaraya (USA) (Shahrastani (USA)) 8.8f **(72)**
Form - 04080
Record 1999 - 1st:0 2nd:0 3rd:0 Ran:5
Win Prizemoney £0 *Total Prizemoney* £321
1999 Turf 0-5: (5f, 6f 3, 8f) (gd 3, g-f, frm)
Average gelding. Turf high 69.
**K A Ryan [0-5] Pendle Inn Partnership.*

DESTINATION RR 55f 5063[9]
2 ch g Deploy 11.4f **(67)** - Veuve (Tirol)
Form - 0
Record 1999 - 1st:0 2nd:0 3rd:0 Ran:1
1999 Turf 0-1: (8f) (gd)
Currently fair gelding. **C A Cyzer [0-1] R M Cyzer.*

DETECTIVE BHB 64f RR 62f 4879[19]
3 ch c Wolfhound (USA) 7.3f **(71)** - Ivoronica (Targowice (USA)) 11.4f **(70)**
Form - 005200
Record 1999 - 1st:0 2nd:1 3rd:0 Ran:6
Pre1999 - 1st:0 2nd:0 3rd:0 Ran:1
Win Prizemoney £0 *Total Prizemoney* £806
1999 Turf 0-6: (6f 2, 7f 2, 8f 2) (gd, g-f 2, frm 3)
Workmanlike, average colt. Turf high 62.
**Dr J D Scargill [0-3] A C Edwards (from J H M Gosden [0-4] Jly 1999).*

DETERMINATION (USA) RR 92f 4974a[4]
2 b c Mystery Storm (USA) - Roxaneka (USA) 00
Form - 414
1999 Turf 1-3: (7f 1-2, 8f) (g-s 1-3)
Currently useful colt. Turf high 92 (began Spt) - 1st of 15 giving 5lb to Sugar Baby (6 Oct Fairyhouse RF 4841a).
**J S Bolger in IRE [1-3] Mrs J M Ryan.*

DE TRAMUNTANA RR 73f 5108[7]
2 b f Alzao (USA) 9.8f **(73)** - Glamour Game (Nashwan (USA))
Form - 07
Record 1999 - 1st:0 2nd:0 3rd:0 Ran:2
1999 Turf 0-2: (7f, 8f) (gd 2)
Currently above-average filly. Turf high 73 (began Oct).
**W Jarvis [0-2] P A Howell.*

DETROIT CITY (IRE) BHB 43f43a RR 32f 43a 5191[14]
4 b g Distinctly North (USA) 7.4f **(63)** - Moyhora (IRE) (Nashamaa) 7.1f **(66)**
Form - 6676071365257000
Record 1999 - 1st:1 2nd:1 3rd:1 Ran:16
Pre1999 - 1st:2 2nd:1 3rd:0 Ran:15
Win Prizemoney £8,006 *Total Prizemoney* £9,814
Wins * **1999** Apr Mussel (G-F) H 7.1f 54 56
* 1998 Jly Beverl (G-F) C 7.5f 62 <
* 1998 Jun Mussel (SFT) 7.1f 57
1999 Turf 1-12: (6f, 7f 1-8, 8f 3) (g-s, gd, g-f 1-5, frm 4, hrd) 1999 AW 0-4: (6f, 7f 2, 8f) (Fibr 4)
Light-framed, moderate gelding, effective 7f, acts on gd to frm, has worn blinkers, prefers right handed tracks, favours tight tracks. Turf high 56 - 1st of 14 getting 8lb from Technician (30 Apr Musselburgh RF 0941). AW high 43. Becoming disappointing.
**B S Rothwell [3-25] Mrs Liz Hunt (from J Berry [0-6] Apr 1998).*

DEVASTATING RR 71f 4328[10]
2 b f Bluebird (USA) 7.9f **(71)** - Winning Appeal (FR) (Law Society (USA)) 9.9f **(70)**
Form - 540
Record 1999 - 1st:0 2nd:0 3rd:0 Ran:3
Win Prizemoney £0 *Total Prizemoney* £365
1999 Turf 0-3: (6f, 7f, 8f) (gd, g-f, frm)
Currently above-average filly. Turf high 71. **R Hannon [0-3] M W Grant & W F Hawkings.*

DEVILETTA (USA) BHB 68f **RR 53f** 4027[13]
3 ch f Trempolino (USA) 11.9f **(77)** - Polish Devil (USA) (Devil's Bag (USA)) 12.4f **(78)**
Form - 100
Record 1999 - 1st:1 2nd:0 3rd:0 Ran:3
Pre1999 - 1st:0 2nd:2 3rd:0 Ran:4
Win Prizemoney £3,572 *Total Prizemoney* £6,006
Wins * 1999 *Feb Lingfi (STD) 6f 70+* <
1999 Turf 0-2: (6f 2) (g-f 2) 1999 AW 1-1: (6f 1-1) (Equi 1-1)
Leggy, above-average filly, effective 5 to 6f, acts on frm. Turf high 53. (1st run). **J H M Gosden [1-7] Sheikh Mohammed.*

DEVIL'S IMP (IRE) BHB 67f **RR 75f** 4989[3]
3 ch f Cadeaux Genereux 7.9f **(76)** - High Spirited (Shirley Heights) 10.3f **(74)**
Form - 213
Record 1999 - 1st:1 2nd:1 3rd:1 Ran:3
Pre1999 - 1st:1 2nd:0 3rd:0 Ran:1
Win Prizemoney £4,458 *Total Prizemoney* £6,398
Wins * 1999 Spt Thirsk (FRM) 6f 66+
*** 1998** Oct Newmar (GD) 7f 70+ <
1999 Turf 1-3: (6f 1-2, 7f) (g-f, frm, hrd 1-1)
Neat, above-average filly. Turf high 75 (1st run) (began Aug) - 2nd of 6 to Modern Era (20 Aug Newcastle 7f g-f RF 3801) - also 1st of 11 getting 7lb from Technician (4 Spt Thirsk RF 4147).
**E A L Dunlop [2-4] Maktoum Al Maktoum.*

DEVILS NIGHT BHB 20f **RR 9f** 3642[14]
4 b g Faustus (USA) 9.1f **(54)** - Up All Night **(6f)** (Green Desert (USA)) 8.6f **(78)**
Form - 00
Record 1999 - 1st:0 2nd:0 3rd:0 Ran:2
Pre1999 - 1st:0 2nd:0 3rd:0 Ran:1
1999 Turf 0-1: (10f) (g-f) 1999 AW 0-1: (8f) (Fibr)
Currently poor gelding. **K Bell [0-3] Brian Footer.*

DEVON DREAM (IRE) RR 49f 4276[10]
3 b g Paris House 5.9f **(64)** - Share The Vision (Vision (USA)) 9f **(64)**
Form - 013633740
Record 1999 - 1st:1 2nd:0 3rd:3 Ran:9
Pre1999 - 1st:0 2nd:0 3rd:0 Ran:3
Win Prizemoney £2,924 *Total Prizemoney* £4,192
Wins * 1999 May Bright (FRM) H 5.3f 54 57 <
1999 Turf 1-9: (5f 1-4, 6f 4, 7f) (g-f 1-3, frm 4, hrd 2)
Workmanlike, moderate gelding, effective 5 to 7f, acts on g-f to frm, best on g-f, prefers left handed tracks, prefers tight tracks. Turf high 57 - 1st of 10 getting 13lb from Lucy Mariella (28 May Brighton RF 1537). Consistent.
**M J Weeden [1-9] Dr Ian Shenkin (from H S Howe [0-3] Oct 1998).*

DEVON REEF RR 1411[13]
4 ch f Bandmaster (USA) - Reef Bay (IRE) (Phardante (FR))
Form - 0
Record 1999 - 1st:0 2nd:0 3rd:0 Ran:1
1999 Turf 0-1: (10f) (g-f)
Neat, currently very poor filly. **R C Spicer [0-2] Joy/L Kasparian.*

DEWI SANT BHB 25f **RR 31f** 1939[15]
5 ch g Nalchik (USA) 12.6f **(44)** - Secret Ingredient (Most Secret) 7.1f **(58)**
Form - 0
Record 1999 - 1st:0 2nd:0 3rd:0 Ran:1
Pre1999 - 1st:0 2nd:0 3rd:0 Ran:2
1999 Turf 0-1: (10f) (g-f)
Very moderate gelding. **D Burchell [0-4] Lyn Phillips.*

DE-WOLF BHB 57f41a **RR 63f 41a** 215[6]
4 gr f Petong 7.6f **(58)** - Doppio (Dublin Taxi) 6.4f **(55)**
Form - 4006
Record 1999 - 1st:0 2nd:0 3rd:0 Ran:2
Pre1999 - 1st:0 2nd:0 3rd:0 Ran:7
Win Prizemoney £0 *Total Prizemoney* £429
1999 AW 0-2: (7f 2) (Fibr 2)
Leggy, average filly, often wears blinkers. AW high 26. Inconsistent. **P J Makin [0-9] D A Poole.*

DIABLENEYEV (USA) RR 106f 1901a[4]
4 b c Nureyev (USA) 8.4f **(84)** - La Pitie (USA) (Devil's Bag (USA)) 12.4f **(78)**
Form - 314
1999 Turf 1-2: (5f, 6f 1-1) (sft 1-1, g-f)
Pattern-class colt. Turf high 106 (1st run) - 1st of 10 from Symboli Kildare (6 Apr Maisons-Laffitte RF 0712a). **Mme C Head in FR [2-5].*

DIABLO DANCER (IRE) BHB 72f **RR 76f** 3993[12]
3 b c Deploy 11.4f **(67)** - Scharade (Lombard (GER)) 10.5f **(66)**
Form - 426P8000
Record 1999 - 1st:0 2nd:1 3rd:0 Ran:8
Pre1999 - 1st:2 2nd:1 3rd:3 Ran:10
Win Prizemoney £6,424 *Total Prizemoney* £16,223
Wins * 1998 Jly Lingfi (G-F) 7f 82 <
*** 1998** Apr Nottin (G-S) 5.1f 75
1999 Turf 0-8: (10f 4, 12f 3, 13f) (g-s, gd, g-f 4, frm 2)
Strong, above-average colt, effective 7 to 10f, best at 10f, acts on gd to frm, best on frm, has worn blinkers, excels at Salisbury. Turf high 90 - 2nd of 11 giving 3lb to Senure (2 May Salisbury 10f frm RF 0985). **B R Millman [2-18] Kentisbeare Quartet.*

DIAGHILEF (IRE) BHB 89f **RR 86f** 3758[12]
7 b g Royal Academy (USA) 7.8f **(77)** - Miss Audimar (USA) (Mr Leader (USA)) 9.8f **(66)**
Form - 01010
Record 1999 - 1st:2 2nd:0 3rd:0 Ran:5
Pre1999 - 1st:2 2nd:3 3rd:1 Ran:13
Win Prizemoney £41,489 *Total Prizemoney* £50,845
Wins * 1999 Jly Leices (G-F) H 11.8f 85 86
*** 1999** May Doncas (G-F) H 12f 77 84
1995 Jun Ascot (G-F) H 12f 99 102 <
1995 May Newcas (GD) 10.1f 74
1999 Turf 2-5: (12f 2-3, 14f 2) (g-s, gd 2, g-f 1-1, frm 1-1)
Useful gelding. Turf high 86. A useful handicapper on his day, he was reported to have died of grass sickness in September. (DEAD)
**M A Buckley [2-9] C C Buckley (from M Johnston [2-9] Aug 1995).*

DIAMOND BEACH BHB 47f **RR 51f** 5168[8]
6 b g Lugana Beach 7f **(63)** - Cannon Boy (USA) (Canonero (USA)) 7.8f **(71)**
Form - 64078
Record 1999 - 1st:0 2nd:0 3rd:0 Ran:5
Pre1999 - 1st:0 2nd:3 3rd:1 Ran:12
Win Prizemoney £0 *Total Prizemoney* £5,684
1999 Turf 0-5: (9f, 10f 2, 11f, 14f) (g-s, gd, g-f, frm 2)
Fair gelding. Turf high 51 (began Aug). Consistent.
**G M Moore [1-16] J & M Leisure / Unos Restaurant (from B W Hills [0-11] Oct 1996).*

DIAMOND BLUSH BHB 43f45a **RR 15f 45a** 600[8]
3 ch f Sure Blade (USA) 10.6f **(66)** - Dawn Ditty (Song) 7.2f **(61)**
Form - 0533208
Record 1999 - 1st:0 2nd:1 3rd:2 Ran:6
Pre1999 - 1st:0 2nd:0 3rd:0 Ran:2
Win Prizemoney £0 *Total Prizemoney* £1,431
1999 AW 0-6: (6f 2, 7f 2, 8f, 9f) (Fibr 6)
Moderate filly, effective 6f, - acts on Fibr, favours tight tracks. AW high 48 - 2nd of 7 to Live To Tell (20 Feb Wolverhampton 6f Fibr RF 0330). Inconsistent.
**N P Littmoden [0-7] Unity Farm Holiday Centre Ltd (from R J Hodges [0-1] Aug 1998).*

DIAMOND CONCORDE (IRE) BHB 46f **RR 57f** 3419[11]
2 b br f Blues Traveller (IRE) - Petova (IRE) **(23f 30a)** (Petorius) 7.3f **(61)**
Form - 532350
Record 1999 - 1st:0 2nd:1 3rd:2 Ran:6
Win Prizemoney £0 *Total Prizemoney* £1,083
1999 Turf 0-3: (5f 2, 6f) (gd 2, frm) 1999 AW 0-3: (6f, 7f 2) (Fibr 3)
Fair filly, has worn blinkers. Turf high 57. AW high 50.
**P D Evans [0-6] Diamond Racing Ltd.*

DIAMOND CROWN (IRE) BHB 36f44a **RR 22f 44a** 4980[11]
8 ch g Kris 10f **(75)** - State Treasure (USA) (Secretariat (USA)) 9f **(79)**
Form - 8432014254800
Record 1999 - 1st:1 2nd:2 3rd:1 Ran:13

Pre1999 - 1st:6 2nd:6 3rd:12 Ran:66
Win Prizemoney £16,782 *Total Prizemoney* £29,065
Wins * **1999** Jly Hamilt (FRM) H 13f 39 42
* 1998 Aug Newcas (GD) S 12.4f 47
* 1998 Jly Ayr (GD) S 10.9f 47
* 1997 Jun Nottin (GD) SH 10f 42 45
* 1996 Oct Newcas (G-F) CH 8f 44 44
* 1995 Aug Beverl (G-F) S 12f 56 <
1999 Turf 1-13: (10f, 12f 2, 13f 1-3, 14f 5, 16f 2) (gd 3, g-f 5, frm 1-5)
Little account gelding, effective 10 to 16f, best at 12f, acts on gd to frm, best on g-f, has worn blinkers, and does well at Catterick and Hamilton. Turf high 45 - also 1st of 8 getting 18lb from Mystagogue (16 Jly Hamilton RF 2873). Becoming disappointing.
**Martyn Wane [7-82] J M Pickup (from P F I Cole [0-2] Jly 1993).*

DIAMOND DECORUM (IRE) BHB 68f70a **RR 61f 70a** 5217[13]
3 ch g Fayruz 6.6f **(63)** - Astra Adastra (Mount Hagen (FR)) 8.4f **(70)**
Form - 0750517247040800
Record 1999 - 1st:1 2nd:1 3rd:0 Ran:16
Pre1999 - 1st:1 2nd:0 3rd:0 Ran:7
Win Prizemoney £10,724 *Total Prizemoney* £17,734
Wins * **1999** Jun Lingfi (GD) H 6f 73 77 <
* 1998 Aug Thirsk (G-F) 5f 77 <
1999 Turf 1-14: (5f 3, 6f 1-2, 7f 7, 8f 2) (g-s 2, gd 5, g-f 3, frm 1-4) 1999 AW 0-2: (7f, 8f) (Fibr 2)
Leggy, average gelding, effective 5 to 7f, best at 7f, acts on g-f to frm, best on g-f, likes tight tracks. Turf high 86 - 2nd of 16 giving 1lb to Petrus (30 Jly Goodwood 7f g-f RF 3233) - also 1st of 11 giving 11lb to Just Wiz (22 Jun Lingfield RF 2198). AW high 61.
**P D Evans [2-23] Diamond Racing Ltd.*

DIAMOND DIANA RR 48f 2002[10]
3 ch f Selkirk (USA) 7.9f **(76)** - Lady Vivienne (Golden Fleece (USA)) 7.9f **(74)**
Form - 40
Record 1999 - 1st:0 2nd:0 3rd:0 Ran:2
1999 Turf 0-2: (7f, 10f) (g-s, frm)
Unfurnished, currently moderate filly. Turf high 48.
**J L Eyre [0-2] Diamond Racing Ltd.*

DIAMOND FLAME BHB 59f78a **RR 59f 78a** 5069[12]
5 b g Suave Dancer (USA) 10.7f **(68)** - Eternal Flame (Primo Dominie) 6.2f **(80)**
Form - 88584057884720
Record 1999 - 1st:0 2nd:1 3rd:0 Ran:13
Pre1999 - 1st:2 2nd:0 3rd:1 Ran:11
Win Prizemoney £6,775 *Total Prizemoney* £8,749
Wins * 1998 *Mar Wolver (STD) 9.4f* 87 <
* 1998 *Feb Lingfi (SLW) 10f* 83+
1999 Turf 0-10: (10f 8, 11f, 12f) (sft, g-s, gd 2, g-f 3, frm 3) 1999 AW 0-3: (9f 2, 12f) (Fibr 3)
Above-average gelding, effective 9 to 10f, best at 10f, acts on g-s - acts on AW, likes left handed tracks, likes tight tracks. Turf high 69. AW high 75. **P W Harris [2-24] The Seven Diamonds.*

DIAMOND GEEZER (IRE) BHB 63f57a **RR 62f 57a** 5199[7]
3 br c Tenby 10.4f **(76)** - Unaria (Prince Tenderfoot (USA)) 9f **(61)**
Form - 0705125842301150257
Record 1999 - 1st:3 2nd:3 3rd:1 Ran:17
Pre1999 - 1st:1 2nd:0 3rd:0 Ran:10
Win Prizemoney £10,808 *Total Prizemoney* £14,099
Wins * **1999** Jly Windso (G-F) H 6f 64 65 <
* **1999** Jly Windso (GD) H 6f 61 62
* **1999** *Jan Lingfi (STD) H 6f 48 57*
* 1998 Spt Sandow (G-S) C 5f 62
1999 Turf 2-11: (6f 2-10, 7f) (gd 3, g-f 2, frm 2-5, hrd) 1999 AW 1-6: (6f 1-3, 7f 3) (Equi 1-6)
Workmanlike, average colt, effective 7f, acts on frm, has worn blinkers, likes right handed tracks. Turf high 65. AW high 57. He was very busy last season, winning on the Lingfield Equitrack in January and adding a couple of handicaps at Windsor in July.
**R Hannon [4-27] J B R Leisure Ltd.*

DIAMOND GEORGIA (IRE) RR 53f 1954[6]
2 ch f Soviet Lad (USA) 9.4f **(63)** - Secret Assignment (Vitiges (FR)) 8.2f **(59)**
Form - 66
Record 1999 - 1st:0 2nd:0 3rd:0 Ran:2
1999 Turf 0-2: (5f, 7f) (gd, g-f)
Currently fair filly. Turf high 53.
**John Berry [0-2] Diamond Racing Ltd.*

DIAMOND ISLE BHB 45f42a **RR 51f 42a** 4929[8]
2 b f Clantime 6.6f **(57)** - Five Islands (Bairn (USA)) 7.7f **(59)**
Form - 5002863008
Record 1999 - 1st:0 2nd:1 3rd:1 Ran:10
Win Prizemoney £0 *Total Prizemoney* £1,032
1999 Turf 0-10: (5f 7, 6f 3) (gd 2, g-f 4, frm 4)
Fair filly, effective 5f, acts on g-f. Turf high 51.
**M Brittain [0-10] Brian Gaynor.*

DIAMOND KISS (IRE) RR 25f 1298[8]
2 b f Perugino (USA) - Kunuz (Ela-Mana-Mou) 10.1f **(70)**
Form - 8
Record 1999 - 1st:0 2nd:0 3rd:0 Ran:1
1999 Turf 0-1: (6f) (gd)
Currently little account filly. **Mrs P N Dutfield [0-1] Harry Dutfield.*

DIAMOND LAD (IRE) BHB 54f **RR 41df** 4726[15]
3 b c Namaqualand (USA) - Eight Mile Rock (Dominion) 8.5f **(63)**
Form - 2316770
Record 1999 - 1st:1 2nd:1 3rd:1 Ran:7
Pre1999 - 1st:0 2nd:0 3rd:0 Ran:5
Win Prizemoney £2,304 *Total Prizemoney* £3,286
Wins * **1999** May Ayr (GD) 13.1f 61 <
1999 Turf 1-7: (12f 2, 13f 1-1, 14f 2, 15f, 16f) (g-s, gd 1-4, g-f, frm)
Scopey, moderate colt, effective 12 to 13f, acts on gd, often wears blinkers, likes left handed tracks, likes tight tracks. Turf high 61 - 1st of 8 getting 20lb from Linea-G (21 May Ayr RF 1365). Inconsistent. **W T Kemp [1-12] Mrs M Irwin.*

DIAMOND LILLY (IRE) BHB 54f50a **RR 58f 50a** 5192[6]
2 b f Namaqualand (USA) - Mousseux (IRE) (Jareer (USA)) 5.9f **(75)**
Form - 8637765606
Record 1999 - 1st:0 2nd:0 3rd:1 Ran:10
Win Prizemoney £0 *Total Prizemoney* £318
1999 Turf 0-8: (6f, 7f 5, 8f 2) (gd 2, g-f 2, frm 4) 1999 AW 0-2: (8f 2) (Fibr 2)
Fair filly, effective 7f, acts on frm, has worn blinkers. Turf high 70 - 3rd of 18 getting 5lb from Anbari (8 Jly Lingfield 7f frm RF 2635). AW high 23 (began Spt).
**J G Portman [0-10] Out To Grass Partnership.*

DIAMOND LOOK (USA) RR 75f 1882[2]
2 b c Dayjur (USA) 6.8f **(79)** - Pedestal (High Line) 10.3f **(70)**
Form - 2
Record 1999 - 1st:0 2nd:1 3rd:0 Ran:1
Win Prizemoney £0 *Total Prizemoney* £1,368
1999 Turf 0-1: (6f) (gd)
Currently above-average colt. (1st run) - 2nd of 14 to With Iris (10 Jun Newbury 6f gd RF 1882). Comes from an excellent family, and looks sure to win races judged on his Newbury debut.
**E A L Dunlop [0-1] Jaber Abdullah.*

DIAMOND OLIVIA BHB 53a **RR 29f 53a** 4705[12]
2 b f Beveled (USA) 6.9f **(64)** - Queen of the Quorn **(51df 45a)** (Governor General)
Form - 3640
Record 1999 - 1st:0 2nd:0 3rd:1 Ran:4
Win Prizemoney £0 *Total Prizemoney* £310
1999 Turf 0-1: (5f) (frm) 1999 AW 0-3: (5f 3) (Fibr 3)
Very moderate filly. AW high 57 (1st run) - 3rd of 11 getting 7lb from Richard Ansdell (29 Apr Wolverhampton 5f Fibr RF 0922).
**W G M Turner [0-4] Diamond Racing Ltd.*

DIAMOND PROMISE (IRE) BHB 62f63a **RR 69f 63a** 4707[3]
2 b f Fayruz 6.6f **(63)** - Cupid Miss (Anita's Prince)
Form - 2512120682123
Record 1999 - 1st:3 2nd:5 3rd:1 Ran:13
Win Prizemoney £6,806 *Total Prizemoney* £11,321
Wins * **1999** Spt Lingfi (HVY) C 6f 69 <
* **1999** May Leices (GD) C 5f 69 <
* **1999** Apr Thirsk (GD) C 5f 69+
1999 Turf 3-12: (5f 2-10, 6f 1-2) (g-s 1-2, gd 1-6, g-f 1-2, frm 2) 1999 AW 0-1: (6f) (Fibr)

Above-average filly, effective 5 to 6f, best at 5f, acts on g-s to g-f, likes Lingfield and Thirsk. Turf high 71 - 2nd of 7 getting 2lb from Pegasus Star (19 Jun Ayr 5f gd RF 2140) - also 1st of 6 from Chorus (31 May Leicester RF 1602). Inconsistent. Nippy sort, effective in claimers. **P D Evans [3-13] Diamond Racing Ltd.*

DIAMOND RACHAEL (IRE) RR 43f 4815[18]

2 b f Shalford (IRE) 7.8f **(63)** - Brown Foam (Horage) 10.3f **(61)**
Form - 0
Record 1999 - 1st:0 2nd:0 3rd:0 Ran:1
1999 Turf 0-1: (7f) (gd)
Currently moderate filly. **Mrs N Macauley [0-1] Diamond Racing Ltd.*

DIAMOND ROAD (IRE) RR 45f 4419[17]

2 b c Dolphin Street (FR) - Tiffany's Case (IRE) **(58f)** (Thatching) 8f **(66)**
Form - 0
Record 1999 - 1st:0 2nd:0 3rd:0 Ran:1
1999 Turf 0-1: (7f) (gd)
Currently moderate colt. **C A Horgan [0-1] John Kelsey-Fry.*

DIAMOND ROUGE BHB 53f46a RR 52f 46a 307[6]

3 b f Puissance 7.1f **(60)** - Maravilla (Mandrake Major) 7.6f **(53)**
Form - 66
Record 1999 - 1st:0 2nd:0 3rd:0 Ran:2
Pre1999 - 1st:0 2nd:0 3rd:1 Ran:3
Win Prizemoney £0 *Total Prizemoney* £415
1999 AW 0-2: (6f 2) (Fibr 2)
Light-framed, fair filly. AW high 29.
**A Bailey [0-5] Diamond Racing Ltd.*

DIAMOND STEALTH BHB 47f RR 42f 2054[16]

3 b f Ardkinglass 5f **(64)** - Alumia (Great Nephew) 9.9f **(64)**
Form - 7080
Record 1999 - 1st:0 2nd:0 3rd:0 Ran:4
Pre1999 - 1st:0 2nd:0 3rd:0 Ran:1
1999 Turf 0-3: (6f, 8f, 10f) (gd 2, g-f) 1999 AW 0-1: (6f) (Fibr)
Scopey, moderate filly. Turf high 42.
**J L Eyre [0-5] Diamond Racing Ltd.*

DIAMOND VANESSA (IRE) RR 49f 5157[12]

2 b f Distinctly North (USA) 7.4f **(63)** - Elegant Act (USA) (Shecky Greene (USA)) 8f **(50)**
Form - 0
Record 1999 - 1st:0 2nd:0 3rd:0 Ran:1
1999 Turf 0-1: (7f) (frm)
Currently moderate filly. **J Hetherton [0-1] Diamond Racing Ltd.*

DIAMOND WHITE BHB 112f100a RR 113f 100a 4871[11]

4 b f Robellino (USA) 9.5f **(68)** - Diamond Wedding (USA) (Diamond Shoal) 9.1f **(66)**
Form - 6256047703235043328232110
Record 1999 - 1st:2 2nd:4 3rd:5 Ran:23
Pre1999 - 1st:4 2nd:2 3rd:5 Ran:26
Win Prizemoney £89,082 *Total Prizemoney* £163,722

Wins								
* **1999**	Oct	Longch	(HVY)	G2	9.3f		113	<
* **1999**	Spt	Goodwo	(HVY)	L	9.9f		108+	
1998	Nov	Doncas	(SFT)		10.3f		91	
1998	Spt	Nottin	(G-F)		10f		90	
1998	Jun	Folkes	(G-F)	H	7f	85	95+	
1997	Aug	Newmar	(G-F)	L	7f		85	

1999 Turf 2-20: (8f, 9f 1-4, 10f 1-13, 12f 2) (sft 2-2, g-s 2, gd 6, g-f 5, frm 5) 1999 AW 0-3: (7f, 9f, 10f) (Equi, Fibr 2)
Neat, Group-class filly, effective 9 to 10f, best at 10f, acts on sft to frm, best on sft, has worn blinkers, likes right handed tracks, likes tight tracks, excels at Goodwood. Turf high 113 - 1st of 11 from Miss Berbere (3 Oct Longchamp RF 4780a) - also 1st of 8 getting 8lb from Prolix (22 Spt Goodwood RF 4492). AW high 89. A model of consistency in an extremely busy campaign, she produced the best form of her life given bottomless ground late in the season, winning a listed race at Goodwood before taking the Group Two Prix de l'Opera at the Arc meeting. Tough and game, she is a credit to her connections' attacking policy.
**M J Ryan [2-22] Peter Scott (from P W D'Arcy [0-1] Mar 1999).*

DIBOLA BHB 28f28a RR 23f 28a 223[7]

4 ch g Dilum (USA) 7.1f **(56)** - Bella Bambola (IRE) **(7f)** (Tate Gallery (USA)) 7.4f **(67)**
Form - 067
Record 1999 - 1st:0 2nd:0 3rd:0 Ran:3
Pre1999 - 1st:0 2nd:0 3rd:0 Ran:9
1999 AW 0-3: (7f, 8f, 10f) (Equi 2, Fibr)
Neat, moderate gelding, has worn blinkers. AW high 43.
**J S Wainwright [0-12] S Pedersen.*

DICK TURPIN (USA) BHB 57f75a RR 52f 75a 3916[8]

5 br g Red Ransom (USA) 8.6f **(83)** - Turn To Money (USA) (Turn To Mars (USA)) 10f **(83)**
Form - 84113355003608
Record 1999 - 1st:2 2nd:0 3rd:3 Ran:13
Pre1999 - 1st:1 2nd:1 3rd:2 Ran:10
Win Prizemoney £9,265 *Total Prizemoney* £13,217

Wins								
* **1999**	*Feb*	*Southw*	*(STD)*	*H*	*11f*	*70*	*75*	<
* **1999**	*Jan*	*Southw*	*(STD)*	*H*	*11f*	*65*	*70*	
* 1998	*Jan*	*Lingfi*	*(STD)*		*10f*		*65*	

1999 Turf 0-8: (10f 3, 12f 4, 13f) (g-s, gd 3, g-f, frm 2, hrd) 1999 AW 2-5: (11f 2-4, 12f) (Equi, Fibr 2-4)
Above-average gelding, has broken blood-vessels, effective 11f, - acts on Fibr, prefers left handed tracks, favours tight tracks. Turf high 78. AW high 75 - 3rd of 12 giving 17lb to Green Bopper (15 Feb Southwell 11f Fibr RF 0293) - also 1st of 15 giving 5lb to Copper Shell (8 Feb Southwell RF 0252). He has become a decent middle-distance performer on Fibresand, and can win more races under those conditions.
**B Smart [3-19] The Dyball Partnership (from Lord Huntingdon [0-5] Oct 1997).*

DIDIFON BHB 83f RR 85f 4710[5]

4 b c Zafonic (USA) 9f **(83)** - Didicoy (USA) (Danzig (USA)) 8.4f **(76)**
Form - 73145
Record 1999 - 1st:1 2nd:0 3rd:1 Ran:5
Pre1999 - 1st:0 2nd:1 3rd:1 Ran:4
Win Prizemoney £3,793 *Total Prizemoney* £6,989
Wins * **1999** Aug Ripon (GD) 10f 85 <
1999 Turf 1-5: (9f, 10f 1-3, 11f) (gd 2, g-f 1-3)
Strong, useful colt, effective 10 to 11f, best at 10f, acts on gd to frm, best on g-f, likes tight tracks. Turf high 85 (began Jly) - 1st of 15 giving 13lb to Ring The Relatives (21 Aug Ripon RF 3822). Consistent. Out of a half-sister to Xaar, he lost his maiden tag when winning a ten-furlong Ripon maiden in good style, galloping his rivals into the ground. He has moved to Noel Meade.
**B W Hills [1-5] K Abdulla (from H R A Cecil [0-4] Jly 1998).*

DIFESA INDIANA (IRE) RR 102f 4661a[5]

5 b m High Estate 10.5f **(66)** - Kunuz (Ela-Mana-Mou) 10.1f **(70)**
Form - 15
1999 Turf 1-2: (8f 1-1, 10f) (gd, g-f 1-1)
Currently very useful filly. Turf high 102 (began Jly). She did not seem to get home behind Zomaradah in a Group 3 in Rome and may be best over a mile.
**M Gasparini in ITY [0-1] (from A Borroni in ITY [1-1] Jly 1999).*

DIFFERENTIAL (USA) BHB 100f RR 87f 4268[12]

2 b br c Known Fact (USA) 8.3f **(72)** - Talk About Home (USA) (Elocutionist (USA)) 8f **(77)**
Form - 1340
Record 1999 - 1st:1 2nd:0 3rd:1 Ran:4
Win Prizemoney £3,647 *Total Prizemoney* £5,958
Wins * **1999** Jly Windso (G-F) 5f 82+ <
1999 Turf 1-4: (5f 1-3, 6f) (gd, g-f 1-2, frm)
Useful colt. Turf high 87 - also 1st of 14 from Melon Place (26 Jly Windsor RF 3149). After making a successful debut at Windsor, he ran well next time and seemed to stay the extra furlong at Ripon on his third start. **B Smart [1-4] Peter Nelson And Partners.*

DIG FOR GOLD BHB 23f RR 27?f 2154[11]

6 ch g Digamist (USA) 8.8f **(56)** - Formidable Task (Formidable (USA)) 9.2f **(63)**
Form - 000
Record 1999 - 1st:0 2nd:0 3rd:0 Ran:3
Pre1999 - 1st:0 2nd:0 3rd:0 Ran:1
1999 Turf 0-3: (8f, 12f, 14f) (gd, frm 2)
Little account gelding. Turf high 27.
**R D E Woodhouse [1-9] R D E Woodhouse (from Miss S E Hall [0-6] Spt 1997).*

DIGITAL IMAGE BHB 90f **RR 92+f** 2901[16]
2 b c Presidium 7.5f **(56)** - Sally Tadpole (Jester)
Form - 1060

Record	**1999** -	1st:1	2nd:0	3rd:0	Ran:4

Win Prizemoney £7,422 *Total Prizemoney* £7,602

Wins	* **1999**	May Cheste	(G-F)	5.1f	92+	<

1999 Turf 1-4: (5f 1-2, 6f 2) (g-f 1-3, frm)
Useful colt. Turf high 92 (1st run) - 1st of 9 from Coco de Mer (4 May Chester RF 1025). Made a winning debut at Chester, though the form does not look anything special, and he was well and truly found out in both the Coventry and July Stakes.
**R Hannon [1-4] Kellco Ltd.*

DIGITAL OPTION (IRE) BHB 29f **RR 32df** 421[8]
5 b g Alzao (USA) 9.8f **(73)** - Elevated (Shirley Heights) 10.3f **(74)**
Form - 08

Record	**1999** -	1st:0	2nd:0	3rd:0	Ran:2
	Pre1999 -	1st:0	2nd:1	3rd:0	Ran:9

Win Prizemoney £0 *Total Prizemoney* £714
1999 AW 0-2: (12f, 16f) (Fibr 2)
Very moderate gelding, has worn blinkers. Inconsistent.
**Mrs N Macauley [0-2] Inthebing Ltd (from J L Spearing [0-1] Oct 1997).*

DIGNIFY (IRE) RR 89f 4776a[7]
2 b f Rainbow Quest (USA) 11.2f **(81)** - Her Ladyship **(115df)** (Polish Precedent (USA)) 10.2f **(60)**
Form - 1317
1999 Turf 2-4: (7f 1-2, 8f 1-2) (sft, gd 2-2, g-f)
Useful filly. Turf high 89 (began Jly) - also 1st of 7 from Well Minded (13 Spt Chantilly RF 4509a). A half-sister to Lord of Men, she won twice, including a Group Three, but was found wanting against the better fillies in the Cherry Hinton and the Prix Marcel Boussac. **D R Loder in FR [2-4] Godolphin.*

DIGON DA BHB 70f **RR 79df** 4583[12]
3 ch g Sparky Lad - Fleur Power (IRE) (The Noble Player (USA)) 6.5f **(67)**
Form - 037400

Record	**1999** -	1st:0	2nd:0	3rd:1	Ran:6

Win Prizemoney £0 *Total Prizemoney* £933
1999 Turf 0-6: (8f 4, 10f 2) (gd 2, frm 4)
Workmanlike, above-average gelding, effective 8f, acts on gd to frm. Turf high 79 (began Jly) - 4th of 17 giving 5lb to Lady Georgia (30 Aug Warwick 8f gd RF 4038).
**B Palling [0-6] Davies and Bridgeman.*

DIHATJUM BHB 63f **RR 71f** 5158[6]
2 b g Mujtahid (USA) 7.4f **(69)** - Rosie Potts (Shareef Dancer (USA)) 9.9f **(73)**
Form - 083385026

Record	**1999** -	1st:0	2nd:1	3rd:2	Ran:9

Win Prizemoney £0 *Total Prizemoney* £1,740
1999 Turf 0-9: (5f, 6f 4, 7f 3, 8f) (g-f, frm 7, hrd)
Above-average gelding, effective 6 to 7f, best at 7f, acts on frm to hrd, best on frm, has worn blinkers. Turf high 71 - 3rd of 17 giving 2lb to Rhodamine (12 Jly Newcastle 6f frm RF 2754). Inconsistent.
**T D Easterby [0-9] The Gordon Partnership.*

DIKTAT BHB 121f **RR 123f** 5014a[5]
4 br c Warning 8.1f **(77)** - Arvola (Sadler's Wells (USA)) 10f **(76)**
Form - 11115

Record	**1999** -	1st:4	2nd:0	3rd:0	Ran:5
	Pre1999 -	1st:3	2nd:1	3rd:0	Ran:5

Win Prizemoney £249,654 *Total Prizemoney* £256,500

Wins							
	* **1999**	Spt Haydoc	(G-F)	G1	6f	120	
	* **1999**	Aug Deauvi	(HVY)	G1	6.5f	123	<
	* **1999**	Jun Newmar	(G-F)	G3	7f	118	
	* **1999**	May Goodwo	(GD)		7f	121+	
	1998	Jun Ascot	(GD)	G3	7f	114	
	1998	May Leices	(GD)		7f	115+	
	1998	Apr Newmar	(SFT)		7f	90+	

1999 Turf 4-5: (6f 1-1, 7f 3-4) (hvy 1-1, gd 1-1, g-f 1-1, frm 1-1)
Scopey, very high-class colt, effective 6 to 7f, best at 7f, acts on frm. Turf high 123 - 1st of 10 from Gold Away (8 Aug Deauville RF 3589a) - also 1st of 10 from Russian Revival (8 May Goodwood RF 1107). Consistent. Developed into a very smart colt in 1998 and, after two impressive victories, was successfully stepped up in class to land the Jersey Stakes at Royal Ascot. He was then just beaten by the battle-hardened Decorated Hero in the Beeswing at Newcastle, but was not seen out again that season. Returned in 1999 to beat a subsequent Group winner in fine style at the Shergar Cup meeting, and followed up in a Newmarket Group Three before landing the Group One Prix Maurice de Gheest. Dropped back to six furlongs, he won the Haydock Park Sprint Cup in style, and ran pretty well from a bad draw in the Prix de la Foret. Arguably the best seven-furlong horse in Europe, he is reportedly heading for Hong Kong in December.
**S bin Suroor [4-5] (from D R Loder [3-5] Jly 1998).*

Diktat (near side) developed into a top-class performer at six and seven furlongs

DIL BHB 63f95a **RR 58f 95a** 4483[8]
4 b g Primo Dominie 7.2f **(67)** - Swellegant (Midyan (USA)) 6f **(60)**
Form - 18010708008
Record 1999 - 1st:2 2nd:0 3rd:0 Ran:11
Pre1999 - 1st:3 2nd:1 3rd:1 Ran:15
Win Prizemoney £22,120 *Total Prizemoney* £24,796
Wins *** 1999** *Apr Wolver (STD) H 5f 90 95 <*
*** 1999** *Mar Southw (SLW) H 5f 83 85*
* 1998 Spt Leices (G-F) H 5f 78 82
* 1998 Jly Doncas (G-F) H 6f 73 76
1998 May Doncas (GD) 5f 74
1999 Turf 0-9: (5f 7, 6f 2) (g-s, gd 4, g-f 2, frm 2) 1999 AW 2-2: (5f 2-2) (Fibr 2-2)
Very useful gelding, effective 5f, - acts on Fibr, has worn blinkers. Turf high 84. AW high 95 - 1st of 13 giving 29lb to Consultant (29 Apr Wolverhampton RF 0926). Effective over five and six furlongs, his turf form tailed-off during the summer. He may prefer All-Weather surfaces nowadays.
**Mrs N Macauley [4-17] Mrs N Macauley (from B Hanbury [1-9] Jun 1998).*

DILETIA RR 77f 4176[7]
2 b f Dilum (USA) 7.1f **(56)** - Miss Laetitia (IRE) **(36f)** (Entitled)
Form - 67
Record 1999 - 1st:0 2nd:0 3rd:0 Ran:2
1999 Turf 0-2: (7f 2) (gd, frm)
Currently above-average filly. Turf high 77 (began Aug).
**N A Graham [0-2] T H Chadney.*

DILETTO (IRE) BHB 47f60a **RR 50f 60a** 4807[6]
3 b f Mujadil (USA) 7.7f **(70)** - Avidal Park (Horage) 10.3f **(61)**
Form - 7300537675360376
Record 1999 - 1st:0 2nd:0 3rd:4 Ran:16
Pre1999 - 1st:0 2nd:2 3rd:2 Ran:12
Win Prizemoney £0 *Total Prizemoney* £5,906
1999 Turf 0-15: (7f 4, 8f 6, 9f, 10f 2, 11f 2) (sft, g-s 2, gd, g-f 5, frm 6) 1999 AW 0-1: (6f) (Fibr)
Lengthy, average filly, effective 5 to 8f, best at 5f, acts on gd to frm, has worn blinkers. Turf high 68 (1st run) - 3rd of 14 giving 4lb to Fallachan (1 Apr Musselburgh 8f g-f RF 0553). Inconsistent.
**E J Alston [0-28] Liam & Tony Ferguson.*

DILIGENCE (IRE) BHB 80f **RR 75?f** 4699[9]
4 b g Dilum (USA) 7.1f **(56)** - Florinda (CAN) (Vice Regent (CAN)) 8.7f **(74)**
Form - 00
Record 1999 - 1st:0 2nd:0 3rd:0 Ran:2
Pre1999 - 1st:1 2nd:1 3rd:0 Ran:4
Win Prizemoney £4,889 *Total Prizemoney* £9,259
Wins 1997 May Goodwo (G-S) 5f 82 <
1999 Turf 0-2: (5f, 6f) (sft, g-f)
Strong, above-average gelding. Turf high 40 (began Spt).
**G B Balding [0-2] Miss Lindsay Bower (from P F I Cole [1-4] Spt 1998).*

DILKUSHA (IRE) BHB 77f75a **RR 76f 75a** 4333[6]
4 b g Indian Ridge 7.6f **(74)** - Crimson Glen (Glenstal (USA)) 10.1f **(64)**
Form - 18150376
Record 1999 - 1st:2 2nd:0 3rd:1 Ran:8
Pre1999 - 1st:1 2nd:1 3rd:1 Ran:14
Win Prizemoney £11,337 *Total Prizemoney* £14,777
Wins *** 1999** Jly Newbur (G-F) H 7f 75 76 <
*** 1999** Jun Kempto (G-F) H 7f 73 75
* 1998 Aug Bright (FRM) H 7f 67 72
1999 Turf 2-8: (7f 2-6, 8f 2) (gd 2, g-f, frm 2-5)
Leggy, above-average gelding, effective 7f, acts on g-f to frm, best on frm, has worn blinkers. Turf high 78 - also 1st of 11 giving 9lb to Compradore (16 Jly Newbury RF 2880). Consistent. A winner at Brighton last term, he showed battling qualities to win at Kempton on his reappearance despite suffering interference and added a Newbury handicap in July. Seven furlongs and fast ground appear to suit him well. **B J Meehan [3-22] Trevor Painting.*

DILLUS BHB 35f **RR 30f** 2807[6]
3 b f Dilum (USA) 7.1f **(56)** - Lismore (Relkino) 8.9f **(65)**
Form - 00066
Record 1999 - 1st:0 2nd:0 3rd:0 Ran:5
Pre1999 - 1st:0 2nd:2 3rd:0 Ran:8
Win Prizemoney £0 *Total Prizemoney* £1,549
1999 Turf 0-5: (6f 2, 7f, 8f 2) (gd, g-f 2, frm 2)
Leggy, very moderate filly, effective 5 to 6f, acts on gd, has worn blinkers. Turf high 38. Consistent. **B S Rothwell [0-13] S P Hudson.*

DILSAA BHB 80f **RR 78f** 4909[5]
2 ch c Night Shift (USA) 8.1f **(73)** - Llia **(86f)** (Shirley Heights) 10.3f **(74)**
Form - 5525
Record 1999 - 1st:0 2nd:1 3rd:0 Ran:4
Win Prizemoney £0 *Total Prizemoney* £1,160
1999 Turf 0-4: (7f 4) (g-s, gd, frm 2)
Above-average colt. Turf high 78 (began Aug).
**P W Harris [0-4] G Knight & D Patel.*

DIMINUTIVE (USA) BHB 69f62a **RR 71f 62a** 5057[6]
6 b g Diesis 9f **(80)** - Graceful Darby (USA) (Darby Creek Road (USA)) 9.5f **(77)**
Form - 308331806
Record 1999 - 1st:1 2nd:0 3rd:3 Ran:9
Pre1999 - 1st:4 2nd:2 3rd:4 Ran:26
Win Prizemoney £21,215 *Total Prizemoney* £29,943
Wins *** 1999** Aug Leices (G-F) 11.8f 71
* 1998 Jly Bath (GD) H 10.2f 71 75
* 1996 Aug Yarmou (G-F) 10.1f 85 <
* 1996 Jly Bath (FRM) 10.2f 75
* 1996 Jun Thirsk (FRM) 8f 66
1999 Turf 1-8: (9f, 10f 4, 12f 1-3) (gd 2, g-f 3, frm 1-2, hrd) 1999 AW 0-1: (12f) (Equi)
Above-average gelding, effective 10 to 12f, best at 10f, acts on gd to frm, best on frm, prefers tight tracks, excels at Leicester. Turf high 71 - 1st of 11 giving 3lb to Totem Dancer (22 Aug Leicester RF 3840). He managed to win a Bath handicap in '98, but endured a long losing run afterwards until regaining winning form at Leicester in August on his first attempt at a mile and a half.
**J W Hills [5-35] Gainsbury Partnership.*

DIMMING OF THE DAY BHB 54f60a **RR 56f 60a** 4705[2]
2 ch f Muhtarram (USA) - Darkness At Noon (USA) (Night Shift (USA)) 7.2f **(69)**
Form - 78322742
Record 1999 - 1st:0 2nd:3 3rd:1 Ran:8
Win Prizemoney £0 *Total Prizemoney* £1,965
1999 Turf 0-6: (5f 6) (g-f 2, frm 3, hrd) 1999 AW 0-2: (5f 2) (Fibr 2)
Average filly, effective 5f, - acts on Fibr, mostly wears blinkers (effectively). Turf high 56 (began Jly). AW high 68 - 2nd of 13 to Pips Star (2 Oct Wolverhampton 5f Fibr RF 4705).
**B J Meehan [0-8] Geoff Howard-Spink & Lindy Regis.*

DIM OFAN BHB 62f **RR 68f** 5146[4]
3 b f Petong 7.6f **(58)** - Wilsonic (Damister (USA)) 9f **(73)**
Form - 30078774
Record 1999 - 1st:0 2nd:0 3rd:1 Ran:8
Pre1999 - 1st:2 2nd:2 3rd:0 Ran:8
Win Prizemoney £6,151 *Total Prizemoney* £9,084
Wins * 1998 Oct Nottin (SFT) 6.1f 84? <
* 1998 Jly Chepst (GD) 6.1f 69
1999 Turf 0-7: (6f 4, 7f, 8f, 10f) (g-s, gd 3, g-f 2, frm) 1999 AW 0-1: (7f) (Fibr)
Average filly, effective 6f, acts on sft. Turf high 71.
**B Palling [2-16] Mrs D J Hughes.*

DIM OTS BHB 83f77a **RR 91f 77a** 369[9]
4 b f Alhijaz 7.7f **(57)** - Placid Pet (Mummy's Pet) 7.7f **(60)**
Form - 00
Record 1999 - 1st:0 2nd:0 3rd:0 Ran:2
Pre1999 - 1st:3 2nd:3 3rd:1 Ran:14
Win Prizemoney £11,463 *Total Prizemoney* £15,220
Wins * 1998 Apr Kempto (HVY) H 6f 80 91 <
* 1997 May Bath (G-S) 5.1f 72
* 1997 Apr Nottin (G-F) 5.1f 72
1999 AW 0-2: (7f 2) (Fibr 2)
Light-framed, useful filly, effective 6f, acts on hvy to g-f, best on g-f, has worn blinkers. **B Palling [3-16] Mrs D J Hughes.*

DINAR (USA) BHB 41f **RR 42f** 5154[7]
4 b c Dixieland Band (USA) 10.1f **(80)** - Bold Jessie (Never so Bold) 6.3f **(66)**

Form - 0003041207
Record 1999 - 1st:1 2nd:1 3rd:1 Ran:10
Win Prizemoney £3,139 *Total Prizemoney* £4,264
Wins * 1999 Spt Kempto (G-F) H 12f 36 42 <
1999 Turf 1-10: (5f, 7f 2, 10f 2, 12f 1-4, 17f) (g-s, gd 2, g-f 2, frm 1-5)
Moderate colt, likes tight tracks. Turf high 53. Improved form in the autumn, winning at Kempton and running well next time.
**P Bowen [1-10] J Rees.*

DING DONG BHB 30f23a **RR 10f 23a** 850[9]

3 b f Librate 10.4f **(37)** - Dawn Bell (Belfort (FR)) 6.8f **(63)**
Form - 000
Record 1999 - 1st:0 2nd:0 3rd:0 Ran:3
Pre1999 - 1st:0 2nd:0 3rd:0 Ran:2
1999 Turf 0-1: (6f) (gd) 1999 AW 0-2: (5f 2) (Fibr 2)
Light-framed, poor filly. **J M Bradley [0-5] J M Bradley.*

DINKY BHB 30f **RR 5f** 5123[11]

2 ch f Floose 16f **(5)** - Marinsky (USA) (Diesis) 9.3f **(69)**
Form - 000
Record 1999 - 1st:0 2nd:0 3rd:0 Ran:3
1999 Turf 0-3: (6f 2, 8f) (g-s, gd 2)
Currently very poor filly. Turf high 5 (began Oct).
**M J Ryan [0-3] M J Ryan.*

DINKY-WINKY BHB 39f **RR 49f** 5187[15]

2 gr f Petong 7.6f **(58)** - Just Julia (Natroun (FR))
Form - 56000
Record 1999 - 1st:0 2nd:0 3rd:0 Ran:5
1999 Turf 0-5: (5f 4, 6f) (gd 3, g-f, frm)
Moderate filly, has worn blinkers. Turf high 49 (began Aug).
**Miss L A Perratt [0-5] T P Finch.*

DINO'S GIRL BHB 42f **RR 30f** 4929[11]

2 ch f Sabrehill (USA) 8.5f **(64)** - Nashya (Rousillon (USA)) 8.2f **(74)**
Form - 580
Record 1999 - 1st:0 2nd:0 3rd:0 Ran:3
1999 Turf 0-3: (6f 2, 7f) (gd 2, g-f)
Currently very moderate filly. Turf high 40 (began Jly).
**W T Kemp [0-3] G Coburn.*

DION DEE BHB 64f **RR 55f** 1325[12]

3 ch f Anshan 8.2f **(63)** - Jade Mistress (Damister (USA)) 9f **(73)**
Form - 0
Record 1999 - 1st:0 2nd:0 3rd:0 Ran:1
Pre1999 - 1st:0 2nd:0 3rd:1 Ran:3
Win Prizemoney £0 *Total Prizemoney* £540
1999 Turf 0-1: (10f) (gd)
Leggy, fair filly. **A P Jarvis [0-4] Mrs Ann Jarvis.*

DIPLOMAT BHB 80f **RR 83f** 5143[6]

3 b g Deploy 11.4f **(67)** - Affair of State (IRE) (Tate Gallery (USA)) 7.4f **(67)**
Form - 17420346
Record 1999 - 1st:1 2nd:1 3rd:1 Ran:8
Pre1999 - 1st:0 2nd:2 3rd:0 Ran:4
Win Prizemoney £2,219 *Total Prizemoney* £11,241
Wins * 1999 Mar Folkes (SFT) 6f 80 <
1999 Turf 1-8: (6f 1-2, 7f 2, 8f 4) (sft 1-1, g-s, gd 2, g-f, frm 2, hrd)
Scopey, decent gelding, effective 6 to 8f, best at 8f, acts on sft to hrd, likes tight tracks, excels at Folkestone and Sandown. Turf high 84 - 2nd of 9 giving 16lb to Pentagon Lad (17 Jun Ripon 8f hrd RF 2078) - also 1st of 5 from Elmhurst Boy (31 Mar Folkestone RF 0533). Consistent. Got off the mark on his reappearance at Folkestone when encountering soft ground for the first time. He does act on fast ground too.
**D W P Arbuthnot [1-8] Stephen Crown (from M R Channon [0-4] Spt 1998).*

DIRECT DEAL BHB 79f **RR 80f** 3549[3]

3 b c Rainbow Quest (USA) 11.2f **(81)** - Al Najah (USA) (Topsider (USA)) 8.3f **(71)**
Form - 000413
Record 1999 - 1st:1 2nd:0 3rd:1 Ran:6
Pre1999 - 1st:0 2nd:0 3rd:1 Ran:1
Win Prizemoney £4,091 *Total Prizemoney* £5,784
Wins * 1999 Jly Bath (G-F) 10.2f 72+ <
1999 Turf 1-6: (9f, 10f 1-4, 11f) (g-f 4, frm, hrd 1-1)
Scopey, decent colt, effective 7f, acts on gd. Turf high 80. A winner on his penultimate start of a fast-ground ten-furlong maiden at Bath, he tried to slip his field again at Leicester, although was legless when the field came to take him.
**E A L Dunlop [1-7] Maktoum Al Maktoum.*

DIRECT REACTION (IRE) BHB 66f72a **RR 51f 72a** 5052[10]

2 b g College Chapel - Mary's Way (GR) **(78df)** (Night Shift (USA)) 7.2f **(69)**
Form - 42750
Record 1999 - 1st:0 2nd:1 3rd:0 Ran:5
Win Prizemoney £0 *Total Prizemoney* £1,284
1999 Turf 0-4: (5f 2, 6f, 7f) (gd, g-f 2, frm) 1999 AW 0-1: (5f) (Equi)
Fair gelding, has worn blinkers. Turf high 71 (1st run) - 4th of 15 giving 5lb to Seraphina (25 Mar Doncaster 5f g-f RF 0464). (1st run) - 2nd of 7 to Paris Star (9 Apr Lingfield 5f Equi RF 0629).
**Miss Gay Kelleway [0-5] A P Griffin.*

DISCERNING AIR BHB 63f **RR 48f** 2464[8]

3 b f Ezzoud (IRE) - Jhansi Ki Rani (USA) (Far North (CAN)) 9.7f **(75)**
Form - 408
Record 1999 - 1st:0 2nd:0 3rd:0 Ran:3
Pre1999 - 1st:0 2nd:1 3rd:1 Ran:3
Win Prizemoney £0 *Total Prizemoney* £1,916
1999 Turf 0-3: (12f, 14f 2) (gd 2, frm)
Leggy, moderate filly. Turf high 48. **E Weymes [0-6] T A Scothern.*

DISCO TEX BHB 39f49a **RR 46f 49a** 2767[7]

4 b g Rambo Dancer (CAN) 8.4f **(59)** - Andbracket (Import) 6.6f **(68)**
Form - 7
Record 1999 - 1st:0 2nd:0 3rd:0 Ran:1
Pre1999 - 1st:1 2nd:0 3rd:3 Ran:17
Win Prizemoney £2,668 *Total Prizemoney* £3,869
Wins * 1998 Jly Hamilt (FRM) H 13f 43 49 <
1999 Turf 0-1: (16f) (frm)
Scopey, moderate gelding, effective 11 to 16f, acts on gd to frm, best on frm, often wears blinkers (extremely effectively), prefers left handed tracks. **M W Easterby [2-27] Mybank Racing.*

DISCRETION (IRE) BHB 33f **RR 47f** 4905[9]

4 b f Alzao (USA) 9.8f **(73)** - Sawaki (Song) 7.2f **(61)**
Form - 070000
Record 1999 - 1st:0 2nd:0 3rd:0 Ran:6
Pre1999 - 1st:0 2nd:0 3rd:0 Ran:6
Win Prizemoney £0 *Total Prizemoney* £250
1999 Turf 0-6: (5f, 6f 2, 8f, 10f, 12f) (gd 2, g-f 2, frm 2)
Workmanlike, moderate filly. Turf high 47.
**S Gollings [0-12] Northern Bloodstock Racing.*

DISHABILLE BHB 36f **RR 39df** 1606[14]

3 b f Dilum (USA) 7.1f **(56)** - Swagger Lady (Tate Gallery (USA)) 7.4f **(67)**
Form - 0400
Record 1999 - 1st:0 2nd:0 3rd:0 Ran:4
Pre1999 - 1st:0 2nd:0 3rd:0 Ran:5
1999 Turf 0-4: (6f, 7f 3) (gd, frm 3)
Leggy, very moderate filly, has worn blinkers. Turf high 39.
**J D Bethell [0-9] R M Chetham.*

DISPOL AQUA (IRE) RR 42f 3003[12]

2 b f Namaqualand (USA) - Easter Morning (FR) (Nice Havrais (USA))
Form - 650
Record 1999 - 1st:0 2nd:0 3rd:0 Ran:3
1999 Turf 0-3: (6f 2, 7f) (gd, g-f, frm)
Currently moderate filly. Turf high 42. **P Calver [0-3] W B Imison.*

DISPOL CLAN BHB 57f54a **RR 59f 54a** 432[7]

3 ch f Clantime 6.6f **(57)** - She's a Breeze (Crofthall) 6.3f **(59)**
Form - 17267
Record 1999 - 1st:0 2nd:1 3rd:0 Ran:4
Pre1999 - 1st:3 2nd:3 3rd:1 Ran:10
Win Prizemoney £6,478 *Total Prizemoney* £9,385
Wins * 1998 *Nov Wolver (STD) S 5f 57*
* 1998 *Oct Wolver (sta) S 5f 67*
1998 Apr Nottin (SFT) 5.1f 69 <
1999 AW 0-4: (5f 4) (Fibr 4)

Scopey, fair filly, effective 5f, acts on g-s to gd - acts on Fibr. AW high 57.
**D J G MurraySmith [2-7] Cardinal Racing (from J L Eyre [0-2] Aug 1998).*

DISPOL DIAMOND BHB 51f RR 50f 5073[4]
6 b m Sharpo 7.5f **(68)** - Fabulous Rina (FR) (Fabulous Dancer (USA)) 9.4f **(70)**
Form - 664504004
Record 1999 - 1st:0 2nd:0 3rd:0 Ran:9
Pre1999 - 1st:3 2nd:2 3rd:5 Ran:32
Win Prizemoney £12,146 *Total Prizemoney* £21,427
Wins 1998 Apr Pontef (G-S) H 8f 58 63+ <
1998 Apr Nottin (G-S) H 8.2f 47 57+
1997 May Redcar (FRM) S 7f 44
1999 Turf 0-9: (8f 4, 9f, 10f 4) (gd 4, g-f, frm 3, hrd)
Fair mare, effective 8 to 9f, best at 8f, acts on g-s to frm. Turf high 56.
**J S Wainwright [0-4] Mrs D Drewery (from N Tinkler [0-8] Jun 1999).*

DISPOL EMMA RR 43f 2454[13]
2 b f Emarati (USA) 6.6f **(63)** - Swift Pursuit (Posse (USA)) 8.9f **(61)**
Form - 0880
Record 1999 - 1st:0 2nd:0 3rd:0 Ran:4
1999 Turf 0-4: (5f 4) (gd 2, g-f, frm)
Moderate filly. Turf high 43. **P Calver [0-4] W B Imison.*

DISPOL JAZZ BHB 72f RR 74f 5023[8]
2 ch f Alhijaz 7.7f **(57)** - Foxtrot Pie (Shernazar) 10.2f **(73)**
Form - 813321652418
Record 1999 - 1st:3 2nd:2 3rd:2 Ran:12
Win Prizemoney £10,075 *Total Prizemoney* £13,875
Wins * 1999 Oct Catter (SFT) H 7f 64 74 <
*** 1999** Jly Carlis (GD) 5.9f 70
*** 1999** May Thirsk (G-F) S 6f 64
1999 Turf 3-12: (5f 3, 6f 2-6, 7f 1-3) (gd 1-4, g-f 2, frm 2-6)
Above-average filly, effective 6 to 7f, best at 6f, acts on gd to frm, best on frm. Turf high 74 - 1st of 15 giving 8lb to Coral Shells (5 Oct Catterick RF 4722) - also 1st of 9 getting 6lb from Islay Mist (3 Jly Carlisle RF 2518). **S E Kettlewell [3-12] W B Imison.*

DISPOL MAGIC (IRE) BHB 60f RR 66f 4901[7]
2 br g Magic Ring (IRE) 6.5f **(64)** - Miss Doody (Gorytus (USA)) 7.8f **(60)**
Form - 8001440157
Record 1999 - 1st:2 2nd:0 3rd:0 Ran:10
Win Prizemoney £4,855 *Total Prizemoney* £5,418
Wins * 1999 Spt Beverl (GD) SH 7.5f 60 66 <
*** 1999** Jun Hamilt (GD) S 6f 63
1999 Turf 2-10: (5f 3, 6f 1-2, 7f 1-4, 8f) (gd 1-3, g-f 1-4, frm 3)
Average gelding, effective 6 to 7f, best at 7f, acts on gd to frm, best on g-f, likes tight tracks. Turf high 66 - 1st of 15 giving 8lb to Portia Lady (15 Spt Beverley RF 4320) - also 1st of 6 giving 5lb to Schatzi (29 Jun Hamilton RF 2393). **P Calver [2-10] W B Imison.*

DISPOL MISS CHIEF BHB 48f RR 38f 4751[18]
2 ch f Be My Chief (USA) 10.2f **(62)** - Tino-Ella (Bustino) 10.4f **(64)**
Form - 500
Record 1999 - 1st:0 2nd:0 3rd:0 Ran:3
1999 Turf 0-3: (7f, 8f 2) (gd, frm 2)
Currently very moderate filly. Turf high 38 (began Aug).
**P Calver [0-3] W B Imison.*

DISPOL PRESIDENT BHB 39f RR 24f 2132[15]
3 b g Presidium 7.5f **(56)** -Sister Hannah (Monseigneur (USA)) 7.7f **(63)**
Form - 0600
Record 1999 - 1st:0 2nd:0 3rd:0 Ran:4
Pre1999 - 1st:0 2nd:0 3rd:0 Ran:3
1999 Turf 0-4: (5f 3, 8f) (gd, frm 3)
Workmanlike, little account gelding, has worn blinkers. Turf high 24. **P Calver [0-7] W B Imison.*

DISPOL ROCK (IRE) BHB 74f RR 72f 5022[7]
3 b g Ballad Rock 7.2f **(63)** - Havana Moon (Ela-Mana-Mou) 10.1f **(70)**
Form - 08322167
Record 1999 - 1st:1 2nd:2 3rd:1 Ran:8
Pre1999 - 1st:1 2nd:0 3rd:1 Ran:3
Win Prizemoney £5,373 *Total Prizemoney* £9,781
Wins * 1999 Aug Ripon (GD) H 10f 69 71+ <
*** 1998** Spt Newcas (GD) 7f 66
1999 Turf 1-8: (8f 3, 9f, 10f 1-4) (gd 2, g-f 1-1, frm 4, hrd)
Workmanlike, above-average gelding, effective 7 to 10f, best at 10f, acts on g-f to frm, best on frm. Turf high 72 - 2nd of 7 getting 11lb from Canta Ke Brave (2 Aug Ripon 9f frm RF 3297) - also 1st of 18 giving 13lb to Hannah Park (30 Aug Ripon RF 4031). Consistent. **P Calver [2-11] W B Imison.*

DISPOL TRUMP BHB 43f36a RR 30f 36a 3989[10]
3 ch f Chilibang 7f **(55)** - Broken Silence (Busted) 10.2f **(61)**
Form - 0720000
Record 1999 - 1st:0 2nd:1 3rd:0 Ran:7
Pre1999 - 1st:0 2nd:0 3rd:0 Ran:4
Win Prizemoney £0 *Total Prizemoney* £804
1999 Turf 0-5: (10f, 12f 4) (gd, g-f, frm 3) 1999 AW 0-2: (7f, 12f) (Fibr 2)
Neat, very moderate filly, effective 12f, acts on frm, likes tight tracks. Turf high 53 - 2nd of 12 giving 1lb to Hi-Jenny (14 Apr Beverley 12f frm RF 0689). AW high 17. Inconsistent.
**J Norton [0-2] T Hurst (from P Calver [0-9] May 1999).*

DISTANT BELLE BHB 38f38a RR 38a 267[6]
3 b f Distant Relative 7f **(69)** - Moments Joy (Adonijah) 10f **(61)**
Form - 0856
Record 1999 - 1st:0 2nd:0 3rd:0 Ran:3
Pre1999 - 1st:0 2nd:0 3rd:0 Ran:1
1999 AW 0-3: (7f 2, 8f) (Equi, Fibr 2)
Scopey, very moderate filly. AW high 32.
**N P Littmoden [0-4] Dead Shark Partnership.*

DISTANT FLAME RR 51f 2537[13]
2 b f Distant Relative 7f **(69)** - Brockton Flame **(65f)** (Emarati (USA))
Form - 0
Record 1999 - 1st:0 2nd:0 3rd:0 Ran:1
1999 Turf 0-1: (6f) (g-f)
Currently fair filly. **N A Graham [0-1] First Millennium Racing.*

DISTANT GUEST BHB 65f RR 73f 5100[7]
2 b c Distant Relative 7f **(69)** - Teacher's Game (Mummy's Game) 8.2f **(60)**
Form - 087
Record 1999 - 1st:0 2nd:0 3rd:0 Ran:3
1999 Turf 0-3: (6f, 8f 2) (g-s, gd, frm)
Currently above-average colt. Turf high 73 (began Aug).
**G G Margarson [0-3] John Guest.*

DISTANT KING BHB 35f RR 58df 5161[8]
6 b g Distant Relative 7f **(69)** - Lindfield Belle (IRE) (Fairy King (USA)) 7.7f **(59)**
Form - 000000600608
Record 1999 - 1st:0 2nd:0 3rd:0 Ran:12
Pre1999 - 1st:3 2nd:0 3rd:1 Ran:26
Win Prizemoney £7,950 *Total Prizemoney* £8,409
Wins * 1998 Jly Beverl (G-F) H 5f 49 54 <
* 1998 Jly Carlis (G-F) H 5f 43 45
* 1998 Jun Beverl (GD) H 5f 31 43
1999 Turf 0-12: (5f 9, 6f 3) (sft, gd, g-f 3, frm 7)
Fair gelding, effective 5f, acts on frm, has worn blinkers. Turf high 58. **G P Kelly [3-37] A Barrett (from S Coathup [0-1] Aug 1995).*

DISTANT MUSIC (USA) RR 113+f 4918[1]
2 b c Distant View (USA) - Musicanti (USA) (Nijinsky (CAN)) 10.3f **(77)**
Form - 111
Record 1999 - 1st:3 2nd:0 3rd:0 Ran:3
Win Prizemoney £182,120 *Total Prizemoney* £182,120
Wins * 1999 Oct Newmar (GD) G1 7f 106+
*** 1999** Spt Doncas (G-F) G2 7f 113+ <
*** 1999** Jly Doncas (G-F) 7f 91++
1999 Turf 3-3: (7f 3-3) (gd 1-1, frm 2-2)
Currently Group-class colt. Turf high 113 (began Jly) - 1st of 6 getting 4lb from Rossini (10 Spt Doncaster RF 4252) - also 1st of 5 from Brahms (16 Oct Newmarket RF 4918). Barry Hills has stated that this colt is potentially the best he has handled and his enthusiasm is easy to understand. Impressive when winning a maiden and the Group 2 Frigidaire Champagne Stakes at Doncaster, he completed his juvenile programme in Newmarket's Dewhurst

Stakes. Not every observer was impressed with his length success over Brahms that day, but he was asked to deliver a challenge sooner than ideal and did well to maintain his rhythm after meeting the rising ground. Out of a mare that won over a mile and three-quarters, he should stay beyond a mile and will have a big say in the outcome of the 2,000 Guineas. However, he makes limited appeal at his current odds for that race and those who intend supporting him for the first colts' Classic are advised to hold fire until next spring. **B W Hills [3-3] K Abdulla.*

Dancer (USA)) 10.3f **(74)**
Form - 662148
Record 1999 - 1st:1 2nd:1 3rd:0 Ran:6
Pre1999 - 1st:6 2nd:6 3rd:0 Ran:32
Win Prizemoney £23,343 *Total Prizemoney* £35,492
Wins * 1999 Jly Haydoc (FRM) 7.1f 73
1997 Spt Kempto (G-F) H 6f 73 79 <
1997 Aug Windso (GD) H 5f 63 70
1997 Jly Southw (STD) H 5f 56 66

Distant Music took over the mantle of the injured Fasliyev as 2000 Guineas favourite

DISTANT PROSPECT (IRE) BHB 68f **RR 76f** 4103[12]
2 b c Namaqualand (USA) - Ukraine's Affair (USA) (The Minstrel (CAN)) 10f **(72)**
Form - 0030
Record 1999 - 1st:0 2nd:0 3rd:1 Ran:4
Win Prizemoney £0 *Total Prizemoney* £428
1999 Turf 0-4: (6f 2, 7f, 8f) (gd, g-f, frm 2)
Above-average colt. Turf high 76.
**J R Arnold [0-4] The Rae Smiths and Pauline Gale.*

DISTANT STORM BHB 53f46a **RR 54f 46a** 1986[2]
6 ch g Pharly (FR) 11.5f **(64)** - Candle in the Wind (Thatching) 8f **(66)**
Form - 8222
Record 1999 - 1st:0 2nd:3 3rd:0 Ran:4
Pre1999 - 1st:1 2nd:3 3rd:3 Ran:14
Win Prizemoney £2,243 *Total Prizemoney* £10,566
Wins 1995 Jly Bright (FRM) S 7f 66 <
1999 Turf 0-3: (16f, 18f 2) (g-s, gd, g-f) 1999 AW 0-1: (16f) (Fibr)
Fair gelding, effective 14 to 18f, acts on sft to g-f - acts on AW, mostly wears blinkers (extremely effectively), excels at Nottingham. Turf high 54 - 2nd of 12 giving 13lb to Urgent Reply (7 Jun Warwick 16f g-s RF 1799).
**B J Llewellyn [4-43] D H Driscoll (from M L W Bell [1-7] Aug 1996).*

DISTINCTIVE DREAM (IRE) BHB 74f68a **RR 76f 68a** 3156[8]
5 b g Distinctly North (USA) 7.4f **(63)** - Green Side (USA) (Green
1997 Jly Windso (G-F) H 6f 49 61
1997 Jly Salisb (FRM) CH 6f 43 53
1997 Jly Windso (GD) H 6f 45 50
1999 Turf 1-6: (6f, 7f 1-4, 8f) (g-f, frm 1-5)
Above-average gelding, effective 6 to 7f, best at 6f, acts on gd to frm, best on gd, mostly wears blinkers (effectively). Turf high 76 - 2nd of 11 giving 2lb to Dilkusha (23 Jun Kempton 7f frm RF 2243). Consistent.
**Lady Herries [1-13] R Bremner (from K T Ivory [6-25] Nov 1997).*

DISTINCTLY BLU (IRE) RR 37f 1502[8]
2 b f Distinctly North (USA) 7.4f **(63)** - Stifen (Burslem) 8.8f **(53)**
Form - 88
Record 1999 - 1st:0 2nd:0 3rd:0 Ran:2
1999 Turf 0-2: (5f 2) (gd, frm)
Currently very moderate filly. Turf high 37.
**K A Ryan [0-2] Hambleton Lodge Equine Premix Ltd.*

DISTINCTLY EAST (IRE) BHB 75f **RR 92?f** 4895[11]
2 b c Distinctly North (USA) 7.4f **(63)** - Raggy (Smoggy) 8f **(50)**
Form - 1456020
Record 1999 - 1st:1 2nd:1 3rd:0 Ran:7
Win Prizemoney £3,146 *Total Prizemoney* £5,754
Wins * 1999 Apr Ripon (G-F) 5f 74 <
1999 Turf 1-7: (5f 1-2, 6f 4, 8f) (g-s, gd 2, g-f 1-3, frm)

Useful colt, effective 6f, acts on g-s. Turf high 92 - 2nd of 4 giving 7lb to Bailey's Whirlwind (16 Spt Yarmouth 6f g-s RF 4354). Made a winning debut at Ripon in April, but did not go on from that.
**M H Tompkins [1-7] P F Riseborough.*

DISTINCTLY WELL (IRE) BHB 67f79a RR 59f 79a 4909[8]

2 b g Distinctly North (USA) 7.4f **(63)** - Brandywell (Skyliner) 7.3f **(53)**
Form - 4222744465516008
Record 1999 - 1st:1 2nd:3 3rd:0 Ran:16
Win Prizemoney £6,092 *Total Prizemoney* £10,313
Wins * **1999** Aug Cheste (G-S) H 7f 70 77 <
1999 Turf 1-15: (5f 6, 6f 3, 7f 1-4, 8f 2) (g-s 2, gd 1-6, g-f 3, frm 4) 1999 AW 0-1: (6f) (Fibr)
Above-average gelding, effective 5 to 7f, acts on gd to g-f - acts on Fibr, has worn blinkers, likes tight tracks. Turf high 81 - 2nd of 8 to Desert Fury (5 May Chester 5f g-f RF 1043) - also 1st of 9 getting 10lb from Water Hunter (20 Aug Chester RF 3789). (1st run) - 2nd of 8 to Random Task (14 May Wolverhampton 6f Fibr RF 1230). Landed a Chester nursery a few days after finishing fifth in a valuable York seller. **P D Evans [1-16] The Bears Syndicate.*

DIVA D'ARGENT BHB 43a RR 43a 108[5]

3 gr f Petong 7.6f **(58)** - Duxyana (IRE) (Cyrano de Bergerac) 6f **(68)**
Form - 0085
Record 1999 - 1st:0 2nd:0 3rd:0 Ran:2
Pre1999 - 1st:0 2nd:0 3rd:0 Ran:2
1999 AW 0-2: (5f, 6f) (Equi 2)
Neat, very moderate filly. AW high 35.
**W R Muir [0-4] D Lancaster-Smith.*

DIVE BHB 54f RR 54f 4482[6]

2 b c Slip Anchor 12.7f **(75)** - Delightful Chime (IRE) (Alzao (USA)) 7.1f **(68)**
Form - 006
Record 1999 - 1st:0 2nd:0 3rd:0 Ran:3
1999 Turf 0-3: (7f 2, 8f) (g-s 2, frm)
Currently fair colt. Turf high 54 (began Spt).
**Sir Mark Prescott [0-3] B Haggas.*

DIVER'S PEARL (FR) RR 80f 4178[3]

2 b f Prince Sabo 6.6f **(64)** - Seek the Pearl **(90df)** (Rainbow Quest (USA)) 10.4f **(75)**
Form - 63
Record 1999 - 1st:0 2nd:0 3rd:1 Ran:2
Win Prizemoney £0 *Total Prizemoney* £374
1999 Turf 0-2: (6f 2) (gd, frm)
Currently decent filly. Turf high 80 (began Aug) - 3rd of 19 to Iftiraas (7 Spt Lingfield 6f frm RF 4178).
**J R Fanshawe [0-2] Cheveley Park Stud.*

DIVIDE AND RULE BHB 35f30a RR 26f 30a 4233[8]

5 b h Puissance 7.1f **(60)** - Indivisible (Remainder Man) 11.2f **(45)**
Form - 03700008
Record 1999 - 1st:0 2nd:0 3rd:0 Ran:6
Pre1999 - 1st:1 2nd:0 3rd:4 Ran:26
Win Prizemoney £3,028 *Total Prizemoney* £5,616
Wins * 1996 Jun Ripon (G-F) 5f 71 <
1999 Turf 0-5: (5f 3, 6f 2) (g-f 2, frm 2, hrd) 1999 AW 0-1: (6f) (Fibr)
Very moderate colt. Turf high 38 (began Aug). Consistent.
**R Hollinshead [1-32] M Johnson.*

DIVIDED HONOURS (IRE) BHB 48f RR 54f 3008[11]

2 b c Sri Pekan (USA) - It's All Academic (IRE) (Mazaad) 7.1f **(45)**
Form - 0640
Record 1999 - 1st:0 2nd:0 3rd:0 Ran:4
Win Prizemoney £0 *Total Prizemoney* £216
1999 Turf 0-4: (5f 2, 6f, 7f) (gd, g-f 2, hrd)
Fair colt. Turf high 54. **D Shaw [0-4] J C Fretwell.*

DIVINATION (FR) RR 107f 4768a[3]

4 ch f Groom Dancer (USA) 9.5f **(75)** - Devalois (FR) (Nureyev (USA)) 8.7f **(78)**
Form - 233
1999 Turf 0-3: (16f, 17f, 20f) (hvy, sft, gd)
Currently Pattern-class filly. Turf high 107 - 3rd of 8 getting 3lb from Tajoun (2 Oct Longchamp 20f hvy RF 4768a). She ran a couple of fine races behind Tajoun, looking a shade unlucky in the Prix Gladiateur. However, she lacks a turn-of-foot even over extreme distances.
**F Head in FR [0-2] (from Mme C Head in FR [0-1] Jun 1999).*

DIVINE HOSTESS BHB 38f RR 42f 3256[12]

2 br f Batshoof 9.5f **(66)** - Divina Mia **(65f)** (Dowsing (USA))
Form - 040
Record 1999 - 1st:0 2nd:0 3rd:0 Ran:3
Win Prizemoney £0 *Total Prizemoney* £266
1999 Turf 0-3: (6f 2, 7f) (g-f, frm 2)
Currently moderate filly. Turf high 42 (began Jly).
**M W Easterby [0-3] W H Jackson.*

DIVINE MISS-P BHB 66f70a RR 75f 70a 5110[17]

6 ch m Safawan 6.6f **(60)** - Faw (Absalom) 7.2f **(58)**
Form - 01036002000
Record 1999 - 1st:1 2nd:1 3rd:1 Ran:11
Pre1999 - 1st:8 2nd:5 3rd:3 Ran:33
Win Prizemoney £32,756 *Total Prizemoney* £44,898

Wins								
* **1999**	May	Bath	(GD)		5.1f		76	
* 1998	Jun	Chepst	(G-S)	H	5.1f	74	81	<
* 1998	May	Bath	(GD)	H	5.1f	69	71	
* 1998	Apr	Folkes	(GD)	H	5f	60	67	
* 1998	*Mar*	*Southw*	*(STD)*	*H*	*5f*	*63*	*69*	
1998	*Feb*	*Wolver*	*(STD)*	*C*	*6f*		*64*	
1997	Aug	Warwic	(G-S)	C	5f		59	
1997	Aug	Yarmou	(G-F)	H	5.2f	50	57	
1997	Apr	Thirsk	(G-F)		6f		64	

1999 Turf 1-11: (5f 1-10, 6f) (sft, g-s 2, gd 3, g-f 1-4, frm)
Above-average mare, effective 5f, acts on gd to g-f, best on gd, excels at Chepstow, does well at Bath. Turf high 76 - 6th of 8 getting 9lb from Speed On (29 Jun Chepstow 5f g-f RF 2388) - also 1st of 8 getting 3lb from Cauda Equina (17 May Bath RF 1271). Inconsistent. Effective on Fibresand or turf, her form last season was patchy, her only victory coming in a Bath classified event in May. She is normally very quick into her stride and possesses plenty of early speed, and though successful over six furlongs, is probably better over five.
**J Cullinan [5-30] Alan Spargo Ltd Toolmakers (from A P Jarvis [4-14] Feb 1998).*

DIVINE PROSPECT (IRE) BHB 74f RR 76f 4899[6]

2 b br f Namaqualand (USA) - Kayu (Tap On Wood) 10.3f **(65)**
Form - 38561586
Record 1999 - 1st:1 2nd:0 3rd:1 Ran:8
Win Prizemoney £4,581 *Total Prizemoney* £5,108
Wins * **1999** Aug Newmar (GD) H 7f 70 76 <
1999 Turf 1-8: (5f, 6f 2, 7f 1-3, 8f 2) (g-s, gd 2, g-f 1-2, frm 3)
Above-average filly, effective 7f, acts on g-f to frm. Turf high 76 - 1st of 9 getting 1lb from Muffin Man (6 Aug Newmarket RF 3428). Consistent. **A P Jarvis [1-8] Christopher Shankland.*

DIVORCE ACTION (IRE) BHB 65f RR 67f 3915[10]

3 b g Common Grounds 8.1f **(66)** - Overdue Reaction (Be My Guest (USA)) 9.3f **(67)**
Form - 550150
Record 1999 - 1st:1 2nd:0 3rd:0 Ran:6
Pre1999 - 1st:0 2nd:0 3rd:1 Ran:4
Win Prizemoney £2,788 *Total Prizemoney* £3,272
Wins 1999 Aug Kempto (G-F) C 9f 67 <
1999 Turf 1-6: (8f, 9f 1-1, 10f 2, 11f, 12f) (gd, g-f 3, frm 1-2)
Strong, average gelding, effective 9 to 11f, acts on g-f to frm, best on g-f, prefers tight tracks. Turf high 67 - 1st of 8 giving 5lb to April Ace (4 Aug Kempton RF 3356). Inconsistent.
**P R Hedger [0-2] J J Whelan (from P F I Cole [1-8] Aug 1999).*

DIXIE FLYER (IRE) BHB 44f RR 41f 4868[9]

2 b f Blues Traveller (IRE) - African Cousin (Kampala) 8.5f **(56)**
Form - 00770
Record 1999 - 1st:0 2nd:0 3rd:0 Ran:5
1999 Turf 0-4: (5f 2, 7f 2) (gd 2, g-f, hrd) 1999 AW 0-1: (5f) (Fibr)
Moderate filly. Turf high 41.
**E J Alston [0-5] The Burlington Partnership.*

DIXIE JAZZ BHB 60f RR 61f 616[5]

3 br f Mtoto 11.5f **(71)** - Dixie Favor (USA) (Dixieland Band (USA)) 7f **(74)**

Form - 5
Record 1999 - 1st:0 2nd:0 3rd:0 Ran:1
Pre1999 - 1st:0 2nd:0 3rd:0 Ran:2
1999 Turf 0-1: (8f) (g-f)
Currently average filly. **Miss J A Camacho [0-3] Elite Racing Club.*

DIXIELAKE (IRE) RR 57f 5208[8]

2 b f Lake Coniston (IRE) - Rathvindon (Realm) 8.1f **(65)**
Form - 8
Record 1999 - 1st:0 2nd:0 3rd:0 Ran:1
1999 Turf 0-1: (7f) (g-s)
Currently fair filly. **H Candy [0-1] C G P Wyatt.*

DIXIE UNION (USA) RR 5229a[5]

2 br c Dixieland Band (USA) 10.1f **(80)** -She's Tops (USA) (Capote (USA))
Form - 5
1999 AW 0-1: (9f) (Dirt)
Currently useful. **R Mandella in USA [0-1].*

DIXXY DANCER (IRE) RR 70f 2550[6]

2 b c Dancing Dissident (USA) 6.8f **(65)** - Biddy Mulligan (Ballad Rock) 7.8f **(63)**
Form - 756
Record 1999 - 1st:0 2nd:0 3rd:0 Ran:3
1999 Turf 0-3: (5f 3) (frm 2, hrd)
Currently above-average colt. Turf high 70.
**M R Channon [0-3] Ken Lock Racing Ltd.*

DIZZY KNIGHT RR 53f 4407[8]

2 b f Distant Relative 7f **(69)** - Top Treat (USA) (Topsider (USA)) 8.3f **(71)**
Form - 8
Record 1999 - 1st:0 2nd:0 3rd:0 Ran:1
1999 Turf 0-1: (6f) (frm)
Currently fair filly.
**M J Fetherston-Godley [0-1] Derek D & Mrs Jean P Clee.*

DIZZY TILLY BHB 50f RR 51f 4822[11]

5 b m Anshan 8.2f **(63)** - Nadema (Artaius (USA)) 9f **(69)**
Form - 0055124536230
Record 1999 - 1st:1 2nd:2 3rd:2 Ran:13
Pre1999 - 1st:2 2nd:1 3rd:3 Ran:25
Win Prizemoney £8,200 *Total Prizemoney* £14,314
Wins * **1999** Jun Windso (G-F) H 11.6f 43 46
1997 Jun Windso (G-S) 10f 66 <
1997 Jun Windso (G-F) H 11.6f 57 64+
1999 Turf 1-13: (9f, 10f 2, 11f, 12f 1-8, 14f) (g-s, gd 2, g-f 1-3, frm 7)
Fair filly, effective 10f, acts on g-f, favours tight tracks. Turf high 51. Consistent. She obviously likes Windsor.
**A J McNae [1-13] Mrs S Leech (from T J Naughton [2-25] Oct 1998).*

DJAIS (FR) BHB 78f RR 56f 1300[6]

10 ch g Vacarme (USA) - Dame de Carreau (FR) (Targowice (USA)) 11.4f **(70)**
Form - 6
Record 1999 - 1st:0 2nd:0 3rd:0 Ran:1
Pre1999 - 1st:1 2nd:1 3rd:3 Ran:14
Win Prizemoney £20,640 *Total Prizemoney* £22,343
1999 Turf 0-1: (18f) (gd)
Fair gelding, has worn blinkers. Becoming disappointing.
**J R Jenkins [3-28] Christopher Shankland (from R T Phillips [0-3] Jly 1995).*

D'MARTI BHB 43f54a RR 34f 54a 4878[16]

4 b f Emarati (USA) 6.6f **(63)** - Hellene (Dominion) 8.5f **(63)**
Form - 7308500000
Record 1999 - 1st:0 2nd:0 3rd:1 Ran:10
Pre1999 - 1st:1 2nd:2 3rd:5 Ran:16
Win Prizemoney £3,533 *Total Prizemoney* £9,695
Wins * 1998 Jly Sandow (G-S) H 5f 65 73 <
1999 Turf 0-9: (5f 6, 6f 3) (gd 5, g-f 3, frm) 1999 AW 0-1: (5f) (Fibr)
Scopey, moderate filly, effective 5f, acts on sft to g-f. Turf high 57.
**C B B Booth [1-26] Mrs Marian Rogers.*

DOBAANDI SECRET BHB 35f RR 34f 1092[11]

3 b g Reprimand 8.2f **(63)**-Secret Dance (Sadler's Wells (USA))10f **(76)**
Form - 800
Record 1999 - 1st:0 2nd:0 3rd:0 Ran:2
Pre1999 - 1st:0 2nd:0 3rd:0 Ran:3
1999 Turf 0-2: (10f, 14f) (g-s, g-f)
Leggy, very moderate gelding. Turf high 34.
**A Bailey [0-2] Smiley Partnership (from P D Evans [0-2] Nov 1998).*

DOBERMAN (IRE) BHB 42f41a RR 40f 41a 5147[4]

4 br g Dilum (USA) 7.1f **(56)** - Switch Blade (IRE) (Robellino (USA)) 7.6f **(80)**
Form - 40852066000427240364
Record 1999 - 1st:0 2nd:3 3rd:1 Ran:17
Pre1999 - 1st:0 2nd:2 3rd:0 Ran:7
Win Prizemoney £0 *Total Prizemoney* £4,417
1999 Turf 0-9: (6f, 7f, 8f 3, 9f, 10f 2, 11f) (g-s, gd 3, frm 5) 1999 AW 0-8: (8f 6, 10f 2) (Equi 3, Fibr 5)
Workmanlike, moderate gelding, effective 5 to 6f, acts on frm to hrd, often wears blinkers. Turf high 55. AW high 55. Consistent.
**P D Evans [0-8] Mrs I M Folkes (from S A Brookshaw [0-5] Jun 1999).*

DOCKLANDS MERC (IRE) BHB 30f34a RR 34a 537[17]

3 b f Common Grounds 8.1f **(66)** - Chouette (Try My Best (USA)) 7.6f **(67)**
Form - 550
Record 1999 - 1st:0 2nd:0 3rd:0 Ran:3
Pre1999 - 1st:0 2nd:0 3rd:0 Ran:1
1999 Turf 0-1: (7f) (gd) 1999 AW 0-2: (7f, 10f) (Equi 2)
Light-framed, very poor filly. AW high 5.
**R T Phillips [0-3] Mrs Lisa Olley (from N Tinkler [0-1] May 1998).*

DOCKSIDER (USA) RR 125f 5226a[3]

4 ch c Diesis 9f **(80)** - Pump (USA) (Forli (ARG)) 9.6f **(67)**
Form - 13121263
Record 1999 - 1st:3 2nd:2 3rd:2 Ran:8
Pre1999 - 1st:2 2nd:3 3rd:0 Ran:9
Win Prizemoney £88,247 *Total Prizemoney* £298,080
Wins * **1999** Jly Hoppeg (GD) G2 8f 123 <
* **1999** May Baden- (G-S) G3 8f 113
* **1999** May Newmar (G-F) 10f 113
* 1998 Aug Sandow (G-F) 8.1f 111
* 1997 Jly Salisb (G-F) 7f 87
1999 Turf 3-8: (8f 2-5, 10f 1-3) (g-s 1-1, gd 1-2, g-f 2, frm 1-3)
Scopey, top-class colt, effective 8f, acts on gd to frm. Turf high 125 - 2nd of 8 giving 8lb to Aljabr (28 Jly Goodwood 8f g-f RF 3209) - also 1st of 6 giving 11lb to Gonlargo (11 Jly Hoppegarten RF 2859a). He was in fine form all season, winning at Newmarket and a couple of German Group races, and running superbly to go down by the narrowest of margins in the Queen Anne and by just a length to Aljabr in the Sussex Stakes. He went to America in the autumn, and ran a cracking race when third in the Breeders' Cup Mile. A genuine Group One performer, he is likely to be retired after keeping a date in Hong Kong.
J W Hills [5-16] (from B W Hills [0-1] Oct 1999).

DOC RYAN'S BHB 63f75a RR 67f 75a 4650[14]

5 b h Damister (USA) 9.1f **(66)** - Jolimo (Fortissimo) 11.8f **(61)**
Form - 24451131113260
Record 1999 - 1st:5 2nd:1 3rd:2 Ran:11
Pre1999 - 1st:2 2nd:3 3rd:4 Ran:25
Win Prizemoney £21,841 *Total Prizemoney* £28,202
Wins * **1999** *Jun Wolver (STD) C 12f 73* <
* **1999** *Jun Wolver (STD) C 16.2f 73* <
* **1999** *Jun Southw (STD) C 14f 73* <
* **1999** *May Southw (STD) H 16f 62 73+*
* **1999** *May Southw (STD) H 14f 62 66+*
* 1998 Jun Mussel (SFT) H 12f 61 68
* 1997 Nov Mussel (G-S) H 12f 61 67
1999 Turf 0-5: (12f 3, 15f, 16f) (hvy, gd 2, g-f, frm) 1999 AW 5-6: (12f 1-1, 14f 2-2, 16f 2-3) (Fibr 5-6)
Above-average colt, effective 12 to 16f, best at 16f, acts on gd to frm - acts on Fibr, often wears blinkers (extremely effectively), likes left handed tracks, favours tight tracks, excels at Wolverhampton and Musselburgh and Southwell. Turf high 67 - 2nd of 5 giving 14lb to Brodessa (5 Jly Musselburgh 16f frm RF 2559). AW high 73 - 1st of 4 giving 16lb to Alakdar (16 Jun Wolverhampton RF 2064) - also 1st of 13 giving 6lb to Time Can Tell (17 May Southwell RF 1282). He is a winner on soft ground on turf, but had a fine time on Fibresand last season, winning a string

of modest staying events. Not many stay as well as him on that surface. **M J Ryan [7-39] Paul Blows.*

DOCTOR BRAVIOUS (IRE) BHB 41f50a **RR 44f 50a** 1770^{27}
6 b g Priolo (USA) 10.9f **(71)** - Sharp Slipper (Sharpo) 7.7f **(59)**
Form - 250
Record 1999 - 1st:0 2nd:1 3rd:0 Ran:3
Pre1999 - 1st:1 2nd:1 3rd:2 Ran:21
Win Prizemoney £3,743 *Total Prizemoney* £7,626
Wins 1996 *Jan Wolver (STD) 8.5f 65 <*
1999 Turf 0-3: (12f 2, 13f) (hvy, g-f 2)
Moderate gelding, effective 7 to 12f, acts on hvy to frm, mostly wears blinkers (effectively), prefers right handed tracks, prefers tight tracks. Turf high 44.
**J R Poulton [2-12] Chris Steward (from B Ellison [0-15] Jly 1998).*

DOCTOR DENNIS (IRE) BHB 69f **RR 68f** 4995^{2}
2 b c Last Tycoon 9.4f **(73)** - Noble Lustre (USA) (Lyphard's Wish (FR)) 9f **(74)**
Form - 0586872
Record 1999 - 1st:0 2nd:1 3rd:0 Ran:7
Win Prizemoney £0 *Total Prizemoney* £890
1999 Turf 0-7: (6f, 7f 3, 8f 2, 10f) (gd 2, g-f 2, frm 3)
Average colt, effective 7f, acts on gd, often wears blinkers, likes tight tracks. Turf high 68 - 2nd of 16 getting 3lb from Villa Romana (21 Oct Brighton 7f gd RF 4995).
**B J Meehan [0-7] Mrs Judith Mendonca.*

DOCTOR KOOL BHB 68f **RR 67f** 2260^{14}
3 ch g Local Suitor (USA) 9.7f **(58)** - Hasty Sarah (Gone Native)
Form - 50
Record 1999 - 1st:0 2nd:0 3rd:0 Ran:2
Pre1999 - 1st:0 2nd:0 3rd:0 Ran:5
Win Prizemoney £0 *Total Prizemoney* £516
1999 Turf 0-2: (8f, 12f) (gd, hrd)
Scopey, average gelding. Turf high 67.
**T P Tate [0-7] The Ivy Syndicate.*

DOCTOR SPIN (IRE) BHB 99f **RR 101f** 2900^{9}
3 b c Namaqualand (USA) - Madam Loving (Vaigly Great) 7f **(58)**
Form - 406340
Record 1999 - 1st:0 2nd:0 3rd:1 Ran:6
Pre1999 - 1st:2 2nd:0 3rd:0 Ran:3
Win Prizemoney £6,460 *Total Prizemoney* £15,983
Wins * 1998 May Lingfi (GD) 5f 93+ <
* 1998 May Windso (G-F) 5f 82
1999 Turf 0-6: (5f, 6f 4, 7f) (g-s, gd 2, g-f 3)
Leggy, very useful colt, effective 5 to 7f, best at 6f, acts on gd to g-f, best on gd. Turf high 101 - 4th of 30 giving 2lb to Deep Space (18 Jun Ascot 6f g-f RF 2105). He ran a cracking race to finish fourth in the Wokingham, but was not seen out after finishing unplaced on fast ground at Newbury in July. He ran well on his only start over seven furlongs and is worth another chance at that trip.
**R F JohnsonHoughton [2-9] Anthony Pye-Jeary.*

DODO (IRE) BHB 79f **RR 81f** 3117^{9}
4 b f Alzao (USA) 9.8f **(73)** - Dead Certain (Absalom) 7.2f **(58)**
Form - 3380
Record 1999 - 1st:0 2nd:0 3rd:2 Ran:4
Pre1999 - 1st:1 2nd:2 3rd:7 Ran:17
Win Prizemoney £3,972 *Total Prizemoney* £17,535
Wins * 1998 Spt Kempto (GD) H 6f 72 78 <
1999 Turf 0-4: (5f, 6f, 7f 2) (gd, g-f, frm 2)
Scopey, decent filly, effective 6 to 8f, best at 7f, acts on gd to frm, best on gd, has worn blinkers, excels at Newmarket. Turf high 81 - 3rd of 10 getting 3lb from Therhea (10 Jun Newbury 7f gd RF 1885). Consistent. A daughter of Dead Certain, she ran well in both her first two starts last season, but found Listed company far too much. **D R C Elsworth [1-21] D R C Elsworth.*

DOLFINESSE (IRE) BHB 58f **RR 58f** 4320^{15}
2 ch f Dolphin Street (FR) - Gortadoo (USA) (Sharpen Up) 8.3f **(67)**
Form - 675750
Record 1999 - 1st:0 2nd:0 3rd:0 Ran:6
1999 Turf 0-6: (6f 3, 7f 3) (gd 3, g-f 2, frm)
Fair filly. Turf high 58 (began Jly). **M Brittain [0-6] Steven Box.*

DOLLAR BIRD (IRE) BHB 86f **RR 84f** 5142^{7}
2 b f Kris 10f **(75)** - High Spirited (Shirley Heights) 10.3f **(74)**
Form - 617
Record 1999 - 1st:1 2nd:0 3rd:0 Ran:3
Win Prizemoney £4,695 *Total Prizemoney* £4,695
Wins * **1999** Spt Nottin (GD) 8.2f 84 <
1999 Turf 1-3: (7f, 8f 1-2) (gd 1-2, frm)
Currently decent filly. Turf high 84 (began Aug) - also 1st of 11 from Purple Heather (25 Spt Nottingham RF 4559). Came into her own on her second run with a fine win at Nottingham over a mile, but was well beaten in a Newmarket Listed event.
**J L Dunlop [1-3] Sir Thomas Pilkington.*

DOLLAR LAW BHB 72f **RR 78df** 4758^{14}
3 ch g Selkirk (USA) 7.9f **(76)** - Western Heights (Shirley Heights) 10.3f **(74)**
Form - 0700
Record 1999 - 1st:0 2nd:0 3rd:0 Ran:4
Pre1999 - 1st:1 2nd:1 3rd:0 Ran:3
Win Prizemoney £4,042 *Total Prizemoney* £5,321
Wins * 1998 Oct Leices (G-S) 8f 81 <
1999 Turf 0-4: (8f, 10f 2, 12f) (gd 3, frm)
Leggy, above-average gelding, effective 7 to 8f, acts on gd to g-f. Turf high 78 (began Aug). **P F I Cole [1-7] N C Kersey.*

DOLLY DAY DREAM (IRE) BHB 44f47a **RR 25f 47a** 2571^{14}
3 ch f Magic Ring (IRE) 6.5f **(64)** - Lariston Gale (Pas de Seul) 9.1f **(67)**
Form - 78634650640050
Record 1999 - 1st:0 2nd:0 3rd:1 Ran:14
Pre1999 - 1st:1 2nd:3 3rd:1 Ran:12
Win Prizemoney £1,882 *Total Prizemoney* £6,054
Wins * 1998 Jly Yarmou (GD) S 6f 44 <
1999 Turf 0-5: (5f 2, 6f 3) (g-s, gd, g-f, frm 2) 1999 AW 0-9: (5f 4, 6f 4, 7f) (Equi 4, Fibr 5)
Neat, very moderate filly, effective 6f, - acts on Fibr, often wears blinkers (effectively). Turf high 50. AW high 57. Consistent.
**K T Ivory [1-26] K T Ivory.*

DOLPHINELLE (IRE) BHB 64f60a **RR 62f 60a** 5058^{4}
3 b c Dolphin Street (FR) - Mamie's Joy (Prince Tenderfoot (USA)) 9f **(61)**
Form - 58301727725474
Record 1999 - 1st:1 2nd:2 3rd:1 Ran:14
Pre1999 - 1st:0 2nd:0 3rd:1 Ran:7
Win Prizemoney £3,972 *Total Prizemoney* £6,939
Wins * **1999** Jun Bright (G-F) H 6f 66 71 <
1999 Turf 1-13: (5f, 6f 1-6, 7f 4, 8f 2) (g-s 3, gd, g-f 1-2, frm 7) 1999 AW 0-1: (7f) (Equi)
Unfurnished, average colt, effective 5 to 7f, acts on g-f to frm, best on frm, has worn blinkers, likes left handed tracks, prefers tight tracks. Turf high 73 - 2nd of 7 getting 5lb from Distinctive Dream (11 Jly Haydock 7f frm RF 2741) - also 1st of 11 getting 3lb from Lucy Mariella (14 Jun Brighton RF 1976). Consistent.
**R Hannon [1-21] Tommy Staunton.*

DOLPHIN FRIENDLY (IRE) BHB 34f **RR 43f** 5050^{9}
3 b f Dolphin Street (FR) - Sound Performance (IRE) (Ahonoora) 8.1f **(73)**
Form - 045082560
Record 1999 - 1st:0 2nd:1 3rd:0 Ran:9
Pre1999 - 1st:0 2nd:1 3rd:0 Ran:4
Win Prizemoney £0 *Total Prizemoney* £1,504
1999 Turf 0-9: (8f 2, 10f 4, 12f 2, 14f) (g-s, gd 3, g-f 2, frm 3)
Leggy, moderate filly, effective 7f, acts on gd. Turf high 44.
**J W Payne [0-13] The Frankland Lodgers.*

DOMAPPEL BHB 74f **RR 76f** 1752^{8}
7 b g Domynsky 7.8f **(58)** - Appelania (Star Appeal) 9.6f **(65)**
Form - 82238
Record 1999 - 1st:0 2nd:2 3rd:1 Ran:5
Pre1999 - 1st:4 2nd:7 3rd:2 Ran:25
Win Prizemoney £22,163 *Total Prizemoney* £39,046
Wins 1998 May Cheste (G-F) H 12.3f 70 72
1996 Jun Thirsk (FRM) H 12f 70 75 <
1995 Spt Yarmou (GD) H 10.1f 65 67
1999 Turf 0-5: (12f 4, 14f) (g-s, g-f 3, frm)
Above-average gelding, effective 12 to 16f, acts on g-f to frm, best

on frm, prefers tight tracks, excels at Chester. Turf high 76 - 2nd of 9 getting 5lb from Bay of Islands (22 May Nottingham 14f g-f RF 1416). Consistent. Suited by front-running tactics, and is hard to peg back when in the mood.

**W Jarvis [1-9] M C Banks (from Mrs J Cecil [6-31] Spt 1998).*

DOMINANT DANCER BHB 86f **RR 85f** 5055[3]

3 ch f Primo Dominie 7.2f **(67)** - Footlight Fantasy (USA) **(66f)** (Nureyev (USA)) 8.7f **(78)**

Form - 20537463

Record 1999 - 1st:0 2nd:1 3rd:2 Ran:8
Pre1999 - 1st:1 2nd:1 3rd:0 Ran:5

Win Prizemoney £4,052 *Total Prizemoney* £11,174

Wins * 1998 Spt Pontef (G-F) 6f 81 <

1999 Turf 0-8: (6f 4, 7f 4) (g-s, gd 2, g-f 3, frm 2)

Workmanlike, useful filly, effective 6 to 7f, acts on frm. Turf high 95 - 3rd of 9 giving 1lb to Juno Marlowe (6 Jly Newmarket 7f frm RF 2578). Consistent. Made all over six furlongs at Pontefract on her fourth start at two, but has not won since and whether she truly gets seven furlongs is still open to conjecture.

**J W Hills [1-13] P F Warren.*

DOMINANT DUCHESS BHB 82f **RR 84f** 4917[2]

5 b m Old Vic 12.8f **(72)** -Andy's Find (USA)(Buckfinder(USA)) 8.1f **(71)**

Form - 15604P22

Record 1999 - 1st:1 2nd:2 3rd:0 Ran:8
Pre1999 - 1st:2 2nd:2 3rd:0 Ran:10

Win Prizemoney £9,573 *Total Prizemoney* £38,072

Wins * 1999 May Kempto (G-F) H 14.4f 75 78 <
* 1997 Apr Nottin (G-F) 10f 73+
* 1997 Mar Warwic (G-F) C 12.5f 61+

1999 Turf 1-8: (12f, 14f 1-1, 16f 3, 17f, 20f 2) (gd 2, g-f 2, frm 1-4)

Decent filly, has broken blood-vessels, effective 14 to 20f, acts on gd to frm, prefers right handed tracks, and excels at Kempton. Turf high 84 - 2nd of 32 getting 14lb from Top Cees (16 Oct Newmarket 17f gd RF 4917) - also 1st of 13 giving 5lb to Random Kindness (16 May Kempton RF 1256). Inconsistent. She stays extreme distances and ran the race of her life when finishing second in the Cesarewitch. Possibly unsuited by soft ground, she is quite high in the handicap and may need to drop a few pounds before scoring again. **J W Hills [3-18] Mrs Diana Patterson.*

DOMINELLE BHB 57f45a **RR 58f 45a** 4989[8]

7 b m Domynsky 7.8f **(58)** - Gymcrak Lovebird (Taufan (USA)) 7f **(57)**

Form - 0200087220347240608

Record 1999 - 1st:0 2nd:4 3rd:1 Ran:19
Pre1999 - 1st:8 2nd:8 3rd:8 Ran:69

Win Prizemoney £27,551 *Total Prizemoney* £50,820

Wins * 1998 Aug Ripon (G-F) H 6f 65 67 <
* 1998 Aug Redcar (G-F) H 6f 53 63
* 1998 Aug Pontef (G-F) H 5f 54 58
* 1998 Jun Doncas (GD) H 6f 48 49
* 1996 Jun Beverl (G-F) H 5f 45 46
1995 Jly Carlis (FRM) H 5f 49 45
1995 Jun Carlis (FRM) H 5f 45 46

1999 Turf 0-19: (5f 9, 6f 9, 7f) (gd 6, g-f, frm 11, hrd)

Fair mare, effective 6f, acts on g-f to frm, best on g-f, has worn blinkers. Turf high 59. Consistent.

**T D Easterby [5-66] Sandmoor Textiles Co Ltd (from M H Easterby [3-22] Oct 1995).*

DOMINO FLYER BHB 55f59a **RR 62df 59a** 852[5]

6 b g Warrshan (USA) 9.7f **(59)** - Great Dilemma (Vaigly Great) 7f **(58)**

Form - 70245

Record 1999 - 1st:0 2nd:1 3rd:0 Ran:5
Pre1999 - 1st:6 2nd:3 3rd:3 Ran:34

Win Prizemoney £14,785 *Total Prizemoney* £19,082

Wins * 1998 *Jun Southw (STD) H 8f 56 61*
* 1997 Mar Newcas (GD) H 10.1f 66 72 <
* 1997 *Jan Southw (STD) H 8f 58 56*
* 1996 *Nov Southw (STD) 8f 62*
* 1996 May Hamilt (SFT) 9.2f 63
* 1996 *Apr Southw (STD) H 7f 52 59*

1999 Turf 0-1: (9f) (hvy) 1999 AW 0-4: (8f 2, 11f 2) (Fibr 4)

Average gelding, effective 7 to 8f, best at 8f, acts on g-s - acts on Fibr, favours tight tracks. AW high 66 - 5th of 16 giving 15lb to Pine Ridge Lad (26 Apr Southwell 8f Fibr RF 0852). Inconsistent. He still has the ability to win modest events under his optimum conditions, a mile on the Southwell Fibresand.

**Mrs A Swinbank [6-40] S Smith.*

DOM MIGUEL (FR) **RR 62f** 3812[5]

2 b c Fairy King (USA) 7.7f **(75)** - Damasquine (USA) (Damascus (USA)) 8.9f **(71)**

Form - 75

Record 1999 - 1st:0 2nd:0 3rd:0 Ran:2

1999 Turf 0-2: (7f 2) (gd, frm)

Currently average colt. Turf high 62 (began Aug).

**P W Harris [0-2] The Fairy Kings.*

DOM SHADEED BHB 50f64a **RR 49f 64a** 2296[12]

4 b g Shadeed (USA) 7.7f **(72)** - Fair Dominion (Dominion) 8.5f **(63)**

Form - 108000

Record 1999 - 1st:0 2nd:0 3rd:0 Ran:5
Pre1999 - 1st:1 2nd:0 3rd:0 Ran:4

Win Prizemoney £2,411 *Total Prizemoney* £2,411

Wins 1998 *Dec Wolver (STD) 8.5f 62* <

1999 Turf 0-4: (9f, 10f, 11f, 12f) (g-s 2, g-f, frm) 1999 AW 0-1: (9f) (Fibr)

Leggy, average gelding, effective 7 to 8f, acts on g-s - acts on Fibr, has worn blinkers. Turf high 49. Becoming disappointing. He showed a little bit of ability before narrowly winning a maiden on the Wolverhampton Fibresand at the end of 1998, but has done nothing since.

**R Charlton [0-5] Exors of the Late D A Shirley (from Lord Huntingdon [1-4] Dec 1998).*

DONA FILIPA BHB 33f32a **RR 24f 32a** 4878[22]

6 ch m Precocious 7.2f **(54)** -Quisissanno(Be My Guest(USA)) 9.3f **(67)**

Form - 062008030000

Record 1999 - 1st:0 2nd:1 3rd:1 Ran:12
Pre1999 - 1st:2 2nd:2 3rd:5 Ran:39

Win Prizemoney £5,176 *Total Prizemoney* £9,625

Wins * 1998 Spt Yarmou (G-S) H 6f 36 41
* 1997 Aug Mussel (G-F) H 5f 39 47 <

1999 Turf 0-4: (5f, 6f 2, 7f) (gd 2, g-f, frm) 1999 AW 0-8: (5f 2, 6f 5, 7f) (Fibr 8)

Little account mare, effective 5 to 6f, best at 5f, acts on gd to frm - acts on Fibr. Turf high 29. AW high 36. She has a pretty awful wins to runs ratio, and is basically inconsistent. She seems equally effective over five and six furlongs.

**Miss L C Siddall [2-51] A Emmerson.*

DONATUS (IRE) BHB 70f **RR 74f** 5197[9]

3 b c Royal Academy (USA) 7.8f **(77)** - La Dame du Lac (USA) (Round Table) 9.5f **(81)**

Form - 7200260

Record 1999 - 1st:0 2nd:2 3rd:0 Ran:7
Pre1999 - 1st:0 2nd:0 3rd:1 Ran:3

Win Prizemoney £0 *Total Prizemoney* £7,204

1999 Turf 0-7: (8f 3, 9f 2, 10f 2) (g-s, gd 2, g-f, frm 3)

Above-average colt, effective 7 to 9f, acts on g-s to frm. Turf high 74 (began Jly) - 2nd of 10 getting 14lb from Tarawan (2 Oct Sandown 8f g-s RF 4698). A maiden, he ran a cracker in a handicap at Glorious Goodwood, but has been disappointing since.

**S Dow [0-7] Michael A J Hall & Miss M Shields (from C O'Brien in IRE [0-3] Oct 1998).*

DON BOSCO (IRE) BHB 72f **RR 72f** 2907[8]

3 ch c Grand Lodge (USA) - Suyayeb (USA) (The Minstrel (CAN)) 10f **(72)**

Form - 618

Record 1999 - 1st:1 2nd:0 3rd:0 Ran:3
Pre1999 - 1st:0 2nd:0 3rd:0 Ran:2

Win Prizemoney £7,132 *Total Prizemoney* £7,132

Wins * 1999 Jun Ripon (G-F) H 6f 68 72 <

1999 Turf 1-3: (6f 1-1, 7f, 8f) (g-f 1-2, frm)

Above-average colt. Turf high 72 - 1st of 11 getting 8lb from Bollin Rita (16 Jun Ripon RF 2060).

**J E Banks [1-5] Mrs Patricia Cunningham.*

DONE AND DUSTED (IRE) BHB 72f66a **RR 83df 66a** 4924[9]

3 ch f Up and At 'em - Florentink (USA) (The Minstrel (CAN)) 10f **(72)**

Form - 41146143315000

Record 1999 - 1st:2 2nd:0 3rd:2 Ran:10
Pre1999 - 1st:2 2nd:1 3rd:2 Ran:12

Win Prizemoney £14,288 *Total Prizemoney* £16,568

Wins * **1999** Apr Windso (GD) H 6f 60 68+
* **1999** *Feb Lingfi (STD) H 7f 62 70* <
* 1998 *Dec Lingfi (STD) C 7f 67*
1998 *Nov Southw (STD) S 7f 54*

1999 Turf 1-4: (6f 1-3, 7f) (gd, frm 1-3) 1999 AW 1-6: (6f 3, 7f 1-2, 8f) (Equi 1-3, Fibr 3)

Light-framed, decent filly, likes left handed tracks, likes tight tracks. Turf high 83. AW high 70. Becoming disappointing. She has shown consistent form in moderate company on sand, but used her fitness to full advantage when winning back on turf at Windsor in April.

**R Brotherton [3-12] Paul Stringer (from J Berry [1-10] Nov 1998).*

DONE WELL (USA) BHB 40f **RR 6f** 5190[11]

7 b g Storm Bird (CAN) 8.5f **(82)** - Suspicious Toosome (USA) (Secretariat (USA)) 9f **(79)**

Form - 0

Record 1999 - 1st:0 2nd:0 3rd:0 Ran:1
Pre1999 - 1st:1 2nd:3 3rd:1 Ran:14

Win Prizemoney £4,557 *Total Prizemoney* £8,762

1999 Turf 0-1: (12f) (g-f)

Very poor gelding. Becoming disappointing.

**P Monteith [2-21] Allan Melville (from E A L Dunlop [0-3] Jly 1995).*

DONNA'S DOUBLE BHB 67f55a **RR 65f 55a** 5217[19]

4 ch g Weldnaas (USA) 8.4f **(55)** - Shadha (Shirley Heights) 10.3f **(74)**

Form - 7026842602286 0110

Record 1999 - 1st:2 2nd:4 3rd:0 Ran:17
Pre1999 - 1st:2 2nd:1 3rd:4 Ran:16

Win Prizemoney £16,676 *Total Prizemoney* £27,102

Wins * **1999** Oct Redcar (SFT) H 8f 62 65 <
* **1999** Oct Catter (GD) H 7f 58 62
* 1998 Spt Hamilt (SFT) H 8.3f 49 54
* 1998 Spt Mussel (GD) H 7.1f 44 54

1999 Turf 2-15: (7f 1-5, 8f 1-6, 9f 4) (g-s 2, gd 2-6, g-f 3, frm 4) 1999 AW 0-2: (7f, 11f) (Fibr 2)

Workmanlike, average gelding, effective 7 to 9f, best at 7f, acts on gd to g-f, best on gd, does well at Newcastle. Turf high 65 - 1st of 16 from Tony Tie (26 Oct Redcar RF 5073) - also 1st of 15 getting 4lb from Inchalong (16 Oct Catterick RF 4914). He comes into his own in the autumn.

**D Eddy [4-24] James Adams (from Don Enrico Incisa [0-5] Jun 1998).*

DON PEPE BHB 56f42a **RR 55f 42a** 3766[11]

8 br g Dowsing (USA) 7f **(61)** - Unique Treasure (Young Generation) 7.7f **(63)**

Form - 558204030

Record 1999 - 1st:0 2nd:1 3rd:1 Ran:9
Pre1999 - 1st:9 2nd:5 3rd:7 Ran:63

Win Prizemoney £30,907 *Total Prizemoney* £40,687

Wins * 1998 Jly Yarmou (G-F) H 7f 55 58
1997 Jun Yarmou (FRM) H 6f 60 65 <
1996 Spt Yarmou (G-F) H 7f 62 65 <
1996 Jun Goodwo (GD) H 6f 56 61
1995 Jun Ayr (G-F) H 7f 67 65 <
1995 Apr Mussel (GD) H 7.1f 64 65 <

1999 Turf 0-9: (6f, 7f 7, 8f) (gd 2, g-f 4, frm 3)

Fair gelding, effective 6 to 8f, best at 7f, acts on gd to frm, has worn blinkers, likes left handed tracks, likes tight tracks, excels at Catterick and Thirsk, does well at Yarmouth. Turf high 57 - 5th of 12 getting 2lb from Lunch Party (15 Jun Thirsk 7f frm RF 2007).

**D Nicholls [1-22] Mrs Elaine Aird (from R Boss [8-50] Oct 1997).*

DON PUCCINI BHB 100f **RR 101f** 2901[1]

2 ch c Piccolo - Baileys by Name (Nomination) 7f **(60)**

Form - 3161

Record 1999 - 1st:2 2nd:0 3rd:1 Ran:4

Win Prizemoney £76,876 *Total Prizemoney* £77,485

Wins * **1999** Jly Newbur (G-F) 5.2f 101 <
* **1999** May Kempto (G-F) 6f 90

1999 Turf 2-4: (5f 1-2, 6f 1-2) (gd, g-f 1-2, frm 1-1)

Very useful colt. Turf high 101 - 1st of 25 giving 11lb to Halland Park Girl (17 Jly Newbury RF 2901). He put up a smashing performance to give Halland Park Girl 11lb and a half-length beating in the Weatherbys Super Sprint. Reported to be fully recovered from a stress fracture that kept him off the track in the second half of the season, he has plenty of scope and will make a smart sprinter in 2000 if recovering from a stress fracture sutained in August. Very genuine when racing, he often gets upset at the start.

**B Smart [2-4] The Tenors.*

DON QUIXOTE (IRE) BHB 47f **RR 42f** 2810[11]

3 b c Waajib 8.9f **(67)** - Maimiti (Goldhill) 8.5f **(55)**

Form - 0030

Record 1999 - 1st:0 2nd:0 3rd:1 Ran:4
Pre1999 - 1st:0 2nd:0 3rd:0 Ran:1

Win Prizemoney £0 *Total Prizemoney* £428

1999 Turf 0-4: (5f, 6f, 7f, 8f) (gd 2, g-f, frm)

Well made, moderate colt. Turf high 42.

**L M Cumani [0-5] M Tabor & Mrs John Magnier.*

DON'T ASK BHB 43f55a **RR 47df 55a** 4938[10]

3 b g Paris House 5.9f **(64)** - Glenfield Portion (Mummy's Pet) 7.7f **(60)**

Form - 5000

Record 1999 - 1st:0 2nd:0 3rd:0 Ran:4
Pre1999 - 1st:0 2nd:0 3rd:0 Ran:2

1999 Turf 0-2: (5f 2) (gd 2) 1999 AW 0-2: (5f, 6f) (Equi, Fibr)

Strong, moderate gelding, effective 5f, acts on g-f. Turf high 6. AW high 46.

**Mrs L C Jewell [0-2] Mrs Linda Jewell (from D J G MurraySmith [0-4] Apr 1999).*

DONTBESOBOLD (IRE) BHB 65f **RR 72f** 4934[14]

2 b g River Falls 8.2f **(56)** - Jarmar Moon **(55f)** (Unfuwain (USA))

Form - 4067040

Record 1999 - 1st:0 2nd:0 3rd:0 Ran:7

Win Prizemoney £0 *Total Prizemoney* £219

1999 Turf 0-7: (5f, 6f 2, 7f 3, 8f) (sft, g-f 4, frm, hrd)

Above-average gelding, effective 7f, acts on sft. Turf high 72 - 4th of 16 giving 1lb to Jamestown (21 Spt Warwick 7f sft RF 4451).

**B S Rothwell [0-7] J Eddings.*

DON'T DROP BOMBS (USA) BHB 22f35a **RR 24f 35a** 2146[13]

10 ch g Fighting Fit (USA) 7.9f **(70)** - Promised Star (USA) (Star de Naskra (USA)) 9.7f **(65)**

Form - 047500

Record 1999 - 1st:0 2nd:0 3rd:0 Ran:6
Pre1999 - 1st:8 2nd:15 3rd:17 Ran:97

Win Prizemoney £20,097 *Total Prizemoney* £37,986

Wins 1997 *Mar Lingfi (STD) H 8f 33 39*
1996 Spt Bright (FRM) H 10f 39 43
1996 Jly Yarmou (G-F) H 10.1f 35 34
1996 *Feb Lingfi (STD) H 8f 34 40*
1995 Aug Bright (FRM) H 10f 31 39
1995 *Jan Lingfi (STD) H 12f 29 37*

1999 Turf 0-2: (11f, 12f) (g-f, hrd) 1999 AW 0-4: (8f, 10f, 12f, 13f) (Equi 3, Fibr)

Very moderate gelding, effective 8 to 12f, - acts on AW, best on Equi, mostly wears blinkers, likes left handed tracks, likes tight tracks. AW high 34.

**H J Collingridge [0-6] Miss J Feilden (from R McGhin [0-14] Spt 1998).*

DONT GO MAD (USA) **RR 82f** 1241[1]

2 b br c Blush Rambler (USA) - Flaming Reason (USA) (Limit To Reason (USA))

Form - 41

Record 1999 - 1st:1 2nd:0 3rd:0 Ran:2

Win Prizemoney £4,425 *Total Prizemoney* £4,828

Wins * **1999** May Newmar (GD) 6f 82 <

1999 Turf 1-2: (5f, 6f 1-1) (g-f 1-2)

Currently decent colt. Turf high 82 - 1st of 12 from Dont Worry Bout Me (15 May Newmarket RF 1241). (DEAD)

**K R Burke [1-2] High Havens Stables.*

DON'T SURRENDER (IRE) BHB 91f **RR 92f** 5134[1]

2 b c Zieten (USA) - St Clair Star (Sallust) 8.4f **(63)**

Form - 2211

Record 1999 - 1st:2 2nd:2 3rd:0 Ran:4

Win Prizemoney £8,521 *Total Prizemoney* £10,901

Wins * **1999** Oct Newmar (G-S) 6f 92 <
* **1999** Oct Lingfi (G-F) 6f 80

1999 Turf 2-4: (6f 2-4) (gd 2-2, g-f, frm)

Useful colt. Turf high 92 (began Jly) - 1st of 11 getting 14lb from Blue Melody (29 Oct Newmarket RF 5134). Lived up to his name by

battling on well to win his last two starts. Should make a decent sprinter at three. **J L Dunlop [2-4] Bob Demuyser.*

DONT WORRY BOUT ME (IRE) BHB 67f **RR 65f** 5124[8]
2 b g Brief Truce (USA) 9.1f **(73)** - Coggle **(65f)** (Kind of Hush) 10.1f **(62)**
Form - 326308
Record 1999 - 1st:0 2nd:1 3rd:2 Ran:6
Win Prizemoney £0 *Total Prizemoney* £2,250
1999 Turf 0-5: (5f, 6f 3, 8f) (g-s, gd, g-f 2, frm) 1999 AW 0-1: (6f) (Fibr)
Average gelding, effective 5 to 6f, acts on g-f to frm. Turf high 78 - 2nd of 12 to Dont Go Mad (15 May Newmarket 6f g-f RF 1241). **T G Mills [0-6] Thorpe Vernon.*

DON'T WORRY MIKE BHB 36f38a **RR 31f 38a** 38[11]
5 ch g Forzando 7.2f **(63)** - Hat Hill (Roan Rocket) 7.8f **(57)**
Form - 0
Record 1999 - 1st:0 2nd:0 3rd:0 Ran:1
Pre1999 - 1st:0 2nd:4 3rd:1 Ran:24
Win Prizemoney £0 *Total Prizemoney* £3,189
1999 AW 0-1: (8f) (Fibr)
Very moderate gelding, has worn blinkers.
**K S Bridgwater [0-8] Miss E E Hill (from J L Spearing [0-13] May 1998).*

DOODLE BUG RR 76f 4006[7]
2 b f Missed Flight - Kaiserlinde (GER) (Frontal) 6.4f **(64)**
Form - 37
Record 1999 - 1st:0 2nd:0 3rd:1 Ran:2
Win Prizemoney £0 *Total Prizemoney* £478
1999 Turf 0-2: (7f, 8f) (gd, g-f)
Currently above-average filly. Turf high 76 (1st run) (began Aug) - 3rd of 11 to Vigour (11 Aug Leicester 7f g-f RF 3546). **T R Watson [0-2] Miss S Hoare.*

DOONAREE (IRE) BHB 95f **RR 96f** 4677[9]
3 b c Sadler's Wells (USA) 11.3f **(87)** - Rosananti (Blushing Groom (FR)) 10.3f **(76)**
Form - 1182340
Record 1999 - 1st:2 2nd:1 3rd:1 Ran:7
Win Prizemoney £10,002 *Total Prizemoney* £13,783
Wins * 1999 Apr Catter (SFT) 12f 78+
*** 1999** Apr Newcas (GD) 12.4f 83+ <
1999 Turf 2-7: (10f 2, 12f 2-5) (gd 2-4, g-f 2, frm)
Scopey, very useful colt, effective 10 to 12f, acts on g-f to frm. Turf high 96 - 3rd of 9 giving 15lb to Sandmoor Chambray (22 Aug Pontefract 12f frm RF 3847). He failed to live up to expectations, developing into a decent middle-distance handicapper rather than a Group horse. Sold for 70,000 guineas at Newmarket in October, he is set to continue his career over hurdles in Ireland. **M Johnston [2-7] M P Burke.*

DOOWALEY (IRE) RR 98f 4652[6]
3 b c Sadler's Wells (USA) - Dwell (USA) (Habitat)
Form - 16
Record 1999 - 1st:1 2nd:0 3rd:0 Ran:2
Win Prizemoney £7,290 *Total Prizemoney* £7,478
Wins * 1999 Spt San Si (GD) 10f 80 <
1999 Turf 1-2: (8f, 10f 1-1) (gd 1-2)
Currently very useful colt. Turf high 98 (began Spt). He belied his inexperience when finishing sixth in a Listed event at Newmarket in September. Already effective over a mile and a quarter, he is entitled to improve but may be difficult to place. **M R Channon [1-2] Luigi Colasanti.*

DORCHESTER RR 92f 4953[4]
2 b c Primo Dominie 7.2f **(67)** - Penthouse Lady (Last Tycoon) 8.5f **(62)**
Form - 801112374
Record 1999 - 1st:3 2nd:1 3rd:1 Ran:9
Win Prizemoney £8,761 *Total Prizemoney* £14,774
Wins * 1999 Jly Doncas (G-F) 5f 86 <
*** 1999** *Jly Southw (STD) H 5f 79*
*** 1999** Jly Nottin (GD) 5.1f 80
1999 Turf 2-8: (5f 2-5, 6f 3) (gd, g-f 2-4, frm 3) 1999 AW 1-1: (5f 1-1) (Fibr 1-1)
Useful colt, effective 5 to 6f, best at 5f, acts on gd to frm, best on frm, excels at Doncaster. Turf high 92 - 7th of 14 giving 5lb to Mrs P (11 Spt Doncaster 5f frm RF 4268) - also 1st of 7 getting 1lb from Shatin Venture (14 Jly Doncaster RF 2813). (1st run). He spoilt his chance in his early starts by starting slowly, but gradually got it together and completed a summer. Third in a French listed race on his first run over six, he is not an easy ride, and disappointed in the Flying Childers. **Sir Mark Prescott [3-9] Cheveley Park Stud.*

DORISSIO (IRE) BHB 64f **RR 66+f** 4718[1]
3 b f Efisio 7.7f **(69)** - Floralia (Auction Ring (USA)) 8.6f **(65)**
Form - 48060011
Record 1999 - 1st:2 2nd:0 3rd:0 Ran:8
Pre1999 - 1st:0 2nd:0 3rd:0 Ran:1
Win Prizemoney £10,599 *Total Prizemoney* £10,797
Wins * 1999 Oct Pontef (SFT) H 8f 54 66+ <
*** 1999** Spt Bath (FRM) SH 8f 50 54
1999 Turf 2-8: (6f 4, 7f 2, 8f 2-2) (sft, gd 1-1, g-f 2, frm 1-4)
Strong, average filly, effective 8f, acts on gd. Turf high 66 - 1st of 19 getting 18lb from Adelphi Boy (4 Oct Pontefract RF 4718). Showed much-improved form when stepped up to a mile for her last two starts, winning both in good style. Suited by middle distances at three. **I A Balding [2-9] Miss A V Hill.*

DOROTHEA SHARP (IRE) BHB 53f **RR 53+f** 4728[14]
2 b br f Foxhound (USA) - Captain's Niece (Vitiges (FR)) 8.2f **(59)**
Form - 080
Record 1999 - 1st:0 2nd:0 3rd:0 Ran:3
1999 Turf 0-3: (6f 2, 8f) (g-s, frm 2)
Currently fair filly. Turf high 53 (began Jly).
**N P Littmoden [0-3] Richard Green (Fine Paintings).*

DOROTHY ALLEN BHB 50f40a **RR 58f 40a** 370[9]
3 b f Mon Tresor 7.9f **(60)** - Anytime Anywhere (Daring March) 7.1f **(61)**
Form - 0
Record 1999 - 1st:0 2nd:0 3rd:0 Ran:1
Pre1999 - 1st:0 2nd:0 3rd:1 Ran:3
Win Prizemoney £0 *Total Prizemoney* £270
1999 AW 0-1: (7f) (Fibr)
Neat, fair filly. **M R Channon [0-4] Malcolm Allen.*

DORRINGTON BHB 50f40a **RR 56df 40a** 37[8]
4 b g Puissance 7.1f **(60)** - Prydwen (Hard Fought) 8.8f **(62)**
Form - 8
Record 1999 - 1st:0 2nd:0 3rd:0 Ran:1
Pre1999 - 1st:0 2nd:0 3rd:0 Ran:3
1999 AW 0-1: (9f) (Fibr)
Workmanlike, fair gelding.
**B P J Baugh [0-2] Mrs J Gill (from M Johnston [0-3] Jly 1998).*

DORTON GRANGE BHB 38f40a **RR 22f 40a** 2088a[6]
4 ch f Absalom 7.1f **(56)** - Stranger to Fear (Never so Bold) 6.3f **(66)**
Form - 00506
Record 1999 - 1st:0 2nd:0 3rd:0 Ran:5
Pre1999 - 1st:0 2nd:0 3rd:1 Ran:10
Win Prizemoney £0 *Total Prizemoney* £413
1999 Turf 0-4: (6f, 7f 2, 8f) (sft, gd, g-f, frm) 1999 AW 0-1: (6f) (Fibr)
Light-framed, little account filly. Turf high 22. Inconsistent.
**H J Manners [0-5] (from N E Berry [0-5] Aug 1998).*

DOUBLE ACTION BHB 67f **RR 66f** 4804[6]
5 br g Reprimand 8.2f **(63)** - Final Shot (Dalsaan) 9.8f **(64)**
Form - 58404000332006
Record 1999 - 1st:0 2nd:1 3rd:2 Ran:14
Pre1999 - 1st:3 2nd:3 3rd:3 Ran:27
Win Prizemoney £27,190 *Total Prizemoney* £65,784
Wins * 1997 Spt York (SFT) H 6f 90 104 <
* 1997 Jun Ripon (GD) H 6f 86 88
* 1996 May Thirsk (G-F) 5f 71
1999 Turf 0-14: (6f 6, 7f 7, 8f) (g-s, gd 6, g-f 6, frm)
Average gelding, effective 6f, acts on gd, has worn blinkers. Turf high 77. **T D Easterby [3-41] C H Stevens.*

DOUBLE BAILEYS BHB 63f60a **RR 71f 60a** 4893[12]
3 b g Robellino (USA) 9.5f **(68)** - Thimblerigger (Sharpen Up) 8.3f **(67)**
Form - 52723050
Record 1999 - 1st:0 2nd:2 3rd:1 Ran:8
Pre1999 - 1st:0 2nd:0 3rd:1 Ran:1
Win Prizemoney £0 *Total Prizemoney* £3,477

1999 Turf 0-7: (11f, 12f 2, 14f, 15f, 16f, 17f) (gd 4, g-f, frm, hrd) 1999 AW 0-1: (13f) (Equi)
Rangy, above-average gelding, effective 11 to 17f, acts on g-f to hrd, has worn blinkers, prefers tight tracks. Turf high 71 - 3rd of 7 getting 12lb from Ten Kingdoms (11 Jly Haydock 12f frm RF 2739). Inconsistent. **M Johnston [0-9] The Double Baileys Partnership.*

DOUBLE BANGER (IRE) RR 75f 4818[4]

2 b c Ela-Mana-Mou 12.7f **(72)** - Penny Banger (IRE) (Pennine Walk) 8.5f **(61)**
Form - 34
Record 1999 - 1st:0 2nd:0 3rd:1 Ran:2
Win Prizemoney £0 *Total Prizemoney* £975
1999 Turf 0-2: (10f 2) (gd 2)
Currently above-average colt. Turf high 75 (began Oct).
**M Johnston [0-2] R W Huggins & P H Wilkerson.*

DOUBLE BLADE BHB 59f RR 61f 3973[7]

4 b g Kris 10f **(75)** - Sesame (Derrylin) 8.8f **(54)**
Form - 047
Record 1999 - 1st:0 2nd:0 3rd:0 Ran:3
Pre1999 - 1st:0 2nd:2 3rd:3 Ran:10
Win Prizemoney £0 *Total Prizemoney* £4,347
1999 Turf 0-3: (12f, 14f, 16f) (g-f 2, frm)
Strong, average gelding, effective 9 to 12f, acts on gd to frm, has worn blinkers, likes tight tracks. Turf high 61 (began Jly).
**Mrs M Reveley [0-3] The Mary Reveley Racing Club (from M Johnston [0-10] Oct 1998).*

DOUBLE BOUNCE BHB 76f RR 76f 3261[27]

9 b g Interrex (CAN) 7.7f **(51)** - Double Gift (Cragador) 6f **(67)**
Form - 060
Record 1999 - 1st:0 2nd:0 3rd:0 Ran:3
Pre1999 - 1st:6 2nd:2 3rd:4 Ran:38
Win Prizemoney £45,874 *Total Prizemoney* £72,646
Wins 1996 Jun Newcas (FRM) H 6f 84 85 <
1995 Oct York (GD) H 6f 77 81
1995 Spt Haydoc (GD) H 6f 70 74
1995 Jly Nottin (G-F) H 6.1f 65 66
1999 Turf 0-3: (6f 3) (gd, g-f, frm)
Above-average gelding, has worn blinkers. Turf high 72.
**H Morrison [0-3] Mrs P Scott-Dunn (from H Candy [0-3] Nov 1998).*

DOUBLE BRANDY BHB 76f RR 77f 4085[7]

4 ch c Elmaamul (USA) 8.1f **(70)** - Brand (Shareef Dancer (USA)) 9.9f **(73)**
Form - 0011067
Record 1999 - 1st:2 2nd:0 3rd:0 Ran:7
Pre1999 - 1st:1 2nd:1 3rd:0 Ran:9
Win Prizemoney £16,437 *Total Prizemoney* £17,259
Wins * **1999** Jun Doncas (G-F) H 8f 73 77
* **1999** Jun Windso (G-F) H 8.3f 70 73
* 1998 May Newbur (G-F) H 6f 74 79 <
1999 Turf 2-7: (7f, 8f 2-6) (gd, g-f 1-2, frm 1-4)
Unfurnished, above-average colt, effective 6 to 8f, best at 8f, acts on g-f to frm, best on frm. Turf high 77 - 1st of 13 giving 16lb to Freedom Quest (27 Jun Doncaster RF 2350) - also 1st of 18 giving 13lb to Daintree (14 Jun Windsor RF 1990). He hit form in June of this year with victories at Windsor and Doncaster. A mile on fast ground seems to suit him admirably.
**I A Balding [3-16] Queen Elizabeth.*

DOUBLE CHOICE (IRE) BHB 60f RR 59f 3434[10]

3 b f Doubletour (USA) 12f **(46)** - Virginia Cottage (Lomond (USA)) 8.8f **(65)**
Form - 000550
Record 1999 - 1st:0 2nd:0 3rd:0 Ran:6
Pre1999 - 1st:2 2nd:0 3rd:0 Ran:5
Win Prizemoney £10,010 *Total Prizemoney* £10,504
Wins * 1998 Jly Goodwo (G-S) H 5f 71 <
* 1998 Jly Leices (GD) H 5f 70
1999 Turf 0-6: (5f 5, 6f) (g-s, gd 2, frm 3)
Workmanlike, fair filly, effective 5f, acts on gd to frm. Turf high 59. Consistent. **R Hannon [2-11] John Homer Racing.*

DOUBLE DESTINY BHB 60f RR 66f 4181[9]

3 b g Anshan 8.2f **(63)** - Double Gift (Cragador) 6f **(67)**
Form - 670
Record 1999 - 1st:0 2nd:0 3rd:0 Ran:3
1999 Turf 0-3: (6f, 7f 2) (g-f, frm 2)
Currently average gelding. Turf high 66 (began Aug).
**H Candy [0-3] Mrs P Scott-Dunn.*

DOUBLE ECHO (IRE) BHB 30f28a RR 38f 28a 450[7]

11 br g Glow (USA) 10.2f **(61)** - Piculet (Morston (FR)) 9.4f **(55)**
Form - 50423757
Record 1999 - 1st:0 2nd:1 3rd:1 Ran:5
Pre1999 - 1st:10 2nd:7 3rd:5 Ran:75
Win Prizemoney £35,964 *Total Prizemoney* £52,814
Wins * 1998 *Jan Southw (STD) H 11f 31 44*
* 1998 *Jan Southw (STD) H 12f 25 45*
* 1998 *Jan Southw (STD) H 11f 25 32*
* 1996 Spt Newbur (G-F) H 12f 46 51
1999 AW 0-5: (11f, 12f 3, 14f) (Fibr 5)
Very moderate gelding, effective 11 to 12f, best at 11f, - acts on Fibr, has worn blinkers, favours left handed tracks.
**J D Bethell [10-80] Mrs John Lee.*

DOUBLE ENTRY BHB 30f RR 21f 4928[8]

2 b c Rambo Dancer (CAN) 8.4f **(59)** - Andbracket (Import) 6.6f **(68)**
Form - 008
Record 1999 - 1st:0 2nd:0 3rd:0 Ran:3
1999 Turf 0-3: (6f 2, 8f) (g-f 2, frm)
Currently little account colt. Turf high 21 (began Jly).
**D Nicholls [0-3] Deeteecee Eff Partnership.*

DOUBLE FAULT (IRE) BHB 55f RR 60f 4103[11]

2 br f Zieten (USA) - Kashapour (Nishapour (FR)) 9.1f **(61)**
Form - 702840
Record 1999 - 1st:0 2nd:1 3rd:0 Ran:6
Win Prizemoney £0 *Total Prizemoney* £1,276
1999 Turf 0-6: (5f 3, 6f, 7f, 8f) (gd 2, frm 4)
Average filly, effective 5f, acts on frm. Turf high 60 - 2nd of 8 getting 5lb from Slick Willie (13 Jly Beverley 5f frm RF 2770).
**T D Easterby [0-6] I Bray.*

DOUBLE FLIGHT BHB 50f55a RR 47f 55a 4429[19]

5 b m Mtoto 11.5f **(71)** - Sariah (Kris) 9.5f **(73)**
Form - 340670
Record 1999 - 1st:0 2nd:0 3rd:0 Ran:5
Pre1999 - 1st:1 2nd:2 3rd:2 Ran:13
Win Prizemoney £4,347 *Total Prizemoney* £7,814
Wins 1996 Spt Ayr (G-F) H 8f 66 <
1999 Turf 0-3: (9f 2, 12f) (g-s, frm 2) 1999 AW 0-2: (12f, 13f) (Equi 2)
Fair filly, has broken blood-vessels, effective 10f, - acts on Equi. Turf high 47. AW high 54. Inconsistent.
**Miss B Sanders [0-8] Mark Champion (from M Johnston [1-12] Spt 1997).*

DOUBLE GUN BHB 75f RR 74f 4942[3]

2 b c Puissance 7.1f **(60)** - Star of Jupiter (Jupiter Island) 14f **(62)**
Form - 843
Record 1999 - 1st:0 2nd:0 3rd:1 Ran:3
Win Prizemoney £0 *Total Prizemoney* £702
1999 Turf 0-3: (6f 3) (gd, frm 2)
Currently above-average colt. Turf high 74 (began Aug).
**R Hannon [0-3] Heathavon Stables Ltd.*

DOUBLE HEART (FR) RR 101f 5009a[3]

3 b c
Form - 3
1999 Turf 0-1: (8f) (hvy)
Currently very useful colt. (1st run) - 3rd of 10 to Spadoun (14 Oct Longchamp 8f hvy RF 5009a). **in FR [0-1].*

DOUBLE IDENTITY BHB 30f RR 35f 4824[10]

4 b f Rudimentary (USA) 8.2f **(66)** - Frivolous Fancy (Piaffer (USA))
Form - 00000
Record 1999 - 1st:0 2nd:0 3rd:0 Ran:5
1999 Turf 0-5: (6f, 8f 2, 10f, 12f) (hvy, gd, g-f 3)
Workmanlike, very moderate filly. Turf high 35.
**T D McCarthy [0-5] & Mrs M A Roberts.*

DOUBLE-J (IRE) BHB 38f **RR 39f** 4448[9]

5 b g Fayruz 6.6f **(63)** - Farriers Slipper (Prince Tenderfoot (USA)) 9f **(61)**

Form - 80550

Record 1999 - 1st:0 2nd:0 3rd:0 Ran:5
Pre1999 - 1st:1 2nd:4 3rd:2 Ran:22

Win Prizemoney £3,059 *Total Prizemoney* £12,362

Wins 1996 Jly Beverl (G-F) 5f 83 <

1999 Turf 0-5: (7f, 8f 3, 10f) (g-s, gd 2, g-f 2)

Very moderate gelding, has worn blinkers. Turf high 39.

**M Brittain [0-12] Northgate Lodge Racing Club (from K McAuliffe [1-15] Oct 1997).*

DOUBLE M BHB 80f **RR 83f** 4043[4]

2 ch c First Trump - Girton Degree (Balliol) 5f **(43)**

Form - 6241474

Record 1999 - 1st:1 2nd:1 3rd:0 Ran:7

Win Prizemoney £3,655 *Total Prizemoney* £5,055

Wins * **1999** Jly Nottin (G-F) 5.1f 83+ <

1999 Turf 1-6: (5f 1-5, 6f) (g-f 3, frm 1-3) 1999 AW 0-1: (5f) (Fibr)

Decent colt, effective 5f, acts on frm, mostly wears blinkers (effectively). Turf high 83 - 1st of 5 from Power Packed (23 Jly Nottingham RF 3067). **J L Spearing [1-7] Bryan Mathieson.*

DOUBLE MARCH BHB 62f60a **RR 66f 60a** 4826[16]

6 b g Weldnaas (USA) 8.4f **(55)** - Double Gift (Cragador) 6f **(67)**

Form - 0050040

Record 1999 - 1st:0 2nd:0 3rd:0 Ran:7
Pre1999 - 1st:3 2nd:2 3rd:3 Ran:25

Win Prizemoney £12,423 *Total Prizemoney* £19,062

Wins 1998 Oct Nottin (SFT) H 6.1f 67 68
1998 Jun Windso (SFT) H 6f 56 58
1998 May Nottin (GF) H 6.1f 50 53

1999 Turf 0-7: (6f 7) (gd 2, g-f 2, frm 2, hrd)

Average gelding, effective 5 to 6f, best at 6f, acts on sft to g-f, best on g-f, excels at Nottingham and Windsor. Turf high 66 - 5th of 11 giving 15lb to Cold Climate (6 Aug Newmarket 6f g-f RF 3426).

**H Candy [0-5] Mrs P Scott-Dunn (from K T Ivory [3-17] May 1999).*

DOUBLE-O BHB 70f73a **RR 68?f 73a** 5212[9]

5 b g Sharpo 7.5f **(68)** - Ktolo (Tolomeo) 5.6f **(60)**

Form - 050036200180

Record 1999 - 1st:1 2nd:1 3rd:1 Ran:10
Pre1999 - 1st:5 2nd:0 3rd:1 Ran:20

Win Prizemoney £23,277 *Total Prizemoney* £25,353

Wins * **1999** Oct Bright (G-S) H 5.3f 64 68?
* 1998 *Feb Wolver (STD) H 5f 79 85* <
* 1998 *Feb Wolver (STD) H 6f 74 75*
* 1997 *Dec Wolver (STD) H 6f 69 75*
* 1997 *Mar Southw (STD) H 6f 70 73*
* 1996 *Dec Wolver (STD) 6f 78*

1999 Turf 1-7: (5f 1-5, 6f 2) (g-s, gd 1-3, g-f 3) 1999 AW 0-3: (6f 3) (Equi, Fibr 2)

Above-average gelding, effective 5 to 6f, - acts on Fibr, has worn blinkers, likes left handed tracks, likes tight tracks. Turf high 68 (began Aug). AW high 73. **W Jarvis [6-30] Canisbay Bloodstock Ltd.*

DOUBLE OSCAR (IRE) BHB 74f93a **RR 68f 93a** 5212[12]

6 ch g Royal Academy (USA) 7.8f **(77)** - Broadway Rosie (Absalom) 7.2f **(58)**

Form - 002060124720004000

Record 1999 - 1st:1 2nd:3 3rd:0 Ran:18
Pre1999 - 1st:10 2nd:7 3rd:10 Ran:64

Win Prizemoney £48,627 *Total Prizemoney* £74,070

Wins * **1999** Jun Ayr (GD) H 5f 74 78
* 1998 Aug Ascot (G-F) H 5f 73 84+
* 1998 Jly Goodwo (G-S) H 5f 73 80
* 1998 *Apr Wolver (STD) H 5f 84 88* <
* 1998 *Jan Lingfi (STD) C 6f 75+*
* 1997 Aug Carlis (FRM) H 5f 75 80
* 1997 Aug Pontef (G-F) H 5f 62 76
* 1997 Aug Catter (G-F) H 5f 62 69
* 1997 Jly Folkes (G-F) H 6f 48 61+
* 1997 Apr Nottin (G-F) C 5.1f 53
1995 Jun Ayr (G-F) 6f 68

1999 Turf 1-18: (5f 1-10, 6f 8) (g-s 2, gd 5, g-f 1-9, frm 2)

Useful gelding, effective 5 to 6f, best at 5f, acts on gd to g-f - acts on AW, best on g-f, often wears blinkers (very effectively), likes left handed tracks, likes tight tracks, excels at Wolverhampton and Lingfield and Goodwood. Turf high 81 - 2nd of 12 giving 7lb to Antonia's Double (24 Jly Newcastle 5f g-f RF 3101). He scored at Ayr in June of this year as well as putting up some fine performances in defeat, but his style of racing means he needs to get the breaks when they are needed, and not getting them cost him dear at least once last season. Alex Greaves rides him particularly well.

**D Nicholls [10-68] Trilby Racing (from M Johnston [1-14] Aug 1996).*

DOUBLE PLATINUM **RR 86f** 4920[8]

2 ch f Seeking the Gold (USA) 7.4f **(80)** - Band (USA) (Northern Dancer) 9.6f **(80)**

Form - 28

Record 1999 - 1st:0 2nd:1 3rd:0 Ran:2

Win Prizemoney £0 *Total Prizemoney* £1,610

1999 Turf 0-2: (6f, 7f) (gd 2)

Currently useful filly. Turf high 86 (began Oct).

**A G Foster [0-1] Lord Lloyd-Webber (from P W Chapple-Hyam [0-1] Oct 1999).*

DOUBLE RED (IRE) **RR 66f** 4934[2]

2 b f Thatching 7.8f **(69)** - Local Custom (IRE) (Be My Native (USA)) 10.2f **(71)**

Form - 08722

Record 1999 - 1st:0 2nd:2 3rd:0 Ran:5

Win Prizemoney £0 *Total Prizemoney* £2,063

1999 Turf 0-5: (5f, 6f 2, 8f, 10f) (g-s, g-f, frm 3)

Average filly. Turf high 66 (began Spt) - 2nd of 19 getting 3lb from Fashion (18 Oct Pontefract 8f g-f RF 4934).

**M L W Bell [0-5] Terry Neill.*

DOUBLE RUSH (IRE) BHB 36f58a **RR 41f 58a** 4648[6]

7 b g Doulab (USA) 7.4f **(61)** - Stanza Dancer (Stanford) 7.9f **(56)**

Form - 3203454376

Record 1999 - 1st:0 2nd:1 3rd:3 Ran:10
Pre1999 - 1st:7 2nd:3 3rd:2 Ran:46

Win Prizemoney £16,518 *Total Prizemoney* £23,575

Wins 1998 Jly Bath (GD) S 11.7f 48
1996 *Nov Lingfi (STD) H 10f 53 61* <
1996 *Nov Lingfi (STD) 10f 59+*
1996 Aug Bright (FRM) H 10f 48 56
1996 Aug Bright (FRM) H 10f 40 48+
1995 *Nov Lingfi (STD) 10f 59*
1995 Mar Folkes (GD) 6.9f 58

1999 Turf 0-9: (12f 4, 14f 2, 15f 2, 16f) (sft, g-s, g-f 3, frm 4) 1999 AW 0-1: (12f) (Fibr)

Moderate gelding, effective 10f, - acts on Equi, has worn blinkers, likes left handed tracks. Turf high 43.

**T Keddy [0-14] The Barneby Partnership (from T G Mills [7-46] Oct 1998).*

DOUBLE SPLENDOUR (IRE) BHB 82f72a **RR 86df 72a** 5160[22]

9 b g Double Schwartz 7f **(60)** - Princess Pamela (Dragonara Palace (USA)) 6.1f **(55)**

Form - 00231657000

Record 1999 - 1st:1 2nd:1 3rd:1 Ran:11
Pre1999 - 1st:8 2nd:7 3rd:3 Ran:43

Win Prizemoney £42,068 *Total Prizemoney* £75,929

Wins * **1999** Jly Newmar (G-F) H 6f 82 86
* 1998 May Newmar (GD) H 6f 95 100 <
* 1996 Jly York (GD) H 6f 82 87
* 1996 Apr Nottin (G-F) H 6.1f 70 83+
* 1995 Oct Newcas (G-F) H 6f 66 70
* 1995 Oct Haydoc (G-S) H 6f 60 64
* 1995 Spt Yarmou (GD) H 6f 51 61+
* 1995 Apr Nottin (G-F) H 6.1f 41 46

1999 Turf 1-11: (6f 1-11) (gd 2, g-f 4, frm 1-5)

Useful gelding, effective 6f, acts on gd to g-f, best on gd. Turf high 86. He proved he was no back number last summer, including a victory at Newmarket.

**P S Felgate [9-54] M Heywood, E Rollinson & J Spooner.*

DOUBLE STAR BHB 35f **RR 42f** 4563[10]

8 b g Soviet Star (USA) 8.6f **(74)** - Startino (Bustino) 10.4f **(64)**

Form - 502030

Record 1999 - 1st:0 2nd:1 3rd:1 Ran:6

Pre1999 - 1st:0 2nd:0 3rd:1 Ran:3
Win Prizemoney £0 *Total Prizemoney* £1,718
1999 Turf 0-6: (12f, 14f 3, 16f, 17f) (g-s, gd, g-f 2, frm 2)
Moderate gelding. Turf high 42 (began Jly).
**J L Harris [1-19] A K Collins.*

DOUBLE STYLE RR 46?f 4145[6]
2 ch c Presidium 7.5f **(56)** - Sorrowful (Moorestyle) 6.9f **(64)**
Form - 06
Record 1999 - 1st:0 2nd:0 3rd:0 Ran:2
1999 Turf 0-2: (6f, 8f) (hrd 2)
Currently moderate colt. Turf high 46 (began Aug).
**J L Eyre [0-2] K Birkinshaw.*

DOUBLE TWO (IRE) BHB 45f **RR 33f** 1725[7]
3 br g Petardia 8.2f **(58)** - Reasonably French (Reasonable (FR))
Form - 07
Record 1999 - 1st:0 2nd:0 3rd:0 Ran:2
Pre1999 - 1st:0 2nd:0 3rd:2 Ran:8
Win Prizemoney £0 *Total Prizemoney* £994
1999 Turf 0-2: (7f, 8f) (gd, frm)
Very moderate gelding, often wears blinkers. Turf high 27. Becoming disappointing. **T D Easterby [0-10] C H Stevens.*

DOUBLE VISION RR 54f 5157[14]
2 ch c Most Welcome 8.6f **(66)** - Two Moons (Bold Lad (IRE)) 8.4f **(68)**
Form - 00
Record 1999 - 1st:0 2nd:0 3rd:0 Ran:2
1999 Turf 0-2: (6f, 7f) (g-f, frm)
Currently fair colt. Turf high 54 (began Spt).
**C W Thornton [0-2] Guy Reed.*

DOUBTLESS RISK BHB 42f **RR 28f** 5186[11]
2 b c Risk Me (FR) 8f **(53)** - Doubtfire (Jalmood (USA)) 10.1f **(52)**
Form - 6540000
Record 1999 - 1st:0 2nd:0 3rd:0 Ran:7
Win Prizemoney £0 *Total Prizemoney* £226
1999 Turf 0-7: (5f, 6f 2, 7f 2, 8f 2) (sft, g-s, gd 2, g-f 2, frm)
Little account colt, has worn blinkers. Turf high 72.
**Miss L A Perratt [0-7] J A Davidson.*

DOUX DELICE BHB 44f **RR 45f** 3834[7]
3 b f Deploy 11.4f **(67)** - Springs Welcome (Blakeney) 10.5f **(64)**
Form - 007
Record 1999 - 1st:0 2nd:0 3rd:0 Ran:3
1999 Turf 0-3: (10f 2, 12f) (g-s, frm 2)
Workmanlike, currently moderate filly. Turf high 45.
**C A Cyzer [0-3] R M Cyzer.*

DOVEBRACE BHB 38f47a **RR 40f 47a** 4488[6]
6 b g Dowsing (USA) 7f **(61)** - Naufrage (Main Reef) 9.6f **(57)**
Form - 830673086
Record 1999 - 1st:0 2nd:0 3rd:2 Ran:9
Pre1999 - 1st:3 2nd:1 3rd:1 Ran:32
Win Prizemoney £17,640 *Total Prizemoney* £21,943
Wins * 1995 Aug Cheste (G-F) 6.1f 95
* 1995 May York (GD) 6f 92
* 1995 May Haydoc (G-F) 5f 98t? <
1999 Turf 0-9: (7f 5, 8f 3, 10f) (g-s, gd, g-f 2, frm 4, hrd)
Average gelding, effective 7f, acts on g-f to frm, has worn blinkers. Turf high 43.
**A Bailey [3-27] Dovebrace Ltd Air-Conditioning-Projects (from T D Barron [0-16] Aug 1998).*

DOVEDON TIMES BHB 34f38a **RR 15f 38a** 3792[12]
3 ch g Timeless Times (USA) 6.1f **(56)** - La Pepper (Workboy) 7.3f **(46)**
Form - 0503258000
Record 1999 - 1st:0 2nd:1 3rd:1 Ran:8
Pre1999 - 1st:0 2nd:0 3rd:0 Ran:2
Win Prizemoney £0 *Total Prizemoney* £984
1999 Turf 0-2: (8f 2) (g-f, frm) 1999 AW 0-6: (6f 2, 7f, 8f 3) (Equi, Fibr 5)
Lengthy, moderate gelding, effective 6f, - acts on Fibr, has worn blinkers. Turf high 15 (began Jly). AW high 45. Becoming disappointing. **H Akbary [0-10] Michael Whatley.*

DOVE'S DOMINION BHB 58f **RR 52f** 5195[9]
2 b c Primo Dominie 7.2f **(67)** - Dame Helene (USA) (Sir Ivor) 10.2f **(70)**
Form - 800
Record 1999 - 1st:0 2nd:0 3rd:0 Ran:3
1999 Turf 0-3: (6f 3) (hvy, gd, g-f)
Currently fair colt. Turf high 52 (began Oct).
**M R Channon [0-3] W A Harrison-Allan.*

DOVIRI (USA) RR 68f 4992[4]
3 ch f Irish River (FR) 9f **(77)** - Storm Dove (USA) (Storm Bird (CAN)) 10.3f **(74)**
Form - 34
Record 1999 - 1st:0 2nd:0 3rd:1 Ran:2
Win Prizemoney £0 *Total Prizemoney* £818
1999 Turf 0-2: (9f, 10f) (g-s, frm)
Scopey, currently average filly. Turf high 68 (began Oct) - 4th of 15 to Anaam (20 Oct Nottingham 10f frm RF 4992).
**R Charlton [0-2] K Abdulla.*

DOWER HOUSE BHB 97f **RR 104?f** 1757[12]
4 ch c Groom Dancer (USA) 9.5f **(75)** - Rose Noble (USA) (Vaguely Noble) 10.1f **(72)**
Form - U450
Record 1999 - 1st:0 2nd:0 3rd:0 Ran:4
Pre1999 - 1st:2 2nd:2 3rd:2 Ran:10
Win Prizemoney £21,505 *Total Prizemoney* £39,283
Wins * 1998 Jun Epsom (GD) H 10.1f 95 97 <
* 1997 Spt Yarmou (FRM) 8f 84+
1999 Turf 0-4: (9f, 10f 3) (g-s, gd 2, g-f)
Scopey, very useful colt, effective 9 to 12f, acts on gd to frm. Turf high 104 - 4th of 10 giving 3lb to Shiva (14 Apr Newmarket 9f gd RF 0693). Inconsistent. He failed to progress after finishing fourth in the Earl Of Sefton Stakes, but hails from a stable that was out of sorts during the summer. Tough and genuine at his best, he stays a mile and a half and goes well on fast ground.
**W Jarvis [2-14] Lord Howard de Walden.*

DOWNLAND (IRE) BHB 83f **RR 82f** 5106[7]
3 b c Common Grounds 8.1f **(66)** - Boldabsa (Persian Bold) 9.3f **(66)**
Form - 210627
Record 1999 - 1st:1 2nd:2 3rd:0 Ran:6
Pre1999 - 1st:0 2nd:0 3rd:0 Ran:1
Win Prizemoney £3,622 *Total Prizemoney* £6,625
Wins * 1999 Jly Lingfi (G-F) 6f 78++ <
1999 Turf 1-6: (6f 1-4, 8f, 10f) (g-s, gd, g-f 2, frm 1-2)
Well made, decent colt, effective 6 to 8f, best at 6f, acts on g-f to frm, best on frm. Turf high 82 - 2nd of 11 giving 13lb to Picture Puzzle (19 Spt Newcastle 8f frm RF 4426) - also 1st of 4 from Elmhurst Boy (7 Jly Lingfield RF 2625). Galloped to the easiest of maiden victories at Lingfield from a moderate and small field but later showed himself to be a very difficult ride.
**G Wragg [1-7] Mollers Racing.*

DRAFT OF VINTAGE (IRE) RR 97f 5091a[7]
6 b g Imperial Frontier (USA) 7f **(65)** - Kelly's Vintage (Persian Bold) 9.3f **(66)**
Form - 823434265087
1999 Turf 0-12: (7f 3, 8f 3, 9f 4, 10f, 11f) (sft 2, g-s 3, gd 3, g-f 4)
Very useful gelding, effective 7 to 10f, best at 9f, acts on g-s to g-f, best on g-f, likes right handed tracks, excels at Fairyhouse and likes Leopardstown. Turf high 101 - 3rd of 11 giving 11lb to Tarry Flynn (18 Apr Leopardstown 7f g-f RF 0787a). Consistent.
**J E Mulhern in IRE [5-34] J E Mulhern.*

DRAGON STAR BHB 57f **RR 51f** 3610[6]
2 b f Rudimentary (USA) 8.2f **(66)** - Nazakat (Known Fact (USA)) 7.4f **(67)**
Form - 36
Record 1999 - 1st:0 2nd:0 3rd:1 Ran:2
Win Prizemoney £0 *Total Prizemoney* £535
1999 Turf 0-2: (5f, 6f) (frm 2)
Currently fair filly. Turf high 51 (began Jly).
**J W Payne [0-2] T H Barma.*

DRAGON TRIUMPH (IRE) RR 91f 3337a[8]
4 b c Alzao (USA) 9.8f **(73)** - Tir-An-Oir (Law Society (USA)) 9.9f **(70)**
Form - 0577P8
1999 Turf 0-5: (10f, 12f 2, 14f 2) (hvy, g-s, gd, g-f 2)
Useful colt, effective 10 to 12f, best at 12f, acts on hvy to hrd,

prefers right handed tracks. Turf high 91. Inconsistent.
**J T Gorman in IRE [2-17] Timothy Beardson.*

DRAKENSBERG BHB 63f **RR 55f** 4836[14]
4 b g Bering 9.6f **(80)** - Theme (IRE) (Sadler's Wells (USA)) 10f **(76)**
Form - 107000
Record 1999 - 1st:1 2nd:0 3rd:0 Ran:6
Pre1999 - 1st:0 2nd:0 3rd:0 Ran:1
Win Prizemoney £3,567 *Total Prizemoney* £3,567
Wins * 1999 Apr Leices (HVY) 10f 75 <
1999 Turf 1-6: (10f 1-3, 11f, 14f 2) (sft 1-1, g-s, gd, frm 3)
Workmanlike, fair gelding, effective 10f, acts on sft, likes tight tracks. Turf high 75 (1st run) - 1st of 9 giving 22lb to Amaretto Flame (24 Apr Leicester RF 0833). Unraced at two and bred to need middle distances, he got off the mark in heavy ground over ten furlongs at Leicester in April, but was disappointing afterwards. **Lady Herries [1-7] Mrs Berta Lazarus.*

DRAMATIC QUEST BHB 100f **RR 105+f** 4252[5]
2 b c Zafonic (USA) 9f **(83)** - Ultra Finesse (USA) (Rahy (USA))
Form - 7115
Record 1999 - 1st:2 2nd:0 3rd:0 Ran:4
Win Prizemoney £11,625 *Total Prizemoney* £11,625
Wins * 1999 Jly Ascot (G-F) 7f 105+ <
*** 1999** May Pontef (G-F) 6f 84+
1999 Turf 2-4: (6f 1-2, 7f 1-2) (g-s, g-f 2-2, frm)
Pattern-class colt. Turf high 105 - 1st of 7 giving 14lb to Meadaaar (10 Jly Ascot RF 2702). A tough and able juvenile, he proved no match for Distant Music and company in the Champagne Stakes at Doncaster. **M Johnston [2-4] Maktoum Al Maktoum.*

DRAMATIC SCENES BHB 48f **RR 49?f** 1642[12]
3 b f Deploy 11.4f **(67)** - Dramatic Mood (Jalmood (USA)) 10.1f **(52)**
Form - 070
Record 1999 - 1st:0 2nd:0 3rd:0 Ran:3
Pre1999 - 1st:0 2nd:0 3rd:0 Ran:1
1999 Turf 0-3: (11f, 12f 2) (hvy, g-f 2)
Unfurnished, moderate filly. Turf high 49. **J S Moore [0-4] P Henley.*

DRAM TIME BHB 47f **RR 42f** 739[6]
3 b g Clantime 6.6f **(57)** - Chablisse (Radetzky) 9.8f **(56)**
Form - 06
Record 1999 - 1st:0 2nd:0 3rd:0 Ran:2
Pre1999 - 1st:0 2nd:0 3rd:0 Ran:4
Win Prizemoney £0 *Total Prizemoney* £230
1999 Turf 0-2: (7f, 8f) (gd, g-f)
Workmanlike, moderate gelding. Turf high 42.
**T D Easterby [0-6] Mrs Jennifer Pallister.*

DRAPLOY (GER) **RR 97f** 4774a[6]
3 f
Form - 6
1999 Turf 0-1: (14f) (sft)
Currently very useful. **A Schutz in GER [0-1].*

DRAWING ROOM (IRE) BHB 54f **RR 63df** 2326[16]
3 b f Grand Lodge (USA) - Wild Abandon (USA) (Graustark) 10.1f **(70)**
Form - 700
Record 1999 - 1st:0 2nd:0 3rd:0 Ran:3
Pre1999 - 1st:0 2nd:0 3rd:0 Ran:2
1999 Turf 0-3: (7f, 8f, 10f) (frm 3)
Light-framed, average filly. Turf high 63.
**R F JohnsonHoughton [0-5] Bob Lanigan.*

DR COOL **RR 39f** 5207[9]
2 b c Ezzoud (IRE) - Vayavaig (Damister (USA)) 9f **(73)**
Form - 0
Record 1999 - 1st:0 2nd:0 3rd:0 Ran:1
1999 Turf 0-1: (7f) (g-s)
Currently very moderate colt.
**W Jarvis [0-1] Canisbay Bloodstock Ltd.*

DR DUKE (IRE) BHB 55f44a **RR 60f 44a** 5148[5]
2 b g Dolphin Street (FR) - Diamond Lake (Kings Lake (USA)) 10.8f **(67)**
Form - 47363320075
Record 1999 - 1st:0 2nd:1 3rd:3 Ran:11
Win Prizemoney £0 *Total Prizemoney* £1,727
1999 Turf 0-9: (5f 4, 6f, 7f 3, 8f) (sft, g-f 3, frm 5) 1999 AW 0-2: (6f, 8f) (Fibr 2)
Average gelding, effective 5 to 7f, best at 7f, acts on frm, has worn blinkers, likes left handed tracks. Turf high 60 - 3rd of 16 to Inch Pincher (21 Aug Sandown 7f frm RF 3823). AW high 31 (began Oct).
**Mrs N Macauley [0-4] Stephen Roots (from R J Hodges [0-7] Spt 1999).*

DREAM CARRIER (IRE) BHB 34f30a **RR 40f 30a** 2649[6]
11 b g Doulab (USA) 7.4f **(61)** - Dream Trader (Auction Ring (USA)) 8.6f **(65)**
Form - 05576
Record 1999 - 1st:0 2nd:0 3rd:0 Ran:5
Pre1999 - 1st:11 2nd:13 3rd:13 Ran:121
Win Prizemoney £37,821 *Total Prizemoney* £59,439
Wins * 1997 *Jun Southw (STD) H 7f 39 45*
1995 *Jan Southw (STD) C 7f 69*
1999 AW 0-5: (7f 3, 8f 2) (Equi, Fibr 4)
Moderate gelding, has worn blinkers. AW high 41.
**R E Peacock [1-41] R E Peacock (from J G M O'Shea [0-9] Jly 1995).*

DREAM CHIEF (USA) **RR 106f** 1901a[2]
3 ch c Holy Bull (USA) - Cheyenne Dream **(102f)** (Dancing Brave (USA)) 8.4f **(76)**
Form - 2
1999 Turf 0-1: (5f) (g-f)
Currently Pattern-class filly. **P Bary in FR [0-1].*

DREAM ON ME BHB 50f58a **RR 50f 58a** 3550[7]
3 b f Prince Sabo 6.6f **(64)** - Helens Dreamgirl (Caerleon (USA)) 8.6f **(71)**
Form - 7116522580137
Record 1999 - 1st:2 2nd:2 3rd:1 Ran:11
Pre1999 - 1st:1 2nd:2 3rd:1 Ran:6
Win Prizemoney £7,278 *Total Prizemoney* £10,217
Wins 1999 Jly Leices (G-F) S 8f 50 <
1999 *Jan Lingfi (STD) H 7f 56 62 <*
1998 *Dec Lingfi (STD) S 8f 58*
1999 Turf 1-4: (7f 2, 8f 1-2) (g-f 2, frm 1-2) 1999 AW 1-7: (6f, 7f 1-4, 8f 2) (Equi 1-7)
Unfurnished, fair filly, effective 5 to 8f, acts on gd - acts on Equi. Turf high 50 (began Jly). AW high 62 - 2nd of 4 getting 13lb from Royal Preview (11 Feb Lingfield 8f Equi RF 0273) - also 1st of 5 getting 1lb from Shabaash (1 Jan Lingfield RF 0005). Won twice on the Lingfield Equitrack during the winter and added a Leicester seller later in the season, but became rather inconsistent.
**H J Manners [0-2] H J Manners (from G L Moore [3-11] Jly 1999).*

DREAM WELL (FR) **RR 124f** 5230a[5]
4 b c Sadler's Wells (USA) 11.3f **(87)** - Soul Dream (USA) (Alleged (USA)) 10f **(76)**
Form - 233135
1999 Turf 1-6: (10f 1-2, 11f, 12f 3) (hvy 1-1, gd 4, frm)
Very high-class colt, effective 10 to 12f, best at 12f, acts on hvy to gd, best on sft, often wears blinkers, likes right handed tracks. Turf high 125 (1st run) - 2nd of 5 to Dark Moondancer (2 May Longchamp 11f gd RF 1072a). Consistent. Winner of the French and Irish Derbies in 1998, he was not at his best after returning from a mid-season break. Touched off in the Prix Ganay on his seasonal debut in 1999, he was third in a tactical Coronation Cup next time, looking unsuited by Epsom's cambers. Beaten fair and square by El Condor Pasa in the Grand Prix de Saint-Cloud, he gained a comfortable success in the Prix Gontaut-Biron. A respectable third behind Daylami over ten furlongs at Leopardstown, he finished a little closer when fifth in the Breeders' Cup Turf. Not an easy ride, he was a top-class colt on his favoured easy ground. **P Bary in FR [4-12].*

DRIVE ASSURED BHB 66f **RR 71f** 2925[11]
5 gr g Mystiko (USA) 7.7f **(59)** - Black Ivor (USA) (Sir Ivor) 10.2f **(70)**
Form - 0
Record 1999 - 1st:0 2nd:0 3rd:0 Ran:1
Pre1999 - 1st:1 2nd:2 3rd:4 Ran:19
Win Prizemoney £2,577 *Total Prizemoney* £7,407
Wins 1998 Oct Bright (GD) H 8f 65 71+ <
1999 Turf 0-1: (8f) (frm)

Above-average gelding, effective 7 to 8f, best at 7f, acts on g-f to frm, best on g-f. Inconsistent.
**K A Morgan [0-6] Mrs J M Penney (from C E Brittain [1-19] Oct 1998).*

DR MARTENS (IRE) BHB 51f **RR 52f** 3916[6]

5 b g Mtoto 11.5f **(71)** - Suyayeb (USA) (The Minstrel (CAN)) 10f **(72)**
Form - 0076
Record 1999 - 1st:0 2nd:0 3rd:0 Ran:4
Pre1999 - 1st:1 2nd:1 3rd:0 Ran:6
Win Prizemoney £3,642 *Total Prizemoney* £4,832
Wins 1997 Aug Windso (G-F) 8.3f 84 <
1999 Turf 0-4: (8f 2, 10f, 12f) (gd, g-f, frm 2)
Fair gelding. Turf high 53. Consistent. Got off the mark at the third attempt at Windsor.
**W J Musson [0-4] R Griggs Group Ltd (from J Glover [0-2] Aug 1998).*

DROWNED IN BUBBLY BHB 30f **RR 32f** 4913[8]

3 b g Tragic Role (USA) 9.4f **(63)** - Champenoise (Forzando) 7.6f **(59)**
Form - 00040078
Record 1999 - 1st:0 2nd:0 3rd:0 Ran:8
Pre1999 - 1st:0 2nd:0 3rd:0 Ran:2
1999 Turf 0-8: (8f 2, 12f, 14f 2, 16f 3) (gd 5, g-f 2, frm)
Leggy, very moderate gelding, has worn blinkers. Turf high 32. Inconsistent. **J L Eyre [0-10] Lovely Bubbly Racing.*

DRURIDGE BAY (IRE) BHB 44f48a **RR 43f 48a** 3862[17]

3 b g Turtle Island (IRE) - Lady of Shalott (Kings Lake (USA)) 10.8f **(67)**
Form - 6224876680
Record 1999 - 1st:0 2nd:0 3rd:0 Ran:5
Pre1999 - 1st:0 2nd:3 3rd:0 Ran:16
Win Prizemoney £0 *Total Prizemoney* £2,048
1999 Turf 0-5: (7f 2, 8f 2, 10f) (sft, g-f, frm 2, hrd)
Workmanlike, fair gelding, effective 7f, acts on frm. Turf high 43.
**K S Bridgwater [0-1] Mrs Mary Bridgwater (from M R Channon [0-20] May 1999).*

DR WILLIE CARSON (USA) **RR 60+f** 4560[7]

2 ch c Carson City (USA) - Always Nettie (USA) (Vice Regent (CAN)) 8.7f **(74)**
Form - 7
Record 1999 - 1st:0 2nd:0 3rd:0 Ran:1
1999 Turf 0-1: (6f) (gd)
Currently average colt.
**H R A Cecil [0-1] The Thoroughbred Corporation.*

DR WOODSTOCK BHB 38f27a **RR 53df 27a** 2190[6]

5 br g Rock City 8.8f **(62)** - Go Tally-Ho (Gorytus (USA)) 7.8f **(60)**
Form - 00323227626
Record 1999 - 1st:0 2nd:4 3rd:2 Ran:11
Pre1999 - 1st:0 2nd:2 3rd:2 Ran:21
Win Prizemoney £0 *Total Prizemoney* £5,932
1999 Turf 0-9: (9f, 10f 2, 11f 2, 12f 4) (g-s, gd 2, g-f 5, frm) 1999 AW 0-2: (7f, 11f) (Fibr 2)
Fair gelding, effective 10f, acts on frm. Turf high 53 - 2nd of 10 getting 5lb from Wafir (18 Jun Redcar 10f frm RF 2128). AW high 16.
**M E Sowersby [0-4] S Mellor (from W Storey [0-22] May 1999).*

DRYAD BHB 49f60a **RR 48f 60a** 4154[3]

4 ch c Risk Me (FR) 8f **(53)** - Lizzy Cantle (Homing) 7.8f **(59)**
Form - 22415223051453
Record 1999 - 1st:2 2nd:2 3rd:2 Ran:12
Pre1999 - 1st:0 2nd:4 3rd:1 Ran:13
Win Prizemoney £5,041 *Total Prizemoney* £11,138
Wins * **1999** *Jun Southw (STD)* *6f* *57*
* **1999** *Jan Wolver (STD)* *6f* *67* <
1999 Turf 0-2: (6f 2) (g-s, g-f) 1999 AW 2-10: (5f, 6f 2-7, 7f 2) (Fibr 2-10)
Workmanlike, fair colt, effective 6 to 7f, best at 7f, - acts on Fibr, has worn blinkers, prefers left handed tracks, prefers tight tracks, excels at Wolverhampton. Turf high 48. AW high 68 - 2nd of 8 giving 3lb to Ron's Pet (3 Mar Wolverhampton 7f Fibr RF 0393) - also 1st of 13 giving 5lb to Love Opera (27 Jan Wolverhampton RF 0174). Consistent. **N P Littmoden [2-25] Miss Vanessa Church.*

DRYING GRASS MOON **RR 65f** 2290[6]

3 b f Be My Chief (USA) 10.2f **(62)** - Sickle Moon (Shirley Heights) 10.3f **(74)**
Form - 46
Record 1999 - 1st:0 2nd:0 3rd:0 Ran:2
Win Prizemoney £0 *Total Prizemoney* £254
1999 Turf 0-2: (10f 2) (gd, frm)
Workmanlike, currently average filly. Turf high 65.
**J R Fanshawe [0-2] The Snailwell Stud Company Ltd.*

DUBAI DOLLY (IRE) BHB 29f32a **RR 28?f 32a** 1231[3]

6 b m Law Society (USA) 11.6f **(71)** - Lola Sharp (Sharpen Up) 8.3f **(67)**
Form - 3
Record 1999 - 1st:0 2nd:0 3rd:1 Ran:1
Pre1999 - 1st:0 2nd:0 3rd:0 Ran:7
Win Prizemoney £0 *Total Prizemoney* £247
1999 AW 0-1: (15f) (Fibr)
Moderate mare, has worn blinkers. (1st run) - 3rd of 6 getting 3lb from Emerald Hunter (14 May Wolverhampton 15f Fibr RF 1231).
**J W Mullins [1-13] Woodford Valley Racing (from D J Reddan in IRE [0-6] Jly 1996).*

DUBAI MILLENNIUM BHB 127f **RR 124+f** 4566[1]

3 b c Seeking the Gold (USA) 7.4f **(80)** - Colorado Dancer (Shareef Dancer (USA)) 9.9f **(73)**
Form - 110111
Record 1999 - 1st:5 2nd:0 3rd:0 Ran:6
Pre1999 - 1st:1 2nd:0 3rd:0 Ran:1
Win Prizemoney £365,916 *Total Prizemoney* £365,916

Wins							
* **1999**	Spt	Ascot	(HVY)	G1	8f	124+	<
* **1999**	Aug	Deauvi	(HVY)	G1	8f	124	
* **1999**	Jly	Maison	(GD)	G2	10f	120	
* **1999**	May	Goodwo	(GD)	L	9.9f	113+	
* **1999**	May	Doncas	(G-F)		8f	114++	
1998	Oct	Yarmou	(SFT)		8f	103++	

1999 Turf 5-6: (8f 3-3, 10f 2-2, 12f) (hvy 1-1, sft 1-1, gd 2-3, hrd 1-1)
Very high-class colt, effective 8 to 10f, best at 8f, acts on hvy to hrd. Turf high 124 - 1st of 4 getting 4lb from Almushtarak (26 Spt Ascot RF 4566) - also 1st of 5 from Slickly (15 Aug Deauville RF 3780a). Impressed onlookers with a fluent debut win at the back-end of 1998, and confirmed the promise by winning at Doncaster and the Predominate at Goodwood at the start of the 1999 season. Even though the bubble was burst in the Derby, he landed a French Group Two over ten furlongs, and gained his biggest success to date with a fine win on heavy ground in the Jacques Le Marois. He followed up in similar going in a sub-standard renewal of the Queen Elizabeth II Stakes at Ascot. Versatile when it comes to going conditions, he looks capable of better yet, and is likely to succeed Daylami as the flagbearer for the 'boys in blue' in 2000. Only going preferences are liable to preclude a series of mouthwatering clashes with Sendawar next year.
**S bin Suroor [5-6] Godolphin (from D R Loder [1-1] Oct 1998).*

DUBAI NURSE BHB 39f **RR 55df** 4986[18]

5 ch m Handsome Sailor 6.6f **(53)** - Lady Eccentric (IRE) (Magical Wonder (USA))
Form - 00
Record 1999 - 1st:0 2nd:0 3rd:0 Ran:2
Pre1999 - 1st:0 2nd:4 3rd:0 Ran:14
Win Prizemoney £0 *Total Prizemoney* £3,126
1999 Turf 0-2: (5f, 6f) (gd, g-f)
Fair filly, effective 5f, acts on g-s to gd. (began Spt). Inconsistent.
**A R Dicken [0-18] John Smith.*

DUBELLE BHB 20f **RR 37f** 1187[12]

9 b m Dubassoff (USA) - Flopsy Mopsy (Full of Hope) 8.5f **(64)**
Form - 0
Record 1999 - 1st:0 2nd:0 3rd:0 Ran:1
Pre1999 - 1st:0 2nd:0 3rd:0 Ran:4
1999 Turf 0-1: (10f) (frm)
Very moderate mare. **J S King [4-34] W J Lee.*

DUBERRA (USA) BHB 48f **RR 62df** 3547[12]

2 b f Defensive Play (USA) - Coffee Ice (Primo Dominie) 6.2f **(80)**
Form - 05350
Record 1999 - 1st:0 2nd:0 3rd:1 Ran:5
Win Prizemoney £0 *Total Prizemoney* £251
1999 Turf 0-5: (6f 2, 7f 3) (gd, g-f 3, frm)
Average filly. Turf high 62. **M L W Bell [0-5] BillionMind Partnership.*

DUBLIN RIVER (USA) BHB 45f **RR 41f** 4869[9]
6 b g Irish River (FR) 9f **(77)** - Vivre Libre (USA) (Honest Pleasure (USA)) 10.4f **(73)**
Form - 76540

Record	**1999** -	1st:0	2nd:0	3rd:0	Ran:5
	Pre1999 -	1st:2	2nd:1	3rd:0	Ran:6

Win Prizemoney £9,674 *Total Prizemoney* £11,850

Wins	1995	Aug	Kempto (G-F)	7f	91 <
	1995	Jly	Yarmou (G-F)	6f	74+

1999 Turf 0-1: (12f) (frm) 1999 AW 0-4: (11f, 12f 3) (Equi, Fibr 3)
Fair gelding, has worn blinkers. AW high 50. Becoming disappointing.
**J G M O'Shea [1-16] K W Bell (from H ThomsonJones [2-6] Spt 1996).*

Dubai Millennium will be a leading flagbearer for Godolphin during 2000

DUBLINTWOTHOUSAND (IRE) BHB 30f **RR 25f** 4923[13]
2 ch f Port Lucaya - Dublin Millennium (Dalsaan) 9.8f **(64)**
Form - 070

Record	**1999** -	1st:0	2nd:0	3rd:0	Ran:3

1999 Turf 0-1: (7f) (g-f) 1999 AW 0-2: (6f, 7f) (Fibr 2)
Currently little account filly. AW high 27 (began Spt).
**M H Tompkins [0-3] Michael Keogh.*

DUCHAMP (USA) BHB 84f **RR 85f** 4762[1]
2 b c Pine Bluff (USA) - Higher Learning (USA) (Fappiano (USA)) 8.7f **(77)**
Form - 66221

Record	**1999** -	1st:1	2nd:2	3rd:0	Ran:5

Win Prizemoney £7,590 *Total Prizemoney* £9,795

Wins	*** 1999**	Oct	York (G-S) H	7.9f	76	85 <

1999 Turf 1-5: (7f, 8f 1-3, 10f) (gd 1-3, frm 2)
Useful colt. Turf high 85 (began Jly) - 1st of 20 getting 4lb from William Barraud (7 Oct York RF 4762).
**I A Balding [1-5] Mrs Paul Mellon.*

DUCIE BHB 68f **RR 66f** 4651[7]
2 b f Distant Relative 7f **(69)** - Ellebanna (Tina's Pet) 6.8f **(59)**
Form - 22827

Record	**1999** -	1st:0	2nd:3	3rd:0	Ran:5

Win Prizemoney £0 *Total Prizemoney* £3,869
1999 Turf 0-5: (5f 5) (g-s, gd 2, g-f, frm)
Average filly. Turf high 66 - 2nd of 6 getting 5lb from Russian Fox (26 Jun Lingfield 5f frm RF 2330). **I A Balding [0-5] Robert Hitchins.*

DUCK OVER BHB 67f **RR 71f** 5003[4]
3 b f Warning 8.1f **(77)** - Waterfowl Creek (IRE) (Be My Guest (USA)) 9.3f **(67)**
Form - 84734

Record	**1999** -	1st:0	2nd:0	3rd:1	Ran:5

Win Prizemoney £0 *Total Prizemoney* £1,077
1999 Turf 0-5: (8f 4, 10f) (gd 2, g-f 2, frm)
Scopey, above-average filly. Turf high 71 - 3rd of 14 to Sheer Harmony (11 Oct Windsor 8f g-f RF 4824). **R Charlton [0-5] A E Oppenheimer.*

DUCK ROW (USA) BHB 108f **RR 109f** 2242[7]
4 ch c Diesis 9f **(80)** - Sunny Moment (USA) (Roberto (USA)) 10f **(76)**
Form - 0167

Record	**1999** -	1st:1	2nd:0	3rd:0	Ran:4
	Pre1999 -	1st:1	2nd:0	3rd:3	Ran:7

Win Prizemoney £15,673 *Total Prizemoney* £44,693

Wins	*** 1999**	Apr	Ascot (GD)	8f	109 <
	* 1997	Spt	Newbur (SFT)	8f	100

1999 Turf 1-4: (8f 1-2, 9f, 10f) (gd 2, g-f 1-1, frm)
Scopey, Pattern-class colt, effective 8f, acts on gd to g-f. Turf high 109 - 1st of 5 from Right Wing (28 Apr Ascot RF 0900). Consistent. Landed a small race at Ascot on his second start but was well beaten in Group One company next time. Spoilt his chances by pulling too hard on his final start.
**J A R Toller [2-11] Duke of Devonshire.*

DUDEEN (IRE) BHB 50f **RR 59f** 2256[8]
4 br f Anshan 8.2f **(63)** - Pipers Pool (IRE) (Mtoto)
Form - 48

Record	**1999** -	1st:0	2nd:0	3rd:0	Ran:2
	Pre1999 -	1st:0	2nd:0	3rd:0	Ran:4

Win Prizemoney £0 *Total Prizemoney* £246
1999 Turf 0-2: (12f 2) (hvy, g-f)
Fair filly. Turf high 59.
**T P McGovern [0-9] N Boyle (from D K Weld in IRE [0-2] Aug 1997).*

DUDLEY ALLEN BHB 45f40a **RR 42f 40a** 159[5]
4 ch g Superlative 8.8f **(57)** - Smooth Flight (Sandhurst Prince) 7.9f **(63)**
Form - 02545

Record	**1999** -	1st:0	2nd:0	3rd:0	Ran:3
	Pre1999 -	1st:0	2nd:1	3rd:0	Ran:11

Win Prizemoney £0 *Total Prizemoney* £518
1999 AW 0-3: (12f 3) (Fibr 3)
Scopey, moderate gelding, effective 11f, - acts on Fibr, likes left handed tracks, likes tight tracks. AW high 39. Consistent.
**T T Clement [0-14] Miss L Davies.*

DUEL ISLAND BHB 53f **RR 46f** 4011[15]
4 b g Jupiter Island 10.4f **(57)** - Duellist (Town Crier) 10.2f **(55)**
Form - 00

Record	**1999** -	1st:0	2nd:0	3rd:0	Ran:2
	Pre1999 -	1st:0	2nd:1	3rd:0	Ran:5

Win Prizemoney £0 *Total Prizemoney* £1,353
1999 Turf 0-2: (8f, 10f) (g-f 2)
Light-framed, moderate gelding, effective 10f, acts on g-f to frm. Turf high 36 (began Aug). **J L Spearing [0-11] C J Hitchings.*

DUELLING GIRL (USA) BHB 84f **RR 85f** 3124[15]
3 b f Dayjur (USA) 6.8f **(79)** - Carduel (USA) (Buckpasser) 10.8f **(80)**
Form - 32100

Record	**1999** -	1st:1	2nd:1	3rd:1	Ran:5
	Pre1999 -	1st:0	2nd:0	3rd:0	Ran:1

Win Prizemoney £4,340 *Total Prizemoney* £6,564

Wins	*** 1999**	Jun	Yarmou (GD)	7f	85 <

1999 Turf 1-5: (7f 1-2, 8f 3) (gd, g-f 1-4)
Scopey, useful filly, effective 6 to 7f, acts on g-f to frm. Turf high 85 - 1st of 9 from Sulalat (10 Jun Yarmouth RF 1890). She was beaten a long way by Gold Academy at Chepstow, but made the most of an easy opportunity at Yarmouth. Well beaten on her handicap debut. **Sir Michael Stoute [1-6] Maktoum Al Maktoum.*

DUELLO BHB 54f70a **RR 62f 70a** 4837[1]

8 b g Sure Blade (USA) 10.6f **(66)** - Royal Loft (Homing) 7.8f **(59)**
Form - 7205857521
Record 1999 - 1st:1 2nd:2 3rd:0 Ran:10
Pre1999 - 1st:4 2nd:11 3rd:8 Ran:76
Win Prizemoney £22,988 *Total Prizemoney* £45,848
Wins * **1999** Oct Leices (GD) C 11.8f 53
* 1998 Spt Nottin (G-F) H 14.1f 56 59
* 1996 Spt Newbur (G-F) H 7.3f 64 66 <
* 1996 May Newbur (SFT) H 7.3f 60 62
* 1995 Spt Epsom (G-S) H 8.5f 55 62
1999 Turf 1-10: (12f 1-5, 14f 5) (g-s, gd 1-4, g-f 3, frm 2)
Average gelding, effective 10 to 14f, best at 12f, acts on g-s to frm, best on gd, has worn blinkers, likes right handed tracks, favours tight tracks, excels at Kempton and Windsor. Turf high 62 - 2nd of 8 getting 4lb from Grief (4 Oct Brighton 12f gd RF 4709) - also 1st of 20 giving 7lb to Port Meadow (12 Oct Leicester RF 4837).
**M Blanshard [6-94] C McKenna.*

DUE RISK (IRE) BHB 71f **RR 75f** 3842[8]
2 b g Kris 10f **(75)** - Dukrame (Top Ville) 11.7f **(68)**
Form - 748
Record 1999 - 1st:0 2nd:0 3rd:0 Ran:3
Win Prizemoney £0 *Total Prizemoney* £260
1999 Turf 0-3: (7f 3) (gd, frm 2)
Currently above-average gelding. Turf high 75.
**J Noseda [0-3] P G Goulandris.*

DUKE OF ASTON (IRE) BHB 93f **RR 83f** 4858[3]
2 ch c Shalford (IRE) 7.8f **(63)** - Glenstal Priory (Glenstal (USA)) 10.1f **(64)**
Form - 1305233
Record 1999 - 1st:1 2nd:1 3rd:3 Ran:7
Win Prizemoney £3,881 *Total Prizemoney* £8,243
Wins * **1999** Jun Goodwo (SFT) 5f 83 <
1999 Turf 1-7: (5f 1-1, 6f 2, 7f 3, 8f) (sft, g-s 1-1, gd 2, g-f, frm 2)
Decent colt, effective 5 to 7f, best at 7f, acts on g-s to frm. Turf high 83 (1st run) - 1st of 9 from Deep Blue (2 Jun Goodwood RF 1678). Made a successful debut at Goodwood before coming up against two high-class juveniles at Newbury. He was held in his subsequent races including when tried in Group company.
**A P Jarvis [1-7] Grant & Bowman Ltd.*

DUKE OF MODENA BHB 79f **RR 65f** 5044[3]
2 ch c Salse (USA) 10.9f **(71)** - Palace Street (USA) (Secreto (USA)) 8.7f **(72)**
Form - 603
Record 1999 - 1st:0 2nd:0 3rd:1 Ran:3
Win Prizemoney £0 *Total Prizemoney* £700
1999 Turf 0-3: (6f 2, 7f) (sft, g-f, frm)
Currently average colt. Turf high 65 (began Spt).
**G B Balding [0-3] Miss B Swire.*

DUKHAN (USA) BHB 68a **RR 49f** 4930[18]
5 b h Silver Hawk (USA) 11.2f **(85)** - Azayim (Be My Guest (USA)) 9.3f **(67)**
Form - 700
Record 1999 - 1st:0 2nd:0 3rd:0 Ran:2
Pre1999 - 1st:1 2nd:0 3rd:2 Ran:15
Win Prizemoney £2,085 *Total Prizemoney* £3,972
Wins * 1998 *Feb Southw (STD) 12f 65* <
1999 Turf 0-1: (10f) (g-f) 1999 AW 0-1: (11f) (Fibr)
Average colt, effective 12f, acts on gd - acts on Fibr, likes left handed tracks. Becoming disappointing.
**E J Alston [1-14] Ms Jan Fletcher (from R W Armstrong [0-3] Spt 1997).*

DULFORD BHB 54f **RR 54f** 4584[10]
3 b g Never so Bold 7.1f **(62)** - Cabra (Red Sunset) 8.2f **(63)**
Form - 77500
Record 1999 - 1st:0 2nd:0 3rd:0 Ran:5
Pre1999 - 1st:0 2nd:0 3rd:1 Ran:2
Win Prizemoney £0 *Total Prizemoney* £455
1999 Turf 0-4: (8f 2, 10f, 11f) (gd 2, g-f, frm) 1999 AW 0-1: (9f) (Fibr)
Workmanlike, fair gelding. Turf high 54.
**B R Millman [0-7] Mrs L S Millman.*

DULZIE **RR 65f** 4815[15]
2 b f Safawan 6.6f **(60)** - Dulzura (Daring March) 7.1f **(61)**
Form - 60
Record 1999 - 1st:0 2nd:0 3rd:0 Ran:2
1999 Turf 0-2: (7f 2) (gd, g-f)
Currently average filly. Turf high 65 (began Aug).
**A P Jarvis [0-2] Mrs D B Brazier.*

DUNA **RR** 4364a[1]
2 b f Turtle Island (IRE) - Hana Marie (Formidable (USA)) 9.2f **(63)**
Form - 1
Record 1999 - 1st:1 2nd:0 3rd:0 Ran:1
Win Prizemoney £5,468 *Total Prizemoney* £5,468
Wins * **1999** Spt Cascin (GD) 7.5f
1999 Turf 1-1: (8f 1-1) (gd 1-1)
Currently unbeaten filly. - 1st of 8 from Fior D'Aprile (12 Spt Cascine RF 4364a).
**M Quinlan [1-1] Paolo Benedetti.*

DUN DISTINCTLY (IRE) BHB 54f **RR 49f** 5076[15]
2 b g Distinctly North (USA) 7.4f **(63)** - Dunbally (Dunphy) 9.4f **(57)**
Form - 4000
Record 1999 - 1st:0 2nd:0 3rd:0 Ran:4
Win Prizemoney £0 *Total Prizemoney* £405
1999 Turf 0-4: (5f, 6f 3) (gd, g-f 2, frm)
Moderate gelding. Turf high 49.
**P C Haslam [0-4] Sir Timothy Kitson & G F Armitage.*

DUNKELD CHAMP **RR 45f** 3750[8]
2 br c Be My Chief (USA) 10.2f **(62)** - Callipoli (USA) (Green Dancer (USA)) 10.3f **(74)**
Form - 08
Record 1999 - 1st:0 2nd:0 3rd:0 Ran:2
1999 Turf 0-2: (6f, 7f) (gd, g-f)
Currently moderate colt. Turf high 45 (began Jly).
**A R Dicken [0-2] J W D Campbell.*

DUNKELLIN HOUSE (IRE) BHB 60f **RR 54f** 5070[11]
2 gr g Petorius 8f **(66)** - More Magnanimous (King Persian)
Form - 600
Record 1999 - 1st:0 2nd:0 3rd:0 Ran:3
1999 Turf 0-3: (5f 3) (gd, frm 2)
Currently fair gelding. Turf high 54 (began Spt).
**R A Fahey [0-3] Tommy Staunton.*

DUNSTON DURGAM (IRE) BHB 16f29a **RR 5f 29a** 74[8]
5 b g Durgam (USA) 12.3f **(53)** - Blazing Sunset (Blazing Saddles (AUS)) 6.7f **(46)**
Form - 050008
Record 1999 - 1st:0 2nd:0 3rd:0 Ran:1
Pre1999 - 1st:0 2nd:0 3rd:1 Ran:15
Win Prizemoney £0 *Total Prizemoney* £285
1999 AW 0-1: (12f) (Fibr)
Poor gelding, effective 11f, - acts on Fibr.
**N P Littmoden [0-16] O A Gunter.*

DURAID (IRE) BHB 76f **RR 75f** 5166[1]
7 ch g Irish River (FR) 9f **(77)** - Fateful Princess (USA) (Vaguely Noble) 10.1f **(72)**
Form - 62176010401
Record 1999 - 1st:3 2nd:1 3rd:0 Ran:11
Pre1999 - 1st:2 2nd:1 3rd:0 Ran:23
Win Prizemoney £32,801 *Total Prizemoney* £42,158
Wins * **1999** Nov Catter (SFT) H 7f 70 75
* **1999** Aug Ripon (GD) H 8f 66 68
* **1999** Jly Beverl (G-F) H 8.5f 65 65
* 1997 Spt Haydoc (GD) H 8.1f 76 82 <
* 1997 Jun Newcas (GD) H 8f 64 73
1999 Turf 3-11: (7f 1-5, 8f 2-6) (g-s 1-1, gd, g-f 1-3, frm 1-6)
Above-average gelding, effective 7 to 8f, best at 8f, acts on g-s to frm, best on g-s, has worn blinkers, likes right handed tracks, excels at Newcastle and Beverley. Turf high 75 - 1st of 15 from Haymaker (2 Nov Catterick RF 5166) - also 1st of 11 getting 8lb from Espada (30 Aug Ripon RF 4028). Scored at Beverley in July after a good effort in the Carlisle Bell, and added to his tally with victories in decent handicaps at Ripon and Catterick. Despite his successes, he is still a bit of a character.
**Denys Smith [9-43] A Suddes.*

DURGAMS DELIGHT (IRE) BHB 30f42a **RR 36f 42a** 4089[7]

4 b f Durgam (USA) 12.3f **(53)** - Miromaid (Simply Great (FR)) 8.2f **(65)**
Form - 7
Record 1999 - 1st:0 2nd:0 3rd:0 Ran:1
Pre1999 - 1st:0 2nd:1 3rd:1 Ran:13
Win Prizemoney £0 *Total Prizemoney* £1,213
1999 Turf 0-1: (16f) (frm)
Leggy, moderate filly, effective 10 to 14f, acts on gd to frm - acts on Fibr, has worn blinkers (effectively). Consistent.
**J L Eyre [0-1] The First Thursday Club (from B W Murray [0-13] Jly 1998).*

DURGAMS FIRST (IRE) BHB 46f36a **RR 51f 36a** 3968[6]
7 ch g Durgam (USA) 12.3f **(53)** -Miromaid (Simply Great(FR)) 8.2f **(65)**
Form - 016
Record 1999 - 1st:1 2nd:0 3rd:0 Ran:3
Pre1999 - 1st:8 2nd:12 3rd:6 Ran:44
Win Prizemoney £23,929 *Total Prizemoney* £35,923
Wins * **1999** Aug Pontef (GD) S 10f 51
* 1997 Aug Carlis (FRM) C 12f 52
* 1997 May Carlis (FRM) H 14.1f 42 47
* 1995 Spt Catter (GD) S 13.8f 45
* 1995 Jly Haydoc (G-F) C 11.9f 66
* 1995 Jun Carlis (GD) C 12f 62
* *1995 Feb Southw (STD) C 8f 62*
* *1995 Jan Southw (STD) S 8f 69* <
1999 Turf 1-2: (10f 1-2) (g-f, frm 1-1) 1999 AW 0-1: (8f) (Fibr)
Fair gelding, effective 10f, acts on frm. Turf high 51 (1st run) (began Aug) - 1st of 14 giving 5lb to Maiella (16 Aug Pontefract RF 3674). **Mrs M Reveley [9-47] The Mary Reveley Racing Club.*

DURHAM BHB 60f58a **RR 63f 58a** 4331[11]
8 ch g Caerleon (USA) 10.9f **(79)** - Sanctuary (Welsh Pageant) 10f **(65)**
Form - 20541632270
Record 1999 - 1st:1 2nd:3 3rd:1 Ran:11
Pre1999 - 1st:6 2nd:9 3rd:8 Ran:46
Win Prizemoney £26,686 *Total Prizemoney* £43,076
Wins * **1999** Jun Goodwo (G-F) H 14f 60 62
* 1998 Jly Sandow (G-F) H 14f 60 64
* 1997 Aug Yarmou (G-F) H 14.1f 59 64
1996 Spt Ayr (G-F) H 13.1f 60 68 <
1996 Spt Kempto (GD) H 14.4f 54 61
1996 Aug Lingfi (G-F) S 14f 55
1996 Jun Nottin (G-F) H 14.1f 48 56
1999 Turf 1-11: (14f 1-7, 15f 2, 16f, 17f) (hvy, sft, g-s, gd 1-3, frm 5)
Average gelding, effective 11 to 17f, best at 14f, acts on gd to frm, best on g-f, mostly wears blinkers (very effectively), likes right handed tracks, excels at Lingfield and Sandown. Turf high 63 - 2nd of 10 getting 1lb from Mane Frame (21 Jly Sandown 14f frm RF 3018) - also 1st of 8 getting 20lb from Tough Act (11 Jun Goodwood RF 1913). Consistent. Something of a character, he is a fair sort in modest staying handicaps, but he needs fast ground and is not one to totally rely on.
**G L Moore [3-34] Matthew Thole (from H S Howe [2-4] Oct 1996).*

DURHAM DANCER BHB 53f **RR 57f** 4147[7]
3 b f Magic Ring (IRE) 6.5f **(64)** - Final Shot (Dalsaan) 9.8f **(64)**
Form - 034877
Record 1999 - 1st:0 2nd:0 3rd:1 Ran:6
Win Prizemoney £0 *Total Prizemoney* £824
1999 Turf 0-6: (5f 3, 6f 3) (gd 3, frm 2, hrd)
Leggy, fair filly. Turf high 57. **T D Easterby [0-6] C H Stevens.*

DURHAM DANDY BHB 37f **RR 34f** 3979[10]
3 b g Inchinor 8.9f **(64)** -Disco Girl (FR)(Green Dancer(USA)) 10.3f **(74)**
Form - 062880
Record 1999 - 1st:0 2nd:1 3rd:0 Ran:6
Pre1999 - 1st:0 2nd:0 3rd:0 Ran:4
Win Prizemoney £0 *Total Prizemoney* £880
1999 Turf 0-6: (9f 2, 10f 2, 12f, 14f) (gd, g-f, frm 4)
Light-framed, very moderate gelding. Turf high 46. Consistent.
**T D Easterby [0-10] C H Stevens.*

DURHAM FLYER BHB 38f35a **RR 34f 35a** 4783[9]
4 b g Deploy 11.4f **(67)** - Hyde Princess (Touch Paper) 6.8f **(57)**
Form - 000000
Record 1999 - 1st:0 2nd:0 3rd:0 Ran:6
Pre1999 - 1st:2 2nd:2 3rd:1 Ran:21

Win Prizemoney £7,050 *Total Prizemoney* £9,662
Wins 1998 Aug Carlis (G-S) C 6.9f 65 <
1998 Jun Redcar (G-S) H 7f 60 61
1999 Turf 0-5: (7f 3, 8f, 10f) (g-s 2, g-f 2, frm) 1999 AW 0-1: (8f) (Equi)
Very moderate gelding, effective 7 to 8f, best at 7f, acts on g-s to frm, best on gd, often wears blinkers (effectively). Turf high 34. Consistent.
**J Cullinan [0-6] Alan Spargo Ltd Toolmakers (from T D Easterby [2-21] Oct 1998).*

DURLSTON BAY RR 22f 5192[15]
2 b c Welsh Captain 7.2f **(54)** - Nelliellamay (Super Splash (USA)) 7.3f **(54)**
Form - 0
Record 1999 - 1st:0 2nd:0 3rd:0 Ran:1
1999 Turf 0-1: (8f) (gd)
Currently little account colt. **R Ingram [0-1] M G Mackenzie.*

DUSHANBE (IRE) BHB 75f **RR 63f** 1028[13]
4 b g Alzao (USA) 9.8f **(73)** - Atyaaf (USA) (Irish River (FR)) 8.6f **(78)**
Form - 000
Record 1999 - 1st:0 2nd:0 3rd:0 Ran:3
Pre1999 - 1st:1 2nd:0 3rd:1 Ran:3
Win Prizemoney £3,715 *Total Prizemoney* £4,709
Wins 1998 Jun Beverl (GD) 7.5f 83 <
1999 Turf 0-3: (7f, 8f, 10f) (gd 2, g-f)
Strong, average gelding, effective 7 to 8f, acts on gd to frm. Turf high 63.
**N A Callaghan [0-3] G C Hartigan (from L M Cumani [1-3] Aug 1998).*

DUSKY VIRGIN BHB 61f **RR 60f** 3347[1]
2 b f Missed Flight - Rosy Sunset (IRE) (Red Sunset) 8.2f **(63)**
Form - 07651
Record 1999 - 1st:1 2nd:0 3rd:0 Ran:5
Win Prizemoney £2,211 *Total Prizemoney* £2,211
Wins * **1999** Aug Bright (FRM) S 7f 59 <
1999 Turf 1-5: (5f, 6f 3, 7f 1-1) (gd, g-f 2, frm 1-2)
Average filly. Turf high 60 - also 1st of 7 from Sally-Ann (4 Aug Brighton RF 3347). **M Quinn [1-5] R M Ellis.*

DUSTY DANCER BHB 38f51a **RR 23f 51a** 3394[14]
3 ch g Risk Me (FR) 8f **(53)** - Eternal Triangle (USA) (Barachois (CAN)) 8.3f **(63)**
Form - 60080
Record 1999 - 1st:0 2nd:0 3rd:0 Ran:5
Pre1999 - 1st:0 2nd:0 3rd:0 Ran:4
Win Prizemoney £0 *Total Prizemoney* £157
1999 Turf 0-3: (7f 3) (g-s, gd, frm) 1999 AW 0-2: (6f, 8f) (Equi 2)
Workmanlike, very moderate gelding. Turf high 23. AW high 33. Becoming disappointing.
**W G M Turner [0-1] T O C S Ltd (from Miss Gay Kelleway [0-8] Jun 1999).*

DUTCH DYANE BHB 34f26a **RR 39f 26a** 1799[3]
6 b m Midyan (USA) 9.9f **(64)** - Double Dutch (Nicholas Bill) 10.1f **(56)**
Form - 03
Record 1999 - 1st:0 2nd:0 3rd:1 Ran:2
Pre1999 - 1st:0 2nd:2 3rd:1 Ran:10
Win Prizemoney £0 *Total Prizemoney* £2,361
1999 Turf 0-2: (15f, 16f) (hvy, g-s)
Very moderate mare, effective 13 to 16f, best at 16f, acts on g-s to frm. Turf high 36 - 3rd of 12 getting 1lb from Urgent Reply (7 Jun Warwick 16f g-s RF 1799). Inconsistent.
**G P Enright [1-21] Miss Fuller, Ross, Neil Kenworthy.*

DUTCH LAD BHB 75f **RR 76f** 2044[17]
4 b g Alnasr Alwasheek 9.4f **(62)** -Double Dutch(Nicholas Bill)10.1f **(56)**
Form - 050
Record 1999 - 1st:0 2nd:0 3rd:0 Ran:3
Pre1999 - 1st:1 2nd:4 3rd:2 Ran:12
Win Prizemoney £2,600 *Total Prizemoney* £10,156
Wins * 1998 Apr Mussel (G-S) 12f 68+ <
1999 Turf 0-3: (10f, 12f 2) (g-f 3)
Workmanlike, above-average gelding, effective 10 to 12f, best at 12f, acts on g-s to g-f, best on g-f, likes tight tracks. Turf high 76 - 5th of 13 giving 6lb to Norcroft Joy (5 Jun Doncaster 12f g-f RF

1752). Inconsistent. **M H Tompkins [1-15] D J Anderson.*

DUTCH NIGHTINGALE BHB 39f **RR 41f** 5154[12]
5 b m Warrshan (USA) 9.7f **(59)** - Double Dutch (Nicholas Bill) 10.1f **(56)**
Form - 60670
Record 1999 - 1st:0 2nd:0 3rd:0 Ran:5
Pre1999 - 1st:0 2nd:0 3rd:0 Ran:2
1999 Turf 0-5: (9f, 10f 4) (g-s 2, gd 2, frm)
Moderate filly, effective 10f, acts on g-s. Turf high 47.
**G P Enright [0-8] B Beagley.*

DUTY SQUADRON (IRE) RR 148[11]
3 b g Mac's Imp (USA) 5.6f **(54)** - Guess Who (Be My Guest (USA)) 9.3f **(67)**
Form - 0
Record 1999 - 1st:0 2nd:0 3rd:0 Ran:1
1999 AW 0-1: (8f) (Equi)
Workmanlike, currently very poor gelding.
**P Mitchell [0-1] W R Mann.*

DUVET BHB 30f **RR 49f** 5198[12]
7 b m Squill (USA) 9.4f **(47)** - Embroideress (Stanford) 7.9f **(56)**
Form - 0000
Record 1999 - 1st:0 2nd:0 3rd:0 Ran:4
1999 Turf 0-3: (8f 3) (gd 2, g-f) 1999 AW 0-1: (13f) (Equi)
Moderate mare. Turf high 49 (began Aug).
**Miss K M George [0-8] R J Matthews.*

D W MCCEE BHB 52f **RR 51f** 5050[14]
3 b g Keen 11.1f **(58)** - Miss Coco (Swing Easy (USA)) 6.5f **(55)**
Form - 6050
Record 1999 - 1st:0 2nd:0 3rd:0 Ran:4
1999 Turf 0-4: (8f 2, 9f, 10f) (gd 2, frm, hrd)
Workmanlike, fair gelding. Turf high 51.
**Miss Gay Kelleway [0-4] A P Griffin.*

DYCE BHB 32f32a **RR 36f 32a** 497[5]
5 b m Green Ruby (USA) 6.9f **(47)** - Miss Display (Touch Paper) 6.8f **(57)**
Form - 77055
Record 1999 - 1st:0 2nd:0 3rd:0 Ran:5
Pre1999 - 1st:1 2nd:0 3rd:0 Ran:8
Win Prizemoney £2,301 *Total Prizemoney* £2,301
Wins * 1998 *Jly Wolver (STD) H 5f 32 34* <
1999 AW 0-5: (5f 4, 6f) (Fibr 5)
Very moderate filly, effective 5f, - acts on Fibr, mostly wears blinkers (effectively), likes left handed tracks, likes tight tracks. AW high 30. **J Balding [1-13] Mrs Gillian Jones.*

DYHIM DIAMOND (IRE) RR 114f 2643[16]
5 ch h Night Shift (USA) 8.1f **(73)** - Happy Landing (FR) (Homing) 7.8f **(59)**
Form - 20
1999 Turf 0-2: (6f 2) (sft, frm)
Group-class colt, effective 6 to 7f, best at 6f, acts on g-s to gd, best on gd. Turf high 100. Consistent. This likeable sprinter seemed a shade below his best in 1999 but can never be written off. Best around six furlongs, he enjoys forcing the pace and is game in a finish. **C Laffon-Parias in FR [3-14] Salem Suhail.*

DYNAMIC DREAM (USA) RR 80f 3913[1]
2 b f Dynaformer (USA) 12f **(82)** -Hip Hip Hur Rahy(USA) (Rahy (USA))
Form - 1
Record 1999 - 1st:1 2nd:0 3rd:0 Ran:1
Win Prizemoney £4,597 *Total Prizemoney* £4,597
Wins * **1999** Aug Folkes (GD) 7f 80 <
1999 Turf 1-1: (7f 1-1) (gd 1-1)
Currently decent filly. (1st run) - 1st of 10 from Ghuffran (26 Aug Folkestone RF 3913). **P W Harris [1-1] Dynamic Dozen.*

DYNAMISM (FR) BHB 85f **RR 88f** 5031[14]
4 b g Caerleon (USA) 10.9f **(79)** - Fextal (USA) (Alleged (USA)) 10f **(76)**
Form - 3P84570
Record 1999 - 1st:0 2nd:0 3rd:1 Ran:7
Pre1999 - 1st:1 2nd:0 3rd:0 Ran:2
Win Prizemoney £3,582 *Total Prizemoney* £6,390
Wins 1998 May Ripon (GD) 10f 77 <
1999 Turf 0-7: (10f 7) (g-s 2, gd 2, g-f, frm 2)
Scopey, useful gelding, effective 10f, acts on g-f, has worn blinkers. Turf high 103 (1st run) - 3rd of 8 to Generous Rosi (5 Apr Kempton 10f g-f RF 0575). Inconsistent. He was sold cheaply at the end of 1998 and failed to score last term. However, he retains plenty of ability and is capable of winning, possibly when stepped-up to a mile and a half.
**Mrs L Stubbs [0-7] M S & C S Griffiths (from H R A Cecil [1-2] May 1998).*

EAGLESHAM (IRE) RR 82f 2062[1]
3 b c Barathea (IRE) - High Hawk (Shirley Heights) 10.3f **(74)**
Form - 561
Record 1999 - 1st:1 2nd:0 3rd:0 Ran:3
Win Prizemoney £3,631 *Total Prizemoney* £3,631
Wins * **1999** Jun Ripon (G-F) 8f 82 <
1999 Turf 1-3: (8f 1-3) (g-s, gd, hrd 1-1)
Leggy, currently decent colt. Turf high 82 - 1st of 9 giving 5lb to Manicure (16 Jun Ripon RF 2062). Got off the mark in a Ripon maiden over a mile, but the form of that race may be worth little, as there was a lot of trouble in running for those behind him.
**B W Hills [1-3] Sheikh Mohammed.*

EARLENE (IRE) RR 98f 4740a[2]
2 b f In The Wings 11.2f **(77)** - Ela Romara (Ela-Mana-Mou) 10.1f **(70)**
Form - 212
1999 Turf 1-3: (6f, 7f, 8f 1-1) (sft, g-s 1-1, gd)
Currently very useful filly. Turf high 98 (began Spt) - 2nd of 7 to Theoretically (2 Oct Curragh 7f sft RF 4740a) - also 1st of 5 from Alluring (18 Spt Curragh RF 4468a). She almost justified her supplementary entry for a Group 3 at The Curragh in October, finishing second after drifting right-handed close home. Beautifully bred, she will stay beyond a mile and is a smart prospect.
**J Oxx in IRE [1-3] Sheikh Mohammed.*

EARLEY SESSION (IRE) BHB 40f **RR 49f** 4825[20]
2 b c Puissance 7.1f **(60)** - Shabby Doll (Northfields (USA)) 9f **(72)**
Form - 70
Record 1999 - 1st:0 2nd:0 3rd:0 Ran:2
1999 Turf 0-2: (6f 2) (g-f 2)
Currently moderate colt. Turf high 49 (began Aug).
**J C Tuck [0-2] The Cat & Custard Partnership.*

EARLY DAISY RR 49f 1406[5]
4 ch f Crofthall 8.6f **(54)** - Heldigvis (Hot Grove) 12.5f **(55)**
Form - 5
Record 1999 - 1st:0 2nd:0 3rd:0 Ran:1
1999 Turf 0-1: (7f) (g-f)
Moderate filly. (1st run) - 5th of 9 getting 7lb from Mamma's Boy (22 May Musselburgh 7f g-f RF 1406). **R Allan [0-5] Robbie Cameron.*

EARP (IRE) BHB 45f **RR 21f** 5190[12]
7 b g Anita's Prince 6f **(62)** - Ottavia Abu (Octavo (USA)) 14.4f **(54)**
Form - 00
Record 1999 - 1st:0 2nd:0 3rd:0 Ran:2
Pre1999 - 1st:0 2nd:3 3rd:0 Ran:10
Win Prizemoney £0 *Total Prizemoney* £2,655
1999 Turf 0-2: (8f, 12f) (gd, g-f)
Little account gelding, effective 7f, acts on gd, has worn blinkers. Turf high 21 (began Oct).
**F P Murtagh [1-11] D Tumelty & D May (from N Meade in IRE [2-19] May 1998).*

EASAAR BHB 105f **RR 105f** 958[10]
3 b c Machiavellian (USA) 9.8f **(83)** -Matila(IRE) (Persian Bold) 9.3f **(66)**
Form - 0
Record 1999 - 1st:0 2nd:0 3rd:0 Ran:1
Pre1999 - 1st:1 2nd:1 3rd:0 Ran:2
Win Prizemoney £8,217 *Total Prizemoney* £9,385
Wins * 1998 Oct Newmar () 7f 91+ <
1999 Turf 0-1: (8f) (frm)
Scopey, currently Pattern-class colt. Finished 10th to stablemate Island Sands in the 2000 Guineas, but did not reappear.
**S bin Suroor [1-3] Godolphin.*

EAST ARRAN STREET **RR 24f** 3418[7]
2 b f Balla Cove - Spy Girl (Tanfirion) 7f **(61)**
Form - 7
Record 1999 - 1st:0 2nd:0 3rd:0 Ran:1
1999 Turf 0-1: (5f) (frm)
Currently little account filly. **Noel Chance [0-1] Mrs M Chance.*

EASTERN CHAMP (USA) BHB 73f71a **RR 75f 71a** 4865[2]
3 ch c Star de Naskra (USA) 8.8f **(63)** - Dance Troupe (USA) (Native Charger) 10.7f **(63)**
Form - 0002214202
Record 1999 - 1st:1 2nd:4 3rd:0 Ran:10
Win Prizemoney £3,387 *Total Prizemoney* £9,253
Wins * 1999 Aug Redcar (GD) 9f 78+ <
1999 Turf 1-9: (8f 5, 9f 1-3, 10f) (gd 3, frm 1-6) 1999 AW 0-1: (8f) (Fibr)
Workmanlike, above-average colt, effective 9f, acts on frm, prefers left handed tracks, prefers tight tracks. Turf high 78 - 1st of 5 giving 5lb to Mouton (8 Aug Redcar RF 3466). He showed better form in the second half of last season, including winning a very modest Redcar maiden in August. A mile plus seems to suit.
**S P C Woods [1-10] P K L Chu.*

EASTERN LYRIC **RR 38f** 4352[R]
4 gr f Petong 7.6f **(58)** - Songlines (Night Shift (USA)) 7.2f **(69)**
Form - 0500050R
Record 1999 - 1st:0 2nd:0 3rd:0 Ran:8
Pre1999 - 1st:4 2nd:1 3rd:1 Ran:18
Win Prizemoney £23,551 *Total Prizemoney* £28,019
Wins 1998 Jly Goodwo (G-S) H 5f 80 85 <
1998 Jly Bath (GD) H 5.1f 75 79
1998 Jun Ayr (G-F) H 5f 70 73
1997 May Warwic (FRM) 5f 65
1999 Turf 0-8: (5f 2, 6f 3, 7f 2, 8f) (g-s, g-f, frm 6)
Light-framed, very moderate filly, effective 5 to 6f, acts on gd to frm, has worn blinkers. Turf high 74. Becoming disappointing.
**D Nicholls [0-2] R Meredith (from C E Brittain [0-6] Jly 1999).*

EASTERN PROJECT (IRE) BHB 62f **RR 50f** 1968[13]
5 b g Project Manager 7.2f **(47)** - Diandra (Shardari) 11f **(46)**
Form - 0
Record 1999 - 1st:0 2nd:0 3rd:0 Ran:1
Pre1999 - 1st:0 2nd:1 3rd:1 Ran:8
Win Prizemoney £0 *Total Prizemoney* £1,247
1999 Turf 0-1: (12f) (gd)
Fair gelding. Consistent.
**M D Hammond [3-20] Steve Semple (from J S Bolger in IRE [0-7] Aug 1997).*

EASTERN PROPHETS BHB 59f59a **RR 59f 59a** 4914[10]
6 b g Emarati (USA) 6.6f **(63)** - Four Love (Pas de Seul) 9.1f **(67)**
Form - 40100802822373270
Record 1999 - 1st:1 2nd:4 3rd:2 Ran:17
Pre1999 - 1st:5 2nd:7 3rd:6 Ran:55
Win Prizemoney £24,805 *Total Prizemoney* £49,115
Wins * 1999 May Nottin (GD) H 6.1f 61 58
1998 May Doncas (G-F) C 6f 70
1997 Mar Kempto (G-F) H 6f 79 82
1995 Jun Beverl (G-S) 5f 86 <
1995 May Bath (G-F) 5.1f 76
1995 May Doncas (G-F) 5f 64
1999 Turf 1-16: (5f 6, 6f 1-7, 7f 3) (gd 3, g-f 5, frm 1-7, hrd) 1999 AW 0-1: (6f) (Fibr)
Fair gelding, effective 5 to 6f, best at 6f, acts on gd to frm - acts on Equi, has worn blinkers (effectively), likes tight tracks, excels at Doncaster and Brighton and Lingfield. Turf high 63 - 2nd of 18 giving 11lb to American Cousin (14 Jly Doncaster 5f g-f RF 2810). Consistent.
**M Dods [1-17] Graham and Barbara Spencer (from G Lewis [5-45] Oct 1998).*

EASTERN PURPLE (IRE) BHB 105f **RR 101f** 4392[28]
4 b c Petorius 8f **(66)** - Broadway Rosie (Absalom) 7.2f **(58)**
Form - 271553000
Record 1999 - 1st:1 2nd:1 3rd:1 Ran:9
Pre1999 - 1st:2 2nd:0 3rd:1 Ran:15
Win Prizemoney £42,731 *Total Prizemoney* £60,872
Wins * 1999 May Currag (GD) G3 6f 111 <
1998 May Haydoc (G-S) LH 6f 93 106
1997 Aug Newcas (G-F) 6f 71+
1999 Turf 1-9: (6f 1-7, 7f 2) (gd 5, g-f 1-3, frm)
Very useful colt, effective 6 to 7f, best at 6f, acts on gd to frm, best on g-f, has worn blinkers. Turf high 111 - 1st of 10 from Gaelic Storm (22 May Curragh RF 1476a). He gained a deserved Group 3 success when landing the Weatherbys Ireland Greenland Stakes at The Curragh in May and went on to run creditably in smart company. A few pounds below the leading sprinters and unlikely to improve, he will be best employed on the continent.
**K A Ryan [1-9] T C Chiang (from R A Fahey [2-15] Nov 1998).*

EASTERN RAINBOW (IRE) BHB 44f **RR 25f** 2236[18]
3 b c Bluebird (USA) 7.9f **(71)** - Insaf (USA) (Raise A Native) 11.2f **(69)**
Form - 6000
Record 1999 - 1st:0 2nd:0 3rd:0 Ran:4
1999 Turf 0-4: (7f, 8f, 10f, 12f) (gd, g-f, frm 2)
Leggy, little account colt, has worn blinkers. Turf high 47.
**K A Ryan [0-4] T C Chiang.*

EASTERN SPICE BHB 77f **RR 79f** 4996[5]
2 b c Polish Precedent (USA) 9f **(73)** - Mithl Al Hawa (Salse (USA)) 7.5f **(66)**
Form - 762035
Record 1999 - 1st:0 2nd:1 3rd:1 Ran:6
Win Prizemoney £0 *Total Prizemoney* £1,755
1999 Turf 0-6: (6f, 7f 4, 8f) (gd 2, g-f, frm 3)
Above-average colt, effective 7f, acts on frm. Turf high 79 - 2nd of 14 to Three Points (4 Aug Kempton 7f frm RF 3353).
**R Hannon [0-6] Mohamed Suhail.*

EASTERN TRUMPETER BHB 61f **RR 57f** 5212[5]
3 b c First Trump - Oriental Air (IRE) **(49f 48a)** (Taufan (USA)) 7f **(57)**
Form - 51743105308703375
Record 1999 - 1st:2 2nd:0 3rd:4 Ran:17
Pre1999 - 1st:0 2nd:1 3rd:0 Ran:2
Win Prizemoney £9,322 *Total Prizemoney* £13,092
Wins * 1999 Jun Ayr (SFT) H 5f 62 62
*** 1999** Apr Folkes (SFT) C 5f 70 <
1999 Turf 2-15: (5f 2-12, 6f 3) (g-s 2-5, gd 6, g-f 3, frm) 1999 AW 0-2: (5f, 6f) (Fibr 2)
Average colt, effective 5f, acts on g-s to g-f. Turf high 70 (1st run) - 1st of 12 giving 2lb to Landican Lane (13 Apr Folkestone RF 0656). AW high 61. Consistent.
**J M Bradley [2-17] R G G Racing (from G Lewis [0-2] Aug 1998).*

EASTERN VENTURE **RR 52f** 5049[18]
2 b c Last Tycoon 9.4f **(73)** - Imperial Jade (Lochnager) 6f **(59)**
Form - 70
Record 1999 - 1st:0 2nd:0 3rd:0 Ran:2
1999 Turf 0-2: (6f, 8f) (gd, g-f)
Currently fair colt. Turf high 52 (began Oct).
**W R Muir [0-2] D J Deer.*

EASTER OGIL (IRE) BHB 82f **RR 78f** 5042[10]
4 ch g Pips Pride 6.7f **(70)** - Piney Pass (Persian Bold) 9.3f **(66)**
Form - 8306076230415770
Record 1999 - 1st:1 2nd:1 3rd:2 Ran:16
Pre1999 - 1st:2 2nd:3 3rd:1 Ran:12
Win Prizemoney £11,624 *Total Prizemoney* £22,898
Wins * 1999 Spt Bath (FRM) H 5.7f 78 85 <
*** 1998** Spt Sandow (GD) 7.1f 83
*** 1998** Apr Beverl (SFT) 5f 83
1999 Turf 1-16: (6f 1-9, 7f 5, 8f, 9f) (hvy, sft, g-s 2, gd 4, g-f 4, frm 1-4)
Workmanlike, above-average gelding, effective 5 to 7f, best at 6f, acts on g-s to frm, often wears blinkers (effectively), likes tight tracks, excels at Lingfield and Sandown. Turf high 85 - 1st of 13 giving 6lb to Kilcullen Lad (6 Spt Bath RF 4161). Consistent. Twice a winner in 1998, he has run some fair races since, and finally rewarded his followers last term with a win at Bath in September. He has won on soft and firm ground, and is particularly suited by a turning course. **I A Balding [3-28] G M Smart.*

EASTLEIGH BHB 27f29a **RR 20f 29a** 1421[9]
10 b g Efisio 7.7f **(69)** - Blue Jane (Blue Cashmere) 6.4f **(54)**
Form - 888620060
Record 1999 - 1st:0 2nd:1 3rd:0 Ran:6

Pre1999 - 1st:9 2nd:15 3rd:9 Ran:137
Win Prizemoney £28,650 *Total Prizemoney* £47,553
Wins * 1997 *Feb Lingfi (STD) H 8f 35 43*
* 1995 *Mar Lingfi (STD) H 8f 50 52*
* 1995 *Feb Lingfi (STD) SH 8f 46 47*
1999 Turf 0-1: (8f) (frm) 1999 AW 0-5: (8f 4, 9f) (Fibr 5)
Little account gelding, effective 8f, - acts on Fibr, has worn blinkers. AW high 26 - 2nd of 9 getting 9lb from Brandon Magic (5 Feb Southwell 8f Fibr RF 0227). **R Hollinshead [9-143] R Hollinshead.*

EASTWAYS BHB 93f RR 91f 5034[2]

2 ch c Efisio 7.7f **(69)** - Helens Dreamgirl (Caerleon (USA)) 8.6f **(71)**
Form - 32132
Record 1999 - 1st:1 2nd:2 3rd:2 Ran:5
Win Prizemoney £8,732 *Total Prizemoney* £13,773
Wins * **1999** Jun Beverl (GD) 5f 80+ <
1999 Turf 1-5: (5f 1-3, 6f, 7f) (g-s, gd 1-3, frm)
Useful colt. Turf high 91 - 2nd of 13 to Avezzano (23 Oct Doncaster 7f g-s RF 5034). Improved in each of his first three starts and won a Beverley maiden very comfortably in June. Given a break after, he was a fast-finishing third in a six-furlong Newmarket nursery on his return and looks as if he will be suited by further.
**M Johnston [1-5] B E P Partnership.*

EASTWELL HALL BHB 81f RR 82f 4917[4]

4 b g Saddlers' Hall (IRE) 10.5f **(65)** -Kinchenjunga(Darshaan) 9.9f **(84)**
Form - 754
Record 1999 - 1st:0 2nd:0 3rd:0 Ran:3
Pre1999 - 1st:3 2nd:2 3rd:1 Ran:13
Win Prizemoney £10,519 *Total Prizemoney* £18,816
Wins 1998 May Warwic (GD) H 12.5f 53 68
1998 Apr Bath (SFT) H 10.2f 53 70+ <
1998 Apr Folkes (GD) H 9.7f 47 52
1999 Turf 0-3: (14f, 17f 2) (gd 3)
Leggy, decent gelding, effective 12 to 17f, best at 12f, acts on gd to g-f, best on gd, likes tight tracks. Turf high 82 (began Spt) - 4th of 32 getting 14lb from Top Cees (16 Oct Newmarket 17f gd RF 4917). Off the track for a year before reappearing in September, he ran his best race since when fourth in the Cesarewitch.
**T P McGovern [0-3] Eastwell Manor Racing (from R Curtis [3-13] Spt 1998).*

EASTWELL STAR RR 33f 4435[9]

3 b f Saddlers' Hall (IRE) 10.5f **(65)** -Kinchenjunga (Darshaan) 9.9f **(84)**
Form - 0
Record 1999 - 1st:0 2nd:0 3rd:0 Ran:1
Pre1999 - 1st:0 2nd:0 3rd:0 Ran:1
1999 Turf 0-1: (12f) (g-s)
Currently very moderate filly.
**Miss Gay Kelleway [0-1] Eastwell Manor Racing (from R Curtis [0-1] Oct 1998).*

EASTWOOD DRIFTER (USA) BHB 65f RR 52f 5001[8]

2 ch c Woodman (USA) 9.7f **(77)** - Mandarina (USA) **(93f)** (El Gran Senor (USA)) 9.6f **(76)**
Form - 608
Record 1999 - 1st:0 2nd:0 3rd:0 Ran:3
1999 Turf 0-3: (7f, 8f 2) (g-s, gd, g-f)
Currently fair colt. Turf high 52 (began Jly).
**W R Muir [0-3] M J Caddy.*

EASYCALL BHB 109f RR 115f 4418[12]

5 b h Forzando 7.2f **(63)** - Up And Going (FR) (Never so Bold) 6.3f **(66)**
Form - 0
Record 1999 - 1st:0 2nd:0 3rd:0 Ran:1
Pre1999 - 1st:7 2nd:3 3rd:2 Ran:25
Win Prizemoney £104,248 *Total Prizemoney* £129,623
Wins 1998 Spt Doncas (GD) L 5f 112
1998 Spt Leices (G-S) 5f 110
1996 Oct Ascot (GD) G3 5f 122 <
1996 Spt Doncas (G-F) G2 5f 116
1996 Aug Goodwo (G-F) G2 6f 111
1996 Jly Newmar (G-F) 5f 96
1996 Jun Leices (GD) 5f 92+
1999 Turf 0-1: (5f) (gd)
High-class colt, effective 5f, acts on hvy to g-f, best on gd, has worn blinkers. Very smart as a two-year-old, he came good in the autumn of 1998, winning at Leicester and Doncaster before running two excellent races in defeat at Longchamp. Retired to stud after his only run this term at Newbury in heavy ground.
**J Noseda [0-1] Easycall Partnership (from B J Meehan [7-25] Oct 1998).*

EASY DOLLAR BHB 89f RR 88f 5030[6]

7 ch g Gabitat 8.5f **(44)** - Burglars Girl (Burglar) 7.2f **(49)**
Form - 56805554602106
Record 1999 - 1st:1 2nd:1 3rd:0 Ran:14
Pre1999 - 1st:2 2nd:6 3rd:5 Ran:32
Win Prizemoney £39,459 *Total Prizemoney* £76,795
Wins * **1999** Spt Nottin (GD) H 6.1f 85 88
* 1995 Jly Goodwo (FRM) H 7f 78 89 <
* 1995 Jly Newmar (GD) 6f 83
1999 Turf 1-14: (5f, 6f 1-9, 7f 4) (g-s, gd 1-5, g-f 5, frm 3)
Useful gelding, effective 6 to 7f, acts on gd to g-f, mostly wears blinkers. Turf high 98. Consistent. He ended a long losing run at Nottingham in September and remains a useful six and seven furlong handicapper. Unsuited by soft ground, he is game.
**B Gubby [3-46] Brian Gubby Ltd.*

EASY TO LOVE (USA) RR 74f 668[5]

3 b f Diesis 9f **(80)** - La Sky (IRE) (Law Society (USA)) 9.9f **(70)**
Form - 5
Record 1999 - 1st:0 2nd:0 3rd:0 Ran:1
1999 Turf 0-1: (10f) (g-f)
Light-framed, currently above-average filly. (1st run) - 5th of 15 getting 5lb from Mirjan (13 Apr Newmarket 10f g-f RF 0668).
**H R A Cecil [0-1] Lordship Stud.*

EATON SQUARE (USA) RR 93f 2352[4]

4 b c Nureyev (USA) 8.4f **(84)** -Jolypha (USA)(Lyphard (USA)) 9.9f **(72)**
Form - 54
Record 1999 - 1st:0 2nd:0 3rd:0 Ran:2
Pre1999 - 1st:2 2nd:0 3rd:0 Ran:3
Win Prizemoney £8,068 *Total Prizemoney* £8,704
Wins * 1998 Jun Goodwo (GD) 9.9f 107 <
* 1998 May Newbur (GD) 8f 95
1999 Turf 0-2: (8f, 10f) (gd 2)
Scopey, useful colt. Turf high 93. **H R A Cecil [2-5] K Abdulla.*

EBBA BHB 93f RR 91f 4518a[5]

2 ch f Elmaamul (USA) 8.1f **(70)** -Strawberry Song(Final Straw)7.9f **(64)**
Form - 1171505
Record 1999 - 1st:3 2nd:0 3rd:0 Ran:7
Win Prizemoney £12,255 *Total Prizemoney* £12,255
Wins * **1999** Jly Yarmou (FRM) 5.2f 83 <
* **1999** Jun Yarmou (GD) 6f 82+
* **1999** May Catter (G-F) 5f 69
1999 Turf 3-7: (5f 2-4, 6f 1-2, 7f) (gd 1-4, g-f 1-2, frm 1-1)
Useful filly, effective 5 to 6f, acts on g-f to frm. Turf high 91 - also 1st of 3 getting 8lb from Dorchester (26 Jly Yarmouth RF 3154). Won a pair of auction events before running poorly in the Chesham, but regained winning form in a fair little three-runner event at Yarmouth, before her form tailed off. **M L W Bell [3-7].*

EBDAA RR 98f 5114a[3]

3 ch f Nashwan (USA) 10.3f **(79)** - Al Theraab (USA) (Roberto (USA)) 10f **(76)**
Form - 3
1999 Turf 0-1: (7f) (gd)
Scopey, currently very useful filly. (1st run) - 3rd of 14 getting 5lb from Capistrano Day (18 Oct Deauville 7f gd RF 5114a).
**in FR [0-1] (from Mrs J Cecil [0-1] Jun 1998).*

EBEN AL HABEEB (IRE) BHB 50f RR 21f 1702[8]

8 ch g Nashwan (USA) 10.3f **(79)** - Family Style (USA) (State Dinner (USA)) 9.4f **(74)**
Form - 08
Record 1999 - 1st:0 2nd:0 3rd:0 Ran:2
Pre1999 - 1st:0 2nd:1 3rd:3 Ran:8
Win Prizemoney £0 *Total Prizemoney* £4,983
1999 Turf 0-1: (12f) (gd) 1999 AW 0-1: (16f) (Fibr)
Little account gelding, has broken blood-vessels. Inconsistent.
**D McCain [4-24] D McCain (from Major W R Hern [0-8] Spt 1995).*

EBINZAYD (IRE) BHB 82f **RR 84f** 4759[5]
3 b c Tenby 10.4f **(76)** - Sharakawa (IRE) (Darshaan) 9.9f **(84)**
Form - 35345
Record 1999 - 1st:0 2nd:0 3rd:2 Ran:5
Pre1999 - 1st:1 2nd:0 3rd:0 Ran:4
Win Prizemoney £3,371 *Total Prizemoney* £7,171
Wins * 1998 Spt Newcas (GD) 8f 83 <
1999 Turf 0-5: (10f, 12f 4) (gd 4, g-f)
Workmanlike, decent colt, effective 8 to 12f, acts on gd to g-f, best on g-f. Turf high 84 (began Aug) - 4th of 9 getting 2lb from Ex Gratia (8 Spt Doncaster 10f gd RF 4211). Consistent. Fetched 44,000 gns at Newmarket sales in October.
**E A L Dunlop [1-9] Hamdan Al Maktoum.*

EBISU (GER) RR 112f 4519a[12]
4 c
Form - 570
1999 Turf 0-3: (10f, 11f 2) (sft, gd 2)
Group-class colt, effective 12f, acts on sft. Turf high 101. He is useful over middle-distances, but consistently outpointed in Group company.
**M Hofer in GER [0-1] (from A Schutz in GER [0-6] Jun 1999).*

EBONY BHB 30f40a **RR 49df 40a** 3440[12]
3 b f Mujtahid (USA) 7.4f **(69)** - Sharia (USA) (Irish River (FR)) 8.6f **(78)**
Form - 00000
Record 1999 - 1st:0 2nd:0 3rd:0 Ran:3
Pre1999 - 1st:0 2nd:1 3rd:0 Ran:5
Win Prizemoney £0 *Total Prizemoney* £548
1999 Turf 0-2: (8f, 10f) (gd, g-f) 1999 AW 0-1: (6f) (Fibr)
Unfurnished, moderate filly, effective 5f, acts on g-f, has worn blinkers, favours left handed tracks, favours tight tracks. Turf high 23. Becoming disappointing.
**B J McMath [0-6] The Happy Go Lucky Partnership (from R Guest [0-2] Spt 1998).*

EBONY HEIGHTS BHB 86f **RR 88df** 4754[13]
3 br c Polar Falcon (USA) 9f **(74)** - Maestrale (Top Ville) 11.7f **(68)**
Form - 2301700
Record 1999 - 1st:1 2nd:1 3rd:1 Ran:7
Pre1999 - 1st:0 2nd:0 3rd:0 Ran:1
Win Prizemoney £8,364 *Total Prizemoney* £10,292
Wins * **1999** Jly Newmar (G-F) H 8f 86 88 <
1999 Turf 1-7: (8f 1-3) (gd 3, g-f, frm 1-3)
Unfurnished, useful colt, effective 8f, acts on gd to frm. Turf high 88 - 1st of 7 giving 12lb to High Hoyland (25 Jly Newmarket RF 3130). **W R Muir [1-8] Mrs E Clowes And Mrs D Edginton.*

E B PEARL BHB 41f45a **RR 33f 45a** 4285[15]
3 ch f Timeless Times (USA) 6.1f **(56)** - Petite Elite (Anfield) 8.5f **(59)**
Form - 76367431564201040000
Record 1999 - 1st:2 2nd:1 3rd:2 Ran:19
Pre1999 - 1st:0 2nd:0 3rd:0 Ran:10
Win Prizemoney £4,364 *Total Prizemoney* £5,652
Wins * **1999** Jly Redcar (FRM) SH 5f 41 44
* **1999** *Apr Southw (STD) C 5f 51* <
1999 Turf 1-10: (5f 1-7, 6f 3) (g-f 2, frm 6, hrd 1-2) 1999 AW 1-9: (5f 1-1, 6f, 7f 5, 8f 2) (Fibr 1-9)
Unfurnished, fair filly, effective 5 to 7f, best at 5f, acts on hrd - acts on Fibr, has worn blinkers. Turf high 44 - 1st of 13 giving 6lb to Lemon Strip (17 Jly Redcar RF 2922). AW high 51 - 1st of 9 getting 5lb from Gochinos (6 Apr Southwell RF 0601).
**N Bycroft [2-29] T Umpleby.*

E B TREASURE BHB 24f **RR 31df** 71[13]
4 b f Precocious 7.2f **(54)** - Petite Elite (Anfield) 8.5f **(59)**
Form - 080
Record 1999 - 1st:0 2nd:0 3rd:0 Ran:3
Pre1999 - 1st:0 2nd:0 3rd:0 Ran:8
1999 AW 0-3: (7f, 8f, 11f) (Fibr 3)
Scopey, very moderate filly, has worn blinkers. AW high 5.
**N Bycroft [0-11] T Umpleby.*

ECLECTIC BHB 46f **RR 56f** 760[7]
3 b f Emarati (USA) 6.6f **(63)** - Great Aim (Great Nephew) 9.9f **(64)**
Form - 07
Record 1999 - 1st:0 2nd:0 3rd:0 Ran:2
Pre1999 - 1st:0 2nd:0 3rd:0 Ran:2
1999 Turf 0-2: (7f, 8f) (g-f, frm)
Workmanlike, fair filly. Turf high 56. **S Dow [0-4] Harold Nass.*

ECO FRIENDLY BHB 92f **RR 84f** 5042[5]
4 ch c Sabrehill (USA) 8.5f **(64)** - Flower Girl (Pharly (FR)) 9.8f **(68)**
Form - 705445
Record 1999 - 1st:0 2nd:0 3rd:0 Ran:5
Pre1999 - 1st:2 2nd:3 3rd:1 Ran:10
Win Prizemoney £28,356 *Total Prizemoney* £53,743
Wins * 1997 Nov Saint- (HVY) G3 8f 99+ <
* 1997 Nov Doncas (G-S) 8f 83
1999 Turf 0-5: (8f 2, 9f, 10f, 11f) (sft, gd 2, g-f, frm)
Decent colt, effective 10 to 15f, acts on sft to g-f, has worn blinkers. Turf high 100 (began Jly). Becoming disappointing. Out of luck since winning a Group 3 at Saint-Cloud in 1997, he showed little last season even when granted his favoured soft ground. Bearing that in mind, connections will have been delighted to pick-up 50,000 guineas when he was sold at Newmarket in October to reportedly race in Singapore.
**B W Hills [2-14] W J Gredley (from J R Fanshawe [0-2] Spt 1997).*

ECSTASY BHB 78f **RR 78f** 4895[10]
2 b f Pursuit of Love 9.5f **(69)** - Gong (Bustino) 10.4f **(64)**
Form - 6214030
Record 1999 - 1st:1 2nd:1 3rd:1 Ran:7
Win Prizemoney £3,214 *Total Prizemoney* £7,225
Wins * **1999** Jly Warwic (G-F) 6.8f 78+ <
1999 Turf 1-7: (5f, 6f 3, 7f 1-3) (gd 3, g-f 1-4)
Above-average filly, effective 6 to 7f, best at 7f, acts on gd to g-f, best on g-f. Turf high 78 - 3rd of 19 getting 11lb from Out of Africa (28 Spt Newmarket 7f g-f RF 4599) - also 1st of 9 getting 2lb from Lees First Step (17 Jly Warwick RF 2933). She got off the mark in a modest Warwick maiden on her third start, but seemed to appreciate the step up to seven furlongs when a close third in a valuable nursery at Newmarket in September.
**P T Walwyn [1-7] A D G Oldrey.*

ECTON PARK (USA) RR 5231a[12]
3 ch c Forty Niner (USA) 8.8f **(73)** - Daring Danzig (USA) (Danzig (USA)) 8.4f **(76)**
Form - 0
1999 AW 0-1: (10f) (Dirt)
Currently very useful, wears blinkers. Looked out of his depth in the Breeders' Cup Classic. **W E Walden in USA [0-1].*

ECUDAMAH (IRE) BHB 60f67a **RR 60f 67a** 5065[4]
3 ch g Mukaddamah (USA) 7.6f **(74)** - Great Land (USA) (Friend's Choice (USA)) 8.6f **(57)**
Form - 3500004
Record 1999 - 1st:0 2nd:0 3rd:1 Ran:7
Pre1999 - 1st:0 2nd:3 3rd:1 Ran:10
Win Prizemoney £0 *Total Prizemoney* £4,535
1999 Turf 0-7: (5f 6, 6f) (sft, g-s, gd 3, g-f, frm)
Strong, average gelding, effective 5 to 6f, best at 5f, acts on sft to frm. Turf high 67. Inconsistent.
**Miss Jacqueline Doyle [0-2] Sanford Racing (from K Bell [0-5] Aug 1999).*

EDABIYA (IRE) RR 110f 4771a[4]
3 ch f Rainbow Quest (USA) 11.2f **(81)** - Ebaziya (IRE) (Darshaan) 9.9f **(84)**
Form - 854
1999 Turf 0-3: (8f, 12f, 15f) (hvy, gd, g-f)
Group-class filly, effective 7 to 8f, acts on gd, has worn blinkers. Turf high 108. This half-sister to Ebadiyla looked a top-class prospect when landing the Moyglare Stud Stakes at two, but things did not go according to plan last term. Her best effort of a light campaign was when she finished fifth behind her owner's more fancied runner Daryaba in the Prix Vermeille.
**J Oxx in IRE [2-6] Aga Khan.*

EDE'IFF BHB 63f **RR 64f** 5192[1]
2 b f Tragic Role (USA) 9.4f **(63)** - Flying Amy (Norwick (USA)) 7.2f **(56)**
Form - 681
Record 1999 - 1st:1 2nd:0 3rd:0 Ran:3
Win Prizemoney £2,326 *Total Prizemoney* £2,326

Wins * **1999** Nov Windso (G-S) S 8.3f 64 <
1999 Turf 1-2: (7f, 8f 1-1) (gd 1-2) 1999 AW 0-1: (8f) (Fibr)
Currently average filly. Turf high 64 (began Aug) - 1st of 17 getting 5lb from Momentous Jones (4 Nov Windsor RF 5192).
**W G M Turner [1-3] Ede's (UK) Ltd.*

EDEN (IRE) BHB 84f **RR 86f** 3984^{8}
3 b f Polish Precedent (USA) 9f **(73)** - Isle of Flame (Shirley Heights) 10.3f **(74)**
Form - 4638
Record **1999** - 1st:0 2nd:0 3rd:1 Ran:4
Pre1999 - 1st:1 2nd:0 3rd:0 Ran:1
Win Prizemoney £4,321 *Total Prizemoney* £6,785
Wins * 1998 Oct Newmar (SFT) 7f 81+ <
1999 Turf 0-4: (8f 3, 10f) (gd, g-f, frm 2)
Scopey, useful filly. Turf high 88 (1st run) - 4th of 7 to Insinuate (28 Apr Ascot 8f g-f RF 0896). **L M Cumani [1-5] L Marinopoulos.*

EDEN DANCER BHB 30f **RR 35?f** 3555^{6}
7 b g Shareef Dancer (USA) 10.1f **(67)** - Dash (Connaught) 7.7f **(63)**
Form - 6
Record **1999** - 1st:0 2nd:0 3rd:0 Ran:1
Pre1999 - 1st:2 2nd:1 3rd:0 Ran:18
Win Prizemoney £6,456 *Total Prizemoney* £7,472
Wins 1995 Jly Hamilt (FRM) H 11.1f 54 59 <
1995 Apr Mussel (GD) 8.1f 56
1999 Turf 0-1: (10f) (gd)
Very moderate gelding.
**M C Pipe [3-6] Geoffrey Hamilton (from Mrs M Reveley [4-31] Aug 1997).*

EDEN MELODY BHB 26f **RR 30f** 2458^{6}
3 b f Noble Patriarch 12.2f **(43)** - Edensong (Lochnager) 6f **(59)**
Form - 686
Record **1999** - 1st:0 2nd:0 3rd:0 Ran:3
1999 Turf 0-3: (10f 2, 14f) (gd, g-f, hrd)
Scopey, currently very moderate filly. Turf high 30.
**J J O'Neill [0-3] T A Horn.*

EDEN ROCK (GER) **RR 112f** $4519a^{11}$
5 b h Dashing Blade 7.9f **(80)** -Eriphyle (GER) (Surumu (GER)) 10f **(83)**
Form - 340
1999 Turf 0-3: (10f 3) (gd 3)
Group-class colt, effective 10f, acts on hvy. Turf high 111 (began Jly). **A Schutz in GER [1-6].*

EDIFICE (JPN) BHB 70f **RR 75f** 5112^{7}
3 ch c Carroll House - Moon Tosho (JPN) (Steel Heart) 8.3f **(58)**
Form - 058407
Record **1999** - 1st:0 2nd:0 3rd:0 Ran:6
Pre1999 - 1st:0 2nd:0 3rd:0 Ran:1
Win Prizemoney £0 *Total Prizemoney* £310
1999 Turf 0-6: (7f, 8f, 10f 3, 12f) (gd, g-f 4, frm)
Workmanlike, above-average colt, effective 8 to 10f, acts on g-f to frm. Turf high 75 - 4th of 10 giving 5lb to Ranelle (7 Spt Leicester 10f g-f RF 4170). **A C Stewart [0-7] Teiji Takasaki.*

EDMO HEIGHTS BHB 59f **RR 43f** 4692^{14}
3 ch g Keen 11.1f **(58)** - Bodham (Bustino) 10.4f **(64)**
Form - 08717185000
Record **1999** - 1st:2 2nd:0 3rd:0 Ran:11
Pre1999 - 1st:1 2nd:2 3rd:0 Ran:7
Win Prizemoney £7,964 *Total Prizemoney* £9,455
Wins * **1999** Jly Beverl (G-F) 9.9f 69
* **1999** Jun Redcar (FRM) H 9f 62 63
* 1998 Spt Beverl (G-F) 7.5f 73 <
1999 Turf 2-11: (8f 2, 9f 1-1, 10f 1-6, 12f 2) (gd 3, g-f 1-5, frm 1-3)
Scopey, moderate gelding, effective 7 to 10f, best at 7f, acts on g-f to frm, best on frm, likes right handed tracks, prefers tight tracks. Turf high 69 - 1st of 6 from Greyfield (19 Jly Beverley RF 2948). Becoming disappointing. He scored on fast ground at Redcar and Beverley, but appeared not to stay when tried at twelve furlongs.
**T D Easterby [3-10] Edmolift UK Ltd.*

EDRAAK (IRE) BHB 94f **RR 95f** 2043^{7}
3 b c Shirley Heights 12.1f **(76)** - Sahara Star (Green Desert (USA)) 8.6f **(78)**
Form - 17
Record **1999** - 1st:1 2nd:0 3rd:0 Ran:2
Pre1999 - 1st:0 2nd:0 3rd:1 Ran:1
Win Prizemoney £3,881 *Total Prizemoney* £4,894
Wins * **1999** Jun Goodwo (G-S) 12f 71+ <
1999 Turf 1-2: (12f 1-1, 16f) (gd 1-1, g-f)
Well made, currently very useful colt. Turf high 95. Out of a Molecomb winner, he failed to stay two miles in the Queen's Vase and will be better over shorter trips.
**S bin Suroor [1-2] Godolphin (from D R Loder [0-1] Oct 1998).*

ED'S FOLLY (IRE) BHB 24f24a **RR 17f 24a** 1455^{5}
6 b g Fayruz 6.6f **(63)** - Tabriya (Nishapour (FR)) 9.1f **(61)**
Form - 05765
Record **1999** - 1st:0 2nd:0 3rd:0 Ran:5
Pre1999 - 1st:0 2nd:2 3rd:5 Ran:30
Win Prizemoney £0 *Total Prizemoney* £4,348
1999 Turf 0-1: (7f) (g-f) 1999 AW 0-4: (7f 2, 8f, 16f) (Equi 3, Fibr)
Very moderate gelding, has worn blinkers. AW high 32.
**L A Dace [0-9] Eddie Davess (from S Dow [0-26] May 1998).*

EDWARDIAN BHB 90f **RR 88+f** 1142^{11}
4 ch g Sanglamore (USA) 12.9f **(67)** - Woodwardia (USA) (El Gran Senor (USA)) 9.6f **(76)**
Form - 0
Record **1999** - 1st:0 2nd:0 3rd:0 Ran:1
Pre1999 - 1st:2 2nd:2 3rd:0 Ran:6
Win Prizemoney £10,562 *Total Prizemoney* £12,882
Wins * 1998 Spt Kempto (GD) 12f 88+ <
* 1998 Spt Goodwo (G-S) 9.9f 82
1999 Turf 0-1: (12f) (gd)
Useful gelding, effective 10 to 12f, best at 10f, acts on g-s to frm.
**Mrs A J Perrett [2-7] K Abdulla.*

EFFANDEMM (IRE) BHB 27a **RR 27a** 348^{6}
3 ch g Up and At 'em - Bermuda Princess (Lord Gayle (USA)) 8.8f **(62)**
Form - 76
Record **1999** - 1st:0 2nd:0 3rd:0 Ran:2
Pre1999 - 1st:0 2nd:0 3rd:0 Ran:2
1999 AW 0-2: (6f, 7f) (Fibr 2)
Poor gelding. AW high 16.
**A Bailey [0-2] F Johnson (from Miss L A Perratt [0-2] Spt 1998).*

EFHARISTO BHB 45f **RR 47f** 5101^{6}
10 b g Dominion 8.9f **(65)** - Excellent Alibi (USA) (Exceller (USA)) 12.5f **(74)**
Form - 06
Record **1999** - 1st:0 2nd:0 3rd:0 Ran:2
Pre1999 - 1st:2 2nd:2 3rd:1 Ran:23
Win Prizemoney £22,348 *Total Prizemoney* £30,225
1999 Turf 0-2: (12f, 14f) (g-s, g-f)
Moderate gelding, has worn blinkers. Turf high 47 (began Oct). Becoming disappointing.
**J Cullinan [1-7] Mrs P A White (from J White [0-7] Jun 1996).*

EHTEFAAL (USA) BHB 50f70a **RR 67f 70a** 4581^{6}
8 b g Alysheba (USA) 12.1f **(78)** - Bolt From The Blue (USA) (Blue Times (USA))
Form - 6
Record **1999** - 1st:0 2nd:0 3rd:0 Ran:1
Pre1999 - 1st:1 2nd:0 3rd:3 Ran:6
Win Prizemoney £3,538 *Total Prizemoney* £5,438
1999 Turf 0-1: (17f) (gd)
Average gelding, often wears blinkers.
**J S King [2-24] Mrs Marygold O'Kelly (from J White [1-7] May 1995).*

EI EI BHB 40f **RR 41f** 5033^{12}
4 b g North Briton 8.2f **(53)** - Branitska (Mummy's Pet) 7.7f **(60)**
Form - 00700
Record **1999** - 1st:0 2nd:0 3rd:0 Ran:5
Pre1999 - 1st:1 2nd:0 3rd:2 Ran:11
Win Prizemoney £1,720 *Total Prizemoney* £2,823
Wins 1998 Apr Folkes (SFT) 7f 86 <
1999 Turf 0-5: (7f 4, 9f) (g-s 2, gd, frm 2)
Leggy, moderate gelding, effective 7f, acts on gd. Turf high 41. Inconsistent.
**G L Moore [0-5] John Hetherington (from B W Hills [1-10] Oct 1998).*

EIFFEL TIGER (IRE) BHB 42f30a **RR 43f 30a** 420[12]
4 b br g Paris House 5.9f **(64)** - Rosa Bengala (Balidar) 7.9f **(63)**
Form - 000
Record 1999 - 1st:0 2nd:0 3rd:0 Ran:2
Pre1999 - 1st:0 2nd:0 3rd:0 Ran:11
1999 AW 0-2: (8f, 11f) (Fibr 2)
Neat, moderate gelding, effective 8f, acts on frm, has worn blinkers, likes left handed tracks, likes tight tracks. Becoming disappointing. **Bob Jones [0-13] Mrs Joan Marioni.*

EIGHT (IRE) BHB 68f **RR 70df** 4213[13]
3 ch c Thatching 7.8f **(69)** - Up To You (Sallust) 8.4f **(63)**
Form - 63300
Record 1999 - 1st:0 2nd:0 3rd:2 Ran:5
Pre1999 - 1st:0 2nd:0 3rd:0 Ran:1
Win Prizemoney £0 *Total Prizemoney* £1,541
1999 Turf 0-5: (7f, 8f 4) (g-f 3, frm 2)
Above-average colt, effective 8f, acts on g-f to frm. Turf high 70 - 3rd of 11 to Black Silk (2 Jly Warwick 8f g-f RF 2506).
**C G Cox [0-2] Mrs Anthony Andrews (from M J Heaton-Ellis [0-4] Jly 1999).*

EIGHTEENTH MSF BHB 45f **RR 55f** 4026[8]
2 b f Presidium 7.5f **(56)** - Peters Pet Girl (Norwick (USA)) 7.2f **(56)**
Form - 745408
Record 1999 - 1st:0 2nd:0 3rd:0 Ran:6
1999 Turf 0-6: (5f 2, 6f 4) (gd, g-f 4, frm)
Fair filly, effective 5 to 6f, acted on g-f, had worn blinkers. Turf high 50 (began Jly) - 5th of 12 getting 5lb from Pertemps Fc (24 Jly Newcastle 6f g-f RF 3102). (DEAD)
**N Tinkler [0-6] The Penniless Partnership.*

EILEAN SHONA BHB 97f **RR 91+f** 5132[1]
3 b f Suave Dancer (USA) 10.7f **(68)** - Moidart **(88f)** (Electric) 10.1f **(61)**
Form - 24311
Record 1999 - 1st:2 2nd:1 3rd:1 Ran:5
Pre1999 - 1st:1 2nd:0 3rd:0 Ran:3
Win Prizemoney £23,574 *Total Prizemoney* £26,974
Wins * **1999** Oct Newmar (G-S) LH 16.1f 87 91 <
* **1999** Spt Redcar (G-F) H 14.1f 84 85
* 1998 Spt Redcar (G-F) 9f 75
1999 Turf 2-5: (12f 2, 14f 1-2, 16f 1-1) (gd 1-1, g-f 3, frm 1-1)
Scopey, useful filly, effective 12 to 16f, best at 14f, acts on gd to frm, excels at Redcar. Turf high 91 - 1st of 12 from Trellis Bay (29 Oct Newmarket RF 5132) - also 1st of 7 giving 8lb to Salford Flyer (24 Spt Redcar RF 4540). Improving.
**J R Fanshawe [3-8] Dr Catherine Wills.*

EIN TRESOR BHB 45a **RR 61f 45a** 92[F]
5 b g Mon Tresor 7.9f **(60)** - Play the Game (Mummy's Game) 8.2f **(60)**
Form - F
Record 1999 - 1st:0 2nd:0 3rd:0 Ran:1
Pre1999 - 1st:0 2nd:2 3rd:0 Ran:16
Win Prizemoney £0 *Total Prizemoney* £2,055
1999 AW 0-1: (12f) (Equi)
Average gelding, effective 11f, acts on sft, has worn blinkers.
**B J Llewellyn [0-3] Thomas Leonard (from J C Hayden in IRE [0-19] Aug 1998).*

EJTITHAAB (IRE) RR 53f 4840[6]
2 ch c Arazi (USA) 9.2f **(74)** - Cunning (Bustino) 10.4f **(64)**
Form - 6
Record 1999 - 1st:0 2nd:0 3rd:0 Ran:1
1999 Turf 0-1: (7f) (gd)
Currently fair colt. **P T Walwyn [0-1] Hamdan Al Maktoum.*

EKRAAR (USA) BHB 100f **RR 105f** 5037[3]
2 b c Red Ransom (USA) 8.6f **(83)** - Sacahuista (USA) (Raja Baba (USA)) 10f **(64)**
Form - 2143
Record 1999 - 1st:1 2nd:1 3rd:1 Ran:4
Win Prizemoney £26,600 *Total Prizemoney* £52,691
Wins * **1999** Jly Goodwo (G-F) G3 7f 99+ <
1999 Turf 1-4: (7f 1-3, 8f) (g-s, frm 1-3)
Pattern-class colt, has worn blinkers. Turf high 105 (began Jly) - 3rd of 9 to Aristotle (23 Oct Doncaster 8f g-s RF 5037) - also 1st of 5 from Sarafan (29 Jly Goodwood RF 3221). He looked top-class when winning a Group 3 at Glorious Goodwood, was slightly disappointing in the Champagne Stakes at Doncaster in September. Fitted with blinkers for the Racing Post Trophy, he seemed assured of victory when hitting the front three furlongs out, but weakened close home and finished third. Unlikely to stay beyond a mile, he should develop into a smart three-year-old.
**M P Tregoning [1-4] Hamdan Al Maktoum.*

ELA AGAPI MOU (USA) BHB 57f50a **RR 58f 50a** 1329[9]
6 b g Storm Bird (CAN) 8.5f **(82)** - Vaguar (USA) (Vaguely Noble) 10.1f **(72)**
Form - 40
Record 1999 - 1st:0 2nd:0 3rd:0 Ran:2
Pre1999 - 1st:1 2nd:1 3rd:1 Ran:12
Win Prizemoney £3,131 *Total Prizemoney* £4,012
Wins * 1998 Apr Folkes (SFT) H 15.4f 48 62+ <
1999 Turf 0-2: (15f, 18f) (hvy, gd)
Fair gelding, has worn blinkers. Turf high 58 (1st run) - 4th of 13 to Needwood Spirit (20 Apr Folkestone 15f hvy RF 0763). Inconsistent. **G L Moore [8-27] Action (from A Moore [0-3] Jan 1997).*

ELAANDO RR 66f 2620[7]
4 b c Darshaan 11.9f **(81)** - Evocatrice (Persepolis (FR)) 6.4f **(67)**
Form - 7
Record 1999 - 1st:0 2nd:0 3rd:0 Ran:1
1999 Turf 0-1: (10f) (frm)
Average colt. **Mrs Merrita Jones [3-8] F J Sainsbury.*

ELA ATHENA BHB 113f **RR 115f** 3757[2]
3 gr f Ezzoud (IRE) - Crodelle (IRE) (Formidable (USA)) 9.2f **(63)**
Form - 1212
Record 1999 - 1st:2 2nd:2 3rd:0 Ran:4
Win Prizemoney £17,445 *Total Prizemoney* £66,091
Wins * **1999** Jly Chepst (G-F) L 10.2f 107 <
* **1999** Apr Newbur (G-F) 10f 79
1999 Turf 2-4: (10f 2-3, 12f) (gd, g-f 1-1, frm 1-2)
Leggy, high-class filly. Turf high 115 - 2nd of 11 to Ramruma (18 Aug York 12f gd RF 3757) - also 1st of 8 getting 10lb from Keld (23 Jly Chepstow RF 3055). Unraced at two, she made a winning debut in a Newbury maiden and, after chasing home Alabaq in the Pretty Polly, landed a Listed event at Chepstow. However, her best performance by far came when she chased home Ramruma in the Yorkshire Oaks. Unfortunately, injury ruled her out for the rest of the season. **M A Jarvis [2-4] Andreas Michael.*

ELAFLAAK (USA) BHB 100f **RR 98f** 4596[14]
2 b f Gulch (USA) 9.6f **(79)** - Catnip (USA) (Flying Paster (USA))
Form - 1110
Record 1999 - 1st:3 2nd:0 3rd:0 Ran:4
Win Prizemoney £20,690 *Total Prizemoney* £20,690
Wins * **1999** Aug Newbur (GD) L 5.2f 98+ <
* **1999** Jly Newbur (G-F) 6f 91+
* **1999** Jly Beverl (G-F) 5f 80+
1999 Turf 3-4: (5f 2-2, 6f 1-2) (gd 1-1, g-f, frm 2-2)
Very useful filly. Turf high 98 (began Jly) - 1st of 8 getting 5lb from Kalindi (14 Aug Newbury RF 3648) - also 1st of 6 giving 11lb to Starlyte Girl (16 Jly Newbury RF 2874). She impressed when winning her first three starts and may have been over the top when disappointing in the Cheveley Park Stakes (she pulled hard to post and in the race). Time may show her to be suited by sprint distances. **M P Tregoning [3-4] Hamdan Al Maktoum.*

ELA-YIE-MOU (IRE) BHB 51f39a **RR 56df 39a** 91[9]
6 ch g Kris 10f **(75)** - Green Lucia (Green Dancer (USA)) 10.3f **(74)**
Form - 00
Record 1999 - 1st:0 2nd:0 3rd:0 Ran:1
Pre1999 - 1st:1 2nd:0 3rd:3 Ran:20
Win Prizemoney £3,622 *Total Prizemoney* £5,720
Wins 1996 May Nottin (G-F) H 14.1f 73 76 <
1999 AW 0-1: (16f) (Equi)
Fair gelding. Becoming disappointing.
**L A Dace [0-4] Luke Dace (from S Dow [0-17] Apr 1998).*

ELBA MAGIC (IRE) BHB 60f59a **RR 60f 59a** 4813[12]
4 b f Faustus (USA) 9.1f **(54)** -Dependable (Formidable (USA)) 9.2f **(63)**
Form - 470325333052180
Record 1999 - 1st:1 2nd:2 3rd:4 Ran:15

Pre1999 - 1st:3 2nd:2 3rd:3 Ran:18
Win Prizemoney £10,091 *Total Prizemoney* £17,530
Wins * **1999** Spt Beverl (GD) H 8.5f 58 60
* 1998 Aug Ripon (G-F) H 10f 63 66 <
* 1998 Jly Yarmou (GD) H 10.1f 60 63
* 1998 *Apr Southw (STD) H 7f 55 63*
1999 Turf 1-14: (8f 1-6, 9f, 10f 7) (g-s 2, gd 1-4, g-f 3, frm 5) 1999 AW 0-1: (9f) (Fibr)
Workmanlike, average filly, effective 7 to 10f, best at 8f, acts on g-s to hrd - acts on Fibr, best on gd, likes left handed tracks, prefers tight tracks, excels at Windsor and Southwell and does well at Lingfield. Turf high 60 - 1st of 16 getting 2lb from Tipperary Sunset (15 Spt Beverley RF 4321).
**C A Dwyer [4-32] Graham Mitchell (from H J Collingridge [0-1] Jly 1997).*

EL CARDINAL (IRE) RR $3596a^{2}$
2 b c Foxhound (USA) - Persian Light (Persian Heights)
Form - 2
Record 1999 - 1st:0 2nd:1 3rd:0 Ran:1
Win Prizemoney £0 *Total Prizemoney* £2,187
1999 Turf 0-1: (8f)
Italian-raced colt. **M Quinlan [0-1].*

EL COMENDADOR (IRE) RR 90f $2608a^{9}$
3 ch c Crafty Prospector (USA) 7f **(72)** - Super Cook (USA) **00**
Form - 18400
1999 Turf 1-5: (7f 1-1, 8f 3, 9f) (sft 1-1, g-s, g-f 2, frm)
Useful colt, effective 7f, acts on sft. Turf high 90 (1st run) - 1st of 14 from Union Project (14 Apr Gowran Park RF 0777a).
**D Hanley in IRE [1-6] F Hinojosa.*

EL CONDOR PASA (USA) RR 135f $4778a^{2}$
4 br c Kingmambo (USA) 10.9f **(85)** - Saddlers Gal (USA) (Sadler's Wells (USA)) 10f **(76)**
Form - 12112
1999 Turf 2-4: (9f, 12f 2-3) (sft, g-s, gd 2-2)
Exceptional colt. Turf high 135 - 2nd of 14 giving 8lb to Montjeu (3 Oct Longchamp 12f sft RF 4778a) - also 1st of 10 from Tiger Hill (4 Jly Saint-Cloud RF 2662a). Japanese-trained, he comfortably landed the Japan Cup in 1998, and did all his racing in France in 1999 with his campaign being geared towards a crack at the Arc. Touched off by Croco Rouge first time, he slammed a top-class field in the Grand Prix de Saint-Cloud before beating Borgia a neck in the three-runner Prix Foy. Reportedly some way short of full fitness before that race, he showed the benefit with a remarkable performance in the Arc. Leading from the outset, he quickened turning for home, and it took the exceptional Montjeu to catch him. He retires to stud in Japan as a very high-class international performer, and was the only horse who could arguably be compared with Daylami among the older generation.
**Y Ninomiya in JPN [3-5] T Watanabe.*

EL CURIOSO (USA) BHB 92f RR 90f 4899^{4}
2 b c El Gran Senor (USA) 8.9f **(85)** - Curious (USA) (Rare Performer (USA))
Form - 215714
Record 1999 - 1st:2 2nd:1 3rd:0 Ran:6
Win Prizemoney £11,454 *Total Prizemoney* £13,083
Wins * **1999** Spt Warwic (SFT) H 7.7f 85 87 <
* **1999** Jly Salisb (G-F) 7f 83
1999 Turf 2-6: (6f, 7f 1-3, 8f 1-2) (sft 1-1, gd 2, frm 1-3)
Useful colt, effective 7 to 8f, best at 7f, acts on sft to frm, best on frm. Turf high 90 - also 1st of 12 giving 14lb to Kanistari (21 Spt Warwick RF 4452). **P W Harris [2-6] The Curious Twelve.*

ELDERBERRY RR 2761^{7}
2 gr f Bin Ajwaad (IRE) - Silver Berry (Lorenzaccio) 10f **(64)**
Form - 7
Record 1999 - 1st:0 2nd:0 3rd:0 Ran:1
1999 Turf 0-1: (6f) (frm)
Currently very poor filly. **B J Meehan [0-1] David Hicks.*

EL DIVINO (GER) RR 110f $4892a^{5}$
4 b c Platini (GER) - Eivissa (GER) (Frontal) 6.4f **(64)**
Form - 3215
1999 Turf 1-4: (8f 1-3, 9f) (sft 1-1, gd 3)
Group-class colt. Turf high 110 - 1st of 7 from Up And Away (25 Spt Cologne RF 4662a). He responded well to an enterprising ride when winning a Group 2 in Cologne during September. He had the Irish 2,000 Guineas runner-up, Mus-If, well beaten off that day and is clearly a smart miler. **M Hofer in GER [1-4].*

EL DOLOR (IRE) BHB 65f RR 71f 4716^{10}
2 br g Elbio 9f **(62)** - Payne's Grey (Godswalk (USA)) 7.3f **(58)**
Form - 2500
Record 1999 - 1st:0 2nd:1 3rd:0 Ran:4
Win Prizemoney £0 *Total Prizemoney* £1,105
1999 Turf 0-4: (6f 4) (g-s, gd 2, frm)
Above-average gelding. Turf high 71 (1st run) (began Jly) - 2nd of 17 getting 2lb from Rhodamine (12 Jly Newcastle 6f frm RF 2754).
**R A Fahey [0-4] Mrs M W Kenyon.*

ELEANOR RIGBY (IRE) BHB 33f RR 10f 336^{8}
3 b f Turtle Island (USA) - Eleanor Antoinette (IRE) (Double Schwartz) 7.9f **(55)**
Form - 768
Record 1999 - 1st:0 2nd:0 3rd:0 Ran:3
Pre1999 - 1st:0 2nd:0 3rd:0 Ran:1
1999 AW 0-3: (7f 2, 8f) (Equi, Fibr 2)
Leggy, very moderate filly. AW high 31.
**M Johnston [0-4] Mark Johnston Racing Ltd.*

ELEGANT DANCE BHB 56f58a RR 43f 58a 3612^{12}
5 ch m Statoblest 6.4f **(63)**-Furry Dance (USA) (Nureyev(USA))8.7f **(78)**
Form - 030000
Record 1999 - 1st:0 2nd:0 3rd:1 Ran:6
Pre1999 - 1st:1 2nd:1 3rd:0 Ran:10
Win Prizemoney £3,096 *Total Prizemoney* £4,492
Wins * 1998 Jun Salisb (G-F) H 6f 61 62 <
1999 Turf 0-5: (6f 3, 7f 2) (g-f 2, frm 3) 1999 AW 0-1: (7f) (Fibr)
Moderate filly, effective 6f, acts on frm. Turf high 61 (1st run) - 3rd of 13 giving 6lb to Mister Tricky (22 May Lingfield 6f frm RF 1403).
**J J Sheehan [1-16] Mrs Christina Dowling.*

ELEGANT FAN (USA) BHB 37f RR 32f 2057^{15}
4 b br c Lear Fan (USA) 10.4f **(80)** - Elegance (USA) (Providential) 10.2f **(72)**
Form - 000
Record 1999 - 1st:0 2nd:0 3rd:0 Ran:3
Pre1999 - 1st:0 2nd:0 3rd:0 Ran:4
1999 Turf 0-3: (8f, 9f, 10f) (gd, frm, hrd)
Very moderate colt. Turf high 26.
**W Storey [0-6] Tony Stafford (from C E Brittain [0-4] Oct 1998).*

ELEGANT FELLOW RR 61f 4784^{5}
2 b c Green Desert (USA) 7.8f **(78)** - Lailati (USA) (Mr Prospector (USA)) 8.8f **(78)**
Form - 35
Record 1999 - 1st:0 2nd:0 3rd:1 Ran:2
Win Prizemoney £0 *Total Prizemoney* £602
1999 Turf 0-2: (6f, 7f) (g-s, g-f)
Currently average colt. Turf high 61 (began Spt).
**Sir Michael Stoute [0-2] Maktoum Al Maktoum.*

ELEGANT LADY RR 83df 5040^{10}
3 ch f Selkirk (USA) 7.9f **(76)** - Prompting (Primo Dominie) 6.2f **(80)**
Form - 13000
Record 1999 - 1st:1 2nd:0 3rd:1 Ran:5
Pre1999 - 1st:0 2nd:1 3rd:0 Ran:4
Win Prizemoney £10,866 *Total Prizemoney* £13,678
Wins * **1999** May Cheste (G-F) H 6.1f 80 82 <
1999 Turf 1-5: (5f 4, 6f 1-1) (g-s, gd 2, g-f 1-2)
Lengthy, decent filly, effective 5 to 6f, best at 5f, acts on gd to g-f, best on g-f. Turf high 83 - 3rd of 16 giving 25lb to Oriel Star (17 May Windsor 5f gd RF 1289) - also 1st of 15 giving 7lb to Luanshya (5 May Chester RF 1042). She got off the mark by winning a six-furlong Chester handicap on her reappearance, and was not disgraced when third in quite a competitive handicap over a furlong less at Windsor. Given a break after a moderate performance at Ascot in June, she failed to recapture her form.
**J H M Gosden [1-9] Platt Promotions Ltd.*

ELEGIA PRIMA BHB 66f **RR 69+f** 4177[11]
2 ch f Mon Tresor 7.9f **(60)** - Miss Milton (Young Christopher) 6f **(61)**
Form - 1600
Record 1999 - 1st:1 2nd:0 3rd:0 Ran:4
Win Prizemoney £2,477 *Total Prizemoney* £2,477
Wins * 1999 Jun Salisb (FRM) 7f 69+ <
1999 Turf 1-4: (7f 1-3, 8f) (g-f, frm 1-3)
Average filly, has worn blinkers. Turf high 69 (1st run) - 1st of 15 from Ribbon Lake (24 Jun Salisbury RF 2278).
**Major D N Chappell [1-4] C V Cruden.*

EL EMPERADOR RR 70f 4560[6]
2 b c Emperor Jones (USA) - Car Stop (USA) (Stop The Music (USA)) 9.2f **(71)**
Form - 6
Record 1999 - 1st:0 2nd:0 3rd:0 Ran:1
1999 Turf 0-1: (6f) (gd)
Currently above-average colt.
**J R Fanshawe [0-1] H R H Prince Fahd Salman.*

ELENII BHB 35f **RR 24f** 747[16]
3 b f Risk Me (FR) 8f **(53)** - Sunday Sport's Pet (Mummy's Pet) 7.7f **(60)**
Form - 050
Record 1999 - 1st:0 2nd:0 3rd:0 Ran:3
1999 Turf 0-2: (7f, 8f) (g-s, gd) 1999 AW 0-1: (6f) (Equi)
Light-framed, currently little account filly. Turf high 24.
**Miss Gay Kelleway [0-3] The Absolutely Fabulous Partnership.*

ELFLAND (IRE) BHB 75f **RR 78f** 4386[14]
8 b g Fairy King (USA) 7.7f **(75)** - Ridge The Times (USA) (Riva Ridge (USA)) 8.2f **(68)**
Form - 600
Record 1999 - 1st:0 2nd:0 3rd:0 Ran:3
Pre1999 - 1st:2 2nd:0 3rd:3 Ran:17
Win Prizemoney £13,951 *Total Prizemoney* £22,187
Wins * 1997 Jun Newmar (G-S) H 7f 81 84 <
* 1995 May Doncas (GD) H 7f 77 82
1999 Turf 0-3: (7f, 8f 2) (frm 3)
Above-average gelding, has broken blood-vessels. Turf high 78 (began Jly).
**Lady Herries [2-15] The High Flying Partnership (from J H M Gosden [0-5] Aug 1994).*

EL FUERTE BHB 35f **RR 18f** 3084[12]
4 b g Perpendicular - Sleekit (Blakeney) 10.5f **(64)**
Form - 80
Record 1999 - 1st:0 2nd:0 3rd:0 Ran:2
Pre1999 - 1st:0 2nd:0 3rd:0 Ran:5
1999 Turf 0-1: (12f) (g-f) 1999 AW 0-1: (16f) (Fibr)
Workmanlike, poor gelding.
**W Clay [0-10] Lee Heath (from P J Makin [0-5] Aug 1998).*

EL GRAN LOVE (USA) BHB 43f **RR 53f** 2888[9]
3 b f El Gran Senor (USA) 8.9f **(85)** - Where Is She (USA) (Cure The Blues (USA)) 9.5f **(63)**
Form - 0800
Record 1999 - 1st:0 2nd:0 3rd:0 Ran:4
1999 Turf 0-4: (8f, 12f 3) (gd 2, frm, hrd)
Small, fair filly, has worn blinkers. Turf high 53.
**T D Easterby [0-4] The Thoroughbred Corporation.*

EL GRAN PAPA (USA) RR 74f 4840[3]
2 b c El Gran Senor (USA) 8.9f **(85)** - Banner Hit (USA) (Oh Say (USA))
Form - 53
Record 1999 - 1st:0 2nd:0 3rd:1 Ran:2
Win Prizemoney £0 *Total Prizemoney* £525
1999 Turf 0-2: (7f 2) (gd, g-f)
Currently above-average colt. Turf high 74 (began Aug).
**J H M Gosden [0-2] Thomas Tatham.*

ELHABUB BHB 69f73a **RR 71f 73a** 2173[6]
4 b g Lion Cavern (USA) 7.5f **(74)** - Million Heiress (Auction Ring (USA)) 8.6f **(65)**
Form - 21682026
Record 1999 - 1st:0 2nd:2 3rd:0 Ran:5
Pre1999 - 1st:1 2nd:6 3rd:0 Ran:12
Win Prizemoney £2,508 *Total Prizemoney* £13,838
Wins 1998 *Dec Lingfi (STD) H 10f 70 77* <
1999 Turf 0-3: (10f 3) (gd, g-f, frm) 1999 AW 0-2: (8f, 10f) (Equi, Fibr)
Scopey, above-average gelding, effective 9 to 10f, best at 10f, acts on sft to g-f - acts on Equi, likes left handed tracks. Turf high 71 - 2nd of 9 giving 1lb to Farmost (11 Jun Chepstow 10f gd RF 1910). AW high 61.
**D Burchell [0-5] Primeshade Contracts Ltd (from Miss Gay Kelleway [1-7] Jan 1999).*

ELHAYQ (IRE) BHB 106f **RR 110f** 4250[3]
4 b c Nashwan (USA) 10.3f **(79)** - Mahasin (USA) (Danzig (USA)) 8.4f **(76)**
Form - 21163
Record 1999 - 1st:2 2nd:1 3rd:1 Ran:5
Pre1999 - 1st:1 2nd:3 3rd:1 Ran:9
Win Prizemoney £19,983 *Total Prizemoney* £32,400
Wins * 1999 May Newbur (G-F) 10f 110 <
*** 1999** May Newmar (G-F) H 10f 95 102
* 1998 Apr Thirsk (G-S) 12f 86
1999 Turf 2-5: (10f 2-4, 12f) (gd, g-f 1-2, frm 1-2)
Rangy, Group-class colt, effective 10f, acts on g-f to frm, best on g-f, likes left handed tracks. Turf high 110 - 3rd of 6 giving 11lb to Timahs (10 Spt Doncaster 10f g-f RF 4250) - also 1st of 4 from Pegnitz (26 May Newbury RF 1499). Improving. He looked a thorough stayer in 1998, but improved when dropped back to a mile and a quarter and ended the season verging on Listed class. Effective on all types of ground despite a markedly round-action, he is very genuine. **J L Dunlop [3-14] Hamdan Al Maktoum.*

ELHIDA (IRE) BHB 92f **RR 93f** 4654[12]
3 ch f Mujtahid (USA) 7.4f **(69)** - Nouvelle Star (AUS) (Luskin Star (AUS)) 6.3f **(71)**
Form - 45730
Record 1999 - 1st:0 2nd:0 3rd:1 Ran:5
Pre1999 - 1st:1 2nd:1 3rd:0 Ran:3
Win Prizemoney £6,937 *Total Prizemoney* £10,404
Wins * 1998 Jly Goodwo (GD) 6f 95+ <
1999 Turf 0-5: (5f 2, 6f 3) (gd 2, frm 3)
Scopey, useful filly, effective 5 to 6f, best at 6f, acts on gd to frm, best on gd. Turf high 93 - 7th of 10 getting 8lb from Cretan Gift (29 Aug Yarmouth 6f gd RF 4001). Consistent.
**M P Tregoning [1-8] Hamdan Al Maktoum.*

EL HIDALGO (IRE) RR 59f 3785a[3]
2 br g Namaqualand (USA) - Dancing Sensation (USA) **(72f 51a)** (Faliraki)
Form - 103
Record 1999 - 1st:1 2nd:0 3rd:1 Ran:3
Win Prizemoney £4,556 *Total Prizemoney* £7,180
Wins * 1999 Jun Livorn (HVY) 5f
1999 Turf 1-3: (5f 1-1, 6f, 8f) (hvy 1-1, gd, frm)
Currently fair gelding. Turf high 59.
**M Quinlan [1-2] (from M G Quinlan [0-1] Jly 1999).*

ELHILMEYA (IRE) RR 91f 1215[3]
3 b f Unfuwain (USA) 11.4f **(74)** - Awayed (USA) (Sir Ivor) 10.2f **(70)**
Form - 13
Record 1999 - 1st:1 2nd:0 3rd:1 Ran:2
Win Prizemoney £3,792 *Total Prizemoney* £5,852
Wins * 1999 May Haydoc (GD) 10.5f 84 <
1999 Turf 1-2: (10f, 11f 1-1) (g-s, g-f 1-1)
Scopey, currently useful filly. Turf high 91 - also 1st of 7 from Zariliya (1 May Haydock RF 0952). Unraced at two, she made up for lost time winning a maiden over the extended ten furlongs at Haydock on good ground on her first start at three. Upped in class a couple of weeks later she ran well in a Listed race over ten furlongs on good to soft ground at Newbury when third to Nasheed, with a decent bunch of rivals surrounding her. Has been off the course since that effort in May.
**M P Tregoning [1-2] Hamdan Al Maktoum.*

ELITE HOPE (USA) BHB 57f69a **RR 47f 69a** 1279[4]
7 ch m Moment of Hope (USA) 6.9f **(80)** - Chervil (USA) (Greenough (USA)) 6.9f **(85)**
Form - 454403112343234
Record 1999 - 1st:2 2nd:2 3rd:4 Ran:12
Pre1999 - 1st:8 2nd:7 3rd:2 Ran:44
Win Prizemoney £25,474 *Total Prizemoney* £36,276

Wins	* 1999	Feb Southw	(STD)	C	7f		66
	* 1999	Feb Southw	(STD)	H	7f	62	67
	* 1998	Apr Wolver	(STD)	C	7f		66
	* 1998	Mar Wolver	(STD)	C	7f		67
	* 1998	Jan Wolver	(STD)	C	7f		77
	* 1997	Nov Wolver	(STD)	C	6f		60
	* 1997	Jan Wolver	(SLW)	H	7f	67	71
	* 1996	Dec Wolver	(STD)	H	7f	64	66
	* 1996	Nov Wolver	(STD)	H	7f	52	60

1999 AW 2-12: (6f, 7f 2-10, 8f) (Fibr 2-12)

Above-average mare, effective 6 to 7f, best at 7f, - acts on Fibr, has worn blinkers. AW high 70 - 2nd of 12 to Storm Cat (24 Apr Wolverhampton 7f Fibr RF 0851). Consistent. She is an effective sort on sand when able to dominate.

**N Tinkler [9-40] Elite Racing Club (from C R Egerton [1-16] Spt 1996).*

ELJARIHA RR 72+f 5060[2]

2 b f Unfuwain (USA) 11.4f **(74)** - Hiwaya **(101f)** (Doyoun) 9f **(69)**

Form - 2

Record 1999 - 1st:0 2nd:1 3rd:0 Ran:1

Win Prizemoney £0 *Total Prizemoney* £1,500

1999 Turf 0-1: (7f) (g-s)

Currently above-average filly. **M P Tregoning [0-1] Hamdan Al Maktoum.*

EL KARIM (USA) BHB 70f RR 71f 1945[12]

3 ch c Storm Cat (USA) 7f **(86)** - Gmaasha (IRE) (Kris) 9.5f **(73)**

Form - 80

Record 1999 - 1st:0 2nd:0 3rd:0 Ran:2
Pre1999 - 1st:0 2nd:0 3rd:1 Ran:2

Win Prizemoney £0 *Total Prizemoney* £807

1999 Turf 0-2: (7f 2) (gd, g-f)

Workmanlike, above-average colt. Turf high 68.

**J L Dunlop [0-4] Hamdan Al Maktoum.*

ELKEYVOR BHB 40f RR 31tf 2584[8]

4 b g Elmaamul (USA) 8.1f **(70)** - Petonica (IRE) (Petoski) 5.7f **(62)**

Form - 8

Record 1999 - 1st:0 2nd:0 3rd:0 Ran:1
Pre1999 - 1st:0 2nd:0 3rd:0 Ran:2

1999 Turf 0-1: (12f) (frm)

Workmanlike, currently very moderate gelding.

**S Gollings [0-1] H Key (from T D Easterby [0-2] Jun 1998).*

ELLE DANZIG (GER) RR 116f 4780a[4]

4 b f Roi Danzig (USA) 10.5f **(62)** - Elegie (GER) (Teotepec (GER))

Form - 2414

1999 Turf 1-4: (9f, 10f 1-2, 11f) (sft 2, g-s 1-1, gd)

High-class filly, effective 8 to 12f, best at 10f, acts on sft to gd, best on sft, likes right handed tracks. Turf high 113 - 1st of 9 giving 5lb to Kalatos (27 Aug Baden-Baden RF 4107a). Consistent. She carried all before her in Germany as a three-year-old, but could only manage a handful of starts last term and was put in her place by Diamond White at Longchamp in October. However, she was victorious in the Group One Premio Roma at Capannelle on her last start in November and, should she stay in training, can continue to be a force to reckon with on home soil.

**A Schutz in GER [6-10].*

ELLEN BE CHIC BHB 28f RR 17f 4945[17]

3 gr f Touch of Grey 8.1f **(47)** - Lingfield Lass (USA) (Advocator) 10.9f **(80)**

Form - 0000

Record 1999 - 1st:0 2nd:0 3rd:0 Ran:4

1999 Turf 0-4: (6f, 7f 2, 8f) (gd, g-f 2, frm)

Scopey, poor filly. Turf high 17 (began Aug).

**R M Flower [0-4] Miss Alyson Marshall.*

ELLENS ACADEMY (IRE) BHB 79f RR 88df 4390[8]

4 b c Royal Academy (USA) 7.8f **(77)** - Lady Ellen (Horage) 10.3f **(61)**

Form - 421841008

Record 1999 - 1st:2 2nd:1 3rd:0 Ran:9
Pre1999 - 1st:0 2nd:1 3rd:1 Ran:5

Win Prizemoney £14,189 *Total Prizemoney* £17,108

Wins	* 1999	Jly Newmar	(G-F)	H	6f	73	78 <
	* 1999	May Newbur	(G-F)	H	6f	63	71+

1999 Turf 2-9: (6f 2-7, 7f 2) (gd 2, g-f 1-2, frm 1-5)

Useful colt, effective 6f, acts on gd to frm, has worn blinkers. Turf high 88. Ran well in his class last term, picking up a competitive event at Newbury in May and a 0-90 at Newmarket. Highly tried after, notably when taking on Arkadian Hero.

**E J Alston [2-11] Mrs Chris Harrington (from D K Weld in IRE [0-3] Jly 1998).*

ELLENS LAD (IRE) BHB 95f RR 94f 5040[2]

5 b g Polish Patriot (USA) 7.8f **(70)** - Lady Ellen (Horage) 10.3f **(61)**

Form - 006362307011412

Record 1999 - 1st:3 2nd:2 3rd:2 Ran:15
Pre1999 - 1st:3 2nd:1 3rd:2 Ran:23

Win Prizemoney £36,847 *Total Prizemoney* £50,829

Wins	* 1999	Oct Newmar	(GD)	H	5f	87	94 <
	* 1999	Spt Haydoc	(G-F)	H	5f	84	86
	* 1999	Aug Newbur	(GD)	H	5.2f	80	81
	1998	Jly Newmar	(G-F)	H	5f	81	86
	1996	Nov Newmar	(GD)	H	5f	77	86
	1996	Spt Folkes	(G-F)	H	5f	72	76

1999 Turf 3-15: (5f 3-10, 6f 5) (g-s 2, gd 2-4, g-f 4, frm 1-5)

Useful gelding, effective 5f, acts on g-s to frm, has worn blinkers, and excels at Doncaster. Turf high 94 - 2nd of 14 to Perryston View (23 Oct Doncaster 5f g-s RF 5040) - also 1st of 9 getting 8lb from Light The Rocket (14 Oct Newmarket RF 4873). Improving. In fine form in the second half of the season in sprint handicaps. He goes particularly well for Pat Eddery.

**W J Musson [3-15]Mrs Rita Brown (from E J Alston [1-10] Oct 1998).*

ELLE QUESTRO BHB 51f RR 49f 4639[11]

3 b f Rainbow Quest (USA) 11.2f **(81)** - Lady Be Mine (USA) (Sir Ivor) 10.2f **(70)**

Form - 37120

Record 1999 - 1st:1 2nd:1 3rd:1 Ran:5
Pre1999 - 1st:0 2nd:0 3rd:0 Ran:3

Win Prizemoney £3,304 *Total Prizemoney* £4,905

Wins	* 1999	Jly Thirsk	(FRM)	H	12f	40	45 <

1999 Turf 1-5: (12f 1-2, 14f 2, 16f) (gd, g-f, frm 1-3)

Scopey, moderate filly, effective 12 to 14f, best at 12f, acts on frm, has worn blinkers. Turf high 49 - 2nd of 12 getting 11lb from Pleasant Mount (28 Aug Redcar 14f frm RF 3979) - also 1st of 9 getting 3lb from Rainbow Raver (30 Jly Thirsk RF 3254). Inconsistent. **J L Dunlop [1-8] Mrs Mark Burrell.*

ELLERBECK BHB 37f RR 56f 4563[17]

4 b f Priolo (USA) 10.9f **(71)** - Cadisa (Top Ville) 11.7f **(68)**

Form - 0

Record 1999 - 1st:0 2nd:0 3rd:0 Ran:1
Pre1999 - 1st:0 2nd:0 3rd:0 Ran:8

1999 Turf 0-1: (14f) (gd)

Leggy, fair filly. Becoming disappointing.

**J M Jefferson [1-14] & Mrs J M Davenport.*

ELLIS BHB 62f RR 65f 4808[13]

3 br f Terimon 8.7f **(58)** - Singing Forever **(49a)** (Chief Singer) 8.9f **(66)**

Form - 4740

Record 1999 - 1st:0 2nd:0 3rd:0 Ran:4

Win Prizemoney £0 *Total Prizemoney* £554

1999 Turf 0-4: (7f, 9f, 10f, 11f) (sft, gd 2, g-f)

Neat, average filly. Turf high 65 - 4th of 8 to Tariyfa (24 Spt Haydock 11f gd RF 4525). **J J O'Neill [0-4] Mrs L R Joughin.*

ELLIS ISLAND RR 35f 3158[11]

3 ch c Most Welcome 8.6f **(66)** - Dry Land (Nonoalco (USA)) 8.5f **(66)**

Form - 5560

Record 1999 - 1st:0 2nd:0 3rd:0 Ran:4

1999 Turf 0-4: (7f, 8f, 10f, 12f) (gd, frm 3)

Scopey, very moderate colt. Turf high 41.

**T D Easterby [0-4] Mrs Sue Tindall.*

ELLOPASSOFF BHB 61f RR 59f 4011[11]

7 b m Librate 10.4f **(37)** - Elena Patino (Dubassoff (USA)) 14.2f **(55)**

Form - 1354158700

Record 1999 - 1st:2 2nd:0 3rd:1 Ran:10
Pre1999 - 1st:2 2nd:0 3rd:0 Ran:7

Win Prizemoney £12,095 *Total Prizemoney* £12,559

Wins	* 1999	Jly Chepst	(G-F)	H	10.2f	63	65 <
	* 1999	May Nottin	(FRM)	H	8.2f	62	64

* 1998 Jun Chepst (G-S) H 10.2f 59 64
* 1998 May Warwic (G-F) H 8f 55 58
1999 Turf 2-10: (8f 1-6, 10f 1-4) (gd 2, g-f 1-3, frm 1-5)
Fair mare, effective 8 to 10f, best at 10f, acts on gd to frm, prefers left handed tracks, favours tight tracks, excels at Chepstow. Turf high 65 - 1st of 11 getting 9lb from La Tiziana (3 Jly Chepstow RF 2526) - also 1st of 14 giving 10lb to Night Dance (21 May Nottingham RF 1385). Consistent. **J M Bradley [4-21] E R Griffiths.*

ELLPEEDEE BHB 54f RR 75f 4929[7]

2 b g Wolfhound (USA) 7.3f **(71)** - Kilvarnet (Furry Glen) 8.9f **(63)**
Form - 737007
Record 1999 - 1st:0 2nd:0 3rd:1 Ran:6
Win Prizemoney £0 *Total Prizemoney* £560
1999 Turf 0-6: (5f 4, 6f 2) (gd 2, g-f 2, frm 2)
Above-average gelding, effective 5f, acts on gd. Turf high 75 - 3rd of 9 giving 5lb to Poker Polka (13 Aug Nottingham 5f gd RF 3623). **N Tinkler [0-6] Leeds Plywood and Doors Ltd.*

EL LUTE (FR) RR 96f 4662a[5]

5 b h Scenic 10.6f **(66)** - Easily (Swing Easy (USA)) 6.5f **(55)**
Form - 25
1999 Turf 0-2: (8f 2) (sft, g-s)
Currently very useful colt. Turf high 96. **D Ilic in GER [0-2].*

ELLWAY DANCER (IRE) BHB 55f RR 47f 2270[7]

3 b f Mujadil (USA) 7.7f **(70)** - Moonlight Partner (IRE) (Red Sunset) 8.2f **(63)**
Form - 7
Record 1999 - 1st:0 2nd:0 3rd:0 Ran:1
Pre1999 - 1st:0 2nd:0 3rd:0 Ran:2
1999 Turf 0-1: (6f) (frm)
Neat, currently moderate filly. **I A Balding [0-3] Ellway Racing.*

ELLWAY PRINCE BHB 41f61a RR 45f 61a 5146[8]

4 b g Prince Sabo 6.6f **(64)** - Star Arrangement (Star Appeal) 9.6f **(65)**
Form - 1223258682050606008
Record 1999 - 1st:0 2nd:1 3rd:0 Ran:14
Pre1999 - 1st:1 2nd:5 3rd:1 Ran:15
Win Prizemoney £2,741 *Total Prizemoney* £9,614
Wins * 1998 *Nov Lingfi (STD) 6f 61* <
1999 Turf 0-8: (6f 6, 7f 2) (gd, g-f 5, frm 2) 1999 AW 0-6: (6f 5, 7f) (Equi 3, Fibr 3)
Workmanlike, average gelding, effective 6 to 7f, best at 6f, - acts on AW, best on Equi, mostly wears blinkers (very effectively), prefers left handed tracks, prefers tight tracks. Turf high 45. AW high 64.
**Mrs N Macauley [1-21] Stephen Roots (from IABalding [0-8] Spt 1998).*

ELLWAY STAR (IRE) BHB 95f RR 96f 4873[7]

3 ch f Night Shift (USA) 8.1f **(73)** - Searching Star (Rainbow Quest (USA)) 10.4f **(75)**
Form - 03732025107
Record 1999 - 1st:1 2nd:2 3rd:2 Ran:11
Pre1999 - 1st:1 2nd:0 3rd:0 Ran:1
Win Prizemoney £9,835 *Total Prizemoney* £18,120
Wins * **1999** Spt Leices (FRM) 5f 96 <
* 1998 Aug Lingfi (G-F) 5f 81+
1999 Turf 1-11: (5f 1-5, 6f 4, 7f 2) (g-s, gd 3, g-f 2, frm 1-5)
Unfurnished, very useful filly, effective 5 to 7f, acts on gd to frm, best on frm, excels at Leicester and Yarmouth. Turf high 96 - 3rd of 6 to Sandova (24 May Leicester 7f frm RF 1430) - also 1st of 7 getting 6lb from Repertory (7 Spt Leicester RF 4173). Best over sprint distances, she is suited by a sound surface and is game in a finish. **B Hanbury [2-12] Ellway Racing.*

ELM DUST BHB 84f RR 87df 1444[8]

3 ch f Elmaamul (USA) 8.1f **(70)** - Galaxie Dust (USA) (Blushing Groom (FR)) 10.3f **(76)**
Form - 08
Record 1999 - 1st:0 2nd:0 3rd:0 Ran:2
Pre1999 - 1st:1 2nd:1 3rd:1 Ran:3
Win Prizemoney £3,099 *Total Prizemoney* £5,725
Wins * 1998 Aug Leices (GD) 7f 82+ <
1999 Turf 0-2: (6f, 7f) (frm 2)
Light-framed, useful filly. Turf high 59. **J L Dunlop [1-5] Hesmonds Stud.*

ELMHURST BOY BHB 76f RR 77f 4696[8]

3 b c Merdon Melody 6.8f **(56)** - Young Whip (Bold Owl) 8.5f **(45)**
Form - 23245323178
Record 1999 - 1st:1 2nd:3 3rd:3 Ran:11
Pre1999 - 1st:0 2nd:0 3rd:1 Ran:2
Win Prizemoney £3,728 *Total Prizemoney* £11,225
Wins * **1999** Aug Epsom (GD) 7f 77 <
1999 Turf 1-11: (6f 3, 7f 1-5, 8f 3) (sft 2, g-s, gd, g-f 1-3, frm 4)
Workmanlike, above-average colt, effective 6 to 8f, best at 8f, acts on sft to frm, has worn blinkers, and excels at Lingfield. Turf high 82 - 3rd of 16 getting 1lb from Petrus (30 Jly Goodwood 7f g-f RF 3233) - also 1st of 4 from Tiger Imp (13 Aug Epsom RF 3604). Consistent. He kept on making the frame in maiden and handicap company early last season, but did not seem too enthusiastic about putting his head in front where it matters. He managed to lose his maiden tag in a four-runner event at Epsom in August, but even then looked reluctant. Suited by fast ground. **S Dow [1-13] R E Anderson.*

EL MOBASHERR (USA) BHB 88f RR 88f 3848[7]

3 b c Machiavellian (USA) 9.8f **(83)** - Sheroog (USA) (Shareef Dancer (USA)) 9.9f **(73)**
Form - 752217
Record 1999 - 1st:1 2nd:2 3rd:0 Ran:6
Win Prizemoney £6,742 *Total Prizemoney* £9,636
Wins * **1999** Jly Ascot (G-F) 10f 85+ <
1999 Turf 1-6: (8f, 10f 1-4, 12f) (gd 1-2, g-f, frm 3)
Tall, useful colt, effective 10f, acts on gd to frm, best on frm. Turf high 91 - 2nd of 17 giving 5lb to Suhaad (11 Jun Sandown 10f frm RF 1925) - also 1st of 5 giving 5lb to Limelighting (23 Jly Ascot RF 3052). **M A Jarvis [1-6] Sheikh Ahmed Al Maktoum.*

EL MONICA (IRE) RR 67f 3595a[2]

2 b f Kahyasi 12.9f **(74)** - Parnala (USA) (Assert) 10.6f **(85)**
Form - 37242
Record 1999 - 1st:0 2nd:2 3rd:1 Ran:5
Win Prizemoney £0 *Total Prizemoney* £3,462
1999 Turf 0-5: (5f, 7f 3, 8f) (gd 2, g-f 3)
Average filly. Turf high 67 - 2nd of 6 getting 3lb from Malenchini (8 Aug Livorno 8f gd RF 3595a).
**M Quinlan [0-1] (from M G Quinlan [0-4] Jly 1999).*

ELMS SCHOOLGIRL BHB 64f68a RR 64f 68a 4078[3]

3 ch f Emarati (USA) 6.6f **(63)** - Ascend (IRE) (Glint of Gold) 9.3f **(66)**
Form - 060181153
Record 1999 - 1st:3 2nd:0 3rd:1 Ran:9
Pre1999 - 1st:0 2nd:0 3rd:1 Ran:3
Win Prizemoney £12,001 *Total Prizemoney* £13,043
Wins * **1999** Aug Bright (G-F) H 11.9f 61 64 <
* **1999** Jly Bright (FRM) H 10f 59 60
* **1999** Jun Bright (G-F) 10f 55
1999 Turf 3-9: (6f, 8f 2, 10f 2-3, 12f 1-3) (gd, g-f 2-4, frm 3, hrd 1-1)
Light-framed, average filly, effective 6 to 12f, best at 12f, acts on g-f to hrd, best on g-f, prefers left handed tracks, likes tight tracks. Turf high 64 - 1st of 4 getting 11lb from Indigo Bay (5 Aug Brighton RF 3386). Inconsistent. Developed into a Brighton specialist last summer and, despite a hat-trick of wins, has not been harshly treated by the Handicapper. It remains to be seen if she is as good away from the Sussex track.
**J M P Eustace [3-12] Park Lodge Racing.*

ELMS SCHOOLPREFECT BHB 50f RR 51f 4358[13]

2 b f Emarati (USA) 6.6f **(63)** - Ascend (IRE) (Glint of Gold) 9.3f **(66)**
Form - 7070
Record 1999 - 1st:0 2nd:0 3rd:0 Ran:4
1999 Turf 0-4: (6f, 7f, 8f 2) (g-s, gd, g-f, frm)
Fair filly. Turf high 48 (began Jly).
**J M P Eustace [0-4] Elms School Racing Partnership.*

ELMUTABAKI BHB 109f RR 107f 4266[8]

3 b c Unfuwain (USA) 11.4f **(74)** - Bawaeth (USA) (Blushing Groom (FR)) 10.3f **(76)**
Form - 4221158
Record 1999 - 1st:2 2nd:2 3rd:0 Ran:7
Pre1999 - 1st:0 2nd:0 3rd:0 Ran:1
Win Prizemoney £49,315 *Total Prizemoney* £54,820
Wins * **1999** Jly Haydoc (G-S) L 11.9f 102+ <

* 1999 Jun Ascot (G-F) H 12f 90 100+
1999 Turf 2-7: (10f, 11f, 12f 2-4, 15f) (gd 1-1, g-f 1-5, frm)
Scopey, Pattern-class colt, effective 12f, acts on gd to g-f. Turf high 107 - also 1st of 4 from Flaming Quest (3 Jly Haydock RF 2533). He showed steady improvement early last season, bolting up in Ascot's King George V Handicap before following up in a listed race. However, he was well held in the Voltigeur and the Leger. **B W Hills [2-8] Hamdan Al Maktoum.*

EL NAFIS (USA) BHB 63f RR 65f 3574^{10}

3 b f Kingmambo (USA) 10.9f **(85)** - Ghashtah (USA) (Nijinsky (CAN)) 10.3f **(77)**
Form - 000
Record 1999 - 1st:0 2nd:0 3rd:0 Ran:3
Pre1999 - 1st:1 2nd:0 3rd:0 Ran:3
Win Prizemoney £3,225 *Total Prizemoney* £3,225
Wins * 1998 Aug Chepst (G-F) 8.1f 80 <
1999 Turf 0-3: (7f, 8f, 10f) (g-f 2, frm)
Scopey, average filly, effective 8f, acts on gd. Turf high 49 (began Jly). **P T Walwyn [1-6] Hamdan Al Maktoum.*

EL NAHRAWAN (USA) BHB 83f RR 81f 4018^{13}

3 br c Red Ransom (USA) 8.6f **(83)** - Woodja (USA) (Woodman (USA)) 9f **(74)**
Form - 32410
Record 1999 - 1st:1 2nd:1 3rd:1 Ran:5
Pre1999 - 1st:0 2nd:1 3rd:0 Ran:2
Win Prizemoney £3,993 *Total Prizemoney* £7,635
Wins * 1999 Aug Chepst (G-F) 7.1f 75 <
1999 Turf 1-5: (7f 1-1, 8f 2, 9f, 10f) (gd, g-f 2, frm 1-2)
Scopey, decent colt, effective 7 to 8f, best at 8f, acts on gd to frm. Turf high 81 - 2nd of 4 giving 5lb to Exit (22 Jun Beverley 8f g-f RF 2193) - also 1st of 11 from Tiger Imp (5 Aug Chepstow RF 3393). Has shown a liking for fast ground in his races so far. Got off the mark after looking a bit of a thinker when a winner over seven furlongs at Chepstow in August.
**M P Tregoning [1-7] Hamdan Al Maktoum.*

EL PICADOR BHB 54f RR 26f 1548^{13}

3 b g Aragon 7.7f **(58)** - Hawaiian Bloom (USA) (Hawaii) 9.4f **(66)**
Form - 5000
Record 1999 - 1st:0 2nd:0 3rd:0 Ran:4
Pre1999 - 1st:0 2nd:0 3rd:0 Ran:2
1999 Turf 0-4: (7f 3, 10f) (g-f 2, frm, hrd)
Scopey, little account gelding. Turf high 64.
**B J Meehan [0-6] Mario Lanfranchi.*

EL RACHA BHB 25f RR 21f 2446^{9}

3 b f Midyan (USA) 9.9f **(64)** - Lady Anfield (Anfield) 8.5f **(59)**
Form - 080
Record 1999 - 1st:0 2nd:0 3rd:0 Ran:3
1999 Turf 0-3: (6f, 7f, 9f) (g-f 3)
Leggy, currently little account filly. Turf high 21.
**T J Naughton [0-3] T J Naughton.*

EL RAFFY (IRE) RR $3594a^{1}$

2 br f Petorius 8f **(66)** - Blues Quartet (Cure The Blues (USA)) 9.5f **(63)**
Form - 1
Record 1999 - 1st:1 2nd:0 3rd:0 Ran:1
Win Prizemoney £1,640 *Total Prizemoney* £1,640
Wins * 1999 Aug Livorn (GD) C 5f
1999 Turf 1-1: (5f 1-1) (gd 1-1)
Currently unbeaten filly - 1st of 5 getting 2lb from Schweitzer (8 Aug Livorno RF 3594a). **M Quinlan [1-1] Mario Lanfranchi.*

ELSA DAWN BHB 30f RR 28f 1747^{12}

4 ch f Weldnaas (USA) 8.4f **(55)** -Agnes Jane (Sweet Monday) 8.3f **(25)**
Form - 0
Record 1999 - 1st:0 2nd:0 3rd:0 Ran:1
Pre1999 - 1st:0 2nd:0 3rd:0 Ran:4
1999 AW 0-1: (8f) (Fibr)
Leggy, little account filly. **N Bycroft [0-6] C Lawson.*

ELSIE BAMFORD BHB 46f45a RR 49f 45a 5056^{12}

3 b f Tragic Role (USA) 9.4f **(63)** - Sara Sprint (Formidable (USA)) 9.2f **(63)**
Form - 400530566B30
Record 1999 - 1st:0 2nd:0 3rd:2 Ran:12
Pre1999 - 1st:0 2nd:0 3rd:0 Ran:4
Win Prizemoney £0 *Total Prizemoney* £724
1999 Turf 0-9: (7f 3, 8f 4, 9f, 12f) (gd 2, g-f 2, frm 3, hrd 2) 1999 AW 0-3: (7f, 10f, 12f) (Equi, Fibr 2)
Leggy, moderate filly. Turf high 53. AW high 45.
**M Johnston [0-3] Mrs Sheila Ramsden (from J Berry [0-13] Aug 1999).*

ELTARS RR 44f 2836^{7}

2 ch c Elmaamul (USA) 8.1f **(70)** - Iradah (USA) **(55df)** (Topsider (USA)) 8.3f **(71)**
Form - 7
Record 1999 - 1st:0 2nd:0 3rd:0 Ran:1
1999 Turf 0-1: (6f) (g-f)
Currently moderate colt. **P T Walwyn [0-1] Hamdan Al Maktoum.*

ELTAWAASUL (USA) BHB 101f RR 104f 1772^{4}

3 ch c Nureyev (USA) 8.4f **(84)** - Grand Falls (USA) (Ogygian (USA))
Form - 4314
Record 1999 - 1st:1 2nd:0 3rd:1 Ran:4
Pre1999 - 1st:2 2nd:0 3rd:2 Ran:4
Win Prizemoney £17,342 *Total Prizemoney* £23,916
Wins * 1999 May Thirsk (G-S) 8f 104 <
* 1998 Jun Doncas (GD) 6f 83
* 1998 Jun Haydoc (GD) 6f 83+
1999 Turf 1-4: (8f 1-3, 10f) (gd 1-4)
Strong, very useful colt, effective 8f, acts on gd. Turf high 104 - 1st of 3 giving 3lb to Date (15 May Thirsk RF 1249). He takes time to hit top gear, but knuckles down well in a finish. A shade disappointing when tried over a mile and a quarter at Newmarket in June, he is better suited by a stiff mile.
**J L Dunlop [3-8] Hamdan Al Maktoum.*

ELTON LEDGER (IRE) BHB 48f65a RR 59f 65a 231^{7}

10 b g Cyrano de Bergerac 7.3f **(58)** - Princess of Nashua (Crowned Prince (USA)) 10.1f **(67)**
Form - 2111143147
Record 1999 - 1st:1 2nd:0 3rd:1 Ran:5
Pre1999 - 1st:16 2nd:24 3rd:7 Ran:100
Win Prizemoney £39,373 *Total Prizemoney* £63,420
Wins * 1999 *Jan Southw (STD) S 6f 64*
* 1998 *Dec Southw (STD) C 5f 63+*
* 1998 *Dec Southw (STD) S 6f 70*
* 1998 *Dec Southw (STD) H 6f 67 69*
* 1998 *Nov Southw (STD) C 5f 67*
* 1998 *Jun Southw (STD) 6f 71* <
* 1998 *Mar Southw (STD) SH 6f 58 64*
* 1997 *Feb Southw (STD) S 6f 71* <
* 1997 *Jan Southw (STD) H 6f 70 69*
* 1996 *Spt Southw (STD) C 5f 71* <
* 1996 *Jun Southw (STD) H 5f 63 66*
* 1996 *Apr Southw (STD) 7f 45*
* 1996 *Mar Southw (STD) H 6f 55 56*
1999 AW 1-5: (6f 1-4, 7f) (Fibr 1-5)
Average gelding, effective 5 to 7f, best at 6f, - acts on Fibr, often wears blinkers (effectively), likes left handed tracks, likes tight tracks, excels at Southwell. AW high 67 - also 1st of 15 giving 5lb to Garnock Valley (25 Jan Southwell RF 0163). Consistent.
**Mrs N Macauley [14-78] The Posse (from A A Scott [2-17] May 1994).*

ELVINGTON BOY BHB 74f RR 73f 5214^{11}

2 ch c Emarati (USA) 6.6f **(63)**-Catherines Well (Junius (USA)) 7.7f **(65)**
Form - 422100
Record 1999 - 1st:1 2nd:2 3rd:0 Ran:6
Win Prizemoney £2,970 *Total Prizemoney* £5,234
Wins * 1999 Aug Ripon (GD) 5f 73 <
1999 Turf 1-6: (5f 1-5, 6f) (g-s, gd, g-f 1-2, frm 2)
Above-average colt, effective 5f, acts on g-f to frm, best on frm. Turf high 73 - 2nd of 12 getting 4lb from Buy Or Sell (28 Jun Pontefract 5f frm RF 2367) - also 1st of 14 getting 3lb from Polar Haze (31 Aug Ripon RF 4039).
**M W Easterby [1-6] K Hodgson & Mrs J Hodgson.*

EL ZITO (IRE) RR $5200a^{2}$

2 b c Mukaddamah (USA) 7.6f **(74)** - Samite (FR) 00
Form - 2
Record 1999 - 1st:0 2nd:1 3rd:0 Ran:1
Win Prizemoney £0 *Total Prizemoney* £3,208

1999 Turf 0-1: (9f) (g-s)
Maiden colt. - 2nd of 9 giving 1lb to Snetterton (30 Oct San Siro 9f g-s RF 5200a). **B J Meehan [0-1].*

EMALI RR 47f 4785[6]
2 b c Emarati (USA) 6.6f **(63)** -Princess Poquito (Hard Fought) 8.8f **(62)**
Form - 06
Record 1999 - 1st:0 2nd:0 3rd:0 Ran:2
1999 Turf 0-2: (7f 2) (g-s, gd)
Currently moderate colt. Turf high 47 (began Spt).
**C E Brittain [0-2] C E Brittain.*

EMARINA BHB 39f43a **RR 24f 43a** 4925[12]
3 b f Emarati (USA) 6.6f **(63)** - Cushina (Sparkler) 8.4f **(55)**
Form - 74560050
Record 1999 - 1st:0 2nd:0 3rd:0 Ran:6
Pre1999 - 1st:0 2nd:0 3rd:0 Ran:3
Win Prizemoney £0 *Total Prizemoney* £201
1999 Turf 0-3: (5f, 6f 2) (gd, g-f, frm) 1999 AW 0-3: (7f 2, 8f) (Fibr 3)
Light-framed, moderate filly. Turf high 24 (began Aug). AW high 39. **J L Spearing [0-9] Steele Nicholls.*

EMBATTLE BHB 55f **RR 51f** 2112[6]
3 ch c Rock City 8.8f **(62)** - Sleepline Princess (Royal Palace) 9f **(56)**
Form - 063756
Record 1999 - 1st:0 2nd:0 3rd:1 Ran:6
Pre1999 - 1st:0 2nd:0 3rd:0 Ran:1
Win Prizemoney £0 *Total Prizemoney* £422
1999 Turf 0-6: (7f 2, 8f 3, 9f) (sft, g-s, g-f 3, frm)
Light-framed, fair colt, effective 8f, acts on frm, has worn blinkers. Turf high 54 - 3rd of 17 getting 12lb from Penang Pearl (24 May Windsor 8f frm RF 1443). **M R Channon [0-7] G Z Mizel.*

EMBEZL BHB 70f **RR 74f** 5111[9]
2 b f Belmez (USA) 11.4f **(65)** - Kiya (USA) (Dominion) 8.5f **(63)**
Form - 822200
Record 1999 - 1st:0 2nd:3 3rd:0 Ran:6
Win Prizemoney £0 *Total Prizemoney* £3,940
1999 Turf 0-6: (5f 3, 6f 2, 7f) (g-s 2, gd 2, frm 2)
Above-average filly, effective 5 to 6f, acts on frm. Turf high 74 - 2nd of 6 giving 3lb to Barakula (28 Jun Windsor 6f frm RF 2382).
**R Hannon [0-6] T A Daniels.*

EMBODY RR 99f 4892a[6]
4 b c Indian Ridge 7.6f **(74)** - Kamakha (ITY) (Natroun (FR))
Form - 4526
1999 Turf 0-3: (8f 2, 10f) (g-s, gd 2)
Very useful colt. Turf high 99 - 2nd of 12 giving 4lb to Rio Napo (19 Spt San Siro 10f g-s RF 4522a). **B Grizzetti in ITY [0-6].*

EMBRACED RR 89+f 4728[1]
2 b f Pursuit of Love 9.5f **(69)** - Tromond **(92f)** (Lomond (USA)) 8.8f **(65)**
Form - 1
Record 1999 - 1st:1 2nd:0 3rd:0 Ran:1
Win Prizemoney £4,402 *Total Prizemoney* £4,402
Wins *** 1999** Oct Nottin (SFT) 8.2f 89+ <
1999 Turf 1-1: (8f 1-1) (g-s 1-1)
Currently useful filly. (1st run) - 1st of 14 from Skimra (5 Oct Nottingham RF 4728). A half-sister to Nowhere To Exit, she looks a useful middle distance prospect.
**J R Fanshawe [1-1] Cheveley Park Stud.*

EMBRYONIC (IRE) BHB 66f **RR 46f** 1980[11]
7 b g Prince Rupert (FR) 10.4f **(60)** - Belle Viking (FR) (Riverman (USA)) 9.1f **(76)**
Form - 60
Record 1999 - 1st:0 2nd:0 3rd:0 Ran:2
Pre1999 - 1st:4 2nd:6 3rd:4 Ran:27
Win Prizemoney £15,658 *Total Prizemoney* £35,307

Wins	* 1997	Jun	Newcas	(FRM)	H	16.1f	78	83	<
	* 1997	May	Doncas	(GD)	H	16.5f	76	81	
	1995	May	Hamilt	(GD)	H	13f	70	78	
	1995	Apr	Newcas	(G-F)		12.4f		71	

1999 Turf 0-2: (12f, 16f) (g-f, frm)
Moderate gelding. Turf high 64. Consistent.
**Martin Todhunter [2-12] Mrs D Miller (from R F Fisher [2-17] Oct 1996).*

EMERALD HEIGHTS BHB 85f **RR 89df** 1699[8]
4 b g Shirley Heights 12.1f **(76)** - Lady In Green (Shareef Dancer (USA)) 9.9f **(73)**
Form - 08
Record 1999 - 1st:0 2nd:0 3rd:0 Ran:2
Pre1999 - 1st:2 2nd:1 3rd:1 Ran:9
Win Prizemoney £11,668 *Total Prizemoney* £21,503

Wins	* 1998	Jun	Haydoc	(GD)	H	10.5f	84	88	<
	* 1998	May	Doncas	(G-F)	H	12f	79	82	

1999 Turf 0-2: (10f, 16f) (gd, g-f)
Tall, useful gelding, effective 12f, acts on g-s. Turf high 71.
**J R Fanshawe [2-11] Peter and Noreen Hodgson.*

EMERALD HUNTER (USA) BHB 42f **RR 13f** 1982[10]
4 b br g Quest for Fame 12.8f **(75)** - In Jubilation (USA) (Isgala) 12.1f **(64)**
Form - 000170
Record 1999 - 1st:1 2nd:0 3rd:0 Ran:6
Pre1999 - 1st:0 2nd:0 3rd:0 Ran:2
Win Prizemoney £1,819 *Total Prizemoney* £1,819
Wins *** 1999** *May Wolver (Std) S 14.8f 54* <
1999 Turf 0-4: (10f, 12f 2, 14f) (hvy, gd, g-f, frm) 1999 AW 1-2: (15f 1-1, 16f) (Fibr 1-2)
Workmanlike, fair gelding, effective 15f, - acts on Fibr, has worn blinkers, favours tight tracks. Turf high 61. AW high 54 (1st run) - 1st of 6 giving 22lb to Crash Call Lady (14 May Wolverhampton RF 1231). Inconsistent.
**P S McEntee [1-6] Racing Thoroughbreds Plc (from J Noseda [0-2] Aug 1998).*

EMERALD IMP (IRE) RR 50f 4806[4]
2 ch f Mac's Imp (USA) 5.6f **(54)** - Lady Montekin (Montekin) 11.1f **(55)**
Form - 04
Record 1999 - 1st:0 2nd:0 3rd:0 Ran:2
Win Prizemoney £0 *Total Prizemoney* £244
1999 Turf 0-2: (6f, 7f) (sft, g-s)
Currently fair filly. Turf high 50 (began Oct).
**M S Saunders [0-2] T Leigh.*

EMERALD PARK (USA) RR 108f 2099a[5]
3 ch c Zilzal (USA) 8.5f **(79)** - Greenland Park (Red God) 8.5f **(65)**
Form - 25
1999 Turf 0-2: (6f, 8f) (hvy, g-s)
Currently Pattern-class colt. Turf high 108 - 5th of 7 getting 3lb from Grazalema (13 Jun Chantilly 8f g-s RF 2099a).
**Mme C Head in FR [0-3].*

EMERALD PEACE (IRE) BHB 100f **RR 94f** 4268[2]
2 b f Green Desert (USA) 7.8f **(78)** - Puck's Castle **(85f)** (Shirley Heights) 10.3f **(74)**
Form - 52112
Record 1999 - 1st:2 2nd:2 3rd:0 Ran:5
Win Prizemoney £9,424 *Total Prizemoney* £20,534

Wins	*** 1999**	Aug	Lingfi	(G-F)	5f	87+	<
	*** 1999**	Aug	Lingfi	(GD)	5f	87+	<

1999 Turf 2-5: (5f 2-5) (gd, g-f 1-1, frm 1-3)
Useful filly. Turf high 94 - 2nd of 14 to Mrs P (11 Spt Doncaster 5f frm RF 4268) - also 1st of 5 getting 5lb from Russian Fox (25 Aug Lingfield RF 3908). A progressive filly, she recorded two all-the-way victories at Lingfield over five furlongs on decent ground in 1999. **M A Jarvis [2-5] M P Burke.*

EMERGING MARKET BHB 91f **RR 93f** 4561[6]
7 b g Emarati (USA) 6.6f **(63)** - Flitteriss Park (Beldale Flutter (USA)) 9.7f **(71)**
Form - 0604366
Record 1999 - 1st:0 2nd:0 3rd:1 Ran:7
Pre1999 - 1st:3 2nd:6 3rd:2 Ran:34
Win Prizemoney £57,059 *Total Prizemoney* £88,592

Wins	* 1996	Jun	Ascot	(G-F)	H	6f	95	98	<
	* 1995	Apr	Folkes	(G-F)		6f		78	

1999 Turf 0-7: (6f 6, 7f) (gd 2, g-f 3, frm 2)
Useful gelding, effective 6f, acts on g-f to frm, best on g-f. Turf high 94 - 6th of 14 getting 1lb from Primo Lara (2 May Newmarket 6f frm RF 0980). Ran some good races in well-contested sprint handicaps last summer, notably when third to Zuhair at York in

August. **J L Dunlop [3-41] Philip Wroughton.*

EMILY'S LUCK CHARM (USA) BHB 100f **RR 102f** 4761[6]
3 b br c Lear Fan(USA)10.4f**(80)**-Emily's Charm(CAN)(Dom Alaric(FR))
Form - 3626
Record 1999 - 1st:0 2nd:1 3rd:1 Ran:4
Pre1999 - 1st:2 2nd:1 3rd:0 Ran:5
Win Prizemoney £10,130 *Total Prizemoney* £16,738
Wins * 1998 Spt Cheste (GD) 7.6f 95+ <
* 1998 Jly Doncas (G-F) 6f 88+
1999 Turf 0-4: (7f 3, 8f) (gd 3, g-f)
Scopey, very useful colt, effective 7 to 8f, acts on gd to g-f. Turf high 103 (1st run) - 3rd of 10 getting 4lb from Late Night Out (1 May Haydock 7f g-f RF 0950). Consistent. He is not an easy ride and hung right when finishing second at Bath in September. Probably best around seven furlongs, he has worn a tongue-tie and is one to have reservations about.
**Sir Michael Stoute [2-9] Maktoum Al Maktoum.*

EMINENCE GRISE (IRE) BHB 92f **RR 91f** 5210[4]
4 b c Sadler's Wells (USA) 11.3f **(87)** - Impatiente (USA) (Vaguely Noble) 10.1f **(72)**
Form - 310424464
Record 1999 - 1st:1 2nd:1 3rd:1 Ran:9
Pre1999 - 1st:0 2nd:1 3rd:1 Ran:4
Win Prizemoney £7,002 *Total Prizemoney* £23,782
Wins * **1999** May Kempto (G-F) H 16f 73 77 <
1999 Turf 1-9: (14f 4, 15f, 16f 1-2, 20f, 22f) (sft, g-s, gd, g-f 2, frm 1-4)
Well made, useful colt, effective 14 to 22f, acts on gd to frm, has worn blinkers. Turf high 91 - 4th of 21 getting 3lb from Vicious Circle (18 Aug York 14f gd RF 3758). Consistent. He looked a progressive sort, but was rather disappointing twice in four days at Royal Ascot. Ran respectably after, including when fourth in the Ebor, and looks an out-and-out stayer.
**H R A Cecil [1-13] Wafic Said.*

EMINENT BLAZE BHB 38f **RR 28f** 1260[17]
3 b g Presidium 7.5f **(56)** - Fair Madame (Monseigneur (USA)) 7.7f **(63)**
Form - 080
Record 1999 - 1st:0 2nd:0 3rd:0 Ran:3
Pre1999 - 1st:0 2nd:0 3rd:0 Ran:3
1999 Turf 0-1: (8f) (gd) 1999 AW 0-2: (7f, 8f) (Fibr 2)
Leggy, little account gelding. AW high 7.
**D Nicholls [0-6] The Eminent Partnership.*

EMLEY BHB 52f **RR 53f** 3661[3]
3 b f Safawan 6.6f **(60)** - Bit of a State (Free State) 8.7f **(61)**
Form - 563
Record 1999 - 1st:0 2nd:0 3rd:1 Ran:3
Win Prizemoney £0 *Total Prizemoney* £515
1999 Turf 0-3: (5f, 7f 2) (gd, frm 2)
Unfurnished, currently fair filly. Turf high 53 (began Jly).
**D Nicholls [0-3] J Wilkins.*

EMMA AMOUR RR 66f 5209[15]
2 b br f Emarati (USA) 6.6f **(63)** - Ella Mon Amour (Ela-Mana-Mou) 10.1f **(70)**
Form - 20
Record 1999 - 1st:0 2nd:1 3rd:0 Ran:2
Win Prizemoney £0 *Total Prizemoney* £584
1999 Turf 0-2: (6f 2) (g-s, frm)
Currently average filly. Turf high 65 (1st run) (began Aug) - 2nd of 10 getting 5lb from Glenrock (13 Aug Lingfield 6f frm RF 3609).
**M W Easterby [0-1] M W Easterby (from J R Fanshawe [0-1] Aug 1999).*

EMMACAN (IRE) RR 4f 2961[6]
5 b m Mazaad 8.5f **(53)** - Minerstown (IRE) (Miner's Lamp)
Form - 6
Record 1999 - 1st:0 2nd:0 3rd:0 Ran:1
1999 Turf 0-1: (11f) (g-f)
Very poor filly. **G A Hubbard [0-6] G A Hubbard.*

EMMAJOUN BHB 50f53a **RR 40f 53a** 3007[8]
4 b f Emarati (USA) 6.6f **(63)** - Parijoun (Manado) 9.6f **(63)**
Form - 18042008
Record 1999 - 1st:1 2nd:1 3rd:0 Ran:8
Pre1999 - 1st:0 2nd:1 3rd:1 Ran:9
Win Prizemoney £3,006 *Total Prizemoney* £4,870
Wins * **1999** *Mar Lingfi (STD)* 5f 57 <
1999 Turf 0-6: (5f 3, 6f 2, 7f) (gd 2, g-f 2, frm 2) 1999 AW 1-2: (5f 1-2) (Equi 1-2)
Workmanlike, moderate filly, effective 5 to 6f, best at 6f, acts on gd - acts on Equi, likes left handed tracks, likes tight tracks. Turf high 55. AW high 57 (1st run) - 1st of 5 from Sharp Hint (4 Mar Lingfield RF 0399). Consistent.
**W G M Turner [1-14] P Nabavi (from A P Jarvis [0-3] Spt 1997).*

EMMA-LYNE BHB 47f **RR 46f** 4906[19]
3 b f Emarati (USA) 6.6f **(63)** - Moreton's Martha (Derrylin) 8.8f **(54)**
Form - 0666650
Record 1999 - 1st:0 2nd:0 3rd:0 Ran:7
Pre1999 - 1st:0 2nd:2 3rd:1 Ran:3
Win Prizemoney £0 *Total Prizemoney* £2,104
1999 Turf 0-7: (6f 2, 7f 3, 8f, 9f) (g-s, gd, g-f 2, frm 3)
Light-framed, moderate filly, effective 6 to 7f, best at 6f, acts on g-f to frm, best on frm, has worn blinkers. Turf high 59.
**A P Jarvis [0-10] Quadrillian Partnership.*

EMMA PEEL BHB 107f **RR 105f** 4418[5]
3 b f Emarati (USA) 6.6f **(63)** - Trigamy (Tribal Chief) 8.5f **(61)**
Form - 24214231125
Record 1999 - 1st:3 2nd:4 3rd:1 Ran:11
Pre1999 - 1st:1 2nd:1 3rd:0 Ran:2
Win Prizemoney £53,099 *Total Prizemoney* £71,078
Wins * **1999** Aug Epsom (GD) H 5f 101 104 <
* **1999** Aug York (GD) H 5f 97 100
* **1999** May Baden- (G-S) L 6f 93
* 1998 Oct Nottin (SFT) 6.1f 87+
1999 Turf 3-11: (5f 2-7, 6f 1-4) (g-s 1-1, gd 1-5, g-f 1-3, frm 2)
Strong, Pattern-class filly, effective 5f, acts on gd to g-f, best on g-f. Turf high 105 - 2nd of 7 giving 3lb to Flanders (9 Spt Doncaster 5f g-f RF 4234) - also 1st of 14 giving 28lb to Angie Baby (30 Aug Epsom RF 4013). Consistent. A progressive sprinter, she was awarded a Listed race at Baden-Baden in the Stewards' Room. She gained a deserved victory in a tough sprint handicap at York in August and followed up with a fine victory at Epsom, before splitting Flanders and Dashing Blue in a Listed event at the Doncaster St Leger meeting. **B J Meehan [4-13] Arthur Smith.*

EMMAS HOPE BHB 35f **RR 31f** 5002[14]
2 b f Emarati (USA) 6.6f **(63)** - Ray of Hope **(47f)** (Rainbow Quest (USA)) 10.4f **(75)**
Form - 0400000
Record 1999 - 1st:0 2nd:0 3rd:0 Ran:7
1999 Turf 0-6: (5f 4, 6f, 8f) (gd 2, g-f 4) 1999 AW 0-1: (5f) (Fibr)
Very moderate filly, has worn blinkers. Turf high 41.
**B P J Baugh [0-7] D E Simpson.*

EMMINNI RR 29f 2524[16]
2 b g Emarati (USA) 6.6f **(63)**-Sheesha(USA)(Shadeed (USA)) 8.2f **(70)**
Form - 700
Record 1999 - 1st:0 2nd:0 3rd:0 Ran:3
1999 Turf 0-3: (6f 2, 7f) (gd, frm 2)
Currently little account gelding. Turf high 29.
**S G Knight [0-3] Mrs Rosemary Bolt.*

EMPEROR NAHEEM (IRE) BHB 76f **RR 70f** 5212[18]
4 b g Imperial Frontier (USA) 7f **(65)**-Desert Gale (Taufan (USA))7f **(57)**
Form - 22878540060
Record 1999 - 1st:0 2nd:2 3rd:0 Ran:11
Pre1999 - 1st:3 2nd:2 3rd:3 Ran:23
Win Prizemoney £9,701 *Total Prizemoney* £21,087
Wins * 1998 Aug Newmar (G-F) H 5f 78 80 <
* 1998 Aug Pontef (G-F) C 5f 76
* 1998 Jly Sandow (G-F) H 5f 71 75
1999 Turf 0-11: (5f 11) (g-s, gd 4, g-f 2, frm 4)
Leggy, above-average gelding, effective 5 to 6f, best at 5f, acts on gd to frm, best on frm, has worn blinkers, excels at Newmarket, likes Sandown. Turf high 82 - 2nd of 13 giving 7lb to That Man Again (6 Jly Newmarket 5f frm RF 2579). Consistent.
**B J Meehan [3-34] Mrs Eithne Meehan.*

EMPEROR'S GOLD BHB 40f46a **RR 34f 46a** 4607[13]
4 gr g Petong 7.6f **(58)** -Tarnside Rosal **(56f)**(Mummy's Game) 8.2f **(60)**
Form - 0
Record 1999 - 1st:0 2nd:0 3rd:0 Ran:1
Pre1999 - 1st:2 2nd:2 3rd:4 Ran:17
Win Prizemoney £3,463 *Total Prizemoney* £6,085
Wins 1998 *Jan Southw (STD) S 8f 68+* <
1997 *Nov Wolver (STD) SH 8.5f 58 64*
1999 AW 0-1: (6f) (Fibr)
Tall, fair gelding, effective 8 to 10f, best at 10f, - acts on AW, best on Equi, has worn blinkers, favours left handed tracks, favours tight tracks.
**M G Quinlan [0-1] Emperor's Gold Partnership (from M J Polglase [0-5] Oct 1998).*

EMPIRE GOLD (USA) BHB 59f **RR 64f** 4930[17]
4 ch g Strike The Gold (USA) 8f **(79)** - Careless Halo (USA) (Sunny's Halo (CAN)) 6.7f **(70)**
Form - 00
Record 1999 - 1st:0 2nd:0 3rd:0 Ran:2
Pre1999 - 1st:1 2nd:0 3rd:0 Ran:8
Win Prizemoney £3,330 *Total Prizemoney* £3,330
Wins 1998 Aug Leices (GD) H 8f 59 64 <
1999 Turf 0-2: (8f, 10f) (gd, g-f)
Light-framed, average gelding, has worn blinkers. Turf high 50. Yet to race over fences, he has enjoyed one success over hurdles, coming at Musselburgh in February on firm ground.
**Andrew Turnell [1-8] Dr John Hollowood (from Mrs J R Ramsden [1-7] Aug 1998).*

EMPIRENEYEV (USA) RR 102f 714a[3]
3 b c Nureyev (USA) 8.4f **(84)** -La Pitie (USA) (Devil's Bag (USA)) 12.4f **(78)**
Form - 33
1999 Turf 0-2: (6f, 7f) (hvy, g-s)
Currently very useful colt. Turf high 102 - 3rd of 7 to Berkoutchi (9 Apr Maisons-Laffitte 7f g-s RF 0714a). **Mme C Head in FR [0-2].*

EMPIRE PARK BHB 65f **RR 61f** 3414[1]
4 b g Tragic Role (USA) 9.4f **(63)** -Millaine (Formidable (USA)) 9.2f **(63)**
Form - 8886031
Record 1999 - 1st:1 2nd:0 3rd:1 Ran:7
Pre1999 - 1st:0 2nd:0 3rd:2 Ran:3
Win Prizemoney £2,981 *Total Prizemoney* £4,729
Wins * 1999 Aug Haydoc (G-S) H 10.5f 57 61 <
1999 Turf 1-7: (8f, 10f 3, 11f 1-1, 12f, 14f) (g-s, gd, g-f 1-3, frm 2)
Average gelding, effective 10f, acts on frm, has worn blinkers. Turf high 69 (1st run) - 8th of 10 giving 1lb to Top Jem (14 Apr Beverley 10f frm RF 0690). Consistent.
**T D Easterby [2-8] T G Holdcroft (from M Johnston [0-3] Aug 1997).*

EMPIRE STATE (IRE) BHB 44f **RR 44f** 5066[7]
4 b g High Estate 10.5f **(66)** - Palm Dove (USA) (Storm Bird (CAN)) 10.3f **(74)**
Form - 080800074227
Record 1999 - 1st:0 2nd:2 3rd:0 Ran:12
Pre1999 - 1st:2 2nd:0 3rd:1 Ran:15
Win Prizemoney £6,074 *Total Prizemoney* £8,224
Wins 1998 Jly Catter (GD) H 6f 63 72 <
1998 Jun Carlis (G-S) H 5.9f 63 68
1999 Turf 0-12: (6f 5, 7f 2, 8f 2, 10f, 11f, 12f) (gd, g-f 4, frm 6, hrd)
Moderate gelding, effective 6 to 8f, best at 6f, acts on gd to frm, best on gd, has worn blinkers, likes right handed tracks, likes tight tracks. Turf high 53. Consistent.
**R A Fahey [0-6] E O'Malley (from P S Felgate [0-6] Jly 1999).*

EMPRESS OF LIGHT BHB 62f **RR 54f** 4595[14]
2 b f Emperor Jones (USA) - Lovely Noor (USA) (Fappiano (USA)) 8.7f **(77)**
Form - 780
Record 1999 - 1st:0 2nd:0 3rd:0 Ran:3
1999 Turf 0-3: (7f 2, 8f) (gd, g-f 2)
Currently fair filly. Turf high 54 (began Aug). **M P Tregoning [0-3] R C C Villers.*

EMWILLGEO (IRE) BHB 45f41a **RR 40f 41a** 61[12]
3 b f Petardia 8.2f **(58)** - Lhotse (IRE) (Shernazar) 10.2f **(73)**
Form - 0
Record 1999 - 1st:0 2nd:0 3rd:0 Ran:1
Pre1999 - 1st:0 2nd:0 3rd:0 Ran:3
1999 AW 0-1: (7f) (Equi)
Workmanlike, moderate filly.
**P C Haslam [0-4] Cunningham/R Popely.*

ENAAQ (USA) BHB 79f **RR 84f** 4384[11]
2 b f Bahri (USA) - Elhasna (USA) (Danzig (USA)) 8.4f **(76)**
Form - 22310
Record 1999 - 1st:1 2nd:2 3rd:1 Ran:5
Win Prizemoney £4,299 *Total Prizemoney* £6,809
Wins * 1999 Aug Chepst (G-S) H 5.1f 75 81 <
1999 Turf 1-5: (5f 1-4, 6f) (gd 1-1, g-f, frm 3)
Decent filly, has worn blinkers. Turf high 84 - 2nd of 7 to Sioux Chef (20 Jly Bath 6f frm RF 2958) - also 1st of 12 getting 1lb from Dancemma (30 Aug Chepstow RF 4008). Somewhat frustrating in her early starts, making the frame in three fast-ground maidens, but finally got off the mark at Chepstow in August when racing on easy ground for the first time. Well beaten in a nursery, she is suited by the minimum trip. **P T Walwyn [1-5] Hamdan Al Maktoum.*

ENBORNE BHB 65f **RR 66f** 2488[3]
4 b c Slip Anchor 12.7f **(75)** - Pris (Priamos (GER)) 11.1f **(61)**
Form - 455836513
Record 1999 - 1st:1 2nd:0 3rd:2 Ran:9
Win Prizemoney £6,908 *Total Prizemoney* £8,317
Wins * 1999 Jun Ayr (SFT) H 15f 58 66 <
1999 Turf 1-9: (10f, 12f 5, 14f 2, 15f 1-1) (g-s 1-1, gd 2, g-f 5, frm)
Average colt, effective 14 to 15f, acted on g-s to g-f, liked left handed tracks. Turf high 66 - 1st of 7 getting 9lb from Fnan (19 Jun Ayr RF 2143). (DEAD)
**D W Barker [2-13] Triple G DA Racing Syndicate.*

ENCHANTED ISLE BHB 45f **RR 49f** 544[10]
3 b f Mujtahid (USA) 7.4f **(69)** - Belle Ile (USA) **(52f)** (Diesis) 9.3f **(69)**
Form - 0
Record 1999 - 1st:0 2nd:0 3rd:0 Ran:1
Pre1999 - 1st:0 2nd:0 3rd:0 Ran:6
Win Prizemoney £0 *Total Prizemoney* £396
1999 AW 0-1: (7f) (Equi)
Unfurnished, moderate filly, has worn blinkers.
**C A Dwyer [0-7] D J Donner.*

ENCOUNTER BHB 51f49a **RR 44f 49a** 4906[12]
3 br g Primo Dominie 7.2f **(67)**-Dancing Spirit (IRE)(Ahonoora) 8.1f **(73)**
Form - 605268008304112607700
Record 1999 - 1st:2 2nd:2 3rd:1 Ran:19
Pre1999 - 1st:0 2nd:0 3rd:1 Ran:7
Win Prizemoney £6,116 *Total Prizemoney* £8,979
Wins * 1999 Aug Hamilt (G-F) H 6f 44 53 <
*** 1999** Aug Ayr (G-F) S 7f 45
1999 Turf 2-18: (6f 1-6, 7f 1-9, 8f 3) (hvy 2, sft, gd 3, g-f 1-5, frm 1-7)
1999 AW 0-1: (7f) (Fibr)
Scopey, moderate gelding. Turf high 56. Consistent.
**J Hetherton [2-21] C D Barber-Lomax (from C E Brittain [0-5] Oct 1998).*

ENDLESS HALL RR 98f 5204a[1]
3 b c Saddlers' Hall (IRE) 10.5f **(65)** - Endless Joy (Law Society (USA)) 9.9f **(70)**
Form - 131
Record 1999 - 1st:2 2nd:0 3rd:1 Ran:3
Pre1999 - 1st:0 2nd:1 3rd:1 Ran:2
Win Prizemoney £32,805 *Total Prizemoney* £53,243
Wins * 1999 Oct San Si (YLD) 12f 98 <
*** 1999** Jly San Si (G-F) L 10f 97
1999 Turf 2-3: (10f 1-1, 12f 1-2) (g-s 1-2, g-f 1-1)
Very useful colt. Turf high 98 (began Jly) - 1st of 6 giving 3lb to Award Academy (31 Oct San Siro RF 5204a) - also 1st of 7 from Timboroa (4 Jly San Siro RF 2661a). He improved when moved to Luca Cumani and has developed into a useful middle-distance performer. Open to further improvement, he is an interesting prospect.
**L M Cumani [2-3] Moro Visconti (from G Verricelli in ITY [0-2] Spt 1998).*

ENDLESS JOURNEY (IRE) BHB 48f **RR 60f** 4169[18]
2 b f Blues Traveller (IRE) - Spinelle (Great Nephew) 9.9f **(64)**
Form - 615580
Record 1999 - 1st:1 2nd:0 3rd:0 Ran:6
Win Prizemoney £1,982 *Total Prizemoney* £1,982
Wins * **1999** Jun Redcar (FRM) S 7f 60 <
1999 Turf 1-6: (6f, 7f 1-4, 8f) (g-f, frm 1-5)
Average filly, effective 7f, acts on frm. Turf high 60 - 1st of 11 from Alabama Wurley (19 Jun Redcar RF 2153).
**N P Littmoden [1-6] Clayton Bigley Partnership Ltd.*

END OF STORY (IRE) BHB 59f **RR 58f** 5026[15]
3 b c Doubletour (USA) 12f **(46)** - Baliana (CAN) (Riverman (USA)) 9.1f **(76)**
Form - 406500
Record 1999 - 1st:0 2nd:0 3rd:0 Ran:6
Pre1999 - 1st:0 2nd:0 3rd:0 Ran:1
Win Prizemoney £0 *Total Prizemoney* £223
1999 Turf 0-6: (7f 4, 8f 2) (gd 2, g-f, frm 3)
Light-framed, fair colt. Turf high 65.
**R Hannon [0-7] High Seas Leisure Ltd.*

ENDORSEMENT BHB 101f **RR 103f** 3408a[6]
3 b f Warning 8.1f **(77)** - Overdrive (Shirley Heights) 10.3f **(74)**
Form - 3116
Record 1999 - 1st:2 2nd:0 3rd:1 Ran:4
Win Prizemoney £39,801 *Total Prizemoney* £40,431
Wins * **1999** Jun Ascot (G-F) G3 16.2f 98 <
* **1999** May Thirsk (G-S) 12f 63+
1999 Turf 2-4: (10f, 12f 1-1, 14f, 16f 1-1) (g-s, gd 1-2, g-f 1-1)
Scopey, very useful filly. Turf high 103 - also 1st of 11 getting 5lb from Time Zone (16 Jun Ascot RF 2043). She put up a smashing performance for an inexperienced filly when winning the Queen's Vase at Royal Ascot. Wrong when disappointing in the Prix de Pomone on her only subsequent start, this likeable filly could develop into a top-class stayer next term. **H R A Cecil [2-4].*

ENDYMION (IRE) BHB 75f **RR 77f** 4694[8]
2 ch f Paris House 5.9f **(64)** - Vaguely Jade (Corvaro (USA)) 9f **(53)**
Form - 0543U038
Record 1999 - 1st:0 2nd:0 3rd:2 Ran:8
Win Prizemoney £0 *Total Prizemoney* £1,656
1999 Turf 0-8: (5f 6, 6f 2) (sft, gd, g-f 3, frm 3)
Above-average filly. Turf high 81. Inconsistent.
**Mrs P N Dutfield [0-8] Matt Tompkins.*

ENEMY ACTION (USA) **RR 99f** 1000[3]
3 b f Forty Niner (USA) 8.8f **(73)** - Sun and Shade(Ajdal(USA)) 9.2f **(89)**
Form - 43
Record 1999 - 1st:0 2nd:0 3rd:1 Ran:2
Pre1999 - 1st:2 2nd:0 3rd:0 Ran:4
Win Prizemoney £7,183 *Total Prizemoney* £13,135
Wins * 1998 Jly Doncas (FRM) 6f 92 <
* 1998 Jun Goodwo (GD) 6f 82+
1999 Turf 0-2: (6f, 7f) (g-f, frm)
Workmanlike, very useful filly, effective 6f, acts on frm. Turf high 99. Like her half-brother Daggers Drawn, she failed to train on.
**H R A Cecil [2-6] Cliveden Stud.*

ENFILADE BHB 75f **RR 79f** 3860[4]
3 b g Deploy 11.4f **(67)** - Bargouzine (Hotfoot) 10.5f **(59)**
Form - 43131444
Record 1999 - 1st:2 2nd:0 3rd:2 Ran:8
Pre1999 - 1st:0 2nd:0 3rd:1 Ran:5
Win Prizemoney £12,477 *Total Prizemoney* £15,875
Wins * **1999** Jly Haydoc (G-S) H 14f 72 75 <
* **1999** May Cheste (G-F) H 12.3f 66 69
1999 Turf 2-8: (7f, 10f, 11f, 12f 1-2, 14f 1-3) (sft, gd 1-2, g-f 1-2, frm 3)
Strong, above-average gelding, effective 7 to 14f, acts on gd to frm, has worn blinkers, prefers tight tracks. Turf high 79 - 4th of 7 getting 5lb from Over To You (17 Jly Ripon 12f frm RF 2926) - also 1st of 8 giving 11lb to Nadisha (1 Jly Haydock RF 2464). Consistent. **B Hanbury [2-13] H Channon.*

ENGLAND'S ROSE (IRE) **RR 60f** 1451[8]
3 b f Alzao (USA) 9.8f **(73)** - Gold Tear (USA) (Tejano (USA))
Form - 28
Record 1999 - 1st:0 2nd:1 3rd:0 Ran:2
Win Prizemoney £0 *Total Prizemoney* £1,156
1999 Turf 0-2: (10f 2) (gd 2)
Leggy, currently average filly. Turf high 60 (1st run) - 2nd of 8 getting 5lb from Evergreen Venture (8 May Lingfield 10f gd RF 1116).
**H R A Cecil [0-2] The Thoroughbred Corporation.*

ENGLISH LADY (IRE) BHB 47f40a **RR 30f 40a** 797[15]
4 b f Fayruz 6.6f **(63)** - Paradise Regained (North Stoke) 10.4f **(55)**
Form - 86770
Record 1999 - 1st:0 2nd:0 3rd:0 Ran:3
Pre1999 - 1st:0 2nd:1 3rd:0 Ran:11
Win Prizemoney £0 *Total Prizemoney* £1,195
1999 Turf 0-1: (6f) (g-s) 1999 AW 0-2: (6f, 8f) (Equi 2)
Unfurnished, very moderate filly, has worn blinkers. AW high 35.
**M J Haynes [0-14] English Lady Classics Ltd.*

EN GRISAILLE BHB 48f **RR 47f** 4448[10]
3 gr f Mystiko (USA) 7.7f **(59)** - Hickleton Lady (IRE) **(60f 60a)** (Kala Shikari) 8.4f **(54)**
Form - 76510
Record 1999 - 1st:1 2nd:0 3rd:0 Ran:5
Pre1999 - 1st:1 2nd:0 3rd:0 Ran:6
Win Prizemoney £4,194 *Total Prizemoney* £4,194
Wins * **1999** Aug Yarmou (GD) C 10.1f 44
1998 Aug Folkes (G-F) S 6f 56 <
1999 Turf 1-5: (8f 3, 10f 1-2) (g-s, gd 1-1, g-f 3)
Scopey, moderate filly, effective 6f, acts on frm. Turf high 47. Consistent.
**John Berry [1-5] H R Moszkowicz (from Sir Mark Prescott [1-6] Spt 1998).*

ENLIGHTEN **RR 54f** 4992[7]
3 br g Zafonic (USA) 9f **(83)** - Seek the Pearl **(90df)** (Rainbow Quest (USA)) 10.4f **(75)**
Form - 07
Record 1999 - 1st:0 2nd:0 3rd:0 Ran:2
1999 Turf 0-2: (10f 2) (g-f, frm)
Scopey, currently fair gelding. Turf high 54 (began Aug).
**J R Fanshawe [0-2] James Fanshawe.*

ENNOBLE BHB 54f50a **RR 52f 50a** 3632[7]
3 b g Highest Honor (FR) 10.9f **(72)** - Villella (Sadler's Wells (USA)) 10f **(76)**
Form - 28077
Record 1999 - 1st:0 2nd:1 3rd:0 Ran:5
Pre1999 - 1st:0 2nd:0 3rd:0 Ran:3
Win Prizemoney £0 *Total Prizemoney* £1,220
1999 Turf 0-4: (12f 3, 13f) (gd 2, g-f, frm) 1999 AW 0-1: (9f) (Fibr)
Workmanlike, fair gelding, effective 13f, acts on frm, likes tight tracks. Turf high 64 (1st run) - 2nd of 13 getting 5lb from Bid Me Welcome (3 May Warwick 13f frm RF 1018). Consistent.
**H Morrison [0-8] The Summerdown Partnership.*

EN RETARD (IRE) **RR 73f** 5087a[4]
4 bb f Petardia 8.2f **(58)** - Regal Society 00
Form - 0037655074
1999 Turf 0-10: (5f 5, 6f 5) (sft, g-s 3, gd 3, frm 3)
Above-average filly, effective 5 to 6f, best at 5f, acts on g-s to gd, best on gd, often wears blinkers (very effectively), and excels at Leopardstown. Turf high 90 - 3rd of 6 giving 7lb to Zilina (19 May Leopardstown 5f gd RF 1463a). Consistent.
**Patrick Prendergast in IRE [4-29] Aidan Walsh.*

ENRIQUE **RR 115f** 3209[5]
3 b c Barathea (IRE) - Gwydion (USA) (Raise A Cup (USA)) 7.6f **(74)**
Form - 12225
Record 1999 - 1st:1 2nd:3 3rd:0 Ran:5
Pre1999 - 1st:2 2nd:0 3rd:0 Ran:3
Win Prizemoney £41,820 *Total Prizemoney* £174,470
Wins * **1999** Apr Newbur (G-F) G3 7f 111
* 1998 Oct Newmar (GD) L 7f 117++ <
* 1998 Jly Goodwo (G-S) 7f 94+
1999 Turf 1-5: (7f 1-2, 8f 3) (gd, g-f 1-3, frm)
Scopey, high-class colt, effective 7 to 8f, best at 8f, acts on gd to frm, does well at Newmarket. Turf high 117 - 2nd of 16 to Island Sands (1 May Newmarket 8f frm RF 0958) - also 1st of 7 from Exeat

(17 Apr Newbury RF 0734). Consistent. A very decent two-year-old, he made a winning reappearance in the Tripleprint Greenham Stakes at Newbury, despite idling towards the finish, but ran on really well to get within a neck of Island Sands in the 2000 Guineas. He reversed the form with the winner in the Irish version, but he was unable to cope with Saffron Walden, and found one too good in the Jersey Stakes. He ran his only poor race when seventh in the Sussex Stakes, which proved to be his swansong for the season. **H R A Cecil [3-8] Niarchos Family.*

Enrique was placed in two Guineas

EN SILENCE (USA) BHB 67f70a **RR 62f 70a** 3113[11]
3 b f Rahy (USA) 9.1f **(80)** - No More Ironing (USA) (Slew O' Gold (USA)) 8f **(75)**
Form - 70432510
Record 1999 - 1st:1 2nd:1 3rd:1 Ran:8
Win Prizemoney £2,696 *Total Prizemoney* £4,271
Wins ** 1999 Jly Wolver (STD) 6f 71* <
1999 Turf 0-5: (6f 2, 7f 3) (sft, gd 2, frm 2) 1999 AW 1-3: (6f 1-1, 7f 2) (Fibr 1-3)
Light-framed, above-average filly, effective 6f, - acts on Fibr, often wears blinkers (very effectively). Turf high 77. AW high 71 - 1st of 10 getting 5lb from Sartorial (9 Jly Wolverhampton RF 2687). She has shown her best form so far on Fibresand, including when getting up in the final stride to win a Wolverhampton maiden in July. Rather disappointing when tried in handicap company.
**J Noseda [1-8] Eddy Stibbe.*

ENTAIL (USA) RR 86f 5020[3]
2 b br f Riverman (USA) 9.7f **(78)** - Estala **(87f)** (Be My Guest (USA)) 9.3f **(67)**
Form - 3
Record 1999 - 1st:0 2nd:0 3rd:1 Ran:1
Win Prizemoney £0 *Total Prizemoney* £572
1999 Turf 0-1: (8f) (gd)
Currently useful filly. (1st run) - 3rd of 18 to Interlude (22 Oct Doncaster 8f gd RF 5020). **J H M Gosden [0-1] K Abdulla.*

ENTERTAINER (IRE) BHB 79f **RR 77f** 2736[2]
3 b g Be My Guest (USA) 10.2f **(66)** - Green Wings (General Assembly (USA)) 10f **(68)**
Form - 252
Record 1999 - 1st:0 2nd:2 3rd:0 Ran:3
Pre1999 - 1st:0 2nd:2 3rd:0 Ran:3
Win Prizemoney £0 *Total Prizemoney* £7,949
1999 Turf 0-3: (10f, 11f 2) (gd 2, frm)
Scopey, above-average gelding, effective 7 to 11f, acts on gd to frm, best on frm. Turf high 77 - 2nd of 5 to Weet For Me (11 Jly Haydock 11f frm RF 2736). He has finished runner-up more often than is desirable and is becoming expensive to follow.
**P W Chapple-Hyam [0-6] The Royal Ascot Racing Club.*

ENTIKAA (IRE) BHB 80f **RR 66f** 2061[3]
3 b c Sadler's Wells (USA) 11.3f **(87)** - Miranisa (Habitat) 9.4f **(70)**
Form - 073
Record 1999 - 1st:0 2nd:0 3rd:1 Ran:3
Win Prizemoney £0 *Total Prizemoney* £555
1999 Turf 0-3: (8f, 10f, 12f) (gd, g-f, hrd)
Well made, currently average colt. Turf high 66.
**Sir Michael Stoute [0-3] Hamdan Al Maktoum.*

ENTITY BHB 72f **RR 70f** 5024[7]
2 ch c Rudimentary (USA) 8.2f **(66)** - Desert Ditty (Green Desert (USA)) 8.6f **(78)**
Form - 85447
Record 1999 - 1st:0 2nd:0 3rd:0 Ran:5
Win Prizemoney £0 *Total Prizemoney* £1,174
1999 Turf 0-5: (6f 4, 8f) (gd 2, g-f, frm, hrd)
Above-average colt. Turf high 70 (began Jly).
**T D Barron [0-5] Mrs J Hazell.*

ENTROPY RR 42f 4440[17]
3 b f Brief Truce (USA) 9.1f **(73)** - Distant Isle (IRE) (Bluebird (USA)) 7.5f **(69)**
Form - 80850000
Record 1999 - 1st:0 2nd:0 3rd:0 Ran:8
Pre1999 - 1st:1 2nd:1 3rd:3 Ran:8
Win Prizemoney £2,723 *Total Prizemoney* £5,620
Wins * 1998 Aug Bath (FRM) H 5.7f 73 73+ <
1999 Turf 0-8: (5f, 6f 5, 7f 2) (gd 3, g-f 3, frm 2)
Light-framed, moderate filly, effective 5 to 6f, best at 6f, acts on gd to frm, likes left handed tracks. Turf high 63.
**R Hannon [1-16] T G Holdcroft.*

ENTWINE BHB 84f **RR 83f** 3062[6]
3 b f Primo Dominie 7.2f **(67)** - Splice **(101f)** (Sharpo) 7.7f **(59)**
Form - 33706
Record 1999 - 1st:0 2nd:0 3rd:2 Ran:5
Pre1999 - 1st:2 2nd:0 3rd:0 Ran:4
Win Prizemoney £12,052 *Total Prizemoney* £14,345
Wins * 1998 Oct Newmar (gd) H 5f 77 83+ <
* 1998 Spt Beverl (G-F) 5f 69+
1999 Turf 0-5: (6f 5) (gd, g-f, frm 3)
Small, decent filly, effective 5 to 6f, best at 6f, acts on gd to frm. Turf high 84 (1st run) - 3rd of 15 getting 4lb from Munjiz (15 Apr Newmarket 6f g-f RF 0702). Consistent.
**J R Fanshawe [2-9] Cheveley Park Stud.*

ENZELI (IRE) RR 120f 4471a[4]
4 b c Kahyasi 12.9f **(74)** - Ebaziya (IRE) (Darshaan) 9.9f **(84)**
Form - 1114
1999 Turf 2-3: (14f 1-2, 20f 1-1) (g-s, gd 1-1, g-f 1-1)
Very high-class colt, effective 20f, acts on g-f. Turf high 120 - 1st of 17 getting 2lb from Invermark (17 Jun Ascot RF 2071). A half-brother to Ebadiyla, he improved through out 1998 and maintained that by making a winning reappearance in a Leopardstown Listed event last season. Stepped up on that by landing a highly competitive renewal of the Ascot Gold Cup, and there seemed to be no vestige of a fluke about it. His only subsequent start resulted in him finishing a below-par fourth of five in the Irish St Leger, and though he had previously won on soft ground, he could not cope with conditions on that occasion. **J Oxx in IRE [5-9] H H Aga Khan.*

EPCOT BOY (IRE) BHB 52f **RR 66f** 3866[7]
2 b g Mukaddamah (USA) 7.6f **(74)** - Lightning Laser (Monseigneur (USA)) 7.7f **(63)**
Form - 6587
Record 1999 - 1st:0 2nd:0 3rd:0 Ran:4
1999 Turf 0-4: (6f, 7f 2, 8f) (g-s, g-f 2, frm)
Average gelding. Turf high 66. **J J O'Neill [0-4] Meadowcrest Ltd.*

EPERNAY RR 67f 4951[5]

3 b f Lion Cavern (USA) 7.5f **(74)** - Decant **(61f)** (Rousillon (USA)) 8.2f **(74)**

Form - 25

Record 1999 - 1st:0 2nd:1 3rd:0 Ran:2

Win Prizemoney £0 *Total Prizemoney* £726

1999 Turf 0-2: (7f, 8f) (sft, g-f)

Light-framed, currently average filly. Turf high 67 (1st run) (began Spt) - 2nd of 14 to Beggars Belief (21 Spt Warwick 8f sft RF 4453).

**J R Fanshawe [0-2] Mrs E Fanshawe.*

EPISTOLAIRE (IRE) RR 120f 3231a[5]

4 b c Alzao (USA) 9.8f **(73)** - Epistolienne (Law Society (USA)) 9.9f **(70)**

Form - 3325

1999 Turf 0-4: (10f, 12f 2, 13f) (hvy, sft, g-s, gd)

Very high-class colt, effective 10 to 13f, best at 12f, acts on hvy to gd. Turf high 120 - 3rd of 5 to Public Purse (24 May Saint-Cloud 12f sft RF 1712a). Consistent. A winner at Group Two and Group Three level in 1998, he did not enjoy the same success last season despite making the frame a few times. Probably his best effort came when he chased home Capri in the Grand Prix de Chantilly.

**A Fabre in FR [2-9].*

EPONA RR 32f 4903[10]

2 ch f Inchinor 8.9f **(64)** - Zelda (USA) (Sharpen Up) 8.3f **(67)**

Form - 0

Record 1999 - 1st:0 2nd:0 3rd:0 Ran:1

1999 Turf 0-1: (6f) (frm)

Currently very moderate filly.

**T D Easterby [0-1] Keith Wills & Middleham Park Racing.*

EPSOM CYCLONE (USA) BHB 83f **RR 89df** 4644[19]

4 ch c Rahy (USA) 9.1f **(80)** - Aneesati (Kris) 9.5f **(73)**

Form - 000

Record 1999 - 1st:0 2nd:0 3rd:0 Ran:3

Pre1999 - 1st:2 2nd:1 3rd:0 Ran:7

Win Prizemoney £11,642 *Total Prizemoney* £14,102

Wins * 1998 Spt Salisb (HVY) H 6f 87 89 <

* 1998 Mar Doncas (GD) 6f 84

1999 Turf 0-3: (6f 2, 7f) (g-s, gd, g-f)

Scopey, useful colt, effective 6f, acts on gd. Turf high 51. Becoming disappointing. **B W Hills [2-10] Salem Bel Obaida.*

EPWORTH BHB 34f39a **RR 35f 39a** 2529[8]

5 b m Unfuwain (USA) 11.4f **(74)**-Positive Attitude(Red Sunset)8.2f **(63)**

Form - 420538

Record 1999 - 1st:0 2nd:1 3rd:1 Ran:6

Pre1999 - 1st:0 2nd:3 3rd:1 Ran:17

Win Prizemoney £0 *Total Prizemoney* £6,725

1999 Turf 0-3: (12f, 17f, 18f) (g-f, frm 2)1999 AW 0-3: (9f, 12f 2) (Fibr 3)

Fair filly, has worn blinkers. Turf high 35. AW high 54.

**L J Barratt [0-13] Ray Bailey (from J A Glover [0-9] Oct 1997).*

EQUERRY BHB 42f59a **RR 42f 59a** 2109[3]

8 b g Midyan (USA) 9.9f **(64)** -Supreme Kingdom(Take A Reef)7.5f **(59)**

Form - 08178453

Record 1999 - 1st:1 2nd:0 3rd:1 Ran:7

Pre1999 - 1st:7 2nd:8 3rd:4 Ran:38

Win Prizemoney £35,248 *Total Prizemoney* £46,104

Wins * 1999 Apr Mussel (GD) SH 9f 38 39

1996 Spt Ayr (G-F) C 8f 70

1996 Jly Newcas (G-F) H 7f 81 82 <

1996 Jun Newcas (FRM) H 8f 79 82 <

1996 Jun Beverl (G-F) H 8.5f 75 79

1995 Jly Thirsk (FRM) H 8f 67 75

1995 Jly Wolver (STD) H 8.5f 58 62

1995 May Beverl (G-F) H 8.5f 60 65

1999 Turf 1-6: (8f 3, 9f 1-2, 10f) (gd, g-f 1-5) 1999 AW 0-1: (8f) (Fibr)

Moderate gelding, effective 8 to 9f, best at 8f, acts on g-f, has worn blinkers, likes left handed tracks, favours tight tracks. Turf high 42 - 4th of 10 giving 7lb to Special-K (28 May Pontefract 8f g-f RF 1554) - also 1st of 16 getting 4lb from Anonym (1 Apr Musselburgh RF 0548).

**M Dods [1-12] A G Watson (from M Johnston [7-21] Spt 1996).*

ERIN ANAM CARA (IRE) BHB 62f **RR 64f** 4169[3]

2 ch f Exit To Nowhere (USA) 8.7f **(77)** - Honey Heather (IRE) (Kris) 9.5f **(73)**

Form - 7675443

Record 1999 - 1st:0 2nd:0 3rd:1 Ran:7

Win Prizemoney £0 *Total Prizemoney* £540

1999 Turf 0-6: (5f, 6f 3, 7f, 8f) (gd 2, g-f 2,frm 2)1999 AW 0-1: (5f) (Fibr)

Average filly, effective 7 to 8f, acts on gd to frm. Turf high 64 - 3rd of 18 getting 4lb from Storm Prince (7 Spt Leicester 8f frm RF 4169). **D J S Cosgrove [0-7] Prayer And A Song Syndicate.*

ERINVALE BHB 49f62a **RR 44f 62a** 3291[10]

3 ch g Mon Tresor 7.9f **(60)** - Honey Mill (Milford) 9f **(61)**

Form - 212331436700

Record 1999 - 1st:2 2nd:2 3rd:3 Ran:12

Pre1999 - 1st:0 2nd:0 3rd:1 Ran:5

Win Prizemoney £4,525 *Total Prizemoney* £8,180

Wins * 1999 *Feb Lingfi (STD) C 7f 68 <*

*** 1999** *Jan Lingfi (STD) 5f 68 <*

1999 Turf 0-4: (6f 3, 7f) (g-s, g-f, frm 2) 1999 AW 2-8: (5f 1-1, 6f 3, 7f 1-3, 8f) (Equi 2-4, Fibr 4)

Scopey, average gelding, effective 5 to 7f, - acts on AW, best on Equi, has worn blinkers, prefers left handed tracks, prefers tight tracks. Turf high 44. AW high 70 (1st run) - 2nd of 10 getting 5lb from Palace Green (2 Jan Southwell 6f Fibr RF 0018) - also 1st of 4 getting 3lb from Melody Queen (13 Feb Lingfield RF 0287). Becoming disappointing. A fair sort on sand at between six and seven furlongs.

**P C Haslam [2-17] Middleham Park, B Cunningham & A Hale.*

ERITH'S CHILL WIND BHB 49f48a **RR 49f 48a** 4632[7]

3 b f Be My Chief (USA) 10.2f **(62)** - William's Bird (USA) (Master Willie) 7f **(70)**

Form - 0022317

Record 1999 - 1st:1 2nd:2 3rd:1 Ran:7

Pre1999 - 1st:0 2nd:0 3rd:1 Ran:5

Win Prizemoney £3,308 *Total Prizemoney* £5,399

Wins * 1999 Aug Bright (G-F) H 10f 43 49 <

1999 Turf 1-7: (8f, 9f, 10f 1-5) (hvy, g-s 2, g-f, frm 1-2, hrd)

Workmanlike, moderate filly, likes left handed tracks, likes tight tracks. Turf high 49. Inconsistent.

**G L Moore [1-8] Wessex House Racing (from S Dow [0-5] Spt 1998).*

ERMINE (IRE) BHB 73f **RR 74f** 5126[9]

3 ch f Cadeaux Genereux 7.9f **(76)** - Nibbs Point (IRE) (Sure Blade (USA)) 11.3f **(67)**

Form - 20232170

Record 1999 - 1st:1 2nd:3 3rd:1 Ran:8

Pre1999 - 1st:0 2nd:0 3rd:0 Ran:2

Win Prizemoney £4,021 *Total Prizemoney* £11,460

Wins * 1999 Spt Newcas (G-F) 8f 64 <

1999 Turf 1-8: (8f 1-3, 9f, 10f 4) (gd 2, g-f 4, frm 1-2)

Light-framed, above-average filly, effective 8 to 10f, best at 10f, acts on gd to frm, best on g-f. Turf high 78 (1st run) - 2nd of 14 to Dahshah (21 May Bath 8f g-f RF 1371).

**L M Cumani [1-10] Lady Halifax.*

ERRO CODIGO BHB 53f60a **RR 52f 60a** 5160[19]

4 b g Formidable (USA) 7.8f **(60)** - Home Wrecker (DEN) (Affiliation Order (USA)) 6f **(70)**

Form - 0007410

Record 1999 - 1st:1 2nd:0 3rd:0 Ran:7

Pre1999 - 1st:1 2nd:4 3rd:4 Ran:20

Win Prizemoney £7,193 *Total Prizemoney* £14,318

Wins * 1999 Oct Lingfi (G-F) H 6f 49 52

* 1998 *Feb Southw (STD) 6f 62 <*

1999 Turf 1-7: (6f 1-4, 7f 2, 9f) (gd 1-1, g-f 3, frm 3)

Strong, fair gelding, effective 6 to 7f, best at 7f, acts on gd to frm - acts on Fibr, has worn blinkers, prefers left handed tracks, prefers tight tracks, likes Catterick. Turf high 52 (began Jly).

**S E Kettlewell [2-20] D Neale (from Mrs J R Ramsden [0-7] Aug 1997).*

ERTLON BHB 63f56a **RR 68f 56a** 355[6]

9 b g Shareef Dancer (USA) 10.1f **(67)** -Sharpina(Sharpen Up) 8.3f **(67)**

Form - 33536

Record 1999 - 1st:0 2nd:0 3rd:3 Ran:5

Pre1999 - 1st:5 2nd:10 3rd:8 Ran:77

Win Prizemoney £21,915 *Total Prizemoney* £46,988

Wins * 1997 *Mar Lingfi (STD) C 7f 76*

* 1995 Apr Bright (G-F) H 7f 75 86 <

1999 AW 0-5: (7f, 8f, 10f 3) (Equi 4, Fibr)
Average gelding, effective 7 to 10f, acts on gd - acts on Equi, has worn blinkers. AW high 66. **C E Brittain [5-82] C E Brittain.*

ERUDITE RR 109f
3408a[10]

4 ch f Generous (IRE) 11.5f **(82)** - Roupala (USA) (Vaguely Noble) 10.1f **(72)**
Form - 40
1999 Turf 0-2: (14f, 16f) (g-s, gd)
Pattern-class filly. Turf high 107 (1st run) - 4th of 9 getting 10lb from Kayf Tara (23 May Longchamp 16f g-s RF 1532a).
**M Zilber in FR [0-4].*

ERUPT BHB 51f41a RR 50f 41a
5191[7]

6 b g Beveled (USA) 6.9f **(64)** - Sparklingsovereign (Sparkler) 8.4f **(55)**
Form - 8278080644002177
Record 1999 - 1st:1 2nd:2 3rd:0 Ran:15
Pre1999 - 1st:2 2nd:3 3rd:1 Ran:32
Win Prizemoney £9,624 *Total Prizemoney* £15,307
Wins * **1999** Spt Newcas (SFT) H 8f 47 50
* 1998 May Mussel (GD) H 7.1f 56 62
1995 Oct Chepst (SFT) H 6.1f 66 73 <
1999 Turf 1-9: (7f 3, 8f 1-6) (gd 1-5, g-f 4) 1999 AW 0-6: (7f 3, 8f 3) (Fibr 6)
Fair gelding, effective 7f, acts on g-f, has worn blinkers. Turf high 50. AW high 50.
**M Brittain [2-25] Sidney Eaton (from G B Balding [1-22] Spt 1997).*

ESCALADE BHB 63f RR 63f
5124[11]

2 b g Green Desert (USA) 7.8f **(78)** -Sans Escale(USA)(Diesis)9.3f **(69)**
Form - 08630
Record 1999 - 1st:0 2nd:0 3rd:1 Ran:5
Win Prizemoney £0 *Total Prizemoney* £435
1999 Turf 0-5: (6f, 7f 2, 8f, 9f) (gd 2, frm 3)
Average gelding. Turf high 63 - 3rd of 16 getting 5lb from Villa Romana (21 Oct Brighton 7f gd RF 4995).
**M A Jarvis [0-5] Mohammed Bin Hendi.*

ESCORT RR 68f
5112[6]

3 b g Most Welcome 8.6f **(66)** - Benazir (High Top) 10.2f **(67)**
Form - 44006
Record 1999 - 1st:0 2nd:0 3rd:0 Ran:5
Pre1999 - 1st:1 2nd:0 3rd:0 Ran:3
Win Prizemoney £3,427 *Total Prizemoney* £4,400
Wins * 1998 Nov Doncas (SFT) 8f 74 <
1999 Turf 0-5: (8f 2, 10f 2, 12f) (gd, g-f 3, frm)
Scopey, average gelding, effective 8f, acts on gd to frm. Turf high 81 (began Aug) - 4th of 7 getting 1lb from Wolf Tooth (20 Aug Sandown 8f g-f RF 3806). **W J Haggas [1-8] J M Greetham.*

ES GO BHB 30f RR 29f
4983[16]

6 ch g Dunbeath (USA) 9.9f **(53)** - Track Angel (Ardoon) 7.3f **(53)**
Form - 0000
Record 1999 - 1st:0 2nd:0 3rd:0 Ran:4
Pre1999 - 1st:1 2nd:2 3rd:1 Ran:12
Win Prizemoney £2,610 *Total Prizemoney* £5,008
Wins * 1998 Oct Newcas (SFT) H 10.1f 36 47 <
1999 Turf 0-4: (10f 2, 12f 2) (sft, gd 2, g-f)
Very moderate gelding, effective 10 to 13f, best at 10f, acts on sft to frm, has worn blinkers. Turf high 29. Becoming disappointing.
**R Bastiman [3-24] Peter Beaton-Brown.*

ESHTIAAL (USA) BHB 70f RR 62f
4709[3]

5 b br h Riverman (USA) 9.7f **(78)** - Lady Cutlass (USA) (Cutlass (USA)) 8.5f **(76)**
Form - 073
Record 1999 - 1st:0 2nd:0 3rd:1 Ran:3
Pre1999 - 1st:4 2nd:1 3rd:2 Ran:9
Win Prizemoney £19,190 *Total Prizemoney* £21,571
Wins 1997 Spt Pontef (G-F) H 10f 94 99 <
1997 Aug Beverl (G-S) H 9.9f 84 94
1997 Aug Haydoc (G-F) H 10.5f 84 94
1997 Jly Ayr (G-F) 10f 72+
1999 Turf 0-3: (10f, 12f 2) (g-s, gd 2)
Average colt, often wears blinkers. Turf high 62. Becoming disappointing.
**G L Moore [1-7] Graham Parker (from J L Dunlop [4-9] May 1998).*

ESPADA (IRE) RR 84f
4921[9]

3 b c Mukaddamah (USA) 7.6f **(74)** - Folk Song (CAN) (The Minstrel (CAN)) 10f **(72)**
Form - 51572150
Record 1999 - 1st:2 2nd:1 3rd:0 Ran:8
Pre1999 - 1st:1 2nd:2 3rd:0 Ran:5
Win Prizemoney £16,042 *Total Prizemoney* £20,612
Wins * **1999** Spt Ayr (G-S) H 7f 83 84 <
* **1999** May Thirsk (G-F) 7f 80
* 1998 Aug Ripon (G-F) 6f 79
1999 Turf 2-8: (7f 2-5, 8f 3) (gd 1-4, g-f 1-2, frm 2)
Decent colt, effective 6 to 8f, best at 7f, acts on gd to frm, best on g-f, excels at Ripon, likes Ayr. Turf high 84 - 1st of 18 giving 14lb to Double Action (17 Spt Ayr RF 4380) - also 1st of 6 getting 14lb from Redoubtable (24 May Thirsk RF 1439). Consistent.
**P Calver [3-13] Mrs Janis MacPherson.*

ESPIONAGE (FR) RR 112f
4370a[4]

3 b c Zafonic (USA) 9f **(83)** - Didicoy (USA) (Danzig (USA)) 8.4f **(76)**
Form - 14
1999 Turf 1-2: (10f 1-1, 12f) (hvy 1-1, gd)
Currently Group-class colt. Turf high 112 (began Aug) - 4th of 4 to Montjeu (12 Spt Longchamp 12f gd RF 4370a) - also 1st of 8 from Christophene (15 Aug Deauville RF 3783a). He had run just twice when asked to tackle Montjeu in the Prix Niel and, in the circumstances, was not disgraced despite finishing last of four. Still unexposed, he deserves another chance and will make a useful four-year-old. **A Fabre in FR [1-2] K Abdullah.*

ESSANDESS (IRE) BHB 40f40a RR 46f 40a
2648[8]

4 b f Casteddu 7.4f **(54)** - Ra Ra (Lord Gayle (USA)) 8.8f **(62)**
Form - 43F4308
Record 1999 - 1st:0 2nd:0 3rd:1 Ran:5
Pre1999 - 1st:0 2nd:0 3rd:2 Ran:17
Win Prizemoney £0 *Total Prizemoney* £1,181
1999 AW 0-5: (8f, 11f, 12f 3) (Fibr 5)
Light-framed, moderate filly, effective 7 to 12f, - acts on Fibr, favours left handed tracks, favours tight tracks. AW high 42 - 3rd of 16 getting 19lb from Such Boldness (18 Jan Southwell 12f Fibr RF 0114). **J L Eyre [0-22] J L Eyre.*

ESSE BHB 32f37a RR 20f 37a
1304[8]

4 ch f Rudimentary (USA) 8.2f **(66)**-School Concert(Music Boy)6.8f **(57)**
Form - 80008
Record 1999 - 1st:0 2nd:0 3rd:0 Ran:4
Pre1999 - 1st:0 2nd:1 3rd:0 Ran:6
Win Prizemoney £0 *Total Prizemoney* £982
1999 Turf 0-3: (5f, 6f, 7f) (gd 3) 1999 AW 0-1: (7f) (Fibr)
Scopey, little account filly. Turf high 20.
**A Smith [0-5] The Rufus Partnership (from J Berry [0-1] Nov 1997).*

ESSIE BHB 54f50a RR 48f 50a
4224[7]

2 b f Ezzoud (IRE) - Safari Park (Absalom) 7.2f **(58)**
Form - 80527
Record 1999 - 1st:0 2nd:1 3rd:0 Ran:5
Win Prizemoney £0 *Total Prizemoney* £575
1999 Turf 0-4: (5f 2, 6f, 7f) (g-f 3, frm) 1999 AW 0-1: (6f) (Fibr)
Moderate filly, has worn blinkers. Turf high 48 - 2nd of 5 getting 5lb from Methodist (9 Aug Nottingham 6f g-f RF 3472).
**C E Brittain [0-5] C E Brittain.*

ESTABELLA (IRE) BHB 57f RR 54f
4294[5]

2 ch f Mujtahid (USA) 7.4f **(69)** - Lady In Green (Shareef Dancer (USA)) 9.9f **(73)**
Form - 0005
Record 1999 - 1st:0 2nd:0 3rd:0 Ran:4
1999 Turf 0-4: (6f 2, 7f 2) (g-f 4)
Fair filly. Turf high 54.
**S P C Woods [0-4] Ben Allen & Mrs Catherine Hine.*

ESTABLISHED RR 45f
4727[9]

2 b g Not in Doubt (USA) - Copper Trader (Faustus (USA)) 10f **(58)**
Form - 6087080
Record 1999 - 1st:0 2nd:0 3rd:0 Ran:7
1999 Turf 0-7: (6f 2, 7f 3, 8f, 10f) (g-s 2, gd, frm 3, hrd)
Moderate gelding. Turf high 65.
**J R Best [0-4] Alan Turner (from H Candy [0-3] Jly 1999).*

ESTABLISHMENT RR 65f 3202[8]
2 b c Muhtarram (USA) - Uncharted Waters **(57f 43a)** (Celestial Storm (USA))
Form - 608
Record 1999 - 1st:0 2nd:0 3rd:0 Ran:3
1999 Turf 0-3: (7f 3) (frm 3)
Currently average colt. Turf high 65 (began Jly).
**C A Cyzer [0-3] R M Cyzer.*

ESTACADO (IRE) BHB 48f **RR 54f** 2572[14]
3 b f Dolphin Street (FR) - Raubritter (Levmoss) 11.4f **(66)**
Form - 80
Record 1999 - 1st:0 2nd:0 3rd:0 Ran:2
Pre1999 - 1st:0 2nd:0 3rd:0 Ran:4
Win Prizemoney £0 *Total Prizemoney* £75
1999 Turf 0-2: (8f, 10f) (frm 2)
Neat, fair filly, has worn blinkers. Turf high 42.
**B Gubby [0-6] Brian Gubby Ltd.*

ESTERAAD (IRE) BHB 84f **RR 84f** 5211[2]
3 ch f Cadeaux Genereux 7.9f **(76)** - Eclipsing (IRE) (Baillamont (USA)) 7f **(78)**
Form - 00402
Record 1999 - 1st:0 2nd:1 3rd:0 Ran:5
Pre1999 - 1st:1 2nd:0 3rd:1 Ran:3
Win Prizemoney £4,695 *Total Prizemoney* £7,780
Wins * 1998 Jly Nottin (G-F) 6.1f 78+ <
1999 Turf 0-5: (7f, 8f, 10f 2, 12f) (sft, g-s, gd, g-f, frm)
Scopey, decent filly, effective 6 to 10f, best at 10f, acts on sft to gd, best on gd. Turf high 84 - 2nd of 5 getting 4lb from Limelighting (5 Nov Doncaster 10f sft RF 5211).
**J L Dunlop [1-8] Khalil Alsayegh.*

ESTERELLE (USA) BHB 29f **RR 34f** 849[9]
4 ch f Trempolino (USA) 11.9f **(77)** - Duck Flighting (USA) (Far North (CAN)) 9.7f **(75)**
Form - 0
Record 1999 - 1st:0 2nd:0 3rd:0 Ran:1
Pre1999 - 1st:0 2nd:0 3rd:0 Ran:4
1999 AW 0-1: (12f) (Fibr)
Neat, very moderate filly.
**H J Manners [0-1] C R Cox (from P S McEntee [0-4] Jly 1998).*

ETERNAL NIGHT (FR) RR 91f 4069a[9]
3 b c Night Shift (USA) 8.1f **(73)** - Echoes Of Eternity (FR)
Form - 43221440
1999 Turf 1-8: (8f 1-5, 9f 2, 10f) (sft, g-s, gd 3, g-f 1-3)
Useful colt, effective 8 to 9f, best at 8f, acts on sft to g-f. Turf high 92 - 2nd of 15 to Union Project (19 May Leopardstown 8f gd RF 1465b). Consistent. **N Meade in IRE [1-10] Mrs Patricia Hunt.*

ETERNAL SPRING (IRE) BHB 98f **RR 89f** 4388[2]
2 b c Persian Bold 10f **(69)** - Emerald Waters (Kings Lake (USA)) 10.8f **(67)**
Form - 2132
Record 1999 - 1st:1 2nd:2 3rd:1 Ran:4
Win Prizemoney £4,107 *Total Prizemoney* £7,155
Wins * 1999 Aug Beverl (GD) 7.5f 80+ <
1999 Turf 1-4: (7f 1-3, 8f) (gd, g-f 1-1, frm 2)
Useful colt. Turf high 89 (began Jly) - 2nd of 9 giving 3lb to Modish (18 Spt Ayr 8f gd RF 4388) - also 1st of 8 from Kathir (11 Aug Beverley RF 3537). Easy winner at Beverley having chased home the hotpot Distant Music first time, but was disappointing when long odds-on at Redcar. Much better run at Ayr.
**E A L Dunlop [1-4] Paul & Jenny Green.*

ETHMAAR (USA) RR 95f 5027[3]
2 b c Silver Hawk (USA) 11.2f **(85)** - Minifah (USA) (Nureyev (USA)) 8.7f **(78)**
Form - 13
Record 1999 - 1st:1 2nd:0 3rd:1 Ran:2
Win Prizemoney £9,269 *Total Prizemoney* £10,407
Wins * 1999 Spt Newbur (G-F) 8f 95+ <
1999 Turf 1-2: (8f 1-2) (g-s, frm 1-1)
Currently very useful colt. Turf high 95 (1st run) (began Spt) - 1st of 8 from Paradise Garden (17 Spt Newbury RF 4385). Tall and scopey, he stayed on strongly to win a competitive event at Newbury in September, but folded tamely when returned to that track on easy ground the following month. Likely to stay middle-distances, he will improve but may fall short of Group class.
**M P Tregoning [1-2] Hamdan Al Maktoum.*

ETISALAT (IRE) BHB 42f **RR 41f** 5151[10]
4 b g Lahib (USA) 8f **(69)** - Sweet Repose (High Top) 10.2f **(67)**
Form - 802100600
Record 1999 - 1st:1 2nd:1 3rd:0 Ran:9
Pre1999 - 1st:0 2nd:0 3rd:0 Ran:3
Win Prizemoney £2,285 *Total Prizemoney* £2,837
Wins * 1999 Jun Yarmou (G-F) SH 8f 40 50+ <
1999 Turf 1-9: (7f 3, 8f 1-5, 9f) (gd 1-6, g-f 3)
Strong, moderate gelding, effective 8f, acts on gd. Turf high 50 - 1st of 18 from Danzas (3 Jun Yarmouth RF 1707).
**J Pearce [1-9] Mrs E M Clarke (from R W Armstrong [0-3] Oct 1998).*

ETIZAAZ (USA) BHB 114f **RR 114df** 4682[5]
3 b f Diesis 9f **(80)** - Alamosa (Alydar (USA)) 9.1f **(76)**
Form - 125
Record 1999 - 1st:1 2nd:1 3rd:0 Ran:3
Pre1999 - 1st:1 2nd:1 3rd:0 Ran:2
Win Prizemoney £21,088 *Total Prizemoney* £59,981
Wins * 1999 Aug Sandow (GD) L 8.1f 108+ <
1998 Jly York (G-F) 7f 91++
1999 Turf 1-3: (8f 1-1, 10f, 12f) (gd 2, frm 1-1)
Rangy, Group-class filly. Turf high 114 (began Aug) - 2nd of 11 to Daryaba (12 Spt Longchamp 12f gd RF 4369a) - also 1st of 8 getting 10lb from Selfish (21 Aug Sandown RF 3826). A market leader for the 1,000 Guineas through the winter, she suffered a few niggling setbacks and did not reappear until making all to win a Listed event at Sandown in late August. Immediately pitched into Group One company, she ran a tremendous race to chase Daryaba home in the Prix Vermeille, staying a mile and a half well but having no answer to the winner's turn-of foot. Unsuited by soft ground in the Sun Chariot Stakes at Newmarket in October, she will be an interesting contender for races like the Nassau Stakes and Yorkshire Oaks if kept in training.
**S bin Suroor [1-3] Godolphin (from J L Dunlop [1-2] Aug 1998).*

ETMA ROSE (IRE) BHB 42f **RR 35f** 87[12]
3 b f Fairy King (USA) 7.7f **(75)** - Lassalia (Sallust) 8.4f **(63)**
Form - 0
Record 1999 - 1st:0 2nd:0 3rd:0 Ran:1
Pre1999 - 1st:0 2nd:0 3rd:0 Ran:4
1999 AW 0-1: (6f) (Fibr)
Light-framed, very moderate filly. **R Hollinshead [0-5] Mrs E Rose.*

ETTERBY PARK (USA) BHB 82f77a **RR 82f 77a** 4917[8]
6 b g Silver Hawk (USA) 11.2f **(85)** - Bonita Francita (CAN) (Devil's Bag (USA)) 12.4f **(78)**
Form - 86518
Record 1999 - 1st:1 2nd:0 3rd:0 Ran:5
Pre1999 - 1st:8 2nd:8 3rd:8 Ran:42
Win Prizemoney £49,202 *Total Prizemoney* £102,661

Wins	*** 1999**	Spt	Mussel	(G-S)	H	16f	80	82	
	* 1998	Oct	Newmar	(G-S)	LH	16f	85	93	<
	* 1998	Spt	Yarmou	(G-S)	H	18.2f	80	81	
	* 1997	Apr	Sandow	(G-F)	H	16.4f	74	83	
	* 1996	Spt	Ayr	(G-F)	H	15f	69	78+	
	* 1996	*Jly*	*Wolver*	*(STD)*	*H*	*14.8f*	*51*	*67+*	
	* 1996	*Jly*	*Wolver*	*(STD)*	*H*	*12f*	*51*	*65*	
	* 1996	Jly	Catter	(G-F)	H	12f	51	60+	
	* 1996	Jun	Carlis	(FRM)	H	12f	44	44+	

1999 Turf 1-5: (16f 1-2, 17f, 19f 2) (gd 1-3, g-f 2)
Decent gelding, effective 16 to 18f, acts on gd to g-f, best on gd, likes right handed tracks. Turf high 82. Consistent. A tough stayer, suited by forcing tactics, he was not at his best early on in the year, but bounced back to form with a narrow defeat of Lord Lamb at Musselburgh in September and finished a respectable eighth in the Cesarewitch. He is tough and genuine.
**M Johnston [9-41] & Mrs G Middlebrook (from Mrs J R Ramsden [0-2] May 1996).*

ETTRICK RR 100f 3444[25]
3 b c Selkirk (USA) 7.9f **(76)** - Lucia Tarditi (FR) (Crystal Glitters (USA)) 11.3f **(79)**
Form - 4240

Record 1999 - 1st:0 2nd:1 3rd:0 Ran:4
Pre1999 - 1st:1 2nd:0 3rd:0 Ran:2
Win Prizemoney £3,486 *Total Prizemoney* £7,221
Wins * 1998 Nov Doncas (SFT) 7f 81 <
1999 Turf 0-4: (7f 2, 8f 2) (gd, g-f, frm, hrd)
Workmanlike, very useful colt, effective 7 to 8f, acts on g-f to frm. Turf high 100 - 4th of 12 giving 7lb to River Times (17 Jly Newmarket 8f frm RF 2910). He was only beaten by lack of stamina in a valuable mile handicap at Newmarket in July. That trip may be within his compass as a four-year-old, when he will surely pick up a decent prize. **A C Stewart [1-6] Lord Hartington.*

ETTY B RR 29f
3836[15]
3 b f Clantime 6.6f **(57)** - Paquerette **(36f)** (Crofthall) 6.3f **(59)**
Form - 70
Record 1999 - 1st:0 2nd:0 3rd:0 Ran:2
1999 Turf 0-2: (7f, 11f) (gd, frm)
Small, currently little account filly. Turf high 29 (began Aug).
**Andrew Turnell [0-2] Paul Downey.*

EUROBOX BOY BHB 69f53a RR 69f 53a
1415[2]
6 ch g Savahra Sound 7.8f **(55)** - Princess Poquito (Hard Fought) 8.8f **(62)**
Form - 0042
Record 1999 - 1st:0 2nd:1 3rd:0 Ran:4
Pre1999 - 1st:5 2nd:8 3rd:6 Ran:43
Win Prizemoney £14,349 *Total Prizemoney* £29,869
Wins 1997 Aug Sandow (GD) H 8.1f 67 72 <
1997 Jly Salisb (FRM) H 8f 61 59
1997 Apr Nottin (G-F) H 8.2f 56 62
1996 Aug Leices (G-F) H 8f 51 59
1996 Jly Newmar (G-F) C 8f 55
1999 Turf 0-4: (7f 2, 8f 2) (gd, g-f 2, frm)
Average gelding, effective 8f, acts on g-s to g-f, best on g-f, has worn blinkers, likes tight tracks. Turf high 69 - 4th of 18 giving 7lb to Taffs Well (6 May Chester 8f g-f RF 1053).
**B A McMahon [0-4] N Coverdale (from A P Jarvis [5-45] Jun 1998).*

EURO DANDY BHB 46f RR 52f
5158[26]
2 b g Rambo Dancer (CAN) 8.4f **(59)** - Kagram Queen **(54df)** (Prince Ragusa)
Form - 0700
Record 1999 - 1st:0 2nd:0 3rd:0 Ran:4
1999 Turf 0-4: (5f 2, 6f, 8f) (gd 2, frm 2)
Fair gelding. Turf high 52. **D Nicholls [0-4] W G Swiers.*

EUROLINK MAYFLY RR 61f
4408[7]
2 b f Night Shift (USA) 8.1f **(73)** -NorthKildare (USA)(Northjet) 10.3f **(74)**
Form - 07
Record 1999 - 1st:0 2nd:0 3rd:0 Ran:2
1999 Turf 0-2: (6f, 7f) (frm 2)
Currently average filly. Turf high 61 (began Spt).
**J L Dunlop [0-2] Eurolink Group Plc.*

EUROLINK MOUSSAKA BHB 60f76a RR 68df 76a
1262[14]
4 b g Superlative 8.8f **(57)** - Albiflora (USA) (Manila (USA)) 9.3f **(71)**
Form - 18100
Record 1999 - 1st:1 2nd:0 3rd:0 Ran:4
Pre1999 - 1st:1 2nd:0 3rd:0 Ran:3
Win Prizemoney £5,000 *Total Prizemoney* £5,000
Wins * **1999** *Feb Southw (STD) H* 8f 65 75 <
* 1998 *Dec Wolver (STD)* 7f 69
1999 Turf 0-2: (7f, 10f) (gd, g-f) 1999 AW 1-2: (8f 1-2) (Fibr 1-2)
Strong, above-average gelding, effective 7 to 8f, - acts on Fibr. Turf high 46. AW high 75 - 1st of 15 giving 13lb to Gain Line (12 Feb Southwell RF 0276).
**J L Eyre [2-5] Peter Watson (from C F Wall [0-2] Spt 1998).*

EUROLINK RAINDANCE (IRE) BHB 100f RR 91f
4201a[5]
2 b f Alzao (USA) 9.8f **(73)** - Eurolink Mischief **(81f)** (Be My Chief (USA))
Form - 21125
Record 1999 - 1st:2 2nd:2 3rd:0 Ran:5
Win Prizemoney £12,631 *Total Prizemoney* £18,100
Wins * **1999** Jun Salisb (FRM) 7f 91+ <
* **1999** Jun Chepst (GD) 6.1f 74+
1999 Turf 2-5: (6f 1-2, 7f 1-3) (gd 1-1, g-f 2, frm 1-2)
Useful filly. Turf high 91 - also 1st of 7 giving 6lb to One Step At A Time (24 Jun Salisbury RF 2274). Convincing winner on her second start at Chepstow, the extra furlong and faster ground did not seem to inconvenience her at Salisbury. Flashed her tail next time, but ran well in a Group One on her final start.
**J L Dunlop [2-5] Eurolink Group Plc.*

EUROLINK WINDSONG (IRE) BHB 29f RR 30f
3903[13]
5 ch m Polish Patriot (USA) 7.8f **(70)**-Delvecchia (Glint of Gold)9.3f **(66)**
Form - 40
Record 1999 - 1st:0 2nd:0 3rd:0 Ran:2
Pre1999 - 1st:0 2nd:1 3rd:0 Ran:11
Win Prizemoney £0 *Total Prizemoney* £547
1999 Turf 0-2: (16f, 17f) (gd, frm)
Very moderate filly. Turf high 30 (began Aug).
**Martyn Wane [0-10] William Graham (from R M McKellar [0-2] May 1997).*

EURO VENTURE BHB 77f71a RR 80f 71a
3076[3]
4 b g Prince Sabo 6.6f **(64)** - Brave Advance (USA) (Bold Laddie (USA)) 5.6f **(69)**
Form - 42152121283
Record 1999 - 1st:3 2nd:4 3rd:1 Ran:11
Pre1999 - 1st:1 2nd:0 3rd:1 Ran:9
Win Prizemoney £18,165 *Total Prizemoney* £31,270
Wins * **1999** Jun Carlis (G-F) H 6.9f 68 70
* **1999** May Thirsk (Sft) H 6f 63 67
* **1999** *Feb Southw (STD) H* 6f 67 72
* 1998 *Jan Wolver (STD)* 6f 75 <
1999 Turf 2-7: (6f 1-6, 7f 1-1) (gd 1-1, g-f, frm 1-4, hrd) 1999 AW 1-4: (6f 1-4) (Fibr 1-4)
Scopey, decent gelding, effective 6 to 7f, best at 6f, acts on frm - acts on Fibr, likes tight tracks. Turf high 80 - 2nd of 19 getting 1lb from Unshaken (26 Jun Newcastle 6f frm RF 2334). AW high 72 - 1st of 10 giving 7lb to Thaayer (12 Feb Southwell RF 0277). Another Dandy Nicholls success story, he won three times last year, one of which was on Fibresand, and he has also run some blinding races in defeat. He did just enough to win over seven furlongs at Carlisle, but is probably better over six.
**D Nicholls [4-20] W G Swiers.*

EURYANTHE (IRE) RR 102f
5017a[2]
3 b f Royal Academy (USA) 7.8f **(77)** - El Gran Flower (GER) (El Gran Senor (USA)) 9.6f **(76)**
Form - 352
1999 Turf 0-3: (8f, 10f 2) (gd, g-f, g-s)
Currently very useful filly. Turf high 102 - 2nd of 15 to Alabaq (17 Oct San Siro 8f g-f RF 5017a). **H Remmert in GER [0-3].*

EVANDER (IRE) BHB 84f RR 85f
5221[4]
4 ch g Indian Ridge 7.6f **(74)** -Heavenly Hope(Glenstal (USA))10.1f **(64)**
Form - 60524
Record 1999 - 1st:0 2nd:1 3rd:0 Ran:5
Pre1999 - 1st:1 2nd:1 3rd:2 Ran:6
Win Prizemoney £5,071 *Total Prizemoney* £12,986
Wins * 1998 May Goodwo (G-F) 8f 79 <
1999 Turf 0-5: (10f 3, 12f 2) (sft, g-s, gd 2, frm)
Scopey, useful gelding, effective 8 to 12f, best at 12f, acts on sft to frm. Turf high 87 (began Spt). Consistent. Off the track for 15 months after running at Royal Ascot in '98, he put up a most creditable performance to finish sixth in the Courage Handicap at Newbury in September and ran another good race in the November Handicap. **P F I Cole [1-11] Anthony Speelman.*

EVANILDA (USA) RR 90f
3337a[6]
3 ch f River Special (USA) - Fair Sousanne (Busted) 10.2f **(61)**
Form - 66421146
1999 Turf 2-8: (8f 2, 10f 2-4, 12f 2) (g-s 1-2, gd 2, g-f, frm 1-3)
Useful filly, effective 10f, acts on g-s to frm. Turf high 90 - also 1st of 6 giving 12lb to Delirious Tantrum (13 Jly Down Royal RF 2977a). **J S Bolger in IRE [2-8] D H W Dobson.*

EVASIVE STEP BHB 60f72a RR 68f 72a
3254[8]
3 b f Batshoof 9.5f **(66)** - Tread Carefully (Sharpo) 7.7f **(59)**
Form - 0588
Record 1999 - 1st:0 2nd:0 3rd:0 Ran:4
Pre1999 - 1st:0 2nd:1 3rd:2 Ran:7

Win Prizemoney £0 *Total Prizemoney* £1,949
1999 Turf 0-4: (8f, 10f 2, 12f) (g-f 2, frm 2)
Workmanlike, average filly, effective 6 to 8f, best at 8f, acts on g-s to g-f, prefers left handed tracks, favours tight tracks. Turf high 68 - 5th of 18 getting 1lb from Untold Riches (16 Jun Nottingham 8f g-f RF 2055). **T D Easterby [0-11] Mrs Ian Wills.*

EVENING PROMISE BHB 103f **RR 105f** 4392[2]
3 b f Aragon 7.7f **(58)** - Rosy Sunset (IRE) (Red Sunset) 8.2f **(63)**
Form - 0030442
Record 1999 - 1st:0 2nd:1 3rd:1 Ran:7
Pre1999 - 1st:2 2nd:1 3rd:0 Ran:6
Win Prizemoney £15,007 *Total Prizemoney* £41,744
Wins * 1998 Spt Ayr (G-S) L 6f 99 <
* 1998 Jly Nottin (G-F) 6.1f 77
1999 Turf 0-7: (6f 4, 7f, 8f 2) (gd 2, g-f 2, frm 3)
Light-framed, Pattern-class filly, effective 6f, acts on sft to g-f. Turf high 105 - 2nd of 28 to Grangeville (18 Spt Ayr 6f gd RF 4392). Consistent. Suited by soft ground and waiting tactics, she finished a long way behind Wince in the Fred Darling and the Guineas, but was in good heart in sprint handicaps in the autumn, beating all bar Grangeville in the Ayr Gold Cup.
**B A McMahon [2-13] Mrs C P Lees-Jones.*

EVENING SCENT BHB 47f44a **RR 50f 44a** 4932[7]
3 b f Ardkinglass 5f **(64)** - Fresh Line (High Line) 10.3f **(70)**
Form - 7040137
Record 1999 - 1st:1 2nd:0 3rd:1 Ran:7
Win Prizemoney £1,982 *Total Prizemoney* £2,384
Wins * **1999** Spt Catter (G-F) S 13.8f 46 <
1999 Turf 1-4: (14f 1-2, 16f, 18f) (gd, g-f, frm 1-2) 1999 AW 0-3: (8f 2, 9f) (Fibr 3)
Small, fair filly, effective 14 to 16f, acts on gd to frm. Turf high 50 - 3rd of 15 getting 12lb from Salvage (5 Oct Catterick 16f gd RF 4726) - also 1st of 12 getting 5lb from Masonic (18 Spt Catterick RF 4396). AW high 43. **J Hetherton [1-7] N Hetherton.*

EVENING STORM (IRE) RR 102f 2660a[15]
3 ch c Acatenango (GER) - Evening Kiss (Kris) 9.5f **(73)**
Form - 200
1999 Turf 0-3: (10f, 11f, 12f) (sft, gd 2)
Currently very useful colt. Turf high 102. He ran a useful race at Munich in May, but disappointed twice afterwards and has plenty to prove. **A Schutz in GER [0-3].*

EVENING WORLD (FR) BHB 99f **RR 92f** 4859[5]
4 ch c Bering 9.6f **(80)** - Pivoine (USA) (Nureyev (USA)) 8.7f **(78)**
Form - 28455
Record 1999 - 1st:0 2nd:1 3rd:0 Ran:5
Pre1999 - 1st:3 2nd:1 3rd:2 Ran:10
Win Prizemoney £23,266 *Total Prizemoney* £38,073
Wins 1998 Jun York (G-S) H 10.4f 99 104 <
1998 May Lingfi (GD) H 10f 91 96
1997 Spt York (SFT) 7.9f 100+
1999 Turf 0-5: (10f 3, 11f, 12f) (sft, g-s, gd 2, g-f)
Useful colt, effective 10f, acts on g-s. Turf high 111 (1st run) - 2nd of 9 to Generous Rosi (24 Apr Sandown 10f g-s RF 0844). Consistent. He carries plenty of condition, races freely and is a useful performer up to a mile and a quarter on soft ground. However, he falls short of Group class and is difficult to place. His future could lie over hurdles.
**M C Pipe [0-5] T M Hely-Hutchinson (from P F I Cole [3-10] Oct 1998).*

EVENTUALITY BHB 69f **RR 72f** 4685[6]
3 b f Petoski 10.4f **(56)** - Queen's Tickle (Tickled Pink) 6.5f **(59)**
Form - 60014146
Record 1999 - 1st:2 2nd:0 3rd:0 Ran:8
Pre1999 - 1st:0 2nd:0 3rd:1 Ran:2
Win Prizemoney £7,979 *Total Prizemoney* £9,588
Wins * **1999** Spt Epsom (GD) H 7f 61 68 <
* **1999** Jly Salisb (FRM) H 7f 56 63
1999 Turf 2-8: (6f, 7f 2-5, 9f, 10f) (gd, g-f 1-3, frm 1-4)
Workmanlike, above-average filly, effective 6 to 7f, best at 7f, acts on g-f to frm, best on g-f. Turf high 72 - 4th of 15 getting 2lb from Brecongill Lad (11 Spt Goodwood 6f g-f RF 4272) - also 1st of 17 giving 4lb to Step On Degas (3 Spt Epsom RF 4121). Seemed to appreciate the drop back to seven furlongs when winning at Salisbury in July, and won very nicely over the same trip at Epsom the following month. Suited by fast ground.
**R F JohnsonHoughton [2-10] Anthony Harrison.*

EVEREST (IRE) RR 76f 4139[2]
2 ch c Indian Ridge 7.6f **(74)**-Reine D'Beaute(Caerleon (USA)) 8.6f **(71)**
Form - 2
Record 1999 - 1st:0 2nd:1 3rd:0 Ran:1
Win Prizemoney £0 *Total Prizemoney* £1,180
1999 Turf 0-1: (7f) (frm)
Currently above-average colt. (1st run) - 2nd of 14 to Hunting Tiger (4 Spt Haydock 7f frm RF 4139). Second to Hunting Tiger in what looked a competitive maiden at Haydock on his only start so far.
**P F I Cole [0-1] H R H Prince Fahd Salman.*

EVERGREEN (IRE) RR 75f 5218[16]
2 ch f Lammtarra (USA) - Nettle (Kris) 9.5f **(73)**
Form - 348730
Record 1999 - 1st:0 2nd:0 3rd:2 Ran:6
Win Prizemoney £0 *Total Prizemoney* £1,277
1999 Turf 0-6: (6f 4, 7f, 8f) (g-s, gd 3, frm, hrd)
Above-average filly, effective 6f, acts on gd. Turf high 75.
**R Hannon [0-6] The Queen.*

EVERGREEN VENTURE BHB 79f **RR 76f** 4351[6]
3 b c Pursuit of Love 9.5f **(69)** - Georgica (USA) (Raise A Native) 11.2f **(69)**
Form - 614033716
Record 1999 - 1st:2 2nd:0 3rd:2 Ran:9
Pre1999 - 1st:0 2nd:0 3rd:0 Ran:1
Win Prizemoney £11,349 *Total Prizemoney* £13,418
Wins * **1999** Aug Pontef (GD) H 8f 74 76 <
* **1999** May Lingfi (G-F) 10f 70
1999 Turf 2-9: (8f 1-4, 9f, 10f 1-4) (g-s, gd 1-3, g-f, frm 1-4)
Above-average colt, effective 8 to 10f, best at 8f, acts on gd to frm, best on frm. Turf high 76 - 1st of 9 giving 1lb to Forum Girl (22 Aug Pontefract RF 3848) - also 1st of 8 giving 5lb to England's Rose (8 May Lingfield RF 1116). Consistent. The maiden he won at Lingfield was a moderate affair, but he has put in some fair efforts in handicap company since and regained winning form in a fair Pontefract handicap in August. **S P C Woods [2-10] Dr Frank Chao.*

EVERLASTING LOVE BHB 100f **RR 89f** 4680[11]
2 b f Pursuit of Love 9.5f **(69)** - Now And Forever (IRE) (Kris) 9.5f **(73)**
Form - 84120
Record 1999 - 1st:1 2nd:1 3rd:0 Ran:5
Win Prizemoney £4,232 *Total Prizemoney* £12,206
Wins * **1999** Aug Redcar (G-F) 7f 77+ <
1999 Turf 1-5: (7f 1-4, 8f) (gd, g-f 2, frm 1-2)
Useful filly. Turf high 89 (began Jly) - 2nd of 12 to Teggiano (9 Spt Doncaster 8f g-f RF 4236). She got off the mark in a four-runner event at Redcar on her third start.
**M L W Bell [1-5] DGH Partnership.*

EVER PUNCTUAL RR 4605[12]
2 b f Timeless Times (USA) 6.1f **(56)** - Vital Witness (Garda's Revenge (USA)) 8.3f **(51)**
Form - 0
Record 1999 - 1st:0 2nd:0 3rd:0 Ran:1
1999 AW 0-1: (7f) (Fibr)
Currently poor filly. **J S Moore [0-1] Terry Pasquale.*

EVER REVIE (IRE) BHB 56f **RR 59f** 4504[7]
2 b f Hamas (IRE) 8f **(72)** - Lucy Limelight (Hot Spark) 7.6f **(62)**
Form - 60187
Record 1999 - 1st:1 2nd:0 3rd:0 Ran:5
Win Prizemoney £2,372 *Total Prizemoney* £2,482
Wins * **1999** Jly Beverl (SFT) S 7.5f 59 <
1999 Turf 1-5: (6f, 7f 1-3, 8f) (gd 1-1, g-f 4)
Fair filly, has worn blinkers. Turf high 59 - 1st of 12 from Blue Legend (3 Jly Beverley RF 2511). Being blinkered and racing on soft ground for the first time resulted in a game victory at Beverley in July, though that stiff extended seven looked barely far enough.
**T D Easterby [1-5] Leeds United Racing Club Ltd.*

EVERY PENNY BHB 33f28a **RR 50f 28a** 457[4]
4 b f Interrex (CAN) 7.7f **(51)** - Shiny Penny (Glint of Gold) 9.3f **(66)**
Form - 04

Record 1999 - 1st:0 2nd:0 3rd:0 Ran:1
Pre1999 - 1st:0 2nd:0 3rd:0 Ran:4
1999 AW 0-1: (8f) (Fibr)
Leggy, fair filly.
**R T Phillips [0-1] Edwin Phillips (from E L James [0-4] Dec 1998).*

EVESHAM (USA) BHB 55f **RR 54f** 3161[11]
3 b g Septieme Ciel (USA) - Evening Air (USA) (J O Tobin (USA)) 9.4f **(67)**
Form - 4440150
Record 1999 - 1st:1 2nd:0 3rd:0 Ran:7
Win Prizemoney £2,087 *Total Prizemoney* £2,806
Wins * **1999** Jly Catter (GD) 13.8f 51 <
1999 Turf 1-7: (10f 2, 12f 3, 13f, 14f 1-1) (sft, g-s, gd, g-f 1-2, frm 2)
Light-framed, fair gelding, has worn blinkers. Turf high 63.
**M Johnston [1-7] Sheikh Mohammed.*

EVEZIO RUFO BHB 35f42a **RR 32f 42a** 1982[5]
7 b g Blakeney 11.9f **(53)** - Empress Corina (Free State) 8.7f **(61)**
Form - 3366253436100616745
Record 1999 - 1st:2 2nd:0 3rd:2 Ran:13
Pre1999 - 1st:5 2nd:7 3rd:8 Ran:55
Win Prizemoney £17,499 *Total Prizemoney* £25,212
Wins * **1999** *Mar Wolver (STD) H 12f 39 44*
* **1999** *Jan Wolver (STD) S 14.8f 45*
* 1998 *Apr Wolver (STD) H 12f 54 57*
* 1998 *Feb Southw (STD) H 12f 44 61*
* 1998 *Jan Lingfi (STD) SH 13f 44 47*
* 1997 *May Southw (STD) H 11f 45 50*
1999 Turf 0-1: (14f) (g-f) 1999 AW 2-12: (11f 3, 12f 1-2, 13f 2, 15f 1-4, 16f) (Equi 2, Fibr 2-10)
Moderate gelding, effective 12 to 13f, best at 12f, acts on gd - acts on AW, best on Fibr, mostly wears blinkers (effectively), does well at Lingfield and Wolverhampton. AW high 45. Has had more runs than Brian Lara in recent seasons. He pops up from time to time in moderate company in Fibresand staying events, but his strike rate is pretty low.
**N P Littmoden [7-81] O A Gunter (from J L Dunlop [1-4] Apr 1995).*

EVIE HONE (IRE) BHB 72f **RR 63f** 2129[U]
3 ch f Royal Academy (USA) 7.8f **(77)** - Tochar Ban (USA) (Assert) 10.6f **(85)**
Form - 5U
Record 1999 - 1st:0 2nd:0 3rd:0 Ran:2
Pre1999 - 1st:0 2nd:0 3rd:0 Ran:3
Win Prizemoney £0 *Total Prizemoney* £270
1999 Turf 0-2: (9f, 14f) (gd, frm)
Scopey, average filly, has worn blinkers. Turf high 61.
**B W Hills [0-5] Jeremy Gompertz.*

EVIL EMPIRE (GER) RR 106f 4769a[4]
3 ch f Acatenango (GER) - Elea (GER) (Dschingis Khan) 11.3f **(75)**
Form - 3314
1999 Turf 1-4: (8f, 11f, 12f 1-1, 13f) (hvy, sft, gd 1-2)
Pattern-class filly. Turf high 106 - 4th of 11 getting 7lb from Fairy Queen (2 Oct Longchamp 13f hvy RF 4769a) - also 1st of 8 from Quebra (12 Spt Hanover RF 4366a). She improved as she was stepped-up in distance. A decisive winner at Hanover in September, she was unlucky in the Prix de Royallieu, being hampered inside the last two furlongs and then prematurely eased as her rider mistook the winning post. Open to further improvement, she should win another Group race or two in 2000.
**A Schutz in GER [1-4] Turf Syndikat 97.*

EWENNY BHB 67f53a **RR 76f 53a** 253[4]
3 b f Warrshan (USA) 9.7f **(59)** - Laleston (Junius (USA)) 7.7f **(65)**
Form - 34
Record 1999 - 1st:0 2nd:0 3rd:1 Ran:2
Pre1999 - 1st:1 2nd:0 3rd:2 Ran:3
Win Prizemoney £3,731 *Total Prizemoney* £4,909
Wins * 1998 May Warwic (GD) 5f 66 <
1999 AW 0-2: (6f, 7f) (Fibr 2)
Unfurnished, above-average filly. AW high 48.
**J M P Eustace [1-5] K J Mercer.*

EXALT BHB 55f60a **RR 53f 60a** 869[15]
3 b g Puissance 7.1f **(60)** -Gild the Lily(Ile de Bourbon (USA)) 10.1f **(67)**
Form - 840
Record 1999 - 1st:0 2nd:0 3rd:0 Ran:3
Pre1999 - 1st:0 2nd:0 3rd:0 Ran:1
1999 Turf 0-2: (8f 2) (sft, g-s) 1999 AW 0-1: (7f) (Fibr)
Scopey, fair gelding. Turf high 53.
**A W Carroll [0-3] Mrs J Coghlan-Everitt (from J Balding [0-1] Jly 1998).*

EXALTED (IRE) BHB 60f77a **RR 60f 77a** 975[7]
6 b g High Estate 10.5f **(66)** - Heavenward (USA) (Conquistador Cielo (USA)) 8.8f **(69)**
Form - 47
Record 1999 - 1st:0 2nd:0 3rd:0 Ran:2
Pre1999 - 1st:1 2nd:1 3rd:3 Ran:15
Win Prizemoney £3,940 *Total Prizemoney* £9,381
Wins 1995 Jly Thirsk (GD) 7f 67+ <
1999 Turf 0-2: (10f, 13f) (g-s, g-f)
Average gelding. Turf high 60.
**T A K Cuthbert [1-10] Railway-Lochmaben (from W Jenks [1-14] Jun 1998).*

EXEAT (USA) RR 108df 4688[3]
3 b br c Dayjur (USA) 6.8f **(79)** - By Your Leave (USA) (Private Account (USA)) 8.5f **(74)**
Form - 2882353
Record 1999 - 1st:0 2nd:2 3rd:2 Ran:7
Pre1999 - 1st:1 2nd:2 3rd:0 Ran:4
Win Prizemoney £3,631 *Total Prizemoney* £55,779
Wins * 1998 Jly Haydoc (G-F) 6f 84+ <
1999 Turf 0-7: (7f 4, 8f 3) (g-s, g-f 5, frm)
Workmanlike, Pattern-class colt, effective 6 to 8f, acts on sft to frm, has worn blinkers. Turf high 110 - 8th of 16 to Island Sands (1 May Newmarket 8f frm RF 0958). He ran a decent race under a moderate ride in the 2,000 Guineas, but failed to progress and seemed to be feeling the effects of a long campaign when performing moderately in a visor during the autumn. He could do with a confidence booster, but is difficult to place.
**J H M Gosden [1-11] Lady Harrison.*

EXECUTIVE CHOICE (IRE) BHB 32f **RR 32f** 2132[12]
5 b g Don't Forget Me 9.5f **(66)** -Shadia (USA) (Naskra (USA)) 8.8f **(69)**
Form - 0500
Record 1999 - 1st:0 2nd:0 3rd:0 Ran:4
Pre1999 - 1st:0 2nd:0 3rd:1 Ran:15
Win Prizemoney £0 *Total Prizemoney* £219
1999 Turf 0-4: (8f, 9f, 10f, 12f) (gd 2, g-f, frm)
Very moderate gelding, has worn blinkers. Turf high 32. Consistent.
**B Ellison [0-10] The Couriers Syndicate (from M J Grassick in IRE [0-11] Jly 1998).*

EX GRATIA (USA) BHB 88f **RR 88f** 4594[4]
3 b g Exbourne (USA) - Populi (USA) (Star Envoy (USA)) 9.6f **(78)**
Form - 0410214
Record 1999 - 1st:2 2nd:1 3rd:0 Ran:7
Win Prizemoney £10,216 *Total Prizemoney* £13,381
Wins * **1999** Spt Doncas (G-F) 10.3f 88 <
* **1999** Jun Haydoc (GD) 8.1f 79
1999 Turf 2-7: (8f 1-4, 10f 1-1, 11f, 12f) (gd 2-4, g-f, frm 2)
Well made, useful gelding, effective 8 to 12f, acts on gd to g-f, best on gd. Turf high 88 - 1st of 9 getting 6lb from Fredora (8 Spt Doncaster RF 4211) - also 1st of 8 from King Midas (5 Jun Haydock RF 1768). A winner over a mile on easy ground in June, he had no problem with being stepped up to ten furlongs, including winning over that trip at Doncaster in September. He has won on fast ground, but looks especially suited by some cut.
**B W Hills [2-7] K Abdulla.*

EXILE BHB 66f **RR 70f** 4672[10]
2 b c Emperor Jones (USA) - Silver Venture (USA) (Silver Hawk (USA)) 8.6f **(70)**
Form - 4460400
Record 1999 - 1st:0 2nd:0 3rd:0 Ran:7
Win Prizemoney £0 *Total Prizemoney* £557
1999 Turf 0-7: (5f 2, 6f 2, 7f 2, 8f) (g-s, gd, g-f 2, frm 3)
Above-average colt, has worn blinkers. Turf high 70.
**W J Haggas [0-2] Highclere Thoroughbred Racing Ltd (from G Lewis [0-5] Aug 1999).*

EXIT BHB 79f **RR 76f** 3055[6]
3 b f Exbourne (USA) - Meteoric (High Line) 10.3f **(70)**
Form - 176
Record 1999 - 1st:1 2nd:0 3rd:0 Ran:3
Pre1999 - 1st:0 2nd:0 3rd:0 Ran:1
Win Prizemoney £3,582 *Total Prizemoney* £3,813
Wins * 1999 Jun Beverl (G-F) 8.5f 76 <
1999 Turf 1-3: (8f 1-2, 10f) (g-f 1-1, frm 2)
Scopey, above-average filly. Turf high 76 (1st run) - 1st of 4 getting 5lb from El Nahrawan (22 Jun Beverley RF 2193).
**B Smart [1-3] John Ford (from M L W Bell [0-1] Jly 1998).*

EXORCET (FR) RR 53f 5137[12]
2 b f Selkirk (USA) 7.9f **(76)** -Stack Rock **(105df)** (Ballad Rock) 7.8f **(63)**
Form - 80
Record 1999 - 1st:0 2nd:0 3rd:0 Ran:2
1999 Turf 0-2: (6f, 7f) (hvy, gd)
Currently fair filly. Turf high 53 (began Oct).
**I A Balding [0-2] J C Smith.*

EXPEDIENT RR 22f 5047[11]
2 ch c Polish Precedent (USA) 9f **(73)** - Widows Walk (Habitat) 9.4f **(70)**
Form - 00
Record 1999 - 1st:0 2nd:0 3rd:0 Ran:2
1999 Turf 0-2: (6f, 7f) (hvy, g-s)
Currently little account colt. Turf high 22 (began Oct).
**J L Dunlop [0-2] Ian Cameron.*

EXPRESS GIFT BHB 42f **RR 44f** 5152[5]
10 br g Bay Express 7.1f **(53)** - Annes Gift (Ballymoss) 8.5f **(55)**
Form - 5
Record 1999 - 1st:0 2nd:0 3rd:0 Ran:1
Pre1999 - 1st:6 2nd:3 3rd:3 Ran:32
Win Prizemoney £23,135 *Total Prizemoney* £29,797
Wins 1997 May Haydoc (G-S) H 14f 52 56
1999 Turf 0-1: (14f) (gd)
Moderate gelding. Consistent.
**M Pitman [0-2] M W Horner, H Young and D S Arnold (from Mrs M Reveley [10-46] Jly 1997).*

EXUDE (IRE) RR 34f 3913[10]
2 br f Namaqualand (USA) - Betelgeuse (Kalaglow) 9.8f **(67)**
Form - 0
Record 1999 - 1st:0 2nd:0 3rd:0 Ran:1
1999 Turf 0-1: (7f) (gd)
Currently very moderate filly. **D J S Cosgrove [0-1] D J S Cosgrove.*

EYEBALLS OUT BHB 72f65a **RR 74f 65a** 4883[6]
3 b c Polar Falcon (USA) 9f **(74)** - Jacquelina (USA) **(70f)** (Private Account (USA)) 8.5f **(74)**
Form - 07716
Record 1999 - 1st:1 2nd:0 3rd:0 Ran:4
Pre1999 - 1st:0 2nd:0 3rd:0 Ran:4
Win Prizemoney £3,844 *Total Prizemoney* £3,844
Wins * 1999 Oct Nottin (SFT) H 10f 70 74 <
1999 Turf 1-3: (10f 1-2, 12f) (g-s 1-2, frm) 1999 AW 0-1: (8f) (Fibr)
Scopey, above-average colt, effective 10f, acts on g-s to frm, prefers left handed tracks, prefers tight tracks. Turf high 74 (began Spt) - 1st of 17 giving 7lb to Admirals Place (5 Oct Nottingham RF 4733). Inconsistent.
**Sir Mark Prescott [1-8] John Brown & Megan Dennis.*

EYELETS ECHO RR 42f 4339[6]
2 b c Inchinor 8.9f **(64)** - Kinkajoo (Precocious) 8.6f **(62)**
Form - 6
Record 1999 - 1st:0 2nd:0 3rd:0 Ran:1
1999 Turf 0-1: (7f) (g-s)
Currently moderate colt. **D Morris [0-1] Mrs G M Peel.*

FABILLION BHB 68f **RR 63f** 3535[3]
7 ch g Deploy 11.4f **(67)** - Kai (Kalamoun) 10.4f **(67)**
Form - 3
Record 1999 - 1st:0 2nd:0 3rd:1 Ran:1
Pre1999 - 1st:1 2nd:5 3rd:0 Ran:19
Win Prizemoney £4,305 *Total Prizemoney* £14,584
Wins 1996 Apr Nottin (GD) H 14.1f 61 70 <
1999 Turf 0-1: (16f) (g-f)
Average gelding. Consistent.
**D Nicholson [0-1] Bill Horton (from C A Smith [1-19] Jly 1998).*

FABLE (USA) RR 106f 3324a[18]
3 b g Hansel (USA) 12.6f **(78)** - Aragon (USA) 0**0**
Form - 242040
1999 Turf 0-6: (6f, 7f, 8f 3, 10f) (sft, gd 3, g-f 2)
Pattern-class gelding, effective 7 to 8f, acts on gd, has worn blinkers. Turf high 106 - 2nd of 5 giving 8lb to Polaire (29 May Naas 7f gd RF 1636a). Inconsistent. **N Meade in IRE [1-9] D P Sharkey.*

FABRICE BHB 47f **RR 39f** 5154[15]
4 b g Pursuit of Love 9.5f **(69)** - Parfum D'Automne (FR) (Sharpen Up) 8.3f **(67)**
Form - 050000
Record 1999 - 1st:0 2nd:0 3rd:0 Ran:6
Pre1999 - 1st:0 2nd:1 3rd:1 Ran:4
Win Prizemoney £0 *Total Prizemoney* £2,465
1999 Turf 0-6: (7f, 8f 2, 10f 3) (gd 4, g-f, frm)
Very moderate gelding. Turf high 54. Becoming disappointing.
**H Candy [0-10] Girsonfield Ltd.*

FACE THE CLASS (IRE) BHB 46f55a **RR 51f 55a** 4816[1]
3 ch f Up and At 'em - Siva (FR) (Bellypha) 9.8f **(73)**
Form - 65260073301
Record 1999 - 1st:1 2nd:1 3rd:2 Ran:11
Pre1999 - 1st:0 2nd:0 3rd:0 Ran:1
Win Prizemoney £2,122 *Total Prizemoney* £3,349
Wins * 1999 Oct Leices (G-S) S 10f 51 <
1999 Turf 1-8: (7f 2, 10f 1-6) (sft 2, g-s, gd 1-2, g-f 3) 1999 AW 0-3: (8f 2, 12f) (Fibr 3)
Scopey, average filly, likes tight tracks. Turf high 51. AW high 62.
**A Kelleway [1-12] Mike Perkins.*

FACILE TIGRE BHB 49f60a **RR 43f 60a** 5128[13]
4 gr g Efisio 7.7f **(69)** - Dancing Diana (Raga Navarro (ITY)) 8f **(64)**
Form - 05708005700200
Record 1999 - 1st:0 2nd:1 3rd:0 Ran:14
Pre1999 - 1st:2 2nd:2 3rd:0 Ran:21
Win Prizemoney £4,650 *Total Prizemoney* £8,301
Wins * 1998 Nov Bright (SFT) H 6f 63 68
* 1998 Jun Bright (FRM) H 5.3f 67 74 <
1999 Turf 0-12: (5f 6, 6f 6) (sft 2, g-s 2, gd 4, g-f, frm 2, hrd) 1999 AW 0-2: (5f, 6f) (Equi 2)
Workmanlike, moderate gelding, effective 5 to 6f, acts on g-s to g-f, likes left handed tracks, likes tight tracks. Turf high 57. AW high 49. **S Dow [2-35] D G Churston.*

FACSIMILE BHB 57f55a **RR 26f 55a** 2753[7]
4 b f Superlative 8.8f **(57)** - Just Julia (Natroun (FR))
Form - 77
Record 1999 - 1st:0 2nd:0 3rd:0 Ran:1
Pre1999 - 1st:0 2nd:2 3rd:1 Ran:6
Win Prizemoney £0 *Total Prizemoney* £1,839
1999 Turf 0-1: (6f) (hrd)
Light-framed, moderate filly, effective 7 to 8f, acts on g-f to frm.
**John Berry [0-6] H R Moszkowicz (from Capt J Wilson [0-1] Jly 1997).*

FADHEL (USA) BHB 62f **RR 59f** 5197[20]
3 b g Zilzal (USA) 8.5f **(79)** - Nice Life (USA) (Sportin' Life (USA)) 11.1f **(75)**
Form - 72550
Record 1999 - 1st:0 2nd:1 3rd:0 Ran:5
Pre1999 - 1st:0 2nd:0 3rd:0 Ran:1
Win Prizemoney £0 *Total Prizemoney* £787
1999 Turf 0-5: (7f, 8f, 9f 2, 10f) (gd 2, g-f 2, frm)
Fair gelding, effective 9f, acts on gd, has worn blinkers. Turf high 80 - 2nd of 6 to Gabby Hayes (13 Jun Gowran Park 9f gd RF 2036a).
**D HaydnJones [0-2] Hugh O'Donnell (from D K Weld in IRE [0-4] Jly 1999).*

FA-EQ (IRE) BHB 111f **RR 112f** 3776[1]
4 ch c Indian Ridge 7.6f **(74)** - Searching Star (Rainbow Quest (USA)) 10.4f **(75)**
Form - 1401
Record 1999 - 1st:2 2nd:0 3rd:0 Ran:4

Pre1999 - 1st:1 2nd:2 3rd:0 Ran:4
Win Prizemoney £30,556 *Total Prizemoney* £76,294
Wins * **1999** Aug York (GD) L 7f 112 <
* **1999** May Kempto (G-F) 7f 103+
* 1998 May Newmar (GD) 8f 96+
1999 Turf 2-4: (6f, 7f 2-2, 8f) (gd 1-1, g-f, frm 1-2)
Lengthy, Group-class colt, effective 7 to 8f, best at 8f, acted on gd to frm, best on gd. Turf high 112 - 1st of 11 getting 8lb from Tumbleweed Ridge (19 Aug York RF 3775). He failed to stay a mile at Royal Ascot and found six furlongs to short in the July Cup. That said, he won a competitive Listed race at York's Ebor Meeting and it was a great shame that he met with a fatal accident on the gallops. (DEAD) **S bin Suroor [3-8] Godolphin.*

FAFESTA (IRE) RR 67f 3196[9]
3 b f Rainbow Quest (USA) 11.2f **(81)** - Dancing Berry (Sadler's Wells (USA)) 10f **(76)**
Form - 40
Record 1999 - 1st:0 2nd:0 3rd:0 Ran:2
Pre1999 - 1st:0 2nd:0 3rd:0 Ran:1
Win Prizemoney £0 *Total Prizemoney* £273
1999 Turf 0-2: (10f, 12f) (frm 2)
Currently average filly. Turf high 67 (began Jly).
**L M Cumani [0-3] Scuderia Rencati Srl.*

FAGIN BHB 75f **RR 81f** 4996[6]
2 b c Formidable (USA) 7.8f **(60)** - Rich Pickings (Dominion) 8.5f **(63)**
Form - 636
Record 1999 - 1st:0 2nd:0 3rd:1 Ran:3
Win Prizemoney £0 *Total Prizemoney* £555
1999 Turf 0-3: (6f, 7f, 8f) (g-s, gd, frm)
Currently decent colt. Turf high 81 (began Aug).
**B J Meehan [0-3] P Heath.*

FAHAN (IRE) BHB 72f **RR 67f** 4950[13]
2 b f Sri Pekan (USA) - Damemill (IRE) (Danehill (USA)) 10f **(72)**
Form - 0430
Record 1999 - 1st:0 2nd:0 3rd:1 Ran:4
Win Prizemoney £0 *Total Prizemoney* £830
1999 Turf 0-4: (6f 2, 7f, 8f) (gd, g-f 3)
Average filly. Turf high 67 (began Aug). **B W Hills [0-4] John Grant.*

FAHRIS (IRE) BHB 117f **RR 119f** 5230a[10]
5 ch h Generous (IRE) 11.5f **(82)** - Janbiya (IRE) (Kris) 9.5f **(73)**
Form - 60
1999 Turf 0-2: (12f 2) (g-f, frm)
High-class colt. Turf high 112.
**K McLaughlin in UAE [0-1] (from S bin Suroor in UAE [0-1] Mar 1999).*

FAHS (USA) BHB 73f78a **RR 72f 78a** 4954[9]
7 b br g Riverman (USA) 9.7f **(78)** - Tanwi (Vision (USA)) 9f **(64)**
Form - 17534122360
Record 1999 - 1st:1 2nd:2 3rd:2 Ran:10
Pre1999 - 1st:3 2nd:3 3rd:10 Ran:37
Win Prizemoney £12,203 *Total Prizemoney* £45,979
Wins * **1999** Jun Yarmou (G-F) H 10.1f 68 71
1998 *Nov Lingfi (STD) H 12f 73 75*
1997 Oct Yarmou (GD) H 10.1f 75 79
1997 May Sandow (G-F) H 10f 70 80 <
1999 Turf 1-10: (10f 1-8, 12f 2) (g-s 2, gd, g-f 1-3, frm 4)
Above-average gelding, effective 10 to 14f, acts on gd to frm - acts on Equi, best on gd, likes right handed tracks, and does well at Sandown. Turf high 76 - 2nd of 9 getting 2lb from Ipledgeallegiance (22 Jly Sandown 10f frm RF 3030). Consistent.
**N Hamilton [1-10] City Industrial Supplies Ltd (from G Lewis [1-15] Nov 1998).*

FAILED TO HIT BHB 37f68a **RR 40f 68a** 4704[3]
6 b g Warrshan (USA) 9.7f **(59)** - Missed Again (High Top) 10.2f **(67)**
Form - 541310526703
Record 1999 - 1st:1 2nd:1 3rd:1 Ran:8
Pre1999 - 1st:7 2nd:3 3rd:6 Ran:41
Win Prizemoney £22,523 *Total Prizemoney* £29,208
Wins * **1999** *Jan Wolver (STD) H 12f 66 71* <
* 1998 *Dec Wolver (STD) H 9.4f 62 65*
* 1998 *Oct Lingfi (STD) 12f 60*
* 1998 *Mar Wolver (STD) H 9.4f 60 66*
* 1998 *Feb Lingfi (SLW) 10f 62*
* 1998 *Feb Wolver (STD) C 8.5f 65+*
* 1998 *Feb Lingfi (STD) H 8f 43 51*
1996 Aug Folkes (G-F) 6f 67
1999 Turf 0-1: (12f) (gd) 1999 AW 1-7: (10f, 12f 1-6) (Equi, Fibr 1-6)
Average gelding, effective 8 to 12f, best at 12f, - acts on AW, best on Fibr, mostly wears blinkers (very effectively), favours left handed tracks, and likes Wolverhampton. AW high 72 - 2nd of 8 giving 7lb to Lysandros (10 Feb Wolverhampton 12f Fibr RF 0265) - also 1st of 6 giving 4lb to Sioux (6 Jan Wolverhampton RF 0040).
**N P Littmoden [7-45] M C S D Racing (from Sir Mark Prescott [1-5] Oct 1996).*

FAIR CESTRIAN (IRE) BHB 39f **RR 39f** 4985[7]
3 b g Petardia 8.2f **(58)** - Fair Chance (Young Emperor) 10.1f **(63)**
Form - 00707
Record 1999 - 1st:0 2nd:0 3rd:0 Ran:5
Pre1999 - 1st:0 2nd:0 3rd:0 Ran:4
1999 Turf 0-5: (7f, 8f, 10f, 11f, 17f) (gd, g-f 3, frm)
Scopey, very moderate gelding, has worn blinkers. Turf high 49. Inconsistent.
**A Bailey [0-7] J R & J Littler (from J Berry [0-4] Spt 1998).*

FAIR FLIGHT BHB 90f **RR 94f** 4028[8]
3 b c Green Desert (USA) 7.8f **(78)** - Barari (USA) (Blushing Groom (FR)) 10.3f **(76)**
Form - 07310308
Record 1999 - 1st:1 2nd:0 3rd:2 Ran:8
Pre1999 - 1st:2 2nd:1 3rd:0 Ran:7
Win Prizemoney £25,297 *Total Prizemoney* £37,234
Wins * **1999** Jun Goodwo (G-S) 8f 95 <
* 1998 Oct Newmar (GD) H 8f 92 94
* 1998 Aug Goodwo (GD) H 7f 80
1999 Turf 1-8: (8f 1-7, 9f) (g-s 1-1, gd, g-f 4, frm 2)
Scopey, useful colt, effective 8f, acts on g-s to hrd, likes right handed tracks, excels at Goodwood. Turf high 95 - 1st of 3 getting 13lb from Silk St John (2 Jun Goodwood RF 1676). He was given little respite by the Handicapper and found life tough. Worth trying beyond a mile, he has shown his best form on a sound surface.
**E A L Dunlop [3-15] Khalifa Sultan.*

FAIR LADY RR 79f 5020[6]
2 b f Machiavellian (USA) 9.8f **(83)** - Just Cause (Law Society (USA)) 9.9f **(70)**
Form - 026
Record 1999 - 1st:0 2nd:1 3rd:0 Ran:3
Win Prizemoney £0 *Total Prizemoney* £1,580
1999 Turf 0-3: (7f 2, 8f) (g-s, gd, frm)
Currently above-average filly. Turf high 79 (began Aug). Came up against a useful sort on her second start at Salisbury but failed to handle softish ground next time.
**B W Hills [0-3] Maktoum Al Maktoum.*

FAIRLEE MIXA (FR) RR 104f 1358a[6]
3 f Linamix (FR) 8.2f **(64)**
Form - 26
1999 Turf 0-2: (7f, 8f) (gd 2)
Currently very useful filly. Turf high 104. **A Fabre in FR [0-3].*

FAIRLY SURE (IRE) BHB 33f26a **RR 35f 26a** 4646[17]
6 b m Red Sunset 9f **(57)** - Mirabiliary (USA) (Crow (FR)) 7.4f **(75)**
Form - 50077160
Record 1999 - 1st:1 2nd:0 3rd:0 Ran:8
Pre1999 - 1st:1 2nd:0 3rd:0 Ran:20
Win Prizemoney £5,013 *Total Prizemoney* £5,211
Wins * **1999** Jly Bath (FRM) H 10.2f 26 35
* 1996 Aug Lingfi (G-F) H 7.6f 46 39 <
1999 Turf 1-4: (10f 1-4) (g-s, g-f, frm 1-2) 1999 AW 0-4: (7f, 8f 2, 10f) (Equi 4)
Very moderate mare, effective 10f, acts on frm. Turf high 35 - 1st of 13 getting 30lb from Twin Time (15 Jly Bath RF 2841). AW high 32.
**N E Berry [2-28] Norman Berry.*

FAIRTOTO BHB 45f **RR 58f** 4863[3]
3 b g Mtoto 11.5f **(71)** - Fairy Feet (Sadler's Wells (USA)) 10f **(76)**
Form - 803
Record 1999 - 1st:0 2nd:0 3rd:1 Ran:3

Pre1999 - 1st:0 2nd:0 3rd:0 Ran:3
Win Prizemoney £0 *Total Prizemoney* £314
1999 Turf 0-1: (10f) (g-s) 1999 AW 0-2: (12f, 15f) (Fibr 2)
Fair gelding. AW high 40 (began Spt).
**D J Wintle [0-3] Mrs Joan Egan (from Mrs J R Ramsden [0-3] Spt 1998).*

FAIR VERONA (USA) RR 28f 4023[8]

3 b f Alleged (USA) 11.8f **(81)** - Just Juliet (USA) (What A Pleasure (USA)) 8.4f **(61)**
Form - 08
Record 1999 - 1st:0 2nd:0 3rd:0 Ran:2
1999 Turf 0-2: (8f 2) (g-f 2)
Leggy, currently little account filly. Turf high 28.
**B W Hills [0-2] D J Deer.*

FAIR WARNING (GER) BHB 92f RR 91f 4876[2]

3 b c Warning 8.1f **(77)** - Fairy Bluebird (Be My Guest (USA)) 9.3f **(67)**
Form - 3313007412
Record 1999 - 1st:2 2nd:1 3rd:3 Ran:10
Pre1999 - 1st:0 2nd:0 3rd:1 Ran:1
Win Prizemoney £10,966 *Total Prizemoney* £18,641
Wins * **1999** Oct York (G-S) 11.9f 91
* **1999** Jun Yarmou (G-F) 8f 95 <
1999 Turf 2-10: (8f 1-6, 9f, 10f, 12f 1-2) (gd 2-5, g-f 2, frm 3)
Workmanlike, useful colt, effective 8 to 12f, best at 12f, acts on gd. Turf high 95 - 1st of 11 giving 5lb to Countess Parker (3 Jun Yarmouth RF 1706) - also 1st of 8 giving 2lb to Dark Trojan (7 Oct York RF 4759). Consistent. He improved when stepped up to middle-distances in the autumn, and was given a moderate ride when finishing a creditable second at Newmarket on his final start. Open to improvement, he should win a decent prize in 2000.
**J W Hills [2-11] Wauchope,Sir Simon D Cottam.*

FAIRY CONTESSA (IRE) BHB 58f55a RR 60f 55a 5147[6]

3 b f Fairy King (USA) 7.7f **(75)** - More Fizz (Morston (FR)) 9.4f **(55)**
Form - 72436
Record 1999 - 1st:0 2nd:1 3rd:1 Ran:5
Win Prizemoney £0 *Total Prizemoney* £2,165
1999 Turf 0-4: (6f 2, 7f 2) (gd, frm 2, hrd) 1999 AW 0-1: (8f) (Fibr)
Lengthy, average filly. Turf high 60 - 2nd of 6 getting 5lb from Molyneux (25 Jun Lingfield 6f frm RF 2294).
**N P Littmoden [0-5] DGH Partnership.*

FAIRY FLAME RR 68f 1489[6]

3 b f Fairy King (USA) 7.7f **(75)** - Favoridge (USA) (Riva Ridge (USA)) 8.2f **(68)**
Form - 46
Record 1999 - 1st:0 2nd:0 3rd:0 Ran:2
Win Prizemoney £0 *Total Prizemoney* £277
1999 Turf 0-2: (6f, 7f) (g-f, frm)
Leggy, average filly. Turf high 68 (1st run) - 4th of 16 to Miss Shema (16 May Kempton 7f frm RF 1259). (DEAD)
**Sir Michael Stoute [0-2] Sheikh Mohammed.*

FAIRY GEM (IRE) BHB 100f RR 91f 4680[10]

2 b f Fairy King (USA) 7.7f **(75)** - Cajo (IRE) (Tirol)
Form - 1206460
Record 1999 - 1st:1 2nd:1 3rd:0 Ran:7
Win Prizemoney £5,157 *Total Prizemoney* £10,243
Wins * **1999** May Salisb (G-F) 5f 83 <
1999 Turf 1-7: (5f 1-3, 6f, 7f 3) (gd 2, g-f 3, frm 1-2)
Useful filly, effective 5f, acts on frm. Turf high 91 - also 1st of 10 getting 3lb from Cotton House (2 May Salisbury RF 0984). By no means disgraced against some high-class rivals, she is worth another try over seven furlongs. **R Hannon [1-7] Jubert Family.*

FAIRY GODMOTHER RR 104+f 1884[1]

3 b f Fairy King (USA) 7.7f **(75)** - Highbrow (Shirley Heights) 10.3f **(74)**
Form - 11
Record 1999 - 1st:2 2nd:0 3rd:0 Ran:2
Win Prizemoney £18,749 *Total Prizemoney* £18,749
Wins * **1999** Jun Newbur (GD) L 10f 104+ <
* **1999** May Newbur (SFT) 10f 97
1999 Turf 2-2: (10f 2-2) (gd 2-2)
Scopey, currently very useful filly. Turf high 104 - 1st of 6 from Ras Shaikh (10 Jun Newbury RF 1884) - also 1st of 14 getting 5lb from Flaming Quest (15 May Newbury RF 1237). From a late-maturing family, she was unbeaten in two starts at Newbury, running out the smooth winner of a Listed event in June. Open to plenty of improvement, she should stay a mile and a half and is an interesting prospect for next season. **R Charlton [2-2] The Queen.*

FAIRY PRINCE (IRE) BHB 61f57a RR 63f 57a 4924[12]

6 b g Fairy King (USA) 7.7f **(75)** - Danger Ahead (Mill Reef (USA)) 10.5f **(78)**
Form - 8087552226200
Record 1999 - 1st:0 2nd:4 3rd:0 Ran:13
Pre1999 - 1st:5 2nd:7 3rd:2 Ran:36
Win Prizemoney £14,337 *Total Prizemoney* £30,570
Wins * 1998 Jly Beverl (GD) 5f 67
* 1997 Jly Doncas (GD) 6f 72 <
* 1997 Jly Nottin (G-F) 5.1f 65
* 1997 Jly Pontef (G-F) 6f 67
* 1996 Jun Carlis (FRM) H 5.9f 54 54
1999 Turf 0-12: (6f 5, 7f 6, 8f) (gd 2, g-f, frm 9) 1999 AW 0-1: (6f) (Fibr)
Average gelding, effective 5 to 6f, best at 6f, acts on gd to frm, best on frm, has worn blinkers, excels at Beverley. Turf high 63 - 2nd of 8 to Bandbox (11 Aug Leicester 6f g-f RF 3551).
**Mrs A L M King [5-49] Aiden Murphy.*

Fairy Queen, a dual Group Two winner, stayed better than her breeding suggested

FAIRY QUEEN (IRE) RR 115f 4769a[1]

3 b f Fairy King (USA) 7.7f **(75)** - Dedicated Lady (IRE) (Pennine Walk) 8.5f **(61)**
Form - 01141
Record 1999 - 1st:3 2nd:0 3rd:0 Ran:5
Pre1999 - 1st:2 2nd:0 3rd:0 Ran:2
Win Prizemoney £139,893 *Total Prizemoney* £148,504
Wins * **1999** Oct Longch (HVY) G2 12.5f 115 <
* **1999** Jun Ascot (G-F) G2 12f 107
* **1999** Jun Epsom (G-S) L 8.5f 104
1998 Jly Sandow (G-F) L 7.1f 101
1998 Jun Doncas (GD) 7f 80+
1999 Turf 3-5: (8f, 9f 1-1, 12f 1-2, 13f 1-1) (hvy 1-1, gd 1-2, g-f 1-1, frm)
Leggy, high-class filly, effective 12 to 13f, acts on hvy to g-f. Turf high 115 - 1st of 11 giving 7lb to Daring Miss (2 Oct Longchamp RF 4769a) - also 1st of 12 from Samoa (17 Jun Ascot RF 2069). A lean, lightly-made filly, she finished in midfield in the 1000 Guineas on her return before taking a Listed event over an extended mile at the Epsom Derby meeting. Stepped up to 12 furlongs, she showed that she had the necessary stamina when battling home to land the Ribblesdale at Royal Ascot and was in good form in the autumn, although she was a lucky winner of Longchamp's Prix de Royallieu after the leader was eased prematurely.
**S bin Suroor [3-5] Godolphin (from D R Loder [2-2] Jly 1998).*

FAIRYTIME BHB 40f RR 27f 4276[9]

3 b f Efisio 7.7f **(69)** - Fairy Flax (IRE) (Dancing Brave (USA)) 8.4f **(76)**
Form - 80000

Record 1999 - 1st:0 2nd:0 3rd:0 Ran:5
Pre1999 - 1st:0 2nd:0 3rd:1 Ran:1
Win Prizemoney £0 *Total Prizemoney* £568
1999 Turf 0-5: (5f 2, 6f, 7f 2) (g-s, gd 3, g-f)
Little account filly. Turf high 27. **J R Arnold [0-6] A H Robinson.*

FAITH AGAIN (IRE) BHB 45f RR 47f 3748[4]
3 b f Namaqualand (USA) - Intricacy (Formidable (USA)) 9.2f **(63)**
Form - 002534
Record 1999 - 1st:0 2nd:1 3rd:1 Ran:6
Pre1999 - 1st:0 2nd:0 3rd:0 Ran:4
Win Prizemoney £0 *Total Prizemoney* £1,612
1999 Turf 0-6: (7f, 8f 2, 9f, 10f 2) (gd, g-f, frm 4)
Moderate filly, effective 8f, acts on g-f, has worn blinkers (very effectively). Turf high 52. Consistent.
**C F Wall [0-10] Prudence Lady Salt.*

FAIT LE JOJO (FR) BHB 80a RR 80a 4603[3]
2 b c Pistolet Bleu (IRE) - Pretty Davis (USA) (Trempolino (USA)) 12f **(71)**
Form - 313
Record 1999 - 1st:1 2nd:0 3rd:2 Ran:3
Win Prizemoney £3,590 *Total Prizemoney* £4,288
Wins * 1999 *Spt Wolver (STD) 8.5f 79+* <
1999 AW 1-3: (8f 1-3) (Fibr 1-3)
Currently above-average colt. AW high 79 (began Spt) - 1st of 8 from Tadreej (18 Spt Wolverhampton RF 4411).
**S P C Woods [1-3] G A Roberts.*

FALCON FLIGHT (FR) RR 104f 1904a[8]
3 b c Persian Bold 10f **(69)** - Flying Circus (FR) (Gay Mecene (USA)) 8.6f **(69)**
Form - 118
1999 Turf 2-3: (10f 1-1, 11f 1-1, 12f) (sft 1-1, gd 1-2)
Currently very useful colt. Turf high 104 - 1st of 5 from State Shinto (9 May Chantilly RF 1204a). **P Bary in FR [2-3] J-L Bouchard.*

FALCONIDAE RR 67f 5195[4]
2 ch c Polar Falcon (USA) 9f **(74)** - Barbary Court (Grundy) 10.3f **(65)**
Form - 64
Record 1999 - 1st:0 2nd:0 3rd:0 Ran:2
Win Prizemoney £0 *Total Prizemoney* £220
1999 Turf 0-2: (6f 2) (sft, gd)
Currently average colt. Turf high 67 (began Oct).
**P J Makin [0-2] A W Schiff.*

FALCON PARTNER (USA) RR 30f 2573[9]
2 ch c Silver Hawk (USA) 11.2f **(85)** - L'Esquimau (USA) (Arctic Tern (USA)) 8.9f **(69)**
Form - 0
Record 1999 - 1st:0 2nd:0 3rd:0 Ran:1
1999 Turf 0-1: (7f) (frm)
Currently very moderate colt.
**H R A Cecil [0-1] The Thoroughbred Corporation.*

FALCON SPIRIT BHB 62f RR 66f 4882[10]
3 b g Polar Falcon (USA) 9f **(74)** - Amina (Brigadier Gerard) 9.3f **(58)**
Form - 83255320
Record 1999 - 1st:0 2nd:2 3rd:2 Ran:8
Win Prizemoney £0 *Total Prizemoney* £2,679
1999 Turf 0-6: (7f, 8f, 9f, 10f 2, 11f) (gd, g-f 3, frm 2) 1999 AW 0-2: (8f, 12f) (Equi, Fibr)
Scopey, average gelding, effective 8 to 12f, acts on g-f - acts on AW, often wears blinkers (extremely effectively). Turf high 66 (began Jly). AW high 61 (1st run) (began Spt) - 3rd of 13 to Mr Perry (18 Spt Wolverhampton 8f Fibr RF 4410). Consistent.
**W J Haggas [0-8] C H Bothway.*

FALKENBERG (FR) BHB 35f29a RR 24f 29a 356[7]
4 ch g Polish Precedent (USA) 9f **(73)** - Mithi Al Gamar (USA) **(60f)** (Blushing Groom (FR)) 10.3f **(76)**
Form - 507847
Record 1999 - 1st:0 2nd:0 3rd:0 Ran:3
Pre1999 - 1st:0 2nd:0 3rd:3 Ran:26
Win Prizemoney £0 *Total Prizemoney* £1,779
1999 AW 0-3: (7f 2, 12f) (Equi, Fibr 2)
Little account gelding, has worn blinkers. AW high 22.
**B A Pearce [0-23] J Salter (from M Johnston [0-8] Jan 1998).*

FALLACHAN (USA) BHB 84f RR 83f 4569[20]
3 ch g Diesis 9f **(80)** - Afaff (USA) (Nijinsky (CAN)) 10.3f **(77)**
Form - 411250220
Record 1999 - 1st:2 2nd:3 3rd:0 Ran:8
Pre1999 - 1st:0 2nd:0 3rd:0 Ran:3
Win Prizemoney £6,067 *Total Prizemoney* £15,160
Wins * 1999 Apr Nottin (G-S) H 8.2f 63 78+ <
*** 1999** Apr Mussel (GD) H 8f 63 68+
1999 Turf 2-8: (7f 2, 8f 2-6) (sft, gd 1-1, g-f 1-2, frm 4)
Lengthy, decent gelding, effective 7 to 8f, best at 7f, acts on gd to frm, best on frm. Turf high 83 - 2nd of 10 getting 2lb from Nice One Clare (4 Aug Kempton 7f frm RF 3355) - also 1st of 17 giving 4lb to It's Our Secret (5 Apr Nottingham RF 0592).
**M A Jarvis [2-11] & Mrs Raymond Anderson Green.*

FALLS O'MONESS (IRE) BHB 45f41a RR 49f 41a 4987[16]
5 b m River Falls 8.2f **(56)** - Sevens Are Wild (Petorius) 7.3f **(61)**
Form - 387644010043050
Record 1999 - 1st:1 2nd:0 3rd:2 Ran:15
Pre1999 - 1st:3 2nd:3 3rd:6 Ran:42
Win Prizemoney £12,100 *Total Prizemoney* £23,056
Wins * 1999 Aug Thirsk (SFT) SH 8f 46 50
* 1998 Spt Hamilt (SFT) H 8.3f 48 50
* 1998 Aug Thirsk (G-F) SH 8f 40 48
1997 Spt Ayr (G-S) C 9f 65 <
1999 Turf 1-15: (8f 1-11, 9f 3, 11f) (g-s, gd 1-8, g-f 2, frm 3, hrd)
Moderate filly, effective 8 to 9f, best at 8f, acts on g-s to frm, has worn blinkers, likes left handed tracks, favours tight tracks. Turf high 50 - 1st of 16 getting 4lb from Fancy A Fortune (9 Aug Thirsk RF 3479).
**E J Alston [3-25] Piquet Opera House Partnership (from K R Burke [1-32] Jun 1998).*

FAL 'N' ME BHB 30f RR 27f 4705[13]
2 b f Cyrano de Bergerac 7.3f **(58)** - Azola (IRE) (Alzao (USA)) 7.1f **(68)**
Form - 80
Record 1999 - 1st:0 2nd:0 3rd:0 Ran:2
1999 Turf 0-1: (5f) (g-f) 1999 AW 0-1: (5f) (Fibr)
Currently little account filly. **J L Eyre [0-2] J Laughton.*

FALSE DAWN BHB 29f RR 25f 2536[13]
4 b f Reprimand 8.2f **(63)** - Mardessa (Ardross) 10.6f **(68)**
Form - 000
Record 1999 - 1st:0 2nd:0 3rd:0 Ran:3
Pre1999 - 1st:0 2nd:0 3rd:0 Ran:3
1999 Turf 0-3: (8f, 12f, 14f) (g-f 2, frm)
Tall, little account filly. Turf high 16. **M Mullineaux [0-6] F H Lee.*

FAME AT LAST (USA) RR 82+f 5021[1]
2 b f Quest for Fame 12.8f **(75)** - Ranales (USA) (Majestic Light (USA)) 10.6f **(75)**
Form - 1
Record 1999 - 1st:1 2nd:0 3rd:0 Ran:1
Win Prizemoney £3,988 *Total Prizemoney* £3,988
Wins * 1999 Oct Doncas (G-S) 7f 82+ <
1999 Turf 1-1: (7f 1-1) (gd 1-1)
Currently decent filly. (1st run) - 1st of 22 getting 5lb from All The Gears (22 Oct Doncaster RF 5021). **B W Hills [1-1] K Abdulla.*

FAMILY MAN BHB 100f RR 106f 5039[2]
6 ch g Indian Ridge 7.6f **(74)** - Auntie Gladys (Great Nephew) 9.9f **(64)**
Form - 0424721122
Record 1999 - 1st:2 2nd:4 3rd:0 Ran:10
Pre1999 - 1st:3 2nd:2 3rd:1 Ran:20
Win Prizemoney £38,004 *Total Prizemoney* £59,952
Wins * 1999 Oct Newmar (G-S) H 7f 90 96 <
*** 1999** Aug Thirsk (G-F) 8f 88
* 1998 Oct Newmar () H 7f 76 81
* 1998 Spt Lingfi (G-S) H 7f 69 77
* 1997 May Newmar (G-F) H 8f 72 78+
1999 Turf 2-10: (6f, 7f 1-7, 8f 1-2) (g-s, gd 1-3, g-f 4, frm, hrd 1-1)
Pattern-class gelding, effective 7f, acts on g-s to gd, has worn blinkers. Turf high 106 - 2nd of 7 giving 7lb to Granny's Pet (23 Oct Doncaster 7f g-s RF 5039). Won twice in '98, including when beating a huge field in a back-end Newmarket handicap, and ran well to finish fourth in the Victoria Cup on his second start of this sea-

son. He has run some more good races since in decent handicap company, and added a nice Newmarket handicap to his win at Thirsk in August. Suited by seven furlongs, he does not want the ground too fast. Fetched 44,000 gns at Nemarket sales in October.
**J R Fanshawe [5-33] Family Man Partnership.*

FAMILY TREE (IRE) BHB 38f38a **RR 17f 38a** 1523[20]
3 ch f Soviet Lad (USA) 9.4f **(63)** - The Woman in Red (Red Regent) 7.2f **(44)**
Form - 000000000
Record 1999 - 1st:0 2nd:0 3rd:0 Ran:7
Pre1999 - 1st:1 2nd:0 3rd:1 Ran:9
Win Prizemoney £3,210 *Total Prizemoney* £3,863
Wins 1998 Spt Ayr (g-s) S 8f 62 <
1999 Turf 0-3: (6f, 8f 2) (gd 2, hrd) 1999 AW 0-4: (7f, 8f 2, 10f) (Equi 2, Fibr 2)
Scopey, poor filly, effective 8f, acts on gd, has worn blinkers, likes tight tracks. Turf high 17. AW high 16.
**D W Chapman [0-10] Michael Hill (from B W Hills [1-6] Spt 1998).*

FAMOUS (FR) BHB 48f42a **RR 48f 42a** 4999[7]
6 b g Tropular - Famous Horse (FR) (Labus (FR)) 12.8f **(52)**
Form - 20882766400000085128107
Record 1999 - 1st:2 2nd:2 3rd:0 Ran:18
Pre1999 - 1st:0 2nd:2 3rd:2 Ran:18
Win Prizemoney £5,592 *Total Prizemoney* £9,391
Wins * 1999 Oct Sandow (SFT) H 10f 43 48 <
*** 1999** Aug Bright (G-S) H 10f 35 39
1999 Turf 2-14: (8f 4, 9f, 10f 2-4, 12f 4, 14f) (sft, g-s 1-2, gd 1-5, g-f, frm 5) 1999 AW 0-4: (8f 3, 10f) (Equi 4)
Fair gelding, effective 8 to 10f, best at 10f, acts on g-s to gd - acts on Equi, has worn blinkers, favours tight tracks. Turf high 48 - 1st of 12 getting 8lb from Smarter Charter (2 Oct Sandown RF 4700). AW high 52 - 2nd of 10 to Teofilio (9 Feb Lingfield 8f Equi RF 0255).
**J J Bridger [2-35] Exors of the late M R Pascall (from G L Moore [0-1] May 1998).*

FANADIYR (IRE) BHB 35f **RR 8f** 2361[7]
7 b g Kahyasi 12.9f **(74)** - Fair Fight (Fine Blade (USA)) 14.8f **(39)**
Form - 1077
Record 1999 - 1st:1 2nd:0 3rd:0 Ran:4
Pre1999 - 1st:0 2nd:0 3rd:0 Ran:6
Win Prizemoney £2,262 *Total Prizemoney* £2,959
Wins * 1999 Apr Mussel (G-F) C 16f 44 <
1999 Turf 1-4: (12f, 16f 1-3) (gd, g-f 1-3)
Very poor gelding. Turf high 44 (1st run) - 1st of 6 getting 4lb from Slasher Jack (30 Apr Musselburgh RF 0938). Becoming disappointing.
**J S Goldie [1-14] D Callaghan (from W Storey [0-6] Jun 1996).*

FANCY A FORTUNE (IRE) BHB 48f54a **RR 42f 54a** 4829[13]
5 b g Fools Holme (USA) 10.3f **(64)** - Fancy's Girl (FR) (Nadjar (FR)) 7.2f **(49)**
Form - 620562752620
Record 1999 - 1st:0 2nd:4 3rd:0 Ran:12
Pre1999 - 1st:3 2nd:3 3rd:6 Ran:31
Win Prizemoney £7,907 *Total Prizemoney* £17,976
Wins * 1998 Jly Beverl (GD) SH 7.5f 52 60
* 1998 May Thirsk (GD) S 7f 56
* 1997 Aug Thirsk (GD) H 7f 60 64 <
1999 Turf 0-12: (7f 3, 8f 8, 9f) (sft, gd 3, g-f 3, frm 3, hrd 2)
Moderate gelding, effective 7 to 8f, best at 7f, acts on gd to g-f, best on gd, often wears blinkers. Turf high 49. Consistent.
**D Nicholls [3-34] G Tuer (from J Pearce [0-9] Oct 1996).*

FANCY DESIGN (IRE) BHB 15f39a **RR 15f 39a** 3851[6]
6 b m Cyrano de Bergerac 7.3f **(58)** - Crimson Robes (Artaius (USA)) 9f **(69)**
Form - 000006
Record 1999 - 1st:0 2nd:0 3rd:0 Ran:6
Pre1999 - 1st:0 2nd:4 3rd:2 Ran:44
Win Prizemoney £0 *Total Prizemoney* £5,008
1999 Turf 0-6: (8f 2, 10f 3, 12f) (g-f 2, frm 4)
Moderate mare, effective 8f, acts on g-f to frm - acts on Equi, has worn blinkers, likes right handed tracks. Turf high 15.
**J M Bradley [0-6] Mrs Kay Blandford (from P Mitchell [0-44] Aug 1998).*

FANCY MY CHANCE BHB 74f **RR 59f** 2619[5]
3 b c Rainbow Quest (USA) 11.2f **(81)** - Yazeanhaa (USA) (Zilzal (USA))
Form - 3075
Record 1999 - 1st:0 2nd:0 3rd:1 Ran:4
Pre1999 - 1st:1 2nd:0 3rd:0 Ran:5
Win Prizemoney £3,183 *Total Prizemoney* £4,055
Wins * 1998 Oct Yarmou (G-S) H 8f 76 84 <
1999 Turf 0-4: (10f 3, 12f) (gd, g-f, frm, hrd)
Neat, fair colt, effective 8 to 10f, acts on gd, has worn blinkers. Turf high 84 (1st run) - 3rd of 17 giving 9lb to Kingston Venture (25 Mar Doncaster 10f gd RF 0465). Consistent.
**E A L Dunlop [1-9] Maktoum Al Maktoum.*

FANDANGO DREAM (IRE) BHB 43f **RR 40f** 5007[9]
3 ch c Magical Wonder (USA) 7.2f **(60)** - Fandikos (IRE) (Taufan (USA)) 7f **(57)**
Form - 874607400000
Record 1999 - 1st:0 2nd:0 3rd:0 Ran:12
Pre1999 - 1st:0 2nd:0 3rd:0 Ran:1
Win Prizemoney £0 *Total Prizemoney* £478
1999 Turf 0-12: (8f 4, 9f, 10f 7) (g-s 2, gd 5, g-f 3, frm 2)
Neat, moderate colt, effective 8f, acts on gd, has worn blinkers. Turf high 73 - 4th of 8 getting 12lb from Yeast (31 May Chepstow 8f gd RF 1592). **M D I Usher [0-13] Midweek Racing.*

FANETTA (IRE) BHB 31f47a **RR 38f 47a** 3138[7]
3 b f Taufan (USA) 8.3f **(65)** - Bold Fille (IRE) (Bold Arrangement)
Form - 600607
Record 1999 - 1st:0 2nd:0 3rd:0 Ran:5
Pre1999 - 1st:0 2nd:0 3rd:0 Ran:5
1999 Turf 0-4: (10f, 11f 2, 12f) (gd, g-f 3) 1999 AW 0-1: (10f) (Equi)
Workmanlike, moderate filly. Turf high 38. Consistent.
**M H Tompkins [0-10] The Hon Mrs Tritton.*

FANFARE RR 76f 5216[15]
2 b f Deploy 11.4f **(67)** - Tashinsky (USA) (Nijinsky (CAN)) 10.3f **(77)**
Form - 50
Record 1999 - 1st:0 2nd:0 3rd:0 Ran:2
1999 Turf 0-2: (8f 2) (g-s, gd)
Currently above-average filly. Turf high 76 (began Oct).
**G A Butler [0-2] T D Holland-Martin.*

FANTASTIC BELLE (IRE) BHB 77f **RR 80f** 4352[12]
3 b f Night Shift (USA) 8.1f **(73)** - Gay Fantastic (Ela-Mana-Mou) 10.1f **(70)**
Form - 5220210
Record 1999 - 1st:1 2nd:3 3rd:0 Ran:7
Pre1999 - 1st:0 2nd:0 3rd:0 Ran:2
Win Prizemoney £3,746 *Total Prizemoney* £7,498
Wins * 1999 Jly Salisb (FRM) 6f 77 <
1999 Turf 1-7: (6f 1-2, 7f 4, 8f) (sft, gd, g-f 2, frm 1-3)
Leggy, decent filly, effective 6 to 8f, acts on g-f to frm, best on frm. Turf high 80 - 2nd of 18 to Sandova (7 May Lingfield 7f g-f RF 1084) - also 1st of 6 getting 5lb from Tomasean (30 Jly Salisbury RF 3246). Inconsistent. **P J Makin [1-9] Dr Carlos Stelling.*

FANTASTIC DANCE (USA) BHB 67f65a **RR 69f 65a** 5026[18]
3 br f Imperial Ballet (IRE) - Fantastic Bid (USA) (Auction Ring (USA)) 8.6f **(65)**
Form - 1400
Record 1999 - 1st:1 2nd:0 3rd:0 Ran:4
Pre1999 - 1st:0 2nd:0 3rd:0 Ran:1
Win Prizemoney £3,550 *Total Prizemoney* £4,033
Wins * 1999 Aug Salisb (SFT) 7f 65+ <
1999 Turf 1-3: (7f 1-2, 8f) (gd, g-f 1-1, frm) 1999 AW 0-1: (7f) (Fibr)
Average filly. Turf high 69 (began Aug) - 4th of 12 getting 8lb from Minetta (28 Aug Windsor 8f frm RF 3985) - also 1st of 10 from Jouet (12 Aug Salisbury RF 3575). **P J Makin [1-5] Dr Carlos Stelling.*

FANTASTIC FANTASY (IRE) BHB 67f **RR 72f** 4839[10]
2 b f Lahib (USA) 8f **(69)** - Gay Fantasy (Troy) 10.4f **(68)**
Form - 370
Record 1999 - 1st:0 2nd:0 3rd:1 Ran:3
Win Prizemoney £0 *Total Prizemoney* £590

1999 Turf 0-3: (8f 3) (gd 2, frm)
Currently above-average filly. Turf high 72 (began Spt).
**J L Dunlop [0-3] Windflower Overseas Holdings Inc.*

FANTASTIC LIGHT (USA) RR 125f 4778a[11]

3 b c Rahy (USA) 9.1f **(80)** - Jood (USA) (Nijinsky (CAN)) 10.3f **(77)**
Form - 1423110
Record 1999 - 1st:3 2nd:1 3rd:1 Ran:7
Pre1999 - 1st:2 2nd:0 3rd:1 Ran:3
Win Prizemoney £134,002 *Total Prizemoney* £203,272
Wins * **1999** Spt Newbur (G-S) L 11f 125 <
* **1999** Aug York (GD) G2 11.9f 121
* **1999** Apr Sandow (SFT) G3 10f 108
* 1998 Aug Sandow (G-F) 8.1f 93
* 1998 Aug Sandow (GD) 7.1f 82+

1999 Turf 3-7: (10f 1-3, 11f 1-2,12f 1-2)(sft, g-s 1-1, gd 1-2, g-f 1-2, frm)
Scopey, top-class colt, effective 10 to 12f, acts on gd to frm, excels at Sandown. Turf high 125 - 1st of 6 getting 2lb from High-Rise (19 Spt Newbury RF 4417) - also 1st of 7 from Bienamado (17 Aug York RF 3695). He won twice at Sandown as a juvenile in 1998, and made a winning reappearance at the same track in the Thresher Classic Trial, despite looking in need of the race. He gave the impression he did not stay when stepped up in trip in the Lingfield Derby Trial but, brought back to ten furlongs, ran a fine second in the Prince Of Wales's Stakes at Royal Ascot. Lost his unbeaten Sandown record in the Eclipse, though he still ran a fine race to finish third, and ran out a clear-cut winner of the Great Voltigeur at the Ebor meeting, proving that he does indeed stay a mile and a half. Followed up by beating High-Rise in soft ground at Newbury in September, but was never in the hunt in the Arc. He is likely to develop into an even better horse in 2000.

Fantastic Light won the Group Two Great Voltigeur at the York Ebor meeting

**Sir Michael Stoute [5-10] Maktoum Al Maktoum.*

FANTASTIC QUEST (IRE) RR 95f 1465a[8]

4 b c Sadler's Wells (USA) 11.3f **(87)** - Fitnah (Kris) 9.5f **(73)**
Form - 28
1999 Turf 0-2: (14f 2) (gd 2)
Currently very useful colt. Turf high 95 (1st run) - 2nd of 5 to Theatreworld (3 May Navan 14f gd RF 1153a).
**T J Taaffe in IRE [0-1] William Lickle (from A Mullins in IRE [0-1] May 1999).*

FANTASY RR 72f 2322[2]

2 ch f Cadeaux Genereux 7.9f **(76)** - Elfin Laughter **(72f)** (Alzao (USA)) 7.1f **(68)**
Form - 42
Record 1999 - 1st:0 2nd:1 3rd:0 Ran:2
Win Prizemoney £0 *Total Prizemoney* £1,262
1999 Turf 0-2: (5f, 7f) (frm 2)
Currently above-average filly. Turf high 72 - 2nd of 4 to Marah (26 Jun Doncaster 7f frm RF 2322). **R Hannon [0-2] Lord Carnarvon.*

FANTASY ADVENTURER BHB 69f62a RR 69f 62a 4703[8]

2 b g Magic Ring (IRE) 6.5f **(64)** - Delicious **(53f)** (Dominion) 8.5f **(63)**
Form - 048
Record 1999 - 1st:0 2nd:0 3rd:0 Ran:3
Win Prizemoney £0 *Total Prizemoney* £210
1999 Turf 0-2: (5f, 6f) (g-f 2) 1999 AW 0-1: (6f) (Fibr)
Currently average gelding. Turf high 69 (began Aug).
**J J Quinn [0-3] The Fantasy Fellowship.*

FANTASY HILL (IRE) BHB 92f RR 89f 5220[2]

3 b c Danehill (USA) 9.1f **(79)** - Gay Fantasy (Troy) 10.4f **(68)**
Form - 41302
Record 1999 - 1st:1 2nd:1 3rd:1 Ran:5
Pre1999 - 1st:0 2nd:0 3rd:1 Ran:3
Win Prizemoney £6,287 *Total Prizemoney* £10,751
Wins * **1999** May Nottin (FRM) H 14.1f 81 87 <

1999 Turf 1-5: (12f, 14f 1-2, 15f, 17f) (sft, gd 2, g-f 1-2)
Unfurnished, useful colt, effective 14 to 17f, best at 14f, acts on sft to g-f, best on g-f. Turf high 89 - 2nd of 15 giving 4lb to Il Principe (6 Nov Doncaster 17f sft RF 5220) - also 1st of 5 giving 4lb to Rum Pointer (28 May Nottingham RF 1550). Won at Nottingham in May and was off the course for more than four months before his next start. **J L Dunlop [1-8] Windflower Overseas Holdings Inc.*

FANTASY NIGHT (IRE) BHB 85f RR 83f 4420[3]

4 b g Night Shift (USA) 8.1f **(73)** - Gay Fantasy (Troy) 10.4f **(68)**
Form - 205413213
Record 1999 - 1st:2 2nd:2 3rd:2 Ran:9
Pre1999 - 1st:1 2nd:2 3rd:1 Ran:10
Win Prizemoney £12,514 *Total Prizemoney* £22,992
Wins * **1999** Aug Cheste (G-S) H 15.9f 80 82 <
* **1999** Jun Warwic (G-F) H 15.8f 70 72+
* 1998 Jly Thirsk (FRM) H 12f 73 75

1999 Turf 2-9: (10f 2, 12f, 14f, 16f 2-5) (gd 1-4, g-f 1-1, frm 4)
Well made, decent gelding, effective 10 to 16f, best at 16f, acts on gd to frm, best on gd, prefers left handed tracks, excels at Chester and Redcar. Turf high 83 - 3rd of 4 to Spunkie (19 Spt Newbury 16f gd RF 4420) - also 1st of 11 giving 10lb to Noufari (21 Aug Chester RF 3815). Improving. Got off the mark in good style at Warwick on his on fifth start this year and has since added a smooth victory at Chester. Obviously useful when things go his way.
**J L Dunlop [3-19] Windflower Overseas Holdings Inc.*

FANTAZIA BHB 86f RR 84f 3964[1]

3 b f Zafonic (USA) 9f **(83)** - Trescalini (IRE) (Sadler's Wells (USA)) 10f **(76)**
Form - 375111
Record 1999 - 1st:3 2nd:0 3rd:1 Ran:6
Pre1999 - 1st:0 2nd:0 3rd:1 Ran:3
Win Prizemoney £22,295 *Total Prizemoney* £24,132
Wins * **1999** Aug Newmar (G-F) H 10f 81 84 <
* **1999** Aug Redcar (GD) H 11f 76 79
* **1999** Jly Redcar (FRM) H 10f 73 79

1999 Turf 3-6: (8f 2, 10f 2-3, 11f 1-1) (gd, g-f, frm 3-4)
Decent filly, effective 10 to 11f, best at 10f, acts on frm. Turf high 84 - 1st of 13 from Wasp Ranger (28 Aug Newmarket RF 3964) - also 1st of 5 getting 7lb from Desdemona (8 Aug Redcar RF 3469). Had shown ordinary form before completing a hat-trick with victories at Redcar (twice) and Newmarket. Suited by fast ground, she probably has a bit more in the locker.
**J R Fanshawe [3-6] Byerley Turf (from M Johnston [0-3] Oct 1998).*

FARAJ RR 67f 5186[P]
2 ch c Mizoram (USA) - Petite Butterfly (Absalom) 7.2f **(58)**
Form - 6P
Record 1999 - 1st:0 2nd:0 3rd:0 Ran:2
1999 Turf 0-2: (7f 2) (g-s, g-f)
Currently average colt. Turf high 67 (began Oct).
**M Johnston [0-2] Ziad Galadari.*

FARAWAY LASS BHB 82f85a **RR 80f 85a** 4272[10]
6 b m Distant Relative 7f **(69)** - Vague Lass (Vaigly Great) 7f **(58)**
Form - 80020
Record 1999 - 1st:0 2nd:1 3rd:0 Ran:4
Pre1999 - 1st:5 2nd:5 3rd:2 Ran:27
Win Prizemoney £25,778 *Total Prizemoney* £45,611

Wins								
1998	Spt	Haydoc	(GD)		6f		86	<
1997	Jly	York	(GD)	H	6f	77	80	
1996	Oct	York	(GD)		6f		76	
1996	Jun	Salisb	(G-F)	H	6f	67	77	
1996	May	Nottin	(G-F)		6.1f		62	

1999 Turf 0-4: (6f 4) (g-f 4)
Decent mare, effective 5 to 6f, best at 6f, acts on gd to frm, best on frm. Turf high 80. Consistent.
**D J Coakley [0-4] J Rose (from Lord Huntingdon [5-27] Nov 1998).*

FARAWAY MOON BHB 63f54a **RR 67f 54a** 4925[9]
3 gr f Distant Relative 7f **(69)** - Moon Magic **(59f)** (Polish Precedent (USA)) 10.2f **(60)**
Form - 530030
Record 1999 - 1st:0 2nd:0 3rd:2 Ran:6
Pre1999 - 1st:0 2nd:0 3rd:0 Ran:1
Win Prizemoney £0 *Total Prizemoney* £1,215
1999 Turf 0-5:(6f, 7f, 8f 2, 10f) (gd 2, g-f, frm 2) 1999 AW 0-1: (7f) (Fibr)
Neat, average filly, effective 7f, acts on frm. Turf high 67 (began Jly) - 3rd of 7 to Naughty Crown (31 Jly Thirsk 7f frm RF 3286).
**Lady Herries [0-7] Lady Sarah Clutton.*

FARCEUR DU MESNIL (FR) RR 2375[7]
6 b g Pharly (FR) 11.5f **(64)** - Grundygold (FR) (Grundy) 10.3f **(65)**
Form - 7
Record 1999 - 1st:0 2nd:0 3rd:0 Ran:1
1999 AW 0-1: (11f) (Fibr)
Fair gelding, always wears blinkers.

Far Cry (rails) held the call in a classic battle for the Northumberland Plate

**K A Morgan [0-8] The French Experience.*

FAR CRY (IRE) BHB 110f90a **RR 105f 90a** 4917[5]
4 b g Pharly (FR) 11.5f **(64)** - Darabaka (IRE) (Doyoun) 9f **(69)**
Form - 711113112115
Record 1999 - 1st:5 2nd:1 3rd:1 Ran:8
Pre1999 - 1st:3 2nd:1 3rd:0 Ran:8
Win Prizemoney £117,938 *Total Prizemoney* £127,463

Wins								
* **1999**	Spt	Doncas	(G-F)	G3	18f		105	<
* **1999**	Jun	Newcas	(G-F)	H	16.1f	89	95	
* **1999**	Apr	Kempto	(GD)	H	16f	85	87	
1999	*Mar*	*Wolver*	*(STD)*	*H*	*16.2f*	*82*	*102*	
1999	*Feb*	*Southw*	*(STD)*	*H*	*16f*	*73*	*89+*	
1998	*Dec*	*Southw*	*(STD)*	*H*	*12f*	*67*	*74*	
1998	*Dec*	*Southw*	*(STD)*		*14f*		*71+*	
1998	*Nov*	*Southw*	*(STD)*		*12f*		*67+*	

1999 Turf 3-5: (16f 2-2, 17f, 18f 1-1, 20f) (gd, g-f 2-3, frm 1-1) 1999 AW 2-3: (16f 2-3) (Equi, Fibr 2-2)
Pattern-class gelding, effective 16 to 18f, acts on gd to frm - acts on Fibr, prefers left handed tracks, likes tight tracks, excels at Southwell. Turf high 105 - 1st of 6 from Rainbow High (9 Spt Doncaster RF 4237). AW high 102 - 1st of 8 getting 6lb from Sudest (13 Mar Wolverhampton RF 0433). Formerly with Sir Mark Prescott, he improved once stepped up in trip, and had a merry old time on Fibresand last winter, winning five times. He did not look quite as suited by Equitrack, but after moving to Martin Pipe, carried his improvement on to turf, recording victories in the Queen's Prize and Northumberland Plate and running a blinder to finish runner-up in the Ascot Stakes. He gained his biggest success to date when putting up a typically gutsy performance to win the Group Three Doncaster Cup from Rainbow High and Celeric and lost little in defeat in the Cesarewitch. None of his victories on turf has been gained by more than a head, which illustrates just how tough he is.
**M C Pipe [3-5] Mrs Nicky Chambers (from Sir Mark Prescott [5-10] Mar 1999).*

FARFALA (FR) RR 98f 4769a[11]
3 gr f Linamix (FR) 8.2f **(64)** - Fragrant Hill (Shirley Heights) 10.3f **(74)**
Form - 3010
1999 Turf 1-4: (11f 2, 12f 1-1, 13f) (hvy, sft, g-s, gd 1-1)
Very useful filly. Turf high 98 - 1st of 13 getting 8lb from Key Academy (13 Spt Chantilly RF 4510a). Not one of her trainer's stars, she stays a mile and a half but falls short of Group class.
**A Fabre in FR [1-4] J-L Lagardere.*

FARFIELDS PRINCE BHB 30f **RR 1f** 4983[14]
7 b g Weldnaas (USA) 8.4f **(55)** - Coca (Levmoss) 11.4f **(66)**
Form - 00
Record 1999 - 1st:0 2nd:0 3rd:0 Ran:2
Pre1999 - 1st:0 2nd:2 3rd:1 Ran:12
Win Prizemoney £0 *Total Prizemoney* £2,167
1999 Turf 0-1: (10f) (gd) 1999 AW 0-1: (11f) (Fibr)
Very poor gelding. Becoming disappointing.
**G M Moore [2-9] Exors of the late Mrs D Bainbridge (from D Nicholls [0-12] Oct 1997).*

FARHAN (USA) BHB 50f **RR 74f** 3114[7]
5 b g Lear Fan (USA) 10.4f **(80)** - Mafatin (IRE) (Sadler's Wells (USA)) 10f **(76)**
Form - 7
Record 1999 - 1st:0 2nd:0 3rd:0 Ran:1
Pre1999 - 1st:0 2nd:2 3rd:0 Ran:5
Win Prizemoney £0 *Total Prizemoney* £2,086
1999 AW 0-1: (12f) (Fibr)
Above-average gelding, has worn blinkers.
**K A Morgan [0-5] Mrs R M Burgess (from P T Walwyn [0-5] Jun 1997).*

FARMOST BHB 77f85a **RR 74f 85a** 4954[10]
6 ch g Pharly (FR) 11.5f **(64)** - Dancing Meg (USA) (Marshua's Dancer (USA)) 8.6f **(75)**
Form - 8000321110
Record 1999 - 1st:3 2nd:1 3rd:1 Ran:10
Pre1999 - 1st:11 2nd:5 3rd:0 Ran:24
Win Prizemoney £82,455 *Total Prizemoney* £91,278

Wins								
* **1999**	Jly	Redcar	(FRM)		9f		74	
* **1999**	Jly	Cheste	(G-F)	H	10.3f	70	71	
* **1999**	Jun	Chepst	(GD)	H	10.2f	67	70	
* 1997	*Dec*	*Wolver*	*(STD)*	*L*	*9.4f*		*100*	<
* 1997	*Nov*	*Wolver*	*(STD)*	*H*	*8.5f*	*82*	*87*	
* 1997	*Spt*	*Wolver*	*(STD)*	*H*	*9.4f*	*70*	*84*	
* 1997	Spt	Bright	(FRM)	H	10f	80	85	
* 1997	Jly	Bath	(FRM)		10.2f		78	
* 1996	*Aug*	*Wolver*	*(STD)*	*H*	*9.4f*	*66*	*71*	
* 1996	Jly	Bright	(FRM)	H	8f	75	79	
* 1996	Jun	Folkes	(G-F)		6.9f		78	
* 1996	May	Bright	(GD)		7f		76	
* 1996	May	Sandow	(GD)	H	7.1f	61	69	
* 1996	*Jan*	*Wolver*	*(STD)*		*6f*		*56*	

1999 Turf 3-10: (8f 3, 9f 1-2, 10f 2-5) (g-s, gd 1-3, g-f 2, frm 2-4)
Very useful gelding, effective 9 to 10f, best at 10f, acts on gd to frm, best on frm, prefers left handed tracks. Turf high 74 - 1st of 6

giving 3lb to Tallulah Belle (17 Jly Redcar RF 2923) - also 1st of 8 giving 15lb to Noukari (10 Jly Chester RF 2708). His victories have been due in no small part to his trainer's skill in placing his horses. He beat Running Stag in a Listed race on the Wolverhampton Fibresand in December 1997, but was disappointing behind that horse in the 1998 Winter Derby and was not seen out again that season. He came back to his best when completing a fine hat-trick during the summer, but has refused to enter the stalls twice since and may have his own ideas about the game.
**Sir Mark Prescott [14-34] Sturt Osborne House II.*

FAR MOUNT BHB 96f **RR 101f** 4354[3]

2 ch c Bluebird (USA) 7.9f **(71)** - One False Move (IRE) **(74f)** (Don't Forget Me) 8.3f **(74)**
Form - 11173
Record 1999 - 1st:3 2nd:0 3rd:1 Ran:5
Win Prizemoney £12,297 *Total Prizemoney* £13,259

Wins	* **1999**	Jly	Doncas	(G-F)	6f	101	<
	* **1999**	Jly	Beverl	(G-F)	5f	97	
	* **1999**	*Jun*	*Wolver*	*(STD)*	*6f*	92+	

1999 Turf 2-4: (5f 1-1, 6f 1-3) (g-s, g-f 1-1, frm 1-2) 1999 AW 1-1: (6f 1-1) (Fibr 1-1)
Very useful colt, has worn blinkers. Turf high 101 (began Jly) - 1st of 4 giving 11lb to Linden Grace (14 Jly Doncaster RF 2811) - also 1st of 6 giving 5lb to Dandy Night (2 Jly Beverley RF 2484). (1st run) - 1st of 6 from First Venture (16 Jun Wolverhampton RF 2065). He did his job in the summer, winning three times over sprint distances. Very free when fitted with blinkers on his final start, he is unlikely to stay beyond seven furlongs and made 23,000 guineas at Newmarket in October. **Sir Mark Prescott [3-5] Cyril Humphris.*

FAR REMOVED (IRE) BHB 75f **RR 80f** 4998[5]

4 b g Distant Relative 7f **(69)**-Cormorant Creek(Gorytus (USA))7.8f **(60)**
Form - 0403401405
Record 1999 - 1st:1 2nd:0 3rd:1 Ran:10
Pre1999 - 1st:2 2nd:3 3rd:2 Ran:15
Win Prizemoney £15,014 *Total Prizemoney* £22,881

Wins	* **1999**	Aug	Redcar	(G-F)	H	8f	71	73	
	* 1998	Aug	Redcar	(G-F)	H	8f	75	79	<
	1997	Spt	Doncas	(G-F)	H	6f	72	79	<

1999 Turf 1-10: (7f 3, 8f 1-6, 10f) (gd, g-f 3, frm 1-6)
Workmanlike, decent gelding, effective 7 to 8f, best at 8f, acts on g-s to frm, has worn blinkers, likes tight tracks, does well at Redcar. Turf high 80 - 4th of 9 giving 6lb to Island House (16 Spt Pontefract 8f frm RF 4351) - also 1st of 11 giving 2lb to Gralmano (28 Aug Redcar RF 3975).
**Mrs V C Ward [2-15] Mrs V C Ward (from Mrs J R Ramsden [1-10] Aug 1998).*

FARRIER'S GAMBLE RR 5198[16]

3 ch f Belmez (USA) 11.4f **(65)** - Chrisanthy (So Blessed) 8.7f **(67)**
Form - 0
Record 1999 - 1st:0 2nd:0 3rd:0 Ran:1
1999 Turf 0-1: (8f) (gd)
Small, currently very poor filly.
**R M Flower [0-1] D Leadbetter & J M Gamble.*

FARRINGDON HILL BHB 43f **RR 55f** 4601[10]

8 b g Minster Son 10.9f **(56)** - Firgrove (Relkino) 8.9f **(65)**
Form - 000735000
Record 1999 - 1st:0 2nd:0 3rd:1 Ran:9
Pre1999 - 1st:4 2nd:1 3rd:4 Ran:24
Win Prizemoney £13,320 *Total Prizemoney* £17,322

Wins	1997	Aug	Redcar	(FRM)	H	11f	69	72+
	1997	Aug	Windso	(G-F)	H	11.6f	65	68
	1996	Jun	Sandow	(FRM)	H	14f	71	77

1999 Turf 0-8: (10f, 11f, 12f 5, 14f) (gd, g-f 4, frm 3) 1999 AW 0-1: (11f) (Fibr)
Fair gelding, effective 10 to 12f, best at 12f, acts on gd to hrd, best on gd, often wears blinkers (very effectively). Turf high 56. Becoming disappointing.
**D Sasse [0-9] Christopher Ranson (from J H M Gosden [2-8] Jun 1998).*

FAR-SO-LA BHB 32f40a **RR 32f 40a** 3792[6]

4 b g Absalom 7.1f **(56)** - Fara (Castle Keep) 8.3f **(57)**
Form - 00481077050666
Record 1999 - 1st:1 2nd:0 3rd:0 Ran:11
Pre1999 - 1st:1 2nd:1 3rd:0 Ran:13
Win Prizemoney £4,067 *Total Prizemoney* £4,835

Wins	* **1999**	*Jan*	*Southw*	*(STD)*	S	*7f*	*50*	<
	1998	Jly	Folkes	(GD)	C	7f	48	

1999 Turf 0-5: (7f, 8f 3, 10f) (hvy, g-f 3, hrd) 1999 AW 1-6: (7f 1-2, 8f 4) (Equi 3, Fibr 1-3)
Moderate gelding, effective 7 to 8f, best at 7f, acts on gd to frm - acts on Fibr, has worn blinkers. Turf high 32. AW high 50 - 1st of 12 from Bicton Park (15 Jan Southwell RF 0103).
**Mrs L C Jewell [1-16] Mrs Linda Jewell (from B A Pearce [0-4] Spt 1998).*

FAS BHB 34f43a **RR 26f 43a** 4723[10]

3 ch g Weldnaas (USA) 8.4f **(55)** - Polly's Teahouse (Shack (USA)) 5.8f **(53)**
Form - 50600000
Record 1999 - 1st:0 2nd:0 3rd:0 Ran:8
1999 Turf 0-6: (6f 5, 7f) (gd 3, frm 3) 1999 AW 0-2: (6f, 8f) (Fibr 2)
Workmanlike, little account gelding, has worn blinkers. Turf high 44. AW high 25. Inconsistent. **J D Bethell [0-8] F & T Walton.*

FASHION BHB 66f **RR 70f** 4934[1]

2 b f Bin Ajwaad (IRE) - New Generation (Young Generation) 7.7f **(63)**
Form - 4331
Record 1999 - 1st:1 2nd:0 3rd:2 Ran:4
Win Prizemoney £3,964 *Total Prizemoney* £4,981

Wins	* **1999**	Oct	Pontef	(GD)	H	8f	62	70	<

1999 Turf 1-2: (8f 1-2) (gd, g-f 1-1) 1999 AW 0-2: (8f 2) (Fibr 2)
Above-average filly. Turf high 70 (began Spt) - 1st of 19 giving 3lb to Double Red (18 Oct Pontefract RF 4934). AW high 63 (began Spt). **Sir Mark Prescott [1-4] H R H Prince Fahd Salman.*

FASHION VICTIM BHB 39f **RR 39f** 4429[12]

4 b g High Estate 10.5f **(66)** - Kirkby Belle (Bay Express) 7.1f **(60)**
Form - 700806000
Record 1999 - 1st:0 2nd:0 3rd:0 Ran:9
Pre1999 - 1st:2 2nd:0 3rd:0 Ran:10
Win Prizemoney £10,792 *Total Prizemoney* £11,042

Wins	* 1997	Spt	Ayr	(G-S)	H	8f	74	79	<
	* 1997	Jly	Beverl	(G-F)		5f	69		

1999 Turf 0-9: (7f 2, 8f 2, 9f 2, 10f 3) (g-s 2, g-f 2, frm 4, hrd)
Workmanlike, very moderate gelding. Turf high 43. Inconsistent.

Unbeaten Fasliyev, top-rated juvenile

**T H Caldwell [2-19] R S G Jones.*

FASLIYEV (USA) RR 120+f 3932a[1]

2 b c Nureyev (USA) 8.4f **(84)** - Mr P's Princess (USA) (Mr Prospector (USA)) 8.8f **(78)**

Form - 11111
1999 Turf 5-5: (5f 2-2, 6f 3-3) (gd 2-2, g-f 3-3)
Very high-class colt. Turf high 120 - 1st of 7 from Warm Heart (22 Aug Deauville RF 3932a). Impressive when winning on his Leopardstown debut, he had to work harder when winning a Listed event at the Curragh next time, but was an impressive winner of the Coventry at Royal Ascot over an extra furlong. Ran out the clear-cut winner of the Heinz 57 Phoenix Stakes, despite hanging violently to the left in the closing stages, but maintained his unbeaten record by smashing a top-class field by an easing-down four lengths in the Prix Morny. That was by far the best performance by a two-year-old last season, and it was therefore a tragedy that he should suffer an injury on the gallops in October that was serious enough to end his racing career.
**A P O'Brien in IRE [5-5] M Tabor.*

FAST AND NEAT (IRE) BHB 52f **RR 52f** 4217[3]
3 ch g Soviet Lad (USA) 9.4f **(63)** - Stop The Cavalry (Relko) 9.9f **(59)**
Form - 023133
Record **1999** - 1st:1 2nd:1 3rd:3 Ran:6
Pre1999 - 1st:0 2nd:0 3rd:0 Ran:6
Win Prizemoney £2,818 *Total Prizemoney* £5,350
Wins * **1999** Aug Salisb (GD) H 12f 47 51 <
1999 Turf 1-6: (10f, 11f, 12f 1-3, 16f) (gd, frm 1-5)
Workmanlike, fair gelding, effective 11 to 12f, best at 12f, acts on frm, prefers tight tracks. Turf high 52 - 3rd of 18 giving 4lb to Dinar (8 Spt Kempton 12f frm RF 4217) - also 1st of 10 getting 21lb from Capriolo (6 Aug Salisbury RF 3431).
**G Lewis [1-12] The Bricklayers Partnership.*

FASTBEAT RACING RR 3413[14]
2 b f Safawan 6.6f **(60)** - Little Vixen (Aragon) 8.1f **(60)**
Form - 0
Record **1999** - 1st:0 2nd:0 3rd:0 Ran:1
1999 Turf 0-1: (7f) (g-f)
Currently very poor filly. **A Senior [0-1] J S Camilleri.*

FASTESTBARBERALIVE RR 5113[U]
4 b g Full Extent (USA) 5.2f **(50)** - Please Please Me (IRE) (Tender King) 6.8f **(54)**
Form - U
Record **1999** - 1st:0 2nd:0 3rd:0 Ran:1
1999 Turf 0-1: (6f) (gd)
Neat, currently very poor gelding. **J J Bridger [0-1] Trevor Mitchell.*

FAST FORWARD FRED BHB 55f44a **RR 57f 44a** 823[7]
8 gr g Sharrood (USA) 11.1f **(67)** - Sun Street (Ile de Bourbon (USA)) 10.1f **(67)**
Form - 7
Record **1999** - 1st:0 2nd:0 3rd:0 Ran:1
Pre1999 - 1st:3 2nd:3 3rd:0 Ran:17
Win Prizemoney £9,697 *Total Prizemoney* £12,298
Wins * 1998 Aug Sandow (G-F) H 16.4f 48 57 <
* 1998 Aug Bath (FRM) H 17.2f 48 52
* 1998 Jly Chepst (GD) H 18f 43 49
1999 Turf 0-1: (16f) (g-s)
Fair gelding, effective 16 to 18f, acts on gd to frm.
**L MontagueHall [3-17] The Straight Forward Partnership (from G Lewis [0-2] Oct 1994).*

FAST FRANC (IRE) BHB 42f43a **RR 14f 43a** 4121[15]
4 ch g Paris House 5.9f **(64)** - Elle Va Bon (Tanfirion) 7f **(61)**
Form - 000000
Record **1999** - 1st:0 2nd:0 3rd:0 Ran:5
Pre1999 - 1st:6 2nd:0 3rd:3 Ran:23
Win Prizemoney £14,583 *Total Prizemoney* £16,522
Wins * 1998 *Feb Lingfi (SLW) H 6f 70 73* <
1998 *Feb Lingfi (SLW) C 7f 64*
1998 *Jan Southw (STD) H 6f 50 66*
1998 *Jan Southw (STD) C 6f 66*
1997 Jly Hamilt (SFT) S 6f 70+
1997 Jun Folkes (SFT) S 5f 55+
1999 Turf 0-2: (6f, 7f) (g-s, g-f) 1999 AW 0-3: (6f 2, 7f) (Equi 2, Fibr)
Workmanlike, poor gelding, effective 6 to 7f, best at 6f, - acts on AW, best on Fibr, has worn blinkers, prefers left handed tracks, prefers tight tracks. Turf high 14. AW high 6.
**T J Naughton [1-14] & Mrs D J Flahive (from S C Williams [5-13] Feb 1998).*

FASTRACK TIME BHB 65f **RR 69f** 4877[9]
2 ch g Clantime 6.6f **(57)** - Bitch **(37f 32a)** (Risk Me (FR)) 5.9f **(53)**
Form - 08080
Record **1999** - 1st:0 2nd:0 3rd:0 Ran:5
1999 Turf 0-5: (5f 3, 6f, 7f) (sft, g-f 2, frm 2)
Average gelding. Turf high 69. **S Mellor [0-5] Mice Group Plc.*

FAST TO LIGHT BHB 30f **RR 5f** 5165[14]
3 ch f Pharly (FR) 11.5f **(64)** - Khadino (Relkino) 8.9f **(65)**
Form - 0
Record **1999** - 1st:0 2nd:0 3rd:0 Ran:1
Pre1999 - 1st:0 2nd:0 3rd:0 Ran:2
1999 Turf 0-1: (12f) (g-s)
Scopey, very poor filly. **N Tinkler [0-6] Philip Grundy.*

FAST TRACK (IRE) RR 87+f 5099[1]
2 b c Doyoun 10.7f **(69)** - Manntika (Kalamoun) 10.4f **(67)**
Form - 1
Record **1999** - 1st:1 2nd:0 3rd:0 Ran:1
Win Prizemoney £3,330 *Total Prizemoney* £3,330
Wins * **1999** Oct Yarmou (G-S) 7f 87+ <
1999 Turf 1-1: (7f 1-1) (gd 1-1)
Currently useful colt. (1st run) - 1st of 12 from Tantalus (27 Oct Yarmouth RF 5099). Should develop into a nice three-year-old.
**Sir Michael Stoute [1-1] Maktoum Al Maktoum.*

FAST TRICK BHB 68f **RR 62f** 4766a[3]
2 b f First Trump - Alacrity **(58df)** (Alzao (USA)) 7.1f **(68)**
Form - 34843
Record **1999** - 1st:0 2nd:0 3rd:2 Ran:5
Win Prizemoney £0 *Total Prizemoney* £3,381
1999 Turf 0-5: (5f 2, 6f 2, 8f) (hvy, gd 3, frm)
Average filly. Turf high 62 - 3rd of 17 getting 7lb from Jean De Luz (2 Oct Longchamp 8f hvy RF 4766a).
**in FR [0-1] (from R M Whitaker [0-4] Aug 1999).*

FASTWAN BHB 28f **RR 33f** 4376[12]
3 ch c Nashwan (USA) 10.3f **(79)** - Jammaayil (IRE) (Lomond (USA)) 8.8f **(65)**
Form - 0884045600
Record **1999** - 1st:0 2nd:0 3rd:0 Ran:10
Pre1999 - 1st:0 2nd:1 3rd:0 Ran:3
Win Prizemoney £0 *Total Prizemoney* £1,429
1999 Turf 0-10: (9f 4, 10f, 11f 3, 12f, 13f) (g-s, gd 2, g-f 6, frm)
Scopey, very moderate colt, effective 9 to 11f, acts on g-f, likes tight tracks. Turf high 33 - 5th of 12 getting 20lb from Pegasus Bay (11 Aug Hamilton 9f g-f RF 3544). Inconsistent.
**J S Goldie [0-13] Frank Brady.*

FATEHALKHAIR (IRE) BHB 63f45a **RR 62f 45a** 4752[9]
7 ch g Kris 10f **(75)** - Midway Lady (USA) (Alleged (USA)) 10f **(76)**
Form - 21013124130
Record **1999** - 1st:4 2nd:2 3rd:2 Ran:11
Pre1999 - 1st:0 2nd:2 3rd:1 Ran:14
Win Prizemoney £18,864 *Total Prizemoney* £25,171
Wins * **1999** Spt Thirsk (FRM) H 12f 58 61 <
* **1999** Jun Catter (G-F) H 12f 49 52
* **1999** Jun Catter (GD) H 12f 45 47
* **1999** Apr Redcar (G-S) H 11f 34 42
1999 Turf 4-10: (10f, 11f 1-1, 12f 3-7, 13f) (gd 1-2, g-f, frm 2-6, hrd 1-1)
1999 AW 0-1: (12f) (Fibr)
Average gelding, effective 12 to 13f, best at 12f, acts on frm to hrd, best on frm, has worn blinkers, prefers left handed tracks, prefers tight tracks, excels at Catterick. Turf high 62 - 3rd of 5 getting 9lb from Chicodove (18 Spt Catterick 12f frm RF 4397) - also 1st of 11 getting 17lb from Baffin Bay (4 Spt Thirsk RF 4146). Consistent. A useful hurdler, he has ability on the Flat too. He has sometimes not appeared to relish being put under pressure, and must have a left-handed track. **B Ellison [11-48] R Wagner.*

FATH (USA) RR 107f 4653[2]
2 b c Danzig (USA) 8.1f **(88)** - Desirable (Lord Gayle (USA)) 8.8f **(62)**
Form - 12
Record **1999** - 1st:1 2nd:1 3rd:0 Ran:2
Win Prizemoney £14,490 *Total Prizemoney* £39,890
Wins * **1999** Aug York (GD) 6f 96++ <

1999 Turf 1-2: (6f 1-2) (gd 1-2)

Currently Pattern-class colt. Turf high 107 (began Aug) - 2nd of 6 to Primo Valentino (30 Spt Newmarket 6f gd RF 4653). A half-brother to 1000 Guineas winner Shadayid, he made a big impression when winning York's Convivial Maiden, and found only the more-experienced Primo Valentino too strong in the Middle Park Stakes. Looks sure to make a high-class three-year-old, although a mile might be stretching his stamina.

Fath showed plenty of promise at two

**M P Tregoning [1-2] Hamdan Al Maktoum.*

FATHER JUNINHO (IRE) BHB 91f RR 84f 5196[2]

2 b c Distinctly North (USA) 7.4f **(63)** - Shane's Girl (IRE) (Marktingo)
Form - 0031012
Record 1999 - 1st:2 2nd:1 3rd:1 Ran:7
Win Prizemoney £9,637 *Total Prizemoney* £11,966
Wins * 1999 Spt Doncas (G-F) H 7f 78 84 <
*** 1999** Jly Redcar (FRM) H 7f 84 <
1999 Turf 2-7: (6f 2, 7f 2-3, 8f 2) (gd 3, frm 2-4)

Decent colt, effective 7 to 8f, best at 7f, acts on gd to frm, best on frm. Turf high 84 - 2nd of 13 giving 2lb to Imperial Rocket (4 Nov Windsor 8f gd RF 5196) - also 1st of 17 getting 4lb from Chimney Dust (11 Spt Doncaster RF 4269). **A P Jarvis [2-7] Mrs Ann Jarvis.*

FATHER MURPHY (IRE) RR 96f 4070a[9]

3 b c Erins Isle 8.3f **(76)** - Heiki 00
Form - 4133020
1999 Turf 1-7: (7f 2, 8f 1-2, 9f 2, 10f) (g-s, gd 1-4, g-f 2)

Very useful colt, effective 7 to 9f, best at 8f, acts on gd to g-f, best on gd. Turf high 96 - 3rd of 11 getting 20lb from Free To Speak (27 Jun Curragh 8f gd RF 2418a) - also 1st of 18 giving 5lb to Hierarchy (8 May Fairyhouse RF 1163a). He developed into a useful handicapper at up to nine furlongs. Probably best on decent ground, he is tough and will continue to run well.

**J S Bolger in IRE [1-10] Mrs J S Bolger.*

FATHER SKY BHB 61f61a RR 60f 61a 4387[17]

8 b g Dancing Brave (USA) 10.4f **(78)** - Flamenco Wave (USA) (Desert Wine (USA)) 9.7f **(80)**
Form - 048057180
Record 1999 - 1st:1 2nd:0 3rd:0 Ran:9
Pre1999 - 1st:1 2nd:0 3rd:1 Ran:4
Win Prizemoney £5,943 *Total Prizemoney* £6,758
Wins * 1999 Aug Yarmou (FRM) H 14.1f 58 60
1997 Spt Goodwo (G-F) H 16f 63 71 <
1999 Turf 1-6: (12f, 14f 1-2, 15f, 16f, 20f) (gd 2, g-f, frm 1-3) 1999 AW 0-3: (16f 3) (Equi 2, Fibr)

Average gelding, effective 14 to 16f, best at 16f, acts on gd to frm - acts on AW, often wears blinkers, likes tight tracks. Turf high 60 - 1st of 7 giving 18lb to Charlie's Gold (4 Aug Yarmouth RF 3377). AW high 63 - 4th of 13 to Harik (9 Feb Lingfield 16f Equi RF 0259). Consistent.

**D L Williams [3-8] Miss L Horner (from O Sherwood [10-38] Mar 1999).*

FATINA RR 91?f 2657a[4]

3 ch f Nashwan (USA) 10.3f **(79)** - Gharam (USA) (Green Dancer (USA)) 10.3f **(74)**
Form - 4
Record 1999 - 1st:0 2nd:0 3rd:0 Ran:1
Pre1999 - 1st:1 2nd:0 3rd:0 Ran:1
Win Prizemoney £4,110 *Total Prizemoney* £4,110
Wins * 1998 Oct Doncas (SFT) 8f 74+ <
1999 Turf 0-1: (10f) (gd)

Scopey, currently useful filly. (1st run) - 4th of 6 to Victory Cry (2 Jly Chantilly 10f gd RF 2657a). She was disappointing on her only start at Chantilly in July. **S bin Suroor [1-2].*

FATOOMAH BHB 43f RR 41f 4789[9]

3 b f Skyliner 6.8f **(51)** - Phantom Singer (Relkino) 8.9f **(65)**
Form - 020502007000
Record 1999 - 1st:0 2nd:2 3rd:0 Ran:12
Win Prizemoney £0 *Total Prizemoney* £2,283
1999 Turf 0-12: (7f 3, 8f 5, 9f, 10f 2, 12f) (g-s 2, g-f 3, frm 7)

Workmanlike, moderate filly, effective 8f, acts on frm, has worn blinkers. Turf high 60 - 2nd of 5 getting 5lb from Through The Rye (26 Jun Newcastle 8f frm RF 2340). Inconsistent. **K Mahdi [0-12] Hamad Al-Mutawa.*

FAUTE DE MIEUX BHB 68f RR 67f 4436[12]

4 ch g Beveled (USA) 6.9f **(64)** - Supreme Rose (Frimley Park) 6.5f **(67)**
Form - 4010228700
Record 1999 - 1st:1 2nd:2 3rd:0 Ran:10
Pre1999 - 1st:0 2nd:2 3rd:0 Ran:6
Win Prizemoney £2,626 *Total Prizemoney* £7,896
Wins * 1999 Jun Windso (SFT) 5f 71+ <
1999 Turf 1-10: (5f 1-9, 6f) (gd 1-4, g-f 2, frm 4)

Leggy, average gelding, effective 5 to 6f, best at 5f, acts on sft to hrd, best on frm. Turf high 73 - 2nd of 10 giving 6lb to That Man Again (3 Jly Sandown 5f frm RF 2547) - also 1st of 6 from Mister Jolson (7 Jun Windsor RF 1805).

**Derrick Morris [1-8] The Lambourn Racing Club (from J G Smyth-Osbourne [0-2] Apr 1999).*

FAVORISIO RR 57f 4881[8]

2 br g Efisio 7.7f **(69)** - Dixie Favor(USA) (Dixieland Band (USA))7f **(74)**
Form - 08
Record 1999 - 1st:0 2nd:0 3rd:0 Ran:2
1999 Turf 0-2: (6f 2) (frm, hrd)

Currently fair gelding. Turf high 57 (began Aug).

**Miss J A Camacho [0-2] Elite Racing Club.*

FAVOURED RR 68f 1290[5]

3 ch f Chief's Crown (USA) 10.2f **(75)** - Barboukh (Night Shift (USA)) 7.2f **(69)**
Form - 65
Record 1999 - 1st:0 2nd:0 3rd:0 Ran:2
Pre1999 - 1st:0 2nd:0 3rd:1 Ran:1
Win Prizemoney £0 *Total Prizemoney* £510
1999 Turf 0-2: (7f, 8f) (g-f 2)

Workmanlike, currently average filly. Turf high 68.

**J H M Gosden [0-3] Sheikh Mohammed.*

FAYEZ BHB 45f RR 54f 2688[2]

4 ch g Interrex (CAN) 7.7f **(51)** -Forest Nymph (Native Bazaar) 6.9f **(62)**
Form - 2

Record 1999 - 1st:0 2nd:1 3rd:0 Ran:1
Pre1999 - 1st:0 2nd:0 3rd:0 Ran:5
Win Prizemoney £0 *Total Prizemoney* £524
1999 AW 0-1: (12f) (Fibr)
Leggy, fair gelding, has worn blinkers. (1st run) - 2nd of 7 to Primeval (9 Jly Wolverhampton 12f Fibr RF 2688).
**K McAuliffe [2-10] A Ezen.*

FAYM (IRE) BHB 43f43a **RR 55f 43a** 4702[8]

5 b m Fayruz 6.6f **(63)** - Lorme (Glenstal (USA)) 10.1f **(64)**
Form - 13512007608
Record 1999 - 1st:1 2nd:1 3rd:0 Ran:9
Pre1999 - 1st:1 2nd:3 3rd:4 Ran:22
Win Prizemoney £3,797 *Total Prizemoney* £9,299
Wins 1999 *Jan Wolver (STD) S* 7f 57
1998 *Dec Wolver (SLW) H* 7f 49 59 <
1999 AW 1-9: (7f 1-8, 8f) (Fibr 1-9)
Fair filly, effective 7f, - acts on Fibr, has worn blinkers, favours left handed tracks, favours tight tracks. AW high 57 - 1st of 12 from Without Friends (23 Jan Wolverhampton RF 0157).
**Miss S J Wilton [0-6] John Pointon and Sons (from J Wharton [2-25] Jan 1999).*

FAYRWAY RHYTHM (IRE) BHB 81f **RR 81f** 5216[4]

2 b c Fayruz 6.6f **(63)** - The Way She Moves (North Stoke) 10.4f **(55)**
Form - 72244
Record 1999 - 1st:0 2nd:2 3rd:0 Ran:5
Win Prizemoney £0 *Total Prizemoney* £3,002
1999 Turf 0-5: (5f, 7f, 8f 3) (g-s, gd, g-f 3)
Decent colt. Turf high 81 (began Jly) - 2nd of 15 to First Truth (23 Spt Pontefract 8f g-f RF 4506). **M A Jarvis [0-5] Yusof Sepiuddin.*

FEAR AND GREED (IRE) RR 99f 4971a[5]

3 b f Brief Truce (USA) 9.1f **(73)** - Zing Ping (IRE) (Thatching) 8f **(66)**
Form - 0045
1999 Turf 0-4: (6f, 7f, 8f 2) (sft, g-s, g-f, frm)
Strong, very useful filly, effective 7f, acts on gd, has worn blinkers. Turf high 99. Consistent. She did not improve on her useful juvenile form. **T Stack in IRE [1-8] M A Begley.*

FEARBY CROSS (IRE) BHB 71f **RR 79f** 4805[6]

3 b c Unblest - Two Magpies (Doulab (USA)) 9.8f **(65)**
Form - 00400006
Record 1999 - 1st:0 2nd:0 3rd:0 Ran:8
Pre1999 - 1st:1 2nd:0 3rd:1 Ran:4
Win Prizemoney £3,824 *Total Prizemoney* £6,949
Wins * 1998 Spt Ayr (G-S) 6f 91+ <
1999 Turf 0-8: (6f 4, 7f 4) (gd 5, g-f, frm 2)
Lengthy, above-average colt, effective 6f, acts on g-s, has worn blinkers. Turf high 85. Becoming disappointing. He was a fast-finishing fourth in York's William Hill Trophy on his third start of last term and, despite being well beaten since, remains one to keep an eye on. Likes soft ground and looks as if he will stay seven furlongs. Has reportedly joined Willie Musson.
**J D Bethell [1-12] Clarendon Thoroughbred Racing.*

FEAST OF ROMANCE BHB 64f **RR 62f** 5061[5]

2 b c Pursuit of Love 9.5f **(69)** - June Fayre (Sagaro) 9.7f **(55)**
Form - 885
Record 1999 - 1st:0 2nd:0 3rd:0 Ran:3
1999 Turf 0-3: (5f 3) (g-s 3)
Currently above-average colt. Turf high 62 (began Spt).
**Miss Gay Kelleway [0-3] K & W Racing Partnership.*

FEATHER 'N LACE (IRE) BHB 62f **RR 62f** 4823[8]

3 b f Green Desert (USA) 7.8f **(78)** - Report 'em (USA) (Staff Writer (USA)) 10f **(54)**
Form - 3308004138
Record 1999 - 1st:1 2nd:0 3rd:3 Ran:10
Pre1999 - 1st:0 2nd:0 3rd:2 Ran:2
Win Prizemoney £4,305 *Total Prizemoney* £7,409
Wins * 1999 Aug Newmar (G-F) C 7f 60 <
1999 Turf 1-10: (6f 3, 7f 1-4, 8f 2, 10f) (gd 2, g-f 4, frm 1-4)
Light-framed, average filly, effective 6 to 8f, acts on g-f to frm, best on g-f, has worn blinkers. Turf high 67 - 3rd of 10 getting 5lb from Blackheath (2 Jun Lingfield 6f g-f RF 1682) - also 1st of 19 getting 3lb from Ruff (27 Aug Newmarket RF 3941).

**C A Cyzer [1-12] R M Cyzer.*

FEATHERSTONE LANE BHB 38f44a **RR 35f 44a** 4606[9]

8 b g Siberian Express (USA) 9f **(58)** - Try Gloria (Try My Best (USA)) 7.6f **(67)**
Form - 670685677632060460
Record 1999 - 1st:0 2nd:1 3rd:1 Ran:16
Pre1999 - 1st:7 2nd:16 3rd:20 Ran:114
Win Prizemoney £16,716 *Total Prizemoney* £41,465
Wins * 1998 *Apr Wolver (STD) C* 5f 67
* 1998 *Apr Wolver (STD) C* 5f 65
* 1998 *Mar Wolver (STD) S* 5f 60
* 1998 *Jan Wolver (STD) H* 5f 49 51
* 1997 *Aug Wolver (STD) S* 5f 44
* 1996 *Feb Wolver (STD) H* 5f 64 65
1999 Turf 0-5: (5f 4, 6f) (frm 5) 1999 AW 0-11: (5f 9, 6f 2) (Fibr 11)
Moderate gelding, effective 5 to 6f, best at 5f, - acts on Fibr, often wears blinkers (effectively), likes left handed tracks, likes tight tracks. Turf high 41. AW high 53. If he is to win again it is most likely going to be in selling company.
**Miss L C Siddall [7-130] Miss L C Siddall.*

FEATHERTIME BHB 54f **RR 55f** 5151[4]

3 b f Puissance 7.1f **(60)** - Midnight Owl (FR) (Ardross) 10.6f **(68)**
Form - 050036514
Record 1999 - 1st:1 2nd:0 3rd:1 Ran:9
Win Prizemoney £2,410 *Total Prizemoney* £2,744
Wins * 1999 Oct Newcas (G-S) CH 8f 45 52 <
1999 Turf 1-7: (6f 2, 7f 2, 8f 1-3) (gd 1-4, g-f, frm, hrd) 1999 AW 0-2: (9f, 10f) (Equi, Fibr)
Neat, fair filly, effective 8f, acts on gd, prefers left handed tracks. Turf high 55 - 4th of 18 giving 8lb to Bunty (1 Nov Nottingham 8f gd RF 5151) - also 1st of 20 giving 1lb to Welcome Heights (20 Oct Newcastle RF 4987). AW high 27.
**Mrs G S Rees [1-8] Brooke Rankin (from P Shakespeare [0-1] Jan 1999).*

FEBRUARY BHB 20f27a **RR 10f 27a** 2522[13]

6 b m Full Extent (USA) 5.2f **(50)** - Foligno (Crofter (USA)) 8.4f **(56)**
Form - 06000
Record 1999 - 1st:0 2nd:0 3rd:0 Ran:4
Pre1999 - 1st:0 2nd:0 3rd:5 Ran:19
Win Prizemoney £0 *Total Prizemoney* £1,842
1999 Turf 0-2: (5f 2) (g-f, frm) 1999 AW 0-2: (5f, 6f) (Equi, Fibr)
Little account mare, has worn blinkers. Turf high 10.
**J P Smith [0-5] M Bishop (from N P Littmoden [0-2] Aug 1997).*

FEEL A LINE BHB 45f49a **RR 23f 49a** 548[13]

5 b g Petong 7.6f **(58)** - Cat's Claw (USA) (Sharpen Up) 8.3f **(67)**
Form - 0830
Record 1999 - 1st:0 2nd:0 3rd:1 Ran:4
Pre1999 - 1st:3 2nd:1 3rd:3 Ran:22
Win Prizemoney £8,231 *Total Prizemoney* £10,847
Wins 1997 Aug Ayr (G-F) SH 7f 46 50
1997 Jly Yarmou (G-S) S 7f 60 <
1997 Jun Bright (FRM) H 7f 43 48
1999 Turf 0-1: (9f) (g-f) 1999 AW 0-3: (8f 3) (Fibr 3)
Fair gelding, effective 8f, acts on g-f - acts on Fibr, often wears blinkers (effectively). AW high 52 - 3rd of 12 getting 6lb from Mutahadeth (20 Feb Wolverhampton 8f Fibr RF 0331). Inconsistent.
**J G Given [0-1] Maltby Sporting Club (from M P Bielby [0-3] Feb 1999).*

FEEL NO FEAR BHB 48f54a **RR 47f 54a** 4783[1]

6 b m Fearless Action (USA) 8f**(44)**-Charm Bird(Daring March) 7.1f **(61)**
Form - 0784521071
Record 1999 - 1st:2 2nd:1 3rd:0 Ran:10
Pre1999 - 1st:1 2nd:2 3rd:2 Ran:17
Win Prizemoney £7,890 *Total Prizemoney* £12,332
Wins * 1999 *Oct Lingfi (STD) S* 8f 50
*** 1999** *Aug Lingfi (STD) SH* 8f 44 48
1998 Jly Newmar (G-F) H 8f 50 55 <
1999 Turf 0-7: (7f 3, 8f 3, 9f) (g-f 5, frm, hrd) 1999 AW 2-3: (7f, 8f 2-2) (Equi 2-2, Fibr)
Fair mare, effective 7 to 8f, best at 8f, acts on gd to frm - acts on Equi, best on frm, has worn blinkers, likes tight tracks. Turf high 47. AW high 50 (began Aug) - 1st of 12 getting 5lb from Dark Menace (8 Oct Lingfield RF 4783). Inconsistent.
**B J Meehan [2-5] Antonio Rovai & Franco Gamma (from R Simpson*

[1-16] Jly 1999).

FEE MAIL BHB 65f **RR 69f** 5112[1]
3 b f Danehill (USA) 9.1f **(79)** - Wizardry (Shirley Heights) 10.3f **(74)**
Form - 760021
Record 1999 - 1st:1 2nd:1 3rd:0 Ran:6
Pre1999 - 1st:0 2nd:0 3rd:1 Ran:2
Win Prizemoney £3,954 *Total Prizemoney* £5,309
Wins * **1999** Oct Windso (SFT) H 11.6f 61 63 <
1999 Turf 1-6: (7f, 8f 3, 11f, 12f 1-1) (g-s, gd 1-2, frm 3)
Neat, average filly, effective 8 to 12f, acts on gd to frm, best on gd. Turf high 69 (began Aug) - 6th of 17 to Lady Georgia (30 Aug Warwick 8f gd RF 4038) - also 1st of 8 getting 13lb from Philatelic Lady (28 Oct Windsor RF 5112). **I A Balding [1-8] Gary Coull.*

FEITICEIRA (USA) BHB 70f **RR 76df** 4729[7]
3 b f Deposit Ticket (USA) - Dogwood Lane (USA) (Alydar (USA)) 9.1f **(76)**
Form - 257
Record 1999 - 1st:0 2nd:1 3rd:0 Ran:3
Win Prizemoney £0 *Total Prizemoney* £968
1999 Turf 0-3: (8f 3) (g-s, g-f 2)
Scopey, currently above-average filly. Turf high 76 (1st run) - 2nd of 14 to First Night (9 Jun Salisbury 8f g-f RF 1871).
**J Noseda [0-3] Goncalo Borges Torrealba.*

FELONA BHB 94f **RR 90+f** 4871[8]
3 b f Caerleon (USA) 10.9f **(79)** - Felawnah (USA) (Mr Prospector (USA)) 8.8f **(78)**
Form - 118
Record 1999 - 1st:2 2nd:0 3rd:0 Ran:3
Win Prizemoney £9,709 *Total Prizemoney* £9,709
Wins * **1999** Spt Chepst (GD) 10.2f 90 <
* **1999** May Kempto (G-F) 9f 80
1999 Turf 2-3: (9f 1-1, 10f 1-2) (gd, frm 2-2)
Scopey, currently useful filly. Turf high 90 - 1st of 4 giving 3lb to Penang Pearl (9 Spt Chepstow RF 4231). Well regarded first foal of the useful Felawnah, she won her first two starts, although there was nearly four months between them, but ran poorly in a Newmarket Listed race. Potentially Pattern class.
**S bin Suroor [2-3] Godolphin.*

FELONY (IRE) BHB 29f28a **RR 14f 28a** 3441[11]
4 ch c Pharly (FR) 11.5f **(64)** - Scales of Justice (Final Straw) 7.9f **(64)**
Form - 0250
Record 1999 - 1st:0 2nd:1 3rd:0 Ran:4
Pre1999 - 1st:0 2nd:0 3rd:3 Ran:10
Win Prizemoney £0 *Total Prizemoney* £1,369
1999 AW 0-4: (11f, 15f, 16f 2) (Fibr 4)
Very moderate colt. AW high 30. Inconsistent.
**R Brotherton [1-10] Baskerville Racing Club (from D J G MurraySmith [0-10] Aug 1998).*

FEMME FATALE RR 100+f 4389[1]
2 b f Fairy King (USA) 7.7f **(75)** - Red Rita (IRE) **(75f)** (Kefaah (USA))
Form - 4231
Record 1999 - 1st:1 2nd:1 3rd:1 Ran:4
Win Prizemoney £12,802 *Total Prizemoney* £17,054
Wins * **1999** Spt Ayr (G-S) L 6f 100+ <
1999 Turf 1-4: (5f, 6f 1-3) (gd 1-2, g-f 2)
Very useful filly. Turf high 100 - 1st of 6 from Roo (18 Spt Ayr RF 4389). She was unlucky to bump into Teggiano, Khasayl and Invincible Spirit on her first three starts, and made no mistake in the Listed Firth Of Clyde Stakes at Ayr in September. An impressive five-length winner there, she may stay a mile and should pick-up a Group race. A sharp type, she could run well in one of the early Classic trials. **W Jarvis [1-4] Anthony Foster.*

FENCER'S QUEST (IRE) BHB 42f **RR 51f** 4586[4]
6 ch g Bluebird (USA) 7.9f **(71)** - Fighting Run (Runnett) 7f **(59)**
Form - 0004
Record 1999 - 1st:0 2nd:0 3rd:0 Ran:4
Pre1999 - 1st:0 2nd:0 3rd:0 Ran:1
1999 Turf 0-4: (5f, 6f, 8f, 10f) (gd, g-f 2, frm)
Fair gelding. Turf high 51 (began Jly).
**J C Tuck [1-10] Mrs Simon Preston (from R Charlton [0-1] Spt 1996).*

FERNY FACTORS BHB 55f49a **RR 56f 49a** 2722[12]
3 ch g King Among Kings 7.4f **(49)** -Market Blues (Porto Bello) 8.9f **(43)**
Form - 041100
Record 1999 - 1st:2 2nd:0 3rd:0 Ran:6
Pre1999 - 1st:1 2nd:0 3rd:0 Ran:7
Win Prizemoney £8,139 *Total Prizemoney* £8,139
Wins * **1999** Jun Beverl (GD) H 12f 54 56
* **1999** May Beverl (GD) S 9.9f 46
* 1998 Jly Beverl (GD) S 7.5f 57 <
1999 Turf 2-5: (10f 1-3, 12f 1-2) (gd 2-3, g-f, frm) 1999 AW 0-1: (12f) (Fibr)
Lengthy, fair gelding, effective 7 to 12f, acts on gd to g-f, has worn blinkers, prefers right handed tracks, prefers tight tracks. Turf high 56 - 1st of 13 giving 2lb to Grandioso (2 Jun Beverley RF 1665). **Ronald Thompson [3-13] B Bruce.*

FERNY HILL (IRE) BHB 91f **RR 88f** 4876[9]
5 b g Danehill (USA) 9.1f **(79)** - Miss Allowed (USA) (Alleged (USA)) 10f **(76)**
Form - 060
Record 1999 - 1st:0 2nd:0 3rd:0 Ran:3
Pre1999 - 1st:4 2nd:3 3rd:2 Ran:13
Win Prizemoney £18,593 *Total Prizemoney* £29,132
Wins * 1998 Aug Windso (G-F) 11.6f 80
1997 Spt Redcar (FRM) H 14.1f 84 89
1997 Spt Kempto (G-F) 12f 90 <
1997 Aug Newcas (G-F) 12.4f 84
1999 Turf 0-3: (12f 3) (gd, g-f, frm)
Useful gelding, effective 13f, acts on frm. Turf high 88 (began Spt). Failed to recapture his form in a truncated season.
**W R Muir [1-9] Mrs Monique Bruce Copp (from Sir Mark Prescott [3-8] Spt 1997).*

FEROCITY BHB 30f **RR 23f** 1490[13]
3 ch f Superlative 8.8f **(57)** - Tantalizing Song (CAN) (The Minstrel (CAN)) 10f **(72)**
Form - 00060
Record 1999 - 1st:0 2nd:0 3rd:0 Ran:3
Pre1999 - 1st:0 2nd:0 3rd:0 Ran:2
1999 Turf 0-3: (6f, 7f, 10f) (sft, g-f 2)
Workmanlike, little account filly. Turf high 23.
**M A Jarvis [0-5] N S Yong.*

FERRET EDDIE (IRE) BHB 52f **RR 62?f** 1523[8]
3 ch g Be My Guest (USA) 10.2f **(66)** -Musical Essence (Song) 7.2f **(61)**
Form - 038
Record 1999 - 1st:0 2nd:0 3rd:1 Ran:3
Pre1999 - 1st:0 2nd:0 3rd:0 Ran:1
Win Prizemoney £0 *Total Prizemoney* £639
1999 Turf 0-3: (8f 2, 9f) (gd 2, hrd)
Scopey, average gelding. Turf high 62. (DEAD)
**T P Tate [0-4] The Ivy Syndicate.*

FESTIVAL FLYER BHB 62f47a **RR 69f 47a** 235[8]
4 b g Alhijaz 7.7f **(57)** - Odilese (Mummy's Pet) 7.7f **(60)**
Form - 078
Record 1999 - 1st:0 2nd:0 3rd:0 Ran:3
Pre1999 - 1st:0 2nd:0 3rd:0 Ran:7
Win Prizemoney £0 *Total Prizemoney* £757
1999 AW 0-3: (8f, 10f, 12f) (Equi 3)
Average gelding. AW high 37. Becoming disappointing.
**Miss Gay Kelleway [0-3] Mrs Joan Root (from R W Armstrong [0-2] Oct 1998).*

FESTIVAL HALL (IRE) RR 104+f 2419a[10]
3 b c Sadler's Wells (USA) 11.3f **(87)** - Handsewn (USA) (Sir Ivor) 10.2f **(70)**
Form - 50
1999 Turf 0-2: (10f, 12f) (g-s, gd)
Very useful colt. Turf high 98. He failed to train on and proved most disappointing. **A P O'Brien in IRE [1-5] Mrs John Magnier.*

FESTIVE RR 71df 4719[3]
3 b f Rudimentary (USA) 8.2f **(66)** - Champagne Season (USA) (Vaguely Noble) 10.1f **(72)**
Form - 41011433
Record 1999 - 1st:3 2nd:0 3rd:2 Ran:7
Pre1999 - 1st:0 2nd:0 3rd:0 Ran:1

Win Prizemoney £13,583 *Total Prizemoney* £15,636

Wins * **1999** Jly Yarmou (GD) H 7f 68 75+ <
* **1999** Jun Redcar (FRM) H 7f 64 66
* **1999** *Jan Wolver (STD) 7f 64*

1999 Turf 2-6: (6f, 7f 2-5) (g-s, gd 1-2, frm 1-3) 1999 AW 1-1: (7f 1-1) (Fibr 1-1)

Tall, above-average filly, effective 7f, acts on gd to frm. Turf high 75 - 1st of 8 giving 5lb to Oriel Girl (1 Jly Yarmouth RF 2468) - also 1st of 9 giving 4lb to Supreme Salutation (18 Jun Redcar RF 2130). (1st run). She looked an improving filly when winning three of her first four starts this season, but was found wanting subsequently.

**W J Haggas [3-8] Cheveley Park Stud.*

FEZ RR 92f 4268[4]

2 ch f Mujtahid (USA) 7.4f **(69)** - Velvet Beret (IRE) (Dominion) 8.5f **(63)**

Form - 52511124

Record 1999 - 1st:3 2nd:2 3rd:0 Ran:8

Win Prizemoney £15,459 *Total Prizemoney* £27,612

Wins * **1999** Jly York (G-F) H 5f 90 <
* **1999** Jun Doncas (G-F) 5f 82
* **1999** Jun Redcar (FRM) 5f 75

1999 Turf 3-8: (5f 3-8) (gd 2, g-f 1-2, frm 2-4)

Useful filly, effective 5f, acts on g-f to frm, best on g-f. Turf high 92 - 4th of 14 to Mrs P (11 Spt Doncaster 5f frm RF 4268) - also 1st of 10 giving 3lb to Singsong (10 Jly York RF 2735). Improving. He suddenly hit form in June, winning at Redcar and Doncaster. Showed real courage on the second occasion, and put in a similarly game effort when holding on for the hat-trick at York. Runner-up to Misty Miss in the Molecomb, she then ran fourth in the Flying Childers and certainly deserves a win in decent company.

**M Johnston [3-8] The Earl of Burlington.*

FHULAAD (USA) RR 68f 4751[11]

2 b c Blush Rambler (USA) - Now That's Funny (USA) (Saratoga Six (USA)) 7f **(73)**

Form - 50

Record 1999 - 1st:0 2nd:0 3rd:0 Ran:2

1999 Turf 0-2: (8f 2) (gd 2)

Currently average colt. Turf high 57 (began Spt).

**M Johnston [0-2] Jaber Abdullah.*

FICKLE BHB 86f RR 84f 4019[1]

3 b f Danehill (USA) 9.1f **(79)** - Fade (Persepolis (FR)) 6.4f **(67)**

Form - 30131

Record 1999 - 1st:2 2nd:0 3rd:2 Ran:5

Win Prizemoney £16,900 *Total Prizemoney* £18,701

Wins * **1999** Aug Newcas (GD) LH 10.1f 80 84 <
* **1999** Jun Bright (GD) 8f 73

1999 Turf 2-5: (8f 1-4, 10f 1-1) (gd 1-1, g-f 1-3, frm)

Scopey, decent filly. Turf high 84 - 1st of 14 getting 14lb from Robin Lane (30 Aug Newcastle RF 4019). Showed progressive form, and sprang a 20/1 surprise in a Listed race at Newcastle.

**M L W Bell [2-5] Lady Carolyn Warren.*

FICTITIOUS BHB 103f RR 102f 3055[5]

3 ch f Machiavellian (USA) 9.8f **(83)** - Trying for Gold (USA) (Northern Baby (CAN)) 11.6f **(71)**

Form - 1615

Record 1999 - 1st:2 2nd:0 3rd:0 Ran:4
Pre1999 - 1st:0 2nd:0 3rd:1 Ran:2

Win Prizemoney £21,740 *Total Prizemoney* £24,479

Wins * **1999** Jun Newcas (G-F) L 10.1f 102+ <
* **1999** May Salisb (G-F) 9.9f 79++

1999 Turf 2-4: (10f 2-3, 12f) (g-f, frm 2-3)

Well made, very useful filly, effective 10f, acts on frm. Turf high 102 - 1st of 9 getting 12lb from Maria Isabella (26 Jun Newcastle RF 2337). Talented but wayward - as was her sister Phantom Gold - she was impressive when winning a maiden and Listed event, but disappointed when partnered by Gary Stevens on her two remaining starts. Best when ridden patiently, she has the ability to win a Group race but is not one to rely on.

**Sir Michael Stoute [2-4] The Queen (from Lord Huntingdon [0-2] Spt 1998).*

FIELDGATE FLYER (IRE) BHB 23f RR 17f 4032[16]

4 b f Sabrehill (USA) 8.5f **(64)** - Orba Gold (USA) (Gold Crest (USA))

Form - 0

Record 1999 - 1st:0 2nd:0 3rd:0 Ran:1
Pre1999 - 1st:0 2nd:0 3rd:0 Ran:2

1999 Turf 0-1: (11f) (gd)

Workmanlike, currently poor filly. **R Hollinshead [0-3] G A Farndon.*

FIELD MASTER (IRE) BHB 72f RR 76f 5048[12]

2 ch c Foxhound (USA) - Bold Avril (IRE) (Persian Bold) 9.3f **(66)**

Form - 74440

Record 1999 - 1st:0 2nd:0 3rd:0 Ran:5

Win Prizemoney £0 *Total Prizemoney* £620

1999 Turf 0-5: (6f 2, 7f 3) (hvy, gd, g-f, frm 2)

Above-average colt. Turf high 76 (began Aug).

**A C Stewart [0-5] Jon Waller, A K Collins & R C Stewart.*

FIELD OF HOPE (IRE) RR 116f 5014a[1]

4 ch f Selkirk (USA) 7.9f **(76)** - Fracci (Raise A Cup (USA)) 7.6f **(74)**

Form - 51161

1999 Turf 3-5: (7f 1-1, 8f 2-4) (hvy, sft 1-1, gd 1-2)

High-class filly, effective 7 to 8f, best at 8f, acts on gd. Turf high 116 - 1st getting 4lb from Keos (17 Oct Longchamp RF 5014a) - also 1st of 4 from Miss Berbere (1 Aug Deauville RF 3409a). She improved throughout the campaign and showed a sharp turn-of-foot to win Deauville's Prix d' Astarte. Far from disgraced behind Sendawar in the Prix du Moulin, she settles well and may stay beyond a mile.

**P Bary in FR [4-7] Grundy Bloodstock Ltd (from G Botti in ITY [0-1] Apr 1998).*

FIELD OF VISION (IRE) BHB 53f55a RR 45f 55a 5071[7]

9 b g Vision (USA) 10.4f **(57)** - Bold Meadows (Persian Bold) 9.3f **(66)**

Form - 47

Record 1999 - 1st:0 2nd:0 3rd:0 Ran:2
Pre1999 - 1st:9 2nd:10 3rd:8 Ran:63

Win Prizemoney £34,812 *Total Prizemoney* £53,781

Wins * 1998 May Beverl (G-F) H 12f 68 74 <
* 1998 May Hamilt (G-S) H 13f 65 66
1996 Apr Hamilt (G-S) C 9.2f 64
1996 *Jan Wolver (STD) H 9.4f 63 72*
1996 *Jan Wolver (STD) H 9.4f 63 65*

1999 Turf 0-2: (11f, 12f) (gd 2)

Fair gelding, effective 11 to 16f, acts on g-s to hrd - acts on Fibr, has worn blinkers, favours tight tracks. Turf high 45 (began Oct).

**Mrs A Swinbank [5-35] Mrs L J Tounsend (from M Johnston [7-40] Apr 1996).*

FIELDS OF OMAGH (USA) BHB 75f83a RR 71+f 83a 182[2]

4 b g Pleasant Tap (USA) 13.1f **(71)** - Brave And True (USA) (Fappiano (USA)) 8.7f **(77)**

Form - 112

Record 1999 - 1st:2 2nd:1 3rd:0 Ran:3
Pre1999 - 1st:1 2nd:0 3rd:1 Ran:11

Win Prizemoney £7,575 *Total Prizemoney* £9,329

Wins * **1999** *Jan Lingfi (STD) H 12f 75 79* <
* **1999** *Jan Lingfi (STD) H 12f 70 73*
* 1998 Spt Bath (GD) H 13.1f 64 71+

1999 AW 2-3: (12f 2-3) (Equi 2-3)

Scopey, decent gelding, effective 12f, - acts on Equi, prefers left handed tracks, favours tight tracks. AW high 82 - 2nd of 6 giving 4lb to Space Race (28 Jan Lingfield 12f Equi RF 0182) - also 1st of 9 giving 1lb to Noukari (16 Jan Lingfield RF 0106).

**I A Balding [3-16] Paul Mellon.*

FIERY WATERS BHB 58f RR 71f 3860[8]

3 b g Rudimentary (USA) 8.2f **(66)** - Idle Waters (Mill Reef (USA)) 10.5f **(78)**

Form - 83708

Record 1999 - 1st:0 2nd:0 3rd:1 Ran:5

Win Prizemoney £0 *Total Prizemoney* £353

1999 Turf 0-5: (10f 4, 14f) (g-f, frm 3, hrd)

Workmanlike, above-average gelding. Turf high 71.

**D W P Arbuthnot [0-5] R Crutchley.*

FIFE AND DRUM (USA) BHB 60f RR 63f 4785[10]

2 b br c Rahy (USA) 9.1f **(80)** - Fife (IRE) (Lomond (USA)) 8.8f **(65)**

Form - 780

Record 1999 - 1st:0 2nd:0 3rd:0 Ran:3

1999 Turf 0-3: (7f 2, 8f) (g-s 2, frm)

Currently average colt. Turf high 63 (began Spt).

**E A L Dunlop [0-3] Maktoum Al Maktoum.*

FIFTEEN REDS BHB 38f44a **RR 58f 44a** 4940[7]
4 b g Jumbo Hirt (USA) 15.8f **(44)** - Dominance (Dominion) 8.5f **(63)**
Form - 850007
Record 1999 - 1st:0 2nd:0 3rd:0 Ran:6
1999 Turf 0-3: (10f, 11f, 14f) (gd 3) 1999 AW 0-3: (9f, 12f, 14f) (Fibr 3)
Fair gelding, has worn blinkers. Turf high 58. AW high 43.
**D Shaw [0-8] J Roundtree.*

FIFTH EDITION BHB 60f **RR 63f** 4446[5]
3 b f Rock Hopper 10.6f **(54)** - Glossary (Reference Point) 6.8f **(70)**
Form - 08405
Record 1999 - 1st:0 2nd:0 3rd:0 Ran:5
Win Prizemoney £0 *Total Prizemoney* £279
1999 Turf 0-5: (7f, 8f 4) (g-s, g-f, frm 3)
Scopey, average filly. Turf high 63 (began Jly) - 4th of 11 getting 5lb from El Nahrawan (5 Aug Chepstow 7f frm RF 3393).
**C F Wall [0-5] M Ng.*

FIGAWIN BHB 46f42a **RR 46f 42a** 208[9]
4 b g Rudimentary (USA) 8.2f **(66)** - Dear Person (Rainbow Quest (USA)) 10.4f **(75)**
Form - 0
Record 1999 - 1st:0 2nd:0 3rd:0 Ran:1
Pre1999 - 1st:1 2nd:1 3rd:2 Ran:23
Win Prizemoney £1,984 *Total Prizemoney* £3,341
Wins 1997 *Jun Southw (STD) S 6f 59 <*
1999 AW 0-1: (8f) (Equi)
Leggy, moderate gelding, effective 8f, acts on gd, has worn blinkers. **Mrs H L Walton [0-10] A E Walton (from S Dow [0-10] Mar 1998).*

FIGHTER SQUADRON BHB 21f33a **RR 25f 33a** 2647[7]
10 ch g Primo Dominie 7.2f **(67)** - Formidable Dancer (Formidable (USA)) 9.2f **(63)**
Form - 00607
Record 1999 - 1st:0 2nd:0 3rd:0 Ran:5
Pre1999 - 1st:4 2nd:5 3rd:8 Ran:72
Win Prizemoney £13,194 *Total Prizemoney* £20,653
1999 AW 0-5: (6f, 7f 2, 8f, 10f) (Equi, Fibr 4)
Little account gelding, mostly wears blinkers. AW high 26.
**R E Peacock [0-24] R E Peacock (from J A Glover [4-53] Nov 1994).*

FIGURE IT OUT BHB 22f **RR 22f** 2949[17]
4 ch g Dilum (USA) 7.1f **(56)** - Count On Me (No Mercy) 8f **(61)**
Form - 000
Record 1999 - 1st:0 2nd:0 3rd:0 Ran:3
Pre1999 - 1st:0 2nd:0 3rd:0 Ran:2
1999 Turf 0-3: (5f, 8f, 12f) (frm 3)
Leggy, little account gelding. Turf high 13.
**R J Hodges [0-5] J W Mursell.*

FILEY BRIGG BHB 28f **RR 28f** 1981[11]
4 b f Weldnaas (USA) 8.4f **(55)** - Dusty's Darling (Doyoun) 9f **(69)**
Form - 000600
Record 1999 - 1st:0 2nd:0 3rd:0 Ran:6
Pre1999 - 1st:2 2nd:1 3rd:3 Ran:22
Win Prizemoney £11,833 *Total Prizemoney* £18,424
Wins * 1997 Jun Beverl (G-F) 5f 84 <
* 1997 Apr Hamilt (G-S) 5f 65
1999 Turf 0-6: (7f 2, 8f, 9f, 10f, 13f) (g-s, gd 2, g-f 3)
Leggy, little account filly. Turf high 31.
**W T Kemp [2-28] Drakemyre Racing.*

FILIAL (IRE) BHB 53f57a **RR 56f 57a** 4913[5]
6 b g Danehill (USA) 9.1f **(79)** - Sephira (Luthier) 9.8f **(71)**
Form - 00035
Record 1999 - 1st:0 2nd:0 3rd:1 Ran:4
Pre1999 - 1st:7 2nd:7 3rd:3 Ran:33
Win Prizemoney £17,844 *Total Prizemoney* £25,396

Wins									
	1998	Oct	Redcar	(SFT)	C	11f		70	
	1998	May	Hamilt	(GD)	H	13f	68	73	
	1998	Apr	Ripon	(SFT)	H	12.3f	60	66	
	1998	*Mar*	*Southw*	*(STD)*	*C*	*12f*		*61*	
	1997	*Nov*	*Wolver*	*(STD)*	*C*	*12f*		*72*	
	1996	*Dec*	*Lingfi*	*(STD)*	*H*	*12f*	*80*	*86*	<
	1996	Aug	Sandow	(G-F)		10f		75	

1999 Turf 0-4: (12f 2, 13f, 14f) (gd 2, g-f, frm)
Average gelding, effective 11 to 13f, best at 12f, acts on sft to gd, best on gd, has worn blinkers, prefers tight tracks. Turf high 56. Becoming disappointing.
**Mrs A Swinbank [1-9] Ann Swinbank Racing Club (from J Pearce [5-18] Oct 1998).*

FILS DE VIANE (FR) RR 108f 2476a[6]
3 ch c Kadounor (FR) - Life On The Road (FR) (Persian Heights)
Form - 526
1999 Turf 0-3: (9f, 10f, 11f) (hvy, g-s, gd)
Currently Pattern-class colt. Turf high 108. **J-C Rouget in FR [0-3].*

FINAL DIVIDEND (IRE) BHB 74f **RR 70f** 4802[25]
3 b g Second Set (IRE) 9.2f **(67)** - Prime Interest (IRE) (Kings Lake (USA)) 10.8f **(67)**
Form - 431006610
Record 1999 - 1st:2 2nd:0 3rd:1 Ran:9
Pre1999 - 1st:0 2nd:0 3rd:1 Ran:6
Win Prizemoney £6,385 *Total Prizemoney* £7,580
Wins * 1999 Spt Beverl (SFT) H 8.5f 69 70 <
*** 1999** May Salisb (G-F) H 8f 67 70+
1999 Turf 2-9: (7f 2, 8f 2-6, 9f) (sft, g-s 1-1, gd, g-f 2, frm 1-4)
Workmanlike, above-average gelding, effective 6 to 8f, best at 8f, acts on sft to frm. Turf high 70 - 1st of 17 giving 7lb to Quedex (13 May Salisbury RF 1189) - also 1st of 16 giving 4lb to Rex Is Okay (21 Spt Beverley RF 4446). Inconsistent.
**M J Fetherston-Godley [2-15] The Kennet House Partnership.*

FINAL KISS (IRE) BHB 52f **RR 50f** 4825[13]
2 b c Dolphin Street (FR) - Mystery Train (Bay Express) 7.1f **(60)**
Form - 0000
Record 1999 - 1st:0 2nd:0 3rd:0 Ran:4
1999 Turf 0-4: (6f 4) (g-f 3, frm)
Fair colt. Turf high 50 (began Jly).
**J R Jenkins [0-4] Mrs Stella Garrad.*

FINAL LAP BHB 74f **RR 82f** 5198[4]
3 b g Batshoof 9.5f **(66)** - Lap of Honour (Final Straw) 7.9f **(64)**
Form - 8424
Record 1999 - 1st:0 2nd:1 3rd:0 Ran:4
Win Prizemoney £0 *Total Prizemoney* £1,716
1999 Turf 0-4: (8f 4) (sft, gd 2, frm)
Workmanlike, decent gelding. Turf high 73 (began Aug) - 2nd of 18 to Zanay (21 Oct Nottingham 8f gd RF 5003).
**W Jarvis [0-4] T C Blackwell And Partners.*

FINAL ROW BHB 99f **RR 89f** 4953[2]
2 b c Indian Ridge 7.6f **(74)**-The Jotter **(88f)**(Night Shift (USA)) 7.2f **(69)**
Form - 2127242
Record 1999 - 1st:1 2nd:4 3rd:0 Ran:7
Win Prizemoney £3,600 *Total Prizemoney* £10,577
Wins * 1999 Jly Catter (GD) 6f 78 <
1999 Turf 1-7: (5f 2, 6f 1-5) (g-s, gd 2, g-f 1-2, frm 2)
Useful colt, effective 5 to 6f, best at 6f, acts on gd to g-f, best on gd. Turf high 89 - 2nd of 5 to Observatory (19 Oct Yarmouth 6f g-f RF 4953). Got off the mark at Catterick on his second start and has been pretty consistent otherwise. Probably best suited by six furlongs, he is suited by cut in the ground.
**W Jarvis [1-7] Exors of the Late Mrs D N Allen.*

FINAL SETTLEMENT (IRE) BHB 61f **RR 65f** 5066[3]
4 b g Soviet Lad (USA) 9.4f **(63)** - Tender Time (Tender King) 6.8f **(54)**
Form - 0433
Record 1999 - 1st:0 2nd:0 3rd:2 Ran:4
Pre1999 - 1st:2 2nd:0 3rd:1 Ran:6
Win Prizemoney £6,242 *Total Prizemoney* £8,080
Wins * 1998 Jly Lingfi (G-F) H 11.5f 60 64 <
* 1998 Jun Windso (GD) H 8.3f 58 60
1999 Turf 0-4: (10f 2, 12f 2) (g-s, gd, g-f, frm)
Leggy, average gelding, effective 8 to 12f, acts on g-s to frm, prefers tight tracks, does well at Windsor. Turf high 65 - 3rd of 17 getting 4lb from Eyeballs Out (5 Oct Nottingham 10f g-s RF 4733). Consistent. **J R Jenkins [2-10] T H Ounsley.*

FINAL STAB (IRE) BHB 43f54a **RR 26f 54a** 4219[4]
6 b g Kris 10f **(75)** - Premier Rose (Sharp Edge) 10f **(56)**
Form - 116604

Record 1999 - 1st:2 2nd:0 3rd:0 Ran:6
Pre1999 - 1st:2 2nd:0 3rd:1 Ran:14
Win Prizemoney £14,051 *Total Prizemoney* £14,308
Wins * **1999** *Jun Southw (STD) H 8f 52 55*
* **1999** *May Wolver (STD) H 9.4f 49 50*
1997 Aug Bath (GD) H 8f 69 74+ <
1995 Spt Salisb (G-S) 7f 74
1999 Turf 0-1: (8f) (gd) 1999 AW 2-5: (8f 1-3, 9f 1-2) (Fibr 2-5)
Moderate gelding, effective 8 to 12f, - acts on Fibr, has worn blinkers. AW high 55 - 1st of 15 giving 9lb to Stravsea (17 Jun Southwell RF 2085) - also 1st of 10 getting 19lb from State Approval (22 May Wolverhampton RF 1422). Consistent. A winner over hurdles in the autumn of '98, he won a couple of modest handicaps on Fibresand in the spring, but was exposed when stepped up in class.
**Miss S J Wilton [3-12] John Pointon and Sons (from P W Harris [2-9] Oct 1997).*

FINAL TRIAL (IRE) BHB 60f **RR 62f** 4980[6]
5 b g Last Tycoon 9.4f **(73)** - Perfect Alibi (Law Society (USA)) 9.9f **(70)**
Form - 03000146
Record 1999 - 1st:1 2nd:0 3rd:1 Ran:8
Pre1999 - 1st:0 2nd:0 3rd:1 Ran:7
Win Prizemoney £3,938 *Total Prizemoney* £7,077
Wins * **1999** Spt Pontef (G-F) H 10f 56 59 <
1999 Turf 1-8: (10f 1-5, 12f 3) (hvy, gd 2, g-f, frm 1-3, hrd)
Average gelding, effective 10f, acts on gd to frm, prefers left handed tracks. Turf high 62 - 4th of 19 getting 4lb from Capriolo (12 Oct Leicester 10f gd RF 4836) - also 1st of 19 giving 8lb to Caerosa (16 Spt Pontefract RF 4350). Inconsistent.
**G Wragg [1-15] Mollers Racing.*

FINAL TRICK **RR 35f** 3613[7]
2 b f Primo Dominie 7.2f **(67)** - Tricky Note (Song) 7.2f **(61)**
Form - 67
Record 1999 - 1st:0 2nd:0 3rd:0 Ran:2
1999 Turf 0-2: (5f 2) (frm 2)
Currently very moderate filly. Turf high 35 (began Aug).
**W J Haggas [0-2] R J Bassett.*

FINCH BHB 49f **RR 39f** 5195[12]
2 b f Inchinor 8.9f **(64)** - Wryneck (Niniski (USA)) 10.6f **(65)**
Form - 000
Record 1999 - 1st:0 2nd:0 3rd:0 Ran:3
1999 Turf 0-3: (6f 2, 7f) (sft, gd 2)
Currently very moderate filly. Turf high 39 (began Oct).
**R Charlton [0-3] Lady Sophia Morrison.*

FINE AND ROSY BHB 24f **RR 19f** 4148[11]
4 b f Petoski 10.4f **(56)** - Vaigly Fine (Vaigly Great) 7f **(58)**
Form - 076000000070
Record 1999 - 1st:0 2nd:0 3rd:0 Ran:12
1999 Turf 0-11: (5f 2, 6f 3, 7f 4, 8f 2) (gd 3, g-f 2, frm 4, hrd 2) 1999 AW 0-1: (9f) (Fibr)
Poor filly, has worn blinkers. Turf high 43.
**M Dods [0-13] Miss J Palmer.*

FINGALS COVE **RR 30f** 1648[9]
2 b f Puissance 7.1f **(60)** - Polar Cove (Polar Falcon (USA))
Form - 0
Record 1999 - 1st:0 2nd:0 3rd:0 Ran:1
1999 Turf 0-1: (6f) (frm)
Currently very moderate filly. **J Berry [0-1] T G & Mrs M E Holdcroft.*

FINGERS HENRY (IRE) BHB 53f **RR 35f** 4224[9]
2 b c Shalford (IRE) 7.8f **(63)** - Running For You (FR) (Pampabird) 7.5f **(73)**
Form - 0826220
Record 1999 - 1st:0 2nd:3 3rd:0 Ran:7
Win Prizemoney £0 *Total Prizemoney* £1,560
1999 Turf 0-2: (5f 2) (gd 2) 1999 AW 0-5: (5f, 6f 3, 7f) (Fibr 5)
Average colt, effective 6 to 7f, - acts on Fibr. Turf high 35. AW high 62 (1st run) - 2nd of 7 to Sporty Mo (17 May Southwell 6f Fibr RF 1283). **Ronald Thompson [0-7] Mrs Janet McCabe.*

FINISHED ARTICLE (IRE) **RR 60f** 5208[9]
2 b c Indian Ridge 7.6f **(74)** - Summer Fashion (Moorestyle) 6.9f **(64)**
Form - 50
Record 1999 - 1st:0 2nd:0 3rd:0 Ran:2
1999 Turf 0-2: (7f, 8f) (g-s 2)
Currently average colt. Turf high 60 (began Spt).
**D R C Elsworth [0-2] Dr D B Davis.*

FINISTERRE (IRE) BHB 68f48a **RR 68f 48a** 773[15]
6 b g Salt Dome (USA) 6.5f **(59)** - Inisfail (Persian Bold) 9.3f **(66)**
Form - 3530
Record 1999 - 1st:0 2nd:0 3rd:1 Ran:2
Pre1999 - 1st:2 2nd:6 3rd:5 Ran:36
Win Prizemoney £5,725 *Total Prizemoney* £14,185
Wins * 1998 May Catter (G-S) 7f 63 <
* 1996 May Ripon (GD) H 6f 57 58
1999 Turf 0-2: (7f, 8f) (sft, gd)
Average gelding, effective 7f, acts on gd to frm, has worn blinkers, likes left handed tracks, likes tight tracks. Turf high 68 (1st run) - 3rd of 18 giving 3lb to Rambo Waltzer (31 Mar Catterick 7f gd RF 0526). **J J O'Neill [3-44] Les Femmes Fatales.*

FIONA'S DREAM (IRE) BHB 32f **RR 37f** 4667[11]
3 b br f Soviet Lad (USA) 9.4f **(63)** - Woody's Colours (USA) (Caro)
Form - 740
Record 1999 - 1st:0 2nd:0 3rd:0 Ran:3
Pre1999 - 1st:0 2nd:0 3rd:0 Ran:2
1999 Turf 0-2: (7f, 8f) (frm 2) 1999 AW 0-1: (13f) (Equi)
Scopey, very moderate filly. Turf high 37 (began Jly).
**Miss Gay Kelleway [0-5] A P Griffin.*

FIONN DE COOL (IRE) BHB 49f **RR 49f** 3852[3]
8 b g Mazaad 8.5f **(53)** - Pink Fondant (Northfields (USA)) 9f **(72)**
Form - 80853
Record 1999 - 1st:0 2nd:0 3rd:1 Ran:5
Pre1999 - 1st:3 2nd:4 3rd:4 Ran:38
Win Prizemoney £17,108 *Total Prizemoney* £28,091
Wins * 1998 Jly Chepst (GD) H 8.1f 58 63
1997 Aug Epsom (GD) H 8.5f 59 64
1995 Aug Salisb (FRM) H 8f 70 75 <
1999 Turf 0-5: (8f 4, 9f) (g-f 2, frm 3)
Moderate gelding, effective 8f, acts on gd.
**J Akehurst [1-14] Canisbay Bloodstock Ltd (from R Akehurst [2-29] Spt 1997).*

FIORI BHB 84f80a **RR 88f 80a** 4590[11]
3 b c Anshan 8.2f **(63)** - Fen Princess (IRE) (Trojan Fen) 8.1f **(62)**
Form - 301311550
Record 1999 - 1st:3 2nd:0 3rd:1 Ran:8
Pre1999 - 1st:0 2nd:4 3rd:3 Ran:9
Win Prizemoney £16,320 *Total Prizemoney* £30,383
Wins * **1999** Jun York (G-S) H 10.4f 80 88 <
* **1999** Jun Beverl (SFT) H 12f 80 85+
* **1999** May Hamilt (G-F) 9.2f 64
1999 Turf 3-8: (8f, 9f 1-1, 10f 1-2, 11f, 12f 1-2, 13f) (g-s 1-1, gd 1-4, g-f 1-1, frm 2)
Scopey, useful colt, effective 8 to 12f, acts on g-s to frm. Turf high 88 - 1st of 7 giving 1lb to Chelsea Barracks (12 Jun York RF 1969) - also 1st of 6 giving 1lb to Nathan's Boy (9 Jun Beverley RF 1850). Showed progressive form last term, winning a valuable rated stakes at York in June. Probably needed the run at Chester in August after a ten-week absence and ran a sound race next time. Has hung left on occasions. **P C Haslam [3-17] S A B Dinsmore.*

FIRECREST (IRE) **RR 46f** 5049[11]
2 b f Darshaan 11.9f **(81)** - Trefoil (FR) (Blakeney) 10.5f **(64)**
Form - 00
Record 1999 - 1st:0 2nd:0 3rd:0 Ran:2
1999 Turf 0-2: (7f, 8f) (gd 2)
Currently moderate filly. Turf high 46 (began Oct).
**J L Dunlop [0-2] Sir Thomas Pilkington.*

FIRE DOME (IRE) BHB 83f92a **RR 81?f 92a** 5167[4]
7 ch g Salt Dome (USA) 6.5f **(59)** - Penny Habit (Habitat) 9.4f **(70)**
Form - 3056023101804
Record 1999 - 1st:2 2nd:1 3rd:2 Ran:13
Pre1999 - 1st:5 2nd:4 3rd:2 Ran:28
Win Prizemoney £52,290 *Total Prizemoney* £68,737
Wins * **1999** Oct Redcar (GD) C 6f 68+

* **1999** Oct Sandow (HVY) C 5f 82
* **1998** Jly Sandow (G-S) L 5f 109 <
* **1998** Apr Thirsk (G-S) 6f 106
1996 Mar Doncas (SFT) L 6f 107

1999 Turf 2-13: (5f 1-6, 6f 1-7) (sft 1-1, g-s 3, gd 3, g-f 3, frm 1-3)

Useful gelding, effective 5 to 6f, acts on g-s to gd, has worn blinkers. Turf high 105. He underlined David Nicholls' skill in revitalising horses when winning a couple of decent conditions races in '98, the latter a Listed event at Sandown. He had struggled a bit since then, until dropped successfully into claiming company. Suited by coming off a fast pace.

**D Nicholls [4-24] J M Ranson (from R Hannon [1-10] May 1996).*

FIREPOWER (IRE) BHB 72f RR 80+f 4857[6]

2 br c Hamas (IRE) 8f **(72)** - Winchester Queen (IRE) (Persian Bold) 9.3f **(66)**

Form - 0330852516

Record 1999 - 1st:1 2nd:1 3rd:2 Ran:10

Win Prizemoney £1,945 *Total Prizemoney* £3,884

Wins * **1999** Spt Bright (SFT) S 5.3f 73+ <

1999 Turf 1-10: (5f 1-7, 6f 3) (g-s 1-3, gd 2, g-f, frm 4)

Decent colt, effective 5f, acts on g-s to frm, best on frm, has worn blinkers. Turf high 77 - 2nd of 12 to Connect (16 Spt Pontefract 5f frm RF 4348) - also 1st of 11 from Itsgottabdun (29 Spt Brighton RF 4626). Inconsistent. **B J Meehan [1-10] Trevor Painting.*

FIRST BACK (IRE) BHB 50f RR 65f 4715[6]

2 b c Fourstars Allstar (USA) - Par Un Nez (IRE) (Cyrano de Bergerac) 6f **(68)**

Form - 076

Record 1999 - 1st:0 2nd:0 3rd:0 Ran:3

1999 Turf 0-3: (7f, 9f, 10f) (gd 2, frm)

Currently average colt. Turf high 65 (began Spt).

**C W Fairhurst [0-3] Twinacre Nurseries Ltd.*

FIRST BALLOT (IRE) BHB 90f RR 89f 4360a[7]

3 b g Perugino (USA) - Election Special **(62f)** (Chief Singer) 8.9f **(66)**

Form - 41617

Record 1999 - 1st:2 2nd:0 3rd:0 Ran:5
Pre1999 - 1st:0 2nd:0 3rd:0 Ran:1

Win Prizemoney £16,796 *Total Prizemoney* £17,066

Wins * **1999** Aug Ascot (GD) H 16.2f 87 89 <
* **1999** Jly Newbur (G-F) 12f 83

1999 Turf 2-5: (10f 2, 12f 1-1, 15f, 16f 1-1) (gd 1-3, frm 1-2)

Workmanlike, useful gelding, effective 10 to 16f, acts on gd to frm, best on gd. Turf high 89 - 1st of 7 giving 13lb to Son of Snurge (7 Aug Ascot RF 3443) - also 1st of 7 from Williamshakespeare (11 Jly Newbury RF 2747). Beat Williamshakespeare by a short head in a Newbury maiden in July, having been stepped up to twelve furlongs, but never figured when stepped back down in trip on his handicap debut at Ayr. Demonstrated a liking for staying distances when beating the useful Son Of Snurge in an Ascot handicap over two miles. **D R C Elsworth [2-6].*

FIRST BLOOD BHB 92f RR 91f 5045[2]

2 b c Rambo Dancer (CAN) 8.4f **(59)** - Bollin Victoria (Jalmood (USA)) 10.1f **(52)**

Form - 11356P2

Record 1999 - 1st:2 2nd:1 3rd:1 Ran:7

Win Prizemoney £7,554 *Total Prizemoney* £11,124

Wins * **1999** Apr Newmar (GD) 5f 89 <
* **1999** Mar Folkes (SFT) 5f 79

1999 Turf 2-7: (5f 2-3, 6f 2, 7f 2) (sft 1-3, gd 2, g-f 1-2)

Useful colt, effective 5f, acts on g-f. Turf high 91 - also 1st of 8 getting 6lb from Barringer (15 Apr Newmarket RF 0705).

**T G Mills [2-7] Goodfellows Racing.*

FIRST CUT (USA) BHB 68f RR 67f 4583[5]

3 b f Diesis 9f **(80)** - Super Jamie (USA) (Nijinsky (CAN)) 10.3f **(77)**

Form - 7724345

Record 1999 - 1st:0 2nd:1 3rd:1 Ran:7

Win Prizemoney £0 *Total Prizemoney* £2,272

1999 Turf 0-7: (8f, 9f, 10f 2, 12f 3) (gd 2, g-f 2, frm 3)

Workmanlike, average filly, effective 10 to 12f, best at 12f, acts on g-f to frm, best on frm. Turf high 67 - 4th of 10 getting 5lb from Guest Island (11 Spt Goodwood 10f g-f RF 4275).

**J W Hills [0-7] K Y Lim.*

FIRST DANCE BHB 48f RR 24f 2883[9]

4 b f Primo Dominie 7.2f **(67)** - Soviet Swan (USA) (Nureyev (USA)) 8.7f **(78)**

Form - 80

Record 1999 - 1st:0 2nd:0 3rd:0 Ran:2
Pre1999 - 1st:1 2nd:1 3rd:0 Ran:7

Win Prizemoney £3,582 *Total Prizemoney* £5,288

Wins 1997 Aug Goodwo (G-F) S 6f 70 <

1999 Turf 0-2: (6f, 7f) (gd, frm)

Scopey, little account filly. Turf high 24 (began Jly). Becoming disappointing.

**Dr J D Scargill [0-3] Mrs Susan Scargill (from R Hannon [1-6] Aug 1997).*

FIRST FANTASY BHB 83f RR 79+f 4335[1]

3 b f Be My Chief (USA) 10.2f **(62)** - Dreams **(80df)** (Rainbow Quest (USA)) 10.4f **(75)**

Form - 082311411

Record 1999 - 1st:4 2nd:1 3rd:1 Ran:9
Pre1999 - 1st:0 2nd:0 3rd:0 Ran:1

Win Prizemoney £22,935 *Total Prizemoney* £24,495

Wins * **1999** Spt Yarmou (G-S) H 10.1f 77 79 <
* **1999** Aug Folkes (G-S) H 9.7f 71 76+
* **1999** Jly Yarmou (FRM) H 10.1f 67 72
* **1999** Jly Warwic (G-F) H 10.5f 62 64

1999 Turf 4-9: (7f, 8f, 10f 3-5, 11f 1-2) (sft, g-s 1-1, gd 1-1, g-f 1-3, frm 1-3)

Scopey, above-average filly, effective 10f, acts on g-s to frm, likes left handed tracks, prefers tight tracks. Turf high 79 - 1st of 8 getting 1lb from Pinchincha (15 Spt Yarmouth RF 4335) - also 1st of 14 giving 1lb to Orbital Star (26 Aug Folkestone RF 3915). She was in fine form in the second half of the season, winning four times at around ten furlongs. Very game.

**J R Fanshawe [4-10]Aylesfield Farms Ltd.*

FIRST FRAME BHB 45f54a RR 21f 54a 5035[17]

4 b g Mukaddamah (USA) 7.6f **(74)** - Point of Law (Law Society (USA)) 9.9f **(70)**

Form - 1560000

Record 1999 - 1st:1 2nd:0 3rd:0 Ran:7
Pre1999 - 1st:0 2nd:1 3rd:1 Ran:8

Win Prizemoney £1,759 *Total Prizemoney* £4,591

Wins * **1999** *Jan Southw (STD) C 7f 66* <

1999 Turf 0-2: (7f 2) (g-s, gd) 1999 AW 1-5: (6f, 7f 1-3, 8f) (Fibr 1-5)

Leggy, little account gelding, effective 7 to 8f, acts on g-f - acts on Fibr, often wears blinkers, likes left handed tracks, likes tight tracks. Turf high 21 (began Oct). AW high 66 (1st run) - 1st of 13 from Royal Cascade (4 Jan Southwell RF 0021). Becoming disappointing. **D Shaw [1-7] J Roundtree (from J L Eyre [0-8] Aug 1998).*

FIRST GOLD BHB 25f36a RR 26f 36a 2649[8]

10 gr g Absalom 7.1f **(56)** - Cindys Gold (Sonnen Gold) 6.6f **(47)**

Form - 008

Record 1999 - 1st:0 2nd:0 3rd:0 Ran:3
Pre1999 - 1st:9 2nd:8 3rd:6 Ran:90

Win Prizemoney £26,175 *Total Prizemoney* £37,046

Wins 1997 Mar Leices (G-F) S 7f 37
1996 May Carlis (G-F) C 6.9f 61
1996 *Jan Southw (STD) S 7f 51*
1995 Spt Yarmou (GD) S 7f 64

1999 Turf 0-2: (7f, 8f) (gd 2) 1999 AW 0-1: (7f) (Fibr)

Little account gelding, has worn blinkers. Turf high 26.

**A Smith [0-10] James Bowden (from J Wharton [9-93] Dec 1997).*

FIRST HUSSAR BHB 48f RR 39f 4835[8]

3 b c Primo Dominie 7.2f **(67)** - Third Movement (Music Boy) 6.8f **(57)**

Form - 03057008

Record 1999 - 1st:0 2nd:0 3rd:1 Ran:8
Pre1999 - 1st:0 2nd:0 3rd:0 Ran:3

Win Prizemoney £0 *Total Prizemoney* £662

1999 Turf 0-8: (7f 2, 8f, 9f 2, 10f 2, 11f) (gd 3, g-f 2, frm 3)

Leggy, very moderate colt, effective 6 to 9f, acts on gd to frm, has worn blinkers. Turf high 63 - 3rd of 8 giving 3lb to Edmo Heights (19 Jun Redcar 9f frm RF 2158). **P Howling [0-11] Laci Nester-Smith.*

FIRST IMPRESSION BHB 69f RR 66f 2904[5]

4 b c Saddlers' Hall (IRE) 10.5f **(65)** - First Sapphire (Simply Great (FR)) 8.2f **(65)**
Form - 245
Record 1999 - 1st:0 2nd:1 3rd:0 Ran:3
Pre1999 - 1st:0 2nd:0 3rd:0 Ran:3
Win Prizemoney £0 *Total Prizemoney* £1,347
1999 Turf 0-3: (10f, 12f, 13f) (sft, g-f, frm)
Workmanlike, average colt, effective 13f, acts on g-f. Turf high 66 - 5th of 9 getting 2lb from Borgia (17 Jly Newbury 13f g-f RF 2904).
**Lady Herries [0-6] Ms Elaine Reffo.*

FIRST LEGACY BHB 40f RR 17f 808[15]
3 ch f First Trump - Loving Legacy **(62f)** (Caerleon (USA)) 8.6f **(71)**
Form - 0
Record 1999 - 1st:0 2nd:0 3rd:0 Ran:1
Pre1999 - 1st:0 2nd:0 3rd:0 Ran:3
1999 Turf 0-1: (5f) (gd)
Unfurnished, poor filly, has worn blinkers.
**M Brittain [0-4] Mel Brittain.*

FIRST MAGNITUDE (IRE) RR 118f 5230a[14]
3 ch c Arazi (USA) 9.2f **(74)** - Crystal Cup (USA) (Nijinsky (CAN)) 10.3f **(77)**
Form - 42310
1999 Turf 1-5: (11f, 12f 1-4) (hvy, g-s, gd, frm)
High-class colt. Turf high 118 - 1st from Zarfoot (17 Oct Longchamp RF 5013a). Improved through the season and, after finishing third of four to Montjeu in the Prix Niel, landed the Group Two Prix du Conseil de Paris. Ended the season by finishing tailed off in the Breeders' Cup Turf. **A Fabre in FR [1-5].*

FIRST MAITE BHB 102f90a RR 103f 90a 5222[13]
6 b g Komaite (USA) 6.9f **(61)** - Marina Plata (Julio Mariner) 7.2f **(57)**
Form - 4471007107021000
Record 1999 - 1st:3 2nd:1 3rd:0 Ran:14
Pre1999 - 1st:8 2nd:8 3rd:5 Ran:51
Win Prizemoney £89,452 *Total Prizemoney* £114,896
Wins * **1999** Spt Ascot (HVY) H 5f 99 103+ <
* **1999** Aug Haydoc (SFT) H 5f 95 101
* **1999** May York (SFT) H 6f 92 97
* 1998 Oct Ascot (SFT) H 5f 85 93
* 1998 *Jly Southw (STD) H 7f 77 83*
* 1998 May Ripon (G-F) H 5f 83 84
* 1997 May Beverl (GD) H 5f 72 75
* 1997 *Apr Wolver (STD) C 5f 67*
* 1996 *Feb Southw (STD) H 6f 70 77*
* 1996 *Feb Southw (STD) H 6f 70 78*
* 1995 Spt Beverl (GD) 5f 70
1999 Turf 3-13: (5f 2-5, 6f 1-8) (sft 1-1, g-s 3, gd 2-5, g-f, frm 3) 1999 AW 0-1: (5f) (Fibr)
Very useful gelding, effective 5 to 6f, best at 5f, acts on sft to gd, best on gd, mostly wears blinkers (effectively), excels at Ascot. Turf high 103 - 1st of 7 giving 2lb to Monkston Point (26 Spt Ascot RF 4572) - also 1st of 11 giving 17lb to Demolition Jo (7 Aug Haydock RF 3451). Best on easy ground and Fibresand, he was impressive when winning three valuable sprint handicaps. He has gained five of his last six victories for Kieren Fallon and together they make a formidable partnership.
**S R Bowring [11-65] S R Bowring.*

FIRST MANASSAS (USA) BHB 84f RR 82f 4378[3]
2 b c Sea Hero (USA) - Ispahan (USA) (Majestic Light (USA)) 10.6f **(75)**
Form - 5213
Record 1999 - 1st:1 2nd:1 3rd:1 Ran:4
Win Prizemoney £2,920 *Total Prizemoney* £4,488
Wins * **1999** Spt Haydoc (G-F) 8.1f 82 <
1999 Turf 1-4: (7f, 8f 1-3) (gd, g-f 1-2, frm)
Decent colt. Turf high 82 (began Jly) - 3rd of 20 giving 6lb to Lonely Place (17 Spt Ayr 8f gd RF 4378) - also 1st of 9 from Tigre (3 Spt Haydock RF 4122). **I A Balding [1-4] Mrs Paul Mellon.*

FIRST MASTER BHB 56f73a RR 57f 73a 2195[8]
4 ch c Primo Dominie 7.2f **(67)** - Bodham (Bustino) 10.4f **(64)**
Form - 2130000558
Record 1999 - 1st:0 2nd:0 3rd:0 Ran:7
Pre1999 - 1st:2 2nd:4 3rd:3 Ran:13
Win Prizemoney £4,979 *Total Prizemoney* £11,687
Wins * 1998 *Nov Lingfi (STD) H 10f 78 81* <
* 1997 Oct Folkes (GD) 6.9f 74
1999 Turf 0-5: (10f, 12f 4) (g-s 2, gd, frm 2) 1999 AW 0-2: (11f, 12f) (Equi, Fibr)
Workmanlike, average colt, effective 10 to 12f, best at 10f, acts on gd to frm - acts on Equi, prefers left handed tracks, likes tight tracks. Turf high 67. AW high 59.
**Miss Gay Kelleway [2-20] Three's Lucky Partnership.*

FIRST MUSICAL BHB 92f RR 89f 5040[4]
3 ch f First Trump - Musical Sally (USA) (The Minstrel (CAN)) 10f **(72)**
Form - 2060004
Record 1999 - 1st:0 2nd:1 3rd:0 Ran:7
Pre1999 - 1st:4 2nd:4 3rd:0 Ran:11
Win Prizemoney £14,771 *Total Prizemoney* £35,861
Wins * 1998 Jly Windso (GD) 6f 89+ <
* 1998 Jun Pontef (GD) 6f 89
* 1998 Jun Ayr (G-F) 5f 83
* 1998 Jun Pontef (G-S) 5f 74+
1999 Turf 0-7: (5f 2, 6f 5) (g-s, gd 4, g-f, frm)
Light-framed, useful filly, effective 6f, acts on gd. Turf high 106 (1st run) - 2nd of 23 giving 14lb to Pepperdine (12 Jun York 6f gd RF 1967). She ran an absolute blinder in the William Hill Trophy on her reappearance when drawn on the wrong side, just being caught in the closing stages. Generally ran well after and has bags of early pace. **M Brittain [4-18] Bob Abson BJK Partnership.*

FIRST NIGHT (IRE) RR 91f 3584a[2]
3 b f Sadler's Wells (USA) 11.3f **(87)** - Morning Devotion (USA) (Affirmed (USA)) 9.3f **(79)**
Form - 412
Record 1999 - 1st:1 2nd:1 3rd:0 Ran:3
Win Prizemoney £3,213 *Total Prizemoney* £8,698
Wins * **1999** Jun Salisb (GD) 8f 84 <
1999 Turf 1-3: (8f 1-2, 10f) (hvy, g-f 1-2)
Leggy, currently useful filly. Turf high 91 - 2nd of 10 to Choice Spirit (5 Aug Deauville 8f hvy RF 3584a) - also 1st of 14 from Feiticeira (9 Jun Salisbury RF 1871). **P W Chapple-Hyam [1-3].*

FIRST TRUTH BHB 90f RR 85f 4931[5]
2 b c Rudimentary (USA) 8.2f **(66)** - Pursuit of Truth (USA) (Irish River (FR)) 8.6f **(78)**
Form - 747215
Record 1999 - 1st:1 2nd:1 3rd:0 Ran:6
Win Prizemoney £4,005 *Total Prizemoney* £7,059
Wins * **1999** Spt Pontef (GD) 8f 81 <
1999 Turf 1-6: (5f, 6f 2, 8f 1-3) (g-s, gd, g-f 1-3, frm)
Useful colt, effective 8f, acts on gd to g-f. Turf high 85 - also 1st of 15 from Fayrway Rhythm (23 Spt Pontefract RF 4506).
**A Bailey [1-6] Ray Bailey.*

FIRST VENTURE BHB 70f74a RR 60f 74a 3670[5]
2 b c Formidable (USA) 7.8f **(60)** - Diamond Wedding (USA) (Diamond Shoal) 9.1f **(66)**
Form - 802235
Record 1999 - 1st:0 2nd:2 3rd:1 Ran:6
Win Prizemoney £0 *Total Prizemoney* £2,056
1999 Turf 0-2: (6f 2) (gd, g-f) 1999 AW 0-4: (6f, 7f 3) (Fibr 4)
Above-average colt, effective 7f, - acts on Fibr, has worn blinkers. Turf high 60. AW high 79. **C N Allen [0-6] Pelicas Partnership.*

FISHER ISLAND (IRE) BHB 54f RR 59f 5158[10]
2 b br f Sri Pekan (USA) - Liberty Song (IRE) (Last Tycoon) 8.5f **(62)**
Form - 45053450
Record 1999 - 1st:0 2nd:0 3rd:1 Ran:8
Win Prizemoney £0 *Total Prizemoney* £754
1999 Turf 0-8: (6f 3, 7f 3, 8f 2) (sft, gd 4, g-f 2, frm)
Fair filly, effective 6f, acts on gd to g-f. Turf high 59 (began Aug) - 3rd of 18 giving 2lb to Cumbrian Princess (4 Oct Pontefract 6f gd RF 4716). Consistent. **R Hollinshead [0-8] P D Savill.*

FISHERMAN'S COVE (USA) RR 67f 4932[11]
4 b g Caerleon (USA) 10.9f **(79)** - Free At Last (Shirley Heights) 10.3f **(74)**
Form - 084020
Record 1999 - 1st:0 2nd:1 3rd:0 Ran:6
Pre1999 - 1st:0 2nd:0 3rd:1 Ran:1
Win Prizemoney £0 *Total Prizemoney* £1,731

1999 Turf 0-6: (10f, 12f 2, 14f, 17f, 18f) (gd, g-f, frm 3, hrd)
Average gelding, effective 12 to 17f, acts on gd to frm. Turf high 67 - 2nd of 16 giving 25lb to Black Ice Boy (4 Oct Pontefract 17f gd RF 4717).
**L Lungo [0-8] Four Clubs (from A P O'Brien in IRE [0-1] Aug 1998).*

FISHERMAN'S CREEK (IRE) RR 93f 4478a[4]

2 b c Fairy King (USA) 7.7f **(75)** - Allorette (Ballymore) 7.3f **(64)**
Form - 14
1999 Turf 1-2: (7f 1-1, 8f) (g-s, g-f 1-1)
Currently useful colt. Turf high 93 - 4th of 8 to Sinndar (19 Spt Curragh 8f g-s RF 4478a). Landed the odds on his Naas debut with the minimum of fuss and finished fourth in a Group One next time, but how he ranks in the Ballydoyle pecking order is anyone's guess at the moment. **A P O'Brien in IRE [1-2] Mrs John Magnier.*

FITZWILLIAM (USA) BHB 79a RR 88f 117[6]

6 b g Rahy (USA) 9.1f **(80)** - Early Lunch (USA) (Noble Table (USA)) 10f **(70)**
Form - 6
Record 1999 - 1st:0 2nd:0 3rd:0 Ran:1
Pre1999 - 1st:1 2nd:1 3rd:1 Ran:5
Win Prizemoney £3,598 *Total Prizemoney* £7,489
Wins * 1996 Jly Pontef (G-F) 10f 77+ <
1999 AW 0-1: (11f) (Fibr)
Useful gelding. **I A Balding [2-10] Paul Mellon.*

FIVE OF WANDS RR 57f 5137[11]

2 b f Caerleon (USA) 10.9f **(79)** - Overact (IRE) **(88f)** (Law Society (USA)) 9.9f **(70)**
Form - 0
Record 1999 - 1st:0 2nd:0 3rd:0 Ran:1
1999 Turf 0-1: (7f) (gd)
Currently fair filly. **J L Dunlop [0-1] Woodcote Stud Ltd.*

FIZZYGIG BHB 64f53a RR 64f 53a 4432[2]

3 br f Efisio 7.7f **(69)** - Buzzbomb (Bustino) 10.4f **(64)**
Form - 8034001432
Record 1999 - 1st:1 2nd:1 3rd:2 Ran:8
Pre1999 - 1st:0 2nd:0 3rd:0 Ran:3
Win Prizemoney £2,612 *Total Prizemoney* £6,336
Wins * **1999** Jun Salisb (GD) H 7f 56 59 <
1999 Turf 1-8: (7f 1-3, 8f 3, 10f 2) (sft, g-s, gd 2, g-f 1-2, frm 2)
Small, average filly, effective 7 to 8f, best at 8f, acts on g-s to frm. Turf high 64 - 2nd of 14 getting 15lb from Floating Charge (20 Spt Kempton 8f g-s RF 4432) - also 1st of 20 giving 2lb to Coughlan's Gift (8 Jun Salisbury RF 1819).
**R F JohnsonHoughton [1-11] T D Holland-Martin.*

FLAG FEN (USA) BHB 68f54a RR 68f 54a 3165[5]

8 b br g Riverman (USA) 9.7f **(78)** - Damascus Flag (USA) (Damascus (USA)) 8.9f **(71)**
Form - 07331805
Record 1999 - 1st:1 2nd:0 3rd:2 Ran:8
Pre1999 - 1st:3 2nd:3 3rd:1 Ran:32
Win Prizemoney £14,870 *Total Prizemoney* £22,269
Wins * **1999** Jly Yarmou (GD) H 10.1f 65 68 <
* 1998 Spt Newmar (GD) H 10f 57 60+
* 1998 Jly Newmar (G-F) H 10f 54 60
1997 May Ripon (G-S) S 8f 65
1999 Turf 1-8: (8f, 10f 1-6, 12f) (gd 1-1, g-f 3, frm 4)
Average gelding, effective 10f, acts on gd to frm, has worn blinkers. Turf high 70 - 3rd of 11 getting 24lb from Brilliant Red (19 Jun Ascot 10f g-f RF 2136) - also 1st of 10 getting 8lb from Fahs (1 Jly Yarmouth RF 2471). Inconsistent. He likes to do it the hard way by trying to make all, and is difficult to catch when able to dominate.
**H J Collingridge [3-14] Mrs Carol Dolan (from J Parkes [1-9] Feb 1998).*

FLAK JACKET BHB 77f RR 79f 4755[10]

4 b g Magic Ring (IRE) 6.5f **(64)** - Vaula (Henbit (USA)) 9f **(61)**
Form - 70002600
Record 1999 - 1st:0 2nd:1 3rd:0 Ran:8
Pre1999 - 1st:2 2nd:0 3rd:1 Ran:5
Win Prizemoney £9,135 *Total Prizemoney* £15,543
Wins * 1998 Jly Haydoc (G-F) H 6f 80 83 <
* 1998 Jun Kempto (HVY) H 6f 70 79

1999 Turf 0-8: (5f 2, 6f 5, 7f) (g-s, gd 4, g-f, frm 2)
Scopey, above-average gelding, effective 6f, acts on gd to frm, has worn blinkers. Turf high 83 (1st run) - 7th of 19 giving 14lb to Delta Soleil (16 May Kempton 6f frm RF 1258). A couple of wins in fair sprint handicaps as a three-year-old were followed by a disappointing start to the last campaign. However, after unsuccessfully trying seven furlongs at Newbury, he got back into the swing of things with a good second to Royal Result over six at Goodwood in August, but failed to land the Silver Cup gamble at Ayr on the back of that performance.
**B J Meehan [2-13] Kennet Valley Thoroughbred II.*

FLAME CUTTER (USA) BHB 71f RR 71f 4629[1]

3 ch f Miswaki (USA) 8.1f **(81)**-Flaming Torch(Rousillon (USA))8.2f **(74)**
Form - 31
Record 1999 - 1st:1 2nd:0 3rd:1 Ran:2
Win Prizemoney £3,382 *Total Prizemoney* £4,197
Wins * **1999** Spt Bright (SFT) 8f 71 <
1999 Turf 1-2: (8f 1-2) (g-s 1-1, frm)
Scopey, currently above-average filly. Turf high 71 (began Spt) - 1st of 8 getting 4lb from Bay View (29 Spt Brighton RF 4629).
**H R A Cecil [1-2] K Abdulla.*

FLAMENCO RED BHB 89f RR 83f 3966[5]

2 b f Warning 8.1f **(77)** - Spanish Wells (IRE) (Sadler's Wells (USA)) 10f **(76)**
Form - 31235
Record 1999 - 1st:1 2nd:1 3rd:2 Ran:5
Win Prizemoney £4,337 *Total Prizemoney* £6,889
Wins * **1999** Jun Nottin (GD) 6.1f 74 <
1999 Turf 1-5: (5f, 6f 1-3, 7f) (g-s, g-f 2, frm 1-2)
Decent filly, has worn blinkers. Turf high 83 - also 1st of 13 getting 5lb from Final Row (21 Jun Nottingham RF 2176).
**R Charlton [1-5] K Abdulla.*

FLAME OF FORTUNE (IRE) RR 4120[9]

3 ch f Nucleon (USA) - Lovely Leitrim (IRE) (Erins Hope)
Form - 0
Record 1999 - 1st:0 2nd:0 3rd:0 Ran:1
1999 Turf 0-1: (9f) (g-f)
Workmanlike, currently very poor filly.
**S Dow [0-1] Mrs Ann Fortune.*

FLAME OF GLORY BHB 30f RR 52f 4789[10]

5 ch g Polish Precedent (USA) 9f **(73)** - Danishkada (Thatch (USA)) 9.8f **(62)**
Form - 00000
Record 1999 - 1st:0 2nd:0 3rd:0 Ran:5
Pre1999 - 1st:0 2nd:0 3rd:0 Ran:1
1999 Turf 0-5: (7f 2, 8f, 9f, 10f) (g-s 3, g-f, frm)
Fair gelding. Turf high 52.
**Miss Z C Davison [0-8] Shovelstrode Racing Club.*

FLAME TOWER (IRE) BHB 54f54a RR 48?f 54a 5055[10]

4 ch g Archway (IRE) 8.5f **(60)** - Guantanamera (USA) (El Gran Senor (USA)) 9.6f **(76)**
Form - 41030
Record 1999 - 1st:0 2nd:0 3rd:1 Ran:2
Pre1999 - 1st:1 2nd:2 3rd:3 Ran:19
Win Prizemoney £2,424 *Total Prizemoney* £6,180
Wins 1998 *Dec Wolver (STD) 8.5f* 55 <
1999 Turf 0-1: (7f) (gd) 1999 AW 0-1: (7f) (Fibr)
Workmanlike, average gelding, effective 7 to 8f, best at 7f, acts on gd to frm - acts on Fibr. (1st run) - 3rd of 13 to First Frame (4 Jan Southwell 7f Fibr RF 0021). **Miss A Stokell [0-1] T J Ford (from R Hannon [1-20] Jan 1999).*

FLAMINGO ROAD (GER) RR 118f 4778a[10]

3 f Acatenango (GER) - Fabula Dancer (Northern Dancer) 9.6f **(80)**
Form - 13320
1999 Turf 1-5: (11f 1-1, 12f 4) (sft 1-3, gd 2)
High-class filly. Turf high 118 - 2nd of 6 getting 15lb from Tiger Hill (5 Spt Baden-Baden 12f gd RF 4245a). A smart German-trained filly, she won the German Oaks and was third in the German Derby. Comfortably held by Tiger Hill in the Grosser Preis von Baden in September, she made no show at all in the Arc.

*A Schutz in GER [1-5].

FLAMING QUEST BHB 103f **RR 98f** 3695[7]
3 b c Rainbow Quest (USA) 11.2f **(81)** - Nearctic Flame (Sadler's Wells (USA)) 10f **(76)**
Form - 211227
Record 1999 - 1st:2 2nd:3 3rd:0 Ran:6
Win Prizemoney £7,349 *Total Prizemoney* £17,181
Wins * **1999** May Chepst (GD) 12.1f 90+ <
* **1999** May Leices (G-F) 11.8f 75+
1999 Turf 2-6: (10f, 12f 2-5) (gd 1-3, g-f 2, frm 1-1)
Scopey, very useful colt, effective 10 to 12f, best at 12f, acts on gd to g-f, best on gd. Turf high 100 (1st run) - 2nd of 14 giving 5lb to Fairy Godmother (15 May Newbury 10f gd RF 1237). He was impressive in a couple of minor heats and poorly ridden when bidding for his hat-trick at Ascot in June. Disappointing in the Great Voltigeur Stakes on his final start, he made 85,000 guineas at Newmarket in October and is to continue his career in America.

Form - 088000
Record 1999 - 1st:0 2nd:0 3rd:0 Ran:5
Pre1999 - 1st:1 2nd:4 3rd:7 Ran:36
Win Prizemoney £2,519 *Total Prizemoney* £10,127
Wins 1995 *Jun Wolver (STD) H 7f 53 47* <
1999 Turf 0-1: (7f) (frm) 1999 AW 0-4: (7f 2, 8f 2) (Fibr 4)
Little account gelding, has worn blinkers. AW high 20.
*P D Purdy [0-7] P D Purdy (from K Bishop [1-14] May 1997).

FLAVIAN BHB 93f **RR 87f** 1245[8]
3 b f Catrail (USA) - Fatah Flare (USA) (Alydar (USA)) 9.1f **(76)**
Form - 8
Record 1999 - 1st:0 2nd:0 3rd:0 Ran:1
Pre1999 - 1st:1 2nd:1 3rd:0 Ran:2
Win Prizemoney £3,687 *Total Prizemoney* £5,269
Wins * 1998 Oct Newmar (G-S) 6f 87 <
1999 Turf 0-1: (6f) (g-f)

Flanders (centre), was a real battler, and gained a deserved victory at Doncaster

*Sir Michael Stoute [2-6] Cheveley Park Stud.

FLANDERS (IRE) RR 102f 4654[6]
3 b f Common Grounds 8.1f **(66)** - Family At War (USA) (Explodent (USA)) 9.4f **(87)**
Form - 72225016
Record 1999 - 1st:1 2nd:3 3rd:0 Ran:8
Pre1999 - 1st:4 2nd:1 3rd:1 Ran:7
Win Prizemoney £115,407 *Total Prizemoney* £230,522
Wins * **1999** Spt Doncas (G-F) L 5f 102 <
* 1998 Jly Newbur (G-F) 5.2f 94
* 1998 Jun Ascot (G-S) 5f 98+
* 1998 Jun Beverl (G-S) 5f 99++
* 1998 May Beverl (G-F) 5f 74+
1999 Turf 1-8: (5f 1-7, 6f) (gd 2, g-f 1-3, frm 3)
Workmanlike, very useful filly, effective 5f, acts on g-f, excels at Beverley and Ascot. Turf high 115 - 2nd of 18 getting 3lb from Mitcham (18 Jun Ascot 5f g-f RF 2106). A very speedy filly at two, she was just touched off in the King's Stand on her second start of last season, proving she had trained on, but could never dominate at Sandown next time when runner-up to Cortachy Castle, or when just beaten at Newmarket. She gained her only victory of the season with a very gutsy victory over Emma Peel and Dashing Blue in a Listed event at Doncaster in September.
*T D Easterby [5-15] Mrs Jean Connew.

FLASHFEET BHB 35f35a **RR 8f 35a** 3435[14]
9 b g Rousillon (USA) 10.4f **(69)**-Miellita (King Emperor (USA)) 9.4f **(58)**

Scopey, currently useful filly. *H Candy [1-3] Major M G Wyatt.

FLAXEN PRIDE (IRE) BHB 40f **RR 41f** 3902[6]
4 ch f Pips Pride 6.7f **(70)** - Fair Chance (Young Emperor) 10.1f **(63)**
Form - 007156
Record 1999 - 1st:1 2nd:0 3rd:0 Ran:6
Pre1999 - 1st:0 2nd:1 3rd:0 Ran:9
Win Prizemoney £3,096 *Total Prizemoney* £3,931
Wins * **1999** Aug Leices (G-F) H 8f 37 41 <
1999 Turf 1-6: (6f, 8f 1-4, 9f) (gd 2, g-f 1-2, frm 2)
Strong, moderate filly, effective 5 to 9f, best at 8f, acts on gd to frm. Turf high 41 - 1st of 10 getting 19lb from La Isla Bonita (4 Aug Leicester RF 3363). *Mrs M Reveley [1-16] G Fawcett And Partners.

FLEETING FANCY RR 49f 5129[12]
2 b f Thatching 7.8f **(69)** - Fleetwood Fancy (Taufan (USA)) 7f **(57)**
Form - 00
Record 1999 - 1st:0 2nd:0 3rd:0 Ran:2
1999 Turf 0-2: (6f, 7f) (gd 2)
Currently moderate filly. Turf high 49 (began Oct).
*S Dow [0-2] N Boyle.

FLETCHER BHB 69f **RR 57f** 5066[13]
5 b g Salse (USA) 10.9f **(71)** - Ballet Classique (USA) (Sadler's Wells (USA)) 10f **(76)**
Form - 0602370
Record 1999 - 1st:0 2nd:1 3rd:1 Ran:7
Pre1999 - 1st:2 2nd:4 3rd:3 Ran:28

Win Prizemoney £8,943 *Total Prizemoney* £19,908
Wins * 1998 Oct Ascot (SFT) H 12f 74 78
1996 Apr Newmar (G-F) 5f 83+ <
1999 Turf 0-7: (10f, 12f 5, 13f) (sft, g-s, gd 3, g-f, frm)
Fair gelding, effective 10 to 16f, best at 12f, acts on g-s to frm, has worn blinkers, prefers right handed tracks, does well at Ascot and Newmarket. Turf high 76 (began Jly) - 2nd of 10 giving 11lb to Tipsy (22 Spt Goodwood 12f g-s RF 4489).
**H Morrison [1-31] Lady Margadale (from P F I Cole [1-7] Oct 1996).*

FLEUR D'OR BHB 40a **RR 47f** 228[13]
3 b f Alhijaz 7.7f **(57)** - Forever Shineing **(35f)** (Glint of Gold) 9.3f **(66)**
Form - 0
Record 1999 - 1st:0 2nd:0 3rd:0 Ran:1
Pre1999 - 1st:0 2nd:0 3rd:0 Ran:6
1999 AW 0-1: (11f) (Fibr)
Light-framed, moderate filly. **M J Polglase [0-7] M J Polglase.*

FLICKER BHB 38f34a **RR 51f 34a** 2505[17]
4 b f Unfuwain (USA) 11.4f **(74)** - Lovers Light (Grundy) 10.3f **(65)**
Form - 400
Record 1999 - 1st:0 2nd:0 3rd:0 Ran:2
Pre1999 - 1st:0 2nd:0 3rd:1 Ran:9
Win Prizemoney £0 *Total Prizemoney* £1,661
1999 Turf 0-2: (8f, 10f) (g-f 2)
Light-framed, fair filly, has worn blinkers. Inconsistent.
**W Clay [0-3] Barry Baggott (from Lord Huntingdon [0-9] Nov 1998).*

FLIGHT ETERNAL (IRE) BHB 41f **RR 39f** 4901[20]
2 ch g Prince of Birds (USA) - Timeless Classic (Ahonoora) 8.1f **(73)**
Form - 07050
Record 1999 - 1st:0 2nd:0 3rd:0 Ran:5
1999 Turf 0-5: (5f 2, 6f 2, 7f) (gd, g-f, frm 3)
Very moderate gelding, always wears blinkers. Turf high 39.
**J L Eyre [0-5] Clayton Bigley Partnership Ltd.*

FLIGHT FOR FREEDOM BHB 50f50a **RR 55f 50a** 1802[7]
4 b f Saddlers' Hall (IRE) 10.5f **(65)** - Anatroccolo (Ile de Bourbon (USA)) 10.1f **(67)**
Form - 7
Record 1999 - 1st:0 2nd:0 3rd:0 Ran:1
Pre1999 - 1st:0 2nd:1 3rd:0 Ran:7
Win Prizemoney £0 *Total Prizemoney* £1,196
1999 Turf 0-1: (10f) (gd)
Scopey, fair filly.
**F Murphy [1-11] Miss Samantha Dare (from J R Fanshawe [0-1] Spt 1997).*

FLIGHT OF DREAMS (IRE) BHB 40f **RR 40f** 4731[14]
2 b f College Chapel - Lady Portobello (Porto Bello) 8.9f **(43)**
Form - 000
Record 1999 - 1st:0 2nd:0 3rd:0 Ran:3
1999 Turf 0-3: (5f, 6f, 8f) (gd 2, frm)
Currently moderate filly. Turf high 40.
**B S Rothwell [0-3] Cable Media Consultancy Ltd.*

FLIGHT PATH RR 5020[6]
2 b c Missed Flight - Songlines (Night Shift (USA)) 7.2f **(69)**
Form -
Record 1999 - 1st:0 2nd:1 3rd:0 Ran:3
Win Prizemoney £0 *Total Prizemoney* £1,580
1999 Turf 0-3: (g-s, gd, frm)
Currently above-average filly. Turf high 79 (began Aug).
**B W Hills [0-3] Maktoum Al Maktoum.*

FLIGHT REFUND RR 52f 5208[17]
2 ch g Missed Flight - Settlement (USA) (Irish River (FR)) 8.6f **(78)**
Form - 00
Record 1999 - 1st:0 2nd:0 3rd:0 Ran:2
1999 Turf 0-2: (7f 2) (g-s, gd)
Currently fair gelding. Turf high 52 (began Oct).
**R Hollinshead [0-2] Mrs A L Wood.*

FLIGHT SEQUENCE BHB 76f **RR 77df** 3676[4]
3 b f Polar Falcon (USA) 9f **(74)** - Doubles (Damister (USA)) 9f **(73)**
Form - 2424
Record 1999 - 1st:0 2nd:2 3rd:0 Ran:4
Win Prizemoney £0 *Total Prizemoney* £2,764
1999 Turf 0-4: (8f 3, 10f) (g-f, frm 3)
Leggy, above-average filly. Turf high 81 (1st run) - 2nd of 12 to Lila (9 Jun Salisbury 8f g-f RF 1872). **Lady Herries [0-4] A J Perkins.*

FLINT KNAPPER BHB 83f **RR 73f** 3432[7]
5 ch g Kris 10f **(75)** - Circe's Isle (Be My Guest (USA)) 9.3f **(67)**
Form - 87
Record 1999 - 1st:0 2nd:0 3rd:0 Ran:2
Pre1999 - 1st:3 2nd:1 3rd:1 Ran:8
Win Prizemoney £17,121 *Total Prizemoney* £19,350
Wins * 1998 May Kempto (G-F) H 10f 83 90 <
* 1997 Spt Newmar (G-F) H 10f 80 83
* 1997 Aug Warwic (G-S) 8f 67
1999 Turf 0-2: (8f, 9f) (g-f, frm)
Above-average gelding. Turf high 73 (began Jly). He did not run at two, but won twice in the autumn of 1997. **G Wragg [3-10] A E Oppenheimer.*

FLINTSTONE RR 53f 2001[3]
2 b c First Trump - South Rock **(97f)** (Rock City)
Form - 03
Record 1999 - 1st:0 2nd:0 3rd:1 Ran:2
Win Prizemoney £0 *Total Prizemoney* £367
1999 Turf 0-2: (6f, 7f) (frm 2)
Currently fair colt. Turf high 53 - 3rd of 12 to Buying A Dream (15 Jun Thirsk 7f frm RF 2001).
**J A Glover [0-2] Mrs Andrea Mallinson.*

FLIQUET BAY (IRE) BHB 60f **RR 64f** 4641[9]
2 b c Namaqualand (USA) - Thatcherite (Final Straw) 7.9f **(64)**
Form - 600
Record 1999 - 1st:0 2nd:0 3rd:0 Ran:3
1999 Turf 0-3: (7f, 8f 2) (g-s, g-f 2)
Currently average colt. Turf high 64 (began Aug).
**Mrs A J Perrett [0-3] Mrs S L Whitehead.*

FLITE OF LIFE BHB 65f61a **RR 62f 61a** 5065[13]
3 gr g Forzando 7.2f **(63)**-Frighten The Life(Kings Lake(USA))10.8f **(67)**
Form - 070
Record 1999 - 1st:0 2nd:0 3rd:0 Ran:3
Pre1999 - 1st:0 2nd:1 3rd:0 Ran:6
Win Prizemoney £0 *Total Prizemoney* £2,470
1999 Turf 0-3: (5f, 6f 2) (gd, g-f 2)
Unfurnished, average gelding, effective 6f, acts on g-f to frm. Turf high 62 (began Spt). Consistent. **W R Muir [0-9] Mrs Irene White.*

FLIT 'N' FLIRT BHB 30f **RR** 5144[6]
2 gr g Most Welcome 8.6f **(66)** - David's Dream (HOL) (Superlative) 7.2f **(56)**
Form - 0006
Record 1999 - 1st:0 2nd:0 3rd:0 Ran:4
1999 Turf 0-3: (5f, 6f, 8f) (gd, g-f, frm) 1999 AW 0-1: (6f) (Fibr)
Poor gelding, has worn blinkers. (began Aug).
**R Brotherton [0-4] K T Carpenter.*

FLOATING CHARGE RR 76f 4432[1]
5 b g Sharpo 7.5f **(68)** - Poyle Fizz (Damister (USA)) 9f **(73)**
Form - 10824361
Record 1999 - 1st:2 2nd:1 3rd:1 Ran:8
Pre1999 - 1st:1 2nd:1 3rd:0 Ran:9
Win Prizemoney £13,284 *Total Prizemoney* £18,652
Wins * **1999** Spt Kempto (HVY) H 8f 71 76 <
* **1999** Apr Windso (GD) H 8.3f 65 69+
* 1998 Jly Redcar (G-F) 9f 62
1999 Turf 2-8: (8f 2-7, 9f) (g-s 1-1, gd 3, g-f 2, frm 1-2)
Above-average gelding, effective 8f, acts on g-s to frm, has worn blinkers, likes tight tracks, excels at Windsor and Newcastle. Turf high 76 - 1st of 14 giving 15lb to Fizzygig (20 Spt Kempton RF 4432) - also 1st of 18 giving 20lb to Desert Warrior (12 Apr Windsor RF 0653). Another handicapper to have benefited from his trainer's magic touch, he did little wrong last term having won twice and ran some solid races in defeat. He looks best at a mile on soft ground, and that was certainly the case when he won in boggy conditions at Kempton.
**J R Fanshawe [3-17] The Leonard Curtis Partnership.*

FLOATING EMBER BHB 45f **RR 41f** 4809[12]
2 b f Rambo Dancer (CAN) 8.4f **(59)** - Spark (IRE) **(62df 47a)** (Flash of Steel) 7.2f **(53)**
Form - 70600
Record 1999 - 1st:0 2nd:0 3rd:0 Ran:5
1999 Turf 0-5: (5f, 6f 3, 8f) (sft, gd 3, g-f)
Moderate filly. Turf high 41. **J L Eyre [0-5] Martin West.*

FLOORSO'THEFOREST (IRE) BHB 65f **RR 63f** 3496[4]
3 ch g Forest Wind (USA) - Ravensdale Rose (IRE) (Henbit (USA)) 9f **(61)**
Form - 46630382014
Record 1999 - 1st:1 2nd:1 3rd:2 Ran:11
Win Prizemoney £4,380 *Total Prizemoney* £6,890
Wins * **1999** Jly Hamilt (G-F) H 9.2f 65 59 <
1999 Turf 1-11: (7f 2, 8f, 9f 1-5, 10f 2, 11f) (g-s, gd 5, g-f 1-3, frm 2)
Workmanlike, average gelding, effective 9 to 10f, acts on g-f to frm, likes left handed tracks, prefers tight tracks. Turf high 71. **Miss L A Perratt [1-11] Jim McLaren.*

FLORA DREAMBIRD BHB 26f **RR 38f** 3903[6]
5 b m Mandalus - Dame Flora (Celtic Cone) 9.8f **(43)**
Form - 6526
Record 1999 - 1st:0 2nd:1 3rd:0 Ran:4
Win Prizemoney £0 *Total Prizemoney* £512
1999 Turf 0-2: (16f, 17f) (frm 2) 1999 AW 0-2: (12f 2) (Fibr 2)
Very moderate filly. Turf high 38 (1st run) (began Aug) - 2nd of 6 giving 15lb to Pretty Obvious (3 Aug Catterick 16f frm RF 3314). AW high 26 (began Jly). **P W Hiatt [0-17] Hywel Davies.*

FLORAL RAJ (IRE) BHB 84f **RR 82f** 4915[4]
3 ch c Indian Ridge 7.6f **(74)** - Spring Daffodil (Pharly (FR)) 9.8f **(68)**
Form - 104
Record 1999 - 1st:1 2nd:0 3rd:0 Ran:3
Pre1999 - 1st:0 2nd:0 3rd:0 Ran:2
Win Prizemoney £3,038 *Total Prizemoney* £4,502
Wins * **1999** Spt Catter (G-F) 7f 75+ <
1999 Turf 1-3: (7f 1-1, 8f 2) (g-s, gd, frm 1-1)
Scopey, decent colt. Turf high 82 (began Spt) - 4th of 20 getting 7lb from Free Option (16 Oct Newmarket 8f gd RF 4915) - also 1st of 7 giving 5lb to Generous Diana (18 Spt Catterick RF 4399). Sold for 60,000 gns in October. **Sir Michael Stoute [1-5] P S Partnership.*

FLORISMART BHB 20f45a **RR 45a** 612[15]
7 b g Never so Bold 7.1f **(62)** - Spoilt Again (Mummy's Pet) 7.7f **(60)**
Form - 0
Record 1999 - 1st:0 2nd:0 3rd:0 Ran:1
Pre1999 - 1st:0 2nd:0 3rd:0 Ran:13
Win Prizemoney £0 *Total Prizemoney* £342
1999 Turf 0-1: (12f) (g-f)
Poor gelding.
**B P J Baugh [0-12] Messrs Chrimes, Winn & Wilson (from J A R Toller [0-5] Spt 1995).*

FLOSSY BHB 86f78a **RR 86f 78a** 5221[1]
3 b f Efisio 7.7f **(69)** - Sirene Bleu Marine (USA)(Secreto(USA))8.7f **(72)**
Form - 54501112211621
Record 1999 - 1st:6 2nd:3 3rd:0 Ran:14
Win Prizemoney £44,206 *Total Prizemoney* £50,960

Wins								
* **1999**	Nov	Doncas	(SFT)	H	12f	82	86	<
* **1999**	Spt	Haydoc	(G-F)	H	11.9f	75	81	
* **1999**	Aug	Newcas	(GD)	H	12.4f	66	70	
* **1999**	Jly	Newbur	(G-F)	H	10f	51	59+	
* **1999**	Jly	Mussel	(G-S)	H	12f	43	57+	
* **1999**	Jly	Beverl	(G-F)	H	9.9f	43	47	

1999 Turf 6-11: (10f 2-4, 12f 4-6, 13f) (sft 1-1, g-s, gd 2, g-f 2-4, frm 3-3) 1999 AW 0-3: (7f 2, 8f) (Fibr 3)
Leggy, useful filly, effective 10 to 12f, best at 12f, acts on sft to g-f, likes left handed tracks, excels at Newbury. Turf high 86 - 1st of 16 getting 2lb from Carlys Quest (6 Nov Doncaster RF 5221) - also 1st of 12 getting 5lb from Little Italy (3 Spt Haydock RF 4126). AW high 49. Improving. Suddenly hit form in July, and passed the post first seven times (disqualified at Ripon) as well as going down by the narrowest of margins at Ascot. Ended the season with a gritty win in the November Handicap. Tough and progressive. **C W Thornton [6-14] Guy Reed.*

FLOTSAM RR 24f 4382[18]
3 ch c Beveled (USA) 6.9f **(64)**-Parrot Fashion(Pieces of Eight)7.8f **(51)**
Form - 0
Record 1999 - 1st:0 2nd:0 3rd:0 Ran:1
1999 Turf 0-1: (8f) (frm)
Leggy, currently little account colt. **M D I Usher [0-1] M D I Usher.*

FLOWERING RR 51f 5208[13]
2 b f Deploy 11.4f **(67)** - Ajuga (USA) (The Minstrel (CAN)) 10f **(72)**
Form - 0
Record 1999 - 1st:0 2nd:0 3rd:0 Ran:1
1999 Turf 0-1: (7f) (g-s)
Currently fair filly. **B W Hills [0-1] K Abdulla.*

FLOWER O'CANNIE (IRE) BHB 74f **RR 75df** 4763[16]
4 b f Mujadil (USA) 7.7f **(70)** - Baby's Smile (Shirley Heights) 10.3f **(74)**
Form - 367014854200
Record 1999 - 1st:1 2nd:1 3rd:1 Ran:12
Pre1999 - 1st:4 2nd:3 3rd:5 Ran:22
Win Prizemoney £25,090 *Total Prizemoney* £36,895

Wins								
* **1999**	Jun	York	(G-S)	H	11.9f	75	76	
* 1998	Nov	Mussel	(SFT)	H	12f	68	81	
* 1998	Oct	Newcas	(SFT)	H	12.4f	68	75	
* 1997	Jly	Beverl	(HVY)		7.5f		89?	<
* 1997	Jun	Hamilt	(SFT)		6f		69	

1999 Turf 1-12: (10f, 11f, 12f 1-8, 13f, 14f) (hvy 2, gd 1-5, g-f 4, frm)
Leggy, above-average filly, effective 11 to 12f, best at 12f, acts on hvy to g-f, best on gd, prefers right handed tracks, does well at Ripon. Turf high 79 (1st run) - 3rd of 9 giving 9lb to The Butterwick Kid (29 Mar Hamilton 11f hvy RF 0503) - also 1st of 16 giving 4lb to Lancer (12 Jun York RF 1968). **M W Easterby [5-35] Mrs E Rhind.*

FLOWERS COVE BHB 26f **RR 51f** 337[7]
4 ch f Then Again 7.4f **(52)** - Lady St Lawrence (USA) (Bering) 7.4f **(61)**
Form - 7
Record 1999 - 1st:0 2nd:0 3rd:0 Ran:1
Pre1999 - 1st:0 2nd:1 3rd:0 Ran:10
Win Prizemoney £0 *Total Prizemoney* £738
1999 AW 0-1: (12f) (Fibr)
Workmanlike, fair filly. Becoming disappointing.
**K S Bridgwater [0-1] Miss S Rudge (from Mrs N Macauley [0-2] Oct 1998).*

FLOWER STATE BHB 68f **RR 69f** 3465[5]
3 b c Sabrehill (USA) 8.5f **(64)** - Flower Arrangement (Lomond (USA)) 8.8f **(65)**
Form - 055
Record 1999 - 1st:0 2nd:0 3rd:0 Ran:3
1999 Turf 0-3: (7f 3) (gd 2, g-f)
Currently average colt. Turf high 69.
**J H M Gosden [0-3] Sheikh Mohammed.*

FLOWINGTON (IRE) BHB 96f **RR 86f** 4680[12]
2 b f Owington - Persian Flower **(50f 42a)** (Persian Heights)
Form - 011380
Record 1999 - 1st:2 2nd:0 3rd:1 Ran:6
Win Prizemoney £4,808 *Total Prizemoney* £8,858
Wins * **1999** Jun Warwic (G-F) 6.8f 71 <
* **1999** *Jun Wolver (STA) S 5f 62*
1999 Turf 1-5: (5f, 6f 2, 7f 1-2) (gd 2, g-f 1-2, frm) 1999 AW 1-1: (5f 1-1) (Fibr 1-1)
Useful filly. Turf high 86. (1st run). Won an Fibresand seller on her second start and followed up in better company at Warwick. She finished a most creditable third in a weak-looking renewal of the Cherry Hinton, but was last in the Princess Margaret. **N P Littmoden [2-6] Linane Racing.*

FLUME RR 74f 4383[4]
2 br f Zafonic (USA) 9f **(83)** - Rainy Sky (Rainbow Quest (USA)) 10.4f **(75)**
Form - 44
Record 1999 - 1st:0 2nd:0 3rd:0 Ran:2
Win Prizemoney £0 *Total Prizemoney* £1,107
1999 Turf 0-2: (6f, 7f) (g-f, frm)
Currently above-average filly. Turf high 74 (began Aug). Fourth in a couple of decent races at Newbury. **B W Hills [0-2] K Abdulla.*

FLUSH (FR) BHB 63f60a **RR 73f 60a** 5146[11]
4 b br f Warning 8.1f **(77)** - Garden Pink (FR) (Bellypha) 9.8f **(73)**
Form - 0
Record 1999 - 1st:0 2nd:0 3rd:0 Ran:1
Pre1999 - 1st:1 2nd:0 3rd:2 Ran:12
Win Prizemoney £2,700 *Total Prizemoney* £4,267
Wins 1998 Oct Leices (SFT) C 8f 73 <
1999 AW 0-1: (7f) (Fibr)
Lengthy, above-average filly, effective 8f, acts on sft to frm.
**R E Peacock [0-1] Jim Ennis (from M C Pipe [0-1] Nov 1998).*

FLY HOME BHB 34f30a **RR 32f 30a** 4032[9]
4 br f Skyliner 6.8f **(51)** - Fille de Phaeton (Sun Prince) 12.4f **(52)**
Form - 5000
Record 1999 - 1st:0 2nd:0 3rd:0 Ran:2
Pre1999 - 1st:0 2nd:0 3rd:1 Ran:5
Win Prizemoney £0 *Total Prizemoney* £497
1999 Turf 0-2: (11f, 12f) (gd 2)
Unfurnished, very moderate filly. Turf high 32 (began Aug).
**H E Haynes [0-4] The Reddown High Explosive Partnership (from A J McNae [0-3] Spt 1998).*

FLYING BOLD (IRE) BHB 46f68a **RR 48f 68a** 4726[10]
4 ch g Persian Bold 10f **(69)** - Princess Reema (USA) (Affirmed (USA)) 9.3f **(79)**
Form - 6730
Record 1999 - 1st:0 2nd:0 3rd:1 Ran:4
Pre1999 - 1st:2 2nd:2 3rd:1 Ran:15
Win Prizemoney £5,816 *Total Prizemoney* £8,608
Wins 1998 Aug Lingfi (G-F) H 11.5f 61 62
1997 Oct Newbur (G-S) H 7.3f 63 71 <
1999 Turf 0-4: (11f, 12f 2, 16f) (g-s, gd, frm 2)
Scopey, average gelding, effective 10 to 12f, acts on frm to hrd, best on frm. Turf high 53.
**L Lungo [0-7] Alan Robson (from W R Muir [2-15] Oct 1998).*

FLYING CARPET RR 48f 1147[7]
2 b f Barathea (IRE) - Flying Squaw **(90f)** (Be My Chief (USA))
Form - 7
Record 1999 - 1st:0 2nd:0 3rd:0 Ran:1
1999 Turf 0-1: (5f) (gd)
Currently moderate filly.
**T D Easterby [0-1] Burton Agnes Bloodstock.*

FLYING EAGLE BHB 75f74a **RR 77f 74a** 4822[3]
8 b g Shaadi (USA) 8.1f **(75)** - Fly Me (FR) (Luthier) 9.8f **(71)**
Form - 050728534153
Record 1999 - 1st:1 2nd:1 3rd:2 Ran:12
Pre1999 - 1st:6 2nd:1 3rd:1 Ran:13
Win Prizemoney £26,507 *Total Prizemoney* £30,286
Wins * **1999** Aug Epsom (GD) H 12f 67 76
1998 Jly Epsom (G-F) H 12f 74 82 <
1998 Jly Nottin (G-F) H 10f 74 75
1998 Jly Bright (GD) C 10f 69+
1998 Jun Warwic (G-S) S 10.8f 65+
1998 Jun Bath (G-S) C 10.2f 65
1998 May Nottin (G-F) S 10f 57+
1999 Turf 1-10: (10f, 12f 1-9) (gd 2, g-f 1-3, frm 4, hrd) 1999 AW 0-2: (10f, 13f) (Equi 2)
Above-average gelding, effective 10 to 12f, best at 12f, acts on g-f to frm, best on g-f, likes left handed tracks, favours tight tracks, and excels at Windsor and Nottingham. Turf high 77 - 3rd of 14 giving 6lb to April Stock (11 Oct Windsor 12f g-f RF 4822) - also 1st of 12 getting 16lb from Hibernate (30 Aug Epsom RF 4014). AW high 48. Easy winner of the 'amateurs' Derby at Epsom.
**G L Moore [1-10] T F Maycock (from R Simpson [7-23] Jan 1999).*

FLYING FLIP BHB 54f44a **RR 60f 44a** 4800[14]
5 b m Rolfe (USA) 11.2f **(46)** - Needwood Sprite (Joshua) 10.5f **(58)**
Form - 51514780
Record 1999 - 1st:2 2nd:0 3rd:0 Ran:8
Pre1999 - 1st:1 2nd:1 3rd:1 Ran:15
Win Prizemoney £9,717 *Total Prizemoney* £11,523
Wins * **1999** May Hamilt (SFT) H 13f 57 60 <
* **1999** Apr Nottin (HVY) H 14.1f 47 54
* 1998 Apr Nottin (SFT) H 10f 48 56
1999 Turf 2-8: (12f, 13f 1-3, 14f 1-3, 16f) (sft 1-1, g-s, gd 1-5, g-f)
Average filly, effective 10 to 14f, acts on sft to frm, best on gd, likes right handed tracks, prefers tight tracks, excels at Nottingham, does well at Hamilton and Leicester. Turf high 60 - 1st of 11 giving 14lb to Philmist (24 May Hamilton RF 1423) - also 1st of 14 giving 8lb to Kintbury (27 Apr Nottingham RF 0871).
**B C Morgan [3-23] Tim Leadbeater.*

FLYING HIGH (IRE) BHB 28f **RR** 5073[15]
4 b g Fayruz 6.6f **(63)** - Shayista **(47f)** (Tap On Wood) 10.3f **(65)**
Form - 0000
Record 1999 - 1st:0 2nd:0 3rd:0 Ran:4
Pre1999 - 1st:0 2nd:0 3rd:0 Ran:3
1999 Turf 0-4: (8f 2, 10f, 12f) (gd 3, frm)
Workmanlike, very poor gelding, has worn blinkers. (began Spt).
**B Ellison [0-4] The Three Twos Partnership (from F Murphy [0-3] Jun 1997).*

FLYING HOME BHB 49f **RR 33f** 1375[10]
4 b g Flying Tyke 7.2f **(42)** - Bellinote (FR) (Noir Et Or) 10f **(38)**
Form - 70
Record 1999 - 1st:0 2nd:0 3rd:0 Ran:2
Pre1999 - 1st:0 2nd:0 3rd:0 Ran:1
1999 Turf 0-2: (12f 2) (g-f, frm)
Very moderate gelding. Turf high 33.
**Mrs M Reveley [0-2] Park Racing Partnership (from J L Eyre [0-1] Jly 1998).*

FLYING MEMORY BHB 37f **RR 40f** 4440[11]
3 b f Greensmith - Flying (Head for Heights) 9.6f **(55)**
Form - 680
Record 1999 - 1st:0 2nd:0 3rd:0 Ran:3
Pre1999 - 1st:0 2nd:0 3rd:0 Ran:3
1999 Turf 0-1: (6f) (g-f) 1999 AW 0-2: (5f, 6f) (Fibr 2)
Leggy, moderate filly. AW high 35.
**N P Littmoden [0-3] Avon & West Racing Club Ltd (from W G M Turner [0-3] Jun 1998).*

FLYING OFFICER BHB 94a **RR 94a** 2475a[8]
3 ch c Efisio 7.7f **(69)** - Area Girl (Jareer (USA)) 5.9f **(75)**
Form - 2214112158
Record 1999 - 1st:3 2nd:1 3rd:0 Ran:6
Pre1999 - 1st:1 2nd:2 3rd:0 Ran:4
Win Prizemoney £16,755 *Total Prizemoney* £20,667
Wins * **1999** *Mar Wolver (STD) 7f 108+* <
* **1999** *Jan Wolver (STD) 6f 106++*
* **1999** *Jan Wolver (STD) H 7f 80 102+*
* 1998 *Dec Lingfi (STD) 6f 88+*
1999 Turf 0-1: (6f) (sft) 1999 AW 3-5: (6f 1-1, 7f 2-2, 8f 2) (Equi, Fibr 3-3, Dirt)
Workmanlike, Pattern-class colt, effective 6 to 7f, best at 7f, - acts on Fibr, prefers left handed tracks, prefers tight tracks. AW high 108 - 1st of 6 getting 10lb from Weetman's Weigh (3 Mar Wolverhampton RF 0394) - also 1st of 6 getting 4lb from Adelphi Boy (20 Jan Wolverhampton RF 0130). Inconsistent. He has looked a very smart performer indeed on sand, especially when beating some useful older horses over six furlongs at Wolverhampton at the start of the year. He is also effective over seven furlongs, but in two attempts at a mile he appeared not to stay. He would be an interesting prospect if he were to continue his career in the US. **Sir Mark Prescott [4-10].*

FLYING PENNANT (IRE) BHB 42f **RR 43f** 4121[9]
6 ch h Waajib 8.9f **(67)**-Flying Beckee (IRE) (Godswalk (USA)) 7.3f **(58)**
Form - 007440050350
Record 1999 - 1st:0 2nd:0 3rd:1 Ran:12
Pre1999 - 1st:2 2nd:3 3rd:4 Ran:29
Win Prizemoney £6,366 *Total Prizemoney* £12,774
Wins * 1998 Jun Chepst (G-S) H 7.1f 50 54
1996 May Salisb (G-F) C 7f 63 <
1999 Turf 0-12: (7f 10, 8f 2) (gd 3, g-f 5, frm 3, hrd)
Moderate horse, effective 7f, acts on gd to frm, best on gd, often wears blinkers (very effectively), does well at Brighton. Turf high 46. **J M Bradley [1-31] E A Hayward (from R Hannon [1-10] Oct 1996).*

FLYING RUN (IRE) BHB 62f **RR 67f** 4256[7]
2 b f Lake Coniston (IRE) - Kaskazi (Dancing Brave (USA)) 8.4f **(76)**
Form - 4507

Record 1999 - 1st:0 2nd:0 3rd:0 Ran:4
Win Prizemoney £0 *Total Prizemoney* £257
1999 Turf 0-4: (6f 4) (gd, g-f 2, frm)
Average filly. Turf high 67. **J R Arnold [0-4] A H Robinson.*

FLYING THE FLAG (IRE) BHB 39f **RR 40f** 4807[7]

3 b f Thatching 7.8f **(69)** - Flagpole (IRE) (Be My Guest (USA)) 9.3f **(67)**
Form - 075753705787

Record		1st	2nd	3rd	Ran
	1999 -	1st:0	2nd:0	3rd:1	Ran:12
	Pre1999 -	1st:0	2nd:1	3rd:1	Ran:4

Win Prizemoney £0 *Total Prizemoney* £2,347
1999 Turf 0-12: (5f, 6f 4, 7f 2, 8f 4, 11f) (sft, gd 2, g-f 3, frm 6)
Moderate filly, effective 5 to 6f, best at 6f, acts on gd to frm, has worn blinkers. Turf high 66. Consistent.
**J J Quinn [0-16] Adams, Bloy, Galloway & Thomas.*

FLYING TOUCH BHB 26a **RR 26a** 352[9]

4 ch f Greensmith - Flying (Head for Heights) 9.6f **(55)**
Form - 7050

Record		1st	2nd	3rd	Ran
	1999 -	1st:0	2nd:0	3rd:0	Ran:4
	Pre1999 -	1st:0	2nd:0	3rd:0	Ran:3

1999 AW 0-4: (6f, 7f 2, 8f) (Fibr 4)
Light-framed, little account filly. AW high 25.
**N P Littmoden [0-4] Avon & West Racing Club Ltd (from W G M Turner [0-3] Mar 1998).*

FLY LIKE A BIRD BHB 60f **RR 64f** 689[7]

3 ch f Keen 11.1f **(58)** - Turtle Dove (Gyr (USA)) 9.5f **(65)**
Form - 67

Record		1st	2nd	3rd	Ran
	1999 -	1st:0	2nd:0	3rd:0	Ran:2
	Pre1999 -	1st:0	2nd:0	3rd:1	Ran:4

Win Prizemoney £0 *Total Prizemoney* £452
1999 Turf 0-2: (12f 2) (gd, frm)
Small, average filly, effective 12f, acts on frm. Turf high 64 - 7th of 12 giving 18lb to Hi-Jenny (14 Apr Beverley 12f frm RF 0689).
**S P C Woods [0-6] One Dream Partnership.*

FLY LIKE THE WIND **RR 56f** 1398[5]

2 br f Cyrano de Bergerac 7.3f **(58)**-Thulium (Mansingh (USA)) 7.4f **(55)**
Form - 5
Record 1999 - 1st:0 2nd:0 3rd:0 Ran:1
1999 Turf 0-1: (5f) (frm)
Currently fair filly.
**M A Jarvis [0-1] Cosmic Greyhound Racing Partnership III.*

FLYNN BHB 45f **RR 45f** 1596[9]

3 b g My Generation 6.5f **(68)** - Sky Mariner (Julio Mariner) 7.2f **(57)**
Form - 800
Record 1999 - 1st:0 2nd:0 3rd:0 Ran:3
1999 Turf 0-3: (6f 2, 8f) (gd 3)
Workmanlike, moderate gelding. Turf high 45.
**N M Babbage [0-3] Alan Craddock.*

FLYOVER **RR 74f** 4672[18]

2 b f Presidium 7.5f **(56)** - Flash-By (Ilium)
Form - 2013770
Record 1999 - 1st:1 2nd:1 3rd:1 Ran:7
Win Prizemoney £2,607 *Total Prizemoney* £3,526

Wins	* **1999**	Jun	Salisb	(GD)		6f		74	<

1999 Turf 1-7: (5f 2, 6f 1-3, 7f 2) (sft, g-s, gd, g-f 1-3, frm)
Above-average filly, effective 6f, acts on g-f to frm. Turf high 74 - 3rd of 12 giving 1lb to Card Games (10 Jly Salisbury 6f frm RF 2712) - also 1st of 13 getting 3lb from Bloody Mary (8 Jun Salisbury RF 1812). **B R Millman [1-7] R J Tory.*

FLY TO THE STARS BHB 122f **RR 125?f** 4246a[8]

5 b h Bluebird (USA) 7.9f **(71)**-Rise and Fall (Mill Reef (USA)) 10.5f **(78)**
Form - 178

Record		1st	2nd	3rd	Ran
	1999 -	1st:1	2nd:0	3rd:0	Ran:3
	Pre1999 -	1st:5	2nd:5	3rd:3	Ran:17

Win Prizemoney £221,956 *Total Prizemoney* £329,252

Wins	Year	Month	Course	Going	Type	Dist			
	* **1999**	May	Newbur	(SFT)	G1	8f		122	
	* 1998	Oct	Longch	(SFT)	G2	8f		125	<
	* 1998	Jly	Deauvi	(G-S)	G3	8f		120	
	1997	Jly	Goodwo	(G-F)	H	8f	106	112	
	1997	Jun	Ascot	(GD)	H	8f	100	105	
	1997	Mar	Doncas	(G-F)		8f		92+	

1999 Turf 1-3: (8f 1-3) (gd 1-2, g-f)
Top-class colt, effective 8f, acts on sft to g-f. Turf high 122 (1st run) - 1st of 6 from Jim And Tonic (15 May Newbury RF 1235). Very effective on soft ground, he made that count when making all in the Lockinge on his 1999 return, but the faster ground in the Queen Anne found him out. In his only other run he acted as Aljabr's pacemaker in the Moulin.
**S bin Suroor [3-7] (from S bin Suroor in UAE [0-2] Mar 1998).*

FNAN BHB 100f **RR 98f** 4917[9]

3 b c Generous (IRE) 11.5f **(82)** - Rafha (Kris) 9.5f **(73)**
Form - 821121210

Record		1st	2nd	3rd	Ran
	1999 -	1st:4	2nd:3	3rd:0	Ran:9
	Pre1999 -	1st:0	2nd:0	3rd:2	Ran:4

Win Prizemoney £17,995 *Total Prizemoney* £24,137

Wins	Year	Month	Course	Going	Type	Dist			
	* **1999**	Aug	Newcas	(GD)	H	16.1f	95	98	<
	* **1999**	Jly	Newbur	(G-F)	H	16f	85	88	
	* **1999**	Jun	Haydoc	(SFT)	H	14f	80	81	
	* **1999**	May	Doncas	(G-F)	H	14.6f	75	81	

1999 Turf 4-9: (10f, 12f, 14f 1-1, 15f 1-2, 16f 2-3, 17f) (g-s, gd 1-4, g-f 1-2, frm 1-1, hrd 1-1)
Workmanlike, very useful colt, effective 16f, acts on g-f to frm, best on g-f, prefers left handed tracks. Turf high 98 - 1st of 5 getting 14lb from Murghem (30 Aug Newcastle RF 4025). Tough and genuine - as was his Classic-winning dam - he developed into a useful staying handicapper. Effective on any ground, he lacks pace and is best when adopting enterprising tactics. He was sold for 74,000 gns in October to join Noel Meade.
**J L Dunlop [4-13] Prince A A Faisal.*

FOE (IRE) BHB 93f **RR 87f** 4268[13]

2 b c Fayruz 6.6f **(63)** - Paryiana (IRE) (Shernazar) 10.2f **(73)**
Form - 0176540
Record 1999 - 1st:1 2nd:0 3rd:0 Ran:7
Win Prizemoney £4,924 *Total Prizemoney* £6,915

Wins	* **1999**	May	Windso	(G-F)		5f		83	<

1999 Turf 1-7: (5f 1-3, 6f 4) (gd 2, g-f, frm 1-4)
Useful colt, effective 5 to 6f, acts on frm. Turf high 87 - 7th of 16 to Bally Pride (25 Jun Curragh 6f frm RF 2404a) - also 1st of 6 from Eastways (24 May Windsor RF 1445). He won a Windsor novice stakes on his second start despite running green, but has been found out in rather better company since. Respectable fifth in the Gimcrack but held back at York. **R Hannon [1-7] Michael Pescod.*

FOIST BHB 52f60a **RR 53f 60a** 3821[14]

7 b g Efisio 7.7f **(69)** - When The Saints (Bay Express) 7.1f **(60)**
Form - 0050

Record		1st	2nd	3rd	Ran
	1999 -	1st:0	2nd:0	3rd:0	Ran:4
	Pre1999 -	1st:8	2nd:1	3rd:3	Ran:39

Win Prizemoney £31,161 *Total Prizemoney* £35,156

Wins	Year	Month	Course	Going	Type	Dist			
	* 1998	May	Warwic	(GD)		6f		65	
	* 1998	May	Hamilt	(G-S)	H	6f	56	61	
	* 1997	May	Hamilt	(SFT)	H	6f	59	68+	<
	* 1997	Apr	Hamilt	(G-S)	H	6f	50	64	
	* 1997	Mar	Catter	(GD)	H	7f	46	50	
	* 1996	*Apr*	*Southw*	*(STD)*	*H*	*6f*	*40*	*58*	
	* 1996	*Apr*	*Wolver*	*(STD)*	*H*	*6f*	*40*	*51+*	
	* 1996	*Mar*	*Southw*	*(STD)*	*H*	*6f*	*30*	*36*	

1999 Turf 0-4: (6f 4) (g-f 3, frm)
Fair gelding, effective 6f, acts on g-s to g-f, has worn blinkers. Turf high 53. **M W Easterby [8-43] D F Spence.*

FOLEY BIGTIME **RR 33f** 2271[16]

2 ch c Timeless Times (USA) 6.1f **(56)** - Trachelium **(44df)** (Formidable (USA)) 9.2f **(63)**
Form - 000
Record 1999 - 1st:0 2nd:0 3rd:0 Ran:3
1999 Turf 0-3: (5f 2, 7f) (sft, gd, frm)
Currently very moderate colt. Turf high 33.
**M Quinn [0-3] Foley Steelstock.*

FOLLOW ME **RR 51f** 1209[1]

3 ch g Keen 11.1f **(58)** - Fairlead **(57f)** (Slip Anchor) 9.8f **(73)**
Form - 1

Record		1st	2nd	3rd	Ran
	1999 -	1st:1	2nd:0	3rd:0	Ran:1
	Pre1999 -	1st:0	2nd:0	3rd:0	Ran:3

Win Prizemoney £2,808 *Total Prizemoney* £2,808

Wins	* **1999**	May	Hamilt	(Sft)	SH	11.1f	48	50	<

1999 Turf 1-1: (11f 1-1) (g-s 1-1)
Lengthy, fair gelding. (1st run) - 1st of 12 getting 11lb from Dr Woodstock (14 May Hamilton RF 1209).
**C W Thornton [1-4] Guy Reed.*

FOLLOW SUIT BHB 81f **RR 79f** 4645[5]

2 ch c First Trump - Indian Lament **(34df)** (Indian Ridge)
Form - 15
Record 1999 - 1st:1 2nd:0 3rd:0 Ran:2
Win Prizemoney £6,524 *Total Prizemoney* £6,524
Wins * 1999 Jly York (G-F) 6f 79 <
1999 Turf 1-2: (6f 1-1, 7f) (g-s, g-f 1-1)
Currently above-average colt. Turf high 79 (1st run) (began Jly) - 1st of 14 giving 5lb to Blue Line Lady (10 Jly York RF 2729). Won a six-furlong York maiden on fast ground on his debut, but did not look the same horse on heavy ground over an extra furlong at Salisbury next time. **J L Dunlop [1-2] The Earl Cadogan.*

FOLLOW THAT DREAM BHB 83f **RR 87tf** 4540[5]

3 b f Darshaan 11.9f **(81)** - Try To Catch Me (USA) (Shareef Dancer (USA)) 9.9f **(73)**
Form - 55651243255
Record 1999 - 1st:1 2nd:2 3rd:1 Ran:11
Win Prizemoney £3,636 *Total Prizemoney* £8,693
Wins * 1999 Jun Cheste (G-F) H 12.3f 74 77 <
1999 Turf 1-11: (8f,10f, 11f, 12f 1-2, 13f, 14f 4, 15f) (gd 3, g-f 4, frm 1-4)
Neat, useful filly, effective 12 to 15f, best at 14f, acts on gd to frm, best on frm. Turf high 87 - 5th of 10 to Mistle Song (8 Spt Doncaster 15f gd RF 4209). Consistent. She has improved since being tried over extended trips, and got off the mark at Chester in June over twelve furlongs. She has continued to run well since. Suited by fast ground. **E A L Dunlop [1-11] Maktoum Al Maktoum.*

FONZY BHB 34f36a **RR 26df 36a** 21[13]

5 b g Phountzi (USA) 9.6f **(60)** - Diavalezza (Connaught) 7.7f **(63)**
Form - 00
Record 1999 - 1st:0 2nd:0 3rd:0 Ran:1
Pre1999 - 1st:4 2nd:1 3rd:1 Ran:14
Win Prizemoney £10,357 *Total Prizemoney* £11,690
Wins 1996 Jly Mussel (GD) C 5f 70 <
1996 Jun Mussel (G-F) C 5f 70 <
1996 May Thirsk (G-F) C 5f 59
1996 May Southw (STD) 5f 54
1999 AW 0-1: (7f) (Fibr)
Little account gelding, has worn blinkers. He failed to give his connections any happy days in 1999.
**M Brittain [0-2] Northgate Lodge Racing Club (from G R Oldroyd [0-2] Spt 1998).*

FOOL ON THE HILL **RR 44f** 5207[6]

2 b c Reprimand 8.2f **(63)** - Stock Hill Lass (Air Trooper) 9.1f **(63)**
Form - 06
Record 1999 - 1st:0 2nd:0 3rd:0 Ran:2
1999 Turf 0-2: (6f, 7f) (g-s, g-f)
Currently moderate colt. Turf high 44 (began Oct).
**L G Cottrell [0-2] E Gadsden.*

FOOTPRINTS (IRE) BHB 75f **RR 75f** 5070[1]

2 b f College Chapel - Near Miracle (Be My Guest (USA)) 9.3f **(67)**
Form - 021
Record 1999 - 1st:1 2nd:1 3rd:0 Ran:3
Win Prizemoney £2,407 *Total Prizemoney* £3,117
Wins * 1999 Oct Redcar (SFT) 5f 75 <
1999 Turf 1-3: (5f 1-3) (gd 1-2, frm)
Currently above-average filly. Turf high 75 (began Oct) - 1st of 16 getting 5lb from Marshall St Cyr (26 Oct Redcar RF 5070).
**M Johnston [1-3] Mrs Joan Keaney.*

FORBEARING (IRE) **RR 62f** 5209[6]

2 b c Bering 9.6f **(80)** - For Example (USA) (Northern Baby (CAN)) 11.6f **(71)**
Form - 56
Record 1999 - 1st:0 2nd:0 3rd:0 Ran:2
1999 Turf 0-2: (6f, 7f) (g-s, gd)
Currently average colt. Turf high 62 (began Oct).
**Sir Mark Prescott [0-2] Eclipse Thoroughbreds - Osborne House IV.*

FORCING BID BHB 60f73a **RR 32f 73a** 1510[12]

5 b g Forzando 7.2f **(63)**-Cox's Pippin (USA)(Cox's Ridge (USA))8f **(68)**
Form - 7000
Record 1999 - 1st:0 2nd:0 3rd:0 Ran:4
Pre1999 - 1st:3 2nd:0 3rd:2 Ran:15
Win Prizemoney £9,004 *Total Prizemoney* £10,392
Wins *1997 Nov Wolver (STD) H 6f 78 83* <
1997 Apr Southw (STD) H 6f 65 75
1997 Apr Wolver (STD) H 6f 65 70
1999 Turf 0-2: (7f, 10f) (gd, g-f) 1999 AW 0-2: (6f, 7f) (Fibr 2)
Moderate gelding, has worn blinkers. Turf high 32. AW high 40.
**John Berry [0-4] H R Moszkowicz (from Sir Mark Prescott [3-15] Dec 1997).*

FOREIGN EDITOR BHB 49f52a **RR 50f 52a** 5068[5]

3 ch g Magic Ring (IRE) 6.5f **(64)** - True Precision **(61f 59a)** (Presidium)
Form - 707665
Record 1999 - 1st:0 2nd:0 3rd:0 Ran:6
Pre1999 - 1st:0 2nd:0 3rd:1 Ran:3
Win Prizemoney £0 *Total Prizemoney* £478
1999 Turf 0-5: (5f, 6f 2, 7f, 8f) (gd 2, g-f, frm 2) 1999 AW 0-1: (6f) (Fibr)
Workmanlike, fair gelding, effective 7f, acts on frm, has worn blinkers. Turf high 50 - 6th of 30 getting 11lb from Intricate Web (15 Oct Redcar 7f frm RF 4906). Consistent.
**R A Fahey [0-9] Pride Of Yorkshire Racing Club.*

FOREIGN RULE (IRE) BHB 60f **RR 59f** 1962[9]

5 b g Danehill (USA) 9.1f **(79)**-Guida Centrale(Teenoso (USA)) 9.9f **(72)**
Form - 00
Record 1999 - 1st:0 2nd:0 3rd:0 Ran:2
Pre1999 - 1st:1 2nd:2 3rd:1 Ran:8
Win Prizemoney £3,556 *Total Prizemoney* £6,300
Wins 1997 Jly Haydoc (G-S) H 14f 72 77 <
1999 Turf 0-2: (14f, 16f) (g-f, frm)
Fair gelding, has worn blinkers. Turf high 59. Inconsistent.
**J R Jenkins [1-14] Mrs Susan McCarthy (from P W Chapple-Hyam [1-6] Jly 1997).*

FOREIGN SECRETARY (USA) **RR 66+f** 4216[4]

2 b c Kingmambo (USA) 10.9f **(85)** - Misinskie (USA) (Nijinsky (CAN)) 10.3f **(77)**
Form - 4
Record 1999 - 1st:0 2nd:0 3rd:0 Ran:1
Win Prizemoney £0 *Total Prizemoney* £425
1999 Turf 0-1: (7f) (frm)
Currently average colt. **Sir Michael Stoute [0-1] W J Gredley.*

FOREST BOY BHB 48f58a **RR 38f 58a** 1794[8]

6 b g Komaite (USA) 6.9f **(61)** - Khadine (Astec) 8.6f **(66)**
Form - 868
Record 1999 - 1st:0 2nd:0 3rd:0 Ran:3
Pre1999 - 1st:4 2nd:1 3rd:0 Ran:13
Win Prizemoney £12,397 *Total Prizemoney* £13,333
Wins *1997 Jan Wolver (STD) H 9.4f 70 70* <
1996 May Hamilt (SFT) H 8.3f 62 70 <
1996 Apr Catter (GD) H 7f 62 68
1996 Apr Hamilt (G-S) 8.3f 60
1999 Turf 0-2: (8f, 11f) (g-s, gd) 1999 AW 0-1: (8f) (Fibr)
Fair gelding, often wears blinkers. Turf high 38. Inconsistent.
**M R Bosley [0-7] Marks (Banbury) (from J R Bosley [1-4] Jan 1997).*

FOREST CALL BHB 53f57a **RR 46f 57a** 2692[2]

4 ch f Wolfhound (USA) 7.3f **(71)** - Balnaha (Lomond (USA)) 8.8f **(65)**
Form - 4802
Record 1999 - 1st:0 2nd:1 3rd:0 Ran:4
Pre1999 - 1st:0 2nd:1 3rd:0 Ran:5
Win Prizemoney £0 *Total Prizemoney* £2,477
1999 Turf 0-3: (7f 2, 8f) (gd, frm 2) 1999 AW 0-1: (5f) (Fibr)
Scopey, fair filly, effective 8f, acts on gd, has worn blinkers, likes left handed tracks, likes tight tracks. Turf high 46. Inconsistent.
**Lady Herries [0-4] Seymour Racing Partnership (from G Wragg [0-5] Oct 1998).*

FOREST CAMP (USA) **RR** 5229a[6]

2 f Deputy Minister (CAN) 9.2f **(71)** - La Paz (USA) (Hold Your Peace (USA)) 9f **(72)**
Form - 6
1999 AW 0-1: (9f) (Dirt)

Currently useful. **B Baffert in USA [0-1].*

FOREST DREAM BHB 58f60a **RR 60f 60a** 5069[2]

4 b f Warrshan (USA) 9.7f **(59)** - Sirenivo (USA) (Sir Ivor) 10.2f **(70)**
Form - 562810022
Record 1999 - 1st:1 2nd:3 3rd:0 Ran:9
Pre1999 - 1st:0 2nd:0 3rd:1 Ran:7
Win Prizemoney £3,088 *Total Prizemoney* £6,190
Wins * **1999** Aug Lingfi (G-F) H 10f 53 56 <
1999 Turf 1-8: (8f 2, 10f 1-4, 12f 2) (gd, g-f 2, frm 1-5) 1999 AW 0-1: (12f) (Fibr)
Workmanlike, average filly, effective 10f, acts on gd to frm, likes left handed tracks, likes tight tracks. Turf high 60 - 2nd of 19 giving 2lb to Inch Perfect (26 Oct Bath 10f gd RF 5069) - also 1st of 7 giving 4lb to Ascari (6 Aug Lingfield RF 3422).
**Lady Herries [1-16] Lord Cowdrey.*

FOREST FIRE (SWE) BHB 80f **RR 85f** 4794[10]

4 b f Never so Bold 7.1f **(62)** - Mango Sampaquita (SWE) (Colombian Friend (USA)) 8.5f **(64)**
Form - 446110560
Record 1999 - 1st:2 2nd:0 3rd:0 Ran:9
Pre1999 - 1st:2 2nd:1 3rd:2 Ran:10
Win Prizemoney £17,615 *Total Prizemoney* £19,865
Wins * **1999** Jly Newmar (G-F) H 12f 78 83 <
* **1999** Jly Newmar (G-F) H 10f 74 79
* 1998 Spt Sandow (GD) H 8.1f 65 69
* 1998 Aug Sandow (G-F) C 9f 58
1999 Turf 2-9: (8f, 9f, 10f 1-3, 12f 1-4) (sft, g-s, gd 3, frm 2-4)
Unfurnished, useful filly, effective 10 to 12f, acts on frm, prefers right handed tracks. Turf high 85 - also 1st of 5 giving 17lb to Turtle Soup (30 Jly Newmarket RF 3245). A winner twice at Sandown in '98, she scored twice at Newmarket on fast ground during the summer, but rose in the handicap as a result and looked held.
**B Hanbury [4-18] Mrs Mette Campbell (from P Mooney [0-1] Oct 1997).*

FOREST FRIENDLY RR 76f 5137[4]

2 b f Unfuwain (USA) 11.4f **(74)** - Butsova (Formidable (USA)) 9.2f **(63)**
Form - 4
Record 1999 - 1st:0 2nd:0 3rd:0 Ran:1
Win Prizemoney £0 *Total Prizemoney* £289
1999 Turf 0-1: (7f) (gd)
Currently above-average filly. (1st run) - 4th of 16 to Garota do Leblon (30 Oct Newmarket 7f gd RF 5137).
**B W Hills [0-1] W J Gredley.*

FOREST GREEN FLYER BHB 38f **RR 33f** 2528[12]

3 b f Syrtos 8.1f **(57)** - Bolton Flyer (Aragon) 8.1f **(60)**
Form - 000
Record 1999 - 1st:0 2nd:0 3rd:0 Ran:3
1999 Turf 0-3: (7f 3) (gd, g-f, frm)
Leggy, very moderate filly. Turf high 33. **O O'Neill [0-3] T Horsley.*

FOREST GREY BHB 24f **RR 25f** 4032[15]

3 gr g Petong 7.6f **(58)** - Holyrood Park (Sharrood (USA)) 10.5f **(72)**
Form - 00760
Record 1999 - 1st:0 2nd:0 3rd:0 Ran:5
Pre1999 - 1st:0 2nd:0 3rd:0 Ran:3
1999 Turf 0-4: (8f, 10f, 11f, 12f) (gd, g-f 2, frm) 1999 AW 0-1: (12f) (Equi)
Unfurnished, little account gelding, has worn blinkers. Turf high 25. **K McAuliffe [0-8] E P Jameson.*

FOREST HEATH (IRE) RR 73f 5104[7]

2 gr g Common Grounds 8.1f **(66)** - Caroline Lady (JPN) (Caro)
Form - 87
Record 1999 - 1st:0 2nd:0 3rd:0 Ran:2
1999 Turf 0-2: (6f, 7f) (gd 2)
Currently above-average gelding. Turf high 73 (began Oct).
**J E Banks [0-2] Forest Heath Partnership.*

FOREST KING (IRE) BHB 54f60a **RR 57f 60a** 5067[8]

3 b g Forest Wind (USA) - Paryiana (IRE) (Shernazar) 10.2f **(73)**
Form - 0404238
Record 1999 - 1st:0 2nd:1 3rd:1 Ran:7
Pre1999 - 1st:0 2nd:0 3rd:0 Ran:2
Win Prizemoney £0 *Total Prizemoney* £1,285
1999 Turf 0-4: (10f 2, 11f, 12f) (gd, g-f, frm 2) 1999 AW 0-3: (10f, 12f, 16f) (Equi 2, Fibr)
Workmanlike, average gelding, effective 10 to 12f, - acts on AW, prefers left handed tracks, favours tight tracks. Turf high 57. AW high 63 (1st run) - 4th of 7 getting 14lb from Herr Trigger (25 May Lingfield 10f Equi RF 1459).
**G A Butler [0-8] R J Styles & R J Tarring (from J W Hills [0-2] Jly 1998).*

FOREST QUEEN BHB 59f **RR 61f** 5076[18]

2 b f Risk Me (FR) 8f **(53)** - Grey Cree (Creetown) 6.9f **(50)**
Form - 042073850
Record 1999 - 1st:0 2nd:1 3rd:1 Ran:9
Win Prizemoney £0 *Total Prizemoney* £2,197
1999 Turf 0-9: (5f 5, 6f 4) (gd 3, g-f 4, frm 2)
Average filly, effective 5f, acts on frm. Turf high 61 - 3rd of 13 getting 4lb from Pertemps Fc (29 Aug Beverley 5f frm RF 3988).
**K W Hogg [0-9] P W Cooper.*

FOREST ROBIN BHB 41f49a **RR 47f 49a** 4935[6]

6 ch g Formidable (USA) 7.8f **(60)** - Blush Rambler (IRE) (Blushing Groom (FR)) 10.3f **(76)**
Form - 872044680626644706
Record 1999 - 1st:0 2nd:2 3rd:0 Ran:16
Pre1999 - 1st:3 2nd:5 3rd:8 Ran:50
Win Prizemoney £9,066 *Total Prizemoney* £24,918
Wins 1998 Aug Newmar (G-F) H 8f 56 63+ <
1998 Jly Redcar (G-F) H 8f 48 52
1998 May Redcar (G-F) H 6f 42 50
1999 Turf 0-11: (7f 5, 8f 5, 9f) (g-s, gd, g-f, frm 7, hrd) 1999 AW 0-5: (8f 5) (Equi 2, Fibr 3)
Fair gelding, effective 7 to 8f, best at 8f, acts on frm to hrd - acts on AW, has worn blinkers, excels at Redcar. Turf high 52. AW high 58 - 4th of 12 giving 2lb to Statistician (18 Mar Lingfield 8f Equi RF 0441).
**Mrs L Stubbs [0-18] Mrs L Stubbs (from Mrs J R Ramsden [3-33] Spt 1998).*

FORESTRY BHB 30f **RR 34f** 2085[13]

5 b g Highest Honor (FR) 10.9f **(72)** - Arboretum (IRE) (Green Desert (USA)) 8.6f **(78)**
Form - 40
Record 1999 - 1st:0 2nd:0 3rd:0 Ran:2
Pre1999 - 1st:0 2nd:0 3rd:0 Ran:4
1999 Turf 0-1: (10f) (g-f) 1999 AW 0-1: (8f) (Fibr)
Very moderate gelding.
**M J Wilkinson [0-9] D Ancil (from J G Smyth-Osbourne [0-4] Spt 1997).*

FORESTRY (USA) RR 5227a[4]

3 f Storm Cat (USA) 7f **(86)** - Shared Interest (USA) (Pleasant Colony (USA)) 7f **(70)**
Form - 4
1999 AW 0-1: (6f) (Dirt)
Currently Group-class. **B Baffert in USA [0-1].*

FOREST SHADOW (IRE) BHB 93f **RR 95f** 1233[5]

3 b c Sadler's Wells (USA) 11.3f **(87)** - Bay Shade (USA) (Sharpen Up) 8.3f **(67)**
Form - 0535
Record 1999 - 1st:0 2nd:0 3rd:1 Ran:3
Pre1999 - 1st:1 2nd:2 3rd:0 Ran:5
Win Prizemoney £4,146 *Total Prizemoney* £14,464
Wins * 1998 Aug Newbur (GD) 7f 84 <
1999 Turf 0-3: (10f 2, 12f) (gd, g-f 2)
Unfurnished, very useful colt, effective 10f, acts on g-s. Turf high 95. He is unlikely to stay beyond a mile and a quarter and falls short of Group and Listed class at home.
**P W Chapple-Hyam [1-8] R E Sangster.*

FOREVER MIDNIGHT (IRE) BHB 100f **RR 91f** 5041[7]

2 b f Night Shift (USA) 8.1f **(73)** - Timeless **(59f 56a)** (Royal Academy (USA))
Form - 1252407
Record 1999 - 1st:1 2nd:2 3rd:0 Ran:7
Win Prizemoney £4,108 *Total Prizemoney* £13,101

Wins * **1999** Jun Goodwo (G-F) 6f 89+ <
1999 Turf 1-7: (6f 1-6, 7f) (sft, gd 1-2, g-f 2, frm 2)
Useful filly, effective 6f, acts on gd to frm. Turf high 91 - 2nd of 6 giving 3lb to Crimplene (2 Spt Salisbury 6f frm RF 4093) - also 1st of 10 from Sailing (11 Jun Goodwood RF 1914). Impressive winner of a useful-looking Goodwood maiden on her debut, she has shown herself to be just short of Pattern class since. Suited by fast ground. **B W Hills [1-7] R E Sangster & P D Savill.*

FORGIE (IRE) BHB 69f **RR 69f** 2709[15]
6 b g Don't Forget Me 9.5f **(66)** - Damia (Vision (USA)) 9f **(64)**
Form - 5060

Record					
1999 -	1st:0	2nd:0	3rd:0	Ran:4	
Pre1999 -	1st:6	2nd:4	3rd:5	Ran:33	

Win Prizemoney £28,484 *Total Prizemoney* £38,135

Wins								
* 1998	Apr	Nottin	(SFT)	H	14.1f	77	82	<
* 1997	Spt	Cheste	(GD)	H	15.9f	70	75	
* 1997	Spt	York	(SFT)	H	13.9f	64	70	
* 1997	Jun	Mussel	(G-S)	H	14f	64	68	
* 1997	Jun	Mussel	(GD)	H	14f	58	64	
* 1996	May	Redcar	(G-F)	H	14.1f	53	56	

1999 Turf 0-4: (14f 2, 15f, 16f) (g-s 3, frm)
Average gelding, effective 14 to 16f, acts on sft to frm, best on frm, excels at Nottingham and Haydock. Turf high 76 (1st run) - 5th of 17 giving 8lb to Nichol Fifty (19 Apr Nottingham 14f g-s RF 0750).
**P Calver [6-37] Mrs Janis MacPherson.*

FORGLORI BHB 36f **RR 36f** 2504[19]
4 b g Formidable (USA) 7.8f **(60)** - Glorietta (USA) (Shadeed (USA)) 8.2f **(70)**
Form - 00

Record				
1999 -	1st:0	2nd:0	3rd:0	Ran:2
Pre1999 -	1st:0	2nd:0	3rd:0	Ran:4

1999 Turf 0-2: (10f, 11f) (g-f, frm)
Very moderate gelding. Turf high 33.
**Miss B Sanders [0-2] R Lamb (from C J Benstead [0-4] Spt 1998).*

FORGOTTEN TIMES (USA) BHB 64f71a **RR 63f 71a** 5212[16]
5 ch m Nabeel Dancer (USA) 6.1f **(65)** - Etoile D'Amore (USA) (The Minstrel (CAN)) 10f **(72)**
Form - 0401155140114010760

Record				
1999 -	1st:6	2nd:0	3rd:0	Ran:19
Pre1999 -	1st:3	2nd:3	3rd:2	Ran:31

Win Prizemoney £27,432 *Total Prizemoney* £32,577

Wins								
* **1999**	Spt	Goodwo	(HVY)	H	5f	60	61+	
* **1999**	Aug	Bright	(G-F)	H	5.3f	51	59	
* **1999**	Aug	Windso	(SFT)	H	5f	51	64	
* **1999**	Jly	Salisb	(G-S)	H	5f	50	50	
* **1999**	May	Folkes	(G-F)	H	5f	43	45	
* **1999**	May	Goodwo	(Gd)	H	5f	43	51	
* 1998	*Feb*	*Lingfi*	*(SLW)*	*H*	*6f*	*67*	*71*	<
1997	*Feb*	*Lingfi*	*(STD)*	*H*	*6f*	*69*	*71*	<
1997	*Jan*	*Lingfi*	*(STD)*		*6f*		*59*	

1999 Turf 6-19: (5f 6-18, 6f) (sft 1-1, g-s 2, gd 2-6, g-f 1-5, frm 2-5)
Above-average filly, effective 5 to 6f, best at 5f, acts on sft to gd - acts on Equi, best on gd, often wears blinkers (very effectively), likes Goodwood. Turf high 64 - 1st of 14 giving 10lb to Miss Dangerous (16 Aug Windsor RF 3685). She was in brilliant form last season, winning six times. Suited by the minimum, she goes very well for an apprentice and can act on Equitrack as well.
**K T Ivory [7-33] John Crook (from T M Jones [2-15] Spt 1997).*

FOR HEAVENS SAKE **RR 55f** 5070[10]
2 b c Rambo Dancer (CAN) 8.4f **(59)** - Angel Fire (Nashwan (USA))
Form - 0
Record **1999** - 1st:0 2nd:0 3rd:0 Ran:1
1999 Turf 0-1: (5f) (gd)
Currently fair colt. **C W Thornton [0-1] Guy Reed.*

FORLORN HOPE BHB 40f **RR 55f** 5002[8]
2 b c Tragic Role (USA) 9.4f **(63)** - Rum N Raisin (Rakaposhi King)
Form - 0008
Record **1999** - 1st:0 2nd:0 3rd:0 Ran:4
1999 Turf 0-4: (5f 2, 6f, 8f) (gd 4)
Fair colt. Turf high 55. **B D Leavy [0-4] A J McMullan.*

FORMAL BID (USA) **RR 72f** 4210[5]
2 b br c Dynaformer (USA) 12f **(82)** - Fantastic Bid (USA) (Auction Ring (USA)) 8.6f **(65)**
Form - 35
Record **1999** - 1st:0 2nd:0 3rd:1 Ran:2
Win Prizemoney £0 *Total Prizemoney* £712
1999 Turf 0-2: (7f, 8f) (gd 2)
Currently above-average colt. Turf high 72 (1st run) (began Aug) - 3rd of 13 to Port Vila (14 Aug Newbury 7f gd RF 3650).
**P W Chapple-Hyam [0-2] Dr Carlos Stelling.*

FORMERIC **RR 32f** 5113[16]
3 ch g Formidable (USA) 7.8f **(60)** - Irish Limerick (Try My Best (USA)) 7.6f **(67)**
Form - 00
Record **1999** - 1st:0 2nd:0 3rd:0 Ran:2
1999 Turf 0-1: (6f) (gd) 1999 AW 0-1: (6f) (Fibr)
Leggy, currently very moderate gelding.
**Miss L C Siddall [0-2] Mrs S E Cooper.*

FORMER LOVE (USA) BHB 36f57a **RR 47df 57a** 1549[10]
4 b f Dynaformer (USA) 12f **(82)** - Love and Legend (USA) (Lyphard's Wish (FR)) 9f **(74)**
Form - 008000

Record				
1999 -	1st:0	2nd:0	3rd:0	Ran:6
Pre1999 -	1st:0	2nd:0	3rd:0	Ran:7

Win Prizemoney £0 *Total Prizemoney* £835
1999 Turf 0-5: (8f 2, 10f 3) (g-s, gd 2, g-f 2) 1999 AW 0-1: (8f) (Fibr)
Unfurnished, moderate filly. Turf high 47. Becoming disappointing.
**T W Donnelly [0-8] Mrs D E Andrews (from P R Webber [0-7] Aug 1998).*

FORMIDABLE FLAME BHB 32f29a **RR 31f 29a** 3835[12]
6 ch g Formidable (USA) 7.8f **(60)** - Madiyla (Darshaan) 9.9f **(84)**
Form - 40370

Record				
1999 -	1st:0	2nd:0	3rd:1	Ran:5
Pre1999 -	1st:0	2nd:0	3rd:2	Ran:16

Win Prizemoney £0 *Total Prizemoney* £961
1999 Turf 0-1: (17f) (frm) 1999 AW 0-4: (12f, 13f, 16f 2) (Equi, Fibr 3)
Moderate gelding, effective 9 to 11f, acts on g-f - acts on Fibr, has worn blinkers, favours left handed tracks, favours tight tracks. AW high 40. Inconsistent.
**G A Ham [0-12] G B J Humphries (from W J Musson [0-17] Jly 1998).*

FORMIDABLE SPIRIT BHB 31f31a **RR 28f 31a** 3901[11]
5 ch g Formidable (USA) 7.8f **(60)** - Hicklam Millie (Absalom) 7.2f **(58)**
Form - 023060

Record				
1999 -	1st:0	2nd:1	3rd:1	Ran:6
Pre1999 -	1st:0	2nd:0	3rd:0	Ran:10

Win Prizemoney £0 *Total Prizemoney* £1,479
1999 Turf 0-6: (6f, 7f, 8f 2, 9f, 11f) (gd, g-f 2, frm 3)
Little account gelding, effective 8f, acts on gd, has worn blinkers, likes right handed tracks. Turf high 33 - 2nd of 13 getting 14lb from Dancing Em (28 Jun Musselburgh 8f gd RF 2366).
**B Mactaggart [0-7] Mrs Hilary MacTaggart (from M J Heaton-Ellis [0-9] Jly 1997).*

FORSAKEN (IRE) **RR 60f** 2530[2]
2 b f Lake Coniston (IRE) -Faakirah (Dragonara Palace (USA)) 6.1f **(55)**
Form - 2
Record **1999** - 1st:0 2nd:1 3rd:0 Ran:1
Win Prizemoney £0 *Total Prizemoney* £1,128
1999 Turf 0-1: (6f) (gd)
Currently average filly. (1st run) - 2nd of 5 to Princess Ria (3 Jly Haydock 6f gd RF 2530). **G Lewis [0-1] Geoff Lewis.*

FORSIO BHB 48f **RR 62f** 4814[18]
3 b g Efisio 7.7f **(69)** - Foreseen (Reform) 8.9f **(62)**
Form - 00000
Record **1999** - 1st:0 2nd:0 3rd:0 Ran:5
1999 Turf 0-5: (7f, 8f, 10f 2, 12f) (gd 2, g-f, frm 2)
Unfurnished, average gelding, has worn blinkers. Turf high 62.
**Lady Herries [0-5] Hesmonds Stud.*

FOR SWAN BHB 30f **RR 25f** 3071[10]
3 ch f Forzando 7.2f **(63)** - My Precious Daisy (Sharpo) 7.7f **(59)**
Form - 6000870

Record 1999 - 1st:0 2nd:0 3rd:0 Ran:5
Pre1999 - 1st:0 2nd:0 3rd:0 Ran:2
1999 Turf 0-5: (5f 2, 7f, 8f, 9f) (g-f, frm 4)
Small, little account filly. Turf high 25. **R A Fahey [0-7] R A Fahey.*

FORTHECHOP BHB 38f **RR 23f** 4715[7]

2 b c Minshaanshu Amad (USA) 11.3f **(53)** - Cousin Jenny (Midyan (USA)) 6f **(60)**
Form - 67
Record 1999 - 1st:0 2nd:0 3rd:0 Ran:2
1999 Turf 0-1: (10f) (gd) 1999 AW 0-1: (8f) (Fibr)
Currently little account colt. **Mrs H L Walton [0-2] A E Walton.*

FORT KNOX (IRE) BHB 33f43a **RR 29f 43a** 1179[10]

8 b g Treasure Kay 6.5f **(53)** - Single Viking (Viking (USA)) 6.7f **(65)**
Form - 080
Record 1999 - 1st:0 2nd:0 3rd:0 Ran:3
Pre1999 - 1st:6 2nd:8 3rd:6 Ran:66
Win Prizemoney £17,084 *Total Prizemoney* £29,431
Wins * 1996 *Mar Lingfi (STD) 7f 66* <
* 1996 *Mar Lingfi (STD) H 8f 56 57*
* 1995 *Nov Lingfi (STD) H 7f 49 47*
* 1995 Aug Newmar (G-F) H 8f 49 55
1999 Turf 0-3: (7f 2, 8f) (g-f, frm, hrd)
Moderate gelding, effective 7f, acts on gd, often wears blinkers, likes left handed tracks, favours tight tracks. Turf high 29.
**R M Flower [7-75] Mrs D M Hickling (from R W Armstrong [0-6] Jan 1994).*

FORT SUMTER (USA) RR 65f 4630[13]

3 b c Sea Hero (USA) - Gray And Red (USA) (Wolf Power (SAF))
Form - 606300
Record 1999 - 1st:0 2nd:0 3rd:1 Ran:6
Pre1999 - 1st:0 2nd:2 3rd:0 Ran:3
Win Prizemoney £0 *Total Prizemoney* £2,516
1999 Turf 0-6: (8f, 10f 2, 12f 3) (g-s, gd 3, g-f 2)
Scopey, average colt, effective 9f, acts on gd, favours tight tracks. Turf high 65.
**P R Hedger [0-6] E Whelan (from I A Balding [0-3] Spt 1998).*

FORTUNE COOKIE BHB 25a **RR 29f** 5145[7]

3 ch f Selkirk (USA) 7.9f **(76)** - Lucky Round (Auction Ring (USA)) 8.6f **(65)**
Form - 000007
Record 1999 - 1st:0 2nd:0 3rd:0 Ran:6
1999 Turf 0-5: (7f 2, 8f, 10f, 14f) (gd 2, g-f, frm 2) 1999 AW 0-1: (12f) (Fibr)
Little account filly, has worn blinkers. Turf high 29.
**R M H Cowell [0-5] Dr St John Collier & Mrs Sherry Collier (from J R Fanshawe [0-1] Apr 1999).*

FORTUNE HOPPER BHB 39f **RR 36f** 2226[7]

5 br g Rock Hopper 10.6f **(54)** - Lots of Luck (Neltino) 7.6f **(54)**
Form - 7
Record 1999 - 1st:0 2nd:0 3rd:0 Ran:1
Pre1999 - 1st:0 2nd:0 3rd:3 Ran:7
Win Prizemoney £0 *Total Prizemoney* £903
1999 Turf 0-1: (17f) (frm)
Very moderate gelding, has worn blinkers. Consistent.
**Martin Todhunter [0-1] UGM Racing Club (from J Pearce [0-7] Jly 1997).*

FORTY FORTE BHB 72f70a **RR 66f 70a** 5166[15]

3 b g Pursuit of Love 9.5f **(69)** - Cominna (Dominion) 8.5f **(63)**
Form - 2231210000
Record 1999 - 1st:2 2nd:3 3rd:1 Ran:10
Win Prizemoney £8,042 *Total Prizemoney* £11,558
Wins * 1999 Apr Beverl (GD) H 7.5f 72 76 <
1999 Mar Nottin (G-S) S 8.2f 76+
1999 Turf 2-7: (6f, 7f 1-4, 8f 1-2) (sft 1-1, g-s, gd 1-3, g-f, frm) 1999 AW 0-3: (7f, 8f 2) (Equi 2, Fibr)
Leggy, average gelding, effective 7 to 8f, best at 8f, acts on sft to frm, prefers tight tracks. Turf high 76 (1st run) - 1st of 11 from Sounds Cool (29 Mar Nottingham RF 0505) - also 1st of 5 getting 17lb from River Times (22 Apr Beverley RF 0806). AW high 64. Becoming disappointing. He made the frame in modest company on sand, but absolutely bolted up in a Nottingham seller on his turf debut. He has since shown himself rather better than that, just holding on to win a fair little handicap at Beverley, but then rather lost his form.
**K R Burke [1-6] Nigel Shields (from M R Channon [1-4] Mar 1999).*

FORUM RR 74f 3203[6]

4 b f Lion Cavern (USA) 7.5f **(74)** - Top Society (High Top) 10.2f **(67)**
Form - 0533816
Record 1999 - 1st:1 2nd:0 3rd:2 Ran:7
Pre1999 - 1st:1 2nd:1 3rd:1 Ran:11
Win Prizemoney £8,282 *Total Prizemoney* £13,854
Wins * **1999** Jly Epsom (G-F) H 8.5f 73 74 <
* 1997 Oct Bright (FRM) 7f 62
1999 Turf 1-7: (7f 2, 8f 4, 9f 1-1) (gd, g-f 4, frm 1-2)
Scopey, above-average filly, likes tight tracks. Turf high 74. Consistent. She was ending a long losing run when winning a handicap at Epsom in July. A mile and fast ground seems to suit.
**C E Brittain [2-18] Wyck Hall Stud.*

FORUM GIRL (USA) BHB 75f **RR 72f** 3848[2]

3 b f Sheikh Albadou 9.2f **(75)** - Brava (GER) (Arratos (FR)) 12.2f **(60)**
Form - 51552
Record 1999 - 1st:1 2nd:1 3rd:0 Ran:5
Win Prizemoney £3,814 *Total Prizemoney* £6,074
Wins * **1999** Jun Ayr (GD) 7f 74+ <
1999 Turf 1-5: (7f 1-2, 8f 3) (gd, g-f 1-3, frm)
Scopey, above-average filly. Turf high 74 - 1st of 5 getting 5lb from Liberty Lines (18 Jun Ayr RF 2113).
**M Johnston [1-5] Mrs Jacqueline Conroy.*

FOR VALOUR (USA) RR 63df 4710[10]

6 b h Trempolino (USA) 11.9f **(77)** - Glitter (FR) (Reliance II) 9.9f **(58)**
Form - 7555000
Record 1999 - 1st:0 2nd:0 3rd:0 Ran:6
Pre1999 - 1st:1 2nd:1 3rd:2 Ran:8
Win Prizemoney £24,691 *Total Prizemoney* £87,275
Wins 1997 Jun Longch (SFT) G3 10f 112 <
1999 Turf 0-6: (10f 4, 12f, 14f) (gd 3, g-f, frm 2)
Average horse, effective 12f, acts on gd to g-f, best on gd, has worn blinkers, prefers left handed tracks. Turf high 91. Becoming disappointing. Had excellent form when trained by Andre Fabre, including finishing fourth behind Silver Patriarch and Swain in the 1998 Coronation Cup. Now trained by Ken Cunningham-Brown, he has run very moderately since coming to England and is a shadow of his former self.
**K O Cunningham-Brown [0-7] A J Richards (from A Fabre in FR [1-7] Jun 1998).*

FOR YOUR EYES ONLY BHB 100f **RR 101f** 4265[6]

5 b g Pursuit of Love 9.5f **(69)** - Rivers Rhapsody (Dominion) 8.5f **(63)**
Form - 006
Record 1999 - 1st:0 2nd:0 3rd:0 Ran:3
Pre1999 - 1st:5 2nd:4 3rd:4 Ran:29
Win Prizemoney £103,641 *Total Prizemoney* £134,575
Wins 1998 Jly Goodwo (G-S) H 8f 102 108 <
1998 Jly Sandow (GD) H 8.1f 97 103
1998 May Sandow (GD) H 8.1f 90 102
1996 Jun Beverl (G-F) 5f 91+
1996 May Ripon (GD) 6f 78
1999 Turf 0-3: (8f 3) (gd, frm 2)
Very useful gelding, effective 8f, acts on gd to g-f, best on gd, often wears blinkers (very effectively). Turf high 101 (began Jly). Consistent. He was not disgraced in three hot handicaps and clearly retains most of his ability. Best around a mile, he acts on any ground and could bounce back to winning form in 2000.
**C E Brittain [0-3] H E Sheikh Rashid Al Maktoum (from T D Easterby [5-29] Oct 1998).*

FORZARA BHB 27f **RR 14f** 3318[13]

6 ch m Risk Me (FR) 8f **(53)** - Valldemosa (Music Boy) 6.8f **(57)**
Form - 50
Record 1999 - 1st:0 2nd:0 3rd:0 Ran:2
Pre1999 - 1st:1 2nd:0 3rd:0 Ran:12
Win Prizemoney £3,078 *Total Prizemoney* £3,078
Wins 1996 Jly Mussel (G-S) H 5f 45 47 <
1999 Turf 0-2: (5f 2) (frm 2)
Poor mare. Turf high 14 (began Jly).

**R Hollinshead [0-2] Mrs Robert Heathcote (from J L Spearing [0-4] Aug 1997).*

FOSTON FOX BHB 55f **RR 58f** 5054[8]

2 b f Foxhound (USA) - Enaam (Shirley Heights) 10.3f **(74)**
Form - 088
Record 1999 - 1st:0 2nd:0 3rd:0 Ran:3
1999 Turf 0-3: (6f 2, 7f) (gd 2, frm)
Currently fair filly. Turf high 58 (began Spt).
**C B B Booth [0-3] The Foston Partnership.*

FOSTON SECOND (IRE) RR 5f 4928[11]

2 ch f Lycius (USA) 8.8f **(71)** - Gentle Guest (IRE) (Be My Guest (USA)) 9.3f **(67)**
Form - 00
Record 1999 - 1st:0 2nd:0 3rd:0 Ran:2
1999 Turf 0-2: (6f, 7f) (gd, g-f)
Currently very poor filly. Turf high 5 (began Spt).
**C B B Booth [0-2] The Foston Partnership.*

FOUCHE (GER) RR 106f 2660a[9]

3 f
Form - 0
1999 Turf 0-1: (12f) (gd)
Currently Pattern-class. **A Lowe in GER [0-1].*

FOUND AT LAST BHB 53f **RR 35f** 4723[5]

3 b g Aragon 7.7f **(58)** - Girton (Balidar) 7.9f **(63)**
Form - 05005
Record 1999 - 1st:0 2nd:0 3rd:0 Ran:5
Pre1999 - 1st:0 2nd:0 3rd:0 Ran:1
1999 Turf 0-5: (6f 3, 7f, 8f) (gd 2, g-f, frm 2)
Scopey, very moderate gelding. Turf high 63.
**G Woodward [0-1] Mrs Jo Hardy (from Miss S E Hall [0-4] Jly 1999).*

FOUND AT SEA RR 28?f 4831[6]

4 ch f Handsome Sailor 6.6f **(53)** - Close Call (Nearly A Hand) 5.6f **(48)**
Form - 6
Record 1999 - 1st:0 2nd:0 3rd:0 Ran:1
Pre1999 - 1st:0 2nd:0 3rd:0 Ran:1
1999 Turf 0-1: (10f) (sft)
Scopey, currently little account filly.
**Miss L A Perratt [0-1] Mrs Patrick Campbell Fraser (from J G Smyth-Osbourne [0-1] Jun 1998).*

FOUNDRY LANE BHB 74f **RR 74f** 4917[22]

8 b g Mtoto 11.5f **(71)** - Eider (Niniski (USA)) 10.6f **(65)**
Form - 53440
Record 1999 - 1st:0 2nd:0 3rd:1 Ran:5
Pre1999 - 1st:4 2nd:3 3rd:4 Ran:24
Win Prizemoney £21,609 *Total Prizemoney* £49,236
Wins * 1998 Oct York (GD) H 13.9f 70 75
* 1995 Aug Haydoc (G-F) H 14f 78 82 <
1999 Turf 0-5: (14f 3, 16f, 17f) (g-s, gd 2, frm 2)
Above-average gelding, effective 14 to 16f, best at 14f, acts on g-s to frm, best on gd, prefers left handed tracks. Turf high 74 (1st run) - 5th of 15 giving 8lb to Swift (12 May York 14f g-s RF 1185). Consistent. Has been running on the Flat, over hurdles and over fences in the last couple of years, but remains a decent staying-handicapper on the level. **Mrs M Reveley [7-40] A Sharratt.*

FOUR COUNTIES RR 8f 3609[10]

2 ch c Elmaamul (USA) 8.1f **(70)** - Joyce's Best (Tolomeo) 5.6f **(60)**
Form - 070
Record 1999 - 1st:0 2nd:0 3rd:0 Ran:3
1999 Turf 0-3: (5f, 6f, 7f) (frm 3)
Currently very poor colt. Turf high 8 (began Jly).
**T J Naughton [0-3] Four Counties Partnership.*

FOURDANED (IRE) BHB 28f30a **RR 37f 30a** 4076[10]

6 b g Danehill (USA) 9.1f **(79)** - Pro Patria (Petingo) 11f **(72)**
Form - 650005040000
Record 1999 - 1st:0 2nd:0 3rd:0 Ran:12
Pre1999 - 1st:0 2nd:3 3rd:1 Ran:27
Win Prizemoney £0 *Total Prizemoney* £3,431
1999 Turf 0-7: (7f, 10f, 11f, 12f 3, 16f) (g-s, gd 2, g-f, frm 2, hrd) 1999 AW 0-5: (10f, 12f, 13f 2, 16f) (Equi 5)
Very moderate gelding, effective 11 to 15f, acts on g-f to frm, has worn blinkers, likes tight tracks. Turf high 41. AW high 33.
**B R Johnson [0-12] Mrs B C Knowles (from T D McCarthy [0-6] Oct 1998).*

FOURGREYS BHB 56f52a **RR 57f 52a** 3376[12]

3 gr g Paris House 5.9f **(64)** - Wild Moon (USA) (Arctic Tern (USA)) 8.9f **(69)**
Form - 05010
Record 1999 - 1st:1 2nd:0 3rd:0 Ran:5
Pre1999 - 1st:0 2nd:0 3rd:0 Ran:3
Win Prizemoney £2,495 *Total Prizemoney* £2,495
Wins * 1999 Jly Beverl (G-F) H 8.5f 54 57 <
1999 Turf 1-4: (8f 1-2, 9f, 10f) (g-f 2, frm 1-2) 1999 AW 0-1: (7f) (Fibr)
Workmanlike, fair gelding, effective 8 to 9f, acts on g-f to frm. Turf high 57 - 1st of 11 giving 14lb to Bunty (13 Jly Beverley RF 2766). Inconsistent. **Miss J A Camacho [1-8] Fourgreys Partnership.*

FOUR MEN (IRE) BHB 49f **RR 45f** 3566[10]

2 b c Nicolotte - Sound Pet (Runnett) 7f **(59)**
Form - 0040
Record 1999 - 1st:0 2nd:0 3rd:0 Ran:4
1999 Turf 0-4: (5f, 6f, 7f 2) (gd, g-f, frm, hrd)
Moderate colt. Turf high 45. **J Berry [0-4] J Hales.*

FOUR OF SPADES BHB 32f32a **RR 7?f 32a** 241[8]

8 ch g Faustus (USA) 9.1f **(54)** - Fall To Pieces (USA) (Forli (ARG)) 9.6f **(67)**
Form - 0P8
Record 1999 - 1st:0 2nd:0 3rd:0 Ran:2
Pre1999 - 1st:8 2nd:12 3rd:7 Ran:70
Win Prizemoney £22,741 *Total Prizemoney* £37,872
Wins 1995 *Dec Lingfi (STD) H 7f 70 69* <
1995 *Aug Wolver (STD) H 6f 68 67*
1995 Jun Mussel (G-F) C 7.1f 55
1995 Jun Lingfi (G-F) SH 7f 48 53
1999 AW 0-2: (10f, 12f) (Equi, Fibr)
Very moderate gelding, effective 10f, - acts on Equi, mostly wears blinkers. Becoming disappointing.
**R J Hodges [0-11] Mrs Anna Sanders (from K R Burke [0-3] Jan 1998).*

FOURTH TIME LUCKY BHB 26f34a **RR 24f 34a** 3991[6]

3 b g Timeless Times (USA) 6.1f **(56)** - Wych Willow (Hard Fought) 8.8f **(62)**
Form - 885520006
Record 1999 - 1st:0 2nd:1 3rd:0 Ran:7
Pre1999 - 1st:0 2nd:0 3rd:0 Ran:8
Win Prizemoney £0 *Total Prizemoney* £748
1999 Turf 0-2: (7f, 8f) (frm 2) 1999 AW 0-5: (7f 2, 8f 3) (Fibr 5)
Very moderate gelding, has worn blinkers. Turf high 24 (began Jly). AW high 39. **B W Murray [0-15] Mrs M Lingwood.*

FOXDALE (FR) RR 50f 2180[8]

2 ch f Emarati (USA) 6.6f **(63)** - Fox Croft (FR) (Bustino) 10.4f **(64)**
Form - 8
Record 1999 - 1st:0 2nd:0 3rd:0 Ran:1
1999 Turf 0-1: (6f) (frm)
Currently fair filly. **H Morrison [0-1] Mrs R Pease & Lady Margadale.*

FOXES TAIL BHB 48f **RR 43f** 1599[14]

5 gr g Batshoof 9.5f **(66)** - Secret Gill (Most Secret) 7.1f **(58)**
Form - 1000
Record 1999 - 1st:1 2nd:0 3rd:0 Ran:4
Pre1999 - 1st:2 2nd:1 3rd:1 Ran:20
Win Prizemoney £13,548 *Total Prizemoney* £15,501
Wins * 1999 Apr Folkes (HVY) H 9.7f 46 53
1996 Spt Ayr (G-F) H 8f 72 77 <
1996 Jly Mussel (G-S) 7.1f 70
1999 Turf 1-4: (10f 1-4) (hvy 1-1, gd, g-f 2)
Moderate gelding, effective 10 to 12f, best at 10f, acts on hvy to g-f, best on g-f, has worn blinkers (extremely effectively), prefers tight tracks. Turf high 53 (1st run) - 1st of 13 getting 20lb from Sweet Reward (13 Apr Folkestone RF 0661).
**R J Hodges [2-7] P Slade (from Miss S E Hall [2-20] Spt 1998).*

FOXIE LADY BHB 49f49a **RR 32f 49a** 1136[15]

4 ch f Wolfhound (USA) 7.3f **(71)** - Final Thought (Final Straw) 7.9f **(64)**

Form - 6000
Record 1999 - 1st:0 2nd:0 3rd:0 Ran:4
Pre1999 - 1st:0 2nd:3 3rd:0 Ran:7
Win Prizemoney £0 *Total Prizemoney* £3,508
1999 Turf 0-3: (7f, 8f, 12f) (sft, gd, g-f) 1999 AW 0-1: (7f) (Fibr)
Scopey, very moderate filly, effective 7f, acts on g-f to frm. Turf high 12. Becoming disappointing.
**P G Murphy [0-4] John Brown & Megan Dennis (from E A L Dunlop [0-7] Oct 1998).*

FOXKEY BHB 59f67a **RR 59f 67a** 4671[13]

2 ch f Foxhound (USA) - Latch Key Lady (USA) **(12f 48a)** (Tejano (USA))
Form - 21100
Record 1999 - 1st:2 2nd:1 3rd:0 Ran:5
Win Prizemoney £3,762 *Total Prizemoney* £4,386
Wins 1999 *Apr Southw (STD) S 5f 59 <*
1999 Apr Catter (SFT) S 5f 59 <
1999 Turf 1-4: (5f 1-3, 6f) (g-s 3, gd 1-1)1999 AW 1-1: (5f 1-1) (Fibr 1-1)
Fair filly. Turf high 59 - 1st of 9 from French Mystery (21 Apr Catterick RF 0791). (1st run) - 1st of 8 giving 1lb to Joely Green (26 Apr Southwell RF 0856).
**Miss Gay Kelleway [0-2] A P Griffin (from E J Alston [2-2] Apr 1999).*

FOX'S IDEA BHB 70f **RR 78f** 4455[14]

2 b f Magic Ring (IRE) 6.5f **(64)** - Lindy Belle **(35f)** (Alleging (USA))
Form - 73340
Record 1999 - 1st:0 2nd:0 3rd:2 Ran:5
Win Prizemoney £0 *Total Prizemoney* £1,106
1999 Turf 0-5: (5f 2, 6f 2, 7f) (sft, gd, g-f, frm 2)
Above-average filly. Turf high 78 - 4th of 7 getting 3lb from Argent Facile (21 Jly Leicester 5f frm RF 3010).
**D HaydnJones [0-5] J S Fox and Sons.*

FOX STAR (IRE) BHB 55f51a **RR 57f 51a** 4625[6]

2 b f Foxhound (USA) - Our Pet (Mummy's Pet) 7.7f **(60)**
Form - 0630476
Record 1999 - 1st:0 2nd:0 3rd:1 Ran:7
Win Prizemoney £0 *Total Prizemoney* £838
1999 Turf 0-7: (5f 2, 6f 3, 7f 2) (g-s 2, g-f 2, frm 2, hrd)
Fair filly. Turf high 67. **R Hannon [0-7] Jubert Family.*

FOXY ALPHA (IRE) RR 2f 4903[12]

2 ch f Foxhound (USA) - Ice Baby (Grundy) 10.3f **(65)**
Form - 0
Record 1999 - 1st:0 2nd:0 3rd:0 Ran:1
1999 Turf 0-1: (6f) (frm)
Currently very poor filly.
**A B Mulholland [0-1] Burtree Racing Partnership.*

FOXY BROWN RR 16f 1788[10]

2 b f Factual (USA) - Miltak **(43f 40a)** (Risk Me (FR)) 5.9f **(53)**
Form - 20
Record 1999 - 1st:0 2nd:1 3rd:0 Ran:2
Win Prizemoney £0 *Total Prizemoney* £663
1999 Turf 0-1: (5f) (gd) 1999 AW 0-1: (5f) (Fibr)
Currently fair filly. (1st run) - 2nd of 11 getting 9lb from Turtle Surprise (10 May Southwell 5f Fibr RF 1133).
**Miss I Foustok [0-2] Miss I Foustok.*

FRAGRANT MIX (FR) RR 124f 5013a[4]

5 gr h Linamix (FR) 8.2f **(64)** - Fragrant Hill (Shirley Heights) 10.3f **(74)**
Form - 4
1999 Turf 0-1: (12f)
Very high-class colt, effective 10 to 12f, best at 12f, acts on gd, best on sft. (1st run) - 4th giving 7lb to First Magnitude (17 Oct Longchamp 12f RF 5013a). Consistent.
**J E Hammond in FR [0-1] (from A Fabre in FR [3-8] Oct 1998).*

FRAGRANT OASIS (USA) BHB 106f **RR 108f** 4896[6]

3 ch f Rahy (USA) 9.1f **(80)**-Raahia (CAN) (Vice Regent(CAN))8.7f **(74)**
Form - 8173326
Record 1999 - 1st:1 2nd:1 3rd:2 Ran:7
Pre1999 - 1st:1 2nd:1 3rd:0 Ran:4
Win Prizemoney £23,236 *Total Prizemoney* £36,326
Wins * 1999 May Newmar (GD) L 7f 101 <
***** 1998 Spt Newbur (gd) 7f 86
1999 Turf 1-7: (6f 4, 7f 1-2, 8f) (gd 2, g-f 1-2, frm 3)
Scopey, Pattern-class filly, effective 6 to 7f, best at 6f, acts on gd to frm, best on frm. Turf high 108 - 2nd of 12 giving 9lb to Two Clubs (1 Oct Newmarket 6f gd RF 4678) - also 1st of 5 from Arctic Char (15 May Newmarket RF 1243). Consistent. She did not run badly in the 1000 Guineas on her return, and won a Newmarket Listed event next time despite hitting the front too soon and suffering cuts to her legs. That was her level, and subsequent events showed that seven furlongs was her trip.
**E A L Dunlop [2-11] Maktoum Al Maktoum.*

FRAME OF MIND (FR) RR 128[9]

4 b g Unfuwain (USA) 11.4f **(74)** - Namatanga (USA) (Foolish Pleasure (USA)) 8.9f **(72)**
Form - 0
Record 1999 - 1st:0 2nd:0 3rd:0 Ran:1
1999 AW 0-1: (12f) (Fibr)
Moderate gelding, always wears blinkers.
**F Jordan [0-4] Birmingham Bloodstock.*

FRAMPANT BHB 68f **RR 65f** 5150[2]

2 ch f Fraam - Potent (IRE) (Posen (USA))
Form - 0081404472
Record 1999 - 1st:1 2nd:1 3rd:0 Ran:10
Win Prizemoney £3,501 *Total Prizemoney* £5,403
Wins * 1999 Aug Windso (SFT) 5f 69 <
1999 Turf 1-10: (5f 1-4, 6f 4, 7f 2) (sft, g-s 3, gd 1-3, g-f 2, frm)
Average filly, effective 5 to 6f, acts on g-s to gd. Turf high 72 - also 1st of 13 getting 2lb from All Night Long (16 Aug Windsor RF 3684). **M Quinn [1-10] The Frampant Fellows.*

FRANCE LAMBERT (ITY) BHB 30f **RR 15f** 2755[19]

3 gr f Tirol 8.1f **(64)** - Filicaia (Sallust) 8.4f **(63)**
Form - 000
Record 1999 - 1st:0 2nd:0 3rd:0 Ran:3
Pre1999 - 1st:0 2nd:0 3rd:0 Ran:5
1999 Turf 0-3: (6f, 7f 2) (gd, frm 2)
Unfurnished, poor filly, has worn blinkers. Turf high 15. Inconsistent. **Don Enrico Incisa [0-8] Razza Dormello Olgiata.*

FRANCESCA'S FOLLY BHB 22f26a **RR 23f 26a** 3385[6]

4 b f Efisio 7.7f **(69)** - Nashville Blues (IRE) **(74f)** (Try My Best (USA)) 7.6f **(67)**
Form - 7800036
Record 1999 - 1st:0 2nd:0 3rd:1 Ran:6
Pre1999 - 1st:2 2nd:1 3rd:1 Ran:16
Win Prizemoney £4,862 *Total Prizemoney* £6,255
Wins 1998 Spt Yarmou (G-S) S 10.1f 44
1997 Spt Leices (G-F) SH 8f 49 55 <
1999 Turf 0-5: (10f, 12f 3, 17f) (gd, g-f 2, frm, hrd) 1999 AW 0-1: (9f) (Fibr)
Small, little account filly, effective 10 to 11f, best at 10f, acts on gd to frm, has worn blinkers. Turf high 23.
**C L Popham [0-9] Brewers Arms Racing Club (from N A Callaghan [0-2] Oct 1998).*

FRANCESCO GUARDI (IRE) RR 91f 5130[2]

2 b c Robellino (USA) 9.5f **(68)**-Lamees (USA)(Lomond (USA))8.8f **(65)**
Form - 12
Record 1999 - 1st:1 2nd:1 3rd:0 Ran:2
Win Prizemoney £3,343 *Total Prizemoney* £5,466
Wins * 1999 Oct Catter (GD,) 7f 86+ <
1999 Turf 1-2: (7f 1-1, 8f) (gd 1-2)
Currently useful colt. Turf high 91 (began Oct) - 2nd of 6 getting 2lb from Autonomy (29 Oct Newmarket 8f gd RF 5130) - also 1st of 12 from Bhutan Prince (16 Oct Catterick RF 4910).
**P F I Cole [1-2] Richard Green (Fine Paintings).*

FRANCO MINA (IRE) BHB 68f **RR 66f** 4276[7]

3 b g Lahib (USA) 8f **(69)**-Play The Queen(IRE)(King of Clubs) 7.1f **(57)**
Form - 4000545707
Record 1999 - 1st:0 2nd:0 3rd:0 Ran:10
Pre1999 - 1st:1 2nd:0 3rd:0 Ran:3
Win Prizemoney £3,452 *Total Prizemoney* £4,240
Wins * 1998 May Salisb (FRM) 5f 72+ <
1999 Turf 0-10: (5f 7, 6f, 7f 2) (gd, g-f 9)
Scopey, average gelding, effective 5 to 6f, best at 5f, acts on g-f to

frm, best on g-f. Turf high 82. Consistent.
**M R Channon [1-13] & Mrs Gary Pinchen.*

FRANCPORT BHB 72f **RR 74f** 4656[15]
3 b c Efisio 7.7f **(69)** - Elkie Brooks (Relkino) 8.9f **(65)**
Form - 517200
Record 1999 - 1st:1 2nd:1 3rd:0 Ran:6
Win Prizemoney £3,991 *Total Prizemoney* £6,021
Wins * 1999 May Beverl (GD) 5f 70 <
1999 Turf 1-6: (5f 1-4, 6f 2) (gd 1-5, g-f)
Scopey, above-average colt, effective 5f, acts on gd to g-f. Turf high 74 - 2nd of 6 getting 7lb from Jackie's Baby (15 Jly Bath 5f g-f RF 2839) - also 1st of 16 giving 5lb to Smoke Signal (8 May Beverley RF 1102). **J Berry [1-6] R A Popely.*

FRANKIE FAIR (IRE) BHB 69f55a **RR 71f 55a** 43[2]
4 b f Red Sunset 9f **(57)** - Animate (IRE) (Tate Gallery (USA)) 7.4f **(67)**
Form - 2
Record 1999 - 1st:0 2nd:1 3rd:0 Ran:1
Pre1999 - 1st:3 2nd:0 3rd:3 Ran:14
Win Prizemoney £7,281 *Total Prizemoney* £9,306
Wins * 1998 Jly Folkes (G-F) H 7f 62 71 <
* 1998 Jun Bright (GD) H 8f 53 60
1998 May Folkes (G-F) C 6.9f 58
1999 AW 0-1: (7f) (Equi)
Scopey, above-average filly, effective 7 to 8f, acts on gd.
**G L Moore [2-6] Joe Bates (Bloodstock) Ltd (from M A Jarvis [1-9] May 1998).*

FRANKINCENSE (IRE) RR 61f 4291[4]
3 gr c Paris House 5.9f **(64)** - Mistral Wood (USA) (Far North (CAN)) 9.7f **(75)**
Form - 544
Record 1999 - 1st:0 2nd:0 3rd:0 Ran:3
Pre1999 - 1st:0 2nd:0 3rd:0 Ran:1
Win Prizemoney £0 *Total Prizemoney* £501
1999 Turf 0-3: (5f, 6f 2) (gd 2, g-f)
Neat, average colt, has worn blinkers. Turf high 61 (began Aug).
**J A R Toller [0-4] G B Partnership.*

FRANKLIN-D BHB 46f **RR 39f** 1945[11]
3 ch g Democratic (USA) - English Mint (Jalmood (USA)) 10.1f **(52)**
Form - 000
Record 1999 - 1st:0 2nd:0 3rd:0 Ran:3
Pre1999 - 1st:0 2nd:0 3rd:0 Ran:3
1999 Turf 0-3: (6f 2, 7f) (gd, g-f, frm)
Scopey, very moderate gelding, has worn blinkers. Turf high 39.
**J R Jenkins [0-6] Mrs Stella Peirce.*

FRANKLIN LAKES BHB 32f **RR 33f** 3435[10]
4 ch c Sanglamore (USA) 12.9f **(67)** - Eclipsing (IRE) (Baillamont (USA)) 7f **(78)**
Form - 7055060750
Record 1999 - 1st:0 2nd:0 3rd:0 Ran:10
Pre1999 - 1st:0 2nd:0 3rd:0 Ran:8
Win Prizemoney £0 *Total Prizemoney* £200
1999 Turf 0-10: (6f 2, 7f 3, 8f 3, 11f, 13f) (sft, g-s, gd 2, g-f, frm 5)
Very moderate colt, effective 6 to 8f, acts on frm, often wears blinkers (extremely effectively). Turf high 34 - 5th of 18 getting 24lb from Eastern Prophets (7 May Nottingham 6f frm RF 1088).
**M R Bosley [0-11] Marks (Banbury) (from C A Horgan [0-8] Aug 1998).*

FRAPPE (IRE) BHB 85f **RR 94df** 4005[4]
3 b f Inchinor 8.9f **(64)**- Glatisant **(95f)**(Rainbow Quest (USA))10.4f **(75)**
Form - 7404
Record 1999 - 1st:0 2nd:0 3rd:0 Ran:4
Pre1999 - 1st:1 2nd:0 3rd:0 Ran:2
Win Prizemoney £3,810 *Total Prizemoney* £4,880
Wins * 1998 Spt Kempto (SFT) 6f 88+ <
1999 Turf 0-4: (7f 2, 8f, 10f) (gd 3, g-f)
Neat, useful filly, effective 6f, acts on gd, has worn blinkers. Turf high 94. Held on her return in the Nell Gwyn and showed little in three runs in the autumn. **G Wragg [1-6] A E Oppenheimer.*

FRATERNITY RR 86f 5100[2]
2 b c Grand Lodge (USA) - Catawba (Mill Reef (USA)) 10.5f **(78)**
Form - 72
Record 1999 - 1st:0 2nd:1 3rd:0 Ran:2
Win Prizemoney £0 *Total Prizemoney* £980
1999 Turf 0-2: (7f, 8f) (gd, g-f)
Currently useful colt. Turf high 86 (began Oct) - 2nd of 10 to King Spinner (27 Oct Yarmouth 8f gd RF 5100).
**W Jarvis [0-2] Exors of the late Lord Howard de Walden.*

FRECCIA ROMANA (ITY) RR 100f 811a[4]
3 f
Form - 4
1999 Turf 0-1: (8f) (hvy)
Currently very useful filly. (1st run) - 4th of 16 to Shenck (18 Apr Capannelle 8f hvy RF 0811a). **F Camici in ITY [0-1].*

FRECKLES BHB 35f40a **RR 25f 40a** 684[12]
4 b f High Kicker (USA) 8.4f **(52)** - Ship of Gold (Glint of Gold) 9.3f **(66)**
Form - 0
Record 1999 - 1st:0 2nd:0 3rd:0 Ran:1
Pre1999 - 1st:1 2nd:0 3rd:0 Ran:16
Win Prizemoney £3,184 *Total Prizemoney* £3,184
Wins * 1998 Jun Bright (GD) H 7f 36 46 <
1999 Turf 0-1: (8f) (frm)
Neat, fair filly, effective 7f, acts on gd, often wears blinkers, likes left handed tracks, likes tight tracks. **M J Ryan [1-24] P E Axon.*

FREDERICK JAMES BHB 62f55a **RR 62f 55a** 4826[12]
5 b g Efisio 7.7f **(69)** - Rare Roberta (USA) (Roberto (USA)) 10f **(76)**
Form - 4453334183420248300
Record 1999 - 1st:1 2nd:2 3rd:5 Ran:18
Pre1999 - 1st:0 2nd:1 3rd:1 Ran:8
Win Prizemoney £3,272 *Total Prizemoney* £12,748
Wins * 1999 Mar Nottin (G-S) H 6.1f 57 65 <
1999 Turf 1-12: (6f 1-11, 8f) (sft 1-1, gd 2, g-f 6, frm 3) 1999 AW 0-6: (6f 5, 7f) (Equi 4, Fibr 2)
Average gelding. Turf high 76. AW high 55. Consistent.
**H E Haynes [1-19] Miss Sally Haynes (from M J Heaton-Ellis [0-7] Oct 1997).*

FREDORA BHB 83f **RR 86df** 4759[7]
4 ch f Inchinor 8.9f **(64)** - Ophrys (Nonoalco (USA)) 8.5f **(66)**
Form - 7731430207
Record 1999 - 1st:1 2nd:1 3rd:2 Ran:10
Pre1999 - 1st:2 2nd:2 3rd:0 Ran:8
Win Prizemoney £16,321 *Total Prizemoney* £25,888
Wins * 1999 Jun Salisb (GD) 9.9f 86
* 1998 Aug Kempto (G-F) H 7f 87 89 <
* 1998 May Kempto (GD) 7f 82
1999 Turf 1-10: (8f 2, 10f 1-7, 12f) (gd 2, g-f 1-4, frm 4)
Leggy, useful filly, effective 7 to 10f, best at 10f, acts on gd to frm, prefers right handed tracks, excels at Kempton and Newmarket and Sandown. Turf high 86 - 1st of 6 giving 6lb to Travelling Star (8 Jun Salisbury RF 1817). **M Blanshard [3-18] Peter Goldring.*

FREE BHB 55f **RR 58f** 4281[3]
4 ch g Gone West (USA) 7.8f **(82)** - Bemissed (USA) (Nijinsky (CAN)) 10.3f **(77)**
Form - 635231223
Record 1999 - 1st:1 2nd:3 3rd:3 Ran:9
Pre1999 - 1st:0 2nd:0 3rd:0 Ran:8
Win Prizemoney £2,815 *Total Prizemoney* £7,845
Wins * 1999 Aug Newcas (FRM) H 16.1f 51 54 <
1999 Turf 1-9: (12f, 14f 2, 16f 1-5, 17f) (gd, g-f 1-2, frm 5, hrd)
Scopey, fair gelding, effective 12 to 17f, best at 16f, acts on g-f to hrd, prefers right handed tracks, excels at Musselburgh. Turf high 58 - 2nd of 6 getting 9lb from Il Principe (18 Aug Musselburgh 16f g-f RF 3755) - also 1st of 3 getting 13lb from Royal Expression (4 Aug Newcastle RF 3368). Consistent. A headstrong sort who lacks finishing pace, he nevertheless keeps galloping and is a winner in ordinary company.
**Mrs M Reveley [3-22] P D Savill (from P F I Cole [0-2] Spt 1997).*

FREEDOM QUEST (IRE) BHB 62f55a **RR 62f 55a** 4752[18]
4 b g Polish Patriot (USA) 7.8f **(70)** - Recherchee (Rainbow Quest (USA)) 10.4f **(75)**
Form - 2404830221332410
Record 1999 - 1st:2 2nd:4 3rd:3 Ran:16
Pre1999 - 1st:0 2nd:3 3rd:0 Ran:7

Win Prizemoney £10,511 *Total Prizemoney* £20,649
Wins *** 1999** Spt Mussel (G-F) H 12f 60 62 <
*** 1999** Jly Beverl (SFT) H 9.9f 57 59
1999 Turf 2-14: (7f 2, 8f 2, 9f 2, 10f 1-5, 12f 1-3) (gd 1-4, g-f 6, frm 1-4)
1999 AW 0-2: (7f, 9f) (Fibr 2)
Light-framed, average gelding, has worn blinkers, likes right handed tracks, likes tight tracks. Turf high 62. AW high 49. Consistent.
**B S Rothwell [2-16] B Valentine (from J M Jefferson [0-2] Spt 1998).*

FREE FINISH (IRE) BHB 40f33a **RR 15f 33a** 1649[23]

3 b f Distinctly North (USA) 7.4f **(63)** - Brave Louise (Brave Shot) 10.3f **(54)**
Form - 080000
Record **1999** - 1st:0 2nd:0 3rd:0 Ran:6
Pre1999 - 1st:0 2nd:0 3rd:0 Ran:2
1999 Turf 0-5: (5f, 6f 3, 7f) (sft, g-s, gd, g-f, frm) 1999 AW 0-1: (7f) (Fibr)
Lengthy, poor filly. Turf high 51. **N Tinkler [0-8] Philip Grundy.*

FREE OPTION (IRE) BHB 94f **RR 93f** 5141[11]

4 ch g Indian Ridge 7.6f **(74)** - Saneena (Kris) 9.5f **(73)**
Form - 05170710610
Record **1999** - 1st:3 2nd:0 3rd:0 Ran:11
Pre1999 - 1st:2 2nd:4 3rd:3 Ran:15
Win Prizemoney £48,914 *Total Prizemoney* £58,638
Wins *** 1999** Oct Newmar (GD) H 8f 88 93
*** 1999** Jly Cheste (G-F) 7f 85
*** 1999** May Kempto (G-F) H 8f 91 92
* 1998 Spt Newbur (gd) H 7.3f 85 94 <
* 1998 Jly Lingfi (G-F) 7.6f 72+
1999 Turf 3-11: (7f 1-5, 8f 2-6) (gd 1-4, g-f 3, frm 2-4)
Workmanlike, useful gelding, effective 7 to 10f, best at 8f, acts on gd to frm, best on frm, likes left handed tracks, excels at Kempton. Turf high 93 - 1st of 20 getting 1lb from Mayaro Bay (16 Oct Newmarket RF 4915) - also 1st of 11 giving 16lb to Parisien Star (16 May Kempton RF 1257). A brave winner at Kempton in May, he then disappointed a few times in some competitive handicaps, but regained winning form when just holding on at Chester in July. Although there appeared to be a significant advantage given to those drawn high, he still beat a useful field in fine style at Newmarket in October. **B Hanbury [5-26] Ahmed Ali.*

FREE RIDER BHB 96f **RR 86f** 5195[1]

2 b c Inchinor 8.9f **(64)** - Forever Roses **(62f)** (Forzando) 7.6f **(59)**
Form - 221
Record **1999** - 1st:1 2nd:2 3rd:0 Ran:3
Win Prizemoney £3,160 *Total Prizemoney* £6,318
Wins *** 1999** Nov Windso (G-S) 6f 85 <
1999 Turf 1-3: (6f 1-3) (sft, gd 1-2)
Currently useful colt. Turf high 86 (began Oct) - 2nd of 14 giving 5lb to Out of Reach (23 Oct Newbury 6f sft RF 5044) - also 1st of 18 from Kathology (4 Nov Windsor RF 5195). Easy winner of a maiden, and looks a useful prospect. **I A Balding [1-3] J C Smith.*

FREE TO SPEAK (IRE) BHB 104f **RR 106f** 4314a[15]

7 ch g Be My Guest (USA) 10.2f **(66)** - Love For Poetry (Lord Gayle (USA)) 8.8f **(62)**
Form - 1701010
1999 Turf 2-6: (7f, 8f 2-5) (sft, g-s 1-1, gd 1-3, g-f)
Pattern-class gelding, effective 7 to 10f, best at 8f, acts on sft to gd, best on gd, often wears blinkers (extremely effectively). Turf high 106 - 1st of 11 giving 12lb to Thats Logic (27 Jun Curragh RF 2418a) - also 1st of 13 giving 16lb to Danse Classique (27 Aug Tralee RF 4058a). He remains capable of winning Listed events at around a mile in his favoured soft ground, but the problem is that he is extremely inconsistent.
**D K Weld in IRE [5-28] Moyglare Stud Farm.*

FREETOWN (IRE) BHB 67f **RR 68f** 4807[1]

3 b c Shirley Heights 12.1f **(76)** - Pageantry (Welsh Pageant) 10f **(65)**
Form - 41
Record **1999** - 1st:1 2nd:0 3rd:0 Ran:2
Win Prizemoney £2,745 *Total Prizemoney* £2,998
Wins *** 1999** Oct Ayr (SFT) C 10.9f 68 <
1999 Turf 1-2: (11f 1-1, 12f) (sft 1-1, gd)
Workmanlike, currently average colt. Turf high 68 (began Spt) - 1st of 7 giving 13lb to Bolt From The Blue (11 Oct Ayr RF 4807).
**P F I Cole [1-2] H R H Prince Fahd Salman.*

FREE-VALLEY-MOU (IRE) BHB 49f **RR 48f** 4583[11]

3 b g Ela-Mana-Mou 12.7f **(72)** - Kilcoy (USA) (Secreto (USA)) 8.7f **(72)**
Form - 000
Record **1999** - 1st:0 2nd:0 3rd:0 Ran:3
1999 Turf 0-3: (10f 2, 12f) (gd 2, g-f)
Strong, currently moderate gelding. Turf high 48.
**P W Harris [0-3] The Mana Team.*

FRENCH CONNECTION **RR 54f** 4808[5]

4 b g Tirol 8.1f **(64)** - Heaven-Liegh-Grey (Grey Desire) 8.7f **(50)**
Form - 077844556505
Record **1999** - 1st:0 2nd:0 3rd:0 Ran:12
Pre1999 - 1st:2 2nd:3 3rd:0 Ran:10
Win Prizemoney £24,491 *Total Prizemoney* £31,143
Wins 1998 May Haydoc (G-S) H 8.1f 77 81 <
1998 May Hamilt (SFT) 9.2f 79
1999 Turf 0-12: (6f, 7f 2, 8f 5, 9f, 10f 3) (sft, g-s, gd 5, g-f 5)
Fair gelding, effective 8 to 10f, best at 10f, acts on hvy to frm, has worn blinkers. Turf high 62.
**D Nicholls [0-6] Peter Dodd (from J Berry [2-16] Jly 1999).*

FRENCH FANCY (IRE) BHB 46f **RR 56f** 4671[4]

2 gr f Paris House 5.9f **(64)** - Clipping (Kris) 9.5f **(73)**
Form - 0374043740574
Record **1999** - 1st:0 2nd:0 3rd:2 Ran:13
Win Prizemoney £0 *Total Prizemoney* £715
1999 Turf 0-13: (5f 4, 6f 7, 7f 2) (sft, g-s 2, gd 2, g-f 5, frm 3)
Fair filly, effective 5 to 6f, acts on sft to g-f, has worn blinkers. Turf high 56 - 5th of 14 getting 5lb from Kirsch (25 Aug Lingfield 6f g-f RF 3907). **C A Dwyer [0-13] R West.*

FRENCH FELLOW (IRE) BHB 100f **RR 104f** 4792[1]

2 b c Suave Dancer (USA) 10.7f **(68)** - Mademoiselle Chloe (Night Shift (USA)) 7.2f **(69)**
Form - 5111211
Record **1999** - 1st:5 2nd:1 3rd:0 Ran:7
Win Prizemoney £51,024 *Total Prizemoney* £59,584
Wins *** 1999** Oct Ascot (G-S) L 8f 104 <
*** 1999** Spt Doncas (G-F) H 8f 95 104 <
*** 1999** Aug York (GD) H 7f 88 93+
*** 1999** Aug Redcar (GD) H 6f 80 87+
*** 1999** Jun Ayr (GD) 6f 83
1999 Turf 5-7: (5f, 6f 2-2, 7f 1-1, 8f 2-3) (gd 1-2, g-f 3-3, frm 1-1, hrd)
Very useful colt, effective 8f, acts on gd to g-f, best on gd. Turf high 104 - 1st of 11 giving 5lb to One Step At A Time (9 Oct Ascot RF 4792) - also 1st of 10 giving 6lb to Minkash (9 Spt Doncaster RF 4238). He justified all his connections' faith and would have completed a six-timer but for being badly hampered at Newcastle in August. Tremendously brave when beating One Step At A Time in a Listed event at Ascot, he should stay a mile and a quarter in 2000 but will need to improve again to land a Group race. That said, he will not fail for a lack of trying.
**T D Easterby [5-7] T H Bennett.*

FRENCH GINGER BHB 28f25a **RR 21f 25a** 2326[13]

8 ch m Most Welcome 8.6f **(66)** - French Plait (Thatching) 8f **(66)**
Form - 05780
Record **1999** - 1st:0 2nd:0 3rd:0 Ran:5
Pre1999 - 1st:1 2nd:1 3rd:1 Ran:28
Win Prizemoney £2,752 *Total Prizemoney* £4,896
Wins * 1997 Spt Mussel (G-F) H 7.1f 45 54 <
1999 Turf 0-5: (7f 3, 8f, 10f) (gd, g-f 2, frm 2)
Little account mare, effective 7f, acts on g-f, has worn blinkers, likes right handed tracks. Turf high 30 - 5th of 14 getting 21lb from Detroit City (30 Apr Musselburgh 7f g-f RF 0941).
**L R Lloyd-James [1-12] L R Lloyd-James (from Don Enrico Incisa [0-9] Spt 1998).*

FRENCH GRIT (IRE) BHB 54f46a **RR 50f 46a** 4355[15]

7 b g Common Grounds 8.1f **(66)** - Charbatte (FR) (In Fijar (USA)) 7.5f **(70)**
Form - 0504055242370
Record **1999** - 1st:0 2nd:2 3rd:1 Ran:13
Pre1999 - 1st:4 2nd:5 3rd:4 Ran:47
Win Prizemoney £21,683 *Total Prizemoney* £40,073
Wins 1997 Jun Pontef (G-F) H 6f 71 75
1997 Apr Ripon (G-F) H 6f 72 78

1995 May Doncas (G-F) 6f 85 <
1999 Turf 0-10: (5f 3, 6f 7) (g-s, gd, g-f, frm 7) 1999 AW 0-3: (6f 3) (Fibr 3)
Fair gelding, effective 6f, acts on frm - acts on Fibr. Turf high 59. AW high 52 - 5th of 15 getting 5lb from Elton Ledger (25 Jan Southwell 6f Fibr RF 0163).
**D W Barker [0-13] Mrs C E Dods (from M Dods [4-47] Spt 1998).*

FRENCH HILL RR 1455[7]
4 br g Dromod Hill - Dear France (USA) (Affirmed (USA)) 9.3f **(79)**
Form - 7
Record 1999 - 1st:0 2nd:0 3rd:0 Ran:1
1999 AW 0-1: (16f) (Equi)
Poor gelding. **G M McCourt [0-3] Christopher Shankland.*

FRENCH HORN BHB 66f **RR 71f** 5052[1]
2 b g Fraam - Runcina (Runnett) 7f **(59)**
Form - 000651
Record 1999 - 1st:1 2nd:0 3rd:0 Ran:6
Win Prizemoney £3,756 *Total Prizemoney* £3,756
Wins * **1999** Oct Leices (SFT) H 7f 64 71 <
1999 Turf 1-6: (6f, 7f 1-5) (g-s, gd 1-1, g-f, frm 3)
Above-average gelding, effective 7f, acts on gd. Turf high 71 (began Jly) - 1st of 20 getting 7lb from Safarando (25 Oct Leicester RF 5052).
**M J Ryan [1-6] The French Horn Hotel Ltd Sonning.*

French Fellow was a prolific scorer in 1999

FRENCH MASTER (IRE) BHB 60f57a **RR 72f 57a** 3598[6]
2 b g Petardia 8.2f **(58)** - Reasonably French (Reasonable (FR))
Form - 746336
Record 1999 - 1st:0 2nd:0 3rd:2 Ran:6
Win Prizemoney £0 *Total Prizemoney* £1,062
1999 Turf 0-6: (6f 3, 7f 3) (g-f 2, frm 4)
Above-average gelding, effective 6 to 7f, acts on frm, has worn blinkers. Turf high 72 - 3rd of 12 giving 4lb to It's Allowed (30 Jly Thirsk 7f frm RF 3256).
**P C Haslam [0-6] Middleham Park Racing XIX.*

FRENCH MYSTERY BHB 58f53a **RR 51f 53a** 1134[4]
2 b f Mystiko (USA) 7.7f **(59)** - La Reine de France (Queen's Hussar) 11.6f **(58)**
Form - 024
Record 1999 - 1st:0 2nd:1 3rd:0 Ran:3
Win Prizemoney £0 *Total Prizemoney* £532
1999 Turf 0-2: (5f 2) (g-s, gd) 1999 AW 0-1: (5f) (Fibr)
Currently fair filly, often wears blinkers. Turf high 51 - 2nd of 9 to Foxkey (21 Apr Catterick 5f gd RF 0791).
**P D Evans [0-3] P D Evans.*

FRENCH SPICE RR 281[7]
3 b f Cadeaux Genereux 7.9f **(76)** - Hot Spice (Hotfoot) 10.5f **(59)**
Form - 67
Record 1999 - 1st:0 2nd:0 3rd:0 Ran:2
1999 AW 0-2: (6f, 7f) (Fibr 2)
Light-framed, currently moderate filly. AW high 41.
**Sir Mark Prescott [0-2] J Morley.*

FRIAR TUCK BHB 68f **RR 74f** 4805[21]
4 ch g Inchinor 8.9f **(64)** - Jay Gee Ell (Vaigly Great) 7f **(58)**
Form - 0000824508000
Record 1999 - 1st:0 2nd:1 3rd:0 Ran:13
Pre1999 - 1st:2 2nd:1 3rd:3 Ran:12
Win Prizemoney £40,967 *Total Prizemoney* £50,591
Wins * 1998 Jun York (G-S) H 6f 95 100 <
* 1997 Jly Ayr (G-F) 6f 81
1999 Turf 0-13: (5f 3, 6f 8, 7f, 9f) (g-s, gd 8, frm 4)
Scopey, above-average gelding, effective 5 to 6f, acts on g-s to g-f. Turf high 84. Becoming disappointing.
**Miss L A Perratt [2-25] Cree Lodge Racing Club.*

FRIEND FOR LIFE BHB 59f **RR 69f** 3662[8]
3 b f Lahib (USA) 8f **(69)** - Hardihostess (Be My Guest (USA)) 9.3f **(67)**
Form - 0468
Record 1999 - 1st:0 2nd:0 3rd:0 Ran:4
Win Prizemoney £0 *Total Prizemoney* £218
1999 Turf 0-4: (8f 2, 10f 2) (gd, g-f 2, hrd)
Light-framed, average filly. Turf high 69. **W R Muir [0-4] P J Deer.*

FRIENDLY ALLIANCE BHB 40f **RR 43f** 3854[6]
3 b g Shareef Dancer (USA) 10.1f **(67)** - Snow Huntress (Shirley Heights) 10.3f **(74)**
Form - 0026
Record 1999 - 1st:0 2nd:1 3rd:0 Ran:4
Pre1999 - 1st:0 2nd:0 3rd:0 Ran:3
Win Prizemoney £0 *Total Prizemoney* £804
1999 Turf 0-4: (7f, 8f, 10f 2) (gd, g-f 2, frm)
Workmanlike, moderate gelding, effective 8f, acts on g-f. Turf high 43 - 2nd of 16 getting 12lb from To The Last Man (9 Jun Salisbury 8f g-f RF 1873). **R M Flower [0-7] The Twitchell Partnership.*

FRIENDLY BRAVE (USA) BHB 43f57a **RR 46f 57a** 850[F]
9 b g Well Decorated (USA) 6.3f **(53)** - Companionship (USA) (Princely Native (USA)) 8.6f **(81)**
Form - 43523465453325F
Record 1999 - 1st:0 2nd:1 3rd:3 Ran:11
Pre1999 - 1st:8 2nd:11 3rd:14 Ran:106
Win Prizemoney £23,790 *Total Prizemoney* £46,159
Wins * 1997 *Dec Lingfi (STD) H 5f 59 60*
* 1996 Aug Bath (G-F) H 5.1f 73 73
* 1996 Jun Folkes (FRM) H 5f 70 70
* 1996 Jun Goodwo (GD) H 6f 67 69
* 1996 Apr Folkes (G-F) 5f 66
* 1995 *Nov Lingfi (STD) H 5f 60 67*
* 1995 *Nov Lingfi (STD) H 5f 60 61*
1999 Turf 0-1: (5f) (sft) 1999 AW 0-10: (5f 4, 6f 5, 7f) (Equi 9, Fibr)
Fair gelding, effective 5 to 6f, best at 5f, - acted on Equi, had worn blinkers (extremely effectively), liked left handed tracks, liked tight tracks, did well at Lingfield. AW high 56 (1st run) - 3rd of 13 getting 1lb from Acid Test (2 Jan Lingfield 6f Equi RF 0013). (DEAD)
**Miss Gay Kelleway [7-83] The Friendly Partnership (from T G Mills [1-29] Jun 1995).*

FRILLY FRONT BHB 59f **RR 58f** 5212[3]
3 ch f Aragon 7.7f **(58)** - So so **(56f)** (Then Again)
Form - 88038840004362303
Record 1999 - 1st:0 2nd:1 3rd:4 Ran:17
Pre1999 - 1st:1 2nd:0 3rd:3 Ran:8
Win Prizemoney £2,770 *Total Prizemoney* £9,838
Wins * 1998 Jun Mussel (SFT) 5f 84+ <
1999 Turf 0-17: (5f 15, 6f 2) (sft 2, g-s 2, gd 4, g-f 2, frm 6, hrd)
Scopey, fair filly, effective 5f, acts on gd to g-f, best on gd, has worn blinkers. Turf high 68. **T D Barron [1-25] M Dalby.*

FRIPPET (IRE) BHB 89f **RR 85df** 1729[10]
3 b br f Ela-Mana-Mou 12.7f **(72)** - Happy Tidings (Hello Gorgeous (USA)) 9.7f **(63)**
Form - 140
Record 1999 - 1st:1 2nd:0 3rd:0 Ran:3
Win Prizemoney £3,663 *Total Prizemoney* £4,626
Wins * **1999** Apr Kempto (G-F) 11.1f 85 <
1999 Turf 1-3: (11f 1-2, 12f) (gd 2, g-f 1-1)
Strong, currently useful filly. Turf high 85 (1st run) - 1st of 13 getting 5lb from Kondoty (5 Apr Kempton RF 0578). She caused a bit of a surprise when winning on her Kempton debut, showing a nice turn of foot, but has been outclassed behind Ramruma at Lingfield and Epsom (last in the Oaks). **S Dow [1-3] Clear Height Epsom.*

FRISKY FOX BHB 40f **RR 47f** 5153[10]
5 b m Risk Me (FR) 8f **(53)** - Hill Vixen (Goldhill) 8.5f **(55)**
Form - 4780400
Record 1999 - 1st:0 2nd:0 3rd:0 Ran:7
Pre1999 - 1st:0 2nd:0 3rd:1 Ran:1
Win Prizemoney £0 *Total Prizemoney* £830
1999 Turf 0-6: (8f 2, 10f 3, 12f)(sft 2, gd 3, g-f) 1999AW 0-1: (12f) (Fibr)
Moderate filly. Turf high 58. Inconsistent.
**R Hollinshead [0-8] Exors of the late Mrs J P Bissill.*

FRISKY SILK RR 392[12]
5 b m Risk Me (FR) 8f **(53)** - Power and Red (Skyliner) 7.3f **(53)**
Form - 0
Record 1999 - 1st:0 2nd:0 3rd:0 Ran:1
1999 AW 0-1: (8f) (Fibr)
Currently very poor filly. **R Guest [0-1] Mrs Christine Wilson.*

FRONTIER BHB 90f **RR 90f** 4784[1]
2 b c Indian Ridge 7.6f **(74)** - Adatiya (IRE) (Shardari) 11f **(46)**
Form - 421
Record 1999 - 1st:1 2nd:1 3rd:0 Ran:3
Win Prizemoney £3,752 *Total Prizemoney* £8,389
Wins * **1999** Oct Lingfi (G-S) 7f 84 <
1999 Turf 1-3: (6f, 7f 1-2) (g-s 1-1, g-f, frm)
Currently useful colt. Turf high 90 (began Jly) - also 1st of 18 from Ansari (8 Oct Lingfield RF 4784).
**R Hannon [1-3] Highclere Thoroughbred Racing Ltd.*

FRONTIER FLIGHT (USA) BHB 30f28a **RR 14f 28a** 3475[5]
9 b g Flying Paster (USA) - Sly Charmer (USA) (Valdez (USA)) 10.7f **(70)**
Form - 005
Record 1999 - 1st:0 2nd:0 3rd:0 Ran:3
Pre1999 - 1st:1 2nd:0 3rd:0 Ran:10
Win Prizemoney £2,553 *Total Prizemoney* £2,771
1999 Turf 0-1: (16f) (g-f) 1999 AW 0-2: (16f 2) (Equi, Fibr)
Little account gelding. Becoming disappointing.
**P W Hiatt [0-9] S F Holder (from Miss L C Siddall [1-14] Aug 1996).*

FROSTED AIRE BHB 63f **RR 62f** 4027[P]
3 ch g Chilibang 7f **(55)** - Suzannah's Song (Song) 7.2f **(61)**
Form - 070P
Record 1999 - 1st:0 2nd:0 3rd:0 Ran:4
1999 Turf 0-4: (6f 2, 8f 2) (gd, g-f, frm 2)
Workmanlike, average gelding, has broken blood-vessels. Turf high 62 (began Jly). **G G Margarson [0-4] The Shambles Partnership.*

FROSTY (IRE) RR 29f 4720[11]
3 ch g Lahib (USA) 8f **(69)** - Chilblains (Hotfoot) 10.5f **(59)**
Form - 70
Record 1999 - 1st:0 2nd:0 3rd:0 Ran:2
Pre1999 - 1st:0 2nd:0 3rd:0 Ran:1
1999 Turf 0-2: (8f, 11f) (gd 2)
Lengthy, currently little account gelding. Turf high 29 (began Spt).
**T D Easterby [0-3] Peter Bourke.*

FROZEN SEA (USA) BHB 32f51a **RR 30f 51a** 3614[2]
8 ch g Diesis 9f **(80)** - Ocean Ballad (Grundy) 10.3f **(65)**
Form - 0022
Record 1999 - 1st:0 2nd:2 3rd:0 Ran:4
Pre1999 - 1st:1 2nd:0 3rd:3 Ran:13
Win Prizemoney £2,660 *Total Prizemoney* £6,438
Wins 1996 Jun Yarmou (FRM) 14.1f 66 <
1999 Turf 0-2: (12f 2) (g-f, frm) 1999 AW 0-2: (12f, 13f) (Equi 2)
Fair gelding. Turf high 30 (began Jly). AW high 51.
**G L Moore [0-4] The Oaks Partners (from G P Enright [2-19] Spt 1997).*

FRUITS OF LOVE (USA) RR 123f 5019a[2]
4 b c Hansel (USA) 12.6f **(78)** - Vallee Secrete (USA) (Secretariat (USA)) 9f **(79)**
Form - 516132
Record 1999 - 1st:2 2nd:1 3rd:1 Ran:5
Pre1999 - 1st:2 2nd:2 3rd:3 Ran:13
Win Prizemoney £265,683 *Total Prizemoney* £478,138
Wins * **1999** Jun Ascot (G-F) G2 12f 123 <
* **1999** Mar Nad Al (G-F) 12f 118
* 1998 Jly Newmar (G-F) G2 12f 114
* 1997 Aug Newcas (G-F) 7f 85+
1999 Turf 2-5: (12f 2-5) (gd 3, g-f 2-2)
Strong, very high-class colt, effective 12 to 13f, best at 12f, acts on hvy to frm, best on gd, has worn blinkers (extremely effectively). Turf high 123 - 3rd of 8 to Daylami (24 Jly Ascot 12f gd RF 3088) - also 1st of 9 getting 2lb from Royal Anthem (18 Jun Ascot RF 2104). Consistent. He looked set to justify his trainer's high opinion of him when winning the Group Two Princess Of Walesis Stakes at the July meeting in 1998, but he did not make the expected progress during the rest of the season. He looked a much-improved sort last term, however. He won a big turf race in Dubai in the spring, but the ground was against him in the Coronation Cup, after which he suffered a freak accident in the horse box on the way home. Thankfully back in one piece and with the faster ground in his favour, he scored a fine victory over Royal Anthem in the Hardwicke at Royal Ascot, but was not suited by the modest pace in the King George, though he ran on to finish a most creditable third. Given a short break, he ran well in the Canadian International, and is now on course for the Japan Cup, where he should get the ground he prefers. **M Johnston [4-18].*

FUDGE BROWNIE RR 62f 1002[9]
3 b g Deploy 11.4f **(67)** - Carte Blanche **(47f 57a)** (Cadeaux Genereux)
Form - 70
Record 1999 - 1st:0 2nd:0 3rd:0 Ran:2
1999 Turf 0-2: (8f, 10f) (frm 2)
Workmanlike, currently average gelding. Turf high 62.
**C A Cyzer [0-2] R M Cyzer.*

FUEGIAN BHB 55f37a **RR 58f 37a** 5033[14]
4 ch g Arazi (USA) 9.2f **(74)** - Well Beyond (IRE) (Don't Forget Me) 8.3f **(74)**
Form - 0480550212660
Record 1999 - 1st:1 2nd:2 3rd:0 Ran:11
Pre1999 - 1st:0 2nd:0 3rd:0 Ran:5
Win Prizemoney £2,934 *Total Prizemoney* £4,514
Wins * **1999** Jly Windso (GD) H 8.3f 48 56 <
1999 Turf 1-10: (7f 2, 8f 1-8) (g-s, g-f 4, frm 1-5) 1999 AW 0-1: (10f) (Equi)
Scopey, fair gelding, effective 8f, acts on g-f to frm, best on frm, often wears blinkers (extremely effectively), prefers right handed tracks, prefers tight tracks. Turf high 58 - 2nd of 17 getting 3lb from Byzantium (2 Aug Windsor 8f frm RF 3302) - also 1st of 18 getting 3lb from Critical Air (5 Jly Windsor RF 2569). He got off the mark at the twelfth attempt when making all at Windsor in July. Forcing tactics suit him.
**M Madgwick [1-15] D Knight (from R Charlton [0-2] Aug 1998).*

FUERO REAL (FR) BHB 40f **RR 40f** 2663[4]
4 b g Highest Honor (FR) 10.9f **(72)** - Highest Pleasure (USA) (Foolish Pleasure (USA)) 8.9f **(72)**
Form - 868224
Record 1999 - 1st:0 2nd:2 3rd:0 Ran:6
Win Prizemoney £0 *Total Prizemoney* £1,286
1999 Turf 0-6: (8f, 10f, 11f, 12f 3) (gd 2, g-f, frm 3)
Moderate gelding, effective 10 to 12f, acts on frm. Turf high 40.
**R J Hodges [0-6] Grandstand Jockeys.*

FUJIYAMA CREST (IRE) BHB 72f **RR 74f** 3626[3]
7 b g Roi Danzig (USA) 10.5f**(62)** - Snoozy Time (Cavo Doro) 10.6f **(57)**
Form - 043
Record 1999 - 1st:0 2nd:0 3rd:1 Ran:3
Pre1999 - 1st:6 2nd:0 3rd:2 Ran:17

Win Prizemoney £44,298 *Total Prizemoney* £48,038
Wins 1996 Spt Ascot (G-F) H 16.2f 86 92 <
1995 Spt Ascot (GD) H 16.2f 79 89
1995 Aug Sandow (G-F) H 14f 64 81
1995 Aug Cheste (G-F) H 15.9f 64 72
1995 May Windso (GD) H 11.6f 55 61+
1995 Apr Folkes (G-F) H 9.7f 55 57
1999 Turf 0-3: (14f, 16f, 20f) (gd, g-f, frm)
Above-average gelding, often wears blinkers. Turf high 74. Becoming disappointing.
**R Curtis [0-6] Glazer, Harris & Swaden (from Sir Michael Stoute [6-17] Spt 1996).*

FULHAM BHB 38f RR 32f 3797[15]
3 ch c Safawan 6.6f **(60)** - Sister Sal (Bairn (USA)) 7.7f **(59)**
Form - 0080
Record 1999 - 1st:0 2nd:0 3rd:0 Ran:4
1999 Turf 0-4: (7f 2, 9f, 10f) (gd, frm 3)
Neat, very moderate colt. Turf high 49.
**M J Haynes [0-4] J P Saunders.*

FULL AHEAD (IRE) RR 71f 4007[5]
2 b c Slip Anchor 12.7f **(75)** - Foulard (IRE) (Sadler's Wells (USA)) 10f **(76)**
Form - 45
Record 1999 - 1st:0 2nd:0 3rd:0 Ran:2
Win Prizemoney £0 *Total Prizemoney* £346
1999 Turf 0-2: (7f, 8f) (gd, frm)
Currently above-average colt. Turf high 71 (began Jly).
**M H Tompkins [0-2] J H Ellis.*

FULL EGALITE BHB 52f RR 36f 3765[8]
3 gr g Ezzoud (IRE) - Milva (Jellaby) 6.4f **(58)**
Form - 486708
Record 1999 - 1st:0 2nd:0 3rd:0 Ran:6
Pre1999 - 1st:1 2nd:0 3rd:0 Ran:3
Win Prizemoney £2,965 *Total Prizemoney* £3,271
Wins * 1998 Nov Bright (SFT) 6f 72 <
1999 Turf 0-6: (7f, 8f, 9f 2, 10f, 11f) (g-s 2, gd 2, frm 2)
Workmanlike, very moderate gelding, effective 6f, acts on g-s, has worn blinkers, favours left handed tracks, likes tight tracks. Turf high 61. Becoming disappointing. **W J Haggas [1-9] S Hassiakos.*

FULL FLOW (USA) RR 94f 3759[8]
2 b c Eagle Eyed (USA) - Fast Flow (USA) (Riverman (USA)) 9.1f **(76)**
Form - 128
Record 1999 - 1st:1 2nd:1 3rd:0 Ran:3
Win Prizemoney £3,517 *Total Prizemoney* £7,536
Wins * 1999 Jun Newcas (G-F) 6f 85+ <
1999 Turf 1-3: (6f 1-2, 7f) (gd, frm 1-2)
Currently useful colt. Turf high 94 - 2nd of 5 giving 3lb to Thady Quill (8 Jly Newmarket 7f frm RF 2645) - also 1st of 5 from Atlantic Rhapsody (26 Jun Newcastle RF 2333). A half-brother to Auction House, he showed a decent turn of foot to win on his Newcastle debut, but ran about at Newmarket next time and was just caught. Beaten a long way in the Gimcrack. **B W Hills [1-3] K Abdulla.*

FULL MOON BHB 27f27a RR 21f 27a 640[7]
4 b g Almoojid 7f **(36)** - High Time (FR) (Adonijah) 10f **(61)**
Form - 004867
Record 1999 - 1st:0 2nd:0 3rd:0 Ran:5
Pre1999 - 1st:0 2nd:0 3rd:0 Ran:4
1999 Turf 0-2: (9f, 11f) (hvy 2) 1999 AW 0-3: (12f, 15f, 16f) (Fibr 3)
Unfurnished, very moderate gelding, has worn blinkers. Turf high 21. AW high 37.
**W M Brisbourne [0-6] Mrs E A Dawson (from P D Evans [0-3] Feb 1998).*

FULL OF MISCHIEF RR 2084[P]
2 b f Be My Chief(USA)10.2f **(62)** -Hafhafah (Shirley Heights) 10.3f **(74)**
Form - P
Record 1999 - 1st:0 2nd:0 3rd:0 Ran:1
1999 AW 0-1: (5f) (Fibr)
Very poor filly. (DEAD) **M J Polglase [0-1] M J Polglase.*

FULLOPEP BHB 63f RR 62f 4400[2]
5 b g Dunbeath (USA) 9.9f **(53)** - Suggia (Alzao (USA)) 7.1f **(68)**
Form - 2
Record 1999 - 1st:0 2nd:1 3rd:0 Ran:1
Pre1999 - 1st:1 2nd:1 3rd:1 Ran:14
Win Prizemoney £2,617 *Total Prizemoney* £5,034
Wins * 1997 May Catter (G-F) 12f 57+ <
1999 Turf 0-1: (16f) (frm)
Average gelding. (1st run) - 2nd of 13 giving 19lb to Rigadoon (18 Spt Catterick 16f frm RF 4400).
**Mrs M Reveley [3-18] & Mrs W J Williams.*

FULL PITCH RR 94f 2512[1]
3 ch g Cadeaux Genereux 7.9f **(76)** - Tricky Note (Song) 7.2f **(61)**
Form - 1
Record 1999 - 1st:1 2nd:0 3rd:0 Ran:1
Win Prizemoney £3,873 *Total Prizemoney* £3,873
Wins * 1999 Jly Beverl (SFT) 5f 94 <
1999 Turf 1-1: (5f 1-1) (gd 1-1)
Rangy, currently useful gelding. (1st run) - 1st of 6 giving 5lb to Cyclone Flyer (3 Jly Beverley RF 2512). Unraced at two due to injury, he bolted home in soft ground on his Beverley debut, though the form of the race is difficult to evaluate.
**W J Haggas [1-1] The Tricky Note Partnership.*

FULL SPATE RR 57f 4240[13]
4 ch c Unfuwain (USA) 11.4f **(74)** - Double River (USA) (Irish River (FR)) 8.6f **(78)**
Form - 531500600000
Record 1999 - 1st:1 2nd:0 3rd:1 Ran:12
Pre1999 - 1st:0 2nd:1 3rd:1 Ran:3
Win Prizemoney £6,775 *Total Prizemoney* £9,232
Wins * 1999 May Thirsk (G-F) H 7f 73 76 <
1999 Turf 1-12: (6f 3, 7f 1-8, 8f) (sft, g-s, gd 4, g-f 1-3, frm 3)
Scopey, fair colt, effective 7 to 8f, best at 7f, acts on gd to frm, best on gd. Turf high 76 - 1st of 16 getting 7lb from Asef Alhind (1 May Thirsk RF 0964). Consistent.
**J M Bradley [1-12] E A Hayward (from R Charlton [0-3] Jun 1998).*

FUN LOVER RR 63f 5054[5]
2 b f Lahib (USA) 8f **(69)** - Funun (USA) (Fappiano (USA)) 8.7f **(77)**
Form - 05
Record 1999 - 1st:0 2nd:0 3rd:0 Ran:2
1999 Turf 0-2: (6f 2) (gd 2)
Currently average filly. Turf high 63 (began Oct).
**D R C Elsworth [0-2] J C Smith.*

FUNNY GIRL (IRE) RR 76f 4559[5]
2 b f Darshaan 11.9f **(81)** - Just For Fun (FR) (Lead on Time (USA)) 8f **(65)**
Form - 45
Record 1999 - 1st:0 2nd:0 3rd:0 Ran:2
Win Prizemoney £0 *Total Prizemoney* £247
1999 Turf 0-2: (8f 2) (gd 2)
Currently above-average filly. Turf high 76 (began Aug).
**W R Muir [0-2] Vicki & David Fleet.*

FURLOUGH (USA) RR 5227a[10]
5 b m Easy Goer (USA) 8.7f **(81)** - Blitey (USA) (Riva Ridge (USA)) 8.2f **(68)**
Form - 0
1999 AW 0-1: (6f) (Dirt)
Currently Pattern-class filly. **C McGaughey in USA [0-2].*

FURNESS BHB 54f RR 57f 5215[10]
2 b g Emarati (USA) 6.6f **(63)** - Thelma (Blakeney) 10.5f **(64)**
Form - 080
Record 1999 - 1st:0 2nd:0 3rd:0 Ran:3
1999 Turf 0-3: (8f 3) (g-s, gd 2)
Currently fair gelding. Turf high 57 (began Oct).
**J G Smyth-Osbourne [0-3] T D Rootes.*

FURSAN (USA) BHB 60f50a RR 55f 50a 4863[11]
6 b g Fred Astaire (USA) 12f **(55)** - Ancient Art (USA) (Tell (USA))
Form - 70
Record 1999 - 1st:0 2nd:0 3rd:0 Ran:2
Pre1999 - 1st:0 2nd:1 3rd:1 Ran:7
Win Prizemoney £0 *Total Prizemoney* £2,385
1999 Turf 0-1: (12f) (g-f) 1999 AW 0-1: (15f) (Fibr)

Fair gelding, has worn blinkers. **R T Phillips [0-3] Richard Phillips (from N A Graham [0-7] Jun 1996).*

FURTHER OUTLOOK (USA) BHB 99f **RR 98f** 3697[11]

5 gr g Zilzal (USA) 8.5f **(79)** - Future Bright (USA) (Lyphard's Wish (FR)) 9f **(74)**

Form - 0012101060

Record 1999 - 1st:3 2nd:1 3rd:0 Ran:10
Pre1999 - 1st:2 2nd:2 3rd:2 Ran:15

Win Prizemoney £50,346 *Total Prizemoney* £67,759

Wins * **1999** Jun Doncas (G-F) H 5f 95 98 <
* **1999** Jun Epsom (GD,) H 6f 88 94
* **1999** Apr Pontef (G-S) H 6f 78 82
1996 Spt Hamilt (GD) 8.3f 96
1996 Aug Beverl (GD) 7.5f 85+

1999 Turf 3-10: (5f 1-2, 6f 2-6, 8f, 10f) (gd 3-6, g-f 4)

Very useful gelding, effective 5 to 6f, best at 6f, acts on gd to g-f, best on gd. Turf high 98 - 1st of 8 giving 11lb to Ziggy's Dancer (27 Jun Doncaster RF 2349) - also 1st of 16 giving 11lb to The Fugative (5 Jun Epsom RF 1763). He turned the corner once dropped down to sprint distances, winning three valuable handicaps. Connections were seriously considering him for the Group One Nunthorpe Stakes, which indicates he can win off his current mark.

**D Nicholls [3-10] Mark Leatham (from Mrs A J Perrett [0-10] Oct 1998).*

FUSUL (USA) BHB 50f **RR 53f** 5058[10]

3 ch c Miswaki (USA) 8.1f **(81)** - Silent Turn (USA) (Silent Cal (USA)) 14.5f **(91)**

Form - 47800

Record 1999 - 1st:0 2nd:0 3rd:0 Ran:5
Pre1999 - 1st:0 2nd:0 3rd:0 Ran:2

Win Prizemoney £0 *Total Prizemoney* £232

1999 Turf 0-4: (7f 3, 8f) (g-f 2, frm 2) 1999 AW 0-1: (7f) (Equi)

Leggy, fair colt. Turf high 65.

**G L Moore [0-2] Dave Allen,Barry Pri Russell (from B Hanbury [0-5] Jun 1999).*

FUTURE COUP (USA) BHB 59f **RR 55+f** 4558[1]

3 b g Lord At War (ARG) 6.6f **(67)** - Holy Moly (USA) (Halo (USA)) 10.6f **(75)**

Form - 31264251

Record 1999 - 1st:2 2nd:2 3rd:1 Ran:8

Win Prizemoney £5,275 *Total Prizemoney* £8,582

Wins * **1999** Spt Nottin (GD) SH 8.2f 51 55+
* **1999** Jly Beverl (G-F) C 7.5f 63 <

1999 Turf 2-8: (7f 1-2, 8f 1-3, 9f, 10f 2) (gd 1-3, frm 1-5)

Fair gelding, effective 7 to 10f, acts on gd to frm, best on frm. Turf high 63 - 2nd of 9 getting 10lb from L S Lowry (25 Jly Newmarket 10f frm RF 3129) - also 1st of 10 giving 3lb to Zechariah (13 Jly Beverley RF 2768). Consistent. **W J Haggas [2-8] Michael Brower.*

FUTURE PROSPECT (IRE) BHB 62f48a **RR 50f 48a** 4689[10]

5 b g Marju (IRE) 9.2f **(76)** - Phazania (Tap On Wood) 10.3f **(65)**

Form - 0485261010748482800

Record 1999 - 1st:2 2nd:2 3rd:0 Ran:18
Pre1999 - 1st:3 2nd:2 3rd:1 Ran:17

Win Prizemoney £14,561 *Total Prizemoney* £21,327

Wins * **1999** Jun Redcar (FRM) H 9f 62 64
* **1999** May Hamilt (G-F) H 8.3f 58 60
1998 *Jly Wolver (STD) C 8.5f 70*
1998 May Pontef (G-F) C 8f 73
1996 Jun Haydoc (G-S) 5f 81+ <

1999 Turf 2-13: (8f 1-8, 9f 1-4, 10f) (gd 3, g-f 1-5, frm 1-5) 1999 AW 0-5: (7f, 8f 4) (Equi, Fibr 4)

Fair gelding, effective 7 to 9f, best at 8f, acts on gd to frm - acts on Fibr, best on frm, has worn blinkers, excels at Redcar, does well at Hamilton. Turf high 66 - 2nd of 20 giving 1lb to Orsay (1 Spt York 9f frm RF 4079) - also 1st of 16 giving 20lb to Tarradale (1 Jun Redcar RF 1654). AW high 52. Consistent.

**M A Buckley [2-21] C C Buckley (from M Johnston [3-15] Spt 1998).*

F-ZERO BHB 76f **RR 76f** 4139[8]

2 b c Bin Ajwaad (IRE) - Saluti Tutti (Trojan Fen) 8.1f **(62)**

Form - 728

Record 1999 - 1st:0 2nd:1 3rd:0 Ran:3

Win Prizemoney £0 *Total Prizemoney* £860

1999 Turf 0-3: (7f 3) (frm 3)

Currently above-average colt. Turf high 76 (began Jly) - 2nd of 5 to Splash Out (10 Aug Ayr 7f frm RF 3491). **C F Wall [0-3] S Fustok*

GABIDIA **RR 74tf** 4214[3]

2 br f Bin Ajwaad (IRE) - Diabaig **(70f)** (Precocious) 8.6f **(62)**

Form - 3

Record 1999 - 1st:0 2nd:0 3rd:1 Ran:1

Win Prizemoney £0 *Total Prizemoney* £939

1999 Turf 0-1: (7f) (frm)

Currently above-average filly. (1st run) - 3rd of 7 to Silent Night (8 Spt Kempton 7f frm RF 4214). **M A Jarvis [0-1] Mrs Beryl Sims.*

GABLESEA BHB 46f49a **RR 50f 49a** 4927[9]

5 b g Beveled (USA) 6.9f **(64)** - Me Spede (Valiyar) 8.5f **(73)**

Form - 02333860607000

Record 1999 - 1st:0 2nd:1 3rd:3 Ran:14
Pre1999 - 1st:4 2nd:4 3rd:4 Ran:33

Win Prizemoney £11,332 *Total Prizemoney* £18,399

Wins * 1998 Aug Haydoc (GD) H 8.1f 50 52
* 1998 Jly Chepst (GD) H 7.1f 44 48
* 1997 *Nov Southw (STD) H 7f 49 56* <
* 1997 *Spt Wolver (STD) H 8.5f 44 47*

1999 Turf 0-12: (7f 4, 8f 8) (g-s, gd 5, g-f 2, frm 3, hrd) 1999 AW 0-2: (8f 2) (Fibr 2)

Fair gelding, effective 7 to 8f, best at 8f, acts on gd to frm - acts on Fibr, does well at Southwell. Turf high 60 - 3rd of 21 giving 3lb to Aberkeen (29 May Doncaster 7f frm RF 1566). AW high 9.

**B P J Baugh [4-47] Messrs Chrimes, Winn & Wilson.*

GABRIEL (IRE) BHB 53f **RR 56f** 4632[17]

3 b f River Falls 8.2f **(56)** -Los Angeles (IRE)(Double Schwartz)7.9f **(55)**

Form - 64650

Record 1999 - 1st:0 2nd:0 3rd:0 Ran:5

Win Prizemoney £0 *Total Prizemoney* £293

1999 Turf 0-5: (8f 3, 9f, 10f) (g-s, gd 2, g-f, frm)

Light-framed, fair filly. Turf high 56.

**M H Tompkins [0-5] www raceworld co uk.*

GADGE BHB 54f50a **RR 44f 50a** 5160[12]

8 br g Nomination 7.3f **(57)** - Queenstyle (Moorestyle) 6.9f **(64)**

Form - 472344000860

Record 1999 - 1st:0 2nd:1 3rd:1 Ran:10
Pre1999 - 1st:9 2nd:6 3rd:9 Ran:80

Win Prizemoney £70,169 *Total Prizemoney* £88,256

Wins * 1998 Oct Bright (GD) 7f 68
* 1997 May Ayr (G-F) H 6f 66 80+ <
* 1997 May Goodwo (G-S) H 7f 66 72
* 1997 May Bath (G-S) H 8f 61 66
* 1997 May Thirsk (G-F) H 8f 58 63
* 1997 Mar Newcas (G-F) SH 8f 50 59
* 1997 *Feb Lingfi (STD) SH 8f 40 44*

1999 Turf 0-4: (6f 3, 7f) (sft, g-f, frm 2) 1999 AW 0-6: (6f, 7f 2, 8f 3) (Equi 2, Fibr 4)

Moderate gelding, effective 6 to 7f, best at 7f, acts on g-f to frm, best on frm, has worn blinkers. Turf high 44 (began Aug). AW high 55. Consistent. He was in brilliant form during the spring of '97, winning races ranging from sellers to valuable handicaps, but shot up the weights as a result and has not had much success since. **A Bailey [7-58] J B Wilcox (from D Morris [1-22] Jun 1996).*

GAD YAKOUN BHB 67f35a **RR 67f 35a** 37[9]

6 ch g Cadeaux Genereux 7.9f **(76)** - Summer Impressions (USA) (Lyphard (USA)) 9.9f **(72)**

Form - 000

Record 1999 - 1st:0 2nd:0 3rd:0 Ran:1
Pre1999 - 1st:1 2nd:0 3rd:1 Ran:10

Win Prizemoney £3,566 *Total Prizemoney* £4,136

Wins * 1996 *Nov Lingfi (STD) 7f 69* <

1999 AW 0-1: (9f) (Fibr)

Average gelding. Becoming disappointing.

**M G Meagher [1-11] M R Johnson.*

GAELIC FORAY (IRE) **RR 12f** 4945[15]

3 b f Unblest - Rich Heiress (IRE) (Last Tycoon) 8.5f **(62)**

Form - 0

Record 1999 - 1st:0 2nd:0 3rd:0 Ran:1

1999 Turf 0-1: (7f) (gd)

Workmanlike, currently poor filly. **R P C Hoad [0-1] Foray Racing.*

GAELIC STORM BHB 111f95a **RR 109f 95a** 5222[6]

5 b g Shavian 7.7f **(67)** - Shannon Princess (Connaught) 7.7f **(63)**

Form - 6235612608113408126

Record	**1999** -	1st:4	2nd:3	3rd:2	Ran:18
	Pre1999 -	1st:8	2nd:1	3rd:4	Ran:28

Win Prizemoney £134,570 *Total Prizemoney* £194,721

Wins								
	*** 1999**	Oct	Newmar (GD)	L	6f		108	
	*** 1999**	Jly	Ovrevo (GD)	L	6.8f		104	
	*** 1999**	Jly	Ovrevo (SFT)		6.8f		97	
	*** 1999**	May	Goodwo (GD)		6f		111	<
	* 1998	Oct	Newbur (HVY)	H	6f	105	109	
	* 1998	Oct	York (GD)	H	7f	102	105	
	* 1998	Jun	Newcas (SFT)	H	6f	95	98	
	* 1998	Jun	York (G-S)	H	6f	86	94	
	* 1997	Spt	Catter (GD)		6f		76+	
	* 1997	Aug	Epsom (GD)	H	5f	81	83	
	* 1997	Aug	Thirsk (G-F)	H	5f	75	78	
	* 1996	Spt	Sandow (G-F)		5f		84	

1999 Turf 4-17: (6f 2-11, 7f 2-6) (sft 1-2, g-s 3, gd 3-8, g-f 2, frm 2)
1999 AW 0-1: (6f) (Dirt)

Pattern-class gelding, effective 6 to 7f, best at 6f, acts on sft to frm, and excels at Curragh and Ovrevoll and Newbury. Turf high 111 - 2nd of 10 to Eastern Purple (22 May Curragh 6f g-f RF 1476a) - also 1st of 6 from Lone Piper (18 May Goodwood RF 1295). Consistent. Almost unrideable before being gelded, this tough customer has gone from strength-to-strength and put up a smart performance when winning a Listed event at Newmarket in October. Best when coming from behind a fast pace on soft ground, he can never be left out of the calculations.

**M Johnston [12-46] H C Racing Club.*

Gaelic Storm was a force to be reckoned with in sprint handicaps

GAILY MILL RR 79f 3574[9]

4 b f Keen 11.1f **(58)** - Island Mill (Mill Reef (USA)) 10.5f **(78)**

Form - 2065150

Record	**1999** -	1st:1	2nd:1	3rd:0	Ran:7
	Pre1999 -	1st:3	2nd:2	3rd:2	Ran:15

Win Prizemoney £16,884 *Total Prizemoney* £24,749

Wins								
	*** 1999**	Jly	Windso (G-F)	H	8.3f	78	79	<
	* 1998	Aug	Epsom (G-F)	H	8.5f	73	78	
	* 1998	Aug	Thirsk (G-F)	H	8f	68	71	
	* 1998	Jun	Salisb (G-S)	H	7f	64	71	

1999 Turf 1-7: (8f 1-5, 9f 2) (gd 2, g-f 3, frm 1-2)

Lengthy, above-average filly, effective 8 to 9f, best at 8f, acts on gd to frm, best on gd, likes left handed tracks, likes tight tracks, excels at Epsom. Turf high 85 (1st run) - 2nd of 14 giving 4lb to Topatori (8 Apr Leicester 8f gd RF 0619) - also 1st of 6 giving 7lb to Coffee Cream (12 Jly Windsor RF 2763). Consistent.

**I A Balding [4-22] Nigel Harris.*

GAIN LINE (USA) BHB 39f45a **RR 37f 45a** 3078[7]

6 b g Dayjur (USA) 6.8f **(79)** - Safe Play (USA) (Sham (USA)) 9.5f **(68)**

Form - 152640077

Record	**1999** -	1st:1	2nd:1	3rd:0	Ran:9
	Pre1999 -	1st:1	2nd:1	3rd:2	Ran:22

Win Prizemoney £5,366 *Total Prizemoney* £9,027

Wins								
	*** 1999**	*Jan*	*Southw (STD)*	*H*	*8f*	*44*	*50*	
	1997	Jly	Yarmou (G-F)	H	7f	51	56	<

1999 Turf 0-2: (7f, 8f) (g-f 2) 1999 AW 1-7: (7f, 8f 1-6) (Fibr 1-7)

Fair gelding, effective 7 to 8f, best at 8f, acts on gd - acts on Fibr, has worn blinkers, likes left handed tracks, prefers tight tracks. Turf high 37. AW high 50 - also 1st of 15 giving 2lb to Tom (11 Jan Southwell RF 0071). Consistent.

**K Bell [1-9] Newhaven Racing Club (from C A Dwyer [0-9] Aug 1998).*

GAIN TIME BHB 68f64a **RR 68f 64a** 5150[3]

2 b g Timeless Times (USA) 6.1f **(56)** - Axed Again **(40a)** (Then Again)

Form - 33202277007623

Record	**1999** -	1st:0	2nd:4	3rd:3	Ran:14

Win Prizemoney £0 *Total Prizemoney* £5,466

1999 Turf 0-13: (5f 3, 6f 10) (sft 2, g-s, gd 2, g-f 4, frm 4) 1999 AW 0-1: (6f) (Fibr)

Average gelding, effective 6f, acts on g-s to frm, has worn blinkers (extremely effectively). Turf high 72 - 2nd of 7 giving 7lb to Anstar (15 Jly Leicester 6f g-f RF 2851). **T D Barron [0-14] Mrs J Hazell.*

GALANTY SHOW BHB 78f **RR 72+f** 4564[1]

3 b f Danehill (USA) 9.1f **(79)** - Sacristy (Godswalk (USA)) 7.3f **(58)**

Form - 321

Record	**1999** -	1st:1	2nd:1	3rd:1	Ran:3

Win Prizemoney £4,467 *Total Prizemoney* £6,209

Wins								
	*** 1999**	Spt	Nottin (GD)		6.1f		72+	<

1999 Turf 1-3: (6f 1-3) (gd 1-1, frm 2)

Workmanlike, currently above-average filly. Turf high 72 (began Jly) - 1st of 20 from Cherish Me (25 Spt Nottingham RF 4564).

**J H M Gosden [1-3] K Abdulla.*

GALAPINO BHB 55f50a **RR 60f 50a** 5220[8]

6 b g Charmer 9f **(59)** - Carousella (Rousillon (USA)) 8.2f **(74)**

Form - 80603313478

Record	**1999** -	1st:1	2nd:0	3rd:3	Ran:11
	Pre1999 -	1st:6	2nd:10	3rd:3	Ran:52

Win Prizemoney £25,664 *Total Prizemoney* £47,941

Wins								
	*** 1999**	Aug	Sandow (G-S)	H	16.4f	56	59	
	1998	Aug	Goodwo (G-F)	CH	9.9f	60	64	
	1997	Jun	Warwic (G-F)	H	12.5f	59	58	
	1997	Mar	Doncas (G-F)	H	12f	48	53	
	1997	*Jan*	*Wolver (STD)*	*C*	*12f*		*66*	
	1996	*Feb*	*Wolver (STD)*	*H*	*9.4f*	*65*	*76+*	<
	1996	*Feb*	*Lingfi (STD)*	*H*	*10f*	*65*	*69*	

1999 Turf 1-10: (12f, 13f, 14f, 16f 1-3, 17f 2, 18f, 20f) (sft, g-s 2, gd, g-f 1-4, frm 2) 1999 AW 0-1: (12f) (Equi)

Average gelding, effective 10 to 20f, acts on g-s to frm, best on gd, has worn blinkers (extremely effectively), likes right handed tracks, likes tight tracks, does well at Sandown. Turf high 60. Consistent.

**J R Poulton [1-11] Glendale Partnership Ltd (from M R Channon [2-12] Jan 1999).*

GALETTE RR 89f 3654[1]

3 b f Caerleon (USA) 10.9f **(79)** - Madame Dubois (Legend of France (USA)) 9.5f **(61)**

Form - 21

Record	**1999** -	1st:1	2nd:1	3rd:0	Ran:2

Win Prizemoney £4,854 *Total Prizemoney* £5,959

Wins								
	*** 1999**	Aug	Newmar (GD)		12f		89	<

1999 Turf 1-2: (10f, 12f 1-1) (g-f 1-1, frm)

Lengthy, currently useful filly. Turf high 89 (began Aug) - 1st of 3 getting 5lb from Dark Trojan (14 Aug Newmarket RF 3654).

**H R A Cecil [1-2] Cliveden Stud.*

GALI BHB 53f **RR 39f** 1921[12]

3 gr c Petong 7.6f **(58)** - Wasimah (Caerleon (USA)) 8.6f **(71)**

Form - 3000

Record	**1999** -	1st:0	2nd:0	3rd:1	Ran:4
	Pre1999 -	1st:0	2nd:0	3rd:0	Ran:2

Win Prizemoney £0 *Total Prizemoney* £501

1999 Turf 0-4: (6f 2, 8f 2) (sft, g-f, frm 2)

Workmanlike, very moderate colt. Turf high 39.

**C A Horgan [0-6] B R Tantoco.*

GALLANT RR 53f 5129[15]

2 b c Rainbow Quest (USA) 11.2f **(81)** - Gay Gallanta (USA) **(106f)** (Woodman (USA)) 9f **(74)**

Form - 0
Record 1999 - 1st:0 2nd:0 3rd:0 Ran:1
1999 Turf 0-1: (6f) (gd)
Currently fair colt. **Sir Michael Stoute [0-1] Cheveley Park Stud.*

GALLANT FELLOW (FR) BHB 40f33a **RR 48f 33a** 4332[7]

4 ch g Cadeaux Genereux 7.9f **(76)** - Hiwaayati (Shadeed (USA)) 8.2f **(70)**
Form - 07705040087550037
Record 1999 - 1st:0 2nd:0 3rd:1 Ran:13
Pre1999 - 1st:0 2nd:0 3rd:0 Ran:7
Win Prizemoney £0 *Total Prizemoney* £563
1999 Turf 0-12: (5f 2, 6f 6, 7f 3, 8f) (sft, gd 4, g-f 3, frm 3, hrd) 1999 AW 0-1: (7f) (Equi)
Scopey, moderate gelding. Turf high 54.
**J J Bridger [0-16] P Cook (from C R Egerton [0-4] Nov 1998).*

GALLANT GLORY (USA) BHB 60f **RR 51f** 759[14]

3 b c Dynaformer (USA) 12f **(82)** - Triomphe (CHI) (Nobloys (FR))
Form - 000
Record 1999 - 1st:0 2nd:0 3rd:0 Ran:3
Pre1999 - 1st:0 2nd:0 3rd:0 Ran:2
1999 Turf 0-3: (8f, 10f, 12f) (g-s, g-f, frm)
Well made, fair colt. Turf high 51.
**J H M Gosden [0-5] Sheikh Mohammed.*

GALLEON BEACH RR 92f 5139[2]

2 b c Shirley Heights 12.1f **(76)** - Music in My Life (IRE) (Law Society (USA)) 9.9f **(70)**
Form - 3132
Record 1999 - 1st:1 2nd:1 3rd:2 Ran:4
Win Prizemoney £3,468 *Total Prizemoney* £9,235
Wins * 1999 Spt Hamilt (G-F) 8.3f 78 <
1999 Turf 1-4: (7f, 8f 1-2, 10f) (g-s, gd, frm 1-2)
Useful colt. Turf high 92 (began Aug) - 2nd of 10 to Monte Carlo (30 Oct Newmarket 10f gd RF 5139). A stayer, he finished second in a ten-furlong listed race on his final start.
**J W Hills [1-4] Christopher Wright.*

GALLERY GOD (FR) BHB 84f **RR 82f** 4759[6]

3 ch c In The Wings 11.2f **(77)** - El Fabulous (FR) (Fabulous Dancer (USA)) 9.4f **(70)**
Form - 0337316
Record 1999 - 1st:1 2nd:0 3rd:3 Ran:7
Pre1999 - 1st:0 2nd:0 3rd:0 Ran:2
Win Prizemoney £5,181 *Total Prizemoney* £7,520
Wins * 1999 Spt Newcas (G-F) 12.4f 82 <
1999 Turf 1-7: (10f 5, 12f 1-2) (sft, gd 2, g-f 2, frm 1-2)
Scopey, decent colt, effective 10 to 12f, best at 10f, acts on sft to frm. Turf high 82 - 1st of 8 giving 3lb to Little Italy (19 Spt Newcastle RF 4425). **G Wragg [1-9] Takashi Watanabe.*

GAMBADER (USA) RR 75f 5000[5]

2 b f Holy Bull (USA) - Now Dance (USA) (Sovereign Dancer (USA)) 11.2f **(68)**
Form - 5
Record 1999 - 1st:0 2nd:0 3rd:0 Ran:1
1999 Turf 0-1: (8f) (gd)
Currently above-average filly.
**J H M Gosden [0-1] Sheikh Mohammed.*

GAME JOHN BHB 25f **RR 3f** 2450[7]

3 b g Sirgame - Raffles Virginia (Whistling Deer) 16.4f **(48)**
Form - 0007
Record 1999 - 1st:0 2nd:0 3rd:0 Ran:4
1999 Turf 0-4: (7f, 8f 2, 10f) (gd 2, frm 2)
Scopey, very poor gelding. Turf high 22. **J Pearce [0-4] G H Tufts.*

GAMEKEEPER BHB 65f **RR 62f** 3690[8]

3 ch c Mujtahid (USA) 7.4f **(69)** - High Tern (High Line) 10.3f **(70)**
Form - 748
Record 1999 - 1st:0 2nd:0 3rd:0 Ran:3
Pre1999 - 1st:0 2nd:0 3rd:0 Ran:1
Win Prizemoney £0 *Total Prizemoney* £542
1999 Turf 0-3: (8f, 12f 2) (gd 2, g-f)
Workmanlike, average colt. Turf high 62.
**C E Brittain [0-4] Sheikh Mohammed Obaid Al Maktoum.*

GAME TUFTY BHB 63f55a **RR 63f 55a** 5197[7]

3 b g Sirgame - Melancolia (Legend of France (USA)) 9.5f **(61)**
Form - 054270030317
Record 1999 - 1st:1 2nd:1 3rd:2 Ran:12
Pre1999 - 1st:0 2nd:0 3rd:1 Ran:4
Win Prizemoney £1,913 *Total Prizemoney* £4,771
Wins * 1999 Oct Windso (SFT) S 10f 51 <
1999 Turf 1-11: (7f, 8f 2, 10f 1-6, 11f 2) (g-s, gd 1-5, g-f 4, hrd) 1999 AW 0-1: (12f) (Fibr)
Workmanlike, average gelding, effective 8 to 10f, acts on g-s to g-f, likes left handed tracks, likes tight tracks. Turf high 64. Inconsistent. **J Pearce [1-16] G H Tufts.*

GARBO BHB 40f40a **RR 30f 40a** 4711[12]

4 b f Superlative 8.8f **(57)** - Valence (BEL) (Sarajevo (FR)) 6f **(48)**
Form - 00
Record 1999 - 1st:0 2nd:0 3rd:0 Ran:2
Pre1999 - 1st:1 2nd:0 3rd:0 Ran:7
Win Prizemoney £2,788 *Total Prizemoney* £2,788
Wins 1998 Jly Bright (GD) H 6f 47 48 <
1999 Turf 0-2: (7f, 8f) (gd, frm)
Scopey, very moderate filly, effective 6f, acts on gd. Turf high 30 (began Spt).
**D W P Arbuthnot [0-2] Nimrod Company (from R Hannon [1-7] Spt 1998).*

GARGOYLE GIRL BHB 58f **RR 63f** 4378[20]

2 b f Be My Chief (USA) 10.2f **(62)** - May Hills Legacy (IRE) (Be My Guest (USA)) 9.3f **(67)**
Form - 0563000
Record 1999 - 1st:0 2nd:0 3rd:1 Ran:7
Win Prizemoney £0 *Total Prizemoney* £530
1999 Turf 0-7: (6f 4, 7f 2, 8f) (g-s, gd 4, g-f, frm)
Average filly, effective 6f, acts on gd. Turf high 63 - 3rd of 7 getting 5lb from Howard's Lad (17 Jly Ayr 6f gd RF 2893).
**J S Goldie [0-7] J S Morrison.*

GARNOCK VALLEY BHB 52f62a **RR 49f 62a** 5032[1]

9 b g Dowsing (USA) 7f **(61)** - Sunley Sinner (Try My Best (USA)) 7.6f **(67)**
Form - 34342112010007821
Record 1999 - 1st:4 2nd:3 3rd:0 Ran:14
Pre1999 - 1st:7 2nd:6 3rd:10 Ran:72
Win Prizemoney £37,360 *Total Prizemoney* £54,451
Wins * 1999 Oct Newbur (SFT) H 5.2f 46 49
*** 1999** *Apr Southw (STD) 7f 62*
*** 1999** *Feb Lingfi (STD) C 7f 60*
*** 1999** *Feb Wolver (STD) C 6f 60*
* 1998 Apr Mussel (G-S) H 5f 60 64
* 1996 Oct Haydoc (SFT) H 6f 74 88 <
* 1996 Jun Ayr (G-F) H 5f 71 74
* 1996 May Mussel (G-S) H 5f 65 70
* 1996 Apr Mussel (GD) 5f 62
1999 Turf 1-7: (5f 1-1, 6f 2, 7f 3, 8f) (sft, g-s 1-1, gd, g-f 2, frm 2) 1999 AW 3-7: (6f 1-3, 7f 2-3, 8f) (Equi 1-2, Fibr 2-5)
Average gelding, effective 5 to 7f, best at 7f, acts on gd - acts on AW, best on Fibr, has worn blinkers (extremely effectively), likes left handed tracks, and excels at Wolverhampton. Turf high 49. AW high 62 - 1st of 15 giving 2lb to Mawkab (6 Apr Southwell RF 0603) - also 1st of 9 getting 6lb from Mike's Double (10 Feb Wolverhampton RF 0262). **J Berry [11-86] Robert Aird.*

GAROTA DO LEBLON (USA) BHB 89f **RR 81f** 5137[1]

2 b f Thunder Gulch (USA) - Smart Angle (USA) (Quadrangle) 5f **(81)**
Form - 251
Record 1999 - 1st:1 2nd:1 3rd:0 Ran:3
Win Prizemoney £4,477 *Total Prizemoney* £6,157
Wins * 1999 Oct Newmar (SFT) 7f 81 <
1999 Turf 1-3: (6f 2, 7f 1-1) (gd 1-2, g-f)
Currently decent filly. Turf high 81 (began Aug) - 1st of 16 from Papabile (30 Oct Newmarket RF 5137).
**J Noseda [1-3] Goncalo Borges Torrealba.*

GARTH POOL (IRE) BHB 71f **RR 72f** 4809[14]

2 b c Sri Pekan (USA) - Millionetta (IRE) (Danehill (USA)) 10f **(72)**
Form - 455335250
Record 1999 - 1st:0 2nd:1 3rd:2 Ran:9

Win Prizemoney £0 *Total Prizemoney* £2,610
1999 Turf 0-9: (5f 5, 6f 4) (sft, gd 4, g-f, frm 3)
Above-average colt, effective 5f, acts on g-f to frm, has worn blinkers. Turf high 72. Consistent. **J Berry [0-9] Lord Mostyn.*

GATECRASHER BHB 81f **RR 83f** 1701[5]
4 b g Suave Dancer (USA) 10.7f **(68)** - Benazir (High Top) 10.2f **(67)**
Form - 7405
Record 1999 - 1st:0 2nd:0 3rd:0 Ran:4
Pre1999 - 1st:1 2nd:1 3rd:0 Ran:3
Win Prizemoney £3,826 *Total Prizemoney* £6,428
Wins * 1998 May Kempto (GD) 8f 77 <
1999 Turf 0-4: (10f 2, 11f, 12f) (gd 3, frm)
Workmanlike, decent gelding, effective 8 to 11f, best at 11f, acted on gd to frm. Turf high 83 - 4th of 20 giving 30lb to Broughtons Error (30 Apr Newmarket 10f frm RF 0943). (DEAD)
**J R Fanshawe [1-7] J M Greetham.*

GATEMAN BHB 100f **RR 93f** 4486[1]
2 b c Owington - Scandalette (Niniski (USA)) 10.6f **(65)**
Form - 5415311
Record 1999 - 1st:3 2nd:0 3rd:1 Ran:7
Win Prizemoney £12,948 *Total Prizemoney* £14,188
Wins * **1999** Spt Cheste (HVY) 7.6f 93 <
* **1999** Aug Epsom (GD) 7f 93 <
* **1999** Jly Haydoc (G-S) 6f 85
1999 Turf 3-7: (5f, 6f 1-3, 7f 1-2, 8f 1-1) (g-s 1-1, gd, g-f 2-4, frm)
Useful colt, effective 6 to 8f, acts on g-s to g-f, best on g-f. Turf high 93 - 1st of 4 giving 3lb to Water Hunter (22 Spt Chester RF 4486) - also 1st of 3 from Kingsdon (30 Aug Epsom RF 4016). Showed battling qualities to win a Haydock auction event in July on easy ground, and later added a three-runner affair at Epsom by two short heads, and a 15-length victory at Chester.
**B J Meehan [3-7] Kennet Valley Thoroughbreds IV.*

GATHERING CLOUD (IRE) BHB 41f **RR 45f** 4586[8]
3 b f Mukaddamah (USA) 7.6f **(74)** - Adocentyn (USA) (Upper Nile (USA)) 8.5f **(75)**
Form - 0588
Record 1999 - 1st:0 2nd:0 3rd:0 Ran:3
Pre1999 - 1st:0 2nd:0 3rd:0 Ran:1
1999 Turf 0-3: (7f, 8f 2) (gd, frm 2)
Light-framed, moderate filly. Turf high 50 (began Jly).
**C G Cox [0-2] Mrs Jane Joynson (from M J Heaton-Ellis [0-2] Jly 1999).*

GAUNTLET (IRE) BHB 82f **RR 81f** 665[4]
3 ch c Suave Dancer (USA) 10.7f **(68)** - Be My Everything (IRE) (Be My Guest (USA)) 9.3f **(67)**
Form - 24
Record 1999 - 1st:0 2nd:1 3rd:0 Ran:2
Pre1999 - 1st:0 2nd:1 3rd:1 Ran:3
Win Prizemoney £0 *Total Prizemoney* £3,643
1999 Turf 0-2: (7f 2) (g-s, g-f)
Leggy, decent colt. Turf high 75. **J Noseda [0-5] M Olden.*

GAVEL (IRE) BHB 66f **RR 70f** 4358[7]
2 b g Rhoman Rule (USA) 15.1f **(64)** - Fall of The Hammer (IRE) (Auction Ring (USA)) 8.6f **(65)**
Form - 0637
Record 1999 - 1st:0 2nd:0 3rd:1 Ran:4
Win Prizemoney £0 *Total Prizemoney* £285
1999 Turf 0-4: (5f, 6f, 8f 2) (g-s, gd, g-f, frm)
Above-average gelding. Turf high 65.
**M H Tompkins [0-4] Flint Fairyhouse Partnership.*

GAY BREEZE BHB 76f **RR 78f** 4911[5]
6 b g Dominion 8.9f **(65)** - Judy's Dowry (Dragonara Palace (USA)) 6.1f **(55)**
Form - 63038522445
Record 1999 - 1st:0 2nd:2 3rd:2 Ran:11
Pre1999 - 1st:5 2nd:5 3rd:1 Ran:19
Win Prizemoney £18,909 *Total Prizemoney* £35,554
Wins 1998 Jun Haydoc (GD) H 5f 61 70+ <
1998 May Doncas (G-F) H 6f 56 60
1998 Apr Nottin (SFT) H 6.1f 49 56
1997 Spt Yarmou (FRM) H 6f 43 48
1997 Aug Leices (GD) H 5f 40 42
1999 Turf 0-11: (5f 10, 6f) (g-s, gd 6, g-f, frm 2, hrd)
Above-average gelding, effective 5f, acts on g-s to frm, best on g-f. Turf high 78 - 2nd of 14 giving 1lb to Sharoura (14 Spt Yarmouth 5f g-f RF 4292). Consistent.
**D Nicholls [0-6] J M Flynn (from P S Felgate [5-24] May 1999).*

GAY LASS (IRE) BHB 68f **RR 76f** 4950[7]
2 ch f Mujtahid (USA) 7.4f **(69)** - Maracuja (USA) (Riverman (USA)) 9.1f **(76)**
Form - 4347
Record 1999 - 1st:0 2nd:0 3rd:1 Ran:4
Win Prizemoney £0 *Total Prizemoney* £349
1999 Turf 0-4: (7f 3, 8f) (gd, g-f 3)
Above-average filly. Turf high 76.
**J R Fanshawe [0-4] Gay Lass Partnership.*

GDANSK (IRE) BHB 71f **RR 62f** 5163[5]
2 b c Pips Pride 6.7f **(70)** - Merry Twinkle (Martinmas) 7.6f **(59)**
Form - 055
Record 1999 - 1st:0 2nd:0 3rd:0 Ran:3
1999 Turf 0-3: (6f 2, 7f) (g-s 2, frm)
Currently average colt. Turf high 62 (began Spt).
**J Berry [0-3] Chris & Antonia Deuters.*

GEE BEE BOY BHB 60f47a **RR 62f 47a** 386[6]
5 ch g Beveled (USA) 6.9f **(64)** - Blue and White (Busted) 10.2f **(61)**
Form - 8406
Record 1999 - 1st:0 2nd:0 3rd:0 Ran:4
Pre1999 - 1st:1 2nd:3 3rd:1 Ran:16
Win Prizemoney £2,448 *Total Prizemoney* £5,537
Wins 1997 Jun Redcar (GD) 11f 68 <
1999 AW 0-4: (10f, 12f 2, 13f) (Equi 3, Fibr)
Average gelding, effective 11 to 12f, best at 12f, acts on g-s to frm, best on g-f. AW high 46.
**G M McCourt [0-7] Daltagh Construction Ltd (from A P Jarvis [1-15] Aug 1998).*

GEEFORCE (IRE) BHB 41f44a **RR 31f 44a** 2159[1]
3 ch f Soviet Lad (USA) 9.4f **(63)** - Great Pleasure (GER) (Star Appeal) 9.6f **(65)**
Form - 801
Record 1999 - 1st:1 2nd:0 3rd:0 Ran:3
Pre1999 - 1st:0 2nd:0 3rd:0 Ran:5
Win Prizemoney £2,155 *Total Prizemoney* £2,155
Wins * **1999** *Jun Wolver (STD) H 9.4f 41 45* <
1999 Turf 0-1: (10f) (gd) 1999 AW 1-2: (7f, 9f 1-1) (Fibr 1-2)
Moderate filly, effective 9f, - acts on Fibr. AW high 45 - 1st of 7 getting 24lb from Heathyards Jake (19 Jun Wolverhampton RF 2159). Inconsistent. She had never been placed in seven previous starts before winning a maiden handicap on the Wolverhampton Fibresand in June. It was a very poor race.
**M Brittain [1-3] Robert Cook (from Miss J F Craze [0-1] Oct 1998).*

GEEGEE EMMARR BHB 35f35a **RR 24f 35a** 3768[10]
6 b m Rakaposhi King 9.3f **(55)** - Fair Sara (McIndoe) 13.8f **(32)**
Form - 04005080
Record 1999 - 1st:0 2nd:0 3rd:0 Ran:8
Pre1999 - 1st:0 2nd:0 3rd:1 Ran:5
Win Prizemoney £0 *Total Prizemoney* £1,240
1999 Turf 0-6: (6f, 7f 2, 8f, 10f 2) (gd, g-f 3, frm 2) 1999 AW 0-2: (7f, 8f) (Fibr 2)
Little account mare. Turf high 34. AW high 17.
**S Gollings [0-13] Mrs Stella Barclay.*

GEMINI GUEST (IRE) BHB 80f **RR 74f** 4685[17]
3 ch c Waajib 8.9f **(67)** - Aldhabyih (General Assembly (USA)) 10f **(68)**
Form - 31300
Record 1999 - 1st:1 2nd:0 3rd:2 Ran:5
Win Prizemoney £3,496 *Total Prizemoney* £5,180
Wins * **1999** May Thirsk (G-F) 7f 74 <
1999 Turf 1-5: (7f 1-3, 8f 2) (gd, g-f 1-4)
Strong, above-average colt. Turf high 81 (1st run) - 3rd of 13 to Date (15 Apr Newmarket 7f g-f RF 0703) - also 1st of 9 from My Pleasure (1 May Thirsk RF 0965). Unraced at two, he made hard work of getting off the mark in a Thirsk maiden on his second start but has been well beaten since. **G G Margarson [1-5] John Guest.*

GEM OF WISDOM BHB 49f55a **RR 49f 55a** 4543^{15}
2 gr c Factual (USA) - Indian Crystal **(45f 42a)** (Petong) 6.6f **(58)**
Form - 55342115360
Record 1999 - 1st:2 2nd:1 3rd:2 Ran:11
Win Prizemoney £3,690 *Total Prizemoney* £4,930
Wins *** 1999** *Jly Southw (STD) S 5f 55* <
*** 1999** *Jun Southw (STD) S 5f 55* <
1999 Turf 0-6: (5f 6) (gd, g-f 2, frm 3) 1999 AW 2-5: (5f 2-4, 6f) (Fibr 2-5)
Fair colt, effective 5f, - acts on Fibr, mostly wears blinkers (very effectively). Turf high 63. AW high 55 - 1st of 8 from Sergeant Slipper (28 Jun Southwell RF 2378) - also 1st of 6 giving 5lb to Mosaic Times (8 Jly Southwell RF 2652). Consistent. Won a couple of sellers on the Southwell Fibresand during the summer, his early toe proving a real asset over the straight five there.
**J Berry [2-11] Mrs B A Matthews.*

GENERAL ACADEMY (IRE) BHB 50f **RR 41f** 4105^{F}
6 g Royal Academy (USA) 7.8f **(77)** - Hastening (Shirley Heights) 10.3f **(74)**
Form - 860F
Record 1999 - 1st:0 2nd:0 3rd:0 Ran:4
Pre1999 - 1st:0 2nd:0 3rd:1 Ran:12
Win Prizemoney £0 *Total Prizemoney* £1,312
1999 Turf 0-4: (7f 2, 8f, 10f) (g-f, frm 3)
Above-average gelding, has worn blinkers. Turf high 41. Becoming disappointing.
**M W Easterby [0-4] M W Easterby (from P A Kelleway [0-11] Jun 1997).*

GENERAL ASSEMBLY (IRE) BHB 59f **RR 74df** 695^{11}
7 b g Pharly (FR) 11.5f **(64)** - Hastening (Shirley Heights) 10.3f **(74)**
Form - 770
Record 1999 - 1st:0 2nd:0 3rd:0 Ran:3
Pre1999 - 1st:1 2nd:1 3rd:1 Ran:14
Win Prizemoney £4,055 *Total Prizemoney* £7,225
Wins 1995 Spt Cheste (G-S) 13.4f 82+ <
1999 Turf 0-1: (12f) (gd) 1999 AW 0-2: (16f 2) (Fibr 2)
Above-average gelding, effective 16 to 19f, acts on gd to g-f, has worn blinkers. AW high 60. Becoming disappointing.
**G G Margarson [0-19] The Craftsmen (from H R A Cecil [1-8] Jun 1997).*

GENERAL EQUATION BHB 39f38a **RR 18f 38a** 154^{6}
6 b g Governor General 6.8f **(45)** - Logarithm (King of Spain) 7.8f **(52)**
Form - 4006
Record 1999 - 1st:0 2nd:0 3rd:0 Ran:3
Pre1999 - 1st:2 2nd:0 3rd:5 Ran:32
Win Prizemoney £5,033 *Total Prizemoney* £7,198
Wins *** 1998** *Jan Wolver (STD) H 5f 33 44*
*** 1996** *Mar Southw (STD) S 5f 67* <
1999 AW 0-3: (5f 3) (Fibr 3)
Moderate gelding, effective 5f, - acts on Fibr, often wears blinkers (effectively), likes left handed tracks, likes tight tracks. AW high 49. **J Balding [2-35] Make Our Day.*

GENERAL KLAIRE BHB 49f75a **RR 48f 75a** 4604^{1}
4 b br f Presidium 7.5f **(56)** - Klairover (Smackover) 6f **(52)**
Form - 2258206370302521
Record 1999 - 1st:1 2nd:4 3rd:2 Ran:15
Pre1999 - 1st:1 2nd:1 3rd:0 Ran:14
Win Prizemoney £5,245 *Total Prizemoney* £10,314
Wins *** 1999** *Spt Southw (STD) H 7f 70 76* <
*** 1998** *Jly Wolver (STD) 6f 70*
1999 Turf 0-7: (6f 5, 7f 2) (g-s, gd 3, g-f 2, frm) 1999 AW 1-8: (6f 5, 7f 1-3) (Fibr 1-8)
Scopey, above-average filly, effective 6 to 7f, best at 6f, - acts on Fibr, prefers left handed tracks, prefers tight tracks, excels at Southwell, likes Wolverhampton. Turf high 50. AW high 76 - 1st of 16 giving 8lb to Rouge (28 Spt Southwell RF 4604). Inconsistent. She is a decent sort in handicaps on Fibresand, though she does not win that often. Probably better over seven furlongs than six.
**B A McMahon [2-29] Tommy Staunton.*

GENERIC (IRE) **RR 82f** 5021^{3}
2 b c Fairy King (USA) 7.7f **(75)** - Wannabe (Shirley Heights) 10.3f **(74)**
Form - 63
Record 1999 - 1st:0 2nd:0 3rd:1 Ran:2
Win Prizemoney £0 *Total Prizemoney* £592
1999 Turf 0-2: (6f, 7f) (g-s, gd)
Currently decent colt. Turf high 82 (began Oct) - 3rd of 22 giving 5lb to Fame At Last (22 Oct Doncaster 7f gd RF 5021).
**A G Foster [0-1] M Tabor (from P W Chapple-Hyam [0-1] Oct 1999).*

GENEROSITY BHB 104f **RR 101f** 5132^{4}
4 ch c Generous (IRE) 11.5f **(82)** - Pageantry (Welsh Pageant) 10f **(65)**
Form - 2503254104
Record 1999 - 1st:1 2nd:2 3rd:1 Ran:10
Pre1999 - 1st:4 2nd:1 3rd:2 Ran:10
Win Prizemoney £39,940 *Total Prizemoney* £80,696
Wins *** 1999** Spt Haydoc (SFT) 14f 100+
*** 1998** Oct San Si (HVY) L 15f 101 <
*** 1998** Aug Goodwo (GD) H 14f 86 92
*** 1998** May Sandow (G-S) H 11.4f 78 85
*** 1997** Spt Hamilt (GD) 8.3f 69
1999 Turf 1-10: (14f 1-2, 16f 4, 17f, 19f 2, 22f) (gd 1-3, g-f 4, frm 3)
Unfurnished, very useful colt, effective 14 to 19f, acts on hvy to frm, best on g-f, prefers left handed tracks, excels at York and Chester. Turf high 106 - 5th of 8 getting 3lb from Celeric (17 Aug York 16f g-f RF 3693) - also 1st of 5 giving 3lb to Adnaan (24 Spt Haydock RF 4523). Consistent. A progressive stayer at three, he ran a fine race on his reappearance, finishing runner-up under a welter burden in the Chester Cup, and ran respectably in useful staying company afterwards before regaining winning form in a Haydock conditions event in September. He enjoys coming off a strong pace and appreciates a bit of cut in the ground.
**P F I Cole [5-20] H R H Prince Fahd Salman.*

GENEROUS DIANA BHB 70f **RR 67f** 4789^{1}
3 ch f Generous (IRE) 11.5f **(82)** - Lypharitissima (FR) (Lightning (FR)) 7.9f **(74)**
Form - 4221
Record 1999 - 1st:1 2nd:2 3rd:0 Ran:4
Win Prizemoney £3,708 *Total Prizemoney* £6,035
Wins *** 1999** Oct Lingfi (SFT) 9f 63 <
1999 Turf 1-4: (7f 3, 9f 1-1) (g-s 1-1, g-f, frm 2)
Neat, average filly. Turf high 67 (began Jly) - 2nd of 4 to Kafhanee (30 Aug Epsom 7f g-f RF 4017) - also 1st of 10 from Bitter Sweet (8 Oct Lingfield RF 4789). **K Mahdi [1-4] Greenfield Stud.*

GENEROUS LIBRA BHB 103f **RR 102f** 5131^{6}
5 b g Generous (IRE) 11.5f **(82)** - Come on Rosi (Valiyar) 8.5f **(73)**
Form - 2333456
Record 1999 - 1st:0 2nd:1 3rd:3 Ran:7
Pre1999 - 1st:4 2nd:4 3rd:3 Ran:20
Win Prizemoney £27,467 *Total Prizemoney* £51,916
Wins * 1998 Oct Newmar (SFT) L 8f 104 <
* 1998 Spt Epsom (GD) H 10.1f 90 97+
* 1998 Aug Epsom (G-F) 10.1f 99+
1997 Jun Beverl (G-F) 7.5f 88+
1999 Turf 0-7: (8f 2, 9f 2, 10f 3) (g-s, gd 2, g-f 2, frm 2)
Very useful gelding, effective 8 to 10f, best at 8f, acts on g-s to frm, prefers left handed tracks, likes tight tracks, excels at Epsom and Doncaster. Turf high 109 - 3rd of 4 giving 3lb to Happy Change (30 Aug Epsom 10f g-f RF 4015). Consistent. Able but exasperating. **J L Dunlop [3-18] Wafic Said (from D R Loder [1-9] Oct 1997).*

GENEROUS PRESENT BHB 30f **RR 28f** 3659^{11}
6 ch g Cadeaux Genereux 7.9f **(76)** - Dance Move (Shareef Dancer (USA)) 9.9f **(73)**
Form - 7600
Record 1999 - 1st:0 2nd:0 3rd:0 Ran:4
Pre1999 - 1st:2 2nd:0 3rd:1 Ran:19
Win Prizemoney £7,084 *Total Prizemoney* £7,523
Wins * 1996 Jly Hamilt (G-F) H 8.3f 50 59 <
* 1996 Jun Carlis (FRM) H 8f 46 51
1999 Turf 0-4: (6f, 7f 2, 8f) (gd, g-f 2, frm)
Little account gelding, has worn blinkers. Turf high 28. Inconsistent. **J W Payne [2-24] Mrs J W Payne.*

GENEROUS ROSI BHB 107f **RR 105f** 5131^{7}
4 b c Generous (IRE) 11.5f **(82)** - Come on Rosi (Valiyar) 8.5f **(73)**
Form - 11284577
Record 1999 - 1st:2 2nd:1 3rd:0 Ran:8
Pre1999 - 1st:1 2nd:7 3rd:0 Ran:9

Win Prizemoney £38,088 *Total Prizemoney* £81,321
Wins * **1999** Apr Sandow (SFT) G3 10f 111 <
* **1999** Apr Kempto (G-F) L 10f 109
* 1998 Jly Newmar (G-F) 10f 90
1999 Turf 2-8: (9f, 10f 2-6, 12f) (sft, g-s 1-1, gd 2, g-f 1-3, frm)
Pattern-class colt, effective 10 to 12f, best at 10f, acts on g-s to frm, has worn blinkers, prefers right handed tracks, prefers tight tracks. Turf high 113 - 2nd of 6 giving 3lb to Chester House (1 Jun Sandown 10f frm RF 1658) - also 1st of 9 from Evening World (24 Apr Sandown RF 0844). Consistent. He had a hard race when winning a Group 3 at Sandown in April and trod water thereafter. From a quirky family, he is best watched until returning to form.
**J L Dunlop [3-16] Wafic Said (from D R Loder [0-1] Oct 1997).*

GENEROUS TERMS BHB 100f **RR 103f** 2272[3]

4 ch c Generous (IRE) 11.5f **(82)** - Time Charter (Saritamer (USA)) 9.5f **(63)**
Form - 403
Record 1999 - 1st:0 2nd:0 3rd:1 Ran:3
Pre1999 - 1st:2 2nd:1 3rd:0 Ran:4
Win Prizemoney £9,296 *Total Prizemoney* £15,698
Wins * 1998 Jun Salisb (G-F) 14.1f 104 <
* 1998 Jun Leices (GD) 11.8f 90
1999 Turf 0-3: (13f, 14f, 16f) (gd, frm 2)
Workmanlike, very useful colt, effective 14f, acts on gd to g-f. Turf high 103. Lightly raced, he looked a promising sort in 1998 but failed to fire last term. He ought to stay two miles, but is one to treat with caution at present.
**H Candy [2-7] H R H Prince Fahd Salman.*

GENEROUS WAYS BHB 60f **RR 58f** 4917[31]

4 ch g Generous (IRE) 11.5f **(82)** - Clara Bow (USA) (Coastal (USA)) 11.5f **(72)**
Form - 00357103550
Record 1999 - 1st:1 2nd:0 3rd:2 Ran:11
Pre1999 - 1st:1 2nd:0 3rd:2 Ran:7
Win Prizemoney £9,008 *Total Prizemoney* £12,137
Wins * **1999** Jun Ascot (G-F) H 16.2f 57 62
1998 Aug Redcar (G-F) H 14.1f 65 70 <
1999 Turf 1-11: (12f 2, 13f, 14f 2, 15f, 16f 1-4, 17f) (g-s, gd 3, g-f 1-5, frm 2)
Workmanlike, fair gelding, effective 14 to 16f, best at 16f, acts on gd to g-f, best on g-f, has worn blinkers, likes right handed tracks. Turf high 62 - 3rd of 16 getting 2lb from Danegold (23 Jly Ascot 16f gd RF 3048) - also 1st of 12 getting 1lb from Height of Fantasy (19 Jun Ascot RF 2139). Rather inconsistent, but won well at Ascot in June from a handy mark. Best on fast ground.
**E J Alston [1-11] Honest Traders (from E A L Dunlop [1-7] Oct 1998).*

GENGHIS KHAN (IRE) RR 99f 4778a[14]

3 b c Sadler's Wells (USA) 11.3f **(87)** - Doff the Derby (USA) (Master Derby (USA)) 9.5f **(69)**
Form - 4101050
1999 Turf 2-7: (10f, 12f 2-4, 14f 2) (sft, g-s 1-2, gd 1-3, g-f)
Very useful colt, effective 12f, acts on g-s to gd. Turf high 108 - 1st of 7 from Larboreus (4 Jun Curragh RF 1836a) - also 1st of 5 giving 5lb to Maid Of Killeen (8 Aug Leopardstown RF 3526a). A winner twice last season, he is a resolute galloper and stays well, but was well beaten in both the Ebor and Irish St Leger. Was sold for 70,000gns in October to join Luke Comer.
**A P O'Brien in IRE [2-7] Tabor/Mrs John Magnier.*

GENIUS (IRE) BHB 33f60a **RR 30f 60a** 2057[18]

4 b g Lycius (USA) 8.8f **(71)** - Once in My Life (IRE) (Lomond (USA)) 8.8f **(65)**
Form - 73001608000
Record 1999 - 1st:1 2nd:0 3rd:0 Ran:9
Pre1999 - 1st:2 2nd:1 3rd:2 Ran:24
Win Prizemoney £7,956 *Total Prizemoney* £10,172
Wins 1999 *Feb Lingfi (STD) H 8f* 64 68
1998 *Feb Lingfi (SLW) H 8f* 69 73 <
1998 *Feb Lingfi (SLW) H 8f* 64 66
1999 Turf 0-3: (7f, 8f 2) (gd, g-f, hrd) 1999 AW 1-6: (7f, 8f 1-4, 10f) (Equi 1-4, Fibr 2)
Well made, very moderate gelding, effective 8f, - acts on Equi, has worn blinkers, likes left handed tracks, likes tight tracks. Turf high 30. AW high 68 - 1st of 11 giving 8lb to Mawkab (25 Feb Lingfield RF 0360). Becoming disappointing.
**D W Chapman [0-6] T S Redman (from S Dow [3-24] Feb 1999).*

GENSCHER BHB 55f **RR 57f** 4980[8]

3 b g Cadeaux Genereux 7.9f **(76)** -Marienbad(FR)(Darshaan) 9.9f **(84)**
Form - 341468
Record 1999 - 1st:1 2nd:0 3rd:1 Ran:6
Pre1999 - 1st:0 2nd:0 3rd:0 Ran:2
Win Prizemoney £4,005 *Total Prizemoney* £5,249
Wins * **1999** Spt Hamilt (G-F) H 12.1f 50 53 <
1999 Turf 1-6: (8f, 9f, 10f, 12f 1-3) (gd 3, g-f, frm 1-2)
Scopey, fair gelding, effective 12f, acts on frm. Turf high 57 (began Jly) - 4th of 13 getting 13lb from Freedom Quest (13 Spt Musselburgh 12f frm RF 4279) - also 1st of 17 getting 4lb from Hasta la Vista (6 Spt Hamilton RF 4166). Inconsistent.
**R Allan [1-6] Robert Miller-Bakewell (from M A Jarvis [0-2] Nov 1998).*

GENTLE ANNE BHB 48f **RR 60f** 5002[6]

2 b f Faustus (USA) 9.1f **(54)** - Gentle Stream (Sandy Creek) 8.9f **(59)**
Form - 4857666
Record 1999 - 1st:0 2nd:0 3rd:0 Ran:7
Win Prizemoney £0 *Total Prizemoney* £260
1999 Turf 0-7: (6f, 7f 4, 8f, 9f) (gd, g-f, frm 5)
Average filly, effective 7f, acts on frm. Turf high 60 (began Jly).
**Ronald Thompson [0-7] B Bruce.*

GENTLE DAME BHB 72f **RR 79f** 3662[9]

3 ch f Kris 10f **(75)** - Cascassi (USA) (Nijinsky (CAN)) 10.3f **(77)**
Form - 653310
Record 1999 - 1st:1 2nd:0 3rd:2 Ran:6
Win Prizemoney £3,647 *Total Prizemoney* £4,805
Wins * **1999** Aug Ripon (G-F) 10f 79 <
1999 Turf 1-6: (7f, 8f, 10f 1-3, 12f) (gd 2, g-f, frm 1-3)
Workmanlike, above-average filly, effective 10f, acts on frm. Turf high 79 - 1st of 9 from Galette (2 Aug Ripon RF 3300).
**B W Hills [1-6] Maktoum Al Maktoum.*

GENTLEMAN VENTURE BHB 76f **RR 81f** 4823[10]

3 b c Polar Falcon (USA) 9f **(74)** -Our Shirley(Shirley Heights)10.3f **(74)**
Form - 317348000
Record 1999 - 1st:1 2nd:0 3rd:2 Ran:9
Win Prizemoney £3,015 *Total Prizemoney* £8,070
Wins * **1999** May Redcar (SFT) 10f 73 <
1999 Turf 1-9: (8f, 10f 1-4, 11f, 12f 3) (sft, g-s 1-1, gd 3, g-f 3, frm)
Workmanlike, decent colt, effective 10 to 12f, best at 12f, acts on g-s to frm, best on g-f. Turf high 82 - 3rd of 13 getting 18lb from Zindabad (7 Jly Newmarket 10f frm RF 2630) - also 1st of 7 giving 5lb to Carefree Cheetah (10 May Redcar RF 1127). Unraced at two, he hung badly when getting off the mark at Redcar in May and did the same thing when last at Haydock next time. He suffered traffic problems when running a blinder to finish third in a competitive handicap at the July meeting, and ran well when stepped up to a mile and a half at Goodwood. Disappointing since however, he has joined John Akehurst. **S P C Woods [1-9] Dr Frank Chao.*

GENUINE JOHN (IRE) BHB 40f40a **RR 36f 40a** 5153[11]

6 b g High Estate 10.5f **(66)** - Fiscal Folly (USA) (Foolish Pleasure (USA)) 8.9f **(72)**
Form - 704107580030
Record 1999 - 1st:1 2nd:0 3rd:1 Ran:12
Pre1999 - 1st:4 2nd:6 3rd:11 Ran:56
Win Prizemoney £14,733 *Total Prizemoney* £23,229
Wins * **1999** Apr Beverl (G-F) S 8.5f 52
* 1998 Jly Ripon (G-F) S 8f 59
* 1998 May Hamilt (GD) H 8.3f 40 50
* 1998 May Mussel (GD) H 8f 40 48
* 1997 *Mar Southw (STD) H 7f* 65 64 <
1999 Turf 1-10: (8f 1-7, 9f 2, 10f) (gd 5, g-f 2, frm 1-3) 1999 AW 0-2: (8f 2) (Fibr 2)
Very moderate gelding, effective 8f, acts on gd to frm, best on g-f, has worn blinkers, prefers right handed tracks, favours tight tracks, excels at Beverley. Turf high 52 - 1st of 17 from Wadi (14 Apr Beverley RF 0684). AW high 31.
**J Parkes [5-57] Mrs G M Z Spink (from K Prendergast in IRE [0-13] Spt 1996).*

GEORDIE LAD BHB 30f22a **RR 4f 22a** 2819[13]

5 ch g Tina's Pet 7.4f **(56)** - Edraianthus (Windjammer (USA)) 7f **(59)**

Form - 400
Record 1999 - 1st:0 2nd:0 3rd:0 Ran:3
Pre1999 - 1st:0 2nd:0 3rd:0 Ran:14
1999 Turf 0-3: (6f, 7f, 9f) (g-f, frm 2)
Poor gelding, has worn blinkers. Turf high 38 (1st run) - 4th of 9 giving 8lb to Keys Seminar (31 May Les Landes 9f g-f RF 2089a).
**M Bradstock [0-4] Miller Place Partnership (from J A Bennett [0-15] Jan 1998).*

GEORGE (IRE) BHB 51f **RR 54f** 4914[11]
4 b g Distinctly North (USA) 7.4f **(63)** -Heather Lark (Red Alert) 7.6f **(66)**
Form - 000082500
Record 1999 - 1st:0 2nd:1 3rd:0 Ran:9
Pre1999 - 1st:1 2nd:3 3rd:0 Ran:12
Win Prizemoney £4,795 *Total Prizemoney* £7,938
Wins 1998 Jun Cork (G-S) H 6f 75 90 <
1999 Turf 0-8: (6f 4, 7f 3, 11f) (sft, g-s, gd 4, g-f, frm) 1999 AW 0-1: (7f) (Fibr)
Fair gelding, effective 5 to 6f, acts on g-s, has worn blinkers. Turf high 54. **S Gollings [0-1] Wild Racing (from B Hanbury [0-6] Oct 1999).*

GEORGETTE (USA) **RR 94f** 2186[6]
3 ch f Geiger Counter (USA) 7.8f **(85)** - Odori (USA) (The Minstrel (CAN)) 10f **(72)**
Form - 66
Record 1999 - 1st:0 2nd:0 3rd:0 Ran:2
Pre1999 - 1st:2 2nd:0 3rd:0 Ran:3
Win Prizemoney £10,100 *Total Prizemoney* £12,271
Wins * 1998 Oct Yarmou (G-S) 6f 94 <
* 1998 Oct Newmar () 6f 84
1999 Turf 0-2: (6f, 8f) (gd, frm)
Unfurnished, useful filly. Turf high 88.
**J H M Gosden [2-5] Sheikh Mohammed.*

GET A LIFE BHB 25f **RR 15f** 4040[13]
6 gr m Old Vic 12.8f **(72)** - Sandstream (Sandford Lad) 7.8f **(54)**
Form - 60P0080
Record 1999 - 1st:0 2nd:0 3rd:0 Ran:7
Pre1999 - 1st:0 2nd:2 3rd:1 Ran:19
Win Prizemoney £0 *Total Prizemoney* £2,365
1999 Turf 0-6: (7f 2, 8f 3, 10f) (gd 2, g-f 3, hrd) 1999 AW 0-1: (8f) (Fibr)
Poor mare, effective 8f, acts on gd, has worn blinkers (effectively), likes right handed tracks, likes tight tracks. Turf high 15.
**G Woodward [0-6] A Jane (from M Brittain [0-12] Feb 1999).*

GET ON GEORGE BHB 28f **RR 16f** 3614[7]
5 b g Rudimentary (USA) 8.2f **(66)** - Glint of Victory (Glint of Gold) 9.3f **(66)**
Form - 007
Record 1999 - 1st:0 2nd:0 3rd:0 Ran:3
1999 Turf 0-1: (8f) (gd) 1999 AW 0-2: (10f, 12f) (Equi 2)
Poor gelding. AW high 16 (began Jly).
**Mrs L C Jewell [0-2] Mrs Linda Jewell (from S A Brookshaw [0-5] May 1999).*

GET STUCK IN (IRE) BHB 85f **RR 85f** 4984[18]
3 b g Up and At 'em - Shoka (FR) (Kaldoun (FR)) 10.3f **(68)**
Form - 3774412651207140
Record 1999 - 1st:3 2nd:2 3rd:1 Ran:16
Pre1999 - 1st:0 2nd:7 3rd:1 Ran:11
Win Prizemoney £30,820 *Total Prizemoney* £44,457
Wins * **1999** Oct York (SFT) H 6f 80 85 <
* **1999** Aug Ripon (GD) H 6f 70 75
* **1999** Jun Hamilt (GD) 6f 68
1999 Turf 3-16: (5f 6, 6f 3-9, 8f) (sft, g-s, gd 1-4, g-f 1-7, frm 1-3)
Scopey, useful gelding, effective 5 to 6f, best at 5f, acts on g-s to g-f, best on gd, has worn blinkers, excels at York, does well at Ripon and likes Musselburgh. Turf high 85 - 1st of 23 getting 10lb from Pepperdine (9 Oct York RF 4803). Has plenty of pace, and showed progressive form last term, making all to win a valuable handicap at York in October. Arguably lucky not to be thrown out, however. **Miss L A Perratt [3-27] David Sutherland.*

GET THE POINT BHB 53f **RR 52f** 871[3]
5 b h Sadler's Wells (USA) 11.3f **(87)** - Tolmi (Great Nephew) 9.9f **(64)**
Form - 3
Record 1999 - 1st:0 2nd:0 3rd:1 Ran:1
Pre1999 - 1st:0 2nd:2 3rd:0 Ran:19
Win Prizemoney £0 *Total Prizemoney* £3,649
1999 Turf 0-1: (14f) (sft)
Fair colt. Consistent.
**S Gollings [2-11] R L Houlton (from R Hollinshead [0-18] Spt 1997).*

GEVITY BHB 72f68a **RR 73f 68a** 4865[12]
3 b f Kris 10f **(75)** - Cephira (FR) (Abdos) 10f **(77)**
Form - 31401420
Record 1999 - 1st:2 2nd:1 3rd:1 Ran:8
Pre1999 - 1st:0 2nd:0 3rd:0 Ran:1
Win Prizemoney £5,693 *Total Prizemoney* £8,053
Wins * **1999** May Bath (GD) H 8f 64 69
* **1999** *Mar Wolver (STD) 8.5f 71 <*
1999 Turf 1-5: (7f, 8f 1-3, 9f) (g-s 2, g-f 1-2, frm) 1999 AW 1-3: (8f 1-3) (Fibr 1-3)
Unfurnished, above-average filly, effective 7 to 8f, best at 8f, acts on g-f to frm - acts on Fibr, best on g-f, favours tight tracks. Turf high 73 - 2nd of 18 giving 1lb to Untold Riches (16 Jun Nottingham 8f g-f RF 2055) - also 1st of 16 giving 1lb to Khibrah (21 May Bath RF 1372). AW high 71 - 1st of 10 getting 18lb from Rouge (13 Mar Wolverhampton RF 0427).
**W Jarvis [2-8] Exors of the late Lord Howard de Walden (from Mrs J Cecil [0-1] Oct 1998).*

GHAAZI BHB 54f **RR 49f** 4946[13]
3 ch g Lahib (USA) 8f **(69)** - Shurooq (USA) (Affirmed (USA)) 9.3f **(79)**
Form - 670
Record 1999 - 1st:0 2nd:0 3rd:0 Ran:3
Pre1999 - 1st:0 2nd:0 3rd:1 Ran:4
Win Prizemoney £0 *Total Prizemoney* £572
1999 Turf 0-3: (8f, 10f 2) (gd, g-f, frm)
Scopey, fair gelding. Turf high 49.
**Miss Gay Kelleway [0-1] A P Griffin (from E A L Dunlop [0-6] Jun 1999).*

GHALIB (IRE) BHB 95f **RR 103f** 4585[6]
5 ch h Soviet Star (USA) 8.6f **(74)** - Nafhaat (USA) (Roberto (USA)) 10f **(76)**
Form - 66
Record 1999 - 1st:0 2nd:0 3rd:0 Ran:2
Pre1999 - 1st:3 2nd:1 3rd:1 Ran:7
Win Prizemoney £13,668 *Total Prizemoney* £18,845
Wins * 1998 Oct Leices (HVY) 7f 103 <
1997 Oct Ascot (HVY) 8f 84
1997 Spt Newbur (SFT) 8f 83
1999 Turf 0-2: (7f, 8f) (gd 2)
Very useful colt, effective 7 to 8f, acts on sft to g-s. Turf high 83.
**M P Tregoning [1-6] Hamdan Al Maktoum (from Major W R Hern [2-3] Oct 1997).*

GHOST PATH BHB 35f **RR 24f** 345[5]
4 gr f Absalom 7.1f **(56)** - Glide Path (Sovereign Path) 9.3f **(55)**
Form - 5
Record 1999 - 1st:0 2nd:0 3rd:0 Ran:1
Pre1999 - 1st:0 2nd:1 3rd:0 Ran:3
Win Prizemoney £0 *Total Prizemoney* £1,040
1999 AW 0-1: (12f) (Equi)
Unfurnished, little account filly.
**R J O'Sullivan [0-5] Jack Joseph (from C E Brittain [0-3] Aug 1998).*

GHUFFRAN (USA) BHB 82f **RR 80f** 4450[3]
2 b f Wild Again (USA) 10.7f **(69)** - Halholah (USA) (Secreto (USA)) 8.7f **(72)**
Form - 42223
Record 1999 - 1st:0 2nd:3 3rd:1 Ran:5
Win Prizemoney £0 *Total Prizemoney* £4,955
1999 Turf 0-5: (6f, 7f 3, 8f) (sft, gd, g-f, frm 2)
Decent filly. Turf high 80 (began Jly) - 2nd of 14 to Cream Tease (6 Aug Salisbury 7f frm RF 3433).
**P T Walwyn [0-5] Hamdan Al Maktoum.*

GHUROOB (IRE) **RR 46f** 755[13]
3 ch f Arazi (USA) 9.2f **(74)** - Tablah (USA) **(77f)** (Silver Hawk (USA)) 8.6f **(70)**
Form - 0
Record 1999 - 1st:0 2nd:0 3rd:0 Ran:1

Pre1999 - 1st:0 2nd:0 3rd:0 Ran:1
1999 Turf 0-1: (8f) (frm)
Scopey, currently moderate filly.
**P T Walwyn [0-2] Hamdan Al Maktoum.*

GHUTAH BHB 35f RR 34f 4987[8]
5 ch g Lycius (USA) 8.8f **(71)** - Barada (USA) (Damascus (USA)) 8.9f **(71)**
Form - 750408
Record 1999 - 1st:0 2nd:0 3rd:0 Ran:6
1999 Turf 0-6: (6f, 7f, 8f 2, 9f 2) (sft, gd, g-f 2, frm 2)
Very moderate gelding, has worn blinkers. Turf high 50.
**Martyn Wane [0-6] Mrs H Wane.*

GIFFOINE BHB 44f RR 32f 3205[10]
3 b f Timeless Times (USA) 6.1f **(56)** -Dear Glenda(Gold Song)5.5f **(61)**
Form - 0070580
Record 1999 - 1st:0 2nd:0 3rd:0 Ran:7
Pre1999 - 1st:1 2nd:0 3rd:0 Ran:5
Win Prizemoney £3,557 *Total Prizemoney* £3,802
Wins * 1998 Aug Folkes (G-F) 5f 78 <
1999 Turf 0-6: (5f 2, 6f 4) (g-f 3, frm 3) 1999 AW 0-1: (5f) (Equi)
Very moderate filly, effective 5f, acts on frm. Turf high 49.
**S Dow [1-12] J & S Kelly.*

GIFT OF GOLD BHB 81f64a RR 77f 64a 5143[4]
4 ch c Statoblest 6.4f **(63)** - Ellebanna (Tina's Pet) 6.8f **(59)**
Form - 6607281500304
Record 1999 - 1st:1 2nd:1 3rd:1 Ran:12
Pre1999 - 1st:2 2nd:2 3rd:2 Ran:19
Win Prizemoney £16,765 *Total Prizemoney* £38,520
Wins * **1999** Jun Goodwo (G-S) H 7f 80 83 <
1998 Jly Lingfi (G-F) H 7f 77 80
1997 Nov Mussel (G-S) 7.1f 73
1999 Turf 1-10: (6f, 7f 1-8, 8f) (gd 1-6, g-f 3, frm) 1999 AW 0-2: (7f, 8f) (Fibr 2)
Above-average colt, effective 6 to 8f, best at 7f, acts on gd to frm, best on gd, likes tight tracks, excels at Goodwood. Turf high 83 - 1st of 7 getting 8lb from Smooth Sailing (4 Jun Goodwood RF 1736). AW high 57. He got off the mark for the season when winning at Goodwood in June, but does not win very often. Seven furlongs looks his trip, though he did not look a natural when tried on sand. **A Bailey [1-15] Classic Gold (from A Kelleway [1-8] Aug 1998).*

GIGETTA (IRE) RR 1776[9]
3 ch f Brief Truce (USA) 9.1f **(73)** - Mrs Fisher (IRE) (Salmon Leap (USA)) 11f **(61)**
Form - 0
Record 1999 - 1st:0 2nd:0 3rd:0 Ran:1
1999 AW 0-1: (7f) (Fibr)
Unfurnished, currently very poor filly.
**N P Littmoden [0-1] Joy and Valentine Feerick.*

GIKO BHB 68f60a RR 56f 60a 2116[8]
5 b g Arazi (USA) 9.2f **(74)** - Gayane (Nureyev (USA)) 8.7f **(78)**
Form - 008
Record 1999 - 1st:0 2nd:0 3rd:0 Ran:3
Pre1999 - 1st:3 2nd:2 3rd:5 Ran:22
Win Prizemoney £12,940 *Total Prizemoney* £28,799
Wins * 1998 Jly Sandow (GD) H 8.1f 63 69
* 1998 Jun Goodwo (G-F) H 9f 55 60
* 1997 Aug Chepst (G-F) 7.1f 71 <
1999 Turf 0-3: (7f, 8f 2) (gd, g-f, frm)
Fair gelding, effective 8f, acts on gd to g-f, best on gd. Turf high 56. Consistent.
**J R Poulton [3-24] V R V Partnership (from Miss Gay Kelleway [0-1] May 1997).*

GILDERSLEVE BHB 42f36a RR 44f 36a 21[11]
4 ch f Gildoran 11.6f **(58)** - Fragrant Hackette (Simply Great (FR)) 8.2f **(65)**
Form - 000
Record 1999 - 1st:0 2nd:0 3rd:0 Ran:1
Pre1999 - 1st:0 2nd:1 3rd:1 Ran:14
Win Prizemoney £0 *Total Prizemoney* £1,191
1999 AW 0-1: (7f) (Fibr)
Neat, moderate filly.
**N E Berry [0-11] Lancing Racing Syndicate (from J W Watts [0-4] Spt 1997).*

GILFOOT BREEZE (IRE) BHB 45f RR 47f 4320[6]
2 b g Forest Wind (USA) - Ma Bella Luna (Jalmood (USA)) 10.1f **(52)**
Form - 00776
Record 1999 - 1st:0 2nd:0 3rd:0 Ran:5
1999 Turf 0-4: (6f, 7f 2, 8f) (gd, g-f 2, frm) 1999 AW 0-1: (7f) (Fibr)
Moderate gelding. Turf high 47.
**J Norton [0-5] All Yorkshire Racing Club.*

GILGAMESH (USA) RR 68f 4170[10]
4 br c Mr Prospector (USA) 8.6f **(88)** - Danzante (USA) (Danzig (USA)) 8.4f **(76)**
Form - 40
Record 1999 - 1st:0 2nd:0 3rd:0 Ran:2
Win Prizemoney £0 *Total Prizemoney* £319
1999 Turf 0-2: (8f, 10f) (g-f, frm)
Strong, currently average colt. Turf high 68 (began Aug).
**J H M Gosden [0-2] K Abdulla.*

GILLY WEET BHB 34f RR 30f 4170[9]
3 b f Almoojid 7f **(36)** - Sindos (Busted) 10.2f **(61)**
Form - 0660
Record 1999 - 1st:0 2nd:0 3rd:0 Ran:4
Pre1999 - 1st:0 2nd:0 3rd:0 Ran:3
1999 Turf 0-4: (10f 2, 12f, 16f) (g-s, g-f, frm 2)
Rangy, very moderate filly. Turf high 30.
**R Hollinshead [0-7] Mrs G A Weetman.*

GILOU BHB 39f RR 43f 3254[5]
3 b f Midyan (USA) 9.9f **(64)** - Lunagraphe (USA) (Time For A Change (USA))
Form - 400044665
Record 1999 - 1st:0 2nd:0 3rd:0 Ran:9
Pre1999 - 1st:0 2nd:0 3rd:0 Ran:5
Win Prizemoney £0 *Total Prizemoney* £652
1999 Turf 0-9: (8f, 9f, 10f, 12f 2, 14f, 16f 2, 17f) (gd 2, g-f 2, frm 5)
Leggy, moderate filly. Turf high 57. Consistent.
**C W Fairhurst [0-14] Richmond & Paxton.*

GIMCO RR 78f 1920[5]
2 b c Pelder (IRE) - Valetta **(35f)** (Faustus (USA)) 10f **(58)**
Form - 5
Record 1999 - 1st:0 2nd:0 3rd:0 Ran:1
1999 Turf 0-1: (7f) (frm)
Currently above-average colt. (1st run) - 5th of 11 to Blue Bolivar (11 Jun Sandown 7f frm RF 1920). **A Kelleway [0-1] Osvaldo Pedroni.*

GINGER FLOWER BHB 25f RR 30f 5071[8]
10 ch m Niniski (USA) 13.2f **(67)** - Monterana (Sallust) 8.4f **(63)**
Form - 00608
Record 1999 - 1st:0 2nd:0 3rd:0 Ran:5
Pre1999 - 1st:1 2nd:2 3rd:0 Ran:8
Win Prizemoney £2,070 *Total Prizemoney* £3,382
1999 Turf 0-4: (11f, 12f, 14f, 17f) (gd, g-f, frm 2) 1999 AW 0-1: (14f) (Fibr)
Very moderate mare, has broken blood-vessels, effective 14f, acts on g-f, has worn blinkers. Turf high 30 (began Aug) - 6th of 14 getting 26lb from I Can't Remember (28 Aug Nottingham 14f g-f RF 3973).
**B W Murray [0-5] Peter Barratt-Atkin (from G P Kelly [0-4] Mar 1998).*

GINGER ROGERS BHB 49f48a RR 53f 48a 5006[10]
5 ch m Gildoran 11.6f **(58)** - Axe Valley (Royben) 7.3f **(60)**
Form - 40430
Record 1999 - 1st:0 2nd:0 3rd:1 Ran:5
Pre1999 - 1st:3 2nd:1 3rd:1 Ran:11
Win Prizemoney £8,239 *Total Prizemoney* £10,487
Wins * 1997 Aug Bath (GD) H 17.2f 58 63 <
* 1997 Jly Nottin (G-F) H 16f 51 63 <
* 1997 Jun Yarmou (GD) H 14.1f 47 48
1999 Turf 0-5: (14f 2, 16f 2, 17f) (gd 4, frm)
Fair filly. Turf high 55 (1st run) (began Jly) - 4th of 7 giving 8lb to Salford Flyer (2 Jly Salisbury 14f gd RF 2497). Consistent.
**D W P Arbuthnot [3-16] W H Ponsonby.*

GINNER MORRIS BHB 45f40a **RR 47f 40a** 1094[5]
4 b g Emarati (USA) 6.6f **(63)** - Just Run (IRE) (Runnett) 7f **(59)**
Form - 4278045
Record 1999 - 1st:0 2nd:0 3rd:0 Ran:4
Pre1999 - 1st:0 2nd:2 3rd:0 Ran:13
Win Prizemoney £0 *Total Prizemoney* £1,151
1999 Turf 0-2: (9f, 10f) (gd, g-f) 1999 AW 0-2: (8f 2) (Fibr 2)
Lengthy, moderate gelding. Turf high 46. AW high 32.
**C B B Booth [0-17] Mrs Marian Rogers.*

GIN OCLOCK (IRE) BHB 76f **RR 86f** 3652[8]
2 b f Bin Ajwaad (IRE) - Suspiria (IRE) (Glenstal (USA)) 10.1f **(64)**
Form - 01248
Record 1999 - 1st:1 2nd:1 3rd:0 Ran:5
Win Prizemoney £2,526 *Total Prizemoney* £3,962
Wins * **1999** Jun Thirsk (G-F) 7f 68 <
1999 Turf 1-5: (6f, 7f 1-4) (gd, g-f 3, frm 1-1)
Useful filly. Turf high 86 - 2nd of 7 getting 7lb from Ginola's Magic (30 Jun Epsom 7f g-f RF 2442). **M R Channon [1-5] Tim Corby.*

GINOLA'S MAGIC (IRE) BHB 100f **RR 98+f** 4215[5]
2 b c Perugino (USA) - Simple Annie (Simply Great (FR)) 8.2f **(65)**
Form - 116305
Record 1999 - 1st:2 2nd:0 3rd:1 Ran:6
Win Prizemoney £7,132 *Total Prizemoney* £11,507
Wins * **1999** Jun Epsom (GD) 7f 95+
* **1999** Jun Kempto (GD) 6f 98+ <
1999 Turf 2-6: (6f 1-5, 7f 1-1) (gd, g-f 2-3, frm 2)
Very useful colt, effective 6 to 7f, best at 6f, acts on g-f to frm, best on g-f. Turf high 98 - 3rd of 7 to Bachir (28 Jly Goodwood 6f frm RF 3208) - also 1st of 16 giving 3lb to Las Ramblas (9 Jun Kempton RF 1861). He is an imposing individual, but lost his way in the second half of the season. Unhappy in the stalls, he is best watched. Sold for 42,000gns at Tattersalls in October.
**R Hannon [2-6] J B R Leisure Ltd.*

GINO'S SPIRITS BHB 96f **RR 96f** 4871[12]
3 ch f Perugino (USA) -Rising Spirits (Cure The Blues (USA)) 9.5f **(63)**
Form - 532303016120
Record 1999 - 1st:2 2nd:2 3rd:3 Ran:12
Pre1999 - 1st:1 2nd:1 3rd:1 Ran:8
Win Prizemoney £21,787 *Total Prizemoney* £42,914
Wins * **1999** Spt Yarmou (G-F) L 10.1f 94 <
* **1999** Aug Lingfi (GD) H 9f 80 81
* 1998 Aug Bright (FRM) 7f 73
1999 Turf 2-12: (8f 2, 9f 1-4, 10f 1-5, 11f) (gd 5, g-f 2-6, frm)
Leggy, very useful filly, effective 10f, acts on g-f, prefers left handed tracks, prefers tight tracks. Turf high 96 - also 1st of 7 from Kittiwake (14 Spt Yarmouth RF 4290). She was given a super ride when winning a Listed event at Yarmouth in September and went on to finish a creditable, if distant, second in the Sun Chariot Stakes. Unlikely to improve on that effort, she is best around a mile and a quarter and acts on any ground. She is to continue her career in the States. **C E Brittain [3-20] R N Khan.*

GINZBOURG BHB 51f43a **RR 75f 43a** 123[6]
5 b g Ferdinand (USA) 9.6f **(82)** - Last Request (Dancers Image (USA)) 9.3f **(71)**
Form - 3456
Record 1999 - 1st:0 2nd:0 3rd:0 Ran:2
Pre1999 - 1st:1 2nd:1 3rd:2 Ran:18
Win Prizemoney £2,936 *Total Prizemoney* £5,181
Wins 1996 Oct Folkes (G-S) 6.9f 81 <
1999 AW 0-2: (12f 2) (Equi 2)
Above-average gelding, has worn blinkers. AW high 38.
**R J O'Sullivan [1-18] Frank Adams & & Mrs Gary Pinchen (from J L Dunlop [1-7] Jly 1997).*

GIPSY ANNA (IRE) **RR 87+f** 1212[1]
2 b f Marju (IRE) 9.2f **(76)** - Anna Comnena (IRE) (Shareef Dancer (USA)) 9.9f **(73)**
Form - 11
Record 1999 - 1st:2 2nd:0 3rd:0 Ran:2
Win Prizemoney £8,689 *Total Prizemoney* £8,689
Wins * **1999** May Newbur (GD) 5.2f 87+ <
* **1999** May Haydoc (GD) 5f 68+
1999 Turf 2-2: (5f 2-2) (gd 1-1, g-f 1-1)
Currently useful filly. Turf high 87 - 1st of 6 giving 6lb to Rowaasi (14 May Newbury RF 1212). Looked a good prospect, but was not seen after May. **B J Meehan [2-2] Mrs K J Crangle.*

GIPSY ROSE LEE (IRE) BHB 90f **RR 93df** 4838[3]
3 b f Marju (IRE) 9.2f **(76)** -Rainstone (Rainbow Quest (USA))10.4f **(75)**
Form - 837463
Record 1999 - 1st:0 2nd:0 3rd:2 Ran:6
Pre1999 - 1st:2 2nd:1 3rd:0 Ran:3
Win Prizemoney £8,118 *Total Prizemoney* £20,388
Wins * 1998 Jun Windso (GD) 6f 84 <
* 1998 Jun Sandow (G-S) 5f 78
1999 Turf 0-6: (6f, 7f 2, 8f 3) (gd 4, g-f, frm)
Leggy, useful filly, effective 6f, acts on gd to g-f. Turf high 100. Consistent. A smart juvenile, she ran moderately on all her starts last term and has not trained on. **B J Meehan [2-9] Mrs K J Crangle.*

GIPSY SPIRIT **RR 29f** 3009[8]
3 b f Alhijaz 7.7f **(57)** - What A Pet (Mummy's Pet) 7.7f **(60)**
Form - 8
Record 1999 - 1st:0 2nd:0 3rd:0 Ran:1
Pre1999 - 1st:0 2nd:0 3rd:0 Ran:1
1999 Turf 0-1: (8f) (frm)
Light-framed, currently little account filly.
**P G Murphy [0-1] Mrs Dianne Abel (from T W Donnelly [0-1] Aug 1998).*

GIRLIE SET (IRE) BHB 73f62a **RR 74f 62a** 2963[7]
4 b f Second Set (IRE) 9.2f **(67)** - Heavenward (USA) (Conquistador Cielo (USA)) 8.8f **(69)**
Form - 4483121117
Record 1999 - 1st:4 2nd:1 3rd:1 Ran:10
Pre1999 - 1st:0 2nd:0 3rd:0 Ran:3
Win Prizemoney £12,665 *Total Prizemoney* £13,998
Wins * **1999** Jly Yarmou (G-F) H 8f 53 74 <
* **1999** Jly Lingfi (G-F) H 9f 53 64
* **1999** Jly Mussel (G-S) H 9f 53 58+
* **1999** Jun Lingfi (G-F) H 9f 47 48
1999 Turf 4-7: (7f, 8f 1-1, 9f 3-3, 11f, 12f) (gd 1-2, g-f 2, frm 2-2, hrd 1-1) 1999 AW 0-3: (8f 2, 9f) (Fibr 3)
Leggy, above-average filly, effective 8 to 9f, acts on gd to frm. Turf high 74 - 1st of 9 giving 25lb to Alberkinnie (14 Jly Yarmouth RF 2831). AW high 50. Well placed by her shrewd trainer, she hit a purple patch in midsummer, winning four from five, although in ordinary company. **Sir Mark Prescott [4-13] J T Stimpson.*

GIRL'S BEST FRIEND BHB 92f **RR 91f** 5142[4]
2 b f Nicolotte - Diamond Princess (Horage) 10.3f **(61)**
Form - 72174
Record 1999 - 1st:1 2nd:1 3rd:0 Ran:5
Win Prizemoney £3,460 *Total Prizemoney* £4,871
Wins * **1999** Oct Lingfi (HVY) 6f 87+ <
1999 Turf 1-4: (6f 1-1, 7f, 8f 2) (g-s 1-1, gd 3) 1999 AW 0-1: (8f) (Fibr)
Useful filly. Turf high 91 (began Aug) - 4th of 10 to Silver Colours (30 Oct Newmarket 8f gd RF 5142) - also 1st of 11 getting 5lb from Leeroy (1 Oct Lingfield RF 4670). Has shown some ability on the Wolverhampton Fibresand, and bettered her second there on turf at Lingfield next time over six furlongs when taking a heavy-ground maiden by nine lengths. The form is probably worth little though, and she has disappointed since.
**D W P Arbuthnot [1-5] Stephen Crown.*

GIVE AN INCH (IRE) BHB 69f **RR 70f** 4553[9]
4 b f Inchinor 8.9f **(64)** - Top Heights (High Top) 10.2f **(67)**
Form - 44231410
Record 1999 - 1st:2 2nd:1 3rd:1 Ran:8
Pre1999 - 1st:3 2nd:2 3rd:1 Ran:15
Win Prizemoney £20,330 *Total Prizemoney* £25,934
Wins * **1999** Spt Ayr (G-S) H 17.5f 65 70 <
* **1999** Jun Pontef (GD) H 18f 62 65
* 1998 Spt Ayr (G-S) H 17.5f 51 61
* 1998 Aug Ayr (G-S) H 15f 44 53+
* 1998 Jly Redcar (G-F) S 11f 45
1999 Turf 2-8: (14f 2, 16f 4, 17f 1-1, 18f 1-1) (g-s, gd 1-3, g-f 1-3, frm)
Leggy, above-average filly, effective 16 to 18f, best at 17f, acts on sft to frm, likes left handed tracks, prefers tight tracks, excels at Ayr. Turf high 70 - 1st of 13 giving 18lb to Home Counties (17 Spt Ayr RF 4381) - also 1st of 13 giving 9lb to Distant Storm (14 Jun

Pontefract RF 1986). **W Storey [5-23] Black Type Racing.*

GIVEN RR 1518[8]
3 b f Minshaanshu Amad (USA) 11.3f **(53)** - Little Morston (Morston (FR)) 9.4f **(55)**
Form - 8
Record 1999 - 1st:0 2nd:0 3rd:0 Ran:1
1999 Turf 0-1: (8f) (hrd)
Leggy, currently very poor filly. **G L Moore [0-1] A Moore.*

GIVE NOTICE RR 54f 5099[9]
2 b c Warning 8.1f **(77)** - Princess Genista (Ile de Bourbon (USA)) 10.1f **(67)**
Form - 60
Record 1999 - 1st:0 2nd:0 3rd:0 Ran:2
1999 Turf 0-2: (7f 2) (gd 2)
Currently fair colt. Turf high 54 (began Oct).
**J L Dunlop [0-2] I H Stewart-Brown.*

GIVE THE SLIP RR 85+f 4898[4]
2 b c Slip Anchor 12.7f **(75)** - Falafil (FR) (Fabulous Dancer (USA)) 9.4f **(70)**
Form - 34
Record 1999 - 1st:0 2nd:0 3rd:1 Ran:2
Win Prizemoney £0 *Total Prizemoney* £1,272
1999 Turf 0-2: (7f, 8f) (gd 2)
Currently useful colt. Turf high 85 (began Spt) - 4th of 13 to Pawn Broker (15 Oct Newmarket 8f gd RF 4898).
**Mrs A J Perrett [0-2] John Bodie.*

GLAMIS (USA) RR 119f 3695[3]
3 b c Silver Hawk (USA) 11.2f **(85)** - Glaze (USA) (Mr Prospector (USA)) 8.8f **(78)**
Form - 13763
Record 1999 - 1st:1 2nd:0 3rd:2 Ran:5
Pre1999 - 1st:1 2nd:2 3rd:2 Ran:5
Win Prizemoney £10,012 *Total Prizemoney* £88,546
Wins * 1999 Apr Kempto (GD) 10f 104+ <
* 1998 Aug Goodwo (G-F) 7f 92+
1999 Turf 1-5: (10f 1-3, 12f 2) (g-s 2, gd, g-f 1-2)
Workmanlike, high-class colt, effective 12f, acts on gd to g-f, has worn blinkers. Turf high 119 - 6th of 16 to Oath (5 Jun Epsom 12f gd RF 1760). A useful two-year-old, if just missing out at the top level, he was the smooth winner of a mile-and-a-quarter conditions event at Kempton on his reappearance last season. Ran a couple of disappointing races in Derby trials, but was a respectable sixth in the big race itself and ran well to finish third in the Great Voltigeur, but that was the last that was seen of him as he fractured a cannon bone when being prepared for the St Leger.
**J H M Gosden [2-10] Sheikh Mohammed.*

GLANCE (IRE) BHB 85f **RR 84f** 2044[12]
4 b c Ela-Mana-Mou 12.7f **(72)** - Cursory Look (USA) (Nijinsky (CAN)) 10.3f **(77)**
Form - 60
Record 1999 - 1st:0 2nd:0 3rd:0 Ran:2
Pre1999 - 1st:1 2nd:0 3rd:0 Ran:2
Win Prizemoney £3,582 *Total Prizemoney* £3,815
Wins * 1998 Jun Doncas (GD) 12f 84+ <
1999 Turf 0-2: (10f, 12f) (sft, g-f)
Scopey, decent colt. Turf high 81.
**L M Cumani [1-4] Sheikh Mohammed.*

GLANWYDDEN (IRE) BHB 74f **RR 79f** 4556[8]
3 ch c Grand Lodge (USA) - Brush Away (Ahonoora) 8.1f **(73)**
Form - 56263878
Record 1999 - 1st:0 2nd:1 3rd:1 Ran:8
Pre1999 - 1st:1 2nd:0 3rd:4 Ran:8
Win Prizemoney £3,296 *Total Prizemoney* £10,296
Wins * 1998 Jly Beverl (GD) 7.5f 81 <
1999 Turf 0-8: (7f 3, 8f 5) (g-s, gd 4, g-f, frm 2)
Workmanlike, above-average colt, effective 7 to 8f, best at 8f, acts on gd to frm, best on gd. Turf high 85 - 2nd of 11 getting 9lb from Ice (13 May York 8f gd RF 1198). **J Berry [1-16] Lord Mostyn.*

GLASHEDY ROSE BHB 52f **RR 47f** 1526[5]
3 br f Hamas (IRE) 8f **(72)** - Arabian Rose (USA) (Lyphard (USA)) 9.9f **(72)**
Form - 005
Record 1999 - 1st:0 2nd:0 3rd:0 Ran:3
1999 Turf 0-3: (7f, 8f, 10f) (gd, g-f, frm)
Neat, currently moderate filly. Turf high 47.
**H J Collingridge [0-3] Dr Conor O'Doherty.*

GLASTONBURY (IRE) BHB 54a **RR 49f** 2650[11]
3 b g Common Grounds 8.1f **(66)** - Harmonious (Sharrood (USA)) 10.5f **(72)**
Form - 8163601074370000870
Record 1999 - 1st:1 2nd:0 3rd:1 Ran:15
Pre1999 - 1st:1 2nd:1 3rd:3 Ran:12
Win Prizemoney £3,592 *Total Prizemoney* £7,123
Wins * 1999 *Jan Lingfi (STD) S 7f 63*
1998 *Nov Lingfi (STD) S 7f 73* <
1999 Turf 0-6: (6f 2, 7f 2, 8f 2) (sft, gd 2, frm 2, hrd) 1999 AW 1-9: (5f, 6f 3, 7f 1-5) (Equi 1-7, Fibr 2)
Fair gelding, effective 7f, - acts on Equi, likes left handed tracks, likes tight tracks. Turf high 49. AW high 63.
**P Howling [1-17] Paul Howling (from M R Channon [1-10] Nov 1998).*

GLENDAMAH (IRE) BHB 76f **RR 80f** 5074[3]
2 b c Mukaddamah (USA) 7.6f **(74)** - Sea Glen (IRE) (Glenstal (USA)) 10.1f **(64)**
Form - 53471372033
Record 1999 - 1st:1 2nd:1 3rd:4 Ran:11
Win Prizemoney £2,452 *Total Prizemoney* £6,524
Wins * 1999 Aug Newcas (FRM) 6f 74 <
1999 Turf 1-11: (5f, 6f 1-7, 7f 2, 8f) (sft, gd 3, g-f 3, frm 3, hrd 1-1)
Decent colt, effective 6f, acts on gd to hrd, best on frm, has worn blinkers. Turf high 80 - 2nd of 18 getting 2lb from Rhode Island (24 Spt Haydock 6f gd RF 4524) - also 1st of 14 giving 5lb to Chiquita (4 Aug Newcastle RF 3364). **E Weymes [1-11] Mrs A Birkett.*

GLENMEAD BHB 92f **RR 90f** 5038[3]
4 ch c Polish Precedent (USA) 9f **(73)** - Fair Country (Town And Country) 8.1f **(68)**
Form - 01023
Record 1999 - 1st:1 2nd:1 3rd:1 Ran:5
Pre1999 - 1st:1 2nd:0 3rd:2 Ran:4
Win Prizemoney £13,055 *Total Prizemoney* £19,145
Wins * 1999 Aug Pontef (G-F) H 12f 85 90 <
*** 1998** Aug Ascot (G-F) 12f 79
1999 Turf 1-5: (12f 1-4, 14f) (g-s, gd 2, frm 1-2)
Leggy, useful colt, effective 12f, acts on frm. Turf high 90 - 1st of 5 giving 10lb to Bullet (4 Aug Pontefract RF 3374). Sold for 70,000gns at Tattersalls in October.
**A C Stewart [2-9] Robin Paterson.*

GLEN PARKER (IRE) BHB 40f **RR 40f** 2872[5]
6 ch h Bluebird (USA) 7.9f **(71)** - Trina's Girl (Nonoalco (USA)) 8.5f **(66)**
Form - 086055
Record 1999 - 1st:0 2nd:0 3rd:0 Ran:6
Pre1999 - 1st:1 2nd:2 3rd:1 Ran:12
Win Prizemoney £3,647 *Total Prizemoney* £7,266
Wins 1996 Aug Pontef (G-F) 8f 73 <
1999 Turf 0-6: (8f 2, 9f, 10f, 11f, 12f) (gd 2, g-f 2, frm, hrd)
Moderate horse, effective 10f, acts on g-f, has worn blinkers, likes tight tracks. Turf high 40.
**D A Lamb [0-8] D G Pryde (from H R A Cecil [1-12] Oct 1998).*

GLENROCK BHB 92f **RR 89f** 4484[3]
2 ch c Muhtarram (USA) - Elkie Brooks (Relkino) 8.9f **(65)**
Form - 227431183
Record 1999 - 1st:2 2nd:2 3rd:2 Ran:9
Win Prizemoney £7,587 *Total Prizemoney* £11,008
Wins * 1999 Aug Cheste (G-S) 6.1f 89 <
*** 1999** Aug Lingfi (GD) 6f 75
1999 Turf 2-9: (5f 4, 6f 2-4, 7f) (g-s, gd 1-1, g-f 2, frm 1-4, hrd)
Useful colt, effective 6f, acts on gd. Turf high 89 - 1st of 4 from Chief Response (21 Aug Chester RF 3811).
**J Berry [2-9] Glenrock Racing Ltd.*

GLEN ROSIE (IRE) BHB 90f **RR 92f** 4797[3]
2 ch f Mujtahid (USA) 7.4f **(69)** - Silver Echo (Caerleon (USA)) 8.6f **(71)**
Form - 13663

Record 1999 - 1st:1 2nd:0 3rd:2 Ran:5
Win Prizemoney £4,198 *Total Prizemoney* £7,035
Wins * 1999 Jly Newbur (G-F) 5.2f 70+ <
1999 Turf 1-5: (5f 1-2, 7f 3) (gd 2, g-f, frm 1-2)
Useful filly. Turf high 92 (began Jly) - 6th of 20 giving 13lb to Out of Africa (8 Spt Doncaster 7f gd RF 4206). Made a winning debut in a Newbury maiden, though it was a pretty uncompetitive event. Has run respectably in better company since.
**B W Hills [1-5] John Grant.*

GLEN VALE WALK (IRE) BHB 62f RR 72f 5002[3]

2 ch g Balla Cove - Winter Harvest (Grundy) 10.3f **(65)**
Form - 883
Record 1999 - 1st:0 2nd:0 3rd:1 Ran:3
Win Prizemoney £0 *Total Prizemoney* £286
1999 Turf 0-3: (7f, 8f 2) (gd 2, hrd)
Currently above-average gelding. Turf high 72 (began Spt) - 3rd of 18 giving 5lb to Unimpeachable (21 Oct Nottingham 8f gd RF 5002). **Mrs G S Rees [0-3] D C Brady.*

GLENWHARGEN (IRE) BHB 62f56a RR 60f 56a 5218[11]

2 b f Polar Falcon (USA) 9f **(74)** - La Veine (USA) (Diesis) 9.3f **(69)**
Form - 46420530
Record 1999 - 1st:0 2nd:1 3rd:1 Ran:8
Win Prizemoney £0 *Total Prizemoney* £3,948
1999 Turf 0-5: (5f 2, 6f, 7f 2) (g-s, gd 3, g-f) 1999 AW 0-3: (6f 2, 8f) (Fibr 3)
Average filly, effective 6f, acts on gd, has worn blinkers. Turf high 59 - 2nd of 16 getting 17lb from Golden Miracle (27 Spt Hamilton 6f gd RF 4589). AW high 54.
**M Johnston [0-8] J S Morrison & W Monteith.*

GLIDER (IRE) BHB 69a RR 49f 1946[20]

4 b f Silver Kite (USA) 10.2f **(51)** -Song of The Glens (Horage)10.3f **(61)**
Form - 000
Record 1999 - 1st:0 2nd:0 3rd:0 Ran:3
Pre1999 - 1st:1 2nd:1 3rd:1 Ran:7
Win Prizemoney £1,906 *Total Prizemoney* £3,384
Wins 1998 *Jan Lingfi (STD) H 8f 61 65* <
1999 Turf 0-2: (8f, 10f) (gd, g-f) 1999 AW 0-1: (7f) (Fibr)
Light-framed, average filly, effective 8f, - acts on Equi, favours left handed tracks, favours tight tracks. Turf high 17. Becoming disappointing.
**R Brotherton [0-3] Paul Stringer (from N P Littmoden [1-5] Jun 1998).*

GLIM TRAIL (IRE) RR 27f 1222[18]

3 b f Catrail (USA) - Glim (USA) (Damascus (USA)) 8.9f **(71)**
Form - 00
Record 1999 - 1st:0 2nd:0 3rd:0 Ran:2
1999 Turf 0-2: (6f, 7f) (gd, g-f)
Light-framed, currently little account filly. Turf high 27.
**A B Mulholland [0-2] S J Parkin.*

GLINT IN HER EYE (USA) BHB 69f60a RR 72f 60a 5067[5]

3 b f Arazi (USA) 9.2f **(74)** - Wind in Her Hair (IRE) **(109f)** (Alzao (USA)) 7.1f **(68)**
Form - 8447445
Record 1999 - 1st:0 2nd:0 3rd:0 Ran:7
Win Prizemoney £0 *Total Prizemoney* £740
1999 Turf 0-6: (10f 2, 12f 3, 13f) (gd 2, frm 3, hrd) 1999 AW 0-1: (13f) (Equi)
Unfurnished, above-average filly, effective 12 to 13f, acts on gd to frm. Turf high 73. **J W Hills [0-7] The Dan Abbott Racing Partnership.*

GLOBAL CONCEPT (USA) BHB 75f85a RR 80f 85a 4865[1]

3 b c Warning 8.1f **(77)** - Sweet Snow (USA) (Lyphard (USA)) 9.9f **(72)**
Form - 382301
Record 1999 - 1st:1 2nd:1 3rd:2 Ran:6
Win Prizemoney £3,077 *Total Prizemoney* £5,508
Wins * 1999 *Oct Wolver (STD) H 8.5f 75 81* <
1999 Turf 0-5: (7f, 8f 3, 9f) (g-s 2, g-f, frm 2) 1999 AW 1-1: (8f 1-1) (Fibr 1-1)
Workmanlike, decent colt, effective 8f, acts on g-s to frm - acts on Fibr. Turf high 84 (1st run) (began Jly) - 3rd of 13 to Sir Effendi (8 Jly Lingfield 8f frm RF 2636). (1st run) - 1st of 13 giving 2lb to Eastern Champ (13 Oct Wolverhampton RF 4865). Showed a bit of ability on turf, but got off the mark with a very impressive win in a handicap on the Wolverhampton Fibresand in October. He can win again on that surface.
**P W Harris [1-6] Smith, Palmer, Yeardley & Hon.*

GLOBAL DRAW (IRE) BHB 28f RR 42f 4442[10]

3 ch g Be My Guest (USA) 10.2f **(66)** - Almost A Lady (IRE) (Entitled)
Form - 003000
Record 1999 - 1st:0 2nd:0 3rd:1 Ran:6
Pre1999 - 1st:0 2nd:0 3rd:0 Ran:2
Win Prizemoney £0 *Total Prizemoney* £412
1999 Turf 0-6: (7f, 8f 2, 10f 2, 12f) (g-s, g-f 2, frm 3)
Workmanlike, moderate gelding, has worn blinkers. Turf high 51. Becoming disappointing.
**J Parkes [0-2] W A Sellers (from M A Jarvis [0-6] Jun 1999).*

GLOBE QUEEN (IRE) RR 42f 3083[10]

2 ch f River Falls 8.2f **(56)** - Kristar (Kris) 9.5f **(73)**
Form - 850
Record 1999 - 1st:0 2nd:0 3rd:0 Ran:3
1999 Turf 0-2: (6f 2) (g-f, frm) 1999 AW 0-1: (7f) (Fibr)
Currently moderate filly. Turf high 42.
**J J O'Neill [0-3] G & P Barker Ltd/Globe Engineering.*

GLOBE RAIDER BHB 30f RR 25f 2556[11]

4 b g Safawan 6.6f **(60)** - Polola (Aragon) 8.1f **(60)**
Form - 80
Record 1999 - 1st:0 2nd:0 3rd:0 Ran:2
Pre1999 - 1st:0 2nd:0 3rd:0 Ran:5
1999 Turf 0-2: (6f, 8f) (sft, frm)
Scopey, little account gelding, has worn blinkers. Turf high 12.
**J J O'Neill [0-7] G & P Barker Ltd/Globe Engineering.*

GLOROSIA (FR) BHB 98f RR 99f 4101[5]

4 ch f Bering 9.6f **(80)** - Golden Sea (FR) (Saint Cyrien (FR)) 8.4f **(80)**
Form - 41455
Record 1999 - 1st:1 2nd:0 3rd:0 Ran:5
Pre1999 - 1st:2 2nd:1 3rd:2 Ran:6
Win Prizemoney £102,963 *Total Prizemoney* £116,886
Wins * 1999 Jun Windso (G-F) 10f 91+
* 1997 Spt Ascot (G-F) G1 8f 111 <
* 1997 Jly Newmar (G-S) 7f 76+
1999 Turf 1-5: (9f 2, 10f 1-3) (gd 2, g-f, frm 1-2)
Strong, very useful filly, effective 10 to 12f, acts on gd. Turf high 99. Consistent. She won a soft race at Windsor, but has basically been disappointing since her two-year-old days.
**L M Cumani [3-11] Baron G Von Ullmann.*

GLORY OF GROSVENOR (IRE) BHB 67f RR 65f 695[13]

4 ch g Caerleon (USA) 10.9f **(79)** - Abury (IRE) (Law Society (USA)) 9.9f **(70)**
Form - 0
Record 1999 - 1st:0 2nd:0 3rd:0 Ran:1
Pre1999 - 1st:0 2nd:1 3rd:0 Ran:5
Win Prizemoney £0 *Total Prizemoney* £1,902
1999 Turf 0-1: (12f) (gd)
Scopey, average gelding, has worn blinkers.
**P W Chapple-Hyam [0-6] R E Sangster.*

GLORY OF LOVE BHB 37f RR 32f 3920[9]

4 b g Belmez (USA) 11.4f **(65)** - Princess Lieven (Royal Palace) 9f **(56)**
Form - 8650
Record 1999 - 1st:0 2nd:0 3rd:0 Ran:4
Pre1999 - 1st:0 2nd:0 3rd:0 Ran:3
1999 Turf 0-4: (12f, 13f, 14f 2) (gd, g-f, frm 2)
Workmanlike, very moderate gelding, has worn blinkers. Turf high 32. **J Hetherton [0-7] Eureka Racing.*

GLORY QUEST (USA) RR 82f 4342[3]

2 b c Quest for Fame 12.8f **(75)** - Sonseri (Prince Tenderfoot (USA)) 9f **(61)**
Form - 33
Record 1999 - 1st:0 2nd:0 3rd:2 Ran:2
Win Prizemoney £0 *Total Prizemoney* £1,516
1999 Turf 0-2: (6f 2) (g-s, frm)
Currently decent colt. Turf high 82 (began Spt) - 3rd of 22 giving 9lb to Avezzano (16 Spt Ayr 6f g-s RF 4342). Despite his stable being in the doldrums, he has shown distinct signs of ability and

there are races to be won with him.
**Miss Gay Kelleway [0-2] Quest To Win Partnership.*

GLOW RR 55f 2529[6]
3 br f Alzao (USA) 9.8f **(73)** - Shimmer (Bustino) 10.4f **(64)**
Form - 8046
Record 1999 - 1st:0 2nd:0 3rd:0 Ran:3
Pre1999 - 1st:0 2nd:0 3rd:0 Ran:2
1999 Turf 0-3: (10f, 12f, 18f) (g-f 2, frm)
Unfurnished, fair filly. Turf high 55 - 4th of 7 getting 5lb from Quedex (12 Jun Bath 12f g-f RF 1943).
**I A Balding [0-3] The Queen (from Lord Huntingdon [0-2] Nov 1998).*

GLOWING BHB 74f **RR 73f** 4755[16]
4 b f Chilibang 7f **(55)** - Juliet Bravo (Glow (USA)) 6.7f **(71)**
Form - 440110
Record 1999 - 1st:2 2nd:0 3rd:0 Ran:6
Pre1999 - 1st:1 2nd:2 3rd:2 Ran:7
Win Prizemoney £10,537 *Total Prizemoney* £13,594
Wins * **1999** Spt Doncas (G-F) H 5f 70 73 <
* **1999** Aug Nottin (G-F) H 6.1f 65 68
* 1998 Aug Folkes (G-F) 6f 67
1999 Turf 2-6: (5f 1-2, 6f 1-4) (gd 3, g-f 1-2, frm 1-1)
Scopey, above-average filly, effective 5 to 6f, best at 6f, acts on gd to frm, and excels at Nottingham. Turf high 73 - 1st of 22 giving 1lb to Surprised (10 Spt Doncaster RF 4255) - also 1st of 15 giving 9lb to Inchalong (28 Aug Nottingham RF 3972). Got off the mark at Folkestone on her final start of 1998, and regained winning form at Nottingham in August. Suited by six furlongs and fast ground, she proved five was not to short for her when following up at Doncaster. **J R Fanshawe [3-13] Peters Friends.*

GO BRITANNIA BHB 70f **RR 56?f** 3207[8]
6 b g Machiavellian (USA) 9.8f **(83)** - Chief Celebrity (USA) (Chief's Crown (USA)) 9.8f **(72)**
Form - 8
Record 1999 - 1st:0 2nd:0 3rd:0 Ran:1
Pre1999 - 1st:1 2nd:1 3rd:3 Ran:12
Win Prizemoney £4,391 *Total Prizemoney* £10,703
Wins 1996 Jly Warwic (G-F) 8f 80+ <
1999 Turf 0-1: (20f) (g-f)
Fair gelding, has worn blinkers. Inconsistent.
**F Jordan [0-15] Fenside Waste Management Ltd (from D R Loder [1-12] Oct 1997).*

GOCHINOS BHB 60f52a **RR 62df 52a** 3375[5]
3 b g Wolfhound (USA) 7.3f **(71)** - Reflection (Mill Reef (USA)) 10.5f **(78)**
Form - 04732140155
Record 1999 - 1st:2 2nd:1 3rd:1 Ran:11
Pre1999 - 1st:0 2nd:0 3rd:1 Ran:6
Win Prizemoney £5,053 *Total Prizemoney* £6,656
Wins * **1999** Jun Mussel (SFT) SH 5f 60 62 <
* **1999** May Bright (FRM) H 5.3f 57 59
1999 Turf 2-7: (5f 2-7) (gd 1-2, g-f 1-3, frm 2) 1999 AW 0-4: (5f 3, 6f) (Fibr 4)
Scopey, average gelding, effective 5f, acts on gd, has worn blinkers. Turf high 62 - 1st of 9 giving 20lb to Silvano's Express (28 Jun Musselburgh RF 2362). AW high 55.
**S C Williams [2-17] Stuart Williams.*

GODLEY (IRE) BHB 49f **RR 50f** 4648[15]
3 b g Fayruz 6.6f **(63)** - Divine Apsara (Godswalk (USA)) 7.3f **(58)**
Form - 8666878200
Record 1999 - 1st:0 2nd:1 3rd:0 Ran:10
Pre1999 - 1st:0 2nd:2 3rd:0 Ran:7
Win Prizemoney £0 *Total Prizemoney* £4,269
1999 Turf 0-10: (8f 4, 10f 2, 12f 2, 13f, 14f) (g-s, gd 3, g-f 2, frm 3, hrd)
Strong, fair gelding, effective 7 to 8f, best at 8f, acts on g-f to frm, best on frm, often wears blinkers. Turf high 65.
**M J Fetherston-Godley [0-17] The Kennet House Partnership.*

GODMERSHAM PARK BHB 44f54a **RR 37f 54a** 3113[6]
7 b g Warrshan (USA) 9.7f **(59)** - Brown Velvet (Mansingh (USA)) 7.4f **(55)**
Form - 4072044086507433346
Record 1999 - 1st:0 2nd:1 3rd:3 Ran:17
Pre1999 - 1st:6 2nd:4 3rd:3 Ran:38
Win Prizemoney £14,414 *Total Prizemoney* £22,159
Wins * 1998 *Feb Wolver (STD) H 8.5f 68* *73* <
* 1998 *Jan Southw (STD) H 8f 54 65*
* 1998 *Jan Southw (STD) H 8f 54 63*
* 1998 *Jan Southw (STD) H 7f 54 59*
* 1997 *Dec Southw (STD) H 7f 50 54*
* 1997 *Nov Southw (STD) H 8f 46 51*
1999 Turf 0-1: (11f) (gd) 1999 AW 0-16: (6f, 7f 6, 8f 7, 9f, 10f) (Equi, Fibr 15)
Moderate gelding, effective 7 to 9f, best at 8f, - acts on Fibr, has worn blinkers, favours left handed tracks. AW high 70 - 2nd of 11 giving 5lb to Theatre Magic (11 Jan Southwell 7f Fibr RF 0072). Consistent.
**P S Felgate [6-45] P S Felgate (from M J Heaton-Ellis [0-10] Oct 1996).*

GOES A TREAT (IRE) BHB 73f **RR 77df** 5166[10]
3 b f Common Grounds 8.1f **(66)** - Just a Treat (IRE) (Glenstal (USA)) 10.1f **(64)**
Form - 031260
Record 1999 - 1st:1 2nd:1 3rd:1 Ran:6
Win Prizemoney £4,270 *Total Prizemoney* £6,072
Wins 1999 Jly Warwic (G-F) 6.8f 82 <
1999 Turf 1-6: (6f, 7f 1-5) (g-s, gd, g-f 1-2, frm 2)
Unfurnished, above-average filly, effective 7f, acts on g-f to frm. Turf high 82 - 1st of 7 getting 5lb from Border Prince (10 Jly Warwick RF 2726).
**A G Foster [0-1] David Brown (from P W Chapple-Hyam [1-5] Spt 1999).*

GOING GLOBAL (IRE) RR 81f 4490[1]
2 ch c Bob Back (USA) 11.5f **(71)** - Ukraine Girl (Targowice (USA)) 11.4f **(70)**
Form - 31
Record 1999 - 1st:1 2nd:0 3rd:1 Ran:2
Win Prizemoney £3,670 *Total Prizemoney* £4,327
Wins * **1999** Spt Goodwo (SFT) 8f 77+ <
1999 Turf 1-2: (8f 1-2) (g-s 1-1, gd)
Currently decent colt. Turf high 81 (1st run) (began Spt) - 3rd of 12 to Shamrock City (8 Spt Doncaster 8f gd RF 4210) - also 1st of 12 from Malleus (22 Spt Goodwood RF 4490). Has run well on firm ground and heavy, over the diverse tracks of Goodwood and Doncaster. After getting boxed-in last time, he showed a nice attitude to win. **S P C Woods [1-2] Dwayne Woods.*

GOING HOME (IRE) BHB 56f **RR 72f** 4589[14]
2 b g Thatching 7.8f **(69)** - Princess of Dance (IRE) (Dancing Dissident (USA))
Form - 05400
Record 1999 - 1st:0 2nd:0 3rd:0 Ran:5
Win Prizemoney £0 *Total Prizemoney* £193
1999 Turf 0-5: (5f 4, 6f) (gd, g-f 2, frm 2)
Above-average gelding, has worn blinkers. Turf high 72 - 4th of 11 to Agua Caballo (10 Jun Carlisle 5f g-f RF 1874).
**J L Eyre [0-5] Steve Macdonald.*

GOING PLACES BHB 37f40a **RR 28f 40a** 599[17]
4 b f Risk Me (FR) 8f **(53)** - Spring High **(37f 55a)** (Miami Springs) 9.9f **(59)**
Form - 207800
Record 1999 - 1st:0 2nd:0 3rd:0 Ran:5
Pre1999 - 1st:1 2nd:1 3rd:3 Ran:16
Win Prizemoney £4,470 *Total Prizemoney* £6,504
Wins * 1997 May Windso (SFT) 5f 70 <
1999 Turf 0-2: (5f 2) (sft, gd) 1999 AW 0-3: (5f 2, 6f) (Equi, Fibr 2)
Neat, moderate filly, effective 5f, - acts on Fibr, often wears blinkers (effectively). Turf high 2. AW high 43. **K T Ivory [1-21] K T Ivory.*

GOLCONDA (IRE) BHB 65a **RR 96f** 4019[10]
3 br f Lahib (USA) 8f **(69)** - David's Star (Welsh Saint) 7.6f **(64)**
Form - 212112360
Record 1999 - 1st:3 2nd:3 3rd:1 Ran:9
Pre1999 - 1st:0 2nd:0 3rd:1 Ran:2
Win Prizemoney £17,201 *Total Prizemoney* £31,565
Wins * **1999** May Lingfi (G-F) H 10f 73 75 <
* **1999** May Kempto (G-F) H 9f 68 72
* **1999** *Feb Wolver (STD) 7f 63*

1999 Turf 2-7: (9f 1-1, 10f 1-5, 12f) (g-s, gd, g-f 3, frm 2-2) 1999 AW 1-2: (7f 1-2) (Equi, Fibr 1-1)

Workmanlike, very useful filly, effective 10f, acts on g-f, prefers left handed tracks, likes tight tracks. Turf high 96 - 3rd of 16 getting 15lb from Achilles (10 Jly York 10f g-f RF 2733). AW high 63. Thoroughly genuine, she developed into a smart handicapper and may have won the John Smith's Cup had her challenge been launched earlier. Unlikely to stay beyond a mile and a quarter, she is probably best on a sound surface and remains fairly treated.

**M L W Bell [3-11] Innlaw Racing.*

Golconda crushed her rivals on three occasions in the spring

GOLD ACADEMY (IRE) BHB 118f **RR 119f** 4919[4]

3 b c Royal Academy (USA) 7.8f **(77)** - Soha (USA) (Dancing Brave (USA)) 8.4f **(76)**

Form - 225138134

Record	**1999** -	1st:2	2nd:2	3rd:2	Ran:9
	Pre1999 -	1st:0	2nd:0	3rd:1	Ran:3

Win Prizemoney £23,809 *Total Prizemoney* £116,847

Wins								
* **1999**	Spt	York	(G-F)	L	8.9f	113+	<
* **1999**	May	Chepst	(GD)		8.1f	98+	

1999 Turf 2-9: (8f 1-6, 9f 1-2, 10f) (sft, gd 1-3, g-f 3, frm 1-2)

Scopey, high-class colt, effective 8 to 10f, acts on gd to frm, best on frm. Turf high 119 - 4th of 13 getting 2lb from Alborada (16 Oct Newmarket 10f gd RF 4919) - also 1st of 7 getting 1lb from Diamond White (2 Spt York RF 4101). He did not win until May, but proved himself a high-class performer when making the frame in the St James's Palace and Champion Stakes. Best on a quick surface, he remains open to some improvement and should win a Group race in 2000. **R Hannon [2-12] George Teo.*

GOLD ANGEL **RR 74f** 1890[5]

3 ch f Machiavellian (USA) 9.8f **(83)** - Dafrah (USA) (Danzig (USA)) 8.4f **(76)**

Form - 05

Record	**1999** -	1st:0	2nd:0	3rd:0	Ran:2

1999 Turf 0-2: (7f 2) (gd, g-f)

Workmanlike, currently above-average filly. Turf high 74.

**E A L Dunlop [0-2] Maktoum Al Maktoum.*

GOLD AWAY (IRE) **RR 125f** 4246a[2]

4 ch c Goldneyev (USA) - Blushing Away (FR) (Blushing Groom (FR)) 10.3f **(76)**

Form - 11322

1999 Turf 2-5: (7f, 8f 2-3, 9f) (hvy 1-2, sft 1-1, g-s, gd)

Top-class horse, effective 7 to 9f, best at 8f, acts on hvy to gd, best on hvy, has worn blinkers, likes right handed tracks, and does well at Longchamp. Turf high 125 - 2nd of 9 giving 5lb to Sendawar (5 Spt Longchamp 8f gd RF 4246a) - also 1st of 8 from Lone Bid (24 Apr Saint-cloud RF 0929a). Consistent. A useful two-year-old, he made a winning 1998 return in the Prix de Guiche. He followed that up with three second places, in the Grand Prix de Paris, the Prix du Moulin, and in the Prix du Rond-Point. He started 1999 by winning twice at Saint-Cloud on soft ground. He was then tried at longer and shorter trips in top company, and ran well. Switched back to his favoured mile trip, he then came up against the mighty Sendawar. A top miler who was placed in five Group Ones without winning one, he now retires to stud in France

**Mme C Head in FR [3-11] (from A Fabre in FR [1-1] Apr 1999).*

GOLD BLADE BHB 47f45a **RR 48f 45a** 4347[5]

10 ch g Rousillon (USA) 10.4f **(69)** - Sharp Girl (FR) (Sharpman) 11.3f **(66)**

Form - 033871125

Record	**1999** -	1st:2	2nd:1	3rd:2	Ran:8
	Pre1999 -	1st:12	2nd:12	3rd:7	Ran:72

Win Prizemoney £39,510 *Total Prizemoney* £55,471

Wins							
* **1999**	Jly	Pontef	(G-S)	H	10f	41	44
* **1999**	Jun	Lingfi	(G-F)	H	11.5f	40	38
* 1996	Aug	Catter	(G-F)	H	12f	67	58+
* 1996	Jly	Beverl	(G-F)	H	9.9f	64	68
* 1996	Jly	Ayr	(G-F)	H	13.1f	60	61
* 1996	Jly	Hamilt	(G-F)	H	9.2f	49	60
* 1996	Jly	Pontef	(G-F)	H	10f	49	61+
* 1996	Apr	Nottin	(GD)	H	10f	44	48
* 1996	*Jan*	*Southw*	*(STD)*	*H*	*12f*	*60*	*67*
* 1995	Jly	Hamilt	(FRM)	H	11.1f	42	49
* 1995	*Jan*	*Wolver*	*(STD)*	*H*	*12f*	*57*	*63*

1999 Turf 2-5: (10f 1-1, 11f 1-3, 12f) (gd, g-f, frm 1-2, hrd 1-1) 1999 AW 0-3: (12f 2, 16f) (Equi, Fibr 2)

Moderate gelding, effective 10 to 11f, best at 11f, acts on gd to hrd, best on frm, has worn blinkers, favours tight tracks. Turf high 48 - 2nd of 10 getting 3lb from China Castle (16 Jly Hamilton 11f frm RF 2868) - also 1st of 13 giving 2lb to Acquittal (6 Jly Pontefract RF 2580). AW high 44.

**J Pearce [11-48] Arthur Old (from N A Graham [3-32] Jly 1994).*

GOLD CAMP (USA) **RR 66f** 4275[6]

3 b c Mr Prospector (USA) 8.6f **(88)** - Dance Colony (USA) (Pleasant Colony (USA)) 7f **(70)**

Form - 6

Record	**1999** -	1st:0	2nd:0	3rd:0	Ran:1

1999 Turf 0-1: (10f) (g-f)

Leggy, currently average colt.

**J H M Gosden [0-1] Sheikh Mohammed.*

GOLD CHANCE (IRE) BHB 50f49a **RR 40f 49a** 3071[9]

3 ch g Fayruz 6.6f **(63)** - Maura Paul (Bonne Noel) 10.7f **(71)**

Form - 07450

Record	**1999** -	1st:0	2nd:0	3rd:0	Ran:5
	Pre1999 -	1st:0	2nd:0	3rd:1	Ran:5

Win Prizemoney £0 *Total Prizemoney* £936

1999 Turf 0-2: (5f, 8f) (g-s, frm) 1999 AW 0-3: (5f 2, 6f) (Fibr 3)

Neat, moderate gelding, has worn blinkers. Turf high 38. AW high 47. **G C H Chung [0-10] Ian Pattle.*

GOLD COAST BHB 58a **RR 65f** 2[9]

3 b g Alhijaz 7.7f **(57)** - Odilese (Mummy's Pet) 7.7f **(60)**

Form - 00

Record	**1999** -	1st:0	2nd:0	3rd:0	Ran:1
	Pre1999 -	1st:0	2nd:0	3rd:0	Ran:5

1999 AW 0-1: (8f) (Equi)

Leggy, average gelding. **S Dow [0-6] G Steinberg.*

GOLD DESIRE BHB 56f44a **RR 55?f 44a** 4714[11]

9 b g Grey Desire 9.3f **(49)** - Glory Gold (Hittite Glory) 8.7f **(50)**

Form - 0

Record	**1999** -	1st:0	2nd:0	3rd:0	Ran:1
	Pre1999 -	1st:9	2nd:7	3rd:8	Ran:75

Win Prizemoney £36,562 *Total Prizemoney* £51,920

Wins								
* 1997	Spt	York	(SFT)	H	10.4f	56	61	<
* 1997	Aug	Ascot	(GD)	H	12f	54	58	
* 1997	May	Ayr	(SFT)	H	10.9f	45	53+	
* 1996	Spt	York	(GD)	H	10.4f	44	49	
* 1996	Aug	Newmar	(GD)	H	10f	33	41	
* 1995	Aug	Newcas	(GD)	H	10.1f	26	32	

1999 Turf 0-1: (12f) (gd)

Fair gelding, has worn blinkers.

**M Brittain [9-76] Northgate Lodge Racing Club.*

GOLD EDGE BHB 34f34a RR 34f 34a 3601[5]
5 ch m Beveled (USA) 6.9f **(64)** - Golden October (Young Generation) 7.7f **(63)**
Form - 00507700005
Record **1999** - 1st:0 2nd:0 3rd:0 Ran:9
Pre1999 - 1st:1 2nd:5 3rd:5 Ran:37
Win Prizemoney £3,631 *Total Prizemoney* £11,335
Wins 1997 Aug Chepst (G-F) H 6.1f 50 59 <
1999 Turf 0-8: (5f 8) (gd 4, g-f, frm 3) 1999 AW 0-1: (5f) (Fibr)
Very moderate filly, effective 5f, acts on sft, has worn blinkers. Turf high 37.
**N Tinkler [0-4] Don Enrico Incisa (from Don Enrico Incisa [0-21] Jun 1999).*

GOLDEN ACE (IRE) BHB 37f32a RR 38f 32a 4837[13]
6 ch g Archway (IRE) 8.5f **(60)** - Gobolino (Don) 7.7f **(64)**
Form - 3614020850
Record **1999** - 1st:1 2nd:1 3rd:1 Ran:10
Pre1999 - 1st:2 2nd:2 3rd:6 Ran:31
Win Prizemoney £10,256 *Total Prizemoney* £18,714
Wins *** 1999** Apr Folkes (SFT) H 12f 39 42
1997 Aug Newmar (GD) S 8f 42
1996 Apr Newbur (G-S) 8f 85 <
1999 Turf 1-9: (10f 2, 12f 1-5, 14f 2) (hvy 1-1, sft 2, g-s 3, gd, g-f 2) 1999 AW 0-1: (14f) (Fibr)
Very moderate gelding, effective 10 to 12f, best at 10f, acts on sft to frm, best on g-s, has worn blinkers. Turf high 45 - 2nd of 5 getting 18lb from Mane Frame (7 Jun Warwick 12f g-s RF 1796).
**R C Spicer [1-32] G D J Linder (from R Hannon [2-9] Aug 1997).*

GOLDEN BIFF (IRE) BHB 60f63a RR 52f 63a 4832[27]
3 ch c Shalford (IRE) 7.8f **(63)** - Capable Kate (IRE) (Alzao (USA)) 7.1f **(68)**
Form - 30830062010
Record **1999** - 1st:1 2nd:1 3rd:1 Ran:9
Pre1999 - 1st:0 2nd:2 3rd:2 Ran:8
Win Prizemoney £2,250 *Total Prizemoney* £5,990
Wins *** 1999** Oct Catter (SFT) 6f 52 <
1999 Turf 1-9: (5f 3, 6f 1-2, 7f 4) (sft, gd 1-2, g-f 4, frm 2)
Scopey, average colt, effective 5 to 6f, acts on g-s to gd, has worn blinkers. Turf high 59. **I Semple [1-17] Patersons of Greenoakhill.*

GOLDEN CHARM (IRE) BHB 39f RR 39f 4945[9]
3 b f Common Grounds 8.1f **(66)** - Credit Crunch (IRE) (Caerleon (USA)) 8.6f **(71)**
Form - 00080600
Record **1999** - 1st:0 2nd:0 3rd:0 Ran:8
Pre1999 - 1st:1 2nd:1 3rd:0 Ran:8
Win Prizemoney £3,366 *Total Prizemoney* £4,981
Wins * 1998 May Nottin (G-F) 6.1f 67 <
1999 Turf 0-7: (6f, 7f 4, 8f, 10f) (sft, gd 2, frm 4) 1999 AW 0-1: (6f) (Fibr)
Scopey, very moderate filly, effective 6 to 7f, acts on g-f to frm, has worn blinkers. Turf high 50.
**J E Banks [1-16] Wild Risk Partnership.*

GOLDEN CHIMES (USA) BHB 61f RR 61f 5028[8]
4 ch c Woodman (USA) 9.7f **(77)** - Russian Ballet (USA) (Nijinsky (CAN)) 10.3f **(77)**
Form - 8060038
Record **1999** - 1st:0 2nd:0 3rd:1 Ran:7
Pre1999 - 1st:1 2nd:0 3rd:0 Ran:4
Win Prizemoney £4,468 *Total Prizemoney* £5,508
Wins 1998 Spt Listow (G-S) 10f 87 <
1999 Turf 0-7: (10f, 11f 2, 12f 3, 16f) (g-s 3, gd, frm 3)
Average colt, effective 10f, acts on g-s, has worn blinkers, likes left handed tracks. Turf high 79. Consistent.
**Major D N Chappell [0-7] R C C Villers (from C O'Brien in IRE [1-4] Oct 1998).*

GOLDEN FAWN BHB 29f46a RR 9f 46a 1175[11]
6 ch m Crowning Honors (CAN) 9.9f **(36)** - Hill of Fare (Brigadier Gerard) 9.3f **(58)**
Form - 000
Record **1999** - 1st:0 2nd:0 3rd:0 Ran:2
Pre1999 - 1st:0 2nd:2 3rd:0 Ran:8
Win Prizemoney £0 *Total Prizemoney* £1,398
1999 Turf 0-1: (12f) (g-f) 1999 AW 0-1: (12f) (Equi)
Little account mare, has worn blinkers. Inconsistent.
**M J Haynes [1-9] Blackmore Stevens Partnership (from N M Babbage [0-2] May 1997).*

GOLDEN FORCE BHB 68f80a RR 41f 80a 1771[9]
3 b g Forzando 7.2f **(63)** - Silverlocks **(82f)** (Sharrood (USA)) 10.5f **(72)**
Form - 7010
Record **1999** - 1st:1 2nd:0 3rd:0 Ran:4
Pre1999 - 1st:0 2nd:0 3rd:2 Ran:3
Win Prizemoney £3,655 *Total Prizemoney* £4,732
Wins *** 1999** *May Wolver (STD) H 7f 72 82* <
1999 Turf 0-3: (6f 2, 8f) (gd 2, g-f) 1999 AW 1-1: (7f 1-1) (Fibr 1-1)
Scopey, decent gelding, effective 6 to 7f, best at 6f, acts on frm - acts on Fibr. Turf high 41. (1st run) - 1st of 8 from Polar Ice (8 May Wolverhampton RF 1119). **R Hannon [1-7] George Teo.*

GOLDENGIRLMICHELLE (IRE) BHB 20f RR 42f 2805[4]
4 b f Project Manager 7.2f **(47)** - Arbour Day (Artaius (USA)) 9f **(69)**
Form - 004
Record **1999** - 1st:0 2nd:0 3rd:0 Ran:3
Pre1999 - 1st:0 2nd:0 3rd:0 Ran:6
1999 Turf 0-3: (12f 3) (g-f, frm 2)
Moderate filly, effective 11f, acts on g-f, has worn blinkers, likes left handed tracks. Turf high 42. Inconsistent.
**J J O'Neill [0-4] The Cartmel Syndicate (from F Murphy [1-6] Apr 1999).*

GOLDEN GLORY BHB 32f RR 37?f 4714[15]
6 b g Grey Desire 9.3f **(49)** - Glory Gold (Hittite Glory) 8.7f **(50)**
Form - 0
Record **1999** - 1st:0 2nd:0 3rd:0 Ran:1
Pre1999 - 1st:0 2nd:0 3rd:0 Ran:3
1999 Turf 0-1: (12f) (gd)
Very moderate gelding. **M Brittain [0-4] Mel Brittain.*

GOLDEN HADEER BHB 32f58a RR 23f 58a 1122[10]
8 ch h Hadeer 8.9f **(58)** - Verchinina (Star Appeal) 9.6f **(65)**
Form - 0000
Record **1999** - 1st:0 2nd:0 3rd:0 Ran:3
Pre1999 - 1st:10 2nd:3 3rd:7 Ran:48
Win Prizemoney £30,870 *Total Prizemoney* £36,764
Wins * 1998 *May Southw (STD) H 14f 63 69*
* 1997 May Warwic (G-F) H 14.9f 47 53
* 1997 May Nottin (GD) H 16f 43 49+
* 1997 May Hamilt (SFT) H 13f 34 44
* 1997 *Feb Southw (STD) H 16f 65 77* <
* 1997 *Jan Wolver (STD) H 16.2f 54 66+*
* 1997 *Jan Wolver (STD) H 14.8f 48 63+*
* 1997 *Jan Southw (STD) H 16f 48 63+*
* 1996 *Nov Southw (STD) H 14f 44 48*
1999 Turf 0-2: (14f, 15f) (hvy, sft) 1999 AW 0-1: (16f) (Fibr)
Average horse, effective 14 to 16f, - acts on Fibr, has worn blinkers, likes left handed tracks, favours tight tracks. Inconsistent.
**M J Ryan [9-48] Doug Fleet (from R Harris [1-5] Mar 1994).*

GOLDEN HARVEST (IRE) BHB 72f RR 76f 5045[17]
2 ch g Vettori (IRE) - Dissidence (IRE) (Dancing Dissident (USA))
Form - 4034200
Record **1999** - 1st:0 2nd:1 3rd:1 Ran:7
Win Prizemoney £0 *Total Prizemoney* £2,230
1999 Turf 0-7: (6f 7) (sft, gd 2, g-f, frm 3)
Above-average gelding, effective 6f, acts on frm. Turf high 76 (began Jly). **B J Meehan [0-7] J S Dunningham.*

GOLDEN HAWK (USA) BHB 50f RR 57f 4000[7]
4 ch g Silver Hawk (USA) 11.2f **(85)** - Crockadore (USA) (Nijinsky (CAN)) 10.3f **(77)**
Form - 7657
Record **1999** - 1st:0 2nd:0 3rd:0 Ran:4
Pre1999 - 1st:0 2nd:1 3rd:1 Ran:5
Win Prizemoney £0 *Total Prizemoney* £2,610
1999 Turf 0-4: (12f, 14f 3) (gd, g-f, frm 2)
Leggy, fair gelding, effective 16f, acts on g-s, favours tight tracks. Turf high 57 (began Jly). **S Dow [0-6] Cazanove Clear Height Racing (from P F I Cole [0-5] Oct 1998).*

GOLDEN LEGEND (IRE) RR 58f 3767[7]
2 b c Last Tycoon 9.4f **(73)** - Adjalisa (IRE) (Darshaan) 9.9f **(84)**
Form - 77
Record 1999 - 1st:0 2nd:0 3rd:0 Ran:2
1999 Turf 0-2: (6f 2) (gd, frm)
Currently fair colt. Turf high 58 (began Jly).
**G Wragg [0-2] Mollers Racing.*

GOLDEN LOCKET RR 71f 5060[11]
2 ch f Beveled (USA) 6.9f **(64)** - Rekindled Flame (IRE) (Kings Lake (USA)) 10.8f **(67)**
Form - 570
Record 1999 - 1st:0 2nd:0 3rd:0 Ran:3
1999 Turf 0-3: (7f 3) (g-s 2, gd)
Currently above-average filly. Turf high 71 (began Spt).
**A G Foster [0-2] Good Connections (from P W Chapple-Hyam [0-1] Spt 1999).*

GOLDEN LYRIC (IRE) BHB 32f40a **RR 27f 40a** 5057[11]
4 ch c Lycius (USA) 8.8f **(71)** - Adjala (Northfields (USA)) 9f **(72)**
Form - 6283332167000
Record 1999 - 1st:1 2nd:1 3rd:3 Ran:11
Pre1999 - 1st:0 2nd:1 3rd:0 Ran:13
Win Prizemoney £2,258 *Total Prizemoney* £4,102
Wins ** 1999 Mar Southw (SLW) H 11f 39 42 <*
1999 Turf 0-3: (8f, 11f 2) (g-f, frm, hrd) 1999 AW 1-8: (8f 5, 10f, 11f 1-1, 12f) (Equi 3, Fibr 1-5)
Scopey, moderate colt, effective 8 to 11f, acts on gd to frm - acts on AW, has worn blinkers, prefers tight tracks, does well at Southwell. Turf high 27. AW high 46 - 6th of 12 getting 8lb from Statistician (18 Mar Lingfield 8f Equi RF 0441) - also 1st of 11 giving 9lb to Super-Gem (10 Mar Southwell RF 0422).
**J Pearce [1-13] Saracen Racing (from G Wragg [0-11] Oct 1998).*

GOLDEN MIRACLE (FR) BHB 83f **RR 78f** 4809[5]
2 b c Cadeaux Genereux 7.9f **(76)** - Cheeky Charm (USA) **(47f)** (Nureyev (USA)) 8.7f **(78)**
Form - 45451315
Record 1999 - 1st:2 2nd:0 3rd:1 Ran:8
Win Prizemoney £14,950 *Total Prizemoney* £15,997
Wins * **1999** Spt Hamilt (SFT) H 6f 77 77 <
* **1999** Spt Hamilt (G-F) H 6f 73 77 <
1999 Turf 2-8: (5f, 6f 2-6, 7f) (sft, gd 1-2, frm 1-5)
Above-average colt, effective 6 to 7f, best at 6f, acts on gd to frm, best on frm. Turf high 77 - 1st of 9 giving 6lb to City Princess (6 Spt Hamilton RF 4164) - also 1st of 16 giving 17lb to Glenwhargen (27 Spt Hamilton RF 4589). Consistent. Both of his wins to date have come at Hamilton, albeit on contrasting ground. The second of those wins came in a valuable nursery. Six furlongs looks as far as he wants at the moment. **M Johnston [2-8] Maktoum Al Maktoum.*

GOLDEN NOTE BHB 71f **RR 72f** 4860[4]
2 ch c Efisio 7.7f **(69)** - Triple Tricks (IRE) **(67f)** (Royal Academy (USA))
Form - 084
Record 1999 - 1st:0 2nd:0 3rd:0 Ran:3
Win Prizemoney £0 *Total Prizemoney* £272
1999 Turf 0-3: (6f, 7f 2) (g-s, gd, frm)
Currently above-average colt. Turf high 72 (began Aug).
**B J Meehan [0-3] Mrs K J Crangle.*

GOLDEN POUND (USA) BHB 48f60a **RR 43f 60a** 5128[6]
7 b g Seeking the Gold (USA) 7.4f **(80)** - Coesse Express (USA) (Dewan (USA)) 7.4f **(65)**
Form - 0674445056
Record 1999 - 1st:0 2nd:0 3rd:0 Ran:10
Pre1999 - 1st:4 2nd:5 3rd:5 Ran:49
Win Prizemoney £14,201 *Total Prizemoney* £27,151
Wins * 1998 May Leices (GD) H 6f 72 77
* 1997 Aug Bright (GD) H 6f 75 78
* 1996 Jly Epsom (G-F) H 6f 77 83 <
* 1996 Apr Thirsk (G-F) 6f 75
1999 Turf 0-10: (6f 10) (g-s, gd 2, g-f 3, frm 3, hrd)
Average gelding, effective 6f, acts on g-f, often wears blinkers (effectively). Turf high 56.
**Miss Gay Kelleway [4-48] A P Griffin (from Mrs L Stubbs [0-7] May 1999).*

GOLDEN PRINCE (IRE) BHB 72f **RR 76f** 4991[1]
3 b c Polish Patriot (USA) 7.8f **(70)** - Cathryn's Song (Prince Tenderfoot (USA)) 9f **(61)**
Form - 70411
Record 1999 - 1st:2 2nd:0 3rd:0 Ran:5
Win Prizemoney £7,179 *Total Prizemoney* £7,416
Wins * **1999** Oct Nottin (FRM) H 8.2f 66 70 <
* **1999** Spt Bright (SFT) 8f 66
1999 Turf 2-5: (7f, 8f 2-4) (g-s 1-1, g-f, frm 1-3)
Leggy, above-average colt. Turf high 76 - also 1st of 15 getting 5lb from Isle Au Haut (20 Oct Nottingham RF 4991).
**R Hannon [2-5] George Teo.*

GOLDEN RAINBOW (IRE) RR 35f 4988[5]
3 b g Rainbows For Life (CAN) 9.3f **(64)** - Nawadder (Kris) 9.5f **(73)**
Form - 00605
Record 1999 - 1st:0 2nd:0 3rd:0 Ran:5
Pre1999 - 1st:0 2nd:1 3rd:0 Ran:6
Win Prizemoney £0 *Total Prizemoney* £1,045
1999 Turf 0-5: (7f, 8f 2, 10f, 14f) (hvy, g-f 2, frm 2)
Light-framed, very moderate gelding, effective 6f, acts on gd, has worn blinkers. Turf high 35.
**Mrs P N Dutfield [0-3] Golden Rainbow Partnership (from B R Millman [0-9] Jun 1999).*

GOLDEN REEF BHB 59f **RR 53f** 2525[12]
3 b g Puissance 7.1f **(60)** - Cloudy Reef (Cragador) 6f **(67)**
Form - 5783600
Record 1999 - 1st:0 2nd:0 3rd:1 Ran:7
Pre1999 - 1st:0 2nd:2 3rd:0 Ran:7
Win Prizemoney £0 *Total Prizemoney* £1,730
1999 Turf 0-7: (6f 4, 7f 2, 8f) (sft 3, gd 2, frm 2)
Scopey, fair gelding, effective 5 to 6f, best at 5f, acts on sft to gd. Turf high 73 - 3rd of 10 to Royal Wave (18 May Pontefract 6f gd RF 1304). **R Hollinshead [0-14] M Johnson.*

GOLDEN RETRIEVER (USA) RR 54f 5129[13]
2 b br c Red Ransom (USA) 8.6f **(83)** - Golden Rhyme (Dom Racine (FR)) 9.2f **(62)**
Form - 0
Record 1999 - 1st:0 2nd:0 3rd:0 Ran:1
1999 Turf 0-1: (6f) (gd)
Currently fair colt. **D R C Elsworth [0-1] P D Savill.*

GOLDEN ROD BHB 71f **RR 68f** 5216[9]
2 ch c Rainbows For Life (CAN) 9.3f **(64)** - Noble Form (Double Form) 7.3f **(58)**
Form - 400
Record 1999 - 1st:0 2nd:0 3rd:0 Ran:3
1999 Turf 0-3: (7f, 8f 2) (g-s, gd, g-f)
Currently average colt. Turf high 68 (began Aug).
**P W Harris [0-3] Neil Rodway.*

GOLDEN SHOT BHB 30f **RR 35f** 5066[16]
3 ch f Pharly (FR) 11.5f **(64)** - Hoop la (Final Straw) 7.9f **(64)**
Form - 0000
Record 1999 - 1st:0 2nd:0 3rd:0 Ran:4
1999 Turf 0-3: (10f 2, 12f) (gd, frm 2) 1999 AW 0-1: (9f) (Fibr)
Scopey, very moderate filly. Turf high 35 (began Jly).
**J L Spearing [0-4] Alan Cadoret.*

GOLDEN SILCA BHB 111f **RR 110f** 2041[2]
3 ch f Inchinor 8.9f **(64)** - Silca-Cisa (Hallgate)
Form - 2722
Record 1999 - 1st:0 2nd:3 3rd:0 Ran:4
Pre1999 - 1st:5 2nd:1 3rd:1 Ran:9
Win Prizemoney £84,415 *Total Prizemoney* £199,725
Wins * 1998 Spt Newbur (GD) G2 6f 106 <
* 1998 Spt Baden- (SFT) G2 6f 97
* 1998 Jly Newbur (G-F) L 6f 97
* 1998 May Newbur (GD) 5.2f 84
* 1998 Apr Newbur (HVY) 5.2f 84+
1999 Turf 0-4: (7f, 8f 3) (g-f 2, frm 2)
Leggy, Group-class filly, effective 6 to 8f, best at 8f, acts on sft to frm, best on g-f, excels at Newbury. Turf high 110 - 2nd of 9 to Balisada (16 Jun Ascot 8f g-f RF 2041). Consistent. She bounced back well from a vigorous juvenile campaign, finishing second in

both the Irish 1,000 Guineas and Coronation Stakes. Unlikely to stay beyond a mile or improve significantly, she will make a smashing broodmare. **M R Channon [5-13] Aldridge Racing Ltd.*

GOLDEN SKY (IRE) BHB 32f **RR 33f** 2262[13]
3 b f Petardia 8.2f **(58)** - Oriental Splendour (Runnett) 7f **(59)**
Form - 0700
Record 1999 - 1st:0 2nd:0 3rd:0 Ran:4
Pre1999 - 1st:0 2nd:0 3rd:0 Ran:4
1999 Turf 0-4: (7f, 8f 2, 10f) (g-s, g-f, frm, hrd)
Leggy, very moderate filly. Turf high 33.
**Don Enrico Incisa [0-6] Don Enrico Incisa (from N Tinkler [0-2] Apr 1998).*

GOLDEN SNAKE (USA) BHB 114f **RR 117f** 4919[10]
3 b c Danzig (USA) 8.1f **(88)** - Dubian (High Line) 10.3f **(70)**
Form - 12160
Record 1999 - 1st:2 2nd:1 3rd:0 Ran:5
Pre1999 - 1st:1 2nd:0 3rd:0 Ran:2
Win Prizemoney £59,565 *Total Prizemoney* £89,790
Wins * **1999** Jun Chanti (SFT) G1 9f 117 <
* **1999** Apr Newmar (GD) L 8.5f 108
* 1998 Spt Doncas (GD) 8f 85+
1999 Turf 2-5: (9f 2-2, 10f 3) (g-s, gd 1-2, g-f 1-2)
Scopey, high-class colt, effective 9 to 10f, best at 10f, acts on g-s to g-f, best on gd. Turf high 117 - 1st of 6 from Slip Stream (6 Jun Chantilly RF 1903a) - also 1st of 9 from Gold Academy (15 Apr Newmarket RF 0700). A progressive colt, he won the Feilden Stakes at Newmarket and the Group One Prix Jean Prat at the beginning of last season, as well as finishing runner-up in the Dante. Rather disappointing in his last two starts, finishing a well-beaten sixth in the Juddmonte International and down the field in the Dubai Champion Stakes. **B W Hills [3-7] Mohamed Obaida.*

Golden Snake developed into a Group One performer last season

GOLDEN SYRUP (IRE) BHB 58f54a **RR 45f 54a** 1382[11]
3 b f Dolphin Street (FR) - Sprint For Gold (USA) (Slew O' Gold (USA)) 8f **(75)**
Form - 12224410050
Record 1999 - 1st:2 2nd:3 3rd:0 Ran:11
Pre1999 - 1st:0 2nd:0 3rd:0 Ran:5
Win Prizemoney £3,941 *Total Prizemoney* £5,501
Wins * **1999** Apr Leices (GD) S 6f 61 <
* **1999** *Jan Southw (STD) S 8f 57*
1999 Turf 1-5: (6f 1-1, 7f 2, 8f 2) (g-s, gd 1-1, g-f, frm 2) 1999 AW 1-6: (7f 2, 8f 1-4) (Equi, Fibr 1-5)
Scopey, fair filly, effective 6 to 8f, best at 6f, acts on gd to frm - acts on Fibr, best on gd, excels at Southwell. Turf high 61 (1st run) - 1st of 16 from Split The Aces (8 Apr Leicester RF 0621). AW high 59 - 2nd of 6 to Alana's Cavalier (11 Jan Southwell 8f Fibr RF 0076) - also 1st of 7 getting 5lb from Nathan's Hero (4 Jan Southwell RF 0026). **P Howling [2-11] Paul Howling (from R Hannon [0-5] Spt 1998).*

GOLDEN WAY (IRE) RR 53f 4681[10]
2 ch f Cadeaux Genereux 7.9f **(76)** - Diavolina (USA) (Lear Fan (USA)) 8.5f **(73)**
Form - 0
Record 1999 - 1st:0 2nd:0 3rd:0 Ran:1
1999 Turf 0-1: (6f) (gd)
Currently fair filly. **E A L Dunlop [0-1] Ahmed Ali.*

GOLDFAW RR 30f 5061[7]
2 ch c Wing Park - Sailors Moon **(33f 46a)** (Indian Ridge)
Form - 07
Record 1999 - 1st:0 2nd:0 3rd:0 Ran:2
1999 Turf 0-2: (5f, 6f) (g-s, frm)
Currently very moderate colt. Turf high 30 (began Aug).
**A T Murphy [0-2] Orby Racing.*

GOLDFINCH RR 57f 4821[12]
2 b f Zilzal (USA) 8.5f **(79)** - Garconniere (Gay Mecene (USA)) 8.6f **(69)**
Form - 0
Record 1999 - 1st:0 2nd:0 3rd:0 Ran:1
1999 Turf 0-1: (6f) (g-f)
Currently fair filly. **J R Fanshawe [0-1] Dr Catherine Wills.*

GOLD HALO (IRE) BHB 33f **RR 40f** 4667[9]
3 b f Strike The Gold (USA) 8f **(79)** - Halo's Charm (USA) (Halo (USA)) 10.6f **(75)**
Form - 670
Record 1999 - 1st:0 2nd:0 3rd:0 Ran:3
1999 Turf 0-2: (7f, 10f) (g-s, frm) 1999 AW 0-1: (13f) (Equi)
Leggy, currently moderate filly. Turf high 40 (began Jly).
**A Kelleway [0-3] L J Rice.*

GOLD HONOR (FR) BHB 57f60a **RR 62f 60a** 1020[2]
3 gr g Highest Honor (FR) 10.9f **(72)** - Golden Sea (FR) (Saint Cyrien (FR)) 8.4f **(80)**
Form - 773432
Record 1999 - 1st:0 2nd:1 3rd:1 Ran:3
Pre1999 - 1st:1 2nd:0 3rd:2 Ran:10
Win Prizemoney £4,240 *Total Prizemoney* £6,396
Wins * 1998 Oct Newmar (SFT) S 8f 73 <
1999 Turf 0-3: (10f, 12f 2) (hvy, gd, hrd)
Scopey, average gelding, effective 8f, acts on gd, often wears blinkers (effectively). Turf high 59.
**B J Meehan [1-13] Mrs Susan Roy.*

GOLD KRIEK RR 13f 5216[16]
2 b g High Kicker (USA) 8.4f **(52)** - Ship of Gold (Glint of Gold) 9.3f **(66)**
Form - 0
Record 1999 - 1st:0 2nd:0 3rd:0 Ran:1
1999 Turf 0-1: (8f) (g-s)
Currently poor gelding. **N A Callaghan [0-1] Norcroft Park Stud.*

GOLD LANCE (USA) BHB 44f35a **RR 40f 35a** 4997[9]
6 ch g Seeking the Gold (USA) 7.4f **(80)** - Lucky State (USA) (State Dinner (USA)) 9.4f **(74)**
Form - 003020060
Record 1999 - 1st:0 2nd:1 3rd:1 Ran:8
Pre1999 - 1st:4 2nd:1 3rd:3 Ran:20
Win Prizemoney £13,264 *Total Prizemoney* £16,568
Wins * 1997 Spt Goodwo (GD) H 8f 56 60 <
* 1997 Aug Windso (G-F) H 8.3f 53 57
* 1997 Jly Chepst (G-F) SH 8.1f 48 53
* 1997 Apr Pontef (G-F) SH 8f 45 53
1999 Turf 0-8: (8f, 9f, 10f 4, 12f 2) (gd, g-f, frm 4, hrd 2)
Moderate gelding, effective 9f, acts on hrd, has worn blinkers, likes left handed tracks. Turf high 49 - 2nd of 13 giving 4lb to Girlie

Set (19 Jun Lingfield 9f hrd RF 2147). Consistent.
**R J O'Sullivan [4-36] Mrs Barbara Marchant (from Sir Michael Stoute [0-2] Jun 1996).*

GOLDLINER GOSSIP (IRE) BHB 32f **RR 26f** 1280[11]
4 b f Pips Pride 6.7f **(70)** - Swift And Early (IRE) (Alzao (USA)) 7.1f **(68)**
Form - 000
Record 1999 - 1st:0 2nd:0 3rd:0 Ran:3
Pre1999 - 1st:0 2nd:0 3rd:0 Ran:3
1999 Turf 0-1: (7f) (gd) 1999 AW 0-2: (7f, 11f) (Fibr 2)
Light-framed, little account filly, has worn blinkers.
**Miss M E Rowland [0-6] Goldliner Racing Club.*

GOLD LODGE BHB 69f **RR 81df** 5067[6]
3 ch g Grand Lodge (USA) - Glimmering Girl (USA) (Spectacular Bid (USA)) 11.2f **(76)**
Form - 283336
Record 1999 - 1st:0 2nd:1 3rd:3 Ran:6
Pre1999 - 1st:0 2nd:1 3rd:0 Ran:3
Win Prizemoney £0 *Total Prizemoney* £3,912
1999 Turf 0-6: (12f 3, 14f 2, 17f) (gd 2, g-f 2, frm, hrd)
Scopey, decent gelding, effective 9 to 14f, best at 14f, acts on gd to frm, best on frm, prefers left handed tracks, favours tight tracks. Turf high 81 - 3rd of 10 to Ashgar (18 Jun Redcar 14f frm RF 2129). Consistent. **S C Williams [0-9] Livingston Trading Ltd.*

GOLD MILLENIUM (IRE) BHB 42f **RR 47f** 4882[12]
5 gr g Kenmare (FR) 9.6f **(76)** - Gold Necklace (Golden Fleece (USA)) 7.9f **(74)**
Form - 7000840
Record 1999 - 1st:0 2nd:0 3rd:0 Ran:7
Pre1999 - 1st:0 2nd:0 3rd:0 Ran:1
1999 Turf 0-7: (7f 2, 8f 2, 11f, 12f, 14f) (gd 2, g-f 3, frm 2)
Moderate gelding. Turf high 58. **C A Horgan [0-8] Mrs L M Horgan.*

GOLD QUEST (IRE) RR 54f 4210[10]
2 ch c Rainbow Quest (USA) 11.2f **(81)** - My Potters (USA) (Irish River (FR)) 8.6f **(78)**
Form - 0
Record 1999 - 1st:0 2nd:0 3rd:0 Ran:1
1999 Turf 0-1: (8f) (gd)
Currently fair colt. **Sir Michael Stoute [0-1] Lady Clague.*

GOLD SEEKER BHB 60f **RR 51f** 4543[18]
2 ch f Superlative 8.8f **(57)** - Goldsearch (IRE) **(56f 53a)** (Fayruz)
Form - 6740
Record 1999 - 1st:0 2nd:0 3rd:0 Ran:4
1999 Turf 0-4: (5f 4) (gd 2, frm 2)
Fair filly. Turf high 51. **D W Barker [0-4] D W Barker.*

GOLDSTAR (IRE) BHB 23f **RR 6f** 2949[12]
4 b g Fayruz 6.6f **(63)** - Scarlet Red (Pas de Seul) 9.1f **(67)**
Form - 8360
Record 1999 - 1st:0 2nd:0 3rd:1 Ran:4
Pre1999 - 1st:0 2nd:0 3rd:0 Ran:5
Win Prizemoney £0 *Total Prizemoney* £248
1999 Turf 0-2: (12f 2) (g-f, frm) 1999 AW 0-2: (9f, 11f) (Fibr 2)
Little account gelding, has worn blinkers. Turf high 6 (began Jly). AW high 27. Inconsistent.
**P Eccles [0-10] D W Watson (from Miss Frances Crowley in IRE [0-3] Oct 1998).*

GOLLACCIA BHB 25f **RR 30f** 4442[12]
5 gr m Mystiko (USA) 7.7f **(59)** - Millie Grey (Grey Ghost) 9.9f **(60)**
Form - 0
Record 1999 - 1st:0 2nd:0 3rd:0 Ran:1
Pre1999 - 1st:0 2nd:0 3rd:0 Ran:5
1999 Turf 0-1: (12f) (g-s)
Very moderate filly.
**B Ellison [0-3] Mrs Susan Ellison (from G M Moore [0-5] May 1997).*

GO MAN (IRE) RR 849[6]
5 b g Mandalus - Cherry Park (Netherkelly) 5.6f **(46)**
Form - 6
Record 1999 - 1st:0 2nd:0 3rd:0 Ran:1
1999 AW 0-1: (12f) (Fibr)
Currently very moderate gelding. **P D Evans [0-3] J E Potter.*

GONE FOR A BURTON (IRE) BHB 60f **RR 60f** 3487[7]
9 ch g Bustino 11f **(64)** - Crimbourne (Mummy's Pet) 7.7f **(60)**
Form - 067
Record 1999 - 1st:0 2nd:0 3rd:0 Ran:3
Pre1999 - 1st:3 2nd:4 3rd:5 Ran:32
Win Prizemoney £8,946 *Total Prizemoney* £26,678
Wins * 1995 Apr Warwic (G-S) H 10.8f 80 86 <
1999 Turf 0-3: (11f, 12f 2) (gd 2, g-f)
Average gelding, effective 11 to 12f, acts on gd to frm, has worn blinkers. Turf high 60. Consistent. **P J Makin [3-42] H P Carrington.*

GONE IN THE WIND (FR) BHB 39f **RR 33f** 5046[11]
3 ch c Sanglamore (USA) 12.9f **(67)** - Miss Silca Key (Welsh Saint) 7.6f **(64)**
Form - 760
Record 1999 - 1st:0 2nd:0 3rd:0 Ran:3
1999 Turf 0-3: (7f, 8f, 10f) (hvy, g-f, frm)
Currently very moderate colt. Turf high 33 (began Aug) - 6th of 20 getting 5lb from Cosmo Jack (9 Spt Chepstow 8f frm RF 4228).
**R Hannon [0-3] J O Eddery.*

GONE SAVAGE BHB 70f65a **RR 74?f 65a** 2383[13]
11 b g Nomination 7.3f **(57)** - Trwyn Cilan (Import) 6.6f **(68)**
Form - 00
Record 1999 - 1st:0 2nd:0 3rd:0 Ran:2
Pre1999 - 1st:11 2nd:11 3rd:5 Ran:79
Win Prizemoney £43,412 *Total Prizemoney* £63,237
Wins * 1997 Jly Newmar (GD) H 5f 80 79
* 1997 Apr Sandow (G-F) H 5f 75 79
* 1996 Oct York (GD) H 5f 69 75
* 1996 Aug Windso (G-F) H 5f 58 62
* 1995 Apr Kempto (G-F) H 6f 62 58
1999 Turf 0-2: (5f, 6f) (frm 2)
Above-average gelding, has worn blinkers. Turf high 16. Becoming disappointing.
**W J Musson [5-56] Broughton Thermal Insulation (from G B Balding [5-16] Jun 1993).*

GOODBYE GATEMEN (IRE) BHB 48f50a **RR 42f 50a** 1083[8]
5 gr g Soviet Lad (USA) 9.4f **(63)** - Simple Love (Simply Great (FR)) 8.2f **(65)**
Form - 08
Record 1999 - 1st:0 2nd:0 3rd:0 Ran:2
Pre1999 - 1st:1 2nd:6 3rd:2 Ran:25
Win Prizemoney £2,469 *Total Prizemoney* £9,159
Wins 1997 Jly Leices (GD) 5f 46 <
1999 Turf 0-2: (5f, 7f) (sft, g-f)
Fair gelding, effective 5 to 7f, best at 6f, - acts on Equi, has worn blinkers, prefers left handed tracks, prefers tight tracks. Turf high 42. Consistent.
**A J McNae [0-2] Mrs E N Nield (from B A Pearce [1-24] Apr 1998).*

GOODBYE GOLDSTONE BHB 73f53a **RR 73f 53a** 1966[10]
3 b c Mtoto 11.5f **(71)** - Shareehan (Dancing Brave (USA)) 8.4f **(76)**
Form - 3861420
Record 1999 - 1st:1 2nd:1 3rd:1 Ran:7
Pre1999 - 1st:0 2nd:0 3rd:1 Ran:1
Win Prizemoney £2,483 *Total Prizemoney* £9,461
Wins * 1999 Apr Folkes (SFT) H 9.7f 62 69 <
1999 Turf 1-4: (9f, 10f 1-2, 12f) (hvy 1-1, gd 2, g-f) 1999 AW 0-3: (8f 2, 11f) (Fibr 3)
Light-framed, above-average colt, effective 10 to 12f, best at 10f, acts on hvy to g-f, prefers tight tracks. Turf high 73 - 2nd of 15 getting 16lb from Tier Worker (4 Jun Epsom 10f gd RF 1732) - also 1st of 14 getting 3lb from Swampy (20 Apr Folkestone RF 0768). AW high 49. A winner on soft ground at Folkestone in April, he ran very well to finish runner-up at Epsom on Oaks Day. Ten furlongs is his trip. **T J Naughton [1-8] Ashley Carr Racing 2.*

GOODENOUGH MOVER BHB 50f **RR 52df** 4628[9]
3 ch g Beveled (USA) 6.9f **(64)** - Rekindled Flame (IRE) (Kings Lake (USA)) 10.8f **(67)**
Form - 67600
Record 1999 - 1st:0 2nd:0 3rd:0 Ran:5
1999 Turf 0-5: (6f, 7f, 8f 3) (g-s, gd, g-f, frm 2)
Unfurnished, fair gelding. Turf high 66.

G F H Charles-Jones [0-5] D Goodenough Removals & Transport.

GOOD EVANS ABOVE BHB 59f64a **RR 51f 64a** 1436[7]
2 br f Tragic Role (USA) 9.4f **(63)** - Dark Amber (Formidable (USA)) 9.2f **(63)**
Form - 04047
Record 1999 - 1st:0 2nd:0 3rd:0 Ran:5
1999 Turf 0-3: (5f 2, 6f) (g-f, frm 2) 1999 AW 0-2: (5f 2) (Fibr 2)
Fair filly. Turf high 46. AW high 51 (1st run) - 4th of 11 getting 9lb from Richard Ansdell (29 Apr Wolverhampton 5f Fibr RF 0922).
P D Evans [0-5] David Evans.

GOOD FRIDAY (IRE) BHB 68f **RR 63f** 4080[11]
2 b f Tenby 10.4f **(76)** - Sign of Peace (IRE) (Posen (USA))
Form - 66530
Record 1999 - 1st:0 2nd:0 3rd:1 Ran:5
Win Prizemoney £0 *Total Prizemoney* £490
1999 Turf 0-5: (6f, 7f 3, 8f) (g-f 4, frm)
Average filly. Turf high 63 - 3rd of 18 getting 7lb from Noble Pursuit (12 Aug Salisbury 7f g-f RF 3570).
Mrs P N Dutfield [0-5] Aidan Walsh.

GOODWOOD BLIZZARD BHB 100f **RR 98f** 4891a[2]
2 ch f Inchinor 8.9f **(64)** - Icecapped (Caerleon (USA)) 8.6f **(71)**
Form - 412132
Record 1999 - 1st:2 2nd:2 3rd:1 Ran:6
Win Prizemoney £16,921 *Total Prizemoney* £33,498

Wins						
* **1999**	Jly	Ascot	(FRM)	7f	93	<
* **1999**	Jun	Salisb	(GD)	6f	84	

1999 Turf 2-6: (6f 1-2, 7f 1-3, 8f) (gd 2, g-f 2-3, frm)
Very useful filly, effective 7 to 8f, best at 7f, acts on gd to g-f, best on g-f. Turf high 98 - 2nd of 11 to Sonda (10 Oct San Siro 8f gd RF 4891a) - also 1st of 7 getting 8lb from Frontier (25 Jly Ascot RF 3118). Like many of her sire's stock, she lacks scope but is game. Touched-off in Group races on her last two starts, she should stay beyond a mile and may be best campaigned on the continent.
J L Dunlop [2-6].

GOODWOOD JAZZ (IRE) BHB 66f **RR 70f** 2149[10]
3 b f Night Shift (USA) 8.1f **(73)** - Wood Violet (USA) (Riverman (USA)) 9.1f **(76)**
Form - 380
Record 1999 - 1st:0 2nd:0 3rd:1 Ran:3
Pre1999 - 1st:0 2nd:1 3rd:2 Ran:6
Win Prizemoney £0 *Total Prizemoney* £2,425
1999 Turf 0-3: (7f, 8f 2) (sft, g-f, hrd)
Unfurnished, above-average filly, effective 7 to 8f, best at 7f, acts on sft to frm, has worn blinkers. Turf high 70 (1st run) - 3rd of 12 giving 5lb to Birth of The Blues (24 Apr Leicester 8f sft RF 0831).
J L Dunlop [0-9] Goodwood Racehorse Owners Group (Four).

GOOMBAYLAND (IRE) BHB 109f **RR 114f** 4250[2]
3 ch g Common Grounds 8.1f **(66)** - House of Fame (USA) (Trempolino (USA)) 12f **(71)**
Form - 4112
Record 1999 - 1st:2 2nd:1 3rd:0 Ran:4
Win Prizemoney £9,812 *Total Prizemoney* £13,044

Wins						
* **1999**	Aug	Windso	(GD)	10f	101+	<
* **1999**	Jun	Epsom	(GD)	10.1f	82	

1999 Turf 2-4: (8f, 10f 2-3) (gd 1-2, g-f 1-2)
Lengthy, Group-class gelding. Turf high 114 - 2nd of 6 giving 6lb to Timahs (10 Spt Doncaster 10f g-f RF 4250). He fractured a bone in his shoulder at two and is still a moderate mover. However, the ability is there and he looked smart when winning minor events at Epsom and Windsor during the summer. Inched out on ground that looked a shade too fast at Doncaster's St Leger Meeting, he will improve and should do well on an easy surface next term.
J Noseda [2-4] Lucayan Stud.

GO ON GRACE **RR 42f** 2511[10]
2 b f Minshaanshu Amad (USA) 11.3f **(53)** - Peach Brandy **(46f)** (Pharly (FR)) 9.8f **(68)**
Form - 070
Record 1999 - 1st:0 2nd:0 3rd:0 Ran:3
1999 Turf 0-3: (6f, 7f 2) (gd 2, g-f)
Currently moderate filly. Turf high 42. *D Morris [0-3] James Brown.*

GORECKI (USA) BHB 93f **RR 84f** 3698[13]
2 b c Hermitage (USA) 8.6f **(84)** - Leading Candidate (USA) (Allen's Prospect (USA))
Form - 441150
Record 1999 - 1st:2 2nd:0 3rd:0 Ran:6
Win Prizemoney £20,552 *Total Prizemoney* £21,511

Wins							
* **1999**	Jun	Epsom	(G-S)	L	6f	84	<
* **1999**	May	Bright	(FRM)		6f	81+	

1999 Turf 2-6: (5f, 6f 2-3, 7f 2) (gd 1-1, g-f 1-3, frm 2)
Decent colt, effective 6f, acts on gd to g-f, best on g-f. Turf high 84 - 1st of 9 from Bee Eight (4 Jun Epsom RF 1726) - also 1st of 4 from Legendaire (28 May Brighton RF 1535). The winner of a Brighton maiden and Epsom's Woodcote Stakes, he has been disappointing since, and was sold for 29,000 gns in the autumn. Obviously suited by a downhill track.
N A Callaghan [2-6] M Tabor.

GORETSKI (IRE) BHB 75f78a **RR 73f 78a** 5212[14]
6 b g Polish Patriot (USA) 7.8f **(70)** - Celestial Path (Godswalk (USA)) 7.3f **(58)**
Form - 78000185113700020
Record 1999 - 1st:3 2nd:1 3rd:1 Ran:17
Pre1999 - 1st:12 2nd:7 3rd:1 Ran:54
Win Prizemoney £56,999 *Total Prizemoney* £68,377

Wins								
* **1999**	Aug	Beverl	(GD)	H	5f	65	73	
* **1999**	Aug	Pontef	(G-F)	H	5f	65	71	
* **1999**	Jun	Hamilt	(GD)	H	5f	59	66	
* 1998	Aug	Beverl	(G-F)	H	5f	70	74	
* 1998	*Jly*	*Southw*	*(STD)*	*H*	*5f*	*74*	*80*	<
* 1998	*Jly*	*Southw*	*(STD)*	*H*	*5f*	*67*	*74*	
* 1998	Jun	Pontef	(SFT)		5f		66	
* 1997	Aug	Beverl	(G-S)	H	5f	71	78	
* 1997	Jly	Catter	(G-F)	H	5f	60	63	
* 1997	Jly	Bath	(GD)	H	5.1f	60	65+	
* 1997	*Jun*	*Southw*	*(STD)*	*H*	*5f*	*59*	*67*	
* 1997	*Jun*	*Southw*	*(STD)*	*H*	*5f*	*59*	*63*	
* 1997	May	Hamilt	(SFT)	H	5f	54	59	
* 1996	Apr	Catter	(GD)	H	5f	58	57+	
* 1995	Aug	Redcar	(FRM)	S	6f		66+	

1999 Turf 3-17: (5f 3-15, 6f 2) (sft, g-s 3, gd 6, g-f, frm 3-6)
Decent gelding, effective 5f, acts on gd to frm - acts on Fibr, has worn blinkers, prefers left handed tracks, prefers tight tracks, excels at Southwell and Beverley and Pontefract. Turf high 76 - 3rd of 13 giving 14lb to Polly Golightly (21 Aug Chester 5f gd RF 3816) - also 1st of 16 giving 18lb to High Carry (11 Aug Beverley RF 3538). He won three times last season, but climbed up the handicap as a result. Virtually invincible over the straight five furlongs at Southwell. *N Tinkler [15-71] P D Savill.*

GORMIRE BHB 24f27a **RR 22f 27a** 319[9]
6 ro m Superlative 8.8f **(57)** - Lady of the Lodge (Absalom) 7.2f **(58)**
Form - 770
Record 1999 - 1st:0 2nd:0 3rd:0 Ran:1
Pre1999 - 1st:0 2nd:1 3rd:0 Ran:15
Win Prizemoney £0 *Total Prizemoney* £1,409
1999 AW 0-1: (6f) (Fibr)
Little account mare, has worn blinkers. Inconsistent.
B W Murray [0-3] P Barron (from J Hetherton [0-13] Aug 1997).

GORSE BHB 113f **RR 111f** 4568[5]
4 b c Sharpo 7.5f **(68)** - Pervenche (Latest Model) 6f **(62)**
Form - 331125
Record 1999 - 1st:2 2nd:1 3rd:2 Ran:6
Pre1999 - 1st:3 2nd:1 3rd:0 Ran:6
Win Prizemoney £86,588 *Total Prizemoney* £115,739

Wins							
* **1999**	Aug	Leopar	(SFT)	G3	6f	103	
* **1999**	Jly	Hambur	(GD)	G3	12f	106+	
* 1998	Nov	Doncas	(SFT)	L	6f	111	<
* 1998	Oct	Newmar	(SFT)		6f	98	
* 1998	May	Salisb	(G-S)		6f	100+	

1999 Turf 2-6: (6f 1-5, 12f 1-1) (sft 2, gd 2-3, g-f)
Group-class colt, effective 6 to 12f, best at 6f, acts on sft to gd, best on gd. Turf high 111 - 2nd of 8 to Keos (1 Spt Baden-Baden 6f gd RF 4243a) - also 1st of 7 from Night Shot (3 Jly Hamburg RF 2658a). Consistent. A late developer, who fractured his near fore as a juvenile, he won Group Three races at Hamburg and Leopardstown during the summer. Best on easy ground, he had everything in his favour at Ascot in September, but could not quicken and had to settle for fifth spot behind Bold Edge. That

suggests he will struggle to win a Group race at home.
**H Candy [5-12] Girsonfield Ltd.*

GO SALLY GO (IRE) BHB 33f **RR 35f** 4985[9]
3 b f Elbio 9f **(62)** - Pollette (Stanford) 7.9f **(56)**
Form - 8580
Record 1999 - 1st:0 2nd:0 3rd:0 Ran:4
Pre1999 - 1st:0 2nd:0 3rd:1 Ran:6
Win Prizemoney £0 *Total Prizemoney* £252
1999 Turf 0-4: (6f, 7f, 8f 2) (gd 2, g-f, frm)
Light-framed, very moderate filly, effective 5f, acts on frm. Turf high 35.
**F Murphy [0-4] The Bitter Fun Partnership (from R Craggs [0-6] Jly 1998).*

GOTHIC REVIVAL (IRE) RR 80f 4839[12]
2 b c Indian Ridge 7.6f **(74)** - Gothic Dream (IRE) **(107df)** (Nashwan (USA))
Form - 40
Record 1999 - 1st:0 2nd:0 3rd:0 Ran:2
Win Prizemoney £0 *Total Prizemoney* £970
1999 Turf 0-2: (7f, 8f) (sft, gd)
Currently decent colt. Turf high 80 (began Spt).
**J L Dunlop [0-2] Lady Clague.*

GO THUNDER (IRE) BHB 43f **RR 51f** 4808[12]
5 b g Nordico (USA) 8.2f **(59)** - Moving Off (Henbit (USA)) 9f **(61)**
Form - 000
Record 1999 - 1st:0 2nd:0 3rd:0 Ran:3
Pre1999 - 1st:1 2nd:2 3rd:2 Ran:21
Win Prizemoney £13,100 *Total Prizemoney* £15,921
Wins 1996 Aug Tralee (Y-S) H 8f 71 90 <
1999 Turf 0-3: (8f, 10f, 13f) (sft, gd 2)
Fair gelding, effective 14f, acts on gd. Turf high 35 (began Spt). Becoming disappointing.
**D A Nolan [0-3] Miss G Joughin (from W P Mullins in IRE [1-25] Spt 1998).*

GOT ONE TOO (FR) BHB 55f **RR 58f** 5024[12]
2 ch g Green Tune (USA) - Gloria Mundi (FR) (Saint Cyrien (FR)) 8.4f **(80)**
Form - 805700
Record 1999 - 1st:0 2nd:0 3rd:0 Ran:6
Win Prizemoney £0 *Total Prizemoney* £192
1999 Turf 0-5: (7f 2, 8f 3) (sft, gd, g-f, frm 2) 1999 AW 0-1: (7f) (Fibr)
Fair gelding, has worn blinkers. Turf high 58 (began Spt).
**D Sasse [0-6] Christopher Ranson.*

GO TOO MOOR (IRE) BHB 40f **RR** 5153[18]
6 b g Posen (USA) 8.6f **(59)** - Gulistan (Sharpen Up) 8.3f **(67)**
Form - 0
Record 1999 - 1st:0 2nd:0 3rd:0 Ran:1
Pre1999 - 1st:0 2nd:1 3rd:0 Ran:2
Win Prizemoney £0 *Total Prizemoney* £707
1999 Turf 0-1: (10f) (gd)
Currently very poor gelding.
**P S McEntee [0-1] R Allder (from G C Bravery [0-2] Nov 1996).*

GOWITHTHEFLOW (IRE) BHB 51f **RR 33f** 1102[13]
3 b g River Falls 8.2f **(56)** - Astral Way (Hotfoot) 10.5f **(59)**
Form - 00
Record 1999 - 1st:0 2nd:0 3rd:0 Ran:2
Pre1999 - 1st:0 2nd:0 3rd:1 Ran:5
Win Prizemoney £0 *Total Prizemoney* £458
1999 Turf 0-2: (5f, 8f) (sft, gd)
Scopey, very moderate gelding. Turf high 33.
**B S Rothwell [0-7] C D Carr.*

GO WITH THE WIND BHB 53f **RR 53f** 4279[3]
6 b g Unfuwain (USA) 11.4f **(74)** - Cominna (Dominion) 8.5f **(63)**
Form - 07612203
Record 1999 - 1st:1 2nd:2 3rd:1 Ran:8
Pre1999 - 1st:1 2nd:3 3rd:3 Ran:19
Win Prizemoney £7,247 *Total Prizemoney* £17,024
Wins * 1999 Jly Beverl (G-F) H 12f 44 48
1996 Spt Nottin (G-F) H 16f 60 67 <
1999 Turf 1-8: (11f, 12f 1-3, 14f 2, 15f, 16f) (g-s, g-f 3, frm 1-4)
Fair gelding, effective 11 to 14f, acts on g-f to frm, best on frm, has worn blinkers, favours tight tracks. Turf high 54 - 2nd of 12 giving 7lb to Stolen Music (3 Aug Catterick 14f frm RF 3316) - also 1st of 13 getting 3lb from Lay The Blame (27 Jly Beverley RF 3161).
**J S Goldie [3-15] Alf Chadwick (from M L W Bell [1-14] Oct 1996).*

GRACE BHB 59a **RR 46f** 5032[2]
5 b m Buzzards Bay 8.9f **(44)** - Bingo Bongo (Petong) 6.6f **(58)**
Form - 00204066008368402
Record 1999 - 1st:0 2nd:2 3rd:1 Ran:17
Pre1999 - 1st:1 2nd:2 3rd:0 Ran:19
Win Prizemoney £3,048 *Total Prizemoney* £7,696
Wins * 1998 Jun Chepst (G-S) H 6.1f 50 60 <
1999 Turf 0-17: (5f 3, 6f 8, 7f 5, 8f) (sft, g-s, gd 6, g-f 3, frm 6)
Moderate filly, effective 6 to 7f, best at 6f, acts on g-s to g-f, has worn blinkers. Turf high 54 - 4th of 20 getting 6lb from Halmanerror (19 May Chepstow 7f gd RF 1328).
**J M Bradley [1-36] Treevale Syndicate.*

GRACE AND POWER (IRE) BHB 83f **RR 78f** 3546[2]
2 b f Brief Truce (USA) 9.1f **(73)** - Tantum Ergo (Tanfirion) 7f **(61)**
Form - 242
Record 1999 - 1st:0 2nd:2 3rd:0 Ran:3
Win Prizemoney £0 *Total Prizemoney* £2,259
1999 Turf 0-3: (6f 2, 7f) (g-f 2, frm)
Currently above-average filly. Turf high 78 - 2nd of 11 to Vigour (11 Aug Leicester 7f g-f RF 3546). **J L Dunlop [0-3] P J Vela.*

GRACE PARK RR 36f 4123[13]
2 gr f Absalom 7.1f **(56)** - Aspark (Sparkler) 8.4f **(55)**
Form - 0
Record 1999 - 1st:0 2nd:0 3rd:0 Ran:1
1999 Turf 0-1: (5f) (g-f)
Currently very moderate filly.
**R F JohnsonHoughton [0-1] Woodway Racing.*

GRACIOUS GIFT BHB 89f **RR 91f** 4803[12]
3 ch f Cadeaux Genereux 7.9f **(76)** - Gentle Persuasion (Bustino) 10.4f **(64)**
Form - 5141230
Record 1999 - 1st:2 2nd:1 3rd:1 Ran:7
Pre1999 - 1st:0 2nd:1 3rd:0 Ran:2
Win Prizemoney £7,621 *Total Prizemoney* £14,701
Wins * 1999 Jly Windso (G-F) H 6f 77 80 <
*** 1999** Jun Salisb (G-F) 7f 75
1999 Turf 2-7: (6f 1-3, 7f 1-4) (gd 2, g-f 2-2, frm 3)
Scopey, useful filly, effective 6f, acts on gd. Turf high 91 - 3rd of 12 getting 6lb from Two Clubs (1 Oct Newmarket 6f gd RF 4678).
**R Hannon [2-7] The Queen (from Lord Huntingdon [0-2] Oct 1998).*

GRACIOUS PLENTY (IRE) BHB 95f **RR 100f** 2069[5]
3 ch f Generous (IRE) 11.5f **(82)** - Formide (USA) (Trempolino (USA)) 12f **(71)**
Form - 15
Record 1999 - 1st:1 2nd:0 3rd:0 Ran:2
Pre1999 - 1st:0 2nd:1 3rd:1 Ran:3
Win Prizemoney £3,521 *Total Prizemoney* £6,206
Wins * 1999 *Apr Lingfi (STD) 10f 69+* <
1999 Turf 0-1: (12f) (g-f) 1999 AW 1-1: (10f 1-1) (Equi 1-1)
Scopey, very useful filly. (1st run) - 5th of 12 to Fairy Queen (17 Jun Ascot 12f g-f RF 2069). (1st run). She won a desperate maiden on the all-weather before finishing a creditable fifth in the Ribblesdale Stakes at Royal Ascot. Probably unsuited by fast ground there - she moves poorly - she remains unexposed and is one to watch on a soft surface in 2000. **B W Hills [1-5] E D Kessly.*

GRALMANO (IRE) BHB 71f85a **RR 71f 85a** 4393[14]
4 b g Scenic 10.6f **(66)** - Llangollen (IRE) (Caerleon (USA)) 8.6f **(71)**
Form - 44400066241120
Record 1999 - 1st:2 2nd:2 3rd:0 Ran:14
Pre1999 - 1st:3 2nd:3 3rd:4 Ran:19
Win Prizemoney £19,407 *Total Prizemoney* £29,351
Wins * 1999 Aug Pontef (GD) H 8f 65 68
*** 1999** Aug Redcar (GD) 8f 67
1998 *Feb Lingfi (SLW) 8f 91*
1997 *Dec Wolver (STD) 7f 94* <
1997 *Nov Wolver (STD) 8.5f 69*

1999 Turf 2-10: (8f 2-4, 10f 4, 12f, 14f) (gd, g-f 6, frm 2-3) 1999 AW 0-4: (8f, 9f, 10f 2) (Equi 3, Fibr)

Workmanlike, useful gelding, effective 8 to 9f, best at 9f, - acts on AW, best on Fibr, has worn blinkers, likes left handed tracks. Turf high 71. AW high 89 - 4th of 7 giving 22lb to Yakareem (13 Mar Wolverhampton 9f Fibr RF 0429). A horse with a history of solid performances on turf and sand, he is now over the back problems that have troubled him, and demonstrated as much by notching up an August double at Redcar and Pontefract. **K A Ryan [2-4] Coleorton Moor Racing (from N P Littmoden [3-29] Jun 1999).*

GRANBY BELL BHB 40f **RR 38f** 1501[10]

8 b g Ballacashtal (CAN) 7.9f **(51)** - Betbellof (Averof) 8.2f **(62)**

Form - 0

Record	**1999** -	1st:0	2nd:0	3rd:0	Ran:1
	Pre1999 -	1st:3	2nd:1	3rd:0	Ran:24

Win Prizemoney £11,208 *Total Prizemoney* £12,697

Wins * 1996 May Newbur (SFT) H 13.3f 48 55 <

1999 Turf 0-1: (13f) (g-f)

Very moderate gelding, has worn blinkers.

**P Hayward [4-34] H A Watton (from M P Muggeridge [0-6] Oct 1993).*

GRAND CHAPEAU (IRE) BHB 53f55a **RR 21f 55a** 5167[12]

7 b g Ballad Rock 7.2f **(63)** - All Hat (Double Form) 7.3f **(58)**

Form - 0770600

Record	**1999** -	1st:0	2nd:0	3rd:0	Ran:7
	Pre1999 -	1st:5	2nd:3	3rd:1	Ran:44

Win Prizemoney £17,257 *Total Prizemoney* £24,211

Wins	* 1998	*Jly*	*Wolver*	*(STD)*	H	*6f*	*59*	*60*	
	* 1997	Aug	Redcar	(G-F)	H	6f	61	63	<
	* 1997	Aug	Thirsk	(GD)	H	6f	50	57	
	* 1996	Spt	Pontef	(GD)	H	6f	55	59	
	1995	Jly	Windso	(G-F)	H	5f	59	58	

1999 Turf 0-2: (5f, 6f) (g-s, frm) 1999 AW 0-5: (6f 5) (Fibr 5)

Moderate gelding, effective 5 to 6f, best at 6f, acts on gd to frm - acts on Fibr, likes left handed tracks, likes tight tracks. Turf high 21 (began Oct). AW high 61 - 7th of 15 getting 7lb from Theatre Magic (18 Jan Southwell 6f Fibr RF 0116). Inconsistent.

**D Nicholls [4-39] David Faulkner (from R Hannon [1-12] Oct 1995).*

GRAND CORONET BHB 53f65a **RR 48f 65a** 4074[2]

3 b f Grand Lodge (USA) - Coronati (IRE) (Bluebird (USA)) 7.5f **(69)**

Form - 31402

Record	**1999** -	1st:1	2nd:1	3rd:1	Ran:5
	Pre1999 -	1st:0	2nd:0	3rd:0	Ran:1

Win Prizemoney £3,648 *Total Prizemoney* £4,944

Wins * **1999** *Jan Lingfi (STD) 7f 64* <

1999 Turf 0-2: (7f 2) (frm 2) 1999 AW 1-3: (7f 1-2, 8f) (Equi 1-3)

Scopey, average filly, effective 7f, - acts on Equi. Turf high 48. AW high 64 - 1st of 6 from Legend Falls (21 Jan Lingfield RF 0137). Got off the mark when winning a very poor maiden on the Lingfield Equitrack in January. **T G Mills [1-6] T G Mills.*

GRAND CRU BHB 37f45a **RR 44f 45a** 5152[3]

8 ch g Kabour 6.1f **(36)** - Hydrangea (Warpath) 12.3f **(52)**

Form - 40087703

Record	**1999** -	1st:0	2nd:0	3rd:1	Ran:6
	Pre1999 -	1st:3	2nd:0	3rd:2	Ran:16

Win Prizemoney £10,407 *Total Prizemoney* £12,055

Wins	* 1997	May	Newbur	(SFT)	H	16f	62	67	<
	1997	*Apr*	*Southw*	*(STD)*	*S*	*12f*		*67*	<
	1997	*Feb*	*Southw*	*(STD)*	*C*	*14f*		*39*	

1999 Turf 0-5: (12f 2, 14f 2, 16f) (sft, gd 3, frm) 1999 AW 0-1: (12f) (Equi)

Moderate gelding, effective 12f, acts on gd - acts on Fibr, has worn blinkers, favours tight tracks. Turf high 44.

**J Cullinan [1-25] Alan Spargo Ltd Toolmakers (from R Craggs [1-2] Apr 1997).*

GRAND ESTATE BHB 65f56a **RR 63f 56a** 4150[5]

4 b g Prince Sabo 6.6f **(64)** - Ultimate Dream (Kafu) 6f **(47)**

Form - 02578117405

Record	**1999** -	1st:2	2nd:1	3rd:0	Ran:11
	Pre1999 -	1st:1	2nd:1	3rd:2	Ran:13

Win Prizemoney £9,187 *Total Prizemoney* £13,662

Wins	* **1999**	Jly	Hamilt	(FRM)	H	6f	57	63	
	* **1999**	Jun	Hamilt	(GD)		6f		55	
	1997	Aug	Thirsk	(G-F)	H	6f	69	75	<

1999 Turf 2-7: (5f 2, 6f 2-5) (gd 2, g-f 1-3, frm 1-2) 1999 AW 0-4: (5f, 6f, 7f 2) (Fibr 4)

Unfurnished, average gelding, effective 5 to 6f, acts on gd to g-f, has worn blinkers. Turf high 63. AW high 57. Won a couple of weak sprint races at Hamilton in the summer but has been out of sorts since.

**D W Chapman [2-10] S B Clark (from T D Easterby [1-14] Apr 1999).*

GRANDIOSO (IRE) BHB 48f **RR 42f** 3412[5]

3 b g High Estate 10.5f **(66)** - Palmyra (GER) (Arratos (FR)) 12.2f **(60)**

Form - 665243605

Record	**1999** -	1st:0	2nd:1	3rd:1	Ran:9
	Pre1999 -	1st:0	2nd:0	3rd:0	Ran:2

Win Prizemoney £0 *Total Prizemoney* £1,732

1999 Turf 0-8: (10f, 12f 5, 13f, 14f) (g-s, gd 3, g-f, frm 3) 1999 AW 0-1: (8f) (Fibr)

Scopey, fair gelding, effective 12 to 13f, best at 12f, acted on gd to frm, best on gd, favoured tight tracks. Turf high 54 - 3rd of 18 getting 4lb from Cupboard Lover (23 Jun Hamilton 12f frm RF 2236). (DEAD) **C W Thornton [0-11] Guy Reed.*

GRAND LAD (IRE) BHB 94f **RR 102?f** 1891[7]

5 ch h Mujtahid (USA) 7.4f **(69)** -Supportive (IRE) (Nashamaa) 7.1f **(66)**

Form - 7

Record	**1999** -	1st:0	2nd:0	3rd:0	Ran:1
	Pre1999 -	1st:2	2nd:1	3rd:2	Ran:6

Win Prizemoney £8,606 *Total Prizemoney* £15,194

Wins	* 1997	Apr	Leices	(FRM)	6f	102	
	* 1996	May	Ripon	(GD)	5f	105+	<

1999 Turf 0-1: (6f) (g-f)

Very useful colt. **R W Armstrong [2-7] Hugh Hart.*

GRAND MAITRE (USA) BHB 90f **RR 87++f** 506[1]

3 gr ro c Gone West (USA) 7.8f **(82)** - La Grande Epoque (USA) (Lyphard (USA)) 9.9f **(72)**

Form - 1

Record	**1999** -	1st:1	2nd:0	3rd:0	Ran:1
	Pre1999 -	1st:0	2nd:0	3rd:1	Ran:3

Win Prizemoney £3,419 *Total Prizemoney* £4,012

Wins * **1999** Mar Nottin (G-S) 8.2f 87++ <

1999 Turf 1-1: (8f 1-1) (sft 1-1)

Scopey, useful colt. (1st run) - 1st of 10 getting 17lb from Algunnaas (29 Mar Nottingham RF 0506). Looked green in his first couple of runs at two, but got off the mark on his Nottingham reappearance when stepped up to a mile but was not seen again. **J L Dunlop [1-4] Robin Scully.*

GRANDMA ULLA (IRE) BHB 75f **RR 73f** 5045[15]

2 b f Muhtarram (USA) - Trojan Lady (USA) (Irish River (FR)) 8.6f **(78)**

Form - 51800

Record	**1999** -	1st:1	2nd:0	3rd:0	Ran:5

Win Prizemoney £3,550 *Total Prizemoney* £3,550

Wins * **1999** Jly Kempto (G-F) 6f 73 <

1999 Turf 1-5: (5f, 6f 1-2, 7f 2) (sft, gd, g-f, frm 1-2)

Above-average filly. Turf high 73 - 1st of 13 from Mrs P (14 Jly Kempton RF 2824). Good winner of a maiden on her second start at Kempton, but disappointed afterwards.

**R J O'Sullivan [1-5] Jack Joseph.*

GRAND ORO **RR 95f** 5215[2]

2 ch c Suave Dancer (USA) 10.7f **(68)** - Hence (USA) (Mr Prospector (USA)) 8.8f **(78)**

Form - 2

Record	**1999** -	1st:0	2nd:1	3rd:0	Ran:1

Win Prizemoney £0 *Total Prizemoney* £975

1999 Turf 0-1: (8f) (g-s)

Currently very useful colt. (1st run) - 2nd of 18 giving 5lb to Blusienka (6 Nov Doncaster 8f g-s RF 5215).

**G C H Chung [0-1] Osvaldo Pedroni.*

GRAND RUN (IRE) **RR 44f** 481[7]

3 ch c Grand Lodge (USA) - Entracte (Henbit (USA)) 9f **(61)**

Form - 7

Record	**1999** -	1st:0	2nd:0	3rd:0	Ran:1

1999 Turf 0-1: (7f) (g-s)

Workmanlike, currently moderate colt.

**J W Hills [0-1] Miss Elizabeth Herbert.*

GRAND SLAM (IRE) BHB 67f **RR 68f** 4260[2]
4 b c Second Set (IRE) 9.2f **(67)** - Lady In The Park (IRE) (Last Tycoon) 8.5f **(62)**
Form - 038562042
Record 1999 - 1st:0 2nd:2 3rd:1 Ran:9
Pre1999 - 1st:1 2nd:3 3rd:0 Ran:9
Win Prizemoney £2,658 *Total Prizemoney* £10,152
Wins * 1998 Spt Warwic (G-F) 8f 76 <
1999 Turf 0-9: (8f 9) (g-s, g-f 3, frm 5)
Strong, average colt, effective 7 to 8f, best at 7f, acts on gd to frm, has worn blinkers, likes right handed tracks, prefers tight tracks, and does well at Brighton. Turf high 68 - 2nd of 13 getting 8lb from Arterxerxes (14 Jly Kempton 8f frm RF 2828). Consistent.
**R Hannon [1-18] Mrs D M Wight.*

GRAND SONNET (IRE) BHB 72f **RR 71f** 4382[11]
3 b c Second Set (IRE) 9.2f **(67)** - Mali (USA) (Storm Bird (CAN)) 10.3f **(74)**
Form - 4243450
Record 1999 - 1st:0 2nd:1 3rd:1 Ran:7
Pre1999 - 1st:0 2nd:0 3rd:0 Ran:1
Win Prizemoney £0 *Total Prizemoney* £3,380
1999 Turf 0-7: (7f, 8f 4, 10f 2) (g-s, g-f 3, frm 3)
Scopey, above-average colt, effective 8 to 10f, acts on g-s to frm, prefers right handed tracks. Turf high 82 - 2nd of 5 getting 4lb from Little Rock (23 Apr Sandown 8f g-s RF 0820). Consistent.
**D R C Elsworth [0-8] Michael Jackson Bloodstock Ltd.*

GRAND VIEW BHB 66f **RR 66f** 4947[17]
3 ch c Grand Lodge (USA) - Hemline (Sharpo) 7.7f **(59)**
Form - 240018300
Record 1999 - 1st:1 2nd:1 3rd:1 Ran:9
Pre1999 - 1st:0 2nd:0 3rd:0 Ran:3
Win Prizemoney £3,013 *Total Prizemoney* £4,544
Wins * **1999** Jly Salisb (G-F) H 6f 65 67 <
1999 Turf 1-9: (5f, 6f 1-8) (sft, gd 2, g-f 3, frm 1-3)
Scopey, average colt, effective 6f, acts on frm. Turf high 78 - 4th of 17 getting 10lb from Loch Laird (2 May Salisbury 6f frm RF 0988). Inconsistent.
**R Hannon [1-12] I A N Wight.*

GRANGEVILLE (USA) BHB 103f **RR 103f** 4392[1]

Grangeville was a dual big race winner

4 b g Gulch (USA) 9.6f **(79)** - Cor Anglais (USA) (Nijinsky (CAN)) 10.3f **(77)**
Form - 38217331
Record 1999 - 1st:2 2nd:1 3rd:3 Ran:8
Pre1999 - 1st:1 2nd:1 3rd:1 Ran:8
Win Prizemoney £90,601 *Total Prizemoney* £103,335
Wins * **1999** Spt Ayr (G-S) H 6f 98 103 <
* **1999** Jly Newmar (G-F) H 7f 92 100
* 1998 Spt Sandow (GD) H 7.1f 77 84+
1999 Turf 2-8: (6f 1-2, 7f 1-6) (gd 1-2, g-f 3, frm 1-3)
Workmanlike, very useful gelding, effective 6 to 7f, best at 7f, acts on gd to frm. Turf high 103 - 1st of 28 from Evening Promise (18 Spt Ayr RF 4392) - also 1st of 19 giving 7lb to Salty Jack (8 Jly Newmarket RF 2644). Consistent. He went from strength-to-strength, winning both the Bunbury Cup and Ayr Gold Cup. Equally effective over six or seven furlongs, he is suited by fast ground and tenacious in a finish. Unraced at two, he does not have many miles on the clock and could make his mark in Listed/Group races next term, although he is likely to continue his career in the United States. **I A Balding [3-16] George Strawbridge.*

GRANITE CITY BHB 51f **RR 49f** 5187[8]
2 ro c Clantime 6.6f **(57)** - Alhargah (Be My Guest (USA)) 9.3f **(67)**
Form - 450350568
Record 1999 - 1st:0 2nd:0 3rd:1 Ran:9
Win Prizemoney £0 *Total Prizemoney* £765
1999 Turf 0-9: (5f 7, 6f 2) (sft, gd 2, g-f 4, frm 2)
Moderate colt, effective 5f, acts on frm. Turf high 54. Consistent.
**J S Goldie [0-9] Aberdeenshire Racing Club.*

GRANNY RICH BHB 38f **RR 39f** 2913[4]
5 ch m Ardross 12.4f **(67)** - Weareagrandmother (Prince Tenderfoot (USA)) 9f **(61)**
Form - 604564
Record 1999 - 1st:0 2nd:0 3rd:0 Ran:6
1999 Turf 0-6: (8f, 10f, 12f 2, 14f, 16f) (gd 2, g-f, frm 3)
Very moderate filly. Turf high 59. Out of a winning hurdler, she showed promise on her bumper debut. **P M Rich [0-12] P M Rich.*

GRANNY'S PET BHB 107f **RR 105f** 5039[1]
5 ch g Selkirk (USA) 7.9f **(76)** - Patsy Western (Precocious) 8.6f **(62)**
Form - 2802113121
Record 1999 - 1st:4 2nd:3 3rd:1 Ran:10
Pre1999 - 1st:2 2nd:4 3rd:2 Ran:21
Win Prizemoney £53,652 *Total Prizemoney* £85,515
Wins * **1999** Oct Doncas (SFT) 7f 101
* **1999** Spt Goodwo (G-F) H 7f 100 103 <
* **1999** Aug Goodwo (GD) H 7f 98 99
* **1999** Aug Cheste (G-S) H 7f 95 98
* 1998 Spt Haydoc (GD) H 7.1f 89 99
* 1996 Jun Epsom (GD) 5f 84
1999 Turf 4-10: (6f, 7f 4-9) (g-s 1-1, gd 2-5, g-f 1-4)
Pattern-class gelding, effective 7f, acts on g-s to frm, best on gd, has worn blinkers, prefers left handed tracks, prefers tight tracks, excels at York, likes Goodwood. Turf high 105 - 2nd of 8 giving 14lb to Omaha City (7 Oct York 7f gd RF 4761) - also 1st of 10 from Kumait (11 Spt Goodwood RF 4270). Consistent. He enjoyed something of a renaissance in 1999, winning four times over his optimum distance of seven furlongs. Seemingly effective on all types of ground nowadays, he goes well for Jimmy Fortune and is capable of landing a Listed race in 2000.
**P F I Cole [6-31] Mrs Denise Margot Arbib.*

GRANNYS RELUCTANCE (IRE) BHB 51f48a **RR 62f 48a** 5068[2]
3 b br f Anita's Prince 6f **(62)** - Dawn is Breaking (Import) 6.6f **(68)**
Form - 0065362
Record 1999 - 1st:0 2nd:1 3rd:1 Ran:7
Pre1999 - 1st:0 2nd:0 3rd:1 Ran:4
Win Prizemoney £0 *Total Prizemoney* £1,562
1999 Turf 0-4: (6f 2, 8f 2) (sft, gd, g-f, frm) 1999 AW 0-3: (6f, 7f, 9f) (Fibr 3)
Neat, average filly, effective 8f, acts on sft, likes left handed tracks. Turf high 62 - 3rd of 14 to Beggars Belief (21 Spt Warwick 8f sft RF 4453). AW high 49 (began Jly).
**B Palling [0-11] Philip Reynolds & Mrs Anita Quinn.*

GRANTED (FR) **RR 76f** 4982[4]

2 b f Cadeaux Genereux 7.9f **(76)** - Germane **(83df)** (Distant Relative)
Form - 54
Record 1999 - 1st:0 2nd:0 3rd:0 Ran:2
Win Prizemoney £0 *Total Prizemoney* £270
1999 Turf 0-2: (6f, 7f) (gd, g-f)
Currently above-average filly. Turf high 76 (began Oct).
**M L W Bell [0-2] E D Kessly.*

GRANTLEY RR 49f 4342[15]

2 b c Deploy 11.4f **(67)** - Matisse **(43f 39a)** (Shareef Dancer (USA)) 9.9f **(73)**
Form - 00
Record 1999 - 1st:0 2nd:0 3rd:0 Ran:2
1999 Turf 0-2: (6f 2) (g-s, gd)
Currently moderate colt. Turf high 49 (began Aug).
**J D Bethell [0-2] Clarendon Thoroughbred Racing II.*

GRASSLANDIK BHB 56f56a RR 51f 56a 5149[5]

3 b c Ardkinglass 5f **(64)** - Sophisticated Baby (Bairn (USA)) 7.7f **(59)**
Form - 132500420805
Record 1999 - 1st:0 2nd:2 3rd:1 Ran:11
Pre1999 - 1st:1 2nd:0 3rd:0 Ran:1
Win Prizemoney £1,934 *Total Prizemoney* £3,655
Wins * 1998 *Dec Southw (STD) S 5f 53* <
1999 Turf 0-5: (5f 4, 6f) (gd 2, g-f, frm 2) 1999 AW 0-6: (5f 3, 6f 3) (Equi 2, Fibr 4)
Fair colt, effective 5f, - acts on Equi. Turf high 51. AW high 69 (1st run) - 3rd of 4 giving 3lb to Erinvale (9 Jan Lingfield 5f Equi RF 0060). **A G Newcombe [1-12] Chris Bradbury.*

GRATE SPARK (IRE) BHB 33f RR 36f 3903[9]

3 b c Posen (USA) 8.6f **(59)** - Linda's Fantasy (Raga Navarro (ITY)) 8f **(64)**
Form - 30
Record 1999 - 1st:0 2nd:0 3rd:1 Ran:2
Pre1999 - 1st:0 2nd:0 3rd:0 Ran:3
Win Prizemoney £0 *Total Prizemoney* £390
1999 Turf 0-2: (16f, 17f) (gd, frm)
Strong, very moderate colt, has worn blinkers. Turf high 36 (1st run) (began Aug) - 3rd of 8 getting 32lb from Pay The Pied Piper (13 Aug Catterick 16f gd RF 3602). **E Weymes [0-5] Mrs M Ashby.*

GRAY PASTEL (IRE) BHB 48f RR 56f 2852[6]

5 gr g Al Nasr (FR) 9.9f **(72)** - Gay Pastel (FR) (No Pass No Sale) 11.9f **(85)**
Form - 6
Record 1999 - 1st:0 2nd:0 3rd:0 Ran:1
Pre1999 - 1st:1 2nd:0 3rd:0 Ran:2
Win Prizemoney £2,259 *Total Prizemoney* £2,259
Wins * 1998 Jly Leices (GD) C 11.8f 56 <
1999 Turf 0-1: (12f) (g-f)
Fair gelding. **M C Pipe [3-14] Harry Saunders.*

GRAZIA RR 95f 4138[16]

4 b f Sharpo 7.5f **(68)** - Dance Machine(Green Dancer (USA))10.3f **(74)**
Form - 6320
Record 1999 - 1st:0 2nd:1 3rd:1 Ran:4
Pre1999 - 1st:2 2nd:1 3rd:0 Ran:4
Win Prizemoney £81,661 *Total Prizemoney* £92,461
Wins * 1998 Jly Newbur (G-F) L 6f 108+ <
* 1997 Oct Redcar (G-F) 6f 97+
1999 Turf 0-4: (6f 3, 7f) (sft, gd, g-f, frm)
Scopey, very useful filly, effective 6f, acts on gd. Turf high 95. She is a useful sprinter and worth another chance over seven furlongs.
**Sir Mark Prescott [2-8] Cyril Humphris.*

GREAT CRUSADER BHB 69f RR 69f 2000[25]

7 ch g Deploy 11.4f **(67)** - Shannon Princess (Connaught) 7.7f **(63)**
Form - 00
Record 1999 - 1st:0 2nd:0 3rd:0 Ran:2
Pre1999 - 1st:1 2nd:1 3rd:3 Ran:14
Win Prizemoney £3,525 *Total Prizemoney* £10,182
1999 Turf 0-2: (14f, 20f) (g-f, frm)
Average gelding, has worn blinkers. Turf high 69. Becoming disappointing.
**R Rowe [0-4] Mrs Barbara Hogan (from C A Cyzer [1-14] Spt 1995).*

GREAT DANE (IRE) BHB 115f RR 119+f 2421a[1]

4 b c Danehill (USA) 9.1f **(79)** - Itching (IRE) (Thatching) 8f **(66)**
Form - 11
Record 1999 - 1st:2 2nd:0 3rd:0 Ran:2
Pre1999 - 1st:5 2nd:1 3rd:1 Ran:8
Win Prizemoney £137,703 *Total Prizemoney* £139,748
Wins * **1999** Jun Currag (GD) G2 9f 117+
* **1999** May Goodwo (GD) L 9.9f 119 <
* 1998 Oct Lyon P (SFT) G3 10f 115
* 1998 Spt York (GD) L 8.9f 115
* 1998 Aug Goodwo (GD) L 8f 118+
* 1998 May Haydoc (GD) 8.1f 119?
* 1998 May Haydoc (GD) 8.1f 83+
1999 Turf 2-2: (9f 1-1, 10f 1-1) (gd 2-2)
Workmanlike, high-class colt, effective 8 to 10f, best at 8f, acts on sft to g-f, best on gd, likes Goodwood and Haydock. Turf high 119 (1st run) - 1st of 8 giving 11lb to Diamond White (20 May Goodwood RF 1344) - also 1st of 5 from Altibr (27 Jun Curragh RF 2421a). Consistent. He enjoyed a very fruitful 1998 season with five wins from seven outings, and won his only two starts last season, a Goodwood Listed event and the Group Two Budweiser International at the Curragh in June. Unfortunately, that was the last that was seen of him, and he has been retired to the National Stud. **H R A Cecil [7-10] Greenbay Stables Ltd.*

GREAT HOPPER BHB 20f RR 17f 5165[13]

4 b f Rock Hopper 10.6f **(54)** - Spun Gold (Thatch (USA)) 9.8f **(62)**
Form - 700
Record 1999 - 1st:0 2nd:0 3rd:0 Ran:3
1999 Turf 0-3: (11f, 12f 2) (g-s, gd, g-f)
Leggy, currently poor filly. Turf high 17. **F Watson [0-3] F Watson.*

GREAT MELODY (IRE) BHB 53f58a RR 50f 58a 3836[11]

4 ch g Pips Pride 6.7f **(70)** - Unbidden Melody (USA) (Chieftain II) 10.4f **(75)**
Form - 48506510
Record 1999 - 1st:1 2nd:0 3rd:0 Ran:8
Pre1999 - 1st:1 2nd:2 3rd:0 Ran:12
Win Prizemoney £5,773 *Total Prizemoney* £11,539
Wins * **1999** Aug Chepst (G-F) S 7.1f 50
* 1998 *Feb Lingfi (STD) 8f 64* <
1999 Turf 1-7: (7f 1-2, 8f 4, 10f) (gd 2, frm 1-5) 1999 AW 0-1: (8f) (Equi)
Workmanlike, average gelding, effective 8f, acts on gd - acts on Equi, often wears blinkers. **D J S Cosgrove [2-17] Crown Pkg & Mailing Svs Ltd (from J M P Eustace [0-3] Oct 1997).*

GREAT NEWS BHB 83f RR 89f 4675[8]

4 b g Elmaamul (USA) 8.1f **(70)** - Amina (Brigadier Gerard) 9.3f **(58)**
Form - 2130138
Record 1999 - 1st:2 2nd:1 3rd:2 Ran:7
Pre1999 - 1st:1 2nd:3 3rd:2 Ran:6
Win Prizemoney £32,291 *Total Prizemoney* £41,914
Wins * **1999** Aug Windso (GD) H 8.3f 80 83 <
* **1999** Apr Ascot (GD) H 7f 77 81
* 1998 Oct Lingfi (SFT) H 7f 69 73
1999 Turf 2-7: (7f 1-5, 8f 1-2) (gd 4, g-f 1-1, frm 1-2)
Scopey, useful gelding, effective 7 to 8f, best at 7f, acts on gd to frm. Turf high 89 - also 1st of 12 getting 3lb from The Prince (28 Aug Windsor RF 3984). Built on a good 1998 with victory in the Victoria Cup second time out last term and regained winning form over the extended mile at Windsor in August. Third to a rejuvenated Tayseer in a warm race at Ayr in September, he was sold for 40,000 gns in the autumn. **I A Balding [3-13] Mrs C H Bothway.*

GREAT ORATION (IRE) BHB 50f47a RR 46f 47a 2267[11]

10 b or br g Simply Great (FR) 11.9f **(61)** - Spun Gold (Thatch (USA)) 9.8f **(62)**
Form - 70
Record 1999 - 1st:0 2nd:0 3rd:0 Ran:2
Pre1999 - 1st:7 2nd:4 3rd:12 Ran:54
Win Prizemoney £25,560 *Total Prizemoney* £37,776
Wins * 1997 Aug Pontef (G-F) H 17.1f 60 66 <
* 1997 Apr Pontef (G-F) H 17.1f 54 58
* 1996 Jly Cheste (G-F) H 15.9f 51 56
* 1996 Jun Pontef (G-F) H 18f 41 50
* 1995 Aug Pontef (G-F) H 17.1f 38 46
1999 Turf 0-2: (16f, 18f) (gd, g-f)
Moderate gelding, has worn blinkers.

**F Watson [7-54] F Watson (from M L W Bell [0-2] Oct 1991).*

GREAT RICHES BHB 40f **RR 30f** 5070[14]

2 b g Mon Tresor 7.9f **(60)** - Glitter of Gold **(56f 52a)** (Glint of Gold) 9.3f **(66)**

Form - 000

Record 1999 - 1st:0 2nd:0 3rd:0 Ran:3

1999 Turf 0-3: (5f, 8f 2) (gd 2, frm)

Currently very moderate gelding. Turf high 30 (began Oct).

**Mrs M Reveley [0-3] Skeltools Ltd.*

GREAT WHITE BHB 66f **RR 78f** 5214[12]

2 gr c Marju (IRE) 9.2f **(76)** - Galava (CAN) (Graustark) 10.1f **(70)**

Form - 353770

Record 1999 - 1st:0 2nd:0 3rd:2 Ran:6

Win Prizemoney £0 *Total Prizemoney* £1,413

1999 Turf 0-6: (5f 5, 6f) (g-s, gd, g-f 2, frm 2)

Above-average colt, effective 5f, acts on g-f to frm. Turf high 78 (1st run) - 3rd of 10 to Alfailak (15 Apr Newmarket 5f g-f RF 0704). He showed ability in his early starts but does not seem to be progressing. **R Hannon [0-6] I A N Wight.*

GRECIAN TALE (IRE) BHB 48f64a **RR 52f 64a** 5199[25]

3 b g Catrail (USA) - Athens Belle (IRE) (Groom Dancer (USA))

Form - 7000530

Record 1999 - 1st:0 2nd:0 3rd:1 Ran:7
Pre1999 - 1st:0 2nd:1 3rd:2 Ran:7

Win Prizemoney £0 *Total Prizemoney* £2,312

1999 Turf 0-6: (5f 2, 6f 3, 7f) (sft, g-s, gd 2, g-f, hrd) 1999 AW 0-1: (6f) (Fibr)

Workmanlike, fair gelding, effective 6f, acts on g-f to frm, best on frm. Turf high 52. Inconsistent. **A P Jarvis [0-14] Ambrose Turnbull.*

Greek Dance was a step ahead of his rivals in the Rose of Lancaster

GREEK DANCE (IRE) BHB 121f **RR 120f** 4919[5]

4 b c Sadler's Wells (USA) 11.3f **(87)** - Hellenic (Darshaan) 9.9f **(84)**

Form - 571265

Record 1999 - 1st:1 2nd:1 3rd:0 Ran:6
Pre1999 - 1st:2 2nd:1 3rd:0 Ran:4

Win Prizemoney £35,989 *Total Prizemoney* £141,107

Wins						
* 1999	Aug	Haydoc	(SFT)	G3	10.5f	114+ <
* 1998	May	York	(GD)		10.4f	112++
* 1998	Apr	Newmar	(G-S)		10f	95+

1999 Turf 1-6: (10f 3, 11f 1-1, 12f 2) (sft, gd 1-3, g-f, frm)

Well made, very high-class colt, effective 10 to 12f, acts on gd to g-f, best on gd. Turf high 120 - also 1st of 5 getting 4lb from Prolix (7 Aug Haydock RF 3452). Consistent. He looked well for his Sandown reappearance last season, but was entitled to need it and finished well beaten. Again disappointing when beaten in France, he recaptured some of his three-year-old sparkle when turning the Rose Of Lancaster Stakes Haydock into a procession. An eight-length runner-up to Royal Anthem in the Juddmonte International, he ran well in the Arc, but despite running well to finish fifth in the Champion Stakes, may still have been feeling the effects of Longchamp. **Sir Michael Stoute [3-10] Lord Weinstock.*

GREEK FAYR (IRE) BHB 39f **RR 49f** 4926[6]

2 b f Fayruz 6.6f **(63)** - Greek Music (Tachypous) 8.6f **(55)**

Form - 445658706

Record 1999 - 1st:0 2nd:0 3rd:0 Ran:9

Win Prizemoney £0 *Total Prizemoney* £189

1999 Turf 0-7: (5f 2, 7f 5) (sft, g-f 2, frm 4) 1999 AW 0-2: (5f, 8f) (Fibr 2)

Moderate filly, often wears blinkers. Turf high 49. AW high 43.

**P D Evans [0-9] P D Evans.*

GREEK MYTH (IRE) **RR 60f** 1546[6]

3 b f Sadler's Wells (USA) 11.3f **(87)** - Greektown (Ela-Mana-Mou) 10.1f **(70)**

Form - 46

Record 1999 - 1st:0 2nd:0 3rd:0 Ran:2

Win Prizemoney £0 *Total Prizemoney* £224

1999 Turf 0-2: (10f, 12f) (gd, frm)

Scopey, currently average filly. Turf high 60.

**R Charlton [0-2] Lord Weinstock.*

GREENAWAY BAY (USA) BHB 58f **RR 57f** 5162[3]

5 ch g Green Dancer (USA) 11.9f **(77)** - Raise 'n Dance (USA) (Raise A Native) 11.2f **(69)**

Form - 50816463

Record 1999 - 1st:1 2nd:0 3rd:1 Ran:8
Pre1999 - 1st:1 2nd:0 3rd:3 Ran:15

Win Prizemoney £7,116 *Total Prizemoney* £12,536

Wins							
* 1999	Aug	Bright	(G-F)	H	8f	54	56
1997	Mar	Kempto	(G-F)		7f		80+ <

1999 Turf 1-8: (8f 1-3, 9f 2, 10f 3) (gd 2, g-f 2, frm 1-4)

Fair gelding, effective 8 to 10f, best at 10f, acts on gd to hrd, best on gd, prefers left handed tracks, excels at Redcar and York. Turf high 58 (1st run) - 5th of 19 giving 1lb to Statajack (27 Apr Windsor 10f gd RF 0877) - also 1st of 15 getting 7lb from Automatic (23 Aug Brighton RF 3852). Consistent.

**K R Burke [1-5] Asterlane Ltd (from W J Musson [0-13] Jly 1999).*

GREEN BOPPER (USA) BHB 68f72a **RR 66f 72a** 5162[11]

6 b g Green Dancer (USA) 11.9f **(77)** - Wayage (USA) (Mr Prospector (USA)) 8.8f **(78)**

Form - 551214013620

Record 1999 - 1st:3 2nd:2 3rd:1 Ran:12
Pre1999 - 1st:4 2nd:1 3rd:1 Ran:18

Win Prizemoney £21,055 *Total Prizemoney* £26,413

Wins							
* 1999	Jly	Haydoc	(G-S)	H	10.5f	56	62
* **1999**	*Mar*	*Southw*	*(STD)*	*H*	*11f*	*65*	*68*
* **1999**	*Feb*	*Southw*	*(STD)*	*H*	*11f*	*59*	*61*
* 1998	*Apr*	*Wolver*	*(STD)*		*8.5f*		*64*
* 1998	*Mar*	*Wolver*	*(STD)*	*H*	*8.5f*	*54*	*62*
* 1998	*Mar*	*Southw*	*(STD)*	*H*	*8f*	*47*	*56*
1996	Apr	Newcas	(GD)		8f		80 <

1999 Turf 1-6: (10f 2, 11f 1-2, 12f 2) (gd 1-3, g-f 3) 1999 AW 2-6: (8f, 9f, 11f 2-2, 12f 2) (Fibr 2-6)

Average gelding, effective 8 to 12f, best at 11f, acts on gd to g-f - acts on Fibr, has worn blinkers, favours left handed tracks, favours tight tracks, and excels at Haydock. Turf high 66 - 3rd of 12 giving 8lb to Empire Park (6 Aug Haydock 11f g-f RF 3414) - also 1st of 6 getting 5lb from Manful (3 Jly Haydock RF 2535). AW high 68 - 1st of 7 from Swift (1 Mar Southwell RF 0385) - also 1st of 12 getting 4lb from Swift (15 Feb Southwell RF 0293).

**G Woodward [6-20] Wetherby Racing Bureau 35 (from C P Morlock [0-6] May 1997).*

GREEN CARD (USA) BHB 95f **RR 100?f** 4136[3]

5 br h Green Dancer (USA) 11.9f **(77)** - Dunkellin (USA) (Irish River (FR)) 8.6f **(78)**

Form - 3555433

Record 1999 - 1st:0 2nd:0 3rd:3 Ran:7
Pre1999 - 1st:3 2nd:2 3rd:3 Ran:18

Win Prizemoney £14,462 *Total Prizemoney* £43,068

Wins					
* 1998	Jly	Doncas	(G-F)	8f	110 <
* 1998	Jun	Nottin	(GD)	8.2f	98
* 1997	Apr	Ripon	(G-F)	8f	81+

1999 Turf 0-7: (8f 4, 9f 2, 12f) (sft, gd 3, frm 3)

Very useful colt, effective 8 to 9f, best at 8f, acts on gd to frm, best on gd, has worn blinkers, and does well at Doncaster. Turf high 105 (1st run) - 3rd of 10 giving 3lb to Shiva (14 Apr Newmarket 9f gd RF 0693). He was very disappointing last term, his lack of a turn of foot all too evident, and a try at twelve furlongs failed to pay off. Becoming frustrating. **S P C Woods [3-25] P K L Chu.*

GREEN CASKET (IRE) RR 77f 5100[6]

2 b c Green Desert (USA) 7.8f **(78)** - Grecian Urn (Ela-Mana-Mou) 10.1f **(70)**
Form - 6
Record 1999 - 1st:0 2nd:0 3rd:0 Ran:1
1999 Turf 0-1: (8f) (gd)
Currently above-average colt.
**Sir Michael Stoute [0-1] Lord Weinstock.*

GREEN GINGER BHB 75f RR 80f 4989[13]

3 ch c Ardkinglass 5f **(64)** - Bella Maggio (Rakaposhi King)
Form - 4443180
Record 1999 - 1st:1 2nd:0 3rd:1 Ran:7
Pre1999 - 1st:0 2nd:0 3rd:0 Ran:3
Win Prizemoney £2,417 *Total Prizemoney* £4,117
Wins * 1999 Aug Nottin (G-F) 6.1f 80 <
1999 Turf 1-7: (6f 1-5, 7f 2) (gd, g-f 1-4, frm 2)
Small, decent colt, effective 6f, acts on gd to g-f. Turf high 80 - 1st of 7 giving 5lb to Tess Too (9 Aug Nottingham RF 3473). Consistent. Won an extremely modest race at Nottingham in August but has otherwise disappointed.
**A Streeter [1-10] B J Garrett.*

GREEN GOD (IRE) RR 65f 4718[15]

3 b c Common Grounds 8.1f **(66)** - Inanna (Persian Bold) 9.3f **(66)**
Form - 02620
Record 1999 - 1st:0 2nd:2 3rd:0 Ran:5
Pre1999 - 1st:0 2nd:0 3rd:0 Ran:1
Win Prizemoney £0 *Total Prizemoney* £2,154
1999 Turf 0-5: (7f 3, 8f 2) (g-s 2, gd 2, frm)
Workmanlike, average colt, effective 7f, acts on g-s. Turf high 65.
**C G Cox [0-1] Mrs Caroline Parker (from M J Heaton-Ellis [0-5] Jun 1999).*

GREEN JACKET BHB 54f34a RR 77f 34a 386[10]

4 b g Green Desert (USA) 7.8f **(78)** - Select Sale (Auction Ring (USA)) 8.6f **(65)**
Form - 8008850
Record 1999 - 1st:0 2nd:0 3rd:0 Ran:5
Pre1999 - 1st:0 2nd:1 3rd:1 Ran:12
Win Prizemoney £0 *Total Prizemoney* £456
1999 AW 0-5: (8f, 10f 2, 13f 2) (Equi 5)
Scopey, above-average gelding, effective 9f, acts on g-f, often wears blinkers, likes left handed tracks. AW high 30.
**R J O'Sullivan [0-11] Jack Joseph (from J L Dunlop [0-10] Jly 1998).*

GREENSAND BHB 95f RR 93f 3625[8]

3 b f Green Desert (USA) 7.8f **(78)** - Totham (Shernazar) 10.2f **(73)**
Form - 0628
Record 1999 - 1st:0 2nd:1 3rd:0 Ran:4
Pre1999 - 1st:1 2nd:0 3rd:1 Ran:4
Win Prizemoney £3,701 *Total Prizemoney* £6,482
Wins * 1998 Aug Salisb (G-F) 6f 86+ <
1999 Turf 0-4: (6f 3, 8f) (gd 2, g-f, frm)
Useful filly, effective 6f, acts on g-f to frm, best on g-f. Turf high 93. After a fair two-year-old season she was thrown in at the deep end in the 1,000 Guineas on her reappearance, where she finished last. Outclassed on her return to six furlongs by Vision of Night, she subsequently put in a good second to Cassandra Go at Newmarket on her favoured fast ground.
**R Hannon [1-8] Lord Carnarvon.*

GREEN SNAKE BHB 80f RR 79df 3198[7]

3 ch f Royal Academy (USA) 7.8f **(77)** - Tigwa **(66f)** (Cadeaux Genereux)
Form - 7
Record 1999 - 1st:0 2nd:0 3rd:0 Ran:1
Pre1999 - 1st:1 2nd:0 3rd:0 Ran:2
Win Prizemoney £3,624 *Total Prizemoney* £3,624
Wins * 1998 Aug Beverl (G-F) 7.5f 79 <
1999 Turf 0-1: (8f) (frm)
Leggy, currently above-average filly.
**C E Brittain [1-3] Mohamed Obaida.*

GREENSPAN (IRE) BHB 70f75a RR 72f 75a 69[P]

7 b g Be My Guest (USA) 10.2f **(66)** - Prima Ballerina (FR) (Nonoalco (USA)) 8.5f **(66)**
Form - P
Record 1999 - 1st:0 2nd:0 3rd:0 Ran:1
Pre1999 - 1st:12 2nd:6 3rd:5 Ran:37
Win Prizemoney £30,287 *Total Prizemoney* £39,936
Wins * 1998 *Jun Wolver (STD) C* *12f* *76* <
1998 *Feb Southw (STD) C* *12f* *75*
1998 *Jan Wolver (STD) C* *12f* *65*
1998 *Jan Southw (STD) C* *12f* *75*
1997 *Dec Southw (STD) C* *14f* *70*
1997 *Mar Southw (STD) C* *12f* *68+*
1997 *Feb Southw (STD) C* *12f* *64*
1997 *Feb Southw (STD) C* *12f* *71+*
1996 *Dec Wolver (STD) C* *9.4f* *72*
1996 *Nov Wolver (STD) S* *12f* *60+*
1996 *Apr Southw (STD) C* *12f* *74*
1996 *Feb Southw (STD) H* *12f* *73* *72*
1999 AW 0-1: (16f) (Fibr)
Above-average gelding, effective 12f, - acts on Fibr. Consistent.
**Miss S J Wilton [1-2] John Pointon and Sons (from W R Muir [12-40] Apr 1998).*

GREENSTONE (IRE) BHB 77f RR 79f 5197[5]

3 b f Green Desert (USA) 7.8f **(78)** - Mahabba (USA) (Elocutionist (USA)) 8f **(77)**
Form - 1073475
Record 1999 - 1st:1 2nd:0 3rd:1 Ran:7
Pre1999 - 1st:0 2nd:1 3rd:0 Ran:4
Win Prizemoney £3,198 *Total Prizemoney* £7,508
Wins * 1999 May Warwic (GD) 8f 78 <
1999 Turf 1-7: (8f 1-4, 9f, 10f 2) (gd 2, g-f, frm 1-4)
Above-average filly, effective 7 to 10f, best at 7f, acts on gd to frm, best on g-f. Turf high 79 - also 1st of 14 from Aqraba (3 May Warwick RF 1017). She got off the mark when just holding on in a Warwick maiden on her reappearance, but has been well beaten in valuable handicaps since. **J W Hills [1-11] David Caruth.*

GREEN TURTLE CAY (IRE) BHB 61f RR 63f 3660[6]

3 b g Turtle Island (IRE) - Pinta (IRE) (Ahonoora) 8.1f **(73)**
Form - 776
Record 1999 - 1st:0 2nd:0 3rd:0 Ran:3
1999 Turf 0-3: (6f, 7f 2) (gd 2, g-f)
Scopey, currently average gelding. Turf high 63.
**J Noseda [0-3] Lucayan Stud.*

GRENADIER (IRE) RR 72f 5049[4]

2 b c Sadler's Wells (USA) 11.3f **(87)** - Sandhurst Goddess (Sandhurst Prince) 7.9f **(63)**
Form - 4
Record 1999 - 1st:0 2nd:0 3rd:0 Ran:1
Win Prizemoney £0 *Total Prizemoney* £310
1999 Turf 0-1: (8f) (gd)
Currently above-average colt.
**W R Muir [0-1] Song And Dance Partnership.*

GREY BIRD (IRE) RR 31f 3313[9]

2 ro f Prince of Birds (USA) - Ganador **(42f 41a)** (Weldnaas (USA))
Form - 00
Record 1999 - 1st:0 2nd:0 3rd:0 Ran:2
1999 Turf 0-2: (7f 2) (frm 2)
Currently very moderate filly. Turf high 31.
**Martyn Wane [0-2] Mrs H Wane.*

GREY BUTTONS BHB 39f RR 45df 2471[10]

4 gr f Norton Challenger 10f **(41)** - Albury Grey (Petong) 6.6f **(58)**
Form - 00
Record 1999 - 1st:0 2nd:0 3rd:0 Ran:2
Pre1999 - 1st:0 2nd:0 3rd:0 Ran:3
1999 Turf 0-2: (10f, 12f) (gd, g-f)
Leggy, moderate filly. Turf high 9.
**D G Bridgwater [0-2] K Powell (from K R Burke [0-3] Jly 1998).*

GREYCOAT BOY BHB 51f **RR 33f** 904^{6}
7 br g Pragmatic - Sirdar Girl (Milford) 9f **(61)**
Form - 6
Record **1999** - 1st:0 2nd:0 3rd:0 Ran:1
Pre1999 - 1st:1 2nd:2 3rd:2 Ran:17
Win Prizemoney £3,969 *Total Prizemoney* £10,334
Wins 1995 Spt Bath (G-F) H 17.2f 61 70 <
1999 Turf 0-1: (22f) (gd)
Very moderate gelding, has worn blinkers. Inconsistent. Stepped up in trip in 1997, showing modest placed form, he has yet to prove himself a stayer.
**J S King [0-7] N W Rimington (from B J Meehan [1-17] Jun 1996).*

GREY COSSACK RR 63f 4721^{4}
2 gr g Kasakov - Royal Rebeka **(24f)** (Grey Desire) 8.7f **(50)**
Form - 4
Record **1999** - 1st:0 2nd:0 3rd:0 Ran:1
Win Prizemoney £0 *Total Prizemoney* £233
1999 Turf 0-1: (5f) (gd)
Currently average gelding. (1st run) - 4th of 14 giving 5lb to Poppy's Song (5 Oct Catterick 5f gd RF 4721).
**M Brittain [0-1] Robert Cook.*

GREY EMINENCE (FR) RR 67f 2573^{5}
2 gr c Indian Ridge 7.6f **(74)** - Rahaam (USA) (Secreto (USA)) 8.7f **(72)**
Form - 5
Record **1999** - 1st:0 2nd:0 3rd:0 Ran:1
1999 Turf 0-1: (7f) (frm)
Currently average colt. **R Hannon [0-1] Jeffen Racing.*

GREYFIELD (IRE) BHB 74f **RR 79f** 4823^{6}
3 b g Persian Bold 10f **(69)** - Noble Dust (USA) (Dust Commander (USA)) 10.3f **(77)**
Form - 22232112381337 6
Record **1999** - 1st:3 2nd:5 3rd:4 Ran:15
Pre1999 - 1st:0 2nd:0 3rd:0 Ran:7
Win Prizemoney £11,968 *Total Prizemoney* £20,549
Wins * **1999** Aug Cheste (G-S) H 10.3f 71 75 <
* **1999** Jly Beverl (G-F) 9.9f 69
* **1999** Jly Folkes (G-F) 9.7f 67
1999 Turf 3-15: (9f 2, 10f 3-9, 11f 2, 12f 2) (gd 2-5, g-f 1-7, frm 3)
Leggy, above-average gelding, effective 10f, acts on gd to frm, likes right handed tracks, likes tight tracks. Turf high 79 - also 1st of 8 getting 16lb from Crystal Creek (20 Aug Chester RF 3791). Consistent. He proved an excellent servant last season, running consistently well. A very honest sort, he is suited by fast ground.
**M R Channon [3-22] Paulton Bloodstock.*

GREY FLYER BHB 56f **RR 63f** 5187^{6}
2 gr g Factual (USA) - Faraway Grey (Absalom) 7.2f **(58)**
Form - 6186
Record **1999** - 1st:1 2nd:0 3rd:0 Ran:4
Win Prizemoney £2,276 *Total Prizemoney* £2,276
Wins * **1999** Spt Mussel (G-F) C 5f 63 <
1999 Turf 1-3: (5f 1-3) (g-s, gd, g-f 1-1) 1999 AW 0-1: (5f) (Fibr)
Average gelding. Turf high 63 (1st run) (began Spt) - 1st of 8 getting 3lb from Shouldhavegonehome (2 Spt Musselburgh RF 4086).
**Mrs L Stubbs [1-4] D M Smith.*

GREY KINGDOM BHB 77f33a **RR 78f 33a** 4803^{16}
8 gr g Grey Desire 9.3f **(49)** - Miss Realm (Realm) 8.1f **(65)**
Form - 0001006080610
Record **1999** - 1st:2 2nd:0 3rd:0 Ran:13
Pre1999 - 1st:9 2nd:3 3rd:9 Ran:60
Win Prizemoney £62,898 *Total Prizemoney* £81,199
Wins * **1999** Spt Ayr (G-S) H 6f 72 78 <
* **1999** Jun York (G-S) H 6f 74 77
* 1998 Jly Ayr (SFT) H 7f 75 77
* 1998 Jun York (G-S) H 6f 68 72
* 1997 Jly Epsom (SFT) H 7f 69 72
* 1997 Jun York (G-S) H 6f 62 67
* 1997 May Mussel (G-F) H 7.1f 42 57
* 1997 Apr Carlis (GD) H 5.9f 41 59
* 1997 Apr Nottin (G-F) H 6.1f 41 52
* 1996 Aug Doncas (G-F) H 7f 41 43
* 1996 Jun Beverl (G-F) H 7.5f 34 39
1999 Turf 2-13: (5f, 6f 2-6, 7f 6) (g-s, gd 2-5, g-f 4, frm 3)
Above-average gelding, effective 6 to 7f, best at 6f, acts on sft to hrd, best on gd, excels at Ayr, likes York and Newcastle. Turf high 78 - 1st of 29 getting 11lb from Princely Dream (18 Spt Ayr RF 4390) - also 1st of 22 giving 7lb to Pigeon (12 Jun York RF 1964). His victory at York in June from a big field was eclipsed by his winning of the Ayr Silver Cup, demonstrating he retains all his ability. **M Brittain [11-73] Mel Brittain.*

Grey Kingdom ruled in the Ayr Silver Cup

GREY MATTER BHB 33f **RR 30f** 2086^{14}
3 gr f Tina's Pet 7.4f **(56)** - Phar Lapa (Grundy) 10.3f **(65)**
Form - 04000
Record **1999** - 1st:0 2nd:0 3rd:0 Ran:5
Pre1999 - 1st:0 2nd:0 3rd:0 Ran:4
1999 Turf 0-3: (6f 2, 8f) (gd 2, g-f) 1999 AW 0-2: (7f 2) (Fibr 2)
Leggy, very moderate filly. Turf high 30. AW high 2.
**T H Caldwell [0-9] R Cabrera-Vargas.*

GREY PRINCESS (IRE) BHB 78f **RR 75f** 3651^{13}
3 gr f Common Grounds 8.1f **(66)** - Miss Goodbody (Castle Keep) 8.3f **(57)**
Form - 0308800
Record **1999** - 1st:0 2nd:0 3rd:1 Ran:7
Pre1999 - 1st:4 2nd:2 3rd:0 Ran:7
Win Prizemoney £11,523 *Total Prizemoney* £15,442
Wins * 1998 Oct Bright (GD) H 5.3f 85 92+ <
* 1998 Spt Bright (FRM) H 5.3f 80 82
* 1998 Jly Salisb (FRM) 6f 78
* 1998 Jun Windso (G-F) 6f 75
1999 Turf 0-7: (5f 5, 6f 2) (gd 3, g-f 4)
Neat, above-average filly, effective 5 to 6f, best at 5f, acts on gd to frm. Turf high 87 - 3rd of 11 giving 15lb to Uplifting (19 May Goodwood 6f gd RF 1330). Inconsistent.
**P W Harris [4-14] The Commitments.*

GREY PROSPECT BHB 34f32a **RR 41f 32a** 2561^{14}
5 b g Grey Desire 9.3f **(49)** - Nicky Mygirl (Chief Singer) 8.9f **(66)**
Form - 80600
Record **1999** - 1st:0 2nd:0 3rd:0 Ran:5
Pre1999 - 1st:0 2nd:1 3rd:0 Ran:7
Win Prizemoney £0 *Total Prizemoney* £684
1999 Turf 0-4: (7f, 8f, 10f 2) (gd 3, g-f) 1999 AW 0-1: (8f) (Fibr)
Moderate gelding, effective 8f, acts on g-f, favours tight tracks. Turf high 41. Inconsistent. **M Brittain [0-12] Mel Brittain.*

GREY STRIKE (IRE) BHB 55f40a **RR 52f 40a** 421^{7}
3 gr g Magical Strike (USA) 5.5f **(61)** - Narrow Band (IRE) (Standaan (FR)) 7f **(55)**
Form - 0767

Record 1999 - 1st:0 2nd:0 3rd:0 Ran:3
Pre1999 - 1st:0 2nd:1 3rd:0 Ran:8
Win Prizemoney £0 *Total Prizemoney* £530
1999 AW 0-3: (5f, 6f 2) (Fibr 3)
Scopey, fair gelding, effective 6f, - acts on Flbr, has worn blinkers, likes left handed tracks, likes tight tracks. AW high 45. Inconsistent. **J Berry [0-11] J Berry.*

GRIEF (IRE) BHB 65f **RR 70f** 4837[3]
6 ch g Broken Hearted 10.1f **(65)** - Crecora (Royal Captive) 10f **(50)**
Form - 4713
Record 1999 - 1st:1 2nd:0 3rd:1 Ran:4
Pre1999 - 1st:2 2nd:4 3rd:1 Ran:17
Win Prizemoney £10,308 *Total Prizemoney* £16,777
Wins * **1999** Oct Bright (G-S) C 11.9f 70
* 1997 Aug Epsom (GD) H 12f 82 87 <
1996 Aug Roscom (GD) 10f 79
1999 Turf 1-4: (12f 1-4) (g-s, gd 1-3)
Above-average gelding. Turf high 80 (began Spt). Consistent.
**D R C Elsworth [2-16] Mike Balcomb (from J Oxx in IRE [1-7] Oct 1996).*

GRINKOV (IRE) BHB 82f **RR 89f** 4683[4]
4 b br g Soviet Lad (USA) 9.4f **(63)** - Tallow Hill (Dunphy) 9.4f **(57)**
Form - 13454
Record 1999 - 1st:1 2nd:0 3rd:1 Ran:5
Pre1999 - 1st:3 2nd:1 3rd:0 Ran:8
Win Prizemoney £22,817 *Total Prizemoney* £32,429
Wins * **1999** Apr Newbur (G-F) H 10f 76 79 <
* 1998 Oct Folkes (SFT) H 9.7f 66 70
* 1998 Jly Windso (GD) H 10f 61 63
* 1998 Jly Windso (G-F) H 10f 57 60
1999 Turf 1-5: (10f 1-3, 12f 2) (gd 3, g-f 1-2)
Workmanlike, useful gelding, effective 10 to 12f, best at 10f, acts on gd to g-f, best on gd, likes Windsor. Turf high 89 - 4th of 33 giving 4lb to She's Our Mare (2 Oct Newmarket 10f gd RF 4683). He made a fine winning reappearance at Newbury, and has run well on a couple of occasions over a mile and a half since, though his winning form has been at ten furlongs. Sold for 62,000 gns in October to join Pat Hughes in Ireland.
**H Morrison [4-13] Rosanne Dobson & Partners.*

GRINLING GIBBONS BHB 53f **RR 61?f** 4630[12]
3 ch c Woodman (USA) 9.7f **(77)** - Saddle Bow (Sadler's Wells (USA)) 10f **(76)**
Form - 80
Record 1999 - 1st:0 2nd:0 3rd:0 Ran:2
Pre1999 - 1st:0 2nd:0 3rd:0 Ran:3
1999 Turf 0-2: (10f, 12f) (g-s, frm)
Unfurnished, average colt. Turf high 47 (began Spt).
**J L Dunlop [0-5] Peter Winfield.*

GRIP FAST BHB 67f **RR 64f** 1741[2]
3 b c Saddlers' Hall (IRE) 10.5f **(65)** - Comic Talent (Pharly (FR)) 9.8f **(68)**
Form - 7212
Record 1999 - 1st:1 2nd:2 3rd:0 Ran:3
Pre1999 - 1st:0 2nd:0 3rd:0 Ran:3
Win Prizemoney £3,027 *Total Prizemoney* £4,925
Wins * **1999** May Nottin (GD) H 14.1f 58 62 <
1999 Turf 1-3: (12f, 14f 1-2) (gd, g-f 1-1, frm)
Scopey, average colt, effective 12 to 14f, best at 14f, acts on gd to frm, has worn blinkers. Turf high 64 - 2nd of 4 getting 15lb from Fnan (4 Jun Haydock 14f gd RF 1741) - also 1st of 12 getting 2lb from Lady Coldunell (7 May Nottingham RF 1092).
**I A Balding [1-6] Nigel Harris.*

GRIZELDA (IRE) BHB 36f53a **RR 35f 53a** 4438[14]
3 ro f Bluebird (USA) 7.9f **(71)** - Phazania (Tap On Wood) 10.3f **(65)**
Form - 2000000
Record 1999 - 1st:0 2nd:1 3rd:0 Ran:7
Pre1999 - 1st:0 2nd:0 3rd:0 Ran:3
Win Prizemoney £0 *Total Prizemoney* £1,063
1999 Turf 0-6: (7f 3, 8f 2, 10f) (gd, g-f 4, hrd) 1999 AW 0-1: (8f) (Fibr)
Neat, very moderate filly, has worn blinkers. Turf high 55. Inconsistent. **J D Bethell [0-10] The Hon Mrs J M Corbett.*

GROESFAEN LAD BHB 75f **RR 81f** 5023[10]
2 b c Casteddu 7.4f **(54)** - Curious Feeling (Nishapour (FR)) 9.1f **(61)**
Form - 5255422000
Record 1999 - 1st:0 2nd:3 3rd:0 Ran:10
Win Prizemoney £0 *Total Prizemoney* £2,830
1999 Turf 0-10: (5f 5, 6f 2, 7f 2, 8f) (sft 2, gd 2, g-f 3, frm 2, hrd)
Decent colt, effective 5 to 7f, best at 7f, acts on gd to hrd, has worn blinkers. Turf high 81 - 2nd of 10 to Bogus Dreams (4 Spt Thirsk 7f hrd RF 4143).
**B Palling [0-10] John Harris and Mrs Sian Harris.*

GROESFAEN LADY (IRE) BHB 46f48a **RR 37f 48a** 4938[2]
3 b f Anita's Prince 6f **(62)** - Out On Her Own (Superlative) 7.2f **(56)**
Form - 34674360642
Record 1999 - 1st:0 2nd:1 3rd:1 Ran:8
Pre1999 - 1st:0 2nd:0 3rd:1 Ran:6
Win Prizemoney £0 *Total Prizemoney* £1,383
1999 Turf 0-4: (5f 3, 6f) (gd 2, frm 2) 1999 AW 0-4: (5f, 6f 3) (Fibr 4)
Unfurnished, moderate filly, has worn blinkers. Turf high 51. AW high 44 (began Jly). Consistent.
**B Palling [0-14] John Harris and Mrs Sian Harris.*

GROOMS GOLD (IRE) BHB 33f47a **RR 35f 47a** 4869[3]
7 ch g Groom Dancer (USA) 9.5f **(75)** - Gortynia (FR) (My Swallow) 9.2f **(71)**
Form - 4357478663433
Record 1999 - 1st:0 2nd:0 3rd:4 Ran:13
Pre1999 - 1st:1 2nd:4 3rd:2 Ran:21
Win Prizemoney £3,280 *Total Prizemoney* £8,076
Wins 1995 Jly Redcar (FRM) H 10f 63 67 <
1999 Turf 0-5: (10f 2, 11f 2, 16f) (gd 3, frm 2) 1999 AW 0-8: (8f 2, 10f, 11f 2, 12f 3) (Equi 3, Fibr 5)
Moderate gelding, effective 8 to 12f, best at 8f, acts on frm - acts on AW, best on Equi, has worn blinkers, excels at Southwell and Lingfield. Turf high 43. AW high 53 - 3rd of 13 giving 6lb to Caernarfon Bay (28 Jan Lingfield 10f Equi RF 0183).
**J Pearce [0-13] Mrs Anne Holman-Chappell (from P W Harris [1-20] Oct 1998).*

GROSVENOR FLYER (IRE) BHB 73f **RR 76f** 5220[10]
3 ch g Dolphin Street (FR) - Kilcsem Eile (IRE) (Commanche Run) 8.5f **(58)**
Form - 73352683220
Record 1999 - 1st:0 2nd:3 3rd:3 Ran:11
Pre1999 - 1st:0 2nd:0 3rd:0 Ran:2
Win Prizemoney £0 *Total Prizemoney* £5,282
1999 Turf 0-11: (9f, 10f 3, 11f, 12f 4, 15f, 17f) (sft 2, g-s, gd 3, g-f 5)
Above-average gelding, effective 9 to 15f, acts on g-s to g-f, has worn blinkers, likes left handed tracks, likes tight tracks, excels at Lingfield. Turf high 83 - 3rd of 10 giving 17lb to Enfilade (5 May Chester 12f g-f RF 1047). He is regularly in the frame, but lacks a turn of foot.
**T D McCarthy [0-1] A D Spence (from A G Foster [0-2] Oct 1999).*

GROVEFAIR LAD (IRE) BHB 26f44a **RR 27f 44a** 2653[9]
5 b g Silver Kite (USA) 10.2f **(51)** - Cienaga (Tarboosh (USA)) 10f **(55)**
Form - 66813540
Record 1999 - 1st:1 2nd:0 3rd:1 Ran:8
Pre1999 - 1st:2 2nd:2 3rd:1 Ran:34
Win Prizemoney £6,204 *Total Prizemoney* £8,511
Wins * **1999** *May Southw (STD) C 11f 54* <
* 1998 *Mar Southw (STD) H 12f 46 53*
* 1998 *Feb Wolver (STD) H 12f 45 47*
1999 Turf 0-4: (12f 4) (g-f 3, hrd) 1999 AW 1-4: (8f, 11f 1-1, 14f, 16f) (Fibr 1-4)
Fair gelding, effective 11 to 12f, best at 12f, - acts on Fibr, has worn blinkers, likes left handed tracks, favours tight tracks. Turf high 27. AW high 54 - 1st of 12 giving 3lb to Hill Farm Dancer (17 May Southwell RF 1280).
**S R Bowring [3-22] David Garner (from Martyn Wane [0-12] Aug 1997).*

GROVE LODGE BHB 47f **RR 53f** 5194[11]
2 b c Donna's Red - Shanuke (IRE) **(12f 20a)** (Contract Law (USA))
Form - 080
Record 1999 - 1st:0 2nd:0 3rd:0 Ran:3
1999 Turf 0-3: (6f 3) (g-s, gd 2)

Currently fair colt. Turf high 53 (began Spt).
**S Woodman [0-3] R Howitt.*

GRUB STREET RR 52f 5003[16]

3 b c Barathea (IRE) - Broadmara (IRE) (Thatching) 8f **(66)**
Form - 50
Record 1999 - 1st:0 2nd:0 3rd:0 Ran:2
1999 Turf 0-2: (8f 2) (gd, g-f)
Scopey, currently fair colt. Turf high 52 (began Aug).
**J H M Gosden [0-2] P D Savill.*

GRUINART (IRE) RR 26f 4033[16]

2 br c Elbio 9f **(62)** - Doppio Filo (Vision (USA)) 9f **(64)**
Form - 0
Record 1999 - 1st:0 2nd:0 3rd:0 Ran:1
1999 Turf 0-1: (7f) (gd)
Currently little account colt.
**H Morrison [0-1] The Gruinart Partnership.*

GUARD DUTY RR 91+f 5215[3]

2 b g Deploy 11.4f **(67)** - Hymne D'Amour (USA) (Dixieland Band (USA)) 7f **(74)**
Form - 33
Record 1999 - 1st:0 2nd:0 3rd:2 Ran:2
Win Prizemoney £0 *Total Prizemoney* £841
1999 Turf 0-2: (8f 2) (g-s, gd)
Currently useful gelding. Turf high 91 (began Oct) - 3rd of 18 giving 5lb to Blusienka (6 Nov Doncaster 8f g-s RF 5215).
**M P Tregoning [0-2] The Earl Cadogan.*

GUARDED SECRET RR 67f 4283[3]

2 ch c Mystiko (USA) 7.7f **(59)** - Fen Dance (IRE) (Trojan Fen) 8.1f **(62)**
Form - 3
Record 1999 - 1st:0 2nd:0 3rd:1 Ran:1
Win Prizemoney £0 *Total Prizemoney* £540
1999 Turf 0-1: (8f) (frm)
Currently average colt. **P J Makin [0-1] D M Ahier.*

GUDLAGE (USA) BHB 93f RR 93f 1401[5]

3 b c Gulch (USA) 9.6f **(79)** - Triple Kiss (Shareef Dancer (USA)) 9.9f **(73)**
Form - 035
Record 1999 - 1st:0 2nd:0 3rd:1 Ran:3
Pre1999 - 1st:1 2nd:1 3rd:0 Ran:3
Win Prizemoney £4,659 *Total Prizemoney* £10,637
Wins * 1998 Jly Newmar (G-F) 7f 81 <
1999 Turf 0-3: (7f, 10f 2) (gd, frm 2)
Scopey, useful colt, effective 10f, acts on gd to frm. Turf high 93 - 3rd of 13 giving 15lb to Tier Worker (11 May York 10f gd RF 1145).
**B Hanbury [1-6] Hilal Salem.*

GUESSTIMATION (USA) BHB 30f37a RR 34f 37a 4997[5]

10 b g Known Fact (USA) 8.3f **(72)** - Best Guess (USA) (Apalachee (USA)) 9.4f **(71)**
Form - 4085460085
Record 1999 - 1st:0 2nd:0 3rd:0 Ran:10
Pre1999 - 1st:16 2nd:17 3rd:14 Ran:100
Win Prizemoney £46,267 *Total Prizemoney* £66,956
Wins * 1998 Aug Nottin (G-F) SH 10f 56 62
* 1998 Jly Yarmou (G-F) S 10.1f 50
* 1997 Aug Bright (G-F) C 10f 63
* 1997 Aug Warwic (SFT) S 10.8f 60
* 1997 Jly Ayr (G-F) S 10.9f 41
* 1997 Jun Warwic (GD) S 10.8f 55
* 1996 Aug Warwic (GD) S 10.8f 53
* 1996 Jly Sandow (G-F) H 10f 57 56
* 1995 Spt Newmar (GD) H 10f 62 67 <
* 1995 Aug Kempto (G-F) S 9f 64
* 1995 Jun Ripon (FRM) SH 8f 57 60
* 1995 May Folkes (G-F) C 9.7f 57
1999 Turf 0-10: (8f, 10f 5, 11f 3, 12f) (sft, gd 5, g-f 2, frm, hrd)
Moderate gelding, effective 10 to 11f, best at 10f, acts on gd to frm, best on g-f, has worn blinkers, likes left handed tracks, prefers tight tracks, does well at Brighton. Turf high 54.
**J Pearce [16-108] The Exclusive Two Partnership (from J H M Gosden [0-2] Jun 1992).*

GUEST ENVOY (IRE) BHB 36f46a RR 31f 46a 4706[13]

4 b f Paris House 5.9f **(64)** - Peace Mission (Dunbeath (USA)) 7.8f **(70)**
Form - 80040443104850
Record 1999 - 1st:1 2nd:0 3rd:1 Ran:14
Pre1999 - 1st:1 2nd:1 3rd:0 Ran:16
Win Prizemoney £6,581 *Total Prizemoney* £7,991
Wins * **1999** *Aug Wolver (STD) H 8.5f 42 50+* <
* 1998 Aug Hamilt (SFT) H 6f 40 46
1999 Turf 0-6: (6f 3, 7f 2, 8f) (gd 2, g-f, frm 2, hrd) 1999 AW 1-8: (6f 2, 7f 4, 8f 1-1, 9f) (Equi, Fibr 1-7)
Small, moderate filly, effective 6 to 8f, best at 6f, acts on gd - acts on Fibr, has worn blinkers. Turf high 31. AW high 50 - also 1st of 13 getting 18lb from Ra Ra Rasputin (14 Aug Wolverhampton RF 3672). **C N Allen [2-30] Mrs Linda Walker.*

GUEST ISLAND (IRE) BHB 80f RR 77f 4677[12]

3 ch g Grand Lodge (USA) - Guest Room (IRE) (Be My Guest (USA)) 9.3f **(67)**
Form - 53610
Record 1999 - 1st:1 2nd:0 3rd:1 Ran:5
Win Prizemoney £4,154 *Total Prizemoney* £4,754
Wins * **1999** Spt Goodwo (G-F) 9.9f 77 <
1999 Turf 1-5: (10f 1-4, 11f) (gd 2, g-f 1-3)
Rangy, above-average gelding, always wears blinkers. Turf high 77 (began Aug) - 1st of 10 from Altichiero (11 Spt Goodwood RF 4275). Got off the mark in fine style when victorious over the extended nine furlongs at Goodwood. First-time blinkers obviously helped that day. **J H M Gosden [1-5] Sheikh Mohammed.*

GUEST OF HONOUR BHB 63a RR 52f 2198[5]

3 gr f Petong 7.6f **(58)** - Special Guest (Be My Guest (USA)) 9.3f **(67)**
Form - 10205
Record 1999 - 1st:1 2nd:1 3rd:0 Ran:5
Pre1999 - 1st:0 2nd:0 3rd:0 Ran:3
Win Prizemoney £2,206 *Total Prizemoney* £3,334
Wins * **1999** Mar Catter (G-S) 5f 60 <
1999 Turf 1-4: (5f 1-1, 6f 2, 7f) (gd 1-3, frm) 1999 AW 0-1: (6f) (Fibr)
Workmanlike, average filly, effective 5 to 6f, acts on gd - acts on Fibr. Turf high 60 (1st run) - 1st of 8 getting 3lb from Off Hire (31 Mar Catterick RF 0523). (1st run) - 2nd of 10 giving 2lb to Night Life (29 Apr Wolverhampton 6f Fibr RF 0924).
**B W Hills [1-8] Major Christopher Hanbury.*

GUILSBOROUGH BHB 50f69a RR 49f 69a 5103[9]

4 br g Northern Score (USA) - Super Sisters (AUS) (Call Report (USA))
Form - 2216260
Record 1999 - 1st:1 2nd:3 3rd:0 Ran:7
Pre1999 - 1st:0 2nd:0 3rd:0 Ran:8
Win Prizemoney £1,987 *Total Prizemoney* £4,669
Wins * **1999** *Jun Southw (STD) H 7f 56 67+* <
1999 Turf 0-4: (7f 4) (gd 3, frm) 1999 AW 1-3: (7f 1-3) (Fibr 1-3)
Above-average gelding, effective 7f, - acts on Fibr, has worn blinkers. Turf high 55. AW high 72 - 2nd of 13 giving 10lb to Almazhar (10 Jly Southwell 7f Fibr RF 2720) - also 1st of 14 giving 4lb to Denbrae (11 Jun Southwell RF 1931).
**D Morris [1-15] Mason Racing Ltd.*

GUILTY SUSPECT RR 1123[10]

2 b f Reprimand 8.2f **(63)** - Island Desert (IRE) (Green Desert (USA)) 8.6f **(78)**
Form - 0
Record 1999 - 1st:0 2nd:0 3rd:0 Ran:1
1999 Turf 0-1: (5f) (gd)
Currently very poor filly. **D Shaw [0-1] J C Fretwell.*

GUINEA HUNTER (IRE) BHB 102f RR 101f 2487[3]

3 b c Pips Pride 6.7f **(70)** - Preponderance (IRE) (Cyrano de Bergerac) 6f **(68)**
Form - 516D03
Record 1999 - 1st:1 2nd:0 3rd:1 Ran:6
Pre1999 - 1st:1 2nd:2 3rd:0 Ran:3
Win Prizemoney £9,044 *Total Prizemoney* £15,102
Wins * **1999** May Haydoc (GD) 6f 101 <
* 1998 Jun Carlis (G-S) 5.9f 80+
1999 Turf 1-6: (6f 1-6) (gd 3, g-f 1-2, frm)
Strong, very useful colt, effective 6f, acts on gd to frm. Turf high

101 - 1st of 6 getting 17lb from Superior Premium (1 May Haydock RF 0953). He did well over the winter, winning at Haydock and looked a shade unlucky when finishing third (demoted to last) in a Listed event at the same track in May. Well held on his two subsequent starts, he could stay beyond six furlongs and goes well on yielding ground. **T D Easterby [2-9] Burke's 5th Family Settlement.*

GULF SHAADI BHB 80f83a **RR 81f 83a** 5143[7]

7 b g Shaadi (USA) 8.1f **(75)** - Ela Meem (USA) (Kris) 9.5f **(73)**
Form - 0003423200067

Record	**1999** -	1st:0	2nd:2	3rd:2	Ran:12
	Pre1999 -	1st:13	2nd:6	3rd:5	Ran:76

Win Prizemoney £104,604 *Total Prizemoney* £139,115

Wins								
1998	*Mar*	*Wolver*	*(STD)*	*H*	*9.4f*	*85*	*90*	*<*
1997	Oct	Newmar	(GD)	H	8f	82	90	<
1997	Spt	Ascot	(G-F)	H	8f	74	81	
1997	Aug	Sandow	(G-F)	H	7.1f	66	71	
1997	Apr	Beverl	(G-F)	H	7.5f	59	62	
1997	*Jan*	*Southw*	*(STD)*	*H*	*8f*	*51*	*67*	
1997	*Jan*	*Southw*	*(STD)*	*H*	*8f*	*55*	*60*	
1995	*May*	*Wolver*	*(STD)*	*C*	*8.5f*		*81+*	
1995	*Mar*	*Lingfi*	*(STD)*	*C*	*7f*		*75*	
1995	*Mar*	*Lingfi*	*(STD)*	*C*	*8f*		*73*	
1995	*Jan*	*Wolver*	*(STD)*	*H*	*7f*	*78*	*79*	
1995	*Jan*	*Lingfi*	*(STD)*	*C*	*7f*		*68*	

1999 Turf 0-12: (7f 2, 8f 9, 10f) (sft, gd 3, g-f 3, frm 5)
Decent gelding, effective 7 to 9f, best at 8f, acts on sft to gd - acts on Fibr, best on gd, has worn blinkers, likes left handed tracks. Turf high 87. He was a cracking handicapper a couple of seasons ago both on turf and sand, but was then disappointing for quite a while and seemed to have lost the plot. However mid-season he was enjoying something of a revival as he was placed three times on consecutive starts at distances around a mile. Disappointing latterly, his hold-up, come-from-behind tactics often make it difficult for him to get his head in front.
**Miss Gay Kelleway [0-12] Wetherby Racing Bureau 40 (from E J Alston [7-55] Nov 1998).*

GULLAND BHB 100f **RR 112?f** 4652[13]

4 b c Unfuwain (USA) 11.4f **(74)** - Spin (High Top) 10.2f **(67)**
Form - 00

Record	**1999** -	1st:0	2nd:0	3rd:0	Ran:2
	Pre1999 -	1st:2	2nd:2	3rd:0	Ran:6

Win Prizemoney £45,479 *Total Prizemoney* £54,850

Wins							
* 1998	May	Cheste	(GD)	G3	12.3f	112	<
* 1997	Oct	Pontef	(G-S)	L	8f	102+	

1999 Turf 0-2: (8f 2) (gd, g-f)
Scopey, Group-class colt. Turf high 62 (began Spt). Inconsistent. He gave Xaar a good race in the Craven on his reappearance at three in what was a muddling affair, and only held on by the skin of his teeth in the Chester Vase, giving the impression that he may not have stayed. He ran poorly in the Derby, sustaining a suspensory injury to a foreleg which sidelined him for the rest of the season, and on his return last term he was understandably disappointing. **G Wragg [2-8] Mollers Racing.*

GUNBOAT DIPLOMACY **RR 39f** 1723[12]

4 b br g Mtoto 11.5f **(71)** - Pepper Star (IRE) (Salt Dome (USA))
Form - 700

Record	**1999** -	1st:0	2nd:0	3rd:0	Ran:3
	Pre1999 -	1st:0	2nd:0	3rd:0	Ran:5

1999 Turf 0-3: (12f 3) (g-f, frm 2)
Leggy, very moderate gelding, has worn blinkers. Turf high 39. Inconsistent.
**Mrs M Reveley [0-3] A Sharratt (from M J Fetherston-Godley [0-5] Jun 1998).*

GUNNER SAM BHB 57f **RR 69f** 4880[25]

3 ch g Emarati (USA) 6.6f **(63)** - Minne Love (Homeric) 9.8f **(67)**
Form - 21000

Record	**1999** -	1st:1	2nd:1	3rd:0	Ran:5
	Pre1999 -	1st:0	2nd:0	3rd:1	Ran:3

Win Prizemoney £2,722 *Total Prizemoney* £3,963

Wins						
* **1999**	Apr	Catter	(SFT)	7f	69	<

1999 Turf 1-5: (6f, 7f 1-4) (gd 1-2, frm 3)
Scopey, average gelding, effective 6 to 7f, acts on gd. Turf high 73 (1st run) - 2nd of 14 giving 5lb to Miss Grapette (31 Mar Catterick 6f gd RF 0527) - also 1st of 9 from The Haka (21 Apr Catterick RF 0795). Becoming disappointing. **B W Hills [1-8] R W Miller.*

GYMCRAK FIREBIRD (IRE) BHB 55f **RR 60f** 4939[2]

2 ch f Petardia 8.2f **(58)** - Fiery Song (Ballad Rock) 7.8f **(63)**
Form - 07602

Record	**1999** -	1st:0	2nd:1	3rd:0	Ran:5

Win Prizemoney £0 *Total Prizemoney* £578
1999 Turf 0-4: (5f 2, 7f 2) (g-f, frm 2, hrd) 1999 AW 0-1: (7f) (Fibr)
Average filly. Turf high 60. (1st run) - 2nd of 14 getting 11lb from Sporty Mo (18 Oct Southwell 7f Fibr RF 4939).
**G Holmes [0-5] The Gymcrak Thoroughbred Racing Club.*

GYMCRAK FLYER BHB 53f65a **RR 52f 65a** 4638[14]

8 b m Aragon 7.7f **(58)** - Intellect (Frimley Park) 6.5f **(67)**
Form - 00507701100

Record	**1999** -	1st:2	2nd:0	3rd:0	Ran:11
	Pre1999 -	1st:10	2nd:5	3rd:5	Ran:55

Win Prizemoney £40,448 *Total Prizemoney* £51,215

Wins								
* **1999**	Spt	Mussel	(G-F)	H	8f	44	52	
* **1999**	Aug	Carlis	(G-F)	H	8f	44	46	
* 1997	Spt	Yarmou	(FRM)	H	8f	62	68	
* 1997	May	Redcar	(GD)	H	7f	60	63	
* 1997	Apr	Pontef	(GD)		8f		62	
* 1996	Jly	Yarmou	(FRM)	H	7f	63	66	
* 1996	Jly	Redcar	(G-F)	H	7f	58	60	
* 1996	Jun	Carlis	(FRM)		8f		61	
* 1995	Spt	Haydoc	(GD)		8.1f		66	
* 1995	Aug	Newcas	(FRM)	H	7f	59	66	

1999 Turf 2-11: (7f 2, 8f 2-9) (sft, gd 4, g-f, frm 2-5)
Fair mare, effective 7 to 8f, best at 8f, acts on gd to frm, best on g-f, has worn blinkers (effectively), excels at Yarmouth and Carlisle. Turf high 52 - 1st of 14 giving 3lb to Kid'z'play (2 Spt Musselburgh RF 4091). Inconsistent.
**G Holmes [12-66] The Gymcrak Thoroughbred Racing Club.*

GYMCRAK MYSTERY BHB 26f26a **RR 18f 26a** 199[5]

4 br f Ballacashtal (CAN) 7.9f **(51)** - Little Unknown (Known Fact (USA)) 7.4f **(67)**
Form - 000885

Record	**1999** -	1st:0	2nd:0	3rd:0	Ran:2
	Pre1999 -	1st:0	2nd:0	3rd:1	Ran:12

Win Prizemoney £0 *Total Prizemoney* £471
1999 AW 0-2: (7f 2) (Fibr 2)
Unfurnished, little account filly, effective 6f, - acts on Fibr, has worn blinkers, favours left handed tracks. AW high 25.
**G Holmes [0-14] The Gymcrak Thoroughbred Racing Club.*

GYPSY (IRE) BHB 68f **RR 69f** 2338[6]

3 b c Distinctly North (USA) 7.4f **(63)** - Winscarlet North (Garland Knight)
Form - 21456

Record	**1999** -	1st:1	2nd:1	3rd:0	Ran:5
	Pre1999 -	1st:1	2nd:0	3rd:1	Ran:8

Win Prizemoney £9,698 *Total Prizemoney* £11,852

Wins								
* **1999**	May	Lingfi	(G-F)	H	9f	67	72	<
* 1998	Jly	Yarmou	(G-F)		7f		68	

1999 Turf 1-5: (9f 1-1, 10f 3, 11f) (gd 1-3, g-f, frm)
Workmanlike, average colt, effective 7 to 11f, acts on gd to g-f, best on gd, prefers left handed tracks, prefers tight tracks. Turf high 72 - 1st of 7 getting 13lb from Gino's Spirits (8 May Lingfield RF 1115). Consistent. A winner over seven furlongs at two, he was only just caught on his Beverley reappearance when stepped up to ten furlongs, but made no mistake back over nine furlongs at Lingfield next time despite not handling the track very well. Sound efforts in defeat since. **M H Tompkins [2-13] Richard Flatt.*

GYPSY HILL BHB 63f **RR 64f** 4011[6]

4 ch f Theatrical Charmer 10.9f **(63)** - Mirkan Honey (Ballymore) 7.3f **(64)**
Form - 6124426

Record	**1999** -	1st:1	2nd:2	3rd:0	Ran:7
	Pre1999 -	1st:1	2nd:1	3rd:1	Ran:12

Win Prizemoney £7,012 *Total Prizemoney* £11,690

Wins								
* **1999**	May	Windso	(G-F)	H	10f	59	61	
* 1997	May	Bath	(G-S)		5.1f		78	<

1999 Turf 1-7: (10f 1-5, 11f, 12f) (gd 2, g-f, frm 1-4)
Leggy, average filly, effective 8 to 12f, acts on gd to frm, best on gd, likes left handed tracks. Turf high 64 - 2nd of 5 getting 6lb from

Water Flower (5 Aug Chepstow 12f frm RF 3395). Consistent. Consistent form in minor handicaps in '99.
**D HaydnJones [2-19] Kevan Kynaston.*

GYPSY MUSIC (IRE) BHB 51f46a **RR 49f 46a** 857[16]
3 b f Treasure Kay 6.5f **(53)** - Mighty Special (IRE) (Head for Heights) 9.6f **(55)**
Form - 00
Record 1999 - 1st:0 2nd:0 3rd:0 Ran:2
Pre1999 - 1st:0 2nd:1 3rd:1 Ran:11
Win Prizemoney £0 *Total Prizemoney* £1,205
1999 Turf 0-1: (6f) (sft) 1999 AW 0-1: (7f) (Fibr)
Unfurnished, moderate filly, effective 6f, acts on frm, has worn blinkers. Inconsistent.
**M Brittain [0-2] Robert Cook (from G R Oldroyd [0-11] Spt 1998).*

GYPSY SINGER (USA) RR 42f 4328[7]
2 b f Kingmambo (USA) 10.9f **(85)** - Zakota (IRE) (Polish Precedent (USA)) 10.2f **(60)**
Form - 77
Record 1999 - 1st:0 2nd:0 3rd:0 Ran:2
1999 Turf 0-2: (7f, 8f) (gd, frm)
Currently moderate filly. Turf high 42 (began Jly).
**P F I Cole [0-2] Lord Lloyd-Webber.*

HAAFIZ (IRE) BHB 102f **RR 102f** 4896[14]
3 b c Green Desert (USA) 7.8f **(78)** - Midway Lady (USA) (Alleged (USA)) 10f **(76)**
Form - 4011650
Record 1999 - 1st:2 2nd:0 3rd:0 Ran:7
Pre1999 - 1st:2 2nd:0 3rd:1 Ran:4
Win Prizemoney £27,625 *Total Prizemoney* £32,450
Wins * **1999** Aug Yarmou (FRM) 6f 94+
* **1999** Jly Newmar (GD) H 6f 100 103 <
* 1998 Aug Pontef (G-F) 6f 103+
* 1998 Jly Newmar (G-F) 6f 99
1999 Turf 2-7: (6f 2-4, 7f 2, 8f) (gd 2, g-f 1-3, frm 1-2)
Well made, very useful colt, effective 6 to 7f, best at 6f, acts on g-f to frm, best on frm, likes Newmarket. Turf high 103 - 1st of 17 giving 1lb to Munjiz (6 Jly Newmarket RF 2577) - also 1st of 4 giving 1lb to Classy Cleo (4 Aug Yarmouth RF 3379). Consistent. He did well when dropped back to six furlongs under waiting tactics and is a high-class sprint handicapper. Usually warm in the preliminaries, he can improve again and make a mark in Listed races next term. **B Hanbury [4-11] Hamdan Al Maktoum.*

HAAMI (USA) BHB 110f **RR 111f** 4241a[3]
4 b c Nashwan (USA) 10.3f **(79)** - Oumaldaaya (USA) (Nureyev (USA)) 8.7f **(78)**
Form - 2742213
Record 1999 - 1st:1 2nd:3 3rd:1 Ran:7
Pre1999 - 1st:4 2nd:2 3rd:1 Ran:9
Win Prizemoney £57,419 *Total Prizemoney* £102,580
Wins * **1999** Aug Currag (GD) G3 8f 111
* 1998 Oct Newmar (GD) L 9f 114 <
* 1997 Oct Newmar (G-F) L 7f 102+
* 1997 Jly Doncas (GD) 7f 95+
* 1997 Jly Newmar (GD) 7f 90++
1999 Turf 1-7: (6f, 7f, 8f 1-3, 9f, 10f) (g-s, gd 4, g-f, frm 1-1)
Well made, Group-class colt, effective 6 to 9f, best at 8f, acts on gd to frm, has worn blinkers, does well at Newmarket. Turf high 111 - 1st of 6 giving 10lb to Castle Quest (14 Aug Curragh RF 3717a). Consistent. He has looked tricky in the past, but did nothing wrong when enterprisingly ridden by John Reid at The Curragh in August. However, he is not one to trust implicitly and normally accepts the silver medal if the going gets tough. **J L Dunlop [5-16].*

HABIBI BHB 51f35a **RR 23f 35a** 396[11]
3 b f Alhijaz 7.7f **(57)** - Balearica (Bustino) 10.4f **(64)**
Form - 0060
Record 1999 - 1st:0 2nd:0 3rd:0 Ran:3
Pre1999 - 1st:1 2nd:1 3rd:0 Ran:6
Win Prizemoney £1,898 *Total Prizemoney* £2,373
Wins 1998 May Catter (G-S) S 6f 58 <
1999 AW 0-3: (5f, 7f, 8f) (Fibr 3)
Little account filly, effective 6f, acts on gd, has worn blinkers, likes left handed tracks, likes tight tracks. AW high 17. Becoming disappointing.
**Mrs N Macauley [0-4] J Teasdale (from J Berry [1-5] Aug 1998).*

HABUB (USA) RR 100df 4270[9]
3 b br c Danzig (USA) 8.1f **(88)** - Cheval Volant (USA) (Kris S (USA)) 7.9f **(71)**
Form - 5750
Record 1999 - 1st:0 2nd:0 3rd:0 Ran:4
Pre1999 - 1st:1 2nd:1 3rd:0 Ran:2
Win Prizemoney £4,402 *Total Prizemoney* £5,786
Wins * 1998 Spt Nottin (G-F) 6.1f 84 <
1999 Turf 0-4: (6f 3, 7f) (gd 3, g-f)
Strong, very useful colt. Turf high 100. A laid-back individual, he proved most disappointing after a promising juvenile campaign. A step-up to a mile might aid his cause.
**J H M Gosden [1-6] Hamdan Al Maktoum.*

HADATH (IRE) BHB 87f **RR 88f** 4833[5]
2 br c Mujtahid (USA) 7.4f **(69)** - Al Sylah (Nureyev (USA)) 8.7f **(78)**
Form - 6425
Record 1999 - 1st:0 2nd:1 3rd:0 Ran:4
Win Prizemoney £0 *Total Prizemoney* £1,667
1999 Turf 0-4: (6f, 7f 3) (g-s, gd, frm 2)
Useful colt. Turf high 88 (began Jly) - 2nd of 6 getting 4lb from Kingsdon (29 Spt Salisbury 7f g-s RF 4645).
**M P Tregoning [0-4] Hamdan Al Maktoum.*

HADEQA BHB 63f **RR 63f** 4930[15]
3 ch g Hadeer 8.9f **(58)** - Heavenly Queen (Scottish Reel) 7f **(61)**
Form - 51654061100
Record 1999 - 1st:3 2nd:0 3rd:0 Ran:11
Pre1999 - 1st:1 2nd:2 3rd:2 Ran:14
Win Prizemoney £13,370 *Total Prizemoney* £17,337
Wins **1999** Jly Carlis (GD) C 6.9f 59
1999 Jun Pontef (GD) S 8f 63+
1999 Apr Catter (SFT) H 7f 66 74+ <
1998 Aug Redcar (G-F) H 6f 61 63
1999 Turf 3-11: (7f 2-3, 8f 1-4, 10f 3, 11f) (sft, g-s, gd 1-4, g-f 1-3, frm 1-2)
Light-framed, average gelding, effective 6 to 8f, acts on gd to frm, best on gd, mostly wears blinkers (extremely effectively). Turf high 74 - 1st of 16 giving 8lb to Grizelda (21 Apr Catterick RF 0792). Consistent. Has pays his way in modest company.
**F Jordan [1-6] The French Connection (from P D Evans [4-23] Jly 1999).*

HADITOVSKI BHB 48f **RR 59f** 1853[7]
3 b g Hatim (USA) 7.8f **(56)** - Grand Occasion (Great Nephew) 9.9f **(64)**
Form - 07
Record 1999 - 1st:0 2nd:0 3rd:0 Ran:2
Pre1999 - 1st:0 2nd:0 3rd:0 Ran:1
1999 Turf 0-2: (7f 2) (g-s, gd)
Fair gelding. Turf high 39. **T P Tate [0-3] T P Tate.*

HADLEIGH (IRE) BHB 72f **RR 70f** 5143[15]
3 b c Perugino (USA) - Risacca (ITY) (Sir Gaylord) 10.6f **(64)**
Form - 00050
Record 1999 - 1st:0 2nd:0 3rd:0 Ran:5
Pre1999 - 1st:1 2nd:0 3rd:1 Ran:5
Win Prizemoney £3,728 *Total Prizemoney* £4,549
Wins * 1998 Aug Kempto (G-F) 6f 83 <
1999 Turf 0-5: (6f, 7f 3, 8f) (g-s, gd, g-f 3)
Workmanlike, above-average colt, effective 6f, acts on frm. Turf high 73. Consistent. **R W Armstrong [1-10] C G Donovan.*

HAIFAA (IRE) RR 48f 4697[5]
3 b br f Doyoun 10.7f **(69)** - Mayaasa (USA) (Lyphard (USA)) 9.9f **(72)**
Form - 05
Record 1999 - 1st:0 2nd:0 3rd:0 Ran:2
1999 Turf 0-2: (8f, 10f) (g-s, frm)
Light-framed, currently moderate filly. Turf high 48 (began Spt).
**R W Armstrong [0-2] Hamdan Al Maktoum.*

HAIKAL RR 51f 4284[7]
2 b c Owington - Magic Milly (Simply Great (FR)) 8.2f **(65)**
Form - 7
Record 1999 - 1st:0 2nd:0 3rd:0 Ran:1
1999 Turf 0-1: (6f) (frm)

Currently fair colt. **N A Graham [0-1] Hamdan Al Maktoum.*

HAIL SHEEVA RR 26f 3419[9]

2 ch f Democratic (USA) - Sun Storm (Sunyboy)
Form - 0
Record 1999 - 1st:0 2nd:0 3rd:0 Ran:1
1999 Turf 0-1: (6f) (frm)
Currently little account filly. **Miss K M George [0-1] R J Matthews.*

HAIL THE CHIEF RR 51f 2278[10]

2 b c Be My Chief (USA) 10.2f **(62)** - Jade Pet **(84df)** (Petong) 6.6f **(58)**
Form - 0
Record 1999 - 1st:0 2nd:0 3rd:0 Ran:1
1999 Turf 0-1: (7f) (frm)
Currently fair colt. **R Hannon [0-1] Peter Crane.*

HAITHEM (IRE) BHB 74f RR 69f 5157[10]

2 b c Mtoto 11.5f **(71)** - Wukk (IRE) (Glow (USA)) 6.7f **(71)**
Form - 420
Record 1999 - 1st:0 2nd:1 3rd:0 Ran:3
Win Prizemoney £0 *Total Prizemoney* £1,392
1999 Turf 0-3: (6f, 7f 2) (frm 3)
Currently average colt. Turf high 69 (began Aug) - 2nd of 10 to Al Towd (19 Spt Newcastle 7f frm RF 4423). **M Johnston [0-3] Ziad Galadari.*

HAJR (IRE) BHB 96f RR 94f 981[4]

5 b g Rainbow Quest (USA) 11.2f **(81)** - Dance by Night (Northfields (USA)) 9f **(72)**
Form - 434
Record 1999 - 1st:0 2nd:0 3rd:1 Ran:3
Pre1999 - 1st:4 2nd:1 3rd:0 Ran:13
Win Prizemoney £41,565 *Total Prizemoney* £48,449

Wins								
* 1998	Jun	Epsom	(GD)	H	12f	90	93	<
* 1998	May	Goodwo	(G-F)	H	12f	85	87	
* 1997	Aug	Newmar	(G-F)	H	10f	82	86+	
* 1997	Jun	Newbur	(GD)		7f		75	

1999 Turf 0-3: (12f 3) (gd 2, frm)
Useful gelding, effective 10 to 12f, best at 12f, acts on gd to frm. Turf high 94 - 4th of 13 giving 4lb to Blueprint (2 May Newmarket 12f frm RF 0981). Consistent. Respectable efforts in a short campaign. **E A L Dunlop [4-16] Maktoum Al Maktoum.*

HAKEEM (IRE) BHB 61f RR 61f 2156[13]

4 ch g Kefaah (USA) 11.2f **(64)** - Masarrah (Formidable (USA)) 9.2f **(63)**
Form - 780710020
Record 1999 - 1st:1 2nd:1 3rd:0 Ran:9
Pre1999 - 1st:1 2nd:0 3rd:1 Ran:10
Win Prizemoney £5,656 *Total Prizemoney* £7,665

Wins								
* 1999	May	Thirsk	(G-F)	H	8f	53	56	
1997	Spt	Folkes	(GD)		6f		78	<

1999 Turf 1-7: (6f 2, 7f 4, 8f 1-1) (sft, gd 2, g-f 1-2, frm 2) 1999 AW 0-2: (8f 2) (Fibr 2)
Scopey, average gelding, has worn blinkers, likes left handed tracks, likes tight tracks. Turf high 61. AW high 42. Scored over a mile at Thirsk in May when racing on fast ground. He is going to need those conditions if he is to score again. **M Brittain [1-9] Mel Brittain (from R W Armstrong [1-10] Spt 1998).*

HALBERD (IRE) BHB 76f RR 73f 4685[18]

3 b c Barathea (IRE) - Hanzala (FR) (Akarad (FR)) 9f **(76)**
Form - 3170
Record 1999 - 1st:1 2nd:0 3rd:1 Ran:4
Win Prizemoney £4,464 *Total Prizemoney* £5,083

Wins							
* 1999	Jly	Newmar	(G-F)	7f		73	<

1999 Turf 1-4: (7f 1-4) (gd 2, frm 1-2)
Scopey, above-average colt. Turf high 80 (began Jly) - also 1st of 10 from Compensation (17 Jly Newmarket RF 2912). **J H M Gosden [1-4] Sheikh Mohammed.*

HALBERT BHB 29f30a RR 17f 30a 179[10]

10 b g Song 6.4f **(63)** - Stoneydale (Tickled Pink) 6.5f **(59)**
Form - 0580
Record 1999 - 1st:0 2nd:0 3rd:0 Ran:4
Pre1999 - 1st:4 2nd:8 3rd:5 Ran:72
Win Prizemoney £11,572 *Total Prizemoney* £23,662

Wins								
* 1996	*Dec*	*Lingfi*	*(STD)*	*H*	*6f*	*40*	*44*	
1995	Aug	Bright	(FRM)	H	5.3f	54	62	<
1995	Jly	Mussel	(G-F)	SH	5f	49	51	
1995	Jun	Hamilt	(FRM)	SH	5f	41	49	

1999 AW 0-4: (6f 4) (Equi 4)
Little account gelding, often wears blinkers. AW high 22.
**P Burgoyne [1-32] Philip Saunders (from M D I Usher [0-4] May 1997).*

HALF MOON BAY RR 88+f 3253[1]

2 b g Cyrano de Bergerac 7.3f **(58)** - Tarnside Rosal **(56f)** (Mummy's Game) 8.2f **(60)**
Form - 15511
Record 1999 - 1st:3 2nd:0 3rd:0 Ran:5
Win Prizemoney £10,467 *Total Prizemoney* £10,467

Wins								
* **1999**	Jly	Thirsk	(FRM)	H	5f		88+	<
* **1999**	Jly	Doncas	(G-F)	H	5f		86	
* **1999**	May	Thirsk	(GD)		5f		80+	

1999 Turf 3-5: (5f 3-5) (gd, g-f 2-2, frm 1-2)
Useful gelding. Turf high 88 - 1st of 7 giving 25lb to Natsmagirl (30 Jly Thirsk RF 3253) - also 1st of 8 giving 25lb to Pape Diouf (15 Jly Doncaster RF 2842). An excitable sort, he has bags of natural pace. **T D Barron [3-5] Mrs Ann Lockhart.*

HALF TIDE BHB 45f49a RR 48f 49a 335[3]

5 ch h Nashwan (USA) 10.3f **(79)** - Double River (USA) (Irish River (FR)) 8.6f **(78)**
Form - 622213
Record 1999 - 1st:1 2nd:2 3rd:1 Ran:4
Pre1999 - 1st:0 2nd:1 3rd:0 Ran:6
Win Prizemoney £2,621 *Total Prizemoney* £5,021

Wins								
* **1999**	*Feb*	*Lingfi*	*(STD)*	*H*	*12f*	*48*	*48*	<

1999 AW 1-4: (10f 2, 12f 1-2) (Equi 1-3, Fibr)
Moderate colt, effective 10f, - acts on Equi, likes left handed tracks, likes tight tracks. AW high 68 (1st run) - 2nd of 9 giving 2lb to Thekryaati (1 Jan Lingfield 10f Equi RF 0003).
**P Mitchell [1-10] The Fruit Cake Partnership.*

HALF TONE BHB 45f64a RR 35f 64a 4713[10]

7 gr h Touch of Grey 8.1f **(47)** - Demilinga (Nishapour (FR)) 9.1f **(61)**
Form - 6067432132222080400050
Record 1999 - 1st:1 2nd:5 3rd:2 Ran:18
Pre1999 - 1st:9 2nd:10 3rd:16 Ran:82
Win Prizemoney £30,680 *Total Prizemoney* £55,225

Wins								
* **1999**	*Jan*	*Lingfi*	*(STD)*	*H*	*5f*	*53*	*56*	
* 1998	Oct	Bath	(HVY)	H	5.1f	54	60	
* 1998	Aug	Sandow	(G-F)	H	5f	51	56	
* 1997	Aug	Sandow	(GD)	H	5f	56	60	
* 1997	May	Goodwo	(G-S)	H	5f	52	53	
* 1996	Aug	Sandow	(G-F)	H	5f	50	54	
* 1996	*Feb*	*Lingfi*	*(STD)*	*H*	*5f*	*64*	*65*	<
* 1995	*Dec*	*Lingfi*	*(STD)*	*H*	*5f*	*53*	*60*	
* 1995	*Nov*	*Lingfi*	*(STD)*	*H*	*5f*	*53*	*52*	
* 1995	*Jan*	*Wolver*	*(STD)*	*H*	*5f*	*48*	*54*	

1999 Turf 0-9: (5f 7, 6f 2) (sft, gd 3, g-f 2, frm 3) 1999 AW 1-9: (5f 1-7, 6f 2) (Equi 1-9)
Average horse, effective 5 to 6f, best at 6f, acts on sft to g-s - acts on Equi, mostly wears blinkers (effectively), prefers left handed tracks, likes tight tracks, likes Lingfield. Turf high 52 (began Jly). AW high 61 - 2nd of 7 giving 24lb to Bowcliffe Grange (2 Mar Lingfield 5f Equi RF 0387). He manages to reach the frame regularly, but does not win that often. Capable of a power-packed finish, he does well over the minimum trip at Sandown and on the Lingfield Equitrack. **R M Flower [10-100] M G Rogers.*

HALHOO LAMMTARRA RR 83f 4274[2]

2 ch c Lammtarra (USA) - Shadha (USA)(Devil's Bag (USA))12.4f **(78)**
Form - 2
Record 1999 - 1st:0 2nd:1 3rd:0 Ran:1
Win Prizemoney £0 *Total Prizemoney* £1,326
1999 Turf 0-1: (8f) (g-f)
Currently decent colt. (1st run) - 2nd of 7 to Air Marshall (11 Spt Goodwood 8f g-f RF 4274). Looks sure to win a race or two in 2000. **M R Channon [0-1] Sheikh Ahmed Al Maktoum.*

HAL HOO YAROOM BHB 57f65a RR 59f 65a 3835[5]

6 b h Belmez (USA) 11.4f **(65)** - Princess Nawaal (USA) (Seattle Slew (USA)) 9.4f **(76)**
Form - 451145

Record 1999 - 1st:2 2nd:0 3rd:0 Ran:6
Pre1999 - 1st:2 2nd:2 3rd:3 Ran:18
Win Prizemoney £13,738 *Total Prizemoney* £17,894
Wins * **1999** Jly Warwic (G-F) H 15.8f 52 59
* **1999** Jun Bath (GD) H 17.2f 50 51
1996 Jly Folkes (FRM) H 15.4f 67 82 <
1996 Jun Yarmou (FRM) 14.1f 67
1999 Turf 2-5: (16f 1-2, 17f 1-2, 20f) (g-f 1-3, frm 1-2) 1999 AW 0-1: (16f) (Equi)

Average horse, effective 13 to 16f, best at 16f, acts on g-f - acts on AW, best on Equi, prefers left handed tracks, likes Lingfield. Turf high 59 - 1st of 10 getting 11lb from Tory Boy (10 Jly Warwick RF 2724). (1st run) - 4th of 6 giving 22lb to Sleave Silk (2 Mar Lingfield 16f Equi RF 0390). Won three times over hurdles last season, and has returned to the Flat in fine fettle, winning two ordinary events at Bath and Warwick.

**J R Jenkins [5-26] R M Ellis (from R Akehurst [0-4] Oct 1997).*

HALLAND PARK GIRL (IRE) BHB 100f RR 106f 5036[1]

2 b f Primo Dominie 7.2f **(67)** - Katsina (USA) (Cox's Ridge (USA)) 8f **(68)**
Form - 41212111
Record 1999 - 1st:5 2nd:2 3rd:0 Ran:8
Win Prizemoney £101,393 *Total Prizemoney* £129,884
Wins * **1999** Oct Doncas (SFT) L 6f 106 <
* **1999** Aug Currag (G-S) 6f 96+
* **1999** Jly Salisb (FRM) 6f 96
* **1999** Jly Ascot (G-F) H 6f 86+
* **1999** May Lingfi (G-F) 5f 75
1999 Turf 5-8: (5f 1-2, 6f 4-6) (g-s 1-1, gd 1-1, g-f 1-2, frm 2-4)

Pattern-class filly, effective 6f, acts on g-s to frm. Turf high 106 - 1st of 8 getting 2lb from Seven No Trumps (23 Oct Doncaster RF 5036). Improving. Bought for just IR5,000 guineas as a yearling, she proved a rare bargain. The winner of four of her seven starts, including the valuable Tattersalls Breeders Stakes in Ireland, she looked better than ever when returning from an eight-week break to win a listed event at Doncaster in October. She should stay seven furlongs, acts on any ground and is a credit to connections.

**R Hannon [5-8] Mrs B Burchett.*

HALLOA BHB 96f RR 84f 1245[6]

Halland Park Girl was a real bargain

3 ch f Wolfhound (USA) 7.3f **(71)** - Fairy Fortune (Rainbow Quest (USA)) 10.4f **(75)**
Form - 6
Record 1999 - 1st:0 2nd:0 3rd:0 Ran:1
Pre1999 - 1st:1 2nd:0 3rd:2 Ran:5
Win Prizemoney £4,012 *Total Prizemoney* £7,255
Wins * 1998 Jun Nottin (GD) 6.1f 81 <
1999 Turf 0-1: (6f) (g-f)

Unfurnished, decent filly, effective 6 to 7f, acts on gd to hrd.

**J R Fanshawe [1-6] T & J Vestey.*

HALMAHERA (IRE) BHB 109f RR 110f 4568[6]

4 b g Petardia 8.2f **(58)** - Champagne Girl (Robellino (USA)) 7.6f **(80)**
Form - 222212406
Record 1999 - 1st:1 2nd:5 3rd:0 Ran:9
Pre1999 - 1st:4 2nd:2 3rd:1 Ran:17
Win Prizemoney £56,673 *Total Prizemoney* £110,758
Wins * **1999** Jun Newcas (G-F) L 6f 110
* 1997 Oct Ascot (HVY) G3 5f 111? <
* 1997 Spt Ayr (G-S) L 5f 96
* 1997 Jly Goodwo (G-F) H 6f 89
* 1997 Jly Chepst (G-S) 6.1f 71
1999 Turf 1-9: (5f, 6f 1-8) (sft, g-s 2, gd, g-f 2, frm 1-3)

Leggy, Group-class gelding, effective 6f, acts on sft to frm, best on g-f, has worn blinkers, does well at Ascot. Turf high 110 - 2nd of 30 giving 15lb to Harmonic Way (31 Jly Goodwood 6f g-f RF 3261) - also 1st of 9 getting 4lb from Nigrasine (26 Jun Newcastle RF 2339). Consistent. He lost his way after winning the Cornwallis Stakes as a juvenile, but bounced back in style last season, running a series of fine races. Unfortunate to finish second in both the Wokingham and Stewards' Cup, he is best at six furlongs, goes on any ground and will continue to give a good account of himself.

**I A Balding [5-26] Robert Hitchins.*

HALMANERROR BHB 62f57a RR 38f 57a 5127[8]

9 gr g Lochnager 6.9f **(50)** - Counter Coup (Busted) 10.2f **(61)**
Form - 241510008
Record 1999 - 1st:2 2nd:1 3rd:0 Ran:9
Pre1999 - 1st:8 2nd:4 3rd:5 Ran:62
Win Prizemoney £46,325 *Total Prizemoney* £55,943
Wins * **1999** Jun Chepst (GD) H 7.1f 63 64
* **1999** May Chepst (GD) H 7.1f 60 62
* 1998 Jun Salisb (G-S) CH 7f 53 59
* 1998 Apr Bright (GD) C 6f 51
1997 May Doncas (G-S) H 6f 57 60
1996 Aug Doncas (G-F) 6f 65
1995 Aug Pontef (G-F) H 6f 67 66 <
1995 Jly Pontef (G-F) H 6f 61 63
1999 Turf 2-8: (6f, 7f 2-7) (sft, g-s, gd 2-4, g-f, frm) 1999 AW 0-1: (8f) (Fibr)

Fair gelding, effective 7f, acts on sft to gd, best on gd. Turf high 64 - 1st of 14 giving 1lb to Akalim (11 Jun Chepstow RF 1908) - also 1st of 20 giving 7lb to Arbenig (19 May Chepstow RF 1328). Becoming disappointing.

**G M McCourt [4-25] Caulkheads Racing (from Mrs J R Ramsden [6-48] Oct 1997).*

HAMARATARA BHB 55f RR 59df 4017[4]

3 b f Sheikh Albadou 9.2f **(75)** - Low Hill (Rousillon (USA)) 8.2f **(74)**
Form - 684
Record 1999 - 1st:0 2nd:0 3rd:0 Ran:3
Win Prizemoney £0 *Total Prizemoney* £262
1999 Turf 0-3: (6f, 7f, 8f) (g-f, frm 2)

Light-framed, currently fair filly. Turf high 59 (began Jly).

**A J McNae [0-3] Eridge Lodge Racing.*

HAMBLEDEN RR 59f 5129[9]

2 b c Vettori (IRE) - Dalu (IRE) **(69f)** (Dancing Brave (USA)) 8.4f **(76)**
Form - 70
Record 1999 - 1st:0 2nd:0 3rd:0 Ran:2
1999 Turf 0-2: (6f, 7f) (gd 2)

Currently fair colt. Turf high 59 (began Oct).

**M A Jarvis [0-2] Stag and Huntsman.*

HAMERKOP BHB 30f RR 33f 4334[5]

4 br f Damister (USA) 9.1f **(66)** - Royal Scene (NZ) (Sovereign Edition)
Form - 85675
Record 1999 - 1st:0 2nd:0 3rd:0 Ran:5
Pre1999 - 1st:0 2nd:0 3rd:0 Ran:6
1999 Turf 0-4: (8f, 10f 2, 14f) (g-s, gd 2, g-f) 1999 AW 0-1: (12f) (Fibr)

Workmanlike, very moderate filly, effective 8f, acts on gd, has worn blinkers. Turf high 33 (1st run) (began Jly) - 5th of 9 getting 12lb from Saifan (1 Jly Yarmouth 8f gd RF 2470).

**John Berry [0-17] John Berry.*

HAMLYN (IRE) RR 62f 5129[8]
2 br c Lure (USA) - Passamaquoddy (USA) (Drone) 10.3f **(74)**
Form - 58
Record 1999 - 1st:0 2nd:0 3rd:0 Ran:2
Win Prizemoney £0 *Total Prizemoney* £435
1999 Turf 0-2: (6f, 7f) (sft, gd)
Currently average colt. Turf high 62 (began Spt).
**D R C Elsworth [0-2] M Tabor.*

HAMMER AND SICKLE (IRE) BHB 97f **RR 97f** 2070[11]
2 b c Soviet Lad (USA) 9.4f **(63)** - Preponderance (IRE) (Cyrano de Bergerac) 6f **(68)**
Form - 1D210
Record 1999 - 1st:2 2nd:1 3rd:0 Ran:5
Win Prizemoney £6,043 *Total Prizemoney* £6,964
Wins *** 1999** May Redcar (FRM) 5f 78+
*** 1999** Apr Ripon (G-S) 5f 82 <
1999 Turf 2-5: (5f 2-5) (gd 1-2, g-f, frm 1-1, hrd)
Very useful colt. Turf high 97. A robust individual, he looked a useful sprinting juvenile in the first half of the season but went missing after Royal Ascot. There must be a doubt about his ability to train on. **M Johnston [2-5] The 4th Middleham Partnership.*

HAMMER AND TONGS (IRE) RR 52f 4951[8]
3 ch g Hamas (IRE) 8f **(72)** - Bag Lady (Be My Guest (USA)) 9.3f **(67)**
Form - 038
Record 1999 - 1st:0 2nd:0 3rd:1 Ran:3
Win Prizemoney £0 *Total Prizemoney* £320
1999 Turf 0-2: (7f, 8f) (g-f, frm) 1999 AW 0-1: (7f) (Fibr)
Scopey, currently fair gelding. Turf high 52 (began Jly). (1st run) - 3rd of 12 to Automatic (16 Oct Wolverhampton 7f Fibr RF 4925).
**M Johnston [0-3] The 4th Middleham Partnership.*

HANA'S PRIDE (IRE) BHB 35f **RR 42f** 3007[11]
3 gr f Pips Pride 6.7f **(70)** - Singhana (IRE) (Mouktar)
Form - 60
Record 1999 - 1st:0 2nd:0 3rd:0 Ran:2
Pre1999 - 1st:0 2nd:0 3rd:0 Ran:1
1999 Turf 0-1: (5f) (g-f) 1999 AW 0-1: (5f) (Fibr)
Tall, currently moderate filly. **Mrs A Swinbank [0-3] Bill Martin.*

HAND CRAFT (IRE) BHB 60f58a **RR 62df 58a** 4927[10]
7 b g Dancing Dissident (USA) 6.8f **(65)** - Fair Flutter (Beldale Flutter (USA)) 9.7f **(71)**
Form - 14114500
Record 1999 - 1st:3 2nd:0 3rd:0 Ran:8
Pre1999 - 1st:3 2nd:0 3rd:1 Ran:10
Win Prizemoney £21,618 *Total Prizemoney* £22,371
Wins *** 1999** Jly Hamilt (FRM) C 9.2f 64
*** 1999** Jun Bright (GD) C 10f 46
*** 1999** *Jun Wolver (STD) C 8.5f 61*
1995 Aug Ripon (G-F) H 9f 78 83 <
1995 Jly Nottin (G-F) H 8.2f 74 73
1995 *Feb Wolver (STD) 7f 75*
1999 Turf 2-6: (8f 2, 9f 1-1, 10f 1-3) (gd 1-1, g-f, frm 1-4) 1999 AW 1-2: (8f 1-2) (Fibr 1-2)
Average gelding, effective 8 to 10f, acts on frm - acts on Fibr, favours tight tracks. Turf high 64 - 1st of 9 giving 6lb to Big Target (16 Jly Hamilton RF 2872). AW high 61 (1st run) - 1st of 10 getting 6lb from The Imposter (19 Jun Wolverhampton RF 2160). Becoming disappointing. He put up a remarkable performance to win at Wolverhampton in June considering he had been off the track for three years. He won twice more on turf but appeared to have lost interest by the end of the season.
**W G M Turner [3-8] E Goody (from W J Haggas [3-10] Oct 1996).*

HANDSOME BEAU BHB 30f **RR 38f** 4228[20]
4 ch g Handsome Sailor 6.6f **(53)** - Chester Belle (Ballacashtal (CAN)) 5.3f **(50)**
Form - 0
Record 1999 - 1st:0 2nd:0 3rd:0 Ran:1
Pre1999 - 1st:0 2nd:0 3rd:0 Ran:2
1999 Turf 0-1: (8f) (frm)
Unfurnished, currently very moderate gelding, has worn blinkers.
**A Bailey [0-3] C W Jenkins.*

HANDSOME DUKE RR 16f 1448[10]
2 ch g Handsome Sailor 6.6f **(53)** - Dutch Girl (Workboy) 7.3f **(46)**
Form - 0780
Record 1999 - 1st:0 2nd:0 3rd:0 Ran:4
1999 Turf 0-3: (5f 2, 6f) (gd 2, frm) 1999 AW 0-1: (5f) (Fibr)
Very moderate gelding. Turf high 16.
**M W Easterby [0-4] C F Buckton.*

HANDSOME RIDGE BHB 117f **RR 121f** 4919[7]
5 ch h Indian Ridge 7.6f **(74)** - Red Rose Garden (Electric) 10.1f **(61)**
Form - 061155767
Record 1999 - 1st:2 2nd:0 3rd:0 Ran:8
Pre1999 - 1st:5 2nd:4 3rd:3 Ran:17
Win Prizemoney £170,805 *Total Prizemoney* £219,245
Wins *** 1999** May Goodwo (GD) 9.9f 121+ <
*** 1999** Apr Sandow (G-S) G2 8.1f 113
* 1998 Nov Saint- (HLD) G3 8f 118+
* 1998 Spt Doncas (GD) G3 8f 116
* 1997 Jly Maison (SFT) G3 9f 101
* 1997 Jun Goodwo (G-S) 9f 104
* 1996 Nov Doncas (SFT) 7f 91+
1999 Turf 2-8: (8f 1-2, 9f 2, 10f 1-4) (hvy, g-s 1-2, gd 1-3, g-f 2)
Very high-class colt, effective 8 to 10f, best at 10f, acts on sft to g-f, likes right handed tracks, likes Longchamp. Turf high 121 - 1st of 10 from Running Stag (8 May Goodwood RF 1108) - also 1st of 9 from On The Ridge (23 Apr Sandown RF 0822). He was in good form in the spring, winning the Group Two Credit Suisse Mile at Sandown, and one of the valuable Shergar Cup races. Things did not go his way in his next two races, and he was subsequently given a break. After his return he ran creditably without being able to rekindle earlier sparkle. He has been a wonderful servant to connections and, if found a place at stud, should be a popular competitively-priced stallion.
**J H M Gosden [7-25] Platt Promotions Ltd.*

Handsome Ridge once again paid his way for connections at Group level

HANNAH PARK (IRE) BHB 54f **RR 54f** 4882[6]
3 b f Lycius (USA) 8.8f **(71)** - Wassl This Then (IRE) (Wassl) 9.7f **(62)**
Form - 44204407236
Record 1999 - 1st:0 2nd:2 3rd:1 Ran:11
Pre1999 - 1st:0 2nd:0 3rd:0 Ran:1
Win Prizemoney £0 *Total Prizemoney* £3,347
1999 Turf 0-11: (7f, 8f 2, 10f 4, 11f 4) (sft, gd, g-f 6, frm 3)
Neat, fair filly, effective 10 to 11f, acts on gd to g-f, has worn blinkers, likes tight tracks. Turf high 63.
**M L W Bell [0-12] Miss Susannah Farr.*

HANNIBAL LAD BHB 58f60a **RR 55f 60a** 2160[4]
3 ch g Rock City 8.8f **(62)** - Appealing (Star Appeal) 9.6f **(65)**

Form - 1004
Record 1999 - 1st:1 2nd:0 3rd:0 Ran:4
Pre1999 - 1st:1 2nd:0 3rd:1 Ran:5
Win Prizemoney £4,100 *Total Prizemoney* £4,985
Wins *** 1999** *Apr Wolver (STD) S 9.4f 64*
* 1998 *Spt Southw (STD) S 7f 68* <
1999 Turf 0-2: (8f, 12f) (gd, g-f) 1999 AW 1-2: (8f, 9f 1-1) (Fibr 1-2)
Leggy, average gelding, effective 7f, acts on frm. Turf high 37. AW high 64 (1st run). His best form to date has been in plating company on Fibresand. **P D Evans [2-9] John Pugh.*

HAPPY CHANGE (GER) RR 110f 4015[1]

5 ch h Surumu (GER) - Happy Gini (USA) (Ginistrelli (USA)) 5.6f **(66)**
Form - 21
Record 1999 - 1st:1 2nd:1 3rd:0 Ran:2
Pre1999 - 1st:1 2nd:1 3rd:2 Ran:10
Win Prizemoney £31,860 *Total Prizemoney* £95,028
Wins *** 1999** Aug Epsom (GD) 10.1f 110 <
1998 Aug Baden- (SFT) G3 10f 108+
1999 Turf 1-2: (10f 1-2) (gd, g-f 1-1)
Group-class colt, effective 10 to 11f, best at 10f, acts on sft to g-f. Turf high 110 (began Aug) - 1st of 4 from Muhib (30 Aug Epsom RF 4015). Consistent. A Group 3 winner in Germany, he has been lightly raced since moving to England, but showed plenty of zip when winning a conditions event at Epsom. Switched to the leading National Hunt trainer Venetia Williams immediately afterwards, much to the chagrin of Mark Johnston, he is capable of winning decent races on the Flat.
**M Johnston [1-2] The Winning Line (from Miss Venetia Williams [0-1] Spt 1998).*

HAPPY DAYS BHB 42f RR 44df 4717[14]

4 b g Primitive Rising (USA) 8.1f **(48)** - Miami Dolphin (Derrylin) 8.8f **(54)**
Form - 051800
Record 1999 - 1st:1 2nd:0 3rd:0 Ran:6
Pre1999 - 1st:0 2nd:3 3rd:1 Ran:16
Win Prizemoney £3,663 *Total Prizemoney* £8,495
Wins *** 1999** May Ripon (G-F) H 16f 38 44 <
1999 Turf 1-6: (12f, 14f, 16f 1-1, 17f 3) (sft, gd 2, g-f 2, frm 1-1)
Unfurnished, moderate gelding, has worn blinkers, likes right handed tracks. Turf high 44. Becoming disappointing.
**D Moffatt [1-28] J W Barrett (from J Berry [0-2] Spt 1998).*

HAPPY DAYS AGAIN (IRE) BHB 44f51a RR 44f 51a 5032[23]

4 b f Elbio 9f **(62)** - Tacheo (Tachypous) 8.6f **(55)**
Form - 40007670
Record 1999 - 1st:0 2nd:0 3rd:0 Ran:8
Pre1999 - 1st:2 2nd:2 3rd:0 Ran:19
Win Prizemoney £6,318 *Total Prizemoney* £8,759
Wins * 1997 Oct Newmar (G-F) H 5f 80 84 <
* 1997 Jly Ripon (GD) 5f 77
1999 Turf 0-6: (5f 6) (g-s 2, gd, g-f 2, hrd) 1999 AW 0-2: (5f 2) (Fibr 2)
Scopey, moderate filly, effective 5f, acts on frm, has worn blinkers. Turf high 54. AW high 41. **J Wharton [2-27] Mrs S M Moore.*

HAPPY DIAMOND (USA) RR 83+f 3283[1]

2 b c Diesis 9f **(80)** - Urus (USA) (Kris S (USA)) 7.9f **(71)**
Form - 21
Record 1999 - 1st:1 2nd:1 3rd:0 Ran:2
Win Prizemoney £4,081 *Total Prizemoney* £5,027
Wins *** 1999** Jly Thirsk (FRM) 5f 83+ <
1999 Turf 1-2: (5f 1-2) (frm 1-2)
Currently decent colt. Turf high 83 - 1st of 10 from Scafell (31 Jly Thirsk RF 3283). **M Johnston [1-2] Jaber Abdullah.*

HAPPY HOOLIGAN RR 79+f 1361[2]

2 b c Ezzoud (IRE) - Continual (USA) (Damascus (USA)) 8.9f **(71)**
Form - 2
Record 1999 - 1st:0 2nd:1 3rd:0 Ran:1
Win Prizemoney £0 *Total Prizemoney* £884
1999 Turf 0-1: (6f) (g-s)
Currently above-average colt. (1st run) - 2nd of 10 to Niagara (21 May Ayr 6f g-s RF 1361). **M Johnston [0-1] Maktoum Al Maktoum.*

HAPPY LADY (FR) BHB 66f RR 60f 4905[5]

3 b f Cadeaux Genereux 7.9f **(76)** - Siwaayib (Green Desert (USA)) 8.6f **(78)**
Form - 83855
Record 1999 - 1st:0 2nd:0 3rd:1 Ran:5
Pre1999 - 1st:0 2nd:0 3rd:0 Ran:1
Win Prizemoney £0 *Total Prizemoney* £466
1999 Turf 0-5: (6f 2, 8f 2, 9f) (gd, g-f 2, frm 2)
Scopey, average filly, effective 8f, acts on g-f. Turf high 75 - 3rd of 12 to Lila (9 Jun Salisbury 8f g-f RF 1872).
**B W Hills [0-6] Maktoum Al Maktoum.*

HAPPY LANDING RR 66df 1084[13]

3 b f Minshaanshu Amad (USA) 11.3f **(53)** - Cee Beat (Bairn (USA)) 7.7f **(59)**
Form - 500
Record 1999 - 1st:0 2nd:0 3rd:0 Ran:3
1999 Turf 0-3: (7f, 8f 2) (gd, g-f, frm)
Workmanlike, currently average filly. Turf high 66.
**E A Wheeler [0-3] Austin Stroud & Co Ltd.*

HAPPY MEDIUM (IRE) BHB 27f28a RR 11f 28a 357[7]

6 b g Fairy King (USA) 7.7f **(75)** - Belle Origine (USA) (Exclusive Native (USA)) 9.1f **(81)**
Form - 67
Record 1999 - 1st:0 2nd:0 3rd:0 Ran:2
Pre1999 - 1st:1 2nd:0 3rd:1 Ran:10
Win Prizemoney £2,763 *Total Prizemoney* £3,503
Wins * 1998 *Aug Southw (STD) H 14f 30 31* <
1999 AW 0-2: (16f 2) (Equi, Fibr)
Very moderate gelding. AW high 17.
**G P Enright [1-14] Dave Howe (from C O'Brien in IRE [0-2] Aug 1996).*

HAPPY OMEN RR 52f 5208[10]

2 b f Warning 8.1f **(77)** - Valika (Valiyar) 8.5f **(73)**
Form - 0
Record 1999 - 1st:0 2nd:0 3rd:0 Ran:1
1999 Turf 0-1: (7f) (g-s)
Currently fair filly. **L M Cumani [0-1] The Romney Partnership.*

HAPPY TIMES BHB 90f RR 88f 4041[1]

2 b g Timeless Times (USA) 6.1f **(56)** - Penny Hasset **(64f)** (Lochnager) 6f **(59)**
Form - 5613421
Record 1999 - 1st:2 2nd:1 3rd:1 Ran:7
Win Prizemoney £6,302 *Total Prizemoney* £8,142
Wins *** 1999** Aug Ripon (GD) H 6f 84 88 <
*** 1999** Jly Mussel (G-S) 5f 82
1999 Turf 2-7: (5f 1-5, 6f 1-2) (gd, g-f 1-4, frm 1-2)
Useful gelding, effective 5 to 6f, best at 5f, acts on g-f to frm, best on g-f. Turf high 88 - 1st of 11 giving 14lb to It's Allowed (31 Aug Ripon RF 4041) - also 1st of 12 from Seven of Spades (5 Jly Musselburgh RF 2555).
**M W Easterby [2-7] Bernard Bargh & John Walsh.*

HAPPY VALENTINE BHB 114f RR 121f 1108[4]

5 b h Rainbow Quest (USA) 11.2f **(81)** - Nearctic Flame (Sadler's Wells (USA)) 10f **(76)**
Form - 4
Record 1999 - 1st:0 2nd:0 3rd:0 Ran:1
Pre1999 - 1st:2 2nd:0 3rd:0 Ran:8
Win Prizemoney £15,353 *Total Prizemoney* £23,378
Wins * 1998 Jly Kempto (G-S) L 10f 108 <
* 1996 Oct Yarmou (GD) 7f 103++
1999 Turf 0-1: (10f) (gd)
Very high-class colt, effective 10 to 12f, acts on sft to gd. (1st run) - 4th of 10 to Handsome Ridge (8 May Goodwood 10f gd RF 1108). Often used as a pacemaker by the Godolphin team, he ran on his own merits when finishing fourth at Goodwood in May.
**S bin Suroor [2-9] Godolphin.*

HARD DAYS NIGHT (IRE) BHB 52f RR 46f 4995[7]

2 b c Mujtahid (USA) 7.4f **(69)** - Oiche Mhaith (Night Shift (USA)) 7.2f **(69)**
Form - 0500067
Record 1999 - 1st:0 2nd:0 3rd:0 Ran:7
1999 Turf 0-7: (6f 4, 7f 2, 8f) (gd 2, g-f 2, frm 2, hrd)
Moderate colt. Turf high 67 (began Jly).
**M Blanshard [0-7] David Sykes.*

HARD LINES (USA) BHB 75f **RR 83?f** 5035[10]
3 b c Silver Hawk (USA) 11.2f **(85)** - Arctic Eclipse (USA) (Northern Dancer) 9.6f **(80)**
Form - 0
Record 1999 - 1st:0 2nd:0 3rd:0 Ran:1
Pre1999 - 1st:1 2nd:0 3rd:0 Ran:1
Win Prizemoney £4,042 *Total Prizemoney* £4,042
Wins * 1998 May Newbur (G-F) 6f 83+ <
1999 Turf 0-1: (7f) (g-s)
Scopey, currently decent colt. **I A Balding [1-2] C H Bothway.*

HARD TO FIGURE BHB 70f74a **RR 72f 74a** 4161[8]
13 gr g Telsmoss 6.7f **(73)** - Count On Me (No Mercy) 8f **(61)**
Form - 0332278
Record 1999 - 1st:0 2nd:2 3rd:2 Ran:7
Pre1999 - 1st:13 2nd:11 3rd:19 Ran:115
Win Prizemoney £136,041 *Total Prizemoney* £221,639
Wins * 1997 Aug Bath (GD) C 5.7f 60
* 1997 Jly Bath (FRM) H 5.7f 73 83
* 1997 Jly Bath (G-F) C 5.1f 57
* 1996 Apr Kempto (GD) 6f 107
* 1995 Jly Newbur (GD) L 6f 109 <
1999 Turf 0-7: (6f 7) (g-f, frm 5, hrd)
Above-average gelding, effective 6 to 7f, best at 6f, acts on sft to frm, best on gd. Turf high 72. Consistent. This much-loved veteran sprinter has earned his retirement.
**R J Hodges [13-123] J W Mursell.*

HARDWICK LODGE BHB 49f **RR 44f** 4324[7]
3 ch f Grand Lodge (USA) - Mrs Musgrove (Jalmood (USA)) 10.1f **(52)**
Form - 067
Record 1999 - 1st:0 2nd:0 3rd:0 Ran:3
Pre1999 - 1st:0 2nd:0 3rd:0 Ran:1
1999 Turf 0-3: (8f, 10f, 12f) (gd 2, frm)
Scopey, moderate filly. Turf high 44.
**M J Ryan [0-4] Norcroft Park Stud.*

HARIK BHB 55f72a **RR 28f 72a** 5028[14]
5 ch g Persian Bold 10f **(69)** - Yaqut (USA) (Northern Dancer) 9.6f **(80)**
Form - 63412200
Record 1999 - 1st:1 2nd:2 3rd:1 Ran:8
Pre1999 - 1st:2 2nd:1 3rd:0 Ran:6
Win Prizemoney £9,024 *Total Prizemoney* £12,142
Wins * **1999** *Feb Lingfi (STD) H 16f 65 70*
* 1998 *Mar Lingfi (SLW) H 13f 65 73* <
* 1998 *Feb Lingfi (SLW) 12f 65*
1999 Turf 0-2: (12f, 16f) (g-s, g-f) 1999 AW 1-6: (12f, 16f 1-5) (Equi 1-6)
Above-average gelding, effective 12 to 16f, best at 16f, - acts on Equi, prefers left handed tracks, prefers tight tracks, excels at Lingfield. Turf high 28 (began Oct). AW high 72 - 2nd of 6 giving 28lb to Sleave Silk (2 Mar Lingfield 16f Equi RF 0390) - also 1st of 13 giving 11lb to Padauk (9 Feb Lingfield RF 0259). He seems to show his best form in staying events on Equitrack.
**G L Moore [4-23] The Best Beech Partnership (from B Hanbury [0-1] Oct 1996).*

HARIYANA (IRE) BHB 65f **RR 67f** 4862[9]
3 br f Kahyasi 12.9f **(74)** - Harouniya (Siberian Express (USA)) 8.8f **(65)**
Form - 60
Record 1999 - 1st:0 2nd:0 3rd:0 Ran:2
Pre1999 - 1st:0 2nd:0 3rd:1 Ran:2
Win Prizemoney £0 *Total Prizemoney* £535
1999 Turf 0-2: (8f, 11f) (sft 2)
Workmanlike, average filly. Turf high 52.
**L M Cumani [0-4] H H Aga Khan.*

HARKNESS WARRIOR (USA) BHB 43f **RR 51f** 204[7]
5 b g Geiger Counter (USA) 7.8f **(85)** - Judaire's Mint (USA) (Key To The Mint (USA)) 9.4f **(75)**
Form - 47
Record 1999 - 1st:0 2nd:0 3rd:0 Ran:2
Pre1999 - 1st:0 2nd:0 3rd:0 Ran:2
1999 AW 0-2: (12f, 16f) (Fibr 2)
Fair gelding, has worn blinkers. AW high 43.
**B S Rothwell [0-5] Brian Rothwell (from A J Martin in IRE [0-12] Nov 1998).*

HARLEQUIN DANCER BHB 82f **RR 76f** 5004[13]
3 b c Distant Relative 7f **(69)** - Proudfoot (IRE) (Shareef Dancer (USA)) 9.9f **(73)**
Form - 45413500
Record 1999 - 1st:1 2nd:0 3rd:1 Ran:8
Win Prizemoney £2,448 *Total Prizemoney* £8,338
Wins * **1999** May Leices (GD) 8f 83 <
1999 Turf 1-8: (8f 1-7, 10f) (gd 3, g-f 1-3, frm 2)
Strong, above-average colt, effective 8f, acts on g-f, often wears blinkers. Turf high 87 - 3rd of 32 getting 9lb from Pythios (15 Jun Ascot 8f g-f RF 1999) - also 1st of 14 giving 5lb to Manicure (31 May Leicester RF 1601). Inconsistent. He got off the mark with a narrow victory at Leicester in May, but ran a blinder to finish third in the Britannia when possibly drawn on the wrong side. Off the track for three months before finishing unplaced at Newbury in September, his Cambridgeshire run was unrevealing and his current ability is hard to assess.
**J H M Gosden [1-8] C T S Racing Partnership.*

HARMONIC (USA) BHB 77f **RR 78f** 4825[4]
2 b f Shadeed (USA) 7.7f **(72)** - Running Melody (Rheingold) 10.4f **(62)**
Form - 6624
Record 1999 - 1st:0 2nd:1 3rd:0 Ran:4
Win Prizemoney £0 *Total Prizemoney* £1,352
1999 Turf 0-4: (6f 3, 7f) (g-f 2, frm 2)
Above-average filly. Turf high 78 (began Jly) - 2nd of 12 to Princess Louise (8 Spt Kempton 6f frm RF 4212).
**D R C Elsworth [0-4] Mrs P J Sheen.*

HARMONIC WAY BHB 101f **RR 101f** 4896[10]
4 ch c Lion Cavern (USA) 7.5f **(74)** - Pineapple (Superlative) 7.2f **(56)**
Form - 72435212200
Record 1999 - 1st:1 2nd:4 3rd:1 Ran:11
Pre1999 - 1st:1 2nd:1 3rd:2 Ran:11
Win Prizemoney £54,694 *Total Prizemoney* £89,843
Wins * **1999** Jly Goodwo (G-F) H 6f 92 99 <
* 1997 Aug Salisb (G-F) 6f 80
1999 Turf 1-11: (6f 1-10, 7f) (gd 6, g-f 1-1, frm 4)
Scopey, very useful colt, effective 6 to 7f, best at 6f, acts on gd to frm, excels at York, likes Newmarket. Turf high 101 - 2nd of 11 getting 2lb from Ho Leng (1 Spt York 6f frm RF 4082) - also 1st of 30 getting 15lb from Halmahera (31 Jly Goodwood RF 3261). Consistent. This perennial bridesmaid finally had his day when winning the Stewards' Cup, where he swept from almost last to first in the final quarter-mile. Best over six furlongs, he benefits from exaggerated waiting tactics and goes well for Richard Hughes. **R Charlton [2-22] Mrs Alexandra Chandris.*

HARMONIZE RR 49f 3163[6]
2 b f Emperor Jones (USA) - Hemline (Sharpo) 7.7f **(59)**
Form - 066
Record 1999 - 1st:0 2nd:0 3rd:0 Ran:3
1999 Turf 0-3: (5f 2, 6f) (gd, frm 2)
Currently moderate filly. Turf high 49.
**Martyn Wane [0-3] Mrs H Wane.*

HARMONY HALL BHB 60f **RR 58f** 4711[9]
5 ch g Music Boy 6.5f **(56)** - Fleeting Affair (Hotfoot) 10.5f **(59)**
Form - 082022256053040
Record 1999 - 1st:0 2nd:4 3rd:1 Ran:15
Pre1999 - 1st:1 2nd:2 3rd:2 Ran:18
Win Prizemoney £5,247 *Total Prizemoney* £16,799
Wins 1998 Jly Nottin (G-F) H 10f 64 69 <
1999 Turf 0-15: (8f 9, 9f 3, 10f 2, 11f) (g-s 2, gd 4, g-f 5, frm 4)
Fair gelding, effective 8 to 12f, acts on gd to frm, best on frm, has worn blinkers, likes right handed tracks, excels at Newmarket, does well at Nottingham. Turf high 71 - 2nd of 12 giving 21lb to Ardent (22 May Kempton 9f frm RF 1392). He does not win that often, but has run some fine races in handicap company in the last couple of seasons. Effective from between a mile and ten furlongs, he needs fast ground.
**J M Bradley [0-15] E A Hayward (from J R Fanshawe [1-21] Aug 1998).*

HARNAGE (IRE) BHB 27f **RR 25f** 1707[13]
4 b g Mujadil (USA) 7.7f **(70)** - Wilderness (Martinmas) 7.6f **(59)**
Form - 5000

Record 1999 - 1st:0 2nd:0 3rd:0 Ran:4
Pre1999 - 1st:0 2nd:0 3rd:1 Ran:8
Win Prizemoney £0 *Total Prizemoney* £259
1999 Turf 0-4: (8f, 10f 3) (sft, gd, g-f 2)
Light-framed, little account gelding. Turf high 28. Inconsistent.
**P Burgoyne [0-7] Ice Cooling Ltd (from M R Channon [0-5] Jly 1997).*

HAROLDON (IRE) BHB 40f37a RR 42f 37a 5153[5]

10 ch g Heraldiste (USA) 8.9f **(54)** - Cordon (Morston (FR)) 9.4f **(55)**
Form - 04800063365023305
Record 1999 - 1st:0 2nd:1 3rd:4 Ran:17
Pre1999 - 1st:7 2nd:5 3rd:4 Ran:67
Win Prizemoney £24,629 *Total Prizemoney* £35,582
Wins * 1998 May Nottin (FRM) SH 10f 52 57
* 1997 Jly Windso (GD) H 10f 65 68
* 1995 Spt Haydoc (GD) H 10.5f 72 76
* 1995 Jly Windso (GD) H 11.6f 68 67
* 1995 May Warwic (FRM) H 10.8f 56 61
1999 Turf 0-17: (8f 2, 10f 10, 11f 2, 12f 3) (sft, gd 6, g-f 5, frm 5)
Moderate gelding, effective 10f, acts on g-f to frm, best on frm, has worn blinkers. **B Palling [8-89] Lamb Brook Associates.*

HARPER'S FERRY (USA) BHB 55f RR 59f 4715[5]

2 b c Eastern Echo (USA) 8f **(61)** - Gray And Red (USA) (Wolf Power (SAF))
Form - 405
Record 1999 - 1st:0 2nd:0 3rd:0 Ran:3
Win Prizemoney £0 *Total Prizemoney* £297
1999 Turf 0-3: (8f 2, 10f) (g-s, gd, g-f)
Currently fair colt, has worn blinkers. Turf high 59 (began Spt).
**I A Balding [0-3] Mrs Paul Mellon.*

HARP PLAYER (IRE) BHB 57f45a RR 57f 45a 2087[7]

3 ch g Pips Pride 6.7f **(70)** - Angelic Sounds (IRE) (The Noble Player (USA)) 6.5f **(67)**
Form - 1578227
Record 1999 - 1st:1 2nd:2 3rd:0 Ran:7
Pre1999 - 1st:0 2nd:0 3rd:0 Ran:3
Win Prizemoney £2,880 *Total Prizemoney* £4,895
Wins * **1999** Apr Warwic (GD) H 10.8f 54 57 <
1999 Turf 1-5: (11f 1-3, 12f 2) (g-s, gd 1-2, frm 2) 1999 AW 0-2: (11f, 12f) (Fibr 2)
Leggy, fair gelding, effective 11 to 12f, best at 11f, acts on g-s to frm, best on frm, prefers tight tracks. Turf high 57 - 5th of 19 giving 3lb to Dalby of York (19 Apr Windsor 12f frm RF 0759) - also 1st of 11 getting 11lb from Azihaam (5 Apr Warwick RF 0595). AW high 43. **M L W Bell [1-10] Billy Maguire.*

HARQUEBUSIER BHB 34f41a RR 27f 41a 4293[15]

3 ch f Keen 11.1f **(58)** - Mainly Me **(17f)** (Huntingdale)
Form - 7036800
Record 1999 - 1st:0 2nd:0 3rd:0 Ran:4
Pre1999 - 1st:0 2nd:0 3rd:3 Ran:8
Win Prizemoney £0 *Total Prizemoney* £804
1999 Turf 0-4: (6f 2, 7f 2) (gd 3, g-f)
Workmanlike, very moderate filly, effective 5f, acts on g-f. Turf high 27. Inconsistent. **J Pearce [0-12] & Mrs J Matthews.*

HARRYANA BHB 79f RR 82f 5214[2]

2 b f Efisio 7.7f **(69)** - Allyana (IRE) **(62df)** (Thatching) 8f **(66)**
Form - 215100742
Record 1999 - 1st:2 2nd:2 3rd:0 Ran:9
Win Prizemoney £9,796 *Total Prizemoney* £11,846
Wins * **1999** Aug Redcar (G-F) 5f 79+ <
* **1999** May Cheste (G-F) 5.1f 79+ <
1999 Turf 2-9: (5f 2-7, 6f 2) (sft, g-s, gd 2, g-f 1-3, frm 1-2)
Decent filly, effective 5 to 6f, best at 5f, acts on g-s to frm. Turf high 82 - 7th of 20 getting 4lb from Magic of Love (15 Oct Newmarket 6f gd RF 4895) - also 1st of 10 from Shining Hour (6 May Chester RF 1052). Very pacey, she won at the big Chester meeting and at Redcar in August after a lengthy break. Never figured in the Flying Childers or the Redcar Two-Year-Old Trophy, but is a decent sort over the minimum on fast ground.
**M Johnston [2-9] S Kimberley.*

HARRY TASTERS RR 72f 4784[12]

2 ch c Efisio 7.7f **(69)** - Laugharne (Known Fact (USA)) 7.4f **(67)**
Form - 50
Record 1999 - 1st:0 2nd:0 3rd:0 Ran:2
1999 Turf 0-2: (6f, 7f) (g-s, frm)
Currently above-average colt. Turf high 72 (began Spt).
**D R C Elsworth [0-2] Sir Stanley and Lady Grinstead.*

HARTSTOWN GIRL (IRE) BHB 65f RR 65?f 4293[11]

4 ch f Common Grounds 8.1f **(66)** - Very Sophisticated (USA) (Affirmed (USA)) 9.3f **(79)**
Form - 070150
Record 1999 - 1st:1 2nd:0 3rd:0 Ran:6
Pre1999 - 1st:1 2nd:1 3rd:2 Ran:9
Win Prizemoney £5,328 *Total Prizemoney* £8,009
Wins **1999** Jly Ballin (SFT) C 6f 63+
1998 Jly Ballin (SFT) 6f 90 <
1999 Turf 1-6: (6f 1-2, 7f 4) (sft 1-1, gd, g-f 4)
Average filly, effective 6 to 8f, acts on sft to gd, best on sft, has worn blinkers. Turf high 65. Inconsistent.
**J C Fox [0-1] Ms Miriam Mulcahy (from E Lynam in IRE [2-14] Jly 1999).*

HARVEY'S FUTURE BHB 43f42a RR 42f 42a 2452[7]

5 b g Never so Bold 7.1f **(62)** - Orba Gold (USA) (Gold Crest (USA))
Form - 1027
Record 1999 - 1st:1 2nd:1 3rd:0 Ran:4
Pre1999 - 1st:0 2nd:2 3rd:1 Ran:14
Win Prizemoney £2,920 *Total Prizemoney* £6,124
Wins * **1999** Apr Bath (SFT) H 5.1f 36 42 <
1999 Turf 1-3: (5f 1-1, 6f 2) (g-s 1-1, gd, g-f) 1999 AW 0-1: (5f) (Fibr)
Moderate gelding, effective 5 to 6f, best at 5f, acts on g-s to g-f - acts on Fibr. Turf high 42 (1st run) - 1st of 18 getting 7lb from Present 'n Correct (27 Apr Bath RF 0863). Consistent.
**P L Gilligan [1-14] Treasure Seekers Partnership (from T T Clement [0-4] Aug 1997).*

HARVEY WHITE (IRE) BHB 31f37a RR 30f 37a 4997[6]

7 b or br g Petorius 8f **(66)** - Walkyria (Lord Gayle (USA)) 8.8f **(62)**
Form - 3722335270870006
Record 1999 - 1st:0 2nd:3 3rd:2 Ran:14
Pre1999 - 1st:4 2nd:3 3rd:9 Ran:48
Win Prizemoney £13,357 *Total Prizemoney* £25,485
Wins * 1997 Jun Lingfi (GD) H 9f 52 55
* 1996 Spt Kempto (GD) H 10f 56 62
* 1996 May Warwic (FRM) H 10.8f 53 62
* 1995 Aug Epsom (G-F) C 10.1f 64 <
1999 Turf 0-8: (9f, 10f 7) (gd 2, g-f, frm 4, hrd) 1999 AW 0-6: (10f, 12f 2, 13f, 16f 2) (Equi 5, Fibr)
Moderate gelding, effective 9f, acts on gd. Turf high 40. AW high 41. **J Pearce [4-62] B & G Racing.*

HASTA LA VISTA BHB 43f39a RR 43f 39a 4563[9]

9 b g Superlative 8.8f **(57)** - Falcon Berry (FR) (Bustino) 10.4f **(64)**
Form - 77085664220
Record 1999 - 1st:0 2nd:2 3rd:0 Ran:11
Pre1999 - 1st:14 2nd:8 3rd:10 Ran:83
Win Prizemoney £45,602 *Total Prizemoney* £64,258
Wins * 1998 Jly Beverl (GD) H 12f 52 55
* 1998 May Catter (G-S) H 13.8f 47 51
* 1998 May Mussel (G-F) H 12f 44 47
* 1997 Aug Ripon (GD) H 12.3f 55 60
* 1997 Aug Catter (G-F) H 13.8f 50 55
* 1997 Jly Catter (SFT) H 15.8f 52 55
* 1997 Jun Hamilt (G-S) H 13f 47 54
* 1997 May Mussel (G-F) H 16f 48 53
* 1996 Apr Catter (GD) H 12f 50 54
* 1995 Aug Ripon (G-F) H 12.3f 41 48
1999 Turf 0-10: (12f 7, 14f 3) (gd 3, g-f, frm 6) 1999 AW 0-1: (11f) (Fibr)
Moderate gelding, effective 12 to 14f, best at 14f, acts on g-s to frm, mostly wears blinkers, likes right handed tracks, favours tight tracks, excels at Musselburgh. Turf high 48.
**M W Easterby [14-97] K Hodgson & Mrs J Hodgson.*

HASTATE BHB 43f38a RR 39f 38a 4648[12]

4 b g Persian Bold 10f **(69)** - Gisarne (USA) (Diesis) 9.3f **(69)**
Form - 08050
Record 1999 - 1st:0 2nd:0 3rd:0 Ran:5
Pre1999 - 1st:1 2nd:1 3rd:1 Ran:9
Win Prizemoney £2,448 *Total Prizemoney* £4,304

Wins 1998 Aug Folkes (G-F) H 16.4f 54 56 <
1999 Turf 0-5: (12f 2, 14f 2, 15f) (hvy, g-s, gd, g-f, hrd)
Well made, very moderate gelding, effective 12 to 16f, acts on g-f to frm, best on frm. Turf high 39.
**J W Mullins [0-1] Mrs Deborah Potter (from W Jarvis [1-13] May 1999).*

HASTENBY (IRE) RR 86f 2073[2]

2 b f Tenby 10.4f **(76)** - Dahsala (Top Ville) 11.7f **(68)**
Form - 222
Record 1999 - 1st:0 2nd:3 3rd:0 Ran:3
Win Prizemoney £0 *Total Prizemoney* £9,210
1999 Turf 0-3: (6f 2, 7f) (gd, g-f 2)
Currently useful filly. Turf high 86 - 2nd of 7 getting 5lb from Bach (17 Jun Ascot 7f g-f RF 2073). Second in her first three starts, going down fighting to Bach in the Chesham Stakes at Ascot, she has since moved to the United States.
**Mrs P N Dutfield [0-3] The Two Legs Partnership.*

HASTY WORDS (IRE) BHB 105f RR 103f 2631[6]

3 b f Polish Patriot (USA) 7.8f **(70)** - Park Elect (Ahonoora) 8.1f **(73)**
Form - 06
Record 1999 - 1st:0 2nd:0 3rd:0 Ran:2
Pre1999 - 1st:1 2nd:1 3rd:2 Ran:6
Win Prizemoney £3,566 *Total Prizemoney* £13,223
Wins * 1998 May Sandow (G-F) 5f 78+ <
1999 Turf 0-2: (8f 2) (frm 2)
Scopey, very useful filly, effective 7f, acts on gd. Turf high 102. Tough and consistent as a juvenile, she ran just twice last term, putting up a fair effort in the Falmouth Stakes at Newmarket in July. She is bred to stay a mile, but races freely and may be better over seven furlongs. **B W Hills [1-8] W J Gredley.*

HATAAB (USA) BHB 100f RR 95f 4931[1]

2 ch c Woodman (USA) 9.7f **(77)** - Miss Mistletoes (IRE) (The Minstrel (CAN)) 10f **(72)**
Form - 121
Record 1999 - 1st:2 2nd:1 3rd:0 Ran:3
Win Prizemoney £20,029 *Total Prizemoney* £21,855
Wins * **1999** Oct Pontef (GD) L 8f 95 <
* **1999** Jly Ascot (G-F) 7f 73+
1999 Turf 2-3: (7f 1-2, 8f 1-1) (gd, g-f 2-2)
Currently very useful colt. Turf high 95 (began Jly) - 1st of 6 from Paradise Garden (18 Oct Pontefract RF 4931). He looks flashy, but knuckled down to the job with gusto when winning a Listed event at Pontefract in October. Likely to stay beyond a mile, he is no world-beater but can win a Group race on the continent.
**E A L Dunlop [2-3] Hamdan Al Maktoum.*

HATHNI KHOUND BHB 50f36a RR 49f 36a 1066[11]

3 b f Reprimand 8.2f **(63)** - Rattle Along (Tap On Wood) 10.3f **(65)**
Form - 0803020
Record 1999 - 1st:0 2nd:1 3rd:1 Ran:6
Pre1999 - 1st:0 2nd:0 3rd:0 Ran:1
Win Prizemoney £0 *Total Prizemoney* £1,161
1999 Turf 0-3: (10f, 11f, 12f) (sft, gd, frm) 1999 AW 0-3: (6f, 8f, 12f) (Fibr 3)
Unfurnished, moderate filly, effective 10 to 11f, acts on sft to gd, prefers left handed tracks. Turf high 49 - 2nd of 12 getting 20lb from Rada's Daughter (27 Apr Bath 10f sft RF 0864). AW high 27.
**D Marks [0-7] G J King.*

HAUNT THE ZOO BHB 40f RR 38f 4002[6]

4 b f Komaite (USA) 6.9f **(61)** - Merryhill Maid (IRE) (M Double M (USA)) 14.1f **(52)**
Form - 3840546
Record 1999 - 1st:0 2nd:0 3rd:1 Ran:7
Pre1999 - 1st:0 2nd:0 3rd:0 Ran:3
Win Prizemoney £0 *Total Prizemoney* £813
1999 Turf 0-6: (6f 2, 7f 3, 8f) (gd, g-f, frm 4) 1999 AW 0-1: (6f) (Fibr)
Lengthy, moderate filly. Turf high 44. **J L Harris [0-10] R Atkinson.*

HAVANA (IRE) RR 69f 2930[3]

3 b f Dolphin Street (FR) - Royaltess (Royal And Regal (USA)) 9.5f **(60)**
Form - 33
Record 1999 - 1st:0 2nd:0 3rd:2 Ran:2
Win Prizemoney £0 *Total Prizemoney* £1,091
1999 Turf 0-2: (8f, 9f) (gd, frm)
Workmanlike, currently average filly. Turf high 62.
**J E Banks [0-2] K J Mercer.*

HAVEN SUNRISE BHB 30f RR 16f 3096[9]

3 b f Chaddleworth (IRE) - Gaynor Goodman (IRE) **(41f)** (Fayruz)
Form - 00
Record 1999 - 1st:0 2nd:0 3rd:0 Ran:2
Pre1999 - 1st:0 2nd:0 3rd:0 Ran:2
1999 Turf 0-2: (6f, 8f) (frm 2)
Unfurnished, poor filly. Turf high 16 (began Jly).
**P R Hedger [0-4] Ian Hutchins.*

HAVENT MADE IT YET BHB 35f RR 40f 5109[12]

2 ch f Be My Guest (USA) 10.2f **(66)** - Onika (Great Nephew) 9.9f **(64)**
Form - 000
Record 1999 - 1st:0 2nd:0 3rd:0 Ran:3
1999 Turf 0-3: (6f, 8f 2) (g-s, gd, g-f)
Currently moderate filly. Turf high 40 (began Aug).
**J R Jenkins [0-3] Operation Solstice.*

HAWA AL NASAMAAT (USA) BHB 48f45a RR 23f 45a 4987[14]

7 b g Houston (USA) 7.7f **(65)** - Barrera Miss (USA) (Barrera (USA)) 7f **(84)**
Form - 3880670
Record 1999 - 1st:0 2nd:0 3rd:1 Ran:7
Pre1999 - 1st:2 2nd:2 3rd:3 Ran:25
Win Prizemoney £10,674 *Total Prizemoney* £16,315
Wins 1996 Aug Goodwo (G-F) 6f 76
1995 Jun Redcar (FRM) H 7f 77 81 <
1999 Turf 0-2: (6f, 8f) (gd 2) 1999 AW 0-5: (6f 2, 7f 3) (Fibr 5)
Fair gelding. Turf high 23. AW high 59. Inconsistent.
**M Brittain [0-16] Mel Brittain (from E A L Dunlop [2-13] Spt 1996).*

HAWAII STORM (FR) BHB 40f35a RR 47f 35a 285[5]

11 b g Plugged Nickle (USA) 7.4f **(70)** - Slewvindaloo (USA) (Seattle Slew (USA)) 9.4f **(76)**
Form - 480005
Record 1999 - 1st:0 2nd:0 3rd:0 Ran:4
Pre1999 - 1st:11 2nd:11 3rd:11 Ran:118
Win Prizemoney £26,013 *Total Prizemoney* £41,191
Wins * 1998 *Jan Lingfi (STD) C 8f* 52+
* 1997 Jly Bright (FRM) S 8f 52?
* 1997 *Feb Lingfi (STD) H 8f* 52 55
* 1997 *Jan Lingfi (STD) S 7f* 55
* 1995 *Dec Lingfi (STD) H 7f* 59 58
1999 AW 0-4: (7f, 8f 3) (Equi 4)
Moderate gelding, effective 8f, - acts on Equi, has worn blinkers, favours left handed tracks, favours tight tracks. AW high 39.
**D J S ffrenchDavis [5-65] Ms Renee Wheeler (from Miss A J Whitfield [6-57] Jan 1995).*

HAWALA (IRE) BHB 88f RR 88f 3770[16]

3 b f Warning 8.1f **(77)** - Halawa (IRE) (Dancing Brave (USA)) 8.4f **(76)**
Form - 16470
Record 1999 - 1st:1 2nd:0 3rd:0 Ran:5
Pre1999 - 1st:0 2nd:0 3rd:1 Ran:1
Win Prizemoney £3,987 *Total Prizemoney* £5,394
Wins * **1999** May Windso (GD) 8.3f 71 <
1999 Turf 1-5: (8f 1-3, 9f 2) (gd 2, g-f 1-2, frm)
Lengthy, useful filly, effective 8f, acts on frm. Turf high 88 - 4th of 15 giving 7lb to Calcutta (8 Jly Newmarket 8f frm RF 2646). Held in Listed company and warm handicaps after winning her maiden.
**Sir Michael Stoute [1-6] H H Aga Khan.*

HAWKSBILL HENRY (USA) BHB 46f60a RR 48f 60a 4387[15]

5 ch g Known Fact (USA) 8.3f **(72)** - Novel Approach (USA) (Codex (USA)) 8.6f **(73)**
Form - 24220425530
Record 1999 - 1st:0 2nd:3 3rd:1 Ran:10
Pre1999 - 1st:1 2nd:3 3rd:2 Ran:15
Win Prizemoney £3,157 *Total Prizemoney* £9,023
Wins * 1998 *Jly Lingfi (STD) H 10f* 48 54 <
1999 Turf 0-4: (9f, 10f, 11f, 12f) (g-f, frm 2, hrd) 1999 AW 0-6: (10f 6) (Equi 6)
Average gelding, effective 10f, - acts on Equi, has worn blinkers,

prefers left handed tracks, favours tight tracks, excels at Lingfield. Turf high 48. AW high 63 - 2nd of 11 giving 1lb to Birthday Venture (29 May Lingfield 10f Equi RF 1585). A fair sort over ten furlongs on Equitrack and turf, but he does not appear to put it all in at the finish. **Mrs A J Perrett [1-25] Miss G Harwood.*

HAWKSBURY (IRE) BHB 64f **RR 59f** 4826[10]

4 b g Simply Great (FR) 11.9f **(61)** - Hawksbill Special (IRE) (Taufan (USA)) 7f **(57)**

Form - 58178500

Record **1999** - 1st:1 2nd:0 3rd:0 Ran:8
Pre1999 - 1st:1 2nd:2 3rd:0 Ran:5

Win Prizemoney £6,690 *Total Prizemoney* £7,871

Wins * **1999** Jly Sandow (G-F) H 5f 65 65
1998 Spt Fairyh (G-S) 6f 84 <

1999 Turf 1-8: (5f 1-4, 6f 4) (gd 3, g-f 1-3, frm 2)

Fair gelding, effective 6 to 7f, best at 6f, acts on g-s to g-f, has worn blinkers. Turf high 65. Consistent.

**N Hamilton [1-8] J L Building Contracts Ltd (from J C Harley in IRE [1-5] Spt 1998).*

HAWRIYAH (USA) BHB 100f **RR 96f** 4796[9]

3 b br f Dayjur (USA) 6.8f **(79)** - Lady Cutlass (USA) (Cutlass (USA)) 8.5f **(76)**

Form - 221080

Record **1999** - 1st:1 2nd:2 3rd:0 Ran:6
Pre1999 - 1st:1 2nd:1 3rd:0 Ran:2

Win Prizemoney £17,847 *Total Prizemoney* £28,684

Wins * **1999** May Goodwo (Gd) L 8f 96 <
* 1998 Oct Leices (G-S) 7f 84

1999 Turf 1-6: (7f 3, 8f 1-3) (gd 1-2, g-f 3, frm)

Scopey, very useful filly, effective 7 to 8f, best at 7f, acts on gd to frm. Turf high 103 (1st run) - 2nd of 11 to Valentine Waltz (13 Apr Newmarket 7f g-f RF 0664) - also 1st of 7 from Balisada (20 May Goodwood RF 1347). She had things her own way when making all at Goodwood in May, but folded tamely on her remaining starts. Unlikely to stay beyond a mile, she has become disappointing.

**J L Dunlop [2-8] Hamdan Al Maktoum.*

HAYAAIN BHB 65f **RR 66f** 4036[3]

6 b h Shirley Heights 12.1f **(76)** - Littlefield (Bay Express) 7.1f **(60)**

Form - 03

Record **1999** - 1st:0 2nd:0 3rd:1 Ran:2
Pre1999 - 1st:1 2nd:0 3rd:1 Ran:7

Win Prizemoney £3,780 *Total Prizemoney* £4,923

Wins 1996 Jun Bath (FRM) 11.7f 81 <

1999 Turf 0-2: (12f, 16f) (g-s, gd)

Average horse, has broken blood-vessels. Turf high 66 (began Aug). Consistent.

**K C Bailey [2-6] Quicksilver Racing Partnership (from Major W R Hern [1-7] Jly 1996).*

HAYDN JAMES (USA) BHB 51f60a **RR 50f 60a** 5057[2]

5 ch g Danzig Connection (USA) 8.2f **(75)** - Royal Fi Fi (USA) (Conquistador Cielo (USA)) 8.8f **(69)**

Form - 17223002038232

Record **1999** - 1st:0 2nd:5 3rd:3 Ran:12
Pre1999 - 1st:3 2nd:2 3rd:1 Ran:22

Win Prizemoney £8,094 *Total Prizemoney* £14,712

Wins * 1998 *Nov Wolver (STD) H 9.4f 57 58* <
* 1998 Aug Windso (G-F) H 10f 54 57
* 1998 May Nottin (FRM) H 10f 51 53

1999 Turf 0-6: (9f, 10f 5) (gd 4, g-f, frm) 1999 AW 0-6: (9f 2, 12f 4) (Equi 4, Fibr 2)

Average gelding, effective 12f, - acts on Equi, often wears blinkers, likes left handed tracks, favour tight tracks. Turf high 51. AW high 69. **P W Harris [3-34] Resplendent Racing Ltd.*

HAYELAH BHB 60f **RR 58f** 4860[8]

2 b f Polish Precedent (USA) 9f **(73)** - Mesaafi (IRE) (Slip Anchor) 9.8f **(73)**

Form - 348

Record **1999** - 1st:0 2nd:0 3rd:1 Ran:3

Win Prizemoney £0 *Total Prizemoney* £751

1999 Turf 0-3: (7f, 8f 2) (g-s 2, frm)

Currently fair filly. Turf high 58 (began Aug).

**M Johnston [0-3] Ziad Galadari.*

HAYMAKER (IRE) RR 69f 5166[2]

3 b g Thatching 7.8f **(69)** - Susie Sunshine (IRE) (Waajib)

Form - 30763202

Record **1999** - 1st:0 2nd:2 3rd:2 Ran:8
Pre1999 - 1st:0 2nd:0 3rd:0 Ran:1

Win Prizemoney £0 *Total Prizemoney* £5,842

1999 Turf 0-8: (7f 5, 8f 3) (sft, g-s 2, gd 3, frm 2)

Well made, average gelding, effective 7f, acts on g-s to frm, best on g-s. Turf high 69 - 2nd of 15 to Duraid (2 Nov Catterick 7f g-s RF 5166). Consistent.

**B S Rothwell [0-1] B Valentine (from I A Balding [0-8] Oct 1999).*

HAYSTACKS (IRE) BHB 56f **RR 58f** 4324[6]

3 b g Contract Law (USA) 8.9f **(54)** - Florissa (FR) (Persepolis (FR)) 6.4f **(67)**

Form - 63362056

Record **1999** - 1st:0 2nd:1 3rd:2 Ran:8
Pre1999 - 1st:0 2nd:1 3rd:1 Ran:9

Win Prizemoney £0 *Total Prizemoney* £3,261

1999 Turf 0-8: (9f, 10f, 11f 3, 12f 3) (g-s, gd 2, g-f 4, hrd)

Leggy, fair gelding, effective 7 to 12f, best at 11f, acts on g-s to g-f, best on gd, often wears blinkers (extremely effectively), prefers left handed tracks, likes tight tracks. Turf high 63. Consistent.

**D Moffatt [0-17] & Mrs A G Milligan.*

HAZARD A GUESS (IRE) BHB 66f **RR 58f** 3162[9]

9 ch g Digamist (USA) 8.8f **(56)** - Guess Who (Be My Guest (USA)) 9.3f **(67)**

Form - 00

Record **1999** - 1st:0 2nd:0 3rd:0 Ran:2
Pre1999 - 1st:10 2nd:6 3rd:7 Ran:60

Win Prizemoney £50,868 *Total Prizemoney* £68,556

Wins 1996 Oct York (GD) C 10.4f 64
* 1996 Aug Newcas (G-F) H 10.1f 82 85 <
* 1996 Apr Kempto (GD) H 10f 76 81
1995 May Beverl (G-F) H 9.9f 72 77
1995 May Pontef (FRM) 10f 79

1999 Turf 0-2: (8f, 10f) (frm 2)

Fair gelding. Turf high 58 (began Jly). Consistent.

**D Nicholls [3-28] J M G Promotions Ltd (from B S Rothwell [1-4] May 1998).*

HEART BHB 79f **RR 77f** 4794[11]

6 ch m Cadeaux Genereux 7.9f **(76)** - Recipe (Bustino) 10.4f **(64)**

Form - 146210

Record **1999** - 1st:2 2nd:1 3rd:0 Ran:6
Pre1999 - 1st:0 2nd:2 3rd:0 Ran:8

Win Prizemoney £14,892 *Total Prizemoney* £19,773

Wins * **1999** Spt Ayr (G-S) H 10f 73 77 <
* **1999** Apr Bath (SFT) H 11.7f 66 77+

1999 Turf 2-6: (10f 1-2, 12f 1-4) (sft 1-1, gd 1-3, g-f, frm)

Above-average mare, effective 10 to 12f, best at 10f, acts on sft to frm, prefers tight tracks. Turf high 77 (1st run) - 1st of 14 giving 18lb to Misconduct (27 Apr Bath RF 0861) - also 1st of 14 giving 8lb to Mindanao (17 Spt Ayr RF 4377). Won four races over hurdles in the winter of 1998/99, and returned to the Flat to score in style at Bath in April. She was particularly well handled to win at Ayr in September when racing on her favoured soft ground. She has won over ten furlongs, but looks better suited by a bit further.

**G A Butler [2-6] Christopher Shirley Brasher (from Miss H C Knight [0-12] Jun 1998).*

HEARTS ABLAZE BHB 42a **RR 42a** 113[10]

4 b g Excelsis - Qualitair Blazer (Blazing Saddles (AUS)) 6.7f **(46)**

Form - 0060

Record **1999** - 1st:0 2nd:0 3rd:0 Ran:1
Pre1999 - 1st:0 2nd:0 3rd:0 Ran:3

1999 AW 0-1: (7f) (Fibr)

Workmanlike, moderate gelding. **K T Ivory [0-4] K Brooke.*

HEARTWOOD (USA) BHB 72f **RR 74f** 3992[5]

3 ch f Woodman (USA) 9.7f **(77)** - Good Example (FR) (Crystal Glitters (USA)) 11.3f **(79)**

Form - 6610055

Record **1999** - 1st:1 2nd:0 3rd:0 Ran:7
Pre1999 - 1st:0 2nd:1 3rd:1 Ran:3

Win Prizemoney £3,788 *Total Prizemoney* £5,884

Wins * **1999** May Beverl (GD) 9.9f 74 <
1999 Turf 1-7: (8f 2, 10f 1-4, 12f) (gd 1-2, g-f 2, frm 3)
Scopey, above-average filly, effective 7 to 10f, best at 7f, acts on sft to gd, best on gd. Turf high 74 - 1st of 8 from Lady In Colour (25 May Beverley RF 1451). Consistent.
**G C Bravery [1-7] Silfield Bloodstock & The Iona Stud (from Sir Michael Stoute [0-3] Oct 1998).*

HEATHER VALLEY BHB 44f RR 40f 4819[12]

3 ch f Clantime 6.6f **(57)** - Sannavally (Sagaro) 9.7f **(55)**
Form - 000
Record 1999 - 1st:0 2nd:0 3rd:0 Ran:3
1999 Turf 0-3: (6f 2, 7f) (gd 2, g-f)
Workmanlike, currently moderate filly. Turf high 40 (began Aug).
**C F Wall [0-3] Miss Vivian Pratt.*

HEATHYARDSBLESSING (IRE) BHB 100f RR 103f 4990[1]

2 b c Unblest - Noble Nadia (Thatching) 8f **(66)**
Form - 0143217521
Record 1999 - 1st:3 2nd:2 3rd:1 Ran:10
Win Prizemoney £8,946 *Total Prizemoney* £50,352
Wins * **1999** Oct Nottin (FRM) 6.1f 103 <
* **1999** Jly Cheste (G-F) H 5.1f 83+
* **1999** May Haydoc (GD) 5f 75
1999 Turf 3-10: (5f 2-6, 6f 1-4) (gd, g-f 2-7, frm 1-2)
Very useful colt, effective 5 to 6f, best at 6f, acts on g-f to frm, best on g-f. Turf high 104 - 5th of 7 getting 14lb from Flanders (9 Spt Doncaster 5f g-f RF 4234) - also 1st of 6 giving 12lb to Dandilum (20 Oct Nottingham RF 4990). Blessed with an iron constitution, he improved throughout a hectic campaign, running his best race when chasing Khasayl home in the NTL Two-Year-Old Trophy at Redcar in October. Unlikely to stay much beyond six furlongs, he looked uncomfortable on a fast surface toward the end of the season and may prefer some give underfoot.
**R Hollinshead [3-10] L A Morgan.*

HEATHYARDS JAKE BHB 47f60a RR 50f 60a 4835[7]

3 b c Nomination 7.3f **(57)** - Safe Bid (Sure Blade (USA)) 11.3f **(67)**
Form - 535323620405528423207
Record 1999 - 1st:0 2nd:5 3rd:3 Ran:18
Pre1999 - 1st:0 2nd:2 3rd:4 Ran:13
Win Prizemoney £0 *Total Prizemoney* £8,316
1999 Turf 0-9: (7f 2, 8f 7) (gd 5, g-f 2, frm, hrd) 1999 AW 0-9: (6f, 7f, 8f 4, 9f 2, 12f) (Fibr 9)
Unfurnished, average colt, effective 6 to 7f, - acts on Fibr, likes left handed tracks, likes tight tracks. Turf high 54. AW high 67. Acts on Fibresand, but must have now found every conceivable method of getting himself beaten. **R Hollinshead [0-31] L A Morgan.*

HEATHYARDS LAD (IRE) BHB 61f77a RR 57f 77a 5024[4]

2 b c Petardia 8.2f **(58)** - Maiden's Dance (Hotfoot) 10.5f **(59)**
Form - 034546354454164
Record 1999 - 1st:1 2nd:0 3rd:2 Ran:15
Win Prizemoney £2,199 *Total Prizemoney* £4,177
Wins * **1999** *Spt Wolver (STD) 8.5f* *62* <
1999 Turf 0-11: (5f 4, 6f 5, 8f 2) (gd 3, g-f 2, frm 5, hrd) 1999 AW 1-4: (5f, 6f, 7f, 8f 1-1) (Fibr 1-4)
Average colt, effective 5 to 8f, acts on gd - acts on Fibr. Turf high 69 - 3rd of 11 giving 5lb to Pipadash (3 Apr Haydock 5f gd RF 0563). AW high 62 - also 1st of 11 giving 5lb to Girl's Best Friend (8 Spt Wolverhampton RF 4220). Consistent. His previous experience of Fibresand proved invaluable when he got off the mark in a Wolverhampton maiden in September.
**R Hollinshead [1-15] L A Morgan.*

HEATHYARDS MATE BHB 59f59a RR 60f 59a 5148[2]

2 b g Timeless Times (USA) 6.1f **(56)** - Quenlyn (Welsh Pageant) 10f **(65)**
Form - 6054300542
Record 1999 - 1st:0 2nd:1 3rd:1 Ran:10
Win Prizemoney £0 *Total Prizemoney* £1,100
1999 Turf 0-7: (5f 3, 6f 2, 7f 2) (gd, g-f 3, frm 3) 1999 AW 0-3: (5f, 7f, 8f) (Fibr 3)
Average gelding, effective 6 to 8f, acts on frm - acts on Fibr. Turf high 60 - 3rd of 12 to Pedro Jack (23 Aug Nottingham 6f frm RF 3857). AW high 57 (began Oct) - 2nd of 12 giving 7lb to Samarardo (30 Oct Wolverhampton 8f Fibr RF 5148).
**R Hollinshead [0-10] L A Morgan.*

HEATHYARDS TIPPLE (IRE) BHB 50f55a RR 50f 55a 3545[5]

3 b f Marju (IRE) 9.2f **(76)** - Nikki's Groom (Shy Groom (USA)) 10f **(66)**
Form - 36453363445
Record 1999 - 1st:0 2nd:0 3rd:4 Ran:11
Pre1999 - 1st:0 2nd:0 3rd:1 Ran:7
Win Prizemoney £0 *Total Prizemoney* £3,055
1999 Turf 0-7: (6f, 7f, 8f 5) (gd 2, g-f 2, frm 2, hrd) 1999 AW 0-4: (6f, 7f, 8f, 9f) (Fibr 4)
Fair filly, effective 7 to 8f, best at 7f, acts on frm to hrd - acts on Fibr, has worn blinkers. Turf high 59. AW high 53 - 3rd of 12 getting 8lb from Tayovullin (14 May Wolverhampton 7f Fibr RF 1232). Consistent. **D McCain [0-18] L A Morgan.*

HEAVENLY ABSTONE BHB 39f63a RR 32f 63a 4127[17]

4 b f Interrex (CAN) 7.7f **(51)** - Heavenly Queen (Scottish Reel) 7f **(61)**
Form - 0070600
Record 1999 - 1st:0 2nd:0 3rd:0 Ran:7
Pre1999 - 1st:2 2nd:7 3rd:6 Ran:31
Win Prizemoney £5,820 *Total Prizemoney* £21,669
Wins * 1997 May Ayr (SFT) 5f 78 <
* 1997 Apr Mussel (G-F) 5f 72
1999 Turf 0-7: (6f 6, 7f) (gd, g-f 3, frm 3)
Scopey, average filly, effective 5 to 7f, best at 5f, acts on gd - acts on AW, best on Fibr, mostly wears blinkers (effectively), likes left handed tracks, likes tight tracks. Turf high 39 (began Jly).
**P D Evans [2-38] J E Abbey.*

HEAVENLY MISS (IRE) BHB 49f49a RR 49f 49a 5160[21]

5 b m Anita's Prince 6f **(62)** - Heavenly Blessed (Monseigneur (USA)) 7.7f **(63)**
Form - 6427811340650210
Record 1999 - 1st:3 2nd:2 3rd:1 Ran:16
Pre1999 - 1st:3 2nd:6 3rd:5 Ran:47
Win Prizemoney £16,932 *Total Prizemoney* £27,390
Wins * **1999** Oct Bath (SFT) H 5.1f 45 49
* **1999** *Apr Wolver (STD) H 5f 42 52*
* **1999** Apr Thirsk (GD) H 6f 45 49
1996 *Dec Lingfi (STD) C 5f 71*
1996 Spt Nottin (FRM) H 6.1f 64 77 <
1996 Aug Leices (G-F) S 6f 63+
1999 Turf 2-8: (5f 1-5, 6f 1-3) (sft, gd 2-2, g-f 3, frm, hrd) 1999 AW 1-8: (5f 1-3, 6f 5) (Equi 4, Fibr 1-4)
Fair filly, effective 5 to 6f, best at 5f, acts on gd to frm - acts on Fibr, has worn blinkers (effectively), does well at Salisbury. Turf high 49 - 1st of 17 getting 12lb from Mammas F-C (26 Oct Bath RF 5065) - also 1st of 24 getting 5lb from Patsy Culsyth (16 Apr Thirsk RF 0731). AW high 53 - 3rd of 12 to La Doyenne (6 May Southwell 5f Fibr RF 1061) - also 1st of 13 getting 22lb from Antonia's Double (24 Apr Wolverhampton RF 0846).
**D Shaw [3-12] E Gray (from J J Bridger [1-43] Feb 1999).*

HEIGHT OF FANTASY (IRE) BHB 90f RR 92?f 4917[P]

3 b f Shirley Heights 12.1f **(76)**-Persian Fantasy (Persian Bold) 9.3f **(66)**
Form - 3121612P
Record 1999 - 1st:3 2nd:2 3rd:1 Ran:8
Pre1999 - 1st:0 2nd:1 3rd:0 Ran:2
Win Prizemoney £14,758 *Total Prizemoney* £20,169
Wins * **1999** Aug Beverl (GD) H 16.2f 85 87 <
* **1999** Jly Chepst (G-F) H 16.2f 80 79+
* **1999** Jun Haydoc (SFT) 14f 75
1999 Turf 3-8: (12f, 14f 1-1, 16f 2-4, 17f, 18f) (g-s, gd 1-4, g-f, frm 2-2)
Neat, useful filly, effective 16 to 18f, acts on g-s to frm. Turf high 92 - 2nd of 5 giving 20lb to Little Brave (16 Spt Yarmouth 18f g-s RF 4356) - also 1st of 6 giving 25lb to Lady Coldunell (29 Aug Beverley RF 3987). A progressive stayer, she won three times on varying types of ground as well as running some fine races in defeat, but was pulled up in the Cesarewitch.
**J L Dunlop [3-10] Windflower Overseas Holdings Inc.*

HELENA JOHN (IRE) RR 50f 4172[7]

2 b f Perugino (USA) - Deirdre's Music (Advocator) 10.9f **(80)**
Form - 87
Record 1999 - 1st:0 2nd:0 3rd:0 Ran:2
1999 Turf 0-2: (7f 2) (frm 2)
Currently fair filly. Turf high 50 (began Aug).
**J L Eyre [0-2] John Michael.*

HELEN ALBADOU (USA) RR 70f 2568[3]
2 b f Sheikh Albadou 9.2f **(75)** - Sister Troy (USA) (Far North (CAN)) 9.7f **(75)**
Form - 3
Record 1999 - 1st:0 2nd:0 3rd:1 Ran:1
Win Prizemoney £0 *Total Prizemoney* £432
1999 Turf 0-1: (5f) (frm)
Currently above-average filly. (1st run) - 3rd of 15 to Passion Flower (5 Jly Windsor 5f frm RF 2568).
**J M P Eustace [0-1] J C Smith.*

HELEN'S STARDUST BHB 40f48a **RR 36f 48a** 3871[6]
3 br f Ballacashtal (CAN) 7.9f **(51)** - Legendary Lady (Reprimand)
Form - 6408606
Record 1999 - 1st:0 2nd:0 3rd:0 Ran:5
Pre1999 - 1st:1 2nd:0 3rd:0 Ran:5
Win Prizemoney £2,973 *Total Prizemoney* £2,973
Wins * 1998 Spt Folkes (G-F) C 6f 65 <
1999 Turf 0-5: (6f 2, 7f 2, 8f) (gd 2, g-f 2, frm)
Unfurnished, moderate filly, effective 6f, acts on g-f. Turf high 44.
**W R Muir [1-10] John Mills.*

HELEN'S WEDDING BHB 30a **RR 30a** 210[4]
3 b f Minshaanshu Amad (USA) 11.3f **(53)** - Doris Doors **(57f 48a)** (Beveled (USA)) 9f **(59)**
Form - 074
Record 1999 - 1st:0 2nd:0 3rd:0 Ran:3
1999 AW 0-3: (6f 2, 9f) (Equi, Fibr 2)
Light-framed, currently poor filly. AW high 18. **J Berry [0-3] J Berry.*

HELLO HOLLY BHB 58f **RR 60f** 4728[11]
2 b f Lake Coniston (IRE) - Amandine (IRE) (Darshaan) 9.9f **(84)**
Form - 070
Record 1999 - 1st:0 2nd:0 3rd:0 Ran:3
1999 Turf 0-3: (7f, 8f 2) (sft, g-s, gd)
Currently average filly. Turf high 60 (began Aug).
**Mrs A L M King [0-3] Mrs Bettina Melliger.*

HELLO SAILOR RR 3290[13]
2 ch f Handsome Sailor 6.6f **(53)** - Miss Marjorie (Swing Easy (USA)) 6.5f **(55)**
Form - 00
Record 1999 - 1st:0 2nd:0 3rd:0 Ran:2
1999 Turf 0-2: (5f 2) (frm 2)
Currently very poor filly. (began Jly).
**Mrs D Thomson [0-2] Mrs Dorothy Thomson.*

HELLO VEGAS RR 59f 5001[6]
2 b c First Trump - Meet Again (Lomond (USA)) 8.8f **(65)**
Form - 6
Record 1999 - 1st:0 2nd:0 3rd:0 Ran:1
1999 Turf 0-1: (8f) (gd)
Currently fair colt. **J H M Gosden [0-1] D H Armitage.*

HELVETIUS BHB 97f **RR 103f** 4674[8]
3 b c In The Wings 11.2f **(77)** - Hejraan (USA) (Alydar (USA)) 9.1f **(76)**
Form - 435133568
Record 1999 - 1st:1 2nd:0 3rd:3 Ran:9
Pre1999 - 1st:0 2nd:1 3rd:0 Ran:1
Win Prizemoney £4,380 *Total Prizemoney* £12,607
Wins * **1999** May Bright (FRM) 11.9f 55+ <
1999 Turf 1-9: (10f 3, 12f 1-5, 13f) (g-s, gd 4, g-f 1-4)
Workmanlike, very useful colt, effective 12f, acts on gd to g-f, has worn blinkers. Turf high 103. Consistent. Aside from when winning a maiden at Brighton, he spent 1999 chasing some elusive shadows. Possibly best over a mile and a quarter, he is not a Group horse and needs his sights lowered.
**C E Brittain [1-10] Sheikh Mohammed Obaid Al Maktoum.*

HENBIRD BHB 20f **RR** 5145[12]
3 b f Henbit (USA) 10.2f **(46)** - View Halloa (Al Sirat (USA))
Form - 000
Record 1999 - 1st:0 2nd:0 3rd:0 Ran:3
1999 Turf 0-2: (10f 2) (gd, frm) 1999 AW 0-1: (12f) (Fibr)
Workmanlike, currently very poor filly, has worn blinkers. (began Oct) - 14th of 15 to Anaam (20 Oct Nottingham 10f frm RF 4992).
**A Senior [0-3] Frank Youds.*

HENBURY DANCER RR 33f 5067[12]
3 br f Teamster 11.4f **(22)** - Record Flight (Record Token) 6.3f **(53)**
Form - 00
Record 1999 - 1st:0 2nd:0 3rd:0 Ran:2
1999 Turf 0-2: (12f 2) (g-s, gd)
Scopey, currently very moderate filly. Turf high 33 (began Spt).
**B R Millman [0-2] Frank Crumpler.*

HENRIETTA HOLMES (IRE) BHB 60f56a **RR 56+f 56a** 4289[1]
3 gr f Persian Bold 10f **(69)** - Faakirah (Dragonara Palace (USA)) 6.1f **(55)**
Form - 0683221
Record 1999 - 1st:1 2nd:2 3rd:1 Ran:7
Pre1999 - 1st:0 2nd:0 3rd:0 Ran:3
Win Prizemoney £2,469 *Total Prizemoney* £4,080
Wins * **1999** Spt Yarmou (G-F) C 11.5f 56 <
1999 Turf 1-7: (8f 4, 10f, 11f 1-2) (gd 3, g-f 1-3, frm)
Scopey, fair filly, effective 11f, acts on gd to g-f, has worn blinkers. Turf high 56 - 1st of 13 giving 5lb to Lucky Nemo (14 Spt Yarmouth RF 4289).
**J R Fanshawe [1-10] William McGregor & Georgia Fanshawe.*

HENRY HALL (IRE) BHB 92f **RR 95f** 5040[12]
3 b c Common Grounds 8.1f **(66)** - Sovereign Grace (IRE) (Standaan (FR)) 7f **(55)**
Form - 2020268700200
Record 1999 - 1st:0 2nd:4 3rd:0 Ran:13
Pre1999 - 1st:3 2nd:1 3rd:1 Ran:8
Win Prizemoney £9,425 *Total Prizemoney* £24,853
Wins 1998 Jly Doncas (G-F) 5f 90 <
* 1998 Jly Beverl (GD) 5f 90 <
* 1998 May Thirsk (G-F) C 5f 79
1999 Turf 0-13: (5f 10, 6f 3) (g-s, gd 6, g-f 2, frm 4)
Very useful colt, effective 5f, acts on gd to frm. Turf high 101 - 2nd of 15 giving 9lb to Pips Magic (19 Jun Ascot 5f g-f RF 2134). Inconsistent. A five-furlong specialist, he ran several creditable races in top-class sprint handicaps, but was always a step behind the weights compiler. Effective when held-up or ridden positively, he is game and deserves to win a decent prize.
**N Tinkler [3-21] J M G Promotions Ltd.*

HENRY ISLAND (IRE) BHB 82f **RR 86f** 723[9]
6 ch g Sharp Victor (USA) 10f **(56)** - Monterana (Sallust) 8.4f **(63)**
Form - 30
Record 1999 - 1st:0 2nd:0 3rd:1 Ran:2
Pre1999 - 1st:3 2nd:2 3rd:1 Ran:16
Win Prizemoney £24,464 *Total Prizemoney* £31,632
Wins 1998 May Goodwo (G-F) H 14f 90 93 <
1996 Oct Doncas (GD) H 12f 88 93 <
1996 May Leices (G-S) 8f 73++
1999 Turf 0-2: (16f, 18f) (g-s, frm)
Useful gelding, effective 14 to 18f, acts on g-s to g-f. Turf high 86 (1st run) - 3rd of 8 giving 22lb to Danegold (26 Mar Doncaster 18f g-s RF 0478).
**M Pitman [0-4] J Hickford & M Hickford (from G Wragg [3-16] Spt 1998).*

HENRY THE HAWK BHB 43f39a **RR 40f 39a** 3871[4]
8 b g Doulab (USA) 7.4f **(61)** - Plum Blossom (USA) (Gallant Romeo (USA)) 8.4f **(64)**
Form - 255605204
Record 1999 - 1st:0 2nd:2 3rd:0 Ran:9
Pre1999 - 1st:5 2nd:5 3rd:9 Ran:67
Win Prizemoney £13,040 *Total Prizemoney* £22,730
Wins * 1998 May Hamilt (SFT) H 5f 40 47
* 1997 Jun Hamilt (G-F) H 6f 42 46
* 1996 May Hamilt (SFT) H 5f 47 51 <
* 1996 Apr Carlis (G-S) H 5.9f 43 47
* 1995 Jun Beverl (G-S) H 5f 41 48
1999 Turf 0-9: (5f 4, 6f 5) (gd 2, g-f 3, frm 4)
Moderate gelding, effective 5 to 6f, best at 5f, acts on sft to frm, has worn blinkers (extremely effectively). Turf high 40.
**M Dods [5-76] S Barras.*

HERECOMESCHARLIE BHB 35f **RR 43f** 3376[14]
3 b g Theatrical Charmer 10.9f **(63)** - Excavator Lady (Most Secret) 7.1f

(58)
Form - 6570
Record 1999 - 1st:0 2nd:0 3rd:0 Ran:4
1999 Turf 0-4: (8f, 10f 2, 12f) (g-s, gd, frm, hrd)
Workmanlike, moderate gelding, has worn blinkers. Turf high 43.
**M G Meagher [0-4] Aim High Partnership.*

HERE COMES HERBIE BHB 62f **RR 62f** 2267[1]
7 ch g Golden Lahab (USA) 14.4f **(32)** - Megan's Move (Move Off) 15f **(41)**
Form - 77031
Record 1999 - 1st:1 2nd:0 3rd:1 Ran:5
Pre1999 - 1st:4 2nd:5 3rd:3 Ran:26
Win Prizemoney £19,113 *Total Prizemoney* £29,506
Wins * **1999** Jun Newcas (GD) H 16.1f 60 62
* 1997 Jly Redcar (G-S) H 16f 62 68 <
* 1997 Apr Ripon (GD) H 16f 51 58
* 1997 Mar Mussel (SFT) H 16f 37 54?
* 1996 Jun Catter (G-F) H 12f 32 42
1999 Turf 1-5: (12f, 15f, 16f 1-2, 22f) (g-s, gd 1-4)
Average gelding, effective 16f, acted on gd. Turf high 62 - 1st of 12 from Ledgendry Line (24 Jun Newcastle RF 2267).(DEAD)
**W Storey [7-41] H S Hutchinson.*

HERE'S TO HOWIE (USA) BHB 51f **RR 58?f** 213[10]
5 b g Hermitage (USA) 8.6f **(84)** - Choice Comment (USA) (Rich Cream (USA))
Form - 0
Record 1999 - 1st:0 2nd:0 3rd:0 Ran:1
Pre1999 - 1st:1 2nd:1 3rd:1 Ran:13
Win Prizemoney £2,277 *Total Prizemoney* £3,624
Wins 1997 Apr Bright (FRM) 10f 63 <
1999 AW 0-1: (12f) (Equi)
Average gelding.
**M R Bosley [0-6] M F Cartwright (from R Hannon [1-13] Oct 1997).*

HERITAGE PARK (IRE) BHB 81f **RR 80f** 4256[6]
2 gr c Paris House 5.9f **(64)** - Caradene (IRE) (Ballad Rock) 7.8f **(63)**
Form - 332156
Record 1999 - 1st:1 2nd:1 3rd:2 Ran:6
Win Prizemoney £3,615 *Total Prizemoney* £5,362
Wins * **1999** Jly Sandow (G-F) 5f 80 <
1999 Turf 1-6: (5f 1-2, 6f 3, 7f) (g-f 1-3, frm 1-3)
Decent colt, effective 5 to 6f, acts on frm. Turf high 80 - 2nd of 12 giving 5lb to Card Games (10 Jly Salisbury 6f frm RF 2712) - also 1st of 11 giving 3lb to Dancing Empress (22 Jly Sandown RF 3027). **R Hannon [1-6] R V Lewis.*

HERMINIUS (IRE) BHB 74f **RR 78f** 510[13]
4 b g Ballad Rock 7.2f **(63)** - Scotia Rose (Tap On Wood) 10.3f **(65)**
Form - 0
Record 1999 - 1st:0 2nd:0 3rd:0 Ran:1
Pre1999 - 1st:1 2nd:0 3rd:0 Ran:7
Win Prizemoney £3,073 *Total Prizemoney* £4,599
Wins 1997 Oct Redcar (G-F) 8f 80 <
1999 Turf 0-1: (10f) (sft)
Workmanlike, above-average gelding.
**G B Balding [0-2] The Roman Legion (from J L Dunlop [1-7] Jun 1998).*

HEROIC BLUE (USA) BHB 86f **RR 88f** 1955[1]
3 ch c Known Fact (USA) 8.3f **(72)** - To Act (USA) (Roberto (USA)) 10f **(76)**
Form - 351
Record 1999 - 1st:1 2nd:0 3rd:1 Ran:3
Win Prizemoney £4,306 *Total Prizemoney* £4,951
Wins * **1999** Jun Lingfi (GD) 6f 88 <
1999 Turf 1-3: (6f 1-2, 7f) (g-f 1-2, frm)
Strong, currently useful colt, has worn blinkers. Turf high 88 - 1st of 18 from Alfath (12 Jun Lingfield RF 1955). Unraced at two, he got off the mark with a battling victory at Lingfield in June but was not seen afterwards. **J Noseda [1-3] Adrian F Nolan & Mrs J M Ryan.*

HEROS FATAL (FR) BHB 82f **RR 83f** 4917[3]
5 ch h Hero's Honor (USA) 9.2f **(76)** - Femme Fatale (FR) (Garde Royale)
Form - 5453
Record 1999 - 1st:0 2nd:0 3rd:1 Ran:4
Pre1999 - 1st:1 2nd:1 3rd:0 Ran:2
Win Prizemoney £20,202 *Total Prizemoney* £31,114
Wins 1998 Spt Toulou () L 8f
1999 Turf 0-4: (6f, 8f, 10f, 17f) (gd, g-f 2, frm)
Decent colt, effective 17f, acts on gd. Turf high 83 (began Jly) - 3rd of 32 getting 14lb from Top Cees (16 Oct Newmarket 17f gd RF 4917). A French import and already a winner over hurdles for the Pipe team, his efforts on the level had been modest until he ran a blinder to finish third in the Cesarewitch.
**M C Pipe [1-9] Frank Farrant (from H-A Pantall in FR [1-2] Spt 1998).*

HER OWN WAY (USA) **RR 58f** 5213[4]
2 b f Danzig (USA) 8.1f **(88)** - Formidable Lady (USA) (Silver Hawk (USA)) 8.6f **(70)**
Form - 4
Record 1999 - 1st:0 2nd:0 3rd:0 Ran:1
Win Prizemoney £0 *Total Prizemoney* £413
1999 Turf 0-1: (8f) (g-s)
Currently fair filly. **J H M Gosden [0-1] George Strawbridge.*

HERR TRIGGER BHB 52f67a **RR 55f 67a** 4836[12]
8 gr g Sharrood (USA) 11.1f **(67)**-Four-Legged Friend(Aragon) 8.1f **(60)**
Form - 70651340
Record 1999 - 1st:1 2nd:0 3rd:1 Ran:8
Pre1999 - 1st:7 2nd:4 3rd:5 Ran:32
Win Prizemoney £30,736 *Total Prizemoney* £43,885
Wins * **1999** *May Lingfi (STD) 10f 68*
* 1998 *Mar Lingfi (SLW) H 10f 75 81* <
* 1995 Jun Newmar (G-F) H 10f 57 68+
* 1995 Jun Ripon (FRM) H 10f 57 61
* 1995 May Newmar (G-F) H 10f 53 60
1999 Turf 0-3: (10f 3) (gd, g-f, frm) 1999 AW 1-5: (10f 1-5) (Equi 1-5)
Average gelding, effective 10f, - acts on Equi, mostly wears blinkers, likes left handed tracks, likes tight tracks. Turf high 55. AW high 68. **Dr J D Scargill [8-40] The Inn Crowd.*

HE'S GOT WINGS (IRE) BHB 54f56a **RR 59f 56a** 1099[9]
6 b g In The Wings 11.2f **(77)** - Mariella (Sir Gaylord) 10.6f **(64)**
Form - 130180
Record 1999 - 1st:2 2nd:0 3rd:1 Ran:6
Pre1999 - 1st:2 2nd:1 3rd:1 Ran:17
Win Prizemoney £11,247 *Total Prizemoney* £12,723
Wins * **1999** Apr Nottin (G-S) H 14.1f 53 59 <
* **1999** *Feb Southw (STD) H 16f 48 54*
1996 Oct Newcas (G-F) H 16.1f 53 57+
1996 Aug Newcas (G-F) S 12.4f 49
1999 Turf 1-3: (14f 1-2, 16f) (g-s, gd 1-2) 1999 AW 1-3: (16f 1-3) (Fibr 1-3)
Fair gelding, effective 14 to 16f, best at 16f, acts on gd - acts on Fibr, has worn blinkers (extremely effectively). Turf high 59 (1st run) - 1st of 18 getting 3lb from Mane Frame (5 Apr Nottingham RF 0591). AW high 56 - 3rd of 10 giving 7lb to Coleridge (19 Feb Southwell 16f Fibr RF 0317) - also 1st of 16 giving 13lb to Old Hush Wing (12 Feb Southwell RF 0283).
**M A Peill [2-9] D J Lever (from Mrs J R Ramsden [1-7] May 1997).*

HETRA HAWK BHB 42f **RR 47f** 4650[11]
3 ch g Be My Guest (USA) 10.2f **(66)** - Silver Ore (FR) (Silver Hawk (USA)) 8.6f **(70)**
Form - 00
Record 1999 - 1st:0 2nd:0 3rd:0 Ran:2
Pre1999 - 1st:0 2nd:0 3rd:0 Ran:2
1999 Turf 0-1: (12f) (gd) 1999 AW 0-1: (8f) (Fibr)
Leggy, moderate gelding. **W J Musson [0-4] B N Fulton.*

HETRA HEIGHTS (USA) BHB 37f **RR 31f** 2966[5]
4 b f Cox's Ridge (USA) 9.4f **(72)** - Top Hope (High Top) 10.2f **(67)**
Form - 005
Record 1999 - 1st:0 2nd:0 3rd:0 Ran:3
Pre1999 - 1st:0 2nd:1 3rd:0 Ran:6
Win Prizemoney £0 *Total Prizemoney* £1,452
1999 Turf 0-3: (12f, 13f, 14f) (gd, g-f 2)
Scopey, very moderate filly, effective 12f, acts on frm. Turf high 31. Consistent. **W J Musson [0-9] K L West.*

HEVER FEVER BHB 30f48a **RR 28f 48a** 1020[11]
4 br f Machiavellian (USA) 9.8f **(83)** - Wanisa (USA) (Topsider (USA))

8.3f **(71)**
Form - 0
Record 1999 - 1st:0 2nd:0 3rd:0 Ran:1
Pre1999 - 1st:0 2nd:1 3rd:1 Ran:10
Win Prizemoney £0 *Total Prizemoney* £1,720
1999 Turf 0-1: (10f) (hrd)
Moderate filly, effective 9f, - acts on Fibr, favours left handed tracks, favours tight tracks. Becoming disappointing.
**T J Naughton [0-11] T J Naughton.*

HEVER GOLF GLORY BHB 41f69a RR 43f 69a 2881[4]

5 b g Efisio 7.7f **(69)** - Zaius (Artaius (USA)) 9f **(69)**
Form - 0861856001706004
Record 1999 - 1st:2 2nd:0 3rd:0 Ran:15
Pre1999 - 1st:1 2nd:2 3rd:1 Ran:23
Win Prizemoney £27,397 *Total Prizemoney* £35,291
Wins * **1999** *May Wolver (Std) H 8.5f 62 72*
* **1999** *Feb Wolver (STD) H 8.5f 53 68*
1997 Jun Taby (GD) 8f 81 <
1999 Turf 0-7: (7f, 8f 5, 9f) (gd 2, g-f 2, frm 3) 1999 AW 2-8: (7f, 8f 2-6, 9f) (Fibr 2-8)
Above-average gelding, effective 8f, - acts on Fibr, likes left handed tracks, likes tight tracks. Turf high 46. AW high 72.
**C N Kellett [2-16] Gemini Associates (from N P Littmoden [0-9] Oct 1998).*

HEVERGOLF PRINCESS (IRE) BHB 47f38a RR 38f 38a 206[12]

4 ch f Petardia 8.2f **(58)** - High Profile (High Top) 10.2f **(67)**
Form - 8060
Record 1999 - 1st:0 2nd:0 3rd:0 Ran:4
Pre1999 - 1st:1 2nd:1 3rd:1 Ran:9
Win Prizemoney £2,190 *Total Prizemoney* £3,209
Wins * 1998 *Feb Lingfi (SLW) 7f 58* <
1999 AW 0-4: (7f, 8f 2, 10f) (Equi 3, Fibr)
Leggy, very moderate filly, effective 7 to 10f, best at 7f, acts on gd - acts on Equi, has worn blinkers, prefers tight tracks. AW high 33.
**T J Naughton [1-13] T J Naughton.*

HEVER GOLF RANGER BHB 75f66a RR 67f 66a 292[9]

4 b c Efisio 7.7f **(69)** - Bold Green (FR) (Green Dancer (USA)) 10.3f **(74)**
Form - 070
Record 1999 - 1st:0 2nd:0 3rd:0 Ran:3
Pre1999 - 1st:1 2nd:2 3rd:1 Ran:10
Win Prizemoney £3,452 *Total Prizemoney* £12,184
Wins * 1998 *Jan Lingfi (STD) 7f 84?* <
1999 AW 0-3: (6f, 7f 2) (Equi, Fibr 2)
Scopey, average colt, effective 7 to 8f, acts on sft - acts on Equi, prefers left handed tracks. AW high 55. Becoming disappointing. He has been below form since winning on the Lingfield Equitrack in January 1998. **T J Naughton [1-13] The Awayday Partnership.*

HEVER ROSINA BHB 53f RR 40f 4879[15]

3 b f Efisio 7.7f **(69)** - Truly Bold (Bold Lad (IRE)) 8.4f **(68)**
Form - 5518000
Record 1999 - 1st:1 2nd:0 3rd:0 Ran:7
Pre1999 - 1st:0 2nd:0 3rd:0 Ran:1
Win Prizemoney £2,714 *Total Prizemoney* £2,714
Wins * **1999** Jun Redcar (FRM) 6f 65 <
1999 Turf 1-7: (5f 2, 6f 1-5) (g-f 3, frm 1-4)
Scopey, moderate filly, effective 6f, acts on frm. Turf high 65 - 1st of 5 getting 3lb from Square Dancer (19 Jun Redcar RF 2152). Becoming disappointing.
**J Berry [1-7] R A Popely (from T J Naughton [0-1] Oct 1998).*

HIBAAT BHB 64f RR 59f 2149[9]

3 ch c Zafonic (USA) 9f **(83)** - Realisatrice (USA) (Raja Baba (USA)) 10f **(64)**
Form - 850
Record 1999 - 1st:0 2nd:0 3rd:0 Ran:3
Pre1999 - 1st:0 2nd:0 3rd:0 Ran:1
1999 Turf 0-3: (7f 2, 8f) (gd 2, hrd)
Scopey, fair colt. Turf high 59.
**P T Walwyn [0-4] Hamdan Al Maktoum.*

HIBERNATE (IRE) BHB 80f77a RR 83?f 77a 4876[13]

5 ch g Lahib (USA) 8f **(69)** - Ministra (USA) (Deputy Minister (CAN)) 7.4f **(80)**
Form - 2155222110140240
Record 1999 - 1st:4 2nd:5 3rd:0 Ran:16
Pre1999 - 1st:0 2nd:0 3rd:1 Ran:1
Win Prizemoney £33,036 *Total Prizemoney* £41,347
Wins * **1999** Jly Bright (FRM) H 11.9f 76 83 <
* **1999** Jun Carlis (G-F) H 12f 68 76
* **1999** Jun Mussel (GD) H 12f 68 73
* **1999** *Feb Lingfi (STD) 12f 68*
1999 Turf 3-13: (10f, 11f 2, 12f 3-10) (gd 3, g-f 1-4, frm 4, hrd 2-2) 1999 AW 1-3: (10f, 12f 1-2) (Equi 1-2, Fibr)
Decent gelding, effective 12f, acts on g-f to hrd, best on hrd, prefers tight tracks. Turf high 83 - also 1st of 8 from Arctic Fancy (12 Jly Brighton RF 2750). AW high 68. In good heart in ordinary handicaps, but he does not have anything in the way of a turn of foot and needs at least a mile and a half.
**K R Burke [4-16] Nigel Shields (from R Charlton [0-1] Spt 1996).*

HI BUDDY BHB 63f RR 60f 5186[2]

2 br g High Kicker (USA) 8.4f **(52)** - Star Thyme (Point North)
Form - 683842
Record 1999 - 1st:0 2nd:1 3rd:1 Ran:6
Win Prizemoney £0 *Total Prizemoney* £1,482
1999 Turf 0-6: (7f 2, 8f 4) (sft, g-f 2, frm 3)
Average gelding, effective 7f, acts on g-f, has worn blinkers. Turf high 60 (began Aug) - 2nd of 13 to Love's Design (3 Nov Musselburgh 7f g-f RF 5186). **Miss L A Perratt [0-6] R M Mitchell.*

HICKLETON MELODY RR 2688[5]

5 b g Sizzling Melody 6.3f **(49)** - Honest Opinion (Free State) 8.7f **(61)**
Form - 5
Record 1999 - 1st:0 2nd:0 3rd:0 Ran:1
1999 AW 0-1: (12f) (Fibr)
Currently poor gelding. **J Pearce [0-3] D Leech.*

HICKORY (IRE) BHB 50f42a RR 63df 42a 388[6]

4 b g Fayruz 6.6f **(63)** - La Mortola (Bold Lad (IRE)) 8.4f **(68)**
Form - 06
Record 1999 - 1st:0 2nd:0 3rd:0 Ran:2
Pre1999 - 1st:0 2nd:0 3rd:0 Ran:5
Win Prizemoney £0 *Total Prizemoney* £226
1999 AW 0-2: (8f, 10f) (Equi 2)
Workmanlike, average gelding. **M J Haynes [0-7] Hickory Partnership.*

HIDDEN BRAVE RR 85+f 5001[2]

2 b c Bin Ajwaad (IRE) - Fire Lily **(48df)** (Unfuwain (USA))
Form - 2
Record 1999 - 1st:0 2nd:1 3rd:0 Ran:1
Win Prizemoney £0 *Total Prizemoney* £1,100
1999 Turf 0-1: (8f) (gd)
Currently useful colt. (1st run) - 2nd of 11 to Alva Glen (21 Oct Nottingham 8f gd RF 5001). **M Johnston [0-1] Salem Suhail.*

HIDDEN ENEMY RR 67f 5193[4]

3 b c Meqdaam (USA) - Orchard Bay (Formidable (USA)) 9.2f **(63)**
Form - 04
Record 1999 - 1st:0 2nd:0 3rd:0 Ran:2
Win Prizemoney £0 *Total Prizemoney* £177
1999 Turf 0-2: (8f 2) (gd 2)
Currently average colt. Turf high 67 (began Oct).
**R Hollinshead [0-2] J Holcombe.*

HIDDEN FORT BHB 82f RR 82f 4651[11]

2 ch c Mujtahid (USA) 7.4f **(69)** - Temple Fortune (USA) (Ziggy's Boy (USA))
Form - 510600
Record 1999 - 1st:1 2nd:0 3rd:0 Ran:6
Win Prizemoney £5,154 *Total Prizemoney* £5,154
Wins * **1999** Jun Windso (G-F) 5f 85 <
1999 Turf 1-6: (5f 1-5, 7f) (g-s, gd, g-f 2, frm 1-2)
Decent colt, effective 5f, acts on frm. Turf high 85 - 1st of 5 from Whistler (14 Jun Windsor RF 1993). Scored in good style at Windsor on his second start, but has been very disappointing since. **S Dow [1-6] A N Solomons.*

HIDDNAH (USA) BHB 100f **RR 82f** 4236[5]
2 ch f Affirmed (USA) 10.3f **(75)** - L'Extra Honor (USA) (Hero's Honor (USA)) 8.2f **(86)**
Form - 2315
Record 1999 - 1st:1 2nd:1 3rd:1 Ran:4
Win Prizemoney £3,663 *Total Prizemoney* £8,218
Wins * 1999 Jly Newcas (FRM) 7f 82 <
1999 Turf 1-4: (6f, 7f 1-2, 8f) (gd, g-f 1-3)
Decent filly. Turf high 82 - also 1st of 5 getting 5lb from Najjm (24 Jly Newcastle RF 3098). Unfortunate to come up against a smart sort in a Hamilton maiden on her debut. she was third in the Chesham next time. Made no mistake when landing the odds on very fast ground at Newcastle, but looked a tricky ride in a Group Three on her final start. **M Johnston [1-4] Jaber Abdullah.*

HI-FALUTIN RR 5147[10]
3 b f Lugana Beach 7f **(63)** - Hitravelscene (Mansingh (USA)) 7.4f **(55)**
Form - 0
Record 1999 - 1st:0 2nd:0 3rd:0 Ran:1
1999 AW 0-1: (8f) (Fibr)
Currently very poor filly. **A T Murphy [0-1] Clayfields Racing.*

HIGH AND MIGHTY BHB 96f **RR 96f** 3207[1]
4 b g Shirley Heights 12.1f **(76)** - Air Distingue (USA) (Sir Ivor) 10.2f **(70)**
Form - 26411
Record 1999 - 1st:2 2nd:1 3rd:0 Ran:5
Pre1999 - 1st:2 2nd:1 3rd:2 Ran:8
Win Prizemoney £55,884 *Total Prizemoney* £63,250
Wins * 1999 Jly Goodwo (G-F) H 20f 92 96 <
*** 1999** Jun Ascot (G-F) H 20f 85 91
* 1998 Aug Sandow (G-F) H 14f 76 76
* 1998 May Cheste (GD) H 12.3f 66 71+
1999 Turf 2-5: (10f, 12f, 14f, 20f 2-2) (g-s, gd, g-f 2-3)
Neat, very useful gelding, effective 12 to 20f, best at 20f, acts on gd to g-f, best on g-f, has worn blinkers (extremely effectively), prefers right handed tracks, prefers tight tracks. Turf high 96 - 1st of 9 giving 20lb to Mutanassib (28 Jly Goodwood RF 3207) - also 1st of 29 getting 4lb from Far Cry (15 Jun Ascot RF 2000). He stays forever and put up improved performances when completing a big race double at Royal Ascot and Glorious Goodwood. Something of a character at home, he is genuine on the track and will be a force to reckon with in marathons next term. **J H M Gosden [4-13] Sheikh Mohammed.*

HIGH BEAUTY BHB 51f **RR 53f** 4450[9]
2 br f High Kicker (USA) 8.4f **(52)** - Tendresse (IRE) **(21f)** (Tender King) 6.8f **(54)**
Form - 000
Record 1999 - 1st:0 2nd:0 3rd:0 Ran:3
1999 Turf 0-3: (6f, 8f 2) (sft, g-s, frm)
Currently fair filly. Turf high 53 (began Spt).
**M J Ryan [0-3] P E Axon.*

HIGHBORN (IRE) BHB 57f62a **RR 58f 62a** 5156[6]
10 b or br g Double Schwartz 7f **(60)** - High State (Free State) 8.7f **(61)**
Form - 001076588036
Record 1999 - 1st:1 2nd:0 3rd:1 Ran:12
Pre1999 - 1st:13 2nd:6 3rd:7 Ran:79
Win Prizemoney £73,344 *Total Prizemoney* £95,156
Wins * 1999 May Ripon (G-F) H 8f 65 70
* 1997 Aug Cheste (G-S) H 7f 92 100 <
* 1997 Aug Ripon (G-F) H 8f 92 94
* 1996 Oct Newmar (G-F) H 7f 89 92
* 1996 May Cheste (GD) H 7.6f 83 88
* 1995 Oct Redcar (FRM) 6f 81
1999 Turf 1-11: (8f 1-9, 9f 2) (gd 5, g-f 3, frm 1-3) 1999 AW 0-1: (8f) (Fibr)
Fair gelding, effective 8f, acts on frm, likes right handed tracks. Turf high 70. Consistent.
**P S Felgate [14-91] Yorkshire Racing Club Owners Group 1990.*

HIGHCAL RR 58f 3353[9]
2 gr c King's Signet (USA) 7f **(51)** - Guarded Expression **(45f)** (Siberian Express (USA)) 8.8f **(65)**
Form - 080
Record 1999 - 1st:0 2nd:0 3rd:0 Ran:3
1999 Turf 0-3: (6f, 7f 2) (gd, frm 2)
Currently fair colt. Turf high 58.
**D R C Elsworth [0-3] The Caledonian Racing Society.*

HIGH CAPACITY (IRE) BHB 47f **RR 46f** 5158[22]
2 b f Dolphin Street (FR) - Foresta Verde (USA) **(24f 42a)** (Green Forest (USA)) 9.9f **(68)**
Form - 6380000
Record 1999 - 1st:0 2nd:0 3rd:1 Ran:7
Win Prizemoney £0 *Total Prizemoney* £502
1999 Turf 0-7: (5f 2, 6f 2, 7f 2, 8f) (gd, g-f 3, frm 3)
Moderate filly, has worn blinkers. Turf high 56.
**T D Easterby [0-7] Edmolift UK Ltd.*

HIGH CARRY BHB 53f **RR 49f** 4755[8]
4 b f Forzando 7.2f **(63)** - Carn Maire (Northern Prospect (USA)) 9.5f **(71)**
Form - 000750332488
Record 1999 - 1st:0 2nd:1 3rd:2 Ran:12
Pre1999 - 1st:2 2nd:5 3rd:1 Ran:26
Win Prizemoney £6,388 *Total Prizemoney* £17,771
Wins * 1997 Aug Sandow (G-S) H 5f 71 87 <
1997 Jly Beverl (G-F) C 5f 71
1999 Turf 0-12: (5f 11, 6f) (gd 3, g-f 4, frm 4, hrd)
Scopey, moderate filly, effective 5f, acts on g-f, has worn blinkers, likes left handed tracks, likes tight tracks. Turf high 53. Consistent.
**N Tinkler [1-35] James Marshall & Mrs Susan Marshall (from J E Banks [1-3] Jly 1997).*

HIGH CHEVIOT BHB 79f **RR 70f** 5139[8]
2 b c Shirley Heights 12.1f **(76)** - Cutleaf (Kris) 9.5f **(73)**
Form - 2218
Record 1999 - 1st:1 2nd:2 3rd:0 Ran:4
Win Prizemoney £3,582 *Total Prizemoney* £5,822
Wins * 1999 Spt Newcas (SFT) 8f 70 <
1999 Turf 1-4: (7f, 8f 1-2, 10f) (gd 1-2, frm 2)
Above-average colt. Turf high 70 (began Jly) - 1st of 7 from King's Mill (29 Spt Newcastle RF 4635). Third time lucky after two second-places, his win came over a mile at Newcastle on soft ground. A stiff track and soggy conditions helped that day.
**M Johnston [1-4] The Duke of Roxburghe & Lord Hartington.*

HIGH COURT RR 51f 4097[10]
2 ch f Unfuwain (USA) 11.4f **(74)** - Lady Barrister (Law Society (USA)) 9.9f **(70)**
Form - 00
Record 1999 - 1st:0 2nd:0 3rd:0 Ran:2
1999 Turf 0-2: (7f 2) (g-s, frm)
Currently fair filly. Turf high 51 (began Aug).
**M L W Bell [0-2] Cheveley Park Stud.*

HIGH DOMAIN (IRE) BHB 32f66a **RR 31f 66a** 4878[24]
8 b g Dominion Royale 7.8f **(63)** - Recline (Wollow) 8.2f **(61)**
Form - 0075000
Record 1999 - 1st:0 2nd:0 3rd:0 Ran:7
Pre1999 - 1st:5 2nd:1 3rd:5 Ran:54
Win Prizemoney £19,756 *Total Prizemoney* £25,026
Wins * 1996 Nov Doncas (SFT) H 5f 64 65
* 1996 Jun Haydoc (GD) H 6f 64 69
* 1996 May Salisb (SFT) H 5f 58 64
1999 Turf 0-7: (5f 2, 6f 4, 8f) (sft, gd, g-f 3, frm 2)
Fair gelding, has worn blinkers. Turf high 31. Inconsistent.
**J L Spearing [3-37] Stephen Borsberry (from T D Barron [0-12] Spt 1995).*

HIGH ESTEEM BHB 53f **RR 54f** 4986[12]
3 b g Common Grounds 8.1f **(66)** - Whittle Woods Girl **(74f 60a)** (Emarati (USA))
Form - 6707440
Record 1999 - 1st:0 2nd:0 3rd:0 Ran:7
Pre1999 - 1st:0 2nd:0 3rd:0 Ran:3
Win Prizemoney £0 *Total Prizemoney* £442
1999 Turf 0-7: (5f 4, 6f 3) (sft, gd, g-f, frm 4)
Workmanlike, fair gelding, effective 5f, acts on sft. Turf high 59.
**M A Buckley [0-10] C C Buckley.*

HIGH FASHION RR 24f 5071[16]
3 b f Puissance 7.1f **(60)** - Superb Fashion (USA) (Topsider (USA)) 8.3f **(71)**
Form - 0070
Record 1999 - 1st:0 2nd:0 3rd:0 Ran:4
Pre1999 - 1st:0 2nd:0 3rd:0 Ran:1
1999 Turf 0-4: (6f 2, 7f, 11f) (gd, g-f, frm 2)
Leggy, little account filly. Turf high 24.
**J S Haldane [0-5] G J Johnston.*

HIGHFIELDER (IRE) BHB 47f42a **RR 49f 42a** 4945[3]
3 br g Unblest - River Low (IRE) (Lafontaine (USA)) 8.7f **(49)**
Form - 04306003
Record 1999 - 1st:0 2nd:0 3rd:2 Ran:8
Pre1999 - 1st:0 2nd:0 3rd:0 Ran:3
Win Prizemoney £0 *Total Prizemoney* £941
1999 Turf 0-5: (5f, 7f 2, 8f 2) (gd 3, frm 2) 1999 AW 0-3: (7f, 8f 2) (Equi, Fibr 2)
Neat, moderate gelding, has worn blinkers. Turf high 58. AW high 50. Inconsistent. **J S Moore [0-11] Mrs Angela Speyer.*

HIGHFIELD FIZZ BHB 45f44a **RR 44f 44a** 1504[5]
7 b m Efisio 7.7f **(69)** - Jendor (Condorcet (FR)) 12.3f **(62)**
Form - 806315
Record 1999 - 1st:1 2nd:0 3rd:1 Ran:6
Pre1999 - 1st:4 2nd:9 3rd:7 Ran:52
Win Prizemoney £16,674 *Total Prizemoney* £30,057

Wins								
* 1999	May	Mussel	(FRM)	H	16f	41	44	
* 1998	Jun	Mussel	(G-F)	H	16f	50	53	
* 1998	Apr	Pontef	(G-S)	H	17.1f	45	50	
* 1996	Oct	Redcar	(G-F)	H	14.1f	36	44	
* 1995	Spt	Redcar	(GD)	S	11f		57	<

1999 Turf 1-6: (14f, 16f 1-4, 17f) (sft, gd 2, g-f 1-2, frm)
Moderate mare, effective 14 to 18f, acts on g-s to frm, best on g-s, excels at Musselburgh, likes Pontefract and Redcar. Turf high 44 - 1st of 9 getting 5lb from Batoutoftheblue (22 May Musselburgh RF 1408). **C W Fairhurst [5-58] Mrs P J Taylor-Garthwaite.*

HIGH HOYLAND BHB 72f68a **RR 64f 68a** 5042[12]
3 b c High Estate 10.5f **(66)** - Waffling (Lomond (USA)) 8.8f **(65)**
Form - 3337022245820
Record 1999 - 1st:0 2nd:4 3rd:3 Ran:13
Win Prizemoney £0 *Total Prizemoney* £7,683
1999 Turf 0-12: (7f 2, 8f 6, 9f 3, 10f) (sft 2, g-s, gd 3, g-f, frm 5) 1999 AW 0-1: (7f) (Fibr)
Scopey, average colt, effective 7 to 9f, acts on gd to frm, best on frm, has worn blinkers, excels at Brighton and Newmarket. Turf high 77 - 3rd of 7 to Nabonassar (12 May Brighton 7f g-f RF 1178). Becoming disappointing. In the frame in varied company, he undoubtedly has ability but is looking a pretty dodgy customer and has spurned chances when they have presented themselves to him. **R Hannon [0-13] J P Hardiman.*

HIGH KING (IRE) RR 104f 3718a[5]
3 b c Fairy King (USA) 7.7f **(75)** - Ploy (Posse (USA)) 8.9f **(61)**
Form - 1303415
1999 Turf 2-7: (9f 1-1, 10f 1-4, 12f 2) (g-s, gd 1-1, g-f 1-3, frm 2)
Very useful colt, effective 9 to 10f, acts on gd to g-f, has worn blinkers. Turf high 104 - also 1st of 8 giving 7lb to Rainbows Forever (8 Aug Leopardstown RF 3530a). He has taken his chance in Group races, but is basically a smart middle-distance handicapper. **A P O'Brien in IRE [2-8] Michael Tabor.*

HIGHLAND BLUE BHB 40f **RR 53f** 1776[8]
3 b f Never so Bold 7.1f **(62)** - Highland Rowena (Royben) 7.3f **(60)**
Form - 608
Record 1999 - 1st:0 2nd:0 3rd:0 Ran:3
1999 Turf 0-2: (5f, 6f) (sft, frm) 1999 AW 0-1: (7f) (Fibr)
Light-framed, currently fair filly. Turf high 53.
**N P Littmoden [0-3] T Clarke.*

HIGHLAND GOLD (IRE) RR 52f 5207[5]
2 ch c Indian Ridge 7.6f **(74)** - Anjuli (Northfields (USA)) 9f **(72)**
Form - 65
Record 1999 - 1st:0 2nd:0 3rd:0 Ran:2
1999 Turf 0-2: (7f 2) (g-s, gd)
Currently fair colt. Turf high 52 (began Oct).
**Miss L A Perratt [0-2] Miss L A Perratt.*

HIGHLAND SPICE (IRE) RR 795[8]
3 b f Fayruz 6.6f **(63)** - Gaelic Song (Mansingh (USA)) 7.4f **(55)**
Form - 78
Record 1999 - 1st:0 2nd:0 3rd:0 Ran:2
1999 Turf 0-1: (7f) (gd) 1999 AW 0-1: (5f) (Fibr)
Neat, currently little account filly. **Miss L A Perratt [0-2] T P Finch.*

HIGHLY FANCIED BHB 48f **RR 46f** 4538[15]
3 b f High Kicker (USA) 8.4f **(52)** - Angie's Darling (Milford) 9f **(61)**
Form - 7076580
Record 1999 - 1st:0 2nd:0 3rd:0 Ran:7
Pre1999 - 1st:0 2nd:3 3rd:2 Ran:9
Win Prizemoney £0 *Total Prizemoney* £4,415
1999 Turf 0-7: (6f 2, 7f 2, 8f 2, 12f) (gd 2, g-f 3, frm 2)
Workmanlike, moderate filly, effective 6f, acts on sft to gd. Turf high 48.
**Miss L A Perratt [0-10] Mrs Anne Bell (from S E Kettlewell [0-6] Jly 1999).*

HIGHLY PLEASED (USA) RR 62f 2235[6]
4 b g Hansel (USA) 12.6f **(78)** - Bint Alfalla (USA) (Nureyev (USA)) 8.7f **(78)**
Form - 080706
Record 1999 - 1st:0 2nd:0 3rd:0 Ran:6
Pre1999 - 1st:0 2nd:1 3rd:2 Ran:4
Win Prizemoney £0 *Total Prizemoney* £1,751
1999 Turf 0-6: (7f 3, 8f 2, 10f) (g-f 3, frm 3)
Workmanlike, average gelding, effective 8f, acts on g-f. Turf high 63.
**P Burgoyne [0-6] Philip Saunders (from E A L Dunlop [0-4] May 1998).*

HIGHLY PRIZED BHB 69f63a **RR 70f 63a** 3251[2]
5 b g Shirley Heights 12.1f **(76)** - On The Tiles (Thatch (USA)) 9.8f **(62)**
Form - 50442
Record 1999 - 1st:0 2nd:1 3rd:0 Ran:5
Pre1999 - 1st:1 2nd:2 3rd:2 Ran:14
Win Prizemoney £3,030 *Total Prizemoney* £8,386

Wins								
* 1998	Jly	Salisb	(G-F)	H	14.1f	70	77	<

1999 Turf 0-5: (12f, 14f 3, 15f) (g-f, frm 4)
Above-average gelding, effective 14 to 17f, best at 14f, acts on g-s to frm, and excels at Newmarket and Nottingham. Turf high 70 (1st run) - 5th of 9 getting 8lb from Bay of Islands (22 May Nottingham 14f g-f RF 1416). Consistent.
**J S King [1-18] Mrs Marygold O'Kelly (from I A Balding [0-5] Jun 1997).*

HIGHLY SOCIABLE BHB 57f **RR 56f** 4524[7]
2 b f Puissance 7.1f **(60)** - Come To Tea (IRE) (Be My Guest (USA)) 9.3f **(67)**
Form - 5307
Record 1999 - 1st:0 2nd:0 3rd:1 Ran:4
Win Prizemoney £0 *Total Prizemoney* £420
1999 Turf 0-4: (6f 2, 7f 2) (gd 3, g-f)
Fair filly. Turf high 56 (began Jly).
**S A Brookshaw [0-4] The Highly Sociable Syndicate.*

HIGH NOON BHB 50f64a **RR 60f 64a** 4930[12]
4 b c Shirley Heights 12.1f **(76)** - Hocus (High Top) 10.2f **(67)**
Form - 06413411214000
Record 1999 - 1st:3 2nd:1 3rd:1 Ran:10
Pre1999 - 1st:1 2nd:1 3rd:0 Ran:12
Win Prizemoney £10,758 *Total Prizemoney* £13,133

Wins								
1999	*Feb*	*Wolver*	*(STD)*	*H*	*9.4f*	*59*	*63*	<
1999	*Feb*	*Wolver*	*(STD)*	*H*	*9.4f*	*50*	*58*	
1999	*Jan*	*Wolver*	*(STD)*	*H*	*9.4f*	*48*	*54*	
1998	*Dec*	*Wolver*	*(STD)*	*H*	*8.5f*	*43*	*53*	

1999 Turf 0-2: (10f 2) (g-s, g-f) 1999 AW 3-8: (8f 4, 9f 3-4) (Equi, Fibr 3-7)
Neat, average colt, likes left handed tracks, favours tight tracks. Turf high 17 (began Spt). AW high 63. Becoming disappointing. Only very modest on turf, but has shown good form on the Wolverhampton Fibresand since winning there on Boxing Day '98. The extended nine furlongs suits him admirably.
**B J Llewellyn [0-2] Alan Williams (from N P Littmoden [4-16] Mar 1999).*

HIGH ON LIFE BHB 37f37a **RR 27?f 37a** 2146^R
5 b g Mazilier (USA) 8.5f **(56)** - Tina Rosa (Bustino) 10.4f **(64)**
Form - 6RR
Record 1999 - 1st:0 2nd:0 3rd:0 Ran:1
Pre1999 - 1st:0 2nd:3 3rd:3 Ran:17
Win Prizemoney £0 *Total Prizemoney* £3,132
1999 Turf 0-1: (11f) (hrd)
Little account gelding, has worn blinkers.
**J Akehurst [0-10] Canisbay Bloodstock Ltd (from A C Stewart [0-8] Spt 1997).*

HIGH POLICY (IRE) BHB 85f **RR 80f** 1375[3]
3 ch c Machiavellian (USA) 9.8f **(83)** - Road To The Top (Shirley Heights) 10.3f **(74)**
Form - 63
Record 1999 - 1st:0 2nd:0 3rd:1 Ran:2
Pre1999 - 1st:0 2nd:0 3rd:0 Ran:1
Win Prizemoney £0 *Total Prizemoney* £395
1999 Turf 0-2: (10f, 12f) (frm 2)
Workmanlike, currently decent colt. Turf high 80 - 3rd of 11 to Sun Hat (21 May Catterick 12f frm RF 1375). **Sir Michael Stoute [0-3] Lord Weinstock.*

HIGH PRIORITY (IRE) BHB 52f **RR 21f** 1992[22]
6 b g Marju (IRE) 9.2f **(76)** - Blinding (IRE) (High Top) 10.2f **(67)**
Form - 00
Record 1999 - 1st:0 2nd:0 3rd:0 Ran:2
Pre1999 - 1st:1 2nd:2 3rd:1 Ran:13
Win Prizemoney £4,198 *Total Prizemoney* £13,254
Wins 1995 Jun Bath (G-F) 5.1f 77 <
1999 Turf 0-2: (6f 2) (g-f, frm)
Little account gelding. Turf high 21. Becoming disappointing.
**J J Sheehan [0-3] Mrs Eileen Sheehan (from M J Haynes [0-1] Oct 1997).*

HIGH PYRENEES BHB 60f **RR 61f** 774[7]
7 b g Shirley Heights 12.1f **(76)** - Twyla (Habitat) 9.4f **(70)**
Form - 37
Record 1999 - 1st:0 2nd:0 3rd:1 Ran:2
Pre1999 - 1st:1 2nd:0 3rd:1 Ran:5
Win Prizemoney £3,647 *Total Prizemoney* £5,795
Wins 1995 Jun Ayr (G-F) 13.1f 74 <
1999 Turf 0-2: (13f, 17f) (hvy, sft)
Average gelding. Turf high 61.
**F Murphy [0-7] J Stephenson (from R Allan [1-4] Jun 1996).*

HIGH REGARD (JPN) BHB 74f **RR 75+f** 805[7]
3 b c Nashwan (USA) 10.3f **(79)** - Hebba (USA) (Nureyev (USA)) 8.7f **(78)**
Form - 7
Record 1999 - 1st:0 2nd:0 3rd:0 Ran:1
Pre1999 - 1st:0 2nd:2 3rd:1 Ran:5
Win Prizemoney £0 *Total Prizemoney* £2,805
1999 Turf 0-1: (10f) (gd)
Light-framed, above-average colt, effective 7 to 10f, acts on gd to frm, best on gd. (1st run) - 7th of 15 to Nathan's Boy (22 Apr Beverley 10f gd RF 0805). **M Johnston [0-1] Sheikh Mohammed (from D R Loder [0-5] Spt 1998).*

HIGH-RISE (IRE) BHB 122f **RR 119f** 4919[6]
4 b c High Estate 10.5f **(66)** - High Tern (High Line) 10.3f **(70)**
Form - 826
Record 1999 - 1st:0 2nd:1 3rd:0 Ran:3
Pre1999 - 1st:4 2nd:1 3rd:0 Ran:6
Win Prizemoney £639,160 *Total Prizemoney* £784,110

Wins							
1998	Jun	Epsom	(GD)	G1	12f	122	<
1998	May	Lingfi	(GD)	G3	11.5f	115	
1998	Apr	Pontef	(G-S)		10f	100+	
1997	Nov	Doncas	(GD)		7f	83+	

1999 Turf 0-2: (10f, 11f) (gd 2) 1999 AW 0-1: (10f) (Dirt)
Strong, high-class colt, effective 10 to 12f, best at 12f, acts on sft to g-f, best on g-f. Turf high 119 (1st run) (began Spt) - 2nd of 6 giving 2lb to Fantastic Light (19 Spt Newbury 11f gd RF 4417). The winner of the 1998 Derby, he joined Godolphin at the end of that year and made his debut for them in the Dubai World Cup, but finished a long last of the eight runners. Given a break after suffering foot problems, he just found the race-fit Fantastic Light too strong in the Dubai Arc Trial, and found the step down to ten furlongs against him in the Champion Stakes. He maintains the unhappy post-Epsom record of recent Derby winners.
**S bin Suroor [0-2] Godolphin (from S bin Suroor in UAE [0-1] Mar 1999).*

HIGH SHOT BHB 65f **RR 68?f** 4836[16]
9 b g Darshaan 11.9f **(81)** - Nollet (High Top) 10.2f **(67)**
Form - 0
Record 1999 - 1st:0 2nd:0 3rd:0 Ran:1
Pre1999 - 1st:0 2nd:1 3rd:1 Ran:7
Win Prizemoney £0 *Total Prizemoney* £2,094
1999 Turf 0-1: (10f) (gd)
Average gelding.
**G L Moore [0-1] The Tuesday Syndicate (from R Rowe [0-4] Jly 1998).*

HIGHSPEED (IRE) BHB 30f23a **RR 43f 23a** 276[10]
7 ch g Double Schwartz 7f **(60)** - High State (Free State) 8.7f **(61)**
Form - 8705080
Record 1999 - 1st:0 2nd:0 3rd:0 Ran:6
Pre1999 - 1st:3 2nd:1 3rd:1 Ran:24
Win Prizemoney £9,204 *Total Prizemoney* £11,093

Wins								
1996	May	Ayr	(GD)	H	8f	52	57	
1996	May	Ayr	(G-S)	H	7f	49	58	<
1995	Aug	Ayr	(FRM)		7f		51	

1999 AW 0-6: (8f 3, 11f, 12f, 16f) (Fibr 6)
Moderate gelding, has worn blinkers. AW high 29.
**P S Felgate [0-13] David Wright (from S E Kettlewell [3-17] Aug 1997).*

HIGH SUN BHB 60f **RR 61f** 5135[1]
3 b c High Estate 10.5f **(66)** - Clyde Goddess (IRE) **(69df)** (Scottish Reel) 7f **(61)**
Form - 008771030411
Record 1999 - 1st:3 2nd:0 3rd:1 Ran:12
Pre1999 - 1st:0 2nd:0 3rd:0 Ran:3
Win Prizemoney £9,287 *Total Prizemoney* £9,937

Wins								
*** 1999**	Oct	Newmar	(G-S)	H	8f	48	61	<
*** 1999**	Oct	Doncas	(G-S)	H	7f	48	54	
*** 1999**	Aug	Leices	(G-F)	C	8f		50	

1999 Turf 3-12: (7f 1-4, 8f 2-5, 10f, 11f, 12f) (g-s, gd 2-3, g-f 1-1, frm 6, hrd)
Unfurnished, average colt, effective 7 to 8f, acts on gd, has worn blinkers. Turf high 61 - 1st of 18 getting 16lb from Kirk (29 Oct Newmarket RF 5135) - also 1st of 20 getting 19lb from Barabaschi (22 Oct Doncaster RF 5026). **S Gollings [3-15] R L Houlton.*

HIGH TATRA (IRE) BHB 86f **RR 90f** 4817[1]
3 b g Polish Patriot (USA) 7.8f **(70)** - Bouffant (High Top) 10.2f **(67)**
Form - 1111316088021
Record 1999 - 1st:6 2nd:1 3rd:1 Ran:13
Pre1999 - 1st:0 2nd:0 3rd:0 Ran:3
Win Prizemoney £26,359 *Total Prizemoney* £28,414

Wins								
*** 1999**	Oct	Leices	(G-S)	H	11.8f	80	90	<
*** 1999**	May	Thirsk	(G-F)	H	12f	83	83	
*** 1999**	Apr	Nottin	(SFT)		10f		83+	
*** 1999**	Apr	Thirsk	(GD)		12f		79+	
*** 1999**	Apr	Ripon	(G-S)	H	12.3f	68	72+	
*** 1999**	Apr	Mussel	(GD)		12f		63	

1999 Turf 6-12: (10f 1-4, 12f 5-8) (g-s 1-1, gd 3-7, g-f 2-3, frm) 1999 AW 0-1: (12f) (Fibr)
Leggy, useful gelding, effective 10 to 12f, best at 12f, acts on g-s to g-f - acts on Fibr, likes left handed trackslikes right handed tracks, prefers tight tracks, excels at Thirsk. Turf high 90 - 1st of 8 getting 5lb from Limelighting (11 Oct Leicester RF 4817) - also 1st of 15 giving 4lb to Warning Reef (24 May Thirsk RF 1440). (1st run) - 2nd of 6 giving 3lb to Altichiero (2 Oct Wolverhampton 12f Fibr RF 4704). Showed little at two, but was in irresistible form early on last season, winning five times and looking well suited by middle distances. Things became tougher once the Handicapper caught up with him, but returned to form at the back-end.
**S P C Woods [6-16] W J P Jackson.*

HIGH TOPPER (FR) **RR 69f** 5102[7]
2 b c Wolfhound (USA) 7.3f **(71)** - Blushing Barada (USA) (Blushing Groom (FR)) 10.3f **(76)**
Form - 7
Record 1999 - 1st:0 2nd:0 3rd:0 Ran:1
1999 Turf 0-1: (8f) (gd)

Currently average colt. **M Johnston [0-1] Maktoum Al Maktoum.*

HIGH WALDEN (USA) BHB 100f **RR 94f** 4680[2]

2 b f El Gran Senor (USA) 8.9f **(85)** - Modena (USA) (Roberto (USA)) 10f **(76)**

Form - 412

Record 1999 - 1st:1 2nd:1 3rd:0 Ran:3

Win Prizemoney £4,110 *Total Prizemoney* £10,027

Wins * **1999** Spt Leices (FRM) 8f 82 <

1999 Turf 1-3: (7f 2, 8f 1-1) (gd, g-f, frm 1-1)

Currently useful filly. Turf high 94 - 2nd of 12 to Agrippina (2 Oct Newmarket 7f gd RF 4680). Came to the Chesham Stakes with a big reputation, but could only finish fourth. She landed long odd-on at Leicester next time in workmanlike style and was runner-up in a Listed race on her third run. She is probably capable of better, though she does have a bit of a problem with the stalls.

**H R A Cecil [1-3] K Abdulla.*

HIGHWAY BHB 39f39a **RR 47f 39a** 187[14]

5 gr g Salse (USA) 10.9f **(71)** - Ivory Lane (USA) (Sir Ivor) 10.2f **(70)**

Form - 50

Record 1999 - 1st:0 2nd:0 3rd:0 Ran:2

Pre1999 - 1st:0 2nd:0 3rd:0 Ran:7

Win Prizemoney £0 *Total Prizemoney* £265

1999 AW 0-2: (7f, 8f) (Fibr 2)

Moderate gelding, had broken blood-vessels. AW high 44. (DEAD)

**Denys Smith [0-2] Denys Smith (from C W Thornton [0-5] Aug 1998).*

HI GUYS (IRE) RR 3572[13]

2 ch f Imp Society (USA) 7.1f **(63)** - Gorgeous Annie (Hello Gorgeous (USA)) 9.7f **(63)**

Form - 0

Record 1999 - 1st:0 2nd:0 3rd:0 Ran:1

1999 Turf 0-1: (7f) (g-f)

Currently very poor filly.

**Mrs P N Dutfield [0-1] The Wheelwright Wanderers.*

HI-JENNY (IRE) BHB 46f **RR 40f** 4031[9]

3 b f High Estate 10.5f **(66)** - Dream of Jenny(Caerleon (USA)) 8.6f **(71)**

Form - 14524770

Record 1999 - 1st:1 2nd:1 3rd:0 Ran:8

Pre1999 - 1st:0 2nd:0 3rd:2 Ran:7

Win Prizemoney £2,889 *Total Prizemoney* £4,524

Wins * **1999** Apr Beverl (G-F) H 12f 46 53 <

1999 Turf 1-8: (10f 2, 11f, 12f 1-5) (gd, g-f 3, frm 1-4)

Light-framed, fair filly, effective 11 to 12f, best at 12f, acts on gd to frm, has worn blinkers, prefers tight tracks. Turf high 53 (1st run) - 1st of 12 getting 1lb from Dispol Trump (14 Apr Beverley RF 0689).

**W Storey [1-9] Tony Stafford (from W G M Turner [0-6] Spt 1998).*

HILL FARM BLUES BHB 78f55a **RR 80f 55a** 4917[10]

6 b m Mon Tresor 7.9f **(60)** - Loadplan Lass (Nicholas Bill) 10.1f **(56)**

Form - 4331125477470

Record 1999 - 1st:2 2nd:1 3rd:2 Ran:13

Pre1999 - 1st:3 2nd:2 3rd:0 Ran:19

Win Prizemoney £19,680 *Total Prizemoney* £37,410

Wins * **1999** Jun Haydoc (G-S) H 16.2f 54 70 <

* **1999** May Haydoc (GD) H 14f 54 58

* 1998 Oct Nottin (SFT) H 16f 51 56

* 1997 Jly Bath (GD) H 10.2f 58 63

* 1997 May Nottin (GD) SH 10f 49 57

1999 Turf 2-13: (12f 3, 14f 1-5, 15f, 16f 1-2, 17f, 19f) (sft 2, gd 1-6, g-f 1-4, frm)

Decent mare, effective 12 to 19f, acts on gd to g-f, best on g-f, prefers left handed tracks, likes tight tracks, excels at Haydock. Turf high 83 - 4th of 6 getting 17lb from Kahtan (25 Jly Chester 19f g-f RF 3125). She is quite a useful stayer, gaining back-to-back victories at Haydock in the spring and, stepped back down to a mile and a half, ran a blinder to finish runner-up in the Old Newton Cup at the same track. She rose in the handicap as a result and was found wanting.

**W M Brisbourne [6-29] Dennis Newton (from J L Eyre [0-4] Spt 1996).*

HILL FARM DANCER BHB 28f30a **RR 27f 30a** 5190[4]

8 ch m Gunner B 11.2f **(45)** - Loadplan Lass (Nicholas Bill) 10.1f **(56)**

Form - 477148324838U86054

Record 1999 - 1st:1 2nd:1 3rd:2 Ran:18

Pre1999 - 1st:9 2nd:8 3rd:9 Ran:63

Win Prizemoney £27,353 *Total Prizemoney* £42,753

Wins * **1999** *Apr Southw (STD) S 12f 54*

* 1998 Jly Mussel (GD) H 12f 45 49

* 1997 *Jan Wolver (STD) H 12f 68 76* <

* 1996 *Nov Wolver (STD) 12f 70*

* 1996 *Nov Wolver (STD) H 12f 53 62*

* 1996 *Mar Wolver (STD) C 12f 57*

* 1996 *Feb Wolver (STD) H 12f 47 53*

* 1995 May Bath (GD) H 11.7f 50

1999 Turf 0-7: (12f 6, 14f) (hvy, g-f 4, frm 2) 1999 AW 1-11: (9f, 11f, 12f 1-7, 14f, 15f) (Fibr 1-11)

Very moderate mare, effective 11 to 12f, best at 12f, acts on gd to frm - acts on Fibr, likes left handed tracks, excels at Southwell. Turf high 29. AW high 54 - 1st of 6 getting 5lb from Artic Courier (6 Apr Southwell RF 0604). **W M Brisbourne [10-78] M E Hughes (from P D Evans [0-3] Jly 1993).*

HILLINSKI (IRE) BHB 27f27a **RR 6f 27a** 1408[9]

5 b g Danehill (USA) 9.1f **(79)** - Llangollen (IRE) (Caerleon (USA)) 8.6f **(71)**

Form - 0800

Record 1999 - 1st:0 2nd:0 3rd:0 Ran:4

Pre1999 - 1st:0 2nd:0 3rd:0 Ran:6

1999 Turf 0-2: (11f, 16f) (g-f, frm) 1999 AW 0-2: (7f, 8f) (Fibr 2)

Little account gelding, has worn blinkers. Turf high 6. AW high 26.

**M Mullineaux [0-10] Birch Vale Racing.*

HILL MAGIC BHB 90f **RR 73f** 4699[5]

4 br g Magic Ring (IRE) 6.5f **(64)** -Stock Hill Lass (Air Trooper) 9.1f **(63)**

Form - 10005

Record 1999 - 1st:1 2nd:0 3rd:0 Ran:5

Pre1999 - 1st:2 2nd:2 3rd:1 Ran:14

Win Prizemoney £45,663 *Total Prizemoney* £55,468

Wins * **1999** Apr Kempto (GD) 6f 100 <

* 1998 May Lingfi (GD) H 6f 89 94

* 1997 Jly Bath (GD) 5.7f 77

1999 Turf 1-5: (5f, 6f 1-4) (sft, gd, g-f 1-3)

Scopey, above-average gelding, effective 6f, acts on g-f. Turf high 100 (1st run) - 1st of 9 from Brave Edge (5 Apr Kempton RF 0574). Becoming disappointing. Seemingly set for a career in Listed and Group races after winning at Kempton, he proved extremely disappointing and was beaten in a claimer at Sandown in October. Best at six furlongs, he is one to treat with caution.

**D R C Elsworth [3-19] Michael Jackson Bloodstock Ltd.*

HILLSIDE ROSE (IRE) BHB 59a **RR 59f** 4869[11]

4 b f Danehill (USA) 9.1f **(79)** - Miss Belgravia (USA) (Smarten (USA))

Form - 00

Record 1999 - 1st:0 2nd:0 3rd:0 Ran:2

Pre1999 - 1st:0 2nd:2 3rd:2 Ran:6

Win Prizemoney £0 *Total Prizemoney* £2,668

1999 Turf 0-1: (10f) (gd) 1999 AW 0-1: (12f) (Fibr)

Fair filly, effective 8f, acts on gd. Becoming disappointing.

**A T Murphy [0-1] Mrs G Goddard (from R G Frost [0-5] May 1999).*

HILL STORM (IRE) BHB 52f48a **RR 64f 48a** 4153[11]

3 b g Mukaddamah (USA) 7.6f **(74)** - Brockley Hill Lass (IRE) (Alzao (USA)) 7.1f **(68)**

Form - 640

Record 1999 - 1st:0 2nd:0 3rd:0 Ran:3

Pre1999 - 1st:0 2nd:0 3rd:0 Ran:4

1999 AW 0-3: (10f, 12f 2) (Equi, Fibr 2)

Workmanlike, average gelding, has worn blinkers. AW high 54.

**K McAuliffe [0-7] K W J McAuliffe.*

HILLSWICK BHB 35f **RR 37f** 3475[3]

8 ch g Norwick (USA) 9.4f **(51)**-Quite Lucky (Precipice Wood) 17.2f **(38)**

Form - 0223

Record 1999 - 1st:0 2nd:2 3rd:1 Ran:4

Pre1999 - 1st:1 2nd:3 3rd:1 Ran:19

Win Prizemoney £3,533 *Total Prizemoney* £9,286

Wins * **1997** Aug Bath (GD) H 17.2f 37 40 <

1999 Turf 0-4: (16f 2, 17f, 18f) (g-s, g-f 2, frm)

Very moderate gelding. Turf high 37 - 2nd of 7 getting 6lb from Island Song (20 Jly Bath 17f frm RF 2959). Consistent.

**J S King [3-31] M G A Court.*

HILLTOP BHB 51f **RR 40f** 5032[25]
3 b f Absalom 7.1f **(56)** - Just Irene (Sagaro) 9.7f **(55)**
Form - 06040
Record 1999 - 1st:0 2nd:0 3rd:0 Ran:5
1999 Turf 0-5: (5f 3, 6f 2) (g-s, gd 2, frm 2)
Workmanlike, moderate filly. Turf high 42 (began Jly).
**R Guest [0-5] G Noble.*

HILLTOP WARNING BHB 82f **RR 85f** 4981[3]
2 b c Reprimand 8.2f **(63)** - Just Irene (Sagaro) 9.7f **(55)**
Form - 223
Record 1999 - 1st:0 2nd:2 3rd:1 Ran:3
Win Prizemoney £0 *Total Prizemoney* £3,067
1999 Turf 0-3: (6f 3) (gd, g-f, frm)
Currently useful colt. Turf high 85 (began Spt).
**S P C Woods [0-3] G Noble.*

HILLZAH (USA) BHB 47f42a **RR 49f 42a** 1057[14]
11 ch g Blushing Groom (FR) 10.2f **(80)** - Glamour Girl (ARG) (Mysolo) 11.9f **(95)**
Form - 743035250
Record 1999 - 1st:0 2nd:1 3rd:1 Ran:6
Pre1999 - 1st:13 2nd:10 3rd:8 Ran:84
Win Prizemoney £49,193 *Total Prizemoney* £65,471
Wins * 1998 *Feb Southw (STD) H 16f 50 55*
* 1995 Jly Haydoc (G-F) H 10.5f 75 78
* 1995 Jun Carlis (GD) H 14.1f 66 69
* 1995 *Jan Wolver (STD) H 12f 80 80*
1999 Turf 0-2: (12f 2) (g-f 2) 1999 AW 0-4: (14f, 15f, 16f 2) (Fibr 4)
Moderate gelding, effective 15 to 16f, - acts on Fibr, has worn blinkers, favours left handed tracks. Turf high 45. AW high 43.
**R Bastiman [11-78] Robin Bastiman (from P T Walwyn [2-12] Oct 1991).*

HILTONS EXECUTIVE (IRE) BHB 38f44a **RR 42f 44a** 4702[10]
5 b m Petorius 8f **(66)** - Theatral (Orchestra) 9.7f **(52)**
Form - 161877667040500
Record 1999 - 1st:0 2nd:0 3rd:0 Ran:12
Pre1999 - 1st:4 2nd:5 3rd:4 Ran:31
Win Prizemoney £9,798 *Total Prizemoney* £15,632
Wins * 1998 *Dec Wolver (STD) H 6f 48 52* <
* 1998 *Nov Southw (STD) H 6f 45 46*
* 1998 May Ayr (G-F) H 5f 41 47
* 1998 *Apr Wolver (STD) H 5f 40 42*
1999 Turf 0-8: (5f 3, 6f 3, 7f 2) (gd 4, g-f, frm 3) 1999 AW 0-4: (5f 2, 6f, 7f) (Fibr 4)
Moderate filly, effective 5 to 6f, best at 5f, acts on gd to g-f - acts on Fibr, best on g-f, has worn blinkers. Turf high 45 (1st run) - 7th of 24 giving 5lb to Heavenly Miss (16 Apr Thirsk 6f gd RF 0731). AW high 45. Inconsistent. **E J Alston [4-43] Derek Hilton.*

HI MUJTAHID (IRE) BHB 30f34a **RR 26f 34a** 3389[12]
5 ch g Mujtahid (USA) 7.4f **(69)** - High Tern (High Line) 10.3f **(70)**
Form - 0016800503870
Record 1999 - 1st:0 2nd:0 3rd:1 Ran:10
Pre1999 - 1st:2 2nd:4 3rd:2 Ran:28
Win Prizemoney £4,828 *Total Prizemoney* £9,740
Wins * 1998 *Dec Wolver (STD) H 8.5f 34 41*
1997 Jly Ayr (G-F) H 7f 44 50 <
1999 Turf 0-3: (8f, 10f 2) (gd, frm 2) 1999 AW 0-7: (6f, 7f, 8f 4, 9f) (Equi, Fibr 6)
Little account gelding, effective 8f, - acts on Fibr, has worn blinkers. Turf high 26 (began Jly). AW high 29.
**Mrs H L Walton [1-16] Mrs Angela Ellis (from S E Kettlewell [1-19] Jun 1998).*

HINDI BHB 66f **RR 66f** 5198[6]
3 b c Indian Ridge 7.6f **(74)** - Tootsiepop (USA) (Robellino (USA)) 7.6f **(80)**
Form - 00456
Record 1999 - 1st:0 2nd:0 3rd:0 Ran:5
Win Prizemoney £0 *Total Prizemoney* £286
1999 Turf 0-5: (8f 4, 10f) (sft, gd 3, frm)
Lengthy, average colt. Turf high 66. **N A Graham [0-5] Paul Jacobs.*

HI NICKY BHB 72f **RR 68f** 2498[13]
3 ch f High Kicker (USA) 8.4f **(52)** - Sharp Top (Sharpo) 7.7f **(59)**
Form - 46030
Record 1999 - 1st:0 2nd:0 3rd:1 Ran:5
Pre1999 - 1st:1 2nd:0 3rd:0 Ran:1
Win Prizemoney £4,503 *Total Prizemoney* £5,486
Wins * 1998 May Newmar (G-F) 6f 60 <
1999 Turf 0-5: (6f, 7f 3, 8f) (gd, g-f 4)
Workmanlike, average filly, effective 6f, acts on frm. Turf high 70. Made a winning debut at Newmarket as a two-year-old. Failed to add to that since and has looked an awkward ride.
**M J Ryan [1-6] D Bell.*

HINT OF MAGIC RR 70f 4715[2]
2 b c Magic Ring (IRE) 6.5f **(64)** - Thames Glow (Kalaglow) 9.8f **(67)**
Form - 52
Record 1999 - 1st:0 2nd:1 3rd:0 Ran:2
Win Prizemoney £0 *Total Prizemoney* £1,166
1999 Turf 0-2: (8f, 10f) (g-s, gd)
Currently above-average colt. Turf high 70 (began Spt).
**J G Portman [0-2] Madhatter Racing.*

HISHMAH BHB 78f **RR 76f** 2673[1]
3 b f Nashwan (USA) 10.3f **(79)** - Na-Ayim (IRE) (Shirley Heights) 10.3f **(74)**
Form - 84281
Record 1999 - 1st:1 2nd:1 3rd:0 Ran:5
Pre1999 - 1st:0 2nd:1 3rd:0 Ran:3
Win Prizemoney £4,250 *Total Prizemoney* £8,374
Wins * 1999 Jly Cheste (G-F) 7.6f 74 <
1999 Turf 1-5: (7f 2, 8f 1-2, 11f) (gd 2, g-f 1-3)
Well made, above-average filly, effective 6 to 8f, acts on g-f to frm, best on g-f. Turf high 76. **E A L Dunlop [1-8] Hamdan Al Maktoum.*

HISTORIC (IRE) BHB 83f **RR 85f** 5165[2]
3 b c Sadler's Wells (USA) 11.3f **(87)** - Urjwan (USA) (Seattle Slew (USA)) 9.4f **(76)**
Form - 422
Record 1999 - 1st:0 2nd:2 3rd:0 Ran:3
Win Prizemoney £0 *Total Prizemoney* £2,455
1999 Turf 0-3: (12f 3) (sft, g-s 2)
Scopey, currently useful colt. Turf high 85 (began Spt) - 2nd of 14 giving 5lb to Just Dreams (2 Nov Catterick 12f g-s RF 5165).
**W J Haggas [0-3] Highclere Thoroughbred Racing Ltd.*

HOH DEAR (IRE) BHB 100f **RR 94f** 2575[2]
2 b f Sri Pekan (USA) - Miss Kristin (IRE) **(58f)** (Alzao (USA)) 7.1f **(68)**
Form - 1312
Record 1999 - 1st:2 2nd:1 3rd:1 Ran:4
Win Prizemoney £15,030 *Total Prizemoney* £24,442
Wins * 1999 Jun Newmar (G-F) L 6f 94 <
*** 1999** Apr Newmar (GD) 5f 82
1999 Turf 2-4: (5f 1-2, 6f 1-2) (gd 1-2, g-f 1-1, frm)
Useful filly. Turf high 94 - 2nd of 12 to Torgau (6 Jly Newmarket 6f frm RF 2575) - also 1st of 8 from Forever Midnight (26 Jun Newmarket RF 2345). Winner of a decent Newmarket maiden on her debut, she then tackled the classy Gipsy Anna and Rowaasi at Newbury where she was not disgraced in finishing a close third. Boosted that form when beating Forever Midnight in a listed event at Newmarket, and returned to Heaquarters to finish second in the Cherry Hinton. She is now in training in the United States.
**M L W Bell [2-4] Highclere Thoroughbred Racing Ltd.*

HOH DISCOVERY (IRE) RR 81f 1139[2]
2 ch c Emarati (USA) 6.6f **(63)** - Sabonis (USA) (The Minstrel (CAN)) 10f **(72)**
Form - 212
Record 1999 - 1st:1 2nd:2 3rd:0 Ran:3
Win Prizemoney £2,742 *Total Prizemoney* £6,806
Wins * 1999 Apr Leices (HVY) 5f 81 <
1999 Turf 1-3: (5f 1-3) (sft 1-1, g-f, frm)
Decent colt. Turf high 81 - 2nd of 6 to Victory Day (10 May Windsor 5f g-f RF 1139) - also 1st of 11 giving 5lb to Turtle Surprise (24 Apr Leicester RF 0829). (DEAD)
**I A Balding [1-3] D F Allport & Alec Tuckerman.*

HOH EXPLORER (IRE) BHB 30f53a **RR 26f 53a** 4726[14]
5 ch g Shahrastani (USA) 11.5f **(69)** - Heart's Harmony (Blushing Groom (FR)) 10.3f **(76)**

Form - 0
Record 1999 - 1st:0 2nd:0 3rd:0 Ran:1
Pre1999 - 1st:0 2nd:0 3rd:1 Ran:10
Win Prizemoney £0 *Total Prizemoney* £604
1999 Turf 0-1: (16f) (gd)
Little account gelding, has worn blinkers.
**D W Barker [0-19] Saltire Racing Syndicate (from I A Balding [0-2] May 1997).*

HOH GEM BHB 40f **RR 45f** 4632[12]

3 b c Be My Chief (USA) 10.2f **(62)** - Jennies' Gem (Sayf El Arab (USA)) 7.1f **(54)**
Form - 8080
Record 1999 - 1st:0 2nd:0 3rd:0 Ran:4
1999 Turf 0-4: (6f 2, 7f, 10f) (g-s, gd, g-f, frm)
Moderate colt. Turf high 45.
**B R Millman [0-3] Brian Lovrey (from Miss Gay Kelleway [0-1] Jun 1999).*

HOH HOH SEVEN (IRE) BHB 62f **RR 72df** 4697[10]

3 b g College Chapel - Fighting Run (Runnett) 7f **(59)**
Form - 6453756500
Record 1999 - 1st:0 2nd:0 3rd:1 Ran:10
Win Prizemoney £0 *Total Prizemoney* £852
1999 Turf 0-10: (6f, 7f 2, 8f 5, 9f, 10f) (sft, g-s, gd, g-f 2, frm 4, hrd)
Rangy, above-average gelding, effective 8f, acts on frm, has worn blinkers. Turf high 72. **N E Berry [0-6] D W Smith (from I A Balding [0-4] Jun 1999).*

HOH NAVIGATOR (IRE) BHB 41f52a **RR 40f 52a** 2667[19]

4 ch g Common Grounds 8.1f **(66)** - Flying Diva (Chief Singer) 8.9f **(66)**
Form - 2063000660
Record 1999 - 1st:0 2nd:0 3rd:1 Ran:8
Pre1999 - 1st:0 2nd:3 3rd:2 Ran:11
Win Prizemoney £0 *Total Prizemoney* £4,395
1999 Turf 0-6: (7f 2, 8f 4) (sft, gd 2, g-f, frm 2) 1999 AW 0-2: (7f, 8f) (Fibr 2)
Workmanlike, fair gelding, effective 6f, acts on g-f to frm, has worn blinkers. Turf high 40. AW high 56.
**D J S ffrenchDavis [0-11] A Rybak (from M L W Bell [0-8] Oct 1998).*

HOH NO BHB 79f **RR 83f** 4954[11]

3 b g Efisio 7.7f **(69)** - Primetta (Precocious) 8.6f **(62)**
Form - 21874700
Record 1999 - 1st:1 2nd:1 3rd:0 Ran:8
Pre1999 - 1st:1 2nd:0 3rd:2 Ran:6
Win Prizemoney £7,352 *Total Prizemoney* £14,414
Wins * 1999 May Nottin (GD) 10f 84 <
* 1998 Spt Goodwo (G-F) H 8f 68 75
1999 Turf 1-8: (9f, 10f 1-6, 12f) (g-f 1-6, frm 2)
Scopey, decent gelding, effective 8 to 10f, best at 10f, acts on g-f to frm, best on g-f, prefers right handed tracks. Turf high 84 - 1st of 12 getting 14lb from Celestial Welcome (7 May Nottingham RF 1093). Won at Goodwood at two, and gained a courageous victory at Nottingham on his second start of the season. He has been tackling some decent company since then and has not been disgraced, if looking to be in the grip of the Handicapper.
**M L W Bell [2-14] M B Hawtin & R P B Michaelson.*

HOH STEAMER (IRE) BHB 93f **RR 93f** 3239[5]

3 br gr g Perugino (USA) - Dane's Lane (IRE) (Danehill (USA)) 10f **(72)**
Form - 4185
Record 1999 - 1st:1 2nd:0 3rd:0 Ran:4
Pre1999 - 1st:3 2nd:1 3rd:0 Ran:8
Win Prizemoney £54,049 *Total Prizemoney* £59,428
Wins * 1999 Jun Ascot (G-F) 8f 82
* 1998 Aug Newcas (GD) H 8f 82 86 <
* 1998 Aug York (G-F) H 7f 70 77
* 1998 Aug Newbur (GD) H 7.3f 70 75
1999 Turf 1-4: (7f, 8f 1-3) (g-f 1-3, frm)
Scopey, useful gelding, effective 7 to 8f, best at 8f, acts on g-f to hrd, best on g-f, excels at Newbury. Turf high 93 (1st run) - 4th of 18 getting 4lb from Date (29 May Haydock 8f g-f RF 1569). Back to winning form in a decent minor event at Ascot in June, but disappointed later. **M L W Bell [4-12] Highclere Thoroughbred Racing Ltd.*

HOLDING COURT BHB 97f **RR 89+f** 5037[8]

2 b c Hernando (FR) - Indian Love Song (Be My Guest (USA)) 9.3f **(67)**
Form - 6218
Record 1999 - 1st:1 2nd:1 3rd:0 Ran:4
Win Prizemoney £5,587 *Total Prizemoney* £7,071
Wins * 1999 Oct Haydoc (HVY) 8.1f 89++ <
1999 Turf 1-4: (7f 2, 8f 1-2) (sft 1-1, g-s, gd, frm)
Useful colt. Turf high 89 (began Spt) - 1st of 4 from Cover Up (13 Oct Haydock RF 4858). Got off the mark in a conditions race over a mile on heavy ground at Haydock, beating a small field. Was unable to handle the step up in class in the Racing Post Trophy, for which he was supplemented. **B J Meehan [1-4] J R Good.*

HO LENG (IRE) BHB 103f **RR 103f** 4915[3]

4 ch g Statoblest 6.4f **(63)** - Indigo Blue (IRE) (Bluebird (USA)) 7.5f **(69)**
Form - 04020210053
Record 1999 - 1st:1 2nd:2 3rd:1 Ran:11
Pre1999 - 1st:3 2nd:1 3rd:0 Ran:9
Win Prizemoney £68,126 *Total Prizemoney* £87,849
Wins * 1999 Spt York (G-F) H 6f 101 103
* 1998 Jly Newmar (FRM) H 7f 102 105 <
* 1998 May York (GD) H 7f 95 100
* 1997 Aug Hamilt (G-F) 6f 88+
1999 Turf 1-11: (6f 1-5, 7f 4, 8f 2) (g-s, gd 5, g-f, frm 1-4)
Scopey, very useful gelding, effective 6 to 8f, best at 6f, acts on gd to frm, best on frm, excels at Newmarket and York. Turf high 103 - 1st of 11 giving 2lb to Harmonic Way (1 Spt York RF 4082). Effective from six furlongs to a mile, this former front-runner goes well when held-up behind a fast pace. Always one to reckon with in handicap company, he is at his best on firm ground.
**Miss L A Perratt [4-20] Alan Guthrie.*

Ho Leng was suited by a change of tactics

HOLLOWAY MELODY BHB 43f45a **RR 44f 45a** 537[3]

6 ch m Cree Song 6.9f **(54)** - Holloway Wonder (Swing Easy (USA)) 6.5f **(55)**
Form - 3
Record 1999 - 1st:0 2nd:0 3rd:1 Ran:1
Pre1999 - 1st:3 2nd:1 3rd:6 Ran:42
Win Prizemoney £6,746 *Total Prizemoney* £9,622
Wins * 1998 Jly Chepst (GD) SH 8.1f 35 44

* 1998	Jly	Warwic	(GD)	SH	8f	35	44	
* 1996	Oct	Nottin	(GD)	C	8.2f		62	<

1999 Turf 0-1: (7f) (gd)

Moderate mare, effective 7 to 8f, best at 8f, acts on gd to g-f - acts on Fibr, best on g-f, has worn blinkers. (1st run) - 3rd of 18 getting 5lb from Adirpour (1 Apr Leicester 7f gd RF 0537). Consistent.

**B A McMahon [3-43] Mrs Rita Gibson.*

HOLLY BLUE BHB 94f RR 97f 4915[15]

3 ch f Bluebird (USA) 7.9f **(71)** - Nettle (Kris) 9.5f **(73)**

Form - 01164220

Record 1999 - 1st:2 2nd:2 3rd:0 Ran:8
Pre1999 - 1st:0 2nd:0 3rd:0 Ran:3

Win Prizemoney £16,904 *Total Prizemoney* £24,322

Wins								
*** 1999**	Jun	Ascot	(G-F)	LH	8f	84	87	<
*** 1999**	Jun	Bath	(GD)	H	8f	75	81+	

1999 Turf 2-8: (7f 2, 8f 2-5, 10f) (gd 3, g-f 2-2, frm 3)

Scopey, very useful filly, effective 7 to 8f, best at 7f, acts on gd to frm. Turf high 97 - 2nd of 15 to Family Man (1 Oct Newmarket 7f gd RF 4675). Very easy winner of a Bath handicap in June, and followed up in the Fern Hill at Ascot on fast ground under a patient ride. Continued to acquit herself well in handicaps.

**R Charlton [2-11] The Queen.*

HOLME FARM BOY (IRE) BHB 37f RR 27f 3979[11]

3 b g River Falls 8.2f **(56)** - Lady Conchita (IRE) (Whistling Deer) 16.4f **(48)**

Form - 04300

Record 1999 - 1st:0 2nd:0 3rd:1 Ran:5

Win Prizemoney £0 *Total Prizemoney* £660

1999 Turf 0-5: (8f, 10f, 12f, 14f 2) (g-f 2, frm 2, hrd)

Lengthy, little account gelding. Turf high 51.

**G M Moore [0-5] M K Roddis.*

HOLY SMOKE BHB 65f70a RR 68f 70a 5217[10]

4 b f Statoblest 6.4f **(63)** - Native Flair (Be My Native (USA)) 10.2f **(71)**

Form - 11814800

Record 1999 - 1st:2 2nd:0 3rd:0 Ran:7
Pre1999 - 1st:4 2nd:0 3rd:1 Ran:13

Win Prizemoney £15,350 *Total Prizemoney* £16,418

Wins								
*** 1999**	Mar	Doncas	(SFT)	H	10.3f	62	70	
*** 1999**	*Jan*	*Southw*	*(STD)*	*H*	*8f*	*63*	*78*	<
* 1998	*Nov*	*Southw*	*(STD)*	*H*	*8f*	*58*	*67*	
* 1998	Nov	Mussel	(SFT)	H	8f	56	63	
* 1998	Aug	Carlis	(G-S)	H	8f	53	58	
* 1998	*Jun*	*Southw*	*(STD)*	*H*	*8f*	*53*	*56*	

1999 Turf 1-4: (8f 3, 10f 1-1) (sft, g-s 1-2, gd) 1999 AW 1-3: (8f 1-2, 9f) (Fibr 1-3)

Workmanlike, above-average filly, effective 8 to 10f, acts on g-s - acts on Fibr, excels at Southwell. Turf high 70 (1st run) - 1st of 20 getting 10lb from King Priam (25 Mar Doncaster RF 0469). AW high 78 (1st run) - 1st of 16 giving 17lb to Mutabari (2 Jan Southwell RF 0015).

**J L Eyre [6-20] John Roberts (Wakefield).*

HOME COUNTIES (IRE) BHB 55f RR 53f 4800[2]

10 ch g Ela-Mana-Mou 12.7f **(72)** - Safe Home (Home Guard (USA)) 9.3f **(66)**

Form - 5232

Record 1999 - 1st:0 2nd:2 3rd:1 Ran:4
Pre1999 - 1st:1 2nd:0 3rd:1 Ran:19

Win Prizemoney £3,468 *Total Prizemoney* £10,361

1999 Turf 0-4: (12f, 14f 2, 17f) (g-s, gd 2, frm)

Fair gelding, has worn blinkers (extremely effectively). Turf high 53 (began Aug) - 2nd of 21 getting 19lb from Il Principe (9 Oct York 14f gd RF 4800). Consistent.

**J Hetherton [0-9] Ms A Hartley (from D Moffatt [6-47] Spt 1997).*

HOME FORCE RR 66f 4640[8]

2 b c Chaddleworth (IRE) -Breed Reference(Reference Point) 6.8f **(70)**

Form - 48

Record 1999 - 1st:0 2nd:0 3rd:0 Ran:2

Win Prizemoney £0 *Total Prizemoney* £264

1999 Turf 0-2: (7f, 8f) (g-s, gd)

Currently average colt. Turf high 66 (began Spt).

**C F Wall [0-2] Induna Racing Partners.*

HOME OFFICE BHB 77f RR 77f 4861[4]

3 b c Danehill (USA) 9.1f **(79)** - Liaison (USA) (Blushing Groom (FR)) 10.3f **(76)**

Form - 34

Record 1999 - 1st:0 2nd:0 3rd:1 Ran:2
Pre1999 - 1st:0 2nd:1 3rd:1 Ran:3

Win Prizemoney £0 *Total Prizemoney* £2,471

1999 Turf 0-2: (10f, 12f) (sft, gd)

Scopey, above-average colt. Turf high 77 (1st run) (began Spt) - 3rd of 12 giving 5lb to Horatia (27 Spt Bath 10f gd RF 4583). Sold for 82,000 gns in October to join Noel Meade.

**Mrs A J Perrett [0-5] K Abdulla.*

HOMESTEAD BHB 58f52a RR 67f 52a 4930[6]

5 ch g Indian Ridge 7.6f **(74)** - Bertrade (Homeboy) 6.6f **(55)**

Form - 0254262114135524086

Record 1999 - 1st:3 2nd:4 3rd:1 Ran:18
Pre1999 - 1st:2 2nd:1 3rd:2 Ran:22

Win Prizemoney £13,833 *Total Prizemoney* £19,435

Wins								
*** 1999**	*May*	*Wolver*	*(STD)*	*H*	*9.4f*	*48*	*54*	
*** 1999**	Apr	Leices	(HVY)	H	10f	53	65+	<
*** 1999**	Apr	Pontef	(Sft)	H	10f	50	61	
* 1997	Aug	Bright	(FRM)		8f		57	
* 1997	Aug	Bright	(GD)	H	7f	45	51	

1999 Turf 2-11: (8f, 9f, 10f 2-9) (sft 2-2, g-s, gd 2, g-f 2, frm 4) 1999 AW 1-7: (7f, 8f 3, 9f 1-2, 10f) (Equi 4, Fibr 1-3)

Average gelding, effective 10f, acts on sft to frm, best on frm, has worn blinkers, excels at Sandown. Turf high 67 - 2nd of 13 giving 28lb to Dark Age (28 Jly Epsom 10f frm RF 3201) - also 1st of 15 giving 9lb to Cross Talk (24 Apr Leicester RF 0830). AW high 56.

**R Hannon [5-40] G H Shoemark.*

HONEST BORDERER BHB 77f RR 79f 4874[6]

4 b g Selkirk (USA) 7.9f **(76)** - Tell No Lies (High Line) 10.3f **(70)**

Form - 358036

Record 1999 - 1st:0 2nd:0 3rd:2 Ran:6
Pre1999 - 1st:1 2nd:1 3rd:1 Ran:8

Win Prizemoney £6,060 *Total Prizemoney* £10,243

Wins								
* 1998	Aug	Ripon	(G-F)	H	9f	78	81	<

1999 Turf 0-6: (8f 3, 10f 3) (gd, g-f 2, frm 3)

Leggy, above-average gelding, effective 8 to 10f, best at 10f, acts on g-s to frm, has worn blinkers, likes tight tracks. Turf high 83 (1st run) - 3rd of 13 giving 19lb to Mutadarra (11 Jun Sandown 10f frm RF 1922). **J L Dunlop [1-14] Mrs A Johnstone.*

HONEST VILLAIN (USA) BHB 68f RR 64f 1560[8]

2 b c St Jovite (USA) 11.8f **(75)** - Villandry (USA) (Lyphard's Wish (FR)) 9f **(74)**

Form - 378

Record 1999 - 1st:0 2nd:0 3rd:1 Ran:3

Win Prizemoney £0 *Total Prizemoney* £499

1999 Turf 0-3: (5f, 6f 2) (gd, frm 2)

Currently average colt. Turf high 64. **P D Evans [0-3] Colin Booth.*

HONESTY FAIR BHB 72f RR 85f 4895[8]

2 b f Reprimand 8.2f **(63)** - Truthful Image **(68df 70a)** (Reesh)

Form - 3688

Record 1999 - 1st:0 2nd:0 3rd:1 Ran:4

Win Prizemoney £0 *Total Prizemoney* £860

1999 Turf 0-4: (5f 2, 6f 2) (gd, g-f, frm 2)

Useful filly. Turf high 85 (began Aug).

**J A Glover [0-4] P and S Partnership.*

HONEY DANCE (FR) RR 2749[8]

4 b f Fabulous Dancer (USA) 10.6f **(81)** - Honey River (GER) (River River (FR))

Form - 8

Record 1999 - 1st:0 2nd:0 3rd:0 Ran:1

1999 Turf 0-1: (8f) (hrd)

Formerly very poor filly, always wears blinkers.

**M C Pipe [0-6] Martin Pipe Racing Club.*

HONEY GUEST (IRE) BHB 35f RR 33f 4453[11]

3 ch f Roi Danzig (USA) 10.5f **(62)** - Kuwah (IRE) (Be My Guest (USA)) 9.3f **(67)**

Form - 0070

Record 1999 - 1st:0 2nd:0 3rd:0 Ran:4

1999 Turf 0-4: (8f 2, 10f 2) (sft, g-f 2, hrd)
Workmanlike, very moderate filly, has worn blinkers. Turf high 33. **G G Margarson [0-4] John Guest.*

HONEY HOUSE (IRE) RR 5f 5198[15]
3 gr f Paris House 5.9f **(64)** - Heather Honey (Insan (USA))
Form - 0
Record 1999 - 1st:0 2nd:0 3rd:0 Ran:1
1999 Turf 0-1: (8f) (gd)
Neat, currently very poor filly. **A W Carroll [0-1] R T C Racing.*

HONG KONG BHB 47f RR 51f 4169[2]
2 b g Sri Pekan (USA) - Sheryl Lynn (Miller's Mate) 7f **(63)**
Form - 400002
Record 1999 - 1st:0 2nd:1 3rd:0 Ran:6
Win Prizemoney £0 *Total Prizemoney* £811
1999 Turf 0-6: (5f 3, 7f 2, 8f) (gd, g-f, frm 3, hrd)
Fair gelding, effective 8f, acts on frm, has worn blinkers. Turf high 55 (began Jly). **M W Easterby [0-6] Guy Reed.*

HONOURABLE CHIEF RR 54f 4560[9]
2 b c Be My Chief (USA) 10.2f **(62)** - Magic Orb **(69f)** (Primo Dominie) 6.2f **(80)**
Form - 0
Record 1999 - 1st:0 2nd:0 3rd:0 Ran:1
1999 Turf 0-1: (6f) (gd)
Currently fair colt. **K Mahdi [0-1] Kamil Mahdi.*

HOPEFUL LIGHT RR 81+f 5207[1]
2 b c Warning 8.1f **(77)** - Hope (IRE) (Dancing Brave (USA)) 8.4f **(76)**
Form - 1
Record 1999 - 1st:1 2nd:0 3rd:0 Ran:1
Win Prizemoney £3,338 *Total Prizemoney* £3,338
Wins * **1999** Nov Doncas (SFT) 7f 81+ <
1999 Turf 1-1: (7f 1-1) (g-s 1-1)
Currently decent colt. (1st run) - 1st of 20 giving 5lb to Love Divine (5 Nov Doncaster RF 5207). Convincing winner of a back-end maiden. **J H M Gosden [1-1] K Abdulla.*

HOPEFUL STAR (IRE) BHB 32f44a RR 34f 44a 4075[6]
4 ch g Pips Pride 6.7f **(70)** - Mijouter (IRE) (Coquelin (USA)) 8.4f **(58)**
Form - 078060066
Record 1999 - 1st:0 2nd:0 3rd:0 Ran:9
Pre1999 - 1st:1 2nd:0 3rd:2 Ran:14
Win Prizemoney £3,460 *Total Prizemoney* £4,390
Wins 1998 *Apr Lingfi (STD) 6f 59* <
1999 Turf 0-8: (5f, 6f 3, 7f 3, 8f) (gd, g-f, frm 5, hrd) 1999 AW 0-1: (7f) (Fibr)
Workmanlike, very moderate gelding, effective 6f, - acts on Equi, has worn blinkers. Turf high 39.
**J R Poulton [0-5] The Hopeful Millionaires (from Miss Gay Kelleway [1-18] May 1999).*

HOPE SPRINGS BHB 48f RR 53f 4877[18]
2 b f Makbul - Sorcha (IRE) (Shernazar) 10.2f **(73)**
Form - 6780
Record 1999 - 1st:0 2nd:0 3rd:0 Ran:4
1999 Turf 0-3: (5f, 7f 2) (gd, g-f, frm) 1999 AW 0-1: (8f) (Fibr)
Fair filly. Turf high 53 (began Jly). **R Hollinshead [0-4] J M Ranson.*

HOPPIT BHB 20f RR 40f 269[13]
4 b f Rock Hopper 10.6f **(54)** - Pellinora (USA) (King Pellinore (USA)) 8.2f **(68)**
Form - 07000
Record 1999 - 1st:0 2nd:0 3rd:0 Ran:4
Pre1999 - 1st:0 2nd:0 3rd:0 Ran:7
1999 AW 0-4: (11f, 12f, 13f, 16f) (Equi 3, Fibr)
Scopey, moderate filly. **P Howling [0-11] P A & M J Reditt.*

HORATIA (IRE) BHB 104f RR 97f 4871[2]
3 b f Machiavellian (USA) 9.8f **(83)** - Ahead (Shirley Heights) 10.3f **(74)**
Form - 32212
Record 1999 - 1st:1 2nd:3 3rd:1 Ran:5
Win Prizemoney £3,460 *Total Prizemoney* £12,484
Wins * **1999** Spt Bath (G-S) 10.2f 76+ <
1999 Turf 1-5: (9f, 10f 1-4) (gd 1-3, frm 2)
Scopey, very useful filly. Turf high 97 - 2nd of 13 to Khibrah (14 Oct Newmarket 10f gd RF 4871). She improved markedly when finishing second in a Listed race at Newmarket in October and promptly went up a stone in the weights. Likely to stay a mile and a half, she is open to further improvement. **L M Cumani [1-5] Gerald Leigh.*

HORMUZ (IRE) BHB 82f80a RR 68f 80a 4954[15]
3 b g Hamas (IRE) 8f **(72)** - Balqis (USA) (Advocator) 10.9f **(80)**
Form - 512100121850
Record 1999 - 1st:4 2nd:2 3rd:0 Ran:11
Pre1999 - 1st:0 2nd:0 3rd:0 Ran:1
Win Prizemoney £15,679 *Total Prizemoney* £18,747
Wins * **1999** Jly Beverl (SFT) H 8.5f 81 86 <
* **1999** Jun Ripon (G-F) 10f 79
* **1999** *Mar Lingfi (STD) H 10f 78 84*
* **1999** *Jan Lingfi (STD) 10f 72*
1999 Turf 2-8: (8f 1-2, 10f 1-5, 11f) (gd 1-2, g-f 2, frm 3, hrd 1-1) 1999 AW 2-3: (10f 2-3) (Equi 2-3)
Rangy, decent gelding, effective 8 to 10f, best at 10f, acts on gd to hrd - acts on Equi, prefers tight tracks, excels at Lingfield. Turf high 86 - 1st of 7 getting 3lb from Nabonassar (3 Jly Beverley RF 2513) - also 1st of 3 from Ledham (17 Jun Ripon RF 2081). AW high 84 - 1st of 4 giving 4lb to Oo Ee Be (4 Mar Lingfield RF 0404). A winter hat-trick on the All-Weather at Lingfield over ten furlongs in the spring was followed by a couple of moderate turf efforts, but he has shown rather better form since then, winning a three-horse event at Ripon and a soft-ground Beverley classified stakes under a fine tactical ride. **M Johnston [4-12] Brian Yeardley Continental Ltd.*

HORNBEAM RR 88f 5141[5]
5 b h Rich Charlie 5.9f **(50)** - Thinkluckybelucky (Maystreak) 8.7f **(53)**
Form - 0005747585
Record 1999 - 1st:0 2nd:0 3rd:0 Ran:10
Pre1999 - 1st:2 2nd:0 3rd:2 Ran:12
Win Prizemoney £14,992 *Total Prizemoney* £29,505
Wins * 1998 Mar Doncas (GD) L 8f 107 <
* 1997 May Newbur (SFT) 7.3f 86
1999 Turf 0-10: (7f, 8f 8, 9f) (sft, gd 7, g-f, frm)
Useful colt, effective 8f, acts on gd, likes left handed tracks. Turf high 96. He acts well on easy ground, but is frustrating and difficult to win with. **J R Jenkins [2-22] K C Payne.*

HORTA (IRE) BHB 63f RR 67f 4589[7]
2 b c Distinctly North (USA) 7.4f **(63)** - Roouan Girl (IRE) (Tremblant)
Form - 86767
Record 1999 - 1st:0 2nd:0 3rd:0 Ran:5
1999 Turf 0-5: (5f, 6f 2, 7f, 8f) (gd 2, frm 3)
Average colt. Turf high 67. **G C Bravery [0-5] The TT Partnership.*

HORTON DANCER RR 48f 2001[4]
2 b g Rambo Dancer (CAN) 8.4f **(59)** - Horton Lady **(43+f)** (Midyan (USA)) 6f **(60)**
Form - 4
Record 1999 - 1st:0 2nd:0 3rd:0 Ran:1
Win Prizemoney £0 *Total Prizemoney* £171
1999 Turf 0-1: (7f) (frm)
Currently moderate gelding. **M Brittain [0-1] Mick Burrowes.*

HORTON LIGHTS BHB 47f RR 43f 2392[11]
3 b g Clantime 6.6f **(57)** - Blue Rhythm (Blue Cashmere) 6.4f **(54)**
Form - 00
Record 1999 - 1st:0 2nd:0 3rd:0 Ran:2
Pre1999 - 1st:0 2nd:0 3rd:0 Ran:2
1999 Turf 0-2: (5f, 6f) (gd, g-f)
Small, moderate gelding. Turf high 43. **Mrs A Swinbank [0-4] Eddie Shotton.*

HOTELIERS PRIDE RR 55f 5208[14]
2 b g Lugana Beach 7f **(63)** - Pride of Britain (CAN) **(64f 53a)** (Linkage (USA)) 9.1f **(82)**
Form - 00
Record 1999 - 1st:0 2nd:0 3rd:0 Ran:2
1999 Turf 0-2: (6f, 7f) (g-s, g-f)
Currently fair gelding. Turf high 55 (began Oct). **L G Cottrell [0-2] Pride of Britain Ltd.*

HOT ICE (IRE) BHB 55f **RR 54f** 4543[10]
2 b f Petardia 8.2f **(58)** - Blackpool Belle (The Brianstan) 5.9f **(55)**
Form - 000310
Record 1999 - 1st:1 2nd:0 3rd:1 Ran:6
Win Prizemoney £4,260 *Total Prizemoney* £4,772
Wins * 1999 Spt Mussel (G-F) H 5f 53 52 <
1999 Turf 1-6: (5f 1-6) (gd, g-f, frm 1-4)
Fair filly, effective 5f, acts on frm. Turf high 52 - 1st of 10 getting 20lb from Garth Pool (13 Spt Musselburgh RF 4280).
**H Morrison [1-6] Sheran Macdonald-Buchanan & Partners.*

HOT LEGS BHB 39f48a **RR 43f 48a** 4285[17]
3 b f Sizzling Melody 6.3f **(49)** - Ra Ra Girl (Shack (USA)) 5.8f **(53)**
Form - 00006060
Record 1999 - 1st:0 2nd:0 3rd:0 Ran:7
Pre1999 - 1st:0 2nd:0 3rd:0 Ran:3
1999 Turf 0-6: (5f 3, 6f 3) (g-s, gd 3, frm 2) 1999 AW 0-1: (6f) (Fibr)
Scopey, moderate filly. Turf high 43. **B A McMahon [0-10] D J Allen.*

HOT PASSION BHB 33f **RR 30df** 3158[14]
3 b g Keen 11.1f **(58)** - Love You Madly (IRE) (Bob Back (USA))
Form - 00
Record 1999 - 1st:0 2nd:0 3rd:0 Ran:2
Pre1999 - 1st:0 2nd:0 3rd:0 Ran:3
1999 Turf 0-2: (10f, 12f) (frm, hrd)
Very moderate gelding, has worn blinkers. (began Jly).
**M L W Bell [0-5] Frank Farrant.*

HOT POTATO BHB 45a **RR 18f** 5135[13]
3 b c Roman Warrior -My Song of Songs **(7f)** (Norwick (USA)) 7.2f **(56)**
Form - 86556000
Record 1999 - 1st:0 2nd:0 3rd:0 Ran:6
Pre1999 - 1st:0 2nd:0 3rd:0 Ran:5
Win Prizemoney £0 *Total Prizemoney* £155
1999 Turf 0-3: (5f, 6f, 8f) (sft, gd, g-f) 1999 AW 0-3: (6f 2, 7f) (Fibr 3)
Moderate colt, effective 6f, - acts on Fibr, has worn blinkers. Turf high 18. AW high 46. Becoming disappointing.
**J S Wainwright [0-3] Mrs S A Donald (from C Smith [0-8] Jan 1999).*

HOT TIN ROOF (IRE) BHB 100f **RR 101f** 4239[11]
3 b f Thatching 7.8f **(69)** - No Reservations (IRE) (Commanche Run) 8.5f **(58)**
Form - 31230
Record 1999 - 1st:1 2nd:1 3rd:2 Ran:5
Win Prizemoney £3,631 *Total Prizemoney* £9,190
Wins * 1999 Jun Newcas (GD) 6f 74+ <
1999 Turf 1-5: (6f 1-2, 7f 3) (gd, g-f 2, frm 1-2)
Unfurnished, very useful filly. Turf high 101 - 3rd of 7 to Wannabe Grand (22 Aug Pontefract 6f frm RF 3846). Unraced at two, she made great strides in a short space of time, putting up a creditable effort when finishing third behind Wannabe Grand and Pipalong in a Listed heat at Pontefract in August. Running on strongly there, she is out of a Commanche Run mare and should stay a mile.
**J E Banks [1-5] Giles Pritchard-Gordon.*

HOUDINI'S HONEY (USA) BHB 84f **RR 78f** 4019[7]
3 ch f Mr Prospector (USA) 8.6f **(88)** - Coup de Folie (USA) (Halo (USA)) 10.6f **(75)**
Form - 4217
Record 1999 - 1st:1 2nd:1 3rd:0 Ran:4
Pre1999 - 1st:0 2nd:0 3rd:0 Ran:1
Win Prizemoney £4,130 *Total Prizemoney* £5,585
Wins * 1999 Aug Windso (G-F) 10f 78 <
1999 Turf 1-4: (7f, 9f, 10f 1-2) (g-f, frm 1-3)
Leggy, above-average filly. Turf high 78 - 1st of 14 from Aegean Dream (2 Aug Windsor RF 3304).
**Sir Michael Stoute [1-5] Niarchos Family.*

HOUGOUMONT RR 47f 1683[6]
3 b g Formidable (USA) 7.8f **(60)** - Sure Victory (IRE) (Stalker)
Form - 026
Record 1999 - 1st:0 2nd:1 3rd:0 Ran:3
Pre1999 - 1st:0 2nd:1 3rd:0 Ran:1
1999 Turf 0-3: (8f 2, 11f) (g-s, g-f, frm)
Moderate gelding. Turf high 47. **P T Walwyn [0-4] P T Walwyn.*

HOUNDS OF LOVE (IRE) RR 30f 5207[10]
2 b f Foxhound (USA) - Foolish Lady (USA) (Foolish Pleasure (USA)) 8.9f **(72)**
Form - 0
Record 1999 - 1st:0 2nd:0 3rd:0 Ran:1
1999 Turf 0-1: (7f) (g-s)
Currently very moderate filly. **R Guest [0-1] A P Davies & Partners.*

HOUND VENTURE BHB 60f60a **RR 60f 60a** 4712[4]
3 ch g Wolfhound (USA) 7.3f **(71)** - Relatively Sharp (Sharpen Up) 8.3f **(67)**
Form - 003021365214
Record 1999 - 1st:2 2nd:2 3rd:2 Ran:12
Pre1999 - 1st:0 2nd:0 3rd:1 Ran:3
Win Prizemoney £4,820 *Total Prizemoney* £7,793
Wins * 1999 Spt Bright (G-F) 7f 58 <
*** 1999** Jun Yarmou (GD) S 7f 53
1999 Turf 2-11: (7f 2-8, 8f 2, 9f) (g-s, gd 1-3, g-f 3, frm 1-2, hrd 2) 1999 AW 0-1: (7f) (Equi)
Small, average gelding. Turf high 60. Consistent.
**S P C Woods [2-15] Dr Frank Chao.*

HOUSEMASTER (IRE) BHB 117f **RR 121df** 2940[2]
3 b c Rudimentary (USA) 8.2f **(66)** - Glenarff (USA) (Irish River (FR)) 8.6f **(78)**
Form - 34462
Record 1999 - 1st:0 2nd:1 3rd:1 Ran:5
Pre1999 - 1st:1 2nd:0 3rd:1 Ran:5
Win Prizemoney £3,130 *Total Prizemoney* £81,043
Wins * 1998 Jun Yarmou (G-F) 6f 80 <
1999 Turf 0-5: (9f, 10f, 12f 3) (g-s, gd, g-f 3)
Scopey, very high-class colt, effective 12f, acts on gd. Turf high 121 - 4th of 16 to Oath (5 Jun Epsom 12f gd RF 1760). Ran his best race in 1998 when third in the Racing Post Trophy, staying on in the testing ground. He was unfortunately disqualified after 'winning' the Chester Vase on his second start of 1999, and confirmed himself a high-class colt when fourth in the Derby. However, he failed to boost the form when well beaten in the King Edward VII Stakes at Ascot, and finishing runner-up in a Group Three at Ayr. He was subsequently reported to have been sold to race in Hong Kong. **M L W Bell [1-10] Highclere Thoroughbred Racing Ltd.*

HOUSE OF DREAMS BHB 53f **RR 56f** 4913[4]
7 b g Darshaan 11.9f **(81)** -Helens Dreamgirl (Caerleon (USA)) 8.6f **(71)**
Form - 5006624
Record 1999 - 1st:0 2nd:1 3rd:0 Ran:7
Pre1999 - 1st:3 2nd:1 3rd:3 Ran:19
Win Prizemoney £13,855 *Total Prizemoney* £19,213
Wins * 1998 Spt Thirsk (GD) H 12f 62 65 <
* 1998 Jly Carlis (G-F) H 14.1f 59 63
* 1998 Jun Catter (G-S) H 12f 54 56
1999 Turf 0-7: (12f 5, 14f 2) (gd 3, g-f 2, frm, hrd)
Fair gelding, effective 12 to 14f, best at 12f, acts on gd to frm, best on frm, favours tight tracks. Turf high 56. Consistent.
**G M Moore [7-42] J & M Leisure / Unos Restaurant (from B W Hills [0-5] Oct 1995).*

HOUT BAY BHB 70f **RR 74f** 4249[17]
2 ch c Komaite (USA) 6.9f **(61)** - Maiden Pool (Sharpen Up) 8.3f **(67)**
Form - 6440
Record 1999 - 1st:0 2nd:0 3rd:0 Ran:4
Win Prizemoney £0 *Total Prizemoney* £454
1999 Turf 0-4: (5f 2, 6f 2) (gd, g-f, frm 2)
Above-average colt. Turf high 74 - 4th of 10 to Nicholas Dudley (26 Jly Ayr 6f gd RF 3134). **S E Kettlewell [0-4] Hout's Partnership.*

HOWABOYS QUEST (USA) BHB 65f **RR 58f** 4634[12]
2 b g Quest for Fame 12.8f **(75)** - Doctor Black (USA) (Family Doctor (USA))
Form - 440
Record 1999 - 1st:0 2nd:0 3rd:0 Ran:3
Win Prizemoney £0 *Total Prizemoney* £523
1999 Turf 0-3: (6f, 7f, 8f) (gd, frm 2)
Currently fair gelding. Turf high 58 (began Aug). **F Murphy [0-3] Winlow Brothers.*

HOWARD'S LAD (IRE) RR 83f 5034[10]
2 b c Reprimand 8.2f **(63)** - Port Isaac (USA) (Seattle Song (USA)) 9f **(77)**
Form - 713400
Record 1999 - 1st:1 2nd:0 3rd:1 Ran:6
Win Prizemoney £3,610 *Total Prizemoney* £4,738
Wins 1999 Jly Ayr (GD) 6f 73 <
1999 Turf 1-6: (6f 1-5, 7f) (g-s, gd 1-2, g-f 2, frm)
Decent colt, effective 6f, acts on gd to g-f, has worn blinkers. Turf high 83 - 3rd of 7 giving 1lb to Smart Ridge (31 Jly Hamilton 6f g-f RF 3268). Decent efforts in nurseries after a 50/1 Ayr victory.
**I Semple [0-2] Gordon McDowall (from Miss L A Perratt [1-4] Aug 1999).*

HOW HIGH BHB 35f **RR 8f** 5151[16]
4 b g Puissance 7.1f **(60)** - Lucky Starkist (Lucky Wednesday) 8f **(50)**
Form - 00
Record 1999 - 1st:0 2nd:0 3rd:0 Ran:2
Pre1999 - 1st:0 2nd:0 3rd:1 Ran:3
Win Prizemoney £0 *Total Prizemoney* £327
1999 Turf 0-2: (8f, 10f) (gd, frm)
Workmanlike, very poor gelding, has worn blinkers. Turf high 8 (began Jly).
**J Neville [0-3] James Bradley (from R Simpson [0-2] Jly 1998).*

HOWQUA RIVER BHB 30f48a **RR 29f 48a** 3576[11]
7 b g Petong 7.6f **(58)** - Deep Blue Sea (Gulf Pearl) 12f **(54)**
Form - 000
Record 1999 - 1st:0 2nd:0 3rd:0 Ran:3
Pre1999 - 1st:1 2nd:1 3rd:2 Ran:19
Win Prizemoney £2,856 *Total Prizemoney* £4,771
Wins 1996 Oct Pontef (GD) H 12f 43 48 <
1999 Turf 0-3: (12f 2, 14f) (g-f 2, frm)
Moderate gelding, has worn blinkers. Turf high 29. Becoming disappointing.
**J S King [0-3] Mrs Jane Chapple-Hyam (from P W Chapple-Hyam [1-22] Nov 1996).*

HOXTON SQUARE (IRE) BHB 70f **RR 66f** 4033[3]
2 ch f Case Law 6f **(64)** - Guv's Joy (IRE) (Thatching) 8f **(66)**
Form - 0223
Record 1999 - 1st:0 2nd:2 3rd:1 Ran:4
Win Prizemoney £0 *Total Prizemoney* £1,757
1999 Turf 0-3: (5f 2, 7f) (gd 2, frm) 1999 AW 0-1: (5f) (Fibr)
Above-average filly. Turf high 66 - 2nd of 15 getting 5lb from Shaw Venture (19 Jly Windsor 5f frm RF 2950). (1st run) - 2nd of 9 getting 2lb from Blue Velvet (17 Jun Southwell 5f Fibr RF 2084).
**N P Littmoden [0-4] Elliott Slone Ltd.*

HUG ME ROB BHB 34f **RR 43f** 4837[15]
3 b f Robellino (USA) 9.5f **(68)** - Hug Me (Shareef Dancer (USA)) 9.9f **(73)**
Form - 04600
Record 1999 - 1st:0 2nd:0 3rd:0 Ran:5
Win Prizemoney £0 *Total Prizemoney* £196
1999 Turf 0-5: (10f 3, 11f, 12f) (sft, gd, g-f 2, frm)
Workmanlike, moderate filly. Turf high 43.
**W R Muir [0-5] C L A Edginton.*

HUGWITY BHB 73f86a **RR 80f 86a** 197[1]
7 ch g Cadeaux Genereux 7.9f **(76)** - Nuit D'Ete (USA) (Super Concorde (USA)) 10.9f **(66)**
Form - 0645411221
Record 1999 - 1st:1 2nd:2 3rd:0 Ran:3
Pre1999 - 1st:6 2nd:3 3rd:0 Ran:27
Win Prizemoney £36,675 *Total Prizemoney* £42,179
Wins * 1999 *Jan Lingfi (STD) H 7f 79 83* <
* 1998 *Dec Lingfi (STD) H 8f 67 74*
* 1998 *Dec Southw (STD) C 8f 66*
* 1998 Jly Yarmou (GD) H 8f 75 80
1996 May Goodwo (GD) H 8f 79 83 <
1996 May Cheste (GD) H 10.3f 75 80
1996 Apr Leices (GD) 10f 73
1999 AW 1-3: (7f 1-1, 8f 2) (Equi 1-2, Fibr)
Decent gelding, effective 7 to 8f, best at 8f, acts on gd to frm - acts on AW, likes left handed tracks, likes tight tracks. AW high 83 - 1st of 7 giving 5lb to Shades of Love (30 Jan Lingfield RF 0197).
**G C Bravery [4-22] Michael Whatley (from B Hanbury [3-8] Jun 1996).*

HULA ANGEL (USA) BHB 112f **RR 110f** 2631[7]
3 b f Woodman (USA) 9.7f **(77)** - Jode (USA) (Danzig (USA)) 8.4f **(76)**
Form - 6187
Record 1999 - 1st:1 2nd:0 3rd:0 Ran:4
Pre1999 - 1st:2 2nd:0 3rd:2 Ran:6
Win Prizemoney £139,247 *Total Prizemoney* £143,964
Wins * 1999 May Currag (GD) G1 8f 110 <
* 1998 Oct Newmar (GD) G2 7f 106
* 1998 Aug Kempto (G-F) 7f 87
1999 Turf 1-4: (8f 1-4) (g-f 1-2, frm 2)
Workmanlike, Group-class filly, effective 7 to 8f, best at 8f, acts on gd to frm. Turf high 110 - 1st of 17 from Golden Silca (23 May Curragh RF 1485a). A Group 3 winner at two, she ran the race of her life when landing the Irish 1,000 Guineas in a tight finish with Golden Silca. That gallant effort may have had a lasting effect, as she showed little on her two subsequent starts and has been retired to stud.
**B W Hills [3-10] J R Fleming.*

HULLBANK BHB 66f60a **RR 67f 60a** 2455[5]
9 b g Uncle Pokey 10f **(43)** - Dubavarna (Dubassoff (USA)) 14.2f **(55)**
Form - 61255
Record 1999 - 1st:1 2nd:1 3rd:0 Ran:5
Pre1999 - 1st:5 2nd:8 3rd:5 Ran:31
Win Prizemoney £20,103 *Total Prizemoney* £33,439
Wins * 1999 May Redcar (FRM) H 14.1f 65 67
1998 Jly Redcar (G-F) H 16f 68 71 <
1998 *Jly Southw (STD) H 14f 55 58*
* 1997 Jun Beverl (G-F) H 16.2f 63 68
* 1996 Jly Beverl (G-F) H 16.2f 55 60
* 1995 Jun Redcar (FRM) 14.1f 68
1999 Turf 1-4: (14f 1-2, 16f 2) (gd, g-f, frm 1-2)1999 AW 0-1: (14f) (Fibr)
Average gelding, effective 14 to 16f, best at 16f, acts on gd to hrd, has worn blinkers, favours left handed tracks, likes tight tracks, excels at Catterick, does well at Redcar. Turf high 67 - 5th of 12 giving 22lb to Whitley Grange Boy (1 Jly Catterick 16f g-f RF 2455) - also 1st of 9 from Bersaglio (31 May Redcar RF 1610). Inconsistent.
**W W Haigh [5-32] Mrs V Haigh (from J M Jefferson [0-3] Oct 1998).*

HUNTERS TWEED BHB 72f **RR 71f** 4345[5]
3 ch c Nashwan (USA) 10.3f **(79)** - Zorette (USA) **(60f)** (Zilzal (USA))
Form - 0431575
Record 1999 - 1st:1 2nd:0 3rd:1 Ran:7
Pre1999 - 1st:0 2nd:0 3rd:0 Ran:1
Win Prizemoney £4,123 *Total Prizemoney* £5,283
Wins * 1999 Jly Doncas (G-F) 12f 74+ <
1999 Turf 1-7: (10f, 12f 1-3, 14f 2, 15f) (g-s, gd 3, g-f 1-2, frm)
Rangy, above-average colt, effective 12f, acts on gd to g-f. Turf high 74 - 1st of 6 from Bellefonte (15 Jly Doncaster RF 2844).
**J D Bethell [1-8] Robert Gibbons.*

HUNTERS WISH RR 14f 4580[14]
2 ch f Wolfhound (USA) 7.3f **(71)** - Pravolo (Fools Holme (USA))
Form - 0
Record 1999 - 1st:0 2nd:0 3rd:0 Ran:1
1999 Turf 0-1: (6f) (gd)
Currently poor filly. **I A Balding [0-1] Park House Partnership.*

HUNTING GROUND BHB 20f25a **RR 29f 25a** 4089[5]
11 b g Dancing Brave (USA) 10.4f **(78)** - Ack's Secret (USA) (Ack Ack (USA)) 12.7f **(82)**
Form - 8305
Record 1999 - 1st:0 2nd:0 3rd:1 Ran:4
Pre1999 - 1st:5 2nd:4 3rd:0 Ran:36
Win Prizemoney £15,481 *Total Prizemoney* £19,003
1999 Turf 0-4: (16f 3, 17f) (g-f, frm 2, hrd)
Little account gelding, effective 16f, acts on g-f to frm, often wears blinkers, prefers left handed tracks. Turf high 29 - 3rd of 9 getting 6lb from Alhesn (26 Jly Yarmouth 16f frm RF 3152). Inconsistent.
**M Mullineaux [0-10] Esprit de Corps Racing (from B P J Baugh [0-4] Jun 1997).*

HUNTING LION (IRE) BHB 100f **RR 99f** 4244a[3]
2 b c Piccolo - Jalopy (Jalmood (USA)) 10.1f **(52)**

Form - 4123
Record 1999 - 1st:1 2nd:1 3rd:1 Ran:4
Win Prizemoney £3,533 *Total Prizemoney* £20,091
Wins * **1999** Jly Bath (G-F) 5.7f 76 <
1999 Turf 1-4: (5f, 6f 1-3) (gd, g-f, frm, hrd 1-1)
Very useful colt. Turf high 99. He ran a fine race to finish second in the Richmond Stakes, but did not perform with the same zest when beaten at Baden-Baden on his final start. Open to improvement, he may struggle to win a Group race at home.
**M R Channon [1-4].*

HUNTING TIGER BHB 88f **RR 86f** 4872[2]

2 ch c Pursuit of Love 9.5f **(69)** - Pernilla (IRE) (Tate Gallery (USA)) 7.4f **(67)**
Form - 50152
Record 1999 - 1st:1 2nd:1 3rd:0 Ran:5
Win Prizemoney £3,902 *Total Prizemoney* £6,098
Wins * **1999** Spt Haydoc (G-F) 7.1f 76 <
1999 Turf 1-5: (6f, 7f 1-3, 8f) (gd 2, g-f, frm 1-2)
Useful colt. Turf high 86 (began Aug) - 2nd of 17 to Russian Fox (14 Oct Newmarket 6f gd RF 4872). Made all the running to win a Haydock maiden on his third start having bolted on his previous outing. He had a hard race there and similar tactics did not pay off in a competitive Newbury nursery next time.
**M R Channon [1-5] Jaber Abdullah.*

HURGILL DANCER BHB 39f39a **RR 42f 39a** 910[4]

5 b g Rambo Dancer (CAN) 8.4f **(59)** - Try Vickers (USA) (Fuzzbuster (USA)) 6.3f **(63)**
Form - 77651504
Record 1999 - 1st:1 2nd:0 3rd:0 Ran:6
Pre1999 - 1st:1 2nd:1 3rd:3 Ran:18
Win Prizemoney £5,517 *Total Prizemoney* £8,440
Wins * **1999** *Feb Lingfi (STD) H 12f 36 43*
1997 Apr Ripon (G-F) H 12.3f 65 68 <
1999 Turf 0-2: (11f, 12f) (gd, frm) 1999 AW 1-4: (10f, 12f 1-2, 16f) (Equi 1-4)
Moderate gelding.
**R J O'Sullivan [1-10] D G & D J Robinson (from J A R Toller [0-4] Aug 1998).*

HURGILL LADY BHB 45f38a **RR 41f 38a** 194[4]

5 ch m Emarati (USA) 6.6f **(63)** - Gitee (FR) (Carwhite) 7.2f **(61)**
Form - 664
Record 1999 - 1st:0 2nd:0 3rd:0 Ran:3
Pre1999 - 1st:0 2nd:5 3rd:0 Ran:14
Win Prizemoney £0 *Total Prizemoney* £3,923
1999 AW 0-3: (5f 2, 6f) (Equi, Fibr 2)
Moderate filly, effective 5 to 6f, best at 6f, - acts on Fibr, has worn blinkers, prefers left handed tracks, prefers tight tracks. AW high 35. **D Nicholls [0-11] G A Harker (from J W Watts [0-6] Jun 1997).*

HURRICANE LOUIS (IRE) **RR 91f** 3227a[8]

3 br c Fabulous Dancer (USA) 10.6f **(81)** - Lobmille (Mill Reef (USA)) 10.5f **(78)**
Form - 1418
Record 1999 - 1st:2 2nd:0 3rd:0 Ran:4
Win Prizemoney £12,758 *Total Prizemoney* £13,010
Wins * **1999** Jun San Si (GD) 8f 91 <
* **1999** Mar San Si (HVY) 7.5f
1999 Turf 2-4: (8f 2-3, 10f) (hvy 1-1, gd 1-2, g-f)
Useful colt. Turf high 91 - 1st of 5 giving 7lb to Tesiano (4 Jun San Siro RF 1898a). **J Noseda [2-4].*

HURRICANE STORM **RR 57f** 4645[6]

2 b g Runnett 6.7f **(56)** - Polar Storm (IRE) **(69f)** (Law Society (USA)) 9.9f **(70)**
Form - 06
Record 1999 - 1st:0 2nd:0 3rd:0 Ran:2
1999 Turf 0-2: (7f 2) (g-s, gd)
Currently fair gelding. Turf high 57 (began Spt).
**B J Meehan [0-2] Miss Howard Evans.*

HURTLE **RR 17f** 791[7]

2 ch f Prince Sabo 6.6f **(64)** - Hurricane Dancer (IRE) **(57f)** (Nabeel Dancer (USA))
Form - 607
Record 1999 - 1st:0 2nd:0 3rd:0 Ran:3
1999 Turf 0-3: (5f 3) (sft, gd, g-f)
Currently poor filly. Turf high 17. **Martyn Wane [0-3] Mrs H Wane.*

HUSH **RR** 1260[20]

4 b f Barrys Gamble 7f **(50)** - Keep Mum (Mummy's Pet) 7.7f **(60)**
Form - 0
Record 1999 - 1st:0 2nd:0 3rd:0 Ran:1
Pre1999 - 1st:0 2nd:0 3rd:0 Ran:1
1999 Turf 0-1: (8f) (gd)
Leggy, currently very poor filly. **L R Lloyd-James [0-2] P G Yewdall.*

HUSH MONEY BHB 56f **RR 68f** 3986[2]

3 b c Aragon 7.7f **(58)** - Penny Blessing (So Blessed) 8.7f **(67)**
Form - 17041152
Record 1999 - 1st:3 2nd:1 3rd:0 Ran:8
Pre1999 - 1st:0 2nd:0 3rd:0 Ran:4
Win Prizemoney £7,164 *Total Prizemoney* £8,361
Wins * **1999** Aug Carlis (FRM) C 6.9f 56
* **1999** Jly Nottin (FRM) C 8.2f 68 <
* **1999** Apr Thirsk (GD) 7f 59
1999 Turf 3-8: (7f 2-6, 8f 1-2) (gd 1-1, g-f 2, frm 2-5)
Workmanlike, average colt, effective 7 to 8f, best at 7f, acts on gd to frm, best on frm, prefers tight tracks. Turf high 68 - 1st of 9 getting 4lb from Tapage (17 Jly Nottingham RF 2917) - also 1st of 7 giving 3lb to Tamgeed (17 Apr Thirsk RF 0745).
**B W Hills [3-12] Kennet Valley Thoroughbreds III.*

HUTCHIES LADY BHB 23f33a **RR 31f 33a** 3863[17]

7 b m Efisio 7.7f **(69)** - Keep Mum (Mummy's Pet) 7.7f **(60)**
Form - 25400
Record 1999 - 1st:0 2nd:1 3rd:0 Ran:5
Pre1999 - 1st:1 2nd:2 3rd:0 Ran:38
Win Prizemoney £3,595 *Total Prizemoney* £6,994
Wins 1996 May Hamilt (HVY) H 8.3f 30 41 <
1999 Turf 0-5: (10f, 12f 4) (frm 5)
Very moderate mare, effective 10f, acts on frm, has worn blinkers. Turf high 37 (1st run) - 2nd of 11 getting 14lb from Pleasant Dreams (28 Jun Pontefract 10f frm RF 2373).
**M A Peill [0-5] Willie Smith (from R M McKellar [1-45] May 1998).*

HUTOON BHB 79f **RR 78f** 4537[3]

2 b c Mizoram (USA) - Mey Madam (Song) 7.2f **(61)**
Form - 043
Record 1999 - 1st:0 2nd:0 3rd:1 Ran:3
Win Prizemoney £0 *Total Prizemoney* £449
1999 Turf 0-3: (8f 2, 9f) (g-f, frm 2)
Currently above-average colt. Turf high 78 (began Aug) - 4th of 12 to Compton Bolter (9 Spt Chepstow 8f frm RF 4227).
**J W Hills [0-3] Ziad Galadari.*

HUYTON HILL BHB 55f **RR 60f** 3541[4]

2 b c Presidium 7.5f **(56)** - Valerle **(63f)** (Never so Bold) 6.3f **(66)**
Form - 00404
Record 1999 - 1st:0 2nd:0 3rd:0 Ran:5
1999 Turf 0-5: (5f 3, 6f 2) (gd, g-f 3, frm)
Average colt. Turf high 60. **K A Ryan [0-5] Lester Metcalf.*

HYDE PARK (IRE) BHB 60f68a **RR 60f 68a** 5073[16]

5 b h Alzao (USA) 9.8f **(73)** - Park Elect (Ahonoora) 8.1f **(73)**
Form - 250258340033340
Record 1999 - 1st:0 2nd:1 3rd:4 Ran:13
Pre1999 - 1st:4 2nd:3 3rd:0 Ran:15
Win Prizemoney £18,275 *Total Prizemoney* £25,446
Wins 1998 Oct Bright (GD) H 8f 67 70
1998 Aug Cheste (G-S) H 7.6f 60 62
1998 Jly Pontef (G-F) H 8f 55 59
1996 *Nov Lingfi (STD) 5f 71* <
1999 Turf 0-8: (7f 2, 8f 4, 9f 2) (gd 2, g-f 3, frm 3) 1999 AW 0-5: (7f 3, 8f 2) (Equi 4, Fibr)
Above-average colt, effective 7 to 9f, best at 8f, acts on gd to frm - acts on AW, has worn blinkers, prefers left handed tracks, prefers tight tracks. Turf high 68 (1st run) - 4th of 20 giving 8lb to Bintang Timor (1 May Newmarket 7f frm RF 0962). AW high 72 - 3rd of 12 giving 2lb to Prodigal Son (27 Mar Wolverhampton 8f Fibr RF 0493). Inconsistent.
**D Nicholls [0-8] David Nicholls Bloodstock Ltd (from Sir Mark Prescott*

[4-20] Mar 1999).

HYPERACTIVE (IRE) BHB 70f **RR 75f** 4951[1]
3 b c Perugino (USA) - Hyannis (FR) (Esprit du Nord (USA))
Form - 1
Record 1999 - 1st:1 2nd:0 3rd:0 Ran:1
Pre1999 - 1st:0 2nd:1 3rd:0 Ran:3
Win Prizemoney £4,306 *Total Prizemoney* £5,642
Wins * 1999 Oct Yarmou (G-F) 7f 70 <
1999 Turf 1-1: (7f 1-1) (g-f 1-1)
Scopey, above-average colt. (1st run) - 1st of 14 from Royal Artist (19 Oct Yarmouth RF 4951). **A C Stewart [1-4] Racing For Gold.*

HYPERICO (IRE) BHB 40f45a **RR 45f 45a** 3671[6]
5 b g Nordico (USA) 8.2f **(59)** - Hype (USA) (Hyperborean (USA))
Form - 8305467060346
Record 1999 - 1st:0 2nd:0 3rd:2 Ran:12
Pre1999 - 1st:0 2nd:1 3rd:1 Ran:12
Win Prizemoney £0 *Total Prizemoney* £1,640
1999 Turf 0-2: (6f, 8f) (sft, g-f) 1999 AW 0-10: (5f 2, 6f 2, 7f, 8f 2, 9f 2, 11f) (Fibr 10)
Fair gelding, effective 8f, - acts on Fibr, has worn blinkers. AW high 51.
**Miss S J Wilton [0-15] John Pointon and Sons (from G Barnett [0-1] Jly 1998).*

HYPERSONIC BHB 82f **RR 76f** 5163[3]
2 b c Marju (IRE) 9.2f **(76)** - Hi-Li (High Top) 10.2f **(67)**
Form - 5423
Record 1999 - 1st:0 2nd:1 3rd:1 Ran:4
Win Prizemoney £0 *Total Prizemoney* £2,065
1999 Turf 0-4: (6f 2, 7f 2) (g-s 2, frm 2)
Above-average colt. Turf high 76 (began Aug).
**G Wragg [0-4] Katsumi Yoshida.*

HYPNOTIZE BHB 100f **RR 93f** 3995[5]
2 b f Machiavellian (USA) 9.8f **(83)** - Belle et Deluree (USA) (The Minstrel (CAN)) 10f **(72)**
Form - 6115
Record 1999 - 1st:2 2nd:0 3rd:0 Ran:4
Win Prizemoney £15,798 *Total Prizemoney* £15,798
Wins * 1999 Jly Sandow (G-F) L 7.1f 93 <
*** 1999** Jly Yarmou (GD) 7f 85+
1999 Turf 2-4: (6f, 7f 2-3) (gd 1-2, g-f, frm 1-1)
Useful filly. Turf high 93 - 5th of 9 giving 3lb to Icicle (29 Aug Goodwood 7f g-f RF 3995) - also 1st of 5 from Perugia (22 Jly Sandown RF 3029). Improving filly, winner of a listed race at Sandown, she then ran a credible fifth in the Prestige Stakes at Goodwood, where she faded in the final furlongs after attempting to make all. **Sir Michael Stoute [2-4] Cheveley Park Stud.*

HYPOTHESIS (IRE) RR 5074[7]
2 b c Sadler's Wells (USA) 11.3f **(87)** - Surmise (USA) (Alleged (USA)) 10f **(76)**
Form - 7
Record 1999 - 1st:0 2nd:0 3rd:0 Ran:1
1999 Turf 0-1: (7f) (gd)
Currently very poor colt. **A Bailey [0-1] M Tabor.*

I CAN'T REMEMBER BHB 60f54a **RR 64f 54a** 5153[9]
5 br g Petong 7.6f **(58)** - Glenfield Portion (Mummy's Pet) 7.7f **(60)**
Form - 316166515100
Record 1999 - 1st:4 2nd:0 3rd:0 Ran:11
Pre1999 - 1st:5 2nd:4 3rd:1 Ran:42
Win Prizemoney £32,015 *Total Prizemoney* £38,843
Wins * 1999 Aug Nottin (G-F) H 14.1f 58 61
*** 1999** Aug Ripon (G-F) H 12.3f 60 64
*** 1999** Jun Pontef (G-S) H 8f 59 64
1999 May Nottin (FRM) S 10f 53
1998 Jun Cheste (G-S) C 10.3f 59
1996 Oct Doncas (GD) H 8f 77 80 <
1996 Aug Cheste (G-S) H 7f 74 79
1996 Aug Cheste (G-F) H 6.1f 70 67
1996 Jly Catter (G-S) S 5f 46
1999 Turf 4-10: (8f 1-2, 10f 1-4, 12f 1-3, 14f 1-1) (gd 1-3, g-f 2-5, frm 1-1, hrd) 1999 AW 0-1: (16f) (Fibr)
Average gelding, effective 8 to 14f, acts on gd to frm - acts on Equi, has worn blinkers, prefers left handed tracks, prefers tight tracks, excels at Nottingham. Turf high 64 - 1st of 14 getting 2lb from Lynton Lad (7 Jun Pontefract RF 1790) - also 1st of 9 getting 5lb from Premier Project (2 Aug Ripon RF 3296).
**S R Bowring [3-10] Roland Wheatley (from M C Pipe [1-5] May 1999).*

ICE BHB 90f **RR 80f** 4393[19]
3 b c Polar Falcon (USA) 9f **(74)** - Sarabah (IRE) (Ela-Mana-Mou) 10.1f **(70)**
Form - 411800040
Record 1999 - 1st:2 2nd:0 3rd:0 Ran:9
Pre1999 - 1st:3 2nd:2 3rd:1 Ran:7
Win Prizemoney £34,009 *Total Prizemoney* £37,951
Wins * 1999 May York (SFT) H 7.9f 92 98 <
*** 1999** Apr Dielsd (HVY) L 8f 95
* 1998 Oct York (GD) H 7.9f 83 95
* 1998 Spt York (GD) H 7.9f 69 80
* 1998 Aug Mussel (GD) H 7.1f 69 74
1999 Turf 2-9: (7f, 8f 2-5, 9f 3) (hvy 1-1, gd 1-4, g-f 4)
Scopey, decent colt, effective 8f, acts on hvy to frm, often wears blinkers (effectively), prefers left handed tracks. Turf high 98 - 1st of 11 giving 9lb to Glanwydden (13 May York RF 1198) - also 1st of 9 from Catchacoma (25 Apr Dielsdorf RF 0931a). Consistent. A soft-ground specialist, he lost his way in the second half of the campaign and is a shade high in the weights.
**M Johnston [5-16] David Abell.*

ICE AGE BHB 42f53a **RR 33f 53a** 2082[7]
5 gr h Chilibang 7f **(55)** - Mazarine Blue (Bellypha) 9.8f **(73)**
Form - 263542184767
Record 1999 - 1st:1 2nd:2 3rd:1 Ran:12
Pre1999 - 1st:4 2nd:1 3rd:2 Ran:28
Win Prizemoney £11,981 *Total Prizemoney* £15,144
Wins * 1999 *Mar Southw (SLW) S 6f 65*
* 1998 Jly Yarmou (GD) H 6f 44 49
* 1998 *May Southw (STD) S 6f 61*
* 1998 *Jan Southw (STD) H 6f 54 59*
* 1996 May Doncas (G-F) 5f 80+ <
1999 Turf 0-3: (5f 2, 6f) (sft, g-f 2) 1999 AW 1-9: (6f 1-9) (Fibr 1-9)
Fair colt, effective 6f, - acts on Fibr, often wears blinkers (effectively), likes left handed tracks, likes tight tracks. Turf high 33. AW high 65 - 1st of 11 from Little Ibnr (10 Mar Southwell RF 0424).
**R J R Williams [5-39] R J R Williams (from J W Payne [0-1] Feb 1998).*

ICENIC (IRE) BHB 58f60a **RR 46f 60a** 3669[5]
3 b g Scenic 10.6f **(66)** - Resiusa (ITY) (Niniski (USA)) 10.6f **(65)**
Form - 424805
Record 1999 - 1st:0 2nd:1 3rd:0 Ran:5
Pre1999 - 1st:0 2nd:0 3rd:0 Ran:1
Win Prizemoney £0 *Total Prizemoney* £754
1999 Turf 0-2: (12f 2) (frm 2) 1999 AW 0-3: (8f 2, 9f) (Equi 2, Fibr)
Scopey, average gelding, effective 8f, - acts on Equi, has worn blinkers. Turf high 46. AW high 69 (1st run) - 2nd of 12 giving 5lb to Three Bay Trees (23 Jan Lingfield 8f Equi RF 0148).
**J M P Eustace [0-6] The MacDougall Partnership.*

ICE PACK BHB 42f58a **RR 43f 58a** 4936[10]
3 gr f Mukaddamah (USA) 7.6f **(74)** - Mrs Gray (Red Sunset) 8.2f **(63)**
Form - 32068220
Record 1999 - 1st:0 2nd:3 3rd:1 Ran:8
Pre1999 - 1st:0 2nd:0 3rd:0 Ran:2
Win Prizemoney £0 *Total Prizemoney* £1,973
1999 Turf 0-3: (10f 2, 12f) (g-f, frm 2) 1999 AW 0-5: (7f, 9f, 11f, 12f 2) (Fibr 5)
Fair filly, effective 11 to 12f, - acts on Fibr, favours left handed tracks, likes tight tracks. Turf high 43. AW high 58 - 2nd of 11 giving 14lb to Basher Jack (14 Aug Wolverhampton 12f Fibr RF 3667).
**N Tinkler [0-1] A Cute Group (from J W Hills [0-10] Spt 1999).*

ICICLE **RR 98f** 4920[4]
2 br f Polar Falcon (USA) 9f **(74)** - Blessed Honour (Ahonoora) 8.1f **(73)**
Form - 16214
Record 1999 - 1st:2 2nd:1 3rd:0 Ran:5
Win Prizemoney £26,360 *Total Prizemoney* £30,214
Wins * 1999 Aug Goodwo (GD) G3 7f 98 <
*** 1999** May Folkes (G-F) 6f 74+
1999 Turf 2-5: (6f 1-3, 7f 1-2) (gd, g-f 2-4)
Very useful filly. Turf high 98 - 4th of 12 giving 3lb to Lahan (16 Oct

Newmarket 7f gd RF 4920) - also 1st of 9 from Croeso Cariad (29 Aug Goodwood RF 3995). A laid-back individual, she overcame trouble in running to win a Group Three at Goodwood in August. Far from disgraced under a penalty in the Rockfel Stakes, she will find life tough in Group races at home next term.
**J R Fanshawe [2-5] Cheveley Park Stud.*

ICICLE QUEEN RR 31f 5138[15]

2 ch f Aragon 7.7f **(58)** - Kristal Diva **(55df 43a)** (Kris) 9.5f **(73)**
Form - 00
Record 1999 - 1st:0 2nd:0 3rd:0 Ran:2
1999 Turf 0-2: (7f, 8f) (gd 2)
Currently very moderate filly. Turf high 31 (began Oct).
**S C Williams [0-2] Cliffe Rowlands.*

I CRIED FOR YOU (IRE) BHB 70f54a RR 65f 54a 4989[14]

4 b g Statoblest 6.4f **(63)** - Fall of The Hammer (IRE) (Auction Ring (USA)) 8.6f **(65)**
Form - 07411207700
Record 1999 - 1st:2 2nd:1 3rd:0 Ran:11
Pre1999 - 1st:1 2nd:0 3rd:4 Ran:17
Win Prizemoney £13,226 *Total Prizemoney* £16,404
Wins * 1999 Jun Windso (G-F) H 6f 67 71
*** 1999** May Nottin (FRM) 6.1f 65
1998 May Bright (FRM) H 5.3f 68 72 <
1999 Turf 2-9: (5f 2, 6f 2-6, 7f) (gd 3, g-f 1-1, frm 1-5) 1999 AW 0-2: (6f, 8f) (Fibr 2)
Light-framed, average gelding, effective 5 to 6f, best at 6f, acts on frm, has worn blinkers, likes tight tracks. Turf high 80 - 2nd of 15 giving 10lb to Cryhavoc (21 Jun Windsor 6f frm RF 2178) - also 1st of 22 giving 11lb to Cold Climate (14 Jun Windsor RF 1992). AW high 43. Six furlongs and fast ground are his ideal conditions, as he ably demonstrated when winning at Nottingham and Windsor last season.
**J G Given [2-11] One Stop Partnership (from R Hannon [1-17] Oct 1998).*

IDA'S COTTAGE (IRE) BHB 38f40a RR 34f 40a 3792[9]

3 b g Fayruz 6.6f **(63)** - Coral Pink (Miramar Reef)
Form - 848880
Record 1999 - 1st:0 2nd:0 3rd:0 Ran:4
Pre1999 - 1st:0 2nd:0 3rd:0 Ran:3
Win Prizemoney £0 *Total Prizemoney* £198
1999 Turf 0-1: (9f) (frm) 1999 AW 0-3: (6f, 7f, 8f) (Equi 3)
Very moderate gelding. AW high 30.
**P R Chamings [0-7] Twenty Twenty Research.*

IDOLIZE BHB 89f RR 78+f 4006[1]

2 ch f Polish Precedent (USA) 9f **(73)** - Knight's Baroness (Rainbow Quest (USA)) 10.4f **(75)**
Form - 821
Record 1999 - 1st:1 2nd:1 3rd:0 Ran:3
Win Prizemoney £3,517 *Total Prizemoney* £4,727
Wins * 1999 Aug Chepst (G-S) 8.1f 78+ <
1999 Turf 1-3: (7f, 8f 1-2) (gd 1-2, frm)
Currently above-average filly. Turf high 78 (began Jly) - 1st of 9 from Sabreon (30 Aug Chepstow RF 4006). Steadily improving, she got off the mark in good style over a mile at Cheptow on her third start. Subsequent events suggest that was a decent event, and she looks sure to make a useful middle-distance filly next season.
**P F I Cole [1-3] H R H Prince Fahd Salman.*

IFTIRAAS BHB 100f RR 100f 5041[2]

2 b f Distant Relative 7f **(69)** - Ideal Home (Home Guard (USA)) 9.3f **(66)**
Form - 2142
Record 1999 - 1st:1 2nd:2 3rd:0 Ran:4
Win Prizemoney £2,790 *Total Prizemoney* £8,237
Wins * 1999 Spt Lingfi (G-F) 6f 83 <
1999 Turf 1-4: (6f 1-3, 7f) (sft, g-s, g-f, frm 1-1)
Very useful filly. Turf high 100 (began Aug) - 2nd of 12 to Corinium (23 Oct Newbury 7f sft RF 5041). Beaten a whisker on her debut, she landed the odds fairly comfortably at Lingfield next time. Did not enjoy the clearest of passages at Ascot, but ran a brave race when touched off on her final start.
**J L Dunlop [1-4] Kuwait Racing Syndicate II.*

IFTITAH (USA) RR 91?f 5039[5]

3 ch c Gone West (USA) 7.8f **(82)** - Mur Taasha (USA) **(103f)** (Riverman (USA)) 9.1f **(76)**
Form - 5
Record 1999 - 1st:0 2nd:0 3rd:0 Ran:1
Pre1999 - 1st:1 2nd:0 3rd:0 Ran:1
Win Prizemoney £6,326 *Total Prizemoney* £6,326
Wins * 1998 Oct Newmar (GD) 7f 91++ <
1999 Turf 0-1: (7f) (g-s)
Strong, currently useful colt. Slammed four rivals to win Newmarket's Houghton Stakes on his sole start at two, but has obviously been hard to train. **S bin Suroor [1-2] Godolphin.*

IGNITE (IRE) BHB 73f RR 78f 5048[8]

2 b g Bluebird (USA) 7.9f **(71)** - Save Me The Waltz (Kings Lake (USA)) 10.8f **(67)**
Form - 6383384348
Record 1999 - 1st:0 2nd:0 3rd:4 Ran:10
Win Prizemoney £0 *Total Prizemoney* £2,816
1999 Turf 0-10: (5f 4, 6f 5, 7f) (hvy, sft, gd 2, g-f 3, frm 3)
Above-average gelding, effective 5 to 6f, best at 6f, acts on gd to frm, best on gd, has worn blinkers. Turf high 78 - 4th of 9 giving 7lb to Golden Miracle (6 Spt Hamilton 6f frm RF 4164).
**M L W Bell [0-4] Highclere Thoroughbred Racing Ltd (from G Lewis [0-6] Jly 1999).*

IHTIMAAM (FR) BHB 26f48a RR 35f 48a 4869[10]

7 b g Polish Precedent (USA) 9f **(73)** - Haebeh (USA) (Alydar (USA)) 9.1f **(76)**
Form - 0
Record 1999 - 1st:0 2nd:0 3rd:0 Ran:1
Pre1999 - 1st:2 2nd:1 3rd:4 Ran:26
Win Prizemoney £4,116 *Total Prizemoney* £6,801
Wins 1996 *Nov Southw (STD) S 11f 63* <
1996 *Jly Southw (STD) C 11f 53*
1999 AW 0-1: (12f) (Fibr)
Average gelding, has worn blinkers.
**H E Haynes [0-5] Mrs H E Haynes (from Mrs A Swinbank [2-24] Aug 1997).*

IJAB (CAN) BHB 30f34a RR 34f 34a 436[4]

9 b g Ascot Knight (CAN) 11.6f **(74)** - Renounce (USA) (Buckpasser) 10.8f **(80)**
Form - 4
Record 1999 - 1st:0 2nd:0 3rd:0 Ran:1
Pre1999 - 1st:3 2nd:8 3rd:4 Ran:35
Win Prizemoney £8,952 *Total Prizemoney* £17,779
Wins * 1996 *Mar Southw (STD) H 16f 49 56* <
*** 1995** *Aug Southw (STD) H 14f 37 43*
*** 1995** *Apr Southw (STD) H 11f 29 35*
1999 AW 0-1: (14f) (Fibr)
Very moderate gelding, often wears blinkers. Becoming disappointing.
**J Parkes [4-52] Mrs Lynn Parkes (from A A Scott [0-8] Aug 1993).*

IKRAM BOY (USA) BHB 40f44a RR 37f 44a 449[4]

5 b g Salem Drive (USA) 10f **(83)** - Vast Domain (CAN) (Vice Regent (CAN)) 8.7f **(74)**
Form - 3233554
Record 1999 - 1st:0 2nd:0 3rd:1 Ran:4
Pre1999 - 1st:0 2nd:1 3rd:2 Ran:12
Win Prizemoney £0 *Total Prizemoney* £1,823
1999 AW 0-4: (7f, 8f, 11f, 12f) (Fibr 4)
Moderate gelding, effective 8 to 10f, - acts on AW, has worn blinkers. AW high 50. Consistent. **A Bailey [0-16] Sandybrow Stables Ltd.*

ILAHABAD (IRE) RR 66f 4523[4]

4 b g Kahyasi 12.9f **(74)** - Ilmiyya (FR) (Kenmare (FR)) 6.5f **(72)**
Form - 4
Record 1999 - 1st:0 2nd:0 3rd:0 Ran:1
Pre1999 - 1st:0 2nd:0 3rd:1 Ran:1
Win Prizemoney £0 *Total Prizemoney* £435
1999 Turf 0-1: (14f) (gd)
Average gelding.
**J G FitzGerald [2-6] Sir Peter O'Sullevan (from A deRoyerDupre in FR [0-1] Apr 1998).*

IL CAPITANO BHB 96f **RR 93+f** 5027[2]
2 ch c Be My Chief (USA) 10.2f **(62)** -Taza **(40f)**(Persian Bold) 9.3f **(66)**
Form - 21662
Record 1999 - 1st:1 2nd:2 3rd:0 Ran:5
Win Prizemoney £3,649 *Total Prizemoney* £7,639
Wins * **1999** Jly Ayr (SFT) 7f 93+ <
1999 Turf 1-5: (6f, 7f 1-2, 8f 2) (g-s 1-2, gd 2, g-f)
Useful colt. Turf high 93 - 2nd of 5 to Island Sound (22 Oct Newbury 8f g-s RF 5027) - also 1st of 5 from Nicholas Dudley (19 Jly Ayr RF 2937). Was beaten by a useful sort on his debut, but appreciated the soft ground when spread-eagling his field at Ayr next time. Found Group company too much at Sandown and was well held back at Ayr, but ran a better race on his final start.
**B W Hills [1-5] Guy Reed.*

IL DESTINO BHB 62f68a **RR 64f 68a** 4288[2]
4 b c Casteddu 7.4f **(54)** - At First Sight (He Loves Me) 7.9f **(55)**
Form - 0342031262
Record 1999 - 1st:1 2nd:3 3rd:1 Ran:7
Pre1999 - 1st:1 2nd:1 3rd:1 Ran:11
Win Prizemoney £9,491 *Total Prizemoney* £14,147
Wins * **1999** Jly Bath (G-F) H 10.2f 56 55
* 1997 *Nov Lingfi (STD) 7f 62* <
1999 Turf 1-6: (8f, 9f, 10f 1-4) (gd, frm 3, hrd 1-2) 1999 AW 0-1: (10f) (Equi)
Scopey, average colt, effective 10f, acts on frm - acts on Equi, likes left handed tracks, prefers tight tracks. Turf high 64 - 2nd of 14 giving 9lb to Otahuna (13 Spt Nottingham 10f frm RF 4288). (1st run) - 2nd of 13 giving 8lb to Confronter (9 Apr Lingfield 10f Equi RF 0633). **P J Makin [2-18] Mrs P J Makin.*

ILE DE LIBRATE BHB 54f50a **RR 61f 50a** 354[6]
5 b g Librate 10.4f **(37)** - Little Missile (Ile de Bourbon (USA)) 10.1f **(67)**
Form - 76
Record 1999 - 1st:0 2nd:0 3rd:0 Ran:2
Pre1999 - 1st:0 2nd:1 3rd:0 Ran:6
Win Prizemoney £0 *Total Prizemoney* £1,060
1999 AW 0-2: (16f 2) (Equi 2)
Average gelding. AW high 49.
**R J O'Sullivan [1-19] Skampcargo Racing Partnership.*

ILE DISTINCT (IRE) BHB 62f **RR 61f** 4088[3]
5 b g Dancing Dissident (USA) 6.8f **(65)** - Golden Sunlight (Ile de Bourbon (USA)) 10.1f **(67)**
Form - 62483
Record 1999 - 1st:0 2nd:1 3rd:1 Ran:5
Pre1999 - 1st:2 2nd:0 3rd:2 Ran:10
Win Prizemoney £5,030 *Total Prizemoney* £7,509
Wins * 1997 Spt Nottin (G-F) 10f 69 <
* 1997 Aug Mussel (G-F) 8f 54
1999 Turf 0-5: (8f, 9f 2, 10f, 12f) (g-f 2, frm 3)
Average gelding, effective 8 to 9f, acts on gd to g-f. Turf high 67 - 2nd of 9 giving 19lb to Impulsive Air (29 Jun Hamilton 9f g-f RF 2394). Consistent. **Mrs A Swinbank [2-15] Windsor Room Syndicate.*

ILE MICHEL BHB 88f **RR 91df** 4953[5]
2 b c Machiavellian (USA) 9.8f **(83)** - Circe's Isle (Be My Guest (USA)) 9.3f **(67)**
Form - 215
Record 1999 - 1st:1 2nd:1 3rd:0 Ran:3
Win Prizemoney £3,057 *Total Prizemoney* £4,593
Wins * **1999** Spt Catter (G-F) 6f 76++ <
1999 Turf 1-3: (6f 1-3) (g-f, frm 1-2)
Currently useful colt. Turf high 91 (1st run) (began Aug) - 2nd of 8 to Las Ramblas (28 Aug Newmarket 6f frm RF 3963).
**G Wragg [1-3] A E Oppenheimer.*

ILEWIN JANINE (IRE) RR 44f 5071[6]
8 b m Soughaan (USA) 8f **(42)** - Mystery Queen (Martinmas) 7.6f **(59)**
Form - 6
Record 1999 - 1st:0 2nd:0 3rd:0 Ran:1
1999 Turf 0-1: (11f) (gd)
Moderate mare. (1st run) - 6th of 17 getting 1lb from A Day On The Dub (26 Oct Redcar 11f gd RF 5071). **P D Evans [0-1] Tom Segrue.*

ILISSUS (USA) RR 75f 1299[U]
3 b c Alleged (USA) 11.8f **(81)** - Reine des Iles (USA) (Nureyev (USA)) 8.7f **(78)**
Form - 32U
Record 1999 - 1st:0 2nd:1 3rd:1 Ran:3
Win Prizemoney £0 *Total Prizemoney* £1,667
1999 Turf 0-3: (7f, 8f, 10f) (gd 3)
Scopey, currently above-average colt. Turf high 75 - 2nd of 18 to Tonic (15 Apr Ripon 8f gd RF 0710).
**M P Tregoning [0-3] Sheikh Mohammed.*

ILJASOOR (USA) RR 41f 5207[8]
2 b c Rainbow Quest (USA) 11.2f **(81)** - Jasoorah (IRE) (Sadler's Wells (USA)) 10f **(76)**
Form - 8
Record 1999 - 1st:0 2nd:0 3rd:0 Ran:1
1999 Turf 0-1: (7f) (g-s)
Currently moderate colt.
**M P Tregoning [0-1] Sheikh Ahmed Al Maktoum.*

ILLUMINATE BHB 49f55a **RR 31f 55a** 1130[P]
6 b g Marju (IRE) 9.2f **(76)** - Light Bee (USA) (Majestic Light (USA)) 10.6f **(75)**
Form - 6P
Record 1999 - 1st:0 2nd:0 3rd:0 Ran:2
Pre1999 - 1st:1 2nd:1 3rd:1 Ran:14
Win Prizemoney £3,257 *Total Prizemoney* £5,349
Wins * 1997 *Feb Lingfi (STD) 12f 64* <
1999 Turf 0-1: (15f) (hvy) 1999 AW 0-1: (14f) (Fibr)
Very moderate gelding, effective 14f, acts on gd, has worn blinkers. Becoming disappointing.
**D C O'Brien [2-27] J S Court (from Miss Gay Kelleway [0-2] Aug 1996).*

ILLUSIVE (IRE) BHB 60f69a **RR 60f 69a** 4937[7]
2 b g Night Shift (USA) 8.1f **(73)** - Mirage (Red Sunset) 8.2f **(63)**
Form - 000517
Record 1999 - 1st:1 2nd:0 3rd:0 Ran:6
Win Prizemoney £3,882 *Total Prizemoney* £3,882
Wins * **1999** *Oct Lingfi (STD) H 6f 56 64* <
1999 Turf 0-4: (5f, 6f 3) (gd 2, g-f 2) 1999 AW 1-2: (6f 1-2) (Equi 1-1, Fibr)
Average gelding, effective 6f, - acts on Equi, has worn blinkers. Turf high 60 (began Aug). AW high 64 (1st run) (began Oct) - 1st of 14 getting 5lb from Browns Delight (8 Oct Lingfield RF 4786). Improved for Equitrack when running away with a Lingfield nursery in October. First-time blinkers seemed to make all the difference.
**W Jarvis [1-6] Noodles Racing.*

IL PRINCIPE (IRE) BHB 81f65a **RR 77f 65a** 5220[1]
5 b g Ela-Mana-Mou 12.7f **(72)** - Seattle Siren (USA) (Seattle Slew (USA)) 9.4f **(76)**
Form - 332356451213534101
Record 1999 - 1st:4 2nd:1 3rd:2 Ran:14
Pre1999 - 1st:6 2nd:3 3rd:4 Ran:25
Win Prizemoney £43,635 *Total Prizemoney* £51,143
Wins * **1999** Nov Doncas (SFT) H 16.5f 75 77 <
* **1999** Oct York (SFT) H 13.9f 69 72
* **1999** Aug Mussel (G-S) H 16f 63 69
* **1999** Aug Haydoc (SFT) H 14f 57 63
* 1998 Oct Redcar (G-S) H 14.1f 58 60
* 1997 Spt Catter (G-F) H 15.8f 54 65
* 1997 Spt Mussel (G-F) H 16f 46 61
* 1997 *Spt Southw (STD) H 14f 50 59*
* 1997 Aug Mussel (G-F) H 12f 35 48
* 1997 Aug Hamilt (GD) H 11.1f 35 40
1999 Turf 4-12: (12f 2, 14f 2-4, 16f 1-3, 17f 1-3) (sft 1-1, g-s, gd 2-6, g-f 1-1, frm 2, hrd) 1999 AW 0-2: (16f 2) (Fibr 2)
Above-average gelding, effective 14 to 17f, best at 14f, acts on sft to frm - acts on Equi, has worn blinkers, likes left handed tracks, excels at Haydock. Turf high 77 - 1st of 15 getting 4lb from Fantasy Hill (6 Nov Doncaster RF 5220) - also 1st of 21 giving 19lb to Home Counties (9 Oct York RF 4800). AW high 61. Consistent. An effective stayer in modest company, he contributed to an excellent season for his underrated trainer. Suited by soft ground.
**John Berry [10-39] The 1997 Partnership.*

IMAD (USA) BHB 46f49a **RR 44f 49a** 904[1]
9 b or br g Al Nasr (FR) 9.9f **(72)** - Blue Grass Field (Top Ville) 11.7f

(68)
Form - 01
Record 1999 - 1st:1 2nd:0 3rd:0 Ran:2
Pre1999 - 1st:1 2nd:1 3rd:0 Ran:8
Win Prizemoney £16,277 *Total Prizemoney* £16,909
Wins * **1999** Apr Pontef (G-S) H 21.6f 41 44
1995 Jly Goodwo (FRM) H 20f 60 64 <
1999 Turf 1-1: (22f 1-1) (gd 1-1) 1999 AW 0-1: (16f) (Fibr)
Moderate gelding, has worn blinkers. (1st run). Inconsistent. A real stayer on the Flat and over hurdles, he appreciated the test of stamina when winning over the extended two-miles-five at Pontefract in April.
**K C Comerford [2-11] Alan Brackley (from J White [3-19] Jun 1996).*

IMANI BHB 76f RR 75f 4954[12]
4 b f Danehill (USA) 9.1f **(79)** - Santarem (USA) (El Gran Senor (USA)) 9.6f **(76)**
Form - 1151282130
Record 1999 - 1st:4 2nd:2 3rd:1 Ran:10
Pre1999 - 1st:1 2nd:0 3rd:0 Ran:9
Win Prizemoney £18,703 *Total Prizemoney* £23,001
Wins * **1999** Aug Beverl (GD) H 9.9f 75 75 <
* **1999** Jun Salisb (GD) H 12f 71 72
* **1999** May Warwic (GD) H 10.8f 66 70
* **1999** Apr Beverl (GD) H 9.9f 61 65
1998 Jly Newbur (G-F) H 10f 57 65
1999 Turf 4-10: (10f 2-3, 11f 1-2, 12f 1-4, 13f) (g-s, gd 1-3, g-f 1-3, frm 2-2, hrd)
Above-average filly, effective 10 to 13f, acts on g-s to frm, likes tight tracks, excels at Beverley and Haydock. Turf high 75 - 1st of 6 giving 2lb to Heart (29 Aug Beverley RF 3992) - also 1st of 8 getting 2lb from Borgia (9 Jun Salisbury RF 1870). She has a successful season, winning four. Likes good ground.
**J L Dunlop [4-10] R N Khan (from G Lewis [1-9] Spt 1998).*

IMARI BHB 62f RR 60f 5192[4]
2 b f Rock City 8.8f **(62)** - Misty Goddess (IRE) **(51df 37a)** (Godswalk (USA)) 7.3f **(58)**
Form - 44464
Record 1999 - 1st:0 2nd:0 3rd:0 Ran:5
Win Prizemoney £0 *Total Prizemoney* £505
1999 Turf 0-5: (6f 4, 8f) (gd 3, frm 2)
Average filly. Turf high 67 (began Aug). **J G Given [0-5] J R Good.*

IMBACKAGAIN (IRE) BHB 56f45a RR 58f 45a 4935[10]
4 b g Mujadil (USA) 7.7f **(70)** - Ballinclogher (IRE) (Creative Plan (USA)) 7.5f **(67)**
Form - 08323600
Record 1999 - 1st:0 2nd:1 3rd:2 Ran:8
Pre1999 - 1st:1 2nd:1 3rd:0 Ran:13
Win Prizemoney £2,085 *Total Prizemoney* £4,290
Wins * 1998 *Jan Southw (STD) H 6f 60 64* <
1999 AW 0-8: (7f 4, 8f 3, 10f) (Equi 2, Fibr 6)
Tall, fair gelding, effective 6 to 9f, acts on frm - acts on Fibr. AW high 56. Inconsistent.
**N P Littmoden [1-18] Turf 2000 Ltd (from P C Haslam [0-3] Aug 1997).*

IMPALDI (IRE) BHB 38f RR 35f 3868[9]
4 b f Imp Society (USA) 7.1f **(63)** - Jaldi (IRE) (Nordico (USA)) 6.5f **(62)**
Form - 064D40248750
Record 1999 - 1st:0 2nd:1 3rd:0 Ran:12
Pre1999 - 1st:0 2nd:0 3rd:0 Ran:9
Win Prizemoney £0 *Total Prizemoney* £1,318
1999 Turf 0-12: (5f 6, 6f 5, 7f) (gd, g-f 3, frm 8)
Very moderate filly, effective 8f, acts on g-s, has worn blinkers. Turf high 45. Consistent.
**B Ellison [0-12] Brian Ellison Racing Club (from M J Grassick in IRE [0-9] Spt 1998).*

IMPELLING (IRE) BHB 57f57a RR 65f 57a 653[18]
4 ch g Imp Society (USA) 7.1f **(63)** - Real Stunner (Chief Singer) 8.9f **(66)**
Form - 58100
Record 1999 - 1st:1 2nd:0 3rd:0 Ran:5
Pre1999 - 1st:0 2nd:0 3rd:0 Ran:3
Win Prizemoney £1,615 *Total Prizemoney* £1,615
Wins * **1999** *Feb Southw (STD) H 8f 60 52* <
1999 Turf 0-1: (8f) (frm) 1999 AW 1-4: (8f 1-3, 10f) (Equi 2, Fibr 1-2)
Scopey, average gelding, favours tight tracks. AW high 52. Inconsistent. **K R Burke [1-8] D M Littlejohn and Partners.*

IMPERATOR (IRE) BHB 39f31a RR 51f 31a 134[10]
4 b g Mac's Imp (USA) 5.6f **(54)** - Secret Hideaway (USA) (Key To The Mint (USA)) 9.4f **(75)**
Form - 600
Record 1999 - 1st:0 2nd:0 3rd:0 Ran:1
Pre1999 - 1st:0 2nd:1 3rd:0 Ran:10
Win Prizemoney £0 *Total Prizemoney* £732
1999 AW 0-1: (10f) (Equi)
Workmanlike, fair gelding, effective 7f, acts on gd. Inconsistent.
**G L Moore [0-3] George Smith Ltd (from Lady Herries [0-8] Oct 1998).*

IMPERIAL BEAUTY (USA) BHB 112f RR 117f 4777a[2]
3 b f Imperial Ballet (IRE) - Multimara (USA) (Arctic Tern (USA)) 8.9f **(69)**
Form - 012812
Record 1999 - 1st:2 2nd:2 3rd:0 Ran:6
Pre1999 - 1st:1 2nd:2 3rd:0 Ran:3
Win Prizemoney £50,381 *Total Prizemoney* £118,630
Wins * **1999** Spt Newbur (G-S) L 5.2f 104+ <
* **1999** Jly York (G-F) L 6f 104
* 1998 Spt Salisb (GD) 6f 90+
1999 Turf 2-6: (5f 1-3, 6f 1-2, 8f) (sft, gd 1-1, frm 1-4)
Scopey, high-class filly, effective 5f, acts on sft. Turf high 117 - 2nd of 14 getting 3lb from Agnes World (3 Oct Longchamp 5f sft RF 4777a). She developed into a high-class sprinter in soft ground, cruising home in a Newbury listed event before failing narrowly to beat the Japanese colt Agnes World in the Prix de l'Abbaye. She began the season when down the field in the Guineas, but the drop in trip soon began to pay dividends.
**P J Makin [3-9] Dr Carlos Stelling.*

IMPERIAL COURT (IRE) BHB 35f RR 61f 4441[19]
4 b g Imperial Frontier (USA) 7f **(65)** - Fandikos (IRE) (Taufan (USA)) 7f **(57)**
Form - 00
Record 1999 - 1st:0 2nd:0 3rd:0 Ran:2
Pre1999 - 1st:0 2nd:0 3rd:0 Ran:4
1999 Turf 0-2: (8f 2) (gd, g-f)
Workmanlike, average gelding, has worn blinkers. Turf high 61 (began Aug).
**A W Carroll [0-2] Itzabuzz Racing (from J G M O'Shea [0-4] Jun 1998).*

IMPERIAL ENVOY BHB 35a RR 35a 328[4]
4 b g Zafonic (USA) 9f **(83)** - Imperial Jade (Lochnager) 6f **(59)**
Form - 784
Record 1999 - 1st:0 2nd:0 3rd:0 Ran:3
Win Prizemoney £0 *Total Prizemoney* £203
1999 AW 0-3: (6f 2, 8f) (Equi 2, Fibr)
Currently very moderate gelding. AW high 32.
**W R Muir [0-3] D J Deer.*

IMPERIAL HONEY (IRE) BHB 44f40a RR 40f 40a 3753[4]
4 b f Imperial Frontier (USA) 7f **(65)** - Indian Honey (Indian King (USA)) 7.4f **(64)**
Form - 7028334
Record 1999 - 1st:0 2nd:1 3rd:2 Ran:7
Pre1999 - 1st:0 2nd:1 3rd:0 Ran:13
Win Prizemoney £0 *Total Prizemoney* £2,102
1999 Turf 0-6: (5f 5, 6f) (g-f 2, frm 4) 1999 AW 0-1: (6f) (Fibr)
Neat, moderate filly, effective 5f, acts on gd. Turf high 40.
**Mrs A Swinbank [0-20] Ann Swinbank Racing Club.*

IMPERIALIST (IRE) RR 90f 4793[11]
2 b f Imperial Frontier (USA) 7f **(65)** - Petrine (IRE) (Petorius) 7.3f **(61)**
Form - 51134360
Record 1999 - 1st:2 2nd:0 3rd:2 Ran:8
Win Prizemoney £6,760 *Total Prizemoney* £21,791
Wins * **1999** Jun Salisb (GD) 5f 99 <
* **1999** May Sandow (GD) 5f 80
1999 Turf 2-8: (5f 2-5, 6f 3) (gd, g-f 2-5, frm 2)
Useful filly, effective 5f, acts on g-f. Turf high 99 - 1st of 5 giving 7lb to Kalindi (9 Jun Salisbury RF 1867). A sharp juvenile, she ran fine races in two valuable sales events in the summer. Unable to match strides with Group horses later in the campaign, she may

be best at five furlongs but is unlikely to improve. **R Hannon [2-8] John Homer Racing.*

IMPERIAL PRINCE BHB 56a RR 42f 4175[14]

4 b g Prince Sabo 6.6f **(64)** - Joli's Girl (Mansingh (USA)) 7.4f **(55)**
Form - 72032054550630
Record 1999 - 1st:0 2nd:1 3rd:1 Ran:10
Pre1999 - 1st:0 2nd:3 3rd:3 Ran:12
Win Prizemoney £0 *Total Prizemoney* £4,519
1999 Turf 0-10: (8f, 9f, 10f 4, 12f 3, 13f) (hvy, gd, g-f 4, frm 3, hrd)
Light-framed, average gelding, effective 8 to 15f, acts on g-s to g-f - acts on AW, has worn blinkers, likes left handed tracks, favours tight tracks, excels at Wolverhampton. Turf high 65 (1st run) - 2nd of 20 getting 3lb from Christiansted (7 Apr Ripon 12f g-f RF 0615).
**S P C Woods [0-14] George Tong (from K McAuliffe [0-8] Jun 1998).*

IMPERIAL ROCKET (USA) BHB 91f RR 83f 5196[1]

2 b br c Northern Flagship (USA) 12.2f **(72)** - Starsawhirl (USA) (Star de Naskra (USA)) 9.7f **(65)**
Form - 0011
Record 1999 - 1st:2 2nd:0 3rd:0 Ran:4
Win Prizemoney £10,714 *Total Prizemoney* £10,714
Wins * 1999 Nov Windso (G-S) H 8.3f 83 83 <
*** 1999** Oct Leices (GD) 8f 83+
1999 Turf 2-4: (7f, 8f 2-3) (gd 2-4)
Decent colt. Turf high 83 (began Spt) - 1st of 13 getting 2lb from Father Juninho (4 Nov Windsor RF 5196) - also 1st of 19 from Shapour (12 Oct Leicester RF 4839). Looked an improving sort at the end of the campaign and could make up into a decent handicapper. **R Hannon [2-4] The Royal Ascot Racing Club.*

IMPETUS BHB 48f RR 57f 4930[14]

5 b g Puissance 7.1f **(60)** - Cold Line (Exdirectory)
Form - 00
Record 1999 - 1st:0 2nd:0 3rd:0 Ran:2
Pre1999 - 1st:0 2nd:2 3rd:1 Ran:10
Win Prizemoney £0 *Total Prizemoney* £2,616
1999 Turf 0-2: (10f, 11f) (g-f, frm)
Fair gelding, effective 10f, acts on g-s to frm. Turf high 44 (began Oct). Inconsistent. **J Hetherton [0-12] N Hetherton.*

IMPREVUE (IRE) BHB 63f62a RR 62f 62a 4993[1]

5 ch m Priolo (USA) 10.9f **(71)** - Las Bela (Welsh Pageant) 10f **(65)**
Form - 00257821131
Record 1999 - 1st:3 2nd:2 3rd:1 Ran:11
Pre1999 - 1st:1 2nd:2 3rd:3 Ran:16
Win Prizemoney £11,278 *Total Prizemoney* £18,775
Wins * 1999 Oct Nottin (FRM) 10f 62
*** 1999** Spt Bright (G-F) H 10f 44 55
*** 1999** *Jly Lingfi (STD) H 10f 47 53*
1997 Oct Currag (SFT) 12f 85 <
1999 Turf 2-9: (9f, 10f 2-2, 11f, 12f 3, 14f, 15f) (hvy, g-s, g-f 3, frm 2-3, hrd) 1999 AW 1-2: (10f 1-1, 12f) (Equi 1-2)
Average filly, effective 10f, acts on gd, has worn blinkers (effectively), prefers left handed tracks, likes tight tracks. Turf high 62. AW high 53 (began Jly). Improving.
**R J O'Sullivan [3-11] Mrs Barbara Marchant (from D P Kelly in IRE [1-8] Oct 1998).*

I'M PROPOSIN (IRE) BHB 109f RR 104?f 4253[5]

4 b c Posen (USA) 8.6f **(59)** - Kitterland (Rheingold) 10.4f **(62)**
Form - 5
Record 1999 - 1st:0 2nd:0 3rd:0 Ran:1
Pre1999 - 1st:3 2nd:0 3rd:0 Ran:3
Win Prizemoney £19,283 *Total Prizemoney* £19,283
Wins * 1998 Oct Newmar (gd) L 8f 104 <
* 1998 Apr Sandow (SFT) 8.1f 95+
* 1998 Apr Leices (SFT) 8f 83+
1999 Turf 0-1: (12f) (g-f)
Lengthy, very useful colt. He looked a most progressive sort at three, winning three times and looking to appreciate a mile and easy ground. He did not make much impression on his belated reappearance at Doncaster and did not seem to handle the fast ground. **J L Dunlop [3-4] Nicholas & Philippa Cooper.*

IMPULSIVE AIR (IRE) BHB 46f58a RR 46f 58a 4985[5]

7 b g Try My Best (USA) 7.8f **(68)** - Tracy's Sundown (Red Sunset) 8.2f **(63)**
Form - 0001020340405
Record 1999 - 1st:1 2nd:1 3rd:1 Ran:13
Pre1999 - 1st:7 2nd:7 3rd:3 Ran:52
Win Prizemoney £30,972 *Total Prizemoney* £51,553
Wins * 1999 Jun Hamilt (GD) H 9.2f 47 48
* 1998 Jun Carlis (G-S) H 8f 65 68 <
* 1998 May Ripon (GD) H 8f 59 65
* 1997 Aug Mussel (G-F) 7.1f 62
* 1997 Aug Redcar (FRM) 8f 63
* 1996 Aug Newcas (G-F) H 8f 60 64
* 1996 Jun Carlis (FRM) H 6.9f 58 57
1999 Turf 1-13: (8f 6, 9f 1-5, 10f 2) (sft, gd 5, g-f 1-2, frm 5)
Moderate gelding, effective 8f, acts on gd to g-f, best on g-f, has worn blinkers, prefers right handed tracks, likes tight tracks. Turf high 50. **E Weymes [8-65] T A Scothern.*

IMSHISHWAY (IRE) BHB 65f RR 59f 3091[8]

4 b c Royal Academy (USA) 7.8f **(77)** - Mama Lucia (Workboy) 7.3f **(46)**
Form - 18
Record 1999 - 1st:1 2nd:0 3rd:0 Ran:2
Pre1999 - 1st:1 2nd:0 3rd:0 Ran:13
Win Prizemoney £7,703 *Total Prizemoney* £7,703
Wins * 1999 Jly Warwic (G-F) H 12.3f 59 59
1997 Spt Goodwo (GD) 7f 83 <
1999 Turf 1-2: (12f 1-2) (gd, g-f 1-1)
Scopey, fair colt, effective 10f, acts on gd, has worn blinkers, prefers tight tracks. Turf high 59 (1st run) (began Jly). Inconsistent.
**M C Pipe [4-9] A S Helaissi (from B J Meehan [1-11] Aug 1998).*

I'M SOPHIE (IRE) RR 73+f 1977[2]

2 ch f Shalford (IRE) 7.8f **(63)** - Caisson **(67f)** (Shaadi (USA))
Form - 2
Record 1999 - 1st:0 2nd:1 3rd:0 Ran:1
Win Prizemoney £0 *Total Prizemoney* £848
1999 Turf 0-1: (5f) (g-f)
Currently above-average filly. (1st run) - 2nd of 10 to Lady-Love (14 Jun Musselburgh 5f g-f RF 1977).
**T D Barron [0-1] Laurence O'Kane.*

I'M TEF BHB 41f42a RR 30f 42a 282[7]

4 b g Noble Patriarch 12.2f **(43)** - Who's That Lady (Nordance (USA)) 7.5f **(52)**
Form - 08067
Record 1999 - 1st:0 2nd:0 3rd:0 Ran:4
Pre1999 - 1st:2 2nd:4 3rd:1 Ran:20
Win Prizemoney £7,025 *Total Prizemoney* £10,807
Wins * *1998 Jan Southw (STD) H 7f 63 73+* <
* *1997 Dec Southw (STD) H 7f 54 64*
1999 AW 0-4: (7f 2, 8f 2) (Fibr 4)
Neat, very moderate gelding, effective 6 to 7f, best at 7f, - acts on Fibr, has worn blinkers, prefers left handed tracks, prefers tight tracks. AW high 36.
**T D Easterby [2-27] T E F Freight (Scarborough) Ltd.*

IN CAHOOTS BHB 30f36a RR 23f 36a 2316[14]

6 gr g Kalaglow 11.2f **(67)** - Royal Celerity (USA) (Riverman (USA)) 9.1f **(76)**
Form - 0
Record 1999 - 1st:0 2nd:0 3rd:0 Ran:1
Pre1999 - 1st:1 2nd:0 3rd:0 Ran:11
Win Prizemoney £2,658 *Total Prizemoney* £2,658
Wins * 1996 Spt Leices (FRM) S 10f 49 <
1999 Turf 0-1: (17f) (hrd)
Very moderate gelding, has worn blinkers.
**A G Newcombe [1-11] Duckhaven Stud (from C J Hill [0-1] May 1997).*

INCA STAR (USA) RR 83+f 5100[3]

2 b c Trempolino (USA) 11.9f **(77)** - Inca Empress (USA) (Sovereign Dancer (USA)) 11.2f **(68)**
Form - 3
Record 1999 - 1st:0 2nd:0 3rd:1 Ran:1
Win Prizemoney £0 *Total Prizemoney* £465
1999 Turf 0-1: (8f) (gd)
Currently decent colt. (1st run) - 3rd of 10 to King Spinner (27 Oct Yarmouth 8f gd RF 5100). **M Johnston [0-1] Jaber Abdullah.*

INCEPTA BHB 54f54a **RR 56f 54a** 653[8]
4 b g Selkirk (USA) 7.9f **(76)** - Ringlet (USA) **(53f 54a)** (Secreto (USA)) 8.7f **(72)**
Form - 2144058
Record 1999 - 1st:0 2nd:0 3rd:0 Ran:5
Pre1999 - 1st:1 2nd:1 3rd:1 Ran:8
Win Prizemoney £2,814 *Total Prizemoney* £4,248
Wins * 1998 *Dec Wolver (STD) 8.5f 61* <
1999 Turf 0-1: (8f) (frm) 1999 AW 0-4: (7f, 8f 3) (Equi 3, Fibr)
Scopey, average gelding, effective 8f, acts on g-f - acts on Fibr, has worn blinkers, likes left handed tracks, likes tight tracks. AW high 62. Becoming disappointing. A mile looks as far as he wants to go.
**P S McEntee [1-9] Racing Thoroughbreds Plc (from B W Hills [0-6] Aug 1998).*

INCHALONG BHB 64f57a **RR 64f 57a** 4914[2]
4 b f Inchinor 8.9f **(64)** - Reshift (Night Shift (USA)) 7.2f **(69)**
Form - 0000080276102
Record 1999 - 1st:1 2nd:2 3rd:0 Ran:13
Pre1999 - 1st:4 2nd:7 3rd:9 Ran:40
Win Prizemoney £25,045 *Total Prizemoney* £44,941
Wins * **1999** Spt Pontef (G-F) H 6f 59 61
* 1998 Aug Ripon (G-F) H 6f 72 75 <
* 1998 Jly Windso (GD) H 6f 69 72
* 1997 Aug Mussel (GD) H 7.1f 64 70
* 1997 Jun Newcas (GD) S 6f 61
1999 Turf 1-12: (6f 1-7, 7f 5) (sft, gd 5, g-f, frm 1-5) 1999 AW 0-1: (6f) (Fibr)
Light-framed, average filly, effective 6 to 7f, best at 7f, acts on gd to hrd, has worn blinkers, excels at Pontefract. Turf high 64. A tough and speedy sprint handicapper, she got back to winning ways when landing a Pontefract sprint in September.
**M Brittain [5-53] Northgate Lodge Partnerships.*

INCHCAILLOCH (IRE) BHB 44f **RR 48f** 4581[8]
10 b g Lomond (USA) 9.9f **(74)** - Glowing With Pride (Ile de Bourbon (USA)) 10.1f **(67)**
Form - 6808
Record 1999 - 1st:0 2nd:0 3rd:0 Ran:4
Pre1999 - 1st:7 2nd:4 3rd:4 Ran:39
Win Prizemoney £75,123 *Total Prizemoney* £87,455
Wins * 1997 Mar Kempto (GD) H 16f 78 85 <
* 1996 Oct Newmar (GD) H 18f 62 78
* 1996 Oct Warwic (FRM) H 16.1f 62 68
* 1995 Jun Bath (GD) H 17.2f 58 61
* 1995 May Bath (FRM) H 17.2f 55 61
1999 Turf 0-4: (16f 2, 17f 2) (gd 2, frm 2)
Moderate gelding. Turf high 48 (began Aug). Becoming disappointing. **J S King [13-64] F J Carter (from R Charlton [2-7] Oct 1992).*

INCHING CLOSER BHB 78f **RR 83f** 4003[4]
2 b c Inchinor 8.9f **(64)** - Maiyaasah (Kris) 9.5f **(73)**
Form - 524
Record 1999 - 1st:0 2nd:1 3rd:0 Ran:3
Win Prizemoney £0 *Total Prizemoney* £1,615
1999 Turf 0-3: (6f 2, 8f) (gd 2, frm)
Currently decent colt. Turf high 83 (began Jly) - 2nd of 11 to Zoning (19 Aug Yarmouth 6f gd RF 3767).
**N A Callaghan [0-3] Gallagher Equine Ltd.*

INCHINNAN BHB 69f **RR 72f** 5138[2]
2 b f Inchinor 8.9f **(64)** - Westering **(29f 38a)** (Auction Ring (USA)) 8.6f **(65)**
Form - 35522552
Record 1999 - 1st:0 2nd:3 3rd:1 Ran:8
Win Prizemoney £0 *Total Prizemoney* £3,946
1999 Turf 0-8: (7f 5, 8f 3) (gd 3, g-f 3, frm 2)
Above-average filly, effective 7 to 8f, best at 7f, acts on gd to frm. Turf high 72 (began Jly) - 2nd of 11 to Lady of Honour (14 Spt Yarmouth 7f g-f RF 4294). **D Morris [0-8] B McAllister.*

INCHLONAIG RR 98+f 4595[1]
2 ch c Nashwan (USA) 10.3f **(79)**- Inchmurrin (Lomond (USA)) 8.8f **(65)**
Form - 1
Record 1999 - 1st:1 2nd:0 3rd:0 Ran:1
Win Prizemoney £166,850 *Total Prizemoney* £166,850
Wins * **1999** Spt Newmar (G-S) 7f 98+ <
1999 Turf 1-1: (7f 1-1) (g-f 1-1)
Currently very useful colt. (1st run) - 1st of 17 giving 5lb to Bedazzling (28 Spt Newmarket RF 4595).
**R Charlton [1-1] A E Oppenheimer.*

INCH PERFECT BHB 65f63a **RR 61+f 63a** 5217[3]
4 b g Inchinor 8.9f **(64)** - Scarlet Veil (Tyrnavos) 10.1f **(55)**
Form - 10743311113
Record 1999 - 1st:5 2nd:0 3rd:3 Ran:11
Pre1999 - 1st:0 2nd:0 3rd:1 Ran:2
Win Prizemoney £14,076 *Total Prizemoney* £16,249
Wins * **1999** Oct Bath (SFT) H 10.2f 47 61++ <
* **1999** Oct Newcas (G-S) H 10.1f 47 59+
* **1999** Oct Pontef (GD) H 10f 47 52
1999 Spt Redcar (G-F) SH 10f 42 43
1999 *Mar Southw (STD) S 8f 54*
1999 Turf 4-7: (8f 2, 10f 4-4, 11f) (g-s, gd 2-3, g-f 1-2, frm 1-1) 1999 AW 1-4: (7f, 8f 1-2, 12f) (Fibr 1-4)
Scopey, average gelding, favours left handed tracks. Turf high 61. AW high 54 (1st run).
**R A Fahey [3-4] Tommy Staunton (from J Hetherton [2-7] Spt 1999).*

INCH PINCHER BHB 64f59a **RR 66f 59a** 5023[9]
2 ch c Inchinor 8.9f **(64)** - Cutpurse Moll **(71f)** (Green Desert (USA)) 8.6f **(78)**
Form - 702204413060
Record 1999 - 1st:1 2nd:2 3rd:1 Ran:12
Win Prizemoney £3,225 *Total Prizemoney* £5,230
Wins * **1999** Aug Sandow (GD) SH 7.1f 58 66 <
1999 Turf 1-12: (5f 2, 6f 2, 7f 1-7, 8f) (g-s 2, gd 2, g-f 5, frm 1-3)
Average colt, effective 6 to 7f, best at 7f, acts on g-f to frm, best on g-f, has worn blinkers (very effectively), prefers tight tracks. Turf high 73 - 2nd of 9 giving 11lb to Blue Legend (13 Jly Brighton 7f frm RF 2772) - also 1st of 16 getting 4lb from Barbados (21 Aug Sandown RF 3823). **M R Channon [1-12] T S M Cunningham.*

INCHTINA BHB 62f59a **RR 66f 59a** 4217[15]
4 b f Inchinor 8.9f **(64)** - Nikitina (Nijinsky (CAN)) 10.3f **(77)**
Form - 608231200
Record 1999 - 1st:1 2nd:2 3rd:1 Ran:9
Pre1999 - 1st:1 2nd:2 3rd:0 Ran:6
Win Prizemoney £7,179 *Total Prizemoney* £11,443
Wins * **1999** Aug Kempto (G-F) H 12f 60 65
1998 Apr Nottin (SFT) 8.2f 71 <
1999 Turf 1-8: (8f 3, 12f 1-4, 14f) (gd 2, g-f 4, frm 1-2) 1999 AW 0-1: (12f) (Fibr)
Light-framed, average filly, likes tight tracks. Turf high 68.
**M A Jarvis [1-9] Peter Stevenson (from H Candy [1-6] Oct 1998).*

INCLUDE ME OUT BHB 60f **RR 55f** 2724[7]
5 ch g Old Vic 12.8f **(72)** - Tafila (Adonijah) 10f **(61)**
Form - 07
Record 1999 - 1st:0 2nd:0 3rd:0 Ran:2
Pre1999 - 1st:1 2nd:2 3rd:0 Ran:9
Win Prizemoney £3,964 *Total Prizemoney* £7,344
Wins 1998 Aug Redcar (G-F) H 10f 62 66 <
1999 Turf 0-2: (8f, 16f) (g-f 2)
Fair gelding, effective 10f, acts on frm. Turf high 55.
**J A Pickering [0-2] J A Pickering (from J Wharton [1-6] Aug 1998).*

INCREDULOUS (FR) RR 48+f 5129[14]
2 ch f Indian Ridge 7.6f **(74)** - Fetlar (Pharly (FR)) 9.8f **(68)**
Form - 0
Record 1999 - 1st:0 2nd:0 3rd:0 Ran:1
1999 Turf 0-1: (6f) (gd)
Currently moderate filly. **J R Fanshawe [0-1] Dr Catherine Wills.*

INDEEDYEDO BHB 87f **RR 84f** 4952[6]
2 b f Efisio 7.7f **(69)** - Bonita **(60f)** (Primo Dominie) 6.2f **(80)**
Form - 635317386
Record 1999 - 1st:1 2nd:0 3rd:3 Ran:9
Win Prizemoney £3,533 *Total Prizemoney* £5,834
Wins * **1999** Jun Hamilt (GD) 6f 75 <
1999 Turf 1-9: (5f 2, 6f 1-4, 7f 3) (sft, gd 3, g-f 2, frm 1-3)
Decent filly, effective 5 to 6f, best at 6f, acts on gd to frm, best on gd. Turf high 84 - also 1st of 6 giving 4lb to Ronni Pancake (23 Jun

Hamilton RF 2234). Consistent. Met some useful juveniles in her first four outings, but nevertheless performed with credit. Deserved her win at Hamilton and ran well in a Group Two event next time. **J Pearce [1-9] Partners Tojamate.*

INDIA (IRE) RR 63df 4814[20]
4 b f Indian Ridge 7.6f **(74)** - Athens Belle (IRE) (Groom Dancer (USA))
Form - 500
Record 1999 - 1st:0 2nd:0 3rd:0 Ran:3
Pre1999 - 1st:0 2nd:0 3rd:1 Ran:2
Win Prizemoney £0 *Total Prizemoney* £755
1999 Turf 0-3: (8f 2, 10f) (gd, frm 2)
Workmanlike, average filly. Turf high 50 (began Jly).
**L M Cumani [0-5] Fittocks Stud.*

INDIANA LEGEND (IRE) BHB 107f **RR 106f** 2039[6]
3 ch c Indian Ridge 7.6f **(74)** - Mardi Gras Belle (USA) (Masked Dancer (USA))
Form - 206
Record 1999 - 1st:0 2nd:1 3rd:0 Ran:3
Pre1999 - 1st:1 2nd:3 3rd:0 Ran:5
Win Prizemoney £3,468 *Total Prizemoney* £35,426
Wins * 1998 Jly Windso (G-F) 6f 85 <
1999 Turf 0-3: (7f 2, 8f) (gd 3)
Workmanlike, Pattern-class colt, effective 6 to 7f, best at 6f, acts on sft to g-f. Turf high 106 (1st run) - 2nd of 6 getting 1lb from Bertolini (14 Apr Newmarket 7f gd RF 0694). Held by Bertolini in the Free Handicap on his return, he never figured in the French Guineas but ran better in the Jersey Stakes at the Royal Meeting. However, he was not seen again. **B J Meehan [1-8] Joe Allbritton.*

INDIANA PRINCESS BHB 65f **RR 65f** 4044[3]
6 b m Warrshan (USA) 9.7f **(59)** - Lovely Greek Lady (Ela-Mana-Mou) 10.1f **(70)**
Form - 34113133
Record 1999 - 1st:3 2nd:0 3rd:4 Ran:8
Pre1999 - 1st:2 2nd:1 3rd:0 Ran:14
Win Prizemoney £14,704 *Total Prizemoney* £17,557
Wins * **1999** Aug Redcar (GD) H 16f 62 65 <
* **1999** Jun Mussel (G-S) H 16f 59 65 <
* **1999** Jun Mussel (GD) H 14f 54 57
* 1998 Jly Pontef (G-F) H 12f 49 59
* 1998 May Pontef (G-F) H 12f 46 47
1999 Turf 3-8: (12f, 13f, 14f 1-1, 16f 2-5) (gd 1-2, g-f 1-3, frm 1-3)
Average mare, effective 12 to 16f, best at 16f, acts on gd to frm, best on frm, and excels at Pontefract. Turf high 65 - 1st of 5 giving 14lb to Whitley Grange Boy (8 Aug Redcar RF 3471) - also 1st of 7 giving 21lb to Select Equiname (28 Jun Musselburgh RF 2361). Consistent. She did well in modest staying handicaps last season, winning three. **Mrs M Reveley [9-32] The Phoenix Racing C O.*

INDIANA SPRINGS (IRE) BHB 50f **RR 49f** 4455[12]
2 b c Foxhound (USA) - Moss Agate (Alias Smith (USA)) 9.8f **(58)**
Form - 700
Record 1999 - 1st:0 2nd:0 3rd:0 Ran:3
1999 Turf 0-3: (7f 2, 8f) (sft, g-f 2)
Currently moderate colt. Turf high 49 (began Jly).
**N P Littmoden [0-3] Plyvine, Guy, Howles & Slater.*

INDIAN BAZAAR (IRE) BHB 40f **RR 37f** 4448[18]
3 ch g Indian Ridge 7.6f **(74)** - Bazaar Promise (Native Bazaar) 6.9f **(62)**
Form - 0230
Record 1999 - 1st:0 2nd:1 3rd:1 Ran:4
Pre1999 - 1st:0 2nd:0 3rd:0 Ran:3
Win Prizemoney £0 *Total Prizemoney* £1,196
1999 Turf 0-3: (6f, 8f, 10f) (g-s, g-f, frm) 1999 AW 0-1: (12f) (Fibr)
Tall, very moderate gelding. Turf high 37 (began Aug).
**Sir Mark Prescott [0-7] Sturt Osborne House.*

INDIAN BLAZE BHB 86f67a **RR 86f 67a** 5141[10]
5 ch g Indian Ridge 7.6f **(74)** - Odile (Green Dancer (USA)) 10.3f **(74)**
Form - 03418001220321010640l0
Record 1999 - 1st:4 2nd:3 3rd:1 Ran:18
Pre1999 - 1st:2 2nd:3 3rd:1 Ran:22
Win Prizemoney £20,153 *Total Prizemoney* £28,246
Wins * **1999** Oct Newmar (GD) H 8f 80 84 <
* **1999** Aug Kempto (G-F) H 8f 74 76+
* **1999** Jly Kempto (G-F) H 7f 69 71
* **1999** Mar Folkes (SFT) H 7f 61 64
** 1998 Dec Wolver (SLW) H 7f 58 63*
* 1998 Nov Bright (SFT) H 6f 55 62
1999 Turf 4-15: (5f, 6f 2, 7f 2-8, 8f 2-4) (sft 1-2, g-s, gd 1-4, g-f 3, frm 2-5) 1999 AW 0-3: (6f 2, 7f) (Fibr 3)
Useful gelding, effective 7 to 8f, best at 8f, acts on gd to frm, best on gd, has worn blinkers, likes right handed tracks, excels at Kempton. Turf high 86 - 6th of 13 getting 9lb from Granny's Pet (28 Aug Goodwood 7f gd RF 3958) - also 1st of 20 getting 2lb from Smooth Sailing (14 Oct Newmarket RF 4874). AW high 52. A winner four times during a busy campaign, he is best over seven furlongs or a mile.
**D R C Elsworth [6-27] The Braves (from P W Harris [0-13] Apr 1998).*

INDIAN BRAVE BHB 59f **RR 65f** 5199[14]
5 b g Indian Ridge 7.6f **(74)** - Supreme Kingdom (Take A Reef) 7.5f **(59)**
Form - 6403356300
Record 1999 - 1st:0 2nd:0 3rd:3 Ran:10
Pre1999 - 1st:0 2nd:3 3rd:2 Ran:13
Win Prizemoney £0 *Total Prizemoney* £7,096
1999 Turf 0-10: (6f 6, 7f 3, 8f) (g-s, gd 4, g-f 2, frm 3)
Average gelding, effective 6f, acts on gd, has worn blinkers. Turf high 65. **John Harris [0-1] Steppey Lane Bloodstock (from N P Littmoden [0-8] Oct 1999).*

INDIAN CITY BHB 48f **RR 44f** 4945[2]
3 ch f Lahib (USA) 8f **(69)** - Alencon (Northfields (USA)) 9f **(72)**
Form - 00502
Record 1999 - 1st:0 2nd:1 3rd:0 Ran:5
Pre1999 - 1st:1 2nd:1 3rd:0 Ran:3
Win Prizemoney £2,024 *Total Prizemoney* £3,274
Wins * 1998 Aug Leices (GD) S 6f 55 <
1999 Turf 0-4: (6f 2, 7f 2) (gd 2, frm 2) 1999 AW 0-1: (7f) (Fibr)
Leggy, moderate filly, effective 6 to 7f, acts on g-f to frm. Turf high 44. Consistent. **R Guest [1-8] Mrs P D Savill.*

INDIAN DANCE BHB 56f **RR 60f** 4536[16]
3 ch c Indian Ridge 7.6f **(74)** - Petronella (USA) (Nureyev (USA)) 8.7f **(78)**
Form - 6560030
Record 1999 - 1st:0 2nd:0 3rd:1 Ran:7
Win Prizemoney £0 *Total Prizemoney* £550
1999 Turf 0-7: (6f, 7f 4, 8f 2) (g-s, g-f 4, frm 2)
Workmanlike, average colt. Turf high 67.
**J W Hills [0-7] George Tong.*

INDIAN FLAG (IRE) BHB 32f25a **RR 33f 25a** 2627[6]
4 ch f Indian Ridge 7.6f **(74)** - Flagpole (IRE) (Be My Guest (USA)) 9.3f **(67)**
Form - 0605036
Record 1999 - 1st:0 2nd:0 3rd:1 Ran:7
Pre1999 - 1st:0 2nd:0 3rd:1 Ran:4
Win Prizemoney £0 *Total Prizemoney* £837
1999 Turf 0-5: (7f, 8f 2, 10f, 11f) (sft, g-s, g-f, frm 2) 1999 AW 0-2: (8f, 12f) (Equi, Fibr)
Lengthy, very moderate filly. Turf high 33. AW high 19. Inconsistent.
**M D I Usher [0-7] P Sweeting (from J J Bridger [0-4] Jly 1998).*

INDIAN LODGE (IRE) BHB 110f **RR 108f** 4894[1]
3 b c Grand Lodge (USA) - Repetitious (Northfields (USA)) 9f **(72)**
Form - 11630211
Record 1999 - 1st:4 2nd:1 3rd:1 Ran:8
Pre1999 - 1st:0 2nd:0 3rd:1 Ran:3
Win Prizemoney £36,775 *Total Prizemoney* £50,902
Wins * **1999** Oct Newmar (GD) L 8.5f 100
* **1999** Spt Newmar (G-S) L 8f 108 <
* **1999** May Yarmou (FRM) 8f 89+
* **1999** May Newbur (Sft) 8f 85+
1999 Turf 4-8: (7f, 8f 3-6, 9f 1-1) (gd 3-4, g-f 1-2, frm 2)
Scopey, Pattern-class colt, effective 8 to 9f, best at 8f, acts on gd to frm, best on frm. Turf high 108 - 1st of 13 giving 5lb to Ras Shaikh (30 Spt Newmarket RF 4652) - also 1st of 9 giving 4lb to Maidaan (15 Oct Newmarket RF 4894). A useful handicapper, touched off in the William Hill Mile at Goodwood, he developed

into a listed performer, winning twice at Newmarket in the autumn. He is genuine and consistent. **Mrs A J Perrett [4-11] Sir Eric Parker.*

Indian Lodge became a useful Pattern race performer in the autumn

INDIAN MUSIC BHB 74f **RR 74df** 5214[1]
2 b c Indian Ridge 7.6f **(74)** -Dagny Juel (USA) (Danzig (USA)) 8.4f **(76)**
Form - 704071
Record 1999 - 1st:1 2nd:0 3rd:0 Ran:6
Win Prizemoney £3,468 *Total Prizemoney* £3,715
Wins * 1999 Nov Doncas (SFT) H 5f 72 74 <
1999 Turf 1-6: (5f 1-2, 6f 4) (sft, g-s 1-3, gd 2)
Above-average colt, effective 5f, acts on g-s to gd. Turf high 74 (began Jly) - 1st of 12 getting 6lb from Harryana (5 Nov Doncaster RF 5214). **J Berry [1-6] Robert Aird.*

INDIAN NECTAR BHB 56f51a **RR 58f 51a** 4646[8]
6 b m Indian Ridge 7.6f **(74)** - Sheer Nectar (Piaffer (USA))
Form - 434131168
Record 1999 - 1st:3 2nd:0 3rd:2 Ran:9
Pre1999 - 1st:0 2nd:0 3rd:0 Ran:11
Win Prizemoney £8,804 *Total Prizemoney* £10,114
Wins * 1999 Aug Chepst (G-S) H 10.2f 46 54 <
*** 1999** Aug Lingfi (G-F) H 10f 46 49
*** 1999** Aug Nottin (G-F) H 10f 40 43
1999 Turf 3-9: (10f 3-6, 11f, 12f 2) (g-s, gd, g-f 3-5, frm 2)
Fair mare, effective 10f, acts on g-f to frm, best on g-f, has worn blinkers, prefers left handed tracks. Turf high 58 - 6th of 14 giving 10lb to Otahuna (13 Spt Nottingham 10f frm RF 4288) - also 1st of 15 giving 5lb to Spring Pursuit (30 Aug Chepstow RF 4011).
**R Brotherton [5-32] Mrs Carol Newman (from G B Balding [0-8] Mar 1997).*

INDIAN PLUME BHB 85f **RR 75f** 3677[14]
3 b c Efisio 7.7f **(69)** - Boo Hoo (Mummy's Pet) 7.7f **(60)**
Form - 3400
Record 1999 - 1st:0 2nd:0 3rd:1 Ran:4
Pre1999 - 1st:1 2nd:0 3rd:0 Ran:3
Win Prizemoney £3,191 *Total Prizemoney* £5,128
Wins * 1998 Aug Pontef (G-F) 6f 77 <
1999 Turf 0-4: (7f, 8f 3) (gd 2, g-f, frm)
Scopey, above-average colt, effective 6 to 8f, acts on gd to frm. Turf high 83 (1st run) - 3rd of 13 giving 10lb to Prairie Wolf (15 Apr Ripon 8f gd RF 0708). **C W Thornton [1-7] Guy Reed.*

INDIAN ROPE TRICK BHB 50f **RR 44f** 4720[7]
3 ch c Kris 10f **(75)** - Lassoo (Caerleon (USA)) 8.6f **(71)**
Form - 077
Record 1999 - 1st:0 2nd:0 3rd:0 Ran:3
1999 Turf 0-3: (7f, 8f, 10f) (g-s, gd 2)
Workmanlike, currently moderate colt. Turf high 44 (began Jly). **C W Thornton [0-3] Guy Reed.*

INDIAN SPARK BHB 78f **RR 72f** 5212[15]
5 ch h Indian Ridge 7.6f **(74)** - Annes Gift (Ballymoss) 8.5f **(55)**
Form - 005534105300000000
Record 1999 - 1st:1 2nd:0 3rd:2 Ran:18
Pre1999 - 1st:5 2nd:5 3rd:0 Ran:32
Win Prizemoney £39,451 *Total Prizemoney* £53,331
Wins * 1999 Jun York (G-S) H 6f 84 87
* 1998 Oct Doncas (HVY) H 5f 84 87
* 1998 Spt Doncas (GD) H 5f 80 84
* 1998 Jly Thirsk (FRM) H 6f 76 82
1997 May Salisb (G-F) H 6f 98 99 <
1996 Mar Doncas (GD) 5f 85+
1999 Turf 1-18: (5f 7, 6f 1-11) (g-s 1-4, gd 9, g-f 4, frm)
Above-average colt, effective 5 to 6f, best at 5f, acts on sft to frm, excels at Thirsk, does well at Doncaster. Turf high 88 - 3rd of 9 giving 22lb to Peppiatt (19 Jly Ayr 6f g-s RF 2941) - also 1st of 7 getting 14lb from Halmahera (11 Jun York RF 1934).
**J S Goldie [4-39] Frank Brady (from W G M Turner [2-11] Spt 1997).*

INDIAN SPLENDOUR (IRE) BHB 37a **RR 37a** 319[12]
4 b f Second Set (IRE) 9.2f **(67)** - Clover Honey (King of Clubs) 7.1f **(57)**
Form - 000
Record 1999 - 1st:0 2nd:0 3rd:0 Ran:1
Pre1999 - 1st:0 2nd:1 3rd:0 Ran:7
Win Prizemoney £0 *Total Prizemoney* £715
1999 AW 0-1: (6f) (Fibr)
Neat, little account filly, effective 5f, - acts on Fibr. Becoming disappointing.
**R F Marvin [0-3] Tobias Barker (from R Guest [0-5] Apr 1998).*

INDIAN STUNNER (IRE) RR 6f 5047[12]
2 ch c Indian Ridge 7.6f **(74)** - Bazaar Promise (Native Bazaar) 6.9f **(62)**
Form - 0
Record 1999 - 1st:0 2nd:0 3rd:0 Ran:1
1999 Turf 0-1: (6f) (hvy)
Currently very poor colt. **D R C Elsworth [0-1] J McGarry.*

INDIAN SUN BHB 81f **RR 74f** 5045[13]
2 ch c Indian Ridge 7.6f **(74)** - Star Tulip **(91f)** (Night Shift (USA)) 7.2f **(69)**
Form - 7610
Record 1999 - 1st:1 2nd:0 3rd:0 Ran:4
Win Prizemoney £3,492 *Total Prizemoney* £3,492
Wins * 1999 Oct Lingfi (HVY) 6f 73+ <
1999 Turf 1-4: (6f 1-4) (sft, g-s 1-1, gd, frm)
Above-average colt. Turf high 74 - also 1st of 11 from Royal Insult (1 Oct Lingfield RF 4669). Uninspiring runs in maidens at Newbury and Goodwood were a prelude to a nice win in a competitive maiden at Lingfield in heavy ground. *J L Dunlop [1-4] James Flower.*

INDIAN SWINGER (IRE) BHB 62f64a **RR 55f 64a** 3672[5]
3 ch c Up and At 'em - Seanee Squaw (Indian Ridge)
Form - 623305
Record 1999 - 1st:0 2nd:1 3rd:2 Ran:5
Pre1999 - 1st:1 2nd:0 3rd:0 Ran:5
Win Prizemoney £3,099 *Total Prizemoney* £5,396
Wins * 1998 *Oct Southw (STD) H 6f* 62 69 <
1999 Turf 0-1: (6f) (g-f) 1999 AW 0-4: (6f, 7f, 8f 2) (Equi 2, Fibr 2)
Workmanlike, average colt, effective 6 to 7f, - acts on AW, likes left handed tracks, likes tight tracks. AW high 69 - 3rd of 5 getting 10lb from Bartholomew (18 Feb Lingfield 7f Equi RF 0314).
**J M P Eustace [1-10] Kissing Tree Partnership.*

INDIAN WARRIOR BHB 62f **RR 59f** 5217^{12}
3 b c Be My Chief (USA) 10.2f **(62)** - Wanton (Kris) 9.5f **(73)**
Form - 687010
Record **1999** - 1st:1 2nd:0 3rd:0 Ran:6
Pre1999 - 1st:1 2nd:2 3rd:1 Ran:5
Win Prizemoney £6,077 *Total Prizemoney* £9,054
Wins **1999** Oct Lingfi (G-F) S 7f 55+
1998 Aug Warwic (G-F) 7f 81 <
1999 Turf 1-6: (7f 1-4, 8f 2) (g-s, gd 1-2, frm 3)
Scopey, fair colt, effective 7f, acts on frm, has worn blinkers. Turf high 75 (began Jly). Consistent.
**W J Musson [0-1] Broughton Thermal Insulation (from J Noseda [2-10] Oct 1999).*

INDIGENOUS (IRE) RR 117f 3088^{6}
6 br g Marju (IRE) 9.2f **(76)** - Sea Port (Averof) 8.2f **(62)**
Form - 126
1999 Turf 0-2: (10f, 12f) (gd, g-f)
High-class gelding. Turf high 117. Improving. He originally raced in Ireland under the name Qualtron (IRE), but the name was amended under Rule 31 with effect from 3rd June 1999. Sent to race in Hong Kong, he held off a strong International field to win the Hong Kong International Vase at the end of 1998 and split Jim And Tonic and Johan Cruyff in the Queen Elizabeth II Cup in the spring. He ran creditably to finish sixth to Daylami in the King George, if never able to land a blow.
**I Allan in HK [1-3] Pang Yuen Hing (from K Prendergast in IRE [2-5] Jun 1996).*

INDIGO BAY (IRE) BHB 66f60a **RR 56f 60a** 4788^{9}
3 b g Royal Academy (USA) 7.8f **(77)** - Cape Heights (Shirley Heights) 10.3f **(74)**
Form - 73183212880
Record **1999** - 1st:2 2nd:2 3rd:2 Ran:11
Pre1999 - 1st:0 2nd:0 3rd:0 Ran:3
Win Prizemoney £4,832 *Total Prizemoney* £8,328
Wins *** 1999** Jly Lingfi (G-F) H 11.5f 66 72 <
*** 1999** May Bright (FRM) SH 11.9f 55 59
1999 Turf 2-10: (10f 2, 11f 1-4, 12f 1-3, 14f) (g-s, g-f 3, frm 1-4, hrd 1-2)
1999 AW 0-1: (10f) (Equi)
Workmanlike, average gelding, effective 11 to 12f, best at 12f, acts on g-f to frm, best on frm, has worn blinkers, prefers left handed tracks, prefers tight tracks. Turf high 72 - 1st of 5 getting 7lb from Ocean Park (31 Jly Lingfield RF 3275).
**S Dow [2-11] Normandy Developments (London) (from A C Stewart [0-3] Oct 1998).*

INDIGO BEACH (IRE) BHB 50f56a **RR 40f 56a** 1140^{11}
3 b g Rainbows For Life (CAN) 9.3f **(64)** - Sandy Maid (Sandy Creek) 8.9f **(59)**
Form - 0
Record **1999** - 1st:0 2nd:0 3rd:0 Ran:1
Pre1999 - 1st:0 2nd:0 3rd:0 Ran:5
1999 Turf 0-1: (12f) (g-f)
Scopey, average gelding.
**Sir Mark Prescott [0-6] Thurcoe Partnership.*

INDIRECT RR 44f 3454^{7}
2 ch f Interrex (CAN) 7.7f **(51)** - To The Point (Sharpen Up) 8.3f **(67)**
Form - 806857
Record **1999** - 1st:0 2nd:0 3rd:0 Ran:6
1999 Turf 0-4: (5f 2, 6f, 7f) (gd, g-f 2, frm) 1999 AW 0-2: (5f, 6f) (Fibr 2)
Moderate filly, has worn blinkers. Turf high 44. AW high 15.
**K A Ryan [0-6] Top of the World Racing (2).*

INDIUM BHB 79f66a **RR 78f 66a** 5141^{15}
5 b g Groom Dancer (USA) 9.5f **(75)** - Gold Bracelet (Golden Fleece (USA)) 7.9f **(74)**
Form - 5024072604100
Record **1999** - 1st:1 2nd:2 3rd:0 Ran:13
Pre1999 - 1st:1 2nd:1 3rd:3 Ran:20
Win Prizemoney £50,375 *Total Prizemoney* £57,810
Wins *** 1999** Spt Ascot (HVY) H 8f 74 78 <
*** 1998** Spt Newbur (GD) H 8f 71 77
1999 Turf 1-13: (7f 2, 8f 1-11) (sft 1-2, gd 2, g-f 2, frm 7)
Above-average gelding, effective 7 to 8f, best at 8f, acts on sft to frm, prefers right handed tracks, likes tight tracks, excels at Newbury and Kempton. Turf high 78 - 1st of 22 getting 2lb from The Whistling Teal (26 Spt Ascot RF 4569). Consistent. Inclined to blow a bit hot and cold, he is quite useful when on song. He showed signs of a revival when fourth in a big field of handicappers at Newbury in September, and appreciated the step back up to a mile when gaining a short-head victory in the Mail On Sunday Series Final at Ascot later the same month.
**W J Musson [2-28] Magnificent Seven (from J H M Gosden [0-5] Jun 1997).*

INDUCEMENT BHB 84f **RR 86f** 4505^{10}
3 ch c Sabrehill (USA) 8.5f **(64)** - Verchinina (Star Appeal) 9.6f **(65)**
Form - 5516480
Record **1999** - 1st:1 2nd:0 3rd:0 Ran:7
Pre1999 - 1st:1 2nd:0 3rd:2 Ran:5
Win Prizemoney £10,545 *Total Prizemoney* £14,201
Wins **1999** Jun Sandow (GD) H 9f 82 85 <
1998 Aug Beverl (G-F) 8.5f 81
1999 Turf 1-7: (8f, 9f 1-2, 10f 4) (gd, g-f 1-4, frm 2)
Leggy, useful colt, effective 6 to 10f, acts on g-s to g-f, best on g-f, likes tight tracks, excels at Beverley. Turf high 86 - 4th of 10 getting 3lb from Ipledgeallegiance (13 Aug Newbury 10f g-f RF 3618) - also 1st of 14 getting 2lb from Tarawan (12 Jun Sandown RF 1961).
**Mrs A J Perrett [0-3] J B Dale (from B W Hills [2-9] Jly 1999).*

INDUNA BHB 56f **RR 56f** 1246^{12}
3 ch f Grand Lodge (USA) - Kerkura (USA) **(71f 67a)** (Riverman (USA)) 9.1f **(76)**
Form - 880
Record **1999** - 1st:0 2nd:0 3rd:0 Ran:3
1999 Turf 0-3: (12f 3) (hvy, g-f, frm)
Workmanlike, currently fair filly. Turf high 56.
**S Dow [0-3] Mrs I P Blance.*

INDY CARR RR 79+f 5138^{1}
2 b f Pyramus (USA) - Miss Adventure (Adonijah) 10f **(61)**
Form - 1
Record **1999** - 1st:1 2nd:0 3rd:0 Ran:1
Win Prizemoney £4,207 *Total Prizemoney* £4,207
Wins *** 1999** Oct Newmar (SFT) S 8f 78+ <
1999 Turf 1-1: (8f 1-1) (gd 1-1)
Currently above-average filly. (1st run) - 1st of 18 from Inchinnan (30 Oct Newmarket RF 5138). **H J Collingridge [1-1] Ashley Carr.*

INDY KNIGHT (IRE) BHB 30f **RR 36f** 2425^{13}
4 ch f Indian Ridge 7.6f **(74)** - Bag Lady (Be My Guest (USA)) 9.3f **(67)**
Form - 000
Record **1999** - 1st:0 2nd:0 3rd:0 Ran:3
Pre1999 - 1st:0 2nd:0 3rd:0 Ran:5
1999 Turf 0-2: (8f, 10f) (sft, frm) 1999 AW 0-1: (12f) (Fibr)
Leggy, very moderate filly. Becoming disappointing.
**R E Peacock [0-3] Derek D & Mrs Jean P Clee (from M J Fetherston-Godley [0-2] Spt 1998).*

INFAMOUS (USA) BHB 52f38a **RR 68f 38a** 333^{3}
6 ch g Diesis 9f **(80)** - Name And Fame (USA) (Arts And Letters (USA)) 12.7f **(68)**
Form - 822253
Record **1999** - 1st:0 2nd:3 3rd:1 Ran:6
Pre1999 - 1st:1 2nd:4 3rd:2 Ran:17
Win Prizemoney £3,595 *Total Prizemoney* £12,108
Wins 1996 Mar Leices (SFT) 11.8f 79 <
1999 AW 0-6: (11f, 12f, 15f 2, 16f 2) (Fibr 6)
Average gelding, effective 12f, acts on g-f, has worn blinkers. AW high 44.
**B J Llewellyn [0-8] David Lewis (from R J O'Sullivan [2-15] Aug 1998).*

INFATUATION BHB 82f **RR 86df** 4788^{4}
6 b g Music Boy 6.5f **(56)** - Fleeting Affair (Hotfoot) 10.5f **(59)**
Form - 008138604
Record **1999** - 1st:1 2nd:0 3rd:1 Ran:9
Pre1999 - 1st:3 2nd:3 3rd:3 Ran:20
Win Prizemoney £34,723 *Total Prizemoney* £45,749
Wins *** 1999** Jun Newmar (G-F) H 10f 83 85
* 1998 Aug Newmar (G-F) H 10f 83 88 <
* 1997 Spt Doncas (G-F) H 10.3f 77 82
* 1997 Jun Beverl (SFT) H 12f 71 77

1999 Turf 1-9: (10f 1-8, 11f) (g-s, gd, g-f 1-2, frm 5)
Useful gelding, effective 10 to 12f, best at 10f, acts on sft to frm, best on frm, prefers right handed tracks, excels at Newmarket. Turf high 87 - 3rd of 8 giving 12lb to Forest Fire (16 Jly Newmarket 10f frm RF 2884) - also 1st of 8 giving 16lb to Hormuz (25 Jun Newmarket RF 2306). **Lady Herries [4-29] Lady Katharine Phillips.*

INFOTEC (IRE) BHB 74f **RR 60f** 4640[2]

2 b br c Shalford (IRE) 7.8f **(63)** - Tomona (Linacre) 6.7f **(40)**
Form - 722
Record 1999 - 1st:0 2nd:2 3rd:0 Ran:3
Win Prizemoney £0 *Total Prizemoney* £1,629
1999 Turf 0-3: (6f, 7f 2) (g-s 2, gd)
Currently average colt. Turf high 60 (began Aug) - 2nd of 11 getting 6lb from Chapel Royale (29 Spt Newcastle 7f gd RF 4640). **H Akbary [0-3] Michael Whatley.*

IN GOOD FAITH BHB 37f42a **RR 52f 42a** 2923[6]

7 b g Beveled (USA) 6.9f **(64)** - Dulcidene (Behistoun) 14.1f **(45)**
Form - 56
Record 1999 - 1st:0 2nd:0 3rd:0 Ran:2
Pre1999 - 1st:3 2nd:1 3rd:3 Ran:25
Win Prizemoney £14,226 *Total Prizemoney* £16,448
1999 Turf 0-2: (9f, 10f) (gd, frm)
Fair gelding, has worn blinkers. Turf high 36.
**R E Barr [2-10] P Cartmell (from J J Quinn [3-33] Jan 1998).*

IN GOOD ORDER (IRE) BHB 25a **RR 25a** 235[12]

4 b f Ajraas (USA) 7f **(53)** - Ponstinia (Yashgan)
Form - 770
Record 1999 - 1st:0 2nd:0 3rd:0 Ran:3
1999 AW 0-3: (10f 2, 12f) (Equi 3)
Very poor filly. AW high 9. **G L Moore [0-3] Mark Barrett.*

INIGO JONES (IRE) BHB 88f **RR 88f** 4540[3]

3 b g Alzao (USA) 9.8f **(73)** - Kindjal (Kris) 9.5f **(73)**
Form - 2322133
Record 1999 - 1st:1 2nd:3 3rd:3 Ran:7
Win Prizemoney £4,163 *Total Prizemoney* £12,544
Wins * 1999 Aug Nottin (G-F) 14.1f 73 <
1999 Turf 1-7: (10f, 11f, 12f 2, 14f 1-2, 15f) (gd 3, g-f 2, frm 1-2)
Workmanlike, useful gelding, effective 10 to 15f, acts on gd to frm, prefers left handed tracks. Turf high 88 - 3rd of 7 giving 4lb to Eilean Shona (24 Spt Redcar 14f frm RF 4540).
**P W Harris [1-7] Mrs P W Harris.*

INITIATIVE BHB 87f **RR 83f** 3832[5]

3 ch c Arazi (USA) 9.2f **(74)** - Dance Quest (FR) (Green Dancer (USA)) 10.3f **(74)**
Form - 15
Record 1999 - 1st:1 2nd:0 3rd:0 Ran:2
Pre1999 - 1st:0 2nd:0 3rd:1 Ran:1
Win Prizemoney £3,873 *Total Prizemoney* £4,717
Wins * 1999 May Thirsk (G-F) 8f 73++ <
1999 Turf 1-2: (8f 1-2) (g-f 1-1, frm)
Scopey, currently decent colt. Turf high 83.
**H R A Cecil [1-3] Exors of the late Lord Howard de Walden.*

INKWELL BHB 40f38a **RR 40f 38a** 5069[13]

5 b g Relief Pitcher 7.6f **(47)** - Fragrant Hackette (Simply Great (FR)) 8.2f **(65)**
Form - 00700220
Record 1999 - 1st:0 2nd:2 3rd:0 Ran:8
Pre1999 - 1st:3 2nd:1 3rd:5 Ran:26
Win Prizemoney £12,478 *Total Prizemoney* £16,540
Wins * 1998 Nov Bright (SFT) C 7f 57 <
* 1998 Aug Bath (GD) •H 8f 38 41
* 1998 Apr Bright (GD) H 8f 34 43
1999 Turf 0-8: (7f, 8f 3, 10f 3, 11f) (sft 2, g-s, gd 2, g-f, frm, hrd)
Moderate gelding, effective 7f, acts on g-s, has worn blinkers, likes left handed tracks, likes tight tracks. Turf high 40. Inconsistent.
**G L Moore [3-24] Phil Collins (from R P C Hoad [0-1] Mar 1999).*

INNER LIGHT BHB 46f40a **RR 35f 40a** 2255[6]

4 b g Slip Anchor 12.7f **(75)** - Radiance (FR) (Blakeney) 10.5f **(64)**
Form - 706
Record 1999 - 1st:0 2nd:0 3rd:0 Ran:2
Pre1999 - 1st:0 2nd:0 3rd:0 Ran:3
1999 Turf 0-1: (16f) (g-f) 1999 AW 0-1: (11f) (Fibr)
Leggy, very moderate gelding, has worn blinkers.
**B A Pearce [0-13] Mrs P Salter.*

INNES BHB 55f **RR 55f** 3863[7]

3 b f Inchinor 8.9f **(64)** - Trachelium **(44df)** (Formidable (USA)) 9.2f **(63)**
Form - 637
Record 1999 - 1st:0 2nd:0 3rd:1 Ran:3
Pre1999 - 1st:0 2nd:0 3rd:0 Ran:1
Win Prizemoney £0 *Total Prizemoney* £307
1999 Turf 0-3: (12f 3) (frm 3)
Unfurnished, fair filly. Turf high 55 (began Jly) - 7th of 18 to Sing And Dance (24 Aug Hamilton 12f frm RF 3863).
**Miss S E Hall [0-4] C Platts.*

INNKEEPER BHB 76f **RR 75f** 4012[7]

2 b c Night Shift (USA) 8.1f **(73)** - Riyoom (USA) (Vaguely Noble) 10.1f **(72)**
Form - 442487
Record 1999 - 1st:0 2nd:1 3rd:0 Ran:6
Win Prizemoney £0 *Total Prizemoney* £2,376
1999 Turf 0-6: (6f 5, 7f) (gd 2, g-f 2, frm 2)
Above-average colt, effective 6f, acts on gd to frm. Turf high 75 - 2nd of 4 to Observatory (30 Jun Yarmouth 6f gd RF 2451).
**Sir Michael Stoute [0-6] The Royal Ascot Racing Club.*

INN ON THE PARK BHB 38f **RR 38f** 58[8]

4 b g Northern Park (USA) 10f **(57)** - Hotel California (IRE) (Last Tycoon) 8.5f **(62)**
Form - 68
Record 1999 - 1st:0 2nd:0 3rd:0 Ran:1
Pre1999 - 1st:0 2nd:0 3rd:0 Ran:5
1999 AW 0-1: (16f) (Equi)
Leggy, very moderate gelding.
**S Dow [0-7] Cazanove Clear Height Racing.*

INNUENDO (IRE) BHB 107f **RR 104f** 4209[4]

4 b f Caerleon (USA) 10.9f **(79)** - Infamy (Shirley Heights) 10.3f **(74)**
Form - 2214
Record 1999 - 1st:1 2nd:2 3rd:0 Ran:4
Pre1999 - 1st:3 2nd:2 3rd:0 Ran:5
Win Prizemoney £40,083 *Total Prizemoney* £66,506
Wins * 1999 Aug York (GD) L 11.9f 97
* 1998 Oct Newmar (GD) L 12f 104 <
* 1998 Jly Salisb (GD) 9.9f 90+
* 1998 Jun Pontef (GD) 10f 70++
1999 Turf 1-4: (12f 1-2, 14f, 15f) (gd 1-3, frm)
Scopey, very useful filly, effective 10 to 15f, acts on gd to frm, best on gd. Turf high 108 (began Jly) - 2nd of 11 to Bimbola (1 Aug Deauville 14f gd RF 3408a). Consistent. Like her dam, Infamy, this scopey filly improved steadily through her three-year-old season. She put in a good run on her seasonal bow at Newmarket and was second in a Deauville Group Two before giving her trainer his eighth winner in the last twelve runnings of York's Galtres Stakes. A little disappointing in the Park Hill Stakes, however.
**L M Cumani [4-9] Gerald Leigh.*

INSATIABLE (IRE) BHB 120f **RR 125f** 4476a[1]

6 b h Don't Forget Me 9.5f **(66)** - Petit Eclair (Major Portion) 6.8f **(75)**
Form - 461
Record 1999 - 1st:1 2nd:0 3rd:0 Ran:3
Pre1999 - 1st:5 2nd:2 3rd:2 Ran:13
Win Prizemoney £123,501 *Total Prizemoney* £233,829
Wins * 1999 Spt Currag (SFT) G3 11f 119+
* 1998 Oct Longch (SFT) G2 9.8f 119
* 1998 May Sandow (G-S) G3 10f 120 <
* 1998 May Newmar (G-S) 10f 109
* 1997 May Sandow (G-F) H 8.1f 96 105
* 1995 Spt Newcas (GD) 7f 78+
1999 Turf 1-3: (10f, 11f 1-2) (g-s 1-1, g-f, frm)
Top-class horse, effective 10 to 11f, best at 10f, acts on sft to gd, best on gd. Turf high 119 - 1st of 5 from Theatreworld (19 Spt Curragh RF 4476a). A top-notch ten-furlong performer at his best, he managed three victories in 1998 and was possibly unlucky not to win the Champion Stakes, as he finished very strongly after meeting trouble in running. He never really hit the same heights last season, but did not have the ground in his favour until the

Curragh in September, when he walked away with a weak renewal of the Group Three Blandford Stakes. He has been retired.
**Sir Michael Stoute [6-16] Sir Evelyn De Rothschild.*

IN SEQUENCE (USA) RR 76f 4178[7]

2 gr f Robyn Dancer (USA) - What Option (USA) (Star de Naskra (USA)) 9.7f **(65)**
Form - 47
Record 1999 - 1st:0 2nd:0 3rd:0 Ran:2
Win Prizemoney £0 *Total Prizemoney* £247
1999 Turf 0-2: (6f 2) (frm 2)
Currently above-average filly. Turf high 76 (1st run) (began Jly) - 4th of 7 to Sioux Chef (20 Jly Bath 6f frm RF 2958).
**J A R Toller [0-2] Michael Hill.*

INSIGHTFUL (IRE) BHB 77f RR 75f 5218[3]

2 b g Desert Style (IRE) - Insight (Ballad Rock) 7.8f **(63)**
Form - 510253
Record 1999 - 1st:1 2nd:1 3rd:1 Ran:6
Win Prizemoney £5,085 *Total Prizemoney* £7,281
Wins 1999 Jly Newmar (GD) S 7f 75 <
1999 Turf 1-6: (6f, 7f 1-2, 8f 3) (g-s, gd 3, frm 1-2)
Above-average gelding, effective 7 to 8f, best at 7f, acts on g-s to frm. Turf high 75 - 3rd of 22 giving 10lb to Omniheat (6 Nov Doncaster 7f g-s RF 5218) - also 1st of 14 giving 5lb to Secret Conquest (7 Jly Newmarket RF 2633).
**R Hannon [0-4] Mrs B Burchett (from B J Meehan [1-2] Jly 1999).*

INSINUATE (USA) BHB 97f RR 96f 2133[3]

3 ch f Mr Prospector (USA) 8.6f **(88)** - All At Sea (USA) (Riverman (USA)) 9.1f **(76)**
Form - 3153
Record 1999 - 1st:1 2nd:0 3rd:2 Ran:4
Win Prizemoney £13,745 *Total Prizemoney* £16,942
Wins * 1999 Apr Ascot (GD) L 8f 96 <
1999 Turf 1-4: (7f, 8f 1-2, 10f) (gd 2, g-f 1-2)
Scopey, very useful filly. Turf high 96 - 3rd of 15 giving 13lb to Holly Blue (19 Jun Ascot 8f g-f RF 2133) - also 1st of 7 from Sweet Emotion (28 Apr Ascot RF 0896). She looked potentially smart when winning a Listed event in the spring, but failed to improve on that effort. Probably best around a mile, she lacks a telling turn-of-foot. **H R A Cecil [1-4] K Abdulla.*

INTEABADUN BHB 26f29a RR 34f 29a 2559[4]

7 ch g Hubbly Bubbly (USA) 9.5f **(43)** - Madam Taylor (Free State) 8.7f **(61)**
Form - 44
Record 1999 - 1st:0 2nd:0 3rd:0 Ran:2
Pre1999 - 1st:0 2nd:0 3rd:0 Ran:5
Win Prizemoney £0 *Total Prizemoney* £196
1999 Turf 0-2: (16f 2) (g-f, frm)
Very moderate gelding. Turf high 34.
**M Mullineaux [0-3] Esprit de Corps Racing (from A Bailey [0-6] Mar 1996).*

INTENSITY BHB 78f RR 79f 5022[1]

3 b c Bigstone (IRE) - Brillante (FR) (Green Dancer (USA)) 10.3f **(74)**
Form - 15001
Record 1999 - 1st:2 2nd:0 3rd:0 Ran:5
Pre1999 - 1st:0 2nd:0 3rd:0 Ran:1
Win Prizemoney £8,223 *Total Prizemoney* £8,223
Wins * 1999 Oct Doncas (G-S) H 10.3f 72 79 <
1999 Aug Newcas (FRM) 9f 70
1999 Turf 2-5: (8f, 9f 1-1, 10f 1-3) (gd 1-1, g-f 1-1, frm 3)
Workmanlike, above-average colt, effective 9 to 10f, best at 10f, acts on gd to frm. Turf high 79 (began Aug) - 1st of 12 giving 4lb to Cut The Spice (22 Oct Doncaster RF 5022) - also 1st of 3 from Falcon Spirit (4 Aug Newcastle RF 3367).
**M H Tompkins [1-2] High Havens Stables (from K R Burke [1-4] Spt 1999).*

INTERDREAM BHB 45f RR 57df 4076[18]

5 b g Interrex (CAN) 7.7f **(51)** - Dreamtime Quest (Blakeney) 10.5f **(64)**
Form - 00
Record 1999 - 1st:0 2nd:0 3rd:0 Ran:2
Pre1999 - 1st:3 2nd:3 3rd:2 Ran:25
Win Prizemoney £8,191 *Total Prizemoney* £12,469
Wins 1997 Aug Kempto (GD) H 9f 70 74 <
1997 Jly Bright (FRM) H 10f 60 62+
1996 Spt Bright (FRM) 7f 69
1999 Turf 0-2: (10f, 12f) (g-f, frm)
Fair gelding.
**C J Mann [2-9] Mark Heaton (from R Hannon [3-25] Jly 1998).*

INTERLUDE RR 88++f 5020[1]

2 b f Sadler's Wells (USA) 11.3f **(87)** - Starlet (Teenoso (USA)) 9.9f **(72)**
Form - 1
Record 1999 - 1st:1 2nd:0 3rd:0 Ran:1
Win Prizemoney £3,858 *Total Prizemoney* £3,858
Wins * 1999 Oct Doncas (G-S) 8f 88++ <
1999 Turf 1-1: (8f 1-1) (gd 1-1)
Currently useful filly. (1st run) - 1st of 18 from Caballe (22 Oct Doncaster RF 5020). Showed a startling turn of foot on her debut, and should be kept on the right side of.
**Sir Michael Stoute [1-1] The Queen.*

INTERNAL AFFAIR (USA) BHB 60a RR 54f 5156[4]

4 b g Nicholas (USA) 6.1f **(63)** - Gdynia (USA) (Sir Ivor) 10.2f **(70)**
Form - 277250006154
Record 1999 - 1st:1 2nd:2 3rd:0 Ran:12
Pre1999 - 1st:1 2nd:0 3rd:0 Ran:8
Win Prizemoney £4,920 *Total Prizemoney* £7,140
Wins * 1999 *Oct Wolver (STD) H 8.5f 60 63* <
1998 Jun Wolver (STD) 5f 62
1999 Turf 0-10: (7f 3, 8f 6, 9f) (hvy, g-s, gd 4, g-f 2, frm 2) 1999 AW 1-2: (8f 1-2) (Fibr 1-2)
Scopey, average gelding, effective 5 to 9f, best at 8f, acts on hvy to g-f - acts on Fibr, likes tight tracks, excels at Wolverhampton. Turf high 60 - 2nd of 20 getting 2lb from Admirals Flame (12 Jun Leicester 8f gd RF 1946). AW high 63 - 1st of 13 giving 8lb to Kafil (16 Oct Wolverhampton RF 4927). He has been more successful on Fibresand than on turf in the last couple of seasons and was given a fine ride when winning over the extended mile at Wolverhampton in October. Sometimes tends to stand still in the stalls.
**T D Barron [1-7] Stephen Woodall (from W J Haggas [1-13] Jun 1999).*

IN THE ARENA (USA) RR 49f 4825[10]

2 ch c Cadeaux Genereux 7.9f **(76)** - Tajfah (USA) (Shadeed (USA)) 8.2f **(70)**
Form - 00
Record 1999 - 1st:0 2nd:0 3rd:0 Ran:2
1999 Turf 0-2: (6f 2) (g-f, frm)
Currently moderate colt. Turf high 49 (began Spt).
**B W Hills [0-2] Maktoum Al Maktoum.*

IN THE NICK (IRE) BHB 60f RR 71f 4877[19]

2 b g Case Law 6f **(64)** - Bridewell Belle (Saulingo) 6.2f **(53)**
Form - 4600
Record 1999 - 1st:0 2nd:0 3rd:0 Ran:4
1999 Turf 0-4: (5f 4) (g-f 2, frm 2)
Above-average gelding. Turf high 71. **J Berry [0-4] J K Brown.*

IN THE STOCKS BHB 52f RR 49f 4948[1]

5 b m Reprimand 8.2f **(63)** - Stock Hill Lass (Air Trooper) 9.1f **(63)**
Form - 4467561
Record 1999 - 1st:1 2nd:0 3rd:0 Ran:7
Pre1999 - 1st:1 2nd:0 3rd:0 Ran:9
Win Prizemoney £5,214 *Total Prizemoney* £5,490
Wins * 1999 Oct Lingfi (G-F) H 11.5f 47 49
* 1998 Spt Bath (GD) SH 8f 47 52 <
1999 Turf 1-7: (8f 3, 10f 2, 11f 1-2) (sft, gd, g-f 1-2, frm 3)
Moderate filly, effective 8 to 11f, best at 8f, acts on gd to frm, best on frm, likes left handed tracks, favours tight tracks. Turf high 52 (1st run) - 4th of 16 getting 10lb from Twin Time (17 May Bath 8f gd RF 1272). Consistent. **L G Cottrell [2-16] E Gadsden.*

INTIAASH (IRE) BHB 44f52a RR 43f 52a 3871[14]

7 br m Shaadi (USA) 8.1f **(75)**-Funun (USA) (Fappiano (USA)) 8.7f **(77)**
Form - 5310205400300470
Record 1999 - 1st:1 2nd:1 3rd:2 Ran:15
Pre1999 - 1st:5 2nd:6 3rd:4 Ran:49
Win Prizemoney £19,734 *Total Prizemoney* £32,183
Wins * 1999 *Jan Southw (STD) H 6f 51 58*

* 1997	*Jly*	*Lingfi*	*(STD)*	*C*	*5f*		*69*
* 1997	May	Bath	(G-S)	H	5.1f	75	79 <
* 1997	Apr	Bath	(G-F)	H	5.1f	68	74
* 1996	*May*	*Wolver*	*(STD)*	*C*	*6f*		*75*
1995	Oct	Redcar	(FRM)		6f		72

1999 Turf 0-7: (5f, 6f 6) (g-f 6, frm) 1999 AW 1-8: (5f, 6f 1-7) (Equi 2, Fibr 1-6)

Fair mare, effective 6f, acts on frm - acts on Fibr, has worn blinkers, likes left handed tracks. Turf high 47. AW high 60 - 2nd of 15 getting 12lb from Theatre Magic (18 Jan Southwell 6f Fibr RF 0116) - also 1st of 15 getting 16lb from General Klaire (4 Jan Southwell RF 0024).

**D HaydnJones [5-53] Howard Thomas (from P T Walwyn [1-11] Oct 1995).*

INTIKHAB (USA) BHB 130f RR 131?f 1235[4]

5 b h Red Ransom (USA) 8.6f **(83)** - Crafty Example (USA) (Crafty Prospector (USA)) 8.2f **(104)**

Form - 4

Record				
1999 -	1st:0	2nd:0	3rd:0	Ran:1
Pre1999 -	1st:7	2nd:5	3rd:0	Ran:12

Win Prizemoney £137,064 *Total Prizemoney* £228,420

Wins						
* 1998	Jun	Ascot	(G-S)	G2	8f	131+ <
* 1998	Jun	Epsom	(GD)	G3	8.5f	121+
1997	Oct	Newmar	(GD)	L	8f	87
1997	Spt	Epsom	(GD)	L	8.5f	108
1997	Jly	Doncas	(GD)		8f	99
1996	Oct	Yarmou	(G-F)		6f	87+
1996	Spt	Pontef	(G-F)		6f	83+

1999 Turf 0-1: (8f) (gd)

High-calibre colt. He was the top miler of 1998 despite not getting the opportunity to prove himself in Group One company, but suffered from a splint problem after his demolition job in the Queen Anne Stakes and was not seen again that season. His only outing in 1999 came in the Lockinge Stakes but, despite looking fit enough, finished a rather tired fourth in the soft ground. Unfortunately, he sustained an injury there, and has been retired to stud.

**S bin Suroor [2-3] Godolphin (from S bin Suroor in UAE [0-1] Mar 1998).*

Intikhab again suffered injury problems

INTIMAA (IRE) BHB 100f RR 107f 4652[5]

3 b f Caerleon (USA) 10.9f **(79)** - Nahilah (Habitat) 9.4f **(70)**

Form - 33035

Record				
1999 -	1st:0	2nd:0	3rd:3	Ran:5
Pre1999 -	1st:1	2nd:1	3rd:1	Ran:3

Win Prizemoney £2,393 *Total Prizemoney* £14,115

Wins * 1998 Aug Yarmou (FRM) 6f 64 <

1999 Turf 0-5: (7f 3, 8f 2) (gd, g-f 4)

Strong, Pattern-class filly, effective 7f, acts on g-f. Turf high 107 - 3rd of 7 getting 15lb from Tumbleweed Ridge (3 Spt Epsom 7f g-f RF 4119). **P T Walwyn [1-8] Hamdan Al Maktoum.*

IN TIME BHB 65f RR 65f 1175[6]

3 ch f Generous (IRE) 11.5f **(82)** - Affection Affirmed (USA) (Affirmed (USA)) 9.3f **(79)**

Form - 6

Record				
1999 -	1st:0	2nd:0	3rd:0	Ran:1
Pre1999 -	1st:0	2nd:0	3rd:1	Ran:4

Win Prizemoney £0 *Total Prizemoney* £682

1999 Turf 0-1: (12f) (g-f)

Leggy, average filly. **P F I Cole [0-5] H R H Prince Fahd Salman.*

INTIZAA (USA) BHB 67f RR 74f 5193[6]

3 b br f Mr Prospector (USA) 8.6f **(88)** - Oumaldaaya (USA) (Nureyev (USA)) 8.7f **(78)**

Form - 25736

Record				
1999 -	1st:0	2nd:1	3rd:1	Ran:5
Pre1999 -	1st:0	2nd:0	3rd:1	Ran:2

Win Prizemoney £0 *Total Prizemoney* £3,123

1999 Turf 0-5: (8f 4, 9f) (gd 2, g-f 2, frm)

Scopey, above-average filly. Turf high 75.

**J L Dunlop [0-7] Hamdan Al Maktoum.*

INTRICATE WEB (IRE) BHB 68f RR 68f 4906[1]

3 b g Warning 8.1f **(77)** - In Anticipation **00**

Form - 5056301

Record				
1999 -	1st:1	2nd:0	3rd:1	Ran:7

Win Prizemoney £4,666 *Total Prizemoney* £5,285

Wins * 1999 Oct Redcar (GD) H 7f 63 68 <

1999 Turf 1-7: (7f 1-4, 8f, 9f, 10f) (sft, gd 3, frm 1-3)

Average gelding, effective 7f, acts on frm, has worn blinkers. Turf high 72 - also 1st of 30 getting 6lb from The Haulier (15 Oct Redcar RF 4906).

**E J Alston [1-5] Morris, Oliver, Pierce (from D K Weld in IRE [0-2] Jun 1999).*

INTRUM MORSHAAN (IRE) BHB 71f RR 83f 4728[3]

2 b br f Darshaan 11.9f **(81)** - Auntie Maureen (IRE) **(65f)** (Roi Danzig (USA))

Form - 863

Record				
1999 -	1st:0	2nd:0	3rd:1	Ran:3

Win Prizemoney £0 *Total Prizemoney* £635

1999 Turf 0-3: (7f, 8f 2) (g-s, gd, frm)

Currently decent filly. Turf high 83 (began Spt) - 3rd of 14 to Embraced (5 Oct Nottingham 8f g-s RF 4728).

**J L Dunlop [0-3] Mrs Maria Mai Goransson.*

INVADER BHB 90f RR 96f 734[5]

3 b c Danehill (USA) 9.1f **(79)** - Donya (Mill Reef (USA)) 10.5f **(78)**

Form - 45

Record				
1999 -	1st:0	2nd:0	3rd:0	Ran:2
Pre1999 -	1st:0	2nd:0	3rd:0	Ran:4

Win Prizemoney £0 *Total Prizemoney* £758

1999 Turf 0-2: (7f, 9f) (g-f 2)

Scopey, very useful colt, effective 7f, acts on gd. Turf high 96. A maiden, he was flattered to finish close up in the Greenham Stakes. Sold for 52,000 gns at Tattersalls in October.

**C E Brittain [0-6] Sheikh Mohammed Obaid Al Maktoum.*

INVENTIVE BHB 87f RR 84f 5061[1]

2 b f Sheikh Albadou 9.2f **(75)** - Ingenuity (Clever Trick (USA)) 6.6f **(77)**

Form - 52151

Record				
1999 -	1st:2	2nd:1	3rd:0	Ran:5

Win Prizemoney £6,992 *Total Prizemoney* £7,678

Wins					
* 1999	Oct	Lingfi	(HVY)	5f	84 <
* 1999	Spt	Lingfi	(HVY)	5f	81

1999 Turf 2-5: (5f 2-2, 6f 3) (g-s 2-2, gd, frm 2)

Decent filly. Turf high 84 (began Jly) - 1st of 7 getting 10lb from With Iris (25 Oct Lingfield RF 5061) - also 1st of 17 getting 5lb from Bond Boy (24 Spt Lingfield RF 4531). Clearly suited by testing ground and the minimum trip. **R Hannon [2-5] The Queen.*

INVER GOLD RR 72+f 5157[6]

2 ch c Arazi (USA) 9.2f **(74)**-Mary Martin (Be My Guest (USA)) 9.3f **(67)**

Form - 6

Record 1999 - 1st:0 2nd:0 3rd:0 Ran:1
1999 Turf 0-1: (7f) (frm)
Currently above-average colt. **M Johnston [0-1] Greenland Park Ltd.*

INVERMARK BHB 116f **RR 119f** 4768a[4]

5 b g Machiavellian (USA) 9.8f **(83)** -Applecross (Glint of Gold) 9.3f **(66)**
Form - 3224
Record 1999 - 1st:0 2nd:2 3rd:1 Ran:4
Pre1999 - 1st:4 2nd:2 3rd:1 Ran:16
Win Prizemoney £76,181 *Total Prizemoney* £154,317
Wins * 1998 Oct Longch (SFT) G1 20f 109 <
* 1998 Aug Cheste (G-S) LH 13.4f 90 100
* 1998 Jly Haydoc (GD) H 14f 82 88
* 1997 Jly Yarmou (G-F) 11.5f 78
1999 Turf 0-4: (15f, 19f, 20f 2) (hvy, gd, g-f 2)
High-class gelding, effective 15 to 20f, best at 20f, acts on hvy to g-f, and excels at Chester. Turf high 119 - 2nd of 17 giving 2lb to Enzeli (17 Jun Ascot 20f g-f RF 2071). Improved significantly in 1998 and returned last season with a terrific third in the Chester Cup, before chasing home Enzeli in the Ascot Gold Cup. He put in a solid effort to chase home Kayf Tara in the Prix Kergorlay, but pulled too hard in the early stages when well beaten in the Prix du Cadran. A grand stayer who has a bright turn of foot.
**J R Fanshawe [4-20] Sir David Wills.*

INVINCIBLE SPIRIT (IRE) BHB 100f **RR 101+f** 4653[6]

2 b c Green Desert (USA) 7.8f **(78)** - Rafha (Kris) 9.5f **(73)**
Form - 3116
Record 1999 - 1st:2 2nd:0 3rd:1 Ran:4
Win Prizemoney £20,376 *Total Prizemoney* £21,718
Wins * **1999** Aug Ripon (GD) L 6f 106+ <
* **1999** Jly Goodwo (G-F) 6f 85+
1999 Turf 2-4: (6f 2-4) (gd, g-f 1-1, frm 1-2)
Very useful colt. Turf high 106 (began Jly) - 1st of 10 giving 5lb to Khasayl (30 Aug Ripon RF 4029). Came on from his debut to win a Goodwood maiden in taking style. Looked good when landing a Ripon Listed event with the minimum of fuss and his last of six in the Middle Park Stakes was disappointing.
**J L Dunlop [2-4] Prince A A Faisal.*

INVIRAMENTAL BHB 48f **RR 44f** 5147[7]

3 b c Pursuit of Love 9.5f **(69)** - Corn Futures (Nomination) 7f **(60)**
Form - 057
Record 1999 - 1st:0 2nd:0 3rd:0 Ran:3
1999 Turf 0-1: (10f) (gd) 1999 AW 0-2: (7f, 8f) (Fibr 2)
Currently moderate colt. AW high 44 (began Oct).
**D HaydnJones [0-3] Hugh O'Donnell.*

INVISIBLE FORCE (IRE) **RR 52f** 4139[14]

2 b c Imperial Frontier (USA) 7f **(65)** - Virginia Cottage (Lomond (USA)) 8.8f **(65)**
Form - 40
Record 1999 - 1st:0 2nd:0 3rd:0 Ran:2
Win Prizemoney £0 *Total Prizemoney* £284
1999 Turf 0-2: (7f 2) (frm 2)
Currently fair colt. Turf high 52 (began Aug).
**B S Rothwell [0-2] Jim Browne.*

INYA LAKE BHB 105f **RR 101f** 3166[14]

3 b f Whittingham (IRE) - Special One (Aragon) 8.1f **(60)**
Form - 127040
Record 1999 - 1st:1 2nd:1 3rd:0 Ran:6
Pre1999 - 1st:4 2nd:0 3rd:1 Ran:9
Win Prizemoney £46,240 *Total Prizemoney* £55,208
Wins * **1999** Apr Haydoc (SFT) L 5f 101 <
* 1998 Jly Goodwo (G-S) G3 5f 97
* 1998 Jun Catter (G-S) 5f 76
* 1998 Apr Hamilt (HVY) 5f 65
* 1998 Mar Doncas (GD) S 5f 47
1999 Turf 1-6: (5f 1-6) (g-s, gd 1-1, g-f 2, frm 2)
Light-framed, very useful filly, effective 5f, acts on gd. Turf high 101 - also 1st of 7 giving 2lb to Henry Hall (3 Apr Haydock RF 0562). Inconsistent. She began her career in sellers and has done connections proud. Successful in a Listed event at Haydock in April, she appreciates easy ground and is raced exclusively over five furlongs. **M R Channon [5-15] Barry Minty.*

IONIAN SECRET BHB 45f **RR 39f** 3387[3]

3 b f Mystiko (USA) 7.7f **(59)** - Hearten (Hittite Glory) 8.7f **(50)**
Form - 0583
Record 1999 - 1st:0 2nd:0 3rd:1 Ran:4
Pre1999 - 1st:0 2nd:0 3rd:0 Ran:1
Win Prizemoney £0 *Total Prizemoney* £394
1999 Turf 0-4: (5f, 6f 2, 10f) (g-f 2, frm 2)
Neat, very moderate filly. Turf high 55.
**M P Tregoning [0-5] The Emotional Partnership.*

IPANEMA BEACH **RR 58f** 5054[6]

2 ch f Lion Cavern (USA) 7.5f **(74)** - Girl From Ipanema **(102df)** (Salse (USA)) 7.5f **(66)**
Form - 6
Record 1999 - 1st:0 2nd:0 3rd:0 Ran:1
1999 Turf 0-1: (6f) (gd)
Currently fair filly. **J W Hills [0-1] Christopher Wright.*

IPCRESS FILLY BHB 48f54a **RR 12f 54a** 1382[17]

3 b f Puissance 7.1f **(60)** - Daymer Bay (Lomond (USA)) 8.8f **(65)**
Form - 266700
Record 1999 - 1st:0 2nd:0 3rd:0 Ran:4
Pre1999 - 1st:0 2nd:1 3rd:1 Ran:7
Win Prizemoney £0 *Total Prizemoney* £1,091
1999 Turf 0-2: (7f, 8f) (gd, g-f) 1999 AW 0-2: (7f, 8f) (Fibr 2)
Light-framed, moderate filly, effective 7f, - acts on Fibr, likes left handed tracks, likes tight tracks. Turf high 12. AW high 43.
**J M P Eustace [0-11] Mrs James Eustace.*

IPLEDGEALLEGIANCE (USA) BHB 93f **RR 93f** 4594[5]

3 b c Alleged (USA) 11.8f **(81)** - Yafill (USA) (Nureyev (USA)) 8.7f **(78)**
Form - 2667113105
Record 1999 - 1st:3 2nd:1 3rd:1 Ran:10
Pre1999 - 1st:0 2nd:0 3rd:0 Ran:2
Win Prizemoney £17,421 *Total Prizemoney* £20,092
Wins * **1999** Aug Newbur (GD) H 10f 91 93 <
* **1999** Jly Sandow (G-F) H 10f 86 89
* **1999** Jun Pontef (GD) 10f 85
1999 Turf 3-10: (9f, 10f 3-7, 12f 2) (g-s, gd, g-f 1-3, frm 2-5)
Light-framed, useful colt, effective 9 to 12f, best at 10f, acts on gd to frm, best on frm, prefers right handed tracks, and excels at Sandown. Turf high 93 - 1st of 10 getting 1lb from Annapurna (13 Aug Newbury RF 3618) - also 1st of 9 giving 2lb to Fahs (22 Jly Sandown RF 3030). **E A L Dunlop [3-12] Maktoum Al Maktoum.*

I PROMISE YOU BHB 70f **RR 70f** 5196[5]

2 b c Shareef Dancer (USA) 10.1f **(67)** - Abuzz (Absalom) 7.2f **(58)**
Form - 064035
Record 1999 - 1st:0 2nd:0 3rd:1 Ran:6
Win Prizemoney £0 *Total Prizemoney* £743
1999 Turf 0-6: (5f, 7f 2, 8f 3) (g-s, gd, g-f 4)
Above-average colt, effective 8f, acts on g-f. Turf high 72.
**C E Brittain [0-6] Mrs C E Brittain.*

IRANOO (IRE) BHB 53f **RR 60f** 4022[2]

2 b c Persian Bold 10f **(69)** - Rose of Summer (IRE) (Taufan (USA)) 7f **(57)**
Form - 0604702
Record 1999 - 1st:0 2nd:1 3rd:0 Ran:7
Win Prizemoney £0 *Total Prizemoney* £760
1999 Turf 0-7: (5f, 6f 3, 7f 2, 8f) (gd 4, g-f 3)
Average colt, effective 8f, acts on g-f. Turf high 60 - 2nd of 11 getting 10lb from Just Bremner (30 Aug Newcastle 8f g-f RF 4022).
**S C Williams [0-7] The Lager Khan.*

I RECALL (IRE) BHB 42f44a **RR 47f 44a** 2504[18]

8 b g Don't Forget Me 9.5f **(66)** - Sable Lake (Thatching) 8f **(66)**
Form - 200
Record 1999 - 1st:0 2nd:1 3rd:0 Ran:3
Pre1999 - 1st:0 2nd:1 3rd:2 Ran:13
Win Prizemoney £0 *Total Prizemoney* £3,399
1999 Turf 0-3: (11f 3) (sft, g-s, g-f)
Moderate gelding, effective 11f, acts on sft, often wears blinkers (effectively). Turf high 47 (1st run) - 2nd of 5 getting 21lb from Musician (29 May Warwick 11f sft RF 1590).
**P Hayward [0-32] Mrs S A Coplestone (from P Hayward [0-1] May 1995).*

IRELAND'S EYE (IRE) BHB 54f **RR 58f** 5168[6]
4 b g Shareef Dancer (USA) 10.1f **(67)** - So Romantic (IRE) (Teenoso (USA)) 9.9f **(72)**
Form - 4070236
Record 1999 - 1st:0 2nd:1 3rd:1 Ran:7
Win Prizemoney £0 *Total Prizemoney* £1,129
1999 Turf 0-7: (12f 2, 14f 4, 16f) (g-s 2, gd 2, frm 2, hrd)
Fair gelding, effective 14 to 16f, acts on gd, prefers left handed tracks. Turf high 65. **J Norton [2-11] Ejam Connection.*

IRISH CREAM (IRE) BHB 40f44a **RR 44f 44a** 5101[3]
3 b f Petong 7.6f **(58)** - Another Baileys **(49f 55a)** (Deploy)
Form - 7311160000500060783
Record 1999 - 1st:3 2nd:0 3rd:2 Ran:18
Pre1999 - 1st:2 2nd:0 3rd:2 Ran:12
Win Prizemoney £11,134 *Total Prizemoney* £13,285

Wins						
1999	*Mar*	*Southw*	*(STD)*	*C*	*8f*	*66*
1999	*Feb*	*Southw*	*(STD)*	*S*	*7f*	*75* <
1999	*Feb*	*Southw*	*(STD)*	*S*	*7f*	*64*
1998	*Jly*	*Southw*	*(STD)*	*C*	*6f*	*67*
1998	Mar	Hamilt	(HVY)		5f	55

1999 Turf 0-7: (6f 2, 7f 2, 8f 2, 14f) (g-s 2, gd 2, g-f, frm, hrd) 1999 AW 3-11: (6f 2, 7f 2-4, 8f 1-4, 12f) (Equi, Fibr 3-10)
Strong, moderate filly, effective 6 to 8f, - acts on Fibr, often wears blinkers, likes left handed tracks, likes tight tracks. Turf high 44. AW high 75 - 1st of 10 from Carrie Pooter (26 Feb Southwell RF 0370) - also 1st of 2 getting 1lb from Sounds Lucky (1 Mar Southwell RF 0380). She completed a hat trick in modest company on the Southwell Fibresand at the start of this year, though one of them was in a match.
**Andrew Reid [0-14] A S Reid (from P D Evans [5-16] Mar 1999).*

IRISH DANCER (IRE) BHB 57f **RR 57f** 5192[7]
2 ch f Lahib (USA) 8f **(69)** - Mazarine Blue (USA) (Chief's Crown (USA)) 9.8f **(72)**
Form - 054607
Record 1999 - 1st:0 2nd:0 3rd:0 Ran:6
Win Prizemoney £0 *Total Prizemoney* £216
1999 Turf 0-6: (6f, 7f 4, 8f) (g-s, gd 2, g-f, frm 2)
Fair filly. Turf high 57. **Miss Gay Kelleway [0-6] Martin Butler.*

IRISH MELODY (IRE) BHB 30f **RR 30f** 4228[14]
3 ch f Mac's Imp (USA) 5.6f **(54)** - Musical Gem (USA) (The Minstrel (CAN)) 10f **(72)**
Form - 00880
Record 1999 - 1st:0 2nd:0 3rd:0 Ran:5
Pre1999 - 1st:0 2nd:0 3rd:0 Ran:4
1999 Turf 0-5: (6f, 7f 2, 8f 2) (g-f 2, frm 3)
Leggy, very moderate filly, has worn blinkers. Turf high 44. Inconsistent.
**A J McNae [0-5] Mrs Ruth Egan (from B J Meehan [0-4] Jly 1998).*

IRISH SEA (USA) BHB 54a **RR 41f** 2529[3]
6 b g Zilzal (USA) 8.5f **(79)** - Dunkellin (USA) (Irish River (FR)) 8.6f **(78)**
Form - 33
Record 1999 - 1st:0 2nd:0 3rd:2 Ran:2
Pre1999 - 1st:0 2nd:1 3rd:1 Ran:10
Win Prizemoney £0 *Total Prizemoney* £2,509
1999 Turf 0-2: (17f, 18f) (frm, hrd)
Moderate gelding, has worn blinkers. Turf high 41.
**B J Llewellyn [3-21] J V Rawlings (from R F Marvin [0-1] Dec 1996).*

IRIS MAY BHB 67f **RR 67f** 4691[9]
4 b f Brief Truce (USA) 9.1f **(73)** - Choire Mhor (Dominion) 8.5f **(63)**
Form - 2043805880
Record 1999 - 1st:0 2nd:1 3rd:1 Ran:10
Pre1999 - 1st:2 2nd:4 3rd:3 Ran:15
Win Prizemoney £7,205 *Total Prizemoney* £25,757

Wins							
* 1998	May	Windso	(G-F)	H	5f	70	74 <
* 1997	Oct	Lingfi	(FRM)		5f		74 <

1999 Turf 0-10: (5f 9, 6f) (g-s 2, gd, g-f 3, frm 4)
Light-framed, average filly, effective 5f, acts on gd to frm, best on gd, has worn blinkers. Turf high 80 (1st run) - 2nd of 14 getting 4lb from Night Flight (12 May York 5f gd RF 1180). Consistent. A useful sprint handicapper, if rather unfortunate not to have won more races than she has done. Suited by fast ground, but ran a cracker on soft ground at York in May. Has done little since though.
**J Berry [2-25] John Brown & Megan Dennis.*

IRON MOUNTAIN (IRE) BHB 72f **RR 74f** 3677[19]
4 b g Scenic 10.6f **(66)** - Merlannah (IRE) (Shy Groom (USA)) 10f **(66)**
Form - 5544142260
Record 1999 - 1st:1 2nd:2 3rd:0 Ran:10
Pre1999 - 1st:4 2nd:4 3rd:2 Ran:27
Win Prizemoney £21,343 *Total Prizemoney* £31,665

Wins							
*** 1999**	Jun	Goodwo	(G-S)	H	9f	66	74 <
* 1998	Oct	Leices	(G-S)	H	10f	67	69
* 1998	Jly	Beverl	(GD)	H	9.9f	65	64
* 1998	Jly	Bright	(GD)	H	10f	63	67
* 1998	Jun	Yarmou	(GD)	H	10.1f	58	61

1999 Turf 1-10: (8f 4, 9f 1-1, 10f 5) (g-s, gd 1-2, g-f 2, frm 5)
Scopey, above-average gelding, effective 8 to 11f, acts on gd to hrd, has worn blinkers, likes left handed tracks, likes tight tracks, and excels at Yarmouth and Windsor. Turf high 74 - 1st of 16 giving 14lb to Tarski (4 Jun Goodwood RF 1733). Consistent.
**N A Callaghan [5-38] Gallagher Equine Ltd.*

IRREPRESSIBLE (IRE) BHB 37f **RR 22f** 4712[12]
8 b g Don't Forget Me 9.5f **(66)** - Lady of Shalott (Kings Lake (USA)) 10.8f **(67)**
Form - 0800
Record 1999 - 1st:0 2nd:0 3rd:0 Ran:4
Pre1999 - 1st:2 2nd:1 3rd:3 Ran:25
Win Prizemoney £4,525 *Total Prizemoney* £7,957

Wins							
* 1998	May	Folkes	(G-F)	C	6.9f		58 <
* 1996	Jun	Yarmou	(FRM)	SH	8f	33	42+

1999 Turf 0-4: (6f, 7f 3) (gd, g-f, frm 2)
Little account gelding, effective 7f, acts on gd, has worn blinkers. Turf high 22. Becoming disappointing.
**R J Hodges [2-18] R Callow (from K Bishop [0-2] Oct 1995).*

IRSAL BHB 35f30a **RR 40f 30a** 5168[13]
5 ch g Nashwan (USA) 10.3f **(79)** - Amwag (USA) (El Gran Senor (USA)) 9.6f **(76)**
Form - 2850600
Record 1999 - 1st:0 2nd:1 3rd:0 Ran:7
Pre1999 - 1st:1 2nd:0 3rd:3 Ran:9
Win Prizemoney £3,730 *Total Prizemoney* £8,435

Wins							
1997	Jly	Salisb	(FRM)	H	12f	75	73 <

1999 Turf 0-5: (12f 4, 14f) (g-s, g-f, frm 3) 1999 AW 0-2: (8f, 14f)(Fibr 2)
Moderate gelding. Turf high 53 (began Jly). AW high 16 (began Jly). Inconsistent.
**D W Chapman [0-7] Michael Hill (from M C Pipe [1-3] Aug 1997).*

ISABELLA GONZAGA BHB 63f74a **RR 65f 74a** 3875[15]
5 b m Rock Hopper 10.6f **(54)** - Lawful (Law Society (USA)) 9.9f **(70)**
Form - 2431313001320
Record 1999 - 1st:3 2nd:1 3rd:4 Ran:11
Pre1999 - 1st:2 2nd:2 3rd:2 Ran:15
Win Prizemoney £13,347 *Total Prizemoney* £20,329

Wins							
*** 1999**	*Jun*	*Wolver*	*(STD)*	*H*	*12f*	*67*	*69+* <
*** 1999**	*Feb*	*Wolver*	*(STD)*	*H*	*12f*	*62*	*64*
*** 1999**	*Jan*	*Lingfi*	*(STD)*	*H*	*12f*	*60*	*63*
* 1998	*Oct*	*Wolver*	*(STD)*	*H*	*12f*	*57*	*60*
* 1998	Jly	Yarmou	(G-F)	H	10.1f	57	60

1999 Turf 0-6: (10f 4, 12f 2) (g-f 2, frm 4) 1999 AW 3-5: (12f 3-5) (Equi 1-3, Fibr 2-2)
Average filly, effective 10 to 15f, best at 12f, acts on g-f to frm - acts on AW, best on Fibr, prefers left handed tracks, and excels at Wolverhampton and Yarmouth. Turf high 65 - 2nd of 7 giving 4lb to First Fantasy (26 Jly Yarmouth 10f frm RF 3157). AW high 69 - 1st of 7 getting 3lb from Top Jem (16 Jun Wolverhampton RF 2063) - also 1st of 11 getting 5lb from Copper Shell (20 Feb Wolverhampton RF 0335).
**R M H Cowell [5-22] John Waugh (from J L Dunlop [0-4] Oct 1997).*

ISABELLA R (IRE) BHB 69f63a **RR 60f 63a** 5123[3]
2 ch f Indian Ridge 7.6f **(74)** - Sun Screen (Caerleon (USA)) 8.6f **(71)**
Form - 253
Record 1999 - 1st:0 2nd:1 3rd:1 Ran:3
Win Prizemoney £0 *Total Prizemoney* £1,572
1999 Turf 0-3: (5f, 6f 2) (gd 2, frm)
Currently average filly. Turf high 60 (began Oct).
**Sir Mark Prescott [0-3] Timothy Rooney.*

ISCAN (IRE) BHB 112f **RR 109f** 4771a[5]
3 b c Caerleon (USA) 10.9f **(79)** - Idraak (Kris) 9.5f **(73)**
Form - 3322275
Record 1999 - 1st:0 2nd:3 3rd:2 Ran:7
Pre1999 - 1st:1 2nd:0 3rd:2 Ran:3
Win Prizemoney £3,745 *Total Prizemoney* £134,357
Wins * 1998 Aug Newcas (GD) 7f 80 <
1999 Turf 0-7: (10f, 12f 3, 14f, 15f 2) (hvy, gd, g-f 4, frm)
Scopey, Pattern-class colt, effective 10 to 14f, acts on gd to g-f, best on g-f. Turf high 109 - 2nd of 10 to Mutafaweq (18 Jun Ascot 12f g-f RF 2103). Ran some fine races in useful compant, notably when runner-up to Mutafaweq in the King Edward VII Stakes at Ascot, but has only a maiden-race success to his name. Looked a Leger type, a view endorsed by an unlucky-in-running effort at Goodwood, but he was well beaten in the Classic, having had to pass a stalls test before he was allowed to take his chance. He is reported likely to continue his career in the Middle East.
**Sir Michael Stoute [1-10] Sheikh Mohammed.*

ISLA (IRE) RR 23f 3857[12]
2 b f Turtle Island (IRE) - State Treasure (USA) (Secretariat (USA)) 9f **(79)**
Form - 0
Record 1999 - 1st:0 2nd:0 3rd:0 Ran:1
1999 Turf 0-1: (6f) (frm)
Currently little account filly. **T R Watson [0-1] Countess of Lonsdale.*

ISLAND HOUSE (IRE) BHB 99f **RR 104f** 5042[2]
3 ch c Grand Lodge (USA) - Fortitude (IRE) (Last Tycoon) 8.5f **(62)**
Form - 7424112
Record 1999 - 1st:2 2nd:2 3rd:0 Ran:7
Pre1999 - 1st:0 2nd:0 3rd:0 Ran:2
Win Prizemoney £10,248 *Total Prizemoney* £17,131
Wins * **1999** Oct Ayr (SFT) 8f 93 <
* **1999** Spt Pontef (G-F) 8f 82
1999 Turf 2-7: (7f, 8f 2-5, 9f) (sft 1-2, gd, g-f 2, frm 1-2)
Well made, very useful colt, effective 9f, acts on sft, prefers left handed tracks. Turf high 104 - 2nd of 15 getting 1lb from Albarahin (23 Oct Newbury 9f sft RF 5042). Gradually found his form and got off the mark in a classified stakes over a mile at Pontefract in September. Followed up in an Ayr conditions event over the same trip and will be even better suited by a step up in distance.
**G Wragg [2-9] Mollers Racing.*

ISLAND PRINCESS (IRE) BHB 80f **RR 77f** 3913[7]
2 b f Turtle Island (IRE) - Classic Dilemma (Sandhurst Prince) 7.9f **(63)**
Form - 50027
Record 1999 - 1st:0 2nd:1 3rd:0 Ran:5
Win Prizemoney £0 *Total Prizemoney* £1,100
1999 Turf 0-5: (5f 2, 7f 3) (g-s, gd 2, g-f, frm)
Above-average filly. Turf high 77 - 2nd of 13 to Naval Affair (18 Aug Kempton 7f g-s RF 3740).
**D R C Elsworth [0-5] Philip J Costello & John F Costello.*

ISLAND SANDS (IRE) BHB 118f **RR 118f** 1477a[5]
3 b br c Turtle Island (IRE) - Tiavanita (USA) (J O Tobin (USA)) 9.4f **(67)**
Form - 15
Record 1999 - 1st:1 2nd:0 3rd:0 Ran:2
Pre1999 - 1st:2 2nd:0 3rd:0 Ran:2
Win Prizemoney £180,209 *Total Prizemoney* £180,209
Wins * **1999** May Newmar (G-F) G1 8f 118 <
1998 Spt Salisb (HVY) 6f 102+
1998 Aug Salisb (G-F) 6f 102+
1999 Turf 1-2: (8f 1-2) (g-f, frm 1-1)
Workmanlike, high-class colt. Turf high 118 (1st run) - 1st of 16 from Enrique (1 May Newmarket RF 0958). Unbeaten in two races at two for David Elsworth, he joined Godolphin afterwards, and started off last season in the best possible fashion with a battling victory in the 2000 Guineas. He then went to the Curragh, but was a comfortably-beaten fifth and there seemed no valid excuse. He was not seen out again due to a foot problem and, judging by the fact that none of the first four home at Newmarket managed to win a race subsequently, he has to go down as a substandard Guineas winner.
**S bin Suroor [1-2] Godolphin (from D R C Elsworth [2-2] Spt 1998).*

Island Sands proved a good purchase for Godolphin

ISLAND SONG (IRE) RR 68f 3987[4]
3 b g Saddlers' Hall (IRE) 10.5f **(65)** - Island Lake (Kalaglow) 9.8f **(67)**
Form - 457111754
Record 1999 - 1st:3 2nd:0 3rd:0 Ran:9
Pre1999 - 1st:0 2nd:0 3rd:0 Ran:2
Win Prizemoney £8,583 *Total Prizemoney* £9,324
Wins * **1999** Jly Folkes (G-F) H 15.4f 57 68 <
* **1999** Jly Bath (FRM) H 17.2f 57 64
* **1999** Jly Lingfi (G-F) H 14f 55 56
1999 Turf 3-9: (11f, 13f, 14f 1-1, 15f 1-2, 16f 3, 17f 1-1) (hvy, gd 3, g-f 1-1, frm 2-3, hrd)
Workmanlike, average gelding, effective 15 to 17f, acts on gd to frm, prefers tight tracks. Turf high 68 - 1st of 5 giving 4lb to Dalby of York (26 Jly Folkestone RF 3143) - also 1st of 7 giving 6lb to Hillswick (20 Jly Bath RF 2959).
**M Johnston [3-11] The 3rd Middleham Partnership.*

ISLAND SOUND BHB 100f **RR 95+f** 5027[1]
2 b g Turtle Island (IRE) - Ballet (Sharrood (USA)) 10.5f **(72)**
Form - 411
Record 1999 - 1st:2 2nd:0 3rd:0 Ran:3
Win Prizemoney £9,570 *Total Prizemoney* £9,858
Wins * **1999** Oct Newbur (G-S) 8f 95+ <
* **1999** Spt Salisb (HVY) 8f 88+
1999 Turf 2-3: (7f, 8f 2-2) (g-s 2-2, gd)
Currently very useful gelding. Turf high 95 (began Spt) - 1st of 5 from Il Capitano (22 Oct Newbury RF 5027) - also 1st of 11 from Master George (29 Spt Salisbury RF 4641). He created quite an impression when bolting home in heavy ground at Salisbury on his second start, and followed up in good style. He looks a very useful prospect, although his options will be limited as he is already a gelding. **D R C Elsworth [2-3] Mrs Michael Meredith.*

ISLAND THYMES BHB 58f **RR 54f** 2377[6]
2 br g Alhijaz 7.7f **(57)**-Harmonious Sound (Auction Ring(USA))8.6f **(65)**
Form - 406
Record 1999 - 1st:0 2nd:0 3rd:0 Ran:3
Win Prizemoney £0 *Total Prizemoney* £345

1999 Turf 0-2: (6f 2) (gd 2) 1999 AW 0-1: (7f) (Fibr)
Currently fair gelding. Turf high 54. **B J Meehan [0-3] R A Bernard.*

ISLAY MIST BHB 88a **RR 80f** 3438[2]

2 b f Distant Relative 7f **(69)** - Finlaggan **(81f 69a)** (Be My Chief (USA))
Form - 112132
Record 1999 - 1st:3 2nd:2 3rd:1 Ran:6
Win Prizemoney £9,564 *Total Prizemoney* £13,154
Wins * 1999 Jly Beverl (G-F) 7.5f 80 <
*** 1999** Jun Mussel (G-F) 7.1f 73+
*** 1999** *Jun Wolver (STA) 6f 73*
1999 Turf 2-4: (6f, 7f 2-3) (g-f 2-3, frm) 1999 AW 1-2: (6f 1-1, 7f) (Fibr 1-2)
Useful filly, effective 7f, acts on g-f. Turf high 80 - also 1st of 4 giving 2lb to The Wife (19 Jly Beverley RF 2945). AW high 89. Won three of her first four starts, one of which was on Fibresand, and has run well since, though seven furlongs on slow ground looks right on the edge of her stamina limitations.
**Sir Mark Prescott [3-6] Mrs C R Philipson.*

ISLE AU HAUT (IRE) BHB 74f **RR 73f** 5166[7]

3 b f Indian Ridge 7.6f **(74)** - Monterana (Sallust) 8.4f **(63)**
Form - 425227
Record 1999 - 1st:0 2nd:3 3rd:0 Ran:6
Win Prizemoney £0 *Total Prizemoney* £4,033
1999 Turf 0-6: (7f, 8f 5) (g-s, gd 2, g-f, frm 2)
Unfurnished, above-average filly, effective 8f, acts on gd to frm. Turf high 73 - 2nd of 15 giving 5lb to Golden Prince (20 Oct Nottingham 8f frm RF 4991). **G Wragg [0-6] Mrs H H Morriss.*

ISLE OF SODOR BHB 59f59a **RR 44f 59a** 1005[18]

3 b f Cyrano de Bergerac 7.3f **(58)** - Costa Verde **(40df)** (King of Spain) 7.8f **(52)**
Form - 0700
Record 1999 - 1st:0 2nd:0 3rd:0 Ran:4
Pre1999 - 1st:1 2nd:0 3rd:2 Ran:7
Win Prizemoney £3,687 *Total Prizemoney* £4,645
Wins * 1998 Spt Leices (G-F) H 6f 58 68 <
1999 Turf 0-3: (6f 2, 7f) (sft, gd, frm) 1999 AW 0-1: (7f) (Fibr)
Scopey, moderate filly, effective 6f, acts on frm. Turf high 44. Inconsistent. **K W Hogg [1-11] Auldyn Stud Ltd.*

I SPY RR 1226[5]

3 b g Distant Relative 7f **(69)** - Singing Nelly (Pharly (FR)) 9.8f **(68)**
Form - 75
Record 1999 - 1st:0 2nd:0 3rd:0 Ran:2
1999 AW 0-2: (8f, 9f) (Fibr 2)
Light-framed, currently little account gelding. AW high 26.
**K McAuliffe [0-2] K W J McAuliffe.*

ISSARA (IRE) BHB 25f **RR 20f** 4626[11]

2 b g Puissance 7.1f **(60)** - Hollia (Touch Boy) 5f **(66)**
Form - 060000
Record 1999 - 1st:0 2nd:0 3rd:0 Ran:6
1999 Turf 0-6: (5f 5, 6f) (g-s, g-f, frm 4)
Little account gelding, often wears blinkers. Turf high 38.
**B A Pearce [0-6] J Salter.*

ISSEY ROSE (IRE) BHB 100f **RR 93?f** 4776a[11]

2 b f Bigstone (IRE) - Aneeda (Rainbow Quest (USA)) 10.4f **(75)**
Form - 23140
Record 1999 - 1st:1 2nd:1 3rd:1 Ran:5
Win Prizemoney £4,495 *Total Prizemoney* £14,929
Wins * 1999 Jly Folkes (G-F) 7f 71+ <
1999 Turf 1-5: (7f 1-3, 8f 2) (sft 2, g-f 1-1, frm 2)
Useful filly. Turf high 93 - 4th of 6 to Teggiano (26 Spt Ascot 8f sft RF 4565). She looks quite useful and, after coming third to some progressive and well-thought of sorts at Newmarket, she won over seven furlongs at Folkestone. Stayed on well in the Fillies' Mile and looks likely to make up into a Group-race filly.
**T G Mills [1-5] T G Mills.*

ISTIKBAL (USA) RR 14f 4583[9]

3 b f Kingmambo (USA) 10.9f **(85)** - Tafrah (IRE) (Sadler's Wells (USA)) 10f **(76)**
Form - 0
Record 1999 - 1st:0 2nd:0 3rd:0 Ran:1
1999 Turf 0-1: (10f) (gd)
Currently poor filly. **M P Tregoning [0-1] Hamdan Al Maktoum.*

ISTINTAJ (USA) BHB 83f **RR 87f** 4905[1]

3 b br c Nureyev (USA) 8.4f **(84)** - Mathkurh (USA) (Riverman (USA)) 9.1f **(76)**
Form - 4231
Record 1999 - 1st:1 2nd:1 3rd:1 Ran:4
Win Prizemoney £3,338 *Total Prizemoney* £4,954
Wins * 1999 Oct Redcar (GD) 6f 84 <
1999 Turf 1-4: (5f, 6f 1-3) (gd 2, g-f, frm 1-1)
Unfurnished, useful colt. Turf high 87 - 2nd of 10 giving 5lb to Treasury Gardens (18 May Pontefract 6f gd RF 1302) - also 1st of 18 from Mukayed (15 Oct Redcar RF 4905).
**M P Tregoning [1-4] Hamdan Al Maktoum.*

ITALIAN ROSE BHB 37f26a **RR 36f 26a** 5153[6]

4 ch f Aragon 7.7f **(58)** - Cayla (Tumble Wind (USA)) 7.5f **(57)**
Form - 0055080006
Record 1999 - 1st:0 2nd:0 3rd:0 Ran:7
Pre1999 - 1st:0 2nd:2 3rd:2 Ran:15
Win Prizemoney £0 *Total Prizemoney* £2,257
1999 Turf 0-3: (6f 2, 10f) (gd, g-f, frm) 1999 AW 0-4:(6f, 7f, 8f 2) (Fibr 4)
Leggy, very moderate filly, effective 7f, acts on gd to frm, has worn blinkers, likes tight tracks. Turf high 36 (began Jly). AW high 28. Inconsistent.
**A W Carroll [0-15] Serafino Agodino (from W J Musson [0-7] Nov 1997).*

ITALIAN SYMPHONY (IRE) BHB 58f95a **RR 57f 95a** 5217[16]

5 b g Royal Academy (USA) 7.8f **(77)** - Terracotta Hut (Habitat) 9.4f **(70)**
Form - 121435370244314541441405525210
Record 1999 - 1st:6 2nd:4 3rd:3 Ran:33
Pre1999 - 1st:11 2nd:8 3rd:9 Ran:52
Win Prizemoney £50,077 *Total Prizemoney* £73,474
Wins * 1999 Nov Mussel (GD) H 8f 53 57
*** 1999** Aug Catter (FRM) H 7f 45 48
*** 1999** Jly Warwic (G-F) H 6.8f 41 45
*** 1999** Jun Newmar (G-F) H 7f 37 41
*** 1999** *Feb Wolver (STD) H 7f 90 95*
*** 1999** *Feb Lingfi (STD) 8f 96* <
* 1998 *Nov Lingfi (STD) 7f 84*
* 1998 *Oct Wolver (sta) C 7f 74*
* 1998 *Spt Wolver (STD) H 6f 69 74*
* 1998 *Jly Southw (STD) C 7f 73*
* 1998 *May Southw (STD) C 7f 73*
* 1998 *Apr Wolver (STD) C 6f 60*
* 1998 *Feb Wolver (STD) C 7f 67*
* 1998 *Feb Lingfi (SLW) H 7f 63 72*
* 1998 *Feb Wolver (STD) C 6f 61*
* 1997 *Dec Lingfi (STD) H 7f 59 63*
* 1997 *Nov Wolver (STD) H 6f 55 60*
1999 Turf 4-23: (6f 3, 7f 3-14, 8f 1-6) (g-s, gd 4, g-f 3-8, frm 1-9, hrd)
1999 AW 2-10: (7f 1-3, 8f 1-5, 9f 2) (Equi 1-4, Fibr 1-6)
Useful gelding, effective 7 to 8f, best at 8f, - acts on AW, best on Equi, mostly wears blinkers (very effectively), likes left handed tracks, likes tight tracks, and does well at Lingfield and Southwell. Turf high 57. AW high 97 - 2nd of 7 giving 4lb to Weetman's Weigh (10 Feb Wolverhampton 8f Fibr RF 0263) - also 1st of 5 giving 17lb to Flying Officer (4 Feb Lingfield RF 0224). Amazingly tough and genuine, he is no better than fair on the turf and capable of much better form on the sand. Effective up to mile, his courage will ensure further success.
**P D Evans [17-75] J E Abbey (from M Johnston [0-10] May 1997).*

IT CAN BE DONE (IRE) RR 52f 3299[6]

2 ch c Case Law 6f **(64)** - Breeze Away **(40f 48a)** (Prince Sabo) 7.2f **(62)**
Form - 7786
Record 1999 - 1st:0 2nd:0 3rd:0 Ran:4
1999 Turf 0-4: (5f 2, 6f 2) (g-f 3, frm)
Fair colt. Turf high 52. **R Hollinshead [0-4] Michael Oliver.*

ITCH BHB 35f **RR 29f** 4832[14]

4 b c Puissance 7.1f **(60)** - Panienka (POL) (Dom Racine (FR)) 9.2f **(62)**
Form - 00000

Record 1999 - 1st:0 2nd:0 3rd:0 Ran:5
Pre1999 - 1st:1 2nd:0 3rd:0 Ran:5
Win Prizemoney £2,248 *Total Prizemoney* £2,248
Wins * 1997 Oct Pontef (G-S) 6f 75 <
1999 Turf 0-5: (5f, 6f, 7f 2, 8f) (sft, g-s, g-f, frm 2)
Scopey, little account colt, has worn blinkers. Turf high 29.
**R Bastiman [1-10] Mrs Jane Smith.*

ITHADTOBEYOU BHB 49f92a **RR 44f 92a** 4699[10]
4 b c Prince Sabo 6.6f **(64)** - Secret Valentine (Wollow) 8.2f **(61)**
Form - 006763600
Record 1999 - 1st:0 2nd:0 3rd:1 Ran:9
Pre1999 - 1st:1 2nd:0 3rd:0 Ran:4
Win Prizemoney £3,420 *Total Prizemoney* £4,269
Wins 1998 *Feb Lingfi (SLW)* *5f* 75+ <
1999 Turf 0-8: (5f 2, 6f 4, 7f 2) (sft, g-f 2, frm 5) 1999 AW 0-1: (5f) (Equi)
Leggy, moderate colt, effective 5f, - acts on Equi, often wears blinkers. Turf high 72. Becoming disappointing.
**G L Moore [0-9] Mrs M McMillan (from P F I Cole [1-4] May 1998).*

I TINA BHB 69f **RR 72f** 5067[4]
3 b f Lycius (USA) 8.8f **(71)** - Tintomara (IRE) (Niniski (USA)) 10.6f **(65)**
Form - 2364
Record 1999 - 1st:0 2nd:1 3rd:1 Ran:4
Win Prizemoney £0 *Total Prizemoney* £2,563
1999 Turf 0-4: (10f, 12f 3) (sft, gd 2, frm)
Leggy, above-average filly. Turf high 72 (1st run) (began Aug) - 2nd of 9 getting 5lb from Makarim (22 Aug Bath 12f frm RF 3834).
**M P Tregoning [0-4] R Axford.*

ITSALLHAPPENING (IRE) BHB 33f43a **RR 39f 43a** 3615[4]
3 b f Second Set (IRE) 9.2f **(67)** - Primo Stampari **(78?f)** (Primo Dominie) 6.2f **(80)**
Form - 8408750006864
Record 1999 - 1st:0 2nd:0 3rd:0 Ran:12
Pre1999 - 1st:0 2nd:1 3rd:0 Ran:6
Win Prizemoney £0 *Total Prizemoney* £542
1999 Turf 0-5: (7f 2, 8f, 12f, 17f) (g-f 2, frm 2, hrd) 1999 AW 0-7: (7f 2, 8f 3, 13f, 16f) (Equi 5, Fibr 2)
Unfurnished, very moderate filly, effective 6f, acts on g-f, has worn blinkers. Turf high 40. AW high 49. Inconsistent.
**T J Naughton [0-19] T J Naughton.*

IT'S ALLOWED BHB 84f **RR 82f** 5164[2]
2 b f Piccolo - Double Flutter **(68df)** (Beldale Flutter (USA)) 9.7f **(71)**
Form - 0543343113220102
Record 1999 - 1st:3 2nd:3 3rd:4 Ran:16
Win Prizemoney £9,976 *Total Prizemoney* £22,546
Wins * **1999** Oct Catter (GD,) H 7f 77 81 <
1999 Aug Lingfi (GD) S 6f 78+
1999 Jly Thirsk (FRM) C 7f 71
1999 Turf 3-16: (6f 1-8, 7f 2-8) (g-s 2, gd 1-3, g-f 6, frm 2-5)
Decent filly, effective 6 to 7f, best at 7f, acts on gd to frm, best on gd, likes tight tracks. Turf high 82 - also 1st of 15 giving 7lb to Safarando (16 Oct Catterick RF 4909).
**T D Easterby [1-6] Ian Armitage (from M R Channon [2-10] Aug 1999).*

ITS ALL RELATIVE BHB 74f **RR 72f** 2077[5]
4 gr f Distant Relative 7f **(69)** - Sharp Anne (Belfort (FR)) 6.8f **(63)**
Form - 305
Record 1999 - 1st:0 2nd:0 3rd:1 Ran:3
Pre1999 - 1st:2 2nd:1 3rd:1 Ran:14
Win Prizemoney £6,273 *Total Prizemoney* £12,796
Wins * 1997 Jly Bath (FRM) 5.1f 89+ <
* 1997 Jun Mussel (GD) 5f 75
1999 Turf 0-3: (5f 3) (gd, g-f 2)
Rangy, above-average filly, effective 5f, acts on g-f, has worn blinkers. Turf high 72. Inconsistent. **J Berry [2-17] R Leah.*

ITS ANOTHER GIFT BHB 66f **RR 71f** 4941[10]
2 b f Primo Dominie 7.2f **(67)** - Margaret's Gift **(92f)** (Beveled (USA)) 9f **(59)**
Form - 5432300
Record 1999 - 1st:0 2nd:1 3rd:2 Ran:7
Win Prizemoney £0 *Total Prizemoney* £2,141
1999 Turf 0-7: (5f 6, 6f) (g-s, gd 2, g-f, frm 3)
Above-average filly, effective 5f, acts on gd to frm. Turf high 71 (began Jly) - 3rd of 13 getting 5lb from Aira Force (3 Spt Haydock 5f g-f RF 4123). **J Berry [0-7] Margaret's Partnership.*

ITSANOTHERGIRL BHB 67f **RR 71f** 4862[5]
3 b f Reprimand 8.2f **(63)** - Tasmim (Be My Guest (USA)) 9.3f **(67)**
Form - 42035
Record 1999 - 1st:0 2nd:1 3rd:1 Ran:5
Pre1999 - 1st:1 2nd:0 3rd:2 Ran:7
Win Prizemoney £3,233 *Total Prizemoney* £6,279
Wins * 1998 Oct Catter (SFT) H 7f 68 74 <
1999 Turf 0-5: (6f, 8f, 9f, 10f, 11f) (sft, g-s 2, frm 2)
Above-average filly, effective 5 to 9f, acts on g-s to frm, best on frm, likes left handed tracks, likes tight tracks. Turf high 71. Consistent. **M W Easterby [1-12] Miss V Foster.*

ITSGOTTABDUN (IRE) BHB 61f **RR 68f** 4707[7]
2 b c Foxhound (USA) - Lady Ingrid (Taufan (USA)) 7f **(57)**
Form - 06655027
Record 1999 - 1st:0 2nd:1 3rd:0 Ran:8
Win Prizemoney £0 *Total Prizemoney* £545
1999 Turf 0-8: (5f 6, 6f 2) (g-s, gd 4, g-f, frm 2)
Average colt, has worn blinkers. Turf high 68.
**K T Ivory [0-8] Stephen Williams.*

IT'S MAGIC BHB 73f **RR 73f** 4679[6]
3 b g Magic Ring (IRE) 6.5f **(64)** - Ryewater Dream (Touching Wood (USA)) 8.2f **(55)**
Form - 706150116
Record 1999 - 1st:3 2nd:0 3rd:0 Ran:9
Pre1999 - 1st:0 2nd:0 3rd:0 Ran:3
Win Prizemoney £10,259 *Total Prizemoney* £10,431
Wins * **1999** Aug Leices (GD) H 8f 62 73+ <
* **1999** Aug Leices (GD) H 8f 62 69
* **1999** May Newcas (G-F) H 8f 55 69
1999 Turf 3-9: (7f, 8f 3-5, 10f, 11f, 12f) (gd 3, g-f 2-3, frm 2, hrd 1-1)
Scopey, above-average gelding, effective 8f, acts on g-f to hrd, best on g-f, often wears blinkers (extremely effectively). Turf high 73 - 1st of 20 giving 15lb to Rendita (18 Aug Leicester RF 3749) - also 1st of 13 giving 18lb to Kissed By Moonlite (11 Aug Leicester RF 3548). He won a handicap at Newcastle in May having never previously been placed, and seemed to appreciate being put back over a mile when winning two handicaps over that trip at Leicester in August. Not the easiest of rides.
**B Hanbury [3-12] Mrs Hazel Barber.*

ITS MY PLEASURE BHB 24f **RR 30f** 1927[7]
5 b m Rock Hopper 10.6f **(54)** - The Fink Sisters (Tap On Wood) 10.3f **(65)**
Form - 7
Record 1999 - 1st:0 2nd:0 3rd:0 Ran:1
Pre1999 - 1st:0 2nd:0 3rd:2 Ran:2
Win Prizemoney £0 *Total Prizemoney* £1,012
1999 AW 0-1: (14f) (Fibr)
Currently very moderate filly. **W S Cunningham [0-3] Mrs Ann Bell.*

IT'S NORMAN **RR 25f** 2760[10]
3 b g Vantastic - Arrogant Daughter (Aragon) 8.1f **(60)**
Form - 0
Record 1999 - 1st:0 2nd:0 3rd:0 Ran:1
1999 Turf 0-1: (12f) (frm)
Workmanlike, currently little account gelding.
**T R Watson [0-1] R P Brett.*

IT'S OUR SECRET (IRE) BHB 63f **RR 45f** 5026[9]
3 ch c Be My Guest (USA) 10.2f **(66)** - Lady Dulcinea (ARG) (General (FR))
Form - 2051600000
Record 1999 - 1st:1 2nd:1 3rd:0 Ran:10
Pre1999 - 1st:0 2nd:0 3rd:0 Ran:3
Win Prizemoney £2,966 *Total Prizemoney* £3,848
Wins * **1999** May Nottin (FRM) 8.2f 70 <
1999 Turf 1-10: (7f 4, 8f 1-6) (g-s, gd 3, g-f 1-2, frm 4)
Scopey, moderate colt, effective 8f, acts on gd to frm, has worn blinkers, likes tight tracks. Turf high 70 - 1st of 9 getting 12lb from Eurobox Boy (22 May Nottingham RF 1415). Becoming disappointing. Other than winning a weak race at Nottingham over a mile in

May, he has been mainly disappointing.
**M H Tompkins [1-13] Mrs M Barwell.*

IVOR'S DEED BHB 43f43a **RR 48f 43a** 3124[16]

6 b g Shadeed (USA) 7.7f **(72)** - Gena Ivor (USA) (Sir Ivor) 10.2f **(70)**
Form - 1753630543000
Record 1999 - 1st:0 2nd:0 3rd:3 Ran:11
Pre1999 - 1st:5 2nd:2 3rd:5 Ran:40
Win Prizemoney £9,272 *Total Prizemoney* £14,349
Wins * 1998 *Dec Lingfi (STD) S 7f 57*
1998 *Feb Lingfi (SLW) C 7f 63* <
1997 *Nov Lingfi (STD) H 7f 59 61*
1997 May Folkes (G-F) C 6.9f 51
1996 Jun Catter (G-F) 7f 59
1999 Turf 0-2: (8f 2) (sft, g-f) 1999 AW 0-9: (6f 3, 7f 4, 8f 2) (Equi 6, Fibr 3)
Moderate gelding, effective 6 to 7f, best at 7f, - acted on Equi, had worn blinkers, favoured left handed tracks, favoured tight tracks. AW high 49. Becoming disappointing. (DEAD)
**P D Evans [1-18] P D Evans (from Miss Gay Kelleway [2-17] Jly 1998).*

IVOR'S FLUTTER BHB 79f **RR 80f** 5132[10]

10 b g Beldale Flutter (USA) 10.2f **(62)** -Rich Line (High Line) 10.3f **(70)**
Form - 400
Record 1999 - 1st:0 2nd:0 3rd:0 Ran:3
Pre1999 - 1st:6 2nd:2 3rd:4 Ran:32
Win Prizemoney £29,925 *Total Prizemoney* £40,635
Wins * 1998 Apr Sandow (SFT) H 16.4f 83 86 <
* 1998 Apr Kempto (HVY) H 16f 77 84
* 1996 Aug Sandow (GD) H 14f 78 84
1999 Turf 0-3: (16f, 17f 2) (gd 3)
Decent gelding, effective 16f, acts on hvy to gd, prefers right handed tracks. Turf high 80 (began Spt). Consistent.
**D R C Elsworth [8-56] W I M Perry.*

IVOR'S INVESTMENT BHB 48f **RR 45f** 5007[11]

3 ch f Forzando 7.2f **(63)** - Abbotswood (Ahonoora) 8.1f **(73)**
Form - 261221240D050
Record 1999 - 1st:2 2nd:4 3rd:0 Ran:13
Pre1999 - 1st:0 2nd:0 3rd:1 Ran:6
Win Prizemoney £5,268 *Total Prizemoney* £9,476
Wins 1999 Jun Epsom (GD) C 8.5f 58 <
1999 Jun Chepst (GD) C 7.1f 58+
1999 Turf 2-13: (6f 2, 7f 1-5, 8f 4, 9f 1-1, 10f) (gd 1-2, g-f 1-4, frm 6, hrd)
Scopey, moderate filly, effective 5 to 8f, best at 6f, acts on gd to hrd, excels at Epsom and Lingfield and Salisbury. Turf high 71 - 2nd of 11 getting 3lb from Ivory Dawn (9 Jly Lingfield 6f frm RF 2685). Consistent.
**B D Leavy [0-5] R Brown (from D R C Elsworth [2-14] Jly 1999).*

IVORY DAWN **RR 61f** 4989[9]

5 b m Batshoof 9.5f **(66)**-Cradle of Love (USA)(Roberto (USA)) 10f **(76)**
Form - 0060450381133003080
Record 1999 - 1st:2 2nd:0 3rd:4 Ran:19
Pre1999 - 1st:3 2nd:5 3rd:5 Ran:37
Win Prizemoney £16,587 *Total Prizemoney* £32,518
Wins * 1999 Jly Lingfi (G-F) H 6f 64 76 <
*** 1999** Jun Bright (GD) H 6f 65 67
* 1998 Jly Lingfi (G-F) H 6f 60 72
* 1998 Jly Bright (GD) H 6f 60 64
* 1997 Jun Goodwo (GD) H 6f 65 70
1999 Turf 2-19: (5f, 6f 2-18) (g-s, gd 1-5, g-f 6, frm 1-7)
Average filly, effective 6f, acts on g-s to frm, best on frm, has worn blinkers, likes left handed tracks, likes tight tracks, and excels at Lingfield and Newmarket and Brighton. Turf high 76 - 1st of 11 giving 3lb to Ivor's Investment (9 Jly Lingfield RF 2685). Consistent. Won back-to-back handicaps in the summer of '98, and did exactly the same thing last term. Suited by six furlongs and fast ground on a downhill track. **K T Ivory [5-56] Dean Ivory.*

IVORY'S GRAB HIRE BHB 45f50a **RR 47f 50a** 3302[11]

6 b g Shavian 7.7f **(67)** - Knees Up (USA) (Dancing Champ (USA)) 8.8f **(80)**
Form - 66672825007744540
Record 1999 - 1st:0 2nd:2 3rd:0 Ran:16
Pre1999 - 1st:7 2nd:8 3rd:11 Ran:85
Win Prizemoney £21,691 *Total Prizemoney* £38,479
Wins * 1998 *Apr Wolver (STD) H 5f 47 52*
* 1997 Aug Bright (G-F) H 5.3f 62 70 <
* 1997 May Bright (FRM) H 6f 55 67
* 1997 May Bright (FRM) H 6f 55 59
* 1997 *Mar Lingfi (STD) H 5f 48 45*
* 1997 *Feb Lingfi (STD) H 5f 43 44*
* 1996 Jun Lingfi (FRM) H 7f 53 62
1999 Turf 0-11: (5f 7, 6f 2, 7f, 8f) (gd 3, g-f 2, frm 4, hrd 2) 1999 AW 0-5: (5f 3, 6f 2) (Equi 5)
Moderate gelding, effective 5 to 6f, best at 5f, acts on gd to frm - acts on Fibr, mostly wears blinkers. Turf high 53 (1st run) - 2nd of 17 giving 17lb to Whizz Kid (15 Apr Ripon 5f gd RF 0711). AW high 47. Consistent. **K T Ivory [7-101] Dean Ivory.*

IVORY'S GUEST (IRE) **RR 19f** 2432[9]

2 gr g Be My Guest (USA) 10.2f **(66)** - Irish Hope (Nishapour (FR)) 9.1f **(61)**
Form - 000
Record 1999 - 1st:0 2nd:0 3rd:0 Ran:3
1999 Turf 0-3: (5f, 6f, 7f) (gd 2, frm)
Currently poor gelding, often wears blinkers. Turf high 19.
**K T Ivory [0-3] Dean Ivory.*

IVORY'S JOY BHB 80f **RR 79f** 5110[16]

4 b f Tina's Pet 7.4f **(56)** - Jacqui Joy (Music Boy) 6.8f **(57)**
Form - 320162885033381200
Record 1999 - 1st:2 2nd:3 3rd:4 Ran:18
Pre1999 - 1st:3 2nd:4 3rd:4 Ran:29
Win Prizemoney £29,116 *Total Prizemoney* £49,350
Wins * 1999 Spt Haydoc (SFT) H 5f 74 76 <
*** 1999** May Thirsk (Sft) H 5f 69 74
* 1997 Spt Newbur (G-S) H 5.2f 70 73
* 1997 Jun Goodwo (SFT) S 6f 73
* 1997 Jun Goodwo (GD) S 5f 65
1999 Turf 2-18: (5f 2-16, 6f 2) (sft, g-s 1-2, gd 1-9, g-f 4, frm 2)
Workmanlike, above-average filly, effective 5 to 6f, best at 5f, acts on g-s to frm, best on gd, has worn blinkers, excels at Thirsk, likes Goodwood. Turf high 79 - 2nd of 23 giving 5lb to Ambitious (6 Oct York 5f gd RF 4755) - also 1st of 20 from Juwwi (25 Spt Haydock RF 4555). She finally ended her long losing run in soft ground at Haydock in September, despite hanging badly left. Best over the minimum trip, she has run with credit on fast ground, but ideally looks suited by some give. **K T Ivory [5-47] K T Ivory.*

IYAVAYA (USA) BHB 94f **RR 87?f** 4765a[5]

2 b f Valiant Nature (USA) - Odori (USA) (The Minstrel (CAN)) 10f **(72)**
Form - 1714055
Record 1999 - 1st:2 2nd:0 3rd:0 Ran:7
Win Prizemoney £7,169 *Total Prizemoney* £7,551
Wins * 1999 Jly Chepst (G-F) 5.1f 85
*** 1999** Jun Warwic (HVY) 5f 87? <
1999 Turf 2-7: (5f 2-5, 6f, 7f) (hvy, g-s 1-2, gd 2, g-f, frm 1-1)
Useful filly, effective 5f, acts on g-s to frm. Turf high 87 (1st run) - 1st of 4 from Out of Africa (7 Jun Warwick RF 1797) - also 1st of 4 giving 7lb to Embezl (9 Jly Chepstow RF 2664). Was found wanting when tackling Listed company. **M R Channon [2-7].*

JACK DAWSON (IRE) BHB 63f **RR 64f** 4996[7]

2 b c Persian Bold 10f **(69)** -Dream of Jenny (Caerleon (USA)) 8.6f **(71)**
Form - 707
Record 1999 - 1st:0 2nd:0 3rd:0 Ran:3
1999 Turf 0-3: (7f, 8f 2) (g-s, gd 2)
Currently average colt. Turf high 64 (began Spt).
**J Noseda [0-3] Paul & Jenny Green.*

JACKERIN (IRE) BHB 52f **RR 49f** 3372[8]

4 b g Don't Forget Me 9.5f **(66)** - Meanz Beanz (High Top) 10.2f **(67)**
Form - 080050508
Record 1999 - 1st:0 2nd:0 3rd:0 Ran:9
Pre1999 - 1st:3 2nd:4 3rd:2 Ran:23
Win Prizemoney £8,828 *Total Prizemoney* £16,517
Wins * 1998 Oct Ayr (G S) H 5f 61 66
* 1997 May Doncas (GD) 5f 79 <
* 1997 Mar Doncas (G-F) S 5f 63
1999 Turf 0-9: (5f 9) (gd 3, g-f 3, frm 3)
Lengthy, moderate gelding, effective 5f, acts on sft to frm, mostly wears blinkers (very effectively). Turf high 52. Consistent.
**B S Rothwell [3-32] J B Young.*

JACK FLUSH (IRE) BHB 39f34a **RR 46f 34a** 112[13]
5 b g Broken Hearted 10.1f **(65)** - Clubhouse Turn (IRE) (King of Clubs) 7.1f **(57)**
Form - 0
Record 1999 - 1st:0 2nd:0 3rd:0 Ran:1
Pre1999 - 1st:1 2nd:2 3rd:2 Ran:24
Win Prizemoney £7,512 *Total Prizemoney* £10,647
Wins * 1997 May Thirsk (G-S) H 8f 58 64 <
1999 AW 0-1: (8f) (Fibr)
Moderate gelding, effective 8f, acts on g-f, has worn blinkers, likes tight tracks. **B S Rothwell [2-28] Derek Smith.*

JACK GOODMAN (IRE) BHB 51f68a **RR 53f 68a** 2819[7]
3 ch g Simply Great (FR) 11.9f **(61)** - Donna Katrina (Kings Lake (USA)) 10.8f **(67)**
Form - 1600407
Record 1999 - 1st:0 2nd:0 3rd:0 Ran:6
Pre1999 - 1st:2 2nd:1 3rd:0 Ran:7
Win Prizemoney £5,202 *Total Prizemoney* £6,282
Wins * 1998 *Dec Lingfi (STD) H 7f 66 69* <
* 1998 Jly Folkes (GD) 7f 68
1999 Turf 0-5: (7f 2, 8f 3) (g-f 2, frm 3) 1999 AW 0-1: (8f) (Equi)
Workmanlike, average gelding, effective 7f, acts on gd to g-f - acts on Equi, best on gd. Turf high 53.
**J S Moore [2-13] Mrs Victoria Goodman.*

JACKIE'S BABY BHB 86f80a **RR 84f 80a** 3238[8]
3 b c Then Again 7.4f **(52)** - Guarded Expression **(45f)** (Siberian Express (USA)) 8.8f **(65)**
Form - 8020002318
Record 1999 - 1st:1 2nd:2 3rd:1 Ran:10
Pre1999 - 1st:3 2nd:1 3rd:3 Ran:9
Win Prizemoney £15,683 *Total Prizemoney* £29,132
Wins * **1999** Jly Bath (FRM) H 5.1f 82 84 <
* 1998 Aug Folkes (G-F) H 5f 77 84 <
* 1998 *Jly Southw (STD) H 5f 76*
* 1998 *May Southw (STD) 5f 68*
1999 Turf 1-9: (5f 1-8, 6f) (gd 3, g-f 1-6) 1999 AW 0-1: (5f) (Equi)
Leggy, decent colt, effective 5 to 6f, best at 5f, acts on g-f to frm - acts on Fibr, best on g-f, excels at Chester and Folkestone and Southwell. Turf high 84 - 1st of 6 giving 7lb to Francport (15 Jly Bath RF 2839). Inconsistent. **W G M Turner [4-19] Mrs J Glover.*

JACK JACKSON BHB 28f **RR 22f** 2636[13]
3 b c Sizzling Melody 6.3f **(49)**-Millfields House(Record Token) 6.3f **(53)**
Form - 000
Record 1999 - 1st:0 2nd:0 3rd:0 Ran:3
1999 Turf 0-3: (7f, 8f 2) (g-f, frm 2)
Workmanlike, currently little account colt. Turf high 22.
**T D McCarthy [0-3] A H Weller.*

JACK THE LAD (IRE) BHB 48f40a **RR 47f 40a** 3674[8]
5 b g Shalford (IRE) 7.8f **(63)** - Indian Honey (Indian King (USA)) 7.4f **(64)**
Form - 055518
Record 1999 - 1st:1 2nd:0 3rd:0 Ran:6
Pre1999 - 1st:4 2nd:2 3rd:2 Ran:30
Win Prizemoney £15,637 *Total Prizemoney* £19,712
Wins * **1999** Jly Hamilt (G-F) S 12.1f 47
* 1997 May Beverl (G-S) H 8.5f 66 77 <
* 1997 May Redcar (GD) H 10f 66 77 <
* 1997 May Carlis (G-S) H 8f 55 61
* 1997 May Redcar (FRM) H 9f 58 69
1999 Turf 1-3: (9f, 10f, 12f 1-1) (hvy, g-f 1-1, frm) 1999 AW 0-3: (9f, 12f 2) (Fibr 3)
Moderate gelding, effective 12f, acts on g-f, has worn blinkers, favours tight tracks. Turf high 47 - 1st of 8 from Ambidextrous (31 Jly Hamilton RF 3266). AW high 32.
**J Hetherton [5-30] Keith West Partnership (from C Murray [0-6] Spt 1996).*

JACK TO A KING BHB 51f52a **RR 35f 52a** 923[5]
4 b g Nawwar - Rudda Flash (General David)
Form - 005
Record 1999 - 1st:0 2nd:0 3rd:0 Ran:3
Pre1999 - 1st:0 2nd:0 3rd:0 Ran:3
1999 Turf 0-1: (6f) (sft) 1999 AW 0-2: (6f, 7f) (Fibr 2)
Very moderate gelding. AW high 37.
**J Balding [0-6] J D and J R Evans.*

JACK TO A QUEEN RR 16f 4032[17]
3 ch f Nawwar - Merry Marion (Goldengazer)
Form - 0
Record 1999 - 1st:0 2nd:0 3rd:0 Ran:1
1999 Turf 0-1: (11f) (gd)
Scopey, currently poor filly. **J Balding [0-1] J D and J R Evans.*

JACMAR (IRE) BHB 42f **RR 27f** 4986[16]
4 br g High Estate 10.5f **(66)** - Inseyab (Persian Bold) 9.3f **(66)**
Form - 003041435570607800000
Record 1999 - 1st:1 2nd:0 3rd:2 Ran:21
Pre1999 - 1st:3 2nd:4 3rd:1 Ran:19
Win Prizemoney £16,931 *Total Prizemoney* £32,474
Wins * **1999** Jun Hamilt (G-S) H 5f 55 60
* 1997 Spt Hamilt (GD) H 6f 90 93+ <
* 1997 Aug Hamilt (GD) H 6f 80 81
* 1997 Jun Hamilt (G-F) 6f 79
1999 Turf 1-21: (5f 1-6, 6f 11, 7f, 8f 3) (hvy, sft, g-s, gd 5, g-f 1-6, frm 7)
Scopey, little account gelding. Turf high 62.
**Miss L A Perratt [4-40] Marett-Sutherland-Hay.*

JACOBINA BHB 52f **RR 45f** 3821[9]
4 b f Magic Ring (IRE) 6.5f **(64)** - Mistitled (USA) (Miswaki (USA)) 9f **(81)**
Form - 00680
Record 1999 - 1st:0 2nd:0 3rd:0 Ran:5
Pre1999 - 1st:1 2nd:2 3rd:2 Ran:13
Win Prizemoney £3,160 *Total Prizemoney* £5,675
Wins 1998 Aug Haydoc (G-S) H 7.1f 59 63 <
1999 Turf 0-5: (6f, 7f 3, 8f) (g-f 2, frm 3)
Unfurnished, moderate filly, effective 7f, acts on gd to frm, likes left handed tracks. Turf high 45. Consistent.
**D Nicholls [0-1] J M Ranson (from B S Rothwell [1-13] Jly 1999).*

JACQUES REPLY BHB 78f **RR 77f** 4877[6]
2 b c Paris House 5.9f **(64)** - Question Ali **(46f)** (Petoski) 5.7f **(62)**
Form - 834366036
Record 1999 - 1st:0 2nd:0 3rd:3 Ran:9
Win Prizemoney £0 *Total Prizemoney* £4,524
1999 Turf 0-9: (5f 7, 6f, 7f) (sft, gd, g-f 2, frm 4, hrd)
Above-average colt, effective 5 to 6f, acts on frm to hrd. Turf high 77 - 3rd of 22 giving 5lb to Kilbrangan Sound (10 Spt Doncaster 6f frm RF 4249).
**K A Ryan [0-6] The Good Hand Racing Club (from J Berry [0-3] Jun 1999).*

JADE CHEQUER BHB 63f **RR 74df** 3873[7]
3 b f Green Desert (USA) 7.8f **(78)** - Draft Board (Rainbow Quest (USA)) 10.4f **(75)**
Form - 47
Record 1999 - 1st:0 2nd:0 3rd:0 Ran:2
Pre1999 - 1st:0 2nd:0 3rd:1 Ran:1
Win Prizemoney £0 *Total Prizemoney* £960
1999 Turf 0-2: (5f, 6f) (gd, g-f)
Workmanlike, currently above-average filly. Turf high 58 (began Aug). **J H M Gosden [0-3] Mark Horton.*

JADE TIGER BHB 62f **RR 69f** 4930[11]
3 ch g Lion Cavern (USA) 7.5f **(74)** - Precious Jade (Northfields (USA)) 9f **(72)**
Form - 773120328460
Record 1999 - 1st:1 2nd:2 3rd:2 Ran:12
Pre1999 - 1st:0 2nd:1 3rd:1 Ran:5
Win Prizemoney £2,574 *Total Prizemoney* £7,260
Wins **1999** Jun Leices (GD) C 8f 58+ <
1999 Turf 1-12: (7f, 8f 1-8, 10f 3) (g-s, gd 2, g-f 1-5, frm 4)
Workmanlike, average gelding, effective 6 to 8f, best at 8f, acts on gd to frm, best on frm, has worn blinkers. Turf high 73 - 3rd of 14 giving 13lb to Pentagon Lad (15 May Thirsk 8f gd RF 1250).
**F Jordan [0-8] Graham Brown (from B J Meehan [1-9] Jun 1999).*

JADIE BHB 46a **RR 46a** 4923[10]
2 ch f Safawan 6.6f **(60)**-Another Jade **(64f 62a)**(Beveled (USA)) 9f **(59)**
Form - 340

Record 1999 - 1st:0 2nd:0 3rd:1 Ran:3
Win Prizemoney £0 *Total Prizemoney* £264
1999 AW 0-3: (6f 2, 7f) (Fibr 3)
Currently fair filly. AW high 57 (began Spt).
**A P Jarvis [0-3] All Four Corners.*

JAGUAR BHB 77f **RR 72f** 1600[14]

3 b g Barathea (IRE) - Oasis (Valiyar) 8.5f **(73)**
Form - 030
Record 1999 - 1st:0 2nd:0 3rd:1 Ran:3
Pre1999 - 1st:0 2nd:0 3rd:1 Ran:4
Win Prizemoney £0 *Total Prizemoney* £1,457
1999 Turf 0-3: (8f 2, 10f) (gd, g-f, frm)
Above-average gelding, effective 7f, acts on gd to frm. Turf high 72.
**N A Twiston-Davies [0-3] Adrian Fitzpatrick (from Miss Gay Kelleway [0-4] Oct 1998).*

JAILHOUSE ROCKET BHB 92f **RR 100f** 5061[3]

2 gr c Petong 7.6f **(58)** - Selvi (Mummy's Pet) 7.7f **(60)**
Form - 0121033
Record 1999 - 1st:2 2nd:1 3rd:2 Ran:7
Win Prizemoney £6,103 *Total Prizemoney* £9,100
Wins * 1999 Spt Beverl (SFT) 5f 100 <
*** 1999** Aug Carlis (G-F) 5f 76+
1999 Turf 2-7: (5f 2-6, 6f) (g-s 1-2, gd, g-f 3, frm 1-1)
Very useful colt, effective 5f, acts on g-s to g-f. Turf high 100 - 1st of 8 getting 5lb from Final Row (21 Spt Beverley RF 4444). He made an inauspicious debut at Leicester, but went on to prove himself a useful sprinting juvenile. Bought back for 31,000 guineas at Newmarket in October, he should stay six furlongs and can win a decent handicap in 2000. **Sir Mark Prescott [2-7] The Speculators.*

JALAD (IRE) BHB 100f **RR 91f** 4570[6]

2 b c Marju (IRE) 9.2f **(76)** - Hamsaat (IRE) **(82+f)** (Sadler's Wells (USA)) 10f **(76)**
Form - 216
Record 1999 - 1st:1 2nd:1 3rd:0 Ran:3
Win Prizemoney £3,241 *Total Prizemoney* £4,573
Wins * 1999 Aug Leices (G-F) 7f 91 <
1999 Turf 1-3: (7f 1-2, 8f) (sft, g-f, frm 1-1)
Currently useful colt. Turf high 91 (began Aug) - 1st of 11 from Air Marshall (22 Aug Leicester RF 3837). Made a good impression when beaten by King's Best on his debut at Newmarket despite running green. Duly obliged at Leicester, albeit narrowly, but was all at sea in the heavy ground when last in the Royal Lodge. He should be able to win more races on better ground.
**B Hanbury [1-3] Hamdan Al Maktoum.*

JALB (IRE) BHB 60f **RR 61f** 3576[8]

5 b g Robellino (USA) 9.5f **(68)** - Adjacent (IRE) (Doulab (USA)) 9.8f **(65)**
Form - 23608
Record 1999 - 1st:0 2nd:1 3rd:1 Ran:5
Pre1999 - 1st:2 2nd:0 3rd:2 Ran:15
Win Prizemoney £6,041 *Total Prizemoney* £9,217
Wins * 1998 Jly Beverl (GD) H 12f 58 66 <
* 1998 Jun Warwic (G-S) H 12.5f 58 64
1999 Turf 0-4: (13f, 14f 3) (g-s, g-f 2, frm) 1999 AW 0-1: (12f) (Fibr)
Average gelding, effective 10 to 14f, best at 12f, acts on g-s to frm - acts on Fibr, likes tight tracks, and excels at Kempton. Turf high 63 (1st run) - 3rd of 7 getting 2lb from Norcroft Joy (27 Mar Warwick 13f g-s RF 0489). (1st run) - 2nd of 9 giving 8lb to Law Dancer (3 Mar Wolverhampton 12f Fibr RF 0398). **P G Murphy [3-21] Family And Friends (from A C Stewart [0-7] Jly 1997).*

JAMAICAN FLIGHT (USA) BHB 75f68a **RR 78f 68a** 4917[26]

6 b h Sunshine Forever (USA) 13.2f **(76)** - Kalamona (USA) (Hawaii) 9.4f **(66)**
Form - 0752414701125650
Record 1999 - 1st:3 2nd:2 3rd:0 Ran:16
Pre1999 - 1st:3 2nd:10 3rd:6 Ran:31
Win Prizemoney £27,234 *Total Prizemoney* £47,816
Wins * 1999 Jly Doncas (G-F) H 16.5f 72 76
*** 1999** Jly Carlis (FRM) H 14.1f 67 71
*** 1999** May Pontef (GD) 18f 72
* 1998 Aug Pontef (G-F) 18f 78
* 1998 *Feb Wolver (STD) H 12f 72 79* <
1996 Jly Beverl (G-F) 16.2f 57
1999 Turf 3-13: (12f, 14f 1-1, 16f 3, 17f 1-3, 18f 1-3, 20f, 22f) (sft, g-s, gd 1-3, g-f 3, frm 2-5) 1999 AW 0-3: (12f 3) (Fibr 3)
Above-average horse, effective 12 to 19f, best at 12f, acts on g-s to hrd - acts on Fibr, prefers tight tracks, excels at Beverley and does well at Pontefract. Turf high 78 - 5th of 9 giving 8lb to Sandmoor Chambray (22 Aug Pontefract 12f frm RF 3847) - also 1st of 5 giving 11lb to Durham (29 Jly Doncaster RF 3214). AW high 65. This front-running stayer is a thorough professional under both codes. He is very effective when able to gain an uncontested early lead.
**Mrs S Lamyman [12-57] P Lamyman (from C Smith [0-2] May 1997).*

JAMAIEL (IRE) RR 4176[11]

2 b f Polish Precedent (USA) 9f **(73)** - Avice Caro (USA) (Caro)
Form - 0
Record 1999 - 1st:0 2nd:0 3rd:0 Ran:1
1999 Turf 0-1: (7f) (frm)
Currently very poor filly. **C E Brittain [0-1] Saeed Manana.*

JAMES DEE (IRE) BHB 61f76a **RR 60f 76a** 4151[1]

3 b g Shalford (IRE) 7.8f **(63)** - Glendale Joy (IRE) (Glenstal (USA)) 10.1f **(64)**
Form - 20441403024481
Record 1999 - 1st:2 2nd:2 3rd:1 Ran:14
Pre1999 - 1st:0 2nd:2 3rd:1 Ran:6
Win Prizemoney £6,556 *Total Prizemoney* £11,494
Wins * 1999 *Spt Wolver (STD) H 7f 68 76* <
*** 1999** May Bright (FRM) C 7f 62
1999 Turf 1-9: (5f, 6f 5, 7f 1-3) (gd, g-f 4, frm 3, hrd 1-1) 1999 AW 1-5: (6f, 7f 1-2, 8f 2) (Equi, Fibr 1-4)
Scopey, above-average gelding, effective 5 to 8f, acts on gd to g-f - acts on Fibr, likes left handed tracks, likes tight tracks. Turf high 63. AW high 76 - 1st of 11 getting 5lb from Locomotion (4 Spt Wolverhampton RF 4151). He was kept busy, managing a victory on very fast ground at Brighton in May. His form on sand had been fairly modest, but he showed tremendous improvement to make all in a pretty good handicap at Wolverhampton in September. Best over seven furlongs. **A P Jarvis [2-20] Mrs Ann Jarvis.*

JAMES STARK (IRE) BHB 80a **RR 71f 80a** 4870[5]

2 b c Up and At 'em - June Maid (Junius (USA)) 7.7f **(65)**
Form - 05
Record 1999 - 1st:0 2nd:0 3rd:0 Ran:2
1999 Turf 0-2: (7f 2) (sft, gd)
Currently useful colt, often wears blinkers. Turf high 71 (began Spt). **N P Littmoden [0-2] Richard Green (Fine Paintings).*

JAMESTOWN BHB 75f **RR 74?f** 4931[6]

2 b c Merdon Melody 6.8f **(56)** - Thabeh (Shareef Dancer (USA)) 9.9f **(73)**
Form - 0520516
Record 1999 - 1st:1 2nd:1 3rd:0 Ran:7
Win Prizemoney £2,839 *Total Prizemoney* £6,337
Wins * 1999 Spt Warwic (SFT) 6.8f 74 <
1999 Turf 1-6: (5f 2, 6f 2, 7f 1-1, 8f) (sft 1-1, gd, g-f 2, frm 2) 1999 AW 0-1: (5f) (Fibr)
Above-average colt, effective 5 to 7f, acts on sft to gd. Turf high 74 - 1st of 16 giving 5lb to Zaffia (21 Spt Warwick RF 4451).
**C Smith [1-7] A E Needham.*

JAMIE ANN RR 33f 2635[16]

2 b f Son Pardo - Taine Sands (Record Run) 8f **(42)**
Form - 70
Record 1999 - 1st:0 2nd:0 3rd:0 Ran:2
1999 Turf 0-2: (7f 2) (g-f, frm)
Currently very moderate filly. Turf high 33.
**J C Poulton [0-2] Gerald West.*

JAMMIE DODGER BHB 44f **RR 47f** 4883[13]

3 b g Ardkinglass 5f **(64)** - Ling Lane (Slip Anchor) 9.8f **(73)**
Form - 8460540
Record 1999 - 1st:0 2nd:0 3rd:0 Ran:7
1999 Turf 0-7: (7f 2, 8f 4, 10f) (gd 2, g-f 2, frm 3)
Neat, moderate gelding, effective 7 to 8f, acts on gd to frm. Turf high 47. **R M Whitaker [0-7] Mrs R M Whitaker.*

JAMORIN DANCER BHB 51f **RR 55f** 4400[5]
4 b g Charmer 9f **(59)** - Geryea (USA) (Desert Wine (USA)) 9.7f **(80)**
Form - 006835
Record 1999 - 1st:0 2nd:0 3rd:1 Ran:6
Pre1999 - 1st:1 2nd:1 3rd:2 Ran:9
Win Prizemoney £2,406 *Total Prizemoney* £5,255
Wins 1998 Jun Lingfi (GD) 9f 72 <
1999 Turf 0-6: (9f, 10f 2, 12f, 14f, 16f) (gd 3, g-f, frm 2)
Workmanlike, fair gelding, effective 9f, acts on frm, has worn blinkers, likes left handed tracks. Turf high 59. Consistent.
**W Jarvis [0-6] M C Banks (from M A Jarvis [1-9] Oct 1998).*

JAMPET BHB 26f **RR 28f** 2316[13]
3 b g No Big Deal - Jealous Lover (Alias Smith (USA)) 9.8f **(58)**
Form - 00000
Record 1999 - 1st:0 2nd:0 3rd:0 Ran:5
Pre1999 - 1st:0 2nd:0 3rd:0 Ran:4
1999 Turf 0-5: (8f 3, 10f, 17f) (sft, g-s, gd, g-f, hrd)
Little account gelding, has worn blinkers. Turf high 28.
**A Barrow [0-9] Don Hazzard.*

JAMRR (IRE) RR 85f 1994[3]
3 b c Barathea (IRE) - Ela Romara (Ela-Mana-Mou) 10.1f **(70)**
Form - 33
Record 1999 - 1st:0 2nd:0 3rd:2 Ran:2
Win Prizemoney £0 *Total Prizemoney* £1,114
1999 Turf 0-2: (10f 2) (frm 2)
Scopey, currently useful colt. Turf high 85.
**S bin Suroor [0-2] Godolphin.*

JANE ANN (IRE) BHB 46f45a **RR 50f 45a** 4223[9]
3 ch f Perugino (USA) -Height of Elegance (Shirley Heights) 10.3f **(74)**
Form - 414530760270
Record 1999 - 1st:1 2nd:1 3rd:1 Ran:12
Pre1999 - 1st:0 2nd:0 3rd:1 Ran:6
Win Prizemoney £2,507 *Total Prizemoney* £3,881
Wins * **1999** *Mar Lingfi (STD) 13f 48+* <
1999 Turf 0-6: (10f, 12f 4, 14f) (gd 2, g-f 3, frm) 1999 AW 1-6: (11f, 12f 4, 13f 1-1) (Equi 1-1, Fibr 5)
Fair filly, effective 7f, acts on gd. Turf high 50. AW high 54.
**A P Jarvis [1-18] Mrs Ann Jarvis.*

JANEFER JOHN (IRE) BHB 64f **RR 64f** 4738a[8]
2 ch f Magical Wonder (USA) 7.2f **(60)** - John's Vision (IRE) (Vision (USA)) 9f **(64)**
Form - 5470068
Record 1999 - 1st:0 2nd:0 3rd:0 Ran:7
Win Prizemoney £0 *Total Prizemoney* £207
1999 Turf 0-7: (5f 2, 6f 4, 7f) (sft, g-s, gd 2, g-f 2, frm)
Average filly. Turf high 66.
**K F O'Brien in IRE [0-4] John Michael (from J L Eyre [0-3] Jun 1999).*

JANE GREY BHB 55f **RR 57f** 4813[11]
3 br f Tragic Role (USA) 9.4f **(63)** -Kind of Shy (Kind of Hush) 10.1f **(62)**
Form - 05530270
Record 1999 - 1st:0 2nd:1 3rd:1 Ran:8
Pre1999 - 1st:0 2nd:0 3rd:0 Ran:3
Win Prizemoney £0 *Total Prizemoney* £1,414
1999 Turf 0-8: (6f 2, 8f 6) (g-s, gd 3, g-f, frm 3)
Workmanlike, fair filly, effective 5f, acts on gd. Turf high 57.
**M Salaman [0-11] J P M & J W Cook.*

JANET RR 67f 1511[2]
2 b f Emperor Jones (USA) - Bid Dancer (Spectacular Bid (USA)) 11.2f **(76)**
Form - 52
Record 1999 - 1st:0 2nd:1 3rd:0 Ran:2
Win Prizemoney £0 *Total Prizemoney* £1,060
1999 Turf 0-2: (6f 2) (g-f 2)
Currently average filly. Turf high 67 - 2nd of 7 getting 5lb from Speedfit Free (26 May Yarmouth 6f g-f RF 1511).
**A Kelleway [0-2] Osvaldo Pedroni.*

JANICELAND (IRE) BHB 65f65a **RR 70f 65a** 5144[2]
2 b f Foxhound (USA) - Rebecca's Girl (IRE) (Nashamaa) 7.1f **(66)**
Form - 52276735022
Record 1999 - 1st:0 2nd:4 3rd:1 Ran:11
Win Prizemoney £0 *Total Prizemoney* £4,581
1999 Turf 0-9: (5f 7, 6f 2) (gd 2, g-f 3, frm 4)1999 AW 0-2: (6f 2) (Fibr 2)
Above-average filly, effective 5 to 6f, best at 5f, acts on gd to frm - acts on Fibr. Turf high 70 - 2nd of 11 giving 3lb to Ebba (21 May Catterick 5f gd RF 1373). AW high 66 (began Oct).
**S E Kettlewell [0-11] Cable Media Consultancy Ltd.*

JARAAB BHB 79f79a **RR 33f 79a** 100[1]
8 b g Sure Blade (USA) 10.6f **(66)** - Ostora (USA) (Blushing Groom (FR)) 10.3f **(76)**
Form - 11
Record 1999 - 1st:1 2nd:0 3rd:0 Ran:1
Pre1999 - 1st:12 2nd:3 3rd:2 Ran:38
Win Prizemoney £37,052 *Total Prizemoney* £40,733

Wins	* **1999**	*Jan*	*Southw*	*(STD)*	*C*	*16f*		*57*	
	* 1998	*Dec*	*Wolver*	*(SLW)*	*C*	*14.8f*		*72*	
	* 1998	*Mar*	*Southw*	*(STD)*	*C*	*14f*		*71*	
	* 1996	*May*	*Southw*	*(STD)*	*C*	*16f*		*67*	
	* 1996	*Apr*	*Wolver*	*(STD)*	*H*	*14.8f*	*82*	*85*	<
	1996	*Apr*	*Southw*	*(STD)*	*C*	*16f*		*79*	
	1996	*Feb*	*Lingfi*	*(STD)*	*H*	*16f*	*70*	*73*	
	1995	*Nov*	*Lingfi*	*(STD)*	*H*	*16f*	*58*	*73+*	
	1995	*Nov*	*Lingfi*	*(STD)*	*H*	*16f*	*58*	*61*	
	1995	*May*	*Wolver*	*(STD)*	*H*	*14.8f*	*58*	*69+*	
	1995	*Apr*	*Wolver*	*(STD)*	*H*	*7f*	*51*	*59*	
	1995	*Mar*	*Lingfi*	*(STD)*	*H*	*16f*	*41*	*51*	
	1995	*Feb*	*Lingfi*	*(STD)*	*H*	*12f*	*41*	*43*	

1999 AW 1-1: (16f 1-1) (Fibr 1-1)
Decent gelding, effective 14 to 15f, best at 15f, - acts on Fibr, mostly wears blinkers (effectively). (1st run).
**Miss S J Wilton [5-11] John Pointon and Sons (from G Lewis [8-25] Apr 1996).*

JARN RR 89+f 5036[8]
2 b c Green Desert (USA) 7.8f **(78)** - Alkariyh (USA) (Alydar (USA)) 9.1f **(76)**
Form - 18
Record 1999 - 1st:1 2nd:0 3rd:0 Ran:2
Win Prizemoney £4,792 *Total Prizemoney* £4,792
Wins * **1999** Spt Newbur (G-F) 6f 97+ <
1999 Turf 1-2: (6f 1-2) (g-s, frm 1-1)
Currently useful colt. Turf high 97 (1st run) (began Spt) - 1st of 15 from Corridor Creeper (18 Spt Newbury RF 4407). He created a favourable impression on his debut, but disappointed on soft ground in a Listed event at Doncaster in October. He should stay a mile and is worth another chance on a sound surface.
**B Hanbury [1-2] Hamdan Al Maktoum.*

JASEUR (USA) BHB 103f **RR 103f** 4247a[6]
6 b g Lear Fan (USA) 10.4f **(80)** - Spur Wing (USA) (Storm Bird (CAN)) 10.3f **(74)**
Form - 2427306
Record 1999 - 1st:0 2nd:2 3rd:1 Ran:7
Pre1999 - 1st:3 2nd:2 3rd:0 Ran:12
Win Prizemoney £27,339 *Total Prizemoney* £56,449

Wins	* 1997	Oct	Ascot	(HVY)	H	16.2f	82	87+	<
	* 1997	Spt	Ascot	(GD)	H	16.2f	74	82+	
	* 1997	Spt	Bath	(GD)	H	13.1f	69	77	

1999 Turf 0-7: (14f 2, 16f 4, 22f) (gd 4, g-f, frm 2)
Very useful gelding, effective 14 to 22f, acts on gd to frm, mostly wears blinkers (very effectively). Turf high 103 - 3rd of 7 getting 5lb from Kayf Tara (29 Jly Goodwood 16f frm RF 3222). Consistent. Gambled on when unplaced in the Ebor, he has plenty of ability but is difficult to win with.
**J H M Gosden [3-19].*

JATHAAB (USA) RR 74f 5124[3]
2 b br c Silver Hawk (USA) 11.2f **(85)** - Best Of Memories (USA) (Halo (USA)) 10.6f **(75)**
Form - 4103
Record 1999 - 1st:1 2nd:0 3rd:1 Ran:4
Win Prizemoney £3,826 *Total Prizemoney* £4,622
Wins * **1999** Spt Haydoc (SFT) 7.1f 74 <
1999 Turf 1-4: (7f 1-2, 8f 2) (g-s 1-1, gd 2, frm)
Above-average colt. Turf high 74 (began Jly) - 1st of 11 from Dilsaa (25 Spt Haydock RF 4551).
**J L Dunlop [1-4] Hamdan Al Maktoum.*

JATHAABEH RR 52f 5208[11]
2 ch f Nashwan (USA) 10.3f **(79)** - Pastorale (Nureyev (USA)) 8.7f **(78)**
Form - 0
Record 1999 - 1st:0 2nd:0 3rd:0 Ran:1
1999 Turf 0-1: (7f) (g-s)
Currently fair filly. **M A Jarvis [0-1] Sheikh Ahmed Al Maktoum.*

JATO DANCER (IRE) BHB 29f29a **RR 6f 29a** 2446[7]
4 b f Mukaddamah (USA) 7.6f **(74)** - Que Tranquila (Dominion) 8.5f **(63)**
Form - 700087
Record 1999 - 1st:0 2nd:0 3rd:0 Ran:4
Pre1999 - 1st:2 2nd:1 3rd:1 Ran:17
Win Prizemoney £4,750 *Total Prizemoney* £6,107
Wins * 1998 May Windso (G-F) C 8.3f 49 <
1997 Jly Bright (FRM) S 7f 49 <
1999 Turf 0-4: (7f, 8f 2, 9f) (g-f 4)
Leggy, very poor filly, effective 7 to 9f, acts on g-f to frm - acts on Equi, has worn blinkers, favours tight tracks. Turf high 24.
**J R Arnold [1-18] Norman Hill (from M R Channon [1-3] Aug 1997).*

JAVA SHRINE (USA) BHB 48f73a **RR 37f 73a** 1599[18]
8 b g Java Gold (USA) 9.3f **(67)** - Ivory Idol (USA) (Alydar (USA)) 9.1f **(76)**
Form - 11163000
Record 1999 - 1st:3 2nd:0 3rd:1 Ran:8
Pre1999 - 1st:3 2nd:2 3rd:3 Ran:23
Win Prizemoney £15,999 *Total Prizemoney* £19,228
Wins 1999 *Jan Lingfi (STD) C 10f 75+* <
1999 *Jan Lingfi (STD) 10f 72*
* **1999** *Jan Lingfi (STD) C 10f 71+*
* 1998 *Spt Lingfi (STA) SH 10f 60 68*
* 1998 Jly Warwic (G-F) SH 10.8f 50 56
1999 Turf 0-3: (10f 2, 11f) (g-f 2, frm) 1999 AW 3-5: (10f 3-4, 12f) (Equi 3-5)
Above-average gelding, effective 10 to 13f, best at 10f, acts on frm - acts on AW, best on Equi, often wears blinkers (extremely effectively), favours left handed tracks, and excels at Lingfield. Turf high 37. AW high 75 - 1st of 8 giving 9lb to Ki Chi Saga (23 Jan Lingfield RF 0149) - also 1st of 6 giving 4lb to Kings Arrow (16 Jan Lingfield RF 0110). Becoming disappointing. An effective sort in modest company, though he is not an easy ride and needs plenty of driving along to keep in touch. He goes particularly well over ten furlongs on the Lingfield Equitrack.
**P Eccles [3-14] Plough Twenty (Ashto Keynes) (from Andrew Reid [2-4] Feb 1999).*

JAWAH (IRE) BHB 78f **RR 79f** 5220[14]
5 br g In The Wings 11.2f **(77)** - Saving Mercy (Lord Gayle (USA)) 8.8f **(62)**
Form - 27810
Record 1999 - 1st:1 2nd:1 3rd:0 Ran:5
Pre1999 - 1st:3 2nd:2 3rd:1 Ran:21
Win Prizemoney £15,688 *Total Prizemoney* £21,418
Wins 1999 Oct Doncas (G-S) H 14.6f 74 79
1997 Oct Nottin (GD) H 14.1f 70 81+ <
1997 Oct Doncas (GD) H 14.6f 70 75
1997 Jly Bellew (G-S) H 14f 66 62
1999 Turf 1-5: (14f 3, 15f 1-1, 17f) (sft, g-s, gd 1-2, frm)
Above-average gelding, effective 14 to 15f, best at 14f, acts on g-s to frm, has worn blinkers, likes left handed tracks, likes tight tracks. Turf high 79 (began Spt) - 1st of 12 giving 10lb to Grosvenor Flyer (22 Oct Doncaster RF 5025). Scored at Doncaster in October, having made a belated return to action. He has a turn of foot and is suited by being covered up.
**J R Jenkins [0-1] R M Ellis (from K Mahdi [3-19] Oct 1999).*

JAWHARI BHB 63f **RR 63df** 4344[11]
5 b g Lahib (USA) 8f **(69)** - Lady of the Land (Wollow) 8.2f **(61)**
Form - 10600
Record 1999 - 1st:1 2nd:0 3rd:0 Ran:5
Pre1999 - 1st:1 2nd:2 3rd:0 Ran:14
Win Prizemoney £9,032 *Total Prizemoney* £11,054
Wins * **1999** Jly Catter (GD) H 5f 62 63
1997 Jly Lingfi (G-F) 7.6f 80 <
1999 Turf 1-5: (5f 1-4, 6f) (g-s, gd, g-f 1-2, frm)
Average gelding, effective 5 to 6f, acts on g-f to frm, has worn blinkers. Turf high 63 (1st run) (began Jly) - 1st of 10 getting 1lb from William's Well (21 Jly Catterick RF 3005).
**D Nicholls [1-13] Geoffrey Thompson (from J L Dunlop [1-6] Oct 1997).*

JAWLA RR 42f 5208[16]
2 ch f Wolfhound (USA) 7.3f **(71)** - Majmu (USA) (Al Nasr (FR)) 9.3f **(68)**
Form - 0
Record 1999 - 1st:0 2nd:0 3rd:0 Ran:1
1999 Turf 0-1: (7f) (g-s)
Currently moderate filly. **J H M Gosden [0-1] Hamdan Al Maktoum.*

JAYANNPEE BHB 74f **RR 69f** 1111[13]
8 ch g Doulab (USA) 7.4f **(61)** - Amina (Brigadier Gerard) 9.3f **(58)**
Form - 0080
Record 1999 - 1st:0 2nd:0 3rd:0 Ran:4
Pre1999 - 1st:10 2nd:4 3rd:6 Ran:57
Win Prizemoney £113,054 *Total Prizemoney* £141,518
Wins * 1998 Jun Bath (G-S) H 5.7f 82 84
* 1996 Spt Taby (GD) L 6f 95
* 1996 Jly Newbur (G-F) L 6f 107 <
* 1996 May York (G-F) H 6f 96 104
* 1996 May Newmar (G-F) H 6f 90 95
1999 Turf 0-4: (6f 3, 7f) (g-s 2, g-f 2)
Average gelding, effective 5 to 6f, best at 6f, acts on gd to g-f, best on gd. Turf high 69. Consistent. He is not the horse he was, and only pops up from time to time now.
**I A Balding [10-61] Mrs Monica Caine.*

JAYBIRD BHB 77f **RR 76f** 4786[9]
2 ch f Common Grounds 8.1f **(66)** - Flight Soundly (IRE) **(70f)** (Caerleon (USA)) 8.6f **(71)**
Form - 4210
Record 1999 - 1st:1 2nd:1 3rd:0 Ran:4
Win Prizemoney £3,501 *Total Prizemoney* £5,037
Wins * **1999** Spt Mussel (G-S) 5f 76 <
1999 Turf 1-3: (5f 1-1, 6f 2) (gd 1-1, g-f, hrd) 1999 AW 0-1: (6f) (Equi)
Above-average filly. Turf high 76 (began Aug) - 1st of 14 getting 5lb from Polar Haze (26 Spt Musselburgh RF 4574).
**Sir Michael Stoute [1-4] Sir Evelyn De Rothschild.*

JAYESAY (IRE) BHB 47f35a **RR 50f 35a** 3092[11]
3 gr g Mystiko (USA) 7.7f **(59)** - Scravels Saran (IRE) (Indian King (USA)) 7.4f **(64)**
Form - 0080
Record 1999 - 1st:0 2nd:0 3rd:0 Ran:4
1999 Turf 0-2: (8f 2) (gd, frm) 1999 AW 0-2: (8f, 10f) (Equi, Fibr)
Scopey, fair gelding. Turf high 50. (began Jly).
**Dr J D Scargill [0-4] Derek Johnson.*

JAY GEE (IRE) RR 46f 2579[12]
4 b f Second Set (IRE) 9.2f **(67)** - Polynesian Goddess (IRE) (Salmon Leap (USA)) 11f **(61)**
Form - 0080
Record 1999 - 1st:0 2nd:0 3rd:0 Ran:4
Pre1999 - 1st:2 2nd:1 3rd:2 Ran:16
Win Prizemoney £21,599 *Total Prizemoney* £27,495
Wins * 1997 Aug Newmar (GD) H 6f 82 92 <
* 1997 Jly Windso (G-F) 6f 84
1999 Turf 0-4: (5f 2, 6f, 7f) (g-f 2, frm 2)
Unfurnished, moderate filly, effective 5f, acts on g-f, has worn blinkers (effectively). Turf high 46.
**G G Margarson [2-20] John Guest.*

JAYNE'S PRINCESS (IRE) RR 5054[13]
2 b f College Chapel - Water Spirit (USA) (Riverman (USA)) 9.1f **(76)**
Form - 0
Record 1999 - 1st:0 2nd:0 3rd:0 Ran:1
1999 Turf 0-1: (6f) (gd)
Currently very poor filly. **B Palling [0-1] Glyn and Albert Yemm.*

JAY-OWE-TWO (IRE) BHB 76f78a **RR 75f 78a** 1543[5]
5 b g Distinctly North (USA) 7.4f **(63)** - Fiery Song (Ballad Rock) 7.8f **(63)**
Form - 1740072475
Record 1999 - 1st:0 2nd:1 3rd:0 Ran:8
Pre1999 - 1st:6 2nd:3 3rd:2 Ran:33
Win Prizemoney £31,945 *Total Prizemoney* £48,268
Wins * 1998 *Dec Wolver (STD) H 8.5f 76 78*

* 1998	Spt	Ayr	(G-S)	H	7f	66	70+	
* 1997	Oct	Newmar	(G-S)	H	8f	71	81	<
* 1997	Oct	Pontef	(G-F)	H	8f	71	77	
* 1997	Apr	Beverl	(G-F)	H	7.5f	75	81	<
* 1996	*Dec*	*Southw*	*(SLW)*		*6f*		*79+*	

1999 Turf 0-6: (7f, 8f 5) (sft, g-s, gd 3, g-f) 1999 AW 0-2: (8f 2) (Fibr 2)
Above-average gelding, effective 7 to 8f, best at 8f, acts on sft to g-f - acts on Fibr, often wears blinkers, likes left handed tracks, likes tight tracks. Turf high 75 - 2nd of 17 getting 16lb from Latalomne (1 May Thirsk 8f g-f RF 0967). AW high 77 (1st run) - 4th of 8 giving 29lb to Windshift (1 Mar Southwell 8f Fibr RF 0381).
**R M Whitaker [6-41] Country Lane Partnership.*

JAYPEECEE BHB 64f RR 44f 2459[11]

3 b g Never so Bold 7.1f **(62)** - Treeline (High Top) 10.2f **(67)**
Form - 1000
Record 1999 - 1st:1 2nd:0 3rd:0 Ran:4
Win Prizemoney £4,100 *Total Prizemoney* £4,100
Wins * **1999** Apr Beverl (GD) 5f 72 <
1999 Turf 1-4: (5f 1-1, 6f 3) (gd 1-1, g-f 2, frm)
Workmanlike, moderate gelding. Turf high 72 (1st run) - 1st of 17 giving 5lb to Twickers (22 Apr Beverley RF 0808).
**J L Eyre [1-4] Billy Parker.*

JAZIL BHB 104f RR 103f 1104[9]

4 b c Nashwan (USA) 10.3f **(79)** - Gracious Beauty (USA) (Nijinsky (CAN)) 10.3f **(77)**
Form - 0
Record 1999 - 1st:0 2nd:0 3rd:0 Ran:1
Pre1999 - 1st:2 2nd:1 3rd:2 Ran:6
Win Prizemoney £11,927 *Total Prizemoney* £16,347
Wins * 1998 Spt Doncas (GD) H 12f 95 98 <
* 1998 Jly Ascot (G-F) 10f 95+
1999 Turf 0-1: (12f) (gd)
Very useful colt, effective 10 to 12f, best at 12f, acts on gd to g-f, best on g-f, often wears blinkers. Big and imposing, he was a decent three-year-old and ran third in a Listed event at Newmarket on his final start, but he ran very poorly in the Shergar Cup on his reappearance at Goodwood in May. His next public appearance was at Tattersalls in October, where he fetched 42,000 gns.
**J H M Gosden [2-7] Hamdan Al Maktoum.*

JAZZ NIGHT RR 41f 4423[9]

2 b g Alhijaz 7.7f **(57)** - Hen Night (Mummy's Game) 8.2f **(60)**
Form - 0
Record 1999 - 1st:0 2nd:0 3rd:0 Ran:1
1999 Turf 0-1: (7f) (frm)
Currently moderate gelding. **G Woodward [0-1] J M Lacey.*

JAZZ TIME BHB 79f RR 82f 4899[14]

2 ch c Clantime 6.6f **(57)** - Real Popcorn (IRE) **(50df 51a)** (Jareer (USA)) 5.9f **(75)**
Form - 82363440
Record 1999 - 1st:0 2nd:1 3rd:2 Ran:8
Win Prizemoney £0 *Total Prizemoney* £2,741
1999 Turf 0-8: (5f 5, 7f, 8f 2) (sft, gd 2, g-f 2, frm 3)
Decent colt, effective 5 to 8f, acts on g-f to frm. Turf high 82 - 4th of 8 giving 15lb to Amoras (6 Spt Bath 8f frm RF 4157).
**A P Jarvis [0-8] Christopher Shankland.*

JAZZ TRACK (IRE) BHB 75f RR 73f 1044[16]

5 b g Sadler's Wells (USA) 11.3f **(87)** - Minnie Hauk (USA) (Sir Ivor) 10.2f **(70)**
Form - 0
Record 1999 - 1st:0 2nd:0 3rd:0 Ran:1
Pre1999 - 1st:1 2nd:1 3rd:2 Ran:7
Win Prizemoney £3,717 *Total Prizemoney* £5,883
Wins 1997 Oct Catter (SFT) H 15.8f 78 80 <
1999 Turf 0-1: (19f) (g-f)
Above-average gelding, has worn blinkers. Consistent.
**M C Pipe [0-10] Malcolm Jones (from P W Chapple-Hyam [1-6] Oct 1997).*

JAZZY BHB 22f RR 12f 1606[12]

4 b f Alhijaz 7.7f **(57)** - Irenic (Mummy's Pet) 7.7f **(60)**
Form - 007700
Record 1999 - 1st:0 2nd:0 3rd:0 Ran:5
Pre1999 - 1st:0 2nd:0 3rd:0 Ran:3
1999 Turf 0-2: (7f, 8f) (gd, frm) 1999 AW 0-3: (7f, 8f 2) (Fibr 3)
Lengthy, poor filly. Turf high 12. AW high 18. **J Norton [0-8] T Hurst.*

JAZZY MILLENNIUM BHB 83f RR 79f 5195[10]

2 ch c Lion Cavern (USA) 7.5f **(74)** - Woodcrest **(82f)** (Niniski (USA)) 10.6f **(65)**
Form - 4220
Record 1999 - 1st:0 2nd:2 3rd:0 Ran:4
Win Prizemoney £0 *Total Prizemoney* £2,837
1999 Turf 0-4: (6f 2, 7f 2) (gd 3, g-f)
Above-average colt. Turf high 79 (began Jly) - 2nd of 7 to Nothing Daunted (28 Aug Goodwood 7f gd RF 3961).
**Miss Gay Kelleway [0-4] Millennium Millionaires Partnership.*

JEAN PIERRE BHB 36f RR 37f 1939[9]

6 b g Anshan 8.2f **(63)** - Astolat (Rusticaro (FR)) 8.2f **(65)**
Form - 00
Record 1999 - 1st:0 2nd:0 3rd:0 Ran:1
Pre1999 - 1st:0 2nd:4 3rd:2 Ran:19
Win Prizemoney £0 *Total Prizemoney* £4,115
1999 Turf 0-1: (10f) (g-f)
Very moderate gelding.
**C L Popham [0-2] Avalon Racing Syndicate (from J E Banks [0-1] Dec 1998).*

JEDI KNIGHT BHB 88f RR 87f 4754[9]

5 b g Emarati (USA) 6.6f **(63)** - Hannie Caulder (Workboy) 7.3f **(46)**
Form - 70152610140
Record 1999 - 1st:3 2nd:1 3rd:0 Ran:11
Pre1999 - 1st:4 2nd:6 3rd:2 Ran:36
Win Prizemoney £36,249 *Total Prizemoney* £55,752

Wins * **1999**	Aug	Hamilt	(G-F)	H	9.2f	84	87	<
* **1999**	Jly	York	(G-F)	H	7.9f	80	84	
* **1999**	May	Beverl	(GD)	H	8.5f	70	84+	
* 1997	Nov	Redcar	(GD)	H	10f	69	74	
* 1997	Aug	Thirsk	(G-F)	H	8f	67	70	
* 1997	Jun	Carlis	(FRM)	H	8f	55	62++	
* 1997	Jun	Doncas	(GD)	H	7f	55	62	

1999 Turf 3-11: (8f 2-7, 9f 1-2, 10f 2) (gd 1-5, g-f, frm 2-5)
Useful gelding, effective 8 to 9f, best at 9f, acts on gd to frm, best on gd, has worn blinkers, likes right handed tracks, likes tight tracks. Turf high 87 - 1st of 8 giving 2lb to Prairie Wolf (24 Aug Hamilton RF 3867) - also 1st of 17 from Kass Alhawa (8 May Beverley RF 1101). Consistent. A winner of three of his eleven starts last term, all victories coming over distances around a mile on decent ground, he showed he was in good terms with himself when, although no match for the principals, he ran on well to finish fourth at Doncaster in September.
**M W Easterby [7-47] K Hodgson & Mrs J Hodgson.*

JEED (IRE) RR 80+f 2304[1]

2 b f Mujtahid (USA) 7.4f **(69)** - Secretary Bird (IRE) (Kris) 9.5f **(73)**
Form - 1
Record 1999 - 1st:1 2nd:0 3rd:0 Ran:1
Win Prizemoney £4,272 *Total Prizemoney* £4,272
Wins * **1999** Jun Newmar (G-F) 6f 80+ <
1999 Turf 1-1: (6f 1-1) (g-f 1-1)
Currently decent filly. (1st run) - 1st of 6 from Mother Molly (25 Jun Newmarket RF 2304). **E A L Dunlop [1-1] Hamdan Al Maktoum.*

JEFFREY ANOTHERRED BHB 76f73a RR 75f 73a 4380[3]

5 b g Emarati (USA) 6.6f **(63)** - First Pleasure (Dominion) 8.5f **(63)**
Form - 03507061514683
Record 1999 - 1st:2 2nd:0 3rd:2 Ran:13
Pre1999 - 1st:5 2nd:4 3rd:4 Ran:37
Win Prizemoney £33,240 *Total Prizemoney* £50,742

Wins * **1999**	Jly	Ayr	(SFT)	H	7f	71	75	
* **1999**	Jun	Ayr	(G-S)	H	7f	68	71	
* 1998	Jly	Ayr	(SFT)	H	6f	70	84	
* 1998	Jly	Carlis	(G-F)		5.9f		70	
1996	Nov	Doncas	(SFT)	H	7f	86	96	<
1996	Spt	Kempto	(GD)	H	6f	78	74	
1996	Aug	Hamilt	(G-F)	H	5f		69	

1999 Turf 2-13: (6f 5, 7f 2-7, 8f) (hvy, g-s 1-3, gd 1-4, g-f 4, frm)
Above-average gelding, effective 6 to 7f, best at 6f, acts on g-s to gd, best on gd, has worn blinkers, likes left handed tracks, excels at Ayr. Turf high 77 - also 1st of 10 giving 10lb to Technician (19

Jly Ayr RF 2942). Consistent. An ordinary handicapper, effective on a variety of ground conditions, he wins in his turn.
**M Dods [4-32] A G Watson (from K McAuliffe [3-18] Oct 1997).*

JELLYBEEN (IRE) BHB 52f54a **RR 56f 54a** 4223[10]
3 ch f Petardia 8.2f **(58)** - Lux Aeterna (Sandhurst Prince) 7.9f **(63)**
Form - 100026350
Record 1999 - 1st:0 2nd:1 3rd:1 Ran:7
Pre1999 - 1st:1 2nd:0 3rd:0 Ran:5
Win Prizemoney £2,179 *Total Prizemoney* £3,341
Wins * 1998 *Nov Wolver (STD) 9.4f 65 <*
1999 Turf 0-5: (10f, 11f, 14f 2, 15f) (gd 2, g-f 2, frm) 1999 AW 0-2: (12f, 16f) (Equi, Fibr)
Lengthy, fair filly, effective 9 to 14f, acts on g-f - acts on Fibr, has worn blinkers, likes left handed tracks, favours tight tracks. Turf high 56 - 2nd of 7 getting 12lb from Salford Flyer (21 Jun Yarmouth 14f g-f RF 2183). (began Aug). **Miss Gay Kelleway [1-12] N Parker.*

JEMALINA (USA) BHB 58f **RR 57f** 5054[12]
2 b f Trempolino (USA) 11.9f **(77)** - Cachondina (Runnett) 7f **(59)**
Form - 800
Record 1999 - 1st:0 2nd:0 3rd:0 Ran:3
1999 Turf 0-3: (6f, 7f 2) (gd, g-f, frm)
Currently fair filly. Turf high 57 (began Aug).
**J Noseda [0-3] B E Nielsen.*

JEMIMA BHB 100f **RR 100f** 4596[5]
2 b f Owington - Poyle Fizz (Damister (USA)) 9f **(73)**
Form - 62121185
Record 1999 - 1st:3 2nd:2 3rd:0 Ran:8
Win Prizemoney £55,244 *Total Prizemoney* £60,981
Wins * **1999** Aug York (GD) G2 6f 100 <
* **1999** Aug Ripon (G-F) 6f 95+
* **1999** Jun York (G-S) 5f 72
1999 Turf 3-8: (5f 1-4, 6f 2-4) (g-s 1-1, gd 1-3, g-f, frm 1-3)
Very useful filly, effective 6f, acts on gd to frm. Turf high 100 - 1st of 9 from Seraphina (19 Aug York RF 3769) - also 1st of 6 from Secret Conquest (2 Aug Ripon RF 3299). Inconsistent. She won a sub-standard renewal of the Lowther Stakes and will find life difficult under a Group Two penalty in 2000. Likely to stay seven furlongs, she has yet to race on extremes of going.
**T D Easterby [3-8] Mrs Jean Connew.*

JEMINAR BHB 57f **RR 56f** 1247[4]
2 b f Clantime 6.6f **(57)** - Bad Payer (Tanfirion) 7f **(61)**
Form - 064
Record 1999 - 1st:0 2nd:0 3rd:0 Ran:3
Win Prizemoney £0 *Total Prizemoney* £201
1999 Turf 0-3: (5f 3) (gd 2, g-f)
Currently fair filly. Turf high 56.
**M W Easterby [0-3] Bernard Bargh & Garry & Linda Owen.*

JENIN RR 24f 3163[11]
2 b f Rambo Dancer (CAN) 8.4f **(59)** - Rich Lass (Broxted) 6.7f **(65)**
Form - 00
Record 1999 - 1st:0 2nd:0 3rd:0 Ran:2
1999 Turf 0-2: (5f 2) (gd, frm)
Currently little account filly. Turf high 24 (began Jly).
**J W Payne [0-2] Sir Simon Lycett Green.*

JENKO (IRE) BHB 53f **RR 68f** 4929[9]
2 b g College Chapel - Flicker of Hope (IRE) (Baillamont (USA)) 7f **(78)**
Form - 0460
Record 1999 - 1st:0 2nd:0 3rd:0 Ran:4
Win Prizemoney £0 *Total Prizemoney* £230
1999 Turf 0-4: (5f, 6f 2, 7f) (gd, g-f, frm 2)
Average gelding. Turf high 59 (began Jly).
**H J Collingridge [0-4] J W Jenkins.*

JENNELLE BHB 70f **RR 67f** 5161[3]
5 b m Nomination 7.3f **(57)** - Its A Romp (Hotfoot) 10.5f **(59)**
Form - 50078724003
Record 1999 - 1st:0 2nd:1 3rd:1 Ran:11
Pre1999 - 1st:5 2nd:3 3rd:2 Ran:25
Win Prizemoney £18,369 *Total Prizemoney* £38,358
Wins * 1998 Apr Redcar (SFT) H 5f 78 83
* 1996 Oct Lingfi (G-S) 5f 89 <
* 1996 Jly Folkes (GD) H 5f 89 <
* 1996 Apr Thirsk (G-F) 5f 73
* 1996 Mar Folkes (G-S) 5f 72
1999 Turf 0-11: (5f 6, 6f 5) (g-s 3, gd 3, g-f 2, frm 3)
Average filly, effective 5 to 6f, acts on sft to frm. Turf high 83. Consistent. **C A Dwyer [5-36] Mrs J A Cornwell.*

JENSENS TALE (IRE) BHB 46f41a **RR 63f 41a** 4939[12]
2 b c Mukaddamah (USA) 7.6f **(74)** - Miss Tagalie (IRE) (Cyrano de Bergerac) 6f **(68)**
Form - 5076236556500
Record 1999 - 1st:0 2nd:1 3rd:1 Ran:13
Win Prizemoney £0 *Total Prizemoney* £914
1999 Turf 0-12: (5f 4, 6f 5, 7f 2, 10f) (sft 2, g-s, gd 2, g-f 2, frm 5) 1999 AW 0-1: (7f) (Fibr)
Average colt, has worn blinkers. Turf high 63.
**Mrs A L M King [0-13] Mrs A Martin.*

JENUIN RR 33f 2061[15]
4 b f High Kicker (USA) 8.4f **(52)** - Absonant (Absalom) 7.2f **(58)**
Form - 00
Record 1999 - 1st:0 2nd:0 3rd:0 Ran:2
1999 Turf 0-2: (10f, 12f) (frm, hrd)
Currently very moderate filly. Turf high 33.
**G M Moore [0-2] Mrs E S Bradley.*

JEPAJE BHB 62f **RR 62f** 4809[11]
2 b g Rambo Dancer (CAN) 8.4f **(59)** - Hi-Hunsley (Swing Easy (USA)) 6.5f **(55)**
Form - 00420
Record 1999 - 1st:0 2nd:1 3rd:0 Ran:5
Win Prizemoney £0 *Total Prizemoney* £1,108
1999 Turf 0-5: (5f, 6f 3, 7f) (sft, g-s 2, gd, hrd)
Average gelding. Turf high 62 (began Aug) - 2nd of 10 getting 4lb from More Magic (4 Oct Brighton 5f gd RF 4707).
**A Bailey [0-5] Mrs V Farrington.*

JEREBOAM BHB 57f **RR 50f** 4668[11]
2 b c Grand Lodge (USA) - Premiere Cuvee (Formidable (USA)) 9.2f **(63)**
Form - 000
Record 1999 - 1st:0 2nd:0 3rd:0 Ran:3
1999 Turf 0-3: (5f 2, 6f) (g-s, gd, g-f)
Currently fair colt. Turf high 45 (began Spt).
**Sir Mark Prescott [0-3] Neil Greig Osborne House III.*

JESSINCA BHB 40f46a **RR 47f 46a** 3025[7]
3 b f Minshaanshu Amad (USA) 11.3f **(53)** - Noble Soul (Sayf El Arab (USA)) 7.1f **(54)**
Form - 4047
Record 1999 - 1st:0 2nd:0 3rd:0 Ran:2
Pre1999 - 1st:0 2nd:0 3rd:0 Ran:11
1999 Turf 0-1: (10f) (frm) 1999 AW 0-1: (8f) (Fibr)
Leggy, moderate filly, effective 8f, - acts on Fibr, likes left handed tracks. (1st run) - 4th of 15 getting 7lb from Stravsea (8 Jly Southwell 8f Fibr RF 2648).
**R T Phillips [0-2] The Lambourn Racing Club (from A P Jones [0-11] Nov 1998).*

JESS REBEC'S PET (IRE) BHB 43f **RR 39f** 5194[15]
2 b f Petorius 8f **(66)** - Jess Rebec **(12f)** (Kala Shikari) 8.4f **(54)**
Form - 8700
Record 1999 - 1st:0 2nd:0 3rd:0 Ran:4
1999 Turf 0-4: (5f, 6f 2, 7f) (sft, gd, g-f, frm)
Very moderate filly. Turf high 39 (began Aug).
**Derrick Morris [0-4] Byron Stokes.*

JET AGE BHB 76f **RR 72f** 2715[P]
3 b g Danehill (USA) 9.1f **(79)** - Fawaayid (USA) (Vaguely Noble) 10.1f **(72)**
Form - 4633P
Record 1999 - 1st:0 2nd:0 3rd:2 Ran:5
Win Prizemoney £0 *Total Prizemoney* £1,361
1999 Turf 0-5: (8f 2, 12f, 13f, 14f) (gd 3, frm 2)
Strong, above-average gelding. Turf high 72. (DEAD)
**E A L Dunlop [0-5] Maktoum Al Maktoum.*

JEUNE PREMIER (FR) RR 46f 4419[16]
2 ch c Jeune Homme (USA) -Misaine (FR) (Saint Cyrien (FR)) 8.4f **(80)**
Form - 0
Record 1999 - 1st:0 2nd:0 3rd:0 Ran:1
1999 Turf 0-1: (7f) (gd)
Currently moderate colt. **B J Meehan [0-1] Mrs E A Lerpiniere.*

JEWEL FIGHTER BHB 42f **RR 64df** 4927[13]
5 br m Good Times (ITY) 8.7f **(53)** - Duellist (Town Crier) 10.2f **(55)**
Form - 340
Record 1999 - 1st:0 2nd:0 3rd:1 Ran:3
Pre1999 - 1st:0 2nd:0 3rd:0 Ran:4
Win Prizemoney £0 *Total Prizemoney* £698
1999 Turf 0-2: (8f, 9f) (sft, g-s) 1999 AW 0-1: (8f) (Fibr)
Average filly. Turf high 64 (began Oct).
**P D Evans [0-3] Weir Investments (from C A Smith [0-4] Oct 1998).*

JIBE (USA) BHB 101f **RR 103f** 1499[3]
4 b f Danzig (USA) 8.1f **(88)** - Slightly Dangerous (USA) (Roberto (USA)) 10f **(76)**
Form - 43
Record 1999 - 1st:0 2nd:0 3rd:1 Ran:2
Pre1999 - 1st:2 2nd:1 3rd:1 Ran:7
Win Prizemoney £14,658 *Total Prizemoney* £61,024
Wins * 1998 May Newbur (GD) L 10f 94 <
* 1997 Spt Lingfi (GD) 7f 92++
1999 Turf 0-2: (10f 2) (g-s, g-f)
Very useful filly, effective 7 to 12f, acts on g-s to g-f. Turf high 103 - 3rd of 4 getting 5lb from Elhayq (26 May Newbury 10f g-f RF 1499). Consistent. Rated a Classic prospect at the start of 1998, she lacks scope and has become disappointing. **H R A Cecil [2-9] K Abdulla.*

JIBEREEN BHB 50f78a **RR 50f 78a** 901[19]
7 b g Lugana Beach 7f **(63)** - Fashion Lover (Shiny Tenth) 9.2f **(56)**
Form - 7212043520
Record 1999 - 1st:1 2nd:2 3rd:1 Ran:8
Pre1999 - 1st:10 2nd:3 3rd:1 Ran:47
Win Prizemoney £32,161 *Total Prizemoney* £40,859

Wins							
* 1999	*Jan*	*Southw*	*(STD)*	*C*	*8f*		*86* <
* 1998	*Jan*	*Southw*	*(STD)*	*H*	*8f*	*72*	*78*
* 1997	Jly	Newmar	(GD)	H	8f	56	62
* 1997	Jun	Newmar	(SFT)	H	7f	53	56
* 1997	*Apr*	*Southw*	*(STD)*	*H*	*8f*	*70*	*75*
* 1997	*Jan*	*Wolver.*	*(STD)*	*C*	*7f*		*73*
* 1997	*Jan*	*Southw*	*(STD)*	*C*	*7f*		*73*
* 1996	*Dec*	*Southw*	*(SLW)*	*H*	*6f*	*67*	*67*
1995	Oct	Chepst	(G-S)	H	7.1f	69	77

1999 Turf 0-2: (8f 2) (gd, g-f) 1999 AW 1-6: (6f, 8f 1-3, 9f 2) (Fibr 1-6)
Above-average gelding, effective 8 to 9f, best at 8f, - acts on Fibr, prefers left handed tracks, prefers tight tracks, excels at Wolverhampton and Southwell. Turf high 50. AW high 86 (1st run) - 1st of 14 from Sualtach (2 Jan Southwell RF 0016). A fair handicapper on his day, his best recent form has been on Fibresand. A mile at Southwell looks to be his ideal conditions.
**P Howling [8-42] Liam Sheridan (from G Lewis [3-13] Apr 1996).*

JIG (IRE) RR 94?f 5211[3]
3 b f Catrail (USA) - River Jig (USA) (Irish River (FR)) 8.6f **(78)**
Form - 5023
Record 1999 - 1st:0 2nd:1 3rd:1 Ran:4
Pre1999 - 1st:1 2nd:0 3rd:0 Ran:2
Win Prizemoney £4,230 *Total Prizemoney* £7,291
Wins * 1998 Apr Newmar (SFT) 5f 87 <
1999 Turf 0-4: (8f 2, 10f 2) (sft, g-s, gd, g-f)
Leggy, useful filly, effective 5 to 8f, acts on sft to gd. Turf high 94 - 2nd of 7 getting 4lb from Alpenglow (12 Oct Leicester 8f gd RF 4838). **P F I Cole [1-6] H R H Prince Fahd Salman.*

JILLYS FLYER (IRE) RR 26f 1971[10]
2 ch f College Chapel - Idle Gossip (Runnett) 7f **(59)**
Form - 0
Record 1999 - 1st:0 2nd:0 3rd:0 Ran:1
1999 Turf 0-1: (6f) (g-f)
Currently little account filly. **J S Moore [0-1] Mrs Victoria Goodman.*

JILLY WOO BHB 27f29a **RR 42f 29a** 152[5]
5 gr m Environment Friend 7.5f **(67)** - William's Bird (USA) (Master Willie) 7f **(70)**
Form - 055
Record 1999 - 1st:0 2nd:0 3rd:0 Ran:3
Pre1999 - 1st:0 2nd:0 3rd:2 Ran:25
Win Prizemoney £0 *Total Prizemoney* £1,833
1999 AW 0-3: (12f 3) (Equi 3)
Moderate filly, effective 11f, acts on g-f, has worn blinkers, likes left handed tracks. AW high 31.
**P Hayward [0-14] Mrs J Wotherspoon (from B A Pearce [0-1] Aug 1997).*

JIM AND TONIC (FR) RR 123f 5226a[9]
5 g g Double Bed (FR) 13.9f **(54)** - Jimka (FR) (Jim French (USA)) 10.3f **(71)**
Form - 1312630
1999 Turf 1-6: (8f 4, 10f 1-2) (g-s, gd, g-f 1-2, frm 2)
Very high-class gelding, effective 7 to 10f, acts on sft to frm, does well at Sha Tin and Deauville and Saint-Cloud. Turf high 123 (1st run) - 3rd of 12 giving 7lb to Barbola (13 Mar Saint-cloud 10f g-s RF 0448a) - also 1st of 12 from Indigenous (18 Apr Sha Tin RF 0810a). Consistent. He is something of a globetrotter these days, and since December 1998 he has won two big prizes in Hong Kong. He has shown near top-class form in Europe and America too, and is effective between seven and ten furlongs. There are more big prizes to be won if this tough individual stays in training in 2000. **F Doumen in FR [4-13].*

JIMGAREEN (IRE) BHB 67f **RR 75f** 4575[14]
2 b br f Lahib (USA) 8f **(69)** - Sharp Circle (IRE) (Sure Blade (USA)) 11.3f **(67)**
Form - 20400
Record 1999 - 1st:0 2nd:1 3rd:0 Ran:5
Win Prizemoney £0 *Total Prizemoney* £1,362
1999 Turf 0-5: (6f 2, 7f 2, 8f) (gd 5)
Above-average filly. Turf high 75 (1st run) (began Jly) - 2nd of 10 getting 5lb from Nicholas Dudley (26 Jly Ayr 6f gd RF 3134).
**Miss L A Perratt [0-5] Dr J Walker.*

JIMMY TOO BHB 77f **RR 76f** 4390[10]
4 b br c Nomination 7.3f **(57)** - Cutlass Princess (USA) (Cutlass (USA)) 8.5f **(76)**
Form - 070065000
Record 1999 - 1st:0 2nd:0 3rd:0 Ran:9
Pre1999 - 1st:2 2nd:3 3rd:3 Ran:17
Win Prizemoney £8,218 *Total Prizemoney* £33,496
Wins * 1997 Aug Cheste (SFT) 6.1f 93 <
* 1997 Jun Cheste (SFT) 5.1f 66
1999 Turf 0-9: (5f, 6f 5, 7f 2, 8f) (sft, gd 5, g-f, frm 2)
Scopey, above-average colt, effective 6f, acts on g-f to frm, has worn blinkers (effectively). Turf high 84. A useful juvenile, beaten only a neck in the Mill Reef Stakes, he has failed to get his head in front since. **B A McMahon [2-26] J D Graham.*

JIVING RR 66f 2433[11]
3 ch f Generous (IRE) 11.5f **(82)** - Kerali (High Line) 10.3f **(70)**
Form - 0
Record 1999 - 1st:0 2nd:0 3rd:0 Ran:1
Pre1999 - 1st:0 2nd:0 3rd:1 Ran:1
Win Prizemoney £0 *Total Prizemoney* £447
1999 Turf 0-1: (8f) (gd)
Leggy, currently average filly. **R Charlton [0-2] K Abdulla.*

JOB RAGE (IRE) BHB 30f **RR 40f** 2486[5]
5 b br g Yashgan 8f **(51)** - Snatchingly (Thatch (USA)) 9.8f **(62)**
Form - 5
Record 1999 - 1st:0 2nd:0 3rd:0 Ran:1
Pre1999 - 1st:0 2nd:0 3rd:0 Ran:4
1999 Turf 0-1: (12f) (g-f)
Moderate gelding.
**R Ford [0-3] Mrs Carrie Ford (from A Bailey [0-4] Jan 1998).*

JOCASTA BHB 80f **RR 82df** 4921[10]
4 b f Warning 8.1f **(77)** - Breed Reference (Reference Point) 6.8f **(70)**
Form - 54571040
Record 1999 - 1st:1 2nd:0 3rd:0 Ran:8

Pre1999 - 1st:2 2nd:2 3rd:0 Ran:8
Win Prizemoney £12,944 *Total Prizemoney* £17,142
Wins * **1999** Aug Yarmou (GD) H 7f 78 82 <
* 1998 Aug Nottin (G-F) H 6.1f 78 82 <
* 1998 Jly Newmar (G-F) H 6f 70 75
1999 Turf 1-8: (6f 2, 7f 1-6) (gd 1-4, g-f 2, frm 2)
Neat, decent filly, effective 6 to 7f, best at 7f, acts on gd to g-f, best on g-f. Turf high 85 - also 1st of 13 giving 12lb to Nobalino (19 Aug Yarmouth RF 3766). She is suited by coming late off a fast pace, and she was able to do just that at Yarmouth in August. Suited by seven furlongs these days.
**C F Wall [3-16] C J A Hughes.*

JOCKO GLASSES RR 18f 3474[5]
2 ch c Inchinor 8.9f **(64)** - Corinthia (USA) (Empery (USA)) 11.2f **(69)**
Form - 5
Record 1999 - 1st:0 2nd:0 3rd:0 Ran:1
1999 Turf 0-1: (6f) (g-f)
Currently poor colt. **C F Wall [0-1] Jocko Partnership.*

JOCK'S DREAM BHB 20f RR 22f 4936[11]
4 b f Noble Patriarch 12.2f **(43)** - Bold Sophie (Bold Owl) 8.5f **(45)**
Form - 00
Record 1999 - 1st:0 2nd:0 3rd:0 Ran:2
Pre1999 - 1st:0 2nd:0 3rd:0 Ran:2
1999 Turf 0-1: (11f) (gd) 1999 AW 0-1: (12f) (Fibr)
Little account filly.
**K Bell [0-2] Mrs Lisa Olley (from B J McMath [0-2] Jan 1998).*

JOCKWEILER (IRE) BHB 28f18a RR 33f 18a 248[13]
4 b g Night Shift (USA) 8.1f **(73)** - Johara (USA) (Exclusive Native (USA)) 9.1f **(81)**
Form - 870
Record 1999 - 1st:0 2nd:0 3rd:0 Ran:2
Pre1999 - 1st:0 2nd:0 3rd:1 Ran:17
Win Prizemoney £0 *Total Prizemoney* £465
1999 AW 0-2: (6f, 7f) (Equi, Fibr)
Neat, very moderate gelding, has worn blinkers. Becoming disappointing.
**D W Chapman [0-17] David Chapman (from Mrs J R Ramsden [0-2] Jly 1997).*

JOEBERTEDY (IRE) RR 23f 611[12]
2 b c Tirol 8.1f **(64)** - Hinari Disk Deck (Indian King (USA)) 7.4f **(64)**
Form - 0
Record 1999 - 1st:0 2nd:0 3rd:0 Ran:1
1999 Turf 0-1: (5f) (g-f)
Currently little account colt. **Ronald Thompson [0-1] B Bruce.*

JOEL ASH BHB 26f RR 24f 2379[10]
4 b g Crofthall 8.6f **(54)** - Lady Carol (Lord Gayle (USA)) 8.8f **(62)**
Form - 070
Record 1999 - 1st:0 2nd:0 3rd:0 Ran:3
Pre1999 - 1st:0 2nd:0 3rd:0 Ran:2
1999 Turf 0-2: (5f, 8f) (g-f, frm) 1999 AW 0-1: (6f) (Fibr)
Leggy, little account gelding. Turf high 22.
**S R Bowring [0-5] Miss Julie Tomkins.*

JOELY GREEN BHB 63f68a RR 68a 4703[6]
2 b c Binary Star (USA) - Comedy Lady (Comedy Star (USA)) 7.5f **(50)**
Form - 026376
Record 1999 - 1st:0 2nd:1 3rd:1 Ran:6
Win Prizemoney £0 *Total Prizemoney* £932
1999 Turf 0-1: (5f) (frm) 1999 AW 0-5: (5f 2, 6f 3) (Fibr 5)
Average colt, effective 5 to 6f, - acts on Fibr, has worn blinkers. AW high 56.
**N P Littmoden [0-4] Paul Dixon (from W G M Turner [0-2] Apr 1999).*

JOEY THE JOLLY BHB 40f RR 10f 1390[15]
3 b g Belfort (FR) 6.7f **(53)** - Divine Penny (Divine Gift) 6.6f **(57)**
Form - 8000
Record 1999 - 1st:0 2nd:0 3rd:0 Ran:4
1999 Turf 0-4: (7f 2, 8f, 10f) (sft, g-s, g-f, frm)
Unfurnished, poor gelding, has worn blinkers. Turf high 24.
**G Woodward [0-4] Mrs Rosemary McNutt Wolstencroft.*

JOEY TRIBBIANI (IRE) BHB 71f RR 68f 4603[4]
2 b c Foxhound (USA) - Mardi Gras Belle (USA) (Masked Dancer (USA))
Form - 763864
Record 1999 - 1st:0 2nd:0 3rd:1 Ran:6
Win Prizemoney £0 *Total Prizemoney* £657
1999 Turf 0-5: (6f 4, 7f) (gd 2, frm 3) 1999 AW 0-1: (8f) (Fibr)
Average colt. Turf high 67 (began Jly).
**C N Allen [0-6] Newmarket Connections Ltd.*

JOHAYRO BHB 65f60a RR 59f 60a 5072[15]
6 ch g Clantime 6.6f **(57)** - Arroganza (Crofthall) 6.3f **(59)**
Form - 5061115452571644 0000
Record 1999 - 1st:4 2nd:1 3rd:0 Ran:20
Pre1999 - 1st:6 2nd:9 3rd:2 Ran:59
Win Prizemoney £36,176 *Total Prizemoney* £53,798
Wins * **1999** Jly Thirsk (FRM) H 6f 68 72
* **1999** May Mussel (FRM) H 5f 52 62+
* **1999** May Ayr (GD) H 5f 52 58
* **1999** May Mussel (G-F) H 7.1f 52 56
* 1998 Jly Ayr (GD) H 5f 60 65
* 1997 Spt Redcar (FRM) H 6f 60 63
* 1997 Apr Catter (GD) 6f 54
* 1997 Apr Ripon (G-F) H 5f 51 61
* 1997 Apr Mussel (G-F) 5f 59
1995 Oct Catter (G-F) 5f 73+ <
1999 Turf 4-20: (5f 2-10, 6f 1-7, 7f 1-3) (sft, gd 1-8, g-f 1-5, frm 2-6)
Average gelding, effective 5 to 6f, best at 5f, acts on gd to frm, best on g-f, has worn blinkers, and excels at Catterick. Turf high 72 - 1st of 13 giving 14lb to French Grit (23 Jly Thirsk RF 3076). Becoming disappointing. Has bags of pace, and gained a fine hat-trick in the spring over trips ranging from five to seven furlongs. He continued to run well and smashed the Thirsk six-furlong course record when regaining winning form in July.
**J S Goldie [9-65] Frank Brady (from W G M Turner [1-14] Jly 1996).*

JOHN BOWDLER MUSIC BHB 63f63a RR 60f 63a 1777[3]
4 b g Soviet Star (USA) 8.6f **(74)** - Arianna Aldini (Habitat) 9.4f **(70)**
Form - 138642685223133
Record 1999 - 1st:2 2nd:3 3rd:4 Ran:15
Pre1999 - 1st:0 2nd:1 3rd:0 Ran:6
Win Prizemoney £4,643 *Total Prizemoney* £10,355
Wins 1999 *May Southw (STD) S 6f 63*
1999 *Jan Lingfi (STD) H 6f 63 68 <*
1999 Turf 0-3: (6f, 7f 2) (gd, g-f, frm) 1999 AW 2-12: (6f 2-9, 7f 2, 8f) (Equi 1-4, Fibr 1-8)
Workmanlike, average gelding, effective 6 to 9f, best at 6f, acts on gd - acts on AW, best on Equi, has worn blinkers, favours left handed tracks, favours tight tracks, likes Southwell and Lingfield and Wolverhampton. Turf high 60 (1st run) - 5th of 18 to Rambo Waltzer (31 Mar Catterick 7f gd RF 0526). AW high 68 - 2nd of 8 getting 16lb from Mukarrab (27 Feb Lingfield 6f Equi RF 0374) - also 1st of 12 getting 1lb from Anokato (1 Jan Lingfield RF 0006). Consistent. He made a successful Equitrack debut on New Year's Day and ran well in fair handicap company afterwards.
**Miss S J Wilton [0-2] John Pointon and Sons (from M Johnston [2-19] May 1999).*

JOHN COMPANY (IRE) RR 79f 4900[2]
2 ch c Indian Ridge 7.6f **(74)** - Good Policy (IRE) (Thatching) 8f **(66)**
Form - 462
Record 1999 - 1st:0 2nd:1 3rd:0 Ran:3
Win Prizemoney £0 *Total Prizemoney* £272
1999 Turf 0-3: (6f 2, 7f) (gd, g-f, frm)
Currently above-average colt. Turf high 79 (began Spt).
**P T Walwyn [0-3] Alan Lillingston.*

JOHN FERNELEY BHB 90f RR 95f 5141[3]
4 b g Polar Falcon (USA) 9f **(74)** - I'll Try (Try My Best (USA)) 7.6f **(67)**
Form - 44133
Record 1999 - 1st:1 2nd:0 3rd:2 Ran:5
Pre1999 - 1st:3 2nd:0 3rd:0 Ran:5
Win Prizemoney £21,325 *Total Prizemoney* £28,021
Wins * **1999** Oct York (G-S) H 7.9f 82 86 <
* 1998 Jly Sandow (G-F) H 7.1f 78 81+
* 1998 Jun Thirsk (GD) 7f 81
* 1998 Apr Folkes (SFT) 7f 75
1999 Turf 1-5: (7f, 8f 1-3, 9f) (sft, gd 1-3, g-f)

Scopey, very useful gelding, effective 8f, acts on gd, has worn blinkers. Turf high 95 - 3rd of 19 giving 6lb to Tayseer (30 Oct Newmarket 8f gd RF 5141) - also 1st of 13 getting 8lb from Weet-A-Minute (6 Oct York RF 4754). Lightly raced since completing a hat-trick in '98, he is talented, and though not always a straightforward ride, there was a lot to like about the way in which he was produced right on the to win a York rates stakes in October. Third in very soft ground at Newbury next time, he seems to have ironed out his quirks. **P F I Cole [4-10] Richard Green (Fine Paintings).*

JOHNNIE THE JOKER BHB 39f48a **RR 46f 48a** 4936[8]
8 gr g Absalom 7.1f **(56)** - Magic Tower (Tower Walk) 10f **(62)**
Form - 6513432706508
Record 1999 - 1st:0 2nd:1 3rd:2 Ran:10
Pre1999 - 1st:10 2nd:8 3rd:5 Ran:73
Win Prizemoney £30,035 *Total Prizemoney* £41,629
Wins * 1998 *Dec Southw (STD) H 12f 53 58*
* 1997 *Jun Wolver (STD) H 8.5f 61 71*
* 1997 *Jun Southw (STD) H 8f 61 68*
* 1997 *May Southw (STD) H 8f 57 61*
* 1996 *Jun Wolver (STD) H 7f 70 73* <
* 1996 May Doncas (GD) H 7f 46 48
1999 Turf 0-3: (10f 2, 12f) (sft, g-s, gd) 1999 AW 0-7: (8f, 9f, 11f, 12f 4) (Fibr 7)
Fair gelding, effective 8 to 12f, best at 12f, - acts on Fibr, mostly wears blinkers, favours left handed tracks, likes Southwell. Turf high 46. AW high 59 (1st run) - 3rd of 13 giving 11lb to Count de Money (26 Feb Southwell 12f Fibr RF 0371). Becoming disappointing. His best form has been at around a mile on Fibresand.
**J P Leigh [10-83] Miss Carrington Smith.*

JOHNNY STACCATO BHB 37f30a **RR 40f 30a** 5128[17]
5 b g Statoblest 6.4f **(63)** - Frasquita (Song) 7.2f **(61)**
Form - 000040250000030
Record 1999 - 1st:0 2nd:1 3rd:1 Ran:13
Pre1999 - 1st:2 2nd:1 3rd:2 Ran:28
Win Prizemoney £7,734 *Total Prizemoney* £12,460
Wins 1997 Jun Sandow (G-F) 5f 88
1996 Aug Windso (G-F) 6f 89+ <
1999 Turf 0-11: (5f 3, 6f 6, 7f 2) (g-s, gd 3, g-f 2, frm 5) 1999 AW 0-2: (6f, 8f) (Fibr 2)
Moderate gelding, effective 6f, acts on sft, has worn blinkers. Turf high 44. AW high 1.
**M Quinn [0-13] W Trezise (from R J O'Sullivan [0-15] Dec 1998).*

JOHN STEED (IRE) BHB 52f **RR 67f** 5138[7]
2 b g Thatching 7.8f **(69)** - Trinity Hall **(62f)** (Hallgate)
Form - 677
Record 1999 - 1st:0 2nd:0 3rd:0 Ran:3
1999 Turf 0-3: (6f, 7f, 8f) (g-s, gd 2)
Currently average gelding. Turf high 67 (began Oct).
**C A Horgan [0-3] Stephen Starkey.*

JOH'S BROTHER BHB 31f **RR 23f** 2922[11]
3 ch c Clantime 6.6f **(57)** - Arroganza (Crofthall) 6.3f **(59)**
Form - 00
Record 1999 - 1st:0 2nd:0 3rd:0 Ran:2
Pre1999 - 1st:0 2nd:0 3rd:0 Ran:5
1999 Turf 0-2: (5f 2) (frm, hrd)
Unfurnished, little account colt. Turf high 11 (began Jly).
**J S Goldie [0-7] Frank Brady.*

JOIN THE PARADE BHB 58f **RR 58f** 5007[14]
3 b f Elmaamul (USA) 8.1f **(70)** - Summer Pageant (Chief's Crown (USA)) 9.8f **(72)**
Form - 05572310
Record 1999 - 1st:1 2nd:1 3rd:1 Ran:8
Win Prizemoney £3,243 *Total Prizemoney* £4,745
Wins * 1999 Spt Leices (FRM) H 10f 54 58 <
1999 Turf 1-8: (8f, 10f 1-4, 11f, 14f 2) (g-s, gd 2, g-f 1-3, frm 2)
Leggy, fair filly, effective 10f, acts on g-f, favours tight tracks. Turf high 64 - also 1st of 18 getting 23lb from Prodigal Son (7 Spt Leicester RF 4174). Inconsistent. **H J Collingridge [1-8] L Westbury.*

JOINT REGENT (CAN) BHB 75f67a **RR 81df 67a** 4917[24]
4 br c St Jovite (USA) 11.8f **(75)** - Ice Fantasy (USA) (It's Freezing (USA)) 10f **(83)**
Form - 0024262530
Record 1999 - 1st:0 2nd:3 3rd:1 Ran:10
Pre1999 - 1st:0 2nd:0 3rd:1 Ran:3
Win Prizemoney £0 *Total Prizemoney* £6,409
1999 Turf 0-9: (10f, 12f, 13f, 14f 2, 15f 2, 16f, 17f) (g-s, gd, g-f 4, frm 3)
1999 AW 0-1: (13f) (Equi)
Scopey, decent colt, effective 13 to 15f, acts on g-f to frm, best on frm, often wears blinkers (extremely effectively). Turf high 81 - 2nd of 5 getting 10lb from Bold Gait (13 Aug Newbury 13f g-f RF 3621). Becoming disappointing. Put in some fair efforts, including narrow defeats by Alhawa and Bold Gait, but is very one-paced and remains a maiden. **B W Hills [0-13] Gainsborough Stud.*

JOLI FLYERS BHB 44f36a **RR 44f 36a** 4936[9]
5 gr h Joli Wasfi (USA) 11.7f **(57)** - Hagen's Bargain (Mount Hagen (FR)) 8.4f **(70)**
Form - 0040520
Record 1999 - 1st:0 2nd:1 3rd:0 Ran:7
Pre1999 - 1st:1 2nd:1 3rd:1 Ran:12
Win Prizemoney £4,416 *Total Prizemoney* £8,473
Wins 1998 Jun Kempto (HVY) H 12f 44 47 <
1999 Turf 0-6: (12f 4, 14f, 16f) (g-s 2, gd 2, g-f, frm) 1999 AW 0-1: (12f) (Fibr)
Moderate colt, effective 10 to 14f, best at 12f, acts on sft to frm, likes right handed tracks. Turf high 44 - 2nd of 20 getting 8lb from Caerosa (7 Oct York 12f gd RF 4763). Inconsistent.
**V Soane [0-7] Joli Racing (from M J Haynes [1-12] Oct 1998).*

JOLI SADDLERS BHB 52f **RR 44f** 5133[18]
3 b f Saddlers' Hall (IRE) 10.5f **(65)** - Vitality (Young Generation) 7.7f **(63)**
Form - 85465600
Record 1999 - 1st:0 2nd:0 3rd:0 Ran:8
Win Prizemoney £0 *Total Prizemoney* £291
1999 Turf 0-8: (10f 2, 11f, 12f 5) (g-s 2, gd 4, g-f 2)
Leggy, moderate filly. Turf high 69. Becoming disappointing.
**M J Haynes [0-8] Joli Racing.*

JOLI'S SON BHB 62f **RR 64f** 4646[12]
6 gr h Joli Wasfi (USA) 11.7f **(57)** - Hagen's Bargain (Mount Hagen (FR)) 8.4f **(70)**
Form - 0032300
Record 1999 - 1st:0 2nd:1 3rd:2 Ran:7
Pre1999 - 1st:1 2nd:0 3rd:0 Ran:10
Win Prizemoney £3,054 *Total Prizemoney* £6,345
Wins 1998 Aug Lingfi (GD) H 11.5f 62 66 <
1999 Turf 0-7: (9f, 10f 6) (g-s 2, g-f 2, frm 3)
Average horse, effective 10 to 11f, best at 10f, acts on g-f to frm, best on g-f. Turf high 64 - 2nd of 8 giving 3lb to Totom (28 Jun Windsor 10f g-f RF 2385). Inconsistent.
**V Soane [0-7] Joli Racing (from M J Haynes [1-10] Oct 1998).*

JOLLY SHARP (USA) RR 78f 5001[4]
2 ch c Diesis 9f **(80)** - Milly Ha Ha **(101f)** (Dancing Brave (USA)) 8.4f **(76)**
Form - 4
Record 1999 - 1st:0 2nd:0 3rd:0 Ran:1
Win Prizemoney £0 *Total Prizemoney* £237
1999 Turf 0-1: (8f) (gd)
Currently above-average colt. **H R A Cecil [0-1] Cliveden Stud.*

JO MAXIMUS BHB 46f46a **RR 38f 46a** 2818[5]
7 b g Prince Sabo 6.6f **(64)** - Final Call (Town Crier) 10.2f **(55)**
Form - 75
Record 1999 - 1st:0 2nd:0 3rd:0 Ran:2
Pre1999 - 1st:3 2nd:4 3rd:8 Ran:41
Win Prizemoney £10,826 *Total Prizemoney* £19,205
Wins 1996 Spt Bright (FRM) H 7f 70 70
1995 Spt Bright (GD) H 7f 68 75 <
1995 Jun Bright (G-F) 6f 70
1999 Turf 0-2: (7f, 8f) (gd, frm)
Very moderate gelding, effective 7f, acts on g-f, has worn blinkers. Turf high 38 (began Jly).
**J G Smyth-Osbourne [0-10] J G Smyth-Osbourne (from S Dow [3-33] Apr 1997).*

JO MELL BHB 89f **RR 87f** 4984[16]
6 b g Efisio 7.7f **(69)** - Militia Girl (Rarity) 10.1f **(60)**
Form - 57778000150
Record 1999 - 1st:1 2nd:0 3rd:0 Ran:11
Pre1999 - 1st:7 2nd:4 3rd:5 Ran:35
Win Prizemoney £185,227 *Total Prizemoney* £214,168
Wins * **1999** Spt Newcas (SFT) 7f 86+
* 1998 Aug Ascot (G-F) H 7f 98 106 <
* 1997 Oct Doncas (GD) 7f 104
* 1997 Spt Ascot (G-F) H 7f 93 103
* 1997 Jly York (GD) H 7.9f 80 92
* 1997 Jly Haydoc (GD) H 7.1f 73 85
* 1997 Jun Newcas (HVY) H 7f 73 80
1995 Spt Ayr (GD) 7f 85+
1999 Turf 1-11: (6f, 7f 1-5, 8f 5) (g-s, gd 1-7, g-f 2, frm)
Useful gelding, effective 7f, acts on g-f to frm, best on frm. Turf high 93. Tim Easterby produced one of the training performances of '98 when saddling this tough gelding to win the inaugural running of the Tote International Handicap at Ascot. He faced some stiff tasks last term and did not recapture his best, although he did win in minor company .
**T D Easterby [7-42] C H Newton Jnr Ltd (from M H Easterby [1-4] Oct 1995).*

JONA HOLLEY BHB 51f49a **RR 51f 49a** 5153[4]
6 b g Sharpo 7.5f **(68)** - Spurned (USA) (Robellino (USA)) 7.6f **(80)**
Form - 540650614
Record 1999 - 1st:1 2nd:0 3rd:0 Ran:9
Pre1999 - 1st:2 2nd:5 3rd:0 Ran:21
Win Prizemoney £7,768 *Total Prizemoney* £13,906
Wins * **1999** Oct Ayr (SFT) S 9.1f 51
1997 Oct Southw (STD) H 8f 47 52 <
1997 Jly Folkes (SFT) H 9.7f 43 50
1999 Turf 1-8: (8f 2, 9f 1-3, 10f 2, 11f) (hvy, sft 1-2, g-s, gd, g-f 2, frm)
1999 AW 0-1: (8f) (Fibr)
Fair gelding, effective 8 to 9f, best at 8f, acts on sft to g-f, best on g-f, has worn blinkers. Turf high 52 - 4th of 10 giving 3lb to Court Express (2 May Hamilton 8f g-f RF 0971) - also 1st of 16 getting 5lb from Tightrope (12 Oct Ayr RF 4829). Consistent.
**A Streeter [1-4] Malt 'N' Hops (from M D Hammond [0-16] Jun 1999).*

JONAS NIGHTENGALE BHB 76f80a **RR 76f 80a** 2000[5]
4 b g Deploy 11.4f **(67)** - Springs Welcome (Blakeney) 10.5f **(64)**
Form - 835
Record 1999 - 1st:0 2nd:0 3rd:1 Ran:3
Pre1999 - 1st:1 2nd:2 3rd:1 Ran:9
Win Prizemoney £3,525 *Total Prizemoney* £9,033
Wins * 1998 *Apr Wolver (STD) 12f 83?* <
1999 Turf 0-3: (14f 2, 20f) (gd, g-f, frm)
Decent gelding, effective 12 to 20f, best at 12f, acts on g-f to frm - acts on Fibr. Turf high 76 - 5th of 29 getting 10lb from High And Mighty (15 Jun Ascot 20f g-f RF 2000). Bred for stamina, his fifth in the Ascot Stakes behind High And Mighty proves that he stays all day. **C A Cyzer [1-12] R M Cyzer.*

JONATHAN'S GIRL BHB 30f39a **RR 31f 39a** 2435[12]
4 b f Thowra (FR) 11.2f **(47)**-Sicilian Vespers(Mummy's Game)8.2f **(60)**
Form - 843534826000
Record 1999 - 1st:0 2nd:1 3rd:1 Ran:9
Pre1999 - 1st:0 2nd:0 3rd:1 Ran:9
Win Prizemoney £0 *Total Prizemoney* £2,410
1999 Turf 0-3: (5f 2, 6f) (gd 2, hrd) 1999 AW 0-6: (5f, 6f 2, 7f 2, 8f) (Equi 6)
Lengthy, very moderate filly, effective 6f, acts on hrd. Turf high 31 (1st run) - 6th of 15 getting 19lb from Lucy Mariella (4 May Brighton 6f hrd RF 1023). AW high 39. **J J Bridger [0-18] J J Bridger.*

JONLOZ BHB 49f **RR 54f** 4907[10]
2 ch c Presidium 7.5f **(56)** - Stratford Lady (Touching Wood (USA)) 8.2f **(55)**
Form - 6000
Record 1999 - 1st:0 2nd:0 3rd:0 Ran:4
1999 Turf 0-4: (5f 2, 8f 2) (sft, g-f, frm 2)
Fair colt. Turf high 54. **G Woodward [0-4] P Appleyard.*

JOONAYH BHB 86f **RR 79+f** 3656[8]
2 b f Warning 8.1f **(77)** - Jumairah Sun (IRE) **(94?f)** (Scenic)
Form - 218
Record 1999 - 1st:1 2nd:1 3rd:0 Ran:3
Win Prizemoney £3,881 *Total Prizemoney* £4,989
Wins * **1999** Jly Thirsk (FRM) 6f 79+ <
1999 Turf 1-3: (6f 1-2, 7f) (g-f, frm 1-2)
Currently above-average filly. Turf high 79 (began Jly) - 1st of 4 from Zagaleta (23 Jly Thirsk RF 3075). She ran quite well to finish runner-up on her Windsor debut, and easily brushed aside her three rivals in a Thirsk maiden next time. Made no show in a Listed race on her final run. **M R Channon [1-3] A Merza.*

JORROCKS (USA) RR 59+f 4880[13]
5 b g Rubiano (USA) 7.1f **(87)** - Perla Fina (USA) (Gallant Man) 10.2f **(68)**
Form - 007005010
Record 1999 - 1st:1 2nd:0 3rd:0 Ran:9
Pre1999 - 1st:3 2nd:2 3rd:4 Ran:18
Win Prizemoney £34,471 *Total Prizemoney* £42,228
Wins * **1999** Spt Beverl (SFT) H 7.5f 51 59+ <
1997 Spt Newbur (SFT) H 7.3f 87 94 <
1997 Aug Goodwo (G-F) H 7f 74 85
1997 Jly Sandow (G-F) H 7.1f 74 77
1999 Turf 1-9: (7f 1-5, 8f 4) (sft, g-s 1-1, gd 3, frm 4)
Fair gelding, effective 7f, acts on sft to gd, has worn blinkers. Turf high 59. Inconsistent. Enjoyed an excellent '97, winning three times, but really seemed to have lost the plot until bolting up from a lenient mark at Beverley.
**M W Easterby [1-9] Stephen Curtis (from I A Balding [3-18] Spt 1998).*

JOSEPH'S WINE (IRE) BHB 44f62a **RR 48f 62a** 352[2]
10 b g Smile (USA) 9.8f **(80)** - Femme Gendarme (USA) (Policeman (FR)) 9.8f **(80)**
Form - 212
Record 1999 - 1st:1 2nd:2 3rd:0 Ran:3
Pre1999 - 1st:13 2nd:2 3rd:4 Ran:45
Win Prizemoney £37,858 *Total Prizemoney* £41,915
Wins * **1999** *Feb Lingfi (STD) S 8f 50+*
** 1997 Dec Southw (STD) C 8f 69*
1997 Feb Lingfi (STD) C 10f 80+ <
1997 Jan Southw (STD) C 8f 66
1995 Jan Southw (STD) H 11f 75 80
1999 AW 1-3: (8f 1-2, 11f) (Equi 1-1, Fibr 2)
Average gelding, has broken blood-vessels, effective 8 to 11f, - acts on AW, best on Fibr, often wears blinkers (effectively), favours left handed tracks, favours tight tracks. AW high 66 - 2nd of 13 to Kingchip Boy (24 Feb Wolverhampton 8f Fibr RF 0352). A regular winner for David Nicholls, he has since done quite well on sand for John Wharton. Effective on either surface, he seems suited by trips of around a mile and a quarter.
**J Wharton [2-10] Wetherby Racing Bureau 22 (from D Nicholls [10-24] Feb 1997).*

JOSEPH VERNET (IRE) RR 41f 4172[6]
2 b br g Owington - Pizziri (Artaius (USA)) 9f **(69)**
Form - 56
Record 1999 - 1st:0 2nd:0 3rd:0 Ran:2
1999 Turf 0-2: (7f, 8f) (g-f, frm)
Currently moderate gelding. Turf high 41 (began Aug).
**P F I Cole [0-2] Richard Green (Fine Paintings).*

JO'S PRINCESS RR 461[12]
3 b f Emarati (USA) 6.6f **(63)** - Daima (Dominion) 8.5f **(63)**
Form - 00
Record 1999 - 1st:0 2nd:0 3rd:0 Ran:2
Pre1999 - 1st:0 2nd:0 3rd:0 Ran:1
1999 AW 0-2: (5f 2) (Fibr 2)
Light-framed, currently very poor filly.
**J R Jenkins [0-3] Miss J L Watson.*

JOSR ALGARHOUD (IRE) BHB 114f **RR 116f** 4916[3]
3 b c Darshaan 11.9f **(81)** - Pont-Aven (Try My Best (USA)) 7.6f **(67)**
Form - 123
Record 1999 - 1st:1 2nd:1 3rd:1 Ran:3
Pre1999 - 1st:1 2nd:0 3rd:1 Ran:2
Win Prizemoney £90,729 *Total Prizemoney* £116,879
Wins * **1999** Jly Newcas (G-F) G3 7f 113
1998 Aug York (G-F) G2 6f 117+ <
1999 Turf 1-3: (7f 1-2, 8f) (gd 2, g-f 1-1)

Scopey, high-class colt. Turf high 116 (began Jly) - 2nd of 5 getting 12lb from Cape Cross (28 Aug Goodwood 8f gd RF 3957) - also 1st of 5 getting 7lb from Haami (24 Jly Newcastle RF 3100). A smart two-year-old when with Mick Channon, he joined Godolphin afterwards and made a belated winning reappearance in a poorly-contested renewal of the Beeswing Stakes. He then failed to beat stable-companion Cape Cross when favourite for the Celebration Mile, but finished a rather unlucky third in the Challenge Stakes after suffering serious interference a furlong out. Hopefully, he will show what he is capable of in 2000.
**S bin Suroor [1-3] Godolphin (from M R Channon [1-2] Aug 1998).*

JOUET BHB 60f **RR 62f** 4180[6]

3 b f Reprimand 8.2f **(63)** - Babycham Sparkle (So Blessed) 8.7f **(67)**
Form - 3266
Record 1999 - 1st:0 2nd:1 3rd:1 Ran:4
Win Prizemoney £0 *Total Prizemoney* £1,667
1999 Turf 0-4: (7f 3, 8f) (g-f 2, frm 2)
Leggy, average filly. Turf high 62 (began Aug) - 2nd of 10 to Fantastic Dance (12 Aug Salisbury 7f g-f RF 3575).
**Miss Gay Kelleway [0-4] David Hicks.*

JOURNALIST (IRE) BHB 100f **RR 89f** 3769[9]

2 b f Night Shift (USA) 8.1f **(73)** - Schlefalora (Mas Media)
Form - 120
Record 1999 - 1st:1 2nd:1 3rd:0 Ran:3
Win Prizemoney £6,004 *Total Prizemoney* £15,004
Wins * 1999 Jly Newmar (G-F) 6f 82+ <
1999 Turf 1-3: (6f 1-3) (gd 2, frm 1-1)
Currently useful filly. Turf high 89 (began Jly) - 2nd of 8 to Saintly Speech (24 Jly Ascot 6f gd RF 3086) - also 1st of 10 from Dancing Mirage (8 Jly Newmarket RF 2642). She looked a smart prospect when winning at Newmarket on her debut, but may not have been suited by the steady pace when just caught in the Princess Margaret. Ran very disappointingly in the Lowther Stakes on her third start. **B W Hills [1-3] Maktoum Al Maktoum.*

JOYEUX PLAYER (USA) BHB 87f **RR 90f** 3297[3]

3 b c St Jovite (USA) 11.8f **(75)** - Play On And On (USA) (Stop The Music (USA)) 9.2f **(71)**
Form - 6643
Record 1999 - 1st:0 2nd:0 3rd:1 Ran:4
Pre1999 - 1st:2 2nd:1 3rd:0 Ran:5
Win Prizemoney £7,801 *Total Prizemoney* £11,539
Wins * 1998 Spt Ayr (G-S) 8f 85+ <
* 1998 Aug Haydoc (GD) 7.1f 78
1999 Turf 0-4: (9f 2, 10f 2) (gd, g-f, frm 2)
Strong, useful colt, effective 8 to 10f, acts on sft to frm, best on frm. Turf high 90 - 3rd of 7 giving 8lb to Canta Ke Brave (2 Aug Ripon 9f frm RF 3297). **J L Dunlop [2-9] S Khaled.*

JOYFUL WELD BHB 28a **RR 28a** 205[12]

3 ch f Weld - Joyfulness (FR) (Cure The Blues (USA)) 9.5f **(63)**
Form - 080
Record 1999 - 1st:0 2nd:0 3rd:0 Ran:1
Pre1999 - 1st:0 2nd:0 3rd:0 Ran:3
1999 AW 0-1: (8f) (Fibr)
Little account filly. **B P J Baugh [0-4] E Bennion.*

JOYRENA BHB 35f **RR 26f** 5215[13]

2 ch f Inchinor 8.9f **(64)** - Depeche (FR) (Kings Lake (USA)) 10.8f **(67)**
Form - 000
Record 1999 - 1st:0 2nd:0 3rd:0 Ran:3
1999 Turf 0-2: (6f, 8f) (g-s, frm) 1999 AW 0-1: (5f) (Fibr)
Currently little account filly. Turf high 26.
**P W D'Arcy [0-3] Mrs Jean Mitchell.*

J R STEVENSON (USA) BHB 100f **RR 103f** 4101[7]

3 ch c Lyphard (USA) 10.6f **(75)** - While it Lasts (USA) (Foolish Pleasure (USA)) 8.9f **(72)**
Form - 355157
Record 1999 - 1st:1 2nd:0 3rd:1 Ran:6
Pre1999 - 1st:1 2nd:0 3rd:0 Ran:1
Win Prizemoney £7,390 *Total Prizemoney* £8,614
Wins * 1999 Jun Goodwo (G-S) 9.9f 97 <
* 1998 Spt Cheste (GD) 7f 87+
1999 Turf 1-6: (9f, 10f 1-3, 12f 2) (g-s 1-1, g-f 2, frm 3)
Light-framed, very useful colt, effective 10f, acts on g-s, often wears blinkers. Turf high 103 - also 1st of 3 from Mirjan (2 Jun Goodwood RF 1679). **P W Chapple-Hyam [2-7] R E Sangster and B V Sangster.*

JUBILEE SCHOLAR (IRE) BHB 28f54a **RR 22f 54a** 4783[5]

6 b g Royal Academy (USA) 7.8f **(77)**-Jaljuli (Jalmood (USA)) 10.1f **(52)**
Form - 1457235245005
Record 1999 - 1st:0 2nd:2 3rd:1 Ran:10
Pre1999 - 1st:3 2nd:2 3rd:3 Ran:36
Win Prizemoney £6,192 *Total Prizemoney* £9,695
Wins * 1998 *Nov Lingfi (STD) H 10f 54 56* <
* 1998 *Apr Lingfi (STD) H 8f 45 51*
* 1997 *Nov Lingfi (STD) H 10f 36 39?*
1999 Turf 0-4: (10f 3, 12f) (g-f, frm, hrd 2) 1999 AW 0-6: (8f 3, 10f 3) (Equi 6)
Fair gelding, effective 8 to 10f, best at 10f, - acts on Equi, mostly wears blinkers (very effectively), excels at Lingfield. Turf high 47. AW high 58 - 5th of 12 giving 4lb to Statistician (18 Mar Lingfield 8f Equi RF 0441). Becoming disappointing.
**G L Moore [3-36] M V Johnston (from K McAuliffe [0-7] Apr 1997).*

JUDIAM BHB 74f **RR 74f** 5105[1]

2 b f Primo Dominie 7.2f **(67)** - Hoist (IRE) **(72df 63a)** (Bluebird (USA)) 7.5f **(69)**
Form - 05303021
Record 1999 - 1st:1 2nd:1 3rd:2 Ran:8
Win Prizemoney £2,906 *Total Prizemoney* £5,132
Wins * 1999 Oct Yarmou (G-S) H 5.2f 62 74 <
1999 Turf 1-8: (5f 1-6, 6f 2) (g-s 2, gd 1-2, g-f 2, frm 2)
Above-average filly, effective 5f, acts on gd. Turf high 74 (began Jly) - 1st of 6 getting 10lb from Blue Holly (27 Oct Yarmouth RF 5105). **C A Dwyer [1-8] R West.*

JUDICIOUS (IRE) RR 55f 5207[18]

2 b c Fairy King (USA) 7.7f **(75)** - Kama Tashoof **(68f)** (Mtoto)
Form - 80
Record 1999 - 1st:0 2nd:0 3rd:0 Ran:2
1999 Turf 0-2: (7f 2) (g-s, gd)
Currently fair colt. Turf high 55 (began Oct).
**G Wragg [0-2] Mollers Racing.*

JUINEVERA (IRE) BHB 31f **RR 28f** 2679[8]

4 b f Tenby 10.4f **(76)** - Atlantic Dream (USA) (Muscovite (USA)) 6f **(109)**
Form - 60668
Record 1999 - 1st:0 2nd:0 3rd:0 Ran:5
Pre1999 - 1st:0 2nd:0 3rd:1 Ran:9
Win Prizemoney £0 *Total Prizemoney* £470
1999 Turf 0-5: (7f 2, 10f 2, 11f) (g-f, frm 4)
Little account filly, effective 8f, acts on gd, has worn blinkers, likes left handed tracks. Turf high 28. Becoming disappointing.
**J S Haldane [0-6] J S Haldane (from T Stack in IRE [0-9] Spt 1998).*

JULIA TITUS (IRE) RR 60f 5020[11]

2 ch f Perugino (USA) - Blue Vista (IRE) (Pennine Walk) 8.5f **(61)**
Form - 80
Record 1999 - 1st:0 2nd:0 3rd:0 Ran:2
1999 Turf 0-2: (7f, 8f) (g-s, gd)
Currently average filly. Turf high 60 (began Spt).
**W R Muir [0-2] Aster Partnership.*

JULIES JEWEL (IRE) BHB 60f52a **RR 77f 52a** 291[2]

4 ch g Simply Great (FR) 11.9f **(61)** - Melungeon (Ardoon) 7.3f **(53)**
Form - 00042
Record 1999 - 1st:0 2nd:1 3rd:0 Ran:4
Pre1999 - 1st:2 2nd:4 3rd:0 Ran:34
Win Prizemoney £7,822 *Total Prizemoney* £17,564
Wins * 1998 Mar Doncas (GD) H 7f 68 73 <
* 1998 *Jan Southw (STD) H 6f 66 70*
1999 AW 0-4: (8f 2, 11f, 12f) (Fibr 4)
Leggy, above-average gelding, effective 6 to 7f, best at 7f, acts on g-s to gd - acts on Fibr, best on g-s, likes tight tracks. AW high 62.
**M C Chapman [2-38] Mrs Julie Lamming.*

JUMBO'S FLYER BHB 63f **RR 71f** 5189[8]
2 ch c Jumbo Hirt (USA) 15.8f **(44)** - Fragrant Princess (Germont)
Form - 508
Record 1999 - 1st:0 2nd:0 3rd:0 Ran:3
1999 Turf 0-3: (7f, 8f, 9f) (gd, g-f, frm)
Currently above-average colt. Turf high 71 (began Spt).
J L Eyre [0-3] T H Littleton.

JUMP (USA) RR 60f 4942[5]
2 b c Trempolino (USA) 11.9f **(77)** - Professional Dance (USA) (Nijinsky (CAN)) 10.3f **(77)**
Form - 75
Record 1999 - 1st:0 2nd:0 3rd:0 Ran:2
1999 Turf 0-2: (6f, 8f) (gd, frm)
Currently average colt. Turf high 60 (began Spt).
D Marks [0-2] Godiva.

JUNIKAY (IRE) BHB 55f52a **RR 56f 52a** 5069[4]
5 b g Treasure Kay 6.5f **(53)** - Junijo (Junius (USA)) 7.7f **(65)**
Form - 051872663255044

Record	**1999** -	1st:1	2nd:2	3rd:1	Ran:15
	Pre1999 -	1st:2	2nd:2	3rd:2	Ran:31

Win Prizemoney £8,972 *Total Prizemoney* £15,505

Wins	*** 1999**	May	Nottin	(GD)	H	10f	52	54
	* 1998	May	Bright	(G-F)	H	7f	53	58
	1996	Jly	Ballin	(GD)		6f		73 <

1999 Turf 1-15: (8f 3, 9f, 10f 1-9, 12f 2) (g-s, gd 2, g-f 1-5, frm 7)
Fair gelding, effective 7 to 12f, best at 10f, acts on g-s to frm, best on gd, has worn blinkers, favours tight tracks, excels at Nottingham and does well at Goodwood. Turf high 56 - 6th of 13 giving 21lb to Dark Age (28 Jly Epsom 10f frm RF 3201) - also 1st of 15 getting 4lb from Arc (7 May Nottingham RF 1094). Consistent.
R Ingram [2-38] Ellangowan Racing Partners (from J S Bolger in IRE [1-9] Jun 1997).

JUNO MARLOWE (IRE) BHB 96f **RR 96f** 3233[7]
3 b f Danehill (USA) 9.1f **(79)**-Why so Silent (Mill Reef (USA)) 10.5f **(78)**
Form - 0817

Record	**1999** -	1st:1	2nd:0	3rd:0	Ran:4
	Pre1999 -	1st:1	2nd:0	3rd:1	Ran:5

Win Prizemoney £12,828 *Total Prizemoney* £15,125

Wins	*** 1999**	Jly	Newmar	(GD)	H	7f	94	96 <
	* 1998	Aug	Kempto	(G-F)		7f		86

1999 Turf 1-4: (7f 1-2, 8f 2) (g-f 3, frm 1-1)
Scopey, very useful filly, effective 7f, acts on frm. Turf high 96 - 1st of 9 giving 13lb to Coffee Cream (6 Jly Newmarket RF 2578). Consistent. Tried in Group company at two, she found her level in decent handicaps. Likely to stay a mile, she seems suited by a sound surface. *P W Harris [2-9] Mrs P W Harris.*

JUST A SNACK (IRE) RR 22f 4142[18]
3 b g Tenby 10.4f **(76)** - Opening Day (Day Is Done) 6.3f **(67)**
Form - 0080

Record	**1999** -	1st:0	2nd:0	3rd:0	Ran:4
	Pre1999 -	1st:0	2nd:0	3rd:0	Ran:3

Win Prizemoney £0 *Total Prizemoney* £215
1999 Turf 0-4: (7f, 8f 2, 12f) (gd, frm 2, hrd)
Unfurnished, little account gelding. Turf high 22.
M A Buckley [0-7] Mrs N W Buckley.

JUST A STROLL BHB 34f **RR 44?f** 5147[11]
4 ch g Clantime 6.6f **(57)** - Willow Walk (Farm Walk) 11.6f **(55)**
Form - 0

Record	**1999** -	1st:0	2nd:0	3rd:0	Ran:1
	Pre1999 -	1st:0	2nd:1	3rd:0	Ran:3

Win Prizemoney £0 *Total Prizemoney* £570
1999 AW 0-1: (8f) (Fibr)
Neat, moderate gelding.
D Burchell [0-1] Simon Lewis (from J S Moore [0-3] Aug 1997).

JUST BOB BHB 49f65a **RR 44f 65a** 4906[17]
10 b g Alleging (USA) 8.8f **(57)** - Diami (Swing Easy (USA)) 6.5f **(55)**
Form - 000032448038862417040

Record	**1999** -	1st:1	2nd:2	3rd:2	Ran:21
	Pre1999 -	1st:18	2nd:12	3rd:10	Ran:115

Win Prizemoney £61,207 *Total Prizemoney* £83,067

Wins	*** 1999**	Spt	Yarmou	(SFT)	H	6f	47	51
	* 1998	Jun	Hamilt	(G-S)		6f		66
	* 1997	Oct	Newcas	(G-F)	H	5f	72	76 <
	* 1997	Spt	Ayr	(G-S)	H	5f	57	67
	* 1997	Spt	Doncas	(G-F)	H	5f	57	62
	* 1996	May	Carlis	(G-F)		5f		66
	* 1996	May	Ayr	(G-S)	H	5f	60	69
	* 1996	May	Hamilt	(SFT)		5f		69?

1999 Turf 1-21: (5f 15, 6f 1-6) (sft, g-s 1-1, gd 5, g-f 10, frm 4)
Fair gelding, effective 5 to 6f, best at 6f, acts on gd to g-f, best on g-f, has worn blinkers. Turf high 51.
S E Kettlewell [19-136] S E Kettlewell.

JUST BREMNER BHB 62f **RR 72f** 4934[19]
2 b c Rudimentary (USA) 8.2f **(66)** - Legal Precedent (Star Appeal) 9.6f **(65)**
Form - 043P100
Record 1999 - 1st:1 2nd:0 3rd:1 Ran:7
Win Prizemoney £2,710 *Total Prizemoney* £3,180

Wins	*** 1999**	Aug	Newcas	(GD)	C	8f		72 <

1999 Turf 1-7: (6f, 7f 3, 8f 1-3) (g-s, gd, g-f 1-3, frm 2)
Above-average colt, effective 8f, acts on g-f. Turf high 72 - 1st of 11 giving 10lb to Iranoo (30 Aug Newcastle RF 4022).
T D Easterby [1-7] Leeds United Racing Club Ltd.

JUST DISSIDENT (IRE) BHB 34f57a **RR 31f 57a** 3910[1]
7 b g Dancing Dissident (USA) 6.8f **(65)** - Betty Bun (St Chad) 6.7f **(67)**
Form - 70088000701

Record	**1999** -	1st:1	2nd:0	3rd:0	Ran:10
	Pre1999 -	1st:5	2nd:5	3rd:7	Ran:69

Win Prizemoney £22,875 *Total Prizemoney* £31,778

Wins	*** 1999**	*Aug*	*Lingfi*	*(STD)*	*H*	*7f*	*51*	*54*
	* 1997	*Dec*	*Lingfi*	*(STD)*	*H*	*5f*	*52*	*56*
	* 1997	Jly	Pontef	(G-F)	H	5f	57	58
	* 1996	Aug	Carlis	(FRM)	H	5f	57	58
	* 1996	Jly	Pontef	(G-F)	H	5f	55	56
	* 1995	Jun	Redcar	(FRM)		6f		69 <

1999 Turf 0-9: (5f 8, 7f) (gd, g-f 4, frm 4) 1999 AW 1-1:(7f 1-1)(Equi 1-1)
Fair gelding, effective 5 to 7f, best at 5f, - acts on Equi, has worn blinkers, prefers left handed tracks, prefers tight tracks. Turf high 39. (1st run) - 1st of 16 getting 5lb from Trojan Wolf (25 Aug Lingfield RF 3910). *R M Whitaker [6-79] Mrs C A Hodgetts.*

JUST DREAMS BHB 79f **RR 80f** 5165[1]
3 ch f Salse (USA) 10.9f **(71)** - Pato (High Top) 10.2f **(67)**
Form - 25071
Record 1999 - 1st:1 2nd:1 3rd:0 Ran:5
Win Prizemoney £2,974 *Total Prizemoney* £4,199

Wins	*** 1999**	Nov	Catter	(SFT)		12f		80 <

1999 Turf 1-5: (10f 2, 12f 1-3) (sft, g-s 1-1, gd 2, g-f)
Scopey, decent filly. Turf high 80 (began Aug) - 1st of 14 getting 5lb from Historic (2 Nov Catterick RF 5165).
R Guest [1-5] Matthews Breeding and Racing.

JUST FOR YOU JANE (IRE) BHB 63f55a **RR 71f 55a** 322[3]
3 b f Petardia 8.2f **(58)** - Steffi (Precocious) 8.6f **(62)**
Form - 03423

Record	**1999** -	1st:0	2nd:1	3rd:2	Ran:4
	Pre1999 -	1st:0	2nd:1	3rd:3	Ran:10

Win Prizemoney £0 *Total Prizemoney* £3,303
1999 AW 0-4: (6f 3, 7f) (Fibr 4)
Unfurnished, above-average filly, effective 6 to 7f, acts on g-f to frm, often wears blinkers, likes left handed tracks, likes tight tracks. AW high 56. *T J Naughton [0-14] The Awayday Partnership.*

JUST GIFTED BHB 65f **RR 67f** 4882[5]
3 b c Rudimentary (USA) 8.2f **(66)** - Parfait Amour **(48f)** (Clantime)
Form - 03043685

Record	**1999** -	1st:0	2nd:0	3rd:2	Ran:8
	Pre1999 -	1st:0	2nd:0	3rd:1	Ran:2

Win Prizemoney £0 *Total Prizemoney* £2,585
1999 Turf 0-8: (8f 2, 10f 4, 11f, 12f) (gd 2, g-f 4, frm 2)
Workmanlike, average colt, effective 10 to 12f, best at 10f, acts on g-f to frm, best on g-f, likes tight tracks. Turf high 67 - 3rd of 14 giving 1lb to Flossy (20 Aug Newcastle 12f g-f RF 3803). Still a maiden, he has run some good races but looks a little high in the handicap. *R M Whitaker [0-10] Mrs C A Hodgetts.*

JUSTINIANUS (IRE) BHB 32f29a **RR 27f 29a** 4035[12]
7 ch h Try My Best (USA) 7.8f **(68)** - Justitia (Dunbeath (USA)) 7.8f **(70)**
Form - 05857805506606070
Record 1999 - 1st:0 2nd:0 3rd:0 Ran:15
Pre1999 - 1st:2 2nd:3 3rd:8 Ran:61
Win Prizemoney £5,558 *Total Prizemoney* £12,638
Wins 1998 Apr Bright (GD) H 6f 41 48 <
1997 *Feb Lingfi (STD) S 6f 44*
1999 Turf 0-9: (5f 5, 6f 3, 7f) (gd 2, g-f, frm 4, hrd 2) 1999 AW 0-6: (6f, 7f 3, 8f 2) (Equi 6)
Very moderate horse, effective 6f, acts on gd to frm, best on frm, has worn blinkers. Turf high 37. AW high 40.
**D L Williams [0-4] D N Carey (from J J Bridger [2-70] Jly 1999).*

JUST IN TIME BHB 88f **RR 89f** 3758[19]
4 b c Night Shift (USA) 8.1f **(73)** - Future Past (USA) (Super Concorde (USA)) 10.9f **(66)**
Form - 4330760
Record 1999 - 1st:0 2nd:0 3rd:2 Ran:7
Pre1999 - 1st:1 2nd:3 3rd:0 Ran:6
Win Prizemoney £3,397 *Total Prizemoney* £15,733
Wins * 1998 Aug Goodwo (G-F) 9.9f 85+ <
1999 Turf 0-7: (12f 4, 14f 2, 16f) (gd 3, g-f, frm 3)
Scopey, useful colt, effective 10 to 14f, best at 12f, acts on gd to frm, best on frm, prefers right handed tracks. Turf high 91 - 3rd of 18 getting 10lb from Blueprint (16 Jun Ascot 12f g-f RF 2044). Mixed form, but ran well when third in the Duke of Edinburgh at Royal Ascot after attempting to make all. Forcing tactics in a big Goodwood handicap over one and three-quarter miles saw him run out of steam, and he has disappointed since.
**T G Mills [1-13] Mrs Pauline Merrick.*

JUST MAC (USA) RR 59f 4881[6]
2 br c Dayjur (USA) 6.8f **(79)** - Play On And On (USA) (Stop The Music (USA)) 9.2f **(71)**
Form - 6
Record 1999 - 1st:0 2nd:0 3rd:0 Ran:1
1999 Turf 0-1: (6f) (frm)
Currently fair colt. **J Noseda [0-1] Michael McDonnell.*

JUST NICK BHB 64f **RR 56f** 4094[7]
5 b g Nicholas (USA) 6.1f **(63)** - Just Never Know (USA) (Riverman (USA)) 9.1f **(76)**
Form - 0348007
Record 1999 - 1st:0 2nd:0 3rd:1 Ran:7
Pre1999 - 1st:1 2nd:4 3rd:4 Ran:14
Win Prizemoney £2,799 *Total Prizemoney* £20,951
Wins * 1996 Nov Folkes (SFT) 6f 74 <
1999 Turf 0-7: (7f 4, 8f 3) (g-s, g-f 3, frm 3)
Fair gelding. Turf high 72. Becoming disappointing. He ran well in some good races in '97 without managing to win, but missed all of '98. A good third to Teofilio at Sandown in June, he has been out of form since.
**W R Muir [1-19] D G Clarke (from M McCormack [0-2] Jun 1996).*

JUST NOBBY BHB 20f31a **RR 25f 31a** 2805[7]
4 b g Totem (USA) 5f **(38)** - Loving Doll (Godswalk (USA)) 7.3f **(58)**
Form - 00007
Record 1999 - 1st:0 2nd:0 3rd:0 Ran:4
Pre1999 - 1st:0 2nd:0 3rd:0 Ran:14
Win Prizemoney £0 *Total Prizemoney* £250
1999 Turf 0-4: (7f, 8f, 10f, 12f) (gd, frm 3)
Little account gelding, has worn blinkers. Turf high 25.
**Don Enrico Incisa [0-13] Don Enrico Incisa (from N Tinkler [0-5] Spt 1997).*

JUST SUNDAY BHB 47f **RR 45f** 1939[14]
3 ch f Then Again 7.4f **(52)** - Striking Image (IRE) (Flash of Steel) 7.2f **(53)**
Form - 0
Record 1999 - 1st:0 2nd:0 3rd:0 Ran:1
Pre1999 - 1st:0 2nd:0 3rd:1 Ran:6
Win Prizemoney £0 *Total Prizemoney* £225
1999 Turf 0-1: (10f) (g-f)
Leggy, moderate filly.
**J W Mullins [0-1] Woodmarsh Racing (from W G M Turner [0-6] Jun 1998).*

JUST THE BLUES BHB 43a **RR 43a** 4220[8]
2 b c Merdon Melody 6.8f **(56)** - Tripolitaine (FR) (Nonoalco (USA)) 8.5f **(66)**
Form - 88878
Record 1999 - 1st:0 2nd:0 3rd:0 Ran:5
1999 AW 0-5: (6f 2, 7f, 8f 2) (Fibr 5)
Very moderate colt. AW high 39. **N P Littmoden [0-5] T Clarke.*

JUSTUPYOURSTREET (IRE) BHB 75f **RR 77df** 2939[5]
3 b g Dolphin Street (FR) - Sure Flyer (IRE) (Sure Blade (USA)) 11.3f **(67)**
Form - 203475
Record 1999 - 1st:0 2nd:1 3rd:1 Ran:6
Pre1999 - 1st:0 2nd:0 3rd:2 Ran:7
Win Prizemoney £0 *Total Prizemoney* £4,919
1999 Turf 0-6: (8f 3, 9f, 10f 2) (g-s, gd 2, g-f, frm 2)
Workmanlike, above-average gelding, effective 8 to 9f, best at 8f, acts on gd to frm. Turf high 77 - 3rd of 18 giving 17lb to Time Temptress (3 May Newcastle 8f frm RF 1007).
**J J O'Neill [0-13] E A Brook.*

JUST WARNING RR 36f 5136[16]
2 br f Warning 8.1f **(77)** - Stardyn (Star Appeal) 9.6f **(65)**
Form - 0
Record 1999 - 1st:0 2nd:0 3rd:0 Ran:1
1999 Turf 0-1: (7f) (gd)
Currently very moderate filly. **M J Ryan [0-1] M F Kentish.*

JUST WIZ BHB 58f77a **RR 60f 77a** 4441[3]
3 b g Efisio 7.7f **(69)** - Jade Pet **(84df)** (Petong) 6.6f **(58)**
Form - 3451520420723
Record 1999 - 1st:1 2nd:3 3rd:1 Ran:10
Pre1999 - 1st:0 2nd:0 3rd:1 Ran:8
Win Prizemoney £2,316 *Total Prizemoney* £6,938
Wins 1999 *Jan Southw (STD) H 7f* 59 72 <
1999 Turf 0-9: (6f, 7f 2, 8f 2, 9f, 10f 3) (g-s, gd, g-f 3, frm 3, hrd) 1999 AW 1-1: (7f 1-1) (Fibr 1-1)
Workmanlike, above-average gelding, effective 7f, - acts on Fibr, often wears blinkers (effectively), likes left handed tracks, likes tight tracks. Turf high 61. (1st run) - 1st of 14 giving 5lb to Baron de Pichon (2 Jan Southwell RF 0017). Has ability on turf, but his only victory to date came in a modest handicap on the Southwell Fibresand in January, though admittedly the form of that race worked out very well.
**R Hannon [0-9] Peter Crane (from Lord Huntingdon [1-9] Jan 1999).*

JUVENIA (USA) RR 111f 4780a[3]
3 br f Trempolino (USA) 11.9f **(77)** - Vintage (CAN) (Foolish Pleasure (USA)) 8.9f **(72)**
Form - 325763
1999 Turf 0-6: (8f, 9f, 10f 2, 11f, 12f) (sft, g-s 3, gd, g-f)
Group-class filly, effective 8 to 11f, acts on sft to g-f, best on g-s, likes Longchamp. Turf high 111 - 3rd of 11 getting 3lb from Diamond White (3 Oct Longchamp 9f sft RF 4780a). Consistent. Successful in the Prix Marcel Boussac as a juvenile, she ran a series of sound races without scoring last term. Probably best around a mile and a quarter, she is genuine but lacks a top-class turn-of-foot. **Mme C Head in FR [1-8].*

JUWWI BHB 77f75a **RR 76f 75a** 5212[6]
5 ch g Mujtahid (USA) 7.4f **(69)** - Nouvelle Star (AUS) (Luskin Star (AUS)) 6.3f **(71)**
Form - 635005041632606218200026
Record 1999 - 1st:2 2nd:4 3rd:1 Ran:21
Pre1999 - 1st:3 2nd:4 3rd:3 Ran:26
Win Prizemoney £17,375 *Total Prizemoney* £38,430
Wins *** 1999** Spt Chepst (GD) H 5.1f 67 72
*** 1999** May Carlis (FRM) H 5.9f 63 70
* 1998 *Apr Lingfi (STD) H 5f 70 80+* <
* 1998 *Mar Wolver (STD) S 5f 64+*
1996 Jun Newbur (G-F) 6f 79+
1999 Turf 2-20: (5f 1-7, 6f 1-13) (g-s 2, gd 8, g-f 5, frm 2-4, hrd) 1999 AW 0-1: (6f) (Fibr)
Above-average gelding, effective 5 to 6f, best at 5f, acts on g-s to frm - acts on AW, does well at Wolverhampton. Turf high 76 - 2nd of 22 getting 7lb from Classy Cleo (1 Nov Redcar 6f frm RF 5160) - also 1st of 18 giving 12lb to Mary Jane (9 Spt Chepstow RF 4233).

A two-year-old winner for Dick Hern, he has been taking in rather more modest fare since those heady days and pops up in his turn. Suited by coming off a strong pace.
**J M Bradley [4-42] J M Bradley (from Major W R Hern [1-5] Jly 1997).*

KAAMEN (IRE) BHB 95f **RR 98f** 2534[4]

3 ch c Mujtahid (USA) 7.4f **(69)** - Zumurrudah (USA) (Spectacular Bid (USA)) 11.2f **(76)**
Form - 300344
Record 1999 - 1st:0 2nd:0 3rd:2 Ran:6
Pre1999 - 1st:1 2nd:0 3rd:1 Ran:3
Win Prizemoney £3,493 *Total Prizemoney* £7,030
Wins * 1998 May Newbur (GD) 5.2f 90 <
1999 Turf 0-6: (5f, 6f 3, 7f, 8f) (gd 4, g-f 2)
Workmanlike, very useful colt, effective 5 to 6f, best at 6f, acts on gd to g-f, best on gd, has worn blinkers. Turf high 98 (1st run) - 3rd of 9 to Mutaakkid (8 Apr Leicester 6f gd RF 0620). He is useful, but does not seem to have a trip. **B Hanbury [1-9] Hamdan Al Maktoum.*

KABOOL RR 120f 4919[3]

4 b c Groom Dancer (USA) 9.5f **(75)** - Sheroog (USA) (Shareef Dancer (USA)) 9.9f **(73)**
Form - 642233
Record 1999 - 1st:0 2nd:2 3rd:2 Ran:6
Pre1999 - 1st:2 2nd:0 3rd:0 Ran:2
Win Prizemoney £52,525 *Total Prizemoney* £121,617
Wins 1998 Aug Deauvi (SFT) G2 10f 112 <
1998 Jly Maison (GD) G3 9f 106
1999 Turf 0-5: (8f, 9f, 10f 3) (hvy, sft, g-s, gd, g-f) 1999 AW 0-1: (10f) (Dirt)
Very high-class colt, effective 8 to 10f, best at 10f, acts on hvy to g-f, favours right handed tracks, likes Deauville and Longchamp. Turf high 120 - 3rd of 13 giving 3lb to Alborada (16 Oct Newmarket 10f gd RF 4919). Consistent. He joined Godolphin before the start of last term, finishing unplaced in the Dubai Duty Free on his debut for them, but then spent the rest of the season playing the bridesmaid in Group company. He was runner-up in a couple of Group Threes, but his best effort was when beating all except Alborada and Shiva in the Dubai Champion Stakes on his final start.
**S bin Suroor [0-5] Godolphin (from S bin Suroor in UAE [0-1] Mar 1999).*

K-ACE THE JOINT RR 4939[14]

2 ch g Savahra Sound 7.8f **(55)** - Be My Sweet (Galivanter) 7.8f **(56)**
Form - 0
Record 1999 - 1st:0 2nd:0 3rd:0 Ran:1
1999 AW 0-1: (7f) (Fibr)
Currently very poor gelding. **S R Bowring [0-1] Ace Racing One.*

KADAKA (IRE) BHB 104f **RR 106f** 4772a[1]

4 b f Sadler's Wells (USA) 11.3f **(87)** - Kadissya (USA) (Blushing Groom (FR)) 10.3f **(76)**
Form - 622421
Record 1999 - 1st:1 2nd:3 3rd:0 Ran:6
Pre1999 - 1st:1 2nd:2 3rd:1 Ran:5
Win Prizemoney £20,123 *Total Prizemoney* £50,388
Wins * **1999** Oct San Si (HVY) L 15f 93+ <
* 1998 Jly Yarmou (GD) 11.5f 81
1999 Turf 1-6: (12f 2, 13f 2, 14f, 15f 1-1) (hvy 1-1, gd 3, g-f, frm)
Scopey, Pattern-class filly, effective 12 to 15f, acts on gd to frm, and does well at York. Turf high 106 (1st run) - 6th of 11 getting 8lb from Silver Patriarch (30 Apr Newmarket 12f frm RF 0945). Consistent. A half-sister to Kahyasi, she appeared to have regressed from her three-year-old days and proved rather one-paced. Her listed-race win came in bottomless ground
**L M Cumani [2-11] Aga Khan.*

KADIR RR 91f 5038[8]

4 b br c Unfuwain (USA) 11.4f **(74)** - Rafif (USA) (Riverman (USA)) 9.1f **(76)**
Form - 1038
Record 1999 - 1st:1 2nd:0 3rd:1 Ran:4
Pre1999 - 1st:0 2nd:3 3rd:0 Ran:5
Win Prizemoney £3,793 *Total Prizemoney* £10,641
Wins * **1999** Jly Sandow (GD) 14f 88 <
1999 Turf 1-4: (12f, 14f 1-3) (g-s, gd 2, g-f 1-1)
Lengthy, useful colt, effective 12 to 14f, best at 14f, acts on gd to g-f, best on gd, has worn blinkers. Turf high 91 (began Jly) - also 1st of 7 giving 15lb to Tanusius (2 Jly Sandown RF 2502). Finally gained a deserved success in a maiden on his reappearance after an eleven-month absence, despite flashing his tail when hit. Although highly tried in the Ebor, he put in a nice performance when highly tried against better horses at Haydock next time. Fetched 44,000 gns at auction in October.
**M P Tregoning [1-8] Hamdan Al Maktoum (from S bin Suroor [0-1] Oct 1997).*

KAFHANEE (USA) BHB 82f **RR 80f** 4017[1]

3 ch f Seeking the Gold (USA) 7.4f **(80)** - Baya (USA) (Nureyev (USA)) 8.7f **(78)**
Form - 21
Record 1999 - 1st:1 2nd:1 3rd:0 Ran:2
Pre1999 - 1st:0 2nd:0 3rd:1 Ran:1
Win Prizemoney £3,712 *Total Prizemoney* £5,756
Wins * **1999** Aug Epsom (GD) 7f 68 <
1999 Turf 1-2: (7f 1-2) (g-f 1-1, frm)
Workmanlike, currently decent filly. Turf high 80 (1st run) - 2nd of 15 to Alpenglow (30 Apr Newmarket 7f frm RF 0948).
**S bin Suroor [1-2] Godolphin (from D R Loder [0-1] Oct 1998).*

KAFI (USA) BHB 63f **RR 66f** 2192[7]

3 b c Gulch (USA) 9.6f **(79)** - Nonoalca (FR) (Nonoalco (USA)) 8.5f **(66)**
Form - 0707
Record 1999 - 1st:0 2nd:0 3rd:0 Ran:4
Pre1999 - 1st:0 2nd:0 3rd:0 Ran:1
1999 Turf 0-4: (7f, 8f, 10f 2) (sft, g-f, frm 2)
Rangy, average colt. Turf high 66.
**M P Tregoning [0-5] Hamdan Al Maktoum.*

KAFIL (USA) BHB 36f55a **RR 31f 55a** 5058[5]

5 b br g Housebuster (USA) 7f **(81)** - Alchaasibiyeh (USA) (Seattle Slew (USA)) 9.4f **(76)**
Form - 700063707024080225
Record 1999 - 1st:0 2nd:3 3rd:1 Ran:14
Pre1999 - 1st:2 2nd:5 3rd:2 Ran:31
Win Prizemoney £5,408 *Total Prizemoney* £12,280
Wins * 1998 *Oct Lingfi (STD)* *7f* *59*
1997 *Nov Lingfi (STD)* *8f* *68* <
1999 Turf 0-4: (7f, 8f 2, 9f) (gd, frm 3) 1999 AW 0-10: (7f, 8f 6, 9f, 10f 2) (Equi 8, Fibr 2)
Fair gelding, effective 7 to 9f, best at 8f, - acts on AW, best on Equi, likes left handed tracks, favours tight tracks, likes Lingfield. Turf high 41. AW high 63 - 2nd of 8 to Nautical Warning (12 Jun Lingfield 8f Equi RF 1956). Inconsistent. Does not win very often these days. Best on Equitrack.
**J J Bridger [1-34] Exors of the late M R Pascall (from G L Moore [1-8] Dec 1997).*

KAGOSHIMA (IRE) BHB 49f **RR 45f** 5165[5]

4 b g Shirley Heights 12.1f **(76)** - Kashteh (IRE) (Green Desert (USA)) 8.6f **(78)**
Form - 65
Record 1999 - 1st:0 2nd:0 3rd:0 Ran:2
Pre1999 - 1st:0 2nd:0 3rd:0 Ran:1
1999 Turf 0-2: (12f 2) (g-s, gd)
Well made, currently moderate gelding. Turf high 45 (began Oct).
**J Norton [0-2] Keep On Running (from L M Cumani [0-1] Jly 1998).*

KAHTAN BHB 106f **RR 107f** 4674[1]

4 b c Nashwan (USA) 10.3f **(79)** - Harmless Albatross (Pas de Seul) 9.1f **(67)**
Form - 343171
Record 1999 - 1st:2 2nd:0 3rd:2 Ran:6
Pre1999 - 1st:2 2nd:1 3rd:2 Ran:7
Win Prizemoney £43,563 *Total Prizemoney* £58,214
Wins * **1999** Oct Newmar (G-S) L 12f 107 <
* **1999** Jly Cheste (G-F) H 18.7f 105 104
* 1998 Jly Newmar (FRM) L 14.8f 103
* 1997 Oct Newcas (G-F) 8f 80+
1999 Turf 2-6: (12f 1-2, 14f 2, 16f, 19f 1-1) (g-s, gd 1-2, g-f 1-3)
Workmanlike, Pattern-class colt, effective 12 to 19f, best at 12f, acts on gd to frm, best on gd, prefers right handed tracks. Turf high 109 - 4th of 5 to Yavana's Pace (12 Jun Leicester 12f gd RF 1947) - also 1st of 11 giving 7lb to Migration (1 Oct Newmarket RF 4674). Consistent. He gradually ran into form last term, and was

successful at Chester in July, appreciating the extended trip. Scored back at a mile and a half in a Listed event at Newmarket in October when the holding ground brought his stamina into play.
**J L Dunlop [4-13] Hamdan Al Maktoum.*

KAHYASI MOLL (IRE) BHB 41f RR 44f 4582[11]

2 b f Brief Truce (USA) 9.1f **(73)** - Deydarika (IRE) (Kahyasi)
Form - 07450
Record 1999 - 1st:0 2nd:0 3rd:0 Ran:5
1999 Turf 0-5: (5f, 6f, 7f, 8f, 10f) (gd 2, frm 2, hrd)
Moderate filly. Turf high 44. **J S Moore [0-5] Mick Green.*

KAIAPOI BHB 67f RR 75f 5218[18]

2 ch c Elmaamul (USA) 8.1f **(70)** - Salanka (IRE) **(65df 56a)** (Persian Heights)
Form - 501700
Record 1999 - 1st:1 2nd:0 3rd:0 Ran:6
Win Prizemoney £3,533 *Total Prizemoney* £3,533
Wins * 1999 Spt Cheste (SFT) 7f 75 <
1999 Turf 1-6: (7f 1-3, 8f 3) (g-s 1-2, gd, g-f 2, frm)
Above-average colt, effective 7f, acts on g-s. Turf high 75 (began Aug) - 1st of 7 giving 5lb to Castanea Sativa (22 Spt Chester RF 4482). **R Hollinshead [1-6] J D Graham.*

KAIBO BHB 87f RR 86f 1999[9]

3 ch c Safawan 6.6f **(60)** - Jay Gee Ell (Vaigly Great) 7f **(58)**
Form - 0250
Record 1999 - 1st:0 2nd:1 3rd:0 Ran:4
Pre1999 - 1st:2 2nd:1 3rd:1 Ran:5
Win Prizemoney £7,424 *Total Prizemoney* £18,289
Wins * 1998 Aug Haydoc (GD) 6f 80 <
* 1998 Jly Bright (G-F) 7f 80 <
1999 Turf 0-4: (7f, 8f 3) (gd, g-f 2, frm)
Scopey, useful colt, effective 6 to 7f, best at 7f, acts on gd to g-f, best on gd. Turf high 86. He did not enjoy the best of luck last term, but seems to have retained his ability.
**R Hannon [2-9] Mrs D M Wight.*

KAID (IRE) BHB 38f RR 51f 3582[12]

4 b g Alzao (USA) 9.8f **(73)** - Very Charming (USA) (Vaguely Noble) 10.1f **(72)**
Form - 06870
Record 1999 - 1st:0 2nd:0 3rd:0 Ran:5
Pre1999 - 1st:0 2nd:0 3rd:1 Ran:4
Win Prizemoney £0 *Total Prizemoney* £752
1999 Turf 0-5: (11f, 14f 3, 16f) (gd, g-f 3, frm)
Workmanlike, fair gelding, has worn blinkers. Turf high 51.
**Mrs Barbara Waring [0-7] Joy and Valentine Feerick (from E A L Dunlop [0-3] Jun 1998).*

KALA BHB 37f RR 31f 3247[6]

4 b f Alhijaz 7.7f **(57)** - Flushing Meadow (USA) (Raise A Native) 11.2f **(69)**
Form - 006
Record 1999 - 1st:0 2nd:0 3rd:0 Ran:3
Pre1999 - 1st:0 2nd:0 3rd:0 Ran:5
Win Prizemoney £0 *Total Prizemoney* £259
1999 Turf 0-3: (7f, 8f, 10f) (frm 3)
Leggy, very moderate filly. Turf high 31. Becoming disappointing.
**V Soane [0-8] David Bayliss.*

KALAHARI FERRARI BHB 50f RR 48f 4429[18]

3 ch g Clantime 6.6f **(57)** - Royal Agnes (Royal Palace) 9f **(56)**
Form - 53532235330
Record 1999 - 1st:0 2nd:2 3rd:5 Ran:11
Pre1999 - 1st:0 2nd:0 3rd:0 Ran:6
Win Prizemoney £0 *Total Prizemoney* £3,743
1999 Turf 0-10: (7f 2, 8f 6, 9f 2) (g-s, gd, g-f 3, frm 5) 1999 AW 0-1: (8f) (Fibr)
Moderate gelding, effective 8f, acts on g-f. Turf high 56 - 2nd of 16 to Jade Tiger (1 Jun Leicester 8f g-f RF 1643). Consistent.
**A G Hobbs [0-1] Furnish With Abbey (from J Berry [0-16] Jly 1999).*

KALANISI (IRE) BHB 106f RR 112f 1577[1]

3 b c Doyoun 10.7f **(69)** - Kalamba (IRE) (Green Dancer (USA)) 10.3f **(74)**
Form - 111
Record 1999 - 1st:3 2nd:0 3rd:0 Ran:3
Win Prizemoney £23,367 *Total Prizemoney* £23,367
Wins * 1999 May Kempto (G-F) L 8f 109
*** 1999** May Newmar (G-F) 7f 112 <
*** 1999** Apr Folkes (SFT) 7f 87+
1999 Turf 3-3: (7f 2-2, 8f 1-1) (sft 1-1, frm 2-2)
Workmanlike, currently Group-class colt. Turf high 112 - 1st of 4 giving 5lb to Hawriyah (2 May Newmarket RF 0976) - also 1st of 6 from Mensa (29 May Kempton RF 1577). He created a big impression when winning three times in a five-week period, shrugging off a lost shoe to land a Listed event at Kempton. Disappointingly absent through the second half of the campaign, he has the makings of a top-class miler. **L M Cumani [3-3] H H Aga Khan.*

KALAR BHB 40f37a RR 42f 37a 5032[12]

10 b g Kabour 6.1f **(36)** -Wind And Reign(Tumble Wind (USA)) 7.5f **(57)**
Form - 0432044206430061000
Record 1999 - 1st:1 2nd:2 3rd:2 Ran:19
Pre1999 - 1st:14 2nd:24 3rd:12 Ran:143
Win Prizemoney £41,511 *Total Prizemoney* £72,128
Wins * 1999 Aug Ripon (G-F) SH 5f 37 42
* 1997 *Feb Lingfi (STD) C 5f 67*
* 1997 *Jan Wolver (STD) C 5f 60*
* 1996 *Dec Southw (SLW) H 6f 70 69* <
* 1996 *Nov Lingfi (STD) H 5f 61 63*
* 1996 Aug Catter (G-F) H 5f 48 49
* 1995 Aug Thirsk (G-F) H 5f 47 45
* 1995 Aug Catter (G-F) H 5f 42 43
* 1995 *Mar Lingfi (STD) H 5f 63 65*
1999 Turf 1-12: (5f 1-10, 6f 2) (g-s, gd 3, g-f 3, frm 1-4, hrd) 1999 AW 0-7: (5f 5, 6f 2) (Equi 3, Fibr 4)
Moderate gelding, effective 5 to 6f, best at 6f, acts on gd to frm - acts on AW, best on Fibr, mostly wears blinkers, prefers left handed tracks, prefers tight tracks. Turf high 42 - 1st of 23 getting 8lb from Tancred Times (2 Aug Ripon RF 3295). AW high 41 - 2nd of 11 getting 2lb from Nite Owler (1 Mar Southwell 6f Fibr RF 0382). A very fast starter when on-song, but he does not win very often these days. **D W Chapman [15-162] David Chapman.*

KALARRAM RR 52f 5074[5]

2 ch f Muhtarram (USA) - Kalandariya (Kris) 9.5f **(73)**
Form - 5
Record 1999 - 1st:0 2nd:0 3rd:0 Ran:1
1999 Turf 0-1: (7f) (gd)
Currently fair filly. **C B B Booth [0-1] The Foston Partnership.*

KALA SUNRISE BHB 77f RR 79f 4874[14]

6 ch h Kalaglow 11.2f **(67)** - Belle of the Dawn (Bellypha) 9.8f **(73)**
Form - 0178578864240
Record 1999 - 1st:1 2nd:1 3rd:0 Ran:13
Pre1999 - 1st:2 2nd:3 3rd:2 Ran:34
Win Prizemoney £15,901 *Total Prizemoney* £31,454
Wins * 1999 Apr Leices (GD) H 7f 79 83
* 1996 Oct York (GD) H 7.9f 83 86 <
* 1995 Apr Pontef (FRM) 5f 77t
1999 Turf 1-13: (7f 1-2, 8f 11) (gd 1-5, g-f 3, frm 5)
Above-average horse, effective 7 to 8f, best at 8f, acts on gd to frm, best on frm. Turf high 83 - 1st of 20 giving 4lb to Great News (8 Apr Leicester RF 0626). He was off the track four nine months before a creditable effort in the Lincoln, and ended a long losing run with a fine victory at Leicester next time when dropped back down to seven furlongs. Although a rise in the handicap appears to have found him out since, he ran some nice races in the autumn. **C Smith [3-47] A E Needham.*

KALIDASA (USA) BHB 100f RR 98f 1106[8]

3 b f Nureyev (USA) 8.4f **(84)** - Aunt Pearl (USA) (Seattle Slew (USA)) 9.4f **(76)**
Form - 738
Record 1999 - 1st:0 2nd:0 3rd:1 Ran:3
Pre1999 - 1st:1 2nd:4 3rd:0 Ran:6
Win Prizemoney £4,289 *Total Prizemoney* £19,555
Wins * 1998 Spt Warwic (G-F) 7f 74 <
1999 Turf 0-3: (7f, 8f 2) (gd 2, g-f)
Strong, very useful filly, effective 6 to 8f, acts on gd. Turf high 97. She did not progress physically and failed to train on.
**P W Chapple-Hyam [1-9] R E Sangster.*

KALINDI BHB 100f **RR 95f** 4596[10]
2 ch f Efisio 7.7f **(69)** - Rohita (IRE) **(83df)** (Waajib)
Form - 5215200
Record 1999 - 1st:1 2nd:2 3rd:0 Ran:7
Win Prizemoney £20,150 *Total Prizemoney* £24,762
Wins * 1999 Jun Ascot (G-F) 5f 98 <
1999 Turf 1-7: (5f 1-5, 6f 2) (g-s, gd 2, g-f 1-3, frm)
Very useful filly, effective 5f, acts on gd to g-f, best on g-f. Turf high 98 - 1st of 17 getting 7lb from Master Fay (18 Jun Ascot RF 2107). She took advantage of favourable conditions to win the Windsor Castle Stakes at Royal Ascot, but did not make the grade in Group and Listed races thereafter. Unlikely to stay beyond six furlongs, she may be difficult to place.
**M R Channon [1-7] Barry Taylor.*

KALUANA COURT BHB 35f **RR 43f** 5135[10]
3 b f Batshoof 9.5f **(66)** - Fairfields Cone (Celtic Cone) 9.8f **(43)**
Form - 800
Record 1999 - 1st:0 2nd:0 3rd:0 Ran:3
Pre1999 - 1st:0 2nd:0 3rd:0 Ran:1
1999 Turf 0-3: (8f, 10f, 12f) (sft, g-s, gd)
Leggy, moderate filly. Turf high 43 (began Oct).
**R Dickin [0-4] Derek & Cheryl Holder.*

KALYPSO KATIE (IRE) RR 100++f 5109[1]
2 gr f Fairy King (USA) 7.7f **(75)** - Miss Toot (Ardross) 10.6f **(68)**
Form - 1
Record 1999 - 1st:1 2nd:0 3rd:0 Ran:1
Win Prizemoney £3,078 *Total Prizemoney* £3,078
Wins * 1999 Oct Windso (SFT) 8.3f 100++ <
1999 Turf 1-1: (8f 1-1) (gd 1-1)
Currently very useful filly. (1st run) - 1st of 13 from Scarletta (28 Oct Windsor RF 5109). A sister to the high-class Kool Kat Katie, she slammed a field of maidens at Windsor and looks set to go places at three. **J Noseda [1-1] Lucayan Stud.*

KAMARAZI (IRE) RR 49f 5064[8]
2 ch c Arazi (USA) 9.2f **(74)** - Marie D'Argonne (FR) (Jefferson) 7.9f **(89)**
Form - 88
Record 1999 - 1st:0 2nd:0 3rd:0 Ran:2
1999 Turf 0-2: (6f, 8f) (gd 2)
Currently moderate colt, often wears blinkers. Turf high 49 (began Aug). **P F I Cole [0-2] Lord Lloyd-Webber.*

KAMAREYAH (IRE) BHB 86f **RR 77f** 4599[16]
2 b f Hamas (IRE) 8f **(72)** - Nur (USA) (Diesis) 9.3f **(69)**
Form - 4310
Record 1999 - 1st:1 2nd:0 3rd:1 Ran:4
Win Prizemoney £3,655 *Total Prizemoney* £5,309
Wins * 1999 Spt Yarmou (G-S) 6f 77 <
1999 Turf 1-4: (6f 1-3, 7f) (g-s 1-1, g-f 2, frm)
Above-average filly. Turf high 77 (began Jly) - 1st of 7 from Bethesda (15 Spt Yarmouth RF 4337).
**R W Armstrong [1-4] Hamdan Al Maktoum.*

KANAKA CREEK (USA) BHB 74f **RR 71f** 5189[5]
2 ch f Thunder Gulch (USA) - Book Collector (USA) (Irish River (FR)) 8.6f **(78)**
Form - 48343235
Record 1999 - 1st:0 2nd:1 3rd:3 Ran:8
Win Prizemoney £0 *Total Prizemoney* £3,681
1999 Turf 0-8: (5f, 6f 2, 7f 3, 8f 2) (g-s 2, g-f 4, frm 2)
Above-average filly, effective 6 to 8f, best at 8f, acts on g-s to g-f, best on g-s. Turf high 71 - 5th of 9 to Littlepacepaddocks (3 Nov Musselburgh 8f g-f RF 5189). Improving. She looks a bit of a handful, but has made the frame in ordinary maidens.
**J Berry [0-8] Chris Deuters.*

KANAWA BHB 35f48a **RR 33f 48a** 2639[U]
5 b m Beveled (USA) 6.9f **(64)** - Kiri Te (Liboi (USA))
Form - 5376541272134U
Record 1999 - 1st:2 2nd:2 3rd:1 Ran:12
Pre1999 - 1st:0 2nd:0 3rd:1 Ran:14
Win Prizemoney £6,016 *Total Prizemoney* £7,996
Wins * 1999 *May Southw (STD) H 8f 44 51+* <
1999 *Feb Southw (STD) H 7f 33 42*
1999 Turf 0-1: (9f) (frm) 1999 AW 2-11: (7f 1-2, 8f 1-7, 9f, 10f) (Equi 5, Fibr 2-6)
Fair filly, effective 7 to 8f, best at 8f, - acted on Equi to Fibr, best on Equi. AW high 51 - 1st of 12 getting 11lb from Birthday Venture (10 May Southwell RF 1132) - also 1st of 8 getting 2lb from River Ensign (22 Feb Southwell RF 0338). (DEAD)
**Derrick Morris [1-4] The Lambourn Racing Club (from A P Jones [1-24] Apr 1999).*

KANISTARI (IRE) BHB 76f **RR 74f** 4762[11]
2 b c Sri Pekan (USA) - Aster Aweke (IRE) (Alzao (USA)) 7.1f **(68)**
Form - 464820
Record 1999 - 1st:0 2nd:1 3rd:0 Ran:6
Win Prizemoney £0 *Total Prizemoney* £2,878
1999 Turf 0-6: (6f 3, 7f, 8f 2) (sft, gd 2, g-f 2, frm)
Above-average colt, effective 8f, acts on sft. Turf high 74 - 2nd of 12 getting 14lb from El Curioso (21 Spt Warwick 8f sft RF 4452).
**S Dow [0-6] P McCarthy.*

KANZ WOOD (USA) BHB 62f **RR 61f** 2762[12]
3 ch c Woodman (USA) 9.7f **(77)** - Kanz (USA) (The Minstrel (CAN)) 10f **(72)**
Form - 050
Record 1999 - 1st:0 2nd:0 3rd:0 Ran:3
Pre1999 - 1st:0 2nd:0 3rd:1 Ran:5
Win Prizemoney £0 *Total Prizemoney* £887
1999 Turf 0-3: (8f, 10f, 12f) (g-f, frm 2)
Scopey, average colt, effective 8f, acts on frm. Turf high 61.
**W R Muir [0-8] D J Deer.*

KARAJAN (IRE) RR 86f 4898[3]
2 b c Fairy King (USA) 7.7f **(75)** - Dernier Cri **(64df)** (Slip Anchor) 9.8f **(73)**
Form - 3
Record 1999 - 1st:0 2nd:0 3rd:1 Ran:1
Win Prizemoney £0 *Total Prizemoney* £1,230
1999 Turf 0-1: (8f) (gd)
Currently useful colt. (1st run) - 3rd of 13 to Pawn Broker (15 Oct Newmarket 8f gd RF 4898). Kept on nicely on his debut, and should make the grade. **J W Hills [0-1] Ken Lim & Chris Wright.*

KARAKUL (IRE) BHB 65f **RR 60f** 4946[9]
3 ch f Persian Bold 10f **(69)** - Cindy's Baby (Bairn (USA)) 7.7f **(59)**
Form - 851211000
Record 1999 - 1st:3 2nd:1 3rd:0 Ran:9
Pre1999 - 1st:1 2nd:0 3rd:1 Ran:8
Win Prizemoney £12,100 *Total Prizemoney* £13,764
Wins * 1999 Aug Beverl (GD) H 9.9f 56 67 <
*** 1999** Aug Leices (G-F) H 10f 56 63+
*** 1999** Jun Windso (G-F) H 10f 50 55
* 1998 Jly Bright (GD) C 7f 62
1999 Turf 3-9: (7f, 8f, 10f 3-7) (gd 2, g-f 2-5, frm 1-2)
Neat, average filly, effective 7 to 10f, best at 10f, acts on gd to g-f, best on g-f, prefers tight tracks. Turf high 67 - 1st of 11 giving 7lb to Admirals Place (11 Aug Beverley RF 3536) - also 1st of 10 getting 7lb from Just Wiz (4 Aug Leicester RF 3359). Consistent.
**M J Fetherston-Godley [4-17] The Karakul Partnership.*

KARALIYFA (IRE) RR 80+f 4383[3]
2 gr f Kahyasi 12.9f **(74)** - Karliyka (IRE) **(97f)** (Last Tycoon) 8.5f **(62)**
Form - 3
Record 1999 - 1st:0 2nd:0 3rd:1 Ran:1
Win Prizemoney £0 *Total Prizemoney* £1,728
1999 Turf 0-1: (7f) (frm)
Currently decent filly. (1st run) - 3rd of 7 getting 5lb from Veil of Avalon (17 Spt Newbury 7f frm RF 4383). A good third in a decent race on her debut, she will come into her own over middle distances. **Sir Michael Stoute [0-1] H H Aga Khan.*

KARAMEG (IRE) BHB 79f **RR 78f** 5143[5]
3 b f Danehill (USA) 9.1f **(79)** - House of Queens (IRE) (King of Clubs) 7.1f **(57)**
Form - 40813523515
Record 1999 - 1st:2 2nd:1 3rd:2 Ran:11
Pre1999 - 1st:0 2nd:0 3rd:0 Ran:3
Win Prizemoney £11,600 *Total Prizemoney* £14,631
Wins * 1999 Oct Newmar (SFT) H 7f 74 78 <

* 1999 Jun Doncas (G-F) H 7f 67 72
1999 Turf 2-11: (6f 3, 7f 2-5, 8f 3) (gd 1-2, g-f 5, frm 1-4)
Light-framed, above-average filly, effective 6 to 7f, best at 7f, acts on gd to frm, excels at Doncaster. Turf high 78 - 1st of 19 getting 12lb from Salty Jack (2 Oct Newmarket RF 4685) - also 1st of 18 giving 2lb to Bollin Roberta (26 Jun Doncaster RF 2326). Consistent. **P W Harris [2-14] and Mrs G Knight.*

KAREEB (FR) BHB 83f **RR 75f** 5164[4]
2 b c Green Desert (USA) 7.8f **(78)** - Braari (USA) **(100f)** (Gulch (USA)) 8f **(81)**
Form - 22324
Record 1999 - 1st:0 2nd:3 3rd:1 Ran:5
Win Prizemoney £0 *Total Prizemoney* £3,855
1999 Turf 0-5: (5f, 6f 4) (g-s, gd, frm 2, hrd)
Above-average colt. Turf high 87 - 2nd of 9 to Proud Chief (27 Jun Goodwood 6f gd RF 2360). Achieved the unwanted distinction of being beaten favourite on each of his five outings.
**W R Muir [0-1] J Bernstein (from B W Hills [0-4] Oct 1999).*

KAREFREE KATIE (USA) BHB 53f38a **RR 67?f 38a** 2561[16]
4 b f Lac Ouimet (USA) 8.1f **(76)** - Dame Cecilia (USA) (Vaguely Noble) 10.1f **(72)**
Form - 407050
Record 1999 - 1st:0 2nd:0 3rd:0 Ran:4
Pre1999 - 1st:0 2nd:1 3rd:0 Ran:4
Win Prizemoney £0 *Total Prizemoney* £1,160
1999 Turf 0-1: (10f) (gd) 1999 AW 0-3: (9f, 12f 2) (Fibr 3)
Scopey, average filly, effective 10f, acts on g-s, has worn blinkers, favours left handed tracks, favours tight tracks. AW high 35. Inconsistent.
**J G Given [0-7] J E Titley (from M Johnston [0-4] Dec 1998).*

KARINGA PRINCE RR 38tf 698[10]
3 gr g Karinga Bay - Silent Sister (Kind of Hush) 10.1f **(62)**
Form - 0
Record 1999 - 1st:0 2nd:0 3rd:0 Ran:1
1999 Turf 0-1: (8f) (gd)
Tall, currently very moderate gelding.
**G L Moore [0-1] C F Sparrowhawk.*

KARINSKA BHB 32f34a **RR 28f 34a** 3241[9]
9 b m Master Willie 9.2f **(67)** - Kaiserchronik (GER) (Cortez (GER)) 8.6f **(75)**
Form - 053634007P0
Record 1999 - 1st:0 2nd:0 3rd:2 Ran:11
Pre1999 - 1st:10 2nd:6 3rd:7 Ran:89
Win Prizemoney £36,988 *Total Prizemoney* £50,609
Wins * 1997 Spt Nottin (GD) H 8.2f 57 63
* 1997 Jly Yarmou (G-F) H 10.1f 56 55
* 1997 Jly Yarmou (G-S) H 7f 51 49
* 1995 Jun Windso (GD) H 8.3f 59 60
* 1995 Jun Catter (GD) H 7f 54 56
* 1995 Apr Thirsk (GD) H 8f 50 53
1999 Turf 0-6: (10f 2, 12f 3, 18f) (g-f 3, frm 3) 1999 AW 0-5: (8f 3, 12f 2) (Fibr 5)
Very moderate mare, effective 12f, acted on g-f. Turf high 49 (1st run) - 4th of 17 to Prince Nicholas (25 Mar Doncaster 12f g-f RF 0463). AW high 39. (DEAD)
**M C Chapman [10-104] Geoff Whiting (from Sir Mark Prescott [1-6] Jun 1993).*

KARISAL (IRE) BHB 62f **RR 54f** 2861[6]
3 b f Persian Bold 10f **(69)** - Pasadena Lady (Captain James) 5f **(59)**
Form - 8006
Record 1999 - 1st:0 2nd:0 3rd:0 Ran:4
Pre1999 - 1st:1 2nd:0 3rd:0 Ran:3
Win Prizemoney £4,162 *Total Prizemoney* £4,675
Wins * 1998 May Haydoc (G-S) 5f 77 <
1999 Turf 0-4: (5f, 6f 2, 7f) (g-f 3, frm)
Light-framed, fair filly, effective 5f, acts on gd, has worn blinkers. Turf high 54. **J Berry [1-7] J E M Hawkins Ltd.*

KARIYADAN (IRE) BHB 45f **RR 64f** 3877a[9]
3 b c Akarad (FR) 9.7f **(73)** - Kadissya (USA) (Blushing Groom (FR)) 10.3f **(76)**
Form - 75430
Record 1999 - 1st:0 2nd:0 3rd:1 Ran:5
Pre1999 - 1st:0 2nd:0 3rd:0 Ran:1
Win Prizemoney £0 *Total Prizemoney* £612
1999 Turf 0-5: (10f, 12f 4) (sft, g-s, gd 2, g-f)
Lengthy, average colt, effective 12f, acts on gd. Turf high 64.
**S Donohoe in IRE [0-3] Ballyjamesduff Racing Club (from L M Cumani [0-3] Jun 1999).*

KARIYFI (IRE) RR 69f 5157[7]
2 b br c Doyoun 10.7f **(69)** - Karamiyna (IRE) **(92f)** (Shernazar) 10.2f **(73)**
Form - 07
Record 1999 - 1st:0 2nd:0 3rd:0 Ran:2
1999 Turf 0-2: (7f, 8f) (gd, frm)
Currently average colt. Turf high 69 (began Oct).
**L M Cumani [0-2] H H Aga Khan.*

KARLAYA (IRE) RR 65df 5165[9]
3 b f Darshaan 11.9f **(81)** - Kalata (Assert) 10.6f **(85)**
Form - 60
Record 1999 - 1st:0 2nd:0 3rd:0 Ran:2
1999 Turf 0-2: (12f 2) (g-s, g-f)
Leggy, currently average filly. Turf high 65.
**H R A Cecil [0-2] Lordship Stud.*

KAROWNA BHB 68f64a **RR 71f 64a** 3439[9]
3 ch f Karinga Bay - Misowni (Niniski (USA)) 10.6f **(65)**
Form - 3543450
Record 1999 - 1st:0 2nd:0 3rd:2 Ran:7
Pre1999 - 1st:0 2nd:0 3rd:0 Ran:3
Win Prizemoney £0 *Total Prizemoney* £1,604
1999 Turf 0-6: (6f, 7f 5) (gd, g-f, frm 4) 1999 AW 0-1: (8f) (Fibr)
Light-framed, above-average filly, effective 7f, acts on gd to frm. Turf high 73 (1st run) - 3rd of 9 to Arctic Char (1 Apr Leicester 7f gd RF 0541). Consistent. **B A McMahon [0-10] Holding Partnership.*

KASHRA (IRE) BHB 95f **RR 87f** 4389[6]
2 b f Dancing Dissident (USA) 6.8f **(65)** - Tudor Loom (Sallust) 8.4f **(63)**
Form - 266121146
Record 1999 - 1st:3 2nd:2 3rd:0 Ran:9
Win Prizemoney £27,170 *Total Prizemoney* £31,182
Wins * **1999** Aug Newmar (G-F) H 6f 81 87+ <
* **1999** Jly Goodwo (G-F) H 6f 72
* **1999** Jly Pontef (G-S) H 6f 58
1999 Turf 3-9: (5f 3, 6f 3-6) (gd 3, g-f 2, frm 3-4)
Useful filly, effective 6f, acts on frm. Turf high 87 - also 1st of 13 giving 5lb to Phoebe Buffay (28 Aug Newmarket RF 3966). She got off the mark in a Pontefract nursery when stepped up to six furlongs for the first time, and chased home a decent sort in a similar event at Ascot. Good winner of a nursery at Glorious Goodwood over the same trip, she followed up again over six furlongs at Newmarket, where she won very easily. Easily dismissed behind Primo Valentino at Kempton and ran as if over the top at Ayr.
**M Johnston [3-9] K Towey.*

KASS ALHAWA BHB 67f54a **RR 65f 54a** 5075[3]
6 b g Shirley Heights 12.1f **(76)** - Silver Braid (USA) (Miswaki (USA)) 9f **(81)**
Form - 22423722520200153400064З
Record 1999 - 1st:1 2nd:5 3rd:3 Ran:22
Pre1999 - 1st:5 2nd:9 3rd:4 Ran:47
Win Prizemoney £20,668 *Total Prizemoney* £38,628
Wins * **1999** Jly Beverl (G-F) H 8.5f 68 71 <
* 1998 Aug Beverl (G-F) H 7.5f 63 66
* 1998 Jun Beverl (G-S) H 7.5f 63 68
* 1998 *Feb Southw (STD) H 6f 31 38*
* 1997 Aug Catter (G-F) H 7f 59 63
* 1997 Jun Redcar (GD) H 8f 53 58
1999 Turf 1-15: (6f, 7f 6, 8f 1-5, 9f, 10f 2) (g-s, gd 5, g-f 5, frm 1-4) 1999 AW 0-7: (6f, 7f 3, 8f 3) (Fibr 7)
Average gelding, effective 6 to 10f, best at 8f, acts on gd to frm, has worn blinkers, likes right handed tracks, excels at Catterick and Redcar, does well at Beverley. Turf high 71 - 1st of 13 giving 6lb to Bollin Frank (27 Jly Beverley RF 3162). AW high 54. Consistent. He seems to like Beverley and won again there in July.
**D W Chapman [6-66] J B Wilcox (from Sir Michael Stoute [0-3] May 1996).*

KASTAWAY BHB 83f **RR 71f** 860[4]
3 b f Distant Relative 7f **(69)** - Flourishing (IRE) (Trojan Fen) 8.1f **(62)**
Form - 4
Record 1999 - 1st:0 2nd:0 3rd:0 Ran:1
Pre1999 - 1st:4 2nd:2 3rd:0 Ran:8
Win Prizemoney £14,937 *Total Prizemoney* £21,537
Wins 1998 Jun Windso (SFT) 5f 88 <
1998 May Doncas (G-F) 5f 86
1998 Apr Thirsk (G-S) 5f 86
1998 Mar Lingfi (STD) 5f 86
1999 Turf 0-1: (5f) (g-s)
Neat, useful filly, effective 5f, acts on g-s to g-f - acts on Equi. Becoming disappointing.
**D R C Elsworth [0-1] C J Harper (from J Berry [4-8] Spt 1998).*

KATHAKALI (IRE) BHB 60f **RR 72f** 4840[10]
2 b c Dancing Dissident (USA) 6.8f **(65)** - Shes A Dancer (IRE) (Alzao (USA)) 7.1f **(68)**
Form - 8065480
Record 1999 - 1st:0 2nd:0 3rd:0 Ran:7
Win Prizemoney £0 *Total Prizemoney* £232
1999 Turf 0-7: (5f, 6f 4, 7f, 8f) (gd 3, g-f, frm 3)
Above-average colt, effective 6f, acts on frm, has worn blinkers. Turf high 72. **V Soane [0-7] The First Timers.*

KATHIES PET BHB 54f49a **RR 53f 49a** 4702[11]
4 b f Tina's Pet 7.4f **(56)** - Unveiled **(54f 48a)** (Sayf El Arab (USA)) 7.1f **(54)**
Form - 0108454500
Record 1999 - 1st:1 2nd:0 3rd:0 Ran:10
Pre1999 - 1st:2 2nd:2 3rd:1 Ran:19
Win Prizemoney £8,873 *Total Prizemoney* £11,101
Wins * 1999 May Bath (GD) H 5.7f 54 55
* 1998 Jun Windso (GD) H 6f 60 66 <
* 1998 May Bright (G-F) H 6f 56 61
1999 Turf 1-9: (5f, 6f 1-3, 7f, 8f 4) (g-s, gd, g-f 1-2, frm 4, hrd) 1999 AW 0-1: (7f) (Fibr)
Workmanlike, fair filly, effective 6f, acts on gd to g-f, likes left handed tracks. Turf high 56. **R J Hodges [3-29] Mrs E A Tucker.*

KATHIR (USA) BHB 85f **RR 73+f** 3969[1]
2 ch c Woodman (USA) 9.7f **(77)** - Alcando (Alzao (USA)) 7.1f **(68)**
Form - 21
Record 1999 - 1st:1 2nd:1 3rd:0 Ran:2
Win Prizemoney £3,915 *Total Prizemoney* £5,151
Wins * 1999 Aug Nottin (G-F) 8.2f 72+ <
1999 Turf 1-2: (7f, 8f 1-1) (g-f 1-2)
Currently above-average colt. Turf high 73 (1st run) (began Aug) - 2nd of 8 to Eternal Spring (11 Aug Beverley 7f g-f RF 3537) - also 1st of 5 from Keltic Bard (28 Aug Nottingham RF 3969).
**A C Stewart [1-2] Hamdan Al Maktoum.*

KATHOLOGY (IRE) BHB 84f **RR 74f** 5195[2]
2 b c College Chapel - Wicken Wonder (IRE) **(56f)** (Distant Relative)
Form - 0422
Record 1999 - 1st:0 2nd:2 3rd:0 Ran:4
Win Prizemoney £0 *Total Prizemoney* £2,365
1999 Turf 0-4: (5f, 6f 2, 7f) (g-s, gd 3)
Above-average colt. Turf high 74 (began Oct).
**D R C Elsworth [0-4] O J McDowell.*

KATHRYN'S PET BHB 73f **RR 70f** 5133[1]
6 b m Blakeney 11.9f **(53)** - Starky's Pet (Mummy's Pet) 7.7f **(60)**
Form - 10841
Record 1999 - 1st:2 2nd:0 3rd:0 Ran:5
Pre1999 - 1st:3 2nd:2 3rd:2 Ran:21
Win Prizemoney £21,241 *Total Prizemoney* £24,749
Wins * 1999 Oct Newmar (G-S) H 12f 66 70 <
*** 1999** Mar Catter (G-S) H 13.8f 66 68
* 1998 Apr Catter (GD) H 13.8f 61 67
* 1997 Jun Cheste (SFT) H 12.3f 60 64
* 1997 Mar Mussel (SFT) 12f 56
1999 Turf 2-5: (10f, 12f 1-3, 14f 1-1) (gd 2-4, g-f)
Above-average mare, effective 10 to 14f, acts on gd to frm, best on gd, prefers left handed tracks. Turf high 70 - 1st of 19 getting 2lb from Sharp Stepper (29 Oct Newmarket RF 5133) - also 1st of 9 giving 10lb to Aldwych Arrow (31 Mar Catterick RF 0525). Inconsistent. **Mrs M Reveley [9-36] Bill Brown.*

KATIE HAWK BHB 23f **RR 13f** 3053[16]
5 b m Buzzards Bay 8.9f **(44)** - Rayne Park (Julio Mariner) 7.2f **(57)**
Form - 00
Record 1999 - 1st:0 2nd:0 3rd:0 Ran:2
Pre1999 - 1st:0 2nd:0 3rd:0 Ran:2
1999 Turf 0-2: (10f, 12f) (g-f, frm)
Poor filly. Turf high 13. **J M Bradley [0-4] Mrs T D Watts.*

KATIE KOMAITE BHB 39f34a **RR 36f 34a** 5162[9]
6 b m Komaite (USA) 6.9f **(61)** - City to City(Windjammer (USA)) 7f **(59)**
Form - 4505880010
Record 1999 - 1st:1 2nd:0 3rd:0 Ran:10
Pre1999 - 1st:2 2nd:5 3rd:4 Ran:42
Win Prizemoney £8,677 *Total Prizemoney* £14,873
Wins * 1999 Oct Newcas (G-S) H 10.1f 35 36
* 1998 Jun Pontef (SFT) H 8f 39 43
1997 Oct Nottin (GD) H 8.2f 39 45 <
1999 Turf 1-10: (8f 5, 9f, 10f 1-4) (g-s, gd 1-3, g-f 3, frm 3)
Very moderate mare, effective 8 to 10f, best at 8f, acts on g-s to g-f, best on g-s, often wears blinkers (effectively). Turf high 42 (1st run) - 4th of 16 getting 14lb from Future Prospect (6 May Hamilton 8f g-f RF 1059). Consistent. She is a difficult type to win with, but often runs with credit. She does not want the ground fast.
**Mrs G S Rees [2-20] Red Rose Partnership (from Capt J Wilson [1-32] Nov 1997).*

KATIE'S CRACKER BHB 16f27a **RR 32f 27a** 5152[10]
4 b f Rambo Dancer (CAN) 8.4f **(59)** - Tea-Pot (Ragstone) 9.6f **(59)**
Form - 063734210616070442800
Record 1999 - 1st:2 2nd:2 3rd:1 Ran:18
Pre1999 - 1st:2 2nd:5 3rd:5 Ran:27
Win Prizemoney £9,180 *Total Prizemoney* £15,990
Wins * 1999 *Mar Southw (STD) C 14f 36*
*** 1999** *Feb Lingfi (STD) SH 13f 36 41*
1998 Oct Nottin (SFT) SH 14.1f 37 46
* 1998 *Mar Southw (STD) H 11f 53 56+* <
1999 Turf 0-5: (13f, 14f 3, 15f) (hvy, sft, gd 2, frm) 1999 AW 2-13: (12f 3, 13f 1-3, 14f 1-3, 16f 4) (Equi 1-8, Fibr 1-5)
Light-framed, very moderate filly, effective 8 to 14f, acts on g-s to frm - acts on AW, best on Fibr, and likes Southwell. Turf high 41. AW high 41. Becoming disappointing. She has done well in selling company on sand, but looks as if she has to dominate in order to show her best.
**M Quinn [4-38] Mrs S G Davies (from M R Channon [0-7] Spt 1997).*

KATIE'S VALENTINE BHB 55a **RR 52f 55a** 4721[8]
2 b f Balnibarbi - Ring Side (IRE) (Alzao (USA)) 7.1f **(68)**
Form - 8
Record 1999 - 1st:0 2nd:0 3rd:0 Ran:1
1999 Turf 0-1: (5f) (gd)
Currently fair filly. **R A Fahey [0-1] G Shiel.*

KATINO BHB 38f **RR 31f** 1987[12]
3 ch f Superpower 6.6f **(58)** - Nikatino (Bustino) 10.4f **(64)**
Form - 640
Record 1999 - 1st:0 2nd:0 3rd:0 Ran:3
1999 Turf 0-3: (6f, 7f, 8f) (g-s, gd, g-f)
Scopey, very moderate filly. Turf high 31. **B D Leavy [0-3] I Norman.*

KATIYKHA (IRE) BHB 105f **RR 102+f** 5205a[2]
3 b f Darshaan 11.9f **(81)** - Katiyfa (Auction Ring (USA)) 8.6f **(65)**
Form - 11650512
Record 1999 - 1st:3 2nd:1 3rd:0 Ran:8
Win Prizemoney £21,739 *Total Prizemoney* £29,406
Wins * 1999 Oct Newmar (GD) H 12f 97 102+ <
*** 1999** Jun Leices (G-S) 11.8f 73+
*** 1999** May Newmar (GD) 12f 79
1999 Turf 3-8: (10f, 12f 3-7) (sft, g-s, gd 2-4, g-f 1-2)
Well made, very useful filly, effective 10 to 12f, best at 12f, acts on g-s to g-f, likes right handed tracks. Turf high 102 - 1st of 14 giving 9lb to Fair Warning (14 Oct Newmarket RF 4876). Made a winning debut in what looked a decent maiden at Newmarket, before beating Doonaree in a two-horse event at Leicester. She was held in Pattern events afterwards, but easily won a competitive handicap at Newmarket. **L M Cumani [3-8].*

KATIYMANN (IRE) BHB 43f **RR 42f** 1599[1]

7 ch g Persian Bold 10f **(69)** - Katiyfa (Auction Ring (USA)) 8.6f **(65)**

Form - 0001

Record 1999 - 1st:1 2nd:0 3rd:0 Ran:4
Pre1999 - 1st:1 2nd:0 3rd:0 Ran:3

Win Prizemoney £4,446 *Total Prizemoney* £4,446

Wins * 1999 May Leices (GD) SH 10f 40 42
1997 Jun Clonme (GD) 10f 66 <

1999 Turf 1-4: (8f, 10f 1-3) (g-s, gd, g-f 1-2)

Moderate gelding. Turf high 42. Inconsistent. He had not won since arriving from Ireland until causing a surprise in a ten-furlong Leicester seller in May.

**B Ellison [1-10] Paul Campbell (from T J Taaffe in IRE [4-17] Aug 1997).*

KATTEGAT BHB 92f **RR 90f** 4830[1]

3 b c Slip Anchor 12.7f **(75)** - Kirsten (Kris) 9.5f **(73)**

Form - 231

Record 1999 - 1st:1 2nd:1 3rd:1 Ran:3
Pre1999 - 1st:1 2nd:0 3rd:0 Ran:2

Win Prizemoney £10,241 *Total Prizemoney* £13,170

Wins * 1999 Oct Ayr (SFT) H 13.1f 88 90 <
*** 1998** Oct Nottin (SFT) 8.2f 81

1999 Turf 1-3: (12f, 13f 1-1, 14f) (sft 1-1, gd 2)

Workmanlike, useful colt. Turf high 90 - 1st of 7 giving 17lb to Spartan Royale (12 Oct Ayr RF 4830). Returned from a five-month break to land a minor event at Ayr.

**W Jarvis [2-5] Exors of the late Lord Howard de Walden.*

KATUN (FR) RR 110f 2071[9]

6 b h Saumarez 15.1f **(87)** - All Found (USA) (Alleged (USA)) 10f **(76)**

Form - 130

1999 Turf 1-3: (16f 1-2, 20f) (g-s, gd 1-1, g-f)

Group-class horse. Turf high 110 (1st run) - 1st of 8 getting 7lb from Tajoun (2 May Longchamp RF 1074a). He was given plenty to do in the Prix Vicomtesse Vigier at Longchamp in May and, under those circumstances, did well to finish third behind Kayf Tara. Bandaged in front when running poorly in the Ascot Gold Cup, he is unlikely to improve at this stage of his career.

**X Nakkachdji in FR [1-3] A Boucher (from FR [0-1] Aug 1997).*

KATY IVORY (IRE) BHB 65f **RR 63f** 4934[11]

2 b f Night Shift (USA) 8.1f **(73)** - Echo Cove (Slip Anchor) 9.8f **(73)**

Form - 778200

Record 1999 - 1st:0 2nd:1 3rd:0 Ran:6

Win Prizemoney £0 *Total Prizemoney* £976

1999 Turf 0-6: (5f, 6f, 7f, 8f 3) (g-f 4, frm 2)

Average filly, effective 8f, acts on g-f. Turf high 63 - 2nd of 16 getting 1lb from Wintzig (23 Spt Pontefract 8f g-f RF 4504).

**P W Harris [0-6] K T Ivory Ltd.*

KATY NOWAITEE BHB 84f **RR 83f** 5004[2]

3 b f Komaite (USA) 6.9f **(61)** - Cold Blow (Posse (USA)) 8.9f **(61)**

Form - 1512

Record 1999 - 1st:2 2nd:1 3rd:0 Ran:4

Win Prizemoney £11,330 *Total Prizemoney* £13,700

Wins * 1999 Oct Redcar (GD) H 8f 77 82 <
*** 1999** Aug Newmar (G-F) 8f 75

1999 Turf 2-4: (8f 2-4) (gd, g-f 1-1, frm 1-2)

Scopey, decent filly. Turf high 83 (began Aug) - 2nd of 13 giving 5lb to Reviewing (21 Oct Nottingham 8f gd RF 5004) - also 1st of 22 giving 10lb to Maiteamia (2 Oct Redcar RF 4689).

**P W Harris [2-4] The Stable Maites.*

KAY EFF ESS (IRE) RR 4147[11]

3 b f Nucleon (USA) -My Silversmith (IRE) (Cyrano de Bergerac) 6f **(68)**

Form - 0

Record 1999 - 1st:0 2nd:0 3rd:0 Ran:1

1999 Turf 0-1: (6f) (hrd)

Light-framed, currently very poor filly. **J L Eyre [0-1] Mrs G Smyth.*

KAYF TARA BHB 119f **RR 123+f** 4471a[1]

5 b h Sadler's Wells (USA) 11.3f **(87)** - Colorspin (FR) (High Top) 10.2f **(67)**

Form - 13111

Record 1999 - 1st:4 2nd:0 3rd:1 Ran:5
Pre1999 - 1st:4 2nd:1 3rd:1 Ran:8

Win Prizemoney £427,596 *Total Prizemoney* £459,251

Wins * 1999 Spt Currag (SFT) G1 14f 123+ <
*** 1999** Aug Deauvi (HVY) G2 15f 123
*** 1999** Jly Goodwo (G-F) G2 16f 113+
*** 1999** May Longch (HVY) G2 15.5f 121
*** 1998** Spt Currag (SFT) G1 14f 123
*** 1998** Jun Ascot (SFT) G1 20f 118
*** 1998** May Haydoc (GD) 11.9f 95+
1997 Jly Ascot (GD) 10f 91

1999Turf 4-5:(14f 1-1, 15f 1-1, 16f 2-2, 20f)(g-s 2-2, gd 1-1, g-f, frm 1-1)

Very high-class colt, effective 14 to 20f, best at 14f, acts on sft to frm, best on gd. Turf high 123 - 1st of 5 from Yavana's Pace (18 Spt Curragh RF 4471a) - also 1st of 5 from Invermark (22 Aug Deauville RF 3933a). Consistent. Winner of the Ascot Gold Cup and the Irish St Leger in 1998, he won the Prix de Vicomtesse Vigier on his 1999 bow before finishing a most creditable third in the Gold Cup on ground faster than he prefers. He proved he was the leading stayer in Europe by scoring a hat-trick in the Goodwood Cup, the Prix Kergorlay at Deauville and the Irish St Leger, but suffered a tendon injury while being prepared for the Melbourne Cup which may well bring his racing career to an end.

**S bin Suroor [7-11] Godolphin (from Sir Michael Stoute [1-2] Jly 1997).*

Kayf Tara proved himself the leading stayer in Europe

KAYO BHB 93f82a **RR 93f 82a** 5055[7]

4 b g Superpower 6.6f **(58)** - Shiny Kay (Star Appeal) 9.6f **(65)**

Form - 46603073051117

Record 1999 - 1st:3 2nd:0 3rd:2 Ran:14
Pre1999 - 1st:6 2nd:2 3rd:0 Ran:21

Win Prizemoney £53,982 *Total Prizemoney* £67,882

Wins * 1999 Oct Newcas (G-S) H 6f 79 93 <
*** 1999** Oct Newmar (GD) H 7f 79 92
*** 1999** Oct Redcar (GD) H 7f 80 83
1998 Oct Warwic (GD) H 8f 91 92
1998 Jun Newbur (HVY) 7f 86
1998 *May Southw (STD) H 7f 73 78*
1998 *Apr Southw (STD) H 6f 67 72*
1997 Oct Ayr (SFT) H 8f 67 71
1997 Spt Mussel (G-F) C 8f 66

1999 Turf 3-13: (6f 1-4, 7f 2-8, 8f) (g-s 2, gd 1-6, g-f 1-4, frm 1-1) 1999 AW 0-1: (7f) (Fibr)

Workmanlike, useful gelding, effective 6 to 8f, acts on g-s to frm, best on g-f, has worn blinkers, and excels at Newcastle. Turf high 93 - 1st of 20 giving 14lb to Pips Song (20 Oct Newcastle RF 4984) - also 1st of 19 getting 8lb from Family Man (16 Oct Newmarket RF 4921). Struck a rich vein of form for his new yard in the autumn.

**M Johnston [3-5] David Abell (from T J Etherington [6-30] Jly 1999).*

KAYO GEE BHB 67f80a **RR 62f 80a** 3238[11]

3 b f Komaite (USA) 6.9f **(61)** - Darling Miss Daisy (Tina's Pet) 6.8f **(59)**

Form - 07111000

Record 1999 - 1st:2 2nd:0 3rd:0 Ran:5

Pre1999 - 1st:1 2nd:0 3rd:0 Ran:5
Win Prizemoney £10,690 *Total Prizemoney* £10,690
Wins * **1999** *Feb Lingfi (STD) H 5f 73 80*
* **1999** *Jan Lingfi (STD) H 5f 60 81* <
* 1998 *Dec Lingfi (STD) 5f 72?*
1999 Turf 0-3: (5f 3) (gd, g-f, frm) 1999 AW 2-2: (5f 2-2) (Equi 2-2)
Light-framed, decent filly, effective 5f, - acts on Equi, often wears blinkers (extremely effectively), prefers left handed tracks, prefers tight tracks. Turf high 62. AW high 81 (1st run) - 1st of 9 getting 4lb from Grasslandik (21 Jan Lingfield RF 0136) - also 1st of 4 getting 3lb from Trojan Girl (20 Feb Lingfield RF 0327). Inconsistent. Dropped in trip to land an Equitrack hat-trick, but held on turf since. **A J McNae [3-10] Mrs E N Nield.*

KAZZOUD (IRE) BHB 38f **RR 38f** 1020[12]
3 b f Ezzoud (IRE) - Kates Cabin (Habitat) 9.4f **(70)**
Form - 00
Record 1999 - 1st:0 2nd:0 3rd:0 Ran:2
Pre1999 - 1st:0 2nd:0 3rd:0 Ran:1
1999 Turf 0-2: (10f 2) (frm, hrd)
Neat, currently very moderate filly. Turf high 38.
**S Dow [0-3] Mrs A M Upsdell.*

KEEBAAR BHB 89f **RR 91f** 3774[3]
3 b c Shirley Heights 12.1f **(76)** - Historiette (Chief's Crown (USA)) 9.8f **(72)**
Form - 322143
Record 1999 - 1st:1 2nd:2 3rd:2 Ran:6
Win Prizemoney £3,766 *Total Prizemoney* £10,591
Wins * **1999** Jun Yarmou (GD) 11.5f 79+ <
1999 Turf 1-6: (10f 2, 11f 1-1, 12f 2, 14f) (sft, gd 1-4, g-f)
Strong, useful colt, effective 14f, acts on gd. Turf high 91. Improving horse who ran well stepped up to fourteen furlongs at the Ebor meeting. **M A Jarvis [1-6] Sheikh Ahmed Al Maktoum.*

KEEN COMPANION BHB 29f29a **RR 20f 29a** 2256[13]
6 b m Keen 11.1f **(58)** - Constant Companion (Pas de Seul) 9.1f **(67)**
Form - 00750
Record 1999 - 1st:0 2nd:0 3rd:0 Ran:4
Pre1999 - 1st:0 2nd:0 3rd:2 Ran:8
Win Prizemoney £0 *Total Prizemoney* £901
1999 Turf 0-1: (12f) (g-f) 1999 AW 0-3: (11f 2, 14f) (Fibr 3)
Little account mare, has worn blinkers. AW high 17.
**T J Naughton [0-12] Drofmor Racing 2.*

KEEN DANCER BHB 52f58a **RR 49f 58a** 3614[8]
5 ch g Keen 11.1f **(58)** - Royal Shoe (Hotfoot) 10.5f **(59)**
Form - 68
Record 1999 - 1st:0 2nd:0 3rd:0 Ran:2
Pre1999 - 1st:0 2nd:0 3rd:0 Ran:11
Win Prizemoney £0 *Total Prizemoney* £449
1999 Turf 0-1: (12f) (frm) 1999 AW 0-1: (12f) (Equi)
Moderate gelding, effective 13f, acts on gd. Inconsistent.
**M C Pipe [1-15] Mrs Alison Farrant (from M L W Bell [0-7] Jun 1997).*

KEEN HANDS BHB 64f68a **RR 42f 68a** 4924[6]
3 ch g Keen 11.1f **(58)** - Broken Vow(IRE) (Local Suitor (USA)) 8.4f **(67)**
Form - 068221582111068036
Record 1999 - 1st:4 2nd:2 3rd:1 Ran:14
Pre1999 - 1st:0 2nd:1 3rd:0 Ran:5
Win Prizemoney £12,811 *Total Prizemoney* £14,860
Wins * **1999** *Apr Southw (STD) H 6f 68 72* <
* **1999** *Mar Southw (STD) S 5f 71*
* **1999** *Mar Southw (STD) S 7f 61*
* **1999** *Jan Wolver (STD) S 5f 55*
1999 Turf 0-1: (6f) (frm) 1999 AW 4-13: (5f 2-3, 6f 1-7, 7f 1-3) (Equi, Fibr 4-12)
Average gelding, effective 5 to 6f, best at 6f, - acts on AW, best on Fibr, mostly wears blinkers (extremely effectively). AW high 72 - 1st of 16 giving 1lb to Carrie Pooter (26 Apr Southwell RF 0855) - also 1st of 12 giving 5lb to Thornaby Girl (22 Mar Southwell RF 0461). Inconsistent. Apparently resents being hit with the whip, but was very successful on Fibresand early in the year, winning at trips ranging from five to seven furlongs.
**Mrs N Macauley [4-19] Andy Peake.*

KEEP IKIS BHB 40f **RR 39f** 4932[3]
5 ch m Anshan 8.2f **(63)** -Santee Sioux (Dancing Brave (USA)) 8.4f **(76)**
Form - 66888023
Record 1999 - 1st:0 2nd:1 3rd:1 Ran:8
Win Prizemoney £0 *Total Prizemoney* £1,363
1999 Turf 0-8: (12f 2, 14f 2, 16f 3, 18f) (gd 3, g-f 2, frm 2, hrd)
Very moderate filly. Turf high 60.
**Mrs M Reveley [0-1] T McGoran (from S Gollings [0-11] Spt 1999).*

KEEPSAKE (IRE) BHB 30f **RR 25f** 4287[12]
5 b m Distinctly North (USA) 7.4f **(63)** - Souveniers (Relko) 9.9f **(59)**
Form - 73224400
Record 1999 - 1st:0 2nd:2 3rd:1 Ran:8
Pre1999 - 1st:1 2nd:2 3rd:2 Ran:30
Win Prizemoney £3,073 *Total Prizemoney* £8,946
Wins * 1997 Aug Salisb (G-F) H 12f 49 54 <
1999 Turf 0-3: (12f, 14f, 16f) (g-f 2, frm) 1999 AW 0-5: (12f, 13f, 16f 3) (Equi 4, Fibr)
Very moderate filly, effective 13f, acts on frm, has worn blinkers (very effectively). Turf high 25 (began Aug). AW high 30.
**M D I Usher [1-38] B Duke.*

KEEP TAPPING (IRE) **RR 80f** 3966[13]
2 b c Mac's Imp (USA) 5.6f **(54)** - Mystery Bid (Auction Ring (USA)) 8.6f **(65)**
Form - 54281030800
Record 1999 - 1st:1 2nd:1 3rd:1 Ran:11
Win Prizemoney £3,403 *Total Prizemoney* £6,525
Wins * **1999** Jun Sandow (GD) 5f 80 <
1999 Turf 1-11: (5f 1-7, 6f 3, 7f) (gd 2, g-f 5, frm 1-4)
Decent colt, effective 5f, acts on gd to frm, has worn blinkers. Turf high 80 - 1st of 7 from Kareeb (11 Jun Sandown RF 1919). He won an ordinary maiden at Sandown in June, but has had his limitations exposed in useful company.
**A P Jarvis [1-11] Ms Julie Greenacre.*

KEE RING BHB 58f **RR 53f** 3917[5]
3 ch c Keen 11.1f **(58)** - Rose And The Ring (Welsh Pageant) 10f **(65)**
Form - 6885035
Record 1999 - 1st:0 2nd:0 3rd:1 Ran:7
Pre1999 - 1st:0 2nd:1 3rd:0 Ran:2
Win Prizemoney £0 *Total Prizemoney* £1,377
1999 Turf 0-7: (6f 3, 7f 2, 8f 2) (gd, g-f 4, frm 2)
Leggy, fair colt, effective 6f, acts on frm. Turf high 64. Consistent.
**P R Chamings [0-9] Mrs J E L Wright.*

KELD (IRE) BHB 100f **RR 103f** 5131[5]
4 b f Lion Cavern (USA) 7.5f **(74)** - Society Ball (Law Society (USA)) 9.9f **(70)**
Form - 352445
Record 1999 - 1st:0 2nd:1 3rd:1 Ran:6
Pre1999 - 1st:2 2nd:0 3rd:0 Ran:3
Win Prizemoney £11,012 *Total Prizemoney* £21,897
Wins * 1998 Oct Newmar (GD) 8f 89 <
* 1998 Jly Sandow (G-F) 8.1f 89 <
1999 Turf 0-6: (8f, 9f, 10f 4) (gd 2, g-f 2, frm 2)
Leggy, very useful filly, effective 10f, acts on gd to frm. Turf high 103 - 2nd of 8 giving 10lb to Ela Athena (23 Jly Chepstow 10f frm RF 3055). Consistent. Given an unorthodox ride when unplaced over an extended seven furlongs at Lingfield in May (her performance was the subject of protracted enquiry), she went on to show useful form over a mile and a quarter. Possibly best when ridden close to the pace, she is capable of winning a Listed event.
**J R Fanshawe [2-9] C I T Racing Ltd.*

KELLING HALL **RR 48f** 5138[16]
2 b c Distant Relative 7f **(69)** - Naulakha **(55f)** (Bustino) 10.4f **(64)**
Form - 00
Record 1999 - 1st:0 2nd:0 3rd:0 Ran:2
1999 Turf 0-2: (8f 2) (gd 2)
Currently moderate colt. Turf high 48 (began Oct).
**D J S ffrenchDavis [0-2] Miss Henrietta Senn.*

KELSO MAGIC (USA) BHB 98f **RR 91f** 5036[6]
2 ch f Distant View (USA) - Bowl of Honey (USA) (Lyphard (USA)) 9.9f **(72)**
Form - 2514210546

Record 1999 - 1st:2 2nd:2 3rd:0 Ran:10
Win Prizemoney £6,831 *Total Prizemoney* £11,389
Wins * 1999 Spt Bright (G-F) H 5.3f 79 89 <
*** 1999** Jun Salisb (G-F) 5f 89 <
1999 Turf 2-10: (5f 2-7, 6f 2, 7f) (g-s, gd 3, g-f 1-2, frm 1-4)
Useful filly, effective 5f, acts on gd to frm. Turf high 91 - 4th of 13 getting 5lb from Kier Park (9 Oct Ascot 5f gd RF 4793) - also 1st of 11 from Enaaq (23 Jun Salisbury RF 2245). Has shaped as if needing further than five furlongs on several occasions, but fails when put over the longer trip. Twice a winner over five furlongs on fastish ground at Salisbury and Brighton, after running poorly over six at Doncaster behind Out Of Africa, she showed her true ability with good placed efforts in competitive juvenile events at Newmarket and Ascot back over the minimum on much softer ground. The Ascot race was a Group Three, and she is deserving of a nice prize given the quality of that effort.
**B J Meehan [2-10] F C T Wilson.*

KELTECH GOLD (IRE) RR 66f 5215[8]

2 b c Petorius 8f **(66)** - Creggan Vale Lass (Simply Great (FR)) 8.2f **(65)**
Form - 58
Record 1999 - 1st:0 2nd:0 3rd:0 Ran:2
1999 Turf 0-2: (8f 2) (g-s, gd)
Currently average colt. Turf high 66 (began Oct).
**B Palling [0-2] D Brennan.*

KELTIC BARD BHB 77f85a RR 69f 85a 4899[10]

2 b c Emperor Jones (USA) - Broughton Singer (IRE) **(49f)** (Common Grounds)
Form - 2210
Record 1999 - 1st:1 2nd:2 3rd:0 Ran:4
Win Prizemoney £2,722 *Total Prizemoney* £4,891
Wins * 1999 *Spt Wolver (STD) 8.5f 89* <
1999 Turf 0-3: (7f, 8f 2) (gd, g-f, frm) 1999 AW 1-1: (8f 1-1) (Fibr 1-1)
Useful colt. Turf high 69 (began Jly). (1st run) - 1st of 8 getting 10lb from Water Hunter (4 Spt Wolverhampton RF 4152). In the frame in turf maidens before getting off the mark in a novice event over an extended mile on the Wolverhampton Fibresand in September. He does not have much in the way of a turn of foot, and looks a real stayer in the making.
**S P C Woods [1-4] G A Roberts.*

KENNET BHB 69f67a RR 71f 67a 5217[8]

4 b g Kylian (USA) 8.1f **(66)** - Marwell Mitzi **(29f)** (Interrex (CAN))
Form - 1037813346318
Record 1999 - 1st:3 2nd:0 3rd:4 Ran:13
Pre1999 - 1st:0 2nd:7 3rd:1 Ran:19
Win Prizemoney £9,967 *Total Prizemoney* £21,744
Wins * 1999 Oct Bright (G-S) 11.9f 71
*** 1999** May Windso (GD) 10f 72
*** 1999** *Feb Lingfi (STD) 10f 73* <
1999 Turf 2-11: (8f 2, 10f 1-7, 11f, 12f 1-1) (sft, g-s, gd 1-3, g-f 1-4, frm 2) 1999 AW 1-2: (10f 1-2) (Equi 1-2)
Neat, above-average gelding, effective 6 to 12f, best at 8f, acts on gd to frm - acts on Equi, prefers tight tracks, excels at Warwick and Sandown, does well at Windsor. Turf high 72 - 1st of 10 from Northern Sun (10 May Windsor RF 1137) - also 1st of 4 giving 8lb to Royal Patron (29 Oct Brighton RF 5125). AW high 73 (1st run) - 1st of 8 from Baajil (4 Feb Lingfield RF 0223).
**P D Cundell [3-32] Miss M C Fraser.*

KENSINGTON PRINCE RR 18f 3745[13]

2 ch g Prince Sabo 6.6f **(64)** - Future Options **(56f)** (Lomond (USA)) 8.8f **(65)**
Form - 0000
Record 1999 - 1st:0 2nd:0 3rd:0 Ran:4
1999 Turf 0-3: (5f 2, 6f) (g-f 2, frm) 1999 AW 0-1: (6f) (Fibr)
Poor gelding, has worn blinkers. Turf high 18 (began Jly).
**J Berry [0-4] Miss Lilo Blum.*

KENT BHB 56a RR 46f 4791[7]

4 b g Kylian (USA) 8.1f **(66)** - Precious Caroline (IRE) **(26a)** (The Noble Player (USA)) 6.5f **(67)**
Form - 7308007
Record 1999 - 1st:0 2nd:0 3rd:1 Ran:7
Win Prizemoney £0 *Total Prizemoney* £481
1999 Turf 0-5: (8f 2, 10f, 12f 2) (sft, gd 2, g-f, frm) 1999 AW 0-2: (8f, 12f) (Fibr 2)
Fair gelding, has worn blinkers. Turf high 58. AW high 50.
**P D Cundell [0-7] P D Cundell.*

KENTISH LAD (IRE) RR 50f 1768[4]

3 ch c Caerleon (USA) 10.9f **(79)** - Jaljuli (Jalmood (USA)) 10.1f **(52)**
Form - 4
Record 1999 - 1st:0 2nd:0 3rd:0 Ran:1
Win Prizemoney £0 *Total Prizemoney* £270
1999 Turf 0-1: (8f) (gd)
Scopey, currently fair colt. **Sir Michael Stoute [0-1] P S Partnership.*

KENTUCKY BULLET (USA) BHB 42f60a RR 33f 60a 5026[7]

3 b g Housebuster (USA) 7f **(81)** - Exactly So (Caro)
Form - 65151060000660007
Record 1999 - 1st:2 2nd:0 3rd:0 Ran:17
Win Prizemoney £7,347 *Total Prizemoney* £7,347
Wins * 1999 Mar Doncas (G-S) H 7f 65 71 <
*** 1999** *Feb Southw (STD) 7f 69*
1999 Turf 1-11: (6f 3, 7f 1-5, 8f 3) (gd 1-5, g-f, frm 5) 1999 AW 1-6: (7f 1-3, 8f 2, 10f) (Equi 3, Fibr 1-3)
Neat, average gelding, effective 7f, acts on gd - acts on Fibr. Turf high 71 (1st run) - 1st of 14 getting 3lb from Top Star (27 Mar Doncaster RF 0488). AW high 69 - 1st of 12 from Heathyards Jake (12 Feb Southwell RF 0281). Did not race at two, but got off the mark by winning on the Southwell Fibresand in February. He transferred his ability on to turf by winning on easy at the Doncaster Lincoln meeting, but has been well beaten on faster ground since. **M Johnston [2-17] Tony Farmer And Partners.*

KEOS (USA) RR 118f 5014a[2]

5 dk h Riverman (USA) 9.7f **(78)** - Konafa (USA) (Damascus (USA)) 8.9f **(71)**
Form - 3816132
1999 Turf 2-7: (5f, 6f 2-3, 7f 3) (hvy, sft, gd 2-3, g-f)
High-class colt, effective 5 to 8f, acts on gd, has worn blinkers, excels at Longchamp and does well at Saint-Cloud. Turf high 118 - 2nd giving 4lb to Field of Hope (17 Oct Longchamp 7f RF 5014a) - also 1st of 8 from Gorse (1 Spt Baden-Baden RF 4243a). Consistent. Probably at his best over six furlongs on good ground, he enjoyed another profitable campaign and is a thoroughly likeable horse. Top-class sprinters are hard to find and he should do well if kept in training as a six-year-old.
**J E Hammond in FR [4-16].*

KEPHREN (USA) BHB 28f40a RR 14?f 40a 1941[P]

10 ch g Kenmare (FR) 9.6f **(76)** - Marie de Russy (FR) (Sassafras (FR)) 9.6f **(69)**
Form - 800P
Record 1999 - 1st:0 2nd:0 3rd:0 Ran:3
Pre1999 - 1st:2 2nd:2 3rd:2 Ran:11
Win Prizemoney £3,938 *Total Prizemoney* £5,696
Wins 1997 May Wexfor (GD) H 16f 44 53 <
1997 May Downpa (GD) H 13f 37 48+
1999 Turf 0-3: (14f, 16f, 17f) (gd 2, g-f)
Poor gelding, had worn blinkers. Turf high 14. Becoming disappointing. (DEAD)
**P Burgoyne [0-5] Philip Saunders (from P J Flynn in IRE [2-9] May 1998).*

KERALBA (USA) RR 20tf 698[12]

3 b f Sheikh Albadou 9.2f **(75)** -Sookera (USA)(Roberto (USA)) 10f **(76)**
Form - 0
Record 1999 - 1st:0 2nd:0 3rd:0 Ran:1
1999 Turf 0-1: (8f) (gd)
Light-framed, currently little account filly. **B W Hills [0-1] K Abdulla.*

KERALIA (IRE) BHB 72f RR 78df 4789[5]

3 b f Doyoun 10.7f **(69)** - Keraka (USA) (Storm Bird (CAN)) 10.3f **(74)**
Form - 22375
Record 1999 - 1st:0 2nd:2 3rd:1 Ran:5
Pre1999 - 1st:0 2nd:0 3rd:0 Ran:2
Win Prizemoney £0 *Total Prizemoney* £2,922
1999 Turf 0-5: (8f 2, 9f 3) (g-s, g-f 3, frm)
Leggy, above-average filly, effective 8 to 9f, acts on g-f, prefers left handed tracks, prefers tight tracks. Turf high 78 - 3rd of 7 getting 1lb from Calldat Seventeen (13 Aug Epsom 9f g-f RF 3605). She is still a maiden, but has plenty of ability and has not had much luck

in some of her races. *Sir Michael Stoute [0-7] H H Aga Khan.*

KERRIDGE CHAPEL (IRE) BHB 49f40a **RR 45f 40a** 4926[12]
2 b f College Chapel - Crimson Ring (Persian Bold) 9.3f **(66)**
Form - 80688570
Record 1999 - 1st:0 2nd:0 3rd:0 Ran:8
1999 Turf 0-5: (5f 4, 6f) (gd 3, frm 2) 1999 AW 0-3: (5f 2, 8f) (Fibr 3)
Moderate filly, has worn blinkers. Turf high 45. AW high 32. Inconsistent. *A Senior [0-8] Kerridge Racing Partnership.*

KERRY RR 39f 1261[13]
2 b c Magic Ring (IRE) 6.5f **(64)** - Sideloader Special (Song) 7.2f **(61)**
Form - 0
Record 1999 - 1st:0 2nd:0 3rd:0 Ran:1
1999 Turf 0-1: (6f) (gd)
Currently very moderate colt. *M W Easterby [0-1] I Bray.*

KESTON POND (IRE) BHB 38f66a **RR 41?f 66a** 2847[5]
9 b g Taufan (USA) 8.3f **(65)** - Maria Renata (Jaazeiro (USA)) 9.2f **(54)**
Form - 5
Record 1999 - 1st:0 2nd:0 3rd:0 Ran:1
Pre1999 - 1st:5 2nd:8 3rd:0 Ran:43
Win Prizemoney £29,699 *Total Prizemoney* £40,821
Wins 1996 Jly York (GD) H 7f 70 74
1995 Spt Ayr (GD) H 6f 65 71
1995 Spt Leices (GD) H 7f 65 71
1995 Jun Yarmou (FRM) H 7f 63 78 <
1999 Turf 0-1: (7f) (g-f)
Moderate gelding, has worn blinkers.
R A Fahey [0-1] Mrs Andrea Mallinson (from Mrs V A Aconley [1-23] Aug 1997).

KESTRAL BHB 44f41a **RR 43f 41a** 5191[12]
3 ch g Ardkinglass 5f **(64)** - Shiny Kay (Star Appeal) 9.6f **(65)**
Form - 74500440070
Record 1999 - 1st:0 2nd:0 3rd:0 Ran:11
Pre1999 - 1st:0 2nd:0 3rd:0 Ran:4
1999 Turf 0-10: (6f 2, 7f 5, 8f 3) (gd 3, g-f 4, frm 3) 1999 AW 0-1: (6f) (Fibr)
Scopey, moderate gelding. Turf high 50.
T J Etherington [0-15] The R and R Partnership.

KEWARRA BHB 72f **RR 65f** 3828[14]
5 b g Distant Relative 7f **(69)** - Shalati (FR) (High Line) 10.3f **(70)**
Form - 30050
Record 1999 - 1st:0 2nd:0 3rd:1 Ran:5
Pre1999 - 1st:4 2nd:2 3rd:5 Ran:26
Win Prizemoney £26,186 *Total Prizemoney* £35,526
Wins * 1998 Apr Epsom (SFT) H 10.1f 85 90 <
* 1997 Oct Newmar (G-F) H 10f 78 84
* 1997 Spt Chepst (GD) H 10.2f 74 78
* 1997 Aug Chepst (G-F) H 10.2f 70 75
1999 Turf 0-5: (10f 4, 12f) (g-s, gd, g-f, frm 2)
Average gelding, effective 10 to 12f, best at 10f, acts on sft to frm, best on g-f, has worn blinkers, likes left handed tracks, prefers tight tracks. Turf high 83. *B R Millman [4-31] G Palmer.*

KEW GARDENS BHB 87f **RR 81f** 5139[6]
2 ch c Arazi (USA) 9.2f **(74)** - Hatton Gardens (Auction Ring (USA)) 8.6f **(65)**
Form - 0416
Record 1999 - 1st:1 2nd:0 3rd:0 Ran:4
Win Prizemoney £3,857 *Total Prizemoney* £4,250
Wins * **1999** Oct Pontef (SFT) 10f 80 <
1999 Turf 1-4: (7f, 8f, 10f 1-2) (g-s, gd 1-2, frm)
Decent colt. Turf high 81 (began Aug) - also 1st of 7 from Hint of Magic (4 Oct Pontefract RF 4715). Comfortable winner at Pontefract over ten furlongs, but seemed not to stay the trip in a better race at Newmarket. *Mrs A J Perrett [1-4] Sir Eric Parker.*

KEY BHB 58f **RR 59f** 5128[15]
3 b f Midyan (USA) 9.9f **(64)** - Diamond Park (IRE) **(60f)** (Alzao (USA)) 7.1f **(68)**
Form - 52454500
Record 1999 - 1st:0 2nd:1 3rd:0 Ran:8
Pre1999 - 1st:1 2nd:1 3rd:1 Ran:9
Win Prizemoney £3,371 *Total Prizemoney* £7,851
Wins 1998 Aug Bright (FRM) H 5.3f 70 78 <
1999 Turf 0-8: (5f, 6f 3, 7f 4) (gd 2, g-f 2, frm 4)
Fair filly, effective 5f, acts on g-f to frm, likes left handed tracks, likes tight tracks. Turf high 65.
C E Brittain [0-2] Wyck Hall Stud (from R Hannon [1-15] Jly 1999).

KEY ACADEMY BHB 95f **RR 94f** 4510a[2]
4 b f Royal Academy (USA) 7.8f **(77)** - Santa Linda (USA) (Sir Ivor) 10.2f **(70)**
Form - 22
Record 1999 - 1st:0 2nd:2 3rd:0 Ran:2
Pre1999 - 1st:1 2nd:2 3rd:1 Ran:4
Win Prizemoney £3,550 *Total Prizemoney* £14,042
Wins * 1998 Spt Bath (GD) 11.7f 70 <
1999 Turf 0-2: (12f 2) (gd 2)
Scopey, useful filly, effective 12f, acts on gd. Turf high 94 (began Aug) - 2nd of 13 giving 8lb to Farfala (13 Spt Chantilly 12f gd RF 4510a). *C A Horgan [1-6].*

KEY TO THE CITY (IRE) BHB 55f59a **RR 63f 59a** 1118[2]
5 b g Shalford (IRE) 7.8f **(63)** - Green Wings (General Assembly (USA)) 10f **(68)**
Form - 2742102
Record 1999 - 1st:1 2nd:3 3rd:0 Ran:7
Pre1999 - 1st:1 2nd:3 3rd:1 Ran:17
Win Prizemoney £4,418 *Total Prizemoney* £10,349
Wins * **1999** Mar Hamilt (HVY) C 9.2f 50
1997 Spt Dundal (SFT) H 9f 63 76 <
1999 Turf 1-2: (9f 1-2) (hvy 1-1, g-f) 1999 AW 0-5: (8f, 9f, 10f, 12f 2) (Equi 3, Fibr 2)
Average gelding, has broken blood-vessels, effective 7f, acts on gd, has worn blinkers. Turf high 50 (1st run). AW high 61.
P Eccles [1-8] West Lancs Antiques Export Racing (from D K Weld in IRE [1-17] Oct 1998).

KEZ BHB 68f **RR 63f** 5022[10]
3 b g Polar Falcon (USA) 9f **(74)** - Briggsmaid (Elegant Air) 13.2f **(61)**
Form - 733321000
Record 1999 - 1st:1 2nd:1 3rd:3 Ran:9
Win Prizemoney £2,684 *Total Prizemoney* £5,622
Wins * **1999** Aug Bright (FRM) 11.9f 63+ <
1999 Turf 1-9: (8f 3, 10f 5, 12f 1-1) (gd 4, g-f 2, frm 1-3)
Lengthy, average gelding, effective 10f, acts on frm. Turf high 79 - 2nd of 6 to Anschluss (12 Jly Newcastle 10f frm RF 2757). Becoming disappointing. *S P C Woods [1-9] Dennis Yardy.*

KHABAR BHB 51f **RR 55f** 4983[15]
6 b g Forzando 7.2f **(63)** - Ella Mon Amour (Ela-Mana-Mou) 10.1f **(70)**
Form - 843632238200
Record 1999 - 1st:0 2nd:3 3rd:3 Ran:12
Pre1999 - 1st:0 2nd:1 3rd:0 Ran:13
Win Prizemoney £0 *Total Prizemoney* £6,878
1999 Turf 0-12: (7f, 8f 7, 9f 2, 10f 2) (g-s, gd 3, g-f 2, frm 6)
Fair gelding, has broken blood-vessels, effective 8 to 9f, best at 8f, acts on g-s to frm, best on frm, prefers tight tracks. Turf high 55 - 2nd of 16 getting 18lb from Prospector's Cove (15 Spt Yarmouth 8f g-s RF 4340). Inconsistent.
R Bastiman [0-21] Mrs P Bastiman (from D Morley [0-4] Spt 1995).

KHALED (IRE) BHB 75a **RR 75df** 479[13]
4 b c Petorius 8f **(66)**-Felin Special (Lyphard's Special (USA)) 10.3f **(72)**
Form - 50
Record 1999 - 1st:0 2nd:0 3rd:0 Ran:2
Pre1999 - 1st:1 2nd:0 3rd:1 Ran:3
Win Prizemoney £3,980 *Total Prizemoney* £4,850
Wins * 1998 Aug Warwic (G-F) 8f 75 <
1999 Turf 0-1: (8f) (g-s) 1999 AW 0-1: (9f) (Fibr)
Workmanlike, above-average colt. *K Mahdi [1-5] Hamad Al-Mutawa.*

KHALIK (IRE) BHB 64f **RR 63df** 5032[21]
5 br g Lear Fan (USA) 10.4f **(80)** - Silver Dollar (Shirley Heights) 10.3f **(74)**
Form - 118020
Record 1999 - 1st:2 2nd:1 3rd:0 Ran:6
Pre1999 - 1st:0 2nd:1 3rd:2 Ran:11
Win Prizemoney £5,541 *Total Prizemoney* £8,952
Wins * **1999** Aug Lingfi (GD) H 6f 58 63+ <

* **1999** Aug Salisb (SFT) H 6f 58 58
1999 Turf 2-6: (5f 3, 6f 2-3) (g-s 3, g-f 2-3)
Average gelding, effective 6f, acts on g-f, has worn blinkers. Turf high 63 (began Aug). Inconsistent. He had been off the track for 11 months before winning handicaps at Salisbury and Lingfield within the space of three days in August. Mixed form subsequently.
**Miss Gay Kelleway [2-6] A P Griffin (from Mrs L Stubbs [0-8] Spt 1998).*

KHALIL BHB 47f **RR 64f** 4224[4]
2 b g Tragic Role (USA) 9.4f **(63)** - T O O Mamma's (IRE) **(36f 50a)** (Classic Secret (USA))
Form - 37064
Record 1999 - 1st:0 2nd:0 3rd:1 Ran:5
Win Prizemoney £0 *Total Prizemoney* £366
1999 Turf 0-4: (6f 2, 7f 2) (gd 2, g-f 2) 1999 AW 0-1: (6f) (Fibr)
Average gelding. Turf high 64 (1st run) - 3rd of 6 getting 1lb from Islay Mist (21 Jun Musselburgh 7f g-f RF 2165).
**J Berry [0-5] J K Brown.*

KHASAYL (IRE) BHB 100f **RR 99f** 4690[1]
2 b f Lycius (USA) 8.8f **(71)** - Maraatib (IRE) (Green Desert (USA)) 8.6f **(78)**
Form - 2114211
Record 1999 - 1st:4 2nd:2 3rd:0 Ran:7
Win Prizemoney £118,284 *Total Prizemoney* £125,070
Wins * **1999** Oct Redcar (GD) 6f 99 <
* **1999** Spt Ayr (G-S) L 5f 99 <
* **1999** Jly Doncas (G-F) 6f 77+
* **1999** Jun Bath (GD) 5.1f 73+
1999 Turf 4-7: (5f 2-3, 6f 2-3, 7f) (g-s 1-1, g-f 2-5, frm 1-1)
Very useful filly, effective 5 to 6f, best at 6f, acts on g-s to g-f, best on g-f. Turf high 99 - 1st of 26 giving 1lb to Heathyardsblessing (2 Oct Redcar RF 4690) - also 1st of 10 getting 5lb from Tara's Girl (16 Spt Ayr RF 4343). She provided her retiring trainer with a final big race win in the NTL Two-Year-Old Trophy at Redcar in October. Impressive in a Listed event on her previous start, she is effective over five or six furlongs and enjoys easy ground. Likely to improve again, she should make a useful sprinter in 2000.
**P T Walwyn [4-7] Hamdan Al Maktoum.*

KHATTAFF (IRE) BHB 30f **RR 32f** 4985[6]
4 ch g Hamas (IRE) 8f **(72)** - Coven (Sassafras (FR)) 9.6f **(69)**
Form - 0076
Record 1999 - 1st:0 2nd:0 3rd:0 Ran:4
Pre1999 - 1st:0 2nd:0 3rd:0 Ran:11
Win Prizemoney £0 *Total Prizemoney* £213
1999 Turf 0-3: (8f 3) (gd 2, g-f) 1999 AW 0-1: (8f) (Fibr)
Very moderate gelding, has worn blinkers. Turf high 32. Inconsistent.
**M Brittain [0-10] Mel Brittain (from Major W R Hern [0-5] Spt 1997).*

KHIBRAH (IRE) BHB 97f **RR 97f** 4871[1]
3 br f Lahib (USA) 8f **(69)** - Sabayik (IRE) **(84f)** (Unfuwain (USA))
Form - 00214111141
Record 1999 - 1st:6 2nd:1 3rd:0 Ran:11
Pre1999 - 1st:0 2nd:0 3rd:2 Ran:2
Win Prizemoney £39,985 *Total Prizemoney* £42,640
Wins * **1999** Oct Newmar (GD) L 10f 97 <
* **1999** Spt Sandow (GD) H 8.1f 85 90
* **1999** Spt Epsom (GD) H 8.5f 79 85+
* **1999** Jly Bright (FRM) H 8f 67 79
* **1999** Jly Bright (FRM) H 8f 67 72
* **1999** Jun Bright (G-F) H 8f 63 65
1999 Turf 6-11: (6f, 7f, 8f 4-6, 9f 1-1, 10f 1-2) (sft, gd 2-4, g-f 1-2, frm 3-4)
Scopey, very useful filly, effective 8 to 10f, best at 10f, acts on gd, prefers tight tracks, excels at Newmarket and Brighton. Turf high 97 - 1st of 13 from Horatia (14 Oct Newmarket RF 4871) - also 1st of 11 giving 5lb to Madam Alison (15 Spt Sandown RF 4329). Improving. She made remarkable progress, winning six times - only once by more than half a length - and improving some 29lbs according to official ratings. Best around a mile, she has a sharp turn-of-foot and is very tough.
**E A L Dunlop [6-13] Hamdan Al Maktoum.*

KHUCHN (IRE) BHB 62f **RR 63?f** 3840[11]
3 b c Unfuwain (USA) 11.4f **(74)** - Stay Sharpe (USA) (Sharpen Up) 8.3f **(67)**
Form - 50010
Record 1999 - 1st:1 2nd:0 3rd:0 Ran:5
Win Prizemoney £2,652 *Total Prizemoney* £2,652
Wins * **1999** Jly Nottin (GD) 10f 63 <
1999 Turf 1-5: (8f, 10f 1-2, 12f 2) (g-f 1-3, frm 2)
Scopey, average colt. Turf high 67 - also 1st of 7 giving 3lb to Street Walker (3 Jly Nottingham RF 2541).
**R W Armstrong [1-5] Hamdan Al Maktoum.*

KIBA (IRE) **RR 60f** 583[4]
3 b f Tirol 8.1f **(64)** - Ornette (IRE) (Bluebird (USA)) 7.5f **(69)**
Form - 4
Record 1999 - 1st:0 2nd:0 3rd:0 Ran:1
Win Prizemoney £0 *Total Prizemoney* £256
1999 Turf 0-1: (8f) (gd)
Angular, currently average filly. **J J O'Neill [0-1] Mrs A R Thompson.*

KI CHI SAGA (USA) BHB 25f43a **RR 8f 43a** 5057[9]
7 ch g Miswaki (USA) 8.1f **(81)** - Cedilla (USA) (Caro)
Form - 35236336503000180
Record 1999 - 1st:1 2nd:1 3rd:4 Ran:16
Pre1999 - 1st:4 2nd:4 3rd:3 Ran:40
Win Prizemoney £9,550 *Total Prizemoney* £15,664
Wins * **1999** *Aug Lingfi (STD) S 12f 54*
1998 *Apr Lingfi (STD) S 10f 64* <
1998 *Mar Lingfi (STD) H 8f 52 57*
1998 *Feb Lingfi (SLW) S 8f 51*
1997 *Mar Lingfi (STD) 8f 61*
1999 Turf 0-6: (10f, 11f 2, 12f 3) (g-s, gd, frm 4) 1999 AW 1-10: (8f, 9f 2, 10f 4, 12f 1-3) (Equi 1-8, Fibr 2)
Little account gelding, effective 10f, - acts on Equi, often wears blinkers, favours left handed tracks. Turf high 45. AW high 60.
**P Burgoyne [1-17] Philip Saunders (from G L Moore [3-19] Oct 1998).*

KICK ON KATOUCHE (IRE) BHB 66f **RR 49f** 1602[5]
2 ch g Forest Wind (USA) - Lapland Lights (USA) (Northern Prospect (USA)) 9.5f **(71)**
Form - 435
Record 1999 - 1st:0 2nd:0 3rd:1 Ran:3
Win Prizemoney £0 *Total Prizemoney* £300
1999 Turf 0-2: (5f 2) (sft, g-f) 1999 AW 0-1: (5f) (Fibr)
Currently average gelding. Turf high 68.
**K R Burke [0-3] Astaire & Partners (Holdings) Ltd.*

KIDNAPPED BHB 49f **RR 66f** 5193[7]
3 b g Emarati (USA) 6.6f **(63)** - Haddon Anna (Dragonara Palace (USA)) 6.1f **(55)**
Form - 007
Record 1999 - 1st:0 2nd:0 3rd:0 Ran:3
Pre1999 - 1st:0 2nd:0 3rd:0 Ran:2
1999 Turf 0-3: (6f 2, 8f) (gd, g-f, frm)
Unfurnished, average gelding. Turf high 66.
**A J McNae [0-1] L R Gotch (from Mrs A L M King [0-4] Jun 1999).*

KIDOLOGY (IRE) BHB 41f **RR 22f** 5165[10]
3 b g Petardia 8.2f **(58)** - Loveville (USA) (Assert) 10.6f **(85)**
Form - 000
Record 1999 - 1st:0 2nd:0 3rd:0 Ran:3
1999 Turf 0-3: (8f 2, 12f) (g-s, gd, frm)
Leggy, currently little account gelding. Turf high 22 (began Spt).
**W Storey [0-3] Foster Watson.*

KID ORY BHB 24f37a **RR 7f 37a** 3459[20]
8 ch g Rich Charlie 5.9f **(50)** - Woomargama (Creetown) 6.9f **(50)**
Form - 8600
Record 1999 - 1st:0 2nd:0 3rd:0 Ran:2
Pre1999 - 1st:3 2nd:5 3rd:10 Ran:65
Win Prizemoney £9,461 *Total Prizemoney* £20,679
Wins * 1998 *Jan Southw (STD) H 6f 37 34*
1995 Spt Redcar (GD) H 7f 65 70 <
1999 Turf 0-2: (6f 2) (frm 2)
Little account gelding, effective 6f, - acts on Fibr, has worn blinkers, likes left handed tracks, likes tight tracks. Turf high 7 (began Jly).
**D W Chapman [1-29] David Chapman (from P Calver [2-38] Spt 1996).*

KID'Z'PLAY (IRE) BHB 54f **RR 53f** 4347[4]

3 b g Rudimentary (USA) 8.2f **(66)** - Saka Saka (Camden Town) 9.3f **(53)**

Form - 4001724

Record 1999 - 1st:1 2nd:1 3rd:0 Ran:7
Pre1999 - 1st:0 2nd:0 3rd:0 Ran:2

Win Prizemoney £2,892 *Total Prizemoney* £3,991

Wins * 1999 Aug Hamilt (G-F) H 8.3f 40 50 <

1999 Turf 1-7: (6f, 7f 2, 8f 1-2, 9f, 11f) (gd 2, g-f 1-3, frm 2)

Fair gelding, effective 11f, acts on gd, prefers tight tracks. Turf high 53 - 4th of 20 getting 10lb from Brandon Court (16 Spt Ayr 11f gd RF 4347). He is suited by forcing the pace and used those tactics to good effect when winning at Hamilton in August.

**J S Goldie [1-7] W M Johnstone (from M Johnston [0-2] Spt 1998).*

KIERANS BRIDGE (IRE) BHB 53f70a **RR 33f 70a** 4218[11]

4 ch f Arcane (USA) 11.6f **(66)** - Rhein Valley (IRE) (Kings Lake (USA)) 10.8f **(67)**

Form - 442800

Record 1999 - 1st:0 2nd:1 3rd:0 Ran:6
Pre1999 - 1st:2 2nd:1 3rd:1 Ran:11

Win Prizemoney £5,229 *Total Prizemoney* £7,673

Wins * 1998 *Mar Wolver (STD) H 12f 67 72* <
* 1998 *Mar Southw (STD) 12f 53+*

1999 Turf 0-4: (14f, 16f 3) (g-s, gd, g-f, frm) 1999 AW 0-2: (12f 2) (Fibr 2)

Above-average filly, effective 12 to 15f, best at 12f, - acts on Fibr, prefers left handed tracks, favours tight tracks. Turf high 61. AW high 64. Becoming disappointing. **A P Jarvis [2-17] G S Bray.*

KIER PARK (IRE) BHB 100f **RR 101f** 4793[1]

2 b c Foxhound (USA) - Merlannah (IRE) (Shy Groom (USA)) 10f **(66)**

Form - 4211

Record 1999 - 1st:2 2nd:1 3rd:0 Ran:4

Win Prizemoney £27,935 *Total Prizemoney* £30,975

Wins * 1999 Oct Ascot (G-S) G3 5f 101 <
*** 1999** Oct Lingfi (HVY) 5f 86+

1999 Turf 2-4: (5f 2-2, 6f 2) (g-s 1-1, gd 1-2, frm)

Very useful colt. Turf high 101 (began Aug) - 1st of 13 from The Tatling (9 Oct Ascot RF 4793). Improved steadily and got off the mark with a comfortable success in a Lingfield maiden in October. Stamped himself a smart juvenile when following up in the Cornwallis Stakes. **M A Jarvis [2-4] H R H Sultan Ahmad Shah.*

KIGEMA (IRE) BHB 59f **RR 65f** 2300[5]

2 ch f Case Law 6f **(64)** - Grace de Bois (Tap On Wood) 10.3f **(65)**

Form - 504415

Record 1999 - 1st:1 2nd:0 3rd:0 Ran:6

Win Prizemoney £1,882 *Total Prizemoney* £2,399

Wins * 1999 Jun Bright (G-F) S 6f 58 <

1999 Turf 1-5: (5f, 6f 1-4) (g-s, gd, g-f 1-2, frm) 1999 AW 0-1: (5f) (Equi)

Average filly, effective 6f, acts on g-f to frm. Turf high 65 - 5th of 12 to Parkside Prospect (25 Jun Newcastle 6f frm RF 2300) - also 1st of 11 from Baytown Melody (14 Jun Brighton RF 1971).

**C N Allen [1-6] Green Square Racing.*

KIKA BHB 9f23a **RR 17f 23a** 5057[10]

6 gr m Niniski (USA) 13.2f **(67)** - Goeswell (Roan Rocket) 7.8f **(57)**

Form - 0828457780070

Record 1999 - 1st:0 2nd:0 3rd:0 Ran:9
Pre1999 - 1st:2 2nd:2 3rd:2 Ran:27

Win Prizemoney £5,621 *Total Prizemoney* £7,907

Wins 1998 Apr Bright (GD) C 11.9f 44 <
1997 Jly Doncas (GD) S 12f 42

1999 Turf 0-5: (12f 5) (gd 2, g-f, frm 2) 1999 AW 0-4: (12f 3, 13f) (Equi 4)

Little account mare, effective 12 to 13f, best at 13f, acts on g-s - acts on Equi, has worn blinkers, likes left handed tracks. Turf high 17 (began Jly). AW high 25.

**J J Bridger [0-26] J J Bridger (from K R Burke [2-10] Apr 1998).*

KILBOWIE HILL BHB 46f56a **RR 40f 56a** 2650[7]

3 b f Never so Bold 7.1f **(62)** - Out of Hours (Lochnager) 6f **(59)**

Form - 0007

Record 1999 - 1st:0 2nd:0 3rd:0 Ran:4
Pre1999 - 1st:2 2nd:0 3rd:1 Ran:10

Win Prizemoney £4,821 *Total Prizemoney* £5,251

Wins 1998 *Jly Wolver (STD) H 6f 68* <
1998 Jly Leices (GD) S 5f 68 <

1999 Turf 0-3: (5f, 6f 2) (frm 3) 1999 AW 0-1: (6f) (Fibr)

Neat, above-average filly, effective 5 to 6f, acts on frm - acts on Fibr. Turf high 34.

**J L Eyre [0-4] The Flowerpot Men (from D McCain [2-10] Oct 1998).*

KILBRANNAN SOUND BHB 78f **RR 80f** 4686[15]

2 b f Makbul - Highland Rowena (Royben) 7.3f **(60)**

Form - 25723210

Record 1999 - 1st:1 2nd:3 3rd:1 Ran:8

Win Prizemoney £25,000 *Total Prizemoney* £28,482

Wins * 1999 Spt Doncas (G-F) 6f 77 <

1999 Turf 1-8: (5f 4, 6f 1-4) (gd 3, g-f 2, frm 1-3)

Decent filly, effective 5 to 6f, best at 5f, acts on gd to frm. Turf high 80 - also 1st of 22 getting 5lb from Zietzig (10 Spt Doncaster RF 4249). Consistent.

**B A McMahon [1-8] Michael Stokes.*

KILCREGGAN BHB 60f **RR 60f** 4904[10]

5 b g Landyap (USA) - Lehmans Lot (Oats) 8.9f **(46)**

Form - 65405364610

Record 1999 - 1st:1 2nd:0 3rd:1 Ran:11

Win Prizemoney £3,315 *Total Prizemoney* £4,387

Wins * 1999 Oct Redcar (GD) H 14.1f 58 60 <

1999 Turf 1-11: (8f, 9f, 10f 3, 11f, 12f 2, 14f 1-3) (gd, g-f 1-1, frm 9)

Average gelding, effective 10 to 14f, acts on g-f to frm, best on frm, favours left handed tracks. Turf high 64 - also 1st of 16 giving 15lb to Stolen Music (2 Oct Redcar RF 4693). Consistent.

**Mrs M Reveley [1-14] C Anderson.*

KILCULLEN LAD (IRE) BHB 70f68a **RR 69f 68a** 5110[9]

5 b g Fayruz 6.6f **(63)** - Royal Home (Royal Palace) 9f **(56)**

Form - 5400601052D060

Record 1999 - 1st:1 2nd:1 3rd:0 Ran:12
Pre1999 - 1st:6 2nd:6 3rd:0 Ran:34

Win Prizemoney £35,783 *Total Prizemoney* £45,628

Wins * 1999 Aug Bright (SFT) H 5.3f 65 74
1998 May Redcar (G-F) H 5f 75 81 <
1997 May Lingfi (G-F) H 6f 67 74
1996 *Dec Lingfi (STD) H 6f 70 75*
1996 *Nov Lingfi (STD) H 5f 61 77*
1996 Spt Redcar (FRM) H 5f 56 53
1996 Jun Lingfi (FRM) S 6f 48

1999 Turf 1-12: (5f 1-7, 6f 5) (g-s 1-1, gd 3, g-f 4, frm 4)

Average gelding, effective 5 to 6f, best at 5f, acts on g-s to frm, best on g-f, often wears blinkers (extremely effectively), likes left handed tracks. Turf high 74 - 1st of 11 giving 5lb to Poetry In Motion (18 Aug Brighton RF 3732). Consistent.

**R Ingram [1-14] George Tobitt (from K T Ivory [1-11] Oct 1998).*

KILDEE GEM BHB 42f **RR 53f** 4701[12]

3 b g Minshaanshu Amad (USA) 11.3f **(53)** - To The Point (Sharpen Up) 8.3f **(67)**

Form - 000

Record 1999 - 1st:0 2nd:0 3rd:0 Ran:3
Pre1999 - 1st:0 2nd:0 3rd:0 Ran:2

1999 Turf 0-2: (5f, 7f) (gd, g-f) 1999 AW 0-1: (6f) (Fibr)

Light-framed, fair gelding. Turf high 25.

**R G Frost [0-3] J F O'Donovan (from A P Jones [0-2] Oct 1998).*

KILKEE BAY (IRE) BHB 62f **RR 65f** 4532[10]

2 ch f Case Law 6f **(64)** - Persian Polly (Persian Bold) 9.3f **(66)**

Form - 06333480

Record 1999 - 1st:0 2nd:0 3rd:3 Ran:8

Win Prizemoney £0 *Total Prizemoney* £1,634

1999 Turf 0-8: (5f 4, 6f 3, 7f) (g-s, gd 2, g-f, frm 4)

Average filly, effective 5 to 6f, acts on gd to g-f. Turf high 65 - 3rd of 12 getting 10lb from Enaaq (30 Aug Chepstow 5f gd RF 4008).

**M R Channon [0-8] Mrs T Burns.*

KILLARNEY JAZZ BHB 55f63a **RR 49f 63a** 1131[4]

4 b c Alhijaz 7.7f **(57)** - Killarney Belle (USA) (Irish Castle (USA)) 11.2f **(75)**

Form - 45434344274

Record 1999 - 1st:0 2nd:1 3rd:2 Ran:10
Pre1999 - 1st:3 2nd:1 3rd:0 Ran:10

Win Prizemoney £6,278 *Total Prizemoney* £9,218
Wins 1998 *May Southw (STD) C* 8f 71+ <
1998 *Mar Southw (STD) C* 8f 69
1998 *Feb Southw (STD) H* 8f 59 62
1999 Turf 0-1: (8f) (gd) 1999 AW 0-9: (7f 2, 8f 6, 9f) (Fibr 9)
Scopey, average colt, effective 6 to 8f, best at 8f, - acts on Fibr, often wears blinkers, favours left handed tracks, favours tight tracks. AW high 61. Consistent.
**G C H Chung [0-5] G C H Chung (from N P Littmoden [1-8] Feb 1999).*

KILLEEN FOX (IRE) BHB 62f RR 67f 4705[5]
2 b g Foxhound (USA) - Charrua (Sharpo) 7.7f **(59)**
Form - 3446875
Record 1999 - 1st:0 2nd:0 3rd:1 Ran:7
Win Prizemoney £0 *Total Prizemoney* £535
1999 Turf 0-5: (5f 4, 6f) (g-f 4, frm) 1999 AW 0-2: (5f 2) (Fibr 2)
Average gelding, has worn blinkers. Turf high 67. AW high 53 (began Spt). **J A Glover [0-7] Sports Mania.*

KILLER INSTINCT BHB 108f RR 112df 2733[5]
3 b c Zafonic (USA) 9f **(83)** - Rappa Tap Tap (FR) (Tap On Wood) 10.3f **(65)**
Form - 21445
Record 1999 - 1st:1 2nd:1 3rd:0 Ran:5
Pre1999 - 1st:0 2nd:1 3rd:0 Ran:1
Win Prizemoney £4,678 *Total Prizemoney* £20,618
Wins * 1999 May Nottin (GD) 8.2f 92+ <
1999 Turf 1-5: (8f 1-4, 10f) (g-f 1-4, frm)
Well made, Group-class colt, effective 8f, acts on frm. Turf high 112. Responsible for filling more column inches than the Royal Family, he worked like a champion at home only to fail time and again on the track. Sent to America after disappointing in the John Smith's Cup at York, he is a one-paced galloper with a questionable attitude. **H R A Cecil [1-6] The Thoroughbred Corporation.*

Killer Instinct eventually moved to America

KILMEENA LAD BHB 72f79a RR 70df 79a 5033[18]
3 b g Minshaanshu Amad (USA) 11.3f **(53)** - Kilmeena Glen (Beveled (USA)) 9f **(59)**
Form - 8038001010
Record 1999 - 1st:2 2nd:0 3rd:1 Ran:10
Pre1999 - 1st:1 2nd:0 3rd:0 Ran:4
Win Prizemoney £10,960 *Total Prizemoney* £11,581
Wins * 1999 *Oct Lingfi (STD) H* 6f 72 75
*** 1999** Aug Newmar (G-F) H 6f 69 70
* 1998 Oct Newbur (HVY) 6f 80 <
1999 Turf 1-9: (5f, 6f 1-7, 7f) (g-s, gd 2, g-f 5, frm 1-1) 1999 AW 1-1: (6f 1-1) (Equi 1-1)
Workmanlike, above-average gelding, effective 6f, acts on sft to frm - acts on Equi. Turf high 75. (1st run) - 1st of 11 giving 17lb to Diamond Geezer (8 Oct Lingfield RF 4787). Inconsistent. He is extremely difficult to predict, and tends to pop up at big prices.
**E A Wheeler [3-14] Mrs J A Cleary.*

KILTING BHB 96f RR 94f 2477a[7]
3 ch f Nashwan (USA) 10.3f **(79)** - Balliasta (USA) (Lyphard (USA)) 9.9f **(72)**
Form - 307
Record 1999 - 1st:0 2nd:0 3rd:1 Ran:3
Pre1999 - 1st:1 2nd:0 3rd:0 Ran:1
Win Prizemoney £4,695 *Total Prizemoney* £6,993
Wins 1998 Oct Doncas (SFT) 7f 87++ <
1999 Turf 0-3: (10f, 12f 2) (gd 2, frm)
Scopey, useful filly. Turf high 94 (1st run) - 3rd of 9 to Alabaq (2 May Newmarket 10f frm RF 0978). Quickened away to win a Doncaster maiden on her only start at two, and wintered in Dubai. Ran an encouraging third in the Pretty Polly, but never got involved in the Oaks next time after pleasing in her preparation. Disappointing on her final start in France, looking as if 12 furlongs is too far. **S bin Suroor [0-3] (from B W Hills [1-1] Oct 1998).*

KIMBERLEY BHB 88f RR 63f 4954[14]
4 b g Shareef Dancer (USA) 10.1f **(67)** - Willowbank (Gay Fandango (USA)) 8.5f **(59)**
Form - 807880
Record 1999 - 1st:0 2nd:0 3rd:0 Ran:6
Pre1999 - 1st:2 2nd:1 3rd:0 Ran:9
Win Prizemoney £10,446 *Total Prizemoney* £12,606
Wins * 1998 Oct Redcar (HVY) H 10f 80 83 <
* 1998 Oct York (GD) 10.4f 82
1999 Turf 0-6: (10f 4, 11f, 12f) (gd 2, g-f 2, frm 2)
Average gelding, effective 10 to 12f, best at 10f, acts on g-s to frm, has worn blinkers, likes left handed tracks. Turf high 69. Becoming disappointing. **G Wragg [2-15] Mrs John Van Geest.*

KINAN (USA) BHB 85f RR 82f 1569[14]
3 b c Dixieland Band (USA) 10.1f **(80)** - Alsharta (USA) (Mr Prospector (USA)) 8.8f **(78)**
Form - 7050
Record 1999 - 1st:0 2nd:0 3rd:0 Ran:4
Pre1999 - 1st:1 2nd:1 3rd:0 Ran:4
Win Prizemoney £3,336 *Total Prizemoney* £4,304
Wins * 1998 Spt Nottin (GD) 6.1f 85 <
1999 Turf 0-4: (6f 2, 7f, 8f) (gd, g-f 2, frm)
Workmanlike, decent colt, effective 6f, acts on gd to frm. Turf high 82. Consistent. **R W Armstrong [1-8] Hamdan Al Maktoum.*

KIND EMPEROR BHB 76f73a RR 73f 73a 5134[10]
2 br c Emperor Jones (USA) - Kind Lady (Kind of Hush) 10.1f **(62)**
Form - 3222574270820
Record 1999 - 1st:0 2nd:5 3rd:1 Ran:13
Win Prizemoney £0 *Total Prizemoney* £8,017
1999 Turf 0-12: (5f 7, 6f 5) (gd 7, g-f 2, frm 2, hrd) 1999 AW 0-1: (6f) (Fibr)
Above-average colt, effective 5 to 6f, best at 5f, acts on gd to frm, best on gd. Turf high 73. Keeps on making the frame, but is the proverbial bridesmaid. Has plenty of early dash.
**M J Polglase [0-13] Emperor Alliance.*

KIND PRINCE BHB 30f45a RR 10f 45a 451[9]
7 b g Kind of Hush 9.6f **(50)** - Silent Princess (King of Spain) 7.8f **(52)**
Form - 0
Record 1999 - 1st:0 2nd:0 3rd:0 Ran:1
Pre1999 - 1st:0 2nd:0 3rd:0 Ran:4
1999 AW 0-1: (8f) (Fibr)
Little account gelding, has worn blinkers.
**R M Whitaker [0-2] The Norking Partnership (from John Harris [0-4] Oct 1994).*

KIND REGARDS (IRE) BHB 86f RR 85f 4599[4]
2 b f Unfuwain (USA) 11.4f **(74)** - Barari (USA) (Blushing Groom (FR)) 10.3f **(76)**
Form - 05214
Record 1999 - 1st:1 2nd:1 3rd:0 Ran:5
Win Prizemoney £3,783 *Total Prizemoney* £6,133
Wins * 1999 Spt Beverl (GD) 7.5f 78 <
1999 Turf 1-5: (6f, 7f 1-3, 8f) (gd 1-1, g-f 2, frm 2)
Useful filly. Turf high 85 (began Jly) - 4th of 19 getting 1lb from Out of Africa (28 Spt Newmarket 7f g-f RF 4599) - also 1st of 9 from Ashjaan (15 Spt Beverley RF 4323). Ran well in a warm nursery

after winning her maiden, and will stay at least a mile.
**M Johnston [1-5] Maktoum Al Maktoum.*

KIND SIR BHB 75f **RR 72f** 404[4]
3 b c Generous (IRE) 11.5f **(82)** - Noble Conquest (USA) (Vaguely Noble) 10.1f **(72)**
Form - 14
Record 1999 - 1st:1 2nd:0 3rd:0 Ran:2
Pre1999 - 1st:0 2nd:0 3rd:0 Ran:2
Win Prizemoney £3,538 *Total Prizemoney* £3,788
Wins * 1999 *Feb Lingfi (STD) 10f 80+* <
1999 AW 1-2: (10f 1-2) (Equi 1-2)
Scopey, decent colt. AW high 80 (1st run) - 1st of 6 getting 22lb from Hibernate (11 Feb Lingfield RF 0271).
**B W Hills [1-4] A D Shead.*

KING ADAM (IRE) BHB 115f **RR 113+f** 3168[6]
3 b c Fairy King (USA) 7.7f **(75)** - Sailor's Mate (Shirley Heights) 10.3f **(74)**
Form - 16
Record 1999 - 1st:1 2nd:0 3rd:0 Ran:2
Pre1999 - 1st:1 2nd:2 3rd:0 Ran:3
Win Prizemoney £18,023 *Total Prizemoney* £20,531
Wins * 1999 Jun Kempto (G-F) L 10f 113+ <
* 1998 Spt Goodwo (G-S) 8f 104+
1999 Turf 1-2: (10f 1-1, 12f) (frm 1-2)
Scopey, Group-class colt. Turf high 113 (1st run) - 1st of 8 getting 15lb from Prolix (23 Jun Kempton RF 2242). He is held in high regard by Sir Michael Stoute and certainly looked the part when making a winning reappearance at Kempton in June. Immediately nominated as a potential St Leger winner, he disappointed in the Gordon Stakes at Goodwood the following month, but can be excused that effort as he finished lame on his near-hind. Still unexposed, he remains a decent prospect and is one to follow on easy ground in 2000. **Sir Michael Stoute [2-5] Lord Weinstock.*

KINGCHIP BOY BHB 40f61a **RR 20f 61a** 5127[10]
10 b g Petong 7.6f **(58)** - Silk St James (Pas de Seul) 9.1f **(67)**
Form - 550101451150410
Record 1999 - 1st:5 2nd:0 3rd:0 Ran:14
Pre1999 - 1st:20 2nd:16 3rd:8 Ran:130
Win Prizemoney £70,983 *Total Prizemoney* £96,399

Wins	*** 1999**	*May Wolver*	*(Std)*	*C*	*9.4f*		*59*	
	*** 1999**	*Mar Southw*	*(STD)*	*C*	*8f*		*64*	
	*** 1999**	*Feb Wolver*	*(STD)*	*S*	*8.5f*		*67*	
	*** 1999**	*Feb Southw*	*(STD)*	*H*	*7f*	*55*	*63*	
	*** 1999**	*Jan Southw*	*(STD)*	*H*	*8f*	*50*	*57*	
	* 1998	*Feb Southw*	*(STD)*	*C*	*7f*		*68+*	
	* 1998	*Feb Southw*	*(STD)*	*H*	*7f*	*65*	*71*	
	* 1998	*Jan Southw*	*(STD)*	*H*	*8f*	*56*	*61*	
	* 1997	*Feb Southw*	*(STD)*	*H*	*8f*	*71*	*79*	<
	* 1997	*Feb Southw*	*(STD)*	*H*	*8f*	*71*	*75*	
	* 1997	*Jan Southw*	*(STD)*	*H*	*7f*	*68*	*68*	
	* 1996	*Apr Southw*	*(STD)*	*H*	*8f*	*64*	*69*	
	* 1996	*Jan Southw*	*(STD)*	*H*	*8f*	*46*	*66+*	
	* 1996	*Jan Southw*	*(STD)*	*H*	*8f*	*46*	*67*	
	* 1996	*Jan Southw*	*(STD)*	*H*	*8f*	*49*	*57*	
	* 1995	May Goodwo	(FRM)	H	8f	72	74	

1999 Turf 0-2: (7f, 8f) (gd, frm) 1999 AW 5-12: (7f 1-3, 8f 3-8, 9f 1-1) (Fibr 5-12)
Average gelding, effective 7 to 8f, best at 7f, - acts on Fibr, often wears blinkers (very effectively), favours left handed tracks, favours tight tracks, excels at Wolverhampton, does well at Southwell. Turf high 20. AW high 67 - 1st of 13 from Joseph's Wine (24 Feb Wolverhampton RF 0352) - also 1st of 13 getting 4lb from Domino Flyer (19 Mar Southwell RF 0451).
**M J Ryan [25-145] Doug Fleet.*

KING CURAN (USA) BHB 46f65a **RR 51f 65a** 752[10]
8 b g Lear Fan (USA) 10.4f **(80)** - Runaway Lady (USA) (Caucasus (USA)) 8.2f **(74)**
Form - 0
Record 1999 - 1st:0 2nd:0 3rd:0 Ran:1
Pre1999 - 1st:8 2nd:1 3rd:3 Ran:43
Win Prizemoney £29,750 *Total Prizemoney* £33,683

Wins	1996	Spt Hamilt	(GD)	H	8.3f	60	70+	
	1996	Jly Ayr	(GD)	H	7f	52	60	
	1995	Jun Ayr	(FRM)	H	10f	61	64	
	1995	Jun Ayr	(G-F)	H	8f	60	59	
	1995	May Hamilt	(G-F)	H	8.3f	57	59	

1999 Turf 0-1: (10f) (g-s)
Fair gelding, often wears blinkers. Inconsistent.
**A G Juckes [0-1] D W Thorne (from P Bowen [1-11] Jly 1998).*

KING DARIUS (IRE) BHB 95f **RR 95f** 4683[14]
4 ch g Persian Bold 10f **(69)** - Valiant Friend (USA) (Shahrastani (USA)) 8.8f **(72)**
Form - 6831102330
Record 1999 - 1st:2 2nd:1 3rd:3 Ran:10
Pre1999 - 1st:3 2nd:0 3rd:2 Ran:16
Win Prizemoney £30,693 *Total Prizemoney* £64,281

Wins	*** 1999**	May Kempto	(G-F)	H	10f	83	85+	<
	*** 1999**	May Cheste	(G-F)	H	10.3f	77	81+	
	* 1998	Aug Windso	(G-F)	H	11.6f	79	84	
	* 1998	May Kempto	(GD)	H	9f	77	82	
	* 1997	Jly Chepst	(G-S)	C	6.1f		74	

1999 Turf 2-10: (8f, 10f 2-7, 11f, 13f) (g-s, gd 2, g-f 1-5, frm 1-2)
Neat, very useful gelding, effective 10 to 11f, best at 10f, acts on g-f to frm, best on g-f, likes right handed tracks, likes tight tracks, and excels at Kempton. Turf high 95 - 3rd of 16 giving 13lb to Komistar (18 Spt Newbury 10f frm RF 4404). Consistent. A smart mile and a quarter handicapper, he runs his best races when coming late from behind a fast pace. Best on a sound surface, he made 48,000 guineas at Newmarket in October and should win a decent prize in 2000. **R Hannon [5-26] John Perry.*

KINGDOM EMPEROR BHB 38f **RR 40f** 2509[7]
5 b g Forzando 7.2f **(63)** - Wrangbrook (Shirley Heights) 10.3f **(74)**
Form - 7
Record 1999 - 1st:0 2nd:0 3rd:0 Ran:1
Pre1999 - 1st:0 2nd:1 3rd:1 Ran:7
Win Prizemoney £0 *Total Prizemoney* £1,188
1999 Turf 0-1: (15f) (g-f)
Moderate gelding, has worn blinkers. Inconsistent.
**W Clay [2-21] Don Walker, F E & Mrs J J Brindley (from M J Camacho [0-7] Jly 1997).*

KINGDOM OF GOLD (USA) BHB 81f **RR 77f** 4378[6]
2 b c Gone West (USA) 7.8f **(82)** - Aviara (USA) (Cox's Ridge (USA)) 8f **(68)**
Form - 416
Record 1999 - 1st:1 2nd:0 3rd:0 Ran:3
Win Prizemoney £3,420 *Total Prizemoney* £3,699
Wins * 1999 Aug Hamilt (G-F) 8.3f 73+ <
1999 Turf 1-3: (7f, 8f 1-2) (gd, g-f, frm 1-1)
Currently above-average colt. Turf high 77 (began Aug) - also 1st of 9 from High Cheviot (24 Aug Hamilton RF 3866).
**Sir Mark Prescott [1-3] Faisal Salman.*

KINGDOM RUBY (IRE) BHB 60f60a **RR 60f 60a** 2269[16]
4 ch f Bluebird (USA) 7.9f **(71)** - Tapestry (Tap On Wood) 10.3f **(65)**
Form - 36200
Record 1999 - 1st:0 2nd:1 3rd:0 Ran:3
Pre1999 - 1st:1 2nd:1 3rd:1 Ran:7
Win Prizemoney £3,485 *Total Prizemoney* £7,116
Wins * 1998 Oct Newcas (SFT) 7f 66 <
1999 Turf 0-3: (6f 2, 7f) (gd 2, frm)
Average filly, effective 6 to 7f, acts on sft to gd. Turf high 60 (1st run) - 2nd of 18 getting 15lb from Further Outlook (28 Apr Pontefract 6f gd RF 0905).
**Miss J A Camacho [1-10] Mrs S Camacho.*

KINGFISHER GOLD (IRE) BHB 46f **RR 41f** 4983[9]
3 b g Perugino (USA) - Cerosia (Pitskelly) 8.5f **(53)**
Form - 800000
Record 1999 - 1st:0 2nd:0 3rd:0 Ran:6
Pre1999 - 1st:0 2nd:0 3rd:0 Ran:2
1999 Turf 0-6: (6f 2, 7f, 8f, 10f 2) (g-s, gd 3, frm 2)
Scopey, moderate gelding. Turf high 64. Consistent.
**T P Tate [0-8] C E Whiteley.*

KINGFISHERS BONNET BHB 42f39a **RR 42f 39a** 5107[4]
3 b f Hamas (IRE) 8f **(72)** - Mainmast (Bustino) 10.4f **(64)**
Form - 050662802624
Record 1999 - 1st:0 2nd:3 3rd:0 Ran:12

Pre1999 - 1st:0 2nd:0 3rd:2 Ran:7
Win Prizemoney £0 *Total Prizemoney* £3,428
1999 Turf 0-11: (6f, 8f, 10f 6, 12f 3) (hvy, g-s, gd 2, g-f 4, frm 3) 1999 AW 0-1: (12f) (Fibr)
Leggy, moderate filly, effective 6f, acts on frm. Turf high 52.
**S G Knight [0-19] P J Wightman.*

KING FLYER (IRE) BHB 67f55a **RR 67f 55a** 4893[8]
3 b g Ezzoud (IRE) - Al Guswa (Shernazar) 10.2f **(73)**
Form - 323612328
Record 1999 - 1st:1 2nd:3 3rd:3 Ran:9
Pre1999 - 1st:0 2nd:0 3rd:0 Ran:4
Win Prizemoney £3,200 *Total Prizemoney* £8,607
Wins * 1999 Jun Newmar (G-F) C 10f 56 <
1999 Turf 1-5: (10f 1-1, 12f 2, 14f, 15f) (gd 2, g-f 1-1, frm 2) 1999 AW 0-4: (8f, 10f 2, 11f) (Equi 3, Fibr)
Small, average gelding, effective 10 to 14f, acts on gd to frm - acts on Equi, has worn blinkers. Turf high 67 - 2nd of 12 getting 2lb from Bid Me Welcome (23 Aug Nottingham 14f frm RF 3860). AW high 62 - 2nd of 8 getting 2lb from An Executive Do (9 Feb Lingfield 10f Equi RF 0256).
**H J Collingridge [1-9] In The Know (2) (from B Hanbury [0-4] Oct 1998).*

KING FOR A DAY BHB 47f **RR 47f** 4563[18]
3 b g Machiavellian (USA) 9.8f **(83)** - Dizzy Heights (USA) (Danzig (USA)) 8.4f **(76)**
Form - 600000
Record 1999 - 1st:0 2nd:0 3rd:0 Ran:6
Pre1999 - 1st:0 2nd:0 3rd:1 Ran:3
Win Prizemoney £0 *Total Prizemoney* £624
1999 Turf 0-6: (8f 2, 9f, 11f, 12f, 14f) (gd, g-f 2, frm 3)
Well made, moderate gelding, has worn blinkers. Turf high 67. Becoming disappointing.
**Bob Jones [0-2] Mrs Joan Marioni (from B W Hills [0-8] Jun 1999).*

KING KATO BHB 79f **RR 79f** 5031[3]
6 b g Unfuwain (USA) 11.4f **(74)** - Sharmood (USA) (Sharpen Up) 8.3f **(67)**
Form - 3
Record 1999 - 1st:0 2nd:0 3rd:1 Ran:1
Pre1999 - 1st:1 2nd:1 3rd:2 Ran:6
Win Prizemoney £2,577 *Total Prizemoney* £6,370
Wins * 1997 Jly Folkes (G-F) 12f 77+ <
1999 Turf 0-1: (10f) (g-s)
Above-average gelding.
**Mrs A J Perrett [1-8] Mrs Jenny Ells (from G Harwood [0-2] Spt 1996).*

KING MIDAS BHB 90f **RR 98f** 4556[10]
3 b c Bluebird (USA) 7.9f **(71)** - Ellebanna (Tina's Pet) 6.8f **(59)**
Form - 21280
Record 1999 - 1st:1 2nd:2 3rd:0 Ran:5
Win Prizemoney £4,188 *Total Prizemoney* £8,008
Wins * 1999 Jly Haydoc (G-S) 7.1f 90 <
1999 Turf 1-5: (7f 1-3, 8f 2) (g-s, gd 1-3, frm)
Workmanlike, very useful colt. Turf high 98 - 2nd of 8 giving 9lb to Al Fahda (6 Aug Salisbury 8f frm RF 3432) - also 1st of 12 giving 5lb to Celtic Fling (1 Jly Haydock RF 2462). He made steady progress until disappointing under testing conditions on his final start. Unlikely to stay beyond a mile, he has plenty of scope and can improve. **E A L Dunlop [1-5] Mohammed Jaber.*

KING OF BABYLON (IRE) BHB 57f47a **RR 44f 47a** 176[11]
7 b g Persian Heights 10.5f **(61)** - My My Marie (Artaius (USA)) 9f **(69)**
Form - 0
Record 1999 - 1st:0 2nd:0 3rd:0 Ran:1
Pre1999 - 1st:0 2nd:0 3rd:0 Ran:4
1999 AW 0-1: (15f) (Fibr)
Moderate gelding.
**F Jordan [1-18] Miss L M Rochford (from Lady Herries [0-9] Apr 1996).*

KING OF MOMMUR (IRE) BHB 46f **RR 43f** 4217[18]
4 b g Fairy King (USA) 7.7f **(75)** - Monoglow (Kalaglow) 9.8f **(67)**
Form - 003507060
Record 1999 - 1st:0 2nd:0 3rd:1 Ran:9
Pre1999 - 1st:0 2nd:0 3rd:2 Ran:6
Win Prizemoney £0 *Total Prizemoney* £1,694
1999 Turf 0-9: (10f 2, 12f 3, 14f, 16f 3) (g-s, g-f 3, frm 5)
Strong, moderate gelding, effective 12f, acts on frm, has worn blinkers, likes left handed tracks, likes tight tracks. Turf high 69.
**B J Meehan [0-15] The Three Bears Racing.*

KING OF PERU BHB 71f84a **RR 67f 84a** 4691[2]
6 b g Inca Chief (USA) 5.6f **(45)** - Julie's Star (IRE) (Thatching) 8f **(66)**
Form - 00008721305368833200022
Record 1999 - 1st:1 2nd:4 3rd:4 Ran:22
Pre1999 - 1st:4 2nd:3 3rd:4 Ran:37
Win Prizemoney £32,195 *Total Prizemoney* £54,029
Wins * 1999 May Bright (FRM) H 6f 60 61
1996 May Goodwo (GD) H 7f 100 97 <
1995 Spt Newmar (G-F) H 6f 86 93
1995 Spt Ayr (GD) H 6f 77 86
1995 Jly Haydoc (G-F) 6f 75+
1999 Turf 1-20: (5f 8, 6f 1-12) (sft 2, gd 8, g-f 6, frm 3, hrd 1-1) 1999 AW 0-2: (5f, 6f) (Fibr 2)
Decent gelding, effective 5f, - acts on Fibr, has worn blinkers, likes left handed tracks, prefers tight tracks. Turf high 67. AW high 80. Suited by the minimum trip, he won at Brighton in May and has made the frame a number of times since. A bit of a character.
**N P Littmoden [1-37] M C S D Racing (from A P Jarvis [4-22] May 1997).*

KING OF TUNES (FR) BHB 56f79a **RR 60f 79a** 5154[16]
7 b h Chief Singer 8.6f **(62)** - Marcotte (Nebos (GER)) 9f **(78)**
Form - 003060700
Record 1999 - 1st:0 2nd:0 3rd:1 Ran:9
Pre1999 - 1st:3 2nd:4 3rd:1 Ran:22
Win Prizemoney £13,858 *Total Prizemoney* £38,006
Wins * 1997 Jun Newmar (GD) H 8f 77 84 <
* 1996 *Jan Lingfi (STD) H 10f 68 71*
* 1995 Oct Ascot (SFT) 8f 75
1999 Turf 0-9: (8f 5, 10f 4) (g-s, gd 2, g-f 3, frm 3)
Above-average horse, effective 8f, acts on gd, has worn blinkers. Turf high 70. Inconsistent. He is a bit of an in-and-out performer, quite capable of putting in a bold show in decent handicap company, but he is very difficult to predict, though he does seem to go well after a layoff.
**J J Sheehan [3-27] Mrs Eileen Sheehan (from M J Haynes [0-4] Oct 1997).*

KING O' THE MANA (IRE) BHB 100f **RR 100+f** 4792[6]
2 b c Turtle Island (IRE) - Olivia Jane (IRE) (Ela-Mana-Mou) 10.1f **(70)**
Form - 61216
Record 1999 - 1st:2 2nd:1 3rd:0 Ran:5
Win Prizemoney £32,982 *Total Prizemoney* £34,852
Wins * 1999 Aug Newcas (GD) H 8f 90 100+ <
*** 1999** Jly Warwic (G-F) 6.8f 84
1999 Turf 2-5: (6f, 7f 1-2, 8f 1-2) (gd 1-4, g-f 1-1)
Very useful colt. Turf high 100 - 1st of 13 getting 5lb from French Fellow (30 Aug Newcastle RF 4020). He put up an improved performance when beating the unlucky-in-running French Fellow at Newcastle in August, but ran poorly behind that colt when they met again at Ascot. Possibly past his best for the season there, he should develop into a useful middle-distance handicapper.
**R Hannon [2-5] D Boocock.*

KING PERI (IRE) BHB 52f **RR 39f** 903[8]
3 b g Fairy King (USA) 7.7f **(75)** - Maria Roberta (USA) (Roberto (USA)) 10f **(76)**
Form - 8
Record 1999 - 1st:0 2nd:0 3rd:0 Ran:1
Pre1999 - 1st:0 2nd:0 3rd:0 Ran:6
Win Prizemoney £0 *Total Prizemoney* £407
1999 Turf 0-1: (12f) (gd)
Leggy, very moderate gelding.
**N Tinkler [0-7] Leeds Plywood and Doors Ltd.*

KING PRIAM (IRE) BHB 80f74a **RR 87f 74a** 5217[D]
4 b g Priolo (USA) 10.9f **(71)** - Barinia (Corvaro (USA)) 9f **(53)**
Form - 72324635123400088205478011135D
Record 1999 - 1st:4 2nd:4 3rd:4 Ran:29
Pre1999 - 1st:1 2nd:2 3rd:2 Ran:13
Win Prizemoney £22,625 *Total Prizemoney* £37,990
Wins * 1999 Oct York (G-S) H 10.4f 70 75 <
*** 1999** Spt Haydoc (SFT) H 8.1f 57 69+

* 1999 Spt Leices (GD) 8f 66
* 1999 *Mar Southw (STD) H 8f 68 72*
1998 Oct Newmar (gd) C 12f 66

1999 Turf 3-20: (7f, 8f 2-4, 9f 2, 10f 1-11, 12f 2) (g-s 2, gd 2-8, g-f 1-6, frm 4) 1999 AW 1-9: (8f 1-2, 9f 2, 11f 3, 12f 2) (Fibr 1-9)

Lengthy, useful gelding, effective 10f, acts on g-s, mostly wears blinkers (effectively). Turf high 87. AW high 72. Kept very busy, he scored on the Southwell Fibresand in March, but went on a long losing run afterwards. Dropped in the handicap as a result, he suddenly found his form with a hat-trick in the autumn.

**M J Polglase [4-34] Ian Puddle (from M C Pipe [1-5] Oct 1998).*

KINGRHUMBA (USA) BHB 60f70a **RR 58+f 70a** 3793[2]

3 b c Kingmambo (USA) 10.9f **(85)** - Lady Ice (CAN) (Vice Regent (CAN)) 8.7f **(74)**

Form - 071543012

Record 1999 - 1st:2 2nd:1 3rd:1 Ran:9
Pre1999 - 1st:0 2nd:0 3rd:0 Ran:2

Win Prizemoney £4,334 *Total Prizemoney* £5,682

Wins * **1999** *Aug Lingfi (STD) H 16f 60 70+* <
* **1999** Jun Redcar (FRM) 11f 67

1999 Turf 1-7: (8f, 10f 2, 11f 1-2, 12f, 14f) (gd 2, g-f 2, frm 1-3) 1999 AW 1-2: (16f 1-2) (Equi 1-2)

Scopey, above-average colt, effective 11 to 16f, best at 16f, acts on frm - acts on Equi, often wears blinkers, prefers left handed tracks, prefers tight tracks. Turf high 67 - 1st of 4 giving 3lb to Maya Cove (18 Jun Redcar RF 2131). AW high 70 (began Aug) - 2nd of 7 giving 7lb to Alhesn (20 Aug Lingfield 16f Equi RF 3793) - also 1st of 6 giving 16lb to Zola (13 Aug Lingfield RF 3615). Won a poor four-runner maiden at Redcar in June, and won over two miles on the Lingfield Equitrack in August. Although he won that race by a distance, the form is suspect as the opposition could hardly put one hoof in front of another, and he was unable to follow up in a better event over course and distance next time, though he still ran well. He can win another race or two on sand. **J Noseda [2-11] K Y Lim.*

KINGS ARROW (IRE) BHB 57f57a **RR 58f 57a** 1585[4]

4 b c Mujadil (USA) 7.7f **(70)** - Great Leighs (Vaigly Great) 7f **(58)**

Form - 351132286804

Record 1999 - 1st:1 2nd:2 3rd:1 Ran:9
Pre1999 - 1st:1 2nd:1 3rd:1 Ran:11

Win Prizemoney £3,804 *Total Prizemoney* £7,772

Wins * **1999** *Jan Lingfi (STD) 10f 63* <
* 1998 *Dec Lingfi (STD) 10f 59*

1999 Turf 0-1: (10f) (g-s) 1999 AW 1-8: (10f 1-8) (Equi 1-8)

Light-framed, fair colt, effective 10f, - acted on Equi, preferred left handed tracks, preferred tight tracks. AW high 70 - 2nd of 6 getting 4lb from Java Shrine (16 Jan Lingfield 10f Equi RF 0110) - also 1st of 8 getting 2lb from Confronter (1 Jan Lingfield RF 0004). (DEAD)

**P Howling [2-13] C Hammond (from M L W Bell [0-7] Jly 1998).*

KING'S BEST (USA) BHB 100f **RR 96+f** 4918[5]

2 b c Kingmambo (USA) 10.9f **(85)** - Allegretta (Lombard (GER)) 10.5f **(66)**

Form - 115

Record 1999 - 1st:2 2nd:0 3rd:0 Ran:3

Win Prizemoney £25,048 *Total Prizemoney* £28,648

Wins * **1999** Aug York (GD) L 7f 96+ <
* **1999** Aug Newmar (GD) 7f 85++

1999 Turf 2-3: (7f 2-3) (gd, g-f 2-2)

Currently very useful colt. Turf high 96 (began Aug) - 1st of 5 giving 3lb to Shamrock City (17 Aug York RF 3692). He hardly put a foot wrong on his first two starts, but got his tongue over the bit and pulled like a train when running poorly in the Dewhurst Stakes. Described as a "head case" by his owner's racing manager after that dismal effort, he has any amount of ability but must learn to relax. **Sir Michael Stoute [2-3] Saeed Suhail.*

KINGS CAY (IRE) BHB 22f **RR 27f** 4166[10]

8 b g Taufan (USA) 8.3f **(65)** - Provocation (Kings Lake (USA)) 10.8f **(67)**

Form - 0088700

Record 1999 - 1st:0 2nd:0 3rd:0 Ran:7
Pre1999 - 1st:5 2nd:4 3rd:4 Ran:33

Win Prizemoney £17,405 *Total Prizemoney* £24,348

Wins * 1996 Jly Hamilt (GD) H 11.1f 51 59
* 1996 Jun Carlis (FRM) 12f 62
* 1996 Jun Ripon (G-F) H 12.3f 46 55

1999 Turf 0-7: (12f 6, 14f) (g-f 2, frm 4, hrd)

Little account gelding, effective 12 to 14f, acts on g-f to frm, best on g-f, has worn blinkers, prefers right handed tracks, likes tight tracks. Turf high 45.

**T H Caldwell [3-36] R S G Jones (from D R Loder [2-6] Jun 1994).*

KINGSCLERE BHB 100f **RR 93+f** 4570[3]

2 b c Fairy King (USA) 7.7f **(75)** - Spurned (USA) (Robellino (USA)) 7.6f **(80)**

Form - 114323

Record 1999 - 1st:2 2nd:1 3rd:2 Ran:6

Win Prizemoney £14,283 *Total Prizemoney* £36,385

Wins * **1999** Jly York (G-F) 7f 93+ <
* **1999** Jun Newbur (GD) 6f 85+

1999 Turf 2-6: (6f 1-1, 7f 1-3, 8f 2) (sft, gd 1-1, g-f 1-3, frm)

Useful colt, effective 6 to 8f, best at 8f, acts on sft to g-f, best on g-f. Turf high 93 - 3rd of 6 to Royal Kingdom (26 Spt Ascot 8f sft RF 4570) - also 1st of 5 giving 7lb to Bella Bellisimo (10 Jly York RF 2730). A half-brother to Hidden Meadow, he made a winning debut, appropriately, in the Kingsclere Stakes at Newbury. Followed up that success when beating Bella Belissimo at York on fast ground, but has not really built on that since, despite making the frame behind some useful sorts. He looks as if he needs a test of stamina. **I A Balding [2-6] M Tabor.*

KINGSDON (IRE) BHB 95f **RR 93f** 4645[1]

2 b c Brief Truce (USA) 9.1f **(73)** - Richly Deserved (IRE) (Kings Lake (USA)) 10.8f **(67)**

Form - 21231

Record 1999 - 1st:2 2nd:2 3rd:1 Ran:5

Win Prizemoney £7,936 *Total Prizemoney* £10,946

Wins * **1999** Spt Salisb (HVY) 7f 93 <
* **1999** Aug Kempto (G-S) 6f 81

1999 Turf 2-5: (6f 1-2, 7f 1-3) (g-s 2-2, gd 2, g-f)

Useful colt. Turf high 93 (began Aug) - 1st of 6 giving 4lb to Hadath (29 Spt Salisbury RF 4645). **R Hannon [2-5] Fieldspring Racing.*

KING'S DRAGOON (IRE) **RR 2f** 2386[10]

3 ch c College Chapel - Indigo Blue (IRE) (Bluebird (USA)) 7.5f **(69)**

Form - 80

Record 1999 - 1st:0 2nd:0 3rd:0 Ran:2

1999 Turf 0-2: (5f, 8f) (g-s, g-f)

Workmanlike, currently very poor colt. Turf high 2.

**M R Channon [0-2] W H Ponsonby.*

KINGSFOLD BLAZE BHB 51f **RR 43f** 2570[6]

4 b f Mazilier (USA) 8.5f **(56)** - Kingsfold Flame (No Loiterer)

Form - 0606

Record 1999 - 1st:0 2nd:0 3rd:0 Ran:4
Pre1999 - 1st:0 2nd:0 3rd:2 Ran:5

Win Prizemoney £0 *Total Prizemoney* £970

1999 Turf 0-4: (9f, 10f, 11f, 12f) (g-s 2, g-f, frm)

Leggy, moderate filly, effective 9f, acts on gd, has worn blinkers, likes tight tracks. Turf high 43. **M J Haynes [0-9] Mrs Pauline Oliver.*

KINGSFOLD PET BHB 43f **RR 47f** 763[8]

10 b g Tina's Pet 7.4f **(56)** - Bella Lisa (River Chanter) 15.4f **(51)**

Form - 8

Record 1999 - 1st:0 2nd:0 3rd:0 Ran:1
Pre1999 - 1st:1 2nd:1 3rd:2 Ran:11

Win Prizemoney £3,080 *Total Prizemoney* £4,720

1999 Turf 0-1: (15f) (hvy)

Moderate gelding. **M J Haynes [10-48] George Nye Partnership.*

KING'S GINGER BHB 69f **RR 69f** 4944[5]

2 ch g King's Signet (USA) 7f **(51)** - Cosset (Comedy Star (USA)) 7.5f **(50)**

Form - 530305

Record 1999 - 1st:0 2nd:0 3rd:2 Ran:6

Win Prizemoney £0 *Total Prizemoney* £787

1999 Turf 0-6: (5f, 7f 3, 8f 2) (gd 2, g-f 4)

Average gelding, effective 7 to 8f, acts on gd to g-f. Turf high 69.

**P R Chamings [0-4] Ralph Peters (from H Candy [0-2] Jly 1999).*

KINGS HARMONY (IRE) BHB 50f57a **RR 61df 57a** 441[11]

6 b g Nordico (USA) 8.2f **(59)** - Kingston Rose (Tudor Music) 6.8f **(59)**

Form - 0200
Record **1999** - 1st:0 2nd:1 3rd:0 Ran:3
Pre1999 - 1st:5 2nd:6 3rd:1 Ran:35
Win Prizemoney £13,790 *Total Prizemoney* £22,318
Wins 1998 *Feb Lingfi (SLW) C 7f 72* <
1997 Jly Bright (FRM) C 7f 63
1996 Aug Bright (FRM) H 7f 66 71
1996 Apr Bright (FRM) 6f 66
1995 *Nov Southw (STD) 6f 69*
1999 AW 0-3: (7f, 8f 2) (Equi 3)
Average gelding, effective 7f, - acts on Equi, has worn blinkers, likes left handed tracks, likes tight tracks. **R Ingram [0-4] Gerry Boyer (from B A Pearce [0-9] Jly 1998).*

KING'S HUSSAR BHB 48f45a RR 54f 45a 612[17]

4 b g Be My Chief (USA) 10.2f **(62)** - Croire (IRE) (Lomond (USA)) 8.8f **(65)**
Form - 0
Record **1999** - 1st:0 2nd:0 3rd:0 Ran:1
Pre1999 - 1st:0 2nd:1 3rd:0 Ran:9
Win Prizemoney £0 *Total Prizemoney* £660
1999 Turf 0-1: (12f) (g-f)
Neat, fair gelding, effective 12f, acts on g-s, has worn blinkers. Becoming disappointing.
**G M Moore [0-6] White Hart In Hawes Partnership (from R F JohnsonHoughton [0-5] Jun 1998).*

KING SLAYER BHB 93f RR 97f 822[5]

4 b c Batshoof 9.5f **(66)** - Top Sovereign (High Top) 10.2f **(67)**
Form - 5
Record **1999** - 1st:0 2nd:0 3rd:0 Ran:1
Pre1999 - 1st:1 2nd:4 3rd:2 Ran:10
Win Prizemoney £2,490 *Total Prizemoney* £30,078
Wins * 1998 Apr Folkes (GD) 7f 72 <
1999 Turf 0-1: (8f) (g-s)
Leggy, very useful colt, effective 7 to 8f, acts on gd to g-f. A smart handicapper, he went missing after running a tidy race on his reappearance. Best up to a mile, he acts on any ground and is usually held-up. **B Smart [1-11] Ahmed Abdel-Khaleq.*

KING'S MILL (IRE) BHB 81f RR 80f 4899[3]

2 b c Doyoun 10.7f **(69)** - Adarika (Kings Lake (USA)) 10.8f **(67)**
Form - 0223
Record **1999** - 1st:0 2nd:2 3rd:1 Ran:4
Win Prizemoney £0 *Total Prizemoney* £3,077
1999 Turf 0-4: (7f 2, 8f 2) (gd 3, frm)
Decent colt. Turf high 80 (began Aug) - 3rd of 20 getting 5lb from Misbehave (15 Oct Newmarket 8f gd RF 4899).
**N A Graham [0-4] First Millennium Racing.*

KING SPINNER (IRE) BHB 84f RR 86+f 5100[1]

2 b c Mujadil (USA) 7.7f **(70)** - Money Spinner (USA) (Teenoso (USA)) 9.9f **(72)**
Form - 3451
Record **1999** - 1st:1 2nd:0 3rd:1 Ran:4
Win Prizemoney £3,297 *Total Prizemoney* £4,123
Wins * **1999** Oct Yarmou (G-S) 8f 86 <
1999 Turf 1-4: (7f 2, 8f 1-2) (gd 1-4)
Useful colt. Turf high 86 (began Aug) - 1st of 10 from Fraternity (27 Oct Yarmouth RF 5100). **A P Jarvis [1-4] A L R Morton.*

KINGSTON BILL BHB 75f RR 72f 4909[12]

2 b c Then Again 7.4f **(52)** - Tricata (Electric) 10.1f **(61)**
Form - 1360
Record **1999** - 1st:1 2nd:0 3rd:1 Ran:4
Win Prizemoney £3,009 *Total Prizemoney* £3,506
Wins * **1999** Mar Newcas (G-S) 5f 72 <
1999 Turf 1-4: (5f 1-2, 7f 2) (hvy, gd 1-3)
Above-average colt. Turf high 72 (1st run) - 1st of 6 giving 5lb to Kashra (30 Mar Newcastle RF 0512).
**W G M Turner [1-4] Miss Corinne Overton.*

KINGSTON VENTURE BHB 93f RR 97f 4434[5]

3 b g Interrex (CAN) 7.7f **(51)** - Tricata (Electric) 10.1f **(61)**
Form - 162105
Record **1999** - 1st:2 2nd:1 3rd:0 Ran:6
Pre1999 - 1st:1 2nd:0 3rd:0 Ran:4
Win Prizemoney £13,537 *Total Prizemoney* £16,498
Wins * **1999** May Lingfi (G-F) 11.5f 97 <
* **1999** Mar Doncas (GD) H 10.3f 74 78
* 1998 Jun Salisb (G-F) 7f 66
1999 Turf 2-6: (10f 1-2, 11f 1-1, 12f 2, 14f) (g-s, gd 1-3, frm 1-2)
Leggy, very useful gelding, effective 11 to 12f, acts on frm. Turf high 97 - 2nd of 5 to Time Zone (13 May Salisbury 12f frm RF 1190) - also 1st of 3 from Sarangani (22 May Lingfield RF 1399). He stays a mile and a half and is a useful front-runner on his day. He has flashed his tail under pressure, but seems genuine.
**W G M Turner [3-10] Miss Corinne Overton.*

KINGS TO OPEN RR 60f 4451[7]

2 b c First Trump - Shadiyama (Nishapour (FR)) 9.1f **(61)**
Form - 7
Record **1999** - 1st:0 2nd:0 3rd:0 Ran:1
1999 Turf 0-1: (7f) (sft)
Currently average colt. **D Marks [0-1] Godiva.*

KINGSTREE BHB 73f RR 74+f 1013[7]

3 b c Distant Relative 7f **(69)** - Sinking (Midyan (USA)) 6f **(60)**
Form - 427
Record **1999** - 1st:0 2nd:1 3rd:0 Ran:3
Pre1999 - 1st:0 2nd:0 3rd:1 Ran:2
Win Prizemoney £0 *Total Prizemoney* £3,065
1999 Turf 0-3: (6f, 7f 2) (g-s, frm 2)
Above-average colt. Turf high 74 - 2nd of 23 giving 11lb to Done And Dusted (12 Apr Windsor 6f frm RF 0650).
**J H M Gosden [0-5] Sheikh Mohammed.*

KING'S VIEW RR 68f 5157[9]

2 b c Distant View (USA) - Migiyas (Kings Lake (USA)) 10.8f **(67)**
Form - 50
Record **1999** - 1st:0 2nd:0 3rd:0 Ran:2
1999 Turf 0-2: (7f, 8f) (gd, frm)
Currently average colt. Turf high 68 (began Oct).
**E A L Dunlop [0-2] The Serendipity Partnership.*

KING TIARA (USA) RR 35f 5049[13]

2 b br c Fairy King (USA) 7.7f **(75)** - Cap of Dignity (Shirley Heights) 10.3f **(74)**
Form - 0
Record **1999** - 1st:0 2nd:0 3rd:0 Ran:1
1999 Turf 0-1: (8f) (gd)
Currently very moderate colt. **H R A Cecil [0-1] S Khaled.*

KING TUT BHB 48f RR 21f 4105[21]

3 ch g Anshan 8.2f **(63)** - Fahrenheit (Mount Hagen (FR)) 8.4f **(70)**
Form - 6800
Record **1999** - 1st:0 2nd:0 3rd:0 Ran:4
1999 Turf 0-4: (7f 2, 8f, 10f) (g-f, frm 3)
Little account gelding. Turf high 57 (began Jly).
**W Jarvis [0-4] William Jarvis.*

KING UNO BHB 60f60a RR 61f 60a 1753[16]

5 b g Be My Chief (USA) 10.2f **(62)** - The Kings Daughter (Indian King (USA)) 7.4f **(64)**
Form - 8480500
Record **1999** - 1st:0 2nd:0 3rd:0 Ran:7
Pre1999 - 1st:5 2nd:2 3rd:3 Ran:31
Win Prizemoney £16,139 *Total Prizemoney* £22,676
Wins * 1998 Spt Leices (G-S) H 7f 59 62 <
* 1998 Aug Pontef (G-F) H 6f 54 58
1998 Jun Nottin (GD) H 6.1f 49 52
1997 Spt Haydoc (G-S) SH 6f 47 50
1997 Jun Pontef (GD) H 6f 43 46
1999 Turf 0-5: (6f, 7f 2, 8f 2) (sft, gd 3, g-f) 1999AW 0-2: (6f, 7f) (Fibr 2)
Average gelding, effective 6 to 8f, best at 7f, acts on gd to frm, best on gd, has worn blinkers, likes left handed tracks. Turf high 61. AW high 53.
**E J Alston [2-14] The Pain And Heartache Partnership (from Mrs J R Ramsden [3-24] Jun 1998).*

KINLANO BHB 57f54a RR 61f 54a 4879[17]

3 b g Cyrano de Bergerac 7.3f **(58)** - Kinlacey (Aragon) 8.1f **(60)**
Form - 0880
Record **1999** - 1st:0 2nd:0 3rd:0 Ran:4

Pre1999 - 1st:0 2nd:0 3rd:0 Ran:5
1999 Turf 0-3: (6f, 7f 2) (gd, frm 2) 1999 AW 0-1: (6f) (Fibr)
Scopey, average gelding, effective 6f, acts on frm, has worn blinkers. Turf high 52. Becoming disappointing.
**W Jarvis [0-4] M C Banks (from Mrs J R Ramsden [0-5] Oct 1998).*

KINNESCASH (IRE) BHB 82f69a **RR 79f 69a** 4134[1]
6 ch g Persian Heights 10.5f **(61)** - Gayla Orchestra (Lord Gayle (USA)) 8.8f **(62)**
Form - 810701
Record 1999 - 1st:2 2nd:0 3rd:0 Ran:5
Pre1999 - 1st:4 2nd:4 3rd:3 Ran:29
Win Prizemoney £32,439 *Total Prizemoney* £39,800
Wins * 1999 Spt Epsom (GD) H 12f 74 79 <
* **1999** Apr Epsom (SFT) H 12f 73 76
* 1997 Jun Windso (G-S) H 11.6f 59 67
* 1997 Apr Leices (G-S) H 10f 53 62
1995 Spt Nottin (G-S) H 10f 65 67
1995 Aug Bath (HRD) S 5.7f 64?
1999 Turf 2-5: (12f 2-4, 17f) (g-s 1-2, g-f, frm 1-2)
Above-average gelding, effective 12f, acts on g-s to frm, best on frm, likes tight tracks, likes Epsom. Turf high 79 - 1st of 7 getting 3lb from Passionate Pursuit (4 Spt Epsom RF 4134) - also 1st of 11 getting 17lb from Montecristo (21 Apr Epsom RF 0799). Inconsistent. Able under both codes, he landed the Great Metropolitan Handicap in soft ground at Epsom in April, and bounced back to form at the Surrey track on his final start.
**P Bowen [12-47] D R James (from M S Saunders [1-12] Jun 1996).*

KINNINO BHB 33f43a **RR 34f 43a** 4997[8]
5 b g Polish Precedent (USA) 9f **(73)** - On Tiptoes (Shareef Dancer (USA)) 9.9f **(73)**
Form - 75300005058
Record 1999 - 1st:0 2nd:0 3rd:1 Ran:10
Pre1999 - 1st:0 2nd:0 3rd:0 Ran:8
Win Prizemoney £0 *Total Prizemoney* £351
1999 Turf 0-6: (7f 3, 8f, 9f, 10f) (gd 2, g-f, frm 3) 1999 AW 0-4: (7f 3, 10f) (Equi 4)
Very moderate gelding, effective 7f, - acts on Equi, has worn blinkers. Turf high 36. AW high 52. **G L Moore [0-18] A Moore.*

KINSAILE RR 58f 754[8]
2 ro f Robellino (USA) 9.5f **(68)** - Snowing **(87f)** (Tate Gallery (USA)) 7.4f **(67)**
Form - 8
Record 1999 - 1st:0 2nd:0 3rd:0 Ran:1
1999 Turf 0-1: (5f) (g-f)
Currently fair filly. **R Charlton [0-1] Lady Bland.*

KINSMAN (IRE) BHB 68f **RR 69f** 4786[5]
2 b g Distant Relative 7f **(69)** - Besito (Wassl) 9.7f **(62)**
Form - 00006215
Record 1999 - 1st:1 2nd:1 3rd:0 Ran:8
Win Prizemoney £3,403 *Total Prizemoney* £4,404
Wins * 1999 Spt Bright (SFT) H 6f 63 69 <
1999 Turf 1-7: (5f 2, 6f 1-4, 7f) (g-s 1-1, gd, g-f 3, frm 2) 1999 AW 0-1: (6f) (Equi)
Average gelding, effective 6f, acts on g-s to frm, often wears blinkers (extremely effectively). Turf high 69 - 1st of 10 getting 14lb from Sarena Pride (29 Spt Brighton RF 4625). Inconsistent.
**I A Balding [1-8] Miss A V Hill.*

KINTAVI BHB 53f **RR 52f** 2325[4]
9 b g Efisio 7.7f **(69)** - Princess Tavi (Sea Hawk II) 10.8f **(63)**
Form - 86134
Record 1999 - 1st:1 2nd:0 3rd:1 Ran:5
Pre1999 - 1st:3 2nd:4 3rd:3 Ran:24
Win Prizemoney £14,016 *Total Prizemoney* £22,129
Wins * 1999 May Catter (FRM) H 13.8f 45 49
* 1998 Apr Leices (SFT) H 11.8f 52 58 <
* 1997 May Hamilt (SFT) H 13f 46 53
* 1995 Jun Warwic (FRM) H 12.5f 36 40
1999 Turf 1-5: (12f 2, 14f 1-2, 15f) (sft, gd, g-f, frm 1-2)
Fair gelding, effective 12 to 14f, best at 12f, acts on sft to frm, likes right handed tracks, prefers tight tracks. Turf high 52 - 3rd of 14 giving 8lb to Fatehalkhair (4 Jun Catterick 12f frm RF 1723) - also 1st of 12 getting 19lb from Bluewain Lady (22 May Catterick RF 1391).
**T W Donnelly [7-38] S Taberner (from J Mackie [0-5] Aug 1993).*

KINTBURY BHB 53a **RR 42f 53a** 1122[1]
4 b g Kylian (USA) 8.1f **(66)** - Easter Baby (Derrylin) 8.8f **(54)**
Form - 474321
Record 1999 - 1st:1 2nd:1 3rd:1 Ran:6
Win Prizemoney £2,242 *Total Prizemoney* £3,797
Wins * 1999 *May Wolver (STD) H 16.2f 41 49* <
1999 Turf 0-2: (12f, 14f) (sft, gd) 1999 AW 1-4: (8f, 10f, 12f, 16f 1-1) (Equi 2, Fibr 1-2)
Fair gelding, effective 16f, - acts on Fibr. Turf high 42. AW high 52 - also 1st of 12 getting 5lb from Another Monk (8 May Wolverhampton RF 1122). **P D Cundell [1-6] Miss M C Fraser.*

KIRBY PRINCESS BHB 36f **RR 38f** 3954[11]
4 ch f Weldnaas (USA) 8.4f **(55)** - Lovely Greek Lady (Ela-Mana-Mou) 10.1f **(70)**
Form - 750
Record 1999 - 1st:0 2nd:0 3rd:0 Ran:3
Pre1999 - 1st:0 2nd:0 3rd:0 Ran:5
1999 Turf 0-3: (10f, 12f 2) (g-f, frm 2)
Leggy, very moderate filly, effective 12f, acts on g-f. Turf high 38. Consistent. **R A Fahey [0-8] Wentdale Const Ltd.*

KIRILOV (IRE) BHB 50f **RR 54?f** 3765[5]
4 b g Roi Danzig (USA) 10.5f **(62)** - Ever so (Mummy's Pet) 7.7f **(60)**
Form - 500705
Record 1999 - 1st:0 2nd:0 3rd:0 Ran:6
Pre1999 - 1st:0 2nd:0 3rd:0 Ran:4
Win Prizemoney £0 *Total Prizemoney* £254
1999 Turf 0-6: (7f, 10f 4, 12f) (gd 2, g-f 2, frm, hrd)
Workmanlike, fair gelding, effective 10f, acts on g-f, has worn blinkers, likes tight tracks. Turf high 67. Consistent.
**R W Armstrong [0-10] R N Bracher.*

KIRISNIPPA BHB 56f **RR 56f** 5103[13]
4 b g Beveled (USA) 6.9f **(64)** - Kiri Te (Liboi (USA))
Form - 74P3U0
Record 1999 - 1st:0 2nd:0 3rd:1 Ran:6
Win Prizemoney £0 *Total Prizemoney* £917
1999 Turf 0-6: (6f, 7f, 8f, 10f 2, 12f) (gd 3, g-f 2, frm)
Scopey, fair gelding, has worn blinkers. Turf high 56 (began Aug).
**Derrick Morris [0-7] Michael Appleby.*

KIRK BHB 71f **RR 76f** 5135[2]
3 b f Selkirk (USA) 7.9f **(76)** - Sancta (So Blessed) 8.7f **(67)**
Form - 06132
Record 1999 - 1st:1 2nd:1 3rd:1 Ran:5
Win Prizemoney £4,842 *Total Prizemoney* £7,203
Wins * 1999 Oct Nottin (SFT) 8.2f 76 <
1999 Turf 1-5: (8f 1-5) (g-s 1-1, gd 3, g-f)
Lengthy, above-average filly. Turf high 76 - 1st of 14 from Silk Daisy (5 Oct Nottingham RF 4729). **W Jarvis [1-5] William Jarvis.*

KIROV PROTEGE (IRE) BHB 23f32a **RR 47?f 32a** 1455[6]
7 b g Dancing Dissident (USA) 6.8f **(65)** - Still River (Kings Lake (USA)) 10.8f **(67)**
Form - 6
Record 1999 - 1st:0 2nd:0 3rd:0 Ran:1
Pre1999 - 1st:2 2nd:4 3rd:4 Ran:50
Win Prizemoney £5,225 *Total Prizemoney* £9,926
Wins * 1997 Jun Warwic (G-F) H 10.8f 24 40
1995 *Jan Southw (STD) SH 8f 46 43* <
1999 AW 0-1: (16f) (Equi)
Moderate gelding, has worn blinkers.
**Mrs L C Jewell [1-22] Richard Dean (from G L Moore [0-5] Oct 1997).*

KIROVSKI (IRE) BHB 68f **RR 66f** 4785[18]
2 b c Common Grounds 8.1f **(66)** - Nordic Doll (IRE) **(71f 59a)** (Royal Academy (USA))
Form - 760
Record 1999 - 1st:0 2nd:0 3rd:0 Ran:3
1999 Turf 0-3: (7f, 8f 2) (g-s, g-f 2)
Currently average colt. Turf high 66 (began Spt).
**P W Harris [0-3] Batten, Bowstead, Gregory & Manning.*

KIRSCH BHB 66f **RR 69f** 4651[10]
2 ch f Wolfhound (USA) 7.3f **(71)** - Pondicherry (USA) (Sir Wimborne (USA)) 10f **(73)**
Form - 323335756140
Record 1999 - 1st:1 2nd:1 3rd:4 Ran:12
Win Prizemoney £2,535 *Total Prizemoney* £5,702
Wins * 1999 Aug Lingfi (G-F) C 6f 69 <
1999 Turf 1-9: (5f 7, 6f 1-2) (gd, g-f 1-5, frm 3) 1999 AW 0-3: (5f 2, 6f) (Equi, Fibr 2)
Average filly, effective 5f, acts on g-f. Turf high 83 (1st run) - 3rd of 9 getting 5lb from Digital Image (4 May Chester 5f g-f RF 1025). AW high 63. **C A Dwyer [1-12] Cedar Lodge Syndicate.*

KIRSTENBOSCH BHB 42f **RR 39f** 2226[9]
12 b g Caerleon (USA) 10.9f **(79)** - Flower Petals (Busted) 10.2f **(61)**
Form - 0
Record 1999 - 1st:0 2nd:0 3rd:0 Ran:1
Pre1999 - 1st:0 2nd:1 3rd:3 Ran:12
Win Prizemoney £0 *Total Prizemoney* £2,106
1999 Turf 0-1: (17f) (frm)
Very moderate gelding. Improving.
**L Lungo [5-31] Mrs Barbara Lungo (from T D Barron [0-11] Spt 1990).*

KISSED BY MOONLITE BHB 44f **RR 48f** 4359[14]
3 gr f Petong 7.6f **(58)** - Rose Bouquet (General Assembly (USA)) 10f **(68)**
Form - 0660280
Record 1999 - 1st:0 2nd:1 3rd:0 Ran:7
Pre1999 - 1st:0 2nd:0 3rd:0 Ran:3
Win Prizemoney £0 *Total Prizemoney* £1,216
1999 Turf 0-7: (7f, 8f 5, 9f) (g-s, gd, g-f 2, frm 2, hrd)
Lengthy, moderate filly, effective 8f, acts on g-f. Turf high 48 - 2nd of 13 getting 18lb from It's Magic (11 Aug Leicester 8f g-f RF 3548). Inconsistent. **P W Harris [0-10] The Musketeers.*

KISSIMMEE BAY (IRE) BHB 36f **RR 40f** 3459[19]
3 b f Brief Truce (USA) 9.1f **(73)** - Deer Emily (Alzao (USA)) 7.1f **(68)**
Form - 8086005640
Record 1999 - 1st:0 2nd:0 3rd:0 Ran:10
Pre1999 - 1st:0 2nd:1 3rd:0 Ran:8
Win Prizemoney £0 *Total Prizemoney* £842
1999 Turf 0-10: (5f 3, 6f 6, 7f) (g-s, g-f 3, frm 5, hrd)
Moderate filly, effective 6f, acts on gd, has worn blinkers. Turf high 51. Inconsistent. **N Tinkler [0-18] Speedlith Group.*

KISSING TIME BHB 78f **RR 80f** 4651[6]
2 b f Lugana Beach 7f **(63)** - Princess Athena (Ahonoora) 8.1f **(73)**
Form - 71506
Record 1999 - 1st:1 2nd:0 3rd:0 Ran:5
Win Prizemoney £4,318 *Total Prizemoney* £4,318
Wins * 1999 Aug Bath (GD) 5.1f 80 <
1999 Turf 1-5: (5f 1-4, 6f) (gd 3, frm 1-2)
Decent filly. Turf high 80 (began Aug) - 1st of 13 getting 2lb from Dancing Empress (22 Aug Bath RF 3830).
**P F I Cole [1-5] W H Ponsonby.*

KISS ME GOODKNIGHT BHB 75f **RR 68f** 2133[15]
3 b f First Trump - Flitteriss Park (Beldale Flutter (USA)) 9.7f **(71)**
Form - 670
Record 1999 - 1st:0 2nd:0 3rd:0 Ran:3
Pre1999 - 1st:1 2nd:0 3rd:0 Ran:4
Win Prizemoney £3,081 *Total Prizemoney* £3,081
Wins 1998 Jly Chepst (GD) 6.1f 76+ <
1999 Turf 0-3: (6f 2, 8f) (g-f 2, frm)
Scopey, average filly, effective 6f, acts on gd. Turf high 66.
**I A Balding [0-3] Derek D & Mrs Jean P Clee (from P W Chapple-Hyam [1-4] Spt 1998).*

KISS ME KATE BHB 67f **RR 64f** 5075[1]
3 b f Aragon 7.7f **(58)** - Ingerence (FR) (Akarad (FR)) 9f **(76)**
Form - 83215368001
Record 1999 - 1st:2 2nd:1 3rd:2 Ran:11
Pre1999 - 1st:0 2nd:0 3rd:0 Ran:8
Win Prizemoney £5,484 *Total Prizemoney* £8,165
Wins * 1999 Oct Redcar (SFT) 10f 64
*** 1999** Jun Ripon (G-F) 10f 67 <
1999 Turf 2-11: (8f, 9f, 10f 2-9) (g-s, gd 1-3, g-f 3, frm 3, hrd 1-1)
Leggy, average filly, effective 10f, acts on gd to hrd, likes tight tracks. Turf high 67 - 3rd of 13 giving 11lb to Flossy (16 Jly Newbury 10f frm RF 2875) - also 1st of 8 from Legacy of Love (17 Jun Ripon RF 2075). Consistent.
**J W Hills [2-19] The Dan Abbott Racing Partnership.*

KISSOGRAM BHB 113f **RR 108f** 3694[9]
4 b f Caerleon (USA) 10.9f **(79)** - Alligram (USA) (Alysheba (USA)) 9f **(84)**
Form - 440
Record 1999 - 1st:0 2nd:0 3rd:0 Ran:3
Pre1999 - 1st:3 2nd:0 3rd:0 Ran:4
Win Prizemoney £50,403 *Total Prizemoney* £60,302
Wins * 1998 Oct Newmar () G2 10f 117+ <
* 1998 Aug Sandow (G-F) L 8.1f 101+
* 1998 Jun Yarmou (GD) 8f 82+
1999 Turf 0-3: (10f 3) (g-f 2, frm)
Leggy, Pattern-class filly, effective 10f, acts on gd to g-f, best on g-f. Turf high 108 - 4th of 8 giving 9lb to Zahrat Dubai (31 Jly Goodwood 10f g-f RF 3260). A well-bred filly, she concluded a successful three-year-old campaign by winning a substandard Sun Chariot. She had a light campaign at four, running her best race when beaten only a length in the Nassau Stakes at Goodwood.
**L M Cumani [3-7] Helena Springfield Ltd.*

KISTY (IRE) BHB 72f **RR 81f** 4728[4]
2 b f Kris 10f **(75)** - Pine Ridge (High Top) 10.2f **(67)**
Form - 854
Record 1999 - 1st:0 2nd:0 3rd:0 Ran:3
Win Prizemoney £0 *Total Prizemoney* £292
1999 Turf 0-3: (7f, 8f 2) (g-s, gd, frm)
Currently decent filly. Turf high 81 (began Spt).
**H Candy [0-3] Capt J Macdonald-Buchanan.*

KITTIWAKE RR 94f 4290[2]
3 b f Barathea (IRE) - Gull Nook (Mill Reef (USA)) 10.5f **(78)**
Form - 340512
Record 1999 - 1st:1 2nd:1 3rd:1 Ran:6
Win Prizemoney £3,891 *Total Prizemoney* £10,021
Wins * 1999 Jun Kempto (G-F) 10f 78+ <
1999 Turf 1-6: (7f, 10f 1-4, 11f) (sft, gd, g-f, frm 1-3)
Workmanlike, useful filly, effective 10f, acts on g-f to frm. Turf high 94 - 2nd of 7 to Gino's Spirits (14 Spt Yarmouth 10f g-f RF 4290). Ran creditably in Pattern events before dropping to maiden company to get off the mark. Just touched off in a listed event at Yarmouth on her first start and deserves to win in that grade.
**G Wragg [1-6] Gestut Schlenderhan.*

KI YASE (USA) RR 56f 5049[15]
2 b c Chief's Crown (USA) 10.2f **(75)** - Questionablevirtue (USA) (Key To The Mint (USA)) 9.4f **(75)**
Form - 00
Record 1999 - 1st:0 2nd:0 3rd:0 Ran:2
1999 Turf 0-2: (7f, 8f) (gd 2)
Currently fair colt. Turf high 56 (began Spt).
**Sir Michael Stoute [0-2] Hamdan Al Maktoum.*

KIZZAZZY RR 4819[P]
3 b f Chilibang 7f **(55)** - River Fire (IRE) (Petong) 6.6f **(58)**
Form - P
Record 1999 - 1st:0 2nd:0 3rd:0 Ran:1
1999 Turf 0-1: (7f) (gd)
Lengthy, currently very poor filly. *J L Harris [0-1] Friends Racing.*

KNAVE'S ASH (USA) BHB 54f **RR 51f** 3691[3]
8 ch g Miswaki (USA) 8.1f **(81)** - Quiet Rendezvous (USA) (Nureyev (USA)) 8.7f **(78)**
Form - 000003213723
Record 1999 - 1st:1 2nd:2 3rd:3 Ran:12
Pre1999 - 1st:6 2nd:2 3rd:3 Ran:38
Win Prizemoney £51,852 *Total Prizemoney* £70,010
Wins * 1999 Jly Redcar (FRM) H 8f 51 53
* 1998 Spt Newcas (GD) H 8f 64 68
* 1998 Jly Thirsk (FRM) H 8f 60 61
1995 Spt Pontef (GD) H 10f 94 98 <
1995 Jly Doncas (G-F) H 10.3f 88 93
1999 Turf 1-12: (7f 4, 8f 1-7, 10f) (gd 5, g-f 5, frm, hrd 1-1)

Fair gelding, effective 8 to 9f, best at 9f, acts on g-f to frm, best on g-f, likes left handed tracks, excels at Newcastle and Redcar. Turf high 53. Consistent.
**D Nicholls [3-34] J P Hames (from Sir Michael Stoute [4-16] Spt 1995).*

KNIGHTHOOD RR 43f 4992[11]

3 b c Highest Honor (FR) 10.9f **(72)** - Picardy (Polish Precedent (USA)) 10.2f **(60)**
Form - 8860
Record 1999 - 1st:0 2nd:0 3rd:0 Ran:4
1999 Turf 0-4: (7f, 8f, 9f, 10f) (g-s, gd, frm 2)
Workmanlike, moderate colt. Turf high 64.
**J W Hills [0-4] Highclere Thoroughbred Racing Ltd.*

KNIGHT OF SILVER BHB 50f RR 67f 5062[11]

2 gr c Presidium 7.5f **(56)** - Misty Rocket (Roan Rocket) 7.8f **(57)**
Form - 0853000
Record 1999 - 1st:0 2nd:0 3rd:1 Ran:7
Win Prizemoney £0 *Total Prizemoney* £510
1999 Turf 0-7: (5f, 6f 4, 7f, 8f) (gd, g-f 2, frm 4)
Average colt. Turf high 58.
**S Mellor [0-7] Silver Knight Exhibitions Ltd.*

KNIGHT'S EMPEROR (IRE) RR 76f 4875[7]

2 b c Grand Lodge (USA) - So Kind (Kind of Hush) 10.1f **(62)**
Form - 7
Record 1999 - 1st:0 2nd:0 3rd:0 Ran:1
1999 Turf 0-1: (6f) (gd)
Currently above-average colt. **J Noseda [0-1] M Olden.*

KNIGHT'S RETURN RR 22f 3598[9]

2 ch c Never so Bold 7.1f **(62)** - Return to Romance (Trojan Fen) 8.1f **(62)**
Form - 080
Record 1999 - 1st:0 2nd:0 3rd:0 Ran:3
1999 Turf 0-3: (6f, 7f 2) (g-f, frm, hrd)
Currently little account colt. Turf high 22 (began Jly).
**P D Evans [0-3] D Pugh.*

KNOBBLEENEEZE BHB 47f69a RR 44f 69a 5191[9]

9 ch g Aragon 7.7f **(58)** - Proud Miss (USA) (Semi-Pro) 7.5f **(70)**
Form - 20300040550
Record 1999 - 1st:0 2nd:1 3rd:1 Ran:11
Pre1999 - 1st:11 2nd:10 3rd:11 Ran:100
Win Prizemoney £49,283 *Total Prizemoney* £76,587

Wins								
* 1998	May	Newbur	(GD)	H	7.3f	62	67	
* 1997	Spt	Ayr	(G-S)	H	7f	65	65	
* 1997	Apr	Ripon	(GD)	H	8f	65	78	<
* 1996	Jun	Cheste	(G-F)	H	7f	67	73	
* 1995	Spt	Goodwo	(GD)		7f		73	
* 1995	Spt	Doncas	(GD)	H	7f	70	76	

1999 Turf 0-11: (7f 2, 8f 8, 9f) (g-s 2, gd 5, g-f 2, frm, hrd)
Moderate gelding, effective 7 to 8f, best at 7f, acts on gd to frm, mostly wears blinkers, likes left handed tracks. Turf high 60 (1st run) - 2nd of 19 to Night Chorus (28 Apr Pontefract 8f gd RF 0906). Consistent. **M R Channon [11-111] Anthony Andrews.*

KNOCKEMBACK NELLIE BHB 66f RR 64f 2275[5]

3 b f Forzando 7.2f **(63)** - Sea Clover (IRE) (Ela-Mana-Mou) 10.1f **(70)**
Form - 55005
Record 1999 - 1st:0 2nd:0 3rd:0 Ran:5
Pre1999 - 1st:0 2nd:2 3rd:0 Ran:9
Win Prizemoney £0 *Total Prizemoney* £1,645
1999 Turf 0-5: (5f, 6f 3, 7f) (gd 2, g-f, frm 2)
Unfurnished, average filly, effective 6f, acts on g-f to frm, best on frm. Turf high 70 - 5th of 17 getting 15lb from Loch Laird (2 May Salisbury 6f frm RF 0988).
**D R C Elsworth [0-14] Notaproperjob Partnership.*

KNOCKHOLT BHB 98f RR 97f 4251[1]

3 b g Be My Chief (USA) 10.2f **(62)** - Saffron Crocus (Shareef Dancer (USA)) 9.9f **(73)**
Form - 61624181
Record 1999 - 1st:3 2nd:1 3rd:0 Ran:8
Win Prizemoney £34,210 *Total Prizemoney* £37,091

Wins								
*** 1999**	Spt	Doncas	(G-F)	H	14.6f	95	97	<
*** 1999**	Jly	Goodwo	(FRM)	H	14f	87	91	
*** 1999**	May	Salisb	(G-F)		12f		83	

1999 Turf 3-8: (10f, 12f 1-1, 14f 1-4, 15f 1-2) (gd 2, g-f 2-4, frm 1-2)
Leggy, very useful gelding, effective 14 to 15f, best at 15f, acts on g-f to frm, best on g-f. Turf high 97 - 1st of 9 getting 14lb from Mardani (10 Spt Doncaster RF 4251) - also 1st of 6 from Loop The Loup (31 Jly Goodwood RF 3262). He proved a tough and progressive young stayer, running his only bad races at York. Likely to stay two miles, he goes well on a sound surface and will improve again. **S P C Woods [3-8] Crawley Racing.*

KNOCKTOPHER ABBEY BHB 81f RR 84f 4686[14]

2 ch c Pursuit of Love 9.5f **(69)** - Kukri (Kris) 9.5f **(73)**
Form - 428331600
Record 1999 - 1st:1 2nd:1 3rd:2 Ran:9
Win Prizemoney £2,794 *Total Prizemoney* £5,580
Wins * 1999 Jly Chepst (G-F) 6.1f 70 <
1999 Turf 1-9: (5f 2, 6f 1-6, 7f) (sft, gd 5, g-f 2, frm 1-1)
Decent colt, effective 5f, acts on gd. Turf high 81.
**B R Millman [1-9] Seasons Holidays.*

KNOTTY HILL BHB 55f60a RR 60df 60a 729[12]

7 b g Green Ruby (USA) 6.9f **(47)** - Esilam (Frimley Park) 6.5f **(67)**
Form - 700
Record 1999 - 1st:0 2nd:0 3rd:0 Ran:2
Pre1999 - 1st:2 2nd:5 3rd:3 Ran:29
Win Prizemoney £6,665 *Total Prizemoney* £14,664

Wins							
* 1998	May	Hamilt	(SFT)	6f	59	
* 1997	*Feb*	*Southw*	*(STD)*	*7f*	*79+*	<

1999 Turf 0-1: (7f) (gd) 1999 AW 0-1: (8f) (Fibr)
Average gelding, effective 6 to 7f, best at 6f, acts on hvy to g-f - acts on Fibr. Inconsistent. **R Craggs [2-31] Ray Craggs.*

KNYSNA LILY (USA) RR 75f 824[9]

3 b f Kris S (USA) 9.3f **(76)** - Kerygma (USA) (Drone) 10.3f **(74)**
Form - 0
Record 1999 - 1st:0 2nd:0 3rd:0 Ran:1
Pre1999 - 1st:0 2nd:0 3rd:1 Ran:1
Win Prizemoney £0 *Total Prizemoney* £540
1999 Turf 0-1: (10f) (g-s)
Scopey, currently above-average filly.
**J H M Gosden [0-2] Sheikh Mohammed.*

KOCAL BHB 45f RR 51f 3136[18]

3 b g Warrshan (USA) 9.7f **(59)** - Jeethgaya (USA) (Critique (USA))
Form - 0700
Record 1999 - 1st:0 2nd:0 3rd:0 Ran:4
1999 Turf 0-4: (7f 3, 8f) (gd 2, g-f, frm)
Leggy, fair gelding. Turf high 51. **D W Barker [0-4] T Calver.*

KOLBY BHB 46f42a RR 43f 42a 384[8]

4 b g Superpower 6.6f **(58)** - Abrasive (Absalom) 7.2f **(58)**
Form - 0308
Record 1999 - 1st:0 2nd:0 3rd:0 Ran:1
Pre1999 - 1st:1 2nd:1 3rd:1 Ran:11
Win Prizemoney £2,355 *Total Prizemoney* £3,286
Wins * 1998 May Mussel (G-F) S 5f 57 <
1999 AW 0-1: (6f) (Fibr)
Workmanlike, moderate gelding, effective 5f, acted on gd, often wore blinkers (effectively). (DEAD)
**A Bailey [1-12] Sandybrow Stables Ltd.*

KOMASEPH BHB 38f35a RR 29f 35a 3115[15]

7 b g Komaite (USA) 6.9f **(61)** - Starkist (So Blessed) 8.7f **(67)**
Form - 000077050
Record 1999 - 1st:0 2nd:0 3rd:0 Ran:6
Pre1999 - 1st:2 2nd:2 3rd:0 Ran:16
Win Prizemoney £4,806 *Total Prizemoney* £6,181

Wins								
* 1998	*Aug*	*Southw*	*(STD)*	*H*	*6f*	*53*	*58*	<
* 1998	*Jan*	*Southw*	*(STD)*		*6f*		*51*	

1999 Turf 0-2: (6f 2) (g-f, frm) 1999 AW 0-4: (5f, 6f 2, 7f) (Fibr 4)
Moderate gelding, effective 6f, - acts on Fibr, has worn blinkers, likes left handed tracks, likes tight tracks. Turf high 29. AW high 42. Inconsistent. **R F Marvin [2-22] J Shine.*

KOMISTAR BHB 88f RR 87f 5042[7]

4 ch g Komaite (USA) 6.9f **(61)** - Rosie's Gold (Glint of Gold) 9.3f **(66)**
Form - 35317617

Record 1999 - 1st:2 2nd:0 3rd:2 Ran:8
Pre1999 - 1st:1 2nd:1 3rd:1 Ran:6
Win Prizemoney £57,225 *Total Prizemoney* £62,958
Wins * **1999** Spt Newbur (G-F) H 10f 82 87
* **1999** Jun Doncas (Gd) H 10.3f 82 85
* 1997 Oct Warwic (G-F) 7f 93+ <
1999 Turf 2-8: (8f 2, 9f, 10f 2-4, 12f) (sft, gd 1-2, g-f 3, frm 1-2)
Neat, useful gelding, effective 8 to 10f, best at 10f, acts on g-s to frm, prefers left handed tracks. Turf high 87 - 1st of 16 getting 4lb from Senure (18 Spt Newbury RF 4404) - also 1st of 9 getting 21lb from Pasternak (27 Jun Doncaster RF 2351). He was given a fine ride to just get up and pip Pasternak in a Doncaster handicap in June, and was equally well ridden when gaining a battling short-head victory in the Courage Handicap at Newbury in September. Despite that, he is not particularly consistent.
**P W Harris [3-14] Class Act.*

KOMLUCKY BHB 42f27a RR 26f 27a 4398[14]

7 b m Komaite (USA) 6.9f **(61)** - Sweet And Lucky (Lucky Wednesday) 8f **(50)**
Form - 5054510030160000
Record 1999 - 1st:2 2nd:0 3rd:1 Ran:16
Pre1999 - 1st:4 2nd:8 3rd:3 Ran:56
Win Prizemoney £16,497 *Total Prizemoney* £25,482
Wins * **1999** Jly Ripon (GD) H 8f 45 48
* **1999** May Beverl (GD) H 7.5f 41 42
* 1998 Jly Catter (GD) H 7f 29 35
1997 May Thirsk (GD) S 7f 55
1996 Spt Catter (G-F) H 7f 48 51
1999 Turf 2-14: (7f 1-6, 8f 1-7, 10f) (gd 2-5, g-f 3, frm 6) 1999 AW 0-2: (8f 2) (Fibr 2)
Moderate mare, effective 7 to 8f, best at 8f, acts on gd to g-f, best on gd, often wears blinkers (very effectively), likes right handed tracks, likes Carlisle. Turf high 48 - 1st of 18 getting 22lb from Prodigal Son (5 Jly Ripon RF 2565) - also 1st of 16 getting 5lb from Miss Eliminator (8 May Beverley RF 1097). AW high 17. Becoming disappointing.
**K A Ryan [3-24] Hambleton Racing Partnership (from A B Mulholland [2-35] Apr 1998).*

KOMREYEV DANCER BHB 52f57a RR 54f 57a 2057[17]

7 b g Komaite (USA) 6.9f **(61)** - L'Ancressaan (Dalsaan) 9.8f **(64)**
Form - 0
Record 1999 - 1st:0 2nd:0 3rd:0 Ran:1
Pre1999 - 1st:4 2nd:9 3rd:5 Ran:52
Win Prizemoney £16,653 *Total Prizemoney* £33,725
Wins 1996 May Ripon (GD) H 10f 71 75 <
1996 Apr Beverl (G-F) H 9.9f 65 70
1995 *Jan Wolver (STD) H 8f 75 74*
1999 Turf 0-1: (8f) (hrd)
Fair gelding, effective 12f, acts on gd, has worn blinkers, likes left handed tracks.
**Mrs L Williamson [0-1] Miss Judy Eaton (from A Bailey [4-53] Jun 1998).*

KONDOTY (USA) BHB 92f RR 90f 578[2]

3 b c Mtoto 11.5f **(71)** - Princess Haifa (USA) (Mr Prospector (USA)) 8.8f **(78)**
Form - 2
Record 1999 - 1st:0 2nd:1 3rd:0 Ran:1
Pre1999 - 1st:0 2nd:1 3rd:1 Ran:2
Win Prizemoney £0 *Total Prizemoney* £2,672
1999 Turf 0-1: (11f) (g-f)
Scopey, currently useful colt. (1st run) - 2nd of 13 giving 5lb to Frippet (5 Apr Kempton 11f g-f RF 0578).
**M R Channon [0-3] Sheikh Ahmed Al Maktoum.*

KONKER BHB 59f RR 58f 690[6]

4 ch g Selkirk (USA) 7.9f **(76)** - Helens Dreamgirl (Caerleon (USA)) 8.6f **(71)**
Form - 76
Record 1999 - 1st:0 2nd:0 3rd:0 Ran:2
Pre1999 - 1st:1 2nd:0 3rd:2 Ran:10
Win Prizemoney £3,168 *Total Prizemoney* £4,215
Wins 1998 May Newbur (GD) C 10f 69 <
1999 Turf 0-2: (10f, 12f) (g-f, frm)
Scopey, fair gelding, effective 9 to 10f, best at 10f, acts on hvy to g-f. Turf high 58.
**G M Moore [0-8] J & M Leisure / Unos Restaurant (from W J Haggas [1-8] Jun 1998).*

KOOKABURRA (FR) BHB 88f RR 87f 5196[4]

2 b c Zafonic (USA) 9f **(83)** - Annoconnor (USA) (Nureyev (USA)) 8.7f **(78)**
Form - 423324
Record 1999 - 1st:0 2nd:2 3rd:2 Ran:6
Win Prizemoney £0 *Total Prizemoney* £5,187
1999 Turf 0-6: (7f 2, 8f 4) (g-s, gd 3, frm 2)
Useful colt, effective 8f, acts on gd. Turf high 87 (began Aug).
**B J Meehan [0-6] Mrs Susan Roy.*

KOOL CAPTAIN BHB 70f RR 74f 3258[13]

2 b c Distant Relative 7f **(69)** - Jhansi Ki Rani (USA) (Far North (CAN)) 9.7f **(75)**
Form - 0510
Record 1999 - 1st:1 2nd:0 3rd:0 Ran:4
Win Prizemoney £2,472 *Total Prizemoney* £2,472
Wins * **1999** Jly Bath (FRM) 5.7f 74 <
1999 Turf 1-4: (6f 1-2, 7f 2) (g-f 1-2, frm 2)
Above-average colt. Turf high 74 - 1st of 11 giving 5lb to Stoney Garnett (15 Jly Bath RF 2836). Bounced off the hard ground when getting off the mark at Bath in July. **S C Williams [1-4] M C North.*

KOSEVO (IRE) BHB 56f53a RR 52f 53a 4255[19]

5 b g Shareef Dancer (USA) 10.1f **(67)** - Kallista (Zeddaan) 9f **(76)**
Form - 522603275573727452563551026070
Record 1999 - 1st:1 2nd:4 3rd:3 Ran:25
Pre1999 - 1st:2 2nd:5 3rd:0 Ran:27
Win Prizemoney £13,132 *Total Prizemoney* £21,379
Wins * **1999** Jly Haydoc (FRM) H 5f 55 58 <
* 1998 *Jly Southw (STD) H 7f 50 54*
1998 *Jly Southw (STD) S 7f 58* <
1999 Turf 1-11: (5f 1-8, 6f 3) (gd, g-f 3, frm 1-6, hrd) 1999 AW 0-14: (6f 5, 7f 8, 8f) (Fibr 14)
Fair gelding, effective 5 to 7f, best at 7f, acts on g-f to frm - acts on AW, best on Fibr, mostly wears blinkers (extremely effectively), likes left handed tracks, likes tight tracks, and excels at Wolverhampton. Turf high 60 - 3rd of 17 getting 3lb from Rum Lad (14 Jun Pontefract 5f g-f RF 1988) - also 1st of 16 getting 15lb from Maladerie (11 Jly Haydock RF 2738). AW high 60 - 2nd of 11 giving 7lb to Mutabari (11 Jan Southwell 7f Fibr RF 0077). Inconsistent. The moment of the season for this horse came over five furlongs at Haydock on the afternoon Manchester United's players were the VIP guests, swooping fast and late to win a decent sprint handicap. **D Shaw [2-39] K Nicholls (from A Kelleway [1-4] Jly 1998).*

KPOLO BHB 22f36a RR 27f 36a 2314[6]

4 b g Polish Precedent (USA) 9f **(73)** - Ktolo (Tolomeo) 5.6f **(60)**
Form - 207847606
Record 1999 - 1st:0 2nd:0 3rd:0 Ran:8
Pre1999 - 1st:0 2nd:1 3rd:0 Ran:6
Win Prizemoney £0 *Total Prizemoney* £436
1999 Turf 0-3: (11f, 12f 2) (gd 2, g-f) 1999 AW 0-5: (8f 2, 13f 2, 16f) (Equi 3, Fibr 2)
Scopey, little account gelding, effective 12f, - acts on Fibr, has worn blinkers, likes left handed tracks. Turf high 27. AW high 29. Inconsistent.
**C N Kellett [0-5] Krishna Promotions Ltd (from B R Johnson [0-6] Feb 1999).*

KRAKING MAGIC BHB 53f48a RR 63f 48a 5148[8]

2 br f Magic Ring (IRE) 6.5f **(64)** - Little Kraker (Godswalk (USA)) 7.3f **(58)**
Form - 67088
Record 1999 - 1st:0 2nd:0 3rd:0 Ran:5
1999 Turf 0-4: (5f 2, 7f, 8f) (g-s, gd, frm 2) 1999 AW 0-1: (8f) (Fibr)
Average filly, has worn blinkers. Turf high 63 (1st run) - 6th of 13 to Pheisty (8 Apr Leicester 5f gd RF 0622).
**J W Mullins [0-5] T K Pearce.*

KRAM BHB 63f RR 68f 4332[1]

5 ch g Kris 10f **(75)** - Balenare (Pharly (FR)) 9.8f **(68)**
Form - 5057404061
Record 1999 - 1st:1 2nd:0 3rd:0 Ran:10
Pre1999 - 1st:2 2nd:3 3rd:3 Ran:27

Win Prizemoney £9,914 *Total Prizemoney* £17,595
Wins * **1999** Spt Sandow (G-S) C 5f 68 <
* 1998 Jun Salisb (G-F) H 5f 57 58
1997 Aug Tralee (G-S) H 5f 61
1999 Turf 1-10: (5f 1-6, 6f 4) (gd 1-3, g-f 4, frm 3)
Average gelding, effective 5 to 6f, best at 5f, acts on gd to frm, has worn blinkers. Turf high 68 - 1st of 13 getting 15lb from Fire Dome (15 Spt Sandown RF 4332).
**Mrs P N Dutfield [2-26] Mrs C A Clarke (from Patrick Prendergast in IRE [1-11] Aug 1997).*

KRIKLES BHB 55f **RR 58f** 2626[17]
3 ch c Selkirk (USA) 7.9f **(76)** - Bumpkin (Free State) 8.7f **(61)**
Form - 00
Record 1999 - 1st:0 2nd:0 3rd:0 Ran:2
Pre1999 - 1st:0 2nd:0 3rd:0 Ran:3
1999 Turf 0-2: (7f, 8f) (frm 2)
Leggy, fair colt. Turf high 28.
**A J McNae [0-2] Mrs Mette Campbell (from C A Horgan [0-3] Oct 1998).*

KRISALIGHT (USA) BHB 55f **RR 51f** 4862[4]
3 b br f Kris S (USA) 9.3f **(76)** - Dancing Grass (USA) (Northern Dancer) 9.6f **(80)**
Form - 464
Record 1999 - 1st:0 2nd:0 3rd:0 Ran:3
Pre1999 - 1st:0 2nd:0 3rd:0 Ran:1
Win Prizemoney £0 *Total Prizemoney* £516
1999 Turf 0-3: (10f, 11f, 12f) (sft 2, g-s)
Scopey, fair filly. Turf high 51 - 4th of 9 getting 22lb from Little Italy (13 Oct Haydock 11f sft RF 4862). **J L Dunlop [0-4] Hesmonds Stud.*

KRISPY KNIGHT BHB 80f **RR 83f** 5042[15]
4 ch c Kris 10f **(75)** - Top Table (Shirley Heights) 10.3f **(74)**
Form - 64700
Record 1999 - 1st:0 2nd:0 3rd:0 Ran:5
Pre1999 - 1st:2 2nd:0 3rd:2 Ran:6
Win Prizemoney £15,463 *Total Prizemoney* £17,334
Wins * 1998 Apr Kempto (HVY) L 8f 97+ <
* 1997 Jly Newmar (G-F) 6f 96
1999 Turf 0-5: (8f 4, 9f) (sft, g-s, gd, g-f, frm)
Scopey, decent colt, effective 8f, acts on hvy. Turf high 83. Inconsistent. Lightly raced since winning the '98 Easter Stakes at Kempton, and well held last season.
**J W Hills [2-11] Derek D & Mrs Jean P Clee.*

KRISSY (USA) BHB 77f **RR 70df** 3676[10]
3 br f Kris S (USA) 9.3f **(76)** - Rascal Rascal (USA) (Ack Ack (USA)) 12.7f **(82)**
Form - 40
Record 1999 - 1st:0 2nd:0 3rd:0 Ran:2
Pre1999 - 1st:0 2nd:0 3rd:0 Ran:1
Win Prizemoney £0 *Total Prizemoney* £291
1999 Turf 0-2: (10f, 11f) (gd, frm)
Scopey, currently above-average filly. Turf high 70 (began Aug).
**J H M Gosden [0-3] Landon Knight.*

KRISTINA BHB 84f **RR 86f** 4273[4]
3 ch f Kris 10f **(75)** - Derniere Danse (Gay Mecene (USA)) 8.6f **(69)**
Form - 6735234
Record 1999 - 1st:0 2nd:1 3rd:2 Ran:7
Pre1999 - 1st:1 2nd:1 3rd:0 Ran:2
Win Prizemoney £3,214 *Total Prizemoney* £10,331
Wins * 1998 Oct Nottin (G-S) 8.2f 82 <
1999 Turf 0-7: (10f 3, 12f 2, 15f, 16f) (g-s, gd 2, g-f 2, frm 2)
Scopey, useful filly, effective 8 to 15f, best at 10f, acts on g-s to frm, has worn blinkers, does well at Newmarket. Turf high 92 - 3rd of 6 giving 12lb to Ligne Gagnante (24 Jun Newcastle 12f gd RF 2266). Consistent. **Sir Michael Stoute [1-9] J H Richmond-Watson.*

KRYSTAL MAX (IRE) BHB 68f78a **RR 69f 78a** 642[2]
6 b g Classic Music (USA) 7.2f **(57)** - Lake Isle (IRE) (Caerleon (USA)) 8.6f **(71)**
Form - 03611113222
Record 1999 - 1st:4 2nd:3 3rd:1 Ran:8
Pre1999 - 1st:9 2nd:2 3rd:3 Ran:32
Win Prizemoney £40,986 *Total Prizemoney* £48,171
Wins * **1999** *Feb Wolver (STD) C 6f 78*
1999 *Jan Lingfi (STD) C 5f 70*
1999 *Jan Lingfi (STD) C 5f 70+*
1999 *Jan Lingfi (STD) C 6f 66*
1998 *Mar Lingfi (STD) H 5f 70 79*
1998 *Mar Southw (STD) H 5f 70 75*
1998 *Feb Lingfi (SLW) H 6f 60 65*
1997 *Jan Lingfi (STD) C 5f 67*
1996 *Feb Lingfi (STD) C 7f 82*
1996 *Jan Lingfi (STD) H 5f 83 82*
1995 *Dec Lingfi (STD) H 6f 80 84* <
1995 *Dec Southw (STD) H 5f 74 84* <
1995 Jun Redcar (FRM) 5f 78+
1999 AW 4-8: (5f 2-3, 6f 2-5) (Equi 3-6, Fibr 1-2)
Decent gelding, effective 5 to 6f, best at 5f, - acts on AW, best on Fibr, has worn blinkers, likes left handed tracks, likes tight tracks. AW high 80 - 2nd of 8 giving 16lb to Trojan Girl (10 Apr Wolverhampton 5f Fibr RF 0642) - also 1st of 7 giving 8lb to Samwar (6 Feb Wolverhampton RF 0243). Consistent. He is an effective sprinter on sand, especially in claiming company. He responds best if left alone and not bullied. He has been particularly well ridden by two female jockeys in recent seasons.
**T G Mills [1-5] Shipman Racing Ltd (from T D Barron [12-29] Jan 1999).*

KUMAIT (USA) BHB 101f **RR 100f** 4688[1]
5 b br g Danzig (USA) 8.1f **(88)** - Colour Chart (USA) (Mr Prospector (USA)) 8.8f **(78)**
Form - 400720221
Record 1999 - 1st:1 2nd:3 3rd:0 Ran:9
Pre1999 - 1st:2 2nd:3 3rd:6 Ran:20
Win Prizemoney £15,957 *Total Prizemoney* £45,643
Wins * **1999** Oct Redcar (GD) 7f 97
* 1998 Spt Yarmou (G-S) 6f 102 <
1996 Nov Newmar (GD) 6f 94
1999 Turf 1-9: (6f 2, 7f 1-7) (gd 4, g-f 1-3, frm 2)
Very useful gelding, effective 6 to 7f, best at 7f, acts on gd to frm, best on gd, and excels at Yarmouth. Turf high 100 - 2nd of 9 giving 3lb to Granny's Pet (20 Aug Chester 7f gd RF 3788) - also 1st of 5 getting 4lb from Black Amber (2 Oct Redcar RF 4688). Consistent. He usually looks well and is at his best when allowed to dominate a small field. Suited by six or seven furlongs on fast ground, he races with tremendous enthusiasm.
**E A L Dunlop [2-18] Maktoum Al Maktoum (from D R Loder [0-3] Spt 1997).*

KUMON EILEEN **RR 46f** 2241[13]
3 ch f Anshan 8.2f **(63)** - Katie Eileen (USA) (Bering) 7.4f **(61)**
Form 80
Record 1999 - 1st:0 2nd:0 3rd:0 Ran:2
1999 Turf 0-2: (9f, 10f) (frm 2)
Scopey, currently moderate filly. Turf high 46.
**J R Jenkins [0-2] The Royston Raiders.*

KURSIANG BHB 44f **RR 51f** 3434[13]
3 gr f Petong 7.6f **(58)** - Bellyphax (Bellypha) 9.8f **(73)**
Form - 00660
Record 1999 - 1st:0 2nd:0 3rd:0 Ran:5
Pre1999 - 1st:0 2nd:0 3rd:1 Ran:8
Win Prizemoney £0 *Total Prizemoney* £691
1999 Turf 0-5: (6f 2, 7f 3) (gd, g-f 2, frm 2)
Lengthy, fair filly, effective 6 to 7f, acts on g-f to hrd, has worn blinkers. Turf high 51. Inconsistent.
**B R Millman [0-9] C I T Racing Ltd (from M Meade [0-4] Jly 1998).*

KUSTER BHB 88f **RR 90f** 5042[11]
3 b c Indian Ridge 7.6f **(74)** - Ustka (Lomond (USA)) 8.8f **(65)**
Form - 120
Record 1999 - 1st:1 2nd:1 3rd:0 Ran:3
Pre1999 - 1st:0 2nd:0 3rd:0 Ran:1
Win Prizemoney £4,279 *Total Prizemoney* £6,142
Wins * **1999** Apr Epsom (SFT) 8.5f 86 <
1999 Turf 1-3: (9f 1-2, 10f) (sft, g-s 1-1, gd)
Scopey, useful colt. Turf high 90 - also 1st of 14 from Border Prince (21 Apr Epsom RF 0801). **L M Cumani [1-4] Lord Vestey.*

KUSTOM KIT KATE BHB 50f43a **RR 50f 43a** 1950[8]
4 b f Tragic Role (USA) 9.4f **(63)** - Wing of Freedom (Troy) 10.4f **(68)**

Form - 770007468
Record 1999 - 1st:0 2nd:0 3rd:0 Ran:9
Pre1999 - 1st:1 2nd:1 3rd:2 Ran:10
Win Prizemoney £3,446 *Total Prizemoney* £5,491
Wins * 1998 Mar Nottin (G-S) H 6.1f 58 64 <
1999 Turf 0-4: (6f, 7f 2, 8f) (g-s, gd 3) 1999 AW 0-5: (5f, 7f 2, 8f 2) (Fibr 5)
Light-framed, fair filly, effective 6 to 7f, best at 7f, acts on g-s - acts on Fibr, has worn blinkers. Turf high 50. AW high 43.
**S R Bowring [1-21] Charterhouse Holdings Plc.*

KUSTOM KIT KEVIN RR 38f 4541[9]
3 b g Local Suitor (USA) 9.7f **(58)** - Sweet Revival (Claude Monet (USA))
Form - 60
Record 1999 - 1st:0 2nd:0 3rd:0 Ran:2
1999 Turf 0-2: (7f, 10f) (frm 2)
Workmanlike, currently very moderate gelding. Turf high 38.
**S R Bowring [0-2] Charterhouse Holdings Plc.*

KUUIPO BHB 57f **RR 57f** 5076[9]
2 b f Puissance 7.1f **(60)** - Yankee Special (Bold Lad (IRE)) 8.4f **(68)**
Form - 46630600
Record 1999 - 1st:0 2nd:0 3rd:1 Ran:8
Win Prizemoney £0 *Total Prizemoney* £1,295
1999 Turf 0-8: (5f 4, 6f 4) (gd 5, g-f, frm 2)
Fair filly. Turf high 61. **B S Rothwell [0-8] S P Hudson.*

KUWAIT BIRD BHB 49f **RR 44f** 4905[11]
3 b c Cosmonaut - Loadplan Lass (Nicholas Bill) 10.1f **(56)**
Form - 00400
Record 1999 - 1st:0 2nd:0 3rd:0 Ran:5
Win Prizemoney £0 *Total Prizemoney* £369
1999 Turf 0-5: (6f 2, 8f 3) (gd, frm 4)
Leggy, moderate colt. Turf high 61. **K Mahdi [0-5] Greenfield Stud.*

KUWAIT DAWN (IRE) BHB 90f **RR 84f** 5039[7]
3 b f Pips Pride 6.7f **(70)** - Red Note (Rusticaro (FR)) 8.2f **(65)**
Form - 170476077007
Record 1999 - 1st:1 2nd:0 3rd:0 Ran:12
Pre1999 - 1st:0 2nd:1 3rd:0 Ran:5
Win Prizemoney £6,775 *Total Prizemoney* £13,187
Wins * **1999** Mar Doncas (G-S) 8f 99 <
1999 Turf 1-12: (7f 5, 8f 1-6, 10f) (g-s, gd 1-8, g-f, frm 2)
Lengthy, decent filly, effective 7 to 8f, acts on gd to frm. Turf high 104 - also 1st of 7 getting 5lb from Gold Academy (27 Mar Doncaster RF 0484). Consistent. Highly tried since winning at Doncaster in March, she does not appear to stay beyond a mile and is just a decent handicapper. **K Mahdi [1-17] Greenfield Stud.*

KUWAIT FLAVOUR (IRE) RR 63f 483[3]
3 b c Bluebird (USA) 7.9f **(71)** - Plume Magique (Kenmare (FR)) 6.5f **(72)**
Form - 3
Record 1999 - 1st:0 2nd:0 3rd:1 Ran:1
Pre1999 - 1st:0 2nd:0 3rd:0 Ran:1
Win Prizemoney £0 *Total Prizemoney* £797
1999 Turf 0-1: (6f) (gd)
Workmanlike, currently average colt. **K Mahdi [0-2] Greenfield Stud.*

KUWAIT ROSE RR 37f 4723[3]
3 b c Inchinor 8.9f **(64)** - Black Ivor (USA) (Sir Ivor) 10.2f **(70)**
Form - 03
Record 1999 - 1st:0 2nd:0 3rd:1 Ran:2
Win Prizemoney £0 *Total Prizemoney* £300
1999 Turf 0-2: (6f, 8f) (sft, gd)
Neat, currently very moderate colt. Turf high 37 (began Spt).
**K Mahdi [0-2] Greenfield Stud.*

KUWAIT SAND RR 62f 4723[7]
3 b c Lugana Beach 7f **(63)** - Soon to Be (Hot Spark) 7.6f **(62)**
Form - 47
Record 1999 - 1st:0 2nd:0 3rd:0 Ran:2
Win Prizemoney £0 *Total Prizemoney* £297
1999 Turf 0-2: (6f 2) (gd 2)
Light-framed, currently average colt. Turf high 62 (began Spt).
**K Mahdi [0-2] Greenfield Stud.*

KUWAIT THUNDER (IRE) BHB 57f **RR 57f** 5217[20]
3 ch c Mac's Imp (USA) 5.6f **(54)** - Romangoddess (IRE) (Rhoman Rule (USA))
Form - 3074850080
Record 1999 - 1st:0 2nd:0 3rd:1 Ran:10
Pre1999 - 1st:0 2nd:0 3rd:2 Ran:4
Win Prizemoney £0 *Total Prizemoney* £2,266
1999 Turf 0-10: (6f 5, 7f 3, 8f 2) (g-s, gd 5, g-f, frm 3)
Workmanlike, fair colt, effective 6f, acts on gd, has worn blinkers. Turf high 76. Inconsistent.
**J L Eyre [0-1] The Flowerpot Men (from K Mahdi [0-13] Oct 1999).*

KWIKPOINT BHB 41f **RR 34f** 2222[6]
5 ch g Never so Bold 7.1f **(62)** - Try the Duchess (Try My Best (USA)) 7.6f **(67)**
Form - 006
Record 1999 - 1st:0 2nd:0 3rd:0 Ran:3
Pre1999 - 1st:0 2nd:0 3rd:0 Ran:8
Win Prizemoney £0 *Total Prizemoney* £252
1999 Turf 0-3: (5f, 6f, 10f) (g-f, frm 2)
Very moderate gelding, effective 6f, acts on g-f, has worn blinkers. Turf high 34. **Martin Todhunter [0-12] R Garside.*

KYLKENNY BHB 55f **RR 54f** 5050[5]
4 b g Kylian (USA) 8.1f **(66)** - Fashion Flow (Balidar) 7.9f **(63)**
Form - 855
Record 1999 - 1st:0 2nd:0 3rd:0 Ran:3
1999 Turf 0-3: (8f, 9f, 10f) (g-s, gd 2)
Workmanlike, currently fair gelding. Turf high 54 (began Spt).
**H Morrison [0-3] Mrs P Payne.*

LAA JADEED (IRE) BHB 32f41a **RR 33f 41a** 4174[14]
4 b g Petorius 8f **(66)** - Sea Mistress (Habitat) 9.4f **(70)**
Form - 001780800800530
Record 1999 - 1st:1 2nd:0 3rd:1 Ran:13
Pre1999 - 1st:0 2nd:0 3rd:0 Ran:10
Win Prizemoney £2,126 *Total Prizemoney* £2,544
Wins * **1999** *Jan Southw (STD) 11f 48* <
1999 Turf 0-7: (10f 5, 12f 2) (g-f 5, frm, hrd) 1999 AW 1-6: (8f 3, 11f 1-2, 12f) (Fibr 1-6)
Scopey, moderate gelding, effective 8 to 11f, acts on gd - acts on Fibr, likes left handed tracks, likes tight tracks. Turf high 38. AW high 48 (1st run) - 1st of 8 giving 2lb to Blue Hopper (4 Jan Southwell RF 0022). Inconsistent.
**M J Polglase [1-14] T A Farrin (from J A Glover [0-9] Nov 1998).*

LAAL YAN BHB 44f **RR 46f** 1363[5]
3 b f Anshan 8.2f **(63)** -Cromarty **(62f)** (Shareef Dancer (USA)) 9.9f **(73)**
Form - 745
Record 1999 - 1st:0 2nd:0 3rd:0 Ran:3
Win Prizemoney £0 *Total Prizemoney* £251
1999 Turf 0-3: (10f, 11f, 12f) (gd 2, g-f)
Unfurnished, moderate filly. Turf high 46.
**J J O'Neill [0-3] Dr Linda Barber.*

LA BELLE MYSTERE RR 48f 3552[11]
2 b f Lycius (USA) 8.8f **(71)** - Mysterious Plans (IRE) (Last Tycoon) 8.5f **(62)**
Form - 80
Record 1999 - 1st:0 2nd:0 3rd:0 Ran:2
1999 Turf 0-2: (6f 2) (gd, frm)
Currently moderate filly. Turf high 48 (began Jly).
**B R Millman [0-2] Richard Withers.*

LA BIRBA (IRE) BHB 48f **RR 49f** 4923[4]
2 b f Prince of Birds (USA) - Ariadne (Bustino) 10.4f **(64)**
Form - 0004
Record 1999 - 1st:0 2nd:0 3rd:0 Ran:4
1999 Turf 0-3: (5f, 6f 2) (gd 2, frm) 1999 AW 0-1: (6f) (Fibr)
Moderate filly, has worn blinkers. Turf high 49 (began Spt).
**B J Meehan [0-4] G Battocchi.*

LABRETT BHB 90f **RR 90f** 5036[7]
2 b c Tragic Role (USA) 9.4f **(63)** - Play the Game (Mummy's Game) 8.2f **(60)**
Form - 54143145007

Record 1999 - 1st:2 2nd:0 3rd:1 Ran:11
Win Prizemoney £5,822 *Total Prizemoney* £8,546
Wins * **1999** Jun Cheste (G-F) 5.1f 82 <
* **1999** May Redcar (SFT) 5f 72
1999 Turf 2-11: (5f 2-7, 6f 4) (g-s 2, gd 1-3, g-f, frm 1-5)
Useful colt, effective 5 to 6f, best at 5f, acts on gd to frm, best on frm, often wears blinkers (effectively). Turf high 90 - 5th of 7 giving 5lb to Tabheej (11 Spt Doncaster 6f frm RF 4263) - also 1st of 9 giving 7lb to Villa Romana (23 Jun Chester RF 2230). A winner at Redcar and Chester on different types of ground, he looks suited by the minimum trip. **B J Meehan [2-11] T G Holdcroft.*

LA CAPRICE (USA) BHB 78f RR 75f 3869[1]
2 ch f Housebuster (USA) 7f **(81)** - Shicklah (USA) (The Minstrel (CAN)) 10f **(72)**
Form - 204521
Record 1999 - 1st:1 2nd:2 3rd:0 Ran:6
Win Prizemoney £3,200 *Total Prizemoney* £5,796
Wins * **1999** Aug Lingfi (G-F) 5f 75 <
1999 Turf 1-6: (5f 1-6) (gd 3, g-f 1-2, frm)
Above-average filly, effective 5f, acts on gd to frm, best on g-f. Turf high 75 - 1st of 9 getting 5lb from Lalando (24 Aug Lingfield RF 3869). **J Berry [1-6] Slatch Farm Stud.*

LACE WING RR 55f 5136[13]
2 ch f Caerleon (USA) 10.9f **(79)** -Capo Di Monte (Final Straw) 7.9f **(64)**
Form - 0
Record 1999 - 1st:0 2nd:0 3rd:0 Ran:1
1999 Turf 0-1: (7f) (gd)
Currently fair filly. **B W Hills [0-1] Maktoum Al Maktoum.*

LA CHARPENTIERE BHB 59f RR 60f 3831[13]
5 b g Robellino (USA) 9.5f **(68)** - Antoinette Jane (Ile de Bourbon (USA)) 10.1f **(67)**
Form - 0870
Record 1999 - 1st:0 2nd:0 3rd:0 Ran:4
Pre1999 - 1st:0 2nd:0 3rd:0 Ran:1
1999 Turf 0-4: (7f, 8f 2, 9f) (g-s, g-f 2, frm)
Average gelding. Turf high 60.
**P Bowen [0-4] Mrs G R Taylor (from G A Cusack in IRE [0-1] Aug 1996).*

LA CHATELAINE BHB 32a RR 28f 2295[3]
5 b m Then Again 7.4f **(52)** - La Domaine (Dominion) 8.5f **(63)**
Form - 878563
Record 1999 - 1st:0 2nd:0 3rd:1 Ran:4
Pre1999 - 1st:2 2nd:2 3rd:0 Ran:26
Win Prizemoney £7,271 *Total Prizemoney* £10,202
Wins * 1998 Jun Epsom (GD) H 12f 39 45
1997 Aug Bright (G-F) H 7f 43 48 <
1999 Turf 0-4: (10f 3, 12f) (g-s, frm 2, hrd)
Little account filly, effective 11 to 12f, best at 11f, acts on gd to frm, has worn blinkers, favours left handed tracks, favours tight tracks. Turf high 28.
**Miss B Sanders [1-19] Blake Wales & Laycock (from G Lewis [1-11] Spt 1997).*

LA CINECITTA (FR) BHB 39f RR 36f 3376[9]
3 ch f Dancing Spree (USA) 8f **(59)** - Cox's Feather (USA) (Cox's Ridge (USA)) 8f **(68)**
Form - 0000
Record 1999 - 1st:0 2nd:0 3rd:0 Ran:4
Pre1999 - 1st:0 2nd:0 3rd:0 Ran:3
1999 Turf 0-4: (6f, 7f, 8f, 10f) (frm 4)
Workmanlike, very moderate filly, has worn blinkers. Turf high 36. **C B B Booth [0-7] David Hutchinson.*

LA DOYENNE (IRE) BHB 52f58a RR 55f 58a 5161[5]
5 ch m Masterclass (USA) 5.9f **(63)** - Sainthill (St Alphage) 6.6f **(60)**
Form - 010326842505
Record 1999 - 1st:1 2nd:2 3rd:1 Ran:11
Pre1999 - 1st:5 2nd:1 3rd:2 Ran:30
Win Prizemoney £15,143 *Total Prizemoney* £19,846
Wins * **1999** *May Southw (STD) H 5f 52 60* <
* 1998 Spt Hamilt (SFT) H 5f 48 53
* 1998 Aug Beverl (G-F) H 5f 36 48
* 1998 *Feb Lingfi (SLW) H 5f 48 49*
* 1997 *Dec Southw (STD) H 5f 32 41*
* 1997 Aug Bright (G-F) 7f 54
1999 Turf 0-7: (5f 7) (gd 4, g-f 2, frm) 1999 AW 1-4: (5f 1-4) (Fibr 1-4)
Average filly, effective 5f, acts on gd to g-f - acts on AW, best on Fibr, does well at Southwell and Lingfield. Turf high 55. AW high 60 (1st run) - 1st of 12 getting 3lb from Rajmata (6 May Southwell RF 1061). She does not win that often, but can be difficult to catch if able to dominate. Suited by the straight Southwell five, she is speedy but has hung right on occasions.
**C B B Booth [6-41] Mrs J B Robinson.*

LADY ALEXANDER (IRE) RR 102f 4313a[12]
4 ch f Night Shift (USA) 8.1f **(73)** - Sandhurst Goddess (Sandhurst Prince) 7.9f **(63)**
Form - 5800
1999 Turf 0-4: (5f 2, 6f 2) (gd 2, g-f 2)
Very useful filly, effective 5 to 6f, acts on gd, has worn blinkers. Turf high 102. Inconsistent. A useful sprinter at two and three, she appeared to lose her way in 1999.
**C Collins in IRE [3-15] Mrs N O'Callaghan.*

LADY ANGHARAD (IRE) BHB 76f RR 80f 4377[14]
3 b f Tenby 10.4f **(76)** - Lavezzola (IRE) (Salmon Leap (USA)) 11f **(61)**
Form - 570060200
Record 1999 - 1st:0 2nd:1 3rd:0 Ran:9
Pre1999 - 1st:2 2nd:0 3rd:0 Ran:7
Win Prizemoney £26,713 *Total Prizemoney* £29,327
Wins * 1998 Jun Salisb (G-F) 7f 88
* 1998 Jun Epsom (GD) L 6f 88 <
1999 Turf 0-9: (8f 2, 10f 6, 12f) (g-s, gd, g-f 3, frm 4)
Workmanlike, decent filly, effective 6 to 7f, acts on gd to frm, has worn blinkers. Turf high 92. Useful as a juvenile, she ran her best race of '99 in a first time visor. **A P Jarvis [2-16] Ambrose Turnbull.*

LADY ANNABEL BHB 44f RR 35f 1606[9]
3 b f Alhijaz 7.7f **(57)** - Anna Rella (IRE) (Danehill (USA)) 10f **(72)**
Form - 0070
Record 1999 - 1st:0 2nd:0 3rd:0 Ran:4
Pre1999 - 1st:0 2nd:0 3rd:0 Ran:2
1999 Turf 0-4: (6f, 7f, 8f 2) (gd, g-f, frm 2)
Leggy, very moderate filly. Turf high 35.
**C W Fairhurst [0-6] M R Handy.*

LADY ARDROSS BHB 34f RR 27f 5153[15]
4 b f Flying Tyke 7.2f **(42)** - Hatshepsut (Ardross) 10.6f **(68)**
Form - 80000
Record 1999 - 1st:0 2nd:0 3rd:0 Ran:5
Pre1999 - 1st:0 2nd:0 3rd:0 Ran:1
1999 Turf 0-4: (5f, 6f, 8f, 10f) (sft, gd 3) 1999 AW 0-1: (6f) (Fibr)
Light-framed, little account filly, has worn blinkers. Turf high 27.
**A Smith [0-6] Alfred Smith.*

LADY BALLA CALM (IRE) BHB 25f RR 5113[19]
3 b f Balla Cove -Across The Ring (IRE) (Auction Ring (USA)) 8.6f **(65)**
Form - 0
Record 1999 - 1st:0 2nd:0 3rd:0 Ran:1
Pre1999 - 1st:0 2nd:0 3rd:0 Ran:3
1999 Turf 0-1: (6f) (gd)
Formerly poor filly.
**J J Bridger [0-1] T S D (from M J Byrne in IRE [0-3] Oct 1998).*

LADY BENSON (IRE) BHB 21f24a RR 27f 24a 3863[15]
6 b m Pennine Walk 8.9f **(64)** - Sit Elnaas (USA) (Sir Ivor) 10.2f **(70)**
Form - 00220057000
Record 1999 - 1st:0 2nd:2 3rd:0 Ran:11
Pre1999 - 1st:0 2nd:0 3rd:0 Ran:10
Win Prizemoney £0 *Total Prizemoney* £2,114
1999 Turf 0-9: (9f, 10f 4, 12f 4) (gd 2, g-f 3, frm 4) 1999 AW 0-2: (5f, 8f) (Fibr 2)
Little account mare, effective 9 to 10f, acts on gd to g-f, likes tight tracks. Turf high 40 - 2nd of 17 getting 18lb from Sunshine Boy (1 Jun Leicester 10f g-f RF 1647). AW high 20.
**W M Brisbourne [0-18] B L Benson (from D J S Cosgrove [0-3] Aug 1996).*

LADY BEWARE BHB 36f RR 33f 4945[11]
3 b f Warning 8.1f **(77)** - Thewaari (USA) (Eskimo (USA))

Form - 00800780
Record 1999 - 1st:0 2nd:0 3rd:0 Ran:8
Pre1999 - 1st:0 2nd:0 3rd:1 Ran:8
Win Prizemoney £0 *Total Prizemoney* £651
1999 Turf 0-8: (5f 3, 6f 3, 7f 2) (sft, gd 3, frm 4)
Workmanlike, very moderate filly, has worn blinkers.
**M R Channon [0-16] W H Ponsonby.*

LADY BOXER BHB 74f RR 75f 5072[14]

3 b f Komaite (USA) 6.9f **(61)** - Lady Broker **(44a)** (Petorius) 7.3f **(61)**
Form - 04100
Record 1999 - 1st:1 2nd:0 3rd:0 Ran:5
Pre1999 - 1st:1 2nd:0 3rd:1 Ran:5
Win Prizemoney £7,366 *Total Prizemoney* £8,783
Wins * **1999** Spt Cheste (SFT) 6.1f 75 <
* 1998 Jun Leices (SFT) 6f 74+
1999 Turf 1-5: (6f 1-4, 7f) (g-s 1-1, gd 2, g-f 2)
Leggy, above-average filly, effective 6f, acts on g-s to gd, best on gd. Turf high 75 (began Aug) - 1st of 10 from Lively Lady (22 Spt Chester RF 4483). After making a belated comeback in July she pulled things together when finishing fourth in the Ayr Silver Cup, and went on from that to score in heavy ground at Chester. Six furlongs and soft conditions bring out the best in her.
**M Mullineaux [2-10] Esprit de Corps Racing.*

LADY BREANNE (IRE) BHB 55f50a RR 63f 50a 4180[2]

3 b f Woods of Windsor (USA) - Tootsie Roll (Comedy Star (USA)) 7.5f **(50)**
Form - 4602
Record 1999 - 1st:0 2nd:1 3rd:0 Ran:4
Pre1999 - 1st:0 2nd:0 3rd:1 Ran:3
Win Prizemoney £0 *Total Prizemoney* £1,991
1999 Turf 0-4: (6f, 7f 2, 8f) (frm 4)
Average filly, effective 7f, acts on frm. Turf high 63 - 2nd of 11 getting 9lb from One Dinar (7 Spt Lingfield 7f frm RF 4180).
**G L Moore [0-4] Royal Palm Racing (from B Lawlor in IRE [0-3] Oct 1998).*

LADYCAKE (IRE) BHB 43f52a RR 38f 52a 2362[6]

3 gr f Perugino (USA) - Olivia's Pride (IRE) (Digamist (USA))
Form - 7335460776
Record 1999 - 1st:0 2nd:0 3rd:1 Ran:8
Pre1999 - 1st:2 2nd:2 3rd:1 Ran:11
Win Prizemoney £5,392 *Total Prizemoney* £7,635
Wins * 1998 Aug Mussel (GD) S 5f 67 <
* 1998 May Mussel (GD) 5f 65+
1999 Turf 0-4: (5f 3, 6f) (gd 3, g-f) 1999 AW 0-4: (5f 3, 6f) (Fibr 4)
Workmanlike, fair filly, effective 5f, acts on g-f to frm, best on g-f, has worn blinkers. **J Berry [2-19] E Nisbet.*

LADY CARBRON (IRE) BHB 52f53a RR 58df 53a 770[18]

3 br f Elbio 9f **(62)** - Smart Turn (His Turn)
Form - 325650
Record 1999 - 1st:0 2nd:1 3rd:0 Ran:5
Pre1999 - 1st:1 2nd:3 3rd:2 Ran:10
Win Prizemoney £1,865 *Total Prizemoney* £4,692
Wins * 1998 *Apr Wolver (STD) S 5f 56* <
1999 Turf 0-1: (6f) (sft) 1999 AW 0-4: (5f 3, 6f) (Equi, Fibr 3)
Leggy, fair filly, effective 5f, acts on gd - acts on Fibr, likes tight tracks. AW high 57. **J Berry [1-15] P Conroy.*

LADY CAROLINE (IRE) BHB 52a RR 37f 4997[12]

3 b f Hamas (IRE) 8f **(72)** - Pericolo (IRE) (Kris) 9.5f **(73)**
Form - 20215563656300000
Record 1999 - 1st:0 2nd:0 3rd:2 Ran:12
Pre1999 - 1st:1 2nd:3 3rd:0 Ran:9
Win Prizemoney £2,832 *Total Prizemoney* £5,873
Wins 1998 *Dec Lingfi (STD) H 6f 65 69* <
1999 Turf 0-5: (5f, 6f 2, 8f, 10f) (sft, gd 3, frm) 1999 AW 0-7: (5f, 6f 2, 7f 2, 8f 2) (Equi 3, Fibr 4)
Scopey, moderate filly, effective 5 to 6f, - acts on AW.
**A T Murphy [0-4] Hertford Offset Ltd (from M Johnston [1-17] Apr 1999).*

LADY COLDUNELL BHB 60f65a RR 62f 65a 5133[5]

3 b f Deploy 11.4f **(67)** - Beau's Delight (USA) (Lypheor) 12f **(71)**
Form - 0722243147152585
Record 1999 - 1st:2 2nd:4 3rd:1 Ran:16
Pre1999 - 1st:0 2nd:0 3rd:0 Ran:2
Win Prizemoney £7,557 *Total Prizemoney* £11,845
Wins * **1999** Aug Epsom (GD) H 12f 55 55
* **1999** *Jly Lingfi (STD) H 12f 52 62* <
1999 Turf 1-12: (12f 1-6, 14f 2, 16f 3, 17f) (hvy, gd 2, g-f 1-5, frm 4)
1999 AW 1-4: (7f, 11f, 12f 1-2) (Equi 1-2, Fibr 2)
Scopey, average filly, effective 12 to 16f, acts on g-f to frm - acts on Equi, likes right handed tracks, prefers tight tracks, excels at Epsom. Turf high 62 - 2nd of 6 getting 25lb from Height of Fantasy (29 Aug Beverley 16f frm RF 3987) - also 1st of 5 getting 30lb from Imani (13 Aug Epsom RF 3606). AW high 62 - 1st of 9 getting 5lb from Imprevue (7 Jly Lingfield RF 2627).
**N A Callaghan [2-18] Peter Crane.*

LADY CONFESS BHB 39f36a RR 41f 36a 4717[5]

9 ch m Backchat (USA) 11.8f **(53)** - Special Branch (Acer)
Form - 31325
Record 1999 - 1st:1 2nd:1 3rd:2 Ran:5
Pre1999 - 1st:1 2nd:1 3rd:0 Ran:11
Win Prizemoney £6,069 *Total Prizemoney* £8,707
Wins * **1999** Aug Pontef (GD) H 17.1f 30 35
1999 Turf 1-5: (11f, 16f 2, 17f 1-2) (gd, frm 1-4)
Moderate mare, has worn blinkers. Turf high 41 (began Jly). Better known as a hurdler these days, she needs an extreme test of stamina on the Flat and had just that when winning nicely at Pontefract in August.
**M W Easterby [3-12] Winton Bloodstock Ltd (from Mrs N Macauley [1-11] Mar 1994).*

LADY CYRANO BHB 53f49a RR 59f 49a 4868[13]

2 b f Cyrano de Bergerac 7.3f **(58)** - Hazy Kay (IRE) (Treasure Kay)
Form - 0033643000
Record 1999 - 1st:0 2nd:0 3rd:3 Ran:10
Win Prizemoney £0 *Total Prizemoney* £892
1999 Turf 0-4: (5f, 6f 2, 8f) (g-f 2, frm 2) 1999 AW 0-6: (5f 5, 6f) (Fibr 6)
Fair filly, effective 6f, acts on g-f, has worn blinkers. Turf high 59. AW high 50. Inconsistent. **Mrs N Macauley [0-10] J Teasdale.*

LADY D'ABO BHB 28f25a RR 25a 313[9]

4 b f Ron's Victory (USA) 9.2f **(52)** - Lady Sabo **(37?f 42a)** (Prince Sabo) 7.2f **(62)**
Form - 000
Record 1999 - 1st:0 2nd:0 3rd:0 Ran:3
Pre1999 - 1st:0 2nd:0 3rd:0 Ran:3
1999 AW 0-3: (5f, 6f, 7f) (Equi, Fibr 2)
Leggy, formerly very poor filly, has worn blinkers.
**Mrs S Lamyman [0-3] John Purcell (from R C Spicer [0-3] Spt 1997).*

LADY DONATELLA BHB 60f RR 60f 4560[10]

2 b f Last Tycoon 9.4f **(73)** - Nekhbet (Artaius (USA)) 9f **(69)**
Form - 680
Record 1999 - 1st:0 2nd:0 3rd:0 Ran:3
1999 Turf 0-3: (6f 2, 7f) (g-s, gd, g-f)
Currently average filly. Turf high 60 (began Aug).
**M L W Bell [0-3] Mrs M Swinburn.*

LADY DORCHESTER RR 44f 3419[6]

2 b f Then Again 7.4f **(52)** - Miramede (Norwick (USA)) 7.2f **(56)**
Form - 5566
Record 1999 - 1st:0 2nd:0 3rd:0 Ran:4
1999 Turf 0-4: (5f, 6f 2, 7f) (gd, frm 3)
Moderate filly. Turf high 44.
**Miss Gay Kelleway [0-4] Dorchester Racing Club.*

LADY EXCALIBER BHB 37f RR 38f 4727[14]

2 b f Sure Blade (USA) 10.6f **(66)** - Bewails (IRE) (Caerleon (USA)) 8.6f **(71)**
Form - 006650
Record 1999 - 1st:0 2nd:0 3rd:0 Ran:6
1999 Turf 0-5: (5f 2, 6f, 8f, 10f) (sft, g-s, gd, g-f, frm) 1999 AW 0-1: (6f) (Fibr)
Very moderate filly, has worn blinkers. Turf high 38.
**J Cullinan [0-6] Turf 2000 Ltd.*

LADY FEARLESS RR 46f 4981[6]

2 b f Cosmonaut - Lady Broker **(44a)** (Petorius) 7.3f **(61)**

Form - 06
Record 1999 - 1st:0 2nd:0 3rd:0 Ran:2
1999 Turf 0-2: (6f, 7f) (g-s, g-f)
Currently moderate filly. Turf high 46 (began Spt).
**M Mullineaux [0-2] Esprit de Corps Racing.*

LADY FLORA RR 44f 2259[6]

3 b f Alflora (IRE) - Lady Marguerrite **(57f)** (Blakeney) 10.5f **(64)**
Form - 6
Record 1999 - 1st:0 2nd:0 3rd:0 Ran:1
1999 Turf 0-1: (6f) (hrd)
Lengthy, currently moderate filly.
**D McCain [0-1] Champ Chicken Co Ltd.*

LADY FROM LUCCA BHB 53f48a RR 62f 48a 4939[5]

2 b f Inchinor 8.9f **(64)** - Play With Me (IRE) (Alzao (USA)) 7.1f **(68)**
Form - 688065
Record 1999 - 1st:0 2nd:0 3rd:0 Ran:6
1999 Turf 0-4: (6f 3, 7f) (gd, g-f 3) 1999 AW 0-2: (6f, 7f) (Fibr 2)
Average filly, has worn blinkers. Turf high 62 (began Aug). AW high 50 (began Spt). **Sir Mark Prescott [0-6] Tessona Racing Ltd.*

LADY GEORGIA BHB 85f RR 987f 4796[10]

3 gr f Arazi (USA) 9.2f **(74)** - Petillante (Petong) 6.6f **(58)**
Form - 5310
Record 1999 - 1st:1 2nd:0 3rd:1 Ran:3
Pre1999 - 1st:0 2nd:2 3rd:1 Ran:10
Win Prizemoney £4,985 *Total Prizemoney* £12,522
Wins * 1999 Aug Warwic (GD) 7.7f 77 <
1999 Turf 1-3: (8f 1-3) (gd 1-2, frm)
Lengthy, very useful filly, effective 8f, acts on sft. Turf high 77 (began Jly). Faced some near-impossible tasks at two, but showed some ability, and finally got off the mark in a Warwick maiden on her second start of this season. **C E Brittain [1-13] A J Richards.*

LADY HELEN (IRE) RR 63f 4378[8]

2 b f Salse (USA) 10.9f **(71)** -Old Domesday Book (High Top) 10.2f **(67)**
Form - 50188
Record 1999 - 1st:1 2nd:0 3rd:0 Ran:5
Win Prizemoney £3,995 *Total Prizemoney* £3,995
Wins * 1999 Jly Beverl (G-F) 7.5f 63 <
1999 Turf 1-5: (6f 2, 7f 1-2, 8f) (gd 2, g-f, frm 1-2)
Average filly. Turf high 63 - also 1st of 5 getting 5lb from High Cheviot (27 Jly Beverley RF 3159). **T D Easterby [1-5] M P Burke.*

LADY ILSLEY (USA) RR 95f 4362a[2]

3 b f Trempolino (USA) 11.9f **(77)** - Sue Warner (USA) (Forli (ARG)) 9.6f **(67)**
Form - 32
1999 Turf 0-2: (8f 2) (gd 2)
Currently very useful filly. Turf high 95 (began Aug) - 2nd of 9 to Oriental Fashion (8 Spt Chantilly 8f gd RF 4362a).
**Mme C Head in FR [0-2].*

LADY IN COLOUR (IRE) RR 69f 1451[2]

3 b f Cadeaux Genereux 7.9f **(76)** - Piffle (Shirley Heights) 10.3f **(74)**
Form - 2
Record 1999 - 1st:0 2nd:1 3rd:0 Ran:1
Win Prizemoney £0 *Total Prizemoney* £1,138
1999 Turf 0-1: (10f) (gd)
Neat, currently average filly. (1st run) - 2nd of 8 to Heartwood (25 May Beverley 10f gd RF 1451).
**J Noseda [0-1] Mrs N Chambers & Mrs J Dye.*

LADY IN WAITING BHB 108f RR 109f 5018a[5]

4 b f Kylian (USA) 8.1f **(66)** - High Savannah (Rousillon (USA)) 8.2f **(74)**
Form - 122015
Record 1999 - 1st:2 2nd:2 3rd:0 Ran:6
Pre1999 - 1st:4 2nd:2 3rd:0 Ran:11
Win Prizemoney £76,240 *Total Prizemoney* £143,240

Wins						
* 1999	Oct	Newmar (SFT)	G2	10f	109	<
* 1999	May	York (SFT)	L	10.4f	102	
* 1998	Oct	Newmar (GD)	L	10f	97	
* 1998	Spt	Chepst (G-S)		10.2f	109+	
* 1997	Jun	Newmar (SFT)	L	6f	92	
* 1997	Jun	Leices (G-F)		5f	86	

1999 Turf 2-6: (10f 2-5, 12f) (g-s 1-1, gd 1-3, g-f 2)
Workmanlike, Pattern-class filly, effective 8 to 12f, best at 10f, acts on g-s to frm, best on gd. Turf high 109 - 1st of 8 giving 5lb to Gino's Spirits (2 Oct Newmarket RF 4682) - also 1st of 6 giving 3lb to Primary Colours (12 May York RF 1181). She was the easy winner of a substandard Sun Chariot Stakes, proving well suited by the ten furlongs and good ground. Runner-up earlier in the Irish Pretty Polly and in a messy race for the Nassau at Goodwood, she was beaten in Canada on her final run. **P F I Cole [6-17].*

Lady in Waiting gained due reward for her efforts in the Sun Chariot

LADY IONA BHB 32f RR 27f 4807[5]

3 ch f Weldnaas (USA) 8.4f **(55)** - Shadha (Shirley Heights) 10.3f **(74)**
Form - 08286785
Record 1999 - 1st:0 2nd:1 3rd:0 Ran:8
Pre1999 - 1st:0 2nd:0 3rd:0 Ran:5
Win Prizemoney £0 *Total Prizemoney* £720
1999 Turf 0-8: (8f 4, 9f, 10f 2, 11f) (sft, gd, g-f 6)
Light-framed, little account filly, effective 8f, acts on g-f, likes left handed tracks, likes tight tracks. Turf high 44 - 2nd of 16 getting 11lb from Hadeqa (14 Jun Pontefract 8f g-f RF 1987).
**Martyn Wane [0-13] Mrs C M Barlow.*

LADY IRENE (IRE) BHB 42f35a RR 41f 35a 5107[2]

3 br f Tirol 8.1f **(64)** - Felsen (IRE) (Ballad Rock) 7.8f **(63)**
Form - 6256004042
Record 1999 - 1st:0 2nd:2 3rd:0 Ran:10
Win Prizemoney £0 *Total Prizemoney* £1,693
1999 Turf 0-6: (10f 4, 12f 2) (hvy, g-s, gd 2, g-f, frm) 1999 AW 0-4: (7f, 8f 2, 9f) (Equi 3, Fibr)
Neat, moderate filly, effective 10 to 12f, acts on g-s to gd. Turf high 41 - 2nd of 12 getting 5lb from Game Tufty (28 Oct Windsor 10f gd RF 5107). AW high 43. **T J Naughton [0-10] G E Archer.*

LADY JO BHB 62f RR 61f 4078[10]

3 ch f Phountzi (USA) 9.6f **(60)** - Lady Kalliste (Another Realm) 6.6f **(55)**
Form - 0331716860
Record 1999 - 1st:2 2nd:0 3rd:2 Ran:10
Pre1999 - 1st:0 2nd:0 3rd:0 Ran:3
Win Prizemoney £6,314 *Total Prizemoney* £7,091

Wins							
* 1999	Jun	Lingfi (G-F)	H	10f	64	66+	<
* 1999	Jun	Yarmou (GD)	H	10.1f	58	65	

1999 Turf 2-9: (8f, 10f 2-6, 11f, 12f) (gd, g-f 1-2, frm 1-6) 1999 AW 0-1: (10f) (Equi)

Workmanlike, average filly, effective 10f, acts on gd to frm, best on g-f, prefers left handed tracks, prefers tight tracks. Turf high 66 - 1st of 4 giving 7lb to Mill Afrique (25 Jun Lingfield RF 2295) - also 1st of 14 getting 1lb from First Fantasy (10 Jun Yarmouth RF 1894). Consistent. Scored twice over ten furlongs on decent ground in June but has disappointed since.
**S Dow [2-13] Ken Butler.*

LADY JONES BHB 53f **RR 57f** 4995[14]
2 b f Emperor Jones (USA) - So Beguiling (USA) (Woodman (USA)) 9f **(74)**
Form - 508100
Record 1999 - 1st:1 2nd:0 3rd:0 Ran:6
Win Prizemoney £2,304 *Total Prizemoney* £2,304
Wins * 1999 Spt Bright (G-F) S 7f 57 <
1999 Turf 1-6: (6f, 7f 1-3, 8f 2) (g-s, gd 2, frm 1-3)
Fair filly, effective 7f, acts on frm. Turf high 57 (began Jly) - 1st of 12 getting 5lb from Dr Duke (1 Spt Brighton RF 4073).
**J Pearce [1-6] Peter Routledge.*

LADY LAUREN BHB 39f **RR 37f** 4905[13]
3 b f Cyrano de Bergerac 7.3f **(58)** - Wandering Stranger (Petong) 6.6f **(58)**
Form - 000000
Record 1999 - 1st:0 2nd:0 3rd:0 Ran:6
Pre1999 - 1st:0 2nd:0 3rd:3 Ran:6
Win Prizemoney £0 *Total Prizemoney* £1,295
1999 Turf 0-6: (5f 3, 6f 2, 7f) (frm 5, hrd)
Light-framed, very moderate filly, effective 5 to 6f, best at 5f, acts on gd to hrd, has worn blinkers. Turf high 47. Inconsistent.
**G Woodward [0-12] Luke Devine.*

LADY LAZARUS BHB 43f **RR 33f** 2841[12]
3 ch f Beveled (USA) 6.9f **(64)** - Swilly Express (Ballacashtal (CAN)) 5.3f **(50)**
Form - 0000
Record 1999 - 1st:0 2nd:0 3rd:0 Ran:4
Pre1999 - 1st:0 2nd:0 3rd:1 Ran:5
Win Prizemoney £0 *Total Prizemoney* £772
1999 Turf 0-4: (6f, 7f, 8f, 10f) (g-f, frm 3)
Scopey, very moderate filly. Turf high 33. Becoming disappointing.
**M Blanshard [0-9] P J Doherty.*

LADY-LOVE BHB 70f **RR 74f** 3751[8]
2 b f Pursuit of Love 9.5f **(69)** - Lady Day (FR) (Lightning (FR)) 7.9f **(74)**
Form - 1768
Record 1999 - 1st:1 2nd:0 3rd:0 Ran:4
Win Prizemoney £2,801 *Total Prizemoney* £2,801
Wins * 1999 Jun Mussel (GD) 5f 74+ <
1999 Turf 1-4: (5f 1-2, 6f 2) (gd, g-f 1-2, frm)
Above-average filly. Turf high 74 (1st run) - 1st of 10 from I'm Sophie (14 Jun Musselburgh RF 1977).
**Denys Smith [1-4] Duke of Sutherland.*

LADY MARGARET BHB 50f **RR 36f** 5068[10]
3 b f Sir Harry Lewis (USA) - Candarela (Damister (USA)) 9f **(73)**
Form - 66660
Record 1999 - 1st:0 2nd:0 3rd:0 Ran:5
1999 Turf 0-4: (8f, 10f, 12f, 15f) (gd, g-f, frm 2) 1999 AW 0-1: (16f) (Equi)
Leggy, very moderate filly. Turf high 40.
**Mrs L Richards [0-1] Ian Murray Tough (from P R Hedger [0-4] Aug 1999).*

LADY MELBOURNE (IRE) BHB 67f58a **RR 47f 58a** 5160[18]
3 b f Indian Ridge 7.6f **(74)** - Gayshuka (Lord Gayle (USA)) 8.8f **(62)**
Form - 8210000
Record 1999 - 1st:1 2nd:1 3rd:0 Ran:6
Pre1999 - 1st:0 2nd:1 3rd:0 Ran:5
Win Prizemoney £3,988 *Total Prizemoney* £6,358
Wins * 1999 Jly Thirsk (FRM) H 6f 68 72 <
1999 Turf 1-5: (5f 2, 6f 1-3) (g-s, g-f, frm 1-3) 1999 AW 0-1: (6f) (Fibr)
Scopey, fair filly, effective 6f, acts on gd to frm. Turf high 72 - 1st of 14 from Morgan Le Fay (31 Jly Thirsk RF 3285). Becoming disappointing.
**M Johnston [1-11] Hertford Offset Ltd.*

LADY MONTDORE BHB 44f **RR 57f** 5158[16]
2 b f Pursuit of Love 9.5f **(69)** - Kentfield (Busted) 10.2f **(61)**
Form - 0670
Record 1999 - 1st:0 2nd:0 3rd:0 Ran:4
1999 Turf 0-3: (5f, 8f 2) (gd, frm 2) 1999 AW 0-1: (7f) (Fibr)
Fair filly. Turf high 57.
**T J Etherington [0-3] David Abell (from M Johnston [0-1] May 1999).*

LADY MOORINGS (IRE) BHB 33f **RR 37f** 3250[9]
3 b f Dolphin Street (FR) - Crimson Ring (Persian Bold) 9.3f **(66)**
Form - 0607660
Record 1999 - 1st:0 2nd:0 3rd:0 Ran:7
Pre1999 - 1st:0 2nd:0 3rd:0 Ran:3
1999 Turf 0-7: (8f 2, 10f 3, 11f, 12f) (hvy, g-f 3, frm 3)
Light-framed, very moderate filly, effective 10f, acted on g-f, had worn blinkers, liked tight tracks. Turf high 37. (DEAD)
**M Blanshard [0-10] David Sykes.*

LADY MUCK (IRE) BHB 49f **RR 46f** 5068[9]
3 b f Shalford (IRE) 7.8f **(63)** - Kept in Style (Castle Keep) 8.3f **(57)**
Form - 08600
Record 1999 - 1st:0 2nd:0 3rd:0 Ran:5
Pre1999 - 1st:1 2nd:2 3rd:0 Ran:8
Win Prizemoney £3,647 *Total Prizemoney* £5,617
Wins * 1998 Jly Epsom (G-F) 7f 72 <
1999 Turf 0-5: (7f, 8f 2, 10f 2) (gd 2, g-f 2, frm)
Light-framed, moderate filly, effective 7 to 8f, acts on g-f to frm, has worn blinkers, likes left handed tracks, likes tight tracks. Turf high 46 (began Jly). Becoming disappointing.
**D J S ffrenchDavis [1-13] Mrs Patrick McCarthy.*

LADY NOOR BHB 70f **RR 71f** 5214[8]
2 b f Lugana Beach 7f **(63)** - Noor El Houdah (IRE) **(49f 48a)** (Fayruz)
Form - 073038
Record 1999 - 1st:0 2nd:0 3rd:2 Ran:6
Win Prizemoney £0 *Total Prizemoney* £1,515
1999 Turf 0-6: (5f 4, 6f 2) (sft, g-s 2, gd 2, frm)
Above-average filly. Turf high 71.
**Mrs P N Dutfield [0-6] Mrs Margaret Sinanan.*

LADY ODDJOB (IRE) BHB 34f50a **RR 27f 50a** 5107[10]
3 gr f Up and At 'em - Thalssa (Rusticaro (FR)) 8.2f **(65)**
Form - 530035700
Record 1999 - 1st:0 2nd:0 3rd:1 Ran:7
Pre1999 - 1st:0 2nd:0 3rd:1 Ran:3
Win Prizemoney £0 *Total Prizemoney* £796
1999 Turf 0-3: (6f, 10f 2) (gd 3) 1999 AW 0-4: (7f, 8f 2, 9f) (Fibr 4)
Neat, moderate filly, effective 8f, - acts on Fibr, has worn blinkers (very effectively), likes left handed tracks, likes tight tracks. Turf high 27. AW high 56 - 3rd of 8 to Delphini (10 Jly Southwell 8f Fibr RF 2717). Inconsistent. **K McAuliffe [0-10] S S M Partnership.*

LADY OF ARAGON BHB 43f **RR 47f** 3398[13]
3 b f Aragon 7.7f **(58)** - Gentle Stream (Sandy Creek) 8.9f **(59)**
Form - 07650
Record 1999 - 1st:0 2nd:0 3rd:0 Ran:5
Pre1999 - 1st:0 2nd:0 3rd:0 Ran:5
Win Prizemoney £0 *Total Prizemoney* £199
1999 Turf 0-5: (8f, 9f, 10f 2, 12f) (gd, g-f, frm 3)
Lengthy, moderate filly, effective 7f, acts on g-f, has worn blinkers, likes left handed tracks, likes tight tracks. Turf high 53.
**M J Heaton-Ellis [0-10] P G Lowe.*

LADY OF CHAD (IRE) RR 108+f 4776a[1]
2 b f Last Tycoon 9.4f **(73)** - Sahara Breeze (Ela-Mana-Mou) 10.1f **(70)**
Form - 11
1999 Turf 2-2: (8f 2-2) (sft 1-1, gd 1-1)
Currently Pattern-class filly. Turf high 108 (began Spt) - 1st of 11 from New Story (3 Oct Longchamp RF 4776a).
**R Gibson in FR [2-2] J D Martin.*

LADY OF GUADALOPE (IRE) BHB 25f30a **RR 16f 30a** 2723[18]
4 b f Tirol 8.1f **(64)** - Gorgeous Annie (Hello Gorgeous (USA)) 9.7f **(63)**
Form - 668000
Record 1999 - 1st:0 2nd:0 3rd:0 Ran:6
Pre1999 - 1st:0 2nd:0 3rd:0 Ran:4

1999 Turf 0-3: (10f 2, 11f) (gd, g-f 2) 1999 AW 0-3: (8f 2, 11f) (Fibr 3)
Little account filly, has worn blinkers. Turf high 16. AW high 29.
**D J S Cosgrove [0-6] Forgotten Travellers (from P J Flynn in IRE [0-5] Spt 1998).*

LADY OF HONOUR (IRE) BHB 73f **RR 73f** 4504[14]

2 b f Bigstone (IRE) - Zabeta (Diesis) 9.3f **(69)**
Form - 38010
Record 1999 - 1st:1 2nd:0 3rd:1 Ran:5
Win Prizemoney £4,378 *Total Prizemoney* £4,939
Wins * 1999 Spt Yarmou (G-F) H 7f 69 73 <
1999 Turf 1-5: (7f 1-4, 8f) (gd 2, g-f 1-2, frm)
Above-average filly. Turf high 73 (began Jly) - 1st of 11 from Inchinnan (14 Spt Yarmouth RF 4294).
**E A L Dunlop [1-5] Khalifa Sultan.*

LADY OF THE DANCE BHB 31f **RR 10f** 4529[10]

4 b f Tragic Role (USA) 9.4f **(63)** - Waltz (Jimmy Reppin) 8.8f **(64)**
Form - 00
Record 1999 - 1st:0 2nd:0 3rd:0 Ran:2
Pre1999 - 1st:0 2nd:0 3rd:0 Ran:4
1999 Turf 0-2: (10f, 14f) (g-s, g-f)
Workmanlike, moderate filly. (began Jly).
**P Eccles [0-1] Andrew Lambert (from J S Wainwright [0-1] Jly 1999).*

LADY OF THE LUNE BHB 20f **RR 18f** 3394[15]

4 b f Skyliner 6.8f **(51)** - Hot Feet (Marching On) 6f **(60)**
Form - 000
Record 1999 - 1st:0 2nd:0 3rd:0 Ran:2
Pre1999 - 1st:0 2nd:0 3rd:0 Ran:5
1999 Turf 0-1: (7f) (frm) 1999 AW 0-1: (6f) (Fibr)
Workmanlike, poor filly, has worn blinkers.
**J M Bradley [0-1] C P Howells (from D HaydnJones [0-6] May 1999).*

LADY OF THE NIGHT (IRE) **RR 63f** 4729[4]

4 b f Night Shift (USA) 8.1f **(73)** - Joma Kaanem (Double Form) 7.3f **(58)**
Form - 74
Record 1999 - 1st:0 2nd:0 3rd:0 Ran:2
Win Prizemoney £0 *Total Prizemoney* £321
1999 Turf 0-2: (7f, 8f) (g-s, frm)
Strong, currently average filly. Turf high 63 (began Spt).
**P W Harris [0-2] The Euro Crew.*

LADY OF WINDSOR (IRE) BHB 70f **RR 73f** 5163[4]

2 ch f Woods of Windsor (USA) - North Lady (Northfields (USA)) 9f **(72)**
Form - 44432240474
Record 1999 - 1st:0 2nd:2 3rd:1 Ran:11
Win Prizemoney £0 *Total Prizemoney* £4,176
1999 Turf 0-11: (5f, 6f 3, 7f 5, 8f 2) (sft, g-s, gd 4, g-f 3, frm, hrd)
Above-average filly, effective 6 to 8f, acts on gd to g-f, best on g-f, mostly wears blinkers (extremely effectively), likes tight tracks. Turf high 73. **I Semple [0-11] Raeburn Brick Ltd.*

LADY PEPPIATT (IRE) BHB 43f50a **RR 34f 50a** 3550[9]

3 b f Tirol 8.1f **(64)** - Kirsova (Absalom) 7.2f **(58)**
Form - 16200600
Record 1999 - 1st:1 2nd:1 3rd:0 Ran:8
Pre1999 - 1st:2 2nd:0 3rd:3 Ran:11
Win Prizemoney £6,309 *Total Prizemoney* £8,542
Wins * 1999 *Jan Southw (STD) C 8f 58*
*** 1998** *Jly Southw (STD) C 6f 64* <
*** 1998** *Jun Southw (STD) S 6f 64* <
1999 Turf 0-3: (6f, 7f, 8f) (g-f, frm 2) 1999 AW 1-5: (6f, 7f 2, 8f 1-2) (Fibr 1-5)
Lengthy, fair filly, effective 5 to 8f, best at 6f, acts on gd to hrd - acts on Fibr, likes left handed tracks, likes tight tracks, excels at Windsor and Southwell. Turf high 34. AW high 58 (1st run) - 1st of 9 getting 11lb from Ultra Calm (25 Jan Southwell RF 0160).
**J S Moore [3-19] West Lancs Antiques Export Racing.*

LADY PETRA BHB 30f **RR 48f** 3748[14]

3 b f Petong 7.6f **(58)** - Miss Clarinet **(8f)** (Pharly (FR)) 9.8f **(68)**
Form - 08000
Record 1999 - 1st:0 2nd:0 3rd:0 Ran:5
Pre1999 - 1st:0 2nd:0 3rd:0 Ran:3
1999 Turf 0-4: (8f 2, 9f, 10f) (gd 2, g-f, frm) 1999 AW 0-1: (8f) (Equi)
Light-framed, moderate filly, has worn blinkers. Turf high 48. Becoming disappointing. **V Soane [0-8] Classic Four Partnership.*

LADY RACHEL (IRE) BHB 46f53a **RR 47f 53a** 5190[7]

4 b f Priolo (USA) 10.9f **(71)** - Alpine Spring (Head for Heights) 9.6f **(55)**
Form - 70276300007
Record 1999 - 1st:0 2nd:1 3rd:1 Ran:11
Pre1999 - 1st:2 2nd:3 3rd:6 Ran:17
Win Prizemoney £6,607 *Total Prizemoney* £17,625
Wins * 1998 Aug Carlis (G-S) H 12f 64 69 <
*** 1998** May Pontef (G-F) H 10f 60 66
1999 Turf 0-10: (12f 3, 13f, 14f 5, 16f) (g-s, gd 4, g-f 3, frm 2) 1999 AW 0-1: (12f) (Fibr)
Neat, average filly, effective 10 to 15f, acts on g-s to frm, best on gd, likes left handed tracks, favours tight tracks. Turf high 64 - 2nd of 17 getting 13lb from Nichol Fifty (19 Apr Nottingham 14f g-s RF 0750). **J L Eyre [2-28] Steve Macdonald.*

LADY ROCKSTAR BHB 75f **RR 75df** 5106[5]

4 b f Rock Hopper 10.6f **(54)** - Silk St James (Pas de Seul) 9.1f **(67)**
Form - 00415254027405
Record 1999 - 1st:1 2nd:2 3rd:0 Ran:14
Pre1999 - 1st:8 2nd:0 3rd:1 Ran:19
Win Prizemoney £28,631 *Total Prizemoney* £37,379
Wins * 1999 May Newbur (G-S) H 10f 76 80
*** 1998** Jun Windso (GD) 10f 86+ <
*** 1998** Jun Folkes (G-F) H 9.7f 65 76+
*** 1998** Jun Windso (GD) H 10f 65 78
*** 1998** Jun Nottin (G-S) H 8.2f 56 75
*** 1998** Jun Yarmou (SFT) H 10.1f 47 61+
*** 1998** Jun Haydoc (GD) H 8.1f 40 55
*** 1998** Jun Folkes (GD) H 9.7f 40 53+
*** 1998** May Ayr (G-F) H 9.1f 40 48
1999 Turf 1-14: (10f 1-13, 11f) (sft, g-s 1-4, gd 2, g-f 3, frm 3, hrd)
Workmanlike, above-average filly, effective 10 to 11f, best at 10f, acts on g-s to frm, best on g-f, has worn blinkers, prefers tight tracks, excels at Windsor , nd Haydock, does well at Folkestone, likes Yarmouth. Turf high 84 - 2nd of 13 giving 18lb to Mutadarra (11 Jun Sandown 10f frm RF 1922) - also 1st of 20 giving 22lb to Sea Danzig (14 May Newbury RF 1216). One of the success stories of '98, she racked up eight consecutive victories in little more than a month. She was given a chance by the Handicapper when scoring at Newbury on her fourth start of last term, but has been held since. **M J Ryan [9-33] The Five Star Partnership.*

LADY SANDROVITCH (IRE) BHB 53f **RR** 1064[4]

2 b f Desert Style (IRE) - Mauras Pride (IRE) (Cadeaux Genereux)
Form - 54
Record 1999 - 1st:0 2nd:0 3rd:0 Ran:2
1999 Turf 0-1: (5f) (gd) 1999 AW 0-1: (5f) (Fibr)
Currently fair filly. **R A Fahey [0-2] P Sandrovitch.*

LADY SANTANA (IRE) BHB 68f **RR 66f** 4178[7]

2 b f Doyoun 10.7f **(69)** - Santana Lady (IRE) **(64df 60a)** (Blakeney) 10.5f **(64)**
Form - 807
Record 1999 - 1st:0 2nd:0 3rd:0 Ran:3
1999 Turf 0-3: (5f 2, 6f) (gd, g-f, frm)
Currently average filly. Turf high 66 (began Jly).
**Mrs Merrita Jones [0-1] F J Sainsbury (from C G Cox [0-1] Aug 1999).*

LADY SARKA (IRE) BHB 91f **RR 88f** 4908[1]

2 b f Lake Coniston (IRE) - Petite Epaulette (Night Shift (USA)) 7.2f **(69)**
Form - 4142021
Record 1999 - 1st:2 2nd:2 3rd:0 Ran:7
Win Prizemoney £7,227 *Total Prizemoney* £10,895
Wins * 1999 Oct Catter (GD,) 5f 85 <
*** 1999** May Warwic (Gd) 5f 81
1999 Turf 2-7: (5f 2-5, 6f 2) (gd 1-4, g-f 2, frm 1-1)
Useful filly, effective 5 to 6f, best at 6f, acts on gd to frm, best on gd. Turf high 88 - 2nd of 9 giving 7lb to Red Letter (19 Jun Ascot 6f g-f RF 2138) - also 1st of 7 getting 2lb from Uncle Exact (16 Oct Catterick RF 4908). Showed herself to be a pacey filly when winning at Warwick on her second start and disproved the view that she cannot stay six when second over that trip in soft ground at

Haydock, but won back at the minimum at Catterick. **R Hannon [2-7] Thurloe Thoroughbreds IV.*

LADY SO BOLD BHB 46f44a **RR 41f 44a** 1020[14]
4 ch f Bold Arrangement 8.7f **(57)** - Lady Blues Singer (Chief Singer) 8.9f **(66)**
Form - 0
Record 1999 - 1st:0 2nd:0 3rd:0 Ran:1
Pre1999 - 1st:0 2nd:0 3rd:0 Ran:7
1999 Turf 0-1: (10f) (hrd)
Leggy, moderate filly. Inconsistent. **Mrs L Stubbs [0-8] A P Griffin.*

LADY STALKER BHB 58f **RR 58f** 5064[15]
2 b f Primo Dominie 7.2f **(67)** - Tarvie (Swing Easy (USA)) 6.5f **(55)**
Form - 74660
Record 1999 - 1st:0 2nd:0 3rd:0 Ran:5
Win Prizemoney £0 *Total Prizemoney* £257
1999 Turf 0-5: (5f 4, 6f) (gd, g-f 2, frm 2)
Fair filly. Turf high 58.
**M J Fetherston-Godley [0-5] P Fetherston-Godley.*

LADY STORM (IRE) RR 100f 1534a[5]
3 b f Mujadil (USA) 7.7f **(70)** - Lady Lord (IRE) (Coquelin (USA)) 8.4f **(58)**
Form - 35
1999 Turf 0-2: (8f, 11f) (hvy, gd)
Currently very useful filly. Turf high 100 (1st run) - 3rd of 16 to Shenck (18 Apr Capannelle 8f hvy RF 0811a). Third in the Italian 1,000 Guineas, she may not stay much beyond a mile.
**B Grizzetti in ITY [0-3].*

LADY TILLY BHB 47f **RR 49df** 5187[13]
2 b f Puissance 7.1f **(60)** - Lady of Itatiba (BEL) (King Of Macedon) 8.1f **(59)**
Form - 67037560
Record 1999 - 1st:0 2nd:0 3rd:1 Ran:8
Win Prizemoney £0 *Total Prizemoney* £550
1999 Turf 0-8: (5f 4, 7f 3, 8f) (sft, gd 4, g-f, frm 2)
Moderate filly, has worn blinkers. Turf high 61. Becoming disappointing. **Martyn Wane [0-8] James S Kennerley and Miss Jenny Hall.*

LADY UPSTAGE (IRE) RR 92f 5041[4]
2 b f Alzao (USA) 9.8f **(73)** - She's the Tops (Shernazar) 10.2f **(73)**
Form - 3014
Record 1999 - 1st:1 2nd:0 3rd:1 Ran:4
Win Prizemoney £3,745 *Total Prizemoney* £5,107
Wins * 1999 Spt Bright (SFT) 7f 86+ <
1999 Turf 1-4: (7f 1-4) (sft, g-s 1-1, g-f, frm)
Useful filly. Turf high 92 - also 1st of 11 getting 5lb from Bhutan Prince (29 Spt Brighton RF 4627). Thrown in at the deep end when contesting the Moyglare Stud Stakes on her second start, she not surprisingly failed to figure, but had little difficulty landing a moderate Brighton maiden next time. Finished well in a Listed race on her final start. **B W Hills [1-4] Mrs E Roberts.*

LADY VETTORI RR 101f 4776a[3]
2 b f Vettori (IRE) - Lady Golconda (Kendor)
Form - 113
1999 Turf 2-3: (6f 1-1, 7f 1-1, 8f) (sft, gd 2-2)
Currently very useful filly. Turf high 101 (began Aug) - 3rd of 11 to Lady Of Chad (3 Oct Longchamp 8f sft RF 4776a).
**Francois Rohaut in FR [2-3] A Crichton.*

LADY VIENNA BHB 50f **RR 60f** 4582[5]
2 ch f Weldnaas (USA) 8.4f **(55)** - Fresh Lady (IRE) (Fresh Breeze (USA))
Form - 0805
Record 1999 - 1st:0 2nd:0 3rd:0 Ran:4
1999 Turf 0-3: (7f 2, 10f) (gd 2, frm) 1999 AW 0-1: (6f) (Fibr)
Average filly. Turf high 60. **W G M Turner [0-4] Mrs J Glover.*

LADY WYN BHB 25f **RR 31f** 4228[17]
4 ch f Mac's Fighter - Wanracine (Dom Racine (FR)) 9.2f **(62)**
Form - 000
Record 1999 - 1st:0 2nd:0 3rd:0 Ran:3
1999 Turf 0-3: (7f, 8f, 10f) (g-f, frm 2)
Leggy, currently very moderate filly. Turf high 26 (began Aug).
**J M Bradley [0-3] Philip Davies.*

LA FAY RR 78f 4815[4]
2 b f Caerleon (USA) 10.9f **(79)** - Fayrooz (USA) **(81df)** (Gulch (USA)) 8f **(81)**
Form - 24
Record 1999 - 1st:0 2nd:1 3rd:0 Ran:2
Win Prizemoney £0 *Total Prizemoney* £2,160
1999 Turf 0-2: (7f 2) (gd, frm)
Currently above-average filly. Turf high 78 (began Spt).
**J L Dunlop [0-2] Capt J Macdonald-Buchanan.*

LAFITE BHB 83f **RR 83+f** 5117a[9]
3 b f Robellino (USA) 9.5f **(68)** - Gorgeous Dancer (IRE) (Nordico (USA)) 6.5f **(62)**
Form - 31348110
Record 1999 - 1st:3 2nd:0 3rd:2 Ran:8
Pre1999 - 1st:0 2nd:0 3rd:1 Ran:3
Win Prizemoney £18,651 *Total Prizemoney* £20,974
Wins * 1999 Oct Bright (G-S) H 10f 79 83 <
*** 1999** Spt Newbur (G-S) H 10f 75 78+
*** 1999** Jly Chepst (G-F) H 8.1f 74 75
1999 Turf 3-8: (8f 1-3, 10f 2-4, 11f) (sft, gd 2-3, frm 1-4)
Strong, decent filly, effective 8 to 11f, best at 10f, acts on gd to frm, best on gd, likes tight tracks. Turf high 83 - 1st of 10 giving 6lb to Dansker (4 Oct Brighton RF 4710) - also 1st of 14 getting 10lb from West Escape (19 Spt Newbury RF 4421). Found her form in the autumn, scoring at Newbury and Brighton. **J W Hills [3-11].*

LAFLEUR (IRE) RR 79f 5020[7]
2 ch f Grand Lodge (USA) - Russian Countess (USA) (Nureyev (USA)) 8.7f **(78)**
Form - 7
Record 1999 - 1st:0 2nd:0 3rd:0 Ran:1
1999 Turf 0-1: (8f) (gd)
Currently above-average filly.
**M R Channon [0-1] Wood Hall Stud Ltd.*

LA GALLERIA BHB 38f **RR 46f** 2424[9]
4 ch f Royal Academy (USA) 7.8f **(77)** - Two and Sixpence (USA) (Chief's Crown (USA)) 9.8f **(72)**
Form - 0
Record 1999 - 1st:0 2nd:0 3rd:0 Ran:1
Pre1999 - 1st:0 2nd:0 3rd:0 Ran:2
1999 Turf 0-1: (12f) (frm)
Scopey, currently moderate filly. **J S Moore [0-3] D J Walker.*

LAGAN BHB 29f44a **RR 24f 44a** 2226[8]
6 b g Shareef Dancer (USA) 10.1f **(67)** - Lagta (Kris) 9.5f **(73)**
Form - 08
Record 1999 - 1st:0 2nd:0 3rd:0 Ran:2
Pre1999 - 1st:0 2nd:1 3rd:1 Ran:15
Win Prizemoney £0 *Total Prizemoney* £1,814
1999 Turf 0-2: (17f, 22f) (gd, frm)
Very moderate gelding, has worn blinkers. Turf high 24. Inconsistent.
**S Gollings [1-8] Wild Racing (from K A Morgan [2-6] Jly 1997).*

L'AGNEAU NOIR BHB 46f **RR 33f** 4156[13]
3 br f Rock City 8.8f **(62)** - Shernborne (Kalaglow) 9.8f **(67)**
Form - 0000
Record 1999 - 1st:0 2nd:0 3rd:0 Ran:4
Pre1999 - 1st:0 2nd:1 3rd:0 Ran:3
Win Prizemoney £0 *Total Prizemoney* £852
1999 Turf 0-4: (6f, 7f 2, 8f) (gd, frm 3)
Very moderate filly. Turf high 33 (began Jly).
**W R Muir [0-7] S Lamb.*

LAGO DI COMO BHB 53f **RR 60f** 5158[13]
2 b c Piccolo - Farmer's Pet (Sharrood (USA)) 10.5f **(72)**
Form - 0870
Record 1999 - 1st:0 2nd:0 3rd:0 Ran:4
1999 Turf 0-4: (7f 2, 8f 2) (sft, g-f, frm 2)
Average colt. Turf high 60 (began Jly).
**T J Naughton [0-4] E J Fenaroli.*

LAGO DI LEVICO RR 47f 3610[8]
2 ch c Pelder (IRE) - Langton Herring (Nearly A Hand) 5.6f **(48)**
Form - 8
Record 1999 - 1st:0 2nd:0 3rd:0 Ran:1
1999 Turf 0-1: (6f) (frm)
Currently moderate colt. **A P Jarvis [0-1] All Four Corners.*

LAGO DI VARANO BHB 81f **RR 86f** 4933[4]
7 b g Clantime 6.6f **(57)** - On the Record (Record Token) 6.3f **(53)**
Form - 000731785367 1800764
Record 1999 - 1st:2 2nd:0 3rd:2 Ran:19
Pre1999 - 1st:7 2nd:11 3rd:5 Ran:71
Win Prizemoney £47,558 *Total Prizemoney* £100,044
Wins * 1999 Aug Sandow (GD) H 5f 80 86
*** 1999** Jun York (G-S) H 5f 77 80
* 1998 Jun Ripon (SFT) H 5f 80 84
* 1997 Jly Newcas (GD) H 5f 79 80
* 1996 Jun Doncas (G-F) H 5f 83 84
1996 Apr Ripon (G-F) C 5f 73
1999 Turf 2-19: (5f 2-12, 6f 6, 7f) (g-s 1-1, gd 7, g-f 3, frm 1-8)
Useful gelding, effective 5 to 6f, best at 6f, acts on sft to frm, mostly wears blinkers (effectively), does well at Ripon and York. Turf high 86 - 1st of 10 getting 10lb from Levelled (21 Aug Sandown RF 3825). A veteran sprint handicapper, he has put in very creditable efforts over six furlongs, but his wins in the last few seasons have been over five.
**R M Whitaker [5-70] The PBT Group (from J Berry [4-20] Apr 1996).*

LAGOON (IRE) BHB 96f **RR 90f** 5036[5]
2 ch c Common Grounds 8.1f **(66)** - Secret Hideaway (USA) (Key To The Mint (USA)) 9.4f **(75)**
Form - 36135
Record 1999 - 1st:1 2nd:0 3rd:2 Ran:5
Win Prizemoney £4,053 *Total Prizemoney* £5,493
Wins * 1999 Spt Pontef (GD) 6f 80 <
1999 Turf 1-5: (5f 2, 6f 1-3) (g-s, gd, g-f 1-2, hrd)
Useful colt. Turf high 90. **B W Hills [1-5] Guy Reed.*

LAGUNA BAY (IRE) BHB 41f34a **RR 40f 34a** 4218[13]
5 b m Arcane (USA) 11.6f **(66)** - Meg Daughter (IRE) (Doulab (USA)) 9.8f **(65)**
Form - 72515540
Record 1999 - 1st:1 2nd:1 3rd:0 Ran:8
Pre1999 - 1st:1 2nd:2 3rd:0 Ran:16
Win Prizemoney £4,969 *Total Prizemoney* £8,266
Wins * 1999 Jun Bath (FRM) SH 17.2f 44 46
1997 Aug Yarmou (G-F) C 10.1f 54 <
1999 Turf 1-8: (12f, 13f, 14f 2, 16f 2, 17f 1-2) (gd, g-f 2, frm 3, hrd 1-2)
Moderate filly, effective 16 to 17f, best at 17f, acts on g-f to hrd, favours left handed tracks. Turf high 46 - 1st of 15 giving 4lb to Children's Choice (26 Jun Bath RF 2316). Consistent.
**G M McCourt [3-27] Christopher Shankland (from A P Jarvis [1-13] Oct 1997).*

LAHAAY RR 72f 5216[5]
2 ch c Lahib (USA) 8f **(69)** - Jasarah (IRE) (Green Desert (USA)) 8.6f **(78)**
Form - 05
Record 1999 - 1st:0 2nd:0 3rd:0 Ran:2
1999 Turf 0-2: (7f, 8f) (g-s 2)
Currently above-average colt. Turf high 72 (began Oct).
**M P Tregoning [0-2] Hamdan Al Maktoum.*

LAHAN RR 100+f 4920[1]
2 b f Unfuwain (USA) 11.4f **(74)** - Amanah (USA) **(96f)** (Mr Prospector (USA)) 8.8f **(78)**
Form - 11
Record 1999 - 1st:2 2nd:0 3rd:0 Ran:2
Win Prizemoney £26,143 *Total Prizemoney* £26,143
Wins * 1999 Oct Newmar (GD) G2 7f 100+ <
*** 1999** Oct Redcar (GD) 7f 83+
1999 Turf 2-2: (7f 2-2) (gd 1-1, g-f 1-1)
Currently very useful filly. Turf high 100 (began Oct) - 1st of 12 from Clog Dance (16 Oct Newmarket RF 4920). Improved from her first outing, where she showed a willingness and eagerness, to go on and gain a battling victory in the Rockfel Stakes. She should take high rank next season.
**J H M Gosden [2-2] Hamdan Al Maktoum.*

LAHAR (AUS) RR 105f 5223a[3]
5 gr m Kenmare (FR) 9.6f **(76)** - Volcanic (AUS) (Pompeii Court (USA))
Form - 3
1999 Turf 0-1: (16f) (gd)
Currently Pattern-class. (1st run) - 3rd of 24 giving 1lb to Rogan Josh (2 Nov Flemington 16f gd RF 5223a). **P Cave in AUS [0-1].*

LAILA MANJA (IRE) BHB 60f52a **RR 59f 52a** 2159[6]
3 b f Diesis 9f **(80)** - London Pride (USA) (Lear Fan (USA)) 8.5f **(73)**
Form - 0706
Record 1999 - 1st:0 2nd:0 3rd:0 Ran:4
Pre1999 - 1st:0 2nd:0 3rd:0 Ran:1
1999 Turf 0-3: (6f, 8f 2) (g-f, frm 2) 1999 AW 0-1: (9f) (Fibr)
Leggy, fair filly. Turf high 59.
**P F I Cole [0-5] H R H Sultan Ahmad Shah.*

LA ISLA BONITA BHB 58f58a **RR 59f 58a** 4814[10]
4 ch f Lion Cavern (USA) 7.5f **(74)** - La Dama Bonita (USA) (El Gran Senor (USA)) 9.6f **(76)**
Form - 0530220
Record 1999 - 1st:0 2nd:2 3rd:1 Ran:7
Pre1999 - 1st:0 2nd:3 3rd:1 Ran:7
Win Prizemoney £0 *Total Prizemoney* £6,785
1999 Turf 0-6: (7f, 8f 4, 9f) (gd 3, g-f 2, frm) 1999 AW 0-1: (8f) (Equi)
Leggy, fair filly, effective 8f, acts on gd to frm, best on frm. Turf high 62 (1st run) - 10th of 16 giving 3lb to Twin Time (17 May Bath 8f gd RF 1272). **J W Hills [0-14] Christopher Wright.*

LAIYL (IRE) BHB 85f **RR 78?f** 5219[7]
3 gr f Nureyev (USA) 8.4f **(84)** - Alydaress (USA) (Alydar (USA)) 9.1f **(76)**
Form - 17
Record 1999 - 1st:1 2nd:0 3rd:0 Ran:2
Win Prizemoney £3,769 *Total Prizemoney* £3,769
Wins * 1999 Oct Ayr (SFT) 10f 74 <
1999 Turf 1-2: (10f 1-1, 12f) (sft 1-2)
Scopey, currently above-average filly. Turf high 78 (began Oct) - also 1st of 6 getting 5lb from Deputise (12 Oct Ayr RF 4831).
**J H M Gosden [1-2] Sheikh Mohammed.*

LAJADHAL (FR) BHB 14f15a **RR 2f 15a** 2497[7]
10 gr g Bellypha 11.9f **(66)** - Rose d'Amour (USA) (Lines of Power (USA))
Form - 07
Record 1999 - 1st:0 2nd:0 3rd:0 Ran:2
Pre1999 - 1st:0 2nd:0 3rd:0 Ran:30
Win Prizemoney £0 *Total Prizemoney* £174
1999 Turf 0-2: (10f, 14f) (gd, g-f)
Very poor gelding, has worn blinkers. Turf high 2.
**P D Purdy [0-12] P D Purdy (from K Bishop [0-12] Aug 1995).*

LA JURISTE (FR) RR 94f 3781a[2]
5 m Homme de Loi (IRE) - Sponte Sua (FR) (Spoleto (IRE))
Form - 2
1999 Turf 0-1: (8f) (hvy)
Currently useful. (1st run) - 2nd of 20 giving 3lb to Orso (15 Aug Deauville 8f hvy RF 3781a). **in FR [0-1].*

LAKABI (USA) RR 57f 5129[6]
2 b br f Nureyev (USA) 8.4f **(84)** - Lakab (USA) (Manila (USA)) 9.3f **(71)**
Form - 6
Record 1999 - 1st:0 2nd:0 3rd:0 Ran:1
1999 Turf 0-1: (6f) (gd)
Currently fair filly. **J H M Gosden [0-1] Sheikh Mohammed.*

LAKE ARIA BHB 16f21a **RR 24df 21a** 4878[18]
6 b m Rambo Dancer (CAN) 8.4f **(59)** - Hinge (Import) 6.6f **(68)**
Form - 80400
Record 1999 - 1st:0 2nd:0 3rd:0 Ran:5
Pre1999 - 1st:0 2nd:1 3rd:0 Ran:14
Win Prizemoney £0 *Total Prizemoney* £585
1999 Turf 0-1: (6f) (frm) 1999 AW 0-4: (7f, 8f, 12f, 14f) (Fibr 4)

Little account mare, has worn blinkers. AW high 12.
**J Balding [0-1] Mrs M P Neatby (from J L Eyre [0-7] Mar 1999).*

LAKE DOMINION BHB 24f29a **RR 25f 29a** 4600[9]
10 b g Primo Dominie 7.2f **(67)** - Piney Lake (Sassafras (FR)) 9.6f **(69)**
Form - 0000
Record 1999 - 1st:0 2nd:0 3rd:0 Ran:4
Pre1999 - 1st:1 2nd:1 3rd:4 Ran:24
Win Prizemoney £1,984 *Total Prizemoney* £4,512
Wins * 1997 *Jly Wolver (STD) H 16.2f 37 36* <
1999 Turf 0-2: (12f, 18f) (g-f 2) 1999 AW 0-2: (14f, 16f) (Fibr 2)
Little account gelding, effective 16 to 17f, acts on gd - acts on Fibr, has worn blinkers, favours left handed tracks, favours tight tracks. Turf high 25. Inconsistent.
**K C Comerford [1-13] Mrs Betty Bate and Mark Campbell (from J White [1-3] Jun 1994).*

LAKELAND PADDY (IRE) BHB 73f **RR 85f** 5048[6]
2 b c Lake Coniston (IRE) - Inshad (Indian King (USA)) 7.4f **(64)**
Form - 7544256
Record 1999 - 1st:0 2nd:1 3rd:0 Ran:7
Win Prizemoney £0 *Total Prizemoney* £1,944
1999 Turf 0-7: (5f 2, 6f 4, 7f) (hvy, gd 4, frm 2)
Useful colt, effective 6f, acts on gd to frm. Turf high 85 - 4th of 8 to Las Ramblas (28 Aug Newmarket 6f frm RF 3963).
**M Blanshard [0-7] Mrs R G Wellman.*

LAKE MEHRA BHB 42f **RR** 331[6]
3 b c Superlative 8.8f **(57)** - Westering **(29f 38a)** (Auction Ring (USA)) 8.6f **(65)**
Form - 0644486
Record 1999 - 1st:0 2nd:0 3rd:0 Ran:5
Pre1999 - 1st:0 2nd:0 3rd:0 Ran:3
1999 AW 0-5: (8f 4, 9f) (Fibr 5)
Scopey, fair colt, effective 8f, - acts on Fibr, has worn blinkers, favours left handed tracks, favours tight tracks. AW high 50 - 4th of 9 getting 3lb from Lady Peppiatt (25 Jan Southwell 8f Fibr RF 0160). **M H Tompkins [0-8] P J M M Racing.*

LAKE SUNBEAM BHB 85f **RR 88f** 4406[7]
3 b c Nashwan (USA) 10.3f **(79)** - Moon Drop (Dominion) 8.5f **(63)**
Form - 6185367
Record 1999 - 1st:1 2nd:0 3rd:1 Ran:7
Pre1999 - 1st:0 2nd:0 3rd:1 Ran:1
Win Prizemoney £5,809 *Total Prizemoney* £9,479
Wins * 1999 Jun Salisb (G-F) 7f 86 <
1999 Turf 1-7: (7f 1-3, 8f 4) (gd 2, g-f 1-1, frm 4)
Scopey, useful colt, effective 7 to 8f, best at 7f, acts on gd to frm. Turf high 88 - 3rd of 18 giving 1lb to Bold King (14 Aug Newbury 7f gd RF 3647) - also 1st of 4 from Zulu Dawn (23 Jun Salisbury RF 2248). He made all in a weak conditions event at Salisbury in June, but had to work hard. Mostly highly tried afterwards, his best effort since came when third in a big field of handicappers at Newbury in August. Best when held up for a late run.
**R Hannon [1-8] Mohamed Suhail.*

LAKE TAAL BHB 42f47a **RR 42f 47a** 2480[12]
4 ch f Prince Sabo 6.6f **(64)** - Calachuchi (Martinmas) 7.6f **(59)**
Form - 2070
Record 1999 - 1st:0 2nd:1 3rd:0 Ran:4
Pre1999 - 1st:0 2nd:0 3rd:1 Ran:6
Win Prizemoney £0 *Total Prizemoney* £1,158
1999 Turf 0-3: (7f 2, 10f) (frm 3) 1999 AW 0-1: (11f) (Fibr)
Leggy, moderate filly, effective 8f, acts on g-f. Turf high 42.
**Miss J A Camacho [0-8] Mrs S Camacho (from M J Camacho [0-2] Oct 1997).*

LA LANDIERE (FR) RR 39f 3790[6]
4 b br f Synefos (USA) - As You Are (FR) (Saint Estephe (FR)) 16.4f **(79)**
Form - 6
Record 1999 - 1st:0 2nd:0 3rd:0 Ran:1
1999 Turf 0-1: (12f) (gd)
Currently very moderate filly. **D Nicholson [0-1] Mrs R J Skan.*

LALANDO BHB 80f **RR 77f** 4531[9]
2 ch c Forzando 7.2f **(63)** - Laleston (Junius (USA)) 7.7f **(65)**
Form - 434220
Record 1999 - 1st:0 2nd:2 3rd:1 Ran:6
Win Prizemoney £0 *Total Prizemoney* £2,866
1999 Turf 0-6: (5f 5, 6f) (g-s, gd, g-f 2, frm 2)
Above-average colt, effective 5f, acts on gd to frm. Turf high 77 - 2nd of 9 giving 5lb to La Caprice (24 Aug Lingfield 5f g-f RF 3869).
**J L Spearing [0-6] The McIntyre Woods Partnership.*

LALA SALAMA (IRE) BHB 55f **RR 56f** 4824[8]
3 br f College Chapel - Sally St Clair (Sallust) 8.4f **(63)**
Form - 878
Record 1999 - 1st:0 2nd:0 3rd:0 Ran:3
1999 Turf 0-3: (8f, 10f 2) (gd, g-f 2)
Leggy, currently fair filly. Turf high 56 (began Spt).
**Lady Herries [0-3] R Bremner.*

LA LYONESSE BHB 55f50a **RR 59f 50a** 59[11]
4 b f Lion Cavern (USA) 7.5f **(74)** - Princess Sioux (Commanche Run) 8.5f **(58)**
Form - 360
Record 1999 - 1st:0 2nd:0 3rd:0 Ran:1
Pre1999 - 1st:0 2nd:0 3rd:2 Ran:12
Win Prizemoney £0 *Total Prizemoney* £842
1999 AW 0-1: (10f) (Equi)
Leggy, fair filly, effective 10 to 11f, best at 10f, acts on g-f to frm - acts on Equi, prefers left handed tracks.
**J W Hills [0-13] Mrs S E Homewood.*

LAMBORGHINI LOZ BHB 60f64a **RR 71df 64a** 4868[2]
2 b c King's Signet (USA) 7f **(51)** - Scented Goddess (IRE) (Godswalk (USA)) 7.3f **(58)**
Form - 753813642
Record 1999 - 1st:1 2nd:1 3rd:2 Ran:9
Win Prizemoney £1,900 *Total Prizemoney* £3,367
Wins * 1999 Jly Lingfi (FRM) S 5f 71+ <
1999 Turf 1-7: (5f 1-7) (sft, g-s, g-f, frm 1-4) 1999 AW 0-2: (5f 2) (Fibr 2)
Above-average colt, effective 5f, acts on frm, often wears blinkers. Turf high 71 - 3rd of 6 to Russian Fox (26 Jun Lingfield 5f frm RF 2330) - also 1st of 6 giving 5lb to Dimming of The Day (24 Jly Lingfield RF 3094). AW high 64 (began Oct). Inconsistent.
**J Berry [1-9] Chris & Antonia Deuters.*

LAMBSON KATOOSHA BHB 22f **RR 21f** 5127[14]
4 b f Weldnaas (USA) 8.4f **(55)** - Lamsonetti **(9f)** (Never so Bold) 6.3f **(66)**
Form - 070
Record 1999 - 1st:0 2nd:0 3rd:0 Ran:3
Pre1999 - 1st:0 2nd:0 3rd:0 Ran:2
1999 Turf 0-3: (7f, 8f, 12f) (g-s, gd, hrd)
Lengthy, little account filly. Turf high 21. **J Pearce [0-5] Ian Hall.*

LAMEH BHB 80f **RR 83f** 5020[5]
2 ch f Mujtahid (USA) 7.4f **(69)** - Tablah (USA) **(77f)** (Silver Hawk (USA)) 8.6f **(70)**
Form - 405
Record 1999 - 1st:0 2nd:0 3rd:0 Ran:3
Win Prizemoney £0 *Total Prizemoney* £260
1999 Turf 0-3: (6f, 7f, 8f) (g-s, gd, frm)
Currently decent filly. Turf high 83 (began Spt) - 5th of 18 to Interlude (22 Oct Doncaster 8f gd RF 5020).
**P T Walwyn [0-3] Hamdan Al Maktoum.*

LAMENT BHB 58a **RR 48f** 5026[11]
3 b f Phountzi (USA) 9.6f **(60)** - Devils Dirge (Song) 7.2f **(61)**
Form - 82160
Record 1999 - 1st:1 2nd:1 3rd:0 Ran:4
Pre1999 - 1st:1 2nd:2 3rd:1 Ran:11
Win Prizemoney £4,959 *Total Prizemoney* £6,915
Wins * 1999 Oct Pontef (SFT) C 6f 48
1998 Aug Lingfi (GD) C 6f 65 <
1999 Turf 1-4: (6f 1-3, 7f) (gd 1-3, frm)
Workmanlike, moderate filly, effective 6f, acts on gd to frm. Turf high 60 (1st run) - 2nd of 14 giving 1lb to Petit Palais (27 Apr Nottingham 6f gd RF 0865).
**Miss Gay Kelleway [1-3] A P Griffin (from Mrs L Stubbs [1-8] Apr 1999).*

LAMERIE (IRE) BHB 86f **RR 86f** 4677[2]
3 b c Roi Danzig (USA) 10.5f **(62)** - Eurosanta (Scorpio (FR))
Form - 6341872112
Record 1999 - 1st:3 2nd:2 3rd:1 Ran:10
Win Prizemoney £11,279 *Total Prizemoney* £15,672
Wins * 1999 Spt Newmar (G-S) H 10f 83 85 <
*** 1999** Spt Chepst (GD) H 10.2f 80 83
*** 1999** Apr Bright (G-F) 10f 76
1999 Turf 3-10: (8f, 10f 3-5, 11f, 12f 3) (g-s, gd 4, g-f 1-2, frm 2-3)
Leggy, useful colt, effective 8 to 12f, best at 10f, acts on gd to frm, excels at Newmarket. Turf high 86 - 2nd of 12 giving 2lb to Be Thankfull (1 Oct Newmarket 10f gd RF 4677) - also 1st of 19 giving 24lb to Badrinath (28 Spt Newmarket RF 4597). A winner three times last season, he improved at the back end and should continue to do well at four. Suited by ten furlongs, he has tended to hang under pressure. **R Hannon [3-10] Stonethorn Stud Farms Ltd.*

LAMMOSKI (IRE) BHB 62f **RR 59f** 4503[9]
2 ch g Hamas (IRE) 8f **(72)** - Penny In My Shoe (USA) (Sir Ivor) 10.2f **(70)**
Form - 0008758700
Record 1999 - 1st:0 2nd:0 3rd:0 Ran:10
1999 Turf 0-10: (5f 4, 6f 4, 7f 2) (gd 3, g-f 2, frm 5)
Fair gelding. Turf high 59. Inconsistent.
**M C Chapman [0-10] Gordon & Julie Lamming.*

LAMORNA BHB 45f45a **RR 48f 45a** 2263[14]
5 ch m Shavian 7.7f **(67)** - Malibasta (Auction Ring (USA)) 8.6f **(65)**
Form - 673740
Record 1999 - 1st:0 2nd:0 3rd:1 Ran:6
Pre1999 - 1st:4 2nd:2 3rd:3 Ran:30
Win Prizemoney £20,554 *Total Prizemoney* £24,337
Wins * 1998 Aug Folkes (G-F) H 7f 43 47
1997 Spt Catter (G-F) H 7f 48 53
1996 Aug York (GD) S 6f 77 <
1996 Jun Warwic (FRM) 6f 64+
1999 Turf 0-5: (6f 2, 7f 2, 8f) (gd 2, frm 2, hrd) 1999 AW 0-1: (10f) (Equi)
Moderate filly, effective 7f, acts on frm, has worn blinkers. Turf high 48.
**D W P Arbuthnot [1-14] W H Ponsonby (from M R Channon [3-22] Oct 1997).*

LAMORRAN BHB 45f55a **RR 41f 55a** 5064[16]
2 b g Son Pardo - Sans Diablo (IRE) (Mac's Imp (USA))
Form - 08000460
Record 1999 - 1st:0 2nd:0 3rd:0 Ran:8
1999 Turf 0-6: (5f, 6f 4, 7f) (gd, g-f 2, frm 2, hrd) 1999 AW 0-2: (6f 2) (Fibr 2)
Moderate gelding, has worn blinkers. Turf high 46. AW high 45 (began Oct). **D HaydnJones [0-8] The Lamorran Partnership.*

LAMZENA (IRE) BHB 100f **RR 95f** 979[22]
3 b f Fairy King (USA) 7.7f **(75)** - Ezana (Ela-Mana-Mou) 10.1f **(70)**
Form - 60
Record 1999 - 1st:0 2nd:0 3rd:0 Ran:2
Pre1999 - 1st:0 2nd:0 3rd:1 Ran:1
Win Prizemoney £0 *Total Prizemoney* £745
1999 Turf 0-2: (7f, 8f) (g-f, frm)
Workmanlike, currently very useful filly. Turf high 95. She was highly tried, finishing sixth in the Nell Gwyn and last in the Guineas, but was not seen again. **G Wragg [0-3] R N Bracher.*

LANCASHIRE LEGEND BHB 31f31a **RR 40f 31a** 524[9]
6 gr g Belfort (FR) 6.7f **(53)** - Peters Pet Girl (Norwick (USA)) 7.2f **(56)**
Form - 605765500
Record 1999 - 1st:0 2nd:0 3rd:0 Ran:5
Pre1999 - 1st:1 2nd:4 3rd:6 Ran:46
Win Prizemoney £3,206 *Total Prizemoney* £8,988
Wins 1996 *Nov Lingfi (STD) 7f* 62 <
1999 Turf 0-1: (7f) (gd) 1999 AW 0-4: (6f 2, 7f 2) (Fibr 4)
Moderate gelding, effective 7f, - acts on Equi, has worn blinkers.
**W M Brisbourne [0-5] Manton Hire Ltd (from N P Littmoden [0-4] Dec 1998).*

LANCER (USA) BHB 65f40a **RR 67f 40a** 5152[2]
7 ch g Diesis 9f **(80)** - Last Bird (USA) (Sea Bird II) 9f **(71)**
Form - 855312865420042
Record 1999 - 1st:1 2nd:3 3rd:1 Ran:15
Pre1999 - 1st:4 2nd:6 3rd:2 Ran:27
Win Prizemoney £18,541 *Total Prizemoney* £33,842
Wins * 1999 May Folkes (G-F) 12f 70
* 1998 Oct York (GD) H 11.9f 66 71 <
* 1998 Jun Folkes (G-F) H 12f 59 63
* 1998 May Leices (GD) H 11.8f 53 60
1999 Turf 1-13: (10f, 12f 1-11, 14f) (g-s, gd 1-5, g-f, frm 5, hrd) 1999 AW 0-2: (12f, 14f) (Equi, Fibr)
Average gelding, effective 10 to 12f, best at 12f, acts on g-s to frm, best on gd, often wears blinkers (very effectively), prefers right handed tracks, excels at York and Newmarket and Folkestone, does well at Newbury. Turf high 71 - 2nd of 16 getting 4lb from Flower O'Cannie (12 Jun York 12f gd RF 1968) - also 1st of 7 from Meteor Strike (26 May Folkestone RF 1495). AW high 34 (began Oct). An able performer at around a mile and a half, he is best held up for a late run, but is not one to rely too much on.
**J Pearce [4-33] Chris Marsh (from R T Juckes [1-16] Feb 1998).*

LAND AHEAD (USA) **RR 72f** 4815[5]
2 ch f Distant View (USA) - Nimble Folly (USA) (Cyane) 8.8f **(67)**
Form - 5
Record 1999 - 1st:0 2nd:0 3rd:0 Ran:1
1999 Turf 0-1: (7f) (gd)
Currently above-average filly. **H R A Cecil [0-1] K Abdulla.*

LANDFALL LIL (IRE) BHB 58f **RR 66f** 4524[14]
2 b f Mujadil (USA) 7.7f **(70)** - Local Belle (Ballymore) 7.3f **(64)**
Form - 8260
Record 1999 - 1st:0 2nd:1 3rd:0 Ran:4
Win Prizemoney £0 *Total Prizemoney* £744
1999 Turf 0-4: (5f 3, 6f) (gd, g-f, frm 2)
Average filly. Turf high 66 (began Aug) - 2nd of 10 getting 6lb from City Princess (11 Aug Hamilton 5f g-f RF 3541).
**I Semple [0-4] Raeburn Brick Ltd.*

LANDFORD LAD (IRE) BHB 59f **RR 54f** 1591[6]
3 ch c Mujtahid (USA) 7.4f **(69)** - Bold And Bright (FR) (Bold Lad (USA)) 10f **(65)**
Form - 06
Record 1999 - 1st:0 2nd:0 3rd:0 Ran:2
Pre1999 - 1st:0 2nd:0 3rd:0 Ran:3
Win Prizemoney £0 *Total Prizemoney* £237
1999 Turf 0-2: (12f, 15f) (sft, g-f)
Scopey, fair colt. Turf high 54.
**B Palling [0-5] J Hackett & D Brennan.*

LANDICAN LANE BHB 43f50a **RR 43f 50a** 5107[3]
3 b g Handsome Sailor 6.6f **(53)** - Harifa (Local Suitor (USA)) 8.4f **(67)**
Form - 06220000003
Record 1999 - 1st:0 2nd:2 3rd:1 Ran:10
Pre1999 - 1st:1 2nd:0 3rd:0 Ran:7
Win Prizemoney £1,955 *Total Prizemoney* £3,855
Wins 1998 Spt Bright (GD) S 5.3f 58 <
1999 Turf 0-9: (5f 4, 6f 3, 7f, 10f) (sft, g-s, gd 5, g-f, frm) 1999 AW 0-1: (6f) (Equi)
Leggy, moderate gelding, effective 5f, acts on g-s, mostly wears blinkers (effectively). Turf high 66 - 2nd of 12 getting 2lb from Eastern Trumpeter (13 Apr Folkestone 5f g-s RF 0656). Inconsistent.
**G L Moore [0-11] A Moore (from R F JohnsonHoughton [1-6] Spt 1998).*

LANDING SLOT (USA) **RR 96f** 4477a[17]
4 b c Personal Hope (USA) - Durability (USA) **00**
Form - 1200010
1999 Turf 2-7: (8f 2, 9f 2-3, 10f, 12f) (g-s, gd 1-2, g-f 1-4)
Very useful colt, effective 10 to 12f, acts on g-s to gd, has worn blinkers, likes right handed tracks. Turf high 96. Inconsistent. He does not appear to stay beyond a mile and a quarter and has run his best races when ridden forcefully.
**D K Weld in IRE [2-11] Moyglare Stud Farm.*

LANDRFUN BHB 32f49a **RR 31f 49a** 4869[4]
4 b g Lugana Beach 7f **(63)** - Basic Fun (Teenoso (USA)) 9.9f **(72)**
Form - 252200086027124

Record 1999 - 1st:1 2nd:4 3rd:0 Ran:13
Pre1999 - 1st:1 2nd:1 3rd:1 Ran:18
Win Prizemoney £3,763 *Total Prizemoney* £7,442
Wins * **1999** *Spt Wolver (STD) SH 12f 44 49*
* 1998 *Apr Wolver (STD) C 8.5f 58* <
1999 Turf 0-5: (8f, 9f, 11f, 12f 2) (gd, g-f 2, frm 2) 1999 AW 1-8: (8f 5, 12f 1-3) (Equi 3, Fibr 1-5)
Workmanlike, moderate gelding, effective 8 to 12f, best at 8f, - acts on AW, best on Fibr, has worn blinkers, likes left handed tracks, likes tight tracks. Turf high 31. AW high 55 - 2nd of 10 giving 4lb to Harpoon Louie (26 Jan Lingfield 8f Equi RF 0166) - also 1st of 12 giving 8lb to Mama-San (4 Spt Wolverhampton RF 4153). Inconsistent. **H J Collingridge [2-31] Group 1 Racing (1994) Ltd.*

LANDROVAL (GER) RR 95f 929a[7]
5 h Big Shuffle (USA) - Latana (GER) **00**
Form - 7
1999 Turf 0-1: (8f) (hvy)
Currently very useful colt. **R Suerland in GER [0-1].*

LANELLE (USA) RR 64f 5137[9]
2 b f Trempolino (USA) 11.9f **(77)** - Laluche (USA) (Alleged (USA)) 10f **(76)**
Form - 0
Record 1999 - 1st:0 2nd:0 3rd:0 Ran:1
1999 Turf 0-1: (7f) (gd)
Currently average filly. **J H M Gosden [0-1] Sheikh Mohammed.*

LANGANS FIGURINE (IRE) BHB 42f **RR 31f** 4586[12]
3 b f Petardia 8.2f **(58)** - Cree's Figurine (Creetown) 6.9f **(50)**
Form - 00748000
Record 1999 - 1st:0 2nd:0 3rd:0 Ran:8
Pre1999 - 1st:0 2nd:0 3rd:1 Ran:4
Win Prizemoney £0 *Total Prizemoney* £468
1999 Turf 0-8: (5f, 6f 6, 8f) (gd 3, g-f 2, frm 3)
Very moderate filly, has worn blinkers.
**M J Fetherston-Godley [0-12] R A Shepherd.*

LANGUAGE OF LOVE BHB 54f **RR 61df** 5191[13]
3 br f Rock City 8.8f **(62)** - Indian Love Song (Be My Guest (USA)) 9.3f **(67)**
Form - 88200
Record 1999 - 1st:0 2nd:1 3rd:0 Ran:5
Win Prizemoney £0 *Total Prizemoney* £1,268
1999 Turf 0-5: (6f, 7f 3, 8f) (sft, gd 3, g-f)
Scopey, average filly. Turf high 61.
**M Johnston [0-3] J R Good (from B J Meehan [0-2] Jun 1999).*

LANIN BHB 28f **RR 19f** 2256[11]
4 b g Shirley Heights 12.1f **(76)** - Minute Waltz (Sadler's Wells (USA)) 10f **(76)**
Form - 000
Record 1999 - 1st:0 2nd:0 3rd:0 Ran:3
Pre1999 - 1st:0 2nd:0 3rd:0 Ran:5
1999 Turf 0-3: (10f, 12f 2) (sft, g-f 2)
Workmanlike, poor gelding. Turf high 19. Becoming disappointing. **D J S Cosgrove [0-8] Darren Croft.*

LANZLO (FR) BHB 61f **RR 63f** 4727[12]
2 b br c Le Balafre (FR) - L'eternite (FR) (Cariellor (FR))
Form - 07580
Record 1999 - 1st:0 2nd:0 3rd:0 Ran:5
1999 Turf 0-5: (6f, 7f 2, 8f, 10f) (g-s, gd, g-f 2, frm)
Average colt. Turf high 63. **P J Hobbs [0-5] Winton Bloodstock Ltd.*

LA PAOLA (IRE) BHB 57f60a **RR 57f 60a** 4440[22]
3 ch f Common Grounds 8.1f **(66)** - Lotte Lenta (Gorytus (USA)) 7.8f **(60)**
Form - 70004100
Record 1999 - 1st:1 2nd:0 3rd:0 Ran:8
Pre1999 - 1st:1 2nd:1 3rd:0 Ran:5
Win Prizemoney £6,652 *Total Prizemoney* £7,630
Wins * **1999** Aug Folkes (G-S) 6f 57
* 1998 Spt Sandow (G-S) 5f 72 <
1999 Turf 1-7: (5f, 6f 1-6) (g-s, gd 1-1, g-f 3, frm 2) 1999 AW 0-1: (6f) (Fibr)
Leggy, fair filly, effective 5f, acts on gd to g-f, has worn blinkers.
**B J Meehan [2-13] G Battocchi.*

LA PASCUA (SWI) RR 94f 1530a[8]
3 f Caerleon (USA) 10.9f **(79)** - La Venta (USA) (Drone) 10.3f **(74)**
Form - 8
1999 Turf 0-1: (10f) (g-s)
Currently useful filly. **N Clement in FR [0-1].*

LA PETITE FLAMECHE BHB 50f45a **RR 39f 45a** 2380[15]
4 b f Cigar 6.3f **(43)** - Little Missile (Ile de Bourbon (USA)) 10.1f **(67)**
Form - 6008000
Record 1999 - 1st:0 2nd:0 3rd:0 Ran:5
Pre1999 - 1st:0 2nd:0 3rd:1 Ran:6
Win Prizemoney £0 *Total Prizemoney* £575
1999 Turf 0-2: (8f, 10f) (hvy, frm) 1999 AW 0-3: (6f, 7f, 8f) (Equi 2, Fibr)
Light-framed, very moderate filly, has worn blinkers. Turf high 26. AW high 32. **R J O'Sullivan [0-14] M T Bevan.*

LA PIAZZA (IRE) BHB 82f69a **RR 82f 69a** 4154[9]
3 ch f Polish Patriot (USA) 7.8f **(70)** - Blazing Glory (IRE) (Glow (USA)) 6.7f **(71)**
Form - 227612211370
Record 1999 - 1st:3 2nd:3 3rd:1 Ran:11
Pre1999 - 1st:0 2nd:1 3rd:0 Ran:1
Win Prizemoney £12,094 *Total Prizemoney* £17,218
Wins * **1999** Aug Lingfi (GD) H 6f 72 79+ <
* **1999** Jly Lingfi (FRM) H 6f 60 70
* **1999** *Jun Wolver (STD) 5f 66*
1999 Turf 2-7: (5f 2, 6f 2-5) (gd 2, g-f, frm 2-3, hrd) 1999 AW 1-4: (5f 1-2, 6f 2) (Equi, Fibr 1-3)
Workmanlike, decent filly, effective 5 to 6f, best at 6f, acts on gd to frm, best on gd. Turf high 82 - 3rd of 20 getting 17lb from Emma Peel (18 Aug York 5f gd RF 3762) - also 1st of 10 from Angie Baby (6 Aug Lingfield RF 3420). AW high 66. Inconsistent. She got off the mark in a modest maiden on the Wolverhampton Fibresand in June, but has shown his ability on turf with two clear-cut victories at Lingfield. She can be forgiven her final run on sand as she stumbled early on. **W J Haggas [3-12] Jolly Farmers Racing.*

LAPU-LAPU BHB 33f48a **RR 22f 48a** 19[12]
6 b m Prince Sabo 6.6f **(64)** - Seleter (Hotfoot) 10.5f **(59)**
Form - 00
Record 1999 - 1st:0 2nd:0 3rd:0 Ran:1
Pre1999 - 1st:3 2nd:1 3rd:2 Ran:27
Win Prizemoney £8,353 *Total Prizemoney* £11,664
Wins 1997 Jly Hamilt (G-S) 8.3f 55
1996 Oct Newcas (G-F) H 10.1f 52 56 <
1996 Aug Pontef (G-F) H 8f 47 53
1999 AW 0-1: (11f) (Fibr)
Little account mare, has worn blinkers. Inconsistent.
**Miss J A Camacho [0-4] Dunstan French (from M J Camacho [3-24] Nov 1997).*

LARAZA RR 71f 4080[3]
2 ch f Arazi (USA) 9.2f **(74)** - Queen Midas (Glint of Gold) 9.3f **(66)**
Form - 03
Record 1999 - 1st:0 2nd:0 3rd:1 Ran:2
Win Prizemoney £0 *Total Prizemoney* £1,052
1999 Turf 0-2: (7f, 8f) (frm 2)
Currently above-average filly. Turf high 71 (began Jly) - 3rd of 20 getting 5lb from Bold State (1 Spt York 8f frm RF 4080). She showed distinct promise over a mile at York on her second start and looks as if she can find a race over that distance at least. **Miss I Foustok [0-2] R & M Fustok.*

LARBOREUS RR 95f 2781a[5]
3 b g Darshaan 11.9f **(81)** - Lypharita (FR) (Lightning (FR)) 7.9f **(74)**
Form - 25
1999 Turf 0-2: (12f, 16f) (g-s, gd)
Currently very useful gelding. Turf high 95. He looks one-paced and will be better employed over hurdles.
**J Oxx in IRE [0-2] Sheikh Mohammed.*

LARGESSE BHB 110f97a **RR 115?f 97a** 5219[5]
5 b h Cadeaux Genereux 7.9f **(76)** - Vilanika (FR) (Top Ville) 11.7f **(68)**
Form - 1023485
Record 1999 - 1st:1 2nd:1 3rd:1 Ran:7

Pre1999 - 1st:6 2nd:2 3rd:1 Ran:21
Win Prizemoney £45,212 *Total Prizemoney* £90,573
Wins * 1999 Mar Doncas (G-S) 12f 102+
* 1998 Spt Ayr (G-S) L 10.9f 107 <
* 1998 May York (GD) H 11.9f 94 98
* 1998 Mar Nottin (G-S) H 10f 82 87
* 1997 Spt Haydoc (GD) H 11.9f 73 77
* 1997 Spt Haydoc (G-S) H 10.5f 67 71
* 1996 Jly Pontef (G-F) 5f 84+
1999 Turf 1-7: (11f, 12f 1-3, 14f, 15f, 20f) (hvy, sft, gd 1-4, g-f)
High-class colt, effective 11 to 15f, acts on sft to gd, best on gd, has worn blinkers, likes left handed tracks, excels at York. Turf high 115 - 3rd of 5 getting 2lb from Kayf Tara (22 Aug Deauville 15f gd RF 3933a). The star of John Berry's small stable, he is a very useful individual granted cut in the ground, as he showed when landing Ayr's Doonside Cup in 1998. He started off last season with a comfortable victory in a Doncaster conditions event, and ran well when second to Churlish Charm in the Yorkshire Cup. Ran on to finish third behind Kayf Tara at Deauville, but never looked like landing last season's Doonside Cup and was well beaten in both the Prix du Cadran and a Doncaster Listed event on his final two starts. **John Berry [7-28] Mrs Rosemary Moszkowicz.*

LARIMAR BAY BHB 50f RR 38f 1704[14]

3 b c Puissance 7.1f **(60)** - Aryaf (CAN) (Vice Regent (CAN)) 8.7f **(74)**
Form - 7400
Record 1999 - 1st:0 2nd:0 3rd:0 Ran:4
Pre1999 - 1st:0 2nd:0 3rd:0 Ran:2
Win Prizemoney £0 *Total Prizemoney* £739
1999 Turf 0-4: (5f, 7f 2, 12f) (gd 4)
Scopey, very moderate colt. Turf high 38.
**W M Brisbourne [0-4] John Oldknow (from B J Meehan [0-2] Oct 1998).*

L'ARITA (FR) BHB 85f RR 75f 5041[8]

2 ch f Arazi (USA) 9.2f **(74)** - Lypharita (FR) (Lightning (FR)) 7.9f **(74)**
Form - 318
Record 1999 - 1st:1 2nd:0 3rd:1 Ran:3
Win Prizemoney £3,925 *Total Prizemoney* £4,527
Wins * 1999 Oct Redcar (GD) 6f 75+ <
1999 Turf 1-3: (6f 1-2, 7f) (sft, gd, frm 1-1)
Currently above-average filly. Turf high 75 (began Oct) - 1st of 12 from Welsh Valley (15 Oct Redcar RF 4903). She showed promise on her Nottingham debut and had little trouble landing the odds at Redcar next time. Well held in a heavy-ground Listed race on her third run. **J H M Gosden [1-3] Sheikh Mohammed.*

LA ROCQUE (IRE) RR 63f 5062[3]

2 b g Rock Hopper 10.6f **(54)** - Unique Treasure (Young Generation) 7.7f **(63)**
Form - 3
Record 1999 - 1st:0 2nd:0 3rd:1 Ran:1
Win Prizemoney £0 *Total Prizemoney* £366
1999 Turf 0-1: (8f) (gd)
Currently average gelding. **P W Harris [0-1] Turf 2000 Ltd.*

LA SOEUR D'ALBERT BHB 37f RR 50f 2585[11]

3 b f Puissance 7.1f **(60)** - Florentynna Bay (Aragon) 8.1f **(60)**
Form - 000
Record 1999 - 1st:0 2nd:0 3rd:0 Ran:3
Pre1999 - 1st:0 2nd:0 3rd:0 Ran:3
1999 Turf 0-2: (6f, 8f) (frm 2) 1999 AW 0-1: (8f) (Fibr)
Tall, fair filly. Turf high 20. **J Berry [0-6] Chris & Antonia Deuters.*

LA SPEZIANA (IRE) BHB 62f RR 67+f 5049[6]

2 b f Perugino (USA) - Election Special **(62f)** (Chief Singer) 8.9f **(66)**
Form - 466
Record 1999 - 1st:0 2nd:0 3rd:0 Ran:3
Win Prizemoney £0 *Total Prizemoney* £271
1999 Turf 0-3: (6f, 7f, 8f) (gd 2, g-f)
Currently average filly. Turf high 67 (1st run) (began Jly) - 4th of 15 getting 5lb from Delphinius (26 Jly Windsor 6f g-f RF 3146). **D R C Elsworth [0-3] Pampas Partnership.*

LAS RAMBLAS (IRE) BHB 85f RR 92f 4686[12]

2 b c Thatching 7.8f **(69)** - Raise a Warning **(43+f)** (Warning)
Form - 3203170
Record 1999 - 1st:1 2nd:1 3rd:2 Ran:7
Win Prizemoney £4,581 *Total Prizemoney* £6,660
Wins * 1999 Aug Newmar (G-F) 6f 92 <
1999 Turf 1-7: (5f 2, 6f 1-5) (g-s, gd, g-f 2, frm 1-3)
Useful colt, effective 6f, acts on g-f to frm. Turf high 92 - 1st of 8 from Ile Michel (28 Aug Newmarket RF 3963).
**R F JohnsonHoughton [1-7] C W Sumner.*

LAST CHANCE BHB 41f38a RR 46f 38a 135[10]

5 b g River Falls 8.2f **(56)** - Little Red Hut (Habitat) 9.4f **(70)**
Form - 80
Record 1999 - 1st:0 2nd:0 3rd:0 Ran:2
Pre1999 - 1st:1 2nd:3 3rd:1 Ran:21
Win Prizemoney £2,973 *Total Prizemoney* £10,802
Wins 1996 Jun Bath (G-F) 5.1f 72 <
1999 AW 0-2: (5f, 8f) (Equi 2)
Moderate gelding, has worn blinkers. AW high 22. Becoming disappointing.
**J S Wainwright [0-3] Darren Barratt (from D J S Cosgrove [0-12] Jly 1998).*

LAST CHRISTMAS BHB 75f RR 91f 11[12]

4 b g Salse (USA) 10.9f **(71)** - State Ball (Dance In Time (CAN)) 8.9f **(59)**
Form - 0
Record 1999 - 1st:0 2nd:0 3rd:0 Ran:1
Pre1999 - 1st:1 2nd:2 3rd:1 Ran:6
Win Prizemoney £3,582 *Total Prizemoney* £8,308
Wins 1997 Spt Haydoc (GD) 7.1f 83 <
1999 AW 0-1: (12f) (Equi)
Leggy, useful gelding. (DEAD)
**J R Jenkins [0-2] Southern Counties Finance & Leasing (from B W Hills [1-6] Aug 1998).*

LAST HAVEN (FR) BHB 80f RR 87f 4526[8]

3 b c Slip Anchor 12.7f **(75)** - Lady Norcliffe (USA) (Norcliffe (CAN)) 14f **(72)**
Form - 8
Record 1999 - 1st:0 2nd:0 3rd:0 Ran:1
Pre1999 - 1st:1 2nd:0 3rd:0 Ran:4
Win Prizemoney £3,779 *Total Prizemoney* £4,106
Wins * 1998 Oct Pontef (GD) 10f 87+ <
1999 Turf 0-1: (12f) (gd)
Scopey, useful colt. **J G FitzGerald [1-5] Marquesa de Moratalla.*

LASTMAN (USA) RR 65f 623[5]

4 b br g Fabulous Dancer (USA) 10.6f **(81)** - Rivala (USA) (Riverman (USA)) 9.1f **(76)**
Form - 5
Record 1999 - 1st:0 2nd:0 3rd:0 Ran:1
Pre1999 - 1st:0 2nd:0 3rd:0 Ran:1
Win Prizemoney £0 *Total Prizemoney* £252
1999 Turf 0-1: (12f) (gd)
Average gelding. Highly tried over hurdles so far, he should find a race. **D Nicholson [0-6] Darren Mercer.*

LAST REPUTATION (IRE) BHB 66f80a RR 66?f 80a 4171[16]

4 b f Zafonic (USA) 9f **(83)** - Reputation (Tower Walk) 10f **(62)**
Form - 14006650130
Record 1999 - 1st:1 2nd:0 3rd:1 Ran:9
Pre1999 - 1st:2 2nd:0 3rd:0 Ran:8
Win Prizemoney £9,511 *Total Prizemoney* £10,487
Wins * 1999 Aug Leices (GD) 7f 62+
* 1998 *Nov Lingfi (STD) H 7f 73 76* <
* 1998 Spt Catter (G-F) 7f 56
1999 Turf 1-9: (6f, 7f 1-8) (gd, g-f 1-2, frm 6)
Scopey, above-average filly, effective 7 to 8f, best at 7f, acts on sft to frm - acts on Equi, does well at Lingfield, excels at Newmarket. Turf high 68 - 6th of 15 giving 1lb to Teofilio (18 Jun Newmarket 7f frm RF 2124). **B W Hills [3-17] R E Sangster.*

LAST WARNING BHB 59f RR 62f 1372[16]

3 b g Warning 8.1f **(77)** - Dancing Crystal (Kris) 9.5f **(73)**
Form - 600
Record 1999 - 1st:0 2nd:0 3rd:0 Ran:3
Pre1999 - 1st:0 2nd:0 3rd:0 Ran:1
1999 Turf 0-3: (8f, 10f 2) (gd, g-f, frm)

Average gelding. Turf high 62.
**E A L Dunlop [0-4] Mohammed Jaber.*

LA SYLPHIDE (SWI) RR 106?f — 4769a[10]
3 b f Barathea (IRE) - Vanishing Prairie (USA) (Alysheba (USA)) 9f **(84)**
Form - 10600
1999 Turf 1-5: (11f 1-2, 12f 2, 13f) (hvy, g-s 1-2, gd 2)
Pattern-class filly. Turf high 106 (1st run) - 1st of 8 from Aubergade (14 Apr Saint-Cloud RF 0809a). Won the Prix Penelope in the spring, but has been well beaten in top French fillies' races since. **N Clement in FR [1-5].*

LA TACHE BHB 59f RR 59f — 4744a[R]
3 b f Namaqualand (USA) - Fabulous Deed (USA) (Shadeed (USA)) 8.2f **(70)**
Form - 224R
Record 1999 - 1st:0 2nd:2 3rd:0 Ran:4
Pre1999 - 1st:0 2nd:0 3rd:0 Ran:6
Win Prizemoney £0 *Total Prizemoney* £1,495
1999 Turf 0-4: (12f 2, 14f 2) (sft, g-s, gd, g-f)
Workmanlike, fair filly, effective 14f, acts on g-s to g-f, has worn blinkers. Turf high 59 (began Jly) - 2nd of 5 to Senora (4 Aug Sligo 14f g-f RF 3518a). Inconsistent.
**L Woods in IRE [0-4] William Brown (from L Woods [0-2] Aug 1999).*

LATALOMNE (USA) BHB 92f RR 92f — 2042[30]
5 ch g Zilzal (USA) 8.5f **(79)** - Sanctuary (Welsh Pageant) 10f **(65)**
Form - 52180
Record 1999 - 1st:1 2nd:1 3rd:0 Ran:5
Pre1999 - 1st:1 2nd:2 3rd:0 Ran:6
Win Prizemoney £15,688 *Total Prizemoney* £22,432
Wins * 1999 May Thirsk (G-F) H 8f 88 92 <
1997 Apr Nottin (G-F) 8.2f 88
1999 Turf 1-5: (7f, 8f 1-4) (g-s 2, gd, g-f 1-1, frm)
Useful gelding, effective 7 to 8f, best at 7f, acts on g-f to frm, best on frm. Turf high 92 - 1st of 17 giving 16lb to Jay-Owe-Two (1 May Thirsk RF 0967). He landed the Thirsk Hunt Cup in May but did not go on from that.
**B Ellison [1-5] Everaldo Partnership (from E A L Dunlop [1-6] Jun 1998).*

LA TAVERNETTA (IRE) BHB 38f46a RR 54f 46a — 4558[16]
3 ch f Magical Wonder (USA) 7.2f **(60)** - Carolina Rua (USA) (L'Emigrant (USA)) 10.5f **(62)**
Form - 057070
Record 1999 - 1st:0 2nd:0 3rd:0 Ran:5
Pre1999 - 1st:2 2nd:1 3rd:1 Ran:11
Win Prizemoney £3,596 *Total Prizemoney* £4,813
Wins 1998 *Jun Wolver (STD) S 7f 70+* <
1998 May Bright (FRM) S 6f 60
1999 Turf 0-3: (8f 2, 10f) (gd 3) 1999 AW 0-2: (6f, 8f) (Fibr 2)
Leggy, fair filly, effective 6 to 7f, acts on frm - acts on Fibr, likes left handed tracks, likes tight tracks. Turf high 33 (began Jly). AW high 38. Inconsistent.
**J A Gilbert [0-4] Terry Connors (from N Tinkler [0-2] Jan 1999).*

LATCH LIFTER BHB 34f RR 30f — 3309[13]
3 b g Prince Sabo 6.6f **(64)** - Thevetia (Mummy's Pet) 7.7f **(60)**
Form - 080
Record 1999 - 1st:0 2nd:0 3rd:0 Ran:3
Pre1999 - 1st:0 2nd:0 3rd:0 Ran:5
1999 Turf 0-3: (5f, 6f 2) (gd, frm 2)
Scopey, very moderate gelding, has worn blinkers. Turf high 30.
**G Lewis [0-8] Nigel Morris.*

LATE ARRIVAL BHB 58f RR 53f — 3413[11]
2 b c Emperor Jones (USA) - Try Vickers (USA) (Fuzzbuster (USA)) 6.3f **(63)**
Form - 040
Record 1999 - 1st:0 2nd:0 3rd:0 Ran:3
Win Prizemoney £0 *Total Prizemoney* £253
1999 Turf 0-3: (6f, 7f 2) (g-s, g-f 2)
Currently fair colt. Turf high 53 (began Jly).
**J J O'Neill [0-3] Meadowcrest Ltd.*

LATEEN BHB 27f RR 38f — 4456[8]
4 b f Midyan (USA) 9.9f **(64)** - Sail Loft (Shirley Heights) 10.3f **(74)**
Form - 80648
Record 1999 - 1st:0 2nd:0 3rd:0 Ran:5
Pre1999 - 1st:0 2nd:0 3rd:0 Ran:5
1999 Turf 0-5: (11f, 12f 3, 16f) (sft 2, g-s, g-f, frm)
Leggy, very moderate filly, effective 12f, acts on gd. Turf high 38. Inconsistent. **Major D N Chappell [0-10] Major D N Chappell.*

LATE NIGHT LADY (IRE) BHB 58f53a RR 62f 53a — 4849a[9]
2 b f Mujadil (USA) 7.7f **(70)** - Riverwave (USA) (Riverman (USA)) 9.1f **(76)**
Form - 56106200
Record 1999 - 1st:1 2nd:1 3rd:0 Ran:8
Win Prizemoney £2,164 *Total Prizemoney* £2,797
Wins * 1999 Jun Hamilt (GD) C 5f 62 <
1999 Turf 1-7: (5f 1-3, 6f, 7f 3) (sft, gd 2, g-f 1-3, frm) 1999 AW 0-1: (7f) (Fibr)
Average filly, effective 5f, acts on gd to g-f. Turf high 62 - 1st of 6 giving 8lb to Schatzi (16 Jun Hamilton RF 2047).
**P C Haslam [1-8] The Jack Of All Trades P'ship.*

LATE NIGHT OUT BHB 105f RR 102f — 5206a[4]
4 b g Lahib (USA) 8f **(69)** - Chain Dance (Shareef Dancer (USA)) 9.9f **(73)**
Form - 3144704524
Record 1999 - 1st:1 2nd:1 3rd:1 Ran:10
Pre1999 - 1st:2 2nd:0 3rd:2 Ran:7
Win Prizemoney £20,930 *Total Prizemoney* £36,848
Wins * 1999 May Haydoc (GD) LH 7.1f 99 99 <
* 1998 Oct Redcar (G-S) 7f 94
* 1997 Oct Nottin (GD) 6.1f 88+
1999 Turf 1-10: (6f, 7f 1-9) (sft, g-s, gd 5, g-f 1-1, frm 2)
Workmanlike, very useful gelding, effective 6 to 7f, best at 7f, acts on sft to frm, best on gd, likes left handed tracks, excels at Haydock. Turf high 109 (1st run) - 3rd of 7 giving 11lb to Warningford (5 Apr Warwick 7f gd RF 0598). Consistent. He won a Listed handicap at Haydock on his second start of the season and has run respectably since. He has given the impression that a step up to a mile would not come amiss. **W Jarvis [3-17].*

LATE PARADE (IRE) RR 110f — 4781a[2]
8 b h Astronef 7.9f **(59)** - Skisette (Malinowski (USA)) 10f **(56)**
Form - 12
1999 Turf 1-2: (5f 1-2) (g-s, gd 1-1)
Group-class horse. Turf high 105 (1st run) (began Jly) - 1st of 10 from Reinaldo (11 Jly Agnano RF 2857a). Despite advancing years, he retains all his speed and can win another Group race.
**A Renzoni in ITY [3-5] (from A Spanu in FR [0-1] Oct 1995).*

LATIN BAY BHB 45f48a RR 42f 48a — 4783[8]
4 b g Superlative 8.8f **(57)** - Hugging (Beveled (USA)) 9f **(59)**
Form - 611700308
Record 1999 - 1st:2 2nd:0 3rd:1 Ran:9
Pre1999 - 1st:1 2nd:0 3rd:1 Ran:15
Win Prizemoney £6,580 *Total Prizemoney* £7,545
Wins 1999 *Jan Lingfi (STD) SH 12f 38 54*
1999 *Jan Lingfi (STD) SH 13f 42 56* <
1998 Aug Kempto (G-F) H 9f 42 45
1999 Turf 0-4: (9f, 11f, 12f, 14f) (gd 2, g-f, hrd) 1999 AW 2-5: (8f, 11f, 12f 1-2, 13f 1-1) (Equi 2-4, Fibr)
Light-framed, moderate gelding, effective 11 to 13f, acts on gd - acts on Equi, likes left handed tracks, favours tight tracks. Turf high 42. AW high 56 - 1st of 14 getting 4lb from Maradi (5 Jan Lingfield RF 0029) - also 1st of 16 getting 1lb from Maradi (14 Jan Lingfield RF 0092).
**D J Wintle [0-4] N A Bulmer (from G Lewis [1-3] Jun 1999).*

LATINO BAY (IRE) BHB 58f RR 60f — 4834[11]
2 ch c Perugino (USA) - Slightly Latin (Ahonoora) 8.1f **(73)**
Form - 070
Record 1999 - 1st:0 2nd:0 3rd:0 Ran:3
1999 Turf 0-3: (6f, 7f, 8f) (gd 2, g-f)
Currently average colt. Turf high 60 (began Aug).
**N P Littmoden [0-3] The Southgate Seven.*

LA TIZIANA BHB 73f **RR 72f** 2526[2]
4 b f Rudimentary (USA) 8.2f **(66)** - Tizona (Pharly (FR)) 9.8f **(68)**
Form - 07672
Record 1999 - 1st:0 2nd:1 3rd:0 Ran:5
Pre1999 - 1st:1 2nd:2 3rd:2 Ran:9
Win Prizemoney £14,720 *Total Prizemoney* £21,158
Wins * 1998 Spt Newbur (GD) H 10f 72 77 <
1999 Turf 0-5: (10f 4, 11f) (g-s, gd, frm 3)
Lengthy, above-average filly, effective 10 to 11f, best at 10f, acts on gd to frm, best on g-f. Turf high 72 - 2nd of 11 giving 9lb to Ellopassoff (3 Jly Chepstow 10f frm RF 2526). A fair handicapper, she is suited by forcing tactics. She sometimes flashes her tail, but seems genuine enough.
**W Jarvis [1-14] The Phantom House Partnership.*

LA TORTUGA BHB 80f **RR 76f** 5218[15]
2 b g Turtle Island (IRE) - Ville Sainte (FR) (Saint Estephe (FR)) 16.4f **(79)**
Form - 71440
Record 1999 - 1st:1 2nd:0 3rd:0 Ran:5
Win Prizemoney £3,260 *Total Prizemoney* £4,135
Wins * 1999 Aug Carlis (FRM) 5f 76 <
1999 Turf 1-5: (5f 1-3, 6f, 7f) (g-s, gd, g-f 2, frm 1-1)
Above-average gelding, has worn blinkers. Turf high 76 - 1st of 13 giving 2lb to Elvington Boy (2 Aug Carlisle RF 3290).
**P D Evans [1-5] Muckleton Racing Partnership.*

L A TOUCH BHB 49f52a **RR 49f 52a** 3459[17]
6 b m Tina's Pet 7.4f **(56)** - Silvers Era (Balidar) 7.9f **(63)**
Form - 53101300
Record 1999 - 1st:2 2nd:0 3rd:2 Ran:8
Pre1999 - 1st:2 2nd:5 3rd:1 Ran:31
Win Prizemoney £11,755 *Total Prizemoney* £17,546
Wins * **1999** Jly Cheste (G-F) H 7.6f 41 48
* **1999** Jun Yarmou (GD) H 6f 41 44
1998 Aug Yarmou (FRM) H 6f 33 42
1995 Aug Leices (G-F) S 6f 61 <
1999 Turf 2-8: (5f, 6f 1-5, 7f, 8f 1-1) (gd 1-1, g-f 1-2, frm 5)
Moderate mare, effective 6 to 8f, acts on gd to frm, best on g-f. Turf high 49 - 3rd of 12 getting 14lb from Sycamore Lodge (21 Jly Catterick 7f g-f RF 3004) - also 1st of 15 getting 1lb from Knave's Ash (9 Jly Chester RF 2669). **M A Peill [2-8] H M de B Lipscomb (from J J Quinn [1-16] Spt 1998).*

LATOUR RR 84f 4687[5]
2 b br f Sri Pekan (USA) - Fenny Rough (Home Guard (USA)) 9.3f **(66)**
Form - 645
Record 1999 - 1st:0 2nd:0 3rd:0 Ran:3
Win Prizemoney £0 *Total Prizemoney* £245
1999 Turf 0-3: (7f 3) (g-f, frm 2)
Currently decent filly. Turf high 84 (began Jly).
**J W Hills [0-3] Wood Hall Stud Ltd.*

LATVIAN BHB 23f **RR 34f** 3898[10]
12 gr g Rousillon (USA) 10.4f **(69)** - Lorelene (FR) (Lorenzaccio) 10f **(64)**
Form - 460
Record 1999 - 1st:0 2nd:0 3rd:0 Ran:3
Pre1999 - 1st:11 2nd:13 3rd:12 Ran:72
Win Prizemoney £35,411 *Total Prizemoney* £59,072
Wins * 1997 May Mussel (G-F) C 12f 52
* 1996 Aug Carlis (FRM) C 12f 63
* 1996 May Newcas (GD) H 12.4f 62 67
* 1995 Aug Pontef (G-F) H 12f 68 75 <
* 1995 Jly Catter (G-F) C 12f 70+
1999 Turf 0-3: (12f 2, 16f) (g-f 2, frm)
Very moderate gelding, effective 16f, acts on frm, has worn blinkers, likes right handed tracks. Turf high 34 (began Jly).
**R Allan [10-70] R Allan (from P Monteith [2-12] Spt 1994).*

LAUGHARNE PARK (IRE) BHB 62f **RR 62f** 3859[7]
2 b c Fourstars Allstar (USA) - Frantesa (Red Sunset) 8.2f **(63)**
Form - 007
Record 1999 - 1st:0 2nd:0 3rd:0 Ran:3
1999 Turf 0-3: (6f, 7f 2) (g-f, frm 2)
Currently average colt. Turf high 62 (began Jly).
**B R Millman [0-3] Seasons Holidays.*

LAUND VIEW LADY BHB 73f **RR 78f** 5023[11]
2 ch f Presidium 7.5f **(56)** - Vickenda (Giacometti) 11.2f **(56)**
Form - 51700
Record 1999 - 1st:1 2nd:0 3rd:0 Ran:5
Win Prizemoney £4,435 *Total Prizemoney* £4,435
Wins * **1999** Aug Ripon (GD) 6f 78 <
1999 Turf 1-5: (5f 2, 6f 1-3) (gd 1-3, frm 2)
Above-average filly. Turf high 78 (began Aug) - 1st of 16 getting 9lb from Trajan (14 Aug Ripon RF 3665).
**Mrs S J Smith [1-5] Laund View Racing.*

LAUNFAL BHB 95f **RR 89f** 5027[5]
2 gr c Rudimentary (USA) 8.2f **(66)** - Laune (AUS) **(50f)** (Kenmare (FR)) 6.5f **(72)**
Form - 13433325
Record 1999 - 1st:1 2nd:1 3rd:4 Ran:8
Win Prizemoney £3,403 *Total Prizemoney* £17,550
Wins * **1999** Apr Windso (G-F) 5f 76 <
1999 Turf 1-8: (5f 1-1, 6f 3, 7f 3, 8f) (g-s 2, gd, g-f 1-2, frm 3)
Useful colt, effective 6 to 7f, acts on g-s to frm. Turf high 89 - 2nd of 7 to Asaal (29 Spt Salisbury 6f g-s RF 4643). Made a winning debut at Windsor in April. He has been running in decent company since, often with credit, but has not been able to gain another win.
**R Hannon [1-8] Exors of the late Lord Howard de Walden.*

LAUREL PRINCE BHB 30f **RR 27f** 4602[3]
3 b g Reprimand 8.2f **(63)** - Laurel Queen (IRE) (Viking (USA)) 6.7f **(65)**
Form - 002000503
Record 1999 - 1st:0 2nd:1 3rd:1 Ran:9
Pre1999 - 1st:0 2nd:0 3rd:0 Ran:7
Win Prizemoney £0 *Total Prizemoney* £1,185
1999 Turf 0-8: (6f, 7f, 8f 3, 9f, 10f, 12f) (gd, g-f, frm 6) 1999 AW 0-1: (11f) (Fibr)
Neat, moderate gelding. Turf high 46. Inconsistent.
**J Berry [0-16] Laurel (Leisure) Ltd.*

LAUREN'S LAD BHB 46f57a **RR 37f 57a** 1446[20]
4 ch g Tachyon Park - Glory Isle (Hittite Glory) 8.7f **(50)**
Form - 0
Record 1999 - 1st:0 2nd:0 3rd:0 Ran:1
Pre1999 - 1st:1 2nd:1 3rd:0 Ran:13
Win Prizemoney £3,746 *Total Prizemoney* £4,542
Wins 1997 Oct Lingfi (FRM) H 7f 45 57+ <
1999 Turf 0-1: (12f) (frm)
Neat, average gelding, often wears blinkers. **B J Llewellyn [0-8] Mackworth Snooker Club PT (from Lady Herries [0-2] Jly 1998).*

LAURENTIAN BHB 31f **RR 26f** 3257[5]
4 b f Shareef Dancer (USA) 10.1f **(67)** - Kiomi **(64f)** (Niniski (USA)) 10.6f **(65)**
Form 083435005
Record 1999 - 1st:0 2nd:0 3rd:2 Ran:9
Pre1999 - 1st:0 2nd:0 3rd:0 Ran:8
Win Prizemoney £0 *Total Prizemoney* £1,150
1999 Turf 0-8: (7f 4, 8f 4) (gd, g-f 2, frm 4, hrd) 1999 AW 0-1: (8f) (Fibr)
Neat, little account filly, effective 7f, acts on hrd, has worn blinkers. Turf high 40. **K R Burke [0-17] Leydens Farm Stud.*

LAURENTIDE (USA) BHB 100f **RR 107f** 2071[16]
4 b c Pleasant Colony (USA) 12.4f **(88)** - Northern Sunset (Northfields (USA)) 9f **(72)**
Form - 870
Record 1999 - 1st:0 2nd:0 3rd:0 Ran:3
Pre1999 - 1st:1 2nd:2 3rd:0 Ran:3
Win Prizemoney £4,476 *Total Prizemoney* £19,309
Wins * 1998 May Newmar (G-F) 14f 87 <
1999 Turf 0-3: (14f, 16f, 20f) (gd, g-f, frm)
Workmanlike, Pattern-class colt, effective 16f, acts on gd. Turf high 107. A brother to St Jovite, he looked out of his depth in Group company, and disappeared after Royal Ascot for the second successive year. A scratchy mover, he will always be suited by easy ground. **H R A Cecil [1-6] Mrs Virginia Kraft Payson.*

LAUTREC RR 62f 2504[6]
3 b g Shareef Dancer (USA) 10.1f **(67)** - Pride of Paris (Troy) 10.4f **(68)**

Form - 4336

Record	**1999** -	1st:0	2nd:0	3rd:2	Ran:4
	Pre1999 -	1st:0	2nd:0	3rd:1	Ran:3

Win Prizemoney £0 *Total Prizemoney* £1,705

1999 Turf 0-4: (10f 2, 11f, 12f) (g-f 2, frm 2)

Neat, average gelding, effective 7f, acts on g-f. Turf high 62.

**R J R Williams [0-7] Mrs S E Homewood.*

LAVACA RIVER BHB 32f RR 30f 328[5]

4 b g Primo Dominie 7.2f **(67)** - Rose Music (Luthier) 9.8f **(71)**

Form - 5

Record	**1999** -	1st:0	2nd:0	3rd:0	Ran:1
	Pre1999 -	1st:0	2nd:0	3rd:0	Ran:2

1999 AW 0-1: (8f) (Equi)

Strong, currently very moderate gelding. **P Howling [0-3] R N Khan.*

LAVERON RR 109f 5119a[1]

4 b c Konigsstuhl (GER) 9f **(115)** - La Virginia (GER) (Surumu (GER)) 10f **(83)**

Form - 1

1999 Turf 1-1: (12f 1-1) (sft 1-1)

Currently Pattern-class colt. (1st run) - 1st of 10 giving 4lb to Montalban (24 Oct Dusseldorf RF 5119a). A soft-ground specialist, he battled on well to win at Dortmund in October and is certainly game. **P Rau in GER [2-3] Stall Mydlinghoven.*

LAVERY (IRE) RR 112f 2643[14]

3 b c Royal Academy (USA) 7.8f **(77)** - Lady Donna (Dominion) 8.5f **(63)**

Form - 100

1999 Turf 1-3: (6f 1-2, 8f) (gd 1-2, frm)

Group-class colt, effective 6f, acts on gd to frm. Turf high 112 (1st run) - 1st of 10 from Sheer Viking (8 May Goodwood RF 1105). He looked a sprinter of real potential after winning at Goodwood in May, but failed to find a yard on that performance and proved disappointing. He did not stay a mile in the French 2,000 Guineas, but is worth another try over seven furlongs.

**A P O'Brien in IRE [2-6] M Tabor & Mrs John Magnier.*

LAW COMMISSION BHB 68f RR 63f 5143[11]

9 ch g Ela-Mana-Mou 12.7f **(72)** - Adjala (Northfields (USA)) 9f **(72)**

Form - 0150006000

Record	**1999** -	1st:1	2nd:0	3rd:0	Ran:10
	Pre1999 -	1st:6	2nd:5	3rd:2	Ran:56

Win Prizemoney £40,741 *Total Prizemoney* £75,749

Wins								
	*** 1999**	May	Newbur	(G-F)	H	7f	81	85
	* 1997	Spt	Goodwo	(G-S)	H	7f	91	93 <
	* 1996	Aug	Ascot	(G-F)	H	7f	88	91
	* 1996	Jly	Kempto	(GD)	C	6f		81
	* 1996	Jun	Folkes	(G-F)	H	6f	79	81
	* 1995	Aug	Salisb	(FRM)	H	6f	77	79

1999 Turf 1-10: (6f, 7f 1-9) (g-s, gd 4, g-f 1-3, frm 2)

Average gelding, effective 8f, acts on g-f. Turf high 85. Not as good as he was, despite winning at Newbury on his second start of the season. Best suited by fast ground, but needs everything to go his way. **D R C Elsworth [7-66] Raymond Tooth.*

LAW DANCER (IRE) BHB 48f60a RR 31f 60a 1454[4]

6 b g Alzao (USA) 9.8f **(73)** - Judicial (USA) (Law Society (USA)) 9.9f **(70)**

Form - 11064

Record	**1999** -	1st:2	2nd:0	3rd:0	Ran:5
	Pre1999 -	1st:3	2nd:6	3rd:1	Ran:36

Win Prizemoney £15,097 *Total Prizemoney* £22,250

Wins								
	*** 1999**	*Mar*	*Wolver*	*(STD)*	*H*	*12f*	*57*	*64+*
	*** 1999**	*Feb*	*Lingfi*	*(STD)*	*C*	*12f*		*58*
	* 1998	*Apr*	*Wolver*	*(STD)*	*H*	*9.4f*	*53*	*56*
	* 1996	*Apr*	*Wolver*	*(STD)*	*H*	*9.4f*	*68*	*74* <
	* 1996	*Mar*	*Wolver*	*(STD)*	*H*	*9.4f*	*60*	*66*

1999 AW 2-5: (9f, 10f, 12f 2-3) (Equi 1-3, Fibr 1-2)

Fair gelding, effective 9 to 12f, best at 12f, - acts on AW, best on Fibr, has worn blinkers. AW high 64 - 1st of 9 getting 8lb from Jalb (3 Mar Wolverhampton RF 0398) - also 1st of 8 giving 8lb to Key To The City (25 Feb Lingfield RF 0356). Rather better on sand than on turf, especially at Wolverhampton. Lisa Hackett gets on very well with him. **T G Mills [5-41] T J Oswin.*

LAW LADY (IRE) BHB 38f RR 46f 4605[14]

2 ch f Port Lucaya - Law Student (Precocious) 8.6f **(62)**

Form - 0000

Record	**1999** -	1st:0	2nd:0	3rd:0	Ran:4

1999 Turf 0-3: (6f 2, 7f) (gd, g-f, frm) 1999 AW 0-1: (7f) (Fibr)

Moderate filly. Turf high 46 (began Jly).

**M H Tompkins [0-4] De Graags Wine Bar Syndicate.*

LAYAN BHB 61f RR 62f 4280[6]

2 b f Puissance 7.1f **(60)** - Most Uppitty **(47f 49a)** (Absalom) 7.2f **(58)**

Form - 624876

Record	**1999** -	1st:0	2nd:1	3rd:0	Ran:6

Win Prizemoney £0 *Total Prizemoney* £912

1999 Turf 0-5: (5f 5) (gd 2, g-f 2, frm) 1999 AW 0-1: (5f) (Fibr)

Average filly, effective 5f, acts on gd. Turf high 67.

**J Berry [0-6] The Sussex Stud Ltd.*

LAY THE BLAME BHB 49f60a RR 48f 60a 3296[6]

6 b g Reprimand 8.2f **(63)** - Rose And The Ring (Welsh Pageant) 10f **(65)**

Form - 005626

Record	**1999** -	1st:0	2nd:1	3rd:0	Ran:6
	Pre1999 -	1st:2	2nd:1	3rd:2	Ran:17

Win Prizemoney £7,830 *Total Prizemoney* £11,201

Wins							
	1995	Oct	Nottin	(G-F)	6.1f	86 <
	1995	Oct	Warwic	(G-S)	6f	73

1999 Turf 0-5: (10f 3, 12f 2) (gd 2, frm 3) 1999 AW 0-1: (8f) (Fibr)

Fair gelding, has worn blinkers. Turf high 48.

**M D Hammond [0-24] J D Gordon & E C Gordon (from W Jarvis [2-9] Aug 1996).*

LAZER MAGIC (USA) BHB 55f RR 56f 4995[16]

2 b f Personal Hope (USA) - La Caleche (USA) (Gregorian (USA))

Form - 0700

Record	**1999** -	1st:0	2nd:0	3rd:0	Ran:4

1999 Turf 0-4: (6f 2, 7f 2) (gd 2, g-f 2)

Fair filly, often wears blinkers. Turf high 56.

**J H M Gosden [0-4] K Doyle.*

LAZY LODE (ARG) RR 114f 4782a[2]

5 ch h Lode (USA) - Lazy Fables (USA) (Babas Fables (USA))

Form - 2

1999 Turf 0-1: (10f) (frm)

Currently Group-class colt. (1st run) - 2nd of 6 to Mash One (3 Oct Santa Anita 10f frm RF 4782a). **R Mandella in USA [0-1].*

LEADING PROSPECTOR (USA) RR 74f 1029[7]

3 b c Mr Prospector (USA) 8.6f **(88)** - Araadh (USA) **(64f)** (Blushing Groom (FR)) 10.3f **(76)**

Form - 7

Record	**1999** -	1st:0	2nd:0	3rd:0	Ran:1
	Pre1999 -	1st:0	2nd:0	3rd:0	Ran:1

1999 Turf 0-1: (10f) (g-f)

Scopey, currently above-average colt.

**C E Brittain [0-2] The Thoroughbred Corporation.*

LEADING ROLE RR 88+f 4595[10]

2 ch f Cadeaux Genereux 7.9f **(76)** - Footlight Fantasy (USA) **(66f)** (Nureyev (USA)) 8.7f **(78)**

Form - 10

Record	**1999** -	1st:1	2nd:0	3rd:0	Ran:2

Win Prizemoney £4,142 *Total Prizemoney* £4,142

Wins							
	*** 1999**	Spt	Lingfi	(G-F)	7f	88+ <

1999 Turf 1-2: (7f 1-2) (g-f, frm 1-1)

Currently useful filly. Turf high 88 (1st run) (began Spt) - 1st of 11 from Ghuffran (7 Spt Lingfield RF 4176). She won nicely over seven furlongs on her Lingfield debut but made no show in a hot race at Newmarket. **Sir Michael Stoute [1-2] Cheveley Park Stud.*

LEADING SPIRIT (IRE) BHB 75f85a RR 46f 85a 2122[R]

7 b g Fairy King (USA) 7.7f **(75)** - Shopping (FR) (Sheshoon) 11.9f **(69)**

Form - 0RR

Record	**1999** -	1st:0	2nd:0	3rd:0	Ran:3
	Pre1999 -	1st:5	2nd:3	3rd:3	Ran:27

Win Prizemoney £22,873 *Total Prizemoney* £31,526

Wins								
	1997	*Feb*	*Wolver*	*(STD)*	*H*	*12f*	*71*	*79+*
	1996	Spt	Kempto	(GD)	H	12f	83	87 <

1996 Jun Kempto (G-F) H 12f 73 83+
1995 Spt Hamilt (GD) H 12.1f 66 74
1995 Spt Sandow (G-S) H 11.4f 60 66
1999 Turf 0-3: (10f, 12f, 14f) (frm 3)
Above-average gelding, effective 12f, acts on g-f, has worn blinkers. Turf high 46. Inconsistent.
**D Sasse [0-3] Christopher Ranson (from R Champion [0-1] Nov 1998).*

LEAPING CHARLIE BHB 59f **RR 57f** 5212[11]

3 b g Puissance 7.1f **(60)** - Impala Lass (Kampala) 8.5f **(56)**
Form - 00701675020

Record	**1999** -	1st:1	2nd:1	3rd:0	Ran:11
	Pre1999 -	1st:0	2nd:0	3rd:1	Ran:4

Win Prizemoney £2,388 *Total Prizemoney* £3,562
Wins * **1999** Jun Hamilt (GD) H 5f 57 58 <
1999 Turf 1-11: (5f 1-8, 6f 3) (sft, g-s, gd 2, g-f 1-3, frm 4)
Leggy, fair gelding, effective 5f, acts on gd. Turf high 58. Consistent. **Mrs A Swinbank [1-15] Starnotes Racing.*

LEAR SPEAR (USA) BHB 118f **RR 120f** 4919[9]

4 b c Lear Fan (USA) 10.4f **(80)** - Golden Gorse (USA) (His Majesty (USA)) 10.9f **(82)**
Form - 54611810

Record	**1999** -	1st:3	2nd:0	3rd:0	Ran:8
	Pre1999 -	1st:2	2nd:1	3rd:5	Ran:13

Win Prizemoney £198,466 *Total Prizemoney* £211,319

Wins	* **1999** Spt Goodwo (G-F)	G3	9.9f		118	
	* **1999** Jun Ascot (G-F)	G2	10f		120	<
	* **1999** Jun Epsom (GD,)	G3	8.5f		110	
	* 1998 Oct Newmar ()	H	9f	90	96	
	* 1998 Aug Sandow (GD)		8.1f		75	

1999 Turf 3-8: (8f, 9f 1-2, 10f 2-5) (g-s, gd 1-4, g-f 2-2, frm)
Scopey, very high-class colt, effective 9 to 10f, best at 10f, acts on gd to g-f, best on g-f, likes right handed tracks. Turf high 120 - 1st of 8 giving 12lb to Fantastic Light (15 Jun Ascot RF 1996) - also 1st of 7 giving 5lb to Kabool (11 Spt Goodwood RF 4271). Winner of the 1998 Cambridgeshire, he put up a most eyecatching performance on his Newmarket reappearance last season, and though finishing well beaten behind Handsome Ridge in his next two starts, gained the Pattern victory that always seemed likely when taking the Diomed Stakes at Epsom. He caused an even bigger shock when pouncing late to win the Prince of Wales's Stakes at Royal Ascot, but finished last in the Eclipse. Returned from a break to win a Group Three at Goodwood, but again found Group One company too much when down the field in the Dubai Champion Stakes on his final start.
**D R C Elsworth [5-21] Raymond Tooth.*

LEA VALLEY EXPRESS (IRE) BHB 54f50a **RR 54f 50a** 4868[7]

2 b f Fayruz 6.6f **(63)** - Fenland Express (IRE) (Reasonable (FR))
Form - 0854037

Record	**1999** -	1st:0	2nd:0	3rd:1	Ran:7

Win Prizemoney £0 *Total Prizemoney* £501
1999 Turf 0-6: (5f 5, 6f) (g-s, g-f, frm 4) 1999 AW 0-1: (5f) (Fibr)
Fair filly, often wears blinkers. Turf high 54.
**J R Jenkins [0-7] Lea Valley.*

LEAVE IT TO ME BHB 70a **RR 67f** 2586[3]

3 b f College Chapel - Enaam (Shirley Heights) 10.3f **(74)**
Form - 4173

Record	**1999** -	1st:1	2nd:0	3rd:1	Ran:4
	Pre1999 -	1st:0	2nd:1	3rd:0	Ran:4

Win Prizemoney £3,738 *Total Prizemoney* £5,560
Wins * **1999** Apr Nottin (HVY) H 8.2f 66 67 <
1999 Turf 1-3: (8f 1-2, 10f) (sft 1-1, gd, frm) 1999 AW 0-1: (10f) (Equi)
Neat, average filly, effective 6 to 8f, acts on sft to frm. Turf high 67 - 1st of 15 getting 4lb from Redouble (27 Apr Nottingham RF 0869).
**S P C Woods [1-8] Mrs Marian Borsberry.*

LEAVE IT TO RODNEY BHB 28f **RR 16f** 4228[16]

4 b g Tina's Pet 7.4f **(56)** - Fivesevenfiveo **(59df)** (Enchantment) 5.4f **(52)**
Form - 000

Record	**1999** -	1st:0	2nd:0	3rd:0	Ran:3
	Pre1999 -	1st:0	2nd:0	3rd:0	Ran:6

1999 Turf 0-3: (5f, 6f, 8f) (gd, frm 2)
Leggy, poor gelding, has worn blinkers. Turf high 16 (began Aug).
**R J Hodges [0-9] B Dennett.*

LEAVE US LEAP (USA) RR 100f 627a[2]

3 b c Summer Squall (USA) 7f **(80)** - Sporades (USA) (Vaguely Noble) 10.1f **(72)**
Form - 2
1999 Turf 0-1: (8f) (hvy)
Currently very useful colt. (1st run) - 2nd of 6 to Le Roi Chic (30 Mar Maisons-Laffitte 8f hvy RF 0627a). **A Fabre in FR [0-1].*

LE CAVALIER (USA) BHB 60f **RR 59f** 5196[11]

2 b c Mister Baileys - Secret Deed (USA) (Shadeed (USA)) 8.2f **(70)**
Form - 50300

Record	**1999** -	1st:0	2nd:0	3rd:1	Ran:5

Win Prizemoney £0 *Total Prizemoney* £702
1999 Turf 0-5: (7f 2, 8f 3) (g-s, gd, g-f, frm 2)
Fair colt, has worn blinkers. Turf high 59 (began Aug).
**C N Allen [0-5] Mrs K A Hyytiainen.*

LEDGENDRY LINE BHB 60f **RR 62f** 4717[7]

6 b g Mtoto 11.5f **(71)** - Eider (Niniski (USA)) 10.6f **(65)**
Form - 503532247

Record	**1999** -	1st:0	2nd:2	3rd:2	Ran:9
	Pre1999 -	1st:1	2nd:2	3rd:3	Ran:16

Win Prizemoney £2,956 *Total Prizemoney* £13,818
Wins * 1997 Jun Ayr (GD) H 13.1f 70 77 <
1999 Turf 0-9: (12f, 14f 4, 16f, 17f 3) (sft, g-s 2, gd 3, g-f 2, frm)
Average gelding, effective 13 to 17f, acts on sft to frm. Turf high 64. Consistent. **Mrs M Reveley [3-30] The Home & Away Partnership.*

LEDHAM (USA) BHB 80f **RR 77f** 3950[4]

3 ch c Diesis 9f **(80)** - First Tracks (USA) (Alleged (USA)) 10f **(76)**
Form - 0222314

Record	**1999** -	1st:1	2nd:3	3rd:1	Ran:7
	Pre1999 -	1st:0	2nd:0	3rd:1	Ran:3

Win Prizemoney £2,738 *Total Prizemoney* £9,164
Wins * **1999** Aug Mussel (G-S) 9f 76+ <
1999 Turf 1-7: (9f 1-1, 10f 3, 11f, 12f 2) (gd, g-f 1-1, frm 4, hrd)
Above-average colt, effective 9 to 12f, acts on gd to hrd, best on frm, prefers tight tracks. Turf high 77 - 2nd of 3 to Hormuz (17 Jun Ripon 10f hrd RF 2081) - also 1st of 7 from Little John (18 Aug Musselburgh RF 3754). Consistent.
**Sir Michael Stoute [1-10] Saeed Suhail.*

LEEN BHB 70f **RR 73f** 4872[9]

2 b f Distant Relative 7f **(69)** - St James's Antigua (IRE) (Law Society (USA)) 9.9f **(70)**
Form - 62140

Record	**1999** -	1st:1	2nd:1	3rd:0	Ran:5

Win Prizemoney £3,571 *Total Prizemoney* £4,868
Wins * **1999** Spt Bath (FRM) 5.1f 73 <
1999 Turf 1-5: (5f 1-2, 6f 3) (gd 2, frm 1-3)
Above-average filly. Turf high 73 (began Jly) - 2nd of 9 getting 6lb from Ogilia (3 Aug Bath 6f frm RF 3308) - also 1st of 10 from Chorus (6 Spt Bath RF 4155). Scored on very fast ground at Bath in September, but did not run badly on much softer ground at Newmarket and may be worth a try beyond six furlongs.
**C G Cox [1-3] Mrs T L Cox (from M J Heaton-Ellis [0-2] Aug 1999).*

LEEROY (IRE) BHB 82f **RR 80f** 4821[4]

2 b c Dancing Dissident (USA) 6.8f **(65)** - Birdhill (IRE) (Petorius) 7.3f **(61)**
Form - 53224

Record	**1999** -	1st:0	2nd:2	3rd:1	Ran:5

Win Prizemoney £0 *Total Prizemoney* £3,283
1999 Turf 0-5: (6f 5) (g-s, gd 2, g-f 2)
Decent colt. Turf high 80 - 4th of 21 giving 5lb to Toleration (11 Oct Windsor 6f g-f RF 4821).
**R Hannon [0-5] Exors of the late D B Gallop.*

LEES FIRST STEP BHB 64f **RR 72f** 4157[7]

2 b f Reprimand 8.2f **(63)** - Classic Coral (USA) (Seattle Dancer (USA))
Form - 0727

Record	**1999** -	1st:0	2nd:1	3rd:0	Ran:4

Win Prizemoney £0 *Total Prizemoney* £892
1999 Turf 0-4: (6f, 7f 2, 8f) (gd, g-f, frm 2)
Above-average filly. Turf high 72 - 2nd of 9 giving 2lb to Ecstasy

(17 Jly Warwick 7f g-f RF 2933). *P G Murphy [0-4] First Step.

LEGACY OF LOVE BHB 62f **RR 64f** 4991[4]
3 b f Distant Relative 7f **(69)** - May Hills Legacy (IRE) (Be My Guest (USA)) 9.3f **(67)**
Form - 521744
Record 1999 - 1st:1 2nd:1 3rd:0 Ran:6
Win Prizemoney £2,476 *Total Prizemoney* £3,483
Wins * **1999** Jly Lingfi (G-F) 7.6f 64 <
1999 Turf 1-6: (7f, 8f 1-4, 10f) (gd, g-f 2, frm 1-2, hrd)
Neat, average filly, effective 8 to 10f, best at 8f, acts on gd to hrd. Turf high 66 - also 1st of 8 from Fatoomah (31 Jly Lingfield RF 3272). *B W Hills [1-6] J Hanson.

LEGAL ISSUE (IRE) BHB 66f55a **RR 66f 55a** 5191[5]
7 b h Contract Law (USA) 8.9f **(54)** - Natuschka (Authi) 8.9f **(89)**
Form - 146215048003705
Record 1999 - 1st:2 2nd:1 3rd:1 Ran:15
Pre1999 - 1st:8 2nd:12 3rd:5 Ran:60
Win Prizemoney £31,583 *Total Prizemoney* £49,383
Wins * **1999** Jun Beverl (GD) H 8.5f 67 81+ <
* **1999** Apr Thirsk (GD) H 8f 62 67
1998 Jun Beverl (G-S) H 8.5f 67 68
1998 Apr Pontef (G-S) 8f 67
1997 *Dec Lingfi (STD) H 10f 55 59*
1997 *Aug Wolver (STD) H 8.5f 51 52*
1996 Jly Catter (G-S) 7f 68
1996 Jun Doncas (GD) H 7f 56 59
1995 Aug Mussel (G-F) H 7.1f 62 69
1995 Jun Mussel (G-F) 7.1f 59
1999 Turf 2-14: (8f 2-9, 9f 3, 10f 2) (gd 2-6, g-f 6, frm 2) 1999 AW 0-1: (9f) (Fibr)
Average horse, effective 8f, acts on gd, has worn blinkers, likes tight tracks. Turf high 81 - 1st of 9 from Harmony Hall (2 Jun Beverley RF 1664).
B S Rothwell [2-15] B Valentine (from J M Jefferson [0-4] Nov 1998).

LEGAL JOUSTING (IRE) RR 96f 5170a[2]
2 b c Indian Ridge 7.6f **(74)** - In Anticipation 00
Form - 2
1999 Turf 0-1: (7f) (sft)
Currently very useful colt. (1st run) - 2nd of 17 to Apollo Victoria (25 Oct Leopardstown 7f sft RF 5170a).
D K Weld in IRE [0-1] Moyglare Stud Farm.

LEGAL LUNCH (USA) BHB 68f **RR 72f** 5038[2]
4 b g Alleged (USA) 11.8f **(81)** - Dinner Surprise (USA) (Lyphard (USA)) 9.9f **(72)**
Form - 00205263500652
Record 1999 - 1st:0 2nd:3 3rd:1 Ran:14
Pre1999 - 1st:1 2nd:1 3rd:1 Ran:9
Win Prizemoney £3,680 *Total Prizemoney* £14,023
Wins * 1998 May Haydoc (G-S) 10.5f 90 <
1999 Turf 0-14: (12f 8, 14f, 16f 5) (g-s 4, gd 2, g-f 4, frm 4)
Scopey, above-average gelding, effective 11 to 16f, acts on g-s to frm, has worn blinkers, likes left handed tracks, likes tight tracks, excels at Haydock. Turf high 83 - 2nd of 13 giving 9lb to Norcroft Joy (5 Jun Doncaster 12f g-f RF 1752). Consistent. He is rather one-paced, and is also in the grip of the Handicapper. His best form of late has been over two miles.
P W Harris [1-23] The Alleged Partnership.

LEGAL SET (IRE) BHB 70f **RR 69f** 1915[7]
3 b br c Second Set (IRE) 9.2f **(67)** - Tiffany's Case (IRE) **(58f)** (Thatching) 8f **(66)**
Form - 0387
Record 1999 - 1st:0 2nd:0 3rd:1 Ran:4
Pre1999 - 1st:0 2nd:0 3rd:0 Ran:2
Win Prizemoney £0 *Total Prizemoney* £810
1999 Turf 0-4: (7f 2, 8f, 10f) (gd, g-f, frm 2)
Workmanlike, average colt, effective 7 to 8f, acts on frm. Turf high 69 - 3rd of 13 getting 2lb from The Whistling Teal (19 Apr Windsor 8f frm RF 0757). *C A Horgan [0-6] John Kelsey-Fry.*

LEGAL VENTURE (IRE) BHB 45f55a **RR 44f 55a** 2810[10]
3 ch g Case Law 6f **(64)** - We Two (Glenstal (USA)) 10.1f **(64)**
Form - 267574323407106020
Record 1999 - 1st:1 2nd:2 3rd:2 Ran:14
Pre1999 - 1st:1 2nd:3 3rd:2 Ran:16
Win Prizemoney £3,565 *Total Prizemoney* £8,681
Wins * **1999** *May Wolver (STD) S 5f 60*
1998 Jly Lingfi (G-F) S 5f 64+ <
1999 Turf 0-4: (5f 4) (gd, g-f 2, frm) 1999 AW 1-10: (5f 1-9, 6f) (Fibr 1-10)
Fair gelding, effective 5f, acts on g-f to frm - acts on Fibr, best on g-f, often wears blinkers.
N P Littmoden [1-19] Hanibel Racing Partnership (from B J Meehan [1-11] Oct 1998).

LEGEND BHB 64f **RR 70?f** 3074[4]
3 b f Belmez (USA) 11.4f **(65)** - Once Upon a Time (Teenoso (USA)) 9.9f **(72)**
Form - 34
Record 1999 - 1st:0 2nd:0 3rd:1 Ran:2
Pre1999 - 1st:0 2nd:0 3rd:1 Ran:2
Win Prizemoney £0 *Total Prizemoney* £1,537
1999 Turf 0-2: (12f 2) (g-s, frm)
Scopey, above-average filly. Turf high 61.
I A Balding [0-2] The Queen (from Lord Huntingdon [0-2] Nov 1998).

LEGENDAIRE (USA) BHB 55f **RR 67f** 4995[12]
2 gr c Fly Till Dawn (USA) - Iolani **(49f)** (Alzao (USA)) 7.1f **(68)**
Form - 6204000
Record 1999 - 1st:0 2nd:1 3rd:0 Ran:7
Win Prizemoney £0 *Total Prizemoney* £1,302
1999 Turf 0-7: (6f 4, 7f 3) (gd 3, g-f 3, frm)
Average colt. Turf high 67. *C A Dwyer [0-7] Legend Racing.*

LEGENDARY LOVER (IRE) BHB 60a **RR 56f** 4413[6]
5 b g Fairy King (USA) 7.7f **(75)** - Broken Romance (IRE) (Ela-Mana-Mou) 10.1f **(70)**
Form - 026066
Record 1999 - 1st:0 2nd:1 3rd:0 Ran:6
Pre1999 - 1st:0 2nd:0 3rd:1 Ran:5
Win Prizemoney £0 *Total Prizemoney* £2,067
1999 Turf 0-5: (11f, 12f 3, 14f) (gd, frm 4) 1999 AW 0-1: (15f) (Fibr)
Fair gelding. Turf high 67. Inconsistent.
J R Jenkins [0-9] Southern Counties Finance & Leasing (from R Charlton [0-5] Spt 1997).

LEGEND FALLS (IRE) BHB 65f53a **RR 68f 53a** 4623a[7]
3 ch f River Falls 8.2f **(56)** - Sister Dympna (Grundy) 10.3f **(65)**
Form - 2527516177
Record 1999 - 1st:2 2nd:2 3rd:0 Ran:10
Pre1999 - 1st:0 2nd:2 3rd:2 Ran:6
Win Prizemoney £6,542 *Total Prizemoney* £10,633
Wins * **1999** Aug Sligo (G-S) H 6.5f 69 68
* **1999** Jun Sligo (G-S) 6.5f 75 <
1999 Turf 2-6: (6f, 7f 2-4, 8f) (hvy, sft, g-s 2-2, g-f 2) 1999 AW 0-4: (7f 2, 8f, 9f) (Equi 2, Fibr 2)
Average filly, effective 6 to 7f, best at 7f, acts on g-s to gd, best on g-s, has worn blinkers, likes right handed tracks, excels at Sligo. Turf high 75 - 1st of 15 from Pip'n Judy (6 Jun Sligo RF 1846a) - also 1st of 11 getting 1lb from Windy Project (5 Aug Sligo RF 3520a). AW high 54.
M J Grassick in IRE [2-12] Blakestown Racing Club (from J Noseda [0-4] Mar 1999).

LEGEND OF LOVE BHB 59f52a **RR 61f 52a** 3214[4]
4 b g Pursuit of Love 9.5f **(69)** - Legendary Dancer (Shareef Dancer (USA)) 9.9f **(73)**
Form - 005022644
Record 1999 - 1st:0 2nd:2 3rd:0 Ran:9
Pre1999 - 1st:1 2nd:1 3rd:4 Ran:17
Win Prizemoney £3,730 *Total Prizemoney* £10,432
Wins * 1998 Oct Catter (G-S) H 15.8f 48 60+ <
1999 Turf 0-8: (16f 4, 17f 3, 18f) (g-s, gd 3, g-f, frm 3) 1999 AW 0-1: (16f) (Fibr)
Workmanlike, average gelding, effective 12 to 17f, best at 16f, acts on g-s to frm, best on gd, has worn blinkers, likes tight tracks, excels at Bath, likes Nottingham. Turf high 61 - 4th of 16 getting 3lb from Danegold (23 Jly Ascot 16f gd RF 3048).
B J Llewellyn [3-20] B J Llewellyn (from J A Glover [0-14] Spt 1998).

LEGEND OF SPRING (USA) RR 102f 4765a3
2 b f Night Shift (USA) 8.1f **(73)** - Dream Season (USA) (Mr Prospector (USA)) 8.8f **(78)**
Form - 23
1999 Turf 0-2: (5f 2) (hvy, gd)
Currently very useful filly. Turf high 102 (began Jly). She is nothing out of the ordinary judged on her third place at Maisons-Laffitte in October. *C Laffon-Parias in FR [0-2] Jly 1999).*

LEGGERA (IRE) BHB 118f **RR 124?f** 5121aD
4 b f Sadler's Wells (USA) 11.3f **(87)** - Lady Ambassador (General Assembly (USA)) 10f **(68)**
Form - 514D

Record	**1999** -	1st:1	2nd:0	3rd:0	Ran:4
	Pre1999 -	1st:4	2nd:3	3rd:2	Ran:11

Win Prizemoney £143,429 *Total Prizemoney* £395,173

Wins							
* **1999**	Spt	Ayr	(G-S)	L	10.9f	102	
* 1998	Spt	Longch	(SFT)	G1	12f	116	<
* 1998	Aug	Deauvi	(SFT)	G2	13.5f	112	
* 1997	Nov	Maison	(HLD)	L	8f	92	
* 1997	Aug	Sandow	(G-F)		7.1f	92+	

1999 Turf 1-4: (11f 1-1, 12f 2, 16f) (hvy, sft 2, gd 1-1)
Scopey, very high-class filly, effective 12f, acts on hvy to sft, prefers right handed tracks. Turf high 118. Really improved during the autumn of '98, winning the Prix Vermeille, and only just caught by Sagamix in the Arc. Ran moderately in a Group Two at Saint-Cloud on her reappearance in May, and was given a break before gaining a clear-cut victory in the Listed Doonside Cup at Ayr in September. Back to something like her best when fourth to Montjeu in the Arc, where the heavy ground suited her admirably, she was retired after finishing third (disqualified) in the Prix Royal-Oak. *J L Dunlop [5-15].*

LEGGY LADY BHB 47f **RR 61f** 4992[8]
3 b f Sir Harry Lewis (USA) - Lady Minstrel (Tudor Music) 6.8f **(59)**
Form - 868

Record	**1999** -	1st:0	2nd:0	3rd:0	Ran:3

1999 Turf 0-3: (10f 3) (g-f, frm 2)
Scopey, currently average filly. Turf high 61 (began Jly). *J A R Toller [0-3] M E Wates.*

LEGS BE FRENDLY (IRE) BHB 65f66a **RR 57f 66a** 4255[22]
4 b c Fayruz 6.6f **(63)** - Thalssa (Rusticaro (FR)) 8.2f **(65)**
Form - 828800

Record	**1999** -	1st:0	2nd:1	3rd:0	Ran:6
	Pre1999 -	1st:1	2nd:6	3rd:1	Ran:14

Win Prizemoney £4,653 *Total Prizemoney* £15,861

Wins							
* 1997	Oct	Lingfi	(GD)		5f	64	<

1999 Turf 0-5: (5f 4, 6f) (g-s, gd, frm 3) 1999 AW 0-1: (5f) (Fibr)
Scopey, fair colt, effective 5f, acts on gd, often wears blinkers. Turf high 71 - 2nd of 19 to Black Army (8 May Beverley 5f gd RF 1100). *K McAuliffe [1-20] BABK Racing.*

LEIGH CROFTER BHB 36f50a **RR 32f 50a** 2233[11]
10 ch g Son of Shaka 6.2f **(29)** - Ganadora (Good Times (ITY)) 6.6f **(54)**
Form - 000

Record	**1999** -	1st:0	2nd:0	3rd:0	Ran:3
	Pre1999 -	1st:12	2nd:11	3rd:8	Ran:123

Win Prizemoney £39,723 *Total Prizemoney* £58,675

Wins							
1997	*Jan*	*Wolver*	*(SLW)*	*H*	*7f*	*62*	*66*
1996	*Dec*	*Wolver*	*(STD)*	*H*	*7f*	*58*	*64*
1996	*Nov*	*Southw*	*(STD)*	*H*	*7f*	*47*	*57*
1996	*Nov*	*Wolver*	*(STD)*		*7f*		*60*
1995	*Jan*	*Wolver*	*(STD)*	*H*	*5f*	*70*	*72*

1999 Turf 0-2: (6f, 8f) (sft, frm) 1999 AW 0-1: (7f) (Fibr)
Fair gelding, effective 6 to 8f, best at 7f, acts on g-s - acts on Fibr, mostly wears blinkers, prefers left handed tracks, prefers tight tracks, does well at Southwell. *J L Harris [0-4] Mrs Annette Harris (from John Harris [0-14] Jun 1998).*

LE KHOUMF (FR) BHB 50f **RR 43f** 5006[5]
8 ch g Son of Silver - Bentry (FR) (Ben Trovato (FR))
Form - 5

Record	**1999** -	1st:0	2nd:0	3rd:0	Ran:1
	Pre1999 -	1st:0	2nd:0	3rd:0	Ran:6

Win Prizemoney £0 *Total Prizemoney* £268
1999 Turf 0-1: (16f) (gd)
Moderate gelding.
J Neville [1-6] George Moore (from J M Bradley [0-9] Jun 1996).

LE LOUP BHB 62f **RR 76f** 4580[9]
2 b c Wolfhound (USA) 7.3f **(71)** - Chandni (IRE) (Ahonoora) 8.1f **(73)**
Form - 030600

Record	**1999** -	1st:0	2nd:0	3rd:1	Ran:6

Win Prizemoney £0 *Total Prizemoney* £567
1999 Turf 0-6: (5f 3, 6f 3) (g-s, gd, g-f, frm 3)
Above-average colt, effective 5f, acts on g-s. Turf high 76 - 3rd of 9 to Duke of Aston (2 Jun Goodwood 5f g-s RF 1678).
Miss E C Lavelle [0-6] The 1st Little Hatherden Partnership.

LEMON BRIDGE (IRE) BHB 77f **RR 76f** 3741[8]
4 b g Shalford (IRE) 7.8f **(63)** - Sharply (Sharpman) 11.3f **(66)**
Form - 228

Record	**1999** -	1st:0	2nd:2	3rd:0	Ran:3
	Pre1999 -	1st:1	2nd:1	3rd:3	Ran:10

Win Prizemoney £3,850 *Total Prizemoney* £10,282

Wins						
1998	Jun	Goodwo	(G-F)	9.9f	79	<

1999 Turf 0-3: (12f 3) (g-s, g-f 2)
Light-framed, above-average gelding, effective 7 to 12f, best at 10f, acts on hvy to frm, excels at Newmarket and Doncaster. Turf high 76 (1st run) - 2nd of 6 giving 7lb to Musician (25 Jun Newmarket 12f g-f RF 2305).
R T Phillips [0-3] Mrs Lisa Olley (from J W Hills [1-10] Spt 1998).

LEMON DROP KID (USA) RR 5231a[6]
3 b c Kingmambo (USA) 10.9f **(85)** - Charming Lassie (USA) (Seattle Slew (USA)) 9.4f **(76)**
Form - 16
1999 AW 1-2: (10f, 12f 1-1) (Dirt 1-2)
Currently very high-class colt. AW high 121 - 6th of 14 to Cat Thief (6 Nov Gulfstream Park 10f Dirt RF 5231a) - also 1st of 12 from Vision And Verse (5 Jun Belmont Park RF 1899a). He was a useful juvenile in the USA in 1998, and proved he had trained on when outstaying his rivals to win the 1999 Belmont Stakes. Finished well, but seemed to find ten furlongs on the short side in the Breeders' Cup Classic. *F Schulhofer in USA [1-3].*

LEMON STRIP BHB 38f40a **RR 45df 40a** 4148[14]
3 ch f Emarati (USA) 6.6f **(63)** - Lon Isa **(39f 47a)** (Grey Desire) 8.7f **(50)**
Form - 007042370

Record	**1999** -	1st:0	2nd:1	3rd:1	Ran:9
	Pre1999 -	1st:0	2nd:0	3rd:0	Ran:3

Win Prizemoney £0 *Total Prizemoney* £946
1999 Turf 0-6: (5f 2, 6f 2, 8f 2) (gd, g-f 2, frm, hrd 2) 1999 AW 0-3: (5f 3) (Fibr 3)
Unfurnished, fair filly, effective 5f, acts on hrd. Turf high 45. AW high 33. *B Palling [0-12] H Weeks.*

LEND A HAND BHB 120f **RR 122f** 5226a[4]
4 b c Great Commotion (USA) 9.2f **(80)** - Janaat (Kris) 9.5f **(73)**
Form - 10124

Record	**1999** -	1st:2	2nd:1	3rd:0	Ran:5
	Pre1999 -	1st:5	2nd:3	3rd:1	Ran:10

Win Prizemoney £150,823 *Total Prizemoney* £319,030

Wins								
* **1999**	Aug	Newbur	(GD)	G3	7.3f		118+	
1999	*Mar*	*Nad Al*	*(FST)*	*L*	*8f*		*123*	<
1997	Oct	San Si	(GD)	G1	8f		115+	
1997	Spt	Doncas	(G-F)	H	8f	94	103+	
1997	Jly	Beverl	(G-F)		7.5f		90	
1997	Jly	Catter	(G-F)		7f		94+	
1997	Jly	Epsom	(G-S)		6f		75	

1999 Turf 1-4: (7f 1-3, 8f) (gd, g-f 1-1, frm 2) 1999 AW 1-1: (8f 1-1) (Dirt 1-1)
Scopey, very high-class colt, effective 7 to 8f, best at 8f, acts on gd to frm - acts on Dirt, excels at Newmarket. Turf high 122 - 4th of 14 to Silic (6 Nov Gulfstream Park 8f frm RF 5226a) - also 1st of 7 from Teapot Row (13 Aug Newbury RF 3619). (1st run) - 1st of 7 getting 7lb from Muhtathir (28 Mar Nad Al Sheba RF 0558a). Consistent. A very smart colt when with Mark Johnston, he finished runner-up to King Of Kings in the 2000 Guineas on his reappearance in 1998, and continued to run well in top company if not managing a win. Switched to Godolphin before the start of 1999, he easily won on sand at Nad Al Sheba, but was well beaten in

Hong Kong next time. He did not race in Europe until August, but showed just what he is capable of when running away with the Group Three Hungerford Stakes at Newbury. Surprisingly, if only narrowly, beaten by Susu in the Challenge Stakes, he ran his heart out in the Breeders' Cup Mile and, after looking the winner inside the final furlong, was caught and run out of the places close home. Although he has won over a mile more than once, this performance suggests that seven may be his optimum trip.

**S bin Suroor [1-4] (from S bin Suroor in UAE [1-1] Mar 1999).*

LENNOX RR 68f 5135[17]

3 b g Bustino 11f **(64)** - Ivory Gull (USA) (Storm Bird (CAN)) 10.3f **(74)**

Form - 3400

Record 1999 - 1st:0 2nd:0 3rd:1 Ran:4

Pre1999 - 1st:0 2nd:0 3rd:0 Ran:3

Win Prizemoney £0 *Total Prizemoney* £618

1999 Turf 0-4: (8f, 10f, 12f 2) (hvy, g-s, gd, frm)

Scopey, average gelding, effective 7f, acts on g-f. Turf high 68.

**P F I Cole [0-7] Sir George Meyrick.*

LENNY THE LION BHB 57f RR 55f 4995[5]

2 b c Bin Ajwaad (IRE) - Patriotic (Hotfoot) 10.5f **(59)**

Form - 0065

Record 1999 - 1st:0 2nd:0 3rd:0 Ran:4

1999 Turf 0-4: (7f 2, 8f 2) (gd, g-f 3)

Fair colt. Turf high 55 (began Aug). **R Hannon [0-4] Lucayan Stud.*

LEOFRIC BHB 45f44a RR 34f 44a 5035[12]

4 b g Alhijaz 7.7f **(57)** - Wandering Stranger (Petong) 6.6f **(58)**

Form - 500105647004045460010000

Record 1999 - 1st:2 2nd:0 3rd:0 Ran:21

Pre1999 - 1st:0 2nd:0 3rd:6 Ran:29

Win Prizemoney £4,489 *Total Prizemoney* £9,329

Wins * 1999 Aug Sandow (G-S) H 8.1f 39 44?

*** 1999** *Jan Southw (STD) C 7f 65 <*

1999 Turf 1-12: (6f, 7f 2, 8f 1-7, 10f 2) (g-s, gd 2, g-f 1-3, frm 6) 1999 AW 1-9: (5f, 6f 4, 7f 1-4) (Equi, Fibr 1-8)

Scopey, moderate gelding, effective 7f, - acts on Fibr, often wears blinkers. Turf high 44. AW high 65 (1st run) - 1st of 11 getting 3lb from Scotland Bay (18 Jan Southwell RF 0113).

**M J Polglase [2-50] Southwell Racing Club.*

LEONATO (FR) BHB 92f RR 96f 1935[5]

7 b g Law Society (USA) 11.6f **(71)** - Gala Parade (Alydar (USA)) 9.1f **(76)**

Form - 25

Record 1999 - 1st:0 2nd:1 3rd:0 Ran:2

Pre1999 - 1st:0 2nd:3 3rd:1 Ran:12

Win Prizemoney £0 *Total Prizemoney* £20,678

1999 Turf 0-2: (12f, 14f) (g-s 2)

Very useful gelding, effective 12 to 19f, acts on gd to g-f. Turf high 96. Consistent. Lightly raced and obviously difficult to train, he stays well and appreciates some give underfoot.

**P D Evans [0-14] Colin Booth.*

LEONIE SAMUAL RR 27f 2246[9]

4 b f Safawan 6.6f **(60)** - Hy Wilma (Jalmood (USA)) 10.1f **(52)**

Form - 00

Record 1999 - 1st:0 2nd:0 3rd:0 Ran:2

1999 Turf 0-2: (5f, 8f) (g-f, frm)

Unfurnished, currently little account filly. Turf high 27.

**R J Hodges [0-2] Mrs Carol Taylor.*

LE PIN BHB 60f RR 63f 3552[9]

2 ch f Persian Bold 10f **(69)** - Red Rose Garden (Electric) 10.1f **(61)**

Form - 5700

Record 1999 - 1st:0 2nd:0 3rd:0 Ran:4

1999 Turf 0-3: (5f, 6f, 7f) (gd, frm 2) 1999 AW 0-1: (7f) (Fibr)

Average filly. Turf high 63 (began Jly).

**M R Channon [0-4] Uplands Bloodstock.*

LE RHONE (FR) RR 103f 3783a[3]

3 b c Pistolet Bleu (IRE) - Petite Soeur (FR) (Lyphard (USA)) 9.9f **(72)**

Form - 43

1999 Turf 0-2: (10f, 12f) (hvy, sft)

Currently very useful colt. Turf high 103 - 3rd of 8 to Espionage (15 Aug Deauville 10f hvy RF 3783a). He acts on easy ground but is a shade one-paced. **E Lellouche in FR [0-2].*

LERMONTOV (USA) RR 106f 5037[2]

2 br c Alleged (USA) 11.8f **(81)** - Prospect Dalia (USA) (Mr Prospector (USA)) 8.8f **(78)**

Form - 112

1999 Turf 2-3: (7f 1-1, 8f 1-2) (g-s 1-2, gd 1-1)

Currently Pattern-class colt. Turf high 106 - 2nd of 9 to Aristotle (23 Oct Doncaster 8f g-s RF 5037) - also 1st of 6 from Barrier Reef (16 Oct Curragh RF 4974a). Just had to be driven out to land the odds on his Gowran Park debut, but faced a much stiffer task at the Curragh next time. Bravely regaining the lead close home in the Group Three Beresford stakes over a mile, there was a lot to like about his performance and attitude. He stepped up on that form when runner-up to stablemate Aristotle in the Racing Post Trophy. He will stay further.

**A P O'Brien in IRE [2-3] M Tabor & Mrs John Magnier.*

LE ROI CHIC (FR) RR 110f 1903a[6]

3 f Balleroy (USA) - Chic Emilie (FR) (Policeman (FR)) 9.8f **(80)**

Form - 1206

1999 Turf 1-4: (8f 1-3, 9f) (hvy 1-1, g-s, gd 2)

Group-class. Turf high 110 - 2nd of 7 to Indian Danehill (25 Apr Longchamp 8f g-s RF 0935a) - also 1st of 6 from Leave Us Leap (30 Mar Maisons-Laffitte RF 0627a). He ran a super race behind Indian Danehill in a Listed event at Longchamp in April, but flopped when supplemented for the French 2,000 Guineas. Similarly disappointing in the Prix Jean Prat, he falls short of the top-class.

**N Clement in FR [1-4] (from J P Despeyroux in FR [1-1] Apr 1998).*

LE SAUVAGE (IRE) BHB 26f37a RR 28f 37a 4717[6]

4 b g Tirol 8.1f **(64)** - Cistus (Sun Prince) 12.4f **(52)**

Form - 328500756

Record 1999 - 1st:0 2nd:1 3rd:0 Ran:8

Pre1999 - 1st:0 2nd:0 3rd:1 Ran:4

Win Prizemoney £0 *Total Prizemoney* £860

1999 Turf 0-6: (16f 3, 17f 3) (gd 3, frm 3) 1999 AW 0-2: (11f, 12f) (Fibr 2)

Scopey, moderate gelding. Turf high 41. AW high 47.

**D W Barker [0-11] The Ebor Partnership (from M R Channon [0-3] Oct 1998).*

LESLEY'S ADVENTURE (IRE) BHB 36f30a RR 38f 30a 365[5]

4 b br f Petardia 8.2f **(58)** - Island Adventure (Touching Wood (USA)) 8.2f **(55)**

Form - 75

Record 1999 - 1st:0 2nd:0 3rd:0 Ran:2

Pre1999 - 1st:0 2nd:0 3rd:0 Ran:9

1999 AW 0-2: (7f, 8f) (Fibr 2)

Light-framed, very moderate filly. AW high 18.

**E J Alston [0-8] Tom Dearden (from Capt J Wilson [0-3] Aug 1997).*

L'ESTABLE FLEURIE (IRE) BHB 65f57a RR 67f 57a 360[7]

4 b f Common Grounds 8.1f **(66)** - Dorado Llave (USA) (Well Decorated (USA)) 7.6f **(64)**

Form - 05547

Record 1999 - 1st:0 2nd:0 3rd:0 Ran:5

Pre1999 - 1st:2 2nd:0 3rd:3 Ran:18

Win Prizemoney £5,135 *Total Prizemoney* £7,485

Wins 1998 *Jun Lingfi (STD) C 7f 78 <*

1998 May Bright (G-F) C 7f 64

1999 AW 0-5: (7f 2, 8f 3) (Equi 4, Fibr)

Average filly, effective 7f, - acts on Equi, has worn blinkers, likes left handed tracks, likes tight tracks. AW high 59.

**B Smart [0-8] Miss N Jefford (from P J Makin [2-6] Jun 1998).*

LET IT RAIN (NZ) BHB 89f RR 93f 4683[15]

5 b g Rainbow Myth (NZ) - Wayside Inn (NZ) (Long Row)

Form - 43557540

Record 1999 - 1st:0 2nd:0 3rd:1 Ran:8

Win Prizemoney £0 *Total Prizemoney* £4,017

1999 Turf 0-8: (5f, 6f, 7f, 8f, 10f 3, 12f) (gd 4, g-f 3, frm)

Useful gelding, effective 10 to 12f, acts on gd to g-f. Turf high 93. Consistent. A winner in his native New Zealand, he should find a race or two in this country when connections fathom out his best trip, which looks to be a mile judged on a good run at York in

August. **M Johnston [0-8] Michael Watt.*

LEVEL HEADED BHB 36f39a **RR 38f 39a** 5128[14]

4 b f Beveled (USA) 6.9f **(64)** - Snowline (Bay Express) 7.1f **(60)**
Form - 0700
Record 1999 - 1st:0 2nd:0 3rd:0 Ran:4
Pre1999 - 1st:0 2nd:0 3rd:0 Ran:4
1999 Turf 0-4: (6f 2, 8f 2) (g-s, gd, g-f 2)
Leggy, moderate filly. Turf high 38.
**E A Wheeler [0-8] Anthony Harrison.*

LEVELLED BHB 89f88a **RR 91f 88a** 4392[23]

5 b g Beveled (USA) 6.9f **(64)** - Baino Charm (USA) (Diesis) 9.3f **(69)**
Form - 501771455506088200070
Record 1999 - 1st:2 2nd:1 3rd:0 Ran:21
Pre1999 - 1st:7 2nd:5 3rd:5 Ran:40
Win Prizemoney £44,200 *Total Prizemoney* £66,226

Wins								
* **1999**	May	Cheste	(G-F)	H	5.1f	93	98	<
* **1999**	Apr	Ripon	(G-F)	H	6f	88	91	
* 1998	Spt	Yarmou	(G-S)	H	5.2f	76	81	
* 1998	Aug	Lingfi	(G-F)		6f		80	
* 1998	Aug	Bright	(FRM)	H	6f	67	71	
* 1997	Spt	Bright	(FRM)	H	5.3f	70	75	
* 1997	Jun	Bright	(FRM)	H	6f	68	69	
* 1997	Apr	Folkes	(G-F)	C	5f		65	
* 1996	Aug	Carlis	(FRM)		5f		58	

1999 Turf 2-20: (5f 1-8, 6f 1-12) (gd 6, g-f 2-8, frm 6) 1999 AW 0-1: (6f) (Equi)
Useful gelding, effective 5 to 6f, best at 5f, acts on gd to frm. Turf high 98 - 1st of 10 giving 17lb to Westcourt Magic (6 May Chester RF 1048) - also 1st of 22 giving 19lb to Pepperdine (7 Apr Ripon RF 0614). Consistent. Best when held-up, he is a tough and genuine sprint handicapper. Effective on any ground, he has dropped to a winning mark and is one to note next spring.
**M R Channon [9-61] & Mrs Gary Pinchen.*

LEVEL PEGGING (IRE) **RR 39f** 1686[6]

2 ch f Common Grounds 8.1f **(66)** - Family At War (USA) (Explodent (USA)) 9.4f **(87)**
Form - 66
Record 1999 - 1st:0 2nd:0 3rd:0 Ran:2
1999 Turf 0-2: (5f 2) (frm 2)
Currently very moderate filly. Turf high 39.
**T D Easterby [0-2] T H Bennett.*

LEXICON (USA) **RR** 5227a[9]

4 f Conquistador Cielo (USA) 9.8f **(67)** - Felidia (USA) (Golden Fleece (USA)) 7.9f **(74)**
Form - 0
1999 AW 0-1: (6f) (Dirt)
Currently very useful. **R Mandella in USA [0-1].*

LIBERTE BELL (IRE) BHB 40f30a **RR 59df 30a** 1014[14]

4 b f Petorius 8f **(66)** - Ransomed (IRE) (Ballad Rock) 7.8f **(63)**
Form - 0000
Record 1999 - 1st:0 2nd:0 3rd:0 Ran:3
Pre1999 - 1st:0 2nd:0 3rd:1 Ran:5
Win Prizemoney £0 *Total Prizemoney* £438
1999 Turf 0-1: (8f) (frm) 1999 AW 0-2: (7f, 10f) (Equi, Fibr)
Fair filly.
**D HaydnJones [0-4] Mrs Judy Mihalop (from Sir Mark Prescott [0-4] Oct 1997).*

LIBERTY LINES (USA) BHB 72f **RR 74f** 5003[11]

3 b g Zilzal (USA) 8.5f **(79)** - Bold 'n Determined (USA) (Bold And Brave)
Form - 3220
Record 1999 - 1st:0 2nd:2 3rd:1 Ran:4
Pre1999 - 1st:0 2nd:1 3rd:0 Ran:2
Win Prizemoney £0 *Total Prizemoney* £4,047
1999 Turf 0-4: (7f 3, 8f) (gd 2, g-f, frm)
Scopey, above-average gelding, effective 6 to 7f, best at 7f, acts on gd to frm. Turf high 74 (1st run) - 3rd of 16 giving 5lb to Miss Shema (16 May Kempton 7f frm RF 1259).
**B W Hills [0-6] Maktoum Al Maktoum.*

LICENCE TO THRILL **RR 26f** 4825[16]

2 ch f Wolfhound (USA) 7.3f **(71)** - Crime of Passion (Dragonara Palace (USA)) 6.1f **(55)**
Form - 0
Record 1999 - 1st:0 2nd:0 3rd:0 Ran:1
1999 Turf 0-1: (6f) (g-f)
Currently above-average filly.
**D W P Arbuthnot [0-1] Christopher Wright.*

LIEUTENANT FANCY BHB 41f **RR 41f** 2943[7]

3 ch g Kris 10f **(75)** - Noirmant (Dominion) 8.5f **(63)**
Form - 8077
Record 1999 - 1st:0 2nd:0 3rd:0 Ran:4
1999 Turf 0-3: (10f, 12f, 16f) (gd, g-f, hrd) 1999 AW 0-1: (11f) (Fibr)
Scopey, moderate gelding. Turf high 41.
**C A Cyzer [0-4] R M Cyzer.*

LIFE IS LIFE (FR) BHB 100f **RR 97f** 5210[2]

3 b f Mansonnien (FR) 12f **(91)** - La Vie Immobile (USA) (Alleged (USA)) 10f **(76)**
Form - 182
Record 1999 - 1st:1 2nd:1 3rd:0 Ran:3
Win Prizemoney £4,070 *Total Prizemoney* £6,030
Wins * **1999** Spt Kempto (HVY) 12f 84++ <
1999 Turf 1-3: (12f 1-2, 15f) (sft, g-s 1-1, gd)
Scopey, currently very useful filly. Turf high 97 (began Spt) - 2nd of 5 getting 10lb from Persian Punch (5 Nov Doncaster 15f sft RF 5210). Formerly trained in France, she absolutely bolted up in a heavy-ground Kempton maiden in September over a mile and a half. Well beaten next time, she ran well when stepped up to fourteen furlongs on her final start.
**M A Jarvis [1-3] & Mrs Raymond Anderson Green.*

LIFE OF RILEY BHB 100f **RR 100f** 4917[19]

5 ch h Caerleon (USA) 10.9f **(79)** - Catina (Nureyev (USA)) 8.7f **(78)**
Form - 13010
Record 1999 - 1st:2 2nd:0 3rd:1 Ran:5
Pre1999 - 1st:3 2nd:2 3rd:1 Ran:13
Win Prizemoney £27,324 *Total Prizemoney* £33,522

Wins								
* **1999**	Aug	Newmar	(G-F)	H	14.8f	94	100	<
* **1999**	Jun	Goodwo	(G-F)	H	14f	86	90	
* 1998	Jly	Sandow	(GD)	H	16.4f	85	89	
* 1998	May	Kempto	(G-F)	H	14.4f	76	81	
1997	Jun	Pontef	(G-F)		10f		74	

1999 Turf 2-5: (14f 1-2, 15f 1-1, 16f, 17f) (gd, frm 2-4)
Very useful colt, effective 14 to 16f, acts on frm, has worn blinkers, favours right handed tracks. Turf high 100 - 1st of 9 giving 13lb to Loop The Loup (27 Aug Newmarket RF 3940). He looked in outstanding condition when making a winning reappearance at Goodwood in June. Best when able to sit in an uncontested lead much as when winning at Newmarket, he raced with his tongue tied in 1999.
**B J Meehan [4-13] John Manley (from G Lewis [1-5] Spt 1997).*

LIFT BOY (USA) BHB 30f24a **RR 43f 24a** 1951[7]

10 b g Fighting Fit (USA) 7.9f **(70)** - Pressure Seat (USA) (Ginistrelli (USA)) 5.6f **(66)**
Form - 6607068007
Record 1999 - 1st:0 2nd:0 3rd:0 Ran:7
Pre1999 - 1st:8 2nd:7 3rd:11 Ran:86
Win Prizemoney £20,846 *Total Prizemoney* £30,215

Wins								
1997	*Feb*	*Lingfi*	*(STD)*	*H*	*7f*	*58*	*60*	
1996	Jun	Folkes	(G-F)	S	5f		50	
1996	*Mar*	*Wolver*	*(STD)*	*H*	*6f*	*61*	*66*	<
1996	*Feb*	*Lingfi*	*(STD)*	*C*	*5f*		*58*	
1996	*Jan*	*Lingfi*	*(STD)*	*C*	*5f*		*53*	
1995	May	Lingfi	(G-F)	SH	5f	42	44	
1995	*Jan*	*Wolver*	*(STD)*	*C*	*6f*		*60*	

1999 Turf 0-1: (7f) (g-f) 1999 AW 0-6: (7f, 8f 3, 10f 2) (Equi 4, Fibr 2)
Moderate gelding, effective 7f, - acts on Equi, has worn blinkers. AW high 28. **P Burgoyne [0-8] Philip Saunders (from G L Moore [1-26] Dec 1998).*

LIFT THE OFFER (IRE) BHB 44f71a **RR 41f 71a** 4355[9]

4 ch g Ballad Rock 7.2f **(63)** - Timissara (USA) (Shahrastani (USA)) 8.8f **(72)**
Form - 008452870

Record 1999 - 1st:0 2nd:1 3rd:0 Ran:9
Pre1999 - 1st:2 2nd:1 3rd:3 Ran:17
Win Prizemoney £6,272 *Total Prizemoney* £10,200
Wins 1997 *Nov Lingfi (STD)* 7f 67+
1997 *Nov Lingfi (STD) H* 8f 68 77 <
1999 Turf 0-9: (6f 4, 7f 2, 8f 3) (g-s, gd 2, g-f 3, frm 3)
Scopey, above-average gelding, effective 8 to 9f, best at 8f, acts on gd to frm, best on frm, has worn blinkers, likes tight tracks.
**J J Quinn [0-9] Bowlers Racing (from R Hannon [2-17] Oct 1998).*

LIGHT BREEZE BHB 37f52a RR 38f 52a 3305[10]

3 b f Hamas (IRE) 8f **(72)** - Fiorini (Formidable (USA)) 9.2f **(63)**
Form - 53145865700
Record 1999 - 1st:1 2nd:0 3rd:1 Ran:10
Pre1999 - 1st:0 2nd:0 3rd:1 Ran:5
Win Prizemoney £1,800 *Total Prizemoney* £2,896
Wins 1999 *Feb Lingfi (STD) S* 6f 52 <
1999 Turf 0-3: (5f 3) (gd, frm 2) 1999 AW 1-7: (5f 4, 6f 1-3) (Equi 1-3, Fibr 4)
Moderate filly, likes left handed tracks, likes tight tracks. Turf high 38. AW high 61. Becoming disappointing.
**N E Berry [0-4] Mrs Karen Moore (from G L Moore [1-7] Apr 1999).*

LIGHT BURNER (ITY) RR 91f 5204a[3]

3 b c Seattle Centre (ITY) - Avuta (ITY) (Viani)
Form - 333
1999 Turf 0-2: (12f, 15f) (hvy, g-s)
Useful colt. Turf high 91. **E Castelli in ITY [1-4].*

LIGHTHOUSE BHB 84f RR 82f 4679[8]

3 br f Warning 8.1f **(77)** - Valika (Valiyar) 8.5f **(73)**
Form - 148
Record 1999 - 1st:1 2nd:0 3rd:0 Ran:3
Win Prizemoney £2,957 *Total Prizemoney* £3,555
Wins * 1999 Aug Windso (HVY) 8.3f 80 <
1999 Turf 1-3: (8f 1-3) (gd 1-2, hrd)
Workmanlike, currently decent filly. Turf high 82 (began Aug) - 4th of 7 getting 5lb from Family Man (27 Aug Thirsk 8f hrd RF 3945) - also 1st of 12 getting 5lb from Tarawan (9 Aug Windsor RF 3485).
**H R A Cecil [1-3] Lord Lloyd-Webber.*

LIGHTNING ARROW (USA) BHB 104f RR 105f 5043[9]

3 br c Silver Hawk (USA) 11.2f **(85)** - Strait Lane (USA) (Chieftain II) 10.4f **(75)**
Form - 220430
Record 1999 - 1st:0 2nd:2 3rd:1 Ran:6
Pre1999 - 1st:1 2nd:2 3rd:0 Ran:4
Win Prizemoney £5,643 *Total Prizemoney* £28,939
Wins * 1998 Oct Newmar (G-S) 8f 90 <
1999 Turf 0-6: (10f, 12f 5) (sft, g-s, gd, g-f 3)
Neat, Pattern-class colt, effective 8 to 12f, best at 12f, acts on g-s to frm, has worn blinkers. Turf high 105 - 3rd of 11 getting 7lb from Kahtan (1 Oct Newmarket 12f gd RF 4674). He finished runner-up in the Blue Riband Trial and Chester Vase in his first two starts of this season. After a summer break, he ran well to finish third in a Newmarket Listed event. A genuine sort.
**J L Dunlop [1-10] Wafic Said.*

LIGHTNING BLAZE BHB 50f RR 48f 4440[20]

3 ch f Cosmonaut - Royal Deed (USA) (Shadeed (USA)) 8.2f **(70)**
Form - 50642500
Record 1999 - 1st:0 2nd:1 3rd:0 Ran:8
Pre1999 - 1st:4 2nd:1 3rd:2 Ran:12
Win Prizemoney £8,524 *Total Prizemoney* £10,842
Wins 1998 Jly Folkes (G-F) C 5f 64
1998 Jly Beverl (G-F) C 5f 64
1998 Jun Folkes (G-F) S 5f 74+ <
1998 *Jun Wolver (STD) S* 5f 62
1999 Turf 0-8: (5f 6, 6f 2) (gd 2, g-f 2, frm, hrd 3)
Average filly, effective 5f, acts on g-f to frm, best on frm.
**D Nicholls [0-2] Mrs K J Crangle (from B J Meehan [0-6] Aug 1999).*

LIGHTNING REBEL BHB 24f18a RR 45df 18a 302[12]

5 b g Rambo Dancer (CAN) 8.4f **(59)** - Ozra (Red Alert) 7.6f **(66)**
Form - 0300000
Record 1999 - 1st:0 2nd:0 3rd:1 Ran:6
Pre1999 - 1st:0 2nd:1 3rd:0 Ran:10
Win Prizemoney £0 *Total Prizemoney* £1,216
1999 AW 0-6: (11f, 12f 5) (Equi 2, Fibr 4)
Moderate gelding. AW high 38. Becoming disappointing.
**P W Hiatt [0-16] P W Hiatt (from C W Thornton [0-7] Aug 1997).*

LIGHT ON THE WAVES BHB 62f RR 65f 3311[1]

3 b f Greensmith - Roof Dancer (Martinmas) 7.6f **(59)**
Form - 15121
Record 1999 - 1st:2 2nd:1 3rd:0 Ran:3
Pre1999 - 1st:1 2nd:1 3rd:0 Ran:4
Win Prizemoney £6,661 *Total Prizemoney* £8,373
Wins * 1999 Aug Bath (HRD) H 17.2f 60 65
*** 1999** Jun Bath (GD) S 11.7f 49
***** 1998 *Nov Wolver (STD) S* 8.5f 69 <
1999 Turf 2-3: (12f 1-1, 16f, 17f 1-1) (frm 2-3)
Light-framed, average filly, effective 8 to 17f, acts on frm - acts on Fibr. Turf high 65 - 1st of 3 giving 12lb to Zola (3 Aug Bath RF 3311). **M C Pipe [3-7] Paul Neczypir.*

LIGHT PROGRAMME BHB 73f RR 62f 5031[13]

5 b g El Gran Senor (USA) 8.9f **(85)** - Nashmeel (USA) (Blushing Groom (FR)) 10.3f **(76)**
Form - 00
Record 1999 - 1st:0 2nd:0 3rd:0 Ran:2
Pre1999 - 1st:1 2nd:1 3rd:0 Ran:2
Win Prizemoney £5,481 *Total Prizemoney* £6,790
Wins 1997 Jly Newmar (G-F) 10f 87 <
1999 Turf 0-2: (10f 2) (g-s, gd)
Average gelding. Turf high 62 (began Oct).
**J G Smyth-Osbourne [0-2] G F T Agricultural Products Ltd (from H R A Cecil [1-2] Jly 1997).*

LIGHT THE ROCKET (IRE) BHB 100f RR 102f 4873[2]

3 ch c Pips Pride 6.7f **(70)** - Coolrain Lady (IRE) (Common Grounds)
Form - 2260772802
Record 1999 - 1st:0 2nd:4 3rd:0 Ran:10
Pre1999 - 1st:2 2nd:1 3rd:0 Ran:7
Win Prizemoney £10,457 *Total Prizemoney* £25,566
Wins * 1998 Aug Ascot (G-F) 5f 90 <
* 1998 Aug Sandow (GD) 5f 83+
1999 Turf 0-10: (5f 5, 6f 5) (g-s, gd 2, frm 7)
Leggy, very useful colt, effective 5 to 6f, best at 6f, acts on g-s to frm, best on frm, excels at Sandown. Turf high 102 - 2nd of 9 giving 8lb to Ellens Lad (14 Oct Newmarket 5f gd RF 4873). Consistent. He ran some tremendous races without getting his head in front last season, but remains in the handicapper's grip. Best at five furlongs, he seems to act on any ground.
**R Hannon [2-17] M Mulholland.*

LIGNE GAGNANTE (IRE) BHB 91f RR 87f 4571[2]

3 b g Turtle Island (IRE) - Lightino (Bustino) 10.4f **(64)**
Form - 1113532
Record 1999 - 1st:3 2nd:1 3rd:2 Ran:7
Pre1999 - 1st:0 2nd:0 3rd:0 Ran:4
Win Prizemoney £19,938 *Total Prizemoney* £38,532
Wins * 1999 Jun Newcas (GD) H 12.4f 79 83
*** 1999** Jun Goodwo (GD) H 12f 77 85 <
*** 1999** May Ayr (GD) 9.1f 72
1999 Turf 3-7: (9f 1-1, 12f 2-4, 13f, 14f) (sft, g-s 1-1, gd 2-2, g-f 2, frm)
Scopey, useful gelding, effective 12 to 14f, best at 12f, acts on sft to frm, excels at Goodwood. Turf high 87 - 2nd of 16 getting 22lb from Vicious Circle (26 Spt Ascot 12f sft RF 4571) - also 1st of 5 getting 14lb from Deploy Venture (2 Jun Goodwood RF 1674). Completed an early-season hat-trick and continued to run with great credit. **W J Haggas [3-11] The Winning Line.*

LILA BHB 85f RR 87f 4562[8]

3 b f Zafonic (USA) 9f **(83)** - Bint Pasha (USA) (Affirmed (USA)) 9.3f **(79)**
Form - 1238
Record 1999 - 1st:1 2nd:1 3rd:1 Ran:4
Win Prizemoney £3,194 *Total Prizemoney* £6,215
Wins * 1999 Jun Salisb (GD) 8f 83+ <
1999 Turf 1-4: (8f 1-1, 10f 3) (gd, g-f 1-1, frm 2)
Leggy, useful filly. Turf high 87 - 3rd of 4 to Felona (9 Spt Chepstow 10f frm RF 4231) - also 1st of 12 from Flight Sequence (9 Jun Salisbury RF 1872). **P F I Cole [1-4] H R H Prince Fahd Salman.*

LILANITA BHB 40f47a **RR 36f 47a** 5050[4]
4 b f Anita's Prince 6f **(62)** - Jimlil (Nicholas Bill) 10.1f **(56)**
Form - 22380000504
Record 1999 - 1st:0 2nd:0 3rd:1 Ran:9
Pre1999 - 1st:1 2nd:3 3rd:1 Ran:15
Win Prizemoney £2,374 *Total Prizemoney* £4,980
Wins * 1998 Jun Chepst (G-S) S 8.1f 53 <
1999 Turf 0-5: (7f, 8f 4) (gd, frm 2, hrd 2) 1999 AW 0-4: (7f, 8f, 10f 2) (Equi 2, Fibr 2)
Neat, moderate filly, effective 7 to 10f, acts on gd to frm - acts on AW, likes left handed tracks, likes tight tracks. Turf high 36 (began Jly). AW high 54 (1st run) - 3rd of 8 getting 7lb from Confronter (7 Jan Lingfield 10f Equi RF 0049). **B Palling [1-24] Mrs M M Palling.*

LILARDO BHB 49f46a **RR 59f 46a** 5148[6]
2 b br f Son Pardo - Jimlil (Nicholas Bill) 10.1f **(56)**
Form - 508046
Record 1999 - 1st:0 2nd:0 3rd:0 Ran:6
1999 Turf 0-4: (6f, 7f 2, 8f) (g-s, g-f 2, frm) 1999 AW 0-2: (8f 2) (Fibr 2)
Fair filly. Turf high 56 (began Aug). AW high 53 (began Oct). **B Palling [0-6] Mrs M M Palling.*

LIL'S BOY (USA) RR 107f 3188a[5]
5 b h Danzig (USA) 8.1f **(88)** - Kentucky Lill (USA) (Raise A Native) 11.2f **(69)**
Form - 51435
1999 Turf 1-5: (8f, 9f 1-2, 10f, 11f) (gd 1-2, g-f 2, frm)
Pattern-class colt, effective 8 to 9f, best at 9f, acts on gd, has worn blinkers. Turf high 107 - 1st of 4 giving 4lb to Twickenham (9 Jun Leopardstown RF 2020a). Consistent. He was found wanting when stepping out of listed company. **J S Bolger in IRE [5-18] Mrs J S Bolger.*

LIMA TANGO BHB 25f **RR** 2063[7]
3 b f Aird Point - Routine (Teenoso (USA)) 9.9f **(72)**
Form - 6687
Record 1999 - 1st:0 2nd:0 3rd:0 Ran:4
1999 Turf 0-2: (14f, 16f) (gd, frm) 1999 AW 0-2: (9f, 12f) (Fibr 2)
Unfurnished, formerly very poor filly, has worn blinkers. **M Waring [0-4] Mrs P M Daniel.*

LIMELIGHTING (USA) BHB 97f **RR 96f** 5211[1]
3 b f Alleged (USA) 11.8f **(81)** - Steal The Thunder (CAN) (Lyphard (USA)) 9.9f **(72)**
Form - 022121
Record 1999 - 1st:2 2nd:3 3rd:0 Ran:6
Win Prizemoney £13,240 *Total Prizemoney* £18,755
Wins * **1999** Nov Doncas (SFT) 10.3f 96 <
* **1999** Spt York (G-F) 10.4f 79
1999 Turf 2-6: (10f 2-5, 12f) (sft 1-1, gd 3, g-f, frm 1-1)
Lengthy, very useful filly, effective 10 to 12f, acts on sft to gd. Turf high 96 - 1st of 5 giving 4lb to Esteraad (5 Nov Doncaster RF 5211). Improving steadily and got off the mark over ten furlongs at York in September. Bolted up on her final start and should continue to progress. **J H M Gosden [2-6] George Strawbridge.*

LIMPID RR 119f 1996[6]
4 b c Soviet Star (USA) 8.6f **(74)** - Isle Of Glass (USA) (Affirmed (USA)) 9.3f **(79)**
Form - 66
Record 1999 - 1st:0 2nd:0 3rd:0 Ran:2
Pre1999 - 1st:2 2nd:0 3rd:0 Ran:4
Win Prizemoney £130,303 *Total Prizemoney* £134,928
Wins 1998 Jun Longch (GD) G1 10f 120 <
1998 Feb Saint- (SFT) 7f 77
1999 Turf 0-2: (10f 2) (g-f 2)
High-class colt, effective 10f, acts on gd to g-f. Turf high 109. Showed high-class form at three, but following a spell in Hong Kong in the spring, he was employed as pacemaker for Xaar at Royal Ascot.
**S bin Suroor [0-1] Godolphin (from S bin Suroor in UAE [0-1] Apr 1999).*

LINCOLN DANCER (IRE) BHB 100f **RR 100f** 1998[10]
2 b c Turtle Island (IRE) - Double Grange (IRE) (Double Schwartz) 7.9f **(55)**
Form - 1310
Record 1999 - 1st:2 2nd:0 3rd:1 Ran:4
Win Prizemoney £11,797 *Total Prizemoney* £12,370
Wins * **1999** May York (SFT) 6f 100 <
* **1999** Apr Warwic (GD) 5f 82
1999 Turf 2-4: (5f 1-2, 6f 1-2) (g-s 1-1, gd 1-2, g-f)
Very useful colt. Turf high 100 - 1st of 8 giving 5lb to Pipadash (12 May York RF 1184). A sharp juvenile, he won twice before the end of May but was not seen out after finishing unplaced in the Coventry Stakes. Workmanlike in appearance, he lacks scope. **G Lewis [2-4] Michael Baker.*

LINCOLN DEAN BHB 48f67a **RR 45f 67a** 3496[7]
3 b c Mtoto 11.5f **(71)** - Play With Me (IRE) (Alzao (USA)) 7.1f **(68)**
Form - 518275047
Record 1999 - 1st:1 2nd:1 3rd:0 Ran:8
Pre1999 - 1st:0 2nd:0 3rd:0 Ran:3
Win Prizemoney £3,543 *Total Prizemoney* £4,959
Wins 1999 *Jan Lingfi (STD) H 8f 61 70* <
1999 Turf 0-5: (8f 2, 9f, 10f 2) (gd, g-f, frm 3) 1999 AW 1-3: (8f 1-2, 10f) (Equi 1-3)
Scopey, above-average colt, effective 8f, - acts on Equi, likes left handed tracks, likes tight tracks. Turf high 61. AW high 72 - 2nd of 6 getting 8lb from Baron de Pichon (23 Feb Lingfield 8f Equi RF 0347) - also 1st of 6 getting 11lb from Love Diamonds (23 Jan Lingfield RF 0151). Becoming disappointing. Showed winning form on Equitrack for Sir Mark Prescott, but has done little for his present yard.
**J S Goldie [0-5] L H Gilmurray & T J Docherty (from Sir Mark Prescott [1-6] Feb 1999).*

LINDAS GEM BHB 43f45a **RR 19?f 45a** 3633[19]
3 ch f Kasakov - Kabella (Kabour)
Form - 070
Record 1999 - 1st:0 2nd:0 3rd:0 Ran:3
Pre1999 - 1st:0 2nd:1 3rd:0 Ran:4
Win Prizemoney £0 *Total Prizemoney* £1,060
1999 Turf 0-2: (5f, 8f) (gd, g-f) 1999 AW 0-1: (6f) (Fibr)
Leggy, poor filly. (began Aug). **B Preece [0-3] Greg Jones (from Mrs L Stubbs [0-4] Spt 1998).*

LINDEN GRACE (USA) BHB 80f **RR 87f** 5048[13]
2 b f Mister Baileys - Gracefully Bold (USA) (Nasty And Bold (USA))
Form - 1250
Record 1999 - 1st:1 2nd:1 3rd:0 Ran:4
Win Prizemoney £3,403 *Total Prizemoney* £5,862
Wins * **1999** Jly Epsom (G-F) 7f 76+ <
1999 Turf 1-4: (6f, 7f 1-3) (hvy, g-f 2, frm 1-1)
Useful filly. Turf high 87 (began Jly) - 2nd of 4 getting 11lb from Far Mount (14 Jly Doncaster 6f g-f RF 2811). Scored in good style over seven furlongs on her Epsom debut, but may not have been suited by dropping back a furlong at Doncaster next time, though splitting Far Mount and Pipadash was by no means a bad effort. Well beaten subsequently, however. **M Johnston [1-4] R C Moules.*

LINEA-G BHB 64f60a **RR 66f 60a** 4693[10]
5 ch m Keen 11.1f **(58)** - Horton Line (High Line) 10.3f **(70)**
Form - 123125120
Record 1999 - 1st:3 2nd:3 3rd:1 Ran:9
Pre1999 - 1st:0 2nd:0 3rd:0 Ran:7
Win Prizemoney £7,095 *Total Prizemoney* £9,605
Wins * **1999** Aug Beverl (GD) 12f 66 <
* **1999** May Newcas (G-F) H 12.4f 49 54
* **1999** *Mar Southw (STD) 12f 57*
1999 Turf 2-7: (12f 2-4, 13f, 14f, 16f) (gd, g-f 2-4, frm 2) 1999 AW 1-2: (12f 1-2) (Fibr 1-2)
Average filly, effective 12 to 13f, best at 12f, acts on gd to frm - acts on Fibr. Turf high 66 - 1st of 7 from Inchtina (11 Aug Beverley RF 3539). AW high 57 (1st run) - 1st of 6 getting 3lb from Chaliapin (1 Mar Southwell RF 0383). Consistent. A half-sister to Angus-G, she is most consistent and won three fairly modest events last season. She does not have much in the way of a turn of foot, but tries hard and is suited by a test of stamina. **Mrs M Reveley [3-23] W Ginzel.*

LINE CALL RR 50f 4724[9]
3 b c Second Set (IRE) 9.2f **(67)** - Misguided (Homing) 7.8f **(59)**
Form - 0574060
Record 1999 - 1st:0 2nd:0 3rd:0 Ran:7

Pre1999 - 1st:0 2nd:0 3rd:0 Ran:1
Win Prizemoney £0 *Total Prizemoney* £499
1999 Turf 0-7: (8f 5, 12f 2) (g-s, gd, g-f 2, frm 3)
Scopey, fair colt. **D W P Arbuthnot [0-8] T D Holland-Martin.*

LINENS GIRL BHB 65f **RR 67f** 4038[10]
3 br f Thowra (FR) 11.2f **(47)** - Stocktina (Tina's Pet) 6.8f **(59)**
Form - P540
Record 1999 - 1st:0 2nd:0 3rd:0 Ran:4
Win Prizemoney £0 *Total Prizemoney* £263
1999 Turf 0-4: (6f, 7f 2, 8f) (gd, g-f 2, frm)
Unfurnished, average filly. Turf high 67 (began Jly).
**R J Hodges [0-4] D & J Newell.*

LINGUISTIC DANCER BHB 29f28a **RR 27f 28a** 457[9]
4 ch f Aragon 7.7f **(58)** - Linguistic (Porto Bello) 8.9f **(43)**
Form - 30
Record 1999 - 1st:0 2nd:0 3rd:1 Ran:2
Pre1999 - 1st:0 2nd:0 3rd:0 Ran:8
Win Prizemoney £0 *Total Prizemoney* £226
1999 AW 0-2: (8f 2) (Fibr 2)
Light-framed, little account filly, effective 8f, - acts on Fibr. AW high 24 (1st run) - 3rd of 9 getting 26lb from Impelling (26 Feb Southwell 8f Fibr RF 0364). Inconsistent.
**A G Newcombe [0-10] Panamarenko,M Ellis, Patel.*

LINK HILL BHB 59f **RR 58f** 5007[4]
3 ch f Generous (IRE) 11.5f **(82)** - Phaleria (USA) (Lyphard (USA)) 9.9f **(72)**
Form - 057384
Record 1999 - 1st:0 2nd:0 3rd:1 Ran:6
Pre1999 - 1st:0 2nd:0 3rd:0 Ran:1
Win Prizemoney £0 *Total Prizemoney* £442
1999 Turf 0-6: (7f, 8f, 10f 3, 12f) (g-s, gd, g-f 2, frm 2)
Strong, fair filly, effective 10f, acts on frm. Turf high 58 - 3rd of 14 getting 3lb from Otahuna (13 Spt Nottingham 10f frm RF 4288).
**Mrs A J Perrett [0-7] K Abdulla.*

LINKSMAN (USA) BHB 25f **RR** 5050[17]
4 b g Diesis 9f **(80)** - Wrap Around (AUS) (Bletchingly (AUS))
Form - 00
Record 1999 - 1st:0 2nd:0 3rd:0 Ran:2
1999 Turf 0-2: (6f, 8f) (gd, frm)
Currently very poor gelding. (began Oct). **D Shaw [0-2] J Doxey.*

LION CUB (IRE) BHB 34f44a **RR 39f 44a** 4936[4]
3 b g Catrail (USA) - Lightly Dancing (FR) (Groom Dancer (USA))
Form - 00004
Record 1999 - 1st:0 2nd:0 3rd:0 Ran:5
Pre1999 - 1st:0 2nd:0 3rd:0 Ran:3
1999 Turf 0-4: (8f 2, 12f, 14f) (gd 4) 1999 AW 0-1: (12f) (Fibr)
Light-framed, fair gelding, effective 12f, - acts on Fibr, likes left handed tracks, likes tight tracks. Turf high 39. (1st run) - 4th of 11 getting 7lb from Count de Money (18 Oct Southwell 12f Fibr RF 4936). Inconsistent.
**R McGhin [0-5] & Mrs G Calder (from J E Banks [0-3] Oct 1998).*

LIONESS BHB 72f **RR 75f** 3199[7]
3 b f Lion Cavern (USA) 7.5f **(74)** - Pidona (Baillamont (USA)) 7f **(78)**
Form - 4437
Record 1999 - 1st:0 2nd:0 3rd:1 Ran:4
Win Prizemoney £0 *Total Prizemoney* £603
1999 Turf 0-4: (8f 2, 9f, 10f) (g-f 2, frm 2)
Workmanlike, above-average filly. Turf high 75 - 4th of 14 getting 5lb from Harlequin Dancer (31 May Leicester 8f g-f RF 1601).
**J R Fanshawe [0-4] Cheveley Park Stud.*

LION GUEST (IRE) RR 62f 5099[6]
2 ch c Lion Cavern (USA) 7.5f **(74)** - Decrescendo (IRE) (Polish Precedent (USA)) 10.2f **(60)**
Form - 06
Record 1999 - 1st:0 2nd:0 3rd:0 Ran:2
1999 Turf 0-2: (7f 2) (gd, g-f)
Currently average colt. Turf high 62 (began Spt).
**G G Margarson [0-2] John Guest.*

LIONHEARTED (IRE) RR 111df 4512a[9]
3 b c Catrail (USA) - Quiche (Formidable (USA)) 9.2f **(63)**
Form - 12250
Record 1999 - 1st:1 2nd:2 3rd:0 Ran:5
Pre1999 - 1st:0 2nd:0 3rd:0 Ran:1
Win Prizemoney £4,467 *Total Prizemoney* £12,236
Wins * 1999 Apr Newmar (GD) 6f 91 <
1999 Turf 1-5: (6f 1-5) (sft, gd, g-f 1-3)
Scopey, Group-class colt, effective 6f, acts on gd to g-f, has worn blinkers. Turf high 111 - 2nd of 10 to Sampower Star (28 Apr Ascot 6f g-f RF 0899). Big and handsome, he looked good when winning a maiden at Newmarket in April but did not score again. He finds little off the bit and is one to have slight reservations about.
**J H M Gosden [1-6].*

LION'S DOMANE RR 27f 5209[17]
2 b g Lion Cavern (USA) 7.5f **(74)** - Vilany (Never so Bold) 6.3f **(66)**
Form - 00
Record 1999 - 1st:0 2nd:0 3rd:0 Ran:2
1999 Turf 0-2: (6f, 7f) (g-s, gd)
Currently little account gelding. Turf high 27 (began Oct).
**P C Haslam [0-2] Mrs C Barclay.*

LISA-B (IRE) BHB 48f55a **RR 60f 55a** 5076[20]
2 b f Case Law 6f **(64)** - Nishiki (USA) (Brogan (USA))
Form - 68751163537080
Record 1999 - 1st:2 2nd:0 3rd:2 Ran:14
Win Prizemoney £3,743 *Total Prizemoney* £4,777
Wins * 1999 *Jun Wolver (STD) S* *6f* *64+* <
*** 1999** *Jun Southw (STD) S* *6f* *62*
1999 Turf 0-10: (5f 3, 6f 5, 7f 2) (sft, gd 3, g-f, frm 5) 1999 AW 2-4: (5f, 6f 2-3) (Fibr 2-4)
Above-average filly, effective 6f, acts on frm - acts on Fibr, often wears blinkers, prefers left handed tracks, prefers tight tracks. Turf high 60 - 3rd of 7 getting 13lb from Secret Conquest (13 Aug Catterick 6f frm RF 3599). AW high 64 - 1st of 6 giving 5lb to Diamond Concorde (16 Jun Wolverhampton RF 2067) - also 1st of 8 from Seasame Park (4 Jun Southwell RF 1749). She did not show a great deal in her early starts on turf, but blinkers and Fibresand brought about significant improvement. The easy winner of two sellers so far, she could make her mark in slightly better company on that surface.
**J A Glover [2-14] Vic Atherton.*

LISALA BHB 41f41a **RR 40f 41a** 2691[7]
3 ch f Beveled (USA) 6.9f **(64)** - Super Style (Artaius (USA)) 9f **(69)**
Form - 53007
Record 1999 - 1st:0 2nd:0 3rd:1 Ran:5
Pre1999 - 1st:0 2nd:0 3rd:1 Ran:4
Win Prizemoney £0 *Total Prizemoney* £513
1999 Turf 0-2: (8f, 10f) (g-s, gd) 1999 AW 0-3: (9f 2, 11f) (Fibr 3)
Leggy, moderate filly, effective 7f, acts on gd. Turf high 40. AW high 43. Becoming disappointing.
**W G M Turner [0-9] Mrs L Wayne.*

LISIEUX ROSE (IRE) RR 101f 4476a[3]
4 ch f Generous (IRE) 11.5f **(82)** - Epicure's Garden (USA) (Affirmed (USA)) 9.3f **(79)**
Form - 33463
1999 Turf 0-5: (9f, 11f, 12f 2, 15f) (g-s 2, gd 2, g-f)
Very useful filly, effective 9 to 12f, acts on gd to g-f, best on gd, has worn blinkers, likes right handed tracks, likes Curragh. Turf high 101. Consistent. A Group Two winner in 1998, she failed to rediscover her best form last term.
**D K Weld in IRE [3-9] Moyglare Stud Farm.*

LISTE ROUGE (USA) RR 847[10]
6 b g Red Ransom (USA) 8.6f **(83)** - Bestseller's List (USA) (Going Straight (USA))
Form - 0
Record 1999 - 1st:0 2nd:0 3rd:0 Ran:1
1999 AW 0-1: (8f) (Fibr)
Currently little account gelding.
**G L Moore [0-1] Charlton Bloodstock Ltd.*

LIT (IRE) RR 90f 1067a[3]
3 b f Danehill (USA) 9.1f **(79)** - Lisheba (USA) (Alysheba (USA)) 9f **(84)**

Form - 3
1999 Turf 0-1: (8f) (sft)
Currently useful filly. (1st run) - 3rd of 5 to Alexis (28 Apr Chantilly 8f sft RF 1067a). **N Clement in FR [0-2] Nov 1998).*

LITERARY SOCIETY (USA) BHB 93f RR 94?f 4207[21]

6 ch h Runaway Groom (CAN) 8.1f **(69)** - Dancing Gull (USA) (Northern Dancer) 9.6f **(80)**
Form - 803U3380

Record	**1999** -	1st:0	2nd:0	3rd:3	Ran:8
	Pre1999 -	1st:7	2nd:4	3rd:3	Ran:26

Win Prizemoney £48,171 *Total Prizemoney* £68,063

Wins							
* 1998	Aug	York	(G-F)	H	6f	90	94 <
* 1998	Jun	Yarmou	(GD)		6f		91
* 1998	May	Newmar	(G-F)	H	5f	83	86
* 1997	Jly	Newbur	(G-F)	H	6f	77	77
* 1997	May	Newmar	(G-F)	H	5f	71	74
* 1996	Aug	Thirsk	(GD)	H	5f	66	67+
* 1996	Jly	Bright	(FRM)		5.3f		61

1999 Turf 0-8: (6f 8) (gd 2, g-f 3, frm 3)
Useful horse, effective 5 to 6f, best at 6f, acts on gd to frm, best on g-f, and likes Ascot. Turf high 94 - 3rd of 30 to Harmonic Way (31 Jly Goodwood 6f g-f RF 3261). Inconsistent. A string of fairly moderate efforts last term was capped with him unseating his rider upon the stalls opening in the Wokingham, though he ran rather better to finish third to Cretan Gift back at Ascot. Built on that effort in some style when third in the Stewards' Cup, having decimated the opposition on the far side. Robbed by the draw that day, he has since disappointed in Listed company. Needs fast ground.
**J A R Toller [7-34] Lady Celina Carter.*

LITTLE AMIN BHB 77f RR 78f 5038[13]

3 b g Unfuwain (USA) 11.4f **(74)** - Ghassanah (Pas de Seul) 9.1f **(67)**
Form - 127344160

Record	**1999** -	1st:2	2nd:1	3rd:1	Ran:9
	Pre1999 -	1st:0	2nd:0	3rd:1	Ran:2

Win Prizemoney £7,569 *Total Prizemoney* £10,672

Wins							
* **1999**	Aug	Haydoc	(G-S)	H	11.9f	72	78 <
1999	Mar	Newcas	(G-S)		7f		73

1999 Turf 2-9: (7f 1-2, 8f 3, 9f, 12f 1-3) (g-s, gd 2-3, g-f 2, frm 2, hrd)
Above-average gelding, effective 7 to 12f, best at 7f, acts on gd to hrd, best on gd, prefers tight tracks. Turf high 78 - 1st of 10 getting 5lb from Angels Venture (5 Aug Haydock RF 3402) - also 1st of 9 from Plutocrat (30 Mar Newcastle RF 0514). **W R Muir [1-3] Sheikh Amin Dahlawi (from J D Bethell [1-8] Jun 1999).*

LITTLE AN (FR) RR 2827[7]

3 b f Sheyrann - Little Miss John (Last Fandango) 7.8f **(61)**
Form - 7

Record	**1999** -	1st:0	2nd:0	3rd:0	Ran:1

1999 Turf 0-1: (12f) (frm)
Currently very poor filly. **G L Moore [0-1] David Humphreys.*

LITTLE BOY BLUE (IRE) BHB 27f RR 26[7]

3 br g Petardia 8.2f **(58)** - Bluebutton (Blue Cashmere) 6.4f **(54)**
Form - 0707

Record	**1999** -	1st:0	2nd:0	3rd:0	Ran:1
	Pre1999 -	1st:0	2nd:0	3rd:0	Ran:4

1999 AW 0-1: (8f) (Fibr)
Leggy, little account gelding, has worn blinkers.
**M Waring [0-4] P B R Abrasives (W'ton) Ltd (from N Tinkler [0-1] Apr 1998).*

LITTLE BRAVE BHB 59f75a RR 60f 75a 4917[25]

4 b g Kahyasi 12.9f **(74)** - Littlemisstrouble (USA) (My Gallant (USA)) 9f **(71)**
Form - 760161100

Record	**1999** -	1st:3	2nd:0	3rd:0	Ran:9
	Pre1999 -	1st:1	2nd:2	3rd:1	Ran:11

Win Prizemoney £17,705 *Total Prizemoney* £20,634

Wins							
* **1999**	Spt	Yarmou	(SFT)	H	18.2f	57	60
* **1999**	Aug	Warwic	(GD)	H	15.8f	55	57
* **1999**	*Jly*	*Lingfi*	*(STD)*		*16f*		*78* <
* 1998	*Mar*	*Southw*	*(STD)*		*8f*		*68*

1999 Turf 2-8: (16f 1-5, 17f 2, 18f 1-1) (g-s 1-2, gd 1-3, g-f 2, frm) 1999 AW 1-1: (16f 1-1) (Equi 1-1)
Workmanlike, above-average gelding, effective 8 to 16f, - acts on AW, prefers left handed tracks, likes tight tracks. Turf high 60. (1st run) - 1st of 6 giving 3lb to Spirit of The Nile (31 Jly Lingfield RF 3274). A fair stayer on both turf and sand, he bolted up in a two-mile classified event on the Lingfield Equitrack in July and has added turf handicaps at Warwick and Yarmouth. He seems to go best in small fields. **J M P Eustace [4-20] Brave Maple Partnership.*

LITTLE CAESAR BHB 30f RR 38f 1514[8]

5 ch g Keen 11.1f **(58)** - Loredana (Grange Melody) 7f **(59)**
Form - 08

Record	**1999** -	1st:0	2nd:0	3rd:0	Ran:2
	Pre1999 -	1st:0	2nd:0	3rd:0	Ran:3

Win Prizemoney £0 *Total Prizemoney* £383
1999 Turf 0-2: (8f, 10f) (gd, frm)
Very moderate gelding. Turf high 21.
**S C Williams [0-5] D A Shekells.*

LITTLE CHAPEL (IRE) BHB 57f RR 52f 4232[17]

3 b f College Chapel - Istaraka (IRE) (Darshaan) 9.9f **(84)**
Form - 48050

Record	**1999** -	1st:0	2nd:0	3rd:0	Ran:5
	Pre1999 -	1st:0	2nd:1	3rd:1	Ran:6

Win Prizemoney £0 *Total Prizemoney* £1,910
1999 Turf 0-5: (6f 3, 7f 2) (gd 2, frm 2, hrd)
Scopey, fair filly, effective 5 to 6f, acts on g-f to hrd. Turf high 67 (1st run) - 4th of 15 giving 5lb to Lucy Mariella (4 May Brighton 6f hrd RF 1023). **D J S ffrenchDavis [0-11] North Social Racing Club.*

LITTLE CHRISTIAN (IRE) BHB 55f48a RR 60f 48a 4939[13]

2 b c Common Grounds 8.1f **(66)** - Alexanders Way (FR) (Persian Heights)
Form - 360673028400

Record	**1999** -	1st:0	2nd:1	3rd:2	Ran:12

Win Prizemoney £0 *Total Prizemoney* £1,280
1999 Turf 0-10: (5f 4, 6f 3, 7f 3) (gd 4, g-f 3, frm 3) 1999 AW 0-2: (5f, 7f) (Fibr 2)
Average colt, effective 6 to 7f, best at 6f, acts on gd to g-f, best on g-f. Turf high 60. AW high 21. **N Tinkler [0-12] J M G Promotions Ltd.*

LITTLE CINNAMON BHB 51f RR 47f 4148[6]

3 ch c Timeless Times (USA) 6.1f **(56)** - Belltina (Belfort (FR)) 6.8f **(63)**
Form - 00706

Record	**1999** -	1st:0	2nd:0	3rd:0	Ran:5
	Pre1999 -	1st:0	2nd:0	3rd:0	Ran:5

Win Prizemoney £0 *Total Prizemoney* £255
1999 Turf 0-5: (5f, 6f 3, 7f) (g-f, frm 3, hrd)
Moderate colt, has broken blood-vessels, has worn blinkers. Turf high 50. Consistent. **J L Eyre [0-10] Ms Kim Jansen.*

LITTLE DOCKER (IRE) RR 75f 3413[4]

2 b c Vettori (IRE) - Fair Maid of Kent (USA) (Diesis) 9.3f **(69)**
Form - 4

Record	**1999** -	1st:0	2nd:0	3rd:0	Ran:1

Win Prizemoney £0 *Total Prizemoney* £283
1999 Turf 0-1: (7f) (g-f)
Currently above-average colt. **T D Easterby [0-1] C H Stevens.*

LITTLEFEATHER (IRE) BHB 100f RR 103f 4793[5]

2 b f Indian Ridge 7.6f **(74)** - Marwell (Habitat) 9.4f **(70)**
Form - 2411135

Record	**1999** -	1st:3	2nd:1	3rd:1	Ran:7

Win Prizemoney £27,832 *Total Prizemoney* £45,097

Wins						
* **1999**	Aug	Cheste	(G-S)		6.1f	103+ <
* **1999**	Jly	Newmar	(G-F)	H	6f	89
* **1999**	Jly	Ripon	(G-F)		5f	86+

1999 Turf 3-7: (5f 1-4, 6f 2-2, 7f) (gd 1-2, g-f, frm 2-4)
Very useful filly, effective 6 to 7f, acts on gd to g-f. Turf high 103 - 1st of 7 giving 3lb to Rythm N Time (20 Aug Chester RF 3787). A progressive and likeable filly, she completed a hat-trick before failing to stay seven furlongs in the Group One Moyglare Stud Stakes. Past her best for the season when unplaced at Ascot in October, she has a useful turn-of-foot and should win a minor Group race over six furlongs in 2000.
**Sir Mark Prescott [3-7] Sir Edmund Loder.*

LITTLE FOX (IRE) BHB 55f60a RR 42f 60a 5057[4]

4 br f Persian Bold 10f **(69)** - Dance Land (IRE) (Nordance (USA)) 7.5f **(52)**

Form - 4824
Record 1999 - 1st:0 2nd:1 3rd:0 Ran:4
Win Prizemoney £0 *Total Prizemoney* £960
1999 Turf 0-2: (12f 2) (frm 2) 1999 AW 0-2: (12f, 13f) (Equi 2)
Fair filly. Turf high 42 (began Aug). AW high 57 (began Oct).
**Mrs L Richards [0-7] C Mussell.*

Littlefeather improved to be a Group-class filly, and should make a sprinter in 2000

LITTLE GEM BHB 72f **RR 68f** 3574[8]
3 b f Night Shift (USA) 8.1f **(73)** - Um Lardaff (Mill Reef (USA)) 10.5f **(78)**
Form - 58
Record 1999 - 1st:0 2nd:0 3rd:0 Ran:2
Pre1999 - 1st:1 2nd:1 3rd:1 Ran:6
Win Prizemoney £3,436 *Total Prizemoney* £5,672
Wins * 1998 Spt Epsom (SFT) 8.5f 75 <
1999 Turf 0-2: (8f 2) (g-f, frm)
Scopey, average filly, effective 7 to 9f, acts on gd to frm. Turf high 68 (began Jly). **R Hannon [1-8] Mohamed Suhail.*

LITTLE GREENBIRD BHB 33f **RR 25f** 5107[8]
3 b f Ardkinglass 5f **(64)** - Hot Money (Mummy's Pet) 7.7f **(60)**
Form - 0078
Record 1999 - 1st:0 2nd:0 3rd:0 Ran:4
Pre1999 - 1st:0 2nd:0 3rd:0 Ran:3
1999 Turf 0-3: (7f, 8f, 10f) (gd 2, frm) 1999 AW 0-1: (6f) (Fibr)
Leggy, very moderate filly. Turf high 25 (began Aug).
**J G Portman [0-4] J G B Portman (from W G M Turner [0-3] Spt 1998).*

LITTLE HENRY BHB 44f42a **RR 46f 42a** 1079[16]
3 ch g My Generation 6.5f **(68)** - White African (Carwhite) 7.2f **(61)**
Form - 7304560
Record 1999 - 1st:0 2nd:0 3rd:1 Ran:7
Pre1999 - 1st:0 2nd:0 3rd:4 Ran:12
Win Prizemoney £0 *Total Prizemoney* £1,388
1999 Turf 0-3: (8f, 12f, 13f) (gd 2, frm) 1999 AW 0-4: (9f, 10f 2, 11f) (Equi 2, Fibr 2)
Scopey, moderate gelding, effective 7 to 8f, acts on g-f, always wears blinkers. Turf high 46. AW high 46. Inconsistent.
**P D Evans [0-19] J G White.*

LITTLE IBNR BHB 46f48a **RR 48f 48a** 1121[6]
8 b g Formidable (USA) 7.8f **(60)** - Zalatia (Music Boy) 6.8f **(57)**
Form - 7660632403720024636
Record 1999 - 1st:0 2nd:3 3rd:3 Ran:15
Pre1999 - 1st:12 2nd:9 3rd:10 Ran:88
Win Prizemoney £35,504 *Total Prizemoney* £52,206
Wins * 1997 *Mar Wolver (STD) S* 5f *58*
* 1997 *Jan Wolver (STD)* 7f *63*
* 1996 *Apr Wolver (STD) H* 6f *68 66*
* 1995 *Dec Wolver (STD) C* 6f *79*
* 1995 Oct Nottin (G-F) 5.1f 62
* 1995 *Feb Wolver (STD) H* 7f *80 81* <
* 1995 *Jan Southw (STD) H* 6f *73 74*
* 1995 *Jan Wolver (STD) H* 7f *67 73*
1999 AW 0-15: (5f 6, 6f 9) (Fibr 15)
Moderate gelding, effective 5 to 6f, best at 6f, - acts on Fibr, has worn blinkers (effectively), favours left handed tracks, favours tight tracks. AW high 60 - 2nd of 8 getting 5lb from Bold Aristocrat (22 Feb Southwell 6f Fibr RF 0340).
**P D Evans [10-81] Swinnerton Transport Ltd (from P D Cundell [0-9] Feb 1998).*

LITTLE IMP (IRE) BHB 37f29a **RR 39f 29a** 22[8]
4 b f Imp Society (USA) 7.1f **(63)** - Poka Poka (FR) (King Of Macedon) 8.1f **(59)**
Form - 8
Record 1999 - 1st:0 2nd:0 3rd:0 Ran:1
Pre1999 - 1st:0 2nd:0 3rd:0 Ran:6
1999 AW 0-1: (11f) (Fibr)
Leggy, very moderate filly, often wears blinkers.
**K R Burke [0-7] Mrs Elaine Burke.*

LITTLE ITALY (IRE) BHB 95f **RR 97f** 5205a[1]
3 b f Common Grounds 8.1f **(66)** - Broken Romance (IRE) (Ela-Mana-Mou) 10.1f **(70)**
Form - 1311152211
Record 1999 - 1st:6 2nd:2 3rd:1 Ran:10
Pre1999 - 1st:0 2nd:0 3rd:0 Ran:2
Win Prizemoney £33,029 *Total Prizemoney* £37,239
Wins * **1999** Oct San Si (YLD) L 12f 97 <
* **1999** Oct Haydoc (HVY) H 10.5f 80 81
* **1999** Jun Lingfi (GD) H 11.5f 68 71+
* **1999** Jun Leices (GD) H 11.8f 54 67+
* **1999** May Leices (G-F) H 11.8f 54 61
* **1999** *Apr Lingfi (STD)* 6f *48*
1999 Turf 5-8: (11f 2-3, 12f 3-5) (sft 1-1, g-s 1-1, g-f 2-3, frm 1-3) 1999 AW 1-2: (6f 1-1, 7f) (Equi 1-1, Fibr)
Light-framed, very useful filly, effective 12f, acts on g-s, likes tight tracks, does well at Lingfield and Leicester. Turf high 97 - 1st of 9 from Katiykha (31 Oct San Siro RF 5205a). AW high 48 (1st run). Improving. She got off the mark when winning a six-furlong maiden on Equitrack on her reappearance, and then took off over middle distances on turf, completing a fine hat-trick. She went up the handicap as a result, but was far from disgraced and was awarded a Listed race at San Siro. **P F I Cole [6-12] Andrea Pecoraro.*

LITTLE JOHN BHB 58f **RR 64f** 5159[6]
3 b g Warrshan (USA) 9.7f **(59)** - Silver Venture (USA) (Silver Hawk (USA)) 8.6f **(70)**
Form - 425503446
Record 1999 - 1st:0 2nd:1 3rd:1 Ran:9
Pre1999 - 1st:0 2nd:0 3rd:0 Ran:3
Win Prizemoney £0 *Total Prizemoney* £2,694
1999 Turf 0-9: (7f, 9f 3, 10f 2, 11f 2, 12f) (sft, gd 2, g-f 2, frm 4)
Lengthy, average gelding, effective 12f, acts on frm. Turf high 72 (began Aug). **Miss L A Perratt [0-12] Mrs A E Robertson.*

LITTLE LAUREN RR 24f 4022[9]
2 b f Northern Elegance - Denby Wood (Lord Bud)
Form - 00
Record 1999 - 1st:0 2nd:0 3rd:0 Ran:2
1999 Turf 0-2: (7f, 8f) (gd, g-f)
Little account filly. Turf high 24 (began Jly). (DEAD)
**J S Wainwright [0-2] Tony Longbottom.*

LITTLE LENA BHB 25f **RR 14f** 3986[9]
3 b f Alhijaz 7.7f **(57)** - Killarney Belle (USA) (Irish Castle (USA)) 11.2f **(75)**
Form - 000000
Record 1999 - 1st:0 2nd:0 3rd:0 Ran:6
1999 Turf 0-5: (6f, 7f 2, 8f, 10f) (g-s, gd 2, frm 2) 1999 AW 0-1: (6f) (Fibr)
Lengthy, poor filly. Turf high 14. **J Wharton [0-6] John Wharton.*

LITTLE MERMAID (IRE) BHB 25f **RR** 2362[8]
3 b f Mac's Imp (USA) 5.6f **(54)** - Aegaen Lady **(42f)** (Lochnager) 6f **(59)**
Form - 088
Record 1999 - 1st:0 2nd:0 3rd:0 Ran:3

Pre1999 - 1st:0 2nd:0 3rd:0 Ran:1
1999 Turf 0-3: (5f, 6f 2) (sft, gd 2)
Unfurnished, formerly very poor filly.
**G Woodward [0-4] Burntwood Sports Ltd.*

LITTLE MIRACLE BHB 30f **RR 30f** 4022[11]
2 b f Skyliner 6.8f **(51)** - Kalvee Dancer (Kalaglow) 9.8f **(67)**
Form - 6080
Record 1999 - 1st:0 2nd:0 3rd:0 Ran:4
1999 Turf 0-4: (5f, 6f 2, 8f) (g-f 2, frm 2)
Very moderate filly. Turf high 30. **Martyn Wane [0-4] J Hamilton.*

LITTLE MISS LUCY BHB 38f **RR 46?f** 2829[7]
5 b m Petoski 10.4f **(56)** - Puki Puki (Roselier (FR))
Form - 7
Record 1999 - 1st:0 2nd:0 3rd:0 Ran:1
Pre1999 - 1st:0 2nd:0 3rd:0 Ran:3
Win Prizemoney £0 *Total Prizemoney* £189
1999 Turf 0-1: (10f) (gd)
Moderate filly, had worn blinkers. (DEAD)
**M J Heaton-Ellis [0-8] Richard Lissack.*

LITTLEPACEPADDOCKS (IRE) RR 78+f 5189[1]
2 b f Accordion 11.3f **(75)** - Lady in Pace (Burslem) 8.8f **(53)**
Form - 1
Record 1999 - 1st:1 2nd:0 3rd:0 Ran:1
Win Prizemoney £3,615 *Total Prizemoney* £3,615
Wins * **1999** Nov Mussel (GD) 8f 78+ <
1999 Turf 1-1: (8f 1-1) (g-f 1-1)
Currently above-average filly. (1st run) - 1st of 9 getting 5lb from Makasseb (3 Nov Musselburgh RF 5189).
**M Johnston [1-1] Mrs Joan Keaney.*

LITTLE PIPPIN BHB 85f **RR 85f** 4759[8]
3 ch f Rudimentary (USA) 8.2f **(66)** - Accuracy (Gunner B) 11.2f **(58)**
Form - 30431148
Record 1999 - 1st:2 2nd:0 3rd:2 Ran:8
Pre1999 - 1st:0 2nd:0 3rd:1 Ran:4
Win Prizemoney £8,013 *Total Prizemoney* £10,913
Wins * **1999** Aug Kempto (SFT) H 12f 73 80 <
* **1999** Aug Salisb (G-S) H 12f 73 75
1999 Turf 2-8: (10f 2, 11f, 12f 2-4, 13f) (g-s 1-1, gd 1-5, g-f 2)
Neat, useful filly, effective 12 to 13f, best at 12f, acts on g-s to gd, best on gd, prefers tight tracks. Turf high 85 - 4th of 9 getting 19lb from Top Cees (18 Spt Ayr 13f gd RF 4394) - also 1st of 14 getting 6lb from Agitando (18 Aug Kempton RF 3741). Took time in getting off the mark, but won two handicaps over a mile and a half in August. Very effective on soft ground.
**G B Balding [2-12] Miss B Swire.*

LITTLE ROCK RR 116f 5131[1]
3 b c Warning 8.1f **(77)** - Much Too Risky (Bustino) 10.4f **(64)**
Form - 12481
Record 1999 - 1st:2 2nd:1 3rd:0 Ran:5
Pre1999 - 1st:1 2nd:0 3rd:0 Ran:1
Win Prizemoney £22,604 *Total Prizemoney* £32,179
Wins * **1999** Oct Newmar (G-S) L 10f 112 <
* **1999** Apr Sandow (G-S) 8.1f 91+
* 1998 Oct Leices (G-S) 7f 86+
1999 Turf 2-5: (8f 1-2, 10f 1-3) (g-s 1-1, gd 1-3, g-f)
Light-framed, high-class colt, effective 10f, acts on gd to g-f, best on gd. Turf high 116 - 8th of 13 getting 2lb from Alborada (16 Oct Newmarket 10f gd RF 4919) - also 1st of 7 from Mujahid (29 Oct Newmarket RF 5131). A half-brother to Whitewater Affair, who was also trained by Michael Stoute, he was second to Oath at Chester's May meeting, and after a five-month break ran well when fourth to Indian Lodge at Newmarket in a Listed race over a mile. Landed a similar race next time, and should continue to pay his way at that level. **Sir Michael Stoute [3-6] J M Greetham.*

LITTLE TARA RR 41f 4942[18]
2 b f Pyramus (USA) - Eastwood Heiress (Known Fact (USA)) 7.4f **(67)**
Form - 00
Record 1999 - 1st:0 2nd:0 3rd:0 Ran:2
1999 Turf 0-2: (6f 2) (g-s, gd)
Currently moderate filly. Turf high 41 (began Oct).
**J C Fox [0-2] Mrs J A Cleary.*

LITTLE TUMBLER (IRE) BHB 47f **RR 49f** 4078[14]
4 b f Cyrano de Bergerac 7.3f **(58)** - Glass Minnow (IRE) (Alzao (USA)) 7.1f **(68)**
Form - 405100
Record 1999 - 1st:1 2nd:0 3rd:0 Ran:6
Pre1999 - 1st:1 2nd:2 3rd:0 Ran:13
Win Prizemoney £5,326 *Total Prizemoney* £7,311
Wins * **1999** Aug Bright (FRM) H 10f 47 49
* 1998 May Lingfi (G-F) H 6f 55 61 <
1999 Turf 1-6: (7f, 8f, 9f, 10f 1-2, 12f) (gd, g-f 2, frm 1-3)
Neat, moderate filly, effective 6f, acts on gd to frm. Turf high 50.
**S Woodman [2-19] Mrs W Edgar.*

LITTLE WHITE HEART BHB 17f **RR 23f** 5127[12]
4 ch f Russian Red - Dip N Dot (Golden Dipper) 6.5f **(42)**
Form - 0000
Record 1999 - 1st:0 2nd:0 3rd:0 Ran:4
1999 Turf 0-4: (6f, 7f 3) (gd 2, g-f, frm)
Neat, little account filly. Turf high 23 (began Aug).
**L A Dace [0-4] Mike D'Arcy Quinn.*

LIVELY JACQ (IRE) BHB 62f53a **RR 54f 53a** 5058[9]
3 ch f Case Law 6f **(64)** - Nordic Living (IRE) (Nordico (USA)) 6.5f **(62)**
Form - 7343045540
Record 1999 - 1st:0 2nd:0 3rd:2 Ran:10
Pre1999 - 1st:2 2nd:3 3rd:0 Ran:8
Win Prizemoney £5,171 *Total Prizemoney* £14,836
Wins * 1998 Aug Yarmou (G-F) H 6f 62 60 <
* 1998 Jly Yarmou (G-F) S 6f 60 <
1999 Turf 0-8: (5f, 6f 5, 7f 2) (gd, g-f 5, frm 2) 1999 AW 0-2: (6f, 7f) (Equi 2)
Lengthy, fair filly, effective 5 to 6f, best at 6f, acts on g-f to hrd, has worn blinkers, excels at Brighton and Newmarket, does well at Yarmouth. Turf high 68 - 3rd of 10 giving 14lb to Devon Dream (28 May Brighton 5f g-f RF 1537). AW high 51 (began Oct). Becoming disappointing. **C N Allen [2-18] J T B Racing.*

LIVELY LADY BHB 81f63a **RR 78f 63a** 5212[1]
3 b f Beveled (USA) 6.9f **(64)** - In the Papers (Aragon) 8.1f **(60)**
Form - 1002102571
Record 1999 - 1st:3 2nd:2 3rd:0 Ran:10
Pre1999 - 1st:1 2nd:2 3rd:1 Ran:9
Win Prizemoney £16,192 *Total Prizemoney* £20,652
Wins * **1999** Nov Doncas (SFT) H 5f 76 78 <
* **1999** Jun Kempto (GD) H 6f 71 75
* **1999** Mar Nottin (G-S) H 6.1f 66 71
* 1998 Apr Folkes (SFT) S 5f 67+
1999 Turf 3-9: (5f 1-3, 6f 2-6) (sft 1-1, g-s 1-1, gd 4, g-f 1-1) 1999 AW 0-1: (6f) (Fibr)
Light-framed, above-average filly, effective 5 to 6f, best at 6f, acts on sft to g-f, best on g-s, often wears blinkers (effectively). Turf high 78 - 1st of 20 giving 6lb to Demolition Jo (5 Nov Doncaster RF 5212) - also 1st of 12 getting 14lb from Danielle's Lad (9 Jun Kempton RF 1865). Looked to have the best of the draw when making a winning reappearance at Nottingham. Added a victory at Kempton in June, when having to battle after looking to be travelling easily, and ended the season with a victory in soft ground at Doncaster. She needs to be produced late.
**J R Jenkins [4-19] S Powell.*

LIVELY MILLIE BHB 56f **RR 64f** 4950[10]
2 b f Ridgewood Ben - Sweet Pleasure (Sweet Revenge) 7.2f **(54)**
Form - 75070
Record 1999 - 1st:0 2nd:0 3rd:0 Ran:5
1999 Turf 0-5: (6f 3, 7f, 8f) (g-s, g-f, frm 3)
Average filly. Turf high 64 (began Aug).
**P T Walwyn [0-5] John Guest.*

LIVELY PROJECT (IRE) BHB 36f **RR 40f** 3366[4]
3 b f Project Manager 7.2f **(47)** - Lovely Ali (IRE) (Dunbeath (USA)) 7.8f **(70)**
Form - 0055024
Record 1999 - 1st:0 2nd:1 3rd:0 Ran:7
Pre1999 - 1st:0 2nd:0 3rd:0 Ran:4
Win Prizemoney £0 *Total Prizemoney* £760
1999 Turf 0-6: (7f, 10f, 11f, 12f 3) (g-f 2, frm 4) 1999 AW 0-1: (7f) (Fibr)

Leggy, moderate filly. Turf high 40.
**M Dods [0-11] Three Plus One Racing 98.*

LIVE PROJECT (IRE) BHB 43f63a **RR 41f 63a** 752[F]

7 b g Project Manager 7.2f **(47)** - Saturday Live (Junius (USA)) 7.7f **(65)**
Form - 023601324F
Record 1999 - 1st:1 2nd:2 3rd:2 Ran:9
Pre1999 - 1st:5 2nd:4 3rd:3 Ran:36
Win Prizemoney £12,325 *Total Prizemoney* £20,381
Wins * **1999** *Mar Southw (STD) H 7f 60 65*
* 1998 *Mar Southw (STD) H 7f 59 68* <
* 1998 *Feb Southw (STD) H 7f 54 59*
* 1997 *Dec Southw (STD) H 7f 50 52*
1997 *Mar Lingfi (STD) H 8f 55 57*
1997 *Feb Southw (STD) H 7f 50 54*
1999 Turf 0-1: (10f) (g-s) 1999 AW 1-8: (7f 1-6, 8f 2) (Fibr 1-8)
Average gelding, effective 7 to 8f, best at 7f, - acted on Fibr, preferred left handed tracks, favoured tight tracks, excelled at Wolverhampton, liked Southwell. AW high 65 (1st run) - 2nd of 16 giving 23lb to Tom (2 Jan Southwell 8f Fibr RF 0014) - also 1st of 10 giving 14lb to Awesome Venture (1 Mar Southwell RF 0379). (DEAD)
**R Craggs [4-26] Mrs Gillian Quinn (from M Johnston [2-19] Apr 1997).*

LIVE TO TELL BHB 61f51a **RR 60f 51a** 5032[17]

3 ch f Primo Dominie 7.2f **(67)** - Dreams Are Free (IRE) (Caerleon (USA)) 8.6f **(71)**
Form - 41608162210
Record 1999 - 1st:3 2nd:2 3rd:0 Ran:11
Win Prizemoney £8,238 *Total Prizemoney* £11,131
Wins * **1999** Oct Ayr (SFT) H 5f 56 60 <
* **1999** Aug Warwic (GD) H 5f 47 49
* **1999** *Feb Wolver (STD) 6f 49*
1999 Turf 2-8: (5f 2-7, 6f) (sft 1-1, g-s 2, gd 1-2, g-f, frm 2) 1999 AW 1-3: (6f 1-3) (Fibr 1-3)
Lengthy, average filly, effective 5f, acts on sft. Turf high 60 - 1st of 15 getting 3lb from Leaping Charlie (11 Oct Ayr RF 4810). AW high 49. **M S Saunders [3-11] Paul Thorman.*

LIVIUS (IRE) BHB 81f **RR 82f** 3447[1]

5 b g Alzao (USA) 9.8f **(73)** - Marie de Beaujeu (FR) (Kenmare (FR)) 6.5f **(72)**
Form - 721
Record 1999 - 1st:1 2nd:1 3rd:0 Ran:3
Pre1999 - 1st:0 2nd:3 3rd:1 Ran:8
Win Prizemoney £5,602 *Total Prizemoney* £11,871
Wins * **1999** Aug Ascot (GD) H 12f 77 82 <
1999 Turf 1-3: (12f 1-3) (gd 1-3)
Decent gelding, effective 10 to 12f, best at 12f, acts on gd to frm, best on gd, has worn blinkers, prefers right handed tracks, excels at Ascot. Turf high 82 (began Jly) - 1st of 12 giving 16lb to Warning Reef (7 Aug Ascot RF 3447). Began the season as a maiden, but ran well twice at Ascot, being narrowly beaten on the first occasion, before finally getting off the mark in a similar event next time under a superb ride from Keiren Fallon. Unfortunately he sustained an injury there which brought his season to a premature end. Providing he is none the worse, he should be able to add to his tally in 2000. **Major D N Chappell [1-11] D J Dickinson.*

LIZOP (IRE) RR 74f 4477a[11]

4 b g Brief Truce (USA) 9.1f **(73)** - High Glider (High Top) 10.2f **(67)**
Form - 043750000
1999 Turf 0-9: (7f 2, 8f 4, 9f, 10f, 11f) (sft, g-s 2, gd, g-f 3, frm 2)
Above-average gelding, effective 8 to 10f, best at 8f, acts on hvy to frm. Turf high 94 - 3rd of 10 giving 17lb to Markskeepingfaith (30 Jly Galway 8f g-f RF 3338a).
**L Comer in IRE [0-8] L Comer (from J S Bolger in IRE [1-6] Mar 1999).*

LIZZIE SIMMONDS (IRE) BHB 60f **RR 59f** 5076[22]

2 b f Common Grounds 8.1f **(66)** - Able Susan (Formidable (USA)) 9.2f **(63)**
Form - 70300
Record 1999 - 1st:0 2nd:0 3rd:1 Ran:5
Win Prizemoney £0 *Total Prizemoney* £594
1999 Turf 0-5: (5f 3, 6f 2) (gd 4, frm)
Fair filly. Turf high 59 - 3rd of 17 getting 5lb from Royal Romeo (15 Spt Beverley 5f gd RF 4325).
**N Tinkler [0-5] J M G Promotions Ltd.*

LOBLITE LEADER (IRE) BHB 60f **RR 60f** 5158[18]

2 b c Tirol 8.1f **(64)** - Cyrano Beauty (IRE) (Cyrano de Bergerac) 6f **(68)**
Form - 0640450
Record 1999 - 1st:0 2nd:0 3rd:0 Ran:7
Win Prizemoney £0 *Total Prizemoney* £447
1999 Turf 0-7: (6f, 7f 4, 8f 2) (gd 2, frm 5)
Average colt. Turf high 60.
**G M Moore [0-7] Montagu Bloodstock Ltd.*

LOBUCHE (IRE) BHB 35f34a **RR 26f 34a** 5151[12]

4 b g Petardia 8.2f **(58)** - Lhotse (IRE) (Shernazar) 10.2f **(73)**
Form - 0067000
Record 1999 - 1st:0 2nd:0 3rd:0 Ran:7
Pre1999 - 1st:1 2nd:3 3rd:1 Ran:23
Win Prizemoney £3,054 *Total Prizemoney* £5,386
Wins * 1998 Jun Yarmou (SFT) H 6f 58 67 <
1999 Turf 0-3: (7f, 8f, 16f) (gd, frm 2) 1999 AW 0-4: (7f 2, 11f, 15f) (Fibr 4)
Very moderate gelding, effective 6 to 10f, acts on g-f - acts on Equi, has worn blinkers. Turf high 26 (began Jly).
**M C Chapman [2-25] K D Blanch (from R Hannon [0-13] Apr 1998).*

LOCHANGEL BHB 110f **RR 115f** 4418[7]

5 ch m Night Shift (USA) 8.1f **(73)** - Peckitts Well (Lochnager) 6f **(59)**
Form - 240747
Record 1999 - 1st:0 2nd:1 3rd:0 Ran:6
Pre1999 - 1st:3 2nd:4 3rd:2 Ran:14
Win Prizemoney £101,505 *Total Prizemoney* £177,804
Wins * 1998 Aug York (FRM) G1 5f 115 <
* 1998 May Bath (GD) L 5.7f 108
* 1996 Spt Ascot (G-F) 6f 91
1999 Turf 0-6: (5f 5, 6f) (gd 3, g-f 2, frm)
High-class filly, effective 5 to 6f, best at 5f, acts on gd to frm, best on g-f, excels at Ascot and Sandown. Turf high 115 - 4th of 18 giving 6lb to Mitcham (18 Jun Ascot 5f g-f RF 2106). Consistent. A half-sister to Lochsong, she developed into a leading sprinter in 1998, including winning York's Nunthorpe Stakes. Apart from one or two creditable efforts, she did not find her best form last season, and she has been retired. **I A Balding [3-20] J C Smith.*

LOCH BERING (USA) RR 86f 4373a[1]

7 ch h Bering 9.6f **(80)** - Passerine (USA) (Dr Fager) 7f **(83)**
Form - 1
1999 AW 1-1: (8f 1-1) (Dirt 1-1)
Very useful horse. (1st run) - 1st of 10 giving 4lb to Daunting Lady (12 Spt Taby RF 4373a).
**A Lund in NOR [1-3] Stall S (from P A Kelleway [0-3] Nov 1994).*

LOCH DANCER BHB 28f **RR 13f** 3416[14]

6 br m Lochnager 6.9f **(50)** - Cute Dancer (Remainder Man) 11.2f **(45)**
Form - 0
Record 1999 - 1st:0 2nd:0 3rd:0 Ran:1
Pre1999 - 1st:0 2nd:0 3rd:0 Ran:3
1999 Turf 0-1: (6f) (g-f)
Poor mare.
**W M Brisbourne [0-1] Mrs Elizabeth Crewe (from D McCain [0-1] Spt 1998).*

LOCHDENE (IRE) BHB 46f **RR 27f** 635[14]

4 b g Robellino (USA) 9.5f **(68)** - Cat's Claw (USA) (Sharpen Up) 8.3f **(67)**
Form - 60
Record 1999 - 1st:0 2nd:0 3rd:0 Ran:2
Pre1999 - 1st:0 2nd:0 3rd:0 Ran:3
Win Prizemoney £0 *Total Prizemoney* £556
1999 Turf 0-2: (8f, 9f) (hvy 2)
Scopey, little account gelding. Turf high 27.
**M Johnston [0-5] J S Morrison.*

LOCH FYNE BHB 59f **RR 55f** 3917[9]

3 b f Ardkinglass 5f **(64)** - Song's Best (Never so Bold) 6.3f **(66)**
Form - 0330
Record 1999 - 1st:0 2nd:0 3rd:2 Ran:4
Pre1999 - 1st:0 2nd:0 3rd:1 Ran:4
Win Prizemoney £0 *Total Prizemoney* £1,165
1999 Turf 0-4: (5f 2, 6f 2) (gd 2, frm 2)
Workmanlike, fair filly, effective 5f, acts on frm. Turf high 55

(began Jly). Inconsistent. **W R Muir [0-8] D J Deer.*

LOCH INCH BHB 90f85a **RR 87f 85a** 5218[12]
2 ch c Inchinor 8.9f **(64)** - Carrie Kool **(61df)** (Prince Sabo) 7.2f **(62)**
Form - 3510460010
Record 1999 - 1st:2 2nd:0 3rd:1 Ran:10
Win Prizemoney £7,253 *Total Prizemoney* £8,145
Wins * 1999 Oct Windso (SFT) H 6f 85 87 <
*** 1999** Aug Nottin (G-F) 6.1f 78
1999 Turf 2-9: (5f, 6f 2-5, 7f 2, 8f) (sft, g-s 2, gd 1-3, g-f, frm 1-2) 1999 AW 0-1: (8f) (Fibr)
Useful colt, effective 6f, acts on gd to frm, has worn blinkers. Turf high 87 - 1st of 10 giving 15lb to Tribal Prince (28 Oct Windsor RF 5111) - also 1st of 11 giving 7lb to Kilbrannan Sound (23 Aug Nottingham RF 3859). Inconsistent.
**K McAuliffe [2-10] Folly Road Racing Partners (1996).*

LOCH LAIRD BHB 79f **RR 83f** 4644[12]
4 b g Beveled (USA) 6.9f **(64)** - Daisy Loch (Lochnager) 6f **(59)**
Form - 17106780
Record 1999 - 1st:2 2nd:0 3rd:0 Ran:8
Pre1999 - 1st:0 2nd:4 3rd:2 Ran:7
Win Prizemoney £7,444 *Total Prizemoney* £12,244
Wins * 1999 Jun Goodwo (SFT) H 6f 78 79
*** 1999** May Salisb (G-F) 6f 81 <
1999 Turf 2-8: (5f, 6f 2-7) (g-s 1-2, gd 2, g-f 2, frm 1-2)
Unfurnished, decent gelding, effective 6f, acts on g-s to frm. Turf high 83 - also 1st of 17 giving 10lb to Blackheath (2 May Salisbury RF 0988). **M Madgwick [2-15] Miss E M L Coller.*

LOCHLASS (IRE) BHB 29f33a **RR 23f 33a** 4159[14]
5 b m Distinctly North (USA) 7.4f **(63)** - Littleton Song (Song) 7.2f **(61)**
Form - P0
Record 1999 - 1st:0 2nd:0 3rd:0 Ran:2
Pre1999 - 1st:0 2nd:0 3rd:4 Ran:19
Win Prizemoney £0 *Total Prizemoney* £1,564
1999 Turf 0-2: (12f, 13f) (frm 2)
Little account filly, has worn blinkers. (began Jly). Inconsistent.
**R J Price [0-9] My Left Foot Racing Syndicate (from S P C Woods [0-15] Oct 1997).*

LOCH MAGIC RR 45f 1814[15]
3 b g Arazi (USA) 9.2f **(74)** - Peckitts Well (Lochnager) 6f **(59)**
Form - 00
Record 1999 - 1st:0 2nd:0 3rd:0 Ran:2
1999 Turf 0-2: (6f, 7f) (g-f, frm)
Tall, currently moderate gelding. Turf high 45.
**I A Balding [0-2] J C Smith.*

LOCHON BHB 25f25a **RR 13f 25a** 2522[14]
8 br g Lochnager 6.9f **(50)** - Sky Mariner (Julio Mariner) 7.2f **(57)**
Form - 087600
Record 1999 - 1st:0 2nd:0 3rd:0 Ran:6
Pre1999 - 1st:3 2nd:4 3rd:7 Ran:52
Win Prizemoney £9,859 *Total Prizemoney* £16,374
Wins 1996 *Jan Lingfi (STD) H 6f 51 52*
1995 Aug Pontef (G-F) H 5f 55 53 <
1999 Turf 0-2: (5f 2) (g-f, frm) 1999 AW 0-4: (6f 3, 7f) (Fibr 4)
Poor gelding, has worn blinkers. AW high 16.
**F Watson [0-6] Linkchallenge Ltd (from Mrs N Macauley [0-13] Jun 1997).*

LOCH SOUND BHB 32f **RR 34f** 4448[13]
3 b g Primitive Rising (USA) 8.1f **(48)** - Lochcross (Lochnager) 6f **(59)**
Form - 00000
Record 1999 - 1st:0 2nd:0 3rd:0 Ran:5
1999 Turf 0-5: (10f 2, 12f 2, 14f) (g-s, gd 2, frm, hrd)
Workmanlike, very moderate gelding. Turf high 34.
**C W Thornton [0-5] Mrs Jill Murphy.*

LOCKERLEY WATER RR 5067[13]
3 ch f Mac's Fighter - Swift Stream (Chief Singer) 8.9f **(66)**
Form - 0
Record 1999 - 1st:0 2nd:0 3rd:0 Ran:1
1999 Turf 0-1: (12f) (gd)
Currently very poor filly.
**W G M Turner [0-1] Alex Taylor.*

LOCOMBE HILL (IRE) BHB 97f **RR 95f** 4594[7]
3 b c Barathea (IRE) - Roberts Pride (Roberto (USA)) 10f **(76)**
Form - 480317
Record 1999 - 1st:1 2nd:0 3rd:1 Ran:6
Pre1999 - 1st:2 2nd:1 3rd:0 Ran:5
Win Prizemoney £14,358 *Total Prizemoney* £18,375
Wins * 1999 Spt Kempto (HVY) 12f 95 <
*** 1998** Jly Newbur (G-F) 6f 95+
*** 1998** Jun Newbur (SFT) 6f 85+
1999 Turf 1-6: (7f 2, 9f, 10f, 12f 1-2) (g-s 1-1, gd, g-f 3, frm)
Very useful colt, effective 6 to 12f, best at 6f, acts on g-s to g-f. Turf high 105. Consistent. Took time to build on the promise of a fine juvenile career last term, but was running better towards the end of the year and won a minor race at Kempton in testing ground having been stepped up to 12 furlongs.
**M Blanshard [3-11] Stanley Hinton.*

LOCOMOTION (IRE) BHB 70f74a **RR 76f 74a** 4696[15]
3 ch g Seattle Dancer (USA) 10.1f **(74)** - Pipe Opener (Prince Sabo) 7.2f **(62)**
Form - 723312820
Record 1999 - 1st:1 2nd:3 3rd:2 Ran:9
Win Prizemoney £2,640 *Total Prizemoney* £6,563
Wins * 1999 *Jun Southw (STD) 8f 67 <*
1999 Turf 0-4: (6f 2, 7f 2) (g-s, gd 2, frm) 1999 AW 1-5: (6f 2, 7f, 8f 1-2) (Fibr 1-5)
Strong, above-average gelding, effective 6 to 8f, acts on frm - acts on Fibr, prefers left handed tracks. Turf high 76. AW high 76 - 2nd of 9 getting 10lb from The Whistling Teal (6 Aug Wolverhampton 8f Fibr RF 3439) - also 1st of 6 giving 5lb to Delphini (11 Jun Southwell RF 1929). Made the frame in Fibresand and turf maidens over six, but did not get off the mark until being stepped up to a mile at Southwell, though he did not look over-keen to go and win his race. **W J Haggas [1-9] Philip Ellick.*

LODEN BLUE BHB 44f **RR 47f** 5150[13]
2 b f Anshan 8.2f **(63)** - Dolly Bevan (Another Realm) 6.6f **(55)**
Form - 6000
Record 1999 - 1st:0 2nd:0 3rd:0 Ran:4
1999 Turf 0-4: (6f 2, 7f, 8f) (sft, g-s 2, gd)
Moderate filly. Turf high 47 (began Spt).
**C A Dwyer [0-1] John Purcell (from M L W Bell [0-3] Oct 1999).*

LOGANLEA (IRE) BHB 51f46a **RR 52f 46a** 655[11]
5 br m Petong 7.6f **(58)** - White's Pet (Mummy's Pet) 7.7f **(60)**
Form - 070
Record 1999 - 1st:0 2nd:0 3rd:0 Ran:3
Pre1999 - 1st:1 2nd:0 3rd:1 Ran:12
Win Prizemoney £2,455 *Total Prizemoney* £2,831
Wins * 1998 Spt Yarmou (G-S) H 6f 48 52 <
1999 Turf 0-1: (6f) (g-s) 1999 AW 0-2: (7f 2) (Equi 2)
Fair filly, effective 6f, acts on frm. AW high 29.
**W J Musson [1-15] Mrs P A Linton.*

LOHAN (IRE) BHB 44f **RR 42f** 4359[17]
3 b g Perugino (USA) - Deep In September (IRE) (Common Grounds)
Form - 44700
Record 1999 - 1st:0 2nd:0 3rd:0 Ran:3
Pre1999 - 1st:0 2nd:0 3rd:0 Ran:4
Win Prizemoney £0 *Total Prizemoney* £197
1999 Turf 0-3: (6f, 7f, 8f) (sft, g-s, frm)
Strong, average gelding. Turf high 42.
**Miss Z C Davison [0-7] Mrs M Flannery.*

LOKOMOTIV BHB 54f **RR 55f** 4991[13]
3 b g Salse (USA) 10.9f **(71)** - Rainbow's End (My Swallow) 9.2f **(71)**
Form - 0085425300
Record 1999 - 1st:0 2nd:1 3rd:1 Ran:10
Pre1999 - 1st:1 2nd:0 3rd:0 Ran:3
Win Prizemoney £1,987 *Total Prizemoney* £3,311
Wins 1998 Jly Yarmou (G-F) S 7f 67+ <
1999 Turf 0-10: (6f, 7f 3, 8f 5, 9f) (gd 3, g-f 2, frm 5)
Scopey, fair gelding, effective 7f, acts on g-f, has worn blinkers. Turf high 56.
**P D Evans [0-10] Mrs H Raw (from M R Channon [1-3] Jly 1998).*

LOLETTE BHB 54f **RR 50df** 2172[7]
3 b f Arazi (USA) 9.2f **(74)** - Wild Pavane (Dancing Brave (USA)) 8.4f **(76)**
Form - 807
Record 1999 - 1st:0 2nd:0 3rd:0 Ran:3
1999 Turf 0-3: (8f, 10f 2) (gd, g-f, frm)
Scopey, currently fair filly. Turf high 50.
**G Wragg [0-3] A E Oppenheimer.*

LOLITA (FR) BHB 62a **RR 24f** 1433[10]
5 b m Hellios (USA) - Silver Dime (FR) (Son of Silver)
Form - 00
Record 1999 - 1st:0 2nd:0 3rd:0 Ran:2
Pre1999 - 1st:0 2nd:0 3rd:0 Ran:5
Win Prizemoney £0 *Total Prizemoney* £329
1999 Turf 0-2: (12f 2) (frm 2)
Little account filly.
**J R Jenkins [0-11] Southern Counties Finance & Leasing.*

LOMAS (IRE) BHB 44f46a **RR 40f 46a** 1423[7]
8 b g Ela-Mana-Mou 12.7f **(72)** - Bold Miss (Bold Lad (IRE)) 8.4f **(68)**
Form - 087
Record 1999 - 1st:0 2nd:0 3rd:0 Ran:3
Pre1999 - 1st:2 2nd:0 3rd:1 Ran:9
Win Prizemoney £7,929 *Total Prizemoney* £11,848
1999 Turf 0-1: (13f) (gd) 1999 AW 0-2: (7f, 9f) (Fibr 2)
Moderate gelding. AW high 30. Becoming disappointing.
**A G Newcombe [0-3] M B Clemence (from Mrs H Parrott [0-5] Jun 1995).*

LOMOND DANCER (IRE) BHB 65f **RR 70f** 3611[6]
2 b c Common Grounds 8.1f **(66)** - Lomond's Breeze (Lomond (USA)) 8.8f **(65)**
Form - 4486
Record 1999 - 1st:0 2nd:0 3rd:0 Ran:4
Win Prizemoney £0 *Total Prizemoney* £250
1999 Turf 0-4: (6f, 7f 3) (gd, frm 3)
Above-average colt. Turf high 70.
**P W Harris [0-4] Friends of Lomond.*

LONDON LIGHTS RR 58f 1848a[10]
5 b g Slip Anchor 12.7f **(75)** - Pageantry (Welsh Pageant) 10f **(65)**
Form - 850
Record 1999 - 1st:0 2nd:0 3rd:0 Ran:3
Pre1999 - 1st:0 2nd:0 3rd:1 Ran:2
Win Prizemoney £0 *Total Prizemoney* £492
1999 Turf 0-3: (9f, 12f, 16f) (sft, g-s, g-f)
Fair gelding. Turf high 58.
**L Woods [0-3] Q & A Syndicate (from P F I Cole [0-2] Spt 1997).*

LONE BID (FR) RR 120f 929a[2]
4 b c Priolo (USA) 10.9f **(71)** - Lobmille (Mill Reef (USA)) 10.5f **(78)**
Form - 72
1999 Turf 0-1: (8f) (hvy) 1999 AW 0-1: (10f) (Dirt)
Currently very high-class colt. (1st run) - 2nd of 8 to Gold Away (24 Apr Saint-Cloud 8f hvy RF 0929a). A fair French-trained colt, his best effort last season was when runner-up to Gold Away in a Saint-Cloud Group Two. **C Laffon-Parias in FR [0-2].*

LONELY PLACE (IRE) BHB 92f **RR 88f** 5024[1]
2 b c Lake Coniston (IRE) - Aimores (IRE) (Persian Heights)
Form - 0877131
Record 1999 - 1st:2 2nd:0 3rd:1 Ran:7
Win Prizemoney £11,113 *Total Prizemoney* £12,213
Wins * 1999 Oct Doncas (G-S) H 8f 85 88 <
*** 1999** Spt Ayr (G-S) H 8f 76 84
1999 Turf 2-7: (6f 3, 8f 2-4) (gd 2-3, g-f 2, frm 2)
Useful colt, effective 8f, acts on gd. Turf high 88 - 1st of 12 giving 8lb to Badr Rainbow (22 Oct Doncaster RF 5024) - also 1st of 20 getting 4lb from First Truth (17 Spt Ayr RF 4378).
**B W Hills [2-7] H R H Prince Fahd Salman.*

LONE PIPER BHB 98f **RR 95f** 2105[24]
4 b c Warning 8.1f **(77)** - Shamisen (Diesis) 9.3f **(69)**
Form - 020
Record 1999 - 1st:0 2nd:1 3rd:0 Ran:3
Pre1999 - 1st:2 2nd:0 3rd:1 Ran:10
Win Prizemoney £24,284 *Total Prizemoney* £27,121
Wins * 1998 Spt York (GD) H 6f 96 101 <
* 1998 May Newmar (GD) 7f 99
1999 Turf 0-3: (6f 3) (gd 2, g-f)
Neat, very useful colt, effective 6 to 7f, best at 7f, acts on gd to frm, best on gd. Turf high 95. Inconsistent. Effective over six and seven furlongs, he showed little in 1999 and went missing after Royal Ascot. **C E Brittain [2-13] Saeed Manana.*

LONESOME BHB 60f **RR 62f** 3985[12]
3 b f Night Shift (USA) 8.1f **(73)** - Pine Ridge (High Top) 10.2f **(67)**
Form - 5700
Record 1999 - 1st:0 2nd:0 3rd:0 Ran:4
Pre1999 - 1st:0 2nd:0 3rd:0 Ran:1
1999 Turf 0-4: (8f, 9f, 10f, 12f) (gd, frm 3)
Workmanlike, average filly, has worn blinkers. Turf high 62.
**Sir Michael Stoute [0-5] Capt J Macdonald-Buchanan.*

LONESOME DUDE (CAN) RR 107f 4657a[11]
4 b c With Approval (CAN) 8.7f **(80)** - Local Lass (Local Suitor (USA)) 8.4f **(67)**
Form - 10210
Record 1999 - 1st:2 2nd:1 3rd:0 Ran:5
Pre1999 - 1st:2 2nd:2 3rd:0 Ran:7
Win Prizemoney £90,066 *Total Prizemoney* £101,894
Wins * 1999 Jly Goodwo (G-F) H 8f 103 107 <
*** 1999** May Sandow (GD) H 8.1f 96 100
* 1998 Jun Goodwo (GD) 9f 94+
* 1998 May Kempto (G-F) 7f 90
1999 Turf 2-5: (8f 2-5) (gd, frm 2-4)
Pattern-class colt, effective 8 to 9f, best at 8f, acts on gd to frm, best on frm, has worn blinkers, prefers right handed tracks, excels at Goodwood and Sandown. Turf high 107 - 1st of 20 giving 11lb to Swallow Flight (29 Jly Goodwood RF 3223) - also 1st of 12 giving 4lb to Brilliant Red (31 May Sandown RF 1614). A very useful handicapper, he landed the valuable William Hill Golden Mile at Glorious Goodwood having been an unlucky loser on his previous start. Made no show in a Grade One event in Canada on his final run, but listed races should be within his compass.
**Sir Michael Stoute [4-12].*

LONGCHAMP LADY BHB 51f **RR 52f** 4543[13]
2 br f Puissance 7.1f **(60)** - Gem of Gold (Jellaby) 6.4f **(58)**
Form - 0558630
Record 1999 - 1st:0 2nd:0 3rd:1 Ran:7
Win Prizemoney £0 *Total Prizemoney* £378
1999 Turf 0-6: (5f 5, 6f) (gd 2, g-f 3, frm) 1999 AW 0-1: (5f) (Fibr)
Fair filly. Turf high 54.
**J Berry [0-7] The Property Racing Partnership.*

LOOP THE LOUP BHB 98f **RR 96f** 4345[2]
3 b g Petit Loup (USA) - Mithi Al Gamar (USA) **(60f)** (Blushing Groom (FR)) 10.3f **(76)**
Form - 50112122
Record 1999 - 1st:3 2nd:3 3rd:0 Ran:8
Pre1999 - 1st:0 2nd:0 3rd:1 Ran:2
Win Prizemoney £26,343 *Total Prizemoney* £34,856
Wins * 1999 Aug York (GD) H 13.9f 89 95 <
*** 1999** Jly Salisb (G-S) H 12f 83 84
*** 1999** Jun Lingfi (G-S) 11.5f 84
1999 Turf 3-8: (8f, 10f, 11f 1-1, 12f 1-1, 14f 1-2, 15f 2) (g-s 1-1, gd 2-5, g-f, frm)
Scopey, very useful gelding, effective 14 to 15f, best at 15f, acts on gd to frm, best on gd. Turf high 96 - 2nd of 9 getting 13lb from Life of Riley (27 Aug Newmarket 15f frm RF 3940) - also 1st of 11 giving 10lb to Who Cares Wins (19 Aug York RF 3774). He improved as he moved up in trip and ended the campaign a useful staying handicapper. Likely to stay two miles, he made 70,000 guineas at Newmarket in October and is expected to continue his career with Micky Hammond. He should do well over hurdles for his new connections. **J L Dunlop [3-10] The Hon Sir David Sieff.*

LORD ADVOCATE BHB 32f38a **RR 53f 38a** 4590[7]
11 br g Law Society (USA) 11.6f **(71)** - Kereolle (Riverman (USA)) 9.1f **(76)**
Form - 045557536425867
Record 1999 - 1st:0 2nd:1 3rd:1 Ran:15
Pre1999 - 1st:12 2nd:17 3rd:13 Ran:130

Win Prizemoney £36,549 *Total Prizemoney* £60,807

Wins * 1998 Jun Hamilt (GD) H 13f 40 44
* 1997 Jun Hamilt (GD) H 13f 46 57
* 1996 Jun Hamilt (GD) H 13f 45 53
* 1996 May Mussel (GD) H 11.1f 42 47
* 1996 May Hamilt (SFT) H 13f 32 43
* 1995 Aug Mussel (G-F) H 12.1f 30 35
* 1995 Jun Hamilt (FRM) H 13f 33 37
* 1995 May Hamilt (G-F) SH 11.1f 26 36

1999 Turf 0-15: (11f 2, 12f 3, 13f 9, 14f) (g-s, gd 4, g-f 5, frm 4, hrd)
Fair gelding, effective 13f, acts on gd to g-f, mostly wears blinkers. Turf high 53. All of his wins since '92 have been in Scotland but he has not won since June 1998
**D A Nolan [8-100] Mrs J McFadyen-Murray (from T Craig [1-5] Jly 1993).*

LORD BANKES BHB 60f55a **RR 63f 55a** 4786[14]
2 b c Presidium 7.5f **(56)** - Marfen (Lochnager) 6f **(59)**
Form - 225004060
Record 1999 - 1st:0 2nd:2 3rd:0 Ran:9
Win Prizemoney £0 *Total Prizemoney* £2,651
1999 Turf 0-8: (5f 6, 6f 2) (g-s 3, gd 2, g-f, frm 2) 1999 AW 0-1: (6f) (Equi)
Average colt, effective 5f, acts on gd to g-f, has worn blinkers. Turf high 75 (1st run) - 2nd of 15 giving 5lb to Seraphina (25 Mar Doncaster 5f g-f RF 0464). Inconsistent.
**W G M Turner [0-9] T Lightbowne.*

LORD BERGERAC BHB 50f59a **RR 52f 59a** 4127[13]
3 b c Cyrano de Bergerac 7.3f **(58)** - Vax Lady (Millfontaine)
Form - 00634600
Record 1999 - 1st:0 2nd:0 3rd:1 Ran:8
Pre1999 - 1st:1 2nd:0 3rd:0 Ran:3
Win Prizemoney £3,582 *Total Prizemoney* £3,987
Wins * 1998 Aug Hamilt (SFT) 6f 78+ <
1999 Turf 0-7: (6f 5, 7f, 8f) (gd 2, g-f 3, frm, hrd) 1999 AW 0-1: (7f) (Fibr) **Strong, fair colt, effective 6f, acts on g-s, often wears blinkers. Turf high 52.** **J L Spearing [1-11] A J & Mrs L Brazier.*

LORD BREX (FR) RR 97f 4771a[3]
3 c Saint Estephe (FR) - Light Moon (FR)
Form - 623
1999 Turf 0-3: (11f, 15f 2) (hvy, g-s, gd)
Currently very useful colt, often wears blinkers. Turf high 97 - 2nd of 7 giving 3lb to Artistique (30 Jly Chantilly 15f gd RF 3405a).
**F Doumen in FR [0-3].*

LORD DISCORD BHB 40f **RR 39f** 4347[12]
5 b g Primo Dominie 7.2f **(67)** - Busted Harmony (Busted) 10.2f **(61)**
Form - 610
Record 1999 - 1st:1 2nd:0 3rd:0 Ran:3
Pre1999 - 1st:0 2nd:1 3rd:1 Ran:10
Win Prizemoney £2,416 *Total Prizemoney* £4,720
Wins 1999 Jly Ayr (GD) S 10.9f 39 <
1999 Turf 1-2: (11f 1-2) (gd, g-f 1-1) 1999 AW 0-1: (15f) (Fibr)
Very moderate gelding, has worn blinkers. Turf high 39 (1st run) (began Jly). Consistent.
**J S Goldie [0-1] Strathayr Publishing Ltd (from J Mackie [1-6] Jly 1999).*

LORD EUROLINK (IRE) BHB 76f **RR 76f** 4758[5]
5 b h Danehill (USA) 9.1f **(79)** - Lady Eurolink (Kala Shikari) 8.4f **(54)**
Form - 6745
Record 1999 - 1st:0 2nd:0 3rd:0 Ran:4
Pre1999 - 1st:1 2nd:0 3rd:3 Ran:6
Win Prizemoney £4,435 *Total Prizemoney* £7,693
Wins 1997 May Doncas (GD) 8f 83 <
1999 Turf 0-4: (10f 3, 11f) (gd 3, g-f)
Above-average colt. Turf high 76 (began Aug). Consistent.
**C A Dwyer [0-4] Roalco Ltd (from J L Dunlop [1-6] May 1998).*

LORD FLASHEART (USA) RR 104+f 4767a[1]
2 b c Blush Rambler (USA) - Miss Henderson Co (USA) (Silver Hawk (USA)) 8.6f **(70)**
Form - 21
1999 Turf 1-2: (7f, 9f 1-1) (hvy 1-1, gd)
Currently very useful colt. Turf high 104 (began Aug) - 1st of 6 from Crystal D'Ass (2 Oct Longchamp RF 4767a).
**A deRoyerDupre in FR [1-2] J C Serroul.*

LORD HARLEY BHB 40f **RR 30f** 5064[10]
2 b c Formidable (USA) 7.8f **(60)** - Nanny Doon (Dominion) 8.5f **(63)**
Form - 000
Record 1999 - 1st:0 2nd:0 3rd:0 Ran:3
1999 Turf 0-3: (6f 2, 7f) (gd 3)
Currently very moderate colt. Turf high 30.
**B R Millman [0-3] H Gooding.*

LORD HIGH ADMIRAL (CAN) BHB 50f **RR 51f** 5032[9]
11 b g Bering 9.6f **(80)** - Baltic Sea (CAN) (Danzig (USA)) 8.4f **(76)**
Form - 3510587220370
Record 1999 - 1st:1 2nd:2 3rd:2 Ran:13
Pre1999 - 1st:10 2nd:8 3rd:4 Ran:65
Win Prizemoney £49,495 *Total Prizemoney* £72,346
Wins 1999 May Doncas (G-F) C 6f 55
1997 Spt Salisb (G-S) H 5f 75 85+
1996 Spt Haydoc (GD) H 5f 82 87
1996 Jly Sandow (G-S) H 5f 82 86
1996 Jun Sandow (G-F) C 5f 70
1995 Jun Sandow (G-F) C 5f 78+
1995 May Haydoc (G-S) H 5f 86 89 <
1999 Turf 1-13: (5f 10, 6f 1-3) (sft, g-s, gd 4, g-f 2, frm 4, hrd 1-1)
Fair gelding, effective 5f, acts on gd to g-f, has worn blinkers. Turf high 65. Seems best over a stiff five with cut in the ground and when able to dominate.
**C G Cox [0-5] Elite Racing Club (from M J Heaton-Ellis [11-62] Aug 1999).*

LORD KINTYRE BHB 98f **RR 103df** 3166[15]
4 b c Makbul - Highland Rowena (Royben) 7.3f **(60)**
Form - 50
Record 1999 - 1st:0 2nd:0 3rd:0 Ran:2
Pre1999 - 1st:2 2nd:4 3rd:2 Ran:14
Win Prizemoney £77,929 *Total Prizemoney* £123,271
Wins * 1997 Jly Newbur (G-F) 5.2f 98 <
* 1997 Jun Windso (G-F) 6f 80
1999 Turf 0-2: (5f, 6f) (g-f, frm)
Workmanlike, very useful colt, effective 5 to 6f, acts on gd to g-f. Turf high 69. Becoming disappointing.
**B R Millman [2-16] M Calvert.*

LORD LAMB BHB 90f **RR 91f** 5221[3]
7 gr g Dunbeath (USA) 9.9f **(53)** - Caroline Lamb (Hotfoot) 10.5f **(59)**
Form - 323
Record 1999 - 1st:0 2nd:1 3rd:2 Ran:3
Pre1999 - 1st:1 2nd:0 3rd:1 Ran:6
Win Prizemoney £7,262 *Total Prizemoney* £15,797
Wins * 1998 Spt Haydoc (G-F) H 14f 69 69+ <
1999 Turf 0-3: (12f 2, 16f) (sft, gd 2)
Useful gelding, effective 12 to 16f, best at 12f, acts on sft to gd, best on gd. Turf high 91 - 3rd of 16 giving 11lb to Flossy (6 Nov Doncaster 12f sft RF 5221). Narrowly beaten on his return to the Flat at Musselburgh in September after a campaign over hurdles, his will to win might just be in question.
**Mrs M Reveley [6-17] A Sharratt & J Renton.*

LORDOFENCHANTMENT (IRE) BHB 63f **RR 67f** 5034[6]
2 ch g Soviet Lad (USA) 9.4f **(63)** - Sauvignon (IRE) (Alzao (USA)) 7.1f **(68)**
Form - 86581566
Record 1999 - 1st:1 2nd:0 3rd:0 Ran:8
Win Prizemoney £2,253 *Total Prizemoney* £2,253
Wins * 1999 Aug Ripon (GD) S 6f 67+ <
1999 Turf 1-7: (5f, 6f 1-5, 7f) (g-s, gd 3, g-f 1-2, frm) 1999 AW 0-1: (6f) (Fibr) **Average gelding, effective 6f, acts on g-f to frm, has worn blinkers. Turf high 67 - 1st of 9 from Late Night Lady (30 Aug Ripon RF 4026).** **N Tinkler [1-8] David Scott.*

LORD OF MEN BHB 110f **RR 112f** 4316a[6]
6 ch h Groom Dancer (USA) 9.5f **(75)** - Upper Strata (Shirley Heights) 10.3f **(74)**
Form - 36
Record 1999 - 1st:0 2nd:0 3rd:1 Ran:2
Pre1999 - 1st:8 2nd:1 3rd:3 Ran:15

Win Prizemoney £128,969 *Total Prizemoney* £258,866
Wins 1998 Spt Maison (GD) G3 10f 112 <
1998 Jly Cheste (G-F) 10.3f 107+
1997 Aug Deauvi (GD) G3 10f 107
1997 Jly Sandow (G-F) 10f 107
1997 Jun Doncas (G-S) 8f 99
1995 Spt Longch (SFT) G1 7f 108+
1995 Aug Lingfi (G-F) 7.6f 95+
1995 Aug Newmar (G-F) 7f 93+
1999 Turf 0-1: (10f) (gd) 1999 AW 0-1: (10f) (Dirt)
Group-class horse, effective 10 to 11f, best at 10f, acts on gd to frm, best on gd, has worn blinkers. Trained by John Gosden in '98, he raced for Godolphin last term and ran a creditable third in the Dubai Duty Free. He was off the track for a long time until carrying out pacemaking duties for Daylami in Ireland.
**S bin Suroor [0-2] Godolphin.*

LORD OMNI (USA) BHB 70f RR 72f 5074[4]
2 ch c El Prado (IRE) 8f **(74)** - Muskoka Ice (USA) (It's Freezing (USA)) 10f **(83)**
Form - 604
Record 1999 - 1st:0 2nd:0 3rd:0 Ran:3
Win Prizemoney £0 *Total Prizemoney* £246
1999 Turf 0-3: (6f 2, 7f) (gd 2, g-f)
Currently above-average colt. Turf high 72 (1st run) (began Aug) - 6th of 21 to Abderian (21 Aug Ripon 6f g-f RF 3818).
**T D Barron [0-3] Peter Jones.*

LORD PACAL (IRE) BHB 92f RR 88df 5061[4]
2 b c Indian Ridge 7.6f **(74)** - Please Believe Me (Try My Best (USA)) 7.6f **(67)**
Form - 14542034
Record 1999 - 1st:1 2nd:1 3rd:1 Ran:8
Win Prizemoney £4,224 *Total Prizemoney* £15,250
Wins * 1999 May Newbur (G-F) 5.2f 95+ <
1999 Turf 1-8: (5f 1-4, 6f 4) (g-s, gd 2, g-f 1-4, frm)
Useful colt, effective 5f, acts on gd to g-f, best on g-f. Turf high 95 - 4th of 13 to Warm Heart (17 Jun Ascot 5f g-f RF 2070) - also 1st of 8 giving 5lb to Out of Africa (26 May Newbury RF 1496). Consistent. He was highly tried in mid-summer, but did not progress. Likely to stay seven furlongs, he will be difficult to place. **N A Callaghan [1-8] Paul & Jenny Green.*

LORD ROCHESTER BHB 58f RR 52f 4128[9]
3 b c Distant Relative 7f **(69)** - Kentfield (Busted) 10.2f **(61)**
Form - 6081670
Record 1999 - 1st:1 2nd:0 3rd:0 Ran:7
Pre1999 - 1st:0 2nd:0 3rd:0 Ran:3
Win Prizemoney £2,318 *Total Prizemoney* £2,318
Wins * 1999 Jun Salisb (FRM) H 8f 58 60 <
1999 Turf 1-7: (8f 1-3, 10f 2, 11f, 12f) (g-s, g-f 4, frm 1-2)
Workmanlike, fair colt, effective 8f, acts on frm. Turf high 60 - 1st of 10 getting 4lb from Lv Girl (24 Jun Salisbury RF 2276). Consistent. **B R Millman [1-10] Lewis, Gudge, Calver Geering.*

LORD STROLLER BHB 39f RR 39f 1911[10]
3 b g Petong 7.6f **(58)** - Breakfast Boogie (Sizzling Melody)
Form - 00880
Record 1999 - 1st:0 2nd:0 3rd:0 Ran:5
Pre1999 - 1st:0 2nd:0 3rd:0 Ran:5
1999 Turf 0-5: (6f, 7f 2, 8f 2) (gd, g-f, frm 3)
Workmanlike, very moderate gelding, effective 6f, acts on frm, has worn blinkers. Turf high 39. Consistent.
**B R Millman [0-10] Gudge, Calvert, Lewi Geering.*

LORD YASMIN (IRE) RR 69f 2466[2]
2 b c Lahib (USA) 8f **(69)** - Adieu Cherie (IRE) (Bustino) 10.4f **(64)**
Form - 02
Record 1999 - 1st:0 2nd:1 3rd:0 Ran:2
Win Prizemoney £0 *Total Prizemoney* £560
1999 Turf 0-2: (6f 2) (gd 2)
Currently average colt. Turf high 69 - 2nd of 7 giving 5lb to Baytown Melody (1 Jly Yarmouth 6f gd RF 2466).
**J Noseda [0-2] L P Calvente.*

LORIANGO (GER) RR 98f 1714a[3]
3 f Acatenango (GER) - Loveria (GER) (Los Santos (FR))
Form - 3
1999 Turf 0-1: (16f) (gd)
Currently very useful. (1st run) - 3rd of 7 getting 7lb from Solo Mio (29 May Baden-Baden 16f gd RF 1714a). **H Steinmetz in GER [0-1].*

LORINER'S LASS BHB 76f RR 83tf 4209[7]
3 b f Saddlers' Hall (IRE) 10.5f **(65)** - Sixslip (USA) (Diesis) 9.3f **(69)**
Form - 45327
Record 1999 - 1st:0 2nd:1 3rd:1 Ran:5
Pre1999 - 1st:0 2nd:0 3rd:0 Ran:2
Win Prizemoney £0 *Total Prizemoney* £1,486
1999 Turf 0-5: (10f, 12f 2, 14f, 15f) (gd 3, g-f 2)
Strong, decent filly, effective 14f, acts on g-f. Turf high 83. She looks slow, and if she is to win it will be over a marathon trip.
**W Jarvis [0-5] Summertree Stud (from I A Balding [0-2] Spt 1998).*

LORINS GOLD BHB 40f RR 42?f 3628[P]
9 ch g Rich Charlie 5.9f **(50)** - Woolcana (Some Hand) 9f **(50)**
Form - P
Record 1999 - 1st:0 2nd:0 3rd:0 Ran:1
Pre1999 - 1st:3 2nd:5 3rd:5 Ran:47
Win Prizemoney £8,534 *Total Prizemoney* £15,817
Wins * 1997 Aug Lingfi (G-F) H 7.6f 36 42 <
* 1997 Jun Warwic (FRM) H 8f 32 40
* 1996 May Bright (FRM) H 6f 28 31
1999 Turf 0-1: (8f) (gd)
Moderate gelding, had worn blinkers. (DEAD)
**Andrew Turnell [3-49] Mrs M R Taylor.*

L'ORPHELINE (FR) BHB 60f RR 67?f 4353[7]
3 b f Seattle Song (USA) 10.6f **(67)** - Buck's Dame (USA) (Damascus (USA)) 8.9f **(71)**
Form - 007
Record 1999 - 1st:0 2nd:0 3rd:0 Ran:3
1999 Turf 0-3: (7f, 10f 2) (frm 3)
Leggy, currently average filly. Turf high 67.
**C E Brittain [0-3] Saeed Manana.*

LOSADA (IRE) BHB 70f RR 71f 2847[14]
3 b g Unblest - Fickle Femme (Hard Fought) 8.8f **(62)**
Form - 4100
Record 1999 - 1st:1 2nd:0 3rd:0 Ran:4
Win Prizemoney £2,967 *Total Prizemoney* £3,202
Wins * 1999 May Catter (FRM) 7f 71 <
1999 Turf 1-4: (6f, 7f 1-3) (gd, g-f 2, frm 1-1)
Above-average gelding. Turf high 73 - also 1st of 17 giving 5lb to Debbie's Hope (22 May Catterick RF 1390).
**P Calver [1-4] Mrs Janis MacPherson.*

LOST IN HOOK (IRE) BHB 85f RR 85f 4384[2]
2 b f Dancing Dissident (USA) 6.8f **(65)** - Rathbawn Realm (Doulab (USA)) 9.8f **(65)**
Form - 16452
Record 1999 - 1st:1 2nd:1 3rd:0 Ran:5
Win Prizemoney £2,762 *Total Prizemoney* £4,642
Wins * 1999 Jly Ripon (GD) 5f 94+ <
1999 Turf 1-5: (5f 1-4, 6f) (gd 1-2, g-f, frm 2)
Useful filly. Turf high 94 (1st run) (began Jly) - 1st of 11 giving 3lb to Desert Safari (5 Jly Ripon RF 2562). Absolutely bolted up in a Ripon maiden auction event on her debut, but was then rather disappointing until a decent effort in a nursery in September.
**A P Jarvis [1-5] Nick Coverdale.*

LOST IN LUCCA BHB 57f52a RR 61f 52a 4936[3]
3 b f Inchinor 8.9f **(64)** - Poyle Fizz (Damister (USA)) 9f **(73)**
Form - 772351603
Record 1999 - 1st:1 2nd:1 3rd:2 Ran:9
Pre1999 - 1st:0 2nd:0 3rd:0 Ran:4
Win Prizemoney £4,698 *Total Prizemoney* £7,075
Wins * 1999 Jly Newmar (G-F) H 12f 46 61 <
1999 Turf 1-8: (10f, 11f, 12f 1-5, 14f) (g-s, gd 2, g-f 2, frm 1-3) 1999 AW 0-1: (12f) (Fibr)
Scopey, average filly, effective 7 to 12f, best at 12f, acts on gd to frm - acts on Fibr, has worn blinkers. Turf high 61 - 1st of 14 getting 6lb from Renaissance Lady (31 Jly Newmarket RF 3279). (1st run) - 3rd of 11 getting 8lb from Count de Money (18 Oct Southwell 12f Fibr RF 4936). She stepped up in trip for an easy Newmarket

victory, having looked a tricky customer on occasions. **J W Hills [1-13] The Jampot Partnership.*

LOST SPIRIT BHB 41f63a **RR 30f 63a** 4166^{13}

3 b g Strolling Along (USA) - Shoag (USA) (Affirmed (USA)) 9.3f **(79)**
Form - 05631153000
Record 1999 - 1st:2 2nd:0 3rd:2 Ran:11
Pre1999 - 1st:0 2nd:1 3rd:0 Ran:3
Win Prizemoney £5,546 *Total Prizemoney* £7,371
Wins * 1999 *Mar Wolver (SLW) H* *12f* *54* *63*
*** 1999** *Feb Southw (STD) C* *12f* *73+* **<**
1999 Turf 0-3: (12f 3) (gd, frm 2) 1999 AW 2-8: (7f 2, 9f, 11f, 12f 2-4) (Equi, Fibr 2-7)
Light-framed, average gelding, effective 12f, - acts on Fibr, has worn blinkers, likes left handed tracks, likes tight tracks. Turf high 50. AW high 73 - 1st of 6 giving 6lb to Crash Call Lady (26 Feb Southwell RF 0367). Becoming disappointing. **P W Hiatt [2-11] Red Lion (Chipping Norton) Partnership (from B Hanbury [0-3] Aug 1998).*

LOTS OF MAGIC BHB 112f **RR 115f** 4916^{10}

3 b c Magic Ring (IRE) 6.5f **(64)** - Pounelta (Tachypous) 8.6f **(55)**
Form - 14140
Record 1999 - 1st:2 2nd:0 3rd:0 Ran:5
Pre1999 - 1st:1 2nd:2 3rd:0 Ran:5
Win Prizemoney £49,121 *Total Prizemoney* £56,192
Wins * 1999 Jun Ascot (G-F) G3 7f 115 **<**
*** 1999** May Lingfi (G-F) 7f 97
* 1998 Spt Epsom (GD) 7f 85
1999 Turf 2-5: (7f 2-4, 8f) (gd 1-2, g-f, frm 1-2)
Leggy, high-class colt, effective 7f, acts on gd to g-f. Turf high 115 - 1st of 12 getting 6lb from Enrique (16 Jun Ascot RF 2039). A winner at Epsom at two, he made a winning reappearance at Lingfield last season, but failed to produce over a mile at Sandown behind Lonesome Dude. Made all for a shock victory in the Jersey Stakes at Royal Ascot, but was off the track for three months afterwards due to a lung infection. He may have needed the run when fourth in an Epsom Listed event on his return, but was disappointing when finishing last in the Challenge Stakes on his final start. Suited by fast ground. **R Hannon [3-10] Peter Valentine.*

LOUDEAC (USA) **RR 110f** $1531a^{7}$

4 b c Riverman (USA) 9.7f **(78)** - Louveterie (USA) (Nureyev (USA)) 8.7f **(78)**
Form - 337
1999 Turf 0-3: (8f 2, 9f) (hvy, sft, g-s)
Group-class colt. Turf high 110. He regressed after finishing third in a Group 3 at Saint-Cloud in April and needs a confidence booster. **A Fabre in FR [0-4].*

LOUGHANLEA (USA) BHB 60f58a **RR 57f 58a** 461^{3}

3 b br g Salt Lake (USA) - Moment Of Flight (USA) (My Favorite Moment (USA))
Form - 4051403
Record 1999 - 1st:1 2nd:0 3rd:1 Ran:7
Pre1999 - 1st:0 2nd:0 3rd:0 Ran:4
Win Prizemoney £1,855 *Total Prizemoney* £2,366
Wins * 1999 *Feb Wolver (STD) S* *6f* *62* **<**
1999 AW 1-7: (5f 2, 6f 1-1, 7f 4) (Equi, Fibr 1-6)
Scopey, fair gelding, effective 6 to 7f, - acts on Fibr, often wears blinkers, likes left handed tracks, prefers tight tracks. AW high 62 - 1st of 8 giving 5lb to Just For You Jane (17 Feb Wolverhampton RF 0307).
**D Nicholls [1-7] Burke's 5th Family Settlement (from M A Jarvis [0-3] Oct 1998).*

LOUGH SWILLY (IRE) BHB 60f **RR 60f** 4628^{10}

3 b g Mukaddamah (USA) 7.6f **(74)** - Flooding (USA) (Irish River (FR)) 8.6f **(78)**
Form - 000040000
Record 1999 - 1st:0 2nd:0 3rd:0 Ran:9
Pre1999 - 1st:2 2nd:0 3rd:1 Ran:5
Win Prizemoney £8,935 *Total Prizemoney* £10,326
Wins * 1998 Spt Goodwo (G-F) 7f 93 **<**
* 1998 Aug Nottin (G-F) 6.1f 93+
1999 Turf 0-9: (8f 5, 9f 3, 10f) (g-s, gd 2, g-f 5, frm)
Workmanlike, average gelding, effective 6 to 7f, acts on gd to frm. Turf high 87. **B W Hills [2-14] John Grant.*

LOU'S WISH BHB 60f54a **RR 63f 54a** 4937^{12}

2 b c Thatching 7.8f **(69)** - Shamaka **(57df 41a)** (Kris) 9.5f **(73)**
Form - 07508600
Record 1999 - 1st:0 2nd:0 3rd:0 Ran:8
1999 Turf 0-6: (5f, 6f 2, 7f, 8f 2) (sft, gd 3, frm 2) 1999 AW 0-2: (6f, 7f) (Fibr 2)
Average colt. Turf high 63. AW high 43.
**M J Polglase [0-8] Ian Puddle.*

LOUVE (USA) **RR 112f** $5228a^{10}$

3 f Irish River (FR) 9f **(77)** - Louveterie (USA) (Nureyev (USA)) 8.7f **(78)**
Form - 4410
1999 Turf 1-4: (10f, 11f 1-3) (g-s 2, frm)
Group-class filly. Turf high 112 - 4th of 14 to Daryaba (13 Jun Chantilly 11f g-s RF 2098a) - also 1st from Marie De Bayeux (23 Oct Saint-Cloud RF 5118a). Reported to work well at home, she caught the eye in both the Prix Saint-Alary and French Oaks, finishing strongly into fourth spot on each occasion. She cut no ice in the Breeders' Cup Mares Turf , and we have not yet seen the best of this filly. **A Fabre in FR [1-4].*

LOUVE MYSTERIEUSE (FR) **RR** $5224a^{7}$

3 f Seeking the Gold (USA) 7.4f **(80)** - Louve Bleue (USA) 0**0**
Form - 7
1999 AW 0-1: (9f) (Dirt)
Currently very useful. **A Fabre in FR [0-1].*

LOVEABLE ROGUE BHB 69f **RR 69f** 3300^{5}

3 b g Simply Great (FR) 11.9f **(61)** - Quick J (Jim J (USA))
Form - 35
Record 1999 - 1st:0 2nd:0 3rd:1 Ran:2
Pre1999 - 1st:0 2nd:0 3rd:0 Ran:1
Win Prizemoney £0 *Total Prizemoney* £318
1999 Turf 0-2: (10f 2) (g-f, frm)
Currently average gelding. Turf high 69 (1st run) (began Jly) - 3rd of 7 giving 5lb to Manicure (15 Jly Leicester 10f g-f RF 2848).
**M A Peill [0-3] Geoff Bonson.*

LOVE ACADEMY BHB 57f77a **RR 51f 77a** $4302a^{18}$

4 b g Royal Academy (USA) 7.8f **(77)** - Quiet Week-End (Town And Country) 8.1f **(68)**
Form - 126107268507002700000
Record 1999 - 1st:0 2nd:2 3rd:0 Ran:16
Pre1999 - 1st:4 2nd:2 3rd:1 Ran:17
Win Prizemoney £14,616 *Total Prizemoney* £21,420
Wins 1998 *Dec Southw (STD) H* *7f* *71* *76*
1998 *Nov Southw (STD) H* *7f* *62* *70*
1998 *Oct Southw (STD) H* *8f* *55* *63*
1997 Oct Newcas (G-F) 6f 86 **<**
1999 Turf 0-12: (6f 2, 7f 5, 8f 3, 9f, 10f) (sft, gd 2, g-f 6, frm 3) 1999 AW 0-4: (7f 4) (Equi 3, Fibr)
Above-average gelding, effective 7f, - acts on AW, best on Fibr, has worn blinkers, prefers left handed tracks, prefers tight tracks. Turf high 56. AW high 76 - 2nd of 12 getting 6lb from Silca Blanka (16 Jan Lingfield 7f Equi RF 0109). Inconsistent. A winner twice on the Southwell Fibresand at the end of the year, he looks best suited by seven furlongs despite having won over a mile.
**L Comer in IRE [0-9] L Comer (from M Johnston [4-24] Jly 1999).*

LOVE ALONE **RR 51f** 4323^{5}

2 b f Barathea (IRE) - Chepstow Vale (USA) (Key To The Mint (USA)) 9.4f **(75)**
Form - 5
Record 1999 - 1st:0 2nd:0 3rd:0 Ran:1
1999 Turf 0-1: (7f) (gd)
Currently fair filly. **J G FitzGerald [0-1] Marquesa de Moratalla.*

LOVE AND KISSES BHB 47f65a **RR 47f 65a** 3808^{12}

6 ch m Salse (USA) 10.9f **(71)** - Soba (Most Secret) 7.1f **(58)**
Form - 60
Record 1999 - 1st:0 2nd:0 3rd:0 Ran:2
Pre1999 - 1st:1 2nd:0 3rd:0 Ran:6
Win Prizemoney £2,070 *Total Prizemoney* £2,070
Wins * 1996 *Aug Southw (STD) H* *14f* *62* *64* **<**
1999 Turf 0-2: (15f, 16f) (g-f, frm)
Average mare. Turf high 47 (began Jly). **C A Cyzer [1-8] R M Cyzer.*

LOVE BLUES (USA) BHB 58f70a **RR 45f 70a** 4991[14]
3 b g Hansel (USA) 12.6f **(78)** - Jolie Bold (USA) (Bold Forbes (USA)) 8.9f **(59)**
Form - 3211420180000
Record 1999 - 1st:3 2nd:2 3rd:0 Ran:12
Pre1999 - 1st:0 2nd:0 3rd:1 Ran:5
Win Prizemoney £8,349 *Total Prizemoney* £11,366
Wins * 1999 Aug Carlis (FRM) H 12f 67 69
*** 1999** *Jan Lingfi (STD) 10f 69*
*** 1999** *Jan Wolver (STD) 9.4f 70* <
1999 Turf 1-8: (8f 2, 10f, 12f 1-5) (g-s, gd 2, g-f, frm 1-4) 1999 AW 2-4: (8f, 9f 1-1, 10f 1-1, 12f) (Equi 1-1, Fibr 1-3)
Strong, above-average gelding, effective 8 to 12f, acts on gd to frm - acts on AW, has worn blinkers, favours tight tracks. Turf high 69 (began Jly) - 1st of 4 giving 16lb to Manzoni (2 Aug Carlisle RF 3292). AW high 70 - 1st of 7 giving 5lb to Scarlet Sceptre (23 Jan Wolverhampton RF 0153) - also 1st of 5 getting 21lb from Roi de Danse (30 Jan Lingfield RF 0195). An improved sort on sand, he won a fair handicap at Carlisle on firm ground over a mile and a half. **M Johnston [3-17] M Doyle.*

LOVE CROWN (CAN) RR 963[P]
3 br c Chief's Crown (USA) 10.2f **(75)** - With Style (CAN) (Smarten (USA))
Form - P
Record 1999 - 1st:0 2nd:0 3rd:0 Ran:1
1999 Turf 0-1: (12f) (g-f)
Workmanlike, currently very poor colt. **M Johnston [0-1] M Doyle.*

LOVE DIAMONDS (IRE) BHB 49f72a **RR 49f 72a** 5135[9]
3 b g Royal Academy (USA) 7.8f **(77)** - Baby Diamonds (Habitat) 9.4f **(70)**
Form - 22132124500002530
Record 1999 - 1st:1 2nd:3 3rd:1 Ran:14
Pre1999 - 1st:1 2nd:2 3rd:1 Ran:8
Win Prizemoney £5,635 *Total Prizemoney* £12,054
Wins 1999 *Jan Lingfi (STD) H 8f 62 76+* <
1998 *Dec Lingfi (STD) H 8f 56 58*
1999 Turf 0-9: (8f 8, 10f) (gd 5, g-f, frm 2, hrd) 1999 AW 1-5: (8f 1-5) (Equi 1-3, Fibr 2)
Scopey, above-average gelding, effective 8f, - acts on AW, best on Equi, has worn blinkers, prefers left handed tracks, favours tight tracks. Turf high 52. AW high 79 - 2nd of 6 giving 11lb to Lincoln Dean (23 Jan Lingfield 8f Equi RF 0151) - also 1st of 6 giving 14lb to Malchik (12 Jan Lingfield RF 0081).
**N P Littmoden [0-1] P L Williams (from M Johnston [2-21] Jly 1999).*

LOVE DIVINE RR 70f 5207[2]
2 b f Diesis 9f **(80)** - La Sky (IRE) (Law Society (USA)) 9.9f **(70)**
Form - 2
Record 1999 - 1st:0 2nd:1 3rd:0 Ran:1
Win Prizemoney £0 *Total Prizemoney* £1,010
1999 Turf 0-1: (7f) (g-s)
Currently above-average filly. (1st run) - 2nd of 20 getting 5lb from Hopeful Light (5 Nov Doncaster 7f g-s RF 5207).
**H R A Cecil [0-1] Lordship Stud.*

LOVE KISS (IRE) BHB 55f **RR 41f** 5075[10]
4 b g Brief Truce (USA) 9.1f **(73)** - Pendulina (Prince Tenderfoot (USA)) 9f **(61)**
Form - 600
Record 1999 - 1st:0 2nd:0 3rd:0 Ran:3
Pre1999 - 1st:0 2nd:0 3rd:1 Ran:4
Win Prizemoney £0 *Total Prizemoney* £1,051
1999 Turf 0-3: (10f, 12f, 14f) (gd, frm 2)
Workmanlike, moderate gelding. Turf high 41 (began Spt).
**W Storey [0-3] K Knox (from M Johnston [0-4] May 1998).*

LOVE LANE (IRE) BHB 80f **RR 82f** 3942[7]
2 b c Mujtahid (USA) 7.4f **(69)** - Ibda (Mtoto)
Form - 573017
Record 1999 - 1st:1 2nd:0 3rd:1 Ran:6
Win Prizemoney £3,624 *Total Prizemoney* £4,179
Wins * 1999 Aug Beverl (GD) H 7.5f 79 82 <
1999 Turf 1-6: (5f 2, 6f 2, 7f 1-1, 8f) (g-f 1-4, frm 2)
Decent colt, effective 7f, acts on g-f, has worn blinkers. Turf high 82 - 1st of 12 giving 6lb to Timaru (12 Aug Beverley RF 3566).

**M Johnston [1-6] M Doyle.*

LOVE LETTERS BHB 85f **RR 91f** 3656[11]
2 ch f Pursuit of Love 9.5f **(69)** - Pinkie Rose (FR) (Kenmare (FR)) 6.5f **(72)**
Form - 23100
Record 1999 - 1st:1 2nd:1 3rd:1 Ran:5
Win Prizemoney £2,613 *Total Prizemoney* £4,258
Wins * 1999 Jly Warwic (G-F) 6.8f 91+ <
1999 Turf 1-5: (5f, 6f, 7f 1-3) (g-f 1-4, frm)
Useful filly. Turf high 91 - 1st of 10 giving 4lb to Annijaz (10 Jly Warwick RF 2727). In the frame in Pontefract maidens in her first two starts, she bolted up in a Warwick maiden auction event on her third start, but was well beaten afterwards.
**J E Banks [1-5] Giles Pritchard-Gordon.*

LOVELY ISLAND (IRE) BHB 48f53a **RR 37f 53a** 1492[6]
3 b f Inchinor 8.9f **(64)** - Lovely Me (IRE) **(56f 57a)** (Vision (USA)) 9f **(64)**
Form - 0404006
Record 1999 - 1st:0 2nd:0 3rd:0 Ran:4
Pre1999 - 1st:0 2nd:0 3rd:0 Ran:7
1999 Turf 0-3: (5f, 6f 2) (gd, g-f, hrd) 1999 AW 0-1: (8f) (Fibr)
Light-framed, fair filly, effective 5f, acts on g-f, has worn blinkers. Turf high 37. **R F JohnsonHoughton [0-11] Mrs J O'Halloran.*

LOVEMAN (USA) RR 87?f 560[4]
5 b g Alleged (USA) 11.8f **(81)** - Love Someone (USA) (Graustark) 10.1f **(70)**
Form - 4
Record 1999 - 1st:0 2nd:0 3rd:0 Ran:1
Win Prizemoney £0 *Total Prizemoney* £604
1999 Turf 0-1: (16f) (gd)
Currently useful gelding. **K A Morgan [1-3] T R Pryke.*

LOVE OPERA BHB 34f50a **RR 46f 50a** 4539[16]
4 ch f Pursuit of Love 9.5f **(69)** - Lets Fall In Love (USA) (Northern Baby (CAN)) 11.6f **(71)**
Form - 302224000
Record 1999 - 1st:0 2nd:3 3rd:0 Ran:7
Pre1999 - 1st:0 2nd:0 3rd:2 Ran:6
Win Prizemoney £0 *Total Prizemoney* £4,024
1999 Turf 0-2: (10f 2) (frm 2) 1999 AW 0-5: (6f 3, 7f 2) (Equi 2, Fibr 3)
Lengthy, fair filly, effective 5 to 7f, acts on g-f - acts on AW, has worn blinkers. Turf high 33 (began Aug). AW high 59 (1st run) - 2nd of 13 getting 5lb from Dryad (27 Jan Wolverhampton 6f Fibr RF 0174). Becoming disappointing.
**Ronald Thompson [0-2] I Fox (from J Berry [0-11] Mar 1999).*

LOVER'S LEAP BHB 81f **RR 81f** 3131[13]
3 b g Pursuit of Love 9.5f **(69)** - Anna Karietta (Precocious) 8.6f **(62)**
Form - 403120
Record 1999 - 1st:1 2nd:1 3rd:1 Ran:6
Pre1999 - 1st:0 2nd:1 3rd:0 Ran:2
Win Prizemoney £4,380 *Total Prizemoney* £8,245
Wins * 1999 Jun Newbur (GD) 7f 78 <
1999 Turf 1-6: (7f 1-3, 8f 2, 9f) (gd 1-2, g-f 2, frm 2)
Leggy, decent gelding, effective 7 to 8f, best at 7f, acts on gd to frm, best on g-f. Turf high 81 - 3rd of 14 to Harlequin Dancer (31 May Leicester 8f g-f RF 1601) - also 1st of 9 from Make Way (10 Jun Newbury RF 1886). Consistent. Made most to land a moderate Newbury maiden in June. **H Candy [1-8] The Earl Cadogan.*

LOVE'S DESIGN (IRE) BHB 75f **RR 67f** 5186[1]
2 b br c Pursuit of Love 9.5f **(69)** - Cephista **(56f 50a)** (Shirley Heights) 10.3f **(74)**
Form - 7631
Record 1999 - 1st:1 2nd:0 3rd:1 Ran:4
Win Prizemoney £3,225 *Total Prizemoney* £3,695
Wins * 1999 Nov Mussel (GD) 7.1f 67 <
1999 Turf 1-4: (6f 2, 7f 1-2) (g-s, g-f 1-1, frm, hrd)
Average colt, has worn blinkers. Turf high 67 (began Aug) - 1st of 13 from Hi Buddy (3 Nov Musselburgh RF 5186).
**J Noseda [1-4] Mrs Caroline Parker.*

LOVE YOU TOO BHB 95f **RR 93f** 4895[16]
2 ch f Be My Chief (USA) 10.2f **(62)** - Nagida **(69f)** (Skyliner) 7.3f **(53)**

Form - 10064540
Record 1999 - 1st:1 2nd:0 3rd:0 Ran:8
Win Prizemoney £3,777 *Total Prizemoney* £4,948
Wins * 1999 Jun Doncas (GD) 6f 64 <
1999 Turf 1-8: (5f 2, 6f 1-6) (gd 6, g-f 1-1, frm)
Useful filly. Turf high 90. She showed battling qualities when making a winning debut by the minimum margin at Doncaster, but has shown little since, albeit mainly in Pattern company.
**A Kelleway [1-8] Mike Perkins.*

LOWNDES COURT BHB 65f **RR 71f** 3834[4]
3 b f Salse (USA) 10.9f **(71)** - Basha (USA) (Chief's Crown (USA)) 9.8f **(72)**
Form - 44634
Record 1999 - 1st:0 2nd:0 3rd:1 Ran:5
Win Prizemoney £0 *Total Prizemoney* £1,336
1999 Turf 0-5: (7f, 10f 3, 12f) (gd, g-f, frm 3)
Light-framed, above-average filly. Turf high 71.
**M P Tregoning [0-5] Sheikh Mohammed.*

LOW ON FUNDS (USA) RR 63f 3353[6]
2 b c Eagle Eyed (USA) - Miss Sanmar (USA) (Recitation (USA))
Form - 676
Record 1999 - 1st:0 2nd:0 3rd:0 Ran:3
1999 Turf 0-3: (6f 2, 7f) (gd 2, frm)
Currently average colt. Turf high 63.
**T G Mills [0-3] Goodfellows Racing.*

LOYAL TOAST (USA) BHB 34f **RR 38f** 4602[7]
4 b g Lyphard (USA) 10.6f **(75)** - Lisieux (USA) (Steady Growth (CAN)) 9.9f **(78)**
Form - 640008007
Record 1999 - 1st:0 2nd:0 3rd:0 Ran:9
Pre1999 - 1st:1 2nd:0 3rd:0 Ran:7
Win Prizemoney £4,854 *Total Prizemoney* £5,162
Wins 1998 Jun Goodwo (G-F) H 9.9f 73 78 <
1999 Turf 0-8: (8f, 9f, 10f 4, 11f, 12f) (g-s, gd, g-f 3, frm 3) 1999 AW 0-1: (11f) (Fibr)
Well made, very moderate gelding, effective 8 to 10f, best at 10f, acts on frm, likes right handed tracks. **N Tinkler [0-7]*
W F Burton (from L M Cumani [1-9] Jun 1999).

L S LOWRY (USA) BHB 77f **RR 74f** 3378[1]
3 b g Thorn Dance (USA) 8.2f **(77)** - Queluz (USA) (Saratoga Six (USA)) 7f **(73)**
Form - 7211211
Record 1999 - 1st:4 2nd:2 3rd:0 Ran:7
Pre1999 - 1st:1 2nd:0 3rd:0 Ran:3
Win Prizemoney £22,717 *Total Prizemoney* £24,305
Wins * 1999 Aug Yarmou (FRM) C 10.1f 70
*** 1999** Jly Newmar (G-F) C 10f 74
*** 1999** Jly Lingfi (G-F) H 11.5f 70 72
*** 1999** May Newbur (G-F) C 10f 73
* 1998 Oct Newmar (GD) S 7f 78 <
1999 Turf 4-7: (8f, 10f 3-4, 11f 1-1, 12f) (hvy, g-f 1-1, frm 3-5)
Strong, above-average gelding, effective 7 to 12f, best at 10f, acts on g-f to frm, best on frm, has worn blinkers, excels at Newmarket. Turf high 74 - 1st of 9 giving 10lb to Future Coup (25 Jly Newmarket RF 3129) - also 1st of 13 giving 8lb to Capriolo (26 May Newbury RF 1500). Consistent.
**P F I Cole [5-10] Richard Green (Fine Paintings).*

LUANSHYA BHB 71f **RR 71f** 3468[13]
3 b f First Trump - Blues Indigo (Music Boy) 6.8f **(57)**
Form - 4210850
Record 1999 - 1st:1 2nd:1 3rd:0 Ran:7
Pre1999 - 1st:0 2nd:2 3rd:2 Ran:7
Win Prizemoney £2,882 *Total Prizemoney* £9,248
Wins * 1999 May Catter (FRM) 6f 79 <
1999 Turf 1-7: (5f, 6f 1-5, 7f) (sft, g-f, frm 1-5)
Scopey, above-average filly, effective 6f, acts on g-f to frm, best on frm. Turf high 79 - 1st of 11 from Bridge Pool (22 May Catterick RF 1387). Consistent. **R M Whitaker [1-14] The PBT Group.*

LUBOHENRIK (IRE) BHB 43f **RR 54f** 4877[21]
2 b f Perugino (USA) - Febian John (FR) (Shafaraz (FR))
Form - 7000
Record 1999 - 1st:0 2nd:0 3rd:0 Ran:4
1999 Turf 0-4: (5f 2, 6f 2) (gd 3, frm)
Fair filly, has worn blinkers. Turf high 54 (began Jly).
**I Semple [0-4] The Friar Tuck Racing Club.*

LUCAYAN BEACH BHB 60f55a **RR 51f 55a** 4805[18]
5 gr g Cyrano de Bergerac 7.3f **(58)** - Mrs Gray (Red Sunset) 8.2f **(63)**
Form - 0070
Record 1999 - 1st:0 2nd:0 3rd:0 Ran:4
Pre1999 - 1st:1 2nd:1 3rd:1 Ran:9
Win Prizemoney £2,866 *Total Prizemoney* £4,803
Wins * 1998 Jly Kempto (G-F) C 6f 68 <
1999 Turf 0-4: (6f 4) (gd, g-f 2, frm)
Fair gelding, effective 6f, acts on frm, has worn blinkers. Turf high 51. Becoming disappointing. **B Gubby [1-13] Brian Gubby Ltd.*

LUCIDO (IRE) BHB 114f **RR 120f** 5013a[3]
3 b c Royal Academy (USA) 7.8f **(77)** - Lady Ambassador (General Assembly (USA)) 10f **(68)**
Form - 11003
Record 1999 - 1st:2 2nd:0 3rd:1 Ran:5
Pre1999 - 1st:1 2nd:0 3rd:1 Ran:3
Win Prizemoney £44,547 *Total Prizemoney* £64,823
Wins * 1999 May Lingfi (G-F) G3 11.5f 120 <
*** 1999** Apr Newbur (G-F) 10f 105+
* 1998 Spt Salisb (HVY) 8f 82
1999 Turf 2-5: (10f 1-1, 11f 1-1, 12f 3) (gd 1-3, g-f 1-1)
Light-framed, very high-class colt, effective 11 to 12f, acts on gd. Turf high 120 - 1st of 5 from Daliapour (8 May Lingfield RF 1112). Inconsistent. A winner on heavy ground at two, he made a winning reappearance on much faster ground when beating Oath at Newbury, and followed up by taking the scalp of Daliapour in the Lingfield Derby Trial. Having been taken out of the Derby in the spring, he was supplemented for Epsom at a cost of £75,000, but beat just one home. Off the track for four months afterwards, he showed little at Newmarket on his return, but ran better when third in a Longchamp Group Two on his final start. There looks to be more to come. **J L Dunlop [3-8].*

Lucido became a real Derby prospect

LUCKY ARCHER BHB 71f **RR 73f** 4689[19]
6 b g North Briton 8.2f **(53)** - Preobrajenska (Double Form) 7.3f **(58)**
Form - 0610751550
Record 1999 - 1st:2 2nd:0 3rd:0 Ran:10
Pre1999 - 1st:3 2nd:4 3rd:3 Ran:26
Win Prizemoney £25,451 *Total Prizemoney* £32,733
Wins * 1999 Aug Bath (HRD) H 8f 71 73 <
*** 1999** Jun Yarmou (GD) H 8f 70 71
* 1998 Jun Carlis (G-S) H 8f 64 71
* 1998 May Yarmou (FRM) H 7f 55 67
* 1998 May Nottin (FRM) H 8.2f 55 59

1999 Turf 2-10: (7f 2, 8f 2-8) (gd 1-2, g-f 3, frm 1-5)
Above-average gelding, effective 7 to 8f, best at 8f, acts on gd to frm, best on frm, has worn blinkers, likes left handed tracks, prefers tight tracks, excels at Beverley, likes Bath and Yarmouth. Turf high 73 - 5th of 15 giving 13lb to Mr Bergerac (22 Aug Bath 8f frm RF 3831) - also 1st of 10 giving 14lb to Sandicliffe (3 Aug Bath RF 3310). He always runs a game race, attacking from the front.
**J M Bradley [5-22] The Parishioners (from C E Brittain [0-14] Oct 1996).*

LUCKY BEGONIA (IRE) BHB 42f70a RR 48f 70a 4597[15]

6 br m Simply Great (FR) 11.9f **(61)** - Hostess (Be My Guest (USA)) 9.3f **(67)**
Form - 753000
Record 1999 - 1st:0 2nd:0 3rd:1 Ran:6
Pre1999 - 1st:4 2nd:5 3rd:0 Ran:23
Win Prizemoney £10,246 *Total Prizemoney* £15,048
Wins * 1998 *Aug Southw (STD) H* *12f* *65* *68* <
* 1998 Jun Mussel (SFT) 12f 46
* 1998 *May Southw (STD) H* *11f* *55* *60*
* 1998 *Mar Southw (STD) H* *8f* *52* *54*
1999 Turf 0-5: (10f 2, 11f, 12f 2) (hvy, gd 2, g-f, frm) 1999 AW 0-1: (12f) (Fibr)
Average mare, effective 11 to 12f, best at 12f, acted on frm - acted on Fibr, liked left handed tracks, preferred tight tracks. Turf high 48. (DEAD)
**A W Carroll [4-17] Serafino Agodino (from W J Musson [0-8] Nov 1997).*

LUCKY COVE BHB 68f64a RR 67f 64a 2311[3]

3 gr c Lugana Beach 7f **(63)** - Port Na Blath (On Your Mark) 7.7f **(58)**
Form - 003083
Record 1999 - 1st:0 2nd:0 3rd:2 Ran:6
Pre1999 - 1st:0 2nd:1 3rd:2 Ran:5
Win Prizemoney £0 *Total Prizemoney* £2,555
1999 Turf 0-5: (5f 5) (sft, gd 3, frm) 1999 AW 0-1: (5f) (Fibr)
Leggy, average colt, effective 5f, acts on gd - acts on Fibr. Turf high 67 - 3rd of 16 to Francport (8 May Beverley 5f gd RF 1102). Becoming disappointing. **B A McMahon [0-11] J R Smith.*

LUCKY DREAM (FR) RR 112f 4245a[5]

5 b h Homme de Loi (IRE) - Lady Of The House (Habitat) 9.4f **(70)**
Form - 115
1999 Turf 2-3: (12f, 13f 1-1, 15f 1-1) (gd 2-3)
Group-class colt, effective 12 to 16f, best at 15f, acts on sft to gd, best on gd, prefers right handed tracks, likes Longchamp and Chantilly. Turf high 111 (1st run) - 1st of 9 giving 4lb to Turbotiere (15 Jun Chantilly RF 2280a) - also 1st of 6 from Palio Sky (24 Jly Maisons-Laffitte RF 3231a). Consistent. Effective from a mile and a half upward, he stops in front and needs to be delivered as late as possible. Those tactics were executed to perfection in the Prix Maurice de Nieuil, and he will continue to hold his own if campaigned outside the top class. **H-A Pantall in FR [2-8].*

LUCKY GITANO (IRE) BHB 81f RR 81f 913[2]

3 b br c Lucky Guest - April Wind (Windjammer (USA)) 7f **(59)**
Form - 32
Record 1999 - 1st:0 2nd:1 3rd:1 Ran:2
Pre1999 - 1st:0 2nd:1 3rd:1 Ran:3
Win Prizemoney £0 *Total Prizemoney* £2,374
1999 Turf 0-2: (9f, 10f) (g-f, frm)
Workmanlike, decent colt. Turf high 81 (1st run) - 3rd of 14 giving 5lb to Tactful Remark (3 Apr Kempton 9f g-f RF 0572).
**J L Dunlop [0-5] Anamoine Ltd.*

LUCKY HEATHER (IRE) RR 59f 2549[9]

2 b f Soviet Lad (USA) 9.4f **(63)** - Idrak (Young Generation) 7.7f **(63)**
Form - 7600
Record 1999 - 1st:0 2nd:0 3rd:0 Ran:4
1999 Turf 0-4: (5f, 6f 3) (gd 2, frm, hrd)
Fair filly. Turf high 59. **R J Hodges [0-4] P Slade.*

LUCKY JUDGE RR 61f 3413[9]

2 b c Saddlers' Hall (IRE) 10.5f **(65)** - Lady Lydia (Ela-Mana-Mou) 10.1f **(70)**
Form - 0
Record 1999 - 1st:0 2nd:0 3rd:0 Ran:1
1999 Turf 0-1: (7f) (g-f)
Currently average colt. **W W Haigh [0-1] Miss M Swinbank.*

LUCKY LEGEND (IRE) RR 102f 2402a[1]

3 b c Fairy King (USA) 7.7f **(75)** - Lucky Dancer (FR) 00
Form - 2371
1999 Turf 1-4: (7f, 8f 1-3) (hvy 2, g-f, frm 1-1)
Very useful colt. Turf high 102. Used as a pacemaker in the Irish 2,000 Guineas, he is a useful miler but not Group class.
**A P O'Brien in IRE [1-4] Mrs John Magnier.*

LUCKY LINDA (IRE) BHB 53f RR 56f 1584[6]

3 b f Bluebird (USA) 7.9f **(71)** - Spectacular Dawn (Spectacular Bid (USA)) 11.2f **(76)**
Form - 06
Record 1999 - 1st:0 2nd:0 3rd:0 Ran:2
Pre1999 - 1st:0 2nd:0 3rd:0 Ran:3
1999 Turf 0-2: (10f 2) (sft, gd)
Scopey, fair filly. Turf high 51. **J L Dunlop [0-5] Peter Winfield.*

LUCKY LOVER (IRE) BHB 56f RR 56f 2277[11]

4 b br g Ballad Rock 7.2f **(63)** - Petticoat Lane (Ela-Mana-Mou) 10.1f **(70)**
Form - 7880
Record 1999 - 1st:0 2nd:0 3rd:0 Ran:4
Pre1999 - 1st:0 2nd:0 3rd:0 Ran:3
Win Prizemoney £0 *Total Prizemoney* £260
1999 Turf 0-4: (7f 2, 8f, 10f) (g-f 2, frm 2)
Scopey, fair gelding, effective 7f, acted on frm. Turf high 60 (1st run) - 7th of 20 giving 2lb to Samara Song (13 May Salisbury 7f frm RF 1191). (DEAD) **G B Balding [0-7] Ms Julia Doveton.*

LUCKY ME (IRE) BHB 34f50a RR 46df 50a 1951[14]

4 gr g Maledetto (IRE) - Silver Heart (Yankee Gold) 7.6f **(55)**
Form - 000
Record 1999 - 1st:0 2nd:0 3rd:0 Ran:3
Pre1999 - 1st:0 2nd:0 3rd:1 Ran:10
Win Prizemoney £0 *Total Prizemoney* £270
1999 Turf 0-2: (7f, 10f) (hvy, g-f) 1999 AW 0-1: (7f) (Equi)
Workmanlike, moderate gelding. Becoming disappointing.
**P Butler [0-3] A J Taaffe (from M H Tompkins [0-10] Oct 1998).*

LUCKY MELODY BHB 41f45a RR 41f 45a 3003[17]

2 b c Suluk (USA) - Impromptu Melody (IRE) **(46f)** (Mac's Imp (USA))
Form - 0330
Record 1999 - 1st:0 2nd:0 3rd:2 Ran:4
Win Prizemoney £0 *Total Prizemoney* £504
1999 Turf 0-2: (6f, 7f) (g-f, frm) 1999 AW 0-2: (5f, 6f) (Fibr 2)
Moderate colt. Turf high 41. AW high 34.
**B S Rothwell [0-4] S P Hudson.*

LUCKY MYST BHB 31f29a RR 35f 29a 2514[7]

4 b g Mystiko (USA) 7.7f **(59)** - Lucky Omen (Queen's Hussar) 11.6f **(58)**
Form - 000443057
Record 1999 - 1st:0 2nd:0 3rd:1 Ran:9
Pre1999 - 1st:0 2nd:0 3rd:1 Ran:5
Win Prizemoney £0 *Total Prizemoney* £808
1999 Turf 0-5: (12f 2, 14f, 16f 2) (hvy, g-s, gd, g-f, hrd) 1999 AW 0-4: (8f, 12f 2, 13f) (Equi 3, Fibr)
Workmanlike, very moderate gelding. Turf high 35. AW high 26.
**C E Brittain [0-14] R N Khan.*

LUCKY NEMO BHB 56f55a RR 46f 55a 4837[16]

3 b c Sabrehill (USA) 8.5f **(64)** - Lucky Omen (Queen's Hussar) 11.6f **(58)**
Form - 6321765180020
Record 1999 - 1st:2 2nd:2 3rd:1 Ran:13
Pre1999 - 1st:0 2nd:0 3rd:0 Ran:2
Win Prizemoney £4,762 *Total Prizemoney* £6,709
Wins 1999 Jun Lingfi (G-F) H 11.5f 63 64 <
1999 Mar Folkes (SFT) H 12f 55 62
1999 Turf 2-10: (10f 2, 11f 1-2, 12f 1-4, 14f, 15f) (hvy 1-2, gd 3, g-f 3, frm 1-2) 1999 AW 0-3: (8f 2, 10f) (Equi 3)
Neat, fair colt, effective 11 to 12f, best at 12f, acts on hvy to frm, likes tight tracks. Turf high 64 - 1st of 5 getting 2lb from Greyfield (26 Jun Lingfield RF 2327) - also 1st of 7 getting 5lb from Lady

Coldunell (31 Mar Folkestone RF 0534). AW high 57.
**Mrs L Richards [0-1] Mrs Lydia Richards (from C E Brittain [2-14] Spt 1999).*

LUCKY RASCAL (IRE) BHB 63a **RR 59f** 2470[8]
3 b g Indian Ridge 7.6f **(74)** - Chesnut Tree (USA) (Shadeed (USA)) 8.2f **(70)**
Form - 04778
Record 1999 - 1st:0 2nd:0 3rd:0 Ran:5
Pre1999 - 1st:0 2nd:0 3rd:0 Ran:2
Win Prizemoney £0 *Total Prizemoney* £214
1999 Turf 0-4: (8f 4) (gd 3, g-f) 1999 AW 0-1: (7f) (Equi)
Unfurnished, fair gelding, has worn blinkers. Turf high 59.
**B Hanbury [0-7] Abdullah Ali.*

LUCKY RED BHB 42f42a **RR 47f 42a** 3659[12]
3 b g Presidium 7.5f **(56)** - Judys Girl (IRE) (Simply Great (FR)) 8.2f **(65)**
Form - 0074700400
Record 1999 - 1st:0 2nd:0 3rd:0 Ran:7
Pre1999 - 1st:0 2nd:1 3rd:3 Ran:10
Win Prizemoney £0 *Total Prizemoney* £1,575
1999 Turf 0-7: (6f, 7f 2, 8f 2, 10f 2) (hvy, g-f, frm 5)
Light-framed, moderate gelding, effective 6 to 7f, acts on g-s to g-f, has worn blinkers. Turf high 47.
**Pat Mitchell [0-11] Mrs G Dunlop (from K McAuliffe [0-6] Oct 1998).*

LUCKY STAR BHB 57f **RR 65f** 4994[6]
2 b f Emarati (USA) 6.6f **(63)** - Child Star (FR) **(32f 39a)** (Bellypha) 9.8f **(73)**
Form - 766
Record 1999 - 1st:0 2nd:0 3rd:0 Ran:3
1999 Turf 0-3: (5f, 6f, 7f) (gd, g-f, frm)
Currently average filly. Turf high 65. **D Marks [0-3] D Marks.*

LUCKY SWEEP RR 58f 4840[4]
2 ch c Cadeaux Genereux 7.9f **(76)** - Phantom Gold **(115f)** (Machiavellian (USA))
Form - 64
Record 1999 - 1st:0 2nd:0 3rd:0 Ran:2
Win Prizemoney £0 *Total Prizemoney* £237
1999 Turf 0-2: (7f, 8f) (g-s, gd)
Currently fair colt. Turf high 58 (began Spt).
**R Hannon [0-2] The Queen.*

LUCKY TOUCH BHB 55a **RR 55a** 261[3]
6 ch g Broadsword (USA) - Solatia (Kalydon)
Form - 323
Record 1999 - 1st:0 2nd:1 3rd:2 Ran:3
Win Prizemoney £0 *Total Prizemoney* £1,430
1999 AW 0-3: (12f 2, 13f) (Equi, Fibr 2)
Fair gelding. AW high 58 (1st run) - 3rd of 7 giving 10lb to Spirit of The Nile (9 Jan Lingfield 13f Equi RF 0062).
**W R Muir [0-8] Ridgebarn Farm Stud.*

LUCKY UNO BHB 41f **RR 45f** 3291[6]
3 b c Rock City 8.8f **(62)** - Free Skip (Free State) 8.7f **(61)**
Form - 603006
Record 1999 - 1st:0 2nd:0 3rd:1 Ran:6
Pre1999 - 1st:0 2nd:0 3rd:0 Ran:3
Win Prizemoney £0 *Total Prizemoney* £533
1999 Turf 0-6: (5f 2, 6f, 7f 2, 10f) (sft, g-s, gd, g-f, frm 2)
Scopey, moderate colt. Turf high 58. **C Smith [0-9] Lucky Racing.*

LUCONIC RR 71f 2704[7]
3 b c Zafonic (USA) 9f **(83)** - Felucca (Green Desert (USA)) 8.6f **(78)**
Form - 67
Record 1999 - 1st:0 2nd:0 3rd:0 Ran:2
1999 Turf 0-2: (8f 2) (g-f 2)
Well made, currently above-average colt. Turf high 71.
**H R A Cecil [0-2] K Abdulla.*

LUCYLIAM (IRE) BHB 30f **RR 12f** 4530[12]
2 b f College Chapel - Style (Homing) 7.8f **(59)**
Form - 000
Record 1999 - 1st:0 2nd:0 3rd:0 Ran:3
1999 Turf 0-2: (6f 2) (g-s, frm) 1999 AW 0-1: (6f) (Fibr)
Currently poor filly. Turf high 12 (began Aug).
**J S Moore [0-3] Mrs H F Prendergast.*

LUCY MARIELLA BHB 69f **RR 71f** 3200[10]
3 b f Mystiko (USA) 7.7f **(59)** - Deanta in Eirinn (Red Sunset) 8.2f **(63)**
Form - 0120240
Record 1999 - 1st:1 2nd:2 3rd:0 Ran:7
Pre1999 - 1st:0 2nd:1 3rd:1 Ran:5
Win Prizemoney £3,184 *Total Prizemoney* £6,797
Wins * 1999 May Bright (FRM) H 6f 64 67 <
1999 Turf 1-7: (5f 3, 6f 1-3, 7f) (gd, g-f 2, frm 3, hrd 1-1)
Above-average filly, effective 5 to 6f, best at 5f, acts on g-f to hrd, best on g-f, has worn blinkers. Turf high 74 - also 1st of 15 giving 3lb to Celestial Bay (4 May Brighton RF 1023). Got off the mark in a modest maiden handicap at Brighton on very fast ground.
**G A Butler [1-7] Terry Barwick (from J R Arnold [0-5] Oct 1998).*

LUDERE (IRE) BHB 36f37a **RR 40f 37a** 2873[7]
4 ch g Desse Zenny (USA) 12f **(53)** - White Jasmin (Jalmood (USA)) 10.1f **(52)**
Form - 022477
Record 1999 - 1st:0 2nd:2 3rd:0 Ran:6
Pre1999 - 1st:1 2nd:1 3rd:2 Ran:17
Win Prizemoney £2,372 *Total Prizemoney* £8,140
Wins 1998 May Mussel (GD) C 12f 40 <
1999 Turf 0-6: (9f, 12f, 13f 2, 14f, 16f) (gd, g-f 3, frm 2)
Moderate gelding, effective 12 to 16f, best at 12f, acts on gd to g-f, best on g-f, has worn blinkers, prefers right handed tracks. Turf high 44 - 2nd of 16 getting 29lb from Hibernate (14 Jun Musselburgh 12f g-f RF 1980).
**P Monteith [0-14] P Monteith (from J Hetherton [1-6] May 1998).*

LUGANA LADY BHB 30f **RR 30f** 2622[11]
3 b f Lugana Beach 7f **(63)** - Mrs Bacon (Balliol) 5f **(43)**
Form - 0000
Record 1999 - 1st:0 2nd:0 3rd:0 Ran:4
Pre1999 - 1st:0 2nd:0 3rd:0 Ran:2
1999 Turf 0-3: (7f 2, 8f) (gd 2, g-f) 1999 AW 0-1: (10f) (Equi)
Scopey, very moderate filly. Turf high 30.
**D HaydnJones [0-6] Stephen Owen.*

LUJAIN (USA) BHB 115f **RR 120df** 2106[12]
3 b c Seeking the Gold (USA) 7.4f **(80)** - Satin Flower (USA) (Shadeed (USA)) 8.2f **(70)**
Form - 50
Record 1999 - 1st:0 2nd:0 3rd:0 Ran:2
Pre1999 - 1st:3 2nd:0 3rd:0 Ran:4
Win Prizemoney £80,199 *Total Prizemoney* £82,249
Wins 1998 Oct Newmar (gd) G1 6f 120++ <
1998 Spt York (GD) 6f 107++
1998 Jly Newmar (GD) 6f 90++
1999 Turf 0-2: (5f, 6f) (gd, g-f)
Well made, very high-class colt, effective 6f, acts on gd. Turf high 110. Like so many recent winners of the Middle Park Stakes, he failed to train on and had a miserable season. It will be interesting to see if connections persevere with him as a four-year-old.
**S bin Suroor [0-2] Godolphin (from D R Loder [3-4] Oct 1998).*

LULLABY RR 37f 3433[13]
2 b f Unfuwain (USA) 11.4f **(74)** - Heart's Harmony (Blushing Groom (FR)) 10.3f **(76)**
Form - 0
Record 1999 - 1st:0 2nd:0 3rd:0 Ran:1
1999 Turf 0-1: (7f) (frm)
Currently very moderate filly.
**J R Fanshawe [0-1] Mrs Denis Haynes.*

LUMINANT BHB 85f **RR 84f** 5048[2]
2 b c Lammtarra (USA) - Shimmering Sea (Slip Anchor) 9.8f **(73)**
Form - 521002
Record 1999 - 1st:1 2nd:2 3rd:0 Ran:6
Win Prizemoney £3,501 *Total Prizemoney* £5,791
Wins * 1999 Jly Cheste (G-F) 7f 84 <
1999 Turf 1-5: (6f, 7f 1-4) (hvy, gd, g-f 1-3) 1999 AW 0-1: (7f) (Fibr)
Decent colt, effective 6 to 7f, best at 7f, acts on hvy to g-f, best on g-f. Turf high 84 (began Jly) - 2nd of 14 giving 5lb to Mentiga (23 Oct Newbury 7f hvy RF 5048) - also 1st of 8 from Tigre (25 Jly

Chester RF 3126). **Sir Mark Prescott [1-6] Sturt Osborne House III.*

LUNAJAZ BHB 46f **RR 41f** 3911[12]

2 ch g Alhijaz 7.7f **(57)** - Lunagraphe (USA) (Time For A Change (USA))
Form - 000
Record 1999 - 1st:0 2nd:0 3rd:0 Ran:3
1999 Turf 0-3: (6f, 7f 2) (gd, g-f, frm)
Currently moderate gelding. Turf high 41.
**T M Jones [0-3] T M Jones.*

LUNALUX BHB 65f **RR 77f** 4895[12]

2 b f Emarati (USA) 6.6f **(63)** - Ragged Moon (Raga Navarro (ITY)) 8f **(64)**
Form - 0675634550
Record 1999 - 1st:0 2nd:0 3rd:1 Ran:10
Win Prizemoney £0 *Total Prizemoney* £551
1999 Turf 0-9: (5f 6, 6f 3) (gd 4, g-f, frm 4) 1999 AW 0-1: (5f) (Fibr)
Above-average filly, has worn blinkers. Turf high 77.
**C Smith [0-10] Mrs Julia Scott.*

LUNAR LORD BHB 41f **RR 40f** 3376[11]

3 b c Elmaamul (USA) 8.1f **(70)** - Cache (Bustino) 10.4f **(64)**
Form - 7750
Record 1999 - 1st:0 2nd:0 3rd:0 Ran:4
Pre1999 - 1st:0 2nd:0 3rd:0 Ran:3
1999 Turf 0-4: (8f 3, 10f) (sft, gd 2, frm)
Small, moderate colt. Turf high 40. **J S Moore [0-7] Alex Gorrie.*

LUNAR MUSIC BHB 40f37a **RR 42f 37a** 24[13]

5 b m Komaite (USA) 6.9f **(61)** - Lucky Candy (Lucky Wednesday) 8f **(50)**
Form - 00
Record 1999 - 1st:0 2nd:0 3rd:0 Ran:1
Pre1999 - 1st:3 2nd:1 3rd:2 Ran:33
Win Prizemoney £8,103 *Total Prizemoney* £9,906

Wins								
* 1998	Aug	Nottin	(G-F)	H	5.1f	34	42	
1996	Aug	Mussel	(G-F)	S	5f		80+	<
1996	Jly	Lingfi	(FRM)	S	5f		65+	

1999 AW 0-1: (6f) (Fibr)
Moderate filly, effective 5f, acts on gd, has worn blinkers (effectively).
**S R Bowring [1-12] Paul Dixon (from Ronald Thompson [0-8] Jly 1997).*

LUNAR PROSPECTOR (IRE) BHB 71f **RR 68df** 1561[6]

3 ch f Second Set (IRE) 9.2f **(67)** - Eastern Aura (IRE) (Ahonoora) 8.1f **(73)**
Form - 6
Record 1999 - 1st:0 2nd:0 3rd:0 Ran:1
Pre1999 - 1st:0 2nd:3 3rd:2 Ran:7
Win Prizemoney £0 *Total Prizemoney* £4,637
1999 Turf 0-1: (5f) (frm)
Scopey, average filly, has broken blood-vessels, effective 5f, acts on gd to g-f, best on g-f.
**M G Quinlan [0-1] Rous Racing Ltd (from C A Dwyer [0-7] Oct 1998).*

LUNCH PARTY BHB 59f **RR 55f** 4914[14]

7 b g Beveled (USA) 6.9f **(64)** - Crystal Sprite (Crystal Glitters (USA)) 11.3f **(79)**
Form - 4511020060
Record 1999 - 1st:2 2nd:1 3rd:0 Ran:10
Pre1999 - 1st:6 2nd:2 3rd:1 Ran:23
Win Prizemoney £24,936 *Total Prizemoney* £28,902

Wins								
* 1999	Jun	Thirsk	(G-F)	H	7f	62	64	<
* 1999	May	Catter	(FRM)		7f		62	
* 1998	Aug	Catter	(G-F)	H	7f	60	63	
* 1998	May	Catter	(G-S)	H	7f	52	57	
* 1998	May	Mussel	(G-F)	H	7.1f	47	49	
1997	Nov	Mussel	(G-S)	H	8f	40	49	
1997	Spt	Yarmou	(FRM)	H	7f	38	42	
1996	May	Thirsk	(G-F)	S	7f		57+	

1999 Turf 2-10: (7f 2-10) (gd 4, g-f 2, frm 2-4)
Fair gelding, effective 7 to 8f, best at 7f, acts on gd to frm, likes left handed tracks, favours tight tracks, excels at Thirsk and likes Catterick. Turf high 65 - 2nd of 12 to Sycamore Lodge (21 Jly Catterick 7f g-f RF 3004) - also 1st of 12 giving 3lb to Hakeem (15 Jun Thirsk RF 2007). He seems to be well suited by a turning seven. **J Berry [5-20] S Aitken (from D Nicholls [3-13] Nov 1997).*

LUVADUCK BHB 70f **RR 73f** 3872[14]

3 b f Pursuit of Love 9.5f **(69)** - Pillowing (Good Times (ITY)) 6.6f **(54)**
Form - 5480
Record 1999 - 1st:0 2nd:0 3rd:0 Ran:4
Win Prizemoney £0 *Total Prizemoney* £204
1999 Turf 0-4: (7f, 8f 3) (g-s, g-f 2, frm)
Workmanlike, above-average filly. Turf high 73 - 4th of 14 to Greenstone (3 May Warwick 8f frm RF 1017).
**C G Cox [0-1] Mrs Zara Campbell Harris & TH Luckock (from M J Heaton-Ellis [0-3] May 1999).*

LUZ BAY (IRE) BHB 73f69a **RR 73f 69a** 4036[7]

3 b g Tenby 10.4f **(76)** - Cabcharge Princess (IRE) **(51f)** (Rambo Dancer (CAN))
Form - 5164322127
Record 1999 - 1st:2 2nd:3 3rd:1 Ran:9
Pre1999 - 1st:0 2nd:0 3rd:0 Ran:3
Win Prizemoney £5,523 *Total Prizemoney* £9,509

Wins								
* 1999	Aug	Leices	(G-F)		11.8f		72	<
* 1999	Apr	Warwic	(GD)	C	12.5f		67+	

1999 Turf 2-9: (10f 2, 11f, 12f 1-4, 13f 1-1, 16f) (sft, gd 1-3, g-f 1-1, frm 4)
Leggy, above-average gelding, effective 10 to 13f, best at 12f, acts on gd to frm, often wears blinkers (extremely effectively), favours tight tracks, excels at Windsor. Turf high 73 - 2nd of 6 getting 6lb from Anemos (13 Aug Nottingham 10f gd RF 3627) - also 1st of 5 giving 3lb to Red May (4 Aug Leicester RF 3362). Consistent.
**R Charlton [2-12] S M De Zoete.*

LUZERN BHB 81f **RR 74f** 573[7]

3 ch c Selkirk (USA) 7.9f **(76)** - Luana **(94f)** (Shaadi (USA))
Form - 7
Record 1999 - 1st:0 2nd:0 3rd:0 Ran:1
Pre1999 - 1st:0 2nd:0 3rd:1 Ran:3
Win Prizemoney £0 *Total Prizemoney* £525
1999 Turf 0-1: (7f) (g-f)
Unfurnished, above-average colt. **C E Brittain [0-4] Saeed Manana.*

LV GIRL (IRE) BHB 51f **RR 49f** 5156[11]

3 ch f Mukaddamah (USA) 7.6f **(74)** - Penny Fan **(34f)** (Nomination) 7f **(60)**
Form - 40425048040
Record 1999 - 1st:0 2nd:1 3rd:0 Ran:11
Pre1999 - 1st:0 2nd:0 3rd:0 Ran:4
Win Prizemoney £0 *Total Prizemoney* £1,617
1999 Turf 0-11: (6f, 7f 4, 8f 6) (sft, g-s, gd 4, g-f 3, frm 2)
Light-framed, moderate filly, effective 6 to 8f, acts on sft to frm, has worn blinkers. Turf high 62 - 2nd of 10 giving 4lb to Lord Rochester (24 Jun Salisbury 8f frm RF 2276). Has been running very consistently this term in moderate events without being able to find an opportunity. All ground comes alike to her.
**G B Balding [0-15] Mrs C A Richardson.*

LYCIAN (IRE) BHB 59f70a **RR 59f 70a** 4094[15]

4 b g Lycius (USA) 8.8f **(71)** - Perfect Time (IRE) (Dance of Life (USA)) 7f **(66)**
Form - 2151530621200
Record 1999 - 1st:2 2nd:2 3rd:1 Ran:11
Pre1999 - 1st:3 2nd:2 3rd:1 Ran:11
Win Prizemoney £17,463 *Total Prizemoney* £23,243

Wins								
* 1999	Jun	Goodwo	(G-F)	H	9f	56	60	
* **1999**	*Jan*	*Lingfi*	*(STD)*	*H*	*8f*	*63*	*70*	<
* 1998	*Dec*	*Lingfi*	*(STD)*	*H*	*8f*	*58*	*63*	
* 1998	Jly	Bright	(G-F)	H	8f	52	57	
* 1998	May	Bath	(G-F)	H	8f	47	48	

1999 Turf 1-7: (8f 5, 9f 1-2) (gd, g-f 2, frm 1-3, hrd) 1999 AW 1-4: (7f, 8f 1-3) (Equi 1-3, Fibr)
Well made, above-average gelding, effective 8 to 9f, best at 8f, acts on frm - acts on Equi, likes left handed tracks, prefers tight tracks, excels at Lingfield. Turf high 60. AW high 70 - 1st of 12 giving 9lb to Teofilio (28 Jan Lingfield RF 0181).
**J A R Toller [5-18] A Ilsley (from Sir Mark Prescott [0-4] Oct 1997).*

LYNDAH CHARLOTTE (IRE) BHB 48f **RR 45f** 5187[14]
2 ch f Case Law 6f **(64)** - Elanmatina (IRE) (Burslem) 8.8f **(53)**
Form - 50000
Record 1999 - 1st:0 2nd:0 3rd:0 Ran:5
1999 Turf 0-5: (5f 4, 8f) (gd 2, frm 3)
Moderate filly. Turf high 50 (began Jly). **J J O'Neill [0-5] J B Gilruth.*

LYNTON LAD BHB 66f57a **RR 65f 57a** 2224[5]
7 b g Superpower 6.6f **(58)** - House Maid (Habitat) 9.4f **(70)**
Form - 737125
Record 1999 - 1st:1 2nd:1 3rd:1 Ran:6
Pre1999 - 1st:2 2nd:4 3rd:1 Ran:23
Win Prizemoney £10,994 *Total Prizemoney* £23,026
Wins * 1999 May Ayr (GD) H 8f 57 56
1999 Turf 1-4: (8f 1-4) (gd 1-3, frm) 1999 AW 0-2: (6f, 8f) (Fibr 2)
Average gelding, effective 8f, acts on gd to frm, best on gd, has worn blinkers (extremely effectively). Turf high 65 - 2nd of 14 giving 2lb to I Can't Remember (7 Jun Pontefract 8f gd RF 1790) - also 1st of 20 giving 24lb to Pipiji (21 May Ayr RF 1366). AW high 38. Inconsistent.
**E J Alston [1-6] Miss Kim Jones (from C P E Brooks [0-20] Jly 1997).*

LYRIC BHB 54f **RR 58f** 4625[8]
2 ch f Lycius (USA) 8.8f **(71)** - River Jig (USA) (Irish River (FR)) 8.6f **(78)**
Form - 46008
Record 1999 - 1st:0 2nd:0 3rd:0 Ran:5
Win Prizemoney £0 *Total Prizemoney* £293
1999 Turf 0-5: (6f 2, 7f 2, 8f) (g-s, g-f 2, frm 2)
Fair filly, has worn blinkers. Turf high 58 (began Jly). **P F I Cole [0-5] H R H Prince Fahd Salman.*

LYRICAL LEGACY (IRE) BHB 49f **RR 33f** 4903[11]
2 ch f Common Grounds 8.1f **(66)** - Lyric Junction (IRE) (Classic Secret (USA))
Form - 070
Record 1999 - 1st:0 2nd:0 3rd:0 Ran:3
1999 Turf 0-3: (5f 2, 6f) (gd, g-f, frm)
Currently very moderate filly. Turf high 33 (began Aug).
**A P Jarvis [0-3] Grant & Bowman Ltd.*

LYRIST BHB 67f **RR 66f** 5133[17]
3 gr f Cozzene (USA) 10.1f **(87)** - La Llave (USA) (Risen Star (USA))
Form - 8400200110
Record 1999 - 1st:2 2nd:1 3rd:0 Ran:10
Pre1999 - 1st:0 2nd:0 3rd:0 Ran:1
Win Prizemoney £6,003 *Total Prizemoney* £7,117
Wins * 1999 Spt Bright (G-F) H 11.9f 62 66 <
*** 1999** Jly Bright (FRM) H 10f 56 63
1999 Turf 2-10: (7f, 8f 2, 9f, 10f 1-3, 11f, 12f 1-2) (g-s, gd 2, g-f, frm 2-6)
Scopey, average filly, effective 10 to 12f, acts on frm, often wears blinkers (extremely effectively), likes tight tracks. Turf high 66 - 1st of 14 giving 16lb to Stepstone (1 Spt Brighton RF 4078) - also 1st of 10 giving 13lb to Erith's Chill Wind (22 Jly Brighton RF 3025). She took time to find her form last term, but has gained two front-running victories at Brighton. **C E Brittain [2-11] Saeed Manana.*

LYSANDROS (IRE) BHB 73f76a **RR 72f 76a** 265[1]
5 b g Lycius (USA) 8.8f **(71)** - Trojan Relation (Trojan Fen) 8.1f **(62)**
Form - 2321
Record 1999 - 1st:1 2nd:2 3rd:1 Ran:4
Pre1999 - 1st:0 2nd:1 3rd:0 Ran:4
Win Prizemoney £3,606 *Total Prizemoney* £8,122
Wins * 1999 *Feb Wolver (STD) H 12f 67 70 <*
1999 AW 1-4: (12f 1-3, 16f) (Fibr 1-4)
Above-average gelding. AW high 70 - 1st of 8 getting 7lb from Failed To Hit (10 Feb Wolverhampton RF 0265). Consistent.
**Noel Chance [1-4] Premier Chance Racing (from J H M Gosden [0-4] Oct 1997).*

MA-ARIF (IRE) BHB 105f **RR 103f** 3928a[7]
3 b f Alzao (USA) 9.8f **(73)** - Taqreem (IRE) **(75df)** (Nashwan (USA))
Form - 1257
Record 1999 - 1st:1 2nd:1 3rd:0 Ran:4
Pre1999 - 1st:0 2nd:0 3rd:0 Ran:3
Win Prizemoney £7,327 *Total Prizemoney* £14,144
Wins * 1999 Jun Newmar (GD) H 7f 81 89 <
1999 Turf 1-4: (7f 1-1, 8f 2, 10f) (gd 1-2, g-f, frm)
Scopey, very useful filly, effective 8f, acts on frm. Turf high 103 - 5th of 8 to Ronda (7 Jly Newmarket 8f frm RF 2631). Upped in class after winning a handicap on her reappearance, she is genuine but not a Group filly. She is bred to stay beyond a mile.
**J H M Gosden [1-7].*

MAAS (IRE) BHB 52f60a **RR 51f 60a** 5113[8]
4 br c Elbio 9f **(62)** - Payne's Grey (Godswalk (USA)) 7.3f **(58)**
Form - 22008
Record 1999 - 1st:0 2nd:0 3rd:0 Ran:3
Pre1999 - 1st:0 2nd:2 3rd:0 Ran:6
Win Prizemoney £0 *Total Prizemoney* £1,651
1999 Turf 0-3: (5f, 6f 2) (gd 2, frm)
Fair colt, effective 6f, - acts on Equi. Turf high 51 (began Jly).
**P J Makin [0-9] Brian Brackpool.*

MABROOKAH BHB 65f **RR 65?f** 4790[4]
3 b f Deploy 11.4f **(67)** - Adorable Cherub (USA) (Halo (USA)) 10.6f **(75)**
Form - 00624
Record 1999 - 1st:0 2nd:1 3rd:0 Ran:5
Win Prizemoney £0 *Total Prizemoney* £1,251
1999 Turf 0-5: (8f 2, 9f, 10f 2) (g-s 3, frm, hrd)
Workmanlike, average filly. Turf high 65 - 2nd of 8 to Shanghai Lady (29 Spt Brighton 8f g-s RF 4631).
**K Mahdi [0-5] Hamad Al-Mutawa.*

MACARI BHB 19f37a **RR 29f 37a** 3565[12]
5 gr g Arzanni - View Halloa (Al Sirat (USA))
Form - 000
Record 1999 - 1st:0 2nd:0 3rd:0 Ran:2
Pre1999 - 1st:0 2nd:0 3rd:2 Ran:19
Win Prizemoney £0 *Total Prizemoney* £643
1999 Turf 0-2: (8f, 10f) (g-f 2)
Very moderate gelding, effective 12f, acts on g-f, likes left handed tracks. Turf high 29. Inconsistent. **B P J Baugh [0-25] Nigel Taylor.*

MAC BE LUCKY BHB 75f **RR 71f** 5209[11]
2 b c Magic Ring (IRE) 6.5f **(64)** - Take Heart (Electric) 10.1f **(61)**
Form - 320
Record 1999 - 1st:0 2nd:1 3rd:1 Ran:3
Win Prizemoney £0 *Total Prizemoney* £1,663
1999 Turf 0-3: (6f, 7f 2) (sft, g-s 2)
Currently above-average colt. Turf high 71 (1st run) (began Spt) - 3rd of 11 to Jathaab (25 Spt Haydock 7f g-s RF 4551).
**J Noseda [0-3] Michael McDonnell.*

MACCA LUNA (IRE) BHB 70f **RR 70f** 5221[9]
4 b f Kahyasi 12.9f **(74)** - Medicosma (USA) (The Minstrel (CAN)) 10f **(72)**
Form - 78262113600
Record 1999 - 1st:2 2nd:2 3rd:1 Ran:11
Pre1999 - 1st:1 2nd:0 3rd:0 Ran:3
Win Prizemoney £9,179 *Total Prizemoney* £11,989
Wins * 1999 Spt Mussel (G-F) 12f 62 <
*** 1999** Aug Beverl (GD) H 12f 61 61
1997 Spt Hamilt (GD) 8.3f 62+
1999 Turf 2-10: (10f 2, 12f 2-7, 14f) (sft, gd 3, frm 2-6) 1999 AW 0-1: (12f) (Fibr)
Scopey, above-average filly, effective 10 to 12f, best at 12f, acts on gd to frm, best on frm, prefers tight tracks. Turf high 70 - 3rd of 14 getting 3lb from Heart (17 Spt Ayr 10f gd RF 4377) - also 1st of 8 from Linea-G (2 Spt Musselburgh RF 4088). She went a long time without winning, but gained consecutive wins at Beverley and Musselburgh during the autumn.
**Miss S E Hall [2-11] B McAllister (from M H Tompkins [1-3] May 1998).*

MAC FLYER (IRE) RR 3588a[3]
2 b c Nicolotte - Ellendellendoo (IRE) (Ela-Mana-Mou) 10.1f **(70)**
Form - 23
Record 1999 - 1st:0 2nd:1 3rd:1 Ran:2
Win Prizemoney £0 *Total Prizemoney* £3,937
1999 Turf 0-2: (7f, 8f) (sft, g-s)
Currently very poor colt. (began Jly) - 3rd of 5 to Iron Eagle (7 Aug Maia 7f sft RF 3588a). **M Quinlan [0-2].*

MACGILLYCUDDY (IRE) BHB 41f **RR 38f** 1813^{15}
10 bb g Petorius 8f **(66)** - My Bonnie (Highland Melody) 6.3f **(55)**
Form - 0
Record 1999 - 1st:0 2nd:0 3rd:0 Ran:1
Pre1999 - 1st:0 2nd:1 3rd:1 Ran:19
Win Prizemoney £0 *Total Prizemoney* £1,288
1999 Turf 0-1: (7f) (g-f)
Very moderate gelding, often wears blinkers. Consistent.
**Mrs P N Dutfield [0-10] Mrs Nerys Dutfield (from Patrick Prendergast in IRE [0-10] Oct 1996).*

MAC HALL RR $2095a^{3}$
2 b c Saddlers' Hall (IRE) 10.5f **(65)** - Irish Impulse (USA) (Irish River (FR)) 8.6f **(78)**
Form - 3
Record 1999 - 1st:0 2nd:0 3rd:1 Ran:1
Win Prizemoney £0 *Total Prizemoney* £1,312
1999 Turf 0-1: (7f) (sft)
Currently very poor colt. **M Quinlan [0-1].*

MACHAMILLION (USA) RR 57f 4382^{14}
3 ch c Machiavellian (USA) 9.8f **(83)** - Gracieuse (USA) (Nureyev (USA)) 8.7f **(78)**
Form - 0
Record 1999 - 1st:0 2nd:0 3rd:0 Ran:1
1999 Turf 0-1: (8f) (frm)
Scopey, currently fair colt. **P W Chapple-Hyam [0-1] John Gunther.*

MACHE BHB 45f **RR 44f** 4901^{19}
2 b g Noble Patriarch 12.2f **(43)** - Shalta (FR) (Targowice (USA)) 11.4f **(70)**
Form - 000
Record 1999 - 1st:0 2nd:0 3rd:0 Ran:3
1999 Turf 0-3: (7f, 8f 2) (gd, g-f, frm)
Currently moderate gelding. Turf high 44 (began Spt).
**R D E Woodhouse [0-3] R D E Woodhouse.*

MACHIAVELLI BHB 69f **RR 65f** 2310^{6}
5 b g Machiavellian (USA) 9.8f **(83)** - Forest Blossom (USA) (Green Forest (USA)) 9.9f **(68)**
Form - 6
Record 1999 - 1st:0 2nd:0 3rd:0 Ran:1
Pre1999 - 1st:1 2nd:0 3rd:1 Ran:9
Win Prizemoney £3,615 *Total Prizemoney* £5,118
Wins 1997 Jly Pontef (GD) 12f 87 <
1999 AW 0-1: (12f) (Fibr)
Average gelding, has worn blinkers.
**G L Moore [3-14] B V & C J Pennick II (from H R A Cecil [1-6] Spt 1997).*

MACH ONE (FR) BHB 37f37a **RR 45f 37a** 498^{8}
4 b g Sanglamore (USA) 12.9f **(67)** - Douceur (USA) (Shadeed (USA)) 8.2f **(70)**
Form - 28708
Record 1999 - 1st:0 2nd:1 3rd:0 Ran:5
Pre1999 - 1st:0 2nd:0 3rd:0 Ran:3
Win Prizemoney £0 *Total Prizemoney* £623
1999 AW 0-5: (12f 4, 16f) (Fibr 5)
Scopey, moderate gelding, effective 12f, - acts on Fibr, has worn blinkers, likes left handed tracks, likes tight tracks. AW high 47 (1st run) - 2nd of 16 getting 16lb from Such Boldness (18 Jan Southwell 12f Fibr RF 0114). Becoming disappointing.
**Sir Mark Prescott [0-8] Mrs Amanda Shelton.*

MACHRIE BAY BHB 85f **RR 88f** 5049^{3}
2 b c Emarati (USA) 6.6f **(63)** - Fleeting Rainbow (Rainbow Quest (USA)) 10.4f **(75)**
Form - 083
Record 1999 - 1st:0 2nd:0 3rd:1 Ran:3
Win Prizemoney £0 *Total Prizemoney* £670
1999 Turf 0-3: (7f 2, 8f) (gd 3)
Currently useful colt. Turf high 88 (began Spt) - 3rd of 19 to Delius (25 Oct Leicester 8f gd RF 5049).
**J L Dunlop [0-3] Mrs Simon Boscawen.*

MACHUDI RR 42f 5005^{7}
2 b f Bluebird (USA) 7.9f **(71)** - Machaera (Machiavellian (USA))
Form - 7
Record 1999 - 1st:0 2nd:0 3rd:0 Ran:1
1999 Turf 0-1: (5f) (gd)
Currently moderate filly. **B A McMahon [0-1] Barouche Stud Ltd.*

MACKOOK (USA) BHB 85f **RR 80f** $555a^{5}$
7 b or br h Seeking the Gold (USA) 7.4f **(80)** - L'Incestueuse (USA) (Lypheor) 12f **(71)**
Form - 5
1999 AW 0-1: (10f) (Dirt)
Very useful horse, has worn blinkers.
**K McLaughlin in UAE [0-1] Saeed Maktoum Al Maktoum (from Sir Michael Stoute [1-7] Spt 1995).*

MACLOUD (IRE) RR 23f 3240^{9}
6 b g Mac's Imp (USA) 5.6f **(54)** - Cloud Nine (Skymaster) 8.7f **(71)**
Form - 00
Record 1999 - 1st:0 2nd:0 3rd:0 Ran:2
1999 Turf 0-2: (6f, 8f) (frm 2)
Currently little account gelding. Turf high 23 (began Jly).
**N A Graham [0-2] Mrs Lesley Graham.*

MAC RIVER (IRE) RR 79f $4511a^{1}$
2 b c Tenby 10.4f **(76)** - Direct Link (USA) (Super Concorde (USA)) 10.9f **(66)**
Form - 2381
Record 1999 - 1st:1 2nd:1 3rd:1 Ran:4
Win Prizemoney £4,556 *Total Prizemoney* £10,879
Wins * 1999 Spt Cascin (GD) 7.5f 78+ <
1999 Turf 1-4: (6f 2, 8f 1-2) (gd 1-3, g-f)
Above-average colt. Turf high 79 - also 1st of 5 from Panthere (16 Spt Cascine RF 4511a).
**M Quinlan [1-3] Dr Angelo Macchi (from M G Quinlan [0-1] Aug 1999).*

MAC'S DREAM (USA) BHB 44f42a **RR 48f 42a** 4156^{5}
4 b g Mister Frisky (USA) - Annie's Dream (USA) (Droll Role (USA))
Form - 0670070037205
Record 1999 - 1st:0 2nd:1 3rd:1 Ran:10
Pre1999 - 1st:0 2nd:0 3rd:0 Ran:7
Win Prizemoney £0 *Total Prizemoney* £976
1999 Turf 0-10: (6f 3, 7f, 8f 5, 9f) (g-s, gd, g-f 2, frm 5, hrd)
Scopey, moderate gelding, effective 8f, acts on g-f. Turf high 48 - 2nd of 16 getting 12lb from Aix En Provence (4 Aug Yarmouth 8f g-f RF 3380). **W Jarvis [0-2] J R Barr (from A W Carroll [0-11] Aug 1999).*

MAC'S EXPRESS (IRE) BHB 78f **RR 77f** 3238^{9}
3 br g Mac's Imp (USA) 5.6f **(54)** - Almasa (Faustus (USA)) 10f **(58)**
Form - 33831700
Record 1999 - 1st:1 2nd:0 3rd:3 Ran:8
Win Prizemoney £4,110 *Total Prizemoney* £5,306
Wins * **1999** Jun Newmar (G-F) H 5f 77 81 <
1999 Turf 1-8: (5f 1-7, 6f) (sft, gd 2, g-f 1-3, frm 2)
Above-average gelding, was effective 5f, acted on sft to frm. Turf high 90 (1st run) - 3rd of 12 to Tayif (5 Apr Nottingham 5f sft RF 0588) - also 1st of 7 getting 1lb from Jackie's Baby (25 Jun Newmarket RF 2307). (DEAD) **A P Jarvis [1-8] Grant & Bowman Ltd.*

MAC TENBY (IRE) RR $4515a^{3}$
2 b c Tenby 10.4f **(76)** - Siva (FR) (Bellypha) 9.8f **(73)**
Form - 3
Record 1999 - 1st:0 2nd:0 3rd:1 Ran:1
Win Prizemoney £0 *Total Prizemoney* £1,750
1999 Turf 0-1: (8f) (g-s)
Juvenile colt. - 3rd of 9 to Stracch (18 Spt San Siro 8f g-s RF 4515a). **M Quinlan [0-1].*

MADAGASCAR BHB 38a **RR 15f** 3550^{14}
3 b f Puissance 7.1f **(60)** - Tabyan (USA) (Topsider (USA)) 8.3f **(71)**
Form - 000400
Record 1999 - 1st:0 2nd:0 3rd:0 Ran:6
1999 Turf 0-5: (6f 2, 7f 2, 8f) (g-f 3, frm 2) 1999 AW 0-1: (8f) (Fibr)
Workmanlike, moderate filly, has worn blinkers. Turf high 38.
**J W Hills [0-6] Mountgrange Stud.*

MADAM ALISON BHB 80f **RR 84f** 4698^{6}
3 b f Puissance 7.1f **(60)** - Copper Burn (Electric) 10.1f **(61)**
Form - 01236526

Record 1999 - 1st:1 2nd:2 3rd:1 Ran:8
Pre1999 - 1st:1 2nd:0 3rd:0 Ran:5
Win Prizemoney £10,228 *Total Prizemoney* £14,757
Wins * **1999** Jun Newmar (G-F) H 8f 72 76 <
* 1998 Oct Leices (HVY) 6f 71
1999 Turf 1-8: (7f 2, 8f 1-6) (g-s, gd, g-f 1-1, frm 5)
Strong, decent filly, effective 8f, acts on gd to frm, best on frm. Turf high 84 - 2nd of 11 getting 5lb from Khibrah (15 Spt Sandown 8f gd RF 4329) - also 1st of 10 getting 23lb from Selfish (26 Jun Newmarket RF 2346). Consistent. Showed improved form to land a fast-ground handicap at Newmarket, having won her maiden as a juvenile in heavy conditions. **R Hannon [2-13] William Kelly.*

MADAME CHINNERY BHB 55f56a RR 30f 56a 78[6]

5 b m Weldnaas (USA) 8.4f **(55)** - Bel Esprit (Sagaro) 9.7f **(55)**
Form - 666
Record 1999 - 1st:0 2nd:0 3rd:0 Ran:1
Pre1999 - 1st:2 2nd:4 3rd:0 Ran:20
Win Prizemoney £6,734 *Total Prizemoney* £10,982
Wins 1998 Jun Haydoc (GD) C 11.9f 67
1996 Spt Yarmou (GD) H 7f 72 77 <
1999 AW 0-1: (13f) (Equi)
Very moderate filly, effective 12 to 14f, acts on gd - acts on Fibr, has worn blinkers, likes left handed tracks, favours tight tracks. Consistent.
**C Weedon [0-7] Atlantic Foods Ltd (from J M P Eustace [2-15] Jly 1998).*

MADAME GENEREUX RR 52f 4408[11]

2 ch f Cadeaux Genereux 7.9f **(76)** - Bright Spells (Salse (USA)) 7.5f **(66)**
Form - 0
Record 1999 - 1st:0 2nd:0 3rd:0 Ran:1
1999 Turf 0-1: (6f) (frm)
Currently fair filly.
**N A Graham [0-1] Association Des Hommes Genereux.*

MADAME MAXI BHB 53f39a RR 56f 39a 4441[9]

5 ch m Ron's Victory (USA) 9.2f **(52)** - New Pastures (Formidable (USA)) 9.2f **(63)**
Form - 056300
Record 1999 - 1st:0 2nd:0 3rd:1 Ran:6
Pre1999 - 1st:1 2nd:1 3rd:0 Ran:7
Win Prizemoney £2,706 *Total Prizemoney* £3,972
Wins * 1998 Spt Bath (G-S) H 8f 52 54 <
1999 Turf 0-3: (8f 3) (g-f 2, frm) 1999 AW 0-3: (8f 3) (Fibr 3)
Fair filly, effective 8f, acts on g-f to frm, best on frm, has worn blinkers, favours tight tracks. Turf high 56 (1st run) (began Aug) - 3rd of 12 getting 16lb from Minetta (28 Aug Windsor 8f frm RF 3985). AW high 27.
**H S Howe [1-12] George Searle (from P R Hedger [0-4] Spt 1998).*

MADAME SISU RR 49f 2950[7]

2 b f Emarati (USA) 6.6f **(63)** - About Face (Midyan (USA)) 6f **(60)**
Form - 07
Record 1999 - 1st:0 2nd:0 3rd:0 Ran:2
1999 Turf 0-2: (5f 2) (frm 2)
Currently moderate filly. Turf high 49.
**A P Jarvis [0-2] Grant & Bowman Ltd.*

MADAM LUCY BHB 30f30a RR 10f 30a 436[9]

5 ch m Efisio 7.7f **(69)** - Our Aisling (Blakeney) 10.5f **(64)**
Form - 00
Record 1999 - 1st:0 2nd:0 3rd:0 Ran:2
Pre1999 - 1st:1 2nd:1 3rd:2 Ran:19
Win Prizemoney £2,007 *Total Prizemoney* £3,270
Wins 1997 *Jly Wolver (STD) C 9.4f 50* <
1999 AW 0-2: (12f, 14f) (Fibr 2)
Poor filly, has worn blinkers. AW high 4. Becoming disappointing.
**Mrs N Macauley [0-2] Inthebing Ltd (from J L Spearing [0-13] Jun 1998).*

MADEMOISELLE PARIS BHB 46f RR 60f 5150[6]

2 gr f Paris House 5.9f **(64)** - Heather Honey (Insan (USA))
Form - 03006
Record 1999 - 1st:0 2nd:0 3rd:1 Ran:5
Win Prizemoney £0 *Total Prizemoney* £314

1999 Turf 0-5: (5f, 6f 2, 7f 2) (sft, g-s, gd 2, frm)
Average filly. Turf high 60. **A W Carroll [0-5] R T C Racing.*

MADGE'S PET BHB 22f RR 7f 5153[16]

5 b m Precious Metal 9.3f **(42)** - Lucky Lena (Leander)
Form - 00
Record 1999 - 1st:0 2nd:0 3rd:0 Ran:2
Pre1999 - 1st:0 2nd:0 3rd:0 Ran:2
1999 Turf 0-2: (10f, 12f) (g-s, gd)
Very poor filly, has worn blinkers. (began Spt).
**B D Leavy [0-3] Mrs C G Heath (from G Barnett [0-2] Jly 1997).*

MADMAN'S MIRAGE (FR) BHB 55f60a RR 55f 60a 14[16]

4 b g Green Desert (USA) 7.8f **(78)** - Layaali (USA) (Diesis) 9.3f **(69)**
Form - 0
Record 1999 - 1st:0 2nd:0 3rd:0 Ran:1
Pre1999 - 1st:1 2nd:2 3rd:0 Ran:13
Win Prizemoney £2,085 *Total Prizemoney* £4,437
Wins 1998 *Feb Southw (STD) H 6f 60 78+* <
1999 AW 0-1: (8f) (Fibr)
Scopey, above-average gelding, effective 6 to 7f, - acts on AW, prefers left handed tracks, likes tight tracks.
**V Thompson [0-3] Mouldshaugh Farms Ltd (from M Johnston [1-11] Jun 1998).*

MADMUN (IRE) BHB 74f RR 74f 5113[1]

5 ch g Cadeaux Genereux 7.9f **(76)** - Kates Cabin (Habitat) 9.4f **(70)**
Form - 45521
Record 1999 - 1st:1 2nd:1 3rd:0 Ran:5
Pre1999 - 1st:0 2nd:1 3rd:2 Ran:5
Win Prizemoney £2,918 *Total Prizemoney* £7,132
Wins * **1999** Oct Windso (SFT) 6f 74 <
1999 Turf 1-5: (6f 1-5) (sft, gd 1-2, g-f, frm)
Above-average gelding, effective 6f, acts on gd to frm, has worn blinkers. Turf high 74 - 1st of 21 giving 1lb to Touch of Fairy (28 Oct Windsor RF 5113). Consistent. Did not make his racecourse debut until four, however he seems to be going the right way for his skillful trainer, having twice run well in big sprint handicaps last term, before ending the season with a victory in a Windsor maiden. He seems effective on most types of ground.
**M P Tregoning [1-10] Hamdan Al Maktoum.*

MAESTEG BHB 32f RR 9f 2667[18]

3 b f Reprimand 8.2f **(63)** - Eluned May **(42df)** (Clantime)
Form - 000
Record 1999 - 1st:0 2nd:0 3rd:0 Ran:3
Pre1999 - 1st:0 2nd:0 3rd:0 Ran:2
1999 Turf 0-3: (6f 2, 8f) (sft, gd, frm)
Light-framed, very poor filly. Turf high 9.
**M J Fetherston-Godley [0-3] Derek D & Mrs Jean P Clee (from J W Hills [0-2] Spt 1998).*

MAESTERSINGER BHB 88f RR 81f 4872[11]

2 b c Piccolo - Madurai **(63f)** (Chilibang)
Form - 22271230
Record 1999 - 1st:1 2nd:4 3rd:1 Ran:8
Win Prizemoney £3,598 *Total Prizemoney* £9,581
Wins * **1999** Aug Windso (G-S) H 6f 78 75 <
1999 Turf 1-8: (6f 1-8) (g-s, gd 1-2, g-f 3, frm 2)
Decent colt, effective 6f, acts on gd to g-f, best on g-f. Turf high 81 - also 1st of 9 getting 15lb from Seven No Trumps (16 Aug Windsor RF 3683). Consistent. He has been very consistent so far, but has just a victory in a Windsor nursery to show for it. Suited by six furlongs. Sold to Macau for 31,000 gns.
**J L Dunlop [1-8] Miss Julia Bradford(Susan Racing).*

MAESTOSO RR 108f 4519a[2]

98 c Dashing Blade 7.9f **(80)** - Mensa (GER) (Lagunas)
Form - 2
1999 Turf 0-1: (10f) (gd)
Currently Pattern-class. (1st run) - 2nd of 12 giving 2lb to Catella (19 Spt Frankfurt 10f gd RF 4519a).
**A Schutz in GER [0-1] Gestut Hof Vesterberg.*

MAFTUN (USA) BHB 45f47a RR 48f 47a 283[P]

7 ch g Elmaamul (USA) 8.1f **(70)** - Allesheny (Be My Guest (USA)) 9.3f **(67)**

Form - 734P
Record 1999 - 1st:0 2nd:0 3rd:1 Ran:3
Pre1999 - 1st:2 2nd:6 3rd:3 Ran:32
Win Prizemoney £5,999 *Total Prizemoney* £14,026
Wins * 1997 *Feb Southw (STD) H 12f 54 62* <
* 1996 Jly Newcas (FRM) H 12.4f 52 57
1999 AW 0-3: (16f 3) (Fibr 3)
Fair gelding, effective 12 to 16f, best at 16f, acted on frm - acted on Fibr, favoured left handed tracks, favoured tight tracks. AW high 51 (1st run) - 3rd of 10 giving 21lb to Turrill House (8 Jan Southwell 16f Fibr RF 0051). (DEAD)
**G M Moore [2-33] Anmaf Partnership (from Major W R Hern [0-4] Spt 1995).*

MAGDA (IRE) BHB 88f **RR 91+f** 1331[6]
3 b f Turtle Island (IRE) - Pennine Drive (IRE) (Pennine Walk) 8.5f **(61)**
Form - 6
Record 1999 - 1st:0 2nd:0 3rd:0 Ran:1
Pre1999 - 1st:1 2nd:0 3rd:0 Ran:3
Win Prizemoney £3,214 *Total Prizemoney* £3,214
Wins * 1998 Oct Nottin (SFT) 8.2f 91+ <
1999 Turf 0-1: (10f) (gd)
Scopey, useful filly. (DEAD) **C E Brittain [1-4] B H Voak.*

MAGELLA BHB 53f **RR 49f** 4039[14]
2 b f Magic Ring (IRE) 6.5f **(64)** - Thatcherella **(65f)** (Thatching) 8f **(66)**
Form - 000
Record 1999 - 1st:0 2nd:0 3rd:0 Ran:3
1999 Turf 0-3: (5f 2, 6f) (gd, g-f, frm)
Moderate filly. Turf high 49 (began Jly). (DEAD)
**B J Meehan [0-3] J H Widdows.*

MAGELTA BHB 79f **RR 83f** 5129[3]
2 b c Magic Ring (IRE) 6.5f **(64)** - Pounelta (Tachypous) 8.6f **(55)**
Form - 043
Record 1999 - 1st:0 2nd:0 3rd:1 Ran:3
Win Prizemoney £0 *Total Prizemoney* £1,054
1999 Turf 0-3: (6f 3) (gd 2, frm)
Currently decent colt. Turf high 83 (began Jly).
**R Hannon [0-3] Peter Valentine.*

MAGENKO (IRE) BHB 54f **RR 48f** 5099[11]
2 ch c Forest Wind (USA) - Bebe Auction (IRE) (Auction Ring (USA)) 8.6f **(65)**
Form - 800
Record 1999 - 1st:0 2nd:0 3rd:0 Ran:3
1999 Turf 0-3: (6f 2, 7f) (gd 3)
Currently moderate colt. Turf high 48 (began Oct).
**M H Tompkins [0-3] Flint Fairyhouse Partnership.*

MAGHAARB BHB 95f **RR 97f** 3939[4]
3 ch f Machiavellian (USA) 9.8f **(83)** - Fida (IRE) (Persian Heights)
Form - 4414
Record 1999 - 1st:1 2nd:0 3rd:0 Ran:4
Pre1999 - 1st:1 2nd:1 3rd:0 Ran:2
Win Prizemoney £10,406 *Total Prizemoney* £13,936
Wins * **1999** Jly Doncas (G-F) 6f 96 <
* 1998 Jun Goodwo (GD) 6f 94
1999 Turf 1-4: (6f 1-2, 7f 2) (g-f, frm 1-3)
Workmanlike, very useful filly, effective 6 to 7f, best at 6f, acts on gd to frm. Turf high 97 - also 1st of 4 getting 8lb from Light The Rocket (28 Jly Doncaster RF 3197). She failed to stay seven furlongs on her first two starts and looked happier when dropped back in trip. Raced only on a sound surface, she is useful but may have to travel abroad to register another victory.
**M P Tregoning [2-6] Hamdan Al Maktoum.*

MAGICAL BAILIWICK (IRE) BHB 70f **RR 77f** 3994[15]
3 ch g Magical Wonder (USA) 7.2f **(60)** - Alpine Dance (USA) (Apalachee (USA)) 9.4f **(71)**
Form - 4530
Record 1999 - 1st:0 2nd:0 3rd:1 Ran:4
Win Prizemoney £0 *Total Prizemoney* £995
1999 Turf 0-4: (7f, 8f 2, 9f) (g-f 4)
Workmanlike, above-average gelding. Turf high 77 - 5th of 7 giving 5lb to Be Thankfull (10 Jly Ascot 8f g-f RF 2704).

**R J Baker [0-4] Islands Racing Connection.*

MAGICAL COLOURS (IRE) BHB 40f **RR 43?f** 1684[8]
4 b f Rainbows For Life (CAN) 9.3f **(64)** - Immediate Impact (Caerleon (USA)) 8.6f **(71)**
Form - 08
Record 1999 - 1st:0 2nd:0 3rd:0 Ran:2
Pre1999 - 1st:0 2nd:0 3rd:0 Ran:4
1999 Turf 0-2: (10f, 12f) (g-s, frm)
Light-framed, moderate filly.
**R Rowe [0-2] Mrs A Pratt (from J L Dunlop [0-4] Apr 1998).*

MAGICAL DANCER (IRE) BHB 42f **RR 26f** 1179[13]
4 b f Magical Wonder (USA) 7.2f **(60)** - Diva Encore (Star Appeal) 9.6f **(65)**
Form - 000
Record 1999 - 1st:0 2nd:0 3rd:0 Ran:3
Pre1999 - 1st:1 2nd:1 3rd:2 Ran:19
Win Prizemoney £2,763 *Total Prizemoney* £4,573
Wins 1998 Aug Warwic (G-F) H 8f 43 45 <
1999 Turf 0-3: (7f, 8f, 12f) (sft, g-f, frm)
Leggy, little account filly, effective 8 to 10f, acts on gd to frm, best on g-f, likes left handed tracks, prefers tight tracks. Turf high 26. Becoming disappointing.
**M R Channon [0-3] The Piccolo Boys (from Mrs P N Dutfield [1-19] Spt 1998).*

MAGICAL JACK RR 4981[11]
2 b c Belfort (FR) 6.7f **(53)** - Gavea (African Sky) 7.9f **(63)**
Form - 0
Record 1999 - 1st:0 2nd:0 3rd:0 Ran:1
1999 Turf 0-1: (6f) (g-f)
Currently very poor colt. **G Woodward [0-1] David Chamley.*

MAGICAL MILLIE BHB 68f **RR 73f** 4901[5]
2 b f Muhtarram (USA) - Milne's Way (The Noble Player (USA)) 6.5f **(67)**
Form - 147405
Record 1999 - 1st:1 2nd:0 3rd:0 Ran:6
Win Prizemoney £2,202 *Total Prizemoney* £2,432
Wins * **1999** Jly Folkes (G-F) C 5f 69+ <
1999 Turf 1-6: (5f 1-2, 6f 2, 7f 2) (g-f 1-4, frm 2)
Above-average filly, effective 5 to 7f, acts on g-f to frm, best on g-f. Turf high 73 (began Jly) - 4th of 17 giving 1lb to Peruvian Jade (20 Spt Leicester 6f g-f RF 4439) - also 1st of 4 giving 3lb to Bolder Alexander (26 Jly Folkestone RF 3140).
**S C Williams [1-6] D A Shekells.*

MAGICAL RIVER BHB 52f52a **RR 48f 52a** 4995[15]
2 ch f Lahib (USA) 8f **(69)** - Awtaar (USA) **(35df)** (Lyphard (USA)) 9.9f **(72)**
Form - 030600
Record 1999 - 1st:0 2nd:0 3rd:1 Ran:6
Win Prizemoney £0 *Total Prizemoney* £510
1999 Turf 0-5: (5f, 6f 2, 7f 2) (gd 3, g-f 2) 1999 AW 0-1: (6f) (Equi)
Moderate filly. Turf high 67. **C E Brittain [0-6] W H Carson.*

MAGICAL SHOT BHB 46f60a **RR 45f 60a** 5146[9]
4 b g Magic Ring (IRE) 6.5f **(64)** - Final Shot (Dalsaan) 9.8f **(64)**
Form - 64133220087600
Record 1999 - 1st:1 2nd:2 3rd:2 Ran:12
Pre1999 - 1st:0 2nd:0 3rd:4 Ran:11
Win Prizemoney £2,788 *Total Prizemoney* £7,096
Wins * **1999** *Jan Wolver (STD) 8.5f 64* <
1999 Turf 0-4: (7f, 9f, 10f 2) (sft, frm 3) 1999 AW 1-8: (7f, 8f 1-4, 9f, 11f 2) (Fibr 1-8)
Moderate gelding, effective 8f, acts on g-s to g-f, has worn blinkers (effectively).
**D Carroll [1-12] J J Devaney (from D Carroll [0-2] Dec 1998).*

MAGIC ARROW (USA) BHB 62f80a **RR 60f 80a** 3576[7]
3 b c Defensive Play (USA) - Magic Blue (USA) (Cure The Blues (USA)) 9.5f **(63)**
Form - 816157
Record 1999 - 1st:2 2nd:0 3rd:0 Ran:6
Win Prizemoney £7,304 *Total Prizemoney* £7,304
Wins * **1999** *May Wolver (STD) H 14.8f 67 72* <

* **1999** *Feb Lingfi (STD) 12f 69*
1999 Turf 0-3: (14f 2, 16f) (g-s, g-f 2) 1999 AW 2-3: (10f, 12f 1-1, 15f 1-1) (Equi 1-2, Fibr 1-1)
Unfurnished, above-average colt, effective 12 to 15f, - acts on AW. Turf high 60. AW high 72 - 1st of 8 getting 32lb from Noufari (22 May Wolverhampton RF 1420) - also 1st of 12 getting 24lb from Robellita (6 Feb Lingfield RF 0235). A Winner twice on sand, he is smart on that surface but has disappointed on turf.
**J Noseda [2-6] K New Partnership.*

MAGIC BABE BHB 55f **RR 63f** 3823[10]

2 b f Magic Ring (IRE) 6.5f **(64)** - Head Turner **(43f 52a)** (My Dad Tom (USA))
Form - 07040000
Record 1999 - 1st:0 2nd:0 3rd:0 Ran:8
Win Prizemoney £0 *Total Prizemoney* £227
1999 Turf 0-8: (5f 3, 6f 3, 7f 2) (g-s, gd, g-f 2, frm 4)
Average filly. Turf high 63. **D R C Elsworth [0-8] Mrs J Wotherspoon.*

MAGIC COMBINATION (IRE) BHB 64f **RR 55f** 3334a[1]

6 b g Scenic 10.6f **(66)** - Etage (Ile de Bourbon (USA)) 10.1f **(67)**
Form - 1
Record 1999 - 1st:1 2nd:0 3rd:0 Ran:1
Pre1999 - 1st:4 2nd:2 3rd:2 Ran:24
Win Prizemoney £17,539 *Total Prizemoney* £24,095
Wins * **1999** Jly Galway (G-F) H 12f 44 55+
* 1997 Jly Sandow (G-S) H 11.4f 69 72
1996 Aug Roscom (GD) H 12f 84 77+ <
1996 Jly Bellew (GD) H 14f 79 73
1996 Jun Leopar (GD) H 9f 75 65
1999 Turf 1-1: (12f 1-1) (g-f 1-1)
Fair gelding, has worn blinkers. (1st run). Inconsistent.
**B J Curley [4-22] Mrs B J Curley (from K Prendergast in IRE [3-10] Nov 1996).*

MAGIC FLUTE **RR 69f** 4711[13]

3 ch f Magic Ring (IRE) 6.5f **(64)** - Megan's Flight (Welsh Pageant) 10f **(65)**
Form - 755P20
Record 1999 - 1st:0 2nd:1 3rd:0 Ran:6
Win Prizemoney £0 *Total Prizemoney* £1,335
1999 Turf 0-6: (7f 3, 8f 3) (g-s, gd 2, g-f, frm 2)
Scopey, average filly, effective 8f, acts on frm. Turf high 69 - 2nd of 19 giving 2lb to Reason Why (8 Spt Kempton 8f frm RF 4213).
**Lady Herries [0-6] Angmering Park Stud.*

MAGIC GLOW BHB 25f **RR** 3072[11]

3 b f Presidium 7.5f **(56)** - Mrs Magic (Magic Mirror)
Form - 50
Record 1999 - 1st:0 2nd:0 3rd:0 Ran:2
1999 Turf 0-2: (6f, 7f) (frm 2)
Scopey, currently very poor filly. **N Bycroft [0-2] M J Bateson.*

MAGIC GRAND BHB 70f **RR 69f** 2676[5]

2 b f Magic Ring (IRE) 6.5f **(64)** - Between the Sticks (Pharly (FR)) 9.8f **(68)**
Form - 021721635
Record 1999 - 1st:2 2nd:2 3rd:1 Ran:9
Win Prizemoney £5,537 *Total Prizemoney* £8,010
Wins * **1999** Jun Hamilt (G-S) 5f 63 <
* **1999** May Hamilt (Sft) 5f 61
1999 Turf 2-9: (5f 2-8, 6f) (g-s, gd 2-2, g-f 2, frm 4)
Average filly, effective 5f, acts on gd to frm, best on gd. Turf high 69 - also 1st of 7 getting 4lb from College Maid (9 Jun Hamilton RF 1859). Consistent. **M R Channon [2-9] Kingsdown Racing.*

MAGIC LEGS **RR 57f** 4531[7]

2 b f Reprimand 8.2f **(63)** - Inherent Magic (IRE) **(92f 84a)** (Magical Wonder (USA))
Form - 7
Record 1999 - 1st:0 2nd:0 3rd:0 Ran:1
1999 Turf 0-1: (5f) (g-s)
Currently fair filly. **W R Muir [0-1] J Bernstein.*

MAGIC MEMORIES BHB 56f45a **RR 60f 45a** 505[9]

3 b f Magic Ring (IRE) 6.5f **(64)** - Bay Runner (Bay Express) 7.1f **(60)**
Form - 8070
Record 1999 - 1st:0 2nd:0 3rd:0 Ran:1
Pre1999 - 1st:1 2nd:2 3rd:0 Ran:11
Win Prizemoney £2,290 *Total Prizemoney* £4,442
Wins 1998 Aug Salisb (G-F) C 7f 73+ <
1999 Turf 0-1: (8f) (sft)
Workmanlike, average filly, effective 5 to 7f, best at 7f, acts on gd to frm. Becoming disappointing.
**Mrs L Stubbs [0-3] O J Williams & Partners (from D R C Elsworth [1-9] Nov 1998).*

MAGIC MILL (IRE) BHB 69f72a **RR 72f 72a** 1543[14]

6 b g Simply Great (FR) 11.9f **(61)** - Rosy O'Leary (Majetta) 6.5f **(58)**
Form - 040
Record 1999 - 1st:0 2nd:0 3rd:0 Ran:3
Pre1999 - 1st:2 2nd:2 3rd:2 Ran:19
Win Prizemoney £7,543 *Total Prizemoney* £13,331
Wins 1998 Apr Newcas (SFT) H 7f 73 87? <
1995 Oct Redcar (FRM) 7f 82+
1999 Turf 0-3: (7f 2, 8f) (gd 2, g-f)
Above-average gelding, effective 7 to 8f, acts on sft to g-s, has worn blinkers. Turf high 72. Inconsistent.
**J S Goldie [0-6] A S Scott (from J L Eyre [1-14] Jun 1998).*

MAGIC MOMENT BHB 54f **RR 58f** 4879[14]

3 b f Magic Ring (IRE) 6.5f **(64)** - Epithet (Mill Reef (USA)) 10.5f **(78)**
Form - 314400
Record 1999 - 1st:1 2nd:0 3rd:1 Ran:6
Pre1999 - 1st:0 2nd:0 3rd:0 Ran:4
Win Prizemoney £2,514 *Total Prizemoney* £3,511
Wins * **1999** Jun Carlis (GD) 5.9f 52 <
1999 Turf 1-6: (6f 1-5, 7f) (gd, g-f 1-2, frm 3)
Neat, fair filly, effective 6f, acts on gd to g-f. Turf high 58 - 4th of 13 to Piggy Bank (5 Jly Ripon 6f gd RF 2564) - also 1st of 16 getting 3lb from Tapaua (10 Jun Carlisle RF 1878).
**E Weymes [1-10] T A Scothern.*

MAGIC MONDAY (IRE) BHB 32f **RR 9f** 4222[13]

3 b f Petardia 8.2f **(58)** - Ultra (Stanford) 7.9f **(56)**
Form - 000000
Record 1999 - 1st:0 2nd:0 3rd:0 Ran:6
Pre1999 - 1st:0 2nd:1 3rd:0 Ran:5
Win Prizemoney £0 *Total Prizemoney* £1,050
1999 Turf 0-4: (6f 3, 7f) (sft, gd, g-f, hrd) 1999 AW 0-2: (5f, 8f) (Fibr 2)
Workmanlike, little account filly, has worn blinkers. Turf high 9. AW high 24 (began Jly).
**L A Dace [0-4] Trojan Racing (from R Hannon [0-7] May 1999).*

MAGIC OF LOVE BHB 100f **RR 93f** 4895[1]

2 b f Magic Ring (IRE) 6.5f **(64)** - Mistitled (USA) (Miswaki (USA)) 9f **(81)**
Form - 1131
Record 1999 - 1st:3 2nd:0 3rd:1 Ran:4
Win Prizemoney £54,027 *Total Prizemoney* £58,902
Wins * **1999** Oct Newmar (GD) 6f 93 <
* **1999** Aug Lingfi (GD) 6f 86+
* **1999** Jly Beverl (G-F) 5f 86+
1999 Turf 3-4: (5f 1-2, 6f 2-2) (gd 2-2, frm 1-2)
Useful filly. Turf high 93 (began Jly) - 1st of 20 giving 2lb to Blue Velvet (15 Oct Newmarket RF 4895) - also 1st of 8 getting 2lb from Ogilia (20 Aug Lingfield RF 3795). Winner of her first two starts, she showed a nice turn of foot on the second occasion and was not beaten far in the Flying Childers. Ended the season by winning a big pot in the Tattersalls Autumn Auction Stakes at Newmarket.
**M L W Bell [3-4] Mrs Maureen Buckley.*

MAGIC POWERS BHB 61f **RR 55f** 770[12]

4 ch g Magical Wonder (USA) 7.2f **(60)** - Kissin' Cousin (Be Friendly) 9.3f **(53)**
Form - 0
Record 1999 - 1st:0 2nd:0 3rd:0 Ran:1
Pre1999 - 1st:0 2nd:0 3rd:1 Ran:6
Win Prizemoney £0 *Total Prizemoney* £633
1999 Turf 0-1: (6f) (sft)
Leggy, fair gelding. **G B Balding [0-7] The Wizards.*

MAGIC RAINBOW BHB 87f93a **RR 91f 93a** 4207[12]

4 b g Magic Ring (IRE) 6.5f **(64)** - Blues Indigo (Music Boy) 6.8f **(57)**

Form - 1456142030

Record	**1999** -	1st:2	2nd:1	3rd:1	Ran:10
	Pre1999 -	1st:3	2nd:0	3rd:0	Ran:13

Win Prizemoney £43,003 *Total Prizemoney* £53,790

Wins	* **1999**	May Kempto (G-F)	H	6f	81	85	
	* ***1999***	*Mar Lingfi (STD)*	*H*	*6f*	*81*	*94*	*<*
	* 1998	May Newmar (G-F)	H	6f	77	84	
	* 1998	*Mar Southw (STD)*	*H*	*6f*	*76*	*80+*	
	* 1997	Jun Leices (GD)		5f		76	

1999 Turf 1-8: (5f 3, 6f 1-5) (gd 2, g-f 3, frm 1-3) 1999 AW 1-2: (6f 1-2) (Equi 1-1, Fibr)

Leggy, useful gelding, effective 5 to 6f, best at 6f, acts on g-f to frm - acts on AW, likes Newmarket. Turf high 91 - 2nd of 10 getting 12lb from Rudi's Pet (23 Jly Ascot 5f g-f RF 3049) - also 1st of 9 giving 7lb to Alegria (29 May Kempton RF 1579). AW high 94 (1st run) - 1st of 6 giving 3lb to Krystal Max (4 Mar Lingfield RF 0402). He is a decent sprinter on both turf and sand.

**M L W Bell [5-23] P T Fenwick.*

MAGIC SISTER RR 56f 5195[6]

2 ch f Cadeaux Genereux 7.9f **(76)** - Gunner's Belle (Gunner B) 11.2f **(58)**

Form - 66

Record 1999 - 1st:0 2nd:0 3rd:0 Ran:2

1999 Turf 0-2: (6f 2) (g-s, gd)

Currently fair filly. Turf high 56 (began Oct).

**M L W Bell [0-2] M Dawson & K J Mercer.*

MAGIC SUNSET RR 72f 4728[7]

2 b f Magic Ring (IRE) 6.5f **(64)** - Run To The Sun (Run The Gantlet (USA)) 12.1f **(59)**

Form - 07

Record 1999 - 1st:0 2nd:0 3rd:0 Ran:2

1999 Turf 0-2: (8f 2) (g-s, gd)

Currently above-average filly. Turf high 72 (began Spt).

**I A Balding [0-2] M E Wates.*

MAGIC WHISPER (FR) RR 97f 1529a[3]

3 b c Subotica (FR) - Fabulous Noble (FR) (Fabulous Dancer (USA)) 9.4f **(70)**

Form - 33

1999 Turf 0-2: (12f 2) (hvy, sft)

Currently very useful colt. Turf high 97.

**D Sepulchre in FR [0-2] Ecurie Noire Et Bleue.*

MAGIQUE ETOILE (IRE) BHB 50f55a RR 49f 55a 5127[3]

3 b f Magical Wonder (USA) 7.2f **(60)** - Shes A Dancer (IRE) (Alzao (USA)) 7.1f **(68)**

Form - 63330552573

Record	**1999** -	1st:0	2nd:1	3rd:1	Ran:7
	Pre1999 -	1st:0	2nd:0	3rd:3	Ran:12

Win Prizemoney £0 *Total Prizemoney* £2,260

1999 Turf 0-6: (5f, 6f 3, 7f, 8f) (gd 2, frm 3, hrd) 1999 AW 0-1: (8f) (Equi)

Workmanlike, fair filly, effective 6 to 8f, best at 7f, - acts on Equi, often wears blinkers (extremely effectively), prefers left handed tracks, prefers tight tracks. Turf high 54. (1st run) - 5th of 8 giving 8lb to Admirals Place (19 Jun Lingfield 8f Equi RF 2151). Consistent. **M P Muggeridge [0-19] Gallery Racing.*

MAGNO (USA) BHB 103f RR 98df 1399[3]

3 b c El Gran Senor (USA) 8.9f **(85)** - Nice Noble (USA) (Vaguely Noble) 10.1f **(72)**

Form - 3

Record	**1999** -	1st:0	2nd:0	3rd:1	Ran:1
	Pre1999 -	1st:1	2nd:1	3rd:2	Ran:4

Win Prizemoney £7,122 *Total Prizemoney* £48,934

Wins * 1998 Oct York (GD) 7.9f 98 <

1999 Turf 0-1: (11f) (frm)

Scopey, very useful colt. Runner-up in the Racing Post Trophy on his final start of 1998. He ran just once and disappointingly last year. **P F I Cole [1-5] H R H Prince Fahd Salman.*

MAHBOOB (IRE) BHB 104f RR 116f 5014a[7]

4 b br c Marju (IRE) 9.2f **(76)** - Miss Gris (USA) (Hail the Pirates (USA)) 11f **(78)**

Form - 147

1999 Turf 1-3: (7f, 8f 1-2) (sft, g-s 1-1)

Scopey, high-class colt. Turf high 113 (began Aug) - 4th of 9 to Trans Island (3 Oct Longchamp 8f sft RF 4779a).

**J E Hammond in FR [1-5] (from D Morley [1-3] Spt 1997).*

MAIDAAN BHB 105f RR 104?f 5140[8]

3 b c Midyan (USA) 9.9f **(64)** - Panache Arabelle **(66f)**(Nashwan (USA))

Form - 28

Record	**1999** -	1st:0	2nd:1	3rd:0	Ran:2
	Pre1999 -	1st:1	2nd:0	3rd:1	Ran:2

Win Prizemoney £24,759 *Total Prizemoney* £30,361

Wins 1998 Spt Newmar (GD) 7f 104+ <

1999 Turf 0-2: (8f, 9f) (gd 2)

Scopey, very useful colt. Turf high 96 (1st run) (began Oct) - 2nd of 9 getting 4lb from Indian Lodge (15 Oct Newmarket 9f gd RF 4894). Beautifully bred, out of a half-sister to Stagecraft, he was trained by Mick Channon at two winning the Tattersalls Houghton Sales Stakes. Now with Godolphin, he did not make his reappearance until October when beaten just a head by Indian Lodge in a Newmarket Listed event. Possibly unsuited by soft ground in a similar event next time, he remains an interesting proposition at four.

**S bin Suroor [0-2] Godolphin (from M R Channon [1-2] Spt 1998).*

MAIDEN'S BLUSH (USA) BHB 82f RR 81f 4377[4]

3 ch f Silver Hawk (USA) 11.2f **(85)** - Barmistress (USA) (Alydar (USA)) 9.1f **(76)**

Form - 1024

Record	**1999** -	1st:1	2nd:1	3rd:0	Ran:4
	Pre1999 -	1st:0	2nd:0	3rd:0	Ran:1

Win Prizemoney £2,879 *Total Prizemoney* £5,658

Wins * **1999** Apr Windso (G-F) 10f 65 <

1999 Turf 1-4: (10f 1-3, 11f) (gd 2, g-f, frm 1-1)

Scopey, decent filly. Turf high 81 - 2nd of 11 giving 15lb to Mindanao (14 Aug Ripon 10f gd RF 3662).

**J H M Gosden [1-5] Sheikh Mohammed.*

MAID OF KILLEEN (IRE) RR 102f 5174a[7]

3 b f Darshaan 11.9f **(81)** - Sovereign Touch 00

Form - 66326207

1999 Turf 0-7: (8f, 10f, 12f 4, 14f) (sft 2, g-s, gd, g-f, frm 2)

Very useful filly, effective 12f, acts on sft. Turf high 102 (began Jly) - 2nd of 7 getting 12lb from Theatreworld (7 Spt Galway 12f sft RF 4299a). **J Oxx in IRE [1-10] Killeen Castle Stud Syndicate.*

MAID PLANS (IRE) BHB 49f35a RR 50f 35a 219[5]

3 br f Petardia 8.2f **(58)** - Ballerina Anna (IRE) (Dance of Life (USA)) 7f **(66)**

Form - 0685

Record	**1999** -	1st:0	2nd:0	3rd:0	Ran:2
	Pre1999 -	1st:0	2nd:0	3rd:0	Ran:6

1999 AW 0-2: (6f 2) (Fibr 2)

Light-framed, fair filly. AW high 30.

**N P Littmoden [0-4] J W C Coxon (from J Akehurst [0-4] Oct 1998).*

MAID TO LOVE (IRE) BHB 62f57a RR 74f 57a 4926[2]

2 ch f Petardia 8.2f **(58)** - Lomond Heights (IRE) (Lomond (USA)) 8.8f **(65)**

Form - 33702

Record 1999 - 1st:0 2nd:1 3rd:2 Ran:5

Win Prizemoney £0 *Total Prizemoney* £1,394

1999 Turf 0-4: (6f 2, 7f 2) (gd, g-f 3) 1999 AW 0-1: (8f) (Fibr)

Above-average filly, has worn blinkers. Turf high 74. (1st run) - 2nd of 12 to Sheerness Essity (16 Oct Wolverhampton 8f Fibr RF 4926).

**G A Butler [0-5] The Travellers.*

MAID TO MEASURE RR 41f 747[15]

3 b f Inchinor 8.9f **(64)** - Walking Saint (Godswalk (USA)) 7.3f **(58)**

Form - 0

Record	**1999** -	1st:0	2nd:0	3rd:0	Ran:1
	Pre1999 -	1st:0	2nd:0	3rd:1	Ran:4

Win Prizemoney £0 *Total Prizemoney* £738

1999 Turf 0-1: (8f) (g-s)

Light-framed, moderate filly. **M Brittain [0-5] Mel Brittain.*

MAIELLA BHB 45f30a RR 46f 30a 3968[1]

4 ch f Salse (USA) 10.9f **(71)** - Forelino (USA) (Trempolino (USA)) 12f

(71)
Form - 07007773421
Record 1999 - 1st:1 2nd:1 3rd:1 Ran:10
Pre1999 - 1st:2 2nd:0 3rd:2 Ran:13
Win Prizemoney £7,083 *Total Prizemoney* £9,305
Wins * **1999** Aug Nottin (G-F) SH 10f 41 44
1998 Aug Salisb (G-F) H 12f 56 60 <
1998 May Bright (FRM) SH 11.9f 52 59
1999 Turf 1-10: (8f, 10f 1-4, 12f, 14f 2, 16f, 17f) (sft, gd 2, g-f 1-2, frm 5)
Light-framed, moderate filly, effective 10 to 12f, best at 12f, acts on g-f to frm, best on g-f, has worn blinkers. Turf high 48.
**T D Easterby [1-11] J M Newbould (from R Hannon [2-13] Nov 1998).*

MAI TAI (IRE) BHB 42f51a **RR 42f 51a** 4604[3]
4 b f Scenic 10.6f **(66)** - Oystons Propweekly (Swing Easy (USA)) 6.5f **(55)**
Form - 0281303160800003
Record 1999 - 1st:2 2nd:1 3rd:3 Ran:15
Pre1999 - 1st:0 2nd:0 3rd:3 Ran:15
Win Prizemoney £9,460 *Total Prizemoney* £12,942
Wins * **1999** May Redcar (SFT) H 7f 48 54
* **1999** *Feb Southw (STD) H 7f 56* <
1999 Turf 1-10: (7f 1-9, 8f) (gd 1-3, g-f 3, frm 4) 1999 AW 1-5: (7f 1-4, 8f) (Fibr 1-5)
Workmanlike, fair filly, effective 6 to 7f, best at 6f, acts on gd to frm - acts on Fibr, has worn blinkers. Turf high 54 - 1st of 18 getting 10lb from Carrie Pooter (10 May Redcar RF 1126). AW high 56 - 1st of 9 from Miss All Alone (1 Feb Southwell RF 0201).
**D W Barker [2-16] P Asquith (from Mrs P N Dutfield [0-14] Oct 1998).*

MAITEAMIA BHB 67f78a **RR 68f 78a** 4880[8]
6 ch g Komaite (USA) 6.9f **(61)** - Mia Scintilla (Blazing Saddles (AUS)) 6.7f **(46)**
Form - 247033521123506003128
Record 1999 - 1st:3 2nd:3 3rd:4 Ran:18
Pre1999 - 1st:4 2nd:9 3rd:4 Ran:39
Win Prizemoney £20,513 *Total Prizemoney* £39,387
Wins * **1999** Spt Redcar (G-F) H 6f 55 67
* **1999** *Mar Southw (STD) H 6f 69 70*
* **1999** *Feb Southw (STD) H 6f 63 67*
* 1996 May Catter (GD) H 5f 63 61
* 1996 May Hamilt (HVY) H 5f 50 68
* 1996 *Apr Southw (STD) H 6f 61 73+* <
* 1996 *Mar Southw (STD) H 6f 50 51*
1999 Turf 1-10: (5f 3, 6f 1-3, 7f 3, 8f) (gd 2, g-f 4, frm 1-4) 1999 AW 2-8: (5f 4, 6f 2-4) (Fibr 2-8)
Above-average gelding, effective 5 to 8f, acts on g-f to frm - acts on Fibr, mostly wears blinkers (effectively), likes left handed tracks, likes tight tracks, excels at Southwell, likes Redcar. Turf high 68 - 2nd of 22 getting 10lb from Katy Nowaitee (2 Oct Redcar 8f g-f RF 4689) - also 1st of 17 getting 22lb from Mungo Park (24 Spt Redcar RF 4538). AW high 74 - 2nd of 13 getting 8lb from Dil (10 Mar Southwell 5f Fibr RF 0423) - also 1st of 12 giving 7lb to Nifty Norman (8 Mar Southwell RF 0415).
**S R Bowring [7-57] Mrs Zoe Grant.*

MAITREYA BHB 46f **RR 49f** 4288[12]
4 ch f Anshan 8.2f **(63)** - Princess Fair (Crowned Prince (USA)) 10.1f **(67)**
Form - 03060
Record 1999 - 1st:0 2nd:0 3rd:1 Ran:5
Pre1999 - 1st:0 2nd:1 3rd:0 Ran:6
Win Prizemoney £0 *Total Prizemoney* £1,769
1999 Turf 0-4: (10f, 12f 3) (frm 4) 1999 AW 0-1: (10f) (Equi)
Workmanlike, moderate filly, effective 7 to 8f, acted on frm, liked left handed tracks, favoured tight tracks. Turf high 49. (DEAD)
**Mrs D Haine [0-1] B Uniacke (from C N Allen [0-10] May 1999).*

MAIYSHA RR 55f 5060[8]
2 b f Contract Law (USA) 8.9f **(54)** - Bint Al Arab (Ahonoora) 8.1f **(73)**
Form - 08
Record 1999 - 1st:0 2nd:0 3rd:0 Ran:2
1999 Turf 0-2: (7f 2) (g-s 2)
Currently fair filly. Turf high 55 (began Oct).
**R M Flower [0-2] Graham Dutnall.*

MAJALIS BHB 39f **RR 42f** 4539[8]
4 b br f Mujadil (USA) 7.7f **(70)** - Rose Barton (Pas de Seul) 9.1f **(67)**
Form - 3007200388
Record 1999 - 1st:0 2nd:1 3rd:2 Ran:10
Pre1999 - 1st:1 2nd:3 3rd:2 Ran:12
Win Prizemoney £3,756 *Total Prizemoney* £10,925
Wins 1998 Jly Beverl (GD) 5f 74 <
1999 Turf 0-10: (6f, 7f 3, 8f 4, 10f 2) (gd 2, g-f, frm 6, hrd)
Workmanlike, moderate filly, effective 5 to 7f, acts on gd to frm, best on g-f. Turf high 60. Consistent.
**J L Eyre [0-11] Whitestonecliffe Racing Partnership (from R Guest [1-11] Spt 1998).*

MAJESTIC (IRE) BHB 68f68a **RR 78f 68a** 4704[6]
4 b g Belmez (USA) 11.4f **(65)** - Noble Lily (USA) (Vaguely Noble) 10.1f **(72)**
Form - 516
Record 1999 - 1st:1 2nd:0 3rd:0 Ran:3
Pre1999 - 1st:0 2nd:1 3rd:2 Ran:8
Win Prizemoney £2,762 *Total Prizemoney* £6,004
Wins * **1999** *Apr Wolver (STD) 12f 75* <
1999 Turf 0-1: (11f) (gd) 1999 AW 1-2: (12f 1-2) (Fibr 1-2)
Workmanlike, above-average gelding, effective 12f, acts on sft to frm - acts on Fibr, has worn blinkers (extremely effectively), likes left handed tracks, favours tight tracks. AW high 75 (1st run) - 1st of 10 giving 4lb to Epworth (24 Apr Wolverhampton RF 0849).
**Ian Williams [1-11] Patrick Kelly.*

MAJESTIC BAY (IRE) RR 85f 4435[3]
3 b c Unfuwain (USA) 11.4f **(74)** - That'll Be the Day (IRE) (Thatching) 8f **(66)**
Form - 52423
Record 1999 - 1st:0 2nd:2 3rd:1 Ran:5
Win Prizemoney £0 *Total Prizemoney* £3,017
1999 Turf 0-5: (10f 2, 12f 3) (g-s, g-f, frm 3)
Unfurnished, useful colt. Turf high 85 - 3rd of 14 giving 5lb to Life Is Life (20 Spt Kempton 12f g-s RF 4435).
**P W Harris [0-5] The Quiet Ones.*

MAJOR ATTRACTION BHB 34f **RR 44f** 3667[4]
4 gr g Major Jacko - My Friend Melody (Sizzling Melody)
Form - 6434
Record 1999 - 1st:0 2nd:0 3rd:1 Ran:4
Pre1999 - 1st:0 2nd:0 3rd:0 Ran:2
Win Prizemoney £0 *Total Prizemoney* £275
1999 AW 0-4: (11f 2, 12f 2) (Fibr 4)
Leggy, moderate gelding, effective 11f, - acts on Fibr. AW high 48 - 4th of 15 getting 5lb from Count de Money (28 Jun Southwell 11f Fibr RF 2375).
**P Eccles [0-5] Positive Partners (from M Mullineaux [0-2] Aug 1998).*

MAJOR BART (IRE) RR 40f 3869[9]
2 gr c Paris House 5.9f **(64)** - Kilnoe (IRE) (Rhoman Rule (USA))
Form - 80
Record 1999 - 1st:0 2nd:0 3rd:0 Ran:2
1999 Turf 0-2: (5f 2) (g-f, frm)
Currently moderate colt. Turf high 40.
**N P Littmoden [0-2] Mrs Linda Miller.*

MAJOR FORCE (USA) RR 113f 5014a[6]
3 b c Woodman (USA) 9.7f **(77)** - Ready For Action (USA) (Riverman (USA)) 9.1f **(76)**
Form - 1116
1999 Turf 3-4: (7f 2-3, 8f 1-1) (hvy 1-1, g-s 2-2)
Group-class colt. Turf high 113 - 6th giving 2lb to Field of Hope (17 Oct Longchamp 7f RF 5014a) - also 1st of 9 giving 7lb to Artistic Blue (18 Spt Curragh RF 4472a). A useful Irish soft-ground performer, he finished in midfield in the Group One Prix de la Foret. He can win more Group races in Ireland. **D K Weld in IRE [3-5].*

MAJOR MORRIS (IRE) RR 3836[17]
4 br g New Express 6.8f **(54)** - Saul Flower (Saulingo) 6.2f **(53)**
Form - 0
Record 1999 - 1st:0 2nd:0 3rd:0 Ran:1
1999 Turf 0-1: (7f) (frm)
Currently very poor gelding. **J Mackie [0-2] N J Sessions.*

MAJOR REBUKE BHB 87f **RR 87f** 5134[9]
2 b c Reprimand 8.2f **(63)** - Ackcontent (USA) (Key To Content (USA))

8f **(54)**
Form - 140
Record 1999 - 1st:1 2nd:0 3rd:0 Ran:3
Win Prizemoney £4,955 *Total Prizemoney* £5,233
Wins * 1999 Spt Goodwo (G-F) 6f 81 <
1999 Turf 1-3: (6f 1-2, 7f) (g-s, gd, g-f 1-1)
Currently useful colt. Turf high 87 (began Spt) - also 1st of 4 from Leeroy (10 Spt Goodwood RF 4261). **S P C Woods [1-3] N A D Thomas.*

MAJOR'S LAW (IRE) BHB 46f63a RR 57f 63a 254[5]
10 b g Law Society (USA) 11.6f **(71)** - Maryinsky (USA) (Northern Dancer) 9.6f **(80)**
Form - 745
Record 1999 - 1st:0 2nd:0 3rd:0 Ran:2
Pre1999 - 1st:1 2nd:4 3rd:1 Ran:20
Win Prizemoney £2,924 *Total Prizemoney* £10,228
1999 AW 0-2: (16f 2) (Equi, Fibr)
Fair gelding. AW high 49.
**R Simpson [3-12] Miss J Rumford (from C E Brittain [1-16] Oct 1992).*

MAJOUNE (FR) RR 107f 1350a[1]
4 gr f Take Risks (FR) - Madame Est Sortie (FR) (Longleat (USA))
Form - 1
1999 Turf 1-1: (11f 1-1) (g-s 1-1)
Currently Pattern-class filly. (1st run) - 1st of 9 from Vissinia (13 May Lyon Parilly RF 1350a). **J-P Pelat in FR [1-1] C Ankri.*

MAKAHU DON BHB 32f28a RR 6f 28a 599[18]
4 ch g Derrylin 12.7f **(38)** - Rockalong (Native Bazaar) 6.9f **(62)**
Form - 0080
Record 1999 - 1st:0 2nd:0 3rd:0 Ran:2
Pre1999 - 1st:1 2nd:2 3rd:0 Ran:15
Win Prizemoney £2,770 *Total Prizemoney* £5,000
Wins 1997 May Mussel (G-F) S 5f 53 <
1999 Turf 0-1: (5f) (gd) 1999 AW 0-1: (5f) (Fibr)
Very poor gelding, has worn blinkers.
**S R Bowring [0-4] J E Reed & P M Sedgwick (from W T Kemp [1-13] Oct 1997).*

MAKAIRA (IRE) BHB 49f RR 52f 4341[9]
2 b g Thatching 7.8f **(69)** - Sharnazad (IRE) (Track Barron (USA))
Form - 068800700
Record 1999 - 1st:0 2nd:0 3rd:0 Ran:9
1999 Turf 0-9: (5f, 6f 4, 7f 2, 8f 2) (gd 5, g-f, frm 3)
Fair gelding, has worn blinkers. Turf high 52. Consistent.
**N Tinkler [0-9] Speedlith Group.*

MAKARIM (IRE) RR 79df 4893[16]
3 ch c Generous (IRE) 11.5f **(82)** - Emmaline (USA) (Affirmed (USA)) 9.3f **(79)**
Form - 46170
Record 1999 - 1st:1 2nd:0 3rd:0 Ran:5
Win Prizemoney £5,836 *Total Prizemoney* £6,112
Wins * 1999 Aug Bath (GD) 11.7f 79 <
1999 Turf 1-5: (10f, 11f, 12f 1-2, 15f) (gd, g-f, frm 1-3)
Scopey, above-average colt, has worn blinkers. Turf high 81 (1st run) - 4th of 15 to Samasakhan (29 May Haydock 11f g-f RF 1572) - also 1st of 9 giving 5lb to I Tina (22 Aug Bath RF 3834).
**N A Graham [1-5] Hamdan Al Maktoum.*

MAKARUKA (USA) RR 108f 554a[5]
4 b c Trempolino (USA) 11.9f **(77)** - Chinguetti (Green Dancer (USA)) 10.3f **(74)**
Form - 5
1999 Turf 0-1: (12f) (g-f)
Pattern-class colt.
**S bin Suroor in UAE [0-1] (from J Cunnington in FR [1-4] Aug 1998).*

MAKASSEB BHB 86f RR 83f 5189[2]
2 ch c Kris 10f **(75)** - Shefoog **(89f)** (Kefaah (USA))
Form - 6322
Record 1999 - 1st:0 2nd:2 3rd:1 Ran:4
Win Prizemoney £0 *Total Prizemoney* £3,303
1999 Turf 0-4: (8f 4) (g-s, gd 2, g-f)
Decent colt. Turf high 83 (began Spt) - 2nd of 9 giving 5lb to Littlepacepaddocks (3 Nov Musselburgh 8f g-f RF 5189).

**M R Channon [0-4] Ahmed Al Shafar.*

MAKATI BHB 37f50a RR 34f 50a 4940[1]
5 b g Efisio 7.7f **(69)** - Seleter (Hotfoot) 10.5f **(59)**
Form - 805023261
Record 1999 - 1st:1 2nd:2 3rd:1 Ran:9
Pre1999 - 1st:2 2nd:3 3rd:0 Ran:12
Win Prizemoney £7,081 *Total Prizemoney* £10,516
Wins * 1999 *Oct Southw (STD) H 14f 43 52 <*
* 1998 *Jly Wolver (STD) H 16.2f 30 41+*
* 1998 *Jly Southw (STD) H 14f 33 36+*
1999 Turf 0-2: (16f, 17f) (sft, gd) 1999 AW 1-7: (14f 1-2, 15f, 16f 4) (Fibr 1-7)
Fair gelding, effective 12 to 16f, - acts on Fibr, favours tight tracks, and excels at Wolverhampton. Turf high 34. AW high 52 - 1st of 9 getting 13lb from Western Command (18 Oct Southwell RF 4940). Improving. He is a consistent performer in modest handicap company over middle distances on Fibresand, but stayed 14 furlongs well when winning at Southwell in October.
**Miss J A Camacho [3-17] Paul Wilson (from M J Camacho [0-4] Jly 1997).*

MAKEIT MUSIC BHB 25f RR 38f 3986[11]
3 b g Komaite (USA) 6.9f **(61)** - Gandoorah (Record Token) 6.3f **(53)**
Form - 0
Record 1999 - 1st:0 2nd:0 3rd:0 Ran:1
Pre1999 - 1st:0 2nd:0 3rd:0 Ran:4
1999 Turf 0-1: (7f) (frm)
Scopey, very moderate gelding.
**Mrs A M Naughton [0-5] Mrs S E Cooper.*

MAKE NO MISTAKE (IRE) RR 118f 3718a[8]
4 b c Darshaan 11.9f **(81)** - Respectfully (USA) (The Minstrel (CAN)) 10f **(72)**
Form - 3718
1999 Turf 1-4: (10f 1-2, 11f, 12f) (g-f 2, frm 1-2)
High-class colt, effective 10 to 11f, best at 10f, acts on g-f to hrd, often wears blinkers (extremely effectively), likes right handed tracks. Turf high 118 - 1st of 7 giving 7lb to Saffron Walden (23 Jly Curragh RF 3188a). He just seems to find Group One company too much for him and was found wanting at that level behind Shiva and Dark Moondancer in his first two runs of last term. However, he then won the Meld stakes over ten furlongs from Saffron Walden, before running disappointingly in the Royal Whip, a race he had won the previous year. Sent to Australia for the Cox Plate, but finished unplaced. **D K Weld in IRE [3-12] Moyglare Stud Farm.*

MAKE READY BHB 67f57a RR 68f 57a 3391[10]
5 b m Beveled (USA) 6.9f **(64)** - Prepare (IRE) (Millfontaine)
Form - 1455210564150
Record 1999 - 1st:3 2nd:1 3rd:0 Ran:13
Pre1999 - 1st:2 2nd:2 3rd:2 Ran:26
Win Prizemoney £15,151 *Total Prizemoney* £19,729
Wins * 1999 Jly Newmar (G-F) H 6f 64 68 <
* **1999** May Chepst (GD) H 6.1f 55 68+
* **1999** *Apr Wolver (STD) H 6f 39 46+*
* 1996 *Spt Southw (STD) SH 5f 60 57*
* 1996 *Jly Southw (STD) S 5f 51*
1999 Turf 2-9: (6f 2-9) (gd 1-1, g-f 3, frm 1-5) 1999 AW 1-4: (5f 3, 6f 1-1) (Fibr 1-4)
Average filly, effective 6f, acts on gd to frm, best on frm, has worn blinkers. Turf high 68 - 1st of 13 giving 6lb to Rambold (31 May Chepstow RF 1597) - also 1st of 9 getting 1lb from My Emily (16 Jly Newmarket RF 2883). AW high 55. She was on a very long losing run before causing a surprise in winning a six-furlong handicap on the Wolverhampton Fibresand in April. She later added turf victories at Chepstow and Newmarket. **J Neville [5-39] J Neville.*

MAKE RINGS RR 37f 3641[6]
3 b f Rainbow Quest (USA) 11.2f **(81)** - Guillem (USA) (Nijinsky (CAN)) 10.3f **(77)**
Form - 6
Record 1999 - 1st:0 2nd:0 3rd:0 Ran:1
1999 Turf 0-1: (14f) (g-f)
Scopey, currently very moderate filly. **H R A Cecil [0-1] K Abdulla.*

MAKEUP A MYSTERY (USA) RR 93f 5015a4
2 b c Mystery Storm (USA) - No Makeup (USA) (Proud Truth (USA))
Form - 14
1999 Turf 1-2: (8f 1-2) (g-f 1-2)
Currently useful colt. Turf high 93 (began Jly) - 4th of 9 to Night Style (17 Oct San Siro 8f g-f RF 5015a). *B Grizzetti in ITY [1-2].*

MAKE WAY (USA) BHB 84f **RR 84f** 44066
3 b c Red Ransom (USA) 8.6f **(83)** - Way of The World (USA) (Dance of Life (USA)) 7f **(66)**
Form - 213436
Record 1999 - 1st:1 2nd:1 3rd:2 Ran:6
Pre1999 - 1st:0 2nd:0 3rd:0 Ran:1
Win Prizemoney £3,870 *Total Prizemoney* £8,087
Wins * 1999 Jun Windso (G-F) 8.3f 85 <
1999 Turf 1-6: (7f, 8f 1-3, 10f 2) (gd 2, g-f, frm 1-3)
Scopey, decent colt, effective 7 to 10f, best at 8f, acts on gd to frm, best on frm, has worn blinkers. Turf high 85 - 1st of 15 from Daytime (21 Jun Windsor RF 2182). *B J Meehan [1-6] Miss J Semple (from I A Balding [0-1] Jly 1998).*

MAKNAAS BHB 49f47a **RR 50f 47a** 50565
3 ch c Wolfhound (USA) 7.3f **(71)** - White-Wash (Final Straw) 7.9f **(64)**
Form - 700345
Record 1999 - 1st:0 2nd:0 3rd:1 Ran:6
Pre1999 - 1st:0 2nd:0 3rd:0 Ran:2
Win Prizemoney £0 *Total Prizemoney* £481
1999 Turf 0-4: (7f, 8f 2, 10f) (g-s 2, g-f, frm) 1999 AW 0-2: (7f, 10f) (Equi 2)
Strong, fair colt, effective 8f, acts on g-s, often wears blinkers (very effectively). Turf high 55 (began Jly). AW high 43 (began Aug). *R W Armstrong [0-8] Mrs Mary-Anne Parker.*

MALAAH (IRE) BHB 55f **RR 49f** 23326
3 gr g Pips Pride 6.7f **(70)** - Lingdale Lass (Petong) 6.6f **(58)**
Form - 78066
Record 1999 - 1st:0 2nd:0 3rd:0 Ran:5
Pre1999 - 1st:0 2nd:0 3rd:0 Ran:1
1999 Turf 0-5: (5f, 6f, 7f 2, 8f) (g-f 2, frm, hrd 2)
Strong, moderate gelding, has worn blinkers. Turf high 57. *R W Armstrong [0-6] Hamdan Al Maktoum.*

MALADERIE (IRE) BHB 61f **RR 56f** 521213
5 b g Thatching 7.8f **(69)** - Native Melody (Tudor Music) 6.8f **(59)**
Form - 006066130023305050000
Record 1999 - 1st:1 2nd:1 3rd:3 Ran:22
Pre1999 - 1st:4 2nd:9 3rd:4 Ran:43
Win Prizemoney £23,388 *Total Prizemoney* £42,790
Wins * 1999 Jun Bath (GD) H 5.7f 66 69
1998 Oct York (GD) H 5f 69 70
1998 Spt Haydoc (GD) H 5f 64 68
1998 Aug Windso (G-F) H 5f 58 60
1996 Jun Windso (G-F) 6f 76 <
1999 Turf 1-22: (5f 15, 6f 1-5, 7f 2) (g-s, gd 6, g-f 1-4, frm 11)
Fair gelding, effective 5 to 7f, best at 5f, acts on gd to frm, best on gd, often wears blinkers (effectively), excels at Carlisle and Haydock. Turf high 71 - 3rd of 12 getting 3lb from Antonia's Double (24 Jly Newcastle 5f g-f RF 3101) - also 1st of 19 getting 15lb from Ellens Lad (12 Jun Bath RF 1944). Consistent.
M Dods [1-24] A G Watson (from M R Channon [4-41] Oct 1998).

MALCHIK BHB 35f36a **RR 41f 36a** 513512
3 ch c Absalom 7.1f **(56)** - Very Good (Noalto) 5.7f **(49)**
Form - 6332433650800265300
Record 1999 - 1st:0 2nd:2 3rd:4 Ran:17
Pre1999 - 1st:1 2nd:0 3rd:2 Ran:15
Win Prizemoney £2,080 *Total Prizemoney* £6,042
Wins * 1998 Spt Leices (G-S) SH 8f 52 59 <
1999 Turf 0-6: (8f 4, 10f, 12f) (sft, gd, g-f 3, frm) 1999 AW 0-11: (8f 5, 9f, 10f 3, 12f, 16f) (Equi 7, Fibr 4)
Scopey, moderate colt, effective 8f, acts on g-f, has worn blinkers. Turf high 41. AW high 47. Inconsistent.
P Howling [1-32] I G Mirzoian.

MALE-ANA-MOU (IRE) BHB 78f **RR 76f** 50282
6 ch g Ela-Mana-Mou 12.7f **(72)** - Glasson Lady (GER) (Priamos (GER)) 11.1f **(61)**
Form - 0010811352
Record 1999 - 1st:3 2nd:1 3rd:1 Ran:10
Pre1999 - 1st:1 2nd:1 3rd:4 Ran:19
Win Prizemoney £14,820 *Total Prizemoney* £22,852
Wins * 1999 Aug Sandow (GD) H 14f 72 74
*** 1999** Aug Salisb (SFT) H 14.1f 63 68
*** 1999** Jun Sandow (GD) H 14f 60 62
1996 Jun Goodwo (G-F) 10f 79 <
1999 Turf 3-10: (14f 3-7, 16f 2, 20f) (g-s, gd, g-f 1-3, frm 2-5)
Above-average gelding, effective 12 to 16f, best at 16f, acts on g-s to frm, likes right handed tracks, likes tight tracks, does well at Salisbury and Sandown. Turf high 76 - 2nd of 17 giving 12lb to Nicely (22 Oct Newbury 16f g-s RF 5028) - also 1st of 9 getting 5lb from Nichol Fifty (21 Aug Sandown RF 3827). He won three modest handicaps over 14 furlongs last term, but has gone up weights as a result. He does not want the ground fast.
J R Poulton [3-10] Oh So Bright Syndicate (from D R C Elsworth [1-19] Aug 1998).

MALEK (CHI) RR 556a2
6 b h Mocito Guapo (CHI) - Condegnito (CHI) (Chairman Walker (CHI))
Form - 2
1999 AW 0-1: (10f) (Dirt)
Currently top-class horse. (1st run) - 2nd of 8 to Almutawakel (28 Mar Nad Al Sheba 10f Dirt RF 0556a). This American-trained horse was a close fourth in the Dubai World Cup in 1998, and finished even closer when runner-up in the 1999 renewal.
R Mandella in USA [0-2] Greet Falls A.

MALIAN (IRE) BHB 61f **RR 63f** 32518
3 b br g Arcane (USA) 11.6f **(66)** - Rhein Valley (IRE) (Kings Lake (USA)) 10.8f **(67)**
Form - 00558
Record 1999 - 1st:0 2nd:0 3rd:0 Ran:5
1999 Turf 0-5: (11f, 12f 2, 14f, 18f) (gd, g-f 2, frm 2)
Workmanlike, average gelding. Turf high 67.
A P Jarvis [0-5] M I Glass.

MALIBU MAN BHB 69f81a **RR 71f 81a** 23175
7 ch g Ballacashtal (CAN) 7.9f **(51)** - National Time (USA) (Lord Avie (USA)) 5.3f **(61)**
Form - 10035
Record 1999 - 1st:1 2nd:0 3rd:1 Ran:5
Pre1999 - 1st:6 2nd:5 3rd:7 Ran:50
Win Prizemoney £21,401 *Total Prizemoney* £31,346
Wins * 1999 Mar Folkes (SFT) H 5f 63 71
* 1997 Aug Bath (GD) H 5.1f 70 75
* 1997 *Jun Wolver (STD) H 5f 69 77* <
* 1997 Mar Folkes (GD) H 5f 65 74+
* 1996 Spt Chepst (G-F) H 5.1f 63 65
1995 *Jly Wolver (STD) H 5f 62 71+*
1995 *Jun Wolver (STD) H 6f 55 58*
1999 Turf 1-4: (5f 1-2, 6f 2) (sft 1-1, frm 2, hrd) 1999 AW 0-1: (5f) (Fibr)
Above-average gelding, effective 5f, acts on sft to g-s - acts on Fibr, has worn blinkers. Turf high 71 (1st run) - 1st of 11 giving 17lb to Landican Lane (31 Mar Folkestone RF 0530). (1st run) - 3rd of 10 giving 21lb to Polar Mist (16 Jun Wolverhampton 5f Fibr RF 2066). Inconsistent. He can blaze from the stalls but has lost the habit and more often than not walks from the gate these days. That did not stop him from winning in soft ground at Folkestone on his reappearance.
E A Wheeler [5-37] Church Racing Partnership (from S Mellor [2-18] Apr 1996).

MALLEUS BHB 80f **RR 76f** 44902
2 ch c Hamas (IRE) 8f **(72)** - Queen Warrior (Daring March) 7.1f **(61)**
Form - 5532
Record 1999 - 1st:0 2nd:1 3rd:1 Ran:4
Win Prizemoney £0 *Total Prizemoney* £1,390
1999 Turf 0-4: (6f, 7f, 8f 2) (g-s, gd, g-f, frm)
Above-average colt. Turf high 76 - 2nd of 12 to Going Global (22 Spt Goodwood 8f g-s RF 4490). *P T Walwyn [0-4] S W E J Slack.*

MALLIA BHB 69f75a **RR 67f 75a** 51604
6 b g Statoblest 6.4f **(63)** - Pronetta (USA) (Mr Prospector (USA)) 8.8f **(78)**
Form - 51523020513271381464802000004

Record 1999 - 1st:3 2nd:4 3rd:3 Ran:25
Pre1999 - 1st:6 2nd:4 3rd:1 Ran:33
Win Prizemoney £63,260 *Total Prizemoney* £82,697
Wins * **1999** Jly Haydoc (G-S) H 6f 70 74
* **1999** *May Wolver (Std) H 6f 70 74*
* **1999** *Mar Wolver (STD) C 6f 69*
* 1998 *Dec Wolver (STD) C 6f 63*
* 1998 Apr Ripon (SFT) H 6f 65 70
* 1997 *Dec Wolver (STD) H 6f 72 77*
* 1997 *Nov Southw (STD) H 6f 64 70+*
* 1996 Jun York (GD) H 6f 76 84 <
* 1995 May Hamilt (GD) 5f 78
1999 Turf 1-16: (5f, 6f 1-15) (sft, g-s, gd 1-6, g-f 4, frm 4) 1999 AW 2-9: (6f 2-9) (Equi, Fibr 2-8)
Above-average gelding, effective 6f, acts on sft to frm - acts on Fibr, best on g-f, often wears blinkers (extremely effectively), likes left handed tracks, likes tight tracks, excels at Wolverhampton and likes York. Turf high 76 - 4th of 13 getting 1lb from Royal Result (10 Jly York 6f g-f RF 2734) - also 1st of 16 getting 3lb from Royal Result (1 Jly Haydock RF 2463). AW high 74 - 3rd of 15 giving 3lb to Theatre Magic (18 Jan Southwell 6f Fibr RF 0116) - also 1st of 10 giving 6lb to Anthony Mon Amour (14 May Wolverhampton RF 1229). Inconsistent. He shows useful form over sprint distances on Fibresand, especially over the Wolverhampton six. Effective on turf too. **T D Barron [9-58] H T Duddin.*

MAMA-SAN (IRE) BHB 47f42a **RR 47f 42a** 4646[3]
4 b f Doyoun 10.7f **(69)** - Avila (Ajdal (USA)) 9.2f **(89)**
Form - 4470708213
Record 1999 - 1st:1 2nd:1 3rd:1 Ran:10
Win Prizemoney £3,204 *Total Prizemoney* £4,386
Wins * **1999** Spt Warwic (SFT) CH 10.5f 41 47 <
1999 Turf 1-6: (8f, 10f 3, 11f 1-2) (sft 1-2, g-s, g-f, frm 2) 1999 AW 0-4: (8f 2, 10f, 12f) (Equi, Fibr 3)
Fair filly, effective 10 to 11f, best at 10f, acted on sft to frm. Turf high 47 - 10th of 20 getting 7lb from Gypsy Hill (24 May Windsor 10f frm RF 1442) - also 1st of 20 giving 2lb to Inkwell (21 Spt Warwick RF 4454). AW high 50. Consistent. (DEAD)
**N A Callaghan [1-10] Andy Smith.*

MAMBLE'S PENSION (IRE) BHB 33f33a **RR 32f 33a** 1431[21]
4 ch f Elmaamul (USA) 8.1f **(70)** - Chance All (FR) (Glenstal (USA)) 10.1f **(64)**
Form - 00
Record 1999 - 1st:0 2nd:0 3rd:0 Ran:1
Pre1999 - 1st:0 2nd:0 3rd:0 Ran:8
1999 Turf 0-1: (6f) (frm)
Light-framed, very moderate filly. Inconsistent.
**A Bailey [0-9] Sandybrow Stables Ltd.*

MAMMA'S BOY BHB 49f66a **RR 60f 66a** 4914[12]
4 b g Rock City 8.8f **(62)** - Henpot (IRE) (Alzao (USA)) 7.1f **(68)**
Form - 000110350634066470
Record 1999 - 1st:2 2nd:0 3rd:2 Ran:18
Pre1999 - 1st:2 2nd:3 3rd:6 Ran:21
Win Prizemoney £12,604 *Total Prizemoney* £19,247
Wins * **1999** May Mussel (FRM) C 7.1f 61
* **1999** May Thirsk (G-S) S 7f 55
* **1998** Spt Sandow (G-S) C 5f 63+
* 1998 Jun Doncas (GD) H 6f 69 72 <
1999 Turf 2-18: (5f 2, 6f 10, 7f 2-6) (hvy, gd 1-4, g-f 1-7, frm 5, hrd)
Strong, average gelding, effective 5 to 6f, best at 6f, acts on gd to frm, best on gd, has worn blinkers, likes left handed tracks, likes tight tracks. Turf high 61. **J Berry [4-39] G Tiribocchi.*

MAMMAS F-C (IRE) BHB 57f52a **RR 58f 52a** 5199[11]
3 ch f Case Law 6f **(64)** - Wasaif (IRE) (Lomond (USA)) 8.8f **(65)**
Form - 4445242411314820
Record 1999 - 1st:3 2nd:3 3rd:1 Ran:16
Pre1999 - 1st:3 2nd:4 3rd:0 Ran:13
Win Prizemoney £17,813 *Total Prizemoney* £24,222
Wins * **1999** Aug Ripon (GD) H 6f 55 58
* **1999** Aug Bath (HRD) C 5.7f 49
* **1999** Jly Folkes (G-F) C 7f 46
1998 Spt Haydoc (GD) C 6f 65
1998 Jun Mussel (G-F) C 5f 60+
1998 *Jun Southw (STD) 5f 66* <
1999 Turf 3-13: (5f 2, 6f 2-8, 7f 1-3) (gd 6, g-f 1-2, frm 2-5) 1999 AW 0-3: (5f 3) (Fibr 3)
Neat, fair filly, effective 5 to 6f, best at 5f, acts on gd to frm - acts on Fibr, excels at Bath, likes Southwell. Turf high 58 - 2nd of 17 giving 12lb to Heavenly Miss (26 Oct Bath 5f gd RF 5065) - also 1st of 15 getting 24lb from Get Stuck In (30 Aug Ripon RF 4027). AW high 45. Consistent.
**J M Bradley [3-16] J M Kearney (from J Berry [3-13] Oct 1998).*

MAMZUG (IRE) **RR 39f** 5099[12]
2 b c Hamas (IRE) 8f **(72)** - Bellissi (IRE) (Bluebird (USA)) 7.5f **(69)**
Form - 0
Record 1999 - 1st:0 2nd:0 3rd:0 Ran:1
1999 Turf 0-1: (7f) (gd)
Currently very moderate colt. **B Hanbury [0-1] Hamdan Al Maktoum.*

MANA D'ARGENT (IRE) BHB 81f **RR 79f** 5047[3]
2 b c Ela-Mana-Mou 12.7f **(72)** - Petite-D-Argent **(52f)** (Noalto) 5.7f **(49)**
Form - 633
Record 1999 - 1st:0 2nd:0 3rd:2 Ran:3
Win Prizemoney £0 *Total Prizemoney* £1,227
1999 Turf 0-3: (6f 2, 7f) (hvy, gd 2)
Currently above-average colt. Turf high 79 (began Aug) - 3rd of 15 giving 5lb to Another Pearl (23 Oct Newbury 6f hvy RF 5047).
**M Johnston [0-3] Daniel Couper.*

MANA-MOU BAY (IRE) **RR 93+f** 3617[1]
2 b c Ela-Mana-Mou 12.7f **(72)** - Summerhill (Habitat) 9.4f **(70)**
Form - 21
Record 1999 - 1st:1 2nd:1 3rd:0 Ran:2
Win Prizemoney £11,795 *Total Prizemoney* £13,915
Wins * **1999** Aug Newbur (GD) L 7f 93+ <
1999 Turf 1-2: (6f, 7f 1-1) (gd, g-f 1-1)
Currently useful colt. Turf high 93 (began Jly) - 1st of 6 from Tioga (13 Aug Newbury RF 3617). Made a very pleasing racecourse debut over six furlongs at Ascot on good to firm ground where he just lost out. The impression he gave that day was that seven furlongs would be beneficial, and he duly took a Listed event in workmanlike style next time. **R Hannon [1-2] N A Woodcock.*

MANCALA BHB 65f **RR 61df** 1518[5]
3 ch f Deploy 11.4f **(67)** - Alghabrah (Lomond (USA)) 8.8f **(65)**
Form - 75
Record 1999 - 1st:0 2nd:0 3rd:0 Ran:2
Pre1999 - 1st:0 2nd:0 3rd:1 Ran:3
Win Prizemoney £0 *Total Prizemoney* £507
1999 Turf 0-2: (8f, 13f) (gd, hrd)
Neat, average filly. Turf high 39. **P F I Cole [0-5] N C Kersey.*

MANCHURIA (IRE) BHB 76f **RR 79df** 2834[2]
3 ch c Indian Ridge 7.6f **(74)** - Shih Ching (USA) (Secreto (USA)) 8.7f **(72)**
Form - 0332
Record 1999 - 1st:0 2nd:1 3rd:2 Ran:4
Win Prizemoney £0 *Total Prizemoney* £2,386
1999 Turf 0-4: (6f 2, 7f 2) (gd 3, g-f)
Workmanlike, above-average colt. Turf high 79 - 3rd of 5 giving 5lb to Corndavon (2 Jly Warwick 6f g-f RF 2508).
**J H M Gosden [0-4] Sheikh Mohammed.*

MANCINI BHB 52f **RR 37f** 1329[10]
6 b br g Nomination 7.3f **(57)** - Roman Blue (Charlottown) 10.9f **(57)**
Form - 0
Record 1999 - 1st:0 2nd:0 3rd:0 Ran:1
Pre1999 - 1st:1 2nd:1 3rd:0 Ran:10
Win Prizemoney £3,245 *Total Prizemoney* £4,719
Wins 1995 Aug Bright (FRM) 7f 84 <
1999 Turf 0-1: (18f) (gd)
Very moderate gelding, has worn blinkers. Inconsistent.
**J A B Old [0-8] Mrs Anne Yearley (from M L W Bell [1-9] Aug 1996).*

MANDAMA (IRE) **RR 96f** 4737a[3]
2 b f Warning 8.1f **(77)** - Dawnsio (IRE) (Tate Gallery (USA)) 7.4f **(67)**
Form - 173
1999 Turf 1-3: (6f, 7f 1-2) (sft, g-s 1-1, g-f)
Currently very useful filly. Turf high 96 (1st run) (began Aug) - 1st of 16 from Alluring (19 Aug Tipperary RF 3883a). She had a tough race on her debut and was a shade disappointing thereafter. Likely

to stay a mile, she has plenty to prove.
**J Oxx in IRE [1-3] Lady Clague.*

MANDOOB RR 57f
4840[5]

2 b c Zafonic (USA) 9f **(83)** - Thaidah (CAN) (Vice Regent (CAN)) 8.7f **(74)**
Form - 5
Record 1999 - 1st:0 2nd:0 3rd:0 Ran:1
1999 Turf 0-1: (7f) (gd)
Currently fair colt. **A C Stewart [0-1] Hamdan Al Maktoum.*

MANE FRAME BHB 67f RR 66f
5220[4]

4 b g Unfuwain (USA) 11.4f **(74)** - Moviegoer (Pharly (FR)) 9.8f **(68)**
Form - 214114264
Record 1999 - 1st:3 2nd:2 3rd:0 Ran:9
Pre1999 - 1st:0 2nd:1 3rd:2 Ran:8
Win Prizemoney £10,175 *Total Prizemoney* £19,295

Wins								
* 1999	Jly	Sandow	(G-F)	H	14f	62	66	<
* 1999	Jun	Warwic	(HVY)	H	12.3f	60	64	
* 1999	Apr	Windso	(G-S)		11.6f		58	

1999 Turf 3-9: (12f 2-2, 13f 2, 14f 1-3, 16f, 17f) (sft, g-s 1-1, gd 1-4, g-f 2, frm 1-1)
Workmanlike, average gelding, effective 12 to 17f, acts on sft to frm, prefers tight tracks, excels at Sandown. Turf high 66 - 2nd of 11 getting 24lb from Montecristo (27 Spt Hamilton 13f gd RF 4590) - also 1st of 10 giving 1lb to Durham (21 Jly Sandown RF 3018). Consistent. He enjoyed a rewarding season and seemed to have no difficulty staying 14 furlongs when winning at Sandown in July.
**H Morrison [3-17] A, J & M Arbib.*

MANFUL BHB 49f37a RR 54f 37a
5071[3]

7 b g Efisio 7.7f **(69)** - Mandrian (Mandamus) 12.6f **(56)**
Form - 30066023301200068403
Record 1999 - 1st:1 2nd:2 3rd:3 Ran:18
Pre1999 - 1st:10 2nd:10 3rd:9 Ran:74
Win Prizemoney £39,738 *Total Prizemoney* £60,306

Wins								
* 1999	Jun	Ayr	(SFT)	H	10.9f	59	64	
* 1998	Aug	Ayr	(G-S)	H	10f	60	62	
* 1997	May	Hamilt	(SFT)	H	11.1f	72	76	
* 1997	Apr	Hamilt	(SFT)	H	11.1f	68	73	
1996	*Dec*	*Southw*	*(SLW)*	*H*	*11f*	*62*	*68*	
1996	*Oct*	*Lingfi*	*(STD)*	*H*	*12f*	*54*	*58*	
1996	Spt	Hamilt	(G-S)	C	11.1f		69	
1996	May	Ayr	(G-S)	H	10.9f	62	67	
1996	Mar	Doncas	(GD)	H	10.3f	54	63	

1999 Turf 1-16: (10f 4, 11f 1-8, 12f 2, 13f 2) (hvy 2, sft, g-s 1-1, gd 7, g-f 2, frm 3) 1999 AW 0-2: (11f 2) (Fibr 2)
Fair gelding, effective 10 to 12f, best at 11f, acts on g-s to frm, often wears blinkers (effectively), and likes Ayr. Turf high 64 - 1st of 17 giving 21lb to Simple Ideals (19 Jun Ayr RF 2145). AW high 22.
**Miss L A Perratt [4-43] C D Barber-Lomax (from J Hetherton [2-39] Mar 1999).*

MANGUS (IRE) BHB 61f76a RR 59f 76a
3796[2]

5 b g Mac's Imp (USA) 5.6f **(54)** - Holly Bird (Runnett) 7f **(59)**
Form - 44200340330272
Record 1999 - 1st:0 2nd:3 3rd:3 Ran:14
Pre1999 - 1st:3 2nd:3 3rd:1 Ran:25
Win Prizemoney £9,435 *Total Prizemoney* £19,833

Wins								
* 1998	*Jun*	*Wolver*	*(STD)*	*H*	*5f*	*72*	*74*	<
* 1998	May	Lingfi	(G-F)	H	5f	67	72	
* 1997	Apr	Warwic	(G-F)	H	5f	70	72	

1999 Turf 0-11: (5f 11) (g-s, gd 4, g-f, frm 5) 1999 AW 0-3: (5f 3) (Equi 2, Fibr)
Above-average gelding, effective 5f, acts on g-f to frm - acts on Fibr, likes tight tracks. Turf high 66. AW high 73.
**K O Cunningham-Brown [3-39] Danebury Racing Stables Ltd.*

MANHATTAN RR 90+f
1820a[1]

2 b c Fairy King (USA) 7.7f **(75)** - Miss Arizona 00
Form - 1
1999 Turf 1-1: (6f 1-1) (gd 1-1)
Currently useful colt. (1st run) - 1st of 10 giving 5lb to Reve De Nuit (2 Jun Fairyhouse RF 1820a).
**A P O'Brien in IRE [1-1] Mrs John Magnier.*

MANICURE (IRE) BHB 68f RR 66f
4829[10]

3 b f Lucky Guest - Mana (GER) (Windwurf (GER)) 12.7f **(72)**
Form - 022180
Record 1999 - 1st:1 2nd:2 3rd:0 Ran:6
Pre1999 - 1st:0 2nd:0 3rd:0 Ran:1
Win Prizemoney £2,406 *Total Prizemoney* £4,184

Wins								
* 1999	Jly	Leices	(G-F)		10f		66	<

1999 Turf 1-6: (6f, 8f 2, 9f, 10f 1-1, 11f) (sft, g-s, g-f 1-2, frm, hrd)
Unfurnished, average filly, effective 8f, acts on g-f to hrd. Turf high 78 - 2nd of 14 getting 5lb from Harlequin Dancer (31 May Leicester 8f g-f RF 1601). **E A L Dunlop [1-7] Anamoine Ltd.*

MANIKATO (USA) BHB 26f37a RR 32f 37a
2934[10]

5 b g Clever Trick (USA) 7.6f **(69)** - Pasampsi (USA) (Crow (FR)) 7.4f **(75)**
Form - 050600
Record 1999 - 1st:0 2nd:0 3rd:0 Ran:5
Pre1999 - 1st:0 2nd:4 3rd:2 Ran:28
Win Prizemoney £0 *Total Prizemoney* £8,702
1999 Turf 0-3: (10f, 11f, 12f) (g-f, frm, hrd) 1999 AW 0-2: (7f 2) (Fibr 2)
Very moderate gelding, effective 7f, - acts on Fibr, has worn blinkers. Turf high 32. AW high 39.
**T T Clement [0-3] Miss A Hutchinson (from D J S Cosgrove [0-30] Feb 1999).*

MANILENO BHB 62f67a RR 35f 67a
2255[8]

5 ch g K-Battery 12.4f **(59)** - Andalucia (Rheingold) 10.4f **(62)**
Form - 511648
Record 1999 - 1st:2 2nd:0 3rd:0 Ran:6
Pre1999 - 1st:5 2nd:0 3rd:3 Ran:11
Win Prizemoney £16,034 *Total Prizemoney* £17,631

Wins								
* 1999	*Feb*	*Wolver*	*(STD)*	*C*	*14.8f*		*62*	
* 1999	*Feb*	*Wolver*	*(STD)*	*S*	*16.2f*		*55*	
* 1998	*Jun*	*Southw*	*(STD)*	*C*	*14f*		*73*	
1998	*Jun*	*Southw*	*(STD)*	*C*	*16f*		*74*	<
1997	Jly	Warwic	(SFT)	H	14.9f	57	65++	
1997	Jun	Lingfi	(GD)	H	11.5f	51	55+	
1997	May	Bright	(FRM)	SH	11.9f	45	48	

1999 Turf 0-1: (16f) (g-f) 1999 AW 2-5: (15f 1-2, 16f 1-3) (Fibr 2-5)
Fair gelding, effective 14 to 16f, - acts on Fibr, has worn blinkers. AW high 62. Consistent. Completed a hat-trick at the start of 1998 before embarking on a successful hurdles campaign at the end of the year. Successfully returned to the level last season with two victories in long-distance Fibresand claimers.
**Miss S J Wilton [3-12] John Pointon and Sons (from M C Pipe [8-14] Jun 1998).*

MANISTIQUE (USA) RR
5224a[8]

4 f Unbridled (USA) - Astaire Step (USA) (Nureyev (USA)) 8.7f **(78)**
Form - 8
1999 AW 0-1: (9f) (Dirt)
Currently useful. **J Shirreffs in USA [0-1].*

MANNDAR (IRE) BHB 110f RR 114f
4513a[3]

3 b c Doyoun 10.7f **(69)** - Madiriya (Diesis) 9.3f **(69)**
Form - 2211433
Record 1999 - 1st:2 2nd:2 3rd:2 Ran:7
Win Prizemoney £16,457 *Total Prizemoney* £36,526

Wins								
* 1999	Jun	Newmar	(GD)	L	10f		110+	<
* 1999	May	Bath	(GD)		10.2f		97+	

1999 Turf 2-7: (8f 2, 10f 2-4, 12f) (sft, gd 2-4, g-f, frm)
Well made, Group-class colt, effective 10 to 12f, best at 10f, acts on sft to g-f, best on gd. Turf high 114 - 3rd of 5 to Dubai Millennium (18 Jly Maisons-Laffitte 10f gd RF 3042a) - also 1st of 5 getting 3lb from Tissifer (5 Jun Newmarket RF 1772). Unraced at two, he made tremendous strides in a short space of time, putting up his best effort when finishing third behind Dubai Millennium and State Shinto in a Group 2 at Maisons-Laffitte during July. Likely to stay a mile and a half in 2000, he has plenty of scope and is a ready-made Group winner. **L M Cumani [2-7] Aga Khan.*

MAN OF COURAGE BHB 78f RR 74f
1752[11]

4 b g Nashwan (USA) 10.3f **(79)** - Dafrah (USA) (Danzig (USA)) 8.4f **(76)**
Form - 230
Record 1999 - 1st:0 2nd:1 3rd:1 Ran:3
Pre1999 - 1st:0 2nd:0 3rd:1 Ran:2

Win Prizemoney £0 *Total Prizemoney* £2,289
1999 Turf 0-3: (12f 3) (gd, g-f 2)
Above-average gelding. Turf high 74 (1st run) - 2nd of 10 giving 20lb to Toto Caelo (8 Apr Leicester 12f gd RF 0623).
**E A L Dunlop [0-5] Maktoum Al Maktoum.*

MAN OF THE NIGHT BHB 50f RR 42f 2521[6]

3 b g Clantime 6.6f **(57)** - Forbidden Monkey (Gabitat) 5f **(44)**
Form - 0806
Record 1999 - 1st:0 2nd:0 3rd:0 Ran:4
Pre1999 - 1st:1 2nd:0 3rd:0 Ran:3
Win Prizemoney £2,556 *Total Prizemoney* £2,556
Wins * 1998 Aug Hamilt (SFT) S 5f 64+ <
1999 Turf 0-4: (7f, 8f, 12f 2) (gd 2, frm, hrd)
Leggy, moderate gelding, effective 5f, acts on gd, has worn blinkers. Turf high 42. **J J O'Neill [1-7] E A Brook.*

MANOLO (FR) BHB 60f65a RR 48f 65a 4380[15]

6 b g Cricket Ball (USA) 7.9f **(75)** - Malouna (FR) (General Holme (USA)) 5.7f **(63)**
Form - 0
Record 1999 - 1st:0 2nd:0 3rd:0 Ran:1
Pre1999 - 1st:4 2nd:4 3rd:1 Ran:27
Win Prizemoney £12,231 *Total Prizemoney* £18,296
Wins 1998 *Feb Lingfi (SLW) H 5f 56 66 <*
1998 *Feb Lingfi (SLW) H 6f 58 65*
1997 Apr Pontef (G-F) H 5f 62 64
1996 Spt Beverl (G-F) 5f 62
1999 Turf 0-1: (7f) (gd)
Average gelding, effective 5 to 6f, - acts on Equi, often wears blinkers (effectively).
**D Nicholls [0-1] Lucayan Stud (from D R Loder [2-5] Apr 1998).*

MAN O'MYSTERY (USA) RR 62f 3937[11]

2 b c Diesis 9f **(80)** - Eurostorm (USA) (Storm Bird (CAN)) 10.3f **(74)**
Form - 0
Record 1999 - 1st:0 2nd:0 3rd:0 Ran:1
1999 Turf 0-1: (7f) (frm)
Currently average colt. **J Noseda [0-1] Ecurie Pharos.*

MANSA MUSA (IRE) BHB 72f70a RR 75f 70a 2046[7]

4 br g Hamas (IRE) 8f **(72)** - Marton Maid (Silly Season) 9.7f **(56)**
Form - 6710647
Record 1999 - 1st:1 2nd:0 3rd:0 Ran:7
Pre1999 - 1st:0 2nd:2 3rd:3 Ran:9
Win Prizemoney £3,745 *Total Prizemoney* £14,110
Wins * 1999 Apr Bright (G-F) 8f 75 <
1999 Turf 1-6: (8f 1-2, 9f 2, 10f, 11f) (g-s, gd 2, g-f, frm 1-2) 1999 AW 0-1: (10f) (Equi)
Unfurnished, above-average gelding, effective 8 to 10f, acts on gd to frm, best on gd, prefers left handed tracks, prefers tight tracks. Turf high 75 - 4th of 14 to Scene (4 Jun Epsom 9f gd RF 1730) - also 1st of 7 from Sky Dome (29 Apr Brighton RF 0911).
**M R Channon [1-16] Surrey Laminators Ltd.*

MANSTAR (IRE) BHB 60f RR 77f 4388[8]

2 b c In The Wings 11.2f **(77)** - Model Village (Habitat) 9.4f **(70)**
Form - 03458
Record 1999 - 1st:0 2nd:0 3rd:1 Ran:5
Win Prizemoney £0 *Total Prizemoney* £792
1999 Turf 0-5: (6f, 7f 2, 8f 2) (gd 2, g-f, frm 2)
Above-average colt. Turf high 77.
**C W Fairhurst [0-5] C D Barber-Lomax.*

MANTILLA RR 78f 5209[3]

2 b f Son Pardo - Well Tried (IRE) (Thatching) 8f **(66)**
Form - 53
Record 1999 - 1st:0 2nd:0 3rd:1 Ran:2
Win Prizemoney £0 *Total Prizemoney* £565
1999 Turf 0-2: (5f, 6f) (g-s, gd)
Currently above-average filly. Turf high 78 (began Oct) - 3rd of 20 getting 5lb from Royal Highlander (5 Nov Doncaster 6f g-s RF 5209). **R Hollinshead [0-2] Exors of the late Mrs J P Bissill.*

MANTLES PRIDE BHB 82f RR 81f 4880[11]

4 b g Petong 7.6f **(58)** - State Romance (Free State) 8.7f **(61)**
Form - 35376101130
Record 1999 - 1st:3 2nd:0 3rd:3 Ran:11
Pre1999 - 1st:1 2nd:2 3rd:3 Ran:17
Win Prizemoney £18,474 *Total Prizemoney* £28,826
Wins *** 1999** Spt Haydoc (G-F) H 7.1f 76 79+
*** 1999** Aug Redcar (GD) H 7f 71 76
*** 1999** Jly Carlis (FRM) H 6.9f 66 69
1997 Spt Folkes (FRM) H 5f 78 83 <
1999 Turf 3-11: (7f 3-9, 8f 2) (g-s, gd 3, g-f 3, frm 3-4)
Neat, decent gelding, effective 7f, acts on gd to frm, best on frm, often wears blinkers (very effectively), likes tight tracks. Turf high 81 - 3rd of 14 giving 18lb to Perfect Peach (26 Spt Musselburgh 7f gd RF 4579) - also 1st of 14 giving 2lb to Amber Fort (4 Spt Haydock RF 4140). Broke his losing run - which dated back to 1997 - at Carlisle in July. He completed a seasonal hat trick by scoring at Redcar and Haydock.
**P Calver [3-22] Kenneth MacPherson (from G Lewis [1-6] Oct 1997).*

MANTLES PRINCESS BHB 41f40a RR 26f 40a 767[13]

4 b f Rock City 8.8f **(62)** - Teslemi (USA) (Ogygian (USA))
Form - 300
Record 1999 - 1st:0 2nd:0 3rd:1 Ran:3
Pre1999 - 1st:0 2nd:0 3rd:0 Ran:1
Win Prizemoney £0 *Total Prizemoney* £454
1999 Turf 0-2: (8f, 12f) (hvy, sft) 1999 AW 0-1: (10f) (Equi)
Scopey, very moderate filly. Turf high 26.
**G Lewis [0-4] David Barker.*

MANTUSIS (IRE) BHB 83f RR 83f 4954[1]

4 ch g Pursuit of Love 9.5f **(69)** - Mana (GER) (Windwurf (GER)) 12.7f **(72)**
Form - 072334001
Record 1999 - 1st:1 2nd:1 3rd:2 Ran:9
Pre1999 - 1st:1 2nd:2 3rd:1 Ran:8
Win Prizemoney £8,862 *Total Prizemoney* £18,658
Wins *** 1999** Oct Yarmou (G-F) H 10.1f 80 83
* 1997 Oct Leices (G-S) 8f 87 <
1999 Turf 1-9: (8f 2, 10f 1-6, 12f) (gd 2, g-f 1-3, frm 4)
Scopey, decent gelding, effective 7 to 10f, acts on g-s to g-f. Turf high 83 - 1st of 15 giving 6lb to Pinchincha (19 Oct Yarmouth RF 4954). **P W Harris [2-17] The Romantics.*

MANUFAN BHB 46f RR 42f 4987[18]

4 b c Sabrehill (USA) 8.5f **(64)** - The Last Empress (IRE) (Last Tycoon) 8.5f **(62)**
Form - 0304300730
Record 1999 - 1st:0 2nd:0 3rd:3 Ran:10
Pre1999 - 1st:0 2nd:2 3rd:1 Ran:9
Win Prizemoney £0 *Total Prizemoney* £4,812
1999 Turf 0-10: (7f 4, 8f 5, 10f) (gd 4, g-f 2, frm 4)
Lengthy, moderate colt, effective 12f, acts on gd, has worn blinkers, likes tight tracks. Turf high 55.
**W R Muir [0-10] Michael Payton (from R F JohnsonHoughton [0-9] Oct 1998).*

MANX SHADOW BHB 45f RR 43f 3990[8]

2 b br f Contract Law (USA) 8.9f **(54)** - Inbisat (Beldale Flutter (USA)) 9.7f **(71)**
Form - 800058
Record 1999 - 1st:0 2nd:0 3rd:0 Ran:6
1999 Turf 0-6: (5f 3, 6f, 7f, 8f) (gd, g-f, frm 4)
Moderate filly. Turf high 43. **K W Hogg [0-6] K W Hogg.*

MANXWOOD (IRE) BHB 64f RR 66f 4358[9]

2 b c Petorius 8f **(66)** - Eliza Wooding **(24f)** (Faustus (USA)) 10f **(58)**
Form - 07460
Record 1999 - 1st:0 2nd:0 3rd:0 Ran:5
Win Prizemoney £0 *Total Prizemoney* £1,450
1999 Turf 0-4: (6f, 7f, 8f 2) (g-s, frm 3) 1999 AW 0-1: (6f) (Fibr)
Average colt. Turf high 66.
**D J S Cosgrove [0-3] P M Mooney (from R Ingram [0-2] Jly 1999).*

MANY HAPPY RETURNS RR 55f 2524[13]

2 br f Bin Ajwaad (IRE) - Daarat Alayaam (IRE) (Reference Point) 6.8f **(70)**
Form - 00
Record 1999 - 1st:0 2nd:0 3rd:0 Ran:2
1999 Turf 0-2: (6f 2) (g-f, frm)

Currently fair filly. Turf high 55.
**G B Balding [0-2] Rex L Mead & S McQueen.*

MANZONI BHB 49a **RR 53f** 3803[2]
3 b g Warrshan (USA) 9.7f **(59)** - Arc Empress Jane (IRE) (Rainbow Quest (USA)) 10.4f **(75)**
Form - 8043122
Record 1999 - 1st:1 2nd:2 3rd:1 Ran:7
Pre1999 - 1st:0 2nd:0 3rd:0 Ran:4
Win Prizemoney £2,263 *Total Prizemoney* £4,853
Wins * 1999 *Jly Southw (STD) H 12f 49 50* <
1999 Turf 0-5: (5f, 6f, 9f, 12f 2) (gd 2, g-f 2, frm) 1999 AW 1-2: (12f 1-2) (Fibr 1-2)
Fair gelding, effective 12f, acts on g-f to frm - acts on Fibr, has worn blinkers, likes left handed tracks. Turf high 53 - 2nd of 14 getting 14lb from Flossy (20 Aug Newcastle 12f g-f RF 3803). AW high 50 - 1st of 14 getting 11lb from Forest King (10 Jly Southwell RF 2722).
**M W Easterby [1-7] Bodfari Stud Ltd (from G Lewis [0-4] Oct 1998).*

MANZOR (FR) RR 110f 5120a[1]
2 b c Cricket Ball (USA) 7.9f **(75)** - Amarige (FR) (Lesotho (USA))
Form - 11
1999 Turf 2-2: (5f 2-2) (hvy 2-2)
Currently Group-class colt. Turf high 110 (began Oct) - 1st of 9 getting 21lb from Nuclear Debate (24 Oct Longchamp RF 5120a).
**X Nakkachdji in FR [2-2] D Wildenstein.*

MAPLE (IRE) BHB 66f **RR 62f** 4696[12]
3 ch g Soviet Lad (USA) 9.4f **(63)** - Little Red Rose (Precocious) 8.6f **(62)**
Form - 0035770680
Record 1999 - 1st:0 2nd:0 3rd:1 Ran:10
Pre1999 - 1st:1 2nd:3 3rd:1 Ran:9
Win Prizemoney £3,980 *Total Prizemoney* £10,153
Wins * 1998 Spt Newbur (GD) 6f 80 <
1999 Turf 0-10: (5f, 6f 5, 7f 4) (g-s 2, gd 3, g-f 2, frm 3)
Workmanlike, average gelding, effective 5 to 7f, best at 6f, acts on gd to frm, best on frm. Turf high 84 - 3rd of 9 giving 1lb to Cubism (2 May Salisbury 6f frm RF 0987).
**D R C Elsworth [1-19] G Steinberg.*

MARADI (IRE) BHB 41f43a **RR 46f 43a** 133[6]
5 b g Marju (IRE) 9.2f **(76)** - Tigora (Ahonoora) 8.1f **(73)**
Form - 226
Record 1999 - 1st:0 2nd:2 3rd:0 Ran:3
Pre1999 - 1st:1 2nd:2 3rd:5 Ran:23
Win Prizemoney £3,371 *Total Prizemoney* £10,628
Wins 1997 *Feb Southw (STD) 12f 53++* <
1999 AW 0-3: (10f, 12f, 13f) (Equi 3)
Fair gelding, effective 10 to 13f, acts on frm - acts on Equi, has worn blinkers, favours left handed tracks, prefers tight tracks. AW high 50 - 2nd of 16 giving 1lb to Latin Bay (14 Jan Lingfield 12f Equi RF 0092).
**B J Curley [1-15] Mrs B J Curley (from M L W Bell [1-10] Oct 1997).*

MARAH BHB 95f **RR 92f** 5041[6]
2 ch f Machiavellian (USA) 9.8f **(83)** - Samheh (USA) **(60f)** (Private Account (USA)) 8.5f **(74)**
Form - 1376
Record 1999 - 1st:1 2nd:0 3rd:1 Ran:4
Win Prizemoney £3,403 *Total Prizemoney* £5,154
Wins * 1999 Jun Doncas (G-F) 7f 73+ <
1999 Turf 1-4: (7f 1-4) (sft, g-f, frm 1-2)
Useful filly. Turf high 92 - 3rd of 5 to Hypnotize (22 Jly Sandown 7f frm RF 3029). Made a winning debut at Doncaster before finishing a close third to Hypnotize in a Sandown Listed race. She had a rough passage in the Group Three Prestige Stakes at Goodwood, but it did not make any difference to the result.
**J L Dunlop [1-4] Hamdan Al Maktoum.*

MARAHA BHB 81f **RR 82f** 5142[8]
2 ch f Lammtarra (USA) - Taroob (IRE) (Roberto (USA)) 10f **(76)**
Form - 618
Record 1999 - 1st:1 2nd:0 3rd:0 Ran:3
Win Prizemoney £3,501 *Total Prizemoney* £3,501
Wins * 1999 Spt Haydoc (SFT) 8.1f 72 <
1999 Turf 1-3: (7f, 8f 1-2) (g-s 1-1, gd, frm)
Currently decent filly. Turf high 82 (began Spt). Winner of a soft ground mile maiden at Haydock in late September, where she ran on really strongly in the final quarter-mile.
**J L Dunlop [1-3] Hamdan Al Maktoum.*

MARAMBA BHB 80f **RR 88f** 5116a[4]
3 b f Rainbow Quest (USA) 11.2f **(81)** - Gayane (Nureyev (USA)) 8.7f **(78)**
Form - 4154
Record 1999 - 1st:1 2nd:0 3rd:0 Ran:4
Win Prizemoney £3,550 *Total Prizemoney* £3,850
Wins 1999 Aug Sandow (GD) 8.1f 76 <
1999 Turf 1-4: (8f 1-2, 9f, 10f) (hvy, g-s, gd, frm 1-1)
Workmanlike, useful filly. Turf high 88 - 4th of 13 to Shemaya (21 Oct Longchamp 9f hvy RF 5116a). Out of a speedy daughter of Roussalka, she made a pleasing debut at three when fourth in a fair ten-furlong maiden at Sandown. Scored on her next outing four months later, before finding a listed race at Chantilly beyond her. Can find further opportunities if not aimed too high.
**G A Butler [0-1] (from P W Chapple-Hyam [1-3] Spt 1999).*

MARASEM RR 77f 3462[7]
3 b f Cadeaux Genereux 7.9f **(76)** - Balaabel (USA) **(76f)** (Sadler's Wells (USA)) 10f **(76)**
Form - 17
Record 1999 - 1st:1 2nd:0 3rd:0 Ran:2
Win Prizemoney £4,416 *Total Prizemoney* £4,416
Wins * 1999 Jly Chepst (G-F) 7.1f 77+ <
1999 Turf 1-2: (7f 1-1, 8f) (gd, frm 1-1)
Scopey, currently above-average filly. Turf high 77 (1st run) (began Jly) - 1st of 15 from Umbrian Gold (3 Jly Chepstow RF 2528). Unraced at two, she won a fillies' maiden at Chepstow in fine style on her debut but was well beaten in an Ascot Listed event. She may not have handled the soft ground.
**M P Tregoning [1-2] Hamdan Al Maktoum.*

MARATHON MAID BHB 55f50a **RR 66f 50a** 294[11]
5 gr m Kalaglow 11.2f **(67)** - El Rabab (USA) (Roberto (USA)) 10f **(76)**
Form - 0
Record 1999 - 1st:0 2nd:0 3rd:0 Ran:1
Pre1999 - 1st:3 2nd:0 3rd:1 Ran:21
Win Prizemoney £12,101 *Total Prizemoney* £14,680
Wins * 1998 Jly Doncas (G-F) H 8f 60 64
* 1996 May Pontef (GD) 6f 84 <
* 1996 Apr Newcas (GD) 5f 67
1999 AW 0-1: (8f) (Fibr)
Average filly, effective 8 to 10f, best at 8f, acts on g-f to frm, best on frm, has worn blinkers.
**R A Fahey [3-22] John Stephenson & Sons (Nelson) Ltd.*

MARAUD BHB 25f **RR 23f** 3844[12]
5 ch g Midyan (USA) 9.9f **(64)** - Peak Squaw (USA) (Icecapade (USA)) 11f **(62)**
Form - 0030
Record 1999 - 1st:0 2nd:0 3rd:1 Ran:4
Pre1999 - 1st:1 2nd:2 3rd:2 Ran:12
Win Prizemoney £3,507 *Total Prizemoney* £6,965
Wins 1996 Oct Leices (G-F) H 7f 69 75 <
1999 Turf 0-4: (14f, 16f, 17f, 18f) (gd, g-f, frm 2)
Little account gelding, has worn blinkers. Turf high 23.
**M E Sowersby [1-9] David Dyer (from L R Lloyd-James [0-1] Oct 1997).*

MARCH GROOM (USA) RR 115f 2284a[3]
5 ro h Runaway Groom (CAN) 8.1f **(69)** - Marfa's Alibi (USA) (Marfa (USA)) 14.9f **(73)**
Form - 33
1999 Turf 0-2: (11f, 12f) (sft, g-f)
High-class colt, effective 11 to 12f, best at 12f, acts on gd to g-f, best on g-f. Turf high 110 - 3rd of 7 to Dark Moondancer (20 Jun San Siro 12f g-f RF 2284a). Consistent.
**O Gervai in GER [1-7] (from A Friebert in HUN [1-1] Aug 1997).*

MARCHING ORDERS (IRE) RR 91f 4979a[9]
3 b c Nashwan (USA) 10.3f **(79)** - Minstrels Folly (USA) (The Minstrel (CAN)) 10f **(72)**

Form - 35214010
1999 Turf 2-8: (8f 1-3, 9f 1-3, 10f, 12f) (hvy, sft 1-2, g-s 3, gd 1-2)
Useful colt, effective 8 to 9f, best at 9f, acts on sft to gd, often wears blinkers (very effectively), favours right handed tracks. Turf high 91 - 9th of 13 getting 10lb from Wray (17 Oct Fairyhouse 9f g-s RF 4979a) - also 1st of 16 getting 4lb from Misniuil (9 Oct Cork RF 4850a). Consistent. **D K Weld in IRE [2-8] Moyglare Stud Farm.*

MARCH PARTY (FR) BHB 40f51a **RR 32tf 51a** 3809[4]

3 ch f Archway (IRE) 8.5f **(60)** - Social Gathering (IRE) (Dance of Life (USA)) 7f **(66)**
Form - 860040074

Record	**1999** -	1st:0	2nd:0	3rd:0	Ran:9
	Pre1999 -	1st:1	2nd:0	3rd:1	Ran:9

Win Prizemoney £1,882 *Total Prizemoney* £2,459
Wins ** 1998 Jly Wolver (STD) S 7f 49 <*
1999 Turf 0-8: (8f 3, 9f, 10f 3, 11f) (hvy, gd, g-f 6) 1999 AW 0-1: (7f) (Fibr)
Unfurnished, moderate filly, effective 7 to 10f, best at 7f, acts on g-f - acts on Fibr, has worn blinkers, likes left handed tracks, likes tight tracks. Turf high 48. **J G Portman [1-18] Madhatter Racing.*

MARCIANO BHB 40f **RR 51f** 2943[10]

3 b g Rock Hopper 10.6f **(54)** - Raintree Venture (Good Times (ITY)) 6.6f **(54)**
Form - 7700

Record	**1999** -	1st:0	2nd:0	3rd:0	Ran:4
	Pre1999 -	1st:0	2nd:0	3rd:0	Ran:1

1999 Turf 0-3: (12f, 16f, 17f) (g-s, g-f, frm) 1999 AW 0-1: (8f) (Fibr)
Workmanlike, fair gelding. Turf high 51. **C W Thornton [0-5] Guy Reed.*

MARCOMIR (USA) BHB 25f64a **RR 4f 64a** 2758[12]

6 b h Dayjur (USA) 6.8f **(79)** - Mariella (USA) (Roberto (USA)) 10f **(76)**
Form - 050000

Record	**1999** -	1st:0	2nd:0	3rd:0	Ran:6
	Pre1999 -	1st:1	2nd:0	3rd:0	Ran:3

Win Prizemoney £4,260 *Total Prizemoney* £4,260
Wins 1995 Spt Hamilt (GD) 6f 71+ <
1999 Turf 0-6: (7f, 8f, 10f, 11f, 12f 2) (g-s, gd 2, g-f, frm 2)
Moderate horse, has worn blinkers. Turf high 42. Becoming disappointing. **W Storey [0-6] R Auld (from E J Alston [0-2] Jan 1998).*

MARCO'S PAL BHB 50f46a **RR 47f 46a** 122[7]

3 ch g Timeless Times (USA) 6.1f **(56)** - Parijoun (Manado) 9.6f **(63)**
Form - 77

Record	**1999** -	1st:0	2nd:0	3rd:0	Ran:2
	Pre1999 -	1st:0	2nd:0	3rd:0	Ran:4

1999 AW 0-2: (8f 2) (Equi 2)
Workmanlike, moderate gelding. AW high 38. **A P Jarvis [0-6] Ambrose Turnbull.*

MARCUS MAXIMUS (USA) BHB 114f **RR 119f** 1524[1]

4 ch c Woodman (USA) 9.7f **(77)** - Star Pastures (Northfields (USA)) 9f **(72)**
Form - 81

Record	**1999** -	1st:1	2nd:0	3rd:0	Ran:2
	Pre1999 -	1st:2	2nd:0	3rd:0	Ran:3

Win Prizemoney £18,815 *Total Prizemoney* £19,187

Wins	*** 1999**	May Newcas (FRM)	12.4f	119	<
	* 1998	Spt Doncas (GD)	10.3f	105	
	* 1998	Jly Yarmou (G-F)	11.5f	77	

1999 Turf 1-2: (12f 1-2) (frm 1-2)
Workmanlike, high-class colt. Turf high 119 - 1st of 5 giving 15lb to Travelmate (27 May Newcastle RF 1524). A winner twice at two, he was totally outclassed in the Jockey Club Stakes on his reappearance last season, but went on to defeat Travelmate and The Fly at Newcastle. Taken out of the Hardwicke at Royal Ascot on the morning of the race, he was not seen again. **H R A Cecil [3-5] Wafic Said.*

MARDANI (IRE) BHB 98f **RR 98f** 4664a[7]

4 b c Fairy King (USA) 7.7f **(75)** - Marmana (USA) (Blushing Groom (FR)) 10.3f **(76)**
Form - 34112027

Record	**1999** -	1st:2	2nd:2	3rd:1	Ran:8
	Pre1999 -	1st:2	2nd:2	3rd:0	Ran:6

Win Prizemoney £24,832 *Total Prizemoney* £47,424

Wins	*** 1999**	Jly York (G-F) H	11.9f	93	94	<
	*** 1999**	Jun Beverl (G-F) H	12f	90	91	
	1998	Aug Leopar (GD)	12f		92+	
	1998	Jly Dundal (G-F)	12f		82+	

1999 Turf 2-8: (12f 2-4, 14f 2, 15f, 16f) (hvy, g-s, gd 2, g-f 1-3, frm 1-1)
Very useful colt, effective 10 to 12f, acts on g-s to gd, excels at Curragh. Turf high 98. Usually tough and reliable, he ran an unaccountably poor race in the Ebor. Possibly happier in small fields, he goes well on fast ground and is best ridden close to the pace. He is unlikely to stay beyond a mile and three-quarters. **M Johnston [2-8] (from J Oxx in IRE [2-6] Spt 1998).*

MARENGO BHB 55a **RR 48f** 5199[8]

5 b g Never so Bold 7.1f **(62)** - Born to Dance (Dancing Brave (USA)) 8.4f **(76)**
Form - 0207007650348

Record	**1999** -	1st:0	2nd:1	3rd:1	Ran:13
	Pre1999 -	1st:3	2nd:2	3rd:3	Ran:22

Win Prizemoney £13,034 *Total Prizemoney* £19,768

Wins	1998	Apr Epsom (SFT) H	6f	62	65	
	1998	*Apr Wolver (STD) H*	*6f*	*57*	*66*	*<*
	1998	*Mar Southw (STD) H*	*6f*	*53*	*53*	

1999 Turf 0-10: (5f 2, 6f 8) (gd 5, g-f 2, frm 3) 1999 AW 0-3: (6f 3) (Equi, Fibr 2)
Moderate gelding, effective 6f, acts on sft to frm - acts on Fibr, has worn blinkers, likes left handed tracks, likes tight tracks, excels at Epsom. Turf high 70 (1st run) - 2nd of 13 giving 8lb to Blushing Grenadier (10 May Redcar 6f gd RF 1124). **M J Polglase [0-2] M J Polglase (from J Berry [0-13] Oct 1999).*

MARGARET'S DANCER BHB 48f44a **RR 50f 44a** 5151[5]

4 b g Rambo Dancer (CAN) 8.4f **(59)** - Cateryne (Ballymoss) 8.5f **(55)**
Form - 7402770655

Record	**1999** -	1st:0	2nd:1	3rd:0	Ran:10
	Pre1999 -	1st:3	2nd:1	3rd:2	Ran:19

Win Prizemoney £8,998 *Total Prizemoney* £11,889

Wins	* 1998	Spt Beverl (G-F) H	8.5f	57	62	<
	* 1998	Spt Thirsk (GD) S	8f		57	
	* 1998	Jun Pontef (SFT) S	8f		49	

1999 Turf 0-9: (8f 8, 9f) (gd 6, g-f, frm, hrd) 1999 AW 0-1: (8f) (Fibr)
Unfurnished, fair gelding, effective 8f, acts on g-s to frm, has worn blinkers, prefers tight tracks, excels at Thirsk. Turf high 60 (1st run) - 4th of 18 to Legal Issue (16 Apr Thirsk 8f gd RF 0728). Inconsistent. **J L Eyre [3-21] Gordon Batty (from C Smith [0-8] Spt 1997).*

MARGARETS FIRST **RR 4f** 2270[8]

3 b f Puissance 7.1f **(60)** - Margaret's Gift **(92f)** (Beveled (USA)) 9f **(59)**
Form - 08

Record	**1999** -	1st:0	2nd:0	3rd:0	Ran:2

1999 Turf 0-2: (6f 2) (frm 2)
Leggy, currently very poor filly. Turf high 4. **J Berry [0-2] Margaret's Partnership.*

MARGARITA MOU **RR 11f** 3163[10]

2 ch f Clantime 6.6f **(57)** - Needle Sharp (Kris) 9.5f **(73)**
Form - 80

Record	**1999** -	1st:0	2nd:0	3rd:0	Ran:2

1999 Turf 0-1: (5f) (frm) 1999 AW 0-1: (5f) (Fibr)
Currently poor filly. **C Smith [0-2] Mrs N Stewart.*

MARGAY (IRE) **RR 97f** 5171a[3]

2 b f Marju - Almarai (USA) (Vaguely Noble) 10.1f **(72)**
Form - 3153
1999 Turf 1-4: (7f 1-4) (sft 1-3, g-s)
Very useful filly. Turf high 97 (began Aug) - 1st of 7 from Alluring (6 Spt Galway RF 4298a). She improved markedly from her debut and will stay beyond seven furlongs. However, she does not look up to winning a Group race. **M J Grassick in IRE [1-4] Mrs C Grassick.*

MARGOSTO (GER) **RR 107f** 2474a[8]

4 c Acatenango (GER) - Margie's Darling (GER) (Alydar (USA)) 9.1f **(76)**
Form - 38
1999 Turf 0-2: (11f, 12f) (gd 2)

Pattern-class colt. Turf high 99.
**P Schiergen in GER [0-2] (from A Schutz in GER [0-1] Jly 1998).*

MARIA FROM CAPLAW BHB 41f **RR 37f** 4277[7]
2 ch f Clantime 6.6f **(57)** - Mary From Dunlow (Nicholas Bill) 10.1f **(56)**
Form - 577
Record 1999 - 1st:0 2nd:0 3rd:0 Ran:3
1999 Turf 0-3: (5f 2, 6f) (g-f, frm 2)
Currently very moderate filly. Turf high 37 (began Aug).
**J J O'Neill [0-3] G P Bernacchi.*

MARIA ISABELLA (USA) RR 96f 2337[2]
4 ch f Kris 10f **(75)** - Korveya (USA) (Riverman (USA)) 9.1f **(76)**
Form - 22
Record 1999 - 1st:0 2nd:2 3rd:0 Ran:2
Pre1999 - 1st:1 2nd:0 3rd:0 Ran:1
Win Prizemoney £4,175 *Total Prizemoney* £15,667
Wins * 1998 Oct Nottin () 8.2f 61 <
1999 Turf 0-2: (9f, 10f) (frm 2)
Scopey, currently very useful filly. Turf high 96 - 2nd of 9 giving 12lb to Fictitious (26 Jun Newcastle 10f frm RF 2337). Very lightly-raced, she stays a mile and a quarter and is capable of winning a Listed event. **L M Cumani [1-3] Gerald Leigh.*

MARIANA BHB 35a **RR 18f** 4987[7]
4 ch f Anshan 8.2f **(63)** - Maria Cappuccini (Siberian Express (USA)) 8.8f **(65)**
Form - 00833404087
Record 1999 - 1st:0 2nd:0 3rd:2 Ran:8
Pre1999 - 1st:0 2nd:2 3rd:1 Ran:19
Win Prizemoney £0 *Total Prizemoney* £2,815
1999 Turf 0-4: (6f, 7f 2, 8f) (g-s, gd 2, frm) 1999 AW 0-4: (7f 2, 8f 2) (Equi, Fibr 3)
Leggy, very moderate filly, effective 7f, - acts on Equi, has worn blinkers, likes left handed tracks, likes tight tracks. Turf high 18. AW high 35.
**T T Clement [0-11] C Holcroft (from R M Whitaker [0-16] Oct 1998).*

MARIDPOUR (IRE) BHB 113f **RR 120+f** 3693[8]
4 b c Shernazar 11.8f **(71)** - Maridana (USA) (Nijinsky (CAN)) 10.3f **(77)**
Form - 8318
Record 1999 - 1st:1 2nd:0 3rd:1 Ran:4
Pre1999 - 1st:2 2nd:1 3rd:1 Ran:7
Win Prizemoney £64,377 *Total Prizemoney* £75,877
Wins * **1999** Jun Currag (GD) G3 14f 108+ <
* 1998 Jun Ascot (G-S) G3 16.2f 105
* 1998 May Hamilt (GD) 12.1f 86+
1999 Turf 1-4: (14f 1-1, 16f 3) (g-f 1-3, frm)
Well made, very high-class colt, effective 16f, acts on g-f to frm, prefers right handed tracks. Turf high 120 - 3rd of 11 getting 4lb from Arctic Owl (31 May Sandown 16f frm RF 1612). Inconsistent. He ran well behind Arctic Owl at Sandown on his second run of last season before making all in the Curragh Cup. Disappointed behind Celeric at York and was not seen again. Best with some cut in the ground. **Sir Michael Stoute [3-11] H H Aga Khan.*

MARIE DE BAYEUX (FR) RR 104f 5118a[2]
3 f Turgeon (USA) - Mandragore (USA) (Slew O' Gold (USA)) 8f **(75)**
Form - 402
1999 Turf 0-3: (11f, 12f, 13f) (hvy, gd)
Currently very useful. Turf high 104 - 2nd to Louve (23 Oct Saint-Cloud 11f RF 5118a). She is usually held-up but lacks a telling turn-of-foot. **R Collet in FR [0-3].*

MARIGLIANO (USA) BHB 61f70a **RR 58f 70a** 5103[6]
6 b g Riverman (USA) 9.7f **(78)** - Mount Holyoke (Golden Fleece (USA)) 7.9f **(74)**
Form - 86
Record 1999 - 1st:0 2nd:0 3rd:0 Ran:2
Pre1999 - 1st:3 2nd:1 3rd:5 Ran:16
Win Prizemoney £7,940 *Total Prizemoney* £12,098
Wins * 1998 *Jly Southw (STD) C 7f 69*
* 1998 Jun Mussel (SFT) C 7.1f 73+ <
1996 May Beverl (G-F) 7.5f 69+
1999 Turf 0-2: (7f, 10f) (g-s, gd)
Average gelding, effective 7f, acts on gd to hrd - acts on Fibr, best on gd. Turf high 57 (began Oct). Consistent.
**K A Morgan [5-28] T R Pryke (from Sir Michael Stoute [1-4] Jun 1996).*

MARILIA (IRE) BHB 56f45a **RR 39f 45a** 2979a[6]
4 ch f River Falls 8.2f **(56)** - Bronze Celtic (Stanford) 7.9f **(56)**
Form - 0876
Record 1999 - 1st:0 2nd:0 3rd:0 Ran:4
Pre1999 - 1st:1 2nd:0 3rd:0 Ran:9
Win Prizemoney £2,740 *Total Prizemoney* £2,880
Wins 1997 Jun Navan (G-S) 5.8f 61 <
1999 Turf 0-2: (5f, 12f) (g-s, gd) 1999 AW 0-2: (7f 2) (Fibr 2)
Very moderate filly, has worn blinkers. Turf high 16 (began Jly). Becoming disappointing.
**H Rogers in IRE [0-2] Thomas Connolly (from Miss Gay Kelleway [0-2] Mar 1999).*

MARINO STREET BHB 46f33a **RR 46f 33a** 4233[11]
6 b m Totem (USA) 5f **(38)** - Demerger (Dominion) 8.5f **(63)**
Form - 65112560
Record 1999 - 1st:2 2nd:1 3rd:0 Ran:8
Pre1999 - 1st:1 2nd:7 3rd:10 Ran:52
Win Prizemoney £8,389 *Total Prizemoney* £18,838
Wins * **1999** Jly Haydoc (G-S) H 5f 34 43+
* **1999** Jun Warwic (G-F) H 5f 34 37
1996 Jly Leices (G-F) 5f 48 <
1999 Turf 2-8: (5f 2-8) (gd, g-f 2-4, frm 3)
Moderate mare, effective 5 to 6f, best at 5f, acts on g-f to frm, best on g-f, often wears blinkers (extremely effectively), excels at Warwick and Yarmouth. Turf high 48 - 2nd of 8 getting 17lb from Dancing Mystery (10 Jly Warwick 5f g-f RF 2725) - also 1st of 10 giving 1lb to Tinker's Surprise (2 Jly Haydock RF 2491).
**B A McMahon [2-8] Roy Penton (from P D Evans [1-52] Aug 1998).*

MARISOL (IRE) BHB 27f **RR 32f** 2872[6]
6 b m Mujtahid (USA) 7.4f **(69)** - Stanerra's Star (Shadeed (USA)) 8.2f **(70)**
Form - 607866
Record 1999 - 1st:0 2nd:0 3rd:0 Ran:6
Pre1999 - 1st:0 2nd:1 3rd:1 Ran:5
Win Prizemoney £0 *Total Prizemoney* £1,055
1999 Turf 0-6: (9f, 11f, 12f 2, 14f, 16f) (g-f 5, frm)
Very moderate mare, effective 9 to 13f, acts on gd to frm, favours right handed tracks. Turf high 38. **P Monteith [0-17] Allan Melville.*

MARITUN LAD RR 5209[18]
2 b g Presidium 7.5f **(56)** - Girl Next Door **(35df 36a)** (Local Suitor (USA)) 8.4f **(67)**
Form - 0
Record 1999 - 1st:0 2nd:0 3rd:0 Ran:1
1999 Turf 0-1: (6f) (g-s)
Currently very moderate gelding. **D Shaw [0-1] M G Vines.*

MARIUS PETIPA (USA) RR 82f 2205a[3]
3 b c Nureyev (USA) 8.4f **(84)** - Starstruck Gal (USA)
Form - 23833
1999 Turf 0-5: (6f, 7f 2, 8f 2) (hvy, g-s, g-f 3)
Decent colt. Turf high 90 (1st run) - 2nd of 10 to Major Force (11 Apr Curragh 8f g-s RF 0682a).
**A P O'Brien in IRE [0-5] Michael Tabor.*

MARJAANA (IRE) BHB 50f **RR 74df** 4914[15]
6 b m Shaadi (USA) 8.1f **(75)** - Funun (USA) (Fappiano (USA)) 8.7f **(77)**
Form - 00
Record 1999 - 1st:0 2nd:0 3rd:0 Ran:2
Pre1999 - 1st:4 2nd:6 3rd:1 Ran:24
Win Prizemoney £11,762 *Total Prizemoney* £23,431
Wins 1997 Aug Beverl (G-S) H 7.5f 70 78
1997 Jun Folkes (G-F) 6.9f 74
1997 May Warwic (G-F) H 8f 62 70
1995 Jly Newbur (GD) 5.2f 80 <
1999 Turf 0-1: (7f) (gd) 1999 AW 0-1: (7f) (Fibr)
Above-average mare, has worn blinkers.
**C Smith [0-2] Mrs Julia Scott (from P T Walwyn [4-24] Oct 1997).*

MARJEUNE BHB 67f **RR 65f** 4727[1]
2 b f Marju (IRE) 9.2f **(76)** - Ann Veronica (IRE) (Sadler's Wells (USA)) 10f **(76)**

Form - 58041
Record 1999 - 1st:1 2nd:0 3rd:0 Ran:5
Win Prizemoney £3,139 *Total Prizemoney* £3,357
Wins * **1999** Oct Nottin (SFT) H 10f 62 65 <
1999 Turf 1-5: (7f 3, 8f, 10f 1-1) (g-s 1-2, g-f 2, frm)
Average filly. Turf high 65 - 1st of 16 giving 5lb to Double Red (5 Oct Nottingham RF 4727). **P W Harris [1-5] The Lords Of The Ring.*

MARJORIE ROSE (IRE) BHB 52f39a RR 33f 39a 846[9]

6 b m Magical Strike (USA) 5.5f **(61)** - Arrapata (Thatching) 8f **(66)**
Form - 000350
Record 1999 - 1st:0 2nd:0 3rd:1 Ran:6
Pre1999 - 1st:3 2nd:3 3rd:2 Ran:30
Win Prizemoney £6,914 *Total Prizemoney* £11,231
Wins 1996 *Dec Wolver (STD) C 6f 53*
1996 Spt Hamilt (GD) SH 5f 53 54 <
1996 *Jly Wolver (STD) H 5f 55 52*
1999 AW 0-6: (5f 3, 6f 3) (Fibr 6)
Very moderate mare, has worn blinkers. AW high 36.
**R Brotherton [0-6] I Jerrard (from A Bailey [3-30] May 1998).*

MARJORY POLLEY BHB 55f RR 52f 4097[9]

2 ch f Timeless Times (USA) 6.1f **(56)** - Rubylee **(59f 63a)** (Persian Bold) 9.3f **(66)**
Form - 400
Record 1999 - 1st:0 2nd:0 3rd:0 Ran:3
1999 Turf 0-2: (6f, 7f) (g-f, frm) 1999 AW 0-1: (5f) (Fibr)
Currently fair filly. Turf high 52 (began Aug).
**P T Walwyn [0-3] John Grist.*

MARJU GUEST (IRE) BHB 72f RR 64f 4323[4]

2 b f Marju (IRE) 9.2f **(76)** - Dance Ahead (Shareef Dancer (USA)) 9.9f **(73)**
Form - 044
Record 1999 - 1st:0 2nd:0 3rd:0 Ran:3
Win Prizemoney £0 *Total Prizemoney* £621
1999 Turf 0-3: (6f, 7f 2) (gd, g-f, frm)
Currently average filly. Turf high 64 (began Jly).
**M R Channon [0-3] John Guest.*

MARKALE (FR) RR 98f 2654a[1]

3 b f Marmato - Kaldounette (FR) (Kaldoun (FR)) 10.3f **(68)**
Form - 1
1999 Turf 1-1: (8f 1-1) (sft 1-1)
Currently very useful filly. (1st run) - 1st of 7 giving 5lb to Choice Spirit (28 Jun Maisons-Laffitte RF 2654a).
**M Pimbonnet in FR [1-2] M Schemoul.*

MARKAN (USA) BHB 102f RR 101f 3223[16]

3 ch c Affirmed (USA) 10.3f **(75)** - Norma (USA) (Procida (USA))
Form - 4730
Record 1999 - 1st:0 2nd:0 3rd:1 Ran:4
Pre1999 - 1st:1 2nd:0 3rd:0 Ran:2
Win Prizemoney £7,924 *Total Prizemoney* £10,879
Wins * 1998 Jly Newbur (G-F) 7f 89 <
1999 Turf 0-4: (8f, 9f, 10f, 12f) (g-f 2, frm 2)
Scopey, very useful colt, effective 10f, acts on frm. Turf high 101 - 3rd of 13 giving 1lb to Zindabad (7 Jly Newmarket 10f frm RF 2630). Highly rated, he had excuses on his first two starts and seemed unsuited by dropping back to a mile at Goodwood in July. From a tough American family, he remains relatively unexposed and should win a decent handicap around a mile and a quarter in 2000. **P F I Cole [1-6] H R H Prince Fahd Salman.*

MARKELLIS (USA) BHB 32f41a RR 41f 41a 4936[6]

3 b g Housebuster (USA) 7f **(81)** - Crimsons Contender (USA) (Monsieur Champlain (USA))
Form - 75606
Record 1999 - 1st:0 2nd:0 3rd:0 Ran:5
Pre1999 - 1st:0 2nd:0 3rd:0 Ran:1
1999 Turf 0-4: (8f 2, 12f 2) (g-s, gd 2, g-f) 1999 AW 0-1: (12f) (Fibr)
Moderate gelding. Turf high 40.
**D Carroll [0-2] Mark Barrett (from Patrick Prendergast in IRE [0-4] Jly 1999).*

MARK TIME BHB 41f RR 45f 652[11]

4 b g Pursuit of Love 9.5f **(69)** - Quiet Harbour (Mill Reef (USA)) 10.5f **(78)**
Form - 64000
Record 1999 - 1st:0 2nd:0 3rd:0 Ran:5
Pre1999 - 1st:0 2nd:0 3rd:1 Ran:8
Win Prizemoney £0 *Total Prizemoney* £811
1999 Turf 0-2: (7f, 8f) (sft, frm) 1999 AW 0-3: (10f 2, 11f) (Equi 2, Fibr)
Scopey, moderate gelding, effective 7 to 8f, acted on g-s to gd. Turf high 30. AW high 37. Becoming disappointing. (DEAD)
**P R Hedger [0-6] Trevor Grist (from M H Tompkins [0-8] Oct 1998).*

MARLENE RR 62f 413[10]

4 b f Komaite (USA) 6.9f **(61)** - Kaiserlinde (GER) (Frontal) 6.4f **(64)**
Form - 0
Record 1999 - 1st:0 2nd:0 3rd:0 Ran:1
Pre1999 - 1st:0 2nd:0 3rd:1 Ran:1
Win Prizemoney £0 *Total Prizemoney* £385
1999 AW 0-1: (12f) (Fibr)
Light-framed, currently average filly.
**M R Channon [0-2] Sheet & Roll Convertors Ltd.*

MARMADUKE (IRE) RR 76f 3806[7]

3 ch c Perugino (USA) - Sympathy (Precocious) 8.6f **(62)**
Form - 555347
Record 1999 - 1st:0 2nd:0 3rd:1 Ran:6
Pre1999 - 1st:1 2nd:0 3rd:0 Ran:2
Win Prizemoney £8,596 *Total Prizemoney* £10,384
Wins 1998 Oct San Si (SFT) 7.5f
1999 Turf 0-6: (6f, 7f 2, 8f, 10f 2) (sft, gd, g-f 2, frm 2)
Above-average colt, effective 6 to 7f, acts on gd to frm. Turf high 76 - 5th of 13 giving 18lb to Piggy Bank (5 Jly Ripon 6f gd RF 2564).
**Miss Gay Kelleway [0-3] Martin Butler (from L M Cumani [1-5] Jly 1999).*

MARNIE BHB 55f RR 61f 5150[10]

2 ch f First Trump - Miss Aboyne (Lochnager) 6f **(59)**
Form - 3050
Record 1999 - 1st:0 2nd:0 3rd:1 Ran:4
Win Prizemoney £0 *Total Prizemoney* £520
1999 Turf 0-4: (6f 3, 7f) (sft, g-s 2, g-f)
Average filly. Turf high 61 (began Spt).
**M J Ryan [0-4] Miss Jacqueline Goodearl.*

MARNOR (USA) BHB 107f RR 107f 2746[3]

3 ch c Diesis 9f **(80)** - Love's Reward (Nonoalco (USA)) 8.5f **(66)**
Form - 213
Record 1999 - 1st:1 2nd:1 3rd:1 Ran:3
Win Prizemoney £4,737 *Total Prizemoney* £7,208
Wins * **1999** Jun Newmar (G-F) 10f 84+ <
1999 Turf 1-3: (10f 1-3) (frm 1-3)
Scopey, currently Pattern-class colt. Turf high 107 - 3rd of 4 getting 11lb from Danish Rhapsody (11 Jly Newbury 10f frm RF 2746).
**H R A Cecil [1-3] M P Burke.*

MAROMITO (IRE) BHB 85f RR 80+f 2676[7]

2 b c Up and At 'em - Amtico (Bairn (USA)) 7.7f **(59)**
Form - 17
Record 1999 - 1st:1 2nd:0 3rd:0 Ran:2
Win Prizemoney £3,817 *Total Prizemoney* £3,817
Wins * **1999** Jun Lingfi (GD) 5f 80+ <
1999 Turf 1-2: (5f 1-2) (frm 1-2)
Currently decent colt. Turf high 80 (1st run) - 1st of 11 getting 2lb from Chief Response (22 Jun Lingfield RF 2197).
**R Bastiman [1-2] Peter Beaton-Brown.*

MARON BHB 63f58a RR 71f 58a 4937[9]

2 b c Puissance 7.1f **(60)** - Will Be Bold (Bold Lad (IRE)) 8.4f **(68)**
Form - 832301443000
Record 1999 - 1st:1 2nd:1 3rd:3 Ran:12
Win Prizemoney £2,626 *Total Prizemoney* £5,287
Wins * **1999** Jly Hamilt (G-F) 5f 71 <
1999 Turf 1-11: (5f 1-8, 6f 3) (gd 3, g-f 1-5, frm 3) 1999 AW 0-1: (6f) (Fibr)
Above-average colt, effective 5f, acts on g-f to frm, best on g-f. Turf high 71 - 1st of 6 giving 1lb to Shatin Beauty (31 Jly Hamilton RF 3267). Has had a very busy first campaign, which yielded just the one win at Hamilton over five furlongs in July. He looks pretty

moderate. **J Berry [1-12] J Berry.*

MARQUANTE (IRE) RR 38tf
2179[3]

4 b f Brief Truce (USA) 9.1f **(73)** - Festive Season (USA) (Lypheor) 12f **(71)**

Form - 3

Record 1999 - 1st:0 2nd:0 3rd:1 Ran:1

Win Prizemoney £0 *Total Prizemoney* £979

1999 Turf 0-1: (10f) (frm)

Very moderate filly. **D J Wintle [0-4] Mrs Joan Egan.*

MARRY ME RR 50f
4632[16]

3 ch f Pursuit of Love 9.5f **(69)** - Perfect Desire (USA) (Green Forest (USA)) 9.9f **(68)**

Form - 430006000

Record 1999 - 1st:0 2nd:0 3rd:1 Ran:9

Win Prizemoney £0 *Total Prizemoney* £637

1999 Turf 0-8: (8f 4, 9f, 10f 3) (g-s 2, gd, g-f 2, frm 3) 1999 AW 0-1: (10f) (Equi)

Neat, fair filly, effective 10f, acts on frm, likes tight tracks. Turf high 60 (1st run) - 3rd of 15 to Maiden's Blush (12 Apr Windsor 10f frm RF 0648). **C E Brittain [0-9] C E Brittain.*

MARSAD (IRE) BHB 92f RR 92f
4921[8]

5 ch g Fayruz 6.6f **(63)** - Broad Haven (IRE) (Be My Guest (USA)) 9.3f **(67)**

Form - 10564338

Record 1999 - 1st:1 2nd:0 3rd:2 Ran:8

Pre1999 - 1st:1 2nd:2 3rd:4 Ran:13

Win Prizemoney £10,671 *Total Prizemoney* £27,881

Wins * **1999** Mar Doncas (G-S) H 6f 82 91+ <

* 1998 Apr Kempto (SFT) H 6f 69 79?

1999 Turf 1-8: (6f 1-7, 7f) (g-s 1-2, gd 5, g-f)

Useful gelding, effective 6f, acts on g-s to gd, best on gd, excels at Kempton. Turf high 92 - 3rd of 23 giving 11lb to Get Stuck In (9 Oct York 6f gd RF 4803) - also 1st of 19 getting 4lb from Mister Rambo (26 Mar Doncaster RF 0480). Consistent. Off the track for ten months until bolting up at Doncaster in March, and obviously goes very well fresh. Knocking on the door afterwards, he goes very well on soft ground.

**J Akehurst [2-11] Canisbay Bloodstock Ltd (from R Akehurst [0-3] Jly 1997).*

MARSAYAS (IRE) BHB 55f50a RR 60f 50a
176[10]

6 ch g Classic Music (USA) 7.2f **(57)** - Babiana (CAN) (Sharpen Up) 8.3f **(67)**

Form - 0

Record 1999 - 1st:0 2nd:0 3rd:0 Ran:1

Pre1999 - 1st:1 2nd:4 3rd:2 Ran:17

Win Prizemoney £3,366 *Total Prizemoney* £7,745

Wins 1996 Aug Catter (G-F) H 15.8f 54 57 <

1999 AW 0-1: (15f) (Fibr)

Average gelding.

**F Jordan [2-12] G Pickering & J P Hames (from M J Camacho [1-17] Aug 1997).*

MARSHALL ST CYR RR 78f
5070[2]

2 ch g Emarati (USA) 6.6f **(63)** - St Helena (Monsanto) 6.5f **(59)**

Form - 02

Record 1999 - 1st:0 2nd:1 3rd:0 Ran:2

Win Prizemoney £0 *Total Prizemoney* £670

1999 Turf 0-2: (5f 2) (gd 2)

Currently above-average gelding. Turf high 78 (began Oct) - 2nd of 16 giving 5lb to Footprints (26 Oct Redcar 5f gd RF 5070). **P D Evans [0-2] D Maloney.*

MARSH MARIGOLD BHB 45f55a RR 16f 55a
511[16]

5 br m Tina's Pet 7.4f **(56)** - Pulga (Blakeney) 10.5f **(64)**

Form - 0

Record 1999 - 1st:0 2nd:0 3rd:0 Ran:1

Pre1999 - 1st:2 2nd:3 3rd:3 Ran:27

Win Prizemoney £4,885 *Total Prizemoney* £9,218

Wins 1997 Jun Pontef (G-F) H 10f 57 65 <

1996 Oct Haydoc (SFT) SH 6f 60 61

1999 Turf 0-1: (14f) (sft)

Very moderate filly. Becoming disappointing.

**G Fierro [1-14] G Fierro (from J Hetherton [1-11] Jly 1997).*

MARSKE MACHINE BHB 66f RR 69f
3802[U]

4 ch f Prince Daniel (USA) 11.4f **(46)** - Ciboure (Norwick (USA)) 7.2f **(56)**

Form - 000146U1007U

Record 1999 - 1st:2 2nd:0 3rd:0 Ran:12

Pre1999 - 1st:5 2nd:3 3rd:2 Ran:29

Win Prizemoney £22,173 *Total Prizemoney* £27,451

Wins * **1999** Jly Pontef (G-S) H 8f 65 69 <

* **1999** May Pontef (G-F) H 10f 63 65

* 1998 Oct Newmar (G-S) H 9f 62 67

* 1998 Spt Newcas (GD) H 9f 58 64

* 1998 Aug Beverl (G-F) H 9.9f 55 61

* 1997 Aug Sandow (SFT) SH 7.1f 59 61

* 1997 Aug Leices (GD) SH 6f 55 56

1999 Turf 2-12: (8f 1-5, 9f 2, 10f 1-4, 11f) (gd 3, g-f 1-4, frm 1-5)

Scopey, average filly, effective 8 to 10f, acts on g-f to frm, best on g-f, mostly wears blinkers (very effectively), likes left handed tracks, likes Pontefract. Turf high 69 - 1st of 13 giving 25lb to Chasetown Cailin (6 Jly Pontefract RF 2585) - also 1st of 14 giving 18lb to Caerosa (28 May Pontefract RF 1555). Inconsistent. She is at her most effective coming late off a strong pace, but does not seem to run two races alike. **N Tinkler [7-41] Marske Machine Co.*

MARTELLO BHB 61f RR 56f
4718[5]

3 b g Polish Precedent (USA) 9f **(73)** - Round Tower (High Top) 10.2f **(67)**

Form - 4786005

Record 1999 - 1st:0 2nd:0 3rd:0 Ran:7

Win Prizemoney £0 *Total Prizemoney* £257

1999 Turf 0-7: (8f 2, 10f 3, 12f 2) (gd 2, g-f, frm 4)

Scopey, fair gelding, has worn blinkers. Turf high 74.

**R Charlton [0-7] Lady Rothschild.*

MARTHA REILLY (IRE) BHB 42f45a RR 44f 45a
4822[14]

3 ch f Rainbows For Life (CAN) 9.3f **(64)** - Debach Delight (Great Nephew) 9.9f **(64)**

Form - 85561308840

Record 1999 - 1st:1 2nd:0 3rd:1 Ran:8

Pre1999 - 1st:0 2nd:0 3rd:0 Ran:9

Win Prizemoney £1,830 *Total Prizemoney* £2,109

Wins * **1999** *Feb Southw (STD) S 8f 59* <

1999 Turf 0-3: (7f, 12f 2) (g-s, g-f, frm) 1999 AW 1-5: (8f 1-2, 10f 2, 11f) (Equi 3, Fibr 1-2)

Leggy, fair filly, effective 8f, - acts on Fibr, has worn blinkers, likes left handed tracks. Turf high 38. AW high 59 - 1st of 8 getting 6lb from Rich Ballerina (15 Feb Southwell RF 0295).

**Mrs Barbara Waring [1-17] J McDonnell, H Shapter & P Haggarty.*

MARTIN (IRE) BHB 53f RR 49f
3919[4]

2 b c Dancing Dissident (USA) 6.8f **(65)** - Martin's Princess (Martin John) 13.1f **(62)**

Form - 0084

Record 1999 - 1st:0 2nd:0 3rd:0 Ran:4

1999 Turf 0-4: (5f 3, 6f) (gd, g-f 3)

Moderate colt. Turf high 49 (began Jly).

**Martyn Wane [0-4] Mrs H Wane.*

MARTINDALE (IRE) BHB 37f32a RR 39df 32a
77[10]

6 b g Fairy King (USA) 7.7f **(75)** - Whist Awhile (Caerleon (USA)) 8.6f **(71)**

Form - 780

Record 1999 - 1st:0 2nd:0 3rd:0 Ran:2

Pre1999 - 1st:1 2nd:1 3rd:0 Ran:17

Win Prizemoney £3,071 *Total Prizemoney* £3,701

Wins * 1998 Jly Ripon (G-F) H 6f 36 39 <

1999 AW 0-2: (6f, 7f) (Fibr 2)

Very moderate gelding, effective 5 to 6f, acts on g-f - acts on Fibr, often wears blinkers.

**R Bastiman [1-15] S R Johnson (from J Hanson [0-2] Jly 1997).*

MARTINE BHB 35f35a RR 29f 35a
1131[10]

5 ch m Clantime 6.6f **(57)** - Marcroft (Crofthall) 6.3f **(59)**

Form - 00

Record 1999 - 1st:0 2nd:0 3rd:0 Ran:2

Pre1999 - 1st:0 2nd:0 3rd:2 Ran:17

Win Prizemoney £0 *Total Prizemoney* £1,395

1999 AW 0-2: (6f, 7f) (Fibr 2)

Little account filly, effective 7f, acts on frm. AW high 6. Becoming disappointing.
**W G M Turner [0-2] Arthur Bevan (from A Bailey [0-17] Nov 1998).*

MARTINEZ (IRE) RR 30f 3949[9]
3 b g Tirol 8.1f **(64)** - Elka (USA) (Val de L'Orne (FR)) 12f **(75)**
Form - 0
Record 1999 - 1st:0 2nd:0 3rd:0 Ran:1
1999 Turf 0-1: (5f) (frm)
Lengthy, currently very moderate gelding.
**C W Thornton [0-1] Guy Reed.*

MARTINO ALONSO (IRE) RR 111f 1906b[3]
5 h Marju (IRE) 9.2f **(76)** - Cheerful Note (Cure The Blues (USA)) 9.5f **(63)**
Form - 283
1999 Turf 0-2: (8f, 10f) (gd 2)
Group-class colt. Turf high 102. Tough and genuine, he struggles to stay a mile and a quarter.
**A Botti in ITY [0-2] (from G Botti in ITY [0-2] Nov 1998).*

MARTON MERE BHB 49f40a RR 63f 40a 2523[6]
3 ch g Cadeaux Genereux 7.9f **(76)** - Hyatti (Habitat) 9.4f **(70)**
Form - 8002056
Record 1999 - 1st:0 2nd:1 3rd:0 Ran:7
Win Prizemoney £0 *Total Prizemoney* £1,106
1999 Turf 0-4: (6f, 7f 2, 8f) (gd, frm 3) 1999 AW 0-3: (7f, 8f 2) (Fibr 3)
Leggy, average gelding. Turf high 63. AW high 40.
**T D Easterby [0-7] T H Bennett.*

MARTON MOSS (SWE) BHB 92f RR 94f 2697[9]
4 b g Polish Patriot (USA) 7.8f **(70)** - Arrastra (Bustino) 10.4f **(64)**
Form - 05811720

Record					
1999 -		1st:2	2nd:1	3rd:0	Ran:8
Pre1999 -		1st:3	2nd:3	3rd:1	Ran:22

Win Prizemoney £26,946 *Total Prizemoney* £49,984

Wins								
*** 1999**	Jun	Haydoc	(SFT)		7.1f		94+	
*** 1999**	May	Doncas	(G-F)	H	7f	89	96	<
* 1998	Jun	Ripon	(SFT)	H	6f	87	94	
* 1997	Aug	Ripon	(G-F)		6f		78	
* 1997	Jun	Pontef	(SFT)		5f		75+	

1999 Turf 2-8: (6f 3, 7f 2-4, 8f) (g-s, gd 1-2, g-f 3, frm 1-2)
Leggy, useful gelding, effective 6 to 7f, best at 7f, acts on sft to frm, best on gd, likes left handed tracks, prefers tight tracks, excels at Haydock, does well at Ripon. Turf high 96 - 1st of 11 giving 1lb to Deep Space (29 May Doncaster RF 1565) - also 1st of 5 giving 10lb to Present Laughter (4 Jun Haydock RF 1742). He handles any ground and seems best over seven furlongs nowadays. Genuine and consistent, he wears bandages and missed the second half of last season. **T D Easterby [5-30] T H Bennett.*

MARVEL BHB 70f RR 63f 5034[9]
2 b f Rudimentary (USA) 8.2f **(66)** - Maravilla (Mandrake Major) 7.6f **(53)**
Form - 610
Record 1999 - 1st:1 2nd:0 3rd:0 Ran:3
Win Prizemoney £3,652 *Total Prizemoney* £3,652
Wins * 1999 Oct Ayr (SFT) 7f 63 <
1999 Turf 1-3: (6f, 7f 1-2) (sft 1-1, g-s, gd)
Currently average filly. Turf high 63 (began Spt) - 1st of 6 getting 5lb from Mac Be Lucky (11 Oct Ayr RF 4806).
**Don Enrico Incisa [1-3] Don Enrico Incisa.*

MARWELL MAGNUS RR 4f 3609[9]
2 b c Beveled (USA) 6.9f **(64)** - Lily of France (Monsanto (FR)) 6.5f **(59)**
Form - 0
Record 1999 - 1st:0 2nd:0 3rd:0 Ran:1
1999 Turf 0-1: (6f) (frm)
Currently very poor colt.
**M Madgwick [0-1] Dorothea Viscountess Kelburn.*

MARX MISTRESS BHB 24f RR 28f 2913[7]
5 b m Batshoof 9.5f **(66)** - No Jazz (Jaazeiro (USA)) 9.2f **(54)**
Form - 457

Record	1st	2nd	3rd	Ran
1999 -	1st:0	2nd:0	3rd:0	Ran:3
Pre1999 -	1st:0	2nd:0	3rd:0	Ran:3

1999 Turf 0-3: (11f, 14f, 15f) (g-s, g-f, frm)
Little account filly, had worn blinkers. Turf high 28 (1st run) - 4th of 17 getting 28lb from Manful (19 Jun Ayr 11f g-s RF 2145). (DEAD)
**P D Evans [1-5] John Pugh (from J G M O'Shea [0-5] Jly 1998).*

MARY RR 32f 2424[7]
3 b f Batshoof 9.5f **(66)** - Outward's Gal (Ashmore (FR)) 8.5f **(65)**
Form - 7
Record 1999 - 1st:0 2nd:0 3rd:0 Ran:1
1999 Turf 0-1: (12f) (frm)
Currently very moderate filly. **A G Newcombe [0-1] M Patel.*

MARY CULI BHB 28f25a RR 39f 25a 4593[13]
5 gr m Liboi (USA) 11.5f **(56)** - Copper Trader (Faustus (USA)) 10f **(58)**
Form - 708375360

Record	1st	2nd	3rd	Ran
1999 -	1st:0	2nd:0	3rd:2	Ran:9
Pre1999 -	1st:1	2nd:0	3rd:3	Ran:19

Win Prizemoney £2,725 *Total Prizemoney* £4,698
Wins 1998 Spt Sandow (GD) H 10f 41 46 <
1999 Turf 0-5: (8f, 10f 2, 11f, 12f) (sft, gd, g-f, frm 2) 1999 AW 0-4: (11f, 12f 3) (Fibr 4)
Very moderate filly, effective 10 to 12f, acts on gd to g-f, best on gd, has worn blinkers (effectively). Turf high 39. AW high 36. Inconsistent.
**G M McCourt [0-7] G Redford (from H Candy [1-21] May 1999).*

MARY HANNAH BHB 47f45a RR 45a 2066[8]
6 b m Lugana Beach 7f **(63)** - Bloomsbury Girl (Weepers Boy)
Form - 08421008

Record	1st	2nd	3rd	Ran
1999 -	1st:1	2nd:0	3rd:0	Ran:4
Pre1999 -	1st:0	2nd:1	3rd:0	Ran:5

Win Prizemoney £2,284 *Total Prizemoney* £2,998
Wins * 1999 *Jan Wolver (STD) H 5f 38 47* <
1999 AW 1-4: (5f 1-3, 6f) (Fibr 1-4)
Moderate mare, effective 5 to 6f, - acts on Fibr, likes left handed tracks, likes tight tracks. AW high 47 (1st run) - 1st of 13 getting 7lb from Sotonian (9 Jan Wolverhampton RF 0064). Becoming disappointing. **A Senior [1-9] A Senior.*

MARY JANE BHB 61f69a RR 59f 69a 4986[5]
4 b f Tina's Pet 7.4f **(56)** - Fair Attempt (IRE) (Try My Best (USA)) 7.6f **(67)**
Form - 1441513734211825215

Record	1st	2nd	3rd	Ran
1999 -	1st:4	2nd:3	3rd:2	Ran:15
Pre1999 -	1st:4	2nd:0	3rd:2	Ran:21

Win Prizemoney £21,193 *Total Prizemoney* £25,539

Wins								
*** 1999**	Spt	Leices	(GD)	H	5f	57	59	
*** 1999**	Jly	Chepst	(G-F)	H	5.1f	48	54	
*** 1999**	*Jly*	*Wolver*	*(STD)*	*H*	*5f*	*64*	*66*	
1999	*Jan*	*Wolver*	*(STD)*	*H*	*5f*	*58*	*62+*	
1998	*Dec*	*Southw*	*(STD)*	*C*	*5f*		*57+*	
1998	*Nov*	*Southw*	*(STD)*	*C*	*6f*		*57*	
1998	*Feb*	*Wolver*	*(STD)*	*C*	*5f*		*54+*	
1997	Oct	Redcar	(G-F)		5f		68	<

1999 Turf 2-10: (5f 2-10) (g-f 1-6, frm 1-4) 1999 AW 2-5: (5f 2-4, 6f) (Fibr 2-5)
Workmanlike, average filly, effective 5 to 6f, best at 5f, acts on g-f - acts on Fibr, has worn blinkers, likes left handed tracks, likes tight tracks, excels at Southwell and Wolverhampton. Turf high 59 - 1st of 16 giving 7lb to La Doyenne (20 Spt Leicester RF 4436). AW high 66 - 1st of 11 giving 11lb to Forest Call (9 Jly Wolverhampton RF 2692) - also 1st of 9 giving 26lb to Opening Range (27 Jan Wolverhampton RF 0171).
**R M H Cowell [3-12] Paradise Partnership (from J Berry [5-24] Feb 1999).*

MARY STUART (IRE) RR 111f 3757[5]
3 b f Nashwan (USA) 10.3f **(79)** - Scots Lass (Shirley Heights) 10.3f **(74)**
Form - 1115

Record	1st	2nd	3rd	Ran
1999 -	1st:3	2nd:0	3rd:0	Ran:4
Pre1999 -	1st:0	2nd:0	3rd:0	Ran:1

Win Prizemoney £46,542 *Total Prizemoney* £49,542

Wins								
*** 1999**	Jly	Goodwo	(G-F)	H	12f	87	92	<
*** 1999**	Jun	Goodwo	(G-F)	H	9.9f	82	84	
*** 1999**	May	Salisb	(G-F)		9.9f		68	

1999 Turf 3-4: (10f 2-2, 12f 1-2) (gd 1-2, g-f 1-1, frm 1-1)
Scopey, Group-class filly. Turf high 111 - 5th of 11 to Ramruma (18

Aug York 12f gd RF 3757). Something of a character at home, she is tough and genuine on the track and completed a hat-trick when landing the valuable Tote Gold Trophy at Goodwood in July. An excellent fifth when stepped-up in class for the Group One Yorkshire Oaks on her only subsequent start, she is the type to do well as a four-year-old. **Sir Michael Stoute [3-5] Lord Weinstock.*

MARZOCCO BHB 25f **RR 26?f** 3104[9]
11 ch g Formidable (USA) 7.8f **(60)** - Top Heights (High Top) 10.2f **(67)**
Form - 800
Record 1999 - 1st:0 2nd:0 3rd:0 Ran:3
Pre1999 - 1st:2 2nd:2 3rd:2 Ran:28
Win Prizemoney £5,314 *Total Prizemoney* £7,358
1999 Turf 0-3: (6f, 7f, 14f) (frm 3)
Little account gelding, has worn blinkers. Turf high 12 (began Jly).
**T A K Cuthbert [0-9] T A K Cuthbert (from J Ffitch-Heyes [2-28] Aug 1993).*

MASH ONE (CHI) RR 117f 4782a[1]
4 ch c Mashkour (USA) - Exing (USA) (Exceller (USA)) 12.5f **(74)**
Form - 1
1999 Turf 1-1: (10f 1-1) (frm 1-1)
Currently high-class colt. (1st run) - 1st of 6 from Lazy Lode (3 Oct Santa Anita RF 4782a).
**R Frankel in USA [1-1] Amerman Racing Stables.*

MASILIA (IRE) RR 68f 5215[4]
2 b f Kahyasi 12.9f **(74)** - Masmouda (Dalsaan) 9.8f **(64)**
Form - 4
Record 1999 - 1st:0 2nd:0 3rd:0 Ran:1
Win Prizemoney £0 *Total Prizemoney* £225
1999 Turf 0-1: (8f) (g-s)
Currently average filly. **L M Cumani [0-1] H H Aga Khan.*

MASONIC (IRE) BHB 42f **RR 48f** 4650[6]
3 ch c Grand Lodge (USA) - Winning Heart (Horage) 10.3f **(61)**
Form - 023404726
Record 1999 - 1st:0 2nd:2 3rd:1 Ran:9
Pre1999 - 1st:0 2nd:0 3rd:0 Ran:3
Win Prizemoney £0 *Total Prizemoney* £1,838
1999 Turf 0-9: (11f, 12f 3, 14f 4, 16f) (gd 2, g-f 5, frm 2)
Rangy, moderate colt, effective 14f, acts on g-f, often wears blinkers (effectively), likes left handed tracks, likes tight tracks. Turf high 60 - 3rd of 7 getting 5lb from Salford Flyer (21 Jun Yarmouth 14f g-f RF 2183). Consistent. **M H Tompkins [0-12] Mrs Beryl Lockey.*

MASSIMO (FR) RR 104f 5206a[3]
5 gr h Lead on Time (USA) 7.5f **(69)** - Mi Longa (FR) (Caro)
Form - 33
1999 Turf 0-2: (7f 2) (g-s, gd)
Currently very useful colt. Turf high 104 (1st run) - 3rd of 10 to Russian Revival (27 May Longchamp 7f gd RF 1713a).
**J-C Rouget in FR [0-2].*

MASTER BEVELED BHB 68f65a **RR 71f 65a** 4752[14]
9 b g Beveled (USA) 6.9f **(64)** - Miss Anniversary (Tachypous) 8.6f **(55)**
Form - 0
Record 1999 - 1st:0 2nd:0 3rd:0 Ran:1
Pre1999 - 1st:11 2nd:8 3rd:9 Ran:93
Win Prizemoney £64,597 *Total Prizemoney* £85,631
Wins * 1998 Spt Ayr (g-s) H 10.9f 69 72
* 1996 Oct Warwic (FRM) 8f 67
* 1996 Oct Haydoc (SFT) 10.5f 74
1999 Turf 0-1: (10f) (gd)
Above-average gelding, effective 10 to 12f, best at 10f, acts on gd to frm, best on g-f, has worn blinkers (extremely effectively). Inconsistent.
**P D Evans [15-108] Mrs E J Williams (from A P Jones [0-9] Aug 1993).*

MASTER CASTER (IRE) BHB 72f64a **RR 75f 64a** 1392[6]
4 b g Night Shift (USA) 8.1f **(73)** - Honourable Sheba (USA) (Roberto (USA)) 10f **(76)**
Form - 54316
Record 1999 - 1st:1 2nd:0 3rd:1 Ran:5
Pre1999 - 1st:2 2nd:4 3rd:2 Ran:17
Win Prizemoney £10,688 *Total Prizemoney* £16,582
Wins * **1999** May Bright (FRM) H 8f 69 74 <
1998 Spt Beverl (G-F) H 8.5f 63 68
1998 Feb Lingfi (SLW) 10f 70
1999 Turf 1-3: (8f 1-1, 9f, 11f) (gd, g-f 1-1, frm) 1999 AW 0-2: (9f, 10f) (Equi, Fibr)
Unfurnished, above-average gelding, effective 7 to 11f, best at 8f, acts on gd to frm - acts on Equi, best on g-f, has worn blinkers, likes right handed tracks, favours tight tracks, likes Beverley. Turf high 75 (1st run) - 3rd of 19 giving 7lb to Swift (5 Apr Warwick 11f gd RF 0596) - also 1st of 13 giving 8lb to Shipley Glen (12 May Brighton RF 1176). AW high 65. Consistent.
**G M McCourt [1-8] "It Might Be Ten" Partnership (from Mrs J R Ramsden [1-10] Spt 1998).*

MASTER FAY (IRE) BHB 100f **RR 103f** 4208[4]
2 b c Fayruz 6.6f **(63)** - Non Dimenticar Me (IRE) **(65f)** (Don't Forget Me) 8.3f **(74)**
Form - 511222414
Record 1999 - 1st:3 2nd:3 3rd:0 Ran:9
Win Prizemoney £18,490 *Total Prizemoney* £45,187
Wins * **1999** Jly Newbur (G-F) L 6f 98 <
* **1999** May Doncas (G-F) 5f 81
* **1999** Apr Newcas (GD) 5f 84+
1999 Turf 3-9: (5f 2-4, 6f 1-5) (sft, gd 1-3, g-f 1-2, frm 2, hrd 1-1)
Very useful colt, effective 5 to 6f, best at 6f, acts on gd to g-f, best on g-f. Turf high 103 - 2nd of 17 giving 7lb to Kalindi (18 Jun Ascot 5f g-f RF 2107) - also 1st of 6 from Watching (17 Jly Newbury RF 2902). On the go from March until September, he is notably tough, genuine and consistent. Already a Listed winner, he promises to stay seven furlongs but may have to travel abroad to find suitable openings next term. **M R Channon [3-9] Mrs J Hills.*

MASTER GEORGE RR 64f 4641[2]
2 b c Mtoto 11.5f **(71)** - Topwinder (USA) (Topsider (USA)) 8.3f **(71)**
Form - 2
Record 1999 - 1st:0 2nd:1 3rd:0 Ran:1
Win Prizemoney £0 *Total Prizemoney* £962
1999 Turf 0-1: (8f) (g-s)
Currently average colt. **I A Balding [0-1] David Watson.*

MASTER HYDE (USA) BHB 40f54a **RR 40f 54a** 3317[4]
10 gr g Trempolino (USA) 11.9f **(77)** - Sandspur (USA) (Al Hattab (USA)) 9.3f **(74)**
Form - 4834
Record 1999 - 1st:0 2nd:0 3rd:1 Ran:4
Pre1999 - 1st:5 2nd:6 3rd:5 Ran:50
Win Prizemoney £14,681 *Total Prizemoney* £23,077
Wins 1995 Jly Carlis (FRM) H 12f 55 62
1999 Turf 0-4: (12f, 14f 3) (gd, frm 3)
Average gelding, has worn blinkers. Turf high 42.
**J S Goldie [2-22] J S Goldie (from W Storey [5-25] Oct 1996).*

MASTER JONES BHB 63f **RR 68f** 4668[6]
2 b g Emperor Jones (USA) - Tight Spin (High Top) 10.2f **(67)**
Form - 7006
Record 1999 - 1st:0 2nd:0 3rd:0 Ran:4
1999 Turf 0-4: (5f 3, 7f) (g-s, gd, g-f, frm)
Average gelding. Turf high 68. **Mrs L Stubbs [0-4] Maurice Parker.*

MASTER LODGE BHB 58f53a **RR 66df 53a** 4729[10]
4 ch c Night Shift (USA) 8.1f **(73)** - Katie Koo (Persian Bold) 9.3f **(66)**
Form - 550
Record 1999 - 1st:0 2nd:0 3rd:0 Ran:3
1999 Turf 0-3: (6f, 7f, 8f) (g-s, g-f, frm)
Scopey, currently average colt. Turf high 66 (began Aug).
**S C Williams [0-3] Lance Lodge.*

MASTER MAC (USA) BHB 58f **RR 46f** 4947[13]
4 br g Exbourne (USA) - Kentucky Blonde (USA) (General Assembly (USA)) 10f **(68)**
Form - 000000
Record 1999 - 1st:0 2nd:0 3rd:0 Ran:6
Pre1999 - 1st:2 2nd:1 3rd:0 Ran:13
Win Prizemoney £9,498 *Total Prizemoney* £12,533
Wins 1997 Jly Lingfi (G-F) H 6f 81 <
1997 Jun Goodwo (G-S) 7f 75
1999 Turf 0-6: (6f, 7f 2, 8f 2, 9f) (gd, g-f 2, frm 3)
Workmanlike, moderate gelding, effective 6f, acts on gd. Turf high

72 (began Jly).
**N Hamilton [0-6] Normandy Developments (London) (from J Akehurst [0-3] Jly 1998).*

MASTER MILLFIELD (IRE) BHB 47f68a **RR 39f 68a** 3689[10]
7 b g Prince Rupert (FR) 10.4f **(60)** - Calash (Indian King (USA)) 7.4f **(64)**
Form - 000
Record 1999 - 1st:0 2nd:0 3rd:0 Ran:3
Pre1999 - 1st:8 2nd:5 3rd:9 Ran:55
Win Prizemoney £24,282 *Total Prizemoney* £35,661

Wins									
	* 1998	Spt	Goodwo	(G-S)	H	8f	49	58	
	* 1998	Spt	Salisb	(GD)	H	8f	49	53	
	1997	Spt	Folkes	(FRM)	H	6.9f	47	54	
	1995	Spt	Bath	(HRD)	H	5.7f	65	65	
	1995	*Feb*	*Lingfi*	*(STD)*	*H*	*7f*	*72*	*73*	<

1999 Turf 0-3: (8f 3) (gd 2, g-f)
Average gelding, effective 8f, acts on gd to frm, has worn blinkers. Turf high 39. Becoming disappointing.
**R J Hodges [5-22] P Slade (from C J Hill [6-38] Oct 1997).*

MASTERMIND (IRE) RR 86f 3278[1]
2 ch c Dolphin Street (FR) - Glenarff (USA) (Irish River (FR)) 8.6f **(78)**
Form - 21
Record 1999 - 1st:1 2nd:1 3rd:0 Ran:2
Win Prizemoney £4,386 *Total Prizemoney* £5,926
Wins * **1999** Jly Newmar (G-F) 6f 86 <
1999 Turf 1-2: (6f 1-2) (frm 1-2)
Currently useful colt. Turf high 86 (began Jly) - 1st of 9 from The Deputy (31 Jly Newmarket RF 3278). Started his career in fine style when second to Boast in a Newmarket maiden over six furlongs at the July meeting, and this half-brother to Housemaster made the expected improvement when scoring at the same track three weeks later. Likely to aim higher next term.
**P F I Cole [1-2] Highclere Thoroughbred Racing Ltd.*

MASTERPIECE BHB 49f **RR 36f** 4094[10]
5 br g Primo Dominie 7.2f **(67)** - Swift Return (Double Form) 7.3f **(58)**
Form - 0
Record 1999 - 1st:0 2nd:0 3rd:0 Ran:1
Pre1999 - 1st:0 2nd:1 3rd:0 Ran:9
Win Prizemoney £0 *Total Prizemoney* £627
1999 Turf 0-1: (8f) (frm)
Very moderate gelding. Becoming disappointing.
**N J Henderson [0-1] Lady Tennant (from R Hannon [0-9] Jun 1998).*

MASTERPIECE (USA) RR 78+f 5059[1]
2 b br c Nureyev (USA) 8.4f **(84)** - Lovely Gemstone (USA) (Alydar (USA)) 9.1f **(76)**
Form - 81
Record 1999 - 1st:1 2nd:0 3rd:0 Ran:2
Win Prizemoney £4,760 *Total Prizemoney* £4,760
Wins * **1999** Oct Lingfi (HVY) 7f 78+ <
1999 Turf 1-2: (7f 1-2) (g-s 1-1, gd)
Currently above-average colt. Turf high 78 (began Spt) - 1st of 12 from Hypersonic (25 Oct Lingfield RF 5059).
**Sir Michael Stoute [1-2] M Tabor & Mrs John Magnier.*

MASTER REX BHB 42f **RR 51f** 2915[12]
4 ch g Interrex (CAN) 7.7f **(51)** - Whose Lady (USA) (Master Willie) 7f **(70)**
Form - 50
Record 1999 - 1st:0 2nd:0 3rd:0 Ran:1
Pre1999 - 1st:0 2nd:0 3rd:0 Ran:4
1999 Turf 0-1: (10f) (frm)
Strong, fair gelding.
**W R Muir [0-1] Miss Louise Challis (from E A Wheeler [0-4] Nov 1998).*

MASTER SODEN (USA) BHB 61f **RR 59f** 5158[1]
2 b c Pembroke (USA) - Lady Member (FR) (Saint Estephe (FR)) 16.4f **(79)**
Form - 0001
Record 1999 - 1st:1 2nd:0 3rd:0 Ran:4
Win Prizemoney £3,640 *Total Prizemoney* £3,640
Wins * **1999** Nov Redcar (G-S) H 8f 48 59 <
1999 Turf 1-4: (6f 2, 7f, 8f 1-1) (g-s, frm 1-2, hrd)
Fair colt. Turf high 59 - 1st of 27 getting 23lb from Mytton's Again (1 Nov Redcar RF 5158). **T G Mills [1-4] Albert Soden Ltd.*

MASTER TIROL (IRE) BHB 45f **RR 39f** 2766[5]
3 ro c Tirol 8.1f **(64)** - Inisfail (Persian Bold) 9.3f **(66)**
Form - 08005
Record 1999 - 1st:0 2nd:0 3rd:0 Ran:5
Pre1999 - 1st:0 2nd:0 3rd:0 Ran:4
1999 Turf 0-5: (8f, 10f 3, 11f) (g-s 2, gd 2, frm)
Scopey, very moderate colt, has worn blinkers. Turf high 54. Becoming disappointing. **R A Fahey [0-9] D A Read.*

MATERIAL WITNESS (IRE) RR 82f 4753[2]
2 b c Barathea (IRE) - Dial Dream (Gay Mecene (USA)) 8.6f **(69)**
Form - 32
Record 1999 - 1st:0 2nd:1 3rd:1 Ran:2
Win Prizemoney £0 *Total Prizemoney* £2,427
1999 Turf 0-2: (6f, 7f) (gd, frm)
Currently decent colt. Turf high 82 (began Spt) - 2nd of 9 to Strahan (6 Oct York 6f gd RF 4753). Outgunned by the game Strahan at York, is still open to plenty of improvement, and is still learning. **W R Muir [0-2] M J Caddy.*

MATTAN RR 49f 2231[4]
3 b g Chaddleworth (IRE) - Gilded Omen (Faustus (USA)) 10f **(58)**
Form - 34
Record 1999 - 1st:0 2nd:0 3rd:1 Ran:2
Win Prizemoney £0 *Total Prizemoney* £778
1999 Turf 0-2: (12f, 13f) (gd, frm)
Light-framed, moderate gelding. Turf high 49.
**B J Llewellyn [0-2] E A Wrighton-Edwards.*

MA VIE BHB 66f **RR 63f** 4812[15]
2 b f Salse (USA) 10.9f **(71)** - One Life (USA) (L'Emigrant (USA)) 10.5f **(62)**
Form - 600
Record 1999 - 1st:0 2nd:0 3rd:0 Ran:3
1999 Turf 0-3: (6f, 7f 2) (gd, g-f, frm)
Currently average filly. Turf high 63 (began Jly).
**J R Fanshawe [0-3] The Earl Of Lonsdale.*

MAWARED (IRE) BHB 107f **RR 99f** 897[9]
6 ch h Nashwan (USA) 10.3f **(79)** - Harmless Albatross (Pas de Seul) 9.1f **(67)**
Form - 0
Record 1999 - 1st:0 2nd:0 3rd:0 Ran:1
Pre1999 - 1st:6 2nd:2 3rd:3 Ran:16
Win Prizemoney £49,012 *Total Prizemoney* £68,259

Wins									
	* 1998	Aug	Cheste	(G-S)	H	18.7f	99	99	<
	* 1998	Jly	Newbur	(GD)	H	16f	93	97	
	* 1997	Aug	Newmar	(GD)	H	14.8f	77	86	
	* 1997	Aug	Newbur	(G-F)	H	16f	77	83+	
	* 1997	Jly	Sandow	(G-F)	H	14f	67	78	
	* 1997	Jly	Sandow	(G-F)	H	14f	67	72	

1999 Turf 0-1: (16f) (g-f)
Very useful horse. **J L Dunlop [6-17] Hamdan Al Maktoum.*

MAWDSLEY RR 12f 3361[12]
2 b f Piccolo - Legendary Dancer (Shareef Dancer (USA)) 9.9f **(73)**
Form - 0
Record 1999 - 1st:0 2nd:0 3rd:0 Ran:1
1999 Turf 0-1: (6f) (g-f)
Currently poor filly. **G Woodward [0-1] P J Carr.*

MAWINGO (IRE) BHB 62f **RR 62f** 4902[5]
6 b g Taufan (USA) 8.3f **(65)** - Tappen Zee (Sandhurst Prince) 7.9f **(63)**
Form - 030035
Record 1999 - 1st:0 2nd:0 3rd:2 Ran:6
Pre1999 - 1st:3 2nd:2 3rd:2 Ran:19
Win Prizemoney £18,412 *Total Prizemoney* £26,939

Wins									
	* 1996	Jun	Newmar	(G-F)	H	8f	75	80	<
	* 1996	Jun	Newmar	(G-F)	H	8f	69	74	
	* 1996	May	Warwic	(FRM)	H	7f	64	65	

1999 Turf 0-6: (7f, 8f 4, 9f) (sft, gd 2, frm 3)
Average gelding, effective 8 to 9f, best at 8f, acts on sft to frm, has worn blinkers. Turf high 66 - 3rd of 19 getting 11lb from Nominator Lad (20 Apr Pontefract 8f sft RF 0773).

G Wragg [3-25] Mrs Claude Lilley.

MAWKAB (USA) BHB 64a **RR 46f** 5058[2]
4 b br g Gulch (USA) 9.6f **(79)** - Up Sail (USA) (Herculean (USA)) 7.5f **(49)**
Form - 6564127562620074012
Record 1999 - 1st:2 2nd:4 3rd:0 Ran:16
Pre1999 - 1st:0 2nd:0 3rd:0 Ran:3
Win Prizemoney £5,606 *Total Prizemoney* £8,542
Wins * **1999** *Oct Wolver (STD) C 7f 60 <*
* **1999** *Jan Lingfi (STD) 8f 59*
1999 Turf 0-6: (6f, 7f, 8f 4) (sft, g-s, gd, frm 3) 1999 AW 2-10: (6f, 7f 1-3, 8f 1-6) (Equi 1-7, Fibr 1-3)
Workmanlike, average gelding, effective 7 to 8f, best at 7f, - acts on AW, best on Fibr, mostly wears blinkers, prefers left handed tracks, prefers tight tracks, and excels at Southwell. Turf high 52. AW high 60 - 1st of 12 from Seven (13 Oct Wolverhampton RF 4866) - also 1st of 11 giving 20lb to Woolly Winsome (12 Jan Lingfield RF 0082). Inconsistent.
Miss Gay Kelleway [2-19] Martin Butler.

MAXIMUM MAKEUP (IRE) RR 74+f 4990[5]
2 b c Mujadil (USA) 7.7f **(70)** - Oileann Carrig (Pitcairn) 9.5f **(60)**
Form - 5
Record 1999 - 1st:0 2nd:0 3rd:0 Ran:1
1999 Turf 0-1: (6f) (frm)
Currently above-average colt.
J R Fanshawe [0-1] Sporting Index Racing Club.

MAX TYSON (IRE) RR 87f 934a[7]
3 b c Sanglamore (USA) 12.9f **(67)** - Ramonda (Fabulous Dancer (USA)) 9.4f **(70)**
Form - 7
1999 Turf 0-1: (11f) (g-s)
Currently useful colt. *P Demercastel in FR [0-2] Ecurie Fabien Ouaki.*

MAYA COVE BHB 68f **RR 66f** 4999[6]
3 b f Caerleon (USA) 10.9f **(79)** - Shining Water (Kalaglow) 9.8f **(67)**
Form - 642166
Record 1999 - 1st:1 2nd:1 3rd:0 Ran:6
Pre1999 - 1st:0 2nd:0 3rd:0 Ran:1
Win Prizemoney £2,836 *Total Prizemoney* £3,882
Wins * **1999** Aug Lingfi (G-F) H 11.5f 65 66 <
1999 Turf 1-6: (11f 1-3, 12f 2, 14f) (gd 3, frm 1-3)
Lengthy, average filly, effective 11 to 12f, best at 11f, acts on frm. Turf high 66 - 6th of 11 giving 1lb to Macca Luna (29 Aug Beverley 12f frm RF 3989) - also 1st of 6 getting 3lb from Copyforce Girl (6 Aug Lingfield RF 3423). *B W Hills [1-7] K Abdulla.*

MAYARO BAY BHB 96f **RR 96f** 4915[2]
3 b f Robellino (USA) 9.5f **(68)** - Down the Valley (Kampala) 8.5f **(56)**
Form - 2021654632
Record 1999 - 1st:1 2nd:3 3rd:1 Ran:10
Pre1999 - 1st:1 2nd:1 3rd:1 Ran:5
Win Prizemoney £35,296 *Total Prizemoney* £58,268
Wins * **1999** May Goodwo (GD) H 7f 85 90 <
* 1998 Oct Warwic (GD) 6f 76+
1999 Turf 1-10: (7f 1-5, 8f 5) (gd 1-6, g-f, frm 3)
Workmanlike, very useful filly, effective 7 to 8f, best at 7f, acts on gd to frm, best on gd, excels at Newmarket. Turf high 96 - 2nd of 20 giving 1lb to Free Option (16 Oct Newmarket 8f gd RF 4915) - also 1st of 14 giving 3lb to Kaibo (19 May Goodwood RF 1332). Consistent. A likeable individual, she ran a series of creditable races in decent seven furlong and mile handicaps in 1999. Yet to race on extremes of going, she has a useful turn-of-foot and is genuine. *R Hannon [2-15] J R Shannon.*

MAYBE'N RR 62f 2817[9]
2 ch c Deploy 11.4f **(67)** - Travel Mystery (Godswalk (USA)) 7.3f **(58)**
Form - U60
Record 1999 - 1st:0 2nd:0 3rd:0 Ran:3
1999 Turf 0-3: (6f, 7f 2) (g-f 2, frm)
Currently average colt. Turf high 62. *C Smith [0-3] P J Turner.*

MAY CONTESSA (USA) RR 74+f 4580[5]
2 b f Bahri (USA) - Copper Creek (Habitat) 9.4f **(70)**
Form - 35
Record 1999 - 1st:0 2nd:0 3rd:1 Ran:2
Win Prizemoney £0 *Total Prizemoney* £592
1999 Turf 0-2: (6f 2) (gd, g-f)
Currently above-average filly. Turf high 74 (began Aug).
D R C Elsworth [0-2] DGH Partnership.

MAYDORO BHB 34f34a **RR 20f 34a** 2678[6]
6 b m Dominion Royale 7.8f **(63)** - Bamdoro (Cavo Doro) 10.6f **(57)**
Form - 508770706
Record 1999 - 1st:0 2nd:0 3rd:0 Ran:7
Pre1999 - 1st:2 2nd:1 3rd:0 Ran:19
Win Prizemoney £3,998 *Total Prizemoney* £4,848
Wins 1998 Jun Newcas (SFT) S 5f 55 <
1998 *Jan Wolver (STD) C 6f 51*
1999 Turf 0-4: (5f, 6f 2, 7f) (hvy, gd, frm 2) 1999 AW 0-3: (5f, 7f 2) (Fibr 3)
Little account mare, effective 5 to 6f, best at 6f, acts on gd to frm - acts on Fibr. Turf high 20. AW high 25. *W M Brisbourne [0-5] Manton Hire Ltd (from M Dods [2-21] Jan 1999).*

MAY I SAY (IRE) BHB 55f **RR 62f** 4993[12]
3 b f Night Shift (USA) 8.1f **(73)** - Monoglow (Kalaglow) 9.8f **(67)**
Form - 0057200
Record 1999 - 1st:0 2nd:1 3rd:0 Ran:7
Pre1999 - 1st:0 2nd:1 3rd:1 Ran:5
Win Prizemoney £0 *Total Prizemoney* £2,278
1999 Turf 0-7: (10f 6, 11f) (g-s, gd 2, frm 4)
Neat, average filly, effective 8f, acts on gd to frm, prefers left handed tracks, favours tight tracks. Turf high 67. Consistent.
P W Harris [0-12] Colairo, Coles & Harris.

MAY KING MAYHEM BHB 42f39a **RR 40f 39a** 2079[6]
6 ch g Great Commotion (USA) 9.2f **(80)** - Queen Ranavalona (Sure Blade (USA)) 11.3f **(67)**
Form - 56670116
Record 1999 - 1st:2 2nd:0 3rd:0 Ran:8
Pre1999 - 1st:3 2nd:1 3rd:6 Ran:38
Win Prizemoney £15,175 *Total Prizemoney* £18,326
Wins * **1999** Jun Newmar (GD) H 12f 34 40
* **1999** May Leices (GD) H 11.8f 37 39
* 1998 Oct Pontef (GD) H 12f 37 42
* 1998 Aug Haydoc (GD) H 11.9f 31 34
* 1997 Jly Carlis (GD) H 12f 36 47 <
1999 Turf 2-6: (12f 2-4, 14f 2) (sft, gd, g-f 2-3, hrd) 1999 AW 0-2: (12f 2) (Fibr 2)
Moderate gelding, effective 12 to 14f, best at 12f, acts on gd to frm, best on g-f, often wears blinkers (extremely effectively). Turf high 40 - 1st of 31 getting 6lb from Double Rush (5 Jun Newmarket RF 1770) - also 1st of 15 getting 26lb from Taarish (31 May Leicester RF 1604). AW high 35.
Mrs A L M King [5-44] S J Harrison (from W R Muir [0-2] Spt 1995).

MAYL RR 2864[P]
3 b f Lion Cavern (USA) 7.5f **(74)** - Possessive Dancer (Shareef Dancer (USA)) 9.9f **(73)**
Form -
Record 1999 - 1st:0 2nd:0 3rd:0 Ran:2
1999 Turf 0-2: (gd, frm)
Currently poor gelding. Turf high 17 (began Jly).
Mrs G S Rees [0-2] Mrs G S Rees.

MAYLAN (IRE) BHB 28f **RR 38f** 4997[10]
4 br f Lashkari 13.1f **(52)** - Miysam (Supreme Sovereign) 9.5f **(53)**
Form - 0000
Record 1999 - 1st:0 2nd:0 3rd:0 Ran:4
Pre1999 - 1st:0 2nd:0 3rd:0 Ran:4
1999 Turf 0-4: (10f 2, 11f, 12f) (sft, gd, frm 2)
Workmanlike, moderate filly, has worn blinkers. Turf high 38 (began Aug).
W de Best-Turner [0-4] The Spanish Connection (from D M Hyde [0-4] Nov 1997).

MAYLANE BHB 106f **RR 109f** 5219[1]
5 b g Mtoto 11.5f **(71)** - Possessive Dancer (Shareef Dancer (USA)) 9.9f **(73)**
Form - 73511
Record 1999 - 1st:2 2nd:0 3rd:1 Ran:5

Pre1999 - 1st:4 2nd:2 3rd:0 Ran:12

Win Prizemoney £84,493 *Total Prizemoney* £96,158

Wins * **1999** Nov Doncas (SFT) L 12f 107+
* **1999** Oct Haydoc (HVY) 11.9f 102
* 1997 Spt Epsom (GD) G3 12f 112 <
* 1997 Jly Goodwo (G-F) H 12f 99 102
* 1997 Jun Goodwo (GD) 9f 93+
* 1996 Oct Lingfi (G-S) 7f 83+

1999 Turf 2-5: (11f, 12f 2-4) (sft 2-2, gd, g-f, frm)

Pattern-class gelding, effective 12 to 20f, best at 12f, acts on sft to frm, has worn blinkers. Turf high 109 (began Jly) - 3rd of 5 to Yavana's Pace (4 Spt Epsom 12f frm RF 4132) - also 1st of 7 giving 11lb to Badaayer (6 Nov Doncaster RF 5219). He is a very talented individual, but he returned to his old habits for the majority of his starts this season, virtually refusing to race every time he turned up at the track. When it seemed that all was lost, Michael Roberts produced a masterly ride to coax him home in a Haydock conditions event, and Richard Hughes repeated the trick on the last day of the turf season.

**A C Stewart [6-15] Sheikh Ahmed Al Maktoum (from S bin Suroor [0-1] Jun 1998).*

MAYO BHB 91f **RR 91f** 2500[19]

3 b c Nashwan (USA) 10.3f **(79)** - Nuryana (Nureyev (USA)) 8.7f **(78)**

Form - 1100

Record 1999 - 1st:2 2nd:0 3rd:0 Ran:4
Pre1999 - 1st:0 2nd:0 3rd:0 Ran:2

Win Prizemoney £9,518 *Total Prizemoney* £9,518

Wins * **1999** May Haydoc (GD) H 10.5f 83 91+ <
* **1999** May Lingfi (G-F) 10f 88

1999 Turf 2-4: (10f 1-2, 11f 1-1, 12f) (gd 2-2, g-f 2)

Well made, useful colt, effective 10 to 11f, acts on gd. Turf high 91 - 1st of 7 getting 11lb from Senure (28 May Haydock RF 1544) - also 1st of 7 from Inigo Jones (8 May Lingfield RF 1109).

**H R A Cecil [2-6] Burke's 5th Family Settlement.*

MA YORAM (USA) BHB 100f **RR 97f** 4405[3]

2 gr c Dayjur (USA) 6.8f **(79)** - Quelle Affaire (USA) (Riverman (USA)) 9.1f **(76)**

Form - 123

Record 1999 - 1st:1 2nd:1 3rd:1 Ran:3

Win Prizemoney £3,468 *Total Prizemoney* £35,918

Wins * **1999** Apr Kempto (GD) 5f 87+ <

1999 Turf 1-3: (5f 1-1, 6f 2) (gd, g-f 1-1, frm)

Currently very useful colt. Turf high 97 - 3rd of 4 to Primo Valentino (18 Spt Newbury 6f frm RF 4405). He was absent for 137-days after making an impressive debut and, in the circumstances, did well to finish placed in the Gimcrack and Mill Reef Stakes. Likely to improve, he should develop into smart sprinter in 2000.

**M R Channon [1-3] Sheikh Ahmed Al Maktoum.*

MAY QUEEN MEGAN BHB 40f38a **RR 42f 38a** 4985[4]

6 gr m Petorius 8f **(66)** - Siva (FR) (Bellypha) 9.8f **(73)**

Form - 50042032685574

Record 1999 - 1st:0 2nd:2 3rd:1 Ran:14
Pre1999 - 1st:3 2nd:3 3rd:4 Ran:37

Win Prizemoney £10,023 *Total Prizemoney* £17,494

Wins * 1998 Jly Lingfi (G-F) H 9f 49 52 <
* 1998 Jun Nottin (GD) H 8.2f 38 48
* 1996 Jly Lingfi (G-F) H 6f 52 52 <

1999 Turf 0-14: (8f 3, 9f 2, 10f 9) (gd 4, g-f 4, frm 5, hrd)

Moderate mare, effective 8 to 10f, acts on gd to frm, best on frm, has worn blinkers, prefers left handed tracks, prefers tight tracks, excels at Lingfield, does well at Pontefract. Turf high 48. Consistent. **Mrs A L M King [3-51] S J Harrison.*

MAYSHIEL (IRE) **RR 108f** 3933a[5]

6 b g Ela-Mana-Mou 12.7f **(72)** - Orillia (Red God) 8.5f **(65)**

Form - 35

1999 Turf 0-2: (12f, 15f) (gd, frm)

Pattern-class gelding. Turf high 108 (began Aug). **J E Hammond in FR [0-4] (from DEN [0-1] Aug 1999).*

MAY SONG **RR 17f** 2864[P]

7 b g Gold Song - Kaymay (Maystreak) 8.7f **(53)**

Form - 0P

Record 1999 - 1st:0 2nd:0 3rd:0 Ran:2

1999 Turf 0-2: (7f, 8f) (gd, frm)

Poor gelding. Turf high 17 (began Jly). (DEAD)

**Mrs G S Rees [0-2] Mrs G S Rees.*

MAYVILLE'S DANCER (IRE) BHB 62f **RR 67f** 1013[20]

3 ch f Up and At 'em - Cutlers Corner (Sharpen Up) 8.3f **(67)**

Form - 00

Record 1999 - 1st:0 2nd:0 3rd:0 Ran:2
Pre1999 - 1st:0 2nd:1 3rd:0 Ran:3

Win Prizemoney £0 *Total Prizemoney* £738

1999 Turf 0-2: (6f, 7f) (sft, frm)

Neat, average filly. **G A Butler [0-5] Jan Stenbeck.*

MAZAYA (IRE) BHB 98f **RR 97f** 4794[12]

3 b f Sadler's Wells (USA) 11.3f **(87)** - Sharaniya (USA) (Alleged (USA)) 10f **(76)**

Form - 2120

Record 1999 - 1st:1 2nd:2 3rd:0 Ran:4

Win Prizemoney £3,714 *Total Prizemoney* £11,719

Wins * **1999** Jun Chepst (GD) 12.1f 77 <

1999 Turf 1-4: (10f, 12f 1-3) (sft, gd 1-2, frm)

Unfurnished, very useful filly. Turf high 97 - 2nd of 8 to Signorina Cattiva (26 Spt Ascot 12f sft RF 4573). She ran a super race when finishing second in a Listed event at Ascot in September, and was probably over the top when disappointing back there the following month. Likely to stay beyond a mile and a half, she goes well on soft ground but must improve to win a Group event at home.

**J L Dunlop [1-4] Hamdan Al Maktoum.*

MAZEED (IRE) BHB 57f57a **RR 35f 57a** 4666[12]

6 ch g Lycius (USA) 8.8f **(71)** - Maraatib (IRE) (Green Desert (USA)) 8.6f **(78)**

Form - 36577000

Record 1999 - 1st:0 2nd:0 3rd:0 Ran:6
Pre1999 - 1st:8 2nd:3 3rd:4 Ran:29

Win Prizemoney £23,075 *Total Prizemoney* £30,851

Wins 1998 Jly Beverl (GD) H 9.9f 71 73
1998 Jun Yarmou (G-F) H 10.1f 58 71
1998 May Yarmou (FRM) H 10.1f 58 68
1998 *Jan Lingfi (STD) 10f 69+*
1997 *Dec Wolver (STD) H 9.4f 57 64+*
1997 *Dec Wolver (STD) H 9.4f 43 56+*
1995 Aug Haydoc (G-F) 6f 84+ <
1995 Jun Newcas (FRM) 6f 81

1999 Turf 0-3: (10f, 11f, 12f) (gd 2, g-f) 1999 AW 0-3: (10f, 12f 2) (Equi 2, Fibr)

Fair gelding, effective 9 to 10f, best at 10f, acts on g-f to frm - acts on AW, best on frm, often wears blinkers (extremely effectively), excels at Yarmouth, does well at Beverley. Turf high 35 (began Jly). AW high 56. Becoming disappointing.

**Miss K M George [0-7] Miss K George (from P D Evans [6-23] Jan 1999).*

MAZILLA BHB 32f28a **RR 38f 28a** 2145[8]

7 b m Mazilier (USA) 8.5f **(56)** - Mo Ceri (Kampala) 8.5f **(56)**

Form - 608

Record 1999 - 1st:0 2nd:0 3rd:0 Ran:3
Pre1999 - 1st:8 2nd:5 3rd:5 Ran:53

Win Prizemoney £20,386 *Total Prizemoney* £26,528

Wins * 1996 Aug Yarmou (GD) H 10.1f 52 59
* 1996 Jly Nottin (G-F) H 10f 46 53+
* 1996 Jly Warwic (G-F) SH 10.8f 40 52
* 1996 Jun Nottin (G-F) SH 10f 37 42
* 1996 *Feb Southw (STD) H 11f 47 51*
* 1996 *Feb Southw (STD) SH 11f 42 45*
1995 *Jan Wolver (STD) S 7f 60* <
1995 *Jan Southw (STD) S 8f 51*

1999 Turf 0-2: (10f, 11f) (g-s, gd) 1999 AW 0-1: (11f) (Fibr)

Moderate mare, effective 10f, acts on gd to frm, best on gd, has worn blinkers (extremely effectively). Turf high 32. Inconsistent.

**A Streeter [7-49] M Rhodes (from A L Forbes [0-1] Jun 1995).*

MAZZELMO BHB 63f50a **RR 58+f 50a** 4485[1]

6 gr m Thethingaboutitis (USA) 16f **(44)** - Nattfari (Tyrnavos) 10.1f **(55)**

Form - 7573054316075301

Record 1999 - 1st:2 2nd:0 3rd:3 Ran:16
Pre1999 - 1st:2 2nd:0 3rd:3 Ran:13

Win Prizemoney £16,232 *Total Prizemoney* £20,949

Wins * **1999** Spt Cheste (HVY) H 15.9f 58 58+

* 1999 Jun Chepst (G-F) H 18f 56 60
* 1998 Aug Cheste (GD) H 15.9f 52 59
* 1998 *Jun Wolver (STD) C 16.2f 64* <

1999 Turf 2-13: (16f 1-8, 17f 2, 18f 1-2, 19f) (sft, g-s 1-2, gd 2, g-f 1-6, frm 2) 1999 AW 0-3: (16f 3) (Fibr 3)

Fair mare, effective 16 to 18f, best at 16f, acts on sft to g-f - acts on Fibr, has worn blinkers, does well at Chester. Turf high 60 - 6th of 12 giving 18lb to Whitley Grange Boy (1 Jly Catterick 16f g-f RF 2455) - also 1st of 14 giving 20lb to Hillswick (29 Jun Chepstow RF 2391). AW high 39. **A Bailey [6-39] Miss E Oats.*

MBELE RR 85+f

5062[2]

2 b c Mtoto 11.5f **(71)** - Majestic Image (Niniski (USA)) 10.6f **(65)**

Form - 2

Record 1999 - 1st:0 2nd:1 3rd:0 Ran:1

Win Prizemoney £0 *Total Prizemoney* £752

1999 Turf 0-1: (8f) (gd)

Currently useful colt. (1st run) - 2nd of 13 to Riddlesdown (26 Oct Bath 8f gd RF 5062). **W R Muir [0-1] & Mrs John Wilson.*

MCFARLINE (IRE) BHB 53f RR 56f

3916[10]

3 b c Ela-Mana-Mou 12.7f **(72)** - Highland Ball (Bold Lad (IRE)) 8.4f **(68)**

Form - 0400

Record 1999 - 1st:0 2nd:0 3rd:0 Ran:4
Pre1999 - 1st:0 2nd:0 3rd:0 Ran:3

1999 Turf 0-4: (12f 4) (gd 2, frm 2)

Scopey, fair colt, has worn blinkers. Turf high 56. Has shown very little on his racecourse outings so far.
**J L Dunlop [0-7] Michael Watt.*

MCGILLYCUDDY REEKS (IRE) BHB 67f74a RR 69f 74a

5162[12]

8 b m Kefaah (USA) 11.2f **(64)** - Kilvarnet (Furry Glen) 8.9f **(63)**

Form - 03050142140307670

Record 1999 - 1st:2 2nd:1 3rd:2 Ran:17
Pre1999 - 1st:8 2nd:4 3rd:9 Ran:59

Win Prizemoney £39,862 *Total Prizemoney* £52,488

Wins *** 1999** Jly Doncas (G-F) H 10.3f 69 73
*** 1999** Jun Beverl (G-F) H 9.9f 65 70
* 1998 Aug Thirsk (GD) H 12f 73 77 <
* 1998 Jun Newcas (SFT) H 10.1f 70 73
* 1997 Oct York (GD) H 10.4f 68 71
* 1997 Aug Nottin (G-F) H 10f 53 65
* 1997 Jly Beverl (GD) H 9.9f 46 59
* 1997 Jly Beverl (G-F) H 9.9f 46 51
* 1997 Jly Pontef (GD) H 8f 38 45

1999 Turf 2-17: (9f 2, 10f 2-11, 11f, 12f 3) (g-s 2, gd 3, g-f 1-8, frm 1-4)

Average mare, effective 8 to 12f, best at 12f, acts on sft to frm, best on g-f, likes right handed tracks, excels at Newcastle, does well at Beverley. Turf high 73 - 1st of 8 getting 7lb from Mister Benjamin (28 Jly Doncaster RF 3199) - also 1st of 10 getting 3lb from Amarice (22 Jun Beverley RF 2192). She picked up a ten-furlong event at Beverley on fast ground in June, and added a nice prize at Doncaster on similar ground in July. Disappointing since, she is too high in the handicap.

**Don Enrico Incisa [9-53] Don Enrico Incisa (from N Tinkler [0-12] Nov 1996).*

MCQUILLAN RR 49f

4910[12]

2 b g Maledetto (IRE) - Macs Maharanee **(71f 70a)** (Indian King (USA)) 7.4f **(64)**

Form - 00

Record 1999 - 1st:0 2nd:0 3rd:0 Ran:2

1999 Turf 0-2: (6f, 7f) (gd 2)

Currently moderate gelding. Turf high 49 (began Spt).
**P S Felgate [0-2] P S Felgate.*

MEADAAAR (USA) BHB 100f RR 92f

4676[3]

2 ch c Diesis 9f **(80)** - Katiba (USA) (Gulch (USA)) 8f **(81)**

Form - 213

Record 1999 - 1st:1 2nd:1 3rd:1 Ran:3

Win Prizemoney £4,560 *Total Prizemoney* £9,280

Wins *** 1999** Aug Yarmou (FRM) 7f 84+ <

1999 Turf 1-3: (7f 1-3) (gd, g-f 1-2)

Currently useful colt. Turf high 92 (began Jly) - also 1st of 3 from Principle Account (4 Aug Yarmouth RF 3381). A neck-second to Dramatic Quest first time up at Ascot, he got on the scorecard when beating two rivals at Yarmouth next time out, despite running green and losing his pilot after crossing the winning line. There is sure to be more to come.
**J L Dunlop [1-3] Hamdan Al Maktoum.*

MEDELAI BHB 33f RR 35f

4988[9]

3 b f Marju (IRE) 9.2f **(76)** - No Islands (Lomond (USA)) 8.8f **(65)**

Form - 8050750

Record 1999 - 1st:0 2nd:0 3rd:0 Ran:7
Pre1999 - 1st:1 2nd:1 3rd:1 Ran:8

Win Prizemoney £2,197 *Total Prizemoney* £3,365

Wins * 1998 Oct Nottin (SFT) S 8.2f 56 <

1999 Turf 0-7: (12f 4, 14f 3) (gd, g-f, frm 5)

Unfurnished, very moderate filly, effective 7 to 10f, acts on gd to g-f, best on gd, likes tight tracks. Turf high 50.
**J D Bethell [1-15] Clarendon Thoroughbred Racing.*

MEDICINE BALL BHB 49f RR 40f

2953[11]

4 b f Rudimentary (USA) 8.2f **(66)** - Morica (Moorestyle) 6.9f **(64)**

Form - 00

Record 1999 - 1st:0 2nd:0 3rd:0 Ran:2
Pre1999 - 1st:0 2nd:0 3rd:0 Ran:3

1999 Turf 0-1: (10f) (frm) 1999 AW 0-1: (8f) (Fibr)

Scopey, moderate filly. **T R Watson [0-5] Newitt and Co Ltd.*

MEDINA DE RIOSECO BHB 58f RR 67df

5164[5]

2 b f Puissance 7.1f **(60)** - Antonia's Folly **(53f 53a)** (Music Boy) 6.8f **(57)**

Form - 436640200665

Record 1999 - 1st:0 2nd:1 3rd:1 Ran:12

Win Prizemoney £0 *Total Prizemoney* £2,222

1999 Turf 0-12: (5f 10, 6f 2) (g-s 2, gd 4, g-f 3, frm 2, hrd)

Average filly, effective 5f, acts on gd to g-f. Turf high 69.
**J Berry [0-12] Slatch Farm Stud.*

MEG BHB 40f40a RR 47df 40a

4289[12]

3 b f Be My Chief (USA) 10.2f **(62)** - Megdale (IRE) **(41f)** (Waajib)

Form - 0035860

Record 1999 - 1st:0 2nd:0 3rd:1 Ran:7
Pre1999 - 1st:0 2nd:0 3rd:1 Ran:4

Win Prizemoney £0 *Total Prizemoney* £805

1999 Turf 0-5: (7f, 8f, 10f 2, 11f) (gd, g-f 2, frm, hrd) 1999 AW 0-2: (8f, 12f) (Fibr 2)

Unfurnished, moderate filly, effective 7f, acts on frm, likes left handed tracks, likes tight tracks. Turf high 47. AW high 45 (began Jly). **C F Wall [0-11] Induna Racing Partners Two.*

MEGA (IRE) BHB 48f RR 59f

4882[15]

3 b f Petardia 8.2f **(58)** - Gobolino (Don) 7.7f **(64)**

Form - 00800

Record 1999 - 1st:0 2nd:0 3rd:0 Ran:5
Pre1999 - 1st:0 2nd:0 3rd:0 Ran:1

1999 Turf 0-5: (7f, 8f, 10f 2, 11f) (g-f 2, frm 3)

Leggy, fair filly, has worn blinkers. Turf high 59.
**M H Tompkins [0-6] Mystic Meg Ltd.*

MEGS PEARL BHB 46f RR 41f

1046[9]

3 gr f Petong 7.6f **(58)** - Heaven-Liegh-Grey (Grey Desire) 8.7f **(50)**

Form - 000

Record 1999 - 1st:0 2nd:0 3rd:0 Ran:3
Pre1999 - 1st:0 2nd:0 3rd:0 Ran:3

1999 Turf 0-3: (7f, 8f, 10f) (g-s, g-f 2)

Scopey, moderate filly, has worn blinkers. Turf high 41.
**P D Evans [0-6] John Pugh.*

MEHMAAS BHB 72f RR 71f

4406[4]

3 b g Distant Relative 7f **(69)** - Guest List (Be My Guest (USA)) 9.3f **(67)**

Form - 2051504

Record 1999 - 1st:1 2nd:0 3rd:0 Ran:6
Pre1999 - 1st:0 2nd:2 3rd:0 Ran:5

Win Prizemoney £2,550 *Total Prizemoney* £5,178

Wins *** 1999** Aug Bright (G-F) 7f 75 <

1999 Turf 1-6: (7f 1-1, 8f 4, 9f) (g-s 2, gd, frm 1-3)

Workmanlike, above-average gelding, effective 7 to 8f, acts on gd to frm, often wears blinkers. Turf high 75 (began Aug) - 1st of 4 from High Hoyland (23 Aug Brighton RF 3853). Inconsistent.

M R Channon [1-6] Dr Paul Prestwich (from Lord Huntingdon [0-1] Nov 1998).

MEILLEUR (IRE) BHB 54f55a **RR 54f 55a** 4948[8]
5 b g Nordico (USA) 8.2f **(59)** - Lucy Limelight (Hot Spark) 7.6f **(62)**
Form - 022158
Record **1999** - 1st:1 2nd:2 3rd:0 Ran:6
Pre1999 - 1st:1 2nd:1 3rd:2 Ran:16
Win Prizemoney £5,126 *Total Prizemoney* £8,855
Wins * **1999** Spt Newbur (G-F) H 12f 52 54 <
* 1998 Aug Hamilt (SFT) H 11.1f 51 52
1999 Turf 1-6: (11f, 12f 1-5) (gd 3, g-f, frm 1-2)
Fair gelding, effective 11 to 12f, best at 11f, acts on gd to frm, best on frm, has worn blinkers. Turf high 54 (began Jly) - 1st of 21 giving 11lb to Dinar (17 Spt Newbury RF 4387).
Lady Herries [2-23] The Cottage Racing Partnership.

MELANZANA RR 85+f 4542[1]
2 b f Alzao (USA) 9.8f **(73)** - Melody Park (Music Boy) 6.8f **(57)**
Form - 31
Record **1999** - 1st:1 2nd:0 3rd:1 Ran:2
Win Prizemoney £3,270 *Total Prizemoney* £3,815
Wins * **1999** Spt Redcar (G-F) 6f 85+ <
1999 Turf 1-2: (6f 1-2) (frm 1-2)
Currently useful filly. Turf high 85 (began Spt) - 1st of 13 from Adamas (24 Spt Redcar RF 4542).
E A L Dunlop [1-2] The Serendipity Partnership.

MELASUS (IRE) BHB 36f48a **RR 34f 48a** 830[14]
7 ch g Nashamaa 8.1f **(58)** - Sweet Camden (Camden Town) 9.3f **(53)**
Form - 855000
Record **1999** - 1st:0 2nd:0 3rd:0 Ran:6
Pre1999 - 1st:2 2nd:0 3rd:0 Ran:6
Win Prizemoney £13,440 *Total Prizemoney* £13,440
1999 Turf 0-3: (8f, 10f, 11f) (sft, gd, frm) 1999 AW 0-3: (7f 2, 8f) (Fibr 3)
Moderate gelding. Turf high 34. AW high 49.
D W P Arbuthnot [2-12] Mrs A Haynes.

MELBA (IRE) RR 65f 5020[14]
2 b f Namaqualand (USA) - Priyanka (Last Tycoon) 8.5f **(62)**
Form - 00
Record **1999** - 1st:0 2nd:0 3rd:0 Ran:2
1999 Turf 0-2: (7f, 8f) (gd 2)
Currently average filly. Turf high 65 (began Oct).
A P Jarvis [0-2] Mrs D B Brazier.

MELBEN RR 148[12]
3 b c Dolphin Street (FR) - Shapely Test (USA) (Elocutionist (USA)) 8f **(77)**
Form - 80
Record **1999** - 1st:0 2nd:0 3rd:0 Ran:2
1999 AW 0-2: (6f, 8f) (Equi 2)
Workmanlike, currently little account colt, often wears blinkers. AW high 21. *J Noseda [0-2] Schmidt-Bodner & The late Mrs Tillman.*

MELLORS (IRE) BHB 58f62a **RR 62f 62a** 2567[7]
6 b h Common Grounds 8.1f **(66)** - Simply Beautiful (IRE) (Simply Great (FR)) 8.2f **(65)**
Form - 8815147
Record **1999** - 1st:2 2nd:0 3rd:0 Ran:6
Pre1999 - 1st:6 2nd:6 3rd:3 Ran:39
Win Prizemoney £21,027 *Total Prizemoney* £27,757
Wins * **1999** May Bright (FRM) H 10f 57 62
* **1999** Apr Bright (G-F) H 8f 53 56
* 1998 May Bright (FRM) H 8f 46 52
* 1998 Apr Bright (GD) H 8f 41 50
* 1998 *Feb Lingfi (SLW) H 8f 51 68* <
* 1998 *Feb Lingfi (SLW) H 8f 51 56*
* 1997 *Jan Lingfi (STD) H 6f 57 60*
1996 Jun Catter (GD) 6f 52
1999 Turf 2-5: (8f 1-2, 10f 1-3) (g-f 1-3, frm 1-2) 1999 AW 0-1: (8f) (Equi)
Average horse, effective 7 to 10f, acts on g-f - acts on Equi, has worn blinkers, favours left handed tracks, and excels at Brighton. Turf high 62 - 1st of 5 giving 9lb to Caernarfon Bay (28 May Brighton RF 1540). *M J Heaton-Ellis [7-36] Alun Williams (from J A R Toller [1-14] Oct 1996).*

MELLOW JAZZ RR 81f 4557[1]
2 b f Lycius (USA) 8.8f **(71)** - Slow Jazz (USA) (Chief's Crown (USA)) 9.8f **(72)**
Form - 1
Record **1999** - 1st:1 2nd:0 3rd:0 Ran:1
Win Prizemoney £3,947 *Total Prizemoney* £3,947
Wins * **1999** Spt Nottin (GD) 6.1f 81 <
1999 Turf 1-1: (6f 1-1) (gd 1-1)
Currently decent filly. (1st run) - 1st of 12 getting 5lb from Lakeland Paddy (25 Spt Nottingham RF 4557). Cosy winner of an ordinary maiden on his debut, she should go on to better things.
E A L Dunlop [1-1] Saeed Abdullah Humaid.

MELLOW MISS BHB 57f54a **RR 57f 54a** 5058[7]
3 b f Danehill (USA) 9.1f **(79)** - Like the Sun (USA) (Woodman (USA)) 9f **(74)**
Form - 0507
Record **1999** - 1st:0 2nd:0 3rd:0 Ran:4
Pre1999 - 1st:0 2nd:0 3rd:0 Ran:2
1999 Turf 0-3: (5f, 6f, 7f) (g-s, g-f, frm) 1999 AW 0-1: (7f) (Equi)
Scopey, fair filly, has worn blinkers. Turf high 57.
R M Flower [0-4] Trevor Lowe (from E A L Dunlop [0-2] Oct 1998).

MELMAC (SWE) RR 96f 1527a[2]
8 br h Diaglyphard (USA) - Sovereign Star (Comedy Star (USA)) 7.5f **(50)**
Form - 2
1999 AW 0-1: (8f) (Dirt)
Currently Pattern-class horse. (1st run) - 2nd of 9 to Sharp Matt (20 May Jagersro 8f Dirt RF 1527a). *H Meisel in SWE [0-2] Aug 1995).*

MELODIAN BHB 54f **RR 54f** 4880[27]
4 b c Grey Desire 9.3f **(49)** - Mere Melody (Dunphy) 9.4f **(57)**
Form - 40213117350
Record **1999** - 1st:3 2nd:1 3rd:2 Ran:11
Pre1999 - 1st:1 2nd:0 3rd:1 Ran:9
Win Prizemoney £14,322 *Total Prizemoney* £17,118
Wins * **1999** Aug Catter (G-F) H 7f 51 53 <
* **1999** Jly Doncas (G-F) H 7f 42 52
* **1999** Jly Beverl (G-F) H 7.5f 41 48
* 1998 Jly Newcas (GD) H 7f 38 41
1999 Turf 3-11: (7f 3-8, 8f 3) (g-s 2, g-f 1-1, frm 2-8)
Leggy, fair colt, effective 7 to 8f, best at 7f, acts on g-s to frm, best on frm, mostly wears blinkers (extremely effectively). Turf high 54 - 3rd of 16 getting 17lb from Prospector's Cove (15 Spt Yarmouth 8f g-s RF 4340) - also 1st of 18 giving 3lb to Dancing Em (13 Aug Catterick RF 3600). Hit form with a vengeance during the summer, winning three modest handicaps, and overcame a poor draw on the third occasion. *M Brittain [4-20] Mel Brittain.*

MELODIC HEIGHTS RR 36f 1780[5]
2 b f Puissance 7.1f **(60)** - Pick a Tune (Music Boy) 6.8f **(57)**
Form - 7075
Record **1999** - 1st:0 2nd:0 3rd:0 Ran:4
1999 Turf 0-2: (5f 2) (g-s, g-f) 1999 AW 0-2: (5f 2) (Fibr 2)
Very moderate filly. Turf high 36. AW high 38.
J Berry [0-4] J Berry.

MELODY BLUES BHB 47f45a **RR 46f 45a** 370[10]
3 b f Merdon Melody 6.8f **(56)** - Hsian (Shantung) 9.8f **(64)**
Form - 70
Record **1999** - 1st:0 2nd:0 3rd:0 Ran:2
Pre1999 - 1st:0 2nd:0 3rd:2 Ran:4
Win Prizemoney £0 *Total Prizemoney* £554
1999 AW 0-2: (6f, 7f) (Fibr 2)
Moderate filly, effective 6 to 7f, - acts on Fibr, has worn blinkers.
M Dods [0-6] M J K Dods.

MELODY LADY BHB 60f **RR 56f** 2805[2]
3 ch f Dilum (USA) 7.1f **(56)** - Ansellady **(62f 60a)** (Absalom) 7.2f **(58)**
Form - 080272
Record **1999** - 1st:0 2nd:2 3rd:0 Ran:5
Pre1999 - 1st:0 2nd:0 3rd:1 Ran:6
Win Prizemoney £0 *Total Prizemoney* £1,691
1999 Turf 0-5: (7f, 8f, 10f, 12f 2) (g-f, frm 4)
Unfurnished, fair filly, effective 6f, acts on g-f, has worn blinkers.

Turf high 56.
**F Murphy [0-5] R Sunter (from Mrs L Stubbs [0-6] Nov 1998).*

MELODY QUEEN BHB 77f87a RR 65f 87a 2337[9]

3 b f Merdon Melody 6.8f **(56)** - Thabeh (Shareef Dancer (USA)) 9.9f **(73)**
Form - 34211060
Record 1999 - 1st:2 2nd:1 3rd:1 Ran:8
Pre1999 - 1st:2 2nd:4 3rd:0 Ran:10
Win Prizemoney £25,355 *Total Prizemoney* £31,246
Wins * **1999** *Mar Lingfi (STD) H 8f 72 86 <*
* **1999** *Feb Lingfi (STD) C 8f 76*
* 1998 Spt Newmar (GD) H 7f 65 73
1998 Aug Bright (FRM) S 7f 60
1999 Turf 0-2: (8f, 10f) (g-s, frm) 1999 AW 2-6: (7f, 8f 2-3, 10f 2) (Equi 2-6)
Unfurnished, useful filly, effective 8f, - acts on Equi, has worn blinkers, likes left handed tracks, likes tight tracks. Turf high 53. AW high 86 - 1st of 5 giving 24lb to Shady Deal (4 Mar Lingfield RF 0401). Becoming disappointing. She gradually found her form on Equitrack through the winter, ultimately winning twice over a mile.
**K R Burke [3-11] Nigel Shields (from Ronald Thompson [1-7] Aug 1998).*

MELOMANIA (USA) BHB 22f40a RR 5f 40a 4864[6]

7 b g Shadeed (USA) 7.7f **(72)** - Medley of Song (USA) (Secretariat (USA)) 9f **(79)**
Form - 100306807006
Record 1999 - 1st:1 2nd:0 3rd:1 Ran:12
Pre1999 - 1st:0 2nd:0 3rd:0 Ran:6
Win Prizemoney £2,220 *Total Prizemoney* £2,705
Wins * **1999** *Feb Lingfi (STD) H 8f 40 43 <*
1999 Turf 0-5: (5f, 7f, 10f, 11f, 12f) (gd, g-f 2, frm 2) 1999 AW 1-7: (7f 3, 8f 1-4) (Equi 1-3, Fibr 4)
Fair gelding, effective 7 to 8f, - acts on AW, likes left handed tracks, likes tight tracks. Turf high 14. AW high 50 - 6th of 12 getting 2lb from Darwell's Folly (13 Oct Wolverhampton 7f Fibr RF 4864) - also 1st of 9 getting 15lb from Gadge (2 Feb Lingfield RF 0208).
**P Howling [1-14] Mrs P Haddow (from S R Bowring [0-1] Apr 1997).*

MELON PLACE (IRE) BHB 99f RR 89+f 3960[1]

2 b c Dancing Dissident (USA) 6.8f **(65)** - Shikari Rose (Kala Shikari) 8.4f **(54)**
Form - 231
Record 1999 - 1st:1 2nd:1 3rd:1 Ran:3
Win Prizemoney £3,761 *Total Prizemoney* £7,366
Wins * **1999** Aug Goodwo (GD) 5f 89+ <
1999 Turf 1-3: (5f 1-3) (gd 1-2, g-f)
Currently useful colt. Turf high 89 (began Jly) - 1st of 7 giving 8lb to Queensmead (28 Aug Goodwood RF 3960). Ran a fine third in a listed race at York on only his second start before getting off the mark. There should be more to come next season.
**K R Burke [1-3] Michael Wilson.*

MELT THE CLOUDS (CAN) BHB 37f45a RR 34f 45a 4586[13]

6 ch g Diesis 9f **(80)** - Population (General Assembly (USA)) 10f **(68)**
Form - 508070
Record 1999 - 1st:0 2nd:0 3rd:0 Ran:6
Pre1999 - 1st:0 2nd:4 3rd:0 Ran:12
Win Prizemoney £0 *Total Prizemoney* £5,714
1999 Turf 0-4: (7f 2, 8f 2) (g-s, gd, g-f, frm) 1999 AW 0-2: (9f, 13f) (Equi, Fibr)
Very moderate gelding, has worn blinkers. Turf high 34. AW high 23. **J Neville [0-5] T Beresford (from M C Pipe [2-10] Jan 1999).*

MELVELLA BHB 50f RR 49f 5133[11]

3 b f Mtoto 11.5f **(71)** - Trojan Desert (Troy) 10.4f **(68)**
Form - 67656370
Record 1999 - 1st:0 2nd:0 3rd:1 Ran:8
Win Prizemoney £0 *Total Prizemoney* £293
1999 Turf 0-7: (10f 3, 12f 4) (gd 4, frm 3) 1999 AW 0-1: (15f) (Fibr)
Unfurnished, moderate filly. Turf high 69. Consistent.
**M L W Bell [0-8] Paddy Barrett.*

MEMORISE (USA) BHB 105f RR 110f 3445[1]

5 b h Lyphard (USA) 10.6f **(75)** - Shirley Valentine (Shirley Heights) 10.3f **(74)**
Form - 321
Record 1999 - 1st:1 2nd:1 3rd:1 Ran:3
Pre1999 - 1st:3 2nd:2 3rd:2 Ran:13
Win Prizemoney £48,787 *Total Prizemoney* £77,218
Wins * **1999** Aug Ascot (GD) 12f 102
* 1998 Jun Currag (HVY) G3 14f 112 <
* 1997 Jly Newmar (G-F) H 10f 86 89
* 1997 May Newcas (GD) 10.1f 82
1999 Turf 1-3: (12f 1-3) (gd 1-1, g-f, frm)
Group-class colt, effective 12 to 14f, best at 13f, acts on sft to frm, best on g-f. Turf high 103 - 2nd of 6 giving 9lb to Adnaan (16 Jly Newmarket 12f frm RF 2882). Consistent. Lightly raced, he is a genuine Group 3 horse and promises to stay two miles. Effective on any ground, he remains open to improvement but does not seem particularly easy to train. **H R A Cecil [4-16] K Abdulla.*

MEMORY'S MUSIC BHB 32f33a RR 31f 33a 92[11]

7 b g Dance of Life (USA) 9.3f **(69)** - Sheer Luck (Shergar) 10.4f **(66)**
Form - 700
Record 1999 - 1st:0 2nd:0 3rd:0 Ran:1
Pre1999 - 1st:1 2nd:1 3rd:1 Ran:21
Win Prizemoney £1,864 *Total Prizemoney* £2,766
Wins * 1998 *Jan Lingfi (STD) SH 12f 34 39 <*
1999 AW 0-1: (12f) (Equi)
Moderate gelding, effective 12f, - acts on Equi, has worn blinkers.
**M Madgwick [2-27] Mrs J Phillips-Hill (from I A Balding [0-8] Spt 1995).*

MEMPHIS DANCER BHB 52f RR 58f 974[6]

4 b f Shareef Dancer (USA) 10.1f **(67)** - Wollow Maid (Wollow) 8.2f **(61)**
Form - 6
Record 1999 - 1st:0 2nd:0 3rd:0 Ran:1
Pre1999 - 1st:0 2nd:2 3rd:0 Ran:8
Win Prizemoney £0 *Total Prizemoney* £1,750
1999 Turf 0-1: (11f) (g-f)
Scopey, fair filly, effective 8f, acts on frm. Consistent.
**Miss Lucinda Russell [0-4] Peter Russell (from J W Hills [0-8] Oct 1998).*

MENDELUCI (IRE) BHB 45f RR 16f 128[5]

7 b g Nordico (USA) 8.2f **(59)** - Favourite Niece (Busted) 10.2f **(61)**
Form - 5
Record 1999 - 1st:0 2nd:0 3rd:0 Ran:1
Pre1999 - 1st:0 2nd:0 3rd:0 Ran:2
1999 AW 0-1: (12f) (Fibr)
Moderate gelding, always wears blinkers.
**L R Lloyd-James [0-4] C Raine (from J G M O'Shea [0-3] Spt 1998).*

MENDOZA BHB 46f46a RR 50f 46a 1024[P]

5 b g Rambo Dancer (CAN) 8.4f **(59)** - Red Poppy (IRE) (Coquelin (USA)) 8.4f **(58)**
Form - 642454P
Record 1999 - 1st:0 2nd:1 3rd:0 Ran:5
Pre1999 - 1st:1 2nd:2 3rd:3 Ran:25
Win Prizemoney £3,290 *Total Prizemoney* £7,170
Wins 1997 *Jan Lingfi (STD) H 8f 55 53 <*
1999 Turf 0-1: (12f) (hrd) 1999 AW 0-4: (10f 2, 12f 2) (Equi 4)
Fair gelding, effective 8 to 12f, best at 8f, acts on frm - acts on Equi, has worn blinkers. AW high 45 (1st run) - 2nd of 11 giving 3lb to Clonoe (21 Jan Lingfield 10f Equi RF 0133).
**P Mitchell [0-14] R Mardell (from D J G MurraySmith [1-17] Apr 1998).*

MENIFEE (USA) RR 119f 1351a[2]

3 b c Harlan (USA) - Anne Cambell (USA) (Never Bend) 13.1f **(70)**
Form - 22
1999 Turf 0-1: (10f) (frm) 1999 AW 0-1: (10f) (Dirt)
Currently very high-class colt. (1st run) - 2nd of 19 to Charismatic (1 May Churchill Downs 10f frm RF 1070a). (1st run) - 2nd of 13 to Charismatic (15 May Pimlico 10f Dirt RF 1351a). A top-class American-trained colt, he had the misfortune to beat all except Charismatic in the first two legs of the American Triple Crown. He came from out of the clouds on the first occasion and would probably have won in a few more strides, but there seemed no excuses second time. **W E Walden in USA [0-2] Mrs A B Hancock Jr.*

MEN OF WICKENBY BHB 31f **RR 27f** 4539[13]
5 b g Shirley Heights 12.1f **(76)** - Radiant Bride (USA) (Blushing Groom (FR)) 10.3f **(76)**
Form - 7481508750
Record 1999 - 1st:1 2nd:0 3rd:0 Ran:10
Pre1999 - 1st:0 2nd:0 3rd:0 Ran:4
Win Prizemoney £2,853 *Total Prizemoney* £2,853
Wins * 1999 Jun Hamilt (G-S) S 9.2f 39? <
1999 Turf 1-10: (9f 1-3, 10f 2, 11f 2, 12f 3) (g-s, gd 1-2, g-f 3, frm 3, hrd)
Little account gelding, effective 9 to 11f, acts on g-s to gd, likes right handed tracks. Turf high 39 - 1st of 6 from Western General (9 Jun Hamilton RF 1858).
**Martyn Wane [1-10] J P Slattery (from R M McKellar [0-4] May 1997).*

MENSA BHB 104f **RR 109f** 2039[5]
3 ch g Rudimentary (USA) 8.2f **(66)** - Musianica (Music Boy) 6.8f **(57)**
Form - 14525
Record 1999 - 1st:1 2nd:1 3rd:0 Ran:5
Pre1999 - 1st:1 2nd:1 3rd:1 Ran:5
Win Prizemoney £12,466 *Total Prizemoney* £21,997
Wins * 1999 Apr Ripon (G-F) 9f 98+ <
* 1998 Jly Sandow (GD) 7.1f 77
1999 Turf 1-5: (7f, 8f 2, 9f 1-1, 10f) (g-s, gd, g-f 1-2, frm)
Tall, Pattern-class gelding, effective 8f, acts on g-f to frm, has worn blinkers. Turf high 109 - 2nd of 6 to Kalanisi (29 May Kempton 8f frm RF 1577). Has ability, but is a character too and no easy ride. Gelded over the winter, he made a winning return, and ran with credit despite being aimed high. Off since finishing fifth in the Jersey Stakes at Royal Ascot.
**M H Tompkins [2-10] Mrs Beryl Lockey.*

MENTEITH (USA) RR 51f 4861[13]
3 b g Dehere (USA) - Bunka Bunka (USA) (Raja Baba (USA)) 10f **(64)**
Form - 80
Record 1999 - 1st:0 2nd:0 3rd:0 Ran:2
1999 Turf 0-2: (12f 2) (sft, gd)
Workmanlike, currently fair gelding. Turf high 51.
**B P J Baugh [0-1] Mrs Joan Chrimes (from P F I Cole [0-1] Apr 1999).*

MENTIGA (IRE) BHB 85f **RR 84f** 5196[3]
2 b g Dancing Dissident (USA) 6.8f **(65)** - Lowtown (Camden Town) 9.3f **(53)**
Form - 22300213
Record 1999 - 1st:1 2nd:3 3rd:2 Ran:8
Win Prizemoney £4,000 *Total Prizemoney* £7,593
Wins * 1999 Oct Newbur (HVY) H 7.3f 77 84 <
1999 Turf 1-8: (5f 2, 6f 2, 7f 1-3, 8f) (hvy 1-1, sft 2, g-s, gd 2, g-f, frm)
Decent gelding, effective 5 to 7f, best at 7f, acts on hvy to sft, best on sft. Turf high 84 - 1st of 14 getting 5lb from Luminant (23 Oct Newbury RF 5048). **B R Millman [1-8] J A Pickford.*

MERANIE GIRL (IRE) BHB 26f **RR 21f** 4035[13]
3 b f Mujadil (USA) 7.7f **(70)** - Christoph's Girl (Efisio)
Form - 0000800
Record 1999 - 1st:0 2nd:0 3rd:0 Ran:7
Pre1999 - 1st:0 2nd:0 3rd:0 Ran:7
1999 Turf 0-7: (5f, 6f 2, 7f, 8f 2, 10f) (gd 2, g-f 3, frm 2)
Light-framed, little account filly, has worn blinkers. Turf high 28.
**J R Arnold [0-14] George Darling.*

MERANTI BHB 40f62a **RR 21f 62a** 3646[12]
6 b g Puissance 7.1f **(60)** - Sorrowful (Moorestyle) 6.9f **(64)**
Form - 0048000
Record 1999 - 1st:0 2nd:0 3rd:0 Ran:7
Pre1999 - 1st:5 2nd:2 3rd:1 Ran:44
Win Prizemoney £17,359 *Total Prizemoney* £21,460
Wins * 1998 Jly Thirsk (GD) H 6f 56 66 <
* 1998 Jly Salisb (FRM) H 6f 51 54
* 1997 Jly Salisb (G-F) H 6f 56 60
* 1997 Apr Thirsk (G-F) H 7f 43 55
* 1997 Apr Nottin (G-F) H 6.1f 43 57
1999 Turf 0-7: (6f 7) (gd, g-f, frm 5)
Little account gelding, effective 6f, acts on g-f. Turf high 49. Becoming disappointing.
**J M Bradley [5-36] John Wallis (from S Dow [0-8] Jly 1996).*

MERCEDE (IRE) RR 44f 5215[12]
2 b f Perugino (USA) - Miss Busybody (IRE) (Phardante (FR))
Form - 00
Record 1999 - 1st:0 2nd:0 3rd:0 Ran:2
1999 Turf 0-2: (8f 2) (g-s, gd)
Currently moderate filly. Turf high 44 (began Oct).
**N P Littmoden [0-2] Josef Fusenich.*

MERCHANT PRINCE BHB 40f **RR 31f** 5151[17]
3 b g Flying Tyke 7.2f **(42)** - Bellinote (FR) (Noir Et Or) 10f **(38)**
Form - 00800
Record 1999 - 1st:0 2nd:0 3rd:0 Ran:5
Pre1999 - 1st:0 2nd:0 3rd:0 Ran:1
1999 Turf 0-5: (5f 2, 6f, 7f, 8f) (gd 3, frm 2)
Scopey, very moderate gelding. Turf high 52.
**A Smith [0-6] Park Racing Partnership.*

MERCURY (IRE) BHB 20f22a **RR 15f 22a** 1280[10]
6 b g Contract Law (USA) 8.9f **(54)** - Monrovia (FR) (Dancers Image (USA)) 9.3f **(71)**
Form - 070778070
Record 1999 - 1st:0 2nd:0 3rd:0 Ran:6
Pre1999 - 1st:1 2nd:2 3rd:0 Ran:28
Win Prizemoney £2,717 *Total Prizemoney* £4,402
Wins 1996 *Jun Southw (STD) 8f* 71+ <
1999 AW 0-6: (8f, 9f, 11f 2, 12f 2) (Fibr 6)
Very moderate gelding, effective 11f, - acts on Fibr, has worn blinkers. AW high 31. Inconsistent.
**B P J Baugh [0-22] Nigel Taylor (from J A Glover [1-14] Aug 1997).*

MERE SLAD BHB 38f39a **RR 11f 39a** 4600[15]
3 b f Beveled (USA) 6.9f **(64)** - Pallomere (Blue Cashmere) 6.4f **(54)**
Form - 5078500
Record 1999 - 1st:0 2nd:0 3rd:0 Ran:6
Pre1999 - 1st:0 2nd:0 3rd:0 Ran:2
1999 Turf 0-3: (8f, 10f, 12f) (gd, frm 2) 1999 AW 0-3: (6f 2, 14f) (Equi, Fibr 2)
Unfurnished, poor filly. Turf high 11 (began Jly). AW high 19.
**Derrick Morris [0-5] K Powell (from A P Jones [0-3] Jan 1999).*

MERLY NOTTY BHB 24f **RR 33f** 3366[5]
3 ch f Inchinor 8.9f **(64)** - Rambadale (Vaigly Great) 7f **(58)**
Form - 0075
Record 1999 - 1st:0 2nd:0 3rd:0 Ran:4
Pre1999 - 1st:0 2nd:0 3rd:0 Ran:3
1999 Turf 0-4: (7f, 8f, 9f, 12f) (g-f 2, frm 2)
Neat, very moderate filly. Turf high 33.
**J S Haldane [0-7] G J Johnston.*

MERRY (IRE) BHB 30f **RR 12f** 4751[25]
2 ch f Ridgewood Ben - Speedy Action (Horage) 10.3f **(61)**
Form - 000
Record 1999 - 1st:0 2nd:0 3rd:0 Ran:3
1999 Turf 0-3: (7f, 8f 2) (gd 2, frm)
Currently poor filly. Turf high 12 (began Spt).
**N Tinkler [0-3] Mrs L Dales.*

MERRY MELODY RR 39f 3968[14]
4 b f Almoojid 7f **(36)** - Merry Marigold (Sonnen Gold) 6.6f **(47)**
Form - 40
Record 1999 - 1st:0 2nd:0 3rd:0 Ran:2
Pre1999 - 1st:0 2nd:0 3rd:0 Ran:3
Win Prizemoney £0 *Total Prizemoney* £293
1999 Turf 0-2: (7f, 10f) (g-f, frm)
Unfurnished, very moderate filly. Turf high 39 (began Jly).
**R J Hodges [0-5] Mrs I E Penfold.*

MERRY MERLIN RR 92f 4676[5]
2 b c Polar Falcon (USA) 9f **(74)** - Bronzewing (Beldale Flutter (USA)) 9.7f **(71)**
Form - 15
Record 1999 - 1st:1 2nd:0 3rd:0 Ran:2
Win Prizemoney £3,915 *Total Prizemoney* £4,455
Wins * 1999 Aug Newmar (G-F) 7f 85+ <
1999 Turf 1-2: (7f 1-2) (gd, frm 1-1)
Currently useful colt. Turf high 92 (began Aug) - also 1st of 16 from Cabriac (27 Aug Newmarket RF 3937). Showed real battling

qualities when getting off the mark by the minimum margin on his Newmarket debut. Ran as though needing further in a listed event next time. Should win races at three.
**M L W Bell [1-2] Sir Thomas Pilkington.*

MERRY PRINCE (IRE) BHB 48f46a **RR 55f 46a** 2949[11]
4 b g Roi Danzig (USA) 10.5f **(62)** - Queen of the Brush (Averof) 8.2f **(62)**
Form - 4583805550
Record 1999 - 1st:0 2nd:0 3rd:1 Ran:9
Pre1999 - 1st:0 2nd:0 3rd:0 Ran:8
Win Prizemoney £0 *Total Prizemoney* £277
1999 Turf 0-4: (10f 2, 12f 2) (g-f, frm 3) 1999 AW 0-5: (10f 2, 11f, 12f 2) (Equi 4, Fibr)
Fair gelding, effective 8f, acts on g-f, often wears blinkers. Turf high 55. AW high 50.
**P R Hedger [1-15] J J Whelan (from M A Jarvis [0-7] Oct 1998).*

MERRYVALE MAN BHB 58f **RR 60f** 5076[21]
2 b c Rudimentary (USA) 8.2f **(66)** - Salu **(58f)** (Ardross) 10.6f **(68)**
Form - 003500
Record 1999 - 1st:0 2nd:0 3rd:1 Ran:6
Win Prizemoney £0 *Total Prizemoney* £615
1999 Turf 0-6: (5f, 6f, 7f 4) (gd 5, frm)
Average colt, effective 7f, acts on gd. Turf high 60 - 3rd of 15 getting 6lb from Vintage Premium (15 Spt Beverley 7f gd RF 4322).
**J G Given [0-6] Arthur Symons Key.*

MERSEY MIRAGE BHB 86f **RR 78f** 3686[2]
2 b c King's Signet (USA) 7f **(51)** - Kirriemuir (Lochnager) 6f **(59)**
Form - 4401372
Record 1999 - 1st:1 2nd:1 3rd:1 Ran:7
Win Prizemoney £3,777 *Total Prizemoney* £6,492
Wins * **1999** Jly Bright (FRM) 6f 74+ <
1999 Turf 1-7: (5f 2, 6f 1-5) (gd 2, g-f 2, frm 1-3)
Above-average colt, effective 6f, acts on gd to frm, best on frm. Turf high 78 - 2nd of 6 giving 12lb to Water Echo (17 Aug Brighton 6f gd RF 3686) - also 1st of 5 from Tumbleweed Inca (13 Jly Brighton RF 2773). **R Hannon [1-7] Speedlith Group.*

METEORITE (IRE) BHB 64f **RR 66f** 5028[7]
3 b c Bigstone (IRE) - Winning Appeal (FR) (Law Society (USA)) 9.9f **(70)**
Form - 55474256047
Record 1999 - 1st:0 2nd:1 3rd:0 Ran:11
Pre1999 - 1st:0 2nd:0 3rd:0 Ran:1
Win Prizemoney £0 *Total Prizemoney* £2,041
1999 Turf 0-11: (10f, 12f 3, 14f 2, 15f 2, 16f 2, 17f) (g-s, gd 5, g-f 2, frm 3)
Scopey, average colt, effective 14 to 16f, best at 14f, acts on gd to frm. Turf high 71 - 2nd of 9 to Little Brave (30 Aug Warwick 16f gd RF 4036). **R Hannon [0-12] W F Hawkings, M W Grant & T E Bucknall.*

METEOR STRIKE (USA) BHB 56f76a **RR 63df 76a** 4758[17]
5 ch g Lomond (USA) 9.9f **(74)** - Meteoric (High Line) 10.3f **(70)**
Form - 512640300
Record 1999 - 1st:0 2nd:1 3rd:1 Ran:7
Pre1999 - 1st:2 2nd:1 3rd:0 Ran:7
Win Prizemoney £9,973 *Total Prizemoney* £12,790
Wins 1998 *Dec Lingfi (STD) H 12f 75 82* <
1997 Jly Bath (GD) 10.2f 75
1999 Turf 0-7: (9f, 10f 3, 12f 2, 14f) (gd 3, g-f, frm 2, hrd)
Decent gelding, effective 12f, - acts on Equi, has worn blinkers, likes left handed tracks, likes tight tracks. Turf high 65. Inconsistent.
**D Nicholls [0-4] V Greaves (from Mrs A J Perrett [2-12] Jun 1999).*

METHODIST (IRE) BHB 79f **RR 74f** 3761[2]
2 b g Rainbows For Life (CAN) 9.3f **(64)** - Pass The Rose (IRE) (Thatching) 8f **(66)**
Form - 712
Record 1999 - 1st:1 2nd:1 3rd:0 Ran:3
Win Prizemoney £2,075 *Total Prizemoney* £5,495
Wins * **1999** Aug Nottin (G-F) S 6.1f 55 <
1999 Turf 1-3: (6f 1-3) (gd, g-f 1-1, frm)
Currently above-average gelding. Turf high 74 (began Jly) - 2nd of 23 to Zietzig (18 Aug York 6f gd RF 3761). Just failed in the seller at the York Ebor meeting, and was claimed to race in France.
**N Tinkler [1-3] The Rovers Club.*

MEXICAN ROCK BHB 90f **RR 95f** 1243[5]
3 b c Rock City 8.8f **(62)** - Pink Mex (Tickled Pink) 6.5f **(59)**
Form - 185
Record 1999 - 1st:1 2nd:0 3rd:0 Ran:3
Win Prizemoney £2,351 *Total Prizemoney* £2,761
Wins * **1999** Apr Folkes (SFT) 6f 95 <
1999 Turf 1-3: (6f 1-2, 7f) (sft 1-1, g-f 2)
Workmanlike, currently very useful colt. Turf high 95 - also 1st of 16 from Cool Temper (20 Apr Folkestone RF 0762).
**J A R Toller [1-3] Magno-Pulse Ltd.*

MEZZORAMIO BHB 46f30a **RR 46?f 30a** 4338[10]
7 ch g Cadeaux Genereux 7.9f **(76)** - Hopeful Search (USA) (Vaguely Noble) 10.1f **(72)**
Form - 0783556314150
Record 1999 - 1st:2 2nd:0 3rd:2 Ran:11
Pre1999 - 1st:4 2nd:5 3rd:5 Ran:42
Win Prizemoney £20,020 *Total Prizemoney* £28,217
Wins * **1999** Jly Yarmou (FRM) H 7f 43 46?
* **1999** Jly Warwic (G-F) SH 7.7f 41 41
* 1997 Jly Yarmou (G-F) H 7f 47 51 <
* 1996 Aug Newmar (G-F) H 8f 46 49
* 1996 Jly Leices (G-F) H 7f 40 45
* 1996 *Feb Southw (STD) H 8f 39 44*
1999 Turf 2-8: (7f 1-4, 8f 1-4) (g-s, gd, g-f 1-2, frm 1-2, hrd 2) 1999 AW 0-3: (7f, 8f, 9f) (Fibr 3)
Moderate gelding, effective 6 to 7f, acts on gd to frm, mostly wears blinkers. Turf high 46 - 1st of 8 getting 17lb from Fairy Prince (26 Jly Yarmouth RF 3156). AW high 37. Consistent.
**K A Morgan [6-52] T R Pryke (from Sir Mark Prescott [0-2] May 1995).*

MHEANMETOO BHB 60f25a **RR 62df 25a** 416[16]
8 ch g Roi Danzig (USA) 10.5f **(62)** - Spinster (Grundy) 10.3f **(65)**
Form - 00
Record 1999 - 1st:0 2nd:0 3rd:0 Ran:2
Pre1999 - 1st:1 2nd:0 3rd:2 Ran:13
Win Prizemoney £3,297 *Total Prizemoney* £4,750
1999 AW 0-2: (8f, 12f) (Equi, Fibr)
Average gelding. Becoming disappointing.
**A P Jones [0-3] P Newell (from D L Williams [0-3] Mar 1995).*

MIAMI BLUES (GER) RR 92f 4110a[1]
3 f
Form - 1
1999 Turf 1-1: (8f 1-1) (gd 1-1)
Currently useful. (1st run) - 1st of 7 getting 6lb from Al Waffi (29 Aug Baden-Baden RF 4110a). **R Suerland in GER [1-1] Stall Peru.*

MI AMIGO RR 55f 5209[7]
2 b c Primo Dominie 7.2f **(67)** - Third Movement (Music Boy) 6.8f **(57)**
Form - 7
Record 1999 - 1st:0 2nd:0 3rd:0 Ran:1
1999 Turf 0-1: (6f) (g-s)
Currently fair colt. **L M Cumani [0-1] M J Dawson.*

MICE IDEAS (IRE) BHB 54f **RR 65f** 4413[4]
3 ch g Fayruz 6.6f **(63)** - Tender Encounter (Prince Tenderfoot (USA)) 9f **(61)**
Form - 854054
Record 1999 - 1st:0 2nd:0 3rd:0 Ran:6
Pre1999 - 1st:0 2nd:1 3rd:0 Ran:6
Win Prizemoney £0 *Total Prizemoney* £1,198
1999 Turf 0-4: (10f, 12f, 13f, 14f) (gd 2, g-f, frm) 1999 AW 0-2: (12f, 15f) (Fibr 2)
Leggy, average gelding, effective 7f, acts on frm, likes tight tracks. Turf high 65. AW high 50 (began Spt).
**S Mellor [0-12] Mice Group Plc.*

MICE WORLD (IRE) BHB 37f **RR 33f** 5049[17]
2 b g River Falls 8.2f **(56)** - Naglaa (USA) (State Dinner (USA)) 9.4f **(74)**
Form - 000
Record 1999 - 1st:0 2nd:0 3rd:0 Ran:3
1999 Turf 0-3: (7f, 8f 2) (gd 2, g-f)

Currently very moderate gelding. Turf high 33 (began Aug).
**S Mellor [0-3] Mice Group Plc.*

MICHELE MARIESCHI BHB 97f **RR 87f** 4695[2]
2 b g Alzao (USA) 9.8f **(73)** - Escape Path (Wolver Hollow) 8f **(56)**
Form - 1622
Record 1999 - 1st:1 2nd:2 3rd:0 Ran:4
Win Prizemoney £4,425 *Total Prizemoney* £9,489
Wins * 1999 Jun Newmar (G-F) 7f 85+ <
1999 Turf 1-4: (7f 1-1, 8f 3) (g-s, gd, g-f 1-1, frm)
Useful gelding, has worn blinkers. Turf high 87 - 2nd of 5 to Sakhee (2 Oct Sandown 8f g-s RF 4695) - also 1st of 8 from Atwaar (26 Jun Newmarket RF 2342). Bred to need middle distances, he created a good impression when winning on his Newmarket debut, but was firmly put in his place in a Deauville Listed event next time. However back on better ground at Haydock he put in a much better effort when a narrow second to Performing Magic.
**P F I Cole [1-4] Richard Green (Fine Paintings).*

MICKLEY (IRE) BHB 77f **RR 86f** 5034[13]
2 b c Ezzoud (IRE) - Dawsha (IRE) **(69f)** (Slip Anchor) 9.8f **(73)**
Form - 85115400
Record 1999 - 1st:2 2nd:0 3rd:0 Ran:8
Win Prizemoney £6,556 *Total Prizemoney* £8,546
Wins * 1999 Jly Cheste (G-F) H 7f 82 <
*** 1999** Jun Mussel (SFT) 7.1f 76
1999 Turf 2-8: (6f 2, 7f 2-4, 8f 2) (g-s, gd 1-4, g-f 2, frm 1-1)
Useful colt, effective 7f, acts on gd to frm. Turf high 86 - also 1st of 9 giving 5lb to True Obsession (10 Jly Chester RF 2705).
**J D Bethell [2-8] Clarendon Thoroughbred Racing II.*

MIDDAY COWBOY (USA) BHB 15f **RR 42?f** 4576[7]
6 b g Houston (USA) 7.7f **(65)** - Perfect Isn't Easy (USA) (Saratoga Six (USA)) 7f **(73)**
Form - 000087
Record 1999 - 1st:0 2nd:0 3rd:0 Ran:6
Pre1999 - 1st:0 2nd:1 3rd:1 Ran:17
Win Prizemoney £0 *Total Prizemoney* £1,849
1999 Turf 0-6: (7f, 9f, 12f, 14f, 16f 2) (gd, g-f 2, frm 3)
Moderate gelding, has worn blinkers. Turf high 42 (began Aug).
**Miss Lucinda Russell [0-13] Stuart Watson (from G Woodward [0-3] Jan 1998).*

MIDDELKERKE BHB 75f70a **RR 77df 70a** 3671[10]
3 b g College Chapel - Andbell (Trojan Fen) 8.1f **(62)**
Form - 2570
Record 1999 - 1st:0 2nd:1 3rd:0 Ran:4
Win Prizemoney £0 *Total Prizemoney* £1,242
1999 Turf 0-3: (8f 3) (gd 2, g-f) 1999 AW 0-1: (9f) (Fibr)
Scopey, above-average gelding. Turf high 77 (1st run) - 2nd of 18 to Barrister (27 Apr Windsor 8f gd RF 0876).
**D J Wintle [0-1] D J Wintle (from P W Chapple-Hyam [0-3] May 1999).*

MIDDLESEX DRIVE (USA) RR 113f 5226a[10]
4 ch c Pine Bluff (USA) - Yoek Woods (USA) (Mining (USA))
Form - 0
1999 Turf 0-1: (8f) (frm)
Currently Group-class colt. **P Hauswald in USA [0-2].*

MIDDLETHORPE BHB 55f **RR 62f** 4575[13]
2 b g Noble Patriarch 12.2f **(43)** - Prime Property (IRE) **(24f 28a)** (Tirol)
Form - 64053300
Record 1999 - 1st:0 2nd:0 3rd:2 Ran:8
Win Prizemoney £0 *Total Prizemoney* £1,423
1999 Turf 0-8: (5f, 6f, 7f 4, 8f 2) (gd 3, g-f 2, frm 2, hrd)
Average gelding, effective 7f, acts on g-f. Turf high 62 - 3rd of 12 getting 19lb from Love Lane (12 Aug Beverley 7f g-f RF 3566).
**M W Easterby [0-8] J H Quickfall & A G Black.*

MIDHISH TWO (IRE) BHB 82f **RR 80f** 4179[6]
3 b g Midhish - Tudor Loom (Sallust) 8.4f **(63)**
Form - 65310606
Record 1999 - 1st:1 2nd:0 3rd:1 Ran:8
Pre1999 - 1st:1 2nd:0 3rd:0 Ran:4
Win Prizemoney £39,830 *Total Prizemoney* £41,828
Wins * 1999 May Lingfi (G-F) H 6f 81 84 <
1998 Jun Newcas (SFT) 6f 71+

1999 Turf 1-7: (5f, 6f 1-3, 7f 3) (g-s, gd, g-f 1-3, frm 2) 1999 AW 0-1: (6f) (Equi)
Workmanlike, decent gelding, effective 5 to 6f, acts on g-s to g-f. Turf high 84 - 1st of 20 getting 13lb from Cubism (8 May Lingfield RF 1113). He was gelded and changed stables before last season, and looked to have improved as a result. Best held up.
**P Mitchell [1-8] Morton,Mrs Cowley,Murray (from Sir Michael Stoute [1-4] Spt 1998).*

MIDNIGHT ALLURE BHB 58f **RR 52f** 4731[9]
2 b f Aragon 7.7f **(58)** - Executive Lady (Night Shift (USA)) 7.2f **(69)**
Form - 500
Record 1999 - 1st:0 2nd:0 3rd:0 Ran:3
1999 Turf 0-3: (5f, 6f 2) (gd, g-f 2)
Currently fair filly. Turf high 52 (began Jly).
**C F Wall [0-3] Mervyn Ayers.*

MIDNIGHT DREAM RR 28f 507[7]
4 ch f Infantry 10f **(54)** - Enterprise Lady (FR) (Gorytus (USA)) 7.8f **(60)**
Form - 7
Record 1999 - 1st:0 2nd:0 3rd:0 Ran:1
1999 Turf 0-1: (8f) (sft)
Currently little account filly. **A Smith [0-1] Alfred Smith.*

MIDNIGHT ESCAPE BHB 87f **RR 88f** 4561[13]
6 b g Aragon 7.7f **(58)** - Executive Lady (Night Shift (USA)) 7.2f **(69)**
Form - 073780040
Record 1999 - 1st:0 2nd:0 3rd:1 Ran:9
Pre1999 - 1st:6 2nd:1 3rd:2 Ran:23
Win Prizemoney £61,847 *Total Prizemoney* £74,920
Wins * 1998 May Kempto (GD) L 5f 110 <
* 1997 Spt Leopar (GD) G3 5f 99+
* 1996 Oct Newmar (GD) H 5f 91 89
* 1996 Jun Ascot (G-F) H 5f 89 91
* 1996 May Windso (GD) H 5f 82 87
* 1995 Jun Lingfi (G-F) 5f
1999 Turf 0-9: (5f 6, 6f 3) (gd 5, frm 4)
Useful gelding, effective 5f, acts on frm. Turf high 97. Consistent. He deteriorated, but gave connections a glimmer of hope when finishing fourth in the Portland Handicap. Well treated on the pick of his form, he has run his best races when forcing the issue over five furlongs. **C F Wall [6-32] Mervyn Ayers.*

MIDNIGHT FOXTROT RR 102f 3781a[4]
3 c Kingmambo (USA) 10.9f **(85)** - Vana Turns (USA) (Wavering Monarch (USA)) 10.4f **(94)**
Form - 214
1999 Turf 1-3: (8f 2, 12f 1-1) (hvy 2, sft 1-1)
Currently very useful colt. Turf high 102 - 4th of 20 giving 7lb to Orso (15 Aug Deauville 8f hvy RF 3781a). **Mme C Head in FR [1-3].*

MIDNIGHT LINE (USA) BHB 115f **RR 113f** 5018a[3]
4 ch f Kris S (USA) 9.3f **(76)** - Midnight Air (USA) (Green Dancer (USA)) 10.3f **(74)**
Form - 3
1999 Turf 0-1: (10f) (gd)
Scopey, Group-class filly. (1st run) - 3rd of 7 to Insight (17 Oct Woodbine 10f gd RF 5018a). A consistent performer for Henry Cecil, she was moved across the Atlantic and won a Grade One event in November. **in CAN [0-1] (from H R A Cecil [4-9] Aug 1998).*

MIDNIGHT MAX RR 44f 3425[10]
2 b c Sure Blade (USA) 10.6f **(66)** - Carpadia (Icecapade (USA)) 11f **(62)**
Form - 050
Record 1999 - 1st:0 2nd:0 3rd:0 Ran:3
1999 Turf 0-3: (6f, 7f 2) (g-f 2, frm)
Currently moderate colt. Turf high 44.
**C A Dwyer [0-3] Mrs Deborah Crowley.*

MIDNIGHT ORCHID (IRE) BHB 60f **RR 49f** 3136[10]
3 b f Petardia 8.2f **(58)** - Rosa Van Fleet (Sallust) 8.4f **(63)**
Form - 80032700
Record 1999 - 1st:0 2nd:1 3rd:1 Ran:8
Pre1999 - 1st:1 2nd:3 3rd:0 Ran:8
Win Prizemoney £3,468 *Total Prizemoney* £9,214
Wins * 1998 Jun Hamilt (G-S) 6f 68 <

1999 Turf 0-7: (6f 2, 7f 5) (g-f 5, frm, hrd) 1999 AW 0-1: (6f) (Fibr)
Scopey, above-average filly, effective 6f, acts on gd to g-f - acts on Fibr. Turf high 64. Despite her undoubted ability, she has shown a tendency to swish her tail under pressure and should be treated with some caution. **J Berry [1-16] T Herbert-Jackson.*

MIDNIGHT WATCH (USA) BHB 50f **RR 30f** 4218[12]

5 b g Capote (USA) 9.1f **(84)** - Midnight Air (USA) (Green Dancer (USA)) 10.3f **(74)**
Form - 80
Record 1999 - 1st:0 2nd:0 3rd:0 Ran:2
Pre1999 - 1st:0 2nd:1 3rd:1 Ran:6
Win Prizemoney £0 *Total Prizemoney* £2,520
1999 Turf 0-2: (12f, 14f) (frm 2)
Very moderate gelding. Turf high 30 (began Aug). Becoming disappointing. **P Winkworth [0-7] The Knowl Hill Billies (from H R A Cecil [0-5] Oct 1997).*

MIDSUMMER NIGHT (IRE) BHB 50f42a **RR 55f 42a** 262[9]

4 b f Fairy King (USA) 7.7f **(75)** - Villota (Top Ville) 11.7f **(68)**
Form - 00
Record 1999 - 1st:0 2nd:0 3rd:0 Ran:2
Pre1999 - 1st:0 2nd:1 3rd:1 Ran:10
Win Prizemoney £0 *Total Prizemoney* £1,912
1999 AW 0-2: (5f, 6f) (Equi, Fibr)
Leggy, fair filly. AW high 16.
**J S Wainwright [0-2] Rosaly Racing (from R Hannon [0-10] Aug 1998).*

MIDSUMMER ROMANCE (IRE) BHB 39f **RR 30f** 4387[18]

4 b f Fairy King (USA) 7.7f **(75)** - Jealous One (USA) (Raise A Native) 11.2f **(69)**
Form - 30000
Record 1999 - 1st:0 2nd:0 3rd:1 Ran:5
Pre1999 - 1st:0 2nd:0 3rd:0 Ran:7
Win Prizemoney £0 *Total Prizemoney* £288
1999 Turf 0-5: (11f, 12f 3, 14f) (gd 2, g-f, frm 2)
Scopey, very moderate filly, effective 11f, acts on gd, has worn blinkers, likes tight tracks. Turf high 53 (1st run) - 3rd of 11 giving 7lb to Vanborough Lad (4 Jun Haydock 11f gd RF 1739). Becoming disappointing.
**B J Meehan [0-12] Theo Waddington & Mrs Theo Waddington.*

MIDYAN CALL BHB 99f **RR 101f** 4892a[3]

5 b h Midyan (USA) 9.9f **(64)** - Early Call (Kind of Hush) 10.1f **(62)**
Form - 163
1999 Turf 0-2: (8f 2) (gd 2)
Very useful colt, effective 6 to 8f, best at 8f, acts on g-s to gd, best on gd. Turf high 101 - 3rd of 6 to Muhtathir (10 Oct San Siro 8f gd RF 4892a). **O Pessi in ITY [1-3] (from M L W Bell [1-10] May 1998).*

MIDYAN QUEEN BHB 38f **RR 36f** 2669[15]

5 b m Midyan (USA) 9.9f **(64)** - Queen of Aragon (Aragon) 8.1f **(60)**
Form - 600
Record 1999 - 1st:0 2nd:0 3rd:0 Ran:3
Pre1999 - 1st:1 2nd:0 3rd:2 Ran:16
Win Prizemoney £4,123 *Total Prizemoney* £5,482
Wins 1997 Jly Warwic (G-F) H 7f 60 60 <
1999 Turf 0-3: (6f, 8f 2) (sft, g-f, frm)
Very moderate filly, has broken blood-vessels. Turf high 36.
**P D Evans [0-3] Mrs Charles Lockhart (from R Hollinshead [1-16] Spt 1998).*

MIGHTY ARTHUR BHB 34f40a **RR 45f 40a** 3797[14]

3 b g Puissance 7.1f **(60)** - Fire Gold (Never so Bold) 6.3f **(66)**
Form - 50700
Record 1999 - 1st:0 2nd:0 3rd:0 Ran:5
1999 Turf 0-3: (7f 2, 9f) (gd 2, g-f) 1999 AW 0-2: (6f, 7f) (Fibr 2)
Leggy, moderate gelding. Turf high 45. AW high 19.
**D Shaw [0-5] D C G Cooper.*

MIGHTY MAGIC BHB 51f **RR 52f** 4711[8]

4 b f Magic Ring (IRE) 6.5f **(64)** - Mighty Flash (Rolfe (USA)) 12.1f **(65)**
Form - 6522308
Record 1999 - 1st:0 2nd:2 3rd:1 Ran:7
Pre1999 - 1st:0 2nd:2 3rd:2 Ran:17
Win Prizemoney £0 *Total Prizemoney* £5,898
1999 Turf 0-7: (6f 3, 7f 2, 8f 2) (gd, g-f 2, frm 4)
Scopey, fair filly, effective 6 to 14f, acts on g-s to frm, best on g-f, has worn blinkers, likes tight tracks. Turf high 54 - 2nd of 12 getting 6lb from Grand View (10 Jly Salisbury 6f frm RF 2714). Consistent.
**Mrs P N Dutfield [0-13] Mrs V A Tory (from D R C Elsworth [0-11] Oct 1998).*

MIGRATION BHB 105f **RR 106f** 4674[2]

3 b c Rainbow Quest (USA) 11.2f **(81)** - Armeria (USA) (Northern Dancer) 9.6f **(80)**
Form - 162
Record 1999 - 1st:1 2nd:1 3rd:0 Ran:3
Win Prizemoney £3,811 *Total Prizemoney* £9,275
Wins * 1999 Apr Bath (SFT) 10.2f 97+ <
1999 Turf 1-3: (10f 1-2, 12f) (sft 1-1, gd 2)
Well made, currently Pattern-class colt. Turf high 106 - 2nd of 11 getting 7lb from Kahtan (1 Oct Newmarket 12f gd RF 4674) - also 1st of 12 from Sarangani (27 Apr Bath RF 0858). Unraced at two, he handled the soft ground well when making a successful debut at Bath in April, but rather disgraced himself when hanging all over the track in similar conditions at York next time. Subsequently off the track for five months before finishing second in a back-end listed race. **R Charlton [1-3] K Abdulla.*

MIGWAR BHB 53f56a **RR 20f 56a** 5145[11]

6 b g Unfuwain (USA) 11.4f **(74)** - Pick of the Pops (High Top) 10.2f **(67)**
Form - 00116400000
Record 1999 - 1st:2 2nd:0 3rd:0 Ran:9
Pre1999 - 1st:2 2nd:2 3rd:0 Ran:12
Win Prizemoney £24,348 *Total Prizemoney* £26,928
Wins * 1999 *Jan Southw (STD) S 12f 64+*
*** 1999** *Jan Southw (STD) S 11f 65+*
1996 May Redcar (G-F) H 10f 89 95 <
1996 May Doncas (G-F) H 10.3f 83 85+
1999 Turf 0-3: (10f 2, 12f) (g-s, gd, g-f) 1999 AW 2-6: (11f 1-3, 12f 1-3) (Fibr 2-6)
Average gelding, effective 11 to 12f, best at 11f, - acts on Fibr, has worn blinkers, likes left handed tracks, likes tight tracks. Turf high 20. AW high 65 (1st run) - 1st of 14 giving 5lb to Areish (2 Jan Southwell RF 0019) - also 1st of 7 giving 5lb to Infamous (18 Jan Southwell RF 0118). Becoming disappointing. The winner of the 1996 Zetland Gold Cup, he has had his problems since and his recent winning form has been in Fibresand sellers.
**N P Littmoden [2-13] Avon & West Racing Club Ltd (from L M Cumani [2-8] Spt 1997).*

MIKE'S DOUBLE (IRE) BHB 36f40a **RR 38f 40a** 5156[14]

5 br g Cyrano de Bergerac 7.3f **(58)** - Glass Minnow (IRE) (Alzao (USA)) 7.1f **(68)**
Form - 476441382753376000085060
Record 1999 - 1st:0 2nd:1 3rd:3 Ran:18
Pre1999 - 1st:4 2nd:5 3rd:7 Ran:49
Win Prizemoney £14,547 *Total Prizemoney* £22,874
Wins * 1998 *Dec Wolver (STD) H* 6f 50 60
* 1998 May Thirsk (GD) H 6f 57 61
* 1998 *Apr Wolver (STD) H* 7f *55 62* <
1997 *Jly Wolver (STD) 6f 62* <
1999 Turf 0-7: (6f 6, 8f) (sft, gd 3, g-f 2, frm) 1999 AW 0-11: (6f 8, 7f 2, 8f) (Equi 2, Fibr 9)
Moderate gelding, effective 6 to 7f, best at 7f, acts on gd - acts on Fibr, mostly wears blinkers (extremely effectively), likes left handed tracks, likes tight tracks, does well at Wolverhampton. Turf high 54. AW high 64 - 3rd of 9 giving 2lb to Mallia (27 Mar Wolverhampton 6f Fibr RF 0494).
**Mrs N Macauley [3-44] Swift Racing (from Miss Gay Kelleway [1-15] Feb 1998).*

MIKE SIMMONS BHB 37f40a **RR 38f 40a** 3053[17]

3 b g Ballacashtal (CAN) 7.9f **(51)** - Lady Crusty (Golden Dipper) 6.5f **(42)**
Form - 070
Record 1999 - 1st:0 2nd:0 3rd:0 Ran:2
Pre1999 - 1st:0 2nd:0 3rd:0 Ran:3
1999 Turf 0-2: (12f 2) (frm 2)
Scopey, very moderate gelding. (began Jly).
**L P Grassick [0-5] L P Grassick.*

MIKES WIFE RR 4982[9]
2 b f Tragic Role (USA) 9.4f **(63)** - Grecian Belle (Ilium)
Form - 0
Record 1999 - 1st:0 2nd:0 3rd:0 Ran:1
1999 Turf 0-1: (7f) (g-f)
Currently very poor filly. **N Bycroft [0-1] Mike Smallman.*

MIKE THE SPUD BHB 52f49a **RR 56f 49a** 5076[8]
2 b g Emarati (USA) 6.6f **(63)** - Zilzilah (USA) **(59f)** (Zilzal (USA))
Form - 00403058
Record 1999 - 1st:0 2nd:0 3rd:1 Ran:8
Win Prizemoney £0 *Total Prizemoney* £429
1999 Turf 0-8: (5f 5, 6f 3) (g-s, gd 4, frm 2, hrd)
Fair gelding, effective 5f, acts on frm. Turf high 56.
**M W Easterby [0-8] T R Beston.*

MILAD (IRE) BHB 66f60a **RR 64f 60a** 852[15]
4 b g Green Desert (USA) 7.8f **(78)** - Arctic Winter (CAN) (Briartic (CAN)) 9.5f **(84)**
Form - 0
Record 1999 - 1st:0 2nd:0 3rd:0 Ran:1
Pre1999 - 1st:0 2nd:0 3rd:1 Ran:9
Win Prizemoney £0 *Total Prizemoney* £708
1999 AW 0-1: (8f) (Fibr)
Average gelding. Inconsistent.
**K Bell [0-4] Mrs Joyce Wood (from K Prendergast in IRE [0-7] Jun 1998).*

MILADY LILLIE (IRE) BHB 58f **RR 58f** 4074[3]
3 b f Distinctly North (USA) 7.4f **(63)** - Millingdale Lillie (Tumble Wind (USA)) 7.5f **(57)**
Form - 44518463673
Record 1999 - 1st:1 2nd:0 3rd:2 Ran:11
Pre1999 - 1st:0 2nd:0 3rd:0 Ran:3
Win Prizemoney £2,859 *Total Prizemoney* £4,625
Wins * 1999 May Bright (FRM) 7f 59 <
1999 Turf 1-10: (6f 2, 7f 1-7, 9f) (gd, g-f 4, frm 3, hrd 1-2) 1999 AW 0-1: (6f) (Fibr)
Neat, fair filly, effective 7f, acts on g-f to hrd, prefers left handed tracks, prefers tight tracks. Turf high 60 - 3rd of 12 giving 6lb to Addition (10 Jly Warwick 7f g-f RF 2728) - also 1st of 8 getting 14lb from One Dinar (27 May Brighton RF 1519). Consistent.
**K T Ivory [1-14] K T Ivory.*

MILDON (IRE) BHB 45f **RR 34f** 2540[16]
3 ch c Dolphin Street (FR) - Lycia (Targowice (USA)) 11.4f **(70)**
Form - 700
Record 1999 - 1st:0 2nd:0 3rd:0 Ran:3
Pre1999 - 1st:0 2nd:0 3rd:0 Ran:1
1999 Turf 0-3: (8f 2, 10f) (gd, g-f 2)
Unfurnished, very moderate colt. Turf high 34.
**E Weymes [0-4] Don Raper.*

MILETRIAN (IRE) BHB 100f **RR 101f** 4776a[4]
2 b f Marju (IRE) 9.2f **(76)** - Warg (Dancing Brave (USA)) 8.4f **(76)**
Form - 72514
Record 1999 - 1st:1 2nd:1 3rd:0 Ran:5
Win Prizemoney £3,111 *Total Prizemoney* £13,552
Wins * 1999 Spt Redcar (G-F) 9f 78+ <
1999 Turf 1-5: (7f, 8f 3, 9f 1-1) (sft, gd, frm 1-3)
Very useful filly. Turf high 101 (began Aug) - 4th of 11 to Lady Of Chad (3 Oct Longchamp 8f sft RF 4776a). Had shown ability before winning her maiden and ran well to be fourth in Prix Marcel Boussac. Improving. **M R Channon [1-5] Miletrian Plc.*

MILFORD FONTENAILLE (FR) RR 95f 5008a[2]
5 ch g Nashamaa 8.1f **(58)** - Miss Fontenailles (Kautokeino (FR))
Form - 2
1999 Turf 0-1: (10f) (gd)
Currently very useful gelding. (1st run) - 2nd of 12 to Kadance Ville (11 Oct Parc-Borely 10f gd RF 5008a). **R Collet in FR [0-1].*

MILL AFRIQUE BHB 45f **RR 56f** 4883[9]
3 b f Mtoto 11.5f **(71)** - Milinetta (Milford) 9f **(61)**
Form - 00244000
Record 1999 - 1st:0 2nd:1 3rd:0 Ran:8
Pre1999 - 1st:0 2nd:0 3rd:0 Ran:3
Win Prizemoney £0 *Total Prizemoney* £1,037
1999 Turf 0-8: (8f, 10f 5, 12f 2) (sft, g-s, gd, g-f 2, frm 3)
Workmanlike, fair filly, has worn blinkers. Turf high 56. Inconsistent.
**Mrs M Reveley [0-3] R Meredith (from C E Brittain [0-8] Jly 1999).*

MILL EMERALD RR 3f 4784[16]
2 b f Old Vic 12.8f **(72)** - Milinetta (Milford) 9f **(61)**
Form - 0
Record 1999 - 1st:0 2nd:0 3rd:0 Ran:1
1999 Turf 0-1: (7f) (g-s)
Currently very poor filly. **R A Fahey [0-1] R Meredith.*

MILLENARY RR 84f 4385[5]
2 b c Rainbow Quest (USA) 11.2f **(81)** - Ballerina (IRE) **(77f)** (Dancing Brave (USA)) 8.4f **(76)**
Form - 35
Record 1999 - 1st:0 2nd:0 3rd:1 Ran:2
Win Prizemoney £0 *Total Prizemoney* £2,053
1999 Turf 0-2: (7f, 8f) (g-f, frm)
Currently decent colt. Turf high 84 (began Aug). Ran a fine third in the Washington Singer Stakes at Newbury on his debut but was a little disappointing on a return visit. **J L Dunlop [0-2] Neil Jones.*

MILL END QUEST BHB 50f **RR 50df** 4436[16]
4 b f King's Signet (USA) 7f **(51)** - Milva (Jellaby) 6.4f **(58)**
Form - 0434166080
Record 1999 - 1st:1 2nd:0 3rd:1 Ran:10
Pre1999 - 1st:1 2nd:0 3rd:1 Ran:15
Win Prizemoney £10,064 *Total Prizemoney* £11,556
Wins * 1999 Jun Pontef (GD) H 6f 50 56
* 1997 Jly Mussel (GD) 5f 66 <
1999 Turf 1-10: (5f 3, 6f 1-7) (gd 3, g-f, frm 1-6)
Neat, fair filly, effective 5 to 6f, best at 6f, acts on gd to frm, best on gd, has worn blinkers. Turf high 56 - 1st of 9 getting 8lb from Dominelle (28 Jun Pontefract RF 2370). Consistent.
**M W Easterby [2-25] W T Allgood.*

MILL END VENTURE (IRE) BHB 43f **RR 40f** 2154[10]
3 b g Namaqualand (USA) - Risk All (Run The Gantlet (USA)) 12.1f **(59)**
Form - 80
Record 1999 - 1st:0 2nd:0 3rd:0 Ran:2
Pre1999 - 1st:0 2nd:0 3rd:0 Ran:3
1999 Turf 0-2: (12f, 14f) (gd, frm)
Lengthy, moderate gelding. Turf high 35.
**M W Easterby [0-5] W T Allgood.*

MILLENIUM MOONBEAM (USA) BHB 100f **RR 100f** 4690[4]
2 ch c Phone Trick (USA) 7f **(62)** - Shywing (USA) (Wing Out (USA))
Form - 614
Record 1999 - 1st:1 2nd:0 3rd:0 Ran:3
Win Prizemoney £3,844 *Total Prizemoney* £11,639
Wins * 1999 Aug Salisb (G-S) 6f 86+ <
1999 Turf 1-3: (6f 1-3) (gd 1-1, g-f, frm)
Currently very useful colt. Turf high 100 - 4th of 26 giving 6lb to Khasayl (2 Oct Redcar 6f g-f RF 4690). He scored an appropriate victory on the day of the eclipse, and went on to run a super race when finishing fourth in the NTL Two-Year-Old Trophy at Redcar. Effective on easy ground, he starts the new campaign on a stiff mark. **M Pitman [1-3] John Harris.*

MILLENNIUM BUG BHB 40f **RR 40f** 2848[6]
3 b f Rock Hopper 10.6f **(54)** - So Precise (FR) (Balidar) 7.9f **(63)**
Form - 066
Record 1999 - 1st:0 2nd:0 3rd:0 Ran:3
1999 Turf 0-3: (8f, 10f 2) (g-f 2, hrd)
Scopey, currently moderate filly. Turf high 40.
**A Streeter [0-3] B E S T Racing.*

MILLESIME (IRE) BHB 33f **RR 35f** 4878[21]
7 ch g Glow (USA) 10.2f **(61)** - Persian Myth (Persian Bold) 9.3f **(66)**
Form - 0854800
Record 1999 - 1st:0 2nd:0 3rd:0 Ran:7
Pre1999 - 1st:2 2nd:2 3rd:2 Ran:29
Win Prizemoney £6,285 *Total Prizemoney* £10,133
Wins 1995 Jly Bath (FRM) 5.1f 64

1995 Jly Chepst (G-F) 5.1f 66 <
1999 Turf 0-7: (5f 4, 6f 3) (gd, g-f 3, frm 3)
Very moderate gelding, effective 6f, acts on frm, has worn blinkers. Turf high 35 - 4th of 8 getting 28lb from Windy Gulch (16 Jly Hamilton 6f frm RF 2871).
**Martyn Wane [0-19] Mrs P E Edmondson (from B Hanbury [2-17] Spt 1996).*

MILLIGAN (FR) RR 66f 4443[10]
4 b g Exit To Nowhere (USA) 8.7f **(77)** - Madigan Mill (Mill Reef (USA)) 10.5f **(78)**
Form - 000
Record 1999 - 1st:0 2nd:0 3rd:0 Ran:3
Pre1999 - 1st:0 2nd:1 3rd:0 Ran:2
Win Prizemoney £0 *Total Prizemoney* £17,957
1999 Turf 0-3: (5f, 6f 2) (g-s 2, gd)
Average gelding. Turf high 66 (began Aug).
**D Nicholls [0-3] G H Leatham (from J E Pease in FR [0-1] Oct 1997).*

MILLING (IRE) BHB 66f **RR 72f** 4822[12]
4 b f In The Wings 11.2f **(77)** - Princess Pati (Top Ville) 11.7f **(68)**
Form - 7747000
Record 1999 - 1st:0 2nd:0 3rd:0 Ran:7
Pre1999 - 1st:1 2nd:2 3rd:1 Ran:9
Win Prizemoney £5,303 *Total Prizemoney* £8,353
Wins * 1998 Aug Hamilt (SFT) H 9.2f 77 80 <
1999 Turf 0-7: (8f, 9f, 10f 3, 11f, 12f) (gd 4, g-f 2, frm)
Workmanlike, above-average filly, effective 9 to 10f, acts on gd. Turf high 76. Inconsistent. **R Guest [1-16] C J Mills.*

MILLIONFORMERTHYR BHB 35f35a **RR 29f 35a** 3484[7]
3 b f Mon Tresor 7.9f **(60)** - Regal Salute (Dara Monarch) 8.8f **(59)**
Form - 574007
Record 1999 - 1st:0 2nd:0 3rd:0 Ran:5
Pre1999 - 1st:0 2nd:1 3rd:2 Ran:10
Win Prizemoney £0 *Total Prizemoney* £1,127
1999 Turf 0-4: (7f 2, 10f, 12f) (gd 2, g-f, frm) 1999 AW 0-1: (7f) (Fibr)
Leggy, very moderate filly, effective 6 to 7f, acts on gd - acts on Fibr, has worn blinkers. Turf high 29. Becoming disappointing.
**B Palling [0-15] Merthyr Motor Auctions.*

MILLIONS BHB 61f **RR 57f** 4506[9]
2 b c Bering 9.6f **(80)** - Miznah (IRE) (Sadler's Wells (USA)) 10f **(76)**
Form - 000
Record 1999 - 1st:0 2nd:0 3rd:0 Ran:3
1999 Turf 0-3: (7f, 8f 2) (g-s, g-f, frm)
Currently fair colt. Turf high 57 (began Aug).
**Sir Michael Stoute [0-3] Abdullah Ali.*

MILLISCENT BHB 46f40a **RR 47f 40a** 2151[7]
3 b f Primo Dominie 7.2f **(67)** - Millaine (Formidable (USA)) 9.2f **(63)**
Form - 4007
Record 1999 - 1st:0 2nd:0 3rd:0 Ran:4
Pre1999 - 1st:0 2nd:0 3rd:0 Ran:3
1999 Turf 0-3: (8f 3) (gd, frm, hrd) 1999 AW 0-1: (8f) (Equi)
Scopey, moderate filly. Turf high 47.
**M Johnston [0-4] T G & Mrs M E Holdcroft (from J Berry [0-3] Oct 1998).*

MILLSEC BHB 59f **RR 56f** 5187[2]
2 b f Petong 7.6f **(58)** - Harmony Park (Music Boy) 6.8f **(57)**
Form - 0862
Record 1999 - 1st:0 2nd:1 3rd:0 Ran:4
Win Prizemoney £0 *Total Prizemoney* £768
1999 Turf 0-4: (5f 2, 6f 2) (gd 2, g-f, hrd)
Fair filly. Turf high 56 (began Aug) - 2nd of 16 giving 12lb to Parkside Prospect (3 Nov Musselburgh 5f gd RF 5187).
**R Bastiman [0-4] Robin Bastiman.*

MILNE'S DREAM BHB 42f **RR 19f** 2819[10]
3 b f Reprimand 8.2f **(63)** - Milne's Way (The Noble Player (USA)) 6.5f **(67)**
Form - 000
Record 1999 - 1st:0 2nd:0 3rd:0 Ran:3
Pre1999 - 1st:0 2nd:0 3rd:1 Ran:4
Win Prizemoney £0 *Total Prizemoney* £278
1999 Turf 0-3: (7f, 8f, 10f) (g-f 2, frm)
Neat, poor filly, effective 6f, acts on sft. Turf high 19.
**M G Quinlan [0-3] Roy Matthews (from G Lewis [0-4] Oct 1998).*

MILTON BHB 54f65a **RR 43f 65a** 5028[15]
6 ch g Groom Dancer (USA) 9.5f **(75)** - Gold Flair (Tap On Wood) 10.3f **(65)**
Form - 00
Record 1999 - 1st:0 2nd:0 3rd:0 Ran:2
Pre1999 - 1st:0 2nd:1 3rd:1 Ran:5
Win Prizemoney £0 *Total Prizemoney* £1,723
1999 Turf 0-2: (11f, 16f) (g-s, frm)
Fair gelding. Turf high 43 (began Oct).
**P T Dalton [0-2] Mrs Julie Martin (from Mrs A Swinbank [0-2] Mar 1998).*

MIMANDI (IRE) RR 34f 4634[8]
2 b f Pips Pride 6.7f **(70)** - Glass Minnow (IRE) (Alzao (USA)) 7.1f **(68)**
Form - 08
Record 1999 - 1st:0 2nd:0 3rd:0 Ran:2
1999 Turf 0-2: (6f 2) (g-s, gd)
Currently very moderate filly. Turf high 34 (began Spt).
**I Semple [0-2] Raeburn Brick Ltd.*

MINALCO BHB 32f **RR 32f** 5165[12]
3 ch f Minster Son 10.9f **(56)** - La Millie (Nonoalco (USA)) 8.5f **(66)**
Form - 5080
Record 1999 - 1st:0 2nd:0 3rd:0 Ran:4
1999 Turf 0-4: (8f 2, 9f, 12f) (g-s, frm 3)
Workmanlike, very moderate filly. Turf high 32 (began Aug).
**R E Barr [0-4] Mrs M J Schoenberg.*

MINDANAO BHB 82f **RR 90f** 4808[1]
3 b f Most Welcome 8.6f **(66)** - Salala (Connaught) 7.7f **(63)**
Form - 0122121
Record 1999 - 1st:3 2nd:3 3rd:0 Ran:7
Pre1999 - 1st:0 2nd:0 3rd:0 Ran:2
Win Prizemoney £18,963 *Total Prizemoney* £23,715
Wins * **1999** Oct Ayr (SFT) H 10f 75 90 <
* **1999** Aug Ripon (GD) H 10f 65 69
* **1999** Jun Newcas (GD) H 9f 53 58
1999 Turf 3-7: (6f, 9f 1-1, 10f 2-5) (sft 1-1, gd 1-3, frm 1-3)
Neat, useful filly, effective 10f, acts on sft. Turf high 90 - 1st of 14 giving 20lb to Caerosa (11 Oct Ayr RF 4808). Improving.
**Miss J A Camacho [3-9] Mrs S Camacho.*

MINDRACE BHB 33f **RR 37f** 2725[6]
6 b g Tina's Pet 7.4f **(56)** - High Velocity (Frimley Park) 6.5f **(67)**
Form - 06006
Record 1999 - 1st:0 2nd:0 3rd:0 Ran:5
Pre1999 - 1st:2 2nd:2 3rd:1 Ran:37
Win Prizemoney £10,087 *Total Prizemoney* £13,711
Wins * 1997 Jly Sandow (G-F) H 5f 59 61
* 1996 Jly Bath (FRM) H 5.1f 59 67 <
1999 Turf 0-5: (5f 4, 6f) (gd, g-f 3, hrd)
Very moderate gelding, effective 6f, acts on frm, has worn blinkers. Turf high 37. **K T Ivory [2-42] D F Abbott.*

MIND THE SILVER BHB 67f **RR 70f** 4941[6]
2 gr c Petong 7.6f **(58)** - Marjorie's Memory (IRE) **(61df)** (Fairy King (USA)) 7.7f **(59)**
Form - 656
Record 1999 - 1st:0 2nd:0 3rd:0 Ran:3
1999 Turf 0-3: (5f, 6f 2) (gd 2, frm)
Currently above-average colt. Turf high 70 (began Spt).
**V Soane [0-3] The Soane Rangers.*

MINERS QUEST RR 73f 2502[6]
3 b g Miner's Lamp - Interrogate (In Fijar (USA)) 7.5f **(70)**
Form - 6
Record 1999 - 1st:0 2nd:0 3rd:0 Ran:1
1999 Turf 0-1: (14f) (g-f)
Workmanlike, currently above-average gelding.
**G A Butler [0-1] J Jones.*

MINETTA RR 76+f 4874[12]
4 ch f Mujtahid (USA) 7.4f **(69)** - Minwah (USA) (Diesis) 9.3f **(69)**
Form - 04701802110

Record 1999 - 1st:3 2nd:1 3rd:0 Ran:11
Pre1999 - 1st:3 2nd:2 3rd:2 Ran:17
Win Prizemoney £29,175 *Total Prizemoney* £35,421
Wins *1999 Spt Thirsk (FRM) H 8f 73 76+ <
***1999** Aug Windso (GD) H 8.3f 71 73
***1999** Jly Windso (G-F) H 8.3f 69 69
*1998 Jly Bath (GD) 8f 75
*1998 Jly Newmar (FRM) H 8f 68 74
*1997 May Carlis (FRM) 5.9f 66
1999 Turf 3-11: (8f 3-10, 9f) (gd 3, g-f 3, frm 2-4, hrd 1-1)
Scopey, above-average filly, effective 7 to 8f, best at 8f, acts on gd to hrd, has worn blinkers, likes left handed tracks, likes tight tracks, excels at Bath and likes Windsor. Turf high 76 - 1st of 5 giving 1lb to Best of All (4 Spt Thirsk RF 4144) - also 1st of 12 giving 14lb to Elba Magic (28 Aug Windsor RF 3985). After quite a long season thing started to go her way, scoring twice at Windsor over a mile on decent ground and at Thirsk.
**M L W Bell [6-28] Mrs G Rowland-Clark.*

MINGLING BHB 79f RR 72f 4346[7]
2 b c Wolfhound (USA) 7.3f **(71)** - On the Tide **(67f)** (Slip Anchor) 9.8f **(73)**
Form - 457
Record 1999 - 1st:0 2nd:0 3rd:0 Ran:3
Win Prizemoney £0 *Total Prizemoney* £288
1999 Turf 0-3: (7f 3) (gd, g-f, frm)
Currently above-average colt. Turf high 72 (began Aug).
**M H Tompkins [0-3] Mrs Beryl Lockey.*

MINI LODGE (IRE) BHB 67f RR 72f 5022[12]
3 ch g Grand Lodge (USA) - Mirea (USA) (The Minstrel (CAN)) 10f **(72)**
Form - 60680
Record 1999 - 1st:0 2nd:0 3rd:0 Ran:5
Pre1999 - 1st:1 2nd:2 3rd:0 Ran:4
Win Prizemoney £3,208 *Total Prizemoney* £7,700
Wins * 1998 Jly Newcas (G-F) 7f 78+ <
1999 Turf 0-5: (8f 2, 9f, 10f 2) (gd 2, frm 3)
Tall, above-average gelding, effective 7f, acts on sft to gd. Turf high 77. Inconsistent. **J G FitzGerald [1-9] Marquesa de Moratalla.*

MINIMUS TIME BHB 42f RR 52f 3094[6]
2 ch f Timeless Times (USA) 6.1f **(56)** - Glenfield Greta **(46f 43a)** (Gabitat) 5f **(44)**
Form - 0306
Record 1999 - 1st:0 2nd:0 3rd:1 Ran:4
Win Prizemoney £0 *Total Prizemoney* £252
1999 Turf 0-4: (5f 3, 6f) (g-f, frm 2, hrd)
Fair filly. Turf high 52. **T M Jones [0-4] Mervyn Evans.*

MINI RED BHB 35f RR 28f 5192[12]
2 ch f Timeless Times (USA) 6.1f **(56)** - Loving Doll (Godswalk (USA)) 7.3f **(58)**
Form - 000
Record 1999 - 1st:0 2nd:0 3rd:0 Ran:3
1999 Turf 0-3: (5f, 6f, 8f) (gd, g-f, frm)
Currently little account filly. Turf high 28. **G L Moore [0-3] A Moore.*

MINIVET RR 85f 5221[5]
4 b g Midyan (USA) 9.9f **(64)** - Bronzewing (Beldale Flutter (USA)) 9.7f **(71)**
Form - 13038642125
Record 1999 - 1st:2 2nd:2 3rd:2 Ran:11
Pre1999 - 1st:1 2nd:4 3rd:4 Ran:11
Win Prizemoney £17,632 *Total Prizemoney* £33,722
Wins 1999 Spt Haydoc (SFT) H 11.9f 82 83+ <
1999 Apr Newmar (GD) H 12f 75 79
1998 Aug Redcar (G-F) 9f 44+
1999 Turf 2-11: (10f, 12f 2-7, 14f, 16f 2) (sft, g-s, gd 2-5, g-f, frm 3)
Neat, useful gelding, effective 10 to 12f, best at 12f, acts on sft to frm, best on gd, prefers left handed tracks, excels at York. Turf high 85 - 5th of 16 giving 11lb to Flossy (6 Nov Doncaster 12f sft RF 5221) - also 1st of 8 giving 21lb to Powder River (24 Spt Haydock RF 4526). Consistent. Running well since being dropped back to a mile and a half, winning at Haydock before going under narrowly in a York claimer.
**T D Easterby [0-1] The Pertemps Professionals (from M L W Bell [3-21] Oct 1999).*

MINJARA BHB 34f RR 36f 3068[9]
4 b g Beveled (USA) 6.9f **(64)** - Honey Mill (Milford) 9f **(61)**
Form - 00040
Record 1999 - 1st:0 2nd:0 3rd:0 Ran:5
Pre1999 - 1st:0 2nd:0 3rd:0 Ran:7
Win Prizemoney £0 *Total Prizemoney* £264
1999 Turf 0-5: (8f 2, 10f 2, 12f) (g-s, gd, g-f, frm 2)
Workmanlike, very moderate gelding, effective 8f, acts on frm, has worn blinkers, likes left handed tracks, likes tight tracks. Turf high 36 - 4th of 8 getting 15lb from Sandicliffe (20 Jly Bath 8f frm RF 2957). Inconsistent.
**Derrick Morris [0-5] The Lambourn Racing Club (from J G Smyth-Osbourne [0-4] Apr 1999).*

MINKASH (IRE) BHB 93f RR 97f 4792[7]
2 b c Caerleon (USA) 10.9f **(79)** - Ingabelle (Taufan (USA)) 7f **(57)**
Form - 41227
Record 1999 - 1st:1 2nd:2 3rd:0 Ran:5
Win Prizemoney £5,952 *Total Prizemoney* £12,759
Wins *1999 Jly York (G-F) 7f 81 <
1999 Turf 1-5: (6f, 7f 1-2, 8f 2) (gd, g-f, frm 1-3)
Very useful colt. Turf high 97 - 2nd of 10 getting 6lb from French Fellow (9 Spt Doncaster 8f g-f RF 4238). He stays a mile well, but is quite high in the handicap and may not be particularly easy to place. **B Hanbury [1-5] Hamdan Al Maktoum.*

MINNESOTA BHB 45f43a RR 43f 43a 4787[8]
3 b g Danehill (USA) 9.1f **(79)** - Santi Sana (Formidable (USA)) 9.2f **(63)**
Form - 00500848
Record 1999 - 1st:0 2nd:0 3rd:0 Ran:8
Pre1999 - 1st:2 2nd:1 3rd:1 Ran:9
Win Prizemoney £7,605 *Total Prizemoney* £9,318
Wins * 1998 Jly Newmar (G-F) H 7f 83 <
* 1998 *Jun Southw (STD) 7f 78*
1999 Turf 0-6: (7f 2, 8f, 10f 3) (gd 2, g-f, frm 3) 1999 AW 0-2: (6f, 8f) (Equi 2)
Light-framed, fair gelding, effective 7f, acts on frm - acts on Fibr, has worn blinkers.
**N A Callaghan [2-17] M Tabor & Mrs John Magnier.*

MINNISAM BHB 39f RR 46f 2959[7]
6 ch g Niniski (USA) 13.2f **(67)** - Wise Speculation (USA) (Mr Prospector (USA)) 8.8f **(78)**
Form - 07
Record 1999 - 1st:0 2nd:0 3rd:0 Ran:2
Pre1999 - 1st:1 2nd:1 3rd:2 Ran:13
Win Prizemoney £2,381 *Total Prizemoney* £4,492
Wins 1996 Jly Folkes (FRM) H 12f 65 71 <
1999 Turf 0-2: (15f, 17f) (sft, frm)
Moderate gelding, has broken blood-vessels, has worn blinkers. Turf high 15. Becoming disappointing.
**G A Ham [3-15] Mike Cornish (from J L Dunlop [1-10] Aug 1996).*

MINTY BHB 40f49a RR 38f 49a 4980[13]
3 b g Be My Chief (USA) 10.2f **(62)** - Mindomica (Dominion) 8.5f **(63)**
Form - 762455050
Record 1999 - 1st:0 2nd:1 3rd:0 Ran:8
Pre1999 - 1st:0 2nd:0 3rd:0 Ran:2
Win Prizemoney £0 *Total Prizemoney* £739
1999 Turf 0-5: (8f, 9f, 10f 2, 12f) (gd 2, g-f, frm 2) 1999 AW 0-3: (11f 2, 12f) (Fibr 3)
Workmanlike, fair gelding, has worn blinkers. Turf high 49. AW high 54.
**N Bycroft [0-2] Mike Smallman (from C W Thornton [0-9] Jly 1999).*

MINUIT NOIR (IRE) BHB 80f RR 84f 4425[8]
3 b g Machiavellian (USA) 9.8f **(83)** - Misbegotten (IRE) **(106f)** (Baillamont (USA)) 7f **(78)**
Form - 3188
Record 1999 - 1st:1 2nd:0 3rd:1 Ran:4
Win Prizemoney £3,566 *Total Prizemoney* £4,601
Wins *1999 Jly Pontef (G-S) 10f 84 <
1999 Turf 1-4: (8f, 10f 1-1, 12f 2) (gd, g-f, frm 1-2)
Workmanlike, decent gelding. Turf high 84 - 1st of 12 from Bellefonte (6 Jly Pontefract RF 2582). Came on from his York debut to gain a battling victory in a Pontefract maiden, but ran

very poorly in his first two starts.
. *J G FitzGerald [1-4] Marquesa de Moratalla.

MIRACLE ISLAND BHB 70f73a **RR 74f 73a** 943[18]
4 b g Jupiter Island 10.4f **(57)** - Running Game (Run The Gantlet (USA)) 12.1f **(59)**
Form - 80
Record 1999 - 1st:0 2nd:0 3rd:0 Ran:2
Pre1999 - 1st:1 2nd:2 3rd:0 Ran:5
Win Prizemoney £3,468 *Total Prizemoney* £5,395
Wins 1998 *Feb Wolver (STD) 9.4f 73* <
1999 Turf 0-2: (10f 2) (g-f, frm)
Neat, above-average gelding, effective 9 to 11f, best at 9f, - acts on Fibr, has worn blinkers. Turf high 68. *D R C Elsworth [0-2] Mrs P T Fenwick (from D R Loder [1-5] Apr 1998).*

MIRACULOUS GUEST BHB 38f **RR 43f** 4819[15]
3 b f Be My Guest (USA) 10.2f **(66)** - Mystery Ship (Decoy Boy) 6.7f **(56)**
Form - 0076060
Record 1999 - 1st:0 2nd:0 3rd:0 Ran:7
Pre1999 - 1st:0 2nd:0 3rd:0 Ran:2
1999 Turf 0-7: (7f, 8f 4, 10f, 12f) (gd 2, g-f 2, frm 3)
Leggy, moderate filly, has worn blinkers. Turf high 43. Inconsistent. *M Kettle [0-9] B H Simpson.*

MIRAGGIO BHB 42f42a **RR 50f 42a** 5112[8]
3 b g Alhijaz 7.7f **(57)** - Doppio (Dublin Taxi) 6.4f **(55)**
Form - 5565884304448
Record 1999 - 1st:0 2nd:0 3rd:1 Ran:12
Pre1999 - 1st:0 2nd:0 3rd:0 Ran:2
Win Prizemoney £0 *Total Prizemoney* £258
1999 Turf 0-10: (10f 4, 11f, 12f 4, 17f) (gd 3, g-f 4, frm 2, hrd) 1999 AW 0-2: (7f, 8f) (Fibr 2)
Light-framed, fair gelding, effective 10 to 17f, best at 10f, acts on gd to hrd, best on gd, has worn blinkers, prefers tight tracks. Turf high 50 - 4th of 14 getting 5lb from Tumbleweed Glen (20 Spt Leicester 10f g-f RF 4438). AW high 51.
B J Llewellyn [0-1] Mrs Vicki Guy (from H Morrison [0-13] Oct 1999).

MIRAKI (USA) RR 81+f 2123[1]
2 b c Miswaki (USA) 8.1f **(81)** - Lady's Truth (USA) (Riverman (USA)) 9.1f **(76)**
Form - 31
Record 1999 - 1st:1 2nd:0 3rd:1 Ran:2
Win Prizemoney £4,347 *Total Prizemoney* £4,983
Wins * 1999 Jun Newmar (G-F) 6f 81+ <
1999 Turf 1-2: (6f 1-2) (gd, frm 1-1)
Currently decent colt. Turf high 81 - 1st of 10 from El Curioso (18 Jun Newmarket RF 2123). *C F Wall [1-2] Peter Pritchard.*

MIRBECK (USA) BHB 79f **RR 83df** 3985[8]
3 ch f Gone West (USA) 7.8f **(82)** - Oakmead (IRE) (Lomond (USA)) 8.8f **(65)**
Form - 21228
Record 1999 - 1st:1 2nd:3 3rd:0 Ran:5
Pre1999 - 1st:0 2nd:0 3rd:0 Ran:1
Win Prizemoney £4,055 *Total Prizemoney* £8,151
Wins * 1999 Jun Thirsk (G-F) 7f 76 <
1999 Turf 1-5: (7f 1-2, 8f 3) (gd, frm 1-4)
Scopey, decent filly, effective 7 to 8f, best at 8f, acts on frm. Turf high 83 - 2nd of 7 giving 3lb to Pilgrim's Way (28 Jly Doncaster 8f frm RF 3198) - also 1st of 12 getting 5lb from Cool Temper (15 Jun Thirsk RF 2002).
P W Chapple-Hyam [1-6] Mrs B V Sangster & B V Sangster.

MIRJAN (IRE) BHB 94f **RR 98f** 5031[4]
3 b c Tenby 10.4f **(76)** - Mirana (IRE) (Ela-Mana-Mou) 10.1f **(70)**
Form - 132404
Record 1999 - 1st:1 2nd:1 3rd:1 Ran:6
Win Prizemoney £4,500 *Total Prizemoney* £9,758
Wins * 1999 Apr Newmar (GD) 10f 84 <
1999 Turf 1-6: (10f 1-4, 12f 2) (g-s 2, gd, g-f 1-2, frm)
Workmanlike, very useful colt, effective 10 to 12f, best at 12f, acts on g-s to frm. Turf high 99 - 3rd of 5 giving 3lb to Time Zone (13 May Salisbury 12f frm RF 1190). He needs every inch of a mile and a half and was banging his head against a brick wall over shorter trips in the autumn. Still lightly raced, he has scope and should do well for Len Lungo, who paid 82,000 guineas for the horse at Newmarket in October. *L M Cumani [1-6] H H Aga Khan.*

MISALLIANCE RR 53f 4448[11]
4 ch f Elmaamul (USA) 8.1f **(70)** - Cabaret Artiste (Shareef Dancer (USA)) 9.9f **(73)**
Form - 8400
Record 1999 - 1st:0 2nd:0 3rd:0 Ran:4
Pre1999 - 1st:1 2nd:0 3rd:1 Ran:12
Win Prizemoney £2,239 *Total Prizemoney* £3,001
Wins * 1997 Oct Newcas (G-F) 7f 71+ <
1999 Turf 0-4: (8f 3, 10f) (g-s, gd, frm 2)
Scopey, fair filly, effective 8f, acts on gd, likes tight tracks. Turf high 53 (began Aug). *C F Wall [1-16] The Lively Partners.*

MISBEHAVE BHB 93f **RR 92f** 5142[9]
2 b f Reprimand 8.2f **(63)** - Princess Moodyshoe (Jalmood (USA)) 10.1f **(52)**
Form - 22110010
Record 1999 - 1st:3 2nd:2 3rd:0 Ran:8
Win Prizemoney £13,572 *Total Prizemoney* £14,906
Wins * 1999 Oct Newmar (GD) H 8f 86 92 <
*** 1999** Jly Windso (G-F) 6f 85
*** 1999** May Warwic (SFT) 5f 75
1999 Turf 3-7: (5f 1-2, 6f 1-3, 8f 1-2) (sft 1-1, gd 1-2, g-f, frm 1-3) 1999 AW 0-1: (5f) (Fibr)
Useful filly, effective 6 to 8f, acts on gd to frm. Turf high 92 - 1st of 20 giving 10lb to Insightful (15 Oct Newmarket RF 4899) - also 1st of 4 giving 2lb to Water Echo (19 Jly Windsor RF 2952). Two wins over five and six furlongs on soft and firm ground respectively were followed by a disappointing effort at Newmarket in a decent nursery. Returning after a two-month break, a moderate effort in the Two Year Old Trophy preceded by a fine success over a mile at Newmarket, where she won in fine style.
M L W Bell [3-8] Frank Farrant.

MISCHIEF BHB 63f55a **RR 68f 55a** 828[3]
3 ch c Generous (IRE) 11.5f **(82)** - Knight's Baroness (Rainbow Quest (USA)) 10.4f **(75)**
Form - 5383
Record 1999 - 1st:0 2nd:0 3rd:2 Ran:4
Win Prizemoney £0 *Total Prizemoney* £1,423
1999 Turf 0-2: (10f, 12f) (sft, gd) 1999 AW 0-2: (10f, 12f) (Equi 2)
Scopey, average colt, has worn blinkers. Turf high 68. AW high 58.
P F I Cole [0-4] H R H Prince Fahd Salman.

MISCONDUCT BHB 48f51a **RR 54f 51a** 1087[8]
5 gr m Risk Me (FR) 8f **(53)** - Grey Cree (Creetown) 6.9f **(50)**
Form - 28
Record 1999 - 1st:0 2nd:1 3rd:0 Ran:2
Pre1999 - 1st:3 2nd:2 3rd:2 Ran:17
Win Prizemoney £7,640 *Total Prizemoney* £12,290
Wins 1998 *Aug Lingfi (STD) H 10f 42 48+* <
1998 Jly Bath (GD) H 10.2f 44 47+
1998 Jun Salisb (G-F) H 9.9f 39 42
1999 Turf 0-1: (12f) (sft) 1999 AW 0-1: (10f) (Equi)
Fair filly, effective 10 to 12f, best at 10f, acts on sft to gd - acts on Equi. (1st run) - 2nd of 14 getting 18lb from Heart (27 Apr Bath 12f sft RF 0861). *Mrs Merrita Jones [3-9] The Playmates (from G L Moore [3-17] Spt 1998).*

MISHOR BHB 67f **RR 69f** 4893[9]
3 b f Slip Anchor 12.7f **(75)** - Miss Up N Go (Gorytus (USA)) 7.8f **(60)**
Form - 0331650
Record 1999 - 1st:1 2nd:0 3rd:2 Ran:7
Win Prizemoney £4,026 *Total Prizemoney* £5,155
Wins * 1999 Jly Newmar (G-F) 14.8f 80 <
1999 Turf 1-7: (8f 2, 12f, 14f, 15f 1-2, 16f) (sft, g-s, gd 2, g-f, frm 1-2)
Light-framed, average filly, effective 8 to 15f, acts on sft to frm. Turf high 80 - 1st of 6 from Precious Persian (25 Jly Newmarket RF 3128). *W Jarvis [1-7] Mrs J A Prescott.*

MISINTERPRETATION (IRE) BHB 52f **RR 55f** 4444[7]
2 b f Perugino (USA) - Steel Tap (IRE) (Flash of Steel) 7.2f **(53)**
Form - 33014087
Record 1999 - 1st:1 2nd:0 3rd:2 Ran:8

Win Prizemoney £2,220 *Total Prizemoney* £2,955
Wins * **1999** Jun Mussel (G-F) C 5f 53 <
1999 Turf 1-8: (5f 1-7, 6f) (g-s, gd 3, g-f 1-3, hrd)
Fair filly, effective 5f, acts on g-f. Turf high 55 - also 1st of 6 giving 4lb to Diamond Isle (21 Jun Musselburgh RF 2166). **N Tinkler [1-8] E A Brook.*

MISMEWMEW BHB 29f28a **RR 37f 28a** 2716[12]
4 b f Weldnaas (USA) 8.4f **(55)** - Joan's Gift (Doulab (USA)) 9.8f **(65)**
Form - 0080007080
Record 1999 - 1st:0 2nd:0 3rd:0 Ran:9
Pre1999 - 1st:0 2nd:0 3rd:0 Ran:10
1999 Turf 0-7: (7f 2, 8f, 10f, 11f, 12f 2) (gd 2, g-f 3, frm, hrd) 1999 AW 0-2: (8f 2) (Equi 2)
Unfurnished, very moderate filly, has worn blinkers. Turf high 37. AW high 28.
**L A Dace [0-13] Eddie Davess (from C J Benstead [0-6] Jly 1998).*

MISPRINT BHB 52f42a **RR 47f 42a** 399[4]
3 b f Minshaanshu Amad (USA) 11.3f **(53)** - Miss Copyforce (Aragon) 8.1f **(60)**
Form - 827363864
Record 1999 - 1st:0 2nd:0 3rd:2 Ran:7
Pre1999 - 1st:0 2nd:1 3rd:0 Ran:7
Win Prizemoney £0 *Total Prizemoney* £1,251
1999 AW 0-7: (5f, 6f, 7f 3, 8f 2) (Equi 6, Fibr)
Neat, moderate filly, often wears blinkers. AW high 44.
**E A Wheeler [0-14] Benham Racing.*

MISRAAH (IRE) RR 92++f 4834[1]
2 ch c Lure (USA) - Dwell (USA) (Habitat) 9.4f **(70)**
Form - 41
Record 1999 - 1st:1 2nd:0 3rd:0 Ran:2
Win Prizemoney £3,687 *Total Prizemoney* £4,250
Wins * **1999** Oct Leices (GD) 7f 92++ <
1999 Turf 1-2: (7f 1-2) (gd 1-2)
Currently useful colt. Turf high 92 (began Spt) - 1st of 15 from Tap (12 Oct Leicester RF 4834). Easy to back before finishing a promising fourth in a big field on his debut, he won his maiden by ten lengths and looks useful.
**Sir Michael Stoute [1-2] Hamdan Al Maktoum.*

MISS ALL ALONE BHB 41f48a **RR 42f 48a** 4604[11]
4 ch f Crofthall 8.6f **(54)** - Uninvited (Be My Guest (USA)) 9.3f **(67)**
Form - 7233205480
Record 1999 - 1st:0 2nd:2 3rd:2 Ran:9
Pre1999 - 1st:0 2nd:4 3rd:2 Ran:10
Win Prizemoney £0 *Total Prizemoney* £6,215
1999 Turf 0-4: (7f, 9f, 10f 2) (g-s, gd 2, g-f) 1999 AW 0-5: (7f 2, 8f 3) (Fibr 5)
Scopey, fair filly, effective 7 to 8f, best at 8f, acts on gd to g-f - acts on Fibr, often wears blinkers (extremely effectively), prefers left handed tracks, prefers tight tracks, excels at Nottingham and Southwell. Turf high 42. AW high 54 - 3rd of 13 giving 2lb to Chinaberry (25 Jan Southwell 8f Fibr RF 0161).
**J A Glover [0-19] Countrywide Classics Ltd.*

MISS AMANPURI BHB 90f **RR 93f** 4871[13]
3 b f Alzao (USA) 9.8f **(73)** - Miss Rinjani **(88f)** (Shirley Heights) 10.3f **(74)**
Form - 0470
Record 1999 - 1st:0 2nd:0 3rd:0 Ran:4
Pre1999 - 1st:1 2nd:0 3rd:0 Ran:4
Win Prizemoney £4,110 *Total Prizemoney* £6,145
Wins * 1998 Aug Newmar (G-F) 7f 90 <
1999 Turf 0-4: (9f, 10f 2, 12f) (gd 3, g-f)
Workmanlike, useful filly, effective 7f, acts on frm. Turf high 93. Has had her limitations exposed last term, and was well beaten in the Oaks. Needs her sights lowered. **G Wragg [1-8] J L C Pearce.*

MISS ARCH (IRE) BHB 36f **RR 39f** 4438[10]
3 ch f Archway (IRE) 8.5f **(60)** - Zanskar (Godswalk (USA)) 7.3f **(58)**
Form - 5053270
Record 1999 - 1st:0 2nd:1 3rd:1 Ran:7
Pre1999 - 1st:0 2nd:0 3rd:0 Ran:4
Win Prizemoney £0 *Total Prizemoney* £1,112
1999 Turf 0-7: (8f 2, 10f 5) (gd, g-f 2, frm 4)
Leggy, very moderate filly. Turf high 39. Consistent.
**M A Buckley [0-7] Will Racing Partnership (from Miss J F Craze [0-1] Oct 1998).*

MISS ASIA QUEST BHB 75f **RR 79f** 5157[5]
2 ch f Rainbow Quest (USA) 11.2f **(81)** - Miss Kuta Beach (Bold Lad (IRE)) 8.4f **(68)**
Form - 035
Record 1999 - 1st:0 2nd:0 3rd:1 Ran:3
Win Prizemoney £0 *Total Prizemoney* £565
1999 Turf 0-3: (6f, 7f 2) (gd, g-f, frm)
Currently above-average filly. Turf high 79 (began Oct) - 3rd of 10 to Ashjaan (20 Oct Newcastle 7f g-f RF 4982).
**G Wragg [0-3] J L C Pearce.*

MISS BANANAS BHB 42f55a **RR 40f 55a** 3744[1]
4 b f Risk Me (FR) 8f **(53)** - Astrid Gilberto (Runnett) 7f **(59)**
Form - 03830005420000205701
Record 1999 - 1st:1 2nd:2 3rd:0 Ran:15
Pre1999 - 1st:1 2nd:2 3rd:3 Ran:19
Win Prizemoney £6,568 *Total Prizemoney* £10,692
Wins * **1999** Aug Leices (GD) H 5f 29 40
1998 *Feb Lingfi (SLW) H 5f 58 63* <
1999 Turf 1-7: (5f 1-2, 6f 4, 7f) (gd, g-f 1-3, frm 3) 1999 AW 0-8: (5f 3, 6f 4, 7f) (Equi 2, Fibr 6)
Neat, fair filly, effective 5 to 6f, best at 5f, - acts on AW, best on Equi. Turf high 40. AW high 58 - 2nd of 9 getting 5lb from C-Harry (19 Jun Wolverhampton 6f Fibr RF 2164). **C N Kellett [1-22] W Meah (from T T Bill [1-12] Aug 1998).*

MISS BERBERE (FR) RR 115f 5264a[3]
4 ch f Bering 9.6f **(80)** - Miss Afrique (FR) (African Song)
Form - 632423
1999 Turf 0-6: (8f 5, 9f) (hvy 2, sft 2, g-s, gd)
High-class filly, effective 8 to 9f, best at 8f, acts on hvy to gd, and likes Deauville. Turf high 111 - 2nd of 11 to Diamond White (3 Oct Longchamp 9f sft RF 4780a). Not at her best in '99, although she put up an improved showing when runner-up in the Prx de l'Opera in heavy ground. **D Smaga in FR [1-11].*

MISS CHIQUITA (IRE) BHB 48f **RR 68?f** 469[15]
4 b f Waajib 8.9f **(67)** - Golden Leap (Salmon Leap (USA)) 11f **(61)**
Form - 0
Record 1999 - 1st:0 2nd:0 3rd:0 Ran:1
Pre1999 - 1st:2 2nd:0 3rd:1 Ran:17
Win Prizemoney £5,317 *Total Prizemoney* £6,038
Wins 1998 Spt Down R (GD) C 12f 68
1998 May Clonme (G-F) C 12f 72 <
1999 Turf 0-1: (10f) (g-s)
Average filly, effective 12 to 14f, best at 12f, acts on gd to g-f, best on g-f, often wears blinkers (extremely effectively).
**J S Moore [0-1] Ernie Houghton (from J C Hayden in IRE [2-17] Oct 1998).*

MISS DANGEROUS BHB 40f44a **RR 38f 44a** 5065[14]
4 b f Komaite (USA) 6.9f **(61)** - Khadine (Astec) 8.6f **(66)**
Form - 00010080588005020
Record 1999 - 1st:1 2nd:1 3rd:0 Ran:14
Pre1999 - 1st:4 2nd:2 3rd:0 Ran:21
Win Prizemoney £17,765 *Total Prizemoney* £20,048
Wins * **1999** *Jan Lingfi (STD) H 7f 56 58*
* 1998 Jun Warwic (G-S) H 5f 57 60
* 1998 *Apr Wolver (STD) H 6f 55 67+* <
* 1998 Apr Folkes (SFT) C 5f 56
* 1998 *Jan Wolver (STD) S 5f 54*
1999 Turf 0-8: (5f 3, 6f 2, 7f 3) (g-s 3, gd 2, g-f 2, frm) 1999 AW 1-6: (5f, 6f, 7f 1-3, 8f) (Equi 1-3, Fibr 3)
Unfurnished, moderate filly, effective 5 to 7f, acts on frm - acts on AW. Turf high 52. AW high 58 (1st run) - 1st of 13 getting 10lb from Roisin Splendour (5 Jan Lingfield RF 0033). **M Quinn [5-30] M Quinn (from M R Channon [0-5] Oct 1997).*

MISS DOODYBUSINESS BHB 23f19a **RR 27f 19a** 4601[7]
3 b f Formidable (USA) 7.8f **(60)** - Miss Doody (Gorytus (USA)) 7.8f **(60)**
Form - 00345000645877
Record 1999 - 1st:0 2nd:0 3rd:1 Ran:12

Pre1999 - 1st:0 2nd:0 3rd:0 Ran:3
Win Prizemoney £0 *Total Prizemoney* £513
1999 Turf 0-6: (10f 2, 11f, 12f 3) (g-f 2, frm 4) 1999 AW 0-6: (7f 2, 8f 3, 11f) (Fibr 6)
Very moderate filly. Turf high 27. AW high 35.
**C W Thornton [0-15] Racegoers Club Spigot Lodge Owners Group.*

MISS ELIMINATOR BHB 33f48a **RR 29f 48a** 3284[14]
4 b f Komaite (USA) 6.9f **(61)** - Northern Line (Camden Town) 9.3f **(53)**
Form - 02000060
Record 1999 - 1st:0 2nd:1 3rd:0 Ran:8
Pre1999 - 1st:1 2nd:0 3rd:1 Ran:10
Win Prizemoney £2,847 *Total Prizemoney* £4,226
Wins 1997 Jly Beverl (GD) 5f 62 <
1999 Turf 0-8: (6f 3, 7f 3, 8f, 10f) (sft, gd 2, g-f, frm 3, hrd)
Lengthy, little account filly, effective 7f, acts on gd, has worn blinkers, likes tight tracks. Turf high 46 - 2nd of 16 giving 5lb to Komlucky (8 May Beverley 7f gd RF 1097). Inconsistent.
**J L Harris [0-12] Mrs R Morley (from M W Easterby [1-6] Aug 1997).*

MISS FARA (FR) BHB 74f **RR 74f** 3304[8]
4 ch f Galetto (FR) 11.7f **(86)** - Faracha (FR) (Kenmare (FR)) 6.5f **(72)**
Form - 28
Record 1999 - 1st:0 2nd:1 3rd:0 Ran:2
Pre1999 - 1st:0 2nd:2 3rd:1 Ran:4
Win Prizemoney £0 *Total Prizemoney* £3,706
1999 Turf 0-2: (10f 2) (frm 2)
Above-average filly, effective 8 to 10f, best at 10f, acts on gd to g-f, best on g-f. Turf high 68. **M C Pipe [0-10] Mrs Christine Painting.*

MISS FIT (IRE) BHB 76f **RR 74f** 4911[3]
3 b f Hamas (IRE) 8f **(72)** - Soucaro (Rusticaro (FR)) 8.2f **(65)**
Form - 564035510275003
Record 1999 - 1st:1 2nd:1 3rd:2 Ran:15
Pre1999 - 1st:3 2nd:1 3rd:0 Ran:5
Win Prizemoney £15,934 *Total Prizemoney* £21,307
Wins * **1999** Jly Cheste (G-F) H 5.1f 79 82 <
* 1998 Aug Redcar (G-F) 5f 76
* 1998 Jly Carlis (G-F) 5.9f 77+
* 1998 *Jun Southw (STD) 5f 70+*
1999 Turf 1-15: (5f 1-10, 6f 5) (g-s 2, gd 3, g-f 1-5, frm 5)
Scopey, above-average filly, effective 5 to 6f, best at 5f, acts on gd to frm. Turf high 86 - 2nd of 12 to Poles Apart (29 Jly Doncaster 6f frm RF 3217) - also 1st of 13 giving 12lb to Shirley Not (9 Jly Chester RF 2674). **Mrs G S Rees [4-20] Mrs G S Rees.*

MISS FLIRTATIOUS BHB 64f **RR 64f** 4439[2]
2 b f Piccolo - By Candlelight (IRE) **(80f)** (Roi Danzig (USA))
Form - 76654002
Record 1999 - 1st:0 2nd:1 3rd:0 Ran:8
Win Prizemoney £0 *Total Prizemoney* £1,308
1999 Turf 0-8: (5f 4, 6f 4) (gd, g-f 2, frm 4, hrd)
Average filly, effective 6f, acts on g-f, has worn blinkers. Turf high 64 - 2nd of 17 getting 10lb from Peruvian Jade (20 Spt Leicester 6f g-f RF 4439). **D HaydnJones [0-8] Jack Brown (Bookmaker) Ltd.*

MISS GRAPETTE (IRE) BHB 49f **RR 47f** 4810[13]
3 b f Brief Truce (USA) 9.1f **(73)** - Grapette (Nebbiolo) 8.1f **(75)**
Form - 1000436800
Record 1999 - 1st:1 2nd:0 3rd:1 Ran:10
Pre1999 - 1st:0 2nd:2 3rd:2 Ran:6
Win Prizemoney £2,901 *Total Prizemoney* £6,657
Wins * **1999** Mar Catter (G-S) 6f 69 <
1999 Turf 1-10: (5f 4, 6f 1-6) (sft, g-s, gd 1-4, frm 4)
Workmanlike, moderate filly, effective 5 to 6f, best at 5f, acts on g-s to frm, best on g-f, prefers left handed tracks. Turf high 69 (1st run) - 1st of 14 getting 5lb from Gunner Sam (31 Mar Catterick RF 0527). **J Berry [1-16] Mrs A E Robertson.*

MISS HAMOUSE (IRE) BHB 30f **RR 22f** 4148[13]
3 b f Hamas (IRE) 8f **(72)** - Highland Warning **(36f 44a)** (Warning)
Form - 8670
Record 1999 - 1st:0 2nd:0 3rd:0 Ran:4
1999 Turf 0-4: (5f 2, 6f 2) (gd, frm, hrd 2)
Scopey, little account filly. Turf high 22.
**J Parkes [0-4] Mrs Lynn Parkes.*

MISS HIT BHB 64f74a **RR 62f 74a** 4826[14]
4 b f Efisio 7.7f **(69)** - Jennies' Gem (Sayf El Arab (USA)) 7.1f **(54)**
Form - 0110845442214000
Record 1999 - 1st:2 2nd:2 3rd:0 Ran:14
Pre1999 - 1st:2 2nd:1 3rd:1 Ran:10
Win Prizemoney £14,660 *Total Prizemoney* £18,546
Wins 1999 Aug Salisb (GD) H 6f 64 68
1999 *Jan Lingfi (STD) H 5f 70 71* <
1998 *Dec Wolver (STD) H 5f 65 71* <
1998 Oct Newmar () H 5f 60 63
1999 Turf 1-11: (5f 6, 6f 1-5) (gd 2, g-f 4, frm 1-5) 1999 AW 1-3: (5f 1-2, 6f) (Equi 1-2, Fibr)
Scopey, above-average filly, effective 5 to 6f, best at 5f, acts on gd to frm - acts on AW, does well at Lingfield. Turf high 68 - 1st of 14 giving 28lb to Calandrella (6 Aug Salisbury RF 3434). AW high 71 (1st run) - 1st of 7 giving 19lb to Ivory's Grab Hire (26 Jan Lingfield RF 0167). **G A Butler [0-1] D R Windebank (from D R C Elsworth [1-7] Spt 1999).*

MISSILE TOE (IRE) BHB 43f48a **RR 46df 48a** 5053[10]
6 b g Exactly Sharp (USA) 8.4f **(66)** - Debach Dust (Indian King (USA)) 7.4f **(64)**
Form - 654201700
Record 1999 - 1st:1 2nd:1 3rd:0 Ran:9
Pre1999 - 1st:1 2nd:5 3rd:3 Ran:34
Win Prizemoney £7,374 *Total Prizemoney* £15,585
Wins * **1999** Jly Newmar (G-F) H 10f 41 46
1995 Jly Newcas (G-F) 6f 65 <
1999 Turf 1-9: (8f 5, 10f 1-4) (gd 5, g-f, frm 1-3)
Moderate gelding, effective 10f, acts on g-f to frm, best on frm, has worn blinkers, likes left handed tracks, likes tight tracks. Turf high 46 - 1st of 12 getting 15lb from Rare Talent (30 Jly Newmarket RF 3241).
**D Morris [1-22] Stag and Huntsman (from J E Banks [1-21] Oct 1996).*

MISS KIRSTY (USA) RR 78f 5137[3]
2 ch f Miswaki (USA) 8.1f **(81)** - Spit Curl (USA) (Northern Dancer) 9.6f **(80)**
Form - 3
Record 1999 - 1st:0 2nd:0 3rd:1 Ran:1
Win Prizemoney £0 *Total Prizemoney* £638
1999 Turf 0-1: (7f) (gd)
Currently above-average filly. (1st run) - 3rd of 16 to Garota do Leblon (30 Oct Newmarket 7f gd RF 5137).
**G A Butler [0-1] D R Windebank.*

MISS LACROIX BHB 20f27a **RR 22f 27a** 4287[15]
4 b f Picea 12.7f **(43)** - Smartie Lee (Dominion) 8.5f **(63)**
Form - 0844800080
Record 1999 - 1st:0 2nd:0 3rd:0 Ran:8
Pre1999 - 1st:0 2nd:0 3rd:0 Ran:4
1999 Turf 0-4: (10f, 11f, 14f, 16f) (frm 3, hrd) 1999 AW 0-4: (12f 2, 16f 2) (Fibr 4)
Tall, little account filly. Turf high 22. AW high 26.
**R Hollinshead [1-20] Mrs Norma Harris.*

MISS LADY LYDIA BHB 20f15a **RR 15a** 299[11]
4 ch f Tina's Pet 7.4f **(56)** - Kinfauns Dancer (Celtic Cone) 9.8f **(43)**
Form - 0
Record 1999 - 1st:0 2nd:0 3rd:0 Ran:1
Pre1999 - 1st:0 2nd:0 3rd:0 Ran:3
1999 AW 0-1: (10f) (Equi)
Light-framed, formerly very poor filly.
**J R Poulton [0-4] Come Racing Ltd.*

MISS LORILAW (FR) RR 75f 4751[1]
2 b f Homme de Loi (IRE) - Miss Lorika (FR) (Bikala) 10.1f **(49)**
Form - 1
Record 1999 - 1st:1 2nd:0 3rd:0 Ran:1
Win Prizemoney £8,162 *Total Prizemoney* £8,162
Wins * **1999** Oct York (G-S) 7.9f 75 <
1999 Turf 1-1: (8f 1-1) (gd 1-1)
Currently above-average filly. (1st run) - 1st of 26 getting 5lb from Muntej (6 Oct York RF 4751). **J W Hills [1-1] David Caruth.*

MISS MAGNUM (IRE) BHB 24f **RR 15f** 3250[10]
4 b f Whitehall Bridge - Illiney Girl (Lochnager) 6f **(59)**

Form - 0
Record 1999 - 1st:0 2nd:0 3rd:0 Ran:1
Pre1999 - 1st:0 2nd:0 3rd:0 Ran:2
1999 Turf 0-1: (10f) (frm)
Workmanlike, poor filly. **J Neville [0-5] Mrs Theresa O'Toole.*

MISS MILLENNIUM RR 44f
862[15]
2 b f Sabrehill (USA) 8.5f **(64)** - Lucky Thing (Green Desert (USA)) 8.6f **(78)**
Form - 80
Record 1999 - 1st:0 2nd:0 3rd:0 Ran:2
1999 Turf 0-2: (5f 2) (g-s, frm)
Currently moderate filly. Turf high 44.
**B W Hills [0-2] Millennium Partnership.*

MISS MONEY SPIDER (IRE) BHB 50f47a RR 45f 47a
4866[6]
4 b f Statoblest 6.4f **(63)** - Dream of Jenny (Caerleon (USA)) 8.6f **(71)**
Form - 0001081310886
Record 1999 - 1st:3 2nd:0 3rd:1 Ran:13
Pre1999 - 1st:1 2nd:0 3rd:2 Ran:11
Win Prizemoney £9,232 *Total Prizemoney* £10,666
Wins * **1999** Aug Lingfi (GD) H 7f 48 51
* **1999** Jly Folkes (G-F) C 7f 45
* **1999** May Folkes (G-F) C 7f 45
* **1998** Spt Yarmou (G-S) S 7f 55 <
1999 Turf 3-12: (6f 3, 7f 3-7, 8f 2) (g-s 2, gd 2, g-f 1-3, frm 2-5) 1999 AW 0-1: (7f) (Fibr)
Neat, above-average filly, effective 7 to 8f, best at 7f, acts on gd to frm, best on frm, has worn blinkers. Turf high 51 - 1st of 16 giving 3lb to Davis Rock (6 Aug Lingfield RF 3421).
**J M Bradley [3-13] E A Hayward (from N A Callaghan [1-9] Oct 1998).*

MISS MONTROSE BHB 48f RR 50f
4175[13]
5 b m Tina's Pet 7.4f **(56)** - Miss Ark Royal (Broadsword (USA))
Form - 60500
Record 1999 - 1st:0 2nd:0 3rd:0 Ran:5
1999 Turf 0-5: (8f, 10f 3, 14f) (g-f 2, frm 3)
Fair filly, has worn blinkers. Turf high 51 (began Jly).
**M Kettle [0-8] Farmers Weakly & Graham Racing.*

MISS ORAH BHB 91f RR 85f
4801[4]
2 b f Unfuwain (USA) 11.4f **(74)** - Massorah (FR) (Habitat) 9.4f **(70)**
Form - 124
Record 1999 - 1st:1 2nd:1 3rd:0 Ran:3
Win Prizemoney £5,225 *Total Prizemoney* £9,791
Wins * **1999** Spt Salisb (G-F) 7f 85+ <
1999 Turf 1-3: (6f, 7f 1-2) (gd, frm 1-2)
Currently useful filly. Turf high 85 (began Spt) - also 1st of 11 from Fair Lady (2 Spt Salisbury RF 4097). She won a Salisbury maiden over seven furlongs in good style on her debut and ran well when second to Veil Of Avalon at Newbury. Dropped back in trip next time, she was not beaten far. Tends to be excitable.
**J Noseda [1-3] G J Beck.*

MISS PETERSHAM (IRE) BHB 50f RR 40f
4531[17]
2 gr f Petong 7.6f **(58)** - Miss Siham (IRE) **(44+f 39a)** (Green Forest (USA)) 9.9f **(68)**
Form - 560
Record 1999 - 1st:0 2nd:0 3rd:0 Ran:3
1999 Turf 0-3: (5f 3) (g-s, frm 2)
Currently moderate filly. Turf high 40 (began Jly). She showed little, and has been retired to the British Racing School.
**Miss E C Lavelle [0-3] The 2nd Little Hatherden Partnership.*

MISS PIN UP BHB 57f50a RR 63f 50a
5025[9]
10 gr m Kalaglow 11.2f **(67)** - Allander Girl (Miralgo) 12.6f **(63)**
Form - 242270
Record 1999 - 1st:0 2nd:3 3rd:0 Ran:6
Pre1999 - 1st:10 2nd:7 3rd:1 Ran:60
Win Prizemoney £33,438 *Total Prizemoney* £49,722
Wins * 1998 Aug Nottin (G-F) H 14.1f 59 63
1995 Jly Yarmou (G-F) H 11.5f 77 81 <
1999 Turf 0-6: (14f 5, 15f) (gd 2, g-f 3, frm)
Average mare, effective 11 to 16f, best at 14f, acts on gd to frm, best on g-f, has worn blinkers, prefers left handed tracks, prefers tight tracks, and excels at Nottingham. Turf high 64 (1st run) - 2nd of 15 getting 9lb from Christiansted (16 Jun Nottingham 14f g-f RF 2051).
**R McGhin [1-15] Ray McGhin (from W J Haggas [2-11] Aug 1995).*

MISS PIPPIN BHB 54f RR 52f
4564[15]
3 ch f Rudimentary (USA) 8.2f **(66)** -Appledorn (Doulab (USA)) 9.8f **(65)**
Form - 440
Record 1999 - 1st:0 2nd:0 3rd:0 Ran:3
Win Prizemoney £0 *Total Prizemoney* £269
1999 Turf 0-3: (5f, 6f 2) (gd 2, g-f)
Light-framed, currently fair filly. Turf high 52 (began Aug).
**B A McMahon [0-3] Michael Sturgess.*

MISS PORTHCAWL (IRE) RR 31f
4414[8]
2 b f Tenby 10.4f **(76)** - Stella Ann (Ahonoora) 8.1f **(73)**
Form - 08
Record 1999 - 1st:0 2nd:0 3rd:0 Ran:2
1999 Turf 0-1: (7f) (frm) 1999 AW 0-1: (7f) (Fibr)
Currently very moderate filly. **M L W Bell [0-2] R P B Michaelson.*

MISS RIMEX (IRE) BHB 77f RR 78f
5050[1]
3 b f Ezzoud (IRE) - Blue Guitar (Cure The Blues (USA)) 9.5f **(63)**
Form - 4608513501
Record 1999 - 1st:2 2nd:0 3rd:1 Ran:10
Pre1999 - 1st:1 2nd:2 3rd:2 Ran:9
Win Prizemoney £11,679 *Total Prizemoney* £16,448
Wins * **1999** Oct Leices (SFT) C 8f 73
* **1999** Jly Newmar (G-F) H 8f 72 78
* **1998** Aug Kempto (G-F) H 6f 75 79 <
1999 Turf 2-10: (7f, 8f 2-4, 9f 2, 10f 3) (gd 1-5, g-f 2, frm 1-3)
Workmanlike, above-average filly, effective 6 to 10f, best at 8f, acts on gd to frm, best on frm, does well at Newmarket. Turf high 78 - 1st of 8 getting 4lb from High Hoyland (31 Jly Newmarket RF 3282) - also 1st of 20 giving 13lb to Swampy (25 Oct Leicester RF 5050). Consistent. **D R C Elsworth [3-19] Nightmare Partnership.*

MISS ROXANNE RR 41f
3569[6]
2 b f Cyrano de Bergerac 7.3f **(58)** - Conquista (Aragon) 8.1f **(60)**
Form - 0006
Record 1999 - 1st:0 2nd:0 3rd:0 Ran:4
1999 Turf 0-4: (5f 4) (gd, frm 3)
Moderate filly. Turf high 41. **K W Hogg [0-4] Michael Burley.*

MISS SCOOTER BHB 45f37a RR 48f 37a
149[8]
4 ch f Beveled (USA) 6.9f **(64)** - Donosa (Posse (USA)) 8.9f **(61)**
Form - 58
Record 1999 - 1st:0 2nd:0 3rd:0 Ran:1
Pre1999 - 1st:0 2nd:2 3rd:0 Ran:10
Win Prizemoney £0 *Total Prizemoney* £1,117
1999 AW 0-1: (10f) (Equi)
Light-framed, moderate filly, effective 5f, acts on sft.
**M P Muggeridge [0-5] Ms Jan Procter (from A P Jones [0-9] Jun 1998).*

MISS SHANNON (IRE) BHB 27a RR
424[11]
4 ch f Mukaddamah (USA) 7.6f **(74)** - Lyphard en (IRE) (Lyphard's Special (USA)) 10.3f **(72)**
Form - 70
Record 1999 - 1st:0 2nd:0 3rd:0 Ran:2
1999 AW 0-2: (6f, 7f) (Fibr 2)
Currently poor filly. AW high 17. **R A Fahey [0-2] Liam Butler.*

MISS SHEMA (USA) BHB 79f RR 75f
1773[10]
3 b f Gulch (USA) 9.6f **(79)** - Fire and Shade (USA) (Shadeed (USA)) 8.2f **(70)**
Form - 3170
Record 1999 - 1st:1 2nd:0 3rd:1 Ran:4
Pre1999 - 1st:0 2nd:0 3rd:0 Ran:1
Win Prizemoney £3,907 *Total Prizemoney* £4,845
Wins * **1999** May Kempto (G-F) 7f 75 <
1999 Turf 1-4: (7f 1-4) (gd, frm 1-3)
Workmanlike, above-average filly, has worn blinkers. Turf high 77 (1st run) - 3rd of 15 to Alpenglow (30 Apr Newmarket 7f frm RF 0948) - also 1st of 16 getting 5lb from Bun Alley (16 May Kempton RF 1259). **B Hanbury [1-5] Abdullah Ali.*

MISS SINCERE (IRE) BHB 53f RR 50f
3745[14]
2 b f Imperial Frontier (USA) 7f **(65)** - Brite Mist (IRE) (Shy Groom (USA)) 10f **(66)**

Form - 0450
Record 1999 - 1st:0 2nd:0 3rd:0 Ran:4
Win Prizemoney £0 *Total Prizemoney* £255
1999 Turf 0-4: (5f 4) (g-f 3, frm)
Fair filly. Turf high 50. **B S Rothwell [0-4] Jim Browne.*

MISS SKYE (IRE) BHB 34f37a RR 24f 37a 1490[7]

4 b f Common Grounds 8.1f **(66)** - Swift Chorus (Music Boy) 6.8f **(57)**
Form - 080007
Record 1999 - 1st:0 2nd:0 3rd:0 Ran:5
Pre1999 - 1st:1 2nd:1 3rd:3 Ran:20
Win Prizemoney £1,850 *Total Prizemoney* £3,276
Wins 1998 *Feb Lingfi (SLW) C 7f 50* <
1999 Turf 0-3: (6f, 7f 2) (g-f 2, frm) 1999 AW 0-2: (7f, 8f) (Equi 2)
Leggy, little account filly, effective 7 to 8f, - acts on Equi, has worn blinkers, favours left handed tracks, favours tight tracks. Turf high 24. AW high 29. **Miss B Sanders [0-6] Mrs Virginia Toft (from B A Pearce [0-5] May 1998).*

MISS SPRINGFIELD BHB 39f RR 40f 4870[14]

2 b f Environment Friend 7.5f **(67)** - Esilam (Frimley Park) 6.5f **(67)**
Form - 000
Record 1999 - 1st:0 2nd:0 3rd:0 Ran:3
1999 Turf 0-3: (5f, 7f 2) (sft, gd 2)
Currently moderate filly. Turf high 40.
**D Morris [0-3] Wacky Racing.*

MISS TAKE (IRE) BHB 40f60a RR 36f 60a 3671[5]

3 ch f Red Sunset 9f **(57)** - Grave Error (Northern Treat (USA)) 6f **(50)**
Form - 242114365633268023170305
Record 1999 - 1st:1 2nd:2 3rd:5 Ran:18
Pre1999 - 1st:3 2nd:3 3rd:1 Ran:19
Win Prizemoney £8,465 *Total Prizemoney* £13,876
Wins * **1999** *Jun Wolver (STD) H 9.4f 53 61+*
* 1998 *Dec Wolver (SLW) S 7f 70+* <
* 1998 *Dec Wolver (STD) 8.5f 69?*
* 1998 *Jun Wolver (STD) S 6f 63*
1999 Turf 0-4: (8f 2, 10f 2) (gd 2, g-f 2) 1999 AW 1-14: (7f 4, 8f 3, 9f 1-3, 10f 3, 12f) (Equi 4, Fibr 1-10)
Light-framed, average filly, effective 6 to 9f, best at 7f, - acts on Fibr, mostly wears blinkers (effectively), likes left handed tracks, likes tight tracks. Turf high 43. AW high 61 - also 1st of 9 giving 14lb to Malchik (16 Jun Wolverhampton RF 2068). She has shown her best form in modest company on the Wolverhampton Fibresand, all of her wins to date have been on that track.
**P D Evans [4-37] Crewe And Nantwich Racing Club.*

MISS TANGO BHB 62f57a RR 63f 57a 4703[5]

2 b f Batshoof 9.5f **(66)** - Spring Flyer (IRE) **(56f 64a)** (Waajib)
Form - 533335
Record 1999 - 1st:0 2nd:0 3rd:4 Ran:6
Win Prizemoney £0 *Total Prizemoney* £1,848
1999 Turf 0-5: (6f 4, 7f) (gd, frm 4) 1999 AW 0-1: (6f) (Fibr)
Average filly, effective 6f, acts on gd to frm. Turf high 63 - 3rd of 6 getting 5lb from Ile Michel (18 Spt Catterick 6f frm RF 4395).
**J Berry [0-6] Codan Trust Company Ltd.*

MISS TOBACCO (USA) RR 107f 3407a[1]

3 ch f Forty Niner (USA) 8.8f **(73)** - Lisaleen (USA) (Northern Dancer) 9.6f **(80)**
Form - 21
1999 Turf 1-1: (8f 1-1) (gd 1-1)
Currently Pattern-class filly. (1st run) - 1st of 9 getting 12lb from El Divino (1 Aug Cologne RF 3407a).
**R Suerland in GER [1-2] R Eisemann.*

MISS TRAXDATA BHB 45f37a RR 40f 37a 318[10]

3 gr f Absalom 7.1f **(56)** - Princess Sharpenup (Lochnager) 6f **(59)**
Form - 00
Record 1999 - 1st:0 2nd:0 3rd:0 Ran:2
Pre1999 - 1st:0 2nd:0 3rd:0 Ran:3
1999 AW 0-2: (8f, 11f) (Fibr 2)
Scopey, moderate filly. AW high 21. **M L W Bell [0-5] Traxdata.*

MISS UNIVERSE (IRE) RR 90f 5030[7]

3 gr f Warning 8.1f **(77)** - Reine D'Beaute (Caerleon (USA)) 8.6f **(71)**
Form - 83677
Record 1999 - 1st:0 2nd:0 3rd:1 Ran:5
Pre1999 - 1st:1 2nd:1 3rd:4 Ran:7
Win Prizemoney £3,766 *Total Prizemoney* £22,095
Wins * 1998 Aug Windso (G-F) 6f 86 <
1999 Turf 0-5: (6f 3, 7f, 8f) (g-s, gd 2, g-f 2)
Neat, useful filly, effective 6 to 7f, best at 6f, acts on sft to frm. Turf high 90. Consistent. **B W Hills [1-12] The Hon Mrs J M Corbett & C Wright.*

MISS UNIVERSITY (USA) RR 27f 2252[9]

3 gr f Beau Genius (CAN) - Gorgeously Divine (USA) (Al Hattab (USA)) 9.3f **(74)**
Form - 00
Record 1999 - 1st:0 2nd:0 3rd:0 Ran:2
1999 Turf 0-2: (7f, 11f) (gd, g-f)
Light-framed, currently little account filly. Turf high 27.
**C N Allen [0-1] Bernard Butt (from C F Wall [0-1] Apr 1999).*

MISS VITA (USA) BHB 33f42a RR 40f 42a 3475[2]

5 b m Alleged (USA) 11.8f **(81)** - Torrid Tango (USA) (Green Dancer (USA)) 10.3f **(74)**
Form - 75620052
Record 1999 - 1st:0 2nd:2 3rd:0 Ran:7
Pre1999 - 1st:1 2nd:2 3rd:2 Ran:15
Win Prizemoney £1,955 *Total Prizemoney* £6,506
Wins * 1998 *Aug Wolver (STD) H 12f 43 48* <
1999 Turf 0-6: (12f 2, 15f 2, 16f 2) (sft, g-s, g-f 3, frm) 1999 AW 0-1: (12f) (Fibr)
Moderate filly, effective 12 to 16f, best at 12f, acts on frm - acts on Fibr. Turf high 40. **R J R Williams [1-22] R J R Williams.*

MISS VIVIEN BHB 37f RR 34f 1879[5]

4 b f Puissance 7.1f **(60)** - Madam Bold (Never so Bold) 6.3f **(66)**
Form - 000385
Record 1999 - 1st:0 2nd:0 3rd:1 Ran:6
Pre1999 - 1st:1 2nd:1 3rd:0 Ran:17
Win Prizemoney £3,665 *Total Prizemoney* £5,342
Wins * 1997 Oct Pontef (G-F) H 6f 72 75 <
1999 Turf 0-6: (5f 4, 6f, 7f) (gd 2, g-f 3, hrd)
Scopey, very moderate filly, effective 7f, acts on frm, likes tight tracks. Turf high 33. Inconsistent. **Miss L A Perratt [1-23] T P Finch.*

MISS WORLD (IRE) BHB 55f64a RR 63f 64a 4995[6]

2 b f Mujadil (USA) 7.7f **(70)** - Great Land (USA) (Friend's Choice (USA)) 8.6f **(57)**
Form - 04604041446
Record 1999 - 1st:1 2nd:0 3rd:0 Ran:11
Win Prizemoney £2,066 *Total Prizemoney* £2,778
Wins * **1999** *Spt Wolver (STD) S 7f 69+* <
1999 Turf 0-8: (5f, 7f 6, 8f) (gd 2, g-f 2, frm 4) 1999 AW 1-3: (6f 2, 7f 1-1) (Equi, Fibr 1-2)
Average filly, effective 7f, - acts on Fibr, likes tight tracks. Turf high 63. AW high 69 (1st run) (began Spt) - 1st of 12 getting 5lb from Seasame Park (18 Spt Wolverhampton RF 4414).
**C N Allen [1-11] Bernard Butt.*

MISTER BENJAMIN (IRE) BHB 74f86a RR 79f 86a 4146[10]

4 b g Polish Patriot (USA) 7.8f **(70)** - Frau Ahuyentante (ARG) (Frari (ARG)) 11.6f **(74)**
Form - 756022320
Record 1999 - 1st:0 2nd:3 3rd:1 Ran:9
Pre1999 - 1st:4 2nd:2 3rd:0 Ran:10
Win Prizemoney £20,312 *Total Prizemoney* £45,239
Wins * 1998 Aug Ascot (G-F) H 10f 82 86 <
* 1998 Jun Haydoc (GD) H 10.5f 79 81
* 1998 Apr Kempto (HVY) H 9f 75 78
* 1997 *Spt Southw (STD) 7f 69+*
1999 Turf 0-9: (10f 5, 11f, 12f 3) (sft, gd 3, g-f 2, frm 2, hrd)
Scopey, above-average gelding, effective 10 to 11f, best at 10f, acts on g-f to frm, best on g-f, has worn blinkers, prefers right handed tracks. Turf high 79. Inconsistent. **S P C Woods [4-19] Mrs Julie Choy.*

MISTER BLOMBERG (IRE) BHB 42f RR 37f 4558[17]

3 b g Distinctly North (USA) 7.4f **(63)** - Ruby Realm (Valiyar) 8.5f **(73)**
Form - 0680
Record 1999 - 1st:0 2nd:0 3rd:0 Ran:4

1999 Turf 0-4: (5f, 6f 2, 8f) (gd, g-f, frm, hrd)
Workmanlike, very moderate gelding. Turf high 37.
**D Nicholls [0-2] Mrs Jan Hopper (from J R Fanshawe [0-2] Jly 1999).*

MISTER CLINTON (IRE) BHB 47f RR 38f 4825[19]
2 ch g Lion Cavern (USA) 7.5f **(74)** - Thewaari (USA) (Eskimo (USA))
Form - 080
Record 1999 - 1st:0 2nd:0 3rd:0 Ran:3
1999 Turf 0-3: (6f 2, 8f) (g-s 2, g-f)
Currently very moderate gelding. Turf high 38 (began Spt).
**K T Ivory [0-3] Miss Lilo Blum.*

MISTER DAMASK RR 22f 2561[17]
4 b g Damister (USA) 9.1f **(66)** - Smelter (Prominer) 5f **(40)**
Form - 0
Record 1999 - 1st:0 2nd:0 3rd:0 Ran:1
Pre1999 - 1st:0 2nd:0 3rd:0 Ran:1
1999 Turf 0-1: (10f) (gd)
Currently little account gelding, often wears blinkers.
**E J Alston [0-2] Peter Onslow.*

MISTER GILL BHB 60f56a RR 63f 56a 4786[10]
2 ch c Suave Dancer (USA) 10.7f **(68)** - Bundled Up (USA) (Sharpen Up) 8.3f **(67)**
Form - 0474300
Record 1999 - 1st:0 2nd:0 3rd:1 Ran:7
Win Prizemoney £0 *Total Prizemoney* £620
1999 Turf 0-6: (5f 3, 6f 2, 7f) (gd 2, g-f 2, frm, hrd) 1999 AW 0-1: (6f) (Equi)
Average colt, effective 6f, acts on hrd. Turf high 63.
**A T Murphy [0-7] Miss G C Young.*

MISTER HARVEY (IRE) BHB 30f RR 18f 1503[14]
3 b g Elbio 9f **(62)** - White Wine (IRE) (Carmelite House (USA))
Form - 000
Record 1999 - 1st:0 2nd:0 3rd:0 Ran:3
1999 Turf 0-3: (8f, 10f, 12f) (gd, g-f, frm)
Scopey, currently poor gelding. Turf high 18.
**M Dods [0-3] C J Payne.*

MISTER JOLSON BHB 56f78a RR 46f 78a 4732[16]
10 br g Latest Model 5.4f **(48)** - Impromptu (My Swanee) 7.6f **(52)**
Form - 7022020070
Record 1999 - 1st:0 2nd:3 3rd:0 Ran:10
Pre1999 - 1st:12 2nd:7 3rd:12 Ran:87
Win Prizemoney £50,558 *Total Prizemoney* £76,501
Wins * 1998 May Bath (FRM) 5.1f 78
* 1997 May Kempto (GD) H 6f 74 76
* 1996 Jun Salisb (G-F) H 5f 75 78
* 1996 Apr Sandow (GD) H 5f 70 73
1999 Turf 0-10: (5f 7, 6f 3) (sft, g-s, gd 4, g-f 2, frm 2)
Moderate gelding, effective 5 to 6f, best at 5f, acts on gd to frm, best on gd, has worn blinkers. Turf high 67. Becoming disappointing. **R J Hodges [12-97] Bob Froome.*

MISTER MAL (IRE) BHB 77f75a RR 74f 75a 5166[3]
3 b g Scenic 10.6f **(66)** - Fashion Parade (Mount Hagen (FR)) 8.4f **(70)**
Form - 33211200313
Record 1999 - 1st:3 2nd:2 3rd:4 Ran:11
Pre1999 - 1st:0 2nd:0 3rd:0 Ran:2
Win Prizemoney £10,195 *Total Prizemoney* £14,732
Wins * **1999** Oct Redcar (SFT) H 7f 70 72 <
* **1999** Jun Leices (G-S) H 7f 61 70+
* **1999** Jun Catter (GD) 7f 61
1999 Turf 3-10: (7f 3-7, 8f 3) (g-s, gd 2-4, g-f, frm 1-3, hrd) 1999 AW 0-1: (7f) (Fibr)
Strong, above-average gelding, effective 7f, acts on g-s to gd - acts on Fibr, best on gd, prefers left handed tracks, likes tight tracks, excels at Catterick. Turf high 74 - 3rd of 15 giving 5lb to Duraid (2 Nov Catterick 7f g-s RF 5166) - also 1st of 18 getting 6lb from Windy Gulch (26 Oct Redcar RF 5072). (1st run) - 2nd of 8 getting 2lb from Polar Ice (25 Jun Wolverhampton 7f Fibr RF 2312).
**J A Glover [3-13] Mrs Andrea Mallinson.*

MISTER MUNNELLY (IRE) BHB 38f30a RR 36f 30a 1385[9]
6 b g Imperial Frontier (USA) 7f **(65)** - Maid of The Ring (Stetchworth (USA))
Form - 0500000
Record 1999 - 1st:0 2nd:0 3rd:0 Ran:4
Pre1999 - 1st:2 2nd:1 3rd:1 Ran:21
Win Prizemoney £7,192 *Total Prizemoney* £8,396
Wins 1997 Jly Killar (G-S) H 8.5f 55 68 <
1996 Jly Leopar (G-F) H 7f 53 52
1999 Turf 0-1: (8f) (g-f) 1999 AW 0-3: (8f 3) (Equi, Fibr 2)
Very moderate gelding, effective 10f, acts on frm, likes left handed tracks. AW high 13.
**J R Jenkins [0-14] Mrs Wendy Jenkins (from C Roche in IRE [1-6] Jly 1997).*

MISTER PQ BHB 46f40a RR 44f 40a 4940[8]
3 ch g Ardkinglass 5f **(64)** - Well Off (Welsh Pageant) 10f **(65)**
Form - 08818548
Record 1999 - 1st:1 2nd:0 3rd:0 Ran:8
Pre1999 - 1st:0 2nd:0 3rd:0 Ran:4
Win Prizemoney £4,900 *Total Prizemoney* £4,900
Wins * **1999** Aug Bright (G-S) H 11.9f 42 51 <
1999 Turf 1-7: (7f, 9f, 10f, 12f 1-4) (gd 1-3, g-f, frm 3) 1999 AW 0-1: (14f) (Fibr)
Light-framed, moderate gelding, likes left handed tracks, likes tight tracks. Turf high 51.
**J G Smyth-Osbourne [1-12] PQ International/Euromedia.*

MISTER RAIDER BHB 37f42a RR 40f 42a 4233[9]
7 ch g Ballacashtal (CAN) 7.9f **(51)** - Martian Melody (Enchantment) 5.4f **(52)**
Form - 0084506040
Record 1999 - 1st:0 2nd:0 3rd:0 Ran:8
Pre1999 - 1st:4 2nd:4 3rd:3 Ran:55
Win Prizemoney £9,920 *Total Prizemoney* £13,924
Wins * 1997 Jun Leices (G-F) SH 6f 44 46
* 1996 *Dec Lingfi (STD) H 5f 50 51* <
* 1996 *Nov Lingfi (STD) H 5f 48 51* <
1996 *Feb Lingfi (STD) 6f 48*
1999 Turf 0-5: (5f 3, 6f 2) (gd 2, g-f, frm 2) 1999 AW 0-3: (6f, 8f 2) (Equi 2, Fibr)
Moderate gelding, effective 6 to 7f, - acts on Equi, mostly wears blinkers, favours left handed tracks, likes tight tracks. Turf high 40. AW high 41. **E A Wheeler [3-42] Raiders Partnership (from S Mellor [1-21] Feb 1996).*

MISTER RAMBO BHB 79f RR 81f 5143[16]
4 b g Rambo Dancer (CAN) 8.4f **(59)** - Ozra (Red Alert) 7.6f **(66)**
Form - 203084717540
Record 1999 - 1st:1 2nd:1 3rd:1 Ran:12
Pre1999 - 1st:2 2nd:1 3rd:0 Ran:11
Win Prizemoney £18,393 *Total Prizemoney* £25,697
Wins * **1999** Jly Ascot (G-F) H 7f 82 84
* 1998 Jun Frankf (GD) L 7.8f 91 <
* 1997 Oct Newbur (GD) 6f 87
1999 Turf 1-12: (6f 3, 7f 1-9) (g-s, gd 1-5, g-f 6)
Well made, decent gelding, effective 6 to 8f, best at 8f, acts on g-s to gd, best on gd, has worn blinkers, excels at Doncaster. Turf high 88 (1st run) - 2nd of 19 giving 4lb to Marsad (26 Mar Doncaster 6f g-s RF 0480) - also 1st of 18 giving 15lb to Zucchero (24 Jly Ascot RF 3089). Consistent.
**B J Meehan [3-23] Abbott Racing Ltd.*

MISTER SUPERB BHB 82f RR 79f 4872[12]
2 ch c Superlative 8.8f **(57)** - Kiveton Komet (Precocious) 8.6f **(62)**
Form - 5640
Record 1999 - 1st:0 2nd:0 3rd:0 Ran:4
Win Prizemoney £0 *Total Prizemoney* £322
1999 Turf 0-4: (5f 2, 6f 2) (gd, frm 3)
Above-average colt. Turf high 79. **V Soane [0-4] Gordon Weston.*

MISTER TRICKY BHB 63f62a RR 66f 62a 4712[1]
4 ch g Magic Ring (IRE) 6.5f **(64)** - Splintering (Sharpo) 7.7f **(59)**
Form - 6021615310165031
Record 1999 - 1st:5 2nd:1 3rd:2 Ran:15
Pre1999 - 1st:2 2nd:0 3rd:1 Ran:9
Win Prizemoney £34,882 *Total Prizemoney* £37,812
Wins * **1999** Oct Bright (G-S) 7f 66 <
* **1999** Jun Goodwo (G-F) H 6f 60 63
* **1999** May Lingfi (G-F) H 6f 56 58
* **1999** Apr Windso (G-S) H 5f 53 54

*** 1999** *Mar Lingfi (STD) 7f 62*
* 1998 *Apr Lingfi (STD) H 7f 53 62*
* 1998 *Mar Lingfi (STD) H 8f 53 56*

1999 Turf 4-11: (5f 1-4, 6f 2-6, 7f 1-1) (gd 3-5, g-f 2, frm 1-4) 1999 AW 1-4: (7f 1-3, 8f) (Equi 1-4)

Workmanlike, average gelding, effective 5 to 8f, best at 7f, acts on gd to frm - acts on Equi, best on gd. Turf high 66 - 1st of 13 from Akalim (4 Oct Brighton RF 4712) - also 1st of 16 getting 19lb from Double Oscar (27 Jun Goodwood RF 2359). AW high 62 - 1st of 4 getting 2lb from Speedy Classic (4 Mar Lingfield RF 0403).

**P Mitchell [7-24] The Magicians.*

MISTER WEBB RR 73f 4587[4]

2 b c Whittingham (IRE) - Ruda (FR) (Free Round (USA)) 11.7f **(70)**

Form - 64

Record 1999 - 1st:0 2nd:0 3rd:0 Ran:2

Win Prizemoney £0 *Total Prizemoney* £232

1999 Turf 0-2: (8f 2) (gd, g-f)

Currently above-average colt. Turf high 62 (began Aug).

**B Smart [0-2] Norman Webb.*

MISTER WESTSOUND BHB 56f50a **RR 57f 50a** 2049[10]

7 b g Cyrano de Bergerac 7.3f **(58)** - Captivate (Mansingh (USA)) 7.4f **(55)**

Form - 603100

Record 1999 - 1st:1 2nd:0 3rd:1 Ran:5
Pre1999 - 1st:6 2nd:10 3rd:9 Ran:72

Win Prizemoney £23,904 *Total Prizemoney* £42,694

Wins * 1999 May Ayr (GD) H 6f 51 57
* 1998 Oct Ayr (HVY) H 6f 46 50
* 1997 Jun Ayr (GD) H 7f 36 49+
* 1997 Jun Hamilt (G-S) H 6f 37 49
* 1995 Aug Hamilt (FRM) H 6f 45 56
* 1995 Aug Ayr (G-F) H 6f 45 51

1999 Turf 1-4: (6f 1-4) (hvy, g-s 1-1, g-f, frm) 1999 AW 0-1: (7f) (Fibr)

Fair gelding, effective 6f, acts on sft to frm, best on sft, mostly wears blinkers. Turf high 57 - 1st of 10 getting 12lb from Anthony Mon Amour (21 May Ayr RF 1362).

**Miss L A Perratt [7-77] David Sutherland.*

Mistle Song called the tune in the Park Hill

MISTLE SONG BHB 107f **RR 110f** 4794[6]

3 b f Nashwan (USA) 10.3f **(79)** - Mistle Thrush (USA) **(86f)** (Storm Bird (CAN)) 10.3f **(74)**

Form - 323426116

Record 1999 - 1st:2 2nd:2 3rd:2 Ran:9
Pre1999 - 1st:0 2nd:0 3rd:0 Ran:1

Win Prizemoney £24,347 *Total Prizemoney* £41,199

Wins * 1999 Spt Doncas (G-F) G3 14.6f 109 <
*** 1999** Aug Ripon (GD) 12.3f 76

1999 Turf 2-9: (10f 2, 12f 1-6, 15f 1-1) (gd 1-5, g-f 1-4)

Rangy, Group-class filly, effective 12 to 15f, best at 12f, acts on gd to g-f, best on gd. Turf high 110 - 6th of 11 to Ramruma (18 Aug York 12f gd RF 3757) - also 1st of 10 from Credit-A-Plenty (8 Spt Doncaster RF 4209). Inconsistent. A bit of a bridesmaid before winning the Park Hill, she was possibly over the top when disappointing at Ascot on her final outing,

**C E Brittain [2-10] Saeed Manana.*

MIST OVER MEUGHER BHB 38f **RR 27f** 5158[23]

2 gr f Thowra (FR) 11.2f **(47)** - Misty View **(12f)** (Absalom) 7.2f **(58)**

Form - 7000

Record 1999 - 1st:0 2nd:0 3rd:0 Ran:4

1999 Turf 0-4: (5f 2, 7f, 8f) (gd 2, frm 2)

Little account filly. Turf high 27.

**C W Fairhurst [0-4] Mrs A M Leggett.*

MISTY BOY BHB 54f **RR 59f** 4430[11]

2 br g Polar Falcon (USA) 9f **(74)** - Misty Silks **(77f 70a)** (Scottish Reel) 7f **(61)**

Form - 760

Record 1999 - 1st:0 2nd:0 3rd:0 Ran:3

1999 Turf 0-3: (5f, 6f, 8f) (g-s, gd 2)

Currently fair gelding. Turf high 59 (began Jly).

**M J Ryan [0-3] Norcroft Park Stud.*

MISTY MAGIC BHB 61f **RR 55f** 4542[10]

2 b f Distinctly North (USA) 7.4f **(63)** - Meadmore Magic (Mansingh (USA)) 7.4f **(55)**

Form - 030

Record 1999 - 1st:0 2nd:0 3rd:1 Ran:3

Win Prizemoney £0 *Total Prizemoney* £277

1999 Turf 0-3: (6f 3) (frm 2, hrd)

Currently fair filly. Turf high 55 (began Aug) - 3rd of 10 to Premier Fois (13 Aug Lingfield 6f frm RF 3610).

**P W Harris [0-3] Grover, Hartshorn, Williams & Willis.*

MISTY MISS BHB 100f **RR 93f** 4389[3]

2 b f Distant Relative 7f **(69)** - Baino Clinic (USA) (Sovereign Dancer (USA)) 11.2f **(68)**

Form - 121103

Record 1999 - 1st:3 2nd:1 3rd:1 Ran:6

Win Prizemoney £45,011 *Total Prizemoney* £48,459

Wins * 1999 *Aug Wolver (STD) 6f 87+*
*** 1999** Jly Goodwo (G-F) G3 5f 93 <
*** 1999** Jly Bath (G-F) S 5.1f 58

1999 Turf 2-5: (5f 2-4, 6f) (gd, g-f 1-1, frm 2, hrd 1-1) 1999 AW 1-1: (6f 1-1) (Fibr 1-1)

Useful filly, effective 5 to 6f, best at 5f, acts on g-f to frm - acts on Fibr. Turf high 93 (began Jly) - also 1st of 10 from Fez (30 Jly Goodwood RF 3236). (1st run) - 1st of 11 giving 8lb to Peruvian Jade (14 Aug Wolverhampton RF 3668). Won a seller on her Bath debut, but has proved herself a lot better than that, winning the Molecomb at 33/1 and following up with a clear-cut victory in the Weatherbys Dash on the Wolverhampton Fibresand. Returned to turf action when disappointing in the Flying Childers but ran a better race at Ayr.

**P D Evans [3-6] Stott-Richmond.*

MISTY ROSE BHB 52f **RR 48f** 4155[6]

2 b f Lugana Beach 7f **(63)** - Rain Splash **(18f)** (Petong) 6.6f **(58)**

Form - 086

Record 1999 - 1st:0 2nd:0 3rd:0 Ran:3

1999 Turf 0-3: (5f 3) (frm 3)

Currently moderate filly. Turf high 48.

**A P Jarvis [0-3] Mrs D B Brazier.*

MITCHAM (IRE) BHB 114f **RR 118f** 4777a[9]

3 br c Hamas (IRE) 8f **(72)** - Arab Scimetar (IRE) (Sure Blade (USA)) 11.3f **(67)**

Form - 23151040

Record 1999 - 1st:2 2nd:1 3rd:1 Ran:8
Pre1999 - 1st:1 2nd:1 3rd:0 Ran:3

Win Prizemoney £105,359 *Total Prizemoney* £115,414

Wins * 1999 Jun Ascot (G-F) G2 5f 118 <

* **1999** May Newmar (GD) H 6f 98 106
* 1998 Spt Warwic (G-F) 6f 81
1999 Turf 2-8: (5f 1-4, 6f 1-4) (sft, gd 2, g-f 2-4, frm)
Workmanlike, high-class colt, effective 5f, acts on g-f. Turf high 118 - 1st of 18 giving 3lb to Flanders (18 Jun Ascot RF 2106). Landed a competitive Newmarket handicap in May and ran well over the very fast five at Epsom on Derby Day. Stepped up on that when coming fast and late to land the King's Stand Stakes at Ascot, but did not quite reach those heights again despite finishing a creditable fourth in a Newbury listed event.
**T G Mills [3-11] T G Mills.*

MITCHELLS MAYHEM RR 25f 629[6]
2 b f Mistertopogigo (IRE) - Mayday Kitty **(51f 40a)** (Interrex (CAN))
Form - 6
Record 1999 - 1st:0 2nd:0 3rd:0 Ran:1
1999 AW 0-1: (5f) (Equi)
Currently little account filly. **W G M Turner [0-1] T Lightbowne.*

MITHAK (USA) BHB 78f **RR 79f** 3815[6]
5 b g Silver Hawk (USA) 11.2f **(85)** - Kapalua Butterfly (USA) (Stage Door Johnny) 10.3f **(84)**
Form - 106
Record 1999 - 1st:1 2nd:0 3rd:0 Ran:3
Pre1999 - 1st:1 2nd:2 3rd:3 Ran:15
Win Prizemoney £7,499 *Total Prizemoney* £20,149
Wins * **1999** May Chepst (GD) H 18f 78 79 <
1997 Mar Doncas (G-F) 10.3f 77+
1999 Turf 1-3: (16f, 18f 1-1, 20f) (gd 1-2, g-f)
Above-average gelding, effective 16 to 19f, acts on sft to g-f, has worn blinkers, prefers left handed tracks. Turf high 79 (1st run) - 1st of 13 giving 29lb to Sharaf (19 May Chepstow RF 1329). Consistent. Fit from hurdling, he became a rare winner on the Flat for his trainer when narrowly landing a staying handicap at Chepstow, but has been well beaten on the level since.
**D Nicholson [3-8] P A Deal & J S Dale (from Mrs J R Ramsden [0-5] Spt 1998).*

MITHRAIC (IRE) BHB 45f **RR 46f** 3597[3]
7 b g Kefaah (USA) 11.2f **(64)** - Persian's Glory (Prince Tenderfoot (USA)) 9f **(61)**
Form - 3313
Record 1999 - 1st:1 2nd:0 3rd:3 Ran:4
Pre1999 - 1st:2 2nd:4 3rd:1 Ran:13
Win Prizemoney £7,025 *Total Prizemoney* £11,736
Wins * **1999** Aug Newcas (FRM) S 12.4f 46
* 1996 Jly Mussel (G-F) 11.1f 59 <
* 1996 Jly Hamilt (G-F) C 11.1f 59 <
1999 Turf 1-4: (11f, 12f 1-2, 14f) (g-f 1-2, frm 2)
Moderate gelding, has worn blinkers. Turf high 46. Consistent.
**W S Cunningham [6-36] A D Tate (from J W Watts [0-5] Aug 1995).*

MITHRAS (USA) RR 87f 4211[5]
3 ch c Theatrical 11.5f **(78)** - Star Glimmer (USA) (General Assembly (USA)) 10f **(68)**
Form - 145
Record 1999 - 1st:1 2nd:0 3rd:0 Ran:3
Win Prizemoney £3,940 *Total Prizemoney* £4,534
Wins * **1999** Jly Sandow (G-F) 10f 87 <
1999 Turf 1-3: (10f 1-2, 12f) (gd 2, frm 1-1)
Scopey, currently useful colt. Turf high 87 (1st run) (began Jly) - 1st of 12 giving 5lb to Whispering (21 Jly Sandown RF 3019).
**J H M Gosden [1-3] Sheikh Mohammed.*

MITIE ACCESS (IRE) BHB 35f **RR 9f** 2125[12]
3 ch f Mujtahid (USA) 7.4f **(69)** - Simply Marilyn (IRE) (Simply Great (FR)) 8.2f **(65)**
Form - 0000
Record 1999 - 1st:0 2nd:0 3rd:0 Ran:4
Pre1999 - 1st:0 2nd:0 3rd:1 Ran:3
Win Prizemoney £0 *Total Prizemoney* £530
1999 Turf 0-3: (7f, 8f, 10f) (g-f, frm 2) 1999 AW 0-1: (8f) (Fibr)
Light-framed, very poor filly, effective 7f, acts on frm. Turf high 9.
**C A Dwyer [0-7] David Bowkett.*

MIXED CURRENCY (USA) BHB 79f **RR 75f** 1047[6]
3 b br c Silver Hawk (USA) 11.2f **(85)** - Copperhead (USA) (Hawaii) 9.4f **(66)**
Form - 786
Record 1999 - 1st:0 2nd:0 3rd:0 Ran:3
Pre1999 - 1st:0 2nd:0 3rd:1 Ran:1
Win Prizemoney £0 *Total Prizemoney* £515
1999 Turf 0-3: (10f 2, 12f) (g-s, g-f 2)
Lengthy, above-average colt. Turf high 75.
**J H M Gosden [0-4] Sheikh Mohammed.*

MIXED OPINION (IRE) BHB 38f **RR 43f** 3475[4]
6 b g Be My Guest (USA) 10.2f **(66)** - Outside Pressure (Shernazar) 10.2f **(73)**
Form - 044
Record 1999 - 1st:0 2nd:0 3rd:0 Ran:3
Pre1999 - 1st:1 2nd:0 3rd:0 Ran:9
Win Prizemoney £2,740 *Total Prizemoney* £3,069
Wins 1997 Jly Down R (G-F) H 12.3f 56 58 <
1999 Turf 0-3: (12f, 15f, 16f) (g-f 2, frm)
Moderate gelding, often wears blinkers. Turf high 43. Inconsistent.
**C F C Jackson [0-12] C F C Jackson (from D K Weld in IRE [1-9] Spt 1997).*

MIXSTERTHETRIXSTER (USA) BHB 96f **RR 90f** 3756[11]
3 b g Alleged (USA) 11.8f **(81)** - Parliament House (USA) (General Assembly (USA)) 10f **(68)**
Form - 540
Record 1999 - 1st:0 2nd:0 3rd:0 Ran:3
Pre1999 - 1st:2 2nd:0 3rd:2 Ran:5
Win Prizemoney £8,410 *Total Prizemoney* £18,521
Wins * 1998 Spt Haydoc (GD) 8.1f 87 <
* 1998 Jun Newcas (GD) 7f 80+
1999 Turf 0-3: (10f 2, 14f) (gd 2, g-f)
Scopey, useful gelding, effective 7 to 8f, best at 7f, acts on gd to frm, best on frm. Turf high 90. Consistent. Tended to pull too hard, and was gelded in an attempt to settle him. Has gone hurdling.
**T D Easterby [2-8] M P Burke.*

MIZHAR (USA) BHB 93f **RR 94df** 1295[6]
3 b br c Dayjur (USA) 6.8f **(79)** - Futuh (USA) (Diesis) 9.3f **(69)**
Form - 006
Record 1999 - 1st:0 2nd:0 3rd:0 Ran:3
Pre1999 - 1st:2 2nd:0 3rd:0 Ran:4
Win Prizemoney £9,310 *Total Prizemoney* £9,680
Wins * 1998 Oct Newmar () H 6f 91 94 <
* 1998 Spt Nottin (GD) 6.1f 82
1999 Turf 0-3: (6f 3) (gd, g-f 2)
Scopey, useful colt, effective 6f, acts on g-f, has worn blinkers. Turf high 75. **E A L Dunlop [2-7] Hamdan Al Maktoum.*

MIZ TAW BHB 46f **RR 14f** 1382[16]
3 b f Mizoram (USA) - Brown Taw (Whistlefield) 5f **(55)**
Form - 000
Record 1999 - 1st:0 2nd:0 3rd:0 Ran:3
Pre1999 - 1st:0 2nd:0 3rd:0 Ran:3
1999 Turf 0-3: (5f, 7f, 8f) (g-s, g-f, frm)
Neat, poor filly. Turf high 14. **J R Jenkins [0-6] Mrs Carol Davis.*

MO-ADDAB (IRE) BHB 45f **RR 41f** 3864[16]
9 b g Waajib 8.9f **(67)** - Tissue Paper (Touch Paper) 6.8f **(57)**
Form - 000
Record 1999 - 1st:0 2nd:0 3rd:0 Ran:3
Pre1999 - 1st:5 2nd:8 3rd:6 Ran:43
Win Prizemoney £47,393 *Total Prizemoney* £80,122
Wins * 1997 May Chepst (GD) 8.1f 69
* 1995 Spt Ascot (G-S) H 8f 73 80 <
* 1995 Aug Pontef (G-F) H 8f 72 72
1999 Turf 0-3: (8f 2, 10f) (gd, frm 2)
Moderate gelding. Turf high 41 (began Jly).
**A C Stewart [5-46] S J Hammond.*

MODEM (IRE) BHB 54f **RR 58f** 4901[11]
2 b c Midhish - Holy Water (Monseigneur (USA)) 7.7f **(63)**
Form - 800
Record 1999 - 1st:0 2nd:0 3rd:0 Ran:3
1999 Turf 0-3: (7f 2, 8f) (g-s, gd, frm)
Currently fair colt. Turf high 58 (began Spt).
**M H Tompkins [0-3] www.raceworld co uk.*

MODERN ERA (USA) RR 79f 5140[6]
3 ch f Diesis 9f **(80)** - Timely (Kings Lake (USA)) 10.8f **(67)**
Form - 106
Record 1999 - 1st:1 2nd:0 3rd:0 Ran:3
Win Prizemoney £3,826 *Total Prizemoney* £3,987
Wins 1999 Aug Newcas (GD) 7f 75 <
1999 Turf 1-3: (7f 1-1, 8f 2) (g-s, gd, g-f 1-1)
Lengthy, currently above-average filly. Turf high 79 (began Aug) - also 1st of 6 from Devil's Imp (20 Aug Newcastle RF 3801). Unraced at two, she battled on well to make a winning debut at Newcastle, but did not seem to handle the heavy ground when well beaten in a Listed event at Saint-Cloud next time.
**A G Foster [0-1] R E Sangster (from P W Chapple-Hyam [1-2] Spt 1999).*

MODEST HOPE (USA) BHB 11f21a **RR 9f 21a** 5101[15]
12 b g Blushing Groom (FR) 10.2f **(80)** - Key Dancer (USA) (Nijinsky (CAN)) 10.3f **(77)**
Form - 8352800880
Record 1999 - 1st:0 2nd:1 3rd:1 Ran:9
Pre1999 - 1st:11 2nd:8 3rd:18 Ran:102
Win Prizemoney £29,709 *Total Prizemoney* £45,698
Wins * 1998 Aug Bright (FRM) SH 11.9f 26 34
1996 *Jan Southw (STD) H 11f 44 48*
1995 *Mar Southw (STD) H 11f 45 49*
1999 Turf 0-3: (12f 2, 14f) (g-s 2, g-f) 1999 AW 0-6: (11f 3, 12f, 13f, 14f) (Equi, Fibr 5)
Little account gelding, effective 11 to 13f, best at 12f, acts on g-f to frm - acts on AW, favours tight tracks. Turf high 9. AW high 28 - 2nd of 10 getting 6lb from Katie's Cracker (6 Feb Lingfield 13f Equi RF 0234).
**Mrs S Lamyman [1-23] P Lamyman (from B Richmond [5-64] Spt 1996).*

MODESTY FORBIDS BHB 41f **RR 22f** 3749[17]
3 b f Formidable (USA) 7.8f **(60)** - Ming Blue (Primo Dominie) 6.2f **(80)**
Form - 000
Record 1999 - 1st:0 2nd:0 3rd:0 Ran:3
Pre1999 - 1st:0 2nd:0 3rd:1 Ran:4
Win Prizemoney £0 *Total Prizemoney* £292
1999 Turf 0-3: (7f 2, 8f) (g-f, frm 2)
Neat, little account filly, effective 7f, acts on frm. Turf high 22 (began Jly).
**J M Bradley [0-3] R D Willis (from P G Murphy [0-4] Oct 1998).*

MODESTY HALL BHB 41f32a **RR 44f 32a** 877[16]
4 b f Saddlers' Hall (IRE) 10.5f **(65)** - Shy Dolly (Cajun) 5.2f **(54)**
Form - 6750
Record 1999 - 1st:0 2nd:0 3rd:0 Ran:4
1999 Turf 0-2: (8f, 10f) (sft, gd) 1999 AW 0-2: (10f, 12f) (Equi 2)
Moderate filly. Turf high 44. AW high 16.
**M Kettle [0-4] Graham Racing.*

MODISH (IRE) BHB 97f **RR 89f** 4931[4]
2 b c Tenby 10.4f **(76)** - Moorfield Daisy (IRE) (Waajib)
Form - 7114
Record 1999 - 1st:2 2nd:0 3rd:0 Ran:4
Win Prizemoney £7,203 *Total Prizemoney* £8,181
Wins * 1999 Spt Ayr (G-S) 8f 89 <
*** 1999** Aug Beverl (GD) 7.5f 82+
1999 Turf 2-4: (7f 1-2, 8f 1-2) (gd 1-1, g-f 1-3)
Useful colt. Turf high 89 - 4th of 6 to Hataab (18 Oct Pontefract 8f g-f RF 4931) - also 1st of 9 getting 3lb from Eternal Spring (18 Spt Ayr RF 4388). Stepped up on his debut to land a Beverley auction race and followed up in decent company at Ayr.
**M H Tompkins [2-4] Mrs Beryl Lockey.*

MODUS OPERANDI (USA) RR 86f 2249[5]
3 b c Known Fact (USA) 8.3f **(72)** - Proud Lou (USA) (Proud Clarion) 8.7f **(82)**
Form - 8415
Record 1999 - 1st:1 2nd:0 3rd:0 Ran:4
Win Prizemoney £2,960 *Total Prizemoney* £3,293
Wins * 1999 Jun Redcar (FRM) 10f 79 <
1999 Turf 1-4: (8f, 10f 1-2, 12f) (gd, g-f, frm 1-2)
Well made, useful colt. Turf high 86 - also 1st of 11 from Raaqi (1 Jun Redcar RF 1653). Made hard work of landing the odds in a Redcar maiden and looks one of the stable's lesser lights.
**H R A Cecil [1-4] K Abdulla.*

MOET (IRE) BHB 43f61a **RR 43f 61a** 3104[10]
4 b f Mac's Imp (USA) 5.6f **(54)** - Comfrey Glen (Glenstal (USA)) 10.1f **(64)**
Form - 16400000
Record 1999 - 1st:0 2nd:0 3rd:0 Ran:6
Pre1999 - 1st:2 2nd:0 3rd:1 Ran:9
Win Prizemoney £7,064 *Total Prizemoney* £8,093
Wins * 1998 *Nov Southw (STD) H 6f 55 66+* <
* 1998 Spt Thirsk (GD) 6f 52
1999 Turf 0-4: (5f, 6f 2, 7f) (gd 3, frm) 1999 AW 0-2: (6f, 7f) (Fibr 2)
Scopey, fair filly, effective 6f, - acts on Fibr. Turf high 43. AW high 56. Becoming disappointing. **J L Eyre [2-15] Mrs Kate Watson.*

MOGIN BHB 31f43a **RR 39f 43a** 3276[7]
6 ch m Komaite (USA) 6.9f **(61)** - Misdevious (USA) (Alleged (USA)) 10f **(76)**
Form - 270747
Record 1999 - 1st:0 2nd:1 3rd:0 Ran:6
Pre1999 - 1st:3 2nd:3 3rd:2 Ran:34
Win Prizemoney £6,463 *Total Prizemoney* £10,651
Wins 1998 *Jan Lingfi (STD) H 10f 42 46*
1998 *Jan Lingfi (STD) H 8f 38 41*
1996 Aug Bright (G-F) 7f 51 <
1999 AW 0-6: (8f 2, 10f 4) (Equi 5, Fibr)
Fair mare, has worn blinkers, favours left handed tracks. AW high 57. Inconsistent.
**A J McNae [0-6] Les Dutton (from T J Naughton [3-26] Aug 1998).*

MOHICAN PRINCESS RR 38f 2617[4]
3 b f Shirley Heights 12.1f **(76)** - Mohican Girl (Dancing Brave (USA)) 8.4f **(76)**
Form - 4
Record 1999 - 1st:0 2nd:0 3rd:0 Ran:1
Win Prizemoney £0 *Total Prizemoney* £265
1999 Turf 0-1: (10f) (frm)
Unfurnished, currently very moderate filly.
**R M H Cowell [0-1] C Hellyer.*

MOIAVA (FR) RR 110f 1358a[11]
3 b f Bering 9.6f **(80)** - Mona Stella (USA) (Nureyev (USA)) 8.7f **(78)**
Form - 00
1999 Turf 0-2: (8f 2) (gd, frm)
Currently Group-class filly. Turf high 93. Looked a very useful prospect when landing the Criterium de Maisons-Laffitte in testing ground on her final start at two. Started favourite for the 1000 Guineas, but was disappointing, and appeared not to have trained on. **Mme C Head in FR [1-3].*

MOI CANARD BHB 34f38a **RR 39f 38a** 43[10]
6 ch g Bold Owl 9.7f **(47)** - Royal Scots Greys (Blazing Saddles (AUS)) 6.7f **(46)**
Form - 0
Record 1999 - 1st:0 2nd:0 3rd:0 Ran:1
Pre1999 - 1st:6 2nd:7 3rd:2 Ran:42
Win Prizemoney £16,644 *Total Prizemoney* £24,252
Wins * 1996 *Mar Lingfi (STD) H 7f 69 70* <
* 1996 *Feb Lingfi (STD) H 7f 62 68*
1995 *Nov Lingfi (STD) C 6f 66*
1995 Aug Hamilt (FRM) C 6f 66
1995 *May Wolver (STD) S 6f 66?*
1995 *May Southw (STD) S 5f 66*
1999 AW 0-1: (7f) (Equi)
Very moderate gelding, has worn blinkers.
**B A Pearce [2-26] Mrs D Crick (from Pat Mitchell [0-4] Apr 1998).*

MOISEYEV (USA) RR 102f 4058a[3]
3 b c Nureyev (USA) 8.4f **(84)** - Madame Premier (USA) **00**
Form - 2133
1999 Turf 1-4: (8f 1-4) (g-s, g-f 1-2, frm)
Very useful colt, effective 8f, acts on g-s to g-f, often wears blinkers. Turf high 102 - also 1st of 4 from Sapphire Trio (1 Aug Galway RF 3345b). He was a shade disappointing and may improve when tried beyond a mile. **A P O'Brien in IRE [2-6] Mrs John Magnier.*

MOJACK RR 791[4]
2 ch f Interrex (CAN) 7.7f **(51)** - Jubilata (USA) (The Minstrel (CAN)) 10f **(72)**
Form - 4
Record 1999 - 1st:0 2nd:0 3rd:0 Ran:1
1999 Turf 0-1: (5f) (gd)
Very poor filly. (DEAD) **W G M Turner [0-1] O J Stokes.*

MOLA (IRE) BHB 45f **RR** 1016[18]
4 b f Robellino (USA) 9.5f **(68)** - Epure (Bellypha) 9.8f **(73)**
Form - 0000
Record 1999 - 1st:0 2nd:0 3rd:0 Ran:4
Pre1999 - 1st:0 2nd:0 3rd:0 Ran:3
Win Prizemoney £0 *Total Prizemoney* £267
1999 Turf 0-3: (11f, 14f, 15f) (hvy, gd, frm) 1999 AW 0-1: (10f) (Equi)
Scopey, poor filly.
**M J Ryan [0-4] Peter Scott (from Mrs J Cecil [0-3] Jly 1998).*

MOLE CREEK BHB 82f **RR 80f** 1346[5]
4 gr f Unfuwain (USA) 11.4f **(74)** -Nicholas Grey (Track Spare) 8.8f **(62)**
Form - 05
Record 1999 - 1st:0 2nd:0 3rd:0 Ran:2
Pre1999 - 1st:1 2nd:6 3rd:0 Ran:9
Win Prizemoney £3,501 *Total Prizemoney* £13,976
Wins * 1998 Oct Warwic (GD) 10.8f 83 <
1999 Turf 0-2: (12f, 14f) (gd, frm)
Leggy, decent filly, effective 10 to 12f, best at 10f, acts on sft to g-f. Turf high 80. **J R Fanshawe [1-11] Lord Vestey.*

MOLLY BROWN BHB 86f **RR 75f** 3415[5]
2 b f Rudimentary (USA) 8.2f **(66)** - Sinking (Midyan (USA)) 6f **(60)**
Form - 105
Record 1999 - 1st:1 2nd:0 3rd:0 Ran:3
Win Prizemoney £3,290 *Total Prizemoney* £3,481
Wins * **1999** Jun Haydoc (GD-) 5f 83+ <
1999 Turf 1-3: (5f 1-2, 6f) (gd 1-1, g-f 2)
Currently above-average filly. Turf high 83 (1st run) - 1st of 7 getting 5lb from Chase The Pennant (5 Jun Haydock RF 1767). She won very easily on her Haydock debut, but was well beaten in the Norfolk. It looks as if the minimum trip is barely adequate and she is bred to need further. **R Hannon [1-3] The Sinking Fast Partnership.*

MOLLY MACK BHB 25f **RR 6f** 4228[13]
3 b f Thowra (FR) 11.2f **(47)** - Gangawayhame (Lochnager) 6f **(59)**
Form - 000
Record 1999 - 1st:0 2nd:0 3rd:0 Ran:3
Pre1999 - 1st:0 2nd:0 3rd:0 Ran:4
1999 Turf 0-3: (6f, 7f, 8f) (g-f, frm 2)
Light-framed, very poor filly. Turf high 6.
**A W Carroll [0-7] R T C Racing.*

MOLLY MUSIC BHB 33f33a **RR 33f 33a** 119[7]
5 b m Music Boy 6.5f **(56)** - Carlton Glory (Blakeney) 10.5f **(64)**
Form - 6857
Record 1999 - 1st:0 2nd:0 3rd:0 Ran:2
Pre1999 - 1st:1 2nd:4 3rd:5 Ran:38
Win Prizemoney £3,096 *Total Prizemoney* £8,049
Wins * 1997 *Jun Southw (STD) H 8f 55 65* <
1999 AW 0-2: (7f, 8f) (Fibr 2)
Very moderate filly, effective 7 to 8f, - acts on Fibr, has worn blinkers, likes left handed tracks, favours tight tracks. AW high 32.
**G G Margarson [1-40] William Hattersley.*

MOLLYTIME BHB 23f **RR 20f** 3817[11]
3 ch f Timeless Times (USA) 6.1f **(56)** - Merry Molly **(22f)** (Deploy)
Form - 00050
Record 1999 - 1st:0 2nd:0 3rd:0 Ran:5
Pre1999 - 1st:0 2nd:0 3rd:0 Ran:3
1999 Turf 0-5: (6f, 8f 2, 10f 2) (gd, g-f 2, frm 2)
Leggy, little account filly. Turf high 20.
**N Bycroft [0-8] G W H Burnett.*

MOLY RR 62f 5193[5]
3 b f Inchinor 8.9f **(64)** - Circe's Isle (Be My Guest (USA)) 9.3f **(67)**
Form - 45
Record 1999 - 1st:0 2nd:0 3rd:0 Ran:2
Win Prizemoney £0 *Total Prizemoney* £242
1999 Turf 0-2: (8f, 10f) (g-s, gd)
Unfurnished, currently average filly. Turf high 62 (began Spt).
**R Charlton [0-2] A E Oppenheimer.*

MOLYNEUX BHB 68f73a **RR 65f 73a** 5022[11]
3 b g Marju (IRE) 9.2f **(76)** - Mahasin (USA) (Danzig (USA)) 8.4f **(76)**
Form - 6011700
Record 1999 - 1st:2 2nd:0 3rd:0 Ran:7
Win Prizemoney £7,110 *Total Prizemoney* £7,110
Wins * **1999** *Jly Southw (STD) H 6f 68 74* <
* **1999** Jun Lingfi (G-F) 6f 65
1999 Turf 1-5: (6f 1-3, 7f, 10f) (gd, g-f 2, frm 1-2) 1999 AW 1-2: (6f 1-1, 7f) (Fibr 1-2)
Workmanlike, above-average gelding, effective 6f, acts on frm - acts on Fibr. Turf high 65 - 1st of 6 giving 5lb to Fairy Contessa (25 Jun Lingfield RF 2294). AW high 74 (1st run) (began Jly) - 1st of 15 giving 6lb to So Willing (8 Jly Southwell RF 2650). Got off the mark with a narrow victory in a modest maiden at Lingfield in June. He followed up on the Southwell Fibresand in July despite not handling the bend very well, but was disappointing when stepped up to seven furlongs at the same track just two days later. Likely to be placed to win a race or two next season.
**Sir Mark Prescott [2-7] Anthony Speelman.*

MOMENTOUS JONES BHB 64f **RR 65f** 5192[2]
2 b g Emperor Jones (USA) - Ivory Moment (USA) (Sir Ivor) 10.2f **(70)**
Form - 0552
Record 1999 - 1st:0 2nd:1 3rd:0 Ran:4
Win Prizemoney £0 *Total Prizemoney* £654
1999 Turf 0-3: (7f, 8f 2) (gd 2, frm) 1999 AW 0-1: (7f) (Fibr)
Average gelding. Turf high 65 (began Spt) - 2nd of 17 giving 5lb to Ede'iff (4 Nov Windsor 8f gd RF 5192).
**M R Channon [0-4] Kingsdown Racing.*

MONACLE BHB 39f37a **RR 38f 37a** 4714[F]
5 b g Saddlers' Hall (IRE) 10.5f **(65)** - Endless Joy (Law Society (USA)) 9.9f **(70)**
Form - 7361D54083F
Record 1999 - 1st:1 2nd:0 3rd:2 Ran:11
Pre1999 - 1st:0 2nd:0 3rd:0 Ran:7
Win Prizemoney £2,070 *Total Prizemoney* £2,678
Wins * **1999** May Yarmou (FRM) H 11.5f 32 39 <
1999 Turf 1-7: (11f 1-3, 12f 3, 16f) (gd 2, g-f, frm 1-3, hrd) 1999 AW 0-4: (12f, 14f, 16f 2) (Fibr 4)
Very moderate gelding, effective 11 to 16f, best at 11f, acts on gd to frm - acts on Fibr, has worn blinkers. Turf high 39 (1st run) - 1st of 10 getting 30lb from Hibernate (26 May Yarmouth RF 1513). AW high 36 - 3rd of 16 getting 15lb from He's Got Wings (12 Feb Southwell 16f Fibr RF 0283).
**John Berry [1-11] Clearview Partnership (from D Morris [0-7] Oct 1997).*

MONACO (IRE) BHB 30f **RR 39f** 4591[16]
5 b g Classic Music (USA) 7.2f **(57)** - Larosterna (Busted) 10.2f **(61)**
Form - 00030
Record 1999 - 1st:0 2nd:0 3rd:1 Ran:5
Pre1999 - 1st:0 2nd:0 3rd:1 Ran:10
Win Prizemoney £0 *Total Prizemoney* £1,359
1999 Turf 0-5: (5f, 8f, 9f 3) (gd 2, g-f 2, frm)
Very moderate gelding, effective 9f, acts on frm, likes right handed tracks, likes tight tracks. Turf high 39 - 3rd of 13 to Murphy's Gold (6 Spt Hamilton 9f frm RF 4163).
**R Allan [0-17] Ian Flannigan (from L M Cumani [0-5] Aug 1997).*

MONACO GOLD (IRE) BHB 44f54a **RR 43f 54a** 2536[11]
7 b g Durgam (USA) 12.3f **(53)** - Monaco Ville (Rheingold) 10.4f **(62)**
Form - 244441410
Record 1999 - 1st:2 2nd:1 3rd:0 Ran:9
Pre1999 - 1st:6 2nd:3 3rd:2 Ran:24
Win Prizemoney £20,549 *Total Prizemoney* £23,685

Wins	* **1999**	*Jun Lingfi*	*(STD)*	*SH*	*13f*	*50*	*57*	
	* **1999**	*May Lingfi*	*(STD)*	*SH*	*16f*	*45*	*56*	
	* 1998	*May Lingfi*	*(STD)*	*SH*	*16f*	*47*	*54*	
	* 1998	*Mar Southw*	*(STD)*	*C*	*14f*		*54*	
	1997	Jly Hamilt	(SFT)	C	11.1f		40	
	1997	Jun Hamilt	(SFT)	C	12.1f		63	<
	1996	Aug Hamilt	(G-F)	H	13f	39	43	
	1996	Jun Ayr	(G-F)	H	13.1f	35	39	

1999 Turf 0-2: (14f, 16f) (g-f 2) 1999 AW 2-7: (12f 2, 13f 1-1, 15f 2, 16f 1-2) (Equi 2-2, Fibr 5)

Fair gelding, has broken blood-vessels, effective 12 to 16f, - acts on AW, best on Equi, has worn blinkers, favours left handed tracks, excels at Lingfield, likes Wolverhampton. Turf high 43. AW high 57 - 1st of 13 giving 20lb to Katie's Cracker (26 Jun Lingfield RF 2329) - also 1st of 12 giving 18lb to Where's Albert (29 May Lingfield RF 1582).

**D J S Cosgrove [4-17] D J S Cosgrove (from Mrs M Reveley [4-13] Aug 1997).*

MONASABA MUBARAKA RR 68[8]

5 b g Rainbow Quest (USA) 11.2f **(81)** - Blessed Event (Kings Lake (USA)) 10.8f **(67)**

Form - 8

Record 1999 - 1st:0 2nd:0 3rd:0 Ran:1

1999 AW 0-1: (12f) (Fibr)

Formerly very poor gelding. **A Barrow [0-8] A P Smith.*

MONASHEE MOUNTAIN (USA) RR 108+f 5171a[1]

2 b c Danzig (USA) 8.1f **(88)** - Prospectors Delite (USA)

Form - 11

1999 Turf 2-2: (6f 1-1, 7f 1-1) (sft 1-1, gd 1-1)

Currently Pattern-class colt. Turf high 108 - 1st of 5 from Bashkir (25 Oct Leopardstown RF 5171a). Powerfully built, he was selected to contest his maiden from an original entry of six from the O'Brien camp. Running a little green that day he nevertheless landed the odds without being extended, and did the same in a soft Group Three next time. He looks open to plenty of improvement, and could prove very useful.

**A P O'Brien in IRE [2-2] Michael Tabor.*

MONAWARA (IRE) RR 82f 2245[3]

2 b f Namaqualand (USA) - Monus (IRE) (Thatching) 8f **(66)**

Form - 3

Record 1999 - 1st:0 2nd:0 3rd:1 Ran:1

Win Prizemoney £0 *Total Prizemoney* £492

1999 Turf 0-1: (5f) (g-f)

Currently decent filly. (1st run) - 3rd of 11 to Kelso Magic (23 Jun Salisbury 5f g-f RF 2245). **M R Channon [0-1] Ahmed Al Shafar.*

MON BRUCE BHB 36f66a RR 23f 66a 2222[14]

5 ch g Beveled (USA) 6.9f **(64)** - Pendona (Blue Cashmere) 6.4f **(54)**

Form - 700000

Record 1999 - 1st:0 2nd:0 3rd:0 Ran:6

Pre1999 - 1st:3 2nd:3 3rd:3 Ran:28

Win Prizemoney £7,531 *Total Prizemoney* £11,912

Wins									
*	1997	Spt	Pontef	(G-F)	H	5f	57	60	
	1997	*Spt*	*Southw*	*(STD)*	*C*	*5f*		*66*	<
	1997	*Apr*	*Wolver*	*(STD)*		*6f*		*53*	

1999 Turf 0-6: (5f 4, 6f 2) (gd, g-f, frm 4)

Average gelding, effective 5f, acts on frm, has worn blinkers. Turf high 53. Becoming disappointing.

**M Dods [1-19] N A Riddell (from W R Muir [2-15] Spt 1997).*

MONCHANIA BHB 60f55a RR 3f 55a 247[10]

4 ch f Mon Tresor 7.9f **(60)** - Sugar Owl (Bold Owl) 8.5f **(45)**

Form - 2100

Record 1999 - 1st:1 2nd:1 3rd:0 Ran:4

Pre1999 - 1st:1 2nd:0 3rd:0 Ran:4

Win Prizemoney £5,136 *Total Prizemoney* £5,557

Wins									
*	**1999**	*Jan*	*Wolver*	*(STD)*	*S*	*8.5f*		*55*	
*	1998	*Jan*	*Wolver*	*(STD)*		*8.5f*		*79+*	<

1999 AW 1-4: (8f 1-2, 9f 2) (Fibr 1-4)

Light-framed, fair filly, effective 8f, - acted on Fibr, had worn blinkers. AW high 55. (DEAD)

**J L Spearing [2-8] The Not So Risky Partnership.*

MONDRAGON BHB 60f60a RR 67?f 60a 2514[4]

9 b g Niniski (USA) 13.2f **(67)** - La Lutine (My Swallow) 9.2f **(71)**

Form - 04

Record 1999 - 1st:0 2nd:0 3rd:0 Ran:2

Pre1999 - 1st:5 2nd:10 3rd:10 Ran:52

Win Prizemoney £15,953 *Total Prizemoney* £37,116

Wins								
*	1998	Aug	Beverl	(G-F)	H	16.2f	59	62
*	1998	Jly	Redcar	(G-F)	H	16f	55	57

1999 Turf 0-2: (14f, 16f) (gd, g-f)

Average gelding, effective 16f, acts on g-s to hrd - acts on Fibr, likes right handed tracks, favours tight tracks, excels at Redcar and Beverley. Turf high 52. **Mrs M Reveley [6-55] D Young.*

MONDURU RR 54f 3645[11]

2 b c Lion Cavern (USA) 7.5f **(74)** - Bint Albadou (IRE) (Green Desert (USA)) 8.6f **(78)**

Form - 0

Record 1999 - 1st:0 2nd:0 3rd:0 Ran:1

1999 Turf 0-1: (6f) (g-f)

Currently fair colt. **W R Muir [0-1] J Haim.*

MONIS (IRE) BHB 38f38a RR 44f 38a 2109[12]

8 ch g Waajib 8.9f **(67)** - Gratify (Grundy) 10.3f **(65)**

Form - 70020

Record 1999 - 1st:0 2nd:1 3rd:0 Ran:5

Pre1999 - 1st:3 2nd:4 3rd:7 Ran:47

Win Prizemoney £7,974 *Total Prizemoney* £17,317

Wins								
*	1998	Oct	Newcas	(SFT)	CH	8f	33	39
*	1997	Oct	Newcas	(G-F)	CH	8f	30	37

1999 Turf 0-5: (8f 3, 9f, 10f) (hvy, gd 2, g-f 2)

Moderate gelding, effective 8f, acts on g-s, has worn blinkers. Turf high 44.

**B Ellison [3-20] C E Sherry (from Ronald Thompson [0-8] Aug 1997).*

MONKEY BUSINESS RR 70f 3913[4]

2 b f Warning 8.1f **(77)** - Rosie Sweetheart (IRE) **(70f)** (Sadler's Wells (USA)) 10f **(76)**

Form - 34

Record 1999 - 1st:0 2nd:0 3rd:1 Ran:2

Win Prizemoney £0 *Total Prizemoney* £832

1999 Turf 0-2: (6f, 7f) (gd, frm)

Currently above-average filly. Turf high 70 (began Jly).

**N A Callaghan [0-2] Wafic Said.*

MONKSTON POINT (IRE) BHB 96f RR 94f 5030[8]

3 b c Fayruz 6.6f **(63)** - Doon Belle (Ardoon) 7.3f **(53)**

Form - 560000208

Record 1999 - 1st:0 2nd:1 3rd:0 Ran:9

Pre1999 - 1st:3 2nd:0 3rd:4 Ran:8

Win Prizemoney £16,493 *Total Prizemoney* £64,048

Wins								
*	1998	Spt	Ayr	(G-S)	L	5f	99+	<
*	1998	Jun	Bath	(G-S)		5.1f	93	
*	1998	Apr	Bath	(SFT)		5.1f	88	

1999 Turf 0-9: (5f 2, 6f 7) (sft, g-s 2, gd 4, g-f 2)

Workmanlike, useful colt, effective 5f, acts on sft to gd, has worn blinkers. Turf high 102. A useful sprinting juvenile, he found life tough in 1999. He has not been done any favours by the Handicapper. **D W P Arbuthnot [3-17] Derrick Broomfield.*

MONO LADY (IRE) BHB 68f75a RR 69f 75a 3696[9]

6 b m Polish Patriot (USA) 7.8f **(70)** - Phylella (Persian Bold) 9.3f **(66)**

Form - 30215420

Record 1999 - 1st:1 2nd:2 3rd:1 Ran:8

Pre1999 - 1st:6 2nd:5 3rd:3 Ran:36

Win Prizemoney £29,148 *Total Prizemoney* £40,129

Wins									
*	**1999**	May	Cheste	(G-F)	H	12.3f	65	68	
*	1998	Aug	Leices	(GD)	H	11.8f	72	74	<
*	1997	Spt	Bright	(G-F)	H	11.9f	60	68	
*	1997	*May*	*Lingfi*	*(STD)*	*H*	*10f*	*63*	*71*	
*	1997	*Jan*	*Southw*	*(STD)*	*H*	*8f*	*54*	*58*	
*	1997	*Jan*	*Wolver*	*(SLW)*	*H*	*9.4f*	*48*	*52*	
*	1996	Oct	Folkes	(G-S)	H	9.7f	51	57	

1999 Turf 1-6: (12f 1-6) (gd, g-f 1-4, frm) 1999 AW 0-2: (8f, 10f) (Equi, Fibr)

Above-average mare, effective 10 to 12f, best at 12f, acts on gd to frm, often wears blinkers (extremely effectively), excels at Chester. Turf high 69 - 2nd of 7 getting 6lb from Rafting (25 Jly Chester 12f g-f RF 3127) - also 1st of 12 getting 9lb from Domappel (6 May Chester RF 1054). AW high 61. Consistent. Won at Chester's May meeting and has generally ran well afterwards.

**D HaydnJones [7-44] Monolithic Refractories Ltd.*

MONSAJEM (USA) BHB 110f RR 110f 5131[3]

4 ch c Woodman (USA) 9.7f **(77)** - Fairy Dancer (USA) (Nijinsky (CAN)) 10.3f **(77)**

Form - 3081013313

Record 1999 - 1st:3 2nd:0 3rd:4 Ran:10
Pre1999 - 1st:3 2nd:0 3rd:2 Ran:11
Win Prizemoney £64,802 *Total Prizemoney* £82,646
Wins * **1999** Oct Ascot (G-S) H 10f 105 109 <
* **1999** Aug Newbur (GD) H 11f 103 103
* **1999** Jun Epsom (GD,) H 10.1f 98 103
* 1998 Oct Yarmou (SFT) 10.1f 89+
* 1998 Oct Yarmou (G-S) H 10.1f 85 88
1997 Aug Chepst (GD) 8.1f 76
1999 Turf 3-10: (10f 2-9, 11f 1-1) (sft, gd 2-4, g-f 1-4, frm)
Scopey, Group-class colt, effective 10 to 11f, best at 10f, acts on gd to g-f, best on gd, has worn blinkers (effectively), likes left handed tracks, likes tight tracks, excels at Epsom and Yarmouth. Turf high 110 - 3rd of 7 giving 5lb to Little Rock (29 Oct Newmarket 10f gd RF 5131) - also 1st of 13 giving 15lb to Backcloth (9 Oct Ascot RF 4798). Improving. A fine third in the Rosebery on his return, he disappointed twice before a visor did the trick at Epsom on Derby Day. A lazy sort, he had excuses when hampered badly at Sandown in the Hong Kong Jockey Club Trophy, before winning a minor event at Newbury. Suited by the yielding ground when adding a decent handicap at Ascot in October.
**E A L Dunlop [5-16] Khalifa Sultan (from S bin Suroor [1-5] Oct 1997).*

MONTAGUE TIGG (IRE) BHB 46f RR 53df 4906[30]

3 b g Common Grounds 8.1f **(66)** - Astra (IRE) (Glenstal (USA)) 10.1f **(64)**
Form - 0000400
Record 1999 - 1st:0 2nd:0 3rd:0 Ran:7
Pre1999 - 1st:1 2nd:1 3rd:1 Ran:8
Win Prizemoney £3,570 *Total Prizemoney* £5,288
Wins * 1998 Oct Pontef (GD) H 6f 63 64 <
1999 Turf 0-7: (6f, 7f 2, 8f 4) (gd, g-f 3, frm 2, hrd)
Tall, fair gelding, effective 6f, acts on frm, has worn blinkers, prefers left handed tracks, prefers tight tracks. Turf high 53.
**N Tinkler [1-15] Boz.*

MONTALBAN (GER) RR 111f 5119a[2]

3 c
Form - 250522
1999 Turf 0-6: (9f, 11f, 12f 3, 14f) (sft 3, gd 3)
Group-class colt, effective 11 to 14f, acts on sft to gd, best on sft. Turf high 111 - 5th of 9 to Silvano (13 Jun Cologne 11f gd RF 2100a). He kept smart company and improved as he was stepped-up in trip. **A Lowe in GER [0-6].*

MONTALCINO (IRE) BHB 92f RR 92f 5038[10]

3 b c Robellino (USA) 9.5f **(68)** - Only Gossip (USA) (Trempolino (USA)) 12f **(71)**
Form - 2145320
Record 1999 - 1st:1 2nd:2 3rd:1 Ran:7
Pre1999 - 1st:0 2nd:0 3rd:0 Ran:1
Win Prizemoney £4,143 *Total Prizemoney* £10,482
Wins 1999 May Goodwo (GD) 12f 78+ <
1999 Turf 1-7: (10f 2, 12f 1-4, 13f) (g-s, gd 1-5, frm)
Scopey, useful colt, effective 10 to 13f, acts on gd to frm, best on gd. Turf high 92 - 2nd of 9 getting 14lb from Top Cees (18 Spt Ayr 13f gd RF 4394). Got off the mark when attempting a mile and a half for the first time at Goodwood. Running quite well since, if held by the Handicapper, his second to Top Cees at Ayr reads well, and another year should bring further improvement.
**P J Makin [0-1] Dr Carlos Stelling (from P W Chapple-Hyam [1-7] Spt 1999).*

MONTE CALVO BHB 74f RR 74f 5220[11]

3 b f Shirley Heights 12.1f **(76)** - Slava (USA) (Diesis) 9.3f **(69)**
Form - 6241160
Record 1999 - 1st:2 2nd:1 3rd:0 Ran:7
Pre1999 - 1st:0 2nd:0 3rd:0 Ran:1
Win Prizemoney £6,643 *Total Prizemoney* £8,020
Wins * **1999** Aug Bath (GD) H 17.2f 74 74 <
* **1999** Jly Catter (GD) 13.8f 70+
1999 Turf 2-7: (10f, 12f, 14f 1-2, 17f 1-3) (sft, gd 2, g-f 1-1, frm 1-3)
Unfurnished, above-average filly, effective 14 to 17f, acts on g-f to frm, prefers left handed tracks, favours tight tracks. Turf high 74 - 1st of 13 giving 17lb to Mu-Tadil (22 Aug Bath RF 3835) - also 1st of 5 from Cape Clear (21 Jly Catterick RF 3006).
**J L Dunlop [2-8] Capt J Macdonald-Buchanan.*

MONTE CARLO (IRE) BHB 100f RR 97f 5139[1]

2 b c Rainbows For Life (CAN) 9.3f **(64)** -Roberts Pride(Roberto (USA)) 10f **(76)**
Form - 43311
Record 1999 - 1st:2 2nd:0 3rd:2 Ran:5
Win Prizemoney £14,674 *Total Prizemoney* £15,816
Wins * **1999** Oct Newmar (SFT) L 10f 97 <
* **1999** Spt Epsom (GD) 8.5f 77
1999 Turf 2-5: (7f 2, 8f, 9f 1-1, 10f 1-1) (gd 1-2, frm 1-3)
Very useful colt. Turf high 97 - 1st of 10 from Galleon Beach (30 Oct Newmarket RF 5139). Gradually stepped up in trip through his career, he finally broke his maiden-tag over the extended mile at Epsom in early September. Looking in need of further that day, and proved that with a real staying performance in the Zetland Stakes. He has a future.
**R Hannon [2-5] Highclere Thoroughbred Racing Ltd.*

MONTECRISTO BHB 87f90a RR 90f 90a 5221[13]

6 br g Warning 8.1f **(77)** - Sutosky (Great Nephew) 9.9f **(64)**
Form - 20871100
Record 1999 - 1st:2 2nd:1 3rd:0 Ran:8
Pre1999 - 1st:12 2nd:1 3rd:7 Ran:37
Win Prizemoney £62,327 *Total Prizemoney* £79,349
Wins * **1999** Spt Hamilt (SFT) H 13f 90 90 <
* **1999** Aug Newbur (GD) 12f 90 <
* 1998 Spt Epsom (SFT) H 12f 83 86
* 1998 Jly Bright (GD) H 11.9f 77 82
* 1998 Mar Warwic (G-S) H 12.5f 73 77
* *1998 Feb Wolver (STD) H 12f 72 71+*
* *1997 Nov Wolver (STD) 12f 73+*
* 1997 Nov Nottin (GD) 14.1f 74
* *1997 Oct Southw (STD) 12f 51*
* 1997 Spt Newbur (SFT) H 12f 66 70
* 1997 Aug Hamilt (G-F) H 11.1f 62 65
* 1996 Apr Beverl (G-F) C 9.9f 65
* *1996 Feb Lingfi (STD) C 12f 54*
* *1996 Feb Lingfi (STD) H 10f 60 70*
1999 Turf 2-8: (12f 1-7, 13f 1-1) (sft, g-s, gd 2-6)
Useful gelding, effective 12 to 13f, best at 12f, acts on g-s to frm, best on gd, prefers tight tracks. Turf high 91 (1st run) - 2nd of 11 giving 17lb to Kinnescash (21 Apr Epsom 12f g-s RF 0799) - also 1st of 7 giving 14lb to Kristina (14 Aug Newbury RF 3653). He is an able handicapper on both Fibresand and on turf, and is suited by coming from off the pace. Goes well for an inexperienced rider.
**R Guest [14-45] Rae Guest.*

MONTE MAYOR BHB 38f RR 34f 4160[8]

3 b f Magic Ring (IRE) 6.5f **(64)** - Giblet Pie (Henbit (USA)) 9f **(61)**
Form - 048
Record 1999 - 1st:0 2nd:0 3rd:0 Ran:3
Pre1999 - 1st:0 2nd:0 3rd:0 Ran:1
1999 Turf 0-3: (5f, 6f 2) (gd, g-f, frm)
Workmanlike, very moderate filly. Turf high 34.
**D HaydnJones [0-4] Mrs E M HaydnJones.*

MONTENDRE BHB 52f RR 49f 5199[12]

12 b g Longleat (USA) 7.2f **(59)** - La Lutine (My Swallow) 9.2f **(71)**
Form - 03635144030
Record 1999 - 1st:1 2nd:0 3rd:3 Ran:11
Pre1999 - 1st:8 2nd:14 3rd:14 Ran:87
Win Prizemoney £61,552 *Total Prizemoney* £161,082
Wins * **1999** Jly Kempto (G-F) C 6f 56
* 1998 Aug Haydoc (GD) C 6f 66
* 1998 Apr Nottin (SFT) C 5.1f 62
1997 Spt Bath (GD) H 5.7f 75 78
1995 Mar Doncas (G-F) L 6f 102
1999 Turf 1-11: (5f, 6f 1-10) (gd 4, g-f 2, frm 1-4, hrd)
Moderate gelding, effective 5 to 6f, best at 6f, acts on sft to frm, has worn blinkers, excels at Nottingham, does well at Kempton. Turf high 63 - 5th of 20 giving 13lb to Selkirk Rose (21 Jun Nottingham 6f frm RF 2175). A marvellous veteran, he remains well capable of winning sprints in modest company.
**R J Hodges [3-32] David Mort (from M J Heaton-Ellis [1-5] Oct 1997).*

MONTFORT (USA) BHB 70a RR 60f 4225[P]

5 b g Manila (USA) 10f **(81)** - Sable Coated (Caerleon (USA)) 8.6f **(71)**
Form - 504024P
Record 1999 - 1st:0 2nd:1 3rd:0 Ran:7

Pre1999 - 1st:3 2nd:0 3rd:1 Ran:6
Win Prizemoney £15,844 *Total Prizemoney* £18,555
Wins * 1997 Jun Salisb (SFT) 14f 92+ <
* 1997 Jun York (G-S) 11.9f 92+ <
* 1997 May Bright (FRM) 11.9f 80
1999 Turf 0-6: (12f 3, 16f 2, 18f) (gd 3, g-f 2, frm) 1999 AW 0-1: (16f) (Fibr)
Average gelding, has worn blinkers. Turf high 74. Inconsistent.
**P F I Cole [3-13] Sir George Meyrick.*

MONTJEU (IRE) RR 135+f 4778a[1]

3 ch c Sadler's Wells (USA) 11.3f **(87)** - Floripedes (FR) (Top Ville) 11.7f **(68)**
Form - 121111
1999 Turf 5-6: (11f 1-2, 12f 4-4) (sft 1-1, g-s 1-1, gd 3-4)
Exceptional colt, effective 12f, acts on sft to gd. Turf high 135 - 1st of 14 getting 8lb from El Condor Pasa (3 Oct Longchamp RF 4778a) - also 1st of 10 from Daliapour (27 Jun Curragh RF 2419a). A progressive juvenile, he beat no less than Sendawar when maintaining his unbeaten record on his seasonal comeback in 1999, but appeared to find the firm ground against him in the Prix Lupin next time. Back on softer ground in the French Derby, he absolutely bolted up, and he was equally impressive in his five-length demolition of Derby runner-up Daliapour in the Irish Derby. Given a break until the Prix Niel in the autumn, he produced a fine turn of foot to cut down Bienamado off a slow pace. He proved he was the best middle-distance three-year-old colt in Europe by producing a turn of foot in atrocious conditions to catch the older Japanese colt El Condor Pasa in the Arc. A magnificent specimen of a thoroughbred, his performances have mostly lived up to his looks, and the treat for racing fans is that he is due to stay in training as a four-year-old. **J E Hammond in FR [5-6] M Tabor.*

MONUMENT BHB 57f50a RR 57f 50a 3968[12]

7 ch g Cadeaux Genereux 7.9f **(76)** - In Perpetuity (Great Nephew) 9.9f **(64)**
Form - 061450
Record 1999 - 1st:1 2nd:0 3rd:0 Ran:5
Pre1999 - 1st:5 2nd:1 3rd:3 Ran:27
Win Prizemoney £18,697 *Total Prizemoney* £21,675
Wins * **1999** Jun Bath (FRM) CH 8f 56 62
* 1998 Aug Kempto (G-F) H 12f 56 58
* 1997 Jly Nottin (G-F) 10f 65
* 1996 Jly Windso (G-F) H 10f 65 64
* 1996 Jun Salisb (G-F) C 8f 62
1995 Aug Kempto (G-F) 8f 79 <
1999 Turf 1-5: (8f 1-1, 10f 2, 12f 2) (g-f 3, frm, hrd 1-1)
Fair gelding, has broken blood-vessels, effective 8 to 12f, acts on frm to hrd, best on frm, likes left handed tracks. Turf high 62 - 1st of 16 giving 13lb to Danzas (26 Jun Bath RF 2319). Inconsistent.
**J S King [5-34] V Askew (from R Charlton [1-5] Spt 1995).*

MOOCHA CHA MAN BHB 72f62a RR 71f 62a 4656[9]

3 b c Sizzling Melody 6.3f **(49)** - Nilu (IRE) (Ballad Rock) 7.8f **(63)**
Form - 205803061240
Record 1999 - 1st:1 2nd:2 3rd:1 Ran:12
Pre1999 - 1st:1 2nd:0 3rd:1 Ran:6
Win Prizemoney £4,472 *Total Prizemoney* £7,534
Wins * **1999** Aug Pontef (G-F) C 5f 65 <
* 1998 *Jly Wolver (STD) 5f 65* <
1999 Turf 1-9: (5f 1-4, 6f 5) (sft 2, g-s, gd 4, frm 1-2) 1999 AW 0-3: (5f, 6f 2) (Fibr 3)
Workmanlike, above-average colt, effective 5 to 6f, best at 6f, acts on sft to frm - acts on Fibr, has worn blinkers (extremely effectively), prefers left handed tracks, prefers tight tracks. Turf high 71 - 2nd of 17 giving 3lb to Venika Vitesse (13 Aug Nottingham 6f gd RF 3624) - also 1st of 8 giving 11lb to Lightning Blaze (4 Aug Pontefract RF 3375). AW high 56.
**B A McMahon [2-18] Mrs J McMahon.*

MOON AT NIGHT BHB 64f RR 60f 4232[12]

4 gr g Pursuit of Love 9.5f **(69)** - La Nureyeva (USA) (Nureyev (USA)) 8.7f **(78)**
Form - 3677110
Record 1999 - 1st:2 2nd:0 3rd:1 Ran:7
Pre1999 - 1st:1 2nd:0 3rd:0 Ran:6
Win Prizemoney £10,229 *Total Prizemoney* £10,655
Wins * **1999** Aug Bright (G-S) H 8f 59 60 <
* **1999** Jly Chepst (G-F) H 7.1f 56 60 <
* 1998 Spt Goodwo (G-F) CH 8f 50 55
1999 Turf 2-7: (6f, 7f 1-3, 8f 1-2, 9f) (gd 1-2, frm 1-5)
Workmanlike, average gelding, effective 6 to 8f, best at 8f, acts on gd to frm, best on frm, and excels at Brighton. Turf high 60 - 1st of 11 giving 12lb to Titan (17 Aug Brighton RF 3689) - also 1st of 17 giving 3lb to Arbenig (23 Jly Chepstow RF 3056). Consistent.
**L G Cottrell [3-10] H C Seymour (from I A Balding [0-3] Jun 1998).*

MOON BLAST BHB 51f RR 53f 3150[9]

5 gr g Reprimand 8.2f **(63)** - Castle Moon (Kalamoun) 10.4f **(67)**
Form - 086000
Record 1999 - 1st:0 2nd:0 3rd:0 Ran:6
Pre1999 - 1st:2 2nd:2 3rd:2 Ran:13
Win Prizemoney £6,882 *Total Prizemoney* £10,686
Wins 1997 Jun Windso (G-F) 8.3f 86 <
1997 Apr Bright (FRM) 8f 71+
1999 Turf 0-6: (10f 2, 12f 4) (g-f 4, frm 2)
Fair gelding, has worn blinkers. Turf high 68. Becoming disappointing.
**M Salaman [0-6] J P M & J W Cook (from Lady Herries [2-14] Aug 1998).*

MOON COLONY BHB 62f RR 55f 4044[5]

6 b g Top Ville 11f **(71)** - Honeymooning (USA) (Blushing Groom (FR)) 10.3f **(76)**
Form - 003065
Record 1999 - 1st:0 2nd:0 3rd:1 Ran:6
Pre1999 - 1st:3 2nd:4 3rd:2 Ran:19
Win Prizemoney £13,837 *Total Prizemoney* £21,609
Wins * 1998 Jly Newmar (G-F) H 12f 76 79
* 1998 Jly Doncas (G-F) H 12f 73 74
* 1997 Oct Nottin (SFT) 14.1f 81 <
1999 Turf 0-6: (12f 3, 14f 2, 16f) (g-s 2, gd, g-f 2, frm)
Fair gelding, effective 12 to 14f, best at 14f, acts on gd to frm, best on gd, likes right handed tracks. Turf high 69. Inconsistent.
**Lady Herries [3-25] Mrs Berta Lazarus.*

MOON DRAGON (IRE) RR 97f 4317a[10]

3 b c Sadler's Wells (USA) 11.3f **(87)** - Moonsilk (Solinus) 9f **(71)**
Form - 1620
1999 Turf 1-4: (12f 1-1, 14f, 15f, 16f) (gd 1-2, g-f, frm)
Very useful colt, effective 12 to 16f, acts on gd to frm, has worn blinkers. Turf high 97 (1st run) - 1st of 10 from Gaudi (9 May Leopardstown RF 1173a). A strapping half-brother to the St Leger winner Moonax, he is one-paced and will always struggle in Group races. Effective on easy ground, he may be better employed over hurdles. **A P O'Brien in IRE [1-7] Mrs John Magnier.*

MOON DREAM BHB 39f RR 30f 5113[13]

3 gr f Interrex (CAN) 7.7f **(51)** - Zamoon (Zambrano) 6.1f **(37)**
Form - 000
Record 1999 - 1st:0 2nd:0 3rd:0 Ran:3
1999 Turf 0-3: (6f 2, 7f) (gd 2, g-f)
Leggy, currently very moderate filly. Turf high 30 (began Oct).
**J G Smyth-Osbourne [0-3] Edenwood Partnership.*

MOON DRIVER (USA) RR 97f 4596[9]

2 b f Mr Prospector (USA) 8.6f **(88)** - East of the Moon (USA) **(120f)** (Private Account (USA)) 8.5f **(74)**
Form - 10
1999 Turf 1-2: (6f 1-2) (gd 1-1, g-f)
Currently very useful filly. Turf high 97 (1st run) (began Spt) - 1st of 8 getting 7lb from Harbour Island (8 Spt Chantilly RF 4361a). Impressive in a Group 3 at Chantilly in September, she was strongly fancied for the Cheveley Park Stakes but ran no sort of race after being slow to get into her stride. Much better than that performance indicates, she may struggle to stay a mile but remains an interesting prospect.
**J E Pease in FR [1-2] Niarchos Family.*

MOON EMPEROR BHB 97f RR 91f 5015a[5]

2 b c Emperor Jones (USA) - Sir Hollow (USA) (Sir Ivor) 10.2f **(70)**
Form - 3545
Record 1999 - 1st:0 2nd:0 3rd:1 Ran:4
Win Prizemoney £0 *Total Prizemoney* £718
1999 Turf 0-4: (7f, 8f 3) (g-s, gd, g-f 2)

Useful colt. Turf high 91 (began Spt) - 5th of 9 to Night Style (17 Oct San Siro 8f g-f RF 5015a). *H Akbary [0-4].*

MOON GLOW (IRE) RR 71f 4422[7]
3 b g Fayruz 6.6f **(63)** - Jarmar Moon **(55f)** (Unfuwain (USA))
Form - 383407
Record 1999 - 1st:0 2nd:0 3rd:2 Ran:6
Pre1999 - 1st:0 2nd:1 3rd:0 Ran:3
Win Prizemoney £0 *Total Prizemoney* £2,688
1999 Turf 0-6: (7f, 8f 4, 9f) (gd, frm 5)
Scopey, above-average gelding, effective 8 to 9f, acts on gd to frm. Turf high 71. *Miss S E Hall [0-9] C Platts.*

MOON GOD (USA) RR 93f 4841a[3]
2 b c Thunder Gulch (USA) - Lyric Fantasy (IRE) (Tate Gallery (USA)) 7.4f **(67)**
Form - 6223
1999 Turf 0-4: (5f, 6f, 7f, 8f) (sft, g-s 2, frm)
Useful colt. Turf high 93 (began Jly) - 2nd of 17 giving 5lb to Sand Partridge (3 Oct Punchestown 8f g-s RF 4748a).
A P O'Brien in IRE [0-4] Mrs John Magnier.

MOONLIGHT (IRE) RR 72df 3431[10]
3 b f Night Shift (USA) 8.1f **(73)** - Local Custom (IRE) (Be My Native (USA)) 10.2f **(71)**
Form - 0300
Record 1999 - 1st:0 2nd:0 3rd:1 Ran:4
Pre1999 - 1st:0 2nd:0 3rd:0 Ran:1
Win Prizemoney £0 *Total Prizemoney* £549
1999 Turf 0-4: (7f, 10f 2, 12f) (g-f 2, frm 2)
Above-average filly. Turf high 72.
B J Meehan [0-4] Mrs R D Peacock (from H R A Cecil [0-1] Aug 1998).

MOONLIGHT FLIT BHB 48a **RR 38f** 2677[11]
4 b f Presidium 7.5f **(56)** - Moonwalker (Night Shift (USA)) 7.2f **(69)**
Form - 3033413300
Record 1999 - 1st:1 2nd:0 3rd:5 Ran:10
Pre1999 - 1st:2 2nd:0 3rd:0 Ran:12
Win Prizemoney £7,629 *Total Prizemoney* £9,598
Wins * **1999** *Mar Southw (STD) H 8f 41 50*
1998 Aug Pontef (G-F) S 10f 38
1997 Spt Beverl (G-F) SH 7.5f 54 63 <
1999 Turf 0-3: (9f 2, 10f) (gd, g-f, frm) 1999 AW 1-7: (8f 1-7) (Fibr 1-7)
Fair filly, effective 8f, - acts on Fibr, has worn blinkers, prefers left handed tracks, favours tight tracks. Turf high 38. AW high 50 - 1st of 10 giving 1lb to River Ensign (22 Mar Southwell RF 0457).
J L Eyre [1-13] The Claire King Partnership (from J G FitzGerald [2-9] Aug 1998).

MOONLIGHT MONTY BHB 53f **RR 59f** 4563[8]
3 ch c Elmaamul (USA) 8.1f **(70)** - Lovers Light (Grundy) 10.3f **(65)**
Form - 58
Record 1999 - 1st:0 2nd:0 3rd:0 Ran:2
Pre1999 - 1st:0 2nd:0 3rd:1 Ran:4
Win Prizemoney £0 *Total Prizemoney* £496
1999 Turf 0-2: (11f, 14f) (gd, frm)
Scopey, fair colt. Turf high 59 (began Spt).
J L Dunlop [0-6] Credit Income Ltd.

MOONLIGHT SEAS BHB 35f **RR 40f** 3667[8]
3 b f Sabrehill (USA) 8.5f **(64)** - Fair Seas (General Assembly (USA)) 10f **(68)**
Form - 0058
Record 1999 - 1st:0 2nd:0 3rd:0 Ran:4
1999 Turf 0-3: (8f 2, 10f) (g-f 3) 1999 AW 0-1: (12f) (Fibr)
Workmanlike, moderate filly, has worn blinkers. Turf high 40.
A W Carroll [0-4] D R Wellicome.

MOONLIT WATER BHB 59f54a **RR 51f 54a** 928[8]
3 b f Rainbow Quest (USA) 11.2f **(81)** - Shimmer (FR) (Green Dancer (USA)) 10.3f **(74)**
Form - 08
Record 1999 - 1st:0 2nd:0 3rd:0 Ran:2
Pre1999 - 1st:0 2nd:0 3rd:0 Ran:2
1999 Turf 0-1: (10f) (frm) 1999 AW 0-1: (12f) (Fibr)
Scopey, fair filly.
J R Fanshawe [0-2] Aylesfield Farms Ltd (from J L Dunlop [0-2] Spt 1998).

MOON MISSION BHB 33f **RR 14f** 1923[16]
4 br f Interrex (CAN) 7.7f **(51)** - Zamoon (Zambrano) 6.1f **(37)**
Form - 00
Record 1999 - 1st:0 2nd:0 3rd:0 Ran:2
Pre1999 - 1st:0 2nd:0 3rd:0 Ran:1
1999 Turf 0-2: (5f, 7f) (frm, hrd)
Light-framed, currently poor filly. Turf high 14.
J G Smyth-Osbourne [0-3] Edenwood Partnership.

MOON OF ALABAMA RR 51f 5137[13]
2 b f Sadler's Wells (USA) 11.3f **(87)** - Military Tune (IRE) (Nashwan (USA))
Form - 50
Record 1999 - 1st:0 2nd:0 3rd:0 Ran:2
1999 Turf 0-2: (7f, 8f) (gd 2)
Currently fair filly. Turf high 51 (began Oct).
J W Hills [0-2] Geoff Howard-Spink & Lindy Regis.

MOONRAKING BHB 35f62a **RR 25f 62a** 3968[9]
6 gr g Rusticaro (FR) 11.3f **(45)** - Lunaire (Try My Best (USA)) 7.6f **(67)**
Form - 0112537050
Record 1999 - 1st:2 2nd:1 3rd:1 Ran:10
Pre1999 - 1st:4 2nd:6 3rd:4 Ran:24
Win Prizemoney £13,685 *Total Prizemoney* £21,608
Wins * **1999** *Feb Southw (STD) C 12f 68+* <
1999 *Feb Southw (STD) C 8f 57*
1998 *Mar Southw (STD) H 8f 58 68*
1998 *Feb Southw (STD) H 11f 58 60*
1997 *Dec Southw (STD) H 11f 50 54*
1997 *Mar Southw (STD) H 12f 50 56*
1999 Turf 0-3: (10f 2, 12f) (sft, gd, g-f) 1999 AW 2-7: (8f 1-1, 11f, 12f 1-5) (Fibr 2-7)
Average gelding, effective 8 to 12f, best at 12f, - acts on Fibr, often wears blinkers, favours left handed tracks, favours tight tracks, excels at Southwell. Turf high 25. AW high 68 - 1st of 5 getting 1lb from Abuljjood (12 Feb Southwell RF 0279). Inconsistent.
Miss S J Wilton [1-9] John Pointon and Sons (from T J Etherington [5-27] Feb 1999).

MOON RIVER WONDER (IRE) BHB 36f **RR 23f** 5190[9]
3 b g Doyoun 10.7f **(69)** - Bayazida (Bustino) 10.4f **(64)**
Form - 80
Record 1999 - 1st:0 2nd:0 3rd:0 Ran:1
Pre1999 - 1st:0 2nd:0 3rd:0 Ran:3
1999 Turf 0-1: (12f) (g-f)
Unfurnished, moderate gelding.
C W Thornton [0-1] Guy Reed (from B W Hills [0-3] Nov 1998).

MOONSHIFT BHB 28f40a **RR 43f 40a** 1514[1]
5 b g Cadeaux Genereux 7.9f **(76)** - Thewaari (USA) (Eskimo (USA))
Form - 01
Record 1999 - 1st:1 2nd:0 3rd:0 Ran:2
Pre1999 - 1st:0 2nd:0 3rd:0 Ran:9
Win Prizemoney £1,986 *Total Prizemoney* £2,244
Wins * **1999** May Yarmou (FRM) H 10.1f 24 28 <
1999 Turf 1-1: (10f 1-1) (frm 1-1) 1999 AW 0-1: (11f) (Fibr)
Moderate gelding, effective 10f, acts on g-f, has worn blinkers. (1st run). Inconsistent.
H J Collingridge [1-10] C V Lines (from Sir Michael Stoute [0-2] May 1997).

MOON SHOT BHB 72f80a **RR 73f 80a** 4946[4]
3 gr g Pistolet Bleu (IRE) - La Luna (USA) (Lyphard (USA)) 9.9f **(72)**
Form - 0251108064
Record 1999 - 1st:2 2nd:1 3rd:0 Ran:10
Pre1999 - 1st:1 2nd:0 3rd:0 Ran:4
Win Prizemoney £11,411 *Total Prizemoney* £13,219
Wins * **1999** Jly Redcar (FRM) H 11f 70 77+ <
* **1999** *Jly Lingfi (STD) H 10f 66 77++*
* 1998 *Oct Wolver (STD) 6f 64+*
1999 Turf 1-9: (10f 5, 11f 1-3, 12f) (g-s 2, gd 2, g-f 3, frm 1-2) 1999 AW 1-1: (10f 1-1) (Equi 1-1)
Strong, above-average gelding, effective 10 to 11f, best at 10f, acts on gd to frm - acts on Equi, favours tight tracks. Turf high 77 - 1st of 5 giving 4lb to Boogy Woogy (17 Jly Redcar RF 2921). (1st run) -

1st of 8 getting 13lb from Castles Burning (9 Jly Lingfield RF 2686).
**Sir Mark Prescott [3-14] Eclipse Thoroughbreds - Osborne House II.*

MOON SOLITAIRE (IRE) RR 60+f 4784[6]
2 b c Night Shift (USA) 8.1f **(73)** - Gay Fantastic (Ela-Mana-Mou) 10.1f **(70)**
Form - 6
Record 1999 - 1st:0 2nd:0 3rd:0 Ran:1
1999 Turf 0-1: (7f) (g-s)
Currently average colt. **E A L Dunlop [0-1] Maktoum Al Maktoum.*

MOONSTONE (IRE) BHB 36f42a RR 37f 42a 4156[15]
4 b f Statoblest 6.4f **(63)** - Opening Day (Day Is Done) 6.3f **(67)**
Form - 0000
Record 1999 - 1st:0 2nd:0 3rd:0 Ran:3
Pre1999 - 1st:1 2nd:1 3rd:0 Ran:20
Win Prizemoney £3,557 *Total Prizemoney* £4,902
Wins 1998 Jly Yarmou (GD) H 7f 63 67 <
1999 Turf 0-2: (8f, 10f) (frm 2) 1999 AW 0-1: (11f) (Fibr)
Scopey, very moderate filly, effective 7f, acts on frm, has worn blinkers. Turf high 10 (began Aug). Becoming disappointing.
**B P J Baugh [0-12] Mrs Sylvia Knobbs (from A P Jarvis [1-19] Spt 1998).*

MOON STRIKE (FR) BHB 87f79a RR 86f 79a 2298[9]
9 b or br g Strike Gold (USA) 5.9f **(99)** - Lady Lamia (USA) (Secreto (USA)) 8.7f **(72)**
Form - 6730
Record 1999 - 1st:0 2nd:0 3rd:1 Ran:4
Pre1999 - 1st:8 2nd:4 3rd:4 Ran:38
Win Prizemoney £53,562 *Total Prizemoney* £65,960

Wins							
1997	Aug	Haydoc (G-F)	H	5f	91	95	<
1997	Jun	Newcas (GD)	H	5f	83	94	
1996	Aug	Newmar (G-S)	H	5f	74	79	
1996	May	Folkes (GD)	C	6.9f		71+	
1995	May	Lingfi (FRM)	H	7f	70	76	
1995	*Jan*	*Lingfi (STD)*	*H*	*7f*	*77*	*79*	

1999 Turf 0-4: (5f 4) (g-s, frm 3)
Useful gelding, effective 5f, acts on g-s to g-f, has worn blinkers. Turf high 86. Consistent.
**Miss I Foustok [0-4] Miss I Foustok (from Mrs A E Johnson [0-6] Oct 1998).*

MOOSE MALLOY BHB 53f RR 43f 5047[7]
2 ch g Formidable (USA) 7.8f **(60)** - Jolimo (Fortissimo) 11.8f **(61)**
Form - 607
Record 1999 - 1st:0 2nd:0 3rd:0 Ran:3
Win Prizemoney £0 *Total Prizemoney* £99
1999 Turf 0-3: (6f, 7f, 8f) (hvy, g-s, frm)
Currently moderate gelding. Turf high 43 (began Spt).
**M J Ryan [0-3] Extraman Ltd.*

MORE BILLS (IRE) BHB 20f28a RR 17?f 28a 2529[9]
7 b g Gallic League 6.3f **(58)** - Lady Portobello (Porto Bello) 8.9f **(43)**
Form - 0
Record 1999 - 1st:0 2nd:0 3rd:0 Ran:1
Pre1999 - 1st:0 2nd:0 3rd:0 Ran:12
1999 Turf 0-1: (18f) (frm)
Poor gelding, has worn blinkers.
**B J Llewellyn [0-12] S Harrison (from J Neville [0-4] May 1997).*

MORE MAGIC BHB 73f RR 74f 4857[7]
2 b g Cyrano de Bergerac 7.3f **(58)** - Maziere **(30f)** (Mazilier (USA))
Form - 704646117
Record 1999 - 1st:2 2nd:0 3rd:0 Ran:9
Win Prizemoney £7,146 *Total Prizemoney* £7,391

Wins							
*** 1999**	Oct	Bright (G-S)	H	5.3f	65	74	<
*** 1999**	Spt	Lingfi (HVY)	H	5f	58	65	

1999 Turf 2-9: (5f 2-6, 6f 2, 7f) (g-s 1-2, gd 1-1, g-f 2, frm 4)
Above-average gelding, effective 5f, acts on g-s to gd. Turf high 74 (began Jly) - 1st of 10 giving 4lb to Jepaje (4 Oct Brighton RF 4707) - also 1st of 11 from Blue Holly (24 Spt Lingfield RF 4532).
**W J Haggas [2-9] Mrs Barbara Bassett.*

MORGAN LE FAY BHB 63f RR 64f 3746[12]
4 b f Magic Ring (IRE) 6.5f **(64)** - Melody Park (Music Boy) 6.8f **(57)**
Form - 5230
Record 1999 - 1st:0 2nd:1 3rd:1 Ran:4
Pre1999 - 1st:0 2nd:3 3rd:2 Ran:11
Win Prizemoney £0 *Total Prizemoney* £5,708
1999 Turf 0-4: (6f, 7f 2, 8f) (g-f 2, frm 2)
Unfurnished, average filly, effective 6 to 8f, best at 7f, acts on g-s to frm, best on frm. Turf high 64 (began Jly) - 2nd of 14 to Lady Melbourne (31 Jly Thirsk 6f frm RF 3285). Inconsistent.
**Don Enrico Incisa [0-3] Don Enrico Incisa (from B J Meehan [0-12] Jly 1999).*

MORGANS ORCHARD (IRE) RR 43f 1795[5]
3 ch g Forest Wind (USA) - Regina St Cyr (IRE) (Doulab (USA)) 9.8f **(65)**
Form - 05
Record 1999 - 1st:0 2nd:0 3rd:0 Ran:2
1999 Turf 0-2: (10f, 11f) (g-s, g-f)
Strong, currently moderate gelding. Turf high 43.
**A G Newcombe [0-2] After Hours Partnership.*

MORNING DAWN (USA) BHB 69f RR 70f 4401[13]
2 b br c Dayjur (USA) 6.8f **(79)** - Istiska (FR) (Irish River (FR)) 8.6f **(78)**
Form - 57232260
Record 1999 - 1st:0 2nd:3 3rd:1 Ran:8
Win Prizemoney £0 *Total Prizemoney* £3,752
1999 Turf 0-8: (5f 5, 6f 2, 7f) (gd 3, g-f 2, frm 3)
Above-average colt, effective 5f, acts on g-f. Turf high 70. Becoming disappointing. **E A L Dunlop [0-8] Khalifa Sultan.*

MORNING GLORY BHB 60f RR 58f 1013[18]
3 b f Polar Falcon (USA) 9f **(74)** -Round Midnight Star Appeal) 9.6f **(65)**
Form - 50
Record 1999 - 1st:0 2nd:0 3rd:0 Ran:2
Pre1999 - 1st:0 2nd:0 3rd:0 Ran:2
1999 Turf 0-2: (6f, 7f) (sft, frm)
Fair filly. Turf high 58. **R A Fahey [0-4] Mrs A Brown & G Patterson.*

MORNING LOVER (IRE) RR 54f 5157[11]
2 b c Ela-Mana-Mou 12.7f **(72)** - The Dawn Trader (USA) (Naskra (USA)) 8.8f **(69)**
Form - 0
Record 1999 - 1st:0 2nd:0 3rd:0 Ran:1
1999 Turf 0-1: (7f) (frm)
Currently fair colt. **K R Burke [0-1] Mrs Elaine Burke.*

MORNING MUSIC BHB 71f RR 72f 4946[3]
3 b f Green Desert (USA) 7.8f **(78)** - Blushing Storm (USA) (Blushing Groom (FR)) 10.3f **(76)**
Form - 783481603
Record 1999 - 1st:1 2nd:0 3rd:2 Ran:9
Pre1999 - 1st:1 2nd:2 3rd:1 Ran:7
Win Prizemoney £6,731 *Total Prizemoney* £11,771

Wins							
*** 1999**	Jly	Bath (FRM)		8f		75	
* 1998	Spt	Kempto (GD)		7f		82	<

1999 Turf 1-9: (8f 1-3, 9f 3, 10f 3) (gd, g-f 4, frm 1-4)
Light-framed, above-average filly, effective 5 to 7f, best at 7f, acts on frm. Turf high 75. Consistent. **R Hannon [2-16] Mohamed Suhail.*

MORNING PRIDE (IRE) RR 115++f 2656a[1]
2 b f Machiavellian (USA) 9.8f **(83)** - Wilayif (USA) (Danzig (USA)) 8.4f **(76)**
Form - 1
1999 Turf 1-1: (5f 1-1) (gd 1-1)
Currently high-class filly. (1st run) - 1st of 6 from Legend Of Spring (2 Jly Chantilly RF 2656a). She made a very big impression when landing a Group Three event at Chantilly in July.
**A Fabre in FR [1-1] Maktoum Al Maktoum.*

MORNINGSIDE (IRE) RR 20f 4642[6]
2 b f Night Shift (USA) 8.1f **(73)** - Recipe (Bustino) 10.4f **(64)**
Form - 6
Record 1999 - 1st:0 2nd:0 3rd:0 Ran:1
1999 Turf 0-1: (8f) (g-s)
Currently little account filly.
**D R C Elsworth [0-1] Mrs Michael Meredith.*

MOROCCO (IRE) BHB 55f **RR 54f** 1813[6]
10 b g Cyrano de Bergerac 7.3f **(58)** - Lightning Laser (Monseigneur (USA)) 7.7f **(63)**
Form - 7006
Record 1999 - 1st:0 2nd:0 3rd:0 Ran:4
Pre1999 - 1st:9 2nd:6 3rd:10 Ran:81
Win Prizemoney £31,748 *Total Prizemoney* £43,812
Wins * 1998 Jly Leices (GD) H 7f 58 58
* 1996 Spt Lingfi (FRM) H 7f 54 56
* 1996 May Salisb (G-F) H 7f 56 52
* 1995 Aug Carlis (HRD) 6.9f 65
* 1995 Jun Mussel (G-F) H 8.1f 55 57
1999 Turf 0-4: (7f 3, 8f) (g-f, frm 2, hrd)
Fair gelding, effective 7 to 8f, best at 7f, acts on gd to frm, best on frm, has worn blinkers. Turf high 54.
**M R Channon [6-67] Martin Myers (from R Charlton [3-18] Jun 1993).*

MORSELL BHB 52f **RR 55f** 2171[3]
3 br f Dilum (USA) 7.1f **(56)** - Count On Me (No Mercy) 8f **(61)**
Form - 60003
Record 1999 - 1st:0 2nd:0 3rd:1 Ran:5
Pre1999 - 1st:0 2nd:1 3rd:0 Ran:1
Win Prizemoney £0 *Total Prizemoney* £1,030
1999 Turf 0-5: (5f, 6f, 7f, 8f 2) (gd 2, g-f 2, frm)
Strong, fair filly, effective 6 to 8f, acted on g-f to frm. Turf high 55. (DEAD)
**R J Hodges [0-5] J W Mursell (from M J Heaton-Ellis [0-1] Aug 1998).*

MORTEENO BHB 37f46a **RR 36df 46a** 4166[17]
3 b g Perpendicular - Petticoat Rule (Stanford) 7.9f **(56)**
Form - 3800
Record 1999 - 1st:0 2nd:0 3rd:1 Ran:4
Pre1999 - 1st:0 2nd:0 3rd:0 Ran:3
Win Prizemoney £0 *Total Prizemoney* £295
1999 Turf 0-3: (7f, 8f, 12f) (g-f, frm 2) 1999 AW 0-1: (9f) (Fibr)
Strong, very moderate gelding. Turf high 36 (began Jly).
**J Mackie [0-4] Four But Five (from Miss L A Perratt [0-3] Oct 1998).*

MORTENS PROSPECT (USA) RR 107f 1527a[3]
5 ch g Prospector's Bid (USA) - Secret Admirer (USA) (Noble Dancer) 7.8f **(101)**
Form - 3
1999 AW 0-1: (8f) (Dirt)
Currently Pattern-class gelding. (1st run) - 3rd of 9 to Sharp Matt (20 May Jagersro 8f Dirt RF 1527a).**Catherine Erichsen in NOR [1-3].*

MOSAIC TIMES RR 2652[2]
2 ch c Timeless Times (USA) 6.1f **(56)** - Pastelle **(57a)** (Tate Gallery (USA)) 7.4f **(67)**
Form - 2
Record 1999 - 1st:0 2nd:1 3rd:0 Ran:1
Win Prizemoney £0 *Total Prizemoney* £521
1999 AW 0-1: (5f) (Fibr)
Currently moderate colt. (1st run) - 2nd of 6 getting 5lb from Gem of Wisdom (8 Jly Southwell 5f Fibr RF 2652).
**Mrs G S Rees [0-1] David Morley.*

MOSCOW MIST (IRE) BHB 63f58a **RR 70df 58a** 967[17]
8 b g Soviet Star (USA) 8.6f **(74)** -Ivory Dawn (USA) (Sir Ivor) 10.2f **(70)**
Form - 0U0
Record 1999 - 1st:0 2nd:0 3rd:0 Ran:3
Pre1999 - 1st:1 2nd:3 3rd:0 Ran:17
Win Prizemoney £48,250 *Total Prizemoney* £52,212
Wins 1996 Aug Goodwo (G-F) H 8f 70 85 <
1999 Turf 0-2: (8f 2) (g-s, g-f) 1999 AW 0-1: (9f) (Fibr)
Above-average gelding, effective 7f, acts on frm. Turf high 4. Becoming disappointing.
**B Palling [0-12] Merthyr Motor Auctions (from Lady Herries [1-9] Spt 1996).*

MOSELLE RR 92f 5142[3]
2 b f Mtoto 11.5f **(71)** -Miquette (FR) (Fabulous Dancer (USA)) 9.4f **(70)**
Form - 3
Record 1999 - 1st:0 2nd:0 3rd:1 Ran:1
Win Prizemoney £0 *Total Prizemoney* £1,934
1999 Turf 0-1: (8f) (gd)
Currently useful filly. (1st run) - 3rd of 10 to Silver Colours (30 Oct Newmarket 8f gd RF 5142). **W J Haggas [0-1] & Mrs G Middlebrook.*

MOSEY ALONG RR 15f 762[16]
3 b f Petong 7.6f **(58)** - Mo's Star **(66f)** (Most Welcome)
Form - 0
Record 1999 - 1st:0 2nd:0 3rd:0 Ran:1
Pre1999 - 1st:0 2nd:0 3rd:0 Ran:1
1999 Turf 0-1: (6f) (sft)
Neat, currently poor filly.
**L A Dace [0-1] Luke Dace (from E L James [0-1] Aug 1998).*

MOSI-OA-TUNYA (IRE) BHB 35f **RR 22f** 1963[7]
3 ch c River Falls 8.2f **(56)** - Heart to Heart (IRE) **(36f)** (Double Schwartz) 7.9f **(55)**
Form - 87
Record 1999 - 1st:0 2nd:0 3rd:0 Ran:2
Pre1999 - 1st:0 2nd:0 3rd:0 Ran:1
1999 Turf 0-1: (7f) (g-f) 1999 AW 0-1: (8f) (Fibr)
Workmanlike, currently little account colt.
**K McAuliffe [0-3] The PBT Group.*

MOSQUERO (USA) BHB 68f **RR 67f** 1018[7]
3 b c Sky Classic (CAN) 10f **(83)** - Mosella (USA) (Lord At War (ARG))
Form - 577
Record 1999 - 1st:0 2nd:0 3rd:0 Ran:3
Pre1999 - 1st:0 2nd:0 3rd:0 Ran:2
Win Prizemoney £0 *Total Prizemoney* £275
1999 Turf 0-2: (10f, 13f) (gd, frm) 1999 AW 0-1: (9f) (Fibr)
Scopey, average colt. Turf high 67.
**J H M Gosden [0-5] Sheikh Mohammed.*

MOSSFLOWER (USA) RR 113f 5228a[7]
5 m Affirmed (USA) 10.3f **(75)** - Chinquetti (USA) (Green Dancer (FR))
Form - 7
1999 Turf 0-1: (11f) (frm)
Currently Group-class. (1st run) - 7th of 14 to Soaring Softly (6 Nov Gulfstream Park 11f frm RF 5228a). **R Schosberg in USA [0-1].*

MOSS ROSE BHB 50f45a **RR 42f 45a** 1814[9]
3 ch f Wolfhound (USA) 7.3f **(71)** - Champagne 'n Roses (Chief Singer) 8.9f **(66)**
Form - 000
Record 1999 - 1st:0 2nd:0 3rd:0 Ran:3
1999 Turf 0-3: (7f 2, 8f) (gd 2, g-f)
Light-framed, currently moderate filly. Turf high 42.
**B W Hills [0-3] Mrs A D Bourne.*

MOSS SIDE MONKEY BHB 23f **RR 31f** 4400[12]
4 b g Presidium 7.5f **(56)** - Lady of Leisure (Record Run) 8f **(42)**
Form - 0008600
Record 1999 - 1st:0 2nd:0 3rd:0 Ran:7
Pre1999 - 1st:0 2nd:1 3rd:0 Ran:7
Win Prizemoney £0 *Total Prizemoney* £725
1999 Turf 0-7: (8f, 12f 3, 13f, 16f 2) (g-f 3, frm 4)
Workmanlike, very moderate gelding, has worn blinkers. Turf high 35. Inconsistent.
**K W Hogg [0-8] K W Hogg (from J Berry [0-7] Spt 1997).*

MOSSY MOOR RR 68+f 5060[4]
2 ch f Sanglamore (USA) 12.9f **(67)** - Moss (Alzao (USA)) 7.1f **(68)**
Form - 4
Record 1999 - 1st:0 2nd:0 3rd:0 Ran:1
Win Prizemoney £0 *Total Prizemoney* £337
1999 Turf 0-1: (7f) (g-s)
Currently average filly. **Mrs A J Perrett [0-1] K Abdulla.*

MOST RESPECTFUL BHB 47f53a **RR 47f 53a** 4878[9]
6 ch g Respect 5.7f **(44)** - Active Movement (Music Boy) 6.8f **(57)**
Form - 4426443850021856060
Record 1999 - 1st:1 2nd:1 3rd:1 Ran:15
Pre1999 - 1st:2 2nd:1 3rd:1 Ran:18
Win Prizemoney £7,642 *Total Prizemoney* £9,795
Wins * **1999** *Jun Southw (STD) SH* 7f 50 54 <
* 1998 *Spt Southw (STD) H* 6f 50 54 <
* 1998 Aug Beverl (G-F) 5f 54 <
1999 Turf 0-7: (6f 6, 7f) (g-s, gd, g-f 2, frm 3) 1999 AW 1-8: (6f 4, 7f 1-4) (Fibr 1-8)

Fair gelding, effective 5 to 7f, best at 7f, acts on frm - acts on Fibr, likes left handed tracks, likes tight tracks, excels at Southwell. Turf high 50. AW high 54 - 1st of 16 giving 9lb to Dark Menace (17 Jun Southwell RF 2086).
**N Tinkler [3-28] D Callaghan (from Denys Smith [0-7] May 1997).*

MOST-SAUCY BHB 77f **RR 79f** 4329[4]
3 br f Most Welcome 8.6f **(66)** - So Saucy **(35f 41a)** (Teenoso (USA)) 9.9f **(72)**
Form - 734821014
Record 1999 - 1st:2 2nd:1 3rd:1 Ran:9
Win Prizemoney £8,114 *Total Prizemoney* £10,743
Wins * 1999 Aug Lingfi (G-F) H 7.6f 72 76 <
*** 1999** Jly Leices (G-F) H 7f 68 72
1999 Turf 2-9: (7f 1-3, 8f 1-3, 9f, 10f 2) (g-s, gd 3, g-f 1-2, frm 1-3)
Unfurnished, above-average filly, effective 7 to 8f, best at 8f, acts on gd to frm. Turf high 79 - 4th of 11 getting 8lb from Khibrah (15 Spt Sandown 8f gd RF 4329) - also 1st of 14 giving 17lb to April Ace (24 Aug Lingfield RF 3872). A winner twice over seven furlongs on fast ground, she ran consistently last term, albeit at a modest level. **B J Meehan [2-9] Wyck Hall Stud.*

MOTECK (FR) RR 112f 4769a[8]
4 b f Last Tycoon 9.4f **(73)** - Sudaka (FR) (Garde Royale)
Form - 3038
1999 Turf 0-4: (11f, 12f, 13f, 14f) (hvy, g-s, gd 2)
Group-class filly, effective 11f, acts on g-s. Turf high 111 (1st run) - 3rd of 9 giving 7lb to Majoune (13 May Lyon Parilly 11f g-s RF 1350a). **E Lellouche in FR [2-6].*

MOTET BHB 82f **RR 84f** 1578[7]
5 b g Mtoto 11.5f **(71)** - Guest Artiste (Be My Guest (USA)) 9.3f **(67)**
Form - 7
Record 1999 - 1st:0 2nd:0 3rd:0 Ran:1
Pre1999 - 1st:3 2nd:2 3rd:4 Ran:15
Win Prizemoney £14,042 *Total Prizemoney* £21,755
Wins 1997 Spt Yarmou (FRM) H 18.2f 85 90 <
1997 Aug Newcas (GD) H 16.1f 82 84
1997 *Mar Lingfi (STD) 10f 66+*
1999 Turf 0-1: (16f) (frm)
Decent gelding, effective 12 to 16f, acts on gd to frm, best on g-f, has worn blinkers. (1st run) - 7th of 9 giving 14lb to Eminence Grise (29 May Kempton 16f frm RF 1578).
**M Pitman [1-7] H J Jarvis (from G Wragg [3-15] Spt 1998).*

MOTHER CORRIGAN (IRE) BHB 60f **RR 62f** 3434[6]
3 gr f Paris House 5.9f **(64)** - Missed Opportunity (IRE) (Exhibitioner) 8.7f **(61)**
Form - 0746
Record 1999 - 1st:0 2nd:0 3rd:0 Ran:4
Pre1999 - 1st:0 2nd:0 3rd:0 Ran:1
Win Prizemoney £0 *Total Prizemoney* £297
1999 Turf 0-4: (6f, 8f, 10f 2) (gd, g-f, frm 2)
Average filly. Turf high 62. **L M Cumani [0-5] Miss Gatto Roissard.*

MOTHER MOLLY (USA) RR 72f 2304[2]
2 b br f Irish River (FR) 9f **(77)** - Charming Molly (USA) (Diesis) 9.3f **(69)**
Form - 2
Record 1999 - 1st:0 2nd:1 3rd:0 Ran:1
Win Prizemoney £0 *Total Prizemoney* £1,280
1999 Turf 0-1: (6f) (g-f)
Currently above-average filly. (1st run) - 2nd of 6 to Jeed (25 Jun Newmarket 6f g-f RF 2304).
**R Guest [0-1] Matthews Breeding and Racing.*

MOTHER OF PEARL (IRE) RR 108f 5018a[6]
3 b f Sadler's Wells (USA) 11.3f **(87)** - Sisania (High Top) 10.2f **(67)**
Form - 12543766
Record 1999 - 1st:0 2nd:1 3rd:1 Ran:7
Pre1999 - 1st:2 2nd:0 3rd:0 Ran:2
Win Prizemoney £27,447 *Total Prizemoney* £47,953
Wins 1998 Nov Saint- (HVY) G3 8f 108 <
1998 Spt Salisb (GD) 7f 77+
1999 Turf 0-7: (10f 4, 12f 2, 13f) (hvy, g-s, gd 4, g-f)
Scopey, Pattern-class filly, effective 8 to 13f, best at 10f, acts on hvy to gd. Turf high 108 - 3rd of 9 to Star Of Akkar (21 Aug Deauville 10f gd RF 3928a). Consistent. Won both of her starts at two, including a French Group Three, but failed to get her head in front in '99 despite running some good races against the top fillies. **A G Foster [0-1] (from P W Chapple-Hyam [2-8] Oct 1999).*

MOTHERS HELP BHB 54f **RR 57f** 1446[17]
4 b f Relief Pitcher 7.6f **(47)** - Laundry Maid (Forzando) 7.6f **(59)**
Form - 0
Record 1999 - 1st:0 2nd:0 3rd:0 Ran:1
Pre1999 - 1st:0 2nd:0 3rd:1 Ran:6
Win Prizemoney £0 *Total Prizemoney* £628
1999 Turf 0-1: (12f) (frm)
Leggy, fair filly, effective 8f, acts on gd to frm.
**D L Williams [1-10] Berkshire Commercial Components Ltd (from H Candy [0-6] Oct 1998).*

MOUJEEDA RR 63f 5136[10]
2 ch f Zafonic (USA) 9f **(83)** - Dafinah (USA) (Graustark) 10.1f **(70)**
Form - 0
Record 1999 - 1st:0 2nd:0 3rd:0 Ran:1
1999 Turf 0-1: (7f) (gd)
Currently average filly. **Sir Michael Stoute [0-1] Mitaab Abdullah.*

MOUNT ABU (IRE) BHB 100f **RR 97f** 3932a[6]
2 b c Foxhound (USA) - Twany Angel (Double Form) 7.3f **(58)**
Form - 41526
Record 1999 - 1st:1 2nd:1 3rd:0 Ran:5
Win Prizemoney £4,965 *Total Prizemoney* £13,806
Wins * 1999 May Newbur (SFT) 6f 70 <
1999 Turf 1-5: (5f, 6f 1-4) (gd 1-3, g-f 2)
Very useful colt. Turf high 97. A pottery mover, he is suited by easy ground. Likely to stay seven furlongs, he must improve in order to win a Group race. **P W Chapple-Hyam [1-5].*

MOUNTAIN BIRD BHB 44f38a **RR 32f 38a** 2648[14]
3 ch f Superlative 8.8f **(57)** - Northern Bird **(60+f)** (Interrex (CAN))
Form - 0700
Record 1999 - 1st:0 2nd:0 3rd:0 Ran:4
Pre1999 - 1st:0 2nd:0 3rd:0 Ran:3
1999 Turf 0-3: (6f 3) (sft, gd, g-f) 1999 AW 0-1: (8f) (Fibr)
Unfurnished, very moderate filly. Turf high 32.
**M Brittain [0-7] Northgate Silver.*

MOUNTAIN DREAM BHB 30f53a **RR 19f 53a** 2559[5]
6 b g Batshoof 9.5f **(66)** - Echoing (Formidable (USA)) 9.2f **(63)**
Form - 5
Record 1999 - 1st:0 2nd:0 3rd:0 Ran:1
Pre1999 - 1st:0 2nd:0 3rd:1 Ran:13
Win Prizemoney £0 *Total Prizemoney* £382
1999 Turf 0-1: (16f) (frm)
Very moderate gelding, has worn blinkers. Becoming disappointing.
**R Allan [0-24] The Border Hotel (from L M Cumani [0-3] Aug 1996).*

MOUNTAIN MAGIC BHB 46f42a **RR 42f 42a** 5050[10]
4 b f Magic Ring (IRE) 6.5f **(64)** - Nevis (Connaught) 7.7f **(63)**
Form - 0040030
Record 1999 - 1st:0 2nd:0 3rd:1 Ran:7
Pre1999 - 1st:1 2nd:0 3rd:0 Ran:14
Win Prizemoney £4,042 *Total Prizemoney* £4,447
Wins * 1998 May Newbur (G-F) H 7.3f 54 61 <
1999 Turf 0-6: (8f 5, 10f) (sft, gd, frm 4) 1999 AW 0-1: (10f) (Equi)
Workmanlike, moderate filly, effective 7f, acts on frm, has worn blinkers, likes left handed tracks. Turf high 46. Inconsistent.
**D J S ffrenchDavis [1-22] Hargood Ltd.*

MOUNTAIN OYSTER (ITY) RR 5122a[5]
2 f
Form - 415
Record 1999 - 1st:1 2nd:0 3rd:0 Ran:3
Win Prizemoney £7,290 *Total Prizemoney* £7,290
Wins * 1999 Oct San Si (GD) 9f
1999 Turf 1-3: (8f, 9f 1-2) (hvy, g-s, gd 1-1)
Currently very poor filly. (began Spt) - 5th of 8 getting 3lb from Dedi Boy (24 Oct San Siro 9f hvy RF 5122a) - also 1st of 13 from Hot Opinion (9 Oct San Siro RF 4885a). **M L W Bell [1-3].*

MOUNTAIN SONG BHB 108f **RR 111f** 1108[8]
4 b c Tirol 8.1f **(64)** - Persian Song (Persian Bold) 9.3f **(66)**
Form - 8
Record 1999 - 1st:0 2nd:0 3rd:0 Ran:1
Pre1999 - 1st:4 2nd:2 3rd:2 Ran:10
Win Prizemoney £22,136 *Total Prizemoney* £50,350
Wins 1998 Oct Ayr (G-S) 8f 84
1998 Aug Windso (G-F) 10f 99 <
1997 Jun Salisb (SFT) 7f 94+
1997 Jun Thirsk (GD) 7f 71+
1999 Turf 0-1: (10f) (gd)
Scopey, Group-class colt, effective 10f, acts on g-f. Very useful up to a mile and a quarter when trained by Sir Mark Prescott, he showed little when racing for Godolphin at Goodwood in May.
**S bin Suroor [0-1] Godolphin (from Sir Mark Prescott [4-10] Oct 1998).*

MOUNT HOLLY (USA) BHB 77f74a **RR 74f 74a** 4685[11]
5 b h Woodman (USA) 9.7f **(77)** -Mount Helena(Danzig (USA)) 8.4f **(76)**
Form - 43020030
Record 1999 - 1st:0 2nd:1 3rd:2 Ran:8
Pre1999 - 1st:2 2nd:1 3rd:4 Ran:16
Win Prizemoney £12,510 *Total Prizemoney* £20,313
Wins * 1998 Jly Newmar (G-F) H 8f 70 77
1997 Oct Yarmou (GD) 8f 81 <
1999 Turf 0-8: (7f 2, 8f 5, 9f) (g-s 2, gd 4, frm 2)
Above-average colt, effective 7 to 8f, best at 8f, acts on g-s to frm, best on frm, likes tight tracks. Turf high 83 - 3rd of 9 getting 11lb from Silk St John (23 Apr Sandown 8f g-s RF 0821). Consistent.
**K Mahdi [1-18] Hamad Al-Mutawa (from J H M Gosden [1-6] Nov 1997).*

MOUNT PARK (IRE) BHB 70f **RR 80f** 5111[3]
2 b f Colonel Collins (USA) - Make Hay (Nomination) 7f **(60)**
Form - 70253
Record 1999 - 1st:0 2nd:1 3rd:1 Ran:5
Win Prizemoney £0 *Total Prizemoney* £1,687
1999 Turf 0-5: (5f, 6f 3, 7f) (sft, gd 2, frm 2)
Decent filly. Turf high 68 (began Aug) - 3rd of 10 getting 17lb from Loch Inch (28 Oct Windsor 6f gd RF 5111).
**H S Howe [0-5] Owen Delargy.*

MOUNTRATH ROCK BHB 60f **RR 55f** 3823[13]
2 b f Rock Hopper 10.6f **(54)** - Point of Law (Law Society (USA)) 9.9f **(70)**
Form - 0220
Record 1999 - 1st:0 2nd:2 3rd:0 Ran:4
Win Prizemoney £0 *Total Prizemoney* £1,151
1999 Turf 0-4: (6f 2, 7f 2) (g-f, frm 3)
Fair filly. Turf high 55 (began Jly) - 2nd of 10 to City Princess (7 Aug Redcar 6f frm RF 3454). **N Tinkler [0-4] Sampower Racing Club.*

MOURAMARA (IRE) RR 67f 5216[3]
2 b f Kahyasi 12.9f **(74)** - Mamoura (IRE) (Lomond (USA)) 8.8f **(65)**
Form - 3
Record 1999 - 1st:0 2nd:0 3rd:1 Ran:1
Win Prizemoney £0 *Total Prizemoney* £472
1999 Turf 0-1: (8f) (g-s)
Currently average filly. **L M Cumani [0-1] H H Aga Khan.*

MOUSEHOLE BHB 75f **RR 77f** 5110[14]
7 b g Statoblest 6.4f **(63)** - Alo Ez (Alzao (USA)) 7.1f **(68)**
Form - 8017423111236060
Record 1999 - 1st:4 2nd:2 3rd:2 Ran:16
Pre1999 - 1st:6 2nd:10 3rd:5 Ran:49
Win Prizemoney £29,434 *Total Prizemoney* £48,143
Wins * **1999** Aug Windso (G-F) H 5f 69 71
* **1999** Jly Nottin (G-F) 5.1f 66
* **1999** Jly Windso (G-F) H 5f 63 65
* **1999** May Nottin (FRM) H 5.1f 57 61
* 1998 Aug Bath (FRM) 5.1f 77 <
* 1998 Jly Carlis (G-F) 5f 70
* 1997 Aug Bath (GD) 5.1f 72
* 1997 Jly Warwic (G-F) 5f 63
* 1996 Jun Windso (G-F) 5f 63
* 1995 Jun Thirsk (G-F) H 6f 63 65
1999 Turf 4-16: (5f 4-16) (gd 6, g-f 1-3, frm 3-7)
Above-average gelding, effective 5f, acts on gd to frm, best on frm, has worn blinkers, likes right handed tracks, excels at Nottingham and Beverley, likes Windsor. Turf high 77 - 3rd of 13 getting 6lb from Ellens Lad (4 Spt Haydock 5f frm RF 4141) - also 1st of 10 giving 5lb to Miss Hit (2 Aug Windsor RF 3305). A useful sprint-handicapper, he won four times last season including a summer hat-trick. Suited by fast ground and the minimum trip.
**R Guest [10-65] Mrs Janet Linskey.*

MOUTAHDDEE (IRE) BHB 106f **RR 104f** 4271[6]
3 b c Alzao (USA) 9.8f **(73)** - Ah Ya Zein (Artaius (USA)) 9f **(69)**
Form - 21311536
Record 1999 - 1st:3 2nd:1 3rd:2 Ran:8
Pre1999 - 1st:1 2nd:0 3rd:0 Ran:3
Win Prizemoney £68,432 *Total Prizemoney* £74,962
Wins * **1999** Jly Sandow (GD) H 10f 95 102 <
* **1999** Jun Goodwo (G-F) H 9.9f 95 97
* **1999** Apr Newmar (GD) H 10f 88 90
* 1998 Spt Thirsk (GD) 8f 82
1999 Turf 3-8: (10f 3-5, 11f 2, 12f) (gd 1-4, g-f 2-4)
Strong, very useful colt, effective 10f, acts on gd to g-f, best on g-f, prefers tight tracks. Turf high 104 - 5th of 17 giving 10lb to Azouz Pasha (30 Jly Goodwood 10f g-f RF 3234) - also 1st of 20 getting 4lb from King Darius (2 Jly Sandown RF 2500). Consistent. He developed into a cracking front-runner, enjoying his finest hour when winning the Hong Kong Jockey Club Trophy at Sandown in July. Slightly below par when tried on soft ground, he deserves another crack at a Group race under favourable conditions.
**M P Tregoning [4-11] Sheikh Ahmed Al Maktoum.*

Moutahddee was a revelation at three

MOUTON (IRE) BHB 63f **RR 73f** 3466[2]
3 b f Dolphin Street (FR) - The Queen of Soul (Chief Singer) 8.9f **(66)**
Form - 5322
Record 1999 - 1st:0 2nd:2 3rd:1 Ran:4
Pre1999 - 1st:0 2nd:1 3rd:0 Ran:2
Win Prizemoney £0 *Total Prizemoney* £3,131
1999 Turf 0-4: (8f 2, 9f 2) (gd, g-f, frm 2)
Workmanlike, above-average filly, effective 8 to 9f, best at 8f, acts on g-f to frm, best on g-f. Turf high 73 (1st run) - 5th of 14 to Dahshah (21 May Bath 8f g-f RF 1371).
**J W Hills [0-6] Uplands Bloodstock.*

MOVE THE MOUSE (IRE) RR 50f 3425[7]
2 b f Foxhound (USA) - Kip's Sister (Cawston's Clown) 8f **(60)**
Form - 607
Record 1999 - 1st:0 2nd:0 3rd:0 Ran:3
1999 Turf 0-3: (5f, 7f 2) (g-f, frm 2)
Currently fair filly. Turf high 50.
**N A Callaghan [0-2] Mrs A M Byrne (from M H Tompkins [0-1] Jun 1999).*

MOVIE STAR (IRE) RR 36f 4819[6]
3 b f Barathea (IRE) - Mary Astor (FR) (Groom Dancer (USA))
Form - 6
Record 1999 - 1st:0 2nd:0 3rd:0 Ran:1
1999 Turf 0-1: (7f) (gd)

Leggy, currently very moderate filly.
**L M Cumani [0-1] Robert Smith.*

MOVING ARROW BHB 52f76a **RR 53f 76a** 2059[4]

8 ch g Indian Ridge 7.6f **(74)** - Another Move (Farm Walk) 11.6f **(55)**

Form - 04

Record 1999 - 1st:0 2nd:0 3rd:0 Ran:2
Pre1999 - 1st:4 2nd:8 3rd:1 Ran:47

Win Prizemoney £26,848 *Total Prizemoney* £55,170

Wins								
1996	Jly	Newmar	(G-F)	H	10f	92	98	<
1995	Oct	York	(GD)	H	7.9f	90	94	
1995	Aug	Haydoc	(G-F)	H	8.1f	87	89	

1999 Turf 0-1: (10f) (hrd) 1999 AW 0-1: (8f) (Fibr)

Fair gelding, effective 8f, acts on frm, has worn blinkers, likes tight tracks. Consistent.
**Mrs M Reveley [0-3] The Three County Partnership (from Miss S E Hall [4-47] Oct 1998).*

MOVING EXPERIENCE (IRE) **RR 56f** 5062[4]

2 b f Nicolotte - Sound Performance (IRE) (Ahonoora) 8.1f **(73)**

Form - 04

Record 1999 - 1st:0 2nd:0 3rd:0 Ran:2

Win Prizemoney £0 *Total Prizemoney* £173

1999 Turf 0-2: (6f, 8f) (gd, g-f)

Currently fair filly. Turf high 56 (began Oct).
**M J Fetherston-Godley [0-2] The Moving Partnership.*

MOVING ON UP **RR 94f** 4620a[1]

5 b g Salse (USA) 10.9f **(71)** - Thundercloud (Electric) 10.1f **(61)**

Form - 5521

1999 Turf 1-3: (10f 1-3) (hvy 1-1, g-s 2)

Useful gelding, effective 9 to 10f, best at 10f, acts on hvy to gd, best on hvy, often wears blinkers (extremely effectively). Turf high 91 - 1st of 9 giving 13lb to Lawz (24 Spt Listowel RF 4620a).
**D K Weld in IRE [6-22] Michael Hilary Burke.*

MOVING PRINCESS BHB 60f54a **RR 69f 54a** 451[10]

4 b f Prince Sabo 6.6f **(64)** - Another Move (Farm Walk) 11.6f **(55)**

Form - 70

Record 1999 - 1st:0 2nd:0 3rd:0 Ran:2
Pre1999 - 1st:0 2nd:2 3rd:3 Ran:13

Win Prizemoney £0 *Total Prizemoney* £4,706

1999 AW 0-2: (8f 2) (Fibr 2)

Lengthy, average filly, effective 8 to 10f, best at 8f, acts on gd to frm, best on g-f. AW high 51. **Miss S E Hall [0-15] G W Westgarth.*

MOWBRAY (USA) BHB 103f **RR 100f** 5210[5]

4 b br g Opening Verse (USA) 11.8f **(70)** - Peppy Raja (USA) (Raja Baba (USA)) 10f **(64)**

Form - 407281375

Record 1999 - 1st:1 2nd:1 3rd:1 Ran:9
Pre1999 - 1st:3 2nd:3 3rd:0 Ran:11

Win Prizemoney £45,646 *Total Prizemoney* £133,492

Wins								
* **1999**	Jly	Goodwo	(G-F)	H	14f	89	94	
* 1998	Oct	Leices	(HVY)		11.8f		100	<
* 1997	Aug	Kempto	(GD)		7f		97	
* 1997	Aug	Catter	(G-F)		7f		77	

1999 Turf 1-9: (12f 4, 14f 1-3, 15f, 20f) (hvy, sft, gd 4, g-f, frm 1-2)

Strong, very useful gelding, effective 10 to 14f, best at 12f, acts on sft to g-f, best on g-f, has worn blinkers, prefers right handed tracks, likes tight tracks, excels at Goodwood. Turf high 100 - 3rd of 21 giving 6lb to Vicious Circle (18 Aug York 14f gd RF 3758). He carries his head high and is a tricky customer. However, the ability is there, as he showed when winning at Goodwood and finishing third in the Ebor. Best around a mile and three-quarters, he is not one to rely on. **P F I Cole [4-20] Sir George Meyrick.*

MOY (IRE) BHB 28f44a **RR 22f 44a** 3864[11]

4 ch f Beveled (USA) 6.9f **(64)** - Exceptional Beauty (Sallust) 8.4f **(63)**

Form - 730848000

Record 1999 - 1st:0 2nd:0 3rd:1 Ran:9
Pre1999 - 1st:0 2nd:1 3rd:1 Ran:18

Win Prizemoney £0 *Total Prizemoney* £1,988

1999 Turf 0-4: (5f, 6f, 7f, 8f) (g-s, g-f 2, frm) 1999 AW 0-5: (6f, 7f 3, 12f) (Fibr 5)

Light-framed, moderate filly, effective 7f, acts on g-f - acts on Fibr, has worn blinkers, likes left handed tracks, likes tight tracks. Turf high 40. AW high 47. Becoming disappointing.
**W M Brisbourne [0-15] Christopher Chell (from M Brittain [0-12] Jun 1998).*

MR BERGERAC (IRE) BHB 64f70a **RR 64f 70a** 5053[6]

8 b g Cyrano de Bergerac 7.3f **(58)** -Makalu (Godswalk (USA)) 7.3f **(58)**

Form - 050550551206

Record 1999 - 1st:1 2nd:1 3rd:0 Ran:12
Pre1999 - 1st:8 2nd:9 3rd:10 Ran:73

Win Prizemoney £41,034 *Total Prizemoney* £77,350

Wins							
* **1999**	Aug	Bath	(GD)	H	8f	60	62
* 1997	Aug	Newmar	(G-F)	H	6f	80	84
* 1997	May	Leices	(GD)	H	6f	80	82
* 1996	Jly	Newmar	(GD)	H	6f	79	83
* 1995	*Nov*	*Wolver*	*(STD)*	*H*	*6f*	*85*	*86*
* 1995	Aug	Sandow	(G-F)	H	5f	76	79
* 1995	Jly	Sandow	(G-F)	H	5f	70	73

1999 Turf 1-12: (6f 5, 7f, 8f 1-6) (g-s, gd 3, g-f 3, frm 1-5)

Average gelding, effective 6 to 7f, acts on gd to g-f, has worn blinkers. Turf high 64. Consistent. Formerly a winning sprint handicapper, he embarked on a long losing run and was stepped up in trip. That policy paid dividends when he scored over a mile at Bath in August. **B Palling [9-85] P R John.*

MR BOMBASTIQUE (IRE) BHB 60f **RR 57f** 2904[7]

5 b g Classic Music (USA) 7.2f **(57)** - Duende (High Top) 10.2f **(67)**

Form - 007

Record 1999 - 1st:0 2nd:0 3rd:0 Ran:3
Pre1999 - 1st:1 2nd:3 3rd:1 Ran:12

Win Prizemoney £2,882 *Total Prizemoney* £7,553

Wins							
1996	Jly	Chepst	(G-F)	6.1f		71	<

1999 Turf 0-3: (10f 2, 13f) (g-s, g-f 2)

Fair gelding, effective 10f, acts on gd. Turf high 49. Becoming disappointing.
**P Bowen [1-4] G Morris (from Mrs J Brown [0-9] Mar 1999).*

MR COSPECTOR BHB 67f **RR 68f** 4037[13]

2 b c Cosmonaut - L'Ancressaan (Dalsaan) 9.8f **(64)**

Form - 5400

Record 1999 - 1st:0 2nd:0 3rd:0 Ran:4

Win Prizemoney £0 *Total Prizemoney* £237

1999 Turf 0-4: (6f 3, 7f) (gd, g-f 2, frm)

Average colt. Turf high 68. **T H Caldwell [0-4] R Cabrera-Vargas.*

MR CUBE (IRE) BHB 39f36a **RR 41f 36a** 4338[2]

9 ch h Tate Gallery (USA) 8.2f **(63)** - Truly Thankful (CAN) (Graustark) 10.1f **(70)**

Form - 04388736034542

Record 1999 - 1st:0 2nd:1 3rd:3 Ran:13
Pre1999 - 1st:8 2nd:9 3rd:11 Ran:94

Win Prizemoney £24,905 *Total Prizemoney* £41,074

Wins								
* 1997	Jly	Epsom	(G-S)	H	7f	49	59	
* 1996	Spt	Folkes	(G-F)	H	6.9f	50	54	
* 1995	Jly	Newcas	(G-F)	H	7f	55	61	<
* 1995	Jly	Kempto	(G-F)	H	7f	53	58	
* 1995	Jun	Warwic	(G-F)	H	7f	49	58	

1999 Turf 0-13: (6f, 7f 7, 8f 5) (g-s, gd, g-f 4, frm 6, hrd)

Moderate horse, effective 7 to 8f, acts on g-f, mostly wears blinkers, likes left handed tracks, likes tight tracks. Turf high 41.
**J M Bradley [6-91] R Miles (from P F I Cole [2-18] Nov 1993).*

MR FORTYWINKS (IRE) BHB 60f70a **RR 59f 70a** 4913[7]

5 ch g Fools Holme (USA) 10.3f **(64)** - Dream on (Absalom) 7.2f **(58)**

Form - 22521811438307

Record 1999 - 1st:3 2nd:3 3rd:2 Ran:14
Pre1999 - 1st:4 2nd:6 3rd:3 Ran:25

Win Prizemoney £17,614 *Total Prizemoney* £32,508

Wins								
* **1999**	Jly	Carlis	(GD)	H	12f	61	62	
* **1999**	Jun	Ripon	(G-F)	H	12.3f	58	61	
* **1999**	May	Hamilt	(Sft)	H	13f	57	57	
* 1998	Apr	Nottin	(SFT)	H	10f	53	58	
* 1998	*Jan*	*Southw*	*(STD)*	*H*	*11f*	*61*	*61+*	
* 1997	*Nov*	*Wolver*	*(STD)*	*H*	*12f*	*49*	*63*	<
* 1997	Aug	Hamilt	(GD)	S	9.2f		44	

1999 Turf 3-13: (11f, 12f 2-3, 13f 1-5, 14f 2, 16f, 17f) (hvy 2, g-s 1-2, gd, g-f 4, frm 1-3, hrd 1-1) 1999 AW 0-1: (12f) (Fibr)

Above-average gelding, effective 11 to 17f, best at 12f, acts on g-f to hrd - acts on Fibr, and excels at Southwell and Wolverhampton.

Turf high 63 - 4th of 8 giving 25lb to Diamond Crown (16 Jly Hamilton 13f frm RF 2873) - also 1st of 12 getting 4lb from Bullet (3 Jly Carlisle RF 2521). (1st run) - 2nd of 7 getting 6lb from Swift (16 Mar Southwell 12f Fibr RF 0438). An able if modest middle-distance performer, he is kept busy, but scored three times last season. He goes particularly well for Diana Jones.
**J L Eyre [7-39] Miss Nuala Cassidy.*

MR GEORGE SMITH BHB 57f RR 59f 4995[11]

2 b c Prince Sabo 6.6f **(64)** - Nellie's Gamble **(36f 59a)** (Mummy's Game) 8.2f **(60)**
Form - 0800
Record 1999 - 1st:0 2nd:0 3rd:0 Ran:4
1999 Turf 0-4: (6f 2, 7f 2) (gd, g-f, frm 2)
Fair colt. Turf high 59. **G L Moore [0-4] George Smith Ltd.*

MR JONES BHB 64f RR 75f 4934[10]

2 b br c Emperor Jones (USA) - Roxy Hart (High Top) 10.2f **(67)**
Form - 307840
Record 1999 - 1st:0 2nd:0 3rd:1 Ran:6
Win Prizemoney £0 *Total Prizemoney* £883
1999 Turf 0-5: (5f, 6f, 7f, 8f 2) (gd, g-f 3, frm) 1999 AW 0-1: (8f) (Fibr)
Above-average colt. Turf high 75. **R Hannon [0-6] Nicholas Hodges.*

MR MAJICA BHB 51f67a RR 58f 67a 4441[11]

5 b h Rudimentary (USA) 8.2f **(66)** - Pellinora (USA) (King Pellinore (USA)) 8.2f **(68)**
Form - 004700
Record 1999 - 1st:0 2nd:0 3rd:0 Ran:6
Pre1999 - 1st:2 2nd:3 3rd:1 Ran:21
Win Prizemoney £6,271 *Total Prizemoney* £12,041
Wins 1998 Jun Salisb (G-F) C 8f 69
1997 Spt Yarmou (G-F) 6f 80 <
1999 Turf 0-6: (7f 2, 8f 4) (g-s, g-f 2, frm 3)
Fair colt, effective 8f, acts on sft to g-f, often wears blinkers. Turf high 62.
**A J McNae [0-7] One Under The Eight (from B J Meehan [2-20] Jly 1998).*

MR MERTON RR 28f 4229[11]

2 b c Distant Relative 7f **(69)** - Merton Mill (Dominion) 8.5f **(63)**
Form - 0
Record 1999 - 1st:0 2nd:0 3rd:0 Ran:1
1999 Turf 0-1: (7f) (frm)
Currently little account colt. **B Hanbury [0-1] Lord Clinton.*

MR MIYAGI BHB 46f42a RR 50f 42a 157[10]

4 b g Full Extent (USA) 5.2f **(50)** - All the Girls (IRE) (Alzao (USA)) 7.1f **(68)**
Form - 0
Record 1999 - 1st:0 2nd:0 3rd:0 Ran:1
Pre1999 - 1st:0 2nd:0 3rd:0 Ran:9
Win Prizemoney £0 *Total Prizemoney* £83
1999 AW 0-1: (7f) (Fibr)
Small, fair gelding, often wears blinkers. Inconsistent.
**A Bailey [0-10] Sandybrow Stables Ltd.*

MR MONTAGUE (IRE) BHB 25f RR 29f 3412[12]

7 b g Pennine Walk 8.9f **(64)** - Ballyewry (Prince Tenderfoot (USA)) 9f **(61)**
Form - 0670
Record 1999 - 1st:0 2nd:0 3rd:0 Ran:4
Pre1999 - 1st:0 2nd:0 3rd:0 Ran:7
1999 Turf 0-4: (11f, 12f, 14f 2) (frm 4)
Little account gelding, has worn blinkers. Turf high 29.
**T W Donnelly [2-28] C I P Racing.*

MR MORIARTY (IRE) BHB 30f29a RR 36f 29a 3973[11]

8 ch g Tate Gallery (USA) 8.2f **(63)** - Bernica (FR) (Caro)
Form - 0
Record 1999 - 1st:0 2nd:0 3rd:0 Ran:1
Pre1999 - 1st:3 2nd:4 3rd:3 Ran:49
Win Prizemoney £11,736 *Total Prizemoney* £15,577
Wins * 1998 Jun Newmar (GD) H 12f 27 36
* *1996 Feb Southw (STD) H 12f 36 41 <*
* *1996 Jan Southw (STD) H 12f 24 40*
1999 Turf 0-1: (14f) (g-f)

Very moderate gelding, has worn blinkers (effectively).
**S R Bowring [10-56] D H Bowring (from A L Forbes [0-7] Jly 1994).*

MR PARADISE (IRE) BHB 62f65a RR 62f 65a 349[5]

5 b g Salt Dome (USA) 6.5f **(59)** -Glowlamp (IRE)(Glow (USA))6.7f **(71)**
Form - 55
Record 1999 - 1st:0 2nd:0 3rd:0 Ran:1
Pre1999 - 1st:3 2nd:9 3rd:4 Ran:34
Win Prizemoney £8,394 *Total Prizemoney* £22,408
Wins 1998 *Jun Southw (STD) H 7f 63 67*
1997 Jun Lingfi (GD) 7f 73 <
1997 Jun Beverl (G-F) 8.5f 73 <
1999 AW 0-1: (7f) (Fibr)
Above-average gelding, effective 7f, - acts on Fibr, has worn blinkers, prefers left handed tracks, prefers tight tracks.
**W R Muir [0-2] Mrs J M Muir (from R M H Cowell [1-15] Oct 1998).*

MR PEABODY BHB 30f RR 4543[21]

2 b g Tigani - Benten **(28f 37a)** (Sharrood (USA)) 10.5f **(72)**
Form - 0000
Record 1999 - 1st:0 2nd:0 3rd:0 Ran:4
1999 Turf 0-3: (5f 2, 6f) (gd, g-f, frm) 1999 AW 0-1: (6f) (Fibr)
Poor gelding. (began Aug). **D W Chapman [0-4] D Kerry.*

MR PERRY (IRE) BHB 57f70a RR 62f 70a 4991[8]

3 br c Perugino (USA) - Elegant Tune (USA) (Alysheba (USA)) 9f **(84)**
Form - 20672041578
Record 1999 - 1st:1 2nd:2 3rd:0 Ran:11
Win Prizemoney £2,967 *Total Prizemoney* £4,767
Wins * 1999 *Spt Wolver (STD) H 8.5f 65 66 <*
1999 Turf 0-8: (7f 3, 8f 4, 10f) (g-s 2, gd 2, g-f 2, frm, hrd) 1999 AW 1-3: (8f 1-3) (Fibr 1-3)
Workmanlike, average colt, effective 7f, acts on g-s. Turf high 77 (1st run) - 2nd of 10 to Mukasol (13 Apr Folkestone 7f g-s RF 0658). AW high 66 (began Jly). He looks a bit better on sand than on turf and got off the mark in a maiden handicap on the Wolverhampton Fibresand in September. **J S Moore [1-11] Raymond Auld.*

MR ROUGH BHB 38f38a RR 41f 38a 3240[7]

8 b g Fayruz 6.6f **(63)** - Rheinbloom (Rheingold) 10.4f **(62)**
Form - 453430543487
Record 1999 - 1st:0 2nd:0 3rd:3 Ran:11
Pre1999 - 1st:5 2nd:7 3rd:12 Ran:67
Win Prizemoney £15,954 *Total Prizemoney* £29,918
Wins * 1998 Jly Bright (GD) S 8f 39
* 1997 Jun Yarmou (FRM) SH 8f 50 57
* 1995 Apr Bright (G-F) H 8f 58 64 <
1999 Turf 0-6: (8f 6) (gd 2, frm 2, hrd 2) 1999 AW 0-5: (8f 4, 10f) (Equi 4, Fibr)
Moderate gelding, effective 8f, acts on gd to hrd - acts on Equi, has worn blinkers (very effectively), likes left handed tracks, excels at Yarmouth, likes Brighton and Lingfield. Turf high 41 - 3rd of 9 getting 7lb from Saifan (1 Jly Yarmouth 8f gd RF 2470). AW high 42 - 3rd of 9 to Joseph's Wine (13 Feb Lingfield 8f Equi RF 0286). **D Morris [5-79] D Morris.*

MRS BOSSY BOOTS BHB 30f RR 36f 2252[6]

3 gr f Mystiko (USA) 7.7f **(59)** - Rich Pickings (Dominion) 8.5f **(63)**
Form - 066
Record 1999 - 1st:0 2nd:0 3rd:0 Ran:3
1999 Turf 0-3: (8f, 10f, 11f) (g-f 2, frm)
Unfurnished, very moderate filly. Turf high 36.
**G A Butler [0-3] Chris Brasher.*

MRS JODI BHB 52f RR 48?f 2170[13]

3 b f Yaheeb (USA) - Knayton Lass **(56f)** (Presidium)
Form - 80380
Record 1999 - 1st:0 2nd:0 3rd:1 Ran:5
Win Prizemoney £0 *Total Prizemoney* £594
1999 Turf 0-5: (7f, 8f 2, 10f, 12f) (gd 2, g-f 2, hrd)
Moderate filly. Turf high 48.
**J M Jefferson [0-5] & Mrs J M Davenport.*

MRS MIDDLE BHB 41f28a RR 46f 28a 355[12]

4 b f Puissance 7.1f **(60)** - Ibadiyya (Tap On Wood) 10.3f **(65)**
Form - 00
Record 1999 - 1st:0 2nd:0 3rd:0 Ran:2

Pre1999 - 1st:1 2nd:2 3rd:0 Ran:18
Win Prizemoney £3,122 *Total Prizemoney* £5,090
Wins 1997 Aug Warwic (G-S) H 6f 62 66 <
1999 AW 0-2: (8f 2) (Equi 2)
Light-framed, moderate filly, effective 8 to 10f, acts on gd to g-f. AW high 1. Becoming disappointing.
**D W Chapman [0-8] Michael Hill (from N A Callaghan [1-12] Jly 1998).*

MRS P BHB 100f **RR 94f** 4268[1]

2 b f First Trump - Zinzi (Song) 7.2f **(61)**
Form - 72223121
Record 1999 - 1st:2 2nd:4 3rd:1 Ran:8
Win Prizemoney £30,233 *Total Prizemoney* £36,212
Wins * 1999 Spt Doncas (G-F) G2 5f 94 <
*** 1999** Aug Sandow (GD) H 5f 75 73
1999 Turf 2-8: (5f 2-3, 6f 5) (gd, g-f 1-1, frm 1-6)
Useful filly, effective 5f, acts on frm. Turf high 94 - 1st of 14 from Emerald Peace (11 Spt Doncaster RF 4268). Improving. Regularly in the frame, she earned her first victory in a Sandown nursery before causing a 33/1 surprise in the Flying Childers.
**Mrs L Stubbs [2-8] Maurice Parker.*

MR SPEAKER (IRE) BHB 61f48a **RR 61f 48a** 5053[12]

6 ch g Statoblest 6.4f **(63)** - Casting Vote (USA) (Monteverdi) 6.5f **(61)**
Form - 300130
Record 1999 - 1st:1 2nd:0 3rd:1 Ran:5
Pre1999 - 1st:2 2nd:2 3rd:2 Ran:26
Win Prizemoney £9,078 *Total Prizemoney* £12,981
Wins * 1999 Oct Bright (G-S) H 8f 54 56
*** 1998** Spt Beverl (G-F) H 7.5f 55 60 <
*** 1996** Jly Chepst (G-F) H 6.1f 60 60 <
1999 Turf 1-5: (7f 2, 8f 1-2, 9f) (g-s, gd 1-2, frm 2)
Average gelding, effective 7 to 9f, acts on gd to frm, prefers tight tracks. Turf high 61 (began Spt) - 3rd of 16 giving 8lb to Swinging The Blues (15 Oct Redcar 9f frm RF 4902) - also 1st of 14 giving 6lb to Ardent (4 Oct Brighton RF 4711). Inconsistent.
**C F Wall [3-30] David Allan (from G C Bravery [0-2] Jan 1998).*

MRS PICKLES BHB 29f36a **RR 36f 36a** 1282[6]

4 gr f Northern Park (USA) 10f **(57)** - Able Mabel (Absalom) 7.2f **(58)**
Form - 41086
Record 1999 - 1st:1 2nd:0 3rd:0 Ran:5
Pre1999 - 1st:0 2nd:1 3rd:0 Ran:11
Win Prizemoney £2,182 *Total Prizemoney* £2,836
Wins * 1999 *Mar Southw (SLW) H 14f 35 40* <
1999 Turf 0-1: (14f) (gd) 1999 AW 1-4: (14f 1-2, 16f 2) (Fibr 1-4)
Strong, moderate filly, effective 9 to 16f, acts on g-f - acts on Fibr, has worn blinkers, likes tight tracks. AW high 40 - 1st of 11 getting 2lb from Shepherds Rest (10 Mar Southwell RF 0419). Becoming disappointing. **M D I Usher [1-19] Midweek Racing.*

MRS SIDDONS (IRE) BHB 70f **RR 72f** 5197[18]

3 ch f Royal Academy (USA) 7.8f **(77)** - White Water (FR) (Pharly (FR)) 9.8f **(68)**
Form - 450
Record 1999 - 1st:0 2nd:0 3rd:0 Ran:3
Pre1999 - 1st:0 2nd:1 3rd:0 Ran:1
Win Prizemoney £0 *Total Prizemoney* £1,489
1999 Turf 0-3: (7f, 8f, 10f) (gd 2, frm)
Strong, above-average filly. Turf high 72 (began Spt).
**G Wragg [0-4] Mrs R Philipps.*

MR STYLISH BHB 71f68a **RR 70f 68a** 4879[4]

3 b g Mazilier (USA) 8.5f **(56)** - Moore Stylish (Moorestyle) 6.9f **(64)**
Form - 05832223404
Record 1999 - 1st:0 2nd:3 3rd:2 Ran:11
Win Prizemoney £0 *Total Prizemoney* £4,339
1999 Turf 0-10: (6f 8, 7f 2) (sft 2, g-s, gd, frm 6) 1999 AW 0-1: (6f) (Equi)
Unfurnished, above-average gelding, effective 6f, acts on frm. Turf high 74. Consistent. **I A Balding [0-11] Miss A V Hill.*

MT SPECULATION (IRE) BHB 70f **RR 68f** 3585a[1]

3 b c Common Grounds 8.1f **(66)** - Blue Alicia (Wolver Hollow) 8f **(56)**
Form - 053021
Record 1999 - 1st:1 2nd:1 3rd:1 Ran:6
Pre1999 - 1st:0 2nd:2 3rd:0 Ran:3

Win Prizemoney £5,382 *Total Prizemoney* £10,012
Wins * 1999 Aug Claire (HVY) C 8f 68 <
1999 Turf 1-6: (7f 3, 8f 1-2, 9f) (hvy 1-1, gd, frm 4)
Scopey, average colt, effective 7f, acts on sft to gd, has worn blinkers. Turf high 68. Winner of a Clairefontaine claimer, he has reportedly begun a hurdling career in France. **P W Chapple-Hyam [1-9] Mrs Jane Chapple-Hyam, A Peacock, Lady S.*

MUARA BAY BHB 40f46a **RR 41f 46a** 1946[15]

5 gr g Absalom 7.1f **(56)** - Inca Girl (Tribal Chief) 8.5f **(61)**
Form - 000
Record 1999 - 1st:0 2nd:0 3rd:0 Ran:3
Pre1999 - 1st:2 2nd:5 3rd:4 Ran:24
Win Prizemoney £5,179 *Total Prizemoney* £10,455
Wins 1998 *Jan Southw (STD) H 8f 46 52* <
1997 Aug Bright (G-F) H 8f 38 47
1999 Turf 0-2: (7f, 8f) (gd, g-f) 1999 AW 0-1: (8f) (Fibr)
Fair gelding, effective 7 to 8f, best at 8f, acts on gd to g-f - acts on Fibr, has worn blinkers, likes left handed tracks, prefers tight tracks. Turf high 7. Becoming disappointing. **J A Glover [0-3] Miss E L Ramsden (from G Lewis [2-23] Oct 1998).*

MUBRIK (IRE) BHB 102f **RR 103+f** 3657[10]

4 b c Lahib (USA) 8f **(69)** - Bequeath (USA) (Lyphard (USA)) 9.9f **(72)**
Form - 520
Record 1999 - 1st:0 2nd:1 3rd:0 Ran:3
Pre1999 - 1st:2 2nd:2 3rd:1 Ran:7
Win Prizemoney £11,363 *Total Prizemoney* £56,627
Wins * 1998 Jly Sandow (GD) H 7.1f 93 96 <
*** 1998** Jun Thirsk (SFT) 7f 83+
1999 Turf 0-3: (7f 3) (gd 2, g-f)
Strong, very useful colt, effective 7 to 8f, best at 7f, acts on gd to frm, best on gd, excels at Ascot. Turf high 103 (began Jly) - 2nd of 27 getting 14lb from Russian Revival (7 Aug Ascot 7f gd RF 3444). He is a big race winner waiting to happen and went close when chasing Russian Revival home in the Tote International Handicap at Ascot in August. Best around seven furlongs, he enjoys some give underfoot and is still open to improvement.
**J H M Gosden [2-10] Hamdan Al Maktoum.*

MUCHANA YETU BHB 70f **RR 76df** 2711[5]

2 b f Mtoto 11.5f **(71)** - Bobbie Dee **(74f)** (Blakeney) 10.5f **(64)**
Form - 3055
Record 1999 - 1st:0 2nd:0 3rd:1 Ran:4
Win Prizemoney £0 *Total Prizemoney* £864
1999 Turf 0-4: (6f 2, 7f 2) (gd, frm 3)
Above-average filly. Turf high 76 (1st run) - 3rd of 15 to Alpine Park (16 May Kempton 6f frm RF 1254).
**Mrs P N Dutfield [0-4] Mrs Nerys Dutfield.*

MUCHMOORE BHB 50f48a **RR 54f 48a** 4220[10]

2 b g Casteddu 7.4f **(54)** - Tassagh Bridge (IRE) **(16df 19a)** (Double Schwartz) 7.9f **(55)**
Form - 8800
Record 1999 - 1st:0 2nd:0 3rd:0 Ran:4
1999 Turf 0-3: (6f, 7f, 8f) (g-f, frm 2) 1999 AW 0-1: (8f) (Fibr)
Fair gelding. Turf high 54. **J S Moore [0-4] S J Beard.*

MUCHO COLOR (IRE) BHB 60f56a **RR 69f 56a** 174[9]

3 ch c Pips Pride 6.7f **(70)** - Aubretia (USA) (Hatchet Man (USA)) 6.3f **(51)**
Form - 70
Record 1999 - 1st:0 2nd:0 3rd:0 Ran:2
Pre1999 - 1st:0 2nd:0 3rd:0 Ran:5
Win Prizemoney £0 *Total Prizemoney* £76
1999 AW 0-2: (6f 2) (Fibr 2)
Workmanlike, average colt, has worn blinkers. AW high 35.
**S R Bowring [0-2] Charterhouse Holdings Plc (from B J Meehan [0-5] Jly 1998).*

MUDAA-EB **RR 100f** 3041a[10]

3 br c Machiavellian (USA) 9.8f **(83)** - Alkaffeyeh (IRE) (Sadler's Wells (USA)) 10f **(76)**
Form - 3351170
1999 Turf 2-7: (8f, 10f 1-3, 12f 1-3) (sft, gd 1-4, g-f 1-2)
Very useful colt, effective 8 to 12f, acts on sft to g-f. Turf high 100 - 1st of 8 from Scottish Memories (22 May Curragh RF 1480a) - also

1st of 6 getting 10lb from Nash House (9 Jun Leopardstown RF 2024a). Consistent. Out of his depth in Group company, he stays a mile and a half but is no more than a useful handicapper.

**K Prendergast in IRE [2-8].*

MUDALAL (USA) BHB 75f **RR 73f** 1142[18]

4 b c Dixieland Band (USA) 10.1f **(80)** - Barakat (Bustino) 10.4f **(64)**

Form - 000

Record 1999 - 1st:0 2nd:0 3rd:0 Ran:3

Pre1999 - 1st:1 2nd:0 3rd:1 Ran:4

Win Prizemoney £4,110 *Total Prizemoney* £4,881

Wins * 1998 May Lingfi (GD) 10f 86 <

1999 Turf 0-3: (10f, 12f 2) (gd, g-f, frm)

Light-framed, above-average colt. Turf high 73.

**B W Hills [1-5] Hamdan Al Maktoum (from D Morley [0-2] Oct 1997).*

MUDDY WATER BHB 52f48a **RR 52f 48a** 3142[2]

3 b f Salse (USA) 10.9f **(71)** - Rainbow Fleet (Nomination) 7f **(60)**

Form - 7623606462

Record 1999 - 1st:0 2nd:2 3rd:1 Ran:8

Pre1999 - 1st:0 2nd:0 3rd:0 Ran:2

Win Prizemoney £0 *Total Prizemoney* £2,378

1999 Turf 0-4: (6f 3, 7f) (g-f, frm 3) 1999 AW 0-4: (6f 3, 9f) (Fibr 4)

Unfurnished, fair filly. Turf high 52 (began Jly). AW high 54.

**D Marks [0-10] R J F Brothers.*

MUDLARK BHB 30f38a **RR 30f 38a** 2226[5]

7 b g Salse (USA) 10.9f **(71)** - Mortal Sin (USA) (Green Forest (USA)) 9.9f **(68)**

Form - 325324805

Record 1999 - 1st:0 2nd:2 3rd:2 Ran:9

Pre1999 - 1st:0 2nd:0 3rd:2 Ran:10

Win Prizemoney £0 *Total Prizemoney* £3,098

1999 Turf 0-3: (17f 2, 22f) (sft, gd, frm) 1999 AW 0-6: (16f 6) (Fibr 6)

Moderate gelding, effective 16 to 17f, best at 16f, acts on sft - acts on Fibr, mostly wears blinkers (extremely effectively), favours left handed tracks, favours tight tracks, excels at Southwell. Turf high 38 (1st run) - 4th of 16 getting 11lb from Old Hush Wing (20 Apr Pontefract 17f sft RF 0774). AW high 40 - 5th of 16 getting 11lb from He's Got Wings (12 Feb Southwell 16f Fibr RF 0283).

**J Norton [0-23] J Norton (from J W Watts [0-6] Jun 1995).*

MUFFIN MAN BHB 66f **RR 75f** 5048[10]

2 b c Timeless Times (USA) 6.1f **(56)** - Allesca **(68f)** (Alleging (USA))

Form - 8544745524800

Record 1999 - 1st:0 2nd:1 3rd:0 Ran:13

Win Prizemoney £0 *Total Prizemoney* £2,852

1999 Turf 0-13: (5f 4, 6f 4, 7f 5) (hvy, gd 2, g-f 6, frm 4)

Above-average colt, effective 7f, acts on g-f. Turf high 75 - 4th of 17 getting 13lb from French Fellow (17 Aug York 7f g-f RF 3698). Inconsistent. **M D I Usher [0-13] Miss D G Kerr.*

MUFFLED (USA) RR 58f 4490[9]

2 ch f Mizaaya - Sound It (USA) (Believe It (USA)) 9.4f **(70)**

Form - 40

Record 1999 - 1st:0 2nd:0 3rd:0 Ran:2

Win Prizemoney £0 *Total Prizemoney* £282

1999 Turf 0-2: (7f, 8f) (g-s, frm)

Currently fair filly. Turf high 58 (began Spt).

**J L Dunlop [0-2] P D Player.*

MUHAAJIM (IRE) BHB 64f **RR 70f** 4995[8]

2 ch c Lake Coniston (IRE) - Maellen (River Beauty) 8.6f **(77)**

Form - 846088

Record 1999 - 1st:0 2nd:0 3rd:0 Ran:6

Win Prizemoney £0 *Total Prizemoney* £259

1999 Turf 0-6: (6f, 7f 5) (g-s, gd 2, frm 3)

Above-average colt, has worn blinkers. Turf high 70.

**J L Dunlop [0-6] Kuwait Racing Syndicate II.*

MUHANDIS BHB 57f65a **RR 47f 65a** 236[1]

6 b h Persian Bold 10f **(69)** - Night At Sea (Night Shift (USA)) 7.2f **(69)**

Form - 0284411

Record 1999 - 1st:2 2nd:0 3rd:0 Ran:5

Pre1999 - 1st:2 2nd:1 3rd:2 Ran:13

Win Prizemoney £9,046 *Total Prizemoney* £10,754

Wins * 1999 *Feb Lingfi (STD) SH 13f 54 75*

*** 1999** *Jan Lingfi (STD) SH 13f 48 57*

* 1997 *Dec Lingfi (STD) H 10f 47 50*

1996 Jly Yarmou (FRM) 7f 77 <

1999 AW 2-5: (12f 3, 13f 2-2) (Equi 2-5)

Above-average horse, effective 13f, - acted on Equi, often wore blinkers (very effectively). AW high 75 - 1st of 8 giving 18lb to Sir Walter (6 Feb Lingfield RF 0236). (DEAD)

**G L Moore [3-14] A Moore (from J H M Gosden [1-4] Spt 1996).*

MUHASSIL (IRE) BHB 46f48a **RR 46f 48a** 2227[8]

6 ch g Persian Bold 10f **(69)** - Nouvelle Star (AUS) (Luskin Star (AUS)) 6.3f **(71)**

Form - 5528

Record 1999 - 1st:0 2nd:1 3rd:0 Ran:4

Pre1999 - 1st:0 2nd:0 3rd:0 Ran:5

Win Prizemoney £0 *Total Prizemoney* £853

1999 Turf 0-3: (10f 3) (g-f 2, frm) 1999 AW 0-1: (11f) (Fibr)

Moderate gelding, often wears blinkers. Turf high 46. Becoming disappointing.

**K A Morgan [0-13] R W Walpole (from Major W R Hern [0-2] Mar 1997).*

MUHIB (USA) BHB 105f **RR 108f** 5051[1]

4 b c Red Ransom (USA) 8.6f **(83)** - Sensorious (CAN) (Vice Regent (CAN)) 8.7f **(74)**

Form - 2333221

Record 1999 - 1st:1 2nd:3 3rd:3 Ran:7

Pre1999 - 1st:2 2nd:1 3rd:1 Ran:7

Win Prizemoney £43,892 *Total Prizemoney* £70,703

Wins * 1999 Oct Leices (SFT) 11.8f 101

* 1998 Jly Goodwo (G-S) H 12f 96 103 <

* 1998 Jun Goodwo (G-F) 9f 85+

1999 Turf 1-7: (10f 2, 12f 1-5) (sft, g-s, gd 1-3, g-f 2)

Scopey, Pattern-class colt, effective 10 to 12f, best at 12f, acts on gd to g-f, best on g-f, has worn blinkers, prefers right handed tracks, prefers tight tracks, excels at Leicester and Goodwood. Turf high 111 - 3rd of 5 getting 3lb from Yavana's Pace (12 Jun Leicester 12f gd RF 1947). A string of placed efforts may look suspicious, but this colt is certainly game. Unfortunately he does lack a turn-of-foot and is always vulnerable to something with a finishing kick. He finally got it right at Leicester on his final start.

**Sir Michael Stoute [3-14] Hamdan Al Maktoum.*

MUHTAFEL BHB 96f **RR 94f** 957[2]

5 b g Nashwan (USA) 10.3f **(79)** - The Perfect Life (IRE) (Try My Best (USA)) 7.6f **(67)**

Form - 62

Record 1999 - 1st:0 2nd:1 3rd:0 Ran:2

Pre1999 - 1st:3 2nd:4 3rd:2 Ran:18

Win Prizemoney £13,052 *Total Prizemoney* £25,023

Wins * 1998 Aug Chepst (G-F) H 10.2f 81 86 <

1998 Jly Newmar (G-F) H 10f 72 77

1997 Jun Redcar (GD) 8f 81

1999 Turf 0-2: (10f 2) (g-f, frm)

Useful gelding, effective 10f, acts on frm, has worn blinkers, likes right handed tracks. Turf high 94 - 2nd of 17 getting 2lb from Elhayq (1 May Newmarket 10f frm RF 0957). Improving.

**J R Jenkins [1-6] R M Ellis (from M Quinn [1-10] Jly 1998).*

MUHTATHIR BHB 118f **RR 116f** 4892a[1]

4 ch c Elmaamul (USA) 8.1f **(70)** - Majmu (USA) (Al Nasr (FR)) 9.3f **(68)**

Form - 2541

Record 1999 - 1st:1 2nd:1 3rd:0 Ran:4

Pre1999 - 1st:5 2nd:2 3rd:1 Ran:12

Win Prizemoney £112,017 *Total Prizemoney* £184,784

Wins * 1999 Oct San Si (GD) G1 8f 107+

1998 Aug Goodwo (G-F) G2 8f 121 <

1998 Aug Newbur (G-F) G3 7.3f 118

1998 Jly Doncas (G-F) 8f 109+

1997 Jly Sandow (G-S) 7.1f 105+

1997 Jun Sandow (G-F) 7.1f 90

1999 Turf 1-3: (8f 1-3) (gd 1-1, g-f) 1999 AW 0-1: (8f) (Dirt)

Scopey, high-class colt, effective 7 to 8f, best at 8f, acts on gd to g-f, best on g-f, excels at Doncaster. Turf high 116 - 4th of 10 giving 6lb to Sugarfoot (9 Spt Doncaster 8f g-f RF 4235). He had a successful 1998, but had run modestly in Dubai and Japan, before returning from a three month lay-off to finish a creditable fourth

behind Sugarfoot in Doncaster's Park Stakes. He made no mistake when a short-priced favourite for a weak-looking Group One event in Italy next time.
**S bin Suroor [1-3] Godolphin (from S bin Suroor in UAE [0-1] Mar 1999).*

MUJAHID (USA) BHB 112f **RR 111f** 5131[2]

3 b c Danzig (USA) 8.1f **(88)** - Elrafa Ah (USA) **(101f)** (Storm Cat (USA))
Form - 535742
Record 1999 - 1st:0 2nd:1 3rd:1 Ran:6
Pre1999 - 1st:3 2nd:0 3rd:0 Ran:4
Win Prizemoney £142,822 *Total Prizemoney* £185,283
Wins * 1998 Oct Newmar (GD) G1 7f 118 <
* 1998 Jly Salisb (G-F) 6f 95+
* 1998 Jly Newmar (G-F) 6f 98+
1999 Turf 0-6: (7f, 8f 4, 10f) (gd 3, g-f 2, frm)
Scopey, Group-class colt, effective 7 to 10f, acts on gd to frm, best on gd, has worn blinkers. Turf high 115 - 3rd of 16 to Island Sands (1 May Newmarket 8f frm RF 0958). Consistent. Caused quite a surprise when winning the 1998 Dewhurst, showing a great turn of foot, but his three-year-old campaign was one big disappointment. It started badly with his defeat in the Craven, though he then ran quite well to finish third in the Guineas and fifth in the French equivalent. First-time blinkers did not seem to make much difference in the St James's Palace, but he did not run badly when fourth in the Challenge Stakes after a four-month break and with the headgear left off. He ended the season with a fair second in a Newmarket Listed event on his first attempt at ten furlongs.
**J L Dunlop [3-10] Hamdan Al Maktoum.*

MUJA'S MAGIC (IRE) BHB 50f59a **RR 48f 59a** 5149[4]

4 b f Mujadil (USA) 7.7f **(70)** - Grave Error (Northern Treat (USA)) 6f **(50)**
Form - 07705622505016534
Record 1999 - 1st:1 2nd:2 3rd:1 Ran:17
Pre1999 - 1st:2 2nd:3 3rd:5 Ran:32
Win Prizemoney £14,284 *Total Prizemoney* £20,978
Wins 1999 Aug Beverl (GD) H 5f 39 45
1998 Jun Bright (GD) H 6f 53 59 <
1997 *Dec Lingfi (STD) H 6f 54 58*
1999 Turf 1-16: (5f 1-6, 6f 9, 7f) (sft, g-s, gd 2, g-f 3, frm 1-8, hrd) 1999 AW 0-1: (6f) (Fibr)
Leggy, fair filly, effective 6 to 7f, best at 7f, acts on gd to g-f - acts on AW, best on Equi, often wears blinkers, likes tight tracks, does well at Lingfield. Turf high 48. (1st run) - 4th of 13 giving 3lb to Days of Grace (30 Oct Wolverhampton 6f Fibr RF 5149).
**Mrs N Macauley [0-1] Miss P Phillips (from K T Ivory [3-48] Spt 1999).*

MUJKARI (IRE) BHB 41f **RR 44f** 4150[7]

3 ch g Mujtahid (USA) 7.4f **(69)** - Hot Curry (USA) (Sharpen Up) 8.3f **(67)**
Form - 060052167
Record 1999 - 1st:1 2nd:1 3rd:0 Ran:9
Pre1999 - 1st:0 2nd:0 3rd:0 Ran:6
Win Prizemoney £3,273 *Total Prizemoney* £3,838
Wins * **1999** Aug Bright (FRM) H 7f 38 41 <
1999 Turf 1-8: (6f, 7f 1-3, 8f 4) (g-s, gd 3, g-f 2, frm 1-2) 1999 AW 0-1: (7f) (Fibr)
Moderate gelding, effective 7f, acts on frm, has worn blinkers (extremely effectively). Turf high 44 - 2nd of 13 getting 7lb from Miss Money Spider (14 Jly Folkestone 7f frm RF 2819) - also 1st of 13 getting 13lb from Ballymorris Boy (4 Aug Brighton RF 3351).
**J M Bradley [1-9] Robert Bailey (from R Hannon [0-6] Oct 1998).*

MUJODA BHB 38f **RR 31f** 4580[12]

2 b f Mizoram (USA) - Titian Beauty (Auction Ring (USA)) 8.6f **(65)**
Form - 000
Record 1999 - 1st:0 2nd:0 3rd:0 Ran:3
1999 Turf 0-3: (6f, 7f 2) (gd, frm 2)
Currently very moderate filly. Turf high 19 (began Aug).
**R Brotherton [0-3] Mrs Sandra Hall.*

MUKAABED (USA) RR 85f 5129[10]

2 ch c Phone Trick (USA) 7f **(62)** - Slick Delivery (USA) (Topsider (USA)) 8.3f **(71)**
Form - 30
Record 1999 - 1st:0 2nd:0 3rd:1 Ran:2
Win Prizemoney £0 *Total Prizemoney* £819
1999 Turf 0-2: (6f 2) (gd 2)
Currently useful colt. Turf high 85 (began Oct).
**M P Tregoning [0-2] Hamdan Al Maktoum.*

MUKARRAB (USA) BHB 50f85a **RR 47f 85a** 4436[5]

5 b br g Dayjur (USA) 6.8f **(79)** - Mahassin (NZ) (Biscay (AUS)) 6.5f **(51)**
Form - 15113132211300532732060530 35
Record 1999 - 1st:4 2nd:4 3rd:7 Ran:25
Pre1999 - 1st:3 2nd:3 3rd:4 Ran:33
Win Prizemoney £20,123 *Total Prizemoney* £35,130
Wins * **1999** *Feb Lingfi (STD) H 6f 76 85* <
* **1999** *Feb Lingfi (STD) H 5f 76 78*
* **1999** *Jan Lingfi (STD) H 6f 67 74*
* **1999** *Jan Lingfi (STD) H 6f 49 74*
* 1998 *Dec Lingfi (STD) H 5f 49 55*
* 1998 *Dec Lingfi (STD) H 6f 42 51*
* 1998 Spt Thirsk (GD) H 5f 47 56
1999 Turf 0-14: (5f 12, 6f 2) (gd 4, g-f 5, frm 5) 1999 AW 4-11: (5f 1-3, 6f 3-8) (Equi 4-7, Fibr 4)
Decent gelding, effective 5 to 6f, best at 5f, - acts on AW, best on Equi, has worn blinkers, prefers left handed tracks, prefers tight tracks, excels at Lingfield and Wolverhampton. Turf high 51. AW high 85 - 1st of 8 giving 16lb to John Bowdler Music (27 Feb Lingfield RF 0374) - also 1st of 5 giving 16lb to Half Tone (25 Feb Lingfield RF 0358). A real trier who is kept very busy, he is an especially useful sprinter on sand and won six times on Equitrack during the winter. He is rated some 35lb inferior on turf.
**D W Chapman [7-52] Ian Armitage (from D K Weld in IRE [0-6] Jly 1997).*

MUKASOL BHB 90f **RR 81f** 4520a[2]

3 b c Mukaddamah (USA) 7.6f **(74)** - So Long Boys (FR) (Beldale Flutter (USA)) 9.7f **(71)**
Form - 110062
Record 1999 - 1st:2 2nd:1 3rd:0 Ran:6
Pre1999 - 1st:0 2nd:0 3rd:2 Ran:3
Win Prizemoney £16,204 *Total Prizemoney* £24,493
Wins * **1999** May San Si (G-F) 8f 77 <
* **1999** Apr Folkes (HVY) 7f 77 <
1999 Turf 2-6: (7f 1-3, 8f 1-3) (g-s 1-2, g-f 1-3, frm)
Decent colt, effective 7 to 8f, best at 7f, acts on sft to frm, best on g-s. Turf high 81 - 2nd of 5 giving 8lb to Onice Nero (19 Spt San Siro 7f g-s RF 4520a) - also 1st of 10 from Mr Perry (13 Apr Folkestone RF 0658). Consistent. **L M Cumani [2-9].*

MUKAYED (IRE) BHB 76f **RR 77f** 4905[2]

3 ro c Cadeaux Genereux 7.9f **(76)** - Al Sylah (Nureyev (USA)) 8.7f **(78)**
Form - 6854332
Record 1999 - 1st:0 2nd:1 3rd:2 Ran:7
Win Prizemoney £0 *Total Prizemoney* £2,522
1999 Turf 0-7: (6f 2, 7f 4, 8f) (gd, g-f 2, frm 4)
Scopey, above-average colt, effective 7f, acts on g-f to frm, best on frm, often wears blinkers. Turf high 81 - 4th of 14 getting 3lb from Nice One Clare (28 Aug Newmarket 7f frm RF 3965).
**J L Dunlop [0-7] Hamdan Al Maktoum.*

MUKHALIF (IRE) BHB 112f **RR 105f** 2660a[10]

3 ch c Caerleon (USA) 10.9f **(79)** - Potri Pe (ARG) (Potrillazo (ARG))
Form - 2210
Record 1999 - 1st:1 2nd:2 3rd:0 Ran:4
Pre1999 - 1st:2 2nd:0 3rd:0 Ran:2
Win Prizemoney £164,451 *Total Prizemoney* £174,045
Wins * **1999** May Capann (G-F) G1 12f 105 <
1998 Spt Ascot (SFT) 7f 102+
1998 Spt Leices (G-S) 7f 97+
1999 Turf 1-4: (10f 2, 12f 1-2) (gd 2, g-f 1-1, frm)
Scopey, Pattern-class colt, effective 7 to 12f, best at 10f, acts on gd to frm. Turf high 105 - also 1st of 13 from Iscan (30 May Capannelle RF 1719a). An easy winner from Zaajer at Ascot on his second start at two, he was sent to winter in Dubai. He started off the season by chasing home Beat All at Newmarket and his old rival Zaajer at York, before running out a clear-cut winner of the Derby Italiano. Well beaten in the German Derby, however, and did not reappear. **S bin Suroor [1-4] (from D R Loder [2-2] Spt 1998).*

MUKHLLES (USA) BHB 50f48a **RR 50f 48a** 3916[13]
6 b g Diesis 9f **(80)** - Serenely (USA) (Alydar (USA)) 9.1f **(76)**
Form - 14500
Record 1999 - 1st:1 2nd:0 3rd:0 Ran:5
Pre1999 - 1st:0 2nd:0 3rd:3 Ran:19
Win Prizemoney £3,272 *Total Prizemoney* £5,177
Wins * **1999** Jun Lingfi (GD) H 10f 43 52 <
1999 Turf 1-5: (10f 1-3, 11f, 12f) (gd 3, g-f 1-1, frm)
Fair gelding, effective 10 to 11f, acts on gd to g-f, likes left handed tracks, likes tight tracks. Turf high 52 (1st run) - 1st of 14 getting 11lb from Junikay (12 Jun Lingfield RF 1953). Caused a big surprise when winning a Lingfield handicap in June when stepped up to ten furlongs.
**Bob Jones [1-22] Mrs Daphne Downey (from Major W R Hern [0-2] Apr 1996).*

MULLAGH HILL LAD (IRE) BHB 48f38a **RR 59?f 38a** 925[8]
6 b g Cyrano de Bergerac 7.3f **(58)** - Fantasise (FR) (General Assembly (USA)) 10f **(68)**
Form - 68508
Record 1999 - 1st:0 2nd:0 3rd:0 Ran:4
Pre1999 - 1st:1 2nd:2 3rd:2 Ran:29
Win Prizemoney £2,085 *Total Prizemoney* £5,181
Wins 1995 *Nov Wolver (STD) S 5f 65* <
1999 AW 0-4: (6f, 7f, 8f 2) (Equi, Fibr 3)
Fair gelding, effective 6f, - acts on Fibr, has worn blinkers (effectively). AW high 31.
**N P Littmoden [0-14] Nick Littmoden (from B A McMahon [1-19] Jly 1997).*

MULLAGHMORE (IRE) BHB 57f **RR 56f** 5191[4]
3 b g Petardia 8.2f **(58)** - Comfrey Glen (Glenstal (USA)) 10.1f **(64)**
Form - 030653674
Record 1999 - 1st:0 2nd:0 3rd:2 Ran:9
Pre1999 - 1st:0 2nd:0 3rd:0 Ran:2
Win Prizemoney £0 *Total Prizemoney* £1,091
1999 Turf 0-9: (8f 8, 9f) (g-s, g-f 4, frm 4)
Scopey, fair gelding, effective 8f, acts on g-f, has worn blinkers (very effectively). Turf high 64 - 3rd of 16 giving 1lb to Gevity (21 May Bath 8f g-f RF 1372). Consistent. **M Kettle [0-11] Greenacres.*

MULLITOVER BHB 64f64a **RR 65f 64a** 4094[17]
9 ch g Interrex (CAN) 7.7f **(51)** - Atlantic Air (Air Trooper) 9.1f **(63)**
Form - 4850270
Record 1999 - 1st:0 2nd:1 3rd:0 Ran:5
Pre1999 - 1st:6 2nd:5 3rd:2 Ran:52
Win Prizemoney £26,862 *Total Prizemoney* £41,386
Wins 1995 Oct Newmar (G-F) H 7f 83 87 <
1995 Spt Lingfi (FRM) H 7f 75 71
1995 Aug Kempto (G-F) H 7f 62 77
1995 Aug Windso (G-F) H 8.3f 62 71
1999 Turf 0-5: (7f 3, 8f 2) (g-f 2, frm 3)
Average gelding, effective 7 to 8f, best at 7f, acts on gd to hrd, best on gd, prefers tight tracks, excels at Kempton. Turf high 65 - 2nd of 16 giving 2lb to Holly Blue (12 Jun Bath 8f g-f RF 1938).
**C G Cox [0-1] Exors of the late M Heaton-Ellis (from M J Heaton-Ellis [6-56] Jun 1999).*

MULL OF KINTYRE (USA) RR 104+f 5229a[4]
2 b c Danzig (USA) 8.1f **(88)** - Retrospective (USA) (Easy Goer (USA))
Form - 1214
1999 Turf 2-3: (6f 2-3) (gd 2-2, frm) 1999 AW 0-1: (9f) (Dirt)
Very useful colt. Turf high 104 - 1st of 10 from Ma Yoram (18 Aug York RF 3759). He learnt little when winning easily on his debut, and looked green when beaten by City On A Hill in the July Stakes at Newmarket. Wiser when justifying strong market support in the Gimcrack Stakes, he is not far behind Europe's top juveniles on a line through Ma Yoram. He finished the season with a really good fourth in the Breeders' Cup Juvenile and should make his mark at the highest level in 2000. **A P O'Brien in IRE [2-4].*

MULTI FRANCHISE BHB 36f27a **RR 39f 27a** 1280[8]
6 ch g Gabitat 8.5f **(44)** - Gabibti (IRE) (Dara Monarch) 8.8f **(59)**
Form - 88
Record 1999 - 1st:0 2nd:0 3rd:0 Ran:2
Pre1999 - 1st:4 2nd:2 3rd:3 Ran:46
Win Prizemoney £10,045 *Total Prizemoney* £13,730
Wins 1997 *Nov Lingfi (STD) H 10f 39 46*
1996 Aug Bright (FRM) C 8f 54
1996 *Feb Lingfi (STD) C 10f 57*
1995 *Jun Wolver (STD) S 7f 65* <
1999 AW 0-2: (10f, 11f) (Equi, Fibr)
Very moderate gelding, effective 8 to 10f, best at 8f, acts on g-f to frm - acts on Equi, has worn blinkers. **Mrs L C Jewell [0-11] Mrs A Emanuel (from R M Flower [1-29] Spt 1998).*

MUMBAI BHB 29f **RR 26f** 2386[8]
3 b g Theatrical Charmer 10.9f **(63)** - Lehzen (Posse (USA)) 8.9f **(61)**
Form - 408
Record 1999 - 1st:0 2nd:0 3rd:0 Ran:3
1999 Turf 0-3: (8f 2, 11f) (g-s, g-f, frm)
Light-framed, currently little account gelding. Turf high 26.
**D J Wintle [0-3] Mrs Joan Egan.*

MUMMY NOSE BEST BHB 34f **RR 30f** 4819[13]
3 b f Cyrano de Bergerac 7.3f **(58)** - Wendy's Way **(44f 41a)** (Merdon Melody)
Form - 6000700
Record 1999 - 1st:0 2nd:0 3rd:0 Ran:7
Pre1999 - 1st:0 2nd:0 3rd:0 Ran:1
1999 Turf 0-6: (5f, 6f 3, 7f 2) (gd 2, g-f, frm 3) 1999 AW 0-1: (7f) (Equi)
Light-framed, very moderate filly. Turf high 43.
**V Soane [0-8] The Fillies Fanciers.*

MUNASIB (IRE) BHB 43f43a **RR 23f 43a** 1437[18]
4 br g Treasure Kay 6.5f **(53)** - Pipe Opener (Prince Sabo) 7.2f **(62)**
Form - 000
Record 1999 - 1st:0 2nd:0 3rd:0 Ran:2
Pre1999 - 1st:0 2nd:0 3rd:1 Ran:10
Win Prizemoney £0 *Total Prizemoney* £411
1999 Turf 0-2: (7f, 8f) (g-f 2)
Little account gelding, effective 7f, acts on hvy. Turf high 23. Becoming disappointing.
**S E Kettlewell [0-6] Cable Media Consultancy Ltd (from D Hanley in IRE [0-6] Aug 1998).*

MUNDAKA (IRE) BHB 59f **RR 72f** 5138[8]
2 ch c Mukaddamah (USA) 7.6f **(74)** - Frau Ahuyentante (ARG) (Frari (ARG)) 11.6f **(74)**
Form - 853708
Record 1999 1st:0 2nd:0 3rd:1 Ran:6
Win Prizemoney £0 *Total Prizemoney* £566
1999 Turf 0-6: (7f 2, 8f 4) (gd 2, g-f, frm 2, hrd)
Above-average colt, effective 8f, acts on hrd. Turf high 72 (began Jly) - 3rd of 6 to Sovereign State (4 Spt Thirsk 8f hrd RF 4145).
**S P C Woods [0-6] Mrs Jan Smith.*

MUNDO RARO BHB 75f **RR 71f** 4689[18]
4 b c Zafonic (USA) 9f **(83)** - Star Spectacle (Spectacular Bid (USA)) 11.2f **(76)**
Form - 620000
Record 1999 - 1st:0 2nd:1 3rd:0 Ran:6
Pre1999 - 1st:1 2nd:2 3rd:1 Ran:6
Win Prizemoney £3,566 *Total Prizemoney* £11,826
Wins * 1998 Aug Pontef (G-F) 8f 87 <
1999 Turf 0-6: (7f 2, 8f 3, 9f) (gd 3, g-f 2, frm)
Lengthy, above-average colt, effective 8f, acts on gd to frm, prefers tight tracks. Turf high 87 - 2nd of 7 getting 4lb from Night of Glass (25 May Beverley 8f gd RF 1450).
**J G FitzGerald [1-12] Marquesa de Moratalla.*

MUNGO DUFF (IRE) BHB 65f **RR 67f** 3999[15]
4 b g Priolo (USA) 10.9f **(71)** - Noble Dust (USA) (Dust Commander (USA)) 10.3f **(77)**
Form - 50
Record 1999 - 1st:0 2nd:0 3rd:0 Ran:2
Pre1999 - 1st:0 2nd:0 3rd:0 Ran:2
1999 Turf 0-2: (8f, 10f) (gd, g-f)
Scopey, average gelding. Turf high 67 (began Aug).
**J R Fanshawe [0-2] & Mrs Jonathan Jay (from P W Harris [0-2] Jun 1998).*

MUNGO PARK BHB 71f **RR 76f** 4933[7]
5 b g Selkirk (USA) 7.9f **(76)** - River Dove (USA) (Riverman (USA)) 9.1f

(76)
Form - 841746020654245207

Record	1999 -	1st:1	2nd:3	3rd:0	Ran:18
	Pre1999 -	1st:6	2nd:2	3rd:4	Ran:34

Win Prizemoney £26,970 *Total Prizemoney* £39,545

Wins	* 1999 Apr Thirsk (GD)		5f	82+	<
	1998 Jly Newcas (G-F)	H	5f	77 80	
	1998 Jun Nottin (G-F)	H	5.1f	75 76	
	1998 May Beverl (GD)	H	5f	70 75	
	1998 Apr Newcas (SFT)	H	5f	64 70	
	1997 Oct Newcas (G-F)	H	5f	53 60	
	1997 May Carlis (FRM)		5f	51	

1999 Turf 1-18: (5f 1-15, 6f 3) (gd 1-7, g-f 4, frm 7)

Above-average gelding, effective 5 to 6f, best at 5f, acts on gd to frm, best on gd, has worn blinkers, and excels at Bath. Turf high 82 - 1st of 9 from Double Oscar (16 Apr Thirsk RF 0726). He is a useful come-from-behind sprinter when in the mood, however, he has looked unco-operative at times and has thrown away races which he ought to have won.

**M Dods [1-18] Mrs H M Carr (from Mrs J R Ramsden [6-34] Oct 1998).*

MUNIF (USA) BHB 69a RR 66f 1863[15]

4 ch g Woodman (USA) 9.7f **(77)** - Garvin's Gal (USA) (Seattle Slew (USA)) 9.4f **(76)**
Form - 36030

Record	1999 -	1st:0	2nd:0	3rd:2	Ran:5
	Pre1999 -	1st:0	2nd:0	3rd:0	Ran:1

Win Prizemoney £0 *Total Prizemoney* £1,144

1999 Turf 0-4: (7f, 8f, 10f, 12f) (g-s, gd, g-f, hrd) 1999 AW 0-1: (9f) Fibr)

Average gelding, effective 10f, acts on g-s. Turf high 66 - 3rd of 9 giving 6lb to Dee Pee Tee Cee (2 Jun Chester 10f g-s RF 1670).

**B Hanbury [0-6] B Hanbury.*

MUNJIZ (IRE) BHB 114f RR 114f 4568[2]

3 b br c Marju (IRE) 9.2f **(76)** - Absaar (USA) (Alleged (USA)) 10f **(76)**
Form - 1626262

Record	1999 -	1st:1	2nd:3	3rd:0	Ran:7
	Pre1999 -	1st:1	2nd:1	3rd:1	Ran:4

Win Prizemoney £12,597 *Total Prizemoney* £49,479

Wins	* 1999 Apr Newmar (GD)	H	6f	90 94	<
	* 1998 Spt Goodwo (G-S)		6f	88	

1999 Turf 1-7: (6f 1-7) (sft, gd, g-f 1-3, frm 2)

Scopey, Group-class colt, effective 6f, acts on sft. Turf high 114 - 2nd of 11 getting 6lb from Bold Edge (26 Spt Ascot 6f sft RF 4568). He improved by a staggering 24lbs according to official figures and enjoyed a cracking season despite winning just once. Short-headed by Bold Edge in the Diadem Stakes at Ascot in September, he should stay seven furlongs and win a Group race.

**B W Hills [2-11] Hamdan Al Maktoum.*

MUNTEJ BHB 85f RR 79f 4994[3]

2 ch c Muhtarram (USA) - El Rabab (USA) (Roberto (USA)) 10f **(76)**
Form - 622223

Record	1999 -	1st:0	2nd:4	3rd:1	Ran:6

Win Prizemoney £0 *Total Prizemoney* £7,148

1999 Turf 0-6: (7f 5, 8f) (gd 3, g-f 3)

Above-average colt, effective 7 to 8f, best at 7f, acts on gd to g-f, best on gd. Turf high 79 - 3rd of 11 to Wurzel (21 Oct Brighton 7f gd RF 4994).

**B W Hills [0-6] Hamdan Al Maktoum.*

MUQTARB (IRE) BHB 92f RR 89?f 5030[13]

3 ch c Cadeaux Genereux 7.9f **(76)** - Jasarah (IRE) (Green Desert (USA)) 8.6f **(78)**
Form - 40

Record	1999 -	1st:0	2nd:0	3rd:0	Ran:2
	Pre1999 -	1st:1	2nd:0	3rd:0	Ran:2

Win Prizemoney £6,775 *Total Prizemoney* £7,796

Wins	* 1998 Jly Ascot (G-F)	6f	89+	<

1999 Turf 0-2: (6f, 7f) (g-s, g-f)

Scopey, useful colt. Turf high 87 (began Oct). Cracked a cannon bone which meant that his reappearance last season was delayed until October, when he ran fairly well up to a point in a Redcar conditions event.

**M P Tregoning [1-4] Hamdan Al Maktoum.*

MUQTARIB (USA) BHB 107f RR 100f 5222[10]

3 b c Gone West (USA) 7.8f **(82)** - Shicklah (USA) (The Minstrel (CAN)) 10f **(72)**
Form - 00

Record	1999 -	1st:0	2nd:0	3rd:0	Ran:2
	Pre1999 -	1st:2	2nd:1	3rd:0	Ran:3

Win Prizemoney £30,748 *Total Prizemoney* £32,152

Wins	* 1998 Jly Goodwo (G-S)	G2	6f	100	<
	* 1998 Jun Goodwo (GD)		6f	84+	

1999 Turf 0-2: (6f 2) (g-s, gd)

Neat, very useful colt. Turf high 100 (1st run) (began Oct) - 9th of 20 getting 1lb from Gaelic Storm (15 Oct Newmarket 6f gd RF 4896). Off the track for 15 months before reappearing in a Newmarket Listed event in October, he caught the eye with the way he finished and is very much one to bear in mind.

**J L Dunlop [2-5] Hamdan Al Maktoum.*

MURAWWI (IRE) RR 95f 4478a[2]

2 bb c Perugino (USA) - Pheopotstown 00
Form - 61042

1999 Turf 1-5: (5f, 6f 1-2, 8f 2) (sft, g-s 1-3, frm)

Very useful colt, has worn blinkers. Turf high 95 - 2nd of 8 to Sinndar (19 Spt Curragh 8f g-s RF 4478a). He ran a cracker at 50-1 in the Group One National Stakes, only being caught close home after leading inside the final furlong. Raised 16lbs as a result of that performance, he will stay beyond a mile but may be difficult to place.

**D K Weld in IRE [1-5] Hamdan Al Maktoum.*

MURCHAN TYNE (IRE) BHB 58f RR 56f 4917[27]

6 ch m Good Thyne (USA) 11.8f **(60)** - Ardnamurchan (Ardross) 10.6f **(68)**
Form - 3085150

Record	1999 -	1st:1	2nd:0	3rd:1	Ran:7
	Pre1999 -	1st:1	2nd:3	3rd:1	Ran:13

Win Prizemoney £6,251 *Total Prizemoney* £12,956

Wins	* 1999 Aug Ripon (GD)	H	16f	53 56	
	* 1998 Jun Leices (GD)	H	11.8f	53 57	<

1999 Turf 1-7: (12f 2, 16f 1-4, 17f) (gd 3, g-f 1-1, frm 3)

Fair mare, effective 11 to 16f, best at 16f, acts on sft to frm, best on gd, likes left handed tracks. Turf high 56 - 1st of 5 getting 5lb from Salestria (31 Aug Ripon RF 4044). Consistent. She has been suited by being stepped up in trip, including when victorious over two miles at Ripon in August.

**E J Alston [3-23] Harrington-Worrall Racing.*

MURGHEM (IRE) BHB 100f RR 100f 5221[10]

4 b c Common Grounds 8.1f **(66)** - Fabulous Pet (Somethingfabulous (USA)) 9.5f **(75)**
Form - 40641327320

Record	1999 -	1st:1	2nd:2	3rd:2	Ran:11
	Pre1999 -	1st:1	2nd:5	3rd:2	Ran:10

Win Prizemoney £10,031 *Total Prizemoney* £48,158

Wins	1999 Aug Sandow (G-S)	H	14f	90 93	<
	1998 Jly Kempto (G-F)		12f	80	

1999 Turf 1-11: (12f 7, 14f 1-3, 16f) (sft, g-s, gd 4, g-f 1-3, frm 2)

Scopey, very useful colt, effective 12 to 16f, acts on sft to g-f, has worn blinkers, likes right handed tracks, excels at York. Turf high 100 - 2nd of 6 to Muhib (25 Oct Leicester 12f gd RF 5051) - also 1st of 8 giving 22lb to Danegold (11 Aug Sandown RF 3560).

**M Johnston [0-3] A Al-Rostamani (from B Hanbury [2-18] Spt 1999).*

MURJAN (FR) BHB 78f RR 80f 4537[4]

2 ch c Lycius (USA) 8.8f **(71)** - Raknah (IRE) **(85df)** (Night Shift (USA)) 7.2f **(69)**
Form - 434

Record	1999 -	1st:0	2nd:0	3rd:1	Ran:3

Win Prizemoney £0 *Total Prizemoney* £1,332

1999 Turf 0-3: (8f 2, 9f) (frm 3)

Currently decent colt. Turf high 80 (began Aug) - 3rd of 8 to Windsor Boy (29 Aug Beverley 8f frm RF 3990).

**M Johnston [0-3] Mohammed Jaber.*

MURMOON BHB 63f67a RR 71f 67a 407[6]

4 b g Danehill (USA) 9.1f **(79)** - Reflection (Mill Reef (USA)) 10.5f **(78)**
Form - 236

Record	1999 -	1st:0	2nd:1	3rd:1	Ran:3
	Pre1999 -	1st:0	2nd:1	3rd:2	Ran:13

Win Prizemoney £0 *Total Prizemoney* £4,384

1999 AW 0-3: (7f, 8f, 9f) (Equi 2, Fibr)

Scopey, above-average gelding, effective 7 to 12f, acts on g-s to frm - acts on Equi, likes tight tracks. AW high 68 - 3rd of 11 getting

1lb from Roisin Splendour (6 Feb Lingfield 7f Equi RF 0240).
**B Hanbury [0-16] A Al-Rostamani.*

MURPHY'S GOLD (IRE) BHB 46f49a **RR 43f 49a** 4349[16]

8 ch g Salt Dome (USA) 6.5f **(59)** - Winter Harvest (Grundy) 10.3f **(65)**
Form - 008304042010

Record	**1999** -	1st:1	2nd:1	3rd:1	Ran:12
	Pre1999 -	1st:6	2nd:3	3rd:5	Ran:57

Win Prizemoney £26,823 *Total Prizemoney* £36,799

Wins								
* **1999**	Spt	Hamilt	(G-F)	S	9.2f		43	
* 1998	Jly	Beverl	(GD)	H	8.5f	50	53	
* 1997	Jun	Beverl	(G-F)	H	8.5f	49	55	<
* 1995	Jly	Beverl	(G-F)	H	8.5f	52	55	<
* 1995	Jun	Beverl	(G-F)	H	7.5f	49	54	

1999 Turf 1-12: (7f 2, 8f 8, 9f 1-2) (gd 2, g-f 2, frm 1-7, hrd)
Moderate gelding, has broken blood-vessels, effective 7 to 9f, best at 8f, acts on gd to frm, best on frm, has worn blinkers, prefers right handed tracks, favours tight tracks, excels at Hamilton and Beverley. Turf high 45. Inconsistent.
**R A Fahey [7-70] D A Read (from M H Easterby [0-1] Jun 1993).*

MURPHY'S LAW BHB 34f **RR 35f** 3412[16]

3 b g High Kicker (USA) 8.4f **(52)** - Mio Mementa (Streak) 10f **(58)**
Form - 0040

Record	**1999** -	1st:0	2nd:0	3rd:0	Ran:4
	Pre1999 -	1st:0	2nd:0	3rd:0	Ran:3

1999 Turf 0-4: (7f, 12f 2, 16f) (gd, frm 3)
Leggy, very moderate gelding. Turf high 35.
**M J Ryan [0-7] Norcroft Park Stud.*

MURRAY RIVER (FR) RR 97f 716a[3]

3 b c Esprit du Nord (USA) - Mulika (USA) (Procida (USA))
Form - 3
1999 Turf 0-1: (11f) (g-s)
Currently very useful colt. (1st run) - 3rd of 7 to Slickly (11 Apr Longchamp 11f g-s RF 0716a).
**B deMontzey in FR [0-1] B deMontzey.*

MUSALSE BHB 40f53a **RR 35f 53a** 4400[7]

4 b g Salse (USA) 10.9f **(71)** - Musical Sally (USA)(The Minstrel (CAN)) 10f **(72)**
Form - 0433400607

Record	**1999** -	1st:0	2nd:0	3rd:2	Ran:9
	Pre1999 -	1st:4	2nd:2	3rd:3	Ran:17

Win Prizemoney £9,912 *Total Prizemoney* £13,137

Wins								
* 1998	Spt	Warwic	(G-F)	H	16.1f	47	57+	<
* 1998	Spt	Catter	(G-F)	H	15.8f	47	54	
* 1998	*Aug*	*Lingfi*	*(STD)*	*H*	*16f*	*42*	*51*	
* 1998	May	Redcar	(G-F)	H	14.1f	35	41	

1999 Turf 0-5: (16f 4, 17f) (sft, gd 2, frm 2) 1999 AW 0-4: (16f 4) (Equi 2, Fibr 2)
Workmanlike, fair gelding, effective 16f, acts on g-f to frm - acts on AW, best on frm, has worn blinkers, favours left handed tracks, excels at Catterick and Lingfield. Turf high 35. AW high 54 - 3rd of 13 getting 17lb from Harik (9 Feb Lingfield 16f Equi RF 0259).
**P C Haslam [4-28] Mrs Barclay/Mid'ham Park Racing/DJones.*

MUSCHANA BHB 75f **RR 86f** 5063[2]

2 ch f Deploy 11.4f **(67)** - Youthful (FR) (Green Dancer (USA)) 10.3f **(74)**
Form - 532

Record	**1999** -	1st:0	2nd:1	3rd:1	Ran:3

Win Prizemoney £0 *Total Prizemoney* £1,287
1999 Turf 0-3: (7f 2, 8f) (g-s, gd 2)
Currently useful filly. Turf high 86 (began Spt) - 2nd of 12 to Top Hand (26 Oct Bath 8f gd RF 5063).
**J L Dunlop [0-3] Aylesfield Farms Ltd.*

MUSH (IRE) RR 61f 4116[3]

2 b c Thatching 7.8f **(69)** - Petite Jameel (IRE) (Ahonoora) 8.1f **(73)**
Form - 83

Record	**1999** -	1st:0	2nd:0	3rd:1	Ran:2

Win Prizemoney £0 *Total Prizemoney* £535
1999 Turf 0-2: (6f, 7f) (gd, g-f)
Currently average colt. Turf high 61 (began Aug).
**P W Harris [0-2] Turf 2000 Ltd.*

MUSICAL FRUITS BHB 35f **RR 33f** 4414[12]

2 b f Tuam - Golden Apple (Athens Wood) 19.6f **(38)**
Form - 000

Record	**1999** -	1st:0	2nd:0	3rd:0	Ran:3

1999 Turf 0-1: (5f) (g-f) 1999 AW 0-2: (6f, 7f) (Fibr 2)
Currently very moderate filly. AW high 17 (began Spt).
**Mrs P N Dutfield [0-2] Edwin Phillips (from R T Phillips [0-1] Jly 1999).*

MUSICAL PURSUIT BHB 102f **RR 102f** 2020a[4]

5 b h Pursuit of Love 9.5f **(69)** - Gay Music (FR) (Gay Mecene (USA)) 8.6f **(69)**
Form - 34
1999 Turf 0-2: (7f, 9f) (gd 2)
Very useful colt. Turf high 102. He is a shadow of the horse that was beaten a head in the 1996 Dewhurst Stakes.
**J G Burns in IRE [0-2] J G Burns (from M H Tompkins [1-7] Spt 1997).*

MUSICAL TONES (USA) BHB 84f **RR 75f** 2897[1]

3 b f Diesis 9f **(80)** - Arsaan (USA) (Nureyev (USA)) 8.7f **(78)**
Form - 524241

Record	**1999** -	1st:1	2nd:2	3rd:0	Ran:6
	Pre1999 -	1st:0	2nd:1	3rd:0	Ran:1

Win Prizemoney £2,867 *Total Prizemoney* £7,499

Wins								
* **1999**	Jly	Ayr	(GD)		8f		75	<

1999 Turf 1-6: (8f 1-4, 10f 2) (gd 1-3, g-f, frm 2)
Leggy, above-average filly, effective 10f, acts on frm. Turf high 93 (1st run) - 5th of 9 to Alabaq (2 May Newmarket 10f frm RF 0978).
**B W Hills [1-7] Maktoum Al Maktoum.*

MUSICAL TREAT (IRE) BHB 92f **RR 99f** 4019[9]

3 ch f Royal Academy (USA) 7.8f **(77)** - Mountain Ash (Dominion) 8.5f **(63)**
Form - 212430

Record	**1999** -	1st:1	2nd:2	3rd:1	Ran:6
	Pre1999 -	1st:0	2nd:1	3rd:0	Ran:1

Win Prizemoney £7,158 *Total Prizemoney* £21,259

Wins								
* **1999**	May	Cheste	(G-F)		7f		73	<

1999 Turf 1-6: (7f 1-2, 10f 4) (gd 2, g-f 1-2, frm 2)
Scopey, very useful filly, effective 10f, acts on gd to frm. Turf high 99 - 2nd of 8 getting 3lb from Claxon (19 May Goodwood 10f gd RF 1331). Connections hoped that she would develop into a Classic contender, but she fell short of that mark. A shade one-paced in Listed events, she barely stays a mile and a quarter and is unlikely to improve. **P W Chapple-Hyam [1-7] R E Sangster.*

MUSIC EXPRESS (IRE) BHB 34f42a **RR 25f 42a** 1566[17]

5 b m Classic Music (USA) 7.2f **(57)** - Hetty Green (Bay Express) 7.1f **(60)**
Form - 000

Record	**1999** -	1st:0	2nd:0	3rd:0	Ran:3
	Pre1999 -	1st:0	2nd:0	3rd:1	Ran:8

Win Prizemoney £0 *Total Prizemoney* £337
1999 Turf 0-3: (7f, 8f 2) (gd 2, frm)
Little account filly, has worn blinkers. Turf high 25.
**J L Eyre [0-9] Watglea Racing (from A Harrison [0-2] Jly 1996).*

MUSICIAN BHB 94f **RR 93+f** 4571[5]

3 b f Shirley Heights 12.1f **(76)** - Rose Alto (Adonijah) 10f **(61)**
Form - 311115

Record	**1999** -	1st:4	2nd:0	3rd:1	Ran:6
	Pre1999 -	1st:0	2nd:0	3rd:1	Ran:2

Win Prizemoney £30,509 *Total Prizemoney* £31,825

Wins								
* **1999**	Spt	Doncas	(G-F)	H	12f	88	93	<
* **1999**	Jun	Newmar	(G-F)	H	12f	79	84	
* **1999**	Jun	Thirsk	(G-F)	H	12f	79	83+	
* **1999**	May	Warwic	(SFT)	H	10.5f	78	79	

1999 Turf 4-6: (8f, 11f 1-1, 12f 3-4) (sft 1-2, g-f 1-1, frm 2-3)
Leggy, useful filly, effective 12f, acts on sft to frm. Turf high 93 - 1st of 11 getting 4lb from Prince Alex (11 Spt Doncaster RF 4264) - also 1st of 6 getting 7lb from Lemon Bridge (25 Jun Newmarket RF 2305). She is a classic case of an improving filly, scoring a fine four-timer on varying ground, before running well in defeat in a competitive race at Ascot. Stays 12 furlongs well.
**J R Fanshawe [4-8] T & J Vestey.*

MUS-IF RR 114f 4662a[4]

3 b c Lahib (USA) 8f **(69)** - Navajo Love Song (IRE) **(43f 37a)** (Dancing

Brave (USA)) 8.4f **(76)**
Form - 2454
1999 Turf 0-4: (8f 3, 9f) (sft, gd, g-f 2)
Group-class colt, effective 8f, acts on g-f, often wears blinkers (extremely effectively). Turf high 114 - 4th of 10 to Saffron Walden (22 May Curragh 8f g-f RF 1477a). He had a tough season under a Group One penalty and clearly falls short of the top class. He has looked short of speed over a mile and should stay further.
**D K Weld in IRE [2-9].*

MUSKETRY BHB 32f **RR 39f** 5006[15]
3 b c Terimon 8.7f **(58)** - Mousquetade (Moulton)
Form - 0000
Record 1999 - 1st:0 2nd:0 3rd:0 Ran:4
1999 Turf 0-4: (8f, 10f 2, 16f) (g-s, gd, frm 2)
Leggy, very moderate colt. Turf high 39 (began Aug).
**N A Graham [0-4] R E S Greenwood.*

MUSTAFHEL BHB 76f **RR 78f** 4720[3]
3 b br c Wolfhound (USA) 7.3f **(71)** - Kadwah (USA) (Mr Prospector (USA)) 8.8f **(78)**
Form - 652233
Record 1999 - 1st:0 2nd:2 3rd:2 Ran:6
Pre1999 - 1st:0 2nd:0 3rd:0 Ran:3
Win Prizemoney £0 *Total Prizemoney* £4,021
1999 Turf 0-6: (8f 6) (gd 3, g-f, frm 2)
Above-average colt, effective 8f, acts on gd to frm. Turf high 79 - 2nd of 5 giving 5lb to Buckle (4 Jun Goodwood 8f gd RF 1737). Consistent. **J H M Gosden [0-9] Hamdan Al Maktoum.*

MUSTANG BHB 42f46a **RR 51f 46a** 360[4]
6 ch g Thatching 7.8f **(69)** - Lassoo (Caerleon (USA)) 8.6f **(71)**
Form - 46484
Record 1999 - 1st:0 2nd:0 3rd:0 Ran:3
Pre1999 - 1st:2 2nd:8 3rd:0 Ran:33
Win Prizemoney £4,899 *Total Prizemoney* £11,993
Wins 1997 *Nov Lingfi (STD) H 7f 33 45* <
1997 *Mar Wolver (STD) H 7f 27 32*
1999 AW 0-3: (7f, 8f 2) (Equi 3)
Fair gelding, effective 6 to 7f, best at 7f, acts on gd to g-f - acts on AW, best on Equi, often wears blinkers (very effectively). AW high 46. **J Pearce [0-3] Paul Jacobs (from C W Thornton [2-33] Nov 1998).*

MUST BE MAGIC **RR 73f** 5196[8]
2 b c Magic Ring (IRE) 6.5f **(64)** - Sequin Lady (Star Appeal) 9.6f **(65)**
Form - 04308
Record 1999 - 1st:0 2nd:0 3rd:1 Ran:5
Win Prizemoney £0 *Total Prizemoney* £780
1999 Turf 0-5: (7f, 8f 4) (sft, g-s, gd 2, frm)
Above-average colt. Turf high 73 (began Aug) - 3rd of 12 to Going Global (22 Spt Goodwood 8f g-s RF 4490).
**H J Collingridge [0-5] The Headquarters Partnership III.*

MUSTN'T GRUMBLE (IRE) BHB 43f39a **RR 33f 39a** 2086[15]
9 b g Orchestra 7.5f **(44)** - Gentle Heiress (Prince Tenderfoot (USA)) 9f **(61)**
Form - 700
Record 1999 - 1st:0 2nd:0 3rd:0 Ran:3
Pre1999 - 1st:7 2nd:10 3rd:6 Ran:63
Win Prizemoney £21,753 *Total Prizemoney* £32,119
Wins * 1998 *Mar Southw (STD) S 8f 47*
* 1996 Spt Leices (FRM) 8f 64 <
1999 Turf 0-1: (7f) (gd) 1999 AW 0-2: (7f 2) (Fibr 2)
Very moderate gelding, has worn blinkers. AW high 37.
**Miss S J Wilton [2-32] John Pointon and Sons (from D Nicholls [0-2] Mar 1996).*

MUTAAHAB (CAN) BHB 105f **RR 105f** 2620[5]
3 b c Dixieland Band (USA) 10.1f **(80)** - Serene Nobility (USA) (His Majesty (USA)) 10.9f **(82)**
Form - 445
Record 1999 - 1st:0 2nd:0 3rd:0 Ran:3
Pre1999 - 1st:4 2nd:0 3rd:0 Ran:6
Win Prizemoney £92,368 *Total Prizemoney* £102,858
Wins * 1998 Spt Ascot (SFT) G2 8f 109 <
* 1998 Spt Goodwo (G-S) L 8f 109 <
* 1998 Aug Redcar (G-F) 7f 69+
* 1998 May Yarmou (FRM) 6f 87+
1999 Turf 0-3: (7f, 10f 2) (g-s, g-f, frm)
Scopey, Pattern-class colt, effective 8f, acts on gd. Turf high 105. Consistent. High-class at two, a game winner of the Royal Lodge, he was found wanting in Classic trials in the spring and had not progressed. Sold for 105,000 gns at Tattersalls in the autumn, reportedly to race in South Africa.
**E A L Dunlop [4-9] Hamdan Al Maktoum.*

MUTAAKKID (USA) BHB 98f **RR 106f** 4392[25]
3 b br c Dayjur (USA) 6.8f **(79)** - Arjuzah (IRE) **(108f)** (Ahonoora) 8.1f **(73)**
Form - 1580430
Record 1999 - 1st:1 2nd:0 3rd:1 Ran:7
Pre1999 - 1st:1 2nd:0 3rd:0 Ran:2
Win Prizemoney £10,050 *Total Prizemoney* £14,324
Wins * 1999 Apr Leices (GD) 6f 102 <
* 1998 Nov Doncas (SFT) 6f 78
1999 Turf 1-7: (6f 1-6, 7f) (gd 1-5, g-f, frm)
Scopey, Pattern-class colt, effective 6f, acts on gd. Turf high 106 - also 1st of 9 giving 5lb to Emma Peel (8 Apr Leicester RF 0620). Made a winning reappearance at Leicester and contested some warm handicaps afterwards without success.
**J H M Gosden [2-9] Hamdan Al Maktoum.*

MUTABARI (USA) BHB 44f57a **RR 43f 57a** 5146[6]
5 ch g Seeking the Gold (USA) 7.4f **(80)** - Cagey Exuberance (USA) (Exuberant (USA)) 7.8f **(84)**
Form - 5721751172506444755056
Record 1999 - 1st:3 2nd:2 3rd:0 Ran:20
Pre1999 - 1st:0 2nd:0 3rd:2 Ran:18
Win Prizemoney £7,107 *Total Prizemoney* £10,941
Wins * 1999 *Mar Wolver (STD) H 7f 57 61* <
*** 1999** *Feb Lingfi (STD) H 7f 50 55*
*** 1999** *Jan Southw (STD) H 7f 46 54*
1999 Turf 0-11: (6f 5, 7f 5, 10f) (sft, gd 3, g-f, frm 6) 1999 AW 3-9: (6f, 7f 3-6, 8f 2) (Equi 1-2, Fibr 2-7)
Fair gelding, effective 7f, - acts on AW, best on Equi, has worn blinkers (effectively), likes left handed tracks, likes tight tracks. Turf high 50. AW high 61 - 1st of 12 giving 9lb to Kass Alhawa (13 Mar Wolverhampton RF 0430) - also 1st of 8 getting 15lb from Acid Test (25 Feb Lingfield RF 0361).
**Mrs S Lamyman [3-21] P Lamyman (from K Mahdi [0-12] Nov 1998).*

MUTABASSIR (IRE) BHB 67f60a **RR 67f 60a** 3689[11]
5 ch g Soviet Star (USA) 8.6f **(74)** - Anghaam (USA) (Diesis) 9.3f **(69)**
Form - 1122124430
Record 1999 - 1st:1 2nd:2 3rd:1 Ran:7
Pre1999 - 1st:5 2nd:3 3rd:1 Ran:15
Win Prizemoney £16,724 *Total Prizemoney* £23,979
Wins * 1999 Apr Bright (G-F) H 8f 60 73+ <
* 1998 *Nov Southw (STD) H 7f 44 53*
* 1998 *Nov Lingfi (STD) H 7f 44 53+*
* 1998 Spt Folkes (G-F) H 7f 53 57
* 1998 Spt Epsom (GD) H 7f 47 52
* 1998 Aug Bright (FRM) H 7f 40 50
1999 Turf 1-6: (7f 4, 8f 1-2) (gd 2, g-f 2, frm 1-1, hrd) 1999 AW 0-1: (7f) (Equi)
Average gelding, effective 7 to 8f, best at 7f, acts on g-f to hrd, prefers left handed tracks, likes tight tracks, excels at Epsom and Brighton. Turf high 73 (1st run) - 1st of 15 giving 14lb to Ardent (29 Apr Brighton RF 0915). Consistent. H
**G L Moore [6-21] Stanley Clarke (from A C Stewart [0-1] Aug 1997).*

MUTADARRA (IRE) BHB 66f64a **RR 72f 64a** 4802[8]
6 ch g Mujtahid (USA) 7.4f **(69)** - Silver Echo (Caerleon (USA)) 8.6f **(71)**
Form - 0217460888
Record 1999 - 1st:1 2nd:1 3rd:0 Ran:10
Pre1999 - 1st:2 2nd:5 3rd:1 Ran:22
Win Prizemoney £15,760 *Total Prizemoney* £26,897
Wins * 1999 Jun Sandow (GD) H 10f 63 66
* 1997 Jly Newmar (G-F) H 10f 62 69
1996 May Pontef (GD) 6f 80 <
1999 Turf 1-10: (9f, 10f 1-8, 12f) (g-s, gd, g-f, frm 1-7)
Above-average gelding, effective 10f, acts on frm to hrd, best on frm, has worn blinkers, likes right handed tracks. Turf high 72 - also 1st of 13 getting 18lb from Lady Rockstar (11 Jun Sandown RF 1922).

**W J Musson [2-26] Mrs Rita Brown (from R W Armstrong [1-6] Jly 1996).*

MU-TADIL BHB 35f **RR 41f** 4581[11]

7 ch g Be My Chief (USA) 10.2f **(62)** - Inveraven (Alias Smith (USA)) 9.8f **(58)**

Form - 745347280

Record	**1999** -	1st:0	2nd:1	3rd:1	Ran:9
	Pre1999 -	1st:0	2nd:1	3rd:2	Ran:12

Win Prizemoney £0 *Total Prizemoney* £3,590

1999 Turf 0-9: (16f 2, 17f 5, 18f 2) (gd 2, g-f 3, frm 3, hrd)

Moderate gelding, effective 16 to 18f, best at 17f, acts on g-f to frm, best on g-f, has worn blinkers. Turf high 45 - 4th of 10 getting 28lb from Ballet-K (12 Jun Bath 17f g-f RF 1941). Consistent.

**R J Baker [0-41] Mrs V W Jones (from Major W R Hern [0-2] Spt 1995).*

Mutafaweq had stamina in abundance

MUTAFAWEQ (USA) BHB 123f **RR 126f** 4266[1]

3bc Silver Hawk(USA)11.2f**(85)**-TheCaretaker(Caerleon(USA))8.6f **(71)**

Form - 11541

Record	**1999** -	1st:3	2nd:0	3rd:0	Ran:5
	Pre1999 -	1st:1	2nd:1	3rd:0	Ran:2

Win Prizemoney £311,885 *Total Prizemoney* £316,989

Wins							
	* **1999**	Spt	Doncas (G-F)	G1	14.6f	126	<
	* **1999**	Jun	Ascot (G-F)	G2	12f	112	
	* **1999**	May	Doncas (G-F)		10.3f	104+	
	* 1998	Oct	Newmar (GD)		8f	87	

1999 Turf 3-5: (10f 1-1, 12f 1-3, 15f 1-1) (gd, g-f 1-2, frm 2-2)

Scopey, top-class colt, effective 12 to 15f, acts on g-f to frm. Turf high 126 - 1st of 9 giving 5lb to Ramruma (11 Spt Doncaster RF 4266). He beat a big field of maidens at Newmarket on his final start at two, and won a conditions event in style on his reappearance. He appreciated the 12 furlongs when a fluent winner of the King Edward VII Stakes at Royal Ascot, but was well beaten in the Irish Derby for which he was a supplementary entry. He ran an interesting trial for the St Leger when fourth in the Great Voltigeur, staying on after looking likely to finish well beaten, and proved that stamina was his forte when outbattling the triple Oaks winner Ramruma in the St Leger. He was completely exhausted afterwards but lives to fight another day. He has a stamina-laden pedigree, but it remains to be seen whether he steps up in trip for the Cup races or has a middle distance campaign in 2000.

**S bin Suroor [4-7] Godolphin.*

MUTAHADETH BHB 44f61a **RR 49f 61a** 4865[8]

5 ch g Rudimentary (USA) 8.2f **(66)** - Music in My Life (IRE) (Law Society (USA)) 9.9f **(70)**

Form - 383641128048

Record	**1999** -	1st:2	2nd:1	3rd:2	Ran:12
	Pre1999 -	1st:2	2nd:4	3rd:4	Ran:32

Win Prizemoney £8,541 *Total Prizemoney* £14,794

Wins								
	* **1999**	*Mar*	*Southw (STD)*	*H*	*8f*	*57*	*60*	
	* **1999**	*Feb*	*Wolver (STD)*	*C*	*8.5f*		*60*	
	* 1998	*Jan*	*Southw (STD)*	*C*	*7f*		*68*	<
	* 1997	*Feb*	*Southw (STD)*	*H*	*8f*	*58*	*60+*	

1999 AW 2-12: (6f, 7f 3, 8f 2-8) (Equi, Fibr 2-11)

Average gelding, effective 7 to 8f, best at 8f, - acts on AW, best on Fibr, often wears blinkers (very effectively), favours left handed tracks, favours tight tracks, likes Southwell. AW high 65 - 2nd of 9 getting 16lb from Sharp Scotch (16 Mar Southwell 8f Fibr RF 0437) - also 1st of 14 getting 18lb from Cool Secret (8 Mar Southwell RF 0412). Inconsistent. His best form has been in modest company at around a mile on Fibresand.

**D Shaw [4-40] K G Radford (from N A Graham [0-4] Spt 1996).*

MUTAMAYYAZ (USA) BHB 100f **RR 99f** 4896[12]

3 b br c Nureyev (USA) 8.4f **(84)** - Ajfan (USA) (Woodman (USA)) 9f **(74)**

Form - 7220

Record	**1999** -	1st:0	2nd:2	3rd:0	Ran:4
	Pre1999 -	1st:1	2nd:1	3rd:0	Ran:2

Win Prizemoney £4,581 *Total Prizemoney* £12,595

Wins * 1998 Aug Newmar (G-F) 6f 85+ <

1999 Turf 0-4: (6f 2, 7f 2) (gd 3, g-f)

Scopey, very useful colt, effective 6 to 7f, acts on gd to g-f. Turf high 99 (began Jly) - 2nd of 19 giving 10lb to Easy Dollar (25 Spt Nottingham 6f gd RF 4561). He belied his inexperience when finishing second against seasoned handicappers at Nottingham in September, and has sufficient pace to be effective over five furlongs. Scopey and open to improvement, he could win a listed event in 2000. **J H M Gosden [1-6] Hamdan Al Maktoum.*

MUTANASSIB (IRE) BHB 74f **RR 75f** 4917[29]

6 b g Mtoto 11.5f **(71)** - Lightning Legacy (USA) (Super Concorde (USA)) 10.9f **(66)**

Form - 1230

Record	**1999** -	1st:1	2nd:1	3rd:1	Ran:4
	Pre1999 -	1st:0	2nd:1	3rd:0	Ran:4

Win Prizemoney £2,827 *Total Prizemoney* £9,389

Wins * **1999** Jly Chepst (G-F) H 18f 65 72+ <

1999 Turf 1-4: (17f 2, 18f 1-1, 20f) (gd 2, g-f, frm 1-1)

Above-average gelding. Turf high 75 (began Jly) - 2nd of 9 getting 20lb from High And Mighty (28 Jly Goodwood 20f g-f RF 3207) - also 1st of 9 giving 32lb to Panto Queen (3 Jly Chepstow RF 2529). He proved a disappointing sort on the Flat for Alex Stewart, and has done little better for Martin Pipe over jumps. However, he was well supported when running away with a maiden handicap at Chepstow in July and has run with credit since, including when runner-up in the Goodwood Stakes.

**M C Pipe [2-16] Malcolm Jones (from A C Stewart [0-4] Oct 1996).*

MUTASADER (IRE) RR 67f 5137[8]

2 b f Unfuwain (USA) 11.4f **(74)** - Bawaeth (USA) (Blushing Groom (FR)) 10.3f **(76)**

Form - 8

Record **1999** - 1st:0 2nd:0 3rd:0 Ran:1

1999 Turf 0-1: (7f) (gd)

Currently average filly. **B W Hills [0-1] Hamdan Al Maktoum.*

MUTASAWWAR BHB 48f61a **RR 49f 61a** 4233[12]

5 ch g Clantime 6.6f **(57)** - Keen Melody (USA) (Sharpen Up) 8.3f **(67)**

Form - 02403570

Record 1999 - 1st:0 2nd:0 3rd:1 Ran:6
Pre1999 - 1st:2 2nd:4 3rd:0 Ran:26
Win Prizemoney £5,486 *Total Prizemoney* £9,271
Wins * 1998 Spt Chepst (G-S) H 5.1f 51 55
* 1998 *Jan Lingfi (STD) H 6f 60 61* <
1999 Turf 0-2: (5f 2) (frm 2) 1999 AW 0-4: (5f, 6f 3) (Equi 2, Fibr 2)
Average gelding, effective 5 to 6f, best at 6f, acts on gd - acts on AW, best on Equi, has worn blinkers, likes tight tracks. Turf high 49 (began Jly). AW high 64 - 3rd of 8 giving 4lb to Palacegate Touch (18 Mar Lingfield 6f Equi RF 0443).
**M S Saunders [2-27] The Med Lex Partnership (from E A L Dunlop [0-5] Jun 1997).*

MUWAKALL (IRE) BHB 65f **RR 67f** 4950[6]
2 b c Doyoun 10.7f **(69)** - Sabayik (IRE) **(84f)** (Unfuwain (USA))
Form - 7386
Record 1999 - 1st:0 2nd:0 3rd:1 Ran:4
Win Prizemoney £0 *Total Prizemoney* £640
1999 Turf 0-4: (7f, 8f 2, 9f) (g-f 2, frm 2)
Average colt. Turf high 67 (began Aug).
**R W Armstrong [0-4] Hamdan Al Maktoum.*

MUYASSIR (IRE) BHB 74f70a **RR 74f 70a** 4085[9]
4 b c Brief Truce (USA) 9.1f **(73)** - Twine (Thatching) 8f **(66)**
Form - 4362140
Record 1999 - 1st:1 2nd:1 3rd:1 Ran:6
Pre1999 - 1st:1 2nd:1 3rd:1 Ran:11
Win Prizemoney £11,507 *Total Prizemoney* £16,668
Wins * **1999** Jly Newmar (GD) H 8f 69 72 <
* 1998 *Oct Lingfi (STD) H 10f 67 69*
1999 Turf 1-6: (8f 1-3, 9f, 10f 2) (gd, g-f, frm 1-4)
Scopey, above-average colt, effective 8 to 10f, best at 8f, acts on gd to frm - acts on Equi, best on frm, excels at Goodwood and Salisbury. Turf high 74 - 4th of 22 getting 2lb from Thekryaati (29 Jly Goodwood 9f frm RF 3226) - also 1st of 20 getting 3lb from Iron Mountain (6 Jly Newmarket RF 2574). Consistent. He performed well in ordinary handicaps on turf last season. Beat a big field at the July Meeting before running another good race at Glorious Goodwood.
**P J Makin [2-13] William Otley (from C J Benstead [0-4] Oct 1997).*

MUZAHEM (IRE) **RR 49f** 3742[4]
2 b c Grand Lodge (USA) - Annsfield Lady (Red Sunset) 8.2f **(63)**
Form - 4
Record 1999 - 1st:0 2nd:0 3rd:0 Ran:1
Win Prizemoney £0 *Total Prizemoney* £419
1999 Turf 0-1: (7f) (g-s)
Currently moderate colt.
**Sir Michael Stoute [0-1] Hamdan Al Maktoum.*

MY ALIBI (USA) **RR 58f** 4359[6]
3 b f Sheikh Albadou 9.2f **(75)** - Fellwaati (USA) (Alydar (USA)) 9.1f **(76)**
Form - 0056
Record 1999 - 1st:0 2nd:0 3rd:0 Ran:4
Pre1999 - 1st:0 2nd:0 3rd:0 Ran:1
1999 Turf 0-4: (8f 2, 10f, 11f) (g-s, g-f 3)
Scopey, fair filly. Turf high 58 - 5th of 20 getting 10lb from It's Magic (18 Aug Leicester 8f g-f RF 3749).
**E A L Dunlop [0-5] Maktoum Al Maktoum.*

MY ANNETTE (USA) BHB 73f **RR 62f** 4677[10]
3 b f Red Ransom (USA) 8.6f **(83)** - Andover Way (USA) (His Majesty (USA)) 10.9f **(82)**
Form - 5630
Record 1999 - 1st:0 2nd:0 3rd:1 Ran:4
Win Prizemoney £0 *Total Prizemoney* £424
1999 Turf 0-4: (10f 3, 11f) (gd 2, g-f, frm)
Scopey, average filly. Turf high 62 - 3rd of 8 getting 5lb from Arawak Prince (16 Aug Windsor 10f gd RF 3680).
**J R Fanshawe [0-4] Joseph Allen.*

MY BOLD BOYO BHB 61f **RR 70f** 4536[14]
4 b g Never so Bold 7.1f **(62)** - My Rosie (Forzando) 7.6f **(59)**
Form - 665800
Record 1999 - 1st:0 2nd:0 3rd:0 Ran:6
Pre1999 - 1st:1 2nd:0 3rd:2 Ran:8
Win Prizemoney £2,070 *Total Prizemoney* £3,424
Wins 1998 Aug Lingfi (GD) 7.6f 76 <
1999 Turf 0-6: (6f, 7f 3, 8f 2) (g-s, g-f 2, frm 3)
Workmanlike, above-average gelding, effective 7 to 9f, acts on gd to frm, has worn blinkers. Turf high 70 - 5th of 5 giving 12lb to Morning Music (15 Jly Bath 8f frm RF 2838). Inconsistent.
**J R Poulton [0-1] Mrs M J Taylor (from D R C Elsworth [1-13] Aug 1999).*

MY BOLD GIRL **RR 45f** 2166[5]
2 ch f Bold Arrangement 8.7f **(57)** - Oh My Oh My (Ballacashtal (CAN)) 5.3f **(50)**
Form - 53855
Record 1999 - 1st:0 2nd:0 3rd:1 Ran:5
Win Prizemoney £0 *Total Prizemoney* £251
1999 Turf 0-3: (5f 2, 6f) (sft, g-f, frm) 1999 AW 0-2: (5f, 6f) (Fibr 2)
Moderate filly. Turf high 45. AW high 37. (DEAD)
**J Berry [0-5] J Berry.*

MYBOTYE BHB 53f52a **RR 31f 52a** 5151[14]
6 br g Rambo Dancer (CAN) 8.4f **(59)** - Sigh (Highland Melody) 6.3f **(55)**
Form - 000
Record 1999 - 1st:0 2nd:0 3rd:0 Ran:3
Pre1999 - 1st:4 2nd:1 3rd:5 Ran:32
Win Prizemoney £15,941 *Total Prizemoney* £20,795
Wins 1997 Spt Chepst (GD) H 7.1f 58 64
1996 Jun Redcar (FRM) H 7f 76 77 <
1995 Aug Redcar (G-F) H 6f 64 65+
1995 Jun Pontef (GD) 5f 61+
1999 Turf 0-3: (7f, 8f 2) (gd 2, frm)
Fair gelding, effective 7f, acts on g-s to g-f, best on gd, has worn blinkers, excels at Thirsk and Doncaster. Turf high 31. Becoming disappointing.
**A B Mulholland [0-3] J F Wright (from R Bastiman [1-20] Jly 1998).*

MY BOY HARRY (IRE) **RR 41f** 2811[4]
2 b c Efisio 7.7f **(69)** - Caroline Connors (Fairy King (USA)) 7.7f **(59)**
Form - 4
Record 1999 - 1st:0 2nd:0 3rd:0 Ran:1
Win Prizemoney £0 *Total Prizemoney* £436
1999 Turf 0-1: (6f) (g-f)
Currently moderate colt. **J Berry [0-1] R A Popely.*

MY BROADSTAIRS JOY BHB 52f **RR 46f** 4724[16]
3 b g Terimon 8.7f **(58)** - Al Raja (Kings Lake (USA)) 10.8f **(67)**
Form - 0
Record 1999 - 1st:0 2nd:0 3rd:0 Ran:1
Pre1999 - 1st:0 2nd:0 3rd:0 Ran:3
1999 Turf 0-1: (12f) (gd)
Unfurnished, moderate gelding. **J J O'Neill [0-4] Mrs Judy Hunt.*

MY BROTHER BHB 34f **RR 44f** 4180[10]
5 b g Lugana Beach 7f **(63)** - Lucky Love (Mummy's Pet) 7.7f **(60)**
Form - 5P700
Record 1999 - 1st:0 2nd:0 3rd:0 Ran:5
Pre1999 - 1st:0 2nd:0 3rd:0 Ran:3
1999 Turf 0-4: (7f 2, 8f 2) (g-f 2, frm 2) 1999 AW 0-1: (7f) (Equi)
Moderate gelding, has worn blinkers. Turf high 50. Inconsistent.
**P Eccles [0-5] Robert & Cora Till (from S Earle [0-3] Jly 1998).*

MY DARLING DODO (IRE) BHB 48f **RR 50f** 5107[6]
3 b f Anita's Prince 6f **(62)** - Seldovia (Charlottown) 10.9f **(57)**
Form - 756
Record 1999 - 1st:0 2nd:0 3rd:0 Ran:3
1999 Turf 0-3: (7f, 10f 2) (gd 3)
Leggy, currently fair filly. Turf high 50 (began Spt).
**B Palling [0-3] Mrs Anita Quinn.*

MY DESPERADO (IRE) BHB 67f **RR 70f** 5217[7]
6 b m Un Desperado (FR) 9.3f **(42)** - Lady Kasbah (Lord Gayle (USA)) 8.8f **(62)**
Form - 77
Record 1999 - 1st:0 2nd:0 3rd:0 Ran:2
Pre1999 - 1st:3 2nd:0 3rd:2 Ran:16
Win Prizemoney £10,527 *Total Prizemoney* £11,786
Wins 1998 Oct Redcar (SFT) 10f 65

1998 Oct Pontef (SFT) H 10f 66 69
1998 Jly Thirsk (GD) 8f 73 <
1999 Turf 0-2: (8f, 10f) (g-s, g-f)
Above-average mare, effective 7 to 12f, acts on g-s to frm, likes left handed tracks, likes tight tracks. Turf high 64 (began Nov). Consistent.
**M A Peill [0-2] Willie Smith (from L R Lloyd-James [3-16] Nov 1998).*

MY DILEMMA BHB 35f **RR 25f** 5135[16]
3 b f Pursuit of Love 9.5f **(69)** - Butosky (Busted) 10.2f **(61)**
Form - 080060
Record 1999 - 1st:0 2nd:0 3rd:0 Ran:6
Pre1999 - 1st:0 2nd:0 3rd:1 Ran:3
Win Prizemoney £0 *Total Prizemoney* £833
1999 Turf 0-4: (7f, 8f, 10f 2) (gd 2, frm 2) 1999 AW 0-2: (8f, 12f) (Fibr 2)
Leggy, moderate filly, has worn blinkers. Turf high 47 (began Aug).
**M J Ryan [0-8] Peter Scott (from K G Wingrove [0-3] Spt 1998).*

MY EMILY BHB 72f **RR 73f** 3624[16]
3 b f King's Signet (USA) 7f **(51)** - Flying Wind **(33f 41a)** (Forzando) 7.6f **(59)**
Form - 01200
Record 1999 - 1st:1 2nd:1 3rd:0 Ran:5
Pre1999 - 1st:0 2nd:1 3rd:1 Ran:5
Win Prizemoney £3,126 *Total Prizemoney* £5,780
Wins * 1999 Jun Bright (G-F) H 7f 63 65+ <
1999 Turf 1-5: (6f 2, 7f 1-2, 8f) (gd, g-f 1-2, frm 2)
Neat, above-average filly, effective 6 to 7f, acts on g-f to frm. Turf high 73 - 2nd of 9 giving 1lb to Make Ready (16 Jly Newmarket 6f frm RF 2883) - also 1st of 16 getting 5lb from Sarah's Song (14 Jun Brighton RF 1975). **G L Moore [1-10] B V and C J Pennick.*

MY FLOOSIE BHB 25f **RR 17f** 2051[8]
4 b f Unfuwain (USA) 11.4f **(74)** - My Chiara (Ardross) 10.6f **(68)**
Form - 0058
Record 1999 - 1st:0 2nd:0 3rd:0 Ran:4
Pre1999 - 1st:0 2nd:0 3rd:1 Ran:5
Win Prizemoney £0 *Total Prizemoney* £512
1999 Turf 0-4: (10f, 12f, 14f 2) (gd 2, g-f, frm)
Unfurnished, poor filly. Turf high 17. Becoming disappointing.
**B D Leavy [0-4] A Eaton (from P J Bevan [0-5] Oct 1998).*

MY FUNNY VALENTINE (IRE) RR 98f 4661a[7]
3 ch f Mukaddamah (USA) 7.6f **(74)** - Imperfect Timing (IRE) (Coquelin (USA)) 8.4f **(58)**
Form - 57
1999 Turf 0-2: (8f, 10f) (hvy, gd)
Currently very useful filly. Turf high 98 (1st run) - 5th of 16 to Shenck (18 Apr Capannelle 8f hvy RF 0811a). **G Botti in ITY [0-3].*

MY HANSEL (USA) RR 93+f 4565[3]
2 b br f Hansel (USA) 12.6f **(78)** - My Shafy (Rousillon (USA)) 8.2f **(74)**
Form - 13
Record 1999 - 1st:1 2nd:0 3rd:1 Ran:2
Win Prizemoney £3,785 *Total Prizemoney* £24,260
Wins * 1999 Aug Newmar (G-F) 7f 93+ <
1999 Turf 1-2: (7f 1-1, 8f) (sft, frm 1-1)
Currently useful filly. Turf high 93 (began Aug) - 3rd of 6 to Teggiano (26 Spt Ascot 8f sft RF 4565) - also 1st of 9 from Abscond (27 Aug Newmarket RF 3936). Got up to beat a long odds-on shot on her Newmarket debut and ran really well in atrocious conditions in the Fillies' mile. Looks very useful.
**B Hanbury [1-2] Hilal Salem.*

MY HEARTS DESIRE BHB 44f **RR 40f** 4288[10]
4 b f Deploy 11.4f **(67)** - Blue Room (Gorytus (USA)) 7.8f **(60)**
Form - 070
Record 1999 - 1st:0 2nd:0 3rd:0 Ran:3
Pre1999 - 1st:0 2nd:0 3rd:0 Ran:3
1999 Turf 0-3: (10f 3) (g-f 2, frm)
Workmanlike, moderate filly. Turf high 40.
**D HaydnJones [0-6] G J Hicks.*

MY KIND BHB 27f54a **RR 29f 54a** 537[18]
6 ch m Mon Tresor 7.9f **(60)** - Kind of Shy (Kind of Hush) 10.1f **(62)**
Form - 0
Record 1999 - 1st:0 2nd:0 3rd:0 Ran:1
Pre1999 - 1st:1 2nd:2 3rd:0 Ran:18
Win Prizemoney £3,132 *Total Prizemoney* £5,889
Wins 1995 Jun Thirsk (GD) S 6f 56 <
1999 Turf 0-1: (7f) (gd)
Very moderate mare, has worn blinkers.
**N M Babbage [0-1] David James (from N Tinkler [0-10] Aug 1996).*

MY LADY RR 53f 3629[7]
2 b f Derrylin 12.7f **(38)** - Brianstan Rose (The Brianstan) 5.9f **(55)**
Form - 7
Record 1999 - 1st:0 2nd:0 3rd:0 Ran:1
1999 Turf 0-1: (8f) (gd)
Currently fair filly. **W M Brisbourne [0-1] E Dytcher-Boon.*

MYLANIA BHB 62f **RR 61f** 4991[9]
3 b f Midyan (USA) 9.9f **(64)** - Appelania (Star Appeal) 9.6f **(65)**
Form - 78420
Record 1999 - 1st:0 2nd:1 3rd:0 Ran:5
Pre1999 - 1st:0 2nd:0 3rd:0 Ran:1
Win Prizemoney £0 *Total Prizemoney* £908
1999 Turf 0-5: (8f 5) (g-s, gd, g-f 2, frm)
Workmanlike, average filly, effective 8f, acts on g-s to gd. Turf high 61. **M H Tompkins [0-6] J Ellis.*

MY LASS BHB 74f60a **RR 92f 60a** 4856a[9]
3 b f Elmaamul (USA) 8.1f **(70)** - Be My Lass (IRE) (Be My Guest (USA)) 9.3f **(67)**
Form - 5133466360
1999 Turf 1-6: (8f, 10f 2, 12f 1-2, 14f) (sft 3, g-s 1-1, gd 2) 1999 AW 0-3: (10f, 12f 2) (Equi, Fibr 2)
Workmanlike, useful filly, likes tight tracks. Turf high 92. AW high 63.
**L Browne in IRE [0-4] John Cullinan (from Sir Mark Prescott [1-8] Jun 1999).*

MY LEGAL EAGLE (IRE) BHB 53f47a **RR 50+f 47a** 5154[4]
5 b g Law Society (USA) 11.6f **(71)** - Majestic Nurse (On Your Mark) 7.7f **(58)**
Form - 476533304258721304
Record 1999 - 1st:1 2nd:2 3rd:4 Ran:17
Pre1999 - 1st:1 2nd:0 3rd:2 Ran:14
Win Prizemoney £5,258 *Total Prizemoney* £11,095
Wins * 1999 Spt Salisb (HVY) H 9.9f 42 49+ <
1998 Jly Thirsk (GD) H 7f 45 47
1999 Turf 1-16: (9f, 10f 1-9, 11f 4, 12f 2) (sft 2, g-s 1-4, gd 4, g-f 3, frm 2, hrd) 1999 AW 0-1: (7f) (Fibr)
Fair gelding, effective 7 to 12f, best at 10f, acts on g-s to frm - acts on Fibr, best on g-s, has worn blinkers, likes left handed tracks, favours tight tracks, excels at Chester, does well at Nottingham. Turf high 50 - 2nd of 13 giving 1lb to River Ensign (22 Spt Chester 10f g-s RF 4488) - also 1st of 16 getting 9lb from Thihn (29 Spt Salisbury RF 4647). Consistent.
**R J Price [1-18] E G Bevan (from J W Hills [1-11] Dec 1998).*

MY LITTLE MAN BHB 51f **RR 62df** 427[5]
4 b g Lugana Beach 7f **(63)** - Gay Ming (Gay Meadow)
Form - 30255
Record 1999 - 1st:0 2nd:1 3rd:0 Ran:3
Pre1999 - 1st:0 2nd:0 3rd:1 Ran:6
Win Prizemoney £0 *Total Prizemoney* £1,453
1999 AW 0-3: (8f, 9f, 10f) (Equi, Fibr 2)
Light-framed, average gelding, has worn blinkers. AW high 52. Inconsistent. **B Smart [0-9] W Clifford.*

MY MAN FRIDAY BHB 47f44a **RR 60df 44a** 4925[8]
3 b g Lugana Beach 7f **(63)** - My Ruby Ring **(61df 50a)** (Blushing Scribe (USA)) 6f **(45)**
Form - 77053408
Record 1999 - 1st:0 2nd:0 3rd:1 Ran:8
Pre1999 - 1st:0 2nd:0 3rd:0 Ran:3
Win Prizemoney £0 *Total Prizemoney* £890
1999 Turf 0-7: (6f 4, 7f 2, 8f) (gd 2, g-f 2, frm 3) 1999 AW 0-1: (7f) (Fibr)
Leggy, average gelding, effective 7f, acts on frm. Turf high 60 - 3rd of 19 giving 1lb to Feather 'n Lace (27 Aug Newmarket 7f frm RF 3941). **W R Muir [0-11] Rams Racing Club.*

MY MOTHER'S DREAM (IRE) BHB 31f48a **RR 39f 48a** 621[15]
3 b f Fayruz 6.6f **(63)** - With Diamonds (Shirley Heights) 10.3f **(74)**
Form - 0600
Record 1999 - 1st:0 2nd:0 3rd:0 Ran:2
Pre1999 - 1st:0 2nd:0 3rd:3 Ran:12
Win Prizemoney £0 *Total Prizemoney* £815
1999 Turf 0-1: (6f) (gd) 1999 AW 0-1: (5f) (Fibr)
Light-framed, moderate filly, effective 5f, acts on g-f, has worn blinkers, likes left handed tracks. Becoming disappointing.
**A T Murphy [0-4] Dulverton Racing Partnership (from M A Buckley [0-10] Aug 1998).*

MYNAH BIRD (IRE) BHB 57f **RR 30f** 2653[13]
3 b f Bluebird (USA) 7.9f **(71)** - Maribiya (FR) (Natroun (FR))
Form - 000
Record 1999 - 1st:0 2nd:0 3rd:0 Ran:3
Pre1999 - 1st:0 2nd:0 3rd:1 Ran:4
Win Prizemoney £0 *Total Prizemoney* £498
1999 Turf 0-2: (10f 2) (g-f 2) 1999 AW 0-1: (14f) (Fibr)
Workmanlike, very moderate filly. Turf high 30.
**J G FitzGerald [0-3] Sir Tatton Sykes (from Mrs J R Ramsden [0-4] Oct 1998).*

MY PETAL BHB 70f **RR 63f** 4272[13]
3 gr f Petong 7.6f **(58)** - Najariya (Northfields (USA)) 9f **(72)**
Form - 0000
Record 1999 - 1st:0 2nd:0 3rd:0 Ran:4
Pre1999 - 1st:2 2nd:1 3rd:0 Ran:4
Win Prizemoney £11,039 *Total Prizemoney* £12,074
Wins * 1998 Jly Goodwo (GD) H 6f 85 <
* 1998 Jly Newbur (G-F) 5.2f 67
1999 Turf 0-4: (6f 2, 7f 2) (gd, g-f 3)
Scopey, average filly, effective 6f, acts on gd. Turf high 67. Consistent. **R Hannon [2-8] Jubert Family.*

MY PLEASURE BHB 81f **RR 83f** 4685[9]
3 b g Cadeaux Genereux 7.9f **(76)** - Raknah (IRE) **(85df)** (Night Shift (USA)) 7.2f **(69)**
Form - 74221410200
Record 1999 - 1st:2 2nd:3 3rd:0 Ran:11
Win Prizemoney £9,483 *Total Prizemoney* £14,605
Wins *** 1999** Jly Salisb (G-F) H 8f 76 81
*** 1999** Jun Haydoc (G-S) 7.1f 82 <
1999 Turf 2-11: (7f 1-6, 8f 1-5) (gd 1-4, g-f 4, frm 1-3)
Scopey, decent gelding, effective 7 to 8f, best at 8f, acts on gd to frm, has worn blinkers, prefers tight tracks. Turf high 83 - 2nd of 7 getting 2lb from Wolf Tooth (20 Aug Sandown 8f g-f RF 3806) - also 1st of 8 from Daytime (3 Jun Haydock RF 1700). He got off the mark when leading in the dying strides to land a Haydock maiden in June on easy ground, and added a Salisbury handicap on faster ground when making all. **E A L Dunlop [2-11] Mohammed Jaber.*

MY PLEDGE (IRE) BHB 55f **RR 59f** 4791[11]
4 b g Waajib 8.9f **(67)** - Pollys Glow (IRE) (Glow (USA)) 6.7f **(71)**
Form - 70450
Record 1999 - 1st:0 2nd:0 3rd:0 Ran:5
Pre1999 - 1st:1 2nd:0 3rd:0 Ran:6
Win Prizemoney £3,668 *Total Prizemoney* £4,279
Wins * 1998 Jun Windso (SFT) H 10f 69 71 <
1999 Turf 0-5: (12f 3, 13f, 14f) (gd, g-f 3, frm)
Fair gelding, effective 10 to 12f, acts on gd to frm, prefers tight tracks. Turf high 59. Consistent. **C A Horgan [1-11] Mrs B Sumner.*

MY POPPET BHB 35f **RR 43df** 1186[12]
4 b f Midyan (USA) 9.9f **(64)** - Pretty Poppy (Song) 7.2f **(61)**
Form - 00
Record 1999 - 1st:0 2nd:0 3rd:0 Ran:2
Pre1999 - 1st:0 2nd:0 3rd:0 Ran:1
1999 Turf 0-2: (6f, 10f) (frm 2)
Leggy, currently moderate filly. Turf high 7.
**S G Knight [0-3] Gordon Fox.*

MY RAMONA RR 1090[U]
2 b f Alhijaz 7.7f **(57)** - Petriece (Mummy's Pet) 7.7f **(60)**
Form - 7U
Record 1999 - 1st:0 2nd:0 3rd:0 Ran:2
1999 Turf 0-2: (5f 2) (gd, frm)
Currently very poor filly, often wears blinkers. Turf high 57.
**C A Dwyer [0-2] Ms B Murphy.*

MY RETREAT (USA) RR 80f 4994[2]
2 b c Hermitage (USA) 8.6f **(84)** -My Jessica Ann (USA) (Native Rythm)
Form - 52
Record 1999 - 1st:0 2nd:1 3rd:0 Ran:2
Win Prizemoney £0 *Total Prizemoney* £838
1999 Turf 0-2: (6f, 7f) (gd, frm)
Currently decent colt. Turf high 80 (began Aug).
**L M Cumani [0-2] Mrs V Shelton.*

MYRMIDON BHB 70f **RR 52f** 918[18]
5 b g Midyan (USA) 9.9f **(64)** - Moorish Idol (Aragon) 8.1f **(60)**
Form - 0
Record 1999 - 1st:0 2nd:0 3rd:0 Ran:1
Pre1999 - 1st:1 2nd:3 3rd:0 Ran:15
Win Prizemoney £3,489 *Total Prizemoney* £10,816
Wins 1996 Nov Doncas (SFT) H 5f 80 98 <
1999 Turf 0-1: (7f) (gd)
Fair gelding, has worn blinkers. Inconsistent.
**Mrs L Stubbs [0-10] R Rayner (from J L Dunlop [1-6] Nov 1996).*

MYSTAGOGUE BHB 54f63a **RR 29f 63a** 5188[12]
4 ch g Mystiko (USA) 7.7f **(59)** -Malibasta(Auction Ring (USA)) 8.6f **(65)**
Form - 71323030132323770
Record 1999 - 1st:2 2nd:3 3rd:6 Ran:16
Pre1999 - 1st:2 2nd:4 3rd:2 Ran:20
Win Prizemoney £9,744 *Total Prizemoney* £18,355
Wins *** 1999** Jun Hamilt (GD) C 11.1f 49
1999 *Jan Lingfi (STD) C 12f 68 <*
1998 *Jan Lingfi (STD) H 10f 64 65+*
1997 *Nov Lingfi (STD) 10f 54*
1999 Turf 1-11: (11f 1-3, 12f 2, 13f, 14f, 15f, 16f 3) (g-s, g-f 1-3, frm 6, hrd) 1999 AW 1-5: (12f 1-3, 13f 2) (Equi 1-5)
Neat, average gelding, effective 8 to 14f, acts on gd to frm - acts on Equi, has worn blinkers, likes left handed tracks, favours tight tracks, excels at Lingfield. Turf high 60. AW high 68 - 2nd of 8 getting 9lb from Prince Danzig (12 Jan Lingfield 13f Equi RF 0078) - also 1st of 7 getting 10lb from Alsahib (2 Jan Lingfield RF 0007). Becoming disappointing.
**J S Goldie [1-14] Marauders Racing Club (from R Hannon [3-25] Feb 1999).*

MYSTERIOUS ECOLOGY BHB 46f **RR 58?f** 5075[12]
4 gr f Mystiko (USA) 7.7f **(59)** -Ecologically Kind (Alleged(USA))10f **(76)**
Form - 0
Record 1999 - 1st:0 2nd:0 3rd:0 Ran:1
Pre1999 - 1st:0 2nd:1 3rd:0 Ran:6
Win Prizemoney £0 *Total Prizemoney* £951
1999 Turf 0-1: (10f) (gd)
Workmanlike, fair filly.
**J L Spearing [0-1] Heathavon Stables Ltd (from B W Hills [0-5] Oct 1998).*

MYSTERIOUS MISS (IRE) BHB 42f **RR 76f** 1118[8]
4 b f Imp Society (USA) 7.1f **(63)** - Hotel Du Lac (Lomond (USA)) 8.8f **(65)**
Form - 8
Record 1999 - 1st:0 2nd:0 3rd:0 Ran:1
Pre1999 - 1st:0 2nd:2 3rd:1 Ran:16
Win Prizemoney £0 *Total Prizemoney* £2,916
1999 AW 0-1: (12f) (Fibr)
Above-average filly, effective 12f, acts on g-f, likes right handed tracks. Becoming disappointing.
**A W Carroll [0-1] Dennis Deacon (from A Leahy in IRE [0-18] Spt 1998).*

MYSTERIUM BHB 44f41a **RR 43f 41a** 5145[4]
5 gr g Mystiko (USA) 7.7f **(59)** - Way to Go (Troy) 10.4f **(68)**
Form - 56343543531574
Record 1999 - 1st:1 2nd:0 3rd:4 Ran:14
Pre1999 - 1st:1 2nd:1 3rd:1 Ran:11
Win Prizemoney £5,849 *Total Prizemoney* £7,923
Wins **1999** Jly Yarmou (G-F) H 11.5f 40 43
* 1997 *Feb Wolver (STD) 7f 59 <*
1999 Turf 1-6: (10f 4, 11f 1-2) (gd 1-2, g-f, frm 3) 1999 AW 0-8: (9f 2,

12f 6) (Fibr 8)

Fair gelding, effective 9 to 11f, best at 11f, acts on gd to g-f - acts on Fibr, has worn blinkers. Turf high 43 - 1st of 11 getting 14lb from Daniel Deronda (14 Jly Yarmouth RF 2835). AW high 50. Consistent.

**N P Littmoden [1-22] Alcester Associates (from J G Given [1-3] Aug 1999).*

MYSTICAL BHB 44f54a **RR 40f 54a** 4035[1]

5 b m Mystiko (USA) 7.7f **(59)** - Midnight Imperial (Night Shift (USA)) 7.2f **(69)**

Form - 4324441

Record	**1999 -**	1st:1	2nd:1	3rd:1	Ran:7
	Pre1999 -	1st:5	2nd:7	3rd:2	Ran:30

Win Prizemoney £16,055 *Total Prizemoney* £24,350

Wins	*** 1999**	Aug Warwic	(GD)	C	5f		34	
	1998	*Mar Lingfi*	*(SLW)*	*C*	*5f*		*73*	<
	1998	*Jan Lingfi*	*(STD)*	*C*	*6f*		*61+*	
	1997	*Dec Lingfi*	*(STD)*	*C*	*6f*		*61*	
	1997	Aug Bright	(G-F)	H	6f	62	64	
	1997	Jun Mussel	(G-S)	SH	5f	51	58	

1999 Turf 1-5: (5f 1-4, 6f) (gd 1-2, g-f, frm, hrd) 1999 AW 0-2: (5f, 6f) (Equi, Fibr)

Moderate filly, effective 5 to 6f, best at 6f, - acts on Equi, mostly wears blinkers (very effectively), prefers left handed tracks, likes tight tracks, excels at Lingfield. Turf high 40 (began Jly). AW high 42 (began Jly). Consistent.

**N Tinkler [1-7] Ian Blakey (from D Nicholls [0-1] Oct 1998).*

MYSTICAL WISDOM BHB 58f **RR 60f** 4169[6]

2 b f Mystiko (USA) 7.7f **(59)** - Surprise Surprise (Robellino (USA)) 7.6f **(80)**

Form - 005606

Record	**1999 -**	1st:0	2nd:0	3rd:0	Ran:6

1999 Turf 0-6: (6f, 7f 4, 8f) (g-f, frm 5)

Average filly. Turf high 60. **P R Chamings [0-6] Mrs J E L Wright.*

MYSTICISM BHB 46f **RR 46df** 3689[5]

4 ch f Mystiko (USA) 7.7f **(59)** - Abuzz (Absalom) 7.2f **(58)**

Form - 0500130305

Record	**1999 -**	1st:1	2nd:0	3rd:2	Ran:10
	Pre1999 -	1st:0	2nd:2	3rd:1	Ran:12

Win Prizemoney £2,210 *Total Prizemoney* £9,082

Wins	*** 1999**	May Bright	(FRM)	H	7f	48	52	<

1999 Turf 1-8: (6f 3, 7f 1-2, 8f 2, 10f) (sft, g-s, gd 2, g-f 1-2, frm, hrd) 1999 AW 0-2: (6f 2) (Equi, Fibr)

Neat, fair filly, effective 7f, acts on g-f, has worn blinkers (effectively), likes left handed tracks, likes tight tracks. Turf high 52 - 1st of 18 getting 10lb from Caversfield (12 May Brighton RF 1179). AW high 51. Inconsistent. **C E Brittain [1-22] Mrs C E Brittain.*

MYSTIC QUEST (IRE) BHB 42f70a **RR 44f 70a** 4650[10]

5 b g Arcane (USA) 11.6f **(66)** - Tales of Wisdom (Rousillon (USA)) 8.2f **(74)**

Form - 830

Record	**1999 -**	1st:0	2nd:0	3rd:1	Ran:3
	Pre1999 -	1st:3	2nd:3	3rd:3	Ran:24

Win Prizemoney £9,941 *Total Prizemoney* £14,580

Wins	* 1998	Jly Folkes	(G-F)	H	12f	50	53	
	* 1997	*Oct Lingfi*	*(STD)*	*H*	*12f*	*70*	*77*	
	* 1996	*Spt Wolver*	*(STD)*		*8.5f*		*83*	<

1999 Turf 0-2: (12f 2) (gd, frm) 1999 AW 0-1: (12f) (Equi)

Fair gelding, effective 12f, - acts on Equi, often wears blinkers (extremely effectively), favours tight tracks. Turf high 44. Inconsistent.

**K McAuliffe [3-29] Delamere Cottage Racing Partners (1996).*

MYSTIC RIDGE BHB 73f66a **RR 71+f 66a** 4179[1]

5 ch g Mystiko (USA) 7.7f **(59)** - Vallauris (Faustus (USA)) 10f **(58)**

Form - 0011131

Record	**1999 -**	1st:4	2nd:0	3rd:1	Ran:7
	Pre1999 -	1st:0	2nd:2	3rd:4	Ran:19

Win Prizemoney £19,924 *Total Prizemoney* £24,398

Wins	*** 1999**	Spt Lingfi	(G-F)	H	7f	68	71+	<
	*** 1999**	Jly Galway	(G-F)	H	7f		68	
	*** 1999**	Jly Leopar	(G-F)	H	8f		58	
	*** 1999**	May Bright	(FRM)	H	8f	42	50+	

1999 Turf 4-6: (7f 2-3, 8f 2-2, 12f) (g-f 1-2, frm 2-3, hrd 1-1) 1999 AW 0-1: (8f) (Equi)

Above-average gelding, effective 7f, acts on g-f to frm, often wears blinkers. Turf high 71 - 1st of 16 getting 8lb from Blakeset (7 Spt Lingfield RF 4179) - also 1st of 17 giving 2lb to Millie's Lily (27 Jly Galway RF 3325a). He won twice in Ireland after scoring at Brighton in May, and scored again at Lingfield in September. Usually travels up with the pace, and looks sure to find further opportunities.

**B J Curley [4-25] P Byrne (from D R C Elsworth [0-5] Jun 1997).*

MYSTIC SPRING (IRE) BHB 65f72a **RR 70f 72a** 3437[1]

3 gr f Royal Academy (USA) 7.8f **(77)** - Secret Sunday (USA) (Secreto (USA)) 8.7f **(72)**

Form - 48341

Record	**1999 -**	1st:1	2nd:0	3rd:1	Ran:5
	Pre1999 -	1st:0	2nd:0	3rd:0	Ran:2

Win Prizemoney £2,878 *Total Prizemoney* £3,674

Wins	*** 1999**	*Aug Wolver*	*(STD)*	*9.4f*		*72*	<

1999 Turf 0-2: (7f, 8f) (g-f 2) 1999 AW 1-3: (8f, 9f 1-2) (Fibr 1-3)

Light-framed, above-average filly, effective 8 to 9f, best at 9f, - acts on Fibr. Turf high 58. AW high 72 (began Jly) - 1st of 13 getting 5lb from Newscaster (6 Aug Wolverhampton RF 3437).

**J Noseda [1-7] Fieldspring Racing.*

MYSTIFY RR 84f 3936[5]

2 b f Batshoof 9.5f **(66)** - Santa Linda (USA) (Sir Ivor) 10.2f **(70)**

Form - 55

Record	**1999 -**	1st:0	2nd:0	3rd:0	Ran:2

1999 Turf 0-2: (7f 2) (frm 2)

Currently decent filly. Turf high 84 (began Aug).

**J H M Gosden [0-2] Lord Hartington.*

MY TESS BHB 61f64a **RR 54f 64a** 5217[6]

3 br f Lugana Beach 7f **(63)** - Barachois Princess (USA) (Barachois (CAN)) 8.3f **(63)**

Form - 6301075306

Record	**1999 -**	1st:1	2nd:0	3rd:2	Ran:10
	Pre1999 -	1st:0	2nd:0	3rd:1	Ran:3

Win Prizemoney £4,356 *Total Prizemoney* £5,974

Wins	*** 1999**	Apr Nottin	(HVY)	8.2f		77	<

1999 Turf 1-9: (8f 1-6, 10f 2, 11f) (sft 1-1, g-s 2, gd 3, g-f, frm 2) 1999 AW 0-1: (8f) (Fibr)

Light-framed, fair filly, effective 8 to 10f, acts on sft to gd, likes left handed tracks, likes tight tracks. Turf high 77 - 1st of 7 from Red Roses (27 Apr Nottingham RF 0868).

**B A McMahon [1-13] J D Graham.*

MYTHICAL GIRL (USA) BHB 108f **RR 106f** 1485a[17]

3 b f Gone West (USA) 7.8f **(82)** - Yousefia (USA) (Danzig (USA)) 8.4f **(76)**

Form - 10

Record	**1999 -**	1st:1	2nd:0	3rd:0	Ran:2
	Pre1999 -	1st:2	2nd:0	3rd:0	Ran:3

Win Prizemoney £54,596 *Total Prizemoney* £55,171

Wins	*** 1999**	May Goodwo	(GD)		8f	106	<
	1998	Jly Ascot	(G-F)	G3	6f	100	
	1998	Jly Newmar	(FRM)		6f	92+	

1999 Turf 1-2: (8f 1-2) (gd 1-1, g-f)

Neat, Pattern-class filly. Turf high 106 (1st run) - 1st of 9 from Choirgirl (8 May Goodwood RF 1106). She was an impressive winner of Shergar Cup Distaff and looked set for a good season, but finished down the field in the Irish Guineas, having given trouble in the preliminaries, and that was that.

**S bin Suroor [1-2] Godolphin (from D R Loder [2-3] Aug 1998).*

MYTHICAL KING (IRE) RR 72f 4840[11]

2 b c Fairy King (USA) 7.7f **(75)** - Whatcombe (USA) **(75df)** (Alleged (USA)) 10f **(76)**

Form - 350

Record	**1999 -**	1st:0	2nd:0	3rd:1	Ran:3

Win Prizemoney £0 *Total Prizemoney* £535

1999 Turf 0-3: (7f 3) (gd 2, frm)

Currently above-average colt. Turf high 72 (1st run) (began Aug) - 3rd of 14 to Three Points (4 Aug Kempton 7f frm RF 3353).

**B Palling [0-3] Glyn and Albert Yemm.*

MYTTON'S AGAIN BHB 77f **RR 73f** 5158[2]
2 b g Rambo Dancer (CAN) 8.4f **(59)** - Sigh (Highland Melody) 6.3f **(55)**
Form - 520585810042
Record 1999 - 1st:1 2nd:2 3rd:0 Ran:12
Win Prizemoney £6,320 *Total Prizemoney* £8,364
Wins * 1999 Spt Cheste (HVY) H 7f 65 72 <
1999 Turf 1-12: (5f, 6f 3, 7f 1-5, 8f 3) (g-s 1-2, gd 6, g-f 2, frm 2)
Above-average gelding, effective 7 to 8f, best at 7f, acts on g-s to frm, often wears blinkers, prefers tight tracks. Turf high 73 - 2nd of 27 giving 23lb to Master Soden (1 Nov Redcar 8f frm RF 5158) - also 1st of 8 getting 19lb from Card Games (22 Spt Chester RF 4484). Inconsistent. **A Bailey [1-12] Gordon Mytton.*

MYTTONS MISTAKE BHB 49f58a **RR 49f 58a** 5128[7]
6 b g Rambo Dancer (CAN) 8.4f **(59)** - Hi-Hunsley (Swing Easy (USA)) 6.5f **(55)**
Form - 003404056081577
Record 1999 - 1st:1 2nd:0 3rd:1 Ran:15
Pre1999 - 1st:8 2nd:7 3rd:12 Ran:65
Win Prizemoney £31,289 *Total Prizemoney* £51,378

Wins								
	1999	Aug	Bright	(G-S)	S	6f		44
	1998	Aug	Kempto	(G-F)	H	7f	68	70
	1998	Jly	Bath	(GD)	H	5.7f	64	67
	1997	Oct	Leices	(GD)	CH	8f	62	78?
	1997	Spt	Sandow	(G-F)	H	7.1f	59	64
	1997	Aug	Beverl	(GD)	H	7.5f	57	60
	1997	Jly	Cheste	(G-F)	H	7.6f	53	58
	1995	Jly	Beverl	(G-F)		5f		85 <
	1995	Jun	Ayr	(FRM)		7f		74+

1999 Turf 1-14: (5f, 6f 1-6, 7f 6, 8f) (sft, gd 1-3, frm 8, hrd 2) 1999 AW 0-1: (6f) (Fibr)
Moderate gelding, effective 6 to 7f, best at 6f, acts on gd to hrd, has worn blinkers, prefers left handed tracks, likes tight tracks, excels at Brighton. Turf high 63 - 4th of 14 giving 21lb to Dark Menace (4 May Brighton 7f hrd RF 1021). Consistent.
**R J Baker [0-2] P Slade (from R J Hodges [3-32] Spt 1999).*

MYTTON'S MOMENT (IRE) BHB 51f **RR 56f** 3398[3]
3 b g Waajib 8.9f **(67)** - Late Swallow (My Swallow) 9.2f **(71)**
Form - 0080185463
Record 1999 - 1st:1 2nd:0 3rd:1 Ran:10
Pre1999 - 1st:0 2nd:0 3rd:0 Ran:7
Win Prizemoney £3,622 *Total Prizemoney* £5,415
Wins * 1999 Jun Newmar (GD) S 8f 69 <
1999 Turf 1-10: (8f 1-6, 10f 3, 11f) (g-s, gd 1-3, g-f 5, frm)
Light-framed, fair gelding, effective 8f, acts on gd, often wears blinkers (effectively). Turf high 69 - 1st of 9 giving 5lb to Aegean Glory (5 Jun Newmarket RF 1771). Inconsistent.
**A Bailey [1-17] Gordon Mytton.*

NABADHAAT (USA) RR 77f 5020[8]
2 b f Mr Prospector (USA) 8.6f **(88)** -Roseate Tern (Blakeney)10.5f **(64)**
Form - 48
Record 1999 - 1st:0 2nd:0 3rd:0 Ran:2
Win Prizemoney £0 *Total Prizemoney* £315
1999 Turf 0-2: (8f 2) (gd 2)
Currently above-average filly. Turf high 77 (1st run) (began Spt) - 4th of 11 to Dollar Bird (25 Spt Nottingham 8f gd RF 4559).
**E A L Dunlop [0-2] Hamdan Al Maktoum.*

NABONASSAR BHB 93f **RR 93f** 3287[1]
3 ch g Lion Cavern (USA) 7.5f **(74)** - Negligent (Ahonoora) 8.1f **(73)**
Form - 21241
Record 1999 - 1st:2 2nd:2 3rd:0 Ran:5
Pre1999 - 1st:0 2nd:1 3rd:0 Ran:1
Win Prizemoney £10,519 *Total Prizemoney* £14,862
Wins * 1999 Jly Thirsk (FRM) H 8f 87 93 <
*** 1999** May Bright (FRM) 7f 84
1999 Turf 2-5: (7f 1-3, 8f 1-2) (gd 3, g-f 1-1, frm 1-1)
Scopey, useful gelding, effective 7 to 8f, best at 8f, acts on gd to frm, best on gd. Turf high 93 - 1st of 6 getting 1lb from Amalia (31 Jly Thirsk RF 3287) - also 1st of 7 from My Pleasure (12 May Brighton RF 1178). Won a Brighton maiden on firm ground in May, and successfully stepped up to a mile to land a Thirsk handicap on his final start. **Sir Michael Stoute [2-6] Sheikh Mohammed.*

NADDER BHB 33f **RR 18f** 4832[26]
4 ch g Lion Cavern (USA) 7.5f **(74)** - Nadia Nerina (CAN) (Northern Dancer) 9.6f **(80)**
Form - 700057580
Record 1999 - 1st:0 2nd:0 3rd:0 Ran:9
1999 Turf 0-6: (5f, 6f 4, 7f) (sft, gd 3, g-f, frm) 1999 AW 0-3: (6f 2, 7f) (Fibr 3)
Very moderate gelding. Turf high 46. AW high 40.
**W M Brisbourne [0-9] K Bennett.*

NADISHA (IRE) BHB 62f **RR 63f** 4730[3]
3 b f Rainbows For Life (CAN) 9.3f **(64)** - Gracieuse Amie (FR) (Gay Mecene (USA)) 8.6f **(69)**
Form - 33621233333
Record 1999 - 1st:1 2nd:2 3rd:7 Ran:11
Win Prizemoney £2,788 *Total Prizemoney* £8,280
Wins * 1999 Jun Ayr (GD) H 13.1f 59 60 <
1999 Turf 1-6: (10f, 13f 1-2, 14f, 16f 2) (sft, g-s, gd, g-f 1-2, frm) 1999 AW 0-5: (10f, 12f, 14f, 15f, 16f) (Equi 2, Fibr 3)
Workmanlike, average filly, effective 10f, - acts on Equi, has worn blinkers, favours left handed tracks. Turf high 63. AW high 74 (1st run) - 3rd of 13 getting 5lb from Scraggys Dream (2 Jan Lingfield 10f Equi RF 0010). Consistent. She ran consistently well all season. **W J Haggas [1-11] Ahmed Farook.*

NAFITH BHB 63f **RR 60f** 1953[11]
3 ch g Elmaamul (USA) 8.1f **(70)** - Wanisa (USA) (Topsider (USA)) 8.3f **(71)**
Form - 65070
Record 1999 - 1st:0 2nd:0 3rd:0 Ran:5
Pre1999 - 1st:0 2nd:0 3rd:0 Ran:2
1999 Turf 0-5: (8f 4, 10f) (sft, g-s, g-f 2, frm)
Scopey, average gelding. Turf high 69.
**M P Tregoning [0-7] Hamdan Al Maktoum.*

NAGOYA (GER) RR 97f 1534a[1]
3 b f Goofalik (USA) 15.4f **(66)** - Nuas (GER) (Aspros (GER))
Form - 1
1999 Turf 1-1: (11f 1-1) (gd 1-1)
Currently very useful filly. (1st run) - 1st of 11 from Janestra (23 May San Siro RF 1534a). **H Blume in GER [1-1] Gestut Rottgen.*

NAILER (IRE) RR 48f 3834[8]
3 b c Darshaan 11.9f **(81)** - Raysiya (Cure The Blues (USA)) 9.5f **(63)**
Form - 08
Record 1999 - 1st:0 2nd:0 3rd:0 Ran:2
1999 Turf 0-1: (12f) (frm) 1999 AW 0-1: (9f) (Fibr)
Tall, currently moderate colt. **E J O'Neill [0-2] Mrs Patrick O'Neill.*

NAISSANT BHB 56f51a **RR 58f 51a** 4832[18]
6 b m Shaadi (USA) 8.1f **(75)** - Nophe (USA) (Super Concorde (USA)) 10.9f **(66)**
Form - 243146373640515000
Record 1999 - 1st:2 2nd:1 3rd:3 Ran:18
Pre1999 - 1st:4 2nd:4 3rd:1 Ran:46
Win Prizemoney £22,470 *Total Prizemoney* £36,946

Wins								
*	1999	Aug	Carlis	(G-F)		6.9f		58
*	1999	May	Hamilt	(Sft)	H	5f	63	66
	1998	Aug	Hamilt	(SFT)	H	6f	55	61
	1998	Jun	Hamilt	(SFT)	H	6f	51	53
	1996	Aug	Carlis	(FRM)		6.9f		61
	1996	Aug	Ripon	(G-S)	H	6f	60	71 <

1999 Turf 2-17: (5f 1-2, 6f 10, 7f 1-5) (hvy, sft, g-s, gd 1-5, g-f 6, frm 1-3) 1999 AW 0-1: (7f) (Fibr)
Fair mare, effective 5 to 7f, best at 5f, acts on hvy to frm, best on gd, and does well at Hamilton. Turf high 66 - 1st of 12 giving 28lb to Kalar (14 May Hamilton RF 1206) - also 1st of 11 getting 3lb from Eastern Prophets (25 Aug Carlisle RF 3901). Becoming disappointing. She won two races last term, both of which were moderate affairs.
**J S Goldie [2-18] William Graham (from Martyn Wane [2-18] Oct 1998).*

NAJJM (USA) BHB 79f **RR 76f** 5024[3]
2 br c Dynaformer (USA) 12f **(82)** - Azusa (USA) (Flying Paster (USA))
Form - 2233
Record 1999 - 1st:0 2nd:2 3rd:2 Ran:4
Win Prizemoney £0 *Total Prizemoney* £3,549
1999 Turf 0-4: (7f, 8f 3) (gd, g-f 2, hrd)

Above-average colt. Turf high 79 (1st run) (began Jly) - 2nd of 5 giving 5lb to Hiddnah (24 Jly Newcastle 7f g-f RF 3098).
**J L Dunlop [0-4] Hamdan Al Maktoum.*

NAKED OAT BHB 53f64a **RR 53f 64a** 2569[17]

4 b g Imp Society (USA) 7.1f **(63)** - Bajina (Dancing Brave (USA)) 8.4f **(76)**

Form - 2324175610600

Record 1999 - 1st:2 2nd:0 3rd:0 Ran:10
Pre1999 - 1st:0 2nd:3 3rd:4 Ran:18

Win Prizemoney £4,655 *Total Prizemoney* £9,189

Wins * 1999 May Warwic (GD) H 8f 50 56
*** 1999** *Feb Wolver (STD)* *9.4f* *69+* <

1999 Turf 1-7: (8f 1-4, 10f 3) (hvy, sft, gd, g-f, frm 1-3) 1999 AW 1-3: (9f 1-2, 10f) (Equi, Fibr 1-2)

Average gelding, effective 8 to 9f, best at 8f, - acts on Fibr, has worn blinkers, prefers left handed tracks. Turf high 56. AW high 69 - 1st of 10 giving 21lb to The Last Word (6 Feb Wolverhampton RF 0245). **B Smart [2-28] The Dyball Partnership.*

NAMAQUALASS (IRE) BHB 39f **RR 47f** 4626[9]

2 b f Namaqualand (USA) - Joyful Lass (USA) (Danzig (USA)) 8.4f **(76)**

Form - 40050320650500

Record 1999 - 1st:0 2nd:1 3rd:1 Ran:14

Win Prizemoney £0 *Total Prizemoney* £1,011

1999 Turf 0-13: (5f 7, 6f 4, 7f, 8f) (g-s 2, gd, g-f 5, frm 4, hrd) 1999 AW 0-1: (5f) (Fibr)

Moderate filly. Turf high 56. She has made the frame in very modest company. **M Quinn [0-14] M Quinn.*

NAME OF OUR FATHER (USA) BHB 44f36a **RR 50f 36a** 4581[16]

6 b g Northern Baby (CAN) 10.2f **(74)** - Ten Hail Marys (USA) (Halo (USA)) 10.6f **(75)**

Form - 0

Record 1999 - 1st:0 2nd:0 3rd:0 Ran:1
Pre1999 - 1st:0 2nd:1 3rd:0 Ran:10

Win Prizemoney £0 *Total Prizemoney* £1,581

1999 Turf 0-1: (17f) (gd)

Fair gelding.
**P Bowen [8-37] T M Morris (from M J Fetherston-Godley [0-1] Apr 1996).*

NAMID **RR 99f** 4971a[3]

3 b c Indian Ridge 7.6f **(74)** - Dawnsio (IRE) (Tate Gallery (USA)) 7.4f **(67)**

Form - 23

1999 Turf 0-2: (6f, 7f) (hvy, g-s)

Very useful colt. Turf high 99 - 3rd of 14 to Rolo Tomasi (16 Oct Curragh 6f g-s RF 4971a). **J Oxx in IRE [1-4] Lady Clague.*

NAMPARA BAY BHB 33f34a **RR 15f 34a** 340[8]

5 b m Emarati (USA) 6.6f **(63)** - Dewberry (Bay Express) 7.1f **(60)**

Form - 88

Record 1999 - 1st:0 2nd:0 3rd:0 Ran:1
Pre1999 - 1st:0 2nd:1 3rd:1 Ran:11

Win Prizemoney £0 *Total Prizemoney* £924

1999 AW 0-1: (6f) (Fibr)

Poor filly, has worn blinkers.
**J Hetherton [0-3] Rowland Hill (from G C Bravery [0-10] Spt 1997).*

NANOUSHKA (IRE) BHB 101f **RR 103f** 4119[5]

4 b f Taufan (USA) 8.3f **(65)** - West Chazy (USA) (Gone West (USA)) 6.5f **(75)**

Form - 616845

Record 1999 - 1st:1 2nd:0 3rd:0 Ran:6
Pre1999 - 1st:3 2nd:0 3rd:2 Ran:10

Win Prizemoney £43,947 *Total Prizemoney* £52,327

Wins * 1999 May Newmar (GD) L 6f 107
*** 1998** Jly York (G-F) L 6f 111? <
*** 1998** May Lingfi (GD) L 7f 100
*** 1997** Aug Ascot (GD) 6f 89+

1999 Turf 1-6: (6f 1-3, 7f 3) (g-f 1-5, frm)

Leggy, very useful filly, effective 6 to 7f, best at 6f, acts on g-f to frm, best on frm. Turf high 107 - 1st of 8 giving 14lb to Aunt Flo (15 May Newmarket RF 1245). Consistent. Capable in listed races, as she showed when winning at Newmarket on her second start, but stumbles when stepped up to Group events. Equally effective at six and seven furlongs, she has seemed not to stay a mile.
**R Hannon [4-16] Thurloe Thoroughbreds II.*

NANSEN (GER) **RR 69df** 3735[5]

6 ch g Orfano (GER) - Nanja (Surumu (GER)) 10f **(83)**

Form - 35

Record 1999 - 1st:0 2nd:0 3rd:1 Ran:2

Win Prizemoney £0 *Total Prizemoney* £428

1999 Turf 0-2: (8f, 12f) (gd, frm)

Average gelding. Turf high 69 (1st run) (began Jly) - 3rd of 11 giving 8lb to Barbason (21 Jly Sandown 8f frm RF 3015).
**Miss E C Lavelle [0-7] S Calvert.*

NANTUCKET (IRE) BHB 83f **RR 79f** 4384[9]

2 b c Turtle Island (IRE) - Pericolo (IRE) (Kris) 9.5f **(73)**

Form - 7U0410

Record 1999 - 1st:1 2nd:0 3rd:0 Ran:6

Win Prizemoney £3,200 *Total Prizemoney* £3,482

Wins * 1999 Aug Lingfi (G-F) 5f 79 <

1999 Turf 1-6: (5f 1-4, 6f 2) (gd, g-f 1-1, frm 4)

Above-average colt, effective 5 to 6f, acts on g-f to frm. Turf high 79 - 1st of 8 giving 5lb to Corblets (24 Aug Lingfield RF 3870). He was slow to find his form, but after a most encouraging effort at Newmarket in July, got off the mark by the narrowest of margins back over the minimum at Lingfield the following month.
**D R C Elsworth [1-6] O J McDowell.*

NANY'S AFFAIR (USA) BHB 52f67a **RR 52f 67a** 2809[3]

3 b f Colonial Affair (USA) 7f **(57)** - Nuryette (USA) (Nureyev (USA)) 8.7f **(78)**

Form - 211253

Record 1999 - 1st:2 2nd:2 3rd:1 Ran:6

Win Prizemoney £5,337 *Total Prizemoney* £7,590

Wins * 1999 *Mar Southw (STD)* *7f* *63* <
*** 1999** *Feb Lingfi (STD)* *7f* *61*

1999 Turf 0-3: (8f, 10f, 12f) (hvy, g-f, frm) 1999 AW 2-3: (7f 2-3) (Equi 1-2, Fibr 1-1)

Workmanlike, average filly, effective 7f, - acts on AW, has worn blinkers. Turf high 52. AW high 63 - 1st of 8 from Carrie Pooter (16 Mar Southwell RF 0435) - also 1st of 7 getting 5lb from Forty Forte (18 Feb Lingfield RF 0311).
**Sir Mark Prescott [2-6] Mrs Chryss O'Reilly.*

NAPIER STAR BHB 33f44a **RR 8f 44a** 4606[10]

6 b m Inca Chief (USA) 5.6f **(45)** - America Star (Norwick (USA)) 7.2f **(56)**

Form - 00

Record 1999 - 1st:0 2nd:0 3rd:0 Ran:2
Pre1999 - 1st:4 2nd:8 3rd:8 Ran:51

Win Prizemoney £9,262 *Total Prizemoney* £18,928

Wins 1997 *May Wolver (STD) H* *5f* *63* *63* <
1996 *Nov Wolver (STD) H* *5f* *60* *61*
1996 *Jly Wolver (STD) H* *5f* *51* *51*
1996 *Apr Southw (STD)* *6f* *57*

1999 AW 0-2: (6f 2) (Fibr 2)

Fair mare, often wears blinkers. AW high 14 (began Jly). Becoming disappointing.
**A B Mulholland [0-2] P M Heaton (from Mrs N Macauley [4-51] Jan 1998).*

NAPOLEON'S RETURN BHB 41f40a **RR 43f 40a** 4591[14]

6 gr g Daring March 9f **(54)** - Miss Colenca (Petong) 6.6f **(58)**

Form - 70220100700

Record 1999 - 1st:1 2nd:2 3rd:0 Ran:9
Pre1999 - 1st:3 2nd:4 3rd:2 Ran:40

Win Prizemoney £11,699 *Total Prizemoney* £17,951

Wins * 1999 Jun Ripon (G-F) SH 8f 39 44
*** 1997** Jly Catter (G-F) H 7f 37 38
1996 Jun Ayr (G-F) H 8f 45 50
1995 Oct Redcar (FRM) C 7f 66 <

1999 Turf 1-9: (8f 1-5, 9f 3, 10f) (g-s, gd, g-f 3, frm 3, hrd 1-1)

Moderate gelding, effective 8f, acts on g-s to hrd, has worn blinkers, prefers right handed tracks. Turf high 46 (1st run) - 2nd of 10 getting 4lb from Court Express (2 May Hamilton 8f g-f RF 0971) - also 1st of 20 getting 1lb from Shontaine (16 Jun Ripon RF 2057).
**J L Eyre [2-27] J E Wilson (from A Harrison [1-11] Jly 1996).*

NAPOLEON STAR (IRE) BHB 32f35a **RR 33f 35a** 4142[14]
8 ch g Mulhollande (USA) 6.6f **(68)** - Lady Portobello (Porto Bello) 8.9f **(43)**
Form - 0708008000
Record 1999 - 1st:0 2nd:0 3rd:0 Ran:10
Pre1999 - 1st:6 2nd:4 3rd:5 Ran:88
Win Prizemoney £16,057 *Total Prizemoney* £23,548
Wins 1997 Jun Catter (GD) H 6f 48 52
1997 Mar Warwic (G-F) H 5f 43 49
1997 Feb Southw (STD) SH 6f 43 43
1999 Turf 0-10: (5f, 7f 3, 8f 5, 10f) (g-s, gd 3, g-f 3, frm, hrd 2)
Very moderate gelding, effective 8f, acts on g-f, has worn blinkers. Turf high 45.
**Miss J F Craze [0-35] S A Pritchard (from S R Bowring [3-20] Aug 1997).*

NASAIEB (IRE) BHB 90f **RR 80f** 4920[12]
2 b f Fairy King (USA) 7.7f **(75)**-Atyaaf (USA) (Irish River (FR)) 8.6f **(78)**
Form - 81340
Record 1999 - 1st:1 2nd:0 3rd:1 Ran:5
Win Prizemoney £3,752 *Total Prizemoney* £6,279
Wins * 1999 May Nottin (FRM) 5.1f 71 <
1999 Turf 1-5: (5f 1-4, 7f) (gd 2, g-f 1-3)
Decent filly. Turf high 80 - also 1st of 6 getting 5lb from Jazz Time (21 May Nottingham RF 1380). Her Nottingham win does not add up to much, and she has been easily dismissed in pattern events since. **C E Brittain [1-5] Saeed Manana.*

NASHCASH (IRE) BHB 103f **RR 106f** 4781a[3]
6 ch h Nashamaa 8.1f **(58)** - Six Penny Express (Bay Express) 7.1f **(60)**
Form - 3
1999 Turf 0-1: (5f) (g-s)
Pattern-class horse.
**F Gang in GER [1-2] (from C Collins in IRE [0-5] Jun 1996).*

NASHEED (USA) BHB 106f **RR 103f** 2098a[10]
3 b br f Riverman (USA) 9.7f **(78)** - Thawakib (IRE) (Sadler's Wells (USA)) 10f **(76)**
Form - 10
Record 1999 - 1st:1 2nd:0 3rd:0 Ran:2
Pre1999 - 1st:2 2nd:0 3rd:1 Ran:3
Win Prizemoney £26,283 *Total Prizemoney* £27,135
Wins * 1999 May Newbur (G-S) L 10f 102 <
*** 1998** Oct Ascot (SFT) H 7f 81 91
*** 1998** Aug Cheste (G-S) 7f 74
1999 Turf 1-2: (10f 1-1, 11f) (g-s 1-2)
Leggy, very useful filly. Turf high 103 - also 1st of 10 from Samoa (14 May Newbury RF 1215). Tough as teak, she fought like a tigress to win at Newbury in May, but cut no ice in the French Oaks. Suited by easy ground, she should stay a mile and a half.
**J L Dunlop [3-5].*

NASH HOUSE (IRE) BHB 83f **RR 94df** 5055[9]
6 b h Nashwan (USA) 10.3f **(79)** - River Dancer (Irish River (FR)) 8.6f **(78)**
Form - 6520700
Record 1999 - 1st:0 2nd:1 3rd:0 Ran:7
Pre1999 - 1st:1 2nd:0 3rd:0 Ran:3
Win Prizemoney £3,492 *Total Prizemoney* £10,134
Wins 1996 Apr Newbur (G-S) 8f 86+ <
1999 Turf 0-7: (7f, 8f, 10f 3, 12f 2) (g-s, gd 4, g-f, frm)
Useful horse. Turf high 97. Inconsistent. A former Classic contender, he has endured his share of problems and looks regressive.
**N P Littmoden [0-2] A1 Racing (from W M Roper in IRE [0-5] Jly 1999).*

NATALIE JAY BHB 65f68a **RR 65f 68a** 4991[5]
3 b f Ballacashtal (CAN) 7.9f **(51)** - Falls of Lora (Scottish Rifle) 10f **(55)**
Form - 060201508525
Record 1999 - 1st:1 2nd:2 3rd:0 Ran:12
Pre1999 - 1st:0 2nd:0 3rd:3 Ran:4
Win Prizemoney £5,589 *Total Prizemoney* £9,001
Wins * 1999 Aug Salisb (SFT) H 8f 63 67 <
1999 Turf 1-11: (7f, 8f 1-5, 9f 3, 10f 2) (sft, g-s, gd, g-f 1-4, frm 4) 1999 AW 0-1: (10f) (Equi)
Lengthy, average filly, effective 7 to 10f, acts on g-s to g-f - acts on Equi, best on g-f, likes left handed tracks. Turf high 67 - 1st of 11 getting 26lb from Saligo (12 Aug Salisbury RF 3574). (1st run) - 2nd of 11 giving 23lb to Tulsa (24 Jly Lingfield 10f Equi RF 3092). Consistent. **M R Channon [1-16] Peter Jolliffe.*

NATALIE TOO (USA) RR 104f 5228a[12]
5 m Irish River (USA) - Likely Split (USA) (Little Current (USA)) 9.6f **(75)**
Form - 0
1999 Turf 0-1: (11f) (frm)
Currently very useful, always wears blinkers.
**D W Lukas in USA [0-1].*

NATASHA RR 44f 3537[7]
2 b f Mujtahid (USA) 7.4f **(69)** - Wakayi (Persian Bold) 9.3f **(66)**
Form - 7
Record 1999 - 1st:0 2nd:0 3rd:0 Ran:1
1999 Turf 0-1: (7f) (g-f)
Currently moderate filly. **T D Easterby [0-1] D Davidson.*

NATHAN'S BOY BHB 74f74a **RR 77f 74a** 4230[13]
3 gr c Tragic Role (USA) 9.4f **(63)** - Gold Belt (IRE) (Bellypha) 9.8f **(73)**
Form - 4177223400
Record 1999 - 1st:1 2nd:2 3rd:1 Ran:10
Pre1999 - 1st:0 2nd:2 3rd:2 Ran:8
Win Prizemoney £4,048 *Total Prizemoney* £12,016
Wins * 1999 Apr Beverl (GD) H 9.9f 75 78 <
1999 Turf 1-10: (10f 1-5, 12f 5) (g-s, gd 1-4, g-f 3, frm 2)
Light-framed, above-average colt, has broken blood-vessels, effective 6 to 12f, best at 10f, acts on g-s to g-f, best on gd, excels at Doncaster and Beverley. Turf high 83 - 2nd of 6 getting 1lb from Fiori (9 Jun Beverley 12f g-s RF 1850) - also 1st of 15 giving 10lb to Gypsy (22 Apr Beverley RF 0805). Had a busy two-year-old campaign, and continued in the same vein last term. A winner at Beverley over ten furlongs in April, he was placed behind some really progressive horses afterwards.
**R Hollinshead [1-18] Mrs J Hughes.*

NATHAN'S HERO (IRE) BHB 38f41a **RR 32f 41a** 5147[12]
3 ch g Forest Wind (USA) - Lapland Lights (USA) (Northern Prospect (USA)) 9.5f **(71)**
Form - 282642444050
Record 1999 - 1st:0 2nd:2 3rd:0 Ran:10
Pre1999 - 1st:0 2nd:1 3rd:2 Ran:12
Win Prizemoney £0 *Total Prizemoney* £2,404
1999 Turf 0-1: (11f) (sft) 1999AW 0-9: (8f 3, 9f 2, 11f, 12f 2, 15f) (Fibr 9)
Light-framed, moderate gelding, effective 8f, - acts on Fibr, has worn blinkers. AW high 61 (1st run) - 2nd of 7 giving 5lb to Golden Syrup (4 Jan Southwell 8f Fibr RF 0026). Becoming disappointing.
**Miss A Stokell [0-8] T J Ford (from R Hollinshead [0-14] Feb 1999).*

NATIONAL ANTHEM BHB 96f **RR 96f** 4404[4]
3 b c Royal Academy (USA) 7.8f **(77)** - Heart's Harmony (Blushing Groom (FR)) 10.3f **(76)**
Form - 423614
Record 1999 - 1st:1 2nd:1 3rd:1 Ran:6
Pre1999 - 1st:0 2nd:1 3rd:0 Ran:2
Win Prizemoney £4,037 *Total Prizemoney* £18,430
Wins * 1999 Aug Sandow (G-S) 10f 80+ <
1999 Turf 1-6: (7f, 10f 1-5) (gd 2, g-f 1-3, frm)
Light-framed, very useful colt, effective 10f, acts on gd to frm. Turf high 96 - 4th of 16 giving 8lb to Komistar (18 Spt Newbury 10f frm RF 4404). An imposing individual, he lacks a decisive turn-of-foot and will improve when stepped-up to a mile and a half. Possibly a shade weak at present, he is likely to make a useful four-year-old.
**Sir Michael Stoute [1-8] Mrs Denis Haynes.*

NATIONAL WISH (USA) BHB 55f **RR 57df** 3310[10]
4 ch g Forty Niner (USA) 8.8f **(73)** - Regent's Walk (CAN) (Vice Regent (CAN)) 8.7f **(74)**
Form - 00500
Record 1999 - 1st:0 2nd:0 3rd:0 Ran:5
Pre1999 - 1st:0 2nd:0 3rd:1 Ran:4
Win Prizemoney £0 *Total Prizemoney* £530
1999 Turf 0-5: (7f 3, 8f 2) (g-f 2, frm 3)
Scopey, fair gelding, effective 8 to 9f, acted on g-f to frm, had worn blinkers. Turf high 57 - 5th of 8 giving 7lb to Sandicliffe (20 Jly Bath 8f frm RF 2957). Inconsistent. (DEAD)

Mrs Merrita Jones [0-5] Louis Jones (from E A L Dunlop [0-4] Jun 1998).

NATIVE JUSTICE (USA) RR 112f 3408a[3]

4 f Alleged (USA) 11.8f **(81)** - Fabulous Native (USA) (Le Fabuleux) 11.4f **(76)**

Form - 23

1999 Turf 0-2: (10f, 14f) (gd 2)

Group-class filly. Turf high 107 - 3rd of 11 to Bimbola (1 Aug Deauville 14f gd RF 3408a). **A Fabre in FR [0-4].*

NATSMAGIRL (IRE) BHB 54f **RR 63f** 4901[23]

2 b f Blues Traveller (IRE) - Top The Rest (Top Ville) 11.7f **(68)**

Form - 653105244263000

Record 1999 - 1st:1 2nd:2 3rd:2 Ran:15

Win Prizemoney £2,722 *Total Prizemoney* £6,466

Wins * 1999 Jun Thirsk (G-F) S 6f 63 <

1999 Turf 1-15: (5f 5, 6f 1-7, 7f 3) (gd, g-f, frm 1-11, hrd 2)

Average filly, effective 5 to 7f, best at 6f, acts on g-f to hrd, best on frm, excels at Thirsk. Turf high 63 - 1st of 14 getting 5lb from Ostara (15 Jun Thirsk RF 2003). Becoming disappointing.

**Martyn Wane [1-15] Darren & Annaley Yates.*

NATURAL (IRE) RR 42f 4655[14]

2 b c Bigstone (IRE) - You Make Me Real (USA) (Give Me Strength (USA))

Form - 0

Record 1999 - 1st:0 2nd:0 3rd:0 Ran:1

1999 Turf 0-1: (7f) (gd)

Currently moderate colt. **J Noseda [0-1] M Tabor.*

NATURAL EIGHT (IRE) BHB 50f **RR 51f** 5006[2]

5 b g In The Wings 11.2f **(77)** - Fenny Rough (Home Guard (USA)) 9.3f **(66)**

Form - 0586464132

Record 1999 - 1st:1 2nd:1 3rd:1 Ran:10

Pre1999 - 1st:0 2nd:1 3rd:2 Ran:8

Win Prizemoney £3,009 *Total Prizemoney* £7,497

Wins * 1999 Spt Bath (FRM) H 13.1f 43 45+ <

1999 Turf 1-10: (11f, 12f 6, 13f 1-1, 14f, 16f) (gd 4, frm 1-6)

Fair gelding, has worn blinkers. Turf high 54. Consistent.

**J R Poulton [1-10] Mrs Melody Siu (from R W Armstrong [0-4] Spt 1998).*

NATURAL PEARL BHB 41f **RR 37f** 4527[10]

3 gr f Petong 7.6f **(58)** - Petriece (Mummy's Pet) 7.7f **(60)**

Form - 078000

Record 1999 - 1st:0 2nd:0 3rd:0 Ran:6

Pre1999 - 1st:0 2nd:0 3rd:0 Ran:1

1999 Turf 0-6: (6f 5, 7f) (gd 4, frm 2)

Very moderate filly, has worn blinkers. Turf high 37.

**J J Quinn [0-2] Robinski Bloodstock Ltd (from C F Wall [0-5] Jly 1999).*

NAUGHTY BUT NICE RR 19f 1588[5]

3 b f Sizzling Melody 6.3f **(49)** - Aldington Peach (Creetown) 6.9f **(50)**

Form - 0005

Record 1999 - 1st:0 2nd:0 3rd:0 Ran:4

1999 Turf 0-2: (10f, 11f) (sft, gd) 1999 AW 0-2: (7f, 9f) (Fibr 2)

Leggy, poor filly. Turf high 19. AW high 5.

**T Wall [0-4] Alexandra Racing.*

NAUGHTY CROWN (USA) BHB 78f **RR 78f** 4230[6]

3 b f Chief's Crown (USA) 10.2f **(75)** - Native Twine (Be My Native (USA)) 10.2f **(71)**

Form - 668652106

Record 1999 - 1st:1 2nd:1 3rd:0 Ran:9

Pre1999 - 1st:0 2nd:0 3rd:1 Ran:2

Win Prizemoney £3,925 *Total Prizemoney* £6,442

Wins * 1999 Jly Thirsk (FRM) 7f 74 <

1999 Turf 1-9: (7f 1-3, 8f 2, 10f 4) (gd 4, g-f, frm 1-4)

Strong, above-average filly, effective 7 to 10f, best at 7f, acts on sft to frm, has worn blinkers. Turf high 79 - 6th of 15 getting 1lb from Holly Blue (19 Jun Ascot 8f g-f RF 2133) - also 1st of 7 from Singing Winds (31 Jly Thirsk RF 3286). **P F I Cole [1-11] G J Beck.*

NAUTICAL STAR BHB 94f **RR 94f** 2355[2]

4 b c Slip Anchor 12.7f **(75)** - Comic Talent (Pharly (FR)) 9.8f **(68)**

Form - 752202

Record 1999 - 1st:0 2nd:3 3rd:0 Ran:6

Pre1999 - 1st:3 2nd:0 3rd:2 Ran:9

Win Prizemoney £20,257 *Total Prizemoney* £38,399

Wins * 1998 Aug Epsom (G-F) H 12f 89 94 <

* 1998 Apr Newmar (SFT) H 10f 83 91

* 1997 Aug Ayr (G-F) 7f 80+

1999 Turf 0-6: (10f, 12f 5) (g-s, gd 3, g-f 2)

Scopey, useful colt, effective 10 to 12f, best at 12f, acts on g-s to g-f, best on gd, has worn blinkers, prefers tight tracks, excels at Goodwood and Epsom. Turf high 96 - 2nd of 5 to Wales (19 May Goodwood 12f gd RF 1336). Consistent. Usually allowed to race up with the pace, he enjoys turning tracks and does particularly well at Epsom. Unlikely to stay beyond a mile and a half, he probably acts on any ground. **J W Hills [3-15] Wauchope,Sir Simon D Cottam.*

NAUTICAL WARNING BHB 55f69a **RR 53f 69a** 3658[4]

4 b c Warning 8.1f **(77)** - Night At Sea (Night Shift (USA)) 7.2f **(69)**

Form - 813512014

Record 1999 - 1st:3 2nd:1 3rd:1 Ran:9

Pre1999 - 1st:1 2nd:0 3rd:0 Ran:10

Win Prizemoney £11,725 *Total Prizemoney* £13,420

Wins * 1999 Jly Lingfi (FRM) H 7.6f 51 53

*** 1999** *Jun Lingfi (STD)* *8f* *71* <

*** 1999** *Feb Lingfi (STD) H* *8f* *58 71* <

1998 *Jan Lingfi (STD) H* *7f* *57 63*

1999 Turf 1-4: (7f, 8f 1-3) (sft, g-f, frm 1-2) 1999 AW 2-5: (7f, 8f 2-4) (Equi 2-5)

Strong, above-average colt, effective 7 to 8f, best at 8f, - acts on Equi, prefers left handed tracks, likes tight tracks. Turf high 53. AW high 73 - 2nd of 7 giving 2lb to Castles Burning (22 Jun Lingfield 8f Equi RF 2199) - also 1st of 8 from Kafil (12 Jun Lingfield RF 1956). He became the first winner trained by Jeremy Noseda when winning a modest apprentice handicap on the Lingfield Equitrack in January '98, and his best form since has been on that surface. He did get a turf win to his name last term however when battling on well over the extended seven furlongs at Lingfield.

**B R Johnson [3-9] The Twenty Five Club (from J Noseda [1-6] Oct 1998).*

NAVAL AFFAIR (IRE) RR 79f 3740[1]

2 b f Last Tycoon 9.4f **(73)** - Sailor's Mate (Shirley Heights) 10.3f **(74)**

Form - 31

Record 1999 - 1st:1 2nd:0 3rd:1 Ran:2

Win Prizemoney £3,631 *Total Prizemoney* £4,182

Wins * 1999 Aug Kempto (G-S) 7f 79 <

1999 Turf 1-2: (7f 1-2) (g-s 1-1, frm)

Currently above-average filly. Turf high 79 (began Aug) - 1st of 13 from Island Princess (18 Aug Kempton RF 3740). Came on from her Salisbury debut and made all at Kempton next time. Still green there, she can improve further.

**Sir Michael Stoute [1-2] Lord Weinstock.*

NAVAN PROJECT (IRE) BHB 44f **RR 46f** 4983[20]

5 gr g Project Manager 7.2f **(47)** - Just Possible (Kalaglow) 9.8f **(67)**

Form - 8050

Record 1999 - 1st:0 2nd:0 3rd:0 Ran:4

Pre1999 - 1st:1 2nd:0 3rd:1 Ran:11

Win Prizemoney £2,911 *Total Prizemoney* £3,667

Wins 1997 Aug Tipper (GD) H 9f 69 79 <

1999 Turf 0-4: (9f, 10f, 12f, 13f) (gd, g-f 2, frm)

Moderate gelding, has worn blinkers. Turf high 52. Becoming disappointing.

**A R Dicken [0-4] Got To Be In It To Win It Partnership (from J S Bolger in IRE [1-11] Oct 1997).*

NAVIASKY (IRE) BHB 84f **RR 81+f** 4569[6]

4 b br g Scenic 10.6f **(66)** - Black Molly (IRE) (High Top) 10.2f **(67)**

Form - 3311816

Record 1999 - 1st:3 2nd:0 3rd:2 Ran:7

Pre1999 - 1st:2 2nd:1 3rd:2 Ran:20

Win Prizemoney £41,595 *Total Prizemoney* £50,967

Wins * 1999 Aug Leices (G-F) H 8f 77 81 <

*** 1999** Jly Goodwo (G-F) H 8f 69 73

*** 1999** Jun Goodwo (G-F) H 8f 66 69

1998 Jun Carlis (G-S) H 8f 60 66

1997 Aug Thirsk (G-F) 5f 79+
1999 Turf 3-7: (7f, 8f 3-5, 9f) (sft, gd 1-3, frm 2-3)
Strong, decent gelding, effective 8f, acts on frm, prefers right handed tracks, likes tight tracks. Turf high 81 - 1st of 20 getting 7lb from Casimir (22 Aug Leicester RF 3838) - also 1st of 17 getting 13lb from Asef Alhind (27 Jly Goodwood RF 3170). In fine form during the summer, winning three times including twice at Goodwood. A mile and fast ground are ideal.
**W R Muir [3-10] Perspicacious Punters Racing Club (from Mrs J R Ramsden [2-19] Aug 1998).*

NEBL BHB 58f55a RR 56+f 55a 4219[6]

4 ch f Persian Bold 10f **(69)** - Maraatib (IRE) (Green Desert (USA)) 8.6f **(78)**
Form - 70075126
Record 1999 - 1st:1 2nd:1 3rd:0 Ran:8
Pre1999 - 1st:1 2nd:0 3rd:1 Ran:5
Win Prizemoney £5,335 *Total Prizemoney* £6,508
Wins * 1999 Aug Lingfi (GD) S 10f 44+
1997 Spt Sandow (G-F) 8.1f 91 <
1999 Turf 1-6: (8f, 10f 1-5) (gd, g-f 1-4, frm) 1999 AW 0-2: (9f, 10f) (Equi, Fibr)
Workmanlike, fair filly, effective 10f, acts on g-f, likes left handed tracks. Turf high 67 (1st run) - 7th of 13 getting 7lb from King Darius (4 May Chester 10f g-f RF 1028). AW high 56 (began Jly).
**N P Littmoden [1-5] Mrs L A Windsor (from P D Evans [0-3] May 1999).*

NEDAWI BHB 122f RR 123f 3088[2]

4 ch c Rainbow Quest (USA) 11.2f **(81)** - Wajd (USA) (Northern Dancer) 9.6f **(80)**
Form - 252
Record 1999 - 1st:0 2nd:2 3rd:0 Ran:3
Pre1999 - 1st:3 2nd:0 3rd:1 Ran:4
Win Prizemoney £221,990 *Total Prizemoney* £428,656
Wins * 1998 Spt Doncas (GD) G1 14.6f 117 <
* 1998 Jly Goodwo (GD) G3 12f 114
* 1998 Jun Goodwo (G-F) 12f 90+
1999 Turf 0-3: (12f 2, 20f) (gd, g-f 2)
Scopey, very high-class colt, effective 12 to 20f, best at 12f, acts on gd to g-f, best on g-f, does well at Ascot and Goodwood. Turf high 123 - 2nd of 8 to Daylami (24 Jly Ascot 12f gd RF 3088). Unraced at two, he dead-heated with Rabah in the Gordon Stakes in 1998 before gaining his biggest victory in the St Leger, despite being hampered and running green. For a Classic, it was a modest race, but he ran well over a trip too short in Dubai in the spring of 1999, and was a respectable fifth in the Gold Cup, not quite seeing out the marathon trip. Brought back to 12 furlongs, he ran possibly his best race to date to finish second in the King George, finding only stable-companion Daylami too good. That was his last race in 1999, as he injured an ankle, but it will be interesting to see what path connections take with him next term.
**S bin Suroor [3-7] Godolphin.*

NEEDWOOD MAESTRO BHB 32f RR 39f 5101[7]

3 b g Sizzling Melody 6.3f **(49)** - Needwood Poppy **(25f 39a)** (Rolfe (USA)) 12.1f **(65)**
Form - 3340000047
Record 1999 - 1st:0 2nd:0 3rd:2 Ran:10
Win Prizemoney £0 *Total Prizemoney* £537
1999 Turf 0-9: (8f 2, 9f, 10f, 12f 3, 14f 2) (sft, g-s 2, gd 2, g-f 2, frm 2)
1999 AW 0-1: (12f) (Fibr)
Light-framed, very moderate gelding, effective 8f, acts on g-s, likes left handed tracks. Turf high 51 - 3rd of 17 giving 5lb to Angie Marinie (19 Apr Nottingham 8f g-s RF 0747). Consistent.
**B C Morgan [0-10] Needwood Racing Ltd.*

NEEDWOOD MERLIN BHB 42f RR 24f 5026[17]

3 b c Sizzling Melody 6.3f **(49)** - Enchanting Kate (Enchantment) 5.4f **(52)**
Form - 0853000
Record 1999 - 1st:0 2nd:0 3rd:1 Ran:7
Pre1999 - 1st:0 2nd:0 3rd:0 Ran:4
Win Prizemoney £0 *Total Prizemoney* £464
1999 Turf 0-7: (7f 5, 8f 2) (gd 5, g-f 2)
Moderate colt. Turf high 47. Becoming disappointing.
**B C Morgan [0-11] Needwood Racing Ltd.*

NEEDWOOD MINSTREL BHB 45f40a RR 46f 40a 4607[16]

3 b g Clantime 6.6f **(57)** - Azubah **(29a)** (Castle Keep) 8.3f **(57)**
Form - 04605760
Record 1999 - 1st:0 2nd:0 3rd:0 Ran:8
Pre1999 - 1st:0 2nd:0 3rd:0 Ran:4
1999 Turf 0-7: (5f 3, 6f 4) (sft, gd, g-f 4, hrd) 1999 AW 0-1: (6f) (Fibr)
Small, moderate gelding. Turf high 48. Becoming disappointing.
**B C Morgan [0-12] Needwood Racing Ltd.*

NEEDWOOD MYSTIC BHB 48f RR 49f 5133[12]

4 b f Rolfe (USA) 11.2f **(46)** - Enchanting Kate (Enchantment) 5.4f **(52)**
Form - 0670813321500
Record 1999 - 1st:2 2nd:1 3rd:2 Ran:13
Pre1999 - 1st:0 2nd:0 3rd:0 Ran:6
Win Prizemoney £5,218 *Total Prizemoney* £7,156
Wins * 1999 Aug Warwic (GD) H 12.3f 43 48 <
*** 1999** Jun Warwic (G-F) H 12.3f 38 40
1999 Turf 2-13: (8f, 10f 4, 12f 2-8) (g-s 2, gd 1-5, g-f 1-4, frm 2)
Small, moderate filly, effective 8f, acts on frm, likes left handed tracks, likes tight tracks. Turf high 49. Consistent.
**B C Morgan [2-19] Needwood Racing Ltd.*

NEEDWOOD SPIRIT BHB 62f56a RR 63f 56a 5220[5]

4 b g Rolfe (USA) 11.2f **(46)** - Needwood Nymph (Bold Owl) 8.5f **(45)**
Form - 4415200345
Record 1999 - 1st:1 2nd:1 3rd:1 Ran:10
Pre1999 - 1st:1 2nd:0 3rd:1 Ran:12
Win Prizemoney £5,750 *Total Prizemoney* £12,036
Wins * 1999 Apr Folkes (SFT) H 15.4f 61 66 <
* 1998 Oct Catter (SFT) 13.8f 61
1999 Turf 1-10: (13f, 14f 5, 15f 1-1, 16f 2, 17f) (hvy 1-2, sft, g-s 4, gd 2, g-f)
Leggy, average gelding, effective 10 to 15f, acts on hvy to frm, has worn blinkers, likes left handed tracks, excels at Catterick. Turf high 67 - 2nd of 15 getting 2lb from Swift (12 May York 14f g-s RF 1185) - also 1st of 13 giving 21lb to Shepherds Rest (20 Apr Folkestone RF 0763). Consistent.
**B C Morgan [2-22] Needwood Racing Ltd.*

NEEDWOOD SPITFIRE BHB 37f RR 36f 5066[8]

4 b f Rolfe (USA) 11.2f **(46)** - Lime Brook (Rapid River) 5.7f **(51)**
Form - 7766003518
Record 1999 - 1st:1 2nd:0 3rd:1 Ran:10
Pre1999 - 1st:0 2nd:0 3rd:2 Ran:7
Win Prizemoney £3,022 *Total Prizemoney* £4,391
Wins * 1999 Spt Bright (SFT) H 11.9f 35 36 <
1999 Turf 1-10: (12f 1-6, 13f, 14f 2, 17f) (hvy, sft, g-s 1-1, gd 2, g-f 2, frm 3)
Light-framed, very moderate filly, effective 12 to 14f, acts on g-s to frm, best on g-f, favours tight tracks. Turf high 40 - also 1st of 14 getting 11lb from Sure Future (29 Spt Brighton RF 4630).
**B C Morgan [1-17] Needwood Racing Ltd.*

NEEDWOOD TRIDENT RR 43f 5209[10]

2 b f Minshaanshu Amad (USA) 11.3f **(53)** - Needwood Nymph (Bold Owl) 8.5f **(45)**
Form - 00
Record 1999 - 1st:0 2nd:0 3rd:0 Ran:2
1999 Turf 0-2: (6f, 7f) (g-s, gd)
Currently moderate filly. Turf high 43 (began Oct).
**B C Morgan [0-2] Needwood Racing Ltd.*

NEEDWOOD TROOPER RR 36f 5005[11]

2 br c Puissance 7.1f **(60)** - Blueit (FR) (Bold Lad (IRE)) 8.4f **(68)**
Form - 0
Record 1999 - 1st:0 2nd:0 3rd:0 Ran:1
1999 Turf 0-1: (5f) (gd)
Currently very moderate colt.
**B C Morgan [0-1] Needwood Racing Ltd.*

NEEDWOOD TRUFFLE (IRE) BHB 78f RR 76f 4857[12]

2 ch f Brief Truce (USA) 9.1f **(73)** - Green Wings (General Assembly (USA)) 10f **(68)**
Form - 6353180
Record 1999 - 1st:1 2nd:0 3rd:2 Ran:7
Win Prizemoney £7,107 *Total Prizemoney* £8,337
Wins * 1999 Jly Goodwo (G-F) H 5f 76 <
1999 Turf 1-7: (5f 1-4, 6f 3) (g-s, gd, g-f 1-2, frm 3)

Above-average filly, effective 5f, acts on g-f. Turf high 76 - 1st of 9 getting 6lb from Coco de Mer (29 Jly Goodwood RF 3225). Got off the mark when winning a Goodwood nursery, and looks best suited by the minimum trip. **B C Morgan [1-7] Needwood Racing Ltd.*

NEEDWOOD TRUMP (IRE) BHB 39f RR 33f 3003[14]
2 br c Marju (IRE) 9.2f **(76)** - Play The Queen (IRE) (King of Clubs) 7.1f **(57)**
Form - 040
Record 1999 - 1st:0 2nd:0 3rd:0 Ran:3
1999 Turf 0-2: (5f, 7f) (g-f, frm) 1999 AW 0-1: (5f) (Fibr)
Currently very moderate colt. Turf high 33.
**B C Morgan [0-3] Needwood Racing Ltd.*

NEELA (IRE) BHB 58f53a RR 61f 53a 5113[4]
3 ch f Bluebird (USA) 7.9f **(71)** - Scammony (IRE) (Persian Bold) 9.3f **(66)**
Form - 04
Record 1999 - 1st:0 2nd:0 3rd:0 Ran:2
Win Prizemoney £0 *Total Prizemoney* £206
1999 Turf 0-2: (6f 2) (gd 2)
Lengthy, currently average filly. Turf high 61 (began Spt) - 4th of 21 getting 6lb from Madmun (28 Oct Windsor 6f gd RF 5113).
**R Hannon [0-2] Ananda Krishnan.*

NEGRONI RR 72f 4559[6]
2 br f Mtoto 11.5f **(71)** - Carousel Music **(36f)** (On Your Mark) 7.7f **(58)**
Form - 6
Record 1999 - 1st:0 2nd:0 3rd:0 Ran:1
1999 Turf 0-1: (8f) (gd)
Currently above-average filly. **J W Hills [0-1] Scott Hardy Partnership.*

NEIGES ETERNELLES (FR) BHB 74f RR 52f 5211[5]
4 b f Exit To Nowhere (USA) 8.7f **(77)** - Nabita (FR) (Akarad (FR)) 9f **(76)**
Form - 855
Record 1999 - 1st:0 2nd:0 3rd:0 Ran:3
Pre1999 - 1st:0 2nd:0 3rd:1 Ran:2
Win Prizemoney £0 *Total Prizemoney* £3,828
1999 Turf 0-3: (10f 2, 14f) (sft, gd, frm)
Fair filly. Turf high 52 (began Jly).
**P R Webber [0-3] Mrs Joan Egan (from H-A Pantall in FR [0-2] Oct 1998).*

NELIA BHB 30f RR 28f 3748[10]
3 b f Local Suitor (USA) 9.7f **(58)** - La Ciotat (IRE) **(28f)** (Gallic League)
Form - 700
Record 1999 - 1st:0 2nd:0 3rd:0 Ran:3
1999 Turf 0-3: (7f, 8f, 10f) (gd, g-f, frm)
Lengthy, little account filly. Turf high 28 (began Jly). (DEAD)
**J G FitzGerald [0-3] J G FitzGerald.*

NELLIE NORTH BHB 26f RR 8f 2554[13]
6 b m Northern State (USA) 12.6f **(45)** - Kimble Princess (Kala Shikari) 8.4f **(54)**
Form - 0000
Record 1999 - 1st:0 2nd:0 3rd:0 Ran:4
Pre1999 - 1st:1 2nd:3 3rd:7 Ran:42
Win Prizemoney £3,647 *Total Prizemoney* £10,492
Wins 1995 Jly Windso (G-F) 5f 75 <
1999 Turf 0-4: (5f 3, 8f) (gd, g-f 2, hrd)
Very poor mare, effective 5 to 6f, best at 5f, acts on frm, often wears blinkers (extremely effectively). Turf high 8. Becoming disappointing.
**A J Chamberlain [0-17] The Old Biddies (from G M McCourt [0-20] Spt 1997).*

NEPTUNE BHB 38f RR 43f 4601[4]
3 b g Dolphin Street (FR) -Seal Indigo(IRE)(Glenstal (USA)) 10.1f **(64)**
Form - 0806054
Record 1999 - 1st:0 2nd:0 3rd:0 Ran:7
1999 Turf 0-6: (7f 2, 9f, 10f 2, 12f) (g-s, gd, g-f 3, frm) 1999 AW 0-1: (11f) (Fibr)
Scopey, moderate gelding. Turf high 51.
**W J Haggas [0-1] Highclere Thoroughbred Racing Ltd (from G Lewis [0-6] Aug 1999).*

NEPTUNE'S BRIDE (USA) RR 99f 5017a[3]
3 ch f Bering 9.6f **(80)** - Wedding of the Sea (USA) (Blushing Groom (FR)) 10.3f **(76)**
Form - 3
1999 Turf 0-1: (8f) (g-f)
Currently very useful filly. (1st run) - 3rd of 15 to Alabaq (17 Oct San Siro 8f g-f RF 5017a). **H-A Pantall in FR [0-1].*

NERONIAN (IRE) BHB 35f RR 40f 4997[15]
5 ch g Mujtahid (USA) 7.4f **(69)** - Nimieza (USA) (Nijinsky (CAN)) 10.3f **(77)**
Form - 72400450
Record 1999 - 1st:0 2nd:1 3rd:0 Ran:8
Pre1999 - 1st:1 2nd:1 3rd:1 Ran:6
Win Prizemoney £2,812 *Total Prizemoney* £5,379
Wins 1997 Jun Beverl (SFT) 8.5f 71 <
1999 Turf 0-8: (8f 2, 10f 5, 11f) (gd 3, g-f, frm 3, hrd)
Moderate gelding, has worn blinkers. Turf high 58.
**K R Burke [0-8] Cheshire Alliance (from B W Hills [1-6] Jun 1997).*

NERO TIROL (IRE) BHB 60f66a RR 54f 66a 3113[14]
3 b br g Tirol 8.1f **(64)** - Saltoki (Ballad Rock) 7.8f **(63)**
Form - 71130005000
Record 1999 - 1st:2 2nd:0 3rd:1 Ran:11
Pre1999 - 1st:0 2nd:0 3rd:0 Ran:3
Win Prizemoney £4,827 *Total Prizemoney* £5,411
Wins * *1999 Feb Southw (STD) H 6f 62 73* <
* *1999 Feb Southw (STD) 6f 72*
1999 Turf 0-4: (6f 2, 7f 2) (sft, gd, frm 2) 1999 AW 2-7: (6f 2-3, 7f 2, 8f 2) (Equi 2, Fibr 2-5)
Scopey, fair gelding, effective 6f, - acts on Fibr, often wears blinkers (extremely effectively), prefers left handed tracks, prefers tight tracks. Turf high 54. AW high 73 - 1st of 14 giving 4lb to Trina's Pet (15 Feb Southwell RF 0296) - also 1st of 5 from Locomotion (8 Feb Southwell RF 0250). **A Kelleway [2-14] Osvaldo Pedroni.*

NERVOUS REX BHB 59f44a RR 61f 44a 21[12]
5 b g Reprimand 8.2f **(63)** - Spinner (Blue Cashmere) 6.4f **(54)**
Form - 0
Record 1999 - 1st:0 2nd:0 3rd:0 Ran:1
Pre1999 - 1st:3 2nd:2 3rd:2 Ran:28
Win Prizemoney £8,305 *Total Prizemoney* £11,976
Wins * 1998 Jly Haydoc (G-S) H 7.1f 55 58 <
* 1998 Jun Leices (GD) SH 6f 50 53
1997 Jun Carlis (FRM) S 5.9f 55
1999 AW 0-1: (7f) (Fibr)
Average gelding, effective 6 to 7f, best at 7f, acts on frm, has worn blinkers. **D Nicholls [2-9] V Greaves (from W R Muir [1-20] Oct 1997).*

NESTING BHB 45f RR 43f 4326[6]
4 ch f Thatching 7.8f **(69)** - Tatouma (USA) (The Minstrel (CAN)) 10f **(72)**
Form - 506
Record 1999 - 1st:0 2nd:0 3rd:0 Ran:3
1999 Turf 0-3: (5f 2, 6f) (gd, frm, hrd)
Rangy, currently moderate filly. Turf high 43 (began Aug).
**J S Wainwright [0-3] J S Wainwright.*

NESYRED (IRE) BHB 73f RR 76f 5134[11]
3 b f Paris House 5.9f **(64)** - Abrika (Dominion) 8.5f **(63)**
Form - 610
Record 1999 - 1st:1 2nd:0 3rd:0 Ran:3
Win Prizemoney £3,315 *Total Prizemoney* £3,315
Wins * **1999** Aug Folkes (GD) 6f 76 <
1999 Turf 1-3: (6f 1-2, 8f) (gd 1-2, frm)
Unfurnished, currently above-average filly. Turf high 76 (began Jly) - 1st of 10 getting 5lb from Democracy (26 Aug Folkestone RF 3914). **Mrs D Haine [1-3] The Matches Group.*

NETHERHALL BHB 41f48a RR 40f 48a 4600[6]
3 ch g Rudimentary (USA) 8.2f **(66)** - Legal Precedent (Star Appeal) 9.6f **(65)**
Form - 432211D56
Record 1999 - 1st:2 2nd:2 3rd:1 Ran:9
Pre1999 - 1st:0 2nd:0 3rd:0 Ran:5
Win Prizemoney £4,539 *Total Prizemoney* £6,146
Wins * **1999** *Jun Southw (STD) H 12f 46 49* <
* **1999** *Jun Wolver (STA) H 14.8f 44 44*

1999 AW 2-9: (7f, 11f, 12f 1-4, 14f, 15f 1-2) (Fibr 2-9)
Scopey, moderate gelding, effective 12 to 15f, best at 12f, - acts on Fibr, prefers left handed tracks, prefers tight tracks. AW high 54 - 2nd of 17 getting 17lb from Sunny Chief (6 May Southwell 12f Fibr RF 1066) - also 1st of 9 getting 24lb from Tragic Dancer (17 Jun Southwell RF 2087). Consistent. **M G Meagher [2-14] M R Johnson.*

NETTA RUFINA (IRE) BHB 59f70a **RR 61f 70a** 5188[3]
4 ch g Night Shift (USA) 8.1f **(73)** - Age of Elegance (Troy) 10.4f **(68)**
Form - 0074313726570253
Record 1999 - 1st:1 2nd:2 3rd:3 Ran:16
Pre1999 - 1st:2 2nd:3 3rd:0 Ran:13
Win Prizemoney £10,489 *Total Prizemoney* £18,660
Wins * **1999** Jun Mussel (SFT) H 14f 62 66
* 1998 Aug Ripon (GD) H 12.3f 65 70
* 1998 *Feb Lingfi (SLW) 10f 74* <
1999 Turf 1-14: (12f 5, 13f, 14f 1-3, 15f 2, 16f 3) (gd 1-3, g-f 5, frm 5, hrd) 1999 AW 0-2: (12f, 15f) (Equi, Fibr)
Average gelding, effective 9 to 16f, acts on gd to frm - acts on AW, has worn blinkers, likes right handed tracks, does well at Musselburgh. Turf high 70 - 2nd of 6 getting 2lb from Alhawa (25 Jly Newmarket 15f frm RF 3133). AW high 52. Consistent. A reasonably talented if quirky individual, he won over a mile and three-quarters at Musselburgh in June, with the first-time visor helping him stay on a straight line. **M Johnston [3-29] Mrs Belinda Strudwick.*

NEUWEST (USA) BHB 57f95a **RR 69f 95a** 4338[13]
7 b h Gone West (USA) 7.8f **(82)** - White Mischief (Dance In Time (CAN)) 8.9f **(59)**
Form - 00600
Record 1999 - 1st:0 2nd:0 3rd:0 Ran:5
Pre1999 - 1st:6 2nd:6 3rd:2 Ran:29
Win Prizemoney £43,911 *Total Prizemoney* £54,954
Wins 1997 Aug Newmar (G-F) H 7f 92 97
1997 Jun Newbur (GD) H 7f 85 92+
1996 Aug Lingfi (G-F) 7f 85
1996 Jun Folkes (FRM) H 6.9f 78 83+
1996 May Lingfi (G-F) H 7f 73 76
1995 Oct Yarmou (G-F) 8f 69
1999 Turf 0-5: (7f 4, 8f) (g-s, gd, g-f 2, frm)
Above-average horse. Turf high 69.
**K R Burke [0-3] Paul Green (from M C Pipe [0-2] Jly 1999).*

NEVER CAN TELL BHB 46f45a **RR 39f 45a** 5153[14]
3 ch g Emarati (USA) 6.6f **(63)** - Farmer's Pet (Sharrood (USA)) 10.5f **(72)**
Form - 500000
Record 1999 - 1st:0 2nd:0 3rd:0 Ran:6
Pre1999 - 1st:0 2nd:1 3rd:0 Ran:5
Win Prizemoney £0 *Total Prizemoney* £1,897
1999 Turf 0-4: (6f, 7f 2, 10f) (gd 2, g-f 2) 1999 AW 0-2: (8f, 9f) (Fibr 2)
Strong, very moderate gelding, effective 6f, acts on sft, has worn blinkers. Turf high 39 (began Aug). AW high 30 (began Spt). Becoming disappointing.
**B P J Baugh [0-6] Brooklands Racing Partnership (from J G FitzGerald [0-6] Aug 1999).*

NEVER DISS MISS BHB 75f **RR 79f** 4895[18]
2 b f Owington - Pennine Pink (IRE) **(75f 60a)** (Pennine Walk) 8.5f **(61)**
Form - 0140300
Record 1999 - 1st:1 2nd:0 3rd:1 Ran:7
Win Prizemoney £3,566 *Total Prizemoney* £4,942
Wins * **1999** Apr Sandow (G-S) 5f 79 <
1999 Turf 1-7: (5f 1-3, 6f 3, 7f) (g-s 1-1, gd 2, g-f, frm 3)
Above-average filly, effective 5f, acts on g-s to frm. Turf high 79 - 4th of 10 giving 3lb to Fairy Gem (2 May Salisbury 5f frm RF 0984) - also 1st of 13 from Charming Lotte (23 Apr Sandown RF 0825). Last on her debut, she was a surprise winner at Sandown next time. She has run a couple of fair races since, but looks exposed. **R J R Williams [1-7] Tim Fenner.*

NEVER LEAVE RR 28f 2058[5]
2 b f Never so Bold 7.1f **(62)** - Leave it to Lib **(41f)** (Tender King) 6.8f **(54)**
Form - 5
Record 1999 - 1st:0 2nd:0 3rd:0 Ran:1
1999 Turf 0-1: (5f) (g-f)
Little account filly. (DEAD) **P Calver [0-1] Hilton Cox.*

NEW ABBEY BHB 101f **RR 100f** 4794[2]
4 b f Sadler's Wells (USA) 11.3f **(87)** - Bahamian (Mill Reef (USA)) 10.5f **(78)**
Form - 132
Record 1999 - 1st:1 2nd:1 3rd:1 Ran:3
Pre1999 - 1st:1 2nd:0 3rd:0 Ran:1
Win Prizemoney £9,590 *Total Prizemoney* £24,725
Wins * **1999** Aug Windso (GD) 11.6f 97 <
* 1998 May Salisb (G-S) 12f 72
1999 Turf 1-3: (12f 1-3) (sft, gd, frm 1-1)
Well made, very useful filly. Turf high 100 (began Aug) - also 1st of 8 giving 2lb to Azouz Pasha (28 Aug Windsor RF 3982). Beautifully bred, she was an odds-on shot when making a successful debut in May 1998, but was not seen again until narrowly beating her stable-companion Azouz Pasha in a Windsor conditions event in August. She has twice had a rear view of Signorina Cattiva in Pattern company since then, but has run well nonetheless. **H R A Cecil [2-4] K Abdulla.*

NEW ASSEMBLY (IRE) RR 68f 5137[7]
2 b f Machiavellian (USA) 9.8f **(83)** - Abbey Strand (USA) (Shadeed (USA)) 8.2f **(70)**
Form - 07
Record 1999 - 1st:0 2nd:0 3rd:0 Ran:2
1999 Turf 0-2: (7f 2) (gd 2)
Currently average filly. Turf high 68 (began Oct).
**Sir Michael Stoute [0-2] The Queen.*

NEW CAPRICORN (USA) BHB 38f **RR 39f** 4987[15]
9 ch g Green Forest (USA) 7.4f **(73)** - Size Six (USA) (Caerleon (USA)) 8.6f **(71)**
Form - 002460
Record 1999 - 1st:0 2nd:1 3rd:0 Ran:6
Pre1999 - 1st:5 2nd:3 3rd:4 Ran:33
Win Prizemoney £36,458 *Total Prizemoney* £51,870
1999 Turf 0-6: (7f, 8f 4, 9f) (gd 4, frm 2)
Very moderate gelding, effective 8f, acts on frm, has worn blinkers, likes tight tracks. Turf high 43 - 2nd of 13 getting 3lb from Time of Night (2 Aug Carlisle 8f frm RF 3289). Consistent.
**C Parker [0-15] & Mrs Raymond Anderson Green (from M A Jarvis [5-28] Jly 1995).*

NEW EARTH MAIDEN RR 39f 2958[7]
2 b f Ezzoud (IRE) - Susie's Baby (Balidar) 7.9f **(63)**
Form - 0077
Record 1999 - 1st:0 2nd:0 3rd:0 Ran:4
1999 Turf 0-4: (6f 2, 7f 2) (gd, frm 3)
Very moderate filly. Turf high 39. **J Cullinan [0-4] Mrs A C Hudson.*

NEW FORTUNE (FR) RR 43f 3132[9]
2 ch f Exit To Nowhere (USA) 8.7f **(77)** - Fortuna Redux (Primo Dominie) 6.2f **(80)**
Form - 0
Record 1999 - 1st:0 2nd:0 3rd:0 Ran:1
1999 Turf 0-1: (7f) (frm)
Currently moderate filly. **W R Muir [0-1] J Bernstein.*

NEWGATE CASTLE RR 1987[15]
3 b f Rambo Dancer (CAN) 8.4f **(59)** - Gemgem (Lochnager) 6f **(59)**
Form - 0
Record 1999 - 1st:0 2nd:0 3rd:0 Ran:1
1999 Turf 0-1: (8f) (g-f)
Unfurnished, currently very poor filly.
**B W Murray [0-1] W P S Johnson.*

NEWLANDS CORNER BHB 47f47a **RR 47f 47a** 912[13]
6 b m Forzando 7.2f **(63)** - Nice Lady (Connaught) 7.7f **(63)**
Form - 0670
Record 1999 - 1st:0 2nd:0 3rd:0 Ran:3
Pre1999 - 1st:4 2nd:3 3rd:1 Ran:36
Win Prizemoney £11,461 *Total Prizemoney* £16,237
Wins * 1997 *Aug Southw (STD) H 6f 54 58* <
* 1996 Aug Bright (G-F) H 6f 44 54
* 1996 Aug Salisb (G-F) CH 6f 44 47
* 1996 Aug Carlis (FRM) H 5.9f 39 40

1999 Turf 0-3: (6f 3) (sft, g-s, frm)
Moderate mare, effective 6f, acts on sft to frm, mostly wears blinkers (effectively). Turf high 47. Inconsistent. **J Akehurst [4-39] The Jolly Skolars.*

NEW MOON BHB 41a RR 33f 1057[11]
3 ch g Good Times (ITY) 8.7f **(53)** - Two Moons (Bold Lad (IRE)) 8.4f **(68)**
Form - 570
Record 1999 - 1st:0 2nd:0 3rd:0 Ran:3
Pre1999 - 1st:0 2nd:0 3rd:0 Ran:3
1999 Turf 0-1: (12f) (g-f) 1999 AW 0-2: (11f, 12f) (Fibr 2)
Scopey, very moderate gelding, has worn blinkers. AW high 32. **C W Thornton [0-6] Guy Reed.*

NEWSCASTER BHB 75f76a RR 73f 76a 3809[1]
3 b g Bluebird (USA) 7.9f **(71)** - Sharp Girl (FR) (Sharpman) 11.3f **(66)**
Form - 65421
Record 1999 - 1st:1 2nd:1 3rd:0 Ran:5
Win Prizemoney £2,801 *Total Prizemoney* £3,894
Wins * 1999 Aug Sandow (GD) C 9f 65 <
1999 Turf 1-4: (6f, 8f 2, 9f 1-1) (gd, g-f 1-1, frm 2) 1999 AW 0-1: (9f) (Fibr)
Workmanlike, above-average gelding. Turf high 73 - 4th of 12 to Commonwealth (26 Jly Windsor 8f frm RF 3151). (1st run) - 2nd of 13 giving 5lb to Mystic Spring (6 Aug Wolverhampton 9f Fibr RF 3437). **P F I Cole [1-5] Casting Partners C.*

NEWSHAN BHB 39f RR 34f 4453[10]
3 b f Anshan 8.2f **(63)** - New Pastures (Formidable (USA)) 9.2f **(63)**
Form - 000
Record 1999 - 1st:0 2nd:0 3rd:0 Ran:3
1999 Turf 0-3: (8f 2, 12f) (sft, frm 2)
Scopey, currently very moderate filly. Turf high 34 (began Aug). **H S Howe [0-3] R J Parish.*

NEW STORY (USA) RR 102f 4776a[2]
2 f Dynaformer (USA) 12f **(82)** - Dancey Kate (USA)
Form - 42
1999 Turf 0-2: (8f 2) (sft, gd)
Currently very useful filly. Turf high 102 (began Aug) - 2nd of 11 to Lady Of Chad (3 Oct Longchamp 8f sft RF 4776a). **R Collet in FR [0-2] J-P Binet.*

NEW VICTORIA (USA) BHB 65f RR 68f 1682[5]
3 b f Colonel Collins (USA) - Distinctiveness (USA) (Distinctive (USA)) 10.7f **(70)**
Form - 535
Record 1999 - 1st:0 2nd:0 3rd:1 Ran:3
Win Prizemoney £0 *Total Prizemoney* £418
1999 Turf 0-2: (6f 2) (g-f, frm) 1999 AW 0-1: (7f) (Fibr)
Light-framed, currently average filly. Turf high 68. **P W Chapple-Hyam [0-3] R E Sangster.*

NEW YORKER (USA) BHB 47f50a RR 50a 16[4]
4 ch c Gilded Time (USA) 7f **(76)** - Doris's Secret (USA) (Nikoli)
Form - 04834
Record 1999 - 1st:0 2nd:0 3rd:0 Ran:1
Pre1999 - 1st:0 2nd:2 3rd:1 Ran:9
Win Prizemoney £0 *Total Prizemoney* £2,515
1999 AW 0-1: (8f) (Fibr)
Strong, fair colt, effective 12f, - acts on Equi, often wears blinkers, favours tight tracks. Inconsistent. **Miss A Stokell [0-8] T J Ford (from P F I Cole [0-4] Mar 1998).*

NIAGARA (IRE) BHB 80f RR 84f 4375[10]
2 b c Rainbows For Life (CAN) 9.3f **(64)** - Highbrook (USA) **(74f)** (Alphabatim (USA))
Form - 421460
Record 1999 - 1st:1 2nd:1 3rd:0 Ran:6
Win Prizemoney £2,940 *Total Prizemoney* £4,636
Wins * 1999 May Ayr (GD) 6f 84 <
1999 Turf 1-6: (5f 2, 6f 1-2, 7f, 8f) (g-s 1-1, gd 3, g-f, frm)
Decent colt, effective 5 to 6f, acts on g-s to frm. Turf high 84 - 1st of 10 from Happy Hooligan (21 May Ayr RF 1361). He got off the mark in an Ayr maiden, and put in a fair effort in a Newbury nursery in August. **M H Tompkins [1-6] Miss D J Merson.*

NICE BALANCE (USA) BHB 40f RR 53f 4291[5]
4 b g Shadeed (USA) 7.7f **(72)** - Fellwaati (USA) (Alydar (USA)) 9.1f **(76)**
Form - 0608505
Record 1999 - 1st:0 2nd:0 3rd:0 Ran:7
1999 Turf 0-6: (6f 2, 7f, 8f, 10f 2) (gd, g-f 3, frm 2) 1999 AW 0-1: (11f) (Fibr)
Scopey, fair gelding, has worn blinkers. Turf high 53. **M C Chapman [0-12] R J Hayward.*

NICE GUY (IRE) RR 44f 2391[9]
4 ch g Persian Bold 10f **(69)** - Flying Bid (Auction Ring (USA)) 8.6f **(65)**
Form - 070
Record 1999 - 1st:0 2nd:0 3rd:0 Ran:3
Pre1999 - 1st:0 2nd:0 3rd:0 Ran:4
Win Prizemoney £0 *Total Prizemoney* £309
1999 Turf 0-3: (12f, 14f, 18f) (g-f 2, frm)
Moderate gelding. Turf high 44. **S Dow [0-4] Ruelles Partners (from F Berry in IRE [0-4] Oct 1998).*

NICELY (IRE) BHB 85f RR 82f 5132[9]
3 gr f Bustino 11f **(64)** - Nichodoula (Doulab (USA)) 9.8f **(65)**
Form - 505650410
Record 1999 - 1st:1 2nd:0 3rd:0 Ran:9
Pre1999 - 1st:1 2nd:0 3rd:0 Ran:2
Win Prizemoney £9,752 *Total Prizemoney* £10,528
Wins * 1999 Oct Newbur (G-S) H 16f 73 80+ <
* 1998 Oct Bath (SFT) 8f 73
1999 Turf 1-9: (10f, 11f 3, 12f, 14f 2, 16f 1-2) (g-s 1-2, gd 4, g-f 2, frm)
Lengthy, decent filly, effective 11 to 16f, acts on g-s to g-f, prefers left handed tracks. Turf high 85 (1st run) - 5th of 9 getting 3lb from Valentine Girl (5 May Chester 11f g-f RF 1045) - also 1st of 17 getting 12lb from Male-Ana-Mou (22 Oct Newbury RF 5028). **J W Hills [2-10] Mrs Claire Smith (from J Hill [0-1] May 1999).*

NICE 'N EASY (IRE) BHB 36f RR 58f 4169[10]
2 b f Perugino (USA) - Oystons Propweekly (Swing Easy (USA)) 6.5f **(55)**
Form - 874007080
Record 1999 - 1st:0 2nd:0 3rd:0 Ran:9
Win Prizemoney £0 *Total Prizemoney* £232
1999 Turf 0-8: (5f, 6f 4, 7f 2, 8f) (g-s, g-f 3, frm 3, hrd) 1999 AW 0-1: (5f) (Fibr)
Fair filly, has worn blinkers. Turf high 58. **K T Ivory [0-9] K T Ivory.*

NICE ONE CLARE (IRE) BHB 89f RR 87+f 3965[1]
3 b f Mukaddamah (USA) 7.6f **(74)** - Sarah-Clare (Reach) 7f **(83)**
Form - 13211
Record 1999 - 1st:3 2nd:1 3rd:1 Ran:5
Win Prizemoney £17,333 *Total Prizemoney* £19,577
Wins * 1999 Aug Newmar (G-F) H 7f 85 87+ <
*** 1999** Aug Kempto (G-F) H 7f 82 86
*** 1999** May Folkes (G-F) 7f 78
1999 Turf 3-5: (7f 3-5) (g-f 1-3, frm 2-2)
Leggy, useful filly. Turf high 87 - 1st of 14 getting 4lb from Holly Blue (28 Aug Newmarket RF 3965) - also 1st of 10 giving 2lb to Fallachan (4 Aug Kempton RF 3355). A winner of three of her five starts, and placed in the other two. All her form has been achieved on fast ground, and her wins have come over seven furlongs. One to follow at four. **J W Payne [3-5] Oremsa Partnership.*

NICHOLAS DUDLEY (USA) BHB 79f RR 81f 4828[6]
2 b c Caerleon (USA) 10.9f **(79)** - Flood (USA) (Riverman (USA)) 9.1f **(76)**
Form - 21376
Record 1999 - 1st:1 2nd:1 3rd:1 Ran:5
Win Prizemoney £3,707 *Total Prizemoney* £5,216
Wins * 1999 Jly Ayr (GD) 6f 81 <
1999 Turf 1-5: (6f 1-1, 7f 3, 8f) (sft, g-s, gd 1-2, frm)
Decent colt. Turf high 81 (began Jly) - 1st of 10 giving 5lb to Jimgareen (26 Jly Ayr RF 3134). **Sir Mark Prescott [1-5] Faisal Salman.*

NICHOLAS MISTRESS BHB 43f47a RR 28f 47a 2171[11]
3 b f Beveled (USA) 6.9f **(64)** - Foreign Mistress (Darshaan) 9.9f **(84)**
Form - 5346443216500000

Record 1999 - 1st:1 2nd:1 3rd:1 Ran:12
Pre1999 - 1st:0 2nd:3 3rd:2 Ran:13
Win Prizemoney £2,558 *Total Prizemoney* £6,489
Wins * **1999** *Feb Lingfi (STD) H 6f 43 52* <
1999 Turf 0-4: (6f, 7f 2, 8f) (gd, g-f 2, frm) 1999 AW 1-8: (5f 2, 6f 1-3, 7f, 8f 2) (Equi 1-4, Fibr 4)
Light-framed, little account filly, effective 5f, acts on gd to frm, best on frm, has worn blinkers. Turf high 36. AW high 52.
**P D Evans [1-25] J E Abbey.*

NICHOL FIFTY BHB 75f RR 78f 5220[9]

5 b g Old Vic 12.8f **(72)** - Jawaher (IRE) (Dancing Brave (USA)) 8.4f **(76)**
Form - 1061022570
Record 1999 - 1st:2 2nd:2 3rd:0 Ran:10
Pre1999 - 1st:2 2nd:1 3rd:1 Ran:11
Win Prizemoney £18,574 *Total Prizemoney* £23,611
Wins * **1999** Jun Kempto (GD) 14.4f 77 <
* **1999** Apr Nottin (SFT) H 14.1f 71 75
* 1997 Oct Leices (GD) 11.8f 73
* 1997 Jly Cheste (G-F) 12.3f 67
1999 Turf 2-10: (13f, 14f 2-5, 16f, 17f 2, 19f) (sft, g-s 1-1, gd 3, g-f 1-3, frm 2)
Above-average gelding, effective 13 to 17f, best at 14f, acts on g-s to frm, best on gd, prefers tight tracks, excels at Haydock. Turf high 79 - 2nd of 9 giving 18lb to Il Principe (7 Aug Haydock 14f gd RF 3450) - also 1st of 6 giving 22lb to Chicodove (9 Jun Kempton RF 1866). He did well after returning to the Flat last season with victories over 14 furlongs at Nottingham and Kempton. Finished seventh in the Cesarewitch after his stamina just appeared to give way. Likes cut in the ground. **M H Tompkins [5-24] Lloyd Bedack.*

NICIARA (IRE) BHB 40f RR 41f 4839[18]

2 b g Soviet Lad (USA) 9.4f **(63)** - Verusa (IRE) (Petorius) 7.3f **(61)**
Form - 000
Record 1999 - 1st:0 2nd:0 3rd:0 Ran:3
1999 Turf 0-3: (6f, 8f 2) (gd, g-f, frm)
Currently moderate gelding. Turf high 32 (began Aug).
**M C Chapman [0-3] W P Gaff.*

NICKLES BHB 53f RR 64df 5167[10]

4 b g Lugana Beach 7f **(63)** - Instinction (Never so Bold) 6.3f **(66)**
Form - 40307130000
Record 1999 - 1st:1 2nd:0 3rd:2 Ran:11
Pre1999 - 1st:0 2nd:0 3rd:2 Ran:3
Win Prizemoney £2,988 *Total Prizemoney* £5,097
Wins * **1999** Aug Lingfi (GD) C 5f 57 <
1999 Turf 1-11: (5f 1-11) (sft, g-s 4, gd 1-3, frm 3)
Neat, average gelding, effective 5f, acts on g-f. Turf high 66. Becoming disappointing. He got off the mark with a comfortable win in a Lingfield claimer in August.
**L G Cottrell [1-14] Inforfivecents.*

NICK'S CHOICE BHB 30f RR 41f 4447[13]

3 b g Sula Bula - Clare's Choice (Pragmatic)
Form - 0707000
Record 1999 - 1st:0 2nd:0 3rd:0 Ran:7
1999 Turf 0-6: (5f, 6f, 7f 3, 10f) (g-s, gd 2, frm 3) 1999 AW 0-1: (8f) (Fibr)
Moderate gelding, has worn blinkers. Turf high 41.
**J M Bradley [0-7] John Brookman.*

NICK'S JULE (IRE) RR 57f 3740[12]

2 ch f Perugino (USA) - Miss Lee Ann (Tumble Wind (USA)) 7.5f **(57)**
Form - 50
Record 1999 - 1st:0 2nd:0 3rd:0 Ran:2
1999 Turf 0-2: (6f, 7f) (g-s, frm)
Currently fair filly. Turf high 57 (began Jly).
**A P Jarvis [0-2] Ms Julie Greenacre.*

NICOBAR BHB 100f RR 99f 4595[5]

2 b c Indian Ridge 7.6f **(74)** - Duchess of Alba **(74f)** (Belmez (USA))
Form - 31525
Record 1999 - 1st:1 2nd:1 3rd:1 Ran:5
Win Prizemoney £4,045 *Total Prizemoney* £8,808
Wins * **1999** Aug Haydoc (G-S) 7.1f 94+ <
1999 Turf 1-5: (7f 1-5) (g-s, gd, g-f 1-2, frm)
Very useful colt. Turf high 99 (began Jly) - 2nd of 5 giving 11lb to Adilabad (15 Spt Sandown 7f gd RF 4330) also 1st of 14 from Nothing Daunted (6 Aug Haydock RF 3413). He is useful and was not seen to best advantage when badly drawn and ridden too forcefully in the £300,000 Tattersalls Houghton Stakes at Newmarket in September. He should stay a mile and can win a Group race in the continent in 2000.
**I A Balding [1-5] Robert Hitchins.*

NICOLA BELLA (IRE) RR 96?f 961[7]

4 b f Sadler's Wells (USA) 11.3f **(87)** - Valley Of Hope (USA) (Riverman (USA)) 9.1f **(76)**
Form - 7
Record 1999 - 1st:0 2nd:0 3rd:0 Ran:1
Pre1999 - 1st:1 2nd:2 3rd:0 Ran:7
Win Prizemoney £3,093 *Total Prizemoney* £4,953
Wins 1998 Jly Gowran (GD) 9.6f 95+ <
1999 Turf 0-1: (10f) (frm)
Very useful filly, effective 10f, acts on gd, likes right handed tracks. Becoming disappointing.
**J L Dunlop [0-1] Neil Jones (from J Oxx in IRE [1-7] Aug 1998).*

NICOLAOS (GER) RR 100f 2859a[5]

3 c
Form - 5
1999 Turf 0-1: (8f) (gd)
Currently very useful colt. **H Steinmetz in GER [0-1].*

NIFTY MAJOR BHB 82f RR 84f 4343[8]

2 b g Be My Chief (USA) 10.2f **(62)** - Nifty Fifty (IRE) (Runnett) 7f **(59)**
Form - 612545158
Record 1999 - 1st:2 2nd:1 3rd:0 Ran:9
Win Prizemoney £5,809 *Total Prizemoney* £7,146
Wins * **1999** Aug Mussel (G-S) H 5f 73 84 <
* **1999** Apr Mussel (G-F) 5f 71
1999 Turf 2-9: (5f 2-9) (g-s, gd 3, g-f 1-3, frm 1-2)
Decent gelding, effective 5f, acts on gd to g-f. Turf high 84 - 1st of 8 getting 8lb from Happy Times (18 Aug Musselburgh RF 3751).
**J Berry [2-9] Roy Peebles.*

NIFTY NORMAN BHB 62f73a RR 61f 73a 5212[19]

5 b g Rock City 8.8f **(62)** - Nifty Fifty (IRE) (Runnett) 7f **(59)**
Form - 05815221305334126040040
Record 1999 - 1st:3 2nd:3 3rd:3 Ran:23
Pre1999 - 1st:2 2nd:3 3rd:1 Ran:20
Win Prizemoney £18,357 *Total Prizemoney* £26,754
Wins * **1999** Jun Cheste (SFT) H 5.1f 57 67
* **1999** *Mar Southw (STD) H 5f 62 69*
* **1999** *Feb Southw (STD) H 6f 52 58*
1997 Jun Ayr (GD) H 5f 72 73
1997 May Beverl (HVY) 5f 82? <
1999 Turf 1-14: (5f 1-12, 6f 2) (g-s 1-3, gd 5, g-f 3, frm 3) 1999 AW 2-9: (5f 1-4, 6f 1-4, 7f) (Equi, Fibr 2-8)
Above-average gelding, effective 5 to 6f, best at 6f, acts on sft to gd - acts on Fibr, likes left handed tracks, likes tight tracks, excels at Southwell. Turf high 67 - 1st of 7 getting 21lb from Westcourt Magic (2 Jun Chester RF 1672). AW high 74 - 3rd of 13 giving 35lb to Breakin Even (22 Mar Southwell 6f Fibr RF 0462) - also 1st of 15 giving 5lb to Polar Mist (16 Mar Southwell RF 0440). A grand old sprinter, he remains best at five furlongs and is capable of scoring on turf or sand.
**D Nicholls [3-23] The Nifty Norman Partnership (from J Berry [2-20] Spt 1998).*

NIGEL'S LAD (IRE) BHB 80f77a RR 87f 77a 3207[7]

7 b g Dominion Royale 7.8f **(63)** - Back To Earth (FR) (Vayrann) 9.7f **(74)**
Form - 7501537
Record 1999 - 1st:1 2nd:0 3rd:1 Ran:7
Pre1999 - 1st:11 2nd:6 3rd:4 Ran:50
Win Prizemoney £49,341 *Total Prizemoney* £64,709
Wins * **1999** Jun Pontef (GD) H 17.1f 75 81+
* 1998 Jun Hamilt (SFT) H 13f 80 84
* 1998 May Ripon (GD) H 16f 75 76+
* 1997 Jun Pontef (G-F) H 17.1f 70 77+
* 1997 May Catter (G-F) H 15.8f 70 79
* 1997 May Ripon (G-F) H 16f 70 85
* 1995 Spt Newmar (GD) H 10f 79 87 <

* 1995	May	Newcas	(GD)	H	8f	81	87 <
* 1995	May	Hamilt	(G-F)	H	9.2f	70	75
* 1995	Apr	Nottin	(GD)		10f		72
* 1995	*Jan*	*Lingfi*	*(STD)*	*H*	*10f*	*67*	*75*
* 1995	*Jan*	*Lingfi*	*(STD)*	*H*	*10f*	*60*	*60*

1999 Turf 1-7: (12f, 14f 2, 16f, 17f 1-1, 19f, 20f) (g-s, gd 2, g-f 3, frm 1-1)

Useful gelding, effective 13 to 19f, acts on g-s to frm, prefers tight tracks. Turf high 87 - 3rd of 6 getting 17lb from Kahtan (25 Jly Chester 19f g-f RF 3125) - also 1st of 5 giving 29lb to Rum Baba (28 Jun Pontefract RF 2369). A decent performer on the Flat and over hurdles, he bounced back to winning form when making all to win at Pontefract in June. Stays well.

**P C Haslam [19-72] N C Dunnington.*

NIGHT ADVENTURE (IRE) BHB 57f **RR 67f** 4564[18]

3 ch g Night Shift (USA) 8.1f **(73)** - Mary Hinge **(96f)** (Dowsing (USA))

Form - 030

Record 1999 - 1st:0 2nd:0 3rd:1 Ran:3

Win Prizemoney £0 *Total Prizemoney* £529

1999 Turf 0-3: (6f, 7f, 8f) (gd, frm 2)

Workmanlike, currently average gelding. Turf high 67 (began Aug) - 3rd of 11 getting 4lb from One Dinar (7 Spt Lingfield 7f frm RF 4180).

**J L Dunlop [0-3] J E Nash.*

NIGHT AUCTION (IRE) BHB 44f46a **RR 18f 46a** 3632[11]

4 b f Night Shift (USA) 8.1f **(73)** - Maria Stuarda (Royal And Regal (USA)) 9.5f **(60)**

Form - 085203460

Record 1999 - 1st:0 2nd:0 3rd:1 Ran:5

Pre1999 - 1st:1 2nd:2 3rd:0 Ran:19

Win Prizemoney £2,416 *Total Prizemoney* £4,489

Wins * 1998 Jly Redcar (G-S) C 6f 46 <

1999 Turf 0-2: (8f, 12f) (gd, g-f) 1999 AW 0-3: (8f, 12f 2) (Equi 2, Fibr)

Scopey, fair filly, effective 6 to 8f, acts on frm - acts on Fibr. Turf high 18 (began Aug). AW high 48. Inconsistent.

**B Palling [1-24] D Brennan.*

NIGHT CHIME (IRE) BHB 40f33a **RR 28f 33a** 2913[16]

4 b f Night Shift (USA) 8.1f **(73)** - Baydon Belle (USA) (Al Nasr (FR)) 9.3f **(68)**

Form - 748778800

Record 1999 - 1st:0 2nd:0 3rd:0 Ran:8

Pre1999 - 1st:0 2nd:0 3rd:0 Ran:1

1999 Turf 0-3: (6f, 7f, 14f) (sft, gd, frm) 1999 AW 0-5: (5f 3, 6f 2) (Fibr 5)

Workmanlike, little account filly. Turf high 28. AW high 32.

**Miss A Stokell [0-8] T J Ford (from R Charlton [0-1] Dec 1998).*

NIGHT CHORUS BHB 75f58a **RR 74f 58a** 2257[1]

5 b g Most Welcome 8.6f **(66)** - Choral Sundown (Night Shift (USA)) 7.2f **(69)**

Form - 1241

Record 1999 - 1st:2 2nd:1 3rd:0 Ran:4

Pre1999 - 1st:2 2nd:2 3rd:3 Ran:27

Win Prizemoney £13,373 *Total Prizemoney* £21,902

Wins	* **1999**	Jun	Warwic	(G-F)	H	7.7f	72	74 <
	* **1999**	Apr	Pontef	(G-S)		8f		67
	* 1998	Jun	Mussel	(SFT)	H	8f	63	67
	* 1997	Apr	Nottin	(GD)	H	8.2f	67	73

1999 Turf 2-4: (8f 2-4) (gd 1-2, g-f 1-1, frm)

Above-average gelding, effective 8f, acts on g-s to frm, has worn blinkers. Turf high 74 - 1st of 12 giving 19lb to Step On Degas (23 Jun Warwick RF 2257) - also 1st of 19 from Knobbleeneeze (28 Apr Pontefract RF 0906). Improving. Comfortable winner of a weak handicap on his favoured easy ground first time out last season. He won a similar event at Warwick in June, but that was it for the season.

**B S Rothwell [4-31] R M J MacNair.*

NIGHT CITY BHB 72f80a **RR 74f 80a** 5126[1]

8 b g Kris 10f **(75)** - Night Secret (Nijinsky (CAN)) 10.3f **(77)**

Form - 12353258221470151

Record 1999 - 1st:3 2nd:3 3rd:1 Ran:14

Pre1999 - 1st:14 2nd:6 3rd:5 Ran:49

Win Prizemoney £80,730 *Total Prizemoney* £95,599

Wins	* **1999**	Oct	Bright	(G-S)	H	10f	65	74
	* **1999**	Oct	York	(G-S)	C	10.4f		71
	* **1999**	Jun	Hamilt	(GD)	C	11.1f		67+
	* 1998	*Dec*	*Lingfi*	*(STD)*	*H*	*12f*	*77*	*84*
	* 1998	Oct	York	(GD)	C	10.4f		77
	* 1998	Oct	Bright	(GD)	C	11.9f		75
	* 1998	Aug	Lingfi	(FRM)	H	11.5f	70	77
	* 1998	Aug	Catter	(GD)	C	12f		66
	* 1998	Jly	Hamilt	(FRM)	C	12.1f		55
	* 1998	May	Thirsk	(GD)	C	12f		71
	* 1998	Mar	Hamilt	(HVY)	H	11.1f	65	75
	* 1998	*Feb*	*Lingfi*	*(SLW)*	*C*	*12f*		*75+*
	* 1998	*Jan*	*Lingfi*	*(STD)*	*C*	*12f*		*83+*
	* 1997	*Dec*	*Lingfi*	*(STD)*	*H*	*13f*	*70*	*73*
	* 1997	*Nov*	*Lingfi*	*(STD)*	*C*	*12f*		*68*
	1996	May	Newbur	(SFT)	H	9f	96	102 <
	1995	Oct	Chepst	(SFT)		8.1f		84

1999 Turf 3-10: (10f 2-4, 11f 1-3, 12f 3) (hvy, g-s, gd 2-4, g-f 2, frm 1-2) 1999 AW 0-4: (8f, 10f, 11f, 12f) (Equi 3, Fibr)

Decent gelding, effective 12 to 13f, best at 12f, - acts on Equi, has worn blinkers, likes right handed tracks, and likes Brighton and York and Hamilton. Turf high 74. AW high 80. He has been a real moneyspinner for connections in recent seasons in middle-distance events on both turf and sand. Kept very busy, he seems as good as ever just now and remains a difficult horse to pass if allowed an uncontested early lead.

**K R Burke [15-48] Nigel Shields (from Lady Herries [2-16] May 1997).*

NIGHT DANCE BHB 53f60a **RR 53f 60a** 1494[8]

7 ch g Weldnaas (USA) 8.4f **(55)** - Shift Over (USA) (Night Shift (USA)) 7.2f **(69)**

Form - 628

Record 1999 - 1st:0 2nd:1 3rd:0 Ran:3

Pre1999 - 1st:5 2nd:2 3rd:1 Ran:28

Win Prizemoney £81,214 *Total Prizemoney* £86,603

Wins	* 1997	Apr	Beverl	(G-F)		7.5f		78
	1995	Oct	Ascot	(SFT)	H	8f	90	97 <
	1995	Spt	Ascot	(GD)	H	7f	81	91
	1995	Jly	Sandow	(GD)	H	7.1f	76	79

1999 Turf 0-3: (7f, 8f 2) (g-f 3)

Fair gelding. Turf high 53. He is useful but one-paced in Group company.

**K A Morgan [3-23] Racecourse Medical Officers Association (from G Lewis [4-19] Oct 1996).*

NIGHTDANCE (GER) **RR 104f** 4661a[4]

3 b f Shareef Dancer (USA) 10.1f **(67)** - Nightrockette (GER) (Rocket)

Form - 34

1999 Turf 0-2: (10f, 12f) (gd 2)

Currently very useful filly. Turf high 104 (began Spt).

**A Schutz in GER [0-2].*

NIGHT DIAMOND BHB 75f **RR 75f** 4269[12]

2 b c Night Shift (USA) 8.1f **(73)** - Dashing Water **(84f)** (Dashing Blade)

Form - 0530

Record 1999 - 1st:0 2nd:0 3rd:1 Ran:4

Win Prizemoney £0 *Total Prizemoney* £637

1999 Turf 0-4: (6f 3, 7f) (gd, frm 2, hrd)

Above-average colt. Turf high 75 (began Jly).

**I A Balding [0-4] J C Smith.*

NIGHT EMPRESS BHB 80f **RR 79f** 5034[11]

2 br f Emperor Jones (USA) - Night Trader (USA) (Melyno) 10.4f **(55)**

Form - 4230

Record 1999 - 1st:0 2nd:1 3rd:1 Ran:4

Win Prizemoney £0 *Total Prizemoney* £1,787

1999 Turf 0-4: (6f 2, 7f 2) (g-s 3, frm)

Above-average filly. Turf high 79 (began Jly) - 3rd of 6 getting 9lb from Kingsdon (29 Spt Salisbury 7f g-s RF 4645).

**J R Fanshawe [0-4] The Woodman Racing Syndicate.*

NIGHT FLIGHT BHB 92f86a **RR 87f 86a** 5040[6]

5 gr g Night Shift (USA) 8.1f **(73)** - Ancestry (Persepolis (FR)) 6.4f **(67)**

Form - 327811341000706

Record 1999 - 1st:3 2nd:1 3rd:2 Ran:15

Pre1999 - 1st:2 2nd:3 3rd:5 Ran:26

Win Prizemoney £67,890 *Total Prizemoney* £89,984

Wins	* **1999**	Jly	Ascot	(G-F)	H	5f	94	100 <
	* **1999**	May	Haydoc	(GD)	H	5f	86	91
	* **1999**	May	York	(SFT)	H	5f	81	85
	* 1998	Jun	Newcas	(GD)	H	6f	71	80+

1997 Apr Pontef (GD) H 6f 72 82

1999 Turf 3-14: (5f 3-10, 6f 4) (g-s 2, gd 1-6, g-f 1-3, frm 1-3) 1999 AW 0-1: (6f) (Fibr)

Useful gelding, effective 5f, acts on gd to frm. Turf high 100 - 1st of 13 from Rudi's Pet (10 Jly Ascot RF 2701) - also 1st of 18 getting 19lb from Tadeo (29 May Haydock RF 1567). Best when forcing the issue over a stiff five furlongs, he was in great form through the first half of the season, but could not beat the Handicapper from August onward. Back on a winning mark, he is one to note next spring.

**R A Fahey [4-27] C H Stevens (from J J O'Neill [1-14] Spt 1997).*

NIGHT FLYER BHB 85f68a RR 82f 68a 4132[5]

Night Flight was in fine form in the first half of the season

4 b c Midyan (USA) 9.9f **(64)** - Scandalette (Niniski (USA)) 10.6f **(65)**

Form - 07302373121845

Record					
1999 -	1st:2	2nd:2	3rd:3	Ran:13
Pre1999 -	1st:1	2nd:3	3rd:1	Ran:16

Win Prizemoney £17,343 *Total Prizemoney* £36,634

Wins								
*** 1999**	Jly	Epsom	(G-F)	H	12f	77	81	<
*** 1999**	Jly	Epsom	(G-F)	H	12f	71	70+	
* 1997	Aug	Epsom	(GD)	H	7f	75	74	

1999 Turf 2-11: (9f, 10f 4, 12f 2-6) (sft, gd 2, g-f 2, frm 2-5, hrd) 1999 AW 0-2: (10f 2) (Equi 2)

Unfurnished, decent colt, effective 8 to 12f, best at 12f, acts on sft to frm, prefers right handed tracks, does well at Epsom. Turf high 82 - 8th of 12 giving 8lb to Livius (7 Aug Ascot 12f gd RF 3447) - also 1st of 8 giving 19lb to Luz Bay (28 Jly Epsom RF 3204). AW high 43. John Hills has done very well with this colt, having placed him well to win two races over twelve furlongs at Epsom during the summer.

**J W Hills [3-29] The Jampot Partnership.*

NIGHTGLADE (IRE) BHB 38f37a RR 37f 37a 3803[14]

3 b c Night Shift (USA) 8.1f **(73)** - Woodland Garden (Godswalk (USA)) 7.3f **(58)**

Form - 7304080650

Record				
1999 -	1st:0	2nd:0	3rd:1	Ran:10
Pre1999 -	1st:0	2nd:0	3rd:0	Ran:3

Win Prizemoney £0 *Total Prizemoney* £668

1999 Turf 0-9: (10f 2, 12f 5, 16f 2) (gd 4, g-f 4, frm) 1999 AW 0-1: (12f) (Fibr)

Unfurnished, very moderate colt, effective 12f, acts on gd, likes right handed tracks, likes tight tracks. Turf high 45.

**M Brittain [0-13] Mel Brittain.*

NIGHTINGALE BHB 51f RR 34f 121[7]

3 ro f Night Shift (USA) 8.1f **(73)** - Grey Angel (Kenmare (FR)) 6.5f **(72)**

Form - 7

Record				
1999 -	1st:0	2nd:0	3rd:0	Ran:1
Pre1999 -	1st:0	2nd:0	3rd:0	Ran:3

1999 AW 0-1: (7f) (Equi)

Workmanlike, very moderate filly.

**P D Evans [0-1] P D Evans (from I A Balding [0-3] Spt 1998).*

NIGHTINGALE SONG BHB 50f60a RR 47f 60a 5032[18]

5 b m Tina's Pet 7.4f **(56)** - Songlines (Night Shift (USA)) 7.2f **(69)**

Form - 0711331060

Record				
1999 -	1st:3	2nd:0	3rd:2	Ran:10
Pre1999 -	1st:1	2nd:1	3rd:4	Ran:21

Win Prizemoney £12,680 *Total Prizemoney* £16,815

Wins								
*** 1999**	Aug	Sandow	(GD)	H	5f	47	47	
*** 1999**	Jun	Leices	(G-S)	H	6f	41	47	
*** 1999**	Jun	Lingfi	(GD)	H	6f	38	41	
1996	Jly	Windso	(GD)	S	6f		63	<

1999 Turf 3-10: (5f 1-4, 6f 2-4, 7f 2) (g-s 2, gd 1-3, g-f 2-2, frm 2, hrd)

Average filly, effective 5 to 6f, best at 6f, acts on gd to g-f, best on gd. Turf high 47 - 1st of 14 getting 2lb from Brevity (20 Aug Sandown RF 3810) - also 1st of 18 getting 18lb from Windy Gulch (12 Jun Leicester RF 1950). Three times a winner last season over sprint distances in low grade races.

**L MontagueHall [3-10] Stephen & Michelle Bayless (from M Meade [1-21] Jly 1998).*

NIGHT LIFE (IRE) BHB 61a RR 68f 4906[10]

3 gr f Night Shift (USA) 8.1f **(73)** - Petula **(94f)** (Petong) 6.6f **(58)**

Form - 33121602460

Record				
1999 -	1st:2	2nd:2	3rd:2	Ran:11
Pre1999 -	1st:1	2nd:0	3rd:0	Ran:5

Win Prizemoney £9,790 *Total Prizemoney* £13,757

Wins								
*** 1999**	May	Catter	(G-F)	H	6f	63	67	<
*** 1999**	*Apr*	*Wolver*	*(STD)*	*H*	*6f*	*61*	*61*	
* 1998	Oct	Yarmou	(SFT)	H	5.2f	54	60	

1999 Turf 1-9: (6f 1-7, 7f 2) (sft, gd 3, g-f 2, frm 1-3) 1999 AW 1-2: (6f

1-2) (Fibr 1-2)
Workmanlike, average filly, effective 5 to 6f, best at 6f, acts on sft to frm - acts on Fibr, does well at Yarmouth. Turf high 68 - 2nd of 16 giving 28lb to Crusty Lily (19 Aug Yarmouth 6f gd RF 3768) - also 1st of 14 giving 2lb to Red Charger (21 May Catterick RF 1378). AW high 63 (1st run) - 3rd of 16 getting 7lb from Keen Hands (26 Apr Southwell 6f Fibr RF 0855) - also 1st of 10 getting 2lb from Guest of Honour (29 Apr Wolverhampton RF 0924).
**M L W Bell [3-16] The Hon Mrs J M Corbett.*

NIGHT MUSIC BHB 61f RR 61f 4943^{10}

2 br f Piccolo - Oribi (Top Ville) 11.7f **(68)**
Form - 480
Record 1999 - 1st:0 2nd:0 3rd:0 Ran:3
Win Prizemoney £0 *Total Prizemoney* £230
1999 Turf 0-3: (7f 2, 8f) (sft, gd, g-f)
Currently average filly. Turf high 61 (began Aug).
**Major D N Chappell [0-3] Super Sprinters.*

NIGHT OF GLASS BHB 90f RR 94f 4761^{4}

6 b g Mazilier (USA) 8.5f **(56)** - Donna Elvira (Chief Singer) 8.9f **(66)**
Form - 3503153758354
Record 1999 - 1st:1 2nd:0 3rd:4 Ran:13
Pre1999 - 1st:8 2nd:4 3rd:8 Ran:43
Win Prizemoney £40,061 *Total Prizemoney* £73,560
Wins * **1999** May Beverl (GD) H 8.5f 90 92 <
* 1998 Spt Mussel (GD) H 7.1f 85 88
* 1998 May Beverl (GD) H 8.5f 84 87
* 1998 May Thirsk (GD) H 7f 78 85
* 1998 Apr Carlis (G-S) H 8f 68 79
* 1998 Apr Thirsk (G-S) H 7f 68 74
* 1998 Apr Catter (GD) H 7f 64 68
* 1997 Oct Catter (SFT) H 7f 61 65
1996 Spt Yarmou (G-F) H 8f 55 58
1999 Turf 1-13: (7f 3, 8f 1-8, 9f, 10f) (g-s, gd 1-6, g-f 4, frm, hrd)
Useful gelding, effective 7 to 8f, best at 8f, acts on g-s to frm, best on gd, mostly wears blinkers (extremely effectively), excels at Beverley and likes Newcastle and Doncaster. Turf high 94 - 3rd of 20 getting 14lb from Sugarfoot (19 Aug York 8f gd RF 3770) - also 1st of 7 giving 4lb to Mundo Raro (25 May Beverley RF 1450). Consistent. He was in irresistible form at the start of '98, completing a nap hand of victories during April and May. He ran a blinder to finish third in the Lincoln on his reappearance last year, and has performed well in some tough handicaps afterwards, though his only victory came at Beverley in May. A mile looks his best trip.
**J L Eyre [8-44] K Silvester and B Silvester (from D Morris [1-12] Nov 1996).*

NIGHT OF GLORY RR 4f 3822^{15}

4 b f Perpendicular - Donna Elvira (Chief Singer) 8.9f **(66)**
Form - 50
Record 1999 - 1st:0 2nd:0 3rd:0 Ran:2
1999 Turf 0-2: (10f, 14f) (g-f 2)
Neat, currently very poor filly. (began Jly).
**J L Eyre [0-2] K Silvester and B Silvester.*

NIGHT OMEN (IRE) RR 59f 3613^{5}

2 ch c Night Shift (USA) 8.1f **(73)** - Propitious (IRE) (Doyoun) 9f **(69)**
Form - 85
Record 1999 - 1st:0 2nd:0 3rd:0 Ran:2
1999 Turf 0-2: (5f, 6f) (frm 2)
Currently fair colt. Turf high 59 (began Jly).
**S C Williams [0-2] D G Burge.*

NIGHT SHIFTER (IRE) BHB 70f RR 77f 4117^{3}

2 b f Night Shift (USA) 8.1f **(73)** - Atsuko (IRE) (Mtoto)
Form - 04071263
Record 1999 - 1st:1 2nd:1 3rd:1 Ran:8
Win Prizemoney £2,912 *Total Prizemoney* £5,344
Wins * **1999** Aug Lingfi (GD) H 5f 63 69 <
1999 Turf 1-8: (5f 1-5, 6f 2, 7f) (gd, g-f 1-4, frm 2, hrd)
Above-average filly, effective 5 to 6f, acts on g-f to hrd. Turf high 77 - 2nd of 9 to Bebe de Cham (27 Aug Thirsk 6f hrd RF 3947) - also 1st of 10 getting 21lb from Coco de Mer (14 Aug Lingfield RF 3644). Inconsistent. **M R Channon [1-8] Glendale Partnership Ltd.*

NIGHT SHOT BHB 108f RR 110df 3970^{3}

4 br g Night Shift (USA) 8.1f **(73)** - Optaria (Song) 7.2f **(61)**
Form - 174322043
Record 1999 - 1st:1 2nd:2 3rd:2 Ran:9
Pre1999 - 1st:3 2nd:4 3rd:2 Ran:16
Win Prizemoney £51,710 *Total Prizemoney* £105,128
Wins * **1999** Mar Doncas (G-S) H 5f 105 110 <
* 1998 Aug York (G-F) H 5f 97 101+
* 1998 Jun Ascot (G-S) H 5f 90 95
* 1998 Mar Warwic (G-S) 5f 85
1999 Turf 1-9: (5f 1-4, 6f 4, 12f) (gd 1-4, g-f 3, frm 2)
Neat, Group-class gelding, effective 5 to 12f, best at 5f, acts on gd to frm, excels at Doncaster. Turf high 110 - also 1st of 17 giving 25lb to Night Flight (25 Mar Doncaster RF 0466). Consistent. He seems best when coming from behind a fast pace and ran a cracker when finishing fourth in the Nunthorpe Stakes. However, he usually finds something to beat him and is difficult to place.
**I A Balding [4-25] J C Smith.*

NIGHT STYLE (FR) BHB 100f RR 98f 5015a^{1}

2 b c Night Shift (USA) 8.1f **(73)** - Style For Life (IRE) (Law Society (USA)) 9.9f **(70)**
Form - 21352011
Record 1999 - 1st:3 2nd:2 3rd:1 Ran:8
Win Prizemoney £52,369 *Total Prizemoney* £55,897
Wins * **1999** Oct San Si (G-F) G1 8f 97
* **1999** Spt Leices (GD) 7f 98 <
* **1999** Jun Ripon (G-F) 6f 80+
1999 Turf 3-8: (6f 1-4, 7f 1-3, 8f 1-1) (gd, g-f 3-4, frm 3)
Very useful colt, effective 7 to 8f, best at 7f, acts on g-f to frm, best on g-f, has worn blinkers. Turf high 98 - 1st of 4 giving 3lb to Cedar Master (20 Spt Leicester RF 4437) - also 1st of 9 from Whyome (17 Oct San Siro RF 5015a). He improved markedly in the autumn, concluding his campaign with a game win in the Gran Criterium at San Siro. Likely to stay a mile and a quarter, he will struggle under a Group One penalty next term.
**E A L Dunlop [3-8] Mohammed Jaber.*

NIGHT VENTURE (USA) BHB 83f RR 88f 4876^{6}

3 b c Dynaformer (USA) 12f **(82)** - Charming Ballerina (Caerleon (USA)) 8.6f **(71)**
Form - 43110506
Record 1999 - 1st:2 2nd:0 3rd:1 Ran:8
Win Prizemoney £10,568 *Total Prizemoney* £12,657
Wins * **1999** Jun Newcas (G-F) H 10.1f 89 89 <
* **1999** May Ripon (G-F) 10f 84
1999 Turf 2-8: (8f, 10f 2-5, 12f 2) (g-s, gd 2, g-f 2, frm 2-3)
Workmanlike, useful colt, effective 10f, acts on g-f to frm, best on frm. Turf high 89 - 1st of 6 giving 12lb to Simply Noble (26 Jun Newcastle RF 2338) - also 1st of 11 giving 5lb to Shikasta (26 May Ripon RF 1506). A progressive handicapper, he won a Ripon maiden and a Newcastle handicap in the spring, but has struggled in decent handicap company since. His wins were on fast ground, though his action suggests he would appreciate some cut.
**B W Hills [2-8] Maktoum Al Maktoum.*

NIGHT WINK (USA) BHB 45f58a RR 42f 58a 4997^{14}

7 ch g Rahy (USA) 9.1f **(80)** - Lady in White (Shareef Dancer (USA)) 9.9f **(73)**
Form - 00000
Record 1999 - 1st:0 2nd:0 3rd:0 Ran:4
Pre1999 - 1st:6 2nd:7 3rd:2 Ran:46
Win Prizemoney £18,815 *Total Prizemoney* £32,687
Wins 1997 Spt Bright (G-F) C 8f 78
1997 Jly Bright (FRM) C 10f 65
1996 Aug Goodwo (G-F) H 9f 76 80
1996 Jly Bright (FRM) H 8f 74 78
1995 Oct Redcar (FRM) H 8f 70 83 <
1995 Oct Leices (GD) 7f 72
1999 Turf 0-4: (7f, 8f, 9f, 10f) (gd 2, g-f, frm)
Moderate gelding, has worn blinkers. Turf high 42 (began Spt). Becoming disappointing.
**Mrs V C Ward [0-17] Mrs J Morgan (from G L Moore [4-26] Spt 1997).*

NIGRASINE BHB 102f100a RR 102f 100a 5222^{7}

5 b h Mon Tresor 7.9f **(60)** - Early Gales (Precocious) 8.6f **(62)**
Form - 00101242430407
Record 1999 - 1st:2 2nd:2 3rd:1 Ran:14

Pre1999 - 1st:4 2nd:4 3rd:3 Ran:27
Win Prizemoney £38,147 *Total Prizemoney* £97,643
Wins * **1999** Jun Yarmou (GD) 6f 114 <
* **1999** Apr Thirsk (GD) 6f 113
* 1998 Jun Haydoc (GD) L 7.1f 107
* 1997 Jly Haydoc (GD) H 6f 99 103
* 1996 Jly Pontef (G-F) 6f 101
* 1996 Jun Redcar (G-F) 6f 73
1999 Turf 2-13: (6f 2-11, 7f, 8f) (g-s, gd 1-8, g-f 1-3, frm) 1999 AW 0-1: (8f) (Fibr)
Very useful colt, effective 6 to 7f, best at 6f, acts on gd to frm, often wears blinkers, likes left handed tracks. Turf high 114 - 1st of 7 giving 11lb to Cretan Gift (10 Jun Yarmouth RF 1891) - also 1st of 8 giving 7lb to Eastern Purple (17 Apr Thirsk RF 0743). Consistent. He is the veteran of many tough battles but retains his enthusiasm and will to win. Best over six and seven furlongs, he does not quite stay a mile, but acts on most types of ground and is notably game. **J L Eyre [6-41] Sunpak Potatoes.*

NIKA NESGODA BHB 70f **RR 75f** 3989[11]
3 b f Suave Dancer (USA) 10.7f **(68)** - Highland Ceilidh (IRE) (Scottish Reel) 7f **(61)**
Form - 2104550
Record 1999 - 1st:1 2nd:1 3rd:0 Ran:7
Pre1999 - 1st:0 2nd:0 3rd:0 Ran:2
Win Prizemoney £2,804 *Total Prizemoney* £3,935
Wins * **1999** Apr Beverl (GD) 12f 79 <
1999 Turf 1-7: (10f, 12f 1-4, 16f 2) (gd 1-3, g-f, frm 3)
Rangy, above-average filly, effective 12f, acts on gd to g-f, prefers tight tracks. Turf high 79 - 1st of 8 getting 5lb from Compton Ace (22 Apr Beverley RF 0807). Inconsistent. She got off the mark with a game victory in a Beverley maiden, but did not go on from there. **J L Dunlop [1-9] Cyril Humphris.*

NIKITA'S STAR (IRE) BHB 41f60a **RR 36f 60a** 2162[3]
6 ch g Soviet Lad (USA) 9.4f **(63)** - Sally Chase (Sallust) 8.4f **(63)**
Form - 4144611202003263
Record 1999 - 1st:2 2nd:3 3rd:2 Ran:14
Pre1999 - 1st:6 2nd:5 3rd:5 Ran:48
Win Prizemoney £21,130 *Total Prizemoney* £32,485
Wins * **1999** *Feb Southw (STD) 12f 68*
* **1999** *Feb Wolver (STD) H 12f 53 58*
* 1998 *Dec Southw (STD) H 12f 55 57*
1996 *Nov Wolver (STD) H 12f 73 75* <
1996 Jly Folkes (G-F) H 12f 60 64
1996 *Jly Southw (STD) C 11f 64*
1996 *Mar Wolver (STD) H 12f 66 69+*
1996 *Feb Wolver (STD) 9.4f 55*
1999 Turf 0-4: (13f, 14f 2, 17f) (sft 2, gd, g-f) 1999 AW 2-10: (12f 2-6, 15f, 16f 3) (Fibr 2-10)
Average gelding, effective 12 to 16f, best at 12f, - acts on Fibr, has worn blinkers, favours left handed tracks, and excels at Southwell. Turf high 52. AW high 68 - also 1st of 5 giving 7lb to Julies Jewel (15 Feb Southwell RF 0291). He had quite a good time of it during the winter when he won three times on Fibresand. Effective in modest company on that surface, twelve furlongs looks his best trip.
**M Brittain [3-23] D Parker (from D J G MurraySmith [5-39] Mar 1998).*

NILOUPHAR RR 12f 2274[7]
2 b f Pharly (FR) 11.5f **(64)** - White African (Carwhite) 7.2f **(61)**
Form - 077
Record 1999 - 1st:0 2nd:0 3rd:0 Ran:3
1999 Turf 0-2: (5f, 7f) (frm, hrd) 1999 AW 0-1: (5f) (Fibr)
Currently very moderate filly. Turf high 12.
**W G M Turner [0-3] G J Bush.*

NIMELLO (USA) BHB 88f **RR 97df** 5141[19]
3 b c Kingmambo (USA) 10.9f **(85)** - Zakota (IRE) (Polish Precedent (USA)) 10.2f **(60)**
Form - 520
Record 1999 - 1st:0 2nd:1 3rd:0 Ran:3
Pre1999 - 1st:1 2nd:0 3rd:0 Ran:1
Win Prizemoney £5,299 *Total Prizemoney* £7,686
Wins * 1998 Jly Newmar (G-F) 7f 87+ <
1999 Turf 0-3: (8f 2, 9f) (sft, gd, frm)
Very useful colt. Turf high 97 (began Spt). Injured on the gallops after a winning debut in 1998, he proved no better than useful last term. **P F I Cole [1-4] C Shiacolas.*

NIMINY-PIMINY (IRE) BHB 31f **RR 32f** 1745[4]
3 ch f Polish Patriot (USA) 7.8f **(70)** - Recherchee (Rainbow Quest (USA)) 10.4f **(75)**
Form - 0004
Record 1999 - 1st:0 2nd:0 3rd:0 Ran:4
Pre1999 - 1st:0 2nd:0 3rd:0 Ran:3
1999 Turf 0-1: (6f) (frm) 1999 AW 0-3: (7f 2, 8f) (Equi, Fibr 2)
Scopey, very moderate filly, often wears blinkers. AW high 10.
**M Johnston [0-7] P D Savill.*

NINEACRES BHB 43f51a **RR 39f 51a** 5032[4]
8 b g Sayf El Arab (USA) 8.2f **(57)** - Mayor (Laxton)
Form - 00804
Record 1999 - 1st:0 2nd:0 3rd:0 Ran:5
Pre1999 - 1st:3 2nd:7 3rd:6 Ran:42
Win Prizemoney £7,989 *Total Prizemoney* £17,994
Wins 1995 *Jan Lingfi (STD) H 5f 57 56* <
1999 Turf 0-5: (5f 4, 6f) (sft, g-s, gd, frm 2)
Moderate gelding, often wears blinkers. Turf high 39 (began Spt).
**J M Bradley [0-5] Mrs P A Wallis (from N M Babbage [0-12] Nov 1997).*

NINETEENNINETYNINE BHB 65f **RR 58f** 5130[6]
2 b c Warning 8.1f **(77)** - Flower Girl (Pharly (FR)) 9.8f **(68)**
Form - 506
Record 1999 - 1st:0 2nd:0 3rd:0 Ran:3
Win Prizemoney £0 *Total Prizemoney* £79
1999 Turf 0-3: (7f 2, 8f) (g-s, gd 2)
Currently fair colt. Turf high 58 (began Spt).
**R W Armstrong [0-3] W J Gredley.*

NINETY DEGREES BHB 75f **RR 83f** 3396[5]
2 ch c Piccolo - Champagne Grandy **(77f 75a)** (Vaigly Great) 7f **(58)**
Form - 5215
Record 1999 - 1st:1 2nd:1 3rd:0 Ran:4
Win Prizemoney £3,525 *Total Prizemoney* £4,765
Wins * **1999** Jly Yarmou (FRM) 5.2f 72 <
1999 Turf 1-4: (5f 1-4) (gd, g-f 1-2, frm)
Decent colt. Turf high 72 - also 1st of 7 from Morning Dawn (20 Jly Yarmouth RF 2965). **J Berry [1-4] The Right Angle Club.*

NISIBIS RR 30f 668[14]
3 b f In The Wings 11.2f **(77)** - Nibabu (FR) (Nishapour (FR)) 9.1f **(61)**
Form - 0
Record 1999 - 1st:0 2nd:0 3rd:0 Ran:1
1999 Turf 0-1: (10f) (g-f)
Light-framed, currently very moderate filly.
**N A Callaghan [0-1] Martin Moore.*

NISR BHB 85f **RR 77f** 4825[2]
2 b c Grand Lodge (USA) - Tharwa (IRE) **(60f)** (Last Tycoon) 8.5f **(62)**
Form - 802
Record 1999 - 1st:0 2nd:1 3rd:0 Ran:3
Win Prizemoney £0 *Total Prizemoney* £1,025
1999 Turf 0-3: (5f, 6f 2) (gd, g-f, hrd)
Currently above-average colt. Turf high 77 (began Aug) - 2nd of 22 to Spencers Wood (11 Oct Windsor 6f g-f RF 4825).
**J W Payne [0-3] C Cotran.*

NITE OWLER BHB 31f58a **RR 45f 58a** 3113[7]
5 b g Saddlers' Hall (IRE) 10.5f **(65)** - Lorne Lady (Local Suitor (USA)) 8.4f **(67)**
Form - 25416301217
Record 1999 - 1st:3 2nd:1 3rd:1 Ran:8
Pre1999 - 1st:1 2nd:1 3rd:0 Ran:14
Win Prizemoney £9,164 *Total Prizemoney* £10,656
Wins * **1999** *Jly Wolver (STD) H 7f 54 56* <
* **1999** *Jun Southw (STD) H 7f 50 52*
* **1999** *Mar Southw (STD) SH 6f 41 47*
* 1998 *Jun Southw (STD) H 6f 34 41*
1999 AW 3-8: (6f 1-5, 7f 2-3) (Fibr 3-8)
Fair gelding, effective 6 to 7f, best at 6f, - acts on Fibr, prefers left handed tracks, prefers tight tracks, excels at Southwell. AW high 60 - 3rd of 11 to John Bowdler Music (6 May Southwell 6f Fibr RF 1065) - also 1st of 12 getting 10lb from C-Harry (9 Jly

Wolverhampton RF 2690). He is an effective sort in modest handicap company on Fibresand at between six and seven furlongs.
**J Balding [4-19] Steer Arms Belton Racing Club (from J O'Reilly [0-2] Spt 1997).*

NITWITTY BHB 47f42a RR 45f 42a 5127[4]

5 b g Nomination 7.3f **(57)** - Dawn Ditty (Song) 7.2f **(61)**
Form - 08041740084
Record 1999 - 1st:1 2nd:0 3rd:0 Ran:11
Pre1999 - 1st:0 2nd:1 3rd:1 Ran:11
Win Prizemoney £2,668 *Total Prizemoney* £4,326
Wins * 1999 Jly Salisb (G-S) CH 6f 48 51 <
1999 Turf 1-10: (6f 1-6, 7f 4) (gd 5, g-f 2, frm 1-3) 1999 AW 0-1: (6f) (Fibr)
Moderate gelding, effective 6 to 7f, acts on gd. Turf high 51.
**R J Hodges [1-21] Unity Farm Holiday Centre Ltd (from P D Cundell [0-1] Oct 1996).*

NO ANIMOSITY (IRE) BHB 58f52a RR 65f 52a 292[10]

6 ch g Ajraas (USA) 7f **(53)** - Arctic Ford (FR) (Arctic Tern (USA)) 8.9f **(69)**
Form - 80
Record 1999 - 1st:0 2nd:0 3rd:0 Ran:2
Pre1999 - 1st:1 2nd:2 3rd:1 Ran:20
Win Prizemoney £73,500 *Total Prizemoney* £76,463
Wins 1995 Spt Currag (G-F) 6f 86+ <
1999 AW 0-2: (6f, 7f) (Fibr 2)
Average gelding, effective 6 to 8f, acted on sft to gd, often wore blinkers. AW high 43. (DEAD)
**W T Kemp [0-7] Langdale Racing (from D Hassett in IRE [0-20] Nov 1998).*

NOBALINO BHB 62f60a RR 56f 60a 5058[3]

5 ch h Sharpo 7.5f **(68)** - Zipperti Do (Precocious) 8.6f **(62)**
Form - 6720073
Record 1999 - 1st:0 2nd:1 3rd:1 Ran:7
Pre1999 - 1st:1 2nd:6 3rd:2 Ran:22
Win Prizemoney £1,944 *Total Prizemoney* £11,322
Wins 1997 *Dec Southw (STD) H 5f 59 67* <
1999 Turf 0-4: (7f 4) (g-s, gd 2, frm) 1999 AW 0-3: (5f 2, 7f) (Equi, Fibr 2)
Average colt, effective 5 to 7f, best at 5f, acts on gd to g-f - acts on Equi, has worn blinkers (effectively). Turf high 64 (1st run) (began Aug) - 2nd of 13 getting 12lb from Jocasta (19 Aug Yarmouth 7f gd RF 3766). AW high 60.
**Mrs V C Ward [0-5] Two Out & Hard Held (from A G Newcombe [0-2] Jun 1999).*

NOBBY BARNES BHB 36f32a RR 33f 32a 4829[7]

10 b g Nordance (USA) 7.4f **(69)** - Loving Doll (Godswalk (USA)) 7.3f **(58)**
Form - 847644053807
Record 1999 - 1st:0 2nd:0 3rd:1 Ran:12
Pre1999 - 1st:7 2nd:15 3rd:17 Ran:145
Win Prizemoney £23,137 *Total Prizemoney* £53,931
Wins * 1998 Jun Hamilt (SFT) H 9.2f 38 45
1999 Turf 0-12: (7f, 8f 8, 9f 3) (sft, gd 3, g-f 4, frm 4)
Very moderate gelding, effective 8 to 9f, best at 9f, acts on sft to gd, best on gd, likes right handed tracks. Turf high 50. Consistent.
**Don Enrico Incisa [1-94] Don Enrico Incisa (from D A Wilson [6-51] Jly 1994).*

NOBLE CALLING (FR) BHB 64f RR 70f 5215[14]

2 b c Caller I D (USA) - Specificity (USA) (Alleged (USA)) 10f **(76)**
Form - 0600
Record 1999 - 1st:0 2nd:0 3rd:0 Ran:4
1999 Turf 0-4: (7f, 8f 3) (g-s, gd, frm 2)
Above-average colt. Turf high 70 (began Aug).
**N A Graham [0-4] Fieldspring Racing.*

NOBLE CHARGER (IRE) BHB 46f38a RR 58f 38a 3115[14]

4 ch g Cadeaux Genereux 7.9f **(76)** - Shawgatny (USA) (Danzig Connection (USA)) 8f **(68)**
Form - 85008080
Record 1999 - 1st:0 2nd:0 3rd:0 Ran:8
Pre1999 - 1st:0 2nd:0 3rd:0 Ran:1
1999 Turf 0-6: (5f, 6f 3, 7f, 8f) (sft, gd, g-f, frm 3) 1999 AW 0-2: (5f, 6f) (Fibr 2)
Scopey, fair gelding, has worn blinkers. Turf high 58. AW high 13. Inconsistent.
**R F Marvin [0-8] R A B Saville (from E A L Dunlop [0-1] May 1998).*

NOBLE CYRANO BHB 56f RR 58f 4350[18]

4 ch g Generous (IRE) 11.5f **(82)** - Miss Bergerac (Bold Lad (IRE)) 8.4f **(68)**
Form - 50100
Record 1999 - 1st:1 2nd:0 3rd:0 Ran:5
Pre1999 - 1st:0 2nd:0 3rd:1 Ran:2
Win Prizemoney £3,018 *Total Prizemoney* £3,538
Wins * 1999 Aug Haydoc (G-S) H 8.1f 55 58 <
1999 Turf 1-5: (7f, 8f 1-3, 10f) (g-s, g-f 1-1, frm 3)
Workmanlike, fair gelding, likes tight tracks. Turf high 58.
**G Woodward [1-5] Wetherby Racing Bureau 38 (from G Wragg [0-2] Spt 1998).*

NOBLE FALCON RR 13f 4992[13]

3 gr g Polar Falcon (USA) 9f **(74)** - Noble Haven (Indian King (USA)) 7.4f **(64)**
Form - 0
Record 1999 - 1st:0 2nd:0 3rd:0 Ran:1
1999 Turf 0-1: (10f) (frm)
Light-framed, currently poor gelding.
**J W Hills [0-1] G Howard-Spink.*

NOBLELY (USA) BHB 57f56a RR 59f 56a 2915[7]

12 b g Lyphard (USA) 10.6f **(75)** - Nonoalca (FR) (Nonoalco (USA)) 8.5f **(66)**
Form - 2187
Record 1999 - 1st:1 2nd:1 3rd:0 Ran:4
Pre1999 - 1st:1 2nd:1 3rd:2 Ran:7
Win Prizemoney £6,381 *Total Prizemoney* £9,334
Wins * 1999 Jun Warwic (HVY) H 10.5f 55 59
1999 Turf 1-3: (8f, 10f, 11f 1-1) (sft, g-s 1-1, frm) 1999 AW 0-1: (8f) (Fibr)
Fair gelding, has worn blinkers. Turf high 59. He is a game old front runner and quite capable of winning another handicap or two if allowed his own way.
**M Tate [1-4] D H Cowgill (from N J H Walker [6-25] Jun 1995).*

NOBLE ONE BHB 99f RR 102df 5222[16]

3 ch f Primo Dominie 7.2f **(67)** - Noble Destiny (Dancing Brave (USA)) 8.4f **(76)**
Form - 1600
Record 1999 - 1st:1 2nd:0 3rd:0 Ran:4
Pre1999 - 1st:1 2nd:0 3rd:0 Ran:1
Win Prizemoney £9,672 *Total Prizemoney* £9,672
Wins * 1999 Jly Newmar (G-F) 5f 102 <
* 1998 Oct Catter (gd,) 5f 92++
1999 Turf 1-4: (5f 1-1, 6f 3) (g-s, gd, frm 1-2)
Scopey, very useful filly. Turf high 102 (1st run) (began Jly) - 1st of 8 from Flanders (23 Jly Newmarket RF 3061). She maintained her unblemished record when beating Flanders at Newmarket in July, but was a shade disappointing when stepped-up to Listed company. Well worth a try over seven furlongs, she is lightly raced ad open to some improvement.
**Sir Mark Prescott [2-5] Cheveley Park Stud.*

NOBLE PASAO (IRE) BHB 70f RR 71f 4762[15]

2 b g Alzao (USA) 9.8f **(73)** - Belle Passe (Be My Guest (USA)) 9.3f **(67)**
Form - 778010
Record 1999 - 1st:1 2nd:0 3rd:0 Ran:6
Win Prizemoney £4,396 *Total Prizemoney* £4,396
Wins * 1999 Spt Mussel (G-S) H 8f 67 71 <
1999 Turf 1-6: (5f 3, 6f, 8f 1-2) (gd 1-3, g-f, frm 2)
Above-average gelding, effective 8f, acts on gd, has worn blinkers. Turf high 71 - 1st of 14 getting 2lb from Springs Eternal (26 Spt Musselburgh RF 4575). **Andrew Turnell [1-6] Mrs Claire Hollowood.*

NOBLE PATRIOT BHB 33f33a RR 49f 33a 5050[15]

4 b g Polish Patriot (USA) 7.8f **(70)** - Noble Form (Double Form) 7.3f **(58)**
Form - 073845728700304000
Record 1999 - 1st:0 2nd:1 3rd:1 Ran:15

Pre1999 - 1st:0 2nd:0 3rd:2 Ran:11
Win Prizemoney £0 *Total Prizemoney* £2,025
1999 Turf 0-6: (5f, 6f 4, 8f) (gd, g-f, frm 3, hrd) 1999 AW 0-9: (5f 2, 6f 3, 7f 3, 9f) (Fibr 9)
Scopey, moderate gelding, effective 5 to 7f, acts on gd - acts on Fibr, has worn blinkers. Turf high 49. AW high 42 - 2nd of 12 getting 12lb from Approachable (6 Mar Wolverhampton 7f Fibr RF 0405). **R Hollinshead [0-26] The Four Dreamers.*

NOBLE PURSUIT BHB 86f **RR 84f** 4012[2]
2 b c Pursuit of Love 9.5f **(69)** - Noble Peregrine (Lomond)
Form - 412
Record 1999 - 1st:1 2nd:1 3rd:0 Ran:3
Win Prizemoney £3,350 *Total Prizemoney* £5,706
Wins * 1999 Aug Salisb (SFT) 7f 76+ <
1999 Turf 1-3: (7f 1-3) (g-f 1-2, frm)
Currently decent colt. Turf high 84 (began Jly) - 2nd of 8 to Queens Bench (30 Aug Epsom 7f g-f RF 4012) - also 1st of 18 getting 4lb from Fayrway Rhythm (12 Aug Salisbury RF 3570). Ran very green on his debut, and came on for the run in some style when landing a competitive Salisbury maiden over seven furlongs on soft ground next time. **T G Mills [1-3] Mrs Stephanie Merrydew.*

NOBLE REEF BHB 63f **RR 66f** 5158[14]
2 b c Deploy 11.4f **(67)** - Penny Mint (Mummy's Game) 8.2f **(60)**
Form - 74736860
Record 1999 - 1st:0 2nd:0 3rd:1 Ran:8
Win Prizemoney £0 *Total Prizemoney* £581
1999 Turf 0-7: (5f 2, 7f 4, 8f) (gd, g-f 2, frm 3, hrd) 1999 AW 0-1: (5f) (Fibr)
Average colt, effective 7f, acts on frm. Turf high 67.
**Mrs G S Rees [0-8] Lady Lilford.*

NOBLE SPLENDOUR BHB 72f **RR 72f** 5034[8]
2 ch c Grand Lodge (USA) - Haskeir (Final Straw) 7.9f **(64)**
Form - 78358
Record 1999 - 1st:0 2nd:0 3rd:1 Ran:5
Win Prizemoney £0 *Total Prizemoney* £972
1999 Turf 0-5: (6f 3, 7f 2) (g-s, gd 2, frm 2)
Above-average colt. Turf high 72 (began Jly) - 3rd of 10 to Akeed (1 Spt York 7f frm RF 4083). **L M Cumani [0-5] M J Dawson.*

NOBLE WATER (FR) BHB 26f41a **RR 21f 41a** 2685[10]
4 b f Noblequest (FR) - Bulle d'Eau (FR) (Faraway Son (USA)) 10.3f **(55)**
Form - 87301508060
Record 1999 - 1st:1 2nd:0 3rd:1 Ran:9
Pre1999 - 1st:0 2nd:0 3rd:0 Ran:5
Win Prizemoney £2,959 *Total Prizemoney* £3,315
Wins * 1999 *Feb Lingfi (STD) H 6f 35 41 <*
1999 Turf 0-5: (5f 2, 6f 3) (g-f 3, frm 2) 1999 AW 1-4: (6f 1-2, 7f 2) (Equi 1-4)
Moderate filly, effective 6f, - acts on Equi, likes left handed tracks, likes tight tracks. Turf high 21. AW high 41 - 1st of 11 getting 15lb from Miss Bananas (23 Feb Lingfield RF 0346).
**J J Bridger [1-14] M Z Tarlowski.*

NOBODY'S FOOL RR 2688[7]
4 ch g St Ninian - Majestic Form (IRE) (Double Schwartz) 7.9f **(55)**
Form - 7
Record 1999 - 1st:0 2nd:0 3rd:0 Ran:1
1999 AW 0-1: (12f) (Fibr)
Workmanlike, currently very poor gelding.
**M G Meagher [0-2] Greengate Lease Syndicate.*

NOCCIOLA RR 39f 1102[12]
3 ch f Cadeaux Genereux 7.9f **(76)** - Norpella (Northfields (USA)) 9f **(72)**
Form - 0
Record 1999 - 1st:0 2nd:0 3rd:0 Ran:1
1999 Turf 0-1: (5f) (gd)
Neat, currently very moderate filly.
**Sir Mark Prescott [0-1] William Fox.*

NOCKSKY (IRE) BHB 60f **RR 59f** 2000[8]
6 b g Niniski (USA) 13.2f **(67)** - Olivana (GER) (Sparkler) 8.4f **(55)**
Form - 08
Record 1999 - 1st:0 2nd:0 3rd:0 Ran:2
Pre1999 - 1st:1 2nd:2 3rd:2 Ran:11
Win Prizemoney £3,767 *Total Prizemoney* £6,565
Wins 1997 Spt Listow (SFT) H 16f 58 73 <
1999 Turf 0-2: (19f, 20f) (g-f 2)
Fair gelding. Turf high 59.
**M C Pipe [1-7] Terry Neill (from L Browne in IRE [2-13] Spt 1997).*

NO CLICHES BHB 57f **RR 59f** 1440[14]
6 ch g Risk Me (FR) 8f **(53)** - Always on a Sunday (Star Appeal) 9.6f **(65)**
Form - 00
Record 1999 - 1st:0 2nd:0 3rd:0 Ran:2
Pre1999 - 1st:2 2nd:6 3rd:4 Ran:36
Win Prizemoney £8,386 *Total Prizemoney* £19,207
Wins 1998 Mar Doncas (GD) H 10.3f 60 66
1995 Spt Doncas (G-F) H 8f 72 79 <
1999 Turf 0-2: (8f, 12f) (g-f 2)
Fair gelding, effective 9 to 12f, best at 10f, acts on gd to frm, best on gd, has worn blinkers, likes tight tracks, likes Beverley. Turf high 44.
**N Tinkler [0-2] J M G Promotions Ltd (from D Nicholls [1-23] Aug 1998).*

NO COMMITMENT (IRE) BHB 38f **RR 42f** 4671[9]
2 b g Brief Truce (USA) 9.1f **(73)** - Pleasant Memories **(54+f)** (Danehill (USA)) 10f **(72)**
Form - 000
Record 1999 - 1st:0 2nd:0 3rd:0 Ran:3
1999 Turf 0-3: (6f, 7f 2) (g-s, gd, g-f)
Currently moderate gelding. Turf high 42 (began Aug).
**H J Collingridge [0-3] L Westbury.*

NOCTURNE (IRE) BHB 53f49a **RR 61f 49a** 22[4]
4 b f Tenby 10.4f **(76)** - Phylella (Persian Bold) 9.3f **(66)**
Form - 34
Record 1999 - 1st:0 2nd:0 3rd:0 Ran:1
Pre1999 - 1st:0 2nd:2 3rd:1 Ran:12
Win Prizemoney £0 *Total Prizemoney* £2,334
1999 AW 0-1: (11f) (Fibr)
Unfurnished, average filly, effective 12 to 16f, best at 12f, acts on g-f - acts on AW, likes left handed tracks.
**S E Kettlewell [0-3] Uncle Jacks Pub (from J W Hills [0-11] Oct 1998).*

NOD'S NEPHEW RR 52f 4981[7]
2 b g Efisio 7.7f **(69)** - Nordan Raider **(58f 67a)** (Domynsky) 8f **(82)**
Form - 07
Record 1999 - 1st:0 2nd:0 3rd:0 Ran:2
1999 Turf 0-2: (6f 2) (g-f 2)
Currently fair gelding. Turf high 52 (began Aug).
**Miss J A Camacho [0-2] Brian Nordan.*

NOEL (GER) RR 113f 5013a[9]
4
Form - 150
1999 Turf 1-3: (11f 1-1, 12f 2) (hvy 1-1, sft)
Group-class. Turf high 113 (began Spt) - 9th giving 9lb to First Magnitude (17 Oct Longchamp 12f RF 5013a) - also 1st of 7 from Zomaradah (5 Spt San Siro RF 4248a).
**H Blume in GER [1-3] (in GER [0-1] Oct 1998).*

NO EXTRAS (IRE) BHB 67f90a **RR 69f 90a** 5126[7]
9 b g Efisio 7.7f **(69)** - Parkland Rose (Sweet Candy (VEN)) 6.4f **(103)**
Form - 00042100056847
Record 1999 - 1st:1 2nd:1 3rd:0 Ran:14
Pre1999 - 1st:9 2nd:12 3rd:10 Ran:80
Win Prizemoney £68,789 *Total Prizemoney* £135,615
Wins * 1999 Jun Windso (SFT) 8.3f 78
* 1998 Jun Newmar (GD) H 7f 87 92
* 1997 Jly Goodwo (G-F) H 8f 72 78
* 1997 Jun Goodwo (G-S) H 8f 62 67
* 1995 Aug Goodwo (G-F) H 6f 89 95 <
1999 Turf 1-14: (7f 4, 8f 1-6, 9f 2, 10f 2) (sft, gd 1-9, g-f 3, frm)
Average gelding, effective 7 to 8f, best at 8f, acts on gd to frm, has worn blinkers, likes right handed tracks, likes tight tracks. Turf high 78. Consistent. A versatile handicapper, he regained winning form in a Windsor classified stakes in June but has been well held

since, and is consequently dropping down the handicap.
**G L Moore [9-84] K Higson (from J Sutcliffe [1-10] Nov 1992).*

NO FOOL (IRE) BHB 28f RR 6f 3009[12]

3 b f Distinctly North (USA) 7.4f **(63)** - Chez Nous (Habitat) 9.4f **(70)**
Form - 070
Record 1999 - 1st:0 2nd:0 3rd:0 Ran:3
1999 Turf 0-3: (8f 3) (g-f, frm, hrd)
Leggy, currently very poor filly. Turf high 6.
**J S Moore [0-3] P Henley.*

NOIRIE BHB 32f RR 33f 4983[8]

5 br g Warning 8.1f **(77)** - Callipoli (USA) (Green Dancer (USA)) 10.3f **(74)**
Form - 004000378
Record 1999 - 1st:0 2nd:0 3rd:1 Ran:9
Pre1999 - 1st:1 2nd:0 3rd:0 Ran:16
Win Prizemoney £2,237 *Total Prizemoney* £3,692
Wins * 1998 Jun Pontef (HVY) H 10f 38 40 <
1999 Turf 0-9: (10f 7, 12f 2) (sft 3, g-s, gd, g-f 3, frm)
Very moderate gelding, effective 8 to 10f, acts on g-s to g-f, has worn blinkers, likes tight tracks. Turf high 33.
**M Brittain [1-25] Miss Debi Woods.*

NO MERCY BHB 76a RR 69f 4018[4]

3 ch c Faustus (USA) 9.1f **(54)** - Nashville Blues (IRE) **(74f)** (Try My Best (USA)) 7.6f **(67)**
Form - 143334
Record 1999 - 1st:1 2nd:0 3rd:3 Ran:6
Pre1999 - 1st:0 2nd:0 3rd:0 Ran:3
Win Prizemoney £2,558 *Total Prizemoney* £6,023
Wins * **1999** *Apr Lingfi (STD) 10f 73 <*
1999 Turf 0-5: (8f 3, 9f, 10f) (g-f 2, frm 2, hrd) 1999 AW 1-1: (10f 1-1) (Equi 1-1)
Workmanlike, above-average colt, effective 8 to 10f, acts on g-f to hrd - acts on Equi, favours tight tracks. Turf high 70 - 3rd of 15 giving 14lb to Pacific Alliance (11 Jun Sandown 8f frm RF 1921). (1st run) - 1st of 4 from Son of Snurge (9 Apr Lingfield RF 0631). Consistent. His only win to date came over ten furlongs on Equitrack in April, though he made the frame in handicap company several times on turf afterwards.
**J W Hills [1-9] Freddy Bienstock.*

NOM FRANCAIS BHB 28f RR 33f 4000[10]

3 b f First Trump - Eastern Ember (Indian King (USA)) 7.4f **(64)**
Form - 07270230
Record 1999 - 1st:0 2nd:2 3rd:1 Ran:8
Pre1999 - 1st:0 2nd:0 3rd:0 Ran:3
Win Prizemoney £0 *Total Prizemoney* £1,561
1999 Turf 0-8: (10f 2, 12f, 14f, 16f 3, 17f) (hvy, gd 2, g-f, frm 3, hrd)
Neat, very moderate filly, has worn blinkers. Turf high 33.
**R Guest [0-10] M Sakal (from Dr J D Scargill [0-1] Apr 1998).*

NOMINATOR LAD BHB 79f72a RR 79f 72a 4683[26]

5 b g Nomination 7.3f **(57)** - Ankara's Princess (USA) (Ankara (USA)) 8f **(71)**
Form - 001028080
Record 1999 - 1st:1 2nd:1 3rd:0 Ran:9
Pre1999 - 1st:4 2nd:2 3rd:1 Ran:25
Win Prizemoney £37,829 *Total Prizemoney* £45,608
Wins * **1999** Apr Pontef (SFT) H 8f 76 82 <
* 1998 Spt Ayr (G-S) H 8f 75 79
* 1998 *Jun Wolver (STD) H 8.5f 70 70*
* 1997 Spt Haydoc (GD) H 7.1f 67 71
* 1997 Jly Nottin (G-F) 8.2f 72
1999 Turf 1-9: (8f 1-7, 10f 2) (sft 1-1, gd 5, g-f, frm 2)
Above-average gelding, effective 8f, acts on sft to gd, best on sft, prefers left handed tracks, prefers tight tracks, excels at Haydock. Turf high 82 - 1st of 19 giving 14lb to Ca'd'oro (20 Apr Pontefract RF 0773). Came with a late run to win a Showcase event at Pontefract on his third start of last season but, although a good second in a similar race at Haydock, he is inconsistent and cannot always be relied upon to reproduce those efforts.
**B A McMahon [5-34] J D Graham.*

NO MORE HASSLE (IRE) BHB 38f40a RR 33f 40a 4726[8]

6 ch g Magical Wonder (USA) 7.2f **(60)** - Friendly Ann (Artaius (USA)) 9f **(69)**
Form - 8
Record 1999 - 1st:0 2nd:0 3rd:0 Ran:1
Pre1999 - 1st:1 2nd:1 3rd:1 Ran:12
Win Prizemoney £2,785 *Total Prizemoney* £3,977
Wins * 1996 Nov Folkes (SFT) CH 16.4f 34 43 <
1999 Turf 0-1: (16f) (gd)
Very moderate gelding. Consistent.
**Mrs M Reveley [6-34] The No Hassle Partnership.*

NOMORE MR NICEGUY BHB 87f97a RR 82f 97a 4915[11]

5 b h Rambo Dancer (CAN) 8.4f **(59)** - Lariston Gale (Pas de Seul) 9.1f **(67)**
Form - 115340024013260652OO
Record 1999 - 1st:1 2nd:3 3rd:2 Ran:18
Pre1999 - 1st:6 2nd:6 3rd:8 Ran:49
Win Prizemoney £43,972 *Total Prizemoney* £102,976
Wins * **1999** Jun Cheste (G-F) H 6.1f 83 86
* 1998 *Dec Lingfi (STD) 8f 94 <*
* 1998 *Nov Wolver (STD) H 7f 90 94 <*
* 1998 Jun Cheste (GD) H 7f 79 90+
* 1997 *Mar Wolver (STD) H 7f 84 88*
* 1996 *Dec Wolver (STD) H 7f 78 84*
* 1996 Jly Hamilt (GD) 5f 67
1999 Turf 1-16: (6f 1-1, 7f 9, 8f 6) (g-s 2, gd 8, g-f 3, frm 1-3) 1999 AW 0-2: (6f, 8f) (Fibr 2)
Very useful colt, effective 6 to 8f, best at 8f, acts on gd - acts on AW, best on Fibr, has worn blinkers, likes left handed tracks, prefers tight tracks, excels at Wolverhampton, likes Chester. Turf high 89. AW high 101 - 3rd of 13 giving 11lb to Captain Scott (13 Mar Wolverhampton 8f Fibr RF 0431). Tough and genuine, he had a solid season in top handicap company. Effective from six furlongs to a mile and on any ground, he takes plenty of stoking and needs a strong rider. **E J Alston [7-67] Mrs Carol McPhail.*

NON VINTAGE (IRE) BHB 35f47a RR 40f 47a 1300[7]

8 ch g Shy Groom (USA) 8.2f **(59)** - Great Alexandra (Runnett) 7f **(59)**
Form - 7
Record 1999 - 1st:0 2nd:0 3rd:0 Ran:1
Pre1999 - 1st:2 2nd:5 3rd:7 Ran:46
Win Prizemoney £9,212 *Total Prizemoney* £21,408
1999 Turf 0-1: (18f) (gd)
Fair gelding, has worn blinkers.
**M C Chapman [6-97] Alan Mann (from M H Easterby [1-17] Aug 1994).*

NOOSHMAN (USA) BHB 81f RR 87+f 4860[2]

2 ch c Woodman (USA) 9.7f **(77)** - Knoosh (USA) (Storm Bird (CAN)) 10.3f **(74)**
Form - 252
Record 1999 - 1st:0 2nd:2 3rd:0 Ran:3
Win Prizemoney £0 *Total Prizemoney* £2,210
1999 Turf 0-3: (7f 3) (g-s, gd 2)
Currently useful colt. Turf high 87 (1st run) (began Aug) - 2nd of 6 to Chinatown (30 Aug Newcastle 7f gd RF 4021).
**Sir Michael Stoute [0-3] Maktoum Al Maktoum.*

NOPALEA BHB 39f58a RR 18f 58a 3871[10]

5 b m Warrshan (USA) 9.7f **(59)** - Nophe (USA) (Super Concorde (USA)) 10.9f **(66)**
Form - 450070
Record 1999 - 1st:0 2nd:0 3rd:0 Ran:6
Pre1999 - 1st:1 2nd:3 3rd:6 Ran:19
Win Prizemoney £3,613 *Total Prizemoney* £10,094
Wins * 1997 Jun Warwic (G-F) H 5f 66 66 <
1999 Turf 0-6: (5f 5, 6f) (sft, g-s, gd, g-f 2, hrd)
Moderate filly, has worn blinkers. Turf high 53. Becoming disappointing.
**T J Naughton [1-19] T J Naughton (from C E Brittain [0-6] Oct 1996).*

NO PASS NO HONOR (FR) RR 46f 5059[11]

2 b c Highest Honor (FR) 10.9f **(72)** - Marzipan (IRE) **(61f)** (Green Desert (USA)) 8.6f **(78)**
Form - 70
Record 1999 - 1st:0 2nd:0 3rd:0 Ran:2
1999 Turf 0-2: (7f 2) (g-s, g-f)
Currently moderate colt. Turf high 46 (began Jly).
**S Dow [0-2] D G Churston.*

NORCROFT JOY BHB 72f **RR 71f** 5221^{6}

4 b f Rock Hopper 10.6f **(54)** - Greenhills Joy (Radetzky) 9.8f **(56)**

Form - 100815436056

Record	**1999** -	1st:2	2nd:0	3rd:1	Ran:12
	Pre1999 -	1st:4	2nd:2	3rd:0	Ran:13

Win Prizemoney £22,980 *Total Prizemoney* £25,554

Wins								
	1999	Jun	Doncas (GD)	H	12f	73	74	<
	1999	Mar	Warwic (G-S)	H	12.5f	70	73	
	1998	Spt	Haydoc (GD)	H	11.9f	61	70	
	1998	Aug	Beverl (G-F)	H	12f	54	57	
	1998	Aug	Hamilt (SFT)	H	12.1f	54	61	
	1998	Jun	Yarmou (SFT)	H	14.1f	52	60	

1999 Turf 2-12: (12f 1-8, 13f 1-3, 14f) (hvy, sft, g-s 1-2, gd 2, g-f 1-3, frm 3)

Leggy, above-average filly, effective 12 to 13f, best at 12f, acts on sft to frm, does well at Doncaster, likes Beverley. Turf high 74 - 1st of 13 getting 9lb from Legal Lunch (5 Jun Doncaster RF 1752) - also 1st of 7 getting 5lb from Chief Cashier (27 Mar Warwick RF 0489). Consistent. She performed much better after being stepped up in trip in 1998, winning four times in all, and began 1999 in similar vein with a victory at Warwick. Has since added a Doncaster victory in June, and is a very tough filly. Suited by hold-up tactics.

**N A Callaghan [0-2] Norcroft Park Stud (from M J Ryan [6-23] Spt 1999).*

NORDANSK BHB 43f44a **RR 50f 44a** 1446^{14}

10 ch g Nordance (USA) 7.4f **(69)** -Free on Board (Free State) 8.7f **(61)**

Form - 0

Record	**1999** -	1st:0	2nd:0	3rd:0	Ran:1
	Pre1999 -	1st:1	2nd:3	3rd:1	Ran:28

Win Prizemoney £3,696 *Total Prizemoney* £8,154

Wins * 1996 Jun Kempto (GD) H 12f 48 55 <

1999 Turf 0-1: (12f) (frm)

Fair gelding. Consistent.

**M Madgwick [7-56] T Smith (from L J Holt [0-6] Nov 1992).*

NORDICAN INCH RR 94f $3586a^{2}$

3 ch f Inchinor 8.9f **(64)** - Fee Des Mers (FR) (Alzao (USA)) 7.1f **(68)**

Form - 2

1999 Turf 0-1: (10f) (hvy)

Currently useful filly. (1st run) - 2nd of 8 to Welluna (7 Aug Deauville 10f hvy RF 3586a). **H-A Pantall in FR [0-1].*

NORDIC STAR RR 15f 2846^{9}

3 b g Cosmonaut - Could Have Been (Nomination) 7f **(60)**

Form - 000

Record	**1999** -	1st:0	2nd:0	3rd:0	Ran:3

1999 Turf 0-3: (7f 2, 8f) (gd 2, g-f)

Workmanlike, currently poor gelding. Turf high 15.

**J J Quinn [0-3] Mrs Marie Taylor.*

NORDINEX (IRE) BHB 32f38a **RR 32f 38a** 4997^{16}

7 b g Nordico (USA) 8.2f **(59)** - Debbie's Next (USA) (Arctic Tern (USA)) 8.9f **(69)**

Form - 878600

Record	**1999** -	1st:0	2nd:0	3rd:0	Ran:3
	Pre1999 -	1st:4	2nd:0	3rd:5	Ran:38

Win Prizemoney £19,947 *Total Prizemoney* £24,095

Wins								
	1996	*Feb*	*Lingfi (STD)*	*H*	*8f*	*65*	*67*	
	1995	Jly	Newmar (G-F)	H	8f	75	78	<
	1995	Jun	Kempto (G-F)	H	8f	70	75	
	1995	*Jan*	*Lingfi (STD)*	*H*	*8f*	*68*	*67*	

1999 Turf 0-3: (8f, 10f, 11f) (gd, g-f 2)

Moderate gelding, effective 8f, acts on g-f, has worn blinkers, likes left handed tracks. Turf high 32 (1st run) (began Jly) - 6th of 19 getting 1lb from Mezzoramio (2 Jly Warwick 8f g-f RF 2505).

**P Hayward [0-17] A J Byrne (from D R C Elsworth [0-5] Nov 1997).*

NO REGRETS BHB 65f60a **RR 64f 60a** 5000^{8}

2 b c Bin Ajwaad (IRE) - Marton Maid (Silly Season) 9.7f **(56)**

Form - 83468

Record	**1999** -	1st:0	2nd:0	3rd:1	Ran:5

Win Prizemoney £0 *Total Prizemoney* £810

1999 Turf 0-5: (6f, 8f 2, 9f, 10f) (gd 3, frm 2)

Average colt. Turf high 64. **M Quinn [0-5] Mrs J M Ferguson.*

NO RESERVE (USA) BHB 65f **RR 65f** 2384^{7}

3 b f Gone West (USA) 7.8f **(82)** - Milly Ha Ha **(101f)** (Dancing Brave (USA)) 8.4f **(76)**

Form - 587

Record	**1999** -	1st:0	2nd:0	3rd:0	Ran:3
	Pre1999 -	1st:0	2nd:0	3rd:0	Ran:1

1999 Turf 0-3: (10f 2, 12f) (gd, g-f 2)

Light-framed, average filly. Turf high 65.

**H R A Cecil [0-4] Cliveden Stud.*

NORFOLK REED (IRE) RR 88f 3966^{12}

2 b c Thatching 7.8f **(69)** - Sawaki (Song) 7.2f **(61)**

Form - 1720

Record	**1999** -	1st:1	2nd:1	3rd:0	Ran:4

Win Prizemoney £3,114 *Total Prizemoney* £4,392

Wins * 1999 May Lingfi (G-F) 5f 69+ <

1999 Turf 1-4: (5f 1-1, 6f 3) (gd, g-f 1-1, frm 2)

Useful colt. Turf high 88 - 2nd of 11 getting 5lb from Our Ambition (4 Aug Kempton 6f frm RF 3354). He made a winning debut over the minimum at Lingfield, but never figured in the Woodcote. Fair effort in a nursery on his third run after a two-month break, but well beaten in a more competitive event at Newmarket next time.

**R Hannon [1-4] The South-Western Partnership.*

NORLING (IRE) BHB 30f39a **RR 26f 39a** 2395^{9}

9 ch g Nashamaa 8.1f **(58)** - Now Then (Sandford Lad) 7.8f **(54)**

Form - 000

Record	**1999** -	1st:0	2nd:0	3rd:0	Ran:3
	Pre1999 -	1st:5	2nd:3	3rd:5	Ran:56

Win Prizemoney £12,211 *Total Prizemoney* £17,403

Wins 1995 Aug Salisb (G-F) CH 6f 47 51

1999 Turf 0-3: (6f 3) (g-f 2, frm)

Moderate gelding. Turf high 26.

**J S Wainwright [0-3] S Pedersen (from K O Cunningham-Brown [2-39] Jly 1998).*

NORTH ARDAR BHB 44f46a **RR 49f 46a** 5151^{9}

9 b g Ardar 9.5f **(63)** - Langwaite (Seaepic (USA)) 9f **(56)**

Form - 805563312300

Record	**1999** -	1st:1	2nd:1	3rd:3	Ran:12
	Pre1999 -	1st:14	2nd:10	3rd:7	Ran:73

Win Prizemoney £41,230 *Total Prizemoney* £55,795

Wins							
*	**1999**	*Jun*	*Southw (STD)*	*S*	*11f*		*50*
	1998	*Feb*	*Lingfi (STD)*	*H*	*12f*	*40*	*46*
	1998	*Jan*	*Lingfi (STD)*	*H*	*10f*	*35*	*41*
	1996	*Spt*	*Southw (STD)*	*H*	*8f*	*52*	*57*
	1996	Aug	Hamilt (G-F)	S	8.3f		60
	1996	Jly	Ripon (GD)	S	10f		57
	1996	Jun	Redcar (FRM)	C	10f		60
	1996	Jun	Pontef (G-F)	S	10f		53
	1996	May	Catter (GD)	S	10.2f		60
	1995	Jly	Mussel (G-F)	H	11.1f	53	58
	1995	Jun	Thirsk (G-F)	H	12f	50	54

1999 Turf 0-3: (8f, 11f, 12f) (gd, g-f, frm) 1999 AW 1-9: (7f, 8f 2, 11f 1-3, 12f 2, 13f) (Equi 2, Fibr 1-7)

Fair gelding, effective 10 to 13f, best at 11f, acts on frm - acts on AW, best on Fibr, has worn blinkers, likes Southwell and Lingfield. Turf high 49 (1st run) - 3rd of 20 to Tajar (24 May Windsor 12f frm RF 1446). AW high 50 - 2nd of 16 to Count de Money (17 Jun Southwell 11f Fibr RF 2083) - also 1st of 13 from Muhassil (11 Jun Southwell RF 1930). Consistent.

**R Brotherton [1-12] Paul Stringer (from N P Littmoden [2-7] Feb 1998).*

NORTHERN ACCORD BHB 45f **RR 45f** 511^{9}

5 b g Akarad (FR) 9.7f **(73)** - Sioux City (Simply Great (FR)) 8.2f **(65)**

Form - 0

Record	**1999** -	1st:0	2nd:0	3rd:0	Ran:1
	Pre1999 -	1st:2	2nd:0	3rd:0	Ran:9

Win Prizemoney £5,222 *Total Prizemoney* £5,520

Wins								
	1998	Spt	Beverl (G-F)	H	9.9f	41	45	<
	1998	Aug	Hamilt (SFT)	H	8.3f	37	39	

1999 Turf 0-1: (14f) (sft)

Moderate gelding, effective 8 to 12f, best at 10f, acts on gd to g-f, best on gd.

**M Dods [0-4] Bernard Hathaway (from Mrs J R Ramsden [2-10] Oct 1998).*

NORTHERN CHARMER BHB 27f28a **RR 45f 28a** 25[9]
7 b g Charmer 9f **(59)** - Trading (Forlorn River) 7.3f **(54)**
Form - 0
Record 1999 - 1st:0 2nd:0 3rd:0 Ran:1
Pre1999 - 1st:0 2nd:0 3rd:0 Ran:7
1999 AW 0-1: (16f) (Fibr)
Moderate gelding.
**E J Alston [1-11] The Bibby Halliday Partnership (from M G Meagher [0-5] May 1995).*

NORTHERN ECHO RR 57f 2221[14]
2 b g Pursuit of Love 9.5f **(69)** - Stop Press (USA) (Sharpen Up) 8.3f **(67)**
Form - 0
Record 1999 - 1st:0 2nd:0 3rd:0 Ran:1
1999 Turf 0-1: (6f) (frm)
Currently fair gelding. **M Dods [0-1] M J K Dods.*

NORTHERN FLEET BHB 68f **RR 69f** 4218[9]
6 b g Slip Anchor 12.7f **(75)** - Kamkova (USA) (Northern Dancer) 9.6f **(80)**
Form - 5170
Record 1999 - 1st:1 2nd:0 3rd:0 Ran:4
Pre1999 - 1st:1 2nd:2 3rd:1 Ran:11
Win Prizemoney £7,153 *Total Prizemoney* £14,268
Wins * **1999** Jly Salisb (FRM) H 14.1f 65 69
1996 Aug Beverl (G-F) 16.2f 72 <
1999 Turf 1-4: (14f 1-3, 16f) (gd, g-f, frm 1-2)
Average gelding, has worn blinkers. Turf high 69 (began Jly). Showed some good form on the Flat in '96, notably when failing by a neck to spoil the Dettori Seven on its last leg. Although he has been campaigned over hurdles for the most part since, he made a pleasing return to action on the level last term, and picked up a modest handicap over a mile and three-quarters at Salisbury on fast ground.
**Mrs A J Perrett [2-19] Cotton, Elliott, Fearn (from G Harwood [1-7] Oct 1996).*

NORTHERN LAW BHB 48f **RR 51f** 2724[10]
7 gr g Law Society (USA) 11.6f **(71)** - Pharland (FR) (Bellypha) 9.8f **(73)**
Form - 70
Record 1999 - 1st:0 2nd:0 3rd:0 Ran:2
Pre1999 - 1st:2 2nd:1 3rd:0 Ran:12
Win Prizemoney £7,453 *Total Prizemoney* £8,789
Wins 1995 Aug Thirsk (FRM) H 16f 69 74
1995 Aug Catter (G-F) H 15.8f 65 75 <
1999 Turf 0-2: (14f, 16f) (g-f 2)
Fair gelding. Turf high 51. Inconsistent.
**J G Smyth-Osbourne [0-2] J G Smyth-Osbourne (from John Berry [0-3] Aug 1996).*

NORTHERN LIFE (IRE) BHB 40f **RR 30f** 4994[8]
2 b f Distinctly North (USA) 7.4f **(63)** - Another Way (Wolverlife) 9.3f **(54)**
Form - 008
Record 1999 - 1st:0 2nd:0 3rd:0 Ran:3
1999 Turf 0-3: (7f 2, 8f) (g-s, gd, g-f)
Currently very moderate filly. Turf high 30 (began Aug).
**P Shakespeare [0-3] Midas Touch.*

NORTHERN LORD BHB 22f **RR 35f** 4438[9]
3 ch g Northern Park (USA) 10f **(57)** - Miss Trilli (Ardoon) 7.3f **(53)**
Form - 00000
Record 1999 - 1st:0 2nd:0 3rd:0 Ran:5
1999 Turf 0-5: (7f, 8f 2, 10f, 11f) (g-f 3, frm 2)
Leggy, very moderate gelding. Turf high 35 (began Jly).
**R J R Williams [0-5] Partners In Percy.*

NORTHERN MOTTO BHB 53f47a **RR 55f 47a** 5188[7]
6 b g Mtoto 11.5f **(71)** - Soulful (FR) (Zino) 12.9f **(54)**
Form - 405311842447
Record 1999 - 1st:2 2nd:1 3rd:1 Ran:12
Pre1999 - 1st:6 2nd:2 3rd:3 Ran:38
Win Prizemoney £44,263 *Total Prizemoney* £52,015
Wins * **1999** Jly Cheste (G-F) H 15.9f 52 54
* **1999** Jun Mussel (G-F) H 16f 50 53
* 1998 Jly Cheste (G-F) H 15.9f 56 60 <
* 1998 May Mussel (G-S) H 16f 55 58
* 1998 Apr Mussel (G-S) H 16f 48 59
* 1997 Jun Doncas (G-F) H 12f 50 55
* *1997 Feb Wolver (STD) H 12f 52 57*
* 1996 Nov Mussel (G-S) H 15.1f 47 54
1999 Turf 2-12: (13f, 15f, 16f 2-9, 18f) (hvy, gd 2, g-f 1-5, frm 1-4)
Fair gelding, effective 15 to 16f, best at 16f, acts on gd to frm, best on gd, likes right handed tracks, excels at Ascot and Chester and does well at Musselburgh. Turf high 55 (1st run) - 4th of 8 giving 13lb to Batoutoftheblue (1 Apr Musselburgh 16f g-f RF 0550) - also 1st of 17 getting 13lb from Salska (10 Jly Chester RF 2709). Consistent. Came good to win over two miles at his beloved Musselburgh on fast ground in June, and followed up in the same Chester handicap that he had won the previous year.
**J S Goldie [8-49] Martin Delaney (from W Storey [0-3] Oct 1996).*

NORTHERN QUEST RR 110f 1072a[5]
4 c
Form - 5
1999 Turf 0-1: (11f) (gd)
Currently Group-class colt, always wears blinkers. He cut no ice against top-class opposition in the Prix Ganay.
**A Fabre in FR [0-1] J-L Legardere.*

NORTHERN SPRING (IRE) BHB 89f **RR 91f** 3355[4]
3 ch c Common Grounds 8.1f **(66)** - North Telstar (Sallust) 8.4f **(63)**
Form - 2212784
Record 1999 - 1st:1 2nd:3 3rd:0 Ran:7
Pre1999 - 1st:0 2nd:1 3rd:0 Ran:2
Win Prizemoney £3,475 *Total Prizemoney* £9,534
Wins * **1999** Apr Redcar (G-S) 7f 89 <
1999 Turf 1-7: (6f, 7f 1-3, 8f 3) (gd 1-3, g-f 2, frm 2)
Scopey, useful colt, effective 6 to 8f, best at 8f, acts on gd to frm. Turf high 91 - 2nd of 7 giving 2lb to Barrister (5 Jun Haydock 8f gd RF 1769) - also 1st of 16 from Nabonassar (29 Apr Redcar RF 0920). Consistent. He showed his best form over seven furlongs including winning at Redcar maiden, but appeared not to stay a mile. **M J Heaton-Ellis [1-9] Fieldspring Racing.*

NORTHERN SUN BHB 68f54a **RR 72f 54a** 1540[3]
5 b g Charmer 9f **(59)** - Princess Dancer (Alzao (USA)) 7.1f **(68)**
Form - 053203
Record 1999 - 1st:0 2nd:1 3rd:2 Ran:5
Pre1999 - 1st:3 2nd:1 3rd:2 Ran:20
Win Prizemoney £11,789 *Total Prizemoney* £16,769
Wins * 1997 Mar Kempto (GD) H 9f 79 85 <
* 1996 Aug Bright (FRM) H 7f 83 77
* 1996 Jly Bright (FRM) 7f 71
1999 Turf 0-4: (8f, 9f, 10f 2) (g-s, g-f 3) 1999 AW 0-1: (13f) (Equi)
Above-average gelding, effective 10f, acts on frm, has worn blinkers, likes left handed tracks. Turf high 72. Inconsistent.
**T G Mills [3-25] John Humphreys (Turf Accountants) Ltd.*

NORTHERN SVENGALI (IRE) BHB 79f78a **RR 83f 78a** 1564[4]
3 b g Distinctly North (USA) 7.4f **(63)** - Trilby's Dream (IRE) (Mansooj)
Form - 53530444
Record 1999 - 1st:0 2nd:0 3rd:0 Ran:4
Pre1999 - 1st:2 2nd:6 3rd:2 Ran:16
Win Prizemoney £6,878 *Total Prizemoney* £16,416
Wins * 1998 Oct Catter (G-S) H 5f 79 82 <
* 1998 Spt Catter (G-F) 6f 80
1999 Turf 0-4: (5f, 6f 3) (hvy, gd, g-f, frm)
Unfurnished, decent gelding, effective 5 to 6f, best at 6f, acts on hvy to frm - acts on AW, excels at Catterick, likes Doncaster. Turf high 83 - 4th of 12 getting 18lb from Mitcham (15 May Newmarket 6f g-f RF 1244). Consistent. **T D Barron [2-20] Timothy Cox.*

NORTHERN TIMES (USA) RR 45f 1261[10]
2 ch c Cahill Road (USA) 8.5f **(82)** - Northern Nation (USA) (Northrop (USA))
Form - 0
Record 1999 - 1st:0 2nd:0 3rd:0 Ran:1
1999 Turf 0-1: (6f) (gd)
Currently moderate colt. **T D Easterby [0-1] Times of Wigan.*

NORTHERNTOWN (USA) RR 110f 5121a[3]
3 b c Manila (USA) 10f **(81)** - Egyptown (FR) (Top Ville) 11.7f **(68)**
Form - 2123
1999 Turf 1-4: (13f, 15f 1-2, 16f) (hvy 2, gd 1-2)
Group-class colt. Turf high 110 - 3rd of 7 to Amilynx (24 Oct Longchamp 16f hvy RF 5121a) - also 1st of 9 from Rhagaas (7 Spt Longchamp RF 4360a). A thorough stayer, he out-battled Rhagaas in the Group 3 Prix de Lutece at Longchamp in September. Connections are reported to be eyeing up the Millennium Ascot Gold Cup, but he will need to improve to figure there.
**F Head in FR [1-4].*

NORTHERN TRIO (FR) BHB 57f **RR 58f** 5209[16]
2 b g Aragon 7.7f **(58)** - Northern Notion (USA) (Northern Baby (CAN)) 11.6f **(71)**
Form - 800
Record 1999 - 1st:0 2nd:0 3rd:0 Ran:3
1999 Turf 0-3: (6f 3) (g-s, gd 2)
Currently fair gelding. Turf high 58 (began Spt).
**D Carroll [0-3] T McCullough & W C Anthony.*

NORTHERN VILLAGE BHB 38f35a **RR 35a** 2108[8]
12 ch g Norwick (USA) 9.4f **(51)** - Merokette (Blast)
Form - 788
Record 1999 - 1st:0 2nd:0 3rd:0 Ran:3
Pre1999 - 1st:0 2nd:0 3rd:0 Ran:7
1999 Turf 0-1: (22f) (g-f) 1999 AW 0-2: (16f 2) (Equi 2)
Very moderate gelding. AW high 33.
**L A Dace [0-15] L P Dace (from S Dow [4-27] Aug 1993).*

NORTH FACE RR 65f 3364[8]
2 ch g Factual (USA) - Northgate Dancer (Ile de Bourbon (USA)) 10.1f **(67)**
Form - 38
Record 1999 - 1st:0 2nd:0 3rd:1 Ran:2
Win Prizemoney £0 *Total Prizemoney* £343
1999 Turf 0-2: (6f 2) (frm, hrd)
Currently average gelding. Turf high 65 (1st run) (began Jly) - 3rd of 9 getting 1lb from Dispol Jazz (3 Jly Carlisle 6f frm RF 2518).
**J J O'Neill [0-2] Mrs L R Joughin.*

NORTHGATE (IRE) BHB 46f **RR 47f** 5026[8]
3 b c Thatching 7.8f **(69)** - Tender Time (Tender King) 6.8f **(54)**
Form - 0447045208
Record 1999 - 1st:0 2nd:1 3rd:0 Ran:10
Pre1999 - 1st:0 2nd:0 3rd:0 Ran:4
Win Prizemoney £0 *Total Prizemoney* £1,377
1999 Turf 0-10: (7f 5, 8f 4, 9f) (sft, gd, g-f 2, frm 5, hrd)
Leggy, moderate colt, often wears blinkers. Turf high 49.
**M Brittain [0-14] Mel Brittain.*

NORTH OF KALA (IRE) BHB 24f28a **RR 37f 28a** 4630[10]
6 b g Distinctly North (USA) 7.4f **(63)** - Hi Kala (Kampala) 8.5f **(56)**
Form - 0500
Record 1999 - 1st:0 2nd:0 3rd:0 Ran:4
Pre1999 - 1st:0 2nd:0 3rd:0 Ran:6
1999 Turf 0-1: (12f) (g-s) 1999 AW 0-3: (11f, 16f 2) (Equi, Fibr 2)
Very moderate gelding, has worn blinkers. AW high 33. Inconsistent.
**G L Moore [0-9] B Lennard (from S J Treacy in IRE [0-15] Jun 1998).*

NORTHWING BHB 44f **RR 49f** 5152[8]
3 b g Minshaanshu Amad (USA) 11.3f **(53)** - Kicking Bird (Bold Owl) 8.5f **(45)**
Form - 008
Record 1999 - 1st:0 2nd:0 3rd:0 Ran:3
Pre1999 - 1st:0 2nd:0 3rd:0 Ran:2
1999 Turf 0-3: (10f 2, 14f) (sft, gd, frm)
Strong, moderate gelding. Turf high 49.
**G B Balding [0-1] Mrs D Claessen-Brierton (from E A Wheeler [0-4] Apr 1999).*

NORTON (IRE) BHB 91f **RR 84+f** 5157[1]
2 ch c Barathea (IRE) - Primrose Valley (Mill Reef (USA)) 10.5f **(78)**
Form - 501
Record 1999 - 1st:1 2nd:0 3rd:0 Ran:3
Win Prizemoney £3,452 *Total Prizemoney* £3,452
Wins * 1999 Nov Redcar (G-S) 7f 84+ <
1999 Turf 1-3: (7f 1-2, 8f) (gd 2, frm 1-1)
Currently decent colt. Turf high 84 (began Spt) - 1st of 15 from Wathbat Mujtahid (1 Nov Redcar RF 5157). Off the mark at Redcar on his third start, and can win races next season.
**T G Mills [1-3] T G Mills.*

NOSEY NATIVE BHB 44f37a **RR 35f 37a** 2716[7]
6 b g Cyrano de Bergerac 7.3f **(58)** - Native Flair (Be My Native (USA)) 10.2f **(71)**
Form - 6553877
Record 1999 - 1st:0 2nd:0 3rd:1 Ran:5
Pre1999 - 1st:5 2nd:3 3rd:5 Ran:50
Win Prizemoney £16,287 *Total Prizemoney* £21,790
Wins * 1998 Aug Catter (G-F) H 12f 44 46
* 1998 Jun Ripon (SFT) H 12.3f 40 41
* 1997 Jun Ripon (GD) H 12.3f 61 58
* 1996 Oct Haydoc (SFT) H 10.5f 51 71
* 1995 Oct Yarmou (G-F) H 8f 74 82 <
1999 Turf 0-3: (7f, 12f 2) (g-s, frm, hrd) 1999 AW 0-2: (13f, 16f) (Equi 2)
Moderate gelding, effective 11 to 17f, acts on g-s to frm - acts on Fibr, has worn blinkers. Turf high 35. AW high 36. Consistent.
**J Pearce [5-55] Mrs Lydia Pearce.*

NO SHOES NO NEWS (IRE) BHB 35f43a **RR 30f 43a** 1610[9]
4 br g Be My Native (USA) 11.2f **(62)** - Buffs Express (Bay Express) 7.1f **(60)**
Form - 130
Record 1999 - 1st:1 2nd:0 3rd:1 Ran:3
Pre1999 - 1st:0 2nd:0 3rd:0 Ran:3
Win Prizemoney £2,190 *Total Prizemoney* £2,614
Wins * 1999 *Jan Southw (STD) 12f 54* <
1999 Turf 0-1: (14f) (frm) 1999 AW 1-2: (12f 1-2) (Fibr 1-2)
Lengthy, fair gelding, effective 12f, - acts on Fibr. AW high 54 (1st run) - 1st of 8 getting 4lb from Lucky Touch (25 Jan Southwell RF 0159).
**M A Buckley [1-9] C C Buckley.*

NOSTALGIC (USA) RR 2126[4]
3 ch g El Gran Senor (USA) 8.9f **(85)** - Chain Fern (USA) (Blushing Groom (FR)) 10.3f **(76)**
Form -
Record 1999 - 1st:0 2nd:0 3rd:0 Ran:1
Win Prizemoney £0 *Total Prizemoney* £309
1999 Turf 0-1: (frm)
Workmanlike, currently above-average filly.
**A C Stewart [0-1] Hamdan Al Maktoum.*

NOTAGAINTHEN BHB 43f **RR 42f** 2663[10]
3 b f Then Again 7.4f **(52)** - Fairy Ballerina (Fairy King (USA)) 7.7f **(59)**
Form - 0060
Record 1999 - 1st:0 2nd:0 3rd:0 Ran:4
Pre1999 - 1st:0 2nd:0 3rd:0 Ran:3
1999 Turf 0-3: (6f, 8f, 12f) (g-f, frm 2) 1999 AW 0-1: (9f) (Fibr)
Lengthy, moderate filly. Turf high 39.
**S G Knight [0-7] Mrs Ginny Withers.*

NOTATION (IRE) BHB 17f28a **RR 11f 28a** 4225[10]
5 b g Arazi (USA) 9.2f **(74)** - Grace Note (FR) (Top Ville) 11.7f **(68)**
Form - 00048000
Record 1999 - 1st:0 2nd:0 3rd:0 Ran:8
Pre1999 - 1st:2 2nd:2 3rd:2 Ran:23
Win Prizemoney £4,238 *Total Prizemoney* £6,484
Wins * 1997 *Dec Southw (STD) H 14f 45 51* <
* 1997 *Nov Southw (STD) H 14f 29 43*
1999 Turf 0-3: (11f, 16f 2) (gd 2, frm) 1999 AW 0-5: (12f, 14f, 16f 3) (Fibr 5)
Little account gelding, effective 14 to 16f, best at 16f, - acts on Fibr, has worn blinkers, likes left handed tracks. Turf high 11. AW high 24.
**D W Chapman [2-31] J M Chapman.*

NOTEWORTHY BHB 65f **RR 67f** 3641[5]
3 br f Saddlers' Hall (IRE) 10.5f **(65)** - Rushing River (USA) (Irish River (FR)) 8.6f **(78)**
Form - 64345
Record 1999 - 1st:0 2nd:0 3rd:1 Ran:5
Pre1999 - 1st:0 2nd:0 3rd:0 Ran:1
Win Prizemoney £0 *Total Prizemoney* £972

1999 Turf 0-5: (10f, 12f, 14f 2, 17f) (gd 2, g-f 2, hrd)

Scopey, average filly, effective 14f, acts on g-f. Turf high 67.

**J Noseda [0-6] Wyck Hall Stud.*

NOT FORGOTTEN (USA) BHB 20f43a **RR 10f 43a** 4709[8]

5 b g St Jovite (USA) 11.8f **(75)** - Past Remembered (USA) (Solford (USA)) 13f **(71)**

Form - 8

Record	**1999** -	1st:0	2nd:0	3rd:0	Ran:1
	Pre1999 -	1st:0	2nd:0	3rd:0	Ran:16

Win Prizemoney £0 *Total Prizemoney* £979

1999 Turf 0-1: (12f) (gd)

Poor gelding, often wears blinkers. Becoming disappointing.

**R P C Hoad [1-14] Jay Byrds Partnership (from P A Kelleway [0-13] Spt 1997).*

NOTHING DAUNTED BHB 95f **RR 95f** 4686[2]

2 ch c Selkirk (USA) 7.9f **(76)** - Khubza (Green Desert (USA)) 8.6f **(78)**

Form - 62132

Record	**1999** -	1st:1	2nd:2	3rd:1	Ran:5

Win Prizemoney £4,440 *Total Prizemoney* £9,824

Wins	* **1999** Aug Goodwo (GD)		7f	85	<

1999 Turf 1-5: (5f, 6f, 7f 1-2, 8f) (gd 1-2, g-f 3)

Very useful colt. Turf high 95 - 2nd of 16 giving 16lb to Cd Flyer (2 Oct Newmarket 6f gd RF 4686). He could develop into a seven furlong specialist and has a bright future in decent handicaps. Probably effective on any ground, he is genuine.

**E A L Dunlop [1-5] Ahmed Ali.*

NOTHING DOING (IRE) BHB 39f20a **RR 37f 20a** 1209[7]

10 b g Sarab 9.2f **(60)** - Spoons (Orchestra) 9.7f **(52)**

Form - 00037

Record	**1999** -	1st:0	2nd:0	3rd:1	Ran:5
	Pre1999 -	1st:4	2nd:8	3rd:4	Ran:39

Win Prizemoney £11,940 *Total Prizemoney* £19,716

Wins	* 1997 Jly Windso (G-F)	SH	11.6f	42	49	<
	* 1996 Oct Salisb (G-S)	CH	14f	34	42	
	* 1995 Jly Windso (G-F)	SH	11.6f	30	38	
	* 1995 *May Southw (STD)*	*H*	*12f*	*33*	*38*	

1999 Turf 0-2: (11f, 12f) (g-s, g-f) 1999 AW 0-3: (13f 2, 16f) (Equi 3)

Very moderate gelding, has worn blinkers. Turf high 37. Inconsistent.

**W J Musson [4-52] Broughton Bloodstock (from W J Haggas [0-1] Jun 1992).*

NOUF BHB 90f **RR 93f** 4838[4]

3 b f Efisio 7.7f **(69)** - Miss Witch (High Line) 10.3f **(70)**

Form - 184

Record	**1999** -	1st:1	2nd:0	3rd:0	Ran:3

Win Prizemoney £4,396 *Total Prizemoney* £4,836

Wins	* **1999** Mar Doncas (G-S)	7f	93++	<

1999 Turf 1-3: (7f 1-2, 8f) (g-s 1-1, gd, g-f)

Scopey, currently useful filly. Turf high 93 (1st run) - 1st of 11 getting 5lb from Gauntlet (26 Mar Doncaster RF 0481). Unraced at two, she put up a breathtaking performance when bolting up in a Doncaster maiden in March, but was found out subsequently.

**K Mahdi [1-3] Solaiman Alsaiary.*

NOUFARI (FR) BHB 73f85a **RR 76f 85a** 5025[8]

8 b g Kahyasi 12.9f **(74)** - Noufiyla (Top Ville) 11.7f **(68)**

Form - 2124436273121578

Record	**1999** -	1st:2	2nd:3	3rd:2	Ran:14
	Pre1999 -	1st:12	2nd:12	3rd:14	Ran:70

Win Prizemoney £46,425 *Total Prizemoney* £83,706

Wins	* **1999** Aug Thirsk (G-F)	H	16f	70	75	
	* **1999** Aug Nottin (G-F)	H	16f	64	69	
	* 1998 *Dec Wolver (STD)*	*S*	*14.8f*		*51+*	
	* 1998 Aug Newcas (GD)	H	16.1f	64	67	
	* 1998 *Apr Wolver (STD)*	*H*	*14.8f*	*78*	*82*	<
	* 1998 *Mar Wolver (STD)*	*H*	*14.8f*	*74*	*77*	
	* 1998 *Feb Southw (STD)*	*H*	*16f*	*70*	*74*	
	* 1998 *Jan Southw (STD)*	*H*	*16f*	*60*	*66*	
	* 1997 Jly Ayr (G-F)		13.1f		74	
	* 1995 *Feb Wolver (STD)*	*H*	*12f*	*80*	*79*	
	* 1995 *Feb Wolver (STD)*	*H*	*12f*	*72*	*78*	
	* 1995 *Jan Wolver (STD)*	*H*	*14f*	*61*	*69+*	

1999 Turf 2-8: (14f, 15f, 16f 2-6) (gd 1-6, frm, hrd 1-1) 1999 AW 0-6: (15f 2, 16f 4) (Fibr 6)

Above-average gelding, effective 15 to 16f, best at 15f, - acts on Fibr, favours left handed tracks, likes tight tracks, excels at Southwell, does well at Wolverhampton. Turf high 76. AW high 87 (1st run) - 2nd of 5 giving 20lb to Sudest (9 Jan Wolverhampton 16f Fibr RF 0069).

**R Hollinshead [14-84] Ed Weetman.*

NOUKARI (IRE) BHB 70f67a **RR 72f 67a** 4666[1]

6 b g Darshaan 11.9f **(81)** - Noufiyla (Top Ville) 11.7f **(68)**

Form - 553443352435223718422163114501

Record	**1999** -	1st:6	2nd:7	3rd:6	Ran:33
	Pre1999 -	1st:2	2nd:3	3rd:2	Ran:13

Win Prizemoney £19,502 *Total Prizemoney* £32,848

Wins	* **1999** *Oct Lingfi (STD)*		*12f*		*69*	<
	* **1999** Aug Pontef (GD)		12f		69	<
	* **1999** Aug Catter (G-F)	H	12f	62	68	
	* **1999** Jly Newmar (G-F)	H	10f	57	63	
	* **1999** Jun Cheste (G-F)	C	10.3f		45	
	* **1999** *Jan Lingfi (STD)*	*H*	*13f*	*62*	*66*	
	* 1998 *Dec Lingfi (STD)*	*H*	*13f*	*58*	*63*	
	* 1998 *Nov Southw (STD)*	*H*	*12f*	*53*	*61*	

1999 Turf 4-20: (10f 2-5, 11f 3, 12f 2-12) (gd 2, g-f 6, frm 4-12) 1999 AW 2-13: (12f 1-11, 13f 1-1, 15f) (Equi 2-5, Fibr 8)

Above-average gelding, effective 10 to 13f, best at 12f, acts on g-f to frm - acts on AW, best on Equi, excels at Lingfield and likes Southwell. Turf high 72 - 4th of 11 giving 6lb to Diminutive (22 Aug Leicester 12f frm RF 3840) - also 1st of 5 giving 9lb to Macca Luna (16 Aug Pontefract RF 3679). AW high 72 - 2nd of 8 giving 8lb to Banbury (19 Jan Lingfield 12f Equi RF 0123) - also 1st of 15 giving 11lb to Falcon Spirit (1 Oct Lingfield RF 4666). Consistent. Very effective over middle-distances on turf and sand. Goes well for an amateur.

**P D Evans [8-44] J E Abbey (from J Oxx in IRE [0-3] May 1997).*

Noushkey found Ramruma too good on more than one occasion

NOUSHKEY BHB 114f **RR 115f** 4266[6]

3 b f Polish Precedent (USA) 9f **(73)** - Top of the League (High Top) 10.2f **(67)**

Form - 32186

Record	**1999** -	1st:1	2nd:1	3rd:1	Ran:5
	Pre1999 -	1st:1	2nd:0	3rd:0	Ran:1

Win Prizemoney £24,401 *Total Prizemoney* £92,698

Wins	* **1999** Jly Haydoc (G-S)	G3	11.9f	115+	<
	* 1998 Oct Newmar (SFT)		7f	83	

1999 Turf 1-5: (11f, 12f 1-3, 15f) (gd 1-4, frm)

Light-framed, high-class filly, has broken blood-vessels, effective

12f, acts on gd. Turf high 116 - 2nd of 10 to Ramruma (4 Jun Epsom 12f gd RF 1729) - also 1st of 7 from Mistle Song (3 Jly Haydock RF 2531). Winner of a Newmarket maiden on her only start at two, she finished third to Ramruma in the Lingfield Oaks Trial on her reappearance before chasing home that filly in the Oaks itself. Upheld the form with a fine display to win the Lancashire Oaks, but broke a small blood-vessel when well held at York. She never figured in the St Leger on her final start of the season. **M A Jarvis [2-6] Sheikh Ahmed Al Maktoum.*

NOUVEAU CHEVAL BHB 62f59a RR 69f 59a 3053[3]

4 b f Picea 12.7f **(43)** - Freeracer (Free State) 8.7f **(61)**

Form - 213

Record 1999 - 1st:1 2nd:1 3rd:1 Ran:3
Pre1999 - 1st:1 2nd:0 3rd:1 Ran:5

Win Prizemoney £6,236 *Total Prizemoney* £8,005

Wins * **1999** Jly Cheste (G-F) 12.3f 69 <
1998 May Leices (GD) C 8f 51

1999 Turf 1-3: (12f 1-3) (g-f 1-1, frm 2)

Light-framed, average filly, effective 12f, acts on g-f to frm. Turf high 69 - 1st of 4 from Inchtina (9 Jly Chester RF 2670). A winner twice on the Flat, she has shown some ability over hurdles.
**M C Pipe [4-12] Knight Hawks Partnership (from J R Jenkins [1-3] May 1998).*

NOVADREAM BHB 30f RR 24f 3905[16]

2 b f Aragon 7.7f **(58)** - Please Please Me (IRE) (Tender King) 6.8f **(54)**

Form - 000

Record 1999 - 1st:0 2nd:0 3rd:0 Ran:3

1999 Turf 0-3: (6f, 7f, 8f) (g-f, frm 2)

Currently little account filly. Turf high 19 (began Jly).
**J J Bridger [0-3] Miss Julie Self.*

NOVELLINI GOLD RR 5f 3021[8]

2 ch g Mystiko (USA) 7.7f **(59)** - Glittering World (USA) (Diesis) 9.3f **(69)**

Form - 8

Record 1999 - 1st:0 2nd:0 3rd:0 Ran:1

1999 Turf 0-1: (7f) (frm)

Currently very poor gelding.
**N M Babbage [0-1] Provex Products Ltd.*

NOVELTY BHB 25f RR 27f 3533[8]

4 b f Primo Dominie 7.2f **(67)** - Nophe (USA) (Super Concorde (USA)) 10.9f **(66)**

Form - 08

Record 1999 - 1st:0 2nd:0 3rd:0 Ran:2
Pre1999 - 1st:0 2nd:0 3rd:0 Ran:2

1999 Turf 0-2: (8f 2) (gd, g-f)

Unfurnished, little account filly. Turf high 23.
**M Brittain [0-4] Mel Brittain.*

NOVITA ECLATANTI RR 98f 4518a[1]

2 f Imp Society (USA) 7.1f **(63)** - Jackie Mendez (Mendez (FR))

Form - 1

1999 Turf 1-1: (5f 1-1) (gd 1-1)

Currently very useful. (1st run) - 1st of 10 giving 7lb to Jennamara (19 Spt Capannelle RF 4518a).
**R Mimmocchi in ITY [1-1] Scuderia Delta.*

NO WARNING BHB 96f RR 99f 4243a[5]

3 b c Warning 8.1f **(77)** - Norgabie (Northfields (USA)) 9f **(72)**

Form - 25

1999 Turf 0-2: (6f 2) (g-s, gd)

Scopey, very useful colt, effective 6f, acts on g-s. Turf high 99.
**M Hofer in GER [0-2] (from Sir Mark Prescott [3-5] Oct 1998).*

NOWELL HOUSE BHB 68f RR 64+f 4883[1]

3 ch g Polar Falcon (USA) 9f **(74)** - Langtry Lady (Pas de Seul) 9.1f **(67)**

Form - 84731211

Record 1999 - 1st:3 2nd:1 3rd:1 Ran:8
Pre1999 - 1st:0 2nd:0 3rd:2 Ran:7

Win Prizemoney £10,006 *Total Prizemoney* £12,367

Wins * **1999** Oct Redcar (GD) H 10f 60 63
* **1999** Oct Pontef (SFT) H 12f 60 64+ <
* **1999** Spt Beverl (GD) H 12f 51 55

1999 Turf 3-8: (5f 2, 6f, 7f, 10f 1-2, 12f 2-2) (g-s, gd 2-2, g-f 2, frm 1-2, hrd)

Light-framed, average gelding, effective 5 to 12f, acts on gd to frm, prefers tight tracks. Turf high 64 - 1st of 17 giving 1lb to House of Dreams (4 Oct Pontefract RF 4714) - also 1st of 16 giving 17lb to Count Frederick (14 Oct Redcar RF 4883).
**M W Easterby [3-15] Bernard Bargh & John Walsh.*

NOWHERE TO EXIT BHB 116f RR 119df 3955[5]

3 b c Exit To Nowhere (USA) 8.7f **(77)** - Tromond **(92f)** (Lomond (USA)) 8.8f **(65)**

Form - 11125

Record 1999 - 1st:3 2nd:1 3rd:0 Ran:5
Pre1999 - 1st:1 2nd:1 3rd:0 Ran:3

Win Prizemoney £48,518 *Total Prizemoney* £157,690

Wins * **1999** May Longch (HVY) G3 12f 108 <
* **1999** Apr Chanti (SFT) L 12f 90
* **1999** Apr Haydoc (SFT) H 10.5f 91 96
* 1998 Oct Bright (G-S) 8f 83

1999 Turf 3-5: (11f 1-1, 12f 2-3, 14f) (hvy 1-1, sft 1-1, gd 1-3)

Light-framed, high-class colt, effective 12f, acts on gd. Turf high 119 - 2nd of 8 to Montjeu (6 Jun Chantilly 12f gd RF 1904a). He looked to be suited by a test of stamina at two, and used that stamina to good effect when winning in soft ground at Haydock on his three-year-old reappearance. He went on to win a Listed event and a Group Three in France, and though swamped by Montjeu in the French Derby, still beat the others by a wide margin. Off the track for three months after that, he failed to shine in Goodwood's March Stakes, finishing a well-beaten last of five. The ground would have been faster than ideal, and he returned with cuts to his hind legs. **J L Dunlop [4-8] & Mrs Gary Pinchen.*

NOW IS THE HOUR BHB 30f RR 24f 3380[12]

3 ch g Timeless Times (USA) 6.1f **(56)** - Macs Maharanee **(71f 70a)** (Indian King (USA)) 7.4f **(64)**

Form - 4800760

Record 1999 - 1st:0 2nd:0 3rd:0 Ran:7
Pre1999 - 1st:0 2nd:0 3rd:0 Ran:6

Win Prizemoney £0 *Total Prizemoney* £480

1999 Turf 0-6: (5f, 6f 3, 8f 2) (g-f 4, frm 2) 1999 AW 0-1: (6f) (Equi)

Neat, little account gelding. Turf high 28.
**P S Felgate [0-13] John Martin.*

NOW LOOK HERE BHB 89f RR 89f 5134[3]

3 b c Reprimand 8.2f **(63)** - Where's Carol (Anfield) 8.5f **(59)**

Form - 1743003033

Record 1999 - 1st:1 2nd:0 3rd:4 Ran:10
Pre1999 - 1st:0 2nd:0 3rd:1 Ran:3

Win Prizemoney £3,598 *Total Prizemoney* £15,984

Wins * **1999** Apr Haydoc (SFT) 7.1f 83 <

1999 Turf 1-10: (6f 6, 7f 1-4) (gd 1-6, g-f 2, frm 2)

Useful colt, effective 6 to 7f, best at 6f, acts on gd to frm, best on gd, excels at Newmarket and York. Turf high 89 - 3rd of 11 giving 19lb to Don't Surrender (29 Oct Newmarket 6f gd RF 5134) - also 1st of 7 from Compatriot (3 Apr Haydock RF 0565). He showed improved form with a narrow victory in a seven-furlong Haydock maiden on his reappearance, but was totally outclassed in the Greenham. He has run a couple of decent races in handicap company since, notably when third to Swallow Flight in a hot York handicap and to Pipalong in the Great St Wilfrid in August.
**B A McMahon [1-13] S L Edwards.*

NOWT FLASH (IRE) BHB 47f RR 51f 4901[9]

2 ch c Petardia 8.2f **(58)** - Mantlepiece (IRE) (Common Grounds)

Form - 60060

Record 1999 - 1st:0 2nd:0 3rd:0 Ran:5

1999 Turf 0-3: (5f 2, 7f) (gd, frm 2) 1999 AW 0-2: (5f, 6f) (Fibr 2)

Fair colt, has worn blinkers. Turf high 51 (began Jly). AW high 43 (began Aug). **B S Rothwell [0-5] David Scott.*

NOYAN BHB 43f49a RR 37f 49a 1408[7]

9 ch g Northern Baby (CAN) 10.2f **(74)** - Istiska (FR) (Irish River (FR)) 8.6f **(78)**

Form - 7

Record 1999 - 1st:0 2nd:0 3rd:0 Ran:1
Pre1999 - 1st:5 2nd:2 3rd:1 Ran:27

Win Prizemoney £28,416 *Total Prizemoney* £40,852

Wins 1995 May Hamilt (G-F) H 13f 48 55

1995 May Hamilt (G-F) H 13f 43 52
1999 Turf 0-1: (16f) (g-f)
Moderate gelding, has worn blinkers. Consistent.
**K A Ryan [0-7] C H McGhie (from D Nicholls [0-10] Apr 1996).*

NOZOMI (IRE) BHB 53f60a **RR 14f 60a** 2429[8]
3 b f Mujadil (USA) 7.7f **(70)** - Crimbourne (Mummy's Pet) 7.7f **(60)**
Form - 5008
Record 1999 - 1st:0 2nd:0 3rd:0 Ran:3
Pre1999 - 1st:1 2nd:0 3rd:0 Ran:5
Win Prizemoney £2,532 *Total Prizemoney* £2,532
Wins * 1998 *Oct Wolver (sta) 6f 77 <*
1999 Turf 0-3: (6f, 7f, 10f) (gd 2, frm)
Neat, fair filly, effective 6f, - acts on Fibr, has worn blinkers. Turf high 51. Inconsistent. **P J Makin [1-8] R P Marchant.*

NUBILE BHB 28f32a **RR 19f 32a** 3441[6]
5 b m Pursuit of Love 9.5f **(69)** - Trojan Lady (USA) (Irish River (FR)) 8.6f **(78)**
Form - 7080016
Record 1999 - 1st:1 2nd:0 3rd:0 Ran:7
Pre1999 - 1st:1 2nd:0 3rd:1 Ran:12
Win Prizemoney £4,546 *Total Prizemoney* £5,248
Wins * **1999** *Jly Southw (STD) H 12f 25 31*
1997 Jly Windso (G-F) S 11.6f 46 <
1999 Turf 0-3: (13f, 14f 2) (sft 2, gd) 1999 AW 1-4: (12f 1-1, 14f 2, 15f) (Fibr 1-4)
Very moderate filly, effective 12f, - acts on Fibr, has worn blinkers, likes left handed tracks. Turf high 19. AW high 31 - 1st of 17 from Amsara (24 Jly Southwell RF 3110). Ended a long losing run when winning an awful handicap on the Southwell Fibresand in July.
**W J Musson [1-18] Broughton Bloodstock (from B W Hills [1-5] Jly 1997).*

NUCLEAR DEBATE (USA) BHB 98f **RR 111f** 5120a[2]
4 b g Geiger Counter (USA) 7.8f **(85)** - I'm An Issue (USA) (Cox's Ridge (USA)) 8f **(68)**
Form - 13312
1999 Turf 2-5: (5f 2-4, 6f) (hvy 1-2, g-s 1-1, gd 2)
Workmanlike, Group-class gelding, effective 5 to 6f, best at 5f, acts on hvy to gd, excels at Deauville. Turf high 111 (began Aug) - 2nd of 9 giving 21lb to Manzor (24 Oct Longchamp 5f hvy RF 5120a) - also 1st of 12 getting 3lb from Late Parade (3 Oct San Siro RF 4781a). A useful sprint handicapper when trained by Lynda Ramsden, he has joined John Hammond's yard in France and was victorious in a listed event at Deauville in August. Finished third in a similar race at Newbury the following month.
**J E Hammond in FR [2-5] (from Mrs J R Ramsden [2-15] Spt 1998).*

NUCLEAR FREEZE (USA) BHB 89f **RR 92+f** 4254[4]
3 b c Danzig (USA) 8.1f **(88)** - Razyana (USA) (His Majesty (USA)) 10.9f **(82)**
Form - 314
Record 1999 - 1st:1 2nd:0 3rd:1 Ran:3
Win Prizemoney £4,040 *Total Prizemoney* £5,088
Wins * **1999** Jly Thirsk (FRM) 8f 92+ <
1999 Turf 1-3: (8f 1-3) (g-f 2, frm 1-1)
Strong, currently useful colt. Turf high 92 (began Jly) - 1st of 8 giving 5lb to Palm Tree (30 Jly Thirsk RF 3255).
**H R A Cecil [1-3] K Abdulla.*

NUIT D'OR (IRE) BHB 69f30a **RR 66?f 30a** 352[13]
4 ch g Night Shift (USA) 8.1f **(73)** - Sister Golden Hair (IRE) (Glint of Gold) 9.3f **(66)**
Form - 78000
Record 1999 - 1st:0 2nd:0 3rd:0 Ran:5
Pre1999 - 1st:1 2nd:1 3rd:0 Ran:10
Win Prizemoney £1,738 *Total Prizemoney* £2,461
Wins 1998 *Feb Wolver (STD) S 8.5f 62 <*
1999 AW 0-5: (8f 2, 9f 2, 12f) (Fibr 5)
Strong, average gelding, effective 8f, - acts on Fibr, has worn blinkers (extremely effectively). AW high 31. Becoming disappointing.
**M Waring [0-4] Foley Steelstock (from W G M Turner [0-2] Jan 1999).*

NULLI SECUNDUS RR 65f 4628[7]
3 b c Polar Falcon (USA) 9f **(74)** - Exclusive Virtue (USA) (Shadeed (USA)) 8.2f **(70)**
Form - 457
Record 1999 - 1st:0 2nd:0 3rd:0 Ran:3
Pre1999 - 1st:0 2nd:0 3rd:0 Ran:1
Win Prizemoney £0 *Total Prizemoney* £285
1999 Turf 0-2: (8f 2) (g-s, frm) 1999 AW 0-1: (8f) (Fibr)
Average colt. Turf high 65 (began Jly).
**J A R Toller [0-4] Duke of Devonshire.*

NUMERATOR BHB 70f78a **RR 69f 78a** 2470[6]
3 ch f Rudimentary (USA) 8.2f **(66)** - Half a Dozen (USA) (Saratoga Six (USA)) 7f **(73)**
Form - 17616
Record 1999 - 1st:2 2nd:0 3rd:0 Ran:5
Pre1999 - 1st:0 2nd:0 3rd:1 Ran:1
Win Prizemoney £6,255 *Total Prizemoney* £6,675
Wins * **1999** Jun Newmar (G-F) C 8f 69
* **1999** *May Wolver (STD) 9.4f 70+ <*
1999 Turf 1-4: (7f, 8f 1-2, 10f) (gd 2, g-f 1-1, frm) 1999 AW 1-1: (9f 1-1) (Fibr 1-1)
Scopey, above-average filly, effective 8 to 9f, best at 8f, acts on sft to g-f - acts on Fibr. Turf high 69 - 1st of 10 giving 16lb to Faith Again (26 Jun Newmarket RF 2341). (1st run) - 1st of 5 from Ice Pack (8 May Wolverhampton RF 1120). Showed ability in her only start at two, and bolted up in a weak Wolverhampton maiden on her reappearance. Added a Newmarket claimer afterwards.
**W J Haggas [2-6] Cheveley Park Stud.*

NUNTHORPE BHB 54f **RR 30f** 2175[18]
4 ch f Mystiko (USA) 7.7f **(59)** - Enchanting Melody (Chief Singer) 8.9f **(66)**
Form - 00
Record 1999 - 1st:0 2nd:0 3rd:0 Ran:2
Pre1999 - 1st:1 2nd:1 3rd:0 Ran:10
Win Prizemoney £4,416 *Total Prizemoney* £5,678
Wins 1998 May Beverl (G-F) H 8.5f 72 77 <
1999 Turf 0-2: (6f, 7f) (gd, frm)
Leggy, very moderate filly, effective 8f, acts on hrd, likes tight tracks. Turf high 30. Becoming disappointing.
**G Woodward [0-2] J M Lacey (from J A Glover [1-10] Oct 1998).*

NUTCHAT BHB 49f **RR 48f** 2667[16]
3 ch g Beveled (USA) 6.9f **(64)** - Shapina (Sharp Edge) 10f **(56)**
Form - 0040
Record 1999 - 1st:0 2nd:0 3rd:0 Ran:4
Pre1999 - 1st:0 2nd:0 3rd:0 Ran:5
Win Prizemoney £0 *Total Prizemoney* £208
1999 Turf 0-4: (8f 4) (g-f 2, frm 2)
Unfurnished, moderate gelding. Turf high 48. (DEAD)
**R G Frost [0-4] J F O'Donovan (from A P Jones [0-5] Spt 1998).*

NUTMEG (IRE) BHB 65f **RR 78f** 5111[5]
2 ch f Lake Coniston (IRE) - Overdue Reaction (Be My Guest (USA)) 9.3f **(67)**
Form - 000845
Record 1999 - 1st:0 2nd:0 3rd:0 Ran:6
Win Prizemoney £0 *Total Prizemoney* £233
1999 Turf 0-6: (5f, 6f 2, 7f 3) (gd 3, g-f, frm 2)
Above-average filly. Turf high 78. Disappointing so far in maidens over sprint distances. **M H Tompkins [0-6] Mystic Meg Ltd.*

NUTS IN MAY (USA) BHB 68f **RR 77f** 4731[15]
2 b f A P Indy (USA) - Regal State (USA) (Affirmed (USA)) 9.3f **(79)**
Form - 020
Record 1999 - 1st:0 2nd:1 3rd:0 Ran:3
Win Prizemoney £0 *Total Prizemoney* £1,240
1999 Turf 0-3: (6f 3) (gd, g-f, frm)
Currently above-average filly. Turf high 77 (began Aug) - 2nd of 12 getting 5lb from Aljawf (13 Spt Nottingham 6f frm RF 4284).
**J L Dunlop [0-3] Robin Scully.*

NUTTY STAN (IRE) BHB 45f **RR 62f** 2083[15]
5 ch g Shahrastani (USA) 11.5f **(69)** - Coconut Grove (What A Guest) 7f **(62)**
Form - 0
Record 1999 - 1st:0 2nd:0 3rd:0 Ran:1
Pre1999 - 1st:0 2nd:0 3rd:1 Ran:7

Win Prizemoney £0 *Total Prizemoney* £400
1999 AW 0-1: (11f) (Fibr)
Average gelding.
**Miss M E Rowland [0-1] Goldliner Racing Club (from P J Flynn in IRE [0-7] May 1997).*

OAKBURY (IRE) BHB 28f70a **RR 27f 70a** 2226[13]
7 ch g Common Grounds 8.1f **(66)** - Doon Belle (Ardoon) 7.3f **(53)**
Form - 0

Record	**1999** -	1st:0	2nd:0	3rd:0	Ran:1
	Pre1999 -	1st:0	2nd:4	3rd:4	Ran:30

Win Prizemoney £0 *Total Prizemoney* £6,471
1999 Turf 0-1: (17f) (frm)
Very moderate gelding, has worn blinkers.
**Miss L C Siddall [4-58] Panther Racing Ltd (from R Hannon [0-14] Oct 1995).*

Wins	*** 1999**	Aug	Leices	(G-F)	S	7f	48	
	* 1998	Oct	Leices	(G-S)		7f	62	<

1999 Turf 1-13: (6f 2, 7f 1-8, 8f 3) (gd 2, g-f 3, frm 1-7, hrd) 1999 AW 0-1: (7f) (Fibr)
Scopey, moderate filly, effective 5 to 8f, acts on gd to frm, best on gd, mostly wears blinkers (very effectively). Turf high 50.
**G L Moore [2-18] Joe Bates (Bloodstock) Ltd (from P T Walwyn [0-11] Aug 1998).*

OARE LINNET BHB 52f **RR 41f** 2525[10]
3 ch f Polish Precedent (USA) 9f **(73)** - Portvasco (Sharpo) 7.7f **(59)**
Form - 7700

Record	**1999** -	1st:0	2nd:0	3rd:0	Ran:4
	Pre1999 -	1st:0	2nd:0	3rd:0	Ran:1

1999 Turf 0-4: (6f 3, 8f) (g-f 2, frm 2)
Scopey, moderate filly. Turf high 63.
**P T Walwyn [0-5] Mrs Henry Keswick.*

Oath was the Epsom hero, but injury curtailed his career

OAKWELL ACE BHB 41f **RR 45f** 5156[3]
3 b f Clantime 6.6f **(57)** - Fardella (ITY) (Molvedo)
Form - 010788003

Record	**1999** -	1st:1	2nd:0	3rd:1	Ran:9

Win Prizemoney £2,521 *Total Prizemoney* £2,952

Wins	*** 1999**	Jun	Warwic	(HVY)	C	6.8f	59	<

1999 Turf 1-9: (6f, 7f 1-2, 8f 5, 10f) (g-s 1-2, gd 4, g-f, frm, hrd)
Neat, moderate filly, effective 7f, acts on g-s, has worn blinkers, likes tight tracks. Turf high 59 - 1st of 11 giving 5lb to September Harvest (7 Jun Warwick RF 1798). Inconsistent.
**J A Glover [1-9] J A Bower.*

OARE KITE BHB 48f44a **RR 46f 44a** 5050[6]
4 b f Batshoof 9.5f **(66)** - Portvasco (Sharpo) 7.7f **(59)**
Form - 06050264140736

Record	**1999** -	1st:1	2nd:1	3rd:1	Ran:14
	Pre1999 -	1st:1	2nd:2	3rd:2	Ran:15

Win Prizemoney £4,852 *Total Prizemoney* £7,831

OARE PINTAIL BHB 67f **RR 67f** 5048[11]
2 b f Distant Relative 7f **(69)** - Oare Sparrow **(71f 61a)** (Night Shift (USA)) 7.2f **(69)**
Form - 6060

Record	**1999** -	1st:0	2nd:0	3rd:0	Ran:4

1999 Turf 0-4: (7f 3, 8f) (hvy, sft, gd, g-f)
Average filly. Turf high 67 (began Spt).
**P T Walwyn [0-4] Mrs Henry Keswick.*

OATH (IRE) BHB 123f **RR 125f** 3088[7]
3 b c Fairy King (USA) 7.7f **(75)** - Sheer Audacity (Troy) 10.4f **(68)**
Form - 2117

Record	**1999** -	1st:2	2nd:1	3rd:0	Ran:4
	Pre1999 -	1st:1	2nd:0	3rd:1	Ran:3

Win Prizemoney £643,437 *Total Prizemoney* £647,418

Wins	*** 1999**	Jun	Epsom	(GD,)	G1	12f	125	<
	*** 1999**	May	Cheste	(G-F)	L	10.3f	115+	
	* 1998	Oct	Nottin	(SFT)		8.2f	89	

1999 Turf 2-4: (10f 1-2, 12f 1-2) (gd 1-2, g-f 1-2)
Leggy, top-class colt, effective 10 to 12f, acts on gd to g-f. Turf high 125 - 1st of 16 from Daliapour (5 Jun Epsom RF 1760). Showed a smart turn of foot to take up the running and stayed on strongly to win the Derby, relishing the step up in trip. A winner on soft ground at two, he was touched off by Lucido at Newbury on his reappearance before running away with the Dee Stakes on his second start on much faster ground. He missed the Irish Derby after some below-par work leading up to the race, but ran very poorly in the King George, though it later transpired he had suffered a knee injury. The original plan was for him to race as a four-year-old, but his injury did not respond quickly to treatment and he was sold as a potential stallion to Japanese interests.
**H R A Cecil [3-6] The Thoroughbred Corporation (from R Charlton [0-1] Jun 1998).*

OBSERVATORY (USA) BHB 100f **RR 91f** 4953[1]

2 ch c Distant View (USA) - Stellaria (USA) (Roberto (USA)) 10f **(76)**
Form - 141
Record 1999 - 1st:2 2nd:0 3rd:0 Ran:3
Win Prizemoney £10,319 *Total Prizemoney* £12,904
Wins ***1999** Oct Yarmou (G-F) 6f 91 <
***1999** Jun Yarmou (GD) 6f 82++
1999 Turf 2-3: (6f 2-3) (gd 1-1, g-f 1-1, frm)
Currently useful colt. Turf high 91 - 1st of 5 from Final Row (19 Oct Yarmouth RF 4953) - also 1st of 4 from Innkeeper (30 Jun Yarmouth RF 2451). Scored an easy win in a four-runner Yarmouth maiden on his debut, and won another small race at the same track on his third start. Outclassed in the Mill Reef in between.
**J H M Gosden [2-3] K Abdulla.*

OBVIOUSLY FUN (FR) **RR 100f** 1359a[3]

3 b c Highest Honor (FR) 10.9f **(72)** - Obviously Eric (FR) (Gay Mecene (USA)) 8.6f **(69)**
Form - 13
1999 Turf 1-2: (8f 1-1, 11f) (gd 1-2)
Currently very useful colt. Turf high 100.
**J E Hammond in FR [1-3] Tsega Ltd.*

OCCAM (IRE) BHB 40f **RR 28f** 4831[5]

5 ch g Sharp Victor (USA) 10f **(56)** - Monterana (Sallust) 8.4f **(63)**
Form - 05
Record 1999 - 1st:0 2nd:0 3rd:0 Ran:2
Pre1999 - 1st:0 2nd:0 3rd:0 Ran:5
Win Prizemoney £0 *Total Prizemoney* £278
1999 Turf 0-2: (10f, 11f) (sft, g-f)
Little account gelding. Turf high 28 (began Jly).
**L J Barratt [0-2] L J Barratt (from G Wragg [0-5] Oct 1997).*

OCEAN DRIVE (IRE) BHB 48f **RR 49f** 4980[14]

3 b br g Dolphin Street (FR) - Blonde Goddess (IRE) (Godswalk (USA)) 7.3f **(58)**
Form - 0605034145460030
Record 1999 - 1st:1 2nd:0 3rd:2 Ran:16
Pre1999 - 1st:0 2nd:0 3rd:1 Ran:3
Win Prizemoney £2,621 *Total Prizemoney* £5,140
Wins ***1999** Jun Hamilt (GD) H 12.1f 58 59 <
1999 Turf 1-16: (7f, 8f, 9f, 10f 3, 11f 2, 12f 1-5, 13f 2, 14f) (gd 6, g-f 1-5, frm 5)
Workmanlike, moderate gelding, likes right handed tracks. Turf high 60. He won over a mile and a half at Hamilton on good ground in June before contesting some pretty tough handicaps.
**Miss L A Perratt [1-19] Sutherland Marett Hay.*

OCEAN LINE (IRE) BHB 43f34a **RR 50f 34a** 4349[13]

4 b g Kefaah (USA) 11.2f **(64)** - Tropic Sea (IRE) (Sure Blade (USA)) 11.3f **(67)**
Form - 000452514130
Record 1999 - 1st:2 2nd:1 3rd:1 Ran:12
Pre1999 - 1st:0 2nd:0 3rd:1 Ran:10
Win Prizemoney £4,781 *Total Prizemoney* £6,696
Wins ***1999** Aug Bright (G-F) C 10f 50 <
***1999** Jly Windso (G-F) SH 11.6f 34 39
1999 Turf 2-11: (8f 2, 10f 1-4, 11f 2, 12f 1-2, 15f) (sft, g-s, g-f 2, frm 2-7)
1999 AW 0-1: (7f) (Equi)
Workmanlike, fair gelding, effective 8 to 10f, best at 10f, acts on gd to frm, favours tight tracks. Turf high 50 - 1st of 7 getting 10lb from Raed (23 Aug Brighton RF 3851).
**G M McCourt [2-10] Christopher Shankland (from K Bell [0-2] Apr 1999).*

OCEAN OF STORMS (IRE) BHB 105f **RR 106f** 1103[3]

4 b c Arazi (USA) 9.2f **(74)** - Moon Cactus (Kris) 9.5f **(73)**
Form - 3
Record 1999 - 1st:0 2nd:0 3rd:1 Ran:1
Pre1999 - 1st:0 2nd:2 3rd:0 Ran:2
Win Prizemoney £0 *Total Prizemoney* £25,202
1999 Turf 0-1: (14f) (gd)
Currently Pattern-class colt. (1st run) - 3rd of 9 giving 6lb to Opera King (8 May Goodwood 14f gd RF 1103). A progressive stayer in '98, he was acquired by Godolphin but appeared just once, finishing third in a Shergar Cup race in May.
**S bin Suroor [0-1] Godolphin (from A Fabre in FR [0-2] Oct 1998).*

OCEAN PARK BHB 64f75a **RR 66f 75a** 3275[2]

8 b g Dominion 8.9f **(65)** - Chiming Melody (Cure The Blues (USA)) 9.5f **(63)**
Form - 412
Record 1999 - 1st:1 2nd:1 3rd:0 Ran:3
Pre1999 - 1st:6 2nd:5 3rd:2 Ran:36
Win Prizemoney £25,088 *Total Prizemoney* £31,857
Wins ***1999** Jun Lingfi (G-F) H 11.5f 57 59
*1998 Aug Warwic (G-F) S 10.8f 59
*1996 Spt Folkes (G-F) 12f 66
*1996 Apr Leices (GD) H 10f 65 66
*1996 *Mar Lingfi (STD) H 10f 80 84* <
*1996 *Feb Lingfi (STD) H 10f 76 77*
*1996 *Jan Wolver (STD) 8.5f 75*
1999 Turf 1-3: (11f 1-2, 12f) (frm 1-2, hrd)
Decent gelding, effective 8 to 11f, acts on frm, has worn blinkers. Turf high 66 - 2nd of 5 giving 7lb to Indigo Bay (31 Jly Lingfield 11f frm RF 3275) - also 1st of 12 giving 18lb to Fuero Real (25 Jun Lingfield RF 2296). Winner of a Warwick seller in 1998, he returned to winning ways in a slightly better event at Lingfield in June.
**Lady Herries [7-30] Lady Herries (from P J Makin [0-6] Oct 1994).*

OCEAN PRINCE (FR) BHB 52f **RR 52f** 1588[3]

3 b g Dolphin Street (FR) - Dumayla (Shernazar) 10.2f **(73)**
Form - 703
Record 1999 - 1st:0 2nd:0 3rd:1 Ran:3
Pre1999 - 1st:0 2nd:0 3rd:0 Ran:2
Win Prizemoney £0 *Total Prizemoney* £296
1999 Turf 0-3: (7f, 11f, 12f) (sft, g-s, g-f)
Scopey, fair gelding, has worn blinkers. Turf high 52.
**W R Muir [0-5] B Bull.*

OCEAN RAIN (IRE) BHB 80f **RR 79f** 5034[5]

2 ch c Lake Coniston (IRE) - Alicedale (USA) (Trempolino (USA)) 12f **(71)**
Form - 82175
Record 1999 - 1st:1 2nd:1 3rd:0 Ran:5
Win Prizemoney £3,060 *Total Prizemoney* £4,068
Wins 1999 Aug Haydoc (G-S) 6f 76+ <
1999 Turf 1-5: (6f 1-3, 7f 2) (g-s, gd 1-1, g-f, frm, hrd)
Above-average colt. Turf high 79 (began Jly) - also 1st of 17 giving 4lb to The Prosecutor (5 Aug Haydock RF 3400).
**C G Cox [0-2] Stephen Barrow (from M J Heaton-Ellis [1-3] Aug 1999).*

OCEANS FRIENDLY (USA) BHB 85f **RR 81f** 4290[5]

3 br f Green Dancer (USA) 11.9f **(77)** - Sedra (Nebbiolo) 8.1f **(75)**
Form - 8681065
Record 1999 - 1st:1 2nd:0 3rd:0 Ran:7
Pre1999 - 1st:0 2nd:0 3rd:0 Ran:2
Win Prizemoney £5,550 *Total Prizemoney* £6,020
Wins ***1999** Jly Nottin (FRM) 10f 72+ <
1999 Turf 1-7: (10f 1-6, 12f) (g-s, g-f 4, frm 1-2)
Workmanlike, decent filly. Turf high 88. Consistent. Completely outclassed in Pattern company, her only win to date came in a Nottingham match at odds of 1/28. **B W Hills [1-9] W J Gredley.*

OCEAN SPRAY **RR 1f** 3138[11]

6 ch g Cadeaux Genereux 7.9f **(76)** - Shore Line (High Line) 10.3f **(70)**
Form - 0
Record 1999 - 1st:0 2nd:0 3rd:0 Ran:1

1999 Turf 0-1: (11f) (g-f)
Currently very poor gelding. **D Eddy [0-3] Robert Gray.*

OCEAN VIEW RR 47f 583^{6}
3 ch f Rope Trick - Nashya (Rousillon (USA)) 8.2f **(74)**
Form - 6
Record 1999 - 1st:0 2nd:0 3rd:0 Ran:1
1999 Turf 0-1: (8f) (gd)
Leggy, currently moderate filly. **W T Kemp [0-1] G Coburn.*

OCHOS RIOS (IRE) BHB 37f60a RR 28f 60a 3565^{9}
8 br g Horage 11.4f **(58)** - Morgiana (Godswalk (USA)) 7.3f **(58)**
Form - 37000
Record 1999 - 1st:0 2nd:0 3rd:1 Ran:5
Pre1999 - 1st:6 2nd:5 3rd:8 Ran:69
Win Prizemoney £27,019 *Total Prizemoney* £40,062
Wins * 1998 Jun Thirsk (SFT) H 7f 40 50
* 1998 Jun Beverl (GD) H 7.5f 40 43
* 1996 Spt York (GD) H 7f 56 59
1999 Turf 0-5: (7f 2, 8f 2, 10f) (gd, g-f 2, frm 2)
Fair gelding, effective 7f, acts on gd, has worn blinkers, likes tight tracks. Turf high 38. **B S Rothwell [6-74] J B Young.*

OCKER (IRE) BHB 97f78a RR 94f 78a 5222^{5}
5 br g Astronef 7.9f **(59)** - Violet Somers (Will Somers) 5.9f **(59)**
Form - 230233261370430503061O137855
Record 1999 - 1st:3 2nd:2 3rd:6 Ran:26
Pre1999 - 1st:4 2nd:8 3rd:4 Ran:39
Win Prizemoney £41,752 *Total Prizemoney* £69,469
Wins * **1999** Spt Haydoc (G-F) 6f 92
* **1999** Aug Nottin (G-F) 5.1f 100 <
* **1999** Apr Thirsk (GD) H 5f 80 84
* 1998 Nov Doncas (SFT) H 5f 74 78
* 1998 Aug Newbur (GD) H 5.2f 74 77
* 1998 Jly Haydoc (G-F) H 5f 68 71
1998 Mar Nottin (G-S) H 6.1f 53 76
1999 Turf 3-21: (5f 2-4, 6f 1-16, 7f) (sft, g-s 4, gd 1-6, g-f 2-3, frm 7)
1999 AW 0-5: (6f 5) (Fibr 5)
Useful gelding, effective 5 to 6f, acts on g-f, has worn blinkers, does well at Haydock and Nottingham. Turf high 100 - also 1st of 7 giving 2lb to Red Prairie (28 Aug Nottingham RF 3970). AW high 78. Consistent. He can give trouble at the start, but is a useful sprinter once underway. Tremendously consistent through another hectic campaign, he is best over five or six furlongs and is proven on everything bar firm ground.
**Mrs N Macauley [6-46] J Teasdale (from M H Tompkins [1-19] Apr 1998).*

OCKERBRIDGE BHB 51f RR 58f 4870^{9}
2 b f Casteddu 7.4f **(54)** - Grey Twig (Godswalk (USA)) 7.3f **(58)**
Form - 060
Record 1999 - 1st:0 2nd:0 3rd:0 Ran:3
1999 Turf 0-2: (6f, 7f) (g-s, gd) 1999 AW 0-1: (6f) (Fibr)
Currently fair filly. Turf high 58 (began Spt).
**J S Moore [0-3] G A Bosley.*

OCTANE (USA) BHB 62f RR 63f 2764^{12}
3 b c Cryptoclearance (USA) - Something True (USA) (Sir Ivor) 10.2f **(70)**
Form - 60500
Record 1999 - 1st:0 2nd:0 3rd:0 Ran:5
1999 Turf 0-5: (8f 3, 10f 2) (gd, g-f, frm 3)
Light-framed, average colt, has worn blinkers. Turf high 63.
**H R A Cecil [0-5] Buckram Oak Holdings.*

OCTAVIUS CAESAR (USA) RR 76f 4506^{7}
2 ch c Affirmed (USA) 10.3f **(75)** - Secret Imperatrice (USA) (Secretariat (USA)) 9f **(79)**
Form - 27
Record 1999 - 1st:0 2nd:1 3rd:0 Ran:2
Win Prizemoney £0 *Total Prizemoney* £1,055
1999 Turf 0-2: (8f, 9f) (g-f, frm)
Currently above-average colt. Turf high 76 (1st run) (began Spt) - 2nd of 8 to Monte Carlo (4 Spt Epsom 9f frm RF 4135). **P F I Cole [0-2] Sir George Meyrick.*

ODDSANENDS BHB 78f77a RR 73?f 77a 2312^{6}
3 b c Alhijaz 7.7f **(57)** - Jans Contessa (Rabdan) 5.9f **(53)**
Form - 46
Record 1999 - 1st:0 2nd:0 3rd:0 Ran:2
Pre1999 - 1st:1 2nd:0 3rd:1 Ran:5
Win Prizemoney £5,550 *Total Prizemoney* £9,283
Wins * 1998 Aug Ascot (G-F) H 7f 63 73? <
1999 AW 0-2: (7f 2) (Fibr 2)
Scopey, above-average colt, effective 6f, - acts on Fibr. AW high 78. **C N Allen [1-7] J T B Racing.*

ODYN DANCER BHB 53f55a RR 46f 55a 4504^{10}
2 b f Minshaanshu Amad (USA) 11.3f **(53)** - Themeda (Sure Blade (USA)) 11.3f **(67)**
Form - 882540
Record 1999 - 1st:0 2nd:1 3rd:0 Ran:6
Win Prizemoney £0 *Total Prizemoney* £603
1999 Turf 0-3: (6f, 7f, 8f) (g-f 3) 1999 AW 0-3: (7f 2, 8f) (Fibr 3)
Fair filly. Turf high 46. AW high 53 (began Jly).
**M D I Usher [0-6] M D I Usher.*

ODYSSEY BHB 57f RR 62f 4993^{11}
3 b g Slip Anchor 12.7f **(75)** - Circe (Main Reef) 9.6f **(57)**
Form - 545335380
Record 1999 - 1st:0 2nd:0 3rd:3 Ran:9
Pre1999 - 1st:0 2nd:0 3rd:0 Ran:3
Win Prizemoney £0 *Total Prizemoney* £1,708
1999 Turf 0-9: (10f 2, 11f, 12f 2, 13f, 14f 2, 16f) (sft, gd, g-f 4, frm 3)
Scopey, average gelding, effective 11 to 16f, acts on g-f to frm, best on frm, has worn blinkers, prefers left handed tracks, prefers tight tracks. Turf high 66. Consistent.
**P T Walwyn [0-12] A D G Oldrey.*

OFFENBURG BHB 42f RR 56f 5002^{16}
2 b c Petong 7.6f **(58)** - Bold County (Never so Bold) 6.3f **(66)**
Form - 5700
Record 1999 - 1st:0 2nd:0 3rd:0 Ran:4
1999 Turf 0-4: (7f, 8f 3) (g-s, gd 2, g-f)
Fair colt, has worn blinkers. Turf high 56 (began Spt).
**J S Moore [0-4] Chris Bradbury.*

OFF HIRE BHB 53f55a RR 60f 55a 4810^{12}
3 b g Clantime 6.6f **(57)** - Lady Pennington (Blue Cashmere) 6.4f **(54)**
Form - 4334200670
Record 1999 - 1st:0 2nd:1 3rd:0 Ran:7
Pre1999 - 1st:1 2nd:0 3rd:2 Ran:7
Win Prizemoney £2,745 *Total Prizemoney* £4,002
Wins * 1998 Nov Mussel (SFT) SH 5f 35 48 <
1999 Turf 0-5: (5f 4, 6f) (sft, gd 3, g-f) 1999 AW 0-2: (6f 2) (Fibr 2)
Unfurnished, average gelding, effective 5 to 6f, best at 5f, acts on gd - acts on Fibr. Turf high 60 (1st run) - 2nd of 8 giving 3lb to Guest of Honour (31 Mar Catterick 5f gd RF 0523). AW high 63 (1st run) - 4th of 9 giving 2lb to Royal Preview (15 Jan Southwell 6f Fibr RF 0104). Becoming disappointing.
**C Smith [1-14] John Martin-Hoyes.*

OFFICE HOURS BHB 24f40a RR 6f 40a 3667^{9}
7 b g Danehill (USA) 9.1f **(79)** - Charmina (FR) (Nonoalco (USA)) 8.5f **(66)**
Form - 000
Record 1999 - 1st:0 2nd:0 3rd:0 Ran:3
Pre1999 - 1st:0 2nd:2 3rd:3 Ran:24
Win Prizemoney £0 *Total Prizemoney* £4,047
1999 Turf 0-2: (5f, 7f) (g-f, hrd) 1999 AW 0-1: (12f) (Fibr)
Moderate gelding, has worn blinkers. Turf high 6 (began Jly).
**R Lee [0-7] Richard Lee (from W G M Turner [0-5] Apr 1997).*

O'GARNEY PARK (IRE) BHB 18a RR 31f 18a 178^{8}
5 b g Shalford (IRE) 7.8f **(63)** - Rince Si (Malinowski (USA)) 10f **(56)**
Form - 068
Record 1999 - 1st:0 2nd:0 3rd:0 Ran:1
Pre1999 - 1st:0 2nd:0 3rd:1 Ran:19
Win Prizemoney £0 *Total Prizemoney* £412
1999 AW 0-1: (13f) (Equi)
Very moderate gelding, often wears blinkers.
**P Mitchell [0-3] D M Murphy (from D Hassett in IRE [0-20] Aug 1998).*

OGILIA BHB 86f **RR 88+f** 5023^{3}
2 b f Bin Ajwaad (IRE) - Littlemisstrouble (USA) (My Gallant (USA)) 9f **(71)**
Form - D123303
Record 1999 - 1st:1 2nd:1 3rd:3 Ran:7
Win Prizemoney £2,814 *Total Prizemoney* £12,344
Wins * **1999** Aug Bath (HRD) 5.7f 83+ <
1999 Turf 1-7: (6f 1-5, 7f 2) (gd 3, g-f 2, frm 1-2)
Useful filly, effective 6 to 7f, best at 6f, acts on gd to frm, best on gd. Turf high 88 (began Jly) - 3rd of 20 giving 4lb to Out of Africa (8 Spt Doncaster 7f gd RF 4206) - also 1st of 9 giving 6lb to Leen (3 Aug Bath RF 3308). First past the past in two races at Bath, she was disqualified on the first occasion, and put in her best effort when placed behind Out Of Africa in a hot Doncaster nursery.
**I A Balding [1-7] G M Smart.*

OH I SAY BHB 54f55a **RR 55f 55a** 1801^{14}
3 b f Primo Dominie 7.2f **(67)** - Isotonic (Absalom) 7.2f **(58)**
Form - 24780
Record 1999 - 1st:0 2nd:1 3rd:0 Ran:5
Pre1999 - 1st:2 2nd:1 3rd:0 Ran:11
Win Prizemoney £8,028 *Total Prizemoney* £9,996
Wins 1998 May Windso (G-F) 5f 71 <
1998 Apr Nottin (G-S) 5.1f 71 <
1999 Turf 0-1: (6f) (gd) 1999 AW 0-4: (5f 2, 6f 2) (Equi 3, Fibr)
Neat, average filly, effective 5f, acts on gd to frm - acts on Equi. AW high 65. Inconsistent.
**Miss Gay Kelleway [0-5] Loose Cannon Racing (from M L W Bell [2-11] Oct 1998).*

OH NO NOT HIM BHB 35f **RR 45f** 4153^{8}
3 b g Reprimand 8.2f **(63)** - Lucky Mill **(23f)** (Midyan (USA)) 6f **(60)**
Form - 088
Record 1999 - 1st:0 2nd:0 3rd:0 Ran:3
Pre1999 - 1st:0 2nd:0 3rd:0 Ran:3
1999 Turf 0-1: (8f) (gd) 1999 AW 0-2: (9f, 12f) (Fibr 2)
Workmanlike, moderate gelding, has worn blinkers. AW high 8 (began Aug).
**M Mullineaux [0-3] Little Stanneylands Stud (from M A Jarvis [0-3] Oct 1998).*

OH SO GRAND BHB 46f53a **RR 43f 53a** 1974^{7}
3 ch f Grand Lodge (USA) - Cutleaf (Kris) 9.5f **(73)**
Form - 823507
Record 1999 - 1st:0 2nd:0 3rd:0 Ran:2
Pre1999 - 1st:0 2nd:1 3rd:1 Ran:7
Win Prizemoney £0 *Total Prizemoney* £792
1999 Turf 0-1: (8f) (g-f) 1999 AW 0-1: (8f) (Fibr)
Workmanlike, fair filly, effective 8f, - acts on Fibr, has worn blinkers, likes left handed tracks, favours tight tracks. Inconsistent.
**R M H Cowell [0-9] R M West.*

OKABANGO RR 111f $5013a^{8}$
3 c
Form - 8
1999 Turf 0-1: (12f)
Currently Group-class. (1st run) - 8th to First Magnitude (17 Oct Longchamp 12f RF 5013a). **J-C Rouget in FR [0-1].*

OK BABE BHB 37f55a **RR 23f 55a** 5128^{18}
4 b f Bold Arrangement 8.7f **(57)** - Celtic Bird (Celtic Cone) 9.8f **(43)**
Form - 0000
Record 1999 - 1st:0 2nd:0 3rd:0 Ran:4
Pre1999 - 1st:2 2nd:1 3rd:1 Ran:13
Win Prizemoney £4,786 *Total Prizemoney* £6,144
Wins 1998 *Feb Southw (STD) H 6f 65 73* <
1997 *Nov Wolver (STD) S 6f 67*
1999 Turf 0-4: (6f, 7f 3) (g-s, gd 2, g-f)
Light-framed, above-average filly, effective 6f, - acts on Fibr, has worn blinkers, likes left handed tracks, likes tight tracks. Turf high 44 (began Aug). Becoming disappointing.
**G P Enright [0-4] OK Partnership (from J Akehurst [2-13] Nov 1998).*

OK JOHN (IRE) BHB 42f56a **RR 40df 56a** $5078a^{17}$
4 b g Mac's Imp (USA) 5.6f **(54)** - Ching A Ling (Pampapaul) 10.9f **(63)**
Form - 022448000
Record 1999 - 1st:0 2nd:1 3rd:0 Ran:7
Pre1999 - 1st:0 2nd:3 3rd:2 Ran:15
Win Prizemoney £0 *Total Prizemoney* £3,298
1999 Turf 0-4: (5f 2, 6f, 8f) (g-s 2, gd 2) 1999 AW 0-3: (6f 3) (Equi 2, Fibr)
Workmanlike, fair gelding, effective 6f, - acts on AW, best on Fibr, has worn blinkers, prefers left handed tracks, prefers tight tracks. Turf high 3 (began Aug). AW high 61 (1st run) - 2nd of 13 getting 3lb from Acid Test (2 Jan Lingfield 6f Equi RF 0013). Becoming disappointing.
**L T Reilly in IRE [0-4] John Casey (from J Akehurst [0-18] Jan 1999).*

OKTAN (IRE) RR 91f $4373a^{3}$
7 h
Form - 3
1999 AW 0-1: (8f) (Dirt)
Currently useful horse. (1st run) - 3rd of 10 to Loch Bering (12 Spt Taby 8f Dirt RF 4373a). **Catherine Erichsen in NOR [0-1].*

OLD FEATHERS (IRE) BHB 67f **RR 69f** 4283^{6}
2 b c Hernando (FR) - Undiscovered (Tap On Wood) 10.3f **(65)**
Form - 666
Record 1999 - 1st:0 2nd:0 3rd:0 Ran:3
1999 Turf 0-3: (6f, 8f 2) (g-f, frm 2)
Currently average colt. Turf high 69 (began Jly).
**J G FitzGerald [0-3] Marquesa de Moratalla.*

OLD GOLD N TAN BHB 20f24a **RR 11f 24a** 1421^{7}
6 ch g Ballacashtal (CAN) 7.9f **(51)** -Raleigh Gazelle(Absalom) 7.2f **(58)**
Form - 7
Record 1999 - 1st:0 2nd:0 3rd:0 Ran:1
Pre1999 - 1st:0 2nd:0 3rd:0 Ran:11
1999 AW 0-1: (8f) (Fibr)
Very moderate gelding, had worn blinkers. (DEAD)
**A G Juckes [0-9] A C W Price (from J R Poulton [0-10] Feb 1998).*

OLD HUSH WING (IRE) BHB 55f38a **RR 53f 38a** 4717^{10}
6 b g Tirol 8.1f **(64)** - Saneena (Kris) 9.5f **(73)**
Form - 32110
Record 1999 - 1st:2 2nd:1 3rd:1 Ran:5
Pre1999 - 1st:1 2nd:2 3rd:2 Ran:17
Win Prizemoney £8,717 *Total Prizemoney* £11,782
Wins * **1999** Apr Pontef (SFT) H 17.1f 50 53 <
* **1999** Mar Newcas (G-S) H 16.1f 43 49
1997 Jly Hamilt (G-F) H 13f 40 44
1999 Turf 2-3: (16f 1-1, 17f 1-2) (sft 1-1, gd 1-2) 1999 AW 0-2: (16f 2) (Fibr 2)
Fair gelding, effective 13 to 17f, acts on sft to gd, best on gd, has worn blinkers. Turf high 53 - 1st of 16 getting 17lb from Jamaican Flight (20 Apr Pontefract RF 0774) - also 1st of 11 getting 13lb from Quezon City (30 Mar Newcastle RF 0515). AW high 38.
**Mrs M Reveley [3-10] Mark Barrett Racing (from P C Haslam [3-24] Jly 1998).*

OLD JOHN (IRE) RR 2804^{6}
2 b c Port Lucaya - Bradwell (IRE) **(49f 47a)** (Taufan (USA)) 7f **(57)**
Form - P6
Record 1999 - 1st:0 2nd:0 3rd:0 Ran:2
1999 Turf 0-2: (6f, 7f) (gd, frm)
Currently very poor colt, often wears blinkers. (began Jly) - 6th of 6 getting 1lb from Courting (14 Jly Catterick 7f frm RF 2804).
**J J O'Neill [0-2] Clayton Bigley Partnership Ltd.*

OLD RED (IRE) BHB 48f65a **RR 48f 65a** 3475^{6}
9 ch g Ela-Mana-Mou 12.7f **(72)** - Sea Port (Averof) 8.2f **(62)**
Form - 26
Record 1999 - 1st:0 2nd:1 3rd:0 Ran:2
Pre1999 - 1st:5 2nd:5 3rd:4 Ran:30
Win Prizemoney £58,733 *Total Prizemoney* £68,860
Wins * 1998 Spt Nottin (GD) H 16f 44 48
* 1998 Aug Nottin (G-F) H 16f 40 42
* 1995 Oct Newmar (G-F) H 18f 66 74 <
1999 Turf 0-2: (16f 2) (gd, g-f)
Average gelding, effective 14 to 16f, best at 16f, acts on gd to frm, best on gd, likes left handed tracks, likes tight tracks. Turf high 46 (1st run) (began Jly) - 2nd of 8 getting 2lb from Tonnerre (3 Jly Beverley 16f gd RF 2514).
**Mrs M Reveley [5-27] A Flannigan (from P F I Cole [0-5] Spt 1993).*

OLD SCHOOL HOUSE BHB 45f52a **RR 19f 52a** 2244[12]
6 ch h Polar Falcon (USA) 9f **(74)** - Farewell Letter (USA) (Arts And Letters (USA)) 12.7f **(68)**
Form - 000
Record 1999 - 1st:0 2nd:0 3rd:0 Ran:3
Pre1999 - 1st:4 2nd:3 3rd:1 Ran:14
Win Prizemoney £11,102 *Total Prizemoney* £14,131
Wins * 1996 *Aug Lingfi (STD) 16f 73* <
* 1996 Aug Bath (G-F) H 17.2f 50 56+
* 1996 Aug Doncas (G-F) H 16.5f 50 62
* 1996 *Jun Wolver (STD) H 14.8f 45 56*
1999 Turf 0-3: (8f 2, 12f) (frm 3)
Above-average horse. Turf high 19. Becoming disappointing.
**T J Naughton [4-13] T J Naughton (from C N Allen [0-4] Oct 1995).*

OLD TRIESTE (USA) RR 5231a[8]
4 ch c A P Indy (USA) - Lovlier Linda (USA) (Vigors (USA)) 10f **(72)**
Form - 8
1999 AW 0-1: (10f) (Dirt)
Currently Group-class. **M Puype in USA [0-1].*

OLIBERI BHB 41f **RR 51f** 3105[1]
3 b g First Trump - Rhiannon (Welsh Pageant) 10f **(65)**
Form - 6281
Record 1999 - 1st:1 2nd:1 3rd:0 Ran:4
Pre1999 - 1st:0 2nd:0 3rd:0 Ran:3
Win Prizemoney £1,982 *Total Prizemoney* £2,876
Wins * **1999** Jly Redcar (FRM) S 11f 45 <
1999 Turf 1-4: (8f, 11f 1-3) (g-f 2, frm 1-2)
Scopey, fair gelding, effective 11f, acts on g-f to frm. Turf high 51 - 2nd of 10 getting 9lb from Mystagogue (29 Jun Hamilton 11f g-f RF 2396) - also 1st of 9 giving 5lb to Lively Project (24 Jly Redcar RF 3105). **J Berry [1-7] Exors of the late J K M Oliver.*

OLIVE THE TWIST (USA) BHB 88f **RR 94f** 4019[8]
4 ch f Theatrical 11.5f **(78)** - Lady of the Light (USA) (The Minstrel (CAN)) 10f **(72)**
Form - 428
Record 1999 - 1st:0 2nd:1 3rd:0 Ran:3
Pre1999 - 1st:1 2nd:0 3rd:0 Ran:3
Win Prizemoney £4,854 *Total Prizemoney* £7,766
Wins * 1998 Jun Newmar (GD) 10f 85+ <
1999 Turf 0-3: (10f 3) (g-f 3)
Leggy, useful filly. Turf high 94 - 2nd of 5 giving 6lb to Sheba Spring (25 Jly Ascot 10f g-f RF 3121). Lightly raced in recent seasons, she has not proved she has really trained on, although she ran better when runner-up at Ascot.
**J H M Gosden [1-6] Landon Knight.*

OLIVIAS CHOICE BHB 64f **RR 65f** 4375[7]
2 b f Pyramus (USA) - Navarino Bay (Averof) 8.2f **(62)**
Form - 515807
Record 1999 - 1st:1 2nd:0 3rd:0 Ran:6
Win Prizemoney £3,442 *Total Prizemoney* £3,442
Wins * **1999** Jun Goodwo (G-S) S 6f 66 <
1999 Turf 1-6: (5f, 6f 1-3, 7f 2) (g-s 1-1, gd 3, g-f 2)
Average filly, effective 6f, acts on g-s, has worn blinkers. Turf high 66 - 1st of 7 getting 5lb from Vipee (2 Jun Goodwood RF 1673).
**K R Burke [1-6] Mrs Elaine Burke.*

OLIVO (IRE) BHB 61f **RR 63f** 4218[6]
5 ch g Priolo (USA) 10.9f **(71)** - Honourable Sheba (USA) (Roberto (USA)) 10f **(76)**
Form - 2006
Record 1999 - 1st:0 2nd:1 3rd:0 Ran:4
Pre1999 - 1st:2 2nd:2 3rd:3 Ran:20
Win Prizemoney £5,808 *Total Prizemoney* £15,150
Wins * 1998 Jly Salisb (FRM) 14.1f 67
* 1997 Jly Bright (FRM) H 8f 67 69 <
1999 Turf 0-4: (12f, 13f, 14f, 16f) (gd 2, g-f, frm)
Average gelding, effective 13 to 16f, best at 16f, acts on g-s to frm, best on frm, prefers right handed tracks. Turf high 63 (1st run) (began Jly) - 2nd of 9 getting 9lb from Borgia (17 Jly Newbury 13f g-f RF 2904). Consistent.
**C A Horgan [2-21] J L Harrison (from P F I Cole [0-3] Oct 1996).*

OLLIE'S CHUCKLE (IRE) BHB 53f45a **RR 42f 45a** 4902[16]
4 b g Mac's Imp (USA) 5.6f **(54)** - Chenya (Beldale Flutter (USA)) 9.7f **(71)**
Form - 5010303000
Record 1999 - 1st:1 2nd:0 3rd:2 Ran:10
Pre1999 - 1st:0 2nd:2 3rd:2 Ran:13
Win Prizemoney £1,881 *Total Prizemoney* £5,448
Wins * **1999** Apr Redcar (G-S) H 9f 55 56 <
1999 Turf 1-8: (7f, 8f 4, 9f 1-3) (g-s, gd 1-4, g-f, frm 2) 1999 AW 0-2: (8f 2) (Fibr 2)
Moderate gelding, effective 7f, acts on gd, likes left handed tracks, favours tight tracks. Turf high 58. AW high 36. Becoming disappointing. A winner over nine furlongs at Redcar on good to soft ground in April, he has been disappointing since.
**J J Quinn [1-21] Mrs S Quinn (from J A Glover [0-2] Aug 1997).*

OMAHA CITY (IRE) BHB 95f **RR 94f** 5039[6]
5 b g Night Shift (USA) 8.1f **(73)** - Be Discreet (Junius (USA)) 7.7f **(65)**
Form - 055174846333106
Record 1999 - 1st:2 2nd:0 3rd:3 Ran:15
Pre1999 - 1st:2 2nd:3 3rd:3 Ran:29
Win Prizemoney £28,667 *Total Prizemoney* £77,730
Wins * **1999** Oct York (G-S) H 7f 90 94
* **1999** Jun Goodwo (G-F) H 8f 82 87
* 1997 Aug Goodwo (G-F) H 7f 100 100 <
* 1996 Jun Cheste (G-F) 5.1f 73
1999 Turf 2-15: (6f, 7f 1-9, 8f 1-5) (g-s, gd 1-8, g-f 1-3, frm 3)
Useful gelding, effective 7f, acts on gd to frm. Turf high 94 - 1st of 8 getting 14lb from Granny's Pet (7 Oct York RF 4761). He is very difficult to win with these days, but he is a different horse at Goodwood and a drop in the handicap helped enable him to regain winning ways at that track in June. After being placed three times at Goodwood since his win, he won in fine style at York over seven furlongs when beating a useful field. He is effective over seven furlongs to a mile. **B Gubby [4-44] Brian Gubby Ltd.*

OMAR DANCER RR 5f 4951[13]
3 b g Shareef Dancer (USA) 10.1f **(67)** - Happydrome (Ahonoora) 8.1f **(73)**
Form - 00
Record 1999 - 1st:0 2nd:0 3rd:0 Ran:2
1999 Turf 0-2: (7f, 8f) (gd, g-f)
Currently very poor gelding. Turf high 5 (began Oct).
**C Smith [0-2] A E Moss.*

OMAR'S ODYSSEY (IRE) BHB 28f **RR 28f** 4182[7]
4 ch g Sharifabad (IRE) - Tales Of Homer (Home Guard (USA)) 9.3f **(66)**
Form - 4057
Record 1999 - 1st:0 2nd:0 3rd:0 Ran:4
Pre1999 - 1st:0 2nd:0 3rd:0 Ran:10
Win Prizemoney £0 *Total Prizemoney* £245
1999 Turf 0-3: (8f, 10f, 11f) (frm 3) 1999 AW 0-1: (13f) (Equi)
Scopey, little account gelding, often wears blinkers. Turf high 28 (began Jly). **P Mitchell [0-15] Richard Cohen.*

OMNIHEAT BHB 71f **RR 67f** 5218[1]
2 b f Ezzoud (IRE) - Lady Bequick (Sharpen Up) 8.3f **(67)**
Form - 5540461
Record 1999 - 1st:1 2nd:0 3rd:0 Ran:7
Win Prizemoney £4,611 *Total Prizemoney* £4,883
Wins * **1999** Nov Doncas (SFT) H 7f 66 67 <
1999 Turf 1-7: (6f, 7f 1-5, 8f) (g-s 1-1, gd 2, g-f, frm 3)
Average filly, effective 7f, acts on g-s. Turf high 67 (began Jly) - 1st of 22 getting 6lb from Slick Willie (6 Nov Doncaster RF 5218).
**M J Ryan [1-7] Mrs E Delaney.*

ONCE MORE FOR LUCK (IRE) BHB 70f65a **RR 75f 65a** 5025[4]
8 b g Petorius 8f **(66)** - Mrs Lucky (Royal Match) 11.8f **(54)**
Form - 3304
Record 1999 - 1st:0 2nd:0 3rd:2 Ran:4
Pre1999 - 1st:8 2nd:8 3rd:7 Ran:47
Win Prizemoney £29,137 *Total Prizemoney* £49,152
Wins * 1998 Oct Catter (SFT) C 12f 78 <
* 1998 Spt Mussel (GD) H 12f 65 67
* 1998 Spt York (GD) H 10.4f 60 67

* 1997 Oct Ayr (SFT) S 13.1f 53+
* 1996 Oct Redcar (G-F) C 11f 67
* 1995 Oct Catter (G-F) C 12f 61+

1999 Turf 0-4: (12f, 14f 2, 15f) (g-s, gd 3)

Above-average gelding, effective 12 to 15f, best at 14f, acts on g-s to gd, best on g-s, likes tight tracks, excels at Catterick. Turf high 76 (1st run) - 3rd of 9 giving 9lb to Kathryn's Pet (31 Mar Catterick 14f gd RF 0525). Consistent.

**Mrs M Reveley [17-73] The Mary Reveley Racing Club (from M Johnston [0-8] Spt 1994).*

ON CREDIT (IRE) RR 57f 5189[7]

2 ch g Magical Wonder (USA) 7.2f **(60)** - Forest Treasure (USA) (Green Forest (USA)) 9.9f **(68)**

Form - 07

Record 1999 - 1st:0 2nd:0 3rd:0 Ran:2

1999 Turf 0-2: (8f 2) (gd, g-f)

Currently fair gelding, often wears blinkers. Turf high 57 (began Oct). **Miss I Foustok [0-2] Buckram Oak Holdings.*

ONE DINAR (FR) BHB 64f57a **RR 72f 57a** 4260[12]

4 b c Generous (IRE) 11.5f **(82)** - Lyphartissima (FR) (Lightning (FR)) 7.9f **(74)**

Form - 423554024610

Record 1999 - 1st:1 2nd:2 3rd:1 Ran:11
Pre1999 - 1st:0 2nd:0 3rd:0 Ran:9

Win Prizemoney £3,744 *Total Prizemoney* £6,908

Wins * 1999 Spt Lingfi (G-F) 7f 72 <

1999 Turf 1-11: (7f 1-3, 8f 6, 9f, 10f) (gd, g-f 5, frm 1-4, hrd)

Workmanlike, above-average colt, effective 7 to 10f, acts on gd to frm, best on gd, has worn blinkers, likes right handed tracks. Turf high 72 - 1st of 11 giving 9lb to Lady Breanne (7 Spt Lingfield RF 4180). In his relatively short career he has been tried over several distances, but appears best at around a mile on fast ground.

**K Mahdi [1-18] Greenfield Stud (from J H M Gosden [0-2] Spt 1997).*

ONE DOMINO BHB 65f **RR 61f** 4635[6]

2 ch c Efisio 7.7f **(69)** - Dom One **(85f)** (Dominion) 8.5f **(63)**

Form - 53406

Record 1999 - 1st:0 2nd:0 3rd:1 Ran:5

Win Prizemoney £0 *Total Prizemoney* £776

1999 Turf 0-5: (7f 2, 8f 3) (g-s, gd 2, frm 2)

Average colt. Turf high 61. **J Berry [0-5] Bernard Hathaway.*

ONE FOR ALL RR 10f 4440[18]

4 gr g Petong 7.6f **(58)** - Go Tally-Ho (Gorytus (USA)) 7.8f **(60)**

Form - 00

Record 1999 - 1st:0 2nd:0 3rd:0 Ran:2

1999 Turf 0-2: (6f, 8f) (g-f, hrd)

Unfurnished, poor gelding. Turf high 10 (began Spt).

**Mrs S J Smith [0-9] Leigh Musketeer Racing Club.*

ONE IN THE EYE BHB 21f31a **RR 41f 31a** 3015[11]

6 br g Arrasas (USA) 14.4f **(37)** - Mingalles (Prince de Galles)

Form - 800

Record 1999 - 1st:0 2nd:0 3rd:0 Ran:3
Pre1999 - 1st:0 2nd:0 3rd:4 Ran:21

Win Prizemoney £0 *Total Prizemoney* £1,672

1999 Turf 0-2: (8f 2) (frm 2) 1999 AW 0-1: (11f) (Fibr)

Moderate gelding, has worn blinkers. Turf high 41.

**J R Poulton [0-29] F Willson.*

ONE OF THE FAMILY BHB 57f **RR 60f** 4993[6]

4 b f Alzao (USA) 9.8f **(73)** - Someone Special (Habitat) 9.4f **(70)**

Form - 055055266

Record 1999 - 1st:0 2nd:1 3rd:0 Ran:9

Win Prizemoney £0 *Total Prizemoney* £858

1999 Turf 0-9: (8f 4, 9f, 10f 2, 11f, 12f) (gd 3, g-f 2, frm 4)

Scopey, average filly, effective 9f, acts on g-f. Turf high 71. Consistent. **J R Fanshawe [0-9] Helena Springfield Ltd.*

ONE QUICK LION BHB 69f **RR 79f** 5198[5]

3 b c Lion Cavern (USA) 7.5f **(74)** - One Quick Bid (USA) (Commemorate (USA))

Form - 065

Record 1999 - 1st:0 2nd:0 3rd:0 Ran:3

1999 Turf 0-3: (7f, 8f 2) (gd, g-f 2)

Leggy, currently above-average colt. Turf high 73 - 6th of 14 giving 5lb to Sheer Harmony (11 Oct Windsor 8f g-f RF 4824).

**R W Armstrong [0-3] R J Arculli.*

ONES ENOUGH BHB 57f **RR 57f** 4673[17]

3 b c Reprimand 8.2f **(63)** - Sea Fairy (Wollow) 8.2f **(61)**

Form - 05000000

Record 1999 - 1st:0 2nd:0 3rd:0 Ran:8
Pre1999 - 1st:2 2nd:0 3rd:2 Ran:7

Win Prizemoney £6,104 *Total Prizemoney* £7,335

Wins * 1998 Oct Lingfi (HVY) 5f 88 <
* 1998 Spt Folkes (G-F) 5f 70

1999 Turf 0-8: (5f 2, 6f 4, 7f 2) (g-s 3, gd, g-f 3, frm)

Leggy, fair colt, effective 5f, acts on sft, has worn blinkers. Turf high 72. Inconsistent.

**G L Moore [2-15] Heart Of The South Racing (3).*

ONE STEP AT A TIME BHB 99f **RR 98f** 4792[2]

2 b f Sabrehill (USA) 8.5f **(64)** - Ghost Tree (IRE) (Caerleon (USA)) 8.6f **(71)**

Form - 21732

Record 1999 - 1st:1 2nd:2 3rd:1 Ran:5

Win Prizemoney £2,148 *Total Prizemoney* £10,449

Wins * 1999 *Jly Southw (STD) 7f* 76+ <

1999 Turf 0-4: (7f 2, 8f 2) (gd 2, g-f, frm) 1999 AW 1-1:(7f 1-1) (Fibr 1-1)

Very useful filly. Turf high 98 - 2nd of 11 getting 5lb from French Fellow (9 Oct Ascot 8f gd RF 4792). (1st run). She pulled too hard after winning a maiden on the All-Weather, but showed improved form when consenting to settle at Ascot in October. Sold for 90,000 gns at Tattersalls in October, reportedly to race in Saudi Arabia. **B W Hills [1-5] Mrs H Theodorou.*

ONE TO GO (IRE) BHB 39f45a **RR 33f 45a** 4712[10]

4 b g Petorius 8f **(66)** - Caroline's Mark (On Your Mark) 7.7f **(58)**

Form - 06000

Record 1999 - 1st:0 2nd:0 3rd:0 Ran:5
Pre1999 - 1st:1 2nd:5 3rd:1 Ran:21

Win Prizemoney £2,304 *Total Prizemoney* £6,491

Wins 1998 Oct Catter (gd,) 6f 51<

1999 Turf 0-3: (6f, 7f, 8f) (gd, g-f, frm) 1999 AW 0-2: (6f, 8f) (Equi, Fibr)

Workmanlike, very moderate gelding, effective 6 to 7f, best at 6f, acts on gd to g-f - acts on Fibr, has worn blinkers, likes left handed tracks, likes tight tracks. Turf high 33 (began Spt). AW high 30. Consistent.

**G F H Charles-Jones [0-7] J M Cook (from J Berry [1-21] Oct 1998).*

ONE WON ONE (USA) BHB 91f **RR 103+f** 5175a[2]

5 b g Naevus (USA) 7.2f **(86)** - Havards Bay (ARG) **00**

Form - 013404608362

1999 Turf 1-12: (5f 2, 6f 1-7, 7f, 8f 2) (sft 3, g-s 1-2, gd 4, g-f 3)

Very useful gelding, effective 5 to 6f, best at 6f, acts on sft to g-f, has worn blinkers, and excels at Leopardstown. Turf high 109 - 3rd of 10 to Eastern Purple (22 May Curragh 6f g-f RF 1476a). He had a super season in '98 and must have given the Irish handicapper nightmares, moving from a rating of 78 to 104. Not quite so effective last season, but a useful tool in listed company and the top Irish handicaps. **Ms J Morgan in IRE [6-29] Heavenly Syndicate.*

ONICE NERO RR 109f 5206a[2]

3 b c Primo Dominie 7.2f **(67)** - Nord's Lucy (IRE) (Nordico (USA)) 6.5f **(62)**

Form - 212

1999 Turf 1-3: (7f 1-2, 8f) (g-s 1-2, g-f)

Pattern-class colt. Turf high 109 (began Jly) - 2nd of 12 getting 5lb from Tertullian (31 Oct San Siro 7f g-s RF 5206a).

**B Grizzetti in ITY [2-4].*

ONLY FOR GOLD BHB 57f54a **RR 55f 54a** 5072[3]

4 b c Presidium 7.5f **(56)** - Calvanne Miss (Martinmas) 7.6f **(59)**

Form - 257660788220233

Record 1999 - 1st:0 2nd:4 3rd:2 Ran:15
Pre1999 - 1st:2 2nd:0 3rd:0 Ran:13

Win Prizemoney £15,660 *Total Prizemoney* £26,554

Wins * 1997 Jun Beverl (G-F) 5f 84 <
* 1997 May Cheste (SFT) 5.1f 84 <

1999 Turf 0-15: (6f 5, 7f 4, 8f 6) (g-s 2, gd 4, g-f 4, frm 5)

Workmanlike, fair colt, effective 6f, acts on sft, has worn blinkers.

Turf high 69. Consistent.
**J Berry [2-28] John Milner & Stephen Milner.*

ONLY JOSH (IRE) BHB 24f42a **RR 9f 42a** 2919[14]
5 gr g Waajib 8.9f **(67)** - Carlyle Suite (USA) (Icecapade (USA)) 11f **(62)**
Form - 00
Record 1999 - 1st:0 2nd:0 3rd:0 Ran:2
Pre1999 - 1st:0 2nd:0 3rd:1 Ran:10
Win Prizemoney £0 *Total Prizemoney* £782
1999 Turf 0-2: (8f 2) (g-f, hrd)
Little account gelding, has worn blinkers. Turf high 9.
**R A Fahey [0-2] Mrs Andrea Mallinson (from J A Glover [0-2] Jun 1998).*

ONLYONEUNITED BHB 71f **RR 73f** 4668[2]
2 b f Pelder (IRE) - Supreme Rose (Frimley Park) 6.5f **(67)**
Form - 052
Record 1999 - 1st:0 2nd:1 3rd:0 Ran:3
Win Prizemoney £0 *Total Prizemoney* £1,230
1999 Turf 0-3: (5f, 6f 2) (g-s 2, frm)
Currently above-average filly. Turf high 73 - 2nd of 13 getting 5lb from Kier Park (1 Oct Lingfield 5f g-s RF 4668).
**M Blanshard [0-3] Aykroyd and Sons Ltd.*

ON PORPOISE BHB 46f **RR 63f** 5198[9]
3 b g Dolphin Street (FR) - Floppie (FR) (Law Society (USA)) 9.9f **(70)**
Form - 000
Record 1999 - 1st:0 2nd:0 3rd:0 Ran:3
1999 Turf 0-3: (8f 2, 10f) (gd 3)
Currently average gelding. Turf high 63 (began Oct).
**P W D'Arcy [0-3] Paul D'Arcy.*

ON SHADE RR 26f 5020[17]
2 ch f Polar Falcon (USA) 9f **(74)** - Vagrant Maid (USA) (Honest Pleasure (USA)) 10.4f **(73)**
Form - 60
Record 1999 - 1st:0 2nd:0 3rd:0 Ran:2
1999 Turf 0-2: (8f 2) (g-s, gd)
Currently little account filly. Turf high 26 (began Spt).
**N Tinkler [0-2] Philip Grundy.*

ON THE RIDGE (IRE) BHB 115f **RR 112f** 1995[8]
4 ch c Risk Me (FR) 8f **(53)** - Star Ridge (USA) (Storm Bird (CAN)) 10.3f **(74)**
Form - 28
Record 1999 - 1st:0 2nd:1 3rd:0 Ran:2
Pre1999 - 1st:1 2nd:1 3rd:2 Ran:4
Win Prizemoney £7,440 *Total Prizemoney* £25,229
Wins * 1998 Jun York (G-S) 7.9f 98+ <
1999 Turf 0-2: (8f 2) (g-s, g-f)
Scopey, Group-class colt, effective 8f, acts on g-s. Turf high 112 (1st run) - 2nd of 9 to Handsome Ridge (23 Apr Sandown 8f g-s RF 0822). Like most of Risk Me's offspring, he enjoys easy ground and ran well when finishing second to Handsome Ridge under testing conditions at Sandown in April. Obviously unhappy when unplaced on a fast surface at Royal Ascot, he did not run during the second half of the campaign.
**H R A Cecil [1-6] Buckram Oak Holdings.*

ON THE TRAIL RR 54f 4942[6]
2 ch c Catrail (USA) - From The Rooftops (IRE) (Thatching) 8f **(66)**
Form - 86
Record 1999 - 1st:0 2nd:0 3rd:0 Ran:2
1999 Turf 0-2: (6f, 7f) (g-s, gd)
Currently fair colt. Turf high 54 (began Oct).
**S Dow [0-2] A N Solomons.*

ON TILL MORNING (IRE) BHB 66f **RR 67f** 4426[10]
3 ch f Never so Bold 7.1f **(62)** - Shamasiya (FR) (Vayrann) 9.7f **(74)**
Form - 45031180
Record 1999 - 1st:2 2nd:0 3rd:1 Ran:8
Pre1999 - 1st:1 2nd:1 3rd:2 Ran:5
Win Prizemoney £9,083 *Total Prizemoney* £12,417
Wins * **1999** Jly Ayr (GD) H 7f 65 67 <
* **1999** Jly Pontef (G-F) 6f 61
* 1998 Spt Mussel (GD) 5f 66
1999 Turf 2-8: (5f, 6f 1-4, 7f 1-2, 8f) (gd 2, g-f 1-2, frm 1-4)
Light-framed, average filly, effective 5 to 7f, acts on gd to frm, best on g-f. Turf high 67 - also 1st of 18 giving 17lb to Thorntoun Gold (26 Jly Ayr RF 3136). Consistent. **P Calver [3-13] D B Stanley.*

ON TIME (IRE) BHB 95f **RR 93+f** 4760[3]
2 b c Blues Traveller (IRE) - Go Flightline (IRE) (Common Grounds)
Form - 113
Record 1999 - 1st:2 2nd:0 3rd:1 Ran:3
Win Prizemoney £7,856 *Total Prizemoney* £9,197
Wins * **1999** Spt Goodwo (SFT) 7f 93+ <
* **1999** Aug Warwic (GD) 6.8f 72+
1999 Turf 2-3: (7f 2-3) (sft 1-1, gd 1-2)
Currently useful colt. Turf high 93 (began Aug) - 1st of 12 getting 2lb from Sir Ninja (22 Spt Goodwood RF 4491). Has plenty of dash, but has shown a tendency to edge off a true line.
**J R Fanshawe [2-3] Mrs David Russell.*

OO EE BE BHB 58f73a **RR 67f 73a** 4823[15]
3 b g Whittingham (IRE) - Miss Derby (USA) (Master Derby (USA)) 9.5f **(69)**
Form - 1232000
Record 1999 - 1st:0 2nd:1 3rd:0 Ran:4
Pre1999 - 1st:1 2nd:1 3rd:2 Ran:12
Win Prizemoney £2,829 *Total Prizemoney* £5,476
Wins * 1998 *Nov Lingfi (STD) H 8f 64 67* <
1999 Turf 0-3: (9f, 10f 2) (g-s, gd, g-f) 1999 AW 0-1: (10f) (Equi)
Strong, above-average gelding, effective 8 to 10f, best at 8f, - acts on Equi, has worn blinkers, prefers left handed tracks, prefers tight tracks. Turf high 54. (1st run) - 2nd of 4 getting 4lb from Hormuz (4 Mar Lingfield 10f Equi RF 0404). Becoming disappointing.
**A T Murphy [1-9] West Down Racing Partnership (from M A Buckley [0-7] Aug 1998).*

OPEN ARMS BHB 75f **RR 80f** 685[3]
3 ch g Most Welcome 8.6f **(66)** - Amber Fizz (USA) (Effervescing (USA)) 8.1f **(79)**
Form - 3
Record 1999 - 1st:0 2nd:0 3rd:1 Ran:1
Pre1999 - 1st:0 2nd:1 3rd:1 Ran:6
Win Prizemoney £0 *Total Prizemoney* £2,051
1999 Turf 0-1: (7f) (frm)
Scopey, decent gelding, effective 7 to 8f, best at 8f, acts on gd to frm. (1st run) - 3rd of 16 giving 5lb to Zulal (14 Apr Beverley 7f frm RF 0685).
**Mrs A L M King [0-1] Aiden Murphy (from C E Brittain [0-6] Oct 1998).*

OPEN GROUND (IRE) RR 42f 5104[9]
2 ch c Common Grounds 8.1f **(66)** - Poplina (USA) (Roberto (USA)) 10f **(76)**
Form - 0
Record 1999 - 1st:0 2nd:0 3rd:0 Ran:1
1999 Turf 0-1: (7f) (gd)
Currently moderate colt. **A C Stewart [0-1] S J Hammond.*

OPENING NIGHT BHB 46a **RR 22f** 2723[17]
4 b g Theatrical Charmer 10.9f **(63)** - First Time Over (Derrylin) 8.8f **(54)**
Form - 0
Record 1999 - 1st:0 2nd:0 3rd:0 Ran:1
Pre1999 - 1st:0 2nd:0 3rd:0 Ran:5
1999 Turf 0-1: (11f) (g-f)
Light-framed, very moderate gelding.
**Miss K M George [0-5] Exterior Profiles Ltd (from R Simpson [0-5] Aug 1998).*

OPENING RANGE BHB 32f32a **RR 31f 32a** 4233[17]
8 b m Nordico (USA) 8.2f **(59)** - Waveguide (Double Form) 7.3f **(58)**
Form - 86286000050460
Record 1999 - 1st:0 2nd:1 3rd:0 Ran:14
Pre1999 - 1st:2 2nd:2 3rd:1 Ran:20
Win Prizemoney £4,648 *Total Prizemoney* £7,190
Wins * 1997 Aug Windso (G-F) H 5f 35 42 <
* 1997 *Jly Wolver (STD) H 5f 35 34*
1999 Turf 0-8: (5f 8) (gd 2, g-f 2, frm 2, hrd 2) 1999 AW 0-6: (5f 4, 6f 2) (Equi 2, Fibr 4)
Very moderate mare, effective 5f, acts on frm - acts on Fibr, has

worn blinkers (effectively). Turf high 31 - 4th of 10 getting 32lb from Mousehole (2 Aug Windsor 5f frm RF 3305). AW high 31 - 2nd of 9 getting 26lb from Mary Jane (27 Jan Wolverhampton 5f Fibr RF 0171). Consistent.

**N E Berry [2-33] The Purple People Racing Partnership (from W J Musson [0-2] Jly 1994).*

OPERA BUFF (IRE) BHB 57f70a **RR 53f 70a** 2774[3]

8 br g Rousillon (USA) 10.4f **(69)** - Obertura (USA) (Roberto (USA)) 10f **(76)**

Form - 32358313010503

Record					
1999 -		1st:2	2nd:0	3rd:3	Ran:9
Pre1999 -		1st:9	2nd:6	3rd:11	Ran:64

Win Prizemoney £34,905 *Total Prizemoney* £51,353

Wins							
* **1999**	May Bright	(FRM)	H	11.9f	58	61	
* **1999**	*Feb Lingfi*	*(STD)*	*C*	*12f*		*79*	
* 1997	Spt Folkes	(FRM)		12f		72	
* 1997	Aug Bright	(G-F)	H	11.9f	65	69	
* 1997	May Bright	(FRM)		11.9f		70	
* 1997	*Jan Wolver*	*(STD)*	*H*	*12f*	*89*	*93*	<
* 1995	*Nov Lingfi*	*(STD)*	*H*	*13f*	*63*	*78*	
* 1995	*Nov Lingfi*	*(STD)*	*H*	*12f*	*50*	*67*	
* 1995	*Nov Wolver*	*(STD)*	*H*	*12f*	*50*	*62+*	
* 1995	Oct Nottin	(G-F)		14.1f		70+	
* 1995	Spt Salisb	(G-S)	CH	14f	50	58	

1999 Turf 1-5: (11f, 12f 1-3, 14f) (frm 4, hrd 1-1) 1999 AW 1-4: (12f 1-4) (Equi 1-3, Fibr)

Average gelding, effective 12 to 16f, best at 12f, - acted on Equi to Fibr, best on Equi, had worn blinkers, preferred left handed tracks, favoured tight tracks, excelled at Wolverhampton, liked Lingfield. Turf high 61. AW high 79 - 1st of 6 giving 11lb to Dellua (18 Feb Lingfield RF 0309). (DEAD)

**Miss Gay Kelleway [11-63] A P Griffin (from M C Pipe [0-6] Jly 1995).*

OPERA KING (USA) BHB 104f **RR 102f** 3445[3]

4 ch c Storm Bird (CAN) 8.5f **(82)** - Jewel In My Crown (CAN) (Secretariat (USA)) 9f **(79)**

Form - 13

Record					
1999 -		1st:1	2nd:0	3rd:1	Ran:2
Pre1999 -		1st:2	2nd:1	3rd:0	Ran:4

Win Prizemoney £34,049 *Total Prizemoney* £36,557

Wins							
* **1999**	May Goodwo	(GD)	H	14f	99	102	<
* 1998	May Lingfi	(GD)		11.5f		98	
* 1997	Jly Doncas	(GD)		7f		85	

1999 Turf 1-2: (12f, 14f 1-1) (gd 1-2)

Well made, very useful colt. Turf high 102 (1st run) - 1st of 9 getting 2lb from Perfect Paradigm (8 May Goodwood RF 1103). Lightly raced - he does sterling work as a lead horse for the Godolphin team at home - he stays a mile and three-quarters and disappointed on his only encounter with soft ground.

**S bin Suroor [3-6] Godolphin.*

OPERATIC BHB 60f58a **RR 57f 58a** 204[6]

4 b f Goofalik (USA) 15.4f **(66)** - Choir Mistress (Chief Singer) 8.9f **(66)**

Form - 054386

Record					
1999 -		1st:0	2nd:0	3rd:0	Ran:2
Pre1999 -		1st:3	2nd:10	3rd:11	Ran:36

Win Prizemoney £6,691 *Total Prizemoney* £20,121

Wins							
1998	*Spt Wolver*	*(STD)*		*14.8f*		*63*	<
1998	May Yarmou	(FRM)	C	16f		57	
1997	*Jly Wolver*	*(STD)*	*S*	*7f*		*54*	

1999 AW 0-2: (16f 2) (Equi, Fibr)

Workmanlike, average filly, effective 12 to 16f, acts on g-s to frm - acts on AW, mostly wears blinkers (extremely effectively), favours left handed tracks, excels at Yarmouth, likes Haydock and Nottingham, does well at Wolverhampton. AW high 36.

**P R Hedger [0-3] R E Greatorex (from P D Evans [2-32] Dec 1998).*

OPERATIONDESERTFOX RR 5137[16]

2 ch f Foxhound (USA) - Scravels Saran (IRE) (Indian King (USA)) 7.4f **(64)**

Form - 0

Record					
1999 -		1st:0	2nd:0	3rd:0	Ran:1

1999 Turf 0-1: (7f) (gd)

Currently very poor filly. **Dr J D Scargill [0-1] Derek Johnson.*

OPERETTA (FR) BHB 42f **RR 41f** 4153[9]

4 b f Lashkari 13.1f **(52)** - Lyric Opera (Sadler's Wells (USA)) 10f **(76)**

Form - 0

Record					
1999 -		1st:0	2nd:0	3rd:0	Ran:1
Pre1999 -		1st:0	2nd:0	3rd:1	Ran:4

Win Prizemoney £0 *Total Prizemoney* £515

1999 AW 0-1: (12f) (Fibr)

Leggy, moderate filly, has worn blinkers.

**Ian Williams [0-5] & Mrs John Poynton.*

OPTIMAITE BHB 100f **RR 98f** 5037[9]

2 b c Komaite (USA) 6.9f **(61)** - Leprechaun Lady (Royal Blend) 11.9f **(58)**

Form - 11002040

Record					
1999 -		1st:2	2nd:1	3rd:0	Ran:8

Win Prizemoney £10,076 *Total Prizemoney* £13,475

Wins							
* **1999**	Apr Ascot	(GD)		5f		94+	<
* **1999**	Apr Windso	(G-F)		5f		81+	

1999 Turf 2-8: (5f 2-4, 6f 2, 8f 2) (g-s, gd 2, g-f 1-3, frm 1-2)

Very useful colt, effective 5 to 8f, acts on gd to g-f. Turf high 98 - 4th of 11 to French Fellow (9 Oct Ascot 8f gd RF 4792) - also 1st of 5 from Bee Eight (28 Apr Ascot RF 0895). He proved more than just an early season juvenile, but rather struggled later in the campaign over longer trips, and was set some stiff tasks.

**B R Millman [2-8] Always Hopeful Partnership.*

OPTIMISTIC BHB 74f **RR 75f** 4377[13]

4 b f Reprimand 8.2f **(63)** - Arminda (Blakeney) 10.5f **(64)**

Form - 00

Record					
1999 -		1st:0	2nd:0	3rd:0	Ran:2
Pre1999 -		1st:2	2nd:0	3rd:0	Ran:6

Win Prizemoney £15,049 *Total Prizemoney* £15,518

Wins							
* 1997	Aug York	(GD)	H	7f	73	81+	<
* 1997	Jly Yarmou	(G-F)		7f		80+	

1999 Turf 0-2: (10f 2) (gd, frm)

Neat, above-average filly. Turf high 68 (began Aug).

**M H Tompkins [2-8] Mystic Meg Ltd.*

OPULENT BHB 51f **RR 60df** 4902[13]

8 b g Robellino (USA) 9.5f **(68)** - One Half Silver (CAN) (Plugged Nickle (USA)) 7.8f **(68)**

Form - 7380

Record					
1999 -		1st:0	2nd:0	3rd:1	Ran:4
Pre1999 -		1st:1	2nd:1	3rd:1	Ran:13

Win Prizemoney £5,466 *Total Prizemoney* £8,175

Wins							
* 1997	Jly Beverl	(HVY)	H	8.5f	71	74	<

1999 Turf 0-4: (8f, 9f, 10f 2) (sft, gd, frm 2)

Average gelding, effective 8 to 10f, acts on g-f to frm, likes tight tracks. Turf high 60 - 3rd of 10 getting 12lb from Top Jem (14 Apr Beverley 10f frm RF 0690).

**Mrs M Reveley [1-14] Mrs Eileen Hawkey (from C A Dwyer [0-2] Oct 1996).*

ORANGE ORDER (IRE) BHB 36f **RR 30f** 3978[13]

6 ch g Generous (IRE) 11.5f **(82)** - Fleur D'Oranger (Northfields (USA)) 9f **(72)**

Form - 0050

Record					
1999 -		1st:0	2nd:0	3rd:0	Ran:4
Pre1999 -		1st:1	2nd:0	3rd:0	Ran:5

Win Prizemoney £2,675 *Total Prizemoney* £2,850

Wins							
1996	Aug Kempto	(G-F)	C	10f		70	<

1999 Turf 0-4: (11f, 12f 2, 14f) (frm 4)

Very moderate gelding. Turf high 42. Inconsistent.

**G M Moore [2-7] Mrs A Roddis (from M Hourigan in IRE [2-13] Jly 1998).*

ORANGE SUNSET (IRE) RR 100f 4299a[5]

3 b f Roanoke (USA) - Classical Flair (USA) 00

Form - 11655

1999 Turf 2-5: (10f 1-2, 12f 1-2, 14f) (sft 1-2, gd 1-1, g-f 2)

Very useful filly. Turf high 100 - 6th of 8 to Polaire (26 Jun Curragh 10f g-f RF 2411a) - also 1st of 6 from Catherina (3 Jun Gowran Park RF 1827a). She is game, but struggled after winning a Listed race at Gowran Park in June. A galloper rather than a quickener, she is worth another try over a mile and three-quarters.

**D K Weld in IRE [0-3] Mrs Chryss O'Reilly (from L Browne in IRE [2-2] Jun 1999).*

ORANGEVILLE (USA) RR 80+f 5208[2]
2 b br c Dynaformer (USA) 12f **(82)** - Orange Sickle (USA) (Rich Cream (USA))
Form - 2
Record 1999 - 1st:0 2nd:1 3rd:0 Ran:1
Win Prizemoney £0 *Total Prizemoney* £1,010
1999 Turf 0-1: (7f) (g-s)
Currently decent colt. (1st run) - 2nd of 20 to Golovin (5 Nov Doncaster 7f g-s RF 5208). **J H M Gosden [0-1] Sheikh Mohammed.*

ORBITAL STAR (IRE) BHB 71f63a **RR 73f 63a** 3915[2]
3 b c Contract Law (USA) 8.9f **(54)** - Sun Gift (Guillaume Tell (USA)) 13.2f **(54)**
Form - 5711602
Record 1999 - 1st:2 2nd:1 3rd:0 Ran:6
Pre1999 - 1st:0 2nd:0 3rd:0 Ran:4
Win Prizemoney £6,838 *Total Prizemoney* £9,693
Wins * **1999** Jun Carlis (GD) H 9.3f 68 68 <
* **1999** May Lingfi (G-F) H 10f 64 67
1999 Turf 2-5: (9f 1-3, 10f 1-2) (gd 1-2, g-f 1-2, frm) 1999 AW 0-1: (10f) (Equi)
Light-framed, above-average colt, effective 9 to 10f, best at 10f, acted on gd to g-f, best on gd, preferred tight tracks. Turf high 73 - 2nd of 14 getting 1lb from First Fantasy (26 Aug Folkestone 10f gd RF 3915) - also 1st of 16 giving 5lb to Greyfield (10 Jun Carlisle RF 1877). (DEAD)**P W Harris [2-10] Hornbuckle, Buckle, Daffey & Knight.*

ORDAINED BHB 44f36a **RR 44f 36a** 5133[10]
6 b m Mtoto 11.5f **(71)** - In the Habit (USA) (Lyphard (USA)) 9.9f **(72)**
Form - 070080
Record 1999 - 1st:0 2nd:0 3rd:0 Ran:6
Pre1999 - 1st:3 2nd:7 3rd:5 Ran:38
Win Prizemoney £10,721 *Total Prizemoney* £22,404
Wins * 1997 Oct Newmar (G-F) H 12f 52 60
* 1996 Aug Redcar (FRM) H 11f 54 61 <
* 1996 Jun Redcar (G-F) H 10f 50 54
1999 Turf 0-5: (10f, 11f, 12f 3) (gd, g-f, frm 3) 1999 AW 0-1: (12f) (Fibr)
Moderate mare, effective 10 to 12f, best at 12f, acts on frm. Turf high 51 (began Jly).
**E J Alston [3-41] Peter Ebdon Racing (from T T Clement [0-3] Feb 1996).*

ORDER IN COURT (IRE) BHB 40a **RR 40a** 261[2]
5 ch m Imp Society (USA) 7.1f **(63)** - Fair Flutter (Beldale Flutter (USA)) 9.7f **(71)**
Form - 862
Record 1999 - 1st:0 2nd:1 3rd:0 Ran:2
Pre1999 - 1st:0 2nd:0 3rd:0 Ran:1
Win Prizemoney £0 *Total Prizemoney* £621
1999 AW 0-2: (9f, 12f) (Fibr 2)
Currently average filly. AW high 60 - 2nd of 7 giving 24lb to Crash Call Lady (10 Feb Wolverhampton 12f Fibr RF 0261).
**A Bailey [0-3] Peter Freeman.*

OREGON DREAM (IRE) BHB 60f **RR 61f** 4814[1]
3 b f Seattle Dancer (USA) 10.1f **(74)** - Ibda (Mtoto)
Form - 5215316001
Record 1999 - 1st:3 2nd:1 3rd:1 Ran:10
Pre1999 - 1st:0 2nd:0 3rd:1 Ran:3
Win Prizemoney £10,393 *Total Prizemoney* £12,068
Wins * **1999** Oct Leices (G-S) 8f 59
* **1999** Jly Nottin (GD) H 8.2f 60 61 <
* **1999** May Mussel (FRM) H 8f 54 60
1999 Turf 3-10: (8f 3-9, 10f) (g-s, gd 1-2, g-f 1-4, frm 1-3)
Leggy, average filly, effective 8f, acts on gd to frm, best on frm. Turf high 61 - 1st of 10 giving 13lb to Trois Elles (3 Jly Nottingham RF 2539) - also 1st of 13 getting 9lb from L S Lowry (17 May Musselburgh RF 1278). She is a fairly modest handicapper, but is effective in her grade and won three times last season.
**M L W Bell [3-11] Desmond Fitzgerald (from M W Easterby [0-2] Jly 1998).*

ORIEL GIRL BHB 50f41a **RR 39f 41a** 5128[11]
4 b f Beveled (USA) 6.9f **(64)** - St Helena (Monsanto (FR)) 6.5f **(59)**
Form - 800060108300284000
Record 1999 - 1st:1 2nd:1 3rd:1 Ran:14
Pre1999 - 1st:4 2nd:3 3rd:3 Ran:33
Win Prizemoney £21,227 *Total Prizemoney* £26,971
Wins 1999 Apr Nottin (HVY) H 6.1f 53 57
1998 Oct Yarmou (SFT) H 7f 49 58
1997 Aug Mussel (G-F) H 5f 66 71 <
1997 Jly Mussel (G-F) C 5f 65
1997 Jly Catter (SFT) S 5f 65
1999 Turf 1-14: (6f 1-11, 7f 2, 8f) (hvy, g-s, gd 1-8, g-f 2, frm 2)
Unfurnished, fair filly, effective 6 to 7f, best at 6f, acts on g-s to g-f, has worn blinkers. Turf high 57 - 1st of 13 getting 9lb from Ameena (27 Apr Nottingham RF 0866).
**N A Callaghan [0-1] Norcroft Park Stud (from M J Ryan [2-23] Spt 1999).*

ORIEL STAR BHB 53f57a **RR 52f 57a** 4344[17]
3 b f Safawan 6.6f **(60)** - Silvers Era (Balidar) 7.9f **(63)**
Form - 08470108000007870
Record 1999 - 1st:1 2nd:0 3rd:0 Ran:17
Pre1999 - 1st:1 2nd:0 3rd:4 Ran:11
Win Prizemoney £10,043 *Total Prizemoney* £12,359
Wins * **1999** May Windso (GD) H 5f 59 63
* 1998 Spt Ripon (SFT) 5f 74 <
1999 Turf 1-16: (5f 1-15, 6f) (sft, g-s 2, gd 1-5, g-f 3, frm 4, hrd) 1999 AW 0-1: (5f) (Fibr)
Unfurnished, fair filly, effective 5f, acts on gd to frm, mostly wears blinkers (effectively). Turf high 63. **P D Evans [2-28] J G White.*

ORIENTAL BHB 88f **RR 95f** 3647[18]
4 b c Inchinor 8.9f **(64)** - Orient (Bay Express) 7.1f **(60)**
Form - 311000
Record 1999 - 1st:2 2nd:0 3rd:1 Ran:6
Win Prizemoney £12,688 *Total Prizemoney* £13,163
Wins * **1999** May Goodwo (GD) H 7f 84 95 <
* **1999** Apr Thirsk (GD) 6f 71+
1999 Turf 2-6: (6f 1-1, 7f 1-4, 8f) (gd 2-4, g-f, frm)
Scopey, very useful colt, effective 7f, acts on gd, has worn blinkers. Turf high 95 - 1st of 18 giving 9lb to Tayseer (20 May Goodwood RF 1345). He proved disappointing after winning twice in the first half of the season. Possibly best over seven furlongs, he is one to have slight reservations about.
**J H M Gosden [2-6] Sheikh Mohammed.*

ORIENTAL FASHION (IRE) BHB 107f **RR 106f** 4362a[1]
3 b f Marju (IRE) 9.2f **(76)** - Wijdan (USA) **(96f)** (Mr Prospector (USA)) 8.8f **(78)**
Form - 3321
Record 1999 - 1st:1 2nd:1 3rd:2 Ran:4
Pre1999 - 1st:1 2nd:1 3rd:0 Ran:2
Win Prizemoney £19,635 *Total Prizemoney* £32,306
Wins * **1999** Spt Chanti (GD) L 8f 100 <
* 1998 Spt Nottin (G-F) 8.2f 92+
1999 Turf 1-4: (8f 1-3, 10f) (sft, gd 1-3)
Neat, Pattern-class filly, effective 8f, acts on sft to gd, best on gd. Turf high 100 - 1st of 9 from Lady Ilsley (8 Spt Chantilly RF 4362a). She races close to the pace and is particularly enthusiastic. Probably best with some give underfoot, she should stay beyond a mile. Won a Listed event. **S bin Suroor [2-6] Godolphin.*

ORIENTAL PRIDE (IRE) BHB 57f **RR 70df** 1449[13]
3 ch g Indian Ridge 7.6f **(74)** - Mercy Bien (IRE) (Be My Guest (USA)) 9.3f **(67)**
Form - 700
Record 1999 - 1st:0 2nd:0 3rd:0 Ran:3
Pre1999 - 1st:0 2nd:0 3rd:0 Ran:2
1999 Turf 0-3: (11f, 12f, 13f) (gd, g-f, frm)
Tall, above-average gelding, has worn blinkers. Turf high 70.
**E A L Dunlop [0-5] H R H Sultan Ahmad Shah.*

ORIGINAL SPIN RR 76f 5108[2]
2 b f Machiavellian (USA) 9.8f **(83)** - Not Before Time (IRE) (Polish Precedent (USA)) 10.2f **(60)**
Form - 42
Record 1999 - 1st:0 2nd:1 3rd:0 Ran:2
Win Prizemoney £0 *Total Prizemoney* £1,175
1999 Turf 0-2: (7f, 8f) (gd 2)
Currently above-average filly. Turf high 76 (began Oct) - 2nd of 13 to Coeur de La Mer (28 Oct Windsor 8f gd RF 5108).
**J L Dunlop [0-2] R Barnett.*

ORIOLE BHB 53f50a **RR 46f 50a** 5072[4]
6 b g Mazilier (USA) 8.5f **(56)** - Odilese (Mummy's Pet) 7.7f **(60)**
Form - 08425050004
Record 1999 - 1st:0 2nd:1 3rd:0 Ran:11
Pre1999 - 1st:6 2nd:4 3rd:4 Ran:55
Win Prizemoney £19,624 *Total Prizemoney* £28,571
Wins * 1998 Aug Redcar (G-F) H 7f 47 49
* 1998 Jun Carlis (G-S) H 6.9f 46 50
* 1997 Aug Redcar (FRM) H 7f 48 52
* 1997 May Redcar (GD) H 8f 33 39
1996 Jly Ayr (G-S) H 7f 46 49
1995 Jly Thirsk (G-F) H 6f 62 <
1999 Turf 0-11: (7f 8, 8f 3) (gd 2, g-f 4, frm 5)
Moderate gelding, effective 7 to 8f, best at 7f, acts on gd to frm, has worn blinkers, likes tight tracks, and does well at Carlisle. Turf high 46. He runs regularly but wins in his turn, and seem to go well at Redcar.
**Don Enrico Incisa [4-39] Don Enrico Incisa (from N Tinkler [2-27] Oct 1996).*

ORLANDO SUNSHINE BHB 58f **RR 61f** 4451[15]
2 ch g Beveled (USA) 6.9f **(64)** - Harvest Rose **(51f 47a)** (Bairn (USA)) 7.7f **(59)**
Form - 20000
Record 1999 - 1st:0 2nd:1 3rd:0 Ran:5
Win Prizemoney £0 *Total Prizemoney* £788
1999 Turf 0-4: (6f 2, 7f 2) (sft, gd, frm, hrd) 1999 AW 0-1: (6f) (Fibr)
Average gelding. Turf high 61. **J L Spearing [0-5] Charles Eden.*

ORMELIE (IRE) BHB 93f **RR 93f** 3165[1]
4 b c Jade Hunter (USA) 10.4f **(72)** - Trolley Song (USA) (Caro)
Form - 6551
Record 1999 - 1st:1 2nd:0 3rd:0 Ran:4
Pre1999 - 1st:2 2nd:0 3rd:2 Ran:7
Win Prizemoney £44,357 *Total Prizemoney* £46,467
Wins * **1999** Jly Goodwo (G-F) H 9.9f 90 93 <
* 1998 Aug Newbur (G-F) H 13.3f 83 88
* 1998 May Ayr (GD) 10f 74
1999 Turf 1-4: (10f 1-1, 12f, 13f 2) (gd, g-f 2, frm 1-1)
Leggy, useful colt, effective 10 to 13f, acts on g-f to frm, best on g-f. Turf high 93 - 1st of 8 getting 5lb from Achilles (27 Jly Goodwood RF 3165). Consistent. He did not show much in his early starts last season like many from his stable but, dropped back to ten furlongs, got up to land a very valuable handicap at Glorious Goodwood. **P W Chapple-Hyam [3-11] K Doyle.*

ORO STREET (IRE) BHB 74f **RR 79f** 3300[4]
3 b c Dolphin Street (FR) - Love Unlimited (Dominion) 8.5f **(63)**
Form - 76474
Record 1999 - 1st:0 2nd:0 3rd:0 Ran:5
Win Prizemoney £0 *Total Prizemoney* £565
1999 Turf 0-5: (8f 3, 10f 2) (gd 2, frm 3)
Workmanlike, above-average colt. Turf high 81.
**G C H Chung [0-1] Osvaldo Pedroni (from A Kelleway [0-4] Jun 1999).*

ORPEN (USA) RR 114df 3589a[10]
3 b c Lure (USA) - Bonita Francita (CAN) (Devil's Bag (USA)) 12.4f **(78)**
Form - 0300
1999 Turf 0-4: (7f, 8f 3) (hvy, g-f 2, frm)
Scopey, Group-class colt, effective 6 to 8f, acts on sft to g-f, has worn blinkers. Turf high 114 - 3rd of 10 to Saffron Walden (22 May Curragh 8f g-f RF 1477a). A superb physical specimen, he failed to improve on his smart two-year-old form and proved disappointing. Tailed-off in the Prix Maurice de Gheest at Deauville in August, he did not train on and has been retired. **A P O'Brien in IRE [2-6].*

ORSAY BHB 73f78a **RR 72f 78a** 4079[1]
7 b g Royal Academy (USA) 7.8f **(77)** - Bellifontaine (FR) (Bellypha) 9.8f **(73)**
Form - 416651
Record 1999 - 1st:2 2nd:0 3rd:0 Ran:6
Pre1999 - 1st:3 2nd:2 3rd:3 Ran:20
Win Prizemoney £25,547 *Total Prizemoney* £33,957
Wins * **1999** Spt York (G-F) C 8.9f 65
* **1999** *Feb Lingfi (STD) C 10f 76*
* 1998 Aug Sandow (G-F) H 10f 76 80 <
* 1997 Jun Sandow (G-F) H 10f 76 79
* 1995 Apr Leices (GD) 8f 69
1999 Turf 1-2: (9f 1-1, 10f) (gd, frm 1-1) 1999 AW 1-4: (10f 1-4) (Equi 1-4)
Decent gelding, effective 10f, acts on g-f - acts on Equi. Turf high 65. AW high 83 - also 1st of 8 from Night City (2 Feb Lingfield RF 0209). He came back to form on the All-Weather last winter, before apparently gurgling when tried over hurdles in the spring. Regained winning form in a claimer at York in September. Nine to ten furlongs on fast ground or Equitrack suits him best.
**W R Muir [5-28] The Four Willies Partnership.*

ORSO (FR) RR 110f 4779a[7]
3 b g Highest Honor (FR) 10.9f **(72)** - Palombella (FR) (Groom Dancer (USA))
Form - 17
1999 Turf 1-2: (8f 1-2) (hvy 1-1, sft)
Currently Group-class gelding. Turf high 110 (began Aug) - 7th of 9 getting 3lb from Trans Island (3 Oct Longchamp 8f sft RF 4779a).
**F Head in FR [1-2].*

OSCAR PEPPER (USA) BHB 53f **RR 52f** 4934[13]
2 b c Brunswick (USA) - Princess Baja (USA) (Conquistador Cielo (USA)) 8.8f **(69)**
Form - 75700
Record 1999 - 1st:0 2nd:0 3rd:0 Ran:5
1999 Turf 0-5: (5f 2, 6f, 7f, 8f) (sft, g-f, frm 2, hrd)
Fair colt. Turf high 52. **T D Barron [0-5] Ian Armitage.*

OSCIETRA BHB 60f **RR 67f** 4791[8]
3 b f Robellino (USA) 9.5f **(68)** - Top Treat (USA) (Topsider (USA)) 8.3f **(71)**
Form - 756514068
Record 1999 - 1st:1 2nd:0 3rd:0 Ran:9
Win Prizemoney £2,739 *Total Prizemoney* £3,362
Wins * **1999** Aug Kempto (G-S) H 9f 63 67 <
1999 Turf 1-9: (7f 2, 8f 2, 9f 1-1, 10f 3, 12f) (g-s 1-1, gd 3, g-f 2, frm 3)
Workmanlike, average filly, effective 8 to 10f, acts on g-s to g-f. Turf high 67 (began Jly) - 1st of 10 giving 18lb to Who Goes There (18 Aug Kempton RF 3738). **G B Balding [1-9] B T Attenborough.*

OSOOD (IRE) BHB 90f **RR 94f** 5074[1]
2 b c Caerleon (USA) 10.9f **(79)** - Ozette (Dancing Brave (USA)) 8.4f **(76)**
Form - 161
Record 1999 - 1st:2 2nd:0 3rd:0 Ran:3
Win Prizemoney £6,872 *Total Prizemoney* £6,959
Wins * **1999** Oct Redcar (SFT) 7f 94 <
* **1999** Spt Salisb (HVY) 8f 70
1999 Turf 2-3: (7f 1-1, 8f 1-1, 10f) (g-s 1-1, gd 1-2)
Currently useful colt. Turf high 94 (began Spt) - 1st of 7 from Secret Agent (26 Oct Redcar RF 5074).
**M P Tregoning [2-3] Sheikh Ahmed Al Maktoum.*

OSOOL (USA) RR 21f 4422[9]
3 b c Danzig (USA) 8.1f **(88)** - Histoire (FR) (Riverman (USA)) 9.1f **(76)**
Form - 0
Record 1999 - 1st:0 2nd:0 3rd:0 Ran:1
1999 Turf 0-1: (8f) (frm)
Rangy, currently little account colt.
**J L Dunlop [0-1] Hamdan Al Maktoum.*

OSTARA (IRE) BHB 59f **RR 63f** 2489[12]
2 b g Petorius 8f **(66)** - Onde de Choc (USA) (L'Enjoleur (CAN)) 8f **(65)**
Form - 800240
Record 1999 - 1st:0 2nd:1 3rd:0 Ran:6
Win Prizemoney £0 *Total Prizemoney* £760
1999 Turf 0-6: (5f, 6f 4, 7f) (gd 2, g-f, frm 3)
Average gelding, effective 6 to 7f, acts on frm, has worn blinkers. Turf high 63 - 4th of 11 giving 5lb to Endless Journey (19 Jun Redcar 7f frm RF 2153). **K A Ryan [0-6] J Nixon.*

OSWALD BHB 38f **RR 33f** 4326[10]
3 b g Distant Relative 7f **(69)** - River Dove (USA) (Riverman (USA)) 9.1f **(76)**
Form - 080
Record 1999 - 1st:0 2nd:0 3rd:0 Ran:3
1999 Turf 0-3: (5f 3) (gd 2, frm)

Workmanlike, currently very moderate gelding. Turf high 33 (began Aug). **C W Thornton [0-3] Guy Reed.*

OTAHUNA BHB 60f **RR 63f** 5007[7]

3 b c Selkirk (USA) 7.9f **(76)** - Stara (Star Appeal) 9.6f **(65)**
Form - 845354581687
Record 1999 - 1st:1 2nd:0 3rd:1 Ran:12
Pre1999 - 1st:0 2nd:1 3rd:0 Ran:3
Win Prizemoney £3,315 *Total Prizemoney* £5,870
Wins * 1999 Spt Nottin (G-F) 10f 63 <
1999 Turf 1-12: (8f 4, 9f, 10f 1-5, 11f, 12f) (g-s, gd 3, g-f 4, frm 1-4)
Lengthy, average colt, effective 7 to 8f, acts on gd to g-f. Turf high 80. He got on the scorecard when successful over ten furlongs at Nottingham in a poor-quality handicap.
**R Hollinshead [1-15] J D Graham.*

OTIME (IRE) BHB 58f66a **RR 45f 66a** 5064[5]

2 b g Mujadil (USA) 7.7f **(70)** - Kick the Habit (Habitat) 9.4f **(70)**
Form - 714075
Record 1999 - 1st:1 2nd:0 3rd:0 Ran:6
Win Prizemoney £2,276 *Total Prizemoney* £2,524
Wins * 1999 Aug Bath (HRD) S 5.1f 66 <
1999 Turf 1-6: (5f 1-3, 6f 3) (g-s 2, gd, g-f, frm 1-2)
Average gelding, effective 5f, acts on frm. Turf high 66 - 1st of 9 giving 5lb to Dimming of The Day (3 Aug Bath RF 3307).
**M R Channon [1-6] Ken Lock Racing Ltd.*

OTTERINGTON GIRL BHB 32f **RR 20f** 3284[7]

3 b f Noble Patriarch 12.2f **(43)** - Bidweaya (USA) (Lear Fan (USA)) 8.5f **(73)**
Form - 00007
Record 1999 - 1st:0 2nd:0 3rd:0 Ran:5
Pre1999 - 1st:0 2nd:0 3rd:0 Ran:5
1999 Turf 0-5: (6f, 8f 3, 9f) (g-f, frm 3, hrd)
Neat, little account filly, has worn blinkers. Turf high 21. Becoming disappointing. **Miss S E Hall [0-10] Mrs Joan Hodgson.*

OTTO BHB 33a **RR 41f** 62[5]

4 b g Sure Blade (USA) 10.6f **(66)** - Nikatino (Bustino) 10.4f **(64)**
Form - 5
Record 1999 - 1st:0 2nd:0 3rd:0 Ran:1
Pre1999 - 1st:0 2nd:0 3rd:0 Ran:4
1999 AW 0-1: (13f) (Equi)
Leggy, moderate gelding, has worn blinkers.
**K McAuliffe [0-5] Mrs H Raw.*

OUDALMUTEENA (IRE) BHB 56f51a **RR 57f 51a** 4814[15]

4 b g Lahib (USA) 8f **(69)** - Roxy Music (IRE) (Song) 7.2f **(61)**
Form - 8644560325670
Record 1999 - 1st:0 2nd:1 3rd:1 Ran:13
Pre1999 - 1st:0 2nd:0 3rd:1 Ran:2
Win Prizemoney £0 *Total Prizemoney* £3,087
1999 Turf 0-10: (7f 2, 8f 4, 9f, 10f 3) (sft, g-s, gd 3, g-f, frm 4) 1999 AW 0-3: (7f, 8f 2) (Equi 3)
Strong, fair gelding, effective 7 to 10f, acts on sft to frm, best on gd. Turf high 64 - 2nd of 7 giving 8lb to Lycian (25 Jun Goodwood 9f frm RF 2286). AW high 35. Consistent.
**V Soane [0-13] Abdallah,D Bayliss,D Parslow (from A C Stewart [0-2] Oct 1998).*

OULTON BROAD BHB 46f50a **RR 38tf 50a** 3809[5]

3 b g Midyan (USA) 9.9f **(64)** - Lady Quachita (USA) (Sovereign Dancer (USA)) 11.2f **(68)**
Form - 3025005
Record 1999 - 1st:0 2nd:1 3rd:1 Ran:7
Pre1999 - 1st:0 2nd:0 3rd:0 Ran:3
Win Prizemoney £0 *Total Prizemoney* £964
1999 Turf 0-4: (8f 2, 9f, 10f) (g-s, g-f 3) 1999 AW 0-3:(8f, 9f, 11f)(Fibr 3)
Unfurnished, fair gelding, effective 8f, acts on g-s, has worn blinkers, likes left handed tracks, likes tight tracks. Turf high 53 (1st run) - 2nd of 17 giving 5lb to Angie Marinie (19 Apr Nottingham 8f g-s RF 0747). AW high 54. **J G Portman [0-10] A Masse-Stamberger.*

OUR AMBITION (IRE) BHB 91f **RR 95f** 4686[16]

2 b c Great Commotion (USA) 9.2f **(80)** - Sea Power (Welsh Pageant) 10f **(65)**
Form - 13761060
Record 1999 - 1st:2 2nd:0 3rd:1 Ran:8
Win Prizemoney £7,803 *Total Prizemoney* £10,678
Wins * 1999 Aug Kempto (G-F) H 6f 90 95 <
*** 1999** May Kempto (GD) 5f 80
1999 Turf 2-8: (5f 1-1, 6f 1-7) (gd 3, frm 2-5)
Very useful colt, effective 6f, acts on frm. Turf high 95 - 1st of 11 giving 5lb to Norfolk Reed (4 Aug Kempton RF 3354). A sprinter, he is not up to Group class and will be difficult to place off his current mark. **B J Meehan [2-8] Jim McCarthy.*

OUR BANDBOX BHB 35f **RR 24f** 3359[9]

3 ch g Risk Me (FR) 8f **(53)** - Treble Top (USA) (Miswaki (USA)) 9f **(81)**
Form - 0007000
Record 1999 - 1st:0 2nd:0 3rd:0 Ran:7
Pre1999 - 1st:0 2nd:0 3rd:0 Ran:5
1999 Turf 0-7: (6f 5, 10f 2) (gd, g-f 3, frm 3)
Leggy, little account gelding. Turf high 35.
**S Mellor [0-12] The Bandbox Brigade.*

OUR FIRST LADY RR 60f 5136[11]

2 b f Alzao (USA) 9.8f **(73)** - Eclipsing (IRE) (Baillamont (USA)) 7f **(78)**
Form - 0
Record 1999 - 1st:0 2nd:0 3rd:0 Ran:1
1999 Turf 0-1: (7f) (gd)
Currently average filly. **D W P Arbuthnot [0-1] Derrick Broomfield.*

OUR FRED BHB 77f **RR 78f** 4625[3]

2 ch c Prince Sabo 6.6f **(64)** - Sheila's Secret (IRE) **(92f)** (Bluebird (USA)) 7.5f **(69)**
Form - 3433
Record 1999 - 1st:0 2nd:0 3rd:3 Ran:4
Win Prizemoney £0 *Total Prizemoney* £1,967
1999 Turf 0-4: (5f 3, 6f) (g-s, gd 2, frm)
Above-average colt. Turf high 78 (began Aug) - 3rd of 10 giving 16lb to Kinsman (29 Spt Brighton 6f g-s RF 4625).
**T G Mills [0-4] Sherwoods Transport Ltd.*

OUR JACK RR 1421[6]

4 ch g Rock City 8.8f **(62)** - Queen Canute (IRE) (Ahonoora) 8.1f **(73)**
Form - 6
Record 1999 - 1st:0 2nd:0 3rd:0 Ran:1
1999 AW 0-1: (8f) (Fibr)
Currently very moderate gelding. **C N Kellett [0-1] Mrs J Salt.*

OUR MAIN MAN BHB 32f47a **RR 28f 47a** 2653[10]

9 ch g Superlative 8.8f **(57)** - Ophrys (Nonoalco (USA)) 8.5f **(66)**
Form - 640
Record 1999 - 1st:0 2nd:0 3rd:0 Ran:3
Pre1999 - 1st:3 2nd:4 3rd:3 Ran:34
Win Prizemoney £9,100 *Total Prizemoney* £13,514
Wins * 1997 *Jun Southw (STD) H* *12f* *50* *57+*
* 1995 Oct Pontef (FRM) H 10f 49 56
* 1995 Jly Mussel (FRM) 11.1f 58 <
1999 AW 0-3: (12f, 14f, 16f) (Fibr 3)
Moderate gelding, effective 12 to 14f, best at 14f, - acts on Fibr, has worn blinkers, favours tight tracks. AW high 43. Inconsistent.
**R M Whitaker [4-52] R M Whitaker.*

OUR MEMOIRS RR 4419[22]

2 ch c Lake Coniston (IRE) - Julip (Track Spare) 8.8f **(62)**
Form - 0
Record 1999 - 1st:0 2nd:0 3rd:0 Ran:1
1999 Turf 0-1: (7f) (gd)
Currently very poor colt. **P R Chamings [0-1] Amity Finance Ltd.*

OUR MONOGRAM BHB 53f **RR 57f** 4639[9]

3 b g Deploy 11.4f **(67)** - Darling Splodge (Elegant Air) 13.2f **(61)**
Form - 00540
Record 1999 - 1st:0 2nd:0 3rd:0 Ran:5
1999 Turf 0-5: (12f 2, 14f, 16f 2) (gd 2, g-f, frm 2)
Workmanlike, fair gelding. Turf high 64.
**A C Stewart [0-5] The Foxons Fillies Partnership.*

OUR PEOPLE BHB 52f43a **RR 50f 43a** 5162[6]

5 ch g Indian Ridge 7.6f **(74)** - Fair and Wise (High Line) 10.3f **(70)**
Form - 806
Record 1999 - 1st:0 2nd:0 3rd:0 Ran:2

Pre1999 - 1st:3 2nd:1 3rd:4 Ran:26
Win Prizemoney £10,529 *Total Prizemoney* £15,265
Wins * 1998 Aug Redcar (G-F) H 11f 56 60
* 1998 Jly Carlis (G-F) H 8f 49 53
* 1996 Oct Leices (G-F) 8f 84 <
1999 Turf 0-2: (10f 2) (sft, g-f)
Fair gelding, effective 8 to 12f, acts on g-s to frm, has worn blinkers, likes left handed tracks, prefers tight tracks. Turf high 50 (began Oct). **M Johnston [3-28] Dr Fuk To Chang.*

OUR POPPET (IRE) RR 67+f 4944[6]
2 b f Warning 8.1f **(77)** - Upend (Main Reef) 9.6f **(57)**
Form - 6
Record 1999 - 1st:0 2nd:0 3rd:0 Ran:1
1999 Turf 0-1: (7f) (gd)
Currently average filly. **R Guest [0-1] Graham Robinson.*

OUR ROBERT BHB 35f48a **RR 5f 48a** 2051[11]
7 b g Faustus (USA) 9.1f **(54)** - Duck Soup (Decoy Boy) 6.7f **(56)**
Form - 0
Record 1999 - 1st:0 2nd:0 3rd:0 Ran:1
Pre1999 - 1st:0 2nd:1 3rd:3 Ran:17
Win Prizemoney £0 *Total Prizemoney* £3,481
1999 Turf 0-1: (14f) (g-f)
Very poor gelding. Becoming disappointing.
**A Streeter [0-6] Principal Racing (from J G FitzGerald [1-15] Jan 1997).*

OURS FOR LIFE RR 53f 2153[9]
2 b f Rainbows For Life (CAN) 9.3f **(64)** - Kaliala (FR) (Pharly (FR)) 9.8f **(68)**
Form - 0880
Record 1999 - 1st:0 2nd:0 3rd:0 Ran:4
1999 Turf 0-4: (5f 3, 7f) (gd, g-f, frm 2)
Fair filly. Turf high 53. **Ronald Thompson [0-4] Ron Holford.*

OUR TIMMY BHB 75f **RR 77f** 4690[22]
2 gr c Petong 7.6f **(58)** - Doppio (Dublin Taxi) 6.4f **(55)**
Form - 6230
Record 1999 - 1st:0 2nd:1 3rd:1 Ran:4
Win Prizemoney £0 *Total Prizemoney* £1,191
1999 Turf 0-4: (6f 3, 7f) (sft, gd, g-f, frm)
Above-average colt. Turf high 77 - 3rd of 16 giving 2lb to William Barraud (21 Spt Warwick 7f sft RF 4455). **P J Makin [0-4] Barrie Whitehouse.*

OUTCRY BHB 45f **RR 53f** 5068[12]
3 b f Caerleon (USA) 10.9f **(79)** - In Full Cry (USA) (Seattle Slew (USA)) 9.4f **(76)**
Form - 0000
Record 1999 - 1st:0 2nd:0 3rd:0 Ran:4
Pre1999 - 1st:0 2nd:0 3rd:0 Ran:2
1999 Turf 0-4: (8f 2, 10f 2) (g-s, gd, g-f, frm)
Scopey, fair filly. Turf high 53 (began Jly). **G Wragg [0-6] A E Oppenheimer.*

OUTER LIMIT (IRE) BHB 95f **RR 96f** 2502[4]
3 b c Caerleon (USA) 10.9f **(79)** - Lady Liberty (NZ) (Noble Bijou (USA))
Form - 33244
Record 1999 - 1st:0 2nd:1 3rd:2 Ran:5
Win Prizemoney £0 *Total Prizemoney* £5,901
1999 Turf 0-5: (11f, 12f 2, 14f, 16f) (g-f 2, frm 3)
Scopey, very useful colt. Turf high 96 - 4th of 11 giving 5lb to Endorsement (16 Jun Ascot 16f g-f RF 2043). Rated a Classic contender at the start of the season, he lacks any speed. Likely to stay beyond two miles, he was sold for 26,000 guineas at Newmarket in October and should make a useful hurdler. **P W Chapple-Hyam [0-5] R E Sangster & A K Collins.*

OUT FOR A CRUISE RR 279[5]
6 ch m Cruise Missile - Real Beauty (Kinglet)
Form - 5
Record 1999 - 1st:0 2nd:0 3rd:0 Ran:1
1999 AW 0-1: (12f) (Fibr)
Very poor mare. **D E Cantillon [0-1] Don Cantillon.*

OUT LIKE MAGIC BHB 38f40a **RR 39f 40a** 4398[5]
4 ch f Magic Ring (IRE) 6.5f **(64)** - Thevetia (Mummy's Pet) 7.7f **(60)**
Form - 540560705
Record 1999 - 1st:0 2nd:0 3rd:0 Ran:7
Pre1999 - 1st:1 2nd:6 3rd:0 Ran:22
Win Prizemoney £3,203 *Total Prizemoney* £12,632
Wins 1997 Apr Ripon (G-F) 5f 74 <
1999 Turf 0-3: (7f, 8f 2) (frm 3) 1999 AW 0-4: (6f, 7f, 8f, 10f) (Equi 4)
Light-framed, very moderate filly, has worn blinkers. Turf high 39 (began Jly). AW high 43. Consistent.
**J L Eyre [0-3] Mrs E A Dawson (from P D Evans [1-26] Jan 1999).*

OUT LINE BHB 87f **RR 94f** 4678[8]
7 gr m Beveled (USA) 6.9f **(64)** - Free Range (Birdbrook) 8.4f **(62)**
Form - 04512814378
Record 1999 - 1st:2 2nd:1 3rd:1 Ran:11
Pre1999 - 1st:4 2nd:3 3rd:3 Ran:28
Win Prizemoney £28,045 *Total Prizemoney* £39,010
Wins * **1999** Jly Goodwo (FRM) 7f 95 <
* **1999** Jun Goodwo (G-F) H 7f 78 82
* 1998 Jly Salisb (G-F) H 7f 78 81
* 1998 Jun Goodwo (GD) H 6f 66 73
* 1997 Jly Lingfi (G-F) H 6f 61 64
* 1997 May Sandow (GD) H 7.1f 57 61
1999 Turf 2-11: (6f 2, 7f 2-6, 8f 3) (gd 2, g-f 2-3, frm 6)
Useful mare, effective 7f, acts on g-f, likes right handed tracks. Turf high 95 - 1st of 8 giving 11lb to Acicula (30 Jly Goodwood RF 3239). Recently retired, she was a useful handicapper who enjoyed a sound surface and went particularly well at Goodwood.
**M Madgwick [6-39] Miss D M Green.*

Out of Africa scored an autumn hat-trick

OUT OF AFRICA (IRE) BHB 97f **RR 92f** 4801[1]
2 b f Common Grounds 8.1f **(66)** - Limpopo (Green Desert (USA)) 8.6f **(78)**
Form - 5223232111
Record 1999 - 1st:3 2nd:4 3rd:2 Ran:10
Win Prizemoney £55,253 *Total Prizemoney* £62,385
Wins * **1999** Oct York (SFT) L 6f 92 <
* **1999** Spt Newmar (G-S) H 7f 86 90
* **1999** Spt Doncas (G-F) H 6.5f 81 85
1999 Turf 3-10: (5f 5, 6f 1-3, 7f 2-2) (g-s, gd 2-3, g-f 1-2, frm 4)
Useful filly, effective 5 to 7f, best at 7f, acts on g-s to g-f, best on gd. Turf high 92 - 1st of 6 getting 8lb from Bally Pride (9 Oct York RF 4801) - also 1st of 19 getting 4lb from Total Love (28 Spt Newmarket RF 4599). A string of excellent placed efforts against some really progressive types had kept her from the winner's enclosure. However she gained compensation for her near misses in some style when winning a quality nursery at Doncaster over six and a half furlongs, a similar event at Newmarket over seven, and a Listed race back over six at York. **B W Hills [3-10] E D Kessly.*

OUT OF REACH RR 81f 5044[1]
2 b f Warning 8.1f **(77)** - Well Beyond (IRE) (Don't Forget Me) 8.3f **(74)**
Form - 1
Record 1999 - 1st:1 2nd:0 3rd:0 Ran:1

Win Prizemoney £4,825 *Total Prizemoney* £4,825
Wins * **1999** Oct Newbur (HVY) 6f 81 <
1999 Turf 1-1: (6f 1-1) (sft 1-1)
Currently decent filly. (1st run) - 1st of 14 getting 5lb from Free Rider (23 Oct Newbury RF 5044). Won a heavy-ground Newbury maiden on her only start, and will surely make her mark at three.
**B W Hills [1-1] K Abdulla.*

OUT OF SIGHT (IRE) BHB 60f RR 50f 5073[13]

5 ch g Salse (USA) 10.9f **(71)** - Starr Danias (USA) (Sensitive Prince (USA)) 9.1f **(60)**
Form - 465800
Record **1999** - 1st:0 2nd:0 3rd:0 Ran:6
Pre1999 - 1st:1 2nd:0 3rd:0 Ran:13
Win Prizemoney £8,285 *Total Prizemoney* £11,714
Wins * 1997 May York (GD) H 7.9f 75 79 <
1999 Turf 0-6: (7f, 8f 5) (gd 3, frm 3)
Fair gelding, effective 8f, acts on sft to frm, prefers tight tracks. Turf high 73 (began Jly) - 6th of 9 getting 9lb from Sweet Pea (7 Aug Haydock 8f gd RF 3453). Becoming disappointing.
**B A McMahon [1-19] D J Allen.*

OUT OF THE WOOD RR 41f 2153[7]

2 ch g Prince Daniel (USA) 11.4f **(46)** - Spring Garden (Silly Prices)
Form - 67
Record **1999** - 1st:0 2nd:0 3rd:0 Ran:2
1999 Turf 0-2: (5f, 7f) (gd, frm)
Currently moderate gelding. Turf high 41.
**M W Easterby [0-2] W T Allgood.*

OUT ON THE LIFFEY (IRE) RR 3641[13]

7 b g West China - Eurotin (Shack (USA)) 5.8f **(53)**
Form - 0
Record **1999** - 1st:0 2nd:0 3rd:0 Ran:1
1999 Turf 0-1: (14f) (g-f)
Formerly very poor gelding. **John Harris [0-1] James Gough.*

OUTSTANDING TALENT BHB 55f RR 63f 5005[10]

2 gr f Environment Friend 7.5f **(67)** - Chaleureuse (Final Straw) 7.9f **(64)**
Form - 84300
Record **1999** - 1st:0 2nd:0 3rd:1 Ran:5
Win Prizemoney £0 *Total Prizemoney* £560
1999 Turf 0-5: (5f 2, 6f 3) (gd 3, g-f, frm)
Average filly. Turf high 63 - 4th of 7 getting 5lb from Blackpool Mamma's (29 Jun Chepstow 6f g-f RF 2387).
**V Soane [0-3] Talent Entertainment (from R Simpson [0-2] Jun 1999).*

OUZO (NZ) RR 91f 554a[7]

6 ch g Interrex (CAN) 7.7f **(51)** - Ville Air (Town Crier) 10.2f **(55)**
Form - 7
1999 Turf 0-1: (12f) (g-f)
Currently useful gelding. **M Thwaites in NZ [0-1].*

OVERCOME RR 21f 2760[8]

4 b f Belmez (USA) 11.4f **(65)** - Olivana (GER) (Sparkler) 8.4f **(55)**
Form - 88
Record **1999** - 1st:0 2nd:0 3rd:0 Ran:2
1999 Turf 0-2: (7f, 12f) (gd, frm)
Little account filly. Turf high 21.
**R G Frost [0-2] Thurlestone Hotel Racing Club.*

OVERENTHUSE (USA) RR 63f 1917[6]

3 b g Alleged (USA) 11.8f **(81)** - Zealous Lady (USA) (Highland Blade (USA)) 6.9f **(67)**
Form - 06
Record **1999** - 1st:0 2nd:0 3rd:0 Ran:2
1999 Turf 0-2: (12f 2) (gd, g-f)
Scopey, currently average gelding, always wears blinkers. Turf high 63. **J H M Gosden [0-2] Sheikh Mohammed.*

OVER KEEN BHB 46f51a RR 47f 51a 2326[17]

5 b m Keen 11.1f **(58)** - Shift Over (USA) (Night Shift (USA)) 7.2f **(69)**
Form - 2700
Record **1999** - 1st:0 2nd:0 3rd:0 Ran:2
Pre1999 - 1st:0 2nd:1 3rd:0 Ran:6
Win Prizemoney £0 *Total Prizemoney* £791
1999 Turf 0-1: (7f) (frm) 1999 AW 0-1: (8f) (Equi)
Fair filly, effective 8f, - acts on Equi, has worn blinkers, likes tight tracks. Becoming disappointing.
**Miss L C Siddall [0-1] Miss J A Challen (from Miss Gay Kelleway [0-7] Jan 1999).*

OVERSMAN BHB 47f60a RR 50f 60a 2375[8]

6 b g Keen 11.1f **(58)** - Jamaican Punch (IRE) (Shareef Dancer (USA)) 9.9f **(73)**
Form - 302338
Record **1999** - 1st:0 2nd:1 3rd:3 Ran:6
Pre1999 - 1st:1 2nd:1 3rd:2 Ran:8
Win Prizemoney £2,900 *Total Prizemoney* £6,920
Wins * 1996 *Feb Southw (STD) 12f 46+* <
1999 Turf 0-4: (10f, 12f, 14f 2) (gd, frm 3)1999AW 0-2: (11f, 12f)(Fibr 2)
Average gelding. Turf high 50. AW high 62.
**J G FitzGerald [4-33] Marquesa de Moratalla.*

OVER THE MARCH BHB 42f RR 47f 4714[7]

3 b f Deploy 11.4f **(67)** - Carn Maire (Northern Prospect (USA)) 9.5f **(71)**
Form - 6033307
Record **1999** - 1st:0 2nd:0 3rd:3 Ran:7
Pre1999 - 1st:0 2nd:0 3rd:0 Ran:3
Win Prizemoney £0 *Total Prizemoney* £1,316
1999 Turf 0-7: (10f, 12f 3, 14f 2, 16f) (hvy, gd, g-f 2, frm 3)
Workmanlike, moderate filly, has worn blinkers. Turf high 47.
**J E Banks [0-10] Giles Pritchard-Gordon.*

OVER THE MOON BHB 45f48a RR 25f 48a 4864[4]

5 ch m Beveled (USA) 6.9f **(64)** - Beyond the Moon (IRE) (Ballad Rock) 7.8f **(63)**
Form - 61063774
Record **1999** - 1st:1 2nd:0 3rd:1 Ran:8
Pre1999 - 1st:3 2nd:0 3rd:2 Ran:20
Win Prizemoney £8,904 *Total Prizemoney* £9,818
Wins * **1999** *Apr Wolver (STD) C 8.5f 55*
1998 *Spt Wolver (STD) C 7f 59*
1998 *Jly Wolver (STD) C 8.5f 56*
1998 *Jun Wolver (STD) C 7f 60* <
1999 AW 1-8: (7f 4, 8f 1-3, 9f) (Fibr 1-8)
Moderate filly, effective 7 to 8f, best at 7f, - acts on Fibr, has worn blinkers, favours left handed tracks. AW high 55 - 1st of 11 getting 11lb from John Bowdler Music (24 Apr Wolverhampton RF 0847). Consistent. She took her time in getting off the mark, but has been very successful in modest events on the Wolverhampton Fibresand. She does not seem to run two consecutive races alike, however.
**Miss S J Wilton [1-9] John Pointon and Sons (from N P Littmoden [3-13] Spt 1998).*

OVER TO YOU (USA) BHB 74f80a RR 75f 80a 4267[17]

5 ch g Rubiano (USA) 7.1f **(87)** - Overnight (USA) (Mr Leader (USA)) 9.8f **(66)**
Form - 186042601551020
Record **1999** - 1st:3 2nd:2 3rd:0 Ran:15
Pre1999 - 1st:1 2nd:1 3rd:3 Ran:15
Win Prizemoney £19,203 *Total Prizemoney* £30,462
Wins * **1999** *Aug Wolver (STD) H 9.4f 76 80*
* **1999** Jly Ripon (G-F) H 12.3f 71 74
* **1999** *Feb Southw (STD) H 12f 70 76*
1996 Oct Nottin (GD) 8.2f 83 <
1999 Turf 1-12: (8f, 10f 2, 12f 1-6, 16f 2, 19f) (gd, g-f 4, frm 1-6, hrd)
1999 AW 2-3: (9f 1-1, 10f, 12f 1-1) (Equi, Fibr 2-2)
Decent gelding, effective 9 to 12f, acts on g-f to hrd - acts on Fibr, has worn blinkers, likes right handed tracks, likes tight tracks. Turf high 75 - 2nd of 12 getting 1lb from Westender (31 Aug Ripon 10f g-f RF 4042) - also 1st of 7 giving 14lb to Wafir (17 Jly Ripon RF 2926). AW high 80 - 1st of 8 getting 3lb from The Whistling Teal (14 Aug Wolverhampton RF 3669) - also 1st of 8 giving 32lb to Fatehalkhair (5 Feb Southwell RF 0233). He is very able on turf, as he showed when winning at Ripon in July and finishing a short-head second in the Cumberland Plate, but he is a very decent performer on Fibresand, wining at both Southwell and Wolverhampton this year. He has been sent over to America to be trained by Michael Dickinson.
**T D Barron [3-21] Nigel Shields (from E A L Dunlop [1-9] Spt 1997).*

OWENBRISTY (IRE) RR 3f 5054[11]
2 b f Ridgewood Ben - Dance In The Wings (In The Wings)
Form - 0
Record 1999 - 1st:0 2nd:0 3rd:0 Ran:1
1999 Turf 0-1: (6f) (gd)
Currently very poor filly. **G A Butler [0-1] F Deely.*

OXBANE BHB 35f37a **RR 42f 37a** 5101[4]
5 b m Soviet Star (USA) 8.6f **(74)** - Oxslip (Owen Dudley) 8.3f **(61)**
Form - 0052738557044
Record 1999 - 1st:0 2nd:1 3rd:1 Ran:12
Pre1999 - 1st:0 2nd:3 3rd:1 Ran:27
Win Prizemoney £0 *Total Prizemoney* £5,028
1999 Turf 0-7: (7f, 8f, 10f 4, 14f) (g-s 4, gd, g-f, frm) 1999 AW 0-5: (8f 3, 10f, 12f) (Equi, Fibr 4)
Moderate filly, effective 8 to 10f, best at 10f, acts on gd to g-f - acts on Fibr, best on gd, has worn blinkers, likes left handed tracks, likes tight tracks. Turf high 42. AW high 42 - 2nd of 13 getting 14lb from Chinaberry (25 Jan Southwell 8f Fibr RF 0161).
**Mrs S Lamyman [0-23] Sotby Farming Company Ltd (from C A Dwyer [0-10] Jan 1998).*

OYSTER CATCHER (IRE) RR 101f 4971a[8]
3 b f Bluebird (USA) 7.9f **(71)** - Brigid (USA)
Form - 8131431638
1999 Turf 3-10: (5f 2, 6f 3-6, 7f 2) (hvy, sft, g-s, gd 2-3, g-f 1-4)
Very useful filly, effective 6f, acts on gd to g-f, best on gd. Turf high 101 - 1st of 16 getting 3lb from Rolo Tomasi (21 Aug Fairyhouse RF 3886a) - also 1st of 12 from Social Harmony (27 Jun Curragh RF 2417a). Unraced at two, she worked overtime in 1999 and developed into a useful sprinter. Possibly unsuited by soft ground, she should stay seven furlongs and is capable of winning a Group race. **A P O'Brien in IRE [3-10] Mrs P J Magnier.*

OZAWA (IRE) RR 51f 3981[12]
2 gr c Brief Truce (USA) 9.1f **(73)** -Classy **(52f 43a)** (Kalaglow) 9.8f **(67)**
Form - 0
Record 1999 - 1st:0 2nd:0 3rd:0 Ran:1
1999 Turf 0-1: (6f) (frm)
Currently fair colt. **J W Payne [0-1] G Jabre.*

OZZIE BHB 25f32a **RR 15f 32a** 3748[12]
3 br f Ezzoud (IRE) - Australia Fair (AUS) (Without Fear (FR)) 5.9f **(55)**
Form - 80008600
Record 1999 - 1st:0 2nd:0 3rd:0 Ran:6
Pre1999 - 1st:0 2nd:0 3rd:0 Ran:2
1999 Turf 0-4: (6f, 8f, 10f, 11f) (gd, g-f, frm 2) 1999 AW 0-2: (7f, 8f) (Fibr 2)
Light-framed, very moderate filly. Turf high 15. AW high 23.
**Mrs N Macauley [0-4] Swift Racing (from M Waring [0-4] Mar 1999).*

PAARL ROCK BHB 47f **RR 52f** 4914[13]
4 ch c Common Grounds 8.1f **(66)** - Markievicz (IRE) (Doyoun) 9f **(69)**
Form - 08703000
Record 1999 - 1st:0 2nd:0 3rd:1 Ran:8
Pre1999 - 1st:0 2nd:0 3rd:0 Ran:3
Win Prizemoney £0 *Total Prizemoney* £414
1999 Turf 0-8: (7f 3, 8f 3, 10f 2) (gd 2, g-f 4, frm 2)
Scopey, fair colt, effective 8f, acts on g-f, has worn blinkers (very effectively), likes left handed tracks, favours tight tracks. Turf high 52 - 3rd of 17 getting 5lb from Noble Cyrano (6 Aug Haydock 8f g-f RF 3417). Becoming disappointing.
**G Barnett [0-8] J C Bradbury (from D R Loder [0-3] Spt 1997).*

PACAERA (GER) BHB 68f **RR 63f** 1381[7]
3 b f Caerleon (USA) 10.9f **(79)** - Pamplona (GER) (Surumu (GER)) 10f **(83)**
Form - 27
Record 1999 - 1st:0 2nd:1 3rd:0 Ran:2
Pre1999 - 1st:0 2nd:0 3rd:0 Ran:1
Win Prizemoney £0 *Total Prizemoney* £1,143
1999 Turf 0-2: (12f, 14f) (hvy, g-f)
Leggy, currently average filly. Turf high 63 (1st run) - 2nd of 11 getting 20lb from April Stock (13 Apr Folkestone 12f hvy RF 0660).
**J L Dunlop [0-3] Mrs H Focke.*

PACIFIC ALLIANCE (IRE) BHB 65f65a **RR 63f 65a** 3130[4]
3 b c Fayruz 6.6f **(63)** - La Gravotte (FR) (Habitat) 9.4f **(70)**
Form - 4130014
Record 1999 - 1st:2 2nd:0 3rd:1 Ran:7
Pre1999 - 1st:0 2nd:0 3rd:0 Ran:2
Win Prizemoney £6,474 *Total Prizemoney* £7,841
Wins * 1999 Jun Sandow (GD) H 8.1f 60 63
*** 1999** *Feb Lingfi (STD) 8f 68* <
1999 Turf 1-4: (8f 1-4) (gd, frm 1-3) 1999 AW 1-3:(8f 1-2, 10f)(Equi 1-3)
Average colt, effective 8f, acts on frm - acts on Equi, has worn blinkers. Turf high 63 - 4th of 7 getting 21lb from Ebony Heights (25 Jly Newmarket 8f frm RF 3130) - also 1st of 15 getting 15lb from Penang Pearl (11 Jun Sandown RF 1921). AW high 68 - 1st of 10 giving 5lb to Legend Falls (16 Feb Lingfield RF 0297). A winner on Equitrack earlier in the year, he responded well to being blinkered for the first time when taking a Sandown handicap in June.
**R W Armstrong [2-9] Horst Geicke.*

PACIFIC PLACE (IRE) RR 50f 5194[12]
2 gr c College Chapel - Kaitlin (IRE) (Salmon Leap (USA)) 11f **(61)**
Form - 00
Record 1999 - 1st:0 2nd:0 3rd:0 Ran:2
1999 Turf 0-2: (6f 2) (sft, gd)
Currently fair colt. Turf high 50 (began Oct).
**M Quinn [0-2] John Breslin.*

PACINO RR 80f 3244[2]
2 b c Zafonic (USA) 9f **(83)** - June Moon (IRE) (Sadler's Wells (USA)) 10f **(76)**
Form - 22
Record 1999 - 1st:0 2nd:2 3rd:0 Ran:2
Win Prizemoney £0 *Total Prizemoney* £2,470
1999 Turf 0-2: (7f 2) (frm 2)
Currently decent colt. Turf high 80 (began Jly) - 2nd of 8 to Reflex Blue (30 Jly Newmarket 7f frm RF 3244).
**J L Dunlop [0-2] Blue Blood And Wentworth Racing.*

PADAUK BHB 34f56a **RR 40f 56a** 2640[6]
5 b h Warrshan (USA) 9.7f **(59)** - Free on Board (Free State) 8.7f **(61)**
Form - 221236506
Record 1999 - 1st:1 2nd:2 3rd:1 Ran:8
Pre1999 - 1st:0 2nd:4 3rd:5 Ran:26
Win Prizemoney £2,772 *Total Prizemoney* £11,256
Wins * 1999 *Jan Lingfi (STD) H 16f 51 56* <
1999 Turf 0-4: (14f, 16f 3) (g-s 2, g-f, frm) 1999 AW 1-4: (16f 1-4) (Equi 1-4)
Fair colt, effective 14 to 16f, best at 14f, acts on g-s to frm - acts on Equi, has worn blinkers, favours tight tracks, excels at Kempton, does well at Sandown and Lingfield. Turf high 40. AW high 57 - 2nd of 13 getting 11lb from Harik (9 Feb Lingfield 16f Equi RF 0259) - also 1st of 11 getting 2lb from Spick And Span (30 Jan Lingfield RF 0198). Becoming disappointing. Comes there on the bridle, but does not usually see it through. His best recent form has been on Equitrack, and he was given a fine ride to win at Lingfield in January. Has a very poor wins-to-runs ratio.
**M J Haynes [1-34] Butler, Bob Pettis, Haynes.*

PADDOCK INSPECTION (IRE) BHB 56f59a **RR 40f 59a** 2199[7]
3 ch g Archway (IRE) 8.5f **(60)** - Lauretta Blue (IRE) (Bluebird (USA)) 7.5f **(69)**
Form - 142307
Record 1999 - 1st:0 2nd:1 3rd:1 Ran:4
Pre1999 - 1st:1 2nd:0 3rd:1 Ran:6
Win Prizemoney £2,085 *Total Prizemoney* £3,480
Wins 1998 *Nov Lingfi (STD) C 6f 65* <
1999 Turf 0-1: (10f) (gd) 1999 AW 0-3: (8f 3) (Equi 3)
Scopey, average gelding, effective 6 to 7f, - acts on Equi, mostly wears blinkers (very effectively), prefers left handed tracks, likes tight tracks. AW high 63. Inconsistent. Narrowly won a poor claimer on the Lingfield Equitrack last November. Bits and pieces of form since and has changed stables.
**Mrs L Stubbs [0-5] J P Spencer (from G Lewis [1-5] Nov 1998).*

PADDY MCGOON (USA) BHB 60f **RR 65df** 4836[15]
4 ch g Irish River (FR) 9f **(77)** - Flame McGoon (USA) (Staff Writer (USA)) 10f **(54)**

Form - 00
Record 1999 - 1st:0 2nd:0 3rd:0 Ran:2
Pre1999 - 1st:0 2nd:0 3rd:1 Ran:6
Win Prizemoney £0 *Total Prizemoney* £840
1999 Turf 0-2: (10f 2) (hvy, gd)
Scopey, average gelding, effective 10 to 12f, acts on gd to g-f. Turf high 48. **D R C Elsworth [0-8] Mrs Ann Shaw.*

PADDY MUL BHB 42f RR 44f 5076[19]

2 ch c Democratic (USA) - My Pretty Niece (Great Nephew) 9.9f **(64)**
Form - 0870
Record 1999 - 1st:0 2nd:0 3rd:0 Ran:4
1999 Turf 0-4: (6f, 7f 2, 8f) (gd 2, frm, hrd)
Moderate colt. Turf high 44 (began Aug).
**W Storey [0-4] Gremlin Racing.*

PADDYWACK (IRE) BHB 58f44a RR 57f 44a 5218[20]

2 b c Bigstone (IRE) - Millie's Return (IRE) (Ballad Rock) 7.8f **(63)**
Form - 000630010
Record 1999 - 1st:1 2nd:0 3rd:1 Ran:9
Win Prizemoney £3,330 *Total Prizemoney* £3,648
Wins * 1999 Oct Redcar (SFT) H 6f 55 57 <
1999 Turf 1-7: (5f 3, 6f 1-3, 7f) (g-s, gd 1-1, g-f, frm 4) 1999 AW 0-2: (5f, 7f) (Fibr 2)
Fair colt, effective 6f, acts on gd, has worn blinkers. Turf high 57 - 1st of 22 getting 11lb from Gain Time (26 Oct Redcar RF 5076). AW high 25 (began Oct). Inconsistent.
**D W Chapman [1-4] J B Wilcox (from G Lewis [0-5] Aug 1999).*

PADHAMS GREEN BHB 62f60a RR 55f 60a 5035[8]

3 b c Aragon 7.7f **(58)** - Double Dutch (Nicholas Bill) 10.1f **(56)**
Form - 0435317688
Record 1999 - 1st:1 2nd:0 3rd:2 Ran:10
Pre1999 - 1st:0 2nd:0 3rd:0 Ran:3
Win Prizemoney £2,658 *Total Prizemoney* £4,435
Wins * 1999 Aug Salisb (GD) H 7f 62 64 <
1999 Turf 1-9: (7f 1-7, 8f, 9f) (g-s, g-f 4, frm 1-4) 1999 AW 0-1: (7f) (Fibr)
Workmanlike, fair colt, effective 7f, acts on g-f to frm. Turf high 64 - 1st of 15 giving 2lb to Bread Winner (6 Aug Salisbury RF 3435). Consistent. **M H Tompkins [1-13] D J Anderson.*

PADOUKI (USA) BHB 45f RR 49f 3646[14]

3 b g Dayjur (USA) 6.8f **(79)** - Gesedeh (Ela-Mana-Mou) 10.1f **(70)**
Form - 7600
Record 1999 - 1st:0 2nd:0 3rd:0 Ran:4
1999 Turf 0-4: (6f, 7f 3) (sft, g-f, frm 2)
Scopey, moderate gelding. Turf high 49.
**B A Pearce [0-4] Stanley Selby.*

PAGAN RR 43f 3903[15]

4 b g Last Tycoon 9.4f **(73)** - Temple Row (Ardross) 10.6f **(68)**
Form - 4060
Record 1999 - 1st:0 2nd:0 3rd:0 Ran:4
Pre1999 - 1st:0 2nd:0 3rd:0 Ran:2
Win Prizemoney £0 *Total Prizemoney* £872
1999 Turf 0-4: (10f, 12f, 16f, 17f) (gd, frm 3)
Lengthy, moderate gelding, has worn blinkers. Turf high 43 (began Jly).
**M W Easterby [0-5] Mrs P A H Hartley (from L M Cumani [0-2] Aug 1998).*

PAGAN KING (IRE) BHB 74f RR 76f 3736[1]

3 b c Unblest - Starinka (Risen Star (USA))
Form - 7747431
Record 1999 - 1st:1 2nd:0 3rd:1 Ran:7
Pre1999 - 1st:1 2nd:0 3rd:0 Ran:3
Win Prizemoney £7,142 *Total Prizemoney* £8,506
Wins * 1999 Aug Bright (SFT) H 7f 71 76
* 1998 Oct Bright (G-S) 7f 78 <
1999 Turf 1-7: (7f 1-1, 8f 4, 10f 2) (g-s 1-1, gd, g-f 2, frm 3)
Leggy, above-average colt, effective 7 to 8f, best at 7f, acts on g-s to frm, best on g-s, prefers tight tracks. Turf high 76 - 1st of 4 getting 4lb from Ajig Dancer (18 Aug Brighton RF 3736). Consistent. Both of his wins to date have come over seven furlongs at Brighton with give in the ground.
**J A R Toller [2-10] The Gap Partnership.*

PAGEANT BHB 74f RR 73f 4944[3]

2 br f Inchinor 8.9f **(64)** - Positive Attitude (Red Sunset) 8.2f **(63)**
Form - 443
Record 1999 - 1st:0 2nd:0 3rd:1 Ran:3
Win Prizemoney £0 *Total Prizemoney* £1,123
1999 Turf 0-3: (7f 3) (g-s, gd, frm)
Currently above-average filly. Turf high 73 (began Spt) - 3rd of 16 getting 2lb from Azur (19 Oct Lingfield 7f gd RF 4944).
**R J R Williams [0-3] R J R Williams.*

PAGEBOY BHB 40f45a RR 36f 45a 4150[10]

10 b g Tina's Pet 7.4f **(56)** - Edwin's Princess (Owen Dudley) 8.3f **(61)**
Form - 07542280500
Record 1999 - 1st:0 2nd:2 3rd:0 Ran:11
Pre1999 - 1st:11 2nd:12 3rd:6 Ran:96
Win Prizemoney £35,667 *Total Prizemoney* £59,198

Wins								
1998	*Jan*	*Lingfi*	*(STD)*	*H*	*6f*	*70*	*75*	<
* 1997	*Jan*	*Lingfi*	*(STD)*	*H*	*6f*	*73*	*75*	<
* 1996	*Spt*	*Wolver*	*(STD)*	*H*	*6f*	*67*	*65*	
* 1996	Aug	Hamilt	(G-F)	H	6f	58	66+	
* 1996	*Jan*	*Lingfi*	*(STD)*	*H*	*6f*	*61*	*63*	
* 1995	*Jan*	*Lingfi*	*(STD)*	*H*	*6f*	*62*	*63+*	

1999 Turf 0-3: (6f 2, 7f) (gd, frm 2) 1999 AW 0-8: (6f 6, 7f 2) (Equi 5, Fibr 3)
Fair gelding, effective 6f, - acts on Equi, has worn blinkers. Turf high 36. AW high 55. A useful sprint-handicapper on his day, as time went on his wins became confined to the first week of the year on the Lingfield Equitrack. However, the sequence was broken soon after his tenth birthday and age may finally have caught up with him. **P C Haslam [11-107] Lord Scarsdale.*

PAGE'S KING RR 106f 4887a[1]

4 b c Konigsstuhl (GER) 9f **(115)** - Page Bleue (GER) (Sadler's Wells (USA)) 10f **(76)**
Form - 1
1999 Turf 1-1: (9f 1-1) (sft 1-1)
Pattern-class colt. (1st run) - 1st of 11 from Catoki (10 Oct Dusseldorf RF 4887a).
**W Himmel in GER [1-1] Stall Muhlgut (from A Lowe in GER [0-2] Oct 1998).*

PAINT IT BLACK BHB 52f40a RR 38f 40a 334[6]

6 ch g Double Schwartz 7f **(60)**-Tableaux (FR)(Welsh Pageant) 10f **(65)**
Form - 06
Record 1999 - 1st:0 2nd:0 3rd:0 Ran:2
Pre1999 - 1st:3 2nd:1 3rd:2 Ran:33
Win Prizemoney £8,539 *Total Prizemoney* £11,063

Wins								
1998	*Jan*	*Lingfi*	*(STD)*	*S*	*7f*		*47*	
1997	Apr	Thirsk	(G-F)	H	8f	50	54+	
1995	Spt	Epsom	(GD)		7f		76	<

1999 AW 0-2: (8f, 9f) (Fibr 2)
Very moderate gelding, effective 7 to 8f, - acts on Equi, has worn blinkers. AW high 15.
**Mrs A Swinbank [0-2] M A Scaife (from D Nicholls [2-19] Jan 1998).*

PAIRUMANI STAR (IRE) BHB 95f RR 95f 5132[12]

4 ch c Caerleon (USA) 10.9f **(79)** - Dawn Star (High Line) 10.3f **(70)**
Form - 46111200
Record 1999 - 1st:3 2nd:1 3rd:0 Ran:8
Pre1999 - 1st:3 2nd:3 3rd:2 Ran:12
Win Prizemoney £41,074 *Total Prizemoney* £61,303

Wins								
*** 1999**	Jly	Newbur	(G-F)	H	16f	90	90	
*** 1999**	Jun	Salisb	(FRM)		14.1f		92+	<
*** 1999**	Jun	York	(G-S)	H	13.9f	87	90	
* 1998	Aug	Goodwo	(G-F)	H	12f	85	87	
* 1998	Jly	Salisb	(GD)	H	12f	80	86	
* 1998	Jun	Haydoc	(GD)	H	14f	78	80	

1999 Turf 3-8: (14f 2-5, 16f 1-3) (g-s 1-1, gd 3, frm 2-4)
Workmanlike, very useful colt, effective 12 to 16f, best at 14f, acts on g-s to frm, best on frm, has worn blinkers, excels at Salisbury and likes Newbury. Turf high 95 - 2nd of 17 giving 3lb to Mowbray (27 Jly Goodwood 14f frm RF 3167) - also 1st of 3 getting 6lb from Mowbray (24 Jun Salisbury RF 2272). He capitalised on some lenient handicapping when completing a hat-trick in the summer and is a smart staying handicapper. Probably best when forcing the pace, he is genuine and open to a touch more improvement.
**J L Dunlop [6-20] Windflower Overseas Holdings Inc.*

PALACEGATE GOLD (IRE) BHB 40f32a **RR 39f 32a** 1923[8]

10 b g Sarab 9.2f **(60)** - Habilite (Habitat) 9.4f **(70)**

Form - 00008

Record	**1999 -**	1st:0	2nd:0	3rd:0	Ran:4
	Pre1999 -	1st:5	2nd:3	3rd:11	Ran:67

Win Prizemoney £13,266 *Total Prizemoney* £21,777

1999 Turf 0-3: (5f 2, 6f) (gd, frm 2) 1999 AW 0-1: (6f) (Fibr)

Very moderate gelding, has worn blinkers. Turf high 39.

**J E Long [0-10] J King (from R J Hodges [3-53] Apr 1996).*

PALACEGATE JACK (IRE) BHB 45f53a **RR 39f 53a** 5167[9]

8 gr g Neshad (USA) 5.5f **(59)** - Pasadena Lady (Captain James) 5f **(59)**

Form - 024002006010407086340

Record	**1999 -**	1st:1	2nd:2	3rd:1	Ran:21
	Pre1999 -	1st:14	2nd:10	3rd:10	Ran:76

Win Prizemoney £129,138 *Total Prizemoney* £148,523

Wins							
	* **1999**	Jun Newcas	(G-F)	S	5f		49
	* 1998	May Catter	(SFT)	C	5f		56
	* 1997	*Nov Lingfi*	*(STD)*	*H*	*5f*	*68*	*72*
	* 1997	*Spt Southw*	*(STD)*	*C*	*5f*		*67*
	* 1997	Jly Mussel	(G-F)	H	5f	65	67
	* 1997	Jun Hamilt	(G-S)	S	5f		55
	* 1997	Jun Newcas	(FRM)	S	5f		49
	1996	Nov Redcar	(G-F)	C	5f		75
	* 1996	*Spt Southw*	*(STD)*	*C*	*5f*		*75*
	* 1995	Jun Catter	(GD)	C	5f		84

1999 Turf 1-14: (5f 1-14) (g-s, gd 4, g-f 5, frm 1-4) 1999 AW 0-7: (5f 7) (Equi 3, Fibr 4)

Very moderate gelding, effective 5f, - acts on AW, best on Equi, often wears blinkers (effectively), likes left handed tracks, likes tight tracks, excels at Lingfield. Turf high 54. AW high 63 - 4th of 7 getting 32lb from Primo Lara (24 Feb Wolverhampton 5f Fibr RF 0351). **J Berry [14-87] J Berry (from C A Dwyer [1-10] Apr 1997).*

PALACEGATE JO (IRE) BHB 22f23a **RR 14f 23a** 1209[11]

8 b m Drumalis 8.8f **(73)** - Welsh Rhyme (Welsh Term) 9.9f **(71)**

Form - 8600

Record	**1999 -**	1st:0	2nd:0	3rd:0	Ran:4
	Pre1999 -	1st:12	2nd:11	3rd:5	Ran:75

Win Prizemoney £35,231 *Total Prizemoney* £46,977

Wins							
	* 1998	*Feb Wolver*	*(STD)*	*H*	*12f*	*24*	*37*
	* 1995	*Jly Wolver*	*(STD)*	*H*	*12f*	*50*	*53*
	1995	*May Southw*	*(STD)*	*C*	*12f*		*65*
	1995	*Feb Southw*	*(STD)*	*H*	*12f*	*57*	*63+*
	1995	*Jan Southw*	*(STD)*	*H*	*11f*	*57*	*57*

1999 Turf 0-2: (11f, 12f) (hvy, g-s) 1999 AW 0-2: (8f, 11f) (Fibr 2)

Poor mare, has broken blood-vessels, effective 12f, - acts on Fibr, has worn blinkers, likes left handed tracks.

**D W Chapman [2-36] David Chapman (from R Hollinshead [3-19] May 1995).*

PALACEGATE TOUCH BHB 50f70a **RR 44f 70a** 5167[6]

9 gr g Petong 7.6f **(58)** - Dancing Chimes (London Bells (CAN)) 5.8f **(53)**

Form - 41331502578307233356876

Record	**1999 -**	1st:2	2nd:2	3rd:6	Ran:23
	Pre1999 -	1st:25	2nd:10	3rd:10	Ran:104

Win Prizemoney £87,083 *Total Prizemoney* £112,216

Wins							
	* **1999**	*Mar Lingfi*	*(STD)*	*C*	*6f*		*67*
	* **1999**	*Jan Lingfi*	*(STD)*	*C*	*6f*		*63*
	* 1998	Jly Catter	(GD)	C	6f		58
	* 1998	Jly Catter	(FRM)	S	6f		55
	* 1998	Jly Hamilt	(FRM)	S	6f		60
	* 1998	Jun Warwic	(GD)	C	6f		64
	* 1998	*Jan Lingfi*	*(STD)*	*C*	*6f*		*72*
	* 1997	*Nov Lingfi*	*(STD)*	*H*	*7f*	*72*	*76*
	* 1997	Aug Haydoc	(G-F)	C	6f		72
	* 1997	Jly Hamilt	(G-S)	H	6f	77	78
	* 1997	May Catter	(G-F)	C	5f		64
	* 1997	May Doncas	(GD)	C	5f		75
	* 1996	Oct Catter	(GD)	H	5f	74	78
	* 1996	Spt Sandow	(G-F)	C	5f		75
	* 1996	Aug Catter	(G-F)	C	5f		65
	* 1996	Jly Warwic	(FRM)		5f		72
	* 1996	*Jly Lingfi*	*(STD)*	*C*	*5f*		*66*
	* 1996	Apr Carlis	(G-S)	C	6.9f		65
	* 1995	Apr Ripon	(G-S)	H	6f	86	90 <

1999 Turf 0-16: (5f 7, 6f 9) (g-s 2, gd 3, g-f 2, frm 7, hrd 2) 1999 AW 2-7: (6f 2-7) (Equi 2-2, Fibr 5)

Average gelding, mostly wears blinkers, likes left handed tracks, likes tight tracks, does well at Lingfield and Catterick. Turf high 54. AW high 87. He can still win in claiming company, either on turf or on Equitrack. **J Berry [27-127] A B Parr.*

PALACE GREEN (IRE) BHB 65f65a **RR 67f 65a** 4154[11]

3 ch f Rudimentary (USA) 8.2f **(66)** - Show Home (Music Boy) 6.8f **(57)**

Form - 6120

Record	**1999 -**	1st:1	2nd:1	3rd:0	Ran:3
	Pre1999 -	1st:2	2nd:4	3rd:3	Ran:17

Win Prizemoney £6,840 *Total Prizemoney* £12,836

Wins							
	* **1999**	*Jan Southw*	*(STD)*	*H*	*6f*	*65*	*75* <
	1998	*May Southw*	*(STD)*	*S*	*6f*		*60*
	1998	*May Southw*	*(STD)*	*S*	*5f*		*60*

1999 AW 1-3: (6f 1-2, 7f) (Fibr 1-3)

Scopey, average filly, effective 5 to 6f, best at 6f, acts on g-f to frm - acts on Fibr, excels at Southwell. AW high 75 (1st run) - 1st of 10 giving 5lb to Erinvale (2 Jan Southwell RF 0018).

**D W Chapman [1-15] J M Chapman (from M R Channon [2-5] May 1998).*

PALACE HOUSE RR 14f 3003[18]

2 b g Never so Bold 7.1f **(62)** - Cardinal Palace (Royal Palace) 9f **(56)**

Form - 0

Record	**1999 -**	1st:0	2nd:0	3rd:0	Ran:1

1999 Turf 0-1: (7f) (g-f)

Currently poor gelding.

**J J O'Neill [0-1] Clayton Bigley Partnership Ltd.*

PALACE ROYALE (IRE) RR 92f 4315a[4]

3 b f Perugino (USA) - Trojan Tale (USA) 00

Form - 1624

1999 Turf 1-4: (8f, 9f 1-2, 10f) (gd 1-3, g-f)

Useful filly. Turf high 92. **M J Grassick in IRE [1-4] J F O'Malley.*

PALAIS (IRE) BHB 36f56a **RR 49f 56a** 4563[16]

4 b g Darshaan 11.9f **(81)** - Dance Festival (Nureyev (USA)) 8.7f **(78)**

Form - 31250540500

Record	**1999 -**	1st:1	2nd:1	3rd:1	Ran:11
	Pre1999 -	1st:0	2nd:0	3rd:0	Ran:5

Win Prizemoney £2,892 *Total Prizemoney* £5,796

Wins							
	* **1999**	*Jan Southw*	*(STD)*		*11f*		*65* <

1999 Turf 0-6: (10f 3, 14f, 16f 2) (gd, g-f, frm 3, hrd) 1999 AW 1-5: (8f, 11f 1-3, 12f) (Fibr 1-5)

Tall, fair gelding, effective 8 to 11f, acts on gd - acts on Fibr, has worn blinkers, favours tight tracks. Turf high 52 (began Jly). AW high 67 - also 1st of 9 giving 21lb to Tragic Dancer (8 Jan Southwell RF 0052). Won a maiden on the Southwell Fibresand at the start of the year, but has occasionally seemed to sulk and lose interest. One to treat with the utmost caution.

**J L Harris [1-11] J South (from Sir Michael Stoute [0-5] Jly 1998).*

PALAWAN BHB 71f **RR 71df** 4326[9]

3 br c Polar Falcon (USA) 9f **(74)** - Krameria (Kris) 9.5f **(73)**

Form - 25220

Record	**1999 -**	1st:0	2nd:3	3rd:0	Ran:5
	Pre1999 -	1st:0	2nd:0	3rd:0	Ran:2

Win Prizemoney £0 *Total Prizemoney* £3,210

1999 Turf 0-5: (5f 2, 6f, 7f 2) (gd 2, g-f 2, frm)

Scopey, above-average colt, effective 7f, acts on g-f. Turf high 71.

**I A Balding [0-7] Robert Hitchins.*

PALERIA (USA) BHB 68f64a **RR 69f 64a** 5026[13]

3 ch f Zilzal (USA) 8.5f **(79)** - Placer Queen (Habitat) 9.4f **(70)**

Form - 050

Record	**1999 -**	1st:0	2nd:0	3rd:0	Ran:3
	Pre1999 -	1st:1	2nd:0	3rd:0	Ran:3

Win Prizemoney £3,647 *Total Prizemoney* £3,647

Wins							
	* 1998	Jly Thirsk	(FRM)		6f		71 <

1999 Turf 0-3: (7f 2, 8f) (gd, g-f, frm)

Leggy, average filly, effective 6 to 8f, acts on g-f to frm. Turf high 68 (began Aug) - 5th of 22 getting 7lb from Katy Nowaitee (2 Oct Redcar 8f g-f RF 4689). **P W Harris [1-6] Resplendent Racing Ltd.*

PALHA BHB 60f **RR 75f** 4727[15]
2 b g Jalmood (USA) 11.1f **(59)** - Alioli **(49f 35a)** (Nishapour (FR)) 9.1f **(61)**
Form - 83500
Record 1999 - 1st:0 2nd:0 3rd:1 Ran:5
Win Prizemoney £0 *Total Prizemoney* £352
1999 Turf 0-5: (7f 4, 10f) (g-s, gd, g-f 2, frm)
Above-average gelding. Turf high 61.
**Sir Mark Prescott [0-5] Thurcoe Partnership.*

PALINISA (FR) RR 99f 1905a[3]
3 ch f Night Shift (USA) 8.1f **(73)** - Palavera (Bikala) 10.1f **(49)**
Form - 3
1999 Turf 0-1: (11f) (gd)
Currently very useful filly. (1st run) - 3rd of 5 to Ronda (6 Jun Chantilly 11f gd RF 1905a). **A Fabre in FR [0-1].*

PALIO SKY BHB 104f **RR 110df** 4096[3]
5 b h Niniski (USA) 13.2f **(67)** - Live Ammo (Home Guard (USA)) 9.3f **(66)**
Form - 45253
Record 1999 - 1st:0 2nd:1 3rd:1 Ran:5
Pre1999 - 1st:5 2nd:3 3rd:1 Ran:16
Win Prizemoney £46,055 *Total Prizemoney* £114,070

Wins							
* 1998	Jly	Chanti	(GD)	L	15f	113	<
* 1997	Spt	Chanti	(SFT)	L	15f	113+	
* 1997	Apr	Epsom	(GD)		12f	96	
* 1997	Mar	Kempto	(GD)		10f	91	
* 1996	Spt	Haydoc	(GD)		8.1f	88	

1999 Turf 0-5: (13f 2, 14f 2, 15f) (gd 3, g-f, frm)
Group-class colt, effective 13 to 15f, best at 15f, acts on sft to g-f, likes right handed tracks. Turf high 110 - 2nd of 6 to Lucky Dream (24 Jly Maisons-Laffitte 13f gd RF 3231a). A lazy individual, he had a hard race when finishing second at Maisons-Laffitte in July and ran poorly thereafter. He is not one to trust implicitly at present. Sold for 13,000 gns at Tattersalls to jumps trainer Paul Rich.
**J L Dunlop [5-21] J E Nash.*

PALLIUM (IRE) BHB 30f59a **RR 23f 59a** 4167[9]
11 b g Try My Best (USA) 7.8f **(68)** - Jungle Gardenia (Nonoalco (USA)) 8.5f **(66)**
Form - 0000500000580
Record 1999 - 1st:0 2nd:0 3rd:0 Ran:13
Pre1999 - 1st:7 2nd:14 3rd:13 Ran:126
Win Prizemoney £21,855 *Total Prizemoney* £46,469

Wins							
* 1997	Jly	Hamilt	(G-F)	H	5f	45	47
1995	Jly	Ripon	(G-F)	SH	5f	55	56
1995	Jly	Mussel	(G-F)	H	5f	52	53

1999 Turf 0-13: (5f 11, 6f 2) (gd 3, g-f 6, frm 4)
Moderate gelding, effective 5f, acts on gd, has worn blinkers. Turf high 25.
**D A Nolan [1-46] Mrs J McFadyen-Murray (from Mrs A M Naughton [2-31] Spt 1996).*

PALMSTEAD BELLE (IRE) BHB 73f **RR 73df** 3799[5]
2 b f Wolfhound (USA) 7.3f **(71)** - Fiction (Dominion) 8.5f **(63)**
Form - 317745
Record 1999 - 1st:1 2nd:0 3rd:1 Ran:6
Win Prizemoney £2,637 *Total Prizemoney* £3,200
Wins * **1999** May Nottin (FRM) 5.1f 80 <
1999 Turf 1-6: (5f 1-6) (gd, g-f 1-4, frm)
Above-average filly, effective 5f, acts on g-f. Turf high 80 - 1st of 12 getting 2lb from Blackpool Mamma's (21 May Nottingham RF 1379). She won a Nottingham novice auction event on very fast ground on her second start, but the form does not amount to much. **C B B Booth [1-6] The Palmstead Partnership.*

PALM TREE BHB 78f **RR 82f** 3822[3]
3 b f Alzao (USA) 9.8f **(73)** - Swan Heights (Shirley Heights) 10.3f **(74)**
Form - 2723
Record 1999 - 1st:0 2nd:2 3rd:1 Ran:4
Win Prizemoney £0 *Total Prizemoney* £3,233
1999 Turf 0-4: (8f 3, 10f) (g-f 2, frm 2)
Neat, decent filly. Turf high 82 (1st run) - 2nd of 9 to Apple of Kent (15 May Newmarket 8f g-f RF 1242).
**Sir Michael Stoute [0-4] Mitaab Abdullah.*

PAL OF MINE BHB 63f **RR 73df** 5050[12]
3 b c Zafonic (USA) 9f **(83)** - Dana Springs (IRE) **(93df)** (Aragon) 8.1f **(60)**
Form - 0644000
Record 1999 - 1st:0 2nd:0 3rd:0 Ran:7
Pre1999 - 1st:1 2nd:1 3rd:0 Ran:3
Win Prizemoney £3,420 *Total Prizemoney* £5,899
Wins * 1998 Spt Epsom (SFT) 6f 78 <
1999 Turf 0-7: (7f 2, 8f 3, 9f, 10f) (gd 3, g-f, frm 3)
Neat, above-average colt, effective 5 to 10f, acts on gd to frm, best on gd, likes left handed tracks, prefers tight tracks. Turf high 73. Becoming disappointing.
**R Hannon [1-10] Geoff Howard-Spink & Lindy Regis.*

PALUA BHB 75f **RR 78f** 4402[10]
2 b c Sri Pekan (USA) - Reticent Bride (IRE) (Shy Groom (USA)) 10f **(66)**
Form - 7730
Record 1999 - 1st:0 2nd:0 3rd:1 Ran:4
Win Prizemoney £0 *Total Prizemoney* £470
1999 Turf 0-4: (6f, 7f 3) (gd, frm 3)
Above-average colt. Turf high 78 (began Jly) - 3rd of 12 to Strasbourg (9 Spt Chepstow 7f frm RF 4226).
**Mrs A J Bowlby [0-4] Robert Hitchins.*

PALVIC LADY BHB 60f **RR 61f** 4507[15]
3 b f Cotation 5f **(52)** - Palvic Grey (Kampala) 8.5f **(56)**
Form - 0636805310
Record 1999 - 1st:1 2nd:0 3rd:2 Ran:10
Pre1999 - 1st:0 2nd:0 3rd:0 Ran:3
Win Prizemoney £3,923 *Total Prizemoney* £5,070
Wins * **1999** Spt Beverl (GD) 5f 61 <
1999 Turf 1-10: (5f 1-6, 6f 3, 8f) (sft 2, gd 1-3, g-f 3, frm 2)
Leggy, average filly, effective 5f, acts on gd. Turf high 61 - 3rd of 17 getting 5lb from Jaypeecee (22 Apr Beverley 5f gd RF 0808) - also 1st of 12 getting 5lb from Antonio Canova (15 Spt Beverley RF 4326). **C Smith [1-13] Alan Pickard.*

PAMELA ANSHAN BHB 42f **RR 36f** 5044[11]
2 b f Anshan 8.2f **(63)** - Have Form (Haveroid) 6f **(48)**
Form - 000
Record 1999 - 1st:0 2nd:0 3rd:0 Ran:3
1999 Turf 0-3: (6f 3) (sft, gd, g-f)
Currently very moderate filly. Turf high 36 (began Oct).
**J Cullinan [0-3] Alan Spargo Ltd Toolmakers.*

PAMS PRINCESS BHB 28f **RR 26f** 2840[16]
3 b br f King's Signet (USA) 7f **(51)** - Good Skills (Bustino) 10.4f **(64)**
Form - 0800
Record 1999 - 1st:0 2nd:0 3rd:0 Ran:4
1999 Turf 0-2: (5f, 7f) (g-f, frm) 1999 AW 0-2: (6f, 7f) (Fibr 2)
Light-framed, little account filly. Turf high 26 (began Jly).
**K Bishop [0-4] K Bishop.*

PANAMA HOUSE BHB 66f **RR 68f** 4267[10]
4 ch g Rudimentary (USA) 8.2f **(66)** - Lustrous (Golden Act (USA)) 8.8f **(67)**
Form - 36441350
Record 1999 - 1st:1 2nd:0 3rd:2 Ran:8
Pre1999 - 1st:3 2nd:4 3rd:1 Ran:16
Win Prizemoney £17,568 *Total Prizemoney* £24,549

Wins							
* **1999**	Aug	Beverl	(GD)	H	9.9f	65	62
* 1998	Oct	Doncas	(SFT)	H	10.3f	69	73
* 1997	Oct	Doncas	(GD)	H	8f	73	81 <
* 1997	Aug	Thirsk	(G-F)		7f	70+	

1999 Turf 1-8: (9f, 10f 1-6, 12f) (gd, g-f 1-5, frm, hrd)
Scopey, average gelding, effective 8 to 10f, best at 10f, acts on gd to hrd, has worn blinkers (effectively), prefers right handed tracks, likes tight tracks, and excels at Beverley. Turf high 71 (1st run) - 3rd of 7 giving 8lb to Sturgeon (16 Jun Ripon 10f hrd RF 2059). Consistent. Blinkered when making all at Beverley, but looked just held by the assessor next time. **T D Easterby [5-26] P England.*

PANCAKE WOOD BHB 55f **RR 61f** 2267[10]
3 b g Saddlers' Hall (IRE) 10.5f **(65)** - Dame Ashfield (Grundy) 10.3f **(65)**
Form - 6600

Record 1999 - 1st:0 2nd:0 3rd:0 Ran:4
1999 Turf 0-4: (12f 2, 14f, 16f) (gd 3, g-f)
Average gelding. Turf high 61.
**M Johnston [0-4] Greenland Park Ltd.*

PANDJOJOE (IRE) BHB 62f **RR 64f** 5212[10]
3 b g Archway (IRE) 8.5f **(60)** - Vital Princess (Prince Sabo) 7.2f **(62)**
Form - 1114500000
Record 1999 - 1st:3 2nd:0 3rd:0 Ran:10
Pre1999 - 1st:0 2nd:0 3rd:0 Ran:5
Win Prizemoney £10,195 *Total Prizemoney* £10,463
Wins * **1999** May Haydoc (GD) H 6f 70 73
* **1999** May Windso (GD) H 6f 56 74+ <
* **1999** May Newcas (G-F) H 6f 56 64+
1999 Turf 3-10: (5f, 6f 3-9) (g-s, gd, g-f 2-3, frm 1-5)
Tall, average gelding, effective 6f, acts on g-f to frm, best on g-f. Turf high 74 - 1st of 24 getting 1lb from Night Life (10 May Windsor RF 1138) - also 1st of 20 giving 19lb to Three Leaders (28 May Haydock RF 1547). **R A Fahey [3-15] J Dixon.*

PANSY BHB 55f **RR 54f** 2626[6]
3 br f Lugana Beach 7f **(63)** - Smah (Mtoto)
Form - 006406
Record 1999 - 1st:0 2nd:0 3rd:0 Ran:6
Pre1999 - 1st:0 2nd:0 3rd:0 Ran:3
Win Prizemoney £0 *Total Prizemoney* £423
1999 Turf 0-6: (6f 2, 7f 3, 8f) (gd, g-f, frm 4)
Neat, fair filly, has worn blinkers. Turf high 54. Consistent.
**H Morrison [0-6] H Morrison (from J M P Eustace [0-3] Aug 1998).*

PANTANAL BHB 64f **RR 68f** 4901[12]
2 b c Wolfhound (USA) 7.3f **(71)** - Forest Blossom (USA) (Green Forest (USA)) 9.9f **(68)**
Form - 74650
Record 1999 - 1st:0 2nd:0 3rd:0 Ran:5
Win Prizemoney £0 *Total Prizemoney* £203
1999 Turf 0-5: (6f, 7f 3, 8f) (g-s, gd, frm 3)
Average colt. Turf high 68 (began Jly). **J L Dunlop [0-5] J L Dunlop.*

PANTAR (IRE) BHB 90f **RR 89f** 4683[25]
4 b c Shirley Heights 12.1f **(76)** - Spring Daffodil (Pharly (FR)) 9.8f **(68)**
Form - 5450560330
Record 1999 - 1st:0 2nd:0 3rd:2 Ran:10
Pre1999 - 1st:1 2nd:1 3rd:3 Ran:12
Win Prizemoney £14,980 *Total Prizemoney* £42,916
Wins * 1998 Jun Goodwo (GD) H 8f 90 96 <
1999 Turf 0-10: (8f 8, 10f 2) (gd 5, g-f 3, frm 2)
Useful colt, effective 8 to 10f, acts on gd to frm, best on g-f, likes right handed tracks. Turf high 102 - 4th of 19 giving 23lb to Bomb Alaska (17 Apr Newbury 8f g-f RF 0735). He was laid-out for the Royal Hunt Cup, but ran poorly there and has become frustrating. Best over a straight mile, he has swished his tail and is one to treat with some caution. **I A Balding [1-22] Robert Hitchins.*

PANTO QUEEN BHB 29f35a **RR 30f 35a** 3475[7]
8 b m Lepanto (GER) - Tyqueen (Tycoon II) 8.7f **(47)**
Form - 027
Record 1999 - 1st:0 2nd:1 3rd:0 Ran:3
Pre1999 - 1st:0 2nd:0 3rd:0 Ran:4
Win Prizemoney £0 *Total Prizemoney* £856
1999 Turf 0-3: (10f, 16f, 18f) (g-f, frm 2)
Very moderate mare. Turf high 30.
**J Neville [0-3] B C Allen (from C R Barwell [0-4] Mar 1997).*

PAPABILE (USA) **RR 78f** 5137[2]
2 b f Chief's Crown (USA) 10.2f **(75)** - La Papagena (Habitat) 9.4f **(70)**
Form - 52
Record 1999 - 1st:0 2nd:1 3rd:0 Ran:2
Win Prizemoney £0 *Total Prizemoney* £1,336
1999 Turf 0-2: (7f 2) (gd, frm)
Currently above-average filly. Turf high 78 (began Jly) - 2nd of 16 to Garota do Leblon (30 Oct Newmarket 7f gd RF 5137).
**W Jarvis [0-2] Exors of the late Lord Howard de Walden.*

PAPAGENA (USA) BHB 60f **RR 53f** 4716[8]
2 b br f Robellino (USA) 9.5f **(68)** - Morning Crown (USA) (Chief's Crown (USA)) 9.8f **(72)**
Form - 0062038
Record 1999 - 1st:0 2nd:1 3rd:1 Ran:7
Win Prizemoney £0 *Total Prizemoney* £2,642
1999 Turf 0-7: (5f 2, 6f 5) (gd 4, g-f, frm 2)
Fair filly. Turf high 53. **C W Thornton [0-7] Simon Brown.*

PAPE DIOUF BHB 61f **RR 62f** 5064[17]
2 b g Prince Sabo 6.6f **(64)** - Born to Dance (Dancing Brave (USA)) 8.4f **(76)**
Form - 80242550
Record 1999 - 1st:0 2nd:2 3rd:0 Ran:8
Win Prizemoney £0 *Total Prizemoney* £1,572
1999 Turf 0-6: (5f 4, 6f 2) (sft, gd, g-f, frm 3) 1999 AW 0-2: (5f 2) (Fibr 2)
Average gelding, effective 5f, acts on g-f to frm - acts on Fibr, has worn blinkers. Turf high 62 - 2nd of 8 getting 25lb from Half Moon Bay (15 Jly Doncaster 5f g-f RF 2842). AW high 63 (1st run) - 2nd of 9 giving 5lb to Walnut Lady (10 May Southwell 5f Fibr RF 1134).
**B Smart [0-1] Willie McKay (from K McAuliffe [0-7] Jly 1999).*

PAPERWEIGHT BHB 69f **RR 71f** 4946[8]
3 b f In The Wings 11.2f **(77)** - Crystal Reay (Sovereign Dancer (USA)) 11.2f **(68)**
Form - 25238
Record 1999 - 1st:0 2nd:2 3rd:1 Ran:5
Win Prizemoney £0 *Total Prizemoney* £3,460
1999 Turf 0-5: (10f 5) (g-s, gd, g-f, frm 2)
Rangy, above-average filly. Turf high 76 (1st run) - 2nd of 9 getting 5lb from Marnor (18 Jun Newmarket 10f frm RF 2126).
**L M Cumani [0-5] Sheikh Mohammed.*

PAPILLON SAUVAGE BHB 34f29a **RR 35f 29a** 3145[9]
4 b f Theatrical Charmer 10.9f **(63)** - Gotcher (Jalmood (USA)) 10.1f **(52)**
Form - 880
Record 1999 - 1st:0 2nd:0 3rd:0 Ran:1
Pre1999 - 1st:0 2nd:0 3rd:0 Ran:3
1999 Turf 0-1: (12f) (g-f)
Lengthy, very moderate filly. **W R Muir [0-4] Paul Bourdon.*

PAPI SPECIAL (IRE) BHB 72f **RR 72f** 4828[2]
2 b c Tragic Role (USA) 9.4f **(63)** - Practical (Ballymore) 7.3f **(64)**
Form - 0422
Record 1999 - 1st:0 2nd:2 3rd:0 Ran:4
Win Prizemoney £0 *Total Prizemoney* £2,446
1999 Turf 0-4: (8f 4) (sft, gd, frm 2)
Above-average colt, mostly wears blinkers. Turf high 72 (began Aug) - 2nd of 11 getting 13lb from Clever Girl (12 Oct Ayr 8f sft RF 4828). **I Semple [0-4] Mrs E Chung & Peter Tsim.*

PAPUA BHB 88a **RR 89f** 129[12]
5 ch g Green Dancer (USA) 11.9f **(77)** - Fairy Tern (Mill Reef (USA)) 10.5f **(78)**
Form - 40
Record 1999 - 1st:0 2nd:0 3rd:0 Ran:2
Pre1999 - 1st:3 2nd:3 3rd:2 Ran:17
Win Prizemoney £32,409 *Total Prizemoney* £52,301
Wins * 1996 Oct Newmar (GD) 7f 93
* 1996 Aug Doncas (G-F) 7f 95 <
* 1996 Jly Lingfi (G-F) 7f 84
1999 AW 0-2: (12f 2) (Equi, Fibr)
Useful gelding, has worn blinkers. AW high 85.
**I A Balding [4-25] Robert Hitchins.*

PARABLE BHB 70f **RR 75f** 5003[6]
3 b c Midyan (USA) 9.9f **(64)** - Top Table (Shirley Heights) 10.3f **(74)**
Form - 656
Record 1999 - 1st:0 2nd:0 3rd:0 Ran:3
1999 Turf 0-3: (8f 2, 11f) (gd 2, g-f)
Strong, currently above-average colt. Turf high 75 (began Spt) - 5th of 14 giving 5lb to Sheer Harmony (11 Oct Windsor 8f g-f RF 4824). **L M Cumani [0-3] Lord De La Warr.*

PARADISE (IRE) **RR 31f** 4342[19]
2 b c Distinctly North (USA) 7.4f **(63)** - Why Not Glow (IRE) (Glow (USA)) 6.7f **(71)**
Form - 0

Record 1999 - 1st:0 2nd:0 3rd:0 Ran:1
1999 Turf 0-1: (6f) (g-s)
Currently very moderate colt.
**J J O'Neill [0-1] Carlton Appointments (Aberdeen) Ltd.*

PARADISE COUNTY BHB 30f RR 19f 4790[7]

3 b f Prince Sabo 6.6f **(64)** - Bold County (Never so Bold) 6.3f **(66)**
Form - 587
Record 1999 - 1st:0 2nd:0 3rd:0 Ran:3
1999 Turf 0-3: (9f, 10f 2) (g-s, gd, frm)
Unfurnished, currently poor filly. Turf high 19 (began Jly).
**Miss B Sanders [0-3] Mrs P J Sheen.*

PARADISE GARDEN (USA) BHB 100f RR 94f 5139[4]

2 b c Septieme Ciel (USA) - Water Course (USA) (Irish River (FR)) 8.6f **(78)**
Form - 31224
Record 1999 - 1st:1 2nd:2 3rd:1 Ran:5
Win Prizemoney £2,253 *Total Prizemoney* £11,875
Wins * **1999** Aug Newcas (GD) 8f 68+ <
1999 Turf 1-5: (7f, 8f 1-3, 10f) (gd, g-f 1-2, frm 2)
Useful colt. Turf high 94 (began Jly) - 2nd of 6 to Hataab (18 Oct Pontefract 8f g-f RF 4931). Showed promise on Epsom's tricky gradients first time out, and bolted up from four rivals in a Newcastle maiden over a mile next time. Runner-up in a warm conditions event at Newbury, he has since filled the same the position at Pontefract. Attempting to make all last time out, he had his rivals in some trouble before being caught close home.
**M Johnston [1-5] David Abell.*

PARADISE LANE BHB 83f RR 84f 3117[13]

3 ch g Alnasr Alwasheek 9.4f **(62)** - La Belle Vie (Indian King (USA)) 7.4f **(64)**
Form - 21158000
Record 1999 - 1st:2 2nd:1 3rd:0 Ran:8
Pre1999 - 1st:0 2nd:0 3rd:0 Ran:1
Win Prizemoney £11,597 *Total Prizemoney* £12,377
Wins * **1999** May Cheste (G-F) H 5.1f 84 91 <
* **1999** Apr Nottin (SFT) 5.1f 88
1999 Turf 2-8: (5f 2-6, 6f 2) (sft, gd 1-2, g-f 1-5)
Neat, decent gelding, effective 5f, acts on sft to g-f. Turf high 91 - 1st of 12 giving 4lb to Jackie's Baby (4 May Chester RF 1030) - also 1st of 12 giving 5lb to Cyclone Flyer (19 Apr Nottingham RF 0749). Becoming disappointing. He looked to be improving, and won in good style over the minimum at Nottingham and Chester in the spring before the handicapper caught up with him. Speedy front-runner. **B R Millman [2-9] Robin Lawson.*

PARADISE NAVY BHB 58f60a RR 61f 60a 4218[10]

10 b g Slip Anchor 12.7f **(75)** - Ivory Waltz (USA) (Sir Ivor) 10.2f **(70)**
Form - 411515463286460
Record 1999 - 1st:1 2nd:1 3rd:1 Ran:11
Pre1999 - 1st:11 2nd:8 3rd:13 Ran:83
Win Prizemoney £38,091 *Total Prizemoney* £62,687
Wins * **1999** *Jan Lingfi (STD) H 16f 61 64*
* 1998 *Dec Wolver (STD) H 16.2f 50 60*
* 1998 *Nov Southw (STD) H 14f 52 55*
* 1998 Aug Salisb (G-F) H 14.1f 67 71
* 1998 May Nottin (FRM) H 16f 63 65
* 1997 Oct Yarmou (FRM) C 14.1f 56
* 1997 Aug Yarmou (G-F) H 14.1f 70 74 <
* 1997 Jly Doncas (GD) H 16.5f 64 66
* 1997 Apr Folkes (G-F) H 15.4f 65 71
* 1996 *Aug Lingfi (STD) H 16f 65 66*
* 1996 Jly Bath (FRM) H 17.2f 64 69+
1999 Turf 0-7: (12f, 14f 4, 16f, 17f) (gd 2, g-f, frm 4) 1999 AW 1-4: (16f 1-4) (Equi 1-2, Fibr 2)
Average gelding, effective 14 to 17f, acts on sft to frm - acts on Equi, best on g-f, mostly wears blinkers (effectively), likes left handed tracks, likes tight tracks, excels at Redcar, does well at Bath , nd Salisbury, likes Nottingham. Turf high 66 (1st run) - 3rd of 15 getting 3lb from Christiansted (16 Jun Nottingham 14f g-f RF 2051). AW high 64 (1st run) - 1st of 9 giving 28lb to Sweet Serenata (9 Jan Lingfield RF 0058). Kept on the go, he pays his way in minor company on turf and sand. He is a very difficult ride who needs to be left to do it his way, and when he is likely to show his best is very difficult to predict.
**C R Egerton [11-90] Elite Racing Club (from M C Pipe [2-7] Apr 1994).*

PARADISE YANGSHUO BHB 55f RR 54f 4280[8]

2 b f Whittingham (IRE) - Poly Static (IRE) **(37f)** (Statoblest)
Form - 8220528608
Record 1999 - 1st:0 2nd:3 3rd:0 Ran:10
Win Prizemoney £0 *Total Prizemoney* £2,419
1999 Turf 0-10: (5f 10) (sft, g-s, gd, g-f 5, frm 2)
Fair filly, effective 5f, acts on sft to frm. Turf high 55.
**E J Alston [0-7] Valley Paddocks Racing Ltd (from M R Channon [0-3] Apr 1999).*

PARDAN BHB 36f34a RR 35f 34a 2913[9]

5 b g Pharly (FR) 11.5f **(64)** - Silent Pool (Relkino) 8.9f **(65)**
Form - 7180
Record 1999 - 1st:1 2nd:0 3rd:0 Ran:4
Pre1999 - 1st:0 2nd:1 3rd:3 Ran:19
Win Prizemoney £2,215 *Total Prizemoney* £3,865
Wins * **1999** Jly Nottin (GD) SH 14.1f 33 35 <
1999 Turf 1-4: (12f, 14f 1-2, 16f) (g-f 1-3, frm)
Very moderate gelding, effective 14 to 16f, acts on gd to g-f, has worn blinkers, likes left handed tracks. Turf high 35. Consistent. He remained a maiden for a long time, but finally got off the mark in a modest Nottingham seller in July.
**B Palling [1-29] Mrs M M Palling.*

PARDY PET (IRE) BHB 51f RR 55f 4286[16]

2 ch f Petardia 8.2f **(58)** - Elite Exhibition (Exhibitioner) 8.7f **(61)**
Form - 0871480
Record 1999 - 1st:1 2nd:0 3rd:0 Ran:7
Win Prizemoney £1,912 *Total Prizemoney* £1,912
Wins 1999 Jly Leices (G-F) S 5f 55 <
1999 Turf 1-7: (5f 1-3, 6f 4) (gd 2, g-f 1-3, frm 2)
Fair filly, effective 5f, acts on g-f. Turf high 55 - 1st of 10 from Bron Hilda (15 Jly Leicester RF 2849).
**C G Cox [0-2] Mel Davies & Partners (from M J Heaton-Ellis [1-5] Aug 1999).*

PARIJAZZ (IRE) BHB 37f48a RR 23?f 48a 1377[10]

5 b m Astronef 7.9f **(59)** - Brandywell (Skyliner) 7.3f **(53)**
Form - 0
Record 1999 - 1st:0 2nd:0 3rd:0 Ran:1
Pre1999 - 1st:1 2nd:2 3rd:0 Ran:11
Win Prizemoney £2,374 *Total Prizemoney* £4,629
Wins 1996 Oct Pontef (GD) 6f 69 <
1999 Turf 0-1: (6f) (frm)
Little account filly. Inconsistent.
**M A Buckley [0-1] J McKinnon (from M Meade [1-11] Aug 1997).*

PARISIAN LADY (IRE) BHB 59f53a RR 57f 53a 4604[9]

4 b f Paris House 5.9f **(64)** - Mia Gigi (Hard Fought) 8.8f **(62)**
Form - 000040
Record 1999 - 1st:0 2nd:0 3rd:0 Ran:6
Pre1999 - 1st:2 2nd:1 3rd:1 Ran:13
Win Prizemoney £5,449 *Total Prizemoney* £14,583
Wins * 1997 Jly Salisb (G-F) 6f 93+ <
* 1997 Jun Salisb (G-F) 6f 80
1999 Turf 0-4: (6f, 7f 3) (sft, g-f, frm 2) 1999 AW 0-2: (6f, 7f) (Fibr 2)
Leggy, fair filly, effective 7f, acts on g-f, has worn blinkers. Turf high 57. AW high 52 (began Spt).
**A G Newcombe [2-19] Advanced Marketing Services Ltd.*

PARISIENNE HILL BHB 20f RR 29f 4988[8]

3 b f Lapierre - Snarry Hill (Vitiges (FR)) 8.2f **(59)**
Form - 0806607008
Record 1999 - 1st:0 2nd:0 3rd:0 Ran:10
Pre1999 - 1st:0 2nd:0 3rd:0 Ran:3
1999 Turf 0-9: (7f, 8f, 10f 2, 12f 3, 14f, 16f) (gd, g-f 2, frm 6) 1999 AW 0-1: (11f) (Fibr)
Light-framed, little account filly. Turf high 38.
**B W Murray [0-10] M E Foxton (from R A Fahey [0-3] Oct 1998).*

PARISIEN STAR (IRE) BHB 82f RR 86df 4528[11]

3 ch g Paris House 5.9f **(64)** - Auction Maid (IRE) (Auction Ring (USA)) 8.6f **(65)**
Form - 5402026000
Record 1999 - 1st:0 2nd:2 3rd:0 Ran:10
Pre1999 - 1st:2 2nd:1 3rd:1 Ran:8
Win Prizemoney £9,155 *Total Prizemoney* £19,383

Wins 1998 Spt Newbur (gd) H 7.3f 80 82 <
1998 Spt Epsom (GD) H 6f 74 76
1999 Turf 0-10: (7f 2, 8f 7, 9f) (g-s, gd 4, g-f 2, frm 3)
Workmanlike, useful gelding, effective 7f, acts on g-s, likes left handed tracks. Turf high 88. Becoming disappointing.
**N Hamilton [0-1] P Elliott (from G Lewis [2-17] Aug 1999).*

PARIS LIGHTS (IRE) BHB 76f **RR 86df** 4125[7]
2 br c Paris House 5.9f **(64)** - Visible Form (Formidable (USA)) 9.2f **(63)**
Form - 341483657
Record 1999 - 1st:1 2nd:0 3rd:2 Ran:9
Win Prizemoney £2,253 *Total Prizemoney* £5,373
Wins * **1999** *Jun Southw (STD) 5f* 73+ <
1999 Turf 0-8: (5f 7, 6f) (g-f 6, frm 2) 1999 AW 1-1: (5f 1-1) (Fibr 1-1)
Useful colt, often wears blinkers (effectively). Turf high 86. (1st run). Placed in maiden company on turf, but bolted up in a very modest maiden on the Southwell Fibresand. Left even that form behind when fourth in the Windsor Castle, and continued to run with credit. **B J Meehan [1-9] Ms A M Cone-Farran.*

PARIS PUDDLES (IRE) BHB 40f **RR 46f** 4722[11]
2 gr f Paris House 5.9f **(64)** - Bright Puddles (IRE) (Bold Arrangement)
Form - 607540
Record 1999 - 1st:0 2nd:0 3rd:0 Ran:6
1999 Turf 0-5: (5f 3, 6f, 7f) (gd 3, g-f, frm) 1999 AW 0-1: (5f) (Fibr)
Moderate filly, has worn blinkers. Turf high 46.
**C W Fairhurst [0-6] J L Young.*

PARIS STAR (IRE) RR 80f 1424[1]
2 gr c Paris House 5.9f **(64)** - Glenista (IRE) **(57f)** (Glenstal (USA)) 10.1f **(64)**
Form - 81851
Record 1999 - 1st:2 2nd:0 3rd:0 Ran:5
Win Prizemoney £5,955 *Total Prizemoney* £6,219
Wins * **1999** May Hamilt (SFT) C 5f 80 <
* **1999** *Apr Lingfi (STD) 5f 77*
1999 Turf 1-4: (5f 1-4) (gd 1-2, g-f 2) 1999 AW 1-1: (5f 1-1) (Equi 1-1)
Decent colt. Turf high 80 - 1st of 3 getting 1lb from Bescaby Blue (24 May Hamilton RF 1424). (1st run) - 1st of 7 from Direct Reaction (9 Apr Lingfield RF 0629). **J Berry [2-5] C F Sparrowhawk.*

PARKER BHB 73f **RR 78f** 4942[4]
2 b c Magic Ring (IRE) 6.5f **(64)** - Miss Loving (Northfields (USA)) 9f **(72)**
Form - 304
Record 1999 - 1st:0 2nd:0 3rd:1 Ran:3
Win Prizemoney £0 *Total Prizemoney* £374
1999 Turf 0-3: (6f, 7f 2) (sft, g-s, gd)
Currently above-average colt. Turf high 78 (1st run) (began Spt) - 3rd of 16 giving 4lb to Jamestown (21 Spt Warwick 7f sft RF 4451).
**B Palling [0-3] J Hamilton-Jones.*

PARKER'S PEACE (IRE) BHB 60f **RR 49f** 5059[9]
2 b c Common Grounds 8.1f **(66)** - Harmer (IRE) (Alzao (USA)) 7.1f **(68)**
Form - 070
Record 1999 - 1st:0 2nd:0 3rd:0 Ran:3
1999 Turf 0-3: (7f 3) (g-s 2, g-f)
Currently moderate colt. Turf high 49 (began Spt).
**M L W Bell [0-3] Exors of the late C M Watt.*

PARK ROYAL BHB 39f **RR 33f** 4629[8]
4 b g Secret Appeal - Mohibbah (USA) (Conquistador Cielo (USA)) 8.8f **(69)**
Form - 8
Record 1999 - 1st:0 2nd:0 3rd:0 Ran:1
Pre1999 - 1st:0 2nd:0 3rd:0 Ran:6
1999 Turf 0-1: (8f) (g-s)
Leggy, very moderate gelding. **P Butler [2-16] Mrs P A Wood.*

PARKSIDE (IRE) BHB 79f **RR 85f** 4874[17]
3 b g Common Grounds 8.1f **(66)** - Warg (Dancing Brave (USA)) 8.4f **(76)**
Form - 56130
Record 1999 - 1st:1 2nd:0 3rd:1 Ran:5
Win Prizemoney £4,334 *Total Prizemoney* £5,991
Wins * **1999** Aug Warwic (GD) 7.7f 85 <
1999 Turf 1-5: (8f 1-5) (g-s, gd 1-3, frm)
Scopey, useful gelding. Turf high 85 - 1st of 3 from Tomasean (13 Aug Warwick RF 3634). Is clearly going the right way, and he capped his win over a mile on decent ground at Warwick in a maiden with a fine third in a Sandown handicap behind Tarawan.
**W R Muir [1-5] The Parkside Partnership.*

PARKSIDE PREMIER RR 10f 3944[9]
2 ch f First Trump - Golden Scissors (Kalaglow) 9.8f **(67)**
Form - 0
Record 1999 - 1st:0 2nd:0 3rd:0 Ran:1
1999 Turf 0-1: (7f) (hrd)
Currently poor filly. **C Grant [0-1] Mrs Jean Keegan.*

PARKSIDE PROSPECT BHB 52f50a **RR 50f 50a** 5187[1]
2 b f Piccolo - Banner (USA) **(75f)** (Known Fact (USA)) 7.4f **(67)**
Form - 8333417005021
Record 1999 - 1st:2 2nd:1 3rd:3 Ran:13
Win Prizemoney £7,942 *Total Prizemoney* £10,169
Wins * **1999** Nov Mussel (GD) SH 5f 46 50
* **1999** Jun Newcas (GD) S 6f 70 <
1999 Turf 2-12: (5f 1-2, 6f 1-8, 7f 2) (g-s 2, gd 1-4, g-f 4, frm 1-2) 1999 AW 0-1: (6f) (Fibr)
Fair filly, effective 5 to 6f, best at 6f, acts on g-f to frm, best on g-f. Turf high 70 - 1st of 12 from Dispol Jazz (25 Jun Newcastle RF 2300). **M R Channon [2-13] Mrs Jean Keegan.*

PARLEZ MOI D'AMOUR (IRE) BHB 30f **RR 17f** 2109[14]
4 gr f Precocious 7.2f **(54)** - Normanby Lass (Bustino) 10.4f **(64)**
Form - 40800
Record 1999 - 1st:0 2nd:0 3rd:0 Ran:5
Pre1999 - 1st:0 2nd:0 3rd:2 Ran:5
Win Prizemoney £0 *Total Prizemoney* £694
1999 Turf 0-4: (6f 2, 7f, 8f) (sft, g-f 3) 1999 AW 0-1: (7f) (Fibr)
Scopey, moderate filly, effective 11 to 12f, acts on gd to g-f, has worn blinkers, favours tight tracks. Turf high 17. Becoming disappointing.
**Denys Smith [0-7] Holdforth Racing (from C W Thornton [0-5] Aug 1998).*

PARONOMASIA BHB 14f20a **RR 26f 20a** 178[15]
7 b g Precocious 7.2f **(54)** - The Crying Game (Manor Farm Boy)
Form - 00
Record 1999 - 1st:0 2nd:0 3rd:0 Ran:2
Pre1999 - 1st:0 2nd:3 3rd:1 Ran:42
Win Prizemoney £0 *Total Prizemoney* £2,597
1999 AW 0-2: (12f, 13f) (Equi 2)
Little account gelding, effective 11f, acts on gd, has worn blinkers.
**J L Harris [0-36] Paddy Barrett (from M L W Bell [0-9] Feb 1996).*

PARTE PRIMA BHB 38f53a **RR 36f 53a** 4090[9]
3 b g Perpendicular - Pendle's Secret (Le Johnstan) 7.4f **(55)**
Form - 833376030
Record 1999 - 1st:0 2nd:0 3rd:4 Ran:9
Win Prizemoney £0 *Total Prizemoney* £1,117
1999 Turf 0-4: (7f 2, 8f, 12f) (g-f, frm 3) 1999 AW 0-5: (7f, 8f 4) (Equi 3, Fibr 2)
Neat, fair gelding, effective 7f, - acts on Fibr, likes left handed tracks. Turf high 36. AW high 56 - 3rd of 9 getting 12lb from Mai Tai (1 Feb Southwell 7f Fibr RF 0201). Becoming disappointing.
**S E Kettlewell [0-9] Franco Fantoni.*

PARTING ECHO BHB 48f53a **RR 49f 53a** 4837[9]
4 ch g Aragon 7.7f **(58)** - Annabrianna (Night Shift (USA)) 7.2f **(69)**
Form - 7006830
Record 1999 - 1st:0 2nd:0 3rd:1 Ran:6
Pre1999 - 1st:0 2nd:0 3rd:1 Ran:7
Win Prizemoney £0 *Total Prizemoney* £1,486
1999 Turf 0-6: (8f 4, 10f, 12f) (gd, g-f 2, frm 3)
Neat, moderate gelding. Turf high 49. Consistent.
**J A R Toller [0-13] Forum Trustees Ltd A/C Rannerdale.*

PARTY GIRL RR 46f 5137[14]
2 b f Unfuwain (USA) 11.4f **(74)** - Prima Domina (FR) (Dominion) 8.5f **(63)**
Form - 0
Record 1999 - 1st:0 2nd:0 3rd:0 Ran:1

1999 Turf 0-1: (7f) (gd)
Currently moderate filly. **E A L Dunlop [0-1] Stars And Stripes.*

PARTY ROMANCE (USA) BHB 69f **RR 71f** 5028[17]

5 gr h Black Tie Affair 10.5f **(64)** - Tia Juanita (USA) (My Gallant (USA)) 9f **(71)**
Form - 0650

Record					
1999 -	1st:0	2nd:0	3rd:0	Ran:4
Pre1999 -	1st:3	2nd:2	3rd:1	Ran:23

Win Prizemoney £12,292 *Total Prizemoney* £21,332

Wins								
1998	May	Ripon	(G-F)	H	10f	85	83	
1997	Jly	Newcas	(GD)	H	10.1f	84	89	<
1997	May	Ayr	(G-F)		10f		85	

1999 Turf 0-4: (10f, 11f, 12f, 16f) (g-s, gd, g-f 2)
Above-average colt, effective 10f, acts on g-f to frm, best on g-f, has worn blinkers, likes right handed tracks. Turf high 71. Consistent.
**R G Frost [3-10] Mrs G A Robarts (from B Hanbury [3-23] Spt 1998).*

PAS DE MEMOIRES (IRE) BHB 86f97a **RR 92f 97a** 5042[6]

4 b g Don't Forget Me 9.5f **(66)** - Bally Pourri (IRE) (Law Society (USA)) 9.9f **(70)**
Form - 5672813156541722645 6

Record					
1999 -	1st:3	2nd:2	3rd:1	Ran:15
Pre1999 -	1st:2	2nd:2	3rd:2	Ran:17

Win Prizemoney £36,106 *Total Prizemoney* £50,859

Wins								
* **1999**	Jun	Carlis	(G-F)	H	8f	76	78	
* **1999**	*Feb*	*Lingfi*	*(STD)*		*10f*		*93*	<
* **1999**	*Jan*	*Wolver*	*(STD)*	*H*	*9.4f*	*83*	*89*	
1997	*Nov*	*Wolver*	*(STD)*	*H*	*7f*	*70*	*91+*	
1997	*Nov*	*Southw*	*(STD)*	*H*	*7f*	*65*	*88+*	

1999 Turf 1-10: (8f 1-6, 9f 2, 10f 2) (sft, gd 4, g-f 2, frm 1-3) 1999 AW 2-5: (8f 2, 9f 1-1, 10f 1-2) (Equi 1-2, Fibr 1-2, Dirt)
Very useful gelding, effective 8 to 10f, acts on gd - acts on Equi to Dirt, likes Wolverhampton. Turf high 92. AW high 93 - 1st of 6 getting 6lb from Refuse To Lose (27 Feb Lingfield RF 0375) - also 1st of 10 giving 3lb to Jibereen (13 Jan Wolverhampton RF 0088). Effective on sand and turf, he beat Refuse To Lose in the Winter Derby Trial at Lingfield in February and landed the valuable Carlisle Bell in June. Suited by forcing tactics over trips between a mile and ten furlongs, he is very tough.
**K R Burke [3-25] Nigel Shields (from M P Bielby [0-1] Jun 1998).*

PAS DE PROBLEME (IRE) **RR 64f** 3741[13]

3 ch c Ela-Mana-Mou 12.7f **(72)** - Torriglia (USA) (Nijinsky (CAN)) 10.3f **(77)**
Form - 66750

Record					
1999 -	1st:0	2nd:0	3rd:0	Ran:5
Pre1999 -	1st:0	2nd:1	3rd:0	Ran:4

Win Prizemoney £0 *Total Prizemoney* £1,692
1999 Turf 0-5: (8f, 9f, 10f, 11f, 12f) (g-s, g-f 2, frm 2)
Neat, average colt, effective 6 to 9f, acts on gd to g-f. Turf high 68 (1st run) - 6th of 14 getting 5lb from Tactful Remark (3 Apr Kempton 9f g-f RF 0572). **M Blanshard [0-9] Capt Francis Burne.*

PASHA BHB 46a **RR 21f** 454[5]

3 b f Ardkinglass 5f **(64)** - Infanta Maria (King of Spain) 7.8f **(52)**
Form - 605

Record					
1999 -	1st:0	2nd:0	3rd:0	Ran:3
Pre1999 -	1st:0	2nd:1	3rd:0	Ran:6

Win Prizemoney £0 *Total Prizemoney* £672
1999 AW 0-3: (5f 2, 7f) (Fibr 3)
Neat, very moderate filly, often wears blinkers. AW high 35.
**Miss J F Craze [0-3] Ms T J Tennison (from N Tinkler [0-6] Jly 1998).*

PASSE PASSE (USA) BHB 77f **RR 80df** 5067[9]

3 b f Lear Fan (USA) 10.4f **(80)** - Madame L'Enjoleur (USA) (L'Enjoleur (CAN)) 8f **(65)**
Form - 43320

Record					
1999 -	1st:0	2nd:1	3rd:2	Ran:5

Win Prizemoney £0 *Total Prizemoney* £2,532
1999 Turf 0-5: (7f, 11f, 12f 3) (gd 3, g-f, frm)
Leggy, decent filly. Turf high 80 - 3rd of 8 to Summer Splendour (28 May Haydock 12f gd RF 1546). **G Wragg [0-5] A E Oppenheimer.*

PASSINETTI (FR) **RR 92f** 2659a[1]

3 b c Slew O' Gold (USA) 10.2f **(73)** - Cloelia (USA) (Lyphard (USA)) 9.9f **(72)**
Form - 1
1999 Turf 1-1: (10f 1-1) (gd 1-1)
Currently useful colt. (1st run) - 1st of 8 from Antinous (3 Jly Le Lion D'angers RF 2659a). **D Sepulchre in FR [1-1] A L M Wend.*

PASSIONATE PURSUIT BHB 76f **RR 76f** 4264[4]

4 b f Pursuit of Love 9.5f **(69)** - Flambera (FR) (Akarad (FR)) 9f **(76)**
Form - 607440724

Record					
1999 -	1st:0	2nd:1	3rd:0	Ran:9
Pre1999 -	1st:1	2nd:0	3rd:0	Ran:5

Win Prizemoney £3,720 *Total Prizemoney* £8,764

Wins								
* 1998	Jun	Lingfi	(G-F)		10f		76	<

1999 Turf 0-9: (10f, 12f 6, 13f, 14f) (gd 2, g-f 2, frm 5)
Scopey, above-average filly, likes left handed tracks. Turf high 90. Consistent. **S Dow [1-14] Mrs A M Upsdell.*

PASSION FLOWER BHB 90f **RR 94?f** 4793[12]

2 b f Forzando 7.2f **(63)** - Carn Maire (Northern Prospect (USA)) 9.5f **(71)**
Form - 11760

Record					
1999 -	1st:2	2nd:0	3rd:0	Ran:5

Win Prizemoney £6,619 *Total Prizemoney* £6,809

Wins								
* **1999**	Jly	Bath	(FRM)		5.1f		94	<
* **1999**	Jly	Windso	(GD)		5f		76	

1999 Turf 2-5: (5f 2-4, 6f) (gd 2, g-f, frm 2-2)
Useful filly. Turf high 94 (began Jly) - 1st of 5 giving 5lb to Misty Miss (20 Jly Bath RF 2955). She showed plenty of speed when winning on her Windsor debut over the minimum, and though she followed up at Bath she was helped by the runner-up getting into all sorts of trouble. Since being thrown into Listed company she has been disappointing. **J E Banks [2-5] Giles Pritchard-Gordon.*

PASSION FOR LIFE BHB 83f **RR 82f** 4644[1]

6 br g Charmer 9f **(59)** - Party Game (Red Alert) 7.6f **(66)**
Form - 130002761

Record					
1999 -	1st:2	2nd:1	3rd:1	Ran:9
Pre1999 -	1st:5	2nd:2	3rd:2	Ran:25

Win Prizemoney £72,919 *Total Prizemoney* £83,815

Wins								
* **1999**	Spt	Salisb	(HVY)	H	6f	78	82	
* **1999**	Apr	Kempto	(GD)	H	6f	79	85	
1996	Jun	Baden-	(GD)	G3	6f		112	
1996	Apr	Newmar	(G-F)	L	6f		115+	<
1996	Apr	Kempto	(GD)	H	6f	86	103+	
1995	Apr	Warwic	(G-F)		5f		74+t	
1995	Apr	Haydoc	(GD)		5f		86+t	

1999 Turf 2-9: (5f 4, 6f 2-5) (g-s 1-2, gd, g-f 1-5, frm)
Decent gelding, effective 6f, acts on g-s to g-f, best on g-f, has worn blinkers. Turf high 85 (1st run) - 1st of 23 giving 3lb to Rififi (5 Apr Kempton RF 0577) - also 1st of 19 getting 7lb from Danielle's Lad (29 Spt Salisbury RF 4644). A one-time smart sprinter, he dropped alarmingly in the weights, but a change of stables helped him rediscover some of his ability at the start of this season and he gained a narrow victory at Kempton on his reappearance. Regained wining form in soft ground at Salisbury in September when racing on the opposite side of the track to the others, and apparently he likes being left to race alone. Despite those wins, he does not look one to totally rely on these days.
**J Akehurst [2-9] Canisbay Bloodstock Ltd (from W Jarvis [0-4] Jun 1998).*

PASSIONS PLAYTHING BHB 75f **RR 74f** 1737[4]

3 ch g Pursuit of Love 9.5f **(69)** - Maiyaasah (Kris) 9.5f **(73)**
Form - 044

Record					
1999 -	1st:0	2nd:0	3rd:0	Ran:3

Win Prizemoney £0 *Total Prizemoney* £558
1999 Turf 0-3: (8f 3) (gd 2, g-f)
Workmanlike, currently above-average gelding. Turf high 74.
**W R Muir [0-3] Delamere Partnership.*

PASS THE REST (IRE) BHB 64f64a **RR 63f 64a** 4528[8]

4 b c Shalford (IRE) 7.8f **(63)** - Brown Foam (Horage) 10.3f **(61)**
Form - 000700708

Record					
1999 -	1st:0	2nd:0	3rd:0	Ran:7
Pre1999 -	1st:2	2nd:3	3rd:1	Ran:12

Win Prizemoney £9,556 *Total Prizemoney* £13,441

Wins								
1998	*Aug*	*Wolver*	*(STD)*	*H*	*8.5f*	*79*	*85*	<
1998	Jun	Ripon	(SFT)	H	8f	76	79	

1999 Turf 0-5: (7f, 8f 2, 11f, 12f) (g-s, gd 3, frm) 1999 AW 0-2: (7f, 8f) (Fibr 2)

Scopey, average colt, effective 8f, acts on g-s - acts on Fibr, has worn blinkers, likes tight tracks. Turf high 64. AW high 55.
**D Shaw [0-9] J Roundtree (from J Noseda [2-7] Spt 1998).*

PASTERNAK BHB 100f96a **RR 106df 96a** 3429^{4}
6 b h Soviet Star (USA) 8.6f **(74)** - Princess Pati (Top Ville) 11.7f **(68)**
Form - 4204
Record 1999 - 1st:0 2nd:1 3rd:0 Ran:3
Pre1999 - 1st:4 2nd:3 3rd:2 Ran:17
Win Prizemoney £124,028 *Total Prizemoney* £164,039
Wins * 1997 Oct Newmar (G-F) H 9f 91 100+ <
* 1997 Jly York (GD) H 10.4f 85 89++
* 1996 Oct York (GD) H 10.4f 75 85
* 1996 Spt Bath (G-S) 10.2f 79
1999 Turf 0-3: (10f 3) (gd, g-f 2)

Pattern-class horse, effective 9 to 10f, best at 10f, acts on gd to frm. Turf high 106 (1st run) - 2nd of 9 giving 21lb to Komistar (27 Jun Doncaster 10f gd RF 2351). A popular and high-class handicapper, he had a light campaign and failed to recapture his best, although in fairness he did not get the true-run races he needs. Retirement may beckon.
**Sir Mark Prescott [4-20] Graham Rock Osborne House.*

PATACAKE PATACAKE (USA) BHB 68f **RR 60f** 4981^{4}
2 b f Bahri (USA) - Chaleur (CAN) (Rouge Sang (USA)) 7f **(118)**
Form - 644
Record 1999 - 1st:0 2nd:0 3rd:0 Ran:3
Win Prizemoney £0 *Total Prizemoney* £494
1999 Turf 0-3: (6f, 8f 2) (sft, gd, g-f)

Currently average filly. Turf high 59 (began Spt).
**M Johnston [0-3] Lightbody Celebration Cakes Ltd.*

PATRINIA BHB 36f **RR 32f** 4527^{11}
3 ch f Superlative 8.8f **(57)** - Dame du Moulin (Shiny Tenth) 9.2f **(56)**
Form - 7000
Record 1999 - 1st:0 2nd:0 3rd:0 Ran:4
Pre1999 - 1st:0 2nd:0 3rd:0 Ran:3
1999 Turf 0-4: (6f, 7f 3) (gd 2, g-f, frm)

Scopey, very moderate filly. Turf high 32. **M J Ryan [0-7] P E Axon.*

PATRIOT BHB 90f **RR 87f** 4009^{5}
3 b c Whittingham (IRE) - Gibaltarik (IRE) **(63f)** (Jareer (USA)) 5.9f **(75)**
Form - 444005
Record 1999 - 1st:0 2nd:0 3rd:0 Ran:6
Pre1999 - 1st:1 2nd:2 3rd:2 Ran:7
Win Prizemoney £2,950 *Total Prizemoney* £42,206
Wins * 1998 May Warwic (G-F) 5f 73 <
1999 Turf 0-6: (5f, 6f 4, 7f) (gd 4, g-f 2)

Leggy, useful colt, effective 6f, acts on gd to g-f. Turf high 95 - 4th of 6 getting 2lb from Red Lion (1 Jun Leicester 6f g-f RF 1646). He found life tough and needs to relax if he is to fulfil his early promise. At present he seems unlikely to stay beyond six furlongs. **B Smart [1-13] W Clifford.*

PATRITA PARK BHB 42f43a **RR 44f 43a** 4648^{7}
5 br m Flying Tyke 7.2f **(42)** - Bellinote (FR) (Noir Et Or) 10f **(38)**
Form - 32223247
Record 1999 - 1st:0 2nd:4 3rd:2 Ran:8
Pre1999 - 1st:1 2nd:0 3rd:1 Ran:18
Win Prizemoney £2,473 *Total Prizemoney* £7,436
Wins 1998 Spt Bright (FRM) H 10f 26 33+ <
1999 Turf 0-8: (9f, 10f 2, 12f 3, 14f 2) (g-s, gd, frm 5, hrd)

Moderate filly, effective 10 to 14f, best at 10f, acts on frm, prefers left handed tracks, excels at Brighton. Turf high 45 - 2nd of 14 getting 19lb from Wait For The Will (10 Jly Salisbury 12f frm RF 2716).
**Mrs P N Dutfield [0-8] Park Racing Partnership (from W G M Turner [1-10] Spt 1998).*

PATSY CULSYTH BHB 38f **RR 27f** 5035^{14}
4 b f Tragic Role (USA) 9.4f **(63)** - Regal Salute (Dara Monarch) 8.8f **(59)**
Form - 2000000
Record 1999 - 1st:0 2nd:1 3rd:0 Ran:7
Pre1999 - 1st:2 2nd:4 3rd:1 Ran:19
Win Prizemoney £4,963 *Total Prizemoney* £9,779
Wins 1998 Aug Ayr (G-S) SH 7f 45 50
1997 Aug Beverl (G-S) C 5f 62 <
1999 Turf 0-7: (5f, 6f 3, 7f 3) (g-s, gd 2, g-f 2, frm, hrd)

Light-framed, little account filly, effective 6 to 7f, acts on gd, has worn blinkers. Turf high 51 (1st run) - 2nd of 24 giving 5lb to Heavenly Miss (16 Apr Thirsk 6f gd RF 0731).
**Don Enrico Incisa [0-7] Don Enrico Incisa (from N Tinkler [1-10] Spt 1998).*

PATSY STONE BHB 61f53a **RR 63f 53a** 4813^{9}
3 b f Jester 8.5f **(43)** - Third Dam **(47f 45a)** (Slip Anchor) 9.8f **(73)**
Form - 456364003460100
Record 1999 - 1st:1 2nd:0 3rd:2 Ran:15
Pre1999 - 1st:0 2nd:2 3rd:2 Ran:9
Win Prizemoney £3,589 *Total Prizemoney* £7,013
Wins * **1999** Spt Yarmou (SFT) H 8f 59 63 <
1999 Turf 1-12: (7f 8, 8f 1-3, 10f) (g-s 1-1, gd 3, g-f 4, frm 4) 1999 AW 0-3: (7f, 8f 2) (Equi, Fibr 2)

Unfurnished, average filly, effective 6 to 8f, best at 6f, acts on g-s to frm. Turf high 66 - 3rd of 24 getting 6lb from Cinnamon Lady (15 May Newbury 7f gd RF 1238) - also 1st of 17 giving 4lb to Riverdance (16 Spt Yarmouth RF 4359). AW high 41.
**W J Musson [1-4] Mrs Valerie Bennett (from M Kettle [0-20] Aug 1999).*

PAWN BROKER RR 87f 4898^{1}
2 ch c Selkirk (USA) 7.9f **(76)** - Dime Bag (High Line) 10.3f **(70)**
Form - 61
Record 1999 - 1st:1 2nd:0 3rd:0 Ran:2
Win Prizemoney £8,545 *Total Prizemoney* £8,545
Wins * **1999** Oct Newmar (GD) 8f 87 <
1999 Turf 1-2: (7f, 8f 1-1) (gd 1-2)

Currently useful colt. Turf high 87 (began Spt) - 1st of 13 from River Bann (15 Oct Newmarket RF 4898).
**D R C Elsworth [1-2] Raymond Tooth.*

PAWSIBLE (IRE) BHB 44f47a **RR 42f 47a** 3918^{6}
3 b f Mujadil (USA) 7.7f **(70)** - Kentucky Wildcat (Be My Guest (USA)) 9.3f **(67)**
Form - 0778316
Record 1999 - 1st:1 2nd:0 3rd:1 Ran:6
Pre1999 - 1st:0 2nd:0 3rd:0 Ran:3
Win Prizemoney £1,955 *Total Prizemoney* £2,266
Wins * **1999** *Aug Wolver (STD) H 14.8f 44 45* <
1999 Turf 0-4: (10f, 12f 2, 16f) (gd, g-f 3) 1999 AW 1-2: (12f, 15f 1-1) (Fibr 1-2)

Light-framed, moderate filly, favours tight tracks. Turf high 48. AW high 45 (began Jly). Consistent. She showed improved form when stepped up in trip on Fibresand, winning nicely at Wolverhampton in August. **D W P Arbuthnot [1-9] The Pawsible Partnership.*

PAX RR 79+f 5129^{1}
2 ch c Brief Truce (USA) 9.1f **(73)** - Child's Play (USA) (Sharpen Up) 8.3f **(67)**
Form - 1
Record 1999 - 1st:1 2nd:0 3rd:0 Ran:1
Win Prizemoney £4,695 *Total Prizemoney* £4,695
Wins * **1999** Oct Newmar (G-S) 6f 79+ <
1999 Turf 1-1: (6f 1-1) (gd 1-1)

Currently average colt. (1st run) - 1st of 19 from Kathology (29 Oct Newmarket RF 5129). **J W Payne [1-1] C Cotran.*

PAY HOMAGE BHB 45f **RR 47f** 4714^{6}
11 ch g Primo Dominie 7.2f **(67)** - Embraceable Slew (USA) (Seattle Slew (USA)) 9.4f **(76)**
Form - 325377253746
Record 1999 - 1st:0 2nd:2 3rd:3 Ran:12
Pre1999 - 1st:11 2nd:11 3rd:12 Ran:102
Win Prizemoney £94,677 *Total Prizemoney* £130,051
Wins * 1998 May Warwic (GD) H 10.8f 64 67
* 1997 Jly Bath (FRM) 11.7f 69
* 1995 May Goodwo (G-F) H 9f 81 83
1999 Turf 0-12: (9f, 10f, 11f 4, 12f 6) (hvy, sft 2, gd 2, g-f, frm 6)

Moderate gelding, effective 11 to 12f, best at 12f, acts on g-f to frm, best on frm, has worn blinkers, likes left handed tracks. Turf high 59 - 2nd of 17 giving 11lb to Caernarfon Bay (29 Apr Brighton 12f frm RF 0910). Consistent. This popular veteran is still capable of

winning modest middle-distance events. A particularly good ride for an inexperienced apprentice. **I A Balding [11-117] Miss A V Hill.*

PAYS D'AMOUR (IRE) BHB 73f **RR 61f** 4686[7]
2 b c Pursuit of Love 9.5f **(69)** - Lady of the Land (Wollow) 8.2f **(61)**
Form - 05617
Record 1999 - 1st:1 2nd:0 3rd:0 Ran:5
Win Prizemoney £5,771 *Total Prizemoney* £5,771
Wins * 1999 Spt Epsom (GD) H 6f 65 61 <
1999 Turf 1-5: (5f, 6f 1-3, 7f) (gd 2, g-f 1-1, frm 2)
Average colt. Turf high 61 (began Jly) - 1st of 4 getting 19lb from Maestersinger (3 Spt Epsom RF 4117). Got off the mark in an Epsom nursery on his fourth start, but suffered a slipping saddle in a similar event at Newmarket next time, an effort which can be safely ignored. **R Hannon [1-5] Mrs M W Bird.*

PAY THE PIED PIPER (USA) BHB 79f **RR 82f** 4893[7]
3 b g Red Ransom (USA) 8.6f **(83)**-Fife (IRE) (Lomond (USA)) 8.8f **(65)**
Form - 7221167
Record 1999 - 1st:2 2nd:2 3rd:0 Ran:7
Pre1999 - 1st:0 2nd:0 3rd:0 Ran:2
Win Prizemoney £6,492 *Total Prizemoney* £8,231
Wins * 1999 Aug Yarmou (GD) H 14.1f 75 82 <
*** 1999** Aug Catter (GD) H 15.8f 70 75
1999 Turf 2-7: (8f, 12f, 14f 1-2, 15f, 16f 1-2) (g-s, gd 2-4, g-f 2)
Scopey, decent gelding, effective 14 to 16f, best at 16f, acts on gd. Turf high 82 - 1st of 10 from Salford Flyer (29 Aug Yarmouth RF 4000) - also 1st of 8 giving 5lb to Salvage (13 Aug Catterick RF 3602). **E A L Dunlop [2-9] Gainsborough Stud.*

PC'S EUROCRUISER (IRE) BHB 41f38a **RR 44f 38a** 2556[U]
3 b g Fayruz 6.6f **(63)** - Kuwait Night (Morston (FR)) 9.4f **(55)**
Form - 0605004U
Record 1999 - 1st:0 2nd:0 3rd:0 Ran:6
Pre1999 - 1st:0 2nd:0 3rd:0 Ran:7
1999 Turf 0-5: (6f 2, 8f 3) (gd, g-f, frm 3) 1999 AW 0-1: (8f) (Fibr)
Workmanlike, moderate gelding. Turf high 45. Inconsistent.
**G Woodward [0-6] P C Smith (from N P Littmoden [0-7] Nov 1998).*

PEACEFUL RR 42f 3217[11]
3 br f Primo Dominie 7.2f **(67)** - Ideal Home (Home Guard (USA)) 9.3f **(66)**
Form - 000
Record 1999 - 1st:0 2nd:0 3rd:0 Ran:3
Pre1999 - 1st:1 2nd:2 3rd:0 Ran:4
Win Prizemoney £2,723 *Total Prizemoney* £4,518
Wins * 1998 Jly Carlis (G-F) 5f 67+ <
1999 Turf 0-3: (6f 2, 8f) (frm 3)
Leggy, moderate filly, effective 5f, acts on frm, has worn blinkers. Turf high 42. **T D Easterby [1-7] C H Stevens.*

PEACEFUL PROMISE RR 66f 4655[10]
2 b c Cadeaux Genereux 7.9f **(76)** - Island Wedding (USA) (Blushing Groom (FR)) 10.3f **(76)**
Form - 0
Record 1999 - 1st:0 2nd:0 3rd:0 Ran:1
1999 Turf 0-1: (7f) (gd)
Currently average colt. **E A L Dunlop [0-1] Maktoum Al Maktoum.*

PEACEFUL SARAH BHB 68f **RR 69f** 4480a[18]
4 b f Sharpo 7.5f **(68)** - Red Gloves (Red God) 8.5f **(65)**
Form - 502070
Record 1999 - 1st:0 2nd:1 3rd:0 Ran:6
Pre1999 - 1st:2 2nd:1 3rd:2 Ran:14
Win Prizemoney £6,857 *Total Prizemoney* £10,313
Wins 1998 Oct Catter (SFT) H 7f 63 73
1998 Aug Epsom (G-F) 7f 74? <
1999 Turf 0-6: (7f 3, 8f 2, 9f) (g-s 3, gd 3)
Leggy, average filly, effective 7 to 9f, best at 7f, acts on g-s to g-f, prefers left handed tracks, likes tight tracks. Turf high 71 (1st run) - 5th of 17 getting 1lb from Bomb Alaska (26 Mar Doncaster 8f g-s RF 0479). Becoming disappointing.
**S Donohoe in IRE [0-2] Mrs Oliver Sheils (from R Ingram [2-10] May 1999).*

PEACE OF MIND BHB 100f **RR 104f** 1577[5]
3 ch c Nashwan (USA) 10.3f **(79)** - De Stael (USA) (Nijinsky (CAN)) 10.3f **(77)**
Form - 275
Record 1999 - 1st:0 2nd:1 3rd:0 Ran:3
Pre1999 - 1st:1 2nd:0 3rd:1 Ran:2
Win Prizemoney £3,468 *Total Prizemoney* £6,394
Wins * 1998 Spt Kempto (GD) 8f 96 <
1999 Turf 0-3: (8f, 10f, 12f) (g-f 2, frm)
Well made, very useful colt. Turf high 104 - 5th of 6 to Kalanisi (29 May Kempton 8f frm RF 1577). Rated a Derby horse at the start of the campaign, he was not seen out after disappointing over a mile at Kempton in May. Bred to stay middle-distances, he has obviously had a problem. **R Charlton [1-5] K Abdulla.*

PEACE PACT BHB 25f **RR 6f** 3296[9]
3 b f Brief Truce (USA) 9.1f **(73)** - Royal Mazi **(25f)** (Kings Lake (USA)) 10.8f **(67)**
Form - 0600000
Record 1999 - 1st:0 2nd:0 3rd:0 Ran:6
Pre1999 - 1st:0 2nd:0 3rd:0 Ran:2
1999 Turf 0-6: (5f, 6f 2, 7f, 9f, 12f) (gd, g-f 2, frm 3)
Unfurnished, very poor filly, effective 5 to 12f, acts on g-s to frm - acts on Fibr, best on frm, has worn blinkers. Turf high 10.
**G P Kelly [0-8] A M McArdle.*

PEACH OUT OF REACH (IRE) RR 92f 5174a[1]
3 b f Sadler's Wells (USA) 11.3f **(87)** - Cocotte (Troy) 10.4f **(68)**
Form - 2234671
1999 Turf 1-7: (8f, 9f, 10f 3, 12f 1-1, 13f) (sft 1-2, g-s, gd 2, g-f 2)
Useful filly, effective 12f, acts on sft, has worn blinkers. Turf high 92 - 1st of 9 getting 15lb from Golden Rule (25 Oct Leopardstown RF 5174a). **A P O'Brien in IRE [1-7] Mrs N Regan.*

PEACOCK ALLEY (IRE) BHB 77f **RR 82f** 5189[3]
2 gr f Salse (USA) 10.9f **(71)** - Tagiki (IRE) (Doyoun) 9f **(69)**
Form - 5023
Record 1999 - 1st:0 2nd:1 3rd:1 Ran:4
Win Prizemoney £0 *Total Prizemoney* £1,690
1999 Turf 0-4: (6f 2, 7f, 8f) (g-f 4)
Decent filly. Turf high 82 (began Aug) - 2nd of 10 to Ashjaan (20 Oct Newcastle 7f g-f RF 4982).
**W J Haggas [0-4] & Mrs G Middlebrook.*

PEACOCK JEWEL RR 87f 4598[1]
2 ch c Rainbow Quest (USA) 11.2f **(81)** - Dafrah (USA) (Danzig (USA)) 8.4f **(76)**
Form - 21
Record 1999 - 1st:1 2nd:1 3rd:0 Ran:2
Win Prizemoney £5,208 *Total Prizemoney* £6,429
Wins * 1999 Spt Newmar (G-S) 8f 84+ <
1999 Turf 1-2: (8f 1-2) (g-s, g-f 1-1)
Currently useful colt. Turf high 87 (1st run) (began Spt) - 2nd of 12 to Beat Hollow (16 Spt Yarmouth 8f g-s RF 4357) - also 1st of 8 from Capa (28 Spt Newmarket RF 4598).
**E A L Dunlop [1-2] Maktoum Al Maktoum.*

PEAJAY (USA) BHB 75f75a **RR 79f 75a** 4667[1]
3 b c Dehere (USA) - Petroleuse (Habitat) 9.4f **(70)**
Form - 3452741
Record 1999 - 1st:1 2nd:1 3rd:1 Ran:7
Pre1999 - 1st:0 2nd:0 3rd:0 Ran:1
Win Prizemoney £2,752 *Total Prizemoney* £4,902
Wins * 1999 *Oct Lingfi (STD) 13f 64* <
1999 Turf 0-6: (10f, 11f, 12f 4) (gd, g-f, frm 3, hrd) 1999 AW 1-1: (13f 1-1) (Equi 1-1)
Neat, above-average colt, effective 10 to 12f, acts on g-f to frm, best on frm, often wears blinkers (very effectively), prefers left handed tracks, favours tight tracks. Turf high 79 - 2nd of 7 to Angels Venture (20 Jly Yarmouth 11f g-f RF 2961). (1st run). Showed a little ability on turf, but got off the mark in a 13-furlong maiden on the Lingfield Equitrack in October. Looks a stayer and may well end up over hurdles. **M A Jarvis [1-8] M P Burke.*

PEAK PATH (IRE) BHB 111f **RR 112f** 945[10]
4 b c Polish Precedent (USA) 9f **(73)** - Road To The Top (Shirley Heights) 10.3f **(74)**
Form - 60
Record 1999 - 1st:0 2nd:0 3rd:0 Ran:2

Pre1999 - 1st:1 2nd:0 3rd:1 Ran:4
Win Prizemoney £3,111 *Total Prizemoney* £8,013
Wins * 1998 Apr Bath (SFT) 10.2f 92 <
1999 Turf 0-2: (12f 2) (g-f, frm)
Scopey, Group-class colt. Turf high 107 (1st run) - 6th of 11 to Sadian (17 Apr Newbury 12f g-f RF 0733). Lightly raced, his season was restricted to just two runs in April, and he changed hands for 32,000 gns in the autumn. **Sir Michael Stoute [1-6] Lord Weinstock.*

PEARL ANNIVERSARY (IRE) BHB 28f28a RR 23f 28a 176[8]
6 ch g Priolo (USA) 10.9f **(71)** - Tony Award (USA) (Kirtling) 10.9f **(54)**
Form - 08
Record 1999 - 1st:0 2nd:0 3rd:0 Ran:1
Pre1999 - 1st:2 2nd:4 3rd:2 Ran:22
Win Prizemoney £4,451 *Total Prizemoney* £7,360
Wins *1996 May Wolver (STD) S 12f 63 <*
1996 May Wolver (STD) S 12f 51
1999 AW 0-1: (15f) (Fibr)
Little account gelding, has worn blinkers.
**Miss S J Wilton [0-11] John Pointon and Sons (from M Johnston [2-13] Spt 1996).*

PEARL BARLEY (IRE) RR 60f 4536[15]
3 ch f Polish Precedent (USA) 9f **(73)** - Pearl Kite (USA) **(101df)** (Silver Hawk (USA)) 8.6f **(70)**
Form - 6767800
Record 1999 - 1st:0 2nd:0 3rd:0 Ran:7
Pre1999 - 1st:0 2nd:0 3rd:0 Ran:1
1999 Turf 0-7: (7f 2, 8f 2, 10f 3) (g-s, gd, g-f 2, frm 3)
Workmanlike, average filly, has worn blinkers. Turf high 79.
**J S Moore [0-2] Ernest Moore (from C E Brittain [0-6] Jly 1999).*

PEARL BUTTON (IRE) BHB 52f RR 48f 1660[13]
3 b f Seattle Dancer (USA) 10.1f **(74)** - Riflelina (Mill Reef (USA)) 10.5f **(78)**
Form - 0780
Record 1999 - 1st:0 2nd:0 3rd:0 Ran:4
1999 Turf 0-4: (8f, 10f 3) (gd, frm 3)
Leggy, moderate filly. Turf high 48. **C A Cyzer [0-4] R M Cyzer.*

PEARL CROWN (USA) BHB 75f RR 86f 5197[14]
3 gr f Diesis 9f **(80)** - Peach Of It (USA) (Navajo (USA)) 10f **(56)**
Form - 0610
Record 1999 - 1st:1 2nd:0 3rd:0 Ran:4
Win Prizemoney £4,666 *Total Prizemoney* £4,666
Wins * **1999** Oct Newbur (HVY) 10f 86 <
1999 Turf 1-4: (10f 1-4) (hvy 1-1, gd, frm 2)
Useful filly, mostly wears blinkers. Turf high 86 - 1st of 11 getting 5lb from Raji (23 Oct Newbury RF 5046).
**J H M Gosden [1-4] Sheikh Mohammed.*

PEARLY QUEEN BHB 42f26a RR 31f 26a 497[8]
4 ch f Superlative 8.8f **(57)** - Miss Kimmy (Tower Walk) 10f **(62)**
Form - 26700578
Record 1999 - 1st:0 2nd:0 3rd:0 Ran:7
Pre1999 - 1st:0 2nd:2 3rd:6 Ran:18
Win Prizemoney £0 *Total Prizemoney* £3,568
1999 AW 0-7: (5f, 6f 3, 7f 2, 8f) (Equi 3, Fibr 4)
Neat, very moderate filly, effective 6 to 7f, best at 7f, - acts on AW, best on Fibr, favours left handed tracks. AW high 32.
**G C Bravery [0-25] R Allder.*

PEARTREE HOUSE (IRE) BHB 84f82a RR 87f 82a 4915[10]
5 b h Simply Majestic (USA) 7.8f **(72)** - Fashion Front (Habitat) 9.4f **(70)**
Form - 000024000
Record 1999 - 1st:0 2nd:1 3rd:0 Ran:7
Pre1999 - 1st:4 2nd:1 3rd:1 Ran:20
Win Prizemoney £16,910 *Total Prizemoney* £32,061
Wins * 1998 May Lingfi (GD) 7.6f 92
* 1997 May Doncas (G-S) 8f 97 <
1996 Aug Catter (G-F) 7f 89
1996 Jun Ayr (G-F) 6f 60+
1999 Turf 0-7: (7f 2, 8f 5) (gd 3, frm 4)
Useful colt, effective 7 to 8f, acts on frm, has worn blinkers. Turf high 87. He showed glimpses of a return to form last season before running a blinder at Newcastle in June when dropped back to seven furlongs, but has again faced stiff tasks since. Has joined David Nicholls.
**W R Muir [2-22] Fayzad Thoroughbred Ltd (from B W Hills [2-5] Spt 1996).*

PEBBLE MOON BHB 60f64a RR 60f 64a 4814[2]
3 gr g Efisio 7.7f **(69)** - Jazz (Sharrood (USA)) 10.5f **(72)**
Form - 20737032
Record 1999 - 1st:0 2nd:2 3rd:2 Ran:8
Pre1999 - 1st:0 2nd:0 3rd:0 Ran:5
Win Prizemoney £0 *Total Prizemoney* £3,124
1999 Turf 0-6: (8f 3, 10f 3) (sft, g-s, gd, g-f 2, frm) 1999 AW 0-2: (9f, 12f) (Fibr 2)
Average gelding, effective 8 to 9f, best at 8f, acts on sft to gd - acts on Fibr, has worn blinkers. Turf high 69 (1st run) - 2nd of 12 getting 2lb from Birth of The Blues (24 Apr Leicester 8f sft RF 0831). AW high 64 (1st run) (began Jly) - 3rd of 11 giving 1lb to The Shadow (23 Jly Wolverhampton 9f Fibr RF 3079).
**M A Jarvis [0-13] Mrs Christine Stevenson.*

PECULIARITY BHB 105f RR 106f 3775[7]
3 b c Perpendicular - Pretty Pollyanna (General Assembly (USA)) 10f **(68)**
Form - 425132537
Record 1999 - 1st:1 2nd:2 3rd:2 Ran:9
Pre1999 - 1st:1 2nd:0 3rd:1 Ran:3
Win Prizemoney £14,007 *Total Prizemoney* £41,664
Wins * **1999** May Nottin (FRM) 8.2f 107 <
* 1998 Oct York (GD) 7.9f 90+
1999 Turf 1-9: (7f 2, 8f 1-6, 10f) (gd 5, g-f 1-3, frm)
Workmanlike, Pattern-class colt, effective 7 to 8f, best at 8f, acts on gd to frm, best on gd, likes Kempton. Turf high 107 - 2nd of 7 getting 15lb from Ramooz (27 Jun Goodwood 8f gd RF 2358) - also 1st of 3 getting 4lb from Tobruk (21 May Nottingham RF 1383). Consistent. His trainer entertained high hopes for him at the start of the season, and although he did not quite live up to expectations he still proved a useful performer in listed company at seven furlongs and a mile. **B Smart [2-12] The Family Partnership.*

PEDRO JACK (IRE) BHB 76f RR 75f 4872[10]
2 b c Mujadil (USA) 7.7f **(70)** - Festival of Light (High Top) 10.2f **(67)**
Form - 7110
Record 1999 - 1st:2 2nd:0 3rd:0 Ran:4
Win Prizemoney £7,215 *Total Prizemoney* £7,215
Wins * **1999** Spt Nottin (G-F) H 6.1f 70 75 <
* **1999** Aug Nottin (G-F) 6.1f 63
1999 Turf 2-4: (6f 2-4) (gd 2, frm 2-2)
Above-average colt. Turf high 75 (began Aug) - 1st of 19 giving 11lb to Kinsman (13 Spt Nottingham RF 4286). Both of his wins to date have been over six furlongs on fast ground at Nottingham, a maiden auction event and a nursery. He has a commendable attitude and still has some scope. **B J Meehan [2-4] Michael Peart.*

PEDRO PETE RR 59f 4227[8]
2 ch g Fraam - Stride Home (Absalom) 7.2f **(58)**
Form - 08
Record 1999 - 1st:0 2nd:0 3rd:0 Ran:2
1999 Turf 0-2: (7f, 8f) (g-f, frm)
Currently fair gelding. Turf high 59 (began Aug).
**M R Channon [0-2] Peter Taplin.*

PEGASUS BAY BHB 60f52a RR 56f 52a 4349[2]
8 b g Tina's Pet 7.4f **(56)** - Mossberry Fair (Mossberry) 7.4f **(51)**
Form - 372211162
Record 1999 - 1st:3 2nd:3 3rd:0 Ran:7
Pre1999 - 1st:2 2nd:3 3rd:3 Ran:14
Win Prizemoney £14,210 *Total Prizemoney* £19,054
Wins * **1999** Aug Hamilt (G-F) SH 8.3f 52 56+
* **1999** Aug Hamilt (G-F) C 9.2f 51
* **1999** Jly Newmar (G-F) S 8f 62
1997 Oct Lingfi (STD) 7f 64 <
1997 Spt Yarmou (FRM) S 10.1f 56+
1999 Turf 3-7: (8f 2-4, 9f 1-1, 11f, 12f) (g-f 1-2, frm 2-5)
Average gelding, effective 8f, acts on frm, has worn blinkers. Turf high 62 (began Jly) - 1st of 12 from Test The Water (30 Jly Newmarket RF 3240) - also 1st of 16 giving 9lb to Murphy's Gold (24 Aug Hamilton RF 3864). He has run over hurdles, fences, on turf and on sand in recent years, achieving some success in the process. In the right grade, his turn of foot is an asset.

**D E Cantillon [4-24] Don Cantillon (from Mrs A E Johnson [2-7] Nov 1997).*

PEGASUS STAR (IRE) BHB 89f RR 81f 2484[3]

2 ch g Lycius (USA) 8.8f **(71)** - Boranwood (IRE) (Exhibitioner) 8.7f **(61)**
Form - 313
Record 1999 - 1st:1 2nd:0 3rd:2 Ran:3
Win Prizemoney £2,756 *Total Prizemoney* £3,701
Wins * 1999 Jun Ayr (G-S) 5f 75 <
1999 Turf 1-3: (5f 1-3) (gd 1-1, frm 2)
Currently decent gelding. Turf high 81 - also 1st of 7 giving 2lb to Diamond Promise (19 Jun Ayr RF 2140). Ran well behind Warm Heart on his debut before scoring at Ayr.
**J S Wainwright [1-3] P Wong & T Leung.*

PEGNITZ (USA) BHB 106f RR 108f 4417[3]

4 b c Lear Fan (USA) 10.4f **(80)** - Likely Split (USA) (Little Current (USA)) 9.6f **(75)**
Form - 452412853
Record 1999 - 1st:1 2nd:2 3rd:1 Ran:9
Pre1999 - 1st:1 2nd:2 3rd:1 Ran:8
Win Prizemoney £9,301 *Total Prizemoney* £36,831
Wins * 1999 Jly Epsom (G-F) 10.1f 93 <
* 1998 Aug Windso () 10f 80
1999 Turf 1-8: (10f 1-6, 11f, 12f) (gd, g-f 4, frm 1-3) 1999 AW 0-1: (10f) (Equi)
Scopey, Pattern-class colt, effective 10 to 12f, best at 10f, acts on g-f to frm, best on g-f, excels at Windsor, does well at Newbury. Turf high 110 - 2nd of 4 to Elhayq (26 May Newbury 10f g-f RF 1499). Consistent. He continues to run bravely, often in the face of impossible tasks, and seems best around a mile and a quarter. At his most dangerous when ridden forcefully, he acts well on undulating tracks. **C E Brittain [2-17] B H Voak.*

PEKAN HEIGHTS (USA) BHB 75f RR 70f 4692[9]

3 b c Green Dancer (USA) 11.9f **(77)** - Battle Drum (USA) (Alydar (USA)) 9.1f **(76)**
Form - 18400
Record 1999 - 1st:1 2nd:0 3rd:0 Ran:5
Pre1999 - 1st:0 2nd:0 3rd:1 Ran:3
Win Prizemoney £4,045 *Total Prizemoney* £4,907
Wins * 1999 Apr Nottin (G-S) H 10f 77 83 <
1999 Turf 1-5: (10f 1-4, 12f) (gd 1-3, g-f, frm)
Rangy, above-average colt, effective 7 to 10f, acts on gd to g-f, has worn blinkers, favours tight tracks. Turf high 83 (1st run) - 1st of 9 giving 1lb to Beryl (5 Apr Nottingham RF 0590). Consistent. He made a successful reappearance in a Nottingham handicap, but has been rather disappointing since, though he did not seem to stay twelve furlongs when tried over it.
**E A L Dunlop [1-8] H R H Sultan Ahmad Shah.*

PEKANSKI (IRE) RR 85f 4680[6]

2 b f Sri Pekan (USA) - Karinski (USA) (Palace Music (USA))
Form - 16
Record 1999 - 1st:1 2nd:0 3rd:0 Ran:2
Win Prizemoney £3,988 *Total Prizemoney* £4,136
Wins * 1999 Aug Goodwo (GD) 6f 83+ <
1999 Turf 1-2: (6f 1-1, 7f) (gd, g-f 1-1)
Currently useful filly. Turf high 85 (began Aug) - also 1st of 11 from Iftiraas (29 Aug Goodwood RF 3997). Came with a sustained run to snatch victory on the line against a number of other debutants at Goodwood, but was well beaten in a Newmarket Listed event. **P W Chapple-Hyam [1-2] R E Sangster.*

PEKAN'S PRIDE RR 79+f 2240[1]

2 b f Sri Pekan (USA) -London Pride (USA) (Lear Fan (USA)) 8.5f **(73)**
Form - 1
Record 1999 - 1st:1 2nd:0 3rd:0 Ran:1
Win Prizemoney £3,533 *Total Prizemoney* £3,533
Wins * 1999 Jun Kempto (G-F) 7f 79+ <
1999 Turf 1-1: (7f 1-1) (frm 1-1)
Currently above-average filly. (1st run) - 1st of 10 from Terra Nova (23 Jun Kempton RF 2240).
**P F I Cole [1-1] H R H Sultan Ahmad Shah.*

PELARGONIUM BHB 39f RR 50f 3954[12]

3 b f Danehill (USA) 9.1f **(79)** - Sweet Jaffa (Never so Bold) 6.3f **(66)**
Form - 6080
Record 1999 - 1st:0 2nd:0 3rd:0 Ran:4
1999 Turf 0-4: (7f 2, 8f, 10f) (gd 2, frm 2)
Small, fair filly. Turf high 50. **C W Thornton [0-4] Guy Reed.*

PEMBA RR 3779a[3]

2 b f First Trump - Western Sal **(71f)** (Salse (USA)) 7.5f **(66)**
Form - 1443
Record 1999 - 1st:1 2nd:0 3rd:1 Ran:4
Win Prizemoney £5,468 *Total Prizemoney* £7,644
Wins * 1999 Jun San Si (SFT) 7f
1999 Turf 1-4: (7f 1-2, 8f 2) (sft 1-2, gd, g-f)
Fair filly. - 3rd of 5 giving 4lb to Naval War (14 Aug Maia 8f gd RF 3779a) - also 1st of 7 from Green Reew (11 Jun San Siro RF 2094a).
**M Quinlan [1-4].*

PENALTY MISS BHB 30f RR 34f 4077[9]

3 gr f Midyan (USA) 9.9f **(64)** - Between the Sticks (Pharly (FR)) 9.8f **(68)**
Form - 000
Record 1999 - 1st:0 2nd:0 3rd:0 Ran:2
Pre1999 - 1st:0 2nd:0 3rd:0 Ran:4
1999 Turf 0-2: (6f, 8f) (g-f, frm)
Very moderate filly.
**A G Newcombe [0-6] John Bain, Nigel Bea Harley.*

PENANG PEARL (FR) BHB 103f RR 104f 4796[1]

3 b f Bering 9.6f **(80)** - Guapa (Shareef Dancer (USA)) 9.9f **(73)**
Form - 12123241
Record 1999 - 1st:3 2nd:3 3rd:1 Ran:8
Pre1999 - 1st:0 2nd:1 3rd:0 Ran:5
Win Prizemoney £23,887 *Total Prizemoney* £32,772
Wins * 1999 Oct Ascot (G-S) L 8f 104 <
*** 1999** Jun Kempto (G-F) H 9f 79 81
*** 1999** May Windso (G-F) H 8.3f 68 72
1999 Turf 3-8: (8f 2-3, 9f 1-1, 10f 3, 11f) (g-s, gd 1-2, g-f, frm 2-4)
Neat, very useful filly, effective 8f, acts on gd, likes right handed tracks. Turf high 104 - 1st of 10 from Ras Shaikh (9 Oct Ascot RF 4796). She was very consistent last season, winning at Windsor and Kempton and gaining her biggest success in an Ascot Listed event. **G A Butler [3-8] Mrs A K H Ooi (from M Quinn [0-5] Oct 1998).*

PENDANT BHB 65f RR 59f 2305[4]

4 b g Warning 8.1f **(77)** - Emerald (USA)(El Gran Senor (USA))9.6f **(76)**
Form - 44
Record 1999 - 1st:0 2nd:0 3rd:0 Ran:2
Pre1999 - 1st:1 2nd:0 3rd:1 Ran:3
Win Prizemoney £3,501 *Total Prizemoney* £4,318
Wins 1998 Aug Yarmou (G-F) 11.5f 72 <
1999 Turf 0-2: (12f 2) (gd, g-f)
Fair gelding, has worn blinkers. Turf high 59.
**K A Morgan [0-2] D & M Cased Hole (from H R A Cecil [1-3] Spt 1998).*

PENDOGGETT (USA) RR 3851[P]

4 b g Alleged (USA) 11.8f **(81)** - Waaria (Shareef Dancer (USA)) 9.9f **(73)**
Form - P
Record 1999 - 1st:0 2nd:0 3rd:0 Ran:1
1999 Turf 0-1: (10f) (frm)
Very poor gelding. (DEAD) **D R C Elsworth [0-2] Mrs M E Slade.*

PENDOLINO (IRE) BHB 27f62a RR 30f 62a 2561[9]

8 b g Thatching 7.8f **(69)** - Pendulina (Prince Tenderfoot (USA)) 9f **(61)**
Form - 700700
Record 1999 - 1st:0 2nd:0 3rd:0 Ran:6
Pre1999 - 1st:2 2nd:0 3rd:1 Ran:16
Win Prizemoney £5,970 *Total Prizemoney* £7,115
Wins 1997 Apr Pontef (G-F) H 10f 37 48 <
1997 Apr Ripon (G-F) SH 12.3f 37 39
1999 Turf 0-6: (10f 3, 11f, 12f 2) (sft, g-s, gd 2, g-f, frm)
Very moderate gelding, has worn blinkers. Turf high 33.
**A B Mulholland [0-6] J F Wright (from M Brittain [2-17] Apr 1997).*

PEN FRIEND RR 54f 1010[8]

5 b g Robellino (USA) 9.5f **(68)** - Nibbs Point (IRE) (Sure Blade (USA)) 11.3f **(67)**
Form - 8

Record 1999 - 1st:0 2nd:0 3rd:0 Ran:1
Pre1999 - 1st:2 2nd:2 3rd:1 Ran:10
Win Prizemoney £5,941 *Total Prizemoney* £8,684
Wins * 1997 Aug Thirsk (G-F) H 16f 47 53 <
* 1997 Jly Beverl (G-F) H 16.2f 43 48
1999 Turf 0-1: (12f) (g-f)
Fair gelding. Consistent. **W J Haggas [2-11] B Haggas.*

PENGAMON BHB 52f77a **RR 59?f 77a** 5103[10]

7 b g Efisio 7.7f **(69)** - Dolly Bevan (Another Realm) 6.6f **(55)**
Form - 00
Record 1999 - 1st:0 2nd:0 3rd:0 Ran:2
Pre1999 - 1st:4 2nd:2 3rd:3 Ran:29
Win Prizemoney £17,453 *Total Prizemoney* £25,462
Wins * 1997 *May Lingfi (STD) H 8f 74 78*
* 1996 *Mar Lingfi (STD) H 8f 74 79*
1999 Turf 0-1: (7f) (gd) 1999 AW 0-1: (8f) (Fibr)
Above-average gelding. Inconsistent.
**H J Collingridge [2-27] Miss Arabella Smallman (from H R A Cecil [2-4] Aug 1994).*

PENMAR BHB 55f50a **RR 56f 50a** 728[14]

7 b g Reprimand 8.2f **(63)** - Latakia (Morston (FR)) 9.4f **(55)**
Form - 0
Record 1999 - 1st:0 2nd:0 3rd:0 Ran:1
Pre1999 - 1st:2 2nd:3 3rd:4 Ran:23
Win Prizemoney £6,196 *Total Prizemoney* £10,599
Wins 1998 Nov Mussel (SFT) H 8f 49 56
1996 *May Wolver (STD) H 9.4f 56 60 <*
1999 Turf 0-1: (8f) (gd)
Average gelding, has worn blinkers (extremely effectively).
**A B Mulholland [0-1] J F Wright (from M A Peill [1-3] Nov 1998).*

PENMAYNE BHB 90f **RR 92f** 4409[6]

3 ch f Inchinor 8.9f **(64)** - Salanka (IRE) **(65df 56a)** (Persian Heights)
Form - 55446
Record 1999 - 1st:0 2nd:0 3rd:0 Ran:5
Pre1999 - 1st:1 2nd:1 3rd:2 Ran:9
Win Prizemoney £3,517 *Total Prizemoney* £11,667
Wins * 1998 Jly Sandow (GD) 7.1f 78 <
1999 Turf 0-5: (7f, 8f 2, 9f 2) (gd, g-f 2, frm 2)
Neat, useful filly, effective 7 to 8f, acts on g-f to frm. Turf high 92 - 5th of 15 giving 11lb to Holly Blue (19 Jun Ascot 8f g-f RF 2133). Showed useful form at two, but falls just short of Listed class and is not proving easy to place. **D R C Elsworth [1-14] Mrs M E Slade.*

PENN **RR 45f** 1259[10]

3 ch f Be My Guest (USA) 10.2f **(66)** - Scribbling (USA) (Secretariat (USA)) 9f **(79)**
Form - 0
Record 1999 - 1st:0 2nd:0 3rd:0 Ran:1
1999 Turf 0-1: (7f) (frm)
Workmanlike, currently moderate filly.
**J H M Gosden [0-1] K Abdulla.*

PENNILESS (IRE) BHB 43f44a **RR 43f 44a** 1428[16]

4 b f Common Grounds 8.1f **(66)** - Tizzy (Formidable (USA)) 9.2f **(63)**
Form - 7870
Record 1999 - 1st:0 2nd:0 3rd:0 Ran:4
Pre1999 - 1st:3 2nd:1 3rd:2 Ran:25
Win Prizemoney £8,561 *Total Prizemoney* £10,538
Wins * 1998 Jun Catter (G-S) H 5f 47 52
* 1997 Jun Beverl (SFT) C 5f 73 <
* 1997 Apr Thirsk (G-F) 5f 68
1999 Turf 0-3: (5f, 6f 2) (gd, g-f, frm) 1999 AW 0-1: (5f) (Fibr)
Leggy, moderate filly, effective 5 to 6f, best at 6f, acts on gd to frm - acts on Fibr, likes left handed tracks, likes tight tracks. Turf high 43. **N Tinkler [3-29] Mrs C M Tinkler.*

PENNY BLACK **RR 37f** 3575[9]

3 br f Cyrano de Bergerac 7.3f **(58)** - Cow Pastures (Homing) 7.8f **(59)**
Form - 00
Record 1999 - 1st:0 2nd:0 3rd:0 Ran:2
1999 Turf 0-2: (7f 2) (g-f, frm)
Scopey, currently very moderate filly. Turf high 37 (began Jly).
**V Soane [0-2] The Four Farthings.*

PENNYGOWN **RR 71+f** 2354[1]

3 b f Rainbow Quest (USA) 11.2f **(81)** - Applecross (Glint of Gold) 9.3f **(66)**
Form - 1
Record 1999 - 1st:1 2nd:0 3rd:0 Ran:1
Win Prizemoney £4,065 *Total Prizemoney* £4,065
Wins * **1999** Jun Doncas (G-S) 12f 71 <
1999 Turf 1-1: (12f 1-1) (gd 1-1)
Neat, currently above-average filly. (1st run) - 1st of 5 getting 5lb from Inigo Jones (27 Jun Doncaster RF 2354). She won a small Doncaster maiden on her only start to date.
**H R A Cecil [1-1] Dr Catherine Wills.*

PENSHIEL (USA) BHB 58f **RR 52f** 4227[11]

2 b c Mtoto 11.5f **(71)** - Highland Ceilidh (IRE) (Scottish Reel) 7f **(61)**
Form - 000
Record 1999 - 1st:0 2nd:0 3rd:0 Ran:3
1999 Turf 0-3: (7f, 8f 2) (g-f 2, frm)
Currently fair colt. Turf high 52 (began Aug).
**J L Dunlop [0-3] Cyril Humphris.*

PENSION FUND BHB 80f **RR 84f** 5004[6]

5 b g Emperor Fountain 10f **(82)** - Navarino Bay (Averof) 8.2f **(62)**
Form - 106
Record 1999 - 1st:1 2nd:0 3rd:0 Ran:3
Pre1999 - 1st:4 2nd:5 3rd:2 Ran:27
Win Prizemoney £34,078 *Total Prizemoney* £48,818
Wins * **1999** Spt York (G-F) H 7.9f 78 81
* 1998 Spt Ripon (HVY) H 10f 77 82 <
* 1997 Aug Beverl (G-S) H 9.9f 69 70
* 1996 Aug York (GD) H 7f 75 72
* 1996 Jly Redcar (G-F) 5f 63
1999 Turf 1-3: (8f 1-2, 10f) (gd 2, frm 1-1)
Decent gelding, effective 8 to 12f, acts on g-s to frm, best on frm, has worn blinkers. Turf high 84 (began Spt) - also 1st of 24 giving 3lb to Arterxerxes (1 Spt York RF 4085). He has a fine record at York, and put up a tremendous performance to win a competitive handicap at that track in September, having been off the track for ten months previously. **M W Easterby [5-30] Stephen Curtis.*

PENTAGONAL (USA) **RR 70f** 4655[7]

2 b c Dynaformer (USA) 12f **(82)** - Pent (USA) (Mr Prospector (USA)) 8.8f **(78)**
Form - 7
Record 1999 - 1st:0 2nd:0 3rd:0 Ran:1
1999 Turf 0-1: (7f) (gd)
Currently above-average colt. Not knocked about in a warm maiden, he is one to keep a close eye on.
**Sir Michael Stoute [0-1] Sheikh Mohammed.*

PENTAGON LAD BHB 67f **RR 67f** 5022[9]

3 ch g Secret Appeal - Gilboa (Shirley Heights) 10.3f **(74)**
Form - 118161064700
Record 1999 - 1st:4 2nd:0 3rd:0 Ran:12
Pre1999 - 1st:0 2nd:0 3rd:0 Ran:3
Win Prizemoney £23,863 *Total Prizemoney* £24,156
Wins * **1999** Jly Cheste (G-F) H 10.3f 69 71 <
* **1999** Jun Ripon (G-F) H 8f 65 69
* **1999** May Thirsk (G-S) H 8f 61 64
* **1999** May Carlis (FRM) H 8f 55 60
1999 Turf 4-12: (8f 3-6, 9f 2, 10f 1-4) (gd 1-5, g-f 1-2, frm 1-3, hrd 1-2)
Scopey, average gelding, effective 8 to 10f, acts on gd to hrd, prefers tight tracks. Turf high 73 - 6th of 22 getting 10lb from Thekryaati (29 Jly Goodwood 9f frm RF 3226) - also 1st of 8 getting 13lb from West Escape (9 Jly Chester RF 2672). Becoming disappointing. He did well early last season, winning three times over a mile, and once over ten furlongs at Chester. Struggled afterwards, and looks very high in the handicap. Likes firm ground.
**J L Eyre [4-15] Creskeld Racing.*

PENYBONT BHB 82f **RR 67f** 5166[8]

3 b f Unfuwain (USA) 11.4f **(74)** - Morgannwg (IRE) (Simply Great (FR)) 8.2f **(65)**
Form - 2054437108
Record 1999 - 1st:1 2nd:1 3rd:1 Ran:10
Pre1999 - 1st:0 2nd:0 3rd:1 Ran:3
Win Prizemoney £3,769 *Total Prizemoney* £6,497

Wins *** 1999** Oct Lingfi (HVY) H 7f 66 67 <
1999 Turf 1-10: (7f 1-4, 8f 5, 12f) (g-s 1-3, gd 3, g-f, frm 3)
Unfurnished, average filly, effective 7 to 8f, best at 7f, acts on sft to gd, best on gd. Turf high 79 (1st run) - 2nd of 9 to Arctic Char (1 Apr Leicester 7f gd RF 0541).
**M L W Bell [1-13] K J Mercer & Mrs S Mercer.*

PEPETA BHB 69f **RR 67f** 4433[6]
2 b f Presidium 7.5f **(56)** - Mighty Flash (Rolfe (USA)) 12.1f **(65)**
Form - 676
Record 1999 - 1st:0 2nd:0 3rd:0 Ran:3
1999 Turf 0-3: (6f 2, 7f) (g-s, g-f 2)
Currently average filly. Turf high 67 (began Jly).
**I A Balding [0-3] Robert Hitchins.*

PEPPERCORN BHB 45f **RR 43f** 4169[9]
2 b f Totem (USA) 5f **(38)** - Sparkling Roberta **(39f 33a)** (Kind of Hush) 10.1f **(62)**
Form - 5050
Record 1999 - 1st:0 2nd:0 3rd:0 Ran:4
1999 Turf 0-2: (7f, 8f) (gd, frm) 1999 AW 0-2: (6f, 7f) (Fibr 2)
Moderate filly. Turf high 43 (began Aug). AW high 27 (began Jly).
**M D I Usher [0-4] Miss D G Kerr.*

PEPPERDINE (IRE) BHB 93f **RR 93+f** 4803[2]
3 b g Indian Ridge 7.6f **(74)** - Rahwah (Northern Baby (CAN)) 11.6f **(71)**
Form - 2021002
Record 1999 - 1st:1 2nd:3 3rd:0 Ran:7
Pre1999 - 1st:1 2nd:2 3rd:0 Ran:6
Win Prizemoney £42,329 *Total Prizemoney* £54,551
Wins *** 1999** Jun York (G-S) H 6f 85 93+ <
1998 Oct Warwic (GD) H 7f 78 83
1999 Turf 1-7: (6f 1-7) (gd 1-3, g-f 3, frm)
Lengthy, useful gelding, effective 6 to 7f, best at 6f, acts on gd to frm, best on gd, has worn blinkers. Turf high 93 - 1st of 23 getting 14lb from First Musical (12 Jun York RF 1967). He had run a couple of fine races in defeat last season before landing the valuable William Hill Trophy at York in fine style. Made no show in the Stewards' Cup, for which he was sent off a warm favourite, but he ran better from a moderate draw in the Ayr Gold Cup. Finished runner-up in a hot race at York in October, when many observers though him unlucky not to be awarded the race.
**D Nicholls [1-7] P D Savill (from W Jarvis [1-6] Oct 1998).*

PEPPERS GIRL BHB 20f **RR 17f** 5071[15]
3 b f Mon Tresor 7.9f **(60)** - Lady of Itatiba (BEL) (King Of Macedon) 8.1f **(59)**
Form - 58000
Record 1999 - 1st:0 2nd:0 3rd:0 Ran:5
1999 Turf 0-5: (8f 2, 10f, 11f, 14f) (gd 2, g-f, frm 2)
Leggy, poor filly, has worn blinkers. Turf high 11 (began Jly).
**Martyn Wane [0-6] James S Kennerley and Miss Jenny Hall.*

PEPPIATT BHB 60f **RR 49f** 5072[13]
5 ch g Efisio 7.7f **(69)** - Fleur du Val (Valiyar) 8.5f **(73)**
Form - 600568071500060 6050
Record 1999 - 1st:1 2nd:0 3rd:0 Ran:19
Pre1999 - 1st:3 2nd:2 3rd:4 Ran:18
Win Prizemoney £29,589 *Total Prizemoney* £36,804
Wins *** 1999** Jly Ayr (SFT) H 6f 68 70
1998 Spt Goodwo (SFT) H 6f 71 77
1997 Jly Lingfi (G-F) H 7f 80 79 <
1997 Apr Folkes (G-F) 6f 75
1999 Turf 1-19: (5f 2, 6f 1-13, 7f 4) (sft, g-s 1-3, gd 9, g-f 5, frm)
Moderate gelding, effective 6 to 7f, best at 6f, acts on g-s to hrd, has worn blinkers. Turf high 71 - 5th of 10 giving 20lb to Mister Westsound (21 May Ayr 6f g-s RF 1362) - also 1st of 9 getting 13lb from Royal Result (19 Jly Ayr RF 2941). Consistent. He has changed stables a few times in his career and is a fair handicapper on his day. Ended a disappointing spell when winning at Ayr in July. Six furlongs and cut in the ground look to be his ideal conditions.
**N Bycroft [1-20] Swinburne/Moore Partnership (from D Nicholls [1-14] Oct 1998).*

PERADVENTURE (IRE) BHB 80f **RR 79df** 4397[5]
4 b g Persian Bold 10f **(69)** - Missed Opportunity (IRE) (Exhibitioner) 8.7f **(61)**
Form - 5
Record 1999 - 1st:0 2nd:0 3rd:0 Ran:1
Pre1999 - 1st:1 2nd:1 3rd:2 Ran:10
Win Prizemoney £6,290 *Total Prizemoney* £9,428
Wins 1998 Spt York (GD) 10.4f 79 <
1999 Turf 0-1: (12f) (frm)
Workmanlike, above-average gelding, effective 10 to 13f, best at 12f, acts on g-s to frm, prefers left handed tracks.
**M D Hammond [0-1] Shirebrook Park Management Ltd (from R Hannon [1-10] Oct 1998).*

PERCHANCER (IRE) BHB 52f55a **RR 53f 55a** 4031[15]
3 ch g Perugino (USA) - Irish Hope (Nishapour (FR)) 9.1f **(61)**
Form - 32307431280
Record 1999 - 1st:1 2nd:2 3rd:3 Ran:11
Pre1999 - 1st:0 2nd:0 3rd:1 Ran:6
Win Prizemoney £2,689 *Total Prizemoney* £5,887
Wins *** 1999** Jly Thirsk (FRM) H 7f 51 53 <
1999 Turf 1-7: (7f 1-1, 8f 2, 9f 2, 10f 2) (g-f 4, frm 1-3) 1999 AW 0-4: (7f, 8f 2, 9f) (Equi 2, Fibr 2)
Scopey, fair gelding, effective 7 to 9f, best at 8f, acts on g-f to frm - acts on AW, best on Equi, has worn blinkers, likes left handed tracks, prefers tight tracks, excels at Lingfield. Turf high 53 - 2nd of 17 getting 11lb from Noble Cyrano (6 Aug Haydock 8f g-f RF 3417) - also 1st of 14 giving 10lb to Pipiji (30 Jly Thirsk RF 3257). AW high 56 - 2nd of 10 giving 23lb to Trois Elles (19 Jan Lingfield 7f Equi RF 0121).
**P C Haslam [1-17] N P Green.*

PERCHCOURT STEEL (IRE) RR 7f 3822[14]
3 b g Grand Lodge (USA) - Scaravie (IRE) (Drumalis) 12f **(54)**
Form - 00
Record 1999 - 1st:0 2nd:0 3rd:0 Ran:2
1999 Turf 0-1: (10f) (g-f) 1999 AW 0-1: (9f) (Fibr)
Scopey, currently poor gelding.
**R M Whitaker [0-2] Christopher Cooke.*

PERECAPA (IRE) BHB 30f39a **RR 37f 39a** 3642[10]
4 b f Archway (IRE) 8.5f **(60)** - Cupid Miss (Anita's Prince)
Form - 1800
Record 1999 - 1st:0 2nd:0 3rd:0 Ran:3
Pre1999 - 1st:1 2nd:0 3rd:4 Ran:11
Win Prizemoney £1,861 *Total Prizemoney* £2,988
Wins * 1998 *Dec Southw (STD)* *11f* *46* <
1999 Turf 0-2: (10f 2) (g-f, frm) 1999 AW 0-1: (12f) (Fibr)
Light-framed, moderate filly, effective 10 to 12f, acts on g-f to frm - acts on Fibr. Turf high 26 (began Jly).
**B Palling [1-15] Davies And Williams Partnership.*

PERFECT MOMENT (IRE) BHB 60f **RR 73f** 4901[10]
2 b f Mujadil (USA) 7.7f **(70)** - Flashing Raven (IRE) (Maelstrom Lake)
Form - 551000
Record 1999 - 1st:1 2nd:0 3rd:0 Ran:6
Win Prizemoney £3,213 *Total Prizemoney* £3,213
Wins *** 1999** Jly Leices (G-F) 7f 73 <
1999 Turf 1-6: (5f, 6f, 7f 1-4) (gd, g-f 3, frm 1-2)
Above-average filly, effective 7f, acts on frm. Turf high 73 - 1st of 16 getting 11lb from Aima (21 Jly Leicester RF 3011). She showed little in her first two starts, but was well supported on her third start when stepped up to seven furlongs at Leicester and obliged accordingly. **A P Jarvis [1-6] Christopher Shankland.*

PERFECT PARADIGM (IRE) BHB 102f **RR 102f** 1103[2]
5 b h Alzao (USA) 9.8f **(73)** - Brilleaux (Manado) 9.6f **(63)**
Form - 2
Record 1999 - 1st:0 2nd:1 3rd:0 Ran:1
Pre1999 - 1st:3 2nd:3 3rd:2 Ran:15
Win Prizemoney £46,172 *Total Prizemoney* £64,946
Wins 1998 Jly Haydoc (G-F) H 11.9f 94 98
1997 May Cheste (SFT) H 12.3f 88 101+ <
1997 Mar Newcas (G-F) 12.4f 82+
1999 Turf 0-1: (14f) (gd)
Very useful colt, effective 12 to 14f, best at 14f, acts on gd to g-f, best on gd, has worn blinkers (extremely effectively), prefers tight tracks. (1st run) - 2nd of 9 giving 2lb to Opera King (8 May Goodwood 14f gd RF 1103). He does most of his racing in Dubai these days, but ran well on his only British start in 1999. He stays

a mile and three quarters and is effective with or without a visor.
**S bin Suroor [0-1] Godolphin (from J H M Gosden [3-15] Spt 1998).*

PERFECT PEACH BHB 69f **RR 68f** 5072[8]
4 b f Lycius (USA) 8.8f **(71)** - Perfect Timing (Comedy Star (USA)) 7.5f **(50)**
Form - 0400002808108
Record 1999 - 1st:1 2nd:1 3rd:0 Ran:13
Pre1999 - 1st:2 2nd:1 3rd:1 Ran:9
Win Prizemoney £13,151 *Total Prizemoney* £17,213
Wins * **1999** Spt Mussel (G-S) H 7.1f 65 68
1997 Aug Beverl (G-S) H 5f 75 78 <
1997 Aug Thirsk (GD) 5f 78 <
1999 Turf 1-13: (5f 5, 6f 2, 7f 1-5, 8f) (gd 1-4, g-f 3, frm 5, hrd)
Workmanlike, average filly, effective 5 to 7f, best at 5f, acts on gd to hrd, best on frm, has worn blinkers. Turf high 69 - 2nd of 15 getting 4lb from Mantles Pride (8 Aug Redcar 7f frm RF 3468) - also 1st of 14 getting 1lb from Automatic (26 Spt Musselburgh RF 4579). She showed a bit of form in sprint handicaps in 1998, but showed little last term until stepped up to seven furlongs Musselburgh in September.
**C W Fairhurst [1-15] Mrs Ann Morris (from D W Chapman [0-2] Jun 1998).*

PERFECT PITCH RR 63tf 4557[6]
2 b f Dashing Blade 7.9f **(80)** - Singer on the Roof (Chief Singer) 8.9f **(66)**
Form - 56
Record 1999 - 1st:0 2nd:0 3rd:0 Ran:2
Win Prizemoney £0 *Total Prizemoney* £182
1999 Turf 0-2: (6f, 7f) (gd, frm)
Currently average filly. Turf high 63 (began Spt).
**I A Balding [0-2] J C Smith.*

PERFECT STING (USA) RR 116f 5228a[6]
3 b f Red Ransom (USA) 8.6f **(83)** - Valid Victress (USA) (Valid Appeal (USA)) 8.9f **(78)**
Form - 16
1999 Turf 1-2: (9f 1-1, 11f) (frm 1-2)
Currently high-class filly. Turf high 116 (began Oct) - 6th of 14 getting 4lb from Soaring Softly (6 Nov Gulfstream Park 11f frm RF 5228a) - also 1st of 9 from Tout Charmant (9 Oct Keeneland RF 4884a).
**J Orseno in USA [1-2].*

PERFECT VINTAGE RR 108f 1995[5]
9 b g Shirley Heights 12.1f **(76)** - Fair Salinia (Petingo) 11f **(72)**
Form - 5
1999 Turf 0-1: (8f) (g-f)
Pattern-class gelding. (1st run) - 5th of 8 getting 5lb from Cape Cross (15 Jun Ascot 8f g-f RF 1995). This sprightly veteran finished an honourable fifth in Royal Ascot's Queen Anne Stakes.
**Mme P Barbe in FR [1-3] N P Bloodstock.*

PERFORMING MAGIC (USA) BHB 97f **RR 88f** 4792[11]
2 ch c Gone West (USA) 7.8f **(82)** - Performing Arts (The Minstrel (CAN)) 10f **(72)**
Form - 32331610
Record 1999 - 1st:2 2nd:1 3rd:3 Ran:8
Win Prizemoney £12,001 *Total Prizemoney* £15,013
Wins * **1999** Spt Haydoc (G-F) 8.1f 88 <
* **1999** Aug Leices (G-F) 5f 73
1999 Turf 2-8: (5f 1-2, 6f 3, 7f, 8f 1-2) (gd 4, g-f 1-1, frm 1-3)
Useful colt, effective 6 to 8f, acts on gd to frm, has worn blinkers. Turf high 88 - 1st of 4 from Michele Marieschi (4 Spt Haydock RF 4137). He became somewhat expensive to follow, and it was not until he was dropped to the minimum trip that he got off the mark at Leicester. However he proved his runs over the minimum to be all wrong by winning a four-runner conditions event over a mile at Haydock in September. Tends to hang under pressure.
**H R A Cecil [2-8] The Thoroughbred Corporation.*

PERICLES BHB 47f48a **RR 46f 48a** 4175[6]
5 b g Primo Dominie 7.2f **(67)** - Egalite (FR) (Luthier) 9.8f **(71)**
Form - 77800723488303456
Record 1999 - 1st:0 2nd:1 3rd:3 Ran:15
Pre1999 - 1st:5 2nd:5 3rd:4 Ran:38
Win Prizemoney £17,104 *Total Prizemoney* £26,431
Wins * 1998 Jun Folkes (GD) 7f 67
1997 *Oct Wolver (STD) C* 7f 85 <
1997 *Jun Wolver (STD) H* 7f 80 80
1997 Jun Leices (GD) H 7f 70 74
1996 *Spt Wolver (STD)* 6f 77+
1999 Turf 0-6: (7f 2, 8f 3, 10f) (gd, g-f, frm 4) 1999 AW 0-9: (7f 8, 8f) (Equi 7, Fibr 2)
Moderate gelding, effective 7 to 8f, best at 7f, acts on gd to frm - acts on Equi, has worn blinkers. Turf high 61 (1st run) - 3rd of 9 giving 1lb to Village Native (23 Jun Salisbury 8f g-f RF 2250). AW high 62 - 4th of 10 giving 5lb to Garnock Valley (23 Feb Lingfield 7f Equi RF 0343). Consistent.
**Miss Gay Kelleway [1-35] Malcolm Spencer (from M Johnston [4-20] Oct 1997).*

PERIGEUX (IRE) BHB 64f70a **RR 63f 70a** 4027[10]
3 b c Perugino (USA) - Rock On (IRE) (Ballad Rock) 7.8f **(63)**
Form - 40632020200
Record 1999 - 1st:0 2nd:3 3rd:1 Ran:11
Pre1999 - 1st:3 2nd:1 3rd:0 Ran:7
Win Prizemoney £11,853 *Total Prizemoney* £14,874
Wins * 1998 *Jly Wolver (STD)* 6f 86 <
* 1998 Jly Ayr (GD) H 6f 79
* 1998 *Jly Southw (STD)* 6f 79
1999 Turf 0-10: (6f 6, 7f 4) (g-s 2, g-f 5, frm 3) 1999 AW 0-1: (7f) (Fibr)
Strong, useful colt, effective 6f, acts on gd - acts on Fibr, has worn blinkers, likes tight tracks. Turf high 63.
**J Berry [3-18] Mrs Valerie Hubbard.*

PERIQUITUM RR 45f 2240[10]
2 br f Dilum (USA) 7.1f **(56)** - Periquito (USA) (Olden Times) 11.4f **(67)**
Form - 50
Record 1999 - 1st:0 2nd:0 3rd:0 Ran:2
Win Prizemoney £0 *Total Prizemoney* £209
1999 Turf 0-2: (6f, 7f) (gd, frm)
Currently moderate filly. Turf high 45. **R Hannon [0-2] J C Smith.*

PERLE DE SAGESSE BHB 63f61a **RR 69f 61a** 4625[5]
2 b f Namaqualand (USA) - Pearl of Dubai (USA) (Red Ransom (USA))
Form - 3300105
Record 1999 - 1st:1 2nd:0 3rd:2 Ran:7
Win Prizemoney £2,372 *Total Prizemoney* £3,232
Wins * **1999** Aug Windso (GD) S 5f 69 <
1999 Turf 1-6: (5f 1-2, 6f 3, 7f) (g-s, gd, g-f 2, frm 1-1, hrd) 1999 AW 0-1: (5f) (Fibr)
Average filly, effective 5f, acts on frm. Turf high 69 - 1st of 13 getting 5lb from Baytown Melody (28 Aug Windsor RF 3980). She was becoming disappointing and did not seem to be getting home over six and seven furlongs, so the drop down to the minimum for a Windsor seller worked the oracle. She won easily, but it was a poor race. **P F I Cole [1-7] Andy Smith.*

PERPETUAL PRIDE (IRE) RR 4f 1778[9]
2 b c Pips Pride 6.7f **(70)** - Miss Springtime **(32f 55a)** (Bluebird (USA)) 7.5f **(69)**
Form - 80
Record 1999 - 1st:0 2nd:0 3rd:0 Ran:2
1999 Turf 0-1: (5f) (frm) 1999 AW 0-1: (6f) (Fibr)
Currently very moderate colt. **E J Alston [0-2] M Pollitt.*

PERRYSTON VIEW BHB 98f **RR 98f** 5040[1]
7 b h Primo Dominie 7.2f **(67)** - Eastern Ember (Indian King (USA)) 7.4f **(64)**
Form - 100407481
Record 1999 - 1st:2 2nd:0 3rd:0 Ran:9
Pre1999 - 1st:9 2nd:1 3rd:3 Ran:34
Win Prizemoney £128,364 *Total Prizemoney* £141,169
Wins * **1999** Oct Doncas (SFT) H 5f 93 98 <
* **1999** May Newmar (G-F) H 6f 89 96
* 1998 Aug Ripon (GD) H 6f 86 92
* 1997 Spt Ayr (GD) H 6f 81 92
* 1997 May Newmar (GD) H 6f 78 80
* 1995 Jly Newmar (G-F) H 6f 86 81
* 1995 Jun Newmar (GD) H 6f 81 82
* 1995 Apr Catter (GD) H 5f 67 76+
* 1995 Apr Newcas (G-F) H 5f 67 72+
1999 Turf 2-9: (5f 1-2, 6f 1-7) (g-s 1-1, gd 5, g-f 2, frm 1-1)

Very useful horse, effective 5 to 6f, best at 6f, acts on g-s to frm, mostly wears blinkers (effectively), excels at Ripon. Turf high 98 - 1st of 14 from Ellens Lad (23 Oct Doncaster RF 5040) - also 1st of 17 giving 9lb to Rushcutter Bay (1 May Newmarket RF 0960). Thoroughly reliable, he has given his connections tremendous fun and is always one to short-list in the top sprint handicaps. Effective on any ground, he races up with the pace and is game. **P Calver [11-43] Mrs Janis MacPherson.*

PERSEPHONE BHB 20f17a **RR 25f 17a** 62^{6}
6 ch m Lycius (USA) 8.8f **(71)** - Elarrih (USA) (Sharpen Up) 8.3f **(67)**
Form - 086
Record 1999 - 1st:0 2nd:0 3rd:0 Ran:2
Pre1999 - 1st:0 2nd:1 3rd:0 Ran:22
Win Prizemoney £0 *Total Prizemoney* £1,115
1999 AW 0-2: (10f, 13f) (Equi 2)
Little account mare, often wears blinkers. AW high 19.
**C N Allen [0-8] The Freddy Partnership (from J L Harris [0-10] Spt 1997).*

PERSIAN FAYRE BHB 61f72a **RR 61f 72a** 5166^{13}
7 b g Persian Heights 10.5f **(61)** - Dominion Fayre (Dominion) 8.5f **(63)**
Form - 0011127070700
Record 1999 - 1st:3 2nd:1 3rd:0 Ran:12
Pre1999 - 1st:6 2nd:8 3rd:4 Ran:52
Win Prizemoney £45,752 *Total Prizemoney* £67,571
Wins * **1999** May Ayr (GD) H 7f 70 80
* **1999** May Carlis (FRM) C 6.9f 57
* **1999** Apr Redcar (G-S) S 7f 66
* 1998 Jun Haydoc (GD) 7.1f 86+ <
* 1996 Nov Newmar (GD) H 7f 79 83
* 1996 Oct York (GD) H 7f 75 78
* 1996 Aug Newcas (GD) H 7f 67 77
* 1995 May Ayr (G-F) 8f 73
1999 Turf 3-12: (6f 2, 7f 3-10) (sft, g-s 2, gd 2-6, g-f, frm 1-2)
Average gelding, effective 7f, acts on gd to frm, best on frm, likes left handed tracks, likes tight tracks, excels at Haydock, likes Ayr. Turf high 80 - 1st of 13 giving 1lb to Taffs Well (20 May Ayr RF 1340). Inconsistent. A veteran handicapper, he completed a hat-trick in the spring but was out of form latterly. A genuine front-runner, seven furlongs is his trip. **J Berry [9-66] Murray Grubb.*

PERSIANO BHB 92f **RR 96f** 4915^{12}
4 ch c Efisio 7.7f **(69)** - Persiandale (Persian Bold) 9.3f **(66)**
Form - 73053050
Record 1999 - 1st:0 2nd:0 3rd:2 Ran:8
Pre1999 - 1st:3 2nd:0 3rd:0 Ran:8
Win Prizemoney £16,823 *Total Prizemoney* £22,297
Wins * 1998 May Doncas (GD) H 7f 90 99+ <
* 1998 May Salisb (FRM) H 7f 75 89+
* 1998 May Warwic (GD) H 7f 75 83
1999 Turf 0-8: (7f, 8f 7) (gd 4, g-f, frm 3)
Lengthy, very useful colt, effective 7 to 8f, best at 8f, acts on g-f to frm, best on frm, has worn blinkers. Turf high 99 - 3rd of 12 giving 2lb to Lonesome Dude (31 May Sandown 8f frm RF 1614). Consistent. He had a disappointing campaign, but remains a useful handicapper when everything slots into pace. Probably best when racing prominently over seven furlongs on a sound surface, he should not be written off. **J R Fanshawe [3-16] Miss A Church.*

PERSIAN POINT BHB 41f **RR 47f** 4983^{18}
3 ch g Persian Bold 10f **(69)** - Kind Thoughts (Kashmir II) 11.7f **(48)**
Form - 7780
Record 1999 - 1st:0 2nd:0 3rd:0 Ran:4
1999 Turf 0-4: (8f 2, 10f 2) (gd, g-f, frm 2)
Leggy, moderate gelding. Turf high 47 (began Aug).
**Mrs A Swinbank [0-4] A C & A D Partners.*

PERSIAN PUNCH (IRE) BHB 110f **RR 114f** 5210^{1}
6 ch g Persian Heights 10.5f **(61)** - Rum Cay (USA) (Our Native (USA)) 11.2f **(63)**
Form - 475401
Record 1999 - 1st:1 2nd:0 3rd:0 Ran:6
Pre1999 - 1st:8 2nd:2 3rd:6 Ran:21
Win Prizemoney £139,667 *Total Prizemoney* £300,253
Wins * **1999** Nov Doncas (SFT) 14.6f 99
* 1998 Aug York (G-F) G3 15.9f 115
* 1998 May Sandow (GD) G3 16.4f 119
* 1998 May Newmar (G-S) G3 16f 120 <
* 1997 May Sandow (G-F) G3 16.4f 115
* 1997 May Newbur (SFT) L 13.3f 116
* 1996 Jly Newmar (GD) L 14.8f 106
* 1996 Jun Salisb (GD) 14f 90
* 1996 May Windso (G-F) 10f 79+
1999 Turf 1-6: (12f 2, 14f, 15f 1-1, 16f, 20f) (sft 1-1, gd, g-f 2, frm 2)
Group-class gelding, effective 12 to 16f, best at 16f, acts on gd to frm, best on gd, prefers left handed tracks, and excels at Sandown. Turf high 114 - 4th of 11 getting 2lb from Arctic Owl (31 May Sandown 16f frm RF 1612). Consistent. A top-class stayer, he was not seen out after flopping in the Ascot Gold Cup (the third time he has run poorly in that event). Connections are reportedly considering a career over hurdles, and he would certainly be an exciting recruit to the winter game. **D R C Elsworth [9-27] J C Smith.*

PERSIAN RULER RR 115f $5013a^{7}$
4 b c Don Roberto (USA)15.6f **(39)** -Kalawelsh (FR)(Kalaglow) 9.8f **(67)**
Form - 11437
1999 Turf 1-4: (12f 1-4) (sft 1-2, g-s)
High-class colt. Turf high 115 - 7th giving 9lb to First Magnitude (17 Oct Longchamp 12f RF 5013a) - also 1st of 6 from Arnaqueur (29 Apr Longchamp RF 1069a). He looked an improving sort when winning a Longchamp Group Three in April, but was just found out when tried in higher Group company. **D Sepulchre in FR [2-5].*

PERSIAN SABRE BHB 40f **RR 44f** 4835^{17}
4 b f Sabrehill (USA) 8.5f **(64)** - Wassl's Sister (Troy) 10.4f **(68)**
Form - 60600
Record 1999 - 1st:0 2nd:0 3rd:0 Ran:5
Pre1999 - 1st:1 2nd:1 3rd:0 Ran:12
Win Prizemoney £2,070 *Total Prizemoney* £2,802
Wins * 1998 Aug Lingfi (G-F) H 10f 54 56 <
1999 Turf 0-5: (7f, 10f 4) (g-s, gd, g-f, frm 2)
Unfurnished, moderate filly, effective 8 to 10f, acts on frm. Turf high 44. **V Soane [1-17] Alan Prestwich,Steve Soane.*

PERSIAN WATERS (IRE) BHB 62f **RR 64f** 4904^{14}
3 b g Persian Bold 10f **(69)** - Emerald Waters (Kings Lake (USA)) 10.8f **(67)**
Form - 7380
Record 1999 - 1st:0 2nd:0 3rd:1 Ran:4
Pre1999 - 1st:1 2nd:0 3rd:0 Ran:5
Win Prizemoney £3,692 *Total Prizemoney* £4,488
Wins 1998 Oct Pontef (SFT) H 8f 64 68 <
1999 Turf 0-4: (12f 2, 14f 2) (gd, g-f 2, frm)
Scopey, average gelding, effective 8f, acts on gd. Turf high 68. Consistent. A winner on soft ground at Pontefract at two, he joined Martin Pipe for last season and stayed on into seventh in Ascot's King George V Handicap, but was rather disappointing subsequently. Now hurdling.
**J R Fanshawe [0-2] Paul & Jenny Green (from M C Pipe [0-2] Jly 1999).*

PERTEMPS CRAIC BHB 30f47a **RR 47a** 2068^{5}
3 b g Gildoran 11.6f **(58)** - Pertemps Partner **(41f 52a)** (Bairn (USA)) 7.7f **(59)**
Form - 400005
Record 1999 - 1st:0 2nd:0 3rd:0 Ran:5
Pre1999 - 1st:0 2nd:0 3rd:0 Ran:2
1999 Turf 0-1: (11f) (gd) 1999 AW 0-4: (8f, 9f, 10f, 11f) (Equi, Fibr 3)
Light-framed, little account gelding, has worn blinkers. AW high 28.
**A Streeter [0-2] Pertemps Group Ltd (from A G Newcombe [0-5] Apr 1999).*

PERTEMPS FC BHB 67f **RR 67f** 4651^{8}
2 b c Prince Sabo 6.6f **(64)** - Top Mouse (High Top) 10.2f **(67)**
Form - 4U012168
Record 1999 - 1st:2 2nd:1 3rd:0 Ran:8
Win Prizemoney £9,068 *Total Prizemoney* £10,074
Wins * **1999** Aug Beverl (GD) H 5f 65 67 <
* **1999** Jly Newcas (G-F) S 6f 62
1999 Turf 2-8: (5f 1-5, 6f 1-3) (gd 3, g-f 1-2, frm 1-3)
Average colt, effective 5 to 6f, acts on g-f to frm, has worn blinkers. Turf high 67 - 1st of 13 getting 16lb from Mrs P (29 Aug Beverley RF 3988) - also 1st of 12 giving 5lb to Mountrath Rock (24 Jly Newcastle RF 3102). Found his level when dropped into selling

company at Newcastle, and has since landed a Beverley nursery. He tends to lose ground at the start and looks best suited by six furlongs. **T D Easterby [2-8] The Pertemps Professionals.*

PERTEMPS MISSION BHB 42f46a **RR 45f 46a** 354[2]
5 b g Safawan 6.6f **(60)** - Heresheis (Free State) 8.7f **(61)**
Form - 61223562
Record 1999 - 1st:0 2nd:2 3rd:1 Ran:5
Pre1999 - 1st:2 2nd:2 3rd:1 Ran:19
Win Prizemoney £4,865 *Total Prizemoney* £8,327
Wins * 1998 *Dec Wolver (SLW) H 14.8f 40 49 <*
* 1998 Aug Catter (G-F) H 15.8f 35 38+
1999 AW 0-5: (16f 5) (Equi 2, Fibr 3)
Fair gelding, effective 15 to 16f, best at 16f, acts on gd to frm - acts on AW, best on Equi, often wears blinkers (very effectively), favours tight tracks, excels at Lingfield. AW high 50 - 3rd of 10 getting 7lb from Red Raja (14 Jan Lingfield 16f Equi RF 0094).
**J Pearce [2-24] Michael Whatley.*

PERTEMPS STAR BHB 40f **RR 20f** 5064[13]
2 b c Imperial Frontier (USA) 7f **(65)** - Stella Royale (Astronef)
Form - 0000
Record 1999 - 1st:0 2nd:0 3rd:0 Ran:4
1999 Turf 0-4: (5f, 6f 3) (gd, g-f, frm, hrd)
Fair colt. Turf high 20.
**A D Smith [0-2] Miss K Smith (from A G Newcombe [0-2] Jun 1999).*

PERU GENIE (IRE) BHB 59f **RR 65f** 4870[16]
2 b g Perugino (USA) - High Concept (IRE) (Thatching) 8f **(66)**
Form - 46600
Record 1999 - 1st:0 2nd:0 3rd:0 Ran:5
Win Prizemoney £0 *Total Prizemoney* £255
1999 Turf 0-5: (6f 2, 7f 3) (gd 2, g-f 2, frm)
Average gelding. Turf high 65. **R Hannon [0-5] Noodles Racing.*

PERUGIA (IRE) BHB 97f **RR 92f** 4920[9]
2 gr f Perugino (USA) - Lightning Bug (Prince Bee) 12f **(46)**
Form - 1200
Record 1999 - 1st:1 2nd:1 3rd:0 Ran:4
Win Prizemoney £4,264 *Total Prizemoney* £7,851
Wins * 1999 May Goodwo (GD) 6f 90+ <
1999 Turf 1-4: (6f 1-1, 7f 2, 8f) (sft, gd 1-2, frm)
Useful filly. Turf high 92 - 2nd of 5 to Hypnotize (22 Jly Sandown 7f frm RF 3029) - also 1st of 11 getting 5lb from Night Style (19 May Goodwood RF 1335). Nudged along when trying to hang to land a fine victory from Night Style in a Goodwood six-furlong maiden, she came back from a two-month absence to run a close second in a listed event at Sandown. She is capable of more, although found the Prix Marcel Boussac too much.
**B W Hills [1-4] The Hon Mrs J M Corbett & C Wright.*

PERUGIA LADY (IRE) RR 35f 1653[11]
3 ch f Perugino (USA) - Love Hurts (IRE) (Broken Hearted)
Form - 00
Record 1999 - 1st:0 2nd:0 3rd:0 Ran:2
1999 Turf 0-2: (7f, 10f) (gd, frm)
Neat, currently very moderate filly. Turf high 35.
**J S Wainwright [0-2] N F Strange.*

PERUGINA (FR) RR 97f 5263a[6]
2 b f Highest Honor (FR) 10.9f **(72)** - Piacenza (FR) (Darshaan) 9.9f **(84)**
Form - 316
1999 Turf 1-3: (5f, 7f 1-2) (hvy 1-1, g-s, gd)
Currently very useful filly. Turf high 97 (began Jly). She produced a sharp burst of speed to win a Group Three at Saint-Cloud in October and is a useful prospect. Likely to stay a mile or beyond, she goes well on easy ground. **Mme C Head in FR [1-3].*

PERUGINO BAY (IRE) BHB 107f **RR 108f** 734[3]
3 b c Perugino (USA) - Dublah (USA) (Private Account (USA)) 8.5f **(74)**
Form - 73
Record 1999 - 1st:0 2nd:0 3rd:1 Ran:2
Pre1999 - 1st:2 2nd:2 3rd:3 Ran:10
Win Prizemoney £10,203 *Total Prizemoney* £36,674
Wins * 1998 Jly York (FRM) H 5f 103 <
* 1998 Apr Ripon (SFT) 5f 85
1999 Turf 0-2: (5f, 7f) (gd, g-f)
Strong, Pattern-class colt, effective 5 to 7f, acts on sft to frm. Turf high 108 - 3rd of 7 to Enrique (17 Apr Newbury 7f g-f RF 0734). Fancied to make a winning return in a Haydock Listed event, he ran so poorly that something must have been amiss, but he ran a cracker stepped up in seven furlongs in the Greenham, staying on well into third and suggesting that he might even stay further. Did not reappear. **B A McMahon [2-12] J C Fretwell.*

PERUGINO PEARL (IRE) RR 25f 2729[13]
2 b f Perugino (USA) - Farnacliffe (Taufan (USA)) 7f **(57)**
Form - 00
Record 1999 - 1st:0 2nd:0 3rd:0 Ran:2
1999 Turf 0-2: (6f 2) (g-f 2)
Currently little account filly. Turf high 25.
**M Brittain [0-2] Mel Brittain.*

PERUGINO'S MALT (IRE) BHB 70f **RR 22f** 4945[10]
3 ch f Perugino (USA) - Malt Leaf (IRE) (Nearly a Nose (USA))
Form - 14380
Record 1999 - 1st:1 2nd:0 3rd:1 Ran:5
Pre1999 - 1st:0 2nd:0 3rd:0 Ran:1
Win Prizemoney £3,953 *Total Prizemoney* £4,809
Wins 1999 Jly Naas (G-F) 8f 70 <
1999 Turf 1-5: (7f, 8f 1-1, 9f, 10f 2) (g-s, gd 2, g-f 1-2)
Little account filly, effective 8 to 10f, acts on g-s to g-f, best on g-f. Turf high 71 (began Jly) - 8th of 11 getting 7lb from Gift Token (4 Spt Cork 10f g-f RF 4196a) - also 1st of 12 getting 7lb from La Serina (21 Jly Naas RF 3180a).
**A T Murphy [0-1] R W Savery (from A P O'Brien in IRE [1-5] Spt 1999).*

PERUVIAN CHIEF (IRE) BHB 76f **RR 40f** 5144[1]
2 b c Foxhound (USA) - John's Ballad (IRE) (Ballad Rock) 7.8f **(63)**
Form - 0021
Record 1999 - 1st:1 2nd:1 3rd:0 Ran:4
Win Prizemoney £2,511 *Total Prizemoney* £3,144
Wins * **1999** *Oct Wolver (STD) 6f 80 <*
1999 Turf 0-2: (6f 2) (g-s, gd) 1999 AW 1-2: (6f 1-2) (Fibr 1-2)
Decent colt. Turf high 40 (began Aug). AW high 80 (began Oct) - 1st of 6 giving 5lb to Janiceland (30 Oct Wolverhampton RF 5144).
**N P Littmoden [1-4] M C S D Racing.*

PERUVIAN JADE BHB 74f **RR 88f** 5111[4]
2 gr f Petong 7.6f **(58)** - Rion River (IRE) (Taufan (USA)) 7f **(57)**
Form - 634211044
Record 1999 - 1st:2 2nd:1 3rd:1 Ran:9
Win Prizemoney £7,532 *Total Prizemoney* £20,264
Wins * **1999** Spt Leices (GD) H 6f 73 74 <
* **1999** Spt Goodwo (G-F) H 6f 70 74 <
1999 Turf 2-6: (5f 2, 6f 2-4) (gd 3, g-f 2-2, frm) 1999 AW 0-3: (5f, 6f 2) (Fibr 3)
Useful filly, effective 6f, acts on gd. Turf high 88 - 4th of 20 getting 4lb from Magic of Love (15 Oct Newmarket 6f gd RF 4895). AW high 60. She had shown ability on Fibresand, but struck form on turf with wins at Goodwood and Leicester in September. She seemed to find the drop to the minimum trip against her at Newmarket. **N P Littmoden [2-9] M C S D Racing.*

PERUVIAN STAR BHB 74f77a **RR 56f 77a** 2312[7]
3 b c Emarati (USA) 6.6f **(63)** - Julie's Star (IRE) (Thatching) 8f **(66)**
Form - 213777
Record 1999 - 1st:0 2nd:0 3rd:0 Ran:3
Pre1999 - 1st:1 2nd:1 3rd:1 Ran:3
Win Prizemoney £2,853 *Total Prizemoney* £3,771
Wins * 1998 *Dec Wolver (SLW) 6f 84+ <*
1999 Turf 0-1: (6f) (g-f) 1999 AW 0-2: (7f 2) (Fibr 2)
Fair colt, effective 6 to 7f, - acts on Fibr. AW high 56. He was very impressive when bolting up in a maiden on the Wolverhampton Fibresand at the end of '98, but was very disappointing last season. **N P Littmoden [1-6] M C S D Racing.*

PESCARA (IRE) BHB 108f **RR 109f** 4239[2]
3 b f Common Grounds 8.1f **(66)** - Mackla (Caerleon (USA)) 8.6f **(71)**
Form - 552
Record 1999 - 1st:0 2nd:1 3rd:0 Ran:3
Pre1999 - 1st:0 2nd:0 3rd:1 Ran:2

Win Prizemoney £0 *Total Prizemoney* £15,810
1999 Turf 0-3: (7f, 8f 2) (g-f 2, frm)
Well made, Pattern-class filly. Turf high 109 - 5th of 9 to Balisada (16 Jun Ascot 8f g-f RF 2041). Trained in France at two, she carried Godolphin's hopes in the 1000 Guineas having come out on top in their private trial. By no means disgraced in finishing fifth at Newmarket, having being drawn on the disadvantageous side, she filled the same position in the Coronation Stakes, only collared inside the last. Reappeared after a summer brreak at Doncaster, but was unfortunate to come up against Susu.
**S bin Suroor [0-3] Godolphin (from Mme C Head in FR [0-2] Aug 1998).*

PESHTIGO (USA) BHB 106f RR 106f 4132[4]

3 b c Kris S (USA) 9.3f **(76)** - Fume (USA) (Secretariat (USA)) 9f **(79)**
Form - 21554
Record 1999 - 1st:1 2nd:1 3rd:0 Ran:5
Pre1999 - 1st:0 2nd:0 3rd:0 Ran:2
Win Prizemoney £35,550 *Total Prizemoney* £38,645
Wins * 1999 May Cheste (G-F) G3 12.3f 105 <
1999 Turf 1-5: (11f, 12f 1-4) (gd, g-f 1-2, frm 2)
Scopey, Pattern-class colt, effective 12f, acts on g-f. Turf high 106 - also 1st of 8 from Lightning Arrow (4 May Chester RF 1027). He was still a maiden when awarded the Chester Vase on the demotion of Housemaster, but looked beaten on merit. Ran a fair race at Royal Ascot next time, but has been comfortably held since.
**B W Hills [1-7] Maktoum Al Maktoum.*

PETAL (IRE) RR 74f 5133[6]

3 b f Common Grounds 8.1f **(66)** - Bayadere (USA) (Green Dancer (USA)) 10.3f **(74)**
Form - 2324036
Record 1999 - 1st:0 2nd:2 3rd:2 Ran:7
Win Prizemoney £0 *Total Prizemoney* £4,162
1999 Turf 0-7: (10f 3, 11f, 12f 2, 13f) (gd 3, g-f 2, frm 2)
Leggy, above-average filly, effective 10 to 11f, best at 10f, acts on gd to frm, best on gd. Turf high 78 (1st run) - 2nd of 13 to Arabis (5 Jun Newmarket 10f gd RF 1775).
**Lady Herries [0-7] Mrs Denis Haynes.*

PETANE (IRE) BHB 22f RR 25f 4287[14]

4 b g Petardia 8.2f **(58)** - Senane (Vitiges (FR)) 8.2f **(59)**
Form - 0800
Record 1999 - 1st:0 2nd:0 3rd:0 Ran:4
Pre1999 - 1st:1 2nd:0 3rd:1 Ran:14
Win Prizemoney £1,725 *Total Prizemoney* £2,256
Wins 1998 Aug Folkes (G-F) S 12f 47 <
1999 Turf 0-4: (11f, 12f, 14f, 16f) (g-f, frm 2, hrd)
Neat, little account gelding, effective 10f, acts on g-f, often wears blinkers (very effectively). Turf high 25. Inconsistent.
**John Harris [0-4] Steppey Lane Bloodstock (from L A Dace [0-1] Oct 1998).*

PETARA (IRE) BHB 40f RR 43f 4539[9]

4 ch g Petardia 8.2f **(58)** - Romangoddess (IRE) (Rhoman Rule (USA))
Form - 070170
Record 1999 - 1st:1 2nd:0 3rd:0 Ran:6
Pre1999 - 1st:1 2nd:1 3rd:3 Ran:24
Win Prizemoney £5,796 *Total Prizemoney* £8,871
Wins * 1999 Spt Lingfi (FRM) SH 10f 38 40
* 1997 Spt Catter (G-F) H 7f 60 65 <
1999 Turf 1-6: (7f, 8f, 9f 2, 10f 1-2) (g-f, frm 1-5)
Workmanlike, moderate gelding, effective 8f, acts on g-f, mostly wears blinkers, likes left handed tracks. Turf high 43 (began Jly).
**J S Wainwright [2-31] Wisma Partnership.*

PETARGA BHB 76f RR 79f 4272[11]

4 b f Petong 7.6f **(58)** - One Half Silver (CAN) (Plugged Nickle (USA)) 7.8f **(68)**
Form - 0370210300
Record 1999 - 1st:1 2nd:1 3rd:2 Ran:10
Pre1999 - 1st:1 2nd:1 3rd:2 Ran:10
Win Prizemoney £6,795 *Total Prizemoney* £12,868
Wins * 1999 Jly Folkes (G-F) H 6f 73 75 <
* 1997 Jun Bath (G-F) 5.1f 72
1999 Turf 1-10: (5f, 6f 1-9) (gd, g-f 5, frm 1-2, hrd 2)
Neat, above-average filly, effective 5 to 6f, best at 6f, acts on g-f to frm, best on frm. Turf high 79 - 3rd of 14 giving 1lb to Alpen Wolf (22 Aug Bath 6f frm RF 3833) - also 1st of 7 giving 18lb to Beyond Calculation (14 Jly Folkestone RF 2820). Consistent. Has had a busy season, and got off the mark in a Folkestone handicap over six furlongs in July. Should have won at Bath the following month, but came too late and looks to need six furlongs now.
**J A R Toller [2-20] Mrs R W Gore-Andrews.*

PETARY BHB 95f RR 91+f 4833[7]

2 gr g Petong 7.6f **(58)** - Daffodil Fields (Try My Best (USA)) 7.6f **(67)**
Form - 13057
Record 1999 - 1st:1 2nd:0 3rd:1 Ran:5
Win Prizemoney £4,581 *Total Prizemoney* £8,943
Wins * 1999 Jly Newmar (G-F) 6f 79t <
1999 Turf 1-5: (6f 1-4, 7f) (gd 2, g-f 2, frm 1-1)
Useful gelding, has worn blinkers. Turf high 91 (began Jly) - 5th of 26 getting 1lb from Khasayl (2 Oct Redcar 6f g-f RF 4690). Had problems with the stalls on his first two visits to the course, being withdrawn first time. However, this did not stop him scoring in a blanket finish to a Newmarket maiden. He was a close third in a Haydock conditions event next time but disappointed when visored in a Group Two. **J H M Gosden [1-5] Sheikh Mohammed.*

PETER PERFECT BHB 25f46a RR 57df 46a 232[9]

5 gr g Chilibang 7f **(55)** - Misdevious (USA) (Alleged (USA)) 10f **(76)**
Form - 87700
Record 1999 - 1st:0 2nd:0 3rd:0 Ran:2
Pre1999 - 1st:0 2nd:3 3rd:1 Ran:17
Win Prizemoney £0 *Total Prizemoney* £3,186
1999 AW 0-2: (11f, 16f) (Fibr 2)
Fair gelding, often wears blinkers. AW high 23.
**Mrs S Lamyman [0-8] P Lamyman (from R Curtis [0-2] Spt 1997).*

PETER'S IMP (IRE) BHB 65f59a RR 62f 59a 5072[18]

4 b g Imp Society (USA) 7.1f **(63)** - Catherine Clare (Sallust) 8.4f **(63)**
Form - 0121206050700
Record 1999 - 1st:2 2nd:2 3rd:0 Ran:13
Pre1999 - 1st:2 2nd:1 3rd:4 Ran:16
Win Prizemoney £13,204 *Total Prizemoney* £19,191
Wins * 1999 Jun Redcar (FRM) 7f 80
*** 1999** May Hamilt (G-F) 6f 67
* 1998 Jly Haydoc (G-F) 7.1f 68
* 1997 Aug Newcas (G-F) H 6f 77 81 <
1999 Turf 2-13: (6f 1-6, 7f 1-6, 8f) (hvy, gd 3, g-f 1-7, frm 1-2)
Scopey, average gelding, effective 6 to 7f, best at 7f, acts on gd to frm, has worn blinkers, likes Redcar. Turf high 82 - 2nd of 10 giving 17lb to Rum Lad (7 Jun Pontefract 6f gd RF 1791) - also 1st of 4 giving 3lb to Three Angels (1 Jun Redcar RF 1650). Consistent.
**J Berry [4-29] & Mrs Peter Foden.*

PETER'S PRINCESS (IRE) BHB 40f RR 45f 5209[20]

2 ch f Lycius (USA) 8.8f **(71)** - Regal Scintilla (King of Spain) 7.8f **(52)**
Form - 0650
Record 1999 - 1st:0 2nd:0 3rd:0 Ran:4
1999 Turf 0-4: (6f 4) (g-s, g-f, frm 2)
Moderate filly. Turf high 45. **J Berry [0-4] & Mrs Peter Foden.*

PETEURESQUE (USA) RR 73f 4751[5]

2 ch c Peteski (CAN) - Miss Ultimo (USA) (Screen King (USA))
Form - 25
Record 1999 - 1st:0 2nd:1 3rd:0 Ran:2
Win Prizemoney £0 *Total Prizemoney* £2,024
1999 Turf 0-2: (7f, 8f) (gd, frm)
Currently above-average colt. Turf high 73 (1st run) (began Spt) - 2nd of 10 to Akeed (1 Spt York 7f frm RF 4083).
**T D Barron [0-2] J Baggott.*

PET EXPRESS FLYER (IRE) BHB 80f RR 67f 3677[17]

3 b g Mukaddamah (USA) 7.6f **(74)** - Take The Option (USA) (Bold Bidder) 8.8f **(67)**
Form - 80
Record 1999 - 1st:0 2nd:0 3rd:0 Ran:2
Pre1999 - 1st:3 2nd:1 3rd:3 Ran:10
Win Prizemoney £8,509 *Total Prizemoney* £11,233
Wins * 1998 Jly Ayr (GD) H 7f 92 <
* 1998 Jun Mussel (G-F) 7.1f 72+
* 1998 Jun Hamilt (GD) 6f 78
1999 Turf 0-2: (8f, 11f) (gd, frm)

Scopey, average gelding, effective 7 to 8f, acts on gd to g-f. Turf high 50 (began Aug). Becoming disappointing.
**P C Haslam [3-12] Pet Express (W&R) Ltd.*

PETITE DANSEUSE BHB 37f39a **RR 34f 39a** 4832[6]
5 b m Aragon 7.7f **(58)** - Let Her Dance (USA) (Sovereign Dancer (USA)) 11.2f **(68)**
Form - 00650835426
Record 1999 - 1st:0 2nd:2 3rd:1 Ran:11
Pre1999 - 1st:4 2nd:6 3rd:7 Ran:48
Win Prizemoney £13,515 *Total Prizemoney* £26,726
Wins 1997 Spt Leices (G-F) C 6f 61
1997 Aug Leices (GD) C 7f 59+
1996 May Windso (GD) 5f 75 <
1996 May Bath (G-F) 5.1f 72
1999 Turf 0-10: (5f 3, 6f 6, 7f) (sft, gd, g-f 3, frm 4, hrd) 1999 AW 0-1: (5f) (Fibr)
Moderate filly, effective 6 to 7f, best at 6f, acts on g-s to frm, has worn blinkers. Turf high 42.
**D W Chapman [0-33] David Chapman (from C A Dwyer [2-14] Spt 1997).*

PETIT MARQUIS (FR) RR 78f 3361[2]
2 b c Lost World (IRE) - Ephemeride (USA) (Al Nasr (FR)) 9.3f **(68)**
Form - 2
Record 1999 - 1st:0 2nd:1 3rd:0 Ran:1
Win Prizemoney £0 *Total Prizemoney* £816
1999 Turf 0-1: (6f) (g-f)
Currently above-average colt. (1st run) - 2nd of 13 to Trinculo (4 Aug Leicester 6f g-f RF 3361). **J R Fanshawe [0-1] Miss A Church.*

PETIT PALAIS (IRE) BHB 55f44a **RR 62f 44a** 2650[8]
3 gr g Paris House 5.9f **(64)** - Renzola (Dragonara Palace (USA)) 6.1f **(55)**
Form - 0180008
Record 1999 - 1st:1 2nd:0 3rd:0 Ran:7
Pre1999 - 1st:0 2nd:0 3rd:0 Ran:1
Win Prizemoney £2,110 *Total Prizemoney* £2,110
Wins 1999 Apr Nottin (HVY) S 6.1f 62 <
1999 Turf 1-5: (6f 1-3, 8f 2) (g-s 2, gd 1-1, g-f, frm) 1999 AW 0-2: (6f 2) (Fibr 2)
Scopey, average gelding, effective 6f, acts on gd, mostly wears blinkers (effectively). Turf high 62 - 1st of 14 getting 1lb from Lament (27 Apr Nottingham RF 0865). AW high 28.
**P D Evans [0-5] Paul Green (Huyton) (from B J Meehan [1-3] Apr 1999).*

PETRACO (IRE) BHB 37f39a **RR 41f 39a** 2496[16]
11 b g Petorius 8f **(66)** - Merrie Moira (Bold Lad (IRE)) 8.4f **(68)**
Form - 70020
Record 1999 - 1st:0 2nd:1 3rd:0 Ran:5
Pre1999 - 1st:9 2nd:8 3rd:11 Ran:117
Win Prizemoney £29,738 *Total Prizemoney* £44,511
Wins * 1998 Jly Salisb (GD) CH 6f 42 45
* 1996 Spt Haydoc (GD) SH 6f 56 60
* 1995 Aug Pontef (G-F) H 5f 59 63
* 1995 Jun Leices (GD) SH 6f 55 62
1999 Turf 0-3: (5f, 6f 2) (gd, frm 2) 1999 AW 0-2: (6f 2) (Fibr 2)
Moderate gelding, effective 5 to 6f, best at 6f, acts on gd to frm - acts on Fibr, has worn blinkers. Turf high 27. AW high 26.
**N A Smith [6-88] Mrs Penny Day (from L J Codd [3-35] May 1993).*

PETRA NOVA BHB 39f **RR 46f** 4723[8]
3 ch f First Trump - Spinner (Blue Cashmere) 6.4f **(54)**
Form - 060008508
Record 1999 - 1st:0 2nd:0 3rd:0 Ran:9
Pre1999 - 1st:0 2nd:1 3rd:0 Ran:4
Win Prizemoney £0 *Total Prizemoney* £1,493
1999 Turf 0-9: (5f 5, 6f 2, 7f 2) (gd 3, g-f, frm 3, hrd 2)
Strong, moderate filly. Turf high 52.
**R M Whitaker [0-13] Mrs Margaret Schofield.*

PETRIE BHB 58f56a **RR 63f 56a** 5064[2]
2 ch g Fraam - Canadian Capers (Ballacashtal (CAN)) 5.3f **(50)**
Form - 05542
Record 1999 - 1st:0 2nd:1 3rd:0 Ran:5
Win Prizemoney £0 *Total Prizemoney* £604
1999 Turf 0-5: (5f 2, 6f 2, 7f) (g-s, gd, g-f, frm 2)
Average gelding. Turf high 56 (began Jly).
**M R Channon [0-5] Peter Taplin.*

PETRISK BHB 30f **RR 10f** 5020[18]
2 b f Risk Me (FR) 8f **(53)** - Bernstein Bette **(35f 44a)** (Petong) 6.6f **(58)**
Form - 000
Record 1999 - 1st:0 2nd:0 3rd:0 Ran:3
1999 Turf 0-3: (6f 2, 8f) (gd, g-f 2)
Currently poor filly. Turf high 10. **T E Powell [0-3] Lawrence Pratt.*

PETROCELLI RR 100f 5201a[2]
2 b g
Form - 2
1999 Turf 0-1: (10f) (hvy)
Currently very useful gelding, always wears blinkers. (1st run) - 2nd of 7 giving 4lb to Goldamix (31 Oct Saint-Cloud 10f hvy RF 5201a). **Mme C Head in FR [0-1].*

PETROSELLI (IRE) RR 90f 4767a[3]
2 b c Grand Lodge (USA) - Will Be Blue (Darshaan) 9.9f **(84)**
Form - 233
1999 Turf 0-3: (8f 2, 9f) (hvy, gd)
Currently useful colt. Turf high 90 (began Aug).
**Mme C Head in FR [0-3].*

PETROVNA (IRE) BHB 65a **RR 71f** 2720[12]
3 ch f Petardia 8.2f **(58)** - Efficient Funding (IRE) (Entitled)
Form - 60800
Record 1999 - 1st:0 2nd:0 3rd:0 Ran:5
Pre1999 - 1st:1 2nd:1 3rd:0 Ran:5
Win Prizemoney £3,290 *Total Prizemoney* £4,499
Wins * 1998 Aug Windso (G-F) 5f 76 <
1999 Turf 0-4: (5f 2, 6f, 7f) (g-s, g-f 3) 1999 AW 0-1: (7f) (Fibr)
Workmanlike, above-average filly, effective 5f, acts on gd to hrd, has worn blinkers. Turf high 71. Becoming disappointing.
**P L Gilligan [1-10] Dr Susan Barnes.*

PETRUS (IRE) BHB 87f **RR 93f** 4915[17]
3 b c Perugino (USA) - Love With Honey (USA) (Full Pocket (USA)) 14.1f **(61)**
Form - 00103011660
Record 1999 - 1st:3 2nd:0 3rd:1 Ran:11
Pre1999 - 1st:0 2nd:0 3rd:0 Ran:4
Win Prizemoney £29,819 *Total Prizemoney* £32,423
Wins * **1999** Jly Goodwo (FRM) H 7f 79 88 <
* **1999** Jly Yarmou (G-F) H 7f 73 80
* **1999** May Kempto (G-F) H 7f 68 73
1999 Turf 3-11: (7f 3-9, 8f 2) (sft, gd 1-5, g-f 1-3, frm 1-1, hrd)
Scopey, useful colt, effective 7f, acts on g-f. Turf high 93 - also 1st of 16 getting 1lb from Diamond Decorum (30 Jly Goodwood RF 3233). A winner three times over seven furlongs on fast ground so far last season including a valuable handicap at Glorious Goodwood, he has faced some stiff tasks since and not quite been up to it. **C E Brittain [3-15] C E Brittain.*

PETRUSHKA (IRE) RR 89++f 4812[1]
2 ch f Unfuwain (USA) 11.4f **(74)** - Ballet Shoes (IRE) (Ela-Mana-Mou) 10.1f **(70)**
Form - 1
Record 1999 - 1st:1 2nd:0 3rd:0 Ran:1
Win Prizemoney £3,785 *Total Prizemoney* £3,785
Wins * **1999** Oct Leices (G-S) 7f 89++ <
1999 Turf 1-1: (7f 1-1) (gd 1-1)
Currently useful filly. (1st run) - 1st of 19 from Shamah (11 Oct Leicester RF 4812). Winner of a Leicester maiden, she looks an interesting prospect.
**Sir Michael Stoute [1-1] Highclere Thoroughbred Racing Ltd.*

PETTY FRANCE (IRE) BHB 60f **RR 71df** 4160[6]
3 b br f Petardia 8.2f **(58)** - Business Centre (IRE) (Digamist (USA))
Form - 46
Record 1999 - 1st:0 2nd:0 3rd:0 Ran:2
Pre1999 - 1st:0 2nd:1 3rd:0 Ran:1
Win Prizemoney £0 *Total Prizemoney* £1,002
1999 Turf 0-2: (6f, 8f) (frm 2)

Neat, currently above-average filly. Turf high 53 (began Jly).
**J A R Toller [0-3] Racing Options.*

PETUNTSE BHB 40f **RR 38f** 4338[8]

5 b g Phountzi (USA) 9.6f **(60)** - Alipampa (IRE) (Glenstal (USA)) 10.1f **(64)**
Form - 6058
Record 1999 - 1st:0 2nd:0 3rd:0 Ran:4
Pre1999 - 1st:1 2nd:1 3rd:1 Ran:9
Win Prizemoney £2,250 *Total Prizemoney* £3,265
Wins 1998 Jun Yarmou (G-F) SH 8f 38 48+ <
1999 Turf 0-4: (7f, 10f 3) (g-s, g-f 3)
Very moderate gelding, effective 8 to 10f, acts on frm, has worn blinkers. Turf high 40. Consistent.
**R G Frost [0-7] Terry Sanders (from J Pearce [1-4] Jun 1998).*

PETURA (IRE) BHB 48f **RR 39f** 5007[16]

3 br g Petardia 8.2f **(58)** - Roman Heights (IRE) (Head for Heights) 9.6f **(55)**
Form - 000
Record 1999 - 1st:0 2nd:0 3rd:0 Ran:3
Pre1999 - 1st:0 2nd:0 3rd:0 Ran:4
Win Prizemoney £0 *Total Prizemoney* £598
1999 Turf 0-3: (9f, 10f 2) (gd 2, frm)
Scopey, very moderate gelding. Turf high 39 (began Oct).
**J S Wainwright [0-7] Mrs Mary Moloney.*

PHANTOM STAR (IRE) BHB 47f **RR 57f** 4900[5]

2 b c Foxhound (USA) - Une Parisienne (FR) (Bolkonski) 7.6f **(64)**
Form - 05040575
Record 1999 - 1st:0 2nd:0 3rd:0 Ran:8
1999 Turf 0-8: (6f 2, 7f 6) (gd 2, g-f 2, frm 3, hrd)
Fair colt, often wears blinkers. Turf high 57.
**Mrs A E Johnson [0-1] Mrs S N J Embiricos (from N Tinkler [0-7] Aug 1999).*

PHANTOM THREEONINE BHB 38f **RR 36f** 2054[17]

3 ch f Hatim (USA) 7.8f **(56)** - Glenrock Dancer (IRE) **(32f)** (Glenstal (USA)) 10.1f **(64)**
Form - 550
Record 1999 - 1st:0 2nd:0 3rd:0 Ran:3
Pre1999 - 1st:0 2nd:0 3rd:0 Ran:8
1999 Turf 0-3: (9f, 10f, 11f) (g-f 3)
Lengthy, very moderate filly, has worn blinkers. Turf high 36. Inconsistent. **W T Kemp [0-11] A J Thurgood.*

PHANTOM WATERS BHB 63f **RR 67f** 4693[9]

4 b f Pharly (FR) 11.5f **(64)** - Idle Waters (Mill Reef (USA)) 10.5f **(78)**
Form - 40034305370
Record 1999 - 1st:0 2nd:0 3rd:3 Ran:11
Pre1999 - 1st:2 2nd:2 3rd:0 Ran:15
Win Prizemoney £10,260 *Total Prizemoney* £15,851
Wins * 1998 Jly Bright (GD) H 11.9f 74 76 <
*** 1998** May Chepst (G-F) H 12.1f 63 68
1999 Turf 0-11: (12f 7, 13f, 14f 3) (sft, g-s, g-f 3, frm 6)
Workmanlike, average filly, effective 12 to 14f, best at 12f, acts on gd to frm, likes left handed tracks, likes tight tracks. Turf high 67 - 3rd of 13 giving 5lb to Shahrur (8 Spt Kempton 14f frm RF 4218). Consistent. **R F JohnsonHoughton [2-26] R Crutchley.*

PHARAOH'S HOUSE (IRE) BHB 55f **RR 63f** 4640[10]

2 b c Desert Style (IRE) - Cellatica (USA) (Sir Ivor) 10.2f **(70)**
Form - 033000
Record 1999 - 1st:0 2nd:0 3rd:2 Ran:6
Win Prizemoney £0 *Total Prizemoney* £1,124
1999 Turf 0-6: (5f, 6f 3, 7f 2) (gd 5, frm)
Average colt, has worn blinkers. Turf high 63.
**T D Easterby [0-6] P England.*

PHARLY REEF BHB 40f30a **RR 46f 30a** 2444[7]

7 b g Pharly (FR) 11.5f **(64)** - Hay Reef (Mill Reef (USA)) 10.5f **(78)**
Form - 547
Record 1999 - 1st:0 2nd:0 3rd:0 Ran:3
Pre1999 - 1st:0 2nd:0 3rd:0 Ran:10
Win Prizemoney £0 *Total Prizemoney* £261
1999 Turf 0-3: (10f, 12f 2) (g-s, g-f, frm)
Moderate gelding, has worn blinkers. Turf high 46 - 4th of 10 getting 16lb from Musician (15 Jun Thirsk 12f frm RF 2005). Inconsistent.
**D Burchell [2-24] Vivian Guy (from I A Balding [0-5] Jly 1995).*

PHARMACIST (IRE) **RR 97f** 3886a[14]

3 b f Machiavellian (USA) 9.8f **(83)** - Pharaoh's Delight (Fairy King (USA)) 7.7f **(59)**
Form - 3280
1999 Turf 0-4: (5f, 6f 3) (gd 3, g-f)
Very useful filly, effective 5 to 6f, best at 6f, acts on gd to g-f, best on g-f, has worn blinkers. Turf high 97 - 2nd of 14 giving 3lb to Timote (11 Jly Curragh 5f g-f RF 2801a). She falls short of Group class and proved difficult to place. Unhappy on soft ground, she is unlikely to improve. **D K Weld in IRE [1-7] Ballylinch Stud.*

PHASE EIGHT GIRL BHB 38f **RR 38f** 3478[3]

3 b f Warrshan (USA) 9.7f **(59)** - Bugsy's Sister (Aragon) 8.1f **(60)**
Form - 887313
Record 1999 - 1st:1 2nd:0 3rd:2 Ran:6
Pre1999 - 1st:0 2nd:0 3rd:0 Ran:4
Win Prizemoney £2,460 *Total Prizemoney* £3,362
Wins * 1999 Jly Beverl (G-F) SH 12f 25 33 <
1999 Turf 1-6: (10f 2, 12f 1-2, 16f 2) (gd 3, g-f, frm 1-2)
Very moderate filly, effective 12 to 16f, best at 16f, acts on gd to frm, prefers tight tracks. Turf high 38 - 3rd of 16 getting 13lb from Pleasant Mount (9 Aug Thirsk 16f gd RF 3478) - also 1st of 14 getting 3lb from Nom Francais (27 Jly Beverley RF 3158).
**J Hetherton [1-10] Peter Urquhart.*

PHAYUHA KIRI LOVE BHB 30a **RR 23f 30a** 235[10]

4 b g Pursuit of Love 9.5f **(69)** - My Moody Girl (IRE) (Alzao (USA)) 7.1f **(68)**
Form - 0
Record 1999 - 1st:0 2nd:0 3rd:0 Ran:1
Pre1999 - 1st:0 2nd:0 3rd:0 Ran:2
Win Prizemoney £0 *Total Prizemoney* £251
1999 AW 0-1: (12f) (Equi)
Strong, little account gelding. (DEAD)
**B R Johnson [0-1] Mrs S Scott (from A G Newcombe [0-2] Jun 1998).*

PHEISTY BHB 75f **RR 70f** 4034[7]

2 b f Faustus (USA) 9.1f **(54)** - Phlirty (Pharly (FR)) 9.8f **(68)**
Form - 13607
Record 1999 - 1st:1 2nd:0 3rd:1 Ran:5
Win Prizemoney £2,388 *Total Prizemoney* £2,739
Wins * 1999 Apr Leices (GD) 5f 70 <
1999 Turf 1-5: (5f 1-4, 6f) (gd 1-4, g-f)
Above-average filly. Turf high 70 (1st run) - 1st of 13 getting 5lb from Bold State (8 Apr Leicester RF 0622).
**R F JohnsonHoughton [1-5] Woodway Racing.*

PHILAGAIN BHB 25f **RR** 4907[13]

2 b f Ardkinglass 5f **(64)** - Andalucia (Rheingold) 10.4f **(62)**
Form - 000
Record 1999 - 1st:0 2nd:0 3rd:0 Ran:3
1999 Turf 0-3: (8f 3) (gd 2, frm)
Currently very poor filly. Turf high 6 (began Spt).
**J Hetherton [0-3] C D Barber-Lomax.*

PHILANTHA (USA) **RR 80f** 4681[1]

2 b f Woodman (USA) 9.7f **(77)** - Tiger Flower (Sadler's Wells (USA)) 10f **(76)**
Form - 1
Record 1999 - 1st:1 2nd:0 3rd:0 Ran:1
Win Prizemoney £5,390 *Total Prizemoney* £5,390
Wins * 1999 Oct Newmar (SFT) 6f 80 <
1999 Turf 1-1: (6f 1-1) (gd 1-1)
Currently decent filly. (1st run) - 1st of 11 from Double Platinum (2 Oct Newmarket RF 4681). **J H M Gosden [1-1] Sheikh Mohammed.*

PHILATELIC LADY (IRE) BHB 79f **RR 79f** 5197[1]

3 ch f Pips Pride 6.7f **(70)** - Gold Stamp (Golden Act (USA)) 8.8f **(67)**
Form - 2151280421
Record 1999 - 1st:2 2nd:2 3rd:0 Ran:7
Pre1999 - 1st:1 2nd:1 3rd:0 Ran:5
Win Prizemoney £13,414 *Total Prizemoney* £17,073
Wins * 1999 Nov Windso (G-S) H 10f 74 79 <

* 1999	Jun Lingfi	(G-S)	H	10f	70	73	
* 1998	*Nov Lingfi*	*(STD)*		*8f*		*74*	

1999 Turf 2-7: (9f, 10f 2-4, 12f 2) (g-s 1-1, gd 1-2, g-f 2, frm 2)
Neat, above-average filly, effective 8 to 12f, best at 10f, acts on g-s to frm - acts on Equi, best on gd, prefers tight tracks, and excels at Windsor. Turf high 79 - 1st of 20 getting 2lb from Spring Pursuit (4 Nov Windsor RF 5197) - also 1st of 8 getting 4lb from Elba Magic (2 Jun Lingfield RF 1684).
**M J Haynes [3-12] Bob Pettis, Gordon F Haynes.*

PHILISTAR BHB 59f75a RR 61f 75a 5053[5]

6 ch h Bairn (USA) 9.4f **(55)** - Philgwyn (Milford) 9f **(61)**
Form - 513528708760063355355

Record	**1999** -	1st:1	2nd:1	3rd:4	Ran:20
	Pre1999 -	1st:8	2nd:4	3rd:6	Ran:50

Win Prizemoney £59,121 *Total Prizemoney* £79,050

Wins							
* 1999	*Jan Lingfi*	*(STD)*	*H*	*10f*	*70*	*75*	
* 1998	Jun Epsom	(GD)	H	8.5f	75	81	<
* 1998	*Apr Lingfi*	*(STD)*	*H*	*7f*	*67*	*71*	
* 1998	*Feb Lingfi*	*(SLW)*		*7f*		*70*	
* 1997	Jun Bright	(FRM)		10f		70	
* 1997	Jun Hamilt	(GD)	H	8.3f	60	70	
* 1997	Jun Epsom	(GD)	H	8.5f	65	77	
* 1997	Jun Newcas	(FRM)		9f		61	
1996	*Jly Lingfi*	*(STD)*	*H*	*10f*	*60*	*65*	

1999 Turf 0-15: (7f, 8f 3, 9f 5, 10f 6) (g-s 2, gd 5, g-f 3, frm 4, hrd) 1999 AW 1-5: (8f, 10f 1-4) (Equi 1-5)
Above-average horse, effective 7 to 10f, best at 9f, acts on gd to frm - acts on Equi, best on gd, has worn blinkers, likes left handed tracks, likes tight tracks, and does well at Lingfield. Turf high 70. AW high 75 (1st run) - 1st of 9 giving 10lb to Key To The City (12 Jan Lingfield RF 0083).
**K R Burke [8-54] Nigel Shields (from J M P Eustace [1-17] May 1997).*

PHILMIST BHB 47f42a RR 48df 42a 2396[4]

7 b m Hard Fought 8.9f **(51)** - Andalucia (Rheingold) 10.4f **(62)**
Form - 81323164

Record	**1999** -	1st:2	2nd:1	3rd:2	Ran:8
	Pre1999 -	1st:6	2nd:6	3rd:5	Ran:51

Win Prizemoney £21,668 *Total Prizemoney* £31,993

Wins							
* **1999**	Jun Hamilt	(GD)	H	13f	46	48	
* **1999**	May Hamilt	(G-F)	SH	12.1f	37	40	
* 1998	Aug Hamilt	(SFT)	S	12.1f		47+	
* 1997	Spt Ayr	(G-S)	H	10.9f	45	50	<
* 1997	Aug Hamilt	(GD)	H	11.1f	40	48	
* 1997	Jly Hamilt	(G-S)	H	11.1f	40	40	
1996	*May Southw*	*(STD)*	*H*	*11f*	*48*	*50*	<
1995	*Jly Southw*	*(STD)*	*H*	*12f*	*48*	*49*	

1999 Turf 2-8: (11f 2, 12f 1-3, 13f 1-3) (hvy, g-s, gd 2, g-f 2-3, hrd)
Fair mare, effective 12 to 13f, acts on gd to g-f, mostly wears blinkers, likes right handed tracks. Turf high 48 - 1st of 8 getting 10lb from Spartan Royale (16 Jun Hamilton RF 2050). Consistent. She always runs in Scotland, mainly at Hamilton, and can win modest races over a mile and a half.
**Miss L A Perratt [6-29] T P Finch (from J Hetherton [0-9] Feb 1997).*

PHILOSOPHIC BHB 49f64a RR 48f 64a 1282[7]

5 b g Be My Chief (USA) 10.2f **(62)** - Metaphysique (FR) (Law Society (USA)) 9.9f **(70)**
Form - 3676207

Record	**1999** -	1st:0	2nd:1	3rd:1	Ran:7
	Pre1999 -	1st:6	2nd:4	3rd:3	Ran:25

Win Prizemoney £16,612 *Total Prizemoney* £23,780

Wins							
* 1998	Spt Folkes	(G-F)	H	15.4f	46	48	
* 1998	*Aug Lingfi*	*(STD)*	*H*	*16f*	*69*	*73*	<
* 1998	*Jly Wolver*	*(STD)*	*H*	*14.8f*	*66*	*69*	
* 1998	*Mar Lingfi*	*(SLW)*	*H*	*16f*	*53*	*65*	
* 1998	*Feb Lingfi*	*(SLW)*	*H*	*16f*	*53*	*59+*	
* 1998	*Jan Lingfi*	*(STD)*	*H*	*13f*	*48*	*49*	

1999 Turf 0-1: (14f) (frm) 1999 AW 0-6: (12f, 13f, 15f, 16f 3) (Equi 3, Fibr 3)
Average gelding, has broken blood-vessels, effective 12 to 16f, - acts on AW, best on Fibr, likes left handed tracks, excels at Wolverhampton, does well at Lingfield. AW high 64.
**Mrs L C Jewell [6-24] Gallagher Equine Ltd (from Sir Mark Prescott [0-9] Oct 1997).*

PHOEBE BUFFAY (IRE) BHB 77f79a RR 75f 79a 4895[15]

2 b f Petardia 8.2f **(58)** - Art Duo (Artaius (USA)) 9f **(69)**
Form - 221270

Record	**1999** -	1st:1	2nd:3	3rd:0	Ran:6

Win Prizemoney £2,262 *Total Prizemoney* £8,466

Wins						
* 1999	*Jly Southw*	*(STD)*	*6f*		*72*	<

1999 Turf 0-4: (6f 2, 7f 2) (gd 3, frm) 1999 AW 1-2: (6f 1-2) (Fibr 1-2)
Above-average filly, effective 6f, acts on frm - acts on Fibr, has worn blinkers. Turf high 75 - 2nd of 13 getting 5lb from Kashra (28 Aug Newmarket 6f frm RF 3966). AW high 75 (1st run) - 2nd of 10 giving 4lb to Islay Mist (5 Jun Wolverhampton 6f Fibr RF 1778) - also 1st of 9 getting 5lb from Cruising (8 Jly Southwell RF 2651). Showed ability in her first two starts and gained many friends when getting off the mark on the Southwell Fibresand in July. She ran a blinder behind Kashra in a valuable nursery at Newmarket, but was a little disappointing in a similar event at Doncaster.
**C N Allen [1-6] Newmarket Connections Ltd.*

PHOEBUS BHB 64f68a RR 56f 68a 5144[4]

2 b c Piccolo - Slava (USA) (Diesis) 9.3f **(69)**
Form - 0004

Record	**1999** -	1st:0	2nd:0	3rd:0	Ran:4

1999 Turf 0-3: (7f 3) (gd 3) 1999 AW 0-1: (6f) (Fibr)
Average colt. Turf high 56 (began Spt).
**W R Muir [0-4] Duncan Wiltshire.*

PHOTOFIRST RR 2715[9]

6 ch g Derrylin 12.7f **(38)** - Fedelm (Celtic Cone) 9.8f **(43)**
Form - 0

Record	**1999** -	1st:0	2nd:0	3rd:0	Ran:1

1999 Turf 0-1: (14f) (frm)
Formerly very poor gelding. **R M Flower [0-2] Photofinish.*

PHYLOZZO BHB 40f35a RR 41f 35a 205[9]

3 ch f Michelozzo (USA) - Phyllida Fox (Healaugh Fox) 10f **(46)**
Form - 67540

Record	**1999** -	1st:0	2nd:0	3rd:0	Ran:3
	Pre1999 -	1st:0	2nd:0	3rd:0	Ran:4

1999 AW 0-3: (7f, 8f 2) (Equi 2, Fibr)
Leggy, moderate filly. AW high 36.
**P D Evans [0-7] Mrs C W Middleton.*

PIAF BHB 42f RR 39f 5056[3]

3 b f Pursuit of Love 9.5f **(69)** - Pippas Song (Reference Point) 6.8f **(70)**
Form - 0640083

Record	**1999** -	1st:0	2nd:0	3rd:1	Ran:7
	Pre1999 -	1st:0	2nd:0	3rd:0	Ran:3

Win Prizemoney £0 *Total Prizemoney* £396

1999 Turf 0-6: (8f, 10f 3, 12f 2) (hvy, g-f, frm 4) 1999 AW 0-1: (10f) (Equi)
Well made, moderate filly, effective 10f, acts on frm, has worn blinkers, likes tight tracks. Turf high 58 - 4th of 13 giving 7lb to Karakul (21 Jun Windsor 10f frm RF 2177). Consistent.
**B W Hills [0-10] S P Tindall.*

PICCADILLY BHB 37f RR 39f 1723[7]

4 ch f Belmez (USA) 11.4f **(65)** - Polly's Pear (USA) (Sassafras (FR)) 9.6f **(69)**
Form - 1007

Record	**1999** -	1st:1	2nd:0	3rd:0	Ran:4
	Pre1999 -	1st:0	2nd:0	3rd:2	Ran:13

Win Prizemoney £2,368 *Total Prizemoney* £3,595

Wins							
* **1999**	Apr Ripon	(G-F)	SH	12.3f	35	39	<

1999 Turf 1-4: (10f, 12f 1-2, 14f) (gd, g-f 1-1, frm 2)
Workmanlike, very moderate filly, effective 12f, acts on gd, has worn blinkers. Turf high 39 (1st run). Inconsistent.
**Miss Kate Milligan [1-4] S Ward (from T J Etherington [0-13] Oct 1998).*

PICCATA RR 29f 3980[10]

2 b c Piccolo - Katya (IRE) **(93f)** (Dancing Dissident (USA))
Form - 00

Record	**1999** -	1st:0	2nd:0	3rd:0	Ran:2

1999 Turf 0-2: (5f, 6f) (g-s, frm)
Currently little account colt. Turf high 29 (began Aug).
**M R Channon [0-2] John Mitchell.*

PICCOLA BELLA BHB 28f **RR** 3641[12]

3 b f Picea 12.7f **(43)** - Blushing Belle (Local Suitor (USA)) 8.4f **(67)**
Form - 800
Record 1999 - 1st:0 2nd:0 3rd:0 Ran:3
1999 Turf 0-3: (10f, 12f, 14f) (g-f 3)
Unfurnished, currently very poor filly.
**J G Portman [0-3] Christopher Shankland.*

PICCOLO CATIVO BHB 43f44a **RR 42f 44a** 4832[8]

4 b f Komaite (USA) 6.9f **(61)** - Malcesine (IRE) **(38f 31a)** (Auction Ring (USA)) 8.6f **(65)**
Form - 815058082504508
Record 1999 - 1st:1 2nd:1 3rd:0 Ran:14
Pre1999 - 1st:3 2nd:2 3rd:0 Ran:22
Win Prizemoney £11,901 *Total Prizemoney* £15,859
Wins * **1999** Apr Catter (SFT) 6f 58
* 1998 Jun Carlis (G-S) H 5f 60 64
* 1998 May Hamilt (GD) H 5f 54 55
1997 *May Southw (STD) 5f 68* <
1999 Turf 1-14: (5f 4, 6f 1-8, 7f 2) (sft, g-s, gd 1-1, g-f 6, frm 5)
Strong, moderate filly, effective 5 to 6f, best at 5f, acts on g-s to g-f, best on gd, and excels at Carlisle. Turf high 58 (1st run) - 1st of 14 getting 3lb from Blushing Grenadier (21 Apr Catterick RF 0790). Consistent.
**Mrs G S Rees [3-31] J W Gittins (from Capt J Wilson [1-5] Jan 1998).*

PICEA'S PAST **RR** 127[9]

5 b g Picea 12.7f **(43)** - Atoka (March Past)
Form - 0
Record 1999 - 1st:0 2nd:0 3rd:0 Ran:1
1999 AW 0-1: (8f) (Fibr)
Formerly very poor gelding. **J Neville [0-6] J Neville.*

PICHON BARON (USA) BHB 36f **RR 16f** 2056[18]

4 ch g Zilzal (USA) 8.5f **(79)** - Flora Lady (USA) (Track Barron (USA))
Form - 00
Record 1999 - 1st:0 2nd:0 3rd:0 Ran:1
Pre1999 - 1st:0 2nd:0 3rd:0 Ran:7
Win Prizemoney £0 *Total Prizemoney* £403
1999 Turf 0-1: (8f) (g-f)
Leggy, poor gelding. Becoming disappointing.
**Andrew Reid [0-3] A S Reid (from M J Ryan [0-4] Dec 1998).*

PICKENS (USA) BHB 60f63a **RR 51f 63a** 279[4]

7 b g Theatrical 11.5f **(78)** - Alchi (USA) (Alleged (USA)) 10f **(76)**
Form - 26814
Record 1999 - 1st:1 2nd:0 3rd:0 Ran:4
Pre1999 - 1st:6 2nd:4 3rd:1 Ran:26
Win Prizemoney £15,180 *Total Prizemoney* £18,051
Wins * **1999** *Feb Southw (STD) S 11f 62*
* 1998 *Feb Southw (STD) H 12f* 54 *66+* <
* 1998 *Feb Southw (STD) S 11f 52*
* 1998 *Jan Southw (STD) S 11f 53*
* 1998 *Jan Southw (STD) S 12f 55+*
* 1997 Oct Redcar (G-F) C 11f 41
1996 Jly Beverl (G-F) S 12f 52
1999 AW 1-4: (11f 1-3, 12f) (Fibr 1-4)
Average gelding, effective 11 to 12f, best at 12f, - acts on Fibr, has worn blinkers. AW high 62 - 1st of 16 from Joseph's Wine (5 Feb Southwell RF 0232).
**Don Enrico Incisa [6-23] Don Enrico Incisa (from N Tinkler [2-16] Nov 1996).*

PICK OF AFFECTION BHB 74f **RR 76df** 3448[13]

3 gr c Salse (USA) 10.9f **(71)** - High Matinee (Shirley Heights) 10.3f **(74)**
Form - 30
Record 1999 - 1st:0 2nd:0 3rd:1 Ran:2
Pre1999 - 1st:0 2nd:0 3rd:0 Ran:2
Win Prizemoney £0 *Total Prizemoney* £594
1999 Turf 0-2: (12f 2) (gd, frm)
Lengthy, above-average colt. Turf high 76 (began Jly).
**E A L Dunlop [0-4] H R H Sultan Ahmad Shah.*

PICOLETTE BHB 59f53a **RR 60f 53a** 5023[14]

2 ch f Piccolo - Poyle Jezebelle **(50f)** (Sharpo) 7.7f **(59)**
Form - 04570
Record 1999 - 1st:0 2nd:0 3rd:0 Ran:5
Win Prizemoney £0 *Total Prizemoney* £247
1999 Turf 0-4: (5f, 6f 2, 7f) (sft, gd, g-f, frm) 1999 AW 0-1: (6f) (Equi)
Average filly. Turf high 60. **W R Muir [0-5] Dulverton Equine.*

PICOT BHB 83f **RR 74f** 5054[1]

2 b br f Piccolo - Special Guest (Be My Guest (USA)) 9.3f **(67)**
Form - 831
Record 1999 - 1st:1 2nd:0 3rd:1 Ran:3
Win Prizemoney £2,700 *Total Prizemoney* £3,305
Wins * **1999** Oct Leices (SFT) 6f 74 <
1999 Turf 1-3: (6f 1-3) (gd 1-1, g-f 2)
Currently above-average filly. Turf high 74 (began Aug) - 1st of 13 from Branston Fizz (25 Oct Leicester RF 5054).
**H Candy [1-3] Major M G Wyatt.*

PICTURE PUZZLE BHB 72f **RR 71f** 4578[6]

3 b f Royal Academy (USA) 7.8f **(77)** - Cloudslea (USA) (Chief's Crown (USA)) 9.8f **(72)**
Form - 41168616
Record 1999 - 1st:3 2nd:0 3rd:0 Ran:8
Pre1999 - 1st:0 2nd:0 3rd:0 Ran:1
Win Prizemoney £12,452 *Total Prizemoney* £12,452
Wins * **1999** Spt Newcas (G-F) H 8f 68 71
* **1999** May Yarmou (FRM) H 8f 68 72 <
* **1999** May Thirsk (G-F) 7f 59
1999 Turf 3-8: (7f 1-4, 8f 2-4) (gd 4, g-f 2-2, frm 1-2)
Leggy, above-average filly, effective 8f, acts on g-f to frm. Turf high 72 - 1st of 15 giving 2lb to Untold Riches (26 May Yarmouth RF 1509) - also 1st of 11 getting 13lb from Downland (19 Spt Newcastle RF 4426). **W J Haggas [3-9] M H Wilson.*

PICULA BIERE (IRE) BHB 28f **RR 33f** 873[9]

4 ch g Balla Cove - Loreo (IRE) (Lord Chancellor (USA))
Form - 0
Record 1999 - 1st:0 2nd:0 3rd:0 Ran:1
Pre1999 - 1st:0 2nd:0 3rd:0 Ran:4
1999 Turf 0-1: (12f) (gd)
Leggy, very moderate gelding, has worn blinkers.
**N M Babbage [0-9] David James.*

PIERPOINT (IRE) BHB 70f67a **RR 69f 67a** 4911[10]

4 ch g Archway (IRE) 8.5f **(60)** - Lavinia (Habitat) 9.4f **(70)**
Form - 00005761311000
Record 1999 - 1st:3 2nd:0 3rd:1 Ran:14
Pre1999 - 1st:2 2nd:5 3rd:2 Ran:19
Win Prizemoney £15,553 *Total Prizemoney* £23,244
Wins * **1999** Aug Pontef (GD) H 6f 68 69
* **1999** Aug Redcar (FRM) H 6f 60 65
* **1999** *Jun Southw (STD) H 6f 60 64*
1997 Jly Hamilt (G-F) H 5f 78 <
1997 Jun Hamilt (G-F) C 5f 69+
1999 Turf 2-12: (5f 3, 6f 2-5, 7f 3, 8f) (gd 4, g-f 2, frm 2-5, hrd) 1999 AW 1-2: (6f 1-2) (Fibr 1-2)
Scopey, average gelding, effective 6 to 8f, best at 7f, acts on gd to frm, best on gd, has worn blinkers (effectively), likes left handed tracks, prefers tight tracks, excels at Chester. Turf high 69 - 1st of 18 giving 8lb to Russian Romeo (16 Aug Pontefract RF 3678). AW high 64 (1st run). Another testament to his trainer's skill with three victories last summer.
**D Nicholls [3-21] J H Knight (from R A Fahey [2-12] Jun 1998).*

PIGEON BHB 68f73a **RR 70f 73a** 2463[15]

4 b f Casteddu 7.4f **(54)** - Wigeon (Divine Gift) 6.6f **(57)**
Form - 70008800270
Record 1999 - 1st:0 2nd:1 3rd:0 Ran:11
Pre1999 - 1st:4 2nd:4 3rd:3 Ran:23
Win Prizemoney £12,181 *Total Prizemoney* £21,722
Wins * 1998 Spt Cheste (GD) H 5.1f 74 78 <
* 1998 Jun Catter (G-S) H 6f 58 71
* 1998 May Catter (SFT) H 6f 58 71
* 1997 May Catter (G-F) S 6f 63
1999 Turf 0-10: (5f 3, 6f 6, 7f) (g-s, gd 6, frm 2, hrd) 1999 AW 0-1: (6f) (Fibr)
Leggy, above-average filly, effective 5 to 6f, best at 5f, acts on gd to frm, best on g-f, likes left handed tracks, likes tight tracks, does well at Ripon, likes Catterick. Turf high 70 - 2nd of 22 getting 7lb

from Grey Kingdom (12 Jun York 6f gd RF 1964).
**D W Barker [4-34] D W Barker.*

PIGGY BANK BHB 60f57a **RR 58f 57a** 4986[4]

3 b f Emarati (USA) 6.6f **(63)** - Granny's Bank (Music Boy) 6.8f **(57)**
Form - 000454100004
Record 1999 - 1st:1 2nd:0 3rd:0 Ran:12
Pre1999 - 1st:1 2nd:2 3rd:0 Ran:12
Win Prizemoney £9,483 *Total Prizemoney* £12,871
Wins * 1999 Jly Ripon (GD) H 6f 61 62
* 1998 Oct Haydoc (SFT) H 5f 60 66 <
1999 Turf 1-12: (5f 10, 6f 1-2) (gd 1-7, g-f 3, frm, hrd)
Tall, fair filly, effective 5 to 6f, best at 5f, acts on sft to gd, best on gd. Turf high 62 - 1st of 13 getting 8lb from Get Stuck In (5 Jly Ripon RF 2564). **M W Easterby [2-24] Stephen Curtis.*

PILGRIM'S WAY (USA) RR 80df 3975[11]

3 br f Gone West (USA) 7.8f **(82)** - Marling (IRE) (Lomond (USA)) 8.8f **(65)**
Form - 21130
Record 1999 - 1st:2 2nd:1 3rd:1 Ran:5
Win Prizemoney £8,097 *Total Prizemoney* £10,262
Wins * 1999 Jly Doncas (G-F) H 8f 76 80 <
* **1999** Jly Carlis (FRM) 6.9f 58+
1999 Turf 2-5: (6f, 7f 1-1, 8f 1-3) (sft, g-f, frm 2-3)
Workmanlike, decent filly. Turf high 80 - 1st of 7 getting 3lb from Mirbeck (28 Jly Doncaster RF 3198). She was off the track for three months after her debut, but came back to win in game style at Carlisle and Doncaster. Handles fast ground very well.
**Sir Mark Prescott [2-5] Sir Edmund Loder.*

PILLAGER RR 7f 4929[10]

2 b c Reprimand 8.2f **(63)** - Emerald Ring (Auction Ring (USA)) 8.6f **(65)**
Form - 0
Record 1999 - 1st:0 2nd:0 3rd:0 Ran:1
1999 Turf 0-1: (6f) (g-f)
Currently very poor colt. **Mrs A J Bowlby [0-1] Mrs J Pitman.*

PILLAR ROCK (USA) RR 93f 3720a[2]

3 b c Alysheba (USA) 12.1f **(78)** - Butterscotch Sauce (USA)
Form - 18422
1999 Turf 1-5: (7f 1-2, 8f, 10f, 11f) (g-s 1-1, gd, g-f, frm 2)
Useful colt, effective 7 to 11f, acts on g-s to frm, best on frm. Turf high 95 (1st run) - 1st from Creux Noir (2 May Gowran Park RF 1041a). He should stay a mile and a half and is tough without possessing much in the way of finishing speed.
**N Meade in IRE [1-8] D P Sharkey.*

PILOT'S HARBOUR BHB 55f **RR 31f** 5190[14]

3 b c Distant Relative 7f **(69)** - Lillemor (Connaught) 7.7f **(63)**
Form - 0508000
Record 1999 - 1st:0 2nd:0 3rd:0 Ran:7
Pre1999 - 1st:2 2nd:1 3rd:1 Ran:6
Win Prizemoney £9,359 *Total Prizemoney* £11,096
Wins 1998 Aug Newmar (G-F) H 8f 83 85 <
1998 Jly Beverl (GD) 7.5f 80
1999 Turf 0-7: (10f 3, 11f, 12f 2, 14f) (gd, g-f 3, frm 3)
Scopey, very moderate colt, effective 6 to 8f, best at 7f, acts on g-f to frm, best on g-f, has worn blinkers. Turf high 68. Becoming disappointing.
**D W Chapman [0-2] Alex Gorrie (from J L Dunlop [2-11] Aug 1999).*

PIMPINELLA (IRE) BHB 36f **RR 38f** 2054[11]

3 b f Reprimand 8.2f **(63)** - Lady Leman (Pitskelly) 8.5f **(53)**
Form - 6070
Record 1999 - 1st:0 2nd:0 3rd:0 Ran:4
1999 Turf 0-3: (8f, 10f 2) (g-s, g-f, frm) 1999 AW 0-1: (8f) (Fibr)
Leggy, very moderate filly. Turf high 38.
**B S Rothwell [0-4] Brian Rothwell.*

PINAKARAL (FR) RR 96f 935a[6]

3 b c Akarad (FR) 9.7f **(73)** - Pinaflore (FR) (Formidable (USA)) 9.2f **(63)**
Form - 6
1999 Turf 0-1: (8f) (g-s)
Currently very useful colt. **A Fabre in FR [0-1] J-L Lagardere.*

PINCHANINCH BHB 63f **RR 65f** 5049[7]

2 ch g Inchinor 8.9f **(64)** - Wollow Maid (Wollow) 8.2f **(61)**
Form - 587
Record 1999 - 1st:0 2nd:0 3rd:0 Ran:3
1999 Turf 0-3: (8f 3) (g-s, gd 2)
Currently average gelding. Turf high 65 (began Spt).
**J G Portman [0-3] A S B Portman.*

PINCHINCHA (FR) BHB 75f76a **RR 77f 76a** 5106[3]

5 b g Priolo (USA) 10.9f **(71)** - Western Heights (Shirley Heights) 10.3f **(74)**
Form - 6508248422023
Record 1999 - 1st:0 2nd:4 3rd:1 Ran:13
Pre1999 - 1st:4 2nd:3 3rd:2 Ran:22
Win Prizemoney £13,611 *Total Prizemoney* £33,813
Wins * 1997 Jun Pontef (G-F) H 10f 75 78 <
* 1997 May Doncas (G-S) 10.3f 71
* 1997 Apr Folkes (G-F) H 9.7f 65 67
* 1996 *Nov Southw (STD) S 8f* 72
1999 Turf 0-13: (9f, 10f 12) (sft, g-s 3, gd 2, g-f 3, frm 3, hrd)
Above-average gelding, effective 10f, acts on g-s to hrd, best on g-f, has worn blinkers, favours left handed tracks, likes tight tracks, excels at Doncaster and Yarmouth. Turf high 77 - 3rd of 7 giving 2lb to Caerau (27 Oct Yarmouth 10f g-s RF 5106). Consistent.
**D Morris [4-35] D & L Racing.*

PINE RIDGE LAD (IRE) BHB 47f47a **RR 46f 47a** 4076[5]

9 gr g Taufan (USA) 8.3f **(65)** - Rosserk (Roan Rocket) 7.8f **(57)**
Form - 006841700726305
Record 1999 - 1st:1 2nd:1 3rd:1 Ran:15
Pre1999 - 1st:16 2nd:15 3rd:12 Ran:102
Win Prizemoney £48,254 *Total Prizemoney* £68,864
Wins * 1999 *Apr Southw (STD) H 8f 44 57*
1998 May Redcar (GD) H 8f 57 62
1998 *Jan Southw (STD) S 7f 59+*
1997 Spt Hamilt (GD) H 8.3f 50 54
1996 Jly Cheste (G-F) H 7.6f 57 65
1996 Mar Beverl (GD) H 7.5f 54 63
1996 *Feb Wolver (STD) H 7f 79 79* <
1996 *Feb Southw (STD) H 8f 71 78*
1995 *Nov Southw (STD) C 8f 61*
1995 Jun Carlis (FRM) H 6.9f 53 56
1995 *Feb Southw (STD) C 7f 66*
1995 *Jan Southw (STD) C 6f 58*
1999 Turf 0-6: (8f 2, 10f 4) (gd, g-f 2, frm 3) 1999 AW 1-9: (7f 3, 8f 1-4, 9f, 12f) (Fibr 1-9)
Moderate gelding, has broken blood-vessels, effective 7 to 8f, best at 8f, acts on gd - acts on Fibr, has worn blinkers. Turf high 51. AW high 57 - 1st of 16 getting 7lb from Tom (26 Apr Southwell RF 0852). A fair performer on his day, he has only shown bits and pieces of form over the past year or so. Effective on turf and Fibresand, his recent victories have been under an amateur rider.
**J L Harris [1-15] Mrs Annette Harris (from J L Eyre [11-59] Jun 1998).*

PINHEIROS DREAM (IRE) BHB 72f **RR 66f** 4599[15]

2 ch f Grand Lodge (USA) - Nikki's Groom (Shy Groom (USA)) 10f **(66)**
Form - 8380
Record 1999 - 1st:0 2nd:0 3rd:1 Ran:4
Win Prizemoney £0 *Total Prizemoney* £426
1999 Turf 0-4: (6f 2, 7f 2) (g-f 3, frm)
Average filly. Turf high 66 (began Jly).
**B J Meehan [0-4] The Chantilly Partnership.*

PINK CORAL (IRE) RR 97f 2784a[10]

3 b f Sadler's Wells (USA) 11.3f **(87)** - Coral Fury (Mill Reef (USA)) 10.5f **(78)**
Form - 20380
1999 Turf 0-5: (8f 3, 10f, 12f) (g-s, gd, g-f 2, frm)
Very useful filly, effective 8f, acts on hvy to gd, has worn blinkers. Turf high 97 (1st run) - 2nd of 6 to Castle Quest (11 Apr Curragh 8f g-s RF 0683a). She was overrated and fell some way short of Group class. **A P O'Brien in IRE [1-11] Mrs T Hyde.*

PINK CRISTAL BHB 104f **RR 106f** 4871[7]

3 b f Dilum (USA) 7.1f **(56)** - Crystal Fountain (Great Nephew) 9.9f **(64)**
Form - 721177

Record 1999 - 1st:2 2nd:1 3rd:0 Ran:6
Win Prizemoney £20,927 *Total Prizemoney* £22,052
Wins * 1999 Aug Ascot (SFT) L 8f 106 <
*** 1999** Jun Salisb (GD) 7f 77
1999 Turf 2-6: (7f 1-3, 8f 1-1, 9f, 10f) (sft, gd 1-2, g-f 1-1, frm 2)
Scopey, Pattern-class filly, effective 8f, acts on gd. Turf high 106 - 1st of 9 getting 7lb from Diamond White (8 Aug Ascot RF 3462). Earned valuable black type when taking a listed event at Ascot, but was out of her depth in the Prix de l'Opera at the Arc meeting.
**H Candy [2-6] D B Clark.*

PINK MOSAIC BHB 59f RR 69f 4656[11]
3 b f Safawan 6.6f **(60)** - Stoneydale (Tickled Pink) 6.5f **(59)**
Form - 0570
Record 1999 - 1st:0 2nd:0 3rd:0 Ran:4
1999 Turf 0-4: (5f 3, 6f) (sft, gd, g-f, frm)
Workmanlike, average filly. Turf high 69.
**J G Smyth-Osbourne [0-4] GFT Agricultural Products And Partners.*

PINMIX (FR) RR 109f 712a[3]
4 gr c Linamix (FR) 8.2f **(64)** - Pinaflore (FR) (Formidable (USA)) 9.2f **(63)**
Form - 3
1999 Turf 0-1: (6f) (sft)
Pattern-class colt. (1st run) - 3rd of 10 to Diableneyev (6 Apr Maisons-Laffitte 6f sft RF 0712a). **A Fabre in FR [1-4].*

PINNACLE RR 88f 1045[3]
3 b f Shirley Heights 12.1f **(76)** - Manhattan Sunset (USA) **(62f)** (El Gran Senor (USA)) 9.6f **(76)**
Form - 3
Record 1999 - 1st:0 2nd:0 3rd:1 Ran:1
Pre1999 - 1st:0 2nd:1 3rd:0 Ran:1
Win Prizemoney £0 *Total Prizemoney* £5,180
1999 Turf 0-1: (11f) (g-f)
Leggy, currently useful filly. (1st run) - 3rd of 9 getting 3lb from Valentine Girl (5 May Chester 11f g-f RF 1045).
**W J Haggas [0-2] Mrs Barbara Bassett.*

PIPA BHB 64f RR 67f 4932[8]
3 b f Suave Dancer (USA) 10.7f **(68)** - Pipitina (Bustino) 10.4f **(64)**
Form - 005228
Record 1999 - 1st:0 2nd:2 3rd:0 Ran:6
Pre1999 - 1st:0 2nd:1 3rd:0 Ran:3
Win Prizemoney £0 *Total Prizemoney* £3,062
1999 Turf 0-6: (12f, 13f, 14f, 16f 2, 18f) (g-s, g-f 2, frm 3)
Workmanlike, average filly, effective 8 to 16f, best at 16f, acts on g-s to g-f, has worn blinkers, prefers tight tracks. Turf high 67 - 2nd of 8 giving 21lb to Bold Cardowan (24 Spt Lingfield 16f g-s RF 4533). Consistent. **J L Dunlop [0-9] Sir Eric Parker.*

PIPADASH (IRE) BHB 98f RR 89f 4690[19]
2 b f Pips Pride 6.7f **(70)** - Petite Maxine **(63f)** (Sharpo) 7.7f **(59)**
Form - 112383150
Record 1999 - 1st:3 2nd:1 3rd:2 Ran:9
Win Prizemoney £14,438 *Total Prizemoney* £26,163
Wins * 1999 Aug Ascot (GD) 5f 87 <
*** 1999** Apr Pontef (G-S) 5f 75
*** 1999** Apr Haydoc (SFT) 5f 73+
1999 Turf 3-9: (5f 3-5, 6f 4) (g-s, gd 3-5, g-f 3)
Useful filly, effective 5 to 6f, best at 5f, acts on g-s to g-f, best on gd, often wears blinkers, does well at Doncaster. Turf high 89 - 5th of 21 to Sheer Hamas (8 Spt Doncaster 6f gd RF 4208) - also 1st of 4 getting 5lb from Lord Pacal (7 Aug Ascot RF 3442). Consistent. Won her first two starts in battling style, but was held in better company afterwards. Regained winning form in a four-runner conditions event at Ascot in August. Best on easy ground.
**T D Easterby [3-9] T H Bennett.*

PIPADOR (IRE) BHB 40f49a RR 31f 49a 5113[17]
3 ch g Pips Pride 6.7f **(70)** - Dorado Llave (USA) (Well Decorated (USA)) 7.6f **(64)**
Form - 80000
Record 1999 - 1st:0 2nd:0 3rd:0 Ran:5
Pre1999 - 1st:0 2nd:0 3rd:0 Ran:3
1999 Turf 0-3: (5f, 6f, 8f) (g-s, gd, frm) 1999 AW 0-2: (5f, 7f) (Fibr 2)
Well made, very moderate gelding, has worn blinkers. Turf high 31 (began Aug). AW high 14.
**R Guest [0-5] Rae Guest (from R Hannon [0-3] Oct 1998).*

PIPALONG (IRE) BHB 105f RR 105f 5222[1]
3 b f Pips Pride 6.7f **(70)** - Limpopo (Green Desert (USA)) 8.6f **(78)**
Form - 4452424120521
Record 1999 - 1st:2 2nd:4 3rd:0 Ran:13
Pre1999 - 1st:3 2nd:2 3rd:0 Ran:6
Win Prizemoney £130,687 *Total Prizemoney* £177,288
Wins * 1999 Nov Doncas (SFT) L 6f 100
*** 1999** Aug Ripon (GD) H 6f 101 106 <
* 1998 Oct Redcar (HVY) 6f 100
* 1998 May York (GD) 5f 95
* 1998 Apr Ripon (SFT) 5f 99+
1999 Turf 2-13: (5f, 6f 2-11, 8f) (g-s 1-1, gd 1-7, g-f 2, frm 3)
Workmanlike, Pattern-class filly, effective 5 to 6f, best at 6f, acts on sft to frm, best on gd, and excels at Ripon and York and Doncaster. Turf high 106 - 1st of 23 giving 8lb to Bon Ami (14 Aug Ripon RF 3663) - also 1st of 20 from Two Clubs (6 Nov Doncaster RF 5222). Consistent. The only filly to lower Bint Allayl's colours as a juvenile, she failed to stay when tried beyond six furlongs but ran consistently well back at sprint distances, gaining deserved victories in the Great St Wilfrid Handicap and a listed race at Doncaster. Admirably game and genuine.
**T D Easterby [5-19] T H Bennett.*

PIPED ABOARD (IRE) BHB 80f RR 83f 1968[8]
4 b g Pips Pride 6.7f **(70)** - Last Gunboat (Dominion) 8.5f **(63)**
Form - 88
Record 1999 - 1st:0 2nd:0 3rd:0 Ran:2
Pre1999 - 1st:1 2nd:4 3rd:0 Ran:10
Win Prizemoney £2,337 *Total Prizemoney* £7,756
Wins 1998 Apr Thirsk (G-S) 7f 71 <
1999 Turf 0-2: (10f, 12f) (gd, g-f)
Scopey, decent gelding, effective 8 to 10f, best at 8f, acts on gd to g-f, best on gd, has worn blinkers, prefers tight tracks. Turf high 79. Consistent.
**M C Pipe [2-10] & Mrs Malcolm B Jones (from J L Dunlop [1-8] Jly 1998).*

PIPE DREAM BHB 52f RR 64df 5199[22]
3 b g King's Signet (USA) 7f **(51)** - Rather Warm (Tribal Chief) 8.5f **(61)**
Form - 066384700
Record 1999 - 1st:0 2nd:0 3rd:1 Ran:9
Win Prizemoney £0 *Total Prizemoney* £481
1999 Turf 0-9: (6f, 7f 2, 8f 4, 9f, 11f) (hvy, g-s 2, gd 4, g-f, frm)
Average gelding, effective 8 to 9f, acts on gd. Turf high 64 - 3rd of 13 to Gin-U-Wine (20 May Gowran Park 9f gd RF 1469a).
**P Burgoyne [0-2] Philip Saunders (from K Prendergast in IRE [0-7] Jly 1999).*

PIPE MUSIC (IRE) BHB 43f64a RR 52f 64a 4225[2]
4 b g Mujadil (USA) 7.7f **(70)** -Sunset Cafe (IRE) (Red Sunset) 8.2f **(63)**
Form - 5232156705002
Record 1999 - 1st:1 2nd:3 3rd:1 Ran:12
Pre1999 - 1st:1 2nd:1 3rd:1 Ran:14
Win Prizemoney £4,433 *Total Prizemoney* £9,142
Wins * 1999 *Feb Southw (STD) H 16f 66 70*
*** 1998** *Feb Southw (STD) H 8f 60 71* <
1999 Turf 0-5: (14f 2, 16f, 17f, 18f) (gd 2, g-f, frm 2) 1999 AW 1-7: (16f 1-7) (Equi 2, Fibr 1-5)
Scopey, average gelding, effective 8 to 16f, acts on gd - acts on AW, best on Fibr, has worn blinkers (extremely effectively), prefers left handed tracks, excels at Southwell and Wolverhampton. Turf high 53. AW high 70 - 1st of 7 giving 22lb to Spa Lane (1 Feb Southwell RF 0204). Inconsistent. A bit in-and-out and not an easy ride, but has enjoyed some success in modest staying events on sand. **P C Haslam [2-26] Lord Scarsdale.*

PIPER'S CLAN RR 289[1]
3 b c Aragon 7.7f **(58)** - Topwinder (USA) (Topsider (USA)) 8.3f **(71)**
Form - 1
Record 1999 - 1st:1 2nd:0 3rd:0 Ran:1
Win Prizemoney £3,504 *Total Prizemoney* £3,504
Wins * 1999 *Feb Lingfi (STD) 5f 70* <
1999 AW 1-1: (5f 1-1) (Equi 1-1)
Workmanlike, currently above-average colt. (1st run) - 1st of 6 giv-

ing 5lb to College Blue (13 Feb Lingfield RF 0289).
**N A Callaghan [1-1] N A Callaghan.*

PIPIJI (IRE) BHB 35f **RR 34f** 3257[2]
4 gr f Pips Pride 6.7f **(70)** - Blue Alicia (Wolver Hollow) 8f **(56)**
Form - 42502
Record 1999 - 1st:0 2nd:2 3rd:0 Ran:5
Pre1999 - 1st:0 2nd:0 3rd:0 Ran:6
Win Prizemoney £0 *Total Prizemoney* £2,024
1999 Turf 0-5: (7f 3, 8f 2) (g-s, gd, frm 3)
Very moderate filly, effective 7 to 8f, acts on gd to frm, likes left handed tracks, favours tight tracks. Turf high 34 - 2nd of 14 getting 10lb from Perchancer (30 Jly Thirsk 7f frm RF 3257).
**Mrs G S Rees [0-11] Brooke Rankin.*

PIPPAS PRIDE (IRE) BHB 33f40a **RR 37f 40a** 4985[17]
4 ch g Pips Pride 6.7f **(70)** - Al Shany (Burslem) 8.8f **(53)**
Form - 6014040
Record 1999 - 1st:1 2nd:0 3rd:0 Ran:5 .
Pre1999 - 1st:0 2nd:0 3rd:0 Ran:8
Win Prizemoney £1,757 *Total Prizemoney* £1,757
Wins * 1999 *Jan Lingfi (STD) H 8f 35 43* <
1999 Turf 0-1: (8f) (gd) 1999 AW 1-4: (6f, 7f, 8f 1-2) (Equi 1-3, Fibr)
Scopey, moderate gelding, effective 8f, - acts on Equi, favours left handed tracks, likes tight tracks. AW high 43 - also 1st of 12 getting 1lb from Clonoe (5 Jan Lingfield RF 0032). Inconsistent.
**M J Fetherston-Godley [1-13] Mrs Anthony Vickers.*

PIP'S BRAVE BHB 44f51a **RR 40f 51a** 5007[15]
3 b g Be My Chief (USA) 10.2f **(62)** - Pipistrelle (Shareef Dancer (USA)) 9.9f **(73)**
Form - 306144600005641570070
Record 1999 - 1st:2 2nd:0 3rd:0 Ran:19
Pre1999 - 1st:0 2nd:0 3rd:1 Ran:4
Win Prizemoney £7,034 *Total Prizemoney* £8,002
Wins * 1999 Jly Warwic (G-F) H 10.5f 50 50
*** 1999** *Jan Southw (STD) 8f 56* <
1999 Turf 1-13: (8f, 10f 5, 11f 1-2, 12f 2, 14f 2, 15f) (gd 2, g-f 1-6, frm 4, hrd) 1999 AW 1-6: (8f 1-6) (Fibr 1-6)
Moderate gelding, effective 8 to 11f, best at 8f, acts on g-f - acts on Fibr, often wears blinkers. Turf high 57 - 4th of 10 getting 7lb from Numerator (26 Jun Newmarket 8f g-f RF 2341) - also 1st of 5 getting 23lb from Signify (17 Jly Warwick RF 2932). AW high 56 (1st run) - 1st of 11 from Suhail (29 Jan Southwell RF 0189). Inconsistent. **M J Polglase [2-23] Pastern Partnership.*

PIPSISEWA (IRE) BHB 56f **RR 49f** 1813[19]
3 ch f Pips Pride 6.7f **(70)** - Algonquin Park (High Line) 10.3f **(70)**
Form - 40000
Record 1999 - 1st:0 2nd:0 3rd:0 Ran:5
Pre1999 - 1st:0 2nd:0 3rd:0 Ran:2
1999 Turf 0-5: (6f 3, 7f, 8f) (sft, g-f 2, frm 2)
Scopey, moderate filly. Turf high 58.
**D R C Elsworth [0-7] Michael Jackson Bloodstock Ltd.*

PIPS MAGIC (IRE) BHB 85f **RR 79df** 4390[29]
3 b c Pips Pride 6.7f **(70)** - Kentucky Starlet (USA) (Cox's Ridge (USA)) 8f **(68)**
Form - 0002301007000
Record 1999 - 1st:1 2nd:1 3rd:1 Ran:13
Pre1999 - 1st:2 2nd:1 3rd:1 Ran:13
Win Prizemoney £21,707 *Total Prizemoney* £36,326
Wins * 1999 Jun Ascot (G-F) H 5f 90 94 <
* 1998 May Ayr (G-F) 5f 84
* 1998 May Ripon (G-F) 6f 66
1999 Turf 1-13: (5f 1-6, 6f 7) (gd 4, g-f 1-6, frm 3)
Scopey, above-average colt, effective 5 to 6f, best at 6f, acts on g-f to frm, best on g-f. Turf high 94 - 1st of 15 getting 9lb from Henry Hall (19 Jun Ascot RF 2134). Becoming disappointing. Put in a couple of useful placed efforts prior to winning a valuable handicap at Ascot's Heath meeting over five furlongs on fast ground. Has disappointed since. **J S Goldie [3-26] Frank Brady.*

PIPSSALIO (SPA) BHB 62f **RR 50f** 5195[7]
2 b c Pips Pride 6.7f **(70)** - Tesalia (SPA) (Finissimo (SPA))
Form - 007
Record 1999 - 1st:0 2nd:0 3rd:0 Ran:3
1999 Turf 0-3: (6f 3) (gd 2, frm)
Currently fair colt. Turf high 50 (began Aug).
**J R Poulton [0-3] Chris Steward.*

PIPS SONG (IRE) BHB 75f77a **RR 78df 77a** 5161[2]
4 ch g Pips Pride 6.7f **(70)** - Friendly Song (Song) 7.2f **(61)**
Form - 88101306822
Record 1999 - 1st:2 2nd:2 3rd:1 Ran:11
Pre1999 - 1st:1 2nd:0 3rd:1 Ran:8
Win Prizemoney £14,994 *Total Prizemoney* £21,909
Wins * 1999 Apr Leices (HVY) H 6f 69 78 <
*** 1999** *Mar Wolver (STD) H 6f 71 76*
* 1998 *Apr Wolver (STD) 6f 63*
1999 Turf 1-7: (5f, 6f 1-6) (hvy, sft 1-1, g-s, gd 2, g-f, frm) 1999 AW 1-4: (6f 1-3, 7f) (Fibr 1-4)
Leggy, above-average gelding, effective 6f, acts on sft to g-f - acts on Fibr, prefers left handed tracks, prefers tight tracks. Turf high 78 - 1st of 20 giving 4lb to Mallia (24 Apr Leicester RF 0827). AW high 76 - 3rd of 10 giving 7lb to Mallia (14 May Wolverhampton 6f Fibr RF 1229) - also 1st of 13 getting 5lb from Ocker (13 Mar Wolverhampton RF 0428). Returned to form when winning a competitive handicap back at Wolverhampton in March of last year, and has since added a heavy-ground handicap at Leicester. Well held in the Ayr Silver Cup after a lengthy absence.
**Dr J D Scargill [3-18] P J Edwards (from I A Balding [0-1] Jly 1997).*

PIPS STAR BHB 62f64a **RR 81f 64a** 4705[1]
2 b f Pips Pride 6.7f **(70)** - Kentucky Starlet (USA) (Cox's Ridge (USA)) 8f **(68)**
Form - 02553071
Record 1999 - 1st:1 2nd:1 3rd:1 Ran:8
Win Prizemoney £1,955 *Total Prizemoney* £4,102
Wins * 1999 *Oct Wolver (STD) S 5f 73* <
1999 Turf 0-7: (5f 7) (g-s, gd 4, g-f 2) 1999 AW 1-1: (5f 1-1) (Fibr 1-1)
Decent filly, effective 5f, acts on gd - acts on Fibr. Turf high 81 - 3rd of 7 getting 2lb from Melon Place (28 Aug Goodwood 5f gd RF 3960). (1st run) - 1st of 13 from Dimming of The Day (2 Oct Wolverhampton RF 4705). Inconsistent. Showed a small amount of ability on turf, but took to Fibresand at the first attempt by winning a seller at Wolverhampton in October despite drifting significantly in the market. **D W P Arbuthnot [1-8] Noel Cronin.*

PIPS TANGO (IRE) RR 36f 3153[8]
2 ch f Pips Pride 6.7f **(70)** - Suppression (Kind of Hush) 10.1f **(62)**
Form - 878
Record 1999 - 1st:0 2nd:0 3rd:0 Ran:3
1999 Turf 0-3: (6f 3) (gd, frm 2)
Currently very moderate filly. Turf high 36.
**M Mullineaux [0-3] P F Youd.*

PIPS WAY (IRE) BHB 77f **RR 77f** 4599[12]
2 ch f Pips Pride 6.7f **(70)** - Algonquin Park (High Line) 10.3f **(70)**
Form - 16830040
Record 1999 - 1st:1 2nd:0 3rd:1 Ran:8
Win Prizemoney £4,533 *Total Prizemoney* £5,863
Wins * 1999 May Ripon (G-S) 6f 67 <
1999 Turf 1-8: (6f 1-3, 7f 3, 8f 2) (gd 1-5, g-f 3)
Above-average filly, effective 6 to 8f, acts on gd, has worn blinkers. Turf high 79. Held in Listed and nursery company after making a winning debut in a Ripon maiden, she seems to have lost her way. **K R Burke [1-8] Paul James McCaughey.*

PIRANESI (IRE) RR 92f 2401a[1]
3 ch c Grand Lodge (USA) - Princess Dixieland (USA) (Dixieland Band (USA)) 7f **(74)**
Form - 22311
1999 Turf 2-5: (9f, 10f, 12f 2-3) (sft, g-s, g-f 1-2, frm 1-1)
Useful colt, effective 8 to 12f, best at 12f, acts on gd to frm, best on g-f. Turf high 92 - 1st of 6 giving 6lb to Playing Hours (25 Jun Curragh RF 2401a) - also 1st of 9 from Trebizond (14 Jun Roscommon RF 2204a). Consistent.
**D Gillespie in IRE [2-9] Mrs Chryss O'Reilly.*

PIRRO (IRE) RR 94f 4854a[6]
4 ch g Persian Bold 10f **(69)** - Kindness Itself
Form - 8765676
1999 Turf 0-7: (7f, 8f 2, 9f 3, 11f) (sft, gd 2, g-f 4)

Useful gelding, effective 8 to 9f, best at 8f, acts on g-s to g-f. Turf high 94 - 5th of 18 getting 5lb from Tiger Shark (27 Jly Galway 8f g-f RF 3324a). Consistent. Has joined Mark Tompkins.
**J Oxx in IRE [1-9] Lady Clague.*

PISCES LAD BHB 52f64a **RR 54f 64a** 4656[13]
3 b g Cyrano de Bergerac 7.3f **(58)** - Tarnside Rosal **(56f)** (Mummy's Game) 8.2f **(60)**
Form - 0320000054780
Record 1999 - 1st:0 2nd:1 3rd:1 Ran:12
Pre1999 - 1st:0 2nd:2 3rd:1 Ran:7
Win Prizemoney £0 *Total Prizemoney* £4,012
1999 Turf 0-10: (5f 4, 6f 4, 7f 2) (sft, gd 3, g-f 3, frm 3) 1999 AW 0-2: (5f, 6f) (Equi 2)
Scopey, average gelding. Turf high 55. AW high 67.
**S Dow [0-19] J Falvey & G Williamson.*

PISTACHIO BHB 100f **RR 105f** 4372a[3]
3 gr c Unblest - Cashew **(77f)** (Sharrood (USA)) 10.5f **(72)**
Form - 23
1999 Turf 0-2: (6f, 7f) (gd 2)
Lengthy, Pattern-class colt, effective 6f, acts on sft to gd, best on gd. Turf high 105 (began Jly) - 3rd of 7 to Proud Native (12 Spt Taby 6f gd RF 4372a). A useful juvenile for James Fanshawe in '98, he is now trained in Norway. **A Lund in NOR [0-2].*

PIX ME UP (IRE) BHB 69f **RR 73f** 5076[16]
2 b f Up and At 'em - Water Pixie (IRE) (Dance of Life (USA)) 7f **(66)**
Form - 68320
Record 1999 - 1st:0 2nd:1 3rd:1 Ran:5
Win Prizemoney £0 *Total Prizemoney* £1,283
1999 Turf 0-5: (6f 3, 7f 2) (gd 2, frm 2, hrd)
Above-average filly. Turf high 73 - 2nd of 5 getting 5lb from Atwaar (17 Jly Redcar 7f hrd RF 2920). **K A Ryan [0-5] Mrs Gillian Quinn.*

PLAN-B BHB 99f **RR 100f** 2042[2]
4 b c Polish Precedent (USA) 9f **(73)** - Draft Board (Rainbow Quest (USA)) 10.4f **(75)**
Form - 062
Record 1999 - 1st:0 2nd:1 3rd:0 Ran:3
Pre1999 - 1st:1 2nd:2 3rd:1 Ran:6
Win Prizemoney £29,700 *Total Prizemoney* £61,902
Wins * 1998 Jun Ascot (G-S) H 8f 88 97 <
1999 Turf 0-3: (7f, 8f 2) (g-s, gd, g-f)
Scopey, very useful colt, effective 8f, acts on gd to frm. Turf high 100. He landed a gamble in the 1998 Britannia Handicap and ran a cracker in the Royal Hunt Cup last term. Suited by a straight mile, he is one to look out for at the Royal Meeting in 2000.
**J H M Gosden [1-9] Sheikh Mohammed.*

PLAS UCHA **RR 52f** 1788[7]
2 b c Forest Wind (USA) - Adivara (Tyrnavos) 10.1f **(55)**
Form - 27
Record 1999 - 1st:0 2nd:1 3rd:0 Ran:2
Win Prizemoney £0 *Total Prizemoney* £612
1999 Turf 0-1: (5f) (gd) 1999 AW 0-1: (5f) (Fibr)
Currently above-average colt. (1st run) - 2nd of 5 giving 2lb to Cookie (22 May Wolverhampton 5f Fibr RF 1419).
**J Berry [0-2] Lord Mostyn.*

PLAYINAROUND BHB 57f52a **RR 60f 52a** 4605[11]
2 ch f Anshan 8.2f **(63)** - Karonga (Main Reef) 9.6f **(57)**
Form - 60145530
Record 1999 - 1st:1 2nd:0 3rd:1 Ran:8
Win Prizemoney £1,819 *Total Prizemoney* £2,089
Wins * 1999 May Bright (FRM) S 6f 45 <
1999 Turf 1-7: (5f 2, 6f 1-4, 7f) (sft, gd, g-f 1-3, frm, hrd) 1999 AW 0-1: (7f) (Fibr)
Average filly, effective 5 to 7f, acts on g-f to hrd. Turf high 60 - 4th of 14 to Safarando (10 Jun Yarmouth 7f g-f RF 1889). Inconsistent. Her Brighton selling win came on very fast ground.
**W G M Turner [1-8] Gongolfin.*

PLAYING HOURS (USA) **RR 98f** 3231a[6]
3 b c Alleged (USA) 11.8f **(81)** - Playlist (CAN)
Form - 3216
1999 Turf 1-4: (10f, 12f, 13f 1-2) (gd 2, g-f 1-1, frm)
Very useful colt. Turf high 98. He stays well, but is not Group class. Lightly raced, he could make a smart hurdler.
**A P O'Brien in IRE [1-4].*

PLAZZOTTA (IRE) **RR 1f** 5047[13]
2 b g Sri Pekan (USA) - Porte des Iles (IRE) **(70?f)** (Kris) 9.5f **(73)**
Form - 0
Record 1999 - 1st:0 2nd:0 3rd:0 Ran:1
1999 Turf 0-1: (6f) (hvy)
Currently very poor gelding. **B J Meehan [0-1] John Manley.*

PLEADING BHB 60a **RR 73f** 4804[8]
6 b g Never so Bold 7.1f **(62)** - Ask Mama (Mummy's Pet) 7.7f **(60)**
Form - 805203043200301088
Record 1999 - 1st:1 2nd:2 3rd:3 Ran:18
Pre1999 - 1st:3 2nd:1 3rd:0 Ran:20
Win Prizemoney £17,695 *Total Prizemoney* £34,001

Wins								
* **1999**	Spt	Chepst	(GD)	H	7.1f	63	73	
* 1998	Apr	Pontef	(G-S)	H	6f	65	70	
1996	May	Leices	(G-S)	H	6f	80	91+	<
1996	May	Salisb	(GD)		6f		77	

1999 Turf 1-14: (6f 8, 7f 1-6) (sft, g-s, gd 6, g-f 2, frm 1-4) 1999 AW 0-4: (6f 3, 7f) (Fibr 4)
Above-average gelding, effective 6 to 7f, best at 6f, acts on sft to frm, has worn blinkers. Turf high 73 - 1st of 20 giving 9lb to Daphne's Doll (9 Spt Chepstow RF 4232). AW high 55. He shaped as if retaining his ability with some good placed efforts in '99, before absolutely sluicing home in a 0-65 over seven furlongs at Chepstow.
**W J Musson [2-25] Lloyd Bennett (from H Candy [2-13] Oct 1997).*

PLEASANT DREAMS BHB 55f39a **RR 55f 39a** 5162[14]
4 ch f Sabrehill (USA) 8.5f **(64)** - Tafila (Adonijah) 10f **(61)**
Form - 70054460104200
Record 1999 - 1st:1 2nd:1 3rd:0 Ran:13
Pre1999 - 1st:2 2nd:1 3rd:0 Ran:15
Win Prizemoney £7,406 *Total Prizemoney* £9,581

Wins								
* **1999**	Jun	Pontef	(GD)	H	10f	50	54	
* 1998	Spt	Ripon	(HVY)	C	8f		56	<
* 1998	Jly	Carlis	(G-F)	H	9.3f	48	55	

1999 Turf 1-11: (8f 5, 9f, 10f 1-4, 12f) (gd 3, g-f 4, frm 1-4) 1999 AW 0-2: (8f 2) (Fibr 2)
Leggy, fair filly, effective 8 to 10f, best at 8f, acts on g-s to frm, prefers right handed tracks, favours tight tracks, excels at Ripon, does well at Pontefract and Carlisle. Turf high 55 - 2nd of 17 giving 11lb to Gymcrak Flyer (25 Aug Carlisle 8f frm RF 3902) - also 1st of 11 giving 14lb to Hutchies Lady (28 Jun Pontefract RF 2373). AW high 25. **Denys Smith [3-29] J A Bianchi.*

PLEASANT MOUNT BHB 63f **RR 60f** 4485[2]
3 b g First Trump - Alo Ez (Alzao (USA)) 7.1f **(68)**
Form - 833231112
Record 1999 - 1st:3 2nd:2 3rd:3 Ran:9
Pre1999 - 1st:0 2nd:0 3rd:0 Ran:2
Win Prizemoney £10,227 *Total Prizemoney* £14,535

Wins								
* **1999**	Aug	Redcar	(G-F)	H	14.1f	56	60	<
* **1999**	Aug	Thirsk	(SFT)	H	16f	51	56	
* **1999**	Jly	Beverl	(G-F)	H	16.2f	48	53	

1999 Turf 3-9: (6f, 10f, 12f, 14f 1-3, 16f 2-3) (g-s 2, gd 1-4, g-f 1-1, frm 1-2)
Tall, average gelding, effective 14 to 16f, best at 16f, acts on g-s to frm, prefers left handed tracks, prefers tight tracks. Turf high 60 - 2nd of 5 getting 7lb from Mazzelmo (22 Spt Chester 16f g-s RF 4485) - also 1st of 12 giving 11lb to Elle Questro (28 Aug Redcar RF 3979). Consistent.
**Miss J A Camacho [3-11] Shangri-La Racing Club.*

PLEASANT TEMPER (USA) **RR 109f** 5228a[8]
5 m Storm Cat (USA) 7f **(86)** - Colonial Witch (USA) (Pleasant Colony (USA)) 7f **(70)**
Form - 8
1999 Turf 0-1: (11f) (frm)
Currently Pattern-class. **W E Walden in USA [0-1].*

PLEASING PROSPECT (USA) **RR 75f** 3120[2]
3 b f Mr Prospector (USA) 8.6f **(88)** - Promising Girl (USA) (Youth (USA)) 9.8f **(64)**

Form - 632
Record 1999 - 1st:0 2nd:1 3rd:1 Ran:3
Pre1999 - 1st:0 2nd:0 3rd:0 Ran:1
Win Prizemoney £0 *Total Prizemoney* £2,292
1999 Turf 0-3: (7f, 8f 2) (g-f 3)
Strong, above-average filly. Turf high 75 - 2nd of 6 to Chambre Separee (25 Jly Ascot 8f g-f RF 3120).
**J H M Gosden [0-4] Sheikh Mohammed.*

PLEASURE BHB 58f52a RR 56f 52a 4445[16]

4 ch f Most Welcome 8.6f **(66)** - Peak Squaw (USA) (Icecapade (USA)) 11f **(62)**
Form - 500001500
Record 1999 - 1st:1 2nd:0 3rd:0 Ran:7
Pre1999 - 1st:1 2nd:0 3rd:1 Ran:8
Win Prizemoney £6,248 *Total Prizemoney* £6,543
Wins * 1999 Jun Beverl (SFT) H 5f 53 56 <
* 1998 Oct Doncas (SFT) H 7f 51 54
1999 Turf 1-7: (5f 1-3, 6f 2, 7f 2) (g-s, gd 1-3, g-f 2, frm)
Fair filly, effective 5 to 7f, best at 5f, acts on gd to frm, has worn blinkers (extremely effectively). Turf high 56 - 1st of 16 giving 3lb to La Doyenne (9 Jun Beverley RF 1854). Inconsistent.
**A Smith [2-14] The Rufus Partnership (from R W Armstrong [0-1] Nov 1997).*

PLEASURE CENTER (USA) RR 83f 5136[4]

2 ch f Diesis 9f **(80)** - Creaking Board (Night Shift (USA)) 7.2f **(69)**
Form - 4
Record 1999 - 1st:0 2nd:0 3rd:0 Ran:1
Win Prizemoney £0 *Total Prizemoney* £289
1999 Turf 0-1: (7f) (gd)
Currently decent filly. (1st run) - 4th of 16 to Premier Prize (30 Oct Newmarket 7f gd RF 5136). **J H M Gosden [0-1] George Strawbridge.*

PLEASURE PRINCESS BHB 40f RR 19f 5163[14]

2 b f Presidium 7.5f **(56)** - Harem Queen (Prince Regent (FR)) 9.8f **(54)**
Form - 700
Record 1999 - 1st:0 2nd:0 3rd:0 Ran:3
1999 Turf 0-3: (5f, 6f, 7f) (g-s, gd, g-f)
Currently poor filly. Turf high 27.
**A Bailey [0-3] www Mark-Kilner-Raci (16).*

PLEASURE TIME BHB 73f65a RR 74f 65a 4911[12]

6 ch g Clantime 6.6f **(57)** - First Experience (Le Johnstan) 7.4f **(55)**
Form - 2100300
Record 1999 - 1st:1 2nd:1 3rd:1 Ran:7
Pre1999 - 1st:5 2nd:5 3rd:5 Ran:40
Win Prizemoney £18,928 *Total Prizemoney* £30,008
Wins * 1999 Jun Bath (FRM) 5.7f 78 <
* 1998 Aug Thirsk (G-F) H 5f 65 70
* 1998 May Nottin (G-F) H 5.1f 60 66
* 1997 May Nottin (GD) H 5.1f 58 63
* 1995 Aug Haydoc (G-F) H 5f 65 67
* 1995 May Redcar (FRM) 5f 71
1999 Turf 1-7: (5f 6, 6f 1-1) (gd 3, g-f, frm 2, hrd 1-1)
Above-average gelding, effective 5 to 6f, best at 5f, acts on g-f to hrd, often wears blinkers (effectively). Turf high 78 - 1st of 8 giving 3lb to Petarga (26 Jun Bath RF 2317). Inconsistent. After running well on his seasonal bow, he knocked over a decent field at Bath, but has shown little form since. Likes five furlongs and fast ground, and goes well fresh. **C Smith [6-47] A E Needham.*

PLEASURE TRICK (USA) BHB 34f46a RR 43f 46a 2264[8]

8 br g Clever Trick (USA) 7.6f **(69)** - Pleasure Garden (USA) (Foolish Pleasure (USA)) 8.9f **(72)**
Form - 676466870588
Record 1999 - 1st:0 2nd:0 3rd:0 Ran:10
Pre1999 - 1st:9 2nd:4 3rd:5 Ran:69
Win Prizemoney £29,818 *Total Prizemoney* £36,003
Wins 1998 *Feb Southw (STD) H 7f 55 58*
1998 *Jan Southw (STD) H 7f 49 50*
1997 Jly Pontef (G-F) H 8f 41 47
1997 *Feb Southw (STD) H 8f 49 56*
1997 *Jan Southw (STD) H 7f 42 46*
1996 *Nov Southw (STD) H 7f 34 43*
* 1995 Jly Pontef (G-F) C 8f 64 <
1999 Turf 0-5: (7f 2, 8f 3) (gd, g-f, frm 2, hrd) 1999 AW 0-5: (7f 3, 8f 2) (Fibr 5)
Moderate gelding, effective 7 to 8f, best at 7f, - acts on Fibr, has worn blinkers, likes left handed tracks, likes tight tracks. Turf high 43. AW high 51.
**N Tinkler [3-18] Don Enrico Incisa (from Don Enrico Incisa [6-57] May 1999).*

PLEIN GAZ (FR) BHB 33f33a RR 44f 33a 1285[11]

6 ch g Lesotho (USA) 6f **(53)** - Gazzara (USA) (Irish River (FR)) 8.6f **(78)**
Form - 00027645780
Record 1999 - 1st:0 2nd:1 3rd:0 Ran:9
Pre1999 - 1st:1 2nd:1 3rd:2 Ran:22
Win Prizemoney £1,830 *Total Prizemoney* £4,493
Wins 1998 *Feb Lingfi (SLW) S 6f 46* <
1999 Turf 0-3: (6f, 10f 2) (gd, g-f, hrd) 1999 AW 0-6: (5f, 6f, 7f, 8f 3) (Equi 6)
Moderate gelding, effective 5f, - acts on Equi. Turf high 44. AW high 42.
**R J O'Sullivan [0-11] The Mayfair Partnership (from J J Bridger [1-17] Jun 1998).*

PLENTY OF SUNSHINE BHB 21f RR 5f 1707[18]

6 ch m Pharly (FR) 11.5f **(64)** - Zipperti Do (Precocious) 8.6f **(62)**
Form - 0
Record 1999 - 1st:0 2nd:0 3rd:0 Ran:1
Pre1999 - 1st:0 2nd:0 3rd:0 Ran:6
1999 Turf 0-1: (8f) (gd)
Little account mare.
**A G Newcombe [0-1] Maurice Kirby (from Mrs N Macauley [0-4] Aug 1998).*

PLUM FIRST BHB 48f43a RR 52f 43a 3104[6]

9 b g Nomination 7.3f **(57)** - Plum Bold (Be My Guest (USA)) 9.3f **(67)**
Form - 000064056
Record 1999 - 1st:0 2nd:0 3rd:0 Ran:9
Pre1999 - 1st:5 2nd:11 3rd:13 Ran:107
Win Prizemoney £18,673 *Total Prizemoney* £43,315
Wins 1995 May Warwic (FRM) 6f 58
1995 Apr Pontef (GD) 5f 56
1999 Turf 0-9: (5f 2, 6f 5, 7f 2) (gd 2, g-f, frm 6)
Fair gelding, effective 5f, acts on gd, has worn blinkers. Turf high 52.
**J S Wainwright [0-15] J B Slatcher (from L R Lloyd-James [2-35] Aug 1998).*

PLURALIST (IRE) BHB 68f RR 69f 4946[2]

3 b c Mujadil (USA) 7.7f **(70)** - Encore Une Fois (IRE) **(75f)** (Shirley Heights) 10.3f **(74)**
Form - 8426562
Record 1999 - 1st:0 2nd:2 3rd:0 Ran:7
Pre1999 - 1st:0 2nd:2 3rd:0 Ran:4
Win Prizemoney £0 *Total Prizemoney* £6,404
1999 Turf 0-7: (9f 2, 10f 3, 11f 2) (gd 3, g-f 4)
Strong, average colt, effective 6 to 10f, acts on g-f to frm, best on g-f. Turf high 72 - 4th of 13 getting 13lb from Moutahddee (15 Apr Newmarket 10f g-f RF 0699). Consistent. Looks a surefire future winner, probably over seven furlongs.
**W Jarvis [0-11] The Pluralist Partnership.*

PLUTOCRAT BHB 69f RR 73f 3921[1]

3 b g Polar Falcon (USA) 9f **(74)** - Choire Mhor (Dominion) 8.5f **(63)**
Form - 20231
Record 1999 - 1st:1 2nd:2 3rd:1 Ran:5
Win Prizemoney £3,046 *Total Prizemoney* £6,036
Wins * 1999 Aug Mussel (G-F) C 9f 56 <
1999 Turf 1-5: (6f, 7f 2, 8f, 9f 1-1) (g-s, gd 2, g-f 1-1, frm)
Unfurnished, above-average gelding. Turf high 73 - 2nd of 11 giving 5lb to Cladantom (23 Jly Thirsk 7f frm RF 3072).
**J Noseda [1-5] Lucayan Stud.*

POCO A POCO (IRE) RR 103f 4737a[1]

2 b f Imperial Frontier (USA) 7f **(65)** - Cut the Red Tape (IRE) **(63f)** (Sure Blade (USA)) 11.3f **(67)**
Form - 2251
1999 Turf 1-4: (5f, 6f 1-3) (sft 1-1, g-s, g-f 2)
Very useful filly. Turf high 103 (began Aug) - 1st of 6 getting 3lb

from Conormara (2 Oct Curragh RF 4737a).
**E Lynam in IRE [1-4] J Carthy.*

PODIUM BHB 44f **RR 30f** 4355[8]

3 b g Presidium 7.5f **(56)** - Sally Tadpole (Jester)
Form - 008
Record 1999 - 1st:0 2nd:0 3rd:0 Ran:3
Pre1999 - 1st:0 2nd:0 3rd:0 Ran:3
1999 Turf 0-3: (6f, 7f 2) (g-s, frm 2)
Neat, very moderate gelding. Turf high 30.
**P W Harris [0-6] The Saboteurs.*

POETRY IN MOTION (IRE) BHB 64f54a **RR 59f 54a** 4986[15]

4 gr f Ballad Rock 7.2f **(63)** - Nasseem (FR) (Zeddaan) 9f **(76)**
Form - 00210872020
Record 1999 - 1st:1 2nd:3 3rd:0 Ran:11
Pre1999 - 1st:0 2nd:1 3rd:0 Ran:8
Win Prizemoney £2,612 *Total Prizemoney* £11,541
Wins * 1999 Jun Mussel (G-F) 5f 72 <
1999 Turf 1-10: (5f 1-8, 6f, 8f) (g-s 3, gd, g-f 1-4, frm, hrd) 1999 AW 0-1: (7f) (Fibr)
Scopey, fair filly, effective 5f, acts on g-s to g-f, best on g-s, has worn blinkers. Turf high 72 - 1st of 7 giving 6lb to Cyclone Flyer (21 Jun Musselburgh RF 2168). She took a while in getting off the mark, but managed it in a fast-ground maiden at Musselburgh in June. She ran her best race since in very contrasting conditions in the Victor Chandler Dash at Brighton in August.
**E J Alston [1-19] Peter Ebdon Racing.*

POETTO BHB 48f50a **RR 49f 50a** 365[6]

4 ch g Casteddu 7.4f **(54)** - Steamy Windows (Dominion) 8.5f **(63)**
Form - 06
Record 1999 - 1st:0 2nd:0 3rd:0 Ran:2
Pre1999 - 1st:0 2nd:3 3rd:2 Ran:22
Win Prizemoney £0 *Total Prizemoney* £4,261
1999 AW 0-2: (8f 2) (Fibr 2)
Leggy, moderate gelding, effective 7 to 8f, - acts on Fibr, has worn blinkers, likes left handed tracks, favours tight tracks. AW high 31.
**Mrs J Brown [0-6] H R Hewitt (from J Hetherton [0-10] Jun 1998).*

POINT OF DISPUTE BHB 79f **RR 79f** 4989[1]

4 b g Cyrano de Bergerac 7.3f **(58)** - Opuntia (Rousillon (USA)) 8.2f **(74)**
Form - 0010001
Record 1999 - 1st:2 2nd:0 3rd:0 Ran:7
Pre1999 - 1st:1 2nd:0 3rd:0 Ran:4
Win Prizemoney £12,761 *Total Prizemoney* £12,761
Wins * 1999 Oct Nottin (FRM) H 6.1f 72 79
*** 1999** Aug Lingfi (GD) H 7f 69 74+
***** 1998 May Salisb (G-S) 6f 82 <
1999 Turf 2-7: (5f, 6f 1-5, 7f 1-1) (gd 3, frm 2-4)
Well made, above-average gelding, effective 6 to 7f, best at 6f, acts on gd to frm, best on frm, often wears blinkers (very effectively). Turf high 79 - 1st of 16 from Madmun (20 Oct Nottingham RF 4989) - also 1st of 15 getting 4lb from Balanita (13 Aug Lingfield RF 3612). Inconsistent. Has reportedly had his share of training problems, but managed to get off the mark in a 0-75 at Lingfield in August over seven furlongs on good ground. Had no problem with the faster ground when winning at Nottingham.
**P J Makin [3-11] Mrs B J Carrington.*

POKEIT BHB 52f41a **RR 51f 41a** 73[12]

3 b g Cyrano de Bergerac 7.3f **(58)** - Entourage (Posse (USA)) 8.9f **(61)**
Form - 050
Record 1999 - 1st:0 2nd:0 3rd:0 Ran:1
Pre1999 - 1st:0 2nd:0 3rd:1 Ran:10
Win Prizemoney £0 *Total Prizemoney* £647
1999 AW 0-1: (6f) (Fibr)
Leggy, fair gelding, has worn blinkers.
**N P Littmoden [0-2] The Pig In A Poke Partnership (from G L Moore [0-9] Nov 1998).*

POKER POLKA BHB 72f **RR 75f** 4384[7]

2 b f Salse (USA) 10.9f **(71)** - Poker Chip **(97df)** (Bluebird (USA)) 7.5f **(69)**
Form - 061557
Record 1999 - 1st:1 2nd:0 3rd:0 Ran:6
Win Prizemoney £3,915 *Total Prizemoney* £3,915
Wins * 1999 Aug Nottin (G-F) 5.1f 75 <
1999 Turf 1-5: (5f 1-2, 6f 3) (gd 1-1, g-f, frm 2, hrd) 1999 AW 0-1: (5f) (Fibr)
Above-average filly, effective 5f, acts on gd. Turf high 75 (began Jly) - 1st of 9 from La Caprice (13 Aug Nottingham RF 3623). Scored by the narrowest margin at Nottingham on her third start and looks best at the minimum trip. **J M P Eustace [1-6] J C Smith.*

POKER SCHOOL (IRE) BHB 37f56a **RR 35f 56a** 1282[3]

5 b g Night Shift (USA) 8.1f **(73)** - Mosaique Bleue (Shirley Heights) 10.3f **(74)**
Form - 173450033
Record 1999 - 1st:1 2nd:0 3rd:3 Ran:9
Pre1999 - 1st:1 2nd:2 3rd:3 Ran:17
Win Prizemoney £4,262 *Total Prizemoney* £8,221
Wins * 1999 *Jan Southw (STD) H 11f 58 64*
1997 May Dundal (GD) 9f 75 <
1999 Turf 0-3: (10f 2, 11f) (g-s, gd 2) 1999 AW 1-6: (11f 1-2, 12f, 14f, 16f 2) (Fibr 1-6)
Average gelding, effective 11 to 16f, best at 12f, - acts on Fibr, has worn blinkers, prefers left handed tracks, favours tight tracks. Turf high 35. AW high 64 (1st run) - 1st of 11 giving 32lb to Sporty Spice (15 Jan Southwell RF 0098). Inconsistent.
**M R Bosley [1-11] Mrs J L Brindley (from N A Callaghan [0-14] Jun 1998).*

POLAIRE (IRE) **RR 108f** 3718a[3]

3 b f Polish Patriot (USA) 7.8f **(70)** - Headrest (Habitat) 9.4f **(70)**
Form - 3011663
1999 Turf 2-7: (7f 1-1, 8f 2, 10f 1-3, 12f) (gd 1-2, g-f 1-3, frm 2)
Pattern-class filly, effective 6 to 10f, acts on gd to frm. Turf high 108 - also 1st of 8 getting 12lb from Lady In Waiting (26 Jun Curragh RF 2411a). Gained a surprise success in the Pretty Polly Stakes at the Curragh, confirming that ten furlongs is her trip, but was in season in the Irish Oaks and lost her way thereafter.
**K Prendergast in IRE [3-13] M J Halligan.*

POLAR CHALLENGE **RR 79f** 3812[4]

2 b c Polar Falcon (USA) 9f **(74)** - Warning Light (High Top) 10.2f **(67)**
Form - 54
Record 1999 - 1st:0 2nd:0 3rd:0 Ran:2
Win Prizemoney £0 *Total Prizemoney* £251
1999 Turf 0-2: (7f 2) (gd, frm)
Currently above-average colt. Turf high 79 (began Aug) - 4th of 6 giving 5lb to Rainbow Melody (21 Aug Chester 7f gd RF 3812).
**Sir Michael Stoute [0-2] Cheveley Park Stud.*

POLAR ECLIPSE BHB 50f76a **RR 52f 76a** 4980[7]

6 ch g Polar Falcon (USA) 9f **(74)** - Princess Zepoli (Persepolis (FR)) 6.4f **(67)**
Form - 0422047
Record 1999 - 1st:0 2nd:2 3rd:0 Ran:7
Pre1999 - 1st:1 2nd:1 3rd:2 Ran:21
Win Prizemoney £4,320 *Total Prizemoney* £10,556
Wins 1995 Oct Haydoc (G-S) 7.1f 89+ <
1999 Turf 0-7: (8f, 9f, 10f 5) (g-s, gd, g-f 2, frm 3)
Fair gelding, effective 8 to 10f, best at 10f, acts on g-f to frm, best on g-f, has worn blinkers, favours left handed tracks, prefers tight tracks. Turf high 53 - 2nd of 17 giving 9lb to Maiella (28 Aug Nottingham 10f g-f RF 3968).
**J G Given [0-4] J R Good (from K R Burke [0-3] May 1999).*

POLAR FAIR BHB 51f58a **RR 59f 58a** 5066[12]

3 ch f Polar Falcon (USA) 9f **(74)** - Fair Country (Town And Country) 8.1f **(68)**
Form - 00030
Record 1999 - 1st:0 2nd:0 3rd:1 Ran:5
Pre1999 - 1st:0 2nd:0 3rd:0 Ran:2
Win Prizemoney £0 *Total Prizemoney* £524
1999 Turf 0-4: (8f 2, 9f, 12f) (g-s, gd, g-f, frm) 1999 AW 0-1: (8f) (Fibr)
Neat, fair filly. Turf high 59. **J Noseda [0-7] Sir Gordon Brunton.*

POLAR HAZE BHB 77f **RR 79f** 5023[6]

2 ch g Polar Falcon (USA) 9f **(74)** - Sky Music **(82f)** (Absalom) 7.2f **(58)**
Form - 2726
Record 1999 - 1st:0 2nd:2 3rd:0 Ran:4

Win Prizemoney £0 *Total Prizemoney* £2,567
1999 Turf 0-4: (5f 2, 6f 2) (g-s, gd 2, g-f)
Above-average gelding. Turf high 79 (began Aug) - 2nd of 14 giving 5lb to Jaybird (26 Spt Musselburgh 5f gd RF 4574).
**Miss S E Hall [0-4] Mrs Joan Hodgson.*

POLAR ICE BHB 83a RR 74+f 3659[10]

3 b c Polar Falcon (USA) 9f **(74)** - Sweet Slew (USA) (Seattle Slew (USA)) 9.4f **(76)**
Form - 4221130
Record **1999** - 1st:2 2nd:2 3rd:1 Ran:7
Pre1999 - 1st:0 2nd:1 3rd:0 Ran:2
Win Prizemoney £6,533 *Total Prizemoney* £10,670
Wins *** 1999** *Jun Wolver (STD) H* 7f 75 79 <
*** 1999** *Jun Wolver (STA)* 7f 76
1999 Turf 0-3: (5f, 7f 2) (gd, g-f, frm) 1999 AW 2-4: (7f 2-3, 8f) (Fibr 2-4)
Workmanlike, above-average colt, effective 6 to 7f, best at 7f, acts on g-f to frm - acts on Fibr. Turf high 74 - 2nd of 20 giving 7lb to Yellow Ribbon (3 May Warwick 7f frm RF 1013). AW high 79 - 1st of 8 giving 2lb to Mister Mal (25 Jun Wolverhampton RF 2312) - also 1st of 9 giving 5lb to En Silence (5 Jun Wolverhampton RF 1776). Consistent. Made the frame on turf and sand before winning a maiden and a handicap over seven furlongs on the Wolverhampton Fibresand in June. Somewhat disappointing when tried over the extended mile on the same track in August and seemed not to stay. **Sir Mark Prescott [2-9] Cheveley Park Stud.*

POLAR LADY RR 62+f 4731[6]

2 ch f Polar Falcon (USA) 9f **(74)** - Soluce (Junius (USA)) 7.7f **(65)**
Form - 6
Record **1999** - 1st:0 2nd:0 3rd:0 Ran:1
1999 Turf 0-1: (6f) (gd)
Currently average filly. **J R Fanshawe [0-1] Cheveley Park Stud.*

POLAR MIST BHB 58f65a RR 61f 65a 4487[10]

4 b g Polar Falcon (USA) 9f **(74)** - Post Mistress (IRE) **(71f)** (Cyrano de Bergerac) 6f **(68)**
Form - 0277203125402131008522162000
Record **1999** - 1st:4 2nd:5 3rd:2 Ran:22
Pre1999 - 1st:1 2nd:3 3rd:1 Ran:12
Win Prizemoney £13,942 *Total Prizemoney* £21,371
Wins *** 1999** *Jun Wolver (STD) H* 5f 59 61
*** 1999** Apr Folkes (HVY) 5f 70
*** 1999** *Mar Wolver (STD) S* 5f 56
*** 1999** *Jan Wolver (STD) C* 6f 64
1998 *Jan Wolver (STD)* 6f 73 <
1999 Turf 1-7: (5f 1-7) (g-s 1-2, gd 3, g-f 2) 1999 AW 3-15: (5f 2-7, 6f 1-7, 7f) (Equi, Fibr 3-14)
Neat, average gelding, effective 5 to 6f, best at 5f, acts on g-s to gd - acts on Fibr, has worn blinkers, and likes Wolverhampton. Turf high 70 - 1st of 9 giving 3lb to Indian Blaze (13 Apr Folkestone RF 0657). AW high 66 - 2nd of 15 giving 5lb to Samwar (24 Jly Southwell 5f Fibr RF 3115) - also 1st of 4 giving 3lb to Ice Age (13 Jan Wolverhampton RF 0086). Becoming disappointing. He is an effective sort in Fibresand sprint handicaps, though he can win on soft ground on turf. He stays six furlongs, but is probably best over a stiff five. At his best when able to dominate.
**Mrs N Macauley [4-29] Stephen Roots (from Sir Mark Prescott [1-5] Spt 1998).*

POLAR RED BHB 74f RR 73f 5158[3]

2 ch g Polar Falcon (USA) 9f **(74)** - Sharp Top (Sharpo) 7.7f **(59)**
Form - 64075123
Record **1999** - 1st:1 2nd:1 3rd:1 Ran:8
Win Prizemoney £3,046 *Total Prizemoney* £4,843
Wins *** 1999** Oct Windso (G-S) H 8.3f 66 73 <
1999 Turf 1-8: (5f, 6f, 7f 2, 8f 1-4) (sft, gd 2, g-f 1-2, frm 3)
Above-average gelding, effective 8f, acts on g-f, has worn blinkers. Turf high 73 (began Jly) - also 1st of 16 getting 8lb from Bremridge (11 Oct Windsor RF 4820). **M J Ryan [1-8] M Byron.*

POLAR REFRAIN BHB 27f25a RR 31f 25a 4593[8]

6 ch m Polar Falcon (USA) 9f **(74)** - Cut No Ice (Great Nephew) 9.9f **(64)**
Form - 08007060458
Record **1999** - 1st:0 2nd:0 3rd:0 Ran:11
Pre1999 - 1st:1 2nd:2 3rd:3 Ran:21
Win Prizemoney £2,010 *Total Prizemoney* £5,039
Wins * 1998 Jun Redcar (G-S) H 8f 25 29 <
1999 Turf 0-8: (7f, 8f 5, 9f, 10f) (gd 2, g-f 2, frm 2, hrd 2) 1999 AW 0-3: (8f 2, 12f) (Fibr 3)
Very moderate mare, effective 7 to 8f, best at 8f, acts on gd to frm, best on gd, has worn blinkers. Turf high 33. AW high 23.
**J L Eyre [1-13] The Flowerpot Men (from J Norton [0-5] Jun 1997).*

POLAR STAR RR 83f 5209[2]

2 b c Polar Falcon (USA) 9f **(74)** - Glowing With Pride (Ile de Bourbon (USA)) 10.1f **(67)**
Form - 02
Record **1999** - 1st:0 2nd:1 3rd:0 Ran:2
Win Prizemoney £0 *Total Prizemoney* £1,155
1999 Turf 0-2: (6f 2) (g-s, gd)
Currently decent colt. Turf high 83 (began Oct) - 2nd of 20 to Royal Highlander (5 Nov Doncaster 6f g-s RF 5209).
**C F Wall [0-2] A E Oppenheimer.*

POLES APART (IRE) BHB 86f RR 90f 3839[10]

3 b c Distinctly North (USA) 7.4f **(63)** - Slightly Latin (Ahonoora) 8.1f **(73)**
Form - 60050010
Record **1999** - 1st:1 2nd:0 3rd:0 Ran:8
Pre1999 - 1st:1 2nd:0 3rd:1 Ran:4
Win Prizemoney £7,223 *Total Prizemoney* £16,729
Wins *** 1999** Jly Doncas (G-F) H 6f 83 86 <
* 1998 Aug Folkes (G-F) 6f 84+
1999 Turf 1-8: (6f 1-4, 7f 3, 8f) (gd 2, g-f 2, frm 1-4)
Scopey, useful colt, effective 6f, acts on gd to g-f. Turf high 90 - 5th of 12 getting 10lb from Mitcham (15 May Newmarket 6f g-f RF 1244). Not beaten far in a valuable sales race at the Curragh at two, he had been generally disappointing until winning a 0-85 at Doncaster on his penultimate start.
**M H Tompkins [2-12] Flint Fairyhouse Partnership.*

POLISHED UP RR 43f 4428[7]

2 b f Polish Precedent (USA) 9f **(73)** - Smarten Up (Sharpen Up) 8.3f **(67)**
Form - 7
Record **1999** - 1st:0 2nd:0 3rd:0 Ran:1
1999 Turf 0-1: (7f) (g-s)
Currently moderate filly.
**P T Walwyn [0-1] Major & Mrs Kennard and Partners.*

POLISH FALCON (IRE) RR 20f 5046[9]

3 b g Polish Patriot (USA) 7.8f **(70)** - Marie de Fresnaye (USA) (Dom Racine (FR)) 9.2f **(62)**
Form - 0
Record **1999** - 1st:0 2nd:0 3rd:0 Ran:1
1999 Turf 0-1: (10f) (hvy)
Scopey, currently little account gelding.
**R Hannon [0-1] Major A M Everett.*

POLISH GIRL RR 4382[19]

3 b f Polish Precedent (USA) 9f **(73)** - Stack Rock **(105df)** (Ballad Rock) 7.8f **(63)**
Form - 0
Record **1999** - 1st:0 2nd:0 3rd:0 Ran:1
1999 Turf 0-1: (8f) (frm)
Scopey, currently very poor filly. **B J Meehan [0-1] F C T Wilson.*

POLISH LEGION BHB 34f32a RR 14f 32a 914[14]

6 b g Polish Precedent (USA) 9f **(73)** - Crystal Bright (Bold Lad (IRE)) 8.4f **(68)**
Form - 000000
Record **1999** - 1st:0 2nd:0 3rd:0 Ran:6
Pre1999 - 1st:1 2nd:0 3rd:0 Ran:6
Win Prizemoney £3,850 *Total Prizemoney* £3,850
Wins 1995 Apr Newbur (G-F) 5.2f 86+t <
1999 Turf 0-2: (8f 2) (frm 2) 1999 AW 0-4: (5f, 6f, 7f, 8f) (Equi 4)
Very moderate gelding. Turf high 14. AW high 33.
**J Akehurst [0-12] R J P J Partnership (from J H M Gosden [1-1] Apr 1995).*

POLISH PANACHE (USA) RR 93f 5171a[5]

2 br c Gone West (USA) 7.8f **(82)** - Polish Style (USA) (Danzig (USA)) 8.4f **(76)**

Form - 41355
1999 Turf 1-5: (7f 1-4, 8f) (sft, g-s, gd, g-f 1-1, frm)
Useful colt, has worn blinkers. Turf high 93 (began Jly) - 1st of 15 from Still Going On (11 Aug Gowran Park RF 3703a).
**J Oxx in IRE [1-5] Sheikh Mohammed.*

POLISH PILOT (IRE) BHB 40f67a **RR 32f 67a** 2667[14]
4 b g Polish Patriot (USA) 7.8f **(70)** - Va Toujours (Alzao (USA)) 7.1f **(68)**
Form - 000
Record 1999 - 1st:0 2nd:0 3rd:0 Ran:3
Pre1999 - 1st:0 2nd:0 3rd:1 Ran:11
Win Prizemoney £0 *Total Prizemoney* £429
1999 Turf 0-3: (8f, 9f, 11f) (g-f, frm 2)
Workmanlike, moderate gelding, effective 9f, acts on frm, has worn blinkers, favours tight tracks. Turf high 32.
**W R Muir [0-14] Mrs Barbara Jean Martin.*

POLISH SPIRIT BHB 59f **RR 60f** 5069[3]
4 b g Emarati (USA) 6.6f **(63)**-Gentle Star(Comedy Star (USA))7.5f **(50)**
Form - 433235410073
Record 1999 - 1st:1 2nd:1 3rd:4 Ran:12
Pre1999 - 1st:1 2nd:0 3rd:0 Ran:7
Win Prizemoney £11,047 *Total Prizemoney* £16,833
Wins * 1999 Aug Windso (HVY) H 8.3f 58 62
* 1998 Jly Warwic (G-F) 7f 69 <
1999 Turf 1-12: (6f, 7f, 8f 1-8, 10f 2) (sft, g-s, gd 1-5, g-f 3, frm 2)
Unfurnished, average gelding, effective 7 to 10f, acts on gd to frm, best on gd, prefers tight tracks. Turf high 62 - 1st of 13 giving 6lb to Warring (9 Aug Windsor RF 3489). Winner of a Warwick maiden over seven furlongs in 1998, he was on a long losing run before winning a tough Windsor handicap over a mile on heavy ground in August. Has disappointed since winning however.
**B R Millman [2-19] Mrs Izabel Palmer.*

POLIZIANO (USA) BHB 78f **RR 78f** 3849[3]
3 ch c Storm Bird (CAN) 8.5f **(82)** - Polemic (USA) (Roberto (USA)) 10f **(76)**
Form - 33
Record 1999 - 1st:0 2nd:0 3rd:2 Ran:2
Pre1999 - 1st:0 2nd:1 3rd:0 Ran:1
Win Prizemoney £0 *Total Prizemoney* £2,408
1999 Turf 0-2: (8f 2) (frm 2)
Scopey, currently above-average colt. Turf high 78 (began Jly).
**H R A Cecil [0-3] K Abdulla.*

POLKA BHB 43f **RR 38f** 1211[5]
4 b g Slip Anchor 12.7f **(75)** - Peace Dance (Bikala) 10.1f **(49)**
Form - 855
Record 1999 - 1st:0 2nd:0 3rd:0 Ran:3
Pre1999 - 1st:0 2nd:0 3rd:0 Ran:1
1999 Turf 0-2: (11f, 13f) (hvy, g-s) 1999 AW 0-1: (9f) (Fibr)
Very moderate gelding. Turf high 38.
**C W Thornton [0-4] Guy Reed.*

POLLY GOLIGHTLY BHB 65f50a **RR 59f 50a** 5212[4]
6 ch m Weldnaas (USA) 8.4f **(55)** - Polly's Teahouse (Shack (USA)) 5.8f **(53)**
Form - 564640005160044
Record 1999 - 1st:1 2nd:0 3rd:0 Ran:15
Pre1999 - 1st:7 2nd:4 3rd:7 Ran:59
Win Prizemoney £35,467 *Total Prizemoney* £51,603
Wins * 1999 Aug Cheste (G-S) H 5.1f 63 68
* 1998 Jun York (G-S) H 5f 56 73
* 1998 Jun Cheste (GD) H 5.1f 56 76?
* 1997 Oct Catter (SFT) H 5f 54 60
* 1997 Jun Goodwo (G-F) H 5f 59 64
* 1997 May Lingfi (G-F) H 5f 54 57
1995 Nov Doncas (G-F) H 5f 77 80 <
1995 May Bath (GD) 5.1f 60
1999 Turf 1-15: (5f 1-15) (g-s 5, gd 1-8, frm 2)
Fair mare, effective 5f, acts on g-s to frm, mostly wears blinkers. Turf high 70 - also 1st of 13 getting 11lb from Gay Breeze (21 Aug Chester RF 3816). Consistent. A speedy mare who runs from the front, she won twice in June '98, but went up the handicap as a result and struggled as a result. Ended a long losing run at Chester in August. Suited by some cut in the ground.
**M Blanshard [6-65] David Sykes (from B Smart [2-9] Nov 1995).*

POLLY MILLS BHB 58f85a **RR 61f 85a** 5199[17]
3 b f Lugana Beach 7f **(63)** - Danseuse Davis (FR) **(46f 42a)** (Glow (USA)) 6.7f **(71)**
Form - 12242453534210736306054 80
Record 1999 - 1st:1 2nd:1 3rd:4 Ran:19
Pre1999 - 1st:2 2nd:4 3rd:1 Ran:20
Win Prizemoney £8,848 *Total Prizemoney* £17,828
Wins * 1999 *Mar Southw (STD) H 6f 79 83* <
* 1998 *Nov Southw (STD) H 5f 72 78*
* 1998 Jun Windso (SFT) S 5f 66
1999 Turf 0-11: (5f 5, 6f 6) (gd 6, g-f, frm 3, hrd) 1999 AW 1-8: (6f 1-5, 7f 3) (Equi 3, Fibr 1-5)
Light-framed, decent filly, effective 5 to 7f, best at 6f, acts on gd to g-f - acts on AW, best on Equi, mostly wears blinkers (effectively), likes left handed tracks, likes tight tracks, excels at Lingfield, likes Southwell. Turf high 68. AW high 83 - 1st of 10 giving 13lb to Ashover Amber (19 Mar Southwell RF 0455). She has been kept very busy during her short career, and is a winner on turf and Fibresand, but has nothing in the way of scope.
**P D Evans [3-39] The Dave Evans Racing Club.*

POLLYOLLY (IRE) BHB 41f **RR 50f** 4941[16]
2 b f Emarati (USA) 6.6f **(63)** - Eurolink Virago (Charmer)
Form - 5000
Record 1999 - 1st:0 2nd:0 3rd:0 Ran:4
1999 Turf 0-4: (5f 2, 6f 2) (gd, g-f, frm 2)
Fair filly. Turf high 50 (began Aug).
**M J Haynes [0-4] Mrs Pauline Oliver.*

POLO BHB 78f **RR 74f** 4377[8]
3 b f Warning 8.1f **(77)** - Peace Dance (Bikala) 10.1f **(49)**
Form - 518
Record 1999 - 1st:1 2nd:0 3rd:0 Ran:3
Win Prizemoney £3,728 *Total Prizemoney* £3,728
Wins * 1999 Aug Pontef (GD) 10f 74 <
1999 Turf 1-3: (8f, 10f 1-2) (gd 2, frm 1-1)
Unfurnished, currently above-average filly. Turf high 74 (began Jly) - 1st of 10 from Horatia (16 Aug Pontefract RF 3676).
**C W Thornton [1-3] Guy Reed.*

POLO VENTURE BHB 58f68a **RR 64f 68a** 4763[19]
4 ch g Polar Falcon (USA) 9f **(74)** - Ceramic (USA) (Raja Baba (USA)) 10f **(64)**
Form - 0
Record 1999 - 1st:0 2nd:0 3rd:0 Ran:1
Pre1999 - 1st:1 2nd:1 3rd:4 Ran:12
Win Prizemoney £2,898 *Total Prizemoney* £5,983
Wins 1998 *May Lingfi (STD) 10f 69* <
1999 Turf 0-1: (12f) (gd)
Leggy, above-average gelding, effective 10 to 12f, best at 12f, acts on frm - acts on Equi.
**M D Hammond [1-10] Mrs Eve Sweetman (from S P C Woods [1-12] Aug 1998).*

POLRUAN BHB 59f **RR 51f** 4718[4]
3 ch g Elmaamul (USA) 8.1f **(70)** - Trelissick (Electric) 10.1f **(61)**
Form - 0685004
Record 1999 - 1st:0 2nd:0 3rd:0 Ran:7
Pre1999 - 1st:1 2nd:2 3rd:0 Ran:7
Win Prizemoney £3,030 *Total Prizemoney* £5,820
Wins 1998 Oct Warwic (GD) 6f 74+ <
1999 Turf 0-7: (5f, 7f 4, 8f 2) (gd 3, g-f 2, frm 2)
Leggy, fair gelding, effective 6 to 7f, best at 6f, acts on gd to g-f, best on gd, likes tight tracks. Turf high 70. Consistent.
**Lady Herries [0-7] Michael WingfieldDigby (from B R Millman [1-7] Nov 1998).*

POLY BLUE (IRE) BHB 63f **RR 40f** 1974[9]
4 ch f Thatching 7.8f **(69)** - Mazarine Blue (USA) (Chief's Crown (USA)) 9.8f **(72)**
Form - 00
Record 1999 - 1st:0 2nd:0 3rd:0 Ran:2
Pre1999 - 1st:1 2nd:1 3rd:1 Ran:14
Win Prizemoney £3,902 *Total Prizemoney* £7,997
Wins * 1997 Spt Newbur (G-S) 6f 80 <
1999 Turf 0-1: (8f) (g-f) 1999 AW 0-1: (8f) (Equi)
Unfurnished, moderate filly, effective 7f, acts on frm, has worn

blinkers. Becoming disappointing.
**Miss Gay Kelleway [1-16] Sheet & Roll Convertors Ltd.*

POLY RULER (IRE) BHB 40f **RR 54f** 4816[14]

3 b g Dancing Dissident (USA) 6.8f **(65)** - Love Me Tight (Tyrant (USA)) 6.6f **(59)**
Form - 0
Record 1999 - 1st:0 2nd:0 3rd:0 Ran:1
Pre1999 - 1st:0 2nd:0 3rd:0 Ran:4
1999 Turf 0-1: (10f) (gd)
Neat, fair gelding.
**Miss K M George [0-3] Miss K George (from M R Channon [0-4] Oct 1998).*

POMME DUCHESSE (USA) BHB 71f **RR 67f** 4790[1]

3 b f Alleged (USA) 11.8f **(81)** - Quilesse (USA) (Fulmar (USA)) 9f **(59)**
Form - 701
Record 1999 - 1st:1 2nd:0 3rd:0 Ran:3
Win Prizemoney £3,672 *Total Prizemoney* £3,672
Wins * 1999 Oct Lingfi (SFT) 9f 67 <
1999 Turf 1-3: (9f 1-1, 12f 2) (g-s 1-1, gd, frm)
Scopey, currently average filly. Turf high 67 (began Jly) - 1st of 9 from Royal Flame (8 Oct Lingfield RF 4790).
**C E Brittain [1-3] A J Richards.*

POMPEII (IRE) BHB 75f **RR 70f** 4996[9]

2 b c Salse (USA) 10.9f **(71)** - Before Dawn (USA) (Raise A Cup (USA)) 7.6f **(74)**
Form - 620
Record 1999 - 1st:0 2nd:1 3rd:0 Ran:3
Win Prizemoney £0 *Total Prizemoney* £1,123
1999 Turf 0-3: (8f 3) (g-s, gd, frm)
Currently above-average colt. Turf high 70 (began Spt) - 2nd of 10 to Osood (29 Spt Salisbury 8f g-s RF 4642). Short-headed at Salisbury on his second start, he should have no trouble winning races.
**P F I Cole [0-2] Highclere Thoroughbred Racing Ltd (from P W Chapple-Hyam [0-1] Spt 1999).*

PONTIKONISI BHB 50f **RR 57f** 4939[11]

2 b c Mistertopogigo (IRE) - Anse Chastanet (Cavo Doro) 10.6f **(57)**
Form - 0000
Record 1999 - 1st:0 2nd:0 3rd:0 Ran:4
1999 Turf 0-3: (6f, 7f 2) (sft, g-s, gd) 1999 AW 0-1: (7f) (Fibr)
Fair colt. Turf high 57 (began Aug). **K McAuliffe [0-4] Alex Fraser.*

POPLAR JAY BHB 29f **RR** 2519[14]

3 gr ro f Totem (USA) 5f **(38)** - Proclaimer (Town Crier) 10.2f **(55)**
Form - 000
Record 1999 - 1st:0 2nd:0 3rd:0 Ran:3
1999 Turf 0-3: (6f, 7f 2) (frm 3)
Light-framed, currently very poor filly. **J R Turner [0-3] D G Clayton.*

POPPADAM **RR 58f** 5137[10]

2 ch f Salse (USA) 10.9f **(71)** - Wanton (Kris) 9.5f **(73)**
Form - 0
Record 1999 - 1st:0 2nd:0 3rd:0 Ran:1
1999 Turf 0-1: (7f) (gd)
Currently fair filly. **L M Cumani [0-1] Lady Halifax.*

POPPY'S SONG BHB 72f **RR 74f** 4721[1]

2 b f Owington - Pretty Poppy (Song) 7.2f **(61)**
Form - 33441
Record 1999 - 1st:1 2nd:0 3rd:2 Ran:5
Win Prizemoney £3,458 *Total Prizemoney* £5,303
Wins * 1999 Oct Catter (SFT) 5f 61 <
1999 Turf 1-5: (5f 1-5) (gd 1-1, g-f 2, frm 2)
Above-average filly. Turf high 74 (began Jly). She has ability but looks a pretty awkward ride.
**H Candy [1-5] Thomas Frost & Partners.*

POP SHOP BHB 85f **RR 77f** 3974[2]

2 b c Owington - Diamond Park (IRE) **(60f)** (Alzao (USA)) 7.1f **(68)**
Form - 441662
Record 1999 - 1st:1 2nd:1 3rd:0 Ran:6
Win Prizemoney £3,150 *Total Prizemoney* £4,254
Wins * 1999 Jun Nottin (GD) 5.1f 68 <
1999 Turf 1-6: (5f 1-6) (gd, g-f 1-3, frm 2)
Above-average colt, effective 5f, acts on g-f to frm, best on g-f. Turf high 77 - 2nd of 7 giving 3lb to Harryana (28 Aug Redcar 5f frm RF 3974) - also 1st of 18 giving 3lb to Baby Barry (16 Jun Nottingham RF 2053). **J W Payne [1-6] Sir Simon Lycett Green.*

POPULOUS **RR** 4365a[2]

2 b c First Trump - Hotel California (IRE) (Last Tycoon) 8.5f **(62)**
Form - 2
Record 1999 - 1st:0 2nd:1 3rd:0 Ran:1
Win Prizemoney £0 *Total Prizemoney* £2,187
1999 Turf 0-1: (8f) (gd)
Colt. - 2nd of 13 to Fox Terraia (12 Spt Cascine 8f gd RF 4365a).
**M Quinlan [0-1].*

PORCINI (IRE) BHB 89f **RR 86f** 4952[4]

2 b c Alzao (USA) 9.8f **(73)** -Zurarah (Siberian Express (USA)) 8.8f **(65)**
Form - 16644
Record 1999 - 1st:1 2nd:0 3rd:0 Ran:5
Win Prizemoney £4,630 *Total Prizemoney* £5,501
Wins * 1999 Apr Newbur (G-F) 5.2f 86 <
1999 Turf 1-5: (5f 1-1, 6f 2, 7f 2) (g-s 2, gd, g-f, frm 1-1)
Useful colt. Turf high 86 (1st run) - 1st of 9 from Hoh Discovery (16 Apr Newbury RF 0717). Made a winning debut, but did not progress from that. **P F I Cole [1-5] Anthony Speelman.*

PORLOCK LADY BHB 32f **RR 20f** 1912[16]

4 b f King's Signet (USA) 7f **(51)** - Miramede (Norwick (USA)) 7.2f **(56)**
Form - 00
Record 1999 - 1st:0 2nd:0 3rd:0 Ran:2
Pre1999 - 1st:0 2nd:0 3rd:0 Ran:3
1999 Turf 0-2: (5f, 6f) (gd, frm)
Light-framed, little account filly.
**R J Hodges [0-5] John Davey Beverton.*

PORT BAYOU (USA) **RR 111f** 3778a[5]

3 b c Ghazi (USA) - Mrs.K. (USA)
Form - 213185
1999 Turf 2-5: (9f 1-1, 10f 1-3, 12f) (hvy 1-1, gd 1-3, g-f)
Strong, Group-class colt, effective 8 to 10f, acted on gd, had worn blinkers. Turf high 111 - 1st of 5 from Tchaikovsky (9 May Leopardstown RF 1169a). He sprang a surprise in the Derrinstown Stud Derby Trial at Leopardstown in May, but plans to send him to America for the Belmont Stakes were scrapped and he ran poorly on his two subsequent starts. Sadly broke a leg on the gallops in September. (DEAD) **D K Weld in IRE [3-9].*

PORTIA LADY BHB 51f **RR 54f** 4727[11]

2 b f Noble Patriarch 12.2f **(43)** - Gymcrak Lovebird (Taufan (USA)) 7f **(57)**
Form - 0864720
Record 1999 - 1st:0 2nd:1 3rd:0 Ran:7
Win Prizemoney £0 *Total Prizemoney* £735
1999 Turf 0-7: (6f, 7f 5, 10f) (g-s, gd, g-f 2, frm 3)
Fair filly, effective 7f, acts on gd to g-f, often wears blinkers, prefers tight tracks. Turf high 54 - 2nd of 15 getting 8lb from Dispol Magic (15 Spt Beverley 7f gd RF 4320).
**T D Easterby [0-7] Mrs Sue Tindall.*

PORTITE SOPHIE BHB 35f29a **RR 46f 29a** 4601[5]

8 b m Doulab (USA) 7.4f **(61)** - Impropriety (Law Society (USA)) 9.9f **(70)**
Form - 356004302365345
Record 1999 - 1st:0 2nd:1 3rd:3 Ran:14
Pre1999 - 1st:3 2nd:10 3rd:6 Ran:65
Win Prizemoney £7,018 *Total Prizemoney* £19,383
Wins * 1998 Spt Hamilt (SFT) S 9.2f 41
** 1997 Jly Southw (STD) C 11f 45* <
** 1996 Jly Wolver (STD) H 8.5f 29 32*
1999 Turf 0-8: (10f 3, 11f 2, 12f 3) (g-s, gd 4, g-f 2, frm) 1999 AW 0-6: (9f 2, 11f 3, 12f) (Fibr 6)
Moderate mare, effective 9 to 12f, acts on gd to g-f, best on gd, has worn blinkers, prefers right handed tracks, excels at Hamilton and Beverley. Turf high 46 - 3rd of 17 getting 5lb from The Wild Widow (30 Aug Warwick 11f gd RF 4032). AW high 40.
**M Brittain [3-79] Ms Maureen Hanlon.*

PORT MEADOW (IRE) RR 56f 4837[2]
3 b g Common Grounds 8.1f **(66)** - Kharimata (IRE) (Kahyasi)
Form - 37502
Record 1999 - 1st:0 2nd:1 3rd:1 Ran:5
Pre1999 - 1st:0 2nd:0 3rd:0 Ran:2
Win Prizemoney £0 *Total Prizemoney* £1,190
1999 Turf 0-4: (10f, 11f, 12f, 16f) (sft, gd 3) 1999 AW 0-1: (9f) (Fibr)
Well made, fair gelding. Turf high 56. **R Charlton [0-7] Lady Vestey.*

PORTRACK JUNCTION (IRE) BHB 53f **RR 52f** 4635[5]
2 b c Common Grounds 8.1f **(66)** - Boldabsa (Persian Bold) 9.3f **(66)**
Form - 0005
Record 1999 - 1st:0 2nd:0 3rd:0 Ran:4
1999 Turf 0-4: (5f, 6f 2, 8f) (g-s, gd, g-f, frm)
Fair colt. Turf high 52 (began Aug).
**N Tinkler [0-4] James Marshall & Mrs Susan Marshall.*

PORT ST CHARLES (IRE) RR 74f 3869[3]
2 b br c Night Shift (USA) 8.1f **(73)** - Safe Haven (Blakeney) 10.5f **(64)**
Form - 33
Record 1999 - 1st:0 2nd:0 3rd:2 Ran:2
Win Prizemoney £0 *Total Prizemoney* £955
1999 Turf 0-2: (5f, 6f) (g-f 2)
Currently above-average colt. Turf high 74 (began Aug) - 3rd of 9 giving 5lb to La Caprice (24 Aug Lingfield 5f g-f RF 3869).
**N A Callaghan [0-2] Mrs Doreen Tabor.*

PORT VILA (FR) BHB 100f **RR 93f** 4918[4]
2 b c Barathea (IRE) - Girouette (USA) (Nodouble (USA)) 8.8f **(68)**
Form - 114
Record 1999 - 1st:2 2nd:0 3rd:0 Ran:3
Win Prizemoney £10,202 *Total Prizemoney* £18,802
Wins * 1999 Spt Kempto (G-F) 7f 92+ <
*** 1999** Aug Newbur (GD) 7f 80+
1999 Turf 2-3: (7f 2-3) (gd 1-2, frm 1-1)
Currently useful colt. Turf high 93 (began Aug) - also 1st of 6 giving 5lb to Sobriety (8 Spt Kempton RF 4216). Winner of his first two races at Newbury and Kempton, he found the company in the Dewhurst too hot. **J H M Gosden [2-3] Hamdan Al Maktoum.*

POSATIVE BHB 36f29a **RR 27f 29a** 1816[10]
5 ch m Charmer 9f **(59)** - Suprette (Superlative) 7.2f **(56)**
Form - 060
Record 1999 - 1st:0 2nd:0 3rd:0 Ran:3
Pre1999 - 1st:0 2nd:0 3rd:0 Ran:4
1999 Turf 0-3: (8f 2, 12f) (gd, g-f 2)
Little account filly. Turf high 27. (DEAD)
**M P Muggeridge [0-3] M J Lewin (from M Salaman [0-4] Spt 1998).*

POSEIDON BHB 99f **RR 109f** 2284a[5]
5 b h Polar Falcon (USA) 9f **(74)** - Nastassia (FR) (Noble Decree (USA)) 10.2f **(76)**
Form - 45
1999 Turf 0-2: (10f, 12f) (gd, g-f)
Pattern-class colt, effective 12f, acts on gd to g-f. Turf high 109 - 5th of 7 to Dark Moondancer (20 Jun San Siro 12f g-f RF 2284a). Consistent. Finished a close-up fifth in the Group One Gran Premio di Milano.
**L Brogi in ITY [0-2] (from M R Channon [3-17] Aug 1998).*

POSIDONAS BHB 115f **RR 121?f** 2104[6]
7 b h Slip Anchor 12.7f **(75)**-Tamassos (Dance In Time (CAN)) 8.9f **(59)**
Form - 06
Record 1999 - 1st:0 2nd:0 3rd:0 Ran:2
Pre1999 - 1st:8 2nd:4 3rd:5 Ran:25
Win Prizemoney £274,583 *Total Prizemoney* £509,602
Wins * 1998 Jun Ascot (G-S) G2 12f 122
* 1998 Apr Newbur (HVY) G3 12f 115
* 1997 Spt Newbur (G-F) L 11f 113
* 1996 Jly Newmar (GD) G2 12f 123 <
* 1995 Spt San Si (SFT) G1 12f 108
* 1995 Spt Goodwo (GD) 12f 105
* 1995 Apr Newbur (GD) 11f 93
1999 Turf 0-2: (12f 2) (g-f, frm)
Very high-class horse, effective 11 to 12f, best at 12f, acts on sft to g-f, best on sft, has worn blinkers. Turf high 103. He was the subject of discouraging reports prior to Royal Ascot, and duly ran poorly in the Hardwicke Stakes (a race he won in 1998). Never particularly consistent, he acts on any ground and is genuine despite an awkward head-carriage. Reportedly retired to stud.
**P F I Cole [8-27] Athos Christodoulou.*

POSITIVE AIR BHB 51f **RR 42f** 4285[16]
4 b f Puissance 7.1f **(60)** - Breezy Day (Day Is Done) 6.3f **(67)**
Form - 00560
Record 1999 - 1st:0 2nd:0 3rd:0 Ran:5
Pre1999 - 1st:1 2nd:3 3rd:2 Ran:21
Win Prizemoney £7,304 *Total Prizemoney* £11,747
Wins * 1998 Jun Pontef (GD) H 6f 75 78 <
1999 Turf 0-5: (6f 2, 7f, 8f, 10f) (gd, g-f, frm 3)
Scopey, moderate filly, effective 6f, acts on g-f to frm, has worn blinkers. Turf high 42. **B A McMahon [1-26] R Thornhill.*

POWDER RIVER BHB 64f67a **RR 61f 67a** 4526[2]
5 b h Alzao (USA) 9.8f **(73)** - Nest (Sharpo) 7.7f **(59)**
Form - 70310077501342
Record 1999 - 1st:2 2nd:1 3rd:2 Ran:14
Pre1999 - 1st:1 2nd:0 3rd:2 Ran:6
Win Prizemoney £14,505 *Total Prizemoney* £21,635
Wins * 1999 Aug Redcar (G-F) H 11f 57 58
1999 *Mar Lingfi (STD) H 10f 62 67*
1996 Jly Epsom (G-F) 6f 77 <
1999 Turf 1-9: (10f 4, 11f 1-1, 12f 4) (g-s, gd, g-f 3, frm 1-4) 1999 AW 1-5: (7f, 8f, 9f, 10f 1-1, 12f) (Equi 1-3, Fibr 2)
Average colt, effective 8 to 12f, best at 10f, acts on gd to frm - acts on Equi, has worn blinkers, prefers left handed tracks. Turf high 67 - also 1st of 14 giving 13lb to Simple Ideals (28 Aug Redcar RF 3978). AW high 67 - 1st of 14 getting 12lb from Philistar (2 Mar Lingfield RF 0389). Improved after joining Karl Burke, and won a competitive event in fine style at Lingfield in March. Now with Tony Newcombe, his turf form was indifferent until he landed a gamble at Redcar in August.
**A G Newcombe [1-7] Alex Gorrie (from K R Burke [1-7] Jun 1999).*

POWER AND DEMAND BHB 51f **RR 47f** 4221[10]
2 b c Formidable (USA) 7.8f **(60)** - Mazurkanova (Song) 7.2f **(61)**
Form - 0060
Record 1999 - 1st:0 2nd:0 3rd:0 Ran:4
1999 Turf 0-3: (5f 3) (gd 3) 1999 AW 0-1: (5f) (Fibr)
Moderate colt. Turf high 47. **D Shaw [0-4] J C Fretwell.*

POWER AND PANACHE (USA) RR 95f 3720a[1]
3 b c Nureyev (USA) 8.4f **(84)** - Clear Issue (USA) (Riverman (USA)) 9.1f **(76)**
Form - 1331
1999 Turf 2-4: (8f 2, 9f 1-1, 11f 1-1) (g-f 1-3, frm 1-1)
Very useful colt, often wears blinkers. Turf high 95 - 1st of 8 from Pillar Rock (14 Aug Curragh RF 3720a) - also 1st of 6 getting 2lb from Serena (27 May Tipperary RF 1628a). He appreciated the step up to middle-distance on his final start and is open to improvement. Yet to race on extremes of ground, he wears blinkers but seems genuine. **D K Weld in IRE [2-4] Moyglare Stud Farm.*

POWER FLAME (GER) RR 116f 2859a[4]
6 ch g Dashing Blade 7.9f **(80)**-Pikante (GER) (Surumu (GER)) 10f **(83)**
Form - 24
1999 Turf 0-2: (8f, 9f) (gd 2)
High-class gelding. Turf high 114 (1st run) - 2nd of 9 giving 18lb to Gonlargo (20 Jun Dortmund 9f gd RF 2281a). A prolific winner in 1997 and 1998, he was not so successful last term and finished a long way behind Docksider at Hoppegarten in July.
**A Wohler in GER [5-7].*

POWER GAME BHB 24f49a **RR 28f 49a** 4591[13]
6 b g Puissance 7.1f **(60)** - Play the Game (Mummy's Game) 8.2f **(60)**
Form - 0600080
Record 1999 - 1st:0 2nd:0 3rd:0 Ran:7
Pre1999 - 1st:6 2nd:3 3rd:9 Ran:40
Win Prizemoney £16,798 *Total Prizemoney* £25,967
Wins 1997 May Mussel (G-F) H 8f 51 59
1997 May Mussel (G-S) S 8f 54
1996 Oct Leices (GD) C 8f 66 <
1996 Spt Hamilt (GD) C 8.3f 64
1996 Spt Thirsk (G-F) S 8f 59

1996 Aug Haydoc (G-F) S 8.1f 58
1999 Turf 0-7: (6f 3, 8f 3, 9f) (gd 2, g-f 3, frm 2)
Little account gelding, often wears blinkers. Turf high 43.
**D A Nolan [0-12] Mrs J McFadyen-Murray (from J Berry [6-35] Jly 1997).*

POWER GLOW BHB 28f RR 20f 3836[9]

3 gr g Puissance 7.1f **(60)** - Kala Rosa (Kalaglow) 9.8f **(67)**
Form - 0000
Record 1999 - 1st:0 2nd:0 3rd:0 Ran:4
Pre1999 - 1st:0 2nd:0 3rd:0 Ran:3
1999 Turf 0-4: (5f, 7f, 8f 2) (gd, g-f, frm 2)
Light-framed, little account gelding, has worn blinkers. Turf high 20. **J M Bradley [0-7] B Paling.*

POWER HIT (USA) BHB 56f RR 54f 3690[2]

3 b g Leo Castelli (USA) - Rajana (USA) (Rajab (USA))
Form - 85053602
Record 1999 - 1st:0 2nd:1 3rd:1 Ran:8
Win Prizemoney £0 *Total Prizemoney* £1,810
1999 Turf 0-8: (10f 3, 12f 4, 16f) (sft, gd, g-f, frm 4, hrd)
Fair gelding, effective 12f, acts on gd to frm, often wears blinkers (extremely effectively). Turf high 62.
**B R Millman [0-8] Avalon Surfacing Ltd.*

POWERLINE RR 61f 4006[6]

2 b f Warning 8.1f **(77)** - Kantikoy (Alzao (USA)) 7.1f **(68)**
Form - 06
Record 1999 - 1st:0 2nd:0 3rd:0 Ran:2
1999 Turf 0-2: (6f, 8f) (gd, g-f)
Currently average filly. Turf high 61 (began Jly).
**R Hannon [0-2] Lord Roborough.*

POWER PACKED BHB 92f RR 88f 4651[2]

2 b c Puissance 7.1f **(60)** - My First Romance **(64f)** (Danehill (USA)) 10f **(72)**
Form - 5212
Record 1999 - 1st:1 2nd:2 3rd:0 Ran:4
Win Prizemoney £5,810 *Total Prizemoney* £9,300
Wins * **1999** Aug Pontef (GD) 5f 80 <
1999 Turf 1-4: (5f 1-3, 6f) (gd, g-f, frm 1-2)
Useful colt. Turf high 88 (began Jly) - 2nd of 16 giving 7lb to Blue Velvet (30 Spt Newmarket 5f gd RF 4651) - also 1st of 12 from Trembley (22 Aug Pontefract RF 3843). Certainly going the right way, he appears best over the minimum trip.
**M A Jarvis [1-4] Mrs Greta Sarfaty Marchant.*

POY POY RR 1906a[3]

2 b c Forzando 7.2f **(63)** - La Domaine (Dominion) 8.5f **(63)**
Form - 13
Record 1999 - 1st:1 2nd:0 3rd:1 Ran:2
Win Prizemoney £5,468 *Total Prizemoney* £8,530
Wins **1999** May San Si (SFT) 5f
1999 Turf 1-2: (5f 1-2) (sft 1-1, gd)
Colt - 3rd of 5 giving 5lb to Jezebel (6 Jun San Siro 5f gd RF 1906a) - also 1st of 7 from Persian Filly (5 May San Siro RF 1202a). Started off his career racing at San Siro, winning in soft ground over the minimum on his debut.
**M Quinlan [0-1] (from M G Quinlan [1-1] May 1999).*

POZARICA BHB 106f RR 106f 4417[6]

4 b c Rainbow Quest (USA) 11.2f **(81)** - Anna Matrushka (Mill Reef (USA)) 10.5f **(78)**
Form - 426
Record 1999 - 1st:0 2nd:1 3rd:0 Ran:3
Pre1999 - 1st:2 2nd:0 3rd:0 Ran:2
Win Prizemoney £52,525 *Total Prizemoney* £65,136
Wins 1998 Jly Maison (GD) G2 15f 106 <
1998 Jly Chanti (GD) G3 15f 99
1999 Turf 0-3: (11f, 14f, 16f) (gd 3)
Pattern-class colt. Turf high 106 - 2nd of 7 getting 3lb from Tajoun (5 Spt Longchamp 16f gd RF 4247a). He won three Pattern races for Nicholas Clement in '98, but is now with Godolphin for whom he is a useful work horse. Finished fourth behind stable companion Opera King in the Shergar Cup Stayers' at Goodwood in May, and found only Tajoun too good in the Prix Gladiateur at Longchamp in September.
**S bin Suroor [0-3] Godolphin (from N Clement in FR [2-2] Jly 1998).*

PRAETORIAN GOLD BHB 72f RR 76f 4758[4]

4 ch g Presidium 7.5f **(56)** - Chinese Princess (Sunny Way) 9f **(53)**
Form - 070260353264
Record 1999 - 1st:0 2nd:2 3rd:2 Ran:12
Pre1999 - 1st:3 2nd:1 3rd:2 Ran:15
Win Prizemoney £12,497 *Total Prizemoney* £24,467
Wins * 1998 Jun Chepst (G-S) H 10.2f 76 80 <
* 1998 Jun Goodwo (GD) H 9.9f 68 75
* 1997 Spt Nottin (GD) 6.1f 66
1999 Turf 0-12: (10f 11, 12f) (g-s, gd 4, g-f 2, frm 5)
Above-average gelding, effective 10f, acts on gd, has worn blinkers, likes left handed tracks. Turf high 78 - 3rd of 9 getting 7lb from Komistar (27 Jun Doncaster 10f gd RF 2351).
**R Hannon [3-27] The Gold Buster Syndicate (2).*

PRAIRIE DOWNS (USA) RR 67f 1662[5]

2 ch f Thunder Gulch (USA) - Tough As Nails (USA) (Majestic Light (USA)) 10.6f **(75)**
Form - 35
Record 1999 - 1st:0 2nd:0 3rd:1 Ran:2
Win Prizemoney £0 *Total Prizemoney* £1,149
1999 Turf 0-2: (5f 2) (gd 2)
Currently average filly. Turf high 67. **J Berry [0-2] Chris Deuters.*

PRAIRIE FALCON (IRE) BHB 88f RR 87f 1044[4]

5 b g Alzao (USA) 9.8f **(73)** - Sea Harrier (Grundy) 10.3f **(65)**
Form - 24
Record 1999 - 1st:0 2nd:1 3rd:0 Ran:2
Pre1999 - 1st:3 2nd:2 3rd:2 Ran:17
Win Prizemoney £10,092 *Total Prizemoney* £19,842
Wins * 1998 Spt Goodwo (G-F) H 12f 81 85 <
* 1998 Spt Haydoc (GD) H 10.5f 80 80
* 1997 May Chepst (GD) 12.1f 80
1999 Turf 0-2: (16f, 19f) (g-f 2)
Useful gelding, effective 11 to 19f, acts on g-f to frm, best on g-f, prefers tight tracks. Turf high 87 - 4th of 16 getting 12lb from Rainbow High (5 May Chester 19f g-f RF 1044).
**B W Hills [3-19] Mrs B W Hills.*

PRAIRIE RUNNER (IRE) RR 106f 3408a[4]

3 b f Arazi (USA) 9.2f **(74)** - Paix Blanche (FR) (Fabulous Dancer (USA)) 9.4f **(70)**
Form - 14
1999 Turf 1-2: (13f 1-1, 14f) (gd 1-2)
Currently Pattern-class filly. Turf high 106 (began Jly) - 4th of 11 getting 12lb from Bimbola (1 Aug Deauville 14f gd RF 3408a) - also 1st of 8 from Keemoon (14 Jly Deauville RF 3037a).
**A Fabre in FR [1-2].*

PRAIRIE WOLF BHB 90f74a RR 93f 74a 4683[17]

3 ch g Wolfhound (USA) 7.3f **(71)** - Bay Queen **(75f)** (Damister (USA)) 9f **(73)**
Form - 13131863210
Record 1999 - 1st:4 2nd:1 3rd:3 Ran:11
Pre1999 - 1st:0 2nd:0 3rd:0 Ran:2
Win Prizemoney £24,972 *Total Prizemoney* £36,197
Wins * **1999** Aug Yarmou (GD) 10.1f 93 <
* **1999** May Nottin (FRM) H 8.2f 78 85+
* **1999** Apr Ripon (G-S) H 8f 73 75
* ***1999*** *Mar Wolver (STD) 8.5f 75*
1999 Turf 3-10: (8f 2-6, 9f, 10f 1-3) (g-s, gd 2-3, g-f 1-3, frm 3) 1999 AW 1-1: (8f 1-1) (Fibr 1-1)
Workmanlike, useful gelding, effective 8 to 10f, best at 10f, acts on gd to frm, prefers tight tracks. Turf high 93 - 1st of 6 getting 2lb from Sharmy (29 Aug Yarmouth RF 4005) - also 1st of 15 giving 3lb to Spy (22 May Nottingham RF 1414). (1st run). He was in fine form last season, winning four times, one of which one was on Fibresand. He was not disgraced in the Britannia, and also ran well when third in a very competitive handicap at Glorious Goodwood. Acts on fast ground and stays ten furlongs.
**M L W Bell [4-13] B J Warren.*

PRALY DE VEZ (FR) RR 92f 7094a[3]
4 f
Form - 3
1999 Turf 0-1: (17f)
Currently useful filly. (1st run) - 3rd of 6 getting 4lb from Arctic (7 Aug Vichy 17f RF 7094a). **in FR [0-1].*

PRASLIN ISLAND BHB 57f67a **RR 59f 67a** 5188[6]
3 ch c Be My Chief (USA) 10.2f **(62)** - Hence (USA) (Mr Prospector (USA)) 8.8f **(78)**
Form - 82264407206
Record 1999 - 1st:0 2nd:3 3rd:0 Ran:11
Win Prizemoney £0 *Total Prizemoney* £2,874
1999 Turf 0-10: (12f, 14f 3, 15f 2, 16f 2, 17f 2) (g-s, gd, g-f 4, frm 4)
1999 AW 0-1: (15f) (Fibr)
Workmanlike, average colt, effective 14 to 17f, acts on g-f to frm - acts on Fibr, has worn blinkers, prefers left handed tracks, prefers tight tracks. Turf high 73 - 2nd of 5 giving 5lb to Tegyra (21 Jun Yarmouth 14f g-f RF 2184). (1st run) - 2nd of 12 giving 10lb to Up And About (13 Oct Wolverhampton 15f Fibr RF 4863). A maiden, he stays well but is very one-paced. **A Kelleway [0-11] Kevin Hudson.*

PRECIOUS MOMENTS RR 3921[1]
3 b f Polar Falcon (USA) 9f **(74)** - Brassy Nell (Dunbeath (USA)) 7.8f **(70)**
Form -
Record 1999 - 1st:1 2nd:2 3rd:1 Ran:5
Win Prizemoney £3,046 *Total Prizemoney* £6,036
Wins * 1999 Aug Mussel (G-F) C 9f 56 <
1999 Turf 1-5: (g-s, gd 2, g-f 1-1, frm)
Unfurnished, above-average gelding. Turf high 73.
**J Noseda [1-5] Lucayan Stud.*

PRECIOUS PERSIAN (IRE) BHB 72f **RR 72f** 5025[6]
3 b f Persian Bold 10f **(69)** - Cliveden Gail (IRE) **(93f)** (Law Society (USA)) 9.9f **(70)**
Form - 343282166
Record 1999 - 1st:1 2nd:2 3rd:2 Ran:9
Win Prizemoney £2,637 *Total Prizemoney* £5,885
Wins * 1999 Spt Warwic (SFT) H 15.8f 70 72+ <
1999 Turf 1-9: (12f 2, 14f 2, 15f 2, 16f 1-3) (sft 1-1, gd 3, g-f 3, frm 2)
Light-framed, above-average filly, effective 14 to 16f, acts on sft to frm, likes tight tracks. Turf high 77 - 3rd of 7 getting 20lb from Kadir (2 Jly Sandown 14f g-f RF 2502) - also 1st of 14 giving 18lb to Couchant (21 Spt Warwick RF 4456). She was consistent last season and seemed to appreciate the soft ground and extended trip when winning at Warwick in September.
**S P C Woods [1-9] George Tong.*

PRECIOUS YEARS BHB 35f **RR 42df** 4148[16]
4 ch g Dilum (USA) 7.1f **(56)** - Tantot (Charlottown) 10.9f **(57)**
Form - 00
Record 1999 - 1st:0 2nd:0 3rd:0 Ran:2
Pre1999 - 1st:0 2nd:0 3rd:0 Ran:2
1999 Turf 0-2: (5f, 10f) (frm, hrd)
Workmanlike, moderate gelding. Turf high 13 (began Aug).
**L R Lloyd-James [0-2] Miss Kate Waddington (from R Simpson [0-2] Oct 1998).*

PRECOCIOUS MISS (USA) BHB 85f **RR 85?f** 1000[7]
3 b f Diesis 9f **(80)** - Kissogram Girl (USA) (Danzig (USA)) 8.4f **(76)**
Form - 7
Record 1999 - 1st:0 2nd:0 3rd:0 Ran:1
Pre1999 - 1st:1 2nd:1 3rd:0 Ran:2
Win Prizemoney £3,310 *Total Prizemoney* £4,448
Wins * 1998 Aug Lingfi (G-F) 6f 71 <
1999 Turf 0-1: (6f) (frm)
Scopey, currently useful filly.
**Sir Michael Stoute [1-3] Maktoum Al Maktoum.*

PREDATOR RR 76f 5005[8]
2 b g Polar Falcon (USA) 9f **(74)** - Red Azalea **(88f)** (Shirley Heights) 10.3f **(74)**
Form - 58
Record 1999 - 1st:0 2nd:0 3rd:0 Ran:2
1999 Turf 0-2: (5f, 6f) (gd, g-f)
Currently above-average gelding. Turf high 76 (began Oct).
**Sir Mark Prescott [0-2] Neil Greig Osborne House.*

PREMIER BARON BHB 80f66a **RR 90f 66a** 5141[14]
4 b g Primo Dominie 7.2f **(67)** - Anna Karietta (Precocious) 8.6f **(62)**
Form - 253146220
Record 1999 - 1st:1 2nd:3 3rd:1 Ran:9
Pre1999 - 1st:0 2nd:1 3rd:2 Ran:9
Win Prizemoney £7,457 *Total Prizemoney* £18,611
Wins * 1999 Aug Sandow (G-S) H 7.1f 75 78 <
1999 Turf 1-8: (7f 1-6, 8f 2) (g-s, gd 5, g-f 1-2) 1999 AW 0-1: (7f) (Fibr)
Leggy, useful gelding, effective 7f, acts on gd. Turf high 90 - 2nd of 10 to Adjutant (25 Oct Leicester 7f gd RF 5055). Fine effort on his seasonal reappearance at Doncaster and may well have won had he not been interfered with. However, he did not lose his maiden tag until he won a handicap in good style at Sandown in August, and perhaps flew too high after that success.
**Pat Mitchell [1-9] Miss T J Fitzgerald (from T T Clement [0-9] Oct 1998).*

PREMIER DANCE BHB 45f57a **RR 47f 57a** 1122[11]
12 ch g Bairn (USA) 9.4f **(55)** - Gigiolina (King Emperor (USA)) 9.4f **(58)**
Form - 21520
Record 1999 - 1st:1 2nd:2 3rd:0 Ran:5
Pre1999 - 1st:12 2nd:18 3rd:21 Ran:124
Win Prizemoney £34,695 *Total Prizemoney* £59,385
Wins * 1999 *Feb Wolver (STD) H 12f 49 55+*
** 1997 May Wolver (STD) H 12f 66 68*
** 1997 Mar Wolver (STD) H 14.8f 60 62*
** 1996 May Wolver (STD) H 12f 68 74* <
** 1996 Feb Wolver (STD) H 12f 65 64*
** 1996 Jan Southw (STD) H 12f 62 61*
** 1995 Dec Wolver (STD) H 12f 56 61*
** 1995 Jan Wolver (STD) H 14f 55 58+*
1999 AW 1-5: (12f 1-3, 15f, 16f) (Fibr 1-5)
Fair gelding, effective 15 to 16f, - acts on Fibr, has worn blinkers, favours left handed tracks. AW high 57.
**D HaydnJones [13-129] J S Fox and Sons.*

PREMIERE DIVISION BHB 40f **RR 33f** 4539[11]
3 b f Be My Chief (USA) 10.2f **(62)** - One Half Silver (CAN) (Plugged Nickle (USA)) 7.8f **(68)**
Form - 073710670
Record 1999 - 1st:1 2nd:0 3rd:1 Ran:9
Pre1999 - 1st:0 2nd:0 3rd:0 Ran:4
Win Prizemoney £2,905 *Total Prizemoney* £3,283
Wins * 1999 Jly Carlis (FRM) H 9.3f 41 45 <
1999 Turf 1-8: (8f 3, 9f 1-1, 10f 2, 11f, 12f) (g-s, g-f 2, frm 1-4, hrd)
1999 AW 0-1: (8f) (Fibr)
Scopey, very moderate filly, effective 8 to 9f, acts on g-f to frm, likes tight tracks. Turf high 45 - 1st of 7 getting 4lb from Durham Dandy (16 Jly Carlisle RF 2865). Inconsistent.
**Miss L A Perratt [1-13] Lostford Manor Stud.*

PREMIERE FOULEE (FR) BHB 32f37a **RR 27f 37a** 5066[11]
4 ch f Sillery (USA) - Dee (Caerleon (USA)) 8.6f **(71)**
Form - 4446020
Record 1999 - 1st:0 2nd:1 3rd:0 Ran:7
Win Prizemoney £0 *Total Prizemoney* £684
1999 Turf 0-5: (8f, 12f 3, 14f) (g-s, gd 2, g-f, frm) 1999 AW 0-2: (12f, 14f) (Fibr 2)
Very moderate filly, has worn blinkers. Turf high 53. AW high 39.
**F Jordan [0-13] Bill Woodward.*

PREMIERE VALENTINO RR 48f 5194[13]
2 b g Tragic Role (USA) 9.4f **(63)** - Mirkan Honey (Ballymore) 7.3f **(64)**
Form - 0
Record 1999 - 1st:0 2nd:0 3rd:0 Ran:1
1999 Turf 0-1: (6f) (gd)
Currently moderate gelding. **D W P Arbuthnot [0-1] Mrs W A Oram.*

PREMIER FOIS BHB 70f **RR 51f** 4379[5]
2 b f Pelder (IRE) - Doris Doors **(57f 48a)** (Beveled (USA)) 9f **(59)**
Form - 15
Record 1999 - 1st:1 2nd:0 3rd:0 Ran:2
Win Prizemoney £2,119 *Total Prizemoney* £2,310
Wins * 1999 Aug Lingfi (GD) 6f 62 <

1999 Turf 1-2: (6f 1-1, 7f) (gd, frm 1-1)
Currently fair filly. Turf high 62 (1st run) (began Aug) - 1st of 10 getting 5lb from Victor's Crown (13 Aug Lingfield RF 3610).
**G C H Chung [1-2] Osvaldo Pedroni.*

PREMIER LEAGUE (IRE) BHB 28f35a RR 38f 35a 3301[5]

9 gr g Don't Forget Me 9.5f **(66)** - Kilmara (USA) (Caro)
Form - 254500045
Record 1999 - 1st:0 2nd:0 3rd:0 Ran:7
Pre1999 - 1st:4 2nd:3 3rd:2 Ran:38
Win Prizemoney £13,262 *Total Prizemoney* £16,741
Wins * 1998 Aug Windso (G-F) H 11.6f 48 52
* 1998 Jly Windso (G-F) SH 11.6f 43 48
1999 Turf 0-4: (10f, 12f 3) (gd 2, frm 2) 1999 AW 0-3: (13f 2, 16f) (Equi 3)
Moderate gelding, effective 12f, acts on g-f to frm - acts on Equi, best on frm, favours tight tracks. Turf high 40. AW high 40. Consistent.
**K O Cunningham-Brown [2-20] The Harkander Partnership (from J E Long [0-19] Apr 1997).*

PREMIER PRIZE RR 87f 5136[1]

2 ch f Selkirk (USA) 7.9f **(76)** - Spot Prize (USA) **(96df)** (Seattle Dancer (USA))
Form - 61
Record 1999 - 1st:1 2nd:0 3rd:0 Ran:2
Win Prizemoney £4,477 *Total Prizemoney* £4,477
Wins * 1999 Oct Newmar (SFT) 7f 87 <
1999 Turf 1-2: (6f, 7f 1-1) (gd 1-2)
Currently useful filly. Turf high 87 (began Oct) - 1st of 16 from Arabesque (30 Oct Newmarket RF 5136).
**D R C Elsworth [1-2] J C Smith.*

PREMIER PROJECT (IRE) BHB 62f RR 68df 3819[13]

7 b g Project Manager 7.2f **(47)** - Lady Beck (FR) (Sir Gaylord) 10.6f **(64)**
Form - 6250
Record 1999 - 1st:0 2nd:1 3rd:0 Ran:4
Pre1999 - 1st:5 2nd:1 3rd:1 Ran:12
Win Prizemoney £15,241 *Total Prizemoney* £17,380
Wins 1997 Apr Currag (GD) H 10f 82 77 <
1996 Jun Currag (GD) H 12f 78 75
1996 May Currag (G-S) H 12f 73
1996 May Killar (G-F) 12f 67
1996 May Limeri (GD) 12f 70
1999 Turf 0-4: (10f 2, 12f 2) (g-f 2, frm 2)
Average gelding. Turf high 68 (began Jly). Inconsistent.
**M Johnston [0-4] Mark Smith (from J S Bolger in IRE [5-13] Jun 1997).*

PREMIUM PRINCESS BHB 61f52a RR 62f 52a 2156[8]

4 b f Distant Relative 7f **(69)** - Solemn Occasion (USA) (Secreto (USA)) 8.7f **(72)**
Form - 500148
Record 1999 - 1st:1 2nd:0 3rd:0 Ran:4
Pre1999 - 1st:0 2nd:4 3rd:2 Ran:19
Win Prizemoney £7,360 *Total Prizemoney* £12,561
Wins * 1999 May Newcas (FRM) H 5f 56 57 <
1999 Turf 1-4: (5f 1-1, 6f 3) (gd, g-f, frm, hrd 1-1)
Lengthy, average filly, effective 5 to 7f, best at 7f, acts on g-f to hrd, best on frm. Turf high 62 - 4th of 15 getting 13lb from Almasi (5 Jun Doncaster 6f g-f RF 1755) - also 1st of 19 getting 4lb from Poetry In Motion (27 May Newcastle RF 1525). She gained her first victory on her second start of the season at Newcastle, appreciating the very fast ground and a forceful ride.
**J J Quinn [1-23] Derrick Bloy.*

PREMIUM PURSUIT BHB 48f RR 31f 2881[9]

4 b g Pursuit of Love 9.5f **(69)** - Music in My Life (IRE) (Law Society (USA)) 9.9f **(70)**
Form - 700
Record 1999 - 1st:0 2nd:0 3rd:0 Ran:3
Pre1999 - 1st:1 2nd:2 3rd:1 Ran:16
Win Prizemoney £3,304 *Total Prizemoney* £6,305
Wins * 1997 Jun Doncas (GD) 6f 81 <
1999 Turf 0-3: (7f, 8f 2) (gd, frm 2)
Very moderate gelding, effective 8f, acts on g-f, has worn blinkers. Turf high 31. Consistent. **R A Fahey [1-19] J C Parsons.*

PREMIUM QUEST BHB 53f53a RR 50f 53a 504[9]

4 b g Forzando 7.2f **(63)** - Sabonis (USA) (The Minstrel (CAN)) 10f **(72)**
Form - 0
Record 1999 - 1st:0 2nd:0 3rd:0 Ran:1
Pre1999 - 1st:1 2nd:1 3rd:2 Ran:13
Win Prizemoney £3,925 *Total Prizemoney* £6,115
Wins * 1997 Oct Pontef (G-S) H 8f 66 70 <
1999 Turf 0-1: (12f) (hvy)
Workmanlike, fair gelding, effective 12f, - acts on Fibr, has worn blinkers (very effectively), favours tight tracks.
**R A Fahey [2-18] J C Parsons.*

PRESELI (IRE) RR 99f 4201a[1]

2 b f Caerleon (USA) 10.9f **(79)** - Hill Of Snow
Form - 111
1999 Turf 3-3: (7f 3-3) (gd 1-1, g-f 2-2)
Currently very useful filly. Turf high 99 (began Jly) - 1st of 12 from Torgau (5 Spt Curragh RF 4201a). She improved with every start and put up a top-class performance when beating Torgau in the Group One Moyglare Stud Stakes. Likely to stay beyond a mile, she is being trained for the Irish 1,000 Guineas and should give a good account of herself in that race.
**M J Grassick in IRE [3-3] Neil Jones.*

PRESELI MAGIC BHB 43f RR 48f 4160[5]

3 gr f Puissance 7.1f **(60)** - Swallow Bay (Penmarric (USA))
Form - 000655
Record 1999 - 1st:0 2nd:0 3rd:0 Ran:6
Pre1999 - 1st:0 2nd:0 3rd:1 Ran:5
Win Prizemoney £0 *Total Prizemoney* £270
1999 Turf 0-6: (5f, 6f 3, 7f 2) (g-f, frm 4, hrd)
Strong, moderate filly, effective 6f, acts on g-f, has worn blinkers. Turf high 48. **D HaydnJones [0-11] The Preseli Partnership.*

PRESENTATION (IRE) BHB 96f RR 87f 4690[3]

2 b f Mujadil (USA) 7.7f **(70)** - Beechwood (USA) (Blushing Groom (FR)) 10.3f **(76)**
Form - 1547633
Record 1999 - 1st:1 2nd:0 3rd:2 Ran:7
Win Prizemoney £5,243 *Total Prizemoney* £26,770
Wins * 1999 May Windso (GD) 5f 72+ <
1999 Turf 1-7: (5f 1-4, 6f 3) (gd 1-3, g-f 3, frm)
Useful filly, effective 6f, acts on g-f. Turf high 89. She may not have beaten much when winning on her Windsor debut, but did it in style. Creditable efforts in Group races since, but she may need her sights lowered a little if she is to win again.
**R Hannon [1-7] Dr A Haloute.*

PRESENT CHANCE BHB 71f64a RR 71f 64a 2164[4]

5 ch g Cadeaux Genereux 7.9f **(76)** - Chance All (FR) (Glenstal (USA)) 10.1f **(64)**
Form - 03601534
Record 1999 - 1st:1 2nd:0 3rd:2 Ran:8
Pre1999 - 1st:1 2nd:4 3rd:6 Ran:25
Win Prizemoney £9,488 *Total Prizemoney* £22,188
Wins * 1999 *Jun Southw (STD) H 5f 58 65*
1998 Jly Goodwo (G-S) 6f 80 <
1999 Turf 0-5: (6f 4, 7f) (g-s, gd 3, hrd) 1999 AW 1-3: (5f 1-1, 6f, 7f) (Fibr 1-3)
Above-average gelding, effective 5 to 6f, best at 6f, acts on g-s to frm, has worn blinkers. Turf high 71. AW high 65. Inconsistent. Came good over the minimum on the Southwell Fibresand, though he hung badly left and may be one to treat with caution.
**D Shaw [1-8] Ian Guise (from B A McMahon [1-25] Oct 1998).*

PRESENT GENERATION BHB 72f RR 71?f 2820[7]

6 ch g Cadeaux Genereux 7.9f **(76)** - Penny Mint (Mummy's Game) 8.2f **(60)**
Form - 07
Record 1999 - 1st:0 2nd:0 3rd:0 Ran:2
Pre1999 - 1st:2 2nd:6 3rd:0 Ran:21
Win Prizemoney £6,953 *Total Prizemoney* £13,943
Wins * 1998 Jly Bright (GD) H 8f 77 83 <
* 1997 Aug Epsom (GD) 7f 77
1999 Turf 0-2: (6f 2) (frm 2)
Above-average gelding, has broken blood-vessels, effective 8f, acts on gd. Inconsistent. **R Guest [2-23] S Lury.*

PRESENT LAUGHTER BHB 85f80a **RR 91f 80a** 4151[8]
3 b c Cadeaux Genereux 7.9f **(76)** - Ever Genial (Brigadier Gerard) 9.3f **(58)**
Form - 182508
Record 1999 - 1st:1 2nd:1 3rd:0 Ran:6
Pre1999 - 1st:0 2nd:1 3rd:0 Ran:1
Win Prizemoney £3,817 *Total Prizemoney* £7,445
Wins * **1999** Mar Warwic (G-S) 5f 79 <
1999 Turf 1-5: (5f 1-2, 6f 2, 7f) (g-s 1-1, gd 3, g-f) 1999 AW 0-1: (7f) (Fibr)
Scopey, useful colt, effective 7f, acts on g-s to gd. Turf high 91 - 2nd of 5 getting 10lb from Marton Moss (4 Jun Haydock 7f gd RF 1742). He has ability and does stay seven furlongs, even though his Warwick victory came in a modest maiden over the minimum. Has not worried the judge since his win.
**P F I Cole [1-7] Penelope, Viscountess Portman.*

PRESENT 'N CORRECT BHB 43f40a **RR 40f 40a** 3622[9]
6 ch g Cadeaux Genereux 7.9f **(76)** - Emerald Eagle (Sandy Creek) 8.9f **(59)**
Form - 104530282545363550
Record 1999 - 1st:0 2nd:2 3rd:3 Ran:15
Pre1999 - 1st:2 2nd:1 3rd:2 Ran:23
Win Prizemoney £5,644 *Total Prizemoney* £10,272
Wins * 1998 *Nov Lingfi (STD) H 7f 33 42*
1996 Spt Thirsk (G-F) H 5f 45 45 <
1999 Turf 0-12: (5f 3, 6f 7, 7f 2) (g-s, g-f 4, frm 7) 1999 AW 0-3: (6f 2, 7f) (Equi 2, Fibr)
Moderate gelding, effective 5 to 7f, best at 6f, acts on g-s to frm - acts on Equi, best on frm. Turf high 47 (1st run) - 2nd of 18 giving 7lb to Harvey's Future (27 Apr Bath 5f g-s RF 0863). AW high 36. Consistent.
**J M Bradley [1-25] M B Clemence (from C B B Booth [1-13] Jly 1997).*

PRESIDENTS LADY RR 32f 4751[19]
2 b f Superpower 6.6f **(58)** - Flirty Lady (Never so Bold) 6.3f **(66)**
Form - 0
Record 1999 - 1st:0 2nd:0 3rd:0 Ran:1
1999 Turf 0-1: (8f) (gd)
Currently very moderate filly.
**J G Smyth-Osbourne [0-1] Mrs J Harmsworth.*

PRESS AGAIN BHB 37f26a **RR 43f 26a** 3985[11]
7 ch m Then Again 7.4f **(52)** - Silver Empress (Octavo (USA)) 14.4f **(54)**
Form - 00070
Record 1999 - 1st:0 2nd:0 3rd:0 Ran:4
Pre1999 - 1st:0 2nd:0 3rd:1 Ran:16
Win Prizemoney £0 *Total Prizemoney* £452
1999 Turf 0-4: (7f, 8f 2, 10f) (gd, frm 3)
Moderate mare, effective 7 to 8f, acts on gd to g-f. Turf high 43 - 7th of 14 getting 16lb from Halmanerror (11 Jun Chepstow 7f gd RF 1908). **P Hayward [0-23] J Sawyer.*

PRESS AHEAD BHB 51f55a **RR 52f 55a** 599[2]
4 b c Precocious 7.2f **(54)** - By Line (High Line) 10.3f **(70)**
Form - 602
Record 1999 - 1st:0 2nd:1 3rd:0 Ran:3
Pre1999 - 1st:1 2nd:1 3rd:0 Ran:10
Win Prizemoney £2,322 *Total Prizemoney* £3,985
Wins * 1998 *Jly Wolver (STD) 6f 65* <
1999 Turf 0-1: (5f) (gd) 1999 AW 0-2: (6f 2) (Fibr 2)
Workmanlike, average colt, effective 5 to 6f, - acts on Fibr, has worn blinkers. AW high 39. **B A McMahon [1-13] R L Bedding.*

PRESS TIMES (USA) BHB 44f **RR 46f** 2766[7]
3 b c Press Card (USA) - Doubling Time (USA) (Timeless Moment (USA)) 6f **(72)**
Form - 6807
Record 1999 - 1st:0 2nd:0 3rd:0 Ran:4
Pre1999 - 1st:0 2nd:0 3rd:0 Ran:1
1999 Turf 0-3: (6f, 8f, 9f) (gd 2, frm) 1999 AW 0-1: (8f) (Fibr)
Workmanlike, moderate colt. Turf high 46.
**T D Easterby [0-5] Times of Wigan.*

PRESSURISE BHB 65f70a **RR 64+f 70a** 2653[1]
4 ch g Sanglamore (USA) 12.9f **(67)** - Employ Force (USA) (Alleged (USA)) 10f **(76)**
Form - 371
Record 1999 - 1st:1 2nd:0 3rd:1 Ran:3
Pre1999 - 1st:2 2nd:0 3rd:0 Ran:5
Win Prizemoney £8,224 *Total Prizemoney* £9,096
Wins * **1999** *Jly Southw (STD) H 14f 63 64* <
* 1998 Jly Nottin (G-F) H 16f 51 64 <
* 1998 Jly Yarmou (G-F) H 14.1f 51 59+
1999 Turf 0-2: (16f, 18f) (g-f 2) 1999 AW 1-1: (14f 1-1) (Fibr 1-1)
Scopey, average gelding. Turf high 62 (1st run) - 3rd of 12 giving 6lb to Generous Ways (19 Jun Ascot 16f g-f RF 2139). (1st run) - 1st of 16 giving 26lb to Makati (8 Jly Southwell RF 2653). Regained winning form on his third start of the season on the Southwell Fibresand in July. He looks the type of improving sort with which his trainer does so well.
**Sir Mark Prescott [3-8] Charles Walker & Jonathon Carroll.*

PRESTO RR 51f 5163[8]
2 b g Namaqualand (USA) - Polish Dancer (USA) (Malinowski (USA)) 10f **(56)**
Form - 78
Record 1999 - 1st:0 2nd:0 3rd:0 Ran:2
1999 Turf 0-2: (6f, 7f) (g-s, gd)
Currently fair gelding. Turf high 51 (began Oct).
**W J Haggas [0-2] & Mrs Peter Lumley.*

PRESUMED (USA) BHB 106f **RR 106f** 4916[8]
3 br f Dynaformer (USA) 12f **(82)** - Prebend (USA) (L'Emigrant (USA)) 10.5f **(62)**
Form - 1174348
Record 1999 - 1st:2 2nd:0 3rd:1 Ran:7
Win Prizemoney £17,711 *Total Prizemoney* £27,675
Wins * **1999** May Lingfi (G-F) L 7f 98 <
* **1999** Apr Newbur (G-F) 7f 88
1999 Turf 2-7: (7f 2-4, 8f 3) (gd 2, g-f 1-3, frm 1-2)
Workmanlike, Pattern-class filly, effective 7 to 8f, best at 8f, acts on gd to frm. Turf high 106 - 7th of 9 to Balisada (16 Jun Ascot 8f g-f RF 2041) - also 1st of 11 getting 12lb from Rich In Love (8 May Lingfield RF 1114). Created a good impression when making a successful debut at Newbury, and stepped up on that to win a Listed event at Lingfield. Not disgraced in the Coronation Stakes, with the mile perhaps stretching her stamina, she has spoilt her chance on several occasions since then by pulling too hard and failing to last home. If she can learn to settle, she could be very good. **P J Makin [2-7] Dr Carlos Stelling.*

PRETENDING BHB 61f **RR 66f** 5052[14]
2 b c Primo Dominie 7.2f **(67)** - Red Salute (Soviet Star (USA))
Form - 620860
Record 1999 - 1st:0 2nd:1 3rd:0 Ran:6
Win Prizemoney £0 *Total Prizemoney* £841
1999 Turf 0-6: (5f, 6f 3, 7f 2) (sft, gd 2, g-f 3)
Average colt, effective 5f, acts on g-f. Turf high 77 - 2nd of 11 to Agua Caballo (10 Jun Carlisle 5f g-f RF 1874).
**J D Bethell [0-6] Mrs John Lee.*

PRETRAIL (IRE) RR 77f 5194[2]
2 b c Catrail (USA) - Pretty Lady (High Top) 10.2f **(67)**
Form - 82
Record 1999 - 1st:0 2nd:1 3rd:0 Ran:2
Win Prizemoney £0 *Total Prizemoney* £955
1999 Turf 0-2: (6f 2) (sft, gd)
Currently above-average colt. Turf high 77 (began Oct).
**A C Stewart [0-2] S J Hammond.*

PRETTY INDULGENT RR 50f 5195[14]
2 b c Mistertopogigo (IRE) - American Beauty (Mill Reef (USA)) 10.5f **(78)**
Form - 00
Record 1999 - 1st:0 2nd:0 3rd:0 Ran:2
1999 Turf 0-2: (6f, 7f) (g-s, gd)
Currently fair colt. Turf high 50 (began Oct).
**B Smart [0-2] Miss N Jefford.*

PRETTY OBVIOUS BHB 57f **RR 61f** 4730[1]
3 ch f Pursuit of Love 9.5f **(69)** - Settlement (USA) (Irish River (FR)) 8.6f **(78)**
Form - 004051611

Record 1999 - 1st:3 2nd:0 3rd:0 Ran:9
Pre1999 - 1st:0 2nd:1 3rd:0 Ran:4
Win Prizemoney £13,174 *Total Prizemoney* £14,302
Wins *** 1999** Oct Nottin (SFT) H 16f 46 61 <
*** 1999** Spt Newcas (SFT) H 16.1f 46 55
*** 1999** Aug Catter (FRM) S 15.8f 43
1999 Turf 3-9: (9f, 10f, 11f, 12f 2, 14f, 16f 3-3) (g-s 1-1, gd 1-3, g-f 2, frm 1-3)
Scopey, average filly, effective 8 to 16f, best at 16f, acts on sft to gd, has worn blinkers, prefers left handed tracks. Turf high 61 - 1st of 8 getting 22lb from Weet For Me (5 Oct Nottingham RF 4730) - also 1st of 11 getting 7lb from Topacio (29 Spt Newcastle RF 4639). Won three times in the second half of the season, and looks a progressive stayer.
**Mrs M Reveley [3-5] H Hurst (from R A Fahey [0-8] Jun 1999).*

PRETTY PRINC (HUN) RR 99f 4887a[3]
3 gr c Western Star - Pretty Pola (HUN) (Ukaab (GER))
Form - 3
1999 Turf 0-1: (9f) (sft)
Currently very useful colt. (1st run) - 3rd of 11 getting 6lb from Page's King (10 Oct Dusseldorf 9f sft RF 4887a). **in GER [0-1].*

PRETTY WOMAN (IRE) BHB 48f RR 47f 4159[12]
3 b f Alzao (USA) 9.8f **(73)** - Simply Gorgeous (Hello Gorgeous (USA)) 9.7f **(63)**
Form - 4465400
Record 1999 - 1st:0 2nd:0 3rd:0 Ran:7
Pre1999 - 1st:0 2nd:0 3rd:0 Ran:2
Win Prizemoney £0 *Total Prizemoney* £1,041
1999 Turf 0-7: (8f, 9f, 11f 2, 12f 2, 13f) (gd 2, frm 5)
Light-framed, moderate filly, effective 9f, acted on gd, had worn blinkers, liked left handed tracks, favoured tight tracks. Turf high 69. (DEAD) **P F I Cole [0-9] Faisal Salman.*

PRICELESS SECOND BHB 55f RR 41f 4503[7]
2 b c Lugana Beach 7f **(63)** - Early Gales (Precocious) 8.6f **(62)**
Form - 067
Record 1999 - 1st:0 2nd:0 3rd:0 Ran:3
1999 Turf 0-3: (6f 3) (gd, g-f 2)
Currently moderate colt. Turf high 41 (began Aug).
**P Calver [0-3] Mrs Janis MacPherson.*

PRICE OF PASSION BHB 73f RR 69f 4436[15]
3 b f Dolphin Street (FR) - Food of Love (Music Boy) 6.8f **(57)**
Form - 87004710
Record 1999 - 1st:1 2nd:0 3rd:0 Ran:8
Pre1999 - 1st:1 2nd:1 3rd:1 Ran:9
Win Prizemoney £7,638 *Total Prizemoney* £9,420
Wins *** 1999** Spt Goodwo (G-F) H 5f 67 69
* 1998 Spt Folkes (G-F) H 5f 77 81 <
1999 Turf 1-8: (5f 1-4, 6f 3, 7f) (gd, g-f 1-4, frm 3)
Workmanlike, average filly, effective 5f, acts on g-f to frm, has worn blinkers. Turf high 73 (began Jly).
**D W P Arbuthnot [2-17] Noel Cronin.*

PRIDE OF BRIXTON BHB 42f49a RR 22f 49a 5149[13]
6 b g Dominion 8.9f **(65)** - Caviar Blini (What A Guest) 7f **(62)**
Form - 13110522475000000
Record 1999 - 1st:0 2nd:2 3rd:0 Ran:12
Pre1999 - 1st:6 2nd:3 3rd:3 Ran:36
Win Prizemoney £18,689 *Total Prizemoney* £24,469
Wins 1998 *Dec Wolver (SLW) H 5f 63 73*
1998 *Dec Wolver (STD) H 6f 63 68*
1998 *Nov Wolver (STD) H 5f 58 62*
1998 *Aug Wolver (STD) S 5f 65*
1998 May Carlis (G-S) 5f 64
1996 May Cheste (GD) H 5.1f 78 81 <
1999 Turf 0-2: (5f 2) (gd, hrd) 1999 AW 0-10: (5f 6, 6f 4) (Equi, Fibr 9)
Very moderate gelding, effective 5 to 6f, best at 5f, - acts on Fibr, has worn blinkers, likes left handed tracks, likes tight tracks, does well at Wolverhampton. Turf high 22. AW high 76 - 2nd of 8 giving 21lb to Trojan Girl (3 Feb Wolverhampton 5f Fibr RF 0216).
**Andrew Reid [0-10] A S Reid (from P D Evans [3-12] Jan 1999).*

PRIDE OF DINGLE (IRE) BHB 72f RR 72f 4696[9]
3 b g Dolphin Street (FR) - Aneeda (Rainbow Quest (USA)) 10.4f **(75)**
Form - 784800710
Record 1999 - 1st:1 2nd:0 3rd:0 Ran:9
Pre1999 - 1st:1 2nd:0 3rd:1 Ran:2
Win Prizemoney £10,980 *Total Prizemoney* £15,531
Wins *** 1999** Aug Mussel (G-S) 7.1f 72 <
* 1998 Spt San Si (HVY) 12f
1999 Turf 1-9: (7f 1-4, 8f 3, 10f 2) (sft, g-s 2, gd 3, g-f 1-3)
Above-average gelding, has worn blinkers. Turf high 84. Inconsistent. **M L W Bell [2-11] Mike Dawson.*

PRIDE OF INDIA (IRE) RR 23f 5215[15]
2 b g Ezzoud (IRE) - Indian Queen (Electric) 10.1f **(61)**
Form - 0
Record 1999 - 1st:0 2nd:0 3rd:0 Ran:1
1999 Turf 0-1: (8f) (g-s)
Currently little account gelding. **J L Dunlop [0-1] Sir Gordon Brunton.*

PRIDE OF PERU (IRE) BHB 52f RR 54f 5023[18]
2 b f Perugino (USA) - Nation's Game (Mummy's Game) 8.2f **(60)**
Form - 400800
Record 1999 - 1st:0 2nd:0 3rd:0 Ran:6
Win Prizemoney £0 *Total Prizemoney* £220
1999 Turf 0-6: (5f 2, 6f 4) (gd 3, g-f, frm 2)
Fair filly. Turf high 54. **M Brittain [0-6] Mel Brittain.*

PRIDEWAY (IRE) BHB 60f70a RR 47f 70a 4151[9]
3 b f Pips Pride 6.7f **(70)** - Up The Gates (Captain James) 5f **(59)**
Form - 167020200
Record 1999 - 1st:1 2nd:2 3rd:0 Ran:9
Pre1999 - 1st:0 2nd:1 3rd:1 Ran:8
Win Prizemoney £2,658 *Total Prizemoney* £6,566
Wins *** 1999** *Feb Wolver (STD) H 7f 68 80* <
1999 Turf 0-7: (7f 4, 8f 3) (gd 2, g-f 2, frm 3) 1999 AW 1-2: (7f 1-2) (Fibr 1-2)
Light-framed, moderate filly, effective 7f, acts on gd - acts on Fibr, has worn blinkers, prefers left handed tracks, likes tight tracks. Turf high 71 - 2nd of 14 giving 5lb to Sharp Edge Boy (3 Jun Haydock 7f gd RF 1704). AW high 80 (1st run) - 1st of 9 giving 19lb to State Wind (10 Feb Wolverhampton RF 0267). Becoming disappointing. **A Bailey [1-17] Nev Jones.*

PRIESTESS (IRE) RR 38f 4038[16]
3 b f Magical Wonder (USA) 7.2f **(60)** - Forest Treasure (USA) (Green Forest (USA)) 9.9f **(68)**
Form - 5070
Record 1999 - 1st:0 2nd:0 3rd:0 Ran:4
1999 Turf 0-4: (5f, 6f, 7f, 8f) (gd, g-f 2, frm)
Lengthy, very moderate filly, has worn blinkers. Turf high 38 (began Jly). **V Soane [0-4] Forest Five.*

PRIESTLAW (USA) RR 5122a[3]
2 ch c El Gran Senor (USA) 8.9f **(85)** - Schwanensee (USA) (Mr Leader (USA)) 9.8f **(66)**
Form - 13
Record 1999 - 1st:1 2nd:0 3rd:1 Ran:2
Win Prizemoney £7,290 *Total Prizemoney* £11,227
Wins **1999** Spt San Si (HVY) 8f
1999 Turf 1-2: (8f 1-1, 9f) (hvy 1-2)
Currently very poor colt. (began Spt) - also 1st of 8 from Grange Heritage (26 Spt San Siro RF 4665a).
**M Quinlan [0-1] (from J L Dunlop [1-1] Spt 1999).*

PRIMA RR 82f 4348[3]
2 b f Primo Dominie 7.2f **(67)** - Phyliel (USA) (Lyphard (USA)) 9.9f **(72)**
Form - 823
Record 1999 - 1st:0 2nd:1 3rd:1 Ran:3
Win Prizemoney £0 *Total Prizemoney* £1,213
1999 Turf 0-3: (5f, 6f 2) (gd, frm 2)
Currently decent filly. Turf high 82 (began Aug) - 2nd of 19 to Iftiraas (7 Spt Lingfield 6f frm RF 4178). Has put in some fair efforts in well-contested sprint-maidens, and given an easier time will surely get off the mark. **W J Haggas [0-3] Cheveley Park Stud.*

PRIMARY COLOURS BHB 88f94a RR 87f 94a 4682[8]
4 b f Saddlers' Hall (IRE) 10.5f **(65)** - Go For Red (IRE) (Thatching) 8f

(66)
Form - 16348826868
Record 1999 - 1st:0 2nd:1 3rd:1 Ran:9
Pre1999 - 1st:5 2nd:2 3rd:1 Ran:14
Win Prizemoney £28,967 *Total Prizemoney* £37,674

Wins								
* 1998	*Nov*	*Wolver*	*(STD)*	*H*	*12f*	*86*	*97*	<
* 1998	Oct	Haydoc	(SFT)	H	10.5f	58	61	
* 1998	*Oct*	*Wolver*	*(sta)*	*H*	*12f*	*83*	*87*	
* 1998	*Aug*	*Wolver*	*(STD)*	*H*	*9.4f*	*75*	*83*	
1997	*Nov*	*Southw*	*(STD)*	*S*	*8f*		*77*	

1999 Turf 0-7: (9f, 10f 4, 11f, 12f) (sft, g-s, gd 3, frm 2) 1999 AW 0-2: (12f 2) (Fibr 2)

Workmanlike, very useful filly, effective 10 to 12f, best at 12f, acts on g-s - acts on Fibr, prefers left handed tracks, likes tight tracks, excels at Wolverhampton. Turf high 95 - 2nd of 6 getting 3lb from Lady In Waiting (12 May York 10f g-s RF 1181). AW high 99 (1st run) - 3rd of 8 giving 4lb to China Castle (3 Feb Wolverhampton 12f Fibr RF 0217). Inconsistent. She ran out of her skin when finishing second in a listed event at York in May, but could not repeat that performance. Virtually impossible to place on the turf off her current mark.

**J Pearce [4-20] Saracen Racing (from W J Haggas [1-3] Nov 1997).*

PRIME MUSIC BHB 63f **RR 62f** 4451[8]

2 ch g Primo Dominie 7.2f **(67)** - Rose Music (Luthier) 9.8f **(71)**
Form - 0808
Record 1999 - 1st:0 2nd:0 3rd:0 Ran:4
1999 Turf 0-4: (5f 2, 6f, 7f) (sft, g-s, frm 2)

Average gelding. Turf high 62 (began Jly).

**S Mellor [0-4] Rod & Sara Barnes.*

PRIME OFFER BHB 66f **RR 67f** 3217[12]

3 b c Primo Dominie 7.2f **(67)** - Single Bid (Auction Ring (USA)) 8.6f **(65)**
Form - 383410
Record 1999 - 1st:1 2nd:0 3rd:2 Ran:6
Pre1999 - 1st:0 2nd:0 3rd:0 Ran:1
Win Prizemoney £3,422 *Total Prizemoney* £4,658
Wins * 1999 Jly Hamilt (FRM) 6f 67 <
1999 Turf 1-6: (5f 2, 6f 1-4) (gd, g-f 2, frm 1-3)

Leggy, average colt, effective 6f, acts on g-f to frm, best on frm. Turf high 67 - 1st of 3 from Palawan (16 Jly Hamilton RF 2870).

**K A Morgan [1-7] D & M Cased Hole.*

PRIME RECREATION BHB 75f **RR 67f** 5005[3]

2 b g Primo Dominie 7.2f **(67)** - Night Transaction (Tina's Pet) 6.8f **(59)**
Form - 003
Record 1999 - 1st:0 2nd:0 3rd:1 Ran:3
Win Prizemoney £0 *Total Prizemoney* £610
1999 Turf 0-3: (5f, 6f 2) (gd 2, g-f)

Currently average gelding. Turf high 67 (began Spt) - 3rd of 15 to The Bull Macabe (21 Oct Nottingham 5f gd RF 5005).

**P S Felgate [0-3] Moneyleague Ltd.*

PRIME SURPRISE BHB 28f36a **RR 14f 36a** 3398[12]

3 b f Primo Dominie 7.2f **(67)** - My Surprise (Welsh Pageant) 10f **(65)**
Form - 840000
Record 1999 - 1st:0 2nd:0 3rd:0 Ran:6
Pre1999 - 1st:0 2nd:0 3rd:0 Ran:3
1999 Turf 0-4: (6f, 8f 2, 11f) (gd, g-f, frm 2) 1999 AW 0-2: (7f 2) (Equi 2)

Unfurnished, very moderate filly. Turf high 14. AW high 34. Becoming disappointing.

**D W Barker [0-5] T Calver (from C A Dwyer [0-4] Jan 1999).*

PRIMEVAL BHB 55f50a **RR 44f 50a** 3084[9]

5 b g Primo Dominie 7.2f **(67)** - Class Adorns (Sadler's Wells (USA)) 10f **(76)**
Form - 5000010
Record 1999 - 1st:1 2nd:0 3rd:0 Ran:7
Pre1999 - 1st:0 2nd:1 3rd:1 Ran:3
Win Prizemoney £1,871 *Total Prizemoney* £3,536
Wins * 1999 *Jly Wolver (STD) S 12f 49+* <
1999 Turf 0-2: (10f, 13f) (g-f, frm) 1999 AW 1-5: (8f 2, 9f, 12f 1-1, 16f) (Fibr 1-5)

Moderate gelding, effective 10f, - acts on Equi, favours left handed tracks, favours tight tracks. Turf high 44. AW high 51.

**K C Comerford [1-7] The Old Style Partnership (from P W Harris [0-3] Apr 1998).*

PRIMO LARA BHB 99f105a **RR 97f 105a** 3261[23]

7 ch h Primo Dominie 7.2f **(67)** - Clara Barton (Youth (USA)) 9.8f **(64)**
Form - 2115104030
Record 1999 - 1st:2 2nd:0 3rd:1 Ran:8
Pre1999 - 1st:6 2nd:4 3rd:6 Ran:32
Win Prizemoney £65,100 *Total Prizemoney* £84,992

Wins								
* **1999**	May	Newmar	(G-F)	H	6f	96	101	
* **1999**	*Feb*	*Wolver*	*(STD)*	*H*	*5f*	*100*	*102*	<
* 1998	*Dec*	*Lingfi*	*(STD)*	*H*	*6f*	*95*	*100*	
* 1998	Oct	York	(GD)	H	6f	90	94	
* 1997	Nov	Redcar	(GD)	H	6f	84	87	
* 1996	Spt	Haydoc	(G-F)	H	7.1f	82	87	
* 1996	Apr	Thirsk	(G-F)	H	7f	65	82+	
* 1996	Apr	Beverl	(G-F)	H	7.5f	65	70+	

1999 Turf 1-7: (5f, 6f 1-6) (gd 2, g-f 2, frm 1-3) 1999 AW 1-1: (5f 1-1) (Fibr 1-1)

Very useful horse, effective 5 to 7f, best at 6f, acts on gd to frm - acts on AW, excels at Wolverhampton and Newmarket. Turf high 101 - 1st of 14 getting 2lb from Halmahera (2 May Newmarket RF 0980). (1st run) - 1st of 7 giving 24lb to Mangus (24 Feb Wolverhampton RF 0351). Inconsistent. He enjoys fast ground, is effective from five to seven furlongs and is a thoroughly likeable handicapper. Very effective on sand too.

**P W Harris [8-39] Resplendent Racing Ltd (from P W Harris [0-1] May 1995).*

PRIMORDIAL (FR) BHB 62a **RR 50f 62a** 97[5]

4 b g Lesotho (USA) 6f **(53)** - Prilly (FR) (Saint Cyrien (FR)) 8.4f **(80)**
Form - 5345
Record 1999 - 1st:0 2nd:0 3rd:0 Ran:2
Pre1999 - 1st:0 2nd:0 3rd:1 Ran:3
Win Prizemoney £0 *Total Prizemoney* £672
1999 AW 0-2: (7f, 10f) (Equi 2)

Workmanlike, fair gelding. AW high 57. **S Dow [0-5] D G Churston.*

Primo Valentino should not be deserted

PRIMO VALENTINO (IRE) BHB 100f **RR 108f** 4653[1]

2 b c Primo Dominie 7.2f **(67)** - Dorothea Brooke (IRE) **(88df)** (Dancing Brave (USA)) 8.4f **(76)**
Form - 2411111
Record 1999 - 1st:5 2nd:1 3rd:0 Ran:7

Win Prizemoney £120,861 *Total Prizemoney* £124,300
Wins * **1999** Spt Newmar (G-S) G1 6f 108 <
* **1999** Spt Newbur (G-F) G2 6f 104+
* **1999** Spt Kempto (G-F) L 6f 104+
* **1999** Jun Goodwo (G-F) 6f 85+
* **1999** Jun Leices (G-S) 6f 83+
1999 Turf 5-7: (5f 2, 6f 5-5) (gd 2-3, g-f, frm 3-3)
Pattern-class colt, effective 6f, acts on gd to frm, best on frm. Turf high 108 - 1st of 6 from Fath (30 Spt Newmarket RF 4653) - also 1st of 4 from Trouble Mountain (18 Spt Newbury RF 4405). One of the season's success stories, he gave his syndicate of owners superb value for money when notching up a five-timer, including the Mill Reef and Middle Park Stakes. Tough and genuine, he will give a good account of himself next season but will probably prove just short of the required class, and stamina, for the 2000 Guineas.
**P W Harris [5-7] Primo Donnas.*

PRINCE ALEX (IRE) BHB 87f RR 88f 4264[2]
5 b g Night Shift (USA) 8.1f **(73)** - Finalist (Star Appeal) 9.6f **(65)**
Form - 811102
Record 1999 - 1st:3 2nd:1 3rd:0 Ran:6
Pre1999 - 1st:1 2nd:0 3rd:1 Ran:5
Win Prizemoney £22,908 *Total Prizemoney* £29,053
Wins * **1999** Jly Ascot (G-F) H 12f 74 78++ <
* **1999** Jun Kempto (GD) H 12f 69 71
* **1999** May Kempto (G-F) H 12f 64 69
1997 Aug Newmar (GD) H 12f 63 68
1999 Turf 3-6: (10f, 12f 3-4, 14f) (gd 1-2, g-f 1-1, frm 1-3)
Useful gelding, effective 12f, acts on gd to frm. Turf high 88 - 2nd of 11 giving 4lb to Musician (11 Spt Doncaster 12f frm RF 4264). He was in fine form last term, landing three consecutive victories over a mile and a half before appearing not to stay the extra two furlongs in the Ebor.
**Mrs A J Perrett [3-6] Dawson, Mercer, Jones (from A C Stewart [1-5] Spt 1997).*

PRINCE AMONG MEN RR 81f 5104[6]
2 b c Robellino (USA) 9.5f **(68)** - Forelino (USA) (Trempolino (USA)) 12f **(71)**
Form - 7633336
Record 1999 - 1st:0 2nd:0 3rd:4 Ran:7
Win Prizemoney £0 *Total Prizemoney* £2,237
1999 Turf 0-7: (6f 2, 7f 5) (sft 2, gd 4, g-f)
Decent colt, effective 6f, acts on sft, has worn blinkers. Turf high 81. **P D Evans [0-1] Jim Ennis (from E Lynam in IRE [0-6] Spt 1999).*

PRINCE BABAR BHB 79f RR 80f 4569[18]
8 b g Fairy King (USA) 7.7f **(75)** - Bell Toll (High Line) 10.3f **(70)**
Form - 677000
Record 1999 - 1st:0 2nd:0 3rd:0 Ran:6
Pre1999 - 1st:4 2nd:7 3rd:4 Ran:28
Win Prizemoney £196,333 *Total Prizemoney* £269,025
Wins * 1998 Oct Newmar (GD) H 7f 85 92 <
* 1996 Oct Ascot (GD) 8f 83
1999 Turf 0-6: (7f, 8f 5) (sft, gd, g-f, frm 3)
Decent gelding, effective 7 to 8f, acts on sft to gd, has worn blinkers. Turf high 80.
**J E Banks [2-28] Giles Pritchard-Gordon (from G A Pritchard-Gordon [2-8] Jun 1994).*

PRINCE BATSHOOF BHB 65f RR 71df 3250[6]
4 b g Batshoof 9.5f **(66)** - Sipsi Fach (Prince Sabo) 7.2f **(62)**
Form - 6
Record 1999 - 1st:0 2nd:0 3rd:0 Ran:1
Pre1999 - 1st:0 2nd:3 3rd:3 Ran:10
Win Prizemoney £0 *Total Prizemoney* £6,973
1999 Turf 0-1: (10f) (frm)
Above-average gelding, effective 8 to 11f, acts on g-s to frm.
**M C Pipe [0-1] Frank Farrant (from M L W Bell [0-10] Aug 1998).*

PRINCE CONSORT BHB 57f54a RR 52df 54a 4835[13]
3 b g Clantime 6.6f **(57)** - Miss Petella (Dunphy) 9.4f **(57)**
Form - 5547574215045100600
Record 1999 - 1st:2 2nd:1 3rd:1 Ran:18
Pre1999 - 1st:0 2nd:2 3rd:0 Ran:7
Win Prizemoney £4,619 *Total Prizemoney* £6,968
Wins * **1999** Aug Leices (GD) C 7f 49 <
* **1999** May Folkes (G-F) C 7f 49 <
1999 Turf 2-15: (6f 3, 7f 2-8, 8f 4) (sft, g-s 2, gd 2, g-f 2-5, frm 4, hrd)
1999 AW 0-3: (8f, 10f, 12f) (Equi 2, Fibr)
Scopey, average gelding, effective 5 to 6f, acts on g-f to frm, has worn blinkers (effectively). Turf high 55. AW high 56.
**S C Williams [2-19] J W Lovitt (from Mrs J R Ramsden [0-6] Spt 1998).*

PRINCE DANZIG (IRE) BHB 50f67a RR 47f 67a 1454[2]
8 ch g Roi Danzig (USA) 10.5f **(62)** - Veldt (High Top) 10.2f **(67)**
Form - 610145372
Record 1999 - 1st:1 2nd:1 3rd:1 Ran:7
Pre1999 - 1st:10 2nd:10 3rd:9 Ran:73
Win Prizemoney £34,111 *Total Prizemoney* £54,472
Wins * **1999** *Jan Lingfi (STD) C 13f 72*
1998 *Dec Lingfi (STD) H 13f 65 70*
1996 *Dec Wolver (STD) H 12f 79 83* <
* 1996 May Bright (FRM) H 11.9f 63 64
* 1996 *Feb Lingfi (STD) H 12f 77 76*
* 1995 Jly Bright (FRM) H 11.9f 54 60
* 1995 *Mar Lingfi (STD) H 12f 77 78*
* 1995 *Jan Lingfi (STD) C 12f 59+*
1999 Turf 0-1: (12f) (hrd) 1999 AW 1-6: (12f 3, 13f 1-1, 15f, 16f) (Equi 1-5, Fibr)
Average gelding, effective 13f, - acts on Equi, has worn blinkers. AW high 72 - 1st of 8 giving 9lb to Mystagogue (12 Jan Lingfield RF 0078). Consistent. Not as good as he once was, but can still make his mark in modest events on Equitrack.
**D J G MurraySmith [11-80] A H Ulrick.*

PRINCE DARKHAN (IRE) BHB 63f RR 57f 4733[7]
3 b g Doyoun 10.7f **(69)** - Sovereign Dona (Sovereign Path) 9.3f **(55)**
Form - 0457
Record 1999 - 1st:0 2nd:0 3rd:0 Ran:4
Win Prizemoney £0 *Total Prizemoney* £248
1999 Turf 0-4: (10f 4) (g-s, gd 2, frm)
Leggy, fair gelding. Turf high 57.
**P W Harris [0-4] Daydream Believers.*

PRINCE ELMAR RR 79f 5215[7]
2 b c Elmaamul (USA) 8.1f **(70)** - Dramatic Mood (Jalmood (USA)) 10.1f **(52)**
Form - 37
Record 1999 - 1st:0 2nd:0 3rd:1 Ran:2
Win Prizemoney £0 *Total Prizemoney* £700
1999 Turf 0-2: (8f 2) (g-s, gd)
Currently above-average colt. Turf high 79 (1st run) (began Oct) - 3rd of 19 to Imperial Rocket (12 Oct Leicester 8f gd RF 4839).
**W R Muir [0-2] Mrs Richard Plummer & Partners.*

PRINCE KINSKY BHB 57f79a RR 58f 79a 2750[3]
6 ch g Master Willie 9.2f **(67)** - Princess Lieven (Royal Palace) 9f **(56)**
Form - 0033
Record 1999 - 1st:0 2nd:0 3rd:2 Ran:4
Pre1999 - 1st:2 2nd:0 3rd:2 Ran:12
Win Prizemoney £8,825 *Total Prizemoney* £12,340
Wins * 1997 Apr Epsom (GD) H 12f 74 80 <
1996 *Apr Lingfi (STD) 10f 61*
1999 Turf 0-4: (12f 3, 14f) (g-s, g-f, frm, hrd)
Above-average gelding. Turf high 58.
**J A B Old [2-13] Mrs Anne Bickel (from Lord Huntingdon [1-8] Nov 1996).*

PRINCELY DREAM (IRE) BHB 86f RR 87f 4803[10]
3 br c Night Shift (USA) 8.1f **(73)** - Princess of Zurich (IRE) (Law Society (USA)) 9.9f **(70)**
Form - 0302001320
Record 1999 - 1st:1 2nd:2 3rd:2 Ran:10
Pre1999 - 1st:1 2nd:2 3rd:0 Ran:5
Win Prizemoney £9,241 *Total Prizemoney* £22,185
Wins * **1999** Aug Ayr (G-F) 6f 85 <
* 1998 Aug Pontef (G-F) 5f 82
1999 Turf 1-10: (5f, 6f 1-8, 7f) (gd 4, g-f 1-5, frm)
Scopey, useful colt, effective 5 to 6f, best at 6f, acts on g-s to frm, best on g-f, has worn blinkers, excels at Haydock, does well at Ayr. Turf high 88 - 3rd of 12 getting 15lb from Mitcham (15 May Newmarket 6f g-f RF 1244) - also 1st of 4 getting 7lb from Tom Tun (10 Aug Ayr RF 3494). Consistent. Landed a four-runner sprint at Ayr in August, but put up by far his best performance when beat-

ing everything apart from Grey Kingdom in the Ayr Silver Cup.
**R A Fahey [2-15] I Bray.*

PRINCELY HEIR (IRE) RR 108?f 2467[4]

4 b c Fairy King (USA) 7.7f **(75)** - Meis El-Reem (Auction Ring (USA)) 8.6f **(65)**
Form - 0474
Record 1999 - 1st:0 2nd:0 3rd:0 Ran:4
Pre1999 - 1st:3 2nd:1 3rd:3 Ran:11
Win Prizemoney £92,430 *Total Prizemoney* £116,591
Wins * 1997 Aug Leopar (G-S) G1 6f 104 <
* 1997 Jly Beverl (HVY) 5f 101+
* 1997 May Ripon (G-F) 5f 76+
1999 Turf 0-4: (6f, 7f, 9f, 10f) (gd 4)
Lengthy, Pattern-class colt, effective 8f, acts on gd to frm, best on gd, has worn blinkers. Turf high 98. Difficult to place, he has been retired to stud. **M Johnston [3-15] David Abell.*

PRINCELY SPARK (IRE) BHB 28f36a RR 37?f 36a 2653[7]

4 ch g Balla Cove - Tigeen (Habitat) 9.4f **(70)**
Form - 004647
Record 1999 - 1st:0 2nd:0 3rd:0 Ran:6
Pre1999 - 1st:1 2nd:1 3rd:1 Ran:11
Win Prizemoney £1,712 *Total Prizemoney* £2,557
Wins 1998 May Downpa (G-F) H 11.9f 52 63 <
1999 Turf 0-1: (12f) (gd) 1999 AW 0-5: (10f, 12f, 14f, 16f 2) (Equi 2, Fibr 3)
Very moderate gelding, effective 10 to 12f, acts on hvy to g-f, often wears blinkers. AW high 34.
**Noel Chance [0-6] Mrs M Chance (from D K Weld in IRE [1-9] Spt 1998).*

PRINCE NICHOLAS BHB 57f RR 53+f 504[1]

4 ch g Midyan (USA) 9.9f **(64)** - Its My Turn (Palm Track) 9.8f **(50)**
Form - 11
Record 1999 - 1st:2 2nd:0 3rd:0 Ran:2
Pre1999 - 1st:0 2nd:2 3rd:0 Ran:9
Win Prizemoney £4,944 *Total Prizemoney* £6,454
Wins * **1999** Mar Hamilt (HVY) H 12.1f 40 49++
* **1999** Mar Doncas (GD) H 12f 40 53 <
1999 Turf 2-2: (12f 2-2) (hvy 1-1, g-f 1-1)
Fair gelding, effective 8 to 12f, acts on hvy to g-f, best on sft. Turf high 53 (1st run) - 1st of 17 getting 10lb from Noukari (25 Mar Doncaster RF 0463) - also 1st of 10 getting 14lb from Clued Up (29 Mar Hamilton RF 0504). A half-brother to Silverdale Fox and Silverdale Knight, he won twice in March, but was not seen again.
**K W Hogg [2-11] Auldyn Stud Ltd.*

PRINCE OF ABACO (USA) RR 201[8]

4 b g Geiger Counter (USA) 7.8f **(85)** - Abala (FR) (Baldric II) 8.1f **(75)**
Form - 08
Record 1999 - 1st:0 2nd:0 3rd:0 Ran:2
1999 AW 0-2: (6f, 7f) (Fibr 2)
Currently little account gelding. AW high 20.
**D Nicholls [0-2] Lhendup Dorji.*

PRINCE OF ARAGON BHB 40f55a RR 37f 55a 5065[12]

3 b g Aragon 7.7f **(58)** - Queens Welcome (Northfields (USA)) 9f **(72)**
Form - 2010600470400
Record 1999 - 1st:1 2nd:1 3rd:0 Ran:13
Pre1999 - 1st:0 2nd:0 3rd:0 Ran:5
Win Prizemoney £2,477 *Total Prizemoney* £3,054
Wins * **1999** Apr Thirsk (GD) 7f 56 <
1999 Turf 1-11: (5f, 6f 5, 7f 1-4, 8f) (sft, g-s, gd 1-3, g-f 2, frm 4) 1999 AW 0-2: (6f 2) (Fibr 2)
Leggy, fair gelding, effective 7f, acts on gd, has worn blinkers, likes left handed tracks, likes tight tracks. Turf high 56 - 1st of 8 getting 10lb from Robeena (17 Apr Thirsk RF 0739). AW high 54.
**K T Ivory [1-18] K T Ivory.*

PRINCE OF DENIAL BHB 100f100a RR 102f 100a 3085[S]

5 b g Soviet Star (USA) 8.6f **(74)** - Gleaming Water (Kalaglow) 9.8f **(67)**
Form - 8454320S
Record 1999 - 1st:0 2nd:1 3rd:1 Ran:8
Pre1999 - 1st:4 2nd:3 3rd:3 Ran:25
Win Prizemoney £42,309 *Total Prizemoney* £93,442
Wins * 1998 May York (GD) H 10.4f 95 97 <
* 1997 Oct Newbur (G-S) H 9f 89 94
* 1997 Spt Newbur (G-S) H 8f 83 89
* 1997 May Kempto (GD) H 9f 76 78
1999 Turf 0-8: (10f 3, 11f, 12f 4) (g-s, gd 4, g-f 2, frm)
Very useful gelding, effective 10 to 12f, best at 10f, acted on g-s to gd, best on g-s, liked right handed tracks, preferred tight tracks, excelled at Goodwood and Sandown. Turf high 108 - 4th of 9 to Generous Rosi (24 Apr Sandown 10f g-s RF 0844). Sadly died after falling and breaking his leg at Ascot in July on King George day. Had been a credit to connections over the years. (DEAD)
**D W P Arbuthnot [4-33] J S Gutkin.*

PRINCE OF MY HEART BHB 88f RR 84f 1701[6]

6 ch h Prince Daniel (USA) 11.4f **(46)** - Blue Room (Gorytus (USA)) 7.8f **(60)**
Form - 6
Record 1999 - 1st:0 2nd:0 3rd:0 Ran:1
Pre1999 - 1st:3 2nd:1 3rd:5 Ran:30
Win Prizemoney £18,589 *Total Prizemoney* £46,544
Wins 1997 May Newbur (SFT) H 9f 100 108? <
1996 Apr Catter (GD) 12f 87++
1995 Oct York (GD) 7.9f 85
1999 Turf 0-1: (11f) (gd)
Decent horse, effective 8f, acts on gd, has worn blinkers.
**D HaydnJones [0-9] G J Hicks (from B W Hills [3-22] Aug 1997).*

PRINCE OF MYSTERY (IRE) BHB 54f RR 72f 3567[8]

2 b br c Shalford (IRE) 7.8f **(63)** - Mary Kate Danagher (Petoski) 5.7f **(62)**
Form - 638
Record 1999 - 1st:0 2nd:0 3rd:1 Ran:3
Win Prizemoney £0 *Total Prizemoney* £1,025
1999 Turf 0-3: (7f 3) (g-f 3)
Currently above-average colt. Turf high 59.
**A P Jarvis [0-3] Select Racing Partnership.*

PRINCE OMID (USA) RR 66f 4943[5]

2 b c Shuailaan (USA) - Matilda The Hun (USA) (Young Bob (USA))
Form - 75
Record 1999 - 1st:0 2nd:0 3rd:0 Ran:2
1999 Turf 0-2: (7f, 8f) (gd 2)
Currently average colt. Turf high 66 (began Oct).
**J R Fanshawe [0-2] Arashan Ali.*

PRINCE POWHATAN (FR) RR 92f 935a[7]

3 ch c Hero's Honor (USA) 9.2f **(76)** - Wish For Diamonds (USA) (Lyphard's Wish (FR)) 9f **(74)**
Form - 7
1999 Turf 0-1: (8f) (g-s)
Currently useful colt. **H-A Pantall in FR [1-2] Mme A Polard.*

PRINCE PROSPECT BHB 77f88a RR 77f 88a 4656[12]

3 b c Lycius (USA) 8.8f **(71)** - Princess Dechtra (IRE) (Bellypha) 9.8f **(73)**
Form - 313347043513640
Record 1999 - 1st:1 2nd:0 3rd:4 Ran:13
Pre1999 - 1st:1 2nd:2 3rd:3 Ran:8
Win Prizemoney £6,461 *Total Prizemoney* £14,393
Wins * **1999** Jly Sandow (G-F) H 5f 73 76
* 1998 *Dec Lingfi (STD) 6f 81* <
1999 Turf 1-11: (5f 1-7, 6f 4) (g-s, gd 2, g-f 4, frm 1-4) 1999 AW 0-2: (5f, 6f) (Equi 2)
Workmanlike, useful colt, effective 6f, acts on frm - acts on Equi, has worn blinkers, prefers left handed tracks. Turf high 77. AW high 89 (1st run) - 3rd of 9 giving 13lb to Bartholomew (7 Jan Lingfield 6f Equi RF 0047).
**Mrs L Stubbs [2-15] Maurice Parker (from J Noseda [0-6] Oct 1998).*

PRINCE ROCK RR 23f 586[8]

2 ch c Rock City 8.8f **(62)** - Masuri Kabisa (USA) **(46f)** (Ascot Knight (CAN))
Form - 08
Record 1999 - 1st:0 2nd:0 3rd:0 Ran:2
1999 Turf 0-2: (5f 2) (sft, g-s)
Currently little account colt, often wears blinkers. Turf high 23.
**M Dods [0-2] A G Watson.*

PRINCE SLAYER BHB 78f **RR 80f** 4592[2]
3 b c Batshoof 9.5f **(66)** - Top Sovereign (High Top) 10.2f **(67)**
Form - 2352
Record 1999 - 1st:0 2nd:2 3rd:1 Ran:4
Pre1999 - 1st:0 2nd:0 3rd:0 Ran:1
Win Prizemoney £0 *Total Prizemoney* £2,634
1999 Turf 0-4: (8f, 9f, 10f 2) (sft 2, gd, frm)
Scopey, decent colt. Turf high 80 - 2nd of 8 to Truant (27 Spt Hamilton 9f gd RF 4592). He has run most creditably in his races to date and deserves to get off the mark. He can cope with fast ground, but looks ideally suited by soft.
**B Smart [0-5] Ahmed Abdel-Khaleq.*

PRINCESS AURORA BHB 58f **RR 63f** 4543[8]
2 ch f Prince Sabo 6.6f **(64)** - Made in Heaven **(68f 67a)** (Primo Dominie) 6.2f **(80)**
Form - 07728
Record 1999 - 1st:0 2nd:1 3rd:0 Ran:5
Win Prizemoney £0 *Total Prizemoney* £1,050
1999 Turf 0-5: (5f 3, 6f 2) (g-f 2, frm 3)
Average filly. Turf high 63. **P W Harris [0-5] The Lightning Twelve.*

PRINCESS BELFORT BHB 35f20a **RR 39f 20a** 4985[8]
6 b m Belfort (FR) 6.7f **(53)** - Domino Rose (Dominion) 8.5f **(63)**
Form - 00000078
Record 1999 - 1st:0 2nd:0 3rd:0 Ran:8
Pre1999 - 1st:0 2nd:0 3rd:0 Ran:5
1999 Turf 0-6: (5f, 6f 2, 7f 2, 8f) (g-s, gd 2, g-f 2, frm) 1999 AW 0-2: (5f, 9f) (Fibr 2)
Very moderate mare, has worn blinkers. Turf high 39. AW high 17.
**B D Leavy [0-8] Paul Hollinshead (from W Clay [0-3] May 1998).*

PRINCESS ELLEN BHB 100f **RR 93f** 4920[5]
2 br f Tirol 8.1f **(64)** - Celt Song (IRE) (Unfuwain (USA))
Form - 1105
Record 1999 - 1st:2 2nd:0 3rd:0 Ran:4
Win Prizemoney £20,270 *Total Prizemoney* £20,920
Wins 1999 Aug Newmar (GD) L 7f 88 <
1999 Jly Ascot (G-F) 6f 86+
1999 Turf 2-4: (6f 1-1, 7f 1-2, 8f) (gd, g-f 2-3)
Useful filly. Turf high 93 (began Jly) - 5th of 12 to Lahan (16 Oct Newmarket 7f gd RF 4920) - also 1st of 11 getting 5lb from Eurolink Raindance (14 Aug Newmarket RF 3656). She won very nicely on her Ascot debut, and had little trouble with the extra furlong when following up in a Newmarket Listed event next time. Did not give her true running when well-beaten at Doncaster, but was not beaten far in a Listed race on her final start.
**G A Butler [0-1] Mrs S Y Thomas (from P W Chapple-Hyam [2-3] Spt 1999).*

PRINCESSE ZELDA (FR) BHB 41f28a **RR 48f 28a** 3422[4]
5 b m Defensive Play (USA) - Brisk Waters (USA) (Saratoga Six (USA)) 7f **(73)**
Form - 600068384
Record 1999 - 1st:0 2nd:0 3rd:1 Ran:7
Pre1999 - 1st:0 2nd:0 3rd:0 Ran:3
Win Prizemoney £0 *Total Prizemoney* £518
1999 Turf 0-5: (8f, 10f 3, 12f) (g-s, g-f 2, frm 2) 1999 AW 0-2: (12f, 16f) (Fibr 2)
Moderate filly, effective 10f, acts on frm, favours tight tracks. Turf high 48. AW high 10. Inconsistent.
**Miss L C Siddall [0-9] Miss J A Challen (from D J G MurraySmith [0-1] Aug 1998).*

PRINCESS FOLEY (IRE) BHB 44f36a **RR 43f 36a** 4925[10]
3 ch f Forest Wind (USA) - Taniokey (Grundy) 10.3f **(65)**
Form - 07370260
Record 1999 - 1st:0 2nd:1 3rd:1 Ran:7
Pre1999 - 1st:0 2nd:0 3rd:2 Ran:7
Win Prizemoney £0 *Total Prizemoney* £1,700
1999 Turf 0-4: (5f, 6f 2, 7f) (gd, g-f 2, frm) 1999 AW 0-3: (5f, 6f, 7f) (Fibr 3)
Workmanlike, moderate filly, effective 5f, acts on g-f. Turf high 43 (began Jly). AW high 38 (began Jly).
**W G M Turner [0-13] Foley Steelstock (from D HaydnJones [0-1] May 1998).*

PRINCESS KALI (IRE) BHB 57a **RR 39f 57a** 4938[3]
3 ch f Fayruz 6.6f **(63)** - Carriglegan Girl (Don) 7.7f **(64)**
Form - 0006753
Record 1999 - 1st:0 2nd:0 3rd:1 Ran:7
Pre1999 - 1st:0 2nd:0 3rd:0 Ran:3
Win Prizemoney £0 *Total Prizemoney* £309
1999 Turf 0-6: (6f, 7f 2, 8f 3) (hvy, gd 3, g-f 2) 1999 AW 0-1: (6f) (Fibr)
Fair filly, has worn blinkers. Turf high 39.
**D Carroll [0-1] Matthew Lee (from J G Coogan in IRE [0-9] Jly 1999).*

PRINCESS LATIFA BHB 59f **RR 63df** 1238[15]
3 b f Wolfhound (USA) 7.3f **(71)** - Moorish Idol (Aragon) 8.1f **(60)**
Form - 50
Record 1999 - 1st:0 2nd:0 3rd:0 Ran:2
Pre1999 - 1st:0 2nd:0 3rd:0 Ran:2
Win Prizemoney £0 *Total Prizemoney* £227
1999 Turf 0-2: (7f 2) (gd, g-f)
Scopey, average filly. Turf high 49. **B J Meehan [0-4] Michael Broke.*

PRINCESS LONDIS BHB 33f **RR 26f** 4076[7]
4 ch f Interrex (CAN) 7.7f **(51)** - Princess Lucianne (Stanford) 7.9f **(56)**
Form - 077
Record 1999 - 1st:0 2nd:0 3rd:0 Ran:3
Pre1999 - 1st:0 2nd:0 3rd:0 Ran:7
Win Prizemoney £0 *Total Prizemoney* £398
1999 Turf 0-3: (7f 2, 10f) (frm 3)
Neat, little account filly, has worn blinkers. Turf high 26 (began Jly). **B deHaan [0-3] C Richards (from N E Berry [0-1] Oct 1998).*

PRINCESS LOUISE RR 78f 4212[1]
2 b f Efisio 7.7f **(69)** - Louis' Queen (IRE) **(100f)** (Tragic Role (USA))
Form - 1
Record 1999 - 1st:1 2nd:0 3rd:0 Ran:1
Win Prizemoney £3,680 *Total Prizemoney* £3,680
Wins * 1999 Spt Kempto (G-F) 6f 78 <
1999 Turf 1-1: (6f 1-1) (frm 1-1)
Currently above-average filly. (1st run) - 1st of 12 from Harmonic (8 Spt Kempton RF 4212). **J L Dunlop [1-1] Peter Winfield.*

PRINCESS MO BHB 38f **RR 31f** 4713[11]
3 b f Prince Sabo 6.6f **(64)** - Morica (Moorestyle) 6.9f **(64)**
Form - 7000
Record 1999 - 1st:0 2nd:0 3rd:0 Ran:4
Pre1999 - 1st:0 2nd:0 3rd:0 Ran:3
1999 Turf 0-4: (5f 2, 7f, 8f) (gd 3, g-f)
Unfurnished, very moderate filly, has worn blinkers. Turf high 49.
**T E Powell [0-3] Peter Crate (from Pat Mitchell [0-4] May 1999).*

PRINCESS OF HEARTS BHB 39f43a **RR 42df 43a** 2723[19]
5 b m Prince Sabo 6.6f **(64)** - Constant Delight (Never so Bold) 6.3f **(66)**
Form - 0
Record 1999 - 1st:0 2nd:0 3rd:0 Ran:1
Pre1999 - 1st:2 2nd:3 3rd:3 Ran:28
Win Prizemoney £4,054 *Total Prizemoney* £9,513
Wins 1997 Apr Nottin (G-F) S 8.2f 59 <
1996 Aug Folkes (G-F) S 6.9f 58
1999 Turf 0-1: (11f) (g-f)
Moderate filly, often wears blinkers. Becoming disappointing.
**Andrew Reid [0-2] A S Reid (from M J Ryan [0-3] Aug 1998).*

PRINCESS RIA (IRE) BHB 69f **RR 71f** 4484[7]
2 b f Petong 7.6f **(58)** - Walking Saint (Godswalk (USA)) 7.3f **(58)**
Form - 13507
Record 1999 - 1st:1 2nd:0 3rd:1 Ran:5
Win Prizemoney £3,733 *Total Prizemoney* £4,251
Wins * 1999 Jly Haydoc (G-S) 6f 61 <
1999 Turf 1-5: (5f, 6f 1-2, 7f 2) (g-s, gd 1-2, g-f, frm)
Above-average filly. Turf high 71 (began Jly). Kicked off things in July with a good win, albeit in a poor race, at Haydock over six furlongs on softish ground. Has yet to better that effort.
**A Bailey [1-5] Mrs M M Johnson.*

PRINCESS TOPAZ BHB 68f **RR 71f** 3840[5]
5 b m Midyan (USA) 9.9f **(64)** - Diamond Princess (Horage) 10.3f **(61)**
Form - 60735
Record 1999 - 1st:0 2nd:0 3rd:1 Ran:5
Pre1999 - 1st:3 2nd:3 3rd:3 Ran:23

Win Prizemoney £11,834 *Total Prizemoney* £24,808
Wins 1998 Jly Newmar (GD) H 14.8f 75 78 <
1997 Aug Sandow (G-F) H 14f 68 72
1997 Aug Newmar (GD) H 12f 61 65
1999 Turf 0-5: (12f 2, 15f, 16f 2) (g-f, frm 4)
Above-average filly, effective 15 to 16f, best at 16f, acts on gd to frm, best on frm. Turf high 71 - 7th of 17 giving 20lb to Northern Motto (10 Jly Chester 16f frm RF 2709). Inconsistent.
**G M McCourt [0-6] Calypso Racing (from C A Cyzer [3-23] Spt 1998).*

PRINCESS VICTORIA BHB 59f **RR 61f** 2633[11]
2 b f Deploy 11.4f **(67)** - Scierpan (USA) (Sharpen Up) 8.3f **(67)**
Form - 10
Record 1999 - 1st:1 2nd:0 3rd:0 Ran:2
Win Prizemoney £2,285 *Total Prizemoney* £2,285
Wins * 1999 May Beverl (GD) S 5f 61 <
1999 Turf 1-2: (5f 1-1, 7f) (gd 1-1, frm)
Currently average filly. Turf high 61 (1st run) - 1st of 12 from Chili Pepper (25 May Beverley RF 1448).
**N A Callaghan [1-2] N A Callaghan.*

PRINCIPAL BOY (IRE) BHB 38f36a **RR 41f 36a** 4987[5]
6 br g Cyrano de Bergerac 7.3f **(58)** - Shenley Lass (Prince Tenderfoot (USA)) 9f **(61)**
Form - 007660384335508577028506465
Record 1999 - 1st:0 2nd:1 3rd:3 Ran:26
Pre1999 - 1st:5 2nd:5 3rd:2 Ran:44
Win Prizemoney £14,319 *Total Prizemoney* £22,762
Wins 1998 *Jan Southw (STD) H 8f 37 40*
1997 Jun Hamilt (G-S) H 9.2f 44 47
1997 May Hamilt (SFT) H 8.3f 35 45
1996 *May Southw (STD) H 7f 52 52* <
1996 *Feb Southw (STD) H 7f 42 45*
1999 Turf 0-19: (5f 2, 6f 6, 7f 5, 8f 5, 9f) (sft 2, gd 6, g-f 2, frm 9) 1999 AW 0-7: (6f 4, 7f, 8f, 11f) (Fibr 7)
Moderate gelding, effective 6 to 7f, best at 7f, acts on gd to frm, best on gd, has worn blinkers. Turf high 51 (1st run) - 3rd of 16 getting 6lb from The Woodcock (31 Mar Catterick 7f gd RF 0524). AW high 42.
**Miss J F Craze [0-28] Chris Cockcroft (from J A Glover [1-7] May 1998).*

PRINCIPAL DANCER BHB 30f **RR 15f** 3380[16]
3 b f Shareef Dancer (USA) 10.1f **(67)** - Little Beaut **(67df 60a)** (Prince Sabo) 7.2f **(62)**
Form - 0000
Record 1999 - 1st:0 2nd:0 3rd:0 Ran:4
Pre1999 - 1st:0 2nd:0 3rd:1 Ran:6
Win Prizemoney £0 *Total Prizemoney* £751
1999 Turf 0-3: (5f, 8f 2) (g-f 3) 1999 AW 0-1: (6f) (Fibr)
Strong, poor filly. Turf high 15.
**R F Marvin [0-4] G S Alcock (from J A Glover [0-6] Oct 1998).*

PRINCIPLE (IRE) **RR 71f** 4943[4]
2 b c Caerleon (USA) 10.9f **(79)** - Point of Honour (Kris) 9.5f **(73)**
Form - 624
Record 1999 - 1st:0 2nd:1 3rd:0 Ran:3
Win Prizemoney £0 *Total Prizemoney* £1,273
1999 Turf 0-2: (7f, 8f) (gd, frm) 1999 AW 0-1: (8f) (Fibr)
Currently above-average colt. Turf high 71 (began Spt).
**Sir Mark Prescott [0-3] Sir Edmund Loder.*

PRINCIPLE ACCOUNT BHB 76f **RR 88f** 4895[6]
2 b c Rudimentary (USA) 8.2f **(66)** - Fairy Story (IRE) **(75f 64a)** (Persian Bold) 9.3f **(66)**
Form - 42386
Record 1999 - 1st:0 2nd:1 3rd:1 Ran:5
Win Prizemoney £0 *Total Prizemoney* £3,133
1999 Turf 0-5: (6f 2, 7f 2, 8f) (gd 3, g-f, frm)
Useful colt. Turf high 88 (began Jly) - 6th of 20 giving 2lb to Magic of Love (15 Oct Newmarket 6f gd RF 4895).
**C A Dwyer [0-5] The Fairy Story Partnership.*

PRINTSMITH (IRE) BHB 58f **RR 61f** 4439[12]
2 br f Petardia 8.2f **(58)** - Black And Blaze (Taufan (USA)) 7f **(57)**
Form - 6717300
Record 1999 - 1st:1 2nd:0 3rd:1 Ran:7
Win Prizemoney £2,010 *Total Prizemoney* £2,520
Wins * 1999 Jly Catter (GD) S 5f 61 <
1999 Turf 1-7: (5f 1-5, 6f 2) (g-f 1-3, frm 4)
Average filly, effective 5f, acts on g-f to frm. Turf high 61 - 1st of 15 getting 5lb from Apple Peeler (1 Jly Catterick RF 2454).
**J Norton [1-7] Ecosse Racing.*

PRIOLETTE (IRE) BHB 35f **RR 33f** 2396[10]
4 b f Priolo (USA) 10.9f **(71)** - Celestial Path (Godswalk (USA)) 7.3f **(58)**
Form - 04040
Record 1999 - 1st:0 2nd:0 3rd:0 Ran:5
Pre1999 - 1st:0 2nd:1 3rd:1 Ran:12
Win Prizemoney £0 *Total Prizemoney* £2,761
1999 Turf 0-5: (8f, 10f 2, 11f, 12f) (gd 2, g-f 2, frm)
Workmanlike, very moderate filly, effective 9f, acts on gd, likes tight tracks. Turf high 33.
**Don Enrico Incisa [0-5] Don Enrico Incisa (from J G FitzGerald [0-12] Spt 1998).*

PRIORS MOOR BHB 46f42a **RR 24f 42a** 3743[15]
4 br g Petong 7.6f **(58)** - Jaziyah (IRE) (Lead on Time (USA)) 8f **(65)**
Form - 003380500
Record 1999 - 1st:0 2nd:0 3rd:2 Ran:7
Pre1999 - 1st:1 2nd:0 3rd:0 Ran:10
Win Prizemoney £2,994 *Total Prizemoney* £3,782
Wins * 1998 Spt Yarmou (G-S) H 8f 48 53 <
1999 Turf 0-3: (7f 3) (g-s, g-f, frm) 1999 AW 0-4: (8f 3, 10f) (Equi 4)
Scopey, moderate gelding, effective 8 to 10f, acts on frm - acts on Equi, has worn blinkers. Turf high 24. AW high 51 (1st run) - 3rd of 9 getting 4lb from Star Turn (7 Jan Lingfield 10f Equi RF 0045).
**R W Armstrong [1-17] Mrs L Alexander.*

PRIORY GARDENS (IRE) BHB 40f **RR 40f** 4121[14]
5 b g Broken Hearted 10.1f **(65)** - Rosy O'Leary (Majetta) 6.5f **(58)**
Form - 064186824850
Record 1999 - 1st:1 2nd:1 3rd:0 Ran:12
Pre1999 - 1st:3 2nd:0 3rd:0 Ran:19
Win Prizemoney £12,441 *Total Prizemoney* £13,950
Wins * 1999 May Leices (GD) H 6f 34 43
* 1998 Jun Carlis (G-S) H 6.9f 30 34
* 1998 Jun Goodwo (GD) H 6f 30 36
* 1997 Jun Thirsk (GD) H 6f 40 47 <
1999 Turf 1-12: (5f, 6f 1-5, 7f 5, 8f) (gd, g-f 1-6, frm 3, hrd 2)
Moderate gelding, effective 6 to 8f, acts on gd to hrd, likes left handed tracks, likes tight tracks, likes Brighton. Turf high 43 - 1st of 17 getting 27lb from Juwwi (31 May Leicester RF 1598).
**J M Bradley [4-31] Gwilym Fry.*

PRIVATE FIXTURE (IRE) BHB 28f53a **RR 36f 53a** 3576[9]
8 ch g The Noble Player (USA) 7.7f **(58)** - Pennyala (Skyliner) 7.3f **(53)**
Form - 087840
Record 1999 - 1st:0 2nd:0 3rd:0 Ran:6
Pre1999 - 1st:4 2nd:5 3rd:5 Ran:39
Win Prizemoney £9,989 *Total Prizemoney* £15,771
Wins * 1997 *Jly Southw (STD) S 12f 72*
* 1997 *Jun Southw (STD) C 11f 67*
1999 Turf 0-5: (12f 3, 14f, 17f) (g-f 2, frm 3) 1999 AW 0-1: (12f) (Fibr)
Moderate gelding, effective 16f, - acts on Fibr, has worn blinkers. Turf high 36.
**D Marks [2-35] John Jackson (from W Jarvis [2-10] Jun 1994).*

PRIVATE SEAL BHB 30f30a **RR 27f 30a** 2818[10]
4 b g King's Signet (USA) 7f **(51)** - Slender (Aragon) 8.1f **(60)**
Form - 4430765800700
Record 1999 - 1st:0 2nd:0 3rd:1 Ran:12
Pre1999 - 1st:1 2nd:2 3rd:3 Ran:16
Win Prizemoney £1,984 *Total Prizemoney* £4,679
Wins 1997 Oct Bright (FRM) S 5.3f 69 <
1999 Turf 0-3: (7f 2, 10f) (g-f, frm, hrd) 1999 AW 0-9: (6f, 7f 5, 8f, 10f, 12f) (Equi 8, Fibr)
Leggy, little account gelding, effective 7f, - acts on Equi, has worn blinkers (very effectively), likes left handed tracks, likes tight tracks. Turf high 27. AW high 46 - 7th of 14 getting 6lb from Alamein (4 Feb Lingfield 7f Equi RF 0222).
**J C Poulton [0-18] Russell Reed & Gerald West (from G L Moore [1-12] Jly 1998).*

PRIX DE CLERMONT (IRE) BHB 29f29a **RR 35f 29a** 92[6]
5 b g Petorius 8f **(66)** - Sandra's Choice (Sandy Creek) 8.9f **(59)**
Form - 306
Record 1999 - 1st:0 2nd:0 3rd:0 Ran:2
Pre1999 - 1st:1 2nd:0 3rd:3 Ran:19
Win Prizemoney £2,453 *Total Prizemoney* £3,281
Wins 1997 *Dec Wolver (STD) H 12f 45 49* <
1999 AW 0-2: (12f, 13f) (Equi 2)
Very moderate gelding, has worn blinkers. AW high 23.
**G L Moore [0-9] R Kiernan (from G Lewis [1-14] Mar 1998).*

PRIX STAR BHB 58f52a **RR 57f 52a** 5199[2]
4 ch g Superpower 6.6f **(58)** - Celestine **(40f 44a)** (Skyliner) 7.3f **(53)**
Form - 00700102870602
Record 1999 - 1st:1 2nd:2 3rd:0 Ran:14
Pre1999 - 1st:1 2nd:3 3rd:2 Ran:13
Win Prizemoney £7,381 *Total Prizemoney* £18,784
Wins * 1999 Jun Catter (GD) H 6f 60 61
* 1997 Jly Hamilt (G-S) 5f 76 <
1999 Turf 1-12: (6f 1-7, 7f 5) (gd 5, g-f, frm 1-6) 1999 AW 0-2: (6f 2) (Fibr 2)
Workmanlike, fair gelding, effective 6f, acts on g-s, often wears blinkers. Turf high 61. AW high 63. Consistent.
**C W Fairhurst [2-27] M J Grace.*

PROCEDURE (USA) BHB 90f **RR 95+f** 3774[6]
3 b br g Strolling Along (USA) - Bold Courtesan (USA) (Bold Bidder) 8.8f **(67)**
Form - 6116
Record 1999 - 1st:2 2nd:0 3rd:0 Ran:4
Pre1999 - 1st:0 2nd:0 3rd:1 Ran:2
Win Prizemoney £14,508 *Total Prizemoney* £15,240
Wins * 1999 Jun Salisb (G-F) H 12f 83 95 <
*** 1999** May Leices (G-F) H 10f 77 84
1999 Turf 2-4: (8f, 10f 1-1, 12f 1-1, 14f) (gd, g-f 1-2, frm 1-1)
Workmanlike, very useful gelding, effective 12f, acts on g-f. Turf high 95 - 1st of 7 getting 11lb from Tabareeh (23 Jun Salisbury RF 2249). He made all when winning a competitive rated stakes at Salisbury in June, but failed to confirm that form when stepped-up to a mile and three-quarters at York's Ebor Meeting. Unable to adopt his favoured front-running tactics that day, he remains a useful prospect and should make a smart middle-distance handicapper in 2000.
**Sir Michael Stoute [2-6] Highclere Thoroughbred Racing Ltd.*

PRODIGAL SON (IRE) BHB 72f73a **RR 72f 73a** 4505[6]
4 b g Waajib 8.9f **(67)** - Nouveau Lady (IRE) (Taufan (USA)) 7f **(57)**
Form - 1112125226
Record 1999 - 1st:4 2nd:4 3rd:0 Ran:10
Pre1999 - 1st:0 2nd:2 3rd:1 Ran:13
Win Prizemoney £10,434 *Total Prizemoney* £18,277
Wins * 1999 Jun Nottin (GD) H 8.2f 62 67
*** 1999** *Mar Wolver (STD) H 8.5f 65 72* <
*** 1999** *Feb Lingfi (STD) H 8f 60 67*
*** 1999** *Feb Wolver (STD) H 7f 51 59*
1999 Turf 1-6: (8f 1-2, 10f 4) (gd, g-f 1-4, frm) 1999 AW 3-4: (7f 1-1, 8f 2-3) (Equi 1-2, Fibr 2-2)
Workmanlike, above-average gelding, effective 8 to 10f, best at 8f, acts on gd to frm - acts on AW, has worn blinkers, prefers tight tracks, excels at Lingfield, does well at Leicester and Wolverhampton. Turf high 72 - 2nd of 18 giving 23lb to Join The Parade (7 Spt Leicester 10f g-f RF 4174) - also 1st of 18 giving 15lb to Artful Dane (16 Jun Nottingham RF 2056). AW high 72 - 1st of 12 giving 13lb to Areish (27 Mar Wolverhampton RF 0493) - also 1st of 12 giving 21lb to Kanawa (25 Feb Lingfield RF 0355). Consistent. It took him a long time to get off the mark, but he has performed very well on sand and showed he could act on turf too, with a victory at Nottingham. Handles Fibresand and Equitrack equally well.
**Mrs V C Ward [4-10] Prodigal Son Partnership (from R J R Williams [0-13] Oct 1998).*

PROFIT ALERT (IRE) RR 96f 4856a[6]
4 b f Alzao (USA) 9.8f **(73)** - Raysiya (Cure The Blues (USA)) 9.5f **(63)**
Form - 3656
1999 Turf 0-4: (8f 3, 9f) (sft, g-s, gd, frm)
Very useful filly, effective 8f, acts on g-s to gd, has worn blinkers. Turf high 96 (1st run) - 3rd of 6 giving 17lb to Castle Quest (11 Apr Curragh 8f g-s RF 0683a).
**D K Weld in IRE [2-7] Moyglare Stud Farm.*

PROKOFIEV (USA) BHB 76f **RR 80f** 2548[10]
3 br c Nureyev (USA) 8.4f **(84)** - Aviara (USA) (Cox's Ridge (USA)) 8f **(68)**
Form - 530
Record 1999 - 1st:0 2nd:0 3rd:1 Ran:3
Pre1999 - 1st:0 2nd:0 3rd:1 Ran:1
Win Prizemoney £0 *Total Prizemoney* £1,007
1999 Turf 0-3: (10f 2, 11f) (frm 3)
Scopey, decent colt, has worn blinkers. Turf high 80.
**Sir Michael Stoute [0-4] M Tabor & Mrs John Magnier.*

PROLIX BHB 114f **RR 115f** 4492[2]
4 ch c Kris 10f **(75)** - Ajuga (USA) (The Minstrel (CAN)) 10f **(72)**
Form - 7121232
Record 1999 - 1st:2 2nd:3 3rd:1 Ran:7
Pre1999 - 1st:2 2nd:4 3rd:2 Ran:10
Win Prizemoney £63,320 *Total Prizemoney* £138,941
Wins * 1999 Jly Ayr (SFT) G3 10f 113 <
*** 1999** Jun Doncas (GD) 10.3f 105+
***** 1998 May Cheste (G-F) L 10.3f 110+
***** 1998 Apr Thirsk (G-S) 8f 107
1999 Turf 2-7: (10f 2-6, 11f) (sft, g-s 1-1, gd 2, g-f 1-1, frm 2)
Scopey, high-class colt, effective 8 to 12f, best at 10f, acts on sft to frm, prefers left handed tracks, likes tight tracks. Turf high 115 - 2nd of 5 giving 4lb to Greek Dance (7 Aug Haydock 11f gd RF 3452) - also 1st of 5 giving 10lb to Housemaster (19 Jly Ayr RF 2940). Consistent. A decent performer at three, he had a rather frustrating 1999 despite victories in a three-runner Doncaster conditions event and a weak Group Three at Ayr. Otherwise it has been a case of being there or thereabouts, finishing runner-up three times. Suited by ten furlongs, he was sold to race in the Middle East in the autumn. **B W Hills [4-17] K Abdulla.*

Prolix continues his career in Saudi Arabia

PROMESSA BHB 64a **RR 60f** 3768[15]
3 b f Reprimand 8.2f **(63)** - Congress (IRE) (Dancing Brave (USA)) 8.4f **(76)**
Form - 5423170
Record 1999 - 1st:1 2nd:1 3rd:1 Ran:7
Win Prizemoney £2,402 *Total Prizemoney* £3,765
Wins * 1999 *Jly Wolver (STD) 6f 68* <
1999 Turf 0-6: (6f 3, 7f 2, 8f) (g-s, gd, frm 3, hrd) 1999 AW 1-1: (6f 1-1) (Fibr 1-1)
Scopey, average filly, effective 6f, acts on hrd - acts on Fibr. Turf high 64 - 2nd of 9 getting 5lb from Square Dancer (24 Jun Carlisle 6f hrd RF 2259). (1st run) - 1st of 12 getting 5lb from Wellow (23 Jly Wolverhampton RF 3081). She showed some ability in her early

starts on turf, but got off the mark in a modest maiden on the Wolverhampton Fibresand in July. **W J Haggas [1-7] Cyril Humphris.*

PROMISE OF GLORY RR 4210P
2 ch c Lammtarra (USA) - Vana Turns (USA) (Wavering Monarch (USA)) 10.4f **(94)**
Form - 0P
Record 1999 - 1st:0 2nd:0 3rd:0 Ran:2
1999 Turf 0-2: (7f, 8f) (gd 2)
Currently very poor colt. (began Aug).
**B W Hills [0-2] Maktoum Al Maktoum.*

PROPER GENT BHB 40f **RR 36f** 5158[27]
2 b g Alhijaz 7.7f **(57)** - Proper Madam (Mummy's Pet) 7.7f **(60)**
Form - 7800
Record 1999 - 1st:0 2nd:0 3rd:0 Ran:4
1999 Turf 0-4: (6f, 7f, 8f 2) (gd 2, frm 2)
Very moderate gelding, has worn blinkers. Turf high 36 (began Aug). **M Brittain [0-4] P Asquith.*

PROPER SQUIRE (USA) RR 84f 5102[2]
2 b c Bien Bien (USA) - La Cumbre (Sadler's Wells (USA)) 10f **(76)**
Form - 362
Record 1999 - 1st:0 2nd:1 3rd:1 Ran:3
Win Prizemoney £0 *Total Prizemoney* £1,364
1999 Turf 0-3: (8f 2, 9f) (hvy, gd, frm)
Currently decent colt. Turf high 84 (began Spt) - 2nd of 10 to Scotty Guest (27 Oct Yarmouth 8f gd RF 5102).
**A G Foster [0-1] J Toffan & T McCaffery (from P W Chapple-Hyam [0-2] Oct 1999).*

PROPHITS PRIDE (IRE) BHB 25f **RR 35df** 3755[4]
7 ch g Carmelite House (USA) 8.2f **(52)**-Asinara (Julio Mariner)7.2f **(57)**
Form - 065007754
Record 1999 - 1st:0 2nd:0 3rd:0 Ran:9
Pre1999 - 1st:1 2nd:1 3rd:0 Ran:5
Win Prizemoney £2,248 *Total Prizemoney* £3,502
Wins * 1998 May Ayr (G-F) C 10f 50 <
1999 Turf 0-9: (9f 4, 11f 2, 12f 2, 16f) (hvy, g-f 6, frm 2)
Very moderate gelding, effective 10 to 12f, acts on gd to g-f. Turf high 35. **P Monteith [1-25] Mrs Maud Monteith.*

PROSPECTOR'S COVE BHB 72f62a **RR 74df 62a** 5053[18]
6 b g Dowsing (USA) 7f **(61)** - Pearl Cove (Town And Country) 8.1f **(68)**
Form - 2251256325532530023021601000
Record 1999 - 1st:2 2nd:4 3rd:4 Ran:23
Pre1999 - 1st:4 2nd:3 3rd:4 Ran:32
Win Prizemoney £22,357 *Total Prizemoney* £32,627
Wins * **1999** Spt Yarmou (G-S) H 8f 71 74
* **1999** Aug Newmar (GD) H 8f 64 69+
* 1998 *Dec Lingfi (STD) H 10f 56 61*
* 1998 Aug Bright (FRM) H 8f 56 62
* 1996 Apr Kempto (GD) 10f 86 <
* 1995 Nov Mussel (SFT) 7.1f 83+
1999 Turf 2-15: (8f 2-13, 9f 2) (g-s 1-2, gd 3, g-f 1-2, frm 8) 1999 AW 0-8: (8f 3, 9f 3, 10f 2) (Equi 2, Fibr 6)
Above-average gelding, effective 8 to 10f, best at 8f, acts on g-s to frm - acts on AW, has worn blinkers, does well at Brighton, likes Lingfield. Turf high 74 - 1st of 16 giving 18lb to Khabar (15 Spt Yarmouth RF 4340) - also 1st of 19 from Byzantium (14 Aug Newmarket RF 3658). AW high 66 - 3rd of 9 giving 15lb to High Noon (23 Jan Wolverhampton 9f Fibr RF 0158). He ran some very creditable races besides his wins, and appears suited by a decent pace. **J Pearce [6-58] Saracen Racing.*

PROSPERITY (IRE) RR 57f 3978[10]
3 b g Catrail (USA) - Bequeath (USA) (Lyphard (USA)) 9.9f **(72)**
Form - 07400
Record 1999 - 1st:0 2nd:0 3rd:0 Ran:5
Pre1999 - 1st:0 2nd:0 3rd:1 Ran:3
Win Prizemoney £0 *Total Prizemoney* £1,238
1999 Turf 0-5: (8f, 9f, 10f, 11f, 12f) (gd, g-f, frm 3)
Scopey, fair gelding, has worn blinkers. Turf high 57.
**T D Easterby [0-8] Reg Griffin and Jim McGrath.*

PROSPERO RR 45f 2139[9]
6 b g Petong 7.6f **(58)** - Pennies to Pounds (Ile de Bourbon (USA)) 10.1f **(67)**
Form - 0
Record 1999 - 1st:0 2nd:0 3rd:0 Ran:1
Pre1999 - 1st:1 2nd:3 3rd:0 Ran:12
Win Prizemoney £3,042 *Total Prizemoney* £6,277
Wins 1996 Oct Leices (GD) 11.8f 69+ <
1999 Turf 0-1: (16f) (g-f)
Moderate gelding, has worn blinkers. Consistent.
**Mrs A J Perrett [0-17] Peter Salsbury (from G Harwood [1-4] Oct 1996).*

PROSPEROUS (IRE) RR 62f 5241a[5]
3 ch f Generous (IRE) 11.5f **(82)** - Amwag (USA) (El Gran Senor (USA)) 9.6f **(76)**
Form - 6325005
Record 1999 - 1st:0 2nd:1 3rd:1 Ran:7
Pre1999 - 1st:0 2nd:1 3rd:0 Ran:1
Win Prizemoney £0 *Total Prizemoney* £2,858
1999 Turf 0-7: (7f, 10f 3, 12f 3) (sft 2, g-s 2, gd 2, frm)
Neat, average filly, effective 7f, acts on sft. Turf high 68. Consistent.
**P Cashman in IRE [0-3] R Scarborough (from B W Hills [0-5] Spt 1999).*

PROTARAS BAY BHB 36f36a **RR 37f 36a** 4539[6]
5 b g Superpower 6.6f **(58)** - Vivid Impression (Cure The Blues (USA)) 9.5f **(63)**
Form - 0606
Record 1999 - 1st:0 2nd:0 3rd:0 Ran:4
Pre1999 - 1st:1 2nd:4 3rd:2 Ran:20
Win Prizemoney £1,668 *Total Prizemoney* £5,815
Wins * 1998 Oct Newcas (SFT) CH 8f 43 44 <
1999 Turf 0-4: (8f, 9f, 10f 2) (gd, frm 2, hrd)
Moderate gelding, effective 8 to 10f, best at 10f, acts on g-s to frm, often wears blinkers (extremely effectively). Turf high 37.
**P L Gilligan [1-21] Treasure Seekers Partnership (from T T Clement [0-3] Jly 1996).*

PROTECTOR RR 63tf 3739[17]
2 b c Be My Chief (USA) 10.2f **(62)** - Clicquot (Bold Lad (IRE)) 8.4f **(68)**
Form - 50
Record 1999 - 1st:0 2nd:0 3rd:0 Ran:2
1999 Turf 0-2: (6f 2) (g-s, gd)
Currently average colt. Turf high 63 (began Jly).
**J W Hills [0-2] Highclere Thoroughbred Racing Ltd.*

PROTOCOL (IRE) BHB 52f55a **RR 60f 55a** 5152[1]
5 ch g Taufan (USA) 8.3f **(65)** - Ukraine's Affair (USA) (The Minstrel (CAN)) 10f **(72)**
Form - 8000734664325251
Record 1999 - 1st:1 2nd:2 3rd:2 Ran:16
Pre1999 - 1st:3 2nd:3 3rd:2 Ran:28
Win Prizemoney £12,084 *Total Prizemoney* £20,930
Wins * **1999** Nov Nottin (SFT) 14.1f 60
* 1998 Apr Leices (SFT) H 10f 79 83 <
* 1998 Mar Doncas (GD) H 12f 73 78
1997 May Sandow (G-F) H 11.4f 73 74
1999 Turf 1-14: (10f 7, 11f 2, 12f 3, 14f 1-2) (gd 1-4, g-f 4, frm 6) 1999 AW 0-2: (11f, 12f) (Fibr 2)
Average gelding, effective 9 to 12f, acts on sft to gd - acts on Fibr, has worn blinkers. Turf high 60. AW high 55.
**Mrs S Lamyman [3-34] P Lamyman (from J W Hills [1-12] Oct 1997).*

PROUD CAVALIER BHB 29f **RR 23f** 1266[14]
3 b g Pharly (FR) 11.5f **(64)** - Midnight Flit (Bold Lad (IRE)) 8.4f **(68)**
Form - 000
Record 1999 - 1st:0 2nd:0 3rd:0 Ran:2
Pre1999 - 1st:0 2nd:0 3rd:0 Ran:1
1999 Turf 0-2: (8f 2) (gd, g-f)
Neat, currently very moderate gelding. Turf high 23.
**K Bell [0-2] S J Edwards (from M R Bosley [0-1] Nov 1998).*

PROUD CHIEF BHB 76f **RR 87f** 4872[7]
2 ch c Be My Chief (USA) 10.2f **(62)** - Fleur de Foret (USA) (Green Forest (USA)) 9.9f **(68)**
Form - 010807
Record 1999 - 1st:1 2nd:0 3rd:0 Ran:6

Win Prizemoney £3,550 *Total Prizemoney* £3,550
Wins * **1999** Jun Goodwo (G-F) 6f 87 <
1999 Turf 1-6: (5f, 6f 1-5) (gd 1-3, g-f 2, frm)
Useful colt, effective 6f, acts on gd. Turf high 87 - 1st of 9 from Kareeb (27 Jun Goodwood RF 2360). Apparently went lame going to the start on his debut, but gained a battling victory at Goodwood on his next start. He has shown very little since then however. **A P Jarvis [1-6] Grant & Bowman Ltd.*

PROUD MONK BHB 28f41a RR 45f 41a 3370[4]

6 gr g Aragon 7.7f **(58)** - Silent Sister (Kind of Hush) 10.1f **(62)**
Form - 84444864044
Record 1999 - 1st:0 2nd:0 3rd:0 Ran:11
Pre1999 - 1st:1 2nd:2 3rd:6 Ran:44
Win Prizemoney £4,146 *Total Prizemoney* £15,218
Wins 1995 Oct Newbur (G-S) H 7.3f 72 82 <
1999 Turf 0-11: (8f, 9f, 10f 4, 11f 2, 12f 3) (g-s, gd 2, g-f 4, frm 4)
Moderate gelding, effective 10 to 11f, acts on frm, has worn blinkers, likes left handed tracks. Turf high 45.
**K Bell [0-11] S J Edwards (from M R Bosley [0-21] Oct 1998).*

PROUD NATIVE (IRE) BHB 111f RR 113f 4372a[1]

5 b g Imp Society (USA) 7.1f **(63)** - Karamana (Habitat) 9.4f **(70)**
Form - 50115331
Record 1999 - 1st:3 2nd:0 3rd:2 Ran:8
Pre1999 - 1st:8 2nd:1 3rd:0 Ran:27
Win Prizemoney £193,872 *Total Prizemoney* £229,719
Wins * **1999** Spt Taby (GD) G3 5.8f 103
* **1999** Jun Leopar (G-S) G3 5f 109 <
* **1999** May Kempto (G-F) L 5f 109 <
* 1998 Aug Nottin (G-F) 5.1f 109 <
* 1998 Aug Haydoc (GD) H 5f 98 103
* 1998 Mar Doncas (GD) H 5f 100 105
1997 Aug Yarmou (G-F) 6f 101
1996 Oct Redcar (G-F) 6f 103
1996 Jun Epsom (GD) L 6f 105
1996 May York (G-F) 6f 84
1996 Apr Ripon (GD) 5f 78
1999 Turf 3-8: (5f 2-7, 6f 1-1) (gd 2-5, g-f, frm 1-2)
Group-class gelding, effective 5 to 6f, best at 5f, acts on gd to frm, excels at Doncaster. Turf high 113 - also 1st of 9 from Almaty (22 May Kempton RF 1395). Consistent. He has done exceptionally well since joining David Nicholls for 40,000 guineas at the end of 1997, winning Group Three races at Leopardstown and Taby last season. Only beaten three lengths when finishing third to Stravinsky and Sainte Marine in the Nunthorpe Stakes, he is like a fine wine and gets better with age.
**D Nicholls [6-20] P D Savill (from A P Jarvis [5-15] Spt 1997).*

PROUD PICTURE (IRE) BHB 46f RR 29f 4826[20]

3 b g Pips Pride 6.7f **(70)** - Mint Addition (Tate Gallery (USA)) 7.4f **(67)**
Form - 000
Record 1999 - 1st:0 2nd:0 3rd:0 Ran:3
Pre1999 - 1st:0 2nd:0 3rd:0 Ran:4
1999 Turf 0-3: (6f 3) (gd, g-f 2)
Scopey, little account gelding, has worn blinkers. Turf high 19 (began Spt). **J G Smyth-Osbourne [0-7] The G N I Partnership.*

PROVOSKY (IRE) RR 91f 4620a[9]

3 ch g Polish Patriot (USA) 7.8f **(70)** - Sheen Falls **00**
Form - 412352350
1999 Turf 1-9: (7f, 9f 1-4, 10f 4) (hvy, sft, g-s 2, gd 3, g-f 1-2)
Useful gelding, effective 9f, acts on gd to g-f, mostly wears blinkers, likes left handed tracks. Turf high 91 - 2nd of 6 giving 16lb to Lucky Cat (17 Jun Tipperary 9f gd RF 2212a).
**Miss I T Oakes in IRE [2-21] O Brady.*

PRU'S VENTURE BHB 29f RR 2768[10]

3 b f Tragic Role (USA) 9.4f **(63)** - Indivisible (Remainder Man) 11.2f **(45)**
Form - 650
Record 1999 - 1st:0 2nd:0 3rd:0 Ran:3
1999 Turf 0-2: (7f, 12f) (frm 2) 1999 AW 0-1: (8f) (Fibr)
Leggy, currently very poor filly. **R Hollinshead [0-3] Jimm Racing.*

PTAH (IRE) BHB 55f RR 60df 4909[14]

2 b c Petardia 8.2f **(58)** - Davenport Goddess (IRE) (Classic Secret (USA))
Form - 405000
Record 1999 - 1st:0 2nd:0 3rd:0 Ran:6
Win Prizemoney £0 *Total Prizemoney* £265
1999 Turf 0-6: (5f 3, 6f, 7f, 8f) (gd 5, frm)
Average colt. Turf high 63.
**J L Eyre [0-6] M Ford, M James & N Tritton.*

PTARMIGAN RIDGE BHB 72f RR 64f 4555[15]

3 b c Sea Raven (IRE) - Panayr (Faraway Times (USA)) 7.4f **(52)**
Form - 72040000
Record 1999 - 1st:0 2nd:1 3rd:0 Ran:8
Pre1999 - 1st:1 2nd:0 3rd:0 Ran:1
Win Prizemoney £3,626 *Total Prizemoney* £6,015
Wins * 1998 Oct Catter (SFT) 5f 80? <
1999 Turf 0-8: (5f 5, 6f 2, 8f) (g-s 3, gd 4, g-f)
Workmanlike, average colt, effective 5f, acts on g-s. Turf high 80 - 2nd of 11 giving 20lb to Eastern Trumpeter (19 Jun Ayr 5f g-s RF 2144). **Miss L A Perratt [1-9] Miss Heather Galbraith.*

PUBLIC PURSE (USA) RR 121f 4113a[3]

5 b h Private Account (USA) 10.1f **(80)** - Prodigious (FR) (Pharly (FR)) 9.8f **(68)**
Form - 3163
1999 Turf 1-4: (12f 1-3, 13f) (sft 1-2, gd 2)
Very high-class colt, effective 12 to 13f, best at 12f, acts on sft to gd, best on sft, does well at Longchamp. Turf high 121 - 1st of 5 giving 5lb to Sestino (24 May Saint-Cloud RF 1712a). Consistent. Once again proved himself useful at Group Two and Three level, but has struggled in the highest class. **A Fabre in FR [3-8].*

PUDDING LANE (IRE) BHB 67f RR 59f 5164[8]

2 b f College Chapel - Fire of London **(73f)** (Shirley Heights) 10.3f **(74)**
Form - 0738
Record 1999 - 1st:0 2nd:0 3rd:1 Ran:4
Win Prizemoney £0 *Total Prizemoney* £570
1999 Turf 0-4: (5f, 6f 3) (g-s, gd 2, frm)
Fair filly. Turf high 59.
**R F JohnsonHoughton [0-4] R F JohnsonHoughton.*

PUISSANTKOOLA BHB 24f RR 19f 5035[19]

3 b g Puissance 7.1f **(60)** - Nikoola Eve (Roscoe Blake) 11f **(66)**
Form - 00000
Record 1999 - 1st:0 2nd:0 3rd:0 Ran:5
1999 Turf 0-4: (7f, 8f 2, 16f) (g-s, gd, frm 2) 1999 AW 0-1: (8f) (Fibr)
Workmanlike, little account gelding, has worn blinkers. Turf high 19. **D Shaw [0-5] D C G Cooper.*

PUIWEE BHB 20f27a RR 30f 27a 5071[13]

4 b f Puissance 7.1f **(60)** - Glow Again (The Brianstan) 5.9f **(55)**
Form - 4400005000
Record 1999 - 1st:0 2nd:0 3rd:0 Ran:9
Pre1999 - 1st:0 2nd:1 3rd:2 Ran:13
Win Prizemoney £0 *Total Prizemoney* £1,535
1999 Turf 0-5: (7f, 8f 2, 11f 2) (gd, g-f 2, frm, hrd) 1999 AW 0-4: (8f, 9f, 11f, 12f) (Fibr 4)
Moderate filly, effective 7 to 8f, acts on gd to frm, has worn blinkers. Turf high 30. AW high 41. Becoming disappointing.
**P T Dalton [0-22] Mrs Julie Martin.*

PULAU PINANG (IRE) BHB 68f RR 72f 4823[9]

3 ch f Dolphin Street (FR) - Inner Pearl (Gulf Pearl) 12f **(54)**
Form - 310
Record 1999 - 1st:1 2nd:0 3rd:1 Ran:3
Win Prizemoney £2,280 *Total Prizemoney* £3,144
Wins * **1999** Spt Lingfi (FRM) 11.5f 64 <
1999 Turf 1-3: (10f, 11f 1-1, 12f) (g-f, frm 1-2)
Leggy, currently above-average filly. Turf high 72 (1st run) (began Aug) - 3rd of 9 getting 5lb from Makarim (22 Aug Bath 12f frm RF 3834) - also 1st of 10 from Another Rainbow (7 Spt Lingfield RF 4182). **G A Butler [1-3] Mrs A K H Ooi.*

PULAU TIOMAN BHB 95f RR 102f 5141[18]

3 b c Robellino (USA) 9.5f **(68)** - Ella Mon Amour (Ela-Mana-Mou) 10.1f **(70)**
Form - 220181570
Record 1999 - 1st:2 2nd:2 3rd:0 Ran:9

Pre1999 - 1st:1 2nd:0 3rd:1 Ran:4
Win Prizemoney £15,561 *Total Prizemoney* £28,672
Wins * **1999** Aug Sandow (G-S) 7.1f 102 <
* **1999** Jly Haydoc (G-S) H 7.1f 92 98
* 1998 Aug Nottin (G-F) 8.2f 82
1999 Turf 2-9: (7f 2-5, 8f 2, 9f 2) (gd 4, g-f 2-4, frm)
Scopey, very useful colt, effective 7f, acts on g-f, prefers tight tracks. Turf high 102 - 1st of 4 getting 6lb from Granny's Pet (11 Aug Sandown RF 3561) - also 1st of 9 getting 7lb from Marton Moss (2 Jly Haydock RF 2490). Mostly ran with credit early on last season without quite managing to get his head in front, until a drop back to seven worked the oracle at Haydock in July. Has since added a conditions race over the same trip at Sandown, and is clearly useful when conditions are right.
**M A Jarvis [3-13] H R H Sultan Ahmad Shah.*

PUNCTUATE RR 102f 4043[1]
2 b c Distant Relative 7f **(69)** - Niggle **(69f)** (Night Shift (USA)) 7.2f **(69)**
Form - 11
Record 1999 - 1st:2 2nd:0 3rd:0 Ran:2
Win Prizemoney £12,135 *Total Prizemoney* £12,135
Wins * **1999** Aug Ripon (GD) 5f 102 <
* **1999** Aug Sandow (G-S) 5f 72+
1999 Turf 2-2: (5f 2-2) (g-f 2-2)
Currently very useful colt. Turf high 102 (began Aug) - 1st of 5 giving 4lb to Jailhouse Rocket (31 Aug Ripon RF 4043). His debut was delayed by sore shins, but he made up for lost time when winning a maiden and minor event within 19 days during August. Held in high regard, he will be best at sprint distances and is a Listed/Group horse in the making.
**W J Haggas [2-2] Wentworth Racing (Pty) Ltd.*

PUNISHMENT BHB 83f89a **RR 85f 89a** 5221[12]
8 b h Midyan (USA) 9.9f **(64)** - In the Shade (Bustino) 10.4f **(64)**
Form - 54636386200430030
Record 1999 - 1st:0 2nd:1 3rd:4 Ran:15
Pre1999 - 1st:1 2nd:4 3rd:0 Ran:23
Win Prizemoney £7,746 *Total Prizemoney* £82,460
Wins * 1998 Oct Leices (SFT) H 10f 94 98 <
1999 Turf 0-12: (10f 6, 11f, 12f 4, 14f) (sft 2, gd 3, g-f 3, frm 4) 1999 AW 0-3: (10f 2, 12f) (Equi 2, Fibr)
Useful horse, effective 8 to 14f, best at 10f, acts on sft to frm. Turf high 99 - 2nd of 11 giving 2lb to Brilliant Red (19 Jun Ascot 10f g-f RF 2136). AW high 90. Usually set stiff tasks, he is capable of useful form but difficult to win with. Effective over middle-distances, he acts on any ground and invariably takes the eye in the paddock.
**K O Cunningham-Brown [1-24] A J Richards (from J E Hammond in FR [0-3] Jly 1998).*

PUNKAH (USA) BHB 45f64a **RR 48f 64a** 877[19]
6 b g Lear Fan (USA) 10.4f **(80)** -Gentle Persuasion (Bustino) 10.4f **(64)**
Form - 00
Record 1999 - 1st:0 2nd:0 3rd:0 Ran:1
Pre1999 - 1st:3 2nd:0 3rd:1 Ran:19
Win Prizemoney £11,267 *Total Prizemoney* £12,844
Wins * 1997 *Feb Lingfi (STD) H 10f 74 76* <
1996 Jun Windso (G-F) H 10f 72 71
1996 *Feb Lingfi (STD) 10f 47*
1999 Turf 0-1: (10f) (gd)
Moderate gelding, has worn blinkers.
**G M McCourt [5-30] McCourt Fine Meats Ltd & D J Rushen (from Lord Huntingdon [2-6] Jun 1996).*

PUP'S PRIDE BHB 53f **RR 54f** 5076[12]
2 b g Efisio 7.7f **(69)** - Moogie (Young Generation) 7.7f **(63)**
Form - 00600
Record 1999 - 1st:0 2nd:0 3rd:0 Ran:5
1999 Turf 0-5: (5f 3, 6f 2) (gd 2, g-f, frm 2)
Fair gelding. Turf high 54. **R A Fahey [0-5] The Slurping Toads.*

PURE BRIEF (IRE) BHB 62f **RR 63f** 4727[13]
2 b g Brief Truce (USA) 9.1f **(73)** - Epure (Bellypha) 9.8f **(73)**
Form - 5080
Record 1999 - 1st:0 2nd:0 3rd:0 Ran:4
1999 Turf 0-4: (7f 3, 10f) (g-s, gd, g-f, frm)
Average gelding. Turf high 63 (began Jly).
**D J G MurraySmith [0-4] The Joiners Arms Racing Club Quarndon.*

PURE COINCIDENCE BHB 81f78a **RR 79f 78a** 5110[8]
4 b g Lugana Beach 7f **(63)** - Esilam (Frimley Park) 6.5f **(67)**
Form - 00401368
Record 1999 - 1st:1 2nd:0 3rd:1 Ran:8
Pre1999 - 1st:2 2nd:2 3rd:2 Ran:15
Win Prizemoney £12,819 *Total Prizemoney* £47,708
Wins * **1999** Aug Carlis (G-F) H 5f 77 78 <
1997 Aug Redcar (FRM) 5f 75+
1997 *Jun Southw (STD) 5f 77+*
1999 Turf 1-7: (5f 1-5, 6f 2) (sft, g-s, gd 2, g-f, frm 1-2) 1999 AW 0-1: (6f) (Fibr)
Scopey, above-average gelding, effective 5f, acts on sft to frm, has worn blinkers. Turf high 79 - 6th of 21 getting 22lb from Superior Premium (9 Oct Ascot 5f gd RF 4795) - also 1st of 12 giving 2lb to Mungo Park (25 Aug Carlisle RF 3900). Changed stables before regaining winning form in a handicap at Carlisle in August and ran a fine third in a competitive Ayr handicap next time.
**K R Burke [1-4] Asterlane Ltd (from W J Musson [0-4] Jly 1999).*

PURE ELEGANCIA BHB 72f **RR 69f** 3762[6]
3 b f Lugana Beach 7f **(63)** - Esilam (Frimley Park) 6.5f **(67)**
Form - 6401516
Record 1999 - 1st:2 2nd:0 3rd:0 Ran:7
Win Prizemoney £11,120 *Total Prizemoney* £11,356
Wins * **1999** Jly Goodwo (G-F) H 5f 58 69 <
* **1999** Jun Catter (GD) H 5f 53 56
1999 Turf 2-7: (5f 2-5, 6f 2) (gd 4, g-f 1-2, frm 1-1)
Leggy, average filly, effective 5f, acts on g-f. Turf high 69 - 1st of 12 getting 7lb from Angie Baby (30 Jly Goodwood RF 3238). In fair form in the summer, winning over the minimum trip at Glorious Goodwood. **D Nicholls [2-7] Mrs Andry Muinos.*

PURNADAS ROAD (IRE) BHB 48f **RR 27f** 1268[16]
4 ch f Petardia 8.2f **(58)** - Choral Park (Music Boy) 6.8f **(57)**
Form - 00
Record 1999 - 1st:0 2nd:0 3rd:0 Ran:2
Pre1999 - 1st:0 2nd:0 3rd:0 Ran:3
1999 Turf 0-2: (5f, 6f) (g-s, g-f)
Workmanlike, little account filly. Turf high 27.
**J A R Toller [0-5] R A C Toller.*

PURPLE DAWN (IRE) BHB 34f34a **RR 39f 34a** 5107[11]
3 b f Tirol 8.1f **(64)** - Tuesday Morning (Sadler's Wells (USA)) 10f **(76)**
Form - 05010506000
Record 1999 - 1st:1 2nd:0 3rd:0 Ran:11
Pre1999 - 1st:0 2nd:1 3rd:0 Ran:9
Win Prizemoney £2,285 *Total Prizemoney* £3,045
Wins * **1999** Jun Nottin (GD) SH 10f 43 45 <
1999 Turf 1-10: (8f 2, 9f, 10f 1-5, 12f, 14f) (sft, gd 2, g-f 1-4, frm 3) 1999 AW 0-1: (11f) (Fibr)
Leggy, very moderate filly, effective 7f, acts on gd, has worn blinkers, likes tight tracks. Turf high 45. Inconsistent.
**J S Moore [1-22] Mrs Angela Speyer.*

PURPLE FLAME (IRE) BHB 55f **RR 59f** 4213[16]
3 b f Thatching 7.8f **(69)** - Polistatic (Free State) 8.7f **(61)**
Form - 706500
Record 1999 - 1st:0 2nd:0 3rd:0 Ran:6
1999 Turf 0-6: (7f 3, 8f 2, 10f) (gd 2, frm 4)
Workmanlike, fair filly. Turf high 63. **C A Horgan [0-6] Mrs B Sumner.*

PURPLE FLING BHB 54f60a **RR 50f 60a** 5149[3]
8 ch g Music Boy 6.5f **(56)** - Divine Fling (Imperial Fling (USA)) 7.1f **(58)**
Form - 54680313
Record 1999 - 1st:1 2nd:0 3rd:2 Ran:8
Pre1999 - 1st:8 2nd:5 3rd:3 Ran:50
Win Prizemoney £29,514 *Total Prizemoney* £40,425
Wins * **1999** *Spt Southw (STD) H 6f 56 58*
1997 Jly Redcar (G-S) 7f 76 <
1997 Jun Salisb (G-F) H 6f 68 70
1996 Oct Folkes (G-S) 6f 68
1995 Jly Carlis (FRM) 6.9f 76 <
1995 Jly Doncas (FRM) 6f 71
1995 *Jun Southw (STD) 6f 67*
1999 Turf 0-6: (5f, 6f 4, 7f) (gd 2, g-f 3, frm) 1999 AW 1-2: (6f 1-2) (Fibr 1-2)
Fair gelding, effective 6f, - acts on Fibr. Turf high 54. AW high 58

(1st run) (began Spt) - 1st of 16 getting 4lb from Aljaz (28 Spt Southwell RF 4607). Consistent. He ended a long losing run when gaining a narrow victory in a handicap on the Southwell Fibresand in September.

**A J McNae [1-16] A J McNae (from D W Chapman [1-6] Mar 1998).*

PURPLE HEATHER (USA) BHB 100f RR 84f 4559[2]

2 b f Rahy (USA) 9.1f **(80)** - Clear Attraction (USA) **(38f)** (Lear Fan (USA)) 8.5f **(73)**

Form - 642

Record 1999 - 1st:0 2nd:1 3rd:0 Ran:3

Win Prizemoney £0 *Total Prizemoney* £3,035

1999 Turf 0-3: (6f, 8f 2) (gd, g-f 2)

Currently decent filly. Turf high 84 (began Aug) - 2nd of 11 to Dollar Bird (25 Spt Nottingham 8f gd RF 4559).

**R Hannon [0-3] The Queen.*

PURPLE LACE BHB 45f RR 55f 4456[13]

7 b m Salse (USA) 10.9f **(71)** - Purple Prose (Rainbow Quest (USA)) 10.4f **(75)**

Form - 0770

Record 1999 - 1st:0 2nd:0 3rd:0 Ran:4
Pre1999 - 1st:0 2nd:0 3rd:0 Ran:1

1999 Turf 0-4: (8f, 10f, 16f, 17f) (sft, gd, frm 2)

Fair mare. Turf high 55 (began Aug).

**H S Howe [0-9] Kevin Daniel Crabb.*

PURSE BHB 69f RR 69f 4729[9]

3 b f Pursuit of Love 9.5f **(69)** - Rose Noble (USA) (Vaguely Noble) 10.1f **(72)**

Form - 3450

Record 1999 - 1st:0 2nd:0 3rd:1 Ran:4

Win Prizemoney £0 *Total Prizemoney* £844

1999 Turf 0-4: (8f 4) (g-s, g-f, frm 2)

Scopey, average filly. Turf high 70 (1st run) - 3rd of 15 to Hawala (17 May Windsor 8f g-f RF 1290).

**H R A Cecil [0-4] Exors of the late Lord Howard de Walden.*

PURSUANT BHB 35f RR 13f 2755[17]

3 b g Puissance 7.1f **(60)** - Payvashooz (Ballacashtal (CAN)) 5.3f **(50)**

Form - 000

Record 1999 - 1st:0 2nd:0 3rd:0 Ran:3
Pre1999 - 1st:0 2nd:0 3rd:0 Ran:3

1999 Turf 0-3: (6f, 7f 2) (gd, g-f, frm)

Scopey, poor gelding. Turf high 13.

**M Brittain [0-6] M J Paver.*

PURSUIVANT BHB 56f63a RR 64df 63a 4700[11]

5 b g Pursuit of Love 9.5f **(69)** - Collapse (Busted) 10.2f **(61)**

Form - 3252370

Record 1999 - 1st:0 2nd:2 3rd:2 Ran:7
Pre1999 - 1st:0 2nd:2 3rd:3 Ran:9

Win Prizemoney £0 *Total Prizemoney* £6,168

1999 Turf 0-4: (8f 3, 10f) (g-s, gd 3) 1999 AW 0-3: (8f 2, 9f) (Fibr 3)

Average gelding, effective 8 to 9f, best at 8f, acts on gd - acts on Fibr, has worn blinkers, prefers tight tracks. Turf high 64 - 2nd of 7 giving 5lb to Van Gurp (9 Jun Hamilton 8f gd RF 1857). AW high 69 (1st run) - 3rd of 16 giving 15lb to Pine Ridge Lad (26 Apr Southwell 8f Fibr RF 0852).

**M D Hammond [0-10] Andy Peake (from N Meade in IRE [0-8] Aug 1998).*

PURSUMI BHB 32f RR 34f 3376[13]

3 b f Pursuit of Love 9.5f **(69)** - Alacrity **(58df)** (Alzao (USA)) 7.1f **(68)**

Form - 0080

Record 1999 - 1st:0 2nd:0 3rd:0 Ran:4
Pre1999 - 1st:0 2nd:0 3rd:0 Ran:2

1999 Turf 0-4: (8f 2, 11f, 12f) (g-f, frm 3)

Scopey, very moderate filly. Turf high 34.

**R M Whitaker [0-6] G F Pemberton.*

PUSSIE WILLOW (IRE) RR 67f 4681[7]

2 b br f Catrail (USA) - Quiche (Formidable (USA)) 9.2f **(63)**

Form - 27

Record 1999 - 1st:0 2nd:1 3rd:0 Ran:2

Win Prizemoney £0 *Total Prizemoney* £1,290

1999 Turf 0-2: (5f, 6f) (gd 2)

Currently average filly. Turf high 80 (1st run) - 2nd of 9 to Hoh Dear (14 Apr Newmarket 5f gd RF 0697).

**P F I Cole [0-2] Major Christopher Hanbury.*

PUSSY GALORE BHB 68f RR 58f 4202a[14]

4 b f Pursuit of Love 9.5f **(69)** - Zinzi (Song) 7.2f **(61)**

Form - 17000

Record 1999 - 1st:1 2nd:0 3rd:0 Ran:5
Pre1999 - 1st:0 2nd:0 3rd:0 Ran:3

Win Prizemoney £3,480 *Total Prizemoney* £3,480

Wins 1999 Apr Folkes (SFT) 7f 61 <

1999 Turf 1-5: (7f 1-2, 8f 3) (g-s 1-2, gd 2, g-f)

Workmanlike, fair filly, has worn blinkers. Turf high 61 (1st run). Becoming disappointing.

**A Slattery in IRE [0-2] John Bernard O'Connor (from D R C Elsworth [1-6] May 1999).*

PUTERI WENTWORTH BHB 70f RR 81df 4381[11]

5 b m Sadler's Wells (USA) 11.3f **(87)** - Sweeping (Indian King (USA)) 7.4f **(64)**

Form - 70

Record 1999 - 1st:0 2nd:0 3rd:0 Ran:2
Pre1999 - 1st:3 2nd:0 3rd:0 Ran:13

Win Prizemoney £21,324 *Total Prizemoney* £27,585

Wins * 1998 Jly Goodwo (GD) H 20f 72 74 <
* 1998 Jun Doncas (GD) H 14.6f 68 72
* 1997 Nov Mussel (G-S) H 12f 60 68

1999 Turf 0-2: (14f, 17f) (gd, frm)

Decent filly, effective 15 to 20f, acts on gd to frm, best on gd, likes right handed tracks. Turf high 53 (began Aug).

**Miss Gay Kelleway [3-15] H R H Sultan Ahmad Shah.*

PUTUNA BHB 91f RR 93f 4683[23]

4 b f Generous (IRE) 11.5f **(82)** -Ivoronica (Targowice (USA)) 11.4f **(70)**

Form - 41634330

Record 1999 - 1st:1 2nd:0 3rd:3 Ran:8
Pre1999 - 1st:2 2nd:1 3rd:3 Ran:11

Win Prizemoney £27,965 *Total Prizemoney* £49,436

Wins *** 1999** Apr Newmar (GD) L 8.5f 94 <
* 1998 Jun Newbur (SFT) L 10f 93+
* 1998 Apr Epsom (SFT) 8.5f 83

1999 Turf 1-8: (8f, 9f 1-1, 10f 6) (g-s, gd 2, g-f 3, frm 1-2)

Useful filly, effective 9 to 11f, best at 10f, acts on g-s to frm, likes tight tracks. Turf high 100 - also 1st of 8 giving 3lb to Maria Isabella (30 Apr Newmarket RF 0947). Consistent. Effective between a mile and a mile and a quarter, she is consistent and always to be feared in fillies' Listed races.

**I A Balding [3-19] Robert Hitchins.*

PUZZLEMENT BHB 71f75a RR 71f 75a 1590[5]

5 gr g Mystiko (USA) 7.7f **(59)** - Abuzz (Absalom) 7.2f **(58)**

Form - 50452645

Record 1999 - 1st:0 2nd:1 3rd:0 Ran:8
Pre1999 - 1st:6 2nd:2 3rd:2 Ran:32

Win Prizemoney £26,027 *Total Prizemoney* £38,689

Wins * 1998 Aug Beverl (G-F) H 9.9f 63 71+
* 1998 Aug Beverl (G-F) H 9.9f 59 61
* 1997 *Nov Lingfi (STD) H 8f 70* 73 <
* 1997 *Nov Lingfi (STD) H 8f 63* 66
* 1997 *Feb Wolver (STD) H 9.4f 52* 60
* 1997 *Feb Lingfi (STD) H 8f 57* 59

1999 Turf 0-4: (10f 2, 11f, 12f) (sft 2, g-f, frm) 1999 AW 0-4: (8f, 9f, 10f, 11f) (Equi 2, Fibr 2)

Above-average gelding, effective 10 to 12f, best at 10f, acts on sft to frm - acts on Equi, likes right handed tracks, excels at Beverley. Turf high 74 (1st run) - 2nd of 14 giving 15lb to Swift (29 Mar Nottingham 10f sft RF 0510). AW high 75 - 4th of 10 giving 2lb to Bank On Him (16 Feb Lingfield 10f Equi RF 0300). Consistent.

**C E Brittain [6-40] Mrs C E Brittain.*

PYJAMA GIRL (USA) BHB 68f60a RR 71f 60a 4786[8]

2 gr ro f Night Shift (USA) 8.1f **(73)** - Permissible Tender (USA) (Al Hattab (USA)) 9.3f **(74)**

Form - 560458

Record 1999 - 1st:0 2nd:0 3rd:0 Ran:6

Win Prizemoney £0 *Total Prizemoney* £283

1999 Turf 0-5: (6f 5) (gd, g-f 2, frm 2) 1999 AW 0-1: (6f) (Equi)

Above-average filly, effective 6f, acts on g-f. Turf high 71.
**P R Chamings [0-6] M A Kirby.*

PYRAMID PRINCESS RR 67f 2944[3]
2 b f Pyramus (USA) - Sancilia (Dalsaan) 9.8f **(64)**
Form - 3
Record 1999 - 1st:0 2nd:0 3rd:1 Ran:1
Win Prizemoney £0 *Total Prizemoney* £330
1999 Turf 0-1: (5f) (gd)
Average filly. (1st run) - 3rd of 14 getting 10lb from Agua Caballo (19 Jly Beverley 5f gd RF 2944). (DEAD)
**J S Wainwright [0-1] Rosaly Racing & Neil Harrison.*

PYROMANIAC (GER) RR 103f 4519a[6]
5 h
Form - 66
1999 Turf 0-2: (10f, 11f) (gd 2)
Currently very useful. Turf high 103. **P Lautner in GER [0-2].*

PYTHAGORAS RR 76f 4792[9]
2 ch c Kris 10f **(75)** - Tricorne **(72f)** (Green Desert (USA)) 8.6f **(78)**
Form - 40
Record 1999 - 1st:0 2nd:0 3rd:0 Ran:2
Win Prizemoney £0 *Total Prizemoney* £252
1999 Turf 0-2: (8f 2) (gd 2)
Currently above-average colt. Turf high 76 (began Aug).
**W R Muir [0-2] R Haim.*

PYTHIOS (IRE) BHB 100f **RR 101f** 1999[1]
3 b c Danehill (USA) 9.1f **(79)** - Pithara (GR) (Never so Bold) 6.3f **(66)**
Form - 131
Record 1999 - 1st:2 2nd:0 3rd:1 Ran:3
Pre1999 - 1st:0 2nd:0 3rd:0 Ran:1
Win Prizemoney £39,741 *Total Prizemoney* £40,791
Wins * 1999 Jun Ascot (G-F) H 8f 92 101 <
*** 1999** May Doncas (G-F) 7f 79
1999 Turf 2-3: (7f 1-2, 8f 1-1) (g-f 1-2, hrd 1-1)
Scopey, very useful colt. Turf high 101 - 1st of 32 getting 7lb from Siege (15 Jun Ascot RF 1999). He beat Siege in a maiden at Doncaster in May and confirmed the form in the Britannia Handicap at Royal Ascot. Missing through the remainder of the season, he has a grand attitude and will stay beyond a mile.
**H R A Cecil [2-4] Mrs H G Cambanis.*

QAMOUS (USA) RR 86f 4655[1]
2 gr c Bahri (USA) - Bel Ray (USA) (Restivo (USA))
Form - 41
Record 1999 - 1st:1 2nd:0 3rd:0 Ran:2
Win Prizemoney £4,980 *Total Prizemoney* £5,706
Wins * 1999 Spt Newmar (G-S) 7f 86 <
1999 Turf 1-2: (7f 1-1, 8f) (gd 1-1, frm)
Currently useful colt. Turf high 86 (began Spt) - 1st of 14 from Holding Court (30 Spt Newmarket RF 4655). Came on for his debut to win a division of Newmarket's Westley Maiden, making most.
**E A L Dunlop [1-2] Hamdan Al Maktoum.*

QANDIL (USA) BHB 32f **RR 53f** 4222[12]
3 ch g Riverman (USA) 9.7f **(78)** - Confirmed Affair (USA) (Affirmed (USA)) 9.3f **(79)**
Form - 00
Record 1999 - 1st:0 2nd:0 3rd:0 Ran:2
Pre1999 - 1st:0 2nd:0 3rd:0 Ran:1
1999 Turf 0-1: (10f) (gd) 1999 AW 0-1: (8f) (Fibr)
Workmanlike, currently fair gelding.
**H J Collingridge [0-2] Mrs S McGuiness (from M P Tregoning [0-1] Oct 1998).*

QHAZEENAH BHB 90f **RR 89f** 4761[8]
3 b f Marju (IRE) 9.2f **(76)** - Nafhaat (USA) (Roberto (USA)) 10f **(76)**
Form - 4158
Record 1999 - 1st:1 2nd:0 3rd:0 Ran:4
Pre1999 - 1st:2 2nd:0 3rd:1 Ran:5
Win Prizemoney £30,762 *Total Prizemoney* £32,005
Wins * 1999 Jly Yarmou (G-F) 7f 89
* 1998 Spt Doncas (GD) H 6.5f 93 99 <
* 1998 Aug Folkes (G-F) 6.9f 82
1999 Turf 1-4: (6f, 7f 1-2, 8f) (gd 1-3, g-f)
Scopey, useful filly, effective 7f, acts on gd. Turf high 89. Wonderfully progressive at two, she regained winning form with a narrow victory in a Yarmouth conditions event on her second start, but found a mile and soft ground all too much for her in an Ascot Listed event next time. **J L Dunlop [3-9] Hamdan Al Maktoum.*

QILIN (IRE) BHB 90f **RR 93f** 5222[3]
4 b f Second Set (IRE) 9.2f **(67)** - Usance (GER) (Kronenkranich (GER)) 6f **(97)**
Form - 28010343
Record 1999 - 1st:1 2nd:1 3rd:2 Ran:8
Pre1999 - 1st:2 2nd:1 3rd:1 Ran:13
Win Prizemoney £21,149 *Total Prizemoney* £32,013
Wins * 1999 Jun Newcas (G-F) H 7f 83 86
* 1998 Jun Newmar (GD) 6f 97 <
* 1997 Oct Newmar (G-F) 6f 91
1999 Turf 1-8: (5f, 6f 3, 7f 1-4) (g-s 2, gd 2, g-f, frm 1-3)
Scopey, useful filly, effective 6f, acts on g-f. Turf high 93. Highly tried as a two and three-year-old, she found her level in handicaps towards the end of her second season. Caught a tartar first time out in '99 before a step up to seven furlongs saw her return to winning ways at Newcastle in June. She ran a couple of fine races in soft ground towards the end of the season.
**M H Tompkins [3-21] Ian Lochhead.*

QOSHEEYYA RR 32f 1853[8]
3 b f Robellino (USA) 9.5f **(68)** - Sharanella (Shareef Dancer (USA)) 9.9f **(73)**
Form - 8
Record 1999 - 1st:0 2nd:0 3rd:0 Ran:1
1999 Turf 0-1: (7f) (g-s)
Lengthy, currently very moderate filly.
**N A Graham [0-1] Hamdan Al Maktoum.*

QUAESTIO (USA) RR 83f 2345[5]
2 b f Seeking the Gold (USA) 7.4f **(80)** - Oscillate (USA) (Seattle Slew (USA)) 9.4f **(76)**
Form - 15
Record 1999 - 1st:1 2nd:0 3rd:0 Ran:2
Win Prizemoney £4,305 *Total Prizemoney* £4,623
Wins * 1999 Jun Newmar (GD) 6f 81 <
1999 Turf 1-2: (6f 1-2) (gd 1-1, g-f)
Currently decent filly. Turf high 83 - also 1st of 8 from Queens Bench (5 Jun Newmarket RF 1774). Winner of a decent Newmarket maiden over six furlongs at Newmarket on her debut, but was beaten in a listed race over the same course and distance.
**J L Dunlop [1-2] Neil Jones.*

QUAINT DESIRE BHB 24f **RR 32f** 4602[10]
6 br g Grey Desire 9.3f **(49)** - Aquainted (Known Fact (USA)) 7.4f **(67)**
Form - 00
Record 1999 - 1st:0 2nd:0 3rd:0 Ran:2
Pre1999 - 1st:0 2nd:0 3rd:0 Ran:4
1999 Turf 0-1: (10f) (g-s) 1999 AW 0-1: (11f) (Fibr)
Very moderate gelding. **M Brittain [0-6] Mel Brittain.*

QUAKERESS (IRE) BHB 36f **RR 44df** 4732[20]
4 b f Brief Truce (USA) 9.1f **(73)** - Deer Emily (Alzao (USA)) 7.1f **(68)**
Form - 0408000
Record 1999 - 1st:0 2nd:0 3rd:0 Ran:7
Pre1999 - 1st:0 2nd:1 3rd:2 Ran:3
Win Prizemoney £0 *Total Prizemoney* £2,056
1999 Turf 0-7: (5f, 6f 3, 8f 2, 9f) (gd, g-f 2, frm 3, hrd)
Workmanlike, moderate filly, effective 6f, acts on hrd, has worn blinkers. Turf high 57 - 4th of 7 getting 1lb from Sweet Charity (12 Jly Brighton 6f hrd RF 2753). Becoming disappointing.
**John Berry [0-10] Mrs Rosemary Moszkowicz.*

QUAKERS FIELD BHB 85f **RR 53f** 5221[15]
6 b h Anshan 8.2f **(63)** - Nosey (Nebbiolo) 8.1f **(75)**
Form - 00
Record 1999 - 1st:0 2nd:0 3rd:0 Ran:2
Pre1999 - 1st:2 2nd:2 3rd:0 Ran:12
Win Prizemoney £11,018 *Total Prizemoney* £18,893
Wins * 1995 Spt Goodwo (GD) 7f 99 <
* 1995 Aug Kempto (G-F) 6f 80
1999 Turf 0-2: (10f, 12f) (sft, g-s)

Fair horse. Turf high 53 (began Oct). Becoming disappointing.
**G L Moore [3-17] Bryan Pennick.*

QUALITAIR SILVER BHB 33f22a **RR 23f 22a** 282[9]
5 gr m Absalom 7.1f **(56)** - Irish Limerick (Try My Best (USA)) 7.6f **(67)**
Form - 0600
Record 1999 - 1st:0 2nd:0 3rd:0 Ran:2
Pre1999 - 1st:0 2nd:0 3rd:3 Ran:11
Win Prizemoney £0 *Total Prizemoney* £1,314
1999 AW 0-2: (6f, 7f) (Fibr 2)
Little account filly, has worn blinkers. AW high 10.
**Miss L C Siddall [0-4] Mrs S E Cooper (from J F Bottomley [0-9] Jly 1997).*

QUALITAIR SURVIVOR BHB 38f **RR 30f** 5071[11]
4 gr g Terimon 8.7f **(58)** - Comtec Princess (Gulf Pearl) 12f **(54)**
Form - 40000
Record 1999 - 1st:0 2nd:0 3rd:0 Ran:5
1999 Turf 0-5: (9f, 10f 2, 11f, 14f) (gd, g-f 3, frm)
Very moderate gelding. Turf high 59 (began Jly).
**J Hetherton [0-4] Qualitair Holdings Ltd (from T J Etherington [0-5] Jly 1999).*

QUEBRA (GER) RR 98f 4366a[2]
3 ch f Surumu (GER) - Quebrada (IRE) (Devil's Bag (USA)) 12.4f **(78)**
Form - 2
1999 Turf 0-1: (12f) (gd)
Currently very useful filly. (1st run) - 2nd of 8 to Evil Empire (12 Spt Hanover 12f gd RF 4366a). **A Wohler in GER [0-1].*

QUEDEX BHB 68f **RR 68f** 2494[4]
3 b c Deploy 11.4f **(67)** - Alwal (Pharly (FR)) 9.8f **(68)**
Form - 2114
Record 1999 - 1st:2 2nd:1 3rd:0 Ran:4
Pre1999 - 1st:0 2nd:0 3rd:0 Ran:6
Win Prizemoney £6,699 *Total Prizemoney* £8,140
Wins * 1999 Jun Bath (GD) 11.7f 68 <
*** 1999** Jun Goodwo (G-S) H 9.9f 62 65
1999 Turf 2-4: (8f, 10f 1-1, 12f 1-2) (gd 1-2, g-f 1-1, frm)
Unfurnished, average colt, effective 8 to 12f, best at 12f, acts on gd to frm, best on gd. Turf high 68 - 1st of 7 giving 2lb to Greyfield (12 Jun Bath RF 1943) - also 1st of 7 giving 2lb to Kiss Me Kate (4 Jun Goodwood RF 1738). A tough performer, he showed progressive form to win twice in June. **E L James [2-10] E James.*

QUEEN FOR A DAY BHB 62f **RR 65f** 4901[15]
2 b f Emperor Jones (USA) - Could Have Been (Nomination) 7f **(60)**
Form - 034200
Record 1999 - 1st:0 2nd:1 3rd:1 Ran:6
Win Prizemoney £0 *Total Prizemoney* £1,545
1999 Turf 0-6: (6f 2, 7f 3, 8f) (g-s 2, g-f 2, frm, hrd)
Average filly, effective 6 to 8f, acts on g-s to g-f. Turf high 65 - 3rd of 14 getting 3lb from Kirsch (25 Aug Lingfield 6f g-f RF 3907).
**C F Wall [0-6] Ettore Landi.*

QUEEN OF THE KEYS BHB 40f **RR 41f** 5056[7]
3 b f Royal Academy (USA) 7.8f **(77)** - Piano Belle (USA) (Fappiano (USA)) 8.7f **(77)**
Form - 007
Record 1999 - 1st:0 2nd:0 3rd:0 Ran:3
Pre1999 - 1st:0 2nd:0 3rd:0 Ran:2
1999 Turf 0-2: (7f, 8f) (gd, g-f) 1999 AW 0-1: (10f) (Equi)
Unfurnished, moderate filly. Turf high 23.
**S Dow [0-5] Mrs A M Upsdell.*

QUEEN OF THE MAY (IRE) RR 75f 4625[4]
2 b f Nicolotte - Varnish (Final Straw) 7.9f **(64)**
Form - 1044044
Record 1999 - 1st:1 2nd:0 3rd:0 Ran:7
Win Prizemoney £3,273 *Total Prizemoney* £4,505
Wins * 1999 May Bright (FRM) 5.3f 66+ <
1999 Turf 1-7: (5f 1-3, 6f 3, 7f) (g-s, gd, g-f, frm 3, hrd 1-1)
Above-average filly, effective 5f, acts on hrd. Turf high 74 - also 1st of 8 from Safari Blues (27 May Brighton RF 1515). She made a winning debut in a modest Brighton maiden.
**M R Channon [1-7] Miss Maggie Worsdell & Mrs Carolyn Wood.*

QUEEN OF TIDES (IRE) BHB 27f28a **RR 17f 28a** 3276[8]
4 b f Soviet Star (USA) 8.6f **(74)** - Tidesong (Top Ville) 11.7f **(68)**
Form - 076088
Record 1999 - 1st:0 2nd:0 3rd:0 Ran:4
Pre1999 - 1st:0 2nd:0 3rd:0 Ran:6
1999 Turf 0-1: (9f) (frm) 1999 AW 0-3: (10f, 13f, 16f) (Equi 3)
Scopey, very moderate filly. AW high 28.
**S Dow [0-8] S Dow (from Sir Michael Stoute [0-2] Spt 1997).*

QUEEN OMAH (IRE) BHB 38f **RR 53df** 4816[11]
3 b f Dolphin Street (FR) - Quilting (Mummy's Pet) 7.7f **(60)**
Form - 744600
Record 1999 - 1st:0 2nd:0 3rd:0 Ran:6
Pre1999 - 1st:0 2nd:0 3rd:0 Ran:3
Win Prizemoney £0 *Total Prizemoney* £730
1999 Turf 0-6: (9f 2, 10f 4) (gd 2, g-f 2, frm 2)
Light-framed, fair filly. Turf high 53. Becoming disappointing.
**R Hannon [0-9] Buddy Hackett.*

QUEENS BENCH (IRE) BHB 87f **RR 85f** 4012[1]
2 ch f Wolfhound (USA) 7.3f **(71)** - Zafaaf **(98df)** (Kris) 9.5f **(73)**
Form - 423311
Record 1999 - 1st:2 2nd:1 3rd:2 Ran:6
Win Prizemoney £10,458 *Total Prizemoney* £13,568
Wins * 1999 Aug Epsom (GD) H 7f 81 85 <
*** 1999** Aug Beverl (GD) 5f 78
1999 Turf 2-6: (5f 1-2, 6f 3, 7f 1-1) (gd 2, g-f 1-2, frm 1-2)
Useful filly, effective 5 to 7f, acts on gd to frm, best on g-f. Turf high 85 - 1st of 8 from Noble Pursuit (30 Aug Epsom RF 4012) - also 1st of 8 from Cibenze (12 Aug Beverley RF 3569). She got off the mark in a weakish maiden at Beverley over five furlongs on good ground, but relished the step up to seven furlongs when winning at Epsom. **B Hanbury [2-6] Abdullah Ali.*

QUEEN'S HAT BHB 40f40a **RR 36f 40a** 2639[10]
4 b f Cadeaux Genereux 7.9f **(76)** - Greenlet (IRE) (Green Desert (USA)) 8.6f **(78)**
Form - 4500000
Record 1999 - 1st:0 2nd:0 3rd:0 Ran:5
Pre1999 - 1st:0 2nd:0 3rd:1 Ran:7
Win Prizemoney £0 *Total Prizemoney* £716
1999 Turf 0-4: (8f 2, 9f 2) (sft, gd, g-f, frm) 1999 AW 0-1: (8f) (Equi)
Well made, very moderate filly, effective 6f, acts on gd. Turf high 36. Inconsistent.
**J J Bridger [0-7] J J Bridger (from B Hanbury [0-5] Jly 1998).*

QUEEN'S LOVE (USA) RR 91f 5174a[8]
3 b f Kingmambo (USA) 10.9f **(85)** - Wiedniu (USA) (Danzig Connection (USA)) 8f **(68)**
Form - 3453318
1999 Turf 1-7: (8f 1-1, 10f 2, 12f 4) (sft 1-4, g-s, gd 2)
Useful filly, effective 8 to 12f, acts on sft to gd, best on sft, has worn blinkers. Turf high 91 - 3rd of 6 getting 5lb from Mudaa-eb (9 Jun Leopardstown 12f gd RF 2024a) - also 1st of 14 from Crystal Downs (10 Oct Naas RF 4856a).
**J S Bolger in IRE [2-9] Henryk de Kwiatkowski.*

QUEENSMEAD BHB 62f **RR 76f** 5105[5]
2 b f Rudimentary (USA) 8.2f **(66)** - Shernborne (Kalaglow) 9.8f **(67)**
Form - 58462625
Record 1999 - 1st:0 2nd:2 3rd:0 Ran:8
Win Prizemoney £0 *Total Prizemoney* £2,251
1999 Turf 0-8: (5f 7, 6f) (gd 6, g-f, frm)
Above-average filly, effective 5f, acts on gd, has worn blinkers. Turf high 77. Has some ability but looks pretty much exposed.
**R Hannon [0-8] Mrs P I Lever.*

QUEEN'S PAGEANT BHB 70f84a **RR 65f 84a** 5166[5]
5 ch m Risk Me (FR) 8f **(53)** - Mistral's Dancer (Shareef Dancer (USA)) 9.9f **(73)**
Form - 10300005
Record 1999 - 1st:1 2nd:0 3rd:1 Ran:8
Pre1999 - 1st:2 2nd:1 3rd:2 Ran:18
Win Prizemoney £19,029 *Total Prizemoney* £23,520
Wins * 1999 Apr Thirsk (GD) H 8f 73 75 <
*** 1998** Oct York (GD) H 7f 70 73
*** 1996** Oct Haydoc (SFT) 5f 68

1999 Turf 1-8: (7f 4, 8f 1-4) (g-s, gd 1-6, g-f)
Decent filly, effective 7 to 8f, best at 8f, acts on gd to g-f, best on gd, has worn blinkers. Turf high 75 (1st run) - 1st of 10 giving 26lb to Time of Night (17 Apr Thirsk RF 0746).
**J L Spearing [3-26] Mrs Robert Heathcote.*

QUEEN'S SIGNET RR 30f 4453[14]

3 ch f King's Signet (USA) 7f **(51)** - Axe Valley (Royben) 7.3f **(60)**
Form - 00
Record 1999 - 1st:0 2nd:0 3rd:0 Ran:2
1999 Turf 0-2: (7f, 8f) (sft, g-f)
Workmanlike, currently very moderate filly. Turf high 30.
**D W P Arbuthnot [0-2] W H Ponsonby.*

QUEEN TITANIA (IRE) BHB 50f60a RR 37f 60a 4632[20]

3 b f Elbio 9f **(62)** - Astania (GER) (Arratos (FR)) 12.2f **(60)**
Form - 7000
Record 1999 - 1st:0 2nd:0 3rd:0 Ran:4
Pre1999 - 1st:0 2nd:0 3rd:0 Ran:3
1999 Turf 0-3: (8f, 10f, 12f) (g-s, gd, frm) 1999 AW 0-1: (7f) (Fibr)
Light-framed, very moderate filly, has worn blinkers. Turf high 37.
**A J McNae [0-7] Racing Post Syndicate.*

QUEEN ZENOBIA BHB 73f RR 70f 2728[8]

3 b f Danehill (USA) 9.1f **(79)** - Persia (IRE) (Persian Bold) 9.3f **(66)**
Form - 1058
Record 1999 - 1st:1 2nd:0 3rd:0 Ran:4
Pre1999 - 1st:0 2nd:0 3rd:0 Ran:2
Win Prizemoney £3,337 *Total Prizemoney* £3,337
Wins * **1999** Apr Windso (G-F) 8.3f 68 <
1999 Turf 1-4: (7f 2, 8f 1-2) (gd, g-f 2, frm 1-1)
Scopey, above-average filly, effective 7 to 8f, acts on frm. Turf high 70 - also 1st of 13 from Tiergarten (19 Apr Windsor RF 0755).
**J H M Gosden [1-6] Mrs Madelyn Jason.*

QUEL SENOR (FR) RR 109f 3228a[3]

4 g Tel Quel (FR) - Bold Senorita (IRE) (Pennine Walk) 8.5f **(61)**
Form - 3
1999 Turf 0-1: (10f) (gd)
Pattern-class gelding. (1st run) - 3rd of 9 giving 10lb to Victory Cry (21 Jly Vichy 10f gd RF 3228a). **F Doumen in FR [2-6].*

QUESTABELLE RR 54f 5211[4]

3 ch f Rainbow Quest (USA)11.2f **(81)** -Bella Colora (Bellypha) 9.8f **(73)**
Form - 54
Record 1999 - 1st:0 2nd:0 3rd:0 Ran:2
Win Prizemoney £0 *Total Prizemoney* £452
1999 Turf 0-2: (10f 2) (hvy, sft)
Scopey, currently fair filly. Turf high 54 (began Oct).
**L M Cumani [0-2] Helena Springfield Ltd.*

QUESTAN BHB 51f42a RR 56f 42a 412[8]

7 b g Rainbow Quest (USA) 11.2f **(81)** - Vallee Dansante (USA) (Lyphard (USA)) 9.9f **(72)**
Form - 8
Record 1999 - 1st:0 2nd:0 3rd:0 Ran:1
Pre1999 - 1st:1 2nd:1 3rd:0 Ran:11
Win Prizemoney £3,011 *Total Prizemoney* £4,151
Wins * 1998 May Bath (FRM) H 8f 51 57 <
1999 AW 0-1: (8f) (Fibr)
Fair gelding, effective 7 to 8f, best at 8f, acts on gd to frm, favours tight tracks. Becoming disappointing. **B Smart [1-12] B Smart.*

QUESTUARY (IRE) BHB 61f59a RR 48f 59a 169[9]

3 b f Rainbow Quest (USA) 11.2f **(81)** - Pelf (USA) (Al Nasr (FR)) 9.3f **(68)**
Form - 140
Record 1999 - 1st:0 2nd:0 3rd:0 Ran:2
Pre1999 - 1st:1 2nd:0 3rd:0 Ran:3
Win Prizemoney £1,737 *Total Prizemoney* £1,927
Wins * 1998 *Dec Lingfi (STD) S 8f 62+* <
1999 AW 0-2: (8f,.10f) (Equi 2)
Scopey, average filly. AW high 57.
**M R Channon [1-3] Mrs T Burns (from M P Tregoning [0-2] Spt 1998).*

QUEZON CITY BHB 60f62a RR 56f 62a 848[6]

5 ch g Keen 11.1f **(58)** - Calachuchi (Martinmas) 7.6f **(59)**
Form - 141226
Record 1999 - 1st:2 2nd:2 3rd:0 Ran:6
Pre1999 - 1st:1 2nd:1 3rd:1 Ran:11
Win Prizemoney £7,710 *Total Prizemoney* £11,227
Wins * **1999** *Mar Southw (STD) H 16f 50 54+*
* **1999** *Feb Southw (STD) H 16f 45 50+*
1997 Jun Hamilt (G-F) 12.1f 61 <
1999 Turf 0-1: (16f) (gd) 1999 AW 2-5: (15f, 16f 2-4) (Fibr 2-5)
Average gelding, effective 16f, acts on gd - acts on Fibr. (1st run) - 2nd of 11 giving 13lb to Old Hush Wing (30 Mar Newcastle 16f gd RF 0515). AW high 64 - 2nd of 12 giving 1lb to Time Can Tell (10 Apr Wolverhampton 16f Fibr RF 0643). He won twice over two miles on the Southwell Fibresand at the start of the year, and looks better on that surface.
**Miss J A Camacho [2-9] Middleham Park Racing XI (from M J Camacho [1-8] Jly 1997).*

QUIBBLING BHB 26f26a RR 34f 26a 3861[6]

5 b m Salse (USA) 10.9f **(71)** - Great Exception (Grundy) 10.3f **(65)**
Form - 57656
Record 1999 - 1st:0 2nd:0 3rd:0 Ran:5
Pre1999 - 1st:0 2nd:1 3rd:2 Ran:15
Win Prizemoney £0 *Total Prizemoney* £1,964
1999 Turf 0-1: (14f) (frm) 1999 AW 0-4: (11f, 12f 2, 16f) (Equi, Fibr 3)
Very moderate filly, effective 12 to 16f, acts on gd to g-f, often wears blinkers. AW high 31. Consistent.
**K C Comerford [0-15] Red & Black Racing (from H Candy [0-9] Oct 1997).*

QUICK SILVER BHB 26f RR 18f 2128[9]

3 b f Anshan 8.2f **(63)** - Tabeeba (Diesis) 9.3f **(69)**
Form - 700
Record 1999 - 1st:0 2nd:0 3rd:0 Ran:2
Pre1999 - 1st:0 2nd:0 3rd:0 Ran:1
1999 Turf 0-1: (10f) (frm) 1999 AW 0-1: (10f) (Equi)
Workmanlike, currently little account filly.
**R E Barr [0-1] R E Barr (from R Hannon [0-2] Jan 1999).*

QUICKSILVER GIRL RR 59f 3575[5]

3 b f Danehill (USA) 9.1f **(79)** - Crime of Passion (Dragonara Palace (USA)) 6.1f **(55)**
Form - 45
Record 1999 - 1st:0 2nd:0 3rd:0 Ran:2
Win Prizemoney £0 *Total Prizemoney* £267
1999 Turf 0-2: (7f 2) (gd, g-f)
Lengthy, currently fair filly. Turf high 59.
**J W Hills [0-2] Christopher Wright.*

QUICKSTEP RR 69f 4813[13]

3 ch f Salse (USA) 10.9f **(71)** - Short And Sharp (Sharpen Up) 8.3f **(67)**
Form - 0776543780
Record 1999 - 1st:0 2nd:0 3rd:1 Ran:10
Pre1999 - 1st:0 2nd:0 3rd:1 Ran:3
Win Prizemoney £0 *Total Prizemoney* £1,654
1999 Turf 0-10: (8f 4, 9f, 10f 3, 11f, 15f) (gd 2, g-f 3, frm 4, hrd)
Average filly, effective 7 to 11f, acts on g-f to frm, best on g-f, prefers left handed tracks. Turf high 72 - 6th of 14 to Dahshah (21 May Bath 8f g-f RF 1371). **R Hannon [0-13] Lady Tennant.*

QUICKTIME BHB 59f RR 60f 4530[4]

2 ch f Timeless Times (USA) 6.1f **(56)** - Sally Weld **(56f 55a)** (Weldnaas (USA))
Form - 004
Record 1999 - 1st:0 2nd:0 3rd:0 Ran:3
1999 Turf 0-3: (6f 3) (g-s, frm 2)
Currently average filly. Turf high 60. **B Smart [0-3] R Lamb.*

QUIDS INN BHB 51f RR 46f 5158[9]

2 br g Timeless Times (USA) 6.1f **(56)** - Waltz on Air (Doc Marten)
Form - 650000
Record 1999 - 1st:0 2nd:0 3rd:0 Ran:6
1999 Turf 0-6: (5f 3, 6f, 8f 2) (gd 4, g-f, frm)
Moderate gelding, has worn blinkers. Turf high 70.
**T D Easterby [0-6] A Arton.*

QUIET AFFAIR RR 84f 3824[3]

2 b f Distant Relative 7f **(69)** -Princess Eboli (Brigadier Gerard) 9.3f **(58)**

Form - 1413
Record 1999 - 1st:2 2nd:0 3rd:1 Ran:4
Win Prizemoney £8,309 *Total Prizemoney* £9,606
Wins * 1999 Jly Newmar (G-F) H 7f 84 <
*** 1999** Jun Lingfi (GD) 6f 71+
1999 Turf 2-4: (6f 1-2, 7f 1-1, 8f) (g-f 1-1, frm 1-3)
Decent filly. Turf high 84 - 1st of 14 giving 2lb to True Obsession (23 Jly Newmarket RF 3063). Won a Lingfield maiden and a Newmarket nursery, but was a bit disappointing when tried over a mile on her final start. **J L Dunlop [2-4] Ian Pilkington.*

QUIET ARCH (IRE) BHB 60f58a RR 63f 58a 126[9]
6 b g Archway (IRE) 8.5f **(60)** - My Natalie (Rheingold) 10.4f **(62)**
Form - 4040
Record 1999 - 1st:0 2nd:0 3rd:0 Ran:2
Pre1999 - 1st:6 2nd:8 3rd:7 Ran:41
Win Prizemoney £17,023 *Total Prizemoney* £30,132
Wins 1998 Jun Bright (FRM) C 10f 63
1998 *Mar Lingfi (STD)* *12f* *73*
1998 *Feb Lingfi (SLW) H* *12f* *70 75* <
1997 *Jan Lingfi (STD) H* *10f* *57 67*
1997 *Jan Lingfi (STD)* *10f* *51*
1996 *Jun Lingfi (STD)* *8f* *69*
1999 AW 0-2: (13f, 16f) (Equi 2)
Average gelding, effective 10 to 12f, best at 12f, - acts on Equi, has worn blinkers, favours left handed tracks, likes Lingfield. AW high 52. Consistent.
**J G M O'Shea [0-3] Gary Roberts (from W R Muir [5-28] Nov 1998).*

QUIET DIGNITY BHB 67f RR 76f 4631[5]
3 b f Unfuwain (USA) 11.4f **(74)** - Docklands (On Your Mark) 7.7f **(58)**
Form - 675555
Record 1999 - 1st:0 2nd:0 3rd:0 Ran:6
1999 Turf 0-6: (8f 4, 10f 2) (g-s, gd, frm 4)
Leggy, above-average filly. Turf high 76.
**B W Hills [0-6] W J Gredley.*

QUIET MILLFIT (USA) BHB 67f RR 78df 4816[3]
3 b g Quiet American (USA) 7.9f **(60)** - Millfit (USA) (Blushing Groom (FR)) 10.3f **(76)**
Form - 0345106453
Record 1999 - 1st:1 2nd:0 3rd:2 Ran:10
Pre1999 - 1st:0 2nd:0 3rd:0 Ran:2
Win Prizemoney £2,200 *Total Prizemoney* £3,706
Wins * 1999 Jun Lingfi (G-F) 9f 85 <
1999 Turf 1-10: (6f, 7f, 8f, 9f 1-4, 10f 3) (gd 5, g-f, frm 1-4)
Workmanlike, above-average gelding, effective 7 to 10f, best at 9f, acts on g-f to frm, best on frm, likes left handed tracks, prefers tight tracks. Turf high 86 - 3rd of 11 to Siege (22 May Kempton 7f frm RF 1393) - also 1st of 9 from Democracy (26 Jun Lingfield RF 2328). **B Hanbury [1-12] Hilal Salem.*

QUIET RESOLVE (USA) RR 120f 5226a[14]
4 b c Affirmed (USA) 10.3f **(75)** - Quiet Cleo (USA) (No Louder (USA))
Form - 10
1999 Turf 1-2: (8f 1-2) (frm 1-2)
Currently very high-class colt. Turf high 120 (1st run) (began Spt) - 1st of 15 getting 2lb from Rob 'N' Gin (19 Spt Woodbine RF 4657a). A useful Canadian-trained miler, he was awarded the Atto Mile at Woodbine in September on the disqualification of Hawksley Hill, but finished well beaten in the Breeders' Cup Mile.
**M Frostad in CAN [1-2].*

QUIET VENTURE BHB 76f87a RR 75f 87a 4688[5]
5 b g Rainbow Quest (USA) 11.2f **(81)** - Jameelaty (USA) (Nureyev (USA)) 8.7f **(78)**
Form - 10023665
Record 1999 - 1st:0 2nd:1 3rd:1 Ran:6
Pre1999 - 1st:4 2nd:0 3rd:1 Ran:13
Win Prizemoney £15,683 *Total Prizemoney* £18,521
Wins * 1998 *Nov Wolver (STD) H* *6f* *81 88* <
* 1998 Aug Newcas (GD) H 7f 76 78
* 1998 Aug Mussel (G-F) 7.1f 74
* 1998 Aug Redcar (G-F) 8f 65
1999 Turf 0-6: (6f, 7f 4, 8f) (g-f 3, frm, hrd 2)
Useful gelding, effective 6 to 7f, best at 7f, acts on hrd - acts on Fibr. Turf high 79 - 2nd of 4 giving 14lb to Windy Gulch (4 Aug Newcastle 7f hrd RF 3369).
**I Semple [4-15] Gee Kay Gee Gees (from E A L Dunlop [0-4] Oct 1997).*

QUILT BHB 50f RR 42f 3110[14]
3 b f Terimon 8.7f **(58)** - Quaranta (Hotfoot) 10.5f **(59)**
Form - 000
Record 1999 - 1st:0 2nd:0 3rd:0 Ran:3
Pre1999 - 1st:0 2nd:1 3rd:0 Ran:3
Win Prizemoney £0 *Total Prizemoney* £702
1999 Turf 0-2: (10f, 12f) (g-f, frm) 1999 AW 0-1: (12f) (Fibr)
Rangy, moderate filly, effective 10f, acts on gd. Turf high 38 (began Jly). **Sir Mark Prescott [0-6] Lord Fairhaven.*

QUINSTARS (IRE) RR 92f 1478a[6]
4 b g Thatching 7.8f **(69)** - Legal Steps 00
Form - 52146
1999 Turf 1-5: (6f 1-2, 7f 2, 8f) (hvy 1-1, sft, gd, g-f 2)
Useful gelding, effective 5 to 7f, best at 6f, acts on hvy to gd, best on gd, has worn blinkers. Turf high 92 - 1st of 8 giving 20lb to Crown Point (25 Apr Curragh RF 0889a).
**Patrick Brady in IRE [1-10] Miss Rita Shah (from J Oxx in IRE [1-6] Spt 1998).*

QUINTRELL DOWNS BHB 39f74a RR 42+f 74a 2376[1]
4 b g Efisio 7.7f **(69)** - Nineteenth of May (Homing) 7.8f **(59)**
Form - 514011
Record 1999 - 1st:3 2nd:0 3rd:0 Ran:6
Pre1999 - 1st:0 2nd:0 3rd:0 Ran:8
Win Prizemoney £7,525 *Total Prizemoney* £7,842
Wins * 1999 *Jun Southw (STD) H* *12f* *62 70+* <
*** 1999** *Jun Wolver (STD) H* *12f* *55 59+*
*** 1999** *May Southw (STD) H* *11f* *41 59+*
1999 Turf 0-3: (9f, 12f 2) (gd, g-f, frm) 1999 AW 3-3: (11f 1-1, 12f 2-2) (Fibr 3-3)
Above-average gelding, effective 12f, - acts on Fibr, has worn blinkers, prefers left handed tracks, prefers tight tracks. Turf high 42. AW high 70 - 1st of 8 getting 8lb from Aspirant Dancer (28 Jun Southwell RF 2376). Inconsistent. He has looked very ordinary on turf since arriving from Ireland, but is a different proposition on Fibresand. Suited by middle distances, there are more races to be won with him on that surface.
**R M H Cowell [3-6] & Mrs D A Gamble (from M Brassil in IRE [0-9] Oct 1998).*

QUINTUS (USA) BHB 83f RR 91f 4854a[1]
4 ch g Sky Classic (CAN) 10f **(83)** - Superbe Dawn (USA) (Grey Dawn II) 11.1f **(72)**
Form - 3131
1999 Turf 2-4: (9f, 10f, 11f 2-2) (sft 1-1, gd 1-2, frm)
Scopey, useful gelding, effective 10 to 11f, best at 10f, acts on sft to g-f, has worn blinkers. Turf high 91 (began Jly) - 1st of 16 giving 8lb to Lawz (10 Oct Naas RF 4854a) - also 1st of 11 giving 28lb to Society Queen (14 Jly Killarney RF 2986a). Improving.
**E J O'Grady in IRE [4-15] David Lloyd (from P F I Cole [2-13] Spt 1998).*

QUITE HAPPY (IRE) BHB 55f RR 58f 4332[9]
4 b f Statoblest 6.4f **(63)** - Four-Legged Friend (Aragon) 8.1f **(60)**
Form - 020070031400
Record 1999 - 1st:1 2nd:1 3rd:1 Ran:12
Pre1999 - 1st:1 2nd:1 3rd:2 Ran:8
Win Prizemoney £5,093 *Total Prizemoney* £7,846
Wins * 1999 Aug Catter (GD) C 5f 58
1998 May Folkes (G-F) H 5f 68 76? <
1999 Turf 1-12: (5f 1-10, 6f 2) (gd 1-5, g-f 2, frm 5)
Scopey, fair filly, effective 5f, acts on gd to g-f, has worn blinkers. Turf high 69 - 2nd of 12 giving 25lb to Forgotten Times (26 May Folkestone 5f g-f RF 1492).
**M H Tompkins [1-12] Mrs B Cross & M Sakal (from Dr J D Scargill [1-8] Jun 1998).*

QUITE INCREDIBLE (USA) BHB 77f RR 69f 3581[12]
3 ch f Anjiz (USA) 7f **(67)** - Jacqueline Alice (USA) (Riverman (USA)) 9.1f **(76)**
Form - 100
Record 1999 - 1st:1 2nd:0 3rd:0 Ran:3
Win Prizemoney £3,225 *Total Prizemoney* £3,225

Wins * **1999** Apr Kempto (G-F) 7f 69+ <
1999 Turf 1-3: (7f 1-3) (g-f 1-3)
Workmanlike, currently average filly. Turf high 69 - also 1st of 13 getting 19lb from Desert Warrior (5 Apr Kempton RF 0573). Made a winning debut at Kempton, but flopped in listed company next time. **E A L Dunlop [1-3] Maktoum Al Maktoum.*

QUITO (IRE) RR 85f
5000[3]

2 b c Machiavellian (USA) 9.8f **(83)** - Qirmazi (USA) (Riverman (USA)) 9.1f **(76)**
Form - 3
Record 1999 - 1st:0 2nd:0 3rd:1 Ran:1
Win Prizemoney £0 *Total Prizemoney* £530
1999 Turf 0-1: (8f) (gd)
Currently useful colt. (1st run) - 3rd of 11 to Western Summer (21 Oct Nottingham 8f gd RF 5000).
**M P Tregoning [0-1] Sheikh Mohammed.*

QUIZ MASTER BHB 33f39a RR 36f 39a
2919[8]

4 ch g Superpower 6.6f **(58)** - Ask Away (Midyan (USA)) 6f **(60)**
Form - 6806658
Record 1999 - 1st:0 2nd:0 3rd:0 Ran:6
Pre1999 - 1st:0 2nd:4 3rd:3 Ran:24
Win Prizemoney £0 *Total Prizemoney* £5,524
1999 Turf 0-6: (5f, 6f, 7f, 8f, 9f, 11f) (g-s, gd 2, g-f, frm, hrd)
Scopey, very moderate gelding, effective 6f, acts on gd, often wears blinkers. Turf high 41. **E Weymes [0-31] Mrs R L Heaton.*

QUWS RR 110f
4479a[3]

5 b h Robellino (USA) 9.5f **(68)** - Fleeting Rainbow (Rainbow Quest (USA)) 10.4f **(75)**
Form - 03
1999 Turf 0-2: (9f, 12f) (g-s, g-f)
Group-class colt, effective 8 to 10f, best at 10f, acts on sft to hrd. Turf high 98. Becoming disappointing. Lightly raced in 1999, he is effective from a mile to a mile and a half and probably acts on any ground.
**K Prendergast in IRE [6-17] Hamdan Al Maktoum (from K P McLaughlin in USA [0-1] Mar 1999).*

RAAQI BHB 90f RR 82f
2739[6]

3 b c Nashwan (USA) 10.3f **(79)** - Mehthaaf (USA) **(122f)** (Nureyev (USA)) 8.7f **(78)**
Form - 23216
Record 1999 - 1st:1 2nd:2 3rd:1 Ran:5
Pre1999 - 1st:0 2nd:0 3rd:0 Ran:2
Win Prizemoney £3,745 *Total Prizemoney* £6,695
Wins * **1999** Jun Ripon (G-F) 12.3f 69 <
1999 Turf 1-5: (8f 2, 10f, 12f 1-2) (gd, g-f, frm 2, hrd 1-1)
Scopey, decent colt, effective 8 to 10f, acts on gd to frm. Turf high 82 (1st run) - 2nd of 6 to Royal Rebel (5 Apr Newcastle 8f gd RF 0583). A winner over a mile and a half at Ripon in a competitive maiden, he is open to some improvement.
**J L Dunlop [1-7] Hamdan Al Maktoum.*

RAASED BHB 42f41a RR 35f 41a
4987[19]

7 b g Unfuwain (USA) 11.4f **(74)** - Sajjaya (USA) (Blushing Groom (FR)) 10.3f **(76)**
Form - 77250411700
Record 1999 - 1st:2 2nd:1 3rd:0 Ran:10
Pre1999 - 1st:2 2nd:3 3rd:3 Ran:25
Win Prizemoney £11,058 *Total Prizemoney* £16,683

Wins	* **1999**	Aug	Nottin	(G-F)	H	8.2f	42	44	
	* **1999**	Jun	Carlis	(G-F)	H	6.9f	38	41	
	* 1998	*Feb*	*Southw*	*(STD)*	*H*	*8f*	*36*	*43*	
	1995	Apr	Bright	(GD)		10f		71	<

1999 Turf 2-10: (7f 1-1, 8f 1-6, 9f 3) (gd 1-2, g-f 5, frm 2, hrd 1-1)
Moderate gelding, effective 7 to 9f, best at 8f, acts on gd to hrd - acts on Fibr, has worn blinkers, favours tight tracks. Turf high 50 - 2nd of 7 getting 1lb from Stone Ridge (2 May Hamilton 9f g-f RF 0972) - also 1st of 17 getting 1lb from Chinaberry (13 Aug Nottingham RF 3628). A first-time visor seemed to work the oracle at Carlisle in June, and he followed that up with a good win over a mile at Nottingham. Both wins came on fast ground.
**F Watson [3-30] F Watson (from J L Dunlop [1-5] Jun 1995).*

RABAH BHB 106f RR 105f
3982[5]

4 b c Nashwan (USA) 10.3f **(79)** - The Perfect Life (IRE) (Try My Best (USA)) 7.6f **(67)**
Form - 085
Record 1999 - 1st:0 2nd:0 3rd:0 Ran:3
Pre1999 - 1st:5 2nd:4 3rd:1 Ran:12
Win Prizemoney £63,065 *Total Prizemoney* £107,142

Wins	* 1998	Jly	Goodwo	(GD)	G3	12f	114	<
	* 1998	Jly	Haydoc	(G-F)	L	11.9f	114	<
	* 1998	May	Goodwo	(G-F)	L	9.9f	106	
	* 1997	Oct	Newmar	(G-F)		8f	94	
	* 1997	Aug	Redcar	(FRM)		7f	78	

1999 Turf 0-3: (12f 3) (g-f, frm 2)
Workmanlike, Pattern-class colt, effective 10 to 12f, best at 12f, acts on gd to g-f, best on gd. Turf high 105. Tough and able as a three-year-old, notably when dead-heating with Nedawi in the Gordon Stakes at Glorious Goodwood, he failed to do himself justice in '99. **J L Dunlop [5-15] Hamdan Al Maktoum.*

RABI (IRE) BHB 113f RR 117f
555a[4]

4 b c Alzao (USA) 9.8f **(73)** - Sharakawa (IRE) (Darshaan) 9.9f **(84)**
Form - 4
1999 AW 0-1: (10f) (Dirt)
Well made, high-class colt.
**S bin Suroor in UAE [0-1] Hamdan Al Maktoum (from S bin Suroor [0-3] Jly 1998).*

RACE LEADER (USA) RR 107f
4514a[2]

2 b c Gone West (USA) 7.8f **(82)** - Dubian (High Line) 10.3f **(70)**
Form - 132
Record 1999 - 1st:1 2nd:1 3rd:1 Ran:3
Win Prizemoney £5,344 *Total Prizemoney* £26,128
Wins * **1999** Jly Newmar (GD) 7f 86+ <
1999 Turf 1-3: (7f 1-3) (sft, g-f, frm 1-1)
Currently Pattern-class colt. Turf high 106 (began Jly) - 2nd of 5 to Giant's Causeway (18 Spt Longchamp 7f sft RF 4514a). A half-brother to 1000 Guineas winner Sayyedati and Group One scorer Golden Snake, he looked a colt with a future when scoring at the July meeting. Impressed with his attitude there, but was a little disappointing when third to King's Best in a listed race at York. Ran a better race in the Prix de la Salamandre, if finding Giant's Causeway too good, and should make a useful three-year-old at up to ten furlongs. **B W Hills [1-3] Mohammed Obaid Al Maktoum.*

RACINGAGAINSTTIME (IRE) RR 30f
4806[6]

2 b f Night Shift (USA) 8.1f **(73)** - Mysistra (FR) (Machiavellian (USA))
Form - 06
Record 1999 - 1st:0 2nd:0 3rd:0 Ran:2
1999 Turf 0-2: (5f, 7f) (sft, gd)
Currently very moderate filly. Turf high 30 (began Spt).
**M Johnston [0-2] Mrs Liz Nelson.*

RACING TELEGRAPH BHB 33f23a RR 34f 23a
252[15]

9 b g Claude Monet (USA) 7.2f **(54)** - Near Enough (English Prince) 10.1f **(61)**
Form - 00
Record 1999 - 1st:0 2nd:0 3rd:0 Ran:2
Pre1999 - 1st:1 2nd:1 3rd:6 Ran:44
Win Prizemoney £3,106 *Total Prizemoney* £7,500
1999 AW 0-2: (8f, 11f) (Fibr 2)
Very moderate gelding, has worn blinkers. AW high 9. Becoming disappointing.
**M Brittain [0-2] Cliff Woof (from C N Allen [0-16] Jan 1998).*

RADAR (IRE) BHB 81f75a RR 84f 75a
4874[10]

4 b c Petardia 8.2f **(58)** - Soignee (Night Shift (USA)) 7.2f **(69)**
Form - 3608520
Record 1999 - 1st:0 2nd:1 3rd:1 Ran:7
Pre1999 - 1st:2 2nd:2 3rd:0 Ran:14
Win Prizemoney £10,527 *Total Prizemoney* £20,488

Wins	* 1998	Jun	Sandow	(SFT)	H	9f	77	81	<
	* 1997	Oct	Nottin	(GD)	H	8.2f	66	79+	

1999 Turf 0-6: (8f 3, 10f 3) (gd, g-f 2, frm 3) 1999 AW 0-1: (8f) (Fibr)
Scopey, decent colt, effective 8 to 10f, acts on g-s to frm, best on g-f, has worn blinkers, prefers left handed tracks, likes tight tracks, does well at Newbury. Turf high 84 - 2nd of 16 giving 17lb

to Atlantic Charter (2 Oct Redcar 10f g-f RF 4692).
**M A Jarvis [2-21] John Sims.*

RADA'S DAUGHTER BHB 94f **RR 92f** 4889a[11]
3 br f Robellino (USA) 9.5f **(68)** - Drama School (Young Generation) 7.7f **(63)**
Form - 7113515610
Record 1999 - 1st:4 2nd:0 3rd:1 Ran:10
Pre1999 - 1st:0 2nd:0 3rd:0 Ran:2
Win Prizemoney £23,536 *Total Prizemoney* £25,128
Wins * 1999 Spt Newmar (G-S) H 12f 90 92 <
*** 1999** Jly Ascot (FRM) H 12f 81 83
*** 1999** May Windso (GD) H 11.6f 75 81
*** 1999** Apr Bath (SFT) H 10.2f 70 74
1999 Turf 4-10: (10f 1-2, 12f 3-8) (hvy, sft 1-1, g-s, gd 2, g-f 3-3, frm 2)
Workmanlike, useful filly, effective 12f, acts on gd to g-f, best on g-f. Turf high 92 - 5th of 8 getting 10lb from Innuendo (19 Aug York 12f gd RF 3771) - also 1st of 10 getting 2lb from Canta Ke Brave (28 Spt Newmarket RF 4594). Consistent. A winner four times in handicap company last term, including when beating multiple winner Flossy at Ascot, she did not run badly when tried in Listed company at York. **I A Balding [4-12].*

RADICAL JACK RR 49f 3750[7]
2 b c Presidium 7.5f **(56)** - Luckifosome (Smackover) 6f **(52)**
Form - R7887
Record 1999 - 1st:0 2nd:0 3rd:0 Ran:5
1999 Turf 0-5: (5f 4, 7f) (gd, g-f, frm 2, hrd)
Moderate colt, has worn blinkers. Turf high 49.
**Denys Smith [0-5] Lord Durham.*

RAED BHB 55f60a **RR 38f 60a** 4983[11]
6 b g Nashwan (USA) 10.3f **(79)** - Awayed (USA) (Sir Ivor) 10.2f **(70)**
Form - 7622102000
Record 1999 - 1st:1 2nd:3 3rd:0 Ran:10
Pre1999 - 1st:3 2nd:8 3rd:1 Ran:27
Win Prizemoney £11,344 *Total Prizemoney* £25,624
Wins * 1999 Aug Windso (HVY) H 10f 60 61
1998 *Feb Southw (STD) H 11f* 62 72 <
1998 *Feb Southw (STD) H 11f* 62 65
1997 *Dec Southw (STD) H 11f* 57 62
1999 Turf 1-8: (10f 1-7, 11f) (g-s, gd 1-5, g-f, frm) 1999 AW 0-2: (11f 2) (Fibr 2)
Average gelding, effective 10 to 12f, acts on g-f - acts on Fibr, favours tight tracks. Turf high 61. AW high 61. Becoming disappointing.
**J Pearce [1-6] Chris Marsh (from Mrs A Swinbank [3-23] Jly 1999).*

RAELEEN BHB 30f **RR 34df** 4790[8]
3 b f Jupiter Island 10.4f **(57)** - Ballintava (Better By Far)
Form - 008
Record 1999 - 1st:0 2nd:0 3rd:0 Ran:3
Pre1999 - 1st:0 2nd:0 3rd:0 Ran:1
1999 Turf 0-3: (8f 2, 9f) (g-s, gd, frm)
Small, very moderate filly. Turf high 34 (began Aug).
**G M McCourt [0-4] D A N Ross.*

RAFAYDA (IRE) RR 101f 1169a[4]
3 b f Doyoun 10.7f **(69)** - Rayseka (IRE) **(111f)** (Dancing Brave (USA)) 8.4f **(76)**
Form - 44
1999 Turf 0-2: (10f 2) (gd, g-f)
Very useful filly. Turf high 101. (DEAD)
**J Oxx in IRE [1-4] H H Aga Khan.*

RAFTERS MUSIC (IRE) BHB 48f **RR 48f** 4947[8]
4 b g Thatching 7.8f **(69)** - Princess Dixieland (USA) (Dixieland Band (USA)) 7f **(74)**
Form - 70051460468
Record 1999 - 1st:1 2nd:0 3rd:0 Ran:11
Pre1999 - 1st:0 2nd:0 3rd:0 Ran:3
Win Prizemoney £2,736 *Total Prizemoney* £3,201
Wins * 1999 Jly Epsom (G-F) C 6f 52 <
1999 Turf 1-11: (5f, 6f 1-6, 7f 2, 8f 2) (sft, gd, g-f 3, frm 1-6)
Workmanlike, moderate gelding, effective 6f, acts on g-f to frm. Turf high 52 - 1st of 10 giving 11lb to Mystical (28 Jly Epsom RF 3205). Consistent. **Mrs A J Perrett [1-14] C Duncan.*

RAFTERY (FR) RR 105f 2099a[3]
3 b c Nashamaa 8.1f **(58)** - Go On Fiddling (FR) (Thatching) 8f **(66)**
Form - 3
1999 Turf 0-1: (8f) (g-s)
Currently Pattern-class colt. (1st run) - 3rd of 7 getting 3lb from Grazalema (13 Jun Chantilly 8f g-s RF 2099a).
**J-C Rouget in FR [0-1].*

RAFTING (IRE) BHB 80f **RR 81f** 5174a[5]
4 b f Darshaan 11.9f **(81)** - White Water (FR) (Pharly (FR)) 9.8f **(68)**
Form - 01644246611045
Record 1999 - 1st:3 2nd:1 3rd:0 Ran:14
Pre1999 - 1st:1 2nd:1 3rd:1 Ran:6
Win Prizemoney £19,710 *Total Prizemoney* £25,820
Wins * 1999 Jly Thirsk (FRM) H 12f 77 81 <
*** 1999** Jly Cheste (G-F) H 12.3f 74 76
*** 1999** Apr Mussel (G-F) H 12f 76 78
* 1998 May Thirsk (G-F) 12f 57+
1999 Turf 3-14: (12f 3-11, 13f 2, 14f) (sft 2, g-s 2, gd, g-f 2-5, frm 1-3, hrd)
Rangy, decent filly, effective 12 to 14f, best at 12f, acts on gd to hrd, best on frm, has worn blinkers, prefers tight tracks, excels at Thirsk. Turf high 81 - 1st of 10 giving 18lb to Freedom Quest (31 Jly Thirsk RF 3288) - also 1st of 9 giving 29lb to Ambidextrous (30 Apr Musselburgh RF 0940). Consistent. Bagged a double in July in races over a mile and a half on firm ground at Chepstow and Thirsk, but has been disappointing since.
**M Johnston [4-20] Alan Lillingston.*

RAGLAN ACCOLADE BHB 39f **RR 36f** 4229[12]
2 b f New Reputation - Ophiuchus (Nader)
Form - 000
Record 1999 - 1st:0 2nd:0 3rd:0 Ran:3
1999 Turf 0-3: (6f 2, 7f) (g-f 2, frm)
Currently very moderate filly. Turf high 36 (began Aug).
**Derrick Morris [0-3] C Munden.*

RAGTIME COWGIRL BHB 15f33a **RR 8f 33a** 1206[12]
6 ch m Aragon 7.7f **(58)** - Echo Chamber (Music Boy) 6.8f **(57)**
Form - 000
Record 1999 - 1st:0 2nd:0 3rd:0 Ran:3
Pre1999 - 1st:3 2nd:0 3rd:7 Ran:32
Win Prizemoney £7,784 *Total Prizemoney* £10,392
Wins * 1997 Jun Hamilt (SFT) H 5f 30 23
1996 Aug Mussel (G-F) C 11.1f 37 <
1996 Jly Pontef (G-F) SH 12f 35 37 <
1999 Turf 0-3: (5f, 9f, 12f) (hvy, gd, g-f)
Very moderate mare.
**D A Nolan [1-24] Mrs J McFadyen-Murray (from C W Thornton [2-11] Aug 1996).*

RAHAYEB BHB 72f **RR 77f** 4489[4]
3 b f Arazi (USA) 9.2f **(74)** - Bashayer (USA) (Mr Prospector (USA)) 8.8f **(78)**
Form - 564214
Record 1999 - 1st:1 2nd:1 3rd:0 Ran:6
Pre1999 - 1st:0 2nd:1 3rd:1 Ran:3
Win Prizemoney £4,224 *Total Prizemoney* £7,794
Wins * 1999 Aug Cheste (G-S) 12.3f 71 <
1999 Turf 1-6: (8f, 10f, 12f 1-4) (g-s 2, gd 1-3, frm)
Light-framed, above-average filly, effective 7 to 12f, best at 12f, acts on g-s to frm, has worn blinkers, likes tight tracks. Turf high 77 - 2nd of 5 giving 7lb to Boogy Woogy (23 Jly Thirsk 12f frm RF 3074) - also 1st of 6 from Prosperous (20 Aug Chester RF 3790). Consistent. **J L Dunlop [1-9] Hamdan Al Maktoum.*

RAHCAK (IRE) BHB 75f **RR 73f** 4756[2]
3 b f Generous (IRE) 11.5f **(82)** - Homage (Ajdal (USA)) 9.2f **(89)**
Form - 52
Record 1999 - 1st:0 2nd:1 3rd:0 Ran:2
Pre1999 - 1st:0 2nd:0 3rd:1 Ran:1
Win Prizemoney £0 *Total Prizemoney* £2,453
1999 Turf 0-2: (10f, 12f) (gd, frm)
Light-framed, currently above-average filly. Turf high 73 (began Spt) - 2nd of 5 to Caerau (6 Oct York 10f gd RF 4756).
**J H M Gosden [0-2] Sheikh Mohammed (from D R Loder [0-1] Oct 1998).*

RAHEEN (USA) BHB 95f92a **RR 101f 92a** 5141[4]
6 b h Danzig (USA) 8.1f **(88)** - Belle de Jour (USA) (Speak John) 10.7f **(72)**
Form - 74613400605454
Record 1999 - 1st:1 2nd:0 3rd:1 Ran:14
Pre1999 - 1st:2 2nd:1 3rd:3 Ran:20
Win Prizemoney £36,021 *Total Prizemoney* £63,762
Wins * **1999** May York (SFT) H 10.4f 89 97 <
* 1998 Oct Newmar (SFT) H 8f 82 93
1996 *Dec Wolver (STD) 8.5f 81+*
1999 Turf 1-13: (8f 6, 10f 1-6, 12f) (sft, gd 1-7, g-f 4, frm) 1999 AW 0-1: (8f) (Fibr)
Very useful horse, effective 8 to 10f, best at 10f, acts on sft to gd, best on gd, has worn blinkers. Turf high 101 - also 1st of 12 giving 3lb to Achilles (13 May York RF 1200). A regular competitor in our top handicaps between a mile and a mile and a quarter, he acts on any ground and can never be discounted, but often leaves himself with too much to do.
**R A Fahey [2-24] Basheer Kielany (from W G M Turner [1-6] Jly 1997).*

RAHIKA ROSE RR 90f 4971a[9]
4 b f Unfuwain (USA) 11.4f **(74)** - Rahik (Wassl) 9.7f **(62)**
Form - 37060
1999 Turf 0-5: (6f, 7f 2, 8f 2) (hvy, g-s 2, gd, g-f)
Useful filly, effective 7f, acts on frm. Turf high 90.
**C Collins in IRE [3-17] John Costello.*

RAILROADER BHB 75f **RR 74f** 5045[9]
2 ch c Piccolo - Poyle Amber (Sharrood (USA)) 10.5f **(72)**
Form - 030340
Record 1999 - 1st:0 2nd:0 3rd:2 Ran:6
Win Prizemoney £0 *Total Prizemoney* £1,533
1999 Turf 0-6: (5f, 6f 5) (sft 2, gd 2, g-f, frm)
Above-average colt, effective 5 to 6f, acts on sft to gd. Turf high 74 - 4th of 17 getting 8lb from Russian Fox (14 Oct Newmarket 6f gd RF 4872). **G B Balding [0-6] Peter Richardson.*

RAINBOW FRONTIER (IRE) BHB 85f **RR 86f** 2000[18]
5 b g Law Society (USA) 11.6f **(71)** - Tatchers Mate (Thatching) 8f **(66)**
Form - 0
Record 1999 - 1st:0 2nd:0 3rd:0 Ran:1
Pre1999 - 1st:3 2nd:5 3rd:3 Ran:17
Win Prizemoney £10,617 *Total Prizemoney* £49,351
Wins 1997 Jly Killar (G-S) H 14f 79 75+
1997 Jun Currag (G-S) H 11f 75 79 <
1997 May Wexfor (GD) 13f 79 <
1999 Turf 0-1: (20f) (g-f)
Useful gelding. Consistent.
**M C Pipe [1-12] Clive Smith (from A P O'Brien in IRE [6-18] Oct 1997).*

RAINBOW HIGH BHB 114f **RR 118f** 4684[1]
4 b c Rainbow Quest (USA) 11.2f **(81)** - Imaginary (IRE) (Dancing Brave (USA)) 8.4f **(76)**
Form - 1120321
Record 1999 - 1st:3 2nd:2 3rd:1 Ran:7
Pre1999 - 1st:1 2nd:2 3rd:0 Ran:9
Win Prizemoney £81,437 *Total Prizemoney* £122,743
Wins * **1999** Oct Newmar (SFT) G3 16.1f 118 <
* **1999** May Cheste (G-F) H 18.7f 103 107
* **1999** Apr Newbur (G-F) H 16f 93 103+
* 1998 Jun Ripon (SFT) 12.3f 76
1999 Turf 3-7: (16f 2-4, 18f, 19f 1-1, 20f) (gd 1-1, g-f 1-4, frm 1-2)
Scopey, high-class colt, effective 16f, acts on gd to frm. Turf high 118 - 1st of 3 getting 5lb from Arctic Owl (2 Oct Newmarket RF 4684). He had a very successful 1999, with his only poor effort coming in the Ascot Gold Cup. Victorious on his Newbury reappearance, he went on to prove himself an improving stayer with an easy success in the Chester Cup. He put up some fine efforts in Pattern company after that, being only narrowly beaten by Arctic Owl in the Henry II Stakes and by Far Cry in the Doncaster Cup, as well as finishing third to Celeric in the Lonsdale. However, he ended the season by gaining his revenge over both Arctic Owl and Celeric in the Jockey Club Cup, though he was in a somewhat distressed state afterwards. **B W Hills [4-16] K Abdulla.*

RAINBOW MELODY (IRE) BHB 83f **RR 82f** 4599[5]
2 ch f Rainbows For Life (CAN) 9.3f **(64)** - Lingering Melody (IRE) **(48f)** (Nordico (USA)) 6.5f **(62)**
Form - 25521045
Record 1999 - 1st:1 2nd:2 3rd:0 Ran:8
Win Prizemoney £3,629 *Total Prizemoney* £7,687
Wins * **1999** Aug Cheste (G-S) 7f 80 <
1999 Turf 1-8: (6f 2, 7f 1-4, 8f 2) (gd 1-3, g-f 5)
Decent filly, effective 7f, acts on gd to g-f. Turf high 82 - 5th of 19 getting 3lb from Out of Africa (28 Spt Newmarket 7f g-f RF 4599) - also 1st of 6 getting 5lb from Bhutan Prince (21 Aug Chester RF 3812). Winner of a Chester maiden over seven furlongs on good to soft ground in August; that run came after a string of placed efforts in Ireland with Kevin Prendergast. She has been a little disappointing since.
**E J Alston [1-4] Mrs Chris Harrington (from K Prendergast in IRE [0-4] Jly 1999).*

RAINBOW RAIN (USA) BHB 67f62a **RR 66f 62a** 4272[12]
5 b g Capote (USA) 9.1f **(84)** - Grana (USA) (Miswaki (USA)) 9f **(81)**
Form - 548236002004510140
Record 1999 - 1st:2 2nd:1 3rd:1 Ran:14
Pre1999 - 1st:2 2nd:3 3rd:2 Ran:35
Win Prizemoney £16,349 *Total Prizemoney* £26,106
Wins * **1999** Jly Bright (FRM) 6f 62
* **1999** Jly Bright (FRM) H 7f 58 65
* 1998 *Aug Lingfi (STD) H 7f 59 69*
1997 Jun Carlis (FRM) H 8f 73 75 <
1999 Turf 2-11: (5f, 6f 1-8, 7f 1-2) (gd 2, g-f 5, frm 2-4) 1999 AW 0-3: (8f 2, 10f) (Equi 3)
Average gelding, effective 6 to 10f, acts on gd to frm - acts on Equi, likes left handed tracks, likes tight tracks. Turf high 66 - 4th of 27 getting 15lb from Royal Result (28 Aug Goodwood 6f gd RF 3956) - also 1st of 15 giving 16lb to Priory Gardens (13 Jly Brighton RF 2777). AW high 60. Consistent. He showed his liking for Brighton by winning twice there last season, and again ran well on a downhill track when fourth to Royal Result in a hot Goodwood handicap in August.
**S Dow [3-38] P McCarthy (from M Johnston [1-11] Jly 1997).*

RAINBOW RAVER (IRE) BHB 44f43a **RR 45f 43a** 4639[5]
3 ch f Rainbows For Life (CAN) 9.3f **(64)** - Foolish Passion (USA) (Secretariat (USA)) 9f **(79)**
Form - 8763022645
Record 1999 - 1st:0 2nd:2 3rd:1 Ran:10
Pre1999 - 1st:0 2nd:0 3rd:0 Ran:7
Win Prizemoney £0 *Total Prizemoney* £2,874
1999 Turf 0-9: (7f, 8f, 10f 2, 12f 4, 16f) (gd 2, g-f 2, frm 5) 1999 AW 0-1: (12f) (Fibr)
Workmanlike, moderate filly, has worn blinkers. Turf high 47.
**J L Eyre [0-7] A E Needham (from C Smith [0-10] May 1999).*

RAINBOW REALM (IRE) BHB 57f **RR 73f** 5052[18]
2 ch f Rainbows For Life (CAN) 9.3f **(64)** - Sakanda (IRE) (Vayrann) 9.7f **(74)**
Form - 5000
Record 1999 - 1st:0 2nd:0 3rd:0 Ran:4
1999 Turf 0-3: (7f 2, 8f) (gd, g-f 2) 1999 AW 0-1: (6f) (Fibr)
Above-average filly. Turf high 73 (1st run) (began Aug) - 5th of 11 to Vigour (11 Aug Leicester 7f g-f RF 3546).
**S C Williams [0-4] Thomas O'Keeffe.*

RAINBOW ROMEO (IRE) BHB 50f48a **RR 48f 48a** 4945[14]
3 br c Rainbows For Life (CAN) 9.3f **(64)** - Splendid Chance (Random Shot) 11.4f **(52)**
Form - 576152878080
Record 1999 - 1st:1 2nd:1 3rd:0 Ran:11
Pre1999 - 1st:0 2nd:0 3rd:0 Ran:7
Win Prizemoney £3,110 *Total Prizemoney* £3,980
Wins * **1999** Apr Folkes (SFT) 7f 70 <
1999 Turf 1-9: (7f 1-4, 8f 5) (sft 1-1, gd 2, frm 6) 1999 AW 0-2: (5f, 8f) (Equi 2)
Neat, moderate colt, effective 7f, acts on sft. Turf high 70 (1st run) - 1st of 9 giving 5lb to Cinnamon Lady (20 Apr Folkestone RF 0765). AW high 44. Consistent.
**J R Poulton [1-12] Eric Perry (from P T Walwyn [0-6] Oct 1998).*

RAINBOWS FOREVER (IRE) RR 92f 3530a[2]
3 ch g Rainbows For Life (CAN) 9.3f **(64)** - Irish Fountain (USA) **(61f)** (Irish River (FR)) 8.6f **(78)**

Form - 86370102
1999 Turf 1-7: (8f, 9f 2, 10f 1-3, 12f) (hvy, g-s, gd 2, g-f 1-3)
Useful gelding, effective 7 to 10f, acts on hvy to g-f, prefers right handed tracks. Turf high 92 - 2nd of 8 getting 7lb from High King (8 Aug Leopardstown 9f gd RF 3530a) - also 1st of 12 giving 13lb to Slightly Swift (26 Jun Curragh RF 2409a).
**K Prendergast in IRE [3-15] Mrs Chryss O'Reilly.*

RAINBOW SPIRIT (IRE) RR 24f 4080[19]

2 b g Rainbows For Life (CAN) 9.3f **(64)** - Merrie Moment (IRE) (Taufan (USA)) 7f **(57)**
Form - 0
Record 1999 - 1st:0 2nd:0 3rd:0 Ran:1
1999 Turf 0-1: (8f) (frm)
Currently little account gelding.
**A P Jarvis [0-1] Mrs Rebecca Caudle.*

RAINBOW VIEW (IRE) BHB 57f RR 57f 4446[3]

3 b g Rainbows For Life (CAN) 9.3f **(64)** - L'Anno d'Oro (Habitat) 9.4f **(70)**
Form - 01008053
Record 1999 - 1st:1 2nd:0 3rd:1 Ran:8
Win Prizemoney £3,038 *Total Prizemoney* £3,522
Wins * 1999 May Redcar (FRM) 6f 52 <
1999 Turf 1-8: (6f 1-2, 7f 2, 8f 3, 11f) (g-s 2, gd, g-f, frm 1-4)
Angular, fair gelding, effective 6 to 8f, acts on gd to frm. Turf high 57 - 5th of 16 getting 3lb from Elba Magic (15 Spt Beverley 8f gd RF 4321) - also 1st of 6 from Blakey (31 May Redcar RF 1609). A winner over six furlongs at Redcar, he was disappointing afterwards. **Mrs G S Rees [1-8] Miss Marjorie Thompson.*

RAINBOW WAYS BHB 98f RR 101f 4251[5]

4 b c Rainbow Quest (USA) 11.2f **(81)** - Siwaayib (Green Desert (USA)) 8.6f **(78)**
Form - 274165
Record 1999 - 1st:1 2nd:1 3rd:0 Ran:6
Pre1999 - 1st:3 2nd:2 3rd:1 Ran:8
Win Prizemoney £36,874 *Total Prizemoney* £48,368
Wins * 1999 Jly York (G-F) LH 13.9f 96 101 <
* 1998 Oct Newmar (GD) H 12f 88 93
* 1998 Spt Haydoc (G-F) H 11.9f 81 84
* 1998 Aug Newmar (G-F) 12f 74
1999 Turf 1-6: (12f, 14f 1-3, 15f, 16f) (gd 3, g-f 1-2, frm)
Light-framed, very useful colt, effective 12 to 16f, acts on gd to frm, best on g-f, has worn blinkers (very effectively), excels at Newmarket. Turf high 101 - 1st of 8 giving 5lb to Banbury (10 Jly York RF 2732). Effective with or without blinkers, he was a shade lucky when winning at York in July (the runner-up went lame) and is probably in the grip of the handicapper. A mile and three-quarters stretches his stamina to breaking point.
**B W Hills [4-14] Maktoum Al Maktoum.*

RAINDROP BHB 53f RR 57f 4814[8]

3 b f Primo Dominie 7.2f **(67)** - Thundercloud (Electric) 10.1f **(61)**
Form - 0048
Record 1999 - 1st:0 2nd:0 3rd:0 Ran:4
Win Prizemoney £0 *Total Prizemoney* £294
1999 Turf 0-3: (7f, 8f 2) (gd 2, frm) 1999 AW 0-1: (8f) (Fibr)
Fair filly. Turf high 57 (began Spt). **H Morrison [0-4] A J Morrison.*

RAIN IN SPAIN BHB 102f RR 105f 2882[3]

3 b c Unfuwain (USA) 11.4f **(74)** - Maria Isabella (FR) (Young Generation) 7.7f **(63)**
Form - 113
Record 1999 - 1st:2 2nd:0 3rd:1 Ran:3
Win Prizemoney £7,579 *Total Prizemoney* £8,595
Wins * 1999 Jly Windso (GD) 11.6f 90+ <
*** 1999** Jun Kempto (GD) 12f 75
1999 Turf 2-3: (12f 2-3) (g-f 1-1, frm 1-2)
Unfurnished, currently Pattern-class colt. Turf high 105. Unraced at two, he made a winning debut in a twelve-furlong Kempton maiden, battling on well for a narrow victory, and followed up in impressive fashion in a Windsor classified event. Ran well in a decent conditions event on his final start, and has more improvement in him. **J Noseda [2-3] Exors of the late B Schmidt-Bodner.*

RAIN RAIN GO AWAY (USA) BHB 53f RR 60df 4359[16]

3 ch c Miswaki (USA) 8.1f **(81)** - Stormagain (USA) (Storm Cat (USA))
Form - 070
Record 1999 - 1st:0 2nd:0 3rd:0 Ran:3
Pre1999 - 1st:0 2nd:0 3rd:1 Ran:1
Win Prizemoney £0 *Total Prizemoney* £446
1999 Turf 0-3: (6f, 8f, 9f) (g-s, g-f 2)
Workmanlike, average colt. Turf high 52.
**D J S Cosgrove [0-2] G G Grayson (from E A L Dunlop [0-2] Apr 1999).*

RAINSHACK BHB 82f RR 77?f 1363[7]

4 ch c Rainbow Quest (USA) 11.2f **(81)** - Suntrap (USA) (Roberto (USA)) 10f **(76)**
Form - 327
Record 1999 - 1st:0 2nd:1 3rd:1 Ran:3
Win Prizemoney £0 *Total Prizemoney* £1,687
1999 Turf 0-3: (10f 3) (gd 2, g-f)
Currently above-average colt. Turf high 77 (1st run) - 3rd of 13 to Algunnaas (8 Apr Leicester 10f gd RF 0624).
**B W Hills [0-3] K Abdulla.*

RAINSTORM BHB 74a RR 48f 4441[18]

4 b c Rainbow Quest (USA) 11.2f **(81)** - Katsina (USA) (Cox's Ridge (USA)) 8f **(68)**
Form - 214450000
Record 1999 - 1st:0 2nd:0 3rd:0 Ran:6
Pre1999 - 1st:1 2nd:1 3rd:0 Ran:6
Win Prizemoney £2,788 *Total Prizemoney* £3,984
Wins 1998 *Dec Lingfi (STD) 7f 64* <
1999 Turf 0-4: (7f 2, 8f 2) (g-f 2, frm 2) 1999 AW 0-2: (7f, 8f) (Equi 2)
Lengthy, above-average colt, effective 7 to 8f, best at 7f, - acts on Equi, has worn blinkers, prefers left handed tracks, prefers tight tracks. Turf high 48 (began Aug). AW high 72. Becoming disappointing.
**E J O'Neill [0-4] Mrs Patrick O'Neill (from C A Dwyer [1-5] Jan 1999).*

RAINWORTH LADY BHB 54f49a RR 50f 49a 3936[9]

2 b f Governor General 6.8f **(45)** - Monongelia (Welsh Pageant) 10f **(65)**
Form - 040
Record 1999 - 1st:0 2nd:0 3rd:0 Ran:3
Win Prizemoney £0 *Total Prizemoney* £277
1999 Turf 0-2: (6f, 7f) (gd, frm) 1999 AW 0-1: (7f) (Fibr)
Currently fair filly. Turf high 49 (began Jly).
**M J Polglase [0-3] Southwell Racing Club.*

RAISE A GRAND (IRE) BHB 107f RR 111f 3561[3]

3 ch c Grand Lodge (USA) - Atyaaf (USA) (Irish River (FR)) 8.6f **(78)**
Form - 852733
Record 1999 - 1st:0 2nd:1 3rd:2 Ran:6
Pre1999 - 1st:3 2nd:1 3rd:1 Ran:6
Win Prizemoney £23,548 *Total Prizemoney* £53,573
Wins * 1998 Aug Sandow (G-F) G3 7.1f 110 <
* 1998 Jly Yarmou (GD) 7f 89+
* 1998 Jun Nottin (GD) 6.1f 79
1999 Turf 0-6: (7f 2, 8f 4) (g-f 6)
Scopey, Group-class colt, effective 7f, acts on gd to g-f, best on g-f. Turf high 111. Consistent. He had a profitable juvenile campaign, but lacks scope and failed to train on satisfactorily.
**J W Payne [3-12] C Cotran.*

RAISE A PRINCE (FR) BHB 104f98a RR 100f 98a 5210[3]

6 b g Machiavellian (USA) 9.8f **(83)** - Enfant D'Amour (USA) (Lyphard (USA)) 9.9f **(72)**
Form - 2138073033
Record 1999 - 1st:1 2nd:1 3rd:4 Ran:10
Pre1999 - 1st:6 2nd:3 3rd:2 Ran:25
Win Prizemoney £76,785 *Total Prizemoney* £105,245
Wins * 1999 Apr Nottin (SFT) 14.1f 106 <
* 1998 Spt Ascot (SFT) H 12f 90 92
* 1998 Spt Ayr (G-S) H 13.1f 89 92
* 1998 Apr Newmar (SFT) H 12f 79 89
* 1997 *Nov Lingfi (STD) 12f 82*
* 1997 Oct Newbur (G-S) C 12f 81+
1997 Jly Nottin (SFT) H 10f 69 69
1999 Turf 1-10: (12f, 13f, 14f 1-1, 15f 2, 16f 4, 17f) (sft 2, g-s 1-2, gd 4, g-f, frm)

Very useful gelding, effective 12 to 16f, acts on sft to gd, has worn blinkers, likes right handed tracks, likes tight tracks, excels at Ascot, likes Newmarket. Turf high 106 - 1st of 7 from The Fly (19 Apr Nottingham RF 0751). Consistent. He faced some stiff tasks in handicaps last term and was found wanting in listed company. A soft-ground specialist, he ran his best race for a while when third in a valuable handicap at the Ascot Festival, a race he had won in '98. **S P C Woods [6-23] George Tong (from J W Hills [1-9] Jly 1997).*

RAJI BHB 79f **RR 91f** 5046[2]

3 b c Green Desert (USA) 7.8f **(78)** - Cancan Madame (USA) (Mr Prospector (USA)) 8.8f **(78)**
Form - 472
Record 1999 - 1st:0 2nd:1 3rd:0 Ran:3
Win Prizemoney £0 *Total Prizemoney* £1,790
1999 Turf 0-3: (8f 2, 10f) (hvy, g-f, frm)
Leggy, currently useful colt. Turf high 91 (began Spt) - 2nd of 11 giving 5lb to Pearl Crown (23 Oct Newbury 10f hvy RF 5046).
**A C Stewart [0-3] Hamdan Al Maktoum.*

RAJMATA (IRE) BHB 55f65a **RR 42f 65a** 3972[12]

3 b f Prince Sabo 6.6f **(64)** - Heart of India (IRE) (Try My Best (USA)) 7.6f **(67)**
Form - 3282502580
Record 1999 - 1st:0 2nd:2 3rd:0 Ran:8
Pre1999 - 1st:0 2nd:1 3rd:1 Ran:7
Win Prizemoney £0 *Total Prizemoney* £2,919
1999 Turf 0-5: (5f 2, 6f 3) (gd 2, g-f 2, frm) 1999 AW 0-3: (5f 2, 6f) (Equi, Fibr 2)
Scopey, average filly, effective 5f, - acts on Fibr, often wears blinkers. Turf high 61. AW high 66 - 2nd of 12 giving 3lb to La Doyenne (6 May Southwell 5f Fibr RF 1061). Becoming disappointing.
**Mrs N Macauley [0-7] Mrs N Macauley (from Sir Mark Prescott [0-8] Jan 1999).*

RAJWHAN (USA) BHB 75f **RR 77f** 4130[7]

3 br g Lear Fan (USA) 10.4f **(80)** - Samra (USA) (Solford (USA)) 13f **(71)**
Form - 3507041537
Record 1999 - 1st:1 2nd:0 3rd:2 Ran:10
Pre1999 - 1st:0 2nd:0 3rd:0 Ran:2
Win Prizemoney £3,013 *Total Prizemoney* £6,349
Wins * 1999 Jly Folkes (G-F) H 9.7f 71 73 <
1999 Turf 1-10: (7f, 8f 4, 9f, 10f 1-4) (gd 4, g-f 1-2, frm 4)
Above-average gelding, effective 7 to 10f, best at 10f, acts on gd to g-f, best on g-f, has worn blinkers. Turf high 83.
**C E Brittain [1-12] Mohammed Jaber.*

RAKEEB (USA) BHB 60f **RR 55f** 5152[4]

4 ch g Irish River (FR) 9f **(77)** - Ice House (Northfields (USA)) 9f **(72)**
Form - 00806704
Record 1999 - 1st:0 2nd:0 3rd:0 Ran:8
Pre1999 - 1st:2 2nd:0 3rd:2 Ran:6
Win Prizemoney £7,083 *Total Prizemoney* £8,188
Wins 1998 Aug Haydoc (G-S) H 11.9f 85 91
1998 Jly Ayr (SFT) 10f 94 <
1999 Turf 0-8: (12f 6, 14f 2) (gd 4, g-f 3, frm)
Fair gelding, effective 10 to 12f, acts on gd to g-f, has worn blinkers, likes left handed tracks, likes tight tracks. Turf high 74. He showed little last term for his new connections. He goes particularly well on soft ground.
**M W Easterby [0-8] Lady Manton (from A C Stewart [2-6] Spt 1998).*

RAKIS (IRE) BHB 50f68a **RR 53df 68a** 4985[15]

9 b or br g Alzao (USA) 9.8f **(73)** - Bristle (Thatch (USA)) 9.8f **(62)**
Form - 475700870
Record 1999 - 1st:0 2nd:0 3rd:0 Ran:8
Pre1999 - 1st:9 2nd:5 3rd:6 Ran:58
Win Prizemoney £40,817 *Total Prizemoney* £55,695
Wins * 1997 *Feb Wolver (STD) H* 7f 87 87 <
* 1996 Spt Sandow (G-F) H 7.1f 75 77
* 1996 Jun Sandow (G-F) H 7.1f 72 79
1996 *Feb Lingfi (STD) H* 7f 82 85
1996 *Jan Lingfi (STD) H* 7f 72 79
1996 *Jan Lingfi (STD) H* 7f 72 77
1996 *Jan Lingfi (STD) H* 7f 64 58
1995 *Dec Wolver (STD) H* 7f 57 65
1999 Turf 0-5: (7f 3, 8f 2) (gd 2, g-f, frm 2) 1999 AW 0-3: (7f, 8f 2) (Equi 2, Fibr)
Average gelding, effective 7f, acts on gd, has worn blinkers, likes right handed tracks, favours tight tracks. Turf high 54. AW high 68. Becoming disappointing. A seven-furlong specialist, but despite numerous efforts he does not look the horse he once was.
**Mrs L Stubbs [3-46] J P Spencer (from M Brittain [5-8] Feb 1996).*

RAMBLING BEAR BHB 110f **RR 106f** 5222[12]

6 ch h Sharrood (USA) 11.1f **(67)** - Supreme Rose (Frimley Park) 6.5f **(67)**
Form - 1458F0350
Record 1999 - 1st:1 2nd:0 3rd:1 Ran:9
Pre1999 - 1st:6 2nd:4 3rd:4 Ran:36
Win Prizemoney £88,985 *Total Prizemoney* £113,449
Wins * 1999 May Newmar (G-F) G3 5f 110
* 1998 May Goodwo (G-F) 6f 109
* 1996 Jly Goodwo (G-F) G3 5f 107
* 1996 Jun Lingfi (G-F) L 6f 114 <
* 1996 May Newbur (G-F) 6f 108
* 1995 Spt Kempto (GD) L 6f 92
* 1995 Jly Windso (G-F) 5f 91
1999 Turf 1-9: (5f 1-6, 6f 3) (g-s, gd 3, g-f, frm 1-4)
Pattern-class horse, effective 5 to 6f, best at 5f, acts on gd to frm, best on frm, has worn blinkers, excels at Newmarket. Turf high 112 - 4th of 9 giving 7lb to Proud Native (22 May Kempton 5f frm RF 1395) - also 1st of 13 giving 9lb to Red Prairie (1 May Newmarket RF 0959). Inconsistent. He invariably looks well and came right back to his best when winning the Group 3 Palace House Stakes at Newmarket in May. Now successful first-time-out in each of the last two seasons, he is obviously one to note on his reappearance.
**M Blanshard [7-45] Mrs Michael Hill.*

RAMBOLD BHB 37f50a **RR 29f 50a** 5128[10]

8 b m Rambo Dancer (CAN) 8.4f **(59)** - Boldie (Bold Lad (IRE)) 8.4f **(68)**
Form - 727076000
Record 1999 - 1st:0 2nd:1 3rd:0 Ran:9
Pre1999 - 1st:7 2nd:4 3rd:4 Ran:56
Win Prizemoney £25,076 *Total Prizemoney* £32,509
Wins * 1998 Jly Bright (G-F) 6f 58
* 1998 May Chepst (G-F) H 6.1f 47 51
* 1996 Aug Yarmou (GD) H 6f 60 65
* 1996 Jun Hamilt (GD) 6f 48
1999 Turf 0-9: (5f, 6f 8) (gd 3, frm 6)
Fair mare, effective 6f, acts on gd to frm. Turf high 47.
**N E Berry [4-44] Ron Collins (from T M Jones [3-21] Jan 1995).*

RAMBO NINE BHB 55f48a **RR 55f 48a** 4220[7]

2 b c Rambo Dancer (CAN) 8.4f **(59)** - Asmarina **(44f 44a)** (Ascendant)
Form - 0567
Record 1999 - 1st:0 2nd:0 3rd:0 Ran:4
1999 Turf 0-2: (5f, 8f) (g-f, frm) 1999 AW 0-2: (6f, 8f) (Fibr 2)
Fair colt. Turf high 55. AW high 47.
**S R Bowring [0-4] J E Reed & P M Sedgwick.*

RAMBO WALTZER BHB 54f73a **RR 42f 73a** 4985[19]

7 b g Rambo Dancer (CAN) 8.4f **(59)** - Vindictive Lady (USA) (Foolish Pleasure (USA)) 8.9f **(72)**
Form - 13217101300800
Record 1999 - 1st:3 2nd:1 3rd:2 Ran:13
Pre1999 - 1st:15 2nd:10 3rd:7 Ran:60
Win Prizemoney £68,372 *Total Prizemoney* £83,912
Wins * 1999 *May Southw (STD) C* 7f 71
*** 1999** Apr Thirsk (GD) H 7f 67 69
*** 1999** Mar Catter (G-S) H 7f 63 67
* 1998 *Dec Southw (STD) C* 8f 73
* 1998 *Apr Southw (STD) H* 8f 81 87 <
* 1998 *Jan Wolver (STD) H* 9.4f 76 78
* 1997 Apr Hamilt (G-S) H 8.3f 65 71
* 1997 *Mar Wolver (STD) H* 8.5f 78 78
* 1997 *Feb Southw (STD) H* 8f 70 76
* 1997 *Jan Southw (STD) C* 7f 70+
* 1997 *Jan Southw (STD) C* 8f 81+
* 1996 Apr Ripon (GD) H 8f 61 68
* 1996 Apr Thirsk (G-F) H 8f 55 64
* 1996 Apr Hamilt (G-S) H 8.3f 55 58
* 1996 *Jan Wolver (STD) C* 7f 78
* 1996 *Jan Southw (STD) C* 8f 75+
1999 Turf 2-10: (7f 2-3, 8f 4, 9f 2, 10f) (gd 2-7, g-f 3) 1999 AW 1-3: (7f

1-1, 8f 2) (Fibr 1-3)

Above-average gelding, effective 8 to 9f, best at 8f, - acts on Fibr, has worn blinkers, favours left handed tracks, prefers tight tracks, excels at Wolverhampton, likes Southwell. Turf high 69. AW high 71. Becoming disappointing. He is a consistent performer, and though most of his wins in recent seasons have been on Fibresand, a surface on which he is particularly effective, he remains perfectly capable of winning on turf as he showed when winning at Catterick and Thirsk in the Spring. A turning track suits him best, and he issometimes prone to lameness.

**D Nicholls [16-66] W G Swiers (from S G Norton [2-15] Nov 1995).*

RAMIN (IRE) RR 4490P

2 b c Night Shift (USA) 8.1f **(73)** - Shady Leaf (IRE) (Glint of Gold) 9.3f **(66)**

Form - P

Record	**1999** -	1st:0	2nd:0	3rd:0	Ran:1

1999 Turf 0-1: (8f) (g-s)

Very poor colt. (DEAD) **S Dow [0-1] G Steinberg.*

RAMOOZ (USA) BHB 111f RR 112f 4472a6

6 b h Rambo Dancer (CAN) 8.4f **(59)** - My Shafy (Rousillon (USA)) 8.2f **(74)**

Form - 3525611446

Record	**1999** -	1st:2	2nd:1	3rd:1	Ran:11
	Pre1999 -	1st:8	2nd:9	3rd:5	Ran:37

Win Prizemoney £146,497 *Total Prizemoney* £256,086

Wins									
	*** 1999**	Jly	Currag	(G-F)	G3	8f		113	
	*** 1999**	Jun	Goodwo	(G-F)	L	8f		113	
	* 1998	Spt	Currag	(SFT)	G3	7f		109+	
	* 1998	May	York	(GD)	LH	7.9f	110	112	
	* 1997	Jly	Currag	(GD)	G3	8f		115	<
	* 1997	Jun	Newmar	(SFT)	G3	7f		108	
	* 1996	Jun	Epsom	(GD)		7f		98	
	* 1996	Apr	Thirsk	(G-F)		8f		94	
	* 1995	Spt	Newbur	(G-S)	H	7.3f	88	100	
	* 1995	Aug	York	(G-F)	H	7.9f	80	79	

1999 Turf 2-11: (7f 5, 8f 2-4, 9f 2) (g-s 3, gd 1-3, g-f 1-3, frm 2)

Group-class horse, effective 7 to 8f, best at 8f, acts on gd to g-f, best on gd, has worn blinkers, likes tight tracks, and excels at Haydock. Turf high 113 - 1st of 6 giving 7lb to Risque Lady (11 Jly Curragh RF 2803a) - also 1st of 7 giving 15lb to Peculiarity (27 Jun Goodwood RF 2358). Consistent. He is as tough as old boots and has won the last two runnings of the Minstrel Stakes at The Curragh. Best when attacking late in a strongly run race over seven furlongs or a mile, he will pay his way again in 2000.

**B Hanbury [10-48] Hilal Salem.*

RAMP AND RAVE (USA) RR 557a1

5 ch h Ramplett (USA) - Turbonative (USA) (Sitzmark (USA))

Form - 1

1999 AW 1-1: (10f 1-1) (Dirt 1-1)

Currently Pattern-class colt. (1st run) - 1st of 9 from Intidab (28 Mar Nad Al Sheba RF 0557a).

**D J Selvaratnam in UAE [1-1] Sheikh Ahmed bin Rashid Al Maktoum.*

RAMPART RR 67f 5207³

2 b c Kris 10f **(75)** - Balliasta (USA) (Lyphard (USA)) 9.9f **(72)**

Form - 03

Record	**1999** -	1st:0	2nd:0	3rd:1	Ran:2

Win Prizemoney £0 *Total Prizemoney* £492

1999 Turf 0-2: (7f 2) (g-s, gd)

Currently average colt. Turf high 67 (began Oct).

**B W Hills [0-2] K Abdulla.*

RAMRUMA (USA) BHB 119f RR 120f 4266²

3 ch f Diesis 9f **(80)** - Princess of Man (Green God) 9.6f **(68)**

Form - 111112

Record	**1999** -	1st:5	2nd:1	3rd:0	Ran:6
	Pre1999 -	1st:0	2nd:1	3rd:1	Ran:2

Win Prizemoney £432,310 *Total Prizemoney* £515,388

Wins								
	*** 1999**	Aug	York	(GD)	G1	11.9f	117	
	*** 1999**	Jly	Currag	(G-F)	G1	12f	118+	
	*** 1999**	Jun	Epsom	(G-S)	G1	12f	120	<
	*** 1999**	May	Lingfi	(G-F)	L	11.5f	104	
	*** 1999**	Apr	Newmar	(GD)		12f	102+	

1999 Turf 5-6: (11f 1-1, 12f 4-4, 15f) (gd 3-3, g-f 2-2, frm)

Leggy, very high-class filly, effective 12 to 15f, best at 12f, acts on gd to frm. Turf high 120 - 1st of 10 from Noushkey (4 Jun Epsom RF 1729) - also 1st of 7 from Sunspangled (11 Jly Curragh RF 2800a). She looked a fair prospect in a couple of maidens at two if nothing out of the ordinary, but was one of the real stars of 1999. She started off the season with an impressive victory in a Newmarket maiden, before gaining a workmanlike success in the Lingfield Oaks Trial. When it came to the Oaks itself, she was given a positive ride to utilise her proven stamina to maximum effect and it did the trick. She had little difficulty in completing the Oaks double at the Curragh, though she had little to beat. An authoritative winner of the Yorkshire Oaks when partnered by Pat Eddery for the first time, she could not quite gain that elusive fourth consecutive Group One win when beaten by Mutafaweq in the St Leger, though she did seem to stay. She will hopefully come back and make her presence felt at four.

**H R A Cecil [5-8] H R H Prince Fahd Salman.*

Ramruma was a triple Oaks winner

RAMSEY HOPE BHB 40f39a RR 41f 39a 384⁷

6 b h Timeless Times (USA) 6.1f **(56)** - Marfen (Lochnager) 6f **(59)**

Form - 45670347

Record	**1999** -	1st:0	2nd:0	3rd:1	Ran:5
	Pre1999 -	1st:7	2nd:8	3rd:4	Ran:78

Win Prizemoney £20,137 *Total Prizemoney* £32,642

Wins									
	1997	*Nov*	*Southw*	*(STD)*	*C*	*6f*		*64*	
	1997	Jun	Carlis	(FRM)	H	5f	59	59	
	1997	*Feb*	*Lingfi*	*(STD)*	*H*	*5f*	*73*	*74*	
	1996	*Nov*	*Lingfi*	*(STD)*	*H*	*5f*	*65*	*69*	
	1996	*Oct*	*Wolver*	*(STD)*	*H*	*5f*	*58*	*60*	
	1995	Aug	Ripon	(G-F)		6f		84	<
	1995	Jun	Hamilt	(FRM)		6f		84	<

1999 AW 0-5: (6f 4, 7f) (Equi, Fibr 4)

Moderate horse, effective 6f, - acts on Equi, often wears blinkers. AW high 42.

**D W Chapman [0-6] T S Redman (from C W Fairhurst [7-77] Nov 1998).*

RANAAN (IRE) BHB 74f RR 73f 4027⁴

3 ch c Brief Truce (USA) 9.1f **(73)** - Ma Minti (Mummy's Pet) 7.7f **(60)**

Form - 18253604

Record 1999 - 1st:0 2nd:1 3rd:1 Ran:6
Pre1999 - 1st:1 2nd:1 3rd:0 Ran:4
Win Prizemoney £2,866 *Total Prizemoney* £7,125
Wins * 1998 *Nov Wolver (STD)* *5f* *67+* <
1999 Turf 0-6: (5f, 6f 5) (gd 2, g-f 4)
Unfurnished, above-average colt, effective 5 to 6f, best at 6f, acts on gd to g-f - acts on Fibr, best on g-f. Turf high 74 (1st run) - 2nd of 14 getting 4lb from Candleriggs (3 Apr Kempton 6f g-f RF 0568).
**M R Channon [1-10] Ahmed Al Shafar.*

RANDOM KINDNESS BHB 64f85a **RR 72df 85a** 3840[9]
6 b g Alzao (USA) 9.8f **(73)** - Lady Tippins (USA) (Star de Naskra (USA)) 9.7f **(65)**
Form - 134762442080
Record 1999 - 1st:0 2nd:2 3rd:0 Ran:9
Pre1999 - 1st:7 2nd:8 3rd:4 Ran:34
Win Prizemoney £23,894 *Total Prizemoney* £40,206
Wins * 1998 *Nov Lingfi (STD)* *12f* *94* <
* 1998 May Bright (FRM) 11.9f 70
* 1998 *Apr Lingfi (STD)* *12f* *84*
* 1997 *Nov Wolver (STD) H* *12f* *77* *82*
* 1997 Oct Lingfi (FRM) 11.5f 62
* 1997 *Apr Wolver (STD) H* *14.8f* *66* *77*
* 1997 *Mar Wolver (STD)* *16.2f* *77*
1999 Turf 0-8: (12f 5, 14f 3) (gd, g-f, frm 6) 1999 AW 0-1: (12f) (Fibr)
Useful gelding, effective 12f, - acts on Equi, likes left handed tracks, likes tight tracks. Turf high 72. Becoming disappointing. He looks very useful on Fibresand, but over the past couple of seasons he has shown that he is perfectly capable of winning races on Equitrack and on turf too. Effective from 12 to 16 furlongs, he is versatile as well as game and genuine.
**R Ingram [7-38] 949 Racing (from P W Harris [0-5] Jly 1996).*

RANDOM TASK (IRE) BHB 78f85a **RR 54f 85a** 3664[4]
2 b c Tirol 8.1f **(64)** - Minami (IRE) (Caerleon (USA)) 8.6f **(71)**
Form - 14
Record 1999 - 1st:1 2nd:0 3rd:0 Ran:2
Win Prizemoney £2,801 *Total Prizemoney* £3,233
Wins * **1999** *May Wolver (Std)* *6f* *81+* <
1999 Turf 0-1: (6f) (gd) 1999 AW 1-1: (6f 1-1) (Fibr 1-1)
Currently decent colt. (1st run) - 1st of 8 from Distinctly Well (14 May Wolverhampton RF 1230). **D Shaw [1-2] J C Fretwell.*

RANEEN NASHWAN BHB 80f **RR 77f** 985[10]
3 b g Nashwan (USA) 10.3f **(79)** - Raneen Alwatar (Sadler's Wells (USA)) 10f **(76)**
Form - 40
Record 1999 - 1st:0 2nd:0 3rd:0 Ran:2
Pre1999 - 1st:1 2nd:0 3rd:0 Ran:4
Win Prizemoney £3,512 *Total Prizemoney* £4,199
Wins * 1998 Nov Mussel (SFT) 8f 77 <
1999 Turf 0-2: (10f, 11f) (gd, frm)
Above-average gelding, effective 8f, acts on g-s to gd. Turf high 70. **M R Channon [1-6] Sheikh Ahmed Al Maktoum.*

RANELLE (USA) BHB 76f **RR 75f** 4425[5]
3 ch f Rahy (USA) 9.1f **(80)** - Aspenelle (CAN) (Vice Regent (CAN)) 8.7f **(74)**
Form - 7215
Record 1999 - 1st:1 2nd:1 3rd:0 Ran:4
Win Prizemoney £4,630 *Total Prizemoney* £6,126
Wins * **1999** Spt Leices (FRM) 10f 74 <
1999 Turf 1-4: (7f, 8f, 10f 1-1, 12f) (gd, g-f 1-1, frm 2)
Scopey, above-average filly, mostly wears blinkers. Turf high 75 (began Aug) - 2nd of 17 to Lady Georgia (30 Aug Warwick 8f gd RF 4038) - also 1st of 10 from Darling Corey (7 Spt Leicester RF 4170). **J Noseda [1-4] Hesmonds Stud.*

RANGATIRA (IRE) BHB 52f **RR 61df** 2235[10]
4 ch g Royal Academy (USA) 7.8f **(77)** - Chief's Quest (USA) (Chief's Crown (USA)) 9.8f **(72)**
Form - 00
Record 1999 - 1st:0 2nd:0 3rd:0 Ran:2
Pre1999 - 1st:0 2nd:0 3rd:1 Ran:3
Win Prizemoney £0 *Total Prizemoney* £882
1999 Turf 0-2: (8f 2) (g-f, frm)
Average gelding. Turf high 36. **M Johnston [0-5] J W Robb.*

RANGER SLOANE BHB 30f26a **RR 29f 26a** 4726[11]
7 ch g Gunner B 11.2f **(45)** - Lucky Amy (Lucky Wednesday) 8f **(50)**
Form - 500
Record 1999 - 1st:0 2nd:0 3rd:0 Ran:3
Pre1999 - 1st:1 2nd:2 3rd:0 Ran:17
Win Prizemoney £3,096 *Total Prizemoney* £4,923
Wins * 1997 Spt Catter (GD) H 15.8f 38 43 <
1999 Turf 0-3: (14f, 16f 2) (gd 3)
Little account gelding, has worn blinkers. Turf high 29.
**G Fierro [4-46] G Fierro.*

RANGOON RUBY (USA) **RR 103f** 3036a[3]
3 ch f Kingmambo (USA) 10.9f **(85)** - Imperfect Circle (USA) (Riverman (USA)) 9.1f **(76)**
Form - 3183
1999 Turf 1-4: (6f, 7f 1-2, 8f) (g-s, gd 1-3)
Very useful filly. Turf high 103 - 3rd of 11 getting 12lb from Keos (13 Jly Deauville 6f gd RF 3036a). **J E Pease in FR [1-4].*

RAPIDASH **RR 33f** 4557[11]
2 gr g Petong 7.6f **(58)** - Join the Clan **(91f)** (Clantime)
Form - 00
Record 1999 - 1st:0 2nd:0 3rd:0 Ran:2
1999 Turf 0-2: (5f, 6f) (gd 2)
Currently very moderate gelding. Turf high 33 (began Aug).
**Mrs N Macauley [0-2] Mrs N Macauley.*

RAPID DEPLOYMENT BHB 71f **RR 79f** 4895[13]
2 b c Deploy 11.4f **(67)** - City Times (IRE) (Last Tycoon) 8.5f **(62)**
Form - 5030
Record 1999 - 1st:0 2nd:0 3rd:1 Ran:4
Win Prizemoney £0 *Total Prizemoney* £268
1999 Turf 0-4: (6f, 7f 3) (gd 2, g-f, frm)
Above-average colt. Turf high 79.
**J G Smyth-Osbourne [0-4] Mrs E T Smyth-Osbourne & Partners.*

RAPID LINER BHB 20f **RR 36f** 4288[11]
6 b g Skyliner 6.8f **(51)** - Stellaris (Star Appeal) 9.6f **(65)**
Form - 000
Record 1999 - 1st:0 2nd:0 3rd:0 Ran:3
Pre1999 - 1st:0 2nd:0 3rd:0 Ran:12
Win Prizemoney £0 *Total Prizemoney* £206
1999 Turf 0-3: (10f, 14f, 17f) (frm 3)
Very moderate gelding, has worn blinkers. Turf high 36 (began Jly). Inconsistent.
**R J Baker [0-17] Mrs V W Jones (from H Oliver [0-4] May 1996).*

RAPID RELIANCE BHB 28f40a **RR 10f 40a** 3394[16]
4 b f Emarati (USA) 6.6f **(63)** - Chiquitita (Reliance II) 9.9f **(58)**
Form - 000
Record 1999 - 1st:0 2nd:0 3rd:0 Ran:3
Pre1999 - 1st:1 2nd:0 3rd:0 Ran:15
Win Prizemoney £2,882 *Total Prizemoney* £3,087
Wins 1997 Spt Sandow (GD) C 5f 68 <
1999 Turf 0-3: (5f, 7f, 12f) (g-f 2, frm)
Neat, fair filly, effective 10f, acts on g-f, has worn blinkers. (began Jly). Becoming disappointing.
**H J Manners [0-3] H J Manners (from K R Burke [0-1] Spt 1998).*

RAPIER BHB 83f **RR 78f** 1701[9]
5 b g Sharpo 7.5f **(68)** - Sahara Breeze (Ela-Mana-Mou) 10.1f **(70)**
Form - 710
Record 1999 - 1st:1 2nd:0 3rd:0 Ran:3
Pre1999 - 1st:2 2nd:2 3rd:4 Ran:17
Win Prizemoney £25,855 *Total Prizemoney* £36,252
Wins * **1999** May Ayr (GD) H 10f 83 78
* 1998 Jun York (G-S) H 8.9f 82 88 <
1996 Spt Bright (FRM) 8f 77
1999 Turf 1-3: (10f 1-2, 11f) (gd 1-3)
Above-average gelding, has broken blood-vessels, effective 9 to 10f, acts on g-s to gd, likes left handed tracks. Turf high 78.
**M D Hammond [3-11] Mrs A Kane (from R Hannon [1-11] Oct 1997).*

RA RA RASPUTIN BHB 38f60a **RR 35f 60a** 5156[17]
4 b g Petong 7.6f **(58)** - Ra Ra Girl (Shack (USA)) 5.8f **(53)**
Form - 00006720
Record 1999 - 1st:0 2nd:1 3rd:0 Ran:8

Pre1999 - 1st:1 2nd:1 3rd:1 Ran:19

Win Prizemoney £18,555 *Total Prizemoney* £21,417

Wins * 1997 *Aug Wolver (STD) 6f 82* <

1999 Turf 0-6: (8f 4, 10f 2) (g-s, gd 3, g-f, frm) 1999 AW 0-2: (8f 2) (Fibr 2)

Scopey, average gelding, effective 7 to 8f, acts on gd - acts on Fibr, has worn blinkers, likes left handed tracks, likes tight tracks. Turf high 43. AW high 64 (began Jly) - 2nd of 13 giving 18lb to Guest Envoy (14 Aug Wolverhampton 8f Fibr RF 3672). Inconsistent. **B A McMahon [1-27] D J Allen.*

RARE GENIUS (USA) BHB 64f **RR 64f** 4904[2]

3 ch c Beau Genius (CAN) - Aunt Nola (USA) (Olden Times) 11.4f **(67)**

Form - 0563052

Record 1999 - 1st:0 2nd:1 3rd:1 Ran:7

Win Prizemoney £0 *Total Prizemoney* £2,014

1999 Turf 0-7: (10f 4, 12f 2, 14f) (g-s, gd, g-f 2, frm 3)

Leggy, average colt, effective 10 to 14f, acts on g-s to frm, prefers tight tracks. Turf high 64 - 2nd of 16 giving 9lb to Simple Ideals (15 Oct Redcar 14f frm RF 4904).

**P W Harris [0-7] Beever,E Long,R Spen Harris.*

RARE TALENT BHB 56f **RR 49f** 4993[10]

5 b g Mtoto 11.5f **(71)** - Bold As Love (Lomond (USA)) 8.8f **(65)**

Form - 586768121262800

Record 1999 - 1st:2 2nd:3 3rd:0 Ran:15

Pre1999 - 1st:4 2nd:1 3rd:3 Ran:26

Win Prizemoney £19,420 *Total Prizemoney* £25,663

Wins *** 1999** Aug Windso (G-F) H 11.6f 48 58

*** 1999** Jly Beverl (G-F) H 9.9f 50 55

***** 1998 Jly Cheste (G-F) H 10.3f 60 63

***** 1998 Jun Doncas (GD) H 10.3f 55 59

1997 Spt Leices (G-F) S 10f 60

1997 Aug Ripon (G-F) SH 10f 60 65 <

1999 Turf 2-15: (8f 2, 10f 1-11, 12f 1-2) (gd 2, g-f 4, frm 2-9)

Moderate gelding, effective 10 to 12f, best at 10f, acts on gd to hrd, best on frm, has worn blinkers, likes right handed tracks, excels at Windsor and Yarmouth and likes Beverley. Turf high 61 - 2nd of 12 giving 15lb to Missile Toe (30 Jly Newmarket 10f frm RF 3241) - also 1st of 9 giving 24lb to Slapy Dam (2 Aug Windsor RF 3301). Consistent.

**S Gollings [4-30] John King, Bill Hobs King (from M R Channon [2-11] Spt 1997).*

RASM **RR 81+f** 4784[3]

2 b c Darshaan 11.9f **(81)** - Northshiel (Northfields (USA)) 9f **(72)**

Form - 3

Record 1999 - 1st:0 2nd:0 3rd:1 Ran:1

Win Prizemoney £0 *Total Prizemoney* £535

1999 Turf 0-1: (7f) (g-s)

Currently decent colt. (1st run) - 3rd of 18 to Frontier (8 Oct Lingfield 7f g-s RF 4784). Showed distinct promise on his debut and is worth watching out for next season.

**A C Stewart [0-1] Hamdan Al Maktoum.*

RASPBERRY SAUCE BHB 52f54a **RR 54f 54a** 2199[6]

5 b m Niniski (USA) 13.2f **(67)** - Sobranie (High Top) 10.2f **(67)**

Form - 00150841506

Record 1999 - 1st:1 2nd:0 3rd:0 Ran:7

Pre1999 - 1st:3 2nd:2 3rd:2 Ran:18

Win Prizemoney £12,757 *Total Prizemoney* £16,038

Wins *** 1999** *May Lingfi (STD) H 10f 50 57+*

* 1998 *Dec Lingfi (STD) H 8f 50 53*

* 1998 Apr Bath (SFT) H 11.7f 58 62 <

* 1998 *Apr Lingfi (STD) 10f 54*

1999 Turf 0-2: (10f, 12f) (sft, g-f) 1999 AW 1-5: (7f, 8f 2, 10f 1-2) (Equi 1-5)

Fair filly, effective 8 to 12f, best at 12f, acts on g-s to g-f - acts on Equi. Turf high 53. AW high 57 - 1st of 8 giving 4lb to Mogin (7 May Lingfield RF 1087). **C A Cyzer [4-25] R M Cyzer.*

RAS SHAIKH (USA) BHB 100f **RR 102f** 5140[5]

3 b f Sheikh Albadou 9.2f **(75)** - Aneesati (Kris) 9.5f **(73)**

Form - 628225

Record 1999 - 1st:0 2nd:3 3rd:0 Ran:6

Pre1999 - 1st:1 2nd:0 3rd:2 Ran:3

Win Prizemoney £2,994 *Total Prizemoney* £20,287

Wins * 1998 Aug Leices (GD) 6f 73 <

1999 Turf 0-6: (7f, 8f 3, 10f 2) (gd 4, frm 2)

Scopey, very useful filly, effective 7 to 10f, acts on gd to frm, best on gd. Turf high 103 (1st run) - 6th of 11 to Wince (16 Apr Newbury 7f frm RF 0719). Inconsistent. She has ability, but is a tricky ride and needs to be produced fast and late past tiring rivals. Best over a mile, she goes well on easy ground.

**B W Hills [1-9] Salem Bel Obaida.*

RATATUIA BHB 88f **RR 87f** 2006[1]

3 b f Zafonic (USA) 9f **(83)** - Refilee (IRE) (Sadler's Wells (USA)) 10f **(76)**

Form - 131

Record 1999 - 1st:2 2nd:0 3rd:1 Ran:3

Pre1999 - 1st:0 2nd:1 3rd:1 Ran:3

Win Prizemoney £9,580 *Total Prizemoney* £12,022

Wins *** 1999** Jun Thirsk (G-F) H 8f 84 87 <

*** 1999** Apr Windso (G-F) 8.3f 86

1999 Turf 2-3: (8f 2-2, 9f) (gd, frm 2-2)

Useful filly, effective 8 to 9f, best at 8f, acts on g-s to frm, best on frm. Turf high 87 - 1st of 13 getting 12lb from Cruinn A Bhord (15 Jun Thirsk RF 2006) - also 1st of 11 from Balladonia (19 Apr Windsor RF 0760). She got up right on the line to make a winning reappearance at Windsor before adding to that success at Thirsk. A mile on fast ground looks ideal.

**L M Cumani [2-6] Scuderia Rencati Srl.*

RATHCLOGHEENDANCER (IRE) BHB 46f **RR 45f** 4341[12]

2 ch g Colonel Collins (USA) - Fleeting Quest (Rainbow Quest (USA)) 10.4f **(75)**

Form - 4870460

Record 1999 - 1st:0 2nd:0 3rd:0 Ran:7

1999 Turf 0-6: (5f 3, 6f, 8f 2) (g-s, gd 3, frm 2) 1999 AW 0-1: (5f) (Fibr)

Moderate gelding, has worn blinkers. Turf high 45.

**K A Ryan [0-7] The Gloria Darley Racing Partnership.*

RATHER DIZZY RR 4631[8]

4 b g Sizzling Melody 6.3f **(49)** - Rather Dark (Nomination) 7f **(60)**

Form - 08

Record 1999 - 1st:0 2nd:0 3rd:0 Ran:2

1999 Turf 0-2: (7f, 8f) (g-s, frm)

Workmanlike, currently very poor gelding. (began Spt) - 8th of 8 giving 9lb to Shanghai Lady (29 Spt Brighton 8f g-s RF 4631).

**P Butler [0-2] Mrs Gill Oakley.*

RATHLEA BHB 38f **RR 38f** 5155[8]

5 b h Risk Me (FR) 8f **(53)** - Star of Jupiter (Jupiter Island) 14f **(62)**

Form - 708

Record 1999 - 1st:0 2nd:0 3rd:0 Ran:3

1999 Turf 0-2: (8f 2) (gd, g-f) 1999 AW 0-1: (7f) (Fibr)

Currently very moderate colt. Turf high 38 (began Oct).

**R Hollinshead [0-3] Mrs Robert Heathcote.*

RATIFIED BHB 52f **RR 43f** 4007[9]

2 b c Not in Doubt (USA) - Festival of Magic (USA) (Clever Trick (USA)) 6.6f **(77)**

Form - 000

Record 1999 - 1st:0 2nd:0 3rd:0 Ran:3

1999 Turf 0-3: (7f 2, 8f) (gd, frm 2)

Currently moderate colt. Turf high 43 (began Jly).

**H Candy [0-3] Mrs David Blackburn.*

RATTLE BHB 25f25a **RR 25f 25a** 5188[15]

6 b g Mazilier (USA) 8.5f **(56)** - Snake Song (Mansingh (USA)) 7.4f **(55)**

Form - 0

Record 1999 - 1st:0 2nd:0 3rd:0 Ran:1

Pre1999 - 1st:0 2nd:1 3rd:4 Ran:25

Win Prizemoney £0 *Total Prizemoney* £2,340

1999 Turf 0-1: (16f) (g-f)

Little account gelding, has worn blinkers. Inconsistent.

**D A Nolan [0-11] Mrs L A Ogilvie (from J J O'Neill [0-16] Jly 1996).*

RAUCOUS LAD RR 112f 4513a[4]

3 b c Warning 8.1f **(77)** - Someone Special (Habitat) 9.4f **(70)**

Form - 14

1999 Turf 1-2: (8f 1-1, 10f) (hvy 1-1, sft)

Currently Group-class colt. Turf high 112 (began Aug) - 4th of 4 to

State Shinto (18 Spt Longchamp 10f sft RF 4513a) - also 1st of 5 from Tobruk (11 Aug Deauville RF 3776a). Very lightly raced, he was not disgraced when finishing fourth in the Prix du Prince d'Orange at Longchamp in September. Open to improvement, he could develop into a useful four-year-old. **A Fabre in FR [1-2].*

RAVENSWOOD (IRE) BHB 78f RR 81f 4899[20]

2 b c Warning 8.1f **(77)** - Green Lucia (Green Dancer (USA)) 10.3f **(74)**
Form - 6100
Record 1999 - 1st:1 2nd:0 3rd:0 Ran:4
Win Prizemoney £2,879 *Total Prizemoney* £2,879
Wins * **1999** Aug Bright (FRM) 7f 81 <
1999 Turf 1-4: (7f 1-2, 8f 2) (sft, gd, frm 1-2)
Decent colt. Turf high 81 (began Jly) - 1st of 7 giving 8lb to Seeking Utopia (4 Aug Brighton RF 3346).
**M C Pipe [1-4] Lord Donoughmore.*

RAVENWOOD LADY BHB 59f RR 62f 2504[11]

3 ch f Unfuwain (USA) 11.4f **(74)** - Sylvatica (Thatching) 8f **(66)**
Form - 3300
Record 1999 - 1st:0 2nd:0 3rd:2 Ran:4
Pre1999 - 1st:0 2nd:0 3rd:0 Ran:1
Win Prizemoney £0 *Total Prizemoney* £1,026
1999 Turf 0-4: (10f, 11f, 12f, 13f) (hvy, g-f, frm 2)
Lengthy, average filly. Turf high 61 (1st run) - 3rd of 11 getting 20lb from April Stock (13 Apr Folkestone 12f hvy RF 0660).
**S C Williams [0-5] W J de Ruiter.*

RAVINE RR 59f 4753[6]

2 ch f Indian Ridge 7.6f **(74)** - Cubby Hole (Town And Country) 8.1f **(68)**
Form - 6
Record 1999 - 1st:0 2nd:0 3rd:0 Ran:1
1999 Turf 0-1: (6f) (gd)
Currently fair filly. **R Hannon [0-1] Lord Carnarvon.*

RAVISHING (IRE) RR 77+f 4928[1]

2 b f Bigstone (IRE) -Dazzling Maid(IRE) (Tate Gallery (USA)) 7.4f **(67)**
Form - 1
Record 1999 - 1st:1 2nd:0 3rd:0 Ran:1
Win Prizemoney £1,955 *Total Prizemoney* £1,955
Wins * **1999** Oct Pontef (GD) 6f 77+ <
1999 Turf 1-1: (6f 1-1) (g-f 1-1)
Currently above-average filly. (1st run) - 1st of 12 getting 4lb from Risky Reef (18 Oct Pontefract RF 4928).
**W J Haggas [1-1] G C Johnston.*

RAWAFED RR 71f 2126[4]

3 b f Arazi (USA) 9.2f **(74)** - Princess Sucree (USA) (Roberto (USA)) 10f **(76)**
Form - 4
Record 1999 - 1st:0 2nd:0 3rd:0 Ran:1
Win Prizemoney £0 *Total Prizemoney* £309
1999 Turf 0-1: (10f) (frm)
Workmanlike, currently above-average filly. (1st run) - 4th of 9 getting 5lb from Marnor (18 Jun Newmarket 10f frm RF 2126).
**A C Stewart [0-1] Hamdan Al Maktoum.*

RAWI BHB 30f45a RR 33f 45a 4076[14]

6 ch g Forzando 7.2f **(63)** - Finally (Final Straw) 7.9f **(64)**
Form - 8705050
Record 1999 - 1st:0 2nd:0 3rd:0 Ran:7
Pre1999 - 1st:3 2nd:4 3rd:6 Ran:38
Win Prizemoney £7,381 *Total Prizemoney* £13,549
Wins 1997 Jly Folkes (G-F) C 6.9f 46
1997 *Jan Lingfi (STD) H 7f 53 56* <
1996 *Dec Lingfi (STD) 7f 50*
1999 Turf 0-6: (8f, 9f, 10f 2, 11f, 12f) (gd, frm 4, hrd) 1999 AW 0-1: (7f) (Fibr)
Very moderate gelding, has worn blinkers. Turf high 33. Had become very disappointing until narrowly winning a Folkestone claimer in July, and continued to run respectably. His three wins have all been over seven furlongs.
**Mrs A J Perrett [0-6] Miss G Harwood (from J I A Charlton [1-9] Feb 1999).*

RAYIK BHB 48f67a RR 50f 67a 5069[17]

4 br g Marju (IRE) 9.2f **(76)** - Matila (IRE) (Persian Bold) 9.3f **(66)**
Form - 36126060000000
Record 1999 - 1st:0 2nd:1 3rd:0 Ran:11
Pre1999 - 1st:1 2nd:0 3rd:1 Ran:6
Win Prizemoney £2,788 *Total Prizemoney* £5,461
Wins 1998 *Dec Lingfi (STD) 10f 69* <
1999 Turf 0-9: (8f, 9f, 10f 5, 11f, 12f) (g-s, gd 2, g-f 3, frm 2, hrd) 1999 AW 0-2: (8f, 12f) (Fibr 2)
Workmanlike, decent gelding, effective 8 to 12f, acts on frm - acts on AW, has worn blinkers, likes left handed tracks. Turf high 75. AW high 80 (1st run) - 2nd of 12 getting 6lb from China Castle (20 Jan Wolverhampton 12f Fibr RF 0129).
**G L Moore [0-1] Lancing Racing Syndicate (from N E Berry [1-13] Aug 1999).*

RAYPOUR (IRE) RR 91f 4960a[2]

2 ch c Barathea - Rayseka 00
Form - 042
1999 Turf 0-3: (7f 2, 8f) (g-s 3)
Currently useful colt. Turf high 91 (began Spt) - 2nd of 14 giving 5lb to Plurabelle (13 Oct Gowran Park 7f g-s RF 4960a).
**J Oxx in IRE [0-3] H H Aga Khan.*

RAYWARE BOY (IRE) BHB 48f65a RR 49f 65a 4906[17]

3 b c Scenic 10.6f **(66)** - Amata (USA) (Nodouble (USA)) 8.8f **(68)**
Form - 114200000
Record 1999 - 1st:2 2nd:1 3rd:0 Ran:9
Pre1999 - 1st:0 2nd:0 3rd:0 Ran:4
Win Prizemoney £5,602 *Total Prizemoney* £6,961
Wins * **1999** *Feb Southw (STD) H 8f 60 60* <
* **1999** *Jan Southw (STD) H 8f 48 57*
1999 Turf 0-4: (7f, 8f, 10f 2) (gd, g-f 2, frm) 1999 AW 2-5: (8f 2-2, 9f, 10f, 12f) (Equi, Fibr 2-4)
Light-framed, average colt, effective 8 to 12f, best at 8f, - acts on Fibr, mostly wears blinkers (extremely effectively), prefers left handed tracks, prefers tight tracks. Turf high 49. AW high 67 - 2nd of 5 giving 7lb to Lost Spirit (6 Mar Wolverhampton 12f Fibr RF 0408) - also 1st of 9 getting 8lb from James Dee (5 Feb Southwell RF 0230). Becoming disappointing. **D Shaw [2-13] Rayton Racing.*

RAYYAAN (IRE) BHB 80f RR 86f 4708[2]

2 ch c Cadeaux Genereux 7.9f **(76)** - Anam **(80df)** (Persian Bold) 9.3f **(66)**
Form - 5422
Record 1999 - 1st:0 2nd:2 3rd:0 Ran:4
Win Prizemoney £0 *Total Prizemoney* £2,637
1999 Turf 0-4: (6f 3, 8f) (sft, gd 3)
Useful colt. Turf high 86 - 2nd of 6 giving 5lb to Trewornan (4 Oct Brighton 6f gd RF 4708). **P T Walwyn [0-4] Hamdan Al Maktoum.*

REACHFORYOURPOCKET (IRE) BHB 50f RR 48df 4790[9]

4 b c Royal Academy (USA) 7.8f **(77)** - Gemaasheh (Habitat) 9.4f **(70)**
Form - 800P0006660
Record 1999 - 1st:0 2nd:0 3rd:0 Ran:11
1999 Turf 0-11: (6f 3, 7f 5, 8f 2, 9f) (g-s 2, g-f 6, frm 3)
Scopey, moderate colt. Turf high 65. Inconsistent.
**K Mahdi [0-11] Bryan Fry & Alan Hall.*

REACTION BALL BHB 65f RR 67f 3024[5]

3 b f Simply Great (FR) 11.9f **(61)** - Empty Purse (Pennine Walk) 8.5f **(61)**
Form - 5U255
Record 1999 - 1st:0 2nd:1 3rd:0 Ran:5
Pre1999 - 1st:0 2nd:0 3rd:0 Ran:1
Win Prizemoney £0 *Total Prizemoney* £1,277
1999 Turf 0-5: (8f 5) (gd 2, g-f, frm 2)
Leggy, average filly, effective 8f, acts on gd to frm. Turf high 67 - 5th of 9 giving 1lb to Khibrah (13 Jly Brighton 8f frm RF 2775).
**T R Watson [0-6] Newitt and Co Ltd.*

READY FONTAINE BHB 37f RR 29f 1923[13]

4 b g Dilum (USA) 7.1f **(56)** - Prepare (IRE) (Millfontaine)
Form - 0
Record 1999 - 1st:0 2nd:0 3rd:0 Ran:1
Pre1999 - 1st:0 2nd:2 3rd:2 Ran:11
Win Prizemoney £0 *Total Prizemoney* £2,494
1999 Turf 0-1: (5f) (frm)
Strong, little account gelding, effective 6f, acts on gd to frm, best

on gd. Becoming disappointing. **J Neville [0-13] T A Wadsworth.*

REAGANESQUE (USA) BHB 43f **RR 51f** 2509[2]

7 b g Nijinsky (CAN) - Basoof (USA) (Believe It (USA)) 9.4f **(70)**
Form - 2
Record 1999 - 1st:0 2nd:1 3rd:0 Ran:1
Pre1999 - 1st:3 2nd:1 3rd:3 Ran:22
Win Prizemoney £9,125 *Total Prizemoney* £13,394
Wins * 1996 Aug Haydoc (G-F) H 11.9f 51 51 <
* 1996 Jun Chepst (G-F) H 12.1f 42 50
* 1996 Jun Warwic (FRM) H 12.5f 42 47
1999 Turf 0-1: (15f) (g-f)
Fair gelding. (1st run) - 2nd of 9 getting 2lb from Burma Baby (2 Jly Warwick 15f g-f RF 2509). Consistent.
**P G Murphy [8-45] Mrs John Spielman (from E A L Dunlop [0-5] Oct 1995).*

REALMS OF GOLD (USA) BHB 46f **RR 59f** 3910[11]

3 ch f Gulch (USA) 9.6f **(79)** - Royal Pageant (USA) (Majestic Light (USA)) 10.6f **(75)**
Form - 6000
Record 1999 - 1st:0 2nd:0 3rd:0 Ran:4
Pre1999 - 1st:0 2nd:0 3rd:0 Ran:2
1999 Turf 0-3: (7f, 9f, 10f) (gd, frm 2) 1999 AW 0-1: (7f) (Equi)
Scopey, fair filly. Turf high 59 (began Jly).
**I A Balding [0-6] & Mrs F C Welch.*

REAL QUIET (USA) **RR 123f** 1716a[3]

4 b c Quiet American (USA) 7.9f **(60)** - Really Blue (USA) (Believe It (USA)) 9.4f **(70)**
Form - 3
1999 AW 0-1: (9f) (Dirt)
Top-class colt. (1st run) - 3rd of 6 giving 3lb to Behrens (29 May Suffolk Downs 9f Dirt RF 1716a). He was a close third to Behrens and Running Stag in the Massachusetts Handicap in 1999 before his career was curtailed by injury. **B Baffert in USA [2-4].*

REAL TING BHB 30f **RR 8f** 461[8]

3 br g Forzando 7.2f **(63)** - St Helena (Monsanto (FR)) 6.5f **(59)**
Form - 88
Record 1999 - 1st:0 2nd:0 3rd:0 Ran:2
Pre1999 - 1st:0 2nd:0 3rd:0 Ran:3
1999 AW 0-2: (5f 2) (Fibr 2)
Very moderate gelding, has worn blinkers. AW high 32.
**P D Evans [0-3] P D Evans (from P C Haslam [0-2] Aug 1998).*

REAMZAFONIC BHB 40f **RR 41f** 4906[7]

3 b f Grand Lodge (USA) - Eye Witness (IRE) (Don't Forget Me) 8.3f **(74)**
Form - 8687
Record 1999 - 1st:0 2nd:0 3rd:0 Ran:4
Pre1999 - 1st:0 2nd:0 3rd:0 Ran:1
1999 Turf 0-4: (7f, 10f 2, 11f) (sft, g-f, frm 2)
Light-framed, moderate filly. Turf high 41 (began Aug).
**E J Alston [0-5] Miss F Fenley.*

REAR GUARD ACTION BHB 37f **RR 23f** 1538[3]

3 b c Almoojid 7f **(36)** - Belle Deirdrie (Mandamus) 12.6f **(56)**
Form - 073
Record 1999 - 1st:0 2nd:0 3rd:1 Ran:2
Pre1999 - 1st:0 2nd:0 3rd:0 Ran:1
Win Prizemoney £0 *Total Prizemoney* £600
1999 Turf 0-2: (12f 2) (gd, g-f)
Workmanlike, currently little account colt. Turf high 23.
**P Butler [0-3] G P Tresidder.*

REAR WINDOW BHB 50f50a **RR 57f 50a** 3441[8]

5 b g Night Shift (USA) 8.1f **(73)** - Last Clear Chance (USA) (Alleged (USA)) 10f **(76)**
Form - 444558
Record 1999 - 1st:0 2nd:0 3rd:0 Ran:6
Pre1999 - 1st:2 2nd:3 3rd:1 Ran:13
Win Prizemoney £5,404 *Total Prizemoney* £9,075
Wins * 1998 May Nottin (G-F) H 10f 54 60
* 1998 *Mar Southw (STD) H 12f 53 61* <
1999 Turf 0-3: (12f, 14f 2) (g-s, gd, g-f) 1999 AW 0-3: (11f, 14f, 15f) (Fibr 3)
Fair gelding, effective 10 to 14f, best at 10f, acts on sft to frm - acts on Fibr, best on frm, has worn blinkers, prefers left handed tracks, favours tight tracks, excels at Nottingham and Southwell. Turf high 57 - 4th of 17 getting 14lb from Nichol Fifty (19 Apr Nottingham 14f g-s RF 0750). AW high 54 (1st run) - 5th of 15 giving 2lb to Count de Money (28 Jun Southwell 11f Fibr RF 2375).
**G M McCourt [2-20] Dawn Build Ltd (from Lord Huntingdon [0-5] Oct 1997).*

REASON WHY (IRE) BHB 69f **RR 69f** 4213[1]

3 b c College Chapel - Stifen (Burslem) 8.8f **(53)**
Form - 008622001
Record 1999 - 1st:1 2nd:2 3rd:0 Ran:9
Win Prizemoney £4,395 *Total Prizemoney* £5,865
Wins * 1999 Spt Kempto (G-F) H 8f 66 68 <
1999 Turf 1-9: (7f 5, 8f 1-4) (gd 2, g-f 2, frm 1-4, hrd)
Lengthy, average colt, effective 7 to 8f, best at 8f, acts on frm, often wears blinkers (extremely effectively). Turf high 71 - 2nd of 16 giving 8lb to Adobe (30 Jun Bath 8f frm RF 2425) - also 1st of 19 getting 2lb from Magic Flute (8 Spt Kempton RF 4213).
**Bob Jones [1-9] The Reason Why Partnership.*

REBECCA JAY BHB 43f49a **RR 28f 49a** 4604[10]

3 b f Rambo Dancer (CAN) 8.4f **(59)** - Having Fun (Hard Fought) 8.8f **(62)**
Form - 2000000
Record 1999 - 1st:0 2nd:1 3rd:0 Ran:7
Pre1999 - 1st:0 2nd:0 3rd:0 Ran:5
Win Prizemoney £0 *Total Prizemoney* £652
1999 Turf 0-3: (6f 2, 7f) (gd, g-f 2) 1999 AW 0-4: (7f 2, 8f 2) (Fibr 4)
Scopey, fair filly. Turf high 28. AW high 55. Inconsistent.
**M G Meagher [0-12] B Collier.*

REBEL COUNTY (IRE) BHB 56f75a **RR 57f 75a** 3677[11]

6 b m Maelstrom Lake 8.8f **(53)** - Haven Bridge (Connaught) 7.7f **(63)**
Form - 4748350020
Record 1999 - 1st:0 2nd:1 3rd:1 Ran:10
Pre1999 - 1st:9 2nd:8 3rd:3 Ran:60
Win Prizemoney £43,971 *Total Prizemoney* £62,506
Wins * 1998 Aug Epsom (G-F) H 8.5f 61 65
* 1998 Jly Bath (GD) H 8f 54 58
* 1996 Oct Haydoc (SFT) H 8.1f 84 88 <
* 1996 Spt Ayr (G-F) H 10f 80 80
* 1996 Aug Epsom (GD) H 8.5f 69 75
1996 Jun Cheste (G-F) C 10.3f 53+
1996 May Leices (G-S) C 8f 60
1996 May Newmar (GD) C 8f 57
1995 Spt Lingfi (G-F) 6f 76
1999 Turf 0-10: (8f 6, 10f 4) (g-s, gd 2, g-f, frm 6)
Average mare, effective 8 to 9f, best at 9f, acts on gd to frm, best on gd, has worn blinkers, likes left handed tracks. Turf high 57 - 2nd of 11 getting 9lb from Ryefield (10 Aug Ayr 8f frm RF 3493).
**A Bailey [5-55] Showtime Ice Cream Concessionaire (from M C Pipe [1-3] Jun 1996).*

REBEL ROSE **RR 8f** 1926[5]

2 ch f Factual (USA) - Ragtime Rose (Ragstone) 9.6f **(59)**
Form - 65
Record 1999 - 1st:0 2nd:0 3rd:0 Ran:2
1999 Turf 0-1: (5f) (hrd) 1999 AW 0-1: (5f) (Fibr)
Currently very moderate filly. **E A Wheeler [0-2] All Four Corners.*

RECADERO (GER) **RR 105f** 1355a[3]

3 b c
Form - 33
1999 Turf 0-2: (8f 2) (sft, gd)
Currently Pattern-class colt. Turf high 105 - 3rd of 11 to Sumitas (16 May Cologne 8f gd RF 1355a). **Uwe Stoltefuss in GER [0-2].*

RECOLETA **RR 37f** 5137[15]

2 b f Ezzoud (IRE) - Hug Me (Shareef Dancer (USA)) 9.9f **(73)**
Form - 00
Record 1999 - 1st:0 2nd:0 3rd:0 Ran:2
1999 Turf 0-2: (6f, 7f) (gd 2)
Currently very moderate filly. Turf high 37 (began Oct).
**D R C Elsworth [0-2] Pampas Partnership.*

RECORD TIME BHB 61f **RR 55f** 4810[9]
3 ch f Clantime 6.6f **(57)** - On the Record (Record Token) 6.3f **(53)**
Form - 765257242410
Record 1999 - 1st:1 2nd:3 3rd:0 Ran:12
Pre1999 - 1st:0 2nd:0 3rd:0 Ran:2
Win Prizemoney £5,088 *Total Prizemoney* £8,270
Wins * **1999** Spt Newmar (G-S) H 5f 53 55 <
1999 Turf 1-12: (5f 1-11, 6f) (sft, gd 1-5, g-f 2, frm 2, hrd 2)
Scopey, fair filly, effective 5f, acts on gd. Turf high 55 - 1st of 20 from Live To Tell (30 Spt Newmarket RF 4656). Consistent.
**E J Alston [1-14] Peter Onslow.*

RED APOLLO BHB 50f54a **RR 54f 54a** 4927[12]
3 gr g Petong 7.6f **(58)** - Scarlet Veil (Tyrnavos) 10.1f **(55)**
Form - 2008248700
Record 1999 - 1st:0 2nd:1 3rd:0 Ran:9
Pre1999 - 1st:0 2nd:1 3rd:0 Ran:3
Win Prizemoney £0 *Total Prizemoney* £1,354
1999 Turf 0-6: (6f, 7f 4, 8f) (gd, g-f 2, frm 3) 1999 AW 0-3: (7f, 8f, 9f) (Fibr 3)
Strong, fair gelding, effective 6f, - acts on Fibr, has worn blinkers. Turf high 55. AW high 55 (began Jly). Inconsistent.
**P Howling [0-5] S J Hammond (from A C Stewart [0-7] Jly 1999).*

RED BARRON (IRE) RR 43f 2166[6]
2 b g Brief Truce (USA) 9.1f **(73)** - Miss Sandman (Manacle) 7.8f **(56)**
Form - 606
Record 1999 - 1st:0 2nd:0 3rd:0 Ran:3
1999 Turf 0-3: (5f 2, 6f) (g-f 2, frm)
Currently moderate gelding, has worn blinkers. Turf high 43.
**J Berry [0-3] The Red Shirt Brigade Ltd.*

RED BORDEAUX BHB 60f **RR 64?f** 511[15]
4 b c Alzao (USA) 9.8f **(73)** - Marie de Flandre (FR) (Crystal Palace (FR)) 12.5f **(76)**
Form - 0
Record 1999 - 1st:0 2nd:0 3rd:0 Ran:1
Pre1999 - 1st:1 2nd:0 3rd:1 Ran:8
Win Prizemoney £2,290 *Total Prizemoney* £3,065
Wins 1998 Oct Catter (G-S) 12f 64 <
1999 Turf 0-1: (14f) (sft)
Average colt, effective 12f, acts on gd, likes left handed tracks, likes tight tracks.
**J Akehurst [0-5] A D Spence (from B W Hills [1-8] Oct 1998).*

REDBRIDGE (USA) BHB 106f **RR 105f** 3235[U]
5 b h Alleged (USA) 11.8f **(81)** - Red Slippers (USA) (Nureyev (USA)) 8.7f **(78)**
Form - 82U
Record 1999 - 1st:0 2nd:1 3rd:0 Ran:3
Pre1999 - 1st:3 2nd:0 3rd:2 Ran:8
Win Prizemoney £20,393 *Total Prizemoney* £28,687
Wins * 1998 Jun Leices (SFT) L 11.8f 102
* 1998 Jun Doncas (GD) 10.3f 115+ <
* *1998 Apr Wolver (STD) 12f 99+*
1999 Turf 0-2: (10f, 12f) (g-f, frm) 1999 AW 0-1: (10f) (Dirt)
Pattern-class colt, effective 10 to 13f, acts on g-f, has worn blinkers, likes left handed tracks, likes tight tracks. Turf high 105 (began Jly). After running in Dubai during the winter he ran quite well in a Newbury conditions event, but he unshipped Dettori on his only subsequent start.
**J H M Gosden [3-10] H E Sheikh Rashid Al Maktoum (from S bin Suroor in UAE [0-1] Mar 1999).*

RED BROOK LAD BHB 38f **RR 36f** 1582[10]
4 ch g Nomadic Way (USA) - Silently Yours (USA) (Silent Screen (USA)) 8.6f **(65)**
Form - 51680
Record 1999 - 1st:1 2nd:0 3rd:0 Ran:4
Pre1999 - 1st:0 2nd:0 3rd:0 Ran:5
Win Prizemoney £1,688 *Total Prizemoney* £1,688
Wins * **1999** *Feb Lingfi (STD) H 16f* 32 44 <
1999 AW 1-4: (16f 1-4) (Equi 1-4)
Workmanlike, very moderate gelding, effective 16f, - acts on Equi, has worn blinkers, likes left handed tracks. AW high 44 (1st run) - 1st of 10 getting 19lb from Pertemps Mission (25 Feb Lingfield RF 0354). Inconsistent. **S Dow [1-16] Miss Michelle Devine.*

RED CANYON (IRE) BHB 63f **RR 66f** 4950[8]
2 b c Zieten (USA) - Bayazida (Bustino) 10.4f **(64)**
Form - 76808
Record 1999 - 1st:0 2nd:0 3rd:0 Ran:5
1999 Turf 0-5: (5f, 6f 3, 8f) (g-s, gd, g-f 3)
Average colt. Turf high 66 (began Jly). **M L W Bell [0-5] Terry Neill.*

RED CASTILE RR 12f 2234[6]
2 ch f Casteddu 7.4f **(54)** - La Fontainova (IRE) (Lafontaine (USA)) 8.7f **(49)**
Form - 56
Record 1999 - 1st:0 2nd:0 3rd:0 Ran:2
1999 Turf 0-1: (6f) (frm) 1999 AW 0-1: (6f) (Fibr)
Currently little account filly. **J Berry [0-2] The Red Shirt Brigade Ltd.*

RED CHARGER (IRE) BHB 66f **RR 62f** 3483[1]
3 ch g Up and At 'em - Smashing Pet (Mummy's Pet) 7.7f **(60)**
Form - 0082558001
Record 1999 - 1st:1 2nd:1 3rd:0 Ran:10
Pre1999 - 1st:3 2nd:0 3rd:2 Ran:10
Win Prizemoney £20,525 *Total Prizemoney* £22,340
Wins * **1999** Aug Thirsk (SFT) H 5f 60 62
1998 Aug York (G-F) S 6f 79
1998 Jly Catter (FRM) 7f 82 <
1998 May Redcar (GD) 5f 67
1999 Turf 1-9: (5f 1-2, 6f 4, 7f 3) (gd 1-3, frm 6) 1999 AW 0-1: (6f) (Fibr)
Scopey, above-average gelding, effective 6 to 7f, acts on frm, has worn blinkers. Turf high 64.
**D Nicholls [1-12] Gemini Upholstery/GR 1980 Ltd (from J Berry [3-8] Aug 1998).*

RED CITY (IRE) RR 57f 4897[4]
2 b c Mujadil (USA) 7.7f **(70)** - Prim (USA) (Diesis) 9.3f **(69)**
Form - 44
Record 1999 - 1st:0 2nd:0 3rd:0 Ran:2
Win Prizemoney £0 *Total Prizemoney* £792
1999 Turf 0-2: (6f, 7f) (g-s, gd)
Currently fair colt. Turf high 57 (began Oct).
**R Hannon [0-2] Terry Neill.*

RED DECEMBER (IRE) BHB 49f **RR 58?f** 747[14]
3 b g Soviet Lad (USA) 9.4f **(63)** - Late Date (Goldhill) 8.5f **(55)**
Form - 00
Record 1999 - 1st:0 2nd:0 3rd:0 Ran:2
Pre1999 - 1st:0 2nd:0 3rd:0 Ran:2
1999 Turf 0-2: (8f, 11f) (g-s, g-f)
Scopey, fair gelding. Turf high 30. **A P Jarvis [0-4] Mrs Ann Jarvis.*

RED DELIRIUM BHB 66f **RR 69f** 5033[17]
3 b g Robellino (USA) 9.5f **(68)** - Made of Pearl (USA) (Nureyev (USA)) 8.7f **(78)**
Form - 000005080
Record 1999 - 1st:0 2nd:0 3rd:0 Ran:9
Pre1999 - 1st:1 2nd:2 3rd:0 Ran:11
Win Prizemoney £4,581 *Total Prizemoney* £7,142
Wins * 1998 May Goodwo (G-F) 6f 88+ <
1999 Turf 0-9: (7f 6, 8f 3) (g-s, gd 2, g-f 3, frm 3)
Average gelding, effective 6 to 7f, best at 7f, acts on g-f to frm, best on g-f, has worn blinkers. Turf high 72.
**R Hannon [1-20] Terry Neill.*

REDEPLOY BHB 50f **RR 49f** 3808[10]
3 b c Deploy 11.4f **(67)** - Baino Clinic (USA) (Sovereign Dancer (USA)) 11.2f **(68)**
Form - 770
Record 1999 - 1st:0 2nd:0 3rd:0 Ran:3
Pre1999 - 1st:0 2nd:0 3rd:0 Ran:3
1999 Turf 0-3: (12f, 14f, 16f) (g-f, frm 2)
Lengthy, moderate colt. Turf high 49 (began Jly).
**B R Millman [0-6] Take Six.*

RED GUARD BHB 76f **RR 66f** 1400[2]
5 ch g Soviet Star (USA) 8.6f **(74)** - Zinzara (USA) (Stage Door Johnny) 10.3f **(84)**
Form - 42
Record 1999 - 1st:0 2nd:1 3rd:0 Ran:2
Pre1999 - 1st:0 2nd:1 3rd:3 Ran:9

Win Prizemoney £0 *Total Prizemoney £5,104*
1999 Turf 0-2: (10f 2) (gd, frm)
Average gelding. Turf high 66. Consistent.
**J T Gifford [1-12] L A Hooper (from G Wragg [0-9] Aug 1997).*

RED HEATHER BHB 35f **RR 35f** 3944[11]
2 b f Mistertopogigo (IRE) - That's Rich (Hot Spark) 7.6f **(62)**
Form - 000
Record 1999 - 1st:0 2nd:0 3rd:0 Ran:3
1999 Turf 0-3: (7f 3) (g-f, frm, hrd)
Currently very moderate filly. Turf high 35 (began Jly).
**J Berry [0-3] The Red Shirt Brigade Ltd.*

RED KING BHB 45f40a **RR 59f 40a** 5158[17]
2 b c King Among Kings 7.4f **(49)** - Market Blues (Porto Bello) 8.9f **(43)**
Form - 00770
Record 1999 - 1st:0 2nd:0 3rd:0 Ran:5
1999 Turf 0-5: (6f, 7f, 8f 3) (gd 3, frm, hrd)
Fair colt. Turf high 59 (began Aug).
**J Berry [0-5] The Red Shirt Brigade Ltd.*

RED LETTER BHB 85f **RR 82f** 4599[10]
2 b f Sri Pekan (USA) - Never Explain (IRE) **(79f)** (Fairy King (USA)) 7.7f **(59)**
Form - 17840
Record 1999 - 1st:1 2nd:0 3rd:0 Ran:5
Win Prizemoney £5,680 *Total Prizemoney £6,388*
Wins * 1999 Jun Ascot (G-F) 6f 82 <
1999 Turf 1-5: (6f 1-4, 7f) (gd 2, g-f 1-2, frm)
Decent filly. Turf high 82 (1st run) - 1st of 9 getting 7lb from Lady Sarka (19 Jun Ascot RF 2138). Made a winning debut in a decent race at Ascot in June, but has been very disappointing since.
**R Hannon [1-5] Terry Neill.*

RED LION BHB 93f **RR 87f** 5040[7]
3 ch g Lion Cavern (USA) 7.5f **(74)** - Fleur Rouge (Pharly (FR)) 9.8f **(68)**
Form - 15081055007
Record 1999 - 1st:2 2nd:0 3rd:0 Ran:11
Pre1999 - 1st:2 2nd:0 3rd:1 Ran:6
Win Prizemoney £19,383 *Total Prizemoney £21,413*
Wins * 1999 Jly Yarmou (FRM) H 6f 93 95
*** 1999** Jun Leices (GD) 6f 101+ <
* 1998 Jun Windso (GD) 5f 83
* 1998 May Redcar (G-F) 5f 89
1999 Turf 2-11: (5f, 6f 2-10) (g-s 2, gd 2, g-f 2-5, frm 2)
Scopey, useful gelding, effective 6f, acts on g-f. Turf high 101 - also 1st of 6 from Sailing Shoes (1 Jun Leicester RF 1646). He goes well when fresh and seems suited by six furlongs nowadays.
**J W Payne [4-17] R G Gibney.*

RED MAY (IRE) BHB 62f60a **RR 64f 60a** 4922[4]
3 b br f Persian Bold 10f **(69)** - Stay That Way (Be My Guest (USA)) 9.3f **(67)**
Form - 45578224404
Record 1999 - 1st:0 2nd:2 3rd:0 Ran:11
Pre1999 - 1st:0 2nd:0 3rd:0 Ran:2
Win Prizemoney £0 *Total Prizemoney £2,664*
1999 Turf 0-10: (10f 2, 12f 8) (gd 2, g-f 3, frm 5) 1999 AW 0-1: (12f) (Fibr)
Workmanlike, average filly, effective 12f, acts on gd to frm, best on g-f, prefers tight tracks. Turf high 69 - 5th of 10 giving 6lb to Enfilade (5 May Chester 12f g-f RF 1047). Consistent.
**R Hannon [0-13] Terry Neill.*

RED MITTENS BHB 52f **RR 57f** 4716[13]
2 ch f Wolfhound (USA) 7.3f **(71)** - Red Gloves (Red God) 8.5f **(65)**
Form - 5600
Record 1999 - 1st:0 2nd:0 3rd:0 Ran:4
1999 Turf 0-4: (5f, 6f 3) (g-s, gd, frm 2)
Fair filly. Turf high 57. **Martyn Wane [0-4] Mrs H Wane.*

RED N' SOCKS (USA) BHB 85f **RR 81f** 5139[7]
2 ch c Devil's Bag (USA) 9.3f **(73)** - Racing Blue (Reference Point) 6.8f **(70)**
Form - 44517
Record 1999 - 1st:1 2nd:0 3rd:0 Ran:5
Win Prizemoney £3,392 *Total Prizemoney £3,873*
Wins * 1999 Oct Yarmou (G-F) H 8f 76 81+ <
1999 Turf 1-5: (7f 3, 8f 1-1, 10f) (gd, g-f 1-1, frm 3)
Decent colt. Turf high 81 (began Aug) - 1st of 14 giving 4lb to Polar Red (19 Oct Yarmouth RF 4950). Bettered three moderate efforts over seven furlongs when winning over a mile at Yarmouth in October. **J L Dunlop [1-5] Mrs H Focke.*

REDOUBLE BHB 58f57a **RR 62f 57a** 4946[5]
3 b c First Trump - Sunflower Seed (Mummy's Pet) 7.7f **(60)**
Form - 052470035455
Record 1999 - 1st:0 2nd:1 3rd:1 Ran:11
Pre1999 - 1st:0 2nd:1 3rd:2 Ran:9
Win Prizemoney £0 *Total Prizemoney £3,335*
1999 Turf 0-10: (8f, 9f 2, 10f 3, 12f 3, 14f) (sft, gd 3, g-f 4, frm 2) 1999 AW 0-1: (7f) (Equi)
Strong, average colt, effective 7 to 8f, acts on g-f to frm. Turf high 70. Consistent.
**N Hamilton [0-8] Normandy Developments (London) (from R Hannon [0-12] May 1999).*

REDOUBTABLE (USA) BHB 79f72a **RR 79f 72a** 3663[20]
8 b h Grey Dawn II 6.8f **(76)** - Seattle Rockette (USA) (Seattle Slew (USA)) 9.4f **(76)**
Form - 00306262702201325405743O
Record 1999 - 1st:1 2nd:5 3rd:3 Ran:24
Pre1999 - 1st:6 2nd:3 3rd:4 Ran:37
Win Prizemoney £45,211 *Total Prizemoney £93,167*
Wins * 1999 May Thirsk (G-S) H 6f 72 79
* 1998 Jun Newcas (SFT) H 7f 72 77
* 1998 May Ayr (G-F) H 7f 68 69
* 1998 *Jan Lingfi (STD) H 7f 67 73+*
* 1997 *Dec Wolver (STD) H 6f 60 65+*
1999 Turf 1-15: (6f 1-6, 7f 8, 8f) (g-s 2, gd 1-6, g-f 3, frm 4) 1999 AW 0-9: (6f 5, 7f 2, 8f 2) (Equi 3, Fibr 6)
Above-average horse, effective 6 to 8f, best at 7f, acts on g-s to frm - acts on Equi, has worn blinkers, does well at Ayr and Lingfield and likes Thirsk and Newcastle. Turf high 81 - 3rd of 13 giving 8lb to Persian Fayre (20 May Ayr 7f gd RF 1340) - also 1st of 18 giving 12lb to Young Bigwig (15 May Thirsk RF 1251). AW high 73 - 2nd of 8 getting 17lb from Welville (27 Feb Lingfield 8f Equi RF 0376). He is an effective sort on turf and sand, but although he has made the frame on several occasions, his only victory came with give in the ground at Thirsk in May.
**D W Chapman [5-49] David Chapman (from R Hannon [2-12] Aug 1994).*

RED PRAIRIE (USA) BHB 98f **RR 99f** 4443[5]
3 b c El Prado (IRE) 8f **(74)** - Kates Delimma (USA) (Tank's Prospect (USA))
Form - 285330245
Record 1999 - 1st:0 2nd:2 3rd:2 Ran:9
Pre1999 - 1st:3 2nd:0 3rd:2 Ran:8
Win Prizemoney £22,489 *Total Prizemoney £54,824*
Wins * 1998 Aug York (G-F) L 5f 93 <
* 1998 May Pontef (G-F) 6f 82
* 1998 May Hamilt (G-S) 5f 78
1999 Turf 0-9: (5f 8, 6f) (g-s, gd 2, g-f 2, frm 4)
Strong, very useful colt, effective 5f, acts on g-f to frm, best on frm, has worn blinkers. Turf high 106 - 5th of 9 getting 4lb from Proud Native (22 May Kempton 5f frm RF 1395). Consistent. Stood up well to a busy juvenile season, and ran a blinder to finish runner-up to Rambling Bear in the Palace House on his return. Highly tried since, he generally performed with credit but could not get his head in front. Sold for 55,000 gns at Tattersalls in October.
**M L W Bell [3-17] Terry Neill.*

RED RAJA BHB 55f50a **RR 59f 50a** 3793[6]
6 b g Persian Heights 10.5f **(61)** - Jenny Splendid (John Splendid) 8.1f **(62)**
Form - 1031U456
Record 1999 - 1st:2 2nd:0 3rd:1 Ran:8
Pre1999 - 1st:0 2nd:1 3rd:0 Ran:11
Win Prizemoney £4,077 *Total Prizemoney £4,934*
Wins * 1999 Jun Lingfi (G-S) H 16f 55 59
*** 1999** *Jan Lingfi (STD) H 16f 52 60 <*
1999 Turf 1-4: (14f, 16f 1-1, 18f, 20f) (g-s 1-1, g-f 2, frm) 1999 AW 1-4: (16f 1-4) (Equi 1-4)

Fair gelding, effective 14 to 16f, best at 16f, acts on g-s to frm - acts on Equi, prefers left handed tracks, favours tight tracks. Turf high 59 (1st run) - 1st of 12 giving 23lb to Coleridge (2 Jun Lingfield RF 1685). AW high 60 (1st run) - 1st of 10 giving 4lb to Padauk (14 Jan Lingfield RF 0094). Inconsistent. Better known as a hurdler, he has been running well on the level, particularly at Lingfield. **P Mitchell [5-36] Mrs Mitchell,Mrs Gerber, Cohen.*

RED RAMONA BHB 85f RR 85f 5221[16]

4 b c Rudimentary (USA) 8.2f **(66)** - Apply(Kings Lake (USA)) 10.8f **(67)**
Form - 03080
Record 1999 - 1st:0 2nd:0 3rd:1 Ran:5
Pre1999 - 1st:1 2nd:1 3rd:0 Ran:7
Win Prizemoney £2,406 *Total Prizemoney* £9,023
Wins 1998 Jun Folkes (GD) 12f 75 <
1999 Turf 0-5: (12f 2, 14f 2, 15f) (sft, g-s, gd, g-f, frm)
Strong, useful colt, effective 12 to 14f, best at 12f, acts on g-s to frm. Turf high 92 - 3rd of 17 giving 1lb to Mowbray (27 Jly Goodwood 14f frm RF 3167). Lightly raced in '99, he ran well when third at Goodwood but has been held in competitive affairs since. Suited by hold-up tactics.
**J Akehurst [0-6] A D Spence (from R Charlton [1-6] Oct 1998).*

RED REVOLUTION (USA) RR 63+f 939[3]

2 ch c Explosive Red (CAN) - Braided Way (USA) (Mining (USA))
Form - 3
Record 1999 - 1st:0 2nd:0 3rd:1 Ran:1
Win Prizemoney £0 *Total Prizemoney* £366
1999 Turf 0-1: (5f) (frm)
Currently average colt. **T D Barron [0-1] Harrowgate Bloodstock Ltd.*

RED RISK BHB 25f41a RR 29f 41a 215[9]

4 ch g Risk Me (FR) 8f **(53)** - Red Sails (Town And Country) 8.1f **(68)**
Form - 00
Record 1999 - 1st:0 2nd:0 3rd:0 Ran:2
Pre1999 - 1st:0 2nd:0 3rd:1 Ran:15
Win Prizemoney £0 *Total Prizemoney* £414
1999 AW 0-2: (7f 2) (Fibr 2)
Light-framed, little account gelding. AW high 16.
**S G Knight [0-5] J F Jones (from P W Harris [0-15] Oct 1998).*

RED ROSES (IRE) RR 49f 5165[6]

3 b f Mukaddamah (USA) 7.6f **(74)** - Roses Red (IRE) (Exhibitioner) 8.7f **(61)**
Form - 278850836
Record 1999 - 1st:0 2nd:1 3rd:1 Ran:9
Pre1999 - 1st:0 2nd:0 3rd:0 Ran:1
Win Prizemoney £0 *Total Prizemoney* £1,744
1999 Turf 0-9: (7f, 8f 2, 10f 2, 11f, 12f 3) (sft, g-s, gd 2, g-f 2, frm 3)
Moderate filly, effective 8f, acts on sft, likes left handed tracks, likes tight tracks. Turf high 74 (1st run) - 2nd of 7 to My Tess (27 Apr Nottingham 8f sft RF 0868).
**Don Enrico Incisa [0-5] Don Enrico Incisa (from L M Cumani [0-5] Jly 1999).*

RED SEA RR 112f 3168[4]

3 b c Barathea (IRE) - Up Anchor (IRE) (Slip Anchor) 9.8f **(73)**
Form - 02344
Record 1999 - 1st:0 2nd:1 3rd:1 Ran:5
Pre1999 - 1st:2 2nd:1 3rd:0 Ran:6
Win Prizemoney £38,175 *Total Prizemoney* £101,959
Wins * 1998 Jun Ascot (G-S) G3 6f 105 <
* 1998 May York (GD) 6f 93+
1999 Turf 0-5: (8f, 10f, 12f 3) (gd 2, g-f, frm 2)
Scopey, Group-class colt, effective 6 to 12f, best at 12f, acts on g-s to frm, has worn blinkers, excels at Goodwood and Ascot. Turf high 112 - 4th of 6 to Compton Ace (27 Jly Goodwood 12f frm RF 3168). Not the easiest horse to deal with, he lost his way in 1999 and has left Paul Cole to continue his career in America.
**P F I Cole [2-11] H R H Prince Fahd Salman.*

RED SEPTEMBER BHB 55f RR 60f 4929[5]

2 b c Presidium 7.5f **(56)** - Tangalooma (Hotfoot) 10.5f **(59)**
Form - 40665
Record 1999 - 1st:0 2nd:0 3rd:0 Ran:5
1999 Turf 0-5: (6f 5) (gd, g-f 3, frm)
Average colt. Turf high 60. **G M Moore [0-5] Dr C I Emmerson.*

RED SHIFT (IRE) BHB 33f RR 31f 3968[16]

4 b g Night Shift (USA) 8.1f **(73)** - Histoire Douce (USA) (Chief's Crown (USA)) 9.8f **(72)**
Form - 800000
Record 1999 - 1st:0 2nd:0 3rd:0 Ran:6
Pre1999 - 1st:0 2nd:0 3rd:0 Ran:3
1999 Turf 0-5: (5f 2, 6f, 8f, 10f) (gd, g-f 2, frm, hrd) 1999 AW 0-1: (8f) (Fibr)
Strong, very moderate gelding, has worn blinkers. Turf high 50. Becoming disappointing.
**C R Egerton [0-6] Mrs R F Lowe (from D R C Elsworth [0-2] Spt 1998).*

RED SONNY (IRE) BHB 60f RR 61f 5070[8]

2 ch g Foxhound (USA) - Olivia's Pride (IRE) (Digamist (USA))
Form - 5708
Record 1999 - 1st:0 2nd:0 3rd:0 Ran:4
Win Prizemoney £0 *Total Prizemoney* £216
1999 Turf 0-4: (5f 2, 6f 2) (gd, g-f, frm 2)
Average gelding. Turf high 61.
**J Berry [0-4] The Red Shirt Brigade Ltd.*

RED SUN BHB 50f RR 59f 4401[9]

2 b g Foxhound (USA) - Superetta (Superlative) 7.2f **(56)**
Form - 308660
Record 1999 - 1st:0 2nd:0 3rd:1 Ran:6
Win Prizemoney £0 *Total Prizemoney* £446
1999 Turf 0-6: (5f 2, 6f 2, 7f 2) (g-s, gd 2, frm 3)
Fair gelding. Turf high 59. **J Berry [0-6] Shine Racing.*

REDSWAN BHB 73f68a RR 71f 68a 4240[1]

4 ch g Risk Me (FR) 8f **(53)** - Bocas Rose (Jalmood (USA)) 10.1f **(52)**
Form - 00653155401
Record 1999 - 1st:2 2nd:0 3rd:1 Ran:11
Pre1999 - 1st:1 2nd:1 3rd:1 Ran:6
Win Prizemoney £15,318 *Total Prizemoney* £18,620
Wins * **1999** Spt Doncas (G-F) H 7f 68 71 <
* **1999** Jly Leices (G-F) H 7f 66 67
* 1998 Jun Newmar (GD) C 8f 67+
1999 Turf 2-11: (7f 2-8, 8f 3) (sft, gd 3, g-f 2-2, frm 5)
Leggy, above-average gelding, effective 7 to 8f, best at 7f, acts on g-f to frm, best on frm, excels at Newmarket. Turf high 71 - 1st of 21 getting 10lb from Fallachan (9 Spt Doncaster RF 4240) - also 1st of 6 giving 15lb to Churchill's Shadow (15 Jly Leicester RF 2850). Consistent. Facile winner of a Newmarket claimer in 1998, he ran well in better company this season and got up to win over seven furlongs at Leicester in July. He added to that victory with a success in a well-contested Doncaster handicap afterwards.
**S C Williams [3-17] P Geoghan.*

RED SYMPHONY BHB 54f RR 52f 4810[3]

3 b f Merdon Melody 6.8f **(56)** - Woodland Steps (Bold Owl) 8.5f **(45)**
Form - 080300703
Record 1999 - 1st:0 2nd:0 3rd:2 Ran:9
Pre1999 - 1st:3 2nd:1 3rd:1 Ran:9
Win Prizemoney £7,144 *Total Prizemoney* £9,210
Wins * 1998 Spt Mussel (GD) H 5f 60 72 <
1998 May Mussel (G-S) S 5f 55
1998 Apr Wolver (STD) S 5f 48+
1999 Turf 0-9: (5f 8, 6f) (sft, g-s, gd, g-f 4, frm 2)
Light-framed, fair filly, effective 5f, acts on frm. Turf high 56.
**I Semple [1-13] W Edward (from J Berry [2-5] Jun 1998).*

RED THATCH RR 2493[6]

2 ch c Pelder (IRE) - Straw Castle (Final Straw) 7.9f **(64)**
Form - 06
Record 1999 - 1st:0 2nd:0 3rd:0 Ran:2
1999 Turf 0-2: (6f, 7f) (frm 2)
Currently very poor colt. **G F H Charles-Jones [0-2] George Smith.*

RED TIARA (USA) BHB 62f RR 52f 3749[20]

3 b br f Mr Prospector (USA) 8.6f **(88)** - Heart of Joy (USA) (Lypheor) 12f **(71)**
Form - 040
Record 1999 - 1st:0 2nd:0 3rd:0 Ran:3
Pre1999 - 1st:0 2nd:0 3rd:0 Ran:1
Win Prizemoney £0 *Total Prizemoney* £290
1999 Turf 0-3: (8f 3) (g-f 2, frm)

Well made, fair filly. Turf high 52.
**Sir Michael Stoute [0-4] Cheveley Park Stud.*

RED TOWER RR 59f
3348[2]

4 b g Damister (USA) 9.1f **(66)** - Tower of Ivory (IRE) (Cyrano de Bergerac) 6f **(68)**
Form - 02
Record 1999 - 1st:0 2nd:1 3rd:0 Ran:2
Win Prizemoney £0 *Total Prizemoney* £812
1999 Turf 0-2: (10f, 12f) (frm 2)
Fair gelding. Turf high 59 (began Jly). **L Wells [0-5] High As Kite.*

RED TYPHOON BHB 77f RR 84f
5023[13]

2 ro f Belfort (FR) 6.7f **(53)** - Dash Cascade (Absalom) 7.2f **(58)**
Form - 45406331610
Record 1999 - 1st:2 2nd:0 3rd:2 Ran:11
Win Prizemoney £5,067 *Total Prizemoney* £6,129
Wins * **1999** Oct Lingfi (HVY) C 6f 84+ <
* **1999** Spt Haydoc (G-F) C 6f 67+
1999 Turf 2-10: (5f 3, 6f 2-4, 7f 3) (g-s 1-1, gd 2, g-f 1-4, frm 2, hrd)
1999 AW 0-1: (5f) (Fibr)
Decent filly, effective 6f, acts on g-s. Turf high 84 - 1st of 19 giving 10lb to Diamond Promise (1 Oct Lingfield RF 4671).
**J Berry [2-11] The Red Shirt Brigade Ltd.*

RED VENUS (IRE) BHB 46f58a RR 45f 58a
4604[4]

3 ch f Perugino (USA) - Reflection Time (IRE) (Fayruz)
Form - 5043126410000654
Record 1999 - 1st:2 2nd:1 3rd:1 Ran:14
Pre1999 - 1st:0 2nd:0 3rd:2 Ran:9
Win Prizemoney £4,135 *Total Prizemoney* £6,029
Wins * **1999** *Apr Southw (STD) H 7f 54 61* <
1999 *Jan Southw (STD) S 7f 50*
1999 Turf 0-5: (7f 4, 8f) (gd 2, g-f, frm 2) 1999 AW 2-9: (6f 2, 7f 2-5, 8f, 10f) (Equi 4, Fibr 2-5)
Average filly, effective 7f, - acts on AW, often wears blinkers, likes left handed tracks, likes tight tracks. Turf high 45. AW high 61 - 1st of 16 getting 4lb from Crystal Lass (26 Apr Southwell RF 0857).
**Miss Gay Kelleway [1-10] Inside Track Racing Club (from J Berry [1-13] Feb 1999).*

RED WOLF BHB 54f RR 51df
4992[10]

3 ch g Timeless Times (USA) 6.1f **(56)** - Stealthy (Kind of Hush) 10.1f **(62)**
Form - 600
Record 1999 - 1st:0 2nd:0 3rd:0 Ran:3
1999 Turf 0-3: (7f, 8f, 10f) (gd 2, frm)
Currently fair gelding. Turf high 51 (began Spt).
**J G Given [0-3] K H Benson.*

REDWOOD GROVE (USA) BHB 69f RR 71f
4381[13]

3 b c Woodman (USA) 9.7f **(77)** - Ikebana (IRE) (Sadler's Wells (USA)) 10f **(76)**
Form - 8051660
Record 1999 - 1st:1 2nd:0 3rd:0 Ran:7
Win Prizemoney £3,473 *Total Prizemoney* £3,473
Wins * **1999** Jly Salisb (G-F) 14.1f 77 <
1999 Turf 1-7: (10f, 12f 2, 14f 1-3, 17f) (gd 3, g-f, frm 1-2, hrd)
Scopey, above-average colt, effective 14f, acts on frm, likes tight tracks. Turf high 77 - 1st of 10 getting 15lb from Copernicus (10 Jly Salisbury RF 2715). Benefited from the step up to fourteen furlongs when winning well at Salisbury on what looks to be his favoured fast ground.
**P W Chapple-Hyam [1-7] R E Sangster & A K Collins.*

REEMATNA RR 76+f
5136[8]

2 b f Sabrehill (USA) 8.5f **(64)** - Reem Albaraari (Sadler's Wells (USA)) 10f **(76)**
Form - 8
Record 1999 - 1st:0 2nd:0 3rd:0 Ran:1
1999 Turf 0-1: (7f) (gd)
Currently above-average filly.
**M A Jarvis [0-1] Sheikh Ahmed Al Maktoum.*

REFERENDUM (IRE) BHB 89f RR 96df
4392[27]

5 b h Common Grounds 8.1f **(66)** - Final Decision (Tap On Wood) 10.3f **(65)**
Form - 446000
Record 1999 - 1st:0 2nd:0 3rd:0 Ran:6
Pre1999 - 1st:1 2nd:4 3rd:1 Ran:12
Win Prizemoney £4,513 *Total Prizemoney* £64,707
Wins 1996 Aug Goodwo (GD) 6f 94 <
1999 Turf 0-6: (6f 5, 7f) (gd 3, g-f 2, frm)
Very useful colt, effective 6f, acts on frm. Turf high 96. Inconsistent. Probably best around six furlongs, he did not progress after an encouraging reappearance and is still a shade high in the handicap.
**D Nicholls [0-6] David Nicholls Bloodstock Ltd (from G Lewis [1-12] Oct 1998).*

REFLEX BLUE BHB 89f RR 84df
4818[5]

2 b c Ezzoud (IRE) - Briggsmaid (Elegant Air) 13.2f **(61)**
Form - 2125
Record 1999 - 1st:1 2nd:2 3rd:0 Ran:4
Win Prizemoney £4,503 *Total Prizemoney* £9,239
Wins * **1999** Jly Newmar (G-F) 7f 82 <
1999 Turf 1-4: (7f 1-2, 8f, 10f) (gd, frm 1-3)
Decent colt. Turf high 82 (1st run) (began Jly) - 2nd of 9 to Umistim (11 Jly Newbury 7f frm RF 2742) - also 1st of 8 from Pacino (30 Jly Newmarket RF 3244). Stayed on for the runner-up spot in a Newbury maiden on his debut and went one better at Newmarket. However, he did not impress with his attitude when beaten at Pontefract on his third start.
**J W Hills [1-4] The Jonathawn Q Partnership.*

REFUSE TO LOSE BHB 97f102a RR 98f 102a
4235[9]

5 ch h Emarati (USA) 6.6f **(63)** - Petrol (Troy) 10.4f **(68)**
Form - 12731000
Record 1999 - 1st:1 2nd:1 3rd:1 Ran:7
Pre1999 - 1st:5 2nd:5 3rd:0 Ran:19
Win Prizemoney £122,039 *Total Prizemoney* £160,447
Wins * **1999** Jly Ascot (G-F) H 8f 95 98 <
* 1998 *Nov Wolver (STD) L 9.4f 98* <
* 1998 Jun Ascot (G-S) H 8f 83 95
* 1998 *May Lingfi (STD) H 8f 90 98* <
* 1998 *Feb Lingfi (SLW) H 8f 76 89*
* 1996 Oct Leices (GD) 6f 73+
1999 Turf 1-5: (7f, 8f 1-4) (gd 1-4, g-f) 1999 AW 0-2: (10f 2) (Equi 2)
Very useful colt, effective 7 to 10f, acts on gd to frm - acts on AW, best on Equi, likes left handed tracks, prefers tight tracks, and excels at Wolverhampton and Lingfield. Turf high 98 - 1st of 10 getting 2lb from Rock Falcon (24 Jly Ascot RF 3087). AW high 98 (1st run) - 2nd of 6 giving 6lb to Pas de Memoires (27 Feb Lingfield 10f Equi RF 0375). Aptly named, this tough front-runner enjoyed another profitable campaign. Effective from seven furlongs to a mile and a quarter, he also showed himself to be suited by sand. Sold in October to race in Saudi Arabia.
**J M P Eustace [6-26] J C Smith.*

REGAL ACADEMY (IRE) BHB 39f RR 37f
4078[4]

5 b m Royal Academy (USA) 7.8f **(77)** - Polistatic (Free State) 8.7f **(61)**
Form - 037704
Record 1999 - 1st:0 2nd:0 3rd:1 Ran:6
Pre1999 - 1st:0 2nd:0 3rd:0 Ran:7
Win Prizemoney £0 *Total Prizemoney* £656
1999 Turf 0-6: (8f, 10f, 11f, 12f 3) (g-f 2, frm 4)
Very moderate filly, effective 12f, acts on g-f to frm, has worn blinkers (extremely effectively). Turf high 46 - 3rd of 11 giving 3lb to Cabcharge Blue (12 May Brighton 12f g-f RF 1175). Consistent.
**C A Horgan [0-13] Mrs B Sumner.*

REGAL BRIDGET BHB 40f RR 42f
4415[12]

4 ch f Gildoran 11.6f **(58)** - Bridge Street Lady (Decoy Boy) 6.7f **(56)**
Form - 4400000
Record 1999 - 1st:0 2nd:0 3rd:0 Ran:7
Pre1999 - 1st:0 2nd:1 3rd:1 Ran:6
Win Prizemoney £0 *Total Prizemoney* £2,443
1999 Turf 0-6: (8f, 10f 4, 12f) (sft, g-s, gd, g-f 2, frm) 1999 AW 0-1: (12f) (Fibr)
Unfurnished, moderate filly, effective 10 to 12f, best at 10f, acts on g-f to frm, best on frm, favours tight tracks. Turf high 58. Inconsistent.
**B A McMahon [0-7] M A Wilkins & J Wilkins (from D R C Elsworth [0-6] Spt 1998).*

REGAL CHARM (IRE) RR 63f 5020[10]
2 b f Sadler's Wells (USA) 11.3f **(87)** - Abury (IRE) (Law Society (USA)) 9.9f **(70)**
Form - 0
Record 1999 - 1st:0 2nd:0 3rd:0 Ran:1
1999 Turf 0-1: (8f) (gd)
Currently average filly. **A G Foster [0-1] R E Sangster.*

REGAL EXIT (FR) BHB 67f **RR 69f** 3806[6]
3 ch g Exit To Nowhere (USA) 8.7f **(77)** - Regalante (Gairloch) 7f **(63)**
Form - 4056356
Record 1999 - 1st:0 2nd:0 3rd:1 Ran:7
Pre1999 - 1st:0 2nd:0 3rd:1 Ran:2
Win Prizemoney £0 *Total Prizemoney* £2,115
1999 Turf 0-7: (7f, 8f 3, 9f, 10f 2) (g-s, gd 3, g-f 2, frm)
Average gelding. Turf high 70. Consistent.
**M L W Bell [0-7] Brian Buckley (from M R Channon [0-2] Oct 1998).*

REGAL GLOW BHB 30f **RR 27f** 3744[18]
3 b c Regal Embers (IRE) - Kimmy's Princess (Prince Sabo) 7.2f **(62)**
Form - 6000
Record 1999 - 1st:0 2nd:0 3rd:0 Ran:4
1999 Turf 0-4: (5f, 7f 2, 8f) (sft, g-f 2, frm)
Workmanlike, little account colt. Turf high 36.
**T Keddy [0-4] Allan Howling.*

REGALO BHB 55f **RR 46f** 2638[12]
4 b c Nalchik (USA) 12.6f **(44)** - Stardrop (Starch Reduced) 11.5f **(52)**
Form - 0
Record 1999 - 1st:0 2nd:0 3rd:0 Ran:1
Pre1999 - 1st:0 2nd:0 3rd:1 Ran:10
Win Prizemoney £0 *Total Prizemoney* £826
1999 Turf 0-1: (5f) (frm)
Workmanlike, moderate colt.
**W de Best-Turner [0-1] The Spanish Connection (from D M Hyde [0-10] May 1998).*

REGAL PHILOSOPHER BHB 88f **RR 91f** 4683[12]
3 b c Faustus (USA) 9.1f **(54)** - Princess Lucy (Local Suitor (USA)) 8.4f **(67)**
Form - 11027420
Record 1999 - 1st:2 2nd:2 3rd:0 Ran:8
Pre1999 - 1st:0 2nd:2 3rd:1 Ran:4
Win Prizemoney £8,230 *Total Prizemoney* £17,187
Wins * 1999 Jun Newcas (G-F) H 8f 83 88 <
*** 1999** May Bath (GD) 8f 84
1999 Turf 2-8: (8f 2-5, 10f 3) (gd 1-3, g-f, frm 1-4)
Well made, useful colt, effective 8 to 10f, best at 10f, acts on gd to frm, best on frm. Turf high 91 - also 1st of 10 giving 7lb to Spy (2 Jun Newcastle RF 1688). Consistent. A brother to the smart Royal Philosopher, he showed ability at two and won his first two starts of last season over a mile. He made no show in the Britannia, but ran well in some decent handicaps. Suited by coming from off the pace. **J W Hills [2-12] Trajan Partners.*

REGAL RAMBLER (CAN) BHB 36f26a **RR 43f 26a** 2653[P]
8 ch g Regal Classic (CAN) - Rushing Rachel (USA) (Breezing On (USA))
Form - P
Record 1999 - 1st:0 2nd:0 3rd:0 Ran:1
Pre1999 - 1st:0 2nd:1 3rd:2 Ran:18
Win Prizemoney £0 *Total Prizemoney* £2,429
1999 AW 0-1: (14f) (Fibr)
Moderate gelding, had worn blinkers. (DEAD)
**L J Barratt [1-27] P L Loake (from G Lewis [0-3] Jly 1993).*

REGAL SONG (IRE) BHB 66f57a **RR 67f 57a** 2048[1]
3 b g Anita's Prince 6f **(62)** - Song Beam (Song) 7.2f **(61)**
Form - 07431
Record 1999 - 1st:1 2nd:0 3rd:1 Ran:5
Pre1999 - 1st:0 2nd:0 3rd:2 Ran:6
Win Prizemoney £2,220 *Total Prizemoney* £3,766
Wins * 1999 Jun Hamilt (GD) 5f 67 <
1999 Turf 1-3: (5f 1-1, 6f 2) (g-f 1-2, frm) 1999 AW 0-2: (6f 2) (Fibr 2)
Workmanlike, average gelding, effective 5 to 6f, acts on gd to g-f, often wears blinkers (extremely effectively). Turf high 67 - 1st of 9 from Blakey (16 Jun Hamilton RF 2048). AW high 50.
**T J Etherington [1-11] Mrs Y Brierley.*

REGAL SPLENDOUR (CAN) BHB 50a **RR 34f** 3565[6]
6 ch g Vice Regent (CAN) 7.3f **(70)** - Seattle Princess (USA) (Seattle Slew (USA)) 9.4f **(76)**
Form - 5626
Record 1999 - 1st:0 2nd:1 3rd:0 Ran:4
Pre1999 - 1st:1 2nd:2 3rd:0 Ran:21
Win Prizemoney £2,427 *Total Prizemoney* £5,527
Wins 1997 *Feb Lingfi (STD) H 8f* 60 62 <
1999 Turf 0-2: (8f 2) (g-f, frm) 1999 AW 0-2: (7f 2) (Fibr 2)
Moderate gelding, effective 8f, acts on frm. Turf high 34 (1st run) (began Jly) - 2nd of 9 getting 9lb from Silver Secret (16 Jly Newmarket 8f frm RF 2881). AW high 43. Inconsistent.
**B A McMahon [0-4] Mrs J McMahon (from J J Bridger [0-11] Spt 1998).*

REGAL THUNDER (USA) BHB 66f **RR 71f** 5227a[8]
5 b h Chief's Crown (USA) 10.2f **(75)** - Summertime Showers (USA) (Raise A Native) 11.2f **(69)**
Form - 8
1999 AW 0-1: (6f) (Dirt)
Very useful colt, has worn blinkers.
**J Canani in USA [0-1] (from Sir Michael Stoute [0-9] Oct 1997).*

REGARDEZ-MOI BHB 64f **RR 65f** 5138[3]
2 b f Distinctly North (USA) 7.4f **(63)** - Tomard (Thatching) 8f **(66)**
Form - 07877366433
Record 1999 - 1st:0 2nd:0 3rd:3 Ran:11
Win Prizemoney £0 *Total Prizemoney* £2,387
1999 Turf 0-10: (5f 5, 6f 2, 7f 2, 8f) (g-s, gd 7, g-f, frm) 1999 AW 0-1: (5f) (Fibr)
Average filly, effective 5 to 7f, acts on gd. Turf high 73 - 3rd of 20 getting 5lb from Castle Sempill (14 Oct Newmarket 7f gd RF 4870).
**A W Carroll [0-11] Mrs B Nash.*

REGENT RR 47f 2880[8]
4 ch g Zafonic (USA) 9f **(83)** - Queen Midas (Glint of Gold) 9.3f **(66)**
Form - 804656408
Record 1999 - 1st:0 2nd:0 3rd:0 Ran:8
Pre1999 - 1st:0 2nd:0 3rd:0 Ran:3
1999 Turf 0-8: (7f, 8f 4, 9f, 10f, 11f) (gd, g-f, frm 5, hrd)
Workmanlike, moderate gelding, effective 8 to 10f, best at 8f, acts on gd to frm, prefers tight tracks. Turf high 56.
**C P Morlock [0-11] P J Morgan.*

REGGIE BUCK (USA) BHB 34f46a **RR 34f 46a** 4539[7]
5 b br g Alleged (USA) 11.8f **(81)** - Hello Memphis (USA) (Super Concorde (USA)) 10.9f **(66)**
Form - 7087
Record 1999 - 1st:0 2nd:0 3rd:0 Ran:3
Pre1999 - 1st:0 2nd:1 3rd:2 Ran:9
Win Prizemoney £0 *Total Prizemoney* £2,521
1999 Turf 0-3: (10f 2, 12f) (g-f 2, frm)
Fair gelding, has worn blinkers. Turf high 34.
**J L Harris [1-13] L Pipe (from R J O'Sullivan [0-6] Mar 1998).*

REGGIE BYRNE RR 2f 4729[12]
3 b g Mon Tresor 7.9f **(60)** - Failand (Kala Shikari) 8.4f **(54)**
Form - 0
Record 1999 - 1st:0 2nd:0 3rd:0 Ran:1
Pre1999 - 1st:0 2nd:0 3rd:0 Ran:1
1999 Turf 0-1: (8f) (g-s)
Currently very poor gelding. **R Dickin [0-2] Mrs Tessa Byrne.*

REINALDO (FR) RR 99f 2857a[2]
7 b h Green Desert (USA) 7.8f **(78)** - Ghariba (Final Straw) 7.9f **(64)**
Form - 32
1999 Turf 0-2: (5f, 6f) (gd 2)
Very useful horse. Turf high 95.
**L Antonacci in ITY [0-1] (from G Botti in ITY [0-3] May 1999).*

REINE DE LA CHASSE (FR) BHB 30a **RR 12f 30a** 5051[6]
7 ch m Ti King (FR) - Hunting Cottage (Pyjama Hunt) 11.1f **(38)**
Form - 06
Record 1999 - 1st:0 2nd:0 3rd:0 Ran:2
1999 Turf 0-2: (12f 2) (gd 2)

Poor mare. Turf high 12 (began Oct).
**N M Babbage [0-2] D G & D J Robinson.*

REKEN BHB 38f **RR 47f** 5058[13]
3 b c Mujtahid (USA) 7.4f **(69)** - Reem Albaraari (Sadler's Wells (USA)) 10f **(76)**
Form - 50000000
Record 1999 - 1st:0 2nd:0 3rd:0 Ran:8
1999 Turf 0-6: (7f, 8f 4, 10f) (gd 3, frm 3) 1999 AW 0-2: (7f, 8f) (Equi, Fibr)
Unfurnished, moderate colt. Turf high 63. (began Spt). Becoming disappointing. **P Burgoyne [0-8] Philip Saunders.*

REMARKABLE STYLE (USA) RR 98f 5175a[6]
4 b f Danzig (USA) 8.1f **(88)** - Ophidian (USA) 00
Form - 40186
1999 Turf 1-5: (5f, 6f 1-3, 7f) (sft, gd, g-f 1-3)
Very useful filly, effective 6f, acts on g-f, often wears blinkers (effectively). Turf high 98 - 1st of 9 giving 3lb to Beckon The King (17 Jly Leopardstown RF 2994a). Inconsistent. She is a useful sprint handicapper, but fully exposed and unlikely to pull up any trees in 2000. **J S Bolger in IRE [3-13] Henryk de Kwiatkowski.*

REMEMBER STAR BHB 28f **RR 15f** 2391[10]
6 ch m Don't Forget Me 9.5f **(66)** - Star Girl Gay (Lord Gayle (USA)) 8.8f **(62)**
Form - 00
Record 1999 - 1st:0 2nd:0 3rd:0 Ran:2
Pre1999 - 1st:0 2nd:0 3rd:0 Ran:4
1999 Turf 0-1: (18f) (g-f) 1999 AW 0-1: (16f) (Fibr)
Poor mare.
**R J Baker [0-7] Duckhaven Stud (from A G Newcombe [0-5] Feb 1999).*

REMURIA (USA) RR 95f 5174a[6]
3 b f Theatrical 11.5f **(78)** - Reloy (USA) (Liloy (FR)) 10f **(85)** -
Form - 21416
1999 Turf 2-5: (9f, 10f 2-2, 12f 2) (sft 1-2, g-s 2, g-f 1-1)
Very useful filly, effective 10f, acts on sft to g-f. Turf high 95 (began Aug) - 1st of 10 from Catherina (2 Oct Curragh RF 4742a) - also 1st of 11 from Sinndiya (5 Spt Curragh RF 4199a). She showed improved form when winning a Listed event at The Curragh in October, seeming well suited by the soft ground. Effective up to a mile and a half, she is unlikely to improve significantly. **J Oxx in IRE [2-7] Sheikh Mohammed.*

RENAISSANCE LADY (IRE) BHB 48f **RR 52f** 4078[11]
3 ch f Imp Society (USA) 7.1f **(63)** - Easter Morning (FR) (Nice Havrais (USA))
Form - 044616P200
Record 1999 - 1st:1 2nd:1 3rd:0 Ran:10
Pre1999 - 1st:0 2nd:0 3rd:0 Ran:2
Win Prizemoney £2,540 *Total Prizemoney* £3,944
Wins * 1999 Jun Bright (G-F) 11.9f 54+ <
1999 Turf 1-10: (7f, 10f 2, 11f, 12f 1-4, 14f, 15f) (sft, g-f 1-4, frm 5)
Scopey, fair filly, effective 12f, acts on g-f, likes tight tracks. Turf high 63 - also 1st of 4 getting 5lb from Vantage Point (14 Jun Brighton RF 1972). Consistent. **T R Watson [1-12] Alan Wright.*

RENAZIG RR 93f 1531a[8]
1805 h Polish Precedent (USA) 9f **(73)** - Renasahaan 00
Form - 8
1999 Turf 0-1: (9f) (g-s)
Currently useful horse. **Mme C Head in FR [0-1].*

RENDITA (IRE) BHB 49f59a **RR 34f 59a** 5053[16]
3 b f Waajib 8.9f **(67)** - Rend Rover (FR) (Monseigneur (USA)) 7.7f **(63)**
Form - 34861002000
Record 1999 - 1st:1 2nd:1 3rd:0 Ran:9
Pre1999 - 1st:0 2nd:0 3rd:1 Ran:2
Win Prizemoney £2,621 *Total Prizemoney* £4,229
Wins * 1999 *Apr Lingfi (STD) H 7f 48 59* <
1999 Turf 0-6: (7f 2, 8f 3, 10f) (gd 2, g-f, frm 3) 1999 AW 1-3: (7f 1-2, 8f) (Equi 1-1, Fibr 2)
Scopey, fair filly, effective 7 to 8f, acts on g-f - acts on Equi, has worn blinkers. Turf high 53 - 2nd of 20 getting 15lb from It's Magic (18 Aug Leicester 8f g-f RF 3749). AW high 59 - 1st of 10 getting 17lb from Compton Akka (1 Apr Lingfield RF 0544). Inconsistent.
**D HaydnJones [1-11] Mrs William Byrne.*

RENDITION BHB 75f **RR 68f** 4812[8]
2 b f Polish Precedent (USA) 9f **(73)** - Rensaler (USA) (Stop The Music (USA)) 9.2f **(71)**
Form - 538
Record 1999 - 1st:0 2nd:0 3rd:1 Ran:3
Win Prizemoney £0 *Total Prizemoney* £766
1999 Turf 0-3: (7f 3) (g-s, gd, frm)
Currently average filly. Turf high 68 (began Aug).
**J H M Gosden [0-3] Cheveley Park Stud.*

RENNYHOLME BHB 33f37a **RR 35f 37a** 936[14]
8 ch g Rich Charlie 5.9f **(50)** - Jacqui Joy (Music Boy) 6.8f **(57)**
Form - 003600
Record 1999 - 1st:0 2nd:0 3rd:1 Ran:6
Pre1999 - 1st:1 2nd:3 3rd:3 Ran:52
Win Prizemoney £2,070 *Total Prizemoney* £7,434
Wins 1996 *Mar Wolver (STD) S 5f 58* <
1999 Turf 0-1: (5f) (frm) 1999 AW 0-5: (5f 2, 6f 2, 7f) (Fibr 5)
Moderate gelding, effective 6f, acts on g-f to frm, has worn blinkers (effectively). AW high 42. He has won only once in his long career, which just about says it all.
**K A Ryan [0-8] The Gloria Darley Racing Partnership (from A B Mulholland [0-14] Apr 1998).*

RENOWN BHB 62f65a **RR 63f 65a** 3959[7]
7 b g Soviet Star (USA) 8.6f **(74)** - Starlet (Teenoso (USA)) 9.9f **(72)**
Form - 1854577
Record 1999 - 1st:1 2nd:0 3rd:0 Ran:7
Pre1999 - 1st:5 2nd:3 3rd:2 Ran:22
Win Prizemoney £22,630 *Total Prizemoney* £27,614

Wins								
	*** 1999**	May Goodwo	(GD)	H	8f	66	69	
	1998	Aug Salisb	(G-F)	H	9.9f	62	68	
	1996	Jun Bright	(FRM)	H	11.9f	64	69	
	1996	*Mar Lingfi*	*(STD)*	*H*	*10f*	*67*	*73*	<
	1995	*Dec Lingfi*	*(STD)*	*H*	*10f*	*65*	*65*	
	1995	*Feb Lingfi*	*(STD)*		*7f*		*51*	

1999 Turf 1-7: (8f 1-2, 9f 4, 10f) (gd 1-3, g-f 2, frm 2)
Above-average gelding, effective 8 to 10f, acts on gd to frm, best on gd, prefers right handed tracks, favours tight tracks. Turf high 69 (1st run) - 1st of 21 getting 10lb from Bold King (19 May Goodwood RF 1334). Getting on in years, he does not have much racing these days, but retains his ability, and seems to go well on undulating tracks.
**I A Balding [1-7] D H Caslon Partners (from Lord Huntingdon [5-22] Aug 1998).*

RENZO (IRE) BHB 60f **RR 60f** 5220[12]
6 b g Alzao (USA) 9.8f **(73)** - Watership (USA) (Foolish Pleasure (USA)) 8.9f **(72)**
Form - 84080000
Record 1999 - 1st:0 2nd:0 3rd:0 Ran:8
Pre1999 - 1st:3 2nd:4 3rd:3 Ran:20
Win Prizemoney £14,996 *Total Prizemoney* £24,395

Wins								
	***** 1998	Nov Doncas	(SFT)	H	16.5f	78	78	
	1997	Spt Kempto	(GD)	H	14.4f	79	86	<
	1996	Nov Redcar	(G-F)	H	11f	77	83	

1999 Turf 0-8: (14f 3, 15f, 16f 3, 17f) (sft, g-s, gd 2, g-f 2, frm 2)
Average gelding, effective 14 to 17f, best at 14f, acts on g-s to frm, has worn blinkers, likes right handed tracks, prefers tight tracks. Turf high 82 - 4th of 10 giving 15lb to Wave of Optimism (23 Apr Sandown 16f g-s RF 0823). Becoming disappointing. He possesses the ability but carries his head awkwardly and is not one to trust entirely. Has fallen considerably in the handicap after a fruitless 99.
**J L Harris [2-16] Cleartherm Ltd (from Mrs A J Perrett [1-13] Oct 1998).*

REPEAT WARNING RR 74f 5198[3]
3 b f Warning 8.1f **(77)** - Reprocolor (Jimmy Reppin) 8.8f **(64)**
Form - 73
Record 1999 - 1st:0 2nd:0 3rd:1 Ran:2
Win Prizemoney £0 *Total Prizemoney* £372
1999 Turf 0-2: (7f, 8f) (gd, g-f)
Well made, currently above-average filly. Turf high 74 (began Oct).
**G Wragg [0-2] Helena Springfield Ltd.*

REPERTORY BHB 107f **RR 107f** 5120a3
6 b g Anshan 8.2f **(63)** - Susie's Baby (Balidar) 7.9f **(63)**
Form - 405600622543
Record 1999 - 1st:0 2nd:2 3rd:1 Ran:12
Pre1999 - 1st:4 2nd:7 3rd:2 Ran:29
Win Prizemoney £59,375 *Total Prizemoney* £119,877
Wins * 1998 Aug Epsom (G-F) H 5f 98 106
* 1998 Jly Currag (G-S) LH 5f 107 <
* 1997 Apr Newbur (G-F) H 5.2f 88 88
1995 May Salisb (GD) 5f 85+
1999 Turf 0-12: (5f 11, 6f) (hvy, sft 2, gd 4, g-f 2, frm 3)
Pattern-class gelding, effective 5 to 6f, best at 5f, acts on hvy to g-f, excels at Newbury. Turf high 107 (1st run) - 4th of 10 giving 4lb to Diableneyev (6 Apr Maisons-Laffitte 6f sft RF 0712a). A real flying machine, he began the season rather disappointingly but generally showed consistent form without getting the rewards.
**M S Saunders [3-33] (from M R Channon [1-8] Oct 1996).*

REPOSE (IRE) BHB 21f **RR 11f** 1260[19]
4 gr f Posen (USA) 8.6f **(59)** - Dream Trader (Auction Ring (USA)) 8.6f **(65)**
Form - 00
Record 1999 - 1st:0 2nd:0 3rd:0 Ran:2
Pre1999 - 1st:0 2nd:0 3rd:0 Ran:8
1999 Turf 0-2: (7f, 8f) (gd, frm)
Neat, poor filly. Turf high 4.
**A B Mulholland [0-2] Ms Janet McLeod (from G R Oldroyd [0-8] Oct 1998).*

REPTON BHB 40f50a **RR 41f 50a** 5066[6]
4 ch g Rock City 8.8f **(62)** - Hasty Key (USA) (Key To The Mint (USA)) 9.4f **(75)**
Form - 330138006
Record 1999 - 1st:1 2nd:0 3rd:1 Ran:7
Pre1999 - 1st:1 2nd:0 3rd:3 Ran:11
Win Prizemoney £4,774 *Total Prizemoney* £5,921
Wins 1999 *Mar Southw (STD) H 12f 47 52*
1998 Jly Redcar (G-S) H 10f 50 58+ <
1999 Turf 0-5: (11f 3, 12f 2) (hvy, g-s, gd 2, g-f) 1999 AW 1-2: (11f, 12f 1-1) (Fibr 1-2)
Leggy, fair gelding, effective 10f, acts on gd, has worn blinkers, likes left handed tracks. Turf high 53. AW high 52. Inconsistent.
**B Smart [0-2] Mrs Julie Martin (from Mrs A Swinbank [2-16] Jun 1999).*

REPUBLIC (IRE) BHB 34f55a **RR 42f 55a** 4938[13]
3 b g Anita's Prince 6f **(62)** - Sweet Finale (Sallust) 8.4f **(63)**
Form - 00630084050
Record 1999 - 1st:0 2nd:0 3rd:1 Ran:11
Pre1999 - 1st:0 2nd:0 3rd:1 Ran:6
Win Prizemoney £0 *Total Prizemoney* £1,098
1999 Turf 0-8: (5f, 6f, 7f 2, 8f 4) (hvy, sft, gd, g-f 2, frm 3) 1999 AW 0-3: (6f 2, 7f) (Fibr 3)
Scopey, moderate gelding, effective 5 to 6f, best at 5f, acts on gd to frm, best on frm. Turf high 55. AW high 19.
**J Hetherton [0-11] Keith West Racing (from R Hannon [0-6] Oct 1998).*

REQUESTOR BHB 62f **RR 59f** 2694[3]
4 br g Distinctly North (USA) 7.4f **(63)** - Bebe Altesse (GER) (Alpenkonig (GER)) 10.8f **(76)**
Form - 080663
Record 1999 - 1st:0 2nd:0 3rd:1 Ran:6
Pre1999 - 1st:0 2nd:3 3rd:2 Ran:8
Win Prizemoney £0 *Total Prizemoney* £6,056
1999 Turf 0-6: (7f, 8f 5) (sft, gd 3, frm 2)
Fair gelding, has worn blinkers. Turf high 68. Consistent.
**J G FitzGerald [0-14] Marquesa de Moratalla.*

RESALAH BHB 80f **RR 80f** 4880[19]
3 ch f Zafonic (USA) 9f **(83)** - Ghzaalh(USA)(Northern Dancer) 9.6f **(80)**
Form - 20
Record 1999 - 1st:0 2nd:1 3rd:0 Ran:2
Pre1999 - 1st:1 2nd:0 3rd:1 Ran:2
Win Prizemoney £3,330 *Total Prizemoney* £6,494
Wins * 1998 Oct Redcar (g-s) 6f 78 <
1999 Turf 0-2: (7f, 8f) (g-f, frm)
Workmanlike, decent filly. Turf high 75 (1st run) (began Jly) - 2nd of 6 getting 11lb from Virtual Reality (17 Jly Warwick 8f g-f RF 2935). **M P Tregoning [1-4] Hamdan Al Maktoum.*

RESEARCH MASTER BHB 60f **RR 62f** 3021[4]
2 br c Primo Dominie 7.2f **(67)** - Nutmeg Point (Nashwan (USA))
Form - 004
Record 1999 - 1st:0 2nd:0 3rd:0 Ran:3
Win Prizemoney £0 *Total Prizemoney* £200
1999 Turf 0-3: (6f 2, 7f) (frm 3)
Currently average colt. Turf high 62.
**P R Chamings [0-3] Twenty Twenty Research.*

RESERVATION (IRE) BHB 71f **RR 71f** 4804[19]
3 ch f Common Grounds 8.1f **(66)** - Chief's Quest (USA) (Chief's Crown (USA)) 9.8f **(72)**
Form - 51400
Record 1999 - 1st:1 2nd:0 3rd:0 Ran:5
Win Prizemoney £3,647 *Total Prizemoney* £4,172
Wins * **1999** Jun Sandow (GD) 7.1f 69+ <
1999 Turf 1-5: (7f 1-3, 8f 2) (gd, g-f 1-3, frm)
Scopey, above-average filly. Turf high 71 - also 1st of 8 getting 5lb from Palawan (12 Jun Sandown RF 1963). Unraced at two, she was the easy winner of a Sandown maiden on her second start before putting in a gallant bid to make all over the same course and distance. Disappointing subsequently.
**A C Stewart [1-5] The Duchess of Roxburghe.*

RESIDUAL VALUE (USA) BHB 103f **RR 100f** 2903[5]
3 b c Lear Fan (USA) 10.4f **(80)** - Riverlyph (USA) (Lyphard (USA)) 9.9f **(72)**
Form - 115
Record 1999 - 1st:2 2nd:0 3rd:0 Ran:3
Pre1999 - 1st:0 2nd:0 3rd:0 Ran:1
Win Prizemoney £10,069 *Total Prizemoney* £10,069
Wins * **1999** Jly Salisb (G-S) 9.9f 97+ <
* **1999** Jun Windso (G-F) 10f 79
1999 Turf 2-3: (10f 2-3) (gd 1-1, g-f, frm 1-1)
Strong, very useful colt. Turf high 100 - 5th of 6 to Rhapsodist (17 Jly Newbury 10f g-f RF 2903) - also 1st of 6 giving 7lb to Annapurna (2 Jly Salisbury RF 2495). A galloping type, he swishes his tail but seems genuine enough. Probably best when forcing the pace, he stays a mile and a quarter and could yet make the jump into Listed class.
**Sir Michael Stoute [2-4] The Thoroughbred Corporation.*

RES JUDICATA (FR) RR 107f 4113a[5]
4 f
Form - 035
1999 Turf 0-3: (10f, 12f, 13f) (hvy, gd 2)
Currently Pattern-class, has worn blinkers. Turf high 107 (began Jly). **J E Pease in FR [0-3].*

RESOUNDING (IRE) BHB 77f **RR 78f** 4731[1]
2 b f Elmaamul (USA) 8.1f **(70)** - Echoing (Formidable (USA)) 9.2f **(63)**
Form - 51
Record 1999 - 1st:1 2nd:0 3rd:0 Ran:2
Win Prizemoney £4,169 *Total Prizemoney* £4,169
Wins * **1999** Oct Nottin (SFT) 6.1f 78 <
1999 Turf 1-2: (6f 1-2) (gd 1-1, frm)
Currently above-average filly. Turf high 78 (began Spt) - 1st of 15 from Dancemma (5 Oct Nottingham RF 4731).
**A C Stewart [1-2] Racing For Gold.*

RESPLENDENT STAR (IRE) BHB 82f87a **RR 85f 87a** 5024[9]
2 b c Northern Baby (CAN) 10.2f **(74)** - Whitethroat (Artaius (USA)) 9f **(69)**
Form - 03210710
Record 1999 - 1st:2 2nd:1 3rd:1 Ran:8
Win Prizemoney £5,812 *Total Prizemoney* £6,830
Wins * **1999** *Spt Southw (STD) 8f 85* <
* **1999** Aug Newcas (FRM) H 7f 80 85 <
1999 Turf 1-7: (6f, 7f 1-4, 8f 2) (gd 2, g-f 2, frm 2, hrd 1-1) 1999 AW 1-1: (8f 1-1) (Fibr 1-1)
Useful colt, effective 7 to 8f, best at 7f, acts on frm to hrd - acts on Fibr, has worn blinkers. Turf high 85 - 1st of 12 giving 22lb to Africa (4 Aug Newcastle RF 3365). (1st run) - 1st of 6 giving 4lb to Storm Prince (28 Spt Southwell RF 4603). Inconsistent. Got off the

mark on fast ground at Newcastle in August despite swerving badly right, but was very impressive in a Southwell novice event on his Fibresand debut in September. He can win again on that surface. **P W Harris [2-8] Resplendent Racing Ltd.*

RESPOND BHB 56f55a **RR 56f 55a** 2195[1]
4 b f Reprimand 8.2f **(63)** - Kina (USA) (Bering) 7.4f **(61)**
Form - 670361
Record 1999 - 1st:1 2nd:0 3rd:1 Ran:6
Pre1999 - 1st:2 2nd:0 3rd:2 Ran:19
Win Prizemoney £7,206 *Total Prizemoney* £8,932
Wins * **1999** Jun Lingfi (GD) H 10f 54 56
* 1998 Jun Salisb (G-F) H 8f 67 74
* 1997 *Dec Lingfi (STD) H 8f 68 78* <
1999 Turf 1-4: (8f, 10f 1-3) (g-s, gd 2, frm 1-1) 1999 AW 0-2: (8f, 12f) (Equi 2)
Leggy, fair filly, effective 8 to 10f, best at 8f, acts on gd to frm, has worn blinkers. Turf high 56. AW high 42. Consistent. A modest handicapper at between eight and ten furlongs, she seems to go well for an inexperienced rider.
**G L Moore [3-25] B V and C J Pennick.*

RESTLESS WAR (FR) RR 108f 714a[2]
3 b c Akarad (FR) 9.7f **(73)** - Restless Girl (FR) (Bolkonski) 7.6f **(64)**
Form - 2
1999 Turf 0-1: (7f) (g-s)
Currently Pattern-class colt. (1st run) - 2nd of 7 to Berkoutchi (9 Apr Maisons-Laffitte 7f g-s RF 0714a). **A Fabre in FR [0-2].*

RESURRECTION (IRE) BHB 25f **RR 20f** 114[14]
4 b f Midyan (USA) 9.9f **(64)** - Tolstoya (Northfields (USA)) 9f **(72)**
Form - 000
Record 1999 - 1st:0 2nd:0 3rd:0 Ran:2
Pre1999 - 1st:0 2nd:0 3rd:0 Ran:8
1999 AW 0-2: (8f, 12f) (Fibr 2)
Light-framed, little account filly.
**M C Chapman [0-6] Mrs N Gidleywright (from R Hannon [0-4] Oct 1997).*

RETALIATOR BHB 69f51a **RR 55f 51a** 5149[10]
3 b f Rudimentary (USA) 8.2f **(66)** - Redgrave Design (Nebbiolo) 8.1f **(75)**
Form - 2031001004750000
Record 1999 - 1st:2 2nd:1 3rd:1 Ran:16
Pre1999 - 1st:1 2nd:0 3rd:3 Ran:8
Win Prizemoney £11,388 *Total Prizemoney* £17,608
Wins * **1999** Jun Cheste (G-F) H 7f 71 76 <
1999 Jun Cheste (SFT) C 6.1f 67+
1998 Jly Leices (GD) H 6f 70
1999 Turf 2-13: (5f, 6f 1-7, 7f 1-5) (g-s 1-2, gd 3, g-f 3, frm 1-4, hrd)
1999 AW 0-3: (6f, 7f 2) (Fibr 3)
Leggy, fair filly, effective 6 to 7f, best at 7f, acts on g-s to frm, best on frm, has worn blinkers, excels at Leicester and Newmarket, likes Chester. Turf high 76 - 1st of 11 giving 5lb to Midnight Orchid (23 Jun Chester RF 2232) - also 1st of 14 giving 1lb to Sweet As A Nut (2 Jun Chester RF 1671). AW high 22 (began Spt). Becoming disappointing.
**P D Evans [1-12] Treble Chance Partnership (from M L W Bell [2-12] Jun 1999).*

RETURN OF AMIN BHB 90f84a **RR 98df 84a** 2335[12]
5 ch h Salse (USA) 10.9f **(71)** - Ghassanah (Pas de Seul) 9.1f **(67)**
Form - 5055500
Record 1999 - 1st:0 2nd:0 3rd:0 Ran:6
Pre1999 - 1st:4 2nd:7 3rd:2 Ran:31
Win Prizemoney £49,114 *Total Prizemoney* £79,694
Wins * 1998 Jun Pontef (SFT) H 6f 85 89 <
* 1997 Jun York (G-S) H 6f 66 78
* 1996 *Nov Southw (STD) H 7f 70 82*
* 1996 Nov Folkes (SFT) H 6.9f 61 68
1999 Turf 0-6: (6f 2, 7f 4) (gd 3, g-f 2, frm)
Very useful colt, effective 6 to 7f, best at 6f, acts on g-s to frm, best on gd, has worn blinkers, excels at York. Turf high 98. Inconsistent. Effective over six or seven furlongs, he ran some fair races last season but was a shade too high in the handicap. Best on easy ground, he is genuine.
**J D Bethell [4-37] Sheikh Amin Dahlawi.*

RETURN TO BASE RR 4325[15]
2 b g Whittingham (IRE) - Isla Bonita (Kings Lake (USA)) 10.8f **(67)**
Form - 0
Record 1999 - 1st:0 2nd:0 3rd:0 Ran:1
1999 Turf 0-1: (5f) (gd)
Currently very poor gelding. **C W Fairhurst [0-1] M R Handy.*

RETURN TO BRIGHTON BHB 21f27a **RR 27f 27a** 3053[11]
7 b m Then Again 7.4f **(52)** - Regency Brighton (Royal Palace) 9f **(56)**
Form - 06780
Record 1999 - 1st:0 2nd:0 3rd:0 Ran:5
Pre1999 - 1st:1 2nd:2 3rd:1 Ran:23
Win Prizemoney £2,837 *Total Prizemoney* £4,821
Wins * 1996 Jun Ripon (G-F) SH 8f 45 47 <
1999 Turf 0-5: (10f 3, 12f 2) (gd 2, g-f 2, frm)
Little account mare, effective 10f, acts on g-f. Turf high 27.
**J M Bradley [1-28] Alan Purvis (from P C Clarke [0-3] May 1995).*

REVENGE RR 71f 3448[4]
3 b g Saddlers' Hall (IRE) 10.5f **(65)** - Classic Heights (Shirley Heights) 10.3f **(74)**
Form - 04
Record 1999 - 1st:0 2nd:0 3rd:0 Ran:2
Win Prizemoney £0 *Total Prizemoney* £273
1999 Turf 0-2: (10f, 12f) (gd, frm)
Workmanlike, currently above-average gelding. Turf high 71 (began Jly). **R T Phillips [0-2] Axom.*

REVERSE CHARGE BHB 24f39a **RR 6f 39a** 3903[8]
7 b g Teenoso (USA) 10.5f **(62)** - Ebb And Flo (Forlorn River) 7.3f **(54)**
Form - 8
Record 1999 - 1st:0 2nd:0 3rd:0 Ran:1
Pre1999 - 1st:0 2nd:0 3rd:0 Ran:4
1999 Turf 0-1: (17f) (frm)
Very poor gelding. **D Nicholls [0-5] Ian Glenton.*

REVIEWING (USA) BHB 80f **RR 78f** 5004[1]
3 ch c Irish River (FR) 9f **(77)** - Be Exclusive (Be My Guest (USA)) 9.3f **(67)**
Form - 31001
Record 1999 - 1st:2 2nd:0 3rd:1 Ran:5
Win Prizemoney £11,828 *Total Prizemoney* £12,484
Wins * **1999** Oct Nottin (GD) H 8.2f 77 78 <
* **1999** Aug Windso (G-F) 8.3f 56+
1999 Turf 2-5: (8f 2-4, 10f) (gd 1-2, g-f, frm 1-2)
Scopey, above-average colt. Turf high 78 - 1st of 13 getting 5lb from Katy Nowaitee (21 Oct Nottingham RF 5004). Unraced at two, he got off the mark in a Windsor maiden on his second start, but was disappointing until gaining a surprise win in a Nottingham handicap. **J H M Gosden [2-5] George Strawbridge.*

REVIVAL RR 66f 4875[9]
2 b f Sadler's Wells (USA) 11.3f **(87)** - Fearless Revival (Cozzene (USA)) 6f **(93)**
Form - 0
Record 1999 - 1st:0 2nd:0 3rd:0 Ran:1
1999 Turf 0-1: (6f) (gd)
Currently average filly. A sister to Pivotal, she should find a maiden over around a mile. **Sir Michael Stoute [0-1] Cheveley Park Stud.*

REVOLUTION BHB 50f **RR 60f** 119[14]
5 b h Suave Dancer (USA) 10.7f **(68)** - Sunny Flower (FR) (Dom Racine (FR)) 9.2f **(62)**
Form - 0
Record 1999 - 1st:0 2nd:0 3rd:0 Ran:1
Pre1999 - 1st:0 2nd:0 3rd:0 Ran:5
Win Prizemoney £0 *Total Prizemoney* £501
1999 AW 0-1: (8f) (Fibr)
Average colt.
**D Nicholls [0-1] W G Swiers (from R J R Williams [0-5] Spt 1998).*

REWARD BHB 52f **RR 15f** 1368[20]
5 gr g Highest Honor (FR) 10.9f **(72)** - Intimate Guest (Be My Guest (USA)) 9.3f **(67)**
Form - 6000
Record 1999 - 1st:0 2nd:0 3rd:0 Ran:4
Pre1999 - 1st:0 2nd:0 3rd:1 Ran:3

Win Prizemoney £0 *Total Prizemoney* £440
1999 Turf 0-4: (5f, 6f, 7f, 10f) (g-s, gd, g-f, frm)
Poor gelding, has worn blinkers. Turf high 57.
**D L Williams [0-5] Berkshire Commercial Components Ltd (from P F I Cole [0-3] Jun 1997).*

REX IS OKAY BHB 70f **RR 70f** 5033[7]
3 ch g Mazilier (USA) 8.5f **(56)** - Cocked Hat Girl (Ballacashtal (CAN)) 5.3f **(50)**
Form - 8808323337
Record 1999 - 1st:0 2nd:1 3rd:4 Ran:10
Pre1999 - 1st:2 2nd:0 3rd:3 Ran:8
Win Prizemoney £12,037 *Total Prizemoney* £18,095
Wins * 1998 Nov Doncas (SFT) H 7f 66 77 <
* 1998 Oct Leices (HVY) H 7f 59 65
1999 Turf 0-10: (5f, 6f, 7f 4, 8f 4) (g-s 4, gd 3, g-f, frm 2)
Workmanlike, above-average gelding, effective 7f, acts on gd, has worn blinkers. Turf high 70 - 3rd of 24 getting 12lb from Canovas Heart (9 Oct York 7f gd RF 4804).
**S R Bowring [2-18] The Belfitt Family.*

REYNOLDS (IRE) BHB 61f **RR 59f** 2907[6]
3 b g Royal Academy (USA) 7.8f **(77)** - In Perpetuity (Great Nephew) 9.9f **(64)**
Form - 866
Record 1999 - 1st:0 2nd:0 3rd:0 Ran:3
Pre1999 - 1st:0 2nd:0 3rd:0 Ran:1
1999 Turf 0-3: (7f 3) (sft, g-f, frm)
Well made, fair gelding. Turf high 59.
**R Charlton [0-4] Lady Rothschild.*

RHAGAAS BHB 106f **RR 115df** 4774a[3]
3 b c Sadler's Wells (USA) 11.3f **(87)** - Darara (Top Ville) 11.7f **(68)**
Form - 23523
Record 1999 - 1st:0 2nd:2 3rd:2 Ran:5
Pre1999 - 1st:1 2nd:0 3rd:0 Ran:1
Win Prizemoney £3,900 *Total Prizemoney* £70,599
Wins 1998 Spt Nottin (GD) 8.2f 94+ <
1999 Turf 0-5: (12f 2, 14f, 15f, 16f) (sft, gd 2, g-f, frm)
Light-framed, high-class colt, often wears blinkers. Turf high 115. Winner of his sole start at two, he did not manage a win in 1999. Stepped up to a mile and a half for his Newmarket reappearance, he looked ill-at-ease on the fast ground, but ran a creditable third behind Montjeu in the French Derby next time. Only fifth in the Queen's Vase over two miles, he ran a bit better when runner-up in the Prix de Lutece, but ended the season by finishing third in a German Group Two.
**S bin Suroor [0-5] (from D R Loder [1-1] Spt 1998).*

RHAPSODIST (USA) BHB 108f **RR 108f** 3983[4]
3 b c Affirmed (USA) 10.3f **(75)** - Secret Rhapsody (USA) (Secreto (USA)) 8.7f **(72)**
Form - 214
Record 1999 - 1st:1 2nd:1 3rd:0 Ran:3
Pre1999 - 1st:1 2nd:2 3rd:1 Ran:5
Win Prizemoney £39,381 *Total Prizemoney* £52,040
Wins * **1999** Jly Newbur (G-F) L 10f 108 <
* 1998 Jun Ascot (SFT) L 7f 87
1999 Turf 1-3: (10f 1-3) (gd, g-f 1-1, frm)
Leggy, Pattern-class colt, effective 7 to 10f, best at 10f, acts on gd to frm, best on frm, has worn blinkers. Turf high 108 - 4th of 8 to Zindabad (28 Aug Windsor 10f frm RF 3983) - also 1st of 6 getting 10lb from Pegnitz (17 Jly Newbury RF 2903). Put up a brave performance to win a Newbury Listed event in July, but has been found out when taking on decent company otherwise.
**J H M Gosden [2-8] H E Sheikh Rashid Al Maktoum.*

RHAPSODY IN BLUE (IRE) BHB 33f **RR 28df** 2237[11]
4 b g Magical Strike (USA) 5.5f **(61)** - Palace Blue (IRE) (Dara Monarch) 8.8f **(59)**
Form - 0
Record 1999 - 1st:0 2nd:0 3rd:0 Ran:1
Pre1999 - 1st:0 2nd:0 3rd:0 Ran:6
1999 Turf 0-1: (11f) (frm)
Leggy, little account gelding.
**Andrew Turnell [0-14] The Eternal Optimists.*

RHAPSODY IN WHITE (IRE) BHB 32f40a **RR 42?f 40a** 3496[8]
5 b g Contract Law (USA) 8.9f **(54)** - Lux Aeterna (Sandhurst Prince) 7.9f **(63)**
Form - 08
Record 1999 - 1st:0 2nd:0 3rd:0 Ran:2
Pre1999 - 1st:1 2nd:1 3rd:2 Ran:11
Win Prizemoney £2,277 *Total Prizemoney* £4,038
Wins 1997 May Bright (FRM) 8f 49+ <
1999 Turf 0-2: (10f, 12f) (g-f, frm)
Moderate gelding, has worn blinkers. (began Jly).
**S E Kettlewell [0-2] J Ross (from M A Jarvis [1-11] Oct 1997).*

RHEINBOLD BHB 59f **RR 60f** 2822[5]
5 br g Never so Bold 7.1f **(62)** - Rheinbloom (Rheingold) 10.4f **(62)**
Form - 2045
Record 1999 - 1st:0 2nd:1 3rd:0 Ran:4
Pre1999 - 1st:1 2nd:2 3rd:2 Ran:17
Win Prizemoney £2,617 *Total Prizemoney* £7,446
Wins 1997 May Mussel (G-S) 12f 64+ <
1999 Turf 0-4: (10f 2, 12f 2) (gd 3, frm)
Average gelding, effective 10f, acts on g-f to frm, likes left handed tracks, favours tight tracks. Turf high 63. Consistent.
**Mrs A E Johnson [0-6] Chasers III (from T J Etherington [1-17] Oct 1998).*

RHODAMINE (IRE) BHB 70f **RR 74f** 4762[4]
2 b c Mukaddamah (USA) 7.6f **(74)** - Persian Empress (IRE) (Persian Bold) 9.3f **(66)**
Form - 00140354
Record 1999 - 1st:1 2nd:0 3rd:1 Ran:8
Win Prizemoney £3,647 *Total Prizemoney* £8,690
Wins * **1999** Jly Newcas (G-F) 6f 73 <
1999 Turf 1-8: (6f 1-3, 7f 2, 8f 3) (gd 2, g-f, frm 1-5)
Above-average colt, effective 6 to 8f, best at 8f, acts on gd to frm. Turf high 74 - 5th of 10 getting 24lb from French Fellow (9 Spt Doncaster 8f g-f RF 4238) - also 1st of 17 giving 2lb to El Dolor (12 Jly Newcastle RF 2754). Held since landing an ordinary Newcastle maiden.
**J L Eyre [1-8] M Gleason.*

RHODE ISLAND (IRE) RR 87f 4524[1]
2 b c Dolphin Street (FR) - Far From Home (Habitat) 9.4f **(70)**
Form - 7441
Record 1999 - 1st:1 2nd:0 3rd:0 Ran:4
Win Prizemoney £3,891 *Total Prizemoney* £4,400
Wins * **1999** Spt Haydoc (SFT) H 6f 80 87 <
1999 Turf 1-4: (6f 1-4) (gd 1-1, frm 3)
Useful colt. Turf high 87 (began Jly) - 1st of 18 giving 2lb to Glendamah (24 Spt Haydock RF 4524).
**N Hamilton [1-1] Mrs John Magnier (from G Lewis [0-3] Spt 1999).*

RHYTHM BAND (USA) RR 105f 2814[1]
3 gr c Cozzene (USA) 10.1f **(87)** - Golden Wave Band (USA) (Dixieland Band (USA)) 7f **(74)**
Form - 1
Record 1999 - 1st:1 2nd:0 3rd:0 Ran:1
Win Prizemoney £6,970 *Total Prizemoney* £6,970
Wins * **1999** Jly Doncas (G-F) 8f 105 <
1999 Turf 1-1: (8f 1-1) (g-f 1-1)
Leggy, currently Pattern-class colt. (1st run) - 1st of 5 getting 9lb from Sunstreak (14 Jly Doncaster RF 2814).
**S bin Suroor [1-1] Godolphin.*

RIBBLE ASSEMBLY BHB 36f **RR 31f** 3864[12]
4 ch g Presidium 7.5f **(56)** - Spring Sparkle (Lord Gayle (USA)) 8.8f **(62)**
Form - 100000000
Record 1999 - 1st:1 2nd:0 3rd:0 Ran:9
Pre1999 - 1st:1 2nd:3 3rd:1 Ran:17
Win Prizemoney £5,269 *Total Prizemoney* £8,401
Wins * **1999** Mar Hamilt (HVY) 8.3f 62 <
1998 May Carlis (G-S) H 8f 52 60
1999 Turf 1-9: (7f, 8f 1-4, 9f 2, 11f 2) (hvy 1-2, gd 2, g-f 2, frm 2, hrd)
Workmanlike, very moderate gelding, effective 8f, acts on hvy to frm, has worn blinkers, likes tight tracks. Turf high 62 (1st run) - 1st of 7 giving 16lb to Nany's Affair (29 Mar Hamilton RF 0502). Inconsistent. He seems to go especially well when fresh, and was winning first time out for the second year in succession when

bolting home in a Hamilton classified stakes in March.
**K A Ryan [1-18] Swan At Whalley Partnership (from R A Fahey [1-8] May 1998).*

RIBBLE PRINCESS BHB 63f **RR 62f** 503[9]

4 b f Selkirk (USA) 7.9f **(76)** - Ricochet Romance (USA) (Shadeed (USA)) 8.2f **(70)**
Form - 0
Record 1999 - 1st:0 2nd:0 3rd:0 Ran:1
Pre1999 - 1st:0 2nd:0 3rd:1 Ran:3
Win Prizemoney £0 *Total Prizemoney* £761
1999 Turf 0-1: (11f) (hvy)
Leggy, average filly. **K A Ryan [0-4] Swan At Whalley Partnership.*

RIBBON LAKE (IRE) BHB 72f **RR 74f** 4899[13]

2 b f Namaqualand (USA) - Topmost (IRE) (Top Ville) 11.7f **(68)**
Form - 321680
Record 1999 - 1st:1 2nd:1 3rd:1 Ran:6
Win Prizemoney £2,937 *Total Prizemoney* £4,241
Wins * 1999 Jly Lingfi (G-F) 6f 74 <
1999 Turf 1-6: (6f 1-3, 7f 2, 8f) (gd 2, g-f, frm 1-3)
Above-average filly, effective 6 to 7f, best at 6f, acts on g-f to frm, best on frm. Turf high 74 - 1st of 18 getting 8lb from Our Timmy (7 Jly Lingfield RF 2624). **Mrs P N Dutfield [1-6] D Bevan.*

RIBERAC BHB 80f **RR 84df** 5160[14]

3 b f Efisio 7.7f **(69)** - Ciboure (Norwick (USA)) 7.2f **(56)**
Form - 0360
Record 1999 - 1st:0 2nd:0 3rd:1 Ran:4
Pre1999 - 1st:1 2nd:0 3rd:1 Ran:5
Win Prizemoney £3,241 *Total Prizemoney* £6,390
Wins 1998 Jly Windso (G-F) 5f 74+ <
1999 Turf 0-4: (6f 4) (frm 4)
Workmanlike, decent filly, effective 5 to 6f, acts on gd to frm. Turf high 84 (began Jly). Consistent.
**M Johnston [0-1] & Mrs G Middlebrook (from W J Haggas [1-8] Aug 1999).*

RICCARTON BHB 50f **RR 47f** 4174[7]

6 b g Nomination 7.3f **(57)** - Legendary Dancer (Shareef Dancer (USA)) 9.9f **(73)**
Form - 4645707
Record 1999 - 1st:0 2nd:0 3rd:0 Ran:7
Pre1999 - 1st:4 2nd:2 3rd:6 Ran:26
Win Prizemoney £12,681 *Total Prizemoney* £18,986
Wins 1998 Jly Doncas (G-F) H 10.3f 60 61 <
1998 Jun Hamilt (GD) H 9.2f 56 57
1998 Apr Redcar (SFT) H 11f 52 55+
1997 Aug Beverl (GD) H 9.9f 46 52
1999 Turf 0-7: (9f 2, 10f 5) (gd, g-f 4, frm 2)
Moderate gelding, effective 9 to 11f, best at 10f, acts on sft to frm, best on g-f, has worn blinkers, likes right handed tracks, excels at Hamilton. Turf high 59 (1st run) - 4th of 17 giving 4lb to Sunshine Boy (1 Jun Leicester 10f g-f RF 1647). Consistent.
**J M Bradley [0-10] Terry Warner (from P Calver [4-26] Oct 1998).*

RICHARD ANSDELL BHB 72f **RR 76f** 4923[5]

2 gr g Absalom 7.1f **(56)** - Reina (Homeboy) 6.6f **(55)**
Form - 1447005
Record 1999 - 1st:1 2nd:0 3rd:0 Ran:7
Win Prizemoney £2,290 *Total Prizemoney* £2,290
Wins * 1999 *Apr Wolver (STD) 5f 68* <
1999 Turf 0-4: (5f 3, 6f) (g-f, frm 3) 1999 AW 1-3: (5f 1-1, 6f 2) (Fibr 1-3)
Above-average gelding, effective 5f, - acts on Fibr, has worn blinkers. Turf high 76. AW high 68 (1st run) - 1st of 11 giving 9lb to Kirsch (29 Apr Wolverhampton RF 0922).
**N P Littmoden [1-7] Richard Green (Fine Paintings).*

RICH BALLERINA (USA) BHB 59a **RR 42f 59a** 454[F]

3 b f Strike The Gold (USA) 8f **(79)** - Corps de Ballet (Green Dancer (USA)) 10.3f **(74)**
Form - 12433F
Record 1999 - 1st:0 2nd:1 3rd:2 Ran:5
Pre1999 - 1st:1 2nd:0 3rd:0 Ran:2
Win Prizemoney £2,827 *Total Prizemoney* £3,930
Wins 1998 *Dec Southw (STD) 7f 75* <
1999 AW 0-5: (7f 3, 8f 2) (Fibr 5)
Average filly, effective 7f, - acts on Fibr, has worn blinkers, likes left handed tracks, likes tight tracks. AW high 63.
**D Carroll [0-5] Miss G O'Ferrall (from D Carroll [1-1] Dec 1998).*

RICH DOMINION BHB 45f38a **RR 39f 38a** 1062[7]

3 ch g First Trump - Tiszta Sharok (Song) 7.2f **(61)**
Form - 74587
Record 1999 - 1st:0 2nd:0 3rd:0 Ran:5
Pre1999 - 1st:0 2nd:0 3rd:0 Ran:8
1999 Turf 0-2: (7f, 8f) (sft, frm) 1999 AW 0-3: (6f, 8f, 9f) (Fibr 3)
Workmanlike, very moderate gelding, has worn blinkers. Turf high 39. AW high 21. Becoming disappointing.
**J D Bethell [0-13] Mrs J E Vickers.*

RICH GLOW BHB 31f45a **RR 33f 45a** 707[9]

8 b g Rich Charlie 5.9f **(50)** - Mayglow (Sparkling Boy) 5f **(36)**
Form - 0
Record 1999 - 1st:0 2nd:0 3rd:0 Ran:1
Pre1999 - 1st:6 2nd:8 3rd:4 Ran:92
Win Prizemoney £20,529 *Total Prizemoney* £36,611
Wins * 1997 May Ayr (SFT) H 5f 46 49
* 1996 Aug Pontef (G-F) H 5f 60 58 <
* 1996 Jly Ayr (G-S) H 5f 53 54
* 1995 Jun Ayr (FRM) H 5f 54 55
* 1995 Jun Ayr (G-F) H 5f 50 47
* 1995 May Ayr (G-F) H 5f 47 47
1999 Turf 0-1: (5f) (gd)
Very moderate gelding, has worn blinkers.
**N Bycroft [6-93] N Bycroft.*

RICH IN LOVE (IRE) BHB 84f **RR 78f** 4270[8]

5 b m Alzao (USA) 9.8f **(73)** - Chief's Quest (USA) (Chief's Crown (USA)) 9.8f **(72)**
Form - 42403564078
Record 1999 - 1st:0 2nd:1 3rd:1 Ran:11
Pre1999 - 1st:4 2nd:6 3rd:0 Ran:31
Win Prizemoney £23,236 *Total Prizemoney* £44,664
Wins * 1998 Aug Yarmou (G-F) H 7f 72 78 <
* 1998 Jly Ascot (G-F) H 7f 65 71
* 1997 Aug Yarmou (G-F) H 7f 69 75
* 1996 Jun Ripon (G-F) 6f 73
1999 Turf 0-11: (6f, 7f 7, 8f 2, 9f) (gd 4, g-f 3, frm 4)
Above-average filly, effective 7f, acts on gd to g-f, best on gd, has worn blinkers. Turf high 97. Inconsistent. She set a personal best when finishing second in a listed event at Lingfield in May, but cut little ice thereafter. Effective from six furlongs to a mile, she prefers a sound surface but is inconsistent.
**C A Cyzer [4-42] R M Cyzer.*

RICH VEIN (IRE) BHB 66f **RR 54f** 5049[14]

2 b c Up and At 'em - Timissara (USA) (Shahrastani (USA)) 8.8f **(72)**
Form - 500
Record 1999 - 1st:0 2nd:0 3rd:0 Ran:3
1999 Turf 0-3: (7f 2, 8f) (g-s, gd 2)
Currently fair colt. Turf high 54 (began Oct).
**S P C Woods [0-3] Arashan Ali.*

RIDDLE BHB 47f **RR 44f** 307[8]

3 ch f Superlative 8.8f **(57)** - Griddle Cake (IRE) **(65df)** (Be My Guest (USA)) 9.3f **(67)**
Form - 0064420388
Record 1999 - 1st:0 2nd:1 3rd:1 Ran:7
Pre1999 - 1st:0 2nd:0 3rd:0 Ran:6
Win Prizemoney £0 *Total Prizemoney* £766
1999 AW 0-7: (5f, 6f 2, 7f 4) (Equi 6, Fibr)
Light-framed, moderate filly, effective 6 to 7f, - acts on Equi, often wears blinkers (very effectively), likes left handed tracks, likes tight tracks. AW high 52 - 2nd of 11 getting 5lb from Glastonbury (12 Jan Lingfield 7f Equi RF 0079). **P D Evans [0-13] P D Evans.*

RIDDLESDOWN (IRE) BHB 93f **RR 86f** 5062[1]

2 ch c Common Grounds 8.1f **(66)** - Neat Dish (CAN) (Stalwart (USA)) 9.9f **(78)**
Form - 321
Record 1999 - 1st:1 2nd:1 3rd:1 Ran:3
Win Prizemoney £2,489 *Total Prizemoney* £4,026
Wins * 1999 Oct Bath (SFT) 8f 85 <

1999 Turf 1-3: (8f 1-3) (g-s, gd 1-1, frm)
Currently useful colt. Turf high 86 (began Spt) - 2nd of 14 giving 5lb to Al Ghabraa (15 Oct Redcar 8f frm RF 4907) - also 1st of 13 from Mbele (26 Oct Bath RF 5062). Has a round knee action, and should make up into a decent middle-distance handicapper at three. **S P C Woods [1-3] The Storm Again Syndicate.*

RIDE THE TIGER (IRE) RR 45f 3553[7]
2 ch c Imp Society (USA) 7.1f **(63)** - Krisdaline (USA) (Kris S (USA)) 7.9f **(71)**
Form - 007
Record 1999 - 1st:0 2nd:0 3rd:0 Ran:3
1999 Turf 0-3: (6f, 7f 2) (gd 2, g-f)
Currently moderate colt. Turf high 45.
**M D I Usher [0-3] M S C Thurgood.*

RIDGECREST BHB 57f **RR 49f** 5064[3]
2 ch c Anshan 8.2f **(63)** - Lady Sabo **(37?f 42a)** (Prince Sabo) 7.2f **(62)**
Form - 003
Record 1999 - 1st:0 2nd:0 3rd:1 Ran:3
Win Prizemoney £0 *Total Prizemoney* £292
1999 Turf 0-3: (5f 2, 6f) (gd, frm, hrd)
Currently average colt. Turf high 49. **R Ingram [0-3] P M Mooney.*

RIDGEWAY (IRE) BHB 105f **RR 110?f** 1542[4]
4 b c Indian Ridge 7.6f **(74)** - Regal Promise (Pitskelly) 8.5f **(53)**
Form - 4
Record 1999 - 1st:0 2nd:0 3rd:0 Ran:1
Pre1999 - 1st:1 2nd:1 3rd:0 Ran:5
Win Prizemoney £4,337 *Total Prizemoney* £10,734
Wins * 1998 Apr Nottin (G-S) 8.2f 90 <
1999 Turf 0-1: (8f) (gd)
Well made, Group-class colt. He must have had his problems as he has been so lightly raced, we have never really seen the best of him. **G Wragg [1-6] Mollers Racing.*

RIDGEWOOD BAY (IRE) BHB 42f **RR 49f** 5192[14]
2 b f Ridgewood Ben - Another Baileys **(49f 55a)** (Deploy)
Form - 00060000
Record 1999 - 1st:0 2nd:0 3rd:0 Ran:8
Win Prizemoney £0 *Total Prizemoney* £87
1999 Turf 0-8: (5f, 6f 3, 7f, 8f 3) (g-s, gd 4, g-f 2, frm)
Moderate filly. Turf high 49. Inconsistent.
**J C Fox [0-8] John Homer Racing.*

RIDGEWOOD RUBY (IRE) BHB 62f **RR 56f** 1923[7]
4 b f Indian Ridge 7.6f **(74)** - Glen Kella Manx (Tickled Pink) 6.5f **(59)**
Form - 07
Record 1999 - 1st:0 2nd:0 3rd:0 Ran:2
Pre1999 - 1st:0 2nd:0 3rd:2 Ran:8
Win Prizemoney £0 *Total Prizemoney* £1,595
1999 Turf 0-2: (5f, 6f) (g-f, frm)
Fair filly, effective 7 to 8f, best at 7f, acts on g-s to gd, best on gd. Turf high 47. Becoming disappointing.
**D R C Elsworth [0-2] D R C Elsworth (from J Oxx in IRE [0-8] Oct 1998).*

RIFIFI BHB 73f78a **RR 63f 78a** 2156[12]
6 ch g Aragon 7.7f **(58)** - Bundled Up (USA) (Sharpen Up) 8.3f **(67)**
Form - 814720080
Record 1999 - 1st:0 2nd:1 3rd:0 Ran:7
Pre1999 - 1st:8 2nd:0 3rd:2 Ran:37
Win Prizemoney £42,107 *Total Prizemoney* £47,744

Wins								
* 1998	*Dec*	*Lingfi*	*(STD)*	*H*	*7f*	*73*	*78*	
* 1998	Aug	Sandow	(G-F)	H	5f	69	72	
* 1998	Aug	Newbur	(G-F)	H	6f	71	72	
* 1997	Aug	Goodwo	(G-F)	H	6f	71	80	<
* 1997	Aug	Newmar	(GD)	H	6f	64	71	
* 1997	Jun	Windso	(G-F)	H	6f	58	61	
* 1997	*Feb*	*Lingfi*	*(STD)*	*H*	*5f*	*60*	*66*	
* 1997	*Feb*	*Lingfi*	*(STD)*		*5f*		*66*	

1999 Turf 0-5: (6f 5) (g-f, frm 4) 1999 AW 0-2: (7f 2) (Equi 2)
Above-average gelding, effective 5 to 7f, best at 6f, acts on g-s to g-f - acts on Equi, and excels at Kempton and Goodwood. Turf high 81 (1st run) - 2nd of 23 getting 3lb from Passion For Life (5 Apr Kempton 6f g-f RF 0577). AW high 75 - 7th of 12 getting 3lb from Silca Blanka (16 Jan Lingfield 7f Equi RF 0109). Becoming disappointing.
**R Ingram [8-42] Gary Williams (from J L Dunlop [0-2] Oct 1995).*

RIGADOON (IRE) BHB 56f **RR 55f** 4400[1]
3 b g Be My Chief (USA) 10.2f **(62)** - Loucoum (FR) (Iron Duke (FR)) 8.8f **(60)**
Form - 000613161
Record 1999 - 1st:3 2nd:0 3rd:1 Ran:9
Pre1999 - 1st:0 2nd:0 3rd:0 Ran:3
Win Prizemoney £7,394 *Total Prizemoney* £7,793

Wins								
*** 1999**	Spt	Catter	(G-F)	H	15.8f	51	55	<
*** 1999**	Jly	Nottin	(G-F)	H	16f	46	53	
*** 1999**	Jun	Carlis	(G-F)	H	17.2f	39	45	

1999 Turf 3-9: (7f, 8f 2, 12f, 14f, 16f 2-3, 17f 1-1) (gd 3, g-f, frm 3-5)
Leggy, fair gelding, effective 16 to 17f, best at 16f, acts on frm, often wears blinkers (extremely effectively), likes left handed tracks. Turf high 55 - 1st of 13 getting 19lb from Fullopep (18 Spt Catterick RF 4400) - also 1st of 6 getting 18lb from Burma Baby (23 Jly Nottingham RF 3070). Inconsistent.
**M W Easterby [3-12] Mybank Racing.*

RIGGING BHB 65f59a **RR 63f 59a** 4813[19]
3 b f Warning 8.1f **(77)** - Pilot (Kris) 9.5f **(73)**
Form - 8080
Record 1999 - 1st:0 2nd:0 3rd:0 Ran:4
Pre1999 - 1st:0 2nd:0 3rd:0 Ran:1
1999 Turf 0-3: (7f, 8f 2) (gd 2, frm) 1999 AW 0-1: (8f) (Equi)
Neat, average filly. Turf high 63. **B W Hills [0-5] R D Hollingsworth.*

RIGHT WING (IRE) BHB 104f **RR 107f** 5155[1]
5 b h In The Wings 11.2f **(77)** - Nekhbet (Artaius (USA)) 9f **(69)**
Form - 1250371
Record 1999 - 1st:2 2nd:1 3rd:1 Ran:7
Pre1999 - 1st:3 2nd:0 3rd:5 Ran:15
Win Prizemoney £76,574 *Total Prizemoney* £101,607

Wins								
*** 1999**	Nov	Nottin	(SFT)		8.2f		101+	
*** 1999**	Mar	Doncas	(G-S)	H	8f	100	107	<
* 1998	Spt	Doncas	(GD)	H	8f	97	100	
1997	Oct	Ayr	(SFT)		8f		88+	
1997	Jun	Ascot	(SFT)		8f		89	

1999 Turf 2-7: (8f 2-4, 10f 3) (g-s, gd 2-4, g-f 2)
Pattern-class colt, effective 8 to 10f, best at 8f, acts on sft to g-f, best on gd, has worn blinkers (effectively), does well at Doncaster. Turf high 107 (1st run) - 1st of 24 giving 10lb to Captain Scott (27 Mar Doncaster RF 0485) - also 1st of 8 from Weet-A-Minute (1 Nov Nottingham RF 5155). Consistent. Something of a tricky customer as he needs to be produced right on the line, he was given a fine ride by Richard Quinn when winning the Lincoln on his reappearance, but did not quite run up to that level afterwards until he was given an absolute peach of a ride by Quinn to win at Nottingham on his final start. He appreciates a bit of cut in the ground.
**J L Dunlop [3-14] The Earl Cadogan (from Major W R Hern [2-8] Oct 1997).*

RIGHTY HO BHB 53f57a **RR 64f 57a** 4758[3]
5 b g Reprimand 8.2f **(63)** - Challanging (Mill Reef (USA)) 10.5f **(78)**
Form - 63246673
Record 1999 - 1st:0 2nd:1 3rd:2 Ran:8
Pre1999 - 1st:2 2nd:1 3rd:1 Ran:16
Win Prizemoney £5,628 *Total Prizemoney* £9,700

Wins								
1997	Aug	Epsom	(GD)	H	10.1f	58	66	<
1997	Jun	Salisb	(SFT)	H	8f	57	62	

1999 Turf 0-8: (10f 3, 11f, 12f 4) (gd 2, g-f 3, frm 3)
Average gelding, effective 10 to 12f, acts on gd to frm, has worn blinkers, prefers left handed tracks. Turf high 64 - 3rd of 17 to Night City (7 Oct York 10f gd RF 4758). The winner of amateur riders' events at Salisbury in June and Epsom in August, he obviously goes well for an inexperienced rider.
**C B B Booth [0-8] W H Tinning (from P T Walwyn [2-16] Nov 1997).*

RIGOLETTO BHB 36f44a **RR 29f 44a** 4456[14]
4 ch g Machiavellian (USA) 9.8f **(83)** - Sally Brown (Posse (USA)) 8.9f **(61)**
Form - 44060
Record 1999 - 1st:0 2nd:0 3rd:0 Ran:5
Pre1999 - 1st:0 2nd:0 3rd:0 Ran:3
1999 Turf 0-2: (16f 2) (sft, frm) 1999 AW 0-3: (8f, 11f, 12f) (Fibr 3)
Strong, very moderate gelding. (began Aug). AW high 38.

Becoming disappointing.
**R Ford [0-2] Dave Teasdale (from C W Thornton [0-6] May 1999).*

RIMATARA RR 69f 2120[6]
3 ch c Selkirk (USA) 7.9f **(76)** -Humble Pie (Known Fact(USA)) 7.4f **(67)**
Form - 6
Record 1999 - 1st:0 2nd:0 3rd:0 Ran:1
1999 Turf 0-1: (9f) (g-f)
Unfurnished, currently average colt.
**I A Balding [0-1] Robert Hitchins.*

RIMBA (USA) BHB 70f **RR 72f** 1708[3]
3 b f Dayjur (USA) 6.8f **(79)** - Ristna (Kris) 9.5f **(73)**
Form - 003
Record 1999 - 1st:0 2nd:0 3rd:1 Ran:3
Pre1999 - 1st:0 2nd:0 3rd:0 Ran:2
Win Prizemoney £0 *Total Prizemoney* £944
1999 Turf 0-3: (7f 3) (gd 3)
Scopey, above-average filly. Turf high 72.
**J H M Gosden [0-5] George Strawbridge.*

RING CHEQUER'S RR 20f 3[9]
4 ch g Magic Ring (IRE) 6.5f **(64)** - Sharp Silk (Sharpo) 7.7f **(59)**
Form - 0
Record 1999 - 1st:0 2nd:0 3rd:0 Ran:1
Pre1999 - 1st:0 2nd:0 3rd:0 Ran:1
1999 AW 0-1: (10f) (Equi)
Light-framed, currently little account gelding.
**T T Clement [0-2] Sackville House Racing.*

RING DANCER BHB 82f **RR 89f** 4644[16]
4 b c Polar Falcon (USA) 9f **(74)** - Ring Cycle (Auction Ring (USA)) 8.6f **(65)**
Form - 00
Record 1999 - 1st:0 2nd:0 3rd:0 Ran:2
Pre1999 - 1st:1 2nd:2 3rd:1 Ran:8
Win Prizemoney £3,223 *Total Prizemoney* £7,727
Wins * 1997 Aug Ripon (GD) 6f 93+ <
1999 Turf 0-2: (6f 2) (g-s, gd)
Lengthy, useful colt, effective 6 to 7f, acts on gd to frm. Turf high 81. **P J Makin [1-10] Mrs Tricia Mitchell.*

RING FENCE BHB 71f **RR 67f** 3559[1]
3 b f Polar Falcon (USA) 9f **(74)** - Ring Cycle (Auction Ring (USA)) 8.6f **(65)**
Form - 431
Record 1999 - 1st:1 2nd:0 3rd:1 Ran:3
Win Prizemoney £3,777 *Total Prizemoney* £4,463
Wins * **1999** Aug Sandow (G-S) 5f 48 <
1999 Turf 1-3: (5f 1-1, 6f 2) (gd 1-2, frm)
Neat, currently average filly. Turf high 67 (1st run) - 4th of 10 getting 5lb from Royal Wave (18 May Pontefract 6f gd RF 1304).
**H Candy [1-3] Major M G Wyatt.*

RING MY MATE RR 52f 5163[6]
2 ch c Komaite (USA) 6.9f **(61)** - My Ruby Ring **(61df 50a)** (Blushing Scribe (USA)) 6f **(45)**
Form - 6
Record 1999 - 1st:0 2nd:0 3rd:0 Ran:1
1999 Turf 0-1: (7f) (g-s)
Currently fair colt. **W R Muir [0-1] Mrs Marion Wickham.*

RING OF LOVE BHB 69f **RR 67f** 4691[5]
3 b f Magic Ring (IRE) 6.5f **(64)** - Fine Honey (USA) (Drone) 10.3f **(74)**
Form - 04872661105
Record 1999 - 1st:2 2nd:1 3rd:0 Ran:11
Pre1999 - 1st:1 2nd:1 3rd:1 Ran:6
Win Prizemoney £10,376 *Total Prizemoney* £13,240
Wins * **1999** Spt Mussel (G-F) H 5f 64 67
* **1999** Aug Mussel (G-F) H 5f 64 65
* 1998 Jly Cheste (G-F) 5.1f 76 <
1999 Turf 2-11: (5f 2-9, 6f 2) (g-s, gd 1-3, g-f 1-4, frm 3)
Neat, average filly, effective 5f, acts on g-f to frm, best on g-f, has worn blinkers. Turf high 67 - 1st of 11 getting 5lb from William's Well (2 Spt Musselburgh RF 4087). Consistent. Seems to like Musselburgh as she won twice there in the space of a week in the autumn. Fast ground and the minimum trip suit her well.
**M L W Bell [3-17] J M Ratcliffe.*

RING OF VISION (IRE) BHB 31f **RR 27f** 1423[8]
7 br g Scenic 10.6f **(66)** - Circus Lady (High Top) 10.2f **(67)**
Form - 708
Record 1999 - 1st:0 2nd:0 3rd:0 Ran:3
Pre1999 - 1st:2 2nd:1 3rd:0 Ran:15
Win Prizemoney £6,198 *Total Prizemoney* £7,920
Wins 1996 Jly Redcar (G-F) H 11f 51 54 <
1995 May Redcar (GD) H 10f 47 46
1999 Turf 0-2: (10f, 13f) (gd 2) 1999 AW 0-1: (12f) (Fibr)
Very moderate gelding. Turf high 27. Becoming disappointing.
**J J Quinn [1-9] Harold Bray (from Mrs M Reveley [2-15] Oct 1996).*

RINGSIDE JACK BHB 64f **RR 66f** 5162[8]
3 b g Batshoof 9.5f **(66)** - Celestine **(40f 44a)** (Skyliner) 7.3f **(53)**
Form - 02087003758
Record 1999 - 1st:0 2nd:1 3rd:1 Ran:11
Pre1999 - 1st:1 2nd:1 3rd:1 Ran:7
Win Prizemoney £3,302 *Total Prizemoney* £7,156
Wins * 1998 Jun Redcar (G-S) 5f 70 <
1999 Turf 0-11: (8f 4, 10f 6, 11f) (gd 3, g-f 3, frm 5)
Scopey, average gelding, effective 7 to 8f, acts on frm, has worn blinkers. Turf high 80 - 2nd of 18 giving 16lb to Time Temptress (3 May Newcastle 8f frm RF 1007). Consistent.
**C W Fairhurst [1-18] M J G Partnership.*

RING THE CHIEF BHB 37f37a **RR 40f 37a** 430[6]
7 b g Chief Singer 8.6f **(62)** - Lomond Ring (Lomond (USA)) 8.8f **(65)**
Form - 0412306
Record 1999 - 1st:1 2nd:1 3rd:1 Ran:5
Pre1999 - 1st:3 2nd:3 3rd:8 Ran:41
Win Prizemoney £7,941 *Total Prizemoney* £14,169
Wins * **1999** *Jan Southw (STD) H 8f 35 42* <
* 1997 Aug Salisb (G-S) H 7f 34 42 <
* 1997 *Jun Southw (STD) SH 7f 33 39*
* 1997 *Feb Southw (STD) H 7f 30 34*
1999 AW 1-5: (7f 3, 8f 1-2) (Fibr 1-5)
Moderate gelding, effective 8f, - acts on Fibr. AW high 42 (1st run) - 1st of 14 getting 17lb from Forest Robin (11 Jan Southwell RF 0070). A modest performer who pops up once in a while on Fibresand.
**M D I Usher [4-36] G A Summers (from R Akehurst [0-7] Aug 1995).*

RING THE RAFTERS BHB 30f20a **RR 51f 20a** 245[9]
4 b f Batshoof 9.5f **(66)** - Soprano (Kris) 9.5f **(73)**
Form - 070
Record 1999 - 1st:0 2nd:0 3rd:0 Ran:2
Pre1999 - 1st:0 2nd:0 3rd:0 Ran:4
1999 AW 0-2: (9f, 12f) (Fibr 2)
Workmanlike, fair filly, has worn blinkers. AW high 1.
**B P J Baugh [0-5] Mrs Joan Chrimes (from I A Balding [0-1] Apr 1997).*

RING THE RELATIVES RR 73f 3822[2]
3 b f Bering 9.6f **(80)** - Relatively Special **(105f)** (Alzao (USA)) 7.1f **(68)**
Form - 42
Record 1999 - 1st:0 2nd:1 3rd:0 Ran:2
Win Prizemoney £0 *Total Prizemoney* £1,435
1999 Turf 0-2: (7f, 10f) (g-f 2)
Workmanlike, currently above-average filly. Turf high 73.
**L M Cumani [0-2] Helena Springfield Ltd.*

RIO NAPO (IRE) RR 105f 5016a[4]
5 b h Law Society (USA) 11.6f **(71)** - My Southern love (ITY) (Southern Arrow (USA))
Form - 414
1999 Turf 1-3: (10f 1-1, 12f 2) (g-s 1-1, g-f, frm)
Pattern-class colt. Turf high 105 - 4th of 6 giving 5lb to Sumati (17 Oct San Siro 12f g-f RF 5016a) - also 1st of 12 getting 4lb from Embody (19 Spt San Siro RF 4522a). **L Camici in ITY [1-8]* .

RIO'S DIAMOND BHB 39f41a **RR 42f 41a** 5158[19]
2 b f Formidable (USA) 7.8f **(60)** - Rio Piedras (Kala Shikari) 8.4f **(54)**
Form - 0787300
Record 1999 - 1st:0 2nd:0 3rd:1 Ran:7
Win Prizemoney £0 *Total Prizemoney* £317

1999 Turf 0-6: (5f 3, 6f, 8f 2) (sft, g-s, gd 2, frm 2) 1999 AW 0-1: (6f) (Fibr)
Moderate filly. Turf high 42. **M J Ryan [0-7] Rettendon Racing.*

RIPARIAN RR 64+f 4139[5]
2 b c Last Tycoon 9.4f **(73)** - La Riveraine (USA) **(81f)** (Riverman (USA)) 9.1f **(76)**
Form - 5
Record 1999 - 1st:0 2nd:0 3rd:0 Ran:1
1999 Turf 0-1: (7f) (frm)
Currently average colt.
**Sir Michael Stoute [0-1] J H Richmond-Watson.*

RIPLEY RR 2003[14]
2 b f Presidium 7.5f **(56)** - Hannie Caulder (Workboy) 7.3f **(46)**
Form - 0
Record 1999 - 1st:0 2nd:0 3rd:0 Ran:1
1999 Turf 0-1: (6f) (frm)
Currently very poor filly, always wears blinkers.
**M W Easterby [0-1] I Bray.*

RIPSNORTER (IRE) BHB 30f26a **RR 34f 26a** 59[8]
10 ch g Rousillon (USA) 10.4f **(69)** - Formulate (Reform) 8.9f **(62)**
Form - 0808
Record 1999 - 1st:0 2nd:0 3rd:0 Ran:2
Pre1999 - 1st:4 2nd:5 3rd:3 Ran:57
Win Prizemoney £9,433 *Total Prizemoney* £15,091
Wins * 1998 *Feb Lingfi (SLW) SH 8f 26 36*
1999 AW 0-2: (8f, 10f) (Equi, Fibr)
Very moderate gelding, effective 8f, - acts on Equi, has worn blinkers. AW high 25.
**P D Purdy [1-16] P D Purdy (from K Bishop [0-8] Aug 1996).*

RISCATTO (USA) BHB 42f30a **RR 41f 30a** 299[9]
5 b g Red Ransom (USA) 8.6f **(83)** - Ultima Cena (USA) (Leonardo da Vinci (FR)) 10f **(55)**
Form - 0040
Record 1999 - 1st:0 2nd:0 3rd:0 Ran:2
Pre1999 - 1st:1 2nd:1 3rd:2 Ran:15
Win Prizemoney £1,984 *Total Prizemoney* £3,202
Wins * 1997 Apr Nottin (G-F) SH 10f 48 46 <
1999 AW 0-2: (10f, 13f) (Equi 2)
Moderate gelding, has worn blinkers. AW high 23. Inconsistent.
**W R Muir [1-18] F Hope.*

RISE 'N SHINE BHB 36f40a **RR 35f 40a** 1581[10]
5 ch m Night Shift (USA) 8.1f **(73)** - Clunk Click (Star Appeal) 9.6f **(65)**
Form - 868824560
Record 1999 - 1st:0 2nd:1 3rd:0 Ran:7
Pre1999 - 1st:1 2nd:5 3rd:5 Ran:26
Win Prizemoney £2,221 *Total Prizemoney* £9,455
Wins * 1998 *Feb Lingfi (SLW) H 5f 42 51* <
1999 Turf 0-2: (5f 2) (gd, g-f) 1999 AW 0-5: (5f 5) (Equi 4, Fibr)
Very moderate filly, effective 5 to 6f, best at 5f, - acts on Equi, has worn blinkers, likes left handed tracks, likes tight tracks. Turf high 35. AW high 38. Consistent. **C A Cyzer [1-33] R M Cyzer.*

RISING SPRAY BHB 67f **RR 69f** 1913[6]
8 ch g Waajib 8.9f **(67)** - Rose Bouquet (General Assembly (USA)) 10f **(68)**
Form - 0206
Record 1999 - 1st:0 2nd:1 3rd:0 Ran:4
Pre1999 - 1st:4 2nd:4 3rd:7 Ran:41
Win Prizemoney £14,201 *Total Prizemoney* £23,753
Wins * 1997 May Salisb (G-F) H 14f 67 71 <
* 1997 Apr Folkes (G-F) H 12f 62 66
* 1996 Aug Folkes (G-F) H 12f 44 53+
* 1996 Aug Folkes (G-F) H 12f 44 52
1999 Turf 0-4: (10f 2, 12f, 14f) (gd, frm 3)
Average gelding, effective 10 to 14f, acts on gd to frm, best on frm, has worn blinkers. Turf high 69 - 2nd of 20 giving 8lb to Gypsy Hill (24 May Windsor 10f frm RF 1442). Consistent.
**C A Horgan [4-37] Exors of the late J T Heritage (from P W Harris [0-8] Spt 1994).*

RISK FREE BHB 85f93a **RR 73f 93a** 4895[20]
2 ch c Risk Me (FR) 8f **(53)** - Princess Lily (Blakeney) 10.5f **(64)**
Form - 818280
Record 1999 - 1st:1 2nd:1 3rd:0 Ran:6
Win Prizemoney £2,304 *Total Prizemoney* £3,052
Wins * **1999** *May Southw (STD) 5f 78* <
1999 Turf 0-4: (5f 2, 6f 2) (gd 2, g-f 2) 1999 AW 1-2: (5f 1-2) (Fibr 1-2)
Above-average colt, effective 5f, - acts on Fibr. Turf high 73. AW high 78 (1st run) - 1st of 11 giving 5lb to Misbehave (17 May Southwell RF 1281). His best form so far has been on Fibresand, including winning a maiden over the minimum at Southwell on his second start. **N P Littmoden [1-6] Mrs P J Sheen.*

RISK MATERIAL (IRE) RR 112f 3718a[7]
4 b c Danehill (USA) 9.1f **(79)** - Spear Dance (Gay Fandango (USA)) 8.5f **(59)**
Form - 62507
1999 Turf 0-5: (8f, 10f 2, 14f 2) (g-s, gd, g-f 2, frm)
Group-class colt, effective 9 to 14f, best at 10f, acts on gd, has worn blinkers. Turf high 112 - 2nd of 9 giving 7lb to Enzeli (19 May Leopardstown 14f gd RF 1465a). He had a disappointing campaign, failing to stay a mile and three-quarters at The Curragh in June. Unlikely to improve at this stage of his career, he might be better employed over hurdles.
**A P O'Brien in IRE [7-18] Castleblake Racing Syndicate.*

RISKNOWT GETNOWT BHB 22f **RR 22f** 242[9]
4 b g Ron's Victory (USA) 9.2f **(52)** - Scottish Tina (Scottish Reel) 7f **(61)**
Form - 0
Record 1999 - 1st:0 2nd:0 3rd:0 Ran:1
Pre1999 - 1st:0 2nd:0 3rd:0 Ran:6
1999 AW 0-1: (12f) (Fibr)
Leggy, little account gelding, had worn blinkers. (DEAD)
**R J Price [0-3] Keith Warrington, Ma Taylor (from T Wall [0-6] Spt 1997).*

RISKY EXPERIENCE BHB 43f42a **RR 42f 42a** 621[13]
3 ch f Risk Me (FR) 8f **(53)** - First Experience (Le Johnstan) 7.4f **(55)**
Form - 05080
Record 1999 - 1st:0 2nd:0 3rd:0 Ran:3
Pre1999 - 1st:0 2nd:1 3rd:1 Ran:12
Win Prizemoney £0 *Total Prizemoney* £1,098
1999 Turf 0-1: (6f) (gd) 1999 AW 0-2: (6f 2) (Fibr 2)
Light-framed, moderate filly, effective 5f, - acts on Fibr, has worn blinkers. AW high 32.
**B P J Baugh [0-5] D E Simpson (from P D Evans [0-10] Spt 1998).*

RISKY GEM BHB 59f66a **RR 70f 66a** 4937[10]
2 ch c Risk Me (FR) 8f **(53)** - Dark Kristal (IRE) (Gorytus (USA)) 7.8f **(60)**
Form - 002710600
Record 1999 - 1st:1 2nd:1 3rd:0 Ran:9
Win Prizemoney £2,801 *Total Prizemoney* £3,349
Wins * **1999** *Jly Wolver (STD) H 6f 56* <
1999 Turf 0-7: (5f 2, 6f 3, 7f 2) (gd 2, g-f 2, frm 3) 1999 AW 1-2: (6f 1-2) (Fibr 1-2)
Above-average colt, effective 5f, acts on frm. Turf high 70 - 2nd of 11 giving 5lb to Breezy Louise (14 Jun Windsor 5f frm RF 1989). AW high 56 (1st run) (began Jly). Got off the mark in a very modest nursery on the Wolverhampton Fibresand in July.
**R Hannon [1-9] J C Smith.*

RISKY MONEY BHB 36f **RR 46f** 1136[14]
4 b c Risk Me (FR) 8f **(53)** - Where's the Money (Lochnager) 6f **(59)**
Form - 0
Record 1999 - 1st:0 2nd:0 3rd:0 Ran:1
Pre1999 - 1st:0 2nd:0 3rd:0 Ran:4
1999 Turf 0-1: (8f) (g-f)
Workmanlike, moderate colt. **V Soane [0-5] The Risky Bunch.*

RISKY REEF RR 73f 4928[2]
2 ch g Risk Me (FR) 8f **(53)** - Pas de Reef (Pas de Seul) 9.1f **(67)**
Form - 52
Record 1999 - 1st:0 2nd:1 3rd:0 Ran:2
Win Prizemoney £0 *Total Prizemoney* £548
1999 Turf 0-2: (6f 2) (g-f 2)
Currently above-average gelding. Turf high 73 (began Oct) - 2nd

of 12 giving 4lb to Ravishing (18 Oct Pontefract 6f g-f RF 4928).
**I A Balding [0-2] Park House Partnership.*

RISKY VALENTINE BHB 60f59a **RR 43f 59a** 4699[12]
3 ch f Risk Me (FR) 8f **(53)** - Mandrake Madam (Mandrake Major) 7.6f **(53)**
Form - 41000
Record 1999 - 1st:1 2nd:0 3rd:0 Ran:5
Pre1999 - 1st:1 2nd:3 3rd:4 Ran:14
Win Prizemoney £5,505 *Total Prizemoney* £8,648
Wins * 1999 Apr Nottin (G-S) H 6.1f 57 65 <
* 1998 *Apr Wolver (STD) 5f 55*
1999 Turf 1-5: (5f, 6f 1-4) (sft 1-3, gd 2)
Light-framed, average filly, effective 5 to 6f, best at 6f, acts on sft to g-s, best on g-s. Turf high 65 - 1st of 20 getting 5lb from Grand View (5 Apr Nottingham RF 0589). She showed some ability on her Nottingham debut, and came fast and late to win on the Wolverhampton Fibresand just four days later. Well beaten afterwards. **J L Spearing [2-19] Kinnersley Racing Club.*

RISKY WAY BHB 44f50a **RR 45f 50a** 1987[8]
3 b g Risk Me (FR) 8f **(53)** - Hot Sunday Sport (Star Appeal) 9.6f **(65)**
Form - 75560758
Record 1999 - 1st:0 2nd:0 3rd:0 Ran:8
Pre1999 - 1st:1 2nd:1 3rd:2 Ran:9
Win Prizemoney £2,024 *Total Prizemoney* £3,493
Wins * 1998 Jly Catter (GD) S 7f 67 <
1999 Turf 0-5: (7f 2, 8f 3) (gd 2, g-f, frm 2) 1999 AW 0-3: (6f, 7f, 8f) (Fibr 3)
Tall, fair gelding, effective 7f, acts on g-f - acts on Fibr, likes left handed tracks, likes tight tracks. Turf high 46. AW high 54.
**B S Rothwell [1-17] J M G Promotions Ltd.*

RISQUE LADY BHB 95f **RR 91f** 4652[10]
4 ch f Kenmare (FR) 9.6f **(76)** - Christine Daae (Sadler's Wells (USA)) 10f **(76)**
Form - 4332124030
Record 1999 - 1st:1 2nd:2 3rd:3 Ran:10
Pre1999 - 1st:3 2nd:1 3rd:4 Ran:13
Win Prizemoney £41,851 *Total Prizemoney* £77,305
Wins * 1999 Jun Newcas (GD) 8f 91
* 1998 Spt Ascot (GD) LH 8f 97 100 <
* 1997 Spt Haydoc (GD) 5f 96
* 1997 Aug Windso (G-F) 5f 83+
1999 Turf 1-10: (8f 1-8, 9f, 10f) (gd 6, g-f 3, frm 1-1)
Neat, useful filly, effective 7 to 9f, best at 8f, acts on gd to frm, best on gd, likes tight tracks, excels at Doncaster and Epsom, likes Goodwood. Turf high 99 - 2nd of 6 getting 7lb from Ramooz (11 Jly Curragh 8f g-f RF 2803a) - also 1st of 5 getting 3lb from Celtic Cross (24 Jun Newcastle RF 2268). Consistent. Suited by fast-run races - she can pull hard - she stays a mile but finds life tough in Listed and Group events. Harshly treated in handicaps, she will continue to be difficult to place.
**P W Harris [4-23] Godwin Hollis Lawren Rice.*

RITA MACKINTOSH (IRE) BHB 50f **RR 56f** 4926[3]
2 b f Port Lucaya - Silver Stream (USA) (Silver Hawk (USA)) 8.6f **(70)**
Form - 630403
Record 1999 - 1st:0 2nd:0 3rd:2 Ran:6
Win Prizemoney £0 *Total Prizemoney* £526
1999 Turf 0-5: (7f 3, 8f, 10f) (g-s, gd, g-f, frm 2) 1999 AW 0-1: (8f) (Fibr)
Fair filly, effective 7 to 8f, acts on frm, has worn blinkers. Turf high 56 (began Aug) - 3rd of 11 to Summertime Joy (13 Aug Catterick 7f frm RF 3598). **M H Tompkins [0-6] Michael Keogh.*

RITA'S ROCK APE BHB 77f54a **RR 79+f 54a** 4933[13]
4 b f Mon Tresor 7.9f **(60)** - Failand (Kala Shikari) 8.4f **(54)**
Form - 3546004111132130
Record 1999 - 1st:5 2nd:1 3rd:2 Ran:13
Pre1999 - 1st:0 2nd:3 3rd:4 Ran:16
Win Prizemoney £13,033 *Total Prizemoney* £21,059
Wins * 1999 Spt Salisb (G-F) H 5f 72 79 <
***1999** Jly Bright (FRM) 5.3f 62+
***1999** Jly Lingfi (G-F) H 5f 50 61
***1999** Jly Bath (G-F) H 5.1f 50 65
***1999** Jun Bright (GD) H 5.3f 50 54
1999 Turf 5-12: (5f 5-12) (g-s, gd 1-1, g-f 5, frm 2-3, hrd 2-2) 1999 AW 0-1: (5f) (Fibr)
Neat, above-average filly, has broken blood-vessels, effective 5f, acts on g-f to frm, best on frm, excels at Brighton. Turf high 79 - 2nd of 8 giving 21lb to Forgotten Times (23 Aug Brighton 5f frm RF 3855) - also 1st of 14 giving 5lb to Juwwi (2 Spt Salisbury RF 4092). She has bags of pace, and rattled up a sparkling four-timer during the summer at Bath, Lingfield and Brighton twice. She has maintained her fine form since, and regained winning form at Salisbury in September. A sharp five furlongs and fast ground are what she needs. **R Brotherton [5-29] Mrs Janet Pearce.*

RITUAL BHB 75a **RR 54f** 2567[8]
4 ch g Selkirk (USA) 7.9f **(76)** - Pure Formality (Forzando) 7.6f **(59)**
Form - 1000800878
Record 1999 - 1st:0 2nd:0 3rd:0 Ran:9
Pre1999 - 1st:1 2nd:0 3rd:1 Ran:6
Win Prizemoney £2,424 *Total Prizemoney* £3,244
Wins * 1998 *Nov Lingfi (STD) 8f 72+* <
1999 Turf 0-8: (8f, 10f 6, 12f) (hvy 2, gd, g-f 2, frm 3) 1999 AW 0-1: (10f) (Equi)
Light-framed, above-average gelding, effective 7 to 8f, best at 7f, acts on g-s to g-f - acts on Equi. Turf high 54.
**S Dow [1-10] G A Jackman (from H Candy [0-5] Jly 1998).*

RITUAL RUN BHB 50f47a **RR 56f 47a** 74[5]
4 b g Rudimentary (USA) 8.2f **(66)** - Roussalka (Habitat) 9.4f **(70)**
Form - 5
Record 1999 - 1st:0 2nd:0 3rd:0 Ran:1
Pre1999 - 1st:0 2nd:0 3rd:0 Ran:5
1999 AW 0-1: (12f) (Fibr)
Well made, fair gelding.
**Ronald Thompson [0-1] Haggswood Partnerships (from R Hannon [0-5] Aug 1998).*

RIVAL BID (USA) BHB 36f25a **RR 32f 25a** 299[10]
11 b g Cannonade (USA) 9.9f **(79)** - Love Triangle (USA) (Nodouble (USA)) 8.8f **(68)**
Form - 80
Record 1999 - 1st:0 2nd:0 3rd:0 Ran:2
Pre1999 - 1st:10 2nd:10 3rd:10 Ran:87
Win Prizemoney £33,591 *Total Prizemoney* £49,418
Wins * 1998 May Leices (GD) SH 10f 37 45
* 1996 Oct Leices (G-F) H 10f 63 67
* 1996 Jun Warwic (FRM) H 10.8f 64 70
* 1996 *Jan Lingfi (STD) 10f 61*
* 1995 Oct Leices (FRM) H 10f 62 68
* 1995 Oct Warwic (G-S) CH 10.8f 57 66
1999 AW 0-2: (10f 2) (Equi 2)
Very moderate gelding, effective 10f, acts on g-f, has worn blinkers. AW high 10.
**Mrs N Macauley [6-55] Mrs N Macauley (from M A Jarvis [4-42] Aug 1995).*

RIVENDELL BHB 28f **RR 26f** 4438[12]
3 b f Saddlers' Hall (IRE) 10.5f **(65)** - Fairy Kingdom (Prince Sabo) 7.2f **(62)**
Form - 0F50
Record 1999 - 1st:0 2nd:0 3rd:0 Ran:4
Pre1999 - 1st:0 2nd:0 3rd:0 Ran:1
1999 Turf 0-4: (8f 3, 10f) (gd, g-f, frm 2)
Workmanlike, little account filly. Turf high 26.
**A G Newcombe [0-4] Maurice Kirby (from Mrs N Macauley [0-1] Spt 1998).*

RIVERA RR 93f 4110a[3]
3 f
Form - 3
1999 Turf 0-1: (8f) (gd)
Currently useful. (1st run) - 3rd of 7 giving 2lb to Miami Blues (29 Aug Baden-Baden 8f gd RF 4110a). **A Schutz in GER [0-1].*

RIVER BANN (USA) RR 87f 4898[2]
2 ch c Irish River (FR) 9f **(77)** - Spiritual Star (USA) (Soviet Star (USA))
Form - 2
Record 1999 - 1st:0 2nd:1 3rd:0 Ran:1
Win Prizemoney £0 *Total Prizemoney* £2,560
1999 Turf 0-1: (8f) (gd)
Currently useful colt. (1st run) - 2nd of 13 to Pawn Broker (15 Oct

Newmarket 8f gd RF 4898). Made a highly pleasing debut when beaten a short-head at Newmarket over a mile. Entitled to have learnt from the run, he looks to have what it takes to establish a name for himself. **P F I Cole [0-1] H R H Prince Fahd Salman.*

RIVER BEAT (IRE) BHB 68f **RR 70f** 5050[8]

4 b g River Falls 8.2f **(56)** - Aughamore Beauty (IRE) (Dara Monarch) 8.8f **(59)**
Form - 000453771758
Record 1999 - 1st:1 2nd:0 3rd:1 Ran:12
Pre1999 - 1st:4 2nd:0 3rd:1 Ran:13
Win Prizemoney £20,155 *Total Prizemoney* £23,235
Wins 1999 Spt Ayr (G-S) C 9.1f 70
1998 Jun Goodwo (GD) H 9.9f 87 88 <
1998 Jun Ayr (GD) H 9.1f 71 85
1998 Jun Carlis (G-S) H 9.3f 64 76
1998 Jun Windso (G-F) H 8.3f 64 71
1999 Turf 1-12: (8f 2, 9f 1-1, 10f 9) (gd 1-4, g-f 5, frm 3)
Workmanlike, above-average gelding, effective 9 to 10f, acts on gd, prefers tight tracks. Turf high 77. This progressive gelding rattled up a four-timer in '98, and after a string of average efforts won a claimer at Ayr in September.
**D Sasse [0-3] High Havens Stables (from K R Burke [1-11] Spt 1999).*

RIVERBIRD (IRE) BHB 71f **RR 68?f** 4406[13]

3 b f Mujadil (USA) 7.7f **(70)** - Ruby River (Red God) 8.5f **(65)**
Form - 7010
Record 1999 - 1st:1 2nd:0 3rd:0 Ran:4
Pre1999 - 1st:0 2nd:0 3rd:0 Ran:2
Win Prizemoney £3,696 *Total Prizemoney* £3,696
Wins * 1999 Aug Goodwo (GD) 7f 68 <
1999 Turf 1-4: (7f 1-3, 8f) (g-f 1-2, frm 2)
Unfurnished, average filly, has broken blood-vessels, effective 7f, acts on g-f. Turf high 68 - 1st of 7 from Vanille (29 Aug Goodwood RF 3998). She contested some very competitive maidens in her early starts, but was suffering with an internal problem which had been operated on before she landed a Goodwood maiden in August. **Major D N Chappell [1-6] R C C Villers.*

RIVER BLEST (IRE) BHB 57f **RR 52f** 3800[6]

3 b g Unblest - Vaal Salmon (IRE) (Salmon Leap (USA)) 11f **(61)**
Form - 08336
Record 1999 - 1st:0 2nd:0 3rd:2 Ran:5
Win Prizemoney £0 *Total Prizemoney* £748
1999 Turf 0-5: (6f 4, 7f) (gd 2, g-f 2, frm)
Workmanlike, fair gelding. Turf high 52 - 3rd of 9 getting 7lb from Grand Estate (29 Jun Hamilton 6f g-f RF 2395).
**Mrs A Swinbank [0-5] J W Haygarth.*

RIVERBLUE (IRE) BHB 81f77a **RR 79f 77a** 5004[4]

3 b c Bluebird (USA) 7.9f **(71)** - La Riveraine (USA) **(81f)** (Riverman (USA)) 9.1f **(76)**
Form - 72050784
Record 1999 - 1st:0 2nd:1 3rd:0 Ran:8
Pre1999 - 1st:2 2nd:1 3rd:1 Ran:6
Win Prizemoney £7,707 *Total Prizemoney* £24,023
Wins 1998 Aug Thirsk (G-F) H 6f 80 91+ <
1998 Aug Catter (GD) 7f 76
1999 Turf 0-8: (8f 7, 10f) (g-s, gd 3, g-f 3, frm)
Scopey, above-average colt, effective 6 to 8f, acts on g-f to frm, has worn blinkers, likes left handed tracks. Turf high 90 - 2nd of 18 getting 10lb from Date (29 May Haydock 8f g-f RF 1569). Consistent. Twice a winner last season, he finished a good second in a valuable handicap at Haydock in May, splitting Date and Swallow Flight. Since then however, he has proved a little disappointing.
**D J Wintle [0-2] Mrs Joan Egan (from M R Channon [0-6] Aug 1999).*

RIVER BOY (IRE) BHB 44f42a **RR 46f 42a** 2760[6]

3 b g River Falls 8.2f **(56)** - Natty Gann (IRE) (Mister Majestic)
Form - 86520666
Record 1999 - 1st:0 2nd:1 3rd:0 Ran:7
Pre1999 - 1st:0 2nd:0 3rd:0 Ran:5
Win Prizemoney £0 *Total Prizemoney* £665
1999 Turf 0-5: (8f, 10f 3, 12f) (gd, g-f 3, frm) 1999 AW 0-2: (11f, 12f) (Fibr 2)
Light-framed, moderate gelding, effective 10f, acts on gd to g-f, has worn blinkers, likes tight tracks. Turf high 46 - 6th of 17 giving 6lb to Purple Dawn (16 Jun Nottingham 10f g-f RF 2054). AW high 27. **P Shakespeare [0-12] Mrs M Shakespeare.*

RIVER CANYON (IRE) **RR 107f** 1486a[4]

3 b c College Chapel - Na-Ammah (IRE) **(84f)** (Ela-Mana-Mou) 10.1f **(70)**
Form - 334
1999 Turf 0-3: (7f, 10f 2) (sft, gd, g-f)
Pattern-class colt, has worn blinkers. Turf high 107 - 3rd of 5 to Port Bayou (9 May Leopardstown 10f gd RF 1169a). He ran creditably on a soft surface in the spring, but was not seen out after disappointing on a faster ground at The Curragh in late May.
**D K Weld in IRE [1-4] Lord Harris.*

RIVER CAPTAIN (USA) BHB 47f57a **RR 29f 57a** 4936[7]

6 ch g Riverman (USA) 9.7f **(78)** - Katsura (USA) (Northern Dancer) 9.6f **(80)**
Form - 0512657
Record 1999 - 1st:1 2nd:1 3rd:0 Ran:7
Pre1999 - 1st:3 2nd:1 3rd:1 Ran:13
Win Prizemoney £9,679 *Total Prizemoney* £11,614
Wins * 1999 *Mar Southw (STD) H 12f 53 61+*
* 1998 *Oct Southw (STD) 12f 61*
* 1998 *Mar Southw (STD) H 12f 54 57*
* 1997 *Mar Southw (STD) 11f 62* <
1999 Turf 0-1: (12f) (gd) 1999 AW 1-6: (11f, 12f 1-4, 14f) (Fibr 1-6)
Average gelding, effective 12f, - acts on Fibr, favours left handed tracks. AW high 61 - 5th of 5 getting 2lb from Nikita's Star (15 Feb Southwell 12f Fibr RF 0291) - also 1st of 11 giving 13lb to Approved Quality (8 Mar Southwell RF 0418). Becoming disappointing. Four times a winner over middle distances at Southwell, he is not particularly consistent, but he may have another race in him under his ideal conditions.
**D J G MurraySmith [4-21] The Joiners Arms Racing Club Quarndon (from J H M Gosden [0-1] Apr 1996).*

RIVER COLN (USA) **RR 57f** 5157[8]

2 b f Irish River (FR) 9f **(77)** - Erwinna (USA) (Lyphard (USA)) 9.9f **(72)**
Form - 78
Record 1999 - 1st:0 2nd:0 3rd:0 Ran:2
1999 Turf 0-2: (7f 2) (frm 2)
Currently fair filly. Turf high 57 (began Spt).
**L M Cumani [0-2] Lord Vestey.*

RIVERDANCE (IRE) **RR 38f** 5068[7]

3 ch g College Chapel - Valmarana (USA) (Danzig Connection (USA)) 8f **(68)**
Form - 75062067
Record 1999 - 1st:0 2nd:1 3rd:0 Ran:8
Pre1999 - 1st:0 2nd:0 3rd:0 Ran:5
Win Prizemoney £0 *Total Prizemoney* £1,257
1999 Turf 0-8: (5f, 6f, 7f, 8f 5) (g-s, gd 3, g-f 2, frm, hrd)
Leggy, very moderate gelding, has worn blinkers. Turf high 58. Consistent.
**P D Evans [0-5] Gallagher Equine Ltd (from Mrs L C Jewell [0-3] Jun 1999).*

RIVER ENSIGN BHB 46f50a **RR 50f 50a** 4922[8]

6 br m River God (USA) 6f **(37)** - Ensigns Kit (Saucy Kit) 6f **(43)**
Form - 673202751277025234188
Record 1999 - 1st:2 2nd:5 3rd:2 Ran:19
Pre1999 - 1st:3 2nd:2 3rd:6 Ran:38
Win Prizemoney £14,821 *Total Prizemoney* £23,837
Wins * 1999 Spt Cheste (HVY) H 10.3f 41 50 <
*** 1999** *Apr Wolver (STD) C 6f 50* <
* 1998 Apr Nottin (SFT) H 6.1f 39 44
* 1998 *Jan Southw (STD) H 6f 35 36*
* 1997 Aug Thirsk (GD) H 6f 35 41
1999 Turf 1-6: (6f 2, 7f, 10f 1-2, 12f) (sft, g-s 1-2, gd 3) 1999 AW 1-13: (6f 1-3, 7f 4, 8f 3, 9f 2, 12f) (Fibr 1-13)
Fair mare, effective 6 to 10f, acts on g-s - acts on Fibr, likes left handed tracks, likes tight tracks. Turf high 50 - 1st of 13 getting 1lb from My Legal Eagle (22 Spt Chester RF 4488). AW high 52 - 2nd of 8 getting 32lb from Tallulah Belle (5 Jun Wolverhampton 9f Fibr RF 1779) - also 1st of 11 getting 7lb from Grand Estate (29 Apr Wolverhampton RF 0923).
**W M Brisbourne [5-57] Crispandave Racing Associates.*

RIVER JUNCTION (IRE) BHB 31f58a **RR 34f 58a** 308[8]
8 b g Cyrano de Bergerac 7.3f **(58)** - Lovestream (Sandy Creek) 8.9f **(59)**
Form - 8
Record 1999 - 1st:0 2nd:0 3rd:0 Ran:1
Pre1999 - 1st:3 2nd:3 3rd:0 Ran:18
Win Prizemoney £8,843 *Total Prizemoney* £11,887
1999 AW 0-1: (12f) (Fibr)
Average gelding.
**B Smart [0-6] The Dyball Partnership (from P C Haslam [3-13] Aug 1994).*

RIVER KEEN (IRE) BHB 83f106a **RR 82f 126a** 5231a[11]
7 ch h Keen 11.1f **(58)** - Immediate Impact (Caerleon (USA)) 8.6f **(71)**
Form - 110
1999 AW 2-3: (9f 1-1, 10f 1-2) (Dirt 2-3)
Top-class horse, has worn blinkers (extremely effectively). AW high 126 (began Spt) - 1st of 8 from Behrens (10 Oct Belmont Park RF 4886a) - also 1st of 7 from Almutawakel (18 Spt Belmont Park RF 4517a). Inconsistent. A particularly smart All-Weather performer when trained by Robert Armstrong in the mid-nineties, his sand handicap mark became so high that further opportunities in that sphere were virtually non-existent. Subsequently sent to race in the USA, he was claimed for $100,000 by present connections, and has not stopped improving since. He beat Almutawakel in the Woodward Stakes before disposing of Behrens and the Godolphin colt again in the Jockey Club Gold Cup. A below-par effort in the Breeders' Cup Classic may have been one race too many, but he remains a serious contender in major US dirt events.
**B Baffert in USA [2-3] (from R W Armstrong [5-18] Mar 1997).*

RIVER SAINT (USA) RR 69df 3752[6]
3 ch f Irish River (FR) 9f **(77)** - Imagining (USA) (Northfields (USA)) 9f **(72)**
Form - 45236
Record 1999 - 1st:0 2nd:1 3rd:1 Ran:5
Pre1999 - 1st:0 2nd:0 3rd:0 Ran:1
Win Prizemoney £0 *Total Prizemoney* £2,403
1999 Turf 0-5: (7f 3, 8f 2) (g-f 2, frm 3)
Light-framed, average filly, effective 7f, acts on frm. Turf high 79 (1st run) - 4th of 11 getting 5lb from Siege (22 May Kempton 7f frm RF 1393). **Sir Michael Stoute [0-6] Cheveley Park Stud.*

RIVERSDALE (IRE) BHB 53f49a **RR 55f 49a** 5191[2]
3 b g Elbio 9f **(62)** - Embustera (Sparkler) 8.4f **(55)**
Form - 34702
Record 1999 - 1st:0 2nd:1 3rd:1 Ran:5
Pre1999 - 1st:0 2nd:0 3rd:0 Ran:2
Win Prizemoney £0 *Total Prizemoney* £1,901
1999 Turf 0-5: (8f 4, 10f) (g-s, g-f 2, frm 2)
Lengthy, fair gelding, effective 8f, acts on g-f to frm. Turf high 62 (1st run) - 3rd of 5 to Through The Rye (26 Jun Newcastle 8f frm RF 2340). **J G FitzGerald [0-7] J G FitzGerald.*

RIVER'S SOURCE (USA) BHB 68f **RR 67f** 4429[16]
5 b g Irish River (FR) 9f **(77)** - Singing (USA) (The Minstrel (CAN)) 10f **(72)**
Form - 7081700
Record 1999 - 1st:1 2nd:0 3rd:0 Ran:7
Pre1999 - 1st:2 2nd:5 3rd:1 Ran:19
Win Prizemoney £11,785 *Total Prizemoney* £18,121

Wins								
	* **1999**	Aug	Pontef	(G-F)	H	10f	64	67
	* 1998	Aug	Pontef	(G-F)	H	10f	68	68
	* 1997	Apr	Newmar	(G-F)	H	10f	82	78 <

1999 Turf 1-7: (9f, 10f 1-3, 11f 2, 12f) (g-s, gd, g-f 3, frm 1-2)
Average gelding, effective 9 to 11f, best at 10f, acts on sft to frm, has worn blinkers, likes left handed tracks, likes tight tracks, excels at Newbury and Pontefract. Turf high 67 - 1st of 9 giving 11lb to Rare Talent (4 Aug Pontefract RF 3370).
**B W Hills [3-26] Mrs B W Hills.*

RIVER'S SPARKLE (IRE) BHB 31f **RR 34f** 4010[5]
3 b f River Falls 8.2f **(56)** - El Zaana (Priamos (GER)) 11.1f **(61)**
Form - 8067405
Record 1999 - 1st:0 2nd:0 3rd:0 Ran:7
Pre1999 - 1st:0 2nd:0 3rd:0 Ran:4
1999 Turf 0-7: (10f, 11f, 12f 5) (gd, g-f 4, frm 2)
Light-framed, very moderate filly. Turf high 38. Consistent.
**G B Balding [0-11] Mrs K L Perrin & Mrs P D Gulliver.*

RIVER TERN BHB 70f63a **RR 68f 63a** 4292[5]
6 b g Puissance 7.1f **(60)** - Millaine (Formidable (USA)) 9.2f **(63)**
Form - 313341802456045
Record 1999 - 1st:2 2nd:1 3rd:3 Ran:15
Pre1999 - 1st:4 2nd:3 3rd:6 Ran:36
Win Prizemoney £24,397 *Total Prizemoney* £37,960

Wins								
	* **1999**	Jly	York	(G-F)	H	5f	65	68 <
	* **1999**	May	Thirsk	(G-F)	H	5f	58	60+
	* 1997	Aug	Catter	(G-F)	C	5f		62
	* 1997	Jly	Warwic	(G-F)	H	5f	63	64
	* 1997	May	Redcar	(GD)	C	6f		65
	1996	Spt	Thirsk	(G-F)		6f		59

1999 Turf 2-15: (5f 2-13, 6f 2) (gd 2, g-f 3, frm 2-10)
Average gelding, effective 5 to 6f, best at 5f, acts on gd to frm, best on frm, has worn blinkers, excels at Bath. Turf high 73 - 5th of 14 getting 3lb from Alpen Wolf (22 Aug Bath 6f frm RF 3833) - also 1st of 7 getting 6lb from Antonia's Double (9 Jly York RF 2693). Consistent.
**J M Bradley [5-39] Martyn James & Pete Smith (from J Berry [1-12] Oct 1996).*

RIVER TIMES (USA) BHB 93f **RR 94f** 4265[8]
3 b c Runaway Groom (CAN) 8.1f **(69)** - Miss Riverton (USA) (Fred Astaire (USA))
Form - 712005158
Record 1999 - 1st:2 2nd:1 3rd:0 Ran:9
Pre1999 - 1st:1 2nd:0 3rd:1 Ran:4
Win Prizemoney £26,141 *Total Prizemoney* £29,826

Wins								
	* **1999**	Jly	Newmar	(G-F)	H	8f	91	94 <
	* **1999**	Apr	Beverl	(G-F)		7.5f		92
	* 1998	Spt	Haydoc	(GD)		8.1f		77

1999 Turf 2-9: (7f 1-2, 8f 1-5, 10f, 11f) (gd 2, g-f 3, frm 2-4)
Lengthy, useful colt, effective 7 to 10f, best at 7f, acts on gd to frm, best on frm, has worn blinkers, likes tight tracks, excels at Beverley. Turf high 94 - 1st of 12 giving 2lb to Calcutta (17 Jly Newmarket RF 2910) - also 1st of 8 getting 11lb from Latalomne (14 Apr Beverley RF 0686). Scored first time out at Beverley, but contested some very competitive handicaps afterwards and failed to sparkle. Regained winning form at Newmarket in July when blinkered for the first time. A mile and fast ground seems to suit.
**T D Easterby [3-13] Times of Wigan.*

RM AGAIN BHB 32f **RR 29f** 4148[18]
3 b g Primo Dominie 7.2f **(67)** - La Cabrilla (Carwhite) 7.2f **(61)**
Form - 007360780
Record 1999 - 1st:0 2nd:0 3rd:1 Ran:9
Pre1999 - 1st:0 2nd:0 3rd:0 Ran:2
Win Prizemoney £0 *Total Prizemoney* £328
1999 Turf 0-9: (5f 8, 6f) (gd 2, g-f 3, frm 2, hrd 2)
Scopey, little account gelding, effective 5f, acts on frm, has worn blinkers. Turf high 39 - 3rd of 17 getting 13lb from Pure Elegancia (4 Jun Catterick 5f frm RF 1724).
**R Guest [0-11] RM Partnership Architectural Consultants.*

ROAR ON TOUR BHB 25f36a **RR 23f 36a** 119[10]
10 b g Dunbeath (USA) 9.9f **(53)** - Tickled Trout (Red Alert) 7.6f **(66)**
Form - 040
Record 1999 - 1st:0 2nd:0 3rd:0 Ran:3
Pre1999 - 1st:8 2nd:3 3rd:3 Ran:44
Win Prizemoney £27,127 *Total Prizemoney* £31,114

Wins								
	1996	*Jly*	*Southw*	*(STD)*	*H*	*8f*	*58*	*62*
	1995	*Feb*	*Southw*	*(STD)*	*H*	*8f*	*55*	*68 <*
	1995	*Feb*	*Southw*	*(STD)*	*H*	*8f*	*55*	*55*
	1995	*Jan*	*Southw*	*(STD)*	*H*	*8f*	*49*	*53*
	1995	*Jan*	*Southw*	*(STD)*	*H*	*8f*	*46*	*45*

1999 AW 0-3: (8f 3) (Fibr 3)
Very moderate gelding, has worn blinkers. AW high 33.
**Mrs P Sly [0-3] Mike Lurcock (from Mrs M Reveley [7-34] May 1997).*

ROBANDELA (USA) RR 55f 4083[9]
2 b c Kingmambo (USA) 10.9f **(85)** - Yemanja (USA) (Alleged (USA)) 10f **(76)**
Form - 0
Record 1999 - 1st:0 2nd:0 3rd:0 Ran:1

1999 Turf 0-1: (7f) (frm)
Currently fair colt. **M Johnston [0-1] Robert Aird.*

ROBANNA BHB 42f **RR 47f** 1816[8]

4 b f Robellino (USA) 9.5f **(68)** - Pounelta (Tachypous) 8.6f **(55)**
Form - 348

Record	**1999** -	1st:0	2nd:0	3rd:1	Ran:3
	Pre1999 -	1st:0	2nd:1	3rd:0	Ran:13

Win Prizemoney £0 *Total Prizemoney* £1,831
1999 Turf 0-3: (12f 2, 13f) (gd 2, g-f)
Light-framed, moderate filly, effective 10 to 14f, acts on g-s to gd, best on gd, prefers left handed tracks, favours tight tracks. Turf high 47 (1st run) - 3rd of 11 getting 5lb from Sound Appeal (17 May Bath 13f gd RF 1270). Consistent.
**J Akehurst [0-13] The Grass is Greener Partnership (from R Akehurst [0-3] Oct 1997).*

ROBBER RED BHB 53f **RR 48f** 4260[18]

3 b g Mon Tresor 7.9f **(60)** - Starisk **(33f)** (Risk Me (FR)) 5.9f **(53)**
Form - 500762757060

Record	**1999** -	1st:0	2nd:1	3rd:0	Ran:12
	Pre1999 -	1st:1	2nd:5	3rd:0	Ran:12

Win Prizemoney £1,972 *Total Prizemoney* £8,410

Wins	1998	Aug Lingfi	(FRM) C	6f	78 <

1999 Turf 0-12: (6f 3, 7f, 8f 8) (g-s, gd 2, g-f 2, frm 7)
Moderate gelding, effective 5 to 6f, best at 6f, acts on gd to frm, best on frm, has worn blinkers. Turf high 64.
**R M Flower [0-12] B C Isitt (from B J Meehan [1-12] Oct 1998).*

ROBBIES DREAM (IRE) BHB 53f **RR 49f** 3548[9]

3 ch g Balla Cove - Royal Golden (IRE) (Digamist (USA))
Form - 800

Record	**1999** -	1st:0	2nd:0	3rd:0	Ran:3
	Pre1999 -	1st:0	2nd:0	3rd:0	Ran:4

1999 Turf 0-3: (8f 3) (g-f 2, hrd)
Light-framed, moderate gelding. Turf high 49.
**D Morris [0-7] James Brown.*

ROBBO BHB 57f70a **RR 57f 70a** 774[6]

5 b g Robellino (USA) 9.5f **(68)** - Basha (USA) (Chief's Crown (USA)) 9.8f **(72)**
Form - 6

Record	**1999** -	1st:0	2nd:0	3rd:0	Ran:1
	Pre1999 -	1st:3	2nd:2	3rd:4	Ran:17

Win Prizemoney £6,039 *Total Prizemoney* £10,015

Wins	1997	*Oct Wolver*	*(STD) H*	*14.8f*	*60*	*70* <
	1997	*Spt Wolver*	*(STD)*	*14.8f*		*63+*
	1997	*Aug Southw*	*(STD) H*	*14f*	*54*	*61*

1999 Turf 0-1: (17f) (sft)
Above-average gelding, often wears blinkers. Consistent.
**Mrs M Reveley [4-17] The Scarth Racing Partnership (from C W Thornton [3-14] Nov 1997).*

ROBEENA BHB 35f43a **RR 39f 43a** 4147[5]

4 b f Robellino (USA) 9.5f **(68)** - Raheena (USA) (Lyphard (USA)) 9.9f **(72)**
Form - 07200007005

Record	**1999** -	1st:0	2nd:1	3rd:0	Ran:10
	Pre1999 -	1st:0	2nd:0	3rd:2	Ran:10

Win Prizemoney £0 *Total Prizemoney* £1,900
1999 Turf 0-10: (6f 3, 7f 4, 8f 3) (hvy, gd, g-f 2, frm 5, hrd)
Neat, very moderate filly, effective 7f, acts on gd, has worn blinkers, likes left handed tracks, likes tight tracks. Turf high 52 - 2nd of 8 giving 10lb to Prince of Aragon (17 Apr Thirsk 7f gd RF 0739).
**J L Eyre [0-12] Village Green Racing (from C N Allen [0-8] Jan 1998).*

ROBELLION BHB 54f67a **RR 52f 67a** 4826[21]

8 b g Robellino (USA) 9.5f **(68)** - Tickled Trout (Red Alert) 7.6f **(66)**
Form - 180000

Record	**1999** -	1st:1	2nd:0	3rd:0	Ran:6
	Pre1999 -	1st:10	2nd:12	3rd:11	Ran:88

Win Prizemoney £32,832 *Total Prizemoney* £53,398

Wins	* **1999**	May Lingfi	(G-F) H	7f	60	58
	1998	*Mar Southw*	*(STD) H*	*7f*	*62*	*67*
	1998	*Feb Lingfi*	*(SLW)*	*8f*		*62*
	1998	*Jan Lingfi*	*(STD) C*	*8f*		*62*
	1997	Oct Salisb	(GD) H	6f	47	53
	1996	Aug Newmar	(GD) H	6f	61	69
	1996	Jly Chepst	(G-F) H	5.1f	61	63
	1996	*Feb Lingfi*	*(STD) H*	*10f*	*63*	*62*
	1996	*Jan Lingfi*	*(STD) H*	*8f*	*58*	*55*
	1995	Jly Chepst	(G-F) H	5.1f	68	69

1999 Turf 1-6: (6f, 7f 1-4, 8f) (g-s, gd, g-f, frm 1-3)
Average gelding, effective 6 to 8f, acts on hvy to frm - acts on AW, often wears blinkers (very effectively), prefers left handed tracks, prefers tight tracks, excels at Lingfield. Turf high 58 (1st run) - 1st of 18 giving 15lb to Present 'n Correct (22 May Lingfield RF 1404).
**Miss E C Lavelle [1-6] The Forty Ninth Partnership (from Mrs L Stubbs [2-10] Aug 1998).*

ROBELLITA BHB 56f62a **RR 57f 62a** 511[1]

5 b g Robellino (USA) 9.5f **(68)** - Miellita (King Emperor (USA)) 9.4f **(58)**
Form - 23211

Record	**1999** -	1st:2	2nd:2	3rd:1	Ran:5
	Pre1999 -	1st:0	2nd:0	3rd:0	Ran:3

Win Prizemoney £6,014 *Total Prizemoney* £8,327

Wins	* **1999**	Mar Nottin	(G-S) H	14.1f	50	57
	* **1999**	*Mar Southw*	*(STD)*	*12f*		*64+* <

1999 Turf 1-1: (14f 1-1) (sft 1-1) 1999 AW 1-4: (12f 1-4) (Equi 2, Fibr 1-2)
Average gelding, effective 12 to 14f, best at 12f, acts on sft - acts on AW, best on Equi, prefers left handed tracks. (1st run) - 1st of 18 giving 4lb to Nikita's Star (29 Mar Nottingham RF 0511). AW high 64 - 1st of 10 giving 2lb to Terrazzo (8 Mar Southwell RF 0413).
**B Smart [2-5] Angels Racing Syndicate (from C P Morlock [0-6] Jun 1998).*

ROBERT ELLIS BHB 55f **RR 37f** 3014[5]

3 ch c Anshan 8.2f **(63)** - Susie's Baby (Balidar) 7.9f **(63)**
Form - 5

Record	**1999** -	1st:0	2nd:0	3rd:0	Ran:1
	Pre1999 -	1st:0	2nd:0	3rd:0	Ran:2

1999 Turf 0-1: (5f) (frm)
Workmanlike, currently very moderate colt.
**J Cullinan [0-3] W H Joyce.*

ROBERTICO **RR 110f** 2284a[6]

4 b c Robellino (USA) 9.5f **(68)** - Dance On The Stage (Dancing Brave (USA)) 8.4f **(76)**
Form - 6
1999 Turf 0-1: (12f) (g-f)
Group-class colt. Landed the German Derby in '98.
**A Schutz in GER [1-4].*

ROBERT'S TOY (IRE) BHB 46f **RR 37f** 2837[4]

8 b g Salt Dome (USA) 6.5f **(59)** - Zazu (Cure The Blues (USA)) 9.5f **(63)**
Form - 444

Record	**1999** -	1st:0	2nd:0	3rd:0	Ran:2
	Pre1999 -	1st:0	2nd:0	3rd:0	Ran:1

1999 Turf 0-1: (12f) (frm) 1999 AW 0-1: (12f) (Equi)
Very moderate gelding, has worn blinkers.
**G A Ham [0-8] Mrs Y J White.*

ROBIN HOOD **RR 45f** 4877[17]

2 b c Komaite (USA) 6.9f **(61)** - Plough Hill (North Briton)
Form - 0

Record	**1999** -	1st:0	2nd:0	3rd:0	Ran:1

1999 Turf 0-1: (5f) (frm)
Currently moderate colt.
**Miss L A Perratt [0-1] Cree Lodge Racing Club.*

ROBIN LANE BHB 88f **RR 89f** 5221[14]

4 b f Tenby 10.4f **(76)** - Hiawatha's Song (USA) (Chief's Crown (USA)) 9.8f **(72)**
Form - 0505720122460

Record	**1999** -	1st:1	2nd:3	3rd:0	Ran:13
	Pre1999 -	1st:5	2nd:2	3rd:0	Ran:19

Win Prizemoney £39,909 *Total Prizemoney* £63,713

Wins	* **1999**	Aug Warwic	(GD)	10.5f		85
	* 1998	Oct Doncas	(HVY) H	12f	85	88 <
	* 1998	Oct Ascot	(SFT) H	12f	81	85
	* 1998	Jly Hamilt	(FRM) H	9.2f	72	79

* 1998	Jun	Hamilt	(G-S)	H	9.2f	70	74
* 1998	May	Redcar	(G-F)		10f		71

1999 Turf 1-13: (10f 3, 11f 1-1, 12f 7, 14f 2) (sft 2, g-s, gd 1-5, g-f 3, frm 2)

Scopey, useful filly, effective 9 to 12f, best at 10f, acts on sft to frm, excels at Hamilton and does well at Newcastle and Doncaster. Turf high 89 - 2nd of 17 giving 2lb to Amalia (11 Spt Doncaster 10f frm RF 4267) - also 1st of 6 getting 3lb from Shadoof (13 Aug Warwick RF 3630). She improved a great deal in '98, winning five times. Tough and genuine, she was not as successful last season, only managing victory in a Warwick classified stakes when able to dominate.

**M Johnston [6-27] & Mrs G Middlebrook (from I A Balding [0-5] Oct 1997).*

ROB 'N' GIN (USA) RR 122f 4657a[2]

5 m

Form - 2

1999 Turf 0-1: (8f) (frm)

Currently very high-class. (1st run) - 2nd of 15 giving 2lb to Quiet Resolve (19 Spt Woodbine 8f frm RF 4657a). **in USA [0-1].*

ROBOASTAR (USA) BHB 80f RR 75f 4135[3]

2 b br c Green Dancer (USA) 11.9f **(77)** - Sweet Alabastar (USA) (Gulch (USA)) 8f **(81)**

Form - 033

Record 1999 - 1st:0 2nd:0 3rd:2 Ran:3

Win Prizemoney £0 *Total Prizemoney* £1,113

1999 Turf 0-3: (7f 2, 9f) (g-f, frm 2)

Currently above-average colt. Turf high 75 (began Jly) - 3rd of 8 to Monte Carlo (4 Spt Epsom 9f frm RF 4135).

**W Jarvis [0-3] The Roboastar Partnership.*

ROBO MAGIC (USA) BHB 39f71a RR 33f 71a 4121[8]

7 b g Tejano (USA) 6.5f **(64)** - Bubble Magic (USA) (Clever Trick (USA)) 6.6f **(77)**

Form - 205037734038

Record 1999 - 1st:0 2nd:0 3rd:3 Ran:9

Pre1999 - 1st:10 2nd:8 3rd:5 Ran:71

Win Prizemoney £34,465 *Total Prizemoney* £46,966

Wins									
	* 1998	*Apr*	*Lingfi*	*(STD)*	*H*	*6f*	*78*	*83*	
	* 1998	*Feb*	*Lingfi*	*(STD)*	*H*	*6f*	*71*	*73*	
	* 1997	*May*	*Wolver*	*(STD)*	*H*	*5f*	*78*	*85*	<
	* 1997	*Jan*	*Lingfi*	*(STD)*	*C*	*6f*		*66*	
	* 1996	*Feb*	*Lingfi*	*(STD)*	*H*	*6f*	*70*	*74*	
	* 1996	*Feb*	*Lingfi*	*(STD)*	*H*	*6f*	*70*	*69*	
	* 1995	*Dec*	*Lingfi*	*(STD)*	*H*	*6f*	*67*	*66*	
	* 1995	Aug	Lingfi	(G-F)	H	6f	54	49	
	1995	*Feb*	*Lingfi*	*(STD)*	*S*	*6f*		*67*	

1999 Turf 0-4: (6f 3, 7f) (g-f 3, frm) 1999 AW 0-5: (5f, 6f 2, 7f 2) (Equi 5)

Above-average gelding, effective 5 to 7f, best at 6f, - acts on Equi, has worn blinkers, prefers left handed tracks, prefers tight tracks, excels at Lingfield. Turf high 43. AW high 75 - 3rd of 8 getting 3lb from Topton (21 Jan Lingfield 7f Equi RF 0138). Inconsistent.

**L MontagueHall [8-66] A D Green and Partners (from A Moore [2-6] Feb 1995).*

ROBORANT BHB 78f RR 80f 800[11]

4 b g Robellino (USA) 9.5f **(68)** - Sunny Davis (USA) (Alydar (USA)) 9.1f **(76)**

Form - 0

Record 1999 - 1st:0 2nd:0 3rd:0 Ran:1

Pre1999 - 1st:2 2nd:0 3rd:3 Ran:13

Win Prizemoney £9,047 *Total Prizemoney* £10,771

Wins									
	1998	Oct	Bright	(GD)	H	10f	76	79	<
	1998	Jun	Beverl	(GD)	H	9.9f	74	76	

1999 Turf 0-1: (10f) (g-s)

Unfurnished, decent gelding, effective 10f, acts on g-f to frm, best on frm, has worn blinkers. Inconsistent.

**J Akehurst [1-6] Fraser Miller (from J L Dunlop [2-13] Oct 1998).*

ROCCIOSO RR 21f 5195[16]

2 br c Pelder (IRE) - Priory Bay (Petong) 6.6f **(58)**

Form - 00

Record 1999 - 1st:0 2nd:0 3rd:0 Ran:2

1999 Turf 0-2: (6f 2) (g-s, gd)

Currently little account colt. Turf high 21 (began Oct).

**J C Fox [0-2] Mrs J A Cleary.*

ROCCO TOWER (IRE) BHB 98f RR 101f 2134[6]

3 b c Thatching 7.8f **(69)** - Tatra (Niniski (USA)) 10.6f **(65)**

Form - 4126

Record 1999 - 1st:1 2nd:1 3rd:0 Ran:4

Win Prizemoney £3,745 *Total Prizemoney* £6,246

Wins									
	* 1999	May	Pontef	(G-F)		6f		87	<

1999 Turf 1-4: (5f 3, 6f 1-1) (gd 2, g-f 1-2)

Workmanlike, very useful colt. Turf high 101 - 2nd of 5 getting 3lb from Dashing Blue (12 Jun Sandown 5f gd RF 1960). (DEAD)

**John Berry [1-4] Dee Jay Bloodstock.*

ROCK FALCON (IRE) BHB 93f RR 93f 4921[3]

6 ch g Polar Falcon (USA) 9f **(74)** - Rockfest (USA) (Stage Door Johnny) 10.3f **(84)**

Form - 8402370003

Record 1999 - 1st:0 2nd:1 3rd:2 Ran:10

Pre1999 - 1st:6 2nd:1 3rd:0 Ran:16

Win Prizemoney £37,892 *Total Prizemoney* £48,794

Wins									
	1998	Spt	Bath	(G-S)		8f		97+	
	1998	Aug	Goodwo	(G-F)	H	7f	97	101	<
	1998	May	Kempto	(G-F)	H	8f	85	93	
	1997	Oct	Ascot	(HVY)	H	8f	80	91	
	1997	Spt	Chepst	(GD)	S	8.1f		67+	
	1997	May	Lingfi	(GD)		7f		80	

1999 Turf 0-10: (6f 2, 7f 3, 8f 5) (gd 5, g-f 2, frm 3)

Useful gelding, effective 7 to 8f, best at 7f, acts on gd to frm, best on gd, mostly wears blinkers (extremely effectively), prefers tight tracks. Turf high 99. Consistent. His is not one to trust and often gives away lengths at the start. Capable of smart form when allowed to make the running, he is best around a mile and acts on any ground.

**D Nicholls [0-6] V Greaves (from Lady Herries [6-20] Jly 1999).*

ROCK ISLAND LINE (IRE) BHB 56f64a RR 34f 64a 3800[14]

5 b g New Express 6.8f **(54)** - Gail's Crystal (Crofter (USA)) 8.4f **(56)**

Form - 1631010

Record 1999 - 1st:3 2nd:0 3rd:1 Ran:7

Pre1999 - 1st:4 2nd:3 3rd:6 Ran:24

Win Prizemoney £16,613 *Total Prizemoney* £21,030

Wins									
	* **1999**	*Jly*	*Southw*	*(STD)*	*H*	*7f*	*60*	*62*	<
	* **1999**	*Jly*	*Southw*	*(STD)*	*C*	*7f*		*58*	
	* **1999**	*Feb*	*Southw*	*(STD)*	*S*	*6f*		*60*	
	1998	*Feb*	*Southw*	*(STD)*	*C*	*8f*		*52*	
	1998	*Jan*	*Southw*	*(STD)*	*C*	*7f*		*58*	
	1997	May	Newcas	(GD)	C	7f		62	<
	1997	Apr	Hamilt	(SFT)	S	8.3f		53	

1999 Turf 0-2: (6f, 7f) (g-f 2) 1999 AW 3-5: (6f 1-2, 7f 2-3) (Fibr 3-5)

Average gelding, effective 6 to 8f, best at 7f, acts on gd - acts on Fibr, prefers left handed tracks, favours tight tracks, excels at Southwell. Turf high 34 (began Jly). AW high 62 - 1st of 15 giving 7lb to Bollin Ethos (24 Jly Southwell RF 3113) - also 1st of 10 from Bold Aristocrat (8 Feb Southwell RF 0253). He runs infrequently on turf these days, but is a regular on the Southwell Fibresand. He boasts quite a good strike-rate at between six furlongs and a mile at that track and can be relied upon to try his best.

**G Woodward [3-7] Burntwood Sports Ltd (from J Berry [4-24] Aug 1998).*

ROCKLANDS LANE BHB 44f RR 20f 4233[18]

3 b c Puissance 7.1f **(60)** - Dancing Daughter (Dance In Time (CAN)) 8.9f **(59)**

Form - 20800000

Record 1999 - 1st:0 2nd:1 3rd:0 Ran:8

Pre1999 - 1st:0 2nd:0 3rd:0 Ran:2

Win Prizemoney £0 *Total Prizemoney* £1,336

1999 Turf 0-8: (5f 3, 6f 4, 7f) (gd 2, g-f 3, frm 3)

Unfurnished, little account colt, effective 6f, acts on gd. Turf high 72 (1st run) - 2nd of 13 giving 5lb to Bollin Rita (16 Apr Thirsk 6f gd RF 0730). Inconsistent.

**R F JohnsonHoughton [0-10] R F JohnsonHoughton.*

ROCK ON ROBIN BHB 45f38a RR 49f 38a 5158[8]

2 br g Rock City 8.8f **(62)** - Volcalmeh (Lidhame) 9.2f **(50)**

Form - 065608

Record 1999 - 1st:0 2nd:0 3rd:0 Ran:6

1999 Turf 0-5: (5f, 7f 2, 8f, 10f) (g-s, gd 2, g-f, frm) 1999 AW 0-1: (8f) (Fibr)

Moderate gelding, effective 10f, acts on g-s, often wears blinkers. Turf high 49. **C W Fairhurst [0-6] C W Fairhurst.*

ROCK TO THE TOP (IRE) BHB 30f35a RR 27f 35a 1417[12]

5 b g Rudimentary (USA) 8.2f **(66)** - Well Bought (IRE) (Auction Ring (USA)) 8.6f **(65)**

Form - 0000

Record 1999 - 1st:0 2nd:0 3rd:0 Ran:4
Pre1999 - 1st:0 2nd:1 3rd:1 Ran:14

Win Prizemoney £0 *Total Prizemoney* £1,258

1999 Turf 0-1: (7f) (hrd) 1999 AW 0-3: (6f 2, 7f) (Fibr 3)

Very moderate gelding, has worn blinkers. AW high 31. **J J Sheehan [0-18] Mrs Christina Dowling.*

ROCKY ISLAND BHB 44f RR 41f 1361[8]

2 b g Rock Hopper 10.6f **(54)** - Queen's Eyot (Grundy) 10.3f **(65)**

Form - 008

Record 1999 - 1st:0 2nd:0 3rd:0 Ran:3

1999 Turf 0-3: (5f 2, 6f) (g-s, gd, g-f)

Currently moderate gelding. Turf high 41. **Mrs M Reveley [0-3] W G McHarg.*

ROCKY STALLONE RR 730[11]

4 b g Rock City 8.8f **(62)** - City Link Pet (Tina's Pet) 6.8f **(59)**

Form - 0

Record 1999 - 1st:0 2nd:0 3rd:0 Ran:1
Pre1999 - 1st:0 2nd:0 3rd:0 Ran:1

1999 Turf 0-1: (6f) (gd)

Light-framed, currently very poor gelding. **W McKeown [0-2] C H Dyne.*

RODERICK HUDSON BHB 38f49a RR 31f 49a 1770[29]

7 b g Elmaamul (USA) 8.1f **(70)** - Moviegoer (Pharly (FR)) 9.8f **(68)**

Form - 2070000

Record 1999 - 1st:0 2nd:0 3rd:0 Ran:5
Pre1999 - 1st:1 2nd:4 3rd:0 Ran:15

Win Prizemoney £3,100 *Total Prizemoney* £6,887

Wins 1995 Jun Newbur (G-F) 7f 77+ <

1999 Turf 0-3: (10f, 12f 2) (g-f 2, frm) 1999 AW 0-2: (8f 2) (Equi 2)

Very moderate gelding, effective 9f, - acts on Fibr, has worn blinkers, favours left handed tracks, favours tight tracks. Turf high 31. AW high 33. Inconsistent. **J R Poulton [0-9] Mrs M Liston (from J A R Toller [2-16] May 1998).*

ROFFEY SPINNEY (IRE) BHB 50f46a RR 24f 46a 5058[6]

5 ch g Masterclass (USA) 5.9f **(63)** - Crossed Line (Thatching) 8f **(66)**

Form - 28167400006

Record 1999 - 1st:1 2nd:0 3rd:0 Ran:9
Pre1999 - 1st:4 2nd:2 3rd:7 Ran:32

Win Prizemoney £11,603 *Total Prizemoney* £15,724

Wins * **1999** *Jan Wolver (STD) S 9.4f 65*
1998 Oct Leices (G-S) SH 7f 54 67
1998 Jly Folkes (GD) C 7f 50
1997 *Feb Lingfi (STD) H 5f 66 69* <
1997 *Feb Lingfi (STD) 6f 63*

1999 Turf 0-2: (7f 2) (gd, g-f) 1999 AW 1-7: (7f, 8f 3, 9f 1-2, 11f) (Equi 2, Fibr 1-5)

Moderate gelding, effective 7 to 9f, acts on gd - acts on AW, has worn blinkers. Turf high 24. AW high 65 (1st run) - 1st of 9 giving 12lb to Monchania (6 Jan Wolverhampton RF 0037). He has picked up a few modest events on turf and sand in his time, but is not particularly consistent. Best when able to dominate. **J Cullinan [1-13] Alan Spargo Ltd Toolmakers (from R Hannon [4-29] Oct 1998).*

ROGAN JOSH (AUS) RR 105f 5223a[1]

7 b g Old Spice (AUS) - Eastern Mystique (AUS) (Hammed (AUS))

Form - 1

1999 Turf 1-1: (16f 1-1) (gd 1-1)

Currently Pattern-class, always wears blinkers. (1st run) - 1st of 24 getting 17lb from Central Park (2 Nov Flemington RF 5223a). Completed the Mackinnon Stakes/Melbourne Cup double in the space of five days. **J B Cummings in AUS [1-1] Mrs W L Green & J P Miller.*

ROGER ROSS BHB 48f49a RR 40f 49a 5053[13]

4 b g Touch of Grey 8.1f **(47)** - Foggy Dew (Smoggy) 8f **(50)**

Form - 0008000070

Record 1999 - 1st:0 2nd:0 3rd:0 Ran:10
Pre1999 - 1st:4 2nd:2 3rd:3 Ran:17

Win Prizemoney £21,863 *Total Prizemoney* £25,227

Wins * 1998 Oct Ascot (SFT) H 8f 71 75 <
* 1998 Jly Salisb (FRM) H 8f 62 69
* 1998 Jun Sandow (G-S) H 8.1f 52 64
* 1998 Jun Salisb (G-S) H 8f 52 65

1999 Turf 0-10: (7f, 8f 8, 10f) (g-s 2, gd 4, g-f 4)

Small, fair gelding, effective 8f, acts on g-s to frm, has worn blinkers, likes right handed tracks, excels at Sandown and Salisbury. Turf high 54. **R M Flower [4-27] H Lawrence.*

ROGUE SPIRIT BHB 73f RR 72f 4805[5]

3 b c Petong 7.6f **(58)** - Quick Profit (Formidable (USA)) 9.2f **(63)**

Form - 710380305

Record 1999 - 1st:1 2nd:0 3rd:2 Ran:9

Win Prizemoney £4,273 *Total Prizemoney* £6,528

Wins * **1999** May Folkes (G-F) 6f 70 <

1999 Turf 1-9: (5f, 6f 1-7, 7f) (gd 4, g-f 1-2, frm 3)

Workmanlike, above-average colt, effective 5 to 6f, best at 6f, acts on gd to frm. Turf high 77 - 3rd of 16 getting 1lb from Mallia (1 Jly Haydock 6f gd RF 2463) - also 1st of 10 giving 5lb to Springtime Lady (26 May Folkestone RF 1489). **P W Harris [1-9] L Grover, P Johns, C Stewart & K Swinden.*

ROI DE DANSE BHB 46f44a RR 37f 44a 5033[21]

4 ch g Komaite (USA) 6.9f **(61)** - Princess Lucy (Local Suitor (USA)) 8.4f **(67)**

Form - 0664422000000600

Record 1999 - 1st:0 2nd:2 3rd:0 Ran:12
Pre1999 - 1st:2 2nd:1 3rd:0 Ran:18

Win Prizemoney £5,411 *Total Prizemoney* £10,875

Wins 1998 Spt Bright (GD) 8f 71
1997 Aug Kempto (GD) 6f 72 <

1999 Turf 0-7: (7f 2, 8f 3, 10f 2) (sft, g-s, gd 2, g-f 2, frm) 1999 AW 0-5: (7f 2, 8f, 10f 2) (Equi 2, Fibr 3)

Scopey, moderate gelding, effective 7 to 9f, acts on gd to frm, has worn blinkers, likes left handed tracks. Turf high 37. AW high 55. **M Quinn [0-16] Miss A Jones (from J W Hills [2-14] Oct 1998).*

ROISIN SPLENDOUR (IRE) BHB 61f69a RR 59f 69a 4179[7]

4 ch f Inchinor 8.9f **(64)** - Oriental Splendour (Runnett) 7f **(59)**

Form - 222515863160507

Record 1999 - 1st:2 2nd:1 3rd:1 Ran:13
Pre1999 - 1st:1 2nd:3 3rd:2 Ran:14

Win Prizemoney £8,992 *Total Prizemoney* £16,066

Wins * **1999** Jun Goodwo (G-F) H 7f 64 66
* ***1999*** *Feb Lingfi (STD) H 7f 67 72*
* 1998 Jly Bright (GD) 7f 77 <

1999 Turf 1-9: (7f 1-7, 8f 2) (gd, g-f 3, frm 1-5) 1999 AW 1-4: (7f 1-2, 8f 2) (Equi 1-3, Fibr)

Workmanlike, above-average filly, effective 7f, acts on gd to g-f - acts on Equi, likes left handed tracks, likes tight tracks. Turf high 69. AW high 72 - 1st of 11 giving 3lb to Acid Test (6 Feb Lingfield RF 0240). She showed improved form when racing on Equitrack during the winter, and was possibly unlucky not to win more than once on that surface. Added a victory on turf at Goodwood in June, and is obviously suited by seven furlongs on a turning track. **S Dow [3-27] Byerley Bloodstock.*

ROKEBY BOWL BHB 103f RR 108f 2044[10]

7 b g Salse (USA) 10.9f **(71)** - Rose Bowl (USA) (Habitat) 9.4f **(70)**

Form - 2370

Record 1999 - 1st:0 2nd:1 3rd:1 Ran:4
Pre1999 - 1st:6 2nd:9 3rd:3 Ran:33

Win Prizemoney £60,288 *Total Prizemoney* £120,017

Wins * 1998 Aug York (FRM) H 11.9f 93 96 <
* 1998 Aug Epsom (G-F) H 12f 90 93
* 1997 Aug Newbur (G-F) 12f 96 <
* 1997 Jly Sandow (G-F) 11.4f 91
* 1995 Jun Sandow (GD) H 9f 84 83
* 1995 Jun Pontef (GD) H 10f 76 83

1999 Turf 0-4: (10f, 12f 2, 13f) (gd, g-f 3)

Pattern-class gelding, effective 10 to 13f, acts on g-f to frm, best on g-f, prefers left handed tracks. Turf high 108 (1st run) - 2nd of 20 giving 8lb to Carry The Flag (5 Apr Kempton 10f g-f RF 0576). Consistent. A smart handicapper in recent seasons, he ran a fine

race in the Ormonde Stakes, but faced stiff tasks in handicaps subsequently. **I A Balding [6-37] Mrs Paul Mellon.*

ROLE MODEL BHB 36f **RR 38f** 4988[2]
3 b f Tragic Role (USA) 9.4f **(63)** - Emerald Gulf (IRE) (Wassl) 9.7f **(62)**
Form - 68047862
Record 1999 - 1st:0 2nd:1 3rd:0 Ran:8
Pre1999 - 1st:0 2nd:0 3rd:0 Ran:1
Win Prizemoney £0 *Total Prizemoney* £575
1999 Turf 0-8: (7f, 8f, 10f 2, 11f, 12f, 14f 2) (g-s, gd 3, g-f, frm 3)
Leggy, very moderate filly, effective 14f, acts on frm, favours tight tracks. Turf high 46. **R M Whitaker [0-9] The PBT Group.*

ROLLER BHB 61f **RR 66f** 4817[5]
3 b c Bluebird (USA) 7.9f **(71)** - Tight Spin (High Top) 10.2f **(67)**
Form - 015308075
Record 1999 - 1st:1 2nd:0 3rd:1 Ran:9
Pre1999 - 1st:0 2nd:0 3rd:1 Ran:2
Win Prizemoney £3,915 *Total Prizemoney* £5,430
Wins * 1999 May Warwic (SFT) 6.8f 75 <
1999 Turf 1-9: (7f 1-2, 8f 4, 10f 2, 12f) (sft 1-1, g-s, gd 2, g-f, frm 4)
Scopey, average colt, effective 6 to 8f, best at 7f, acts on sft to frm, often wears blinkers (extremely effectively). Turf high 75 - 1st of 7 giving 5lb to Fantastic Belle (29 May Warwick RF 1589). Consistent. He looks suited by seven furlongs and a bit of cut in the ground. **H Candy [1-11] H R H Prince Fahd Salman.*

ROLLING RIO BHB 56f59a **RR 36f 59a** 4223[11]
3 b g Chaddleworth (IRE) - Broughton's Gold (IRE) **(18f)** (Trojan Fen) 8.1f **(62)**
Form - 2000
Record 1999 - 1st:0 2nd:1 3rd:0 Ran:4
Pre1999 - 1st:0 2nd:0 3rd:0 Ran:5
Win Prizemoney £0 *Total Prizemoney* £941
1999 Turf 0-1: (8f) (g-f) 1999 AW 0-3: (10f 2, 12f) (Equi 2, Fibr)
Workmanlike, very moderate gelding, effective 10f, - acts on Equi. AW high 63 (1st run) - 2nd of 10 giving 5lb to Chalcedony (5 Jan Lingfield 10f Equi RF 0034). Becoming disappointing.
**Ronald Thompson [0-1] Haggswood Partnerships (from P C Haslam [0-8] Jun 1999).*

ROLLING STONE BHB 90f **RR 82+f** 4584[1]
5 b h Northern Amethyst 10.2f **(81)** -First Sapphire(Simply Great (FR)) 8.2f **(65)**
Form - 431
Record 1999 - 1st:1 2nd:0 3rd:1 Ran:3
Pre1999 - 1st:0 2nd:0 3rd:1 Ran:1
Win Prizemoney £3,460 *Total Prizemoney* £4,876
Wins * 1999 Spt Bath (SFT) 10.2f 82+ <
1999 Turf 1-3: (10f 1-2, 12f) (gd 1-1, frm 2)
Decent colt. Turf high 82 (began Aug) - 1st of 11 giving 6lb to Total Delight (27 Spt Bath RF 4584).
**Mrs A J Perrett [1-3] Brian Cooper (from Lady Herries [0-1] Jun 1997).*

ROLO TOMASI (IRE) RR 106+f 4971a[1]
3 b g Mujtahid (USA) 7.4f **(69)** - Elegant Bloom (Be My Guest (USA)) 9.3f **(67)**
Form - 465727221
1999 Turf 1-9: (5f 4, 6f 1-4, 7f) (sft, g-s 1-3, gd 3, g-f 2)
Pattern-class gelding, effective 5 to 6f, best at 6f, acts on sft to gd, best on g-s, does well at Curragh. Turf high 106 - 1st of 14 getting 1lb from Social Harmony (16 Oct Curragh RF 4971a). Consistent. He saved the best till last, producing a sharp burst of speed to win a Listed event at The Curragh in October. Suited by waiting tactics, he is a useful sprinter on soft ground. Sold for 150,000 gns to race in Scandinavia. **E Lynam in IRE [3-13] Gerard Purcell.*

ROMA BHB 45f47a **RR 45f 47a** 5190[10]
4 b f Second Set (IRE) 9.2f **(67)** - Villasanta (Corvaro (USA)) 9f **(53)**
Form - 265000120
Record 1999 - 1st:1 2nd:1 3rd:0 Ran:7
Pre1999 - 1st:0 2nd:1 3rd:1 Ran:6
Win Prizemoney £2,668 *Total Prizemoney* £4,546
Wins * 1999 Jun Mussel (G-F) H 12f 43 45 <
1999 Turf 1-5: (9f, 10f, 12f 1-3) (g-f 1-4, frm) 1999 AW 0-2: (9f, 12f) (Fibr 2)
Rangy, fair filly, effective 9 to 12f, acts on g-s - acts on Fibr, favours tight tracks. Turf high 45. AW high 49. Inconsistent.
**A R Dicken [1-3] J W D Campbell (from C W Thornton [0-10] May 1999).*

ROMAN CANDLE (IRE) RR 71+f 4822[7]
3 b c Sabrehill (USA) 8.5f **(64)** - Penny Banger (IRE) (Pennine Walk) 8.5f **(61)**
Form - 06521157
Record 1999 - 1st:2 2nd:1 3rd:0 Ran:8
Win Prizemoney £7,865 *Total Prizemoney* £8,697
Wins * 1999 Jly Ripon (GD) H 12.3f 70 71+ <
*** 1999** Jun Windso (G-F) H 11.6f 62 68
1999 Turf 2-8: (8f, 10f 2, 12f 2-5) (sft, g-s, gd 1-3, g-f 2, frm 1-1)
Scopey, above-average colt, effective 12f, acts on gd to frm, favours tight tracks. Turf high 71 - 1st of 8 giving 5lb to Love Blues (5 Jly Ripon RF 2563) - also 1st of 10 getting 8lb from Luz Bay (21 Jun Windsor RF 2181). He won nicely at Windsor and Ripon during the summer. Suited by a mile and a half, he can continue to improve. **C F Wall [2-8] Exors of the Late Sir W R Stuttaford.*

ROMANECH (IRE) BHB 58f **RR 58f** 4950[14]
2 b c Nicolotte - O La Bamba (IRE) (Commanche Run) 8.5f **(58)**
Form - 7500
Record 1999 - 1st:0 2nd:0 3rd:0 Ran:4
1999 Turf 0-4: (5f, 6f, 7f, 8f) (gd 2, g-f, frm)
Fair colt. Turf high 58 (began Jly).
**J G Smyth-Osbourne [0-4] Deauville Daze Partnership.*

ROMAN EMPEROR BHB 49f **RR 56f** 5076[17]
2 ch g Lycius (USA) 8.8f **(71)** - Subya **(99f)** (Night Shift (USA)) 7.2f **(69)**
Form - 600080
Record 1999 - 1st:0 2nd:0 3rd:0 Ran:6
1999 Turf 0-6: (5f 2, 6f 3, 7f) (gd 3, frm 3)
Fair gelding. Turf high 56. **M W Easterby [0-6] M W Easterby.*

ROMAN HOLIDAY (IRE) BHB 50f **RR 41f** 4564[17]
3 ch g Lahib (USA) 8f **(69)** - Beneficiary **(56f)** (Jalmood (USA)) 10.1f **(52)**
Form - 660
Record 1999 - 1st:0 2nd:0 3rd:0 Ran:3
1999 Turf 0-3: (5f, 6f 2) (gd 2, g-f)
Moderate gelding. Turf high 41. (DEAD)
**M A Buckley [0-3] Mrs N W Buckley.*

ROMAN KING (IRE) BHB 86f **RR 87f** 4861[1]
4 b c Sadler's Wells (USA) 11.3f **(87)** - Romantic Feeling (Shirley Heights) 10.3f **(74)**
Form - 541
Record 1999 - 1st:1 2nd:0 3rd:0 Ran:3
Win Prizemoney £4,208 *Total Prizemoney* £4,403
Wins * 1999 Oct Haydoc (HVY) 11.9f 87 <
1999 Turf 1-3: (12f 1-3) (sft 1-1, gd, g-f)
Currently useful colt. Turf high 87 (began Aug) - 1st of 14 giving 7lb to Historic (13 Oct Haydock RF 4861). Unraced at two or three, he ran fairly well in his first two starts and got off the mark in a Haydock maiden over a mile and a half. Still has some scope. Sold for 95,000 gns in the autumn, reportedly to join Micky Hammond.
**J H M Gosden [1-3] Mrs John Magnier & Ms Rachel D S Hood.*

ROMAN LEGIONNAIRE BHB 71f **RR 73f** 4672[14]
2 b c Ezzoud (IRE) - Zalfa (Luthier) 9.8f **(71)**
Form - 776370
Record 1999 - 1st:0 2nd:0 3rd:1 Ran:6
Win Prizemoney £0 *Total Prizemoney* £490
1999 Turf 0-6: (6f, 7f 5) (g-s, g-f 4, frm)
Above-average colt, effective 7f, acts on g-f. Turf high 71 - 7th of 9 getting 1lb from Common Place (29 Aug Goodwood 7f g-f RF 3996). **G B Balding [0-6] The Roman Legion.*

ROMAN REEL (USA) BHB 38f53a **RR 35f 53a** 4666[4]
8 ch g Sword Dance 9.4f **(67)** - Our Mimi (USA) (Believe It (USA)) 9.4f **(70)**
Form - 2005007004
Record 1999 - 1st:0 2nd:0 3rd:0 Ran:8
Pre1999 - 1st:11 2nd:9 3rd:10 Ran:75
Win Prizemoney £26,660 *Total Prizemoney* £37,512
Wins * 1998 Aug Bright (FRM) H 10f 55 59

* 1998	*Mar Lingfi*	*(STD)*	*H*	*8f*	*56*	*63*
* 1998	*Jan Lingfi*	*(STD)*	*H*	*10f*	*53*	*65*
* 1997	Spt Bright	(G-F)	H	10f	47	52
* 1997	Jun Bright	(FRM)	C	10f		55
* 1997	*Mar Lingfi*	*(STD)*	*H*	*8f*	*54*	*58*
* 1996	Jun Bright	(FRM)	C	10f		70 <
* 1996	May Bright	(FRM)	S	10f		61
* 1995	Jly Chepst	(G-F)	H	8.1f	62	69
* 1995	*Feb Lingfi*	*(STD)*	*H*	*10f*	*57*	*57*

1999 Turf 0-5: (10f 4, 12f) (g-f, frm 4) 1999 AW 0-3: (10f, 12f 2) (Equi 3)
Fair gelding, effective 8 to 12f, best at 10f, acts on g-f to frm - acts on Equi, likes left handed tracks, likes tight tracks, likes Lingfield. Turf high 46 (began Jly). AW high 51. Pays his way at a low level, and goes particularly well on the Lingfield Equitrack and at Brighton. He is not very consistent, but is a good ride for an inexperienced pilot. **G L Moore [11-83] Mrs J Moore.*

ROMANTIC AFFAIR (IRE) BHB 71f **RR 80f** 5052[3]
2 ch g Persian Bold 10f **(69)** - Broken Romance (IRE) (Ela-Mana-Mou) 10.1f **(70)**
Form - 813
Record 1999 - 1st:1 2nd:0 3rd:1 Ran:3
Win Prizemoney £1,819 *Total Prizemoney* £2,363
Wins * **1999** Spt Newcas (SFT) 7f 80+ <
1999 Turf 1-3: (7f 1-3) (gd 1-2, frm)
Currently decent gelding. Turf high 80 (began Spt) - 1st of 11 giving 8lb to Alpathar (29 Spt Newcastle RF 4633).
**J L Dunlop [1-3] The Earl Cadogan.*

ROMERO BHB 62f **RR 62f** 4904[12]
3 b g Robellino (USA) 9.5f **(68)** - Casamurrae (Be My Guest (USA)) 9.3f **(67)**
Form - 22360
Record 1999 - 1st:0 2nd:2 3rd:1 Ran:5
Pre1999 - 1st:0 2nd:0 3rd:1 Ran:3
Win Prizemoney £0 *Total Prizemoney* £3,131
1999 Turf 0-5: (10f, 12f 2, 14f, 15f) (gd 3, frm, hrd)
Average gelding, effective 10f, acts on gd. Turf high 66 (1st run) - 2nd of 17 getting 9lb from Kingston Venture (25 Mar Doncaster 10f gd RF 0465). Consistent.
**J Akehurst [0-1] Fraser Miller (from C W Thornton [0-7] May 1999).*

ROMNEY RR 47f 4839[15]
2 ch g Timeless Times (USA) 6.1f **(56)** - Ewe Lamb (Free State) 8.7f **(61)**
Form - 00
Record 1999 - 1st:0 2nd:0 3rd:0 Ran:2
1999 Turf 0-2: (7f, 8f) (gd, hrd)
Currently moderate gelding. Turf high 47 (began Spt).
**Mrs P Sly [0-2] Mrs P M Sly.*

ROMOLA BHB 72f **RR 73f** 5133[16]
3 b f Wolfhound (USA) 7.3f **(71)** - Myth (Troy) 10.4f **(68)**
Form - 043620
Record 1999 - 1st:0 2nd:1 3rd:1 Ran:6
Win Prizemoney £0 *Total Prizemoney* £1,524
1999 Turf 0-6: (8f 3, 10f, 12f 2) (gd 2, g-f 2, frm 2)
Unfurnished, above-average filly, effective 12f, acts on gd. Turf high 73 - 2nd of 7 to Zariliya (26 Spt Musselburgh 12f gd RF 4576).
**L M Cumani [0-6] The Speculators.*

RONDA RR 110+f 2631[1]
3 b f Bluebird (USA) 7.9f **(71)** - Memory's Gold (USA) **(61f)** (Java Gold (USA))
Form - 2211
1999 Turf 2-4: (7f, 8f 1-2, 11f 1-1) (g-s, gd 1-2, frm 1-1)
Group-class filly. Turf high 110 - 1st of 8 getting 6lb from Balisada (7 Jly Newmarket RF 2631) - also 1st of 5 getting 4lb from Venize (6 Jun Chantilly RF 1905a). She provided her trainer with his first winner in England when landing the Group 2 Falmouth Stakes at Newmarket's July Meeting. Improving with every start and blessed with a useful turn-of-foot, she is expected to continue her career in America. **C Laffon-Parias in FR [2-5] D Hinojosa.*

RONNI PANCAKE BHB 63f **RR 67f** 4944[7]
2 b f Mujadil (USA) 7.7f **(70)** - Funny Choice (IRE) **(55f)** (Commanche Run) 8.5f **(58)**
Form - 072067
Record 1999 - 1st:0 2nd:1 3rd:0 Ran:6
Win Prizemoney £0 *Total Prizemoney* £1,070
1999 Turf 0-5: (6f 3, 7f 2) (sft, gd, g-f 2, frm) 1999 AW 0-1: (7f) (Fibr)
Average filly, effective 6f, acts on frm. Turf high 67 - 2nd of 6 getting 4lb from Indeedyedo (23 Jun Hamilton 6f frm RF 2234).
**J S Moore [0-6] J Laughton.*

RONQUISTA D'OR BHB 48f49a **RR 49f 49a** 3632[3]
5 b g Ron's Victory (USA) 9.2f **(52)** - Gild the Lily (Ile de Bourbon (USA)) 10.1f **(67)**
Form - 132334253
Record 1999 - 1st:0 2nd:2 3rd:4 Ran:8
Pre1999 - 1st:3 2nd:3 3rd:1 Ran:24
Win Prizemoney £6,641 *Total Prizemoney* £12,504

Wins	* 1998	*Dec Wolver*	*(STD)*	*H*	*12f*	*47*	*51*
	* 1998	Jly Warwic	(G-F)	SH	12.5f	43	52
	* 1998	*Jan Southw*	*(STD)*	*H*	*12f*	*46*	*56+* <

1999 Turf 0-3: (12f 3) (gd, frm 2) 1999 AW 0-5: (11f, 12f 3, 16f) (Fibr 5)
Fair gelding, effective 12 to 13f, best at 13f, acts on gd to frm - acts on AW, often wears blinkers (extremely effectively), prefers left handed tracks, excels at Warwick, does well at Wolverhampton. Turf high 49 - 3rd of 12 giving 5lb to Needwood Mystic (13 Aug Warwick 12f gd RF 3632). AW high 51 - 3rd of 12 giving 11lb to Evezio Rufo (27 Mar Wolverhampton 12f Fibr RF 0498). Consistent.
**G A Ham [3-32] D M Drury.*

RON'S PET BHB 62f74a **RR 61df 74a** 1519[8]
4 ch g Ron's Victory (USA) 9.2f **(52)** - Penny Mint (Mummy's Game) 8.2f **(60)**
Form - 14146008
Record 1999 - 1st:2 2nd:0 3rd:0 Ran:8
Pre1999 - 1st:1 2nd:4 3rd:1 Ran:16
Win Prizemoney £8,855 *Total Prizemoney* £16,010

Wins	* **1999**	*Mar Wolver*	*(STD)*	*H*	*7f*	*68*	*74*
	1999	*Mar Wolver*	*(STD)*	*C*	*7f*		*67*
	1997	Aug Bright	(GD)		7f		79 <

1999 Turf 0-3: (6f, 7f, 8f) (g-s, g-f, hrd) 1999 AW 2-5: (7f 2-2, 8f 3) (Equi, Fibr 2-4)
Scopey, above-average gelding, effective 7 to 8f, best at 7f, acts on frm - acts on Fibr, has worn blinkers. Turf high 61. AW high 74 - 1st of 9 giving 19lb to Kosevo (27 Mar Wolverhampton RF 0496) - also 1st of 8 getting 3lb from Dryad (3 Mar Wolverhampton RF 0393). Formerly a fair handicapper for Richard Hannon, he is now with Karl Burke and has shown improved form since being tried on sand. He looks best suited by seven furlongs.
**K R Burke [1-7] Nigel Shields (from R Hannon [2-18] Mar 1999).*

ROO BHB 95f **RR 87f** 5041[11]
2 b f Rudimentary (USA) 8.2f **(66)** - Shall We Run (Hotfoot) 10.5f **(59)**
Form - 1832621420
Record 1999 - 1st:2 2nd:3 3rd:1 Ran:10
Win Prizemoney £6,690 *Total Prizemoney* £17,074
Wins * **1999** Aug Haydoc (SFT) 6f 86 <
* **1999** Apr Bath (SFT) 5.1f 82+
1999 Turf 2-10: (5f 1-5, 6f 1-4, 7f) (sft, g-s 1-1, gd 1-3, g-f 3, frm 2)
Useful filly, effective 5 to 6f, best at 6f, acts on g-s to frm, best on frm. Turf high 87 - also 1st of 10 getting 3lb from Lady Sarka (7 Aug Haydock RF 3449). Consistent. She paid her way through a busy season with victories at Bath and Haydock and finishing in the frame on several other occasions, including in Listed company. Very much suited by soft ground.
**R F JohnsonHoughton [2-10] Mrs H JohnsonHoughton.*

ROOFTOP PROTEST (IRE) RR 55f 3537[5]
2 b g Thatching 7.8f **(69)** - Seattle Siren (USA) (Seattle Slew (USA)) 9.4f **(76)**
Form - 065
Record 1999 - 1st:0 2nd:0 3rd:0 Ran:3
1999 Turf 0-3: (6f, 7f 2) (g-f, frm 2)
Currently fair gelding. Turf high 55 (began Jly).
**N Tinkler [0-3] P D Savill.*

ROOKIE BHB 44f47a **RR 47f 47a** 5056[2]
3 b g Magic Ring (IRE) 6.5f **(64)** - Shot At Love (IRE) **(83f)** (Last Tycoon) 8.5f **(62)**
Form - 2280572
Record 1999 - 1st:0 2nd:3 3rd:0 Ran:7

Pre1999 - 1st:0 2nd:0 3rd:0 Ran:1
Win Prizemoney £0 *Total Prizemoney* £2,792
1999 Turf 0-4: (7f, 8f, 10f 2) (gd 2, frm 2) 1999 AW 0-3: (10f 2, 16f) (Equi 3)
Leggy, moderate gelding, effective 10f, - acts on Equi, favours left handed tracks, favours tight tracks. Turf high 57 (began Jly). AW high 49. **C A Cyzer [0-8] R M Cyzer.*

ROONAH QUAY (IRE) BHB 33f **RR 38f** 3671[11]

3 br f Soviet Lad (USA) 9.4f **(63)** - Piney Lake (Sassafras (FR)) 9.6f **(69)**
Form - 7866700
Record 1999 - 1st:0 2nd:0 3rd:0 Ran:7
1999 Turf 0-4: (7f, 8f, 10f, 12f) (gd 2, g-f, frm) 1999 AW 0-3: (6f, 8f, 9f) (Fibr 3)
Light-framed, very moderate filly. Turf high 38. AW high 33.
**D McCain [0-4] Helshaw Food Products Ltd (from J L Eyre [0-3] May 1999).*

ROOSTER BHB 55f **RR 44f** 1937[4]

4 b g Roi Danzig (USA) 10.5f **(62)** - Jussoli (Don) 7.7f **(64)**
Form - 84
Record 1999 - 1st:0 2nd:0 3rd:0 Ran:2
Pre1999 - 1st:0 2nd:0 3rd:0 Ran:3
Win Prizemoney £0 *Total Prizemoney* £597
1999 Turf 0-2: (11f, 12f) (g-s, g-f)
Workmanlike, moderate gelding. Turf high 31.
**Miss S E Hall [0-7] C Platts.*

ROSA CANINA BHB 73f **RR 82f** 5132[8]

3 b f Bustino 11f **(64)** - Moon Spin (Night Shift (USA)) 7.2f **(69)**
Form - 031113118
Record 1999 - 1st:5 2nd:0 3rd:2 Ran:9
Pre1999 - 1st:0 2nd:0 3rd:0 Ran:2
Win Prizemoney £15,853 *Total Prizemoney* £16,640

Wins									
*	**1999**	Oct	Pontef	(GD)	H	18f	69	71	<
*	**1999**	Spt	Nottin	(G-F)	H	16f	65	70	
*	**1999**	Jly	Lingfi	(FRM)	H	16f	64	67	
*	**1999**	Jly	Beverl	(G-F)	H	16.2f	60	63	
*	**1999**	Jun	Redcar	(FRM)	H	14.1f	57	58	

1999 Turf 5-9: (10f, 14f 1-2, 16f 3-5, 18f 1-1) (gd, g-f 1-3, frm 4-5)
Light-framed, decent filly, prefers left handed tracks, prefers tight tracks. Turf high 82. Improving. Followed the familiar pattern of improving a pace once upped in trip. Well held in a Listed race on her final start. **J L Dunlop [5-11] J L Dunlop.*

ROSA ROYALE BHB 41f43a **RR 45f 43a** 3289[12]

5 b m Arazi (USA) 9.2f **(74)** - Gussy Marlowe (Final Straw) 7.9f **(64)**
Form - 4250
Record 1999 - 1st:0 2nd:1 3rd:0 Ran:4
Pre1999 - 1st:0 2nd:1 3rd:2 Ran:14
Win Prizemoney £0 *Total Prizemoney* £2,634
1999 Turf 0-2: (8f, 10f) (frm 2) 1999 AW 0-2: (8f, 10f) (Equi, Fibr)
Moderate filly, effective 8 to 12f, acts on gd - acts on Fibr. Turf high 37 (began Jly). AW high 43 (1st run) (began Jly) - 2nd of 15 getting 2lb from Stravsea (8 Jly Southwell 8f Fibr RF 2648).
**Mrs L Stubbs [0-4] Mrs V A Ward (from W Storey [0-10] Oct 1998).*

ROSEAU RR 69f 5165[7]

3 b f Nashwan (USA) 10.3f **(79)** - Fair Rosamunda (Try My Best (USA)) 7.6f **(67)**
Form - 47
Record 1999 - 1st:0 2nd:0 3rd:0 Ran:2
Win Prizemoney £0 *Total Prizemoney* £280
1999 Turf 0-2: (10f, 12f) (g-s, g-f)
Scopey, currently average filly. Turf high 69 (began Aug).
**J H M Gosden [0-2] Sheikh Mohammed.*

ROSE BAY BHB 57f **RR 61f** 3254[4]

3 b f Shareef Dancer (USA) 10.1f **(67)** - Cormorant Bay (Don't Forget Me) 8.3f **(74)**
Form - 554554
Record 1999 - 1st:0 2nd:0 3rd:0 Ran:6
Pre1999 - 1st:0 2nd:0 3rd:0 Ran:1
Win Prizemoney £0 *Total Prizemoney* £226
1999 Turf 0-6: (9f, 10f 2, 11f, 12f 2) (hvy, gd, frm 4)
Light-framed, average filly. Turf high 64.
**C E Brittain [0-7] Saeed Manana.*

ROSE HILL BHB 72f **RR 77f** 864[8]

3 b f Sabrehill (USA) 8.5f **(64)** - Petite Rosanna (Ile de Bourbon (USA)) 10.1f **(67)**
Form - 8
Record 1999 - 1st:0 2nd:0 3rd:0 Ran:1
Pre1999 - 1st:1 2nd:0 3rd:0 Ran:3
Win Prizemoney £2,203 *Total Prizemoney* £2,285
Wins * 1998 Aug Warwic (G-F) 7f 68+ <
1999 Turf 0-1: (10f) (sft)
Unfurnished, above-average filly.
**T G Mills [1-4] Chancery Bourse Inv Stud).*

ROSE OF HYMUS RR 49f 4451[12]

2 ch f Rudimentary (USA) 8.2f **(66)** - Green's Cassatt (USA) (Apalachee (USA)) 9.4f **(71)**
Form - 0
Record 1999 - 1st:0 2nd:0 3rd:0 Ran:1
1999 Turf 0-1: (7f) (sft)
Currently moderate filly. **J E Banks [0-1] Mrs P A Ovenden.*

ROSE OF MOONCOIN (IRE) BHB 93f **RR 72?f** 4290[7]

3 b f Brief Truce (USA) 9.1f **(73)** - Sharp Deposit (Sharpo) 7.7f **(59)**
Form - 77
Record 1999 - 1st:0 2nd:0 3rd:0 Ran:2
Pre1999 - 1st:1 2nd:0 3rd:0 Ran:3
Win Prizemoney £4,308 *Total Prizemoney* £5,958
Wins * 1998 Jun Newmar (GD) 6f 79 <
1999 Turf 0-2: (8f, 10f) (g-f, frm)
Light-framed, above-average filly. Turf high 70 (began Aug). Last in Listed races. **J E Banks [1-5] P Cunningham.*

ROSE OF TARA (IRE) RR 78+f 4476a[5]

3 ch f Generous - Flame of Tara (Artaius (USA)) 9f **(69)**
Form - 072215
1999 Turf 1-6: (10f, 11f, 12f 1-3, 14f) (g-s 3, gd 1-1, g-f, frm)
Above-average filly. Turf high 96. Beautifully bred, she took a while to learn the ropes but was still improving when finishing lame on her final start. Likely to stay well, she seems suited by easy ground. **M J Grassick in IRE [1-6] Miss P F O'Kelly.*

ROSE OF ZOLLERN (IRE) RR 112f 3411a[3]

3 b f Seattle Dancer (USA) 10.1f **(74)** - Kalisha (Rainbow Quest (USA)) 10.4f **(75)**
Form - 1203
1999 Turf 1-4: (8f 1-1, 10f, 11f, 12f) (sft, gd 1-3)
Group-class filly. Turf high 112 - 3rd of 6 getting 13lb from Tiger Hill (1 Aug Munich 10f gd RF 3411a). She put up an excellent effort when beating Ronda in the German 1,000 Guineas, but did not prove quite as effective when stepped-up in trip. She remains an interesting prospect back over a mile. **P Rau in GER [1-4].*

ROSE'S TREASURE (IRE) BHB 50f **RR 38f** 4656[10]

3 b f Treasure Kay 6.5f **(53)** - Euro Miss (IRE) (Double Schwartz) 7.9f **(55)**
Form - 0270058000
Record 1999 - 1st:0 2nd:1 3rd:0 Ran:10
Pre1999 - 1st:1 2nd:3 3rd:0 Ran:9
Win Prizemoney £4,305 *Total Prizemoney* £8,720
Wins * 1998 Mar Doncas (GD) 5f 76 <
1999 Turf 0-10: (5f 7, 6f 3) (gd 4, frm 6)
Lengthy, very moderate filly, effective 5f, acts on g-s to g-f, often wears blinkers. Turf high 65. **B S Rothwell [1-19] Jack Kee.*

ROSETTA BHB 55f **RR 55f** 4671[14]

2 b f Fraam - Starawak (Star Appeal) 9.6f **(65)**
Form - 064354550
Record 1999 - 1st:0 2nd:0 3rd:1 Ran:9
Win Prizemoney £0 *Total Prizemoney* £905
1999 Turf 0-9: (5f 2, 6f 3, 7f 3, 8f) (g-s 2, gd, g-f 3, frm 2, hrd)
Fair filly, effective 5 to 7f, acts on g-f to hrd, best on g-f. Turf high 55. **R J Hodges [0-9] Unity Farm Holiday Centre Ltd.*

ROSEUM BHB 92f **RR 92f** 2534[1]

3 b f Lahib (USA) 8f **(69)** - Rose Barton (Pas de Seul) 9.1f **(67)**

Form - 1101
Record 1999 - 1st:3 2nd:0 3rd:0 Ran:4
Pre1999 - 1st:0 2nd:0 3rd:0 Ran:1
Win Prizemoney £17,018 *Total Prizemoney* £17,018
Wins * **1999** Jly Haydoc (G-S) H 6f 85 92 <
* **1999** May Newbur (SFT) H 6f 80 83
* **1999** Apr Pontef (SFT) 6f 68+
1999 Turf 3-4: (6f 3-3, 7f) (sft 1-1, gd 2-3)
Scopey, useful filly. Turf high 92 - 1st of 8 giving 1lb to Princely Dream (3 Jly Haydock RF 2534) - also 1st of 13 getting 4lb from Candleriggs (15 May Newbury RF 1239). A likeable filly, winner of two small events on soft ground in the spring, she did not stay at Epsom, but scored back over six at Haydock.
**R Guest [3-5] Mrs B Mills.*

ROSHANI (IRE) BHB 80f **RR 80f** 4595[15]
2 b f Kris 10f **(75)** - Maratona (Be My Guest (USA)) 9.3f **(67)**
Form - 530
Record 1999 - 1st:0 2nd:0 3rd:1 Ran:3
Win Prizemoney £0 *Total Prizemoney* £665
1999 Turf 0-3: (6f, 7f 2) (gd 2, g-f)
Currently decent filly. Turf high 80 - 3rd of 10 to Dynamic Dream (26 Aug Folkestone 7f gd RF 3913).
**M R Channon [0-3] Sheikh Ahmed Al Maktoum.*

ROSIE DREAM BHB 57f **RR 52f** 4712[5]
3 ch f Cadeaux Genereux 7.9f **(76)** - Impudent Miss (Persian Bold) 9.3f **(66)**
Form - 2363075
Record 1999 - 1st:0 2nd:1 3rd:2 Ran:7
Win Prizemoney £0 *Total Prizemoney* £2,048
1999 Turf 0-7: (7f, 8f 5, 9f) (gd 2, g-f 2, frm 3)
Unfurnished, fair filly, effective 8f, acts on frm. Turf high 71 - 3rd of 15 to West Escape (3 May Warwick 8f frm RF 1014).
**E A L Dunlop [0-7] Salem Suhail.*

ROSIE JAQUES BHB 38f38a **RR 45f 38a** 457[7]
4 b f Doyoun 10.7f **(69)** - Premier Princess (Hard Fought) 8.8f **(62)**
Form - 767
Record 1999 - 1st:0 2nd:0 3rd:0 Ran:3
Pre1999 - 1st:1 2nd:0 3rd:0 Ran:7
Win Prizemoney £1,773 *Total Prizemoney* £1,773
Wins * 1998 *Jly Wolver (STD) C 9.4f 38* <
1999 AW 0-3: (8f, 10f, 12f) (Equi, Fibr 2)
Workmanlike, moderate filly, effective 9f, - acts on Fibr, has worn blinkers, likes left handed tracks. AW high 24.
**N P Littmoden [1-10] La Piette Partnership.*

ROSIES ALL THE WAY BHB 43f **RR 44f** 4324[10]
3 b f Robellino (USA) 9.5f **(68)** - No More Rosies (Warpath) 12.3f **(52)**
Form - 0470
Record 1999 - 1st:0 2nd:0 3rd:0 Ran:4
Win Prizemoney £0 *Total Prizemoney* £244
1999 Turf 0-4: (7f, 10f 2, 12f) (g-s, gd 2, g-f)
Light-framed, moderate filly. Turf high 44 (began Jly).
**C W Thornton [0-4] Guy Reed.*

ROSSE **RR 57f** 5129[7]
2 ch f Kris 10f **(75)** - Nuryana (Nureyev (USA)) 8.7f **(78)**
Form - 7
Record 1999 - 1st:0 2nd:0 3rd:0 Ran:1
1999 Turf 0-1: (6f) (gd)
Currently fair filly. **G Wragg [0-1] A E Oppenheimer.*

ROSSEL (USA) BHB 65f **RR 62+f** 5190[1]
6 b g Blushing John (USA) 8.9f **(75)** - Northern Aspen (USA) (Northern Dancer) 9.6f **(80)**
Form - 4061
Record 1999 - 1st:1 2nd:0 3rd:0 Ran:4
Pre1999 - 1st:2 2nd:2 3rd:4 Ran:20
Win Prizemoney £12,225 *Total Prizemoney* £18,846
Wins * **1999** Nov Mussel (GD) H 12f 59 62+
* 1998 Apr Hamilt (HVY) H 13f 57 62
1996 Jly Mussel (GD) C 12.1f 63 <
1999 Turf 1-4: (11f, 12f 1-1, 13f 2) (hvy 2, gd, g-f 1-1)
Average gelding, effective 11 to 13f, best at 12f, acts on hvy to g-f, has worn blinkers, prefers right handed tracks. Turf high 62 - 1st of 14 giving 6lb to Beau Roberto (3 Nov Musselburgh RF 5190). A fair sort over jumps, he looks best suited by a trip short of two miles on the Flat.
**P Monteith [10-45] Allan Melville (from Sir Michael Stoute [1-6] Jly 1996).*

ROSSELLI (USA) BHB 106f **RR 103f** 4418[11]
3 b c Puissance 7.1f **(60)** - Miss Rossi (Artaius (USA)) 9f **(69)**
Form - 0050
Record 1999 - 1st:0 2nd:0 3rd:0 Ran:4
Pre1999 - 1st:3 2nd:0 3rd:1 Ran:5
Win Prizemoney £42,917 *Total Prizemoney* £47,292
Wins * 1998 Jun Ascot (SFT) G3 5f 102 <
* 1998 Jun Beverl (G-S) 5f 94
* 1998 May Newcas (G-F) 5f 78+
1999 Turf 0-4: (5f 3, 6f) (gd 3, frm)
Scopey, very useful colt, effective 5 to 6f, best at 5f, acts on g-s to gd, best on gd. Turf high 103 (began Aug). Very lightly raced in 1999, he failed to fulfil his juvenile promise and seems to find five furlongs too sharp. **J Berry [3-9] T G Holdcroft.*

ROSSINI (USA) **RR 111f** 4252[2]
2 b c Miswaki (USA) 8.1f **(81)** - Touch of Greatness (USA) (Hero's Honor (USA)) 8.2f **(86)**
Form - 1112
1999 Turf 3-4: (5f 1-1, 6f 2-2, 7f) (hvy 1-1, gd 1-1, g-f 1-1, frm)
Group-class colt. Turf high 111 - 2nd of 6 giving 4lb to Distant Music (10 Spt Doncaster 7f frm RF 4252) - also 1st of 5 from Auenklang (24 Jly Maisons-Laffitte RF 3230a). Withdrawn after getting stirred-up before the Windsor Castle Stakes at Royal Ascot, he did nothing wrong on his four remaining starts, slamming a sub-standard field in the Prix Robert Papin. Readily outpaced when attempting to concede Distant Music four pounds in the Frigidaire Champagne Stakes at Doncaster, he has the scope to train on and will do well outside the highest class in 2000. Out of an unraced half-sister to the middle-distance stayer Gold And Ivory, he should have little trouble staying a mile.
**A P O'Brien in IRE [3-4] M Tabor & Mrs John Magnier.*

ROSSLYN CHAPEL BHB 41f **RR 60df** 4707[10]
2 b c Petong 7.6f **(58)** - Stoneydale (Tickled Pink) 6.5f **(59)**
Form - 7000
Record 1999 - 1st:0 2nd:0 3rd:0 Ran:4
1999 Turf 0-4: (5f 3, 6f) (gd 2, frm, hrd)
Average colt. Turf high 60. **Bob Jones [0-4] G Price & D Myers.*

ROTHERHITHE **RR 38f** 5003[17]
3 ch g Lycius (USA) 8.8f **(71)** - Cariellor's Miss (FR) (Cariellor (FR))
Form - 00
Record 1999 - 1st:0 2nd:0 3rd:0 Ran:2
1999 Turf 0-2: (6f, 8f) (gd 2)
Light-framed, currently very moderate gelding. Turf high 38 (began Spt). **T J Naughton [0-2] G E Archer.*

ROTOR MAN (IRE) BHB 52f45a **RR 48f 45a** 303[10]
5 b g River Falls 8.2f **(56)** - Need For Cash (USA) (Raise A Native) 11.2f **(69)**
Form - 0
Record 1999 - 1st:0 2nd:0 3rd:0 Ran:1
Pre1999 - 1st:0 2nd:0 3rd:1 Ran:10
Win Prizemoney £0 *Total Prizemoney* £520
1999 AW 0-1: (9f) (Fibr)
Moderate gelding, has worn blinkers. Becoming disappointing.
**J D Bethell [0-11] Mrs John Lee.*

ROTOSTAR BHB 40f **RR 38f** 2556[6]
3 ch f Aragon 7.7f **(58)** - Davinia (Gold Form) 5.6f **(55)**
Form - 086
Record 1999 - 1st:0 2nd:0 3rd:0 Ran:3
Pre1999 - 1st:0 2nd:0 3rd:0 Ran:6
1999 Turf 0-3: (6f, 8f 2) (frm 3)
Light-framed, very moderate filly, effective 6f, acts on frm. Turf high 38. Consistent. **P D Evans [0-9] Treble Chance Partnership.*

ROUBLES GALORE (IRE) **RR 32f** 1798[7]
3 b g Unblest - Cut the Red Tape (IRE) **(63f)** (Sure Blade (USA)) 11.3f **(67)**

Form - 47
Record 1999 - 1st:0 2nd:0 3rd:0 Ran:2
1999 Turf 0-1: (7f) (g-s) 1999 AW 0-1: (8f) (Fibr)
Lenthy, currently fair gelding.
**Dr J D Scargill [0-2] Mrs Susan Scargill.*

ROUGE BHB 49f72a **RR 50f 72a** 5146[1]
4 gr f Rudimentary (USA) 8.2f **(66)** - Couleur de Rose (Kalaglow) 9.8f **(67)**
Form - 2222560231
Record 1999 - 1st:1 2nd:5 3rd:1 Ran:10
Pre1999 - 1st:0 2nd:0 3rd:1 Ran:3
Win Prizemoney £3,106 *Total Prizemoney* £7,878
Wins ** 1999 Oct Wolver (STD) H 7f 64 69* <
1999 Turf 0-2: (7f, 8f) (g-s, gd) 1999 AW 1-8: (7f 1-2, 8f 6) (Fibr 1-8)
Average filly, effective 7 to 8f, best at 7f, - acts on Fibr, prefers left handed tracks, favours tight tracks, does well at Wolverhampton and Southwell. Turf high 50. AW high 69 - 1st of 12 getting 5lb from Young Bigwig (30 Oct Wolverhampton RF 5146). She has been a bit unlucky in most of her efforts on sand this year, always seeming to find one or two to beat her. There was no evidence to suggest lack of enthusiasm, and she gained a long overdue win at Wolverhampton in October. **J P Leigh [1-14] J M Greetham.*

ROUGE ETOILE RR 65f 3915[14]
3 b f Most Welcome 8.6f **(66)** - Choral Sundown (Night Shift (USA)) 7.2f **(69)**
Form - 7080
Record 1999 - 1st:0 2nd:0 3rd:0 Ran:4
Pre1999 - 1st:1 2nd:0 3rd:1 Ran:2
Win Prizemoney £2,763 *Total Prizemoney* £3,458
Wins * 1998 Oct Folkes (G-S) 6f 80 <
1999 Turf 0-4: (7f 3, 10f) (gd 2, g-f, frm)
Light-framed, average filly, effective 6f, acts on g-s. Turf high 74.
**A J McNae [1-6] Astaire & Partners (Holdings) Ltd.*

ROUSING THUNDER BHB 78f **RR 77f** 4210[6]
2 b c Theatrical 11.5f **(78)** - Moss (USA) (Woodman (USA)) 9f **(74)**
Form - 336
Record 1999 - 1st:0 2nd:0 3rd:2 Ran:3
Win Prizemoney £0 *Total Prizemoney* £1,035
1999 Turf 0-3: (7f 2, 8f) (gd, frm 2)
Currently above-average colt. Turf high 77 (began Jly).
**E A L Dunlop [0-3] Abdullah Ali.*

ROUTE SIXTY SIX (IRE) BHB 75f **RR 74f** 5143[20]
3 b f Brief Truce (USA) 9.1f **(73)** - Lyphards Goddess (IRE) (Lyphard's Special (USA)) 10.3f **(72)**
Form - 017477050280
Record 1999 - 1st:1 2nd:1 3rd:0 Ran:12
Pre1999 - 1st:1 2nd:1 3rd:0 Ran:6
Win Prizemoney £18,163 *Total Prizemoney* £22,002
Wins * **1999** May Newmar (G-F) H 8f 77 82 <
* 1998 Oct Bright (G-S) H 7f 72 72
1999 Turf 1-12: (7f 6, 8f 1-6) (sft, g-s, gd 4, g-f 3, frm 1-3)
Scopey, above-average filly, effective 7 to 8f, best at 8f, acts on g-s to frm, best on frm, prefers right handed tracks, prefers tight tracks. Turf high 82 - 1st of 22 getting 1lb from Fallachan (2 May Newmarket RF 0977). She won a Newmarket handicap in good style on her second start of last season. A little high in the weights as a result, she had been a little disappointing until coming second in a decent handicap in early October.
**G L Moore [2-18] J B R Leisure Ltd.*

ROWA (USA) RR 81f 4236[6]
2 ch f Cozzene (USA) 10.1f **(87)** - Met Her Dream (USA) (Mehmet (USA)) 9.7f **(71)**
Form - 6126
Record 1999 - 1st:1 2nd:1 3rd:0 Ran:4
Win Prizemoney £3,018 *Total Prizemoney* £4,198
Wins * **1999** Aug Redcar (FRM) 7f 80+ <
1999 Turf 1-4: (7f 1-2, 8f 2) (g-f, frm 1-3)
Decent filly. Turf high 81 (began Jly) - also 1st of 5 from Ashjaan (7 Aug Redcar RF 3455). She got off the mark on very fast ground at Redcar on her second start, but ran up against a useful colt at Nottingham next time.
**H R A Cecil [1-4] The Thoroughbred Corporation.*

ROWAASI BHB 100f **RR 102?f** 3769[4]
2 gr f Green Desert (USA) 7.8f **(78)** - Pamela Peach (Habitat) 9.4f **(70)**
Form - 2124
Record 1999 - 1st:1 2nd:2 3rd:0 Ran:4
Win Prizemoney £11,477 *Total Prizemoney* £29,231
Wins * **1999** Jun Sandow (GD) L 5f 102++ <
1999 Turf 1-4: (5f 1-3, 6f) (gd 3, g-f 1-1)
Very useful filly. Turf high 102 - 1st of 7 getting 5lb from Fairy Gem (1 Jun Sandown RF 1657). She evoked memories of her late stable-mate Bint Allayl when winning the National Stakes at Sandown in June, but failed to fulfil that promise in the Queen Mary or Lowther Stakes. She may prove best over a stiff five furlongs.
**M R Channon [1-4] Sheikh Ahmed Al Maktoum.*

Rowaasi was surprisingly beaten in the Queen Mary at Royal Ascot

ROWLANDSONS CHARM (IRE) BHB 37f40a **RR 38f 40a** 357[8]
6 b m Fayruz 6.6f **(63)** - Magic Gold (Sallust) 8.4f **(63)**
Form - 558
Record 1999 - 1st:0 2nd:0 3rd:0 Ran:3
Pre1999 - 1st:4 2nd:7 3rd:4 Ran:32
Win Prizemoney £9,928 *Total Prizemoney* £17,602
Wins * 1998 *Feb Lingfi (SLW) SH 13f 40 40*
1996 *Mar Lingfi (STD) C 8f 46*
1996 *Jan Lingfi (STD) S 8f 64* <
1996 *Jan Lingfi (STD) C 8f 58*
1999 AW 0-3: (13f, 16f 2) (Equi 3)
Moderate mare, effective 13 to 16f, best at 13f, - acts on Equi, mostly wears blinkers (effectively), prefers left handed tracks. AW high 41.
**Miss B Sanders [1-18] J M Quinn (from A Moore [0-1] May 1996).*

ROYAL ALIBI BHB 45f **RR 30tf** 2061[14]
5 b g Royal Academy (USA) 7.8f **(77)** - Excellent Alibi (USA) (Exceller (USA)) 12.5f **(74)**
Form - 70
Record 1999 - 1st:0 2nd:0 3rd:0 Ran:2
Pre1999 - 1st:0 2nd:0 3rd:0 Ran:1
Win Prizemoney £0 *Total Prizemoney* £240
1999 Turf 0-1: (12f) (hrd) 1999 AW 0-1: (13f) (Equi)
Currently very moderate gelding.
**D J G MurraySmith [0-2] Cardinal Racing (from H Cecil [0-1] Jly 1998).*

ROYAL AMARETTO (IRE) BHB 98f **RR 100f** 4798[13]
5 b g Fairy King (USA) 7.7f **(75)** - Melbourne Miss (Chaparral (FR)) 13.7f **(90)**
Form - 72070200
Record 1999 - 1st:0 2nd:2 3rd:0 Ran:8
Pre1999 - 1st:2 2nd:1 3rd:3 Ran:12
Win Prizemoney £11,799 *Total Prizemoney* £30,151
Wins * 1997 Apr Newbur (G-F) 10f 110+ <
* 1996 Spt Chepst (G-F) 7.1f 86
1999 Turf 0-8: (10f 4, 11f, 12f 3) (g-s, gd 3, g-f 4)
Very useful gelding, effective 10 to 11f, best at 10f, acts on g-s to g-f. Turf high 107 - 2nd of 12 giving 27lb to Chief Cashier (21 Apr Epsom 10f g-s RF 0800). Inconsistent. Remains a useful performer, but despite finishing runner-up on a couple of occasions last season is frustrating and difficult to win with. Often employs front-running tactics. **B J Meehan [2-20] The Harlequin Partnership.*

ROYAL ANTHEM (USA) BHB 134f **RR 132?f** 5230a[2]
4 b c Theatrical 11.5f **(78)** - In Neon (USA) (Ack Ack (USA)) 12.7f **(82)**
Form - 22152
1999 Turf 1-5: (10f 1-2, 12f 3) (gd 2, g-f 1-2, frm)
Well made, high-calibre colt, effective 10 to 12f, best at 12f, acts on gd to frm, best on frm. Turf high 132 - 2nd of 14 to Daylami (6 Nov Gulfstream Park 12f frm RF 5230a) - also 1st of 12 from Greek Dance (17 Aug York RF 3694). A fabulous-looking racehorse who never stopped improving as a three-year-old in 1998, he failed to live up to his sky-high reputation on his first two starts in 1999, finding one too good for him in both the Coronation Cup and the Hardwicke Stakes. However, his eight-length victory in the Juddmonte International suggested he was one of the best middle-distance horses of recent years. Pitched against a genuine champion in Daylami on his next start in the Irish Champion Stakes, he was most disappointing, folding tamely once headed. He was subsequently transferred to race in the USA and, on his first start there, met his grey nemesis in the Breeders' Cup Turf. Although undoubtedly top class, he was not the super-horse that some sources suggested after York. Nevertheless, he should win his share of good races in America.
**W Mott in USA [0-1] (from H R A Cecil [5-10] Spt 1999).*

Royal Anthem was devastating at York, but failed to live up to the hype afterwards

ROYAL ARROW (USA) RR 86f 3775[9]
3 b c Dayjur (USA) 6.8f **(79)** - Buy The Firm (USA) (Affirmed (USA)) 9.3f **(79)**
Form - 800
Record 1999 - 1st:0 2nd:0 3rd:0 Ran:3
Pre1999 - 1st:0 2nd:0 3rd:0 Ran:1
1999 Turf 0-3: (6f 2, 7f) (gd 2, g-f)
Useful colt. Turf high 86 (began Jly).
**F Murphy [0-3] K Lee (from A Fabre in FR [0-1] Aug 1998).*

ROYAL ARTIST BHB 68f **RR 69f** 5113[3]
3 b g Royal Academy (USA) 7.8f **(77)** - Council Rock (General Assembly (USA)) 10f **(68)**
Form - 7423
Record 1999 - 1st:0 2nd:1 3rd:1 Ran:4
Win Prizemoney £0 *Total Prizemoney* £1,997
1999 Turf 0-4: (5f, 6f 2, 7f) (gd 2, g-f 2)
Workmanlike, average gelding. Turf high 69 - 3rd of 21 getting 1lb from Madmun (28 Oct Windsor 6f gd RF 5113).
**W J Haggas [0-4] Tony Hirschfeld.*

ROYAL AXMINSTER BHB 49f **RR 58f** 4159[6]
4 b g Alzao (USA) 9.8f **(73)** - Number One Spot (Reference Point) 6.8f **(70)**
Form - 00506
Record 1999 - 1st:0 2nd:0 3rd:0 Ran:5
Pre1999 - 1st:0 2nd:0 3rd:0 Ran:1
1999 Turf 0-5: (10f 2, 13f, 14f, 17f) (g-f, frm 4)
Workmanlike, fair gelding. Turf high 58 - 5th of 5 giving 13lb to Hal Hoo Yaroom (30 Jun Bath 17f frm RF 2427).
**Mrs P N Dutfield [0-6] Axminster Carpets Ltd.*

ROYAL BLUE BHB 35f30a **RR 38f 30a** 1015[19]
4 ch g Ron's Victory (USA) 9.2f **(52)** - Angels Are Blue (Stanford) 7.9f **(56)**
Form - 060
Record 1999 - 1st:0 2nd:0 3rd:0 Ran:2
Pre1999 - 1st:0 2nd:0 3rd:0 Ran:10
Win Prizemoney £0 *Total Prizemoney* £251
1999 Turf 0-1: (8f) (frm) 1999 AW 0-1: (7f) (Fibr)
Leggy, very moderate gelding.
**M D I Usher [0-12] The Ridgeway Partnership.*

ROYAL CANARY (IRE) BHB 58f **RR 59df** 2047[5]
2 ch c Prince of Birds (USA) - Inesse (Simply Great (FR)) 8.2f **(65)**
Form - 7205
Record 1999 - 1st:0 2nd:1 3rd:0 Ran:4
Win Prizemoney £0 *Total Prizemoney* £632
1999 Turf 0-4: (5f 3, 6f) (gd, g-f 2, hrd)
Fair colt. Turf high 59 - 2nd of 7 giving 5lb to Vita Spericolata (22 May Musselburgh 5f g-f RF 1405).
**Miss L A Perratt [0-4] Clayton Bigley Partnership Ltd.*

ROYAL CARLTON (IRE) BHB 30f47a **RR 44f 47a** 2505[16]
7 b g Mulhollande (USA) 6.6f **(68)** - Saintly Angel (So Blessed) 8.7f **(67)**
Form - 0
Record 1999 - 1st:0 2nd:0 3rd:0 Ran:1
Pre1999 - 1st:3 2nd:1 3rd:1 Ran:29
Win Prizemoney £8,661 *Total Prizemoney* £10,682
Wins 1997 *Jan Lingfi (STD) H* 8f 65 68
1997 *Jan Lingfi (STD) H* 7f 60 70 <
1996 *Dec Lingfi (STD)* 8f 59
1999 Turf 0-1: (8f) (g-f)
Moderate gelding.
**K C Comerford [0-4] A Kimber (from G L Moore [3-21] Jly 1998).*

ROYAL CASCADE (IRE) BHB 41f83a **RR 31f 83a** 3952[11]
5 b g River Falls 8.2f **(56)** - Relative Stranger (Cragador) 6f **(67)**
Form - 2120111070
Record 1999 - 1st:3 2nd:1 3rd:0 Ran:8
Pre1999 - 1st:5 2nd:3 3rd:0 Ran:24
Win Prizemoney £19,261 *Total Prizemoney* £21,902
Wins * **1999** *Feb Southw (STD) H* 7f 72 81+ <
* **1999** *Feb Wolver (STD) H* 6f 66 71
* **1999** *Jan Southw (STD) C* 7f 70
* 1998 *Dec Wolver (STD) C* 6f 57
* 1998 *Mar Wolver (STD) C* 6f 65
* 1998 *Feb Southw (STD) C* 6f 69
* 1998 *Jan Southw (STD) S* 6f 53
* 1997 *Feb Wolver (STD) S* 6f 51
1999 Turf 0-2: (7f 2) (g-s, frm) 1999 AW 3-6:(6f 1-2, 7f 2-3, 8f) (Fibr 3-6)
Decent gelding, effective 6 to 7f, - acts on Fibr, often wears blink-

ers (extremely effectively), prefers left handed tracks, prefers tight tracks, does well at Southwell, likes Wolverhampton. Turf high 31. AW high 81 - 1st of 10 giving 10lb to Waiting Knight (26 Feb Southwell RF 0369). Inconsistent. A winner three times on the Fibresand last term, he has a powerful finishing kick, although his turf form is indifferent. **B A McMahon [8-32] R L Bedding.*

ROYAL CASTLE (IRE) BHB 75f **RR 78f** 2000[22]
5 b g Caerleon (USA) 10.9f **(79)** - Sun Princess (English Prince) 10.1f **(61)**
Form - 530
Record 1999 - 1st:0 2nd:0 3rd:1 Ran:3
Pre1999 - 1st:2 2nd:1 3rd:1 Ran:11
Win Prizemoney £7,252 *Total Prizemoney* £11,786
Wins 1997 Oct Redcar (G-F) H 14.1f 74 80 <
1997 Jun Pontef (G-F) H 12f 70 73
1999 Turf 0-3: (16f, 19f, 20f) (g-f 2, frm)
Above-average gelding, effective 12 to 16f, acts on frm. Turf high 78.
**M H Tompkins [0-6] Mrs B Cross & M Sakal (from M P Tregoning [0-3] Oct 1998).*

ROYAL CAVALIER RR 76f 5216[2]
2 b g Prince of Birds (USA) - Gold Belt (IRE) (Bellypha) 9.8f **(73)**
Form - 4342
Record 1999 - 1st:0 2nd:1 3rd:1 Ran:4
Win Prizemoney £0 *Total Prizemoney* £2,366
1999 Turf 0-4: (5f, 8f 3) (g-s, gd, frm 2)
Above-average gelding. Turf high 76 (began Spt) - 2nd of 18 to Summoner (6 Nov Doncaster 8f g-s RF 5216).
**R Hollinshead [0-4] The Three R's.*

ROYAL CIRCUS BHB 29f21a **RR 42tf 21a** 4666[15]
10 b g Kris 10f **(75)** - Circus Ring (High Top) 10.2f **(67)**
Form - 077050
Record 1999 - 1st:0 2nd:0 3rd:0 Ran:4
Pre1999 - 1st:7 2nd:6 3rd:5 Ran:60
Win Prizemoney £19,286 *Total Prizemoney* £28,199
Wins 1997 Jly Bath (GD) SH 13.1f 37 43
1996 Jan Lingfi (STD) H 12f 39 44 <
1995 Feb Lingfi (STD) H 13f 35 35
1995 Jan Lingfi (STD) H 13f 33 37
1999 Turf 0-2: (12f, 16f) (gd, g-f) 1999 AW 0-2: (12f, 16f) (Equi 2)
Moderate gelding, effective 13f, - acts on Equi, has worn blinkers. Turf high 42. Inconsistent.
**P W Hiatt [7-67] P W Hiatt (from Ian Williams [1-4] Aug 1997).*

ROYAL COMMAND (IRE) RR 95f 1172a[5]
3 b c Green Desert (USA) 7.8f **(78)** - Elegance in Design (Habitat) 9.4f **(70)**
Form - 15
1999 Turf 1-2: (8f 1-2) (hvy 1-1, gd)
Currently very useful colt. Turf high 95 (1st run) - 1st of 16 giving 5lb to Morning Breeze (25 Apr Curragh RF 0893a). Highly regarded, he went missing after running poorly in a listed event at Leopardstown in May. **D K Weld in IRE [1-2] Moyglare Stud Farm.*

ROYAL DANCE (USA) BHB 76f **RR 78f** 4133[8]
3 b c Trempolino (USA) 11.9f **(77)** - Rosey Ramble (USA) (Chieftain II) 10.4f **(75)**
Form - 674348
Record 1999 - 1st:0 2nd:0 3rd:1 Ran:6
Win Prizemoney £0 *Total Prizemoney* £1,099
1999 Turf 0-6: (8f 3, 9f, 11f, 12f) (gd, g-f, frm 4)
Workmanlike, above-average colt, effective 8f, acts on gd, has worn blinkers. Turf high 78 - 4th of 6 to Waabl (11 Jun Goodwood 8f gd RF 1916). **C E Brittain [0-6] Mohammed Jaber.*

ROYAL DOLPHIN (IRE) BHB 38f **RR 40f** 4448[14]
3 b c Dolphin Street (FR) - Diamond Lake (Kings Lake (USA)) 10.8f **(67)**
Form - 07680
Record 1999 - 1st:0 2nd:0 3rd:0 Ran:5
Pre1999 - 1st:0 2nd:0 3rd:0 Ran:1
1999 Turf 0-4: (6f 2, 10f 2) (g-s, gd, g-f 2) 1999 AW 0-1: (9f) (Fibr)
Workmanlike, moderate colt. Turf high 40.
**B A McMahon [0-6] R L Bedding.*

ROYAL DOME (IRE) BHB 54f75a **RR 49f 75a** 3101[7]
7 b g Salt Dome (USA) 6.5f **(59)** - Brook's Dilemma (Known Fact (USA)) 7.4f **(67)**
Form - 00040867
Record 1999 - 1st:0 2nd:0 3rd:0 Ran:8
Pre1999 - 1st:9 2nd:9 3rd:4 Ran:59
Win Prizemoney £44,615 *Total Prizemoney* £57,785
Wins * 1998 Spt Newcas (GD) H 5f 66 66
* 1998 Aug Carlis (G-S) H 5f 61 65
* 1997 Jly Beverl (GD) 5f 76 <
* 1997 Jun Pontef (GD) 5f 61
* 1996 Aug Haydoc (G-F) H 5f 70 73
* 1996 Jly Beverl (G-F) 5f 68
* 1995 Oct York (GD) H 5f 67 70
* 1995 Spt Pontef (GD) H 5f 64 64
* 1995 Aug Nottin (G-F) H 5.1f 54 60+
1999 Turf 0-8: (5f 7, 6f) (gd 2, g-f 2, frm 4)
Moderate gelding, effective 5f, acted on gd to frm, had worn blinkers (effectively). Turf high 59 - 4th of 17 getting 3lb from Rum Lad (14 Jun Pontefract 5f g-f RF 1988). (DEAD)
**Martyn Wane [9-66] James S Kennerley and Miss Jenny Hall (from M W Easterby [0-1] Jun 1994).*

ROYAL EAGLE (USA) BHB 98f **RR 77f** 3556[2]
2 b c Eagle Eyed (USA) - Accountinquestion (USA) (Classic Account (USA))
Form - 2412
Record 1999 - 1st:1 2nd:2 3rd:0 Ran:4
Win Prizemoney £3,501 *Total Prizemoney* £6,367
Wins * 1999 Jly Epsom (G-F) 7f 76+ <
1999 Turf 1-4: (6f 2, 7f 1-2) (gd 2, g-f, frm 1-1)
Above-average colt. Turf high 77 - 2nd of 5 getting 3lb from Barathea Guest (11 Aug Salisbury 7f gd RF 3556) - also 1st of 11 from Sir Ninja (28 Jly Epsom RF 3202). Consistent, he got off the mark in an Epsom maiden in July despite finding plenty of trouble.
**P F I Cole [1-4] Luciano Gaucci.*

ROYAL EXPRESSION BHB 70f65a **RR 71f 65a** 5028[13]
7 b g Sylvan Express 9.6f **(45)** - Edwin's Princess (Owen Dudley) 8.3f **(61)**
Form - 03700214620
Record 1999 - 1st:1 2nd:2 3rd:1 Ran:11
Pre1999 - 1st:4 2nd:6 3rd:4 Ran:24
Win Prizemoney £14,438 *Total Prizemoney* £26,615
Wins * 1999 Aug Nottin (G-F) H 16f 64 71
1997 Jun Redcar (FRM) C 16f 55
1996 May Carlis (GD) H 14.1f 65 72 <
1996 May Beverl (G-F) H 16.2f 59 67
1995 Jun Hamilt (FRM) 11.1f 60
1999 Turf 1-11: (14f, 16f 1-8, 17f, 18f) (g-s, gd 5, g-f 1-4, frm)
Above-average gelding, effective 14 to 17f, acts on gd to frm, best on g-f, has worn blinkers, likes left handed tracks, prefers tight tracks, excels at Chester. Turf high 71 - 1st of 7 giving 32lb to Miss Vita (9 Aug Nottingham RF 3475). Consistent. He ran generally well in modest staying handicaps in the second half of the season, including winning over two miles at Nottingham in August.
**F Jordan [3-14] Mrs A Roddis (from Mrs M Reveley [6-23] Jun 1997).*

ROYAL FLAME (IRE) BHB 68f65a **RR 70f 65a** 5056[6]
3 b f Royal Academy (USA) 7.8f **(77)** - Samnaun (USA) (Stop The Music (USA)) 9.2f **(71)**
Form - 6554426
Record 1999 - 1st:0 2nd:1 3rd:0 Ran:7
Win Prizemoney £0 *Total Prizemoney* £1,693
1999 Turf 0-6: (8f 2, 9f, 10f 2, 12f) (g-s, gd, frm 4) 1999 AW 0-1: (10f) (Equi)
Workmanlike, above-average filly, effective 8 to 10f, acts on g-s to frm. Turf high 71 (1st run) - 6th of 14 to Kittiwake (23 Jun Kempton 10f frm RF 2241). **J W Hills [0-7] Willy Coleman.*

ROYAL FONTAINE (IRE) BHB 70f **RR 72df** 2081[3]
4 b f Royal Academy (USA) 7.8f **(77)** - Bellifontaine (FR) (Bellypha) 9.8f **(73)**
Form - 703
Record 1999 - 1st:0 2nd:0 3rd:1 Ran:3
Pre1999 - 1st:1 2nd:3 3rd:0 Ran:4
Win Prizemoney £3,696 *Total Prizemoney* £8,306
Wins * 1998 Spt Sandow (GD) 10f 72 <

1999 Turf 0-3: (10f 3) (g-f, frm, hrd)
Workmanlike, above-average filly, effective 8 to 10f, best at 10f, acts on gd to frm. Turf high 72. **J W Hills [1-7] D J Deer.*

ROYAL FUSILIER (IRE) BHB 63f **RR 66f** 3854[5]

3 b g Case Law 6f **(64)** - Tropical Rain (Rainbow Quest (USA)) 10.4f **(75)**
Form - 1025
Record 1999 - 1st:1 2nd:1 3rd:0 Ran:4
Pre1999 - 1st:0 2nd:1 3rd:0 Ran:5
Win Prizemoney £2,304 *Total Prizemoney* £4,205
Wins * 1999 Jun Hamilt (GD) 8.3f 61 <
1999 Turf 1-4: (8f 1-2, 9f, 10f) (g-f 1-2, frm, hrd)
Light-framed, average gelding, effective 7 to 9f, acted on g-f. Turf high 66 - 2nd of 7 getting 13lb from Calldat Seventeen (13 Aug Epsom 9f g-f RF 3605) - also 1st of 7 giving 3lb to Swynford Pleasure (16 Jun Hamilton RF 2045). (DEAD)
**M L W Bell [1-9] W H Ponsonby.*

ROYAL HIGHLANDER (IRE) RR 97++f 5209[1]

2 b c Foxhound (USA) - Sky Lover (Ela-Mana-Mou) 10.1f **(70)**
Form - 1
Record 1999 - 1st:1 2nd:0 3rd:0 Ran:1
Win Prizemoney £3,810 *Total Prizemoney* £3,810
Wins * 1999 Nov Doncas (SFT) 6f 97++ <
1999 Turf 1-1: (6f 1-1) (g-s 1-1)
Currently very useful colt. (1st run) - 1st of 20 from Polar Star (5 Nov Doncaster RF 5209). He won a soft-ground Doncaster maiden- with his head in his chest, and we will be hearing much more of him next season. **A G Foster [1-1] R E Sangster & Mrs J Ramsden.*

ROYAL HUSSAR BHB 58f55a **RR 55f 55a** 4905[7]

3 gr c Efisio 7.7f **(69)** - Altaia (FR) (Sicyos (USA))
Form - 057
Record 1999 - 1st:0 2nd:0 3rd:0 Ran:3
1999 Turf 0-3: (6f 2, 7f) (gd 2, frm)
Strong, currently fair colt. Turf high 55 (began Spt).
**P Howling [0-3] P Gwilliam.*

ROYAL INSULT BHB 85f **RR 77f** 4881[1]

2 ch c Lion Cavern (USA) 7.5f **(74)** - Home Truth (Known Fact (USA)) 7.4f **(67)**
Form - 21
Record 1999 - 1st:1 2nd:1 3rd:0 Ran:2
Win Prizemoney £3,247 *Total Prizemoney* £4,287
Wins * 1999 Oct Redcar (GD) 6f 77 <
1999 Turf 1-2: (6f 1-2) (g-s, frm 1-1)
Currently above-average colt. Turf high 77 (began Oct) - 1st of 13 from Kareeb (14 Oct Redcar RF 4881).
**K R Burke [1-2] Ms Julie Greenacre.*

ROYAL IVY BHB 70f **RR 70f** 4828[3]

2 ch f Mujtahid (USA) 7.4f **(69)** - Royal Climber (Kings Lake (USA)) 10.8f **(67)**
Form - 4445473
Record 1999 - 1st:0 2nd:0 3rd:1 Ran:7
Win Prizemoney £0 *Total Prizemoney* £1,865
1999 Turf 0-7: (5f 2, 6f 2, 7f 2, 8f) (sft, g-s, g-f 4, frm)
Above-average filly, effective 6 to 8f, best at 7f, acts on sft to frm. Turf high 70 - 3rd of 11 getting 12lb from Clever Girl (12 Oct Ayr 8f sft RF 4828). **B W Hills [0-7] Lady Richard Wellesley.*

ROYAL KINGDOM (IRE) RR 99f 5201a[5]

2 b c Fairy King (USA) 7.7f **(75)** - Allicance (USA) (Alleged (USA)) 10f **(76)**
Form - 1115
1999 Turf 3-4: (7f 2-2, 8f 1-1, 10f) (hvy, sft 1-1, frm 2-2)
Very useful colt. Turf high 99 (1st run) (began Jly) - 1st of 7 giving 5lb to Storm Dream (23 Jly Curragh RF 3185a) - also 1st of 6 getting 3lb from Best of The Bests (26 Spt Ascot RF 4570). He was far from the finished article last term and endured a punishing race when getting up to win the Group Two Royal Lodge Stakes at Ascot in September. Probably feeling the effects of that when disappointing at Saint-Cloud the following month, he seems indifferent to the state of the ground and should stay well. That said, he may lack the turn-of-foot required to beat the best of his generation. **A P O'Brien in IRE [3-4].*

ROYAL LEGEND BHB 57f55a **RR 48f 55a** 2117[9]

7 b g Fairy King (USA) 7.7f **(75)** - Legend of Arabia (Great Nephew) 9.9f **(64)**
Form - 000
Record 1999 - 1st:0 2nd:0 3rd:0 Ran:3
Pre1999 - 1st:3 2nd:1 3rd:6 Ran:22
Win Prizemoney £11,014 *Total Prizemoney* £14,881
Wins * 1998 Jun Goodwo (G-F) H 9.9f 51 60 <
* 1998 Jun Lingfi (G-S) H 10f 51 54
1997 *May Southw (STD) C 11f 51*
1999 Turf 0-3: (10f 3) (g-s, g-f 2)
Fair gelding, effective 10f, acts on gd to frm, best on gd, has worn blinkers, prefers right handed tracks, prefers tight tracks. Turf high 48. **R M Flower [2-14] Jan Rieck (from J Pearce [1-10] Jun 1997).*

ROYAL LINE RR 98f 3405a[4]

3 b c Saint Estephe (FR) - Double Line (FR) (What A Guest) 7f **(62)**
Form - 14
Record 1999 - 1st:1 2nd:0 3rd:0 Ran:2
Win Prizemoney £13,304 *Total Prizemoney* £13,304
Wins * 1999 Jly Newmar (GD) L 14.8f 98 <
1999 Turf 1-2: (15f 1-2) (gd, frm 1-1)
Unfurnished, currently very useful colt. Turf high 98 (1st run) (began Jly) - 1st of 4 from Moon Dragon (7 Jly Newmarket RF 2628). He had a hard race when winning a Listed event at Newmarket in July (subsequently failed a drugs test) and disappointed connections when well beaten at Chantilly later that month. They have since intimated that this thorough stayer may lack courage. **S bin Suroor [1-2] Godolphin.*

ROYAL MARK (IRE) BHB 69f **RR 64f** 3900[4]

6 b g Fairy King (USA) 7.7f **(75)** - Take Your Mark (USA) (Round Table) 9.5f **(81)**
Form - 00604
Record 1999 - 1st:0 2nd:0 3rd:0 Ran:5
Pre1999 - 1st:4 2nd:3 3rd:2 Ran:29
Win Prizemoney £19,439 *Total Prizemoney* £31,999
Wins 1998 Jly Newcas (GD) H 7f 81 84
1997 Aug Newcas (GD) H 7f 82 86 <
1995 Aug Newmar (G-F) H 7f 78 85+
1995 Jly Ayr (GD) 7f 84
1999 Turf 0-5: (5f, 6f, 7f 3) (gd 2, g-f 2, frm)
Average gelding, effective 7 to 8f, best at 7f, acts on gd to frm, has worn blinkers. Turf high 64. Inconsistent. A winner at Newcastle in July 1998 for Tim Easterby, he is now with Dandy Nicholls and showed distinct signs of a return to form at Carlisle in August. He should be watched like a hawk.
**D Nicholls [0-5] M P Burke (from T D Easterby [1-11] Oct 1998).*

ROYAL MEASURE BHB 46f44a **RR 56f 44a** 3854[8]

3 b c Inchinor 8.9f **(64)** - Sveltissima (Dunphy) 9.4f **(57)**
Form - 56450778
Record 1999 - 1st:0 2nd:0 3rd:0 Ran:8
Win Prizemoney £0 *Total Prizemoney* £258
1999 Turf 0-6: (10f 2, 12f 4) (sft, gd 2, g-f, frm 2) 1999 AW 0-2: (9f 2) (Fibr 2)
Leggy, fair colt. Turf high 68. AW high 38.
**B R Millman [0-8] The Royal Partnership.*

ROYAL MINSTREL (IRE) RR 74f 4598[4]

2 ch c Be My Guest (USA) 10.2f **(66)** - Shanntabariya (IRE) (Shernazar) 10.2f **(73)**
Form - 664
Record 1999 - 1st:0 2nd:0 3rd:0 Ran:3
Win Prizemoney £0 *Total Prizemoney* £336
1999 Turf 0-3: (7f, 8f 2) (gd, g-f 2)
Currently above-average colt. Turf high 74 (began Aug).
**M H Tompkins [0-3] Mrs Debbie Sakal.*

ROYAL OCCASION (USA) RR 37f 5207[7]

2 b f El Gran Senor (USA) 8.9f **(85)** - Hot Princess (Hot Spark) 7.6f **(62)**
Form - 67
Record 1999 - 1st:0 2nd:0 3rd:0 Ran:2
Win Prizemoney £0 *Total Prizemoney* £160
1999 Turf 0-2: (7f 2) (g-s, frm)

Currently very moderate filly. Turf high 37.
**A G Foster [0-1] R E Sangster (from P W Chapple-Hyam [0-1] Jun 1999).*

ROYAL ORIGINE (IRE) BHB 55f **RR 54f** 4787[11]
3 b g Royal Academy (USA) 7.8f **(77)** - Belle Origine (USA) (Exclusive Native (USA)) 9.1f **(81)**
Form - 00600
Record 1999 - 1st:0 2nd:0 3rd:0 Ran:5
Pre1999 - 1st:0 2nd:0 3rd:2 Ran:3
Win Prizemoney £0 *Total Prizemoney* £1,915
1999 Turf 0-4: (6f, 7f, 8f 2) (g-s 2, g-f, frm) 1999 AW 0-1: (6f) (Equi)
Light-framed, fair gelding, effective 5 to 6f, acts on g-f. Turf high 54. Inconsistent.
**M Quinn [0-2] R M Ellis (from M R Channon [0-6] Jly 1999).*

ROYAL PARADE (IRE) BHB 20f **RR 33f** 2316[11]
4 b g Pips Pride 6.7f **(70)** - Route Royale (Roi Soleil) 8.7f **(57)**
Form - 00700
Record 1999 - 1st:0 2nd:0 3rd:0 Ran:5
Pre1999 - 1st:0 2nd:0 3rd:0 Ran:7
1999 Turf 0-5: (6f 2, 10f, 12f, 17f) (gd, g-f 2, hrd 2)
Strong, very moderate gelding, has worn blinkers. Turf high 33.
**J M Bradley [0-12] Craftbook Ltd.*

ROYAL PASTIMES BHB 48f **RR 50f** 3944[12]
2 b f Ezzoud (IRE) - Royal Recreation (USA) (His Majesty (USA)) 10.9f **(82)**
Form - 76500
Record 1999 - 1st:0 2nd:0 3rd:0 Ran:5
1999 Turf 0-5: (5f, 7f 4) (gd, g-f 2, frm, hrd)
Fair filly. Turf high 50. **Martyn Wane [0-5] Mrs H Wane.*

ROYAL PATRON BHB 70f **RR 70f** 5125[2]
3 ch f Royal Academy (USA) 7.8f **(77)** - Indian Queen (Electric) 10.1f **(61)**
Form - 615562
Record 1999 - 1st:1 2nd:1 3rd:0 Ran:6
Pre1999 - 1st:0 2nd:0 3rd:0 Ran:1
Win Prizemoney £3,013 *Total Prizemoney* £3,823
Wins * 1999 Aug Lingfi (GD) 14f 75 <
1999 Turf 1-6: (10f, 12f, 14f 1-3, 16f) (gd 3, g-f 1-2, frm)
Leggy, above-average filly, effective 12 to 16f, acts on gd to frm, best on gd. Turf high 75 - 1st of 14 from Loriner's Lass (14 Aug Lingfield RF 3641). **J L Dunlop [1-7] Sir Gordon Brunton.*

ROYAL PREVIEW (IRE) BHB 64f78a **RR 62f 78a** 4702[3]
3 b f Prince Sabo 6.6f **(64)** - Visible Form (Formidable (USA)) 9.2f **(63)**
Form - 11121670465043
Record 1999 - 1st:4 2nd:1 3rd:1 Ran:14
Pre1999 - 1st:0 2nd:0 3rd:0 Ran:3
Win Prizemoney £10,595 *Total Prizemoney* £12,054
Wins * 1999 *Feb Lingfi (STD) H* 8f 67 82 <
*** 1999** *Feb Wolver (STD) H* 6f 67 82+
*** 1999** *Jan Southw (STD) H* 6f 55 65
*** 1999** *Jan Lingfi (STD) H* 7f 55 64
1999 Turf 0-8: (5f 4, 6f 4) (gd 2, g-f 3, frm 2, hrd) 1999 AW 4-6: (6f 2-3, 7f 1-2, 8f 1-1) (Equi 2-3, Fibr 2-3)
Leggy, average filly, effective 6 to 8f, best at 6f, - acts on AW, best on Equi, prefers left handed tracks, prefers tight tracks. Turf high 71. AW high 82 - 1st of 4 giving 13lb to Dream On Me (11 Feb Lingfield RF 0273) - also 1st of 9 getting 1lb from Indian Swinger (3 Feb Wolverhampton RF 0220). She really took to sand when winning four of her five starts on that surface at the start of the year, but she has yet to show that sort of form on turf.
**M L W Bell [4-17] Sir Peter Davis.*

ROYAL REBEL BHB 106f **RR 118f** 4374a[7]
3 b c Robellino (USA) 9.5f **(68)** - Greenvera (USA) (Riverman (USA)) 9.1f **(76)**
Form - 31237017
Record 1999 - 1st:2 2nd:1 3rd:2 Ran:8
Pre1999 - 1st:0 2nd:0 3rd:0 Ran:3
Win Prizemoney £19,881 *Total Prizemoney* £38,107
Wins * 1999 Aug Leopar (GD) L 14f 103+ <
*** 1999** Apr Newcas (GD) 8f 82
1999 Turf 2-8: (8f 1-2, 10f 2, 11f, 12f 2, 14f 1-1) (g-s, gd 1-4, g-f 1-3)
Well made, high-class colt, effective 11f, acts on gd, has worn blinkers (extremely effectively), prefers left handed tracks. Turf high 118 - 3rd of 5 to Lucido (8 May Lingfield 11f gd RF 1112). Got off the mark in a Newcastle maiden on his second start, and though he faced some stiff tasks in Pattern company after that, he was far from disgraced when in the frame behind Cupid at Leopardstown and Lucido in the Lingfield Derby Trial. He was well beaten in each of his subsequent starts with one notable exception, gaining a fine victory in a 14-furlong Listed event at Leopardstown, the longest trip he attempted. **M Johnston [2-11].*

ROYAL REPRIMAND (IRE) BHB 36f **RR 33f** 4980[5]
4 b g Reprimand 8.2f **(63)** - Lake Ormond(Kings Lake (USA)) 10.8f **(67)**
Form - 0660054545
Record 1999 - 1st:0 2nd:0 3rd:0 Ran:10
Pre1999 - 1st:0 2nd:1 3rd:0 Ran:3
Win Prizemoney £0 *Total Prizemoney* £1,262
1999 Turf 0-10: (7f, 8f 4, 9f 3, 10f 2) (g-s, gd 2, g-f 3, frm 3, hrd)
Tall, very moderate gelding, effective 9f, acts on gd to frm, has worn blinkers, likes left handed tracks, likes tight tracks. Turf high 47 - 6th of 15 getting 5lb from Ollie's Chuckle (29 Apr Redcar 9f gd RF 0917). **R E Barr [0-13] J C Garbutt.*

ROYAL RESULT (USA) BHB 92f **RR 94f** 4561[10]
6 b br g Gone West(USA) 7.8f **(82)** - Norette (Northfields (USA)) 9f **(72)**
Form - 008021320130
Record 1999 - 1st:2 2nd:2 3rd:2 Ran:12
Pre1999 - 1st:4 2nd:2 3rd:3 Ran:31
Win Prizemoney £63,217 *Total Prizemoney* £83,487
Wins * 1999 Aug Goodwo (GD) H 6f 82 86 <
*** 1999** Jly York (G-F) H 6f 75 81
*** 1998** Spt Ayr (G-S) H 6f 76 80
*** 1998** Spt York (GD) H 7f 70 75
1997 Oct Newmar (G-F) H 7f 65 72
1996 Aug Thirsk (G-F) 8f 56
1999 Turf 2-12: (6f 2-10, 7f 2) (g-s, gd 1-5, g-f 1-3, frm 2, hrd)
Useful gelding, effective 6f, acts on gd, has worn blinkers. Turf high 94 - 3rd of 28 getting 9lb from Grangeville (18 Spt Ayr 6f gd RF 4392) - also 1st of 27 giving 6lb to Flak Jacket (28 Aug Goodwood RF 3956). A very useful sprint handicapper, winner of the Ayr Silver Cup in '98 and third in the Ayr Gold Cup in '99. Has also landed competitive races at York and Goodwood. Suited by patient tactics.
**D Nicholls [4-19] M P Burke (from M W Easterby [1-12] Jly 1998).*

ROYAL ROMEO BHB 74f **RR 69f** 4325[1]
2 ch g Timeless Times (USA) 6.1f **(56)** - Farinara (Dragonara Palace (USA)) 6.1f **(55)**
Form - 60531
Record 1999 - 1st:1 2nd:0 3rd:1 Ran:5
Win Prizemoney £4,056 *Total Prizemoney* £4,426
Wins * 1999 Spt Beverl (GD) 5f 69 <
1999 Turf 1-5: (5f 1-4, 6f) (gd 1-2, frm 3)
Average gelding. Turf high 69 - 1st of 17 giving 5lb to Ducie (15 Spt Beverley RF 4325). **T D Easterby [1-5] Peter Bourke.*

ROYAL ROULETTE BHB 51f74a **RR 52f 74a** 3808[11]
5 ch m Risk Me (FR) 8f **(53)** - Princess Lily (Blakeney) 10.5f **(64)**
Form - 532131807530
Record 1999 - 1st:1 2nd:0 3rd:2 Ran:8
Pre1999 - 1st:3 2nd:3 3rd:5 Ran:24
Win Prizemoney £9,452 *Total Prizemoney* £13,974
Wins * 1999 *Jan Lingfi (STD) H* 16f 65 72 <
* 1998 *Dec Lingfi (STD) H* 16f 52 61
* 1997 *Nov Lingfi (STD) H* 12f 59 60
1997 *Jan Southw (STD) S* 8f 58
1999 Turf 0-5: (14f, 16f 4) (sft, g-f 2, frm 2) 1999 AW 1-3: (16f 1-3) (Equi 1-3)
Above-average filly, effective 16f, - acts on Equi, has worn blinkers, prefers left handed tracks, favours tight tracks. Turf high 53. AW high 72 - 1st of 9 getting 10lb from Sheriff (19 Jan Lingfield RF 0126). She has shown herself to be an effective sort in modest staying events on sand.
**Miss B Sanders [3-17] Mrs P J Sheen (from S P C Woods [1-15] Oct 1997).*

ROYAL SIGNET BHB 37f **RR 34f** 3835[9]
4 ch f King's Signet (USA) 7f **(51)** - Ladiz (Persian Bold) 9.3f **(66)**

Form - 046580
Record **1999** - 1st:0 2nd:0 3rd:0 Ran:6
Pre1999 - 1st:0 2nd:0 3rd:0 Ran:5
Win Prizemoney £0 *Total Prizemoney* £258
1999 Turf 0-6: (12f 2, 13f, 16f, 17f 2) (sft, g-s, gd 2, frm 2)
Scopey, very moderate filly, effective 13f, acts on gd, likes left handed tracks, likes tight tracks. Turf high 48 - 4th of 11 getting 5lb from Sound Appeal (17 May Bath 13f gd RF 1270). Inconsistent. **M J Weeden [0-11] M J Weeden.*

ROYAL SOUTH (IRE) BHB 33f RR 89f 5091a[10]
6 b g Common Grounds 8.1f **(66)** - Arkadina's Million (King of Clubs) 7.1f **(57)**
Form - 1337208344200
1999 Turf 0-12: (7f 3, 8f 3, 9f 5, 10f) (g-s 2, gd 4, g-f 5, frm)
Useful gelding, effective 8 to 9f, best at 8f, acts on g-f, likes left handed tracks, and excels at Dundalk. Turf high 91 - 4th of 13 getting 4lb from Landing Slot (22 Aug Leopardstown 9f g-f RF 3893a). Inconsistent.
**D McDonogh in IRE [6-27] Stephen Curran (from P S Felgate [0-9] Aug 1997).*

ROYAL TARRAGON BHB 29f33a RR 18f 33a 3550[15]
3 b f Aragon 7.7f **(58)** - Lady Philippa (IRE) (Taufan (USA)) 7f **(57)**
Form - 0000000
Record **1999** - 1st:0 2nd:0 3rd:0 Ran:5
Pre1999 - 1st:0 2nd:0 3rd:0 Ran:9
1999 Turf 0-4: (5f, 6f, 7f, 8f) (g-f 3, frm) 1999 AW 0-1: (7f) (Equi)
Light-framed, little account filly, often wears blinkers. Turf high 18. **J R Arnold [0-14] Prof Green.*

ROYAL TIPPLE BHB 64f RR 71f 4882[11]
3 b g Noble Patriarch 12.2f **(43)** - Mashin Time (Palm Track) 9.8f **(50)**
Form - 0750
Record **1999** - 1st:0 2nd:0 3rd:0 Ran:4
1999 Turf 0-4: (10f 2, 11f, 12f) (g-f 2, frm 2)
Rangy, above-average gelding. Turf high 71 (began Aug).
**T D Easterby [0-4] B E W Higgins.*

ROYAL WAVE (IRE) BHB 58f RR 36f 5026[14]
3 b br g Polish Precedent (USA) 9f **(73)** - Mashmoon (USA) (Habitat) 9.4f **(70)**
Form - 10000
Record **1999** - 1st:1 2nd:0 3rd:0 Ran:5
Pre1999 - 1st:0 2nd:0 3rd:0 Ran:1
Win Prizemoney £2,463 *Total Prizemoney* £2,463
Wins 1999 May Pontef (GD) 6f 80 <
1999 Turf 1-5: (6f 1-1, 7f 3, 8f) (gd 1-4, frm)
Scopey, very moderate gelding, effective 6f, acts on gd. Turf high 80 (1st run) - 1st of 10 giving 5lb to Weaver of Words (18 May Pontefract RF 1304). A winner of a Pontefract maiden in May, he disappointed subsequently.
**J L Eyre [0-2] Messrs Cunningham,Hardy,Mason,Jordan (from Mrs A Swinbank [1-3] Spt 1999).*

ROYRACE BHB 30f25a RR 30f 25a 4830[6]
7 b g Wace (USA) - Royal Tycoon (Tycoon II) 8.7f **(47)**
Form - 6
Record **1999** - 1st:0 2nd:0 3rd:0 Ran:1
Pre1999 - 1st:0 2nd:0 3rd:0 Ran:13
1999 Turf 0-1: (13f) (sft)
Very moderate gelding, has worn blinkers. This Royrace is Doncaster Rovers standard. **W M Brisbourne [0-33] Andrew Evans.*

ROYS SUPER CLAN RR 1502[10]
2 ch c Clantime 6.6f **(57)** - Hello Hobson's (IRE) **(49f 46a)** (Fayruz)
Form - 0
Record **1999** - 1st:0 2nd:0 3rd:0 Ran:1
1999 Turf 0-1: (5f) (frm)
Very poor colt. (DEAD) **R Bastiman [0-1] E D Atkinson.*

RUACANA FALLS (USA) BHB 87f RR 83f 2910[7]
3 b f Storm Bird (CAN) 8.5f **(82)** - Obeah (Cure The Blues (USA)) 9.5f **(63)**
Form - 40437
Record **1999** - 1st:0 2nd:0 3rd:1 Ran:5
Pre1999 - 1st:1 2nd:0 3rd:0 Ran:3
Win Prizemoney £3,745 *Total Prizemoney* £7,925
Wins * 1998 Spt Haydoc (G-F) 8.1f 72 <
1999 Turf 0-5: (8f 2, 10f, 11f 2) (gd 2, g-f 2, frm)
Scopey, decent filly, effective 7 to 11f, acts on gd to g-f. Turf high 88 (1st run) - 4th of 9 getting 3lb from Valentine Girl (5 May Chester 11f g-f RF 1045). Consistent. Highly tried last term, she failed to get the trip in the Italian Oaks.
**P W Chapple-Hyam [1-8] R E Sangster.*

RUBAMMA BHB 55f46a RR 37f 46a 420[6]
4 b g Kris 10f **(75)** - Idle Gossip (USA) (Lyphard (USA)) 9.9f **(72)**
Form - 06
Record **1999** - 1st:0 2nd:0 3rd:0 Ran:2
Pre1999 - 1st:0 2nd:0 3rd:3 Ran:15
Win Prizemoney £0 *Total Prizemoney* £1,964
1999 AW 0-2: (8f, 11f) (Fibr 2)
Neat, very moderate gelding, effective 10f, acts on gd to frm, has worn blinkers. AW high 30. Becoming disappointing.
**D J G MurraySmith [0-3] Miss N J Spencer (from P T Walwyn [0-17] Spt 1998).*

RUBIES FROM BURMA (USA) RR 99f 4470a[9]
3 ch f Forty Niner (USA) 8.8f **(73)** - Perfect Example (USA) (Far North (CAN)) 9.7f **(75)**
Form - 6011310
1999 Turf 3-7: (5f 2-3, 6f 1-3, 7f) (g-s 2, gd 2, g-f 2-2, frm 1-1)
Very useful filly, effective 5 to 6f, acts on gd to g-f. Turf high 99 - 1st of 10 giving 32lb to Suzy Street (5 Spt Curragh RF 4200a). Very speedy, she is unlikely to stay beyond six furlongs and is capable of winning a listed event. **A P O'Brien in IRE [3-7] Mrs T Hyde.*

RUBY BEAR BHB 28f30a RR 27f 30a 1209[6]
4 gr f Thethingaboutitis (USA) 16f **(44)** - Hitravelscene (Mansingh (USA)) 7.4f **(55)**
Form - 03060
Record **1999** - 1st:0 2nd:0 3rd:1 Ran:5
Pre1999 - 1st:0 2nd:4 3rd:3 Ran:14
Win Prizemoney £0 *Total Prizemoney* £4,889
1999 Turf 0-4: (9f, 11f 2, 12f) (hvy 2, g-s, g-f) 1999 AW 0-1: (12f) (Fibr)
Leggy, little account filly, effective 8 to 14f, acts on sft to g-f, has worn blinkers, likes right handed tracks. Turf high 27. Inconsistent. **W M Brisbourne [0-25] D J Kirkland.*

RUBY LASER BHB 47f RR 56f 4648[3]
3 b f Bustino 11f **(64)** - Ower (IRE) (Lomond (USA)) 8.8f **(65)**
Form - 07403
Record **1999** - 1st:0 2nd:0 3rd:1 Ran:5
Win Prizemoney £0 *Total Prizemoney* £733
1999 Turf 0-5: (12f, 13f, 14f 3) (g-s, g-f, frm 3)
Leggy, fair filly. Turf high 56 (began Jly).
**R F JohnsonHoughton [0-5] Dr J A E Hobby.*

RUBYS REPLY BHB 61f RR 66f 2962[1]
2 ch f Deploy 11.4f **(67)** - Ruby Venture **(61f)** (Ballad Rock) 7.8f **(63)**
Form - 001
Record **1999** - 1st:1 2nd:0 3rd:0 Ran:3
Win Prizemoney £2,022 *Total Prizemoney* £2,022
Wins *** 1999** Jly Yarmou (FRM) S 7f 64 <
1999 Turf 1-3: (6f, 7f 1-2) (gd, g-f 1-1, frm)
Currently average filly. Turf high 66 - also 1st of 12 getting 5lb from Shaman (20 Jly Yarmouth RF 2962).
**S C Williams [1-3] Bainey Racing Partnership.*

RUDE AWAKENING BHB 40f46a RR 39f 46a 3948[6]
5 b g Rudimentary (USA) 8.2f **(66)** - Final Call (Town Crier) 10.2f **(55)**
Form - 842807345506
Record **1999** - 1st:0 2nd:1 3rd:1 Ran:12
Pre1999 - 1st:2 2nd:4 3rd:3 Ran:36
Win Prizemoney £7,367 *Total Prizemoney* £16,668
Wins * 1998 *Feb Southw (STD) H 6f 44 49*
1996 Apr Pontef (G-F) 5f 94 <
1999 Turf 0-6: (5f 6) (gd, g-f, frm 3, hrd) 1999 AW 0-6: (5f, 6f 5) (Fibr 6)
Fair gelding, effective 5 to 6f, best at 6f, acts on frm - acts on Fibr, has worn blinkers, likes left handed tracks, likes tight tracks. Turf high 43 (began Jly). AW high 51 - 2nd of 9 getting 24lb from Cool Secret (26 Feb Southwell 6f Fibr RF 0368).
**C W Fairhurst [1-42] William Hill (from G Lewis [1-6] Oct 1996).*

RUDIK (USA) BHB 100f **RR 97f** 4801^{3}
2 b br c Nureyev (USA) 8.4f **(84)** - Nervous Baba (USA) (Raja Baba (USA)) 10f **(64)**
Form - 2313
Record 1999 - 1st:1 2nd:1 3rd:2 Ran:4
Win Prizemoney £3,598 *Total Prizemoney* £7,759
Wins * 1999 Spt Newcas (SFT) 6f 96+ <
1999 Turf 1-4: (6f 1-3, 7f) (gd 1-2, frm 2)
Very useful colt. Turf high 97 (began Spt) - 3rd of 6 giving 5lb to Out of Africa (9 Oct York 6f gd RF 4801) - also 1st of 15 from Hilltop Warning (29 Spt Newcastle RF 4634). He proved a costly failure on his first two starts, but improved once united with Kieren Fallon. Touched-off in a Listed event at Doncaster in October, he should stay beyond sprint distances and has a useful turn-of-foot. **Sir Michael Stoute [1-4] Mrs John Magnier & M Tabor.*

RUDI'S PET (IRE) BHB 116f **RR 112+f** 3166^{1}
5 ch g Don't Forget Me 9.5f **(66)** - Pink Fondant (Northfields (USA)) 9f **(72)**
Form - 441861211
Record 1999 - 1st:4 2nd:1 3rd:0 Ran:9
Pre1999 - 1st:4 2nd:1 3rd:2 Ran:35
Win Prizemoney £88,764 *Total Prizemoney* £107,322
Wins * 1999 Jly Goodwo (G-F) G3 5f 112+ <
*** 1999** Jly Ascot (G-F) H 5f 97 109+
*** 1999** Jun Newcas (GD) H 5f 82 90+
*** 1999** May Thirsk (GD) H 5f 73 79+
1997 Oct Doncas (GD) H 5f 88 97
1997 Aug Sandow (SFT) H 5f 80 88
1996 Aug Sandow (GD) H 5f 92 99
1996 Jly Windso (GD) 5f 74
1999 Turf 4-9: (5f 4-9) (gd 3, g-f 2-3, frm 2-3)
Group-class gelding, effective 5f, acts on g-f to frm, often wears blinkers (effectively). Turf high 112 - 1st of 15 giving 7lb to Imperial Beauty (27 Jly Goodwood RF 3166) - also 1st of 10 giving 12lb to Magic Rainbow (23 Jly Ascot RF 3049). Improving. Described as being like "Dennis The Menace" upon joining David Nicholls, he improved immeasurably once gelded and showed blinding speed to win the Group 3 King George Stakes at Goodwood in July. Quite capable of holding his own in any company over five furlongs on that form, he acts particularly well on fast ground and could surprise a few established stars in 2000.
**D Nicholls [4-9] G H Leatham (from Mrs J R Ramsden [0-14] Nov 1998).*

RUFF BHB 55f **RR 63f** 4951^{10}
3 b f First Trump - Hotel California (IRE) (Last Tycoon) 8.5f **(62)**
Form - 260
Record 1999 - 1st:0 2nd:1 3rd:0 Ran:3
Win Prizemoney £0 *Total Prizemoney* £1,290
1999 Turf 0-3: (6f, 7f 2) (gd, g-f, frm)
Workmanlike, currently average filly. Turf high 63 (1st run) (began Aug) - 2nd of 19 giving 3lb to Feather 'n Lace (27 Aug Newmarket 7f frm RF 3941). **W Jarvis [0-3] Major C R Philipson.*

RULE OF THUMB BHB 84f **RR 83f** 5134^{6}
2 ch g Inchinor 8.9f **(64)** - Rockin' Rosie (Song) 7.2f **(61)**
Form - 16
Record 1999 - 1st:1 2nd:0 3rd:0 Ran:2
Win Prizemoney £1,945 *Total Prizemoney* £2,043
Wins * 1999 Oct Pontef (GD) 6f 74+ <
1999 Turf 1-2: (6f 1-2) (gd, g-f 1-1)
Currently decent gelding. Turf high 83 (began Oct) - also 1st of 11 giving 9lb to Boadicea The Red (18 Oct Pontefract RF 4929).
**G L Moore [1-2] Brighthelm Racing.*

RUM BABA (IRE) BHB 42f **RR 43f** 2369^{2}
5 b g Tirol 8.1f **(64)** - Rum Cay (USA) (Our Native (USA)) 11.2f **(63)**
Form - 04402
Record 1999 - 1st:0 2nd:1 3rd:0 Ran:5
Pre1999 - 1st:1 2nd:1 3rd:6 Ran:22
Win Prizemoney £3,425 *Total Prizemoney* £8,876
Wins 1997 Aug Tralee (HVY) 12f 76 <
1999 Turf 0-5: (12f, 13f, 16f 2, 17f) (g-s, g-f 2, frm 2)
Moderate gelding, effective 11 to 13f, acts on gd, has worn blinkers. Turf high 46.
**Mrs M Reveley [0-5] P D Savill (from C Collins in IRE [1-22] Oct 1998).*

RUM LAD BHB 63f66a **RR 60f 66a** 4538^{9}
5 gr g Efisio 7.7f **(69)** - She's Smart (Absalom) 7.2f **(58)**
Form - 52403114054570
Record 1999 - 1st:2 2nd:1 3rd:1 Ran:14
Pre1999 - 1st:4 2nd:2 3rd:4 Ran:35
Win Prizemoney £21,663 *Total Prizemoney* £30,879
Wins * 1999 Jun Pontef (GD) 5f 66
*** 1999** Jun Pontef (SFT) H 6f 62 68
* 1998 *Oct Wolver (sta) H 6f 64 66*
* 1997 Jly Catter (SFT) H 6f 55 69 <
* 1997 Jun Carlis (GD) H 5f 56 61
* 1997 May Catter (G-F) 6f 53
1999 Turf 2-13: (5f 1-2, 6f 1-10, 7f) (sft, gd 1-3, g-f 1-4, frm 4, hrd) 1999 AW 0-1: (6f) (Fibr)
Average gelding, effective 5 to 7f, best at 5f, acts on sft to hrd - acts on Fibr, best on gd, prefers left handed tracks, likes tight tracks, excels at Pontefract, does well at Leicester. Turf high 68 - 1st of 10 getting 17lb from Peter's Imp (7 Jun Pontefract RF 1791) - also 1st of 17 giving 3lb to Sealed By Fate (14 Jun Pontefract RF 1988). Consistent. In fine form in June with two wins at Pontefract, and though the second one came on fast ground over five furlongs, he looks better on soft ground over six.
**J J Quinn [6-49] B Shaw.*

RUM LASS BHB 62f **RR 57f** 4721^{14}
2 gr f Distant Relative 7f **(69)** - She's Smart (Absalom) 7.2f **(58)**
Form - 650
Record 1999 - 1st:0 2nd:0 3rd:0 Ran:3
1999 Turf 0-3: (5f 3) (gd 2, g-f)
Currently fair filly. Turf high 57 (began Jly) - 5th of 17 getting 5lb from Royal Romeo (15 Spt Beverley 5f gd RF 4325).
**J J Quinn [0-3] B Shaw.*

RUM POINTER (IRE) BHB 94f **RR 90f** 5132^{7}
3 b g Turtle Island (IRE) - Osmunda (Mill Reef (USA)) 10.5f **(78)**
Form - 1821214345107
Record 1999 - 1st:4 2nd:2 3rd:1 Ran:13
Pre1999 - 1st:0 2nd:0 3rd:0 Ran:5
Win Prizemoney £23,315 *Total Prizemoney* £30,918
Wins * 1999 Spt Ayr (G-S) H 15f 86 90 <
*** 1999** Jun Haydoc (GD-) H 11.9f 80 84
*** 1999** May Ripon (G-S) H 12.3f 71 79
*** 1999** Mar Catter (G-S) H 12f 64 73
1999 Turf 4-13: (10f, 12f 3-6, 14f 2, 15f 1-2, 16f, 17f) (gd 4-8, g-f 2, frm 2, hrd)
Scopey, useful gelding, effective 12 to 15f, best at 12f, acts on gd to frm, best on gd, has worn blinkers, prefers left handed tracks, prefers tight tracks. Turf high 90 - 1st of 7 getting 9lb from Loop The Loup (16 Spt Ayr RF 4345) - also 1st of 6 getting 2lb from Tanusius (5 Jun Haydock RF 1764). Consistent. Very game, he did very well last season, winning four times, and found the step up to 15 furlongs no problem at Ayr in September. He appreciates the ground just on the soft side of good. **T D Easterby [4-18] M P Burke.*

RUM PUNCH RR 72f 4898^{9}
2 b c Shirley Heights 12.1f **(76)** - Gentle Persuasion (Bustino) 10.4f **(64)**
Form - 0
Record 1999 - 1st:0 2nd:0 3rd:0 Ran:1
1999 Turf 0-1: (8f) (gd)
Currently above-average colt. **Sir Michael Stoute [0-1] The Queen.*

RUNAWAY BAY RR 55f 2362^{7}
3 gr g Lugana Beach 7f **(63)** - Absaloui (Absalom) 7.2f **(58)**
Form - 7
Record 1999 - 1st:0 2nd:0 3rd:0 Ran:1
Pre1999 - 1st:0 2nd:0 3rd:0 Ran:4
1999 Turf 0-1: (5f) (gd)
Neat, fair gelding. **Mrs L Stubbs [0-5] Ian Blakey.*

RUN FOR GLORY (IRE) RR 33f 4668^{12}
2 ch c Lahib (USA) 8f **(69)** - Blazing Glory (IRE) (Glow (USA)) 6.7f **(71)**
Form - 0
Record 1999 - 1st:0 2nd:0 3rd:0 Ran:1
1999 Turf 0-1: (5f) (g-s)
Currently very moderate colt.
**D R C Elsworth [0-1] Everyone's A Winner Partnership.*

RUNIN CIRCLES BHB 57f **RR 51f** 4981[8]
2 b g Presidium 7.5f **(56)** - True Ring (High Top) 10.2f **(67)**
Form - 008
Record 1999 - 1st:0 2nd:0 3rd:0 Ran:3
1999 Turf 0-3: (6f 2, 8f) (gd, g-f 2)
Currently fair gelding. Turf high 51 (began Spt).
**M W Easterby [0-3] Mrs Christopher Hanbury.*

RUN MACHINE (IRE) BHB 48f **RR 39f** 4327[11]
2 ch c Fayruz 6.6f **(63)** - Anita's Love (IRE) (Anita's Prince)
Form - 000
Record 1999 - 1st:0 2nd:0 3rd:0 Ran:3
1999 Turf 0-3: (5f 3) (gd, g-f, frm)
Currently very moderate colt. Turf high 39.
**Mrs P N Dutfield [0-3] The Two Legs Partnership.*

RUNNING BEAR BHB 25f **RR 28f** 2379[8]
5 ch g Sylvan Express 9.6f **(45)** - Royal Girl **(55f)** (Kafu) 6f **(47)**
Form - 088
Record 1999 - 1st:0 2nd:0 3rd:0 Ran:3
Pre1999 - 1st:0 2nd:0 3rd:0 Ran:4
Win Prizemoney £0 *Total Prizemoney* £201
1999 Turf 0-2: (6f, 7f) (gd, frm) 1999 AW 0-1: (6f) (Fibr)
Little account gelding. Turf high 28.
**Mrs A M Naughton [0-3] Mrs S E Cooper (from Miss S E Hall [0-4] Jly 1998).*

RUNNING STAG (USA) BHB 117f120a **RR 120f 120a** 4517a[4]
5 b h Cozzene (USA) 10.1f **(87)** - Fruhlingstag (FR) (Orsini) 10f **(71)**
Form - 47221514
Record 1999 - 1st:2 2nd:2 3rd:0 Ran:7
Pre1999 - 1st:3 2nd:5 3rd:2 Ran:21
Win Prizemoney £295,497 *Total Prizemoney* £506,786

Wins							
*** 1999**	*Aug*	*Sarato*	*(FST)*	*G2H*	*10f*	*119*	
*** 1999**	*Jun*	*Belmon*	*(FST)*	*G2H*	*9f*	*120*	<
* 1998	Aug	Deauvi	(SFT)	G3	10f	115	
* 1998	*Mar*	*Lingfi*	*(STD)*		*10f*	*104+*	
* 1997	*Feb*	*Lingfi*	*(STD)*		*10f*	*59++*	

1999 Turf 0-2: (10f 2) (gd, frm) 1999 AW 2-5: (9f 1-3, 10f 1-2) (Dirt 2-5)
Very high-class colt, effective 9 to 10f, best at 10f, acts on gd to frm - acts on Dirt. Turf high 120 (1st run) - 2nd of 10 to Handsome Ridge (8 May Goodwood 10f gd RF 1108). AW high 120 - 1st of 8 giving 4lb to Deputy Diamond (12 Jun Belmont Park RF 2096a) - also 1st of 8 giving 7lb to Catienus (29 Aug Saratoga RF 4115a). Consistent. The star of Philip Mitchell's stable, he was disappointing in the Dubai World Cup on his first start of last season, having suffered a minor injury earlier in the year, but returned to his best afterwards. Chased home Handsome Ridge at Goodwood before going back on another adventurous mission to the States and, after running a blinder to split Behrens and Real Quiet at Suffolk Downs, he romped away with a Grade Two at Belmont Park. Having obviously come to himself in the States, he somewhat surprisingly returned to these shores for the Eclipse in which he ran a fair fifth, but returned to America and picked up another Grade Two event at Saratoga. A little disappointing when only fourth in the Woodward, but remains a credit to his trainer. **P Mitchell [5-28].*

RUNNING TIMES (USA) BHB 68f **RR 66f** 4378[17]
2 b c Brocco (USA) - Concert Peace (USA) (Hold Your Peace (USA)) 9f **(72)**
Form - 34480
Record 1999 - 1st:0 2nd:0 3rd:1 Ran:5
Win Prizemoney £0 *Total Prizemoney* £1,060
1999 Turf 0-5: (7f 4, 8f) (gd 2, g-f 2, frm)
Average colt. Turf high 70 (1st run) (began Jly) - 3rd of 8 getting 18lb from Sarafan (3 Jly Beverley 7f gd RF 2517).
**T D Easterby [0-5] Times of Wigan.*

RUN SILENT (IRE) BHB 60f **RR 74f** 4863[4]
3 b c Sadler's Wells (USA) 11.3f **(87)** - Fair of the Furze (Ela-Mana-Mou) 10.1f **(70)**
Form - 78374
Record 1999 - 1st:0 2nd:0 3rd:1 Ran:5
Win Prizemoney £0 *Total Prizemoney* £537
1999 Turf 0-4: (12f 2, 14f 2) (gd 2, g-f, frm) 1999 AW 0-1: (15f) (Fibr)
Scopey, above-average colt. Turf high 74 - 3rd of 8 giving 5lb to Height of Fantasy (4 Jun Haydock 14f gd RF 1744).
**J W Hills [0-5] Freddy Bienstock.*

RUSHCUTTER BAY BHB 77f **RR 78f** 4933[9]
6 br g Mon Tresor 7.9f **(60)** - Llwy Bren (Lidhame) 9.2f **(50)**
Form - 201055750
Record 1999 - 1st:1 2nd:1 3rd:0 Ran:9
Pre1999 - 1st:3 2nd:1 3rd:2 Ran:29
Win Prizemoney £20,692 *Total Prizemoney* £36,754

Wins								
*** 1999**	May	Windso	(G-F)		6f		90	<
* 1998	Jly	Newmar	(G-F)	H	6f	77	81	
1996	Jun	Nottin	(G-F)	H	5.1f	79	83	
1995	Jly	Windso	(GD)		5f		63	

1999 Turf 1-9: (5f 3, 6f 1-6) (gd, g-f 4, frm 1-4)
Above-average gelding, effective 5 to 6f, best at 6f, acts on frm, has worn blinkers. Turf high 90 - 1st of 8 from Classy Cleo (24 May Windsor RF 1444). Consistent. In good heart during the spring, including scoring well at Windsor, he gave little encouragement afterwards.
**P L Gilligan [2-20] Treasure Seekers Partnership (from T T Clement [2-18] Jly 1997).*

RUSHED (IRE) BHB 22f37a **RR 11f 37a** 2949[10]
4 b g Fairy King (USA) 7.7f **(75)** - Exotic Bride (USA) (Blushing Groom (FR)) 10.3f **(76)**
Form - 3602000
Record 1999 - 1st:0 2nd:1 3rd:0 Ran:5
Pre1999 - 1st:0 2nd:0 3rd:1 Ran:3
Win Prizemoney £0 *Total Prizemoney* £959
1999 Turf 0-3: (12f 3) (frm 2, hrd) 1999 AW 0-2: (10f, 12f) (Equi 2)
Neat, moderate gelding, effective 12f, - acts on Equi, likes left handed tracks, favours tight tracks. Turf high 11. AW high 41 - 2nd of 13 getting 5lb from Hurgill Dancer (16 Feb Lingfield 12f Equi RF 0302). Becoming disappointing.
**G P Enright [0-7] Anne Ross And The Supremes (from Sir Michael Stoute [0-1] Apr 1998).*

RUSHEN RAIDER BHB 40f **RR 39f** 4400[8]
7 br g Reprimand 8.2f **(63)** - Travel Storm (Lord Gayle (USA)) 8.8f **(62)**
Form - 0008138
Record 1999 - 1st:1 2nd:0 3rd:1 Ran:7
Pre1999 - 1st:6 2nd:1 3rd:0 Ran:31
Win Prizemoney £21,078 *Total Prizemoney* £23,585

Wins								
*** 1999**	Aug	Beverl	(GD)	SH	16.2f	34	37	
* 1996	Aug	Beverl	(GD)	H	16.2f	63	73	<
* 1996	Aug	Catter	(G-F)	C	12f		65	
* 1996	Jly	Doncas	(G-F)	S	12f		66	
* 1996	Jly	Leices	(G-F)	C	11.8f		66	
* 1995	Aug	Redcar	(FRM)	C	10f		65	
* 1995	May	Thirsk	(G-F)	S	7f		45+	

1999 Turf 1-7: (14f, 16f 1-4, 18f, 22f) (gd 2, g-f 1-2, frm 3)
Very moderate gelding, has broken blood-vessels, effective 14 to 16f, best at 16f, acts on gd to frm, best on frm, likes left handed tracks, excels at Redcar. Turf high 39.
**K W Hogg [9-50] Mrs Thelma White.*

RUSHMORE (USA) **RR 72f** 4753[3]
2 ch c Mt Livermore (USA) 7.7f **(90)** - Crafty Nan (USA) (Crafty Prospector (USA)) 8.2f **(104)**
Form - 3
Record 1999 - 1st:0 2nd:0 3rd:1 Ran:1
Win Prizemoney £0 *Total Prizemoney* £940
1999 Turf 0-1: (6f) (gd)
Currently above-average colt. **P F I Cole [0-1] J S Gutkin.*

RUSSIAN ABOUT (IRE) BHB 48f44a **RR 46f 44a** 5103[12]
4 b f Polish Patriot (USA) 7.8f **(70)** -Molly Carter (IRE)(Dr Carter (USA))
Form - 30
Record 1999 - 1st:0 2nd:0 3rd:1 Ran:2
Pre1999 - 1st:0 2nd:1 3rd:0 Ran:9
Win Prizemoney £0 *Total Prizemoney* £909
1999 Turf 0-2: (7f, 8f) (gd 2)
Leggy, moderate filly. Turf high 46 (began Spt).
**H J Collingridge [0-2] Ms D A Stevens (from D T Thom [0-2] Apr 1998).*

RUSSIAN FOX (IRE) BHB 92f **RR 89f** 4872[1]
2 ch c Foxhound (USA) - La Petruschka (Ballad Rock) 7.8f **(63)**

Form - 342341173201
Record 1999 - 1st:3 2nd:2 3rd:3 Ran:12
Win Prizemoney £14,497 *Total Prizemoney* £20,679
Wins * **1999** Oct Newmar (GD) H 6f 85 89 <
* **1999** Jly Lingfi (G-F) H 5f 77
* **1999** Jun Lingfi (G-F) 5f 77
1999 Turf 3-12: (5f 2-11, 6f 1-1) (g-s, gd 1-4, g-f 3, frm 2-3, hrd)
Useful colt, effective 5 to 6f, acts on gd to g-f. Turf high 89 - 1st of 17 from Hunting Tiger (14 Oct Newmarket RF 4872). Improving. He has run with credit on many occasions and is very consistent. He gained back-to-back victories at Lingfield during the summer, and ended the season with a game victory in a decent Newmarket nursery. **R Hannon [3-12] Nicholas Hodges.*

RUSSIAN HOPE (IRE) RR 107f 1532a[9]

4 ch c Rock Hopper 10.6f **(54)** - Dievotchka (GER) (Dancing Brave (USA)) 8.4f **(76)**
Form - 0
1999 Turf 0-1: (16f) (g-s)
Currently Pattern-class colt. **H-A Pantall in FR [1-3].*

RUSSIAN MUSIC BHB 65f100a RR 71df 100a 5103[14]

6 b g Forzando 7.2f **(63)** - Sunfleet (Red Sunset) 8.2f **(63)**
Form - 004000
Record 1999 - 1st:0 2nd:0 3rd:0 Ran:6
Pre1999 - 1st:3 2nd:7 3rd:9 Ran:34
Win Prizemoney £21,772 *Total Prizemoney* £72,915
Wins * 1997 Spt Doncas (G-F) H 8f 100 105
* 1997 Mar Warwic (G-F) 7f 108 <
* 1996 May Lingfi (G-F) 7f 70
1999 Turf 0-6: (7f 5, 8f) (g-s 2, gd 4)
Useful gelding, effective 8f, acts on gd, has worn blinkers. Turf high 72. Becoming disappointing.
**Miss Gay Kelleway [3-38] The Seventh Heaven Partnership (from P C Haslam [0-2] Aug 1995).*

RUSSIAN RELATION (IRE) RR 28f 3435[12]

5 ch g Soviet Star (USA) 8.6f **(74)** - Anjaab (USA) (Alydar (USA)) 9.1f **(76)**
Form - 006700
Record 1999 - 1st:0 2nd:0 3rd:0 Ran:6
Pre1999 - 1st:0 2nd:3 3rd:0 Ran:12
Win Prizemoney £0 *Total Prizemoney* £2,858
1999 Turf 0-6: (6f, 7f, 8f 4) (g-f, frm 5)
Little account gelding, has worn blinkers. Turf high 39.
**Mrs P N Dutfield [0-13] Mrs Jan Fuller (from J S Bolger in IRE [0-5] Oct 1997).*

RUSSIAN REVIVAL (USA) BHB 120f RR 122f 3444[1]

6 ch h Nureyev (USA) 8.4f **(84)** - Memories (USA) (Hail the Pirates (USA)) 11f **(78)**
Form - 2121
Record 1999 - 1st:2 2nd:2 3rd:0 Ran:4
Pre1999 - 1st:5 2nd:5 3rd:3 Ran:22
Win Prizemoney £199,329 *Total Prizemoney* £414,607
Wins * **1999** Aug Ascot (GD) H 7f 114 122 <
* **1999** May Longch (GD) G3 7f 111
* 1998 Spt Newbur (GD) L 7.3f 115
* 1997 Spt Newbur (G-F) L 7f 117
1996 Oct Newmar (GD) L 6f 114
1996 Spt Yarmou (G-F) 6f 110?
1995 May Newbur (G-F) 6f 97+
1999 Turf 2-4: (6f, 7f 2-3) (gd 2-3, g-f)
Very high-class horse, effective 6 to 7f, best at 7f, acts on gd to g-f, best on gd, and excels at Longchamp. Turf high 122 - 1st of 27 giving 14lb to Mubrik (7 Aug Ascot RF 3444). Consistent. A very useful performer at between six and seven furlongs for several seasons, he landed a Longchamp Group Three in May before finishing a good second in the Cork and Orrery at Ascot. He finished his season when putting up an especially fine performance back at Ascot to win the Tote International Handicap under top weight.
**J H M Gosden [4-14] Maktoum Al Maktoum (from S bin Suroor [2-9] May 1997).*

RUSSIAN ROMEO (IRE) BHB 62f69a RR 61f 69a 4755[12]

4 b g Soviet Lad (USA) 9.4f **(63)** - Aotearoa (IRE) (Flash of Steel) 7.2f **(53)**
Form - 0011230
Record 1999 - 1st:2 2nd:1 3rd:1 Ran:5
Pre1999 - 1st:3 2nd:2 3rd:0 Ran:28
Win Prizemoney £12,608 *Total Prizemoney* £15,964
Wins * **1999** *Jly Southw (STD)* *6f* *70*
* **1999** *Jun Wolver (STD) H* *6f* *54 57*
* 1998 Jun Cheste (GD) C 6.1f 72
* 1997 *Oct Wolver (STD) C* *6f* *74* <
* 1997 Aug Leices (GD) S 6f 74 <
1999 Turf 0-2: (5f, 6f) (gd, frm) 1999 AW 2-3: (6f 2-3) (Fibr 2-3)
Light-framed, above-average gelding, effective 6f, acts on gd - acts on Fibr, often wears blinkers (very effectively), prefers left handed tracks, prefers tight tracks. Turf high 61 (began Aug). AW high 70 - 1st of 9 from Aljaz (10 Jly Southwell RF 2719). Has shown his best form on Fibresand and bounced back to his best when encountering that surface after a six-month break, winning over six furlongs at Wolverhampton and Southwell. **B A McMahon [5-33] R L Bedding.*

RUSSIAN ROUGE (IRE) BHB 28f RR 33f 3674[9]

4 b f Soviet Lad (USA) 9.4f **(63)** - Red Lory (Bay Express) 7.1f **(60)**
Form - 007500
Record 1999 - 1st:0 2nd:0 3rd:0 Ran:5
Pre1999 - 1st:0 2nd:0 3rd:0 Ran:1
1999 Turf 0-4: (6f, 7f, 8f, 10f) (sft, frm 3) 1999 AW 0-1: (11f) (Fibr)
Neat, very moderate filly. Turf high 33.
**M Brittain [0-6] Northgate Lodge Racing Club.*

RUSSIAN SILVER (USA) BHB 72f RR 82f 4294[8]

2 ch f Red Bishop (USA) - Russian Maid **(81f)** (Cadeaux Genereux)
Form - 8348
Record 1999 - 1st:0 2nd:0 3rd:1 Ran:4
Win Prizemoney £0 *Total Prizemoney* £950
1999 Turf 0-4: (6f, 7f 3) (gd 2, g-f 2)
Decent filly. Turf high 82 - 4th of 11 to Scottish Spice (26 Aug Folkestone 7f gd RF 3912). **C E Brittain [0-4] Ali Saeed.*

RUSSIAN VELVET (IRE) BHB 35f33a RR 33f 33a 205[11]

3 br f Soviet Lad (USA) 9.4f **(63)** - Ballylesson Girl (IRE) (Nashamaa) 7.1f **(66)**
Form - 867700
Record 1999 - 1st:0 2nd:0 3rd:0 Ran:3
Pre1999 - 1st:0 2nd:0 3rd:0 Ran:5
1999 AW 0-3: (5f, 6f, 8f) (Equi, Fibr 2)
Neat, very moderate filly. AW high 23.
**M Quinn [0-8] Glendale Partnership Ltd.*

RUSTIC (IRE) BHB 84f RR 90f 3647[10]

3 b f Grand Lodge (USA) - Style Of Life (USA) (The Minstrel (CAN)) 10f **(72)**
Form - 624030
Record 1999 - 1st:0 2nd:1 3rd:1 Ran:6
Pre1999 - 1st:1 2nd:0 3rd:1 Ran:3
Win Prizemoney £3,647 *Total Prizemoney* £12,851
Wins * 1998 Jly Haydoc (G-F) 6f 80+ <
1999 Turf 0-6: (6f, 7f 4, 8f) (gd, g-f 2, frm 3)
Workmanlike, useful filly, effective 6 to 7f, best at 7f, acts on g-f to frm, best on g-f, often wears blinkers. Turf high 96 - 2nd of 6 to Sandova (24 May Leicester 7f frm RF 1430). Consistent.
**R Charlton [1-9] K Abdulla.*

RUTLAND CHANTRY (USA) BHB 70f73a RR 57f 73a 5162[10]

5 b g Dixieland Band (USA) 10.1f **(80)** - Christchurch (FR) (So Blessed) 8.7f **(67)**
Form - 41022520700
Record 1999 - 1st:1 2nd:3 3rd:0 Ran:11
Pre1999 - 1st:2 2nd:2 3rd:0 Ran:9
Win Prizemoney £15,076 *Total Prizemoney* £20,653
Wins * **1999** Jun Beverl (SFT) H 9.9f 71 75 <
1998 Apr Newbur (HVY) H 10f 66 72
1997 Oct Pontef (G-S) H 10f 60 66
1999 Turf 1-11: (10f 1-8, 12f 3) (g-s 1-1, gd 5, g-f 3, frm 2)
Average gelding, effective 10 to 12f, best at 10f, acts on sft to frm, best on gd, excels at Beverley. Turf high 78 - 2nd of 6 giving 32lb to Ambidextrous (20 Aug Chester 12f gd RF 3786) - also 1st of 9 giving 14lb to Zaha (9 Jun Beverley RF 1852). Becoming disappointing.
**S Gollings [1-11] Five Go Racing (from Lord Huntingdon [2-9] Oct 1998).*

RUZEN (IRE) BHB 53f70a **RR 44f 70a** 4332[11]
4 b g Fayruz 6.6f **(63)** - Stifen (Burslem) 8.8f **(53)**
Form - 40700070
Record 1999 - 1st:0 2nd:0 3rd:0 Ran:6
Pre1999 - 1st:3 2nd:1 3rd:1 Ran:14
Win Prizemoney £12,209 *Total Prizemoney* £15,031
Wins * 1998 May Leices (GD) 6f 89 <
* 1998 May Windso (G-F) H 6f 78 88
* 1997 Apr Leices (G-S) 5f 84
1999 Turf 0-5: (5f 4, 6f) (gd 3, frm 2) 1999 AW 0-1: (5f) (Equi)
Workmanlike, decent gelding, effective 6f, acts on g-f to frm - acts on Equi, has worn blinkers. Turf high 44. Becoming disappointing.
**B Palling [3-20] Mrs D J Hughes & Mrs M M Palling.*

RYEFIELD BHB 58f **RR 58f** 5217[15]
4 b g Petong 7.6f **(58)** - Octavia (Sallust) 8.4f **(63)**
Form - 2805151008060
Record 1999 - 1st:2 2nd:1 3rd:0 Ran:13
Pre1999 - 1st:1 2nd:3 3rd:1 Ran:13
Win Prizemoney £17,905 *Total Prizemoney* £23,063
Wins * **1999** Aug Ayr (G-F) H 8f 65 66
* **1999** Jly Newcas (G-F) H 8f 62 64
* 1998 Jly Carlis (G-F) 6.9f 76 <
1999 Turf 2-13: (7f 4, 8f 2-9) (g-s 2, gd 3, g-f 1-4, frm 1-4)
Rangy, fair gelding, effective 6 to 7f, best at 6f, acts on gd to frm, best on gd. Turf high 66. Consistent. A winner twice during the summer, he is very much suited by a strongly-run race over a mile on fast ground. **Miss L A Perratt [3-26] Mrs Elaine Aird.*

RYEFIELD STAR BHB 38f34a **RR 13f 34a** 1421[10]
4 b g Marju (IRE) 9.2f **(76)** - Awayed (USA) (Sir Ivor) 10.2f **(70)**
Form - 00600
Record 1999 - 1st:0 2nd:0 3rd:0 Ran:5
Pre1999 - 1st:0 2nd:0 3rd:1 Ran:10
Win Prizemoney £0 *Total Prizemoney* £615
1999 Turf 0-1: (7f) (gd) 1999 AW 0-4: (6f, 8f 2, 12f) (Fibr 4)
Strong, little account gelding, often wears blinkers. AW high 21. Inconsistent.
**D McCain [0-7] Champ Chicken Co Ltd (from J Berry [0-9] Jun 1998).*

RYELAND RR 53f 3676[7]
3 b f Presidium 7.5f **(56)** - Ewe Lamb (Free State) 8.7f **(61)**
Form - 87
Record 1999 - 1st:0 2nd:0 3rd:0 Ran:2
1999 Turf 0-2: (7f, 10f) (g-f, frm)
Leggy, currently fair filly. Turf high 53. **Mrs P Sly [0-2] Mrs P M Sly.*

RYMER'S RASCAL BHB 60f55a **RR 62f 55a** 5073[8]
7 b g Rymer - City Sound (On Your Mark) 7.7f **(58)**
Form - 0027435136050508
Record 1999 - 1st:1 2nd:1 3rd:2 Ran:16
Pre1999 - 1st:5 2nd:4 3rd:8 Ran:54
Win Prizemoney £36,299 *Total Prizemoney* £48,406
Wins * **1999** Jly Cheste (G-F) H 7.6f 60 62
* 1998 Oct Redcar (SFT) H 7f 59 61
* 1997 Spt York (SFT) H 7f 60 64 <
* 1997 Aug Catter (G-F) H 7f 56 61
* 1997 Jly Beverl (G-F) H 7.5f 54 60
1999 Turf 1-16: (6f 2, 7f 8, 8f 1-6) (sft, g-s, gd 4, g-f 1-2, frm 8)
Average gelding, effective 7 to 8f, best at 8f, acts on gd to frm, best on frm, likes left handed tracks, likes tight tracks, excels at Ayr, does well at Redcar, likes York and Catterick. Turf high 66 - 6th of 24 getting 11lb from Pension Fund (1 Spt York 8f frm RF 4085) - also 1st of 16 giving 1lb to Toblersong (25 Jly Chester RF 3124). Showed signs of a revival when winning at Chester over seven furlongs in July, but failed to build on that.
**E J Alston [6-66] Brian Chambers (from P C Haslam [0-4] Jun 1994).*

RYTHM N TIME BHB 77f **RR 75f** 5218[9]
2 b f Timeless Times (USA) 6.1f **(56)** - Primum Tempus **(42df)** (Primo Dominie) 6.2f **(80)**
Form - 0531230430
Record 1999 - 1st:1 2nd:1 3rd:3 Ran:10
Win Prizemoney £3,510 *Total Prizemoney* £9,743
Wins * **1999** Aug Beverl (GD) H 5f 72 80+ <
1999 Turf 1-10: (5f 1-3, 6f 4, 7f 3) (g-s 2, gd 3, frm 1-4, hrd)
Above-average filly, effective 5f, acts on frm. Turf high 87 - also 1st of 8 getting 4lb from Savannah Belle (11 Aug Beverley RF 3534). Consistent. Scored at Beverley despite hanging badly left at the course intersection, and ran well behind Littlefeather in a decent race at Chester. **T D Easterby [1-10] Springs Equestrian Ltd.*

SAAFEND BOY BHB 75f **RR 78f** 4899[16]
2 b c Marju (IRE) 9.2f **(76)** - Perfect Alibi (Law Society (USA)) 9.9f **(70)**
Form - 360735140
Record 1999 - 1st:1 2nd:0 3rd:2 Ran:9
Win Prizemoney £6,319 *Total Prizemoney* £8,585
Wins * **1999** Aug Newmar (G-F) H 8f 72 73 <
1999 Turf 1-9: (5f 2, 6f, 7f 3, 8f 1-3) (gd 3, g-f 4, frm 1-2)
Above-average colt, effective 7 to 8f, best at 8f, acts on g-f to frm, best on g-f. Turf high 78 - 4th of 10 getting 20lb from French Fellow (9 Spt Doncaster 8f g-f RF 4238) - also 1st of 10 giving 2lb to Service Star (27 Aug Newmarket RF 3942). Gradually stepped up in distance during his races so far, he seems to be progressing fairly well and, after a troubled passage in a Chester nursery in August, made no mistake over a mile at Newmarket next time.
**R Hannon [1-9] J B R Leisure/South-Western Partnership.*

SAANEN (IRE) BHB 60f **RR 61f** 5158[7]
2 b c Port Lucaya - Ziffany **(60f)** (Taufan (USA)) 7f **(57)**
Form - 8407
Record 1999 - 1st:0 2nd:0 3rd:0 Ran:4
1999 Turf 0-4: (6f 3, 8f) (gd, frm, hrd 2)
Average colt. Turf high 61 (began Jly).
**Mrs A Swinbank [0-4] Miss Betty Duxbury.*

SABADILLA (USA) BHB 112f **RR 111f** 554a[4]
5 b h Sadler's Wells (USA) 11.3f **(87)** - Jasmina (USA) (Forli (ARG)) 9.6f **(67)**
Form - 4
1999 Turf 0-1: (12f) (g-f)
Group-class colt. Now with Godolphin, he finished fourth behind Fruits Of Love in the big turf race in Dubai.
**S bin Suroor in UAE [0-1] (from J H M Gosden [3-9] Jly 1998).*

SABANG BHB 35f **RR 21f** 1220[16]
3 ch f Sabrehill (USA) 8.5f **(64)** - Seleter (Hotfoot) 10.5f **(59)**
Form - 000
Record 1999 - 1st:0 2nd:0 3rd:0 Ran:3
1999 Turf 0-2: (8f 2) (gd 2) 1999 AW 0-1: (8f) (Fibr)
Leggy, currently little account filly. Turf high 21.
**Miss J A Camacho [0-3] Stuart Postill.*

SABICA RR 56f 4903[8]
2 b f Prince Sabo 6.6f **(64)** - Mindomica (Dominion) 8.5f **(63)**
Form - 08
Record 1999 - 1st:0 2nd:0 3rd:0 Ran:2
1999 Turf 0-2: (6f 2) (frm 2)
Currently fair filly. Turf high 56 (began Spt).
**C W Thornton [0-2] Ailsa Daniels & Guy Reed.*

SABOT BHB 47f58a **RR 52f 58a** 5156[5]
6 b g Polar Falcon (USA) 9f **(74)** - Power Take Off (Aragon) 8.1f **(60)**
Form - 8268040055
Record 1999 - 1st:0 2nd:1 3rd:0 Ran:9
Pre1999 - 1st:1 2nd:6 3rd:0 Ran:18
Win Prizemoney £3,821 *Total Prizemoney* £16,098
Wins 1996 Jun Thirsk (FRM) 7f 65 <
1999 Turf 0-7: (7f 2, 8f 2, 9f 3) (g-s 2, gd 3, g-f 2) 1999 AW 0-2: (7f, 8f) (Fibr 2)
Fair gelding. Turf high 56. AW high 58 (began Jly).
**John Harris [0-3] Steppey Lane Bloodstock (from C W Thornton [0-16] Jly 1999).*

SABRE BUTT BHB 39f42a **RR 42f 42a** 3735[6]
4 gr g Sabrehill (USA) 8.5f **(64)** - Butsova (Formidable (USA)) 9.2f **(63)**
Form - 04036
Record 1999 - 1st:0 2nd:0 3rd:1 Ran:4
Pre1999 - 1st:0 2nd:0 3rd:0 Ran:10
Win Prizemoney £0 *Total Prizemoney* £357
1999 Turf 0-3: (9f, 10f, 12f) (gd 2, g-f) 1999 AW 0-1: (10f) (Equi)
Workmanlike, moderate gelding, effective 10f, - acts on Equi, often wears blinkers (effectively). Turf high 42. (1st run) - 4th of 8 getting

13lb from Confronter (7 Jan Lingfield 10f Equi RF 0049). **M H Tompkins [1-22] www raceworld co uk.*

SABRE LADY BHB 83f **RR 80f** 4589[12]
2 ch f Sabrehill (USA) 8.5f **(64)** - Cal Norma's Lady (IRE) (Lyphard's Special (USA)) 10.3f **(72)**
Form - 1230
Record 1999 - 1st:1 2nd:1 3rd:1 Ran:4
Win Prizemoney £3,501 *Total Prizemoney* £5,681
Wins * 1999 Jly Hamilt (FRM) 5f 60+ <
1999 Turf 1-4: (5f 1-1, 6f 3) (gd 2, frm 1-2)
Decent filly. Turf high 80 (began Jly) - 3rd of 14 giving 20lb to Top of The Class (17 Spt Ayr 6f gd RF 4375).
**Miss L A Perratt [1-4] David Sutherland.*

SABREON BHB 85f **RR 74f** 5196[9]
2 b f Caerleon (USA) 10.9f **(79)** - Sabria (USA) (Miswaki (USA)) 9f **(81)**
Form - 42220
Record 1999 - 1st:0 2nd:3 3rd:0 Ran:5
Win Prizemoney £0 *Total Prizemoney* £3,647
1999 Turf 0-5: (7f, 8f 4) (sft 2, gd 2, frm)
Above-average filly. Turf high 74 (began Aug) - 2nd of 9 to Idolize (30 Aug Chepstow 8f gd RF 4006). **J L Dunlop [0-5] Eurostrait Ltd.*

SACRED HEART (IRE) RR 44f 5192[8]
2 b f Catrail (USA) - Merry Devil (IRE) (Sadler's Wells (USA)) 10f **(76)**
Form - 8
Record 1999 - 1st:0 2nd:0 3rd:0 Ran:1
1999 Turf 0-1: (8f) (gd)
Currently moderate filly. **K McAuliffe [0-1] Mrs H Raw.*

SACRED SONG (USA) RR 79+f 2914[1]
2 b f Diesis 9f **(80)** - Ruby Ransom (CAN) (Red Ransom (USA))
Form - 1
Record 1999 - 1st:1 2nd:0 3rd:0 Ran:1
Win Prizemoney £4,207 *Total Prizemoney* £4,207
Wins * 1999 Jly Nottin (FRM) 6.1f 79+ <
1999 Turf 1-1: (6f 1-1) (gd 1-1)
Currently above-average filly. (1st run) - 1st of 4 from Yazmin (17 Jly Nottingham RF 2914). **H R A Cecil [1-1] Niarchos Family.*

SADAKA (USA) RR 71f 4560[8]
2 ch f Kingmambo (USA) 10.9f **(85)** - Basma (USA) (Grey Dawn II) 11.1f **(72)**
Form - 38
Record 1999 - 1st:0 2nd:0 3rd:1 Ran:2
Win Prizemoney £0 *Total Prizemoney* £595
1999 Turf 0-2: (6f, 7f) (gd, frm)
Currently above-average filly. Turf high 71 (began Spt).
**E A L Dunlop [0-2] Hamdan Al Maktoum.*

SADDLE MOUNTAIN RR 68f 5198[7]
3 b f Saddlers' Hall (IRE) 10.5f **(65)** - Rainbow Mountain **(75f)** (Rainbow Quest (USA)) 10.4f **(75)**
Form - 7
Record 1999 - 1st:0 2nd:0 3rd:0 Ran:1
1999 Turf 0-1: (8f) (gd)
Scopey, currently average filly. **Lady Herries [0-1] Hesmonds Stud.*

SADDLERS' GLORY BHB 53f **RR 46f** 689[12]
3 b f Saddlers' Hall (IRE) 10.5f **(65)** - Hope and Glory (USA) (Well Decorated (USA)) 7.6f **(64)**
Form - 00
Record 1999 - 1st:0 2nd:0 3rd:0 Ran:2
Pre1999 - 1st:0 2nd:0 3rd:0 Ran:3
1999 Turf 0-2: (12f 2) (gd, frm)
Lengthy, moderate filly. Turf high 41.
**C W Fairhurst [0-5] Tony Sweetman.*

SADDLER'S QUEST RR 88+f 4582[1]
2 b c Saddlers' Hall (IRE) 10.5f **(65)** - Seren Quest **(81f)** (Rainbow Quest (USA)) 10.4f **(75)**
Form - 1
Record 1999 - 1st:1 2nd:0 3rd:0 Ran:1
Win Prizemoney £3,550 *Total Prizemoney* £3,550
Wins * 1999 Spt Bath (G-S) 10.2f 88+ <
1999 Turf 1-1: (10f 1-1) (gd 1-1)
Currently useful colt. (1st run) - 1st of 12 from Duchamp (27 Spt Bath RF 4582). **G A Butler [1-1] The Fairy Story Partnership.*

SADEEBAH BHB 40f **RR 46f** 2145[17]
4 b g Prince Sabo 6.6f **(64)** - Adeebah (USA) (Damascus (USA)) 8.9f **(71)**
Form - 0
Record 1999 - 1st:0 2nd:0 3rd:0 Ran:1
Pre1999 - 1st:0 2nd:1 3rd:0 Ran:11
Win Prizemoney £0 *Total Prizemoney* £625
1999 Turf 0-1: (11f) (g-s)
Unfurnished, moderate gelding, effective 8f, acts on gd to frm, has worn blinkers.
**Martin Todhunter [0-2] G C G Racing Partnership (from M Johnston [0-10] Jly 1998).*

SADIAN BHB 114f **RR 114f** 4113a[4]
4 b c Shirley Heights 12.1f **(76)** - Rafha (Kris) 9.5f **(73)**
Form - 11734
Record 1999 - 1st:2 2nd:0 3rd:1 Ran:5
Pre1999 - 1st:4 2nd:1 3rd:0 Ran:8
Win Prizemoney £75,810 *Total Prizemoney* £115,267
Wins * 1999 May Cheste (G-F) G3 13.4f 112
*** 1999** Apr Newbur (G-F) G3 12f 114 <
***** 1998 Spt Salisb (GD) 14.1f 109
***** 1998 Aug Ascot (G-F) 12f 109
1998 Apr Bath (SFT) 10.2f 99
1997 Aug Lingfi (G-S) 7.6f 83+
1999 Turf 2-5: (12f 1-2, 13f 1-3) (gd 2, g-f 2-3)
Scopey, Group-class colt, effective 11 to 15f, acts on gd to g-f, best on g-f, likes left handed tracks, excels at Newbury. Turf high 114 (1st run) - 1st of 11 from The Glow-Worm (17 Apr Newbury RF 0733) - also 1st of 7 giving 3lb to Secret Saver (6 May Chester RF 1050). Consistent. Small in stature, he is all heart and fought hard to win the John Porter and Ormonde Stakes in the spring. Far from disgraced in smart company thereafter, he stays well and could develop into a Cup horse.
**J L Dunlop [4-8] (from H R A Cecil [2-5] Jun 1998).*

SADLER'S REALM BHB 71f **RR 70f** 2000[27]
6 b g Sadler's Wells (USA) 11.3f **(87)** - Rensaler (USA) (Stop The Music (USA)) 9.2f **(71)**
Form - 10
Record 1999 - 1st:1 2nd:0 3rd:0 Ran:2
Pre1999 - 1st:0 2nd:1 3rd:1 Ran:5
Win Prizemoney £3,616 *Total Prizemoney* £5,346
Wins * 1999 May Haydoc (GD) H 14f 65 70 <
1999 Turf 1-2: (14f 1-1, 20f) (g-f 1-2)
Above-average gelding. Turf high 70 (1st run) - 1st of 10 from Aldwych Arrow (1 May Haydock RF 0954). Better known as a hurdler, he was quite impressive when winning a Haydock handicap over fourteen furlongs in April.
**P J Hobbs [6-21] B D Racing (from Sir Michael Stoute [0-5] Aug 1996).*

SADLER'S SONG BHB 53f **RR 55f** 4022[5]
2 b f Saddlers' Hall (IRE) 10.5f **(65)** - Life Watch (USA) (Highland Park (USA))
Form - 6005
Record 1999 - 1st:0 2nd:0 3rd:0 Ran:4
1999 Turf 0-4: (5f, 6f, 7f, 8f) (g-f 3, frm)
Fair filly. Turf high 55. **P C Haslam [0-4] The Drumpellier Partnership.*

SADLERS SWING (USA) RR 54f 3032[8]
3 b c Red Ransom (USA) 8.6f **(83)** - Noblissima (IRE) **(77f)** (Sadler's Wells (USA)) 10f **(76)**
Form - 8
Record 1999 - 1st:0 2nd:0 3rd:0 Ran:1
1999 Turf 0-1: (8f) (frm)
Workmanlike, currently fair colt.
**J J Sheehan [0-1] Mrs Eileen Sheehan.*

SAD MAD BAD (USA) BHB 59f48a **RR 58f 48a** 5168[1]
5 b g Sunny's Halo (CAN) 8f **(80)** - Quite Attractive (USA) (Well Decorated (USA)) 7.6f **(64)**
Form - 1
Record 1999 - 1st:1 2nd:0 3rd:0 Ran:1
Pre1999 - 1st:1 2nd:3 3rd:2 Ran:17

Win Prizemoney £6,353 *Total Prizemoney* £10,652
Wins * **1999** Nov Catter (SFT) H 13.8f 56 58
1996 Aug Lingfi (G-S) 7.6f 80 <
1999 Turf 1-1: (14f 1-1) (g-s 1-1)
Fair gelding. (1st run) - 1st of 14 giving 11lb to Semi Circle (2 Nov Catterick RF 5168). **Mrs M Reveley [8-23]*
P D Savill (from M Johnston [1-8] Jun 1997).

SAFARANDO (IRE) BHB 72f **RR 78f** 5218[8]

2 b c Turtle Island (IRE) - Hertford Castle **(31f)** (Reference Point) 6.8f **(70)**
Form - 451523363571228
Record 1999 - 1st:2 2nd:3 3rd:3 Ran:15
Win Prizemoney £5,896 *Total Prizemoney* £11,369
Wins * **1999** Oct Lingfi (HVY) H 7f 65 69 <
1999 Jun Yarmou (GD) S 7f 64
1999 Turf 2-15: (6f 2, 7f 2-10, 8f 3) (g-s 1-3, gd 3, g-f 1-5, frm 4)
Above-average colt, effective 7f, acts on g-s to frm, best on gd. Turf high 78 - 2nd of 20 giving 7lb to French Horn (25 Oct Leicester 7f gd RF 5052) - also 1st of 18 getting 7lb from Safari Blues (1 Oct Lingfield RF 4672). He seemed to appreciate the seventh furlong when winning a Yarmouth seller in June, and has been kept busy since winning a Lingfield nursery.
**N P Littmoden [1-12] Paul Dixon (from R Hannon [1-3] Jun 1999).*

SAFARASIKNOW BHB 60f55a **RR 70f 55a** 4941[7]

2 ch c Safawan 6.6f **(60)** - Lutine Royal (Formidable (USA)) 9.2f **(63)**
Form - 8777
Record 1999 - 1st:0 2nd:0 3rd:0 Ran:4
1999 Turf 0-4: (5f, 6f 3) (g-s, gd, g-f, frm)
Above-average colt. Turf high 70 (began Jly).
**Major D N Chappell [0-4] Dr Melvyn Walters.*

SAFARI BLUES (IRE) BHB 78f84a **RR 75f 84a** 4672[2]

2 b f Blues Traveller (IRE) - North Hut (Northfields (USA)) 9f **(72)**
Form - 04244352
Record 1999 - 1st:0 2nd:2 3rd:1 Ran:8
Win Prizemoney £0 *Total Prizemoney* £2,863
1999 Turf 0-8: (5f 3, 6f 2, 7f 3) (g-s 2, g-f 2, frm 3, hrd)
Useful filly, effective 7f, acts on g-s to frm. Turf high 75 - 2nd of 18 giving 7lb to Safarando (1 Oct Lingfield 7f g-s RF 4672).
**R Hannon [0-8] T J Dale.*

SAFECRACKER BHB 53f36a **RR 44df 36a** 450[8]

6 ch g Sayf El Arab (USA) 8.2f **(57)** - My Polished Corner (IRE) (Tate Gallery (USA)) 7.4f **(67)**
Form - 808
Record 1999 - 1st:0 2nd:0 3rd:0 Ran:3
Pre1999 - 1st:1 2nd:1 3rd:0 Ran:10
Win Prizemoney £3,261 *Total Prizemoney* £3,992
Wins 1996 Apr Folkes (FRM) H 9.7f 58 65 <
1999 AW 0-3: (8f, 12f 2) (Fibr 3)
Moderate gelding, has worn blinkers. AW high 39.
**T J Etherington [0-7] Mrs J E Todd (from C P Morlock [1-13] Nov 1997).*

SAFERJEL BHB 44f **RR 49df** 2303[6]

3 b f Elmaamul (USA) 8.1f **(70)** - Band of Fire (USA) (Chief's Crown (USA)) 9.8f **(72)**
Form - 066
Record 1999 - 1st:0 2nd:0 3rd:0 Ran:3
1999 Turf 0-3: (8f, 10f 2) (g-f 3)
Lengthy, currently moderate filly. Turf high 49.
**J W Hills [0-3] Ziad Galadari.*

SAFE SHARP JO (IRE) BHB 39f **RR 61df** 173[11]

4 ch g Case Law 6f **(64)** - Kentucky Wildcat (Be My Guest (USA)) 9.3f **(67)**
Form - 00
Record 1999 - 1st:0 2nd:0 3rd:0 Ran:1
Pre1999 - 1st:0 2nd:0 3rd:0 Ran:7
Win Prizemoney £0 *Total Prizemoney* £204
1999 AW 0-1: (7f) (Fibr)
Workmanlike, average gelding.
**M A Jarvis [0-8] Mrs Greta Sarfaty Marchant.*

SAFEY ANA (USA) BHB 56f **RR 54f** 3628[6]

8 b g Dixieland Band (USA) 10.1f **(80)** - Whatsoraire (USA) (Mr Prospector (USA)) 8.8f **(78)**
Form - 006086
Record 1999 - 1st:0 2nd:0 3rd:0 Ran:6
Pre1999 - 1st:7 2nd:3 3rd:5 Ran:49
Win Prizemoney £25,929 *Total Prizemoney* £34,628
Wins * 1998 Aug Salisb (G-F) H 8f 70 75 <
* 1997 Spt Lingfi (GD) H 7f 66 71
* 1997 Jly Lingfi (G-F) H 7.6f 64 69
* 1997 May Yarmou (G-F) H 7f 61 67
* 1997 Apr Bright (FRM) H 8f 59 65
* 1995 Jly Newbur (GD) H 7f 70 71
* 1995 May Redcar (FRM) 7f 69
1999 Turf 0-6: (7f, 8f 4, 10f) (gd 2, g-f 2, frm 2)
Fair gelding, effective 7 to 8f, best at 8f, acts on g-f to frm, best on g-f, has worn blinkers. Turf high 59. **B Hanbury [7-55]*
The Optimists Racing Partnership.

SAFFIZZ BHB 85f **RR 80f** 4375[12]

2 ch g Safawan 6.6f **(60)** - Polar Fizz (Polar Falcon (USA))
Form - 128363300
Record 1999 - 1st:1 2nd:1 3rd:3 Ran:9
Win Prizemoney £2,697 *Total Prizemoney* £6,805
Wins * **1999** Mar Hamilt (HVY) 5f 80 <
1999 Turf 1-9: (5f 1-3, 6f 6) (sft 1-1, g-s, gd 3, g-f 2, frm 2)
Decent gelding, effective 5 to 6f, best at 6f, acts on sft to frm. Turf high 80 - 3rd of 7 giving 2lb to Dramatic Quest (28 May Pontefract 6f g-f RF 1556) - also 1st of 7 giving 6lb to Harryana (29 Mar Hamilton RF 0499). Inconsistent. He is to continue his career in Macau. **K A Ryan [1-9] Swan At Whalley Racing Elite Partnership.*

SAFFRON BHB 70a **RR 50f** 3902[12]

3 ch f Alhijaz 7.7f **(57)** - Silver Lodge (Homing) 7.8f **(59)**
Form - 004800
Record 1999 - 1st:0 2nd:0 3rd:0 Ran:6
Pre1999 - 1st:1 2nd:3 3rd:1 Ran:8
Win Prizemoney £3,246 *Total Prizemoney* £7,513
Wins * 1998 Spt Catter (G-F) H 7f 70 74 <
1999 Turf 0-6: (7f 2, 8f 4) (gd, g-f 3, frm 2)
Above-average filly, effective 6 to 8f, best at 6f, acts on g-f to frm - acts on Fibr, likes left handed tracks. Turf high 67 - 4th of 7 getting 8lb from Pilgrim's Way (28 Jly Doncaster 8f frm RF 3198). Becoming disappointing.
**J A Glover [1-14] Ernest Bennett.*

SAFFRON ROSE BHB 54f50a **RR 53f 50a** 4219[10]

5 b m Polar Falcon (USA) 9f **(74)** - Tweedling (USA) (Sir Ivor) 10.2f **(70)**
Form - 50860
Record 1999 - 1st:0 2nd:0 3rd:0 Ran:5
Pre1999 - 1st:2 2nd:1 3rd:1 Ran:23
Win Prizemoney £6,660 *Total Prizemoney* £9,320
Wins * 1997 Jly Nottin (SFT) H 8.2f 70 73 <
* 1997 Jun Nottin (GD) H 8.2f 63 70
1999 Turf 0-3: (8f, 12f 2) (g-f, frm 2) 1999 AW 0-2: (9f 2) (Fibr 2)
Fair filly, effective 8 to 10f, best at 8f, acts on g-s to frm, best on g-s, likes tight tracks. **M Blanshard [2-30]*
The Lower Bowden II Syndicate.

SAFFRON WALDEN (FR) **RR 117f** 3694[12]

3 b c Sadler's Wells (USA) 11.3f **(87)** - Or Vision (USA) (Irish River (FR)) 8.6f **(78)**
Form - 111720
1999 Turf 3-6: (8f 3-3, 10f 2, 12f) (sft 1-1, gd, g-f 2-3, frm)
High-class colt, effective 8 to 10f, acts on g-f to frm, has worn blinkers. Turf high 121 - 1st of 10 from Enrique (22 May Curragh RF 1477a). He ran as Saffron Waldon for his first four starts before permission was given for the spelling to be changed. Made a winning reappearance in a Curragh maiden before scrambling home in the Leopardstown 2000 Guineas Trial. Ran out the clear-cut winner of the Irish 2000 Guineas itself before finishing a never-nearer seventh in the Derby, reportedly unsuited by the track. He disappointed afterwards, returning slightly lame when second to Make No Mistake in the Meld Stakes and finishing last when visored in the Juddmonte International. He remains in training, and should be able to win further Group races.
**A P O'Brien in IRE [3-7] Mrs Magnier/M Tabor/Niar Family.*

SAFI BHB 48f44a **RR 32f 44a** 3597[9]

4 b g Generous (IRE) 11.5f **(82)** - Jasarah (IRE) (Green Desert (USA)) 8.6f **(78)**
Form - 06050702600
Record 1999 - 1st:0 2nd:1 3rd:0 Ran:11
Pre1999 - 1st:0 2nd:0 3rd:1 Ran:4
Win Prizemoney £0 *Total Prizemoney* £1,852
1999 Turf 0-8: (7f, 8f, 10f, 11f 3, 12f 2) (gd, g-f 3, frm 3, hrd) 1999 AW 0-3: (8f, 9f, 11f) (Fibr 3)
Workmanlike, fair gelding, has worn blinkers. Turf high 54. AW high 53. Becoming disappointing.
**D McCain [0-17] D McCain.*

SAFRANINE (IRE) BHB 96f **RR 92?f** 3787[7]
2 b f Dolphin Street (FR) - Webbiana (African Sky) 7.9f **(63)**
Form - 0127
Record 1999 - 1st:1 2nd:1 3rd:0 Ran:4
Win Prizemoney £2,994 *Total Prizemoney* £3,843
Wins * 1999 Jly Redcar (FRM) 6f 92? <
1999 Turf 1-3: (6f 1-3) (gd, g-f, frm 1-1) 1999 AW 0-1: (5f) (Fibr)
Useful filly. Turf high 92 (1st run) (began Jly) - 1st of 5 from Mrs P (24 Jly Redcar RF 3107).
**J L Eyre [1-4] M Gleason.*

SAGAMIX (FR) RR 127f 2662a[4]
4 br c Linamix (FR) 8.2f **(64)** - Saganeca (USA) (Sagace (FR)) 8f **(124)**
Form - 44
1999 Turf 0-2: (11f, 12f) (gd 2)
Top-class colt. Turf high 122 - 4th of 10 to El Condor Pasa (4 Jly Saint-Cloud 12f gd RF 2662a). Beat Dream Well on heavy ground in the spring of 1998 and, following a mid-term break, returned to take the scalps of both Croco Rouge and Dream Well in the Prix Niel. Confirmed himself a top-notch colt with victory in the Arc, catching Leggera well inside the final furlong but winning a shade comfortably in the end. Suited by 12 furlongs and soft ground, he did not look to be at his best in the 1999 season, but did not have conditions in his favour. He was sold to Godolphin in September and missed the Arc as a result.
**A Fabre in FR [3-5].*

SAGE ET JOLIE RR 108f 3928a[2]
3 gr f Linamix (FR) 8.2f **(64)** - Saganeca (USA) (Sagace (FR)) 8f **(124)**
Form - 312
1999 Turf 1-3: (10f, 12f 1-2) (gd 1-2, g-f)
Currently Pattern-class filly. Turf high 108 - 2nd of 9 to Star Of Akkar (21 Aug Deauville 10f gd RF 3928a) - also 1st of 8 from Side Saddle (27 Jun Longchamp RF 2477a). A full sister to Sagamix, she landed the Prix de Malleret and was short-headed in heavy in a Deauville Group Three.
**A Fabre in FR [1-3].*

SAGUARO BHB 42f77a **RR 39f 77a** 4091[9]
5 b g Green Desert (USA) 7.8f **(78)** - Badawi (USA) (Diesis) 9.3f **(69)**
Form - 11480000
Record 1999 - 1st:2 2nd:0 3rd:0 Ran:8
Pre1999 - 1st:0 2nd:1 3rd:0 Ran:5
Win Prizemoney £4,465 *Total Prizemoney* £5,425
Wins * 1999 *Mar Wolver (SLW) H 9.4f 72 75*
*** 1999** *Feb Southw (STD) H 8f 54 82* <
1999 Turf 0-4: (8f 4) (gd, g-f 2, frm) 1999 AW 2-4: (8f 1-3, 9f 1-1) (Fibr 2-4)
Above-average gelding, effective 8 to 9f, - acts on Fibr, has worn blinkers, likes left handed tracks, likes tight tracks. Turf high 39. AW high 82 (1st run) - 1st of 9 giving 15lb to Golden Lyric (26 Feb Southwell RF 0365) - also 1st of 13 giving 16lb to The Wild Widow (6 Mar Wolverhampton RF 0407). Becoming disappointing. Formerly trained by John Gosden, he got off the mark for Kevin Morgan with a wide-margin victory in a very poor maiden handicap at Southwell, but followed up in a much better race at Wolverhampton. Has shown little on turf.
**K A Morgan [2-9] Rex Norton (from J H M Gosden [0-5] Jun 1998).*

SAHARA SPIRIT (IRE) BHB 76f **RR 69f** 5021[20]
2 b c College Chapel - Desert Palace (Green Desert (USA)) 8.6f **(78)**
Form - 340
Record 1999 - 1st:0 2nd:0 3rd:1 Ran:3
Win Prizemoney £0 *Total Prizemoney* £690
1999 Turf 0-3: (6f, 7f 2) (g-s, gd 2)
Currently average colt. Turf high 69 - 4th of 11 to Jathaab (25 Spt Haydock 7f g-s RF 4551).
**E A L Dunlop [0-3] Stars And Stripes.*

SAIFAN BHB 56f65a **RR 54f 65a** 5053[17]
10 ch g Beveled (USA) 6.9f **(64)** - Superfrost (Tickled Pink) 6.5f **(59)**
Form - 00030108160060
Record 1999 - 1st:2 2nd:0 3rd:1 Ran:13
Pre1999 - 1st:10 2nd:5 3rd:10 Ran:76
Win Prizemoney £92,751 *Total Prizemoney* £114,751
Wins * 1999 Jly Yarmou (FRM) H 7f 58 62
*** 1999** Jly Yarmou (GD) C 8f 51+
* 1997 Aug Redcar (G-F) H 8f 83 87
* 1996 Nov Newmar (GD) H 8f 83 88 <
* 1996 Jly Yarmou (FRM) H 8f 77 82
* 1996 Jun Newmar (G-F) H 8f 72 77
* 1995 Aug Leices (GD) H 7f 72 78
* 1995 Jly Yarmou (G-F) H 8f 66 73
1999 Turf 2-13: (7f 1-3, 8f 1-10) (g-s, gd 1-3, g-f 1-3, frm 6)
Fair gelding, has broken blood-vessels, effective 8f, acts on frm, mostly wears blinkers. Turf high 62. Inconsistent. He is not getting any younger, and had only shown glimpses of form since winning in August 1997, before scoring twice at Yarmouth in July. Out of form since however.
**D Morris [12-82] D Morris (from J C Fox [0-7] Nov 1991).*

SAILING BHB 93f **RR 88f** 5041[5]
2 ch f Arazi (USA) 9.2f **(74)** - Up Anchor (IRE) (Slip Anchor) 9.8f **(73)**
Form - 21105
Record 1999 - 1st:2 2nd:1 3rd:0 Ran:5
Win Prizemoney £9,176 *Total Prizemoney* £10,416
Wins * 1999 Aug Sandow (GD) 8.1f 84+ <
*** 1999** Jun Goodwo (G-F) 7f 78+
1999 Turf 2-5: (6f, 7f 1-2, 8f 1-2) (sft, gd, g-f, frm 2-2)
Useful filly. Turf high 88 - also 1st of 6 giving 3lb to Miletrian (21 Aug Sandown RF 3824). Only narrowly beaten over six furlongs on her Goodwood debut, she landed long odds-on with the minimum of fuss over an extra furlong on the same track next time. Followed up with a clear-cut victory over a mile at Sandown, but was well beaten in the May Hill.
**P F I Cole [2-5] H R H Prince Fahd Salman.*

SAILING SHOES (IRE) BHB 87f **RR 86f** 5134[8]
3 b c Lahib (USA) 8f **(69)** - Born To Glamour (Ajdal (USA)) 9.2f **(89)**
Form - 3240758
Record 1999 - 1st:0 2nd:1 3rd:1 Ran:7
Pre1999 - 1st:1 2nd:1 3rd:0 Ran:6
Win Prizemoney £3,434 *Total Prizemoney* £38,904
Wins * 1998 Jun Cheste (GD) 5.1f 85+ <
1999 Turf 0-7: (5f 2, 6f 5) (sft, g-s, gd 3, g-f 2)
Scopey, useful colt, effective 6f, acts on frm. Turf high 99. He found life tough off a stiff mark, but did show signs of a return to form in the autumn. Probably best over six furlongs, he needs to drop a few pounds in the handicap.
**R Hannon [1-13] Hippodrome Racing.*

SAIL-ON BUN BHB 42f **RR 54f** 4563[15]
3 gr f Beveled (USA) 6.9f **(64)** - Sea Farer Lake (Gairloch) 7f **(63)**
Form - 080
Record 1999 - 1st:0 2nd:0 3rd:0 Ran:3
Pre1999 - 1st:0 2nd:0 3rd:0 Ran:3
1999 Turf 0-2: (12f, 14f) (gd 2) 1999 AW 0-1: (11f) (Fibr)
Leggy, fair filly. Turf high 54.
**K McAuliffe [0-6] Mrs S D Fidler.*

SAIL ON SALLY BHB 36f **RR 55f** 4905[16]
3 ch f Clantime 6.6f **(57)** - Croft Sally (Crofthall) 6.3f **(59)**
Form - 0
Record 1999 - 1st:0 2nd:0 3rd:0 Ran:1
Pre1999 - 1st:0 2nd:0 3rd:0 Ran:2
1999 Turf 0-1: (6f) (frm)
Unfurnished, currently fair filly.
**C F Wall [0-1] Miss Vivian Pratt (from J Akehurst [0-2] Nov 1998).*

SAILOR A'HOY BHB 73f **RR 78df** 3834[5]
3 b c Handsome Sailor 6.6f **(53)** - Eye Sight (Roscoe Blake) 11f **(66)**
Form - 462555
Record 1999 - 1st:0 2nd:1 3rd:0 Ran:6
Win Prizemoney £0 *Total Prizemoney* £1,534

1999 Turf 0-6: (8f, 10f 3, 12f 2) (gd, g-f 2, frm 3)
Scopey, above-average colt, effective 12f, acts on gd. He has shown fair maiden form but his attitude is in question.
**R F JohnsonHoughton [0-6] Lord Leverhulme.*

SAILOR JACK (USA) BHB 38f **RR 39f** 4949[6]

3 b g Green Dancer (USA) 11.9f **(77)** - Chateaubrook (USA) (Alleged (USA)) 10f **(76)**
Form - 885630406
Record 1999 - 1st:0 2nd:0 3rd:1 Ran:9
Pre1999 - 1st:0 2nd:0 3rd:0 Ran:2
Win Prizemoney £0 *Total Prizemoney* £552
1999 Turf 0-9: (10f 3, 11f, 12f 3, 14f 2) (g-s, gd, g-f 6, frm)
Leggy, very moderate gelding, mostly wears blinkers. Turf high 59. Consistent.
**C E Brittain [0-11] R A Pledger.*

SAIL WITH THE WIND RR 53f 5216[13]

2 b f Saddlers' Hall (IRE) 10.5f **(65)** - Shesadelight (Shirley Heights) 10.3f **(74)**
Form - 00
Record 1999 - 1st:0 2nd:0 3rd:0 Ran:2
1999 Turf 0-2: (8f 2) (g-s, gd)
Currently fair filly. Turf high 53 (began Oct).
**T D McCarthy [0-2] Hesmonds Stud.*

SAINT ALBERT BHB 66f **RR 67f** 1733[6]

4 ch g Keen 11.1f **(58)** - Thimbalina (Salmon Leap (USA)) 11f **(61)**
Form - 6
Record 1999 - 1st:0 2nd:0 3rd:0 Ran:1
Pre1999 - 1st:2 2nd:4 3rd:1 Ran:12
Win Prizemoney £4,822 *Total Prizemoney* £8,224
Wins * 1998 Jly Doncas (G-F) H 16.5f 61 67 <
* 1998 Jly Salisb (FRM) H 12f 55 59
1999 Turf 0-1: (9f) (gd)
Scopey, average gelding, effective 12 to 17f, acts on g-f to frm, best on g-f, has worn blinkers.
**P T Walwyn [2-13] Mrs D C Samworth.*

SAINTE MARINE (IRE) RR 115f 4777a[6]

4 b f Kenmare (FR) 9.6f **(76)** - Pont-Aven (Try My Best (USA)) 7.6f **(67)**
Form - 1326
1999 Turf 1-4: (5f 1-4) (sft, gd, g-f 1-2)
High-class filly, effective 5f, acts on sft to frm, best on g-f, and does well at Chantilly and York. Turf high 115 (1st run) - 1st of 7 giving 6lb to Dream Chief (5 Jun Chantilly RF 1901a). Consistent. One of France's leading sprinters, although that is not a strong division, she possesses lightning pace and is suited by an easy five furlongs. The easy winner of the Group Two Prix du Gros-Chene at Chantilly in June, she then finished third in the King's Stand Stakes at Ascot when less than positively ridden. She was the only one to get anywhere near Stravinsky in the Nunthorpe, but was unable to utilise her blinding speed in the heavy ground when well beaten in the Prix de l'Abbaye on her final start.
**R Collet in FR [4-12] R C Strauss.*

SAINT EXPRESS BHB 72f **RR 63f** 2731[10]

9 ch g Clantime 6.6f **(57)** - Redgrave Design (Nebbiolo) 8.1f **(75)**
Form - 000
Record 1999 - 1st:0 2nd:0 3rd:0 Ran:3
Pre1999 - 1st:7 2nd:11 3rd:10 Ran:73
Win Prizemoney £32,831 *Total Prizemoney* £87,395
Wins * 1998 Aug Redcar (G-F) H 8f 80 83
* 1997 Oct Redcar (G-F) H 7f 80 83
* 1995 Jun York (G-F) H 5f 94 100 <
1999 Turf 0-3: (6f 2, 7f) (gd, g-f, frm)
Average gelding, effective 6 to 8f, best at 7f, acts on gd to frm, best on frm, has worn blinkers. Turf high 63. Consistent.
**Mrs M Reveley [3-49] D S Hall (from N Tinkler [0-1] Jun 1994).*

SAINT GEORGE (IRE) BHB 49f **RR 56f** 1819[19]

3 b g Unblest - Jumana (Windjammer (USA)) 7f **(59)**
Form - 00
Record 1999 - 1st:0 2nd:0 3rd:0 Ran:2
Pre1999 - 1st:0 2nd:0 3rd:0 Ran:4

1999 Turf 0-2: (6f, 7f) (g-f, frm)
Unfurnished, fair gelding. Turf high 44.
**G B Balding [0-6] Russell Publishing Ltd.*

SAINTLY SPEECH (USA) RR 90f 3086[1]

2 br f Southern Halo (USA) - Eloquent Minister (USA) (Deputy Minister (CAN)) 7.4f **(80)**
Form - 11
Record 1999 - 1st:2 2nd:0 3rd:0 Ran:2
Win Prizemoney £27,756 *Total Prizemoney* £27,756
Wins * **1999** Jly Ascot (G-F) G3 6f 90+ <
* **1999** May Pontef (GD) 6f 90
1999 Turf 2-2: (6f 2-2) (gd 2-2)
Currently useful filly. Turf high 90 - 1st of 8 from Journalist (24 Jly Ascot RF 3086) - also 1st of 10 from Crimplene (18 May Pontefract RF 1298). Ran green on her Pontefract debut, but still managed to prevail, and stepped up considerably on that when coming with a strong late run to win the Princess Margaret. She was not seen again. **P W Chapple-Hyam [2-2] R E Sangster.*

SAKHA BHB 104f **RR 105f** 5120a[5]

3 ch f Wolfhound (USA) 7.3f **(71)** - Harmless Albatross (Pas de Seul) 9.1f **(67)**
Form - 54115
Record 1999 - 1st:2 2nd:0 3rd:0 Ran:5
Pre1999 - 1st:2 2nd:0 3rd:1 Ran:3
Win Prizemoney £28,307 *Total Prizemoney* £29,893
Wins * **1999** Spt Newmar (G-S) L 5f 100+
* **1999** Spt Yarmou (G-S) 6f 96
* 1998 Aug Haydoc (GD) 6f 102+ <
* 1998 Jly Kempto (G-F) 6f 84
1999 Turf 2-5: (5f 1-2, 6f 1-2, 7f) (hvy, g-s 1-1, gd 1-1, frm 2)
Neat, Pattern-class filly, effective 5 to 7f, best at 6f, acts on g-s to frm, best on frm. Turf high 105 (1st run) - 5th of 11 to Wince (16 Apr Newbury 7f frm RF 0719) - also 1st of 15 getting 6lb from Andreyev (30 Spt Newmarket RF 4654). An improving sort, she did not run too badly in the Fred Darling on her reappearance, and showed just how talented she is when, on her second start since a mid-season break, she won a conditions race at Yarmouth with the minimum of fuss. Has since added a Listed event at Newmarket but was not at her best in France on her final start.
**J L Dunlop [4-8] Hamdan Al Maktoum.*

SAKHEE (USA) BHB 100f **RR 94f** 4695[1]

2 b c Bahri (USA) - Thawakib (IRE) (Sadler's Wells (USA)) 10f **(76)**
Form - 411
Record 1999 - 1st:2 2nd:0 3rd:0 Ran:3
Win Prizemoney £9,999 *Total Prizemoney* £10,225
Wins * **1999** Oct Sandow (SFT) 8.1f 94 <
* **1999** Spt Nottin (G-F) 8.2f 82+
1999 Turf 2-3: (7f, 8f 2-2) (g-s 1-1, frm 1-2)
Currently useful colt. Turf high 94 (began Aug) - 1st of 5 from Michele Marieschi (2 Oct Sandown RF 4695). An impressive looking colt, there has been plenty to like about his two successes to date, at Nottingham and Sandown, as he has showed a really nice attitude on both occasions. He won with something in hand at Sandown, and there looks to be more to come.
**J L Dunlop [2-3] Hamdan Al Maktoum.*

SALABUE (USA) RR 54f 5049[16]

2 b c Affirmed (USA) 10.3f **(75)** - Parliament House (USA) (General Assembly (USA)) 10f **(68)**
Form - 50
Record 1999 - 1st:0 2nd:0 3rd:0 Ran:2
1999 Turf 0-2: (7f, 8f) (g-s, gd)
Currently fair colt. Turf high 54 (began Oct).
**J L Dunlop [0-2] Benny Andersson.*

SALALAH BHB 51f **RR 51f** 5156[12]

3 gr f Lion Cavern (USA) 7.5f **(74)** - Sea Fret (Habat) 7.6f **(61)**
Form - 86610030
Record 1999 - 1st:1 2nd:0 3rd:1 Ran:8
Win Prizemoney £2,472 *Total Prizemoney* £2,832
Wins * **1999** Spt Mussel (G-F) H 7.1f 50 52 <
1999 Turf 1-8: (7f 1-3, 8f 5) (gd 3, g-f, frm 1-4)
Scopey, fair filly, effective 7 to 8f, acts on gd to frm. Turf high 52 (began Aug) - 1st of 14 giving 4lb to Northgate (13 Spt Musselburgh RF 4282). Consistent.

**H Morrison [1-8] The Salalah Partnership.*

SALAMAN (FR) BHB 48f **RR 57f** 2139[7]
7 b g Saumarez 15.1f **(87)** - Merry Sharp (Sharpen Up) 8.3f **(67)**
Form - 007
Record **1999** - 1st:0 2nd:0 3rd:0 Ran:3
Pre1999 - 1st:4 2nd:0 3rd:5 Ran:20
Win Prizemoney £21,144 *Total Prizemoney* £25,420
Wins 1995 Aug Pontef (G-F) 18f 56+
1995 Jly Cheste (GD) H 18.7f 78 85+ <
1995 Jly Beverl (G-F) H 16.2f 72 77+
1995 Jun Warwic (FRM) H 14.9f 67 73+
1999 Turf 0-3: (16f 3) (g-s, g-f 2)
Fair gelding, has worn blinkers. Turf high 57. Becoming disappointing.
**D C O'Brien [1-18] Graham Pasquill (from J L Dunlop [4-18] Spt 1996).*

SALEE (IRE) RR 68f 5137[6]
2 b f Caerleon (USA) 10.9f **(79)** - Almaaseh (IRE) (Dancing Brave (USA)) 8.4f **(76)**
Form - 6
Record **1999** - 1st:0 2nd:0 3rd:0 Ran:1
1999 Turf 0-1: (7f) (gd)
Currently average filly.
**A G Foster [0-1] M Stewkesbury & Mrs J Magnier.*

SALESTRIA BHB 70f **RR 69f** 4999[5]
3 b f Salse (USA) 10.9f **(71)** - Lydia Maria (Dancing Brave (USA)) 8.4f **(76)**
Form - 054242625
Record **1999** - 1st:0 2nd:3 3rd:0 Ran:9
Pre1999 - 1st:0 2nd:1 3rd:2 Ran:4
Win Prizemoney £0 *Total Prizemoney* £6,613
1999 Turf 0-9: (8f, 10f, 12f 4, 15f, 16f 2) (gd 3, g-f 4, frm 2)
Average filly, effective 7 to 16f, best at 7f, acts on gd to frm, has worn blinkers, likes right handed tracks, likes tight tracks, excels at Beverley. Turf high 76. Consistent.
**P W Harris [0-13] Mrs P W Harris.*

SALFORD EXPRESS (IRE) BHB 110f **RR 109f** 5043[2]
3 ch c Be My Guest (USA) 10.2f **(66)** - Summer Fashion (Moorestyle) 6.9f **(64)**
Form - 11050402
Record **1999** - 1st:2 2nd:1 3rd:0 Ran:8
Pre1999 - 1st:0 2nd:1 3rd:0 Ran:2
Win Prizemoney £82,010 *Total Prizemoney* £93,325
Wins *** 1999** May York (SFT) G2 10.4f 115 <
*** 1999** Apr Newbur (G-F) 11f 86
1999 Turf 2-8: (10f 1-4, 11f 1-2, 12f 2) (sft, g-s 1-1, gd 4, g-f, frm 1-1)
Workmanlike, Pattern-class colt, effective 10f, acts on g-s, has worn blinkers, prefers left handed tracks. Turf high 115 - 1st of 8 from Golden Snake (12 May York RF 1182). After making a winning reappearance in a Newbury maiden he stepped up to win a moderate renewal of the Dante, However, he was subsequently very disappointing, making no impact at all at Group level, including in the Derby, the Juddmonte International and the Champion Stakes. He ended the season with a better performance, chasing home the progressive Signorina Cattiva in the St Simon Stakes. That race was on heavy ground and, as the Dante was run on soft, easy ground may be the key to him. **D R C Elsworth [2-10] A J Thompson.*

SALFORD FLYER BHB 76f **RR 78f** 4730[5]
3 b g Pharly (FR) 11.5f **(64)** - Edge of Darkness **(52f)** (Vaigly Great) 7f **(58)**
Form - 06131144225
Record **1999** - 1st:3 2nd:2 3rd:1 Ran:11
Pre1999 - 1st:0 2nd:1 3rd:0 Ran:6
Win Prizemoney £8,349 *Total Prizemoney* £14,964
Wins *** 1999** Jly Salisb (G-S) 14.1f 68 <
*** 1999** Jun Yarmou (G-F) H 14.1f 65 68 <
*** 1999** Jun Haydoc (G-S) C 11.9f 68 <
1999 Turf 3-11:(10f, 12f 1-3, 14f 2-4, 16f 3)(g-s 2, gd 2-5, g-f 1-2, frm 2)
Workmanlike, above-average gelding, effective 12 to 16f, best at 14f, acts on gd to frm, best on gd, likes left handed tracks, prefers tight tracks. Turf high 78 - 2nd of 10 to Pay The Pied Piper (29 Aug Yarmouth 14f gd RF 4000). He flashed his tail and looks a tricky ride, but is an able sort in the right grade.
**G Wragg [3-17] A J Thompson.*

SALFORD LAD BHB 24f35a **RR 33f 35a** 89[7]
5 b h Don't Forget Me 9.5f **(66)** - Adjusting (IRE) (Busted) 10.2f **(61)**
Form - 7
Record **1999** - 1st:0 2nd:0 3rd:0 Ran:1
Pre1999 - 1st:0 2nd:0 3rd:0 Ran:9
1999 AW 0-1: (8f) (Fibr)
Very moderate colt.
**J Pearce [0-7] Jeff Pearce (from G Wragg [0-5] May 1998).*

SALIGO (IRE) BHB 75f **RR 81df** 5143[12]
4 b f Elbio 9f **(62)** - Doppio Filo (Vision (USA)) 9f **(64)**
Form - 058254273000
Record **1999** - 1st:0 2nd:2 3rd:1 Ran:12
Pre1999 - 1st:3 2nd:2 3rd:1 Ran:14
Win Prizemoney £26,926 *Total Prizemoney* £35,100
Wins 1998 Oct York (GD) H 8.9f 76 79 <
1998 Jun Leices (GD) H 10f 73 77
1998 May Salisb (FRM) H 8f 67 73
1999 Turf 0-12: (7f, 8f 6, 10f 5) (g-s, gd 5, g-f 2, frm 4)
Unfurnished, decent filly, effective 8 to 10f, best at 8f, acts on gd to frm, best on g-f, has worn blinkers, excels at Salisbury. Turf high 82. Becoming disappointing. Failed to get her head in front despite some encouraging performances.
**N Tinkler [0-1] Arthur Plant (from H Morrison [3-25] Oct 1999).*

SALIM RR 65f 5104[8]
2 b c Salse (USA) 10.9f **(71)** - Moviegoer (Pharly (FR)) 9.8f **(68)**
Form - 8
Record **1999** - 1st:0 2nd:0 3rd:0 Ran:1
1999 Turf 0-1: (7f) (gd)
Currently average colt. **Sir Michael Stoute [0-1] Hamdan Al Maktoum.*

SALLYANDAR RR 37f 4376[P]
3 b f Milieu - Megan's Move (Move Off) 15f **(41)**
Form - P
Record **1999** - 1st:0 2nd:0 3rd:0 Ran:1
Pre1999 - 1st:0 2nd:0 3rd:0 Ran:2
1999 Turf 0-1: (9f) (gd)
Unfurnished, currently very moderate filly.
**W Storey [0-3] H S Hutchinson.*

SALLY-ANN (IRE) BHB 38f **RR 51f** 5064[11]
2 b f Petardia 8.2f **(58)** - Curie Express (IRE) **(60f 48a)** (Fayruz)
Form - 05054200750
Record **1999** - 1st:0 2nd:1 3rd:0 Ran:11
Win Prizemoney £0 *Total Prizemoney* £621
1999 Turf 0-11: (5f 5, 6f 3, 7f 3) (gd 4, g-f, frm 4, hrd 2)
Fair filly, effective 5 to 7f, acts on frm to hrd. Turf high 51 - 2nd of 7 to Dusky Virgin (4 Aug Brighton 7f frm RF 3347).
**Mrs P N Dutfield [0-11] The Wheelwright Wanderers.*

SALLY GARDENS BHB 57f65a **RR 62f 65a** 5052[17]
2 b f Alzao (USA) 9.8f **(73)** - Polina **(62f)** (Polish Precedent (USA)) 10.2f **(60)**
Form - 575150
Record **1999** - 1st:1 2nd:0 3rd:0 Ran:6
Win Prizemoney £1,934 *Total Prizemoney* £1,934
Wins **1999** *Jly Wolver (STD) S 7f 62* <
1999 Turf 0-5: (6f 2, 7f 3) (gd 2, g-f, frm 2) 1999 AW 1-1: (7f 1-1) (Fibr 1-1)
Average filly, effective 7f, - acts on Fibr. Turf high 62. (1st run) - 1st of 11 from Alabama Wurley (23 Jly Wolverhampton RF 3083).
**T J Naughton [0-2] Ashley Carr Racing 3 (from M R Channon [1-4] Jly 1999).*

SALLY HOPPER BHB 41f **RR 54f** 2075[5]
3 b f Rock Hopper 10.6f **(54)** - Super Sally (Superlative) 7.2f **(56)**
Form - 575
Record **1999** - 1st:0 2nd:0 3rd:0 Ran:3
1999 Turf 0-3: (8f, 10f, 11f) (gd, g-f, hrd)
Leggy, currently fair filly. Turf high 54.
**J J O'Neill [0-3] Miss G Joughin.*

SALMON LADDER (USA) BHB 102f **RR 101f** 5219[3]
7 b h Bering 9.6f **(80)** - Ballerina Princess (USA) (Mr Prospector (USA))

8.8f **(78)**
Form - 27100133
Record 1999 - 1st:2 2nd:1 3rd:2 Ran:8
Pre1999 - 1st:8 2nd:6 3rd:2 Ran:29
Win Prizemoney £127,404 *Total Prizemoney* £188,829
Wins * **1999** Aug Cheste (G-S) LH 13.4f 96 101
* **1999** May Goodwo (GD) H 14f 92 96
* 1998 May Bath (GD) 10.2f 106
* 1998 May Hamilt (G-S) 9.2f 79+
* 1997 Aug Windso (G-F) 10f 106
* 1996 Oct Newbur (SFT) G3 12f 115 <
* 1996 Aug Goodwo (G-F) LH 12f 108 113
* 1996 Jun Ascot (G-F) H 10f 102 107
* 1996 Jun Hamilt (GD) 9.2f 88+
1999 Turf 2-8: (10f, 12f 3, 13f 1-1, 14f 1-2, 16f) (sft 2, gd 2-4, frm 2)
Very useful horse, effective 10 to 14f, acts on sft to frm, has worn blinkers, prefers tight tracks. Turf high 101 - 1st of 5 getting 8lb from Kadaka (21 Aug Chester RF 3813). He proved suited by a step-up to a mile and three-quarters, winning decent races at Goodwood and Chester. Best when ridden forcefully, he seems to act on any ground. **P F I Cole [10-37] M Arbib.*

SALORY BHB 48f RR 65f 5193[8]

3 b c Salse (USA) 10.9f **(71)** - Mory Kante (USA) (Icecapade (USA)) 11f **(62)**
Form - 088
Record 1999 - 1st:0 2nd:0 3rd:0 Ran:3
Pre1999 - 1st:0 2nd:0 3rd:0 Ran:2
1999 Turf 0-3: (8f, 10f, 12f) (hvy, sft, gd)
Workmanlike, average colt. Turf high 65 (began Oct).
**Miss Jacqueline Doyle [0-3] Sanford Racing (from R T Phillips [0-2] Oct 1998).*

SALSA DANCER (IRE) BHB 72f RR 76f 4823[19]

3 b f Seattle Dancer (USA) 10.1f **(74)** - Rince Deas (IRE) (Alzao (USA)) 7.1f **(68)**
Form - 43570
Record 1999 - 1st:0 2nd:0 3rd:1 Ran:5
Win Prizemoney £0 *Total Prizemoney* £748
1999 Turf 0-5: (8f 3, 10f 2) (gd, g-f 3, frm)
Workmanlike, above-average filly, has worn blinkers. Turf high 76. **P J Makin [0-5] Dr J P Ryan.*

SALSIFY RR 61f 536[8]

3 b c Salse (USA) 10.9f **(71)** - Amaranthus (Shirley Heights) 10.3f **(74)**
Form - 8
Record 1999 - 1st:0 2nd:0 3rd:0 Ran:1
Pre1999 - 1st:0 2nd:0 3rd:0 Ran:1
1999 Turf 0-1: (8f) (gd)
Scopey, currently average colt.
**R Charlton [0-2] Highclere Thoroughbred Racing Ltd.*

SALSKA BHB 67f45a RR 71f 45a 4917[20]

8 b m Salse (USA) 10.9f **(71)** - Anzeige (GER) (Soderini) 13.5f **(68)**
Form - 762186770
Record 1999 - 1st:1 2nd:1 3rd:0 Ran:9
Pre1999 - 1st:7 2nd:6 3rd:3 Ran:49
Win Prizemoney £27,592 *Total Prizemoney* £41,225
Wins * **1999** Jly Redcar (FRM) H 16f 67 64
* 1998 Jun Newcas (GD) H 16.1f 60 66 <
* 1998 Jun Nottin (GD) H 14.1f 60 66 <
* 1997 Jly Redcar (G-F) H 16f 58 61
* 1997 Jun Nottin (G-F) H 14.1f 56 61
* 1996 Jly Redcar (G-F) H 14.1f 46 57+
* 1996 Jly Warwic (G-F) H 14.9f 46 54+
* 1995 Spt Haydoc (GD) H 14f 43 50
1999 Turf 1-9: (14f 2, 15f, 16f 1-5, 17f) (gd 4, g-f, frm 1-4)
Above-average mare, effective 14 to 16f, best at 16f, acts on gd to hrd, best on frm, has worn blinkers, prefers left handed tracks, excels at Newcastle, does well at Redcar. Turf high 71 - also 1st of 7 getting 7lb from Star Rage (17 Jly Redcar RF 2924).
**A Streeter [8-40] P L Clinton (from A L Forbes [0-4] Aug 1995).*

SALTENBY (IRE) BHB 17f RR 27f 4396[9]

3 b g Tenby 10.4f **(76)** - Salt (Sallust) 8.4f **(63)**
Form - 085000
Record 1999 - 1st:0 2nd:0 3rd:0 Ran:6
1999 Turf 0-5: (8f 2, 10f, 11f, 14f) (gd 2, g-f, frm 2) 1999 AW 0-1: (12f) (Fibr)
Little account gelding, often wears blinkers. Turf high 27.
**P T Dalton [0-6] Messinger Stud Ltd.*

SALTY BEHAVIOUR (IRE) BHB 67f62a RR 71f 62a 15[12]

5 ch h Salt Dome (USA) 6.5f **(59)** - Good Behaviour (Artaius (USA)) 9f **(69)**
Form - 216D240
Record 1999 - 1st:0 2nd:0 3rd:0 Ran:1
Pre1999 - 1st:7 2nd:4 3rd:1 Ran:26
Win Prizemoney £20,523 *Total Prizemoney* £24,768
Wins * 1998 *Dec Southw (STD) S* *7f* *62*
1998 Aug Chepst (G-F) S 7.1f 68
1998 Jly Epsom (G-F) C 6f 70
1997 *Dec Lingfi (STD) C* *8f* *70*
1997 Aug Salisb (G-F) C 6f 70
1996 Nov Folkes (SFT) 5f 76 <
1996 Jly Salisb (G-F) 6f 76 <
1999 AW 0-1: (8f) (Fibr)
Above-average colt, effective 6 to 7f, best at 6f, acts on gd to frm - acts on Fibr, has worn blinkers. Inconsistent. He is only a plater on turf and sand, albeit an effective one.
**P D Evans [1-6] Men Behaving Badly (from R Hannon [6-21] Nov 1998).*

SALTY JACK (IRE) BHB 86f74a RR 85f 74a 4921[15]

5 b h Salt Dome (USA) 6.5f **(59)** - Play The Queen (IRE) (King of Clubs) 7.1f **(57)**
Form - 8040280020
Record 1999 - 1st:0 2nd:2 3rd:0 Ran:10
Pre1999 - 1st:6 2nd:3 3rd:7 Ran:26
Win Prizemoney £30,358 *Total Prizemoney* £49,379
Wins * 1998 Oct Newmar (GD) H 7f 85 90 <
* 1998 Spt Doncas (GD) H 7f 81 84
* 1998 Jly Epsom (G-F) H 7f 75 78
* 1998 Apr Folkes (SFT) 6.9f 74
* 1997 *Dec Lingfi (STD) H* *7f* *65* *69*
1996 Aug Salisb (GD) 6f 75
1999 Turf 0-10: (7f 9, 8f) (gd 3, g-f 3, frm 4)
Useful colt, effective 7f, acts on gd to frm, best on gd, likes Newmarket. Turf high 90 - 2nd of 19 getting 7lb from Grangeville (8 Jly Newmarket 7f frm RF 2644). Suited by being held up in a fast-run race, those tactics worked to perfection three times in the second half of '98. Largely below form last season, like most of his stablemates, but was a good second to Grangeville in the Bunbury Cup. **V Soane [5-30] Salts Of The Earth (from S Dow [1-6] Spt 1996).*

SALVA RR 74f 4382[9]

3 b f Grand Lodge (USA) - Salvezza (IRE) **(83df)** (Superpower)
Form - 30
Record 1999 - 1st:0 2nd:0 3rd:1 Ran:2
Win Prizemoney £0 *Total Prizemoney* £720
1999 Turf 0-2: (8f 2) (gd, frm)
Unfurnished, currently above-average filly. Turf high 74 (1st run) (began Aug) - 3rd of 17 to Lady Georgia (30 Aug Warwick 8f gd RF 4038). **P J Makin [0-2] Mrs P J Makin.*

SALVAGE BHB 51f RR 53f 5006[7]

4 b g Kahyasi 12.9f **(74)** - Storm Weaver (USA) (Storm Bird (CAN)) 10.3f **(74)**
Form - 78624617
Record 1999 - 1st:1 2nd:1 3rd:0 Ran:8
Win Prizemoney £2,967 *Total Prizemoney* £3,777
Wins * **1999** Oct Catter (SFT) H 15.8f 49 53 <
1999 Turf 1-8: (10f, 12f, 14f, 16f 1-4, 17f) (gd 1-3, frm 5)
Fair gelding, effective 16f, acts on gd, prefers left handed tracks, favours tight tracks. Turf high 54 - also 1st of 15 getting 5lb from Ireland's Eye (5 Oct Catterick RF 4726). Consistent.
**W W Haigh [2-12] Arnie Flower.*

SALVIATI (USA) BHB 85f RR 73+f 2816[1]

2 b c Lahib (USA) 8f **(69)** - Mother Courage (Busted) 10.2f **(61)**
Form - 31
Record 1999 - 1st:1 2nd:0 3rd:1 Ran:2
Win Prizemoney £3,687 *Total Prizemoney* £4,351
Wins * **1999** Jly Folkes (G-F) 6f 73 <
1999 Turf 1-2: (6f 1-2) (gd, frm 1-1)
Currently above-average colt. Turf high 73 - 1st of 7 from Zafoir (14

Jly Folkestone RF 2816). Showed plenty of promise on his Newbury debut before winning an ordinary maiden.
**Mrs A J Perrett [1-2] Cyril Humphris.*

SALZGITTER RR 73f 4812[5]
2 b f Salse (USA) 10.9f **(71)** - Anna of Brunswick **(71f)** (Rainbow Quest (USA)) 10.4f **(75)**
Form - 5
Record 1999 - 1st:0 2nd:0 3rd:0 Ran:1
1999 Turf 0-1: (7f) (gd)
Currently above-average filly. **H Candy [0-1] Major M G Wyatt.*

SAMANGIE RR 44f 2294[4]
3 b f Sure Blade (USA) 10.6f **(66)** - Beauchamp Queen (Known Fact (USA)) 7.4f **(67)**
Form - 04
Record 1999 - 1st:0 2nd:0 3rd:0 Ran:2
Win Prizemoney £0 *Total Prizemoney* £275
1999 Turf 0-2: (6f, 7f) (gd, frm)
Scopey, currently moderate filly. Turf high 44.
**R Simpson [0-2] Miss S Godfrey.*

SAMARARDO BHB 52f56a RR 50f 56a 5148[1]
2 b g Son Pardo - Kinlet Vision (IRE) (Vision (USA)) 9f **(64)**
Form - 0085061
Record 1999 - 1st:1 2nd:0 3rd:0 Ran:7
Win Prizemoney £2,110 *Total Prizemoney* £2,110
Wins * 1999 *Oct Wolver (STD) SH 8.5f 49 54 <*
1999 Turf 0-5: (5f 2, 6f 3) (gd 2, g-f, frm 2) 1999 AW 1-2: (7f, 8f 1-1) (Fibr 1-2)
Fair gelding, effective 8f, - acts on Fibr, has worn blinkers. Turf high 52. AW high 54 (began Spt) - 1st of 12 getting 7lb from Heathyards Mate (30 Oct Wolverhampton RF 5148).
**N P Littmoden [1-7] A1 Racing Partnership.*

SAMARA SONG BHB 64f47a RR 63f 47a 4689[22]
6 ch g Savahra Sound 7.8f **(55)** - Hosting (Thatching) 8f **(66)**
Form - 00106201500000
Record 1999 - 1st:2 2nd:1 3rd:0 Ran:14
Pre1999 - 1st:2 2nd:8 3rd:4 Ran:36
Win Prizemoney £25,838 *Total Prizemoney* £39,060

Wins							
* 1999	Jly York	(G-F)	H	7.9f	66	68	<
* 1999	May Salisb	(G-F)	H	7f	63	65	
* 1998	Aug Sandow	(GD)	H	7.1f	59	63	
* 1997	Spt Leices	(G-F)	H	7f	53	54	

1999 Turf 2-10: (7f 1-4, 8f 1-6) (g-s, gd, g-f 2, frm 2-6) 1999 AW 0-4: (7f 3, 8f) (Equi, Fibr 3)
Average gelding, effective 7 to 8f, best at 7f, acts on gd to frm, has worn blinkers, does well at York. Turf high 68 - 1st of 13 getting 14lb from Pas de Memoires (9 Jly York RF 2694) - also 1st of 20 getting 17lb from Silca Blanka (13 May Salisbury RF 1191).
**Ian Williams [4-39] R J Turton (from W G M Turner [0-10] Oct 1996).*

SAMASAKHAN (IRE) BHB 86f RR 89f 4540[6]
3 b c Slip Anchor 12.7f **(75)** - Samarzana (USA) (Blushing Groom (FR)) 10.3f **(76)**
Form - 610536
Record 1999 - 1st:1 2nd:0 3rd:1 Ran:6
Win Prizemoney £3,948 *Total Prizemoney* £5,751
Wins * 1999 May Haydoc (GD) 10.5f 89 <
1999 Turf 1-6: (10f, 11f 1-1, 14f 3, 16f) (gd 2, g-f 1-2, frm 2)
Scopey, useful colt, effective 11 to 14f, best at 14f, acts on g-f to frm, best on frm, has worn blinkers. Turf high 89 - also 1st of 15 from Elmutabaki (29 May Haydock RF 1572). Came on from his debut to land a ten-furlong Haydock maiden next time. He has not seemed to stay since being tried over extended trips and looks as though he will be suited by a drop back to a mile and a half. Sold for 55,000 gns at Newmarket in October.
**Sir Michael Stoute [1-6] H H Aga Khan.*

SAMATA ONE (IRE) BHB 58f39a RR 62f 39a 2374[16]
4 b c River Falls 8.2f **(56)** - Abadila (IRE) (Shernazar) 10.2f **(73)**
Form - 600
Record 1999 - 1st:0 2nd:0 3rd:0 Ran:3
Pre1999 - 1st:0 2nd:2 3rd:0 Ran:8
Win Prizemoney £0 *Total Prizemoney* £2,170
1999 AW 0-3: (8f 3) (Fibr 3)

Light-framed, average colt, effective 7 to 8f, acts on gd to g-f, often wears blinkers, prefers left handed tracks, likes tight tracks. AW high 12. Becoming disappointing.
**D G Bridgwater [0-1] S Hassiakos (from W J Haggas [0-10] Feb 1999).*

SAMBAKONIG (GER) RR 106f 4519a[7]
6 h
Form - 437
1999 Turf 0-3: (10f 2, 11f) (g-s, gd 2)
Pattern-class horse, effective 9 to 11f, best at 10f, acts on hvy to gd, excels at Baden-Baden. Turf high 103 - 3rd of 9 getting 5lb from Elle Danzig (27 Aug Baden-Baden 10f g-s RF 4107a). Consistent. He is tough, but regularly found out in Group company. **H Horwart in GER [0-12].*

SAMBAREY (GER) RR 96f 1355a[9]
3 f
Form - 0
1999 Turf 0-1: (8f) (gd)
Currently very useful. **H Horwart in GER [0-1].*

SAMEEAH (IRE) RR 33f 3069[5]
3 br f Perugino (USA) - Kayrava (Irish River (FR)) 8.6f **(78)**
Form - 5
Record 1999 - 1st:0 2nd:0 3rd:0 Ran:1
1999 Turf 0-1: (8f) (frm)
Lengthy, currently very moderate filly.
**K Mahdi [0-1] Hamad Al-Mutawa.*

SAMIYAH (IRE) BHB 45f RR 52f 3968[10]
3 b f Anshan 8.2f **(63)** - Fujaiyrah (In Fijar (USA)) 7.5f **(70)**
Form - 548800
Record 1999 - 1st:0 2nd:0 3rd:0 Ran:6
Win Prizemoney £0 *Total Prizemoney* £219
1999 Turf 0-5: (7f 2, 10f 3) (sft, g-s, g-f 3) 1999 AW 0-1: (8f) (Fibr)
Leggy, fair filly. Turf high 52. **Miss I Foustok [0-6] A Foustok.*

SAMMAL (IRE) BHB 56f RR 52f 2922[3]
3 b g Petardia 8.2f **(58)** - Prime Site (IRE) (Burslem) 8.8f **(53)**
Form - 006043
Record 1999 - 1st:0 2nd:0 3rd:1 Ran:6
Pre1999 - 1st:1 2nd:1 3rd:1 Ran:7
Win Prizemoney £3,195 *Total Prizemoney* £5,052
Wins * 1998 Apr Carlis (G-S) 5f 74 <
1999 Turf 0-6: (5f 6) (gd 2, g-f 2, hrd 2)
Leggy, fair gelding, effective 5f, acts on gd to frm, has worn blinkers. **J A Glover [1-13] Mrs Andrea Mallinson.*

SAMMIE DUROSE (IRE) BHB 43f RR 47f 3256[11]
2 b g Forest Wind (USA) - La Calera (Corvaro (USA)) 9f **(53)**
Form - 070
Record 1999 - 1st:0 2nd:0 3rd:0 Ran:3
1999 Turf 0-3: (5f, 6f, 7f) (frm 2, hrd)
Currently moderate gelding. Turf high 47.
**R A Fahey [0-3] Mrs Elizabeth Pettinger.*

SAMMY'S SHUFFLE BHB 38f53a RR 42f 53a 4076[4]
4 b c Touch of Grey 8.1f **(47)** - Cabinet Shuffle (Thatching) 8f **(66)**
Form - 132540674
Record 1999 - 1st:0 2nd:1 3rd:1 Ran:8
Pre1999 - 1st:3 2nd:1 3rd:0 Ran:17
Win Prizemoney £7,645 *Total Prizemoney* £9,696

Wins							
1998	*Dec Lingfi*	*(STD)*	*H*	*10f*	*37*	*47*	*<*
1998	Spt Bright	(GD)	H	10f	43	47	<
1998	Jly Bright	(G-F)	H	10f	30	35	

1999 Turf 0-4: (10f 3, 12f) (gd, frm 3) 1999 AW 0-4: (10f, 12f 3) (Equi 4)
Neat, fair colt, effective 10 to 12f, best at 12f, acts on g-f to frm - acts on Equi, mostly wears blinkers (extremely effectively), prefers left handed tracks, favours tight tracks, likes Lingfield and Brighton. Turf high 42 (began Jly). AW high 49 - 2nd of 8 getting 24lb from Fields of Omagh (9 Jan Lingfield 12f Equi RF 0063).
**J R Poulton [0-4] Mrs G M Temmerman (from R M Flower [3-21] Feb 1999).*

SAMOA BHB 105f RR 106f 2531[7]
3 b f Rainbow Quest (USA) 11.2f **(81)** - Sardegna (Pharly (FR)) 9.8f **(68)**

Form - 1227
Record 1999 - 1st:1 2nd:2 3rd:0 Ran:4
Win Prizemoney £4,260 *Total Prizemoney* £35,240
Wins * **1999** Apr Sandow (G-S) 10f 84 <
1999 Turf 1-4: (10f 1-2, 12f 2) (g-s 1-2, gd, g-f)
Leggy, Pattern-class filly. Turf high 106 - 2nd of 12 to Fairy Queen (17 Jun Ascot 12f g-f RF 2069). Out of a Group-race winning daughter of Ribblesdale winner Sandy Island, this leggy sort made an impressive debut before running a close second in a Newbury listed event. Lost little in defeat when runner-up in the Ribblesdale, but finished tailed off in the Lancashire Oaks and that was the last we saw of her.
**H R A Cecil [1-4] Lady Howard de Walden.*

SAMOL RR 4908[7]

2 ch f Timeless Times (USA) 6.1f **(56)** - Le Bal **(38f 22a)** (Rambo Dancer (CAN))
Form - 07
Record 1999 - 1st:0 2nd:0 3rd:0 Ran:2
1999 Turf 0-2: (5f, 6f) (gd 2)
Currently very poor filly. (began Spt).
**A B Mulholland [0-2] J Lomas & Son.*

SAMPOWER STAR BHB 114f82a RR 115f 82a 4777a[4]

3 b c Cyrano de Bergerac 7.3f **(58)** - Green Supreme (Primo Dominie) 6.2f **(80)**
Form - 2311148725644
Record 1999 - 1st:3 2nd:2 3rd:1 Ran:13
Pre1999 - 1st:2 2nd:1 3rd:1 Ran:9
Win Prizemoney £57,239 *Total Prizemoney* £86,103
Wins * **1999** May York (SFT) G3 6f 113+
* **1999** Apr Ascot (GD) L 6f 119+ <
* **1999** Apr Windso (G-F) 6f 90
1998 Jly Salisb (GD) 7f 82
1998 Jly Folkes (G-F) 6f 71+
1999 Turf 3-13: (5f 2, 6f 3-8, 7f, 8f 2) (hvy, sft 3, g-s, gd 1-2, g-f 2-3, frm 3)
Strong, high-class colt, effective 5 to 6f, best at 6f, acts on sft to frm. Turf high 119 - 1st of 10 from Lionhearted (28 Apr Ascot RF 0899) - also 1st of 14 getting 14lb from Warningford (13 May York RF 1195). Consistent. He won races at Folkestone and Salisbury for Rod Simpson at two, but proved a revelation for Richard Hannon last season. Stepped back to six furlongs from a mile after his first two starts, he improved out of all recognition. Landed a Windsor classified event on his third start before bolting up in an Ascot Listed event, and then made the breakthrough to Group company with success in the Duke Of York Stakes. He spent the rest of a busy season taking on the best, usually running with great credit with his fourth place in the Prix de l'Abbaye being a case in point. He has reportedly joined the Godolphin operation, so even better things are obviously expected next season.
**R Hannon [3-13] Sampower Racing Club (from R Simpson [2-9] Oct 1998).*

SAMRAAN (USA) BHB 107f RR 111f 897[6]

6 br h Green Dancer (USA) 11.9f **(77)** - Sedra (Nebbiolo) 8.1f **(75)**
Form - 16
Record 1999 - 1st:1 2nd:0 3rd:0 Ran:2
Pre1999 - 1st:5 2nd:3 3rd:4 Ran:25
Win Prizemoney £75,160 *Total Prizemoney* £144,992
Wins * **1999** Apr Haydoc (SFT) 16.2f 97
* 1997 Oct San Si (G-F) L 15f 111+ <
* 1996 Spt Salisb (FRM) 14f 110
* 1996 Jun Ascot (G-F) H 12f 94 99
* 1996 May Newbur (GD) H 12f 90 95
* 1996 Apr Kempto (GD) 10f 85+
1999 Turf 1-2: (16f 1-2) (gd 1-1, g-f)
Group-class horse, effective 16f, acts on gd to g-f, best on g-f. Turf high 105. Consistent. A little below the top stayers, he landed a minor event at Haydock at the start of the season but did not run after April. **J L Dunlop [6-27] K M Al-Mudhaf.*

SAMSAAM (IRE) BHB 66f RR 70f 4839[7]

2 b c Sadler's Wells (USA) 11.3f **(87)** - Azyaa (Kris) 9.5f **(73)**
Form - 087
Record 1999 - 1st:0 2nd:0 3rd:0 Ran:3
1999 Turf 0-3: (7f, 8f 2) (g-s, gd 2)
Currently above-average colt. Turf high 70 (began Aug).
**J L Dunlop [0-3] Hamdan Al Maktoum.*

SAMUEL WHISKERS BHB 46f51a RR 49f 51a 4818[8]

2 b c Son Pardo - Yah Dancer **(32f)** (Shareef Dancer (USA)) 9.9f **(73)**
Form - 066508
Record 1999 - 1st:0 2nd:0 3rd:0 Ran:6
Win Prizemoney £0 *Total Prizemoney* £295
1999 Turf 0-2: (6f, 10f) (g-s, gd) 1999 AW 0-4: (5f 2, 6f, 8f) (Fibr 4)
Fair colt. Turf high 49 (began Oct). AW high 52.
**R T Phillips [0-6] Wilwyn Racing.*

SAMUT (IRE) BHB 88f RR 89f 3462[8]

3 b f Danehill (USA) 9.1f **(79)** - Simaat (USA) (Mr Prospector (USA)) 8.8f **(78)**
Form - 468
Record 1999 - 1st:0 2nd:0 3rd:0 Ran:3
Pre1999 - 1st:1 2nd:0 3rd:0 Ran:3
Win Prizemoney £3,829 *Total Prizemoney* £5,026
Wins * 1998 Spt Beverl (G-F) 7.5f 89+ <
1999 Turf 0-3: (7f, 8f 2) (gd, g-f, frm)
Neat, useful filly, effective 7 to 8f, best at 7f, acts on g-f to frm, best on frm, has worn blinkers. Turf high 89 (1st run) - 4th of 15 giving 8lb to Holly Blue (19 Jun Ascot 8f g-f RF 2133). Promising reappearance at Ascot, but did not improve on that.
**J H M Gosden [1-6] Hamdan Al Maktoum.*

SAMWAR BHB 55f69a RR 50f 69a 4732[10]

7 b g Warning 8.1f **(77)** - Samaza (USA) (Arctic Tern (USA)) 8.9f **(69)**
Form - 22443632032530153511006
Record 1999 - 1st:3 2nd:3 3rd:5 Ran:23
Pre1999 - 1st:2 2nd:4 3rd:2 Ran:38
Win Prizemoney £29,760 *Total Prizemoney* £48,757
Wins * **1999** *Aug Wolver (STD) H 5f 62 68*
* **1999** *Jly Southw (STD) H 5f 59 61*
* **1999** *Jun Wolver (STD) S 5f 57+*
1996 Aug Ripon (GD) H 6f 78 89 <
1995 *Dec Lingfi (STD) 7f 70+*
1999 Turf 0-5: (5f 4, 6f) (g-s, gd, g-f 2, frm) 1999 AW 3-18: (5f 3-10, 6f 6, 7f 2) (Fibr 3-18)
Average gelding, effective 5 to 6f, best at 6f, acts on sft to frm - acts on Fibr, best on frm, often wears blinkers. Turf high 50. AW high 70 (1st run) - 2nd of 7 getting 8lb from Krystal Max (6 Feb Wolverhampton 6f Fibr RF 0243) - also 1st of 13 giving 8lb to Superbit (6 Aug Wolverhampton RF 3436). He is hardly the same horse he once was and runs mainly on Fibresand these days. Ended an extraordinarily long losing run when bolting up in a Wolverhampton seller in June, but has enjoyed further success in rather better races since. Looks best over the minimum trip now.
**Mrs N Macauley [3-30] Andy Peake (from Miss Gay Kelleway [2-20] Jly 1998).*

SANAKA (IRE) RR 91f 4473a[12]

4 b f Kahyasi 12.9f **(74)** - Sanamia (Top Ville) 11.7f **(68)**
Form - 843200
1999 Turf 0-6: (12f 3, 14f 3) (g-s 2, gd, g-f 3)
Useful filly, effective 12 to 14f, best at 14f, acts on gd to hrd, best on gd, has worn blinkers, favours right handed tracks. Turf high 93 - 4th of 9 giving 5lb to Khatani (13 Jun Gowran Park 14f gd RF 2038a). Inconsistent. **J Oxx in IRE [1-11] H H Aga Khan.*

SANARIYA (IRE) BHB 60f60a RR 56f 60a 4862[7]

3 b br f Darshaan 11.9f **(81)** - Sanamia (Top Ville) 11.7f **(68)**
Form - 72657
Record 1999 - 1st:0 2nd:1 3rd:0 Ran:5
Win Prizemoney £0 *Total Prizemoney* £1,452
1999 Turf 0-4: (10f, 11f, 12f 2) (sft, gd 2, g-f) 1999 AW 0-1: (9f) (Fibr)
Strong, fair filly. Turf high 56.
**Sir Michael Stoute [0-5] H H Aga Khan.*

SANDABAR BHB 60f RR 57f 5162[4]

6 b g Green Desert (USA) 7.8f **(78)** - Children's Corner (FR) (Top Ville) 11.7f **(68)**
Form - 030441804
Record 1999 - 1st:1 2nd:0 3rd:1 Ran:9
Pre1999 - 1st:1 2nd:0 3rd:0 Ran:6
Win Prizemoney £8,164 *Total Prizemoney* £9,626
Wins * **1999** Jly Ripon (G-F) H 10f 58 63

1996 Apr Folkes (G-F) 6.9f 75 <
1999 Turf 1-9: (8f 2, 9f 2, 10f 1-5) (gd 2, g-f 3, frm 1-4)
Fair gelding, effective 8 to 10f, best at 10f, acts on g-f to frm, best on frm, favours tight tracks. Turf high 63 - 3rd of 6 to Bowcliffe (30 Apr Musselburgh 8f g-f RF 0937) - also 1st of 12 giving 1lb to Dispol Rock (17 Jly Ripon RF 2929). *Mrs M Reveley [6-19] W Williams (from Sir Michael Stoute [1-6] Jun 1997).*

SANDBAGGEDAGAIN BHB 76f **RR 76f** 3847[9]

5 b g Prince Daniel (USA) 11.4f **(46)** - Paircullis (Tower Walk) 10f **(62)**
Form - 0
Record 1999 - 1st:0 2nd:0 3rd:0 Ran:1
Pre1999 - 1st:4 2nd:3 3rd:8 Ran:25
Win Prizemoney £26,393 *Total Prizemoney* £41,059
Wins * 1998 Spt Cheste (GD) H 15.9f 74 76 <
* 1998 Jly Ascot (G-F) H 16.2f 64 68
* 1998 Jly Catter (GD) H 15.8f 62 63
* 1997 Jun York (G-S) 11.9f 76+
1999 Turf 0-1: (12f) (frm)
Above-average gelding, effective 16f, acts on gd to frm, best on gd, has worn blinkers, likes left handed tracks. A useful staying handicapper, he won three times in the second half of '98 but was tailed off on his belated reappearance at Pontefract
**M W Easterby [4-28] Mrs Christopher Hanbury.*

SAND CAY (USA) BHB 45f43a **RR 51f 43a** 234[8]

5 ch g Geiger Counter (USA) 7.8f **(85)** - Lily Lily Rose (USA) (Lypheor) 12f **(71)**
Form - 01057778
Record 1999 - 1st:0 2nd:0 3rd:0 Ran:4
Pre1999 - 1st:1 2nd:1 3rd:0 Ran:19
Win Prizemoney £1,550 *Total Prizemoney* £2,541
Wins 1998 *Nov Lingfi (STD) S 10f 61* <
1999 AW 0-4: (10f 2, 13f 2) (Equi 4)
Fair gelding, effective 10 to 12f, acts on frm - acts on Equi. AW high 34.
**Miss Gay Kelleway [0-5] Greyhound At Lingfield (from R J O'Sullivan [1-13] Dec 1998).*

SANDERLING (IRE) BHB 63f **RR 63f** 1656[10]

3 b f Exit To Nowhere (USA) 8.7f **(77)** - Tartique Twist (USA) (Arctic Tern (USA)) 8.9f **(69)**
Form - 0
Record 1999 - 1st:0 2nd:0 3rd:0 Ran:1
Pre1999 - 1st:0 2nd:0 3rd:0 Ran:3
1999 Turf 0-1: (11f) (frm)
Scopey, average filly. **J L Dunlop [0-4] Sir Thomas Pilkington.*

SAND FALCON RR 116f 4779a[3]

4 ch g Polar Falcon (USA) 9f **(74)** - Sand Grouse (USA) (Arctic Tern (USA)) 8.9f **(69)**
Form - 233
1999 Turf 0-3: (7f, 8f 2) (sft 2, gd)
High-class gelding. Turf high 116 - 3rd of 9 to Trans Island (3 Oct Longchamp 8f sft RF 4779a). Especially effective in easy ground, he was a good third to Trans Island in a competitive event at Longchamp's Arc weekend. **P Bary in FR [1-5].*

SAND HAWK BHB 41f43a **RR 38f 43a** 4606[5]

4 ch g Polar Falcon (USA) 9f **(74)** - Ghassanah (Pas de Seul) 9.1f **(67)**
Form - 204820607580845
Record 1999 - 1st:0 2nd:1 3rd:0 Ran:13
Pre1999 - 1st:0 2nd:2 3rd:2 Ran:10
Win Prizemoney £0 *Total Prizemoney* £3,351
1999 Turf 0-9: (6f 2, 7f 2, 8f 4, 9f) (gd 4, g-f 2, frm 3) 1999 AW 0-4: (6f, 8f 3) (Equi, Fibr 3)
Leggy, moderate gelding, effective 7 to 9f, acts on gd to g-f - acts on Fibr, often wears blinkers, likes left handed tracks. Turf high 47. AW high 41. Consistent. **D Shaw [0-23] J C Fretwell.*

SANDICLIFFE (USA) BHB 58f50a **RR 58f 50a** 3310[2]

6 b m Imp Society (USA) 7.1f **(63)** - Sad Song (USA) (Roberto (USA)) 10f **(76)**
Form - 12
Record 1999 - 1st:1 2nd:1 3rd:0 Ran:2
Pre1999 - 1st:2 2nd:0 3rd:1 Ran:18
Win Prizemoney £10,024 *Total Prizemoney* £13,055
Wins * **1999** Jly Bath (FRM) H 8f 53 57
* 1997 Aug Newmar (G-F) H 8f 50 60 <
1997 May Folkes (G-F) C 6.9f 52
1999 Turf 1-2: (8f 1-2) (frm 1-2)
Fair mare, effective 8f, acts on g-f to hrd, best on frm. Turf high 58 (began Jly) - 2nd of 10 getting 14lb from Lucky Archer (3 Aug Bath 8f frm RF 3310) - also 1st of 8 giving 2lb to Adobe (20 Jly Bath RF 2957).
**J A R Toller [2-10] Ash Partnership (from B W Hills [1-10] May 1997).*

SAN DIMAS (USA) RR 56f 5049[9]

2 gr c Distant View (USA) - Chrystophard (USA) (Lypheor) 12f **(71)**
Form - 00
Record 1999 - 1st:0 2nd:0 3rd:0 Ran:2
1999 Turf 0-2: (6f, 8f) (gd 2)
Currently fair colt. Turf high 56 (began Oct).
**Andrew Turnell [0-2] Dr John Hollowood.*

SANDMASON RR 78+f 4430[1]

2 ch c Grand Lodge (USA) - Sandy Island (Mill Reef (USA)) 10.5f **(78)**
Form - 1
Record 1999 - 1st:1 2nd:0 3rd:0 Ran:1
Win Prizemoney £3,615 *Total Prizemoney* £3,615
Wins * **1999** Spt Kempto (HVY) 8f 78+ <
1999 Turf 1-1: (8f 1-1) (g-s 1-1)
Currently above-average colt. (1st run) - 1st of 12 from Spirit of Light (20 Spt Kempton RF 4430). Comes from an excellent family and should pay his way over middle distances at three.
**H R A Cecil [1-1] Exors of the late Lord Howard de Walden.*

SANDMOOR CHAMBRAY BHB 73f **RR 73f** 5038[11]

8 ch g Most Welcome 8.6f **(66)** - Valadon (High Line) 10.3f **(70)**
Form - 0750000301700
Record 1999 - 1st:1 2nd:0 3rd:1 Ran:13
Pre1999 - 1st:7 2nd:12 3rd:7 Ran:52
Win Prizemoney £52,009 *Total Prizemoney* £95,333
Wins * **1999** Aug Pontef (GD) H 12f 72 73
* 1997 Spt Epsom (GD) H 10.1f 92 96+ <
* 1997 Aug Newcas (G-F) H 10.1f 80 85
* 1997 Jly Ripon (G-F) H 10f 77 81
* 1996 Jun York (GD) H 8.9f 73 77
1995 Apr Beverl (G-F) H 7.5f 71 73
1999 Turf 1-13: (8f 2, 9f, 10f 4, 12f 1-5, 14f) (g-s, gd 5, g-f 3, frm 1-3, hrd)
Above-average gelding, effective 12f, acts on frm, has worn blinkers (effectively), likes left handed tracks, likes tight tracks. Turf high 78 - also 1st of 9 giving 5lb to Lancer (22 Aug Pontefract RF 3847). Had a fine season in 1997, but missed the whole of 1998. He has not recaptured his best since returning but did win well at Pontefract in August when the visor was reapplied.
**T D Easterby [5-44] Sandmoor Textiles Co Ltd (from M H Easterby [3-21] Spt 1995).*

SANDMOOR DENIM BHB 44f30a **RR 33f 30a** 112[12]

12 b g Red Sunset 9f **(57)** - Holernzaye (Sallust) 8.4f **(63)**
Form - 08000
Record 1999 - 1st:0 2nd:0 3rd:0 Ran:3
Pre1999 - 1st:14 2nd:23 3rd:14 Ran:129
Win Prizemoney £45,717 *Total Prizemoney* £70,225
Wins * 1996 *May Wolver (STD) C 9.4f 63*
* 1995 Mar Leices (SFT) H 7f 64 66 <
1999 AW 0-3: (8f 2, 11f) (Fibr 3)
Very moderate gelding. AW high 22.
**S R Bowring [14-134] S R Bowring.*

SANDOVA (IRE) BHB 99f **RR 102?f** 3220[6]

3 b f Green Desert (USA) 7.8f **(78)** - Alinova (USA) (Alleged (USA)) 10f **(76)**
Form - 1146
Record 1999 - 1st:2 2nd:0 3rd:0 Ran:4
Pre1999 - 1st:0 2nd:0 3rd:0 Ran:1
Win Prizemoney £10,047 *Total Prizemoney* £11,692
Wins * **1999** May Leices (G-F) 7f 102+ <
* **1999** May Lingfi (G-F) 7f 88
1999 Turf 2-4: (7f 2-4) (gd, g-f 1-1, frm 1-2)
Scopey, very useful filly. Turf high 102 - 1st of 6 from Rustic (24 May Leicester RF 1430). From the family of Zilzal, she has her quirks and was most disappointing after winning at Leicester in

May. Unlikely to stay much beyond seven furlongs, she is one to leave alone. **Sir Michael Stoute [2-5] Sheikh Mohammed.*

SAND PARTRIDGE (IRE) RR 90f
5089a^{8}

2 b f Desert Style (IRE) - Pipe Opener (Prince Sabo) 7.2f **(62)**
Form - 72450518
1999 Turf 1-8: (6f 3, 7f 2, 8f 1-3) (g-s 1-3, gd 2, g-f 2, frm)
Useful filly, effective 6 to 8f, acts on g-s to gd. Turf high 90 - 1st of 17 getting 5lb from Moon God (3 Oct Punchestown RF 4748a). Inconsistent. **K Prendergast in IRE [1-8] Mrs K Prendergast.*

SANDPOINT BHB 39f RR 31f
5032^{14}

3 b f Lugana Beach 7f **(63)** - Instinction (Never so Bold) 6.3f **(66)**
Form - 87060
Record 1999 - 1st:0 2nd:0 3rd:0 Ran:5
Pre1999 - 1st:0 2nd:0 3rd:0 Ran:1
1999 Turf 0-5: (5f 4, 6f) (sft, g-s, gd, frm 2)
Neat, very moderate filly. Turf high 31 (began Jly). **L G Cottrell [0-6] L G Cottrell.*

SAND STORM (IRE) BHB 38a RR 38a
1121^{8}

3 ch f Forest Wind (USA) - Clifton Beach (Auction Ring (USA)) 8.6f **(65)**
Form - 34100088
Record 1999 - 1st:1 2nd:0 3rd:1 Ran:8
Win Prizemoney £1,822 *Total Prizemoney £2,175*
Wins 1999 *Feb Wolver (STD) S 5f 50 <*
1999 AW 1-8: (5f 1-4, 6f 4) (Equi, Fibr 1-7)
Workmanlike, very moderate filly, effective 5f, - acts on Fibr, often wears blinkers (very effectively). AW high 50 - 1st of 7 getting 7lb from Dispol Clan (10 Feb Wolverhampton RF 0266).
**M Waring [0-5] P B R Abrasives (W'ton) Ltd (from B J Meehan [1-3] Feb 1999).*

SANDY FLOSS (IRE) BHB 43f RR 33f
3808^{14}

6 b g Green Desert (USA) 7.8f **(78)** - Mill on the Floss (Mill Reef (USA)) 10.5f **(78)**
Form - 80
Record 1999 - 1st:0 2nd:0 3rd:0 Ran:2
Pre1999 - 1st:0 2nd:2 3rd:2 Ran:13
Win Prizemoney £0 *Total Prizemoney £4,498*
1999 Turf 0-2: (14f, 16f) (g-f, frm)
Very moderate gelding. Turf high 33 (began Jly). Inconsistent. **P R Hedger [0-2] Mrs S Livesey (from J S King [0-2] Spt 1997).*

SANDY SHORE BHB 46f51a RR 28f 51a
866^{12}

4 b f Lugana Beach 7f **(63)** - City Link Lass (Double Jump) 9.4f **(58)**
Form - 00
Record 1999 - 1st:0 2nd:0 3rd:0 Ran:2
Pre1999 - 1st:0 2nd:2 3rd:1 Ran:10
Win Prizemoney £0 *Total Prizemoney £2,394*
1999 Turf 0-2: (6f, 7f) (gd 2)
Light-framed, little account filly, has worn blinkers. **J Wharton [0-9] J Rose (from J Hetherton [0-3] Jly 1998).*

SANGRA (USA) BHB 69f RR 77f
4728^{6}

2 b f El Gran Senor (USA) 8.9f **(85)** - Water Song (CAN) (Clever Trick (USA)) 6.6f **(77)**
Form - 356
Record 1999 - 1st:0 2nd:0 3rd:1 Ran:3
Win Prizemoney £0 *Total Prizemoney £642*
1999 Turf 0-3: (7f 2, 8f) (g-s, gd, frm)
Currently above-average filly. Turf high 77 (began Jly). **N A Callaghan [0-3] M Tabor & Mrs John Magnier.*

SANGUINE BHB 79f RR 82f
4899^{8}

2 gr c Sanglamore (USA) 12.9f **(67)** - Sacristy (Godswalk (USA)) 7.3f **(58)**
Form - 321568
Record 1999 - 1st:1 2nd:1 3rd:1 Ran:6
Win Prizemoney £2,940 *Total Prizemoney £4,710*
Wins * 1999 Aug Catter (FRM) 7f 77 <
1999 Turf 1-6: (7f 1-4, 8f 2) (gd, g-f 3, frm 1-2)
Decent colt, effective 7f, acts on g-f to frm, best on frm. Turf high 82 - also 1st of 9 from Dance In Tune (3 Aug Catterick RF 3313). Sold for 37,000 gns at Tattersalls in October. **B W Hills [1-6] K Abdulla.*

SANIBEL (GER) RR 92f
5117a^{3}

3 b f Seattle Dancer (USA) 10.1f **(74)** - Septima (GER) (Touching Wood (USA)) 8.2f **(55)**
Form - 3
1999 Turf 0-1: (10f) (sft)
Currently useful filly. (1st run) - 3rd of 11 getting 5lb from Bela-M (23 Oct Gelsenkirchen-Horst 10f sft RF 5117a). **in GER [0-1].*

SANKATY LIGHT (USA) BHB 51f47a RR 54f 47a
5068^{13}

3 b f Summer Squall (USA) 7f **(80)** - Brave And True (USA) (Fappiano (USA)) 8.7f **(77)**
Form - 48080
Record 1999 - 1st:0 2nd:0 3rd:0 Ran:5
Pre1999 - 1st:0 2nd:0 3rd:0 Ran:2
Win Prizemoney £0 *Total Prizemoney £241*
1999 Turf 0-4: (7f 3, 8f) (gd 2, g-f, hrd) 1999 AW 0-1: (9f) (Fibr)
Leggy, fair filly. Turf high 54. **I A Balding [0-7] Lord Halifax.*

SAN MICHEL (IRE) BHB 47f50a RR 41f 50a
4832^{5}

7 b g Scenic 10.6f **(66)** - The Top Diesis (USA) (Diesis) 9.3f **(69)**
Form - 005388005
Record 1999 - 1st:0 2nd:0 3rd:1 Ran:9
Pre1999 - 1st:1 2nd:3 3rd:4 Ran:31
Win Prizemoney £3,082 *Total Prizemoney £10,948*
Wins 1996 Jly Leopar (GD) H 5f 66 58 <
1999 Turf 0-7: (6f 4, 7f 3) (hvy, sft, g-s, gd 3, frm) 1999 AW 0-2: (7f 2) (Fibr 2)
Moderate gelding, effective 5f, acts on gd, mostly wears blinkers. Turf high 55. AW high 38. Inconsistent.
**J L Eyre [0-9] John Michael (from K O'Sullivan in IRE [1-27] Oct 1998).*

SAN SEBASTIAN RR 113f
4768a^{2}

5 ch g Niniski (USA) 13.2f **(67)** -Top of the League (High Top)10.2f **(67)**
Form - 7315442
1999 Turf 1-7: (14f 3, 16f, 18f, 20f, 22f 1-1) (hvy, gd, g-f 1-5)
Group-class gelding, effective 14 to 20f, best at 14f, acts on hvy to g-f, mostly wears blinkers (extremely effectively), and excels at Longchamp. Turf high 113 - 2nd of 8 to Tajoun (2 Oct Longchamp 20f hvy RF 4768a). Showed smart form in top staying events in '98, and landed the Queen Alexandra at Ascot on his third start of last season. He ran his best race since when just beaten in the Prix du Cadran, though the very slow early pace was all against him as he is suited by an extreme test of stamina. Sold for 170,000 gns at Tattersalls in October, he is likely to go hurdling. **M J Grassick in IRE [7-23].*

SANS RIVALE BHB 28f47a RR 21f 47a
3284^{8}

4 ch f Elmaamul (USA) 8.1f **(70)** - Strawberry Song (Final Straw) 7.9f **(64)**
Form - 07000008
Record 1999 - 1st:0 2nd:0 3rd:0 Ran:7
Pre1999 - 1st:2 2nd:2 3rd:1 Ran:16
Win Prizemoney £4,818 *Total Prizemoney £6,537*
Wins 1998 Apr Catter (GD) 5f 60
1997 Aug Mussel (GD) S 5f 71 <
1999 Turf 0-7: (5f 5, 6f, 7f) (gd 2, g-f, frm 4)
Neat, moderate filly, effective 5f, acts on gd to frm. Turf high 28. **D W Chapman [0-4] David Mann (from J L Eyre [1-14] Apr 1999).*

SAN SURU (GER) RR 98f
4519a^{10}

5 b h Surumu (GER) - Sweet Virtue (USA) (Halo (USA)) 10.6f **(75)**
Form - 0
1999 Turf 0-1: (10f) (gd)
Very useful colt, has worn blinkers. **C Von der Recke in GER [0-4] (from P Rau in GER [0-2] Jly 1997).*

SANTA COURT BHB 55f RR 54f
1881^{7}

4 b g Be My Native (USA) 11.2f **(62)** - Christmas Show (Petorius) 7.3f **(61)**
Form - 7527
Record 1999 - 1st:0 2nd:1 3rd:0 Ran:4
Pre1999 - 1st:0 2nd:1 3rd:0 Ran:9
Win Prizemoney £0 *Total Prizemoney £1,839*
1999 Turf 0-4: (10f 3, 11f) (gd 2, g-f, frm)
Neat, fair gelding. Turf high 54. Consistent. **R Dickin [0-16] Derek & Cheryl Holder.*

SANTA LUCIA BHB 63f53a **RR 62f 53a** 5159[2]
3 b f Namaqualand (USA) - Villasanta (Corvaro (USA)) 9f **(53)**
Form - 66602
Record 1999 - 1st:0 2nd:1 3rd:0 Ran:5
Win Prizemoney £0 *Total Prizemoney* £1,300
1999 Turf 0-5: (8f 3, 10f, 11f) (gd, g-f 2, frm 2)
Workmanlike, average filly. Turf high 62 (began Aug) - 2nd of 7 getting 3lb from Archie Babe (1 Nov Redcar 11f g-f RF 5159).
**C W Thornton [0-5] Guy Reed.*

SANTANDRE BHB 56f72a **RR 55f 72a** 5199[15]
3 ch g Democratic (USA) - Smartie Lee (Dominion) 8.5f **(63)**
Form - 0305404510030
Record 1999 - 1st:1 2nd:0 3rd:2 Ran:13
Pre1999 - 1st:1 2nd:1 3rd:1 Ran:11
Win Prizemoney £6,544 *Total Prizemoney* £10,352
Wins * **1999** *Spt Wolver (STD) H* *6f* *68* *70*
* 1998 Jly Thirsk (GD) H 5f 75+ <
1999 Turf 0-10: (5f 2, 6f 4, 7f 3, 8f) (gd 5, g-f 2, frm 2, hrd) 1999 AW 1-3: (6f 1-1, 7f 2) (Fibr 1-3)
Light-framed, above-average gelding, effective 5 to 7f, acts on g-s to frm - acts on Fibr. Turf high 59. AW high 70 - 1st of 12 from General Klaire (4 Spt Wolverhampton RF 4154). Dropped down the weights gradually, and returned to form with a game success over six furlongs on the Wolverhampton Fibresand in September.
**R Hollinshead [2-24] Geoff Lloyd.*

SANTARENE (IRE) BHB 38f26a **RR 40f 26a** 4334[4]
4 b f Scenic 10.6f **(66)** - Rising Spirits (Cure The Blues (USA)) 9.5f **(63)**
Form - 563305500710534
Record 1999 - 1st:1 2nd:0 3rd:3 Ran:14
Pre1999 - 1st:0 2nd:1 3rd:0 Ran:10
Win Prizemoney £1,970 *Total Prizemoney* £3,469
Wins * **1999** Jly Yarmou (G-F) S 10.1f 42 <
1999 Turf 1-8: (8f, 9f, 10f 1-5, 12f) (g-s, gd 1-1, g-f 2, frm 4) 1999 AW 0-6: (10f, 11f, 12f, 13f 3) (Equi 5, Fibr)
Leggy, moderate filly, effective 10f, acts on gd to frm, best on frm, likes tight tracks. Turf high 42 - 1st of 9 getting 11lb from Pine Ridge Lad (14 Jly Yarmouth RF 2829). AW high 33.
**P Howling [1-24] Paul Howling.*

SANTIBURI GIRL BHB 75f **RR 80f** 4872[13]
2 b f Casteddu 7.4f **(54)** - Lake Mistassiu (Tina's Pet) 6.8f **(59)**
Form - 30722134565400
Record 1999 - 1st:1 2nd:2 3rd:2 Ran:14
Win Prizemoney £3,629 *Total Prizemoney* £7,912
Wins * **1999** Jly Salisb (G-S) 7f 80 <
1999 Turf 1-14: (5f 3, 6f 2, 7f 1-8, 8f) (g-s 2, gd 2, g-f 6, frm 1-4)
Decent filly, effective 7 to 8f, best at 7f, acts on gd to frm. Turf high 80 - also 1st of 6 getting 4lb from Goodwood Blizzard (2 Jly Salisbury RF 2493). She has been kept busy and put up several creditable efforts including a narrow success over seven furlongs at Salisbury in July, but did not perform so well in the second half of the season.
**J R Best [1-13] Alan Turner (from J J O'Neill [0-1] Mar 1999).*

SANTONE (IRE) BHB 62f40a **RR 72f 40a** 352[11]
4 b c Fairy King (USA) 7.7f **(75)** - Olivia Jane (IRE) (Ela-Mana-Mou) 10.1f **(70)**
Form - 07660
Record 1999 - 1st:0 2nd:0 3rd:0 Ran:3
Pre1999 - 1st:0 2nd:0 3rd:0 Ran:8
Win Prizemoney £0 *Total Prizemoney* £225
1999 AW 0-3: (7f, 8f, 10f) (Equi, Fibr 2)
Neat, above-average colt. AW high 50. Inconsistent.
**R Hannon [0-11] Stonethorn Stud Farms Ltd.*

SANTOVITO (IRE) **RR 92f** 1151a[4]
3 bb c Project Manager 7.2f **(47)** - Nordic Pageant (IRE) (Nordico (USA)) 6.5f **(62)**
Form - 1324
1999 Turf 1-4: (7f 1-1, 10f 3) (hvy, sft 1-1, g-s, gd)
Useful colt, effective 7 to 10f, acts on sft to gd. Turf high 92 (1st run) - 1st of 11 giving 24lb to Ballintry Guest (28 Mar Curragh RF 0518a).
**J S Bolger in IRE [1-8] D H W Dobson.*

SAO (FR) **RR 91f** 1358a[11]
3 f
Form - 110
1999 Turf 2-3: (8f 2-3) (sft 1-1, g-s 1-1, gd)
Currently useful. Turf high 91. **D Smaga in FR [2-3].*

SAPHIRE BHB 82f **RR 72f** 5222[20]
3 ch f College Chapel - Emerald Eagle (Sandy Creek) 8.9f **(59)**
Form - 5830080
Record 1999 - 1st:0 2nd:0 3rd:1 Ran:7
Pre1999 - 1st:2 2nd:2 3rd:1 Ran:10
Win Prizemoney £8,667 *Total Prizemoney* £18,275
Wins * 1998 Jun York (G-S) 6f 73 <
* 1998 Jun Newcas (SFT) 5f 73 <
1999 Turf 0-7: (5f 4, 6f 3) (g-s 3, gd 4)
Scopey, above-average filly, effective 5 to 6f, best at 5f, acts on g-s to gd, best on gd. Turf high 94 - 3rd of 5 to Antinnaz (5 Jun Haydock 6f gd RF 1765). Inconsistent. After a good juvenile season in which she ran well in Listed company, she struggled last term, despite a couple of good efforts on an easy surface.
**C B B Booth [2-17] Mrs Marian Rogers.*

SAPIENTIA (FR) **RR 104f** 2100a[7]
3 c
Form - 77
1999 Turf 0-2: (8f, 11f) (gd 2)
Currently very useful colt. Turf high 104. **N Sauer in GER [0-2].*

SAPPHIRE SON (IRE) BHB 27f27a **RR 33f 27a** 4666[14]
7 ch g Maelstrom Lake 8.8f **(53)** - Gluhwein (Ballymoss) 8.5f **(55)**
Form - 280800
Record 1999 - 1st:0 2nd:0 3rd:0 Ran:4
Pre1999 - 1st:3 2nd:9 3rd:4 Ran:51
Win Prizemoney £8,604 *Total Prizemoney* £17,027
Wins 1997 Aug Lingfi (G-F) H 11.5f 46 48
1999 Turf 0-1: (12f) (frm) 1999 AW 0-3: (12f 2, 13f) (Equi 3)
Very moderate gelding, effective 12f, acts on g-f - acts on Equi, has worn blinkers.
**P Butler [0-1] D Cobb (from P C Clarke [1-36] Jly 1999).*

SAPPHIRE TRIO **RR 74f** 5090a[5]
3 b c Bluebird (USA) 7.9f **(71)** - Triode (USA) (Sharpen Up) 8.3f **(67)**
Form - 2412430857705
1999 Turf 1-13: (6f, 8f 1-6, 9f 3, 10f, 12f 2) (sft, g-s 4, gd 2, g-f 1-5, frm)
Strong, above-average colt, effective 8f, acts on g-f, has worn blinkers, likes right handed tracks. Turf high 91 - 2nd of 4 to Moiseyev (1 Aug Galway 8f g-f RF 3345b). Becoming disappointing.
**L Comer in IRE [1-13] L Comer (from Sir Michael Stoute [0-2] Jly 1999).*

SARAFAN (USA) BHB 100f **RR 96f** 4257[1]
2 b c Lear Fan (USA) 10.4f **(80)** - Saraa Ree (USA) (Caro)
Form - 111221
Record 1999 - 1st:4 2nd:2 3rd:0 Ran:6
Win Prizemoney £26,237 *Total Prizemoney* £42,272
Wins * **1999** Spt Goodwo (G-F) L 8f 96+ <
* **1999** Jly Beverl (SFT) 7.5f 94
* **1999** Jun Pontef (GD) 6f 93+
* **1999** Jun Hamilt (G-S) 6f 77+
1999 Turf 4-6: (6f 2-2, 7f 1-3, 8f 1-1) (gd 2-2, g-f 1-2, frm 1-2)
Very useful colt, effective 6 to 8f, best at 7f, acts on gd to frm, best on g-f. Turf high 96 - 1st of 5 from Kingsclere (10 Spt Goodwood RF 4257) - also 1st of 8 giving 14lb to Splash Out (3 Jly Beverley RF 2517). He improved for waiting tactics when winning a listed event at Goodwood in September. Capable of landing a Group race on that form, he should stay a mile and a quarter and probably acts on any ground.
**Sir Mark Prescott [4-6] Mrs Burnet Osborne House II.*

SARAH'S SONG (IRE) BHB 69f **RR 67f** 2457[3]
3 b f Warning 8.1f **(77)** - Two and Sixpence (USA) (Chief's Crown (USA)) 9.8f **(72)**
Form - 5605213
Record 1999 - 1st:1 2nd:1 3rd:1 Ran:7
Win Prizemoney £3,076 *Total Prizemoney* £4,646
Wins * **1999** Jun Lingfi (G-F) 7f 65 <

1999 Turf 1-7: (7f 1-6, 8f) (gd, g-f 2, frm 3, hrd 1-1)
Workmanlike, average filly, effective 7f, acts on g-f to hrd. Turf high 67 - 2nd of 16 giving 5lb to My Emily (14 Jun Brighton 7f g-f RF 1975) - also 1st of 11 getting 3lb from Ivor's Investment (19 Jun Lingfield RF 2149). She suddenly found her form in June, landing a Lingfield classified stakes with much more in hand than the official margin suggests. Acts well on fast ground.
**B J Meehan [1-7] Mrs Susan Roy.*

SARA MOON CLASSIC (IRE) BHB 48f46a **RR 44f 46a**
5050[3]
4 b g Fayruz 6.6f **(63)** - Irish Affaire (IRE) (Fairy King (USA)) 7.7f **(59)**
Form - 80063
Record 1999 - 1st:0 2nd:0 3rd:1 Ran:5
Pre1999 - 1st:0 2nd:1 3rd:3 Ran:18
Win Prizemoney £0 *Total Prizemoney* £3,223
1999 Turf 0-3: (7f, 8f 2) (gd 2, frm) 1999 AW 0-2: (7f, 9f) (Fibr 2)
Unfurnished, moderate gelding, effective 6f, - acts on Fibr, often wears blinkers, likes left handed tracks, likes tight tracks. Turf high 44 (began Spt). AW high 19. Inconsistent.
**K McAuliffe [0-23] Highgrove Developments Ltd.*

SARANGANI BHB 98f **RR 97f**
2266[2]
3 b c Polish Precedent (USA) 9f **(73)** - Height of Folly (Shirley Heights) 10.3f **(74)**
Form - 24212
Record 1999 - 1st:1 2nd:3 3rd:0 Ran:5
Win Prizemoney £3,858 *Total Prizemoney* £11,322
Wins * **1999** Jun Goodwo (G-F) 12f 76 <
1999 Turf 1-5: (10f 2, 11f, 12f 1-2) (sft, gd 1-3, frm)
Scopey, very useful colt. Turf high 97 - 2nd of 6 giving 15lb to Ligne Gagnante (24 Jun Newcastle 12f gd RF 2266). He was given a canny ride when winning his maiden and is developing into a smart handicapper. Fairly treated for a horse that held Group entries, he could stay beyond a mile and a half and is open to improvement. **I A Balding [1-5] Robert Hitchins.*

SARATOGA RED (USA) BHB 40f55a **RR 29f 55a**
1702[7]
5 ch g Saratoga Six (USA) 8.7f **(74)** - Wajibird (USA) (Storm Bird (CAN)) 10.3f **(74)**
Form - 4366077
Record 1999 - 1st:0 2nd:0 3rd:1 Ran:7
Pre1999 - 1st:2 2nd:2 3rd:4 Ran:23
Win Prizemoney £6,295 *Total Prizemoney* £10,643
Wins 1998 Aug Hamilt (SFT) SH 9.2f 44 44
1997 Nov Lingfi (STD) 7f 65 <
1999 Turf 0-3: (8f, 10f, 12f) (sft, gd, g-f) 1999 AW 0-4: (8f 2, 9f, 11f) (Fibr 4)
Fair gelding, effective 8f, - acts on Fibr, often wears blinkers, likes tight tracks.
**E J Alston [0-7] Valley Paddocks Racing Ltd (from M J Ryan [1-2] Aug 1998).*

SARAYAN (IRE) **RR 95f**
2422a[2]
4 b c Lahib (USA) 8f **(69)** - Yaqatha
Form - 007672
1999 Turf 0-6: (8f, 10f, 11f, 12f 3) (sft, g-s 2, gd 2, g-f)
Very useful colt, effective 10 to 12f, acts on g-s to gd, likes right handed tracks. Turf high 95. Inconsistent. He returned to form under an aggressive ride at The Curragh in June. Worth a try over extended distances, he has slipped down to a winning mark.
**K Prendergast in IRE [1-16] Hamdan Al Maktoum.*

SARDAUKAR **RR 117f**
4770a[5]
3 br c Royal Academy (USA) 7.8f **(77)** - En Public (Rainbow Quest (USA)) 10.4f **(75)**
Form - 345
1999 Turf 0-3: (10f 3) (hvy, gd 2)
Currently high-class colt. Turf high 117 (1st run) - 3rd of 8 to Slickly (27 Jun Longchamp 10f gd RF 2476a). French-trained colt, with his third place behind Slickly and Indian Danehill in the Prix Eugene Adam being his best effort of 1999. **E Lellouche in FR [0-3].*

SARENA PRIDE (IRE) BHB 76f **RR 78f**
5048[7]
2 b f Persian Bold 10f **(69)** - Avidal Park (Horage) 10.3f **(61)**
Form - 0165127
Record 1999 - 1st:2 2nd:1 3rd:0 Ran:7
Win Prizemoney £6,714 *Total Prizemoney* £7,744
Wins * **1999** Aug Warwic (GD) H 6f 70 75
* **1999** Jun Windso (SFT) 6f 78+ <
1999 Turf 2-7: (5f, 6f 2-5, 7f) (hvy, g-s, gd 2-3, g-f, frm)
Above-average filly, effective 6f, acts on g-s to gd, best on gd. Turf high 78 - 2nd of 10 giving 14lb to Kinsman (29 Spt Brighton 6f g-s RF 4625) - also 1st of 18 giving 2lb to Baytown Rhapsody (7 Jun Windsor RF 1804). **R J O'Sullivan [2-7] Sarena Mfg Ltd.*

SARENA SPECIAL BHB 75f **RR 79f**
3054[6]
2 b c Lucky Guest - Lariston Gale (Pas de Seul) 9.1f **(67)**
Form - 02426
Record 1999 - 1st:0 2nd:2 3rd:0 Ran:5
Win Prizemoney £0 *Total Prizemoney* £3,034
1999 Turf 0-5: (6f 3, 7f 2) (gd 2, g-f, frm 2)
Above-average colt. Turf high 79 - 2nd of 12 to Tioga (29 May Lingfield 6f gd RF 1580). **R J O'Sullivan [0-5] Sarena Mfg Ltd.*

SARI BHB 76f73a **RR 75f 73a**
4804[11]
3 b f Faustus (USA) 9.1f **(54)** - Fire Lily **(48df)** (Unfuwain (USA))
Form - 82004810
Record 1999 - 1st:1 2nd:1 3rd:0 Ran:8
Pre1999 - 1st:1 2nd:2 3rd:1 Ran:6
Win Prizemoney £10,775 *Total Prizemoney* £14,999
Wins * **1999** Oct Sandow (SFT) H 7.1f 71 75
* 1998 Oct Catter (G-S) 7f 80 <
1999 Turf 1-8: (7f 1-5, 8f 3) (g-s 1-1, gd 4, g-f, frm 2)
Workmanlike, above-average filly, effective 6 to 8f, best at 7f, acts on g-s to frm, likes tight tracks. Turf high 80 - 2nd of 24 giving 8lb to Cinnamon Lady (15 May Newbury 7f gd RF 1238) - also 1st of 15 getting 3lb from Route Sixty Six (2 Oct Sandown RF 4696).
**P F I Cole [2-14] R A Instone.*

SARPEDON (IRE) BHB 28a **RR 27f**
4938[9]
3 ch g Be My Chief (USA) 10.2f **(62)** - Sariza (Posse (USA)) 8.9f **(61)**
Form - 0000
Record 1999 - 1st:0 2nd:0 3rd:0 Ran:4
1999 Turf 0-3: (8f, 9f, 10f) (gd, g-f, frm) 1999 AW 0-1: (6f) (Fibr)
Workmanlike, very moderate gelding. Turf high 27.
**M C Chapman [0-3] R J Hayward (from L M Cumani [0-2] May 1999).*

SARSON BHB 83f **RR 67f**
4644[13]
3 b c Efisio 7.7f **(69)** - Sarcita (Primo Dominie) 6.2f **(80)**
Form - 565000
Record 1999 - 1st:0 2nd:0 3rd:0 Ran:6
Pre1999 - 1st:1 2nd:4 3rd:0 Ran:5
Win Prizemoney £10,308 *Total Prizemoney* £29,335
Wins * 1998 Jly Sandow (G-S) L 5f 95 <
1999 Turf 0-6: (6f 3, 7f 2, 8f) (g-s, gd, g-f 4)
Workmanlike, average colt, effective 5 to 6f, best at 5f, acts on g-s to gd, best on gd. Turf high 96 (began Jly). Becoming disappointing. He showed no interest last term and is one to leave alone.
**R Hannon [1-11] Raymond Tooth.*

SARTEANO BHB 24f **RR 4f**
3954[17]
5 ch m Anshan 8.2f **(63)** - Daisy Girl (Main Reef) 9.6f **(57)**
Form - 0
Record 1999 - 1st:0 2nd:0 3rd:0 Ran:1
Pre1999 - 1st:0 2nd:0 3rd:1 Ran:5
Win Prizemoney £0 *Total Prizemoney* £524
1999 Turf 0-1: (10f) (frm)
Very poor filly.
**D Shaw [0-1] S Taberner (from T W Donnelly [0-3] Jly 1998).*

SARTORIAL (IRE) BHB 86f77a **RR 89df 77a**
2687[2]
3 b c Elbio 9f **(62)** - Madam Slaney (Prince Tenderfoot (USA)) 9f **(61)**
Form - 232
Record 1999 - 1st:0 2nd:2 3rd:1 Ran:3
Pre1999 - 1st:0 2nd:0 3rd:0 Ran:1
Win Prizemoney £0 *Total Prizemoney* £2,806
1999 Turf 0-2: (6f 2) (g-f, frm) 1999 AW 0-1: (6f) (Fibr)
Useful colt. Turf high 89 (1st run) - 2nd of 11 to Lionhearted (13 Apr Newmarket 6f g-f RF 0666).
**P J Makin [0-4] Mrs Greta Sarfaty Marchant.*

SARUM BHB 20f25a RR 14f 25a 2146[14]
13 b g Tina's Pet 7.4f **(56)** - Contessa (HUN) (Peleid) 7.6f **(37)**
Form - 007880
Record 1999 - 1st:0 2nd:0 3rd:0 Ran:6
Pre1999 - 1st:8 2nd:10 3rd:13 Ran:109
Win Prizemoney £19,785 *Total Prizemoney* £34,778
Wins 1996 *Mar Lingfi (STD) H 8f 50 49*
1999 Turf 0-1: (11f) (hrd) 1999 AW 0-5: (7f, 8f 3, 10f) (Equi 3, Fibr 2)
Very moderate gelding, effective 8f, - acts on Equi, has worn blinkers. AW high 36. Inconsistent.
**J E Long [0-36] Terry Waters (from C P Wildman [8-79] May 1996).*

SASEEDO (USA) BHB 32f47a RR 35f 47a 5127[6]
9 ch g Afleet (CAN) 6.2f **(83)** - Barbara's Moment (USA) (Super Moment (USA)) 6.2f **(92)**
Form - 526771006300700006006
Record 1999 - 1st:1 2nd:1 3rd:1 Ran:21
Pre1999 - 1st:7 2nd:2 3rd:6 Ran:60
Win Prizemoney £60,859 *Total Prizemoney* £72,339

Wins								
* **1999**	*Apr*	*Lingfi*	*(STD)*	*S*	*10f*		*54*	
1996	Jly	Haydoc	(GD)	H	7.1f	86	90	
1996	Jly	Pontef	(G-F)	H	6f	86	90	
1996	May	Newmar	(GD)	H	7f	86	91	<
1995	Oct	Yarmou	(FRM)		6f		75	
1995	May	Newmar	(GD)	H	6f	84	88	

1999 Turf 0-14: (7f, 9f, 10f 9, 12f 3) (g-s 2, gd 5, g-f 4, frm 3) 1999 AW 1-7: (7f, 8f 4, 10f 1-2) (Equi 1-6, Fibr)
Fair gelding, has worn blinkers. Turf high 49. AW high 54. Once a useful sprinter for Bill O'Gorman, he has been in the doldrums for quite a while, but caused a 25/1 surprise when winning a ten-furlong seller on the Lingfield Equitrack in April.
**J J Bridger [1-19] W Wood (from K A Morgan [0-2] Feb 1999).*

SASHA RR 35f 4348[9]
2 ch c Factual (USA) - Twice in Bundoran (IRE) **(47f 44a)** (Bold Arrangement)
Form - 0
Record 1999 - 1st:0 2nd:0 3rd:0 Ran:1
1999 Turf 0-1: (5f) (frm)
Currently very moderate colt. **J L Eyre [0-1] Ms Kim Jansen.*

SASSY (IRE) BHB 23f30a RR 20f 30a 3145[4]
4 b f Imp Society (USA) 7.1f **(63)** - Merrie Moment (IRE) (Taufan (USA)) 7f **(57)**
Form - 0007064
Record 1999 - 1st:0 2nd:0 3rd:0 Ran:6
Pre1999 - 1st:2 2nd:2 3rd:2 Ran:24
Win Prizemoney £4,370 *Total Prizemoney* £6,683

Wins							
1998	*Spt*	*Southw*	*(STD)*	*C*	*11f*	*45*	
1997	Jly	Windso	(G-F)	S	6f	65	<

1999 Turf 0-3: (12f 3) (g-f 2, hrd) 1999 AW 0-3: (10f, 11f 2) (Equi, Fibr 2)
Workmanlike, little account filly, effective 11f, - acts on Fibr, has worn blinkers.
**Mrs L C Jewell [0-6] The Headquarters Partnership I (from B J McMath [0-3] Nov 1998).*

SATIN SLIPPER (IRE) BHB 55f55a RR 52f 55a 865[9]
3 ch f Petardia 8.2f **(58)** - Lomond Heights (IRE) (Lomond (USA)) 8.8f **(65)**
Form - 5670
Record 1999 - 1st:0 2nd:0 3rd:0 Ran:4
Pre1999 - 1st:1 2nd:0 3rd:1 Ran:6
Win Prizemoney £2,529 *Total Prizemoney* £3,238
Wins * 1998 Jly Bright (GD) 5.3f 71 <
1999 Turf 0-2: (6f, 8f) (sft, gd) 1999 AW 0-2: (7f, 8f) (Equi 2)
Neat, fair filly, effective 5f, acts on gd, likes left handed tracks. Turf high 20. AW high 40. Becoming disappointing.
**K T Ivory [1-10] Mrs G E Maloney.*

SATIRE RR 4907[11]
2 br f Terimon 8.7f **(58)** - Salchow (Niniski (USA)) 10.6f **(65)**
Form - 0
Record 1999 - 1st:0 2nd:0 3rd:0 Ran:1
1999 Turf 0-1: (8f) (frm)
Currently very poor filly.
**T J Etherington [0-1] R V Hughes and Partners.*

SATRIA (IRE) BHB 40f45a RR 26f 45a 631[3]
3 b c Shareef Dancer (USA) 10.1f **(67)** - Inderaputeri **(68f 60a)** (Bold Fort)
Form - 643803
Record 1999 - 1st:0 2nd:0 3rd:2 Ran:6
Pre1999 - 1st:0 2nd:0 3rd:0 Ran:1
Win Prizemoney £0 *Total Prizemoney* £885
1999 Turf 0-1: (10f) (hvy) 1999 AW 0-5: (9f, 10f 3, 11f) (Equi 3, Fibr 2)
Little account colt. AW high 58.
**Miss Gay Kelleway [0-7] H R H Sultan Ahmad Shah.*

SATZUMA (IRE) RR 5209[19]
2 ch c Lycius (USA) 8.8f **(71)** - Satz (USA) (The Minstrel (CAN)) 10f **(72)**
Form - 0
Record 1999 - 1st:0 2nd:0 3rd:0 Ran:1
1999 Turf 0-1: (6f) (g-s)
Currently very poor colt. **C F Wall [0-1] Islanmore Stud.*

SAUCY DANCER RR 1501[14]
6 ch m Chilibang 7f **(55)** - Silent Dancer (Quiet Fling (USA)) 11.8f **(36)**
Form - 0
Record 1999 - 1st:0 2nd:0 3rd:0 Ran:1
Pre1999 - 1st:0 2nd:0 3rd:1 Ran:3
Win Prizemoney £0 *Total Prizemoney* £502
1999 Turf 0-1: (13f) (g-f)
Little account mare.
**G A Ham [0-5] Miss S J Burgin.*

SAUCY NIGHT RR 30f 2768[8]
3 ch g Anshan 8.2f **(63)** - Kiss in the Dark **(36df 41a)** (Starry Night (USA))
Form - 08
Record 1999 - 1st:0 2nd:0 3rd:0 Ran:2
1999 Turf 0-2: (7f, 10f) (frm 2)
Leggy, currently very moderate gelding. Turf high 23 (began Jly).
**M Dods [0-2] A F Monk.*

SAUGERTIES (USA) RR 119f 4663a[9]
5 ch h Trempolino (USA) 11.9f **(77)** - Stalwart Moment (USA) (Stalwart (USA)) 9.9f **(78)**
Form - 0260
1999 Turf 0-4: (10f, 12f 3) (sft, gd 3)
High-class colt, effective 10 to 12f, acts on gd. Turf high 119 (began Jly) - 2nd of 6 to Tiger Hill (1 Aug Munich 10f gd RF 3411a). Trained in Germany, he struggled in Group One company throughout 1999, with his length second to Tiger Hill at Munich his best effort.
**P Schiergen in GER [0-9] (from H Jentzsch in GER [1-3] Oct 1997).*

SAUSALITO BAY BHB 91f RR 91f 4788[1]
5 b g Salse (USA) 10.9f **(71)** - Cantico (Green Dancer (USA)) 10.3f **(74)**
Form - 833181
Record 1999 - 1st:2 2nd:0 3rd:2 Ran:6
Pre1999 - 1st:3 2nd:1 3rd:1 Ran:18
Win Prizemoney £49,193 *Total Prizemoney* £61,355

Wins								
* **1999**	Oct	Lingfi	(SFT)	H	11.5f	88	91	
* **1999**	Jly	Sandow	(G-F)	H	11.4f	84	88	
* 1997	Spt	Doncas	(G-F)	H	14.6f	92	100	<
* 1997	Aug	York	(GD)	H	13.9f	85	92	
* 1996	Oct	Chepst	(SFT)		8.1f		82	

1999 Turf 2-6: (11f 2-2, 12f, 14f 2, 16f) (g-s 1-2, g-f, frm 1-3)
Useful gelding, effective 13 to 16f, acts on sft to frm, has worn blinkers (extremely effectively). Turf high 91. He went backwards in 1998, and as a result became extremely well handicapped. Taking on lesser rivals than he has been used to helped him gain a game front-running victory at Sandown in July. Sold for 66,000 gns after winning at Lingfield in October, he has joined Noel Meade. **I A Balding [5-24] J C Smith.*

SAVANNAH BELLE BHB 87f RR 83f 4651[15]
2 b f Green Desert (USA) 7.8f **(78)** - Third Watch (Slip Anchor) 9.8f **(73)**
Form - 33412560
Record 1999 - 1st:1 2nd:1 3rd:2 Ran:8
Win Prizemoney £2,766 *Total Prizemoney* £5,935

Wins *** 1999** Aug Haydoc (GD) H 5f 69 83+ <
1999 Turf 1-8: (5f 1-7, 6f) (g-s 2, gd, g-f 1-2, frm 3)
Decent filly, effective 5f, acts on g-f to frm. Turf high 83 - 1st of 11 giving 6lb to Pertemps Fc (5 Aug Haydock RF 3396). Not disgraced in Listed races since winning a nursey.
**J A Glover [1-8] Lady Bamford.*

SAVMO ONE BHB 30f **RR 40f** 3986[10]
3 b f Distinctly North (USA) 7.4f **(63)** - Dear Heart (Blakeney) 10.5f **(64)**
Form - 00
Record **1999** - 1st:0 2nd:0 3rd:0 Ran:2
Pre1999 - 1st:0 2nd:0 3rd:0 Ran:3
1999 Turf 0-2: (7f, 10f) (g-f, frm)
Leggy, moderate filly. (began Aug).
**D Shaw [0-2] M F R S Racing Partnership (from C Smith [0-3] Oct 1998).*

SAVOIR FAIRE (IRE) BHB 48f **RR 57?f** 5165[11]
3 b f College Chapel - Arctic Splendour (USA) (Arctic Tern (USA)) 8.9f **(69)**
Form - 0
Record **1999** - 1st:0 2nd:0 3rd:0 Ran:1
Pre1999 - 1st:0 2nd:0 3rd:0 Ran:3
1999 Turf 0-1: (12f) (g-s)
Leggy, fair filly. **M A Buckley [0-4] Mrs D J Buckley.*

SAWLAJAN (USA) BHB 52f48a **RR 37f 48a** 2774[6]
8 ch g Woodman (USA) 9.7f **(77)** - Crafty Satin (USA) (Crimson Satan) 8f **(67)**
Form - 06
Record **1999** - 1st:0 2nd:0 3rd:0 Ran:2
Pre1999 - 1st:2 2nd:0 3rd:2 Ran:10
Win Prizemoney £10,237 *Total Prizemoney* £11,774
1999 Turf 0-1: (12f) (frm) 1999 AW 0-1: (10f) (Equi)
Very moderate gelding. Becoming disappointing.
**T R Watson [0-8] Miss S Hoare (from J L Dunlop [2-9] Spt 1994).*

SAWWAAH (IRE) **RR 91f** 4649[2]
2 b c Marju (IRE) 9.2f **(76)** - Just a Mirage (Green Desert (USA)) 8.6f **(78)**
Form - 32
Record **1999** - 1st:0 2nd:1 3rd:1 Ran:2
Win Prizemoney £0 *Total Prizemoney* £2,073
1999 Turf 0-2: (7f 2) (gd, frm)
Currently useful colt. Turf high 91 (began Spt) - 2nd of 14 to Zentsov Street (30 Spt Newmarket 7f gd RF 4649). A highly-promising third on his debut at Haydock behind Hunting Tiger after losing ground at the start, he ran Zentsov Street to a head next time and is a ready-made winner.
**E A L Dunlop [0-2] Hamdan Al Maktoum.*

SAYARSHAN (FR) **RR 113f** 628a[4]
4 b c Darshaan 11.9f **(81)** - Sayyara (Kris) 9.5f **(73)**
Form - 4
1999 Turf 0-1: (10f) (hvy)
Currently Group-class colt. (1st run) - 4th of 4 giving 3lb to Dark Moondancer (4 Apr Longchamp 10f hvy RF 0628a). Found to be coughing after disappointing in the 1998 French Derby, he attracted plenty of support on his reappearance in the Prix d'Harcourt, but failed to quicken and finished fourth. **P Bary in FR [1-3].*

SAYEDATI ELJAMILAH (USA) **RR 57f** 5136[14]
2 b br f Mr Prospector (USA) 8.6f **(88)** - Histoire (FR) (Riverman (USA)) 9.1f **(76)**
Form - 00
Record **1999** - 1st:0 2nd:0 3rd:0 Ran:2
1999 Turf 0-2: (6f, 7f) (gd 2)
Currently fair filly. Turf high 57 (began Oct).
**J L Dunlop [0-2] Hamdan Al Maktoum.*

SAYEH (IRE) BHB 74f **RR 73f** 4267[3]
7 b g Fools Holme (USA) 10.3f **(64)** - Piffle (Shirley Heights) 10.3f **(74)**
Form - 03
Record **1999** - 1st:0 2nd:0 3rd:1 Ran:2
Pre1999 - 1st:3 2nd:1 3rd:2 Ran:10
Win Prizemoney £14,849 *Total Prizemoney* £26,805
Wins 1995 Spt Epsom (GD) H 10.1f 92 97 <
1995 Aug Yarmou (G-F) 10.1f 89
1999 Turf 0-2: (8f, 10f) (frm 2)
Above-average gelding. Turf high 73 (began Aug).
**P Bowen [4-7] The Galloping Punters (from Major W R Hern [0-2] Spt 1996).*

SAYSO **RR 45f** 2764[8]
3 b f Anshan 8.2f **(63)** - Total Sa (IRE) **(26f 59a)** (Gallic League)
Form - 8
Record **1999** - 1st:0 2nd:0 3rd:0 Ran:1
1999 Turf 0-1: (10f) (frm)
Leggy, currently moderate filly. **P J Hobbs [0-1] P J Hobbs.*

SCAFELL BHB 74f **RR 75f** 4039[7]
2 b c Puissance 7.1f **(60)** - One Half Silver (CAN) (Plugged Nickle (USA)) 7.8f **(68)**
Form - 62733257
Record **1999** - 1st:0 2nd:2 3rd:2 Ran:8
Win Prizemoney £0 *Total Prizemoney* £3,385
1999 Turf 0-8: (5f 6, 6f 2) (gd, g-f 3, frm 3, hrd)
Above-average colt, effective 5 to 6f, best at 5f, acts on g-f to frm, best on frm. Turf high 75 - 3rd of 14 to Follow Suit (10 Jly York 6f g-f RF 2729). **C Smith [0-8] T I Gourley.*

SCARLET CRESCENT BHB 47f39a **RR 47f 39a** 178[10]
5 b m Midyan (USA) 9.9f **(64)** - Scarlet Veil (Tyrnavos) 10.1f **(55)**
Form - 05070
Record **1999** - 1st:0 2nd:0 3rd:0 Ran:2
Pre1999 - 1st:2 2nd:0 3rd:4 Ran:18
Win Prizemoney £6,589 *Total Prizemoney* £8,907
Wins 1997 Jun Nottin (G-F) H 8.2f 70 70 <
1996 Aug Warwic (GD) 7f 67
1999 AW 0-2: (12f, 13f) (Equi 2)
Moderate filly, had broken blood-vessels, effective 10 to 13f, acted on gd - acted on Equi, had worn blinkers, preferred tight tracks. AW high 33. (DEAD)
**M D I Usher [0-12] Midweek Racing (from P T Walwyn [2-13] Oct 1997).*

SCARLET LIVERY BHB 54f **RR 54f** 5007[8]
3 b f Saddlers' Hall (IRE) 10.5f **(65)** - Go For Red (IRE) (Thatching) 8f **(66)**
Form - 67340068
Record **1999** - 1st:0 2nd:0 3rd:1 Ran:8
Win Prizemoney £0 *Total Prizemoney* £887
1999 Turf 0-8: (7f 3, 8f 3, 10f 2) (sft, gd 3, frm 4)
Fair filly, effective 7f, acts on frm, likes tight tracks. Turf high 68 - 3rd of 12 to Mirbeck (15 Jun Thirsk 7f frm RF 2002).
**C B B Booth [0-4] W H Tinning (from R M H Cowell [0-4] Jly 1999).*

SCARLET RAIDER (USA) BHB 83f **RR 83f** 4677[11]
3 b f Red Ransom (USA) 8.6f **(83)** - Dariela (USA) (Manila (USA)) 9.3f **(71)**
Form - 660
Record **1999** - 1st:0 2nd:0 3rd:0 Ran:3
Pre1999 - 1st:1 2nd:0 3rd:0 Ran:2
Win Prizemoney £6,810 *Total Prizemoney* £8,166
Wins *** 1998** Spt York (GD) 7f 74 <
1999 Turf 0-3: (7f, 10f 2) (gd 2, frm)
Workmanlike, decent filly. Turf high 83. **P F I Cole [1-5] M Arbib.*

SCARLET SCEPTRE (USA) BHB 58f56a **RR 59f 56a** 3904[2]
3 b f Red Ransom (USA) 8.6f **(83)** - Wand (IRE) (Reference Point) 6.8f **(70)**
Form - 423032
Record **1999** - 1st:0 2nd:2 3rd:2 Ran:5
Pre1999 - 1st:0 2nd:0 3rd:0 Ran:2
Win Prizemoney £0 *Total Prizemoney* £2,372
1999 Turf 0-2: (12f 2) (frm 2) 1999 AW 0-3: (9f 2, 16f) (Equi, Fibr 2)
Leggy, fair filly, effective 9f, - acts on Fibr, likes tight tracks. Turf high 54. AW high 58 (1st run) - 2nd of 7 getting 5lb from Love Blues (23 Jan Wolverhampton 9f Fibr RF 0153).
**R Charlton [0-7] Mrs M Bryce-Smith.*

SCARLETTA (USA) **RR 88f** 5109[2]
2 b f Red Ransom (USA) 8.6f **(83)** - Snowtown (IRE) **(99f)** (Alzao (USA)) 7.1f **(68)**

Form - 22
Record 1999 - 1st:0 2nd:2 3rd:0 Ran:2
Win Prizemoney £0 *Total Prizemoney* £2,050
1999 Turf 0-2: (7f, 8f) (gd 2)
Currently useful filly. Turf high 88 (began Oct).
**A G Foster [0-2] R E Sangster.*

SCARLETT RIBBON RR 96+f 5194[1]

2 b f Most Welcome 8.6f **(66)** - Scarlett Holly (Red Sunset) 8.2f **(63)**
Form - 1
Record 1999 - 1st:1 2nd:0 3rd:0 Ran:1
Win Prizemoney £3,160 *Total Prizemoney* £3,160
Wins * 1999 Nov Windso (G-S) 6f 96+ <
1999 Turf 1-1: (6f 1-1) (gd 1-1)
Currently very useful filly. (1st run) - 1st of 18 getting 5lb from Pretrail (4 Nov Windsor RF 5194). **P J Makin [1-1] R Angelini-Hurll.*

SCARLETT'S BOY BHB 58f62a RR 40f 62a 5146[10]

3 b g Emarati (USA) 6.6f **(63)** - Katie Scarlett (Lochnager) 6f **(59)**
Form - 1586600
Record 1999 - 1st:0 2nd:0 3rd:0 Ran:6
Pre1999 - 1st:1 2nd:1 3rd:0 Ran:3
Win Prizemoney £2,717 *Total Prizemoney* £3,814
Wins * 1998 *Dec Wolver (STD) C 6f 83* <
1999 Turf 0-2: (5f, 6f) (g-s, g-f) 1999 AW 0-4: (6f 2, 7f 2) (Equi, Fibr 3)
Light-framed, fair gelding, effective 6f, - acts on Fibr. Turf high 40 (began Spt). **N P Littmoden [1-9] John Pugh.*

SCARTEEN FOX (IRE) BHB 100f RR 101f 5037[7]

2 ch c Foxhound (USA) - Best Swinger (IRE) (Ela-Mana-Mou) 10.1f **(70)**
Form - 3117
Record 1999 - 1st:2 2nd:0 3rd:1 Ran:4
Win Prizemoney £25,451 *Total Prizemoney* £26,434
Wins * 1999 Oct Newmar (G-S) L 7f 101 <
*** 1999** Spt Newbur (G-S) 7f 89
1999 Turf 2-4: (7f 2-3, 8f) (g-s, gd 2-2, frm)
Very useful colt. Turf high 101 (began Spt) - 1st of 5 from Winning Venture (1 Oct Newmarket RF 4676). A handsome chestnut - he has been nicknamed Tom Cruise - this colt is held in high regard by his shrewd trainer and looked the part when winning at Newbury and Newmarket. He was heavily backed after being supplemented for the Group 1 Racing Post Trophy at Doncaster, but ran no sort of race and was beaten with fully three furlongs to run. Better than that effort implies, he may not stay much beyond a mile and should win a Group race in 2000.
**D R C Elsworth [2-4] O J McDowell.*

SCATHEBURY BHB 37f52a RR 34f 52a 4987[10]

6 b g Aragon 7.7f **(58)** - Lady Bequick (Sharpen Up) 8.3f **(67)**
Form - 4760803000
Record 1999 - 1st:0 2nd:0 3rd:1 Ran:10
Pre1999 - 1st:7 2nd:11 3rd:6 Ran:62
Win Prizemoney £19,870 *Total Prizemoney* £33,961

Wins	1998	Oct	Newcas	(SFT)	S	8f		54	
	1998	Apr	Catter	(GD)	S	7f		64+	
	1997	Oct	Leices	(G-S)	SH	7f	47	54	
	1997	May	Windso	(SFT)	C	8.3f		64	
	1997	Apr	Mussel	(G-F)	SH	8f	55	60	
	1996	Aug	Mussel	(G-F)	H	7.1f	55	58	
	1995	*Jly*	*Wolver*	*(STD)*		*6f*		*71*	<

1999 Turf 0-8: (6f, 7f 2, 8f 5) (gd 4, frm 2, hrd 2) 1999 AW 0-2: (7f, 8f) (Fibr 2)
Fair gelding, effective 7 to 8f, best at 7f, acts on sft to g-f, has worn blinkers.
**R Craggs [0-7] Prince Bishop Racing (from K R Burke [6-53] Mar 1999).*

SCENE (IRE) BHB 76f RR 72f 5154[1]

4 b f Scenic 10.6f **(66)** - Avebury Ring (Auction Ring (USA)) 8.6f **(65)**
Form - 037142310000041
Record 1999 - 1st:3 2nd:1 3rd:2 Ran:15
Pre1999 - 1st:3 2nd:1 3rd:4 Ran:23
Win Prizemoney £41,642 *Total Prizemoney* £54,163

Wins	*** 1999**	Nov	Nottin	(SFT)	H	10f	70	72	
	*** 1999**	Jun	Epsom	(G-S)	H	8.5f	74	81	< •
	*** 1999**	Apr	Ascot	(GD)	H	8f	70	75	
	* 1998	Jly	Haydoc	(G-F)	H	8.1f	72	77	
	* 1998	Jun	Thirsk	(SFT)	H	8f	68	76	
	1997.	Nov	Doncas	(G-S)	H	7f	63	70	

1999 Turf 3-15: (8f 1-11, 9f 1-1, 10f 1-3) (sft, g-s, gd 2-8, g-f 1-3, frm 2)
Light-framed, above-average filly, effective 8 to 10f, best at 8f, acts on gd to frm, has worn blinkers, likes left handed tracks, prefers tight tracks, excels at Nottingham and Ripon. Turf high 81 - 1st of 14 getting 4lb from Jedi Knight (4 Jun Epsom RF 1730) - also 1st of 29 giving 5lb to Harmony Hall (28 Apr Ascot RF 0901).
**J A Glover [5-26] Paul Dixon (from M Meade [1-12] Apr 1998).*

SCENIC LADY (IRE) BHB 25f RR 34df 4289[6]

3 b f Scenic 10.6f **(66)** -Tu Tu Maori (IRE)(Kings Lake (USA)) 10.8f **(67)**
Form - 520588606
Record 1999 - 1st:0 2nd:1 3rd:0 Ran:9
Pre1999 - 1st:0 2nd:0 3rd:0 Ran:2
Win Prizemoney £0 *Total Prizemoney* £707
1999 Turf 0-8: (7f, 10f 2, 11f 2, 12f 2, 14f) (sft, gd 2, g-f 4, frm) 1999 AW 0-1: (16f) (Equi)
Neat, very moderate filly. Turf high 44. Inconsistent.
**L A Dace [0-9] Eddie Davess (from J J Sheehan [0-2] Spt 1998).*

SCHATZI BHB 55f50a RR 57f 50a 5187[5]

2 gr f Chilibang 7f **(55)** - Fluorescent Flo (Ballad Rock) 7.8f **(63)**
Form - 37222735005
Record 1999 - 1st:0 2nd:3 3rd:2 Ran:11
Win Prizemoney £0 *Total Prizemoney* £2,466
1999 Turf 0-10: (5f 6, 6f 4) (gd 5, g-f 3, frm, hrd) 1999 AW 0-1: (6f) (Fibr)
Fair filly, effective 5 to 6f, best at 5f, acts on gd to g-f, best on g-f. Turf high 57 - 5th of 14 to Poppy's Song (5 Oct Catterick 5f gd RF 4721). **D Moffatt [0-11] Mrs Jennie Moffatt.*

SCHICHT (IRE) BHB 100a RR 4867[2]

3 ch f Fayruz 6.6f **(63)** - Bobby Hays (IRE) (Bob Back (USA))
Form -
Record 1999 - 1st:1 2nd:1 3rd:2 Ran:7
Win Prizemoney £2,857 *Total Prizemoney* £7,481
Wins * 1999 Jun Carlis (G-F) 5f 78+ <
1999 Turf 1-6: (g-s, g-f 3, frm, hrd 1-1) 1999 AW 0-1: (Fibr)
Useful colt, acts on hrd. Turf high 87 - also 1st of 13 from Corunna (24 Jun Carlisle RF 2258). **K R Burke [1-7] Nigel Shields.*

SCHIEHALLION RR 68f 5150[7]

2 b f Polar Falcon (USA) 9f **(74)** - Frisson (Slip Anchor) 9.8f **(73)**
Form - 04067
Record 1999 - 1st:0 2nd:0 3rd:0 Ran:5
Win Prizemoney £0 *Total Prizemoney* £222
1999 Turf 0-5: (5f 2, 6f 3) (g-s, gd, frm 3)
Average filly. Turf high 68. **W J Musson [0-5] Saville House Racing.*

SCHNITZEL (IRE) BHB 75f75a RR 75f 75a 4998[4]

3 b f Tirol 8.1f **(64)** - Good Reference (IRE) (Reference Point) 6.8f **(70)**
Form - 4204481004
Record 1999 - 1st:1 2nd:1 3rd:0 Ran:10
Pre1999 - 1st:2 2nd:1 3rd:0 Ran:6
Win Prizemoney £9,852 *Total Prizemoney* £21,150

Wins	*** 1999**	Spt	Sandow	(G-S)		7.1f		75	<
	1998	Spt	Goodwo	(G-S)	H	7f	71	73	
	* 1998	*Jly*	*Southw*	*(STD)*		*7f*		*71*	

1999 Turf 1-10: (7f 1-7, 8f 3) (g-s, gd 1-5, g-f 2, frm 2)
Neat, above-average filly, effective 7 to 8f, best at 8f, acts on gd to frm - acts on Fibr, best on g-f, likes left handed tracks, prefers tight tracks, excels at Goodwood. Turf high 80 - 2nd of 15 getting 17lb from Sporting Lad (4 May Chester 8f g-f RF 1026) - also 1st of 7 getting 7lb from Temeraire (15 Spt Sandown RF 4333). A winner over seven furlongs on Fibresand and easy ground at two, she took time to find her form last season, but gained a game success at Sandown in September. Needs a bit of give in the ground.
**M L W Bell [3-16] Mrs G Rowland-Clark.*

SCINTILATING SOUND BHB 33f41a RR 29f 41a 2692[8]

4 ch f Savahra Sound 7.8f **(55)** - Mia Scintilla (Blazing Saddles (AUS)) 6.7f **(46)**
Form - 6305283830008
Record 1999 - 1st:0 2nd:1 3rd:2 Ran:11
Pre1999 - 1st:0 2nd:0 3rd:2 Ran:8
Win Prizemoney £0 *Total Prizemoney* £2,277

1999 Turf 0-3: (5f 3) (g-f 2, hrd) 1999 AW 0-8: (5f 2, 6f 2, 7f 3, 8f) (Fibr 8)
Unfurnished, moderate filly, effective 6 to 7f, best at 7f, - acts on Fibr, has worn blinkers, likes left handed tracks, likes tight tracks. Turf high 29. AW high 43 - 3rd of 12 getting 8lb from Approachable (6 Mar Wolverhampton 7f Fibr RF 0405).
**S R Bowring [0-19] Mrs Zoe Grant.*

SCISSOR RIDGE BHB 44f57a **RR 42f 57a** 5033[4]
7 ch g Indian Ridge 7.6f **(74)** - Golden Scissors (Kalaglow) 9.8f **(67)**
Form - 0600453530058780544
Record 1999 - 1st:0 2nd:0 3rd:2 Ran:18
Pre1999 - 1st:7 2nd:14 3rd:7 Ran:94
Win Prizemoney £23,004 *Total Prizemoney* £45,828
Wins * 1998 Jly Folkes (GD) H 6f 50 56
* 1996 *Dec Lingfi (STD) H 5f 60 65* <
* 1996 *Nov Lingfi (STD) H 6f 60 65* <
* 1996 Spt Goodwo (G-F) H 5f 58 60
* 1996 Jun Goodwo (G-F) H 6f 43 52
* 1995 *Dec Lingfi (STD) H 7f 46 47*
1999 Turf 0-7: (5f, 6f, 7f 4, 8f) (g-s, g-f 2, frm 4) 1999 AW 0-11: (5f, 6f 4, 7f 5, 8f) (Equi 9, Fibr 2)
Fair gelding, effective 6 to 7f, best at 7f, - acts on Equi, has worn blinkers, likes left handed tracks, likes tight tracks, does well at Lingfield. Turf high 44 (began Jly). AW high 61 - 9th of 12 getting 16lb from Silca Blanka (16 Jan Lingfield 7f Equi RF 0109).
**J J Bridger [6-104] Donald Smith (from M R Channon [1-8] Aug 1994).*

SCOLD · BHB 32f25a **RR 18f 25a** 458[10]
4 gr f Reprimand 8.2f **(63)** - Hopea (USA) (Drone) 10.3f **(74)**
Form - 0
Record 1999 - 1st:0 2nd:0 3rd:0 Ran:1
Pre1999 - 1st:0 2nd:0 3rd:0 Ran:3
1999 AW 0-1: (7f) (Fibr)
Unfurnished, poor filly, has worn blinkers.
**G P Kelly [0-3] A M McArdle (from J S Wainwright [0-3] Jun 1998).*

SCOLDING BHB 30f **RR 37f** 4142[11]
4 b f Reprimand 8.2f **(63)** - Tinkerbird (Music Boy) 6.8f **(57)**
Form - 00600
Record 1999 - 1st:0 2nd:0 3rd:0 Ran:5
Pre1999 - 1st:1 2nd:0 3rd:0 Ran:14
Win Prizemoney £2,910 *Total Prizemoney* £2,910
Wins * 1998 Aug Pontef (G-F) H 8f 44 48 <
1999 Turf 0-5: (8f 3, 9f, 10f) (gd, frm 2, hrd 2)
Lengthy, very moderate filly, effective 8f, acts on g-s to frm, prefers left handed tracks. Turf high 37 (began Jly).
**G Woodward [1-14] Michael Worth (from K A Morgan [0-5] Aug 1997).*

SCONCED (USA) BHB 32f **RR 34f** 4940[3]
4 ch g Affirmed (USA) 10.3f **(75)** - Quaff (USA) (Raise A Cup (USA)) 7.6f **(74)**
Form - 68040053
Record 1999 - 1st:0 2nd:0 3rd:1 Ran:8
Pre1999 - 1st:1 2nd:0 3rd:1 Ran:6
Win Prizemoney £3,468 *Total Prizemoney* £5,432
Wins 1998 Spt Hamilt (SFT) 9.2f 73 <
1999 Turf 0-6: (10f, 11f, 12f, 13f 2, 17f) (gd, g-f, frm 4) 1999 AW 0-2: (14f 2) (Fibr 2)
Well made, very moderate gelding, effective 9 to 10f, acts on g-s to gd, likes right handed tracks, favours tight tracks. Turf high 65. AW high 29 (began Spt). Consistent.
**Martyn Wane [0-8] James S Kennerley and Miss Jenny Hall (from G Wragg [1-6] Oct 1998).*

SCOOP (IRE) **RR 35f** 4985[16]
3 b f Scenic 10.6f **(66)** - Big Story (Cadeaux Genereux)
Form - 04463440630
Record 1999 - 1st:0 2nd:0 3rd:2 Ran:11
Pre1999 - 1st:1 2nd:0 3rd:3 Ran:8
Win Prizemoney £3,386 *Total Prizemoney* £6,069
Wins 1998 Jly Pontef (G-F) 6f 76 <
1999 Turf 0-11: (8f 7, 9f, 10f, 12f, 14f) (g-s, gd 3, g-f, frm 4, hrd 2)
Scopey, very moderate filly, effective 6f, acts on frm, has worn blinkers. Turf high 55. Becoming disappointing.
**S E Kettlewell [0-13] J Tennant (from Mrs J R Ramsden [1-6] Spt 1998).*

SCORCHED AIR BHB 28f22a **RR 8f 22a** 4128[11]
9 b m Elegant Air 9.6f **(64)** - Misfire (Gunner B) 11.2f **(58)**
Form - 8000
Record 1999 - 1st:0 2nd:0 3rd:0 Ran:4
Pre1999 - 1st:2 2nd:3 3rd:6 Ran:27
Win Prizemoney £6,511 *Total Prizemoney* £13,679
1999 Turf 0-2: (11f, 12f) (g-f, frm) 1999 AW 0-2: (12f, 16f) (Fibr 2)
Poor mare, has worn blinkers. Turf high 8. AW high 17.
**Mrs S Lamyman [1-19] P Lamyman (from J G M O'Shea [0-5] Spt 1995).*

SCOTLAND BAY BHB 50f52a **RR 39f 52a** 915[14]
4 b f Then Again 7.4f **(52)** - Down the Valley (Kampala) 8.5f **(56)**
Form - 48254880
Record 1999 - 1st:0 2nd:1 3rd:0 Ran:7
Pre1999 - 1st:2 2nd:1 3rd:2 Ran:14
Win Prizemoney £4,260 *Total Prizemoney* £6,471
Wins 1998 Oct Folkes (G-S) S 7f 60 <
1998 *Jan Lingfi (STD) H 7f 54 59*
1999 Turf 0-2: (7f, 8f) (g-s, frm) 1999 AW 0-5: (7f 4, 10f) (Equi 4, Fibr)
Workmanlike, moderate filly, effective 7f, acts on g-s - acts on Equi.
**P Butler [0-9] Christopher Wilson (from R Hannon [2-12] Oct 1998).*

SCOTTIE YORK BHB 43f **RR 36f** 4448[5]
3 b g Noble Patriarch 12.2f **(43)** - Devon Dancer (Shareef Dancer (USA)) 9.9f **(73)**
Form - 40305
Record 1999 - 1st:0 2nd:0 3rd:1 Ran:5
Win Prizemoney £0 *Total Prizemoney* £720
1999 Turf 0-5: (9f 2, 10f 2, 17f) (g-s, frm 4)
Workmanlike, very moderate gelding. Turf high 36 (began Jly).
**T D Easterby [0-5] James Glass.*

SCOTTISH MEMORIES (IRE) **RR 99f** 4479a[1]
3 ch g Houmayoun (FR) 7.1f **(79)** - Interj 00
Form - 262121
1999 Turf 2-6: (9f 2-2, 10f 3, 13f) (g-s 1-1, gd 1-3, g-f, frm)
Very useful gelding, effective 9 to 10f, best at 9f, acts on g-s to g-f, prefers right handed tracks. Turf high 99 - 1st of 9 getting 5lb from Wray (19 Spt Curragh RF 4479a). He stays 13 furlongs, but seems better forcing the pace over shorter trips. Raced mainly on good ground or softer, he could do well over hurdles.
**J E Mulhern in IRE [2-5] Mrs Chryss O'Reilly (from F Ennis in IRE [0-4] May 1999).*

SCOTTISH SPICE BHB 89f **RR 87f** 4402[1]
2 b f Selkirk (USA) 7.9f **(76)** - Dilwara (IRE) (Lashkari) 9.8f **(67)**
Form - 6411
Record 1999 - 1st:2 2nd:0 3rd:0 Ran:4
Win Prizemoney £10,885 *Total Prizemoney* £11,809
Wins * **1999** Spt Newbur (G-F) H 7f 85 87 <
* **1999** Aug Folkes (G-S) 7f 87 <
1999 Turf 2-4: (7f 2-4) (gd 1-1, g-f, frm 1-2)
Useful filly. Turf high 87 (began Jly) - 1st of 13 giving 7lb to Travelling Lite (18 Spt Newbury RF 4402) - also 1st of 11 from Ashjaan (26 Aug Folkestone RF 3912). Got off the mark on easy ground at Folkestone on her third start, but had to work hard. Maintained her progress to follow up at Newbury.
**I A Balding [2-4] J C Smith.*

SCOTTY GUEST (IRE) BHB 80f **RR 92+f** 5102[1]
2 b c Distinctly North (USA) 7.4f **(63)** - Tartan Lady (IRE) (Taufan (USA)) 7f **(57)**
Form - 01
Record 1999 - 1st:1 2nd:0 3rd:0 Ran:2
Win Prizemoney £3,297 *Total Prizemoney* £3,297
Wins * **1999** Oct Yarmou (G-S) 8f 92+ <
1999 Turf 1-2: (8f 1-2) (gd 1-1, g-f)
Currently useful colt. Turf high 92 (began Spt) - 1st of 10 from Proper Squire (27 Oct Yarmouth RF 5102).
**G G Margarson [1-2] John Guest.*

SCRAGGYS DREAM (IRE) BHB 85f94a **RR 89f 94a** 4404[14]
3 ch c Shalford (IRE) 7.8f **(63)** - Massive Powder (Caerleon (USA)) 8.6f **(71)**
Form - 1211030

Record 1999 - 1st:3 2nd:1 3rd:1 Ran:7
Pre1999 - 1st:0 2nd:0 3rd:0 Ran:1
Win Prizemoney £14,193 *Total Prizemoney* £17,559
Wins *** 1999** *Mar Lingfi (STD) H 10f 85 91* <
*** 1999** *Feb Lingfi (STD) H 10f 75 82*
*** 1999** *Jan Lingfi (STD) 10f 87*
1999 Turf 0-3: (10f 2, 12f) (gd, g-f, frm) 1999 AW 3-4: (10f 3-4) (Equi 3-4)
Workmanlike, useful colt, effective 10f, acts on gd - acts on Equi, favours left handed tracks, favours tight tracks. Turf high 89 (began Jly) - 3rd of 6 to Prairie Wolf (29 Aug Yarmouth 10f gd RF 4005). AW high 91 - 1st of 12 getting 14lb from Thekryaati (18 Mar Lingfield RF 0445) - also 1st of 13 giving 5lb to Sky City (2 Jan Lingfield RF 0010). Caused a bit of a surprise when winning his maiden on the Lingfield Equitrack in January, but proved that effort to be no fluke on that surface afterwards with two more victories. He ran his best race on turf to date when third in a Yarmouth classified event in August, but looks another interesting sand prospect for his trainer. **P Mitchell [3-8] The O'Keeffe Family.*

SCROOGE (IRE) BHB 43f **RR 42f** 5153[13]

3 b g Tirol 8.1f **(64)** - Gay Appeal (Star Appeal) 9.6f **(65)**
Form - 886600750
Record 1999 - 1st:0 2nd:0 3rd:0 Ran:9
Pre1999 - 1st:0 2nd:0 3rd:0 Ran:3
1999 Turf 0-9: (6f 6, 7f, 10f 2) (sft, gd 3, g-f 2, frm 3)
Scopey, moderate gelding, has worn blinkers. Turf high 63.
**M H Tompkins [0-12] Richard Flatt.*

SCURRILOUS BHB 44f **RR 25f** 440[14]

4 ch f Sharpo 7.5f **(68)** - Tea and Scandals (USA) (Key to the Kingdom (USA)) 8.3f **(65)**
Form - 0735630
Record 1999 - 1st:0 2nd:0 3rd:2 Ran:6
Pre1999 - 1st:0 2nd:1 3rd:0 Ran:5
Win Prizemoney £0 *Total Prizemoney* £2,045
1999 AW 0-6: (5f 2, 6f 4) (Equi 3, Fibr 3)
Light-framed, moderate filly, effective 6f, - acts on Fibr, favours left handed tracks, favours tight tracks. AW high 50. Inconsistent.
**J L Harris [0-6] Paddy Barrett (from D Nicholls [0-1] Nov 1998).*

SEA-BELLE (IRE) BHB 31f46a **RR 43f 46a** 4438[13]

3 ch f Mukaddamah (USA) 7.6f **(74)** - Blue Bell Lady (Dunphy) 9.4f **(57)**
Form - 27700304070
Record 1999 - 1st:0 2nd:1 3rd:1 Ran:11
Pre1999 - 1st:0 2nd:0 3rd:1 Ran:4
Win Prizemoney £0 *Total Prizemoney* £2,191
1999 Turf 0-7: (8f 3, 10f 2, 11f, 12f) (g-s, gd 2, g-f, frm 3) 1999 AW 0-4: (6f, 7f 2, 9f) (Fibr 4)
Leggy, moderate filly, effective 6f, acts on frm, has worn blinkers. Turf high 44. AW high 60. Inconsistent.
**J G Portman [0-7] Christopher Shankland (from K Bell [0-4] Apr 1999).*

SEABOUND **RR 63f** 3485[4]

3 b f Prince Sabo 6.6f **(64)** - Shore Line (High Line) 10.3f **(70)**
Form - 074
Record 1999 - 1st:0 2nd:0 3rd:0 Ran:3
Win Prizemoney £0 *Total Prizemoney* £209
1999 Turf 0-3: (6f, 7f, 8f) (gd, g-f, frm)
Unfurnished, currently average filly. Turf high 63.
**J R Fanshawe [0-3] Cheveley Park Stud.*

SEA DANE BHB 90f **RR 103f** 4372a[2]

6 b h Danehill (USA) 9.1f **(79)** - Shimmering Sea (Slip Anchor) 9.8f **(73)**
Form - 12
1999 Turf 1-2: (6f 1-2) (sft 1-1, gd)
Very useful horse. Turf high 103 - 2nd of 7 to Proud Native (12 Spt Taby 6f gd RF 4372a). Inconsistent. A smart sprinter, he has done well since being exported to Denmark and went close in a Group 3 at Taby. **B Bjorkman in DEN [1-2] (from P W Harris [3-17] Jly 1997).*

SEA DANZIG BHB 57f65a **RR 59f 65a** 4993[7]

6 ch g Roi Danzig (USA) 10.5f **(62)** - Tosara (Main Reef) 9.6f **(57)**
Form - 55063203727431077
Record 1999 - 1st:1 2nd:2 3rd:3 Ran:17
Pre1999 - 1st:7 2nd:7 3rd:5 Ran:63
Win Prizemoney £27,234 *Total Prizemoney* £44,745
Wins *** 1999** Spt Epsom (GD) H 10.1f 55 59
* 1998 Jly Folkes (G-F) 9.7f 63
* 1998 Jun Goodwo (G-F) H 9f 52 61
* 1998 *Jan Lingfi (STD) H 10f 68 73* <
* 1998 *Jan Lingfi (STD) H 10f 68 73* <
* 1997 *Nov Lingfi (STD) H 10f 67 69*
* 1997 *Jan Lingfi (STD) H 7f 63 58*
* 1996 Oct Lingfi (GD) H 7f 62 66
1999 Turf 1-14: (10f 1-11, 11f, 12f 2) (g-s 2, gd 3, g-f 3, frm 1-5, hrd)
1999 AW 0-3: (8f, 10f 2) (Equi 2, Fibr)
Average gelding, effective 8 to 10f, best at 10f, acts on g-f to frm - acts on Equi, likes Lingfield. Turf high 59. AW high 67.
**J J Bridger [8-69] P Cook (from P Howling [0-11] Jly 1996).*

SEA-DEER BHB 77f75a **RR 76f 75a** 4804[13]

10 ch g Hadeer 8.9f **(58)** - Hi-Tech Girl (Homeboy) 6.6f **(55)**
Form - 470240430341100
Record 1999 - 1st:2 2nd:1 3rd:2 Ran:15
Pre1999 - 1st:14 2nd:11 3rd:12 Ran:87
Win Prizemoney £62,775 *Total Prizemoney* £95,574
Wins *** 1999** Spt Yarmou (G-S) H 7f 66 76
*** 1999** Spt Yarmou (G-F) S 7f 51
* 1998 Jly Newmar (G-F) H 6f 69 73
* 1997 Jun Yarmou (GD) 6f 87
* 1996 *Aug Wolver (STD) H 6f 74 77*
* 1996 Jly Newmar (GD) 5f 96 <
* 1996 Jun Yarmou (FRM) H 6f 73 71
* 1996 Jun Yarmou (FRM) H 6f 67 72
1996 May Catter (GD) C 5f 49
1996 May Newcas (GD) S 5f 60
1999 Turf 2-15: (6f 8, 7f 2-7) (g-s 1-2, gd 3, g-f 1-5, frm 5)
Above-average gelding, effective 6 to 7f, best at 6f, acts on g-s to frm, and likes Newmarket. Turf high 76 - 1st of 14 giving 34lb to Mr Cube (15 Spt Yarmouth RF 4338). A useful sprinter on both turf and the All-Weather, he scored twice at Yarmouth in September on consecutive days, although may have had the best of it for the time being given his age.
**C A Dwyer [8-60] Francis Barnes (from D W Chapman [2-12] May 1996).*

SEA DRIFT (FR) **RR 62f** 3971[7]

2 gr f Warning 8.1f **(77)** - Night At Sea (Night Shift (USA)) 7.2f **(69)**
Form - 7
Record 1999 - 1st:0 2nd:0 3rd:0 Ran:1
1999 Turf 0-1: (6f) (g-f)
Currently average filly. **L M Cumani [0-1] Lady Juliet Tadgell.*

SEA EMPEROR **RR 58f** 3400[13]

2 br g Emperor Jones (USA) - Blumarin (IRE) (Scenic)
Form - 770
Record 1999 - 1st:0 2nd:0 3rd:0 Ran:3
1999 Turf 0-3: (6f 3) (gd, g-f, frm)
Currently fair gelding. Turf high 58 (began Jly).
**Mrs G S Rees [0-3] Cross Farm Partnership.*

SEA FIG BHB 33f40a **RR 40f 40a** 2277[16]

4 gr f Robellino (USA) 9.5f **(68)** - Aimee Jane (USA) (Our Native (USA)) 11.2f **(63)**
Form - 7000
Record 1999 - 1st:0 2nd:0 3rd:0 Ran:2
Pre1999 - 1st:0 2nd:3 3rd:0 Ran:18
Win Prizemoney £0 *Total Prizemoney* £2,663
1999 Turf 0-2: (10f 2) (g-f, frm)
Fair filly, has broken blood-vessels, effective 6f, - acts on Fibr, has worn blinkers.
**S G Knight [0-8] Malcolm Enticott (from T D Barron [0-16] Aug 1998).*

SEA FREEDOM BHB 57f **RR 66f** 2546[8]

8 b h Slip Anchor 12.7f **(75)** - Rostova (Blakeney) 10.5f **(64)**
Form - 4073508
Record 1999 - 1st:0 2nd:0 3rd:1 Ran:7
Pre1999 - 1st:4 2nd:8 3rd:8 Ran:49
Win Prizemoney £39,525 *Total Prizemoney* £65,825
Wins * 1998 Jun Chepst (G-S) H 18f 67 71 <
* 1997 Jun Ascot (GD) H 20f 65 71 <
* 1997 Apr Nottin (GD) H 14.1f 63 71 <
* 1997 Apr Hamilt (G-S) H 13f 58 66
1999 Turf 0-7: (12f, 16f 4, 18f, 20f) (g-s 2, g-f 3, frm 2)

Average horse, effective 14 to 20f, acts on sft to gd, best on gd, often wears blinkers (very effectively), excels at Doncaster, does well at Sandown. Turf high 66 - 3rd of 10 getting 3lb from Wave of Optimism (23 Apr Sandown 16f g-s RF 0823). Consistent. The winner of the 1997 Ascot Stakes, he stays particularly well when on song, but is finding winning difficult these days and is not an easy ride. **G B Balding [4-60] Miss B Swire.*

SEA GOD BHB 18f32a **RR 11f 32a** 1710[10]

8 ch g Rainbow Quest (USA) 11.2f **(81)** - Sea Pageant (Welsh Pageant) 10f **(65)**
Form - 0
Record 1999 - 1st:0 2nd:0 3rd:0 Ran:1
Pre1999 - 1st:1 2nd:3 3rd:2 Ran:35
Win Prizemoney £3,077 *Total Prizemoney* £6,122
Wins * 1996 *Feb Southw (STD) H 11f 44 48* <
1999 Turf 0-1: (10f) (gd)
Little account gelding.
**M C Chapman [1-53] McCann Ltd (from B W Hills [0-3] May 1994).*

SEAGREEN (IRE) **RR 6f** 3856[6]

2 b f Green Desert (USA) 7.8f **(78)** - Ocean Ballad (Grundy) 10.3f **(65)**
Form - 06
Record 1999 - 1st:0 2nd:0 3rd:0 Ran:2
1999 Turf 0-2: (6f, 8f) (gd, frm)
Currently very poor filly. (began Aug).
**Mrs A L M King [0-2] Aiden Murphy.*

SEA HAZE BHB 74f **RR 76?f** 4249[21]

2 ch c Emarati (USA) 6.6f **(63)** - Unveiled **(54f 48a)** (Sayf El Arab (USA)) 7.1f **(54)**
Form - 06815340
Record 1999 - 1st:1 2nd:0 3rd:1 Ran:8
Win Prizemoney £2,808 *Total Prizemoney* £3,564
Wins * **1999** Jun Bath (FRM) 5.7f 62 <
1999 Turf 1-8: (5f 2, 6f 1-6) (gd 3, g-f 2, frm 2, hrd 1-1)
Above-average colt. Turf high 76. Inconsistent.
**R J Hodges [1-8] P Slade.*

SEA ISLE BHB 64f **RR 68f** 5073[11]

3 ch f Selkirk (USA) 7.9f **(76)** - Miss Blitz (Formidable (USA)) 9.2f **(63)**
Form - 56350
Record 1999 - 1st:0 2nd:0 3rd:1 Ran:5
Win Prizemoney £0 *Total Prizemoney* £495
1999 Turf 0-5: (7f 2, 8f 3) (g-s, gd, g-f, frm 2)
Scopey, average filly. Turf high 68 (began Aug) - 6th of 19 getting 5lb from Zulu Dawn (17 Spt Newbury 8f frm RF 4382).
**I A Balding [0-5] George Strawbridge.*

SEALED BY FATE (IRE) BHB 54f51a **RR 56f 51a** 4805[19]

4 b g Mac's Imp (USA) 5.6f **(54)** - Fairy Don (Don) 7.7f **(64)**
Form - 0372321260464260080
Record 1999 - 1st:1 2nd:4 3rd:2 Ran:19
Pre1999 - 1st:0 2nd:1 3rd:3 Ran:20
Win Prizemoney £2,430 *Total Prizemoney* £8,378
Wins * **1999** Jun Carlis (GD) H 5f 58 61 <
1999 Turf 1-19: (5f 1-15, 6f 4) (gd 4, g-f 1-5, frm 9, hrd)
Strong, fair gelding, effective 5f, acts on g-f to frm, best on g-f, mostly wears blinkers. Turf high 68 - 2nd of 6 to Torrent (27 Jly Beverley 5f frm RF 3164) - also 1st of 14 giving 15lb to Chakra (10 Jun Carlisle RF 1879). **J S Wainwright [1-39] Neil Harrison.*

SEA MARK BHB 84f **RR 83f** 4819[1]

3 br c Warning 8.1f **(77)** - Mettlesome (Lomond (USA)) 8.8f **(65)**
Form - 1
Record 1999 - 1st:1 2nd:0 3rd:0 Ran:1
Pre1999 - 1st:0 2nd:1 3rd:0 Ran:2
Win Prizemoney £2,389 *Total Prizemoney* £4,209
Wins * **1999** Oct Leices (G-S) 7f 67 <
1999 Turf 1-1: (7f 1-1) (gd 1-1)
Scopey, currently decent colt. (1st run). Off the track until landing an apprentice maiden in October, he is unexposed an should progress. **B W Hills [1-3] K Abdulla.*

SEA MINSTREL BHB 32f **RR 16f** 5167[11]

3 b f Sea Raven (IRE) - Give Us a Treat (Cree Song)
Form - 00000P0
Record 1999 - 1st:0 2nd:0 3rd:0 Ran:7
Pre1999 - 1st:0 2nd:0 3rd:1 Ran:7
Win Prizemoney £0 *Total Prizemoney* £756
1999 Turf 0-7: (5f, 6f 3, 8f, 10f, 12f) (g-s, gd, g-f, frm 4)
Scopey, poor filly. Turf high 28. **M E Sowersby [0-17] T W Heseltine.*

SEAMUS BHB 20f **RR 26?f** 2316[15]

5 ch g Almoojid 7f **(36)** -Royal Celerity(USA)(Riverman (USA)) 9.1f **(76)**
Form - 0
Record 1999 - 1st:0 2nd:0 3rd:0 Ran:1
Pre1999 - 1st:0 2nd:0 3rd:0 Ran:9
1999 Turf 0-1: (17f) (hrd)
Little account gelding.
**A G Newcombe [0-2] Duckhaven Stud (from C J Hill [0-8] Aug 1997).*

SEA PICTURE (IRE) BHB 79f **RR 85df** 2346[5]

3 b f Royal Academy (USA) 7.8f **(77)** - Grecian Sea (FR) (Homeric) 9.8f **(67)**
Form - 6575
Record 1999 - 1st:0 2nd:0 3rd:0 Ran:4
Pre1999 - 1st:0 2nd:1 3rd:0 Ran:1
Win Prizemoney £0 *Total Prizemoney* £2,013
1999 Turf 0-4: (8f 2, 10f 2) (g-s, gd 2, g-f)
Workmanlike, useful filly. Turf high 85.
**Sir Michael Stoute [0-5] Lord Weinstock.*

SEASAME PARK BHB 53f56a **RR 51f 56a** 4414[2]

2 b f Elmaamul (USA) 8.1f **(70)** - Holyrood Park (Sharrood (USA)) 10.5f **(72)**
Form - 321402
Record 1999 - 1st:1 2nd:2 3rd:1 Ran:6
Win Prizemoney £1,871 *Total Prizemoney* £3,279
Wins * **1999** *Jun Wolver (STD) S 7f 60* <
1999 Turf 0-3: (6f, 7f, 8f) (gd 2, frm) 1999 AW 1-3: (6f, 7f 1-2) (Fibr 1-3)
Average filly, effective 7f, - acts on Fibr. Turf high 51. AW high 60 - also 1st of 7 getting 5lb from Fingers Henry (25 Jun Wolverhampton RF 2313). She seemed to appreciate the seventh furlong when getting off the mark in a seller on the Wolverhampton Fibresand in June.
**B Palling [1-6] D Egan & T H Stuart.*

SEASONAL STYLE (IRE) **RR 92f** 4742a[4]

3 ch f Generous - Just Society (USA) 00
Form - 11624
1999 Turf 2-5: (9f 1-2, 10f 1-3) (sft, g-s, gd 1-2, g-f 1-1)
Useful filly, has worn blinkers. Turf high 92 - 1st of 4 giving 14lb to Sukeena (2 Aug Cork RF 3500a).
**D K Weld in IRE [2-5] Moyglare Stud Farm.*

SEASON OF HOPE BHB 35f33a **RR 38f 33a** 3092[4]

3 ch f Komaite (USA) 6.9f **(61)** - Honour and Glory (Hotfoot) 10.5f **(59)**
Form - 3807554
Record 1999 - 1st:0 2nd:0 3rd:1 Ran:7
Pre1999 - 1st:0 2nd:0 3rd:0 Ran:3
Win Prizemoney £0 *Total Prizemoney* £244
1999 Turf 0-4: (8f, 10f 2, 12f) (g-f 2, frm, hrd) 1999 AW 0-3: (9f 2, 10f) (Equi, Fibr 2)
Leggy, moderate filly, effective 10f, acts on g-f, has worn blinkers, likes left handed tracks, likes tight tracks. Turf high 38 - 7th of 17 getting 1lb from Purple Dawn (16 Jun Nottingham 10f g-f RF 2054). AW high 44.
**D E Cantillon [0-7] Mrs Christine Willmott (from D J S Cosgrove [0-3] Jly 1998).*

SEA SPOUSE BHB 29f44a **RR 27f 44a** 4783[7]

8 ch g Jalmood (USA) 11.1f **(59)** - Bambolona (Bustino) 10.4f **(64)**
Form - 000740302368607
Record 1999 - 1st:0 2nd:1 3rd:2 Ran:15
Pre1999 - 1st:9 2nd:5 3rd:8 Ran:62
Win Prizemoney £23,378 *Total Prizemoney* £33,438
Wins * 1998 *Jun Lingfi (STD) 8f 74* <
* 1998 *Jun Lingfi (STD) 8f 63*
* 1998 *Mar Southw (STD) H 8f 58 61*
* 1997 *Jan Southw (STD) H 8f 61 66*
* 1997 *Jan Southw (STD) H 8f 61 66*
* 1996 *Jun Southw (STD) H 7f 57 64*
* 1996 Mar Folkes (G-S) H 6.9f 41 45
* 1996 *Feb Southw (STD) H 8f 48 59*

* 1995 *Apr Southw (STD) S 12f 61*
1999 Turf 0-3: (8f 2, 10f) (g-s, frm 2) 1999 AW 0-12: (7f, 8f 3, 9f 3, 10f 2, 11f 2, 12f) (Equi 4, Fibr 8)
Very moderate gelding, effective 8f, - acts on AW, likes left handed tracks, favours tight tracks. **M Blanshard [9-77] Seven Seas Racing.*

SEA SQUIRT (IRE) RR 74f 5163[2]
2 b c Fourstars Allstar (USA) - Polynesian Goddess (IRE) (Salmon Leap (USA)) 11f **(61)**
Form - 62
Record 1999 - 1st:0 2nd:1 3rd:0 Ran:2
Win Prizemoney £0 *Total Prizemoney* £866
1999 Turf 0-2: (7f, 8f) (g-s, frm)
Currently above-average colt. Turf high 74 (began Oct) - 2nd of 14 to Chem's Truce (2 Nov Catterick 7f g-s RF 5163).
**M Johnston [0-2] M J Pilkington.*

SEATTLE ALLEY (USA) BHB 56f52a **RR 37f 52a** 1368[14]
6 b g Seattle Dancer (USA) 10.1f **(74)** - Alyanaabi (USA) (Roberto (USA)) 10f **(76)**
Form - 0
Record 1999 - 1st:0 2nd:0 3rd:0 Ran:1
Pre1999 - 1st:2 2nd:0 3rd:1 Ran:15
Win Prizemoney £8,684 *Total Prizemoney* £9,396
Wins 1996 Jun Pontef (G-F) H 10f 58 68 <
1996 Jun Pontef (G-F) H 10f 58 63
1999 Turf 0-1: (10f) (g-f)
Average gelding.
**P R Webber [2-24] L & P Partnership (from Mrs J R Ramsden [2-10] Jun 1996).*

SEATTLE ART (USA) BHB 55f **RR 59f** 4576[6]
5 b g Seattle Slew (USA) 7.8f **(64)** - Artiste (Artaius (USA)) 9f **(69)**
Form - 66
Record 1999 - 1st:0 2nd:0 3rd:0 Ran:2
Pre1999 - 1st:0 2nd:2 3rd:1 Ran:5
Win Prizemoney £0 *Total Prizemoney* £2,785
1999 Turf 0-2: (12f, 13f) (gd, g-f)
Fair gelding. **P Monteith [0-5] I Bell (from H R A Cecil [0-5] Aug 1997).*

SEATTLE BAY (USA) RR 92f 5115a[3]
2 b f Opening Verse (USA) 11.8f **(70)** - Seattle Ways (FR) (Seattle Slew (USA)) 9.4f **(76)**
Form - 3
1999 Turf 0-1: (8f) (gd)
Currently useful filly. (1st run) - 3rd of 7 to Volvoreta (19 Oct Deauville 8f gd RF 5115a). **J E Pease in FR [0-1].*

SEA WAVE (IRE) BHB 120f **RR 122f** 2576[4]
4 b c Sadler's Wells (USA) 11.3f **(87)** - Three Tails (Blakeney) 10.5f **(64)**
Form - 34
Record 1999 - 1st:0 2nd:0 3rd:1 Ran:2
Pre1999 - 1st:3 2nd:1 3rd:0 Ran:7
Win Prizemoney £65,617 *Total Prizemoney* £84,571
Wins * 1998 Aug York (G-F) G2 11.9f 119+ <
* 1998 Jun Leices (SFT) 11.8f 109+
* 1998 May Lingfi (GD) 10f 84
1999 Turf 0-2: (12f 2) (g-f, frm)
Workmanlike, very high-class colt, effective 12f, acts on sft to frm. Turf high 117 - 4th of 8 giving 3lb to Craigsteel (6 Jly Newmarket 12f frm RF 2576). Inconsistent. Very much an improving sort in 1998, apart from depositing Frankie Dettori leaving the stalls in the Prix Niel. He was limited to just two starts last season, running a fine third to Fruits Of Love in the Hardwicke, but rather disappointing in the Princess Of Wales's Stakes at the July meeting.
**S bin Suroor [3-9] Godolphin.*

SEA YA MAITE BHB 32f55a **RR 31f 55a** 4935[2]
5 b g Komaite (USA) 6.9f **(61)** - Marina Plata (Julio Mariner) 7.2f **(57)**
Form - 70260688005072
Record 1999 - 1st:0 2nd:2 3rd:0 Ran:12
Pre1999 - 1st:3 2nd:1 3rd:6 Ran:27
Win Prizemoney £6,950 *Total Prizemoney* £12,774
Wins * 1998 *May Southw (STD) H 8f 63 67* <
* 1997 *Oct Wolver (STD) H 8.5f 58 65*
* 1997 *Jly Southw (STD) H 6f 52 56*
1999 Turf 0-3: (8f 3) (gd, g-f 2) 1999 AW 0-9: (6f 2, 7f 2, 8f 3, 9f 2) (Fibr 9)
Fair gelding, effective 7 to 8f, best at 8f, - acts on Fibr, has worn blinkers, likes left handed tracks, favours tight tracks. Turf high 31. AW high 64 (1st run) - 2nd of 10 getting 22lb from Weetman's Weigh (8 Jan Southwell 7f Fibr RF 0055).
**S R Bowring [3-39] S R Bowring.*

SEAZUN (IRE) BHB 100f **RR 107f** 4596[1]
2 b f Zieten (USA) - Sunset Cafe (IRE) (Red Sunset) 8.2f **(63)**
Form - 6121
Record 1999 - 1st:2 2nd:1 3rd:0 Ran:4
Win Prizemoney £81,326 *Total Prizemoney* £84,870
Wins * **1999** Spt Newmar (G-S) G1 6f 107 <
* **1999** Apr Bright (GD) 5.3f 77+
1999 Turf 2-4: (5f 1-2, 6f 1-2) (gd, g-f 1-1, frm 1-2)
Pattern-class filly. Turf high 107 - 1st of 15 from Torgau (28 Spt Newmarket RF 4596). She was a game winner of what did not look a strong renewal of the Cheveley Park Stakes in October, and does not appeal as a Guineas prospect at this stage. That said, she was returning from more than four months off the track when running Primo Valentino to half a length in a Kempton listed race, form which was soon to receive a big boost when the winner landed the Middle Park Stakes, and she is clearly a progressive filly.
**M R Channon [2-4] John Breslin.*

SECOND EMPIRE (IRE) RR 121f 2023a[7]
4 b c Fairy King (USA) 7.7f **(75)** - Welsh Love (Ela-Mana-Mou) 10.1f **(70)**

Seazun had the summer off, but returned to win the Cheveley Park

Form - 67
1999 Turf 0-2: (7f, 11f) (gd, g-f)
Very high-class colt, effective 8f, acts on gd to hrd. Turf high 99. He has regressed since his two-year-old days and was retired after finishing unplaced at Leopardstown in June.
**A P O'Brien in IRE [4-11] Michael Tabor.*

SECOND PAIGE (IRE) BHB 60f **RR 65f** 4944[9]
2 b c Nicolotte - My First Paige (IRE) **(41f 48a)** (Runnett) 7f **(59)**
Form - 800
Record 1999 - 1st:0 2nd:0 3rd:0 Ran:3
1999 Turf 0-2: (7f 2) (gd, frm) 1999 AW 0-1: (8f) (Fibr)
Currently average colt. Turf high 65 (began Jly).

N A Graham [0-3] Coronation Partnership.

SECONDS AWAY BHB 32f22a RR 30f 22a 4163[8]

8 b g Hard Fought 8.9f **(51)** - Keep Mum (Mummy's Pet) 7.7f **(60)**
Form - 08223703208
Record 1999 - 1st:0 2nd:3 3rd:2 Ran:11
Pre1999 - 1st:2 2nd:4 3rd:8 Ran:54
Win Prizemoney £4,964 *Total Prizemoney* £15,443
Wins * 1998 Jun Ayr (GD) SH 8f 31 36 <
* 1997 Jly Mussel (G-F) H 8f 30 35
1999 Turf 0-11: (5f, 8f 4, 9f 4, 10f, 11f) (gd, g-f 5, frm 4, hrd)
Very moderate gelding, effective 8 to 11f, best at 8f, acts on gd to frm, best on g-f, has worn blinkers, and excels at Ayr. Turf high 39 - 2nd of 10 getting 15lb from Burning (27 Jun Doncaster 10f g-f RF 2348). Consistent.
J S Goldie [2-71] J S Goldie (from A Harrison [0-9] Apr 1995).

SECOND TERM (IRE) BHB 26f RR 40f 337[6]

4 b f Second Set (IRE) 9.2f **(67)** - Trinida (Jaazeiro (USA)) 9.2f **(54)**
Form - 06
Record 1999 - 1st:0 2nd:0 3rd:0 Ran:2
Pre1999 - 1st:0 2nd:1 3rd:0 Ran:10
Win Prizemoney £0 *Total Prizemoney* £1,285
1999 AW 0-2: (11f, 12f) (Fibr 2)
Leggy, moderate filly, has worn blinkers. Becoming disappointing.
W Storey [0-14] Black Type Racing.

SECOND TIME AROUND (IRE) BHB 39f RR 32f 4901[18]

2 b f Mukaddamah (USA) 7.6f **(74)** - Up The Gates (Captain James) 5f **(59)**
Form - 80000730
Record 1999 - 1st:0 2nd:0 3rd:1 Ran:8
Win Prizemoney £0 *Total Prizemoney* £275
1999 Turf 0-7: (5f, 6f 3, 7f 3) (gd, g-f 4, frm 2) 1999 AW 0-1: (5f) (Fibr)
Very moderate filly. Turf high 32.
M C Chapman [0-8] Eric Knowles.

SECOND WIND BHB 70f RR 71f 5035[4]

4 ch g Kris 10f **(75)** - Rimosa's Pet (Petingo) 11f **(72)**
Form - 07660118806304
Record 1999 - 1st:2 2nd:0 3rd:1 Ran:14
Pre1999 - 1st:1 2nd:1 3rd:0 Ran:9
Win Prizemoney £11,705 *Total Prizemoney* £16,798
Wins * **1999** Jly Epsom (G-F) H 7f 61 70
1999 Jly Bright (FRM) C 7f 66
1997 Apr Newmar (G-F) 5f 79 <
1999 Turf 2-14: (5f 2, 6f 2, 7f 2-7, 8f 3) (g-s, gd 2, g-f 3, frm 2-8)
Scopey, above-average gelding, effective 6f, acts on frm, likes left handed tracks. Turf high 71. Consistent. Does not appear to stay a mile, and seems better over six or an easy seven furlongs, and he obviously has a fondness for downhill courses.
C A Dwyer [1-8] John Purcell (from Miss Gay Kelleway [1-6] Jly 1999).

SECRET AGENT RR 92f 5074[2]

2 b c Machiavellian (USA) 9.8f **(83)** - Secret Obsession (USA) (Secretariat (USA)) 9f **(79)**
Form - 12
Record 1999 - 1st:1 2nd:1 3rd:0 Ran:2
Win Prizemoney £4,142 *Total Prizemoney* £5,246
Wins * **1999** Spt Warwic (SFT) 7.7f 86+ <
1999 Turf 1-2: (7f, 8f 1-1) (sft 1-1, gd)
Currently useful colt. Turf high 92 (began Spt) - 2nd of 7 to Osood (26 Oct Redcar 7f gd RF 5074) - also 1st of 12 from Rayyaan (21 Spt Warwick RF 4449). Looked good first time, but his attitude looked questionable on his second run.
Sir Michael Stoute [1-2] Cheveley Park Stud.

SECRET ARCHIVE BHB 86f RR 92f 3653[5]

4 b c Salse (USA) 10.9f **(71)** - Lycia (USA) (Lyphard (USA)) 9.9f **(72)**
Form - 0630505
Record 1999 - 1st:0 2nd:0 3rd:1 Ran:7
Pre1999 - 1st:3 2nd:2 3rd:1 Ran:9
Win Prizemoney £16,142 *Total Prizemoney* £22,914
Wins * 1998 Aug Newbur (G-F) H 11f 100 105 <
* 1998 May Salisb (FRM) 12f 104
* 1997 Aug Kempto (GD) 7f 79
1999 Turf 0-7: (12f 5, 13f, 14f) (g-s, gd 2, g-f 2, frm 2)
Scopey, useful colt, effective 11 to 14f, acts on gd to frm, best on frm, has worn blinkers, likes tight tracks, excels at Salisbury and Haydock. Turf high 94. Consistent. A very game winner at Newbury in August '98, he is not quite Group class and struggled to find his form last term. *R Hannon [3-16] Mohamed Suhail.*

SECRETARIO RR 63f 4982[8]

2 b f Efisio 7.7f **(69)** - Lucidity **(59f 43a)** (Vision (USA)) 9f **(64)**
Form - 78
Record 1999 - 1st:0 2nd:0 3rd:0 Ran:2
1999 Turf 0-2: (6f, 7f) (g-f, frm)
Currently average filly. Turf high 63 (began Spt).
C W Thornton [0-2] Guy Reed.

SECRET CONQUEST BHB 82f RR 88?f 4375[11]

2 b f Secret Appeal - Mohibbah (USA) (Conquistador Cielo (USA)) 8.8f **(69)**
Form - 3801212100
Record 1999 - 1st:3 2nd:2 3rd:1 Ran:10
Win Prizemoney £11,186 *Total Prizemoney* £14,284
Wins * 1999 Aug Catter (G-F) H 6f 72 79 <
* **1999** Jly Catter (GD) H 7f 69
* **1999** Jly Haydoc (G-S) S 6f 65
1999 Turf 3-10: (6f 2-8, 7f 1-2) (gd 1-3, g-f 1-2, frm 1-5)
Useful filly, effective 6f, acts on frm. Turf high 88 - 2nd of 6 to Jemima (2 Aug Ripon 6f frm RF 3299) - also 1st of 7 giving 13lb to Natsmagirl (13 Aug Catterick RF 3599). *D W Barker [3-10] P Asquith.*

SECRET DELL (IRE) BHB 68f RR 69f 4381[12]

3 b g Doyoun 10.7f **(69)** - Summer Silence (USA) (Stop The Music (USA)) 9.2f **(71)**
Form - 26344610
Record 1999 - 1st:1 2nd:1 3rd:1 Ran:8
Pre1999 - 1st:0 2nd:0 3rd:0 Ran:3
Win Prizemoney £2,405 *Total Prizemoney* £4,358
Wins * 1999 Aug Folkes (G-S) H 16.4f 63 69 <
1999 Turf 1-8: (10f, 11f, 12f 3, 14f, 16f 1-1, 17f) (hvy, gd 1-4, g-f, frm 2)
Light-framed, average gelding, effective 10 to 16f, acts on hvy to frm, has worn blinkers, prefers tight tracks. Turf high 69 - 1st of 7 getting 6lb from Precious Persian (26 Aug Folkestone RF 3918).
E A L Dunlop [1-11] Ahmed Ali.

SECRET DESTINY (USA) BHB 88f RR 84+f 5136[3]

2 b f Cozzene (USA) 10.1f **(87)** - Dramatrix (USA) (Forty Niner (USA))
Form - 033
Record 1999 - 1st:0 2nd:0 3rd:2 Ran:3
Win Prizemoney £0 *Total Prizemoney* £1,178
1999 Turf 0-3: (7f 3) (gd 2, frm)
Currently decent filly. Turf high 84 (began Jly) - 3rd of 16 to Premier Prize (30 Oct Newmarket 7f gd RF 5136).
A G Foster [0-2] R E Sangster and B V Sangster (from P W Chapple-Hyam [0-1] Jly 1999).

SECRET DROP BHB 65f63a RR 69f 63a 5133[7]

3 b f Bustino 11f **(64)** - Safe House (Lyphard (USA)) 9.9f **(72)**
Form - 60367
Record 1999 - 1st:0 2nd:0 3rd:1 Ran:5
Win Prizemoney £0 *Total Prizemoney* £540
1999 Turf 0-4: (8f, 10f, 11f, 12f) (g-s, gd, frm 2) 1999 AW 0-1: (12f) (Fibr)
Scopey, average filly, has worn blinkers. Turf high 69 (began Spt) - 3rd of 11 to Audition (24 Spt Lingfield 10f g-s RF 4529).
K McAuliffe [0-5] G E Amey.

SECRET RENDEZVOUS (IRE) BHB 60f RR 63f 4439[17]

2 br f Petong 7.6f **(58)** - Heaven-Liegh-Grey (Grey Desire) 8.7f **(50)**
Form - 0670
Record 1999 - 1st:0 2nd:0 3rd:0 Ran:4
1999 Turf 0-4: (5f, 6f 2, 7f) (g-s, gd 2, g-f)
Average filly. Turf high 63. *A T Murphy [0-4] Peter Dodd.*

SECRET SAVER (USA) BHB 106f RR 105f 5043[4]

4 ch c Green Dancer (USA) 11.9f **(77)** - Vachti (FR) (Crystal Palace (FR)) 12.5f **(76)**
Form - 5258344
Record 1999 - 1st:0 2nd:1 3rd:1 Ran:7
Pre1999 - 1st:2 2nd:1 3rd:0 Ran:4

Win Prizemoney £15,623 *Total Prizemoney* £34,816
Wins * 1998 Jun Newcas (GD) H 12.4f 94 103++ <
* 1998 May Hamilt (G-S) 11.1f 83+
1999 Turf 0-7: (10f, 12f 5, 13f) (sft, g-s, gd, g-f 3, frm)
Well made, Pattern-class colt, effective 10 to 13f, best at 12f, acts on g-s to g-f, best on g-f. Turf high 111. Consistent. He lost his way in mid-summer, pulling hard and seeming to resent Gary Stevens's technique. Back to form when placed under John Reid and Kieren Fallon in the autumn, he will continue his career in the United States, having been sold at Tattersalls for 105,000 gns.
**Sir Michael Stoute [2-11] Saeed Suhail.*

SECRET'S OUT BHB 86f RR 87f 1292[11]

3 b g Polish Precedent (USA) 9f **(73)** - Secret Obsession (USA) (Secretariat (USA)) 9f **(79)**
Form - 100
Record 1999 - 1st:1 2nd:0 3rd:0 Ran:3
Pre1999 - 1st:0 2nd:4 3rd:0 Ran:4
Win Prizemoney £3,831 *Total Prizemoney* £9,013
Wins * **1999** Apr Windso (G-F) 10f 87 <
1999 Turf 1-3: (9f, 10f 1-1, 12f) (gd, g-f, frm 1-1)
Scopey, useful gelding, effective 8 to 10f, best at 8f, acts on gd to frm, has worn blinkers. Turf high 87 (1st run) - 1st of 17 from Montalcino (19 Apr Windsor RF 0758).
**Sir Michael Stoute [1-7] Sir Evelyn De Rothschild.*

SECRET SPICE RR 4766a[8]

2 br g Dilum (USA) 7.1f **(56)** - Ancient Secret (Warrshan (USA))
Form - 18
Record 1999 - 1st:1 2nd:0 3rd:0 Ran:2
Win Prizemoney £1,968 *Total Prizemoney* £1,968
Wins 1999 *Spt Wolver (STD) S 6f* 87+ <
1999 Turf 0-1: (8f) (hvy) 1999 AW 1-1: (6f 1-1) (Fibr 1-1)
Currently useful gelding. (1st run) - 1st of 13 from Diamond Promise (8 Spt Wolverhampton RF 4224).
**S C Williams [0-1] (from J M P Eustace [1-1] Spt 1999).*

SECRET SPRING (FR) BHB 80f84a RR 82f 84a 4874[16]

7 b g Dowsing (USA) 7f **(61)** - Nordica (Northfields (USA)) 9f **(72)**
Form - 7032440
Record 1999 - 1st:0 2nd:1 3rd:1 Ran:7
Pre1999 - 1st:4 2nd:6 3rd:3 Ran:25
Win Prizemoney £16,796 *Total Prizemoney* £39,155
Wins 1998 Jly Kempto (G-F) H 10f 82 87 <
1997 Oct Bright (G-F) 8f 81
1996 *Feb Lingfi (STD) H 8f 82 83*
1996 *Feb Lingfi (STD) 8f 81*
1999 Turf 0-6: (8f, 9f, 10f 3, 12f) (gd 2, g-f, frm 3) 1999 AW 0-1: (8f) (Equi)
Decent gelding, effective 8 to 10f, best at 10f, acts on gd to frm, best on frm, likes left handed tracks, likes tight tracks, and likes Lingfield. Turf high 85.
**Mrs L Richards [0-7] M K George (from P R Hedger [6-28] Oct 1998).*

SECRET STYLE BHB 78f RR 74f 3034a[1]

4 b g Shirley Heights 12.1f **(76)** - Rosie Potts (Shareef Dancer (USA)) 9.9f **(73)**
Form - 7608411
Record 1999 - 1st:2 2nd:0 3rd:0 Ran:7
Pre1999 - 1st:0 2nd:0 3rd:0 Ran:2
Win Prizemoney £3,327 *Total Prizemoney* £4,435
Wins * **1999** Jly Les La (G-F) H 15f 73 <
1999 Jun Nottin (GD) C 16f 70+
1999 Turf 2-7: (14f 5, 15f 1-1, 16f 1-1) (g-s 2, g-f 2-4, frm)
Scopey, above-average gelding, effective 12 to 15f, acts on g-f, has worn blinkers. Turf high 83. Consistent.
**Mrs A Malzard in JER [1-1] Mrs B Ramsden (from E A L Dunlop [1-8] Jun 1999).*

SECRET TANGO BHB 29f RR 27f 3394[13]

4 ch f Interrex (CAN) 7.7f **(51)** - Seymour Ann (Krayyan) 8.5f **(49)**
Form - 8680660
Record 1999 - 1st:0 2nd:0 3rd:0 Ran:7
Pre1999 - 1st:0 2nd:0 3rd:0 Ran:5
1999 Turf 0-4: (7f 3, 8f) (g-f, frm 3) 1999 AW 0-3: (6f 2, 8f) (Equi 3)
Leggy, very moderate filly. Turf high 27. AW high 32. Inconsistent.
**J R Best [0-10] Alan Turner (from A P Jones [0-5] Feb 1998).*

SECRET TREASURE BHB 49f RR 55f 4819[14]

3 b f Dilum (USA) 7.1f **(56)** - Surprise Surprise (Robellino (USA)) 7.6f **(80)**
Form - 06050
Record 1999 - 1st:0 2nd:0 3rd:0 Ran:5
Pre1999 - 1st:0 2nd:0 3rd:0 Ran:3
1999 Turf 0-5: (7f 3, 8f, 10f) (g-s, gd 2, g-f, frm)
Unfurnished, fair filly. Turf high 55. Inconsistent.
**H Candy [0-8] Amanda Dixon and Partners.*

SEDONA (IRE) RR 32f 3818[18]

2 b c Namaqualand (USA) - Talahari (IRE) (Roi Danzig (USA))
Form - 00
Record 1999 - 1st:0 2nd:0 3rd:0 Ran:2
1999 Turf 0-2: (5f, 6f) (g-f 2)
Currently very moderate colt. Turf high 32.
**Andrew Turnell [0-2] Mrs Claire Hollowood.*

SEDRAH (USA) BHB 79f RR 73?f 3245[5]

3 ch f Dixieland Band (USA) 10.1f **(80)** - Madame Secretary (USA) (Secretariat (USA)) 9f **(79)**
Form - 2415
Record 1999 - 1st:1 2nd:1 3rd:0 Ran:4
Pre1999 - 1st:0 2nd:0 3rd:0 Ran:2
Win Prizemoney £2,617 *Total Prizemoney* £4,214
Wins * **1999** Jun Catter (G-F) 12f 73 <
1999 Turf 1-4: (9f 2, 12f 1-2) (gd, g-f, frm 1-2)
Workmanlike, above-average filly, effective 9 to 12f, best at 9f, acts on gd to frm. Turf high 79 (1st run) - 2nd of 8 to Balladonia (20 May Goodwood 9f gd RF 1343) - also 1st of 5 from Brightest Star (30 Jun Catterick RF 2440). **E A L Dunlop [1-6] Hamdan Al Maktoum.*

SEEFINN RR 92f 5091a[12]

4 b f Night Shift (USA) 8.1f **(73)** - Adjusting (IRE) (Busted) 10.2f **(61)**
Form - 10340
1999 Turf 1-5: (7f, 8f 1-2, 9f 2) (sft, g-s 2, gd, g-f 1-1)
Useful filly, effective 8 to 10f, best at 9f, acts on sft to frm, best on g-s, and excels at Cork. Turf high 92 (began Spt) - 4th of 13 getting 8lb from Wray (17 Oct Fairyhouse 9f g-s RF 4979a) - also 1st of 14 from Royal South (5 Spt Curragh RF 4202a).
**D Hanley in IRE [2-12] McLoughlin Family Syndicate.*

SEEK RR 75+f 2584[1]

3 br c Rainbow Quest (USA) 11.2f **(81)** -Souk(IRE) (Ahonoora) 8.1f **(73)**
Form - 21
Record 1999 - 1st:1 2nd:1 3rd:0 Ran:2
Win Prizemoney £3,566 *Total Prizemoney* £4,701
Wins * **1999** Jly Pontef (G-S) 12f 75 <
1999 Turf 1-2: (12f 1-2) (frm 1-1, hrd)
Workmanlike, currently above-average colt. Turf high 75 - 1st of 8 giving 5lb to Salestria (6 Jly Pontefract RF 2584). Unraced at two, he showed promise on his Redcar debut and seemed to appreciate the easier ground when going one better in a Pontefract maiden. Should make a useful handicapper at least in 2000.
**L M Cumani [1-2] Fittocks Stud.*

SEEKING SANCTUARY RR 23f 4812[18]

2 ch f Most Welcome 8.6f **(66)** - Tjakka (USA) (Little Missouri (USA))
Form - 0
Record 1999 - 1st:0 2nd:0 3rd:0 Ran:1
1999 Turf 0-1: (7f) (gd)
Currently little account filly. **Dr J D Scargill [0-1] Mrs Susan Scargill.*

SEEKING THE PEARL (USA) RR 118f 2101a[3]

5 b m Seeking the Gold (USA) 7.4f **(80)** - Page Proof (USA) (Seattle Slew (USA)) 9.4f **(76)**
Form - 3
1999 Turf 0-1: (8f)
Currently high-class filly. (1st run) - 3rd of 14 getting 4lb from Air Jihad (13 Jun Fuchu 8f RF 2101a). The first ever Japanese-trained horse to win a Group One race in Europe when landing the 1998 Prix Maurice de Gheest, she had Muhtathir behind her when third in last season's Yasuda Kinen. **H Mori in JPN [1-3].*

SEEKING UTOPIA BHB 78f RR 80f 4899[5]

2 b f Wolfhound (USA) 7.3f **(71)** - Sakura Queen (IRE) (Woodman (USA)) 9f **(74)**
Form - 3221205

Record 1999 - 1st:1 2nd:3 3rd:1 Ran:7
Win Prizemoney £2,612 *Total Prizemoney* £6,929
Wins * 1999 Aug Mussel (G-S) 7.1f 73 <
1999 Turf 1-7: (7f 1-4, 8f 3) (gd, g-f 1-2, frm 4)
Decent filly, effective 7 to 8f, best at 7f, acts on g-f to frm, best on frm. Turf high 80 - 2nd of 8 giving 9lb to Amoras (6 Spt Bath 8f frm RF 4157) - also 1st of 8 getting 7lb from Bold State (18 Aug Musselburgh RF 3750). Consistent in her early starts, she got off the mark with a narrow victory in a Musselburgh maiden auction event on her fourth start. **S P C Woods [1-7] Mrs J Roberts.*

SEE YOU LATER BHB 95f **RR 93f** 4093[3]
2 b f Emarati (USA) 6.6f **(63)** - Rivers Rhapsody (Dominion) 8.5f **(63)**
Form - 133
Record 1999 - 1st:1 2nd:0 3rd:2 Ran:3
Win Prizemoney £3,468 *Total Prizemoney* £6,888
Wins * 1999 Jun Sandow (GD) 5f 77+ <
1999 Turf 1-3: (5f 1-2, 6f) (gd 1-2, frm)
Currently useful filly. Turf high 90. Bolted up over the minimum on her Sandown debut in June, and ran well to finish third in a Newbury Listed event next time. She looked as though she would appreciate six furlongs, but ran moderately over that trip at Salisbury. Making the running that day did not suit her at all.
**Major D N Chappell [1-3] Rex Mead.*

SEGAVIEW (IRE) BHB 66f **RR 70f** 4817[6]
3 b g Scenic 10.6f **(66)** - Little Sega (FR) (Bellypha) 9.8f **(73)**
Form - 4021786
Record 1999 - 1st:1 2nd:1 3rd:0 Ran:7
Pre1999 - 1st:0 2nd:0 3rd:0 Ran:4
Win Prizemoney £5,432 *Total Prizemoney* £7,151
Wins * 1999 Jun York (G-S) 11.9f 63 <
1999 Turf 1-7: (10f 2, 12f 1-5) (g-s 1-1, gd 4, g-f, hrd)
Leggy, above-average gelding, effective 12f, acts on g-s to gd. Turf high 73. **Mrs P Sly [1-11] Thorney Racing Club.*

SEIGNORIAL (USA) BHB 86f **RR 88f** 3222[7]
4 b c Kingmambo (USA) 10.9f **(85)** - Suavite (USA) (Alleged (USA)) 10f **(76)**
Form - 107677
Record 1999 - 1st:0 2nd:0 3rd:0 Ran:5
Pre1999 - 1st:3 2nd:0 3rd:0 Ran:7
Win Prizemoney £53,111 *Total Prizemoney* £53,111
Wins * 1998 Nov Maison (HLD) L 15f 94
* 1998 Jly Goodwo (GD) H 14f 95 99 <
* 1998 Apr Beverl (SFT) 12f 81
1999 Turf 0-5: (12f, 14f 2, 16f 2) (gd, g-f 3, frm)
Rangy, useful colt, effective 14 to 15f, acts on g-s to gd, has worn blinkers, prefers right handed tracks, likes tight tracks. Turf high 97. Unlike his half-brother Suave Dancer, he proved disappointing and seems to lack any speed.
**P W Chapple-Hyam [3-12] John Gunther.*

SELECT EQUINAME BHB 38f **RR 43f** 2867[8]
4 b g Soviet Star (USA) 8.6f **(74)** - Dame Ashfield (Grundy) 10.3f **(65)**
Form - 5550028
Record 1999 - 1st:0 2nd:1 3rd:0 Ran:7
Win Prizemoney £0 *Total Prizemoney* £612
1999 Turf 0-7: (12f 3, 14f, 16f 3) (g-s, gd 2, g-f 2, frm 2)
Moderate gelding, effective 16f, acts on g-f, has worn blinkers, likes right handed tracks, likes tight tracks. Turf high 55 - 5th of 6 giving 10lb to Fanadiyr (30 Apr Musselburgh 16f g-f RF 0938).
**D Eddy [0-7] Equiname Ltd.*

SELFISH BHB 104f **RR 110f** 5039[3]
5 ch m Bluebird (USA) 7.9f **(71)** - Sariza (Posse (USA)) 8.9f **(61)**
Form - 2112253
Record 1999 - 1st:2 2nd:3 3rd:1 Ran:7
Pre1999 - 1st:1 2nd:2 3rd:2 Ran:6
Win Prizemoney £32,923 *Total Prizemoney* £49,202
Wins * 1999 Jly Goodwo (G-F) L 7f 106 <
*** 1999** Jly Lingfi (G-F) 7.6f 83
* 1998 May Lingfi (GD) 7f 67+
1999 Turf 2-7: (7f 1-4, 8f 1-3) (g-s, g-f 3, frm 2-3)
Group-class filly, effective 7 to 8f, best at 7f, acts on g-s to frm, best on frm, likes Doncaster and Lingfield. Turf high 110 - 2nd of 7 getting 8lb from Tumbleweed Ridge (3 Spt Epsom 7f g-f RF 4119) - also 1st of 6 giving 7lb to Wannabe Grand (29 Jly Goodwood RF 3220). Kept in training for a third season, she proved herself a useful performer, beating Wannabe Grand in a Listed race at Goodwood in July. Likely to be effective from six furlongs to a mile, she has probably reached her peak.
**H R A Cecil [3-13] L Marinopoulos.*

SELHURSTPARK FLYER (IRE) BHB 83f **RR 73f** 4082[11]
8 b g Northiam (USA) 6f **(69)** - Wisdom to Know (Bay Express) 7.1f **(60)**
Form - 6660000
Record 1999 - 1st:0 2nd:0 3rd:0 Ran:7
Pre1999 - 1st:10 2nd:5 3rd:6 Ran:54
Win Prizemoney £173,835 *Total Prizemoney* £203,805
Wins * 1998 Jun Ascot (G-S) H 6f 92 105 <
* 1998 Jun Epsom (GD) H 6f 92 105 <
* 1997 Jun Ascot (G-S) H 6f 94 105 <
* 1996 Spt Epsom (G-F) 6f 94+
* 1996 Jun Epsom (GD) H 6f 79 86
* 1996 May Carlis (G-F) H 5.9f 70 75
1999 Turf 0-7: (6f 7) (gd 3, g-f 3, frm)
Above-average gelding, effective 6f, acts on gd to g-f, has worn blinkers. Turf high 87. He became the first horse in 65 years to win successive runnings of the Wokingham Handicap ('97 & '98) but could not land the hat-trick despite showing plenty of dash. Below par otherwise in '99. **J Berry [10-61] Chris & Antonia Deuters.*

SELIANA **RR 75f** 5165[3]
3 b f Unfuwain (USA) 11.4f **(74)** - Anafi (Slip Anchor) 9.8f **(73)**
Form - 3
Record 1999 - 1st:0 2nd:0 3rd:1 Ran:1
Pre1999 - 1st:0 2nd:0 3rd:0 Ran:1
Win Prizemoney £0 *Total Prizemoney* £428
1999 Turf 0-1: (12f) (g-s)
Lengthy, currently above-average filly. (1st run) - 3rd of 14 to Just Dreams (2 Nov Catterick 12f g-s RF 5165).
**G Wragg [0-2] L Marinopoulos.*

SELKING (IRE) BHB 100f95a **RR 87f 95a** 4867[2]
2 ch c Selkirk (USA) 7.9f **(76)** - Stay That Way (Be My Guest (USA)) 9.3f **(67)**
Form - 3413402
Record 1999 - 1st:1 2nd:1 3rd:2 Ran:7
Win Prizemoney £2,857 *Total Prizemoney* £7,481
Wins * 1999 Jun Carlis (G-F) 5f 78+ <
1999 Turf 1-6: (5f 1-4, 6f 2) (g-s, g-f 3, frm, hrd 1-1) 1999 AW 0-1: (6f) (Fibr)
Useful colt, effective 5 to 6f, best at 5f, acts on g-f to hrd - acts on Fibr. Turf high 87 - also 1st of 13 from Corunna (24 Jun Carlisle RF 2258). (1st run) - 2nd of 6 giving 2lb to Shouf Al Badou (13 Oct Wolverhampton 6f Fibr RF 4867). Got off the mark when winning a modest Carlisle maiden in June, and has run pleasingly in Listed races since. Ran well against a decent sort on his Fibresand debut and can surely win races on sand. **K R Burke [1-7] Nigel Shields.*

SELKIRK ROSE (IRE) BHB 49f48a **RR 47f 48a** 4835[15]
4 b f Pips Pride 6.7f **(70)** - Red Note (Rusticaro (FR)) 8.2f **(65)**
Form - 704778040474127406360
Record 1999 - 1st:1 2nd:1 3rd:1 Ran:21
Pre1999 - 1st:1 2nd:1 3rd:0 Ran:15
Win Prizemoney £5,865 *Total Prizemoney* £9,904
Wins * 1999 Jun Nottin (GD) H 6.1f 49 52
1997 Aug Carlis (G-F) 5f 75+ <
1999 Turf 1-14: (6f 1-8, 7f 6) (gd 5, g-f 2, frm 1-7) 1999 AW 0-7: (5f 4, 6f 3) (Fibr 7)
Scopey, moderate filly, effective 7 to 8f, best at 8f, acts on g-f, has worn blinkers, likes tight tracks. Turf high 55. AW high 56. Consistent.
**J G Given [1-21] Probe Racing Syndicate (from Miss L A Perratt [1-15] Oct 1998).*

SELTITUDE (IRE) **RR 103f** 5014a[9]
3 b f Fairy King (USA) 7.7f **(75)** - Dunoof (Shirley Heights) 10.3f **(74)**
Form - 10
1999 Turf 1-2: (6f 1-1, 7f) (sft 1-1)
Currently very useful filly. Turf high 103 (began Spt) - also 1st of 11 getting 2lb from Stella Berine (17 Spt Chantilly RF 4512a).
**J E Hammond in FR [1-2].*

SELTON HILL (IRE) BHB 61f **RR 62f** 5124[4]
2 b c Bin Ajwaad (IRE) -Ivory Gull (USA) (Storm Bird (CAN)) 10.3f **(74)**
Form - 75644
Record 1999 - 1st:0 2nd:0 3rd:0 Ran:5
Win Prizemoney £0 *Total Prizemoney* £476
1999 Turf 0-5: (8f 4, 9f) (sft, gd, g-f, frm 2)
Average colt. Turf high 62 (began Spt).
**N A Callaghan [0-5] Gallagher Equine Ltd.*

SEMI CIRCLE BHB 46f **RR 46f** 5168[2]
4 b f Noble Patriarch 12.2f **(43)** - True Ring (High Top) 10.2f **(67)**
Form - 808444314042
Record 1999 - 1st:1 2nd:1 3rd:1 Ran:12
Pre1999 - 1st:4 2nd:1 3rd:1 Ran:17
Win Prizemoney £15,801 *Total Prizemoney* £20,533

Wins									
* **1999**	Aug	Mussel	(G-F)	H	14f	40	44	
* 1998	Jly	Ripon	(GD)	H	12.3f	52	61	<
* 1998	Jly	Redcar	(G-S)	H	14.1f	52	56	
* 1998	Jun	Beverl	(G-S)	H	12f	49	54	
* 1997	Jly	Catter	(G-F)	S	7f		60	

1999 Turf 1-12: (12f 4, 14f 1-3, 16f 5) (g-s, gd, g-f 1-5, frm 5)
Scopey, moderate filly, effective 11 to 14f, best at 12f, acts on g-s to frm, often wears blinkers (effectively), prefers right handed tracks, favours tight tracks, excels at Redcar and Beverley, does well at Ripon. **T D Easterby [5-29] C H Stevens.*

SEMIRAMIS BHB 63f61a **RR 64f 61a** 4950[12]
2 b f Darshaan 11.9f **(81)** -Sulitelma (USA)(The Minstrel (CAN))10f **(72)**
Form - 4670
Record 1999 - 1st:0 2nd:0 3rd:0 Ran:4
Win Prizemoney £0 *Total Prizemoney* £207
1999 Turf 0-4: (6f 2, 7f, 8f) (g-f 2, frm 2)
Average filly. Turf high 64 (began Spt).
**Sir Mark Prescott [0-4] Miss K Rausing.*

SENA DESERT BHB 82f **RR 84f** 4954[6]
3 b f Green Desert (USA) 7.8f **(78)** - Sueboog (IRE) (Darshaan) 9.9f **(84)**
Form - 60222137026
Record 1999 - 1st:1 2nd:4 3rd:1 Ran:11
Pre1999 - 1st:0 2nd:0 3rd:1 Ran:3
Win Prizemoney £3,733 *Total Prizemoney* £10,954
Wins * **1999** Jun Chepst (G-F) 10.2f 82 <
1999 Turf 1-11: (8f, 9f 2, 10f 1-5, 12f 3) (gd 3, g-f 1-7, frm)
Decent filly, effective 9 to 12f, best at 10f, acts on gd to g-f, best on g-f, has worn blinkers, prefers tight tracks. Turf high 88 - also 1st of 6 from Whispering (29 Jun Chepstow RF 2389). Consistent. Won a weak Chepstow maiden in June after a number of placed efforts in similar events. Has been found wanting when tried in Listed company. **C E Brittain [1-14] Mohamed Obaida.*

SENDAWAR (IRE) RR 128f 4246a[1]
3 b c Priolo (USA) 10.9f **(71)** - Sendana (FR) (Darshaan) 9.9f **(84)**
Form - 12111
1999 Turf 4-5: (8f 3-3, 10f 1-1, 11f) (hvy 1-1, g-s, gd 2-2, g-f 1-1)
Top-class colt. Turf high 128 - 1st of 9 getting 5lb from Gold Away (5 Spt Longchamp RF 4246a) - also 1st of 11 from Aljabr (15 Jun Ascot RF 1997). A very smart French-trained colt who finished runner-up to subsequent Prix du Jockey-Club, Irish Derby and Arc winner Montjeu in the Prix Greffulhe, he then ran out an impressive winner of the French Guineas, a race in which he and runner-up Dansili came away from the rest. He laid claim to the title of top European three-year-old miler with an equally impressive victory over Aljabr and company in the St James's Palace Stakes at Royal Ascot and, despite a three-month break, was again impressive in winning the Prix du Moulin in September. Missed the Queen Elizabeth II Stakes due to the bottomless ground but he will stay in training as a four-year-old, and will be the benchmark against which all other European milers are measured.
**A deRoyerDupre in FR [4-5] Aga Khan.*

SEND IT TO PENNY (IRE) BHB 49f **RR 42f** 4026[4]
2 b f Marju (IRE) 9.2f **(76)** - Sparkish (IRE) (Persian Bold) 9.3f **(66)**
Form - 0504
Record 1999 - 1st:0 2nd:0 3rd:0 Ran:4
1999 Turf 0-4: (5f 3, 6f) (g-f, frm 3)
Moderate filly. Turf high 42. **M W Easterby [0-4] Guy Reed.*

SEND ME AN ANGEL (IRE) RR 59f 4815[7]
2 ch f Lycius (USA) 8.8f **(71)** - Niamh Cinn Oir (IRE) (King of Clubs) 7.1f **(57)**
Form - 7
Record 1999 - 1st:0 2nd:0 3rd:0 Ran:1
1999 Turf 0-1: (7f) (gd)
Currently fair filly.
**S P C Woods [0-1] Kaniz Bloodstock Investments Ltd.*

SENOR HURST BHB 42f **RR 46f** 2470[9]
4 b g Young Senor (USA) 8f **(43)** - Broadhurst (Workboy) 7.3f **(46)**
Form - 300
Record 1999 - 1st:0 2nd:0 3rd:1 Ran:3
Pre1999 - 1st:1 2nd:1 3rd:0 Ran:6
Win Prizemoney £2,700 *Total Prizemoney* £3,792
Wins * 1998 Jly Yarmou (GD) C 8f 49 <
1999 Turf 0-3: (8f 2, 10f) (gd 3)
Scopey, moderate gelding, effective 8 to 11f, best at 8f, acts on gd to hrd. Turf high 46 (1st run) - 3rd of 20 getting 5lb from Antarctic Storm (16 May Ripon 8f gd RF 1260). Inconsistent.
**Mrs P Sly [1-14] Mrs P M Sly.*

SENURE (USA) BHB 97f **RR 97f** 4683[18]
3 b c Nureyev (USA) 8.4f **(84)** - Diese (USA) (Diesis) 9.3f **(69)**
Form - 312520
Record 1999 - 1st:1 2nd:2 3rd:1 Ran:6
Pre1999 - 1st:1 2nd:0 3rd:0 Ran:3
Win Prizemoney £9,972 *Total Prizemoney* £30,076
Wins * **1999** May Salisb (G-F) H 9.9f 87 92 <
* 1998 Oct Leices (G-S) 7f 87
1999 Turf 1-6: (8f, 10f 1-4, 11f) (gd 3, frm 1-3)
Well made, very useful colt, effective 7 to 11f, best at 10f, acts on gd to frm, best on frm. Turf high 97 - 2nd of 16 giving 4lb to Komistar (18 Spt Newbury 10f frm RF 4404) - also 1st of 11 getting 3lb from Diablo Dancer (2 May Salisbury RF 0985). He stays a mile and a quarter and developed into a leading fancy for the Cambridgeshire. Disappointing on soft ground there, he is quick actioned and worth another chance on a better surface.
**R Charlton [2-9] K Abdulla.*

SEPTEMBER HARVEST (USA) BHB 50f **RR 43f** 5197[16]
3 ch g Mujtahid (USA) 7.4f **(69)** - Shawgatny (USA) (Danzig Connection (USA)) 8f **(68)**
Form - 0062246518564000

Sendawar was a superstar at a mile

Record 1999 - 1st:1 2nd:2 3rd:0 Ran:16
Pre1999 - 1st:0 2nd:0 3rd:2 Ran:9
Win Prizemoney £3,730 *Total Prizemoney* £6,927
Wins * 1999 Aug Pontef (G-F) H 8f 54 56 <
1999 Turf 1-16: (5f, 6f, 7f, 8f 1-5, 10f 6, 12f, 16f) (g-s 3, gd 4, g-f 3, frm 1-6)
Workmanlike, moderate gelding, effective 7 to 8f, best at 7f, acts on g-f to frm, best on frm, has worn blinkers. Turf high 64. Consistent.
**Mrs S Lamyman [1-10] P Lamyman (from B J Meehan [0-15] Jun 1999).*

SERAPE BHB 29f30a **RR 33f 30a** 4541^{6}

6 b m Primo Dominie 7.2f **(67)** - Absaloute Service (Absalom) 7.2f **(58)**
Form - 786
Record 1999 - 1st:0 2nd:0 3rd:0 Ran:3
Pre1999 - 1st:0 2nd:4 3rd:1 Ran:25
Win Prizemoney £0 *Total Prizemoney* £3,642
1999 Turf 0-3: (6f, 7f, 8f) (g-f, frm 2)
Very moderate mare, effective 6 to 7f, best at 6f, acts on gd to g-f, best on g-f. Turf high 33. Inconsistent.
**M A Peill [0-19] Mrs Shirley France (from Mrs L Stubbs [0-10] Jly 1997).*

SERAPHINA (IRE) BHB 100f **RR 99f** 4596^{4}

2 ch f Pips Pride 6.7f **(70)** - Angelic Sounds (IRE) (The Noble Player (USA)) 6.5f **(67)**
Form - 13808204
Record 1999 - 1st:1 2nd:1 3rd:1 Ran:8
Win Prizemoney £5,303 *Total Prizemoney* £29,138
Wins * 1999 Mar Doncas (GD) 5f 74 <
1999 Turf 1-8: (5f 1-5, 6f 3) (gd 5, g-f 1-3)
Very useful filly, effective 6f, acts on gd. Turf high 99 - 2nd of 9 to Jemima (19 Aug York 6f gd RF 3769). She improved throughout the campaign, running her best races when held up over six furlongs. Unlikely to stay much beyond that trip, she could find life tough in 2000. **B A McMahon [1-8] J D Graham.*

SERDAL (USA) **RR 64f** 1127^{3}

3 b g Gulch (USA) 9.6f **(79)** - Ginny Dare (USA) (Pilgrim (USA))
Form - 33
Record 1999 - 1st:0 2nd:0 3rd:2 Ran:2
Win Prizemoney £0 *Total Prizemoney* £909
1999 Turf 0-2: (7f, 10f) (g-s, g-f)
Light-framed, average gelding, always wears blinkers. Turf high 64. **Sir Michael Stoute [0-2] Hamdan Al Maktoum.*

SERENA (IRE) **RR 91f** $4479a^{5}$

3 ch f Rainbow Quest (USA) 11.2f **(81)** - Green Lucia (Green Dancer (USA)) 10.3f **(74)**
Form - 13228065
1999 Turf 1-8: (8f 2, 9f 2, 10f 1-4) (g-s 1-2, gd 2, g-f 3, frm)
Useful filly, effective 8 to 9f, best at 9f, acts on hvy to g-f. Turf high 91 - 5th of 9 getting 3lb from Scottish Memories (19 Spt Curragh 9f g-s RF 4479a). Consistent. **C Collins in IRE [1-10] Gerald Jennings.*

SEREN HILL BHB 87f **RR 83f** 5220^{3}

3 ch f Sabrehill (USA) 8.5f **(64)** - Seren Quest **(81f)** (Rainbow Quest (USA)) 10.4f **(75)**
Form - 323313
Record 1999 - 1st:1 2nd:1 3rd:4 Ran:6
Pre1999 - 1st:1 2nd:0 3rd:0 Ran:4
Win Prizemoney £10,787 *Total Prizemoney* £16,178
Wins * 1999 Spt Haydoc (SFT) H 14f 77 82+ <
* 1998 Nov Redcar (G-S) H 8f 69 76
1999 Turf 1-6: (12f 3, 13f, 14f 1-1, 17f) (sft, g-s 1-1, gd 2, g-f, frm)
Unfurnished, decent filly, effective 8 to 17f, acts on sft to frm, prefers tight tracks. Turf high 83 - 3rd of 15 getting 2lb from Il Principe (6 Nov Doncaster 17f sft RF 5220) - also 1st of 17 getting 4lb from Jawah (25 Spt Haydock RF 4553). Consistent. Suited by the step up to 14 furlongs when scoring in soft ground at Haydock.
**G A Butler [2-7] The Fairy Story Partnership (from J W Hills [0-3] Aug 1998).*

SEREN TEG BHB 57f77a **RR 42f 77a** 5199^{21}

3 ch f Timeless Times (USA) 6.1f **(56)** - Hill of Fare (Brigadier Gerard) 9.3f **(58)**
Form - 14124202353450000
Record 1999 - 1st:0 2nd:3 3rd:2 Ran:14
Pre1999 - 1st:2 2nd:0 3rd:1 Ran:9
Win Prizemoney £3,977 *Total Prizemoney* £10,427
Wins 1998 *Dec Lingfi (STD)* C 6f *73* <
1998 *Nov Wolver (STD)* 6f *69*
1999 Turf 0-12: (5f 3, 6f 8, 7f) (gd 8, g-f 2, frm 2) 1999 AW 0-2: (6f 2) (Equi, Fibr)
Workmanlike, above-average filly, effective 5 to 6f, best at 6f, acts on gd to hrd - acts on AW, best on Equi, likes tight tracks, excels at Lingfield, does well at Windsor. Turf high 73 - 2nd of 10 giving 1lb to Clunie (11 Jun Goodwood 6f gd RF 1918). AW high 77 (1st run) - 2nd of 9 getting 1lb from Bartholomew (7 Jan Lingfield 6f Equi RF 0047).
**R M Flower [0-5] K & D Computers Ltd (from B Palling [2-18] Jly 1999).*

SERENUS (USA) BHB 74f **RR 76?f** 1256^{8}

6 b g Sunshine Forever (USA) 13.2f **(76)** - Curl And Set (USA) (Nijinsky (CAN)) 10.3f **(77)**
Form - 18
Record 1999 - 1st:1 2nd:0 3rd:0 Ran:2
Pre1999 - 1st:0 2nd:1 3rd:2 Ran:4
Win Prizemoney £7,360 *Total Prizemoney* £10,748
Wins * 1999 May Kempto (G-F) H 12f 70 72 <
1999 Turf 1-2: (12f 1-1, 14f) (frm 1-2)
Above-average gelding. Turf high 72 (1st run) - 1st of 16 getting 1lb from Borgia (3 May Kempton RF 0998).
**N J Henderson [6-20] W V M W & Mrs E S Robins (from Lord Huntingdon [0-4] Spt 1996).*

SERGEANT IMP (IRE) BHB 35f41a **RR 31f 41a** 5127^{11}

4 b g Mac's Imp (USA) 5.6f **(54)** - Genzyme Gene (Riboboy (USA)) 14f **(54)**
Form - 64882888060
Record 1999 - 1st:0 2nd:1 3rd:0 Ran:11
Pre1999 - 1st:1 2nd:0 3rd:0 Ran:22
Win Prizemoney £2,550 *Total Prizemoney* £3,910
Wins * 1998 Apr Bright (GD) 6f 48 <
1999 Turf 0-11: (7f 3, 8f 6, 9f, 10f) (gd 2, g-f 2, frm 5, hrd 2)
Strong, very moderate gelding, effective 6 to 10f, acts on g-s to frm, has worn blinkers, likes tight tracks. Turf high 47 - 2nd of 10 getting 18lb from Roisin Splendour (25 Jun Goodwood 7f frm RF 2285). **P Mitchell [1-33] W R Mann.*

SERGEANT SLIPPER BHB 49f51a **RR 46f 51a** 5187^{4}

2 ch c Never so Bold 7.1f **(62)** - Pretty Scarce **(23a)** (Handsome Sailor)
Form - 006525004
Record 1999 - 1st:0 2nd:1 3rd:0 Ran:9
Win Prizemoney £0 *Total Prizemoney* £512
1999 Turf 0-6: (5f 5, 6f) (gd 4, g-f 2) 1999 AW 0-3: (5f 3) (Fibr 3)
Fair colt, effective 5f, acts on gd - acts on Fibr, often wears blinkers (extremely effectively). Turf high 46 - 4th of 16 giving 3lb to Parkside Prospect (3 Nov Musselburgh 5f gd RF 5187). AW high 47 - 2nd of 8 to Gem of Wisdom (28 Jun Southwell 5f Fibr RF 2378).
**C Smith [0-9] C Smith.*

SERGEANT YORK BHB 80f **RR 87df** 4758^{9}

3 b c Be My Chief (USA) 10.2f **(62)** - Metaphysique (FR) (Law Society (USA)) 9.9f **(70)**
Form - 626506260370
Record 1999 - 1st:0 2nd:2 3rd:1 Ran:12
Pre1999 - 1st:1 2nd:1 3rd:2 Ran:7
Win Prizemoney £3,436 *Total Prizemoney* £12,811
Wins * 1998 May Hamilt (SFT) 5f 69 <
1999 Turf 0-12: (8f 6, 9f, 10f 5) (gd 4, g-f 5, frm 3)
Workmanlike, useful colt, effective 6 to 9f, acts on g-s to g-f. Turf high 93 - 2nd of 7 to Mensa (7 Apr Ripon 9f g-f RF 0613). Rather disappointing, albeit in the face of some stiff opposition.
**C Smith [1-19] A E Needham.*

SERPENTINE **RR 100f** 4102^{1}

3 ch c Grand Lodge (USA) - Lake Pleasant (IRE) (Elegant Air) 13.2f **(61)**
Form - 4811631

Record 1999 - 1st:3 2nd:0 3rd:1 Ran:7
Pre1999 - 1st:1 2nd:0 3rd:2 Ran:3
Win Prizemoney £32,532 *Total Prizemoney* £35,079
Wins * 1999 Spt York (G-F) H 11.9f 96 100 <
*** 1999** Jly Doncas (G-F) H 10.3f 83 94
*** 1999** Jly Lingfi (G-F) 10f 88
* 1998 Spt Warwic (G-F) 7f 82
1999 Turf 3-7: (7f, 8f, 10f 2-4, 12f 1-1) (gd, g-f 1-2, frm 2-4)
Small, very useful colt, effective 10 to 12f, best at 10f, acts on gd to frm. Turf high 100 - 1st of 7 giving 8lb to Toto Caelo (2 Spt York RF 4102) - also 1st of 6 giving 12lb to Ermine (15 Jly Doncaster RF 2845). He improved as he was stepped-up in trip, putting up a game performance when winning at York in September. Raced only on quick ground, he is open to improvement and could develop into an Ebor candidate in 2000.
**J R Fanshawe [4-10] Lord Vestey.*

SERRA NEGRA RR 56f
5136[12]
2 b f Kris 10f **(75)** - Congress (IRE) (Dancing Brave (USA)) 8.4f **(76)**
Form - 0
Record 1999 - 1st:0 2nd:0 3rd:0 Ran:1
1999 Turf 0-1: (7f) (gd)
Currently fair filly. **W J Haggas [0-1] Cyril Humphris.*

SERRATE BHB 26f28a RR 2f 28a
1649[17]
5 ch m Sharpo 7.5f **(68)** - Baino Clinic (USA) (Sovereign Dancer (USA)) 11.2f **(68)**
Form - 0058680
Record 1999 - 1st:0 2nd:0 3rd:0 Ran:7
Pre1999 - 1st:0 2nd:0 3rd:0 Ran:6
1999 Turf 0-1: (6f) (frm) 1999 AW 0-6: (5f 2, 6f, 7f, 8f 2) (Fibr 6)
Little account filly, often wears blinkers. AW high 29.
**R F Marvin [0-7] Plus Print (from D Shaw [0-6] May 1998).*

SERVICE CHARGE BHB 52f55a RR 59df 55a
4719[14]
3 ch f Pharly (FR) 11.5f **(64)** - Absaloute Service (Absalom) 7.2f **(58)**
Form - 03450
Record 1999 - 1st:0 2nd:0 3rd:1 Ran:5
Win Prizemoney £0 *Total Prizemoney* £537
1999 Turf 0-4: (5f, 6f 2, 7f) (gd 2, g-f, frm) 1999 AW 0-1: (6f) (Fibr)
Fair filly. Turf high 59.
**J M P Eustace [0-5] Major M G Wyatt.*

SERVICE STAR (IRE) BHB 74f RR 80f
5215[9]
2 b br c Namaqualand (USA) - Shenley Lass (Prince Tenderfoot (USA)) 9f **(61)**
Form - 744220
Record 1999 - 1st:0 2nd:2 3rd:0 Ran:6
Win Prizemoney £0 *Total Prizemoney* £4,645
1999 Turf 0-5: (6f, 7f, 8f 3) (g-s, g-f, frm 3) 1999 AW 0-1: (7f) (Fibr)
Decent colt, effective 8f, acts on frm. Turf high 80 - 2nd of 20 to Bold State (1 Spt York 8f frm RF 4080). Has ability, but looks less than enthusiatic. **M A Jarvis [0-6] N S Yong.*

SESTINO (FR) RR 115f
2097a[3]
4 b c Shirley Heights 12.1f **(76)** - Stellina (IRE) (Caerleon (USA)) 8.6f **(71)**
Form - 23
1999 Turf 0-2: (12f 2) (sft, g-s)
High-class colt, effective 10 to 12f, best at 12f, acts on hvy to gd, best on sft. Turf high 115 (1st run) - 2nd of 5 getting 5lb from Public Purse (24 May Saint-Cloud 12f sft RF 1712a). He ran well to finish runner-up in the Prix Jean de Chaudenay on his reappearance last season, but was a disappointing odds-on shot behind Capri in the Grand Prix de Chantilly.
**Mme C Head in FR [0-6] G A Oldham.*

SET AND MATCH (IRE) BHB 48f RR 55f
4948[15]
3 ch g Second Set (IRE) 9.2f **(67)** - Kate Labelle (Teenoso (USA)) 9.9f **(72)**
Form - 000
Record 1999 - 1st:0 2nd:0 3rd:0 Ran:3
Pre1999 - 1st:0 2nd:0 3rd:0 Ran:1
1999 Turf 0-3: (10f, 11f, 12f) (g-f, frm 2)
Scopey, fair gelding. Turf high 55.
**Miss Gay Kelleway [0-4] A P Griffin.*

SET SAIL RR 70f
5194[6]
2 b f Distant Relative 7f **(69)** - Sail Loft (Shirley Heights) 10.3f **(74)**
Form - 46
Record 1999 - 1st:0 2nd:0 3rd:0 Ran:2
1999 Turf 0-2: (5f, 6f) (gd 2)
Currently above-average filly. Turf high 70 (began Oct).
**D R C Elsworth [0-2] C J Harper.*

SEVEN BHB 60f63a RR 61f 63a
5035[6]
4 ch g Weldnaas (USA) 8.4f **(55)** - Polly's Teahouse (Shack (USA)) 5.8f **(53)**
Form - 1024326
Record 1999 - 1st:1 2nd:2 3rd:1 Ran:7
Pre1999 - 1st:0 2nd:1 3rd:0 Ran:10
Win Prizemoney £2,172 *Total Prizemoney* £4,231
Wins 1999 *Mar Southw (STD) C 7f 71 <*
1999 Turf 0-2: (7f 2) (g-s, frm) 1999 AW 1-5: (7f 1-4, 8f) (Fibr 1-5)
Workmanlike, average gelding, effective 7 to 8f, best at 7f, acts on g-f - acts on Fibr, mostly wears blinkers (very effectively), likes left handed tracks, likes tight tracks. Turf high 61 (began Spt). AW high 71 (1st run) - 1st of 10 giving 2lb to Abtaal (22 Mar Southwell RF 0458). Consistent.
**Miss S J Wilton [0-6] John Pointon and Sons (from B Smart [1-11] Mar 1999).*

SEVEN NO TRUMPS BHB 100f RR 106f
5036[2]
2 ch c Pips Pride 6.7f **(70)** - Classic Ring (IRE) (Auction Ring (USA)) 8.6f **(65)**
Form - 0115520322
Record 1999 - 1st:2 2nd:3 3rd:1 Ran:10
Win Prizemoney £6,648 *Total Prizemoney* £16,226
Wins * 1999 May Newcas (G-F) 5f 78 <
*** 1999** May Nottin (FRM) 6.1f 78 <
1999 Turf 2-10: (5f 1-3, 6f 1-7) (g-s 2, gd 5, g-f 1-2, hrd 1-1)
Pattern-class colt, effective 6f, acts on g-s to gd. Turf high 106 - 2nd of 8 giving 2lb to Halland Park Girl (23 Oct Doncaster 6f g-s RF 5036). A tough colt, he made all to win at Nottingham and Newcastle, and has stepped up on that form since. He is effective over five or six and looks worth a try over further.
**B W Hills [2-10] Paul McNamara.*

SEVEN OF SPADES BHB 68f61a RR 70f 61a
5214[5]
2 b c Mistertopogigo (IRE) - Misty Arch (Starch Reduced) 11.5f **(52)**
Form - 520035
Record 1999 - 1st:0 2nd:1 3rd:1 Ran:6
Win Prizemoney £0 *Total Prizemoney* £1,170
1999 Turf 0-4: (5f 4) (g-s, gd, g-f, frm) 1999 AW 0-2: (5f, 6f) (Fibr 2)
Above-average colt, effective 5f, acts on frm. Turf high 74 - 2nd of 12 to Happy Times (5 Jly Musselburgh 5f frm RF 2555). AW high 42 (began Oct). **R A Fahey [0-6] B L Cassidy.*

SEVEN O SEVEN BHB 50f48a RR 8f 48a
4863[12]
6 b g Skyliner 6.8f **(51)** - Fille de Phaeton (Sun Prince) 12.4f **(52)**
Form - 434400
Record 1999 - 1st:0 2nd:0 3rd:1 Ran:6
Win Prizemoney £0 *Total Prizemoney* £1,196
1999 Turf 0-1: (10f) (gd) 1999 AW 0-5: (8f 2, 10f, 12f, 15f) (Equi 2, Fibr 3)
Average gelding, effective 10f, - acts on Equi. AW high 61 - 3rd of 11 giving 2lb to Shogun (14 Jan Lingfield 10f Equi RF 0096).
**P D Cundell [0-10] John Davies (Stonehill).*

SEVEN SPRINGS (IRE) BHB 51f RR 46f
5149[9]
3 b c Unblest - Zaydeen (Sassafras (FR)) 9.6f **(69)**
Form - 10800045000000
Record 1999 - 1st:0 2nd:0 3rd:0 Ran:13
Pre1999 - 1st:1 2nd:1 3rd:0 Ran:3
Win Prizemoney £1,882 *Total Prizemoney* £2,795
Wins * 1998 *Nov Wolver (STD) 6f 76 <*
1999 Turf 0-7: (5f 2, 6f 3, 7f 2) (gd 2, g-f 3, frm, hrd) 1999 AW 0-6: (6f 5, 7f) (Fibr 6)
Workmanlike, moderate colt, effective 6f, - acts on Fibr, likes left handed tracks, likes tight tracks. Turf high 61. AW high 59. Becoming disappointing. **R Hollinshead [1-16] N Chapman.*

SEVEN STARS BHB 42a RR 26f
5071[14]
3 b g Rudimentary (USA) 8.2f **(66)** - Carlton Glory (Blakeney) 10.5f **(64)**

Form - 07000
Record 1999 - 1st:0 2nd:0 3rd:0 Ran:5
Pre1999 - 1st:0 2nd:0 3rd:0 Ran:3
1999 Turf 0-4: (6f, 8f 2, 11f) (gd 2, g-f, frm) 1999 AW 0-1: (7f) (Fibr)
Workmanlike, little account gelding, has worn blinkers. Turf high 32. **W Storey [0-1] W Storey (from M H Tompkins [0-7] Jly 1999).*

SEVENTH HEAVEN BHB 43f **RR 68f** 4427^{14}
4 ch g Clantime 6.6f **(57)** - Portvally (Import) 6.6f **(68)**
Form - 0
Record 1999 - 1st:0 2nd:0 3rd:0 Ran:1
Pre1999 - 1st:0 2nd:0 3rd:0 Ran:8
Win Prizemoney £0 *Total Prizemoney* £238
1999 Turf 0-1: (5f) (frm)
Average gelding, has worn blinkers. Inconsistent.
**J S Wainwright [0-1] J S Wainwright (from D Nicholls [0-4] Spt 1997).*

SEWARDS FOLLY BHB 56f **RR 62f** 3737^{5}
3 b f Rudimentary (USA) 8.2f **(66)** - Anchorage (IRE) (Slip Anchor) 9.8f **(73)**
Form - 047675
Record 1999 - 1st:0 2nd:0 3rd:0 Ran:6
Pre1999 - 1st:0 2nd:0 3rd:0 Ran:1
Win Prizemoney £0 *Total Prizemoney* £258
1999 Turf 0-6: (6f 3, 7f 2, 8f) (g-s, g-f 3, frm 2)
Light-framed, average filly. Turf high 66.
**J A R Toller [0-7] G M Cobey.*

SHAAN MADARY (FR) RR 53f 4655^{13}
2 b br f Darshaan 11.9f **(81)** - Madary (CAN) **(89f)** (Green Desert (USA)) 8.6f **(78)**
Form - 0
Record 1999 - 1st:0 2nd:0 3rd:0 Ran:1
1999 Turf 0-1: (7f) (gd)
Currently fair filly. **B W Hills [0-1] Hilal Salem.*

SHAANXI ROMANCE (IRE) BHB 53f60a **RR 49f 60a** 4165^{8}
4 b g Darshaan 11.9f **(81)** - Easy Romance (USA) (Northern Jove (CAN)) 9.7f **(66)**
Form - 070061408
Record 1999 - 1st:1 2nd:0 3rd:0 Ran:8
Pre1999 - 1st:1 2nd:1 3rd:1 Ran:6
Win Prizemoney £5,577 *Total Prizemoney* £8,691
Wins * 1999 Aug Carlis (FRM) 6.9f 57
1998 *Mar Wolver (STD) 8.5f 67* <
1999 Turf 1-8: (7f 1-3, 8f 5) (gd 2, g-f, frm 1-5)
Scopey, average gelding, effective 8f, acts on g-s, often wears blinkers, likes left handed tracks, favours tight tracks. Turf high 57. **I Semple [1-9] Andy Dickie (from J Noseda [0-1] Oct 1998).*

SHABAASH (IRE) BHB 46f42a **RR 53f 42a** 5056^{9}
3 b c Mujadil (USA) 7.7f **(70)** - Folly Vision (IRE) (Vision (USA)) 9f **(64)**
Form - 5256146000343800
Record 1999 - 1st:1 2nd:1 3rd:2 Ran:15
Pre1999 - 1st:1 2nd:0 3rd:1 Ran:10
Win Prizemoney £5,004 *Total Prizemoney* £7,946
Wins * 1999 *Feb Lingfi (STD) C 7f 59*
1998 Jly Folkes (G-F) H 5f 70 <
1999 Turf 0-4: (7f, 8f 3) (frm 2, hrd 2) 1999 AW 1-11: (7f 1-5, 8f 5, 10f) (Equi 1-10, Fibr)
Fair colt, effective 5 to 7f, acts on g-f - acts on Equi. Turf high 53. AW high 62 (1st run) - 2nd of 5 giving 1lb to Dream On Me (1 Jan Lingfield 7f Equi RF 0005). Becoming disappointing. He is a winner on turf and Equitrack in modest company, but looks inconsistent.
**P Howling [1-16] S J Hammond (from G Lewis [1-9] Spt 1998).*

SHABBY CHIC (USA) RR 110f 3039a^{3}
3 f Red Ransom (USA) 8.6f **(83)** - Style Setter (USA)
Form - 163
1999 Turf 1-3: (9f, 10f 1-2) (sft 1-1, g-s, gd)
Currently Group-class filly. Turf high 110 - 3rd of 4 getting 3lb from Star Of Akkar (16 Jly Chantilly 9f gd RF 3039a). Capable of smart form, she stays a mile and a quarter and acts on most types of ground. **J deRoualle in FR [1-3].*

SHABLAM (USA) RR 90+f 4379^{1}
2 b c Lear Fan (USA) 10.4f **(80)** - Awestamind (USA) (Flying Paster (USA))
Form - 31
Record 1999 - 1st:1 2nd:0 3rd:1 Ran:2
Win Prizemoney £5,691 *Total Prizemoney* £6,345
Wins * 1999 Spt Ayr (G-S) 7f 79 <
1999 Turf 1-2: (6f, 7f 1-1) (gd 1-1, frm)
Currently useful colt. Turf high 90 (1st run) (began Aug) - 3rd of 8 to Las Ramblas (28 Aug Newmarket 6f frm RF 3963).
**Sir Michael Stoute [1-2] Saeed Suhail.*

SHADE D'AMETHYSTE (FR) BHB 44f **RR 40f** 2667^{7}
4 ch f Shadeed (USA) 7.7f **(72)** - Coastal Jewel (IRE) (Kris) 9.5f **(73)**
Form - 2067
Record 1999 - 1st:0 2nd:0 3rd:0 Ran:2
Pre1999 - 1st:0 2nd:1 3rd:0 Ran:2
Win Prizemoney £0 *Total Prizemoney* £732
1999 Turf 0-2: (8f 2) (g-f, frm)
Moderate filly, has worn blinkers. Turf high 40.
**M C Pipe [1-12] Andrew John Crabb.*

SHADES OF LOVE BHB 43f75a **RR 35f 75a** 4121^{5}
5 b h Pursuit of Love 9.5f **(69)** - Shadiliya (Red Alert) 7.6f **(66)**
Form - 146123705
Record 1999 - 1st:1 2nd:1 3rd:1 Ran:7
Pre1999 - 1st:2 2nd:1 3rd:1 Ran:18
Win Prizemoney £8,673 *Total Prizemoney* £11,555
Wins * 1999 *Jan Lingfi (STD) H 7f 70 71* <
* 1998 *Nov Lingfi (STD) H 7f 65 68*
* 1998 *Mar Southw (STD) H 7f 57 64*
1999 Turf 0-3: (7f 2, 8f) (gd, g-f, frm) 1999 AW 1-4: (7f 1-4) (Equi 1-4)
Above-average colt, effective 7f, - acts on AW, best on Equi, prefers left handed tracks, prefers tight tracks. Turf high 35. AW high 71 - 2nd of 7 getting 5lb from Hugwity (30 Jan Lingfield 7f Equi RF 0197) - also 1st of 14 giving 8lb to Ajig Dancer (14 Jan Lingfield RF 0097). Becoming disappointing.
**V Soane [3-25] The Pursuers.*

SHADIANN (IRE) BHB 73f **RR 73f** 3696^{11}
5 b g Darshaan 11.9f **(81)** - Shakanda (IRE) (Shernazar) 10.2f **(73)**
Form - 54280
Record 1999 - 1st:0 2nd:1 3rd:0 Ran:5
Pre1999 - 1st:0 2nd:2 3rd:1 Ran:5
Win Prizemoney £0 *Total Prizemoney* £5,606
1999 Turf 0-5: (12f 4, 13f) (gd 2, g-f 2, frm)
Above-average gelding. Turf high 73 (1st run) - 5th of 16 giving 5lb to Serenus (3 May Kempton 12f frm RF 0998). Consistent. Probably better known as a hurdler, but he ran a couple of fair races in handicap company on the Flat last season.
**P G Murphy [3-18] Michael Blackburn & John Brown (from L M Cumani [0-5] Oct 1997).*

SHADOOF BHB 97f **RR 100f** 5031^{1}
5 b h Green Desert (USA) 7.8f **(78)** - Bermuda Classic (Double Form) 7.3f **(58)**
Form - 302131
Record 1999 - 1st:2 2nd:1 3rd:2 Ran:6
Pre1999 - 1st:3 2nd:2 3rd:3 Ran:18
Win Prizemoney £65,759 *Total Prizemoney* £89,290
Wins * 1999 Oct Newbur (G-S) H 10f 92 96 <
*** 1999** Spt Epsom (GD) H 10.1f 84 89
* 1998 Jun Epsom (GD) H 10.1f 84 88
* 1998 May Redcar (G-F) H 10f 77 85
* 1997 Jun Haydoc (G-F) H 10.5f 75 78
1999 Turf 2-6: (10f 2-5, 11f) (g-s 1-1, gd 4, g-f 1-1)
Very useful colt, effective 10f, acts on g-s to gd, likes left handed tracks. Turf high 100 - 3rd of 33 giving 11lb to She's Our Mare (2 Oct Newmarket 10f gd RF 4683) - also 1st of 16 giving 15lb to Flossy (22 Oct Newbury RF 5031). In fine form in the second half of the season, winning twice in good style and finishing third in the Cambridgeshire, he was sold for 105,000 gns at Tattersalls in the autumn to race in Saudi Arabia. **W R Muir [5-24] J Bernstein.*

SHADOW PRINCE RR 50f 4229^{6}
2 ch c Machiavellian (USA) 9.8f **(83)** - Shadywood (Habitat) 9.4f **(70)**
Form - 6
Record 1999 - 1st:0 2nd:0 3rd:0 Ran:1

1999 Turf 0-1: (7f) (frm)
Currently fair colt. **R Charlton [0-1] Hippodrome Racing.*

SHADY DEAL BHB 54a **RR 54f** 4673[15]
3 b c No Big Deal - Taskalady (Touching Wood (USA)) 8.2f **(55)**
Form - 54422030600800
Record 1999 - 1st:0 2nd:2 3rd:1 Ran:13
Pre1999 - 1st:0 2nd:0 3rd:0 Ran:4
Win Prizemoney £0 *Total Prizemoney* £2,943
1999 Turf 0-8: (6f 5, 7f 3) (g-s, gd 3, g-f 2, frm 2) 1999 AW 0-5: (6f, 7f 2, 8f 2) (Equi 4, Fibr)
Neat, fair colt, effective 6f, acts on gd to frm. Turf high 66 (1st run) - 3rd of 13 getting 13lb from Roseum (15 May Newbury 6f gd RF 1239). AW high 57. Inconsistent.
**M D I Usher [0-17] The Sundial Partnership.*

SHADY POINT (IRE) RR 76f 4097[3]
2 b f Unfuwain (USA) 11.4f **(74)** - Warning Shadows (IRE) **(110f)** (Cadeaux Genereux)
Form - 73
Record 1999 - 1st:0 2nd:0 3rd:1 Ran:2
Win Prizemoney £0 *Total Prizemoney* £770
1999 Turf 0-2: (7f 2) (frm 2)
Currently above-average filly. Turf high 76 (began Jly). She has shown ability and will come into her own over at least a mile.
**C E Brittain [0-2] Sheikh Marwan Al Maktoum.*

SHAFAQ (USA) BHB 82f **RR 76f** 3060[3]
2 b f Dayjur (USA) 6.8f **(79)** - Shemaq (USA) **(94f)** (Blushing John (USA))
Form - 13
Record 1999 - 1st:1 2nd:0 3rd:1 Ran:2
Win Prizemoney £3,850 *Total Prizemoney* £4,480
Wins * **1999** Jly Lingfi (G-F) 6f 76+ <
1999 Turf 1-2: (6f 1-2) (frm 1-2)
Currently above-average filly. Turf high 76 (1st run) (began Jly) - 1st of 6 getting 5lb from Don't Surrender (9 Jly Lingfield RF 2683). She made all and battled on well to win on her Lingfield debut, but pulled too hard next time and paid the price.
**R W Armstrong [1-2] Hamdan Al Maktoum.*

SHAFFISHAYES BHB 66f65a **RR 68f 65a** 5168[5]
7 ch g Clantime 6.6f **(57)** - Mischievous Miss (Niniski (USA)) 10.6f **(65)**
Form - 23305814455
Record 1999 - 1st:1 2nd:1 3rd:2 Ran:11
Pre1999 - 1st:6 2nd:7 3rd:5 Ran:34
Win Prizemoney £27,353 *Total Prizemoney* £42,364
Wins * **1999** Aug Ripon (GD) H 12.3f 62 67
* 1998 Spt Nottin (GD) 10f 73 <
* 1998 Apr Thirsk (G-S) 12f 73 <
* 1997 Jun Newmar (SFT) H 12f 68 70
* 1997 May Newcas (GD) H 12.4f 65 69
* 1996 Apr Pontef (G-F) 8f 66
* 1995 Apr Mussel (GD) 7.1f 45
1999 Turf 1-11: (10f 2, 12f 1-6, 14f 2, 15f) (g-s, gd 3, g-f 1-5, frm 2)
Average gelding, effective 10 to 14f, best at 12f, acts on sft to frm, best on gd, prefers left handed tracks, prefers tight tracks, excels at Thirsk, likes Pontefract. Turf high 73 (1st run) - 2nd of 4 giving 16lb to High Tatra (17 Apr Thirsk 12f gd RF 0740) - also 1st of 13 getting 13lb from Flower O'Cannie (21 Aug Ripon RF 3819).
**Mrs M Reveley [7-45] P Davidson-Brown.*

SHAFTESBURY (IRE) RR 4697[12]
3 b c Sadler's Wells (USA) 11.3f **(87)** - Surmise (USA) (Alleged (USA)) 10f **(76)**
Form - 0
Record 1999 - 1st:0 2nd:0 3rd:0 Ran:1
1999 Turf 0-1: (10f) (g-s)
Scopey, very poor colt. (DEAD)
**Sir Michael Stoute [0-1] Mrs John Magnier.*

SHAHED BHB 79f **RR 72f** 5059[3]
2 ch c Arazi (USA) 9.2f **(74)** - Nafhaat (USA) (Roberto (USA)) 10f **(76)**
Form - 443
Record 1999 - 1st:0 2nd:0 3rd:1 Ran:3
Win Prizemoney £0 *Total Prizemoney* £1,155
1999 Turf 0-3: (7f 3) (g-s 2, frm)
Currently above-average colt. Turf high 72 (began Spt) - 3rd of 12 to Masterpiece (25 Oct Lingfield 7f g-s RF 5059).
**M P Tregoning [0-3] Hamdan Al Maktoum.*

SHAHIK (USA) BHB 50f51a **RR 58?f 51a** 3301[8]
9 b g Spectacular Bid (USA) 10.8f **(63)** - Sham Street (USA) (Sham (USA)) 9.5f **(68)**
Form - 08
Record 1999 - 1st:0 2nd:0 3rd:0 Ran:2
Pre1999 - 1st:2 2nd:4 3rd:2 Ran:28
Win Prizemoney £6,782 *Total Prizemoney* £9,395
Wins 1996 *Nov Wolver (STD) H 9.4f 60 65*
1996 Oct Salisb (G-S) H 10f 61 68 <
1999 Turf 0-2: (12f 2) (g-f, frm)
Fair gelding, has worn blinkers. Turf high 37 (began Jly).
**K C Comerford [0-9] A Kimber (from D HaydnJones [2-14] Aug 1997).*

SHAHRANI BHB 25f23a **RR 23f 23a** 774[12]
7 b g Lear Fan (USA) 10.4f **(80)** - Windmill Princess (Gorytus (USA)) 7.8f **(60)**
Form - 74300
Record 1999 - 1st:0 2nd:0 3rd:1 Ran:5
Pre1999 - 1st:0 2nd:1 3rd:0 Ran:13
Win Prizemoney £0 *Total Prizemoney* £1,109
1999 Turf 0-1: (17f) (sft) 1999 AW 0-4: (12f, 16f 3) (Fibr 4)
Little account gelding, effective 16f, acted on g-f. AW high 25. (DEAD)
**M C Chapman [1-16] Mrs E C Rosbottom (from M C Pipe [2-8] Jly 1996).*

SHAHRUR (USA) BHB 63f **RR 63f** 5220[13]
6 b br g Riverman (USA) 9.7f **(78)** - Give Thanks (Relko) 9.9f **(59)**
Form - 0510
Record 1999 - 1st:1 2nd:0 3rd:0 Ran:4
Pre1999 - 1st:1 2nd:1 3rd:1 Ran:9
Win Prizemoney £4,669 *Total Prizemoney* £6,522
Wins * **1999** Spt Kempto (G-F) H 14.4f 62 63
1997 May Down R (Y-S) 14f 77 <
1999 Turf 1-4: (14f 1-3, 17f) (sft, g-f, frm 1-2)
Average gelding, effective 14 to 16f, acts on gd to frm, prefers right handed tracks. Turf high 63 (began Jly) - 1st of 13 from Miss Pin Up (8 Spt Kempton RF 4218). Consistent. A decent hurdler, he has reverted to jumping since winning at Kempton.
**G L Moore [5-22] Mrs Elizabeth Kiernan (from D K Weld in IRE [1-5] Jun 1997).*

SHAIBANI RR 86+f 5104[1]
2 b c Muhtarram (USA) - Haboobti (Habitat) 9.4f **(70)**
Form - 1
Record 1999 - 1st:1 2nd:0 3rd:0 Ran:1
Win Prizemoney £3,297 *Total Prizemoney* £3,297
Wins * **1999** Oct Yarmou (G-S) 7f 86+ <
1999 Turf 1-1: (7f 1-1) (gd 1-1)
Currently useful colt. (1st run) - 1st of 11 giving 5lb to Fair Impression (27 Oct Yarmouth RF 5104).
**B W Hills [1-1] H R H Prince Fahd Salman.*

SHAKIEYL (IRE) BHB 78f **RR 77f** 1732[15]
3 b c Grand Lodge (USA) - Frill (Henbit (USA)) 9f **(61)**
Form - 51570
Record 1999 - 1st:1 2nd:0 3rd:0 Ran:5
Win Prizemoney £2,723 *Total Prizemoney* £2,913
Wins * **1999** Apr Hamilt (HVY) 11.1f 77 <
1999 Turf 1-5: (10f 2, 11f 1-1, 12f 2) (hvy 1-1, g-s, gd 2, frm)
Workmanlike, above-average colt, has worn blinkers. Turf high 77 - 1st of 9 getting 20lb from Bullet (10 Apr Hamilton RF 0640).
**M R Channon [1-5] A Merza.*

SHAKIYR (FR) BHB 28f60a **RR 30f 60a** 4717[11]
8 gr g Lashkari 13.1f **(52)** - Shakamiyn (Nishapour (FR)) 9.1f **(61)**
Form - 800
Record 1999 - 1st:0 2nd:0 3rd:0 Ran:3
Pre1999 - 1st:6 2nd:6 3rd:6 Ran:50
Win Prizemoney £18,775 *Total Prizemoney* £29,716
Wins * *1998 Jan Wolver (STD) H 16.2f 60 63*
* *1997 Jan Wolver (STD) S 14.8f 59*
* *1996 Jan Wolver (STD) H 16.2f 65 70* <

* 1995 *Apr Wolver (STD) H 12f 61 66*
* 1995 *Feb Wolver (STD) H 12f 55 57*
* 1995 *Jan Southw (STD) 11f 48*

1999 Turf 0-2: (16f, 17f) (gd, frm) 1999 AW 0-1: (16f) (Fibr)

Average gelding, effective 16f, - acts on Fibr, has worn blinkers, likes left handed tracks. Turf high 8 (began Spt).

**R Hollinshead [6-53] R Hollinshead.*

SHALAD'OR BHB 70f **RR 74f** 3862^{15}

4 b f Golden Heights 7.1f **(50)** - Shalati (FR) (High Line) 10.3f **(70)**
Form - 70450560

Record	**1999 -**	1st:0	2nd:0	3rd:0	Ran:8
	Pre1999 -	1st:3	2nd:4	3rd:1	Ran:14

Win Prizemoney £12,500 *Total Prizemoney* £24,197

Wins	* 1998	Jly	Windso	(GD)	H	8.3f	83	91+	<
	* 1998	Jun	Bath	(G-S)	H	8f	79	83	
	* 1997	Jly	Leices	(GD)		7f		61	

1999 Turf 0-8: (8f 3, 10f 4, 11f) (g-s, gd 2, g-f 2, frm 3)

Light-framed, above-average filly, effective 8 to 10f, best at 8f, acts on gd to frm, best on g-f, likes right handed tracks, prefers tight tracks. Turf high 79. **B R Millman [3-22] G Palmer.*

SHALARI (IRE) BHB 37f37a **RR 34f 37a** 1987^{16}

3 b f Shalford (IRE) 7.8f **(63)** - Hinari Disk Deck (Indian King (USA)) 7.4f **(64)**
Form - 080

Record	**1999 -**	1st:0	2nd:0	3rd:0	Ran:3
	Pre1999 -	1st:0	2nd:0	3rd:0	Ran:8

1999 Turf 0-2: (5f, 8f) (gd, g-f) 1999 AW 0-1: (7f) (Fibr)

Leggy, very moderate filly. Turf high 34.

**Miss Kate Milligan [0-1] Wetherby Racing Bureau 33 (from J L Eyre [0-10] Apr 1999).*

SHALARISE (IRE) BHB 69f66a **RR 70f 66a** 4221^{11}

2 ch f Shalford (IRE) 7.8f **(63)** - Orthorising (Aragon) 8.1f **(60)**
Form - 45224310

Record	**1999 -**	1st:1	2nd:2	3rd:1	Ran:8

Win Prizemoney £3,403 *Total Prizemoney* £8,896

Wins * 1999 Aug Newcas (GD) 5f 70 <

1999 Turf 1-6: (5f 1-6) (gd 2, g-f 1-1, frm 3) 1999 AW 0-2: (5f, 6f)(Fibr 2)

Above-average filly, effective 5f, acts on g-f to frm, best on frm, has worn blinkers. Turf high 70 - 1st of 7 giving 4lb to Boadicea The Red (20 Aug Newcastle RF 3799). AW high 56 (began Aug).

**Miss L A Perratt [1-8] Third Estate Racing Club.*

SHALATEENO BHB 65f **RR 63f** 3916^{3}

6 b m Teenoso (USA) 10.5f **(62)** - Shalati (FR) (High Line) 10.3f **(70)**
Form - 72065523

Record	**1999 -**	1st:0	2nd:2	3rd:1	Ran:8
	Pre1999 -	1st:3	2nd:6	3rd:5	Ran:31

Win Prizemoney £9,993 *Total Prizemoney* £27,385

Wins	* 1998	Jun	Salisb	(G-S)	H	12f	72	80	<
	* 1997	Jun	Salisb	(G-F)	H	12f	64	62	
	* 1996	Aug	Chepst	(GD)	H	10.2f	56	63	

1999 Turf 0-8: (12f 5, 14f 2, 18f) (gd 2, g-f 2, frm 4)

Average mare, has broken blood-vessels, effective 10 to 16f, acts on gd to frm, best on gd, likes left handed tracks, prefers tight tracks. Turf high 70.

**B R Millman [3-31] G Palmer (from M R Channon [0-8] Jly 1996).*

SHALIMAR (IRE) **RR 82f** 5136^{6}

2 b f Indian Ridge 7.6f **(74)** - Athens Belle (IRE) (Groom Dancer (USA))
Form - 26

Record	**1999 -**	1st:0	2nd:1	3rd:0	Ran:2

Win Prizemoney £0 *Total Prizemoney* £989

1999 Turf 0-2: (7f 2) (gd, g-f)

Currently decent filly. Turf high 82 (began Oct) - 6th of 16 to Premier Prize (30 Oct Newmarket 7f gd RF 5136).

**A G Foster [0-1] Lady Bamford (from P W Chapple-Hyam [0-1] Oct 1999).*

SHALLOW GROUND (IRE) **RR 90f** $4470a^{8}$

3 b f Common Grounds 8.1f **(66)** - Shabarana (FR) (Nishapour (FR)) 9.1f **(61)**
Form - 1627738

1999 Turf 1-7: (5f, 6f 1-4, 7f 2) (sft 1-2, g-s 2, gd 2, g-f)

Useful filly, has broken blood-vessels, effective 6 to 7f, acts on sft to g-s. Turf high 91 - 2nd getting 10lb from Immovable Option (1 May Cork 6f sft RF 1035a). Inconsistent.

**M Halford in IRE [1-8] S R Mullion.*

SHALL WE DANCE **RR 77f** 4718^{12}

3 b f Rambo Dancer (CAN) 8.4f **(59)** - Angel Fire (Nashwan (USA))
Form - 5412640

Record	**1999 -**	1st:1	2nd:1	3rd:0	Ran:7

Win Prizemoney £3,598 *Total Prizemoney* £6,520

Wins * 1999 Jly Ripon (GD) 8f 84 <

1999 Turf 1-7: (6f, 7f, 8f 1-4, 10f) (gd 1-4, g-f, frm 2)

Workmanlike, above-average filly, effective 8f, acts on gd to frm, best on gd. Turf high 84 - 1st of 10 getting 5lb from Zaman (5 Jly Ripon RF 2566). **C W Thornton [1-7] Guy Reed.*

SHALYAH (IRE) BHB 43f43a **RR 48f 43a** 619^{11}

4 ch f Shalford (IRE) 7.8f **(63)** - Baheejah (Northfields (USA)) 9f **(72)**
Form - 0680

Record	**1999 -**	1st:0	2nd:0	3rd:0	Ran:1
	Pre1999 -	1st:0	2nd:3	3rd:2	Ran:19

Win Prizemoney £0 *Total Prizemoney* £4,563

1999 Turf 0-1: (8f) (gd)

Workmanlike, moderate filly, effective 8f, acts on g-f to frm, best on g-f, has worn blinkers.

**N P Littmoden [0-6] Ciaran McClintock (from Mrs V C Ward [0-1] Aug 1998).*

SHAMAH **RR 87f** 4812^{2}

2 ch f Unfuwain (USA) 11.4f **(74)** - Shurooq (USA) (Affirmed (USA)) 9.3f **(79)**
Form - 22

Record	**1999 -**	1st:0	2nd:2	3rd:0	Ran:2

Win Prizemoney £0 *Total Prizemoney* £2,360

1999 Turf 0-2: (7f, 8f) (gd, frm)

Currently useful filly. Turf high 87 (began Spt) - 2nd of 19 to Petrushka (11 Oct Leicester 7f gd RF 4812). She made hotpot High Walden work very hard on her Leicester debut over a mile, but was just beaten over a furlong shorter at the same track next time.

**B W Hills [0-2] Hamdan Al Maktoum.*

SHAMAN BHB 61f **RR 68f** 4870^{11}

2 b c Fraam - Magic Maggie (Beveled (USA)) 9f **(59)**
Form - 72241030

Record	**1999 -**	1st:1	2nd:2	3rd:1	Ran:8

Win Prizemoney £2,635 *Total Prizemoney* £4,423

Wins 1999 Aug Folkes (G-S) S 7f 68 <

1999 Turf 1-8: (6f 2, 7f 1-6) (g-s, gd 1-2, g-f 2, frm 3)

Average colt, effective 6 to 7f, best at 6f, acts on g-s to frm. Turf high 68 (began Jly) - 2nd of 3 giving 4lb to Sontime (31 Jly Lingfield 6f frm RF 3273) - also 1st of 16 giving 5lb to All Roses (26 Aug Folkestone RF 3911). Consistent.

**G L Moore [0-3] C F Sparrowhawk (from M R Channon [1-5] Aug 1999).*

SHAMANARA (IRE) **RR 94f** $4362a^{3}$

3 b f Danehill (USA) 9.1f **(79)** - Shamaniya (IRE) **(96f)** (Doyoun) 9f **(69)**
Form - 3

1999 Turf 0-1: (8f) (gd)

Currently useful filly. (1st run) - 3rd of 9 to Oriental Fashion (8 Spt Chantilly 8f gd RF 4362a). **A deRoyerDupre in FR [0-1].*

SHAMAYNE BHB 54f **RR 68f** 5193^{12}

3 ch f Most Welcome 8.6f **(66)** -La Primavera (Northfields(USA)) 9f **(72)**
Form - 800

Record	**1999 -**	1st:0	2nd:0	3rd:0	Ran:3

1999 Turf 0-3: (8f 3) (sft, gd 2)

Scopey, currently average filly. Turf high 68 (began Aug).

**P J Makin [0-3] T G Warner.*

SHAMBLES BHB 31f29a **RR 41f 29a** 538^{10}

4 ch f Elmaamul (USA) 8.1f **(70)** - Rambadale (Vaigly Great) 7f **(58)**
Form - 0

Record	**1999 -**	1st:0	2nd:0	3rd:0	Ran:1
	Pre1999 -	1st:0	2nd:1	3rd:3	Ran:16

Win Prizemoney £0 *Total Prizemoney* £1,573

1999 Turf 0-1: (12f) (gd)

Light-framed, moderate filly, effective 11 to 14f, acts on g-s to hrd,

prefers tight tracks, excels at Beverley and Windsor, likes Yarmouth. **G G Margarson [0-17] G G Margarson.*

SHAMEL BHB 73f **RR 74f** 3058[4]
3 b c Unfuwain (USA) 11.4f **(74)** - Narjis (USA) (Blushing Groom (FR)) 10.3f **(76)**
Form - 53134
Record 1999 - 1st:1 2nd:0 3rd:2 Ran:5
Pre1999 - 1st:0 2nd:1 3rd:0 Ran:3
Win Prizemoney £3,054 *Total Prizemoney* £5,450
Wins 1999 Jun Yarmou (GD) H 14.1f 66 69+ <
1999 Turf 1-5: (10f, 12f 2, 14f 1-1, 16f) (g-s, g-f 1-2, frm, hrd)
Scopey, above-average colt, effective 7 to 14f, acts on g-f to frm. Turf high 74 - also 1st of 9 giving 7lb to Masonic (10 Jun Yarmouth RF 1888). An improving colt, he seemed to appreciate the step up to fourteen furlongs when scoring at Yarmouth.
**D Shaw [0-1] J C Fretwell (from J L Dunlop [1-7] Jun 1999).*

SHAMOKIN BHB 27f44a **RR 36df 44a** 3978[7]
7 b g Green Desert (USA) 7.8f **(78)** - Shajan (Kris) 9.5f **(73)**
Form - 243756067
Record 1999 - 1st:0 2nd:1 3rd:1 Ran:9
Pre1999 - 1st:0 2nd:0 3rd:2 Ran:20
Win Prizemoney £0 *Total Prizemoney* £1,456
1999 Turf 0-6: (7f 3, 8f 2, 11f) (gd, g-f, frm 4) 1999 AW 0-3: (7f 2, 8f) (Fibr 3)
Moderate gelding, effective 7 to 8f, - acts on Fibr, has worn blinkers, likes left handed tracks, likes tight tracks. Turf high 37. AW high 49 (1st run) - 2nd of 10 to Abtaal (12 Feb Southwell 7f Fibr RF 0282). Becoming disappointing. **F Watson [0-29] F Watson.*

SHAMROCK CITY (IRE) BHB 100f **RR 88+f** 4210[1]
2 b c Rock City 8.8f **(62)** - Actualite (Polish Precedent (USA)) 10.2f **(60)**
Form - 421
Record 1999 - 1st:1 2nd:1 3rd:0 Ran:3
Win Prizemoney £4,435 *Total Prizemoney* £12,357
Wins * 1999 Spt Doncas (G-F) 8f 88+ <
1999 Turf 1-3: (7f 2, 8f 1-1) (gd 1-1, g-f 2)
Currently useful colt. Turf high 88 (began Jly) - 1st of 12 from Capa (8 Spt Doncaster RF 4210). Ran encouragingly behind Hataab at Ascot on his debut, and was a fine second to King's Best in the Acomb next time. A comfortable winner on his final start, he will stay further and is an interesting prospect for his small stable. **P Howling [1-3] Liam Sheridan.*

SHAMSAN (IRE) RR 58f 2965[6]
2 ch c Night Shift (USA) 8.1f **(73)** - Awayil (USA) **(78f)** (Woodman (USA)) 9f **(74)**
Form - 06
Record 1999 - 1st:0 2nd:0 3rd:0 Ran:2
1999 Turf 0-2: (5f, 6f) (g-f 2)
Currently fair colt. Turf high 58. **B Hanbury [0-2] A Al-Rostamani.*

SHAMSAT MTOTO BHB 69f **RR 71f** 3196[5]
3 b f Mtoto 11.5f **(71)** - Jasoorah (IRE) (Sadler's Wells (USA)) 10f **(76)**
Form - 455
Record 1999 - 1st:0 2nd:0 3rd:0 Ran:3
Win Prizemoney £0 *Total Prizemoney* £188
1999 Turf 0-3: (10f, 12f 2) (gd, frm 2)
Tall, currently above-average filly. Turf high 71 - 5th of 14 to Kittiwake (23 Jun Kempton 10f frm RF 2241).
**M A Jarvis [0-3] Sheikh Ahmed Al Maktoum.*

SHAM SHARIF RR 48f 4419[13]
2 b f Be My Chief (USA) 10.2f **(62)** - Syrian Queen **(76f)** (Slip Anchor) 9.8f **(73)**
Form - 00
Record 1999 - 1st:0 2nd:0 3rd:0 Ran:2
1999 Turf 0-2: (7f 2) (gd 2)
Currently moderate filly. Turf high 48 (began Aug).
**B W Hills [0-2] Wafic Said.*

SHAMWARI SONG BHB 45f45a **RR 42f 45a** 2446[6]
4 b g Sizzling Melody 6.3f **(49)** - Spark Out (Sparkler) 8.4f **(55)**
Form - 885000086
Record 1999 - 1st:0 2nd:0 3rd:0 Ran:7
Pre1999 - 1st:3 2nd:1 3rd:1 Ran:20
Win Prizemoney £7,984 *Total Prizemoney* £10,392
Wins 1998 May Newcas (G-F) H 8f 67 72 <
1998 May Beverl (G-F) C 7.5f 57
1997 Oct Newcas (G-F) 7f 63
1999 Turf 0-5: (8f 3, 9f, 10f) (g-f 3, frm, hrd) 1999 AW 0-2: (7f, 10f) (Equi, Fibr)
Scopey, moderate gelding, effective 8f, acts on g-f to frm, has worn blinkers. Turf high 42. AW high 42.
**Mrs L C Jewell [0-7] Gallagher Equine Ltd (from N A Callaghan [0-8] Jan 1999).*

SHANAZ BHB 28f **RR 13f** 4228[10]
4 b f Then Again 7.4f **(52)** - Trecauldah (Treboro (USA))
Form - 00
Record 1999 - 1st:0 2nd:0 3rd:0 Ran:2
Pre1999 - 1st:0 2nd:0 3rd:0 Ran:6
1999 Turf 0-2: (8f, 10f) (frm 2)
Unfurnished, poor filly. Turf high 13 (began Jly). Inconsistent.
**D Burchell [0-9] The Valleys Partners.*

SHANGHAI CRAB (USA) BHB 60f70a **RR 61f 70a** 4865[5]
3 b c Manila (USA) 10f **(81)** - Saraa Ree (USA) (Caro)
Form - 1430420505
Record 1999 - 1st:1 2nd:1 3rd:1 Ran:10
Win Prizemoney £2,773 *Total Prizemoney* £5,079
Wins * 1999 *Mar Southw (STD)* *8f* *74* <
1999 Turf 0-8: (8f 3, 9f, 10f 4) (g-s, g-f 3, frm 4) 1999 AW 1-2: (8f 1-2) (Fibr 1-2)
Above-average colt, effective 8f, acts on frm - acts on Fibr. Turf high 66 - 3rd of 17 giving 1lb to Final Dividend (13 May Salisbury 8f frm RF 1189). AW high 74 (1st run) - 1st of 9 from Heathyards Jake (22 Mar Southwell RF 0459). **M L W Bell [1-10] Christopher Wright.*

SHANGHAI LADY RR 68f 5217[17]
3 b f Sabrehill (USA) 8.5f **(64)** - Session (Reform) 8.9f **(62)**
Form - 04100
Record 1999 - 1st:1 2nd:0 3rd:0 Ran:5
Pre1999 - 1st:0 2nd:0 3rd:0 Ran:1
Win Prizemoney £3,382 *Total Prizemoney* £3,632
Wins * 1999 Spt Bright (SFT) 8f 68+ <
1999 Turf 1-5: (8f 1-5) (g-s 1-2, g-f, frm 2)
Workmanlike, average filly, effective 8f, acts on g-s. Turf high 68 - also 1st of 8 from Mabrookah (29 Spt Brighton RF 4631).
**J H M Gosden [1-6] Pacific Hawk (HK) Ltd.*

SHANGHAI LIL BHB 28f50a **RR 31f 50a** 5145[10]
7 b m Petong 7.6f **(58)** - Toccata (USA) (Mr Leader (USA)) 9.8f **(66)**
Form - 071137048610
Record 1999 - 1st:3 2nd:0 3rd:1 Ran:12
Pre1999 - 1st:6 2nd:4 3rd:3 Ran:44
Win Prizemoney £22,918 *Total Prizemoney* £27,584
Wins * 1999 *Oct Wolver (STD) H 12f 46 48*
*** 1999** *Feb Lingfi (STD) H 10f 41 50*
*** 1999** *Feb Lingfi (STD) H 12f 41 45*
***** *1998 Jun Wolver (STD) H 12f 44 46*
***** *1998 Mar Wolver (STD) C 12f 47*
***** *1998 Feb Lingfi (SLW) 10f 41*
***** *1997 Jan Lingfi (STD) H 8f 46 51* <
***** *1996 Dec Lingfi (STD) H 8f 40 45*
***** *1995 Apr Wolver (STD) H 6f 40 42*
1999 Turf 0-2: (12f 2) (sft, frm) 1999 AW 3-10: (10f 1-1, 12f 2-7, 13f 2) (Equi 2-5, Fibr 1-5)
Moderate mare, has broken blood-vessels, effective 10 to 13f, - acts on AW, best on Equi, has worn blinkers, favours left handed tracks, favours tight tracks, and excels at Lingfield. AW high 50 - 1st of 6 giving 14lb to Wild Nettle (18 Feb Lingfield RF 0312) - also 1st of 9 getting 9lb from Forest Dream (16 Oct Wolverhampton RF 4922). **M J Fetherston-Godley [9-56] M J Fetherston-Godley.*

SHANILLO BHB 47f **RR 48f** 4591[3]
4 gr g Anshan 8.2f **(63)** - Sea Fret (Habat) 7.6f **(61)**
Form - 000008253
Record 1999 - 1st:0 2nd:1 3rd:1 Ran:9
Pre1999 - 1st:1 2nd:0 3rd:0 Ran:4
Win Prizemoney £3,209 *Total Prizemoney* £4,341
Wins * 1998 Apr Folkes (SFT) 6f 75 <
1999 Turf 0-9: (6f 3, 7f 4, 8f 2) (sft, g-s, gd 3, g-f 2, frm, hrd)

Moderate gelding, effective 6f, acts on sft.
**M R Channon [1-13] The Piccolo Boys.*

SHANNON DORE (IRE) BHB 84f **RR 78f** 4680[9]
2 b f Turtle Island (IRE) - Solas Abu (IRE) (Red Sunset) 8.2f **(63)**
Form - 222010
Record 1999 - 1st:1 2nd:3 3rd:0 Ran:6
Win Prizemoney £3,947 *Total Prizemoney* £8,746
Wins * **1999** Spt Nottin (GD) 6.1f 78 <
1999 Turf 1-6: (5f 2, 6f 1-2, 7f 2) (gd 1-3, g-f, frm 2)
Above-average filly, effective 5 to 6f, best at 6f, acts on gd to frm. Turf high 78 (began Jly) - 1st of 12 getting 5lb from Strahan (25 Spt Nottingham RF 4560). **B Hanbury [1-6] B Hanbury.*

SHANTUNG (IRE) BHB 38a **RR 54f** 223[8]
4 ch f Anshan 8.2f **(63)** - Bamian (USA) (Topsider (USA)) 8.3f **(71)**
Form - 058
Record 1999 - 1st:0 2nd:0 3rd:0 Ran:1
Pre1999 - 1st:0 2nd:0 3rd:0 Ran:11
Win Prizemoney £0 *Total Prizemoney* £198
1999 AW 0-1: (10f) (Equi)
Neat, fair filly, has worn blinkers.
**K McAuliffe [0-12] K & B Wetherell, Mrs Burke, C Krosinsky.*

SHANUKE (IRE) BHB 19f20a **RR 12f 20a** 3023[9]
7 b m Contract Law (USA) 8.9f **(54)** - Auntie Ponny (Last Fandango) 7.8f **(61)**
Form - 560700
Record 1999 - 1st:0 2nd:0 3rd:0 Ran:6
Pre1999 - 1st:1 2nd:0 3rd:0 Ran:17
Win Prizemoney £2,040 *Total Prizemoney* £2,453
Wins * 1998 Jly Bright (G-F) SH 11.9f 30 30 <
1999 Turf 0-4: (12f 4) (gd, g-f, frm, hrd) 1999 AW 0-2: (13f, 16f) (Equi 2)
Poor mare, effective 12f, acts on gd, has worn blinkers, likes left handed tracks. Turf high 12. AW high 12.
**S Woodman [1-19] R Howitt (from J S Moore [0-9] Jun 1995).*

SHAPOUR (IRE) RR 80f 4839[2]
2 b c Sadler's Wells (USA) 11.3f **(87)** - Sharamana (IRE) **(97+f)** (Darshaan) 9.9f **(84)**
Form - 82
Record 1999 - 1st:0 2nd:1 3rd:0 Ran:2
Win Prizemoney £0 *Total Prizemoney* £1,450
1999 Turf 0-2: (7f, 8f) (gd, frm)
Currently decent colt. Turf high 80 (began Aug) - 2nd of 19 to Imperial Rocket (12 Oct Leicester 8f gd RF 4839).
**Sir Michael Stoute [0-2] H H Aga Khan.*

SHARAF (IRE) BHB 46f53a **RR 46f 53a** 4413[5]
6 b g Sadler's Wells (USA) 11.3f **(87)** - Marie de Flandre (FR) (Crystal Palace (FR)) 12.5f **(76)**
Form - 2873045
Record 1999 - 1st:0 2nd:1 3rd:1 Ran:7
Pre1999 - 1st:2 2nd:5 3rd:3 Ran:30
Win Prizemoney £6,918 *Total Prizemoney* £17,123
Wins * 1998 Jly Bath (GD) H 17.2f 47 51
1996 Apr Folkes (G-F) 12f 80+ <
1999 Turf 0-5: (16f 4, 18f) (g-s, gd 2, g-f, frm) 1999 AW 0-2: (15f 2) (Fibr 2)
Moderate gelding, effective 14 to 18f, best at 17f, acts on gd to frm - acts on Fibr, has worn blinkers, likes left handed tracks, likes tight tracks, does well at Bath. Turf high 50 (1st run) - 2nd of 13 getting 29lb from Mithak (19 May Chepstow 18f gd RF 1329). AW high 47 (1st run) (began Aug) - 3rd of 12 giving 18lb to Pawsible (6 Aug Wolverhampton 15f Fibr RF 3441).
**W R Muir [1-31] Mrs A E Chapman (from J L Dunlop [1-7] Jly 1996).*

SHARAVAWN (IRE) BHB 40f **RR 35f** 5123[10]
2 b f College Chapel - My My Marie (Artaius (USA)) 9f **(69)**
Form - 0000
Record 1999 - 1st:0 2nd:0 3rd:0 Ran:4
1999 Turf 0-4: (5f, 6f, 7f 2) (gd 3, frm)
Very moderate filly. Turf high 35 (began Aug).
**N P Littmoden [0-4] Tallulah Racing.*

SHARAZAN (IRE) BHB 55f45a **RR 61f 45a** 5152[12]
6 b g Akarad (FR) 9.7f **(73)** - Sharaniya (USA) (Alleged (USA)) 10f **(76)**
Form - 86760
Record 1999 - 1st:0 2nd:0 3rd:0 Ran:5
Pre1999 - 1st:2 2nd:3 3rd:1 Ran:11
Win Prizemoney £10,960 *Total Prizemoney* £16,568
Wins 1997 Jly Currag (GD) H 16f 94 109 <
1996 May Leopar (GD) 12f 70
1999 Turf 0-3: (12f, 14f, 17f) (gd, g-f, frm) 1999 AW 0-2: (12f 2) (Equi, Fibr)
Average gelding, has worn blinkers. Turf high 61. AW high 47. Inconsistent.
**O O'Neill [0-12] Frank Clarke (from J Oxx in IRE [2-9] Aug 1997).*

SHAREEF KHAN (FR) RR 27f 5207[12]
2 b c Alzao (USA) 9.8f **(73)** - Sharenara (USA) (Vaguely Noble) 10.1f **(72)**
Form - 0
Record 1999 - 1st:0 2nd:0 3rd:0 Ran:1
1999 Turf 0-1: (7f) (g-s)
Currently little account colt. **N A Graham [0-1] Fieldspring Racing.*

SHARH BHB 80f **RR 83f** 4526[6]
3 ch c Elmaamul (USA) 8.1f **(70)** - Depeche (FR) (Kings Lake (USA)) 10.8f **(67)**
Form - 3214617666
Record 1999 - 1st:2 2nd:1 3rd:1 Ran:10
Pre1999 - 1st:0 2nd:0 3rd:0 Ran:1
Win Prizemoney £6,324 *Total Prizemoney* £8,902
Wins * **1999** Jly Ayr (GD) 10f 86 <
* **1999** May Newcas (FRM) 10.1f 83
1999 Turf 2-10: (8f 2, 9f, 10f 2-6, 12f) (gd 1-6, g-f, frm 1-3)
Scopey, decent colt, effective 8 to 10f, best at 10f, acts on gd to frm, best on gd, likes left handed tracks, prefers tight tracks. Turf high 86 - 1st of 6 getting 10lb from Bering Gifts (17 Jly Ayr RF 2896) - also 1st of 6 from Blankenberge (27 May Newcastle RF 1526). Consistent. Twice a winner over ten furlongs in modest company, he is an edgy sort who struggled when tried in handicaps.
**B Hanbury [2-10] Hamdan Al Maktoum (from Mrs J Cecil [0-1] Aug 1998).*

SHARMY (IRE) RR 93f 4005[2]
3 b c Caerleon (USA) 10.9f **(79)** - Petticoat Lane (Ela-Mana-Mou) 10.1f **(70)**
Form - 12
Record 1999 - 1st:1 2nd:1 3rd:0 Ran:2
Win Prizemoney £3,858 *Total Prizemoney* £6,512
Wins * **1999** Aug Sandow (G-S) 8.1f 82++ <
1999 Turf 1-2: (8f 1-1, 10f) (gd, g-f 1-1)
Scopey, currently useful colt. Turf high 93 (began Aug) - 2nd of 6 giving 2lb to Prairie Wolf (29 Aug Yarmouth 10f gd RF 4005).
**Sir Michael Stoute [1-2] Saeed Suhail.*

SHAROURA BHB 80f **RR 79f** 5040[11]
3 ch f Inchinor 8.9f **(64)** - Kinkajoo (Precocious) 8.6f **(62)**
Form - 1660050100
Record 1999 - 1st:2 2nd:0 3rd:0 Ran:10
Pre1999 - 1st:0 2nd:1 3rd:0 Ran:1
Win Prizemoney £11,626 *Total Prizemoney* £12,730
Wins * **1999** Spt Yarmou (G-F) H 5.2f 76 79
* **1999** Mar Doncas (G-S) 6f 83 <
1999 Turf 2-10: (5f 1-3, 6f 1-5, 7f, 8f) (g-s 2, gd 1-2, g-f 1-3, frm 3)
Scopey, above-average filly, effective 5 to 6f, acts on gd to g-f. Turf high 83 - also 1st of 8 getting 5lb from Northern Spring (27 Mar Doncaster RF 0483). She showed battling qualities to get off the mark over six furlongs at Doncaster on her reappearance, but disappointed subsequently until gaining a surprise success in a handicap over the minimum at Yarmouth in September.
**K Mahdi [2-11] Solaiman Alsaiary.*

SHARP CATCH (IRE) RR 98f 2801a[13]
4 b f Common Grounds 8.1f **(66)** - Dear Lorraine (FR) (Nonoalco (USA)) 8.5f **(66)**
Form - 030370
1999 Turf 0-5: (5f 2, 6f 2, 7f) (gd 3, g-f 2)
Strong, very useful filly, effective 5 to 6f, best at 5f, acts on gd to frm, best on gd, has worn blinkers. Turf high 98 - 3rd of 7 getting 6lb from Proud Native (7 Jun Leopardstown 5f gd RF 2011a). Inconsistent. She is difficult to place off her current mark.

**J Oxx in IRE [0-5] Mrs H M Keaveney (from A P O'Brien in IRE [2-9] Nov 1998).*

SHARP EDGE BOY BHB 62f49a **RR 47f 49a** 4719[11]
3 gr g Mystiko (USA) 7.7f **(59)** - Leap Castle (Never so Bold) 6.3f **(66)**
Form - 051023160354070
Record 1999 - 1st:2 2nd:1 3rd:2 Ran:15
Pre1999 - 1st:0 2nd:0 3rd:1 Ran:7
Win Prizemoney £5,748 *Total Prizemoney* £8,534
Wins * **1999** Jun Haydoc (G-S) H 7.1f 62 66 <
* **1999** Mar Hamilt (HVY) H 6f 56 59
1999 Turf 2-13: (6f 1-7, 7f 1-6) (sft 1-1, g-s, gd 1-6, g-f, frm 4) 1999 AW 0-2: (5f, 6f) (Fibr 2)
Workmanlike, moderate gelding, effective 6 to 7f, acts on gd to frm, has worn blinkers. Turf high 67 - 3rd of 12 getting 18lb from Poles Apart (29 Jly Doncaster 6f frm RF 3217) - also 1st of 14 getting 5lb from Prideway (3 Jun Haydock RF 1704).
**E J Alston [2-22] N Gilbert & A Shandley.*

SHARP ENDING (IRE) BHB 48f **RR 50f** 1092[8]
3 b g Keen 11.1f **(58)** - Last Finale (USA) (Stop The Music (USA)) 9.2f **(71)**
Form - 388
Record 1999 - 1st:0 2nd:0 3rd:1 Ran:3
Pre1999 - 1st:0 2nd:0 3rd:0 Ran:4
Win Prizemoney £0 *Total Prizemoney* £350
1999 Turf 0-3: (12f 2, 14f) (gd, g-f 2)
Fair gelding, has worn blinkers. Turf high 50.
**A P Jarvis [0-7] Ambrose Turnbull.*

SHARPEN THE ARROW (IRE) BHB 50f **RR 46f** 4819[9]
3 br g Elbio 9f **(62)** - Clodianus (Bay Express) 7.1f **(60)**
Form - 000
Record 1999 - 1st:0 2nd:0 3rd:0 Ran:3
1999 Turf 0-2: (6f, 7f) (gd 2) 1999 AW 0-1: (6f) (Fibr)
Workmanlike, moderate gelding. Turf high 46 (began Spt). (DEAD)
**N P Littmoden [0-3] Arrow Mushroom And Pea Partnership.*

SHARP FOCUS (USA) RR 96f 5201a[6]
2 b c Lear Fan (USA) 10.4f **(80)** - Spark of Success (USA) (Topsider (USA)) 8.3f **(71)**
Form - 413136
1999 Turf 2-6: (7f 1-3, 8f 1-2, 10f) (hvy, g-s, gd 1-2, g-f 1-1, frm)
Very useful colt, effective 7 to 8f, acts on g-s to gd, mostly wears blinkers (extremely effectively). Turf high 96 - 3rd of 6 to Lermontov (16 Oct Curragh 8f g-s RF 4974a) - also 1st of 10 giving 23lb to Echo Island (11 Spt Leopardstown RF 4319a). He should stay middle-distances, but does not look up to Group class and will be hard to place next term. **D K Weld in IRE [2-6].*

SHARP HAT BHB 57f **RR 68f** 4924[8]
5 ch g Shavian 7.7f **(67)** - Madam Trilby (Grundy) 10.3f **(65)**
Form - 677000008
Record 1999 - 1st:0 2nd:0 3rd:0 Ran:9
Pre1999 - 1st:3 2nd:3 3rd:2 Ran:27
Win Prizemoney £13,908 *Total Prizemoney* £31,942
Wins 1997 May Newbur (SFT) H 6f 85 90 <
1996 Spt Doncas (G-F) H 6f 78 83
1996 Aug Warwic (GD) H 6f 70 67
1999 Turf 0-8: (5f 3, 6f 5) (gd 3, g-f 2, frm 3) 1999 AW 0-1: (6f) (Fibr)
Average gelding, effective 6f, acts on g-f, has worn blinkers. Turf high 71.
**T J Etherington [0-9] J C Smith (from R Hannon [3-27] Spt 1998).*

SHARP HINT BHB 48f48a **RR 59f 48a** 399[2]
4 ch f Sharpo 7.5f **(68)** - May Hinton (Main Reef) 9.6f **(57)**
Form - 30302
Record 1999 - 1st:0 2nd:1 3rd:1 Ran:4
Pre1999 - 1st:0 2nd:0 3rd:1 Ran:8
Win Prizemoney £0 *Total Prizemoney* £1,691
1999 AW 0-4: (5f 3, 6f) (Equi 3, Fibr)
Workmanlike, fair filly, effective 5f, - acts on Equi, likes left handed tracks. AW high 53 - 2nd of 5 to Emmajoun (4 Mar Lingfield 5f Equi RF 0399). Inconsistent.
**D Nicholls [0-8] P D Forster & J S Herrington (from J L Dunlop [0-4] Jun 1998).*

SHARP HOLLY (IRE) BHB 29f29a **RR 28f 29a** 2089a[8]
7 b m Exactly Sharp (USA) 8.4f **(66)** - Children's Hour (Mummy's Pet) 7.7f **(60)**
Form - 05008
Record 1999 - 1st:0 2nd:0 3rd:0 Ran:5
Pre1999 - 1st:0 2nd:1 3rd:4 Ran:29
Win Prizemoney £0 *Total Prizemoney* £3,227
1999 Turf 0-1: (9f) (g-f) 1999 AW 0-4: (5f, 6f, 7f 2) (Equi 2, Fibr 2)
Little account mare, has worn blinkers. AW high 28. Inconsistent.
**M Bradstock [0-5] (from J A Bennett [0-33] Jun 1997).*

SHARP IMP BHB 45f45a **RR 38f 45a** 4161[9]
9 b g Sharpo 7.5f **(68)** - Implore (Ile de Bourbon (USA)) 10.1f **(67)**
Form - 05574700
Record 1999 - 1st:0 2nd:0 3rd:0 Ran:5
Pre1999 - 1st:9 2nd:18 3rd:11 Ran:102
Win Prizemoney £23,615 *Total Prizemoney* £45,146
Wins 1998 *Jan Lingfi (STD) H 6f 49 50*
1997 Aug Folkes (G-F) 6f 63 <
1997 *Jan Lingfi (STD) H 6f 59 62*
1996 Aug Bright (RFM) 7f 60
1996 Jun Bright (FRM) H 6f 48 51
1996 *Jan Lingfi (STD) H 6f 50 54*
1995 Aug Folkes (FRM) 6f 50
1995 Jly Bright (FRM) H 6f 33 38
1999 Turf 0-3: (5f 2, 6f) (frm 3) 1999 AW 0-2: (6f 2) (Equi 2)
Moderate gelding, effective 6 to 7f, acts on g-f to frm, mostly wears blinkers, likes left handed tracks, likes tight tracks. Turf high 38 (began Aug).
**J R Poulton [0-3] Mrs G M Temmerman (from R M Flower [9-97] Jan 1999).*

SHARP LOVE BHB 40f **RR 42f** 4835[19]
3 b f Pursuit of Love 9.5f **(69)** - Sweet Decision (IRE) **(64f 66a)** (Common Grounds)
Form - 0000
Record 1999 - 1st:0 2nd:0 3rd:0 Ran:4
Pre1999 - 1st:0 2nd:0 3rd:0 Ran:4
1999 Turf 0-4: (7f 2, 8f, 10f) (hvy, gd 2, frm)
Neat, moderate filly. Turf high 42. Becoming disappointing.
**N A Callaghan [0-1] Norcroft Park Stud (from M J Ryan [0-7] Apr 1999).*

SHARP MATT RR 104f 1527a[1]
8 ch h Sharpo 7.5f **(68)** - Matoa (USA)
Form - 1
1999 AW 1-1: (8f 1-1) (Dirt 1-1)
Currently Pattern-class horse - 1st of 9 from Melmac (20 May Jagersro RF 1527a). **M Kahn in SWE [2-3] Stall Kebo.*

SHARP MONKEY BHB 39f39a **RR 10f 39a** 451[12]
4 b g Man Among Men (IRE) 8f **(47)** - Sharp Thistle (Sharpo) 7.7f **(59)**
Form - 5877483750
Record 1999 - 1st:0 2nd:0 3rd:1 Ran:6
Pre1999 - 1st:2 2nd:4 3rd:3 Ran:28
Win Prizemoney £4,171 *Total Prizemoney* £7,394
Wins * 1998 *Feb Southw (STD) SH 8f 54 63* <
* 1998 *Jan Southw (STD) C 8f 63* <
1999 AW 0-6: (8f 5, 11f) (Fibr 6)
Leggy, moderate gelding, effective 7 to 9f, best at 8f, - acts on Fibr, mostly wears blinkers (very effectively), favours left handed tracks, favours tight tracks, likes Southwell.
**Mrs N Macauley [2-34] J Teasdale.*

SHARP MOVE BHB 30f21a **RR 45f 21a** 302[13]
7 ch m Night Shift (USA) 8.1f **(73)** - Judeah (Great Nephew) 9.9f **(64)**
Form - 0
Record 1999 - 1st:0 2nd:0 3rd:0 Ran:1
Pre1999 - 1st:0 2nd:0 3rd:0 Ran:11
1999 AW 0-1: (12f) (Equi)
Moderate mare.
**Miss H C Knight [0-7] Miss Caroline Spurrier (from B A Pearce [0-3] Jan 1998).*

SHARP PEARL BHB 62f54a **RR 45f 54a** 626[14]
6 ch g Sharpo 7.5f **(68)** - Silent Pearl (USA) (Silent Screen (USA)) 8.6f

(65)
Form - 8600
Record 1999 - 1st:0 2nd:0 3rd:0 Ran:4
Pre1999 - 1st:3 2nd:3 3rd:4 Ran:36
Win Prizemoney £9,944 *Total Prizemoney* £17,691
Wins 1997 Aug Newmar (G-F) H 5f 77 79 <
1997 Apr Bright (FRM) H 5.3f 70 75
1996 Jun Bright (FRM) H 5.3f 70 75
1999 Turf 0-1: (7f) (gd) 1999 AW 0-3: (6f 2, 7f) (Equi 2, Fibr)
Fair gelding, effective 5f, acts on gd, often wears blinkers.
**D J S Cosgrove [0-7] Dennis Yardy (from P R Webber [1-11] Spt 1998).*

SHARP REBUFF BHB 84f78a **RR 83f 78a** 5143^{10}
8 b h Reprimand 8.2f **(63)** - Kukri (Kris) 9.5f **(73)**
Form - 00542350
Record 1999 - 1st:0 2nd:1 3rd:1 Ran:7
Pre1999 - 1st:5 2nd:5 3rd:4 Ran:31
Win Prizemoney £21,511 *Total Prizemoney* £40,293
Wins * 1998 Jun Sandow (G-S) H 7.1f 85 90 <
* 1997 Jun Warwic (GD) H 8f 79 83
* 1996 Jly Kempto (GD) H 8f 74 81
* 1995 Jun Warwic (GD) H 8f 69 73
1999 Turf 0-7: (7f 5, 8f 2) (g-s 2, gd 4, g-f)
Decent horse, effective 7 to 8f, best at 7f, acts on gd to frm, best on gd, prefers tight tracks. Turf high 83 - 2nd of 14 giving 8lb to Premier Baron (12 Aug Sandown 7f g-f RF 3581). Inconsistent. Suited by seven furlongs to a mile with cut in the ground, he is on a losing run dating back to June '98 although he has run some game races in defeat. **P J Makin [5-38] D M Ahier.*

SHARP RHYTHM (IRE) BHB 48f44a **RR 37f 44a** 425^{12}
3 b f Mujadil (USA) 7.7f **(70)** - Welsh Note (USA) (Sharpen Up) 8.3f **(67)**
Form - 5438270
Record 1999 - 1st:0 2nd:1 3rd:1 Ran:7
Pre1999 - 1st:0 2nd:0 3rd:0 Ran:4
Win Prizemoney £0 *Total Prizemoney* £902
1999 AW 0-7: (5f, 6f 2, 7f 2, 8f 2) (Equi, Fibr 6)
Leggy, moderate filly, effective 8f, - acts on Fibr, likes left handed tracks, likes tight tracks. AW high 43 - 3rd of 14 getting 10lb from Bamboo Garden (1 Feb Southwell 8f Fibr RF 0205).
**M Johnston [0-11] Mrs I Bird.*

SHARP SCOTCH BHB 50f83a **RR 53f 83a** 5151^{3}
6 b g Sharpo 7.5f **(68)** - Scotch Thistle (Sassafras (FR)) 9.6f **(69)**
Form - 31337111150000083
Record 1999 - 1st:4 2nd:0 3rd:1 Ran:13
Pre1999 - 1st:2 2nd:1 3rd:3 Ran:14
Win Prizemoney £14,682 *Total Prizemoney* £16,515
Wins * **1999** *Mar Southw (STD) H 8f 79 84* <
* **1999** *Feb Southw (STD) H 8f 75 75*
* **1999** *Jan Southw (STD) H 8f 62 73*
* **1999** *Jan Southw (STD) H 8f 62 69*
1998 *Nov Wolver (STD) H 9.4f 57 59*
1998 Jun Naas (SFT) H 8f 54 76
1999 Turf 0-7: (5f, 6f 2, 8f, 10f 3) (sft 2, gd 3, g-f 2) 1999 AW 4-6: (7f, 8f 4-5) (Equi, Fibr 4-5)
Decent gelding, effective 8f, acts on sft - acts on Fibr, has worn blinkers, prefers left handed tracks, likes tight tracks, excels at Southwell. Turf high 53. AW high 84 - 1st of 9 giving 16lb to Mutahadeth (16 Mar Southwell RF 0437) - also 1st of 9 giving 4lb to Butrinto (8 Feb Southwell RF 0251). He has become a very effective performer on Fibresand. A winner over the extended nine furlongs at Wolverhampton in November '98, he completed a hat trick over the Southwell mile at the start of the year. He is a real battler.
**D Carroll [4-14] J J Devaney (from D Carroll [1-3] Dec 1998).*

SHARP SHOOTER (IRE) BHB 26f **RR 30f** 3863^{18}
4 b g Sabrehill (USA) 8.5f **(64)** - Kermesse (IRE) (Reference Point) 6.8f **(70)**
Form - 00
Record 1999 - 1st:0 2nd:0 3rd:0 Ran:2
Pre1999 - 1st:0 2nd:1 3rd:1 Ran:10
Win Prizemoney £0 *Total Prizemoney* £1,024
1999 Turf 0-2: (12f 2) (frm 2)
Scopey, very moderate gelding, effective 10 to 12f, acts on g-f to frm. (began Aug). Inconsistent.
**B Ellison [0-2] Alan Thompson (from S E Kettlewell [0-4] Jly 1998).*

SHARP SHUFFLE (IRE) BHB 60f60a **RR 60f 60a** 4935^{11}
6 ch g Exactly Sharp (USA) 8.4f **(66)** - Style (Homing) 7.8f **(59)**
Form - 204020
Record 1999 - 1st:0 2nd:1 3rd:0 Ran:5
Pre1999 - 1st:5 2nd:10 3rd:7 Ran:42
Win Prizemoney £20,233 *Total Prizemoney* £38,566
Wins 1998 Aug Newmar (G-F) C 7f 71+
1998 Jly Newmar (G-F) S 8f 61
1997 Jun Goodwo (G-F) H 8f 75 78+ <
1997 Apr Bright (FRM) 8f 74
1996 Spt Kempto (GD) H 7f 68 74
1999 Turf 0-2: (7f 2) (g-s, frm) 1999 AW 0-3: (7f, 8f, 9f) (Fibr 3)
Average gelding, effective 7 to 8f, best at 7f, acts on frm to hrd - acts on AW. Turf high 60 (began Spt). AW high 65 - 2nd of 12 getting 4lb from Takhlid (2 Oct Wolverhampton 7f Fibr RF 4702).
**Ian Williams [0-4] G A Gilbert (from J G M O'Shea [0-3] May 1999).*

SHARP SMOKE RR 38f 2058^{4}
2 gr f Cigar 6.3f **(43)** - Abrasive (Absalom) 7.2f **(58)**
Form - 4
Record 1999 - 1st:0 2nd:0 3rd:0 Ran:1
Win Prizemoney £0 *Total Prizemoney* £190
1999 Turf 0-1: (5f) (g-f)
Currently very moderate filly. **D W Barker [0-1] Mrs S J Barker.*

SHARP SPICE BHB 62f57a **RR 60f 57a** 5022^{4}
3 b f Lugana Beach 7f **(63)** - Ewar Empress (IRE) **(11f 35a)** (Persian Bold) 9.3f **(66)**
Form - 060775814334
Record 1999 - 1st:1 2nd:0 3rd:2 Ran:11
Pre1999 - 1st:0 2nd:0 3rd:0 Ran:3
Win Prizemoney £4,200 *Total Prizemoney* £6,680
Wins * **1999** Aug Goodwo (GD) H 9.9f 55 58 <
1999 Turf 1-11: (7f 4, 8f 2, 10f 1-4, 11f) (sft 2, gd 4, g-f 1-2, frm 3)
Light-framed, average filly, effective 10 to 11f, best at 10f, acts on sft to frm, likes left handed tracks, prefers tight tracks. Turf high 60 - also 1st of 17 giving 9lb to Briery Mec (29 Aug Goodwood RF 3999). Consistent.
**D J Coakley [1-11] The Nags Head Racing Syndicate (from Lord Huntingdon [0-3] Nov 1998).*

SHARP STEEL BHB 48f53a **RR 26f 53a** 2374^{9}
4 ch g Beveled (USA) 6.9f **(64)** - Shift Over (USA) (Night Shift (USA)) 7.2f **(69)**
Form - 3500
Record 1999 - 1st:0 2nd:0 3rd:1 Ran:4
Pre1999 - 1st:1 2nd:1 3rd:0 Ran:7
Win Prizemoney £1,922 *Total Prizemoney* £3,015
Wins 1998 *Mar Southw (STD) S 7f 61* <
1999 Turf 0-1: (8f) (g-f) 1999 AW 0-3: (7f 2, 8f) (Fibr 3)
Leggy, moderate gelding, effective 7f, - acts on Fibr. AW high 58 (1st run) - 3rd of 15 getting 4lb from Garnock Valley (6 Apr Southwell 7f Fibr RF 0603).
**Miss S J Wilton [0-5] John Pointon and Sons (from G L Moore [1-6] Mar 1998).*

SHARP STEPPER BHB 77f **RR 78f** 5133^{2}
3 b f Selkirk (USA) 7.9f **(76)** - Awtaar (USA) **(35df)** (Lyphard (USA)) 9.9f **(72)**
Form - 4056332
Record 1999 - 1st:0 2nd:1 3rd:2 Ran:7
Win Prizemoney £0 *Total Prizemoney* £3,782
1999 Turf 0-7: (10f 6, 12f) (gd 2, g-f 2, frm 3)
Scopey, above-average filly, effective 10 to 12f, best at 10f, acts on gd to frm, best on g-f. Turf high 78 - 3rd of 20 giving 7lb to Spring Pursuit (11 Oct Windsor 10f g-f RF 4823).
**J H M Gosden [0-7] Mrs Diane Snowden.*

SHARP STOCK BHB 57f **RR 58f** 4493^{13}
6 b g Tina's Pet 7.4f **(56)** - Mrewa (Runnymede) 9.3f **(50)**
Form - 0010700
Record 1999 - 1st:1 2nd:0 3rd:0 Ran:7
Pre1999 - 1st:2 2nd:1 3rd:1 Ran:22
Win Prizemoney £14,541 *Total Prizemoney* £16,393
Wins * **1999** Jun Haydoc (G-S) H 5f 56 58 <
* 1998 Jun Salisb (G-S) H 5f 50 56

* 1998 May Goodwo (G-F) H 5f 44 46
1999 Turf 1-7: (5f 1-7) (sft, gd 1-4, g-f, frm)
Fair gelding, effective 5f, acts on gd, has worn blinkers. Turf high 58 - 1st of 12 getting 7lb from Nifty Norman (3 Jun Haydock RF 1703).
**R J Hodges [3-25] Mrs M Fairbairn (from B J Meehan [0-4] May 1996).*

SHARVIE RR 17f 4996^{10}

2 b g Rock Hopper 10.6f **(54)** - Heresheis (Free State) 8.7f **(61)**
Form - 0
Record 1999 - 1st:0 2nd:0 3rd:0 Ran:1
1999 Turf 0-1: (8f) (gd)
Currently poor gelding. **J Pearce [0-1] Mrs Jennifer Marsh.*

SHATIN BEAUTY BHB 67f RR 69f 4589^{15}

2 b f Mistertopogigo (IRE) - Starisk **(33f)** (Risk Me (FR)) 5.9f **(53)**
Form - 124440
Record 1999 - 1st:1 2nd:1 3rd:0 Ran:6
Win Prizemoney £2,737 *Total Prizemoney* £3,991
Wins * **1999** Jly Hamilt (FRM) 5f 69 <
1999 Turf 1-6: (5f 1-5, 6f) (gd, g-f 2, frm 1-3)
Average filly, effective 5f, acts on g-f to frm, best on frm. Turf high 69 (began Jly) - 4th of 21 giving 14lb to Branston Lucy (24 Spt Redcar 5f frm RF 4543) - also 1st of 8 giving 3lb to Shalarise (9 Jly Hamilton RF 2676). **Miss L A Perratt [1-6] Shatin Racing Group.*

SHATIN LAD RR 34f 3134^{10}

2 b c Timeless Times (USA) 6.1f **(56)** - Fauve (Dominion) 8.5f **(63)**
Form - 0
Record 1999 - 1st:0 2nd:0 3rd:0 Ran:1
1999 Turf 0-1: (6f) (gd)
Currently very moderate colt.
**Miss L A Perratt [0-1] Shatin Racing Group.*

SHATIN VENTURE (IRE) BHB 94f RR 91?f 3442^{4}

2 b c Lake Coniston (IRE) - Justitia (Dunbeath (USA)) 7.8f **(70)**
Form - 1424
Record 1999 - 1st:1 2nd:1 3rd:0 Ran:4
Win Prizemoney £3,072 *Total Prizemoney* £5,410
Wins * **1999** May Ayr (GD) 5f 91+ <
1999 Turf 1-4: (5f 1-4) (gd 1-3, g-f)
Useful colt. Turf high 91 (1st run) - 1st of 5 getting 7lb from Hammer And Sickle (20 May Ayr RF 1337).
**Miss L A Perratt [1-4] Shatin Racing Group.*

SHAUBAN (IRE) BHB 45f RR 43f 3547^{14}

2 b f Dolphin Street (FR) - Boristova (IRE) (Royal Academy (USA))
Form - 08380
Record 1999 - 1st:0 2nd:0 3rd:1 Ran:5
Win Prizemoney £0 *Total Prizemoney* £247
1999 Turf 0-4: (5f, 6f 3) (g-f 3, frm) 1999 AW 0-1: (5f) (Fibr)
Moderate filly. Turf high 43. **N A Callaghan [0-5] Martin Moore.*

SHAWDON BHB 99f RR 102f 1895a[2]

4 b c Inchinor 8.9f **(64)** - Play With Me (IRE) (Alzao (USA)) 7.1f **(68)**
Form - 2
1999 Turf 0-1: (10f) (frm)
Neat, very useful colt. (1st run) - 2nd of 11 to Superior Premium (1 Jun Taby 10f frm RF 1895a).
**M Kahn in SWE [1-2] (from Sir Mark Prescott [4-10] Oct 1997).*

SHAW VENTURE BHB 68f RR 73f 5023^{17}

2 ch c Whittingham (IRE) - Al Shany (Burslem) 8.8f **(53)**
Form - 054516060
Record 1999 - 1st:1 2nd:0 3rd:0 Ran:9
Win Prizemoney £2,827 *Total Prizemoney* £2,827
Wins * **1999** Jly Windso (G-F) 5f 73 <
1999 Turf 1-9: (5f 1-7, 6f 2) (sft, gd 4, g-f, frm 1-3)
Above-average colt, effective 5f, acts on frm, has worn blinkers. Turf high 73 - 1st of 15 giving 5lb to Hoxton Square (19 Jly Windsor RF 2950). **B Palling [1-9] Mrs A L Stacey.*

SHAYA BHB 105f RR 110f 2882^{4}

5 ch h Nashwan (USA) 10.3f **(79)** - Gharam (USA) (Green Dancer (USA)) 10.3f **(74)**
Form - 2325734
Record 1999 - 1st:0 2nd:2 3rd:2 Ran:7
Pre1999 - 1st:1 2nd:4 3rd:0 Ran:8
Win Prizemoney £3,533 *Total Prizemoney* £36,234
Wins 1997 Aug Sandow (GD) 10f 76 <
1999 Turf 0-7: (10f, 12f 2, 14f, 15f, 16f, 20f) (sft, gd, g-f 4, frm)
Group-class colt, effective 10 to 16f, acts on sft to g-f, best on g-f. Turf high 111 - 3rd of 11 giving 1lb to Sadian (17 Apr Newbury 12f g-f RF 0733). He proved well worth the 5,500 guineas he cost out of Marcus Tregoning's yard, finishing placed in four Group or Listed races. Effective from a mile and a quarter to two miles, he lacks a telling turn-of-foot and would benefit from a return to forcing tactics.
**G C Bravery [0-7] Sawyer Whatley Partnership (from M P Tregoning [0-1] Aug 1998).*

SHAYLAN (IRE) BHB 90f RR 90f 4683^{28}

3 br c Primo Dominie 7.2f **(67)** - Shayraz (Darshaan) 9.9f **(84)**
Form - 41363010
Record 1999 - 1st:2 2nd:0 3rd:2 Ran:8
Pre1999 - 1st:0 2nd:1 3rd:0 Ran:1
Win Prizemoney £12,058 *Total Prizemoney* £17,183
Wins * **1999** Spt Newcas (G-F) H 10.1f 86 90+ <
* **1999** May Thirsk (G-S) 8f 80
1999 Turf 2-8: (8f 1-4, 10f 1-4) (gd 1-3, g-f, frm 1-4)
Scopey, useful colt, effective 8 to 10f, best at 8f, acts on gd to frm, best on frm. Turf high 90 - 1st of 10 getting 4lb from Regal Philosopher (19 Spt Newcastle RF 4424). Won at Thirsk on his second start of this term, and ran well on several other occasions. Back to his best when bolting up in a ten-furlong handicap at Newcastle in September, he was sold for 110,000 gns in October to race for Jim Old. **Sir Michael Stoute [2-9] H H Aga Khan.*

SHAYZAN (USA) BHB 62f RR 57f 5163^{7}

2 b c Shadeed (USA) 7.7f **(72)** - Espuela (USA) (Gone West (USA)) 6.5f **(75)**
Form - 07
Record 1999 - 1st:0 2nd:0 3rd:0 Ran:2
1999 Turf 0-2: (7f 2) (g-s, gd)
Currently fair colt. Turf high 57 (began Spt).
**W R Muir [0-2] Fayzad Thoroughbred Ltd.*

SHEATH KEFAAH BHB 37f RR 49f 3642^{3}

6 ch h Kefaah (USA) 11.2f **(64)** - Wasslaweyeh (USA) (Damascus (USA)) 8.9f **(71)**
Form - 03
Record 1999 - 1st:0 2nd:0 3rd:1 Ran:2
Pre1999 - 1st:0 2nd:0 3rd:0 Ran:3
Win Prizemoney £0 *Total Prizemoney* £280
1999 Turf 0-2: (10f, 12f) (g-f 2)
Moderate horse. Turf high 44.
**J R Jenkins [1-6] K C Payne (from W J Haggas [0-2] Oct 1995).*

SHEBANE (USA) RR 107f 5121a[4]

3 b f Alysheba (USA) 12.1f **(78)** - Belle Sultane (USA) (Seattle Slew (USA)) 9.4f **(76)**
Form - 214
1999 Turf 1-3: (10f, 12f 1-1, 16f) (hvy 1-2, gd)
Currently Pattern-class filly. Turf high 107 (began Jly) - also 1st of 11 from Glaoutchika (10 Oct Longchamp RF 4889a). She stays well and could win a weak Group race on soft ground.
**Mme C Head in FR [1-3].*

SHEBA SPRING (IRE) BHB 95f RR 100f 4796^{4}

3 b f Brief Truce (USA) 9.1f **(73)** - Shebasis (USA) (General Holme (USA)) 5.7f **(63)**
Form - 811464
Record 1999 - 1st:2 2nd:0 3rd:0 Ran:6
Win Prizemoney £12,474 *Total Prizemoney* £14,937
Wins * **1999** Jly Ascot (FRM) 10f 100 <
* **1999** Jly Windso (GD) 8.3f 85+
1999 Turf 2-6: (8f 1-4, 10f 1-2) (gd 3, g-f 1-2, frm 1-1)
Scopey, very useful filly, effective 10f, acts on gd to g-f. Turf high 100 - 1st of 5 getting 6lb from Olive The Twist (25 Jly Ascot RF 3121). Well thought of, she looked useful in the summer but failed to progress on easy ground in the second half of the season. Probably best over a mile and a quarter, she deserves another chance on a sound surface. **R Charlton [2-6] Fieldspring Racing.*

SHEBEG RR 38f 4941^{13}

2 ch f Rudimentary (USA) 8.2f **(66)** - Oakbrook Tern (USA) (Arctic Tern (USA)) 8.9f **(69)**
Form - 0
Record 1999 - 1st:0 2nd:0 3rd:0 Ran:1
1999 Turf 0-1: (5f) (gd)
Currently very moderate filly.
**Mrs L C Jewell [0-1] Gallagher Equine Ltd.*

SHEEP STEALER BHB 54f26a RR 48?f 26a 436[7]

11 gr g Absalom 7.1f **(56)** - Kilroe's Calin (Be Friendly) 9.3f **(53)**
Form - 07
Record 1999 - 1st:0 2nd:0 3rd:0 Ran:2
Pre1999 - 1st:0 2nd:0 3rd:0 Ran:7
1999 AW 0-2: (13f, 14f) (Equi, Fibr)
Moderate gelding. AW high 15. Becoming disappointing.
**R E Peacock [1-20] R E Peacock.*

SHEER FACE BHB 65f70a RR 68f 70a 3689[8]

5 b g Midyan (USA) 9.9f **(64)** - Rock Face (Ballad Rock) 7.8f **(63)**
Form - 346763448
Record 1999 - 1st:0 2nd:0 3rd:2 Ran:9
Pre1999 - 1st:3 2nd:4 3rd:3 Ran:30
Win Prizemoney £14,636 *Total Prizemoney* £27,870
Wins * 1998 Jun Goodwo (G-F) H 8f 69 74
* 1996 Spt Bath (G-F) H 8f 86 90 <
* 1996 Aug Bright (FRM) 7f 81+
1999 Turf 0-9: (7f, 8f 7, 10f) (gd 2, g-f 3, frm 4)
Average gelding, effective 7 to 8f, best at 8f, acts on gd to frm, best on gd, has worn blinkers, likes left handed tracks, likes tight tracks, excels at Bath and likes Brighton. Turf high 74 (1st run) - 3rd of 13 giving 3lb to Master Caster (12 May Brighton 8f g-f RF 1176). Consistent. **W R Muir [3-39] A J de V Patrick.*

SHEER HAMAS (IRE) BHB 100f RR 95f 4208[1]

2 b c Hamas (IRE) 8f **(72)** - Kilcoy (USA) (Secreto (USA)) 8.7f **(72)**
Form - 311
Record 1999 - 1st:2 2nd:0 3rd:1 Ran:3
Win Prizemoney £157,548 *Total Prizemoney* £158,202
Wins * 1999 Spt Doncas (G-F) 6f 95 <
*** 1999** Jly Yarmou (FRM) 7f 79+
1999 Turf 2-3: (6f 1-2, 7f 1-1) (gd 1-1, frm 1-2)
Currently very useful colt. Turf high 95 (began Jly) - 1st of 21 from Blue Bolivar (8 Spt Doncaster RF 4208). A good-looker, he put up a cracking performance for an inexperienced individual when winning the £200,000 St Leger Yearling Stakes at Doncaster. Raced only on a sound surface, he should stay a mile and can win a Group event. **B W Hills [2-3] R J Arculli.*

SHEER HARMONY (USA) BHB 73f RR 73f 5197[13]

3 b br f Woodman (USA) 9.7f **(77)** - Memories Of Pam (USA) (Graustark) 10.1f **(70)**
Form - 2210
Record 1999 - 1st:1 2nd:2 3rd:0 Ran:4
Pre1999 - 1st:0 2nd:0 3rd:0 Ran:1
Win Prizemoney £3,048 *Total Prizemoney* £4,929
Wins * 1999 Oct Windso (G-S) 8.3f 71 <
1999 Turf 1-4: (8f 1-3, 10f) (gd 2, g-f 1-1, frm)
Scopey, above-average filly. Turf high 73 - 2nd of 14 getting 5lb from Torch Song (4 Oct Pontefract 8f gd RF 4720) - also 1st of 14 getting 5lb from Stromsholm (11 Oct Windsor RF 4824).
**Sir Michael Stoute [1-5] Lordship Stud.*

SHEER NATIVE BHB 60f70a RR 46f 70a 4376[10]

3 b f In The Wings 11.2f **(77)** - Native Magic (Be My Native (USA)) 10.2f **(71)**
Form - 1380
Record 1999 - 1st:1 2nd:0 3rd:1 Ran:4
Pre1999 - 1st:0 2nd:0 3rd:0 Ran:4
Win Prizemoney £3,081 *Total Prizemoney* £3,609
Wins * 1999 *Mar Lingfi (STD) 10f 64++* <
1999 Turf 0-2: (9f 2) (gd, frm) 1999 AW 1-2: (10f 1-1, 12f) (Equi 1-2)
Unfurnished, above-average filly, effective 10 to 12f, - acts on Equi. Turf high 46 (began Spt). AW high 72 - 3rd of 4 getting 25lb from Banbury (18 Mar Lingfield 12f Equi RF 0446) - also 1st of 8 getting 21lb from Wild Nettle (2 Mar Lingfield RF 0388).
**B W Hills [1-8] R J Arculli.*

SHEERNESS ESSITY BHB 60f RR 68f 5148[10]

2 b f Fraam - Reclusive (Sunley Builds)
Form - 072410
Record 1999 - 1st:1 2nd:1 3rd:0 Ran:6
Win Prizemoney £1,966 *Total Prizemoney* £2,926
Wins 1999 *Oct Wolver (STD) S 8.5f 68* <
1999 Turf 0-3: (6f 2, 8f) (gd, frm 2) 1999 AW 1-3: (7f, 8f 1-2) (Fibr 1-3)
Average filly, effective 7 to 8f, best at 8f, acts on gd - acts on Fibr. Turf high 68 (began Aug) - 2nd of 15 getting 5lb from Timaru (16 Spt Ayr 8f gd RF 4341). AW high 68 (began Spt) - 1st of 12 from Maid To Love (16 Oct Wolverhampton RF 4926). Landed a seller over the extended mile on the Wolverhampton Fibresand in October for Mick Channon.
**M Dods [0-1] C A Lynch (from M R Channon [1-5] Oct 1999).*

SHEER SABO RR 79f 1361[3]

2 b c Prince Sabo 6.6f **(64)** - Sunfleet (Red Sunset) 8.2f **(63)**
Form - 233
Record 1999 - 1st:0 2nd:1 3rd:2 Ran:3
Win Prizemoney £0 *Total Prizemoney* £2,795
1999 Turf 0-3: (5f 2, 6f) (g-s, g-f 2)
Currently above-average colt. Turf high 79 - 3rd of 10 to Niagara (21 May Ayr 6f g-s RF 1361). **B W Hills [0-3] R J Arculli.*

SHEER VIKING (IRE) BHB 90f RR 84f 5030[11]

3 b c Danehill (USA) 9.1f **(79)** - Schlefalora (Mas Media)
Form - 2000800
Record 1999 - 1st:0 2nd:1 3rd:0 Ran:7
Pre1999 - 1st:2 2nd:1 3rd:1 Ran:7
Win Prizemoney £34,133 *Total Prizemoney* £58,036
Wins * 1998 Spt Doncas (GD) G2 5f 105 <
* 1998 May Newmar (G-S) 5f 90+
1999 Turf 0-7: (5f 3, 6f 4) (sft, g-s, gd 3, g-f, frm)
Scopey, decent colt, effective 5 to 6f, best at 6f, acts on gd to frm, has worn blinkers. Turf high 105 (1st run) - 2nd of 10 to Lavery (8 May Goodwood 6f gd RF 1105). Inconsistent. Winner of the Group Two Flying Childers Stakes as a juvenile, he ran an encouraging second in a Shergar Cup race on his reappearance, but has struggled badly against the top sprinters since.
**B W Hills [2-14] R J Arculli.*

SHEER WARNING (IRE) BHB 34f RR 17f 1209[12]

5 b g Warning 8.1f **(77)** - Native Magic (Be My Native (USA)) 10.2f **(71)**
Form - 8000
Record 1999 - 1st:0 2nd:0 3rd:0 Ran:3
Pre1999 - 1st:0 2nd:0 3rd:0 Ran:5
1999 Turf 0-3: (7f, 8f, 11f) (g-s, g-f 2)
Little account gelding, has worn blinkers. Turf high 17. Inconsistent.
**I Semple [0-4] Andy Dickie (from R W Armstrong [0-4] Oct 1998).*

SHEHAB (IRE) BHB 58f RR 49f 2953[13]

6 b g Persian Bold 10f **(69)** - Fenjaan (Trojan Fen) 8.1f **(62)**
Form - 00
Record 1999 - 1st:0 2nd:0 3rd:0 Ran:2
Pre1999 - 1st:1 2nd:1 3rd:0 Ran:4
Win Prizemoney £2,736 *Total Prizemoney* £3,804
Wins 1996 Jun Sandow (FRM) C 10f 83+ <
1999 Turf 0-2: (10f, 12f) (frm 2)
Moderate gelding.
**P R Hedger [1-6] J J Whelan (from W J Haggas [1-2] Jun 1996).*

SHEILA-B BHB 45f RR 34f 2319[14]

4 ch f Formidable (USA) 7.8f **(60)** - Good Woman (Good Times (ITY)) 6.6f **(54)**
Form - 8000
Record 1999 - 1st:0 2nd:0 3rd:0 Ran:4
Pre1999 - 1st:0 2nd:0 3rd:0 Ran:2
1999 Turf 0-4: (6f 2, 7f, 8f) (g-f 2, frm, hrd)
Very moderate filly. Turf high 60.
**P J Makin [0-5] D L C Hodges (from B R Millman [0-1] Mar 1998).*

SHEILAS DREAM BHB 30f39a RR 16f 39a 1881[9]

6 b m Inca Chief (USA) 5.6f **(45)** - Windlass (Persian Bold) 9.3f **(66)**
Form - 00
Record 1999 - 1st:0 2nd:0 3rd:0 Ran:2
Pre1999 - 1st:0 2nd:2 3rd:0 Ran:11
Win Prizemoney £0 *Total Prizemoney* £1,452

1999 Turf 0-2: (10f, 12f) (gd, g-f)
Poor mare, has worn blinkers. Turf high 16. Becoming disappointing. **H S Howe [1-12] George Searle (from G L Moore [0-6] Aug 1997).*

SHENCK RR 111f 1358a[4]
3 b f Zafonic (USA) 9f **(83)** -Buckwig (USA) (Buckfinder (USA)) 8.1f **(71)**
Form - 14
1999 Turf 1-2: (8f 1-2) (hvy 1-1, gd)
Currently Group-class filly. Turf high 111 - 4th of 14 to Valentine Waltz (16 May Longchamp 8f gd RF 1358a). She fought like a tigress to win the Italian 1,000 Guineas, and ran creditably when finishing fourth in the French equivalent. Effective on all types of ground, she is tough, genuine and consistent.
**B Grizzetti in ITY [1-3].*

SHEPHERDS REST (IRE) BHB 39f46a **RR 40f 46a** 904[13]
7 b g Accordion 11.3f **(75)** - Mandy's Last (Krayyan) 8.5f **(49)**
Form - 22320
Record 1999 - 1st:0 2nd:3 3rd:1 Ran:5
Pre1999 - 1st:0 2nd:0 3rd:2 Ran:9
Win Prizemoney £0 *Total Prizemoney* £3,180
1999 Turf 0-3: (14f, 15f, 22f) (hvy, gd 2) 1999 AW 0-2: (12f, 14f) (Fibr 2)
Moderate gelding, has worn blinkers. Turf high 40 (1st run) - 3rd of 18 getting 17lb from He's Got Wings (5 Apr Nottingham 14f gd RF 0591). AW high 46 - 2nd of 9 getting 9lb from Repton (19 Mar Southwell 12f Fibr RF 0449). **S Mellor [2-40] The Odd Dozen.*

SHERATON HEIGHTS BHB 54f **RR 50f** 4687[12]
2 b f Deploy 11.4f **(67)** - Norbella (Nordico (USA)) 6.5f **(62)**
Form - 560
Record 1999 - 1st:0 2nd:0 3rd:0 Ran:3
1999 Turf 0-2: (6f, 7f) (g-f 2) 1999 AW 0-1: (8f) (Fibr)
Currently fair filly. Turf high 50 (began Aug).
**K R Burke [0-3] Philip Harvey.*

SHERGANZAR BHB 69f **RR 73df** 4489[10]
4 b g Shernazar 11.8f **(71)** - Victory Kingdom (CAN) (Viceregal (CAN)) 6.8f **(64)**
Form - 30
Record 1999 - 1st:0 2nd:0 3rd:1 Ran:2
Pre1999 - 1st:0 2nd:2 3rd:1 Ran:12
Win Prizemoney £0 *Total Prizemoney* £3,082
1999 Turf 0-2: (12f 2) (g-s, g-f)
Scopey, above-average gelding, effective 9 to 12f, best at 11f, acts on g-s to g-f, best on gd.
**G L Moore [0-2] Antony Sofroniou (from R Hannon [0-7] Jly 1998).*

SHERIFF BHB 55f74a **RR 51f 74a** 324[4]
8 b g Midyan (USA) 9.9f **(64)** - Daisy Warwick (USA) (Ribot) 15.4f **(65)**
Form - 24
Record 1999 - 1st:0 2nd:1 3rd:0 Ran:2
Pre1999 - 1st:5 2nd:3 3rd:3 Ran:27
Win Prizemoney £13,508 *Total Prizemoney* £19,527
Wins * 1998 *Feb Lingfi (SLW) H* *16f* *70* *76* <
* 1998 *Feb Lingfi (SLW) H* *16f* *60* *75+*
* 1998 *Jan Lingfi (STD) H* *16f* *53* *59*
* 1996 *Feb Lingfi (STD) H* *16f* *52* *56+*
1999 AW 0-2: (16f 2) (Equi 2)
Above-average gelding, effective 16f, - acts on Equi, has worn blinkers. AW high 77 (1st run) - 2nd of 9 giving 10lb to Royal Roulette (19 Jan Lingfield 16f Equi RF 0126).
**J W Hills [11-51] Terry Milson.*

SHERIFF OFFICER (IRE) RR 25f 4503[12]
2 b g Distinctly North (USA) 7.4f **(63)** - Skip The Nonsense (IRE) (Astronef)
Form - 00
Record 1999 - 1st:0 2nd:0 3rd:0 Ran:2
1999 Turf 0-2: (6f 2) (g-f, frm)
Currently little account gelding. Turf high 25 (began Aug).
**P Calver [0-2] Mrs Janis MacPherson.*

SHERZABAD (IRE) RR 49f 4840[9]
2 b br c Doyoun 10.7f **(69)** - Sheriya (USA) (Green Dancer (USA)) 10.3f **(74)**
Form - 00
Record 1999 - 1st:0 2nd:0 3rd:0 Ran:2
1999 Turf 0-2: (7f 2) (gd 2)
Currently moderate colt. Turf high 49 (began Spt).
**Sir Michael Stoute [0-2] H H Aga Khan.*

SHE'S A GEM BHB 47f55a **RR 58f 55a** 4864[7]
4 b f Robellino (USA) 9.5f **(68)** -Rose Gem (IRE) (Taufan (USA)) 7f **(57)**
Form - 7405547
Record 1999 - 1st:0 2nd:0 3rd:0 Ran:7
Pre1999 - 1st:3 2nd:0 3rd:3 Ran:17
Win Prizemoney £6,788 *Total Prizemoney* £8,146
Wins 1998 *Mar Southw (STD) H* *7f* *64* *68* <
1998 *Jan Wolver (STD) H* *7f* *58* *63*
1998 *Jan Southw (STD) S* *7f* *52*
1999 Turf 0-5: (5f, 6f 4) (gd 2, g-f 2, frm) 1999 AW 0-2: (6f, 7f) (Fibr 2)
Light-framed, fair filly, effective 7f, - acts on Fibr, has worn blinkers, prefers left handed tracks, prefers tight tracks.
**Mrs V C Ward [0-4] Two Out & Hard Held (from A G Newcombe [0-3] Jun 1999).*

SHE'S MAGIC RR 39f 2008[11]
2 b f Magic Ring (IRE) 6.5f **(64)** - Norfolk Serenade (Blakeney) 10.5f **(64)**
Form - 00
Record 1999 - 1st:0 2nd:0 3rd:0 Ran:2
1999 Turf 0-2: (6f, 7f) (g-f, frm)
Currently very moderate filly. Turf high 39.
**M Brittain [0-2] Northgate Magic.*

SHE'S OUR MARE (IRE) BHB 72f **RR 93f** 4683[1]
6 b m Commanche Run 10.3f **(63)** - Miss Polymer (Doulab (USA)) 9.8f **(65)**
Form - 135711
1999 Turf 3-6: (8f 2-2, 9f, 10f 1-1, 12f 2) (g-s 1-1, gd 1-2, g-f 1-3)
Useful mare, effective 10f, acts on gd, likes left handed tracks. Turf high 93 - 1st of 33 getting 17lb from Bomb Alaska (2 Oct Newmarket RF 4683). Showed a fine turn of foot to win the Cambridgeshire and is capable of winning in Listed company. Equally effective over hurdles, she is a credit to her trainer.
**A J Martin in IRE [12-31] Exors of the late Mrs Denise Reddan.*

SHE-WOLFF (IRE) BHB 96f **RR 98f** 3825[9]
3 b f Pips Pride 6.7f **(70)** -Royal Wolff (Prince Tenderfoot (USA)) 9f **(61)**
Form - 320
Record 1999 - 1st:0 2nd:1 3rd:1 Ran:3
Pre1999 - 1st:1 2nd:1 3rd:0 Ran:3
Win Prizemoney £3,273 *Total Prizemoney* £12,266
Wins * 1998 May Bath (G-F) 5.7f 80+ <
1999 Turf 0-3: (5f 3) (hvy, g-f, frm)
Workmanlike, very useful filly, effective 5f, acts on g-f. Turf high 98 (1st run) - 3rd of 15 giving 6lb to Pips Magic (19 Jun Ascot 5f g-f RF 2134). **P J Makin [1-6] P E Cooper.*

SHIFTING BHB 42f42a **RR 29f 42a** 335[P]
4 ch f Night Shift (USA) 8.1f **(73)** - Preening (Persian Bold) 9.3f **(66)**
Form - 0354P
Record 1999 - 1st:0 2nd:0 3rd:1 Ran:4
Pre1999 - 1st:0 2nd:0 3rd:2 Ran:10
Win Prizemoney £0 *Total Prizemoney* £1,399
1999 AW 0-4: (7f, 9f 2, 12f) (Fibr 4)
Scopey, moderate filly, had worn blinkers. AW high 48. (DEAD)
**B A McMahon [0-4] Michael Sturgess (from C W Thornton [0-10] Nov 1998).*

SHIFTING MOON BHB 57f **RR 56f** 4648[14]
7 b g Night Shift (USA) 8.1f **(73)** - Moonscape (Ribero) 9.3f **(56)**
Form - 0
Record 1999 - 1st:0 2nd:0 3rd:0 Ran:1
Pre1999 - 1st:1 2nd:3 3rd:1 Ran:14
Win Prizemoney £3,787 *Total Prizemoney* £9,340
Wins 1995 Jly Chepst (G-F) H 8.1f 72 75 <
1999 Turf 0-1: (14f) (g-s)
Fair gelding, has worn blinkers. Becoming disappointing.
**F Jordan [6-34] Mrs K Roberts-Hindle (from I A Balding [1-12] Jly 1995).*

SHIKASTA (IRE) BHB 74f **RR 77f** 2617[3]
3 ch f Kris 10f **(75)** - India Atlanta (Ahonoora) 8.1f **(73)**

Form - 263
Record 1999 - 1st:0 2nd:1 3rd:1 Ran:3
Win Prizemoney £0 *Total Prizemoney* £1,655
1999 Turf 0-3: (10f 2, 12f) (gd, frm 2)
Unfurnished, currently above-average filly. Turf high 77 (1st run) - 2nd of 11 getting 5lb from Night Venture (26 May Ripon 10f frm RF 1506). **H R A Cecil [0-3] L Marinopoulos.*

SHINBONE ALLEY BHB 97f RR 91f 3760[5]

2 b c Lake Coniston (IRE) - Villota (Top Ville) 11.7f **(68)**
Form - 27285
Record 1999 - 1st:0 2nd:2 3rd:0 Ran:5
Win Prizemoney £0 *Total Prizemoney* £2,050
1999 Turf 0-5: (5f 4, 6f) (gd, g-f 2, frm 2)
Useful colt. Turf high 91. Should win his share of races, but he has shown a tendency to hang quite badly on occasions.
**J Berry [0-5] J Hanson.*

SHINEROLLA BHB 68f78a RR 71f 78a 4165[9]

7 b g Thatching 7.8f **(69)** - Primrolla (Relko) 9.9f **(59)**
Form - 00
Record 1999 - 1st:0 2nd:0 3rd:0 Ran:2
Pre1999 - 1st:3 2nd:6 3rd:3 Ran:29
Win Prizemoney £12,841 *Total Prizemoney* £39,904
Wins 1995 Oct Pontef (G-F) H 8f 75 79 <
1995 May Pontef (GD) H 8f 66 65+
1995 May Pontef (FRM) 8f 63
1999 Turf 0-2: (8f, 12f) (gd, frm)
Decent gelding, has worn blinkers. Turf high 53.
**C Parker [2-24] & Mrs Raymond Anderson Green (from Mrs J R Ramsden [3-16] Oct 1995).*

SHINING DANCER BHB 52f53a RR 54f 53a 3251[11]

7 b m Rainbow Quest (USA) 11.2f **(81)** - Strike Home (Be My Guest (USA)) 9.3f **(67)**
Form - 584343230
Record 1999 - 1st:0 2nd:1 3rd:3 Ran:9
Pre1999 - 1st:3 2nd:2 3rd:6 Ran:37
Win Prizemoney £13,080 *Total Prizemoney* £23,270
Wins * 1998 Spt Sandow (GD) H 14f 47 51
* 1997 May Kempto (GD) H 16f 60 64 <
* 1996 Jun Windso (G-F) H 10f 55 60
1999 Turf 0-9: (12f, 14f 5, 16f 3) (gd, g-f 2, frm 6)
Fair mare, effective 12 to 16f, best at 14f, acts on gd to frm, best on g-f, likes right handed tracks, prefers tight tracks, excels at Sandown. Turf high 54 - 2nd of 8 giving 14lb to Island Song (8 Jly Lingfield 14f frm RF 2640). Consistent. She is quite an effective stayer and was running well in staying handicaps during the summer, but has only a solitary Sandown victory over fourteen furlongs to her name in the last couple of seasons.
**S Dow [3-44] Mrs I P Blance (from Sir Michael Stoute [0-3] Jly 1995).*

SHINING DESERT (IRE) BHB 75f RR 61f 3631[7]

3 b f Green Desert (USA) 7.8f **(78)** - Riyoom (USA) (Vaguely Noble) 10.1f **(72)**
Form - 67
Record 1999 - 1st:0 2nd:0 3rd:0 Ran:2
Pre1999 - 1st:1 2nd:0 3rd:1 Ran:5
Win Prizemoney £3,533 *Total Prizemoney* £4,393
Wins 1998 Jun Haydoc (GD) 5f 85++ <
1999 Turf 0-2: (6f, 7f) (gd, g-f)
Neat, average filly, effective 5f, acts on frm.
**J Berry [0-5] Shine Racing (from M Johnston [1-2] Jun 1998).*

SHINING HOUR (USA) RR 94f 2040[1]

2 b f Red Ransom (USA) 8.6f **(83)** - Timely (Kings Lake (USA)) 10.8f **(67)**
Form - 211
Record 1999 - 1st:2 2nd:1 3rd:0 Ran:3
Win Prizemoney £36,402 *Total Prizemoney* £38,512
Wins * 1999 Jun Ascot (G-F) G3 5f 94 <
* 1999 May Bath (GD) 5.7f 80
1999 Turf 2-3: (5f 1-2, 6f 1-1) (gd 2-2, g-f)
Currently useful filly. Turf high 94 - 1st of 13 from Rowaasi (16 Jun Ascot RF 2040). Runner-up on her Chester debut, she was not convincing when landing the odds at Bath next time. However she left that form behind when coming late to beat Rowaasi in the Queen Mary at Royal Ascot. Suffered a muscle injury in July and did not reappear. **P W Chapple-Hyam [2-3] R E Sangster.*

SHINING STAR RR 65f 4574[5]

2 ch f Selkirk (USA) 7.9f **(76)** - Mystery Ship (Decoy Boy) 6.7f **(56)**
Form - 7565
Record 1999 - 1st:0 2nd:0 3rd:0 Ran:4
1999 Turf 0-4: (5f 2, 6f 2) (gd 2, g-f, frm)
Average filly. Turf high 65. **J Berry [0-4] Shine Racing.*

SHINNING WAR (FR) RR 92?f 2657a[3]

3 b f Shining Steel 7f **(46)** - Guerre de Troie (Risk Me (FR)) 5.9f **(53)**
Form - 3
1999 Turf 0-1: (10f) (gd)
Currently useful filly. (1st run) - 3rd of 6 to Victory Cry (2 Jly Chantilly 10f gd RF 2657a). **E Lellouche in FR [0-2].*

SHIPLEY GLEN BHB 60f73a RR 60df 73a 3533[5]

4 b c Green Desert (USA) 7.8f **(78)** - Lady Shipley (Shirley Heights) 10.3f **(74)**
Form - 124135
Record 1999 - 1st:2 2nd:1 3rd:1 Ran:6
Pre1999 - 1st:1 2nd:1 3rd:0 Ran:6
Win Prizemoney £8,509 *Total Prizemoney* £11,282
Wins * **1999** *Jly Wolver (STD) H 8.5f 62 77* <
* **1999** May Carlis (FRM) H 9.3f 55 63+
* 1998 *Jun Wolver (STD) H 9.4f 51 57+*
1999 Turf 1-5: (8f 2, 9f 1-2, 10f) (gd 1-2, g-f 3) 1999 AW 1-1: (8f 1-1) (Fibr 1-1)
Above-average colt, effective 8f, - acts on Fibr. Turf high 65. (1st run) - 1st of 8 giving 17lb to The Last Word (9 Jly Wolverhampton RF 2689). He has shown good consistent form on turf, including winning on very fast ground at Carlisle in the spring, but looks a rather better performer on Fibresand having won twice at Wolverhampton. **Sir Mark Prescott [3-12] Mrs Bumet Osborne House.*

SHIRLEY NOT BHB 67f RR 67f 4879[18]

3 gr g Paris House 5.9f **(64)** - Hollia (Touch Boy) 5f **(66)**
Form - 064223000
Record 1999 - 1st:0 2nd:2 3rd:1 Ran:9
Pre1999 - 1st:2 2nd:3 3rd:0 Ran:7
Win Prizemoney £5,390 *Total Prizemoney* £12,511
Wins * 1998 Aug Cheste (G-S) H 5.1f 73 <
1998 *Apr Southw (STD) S 5f 51*
1999 Turf 0-9: (5f 8, 6f) (g-s, gd 3, g-f, frm 3, hrd)
Leggy, average gelding, effective 5f, acts on gd to frm, best on g-f, excels at Chester and Thirsk. Turf high 68 - 2nd of 13 getting 12lb from Miss Fit (9 Jly Chester 5f g-f RF 2674). Ran some good races, but was unfortunate enough to come up against some really in-form sprinters last term. Likes the minimum trip on fast ground.
**S Gollings [1-13] Whinham-P Brown-J Stelling (from J Berry [1-3] May 1998).*

SHIVA (JPN) BHB 121f RR 117f 4919[2]

4 ch f Hector Protector (USA) 9f **(89)** - Lingerie (Shirley Heights) 10.3f **(74)**
Form - 1172
Record 1999 - 1st:2 2nd:1 3rd:0 Ran:4
Pre1999 - 1st:1 2nd:0 3rd:0 Ran:1
Win Prizemoney £85,680 *Total Prizemoney* £169,880
Wins * **1999** May Currag (GD) G1 10.5f 117 <
* **1999** Apr Newmar (GD) G3 8.5f 106
* 1998 May Kempto (GD) 9f 89
1999 Turf 2-4: (9f 1-1, 10f 2, 11f 1-1) (gd 1-2, g-f 1-2)
Well made, high-class filly. Turf high 117 - 2nd of 13 to Alborada (16 Oct Newmarket 10f gd RF 4919) - also 1st of 6 getting 3lb from Daylami (23 May Curragh RF 1483a). A comfortable winner of a maiden on her only start in 1998, she improved over the winter and was very impressive when winning the Earl Of Sefton on her return. She gained her biggest success to date when beating Daylami in the Tattersalls Gold Cup, but looked totally ill-at-ease on the very fast ground at Royal Ascot and jarred herself up. Given a break, she came back to run a fine second to Alborada in the Champion Stakes, though her trainer would like to have had another week to get her fully fit. **H R A Cecil [3-5] Niarchos Family.*

SHOESTRING BHB 37f RR 26f 4584[11]

3 br g Petong 7.6f **(58)** - Wantage Park (Pas de Seul) 9.1f **(67)**

Form - 070
Record 1999 - 1st:0 2nd:0 3rd:0 Ran:3
1999 Turf 0-3: (6f 2, 10f) (gd 2, frm)
Leggy, currently little account gelding. Turf high 26 (began Aug).
**D W P Arbuthnot [0-3] The Second Kennet Partnership.*

SHOGUN (IRE) BHB 56f65a RR 40f 65a 5154[10]

4 b g Zafonic (USA) 9f **(83)** - Sheriyna (FR) (Darshaan) 9.9f **(84)**
Form - 104000
Record 1999 - 1st:1 2nd:0 3rd:0 Ran:6
Pre1999 - 1st:0 2nd:2 3rd:0 Ran:4
Win Prizemoney £3,648 *Total Prizemoney* £6,877
Wins 1999 *Jan Lingfi (STD) 10f 65 <*
1999 Turf 0-3: (10f 2, 14f) (g-s 2, gd) 1999 AW 1-3: (10f 1-1, 11f, 12f) (Equi 1-2, Fibr)
Scopey, average gelding, effective 8f, acts on frm, has worn blinkers.
**B A McMahon [0-2] Mrs B B Whitehorn (from K R Burke [1-4] Apr 1999).*

SHONTAINE BHB 41f40a RR 41f 40a 5151[7]

6 b g Pharly (FR) 11.5f **(64)** - Hinari Televideo (Caerleon (USA)) 8.6f **(71)**
Form - 00000043604500821432863080207
Record 1999 - 1st:1 2nd:3 3rd:3 Ran:25
Pre1999 - 1st:10 2nd:6 3rd:9 Ran:69
Win Prizemoney £29,884 *Total Prizemoney* £43,122
Wins * 1999 Jun Ayr (GD) SH 8f 40 44
* 1998 *Feb Southw (STD) H 8f 60 63*
* 1998 *Jan Southw (STD) H 8f 51 56*
* 1997 Spt Hamilt (GD) H 8.3f 55 59
* 1997 Aug Thirsk (G-F) SH 8f 51 57
* 1997 May Carlis (FRM) H 6.9f 50 56
* 1997 *Mar Lingfi (STD) C 6f 52*
* 1996 *Nov Southw (STD) H 7f 60 67*
* 1996 Jly Catter (GD) SH 7f 60 64
* 1995 Jly Newcas (G-F) 6f 78 <
* 1995 Jly Doncas (GD) 6f 74
1999 Turf 1-19: (7f 5, 8f 1-14) (sft, g-s, gd 5, g-f 1-2, frm 9, hrd) 1999 AW 0-6: (7f 4, 8f 2) (Equi 2, Fibr 4)
Moderate gelding, effective 8f, - acts on Fibr, has worn blinkers, likes left handed tracks. **M Johnston [11-94] Paul Dean.*

SHOOFHA (IRE) RR 72f 5108[8]

2 b f Bluebird (USA) 7.9f **(71)** - Courtesane (USA) (Majestic Light (USA)) 10.6f **(75)**
Form - 8
Record 1999 - 1st:0 2nd:0 3rd:0 Ran:1
1999 Turf 0-1: (8f) (gd)
Currently above-average filly.
**M P Tregoning [0-1] Sheikh Ahmed Al Maktoum.*

SHOOGLE (USA) BHB 77f RR 77f 4954[13]

3 ch f A P Indy (USA) - Dokki (USA) (Northern Dancer) 9.6f **(80)**
Form - 330
Record 1999 - 1st:0 2nd:0 3rd:2 Ran:3
Pre1999 - 1st:1 2nd:0 3rd:0 Ran:3
Win Prizemoney £3,642 *Total Prizemoney* £5,424
Wins * 1998 Jly Salisb (FRM) 7f 72+ <
1999 Turf 0-3: (8f, 10f 2) (g-f 3)
Tall, above-average filly, effective 7 to 10f, acts on g-f to frm. Turf high 77 - 3rd of 8 giving 11lb to Pentagon Lad (9 Jly Chester 10f g-f RF 2672). **J H M Gosden [1-6] K Abdulla.*

SHOO-IN RR 1800[14]

3 b f Minshaanshu Amad (USA) 11.3f **(53)** - Heavenly State (Enchantment) 5.4f **(52)**
Form - 70
Record 1999 - 1st:0 2nd:0 3rd:0 Ran:2
1999 Turf 0-2: (8f, 12f) (gd, hrd)
Workmanlike, currently very poor filly.
**M Madgwick [0-2] Gail Gaisford And Friends.*

SHOP WINDOW BHB 47f49a RR 49f 49a 2480[10]

3 b f Noble Patriarch 12.2f **(43)** - Warning Bell (Bustino) 10.4f **(64)**
Form - 4000830
Record 1999 - 1st:0 2nd:0 3rd:1 Ran:7
Pre1999 - 1st:0 2nd:0 3rd:1 Ran:4
Win Prizemoney £0 *Total Prizemoney* £685
1999 Turf 0-6: (7f, 8f, 9f, 12f 3) (gd 2, g-f 2, frm 2) 1999 AW 0-1: (12f) (Fibr)
Neat, moderate filly, effective 6 to 12f, acts on frm, has worn blinkers. Turf high 60 (1st run) - 4th of 12 giving 12lb to Hi-Jenny (14 Apr Beverley 12f frm RF 0689). **T D Easterby [0-11] A Arton.*

SHORT ROMANCE (IRE) BHB 49f RR 50f 4837[5]

4 b f Brief Truce (USA) 9.1f **(73)** - Lady's Turn (Rymer)
Form - 62728505
Record 1999 - 1st:0 2nd:2 3rd:0 Ran:8
Pre1999 - 1st:1 2nd:0 3rd:2 Ran:12
Win Prizemoney £3,494 *Total Prizemoney* £7,436
Wins * 1998 Aug Folkes (G-F) H 12f 58 60 <
1999 Turf 0-8: (12f 3, 13f, 14f 2, 16f 2) (g-s, gd 4, g-f, frm 2)
Fair filly, effective 10 to 16f, acts on gd to frm, likes right handed tracks, favours tight tracks, excels at Folkestone. Turf high 59 - 2nd of 11 giving 4lb to Sound Appeal (17 May Bath 13f gd RF 1270). **J W Hills [1-20] Abbott Racing Partners.*

SHOTACROSS THE BOW (IRE) BHB 77f RR 78f 4129[1]

2 b c Warning 8.1f **(77)** - Nordica (Northfields (USA)) 9f **(72)**
Form - 041
Record 1999 - 1st:1 2nd:0 3rd:0 Ran:3
Win Prizemoney £3,468 *Total Prizemoney* £3,736
Wins * 1999 Spt Epsom (G-F) 6f 78 <
1999 Turf 1-3: (6f 1-3) (gd, frm 1-2)
Currently above-average colt. Turf high 78 (began Jly) - 1st of 7 from Golden Harvest (4 Spt Epsom RF 4129).
**B W Hills [1-3] C Wright & The Hon Mrs J M Corbett.*

SHOTLEY MARIE (IRE) BHB 22f RR 10f 5035[18]

4 b f Scenic 10.6f **(66)** - Hana Marie (Formidable (USA)) 9.2f **(63)**
Form - 080800
Record 1999 - 1st:0 2nd:0 3rd:0 Ran:6
Pre1999 - 1st:0 2nd:0 3rd:0 Ran:7
1999 Turf 0-4: (7f, 9f, 12f 2) (sft, g-s, g-f 2) 1999 AW 0-2: (12f, 16f) (Fibr 2)
Light-framed, very moderate filly, has worn blinkers. Turf high 10.
**N Bycroft [0-13] J A Swinburne.*

SHOUF AL BADOU (USA) BHB 97f RR 90+f 5213[1]

2 b c Sheikh Albadou 9.2f **(75)** - Millfit (USA) (Blushing Groom (FR)) 10.3f **(76)**
Form - 34111
Record 1999 - 1st:3 2nd:0 3rd:1 Ran:5
Win Prizemoney £11,082 *Total Prizemoney* £12,132
Wins * 1999 Nov Doncas (SFT) 8f 90+ <
*** 1999** *Oct Wolver (STD) 6f 90*
*** 1999** *Oct Wolver (STD) 6f 72+*
1999 Turf 1-3: (6f, 7f, 8f 1-1) (g-s 1-1, g-f 2) 1999 AW 2-2: (6f 2-2) (Fibr 2-2)
Useful colt. Turf high 90 (began Jly) - 1st of 5 giving 4lb to French Lieutenant (5 Nov Doncaster RF 5213). AW high 90 (began Oct) - 1st of 6 getting 2lb from Selking (13 Oct Wolverhampton RF 4867). His sire won the Breeders' Cup Sprint and he took to Fibresand like a duck to water, easily winning a maiden at Wolverhampton in October but having to work just a bit harder to land a conditions event next time. Showed a similar level of form on turf when scoring at Doncaster and is a useful prospect. **B W Hills [3-5] Hilal Salem.*

SHOULDHAVEGONEHOME (IRE) BHB 52f57a RR 45f 57a 5187[12]

2 ch f Up and At 'em - Gentle Papoose (Commanche Run) 8.5f **(58)**
Form - 04254012430700
Record 1999 - 1st:1 2nd:2 3rd:1 Ran:14
Win Prizemoney £2,766 *Total Prizemoney* £4,698
Wins * 1999 Aug Mussel (G-F) S 5f 65 <
1999 Turf 1-12: (5f 1-10, 6f 2) (g-s, gd 1-5, g-f 5, frm) 1999 AW 0-2: (5f, 6f) (Fibr 2)
Average filly, effective 5f, acts on gd to g-f, best on g-f, has worn blinkers. Turf high 65 - 1st of 12 from Cosmena (26 Aug Musselburgh RF 3919). AW high 60 (began Oct). Becoming disappointing. **P D Evans [1-14] Men Behaving Badly.*

SHOWBOAT BHB 108f **RR 113f** 4919[11]
5 b h Warning 8.1f **(77)** - Boathouse (Habitat) 9.4f **(70)**
Form - 10231424610
Record 1999 - 1st:3 2nd:2 3rd:1 Ran:11
Pre1999 - 1st:2 2nd:0 3rd:3 Ran:15
Win Prizemoney £96,448 *Total Prizemoney* £122,689
Wins * **1999** Spt Newbur (G-F) 9f 110
* **1999** Jun Ascot (G-F) H 8f 92 108
* **1999** Apr Newmar (GD) H 7f 86 90
* 1997 Aug Salisb (G-F) 8f 93
* 1996 Oct Leices (G-F) 7f 93+
1999 Turf 3-11: (7f 1-4, 8f 1-4, 9f 1-2, 10f) (gd 2-6, g-f, frm 1-4)
Group-class colt, effective 8 to 9f, best at 8f, acts on gd to frm, best on frm. Turf high 113 - also 1st of 7 giving 5lb to Diamond White (18 Spt Newbury RF 4409). Consistent. He looked unlucky on a couple of occasions before turning the Royal Hunt Cup into a procession. That impressive success rather forced his trainer's hand, and he was campaigned almost exclusively in conditions races thereafter, winning at Newbury in September. Effective up to nine furlongs, he bounces off fast ground and has an excellent turn-of-foot on his day. While handicaps are probably out of the question, it would not be a great surprise if he landed a Listed race in 2000. **B W Hills [5-26] R D Hollingsworth.*

SHOWING RR 52f 5129[19]
2 b c Owington - Sharanella (Shareef Dancer (USA)) 9.9f **(73)**
Form - 00
Record 1999 - 1st:0 2nd:0 3rd:0 Ran:2
1999 Turf 0-2: (6f 2) (gd 2)
Currently fair colt. Turf high 52 (began Oct).
**N A Graham [0-2] First Millennium Racing.*

SHOW ME HEAVEN RR 28f 3111[6]
2 b f Rock City 8.8f **(62)** - Tufty Lady (Riboboy (USA)) 14f **(54)**
Form - 06
Record 1999 - 1st:0 2nd:0 3rd:0 Ran:2
1999 Turf 0-1: (5f) (gd) 1999 AW 0-1: (6f) (Fibr)
Currently little account filly. **J P Leigh [0-2] Mrs D Dukes.*

SHOW ME THE MONEY (IRE) RR 108f 4848a[6]
3 b f Mujadil (USA) 7.7f **(70)** - Snappy Dresser (Nishapour (FR)) 9.1f **(61)**
Form - 100336
1999 Turf 1-6: (5f, 6f, 7f 1-3, 8f) (sft 2, g-s, gd, g-f 1-2)
Pattern-class filly, effective 5 to 7f, acts on sft to g-f, excels at Ascot, does well at Cork. Turf high 108 (1st run) - 1st of 7 giving 5lb to Apparatchik (18 Apr Leopardstown RF 0784a). Inconsistent. Winner of the Cornwallis Stakes at two, she was stepped up to seven furlongs for her reappearance and ran out the convincing winner of the Leopardstown 1000 Guineas Trial. She incurred sore shins in the Irish 1000 Guineas itself and was off the course a long time, but recaptured some form in soft ground at the end of the campaign. Ran poorly on her final start, however.
**N Meade in IRE [5-13] L Queally.*

SHRIVAR (IRE) BHB 72f **RR 75f** 5104[5]
2 b c Sri Pekan (USA) - Kriva **(72df 61a)** (Reference Point) 6.8f **(70)**
Form - 605
Record 1999 - 1st:0 2nd:0 3rd:0 Ran:3
1999 Turf 0-3: (7f 3) (g-s, gd 2)
Currently above-average colt. Turf high 75 (began Spt).
**M R Channon [0-3] P D Savill.*

SHTURM (RUS) RR 99f 4664a[3]
6 ch h Raut (RUS) - Askanija (RUS)
Form - 3
1999 Turf 0-1: (12f) (hvy)
Very useful horse. (1st run) - 3rd of 11 getting 5lb from Trait De Genie (26 Spt Dielsdorf 12f hvy RF 4664a).
**M Weiss in SWI [2-10] Spt 1998).*

SHUDDER BHB 68f **RR 56f** 5065[17]
4 b c Distant Relative 7f **(69)** - Oublier L'Ennui (FR) (Bellman (FR)) 8.4f **(77)**
Form - 5158070
Record 1999 - 1st:1 2nd:0 3rd:0 Ran:7
Pre1999 - 1st:1 2nd:1 3rd:2 Ran:5
Win Prizemoney £5,885 *Total Prizemoney* £28,201
Wins 1999 Aug Haydoc (G-S) C 6f 80
1997 Aug Goodwo (G-F) 6f 85+ <
1999 Turf 1-7: (5f 2, 6f 1-4, 7f) (gd 3, g-f 1-3, frm)
Workmanlike, fair colt, has worn blinkers (very effectively). Turf high 80 (began Jly). Becoming disappointing.
**R J Hodges [0-5] Mrs Anna Sanders (from W J Haggas [2-7] Aug 1999).*

SHURUK BHB 83f **RR 78f** 4383[7]
2 ch f Cadeaux Genereux 7.9f **(76)** - Harmless Albatross (Pas de Seul) 9.1f **(67)**
Form - 717
Record 1999 - 1st:1 2nd:0 3rd:0 Ran:3
Win Prizemoney £4,207 *Total Prizemoney* £4,207
Wins * **1999** Aug Nottin (G-F) 6.1f 78 <
1999 Turf 1-3: (6f 1-2, 7f) (g-f 1-2, frm)
Currently above-average filly. Turf high 78 (began Aug) - 1st of 13 from Banafsajyh (28 Aug Nottingham RF 3971). Just got up to win over six furlongs at Nottingham on her second start, but was well held when tackling better fillies next time.
**J L Dunlop [1-3] Hamdan Al Maktoum.*

SHUTTLECOCK BHB 24f20a **RR 22f 20a** 323[5]
8 ch g Pharly (FR) 11.5f **(64)** - Upper Sister (Upper Case (USA)) 8.2f **(55)**
Form - 648705
Record 1999 - 1st:0 2nd:0 3rd:0 Ran:5
Pre1999 - 1st:4 2nd:7 3rd:9 Ran:76
Win Prizemoney £10,088 *Total Prizemoney* £18,974
Wins 1995 *Jan Southw (STD) C 8f 69* <
1995 *Jan Southw (STD) C 8f 53*
1999 AW 0-5: (12f, 13f, 16f 3) (Equi 2, Fibr 3)
Little account gelding, effective 12 to 16f, best at 12f, acts on hvy - acts on Fibr, has worn blinkers. AW high 29 (1st run) - 4th of 10 to Turrill House (8 Jan Southwell 16f Fibr RF 0051). Becoming disappointing.
**D W Chapman [0-24] David Chapman (from Mrs N Macauley [2-35] Feb 1997).*

SIANA SPRINGS (IRE) BHB 61f **RR 47f** 4524[13]
2 b f Emarati (USA) 6.6f **(63)** - Psylla (Beldale Flutter (USA)) 9.7f **(71)**
Form - 58162800
Record 1999 - 1st:1 2nd:1 3rd:0 Ran:8
Win Prizemoney £1,982 *Total Prizemoney* £2,848
Wins * **1999** May Haydoc (GD) S 5f 63 <
1999 Turf 1-8: (5f 1-6, 6f, 7f) (gd 3, g-f 1-3, frm 2)
Moderate filly, effective 5f, acts on g-f to frm. Turf high 71 - 2nd of 7 getting 13lb from Argent Facile (21 Jly Leicester 5f frm RF 3010) - also 1st of 9 from Step Ahead (28 May Haydock RF 1545).
**J J Quinn [1-8] Robinski Bloodstock Ltd.*

SIAN'S MILLENNIUM BHB 66f **RR 63f** 2245[9]
2 b f Whittingham (IRE) - Special One (Aragon) 8.1f **(60)**
Form - 564600
Record 1999 - 1st:0 2nd:0 3rd:0 Ran:6
Win Prizemoney £0 *Total Prizemoney* £229
1999 Turf 0-6: (5f 5, 6f) (gd, g-f 4, frm)
Average filly, effective 5f, acted on g-f, had worn blinkers. Turf high 63. (DEAD) **B Palling [0-6] John Harris and Mrs Sian Harris.*

SIBERIAN MYSTIC BHB 41f **RR 31f** 1270[11]
6 gr m Siberian Express (USA) 9f **(58)** - Mystic Crystal (IRE) (Caerleon (USA)) 8.6f **(71)**
Form - 0
Record 1999 - 1st:0 2nd:0 3rd:0 Ran:1
Pre1999 - 1st:2 2nd:3 3rd:1 Ran:17
Win Prizemoney £5,239 *Total Prizemoney* £8,848
Wins * 1997 Oct Pontef (G-F) H 12f 35 43 <
* 1996 Aug Beverl (G-F) H 9.9f 30 36
1999 Turf 0-1: (13f) (gd)
Very moderate mare, effective 12 to 14f, best at 12f, acts on gd to hrd. **P G Murphy [8-38] Glenferry And Partners.*

SIBERTIGO RR 48f 2636[11]
3 b g Touch of Grey 8.1f **(47)** - Young Lady (Young Generation) 7.7f **(63)**

Form - 80
Record 1999 - 1st:0 2nd:0 3rd:0 Ran:2
1999 Turf 0-2: (7f, 8f) (frm 2)
Workmanlike, currently moderate gelding. Turf high 48.
**R M Flower [0-2] Richard Gurr.*

SIBLING RIVAL (USA) RR 114f 2071[14]

5 b h Quest for Fame 12.8f **(75)** - Perfect Sister (USA) (Perrault)
Form - 00
Record 1999 - 1st:0 2nd:0 3rd:0 Ran:2
Pre1999 - 1st:0 2nd:2 3rd:0 Ran:2
Win Prizemoney £0 *Total Prizemoney* £34,343
1999 Turf 0-2: (12f, 20f) (g-f 2)
Group-class colt. Turf high 87. Now with Godolphin, this game colt won in Dubai in February but proved hard to place in Europe.
**S bin Suroor [0-1] Godolphin (from S bin Suroor in UAE [0-1] Mar 1999).*

SICK AS A PARROT BHB 73f93a RR 67f 93a 4335[5]

4 ch g Casteddu 7.4f **(54)** - Sianiski (Niniski (USA)) 10.6f **(65)**
Form - 32005035005
Record 1999 - 1st:0 2nd:1 3rd:2 Ran:11
Pre1999 - 1st:5 2nd:3 3rd:1 Ran:16
Win Prizemoney £21,025 *Total Prizemoney* £40,444

Wins							
* 1998	Aug	Redcar	(G-F)	H	11f	84	84
* 1998	May	Beverl	(GD)	H	8.5f	80	85 <
* 1997	Oct	Yarmou	(GD)	H	8f	75	79
* 1997	Spt	Yarmou	(FRM)	H	8f	70	72
* 1997	Jun	Yarmou	(FRM)	S	7f		58

1999 Turf 0-9: (8f 2, 9f 2, 10f 5) (g-s 2, gd 2, g-f 2, frm 3) 1999 AW 0-2: (10f 2) (Equi 2)
Unfurnished, very useful gelding, effective 10f, - acts on Equi, has worn blinkers, likes left handed tracks, likes tight tracks. Turf high 82. AW high 97 - 2nd of 14 to Supreme Sound (20 Mar Lingfield 10f Equi RF 0456). Ran a cracker in the winter Derby, but only showed glimpses of form on turf. **C A Dwyer [5-27] First Class Mobile.*

SICNEE (USA) BHB 111f RR 107f 4009[1]

3 gr c Rubiano (USA) 7.1f **(87)** - Lets Be Personal (CAN) (Grey Dawn II) 11.1f **(72)**
Form - 71
Record 1999 - 1st:1 2nd:0 3rd:0 Ran:2
Pre1999 - 1st:2 2nd:2 3rd:0 Ran:4
Win Prizemoney £23,530 *Total Prizemoney* £32,275

Wins							
* 1999	Aug	Chepst	(G-S)		7.1f		107 <
1998	Aug	Deauvi	(GD)	L	7f		91+
1998	Jly	Redcar	(G-F)		7f		84+

1999 Turf 1-2: (7f 1-2) (gd 1-2)
Well made, Pattern-class colt, effective 7f, acts on sft to gd. Turf high 107 - 1st of 8 getting 5lb from Trans Island (30 Aug Chepstow RF 4009). This striking individual was touched off in America on his return to action, but came on for his run in the Jersey Stakes to land a Chepstow conditions event in good style. That was the first victory in Wales for Godolphin, for whom he is a valuable work horse.
**S bin Suroor [1-2] Godolphin (from D R Loder [2-4] Oct 1998).*

SIDDONS COMMON (IRE) BHB 54f RR 57f 4882[17]

3 b c Common Grounds 8.1f **(66)** - Miss Siddons (Cure The Blues (USA)) 9.5f **(63)**
Form - 07070
Record 1999 - 1st:0 2nd:0 3rd:0 Ran:5
1999 Turf 0-5: (8f, 10f 3, 11f) (gd, g-f 2, frm 2)
Scopey, fair colt. Turf high 57.
**J W Hills [0-5] Racegoers Club Owners Group (1997).*

SIDE SADDLE (IRE) RR 107f 4769a[7]

3 f Saddlers' Hall (IRE) 10.5f **(65)** - Athene (IRE) **(81f)** (Rousillon (USA)) 8.2f **(74)**
Form - 3212587
1999 Turf 1-7: (9f, 11f, 12f 1-3, 13f, 14f) (hvy, sft, gd 4, g-f 1-1)
Pattern-class, effective 12 to 14f, best at 12f, acts on hvy to g-f, best on gd, prefers right handed tracks. Turf high 107 - also 1st of 6 from White Star (5 Jun Chantilly RF 1900a). Showed useful form in French group races in the spring and, although unplaced, did not run badly in top fillies' races later in the season.
**D Smaga in FR [1-7] Lord Weinstock.*

SIDNEY THE KIDNEY BHB 26f17a RR 30f 17a 185[10]

5 b m Mystiko (USA) 7.7f **(59)** - Martin-Lavell Mail (Dominion) 8.5f **(63)**
Form - 6080
Record 1999 - 1st:0 2nd:0 3rd:0 Ran:4
Pre1999 - 1st:0 2nd:1 3rd:5 Ran:22
Win Prizemoney £0 *Total Prizemoney* £2,337
1999 AW 0-4: (11f, 12f 3) (Equi, Fibr 3)
Very moderate filly, effective 12f, - acts on Fibr. AW high 35.
**M J Ryan [0-26] Norcroft Park Stud.*

SIEGE (IRE) BHB 103f RR 111+f 2733[2]

3 br c Indian Ridge 7.6f **(74)** - Above Water (IRE) (Reference Point) 6.8f **(70)**
Form - 2122
Record 1999 - 1st:1 2nd:3 3rd:0 Ran:4
Pre1999 - 1st:0 2nd:1 3rd:2 Ran:4
Win Prizemoney £3,712 *Total Prizemoney* £42,780
Wins * **1999** May Kempto (G-F) 7f 89 <
1999 Turf 1-4: (7f 1-2, 8f, 10f) (g-f 2, frm 1-1, hrd)
Scopey, Group-class colt, effective 8 to 10f, acts on g-f. Turf high 111 - 2nd of 16 getting 2lb from Achilles (10 Jly York 10f g-f RF 2733). Fitted with a net muzzle when breaking his duck at Kempton in May, he went on to finish second in both the Britannia Handicap and John Smith's Cup. A shade unlucky in the latter event, in which he was struck in the face by the winner's whip, he will continue his career in America and should do well.
**Sir Michael Stoute [1-8] The Royal Ascot Racing Club.*

SIEGE PERILOUS (IRE) BHB 67f57a RR 68f 57a 1578[9]

6 b g Taufan (USA) 8.3f **(65)** - Carado (Manado) 9.6f **(63)**
Form - 560
Record 1999 - 1st:0 2nd:0 3rd:0 Ran:3
Pre1999 - 1st:4 2nd:4 3rd:4 Ran:21
Win Prizemoney £13,599 *Total Prizemoney* £28,022

Wins							
* 1997	Aug	Sandow	(G-S)	H	16.4f	70	75 <
* 1997	Jun	Sandow	(G-F)	H	14f	69	72
* 1996	Apr	Nottin	(G-F)	H	14.1f	58	59
* 1996	Mar	Folkes	(G-S)	H	12f	50	52

1999 Turf 0-3: (16f 3) (g-s, gd, frm)
Average gelding. Turf high 68 - 6th of 13 giving 8lb to Yes Keemo Sabee (14 May Thirsk 16f gd RF 1224).
**S C Williams [4-21] S Demanuele (from Bob Jones [0-3] Oct 1995).*

SIEGFRIED BHB 59f RR 67f 1776[5]

3 ch g Magic Ring (IRE) 6.5f **(64)** - Spirit of The Wind (USA) (Little Current (USA)) 9.6f **(75)**
Form - 085
Record 1999 - 1st:0 2nd:0 3rd:0 Ran:3
1999 Turf 0-2: (7f, 8f) (frm 2) 1999 AW 0-1: (7f) (Fibr)
Leggy, currently average gelding. Turf high 67.
**B W Hills [0-3] H R H Princess Michael of Kent.*

SIFAT BHB 55f RR 62f 5133[15]

4 b f Marju (IRE) 9.2f **(76)** - Reine Maid (USA) (Mr Prospector (USA)) 8.8f **(78)**
Form - 0075740
Record 1999 - 1st:0 2nd:0 3rd:0 Ran:7
Pre1999 - 1st:1 2nd:0 3rd:2 Ran:7
Win Prizemoney £3,647 *Total Prizemoney* £5,066
Wins 1998 Oct Pontef (G-S) 8f 76 <
1999 Turf 0-7: (8f 2, 10f 4, 12f) (sft, g-s, gd, g-f 2, frm, hrd)
Scopey, average filly, effective 8f, acts on g-s to gd, best on gd, has worn blinkers, prefers tight tracks. Turf high 62.
**N A Graham [0-7] C N & Mrs J C Wright (from M P Tregoning [1-7] Oct 1998).*

SIFT BHB 55f RR 62f 4341[3]

2 b f Salse (USA) 10.9f **(71)** - Lake Pleasant (IRE) (Elegant Air) 13.2f **(61)**
Form - 373603
Record 1999 - 1st:0 2nd:0 3rd:3 Ran:6
Win Prizemoney £0 *Total Prizemoney* £1,124
1999 Turf 0-6: (6f 2, 7f 3, 8f) (gd, g-f 3, frm 2)
Average filly, effective 6 to 8f, acts on gd to frm. Turf high 62 - 3rd of 15 getting 5lb from Timaru (16 Spt Ayr 8f gd RF 4341).
**D HaydnJones [0-4] Hugh O'Donnell (from Sir Mark Prescott [0-2] Jun 1999).*

SIGGIEWI BHB 25f **RR 19f** 2051[14]

5 ro m Mystiko (USA) 7.7f **(59)** - Shadiyama (Nishapour (FR)) 9.1f **(61)**

Form - 480

Record					
1999 -	1st:0	2nd:0	3rd:0	Ran:3
Pre1999 -	1st:0	2nd:0	3rd:0	Ran:4

Win Prizemoney £0 *Total Prizemoney* £206

1999 Turf 0-3: (12f 2, 14f) (g-f 2, frm)

Poor filly. Turf high 19. **N M Babbage [0-8] B Babbage.*

SIGNET RING BHB 38f **RR 45f** 4438[8]

3 ch f King's Signet (USA) 7f **(51)** -Geoffreys Bird (Master Willie) 7f **(70)**

Form - 00008

Record 1999 - 1st:0 2nd:0 3rd:0 Ran:5

1999 Turf 0-5: (7f 2, 8f 2, 10f) (g-f, frm 4)

Light-framed, moderate filly, has worn blinkers. Turf high 48.

**H Candy [0-5] Henry Candy & Partners.*

SIGNIFY BHB 72f **RR 69f** 3549[6]

3 b c Marju (IRE) 9.2f **(76)** - Windmill Princess (Gorytus (USA)) 7.8f **(60)**

Form - 05326

Record 1999 - 1st:0 2nd:1 3rd:1 Ran:5

Win Prizemoney £0 *Total Prizemoney* £1,843

1999 Turf 0-5: (8f, 10f 2, 11f, 12f) (gd, g-f 2, frm 2)

Average colt. Turf high 69 - 2nd of 5 giving 23lb to Pip's Brave (17 Jly Warwick 11f g-f RF 2932). **L M Cumani [0-5] M J Dawson.*

SIGN OF HOPE BHB 70f **RR 74+f** 4934[3]

2 ch c Selkirk (USA) 7.9f **(76)** - Rainbow's End (My Swallow) 9.2f **(71)**

Form - 84703

Record 1999 - 1st:0 2nd:0 3rd:1 Ran:5

Win Prizemoney £0 *Total Prizemoney* £876

1999 Turf 0-5: (7f 3, 8f 2) (g-s, gd, g-f 3)

Above-average colt, has worn blinkers. Turf high 74 (began Aug) - 3rd of 19 giving 5lb to Fashion (18 Oct Pontefract 8f g-f RF 4934).

**I A Balding [0-5] George Strawbridge.*

SIGN OF THE TIGER BHB 56f **RR 45f** 4937[4]

2 b g Beveled (USA) 6.9f **(64)** - Me Spede (Valiyar) 8.5f **(73)**

Form - 0004

Record 1999 - 1st:0 2nd:0 3rd:0 Ran:4

Win Prizemoney £0 *Total Prizemoney* £201

1999 Turf 0-3: (5f, 6f 2) (gd 2, frm) 1999 AW 0-1: (6f) (Fibr)

Fair gelding. Turf high 45. **P C Haslam [0-4] Middleham Park Racing.*

SIGNORINA CATTIVA (USA) BHB 114f **RR 113+f** 5043[1]

3 b f El Gran Senor (USA) 8.9f **(85)** - Assez Cuite (USA) (Graustark) 10.1f **(70)**

Form - 2340111

Record					
1999 -	1st:3	2nd:1	3rd:1	Ran:7
Pre1999 -	1st:1	2nd:0	3rd:0	Ran:2

Win Prizemoney £77,536 *Total Prizemoney* £115,366

Wins							
* **1999**	Oct	Newbur	(HVY)	G3	12f	113+	<
* **1999**	Oct	Ascot	(G-S)	G3	12f	109	
* **1999**	Spt	Ascot	(HVY)	L	12f	98	
* 1998	Oct	Leices	(SFT)		8f	91+	

1999 Turf 3-7: (10f, 11f 2, 12f 3-4) (sft 2-2, gd 1-2, g-f 3)

Light-framed, Group-class filly, effective 12f, acts on sft to gd. Turf high 113 - 1st of 10 getting 5lb from Salford Express (23 Oct Newbury RF 5043) - also 1st of 12 getting 7lb from New Abbey (9 Oct Ascot RF 4794). The winner of a soft-ground Leicester maiden by ten lengths at two, she ran with credit earlier on this season, including when third in the Italian Oaks. However, it was not until she encountered softer conditions again that she really found her form, winning Princess Royal Stakes and St Simon Stakes. Concluded her career by finishing third in the Group One Premio Roma in November. **J L Dunlop [4-9] Mrs Maria Mai Goransson.*

SIGNS AND WONDERS BHB 58f66a **RR 59f 66a** 5103[16]

5 b m Danehill (USA) 9.1f **(79)** - Front Line Romance (Caerleon (USA)) 8.6f **(71)**

Form - 7376420

Record					
1999 -	1st:0	2nd:1	3rd:1	Ran:7
Pre1999 -	1st:1	2nd:5	3rd:2	Ran:25

Win Prizemoney £3,460 *Total Prizemoney* £12,275

Wins							
* 1998	*Mar*	*Lingfi*	*(STD)*	*H*	*10f*	*62*	*66* <

1999 Turf 0-7: (7f 2, 8f 5) (gd 2, g-f, frm 4)

Average filly, effective 8 to 10f, best at 8f, acts on frm - acts on Equi, likes right handed tracks, likes tight tracks. Turf high 62 (began Jly) - 3rd of 6 giving 14lb to Nautical Warning (24 Jly Lingfield 8f frm RF 3095). **C A Cyzer [1-32] R M Cyzer.*

SIHAFI (USA) BHB 56f80a **RR 44f 80a** 4832[25]

6 ch g Elmaamul (USA) 8.1f **(70)** - Kit's Double (USA) (Spring Double) 6.8f **(76)**

Form - 7272858050335600000

Record					
1999 -	1st:0	2nd:0	3rd:2	Ran:14
Pre1999 -	1st:11	2nd:9	3rd:2	Ran:57

Win Prizemoney £41,320 *Total Prizemoney* £53,455

Wins							
* 1998	*Oct*	*Wolver*	*(STD)*	*H*	*6f*	*75*	*77* <
* 1998	Spt	Haydoc	(G-F)	H	5f	70	71
* 1998	Jly	Sandow	(G-F)	H	5f	60	70+
* 1998	Jly	Salisb	(GD)	H	5f	56	64
* 1998	Jly	Lingfi	(G-F)	H	5f	46	53+
* 1998	Jly	Folkes	(G-F)	H	5f	46	51+
* 1998	Jly	Bath	(GD)	H	5.1f	46	61
* 1998	Jun	Windso	(GD)	H	6f	41	54+
* 1998	*Jan*	*Lingfi*	*(STD)*	*H*	*6f*	*61*	*64*
1997	*Feb*	*Lingfi*	*(STD)*	*H*	*6f*	*56*	*57*
1996	*Dec*	*Lingfi*	*(STD)*	*H*	*6f*	*50*	*51*

1999 Turf 0-14: (5f 10, 6f 4) (sft, g-s, gd 3, g-f 4, frm 5)

Decent gelding, has broken blood-vessels, effective 5 to 6f, best at 5f, - acts on AW, best on Fibr, likes left handed tracks, excels at Wolverhampton, likes Lingfield. Turf high 68. He had a brilliant 1998, and equalled the twentieth century record of nine handicap wins in a season, but was below-par last term. Has dropped to a handy mark as a result.

**D Nicholls [9-47] John Gilbertson (from J M Carr [2-17] Aug 1997).*

SILCA BLANKA (IRE) BHB 75f84a **RR 70f 84a** 5166[12]

7 b h Law Society (USA) 11.6f **(71)** - Reality (Known Fact (USA)) 7.4f **(67)**

Form - 201002282100448070

Record					
1999 -	1st:2	2nd:3	3rd:0	Ran:17
Pre1999 -	1st:4	2nd:3	3rd:2	Ran:33

Win Prizemoney £48,048 *Total Prizemoney* £78,511

Wins							
* **1999**	Jun	Epsom	(GD)	H	7f	84	87
* **1999**	*Jan*	*Lingfi*	*(STD)*	*H*	*7f*	*82*	*83*
* 1998	Jly	Warwic	(G-F)		7f		86
1995	Jun	Epsom	(FRM)		7f		98

1999 Turf 1-12: (6f 2, 7f 1-8, 8f 2) (g-s 3, gd 5, g-f 1-2, frm 2) 1999 AW 1-5: (7f 1-2, 8f 3) (Equi 1-4, Fibr)

Decent horse, effective 7 to 8f, best at 7f, acts on sft to frm - acts on Equi, likes left handed tracks, does well at Lingfield. Turf high 87 - 1st of 11 giving 18lb to Samara Song (30 Jun Epsom RF 2445). AW high 83 - also 1st of 12 giving 6lb to Love Academy (16 Jan Lingfield RF 0109). He is a somewhat moody individual, but is a fair handicapper on turf and Equitrack. A sharp left-handed seven furlongs is absolutely ideal.

**A G Newcombe [3-30] Duckhaven Stud (from M R Channon [3-20] Aug 1996).*

SILCA FANTASY **RR 31f** 1236[9]

2 b f Piccolo - Fantasy Racing (IRE) **(75f)** (Tirol)

Form - 0

Record 1999 - 1st:0 2nd:0 3rd:0 Ran:1

1999 Turf 0-1: (6f) (gd)

Currently very moderate filly.

**M R Channon [0-1] Aldridge Racing Ltd.*

SILENTLY BHB 45f **RR 43f** 4563[11]

7 b g Slip Anchor 12.7f **(75)** - Land of Ivory (USA) (The Minstrel (CAN)) 10f **(72)**

Form - 6008073660

Record					
1999 -	1st:0	2nd:0	3rd:1	Ran:10
Pre1999 -	1st:6	2nd:9	3rd:7	Ran:46

Win Prizemoney £23,389 *Total Prizemoney* £45,792

Wins							
* 1998	Spt	Mussel	(GD)	H	16f	78	85 <
* 1998	Aug	Mussel	(GD)	H	14f	72	76
1998	Aug	Redcar	(G-F)	C	14.1f		63
1995	Jly	Bath	(HRD)	H	10.2f	72	83+
1995	Jly	Pontef	(G-F)	H	10f	72	76
1995	Apr	Ripon	(G-S)	H	10f	70	70+

1999 Turf 0-10: (12f 2, 14f 3, 16f 4, 19f) (gd 2, g-f 4, frm 4)

Moderate gelding, effective 14 to 16f, best at 14f, acts on g-f to frm, best on g-f, has worn blinkers. Turf high 68.

**K A Ryan [2-18] The Gloria Darley Racing Partnership (from J S King [1-11] Aug 1998).*

SILENT NIGHT BHB 82f **RR 80f** 5041[10]

2 gr f Night Shift (USA) 8.1f **(73)** - Catch The Sun (Kalaglow) 9.8f **(67)**

Form - 150

Record 1999 - 1st:1 2nd:0 3rd:0 Ran:3

Win Prizemoney £5,122 *Total Prizemoney* £5,342

Wins * **1999** Spt Kempto (G-F) 7f 80+ <

1999 Turf 1-3: (7f 1-2, 8f) (sft, g-s, frm 1-1)

Currently decent filly. Turf high 80 (1st run) (began Spt) - 1st of 7 from La Fay (8 Spt Kempton RF 4214). She made a winning debut at Kempton in September, but was all at sea in testing ground on two subsequent starts. **D R C Elsworth [1-3] C J Harper.*

SILENT PRIDE (IRE) BHB 30f34a **RR 41f 34a** 222[10]

4 ch f Pips Pride 6.7f **(70)** - Suppression (Kind of Hush) 10.1f **(62)**

Form - 255060

Record 1999 - 1st:0 2nd:0 3rd:0 Ran:3
Pre1999 - 1st:0 2nd:3 3rd:1 Ran:27

Win Prizemoney £0 *Total Prizemoney* £3,073

1999 AW 0-3: (6f, 7f, 8f) (Equi 3)

Light-framed, moderate filly, effective 8 to 10f, acts on frm - acts on Equi, favours tight tracks.

**G L Moore [0-6] A Moore (from M D I Usher [0-24] Aug 1998).*

SILENT SOUND (IRE) BHB 54f **RR 52f** 4883[10]

3 b g Be My Guest (USA) 10.2f **(66)** - Whist Awhile (Caerleon (USA)) 8.6f **(71)**

Form - 047723166820

Record 1999 - 1st:1 2nd:2 3rd:1 Ran:12
Pre1999 - 1st:0 2nd:0 3rd:0 Ran:4

Win Prizemoney £4,289 *Total Prizemoney* £6,653

Wins * **1999** Aug Redcar (FRM) H 10f 51 53 <

1999 Turf 1-12: (10f 1-4, 11f, 12f 5, 14f, 16f) (g-s, gd, g-f 2, frm 1-8)

Workmanlike, fair gelding, often wears blinkers (effectively), likes left handed tracks. Turf high 54. Consistent.

**P Calver [1-16] Mrs Janis MacPherson.*

SILENT VALLEY BHB 48a **RR 41f** 2915[13]

5 b m Forzando 7.2f **(63)** - Tremmin (Horage) 10.3f **(61)**

Form - 00

Record 1999 - 1st:0 2nd:0 3rd:0 Ran:2
Pre1999 - 1st:1 2nd:2 3rd:3 Ran:25

Win Prizemoney £2,940 *Total Prizemoney* £5,431

Wins * 1997 Jly Nottin (G-F) 10f 56 <

1999 Turf 0-2: (10f, 12f) (frm 2)

Moderate filly, often wears blinkers. Turf high 14 (began Jly). Inconsistent.

**Miss L C Siddall [3-26] Mrs S E Cooper (from D Nicholls [0-4] Jan 1997).*

SILENT WARNING BHB 82f85a **RR 83f 85a** 4917[15]

4 b c Ela-Mana-Mou 12.7f **(72)** - Buzzbomb (Bustino) 10.4f **(64)**

Form - 1730

Record 1999 - 1st:0 2nd:0 3rd:1 Ran:3
Pre1999 - 1st:4 2nd:0 3rd:0 Ran:9

Win Prizemoney £15,402 *Total Prizemoney* £17,277

Wins * 1998 *Nov Southw (STD) H 14f 73 87+* <
* 1998 Nov Mussel (SFT) H 16f 73 79+
* 1998 Oct Leices (SFT) 11.8f 83
* 1998 *Oct Southw (STD) H 14f 69 75*

1999 Turf 0-3: (13f, 16f, 17f) (gd 3)

Workmanlike, useful colt, effective 12 to 16f, acts on sft to gd - acts on Fibr, favours tight tracks. Turf high 82 (began Spt) - 3rd of 7 giving 2lb to Etterby Park (26 Spt Musselburgh 16f gd RF 4577). Completed a four-timer at the end of '98, two on soft ground and two on Fibresand. He made a belated return last season with the Cesarewitch his target, but ran moderately in the race itself.

**Sir Mark Prescott [4-12] Eclipse Thoroughbreds - Osborne House.*

SILIC (FR) RR 123f 5226a[1]

4 c Sillery (USA) - Balletomane (IRE) (Sadler's Wells (USA)) 10f **(76)**

Form - 1

1999 Turf 1-1: (8f 1-1) (frm 1-1)

Very high-class colt. (1st run) - 1st of 14 giving 3lb to Tuzla (6 Nov Gulfstream Park RF 5226a). Game winner of the Breeders' Cup Mile.

**J Canani in USA [1-1] Mrs Elena Lanni (from P Bary in FR [1-3] Oct 1998).*

SILK COTTAGE BHB 52f55a **RR 49f 55a** 1324[9]

7 b g Superpower 6.6f **(58)** - Flute Royale (Horage) 10.3f **(61)**

Form - 51782641320

Record 1999 - 1st:1 2nd:2 3rd:1 Ran:8
Pre1999 - 1st:3 2nd:13 3rd:8 Ran:80

Win Prizemoney £10,984 *Total Prizemoney* £28,698

Wins * **1999** Apr Newcas (GD) H 5f 47 48
* 1998 *Dec Wolver (SLW) H 5f 52 54*
1997 *Mar Wolver (STD) S 5f 48*
1996 Jly Mussel (GD) H 5f 54 57 <

1999 Turf 1-5: (5f 1-5) (gd 1-3, g-f, frm) 1999 AW 0-3: (5f 2, 6f) (Fibr 3)

Fair gelding, effective 5 to 6f, best at 5f, acted on g-s to frm - acted on Fibr, often wore blinkers (extremely effectively), excelled at Newcastle, did well at Wolverhampton. Turf high 49 - also 1st of 14 getting 7lb from Sweet Magic (5 Apr Newcastle RF 0581). AW high 53 - 2nd of 8 giving 5lb to Sotonian (27 Jan Wolverhampton 5f Fibr RF 0172). (DEAD)

**R Bastiman [2-30] Mrs W Walmsley (from R M Whitaker [2-58] Jan 1998).*

SILK DAISY BHB 64f **RR 74f** 5193[3]

3 b f Barathea (IRE) - Scene Galante (FR) (Sicyos (USA))

Form - 533023

Record 1999 - 1st:0 2nd:1 3rd:3 Ran:6

Win Prizemoney £0 *Total Prizemoney* £2,982

1999 Turf 0-6: (6f, 7f 2, 8f 3) (g-s, gd 2, g-f, frm 2)

Leggy, above-average filly, effective 7 to 8f, best at 7f, acts on g-s to frm. Turf high 74 - 3rd of 6 to Modern Era (20 Aug Newcastle 7f g-f RF 3801). **H Candy [0-6] Mrs C M Poland.*

SILKEN BHB 81f **RR 80f** 3993[6]

3 b f Danehill (USA) 9.1f **(79)** - Our Reverie (USA) (J O Tobin (USA)) 9.4f **(67)**

Form - 3231436

Record 1999 - 1st:1 2nd:1 3rd:3 Ran:7
Pre1999 - 1st:0 2nd:0 3rd:0 Ran:2

Win Prizemoney £3,745 *Total Prizemoney* £7,499

Wins * **1999** Jly Epsom (G-F) 10.1f 79 <

1999 Turf 1-7: (7f, 8f, 9f 2, 10f 1-1, 12f 2) (gd 2, g-f 3, frm 1-2)

Scopey, decent filly, effective 8 to 10f, acts on gd to frm, prefers tight tracks. Turf high 80 - also 1st of 5 from Aegean Dream (7 Jly Epsom RF 2617). Consistent. She showed some ability before getting off the mark in an Epsom maiden in July, but has not made much impression in handicaps since. Does not seem to stay 12 furlongs and will be suited by a return to shorter.

**Mrs A J Perrett [1-9] K J Buchanan.*

SILKEN DALLIANCE BHB 80f80a **RR 83f 80a** 4915[16]

4 b f Rambo Dancer (CAN) 8.4f **(59)** - A Sharp (Sharpo) 7.7f **(59)**

Form - 80255000

Record 1999 - 1st:0 2nd:1 3rd:0 Ran:7
Pre1999 - 1st:4 2nd:3 3rd:0 Ran:13

Win Prizemoney £72,437 *Total Prizemoney* £79,480

Wins 1998 Oct Newmar (GD) H 8f 79 83 <
1998 Spt Ascot (SFT) H 8f 74 76
1998 Spt Kempto (SFT) H 8f 67 74+
1998 *Mar Southw (STD) 6f 56*

1999 Turf 0-7: (8f 7) (sft, gd 2, g-f, frm 3)

Lengthy, decent filly, effective 8f, acts on gd to frm, best on frm. Turf high 86 - 2nd of 9 giving 4lb to Jedi Knight (9 Jly York 8f frm RF 2697). Enjoyed a fine season in '98, but could not repeat that last term despite some sound efforts in the summer.

**I A Balding [0-7] The C H F Partnership (from Lord Huntingdon [4-13] Nov 1998).*

SILKEN FOX (IRE) BHB 48f **RR 41f** 5104[10]

2 b g Foxhound (USA) - Crown Witness (Crowned Prince (USA)) 10.1f **(67)**

Form - 000

Record 1999 - 1st:0 2nd:0 3rd:0 Ran:3

1999 Turf 0-3: (6f, 7f 2) (g-s, gd 2)

Currently moderate gelding. Turf high 41 (began Oct).
**J S Moore [0-3] Mrs Angela Speyer.*

SILKEN LADY RR 26f 4525[8]
3 br f Rock Hopper 10.6f **(54)** - Silk St James (Pas de Seul) 9.1f **(67)**
Form - 008
Record 1999 - 1st:0 2nd:0 3rd:0 Ran:3
1999 Turf 0-3: (8f, 10f, 11f) (gd, g-f, frm)
Workmanlike, currently little account filly. Turf high 26 (began Jly).
**M J Ryan [0-3] Sez Les Partnership.*

SILK PRINCESS BHB 46f43a RR 59df 43a 2686[5]
4 gr f Touch of Grey 8.1f **(47)** - Young Lady (Young Generation) 7.7f **(63)**
Form - 0005
Record 1999 - 1st:0 2nd:0 3rd:0 Ran:4
Pre1999 - 1st:0 2nd:0 3rd:0 Ran:3
1999 Turf 0-3: (10f 2, 12f) (g-s, g-f, frm) 1999 AW 0-1: (10f) (Equi)
Workmanlike, fair filly. Turf high 48. **R M Flower [0-7] Richard Gurr.*

SILK ST BRIDGET BHB 58f RR 49f 4903[7]
2 b f Rock Hopper 10.6f **(54)** - Silk St James (Pas de Seul) 9.1f **(67)**
Form - 707
Record 1999 - 1st:0 2nd:0 3rd:0 Ran:3
1999 Turf 0-3: (6f 3) (g-s 2, frm)
Currently moderate filly. Turf high 49 (began Spt).
**M J Ryan [0-3] L Audus.*

SILK ST JOHN BHB 90f81a RR 95df 81a 5141[9]
5 b g Damister (USA) 9.1f **(66)** - Silk St James (Pas de Seul) 9.1f **(67)**
Form - 0010440204164348300
Record 1999 - 1st:2 2nd:1 3rd:2 Ran:19
Pre1999 - 1st:5 2nd:6 3rd:4 Ran:32
Win Prizemoney £37,320 *Total Prizemoney* £71,616

Wins								
* 1999	Jly	Newbur	(G-F)	H	8f	92	93	
* 1999	Apr	Sandow	(G-S)	H	8.1f	92	95	<
* 1998	Aug	Windso	(G-F)	H	8.3f	86	90	
* 1998	Jly	Newbur	(GD)	H	8f	82	87	
* 1998	Jun	Windso	(GD)		8.3f		83	
* 1998	May	Chepst	(G-F)		8.1f		83	
* 1997	Aug	Newmar	(GD)	H	8f	74	78	

1999 Turf 2-19: (8f 2-17, 9f 2) (sft 2, g-s 1-3, gd 7, g-f, frm 1-6)
Very useful gelding, effective 8 to 9f, best at 8f, acts on g-s to frm, best on g-s, prefers right handed tracks, likes tight tracks, excels at Windsor and Sandown, likes Newbury. Turf high 95 - 1st of 9 getting 3lb from Al Azhar (23 Apr Sandown RF 0821) - also 1st of 9 giving 8lb to Gulf Shaadi (11 Jly Newbury RF 2744). A game sort, suited by coming late of a strong pace, he was ridden with the utmost confidence when getting up in the shadow of the post at Sandown on his third start of the season. Found life a bit tougher afterwards, but everything went right for him when he returned to winning form at Newbury in July and he ran a blinder when third in Newmarket Listed event in October.
**M J Ryan [7-51] C R S Partners.*

SILK WING BHB 28f25a RR 32f 25a 803[11]
3 b f Wing Park - Little Park (Cragador) 6f **(67)**
Form - 080070
Record 1999 - 1st:0 2nd:0 3rd:0 Ran:6
Pre1999 - 1st:0 2nd:0 3rd:0 Ran:3
1999 Turf 0-2: (6f, 10f) (sft, gd) 1999 AW 0-4: (6f, 7f 2, 8f) (Equi 3, Fibr)
Unfurnished, very moderate filly, has worn blinkers. Turf high 2. AW high 16. **T T Clement [0-9] J Burns.*

SILVANO (GER) RR 115f 3232a[4]
3 b c Lomitas - Spirit of Eagals (Beau's Eagle (USA))
Form - 144
1999 Turf 1-3: (11f 1-1, 12f 2) (gd 1-3)
Currently high-class colt. Turf high 115 (1st run) - 1st of 9 from Karakal (13 Jun Cologne RF 2100a). German-trained, he landed a Group Two event at Cologne last season, but was just found out in Group One company behind the likes of Belenus and Ungaro.
**A Wohler in GER [1-3].*

SILVANO'S EXPRESS BHB 35f RR 26f 4985[18]
3 b g Sizzling Melody 6.3f **(49)** -Penny Hasset **(64f)** (Lochnager) 6f **(59)**
Form - 0000027000860

Record 1999 - 1st:0 2nd:1 3rd:0 Ran:14
Win Prizemoney £0 *Total Prizemoney* £644
1999 Turf 0-14: (5f 8, 6f 3, 7f 2, 8f) (g-s, gd 5, g-f, frm 5, hrd 2)
Scopey, little account gelding, effective 5f, acts on gd, often wears blinkers (effectively). Turf high 34 - 2nd of 9 getting 20lb from Gochinos (28 Jun Musselburgh 5f gd RF 2362).
**Miss J F Craze [0-14] Silvano Scanu.*

SILVER APPLE (IRE) BHB 89f RR 88f 3392[1]
3 gr c Danehill (USA) 9.1f **(79)** - Moon Festival (Be My Guest (USA)) 9.3f **(67)**
Form - 4046311
Record 1999 - 1st:2 2nd:0 3rd:1 Ran:7
Pre1999 - 1st:0 2nd:1 3rd:0 Ran:1
Win Prizemoney £10,455 *Total Prizemoney* £13,558

Wins								
* 1999	Aug	Chepst	(G-F)	H	8.1f	85	88	<
* 1999	Jly	Sandow	(G-F)		8.1f		81	

1999 Turf 2-7: (8f 2-3, 10f 2, 12f 2) (gd 2, frm 2-5)
Scopey, useful colt, effective 8f, acts on frm, has worn blinkers. Turf high 88 - 1st of 7 getting 5lb from Regal Philosopher (5 Aug Chepstow RF 3392) - also 1st of 10 giving 5lb to Audition (22 Jly Sandown RF 3032). **P F I Cole [2-8] Anthony Speelman.*

SILVER ARROW (USA) RR 55f 1957[4]
2 b br f Shadeed (USA) 7.7f **(72)** - Aneesati (Kris) 9.5f **(73)**
Form - 4
Record 1999 - 1st:0 2nd:0 3rd:0 Ran:1
Win Prizemoney £0 *Total Prizemoney* £243
1999 Turf 0-1: (5f) (gd)
Currently fair filly. **B W Hills [0-1] Mohamed Obaida.*

SILVER BLADE RR 14f 2536[17]
3 gr f Mystiko (USA) 7.7f **(59)** - Blade of Grass (Kris) 9.5f **(73)**
Form - 00
Record 1999 - 1st:0 2nd:0 3rd:0 Ran:2
Pre1999 - 1st:0 2nd:0 3rd:0 Ran:5
1999 Turf 0-2: (10f, 14f) (g-f, frm)
Neat, poor filly. Turf high 14.
**A T Murphy [0-3] D M Beresford (from M A Buckley [0-1] Aug 1998).*

SILVER BULLET RR 35f 4142[15]
3 gr g Grey Desire 9.3f **(49)** - Spanish Realm (King of Spain) 7.8f **(52)**
Form - 600
Record 1999 - 1st:0 2nd:0 3rd:0 Ran:3
1999 Turf 0-3: (6f, 7f, 8f) (g-f, frm, hrd)
Leggy, currently very moderate gelding. Turf high 35 (began Jly).
**W W Haigh [0-3] Des Redhead.*

SILVERBULLETDAY (USA) RR 112t 5224a[6]
3 b f Silver Deputy (CAN) - Rokeby Rose (USA) (Tom Rolfe) 9.4f **(75)**
Form - 6
1999 AW 0-1: (9f) (Dirt)
Top-class filly. Disappointing in the Breeders' Cup Distaff Cup . **B Baffert in USA [1-2].*

SILVER CASTOR (IRE) BHB 44f49a RR 40f 49a 2640[5]
4 b f Indian Ridge 7.6f **(74)** - Bayazida (Bustino) 10.4f **(64)**
Form - 06065
Record 1999 - 1st:0 2nd:0 3rd:0 Ran:3
Pre1999 - 1st:0 2nd:0 3rd:0 Ran:6
Win Prizemoney £0 *Total Prizemoney* £255
1999 Turf 0-3: (12f, 14f, 16f) (g-s, g-f, frm)
Lengthy, fair filly. Turf high 40. **P W Harris [0-9] John Hamshaw.*

SILVER CHARM (USA) RR 118f 556a[6]
5 ro h Silver Buck (USA) - Bonnie's Poker (USA) (Poker (USA))
Form - 16
1999 AW 0-1: (10f) (Dirt)
Top-class colt. Disappointing in the Dubai World Cup, he has been retired. **B Baffert in USA [4-7] Robert Lewis.*

SILVER COLOURS (USA) RR 96+f 5142[1]
2 b br f Silver Hawk (USA) 11.2f **(85)** - Team Colors (USA) (Mr Prospector (USA)) 8.8f **(78)**
Form - 61
Record 1999 - 1st:1 2nd:0 3rd:0 Ran:2
Win Prizemoney £10,841 *Total Prizemoney* £10,841

Wins * 1999 Oct Newmar (SFT) L 8f 96+ <
1999 Turf 1-2: (7f, 8f 1-1) (gd 1-2)
Currently very useful filly. Turf high 96 (began Oct) - 1st of 10 from Bedara (30 Oct Newmarket RF 5142). Not knocked about on her first start when sixth at Leicester, she stepped up greatly on that to win a back-end Listed race.
**L M Cumani [1-2] Christopher Wright.*

SILVERDALE LAD RR 43f 3976[5]

8 b g Presidium 7.5f **(56)** - Its My Turn (Palm Track) 9.8f **(50)**
Form - 75
Record 1999 - 1st:0 2nd:0 3rd:0 Ran:2
1999 Turf 0-2: (12f, 14f) (frm 2)
Moderate gelding. Turf high 43 (began Aug).
**K W Hogg [2-20] Anthony White.*

SILVER GROOM (IRE) BHB 47f RR 61f 690[10]

9 gr g Shy Groom (USA) 8.2f **(59)** - Rustic Lawn (Rusticaro (FR)) 8.2f **(65)**
Form - 50
Record 1999 - 1st:0 2nd:0 3rd:0 Ran:1
Pre1999 - 1st:3 2nd:8 3rd:3 Ran:54
Win Prizemoney £40,798 *Total Prizemoney* £69,389
Wins 1995 Jly Goodwo (FRM) H 10f 65 73+ <
1999 Turf 0-1: (10f) (frm)
Average gelding, has worn blinkers. Has been a useful handicapper in his day under both codes, but is hard to win with nowadays.
**M R Channon [0-15] Alan Leiper (from R Akehurst [4-36] Spt 1997).*

SILVER GYRE (IRE) BHB 56f RR 56f 5006[11]

3 b f Silver Hawk (USA) 11.2f **(85)** - Kraemer (USA) (Lyphard (USA)) 9.9f **(72)**
Form - 707621400
Record 1999 - 1st:1 2nd:1 3rd:0 Ran:9
Pre1999 - 1st:0 2nd:0 3rd:0 Ran:3
Win Prizemoney £2,775 *Total Prizemoney* £3,690
Wins * 1999 Jly Bath (G-F) H 17.2f 54 56 <
1999 Turf 1-9: (7f, 8f, 12f 3, 16f 2, 17f 1-2) (hvy, sft, gd 3, g-f 2, frm, hrd 1-1)
Light-framed, fair filly, likes left handed tracks, likes tight tracks. Turf high 59.
**D J Wintle [1-9] Mrs Joan Egan (from Mrs J R Ramsden [0-3] Oct 1998).*

SILVER MIST BHB 42f RR 21f 4293[18]

3 b f Lugana Beach 7f **(63)** - Highland Bonnie (Dreams to Reality (USA)) 6.4f **(73)**
Form - 0010000
Record 1999 - 1st:1 2nd:0 3rd:0 Ran:7
Pre1999 - 1st:0 2nd:0 3rd:0 Ran:4
Win Prizemoney £2,442 *Total Prizemoney* £2,834
Wins * 1999 Jly Newcas (G-F) H 7f 44 47 <
1999 Turf 1-7: (7f 1-4, 8f 2, 10f) (g-f 4, frm 1-3)
Unfurnished, little account filly, effective 7f, acts on frm, often wears blinkers (very effectively). Turf high 47 - 1st of 19 getting 4lb from Annie Apple (12 Jly Newcastle RF 2755).
**G G Margarson [1-7] Dr Neil Dorward (from B A McMahon [0-4] Oct 1998).*

SILVER PATRIARCH (IRE) BHB 121f RR 122f 5016a[2]

5 gr h Saddlers' Hall (IRE) 10.5f **(65)** - Early Rising (USA) (Grey Dawn II) 11.1f **(72)**
Form - 144132
Record 1999 - 1st:2 2nd:1 3rd:1 Ran:6
Pre1999 - 1st:6 2nd:5 3rd:1 Ran:17
Win Prizemoney £501,222 *Total Prizemoney* £907,195

Wins * 1999	Aug	Newbur	(GD)	G2	13.3f	122	<
* 1999	Apr	Newmar	(GD)	G2	12f	118	
* 1998	Oct	San Si	(SFT)	G1	12f	122	<
* 1998	Jun	Epsom	(GD)	G1	12f	122	<
* 1997	Spt	Doncas	(G-F)	G1	14.6f	121	
* 1997	May	Lingfi	(SFT)	G3	11.5f	102+	
* 1996	Nov	Newmar	(GD)	L	10f	105	
* 1996	Oct	Pontef	(GD)		10f	82+	

1999 Turf 2-6: (12f 1-4, 13f 1-1, 14f) (g-s, gd 1-3, g-f, frm 1-1)
Very high-class colt, effective 12 to 14f, best at 12f, acts on sft to frm, best on gd, excels at Epsom and Newmarket and Newbury. Turf high 122 - 1st of 4 giving 3lb to Craigsteel (14 Aug Newbury RF 3649) - also 1st of 11 giving 8lb to Silver Rhapsody (30 Apr Newmarket RF 0945). Consistent. Still going strong two seasons after his Classic win, this popular grey enjoyed another profitable campaign in 1999, winning the Jockey Club Stakes and the Geoffrey Freer Stakes. He seems to dislike soft ground nowadays, as his only poor run came in those conditions. Best on tracks with a long home straight, if he stays in training he is worth a try over two miles.
**J L Dunlop [8-23]the late Peter S Winfield.*

SILVER PREY (USA) BHB 52f RR 49f 2837[1]

6 b g Silver Hawk (USA) 11.2f **(85)** - Truly My Style (USA) (Mount Hagen (FR)) 8.4f **(70)**
Form - 0061
Record 1999 - 1st:1 2nd:0 3rd:0 Ran:4
Pre1999 - 1st:1 2nd:0 3rd:2 Ran:12
Win Prizemoney £7,200 *Total Prizemoney* £9,418
Wins * 1999 Jly Bath (FRM) S 11.7f 49
1995 Aug Newbur (G-F) 7f 80 <
1999 Turf 1-4: (7f 2, 10f, 12f 1-1) (g-f, frm 1-3)
Moderate gelding, effective 7f, acted on gd, preferred tight tracks. Turf high 49. (DEAD)
**M J Bolton [1-12] A R M Galbraith (from E A L Dunlop [1-4] Oct 1996).*

SILVER PRINCE BHB 35f RR 17f 724[12]

4 gr g Mystiko (USA) 7.7f **(59)** - Hawaiian Song (Henbit (USA)) 9f **(61)**
Form - 800
Record 1999 - 1st:0 2nd:0 3rd:0 Ran:3
1999 Turf 0-3: (6f, 7f, 8f) (gd 2, g-f)
Workmanlike, currently poor gelding. Turf high 17.
**D Nicholls [0-3] John Gilbertson.*

SILVER QUEEN BHB 75f RR 65f 4323[7]

2 ch f Arazi (USA) 9.2f **(74)** - Love of Silver (USA) (Arctic Tern (USA)) 8.9f **(69)**
Form - 55447
Record 1999 - 1st:0 2nd:0 3rd:0 Ran:5
Win Prizemoney £0 *Total Prizemoney* £651
1999 Turf 0-5: (5f, 6f 2, 7f, 8f) (gd, frm 4)
Average filly. Turf high 65. **C E Brittain [0-5] Ali Saeed.*

SILVER RHAPSODY (USA) BHB 110f RR 113f 4794[5]

4 b f Silver Hawk (USA) 11.2f **(85)** - Sister Chrys (USA) (Fit To Fight (USA)) 9.7f **(45)**
Form - 243365
Record 1999 - 1st:0 2nd:1 3rd:2 Ran:6
Pre1999 - 1st:2 2nd:1 3rd:1 Ran:5
Win Prizemoney £35,414 *Total Prizemoney* £82,328
Wins * 1998 Oct Ascot (SFT) G3 12f 110 <
* 1998 Jun Newmar (GD) 10f 85
1999 Turf 0-6: (12f 6) (sft 2, gd 2, frm 2)
Lengthy, Group-class filly, effective 12f, acts on sft to frm, best on frm. Turf high 113 - 3rd of 11 giving 10lb to Ramruma (18 Aug York 12f gd RF 3757). She had a hard race when chasing Silver Patriarch home on her reappearance and proved a shade disappointing later in the campaign. A shade one-paced, she is crying out for a step-up to a mile and three-quarters.
**H R A Cecil [2-11] Lordship Stud.*

SILVER ROBIN (USA) RR 98f 944[3]

3 b br c Silver Hawk (USA) 11.2f **(85)** - Wedge Musical (What A Guest) 7f **(62)**
Form - 3
Record 1999 - 1st:0 2nd:0 3rd:1 Ran:1
Pre1999 - 1st:0 2nd:1 3rd:0 Ran:1
Win Prizemoney £0 *Total Prizemoney* £3,354
1999 Turf 0-1: (10f) (frm)
Scopey, currently very useful colt. He went missing after finishing third in a Listed event at the Guineas Meeting. Likely to stay well, he made 14,000 guineas at Newmarket in October and obviously has his problems.
**L M Cumani [0-2] W V M W & Mrs E S Robins.*

SILVER SECRET BHB 40f RR 40f 4262[3]

5 ro g Absalom 7.1f **(56)** - Secret Dance (Sadler's Wells (USA)) 10f **(76)**
Form - 737441647463
Record 1999 - 1st:1 2nd:0 3rd:2 Ran:12
Pre1999 - 1st:1 2nd:0 3rd:1 Ran:17
Win Prizemoney £6,094 *Total Prizemoney* £9,599

Wins * **1999** Jly Newmar (G-F) H 8f 42 43
1997 Aug Folkes (G-F) 6f 60 <
1999 Turf 1-12: (7f 2, 8f 1-5, 10f 2, 11f, 12f 2) (gd, g-f 7, frm 1-4)
Moderate gelding, effective 7f, acts on frm, has worn blinkers.
**S Gollings [1-18] R Attwood (from M J Heaton-Ellis [1-11] Spt 1997).*

SILVER SKY BHB 47f RR 45f 5198[11]
3 gr f Chilibang 7f **(55)** - Sizzling Sista (Sizzling Melody)
Form - 000
Record 1999 - 1st:0 2nd:0 3rd:0 Ran:3
1999 Turf 0-3: (6f 2, 8f) (gd 3)
Scopey, currently moderate filly. Turf high 45 (began Spt).
**M D I Usher [0-3] Bryan Fry.*

SILVERSMITH (FR) BHB 46a RR 199[4]
4 b g Always Fair (USA) 14f **(61)** - Phargette (USA) (Lyphard (USA)) 9.9f **(72)**
Form - 06054
Record 1999 - 1st:0 2nd:0 3rd:0 Ran:3
Pre1999 - 1st:0 2nd:2 3rd:0 Ran:11
Win Prizemoney £0 *Total Prizemoney* £2,120
1999 AW 0-3: (7f, 8f, 12f) (Equi 2, Fibr)
Workmanlike, moderate gelding, has worn blinkers. AW high 42.
**S Dow [0-14] D G Churston.*

SILVER SNAKE (IRE) RR 50f 4629[6]
3 b c Salse (USA) 10.9f **(71)** - Ibtisamm (USA) (Caucasus (USA)) 8.2f **(74)**
Form - 6
Record 1999 - 1st:0 2nd:0 3rd:0 Ran:1
Pre1999 - 1st:0 2nd:0 3rd:0 Ran:1
Win Prizemoney £0 *Total Prizemoney* £170
1999 Turf 0-1: (8f) (g-s)
Fair colt. (DEAD) **C E Brittain [0-2] Mohamed Obaida.*

SILVER SOCKS BHB 53f RR 56f 4716[15]
2 gr g Petong 7.6f **(58)** - Tasmim (Be My Guest (USA)) 9.3f **(67)**
Form - 5700
Record 1999 - 1st:0 2nd:0 3rd:0 Ran:4
1999 Turf 0-4: (5f, 6f 2, 7f) (gd 2, frm, hrd)
Fair gelding. Turf high 67 (began Jly).
**M W Easterby [0-4] Miss V Foster.*

SILVER SPIDER BHB 28f RR 36f 228[9]
4 gr g Terimon 8.7f **(58)** - Quetta's Girl (Orchestra) 9.7f **(52)**
Form - 60
Record 1999 - 1st:0 2nd:0 3rd:0 Ran:2
Pre1999 - 1st:0 2nd:0 3rd:0 Ran:2
1999 AW 0-2: (11f, 12f) (Fibr 2)
Scopey, very moderate gelding. AW high 22.
**Mrs S Lamyman [0-4] P Lamyman.*

SILVER STAR (FR) RR 103f 4764a[3]
3 b f Zafonic (USA) 9f **(83)** - Monroe (USA) (Sir Ivor) 10.2f **(70)**
Form - 03
1999 Turf 0-2: (8f 2) (g-s, gd)
Currently very useful filly. **A Fabre in FR [0-3] May 1999).*

SILVER SUN BHB 79f62a RR 75f 62a 2495[4]
4 gr f Green Desert (USA) 7.8f **(78)** - Catch The Sun (Kalaglow) 9.8f **(67)**
Form - 62134
Record 1999 - 1st:1 2nd:1 3rd:1 Ran:4
Pre1999 - 1st:0 2nd:2 3rd:1 Ran:11
Win Prizemoney £4,063 *Total Prizemoney* £9,399
Wins * **1999** Jun Goodwo (G-F) 9f 72 <
1999 Turf 1-4: (8f, 9f 1-2, 10f) (gd, g-f 1-2, frm)
Light-framed, above-average filly, effective 8 to 10f, acts on g-f to frm, best on g-f, likes tight tracks. Turf high 75 - also 1st of 9 giving 11lb to Sena Desert (18 Jun Goodwood RF 2120). Belatedly got off the mark in a Goodwood maiden.
**D R C Elsworth [1-15] C J Harper.*

SILVER SYMPHONY BHB 43f RR 47f 3582[5]
4 gr f Kylian (USA) 8.1f **(66)** - Brave Maiden (Three Legs) 11.1f **(54)**
Form - 076635
Record 1999 - 1st:0 2nd:0 3rd:1 Ran:6
Pre1999 - 1st:0 2nd:0 3rd:0 Ran:1
Win Prizemoney £0 *Total Prizemoney* £428
1999 Turf 0-6: (10f 2, 12f, 14f, 16f, 17f) (sft, gd 2, g-f 2, frm)
Scopey, moderate filly. Turf high 64. **B R Millman [0-7] G Palmer.*

SILVER TONGUED BHB 48f RR 43f 4232[15]
3 b c Green Desert (USA) 7.8f **(78)** - Love of Silver (USA) (Arctic Tern (USA)) 8.9f **(69)**
Form - 80500
Record 1999 - 1st:0 2nd:0 3rd:0 Ran:5
1999 Turf 0-5: (7f 2, 8f 2, 10f) (g-f 2, frm 3)
Lengthy, moderate colt. Turf high 43. **C E Brittain [0-5] Ali Saeed.*

SILVERTOWN BHB 53f47a RR 53df 47a 5154[14]
4 b g Danehill (USA) 9.1f **(79)** - Docklands (USA) (Theatrical)
Form - 563131000
Record 1999 - 1st:2 2nd:0 3rd:2 Ran:9
Pre1999 - 1st:0 2nd:2 3rd:1 Ran:12
Win Prizemoney £9,637 *Total Prizemoney* £13,585
Wins * **1999** Spt York (G-F) H 10.4f 51 53 <
* **1999** Aug Epsom (GD) H 10.1f 45 49
1999 Turf 2-8: (10f 2-4, 11f 2, 12f 2) (gd 2, g-f 1-3, frm 1-3) 1999 AW 0-1: (12f) (Fibr)
Scopey, fair gelding, effective 10 to 12f, acts on g-f to frm. Turf high 53.
**B J Curley [2-16] Mrs B J Curley (from J H M Gosden [0-5] Jun 1998).*

SILVER VEIL (IRE) RR 42f 3680[7]
3 gr f Shirley Heights 12.1f **(76)** - Papago (IRE) **(106f)** (Sadler's Wells (USA)) 10f **(76)**
Form - 7
Record 1999 - 1st:0 2nd:0 3rd:0 Ran:1
1999 Turf 0-1: (10f) (gd)
Scopey, currently moderate filly.
**M P Tregoning [0-1] Sheikh Mohammed.*

SIMBATU BHB 62f RR 72f 5186[7]
2 b f Muhtarram (USA) - Kantado (Saulingo) 6.2f **(53)**
Form - 537
Record 1999 - 1st:0 2nd:0 3rd:1 Ran:3
Win Prizemoney £0 *Total Prizemoney* £414
1999 Turf 0-3: (5f 2, 7f) (g-f 3)
Currently above-average filly. Turf high 72 - 3rd of 10 to Lady-Love (14 Jun Musselburgh 5f g-f RF 1977). **Miss I Foustok [0-3] A Foustok.*

SIMPLE IDEALS (USA) BHB 48f RR 48f 5168[3]
5 bb g Woodman (USA) 9.7f **(77)** - Comfort and Style (Be My Guest (USA)) 9.3f **(67)**
Form - 587444423631124563133
Record 1999 - 1st:3 2nd:2 3rd:5 Ran:21
Pre1999 - 1st:0 2nd:0 3rd:2 Ran:15
Win Prizemoney £10,443 *Total Prizemoney* £17,582
Wins * **1999** Oct Redcar (GD) H 14.1f 43 46 <
* **1999** Aug Ayr (G-F) H 15f 33 41
* **1999** Aug Haydoc (G-S) H 11.9f 36 39
1999 Turf 3-21: (9f, 11f 3, 12f 1-8, 14f 1-7, 15f 1-2) (g-s 3, gd 4, g-f 4, frm 3-10)
Moderate gelding, has worn blinkers, likes left handed tracks, likes tight tracks.
**Don Enrico Incisa [3-17] Don Enrico Incisa (from N Tinkler [0-11] May 1999).*

SIMPLY MAGICAL BHB 54f70a RR 58f 70a 4586[7]
3 b f Magic Ring (IRE) 6.5f **(64)** - Naulakha **(55f)** (Bustino) 10.4f **(64)**
Form - 424067
Record 1999 - 1st:0 2nd:0 3rd:0 Ran:4
Pre1999 - 1st:0 2nd:1 3rd:0 Ran:5
Win Prizemoney £0 *Total Prizemoney* £1,094
1999 Turf 0-3: (7f, 8f, 9f) (gd 2, g-f) 1999 AW 0-1: (10f) (Equi)
Workmanlike, above-average filly, effective 8f, - acts on Equi, likes left handed tracks, likes tight tracks. Turf high 58 (began Aug).
**P Mitchell [0-9] The Chint Racing Club.*

SIMPLY NOBLE BHB 75f RR 77f 4264[10]
3 b c Noble Patriarch 12.2f **(43)** - Simply Candy (IRE) (Simply Great (FR)) 8.2f **(65)**

Form - 502630
Record 1999 - 1st:0 2nd:1 3rd:1 Ran:6
Pre1999 - 1st:1 2nd:0 3rd:0 Ran:3
Win Prizemoney £2,738 *Total Prizemoney* £5,978
Wins * 1998 Spt Hamilt (SFT) 8.3f 81 <
1999 Turf 0-6: (10f 2, 12f 4) (g-s, gd, g-f 2, frm 2)
Lengthy, above-average colt, effective 8 to 12f, acts on g-s to frm. Turf high 77 - 2nd of 6 getting 12lb from Night Venture (26 Jun Newcastle 10f frm RF 2338). **K McAuliffe [1-9] MCKPS Equine Ltd.*

SIMPSON'S DOMAIN (IRE) BHB 30f33a **RR 23f 33a** 4076[15]
3 b f Woods of Windsor (USA) - Admiralella **(62f)** (Dominion) 8.5f **(63)**
Form - 8564645006400040
Record 1999 - 1st:0 2nd:0 3rd:0 Ran:13
Pre1999 - 1st:0 2nd:0 3rd:2 Ran:14
Win Prizemoney £0 *Total Prizemoney* £1,514
1999 Turf 0-9: (6f, 8f 3, 10f 3, 12f 2) (frm 9) 1999 AW 0-4: (8f, 10f 2, 12f) (Equi 2, Fibr 2)
Light-framed, very moderate filly, has worn blinkers. Turf high 42. AW high 36.
**S Earle [0-10] P J Jones (from J S Moore [0-18] Feb 1999).*

SING AND DANCE BHB 50f **RR 52f** 4913[2]
6 b m Rambo Dancer (CAN) 8.4f **(59)** - Musical Princess (Cavo Doro) 10.6f **(57)**
Form - 4145363731202
Record 1999 - 1st:2 2nd:2 3rd:3 Ran:13
Pre1999 - 1st:4 2nd:3 3rd:5 Ran:39
Win Prizemoney £20,571 *Total Prizemoney* £30,724
Wins * **1999** Aug Hamilt (G-F) H 12.1f 50 52 <
* **1999** May Mussel (G-F) H 12f 48 52 <
* 1998 Oct Catter (G-S) H 12f 47 50
* 1998 Jly Newcas (GD) H 12.4f 44 46
* 1998 Jun Mussel (G-F) H 12f 39 42
* 1997 Aug Redcar (G-F) H 10f 38 44
1999 Turf 2-13: (11f 2, 12f 2-9, 14f 2) (g-s, gd 2, g-f 3, frm 2-7)
Fair mare, effective 11 to 14f, best at 12f, acts on gd to frm, best on frm, has worn blinkers, and excels at Newcastle and Hamilton. Turf high 53 - 4th of 5 to Dellua (2 Jun Newcastle 12f frm RF 1690) - also 1st of 16 getting 12lb from Noukari (17 May Musselburgh RF 1276). **E Weymes [6-52] Mrs N Napier.*

SING CHEONG (IRE) BHB 60f58a **RR 67f 58a** 4938[8]
3 b c Forest Wind (USA) - Lady Counsel (IRE) (Law Society (USA)) 9.9f **(70)**
Form - 753078
Record 1999 - 1st:0 2nd:0 3rd:1 Ran:6
Win Prizemoney £0 *Total Prizemoney* £374
1999 Turf 0-5: (7f 3, 8f, 9f) (g-s, gd, g-f 2, frm) 1999 AW 0-1: (6f) (Fibr)
Unfurnished, average colt, effective 7f, acts on g-f. Turf high 74 (1st run) - 7th of 13 to Date (15 Apr Newmarket 7f g-f RF 0703).
**G C H Chung [0-6] H C Chung.*

SING FOR ME (IRE) BHB 36f30a **RR 32f 30a** 5167[5]
4 b br f Songlines (FR) 5f **(68)** - Running For You (FR) (Pampabird) 7.5f **(73)**
Form - 05875865857805666005
Record 1999 - 1st:0 2nd:0 3rd:0 Ran:17
Pre1999 - 1st:1 2nd:1 3rd:3 Ran:30
Win Prizemoney £1,738 *Total Prizemoney* £3,226
Wins * 1998 *Feb Wolver (STD) S 5f 53* <
1999 Turf 0-6: (5f 4, 6f 2) (g-s, gd 2, g-f 2, frm) 1999 AW 0-11: (5f, 6f 2, 7f 3, 8f 5) (Fibr 11)
Very moderate filly, effective 5f, - acts on Fibr, has worn blinkers.
**R Hollinshead [1-47] Miss Sarah Hollinshead.*

SINGING WINDS (IRE) BHB 72f **RR 74f** 4578[7]
3 b f Turtle Island (IRE) - Shamiyda (USA) (Sir Ivor) 10.2f **(70)**
Form - 2427
Record 1999 - 1st:0 2nd:2 3rd:0 Ran:4
Win Prizemoney £0 *Total Prizemoney* £2,626
1999 Turf 0-4: (7f 2, 8f 2) (gd, g-f 2, frm)
Lengthy, above-average filly. Turf high 74 (1st run) (began Jly) - 2nd of 7 to Naughty Crown (31 Jly Thirsk 7f frm RF 3286).
**M Johnston [0-4] Sheikh Mohammed.*

SINGLE CURRENCY **RR 72f** 4525[3]
3 b c Barathea (IRE) - Kithanga (IRE) **(109f)** (Darshaan) 9.9f **(84)**
Form - 3
Record 1999 - 1st:0 2nd:0 3rd:1 Ran:1
Win Prizemoney £0 *Total Prizemoney* £625
1999 Turf 0-1: (11f) (gd)
Well made, currently above-average colt. (1st run) - 3rd of 8 giving 5lb to Tariyfa (24 Spt Haydock 11f gd RF 4525).
**P F I Cole [0-1] P S Partnership.*

SINGLE SHOT (USA) BHB 80f **RR 81f** 4998[1]
3 b c Hermitage (USA) 8.6f **(84)** - Bourbon Miss (USA) (Smile (USA))
Form - 6633801
Record 1999 - 1st:1 2nd:0 3rd:2 Ran:7
Pre1999 - 1st:1 2nd:3 3rd:1 Ran:6
Win Prizemoney £7,025 *Total Prizemoney* £12,855
Wins * **1999** Oct Bright (GD) 8f 78 <
* 1998 Nov Mussel (SFT) 7.1f 72
1999 Turf 1-7: (7f 3, 8f 1-3, 9f) (gd 1-2, g-f, frm 4)
Scopey, decent colt, effective 6 to 8f, best at 7f, acts on sft to frm, best on frm, excels at Musselburgh. Turf high 84 - 6th of 11 getting 17lb from Marton Moss (29 May Doncaster 7f frm RF 1565) - also 1st of 10 getting 3lb from Abajany (21 Oct Brighton RF 4998).
**L M Cumani [2-13] Donald Kahn.*

SINGSONG BHB 90f **RR 87f** 3281[10]
2 b g Paris House 5.9f **(64)** - Miss Whittingham (IRE) **(53f 55a)** (Fayruz)
Form - 13471520
Record 1999 - 1st:2 2nd:1 3rd:1 Ran:8
Win Prizemoney £6,455 *Total Prizemoney* £9,777
Wins * **1999** Jun Ripon (G-F) 5f 87 <
* **1999** Mar Doncas (G-S) 5f 80
1999 Turf 2-8: (5f 2-7, 6f) (gd 1-2, g-f 1-3, frm 2, hrd)
Useful gelding, effective 5f, acts on gd to g-f, best on g-f. Turf high 87 - 1st of 6 giving 7lb to Alustar (16 Jun Ripon RF 2058) - also 1st of 15 giving 5lb to Diamond Promise (27 Mar Doncaster RF 0482). He made a winning debut in a Doncaster maiden auction event, and has run credibly since, including a victory at Ripon. Suited by the minimum trip. **J Berry [2-8] G L Tanner.*

SINNDAR (IRE) **RR 95f** 4478a[1]
2 b c Grand Lodge (USA) - Sinntara 00
Form - 11
1999 Turf 2-2: (8f 2-2) (g-s 1-1, g-f 1-1)
Currently very useful colt. Turf high 95 (began Spt) - 1st of 8 from Murawwi (19 Spt Curragh RF 4478a) - also 1st of 13 from Garcia Marquez (5 Spt Curragh RF 4204a). He kept on bravely when winning the National Stakes at The Curragh in September and is a likeable individual. While open to improvement and certain to stay well, that was a weak Group One and he could find life tough under a penalty next term. **J Oxx in IRE [2-2] H H Aga Khan.*

SINNDIYA (IRE) **RR 91f** 5176a[1]
3 b f Pharly (FR) 11.5f **(64)** - Sinntara 00
Form - 2421
1999 Turf 1-4: (9f, 10f, 13f 1-2) (g-s 1-3, g-f)
Useful filly. Turf high 91 (began Spt) - 1st of 11 from Perugino Lady (28 Oct Thurles RF 5176a). **J Oxx in IRE [1-4] H H Aga Khan.*

SINON (IRE) BHB 95f **RR 102?f** 4917[23]
4 ch g Ela-Mana-Mou 12.7f **(72)** - Come In (Be My Guest (USA)) 9.3f **(67)**
Form - 0
Record 1999 - 1st:0 2nd:0 3rd:0 Ran:1
Pre1999 - 1st:2 2nd:0 3rd:0 Ran:5
Win Prizemoney £13,134 *Total Prizemoney* £17,004
Wins * 1998 May York (GD) 13.9f 96 <
* 1997 Spt Redcar (FRM) 9f 85+
1999 Turf 0-1: (17f) (gd)
Scopey, very useful gelding. A winner first time out at two and three, he looked a smart staying proposition, but has had his problems since. **M Johnston [2-6] Ridings Racing.*

SIOUX BHB 55f62a **RR 63f 62a** 40[2]
5 ch m Kris 10f **(75)** - Lassoo (Caerleon (USA)) 8.6f **(71)**
Form - 102
Record 1999 - 1st:0 2nd:1 3rd:0 Ran:1
Pre1999 - 1st:1 2nd:0 3rd:2 Ran:12
Win Prizemoney £2,326 *Total Prizemoney* £4,332

Wins * 1998 *Nov Wolver (STD) H* *12f* *52* *63* <
1999 AW 0-1: (12f) (Fibr)
Average filly, effective 12f, acts on frm - acts on Fibr. (1st run) - 2nd of 6 getting 4lb from Failed To Hit (6 Jan Wolverhampton 12f Fibr RF 0040). Inconsistent. **C W Thornton [1-13] Guy Reed.*

SIOUX CHEF BHB 76f **RR 84f** 2958[1]
2 b f Be My Chief (USA) 10.2f **(62)** - Sea Fret (Habat) 7.6f **(61)**
Form - 41
Record 1999 - 1st:1 2nd:0 3rd:0 Ran:2
Win Prizemoney £3,571 *Total Prizemoney* £3,821
Wins * **1999** Jly Bath (FRM) 5.7f 84 <
1999 Turf 1-2: (6f 1-2) (frm 1-2)
Currently decent filly. Turf high 84 (began Jly) - 1st of 7 from Enaaq (20 Jly Bath RF 2958). **M R Channon [1-2] Mountgrange Stud.*

SIOUX WARRIOR BHB 35f **RR 32f** 1744[7]
7 br g Mandrake Major - Seminole (Amber Rama (USA)) 10.2f **(45)**
Form - 007
Record 1999 - 1st:0 2nd:0 3rd:0 Ran:3
1999 Turf 0-3: (10f, 12f, 14f) (gd, g-f, frm)
Very moderate gelding, has worn blinkers. Turf high 32.
**N Tinkler [0-11] Philip Grundy.*

SIR BEAR (USA) **RR** 2096a[3]
6 br g Sir Leaon (USA) - Spicy Pearl (USA) (Bet Big (USA))
Form - 3
1999 AW 0-1: (9f) (Dirt)
Currently Pattern-class gelding. **R Ziadie in USA [0-1].*

SIRDHANA **RR** 5203a[2]
2 ch f Selkirk (USA) 7.9f **(76)** - Vicky Dolman (USA) (Slew O' Gold (USA)) 8f **(75)**
Form - 2
Record 1999 - 1st:0 2nd:1 3rd:0 Ran:1
Win Prizemoney £0 *Total Prizemoney* £4,010
1999 Turf 0-1: (8f) (g-s)
Currently poor filly - 2nd of 7 to Green Reew (31 Oct San Siro 8f g-s RF 5203a). **L M Cumani [0-1].*

SIR ECHO (FR) BHB 85f **RR 85f** 2266[5]
3 b g Saumarez 15.1f **(87)** - Echoes (FR) (Niniski (USA)) 10.6f **(65)**
Form - 4215
Record 1999 - 1st:1 2nd:1 3rd:0 Ran:4
Pre1999 - 1st:0 2nd:0 3rd:0 Ran:4
Win Prizemoney £3,753 *Total Prizemoney* £5,925
Wins * **1999** Jun Newbur (GD) H 12f 78 85 <
1999 Turf 1-4: (12f 1-4) (sft, gd 1-2, g-f)
Workmanlike, useful gelding, effective 12f, acts on gd to g-f, best on gd. Turf high 85 - 1st of 6 giving 11lb to Thames Dancer (10 Jun Newbury RF 1887). Got off the mark when making all in an uncompetitive Newbury handicap, and proved unable to compete in stiffer company last time. **H Candy [1-8] P A Deal.*

SIR EFFENDI (IRE) BHB 90f **RR 101f** 3832[2]
3 ch c Nashwan (USA) 10.3f **(79)** - Jeema (Thatch (USA)) 9.8f **(62)**
Form - 012
Record 1999 - 1st:1 2nd:1 3rd:0 Ran:3
Win Prizemoney £4,129 *Total Prizemoney* £7,390
Wins * **1999** Jly Lingfi (G-F) 7.6f 88 <
1999 Turf 1-3: (8f 1-3) (gd, frm 1-2)
Currently very useful colt. Turf high 101 - 2nd of 5 getting 5lb from Bathwick (22 Aug Bath 8f frm RF 3832). Disappointing on soft ground on his debut, he looked useful when allowed the chance to race on a quicker surface. A big colt with plenty of scope, he will stay beyond a mile and is an interesting prospect for decent handicaps in 2000. **M P Tregoning [1-3] Hadi Al-Tajir.*

SIRENE BHB 50f **RR 50f** 5163[13]
2 ch f Mystiko (USA) 7.7f **(59)** - Breakaway (Song) 7.2f **(61)**
Form - 000
Record 1999 - 1st:0 2nd:0 3rd:0 Ran:3
1999 Turf 0-3: (6f, 7f 2) (sft, g-s, g-f)
Currently fair filly. Turf high 50 (began Spt).
**M J Polglase [0-3] Mark Bury.*

SIR FERBET (IRE) **RR 86f** 4821[3]
2 b c Mujadil (USA) 7.7f **(70)** - Mirabiliary (USA) (Crow (FR)) 7.4f **(75)**
Form - 43
Record 1999 - 1st:0 2nd:0 3rd:1 Ran:2
Win Prizemoney £0 *Total Prizemoney* £758
1999 Turf 0-2: (6f 2) (gd, g-f)
Currently useful colt. Turf high 86 (began Oct) - 3rd of 21 giving 5lb to Toleration (11 Oct Windsor 6f g-f RF 4821).
**B W Hills [0-2] R J C Upton & International Plywood Plc.*

SIR FOLEY BHB 45a **RR 45a** 2721[7]
2 ch g Elmaamul (USA) 8.1f **(70)** - Light Fantastic **(66f)** (Deploy)
Form - 74357
Record 1999 - 1st:0 2nd:0 3rd:1 Ran:5
Win Prizemoney £0 *Total Prizemoney* £254
1999 AW 0-5: (5f, 6f 3, 7f) (Fibr 5)
Moderate gelding. AW high 46. **W G M Turner [0-5] Foley Steelstock.*

SIRIUS PROSPECT BHB 52f **RR 52f** 2277[4]
3 b g Sanglamore (USA) 12.9f **(67)** - Star of the Future (USA) (El Gran Senor (USA)) 9.6f **(76)**
Form - 6074
Record 1999 - 1st:0 2nd:0 3rd:0 Ran:4
1999 Turf 0-4: (10f 3, 12f) (sft, gd 2, frm)
Rangy, fair gelding. Turf high 52 - 4th of 17 getting 8lb from Capriolo (24 Jun Salisbury 10f frm RF 2277).
**H J Collingridge [0-4] The Headquarters Partnership.*

SIR JACK BHB 80f **RR 85df** 2243[10]
3 b c Distant Relative 7f **(69)** - Frasquita (Song) 7.2f **(61)**
Form - 700
Record 1999 - 1st:0 2nd:0 3rd:0 Ran:3
Pre1999 - 1st:1 2nd:1 3rd:0 Ran:3
Win Prizemoney £3,371 *Total Prizemoney* £4,356
Wins 1998 Spt Newcas (GD) 6f 75 <
1999 Turf 0-3: (6f 2, 7f) (gd, g-f, frm)
Useful colt, effective 6f, acts on gd to g-f, has worn blinkers.
**J Noseda [0-3] Lucayan Stud (from D R Loder [1-3] Oct 1998).*

SIR LEGEND (USA) BHB 63f **RR 62df** 4289[5]
3 br c El Gran Senor (USA) 8.9f **(85)** - Tadkiyra (IRE) (Darshaan) 9.9f **(84)**
Form - 05355
Record 1999 - 1st:0 2nd:0 3rd:1 Ran:5
Win Prizemoney £0 *Total Prizemoney* £567
1999 Turf 0-5: (10f, 11f, 12f 2, 14f) (gd 2, g-f 2, frm)
Well made, average colt. Turf high 67 - 5th of 6 to Flaming Quest (24 May Leicester 12f frm RF 1435).
**E A L Dunlop [0-5] Gainsborough Stud.*

SIR NICHOLAS BHB 100f **RR 97+f** 2629[3]
2 b c Cadeaux Genereux 7.9f **(76)** - Final Shot (Dalsaan) 9.8f **(64)**
Form - 123
Record 1999 - 1st:1 2nd:1 3rd:1 Ran:3
Win Prizemoney £3,728 *Total Prizemoney* £20,478
Wins * **1999** May Doncas (G-F) 6f 90+ <
1999 Turf 1-3: (6f 1-3) (g-f, frm 1-2)
Currently very useful colt. Turf high 97 - 3rd of 7 getting 3lb from City On A Hill (7 Jly Newmarket 6f frm RF 2629) - also 1st of 13 from Day Journey (29 May Doncaster RF 1560). A sharp juvenile, he chased Fasliyev home in the Coventry Stakes but was unable to improve on that effort after moving poorly to post before the July Stakes. Missing during the second half of the campaign, he is not particularly scopey and may be overtaken by his contemporaries next term. **J Noseda [1-3] Lucayan Stud.*

SIR NINJA (IRE) BHB 100f **RR 92f** 5029[7]
2 b c Turtle Island (IRE) - The Poachers Lady (IRE) (Salmon Leap (USA)) 11f **(61)**
Form - 462120217
Record 1999 - 1st:2 2nd:3 3rd:0 Ran:9
Win Prizemoney £12,926 *Total Prizemoney* £19,728
Wins * **1999** Oct Ascot (G-S) 7f 92 <
* **1999** Aug Thirsk (SFT) 7f 87+
1999 Turf 2-9: (6f 2, 7f 2-6, 8f) (sft, g-s, gd 2-5, g-f, frm)
Useful colt, effective 7f, acts on gd to g-f, best on gd. Turf high 92 - 1st of 7 from Compton Bolter (9 Oct Ascot RF 4797) - also 1st of 9 giving 5lb to Lady of Windsor (9 Aug Thirsk RF 3481). Got off the

mark at Thirsk in August and won the Hyperion at Ascot in fine style in October. Suited by soft ground.
**D J S ffrenchDavis [2-9] Hargood Ltd.*

SIR PERSE BHB 40f60a **RR 35f 60a** 4946[12]
3 b g Precocious 7.2f **(54)** - Anne's Bank (IRE) (Burslem) 8.8f **(53)**
Form - 82047800
Record 1999 - 1st:0 2nd:0 3rd:0 Ran:6
Pre1999 - 1st:0 2nd:1 3rd:0 Ran:5
Win Prizemoney £0 *Total Prizemoney* £761
1999 Turf 0-5: (6f, 8f 2, 10f 2) (gd, g-f 3, frm) 1999 AW 0-1: (8f) (Equi)
Strong, average gelding, effective 7 to 8f, - acts on Equi, has worn blinkers, prefers left handed tracks, likes tight tracks. Turf high 50. (1st run) - 4th of 8 giving 12lb to Admirals Place (19 Jun Lingfield 8f Equi RF 2151). Becoming disappointing.
**J R Poulton [0-1] Robert Townsend (from G L Moore [0-10] Aug 1999).*

SIR SANDROVITCH (IRE) BHB 71f **RR 72f** 4427[11]
3 b g Polish Patriot (USA) 7.8f **(70)** - Old Downie (Be My Guest (USA)) 9.3f **(67)**
Form - 017024600
Record 1999 - 1st:1 2nd:1 3rd:0 Ran:9
Pre1999 - 1st:0 2nd:0 3rd:0 Ran:1
Win Prizemoney £2,710 *Total Prizemoney* £4,470
Wins * **1999** May Mussel (FRM) 5f 70 <
1999 Turf 1-9: (5f 1-8, 6f) (g-s 2, gd 2, g-f 1-4, frm)
Workmanlike, above-average gelding, effective 5f, acts on g-f. Turf high 75 - 2nd of 12 getting 2lb from Cartmel Park (2 Jly Sandown 5f g-f RF 2503) - also 1st of 11 from Upper Chamber (22 May Musselburgh RF 1409). He put up an amazing performance to win a Musselburgh maiden on very fast ground in May, coming from last to first in a matter of strides, and has shown mixed form otherwise. **R A Fahey [1-10] The Sandrovitch 4.*

SIR WALTER (IRE) BHB 33f38a **RR 39f 38a** 5145[6]
6 b g The Bart (USA) - Glenbalda (Kambalda)
Form - 55043276344706
Record 1999 - 1st:0 2nd:1 3rd:2 Ran:12
Pre1999 - 1st:1 2nd:0 3rd:0 Ran:8
Win Prizemoney £2,750 *Total Prizemoney* £3,934
Wins 1998 Aug Tramor (G-F) H 9f 40 49 <
1999 Turf 0-2: (10f, 11f) (g-f, frm) 1999 AW 0-10: (8f, 9f, 10f 2, 12f 3, 13f 2, 14f) (Equi 5, Fibr 5)
Moderate gelding. Turf high 39. AW high 49.
**A T Murphy [0-19] A J Oliver (from Seamus Cotter in IRE [1-10] Aug 1998).*

SISAO (IRE) BHB 52f49a **RR 53f 49a** 5113[7]
3 ch c College Chapel - Copt Hall Princess (Crowned Prince (USA)) 10.1f **(67)**
Form - 007
Record 1999 - 1st:0 2nd:0 3rd:0 Ran:3
1999 Turf 0-3: (6f 3) (gd 2, frm)
Workmanlike, currently fair colt, has worn blinkers. Turf high 53 (began Spt). **Miss Gay Kelleway [0-3] Stable Investments Ltd.*

SISTER BELLA (IRE) RR 108f 2800a[3]
3 b f Sadler's Wells (USA) 11.3f **(87)** - Valley Of Hope (USA) (Riverman (USA)) 9.1f **(76)**
Form - 143
1999 Turf 1-3: (10f 1-2, 12f) (gd 1-1, g-f 2)
Pattern-class filly. Turf high 108. Ran the race of her life to finish third to Ramruma in the Irish Oaks. **J Oxx in IRE [2-5] Neil Jones.*

SISTER KATE RR 4799[6]
2 b f Barathea (IRE) - Norpella (Northfields (USA)) 9f **(72)**
Form - 6
Record 1999 - 1st:0 2nd:0 3rd:0 Ran:1
1999 Turf 0-1: (8f) (gd)
Currently very poor filly. **N Tinkler [0-1] Mrs D Wright.*

SISTER PATRICE (IRE) BHB 40f **RR 22f** 1192[15]
3 b f Petorius 8f **(66)** - Top Nurse (High Top) 10.2f **(67)**
Form - 00
Record 1999 - 1st:0 2nd:0 3rd:0 Ran:2
Pre1999 - 1st:0 2nd:0 3rd:0 Ran:8
1999 Turf 0-2: (7f, 11f) (gd, frm)
Workmanlike, little account filly, has worn blinkers. Turf high 21. Becoming disappointing. **Mrs P N Dutfield [0-10] In For The Crack.*

SITTING PRETTY BHB 32f **RR 30f** 3255[8]
3 b f Presidium 7.5f **(56)** - Malvern Madam (Reesh)
Form - 008
Record 1999 - 1st:0 2nd:0 3rd:0 Ran:3
1999 Turf 0-3: (7f, 8f, 10f) (frm 3)
Unfurnished, currently very moderate filly. Turf high 30 (began Jly). **D Nicholls [0-3] Green Bull Partnership.*

SIX FOR LUCK BHB 24f **RR 33f** 4588[7]
7 b g Handsome Sailor 6.6f **(53)** - Fire Sprite (Mummy's Game) 8.2f **(60)**
Form - 0007
Record 1999 - 1st:0 2nd:0 3rd:0 Ran:4
Pre1999 - 1st:1 2nd:2 3rd:2 Ran:39
Win Prizemoney £2,348 *Total Prizemoney* £5,242
1999 Turf 0-4: (5f 2, 6f 2) (gd 2, g-f 2)
Very moderate gelding, has worn blinkers. Turf high 33.
**D A Nolan [0-37] Mrs J McFadyen-Murray (from J Berry [1-6] Jun 1995).*

SIZZLING BHB 49f46a **RR 51df 46a** 181[8]
7 b g Sizzling Melody 6.3f **(49)** - Oriental Splendour (Runnett) 7f **(59)**
Form - 3568
Record 1999 - 1st:0 2nd:0 3rd:0 Ran:3
Pre1999 - 1st:4 2nd:2 3rd:4 Ran:36
Win Prizemoney £12,626 *Total Prizemoney* £16,685
Wins * 1998 May Bright (FRM) H 6f 48 53
* 1997 Apr Bright (FRM) C 6f 56
* 1995 Oct Leices (FRM) H 6f 59 63 <
* 1995 May Bath (G-F) 5.1f 61
1999 AW 0-3: (6f, 7f, 8f) (Equi 3)
Fair gelding, effective 6 to 7f, best at 6f, acts on gd to frm - acts on Equi, has worn blinkers, favours left handed tracks, favours tight tracks. AW high 44. **R Hannon [4-39] Jubert Family.*

SKELTON MONARCH (IRE) BHB 46f **RR 51f** 5207[20]
2 ch c Prince of Birds (USA) - Toda (Absalom) 7.2f **(58)**
Form - 07800
Record 1999 - 1st:0 2nd:0 3rd:0 Ran:5
1999 Turf 0-4: (5f, 6f, 7f 2) (g-s, gd, frm, hrd) 1999 AW 0-1: (6f) (Fibr)
Fair colt. Turf high 42. **R Hollinshead [0-5] G Bailey.*

SKEPTICAL (USA) BHB 80f **RR 72tf** 3961[6]
2 br c Kris S (USA) 9.3f **(76)** - Skep (USA) (Fappiano (USA)) 8.7f **(77)**
Form - 656
Record 1999 - 1st:0 2nd:0 3rd:0 Ran:3
1999 Turf 0-3: (6f, 7f 2) (gd, g-f, frm)
Currently above-average colt. Turf high 72 (1st run) (began Jly) - 6th of 7 to Petary (17 Jly Newmarket 6f frm RF 2906).
**Sir Michael Stoute [0-3] Maktoum Al Maktoum.*

SKERRAY BHB 66f **RR 59f** 1415[6]
4 b f Soviet Star (USA) 8.6f **(74)** - Reuval (Sharpen Up) 8.3f **(67)**
Form - 6
Record 1999 - 1st:0 2nd:0 3rd:0 Ran:1
Pre1999 - 1st:0 2nd:0 3rd:2 Ran:4
Win Prizemoney £0 *Total Prizemoney* £1,164
1999 Turf 0-1: (8f) (g-f)
Scopey, fair filly. Rather disappointing on her second run.
**J R Fanshawe [0-5] Dr Catherine Wills.*

SKIBO (JPN) RR 80f 5021[4]
2 b c Carnegie (IRE) - Dyna Avenue (JPN) (Northern Taste (CAN))
Form - 44
Record 1999 - 1st:0 2nd:0 3rd:0 Ran:2
Win Prizemoney £0 *Total Prizemoney* £608
1999 Turf 0-2: (7f, 8f) (gd 2)
Currently decent colt. Turf high 80 (began Oct) - 4th of 22 giving 5lb to Fame At Last (22 Oct Doncaster 7f gd RF 5021).
**M P Tregoning [0-2] Sheikh Mohammed.*

SKIFFLE MAN RR 20f 3822[13]
3 b g Alhijaz 7.7f **(57)** - Laundry Maid (Forzando) 7.6f **(59)**
Form - 30

Record 1999 - 1st:0 2nd:0 3rd:1 Ran:2
Win Prizemoney £0 *Total Prizemoney* £394
1999 Turf 0-1: (10f) (g-f) 1999 AW 0-1: (9f) (Fibr)
Workmanlike, currently average gelding.
**C G Cox [0-1] Mrs M Howlett (from M J Heaton-Ellis [0-1] Aug 1999).*

SKI FREE BHB 48f45a **RR 58f 45a** 2378[6]
2 b f Factual (USA) - Ski Blade **(16f)** (Niniski (USA)) 10.6f **(65)**
Form - 536
Record 1999 - 1st:0 2nd:0 3rd:1 Ran:3
Win Prizemoney £0 *Total Prizemoney* £250
1999 Turf 0-2: (5f 2) (frm, hrd) 1999 AW 0-1: (5f) (Fibr)
Currently fair filly. Turf high 58. **R Guest [0-3] Zmile Partnership.*

SKI LODGE (IRE) BHB 88f **RR 82f** 1331[8]
3 br f Persian Bold 10f **(69)** - Place of Honour (Be My Guest (USA)) 9.3f **(67)**
Form - 068
Record 1999 - 1st:0 2nd:0 3rd:0 Ran:3
Pre1999 - 1st:1 2nd:0 3rd:0 Ran:3
Win Prizemoney £3,509 *Total Prizemoney* £3,509
Wins * 1998 Oct Leices (G-S) 7f 82 <
1999 Turf 0-3: (7f, 10f, 11f) (gd, g-f 2)
Leggy, decent filly, effective 7f, acts on gd. Turf high 82.
**C E Brittain [1-6] Mrs Sean Collins.*

SKIMRA RR 87f 5108[6]
2 b f Hernando (FR) - Skuld (Kris) 9.5f **(73)**
Form - 26
Record 1999 - 1st:0 2nd:1 3rd:0 Ran:2
Win Prizemoney £0 *Total Prizemoney* £1,320
1999 Turf 0-2: (8f 2) (g-s, gd)
Currently useful filly. Turf high 87 (1st run) (began Oct) - 2nd of 14 to Embraced (5 Oct Nottingham 8f g-s RF 4728).
**R Guest [0-2] Miss K Rausing.*

SKI RUN RR 74f 5067[1]
3 b f Petoski 10.4f **(56)** - Cut and Run **(54f)** (Slip Anchor) 9.8f **(73)**
Form - 881
Record 1999 - 1st:1 2nd:0 3rd:0 Ran:3
Win Prizemoney £4,110 *Total Prizemoney* £4,110
Wins * 1999 Oct Bath (SFT) 11.7f 74 <
1999 Turf 1-3: (12f 1-3) (sft, g-s, gd 1-1)
Scopey, currently above-average filly. Turf high 74 (began Spt) - 1st of 15 from Wedoudah (26 Oct Bath RF 5067).
**R F JohnsonHoughton [1-3] T D Holland-Martin.*

SKY BELLE (IRE) BHB 48f **RR 56f** 4530[8]
2 b f Mujadil (USA) 7.7f **(70)** - Astronomer Lady (IRE) (Montekin) 11.1f **(55)**
Form - 087688
Record 1999 - 1st:0 2nd:0 3rd:0 Ran:6
1999 Turf 0-6: (5f, 6f 4, 7f) (g-s, g-f 4, frm)
Fair filly. Turf high 56. (DEAD)
**J L Spearing [0-6] The McIntyre Woods Partnership.*

SKY CITY BHB 42f47a **RR 16f 47a** 5135[18]
3 b f Be My Chief (USA) 10.2f **(62)** - Pellinora (USA) (King Pellinore (USA)) 8.2f **(68)**
Form - 026000
Record 1999 - 1st:0 2nd:1 3rd:0 Ran:5
Pre1999 - 1st:0 2nd:0 3rd:0 Ran:1
Win Prizemoney £0 *Total Prizemoney* £1,140
1999 Turf 0-2: (8f, 10f) (gd 2) 1999 AW 0-3: (8f, 10f, 12f) (Equi, Fibr 2)
Leggy, very moderate filly, effective 10f, - acts on Equi. Turf high 16 (began Aug). AW high 77 (1st run) - 2nd of 13 getting 5lb from Scraggys Dream (2 Jan Lingfield 10f Equi RF 0010).
**P Howling [0-6] Manor Farm Packers Ltd.*

SKY DOME (IRE) BHB 77f **RR 77f** 4874[11]
6 ch g Bluebird (USA) 7.9f **(71)** - God Speed Her (Pas de Seul) 9.1f **(67)**
Form - 3221060
Record 1999 - 1st:1 2nd:2 3rd:1 Ran:7
Pre1999 - 1st:4 2nd:1 3rd:0 Ran:27
Win Prizemoney £33,287 *Total Prizemoney* £42,301
Wins * 1999 May Newmar (GD) H 8f 74 77
* 1996 Aug Goodwo (GD) H 8f 84 89 <
* 1996 Aug Newmar (GD) H 8f 78 86
* 1996 Apr Newmar (G-F) H 7f 75 80
* 1995 Apr Carlis (GD) 5f 74t
1999 Turf 1-7: (7f 2, 8f 1-5) (g-s, gd 3, g-f 1-1, frm 2)
Above-average gelding, effective 7 to 10f, best at 8f, acts on sft to frm, likes Newmarket. Turf high 77 - 1st of 17 giving 27lb to Alfahaal (15 May Newmarket RF 1240). A tough and genuine performer at his best, he gained a well-deserved success in May at Newmarket after some fair placed efforts. Off the track between June and October, he was below form in his last few starts.
**M H Tompkins [5-34] www raceworld co uk.*

SKYE RR 59f 5070[7]
2 ch f Timeless Times (USA) 6.1f **(56)** - Excavator Lady (Most Secret) 7.1f **(58)**
Form - 007
Record 1999 - 1st:0 2nd:0 3rd:0 Ran:3
1999 Turf 0-3: (5f 3) (gd, frm 2)
Currently fair filly. Turf high 59 (began Spt).
**J Balding [0-3] Mrs Gillian Jones.*

SKYE BLUE (IRE) RR 38f 5044[5]
2 b g Blues Traveller (IRE) - Hitopah (Bustino) 10.4f **(64)**
Form - 5
Record 1999 - 1st:0 2nd:0 3rd:0 Ran:1
1999 Turf 0-1: (6f) (sft)
Currently very moderate gelding.
**M R Channon [0-1] W H Ponsonby.*

SKYERS A KITE BHB 43f32a **RR 43f 32a** 4983[7]
4 b f Deploy 11.4f **(67)** - Milady Jade (IRE) (Drumalis) 12f **(54)**
Form - 706360137
Record 1999 - 1st:1 2nd:0 3rd:2 Ran:9
Pre1999 - 1st:2 2nd:2 3rd:2 Ran:11
Win Prizemoney £9,096 *Total Prizemoney* £11,773
Wins * 1999 Spt Beverl (SFT) H 9.9f 40 43
* 1998 Oct Catter (gd,) H 12f 42 45 <
* 1998 Jly Beverl (GD) SH 12f 40 45 <
1999 Turf 1-7: (10f 1-2, 12f 2, 14f, 16f, 17f) (g-s 1-1, gd 2, g-f 2, frm 2)
1999 AW 0-2: (12f, 14f) (Fibr 2)
Unfurnished, moderate filly, effective 10 to 12f, best at 12f, acts on g-s to hrd, best on g-f, favours tight tracks. Turf high 43 - 1st of 18 getting 11lb from Nowell House (21 Spt Beverley RF 4447). AW high 23. **Ronald Thompson [3-20] G A W Racing Partnership.*

SKYERS FLYER (IRE) BHB 46f65a **RR 38f 65a** 5128[3]
5 b br m Magical Wonder (USA) 7.2f **(60)** - Siwana (IRE) (Dom Racine (FR)) 9.2f **(62)**
Form - 00512004503
Record 1999 - 1st:1 2nd:1 3rd:1 Ran:11
Pre1999 - 1st:4 2nd:5 3rd:7 Ran:41
Win Prizemoney £13,419 *Total Prizemoney* £24,851
Wins * 1999 Jly Carlis (GD) H 5.9f 42 46
* 1997 Aug Newcas (G-F) S 6f 48
* 1997 Apr Nottin (GD) S 6.1f 68
* 1996 Aug Bright (FRM) H 5.3f 85 72 <
* 1996 May Beverl (G-F) S 5f 47
1999 Turf 1-10: (5f 4, 6f 1-5, 7f) (gd, g-f 2, frm 1-7) 1999 AW 0-1: (6f) (Fibr)
Very moderate filly, effective 6 to 7f, best at 7f, acts on gd to g-f, best on gd. Turf high 51. Consistent.
**Ronald Thompson [5-36] A Bell (from Martyn Wane [0-16] Oct 1998).*

SKY HOOK BHB 59f53a **RR 61f 53a** 5150[9]
2 ch c Superlative 8.8f **(57)** - Lady Eccentric (IRE) (Magical Wonder (USA))
Form - 705830
Record 1999 - 1st:0 2nd:0 3rd:1 Ran:6
Win Prizemoney £0 *Total Prizemoney* £487
1999 Turf 0-4: (6f 3, 7f) (g-s, gd, frm, hrd) 1999 AW 0-2: (6f 2) (Fibr 2)
Average colt, effective 6f, acts on gd. Turf high 61 (began Aug). AW high 42 (began Jly). **N P Littmoden [0-6] A1 Racing.*

SKYLARK BHB 76f **RR 72f** 5129[11]
2 ch f Polar Falcon (USA) 9f **(74)** - Boozy (Absalom) 7.2f **(58)**
Form - 23300

Record 1999 - 1st:0 2nd:1 3rd:2 Ran:5
Win Prizemoney £0 *Total Prizemoney* £2,367
1999 Turf 0-5: (5f 2, 6f 3) (gd, g-f, frm 3)
Above-average filly. Turf high 72 (began Jly) - 3rd of 13 to Yazmin (2 Aug Windsor 6f frm RF 3303). She showed ability when making the frame in maiden company in each of her first three starts, but was well beaten at Newmarket on her nursery debut.
**R Hannon [0-5] Heathavon Stables Ltd.*

SKY OF HOPE (FR) BHB 72f RR 76f 5035[2]

3 b c Zieten (USA) - Rain Or Shine (FR) (Nonoalco (USA)) 8.5f **(66)**
Form - 835472
Record 1999 - 1st:0 2nd:1 3rd:1 Ran:6
Pre1999 - 1st:0 2nd:0 3rd:0 Ran:3
Win Prizemoney £0 *Total Prizemoney* £2,620
1999 Turf 0-6: (7f 5, 8f) (g-s, g-f, frm 4)
Scopey, above-average colt, effective 7f, acts on g-s to frm, best on frm. Turf high 76 - 4th of 14 giving 7lb to Avanti (31 May Sandown 7f frm RF 1616). Consistent. Still a maiden, but does have ability and looks as if a trip of at least a mile will suit.
**R Hannon [0-9] Lucayan Stud.*

SKY STORM BHB 50f RR 59f 4128[12]

3 ch g Lycius (USA) 8.8f **(71)** - Beijing (USA) (Northjet) 10.3f **(74)**
Form - 470
Record 1999 - 1st:0 2nd:0 3rd:0 Ran:3
Pre1999 - 1st:0 2nd:0 3rd:0 Ran:2
1999 Turf 0-1: (11f) (g-f) 1999 AW 0-2: (7f, 8f) (Equi, Fibr)
Workmanlike, fair gelding, has worn blinkers. AW high 51.
**J Norton [0-1] Congleton Racing Club (from B J Meehan [0-4] Feb 1999).*

SLAM BID RR 60f 3981[8]

2 b c First Trump - Nadema (Artaius (USA)) 9f **(69)**
Form - 08
Record 1999 - 1st:0 2nd:0 3rd:0 Ran:2
1999 Turf 0-2: (6f 2) (g-s, frm)
Currently average colt. Turf high 60 (began Aug).
**R Charlton [0-2] Thurloe Thoroughbreds IV.*

SLANDER (USA) RR 38f 87[6]

3 ch f Miswaki (USA) 8.1f **(81)** - Slam Bid (USA) (Forli (ARG)) 9.6f **(67)**
Form - 6
Record 1999 - 1st:0 2nd:0 3rd:0 Ran:1
Pre1999 - 1st:0 2nd:0 3rd:0 Ran:1
1999 AW 0-1: (6f) (Fibr)
Currently very moderate filly.
**Sir Mark Prescott [0-1] Mrs Chryss O'Reilly (from D K Weld in IRE [0-1] Jun 1998).*

SLAPY DAM BHB 46f50a RR 24f 50a 4709[5]

7 b g Deploy 11.4f **(67)** - Key to the River (USA) (Irish River (FR)) 8.6f **(78)**
Form - 4211005
Record 1999 - 1st:2 2nd:1 3rd:0 Ran:7
Pre1999 - 1st:3 2nd:1 3rd:1 Ran:32
Win Prizemoney £16,406 *Total Prizemoney* £19,326

Wins									
	1999	Aug	Chepst	(G-S)	C	12.1f		56	
	1999	Aug	Bright	(SFT)	C	11.9f		47	
	1995	Oct	Leices	(GD)	H	11.8f	57	60	<
	1995	Spt	Folkes	(SFT)	H	12f	48	59	
	1995	Apr	Mussel	(GD)	H	11.1f	48	53	

1999 Turf 2-7: (11f, 12f 2-6) (sft, gd 1-2, g-f 1-1, frm 3)
Fair gelding, effective 12f, acts on gd to g-f, has worn blinkers, favours left handed tracks, favours tight tracks. Turf high 56 (began Jly) - 1st of 7 from Summer Bounty (30 Aug Chepstow RF 4010) - also 1st of 6 getting 14lb from Montfort (18 Aug Brighton RF 3735).
**J M Bradley [0-3] David Lewis (from D Burchell [2-4] Aug 1999).*

SLASHER JACK (IRE) BHB 60f54a RR 59f 54a 938[2]

8 b g Alzao (USA) 9.8f **(73)** - Sherkraine (Shergar) 10.4f **(66)**
Form - 2
Record 1999 - 1st:0 2nd:1 3rd:0 Ran:1
Pre1999 - 1st:6 2nd:3 3rd:2 Ran:35
Win Prizemoney £24,031 *Total Prizemoney* £40,195

Wins									
	1998	Jly	Haydoc	(GD)	C	11.9f		59	
	1995	May	Haydoc	(G-F)	H	11.9f	78	87	<

1999 Turf 0-1: (16f) (g-f)
Fair gelding, effective 12f, acts on sft to frm, has worn blinkers, likes tight tracks. Consistent.
**K A Ryan [0-1] T C Chiang (from R A Fahey [1-13] Jly 1998).*

SLAVE TO THE RYTHM (IRE) RR 72f 4178[14]

2 br f Hamas (IRE) 8f **(72)** - Silver Singing (USA) (Topsider (USA)) 8.3f **(71)**
Form - 60
Record 1999 - 1st:0 2nd:0 3rd:0 Ran:2
1999 Turf 0-2: (6f 2) (gd, frm)
Currently above-average filly. Turf high 72.
**J L Dunlop [0-2] Mrs Philippa Cooper.*

SLEAVE SILK (IRE) BHB 39f48a RR 39f 48a 3084[4]

4 b f Unfuwain (USA) 11.4f **(74)** - Shanira (Shirley Heights) 10.3f **(74)**
Form - 312211864
Record 1999 - 1st:3 2nd:2 3rd:0 Ran:8
Pre1999 - 1st:0 2nd:0 3rd:1 Ran:4
Win Prizemoney £7,412 *Total Prizemoney* £9,311

Wins									
	* **1999**	*Mar*	*Lingfi*	*(STD)*	*H*	*16f*	*39*	*49*	<
	* **1999**	*Feb*	*Lingfi*	*(STD)*	*H*	*16f*	*39*	*47*	
	* **1999**	*Jan*	*Lingfi*	*(STD)*	*H*	*12f*	*32*	*37*	

1999 Turf 0-2: (14f, 16f) (gd 2) 1999 AW 3-6: (12f 1-3, 16f 2-3) (Equi 3-5, Fibr)
Workmanlike, moderate filly, effective 16f, - acts on Equi, favours left handed tracks, prefers tight tracks. Turf high 39. AW high 49 - 1st of 6 getting 28lb from Harik (2 Mar Lingfield RF 0390) - also 1st of 9 getting 12lb from Behind The Scenes (25 Feb Lingfield RF 0357). Consistent. She showed much-improved form when stepped up to middle distances on Equitrack, and has proved that she gets two miles on that surface.
**W J Musson [3-12] Broughton Bloodstock.*

SLEEPLESS BHB 90f RR 91f 1731[3]

5 b m Night Shift (USA) 8.1f **(73)** - Late Evening (USA) (Riverman (USA)) 9.1f **(76)**
Form - 003
Record 1999 - 1st:0 2nd:0 3rd:1 Ran:3
Pre1999 - 1st:3 2nd:1 3rd:2 Ran:16
Win Prizemoney £14,771 *Total Prizemoney* £22,863

Wins									
	* 1998	Spt	Newcas	(GD)		7f		76	
	* 1998	Apr	Leices	(SFT)	H	7f	84	94+	<
	* 1997	May	Newbur	(SFT)	H	7.3f	78	90	

1999 Turf 0-3: (7f, 8f, 9f) (gd 2, g-f)
Useful filly, effective 7f, acts on sft, has worn blinkers. Turf high 91. Showed little in handicaps on her first two runs of '99, but ran better when third in an Epsom listed race.
**N A Graham [3-19] Mrs Audrey Scotney.*

SLEEPTITE (FR) BHB 35f49a RR 4f 49a 234[10]

9 gr g Double Bed (FR) 13.9f **(54)** - Rajan Grey (Absalom) 7.2f **(58)**
Form - 0
Record 1999 - 1st:0 2nd:0 3rd:0 Ran:1
Pre1999 - 1st:2 2nd:4 3rd:5 Ran:28
Win Prizemoney £5,246 *Total Prizemoney* £10,748

Wins									
	1995	*Feb*	*Lingfi*	*(STD)*	*SH*	*13f*	*53*	*57*	<

1999 AW 0-1: (13f) (Equi)
Poor gelding. Inconsistent. (DEAD)
**Mrs S D Williams [0-1] Christopher Shirley Brasher (from W G M Turner [3-18] Nov 1996).*

SLICKLY (FR) RR 121f 4246a[5]

3 gr c Linamix (FR) 8.2f **(64)** - Slipstream Queen (FR) (Conquistador Cielo (USA)) 8.8f **(69)**
Form - 14125
1999 Turf 2-5: (8f 2, 10f 1-1, 11f 1-1, 12f) (hvy, g-s 1-1, gd 1-3)
Very high-class colt, effective 8 to 10f, acts on hvy to gd. Turf high 121 - 1st of 8 from Indian Danehill (27 Jun Longchamp RF 2476a). A game winner of the Prix la Rochette as a juvenile, he maintained his winning run by taking the Prix Noailles on his 1999 return. He may have found the trip too far in the Prix du Jockey-Club, and was subsequently returned to shorter trips. He returned to form next time, taking the Grand Prix de Paris, but found the top milers too good later in the season. He has been purchased by Godolphin, and may well be campaigned back at ten furlongs in 2000.
**A Fabre in FR [3-6].*

SLICK WILLIE (IRE) BHB 75f **RR 73f** 5218[2]
2 b g Up and At 'em - Perfectly Entitled (IRE) (Entitled)
Form - 335741036772232
Record 1999 - 1st:1 2nd:3 3rd:4 Ran:15
Win Prizemoney £2,843 *Total Prizemoney* £9,021
Wins * 1999 Jly Beverl (G-F) 5f 71 <
1999 Turf 1-15: (5f 1-5, 6f 6, 7f 4) (sft, g-s 2, gd, g-f 4, frm 1-7)
Above-average gelding, effective 5 to 7f, best at 7f, acts on sft to frm, best on g-s, has worn blinkers (extremely effectively). Turf high 73 - 2nd of 22 giving 6lb to Omniheat (6 Nov Doncaster 7f g-s RF 5218) - also 1st of 8 giving 5lb to Double Fault (13 Jly Beverley RF 2770). Consistent. **T D Easterby [1-15] D H Brown.*

SLIGHTLY DUSTY BHB 45f43a **RR 42f 43a** 927[7]
3 b f Deploy 11.4f **(67)** - Dusty's Darling (Doyoun) 9f **(69)**
Form - 400407
Record 1999 - 1st:0 2nd:0 3rd:0 Ran:6
Pre1999 - 1st:0 2nd:0 3rd:0 Ran:1
1999 Turf 0-3: (8f 2, 11f) (g-s 2, gd) 1999 AW 0-3: (6f, 7f, 9f) (Fibr 3)
Neat, moderate filly, often wears blinkers. Turf high 42. AW high 42. **P D Evans [0-7] D Maloney.*

SLIMS LADY BHB 59f56a **RR 53f 56a** 5066[4]
3 b f Theatrical Charmer 10.9f **(63)** - Lady Antoinette (Pharly (FR)) 9.8f **(68)**
Form - 055302334
Record 1999 - 1st:0 2nd:1 3rd:3 Ran:8
Pre1999 - 1st:0 2nd:0 3rd:3 Ran:6
Win Prizemoney £0 *Total Prizemoney* £3,315
1999 Turf 0-8: (10f 3, 11f 2, 12f 3) (g-s, gd 3, g-f 2, frm 2)
Leggy, fair filly, effective 7 to 8f, acts on g-s to gd, likes left handed tracks, likes tight tracks. Turf high 54. Consistent. **K R Burke [0-14] Stuart Prior.*

SLIP JIG (IRE) BHB 53f53a **RR 69df 53a** 638[17]
6 b g Marju (IRE) 9.2f **(76)** - Taking Steps (Gay Fandango (USA)) 8.5f **(59)**
Form - 503734452430
Record 1999 - 1st:0 2nd:1 3rd:3 Ran:10
Pre1999 - 1st:2 2nd:4 3rd:3 Ran:24
Win Prizemoney £6,713 *Total Prizemoney* £15,506
Wins 1997 *Jan Lingfi (STD) C 12f 72+* <
1996 May Salisb (SFT) 7f 71
1999 Turf 0-1: (13f) (hvy) 1999 AW 0-9: (8f 3, 10f 2, 11f 2, 12f 2) (Equi 4, Fibr 5)
Average gelding, effective 8 to 12f, - acted on Equi to Fibr, best on Equi, had worn blinkers, favoured left handed tracks, and did well at Southwell. AW high 58 - 3rd of 11 giving 20lb to Clonoe (21 Jan Lingfield 10f Equi RF 0133). (DEAD) **K R Burke [0-22] Nigel Shields (from R Hannon [2-13] Jan 1997).*

SLIP KILLICK BHB 57f **RR 59f** 5186[8]
2 b f Cosmonaut - Killick **(64f 55a)** (Slip Anchor) 9.8f **(73)**
Form - 548
Record 1999 - 1st:0 2nd:0 3rd:0 Ran:3
Win Prizemoney £0 *Total Prizemoney* £265
1999 Turf 0-3: (6f, 7f 2) (g-s, g-f, frm)
Currently fair filly. Turf high 59 (began Spt). **M Mullineaux [0-3] Esprit de Corps Racing.*

SLIP OF THE TONGUE BHB 37f37a **RR 38f 37a** 4988[1]
3 b f Slip Anchor 12.7f **(75)** - Plaything (High Top) 10.2f **(67)**
Form - 00056200341
Record 1999 - 1st:1 2nd:1 3rd:1 Ran:10
Pre1999 - 1st:0 2nd:0 3rd:0 Ran:1
Win Prizemoney £2,075 *Total Prizemoney* £3,258
Wins * 1999 Oct Nottin (FRM) SH 14.1f 35 38 <
1999 Turf 1-7: (7f, 10f, 14f 1-3, 16f 2) (gd, g-f 3, frm 1-3) 1999 AW 0-3: (7f, 12f, 16f) (Equi, Fibr 2)
Lengthy, very moderate filly, effective 14 to 16f, best at 16f, acts on g-f to frm - acts on Equi, has worn blinkers. Turf high 44 - 2nd of 13 getting 8lb from Pleasant Mount (19 Jly Beverley 16f g-f RF 2943) - also 1st of 14 from Role Model (20 Oct Nottingham RF 4988). AW high 36 - 3rd of 6 getting 2lb from Zola (25 Aug Lingfield 16f Equi RF 3904). **S C Williams [1-11] Alasdair Simpson.*

SLIPSTREAM BHB 58a **RR 59f** 100[4]
5 b g Slip Anchor 12.7f **(75)** - Butosky (Busted) 10.2f **(61)**
Form - 04
Record 1999 - 1st:0 2nd:0 3rd:0 Ran:2
Pre1999 - 1st:1 2nd:1 3rd:1 Ran:11
Win Prizemoney £2,234 *Total Prizemoney* £3,923
Wins 1998 May Ayr (GD) 13.1f 60+ <
1999 AW 0-2: (13f, 16f) (Equi, Fibr)
Fair gelding, effective 13 to 14f, best at 14f, acts on g-s to gd, best on g-s, has worn blinkers, favours tight tracks. AW high 3. Becoming disappointing.
**G M McCourt [0-4] Matthews Breeding and Racing (from R Guest [1-11] Jly 1998).*

SLIP STREAM (USA) BHB 113f **RR 117f** 4779a[5]
3 ch c Irish River (FR) 9f **(77)** - Sous Entendu (USA) (Shadeed (USA)) 8.2f **(70)**
Form - 32155
Record 1999 - 1st:1 2nd:1 3rd:1 Ran:5
Pre1999 - 1st:1 2nd:0 3rd:0 Ran:1
Win Prizemoney £20,469 *Total Prizemoney* £51,492
Wins * 1999 Jly Goodwo (FRM) L 8f 116+ <
1998 Oct Leices (SFT) 7f 88++
1999 Turf 1-5: (8f 1-3, 9f, 10f) (sft, g-s, gd, g-f 1-2)
Scopey, high-class colt, effective 8 to 9f, best at 8f, acts on sft to g-f. Turf high 117 - 2nd of 6 to Golden Snake (6 Jun Chantilly 9f gd RF 1903a) - also 1st of 4 from Bahamian Bandit (31 Jly Goodwood RF 3259). Won his only race in 1998, and took on good sorts in the Dante on his 1999 debut. That may have been stretching his stamina a little, and he seemed to benefit from the drop back in trip when narrowly beaten in the Prix Jean Prat. Dropped back further to a mile, he had little trouble in seeing off his three opponents in a Goodwood Listed event, though his limitations were latterly exposed in Doncaster's Park Stakes and in the Prix du Rond-Point. **S bin Suroor [1-5] (from D R Loder [1-1] Oct 1998).*

SLOANE BHB 80f **RR 69f** 5003[10]
3 ch c Machiavellian (USA) 9.8f **(83)** - Gussy Marlowe (Final Straw) 7.9f **(64)**
Form - 4620
Record 1999 - 1st:0 2nd:1 3rd:0 Ran:4
Win Prizemoney £0 *Total Prizemoney* £1,501
1999 Turf 0-4: (8f 4) (gd, frm 3)
Scopey, average colt. Turf high 69 (began Aug) - 2nd of 11 giving 5lb to Ermine (19 Spt Newcastle 8f frm RF 4422). **G Wragg [0-4] Mrs John Van Geest.*

SLOWIN RR 107f 1532a[5]
7 g In The Wings 11.2f **(77)** -Louange (Green Dancer (USA)) 10.3f **(74)**
Form - 5
1999 Turf 0-1: (16f) (g-s)
Currently Pattern-class gelding, always wears blinkers. (1st run) - 5th of 9 getting 7lb from Kayf Tara (23 May Longchamp 16f g-s RF 1532a). **X Betron in FR [0-1].*

SLUMBERING (IRE) BHB 84f **RR 88f** 1332[6]
3 b c Thatching 7.8f **(69)** - Bedspread (USA) (Seattle Dancer (USA))
Form - 076
Record 1999 - 1st:0 2nd:0 3rd:0 Ran:3
Pre1999 - 1st:1 2nd:0 3rd:0 Ran:5
Win Prizemoney £6,914 *Total Prizemoney* £7,368
Wins * 1998 Oct York (GD) 6f 84 <
1999 Turf 0-3: (7f 2, 8f) (gd, frm 2)
Leggy, useful colt. Turf high 80. **B J Meehan [1-8] Mrs Christine Painting.*

SMALL RISK BHB 32f **RR 1f** 43[14]
5 b m Risk Me (FR) 8f **(53)** - Small Double (IRE) (Double Schwartz) 7.9f **(55)**
Form - 0
Record 1999 - 1st:0 2nd:0 3rd:0 Ran:1
Pre1999 - 1st:0 2nd:1 3rd:1 Ran:6
Win Prizemoney £0 *Total Prizemoney* £1,085
1999 AW 0-1: (7f) (Equi)
Poor filly, has worn blinkers.
**J W Hills [0-2] Miss Elizabeth Herbert (from T T Clement [0-2] Jun 1997).*

SMART (IRE) BHB 41a **RR** 3747[8]
4 b f Last Tycoon 9.4f **(73)** - Belle Origine (USA) (Exclusive Native (USA)) 9.1f **(81)**
Form - 808
Record 1999 - 1st:0 2nd:0 3rd:0 Ran:3
Pre1999 - 1st:0 2nd:0 3rd:0 Ran:3
1999 Turf 0-2: (8f, 12f) (gd, g-f) 1999 AW 0-1: (7f) (Fibr)
Very moderate filly. (began Aug).
**Andrew Reid [0-3] A S Reid (from Sir Mark Prescott [0-3] Mar 1998).*

SMART BOY (IRE) BHB 61f70a **RR 59?f 70a** 177[P]
5 ch g Polish Patriot (USA) 7.8f **(70)** - Bouffant (High Top) 10.2f **(67)**
Form - 0P
Record 1999 - 1st:0 2nd:0 3rd:0 Ran:2
Pre1999 - 1st:4 2nd:2 3rd:1 Ran:19
Win Prizemoney £11,974 *Total Prizemoney* £14,799
Wins 1998 *Feb Wolver (STD) H 12f 70 77* <
1997 *May Lingfi (STD) 10f 69*
1997 *May Lingfi (STD) 10f 69*
1996 May Lingfi (G-F) 5f 60t
1999 AW 0-2: (9f, 11f) (Fibr 2)
Fair gelding, effective 12 to 14f, best at 12f, acts on g-s - acts on Fibr, has worn blinkers, favours left handed tracks, favours tight tracks.
**M P Bielby [0-7] The Mariner Racing Syndicate (from P F I Cole [4-19] Oct 1998).*

SMARTER CHARTER BHB 50f46a **RR 51f 46a** 5191[3]
6 br g Master Willie 9.2f **(67)** - Irene's Charter (Persian Bold) 9.3f **(66)**
Form - 030417505034842463
Record 1999 - 1st:1 2nd:1 3rd:3 Ran:18
Pre1999 - 1st:4 2nd:4 3rd:3 Ran:33
Win Prizemoney £18,306 *Total Prizemoney* £27,978
Wins * **1999** Jun Mussel (GD) H 9f 53 54
* 1998 Jly Beverl (G-F) H 7.5f 60 65
* 1998 Jly Kempto (G-F) H 8f 56 57
1996 Jly Beverl (G-F) H 8.5f 70 75 <
1996 May Beverl (G-F) H 7.5f 58 61
1999 Turf 1-18: (8f 14, 9f 1-1, 10f 3) (g-s, gd 7, g-f 1-5, frm 4, hrd)
Fair gelding, effective 7 to 8f, best at 8f, acts on frm, likes tight tracks. **Mrs L Stubbs [3-37] O J Williams (from Mrs J R Ramsden [2-14] Aug 1996).*

SMART KID (IRE) BHB 68f75a **RR 67f 75a** 111[7]
5 b g Lahib (USA) 8f **(69)** -Diamond Lake (Kings Lake (USA)) 10.8f **(67)**
Form - 1167
Record 1999 - 1st:0 2nd:0 3rd:0 Ran:1
Pre1999 - 1st:3 2nd:0 3rd:0 Ran:11
Win Prizemoney £7,354 *Total Prizemoney* £7,354
Wins * 1998 *Dec Lingfi (STD) H 8f 70 76* <
* 1998 *Nov Lingfi (STD) C 8f 68*
1997 May Salisb (G-F) 6f 70
1999 AW 0-1: (8f) (Equi)
Above-average gelding, effective 8f, - acts on Equi, favours tight tracks. A fair sort over a mile on Equitrack, he sometimes carries his head awkwardly and tends to hang.
**Miss Gay Kelleway [2-8] Tommy Breen (from P F I Cole [1-4] Oct 1997).*

SMART PREDATOR BHB 76f **RR 81f** 5072[6]
3 gr g Polar Falcon (USA) 9f **(74)** - She's Smart (Absalom) 7.2f **(58)**
Form - 4428221006
Record 1999 - 1st:1 2nd:3 3rd:0 Ran:10
Win Prizemoney £6,758 *Total Prizemoney* £11,520
Wins * **1999** Spt York (G-F) 7.9f 81 <
1999 Turf 1-10: (6f 2, 7f 5, 8f 1-3) (g-s, gd 4, g-f, frm 1-4)
Workmanlike, decent gelding, effective 7 to 8f, best at 8f, acts on frm. Turf high 81 - 1st of 7 giving 5lb to Ermine (2 Spt York RF 4104). He had finished runner-up on three occasions before winning a York maiden in good style in September, although he was held subsequently. A mile looks to be his trip.
**J J Quinn [1-10] B Shaw.*

SMART RIDGE BHB 100f **RR 86f** 4690[14]
2 ch c Indian Ridge 7.6f **(74)** - Guanhumara (Caerleon (USA)) 8.6f **(71)**
Form - 0215506110
Record 1999 - 1st:3 2nd:1 3rd:0 Ran:10
Win Prizemoney £12,154 *Total Prizemoney* £13,440
Wins 1999 Aug Bright (G-F) H 5.3f 84 86 <
1999 Jly Hamilt (G-F) H 6f 86 <
1999 May Bright (FRM) 5.3f 79
1999 Turf 3-10: (5f 2-6, 6f 1-4) (g-s, g-f 2-7, frm, hrd 1-1)
Useful colt, effective 5 to 6f, best at 5f, acts on g-f to hrd, best on g-f. Turf high 86 - 1st of 6 giving 14lb to Morning Dawn (5 Aug Brighton RF 3383) - also 1st of 7 giving 11lb to Lady of Windsor (31 Jly Hamilton RF 3268). Added a couple of nurseries to his maiden win, and goes particularly well at Brighton where he has won twice. Likes the ground firm.
**K R Burke [0-1] Achilles International (from M R Channon [3-9] Aug 1999).*

SMART SAVANNAH BHB 94f **RR 91f** 5031[7]
3 b c Primo Dominie 7.2f **(67)** - High Savannah (Rousillon (USA)) 8.2f **(74)**
Form - 600010577
Record 1999 - 1st:1 2nd:0 3rd:0 Ran:9
Pre1999 - 1st:1 2nd:0 3rd:1 Ran:3
Win Prizemoney £11,023 *Total Prizemoney* £12,163
Wins * **1999** Aug Ascot (SFT) H 8f 93 99 <
* 1998 Spt Sandow (GD) 7.1f 88+
1999 Turf 1-9: (8f 1-7, 10f 2) (sft, g-s, gd 1-2, g-f, frm 4)
Well made, useful colt, effective 8 to 10f, best at 8f, acts on gd to frm, best on frm. Turf high 99 - 1st of 15 giving 2lb to Pas de Memoires (8 Aug Ascot RF 3463). Consistent. He kept good company and put up his best performances on soft ground over a mile. Worth another chance beyond that trip, he is probably in the Handicapper's grasp. **R Charlton [2-12] George Ward.*

SMARTS MEGAN RR 32f 4435[14]
3 b f Marju (IRE) 9.2f **(76)** - Taschkent (IRE) (Sure Blade (USA)) 11.3f **(67)**
Form - 80
Record 1999 - 1st:0 2nd:0 3rd:0 Ran:2
1999 Turf 0-2: (10f, 12f) (g-s, g-f)
Workmanlike, currently very moderate filly. Turf high 32 (began Spt). **Ian Williams [0-2] & Mrs D J Smart.*

SMART SPIRIT (IRE) BHB 47f **RR 47f** 4350[10]
5 b m Persian Bold 10f **(69)** - Sharp Ego (USA) (Sharpen Up) 8.3f **(67)**
Form - 41440
Record 1999 - 1st:1 2nd:0 3rd:0 Ran:5
Pre1999 - 1st:0 2nd:2 3rd:2 Ran:18
Win Prizemoney £2,868 *Total Prizemoney* £6,421
Wins * **1999** May Nottin (GD) H 10f 43 45+ <
1999 Turf 1-5: (10f 1-5) (gd, g-f 1-3, frm)
Moderate filly, effective 10 to 11f, best at 10f, acts on gd to g-f, best on g-f, prefers left handed tracks, prefers tight tracks. Turf high 47 - 4th of 8 giving 10lb to Indian Nectar (9 Aug Nottingham 10f g-f RF 3477) - also 1st of 16 getting 4lb from Polar Eclipse (7 May Nottingham RF 1095).
**Mrs M Reveley [3-29] Mrs Stephanie Smith.*

SMART SQUALL (USA) BHB 107f **RR 107f** 4674[11]
4 b c Summer Squall (USA) 7f **(80)** - Greek Wedding (USA) (Blushing Groom (FR)) 10.3f **(76)**
Form - 0
Record 1999 - 1st:0 2nd:0 3rd:0 Ran:1
Pre1999 - 1st:3 2nd:2 3rd:1 Ran:10
Win Prizemoney £26,668 *Total Prizemoney* £59,555
Wins 1997 Dec Toulou (HVY) L 8f 99 <
1997 Oct Ascot (HVY) H 7f 83 95+
1997 Spt Chepst (GD) 7.1f 81
1999 Turf 0-1: (12f) (gd)
Small, Pattern-class colt, effective 10 to 14f, acts on sft to g-f.
**D J Coakley [0-1] George Ward (from Lord Huntingdon [3-10] Oct 1998).*

SMOKE SIGNAL (IRE) BHB 62a **RR 56f** 5007[13]
3 ch f College Chapel - Indian Express **(59f)** (Indian Ridge)
Form - 75220466050200
Record 1999 - 1st:0 2nd:3 3rd:0 Ran:14
Win Prizemoney £0 *Total Prizemoney* £3,168
1999 Turf 0-12: (5f 4, 6f 6, 7f, 10f) (sft, gd 2, g-f 2, frm 6, hrd) 1999 AW 0-2: (8f 2) (Fibr 2)
Leggy, average filly, effective 5 to 8f, acts on gd to frm - acts on

Fibr. Turf high 67 - 2nd of 22 giving 10lb to Ballina Lad (26 May Ripon 6f frm RF 1507). AW high 60 (1st run) (began Spt) - 2nd of 13 getting 2lb from Charter Flight (4 Spt Wolverhampton 8f Fibr RF 4149). **M Johnston [0-14] The 3rd Middleham Partnership.*

SMOKEY FROM CAPLAW BHB 51f **RR 37f** 2863[13]

5 b g Sizzling Melody 6.3f **(49)** - Mary From Dunlow (Nicholas Bill) 10.1f **(56)**

Form - 0500000

Record	**1999 -**	1st:0	2nd:0	3rd:0	Ran:7
	Pre1999 -	1st:5	2nd:3	3rd:1	Ran:29

Win Prizemoney £16,780 *Total Prizemoney* £21,570

Wins								
* 1998	Jly	Carlis	(G-F)	H	6.9f	67	69	
* 1997	Oct	Redcar	(G-F)	H	7f	65	67	
* 1997	May	Thirsk	(GD)	H	6f	62	70	<
* 1997	May	Newcas	(GD)	H	6f	62	64	
* 1996	May	Hamilt	(G-F)	C	6f		66	

1999 Turf 0-7: (6f, 7f 4, 8f 2) (gd 2, g-f 2, frm 3)

Very moderate gelding, effective 7 to 8f, best at 7f, acts on g-f to frm, best on g-f, has worn blinkers, likes tight tracks. Turf high 63 - 5th of 10 giving 19lb to Court Express (2 May Hamilton 8f g-f RF 0971). **J J O'Neill [5-36] G P Bernacchi.*

SMOKIN BEAU BHB 74f **RR 77f** 5194[3]

2 b g Cigar 6.3f **(43)** - Beau Dada (IRE) (Pine Circle (USA))

Form - 743

Record	**1999 -**	1st:0	2nd:0	3rd:1	Ran:3

Win Prizemoney £0 *Total Prizemoney* £745

1999 Turf 0-3: (5f, 6f 2) (g-s, gd 2)

Currently above-average gelding. Turf high 77 (began Oct). **J Cullinan [0-3] Alan Spargo Ltd Toolmakers.*

SMOOTH SAILING BHB 85f73a **RR 86f 73a** 5141[8]

4 gr g Beveled (USA) 6.9f **(64)** - Sea Farer Lake (Gairloch) 7f **(63)**

Form - 0737208070028

Record	**1999 -**	1st:0	2nd:2	3rd:1	Ran:12
	Pre1999 -	1st:2	2nd:5	3rd:2	Ran:27

Win Prizemoney £7,778 *Total Prizemoney* £26,093

Wins								
* 1998	Jun	Leices	(SFT)	H	7f	78	80	<
* 1997	Apr	Sandow	(GD)		5f		78	

1999 Turf 0-12: (6f, 7f 7, 8f 3, 10f) (gd 6, g-f 5, frm)

Leggy, useful gelding, effective 7 to 8f, best at 7f, acts on g-s to frm, has worn blinkers, likes right handed tracks, and excels at Leicester. Turf high 88 - 2nd of 7 giving 8lb to Gift of Gold (4 Jun Goodwood 7f gd RF 1736). **K McAuliffe [2-39] A R Parrish.*

SMOOTH SAND (USA) BHB 67f **RR 79f** 4821[16]

2 b c Desert Secret (IRE) - Baby Smooth (USA) (Apalachee (USA)) 9.4f **(71)**

Form - 040

Record	**1999 -**	1st:0	2nd:0	3rd:0	Ran:3

Win Prizemoney £0 *Total Prizemoney* £257

1999 Turf 0-3: (6f 2, 8f) (gd, g-f, frm)

Currently above-average colt. Turf high 79 (began Spt) - 4th of 12 giving 5lb to Mellow Jazz (25 Spt Nottingham 6f gd RF 4557). **M A Jarvis [0-3] Mrs B Sadowska.*

SMUDGER SMITH BHB 63f **RR 57f** 4633[8]

2 ch g Deploy 11.4f **(67)** - Parfait Amour **(48f)** (Clantime)

Form - 38208

Record	**1999 -**	1st:0	2nd:1	3rd:1	Ran:5

Win Prizemoney £0 *Total Prizemoney* £1,241

1999 Turf 0-5: (7f 3, 8f 2) (gd 2, g-f 3)

Fair gelding. Turf high 57 (began Jly). **B S Rothwell [0-5] S P Hudson.*

SNAP CRACKER BHB 66f **RR 83df** 5199[20]

3 b f Inchinor 8.9f **(64)** - Valkyrie (Bold Lad (IRE)) 8.4f **(68)**

Form - 0407004040

Record	**1999 -**	1st:0	2nd:0	3rd:0	Ran:10
	Pre1999 -	1st:3	2nd:1	3rd:2	Ran:12

Win Prizemoney £9,397 *Total Prizemoney* £13,945

Wins								
1998	Jun	Cheste	(G-S)		5.1f		78	<
1998	Jun	Leices	(SFT)		5f		64+	
1998	Apr	Sandow	(HVY)		5f		65	

1999 Turf 0-10: (5f 5, 6f 5) (g-s, gd 5, frm 4)

Scopey, decent filly, effective 5 to 6f, best at 5f, acts on gd. Turf high 83 - 4th of 11 giving 14lb to Don't Surrender (29 Oct Newmarket 6f gd RF 5134). **H S Howe [0-10] Owen Delargy (from M Quinn [3-12] Spt 1998).*

SNOW PARTRIDGE (USA) BHB 46f **RR 50f** 2296[6]

5 ch g Arctic Tern (USA) 12.2f **(71)** - Lady Sharp (FR) (Sharpman) 11.3f **(66)**

Form - 06

Record	**1999 -**	1st:0	2nd:0	3rd:0	Ran:2
	Pre1999 -	1st:1	2nd:4	3rd:4	Ran:20

Win Prizemoney £3,011 *Total Prizemoney* £11,349

Wins								
1998	Spt	Bright	(GD)	H	11.9f	48	50	<

1999 Turf 0-2: (11f, 12f) (g-f, frm)

Fair gelding, effective 10f, acts on gd, has worn blinkers, favours tight tracks. **R T Phillips [0-2] Col Lt Young (from P F I Cole [1-20] Oct 1998).*

SNOWY MANTLE BHB 35f35a **RR 22f 35a** 1566[21]

6 b m Siberian Express (USA) 9f **(58)** - Mollified (Lombard (GER)) 10.5f **(66)**

Form - 48040000

Record	**1999 -**	1st:0	2nd:0	3rd:0	Ran:6
	Pre1999 -	1st:1	2nd:2	3rd:3	Ran:18

Win Prizemoney £3,772 *Total Prizemoney* £7,996

Wins								
* 1997	Jly	Nottin	(G-F)	H	8.2f	37	48+	<

1999 Turf 0-3: (7f, 8f, 10f) (gd 2, frm) 1999 AW 0-3: (8f 3) (Fibr 3)

Very moderate mare, effective 8f, acts on g-f - acts on Fibr, has worn blinkers, prefers left handed tracks, prefers tight tracks. Turf high 22. AW high 37 - 4th of 15 getting 1lb from The Barnsley Belle (1 Feb Southwell 8f Fibr RF 0206). Inconsistent. **J D Bethell [1-24] Mrs G Fane.*

SNOWY RANGE (USA) BHB 72f **RR 77f** 4181[1]

3 b f Seattle Slew (USA) 7.8f **(64)** - November Snow (USA) (Storm Cat (USA))

Form - 341

Record	**1999 -**	1st:1	2nd:0	3rd:1	Ran:3

Win Prizemoney £3,708 *Total Prizemoney* £4,663

Wins							
*** 1999**	Spt	Lingfi	(G-F)	7f		77	<

1999 Turf 1-3: (7f 1-1, 8f 2) (gd, frm 1-2)

Light-framed, currently above-average filly. Turf high 77 - 1st of 11 from Cajole (7 Spt Lingfield RF 4181). **J Noseda [1-3] Hesmonds Stud.*

SNUGFIT ROSIE (GER) BHB 65f **RR 66f** 4730[8]

3 ch f Kris 10f **(75)** - Sorceress (FR) (Fabulous Dancer (USA)) 9.4f **(70)**

Form - 563U43738

Record	**1999 -**	1st:0	2nd:0	3rd:3	Ran:9

Win Prizemoney £0 *Total Prizemoney* £1,599

1999 Turf 0-9: (10f 2, 12f, 13f, 14f 2, 16f 3) (g-s 2, gd 2, g-f 2, frm 3)

Scopey, average filly, effective 12 to 16f, acts on gd to frm. Turf high 71 - 3rd of 8 to Mazaya (11 Jun Chepstow 12f gd RF 1909). **M R Channon [0-9] A Greenwood.*

SO BHB 44f **RR 49f** 1937[5]

3 b f Mystiko (USA) 7.7f **(59)** - High and Bright (Shirley Heights) 10.3f **(74)**

Form - 005

Record	**1999 -**	1st:0	2nd:0	3rd:0	Ran:3

1999 Turf 0-3: (8f, 10f, 12f) (g-s, gd, frm)

Scopey, moderate filly. Turf high 49. **B W Hills [0-3] W J Gredley.*

SOAKED BHB 56f84a **RR 52f 84a** 3924[4]

6 b g Dowsing (USA) 7f **(61)** -Water Well(Sadler's Wells (USA)) 10f **(76)**

Form - 2114601343705604

Record	**1999 -**	1st:1	2nd:0	3rd:2	Ran:10
	Pre1999 -	1st:9	2nd:4	3rd:2	Ran:45

Win Prizemoney £32,108 *Total Prizemoney* £38,493

Wins								
*** 1999**	*Jan*	*Lingfi*	*(STD)*	*H*	*5f*	*80*	*84*	<
* 1998	*Nov*	*Lingfi*	*(STD)*	*H*	*6f*	*70*	*82*	
* 1998	*Nov*	*Lingfi*	*(STD)*	*H*	*5f*	*70*	*75+*	
* 1998	Spt	Pontef	(G-F)	H	5f	56	63	
* 1998	*Jun*	*Southw*	*(STD)*	*H*	*5f*	*50*	*67*	
* 1998	*Jun*	*Southw*	*(STD)*	*H*	*5f*	*48*	*63+*	
* 1998	Jun	Hamilt	(GD)	H	6f	46	56	
* 1998	May	Mussel	(G-S)	H	5f	46	57	
* 1998	May	Mussel	(GD)	H	5f	35	44	

* 1998 *Mar Southw (STD) SH 6f 41 49*
1999 Turf 0-6: (5f 5, 6f) (g-s, gd 2, g-f 2, frm) 1999 AW 1-4: (5f 1-3, 6f) (Equi 1-4)
Decent gelding, effective 5 to 6f, best at 5f, - acts on Equi, has worn blinkers, excels at Lingfield, likes Musselburgh and Southwell. Turf high 52. AW high 84 (1st run) - 1st of 8 giving 11lb to Tear White (2 Jan Lingfield RF 0009). A real speedster from the stalls, he is effective on turf, Equitrack and Fibresand, and equalled the 20th century record of ten handicap wins in a season in '98. Very effective when gaining an uncontested early lead, though six furlongs looks to be right on the limit of his stamina, he will come back into his own over the winter.
**D W Chapman [10-50] David Chapman (from J R Fanshawe [0-5] Jly 1996).*

SOAKING BHB 38f44a RR 27f 44a 4783[12]

9 b g Dowsing (USA) 7f **(61)** - Moaning Low (Burglar) 7.2f **(49)**
Form - 301728406760
Record 1999 - 1st:1 2nd:1 3rd:0 Ran:10
Pre1999 - 1st:10 2nd:7 3rd:4 Ran:73
Win Prizemoney £32,573 *Total Prizemoney* £42,097
Wins * **1999** *Jan Lingfi (STD) C 8f 47*
* 1998 *Aug Lingfi (STD) SH 8f 39 51*
* 1997 *Jan Lingfi (STD) C 8f 64*
* 1996 *Dec Lingfi (STD) H 8f 66 74*
* 1996 Jly Kempto (GD) H 7f 47 51
* 1996 *Jan Lingfi (STD) H 7f 63 66*
1995 Jly Chepst (G-F) S 7.1f 62
1999 Turf 0-2: (8f 2) (frm 2) 1999 AW 1-8: (8f 1-8) (Equi 1-8)
Fair gelding, effective 8f, - acted on Equi, had worn blinkers, liked left handed tracks, favoured tight tracks. Turf high 27. AW high 57 - 2nd of 6 getting 8lb from Barbason (20 Feb Lingfield 8f Equi RF 0326). (DEAD)
**P Burgoyne [6-41] Image Office Supplies Ltd (from M D I Usher [0-12] Feb 1998).*

SOAP STONE BHB 25f RR 29f 3903[14]

4 b f Gunner B 11.2f **(45)** - Tzarina (USA) (Gallant Romeo (USA)) 8.4f **(64)**
Form - 0
Record 1999 - 1st:0 2nd:0 3rd:0 Ran:1
Pre1999 - 1st:0 2nd:0 3rd:0 Ran:4
1999 Turf 0-1: (17f) (frm)
Light-framed, little account filly. **A Bailey [0-7] G V Gann.*

SOARING SOFTLY (USA) RR 119f 5228a[1]

4 f Kris S (USA) 9.3f **(76)** - Wings Of Grace (USA) (Key To The Mint (USA)) 9.4f **(75)**
Form - 1
1999 Turf 1-1: (11f 1-1) (frm 1-1)
Currently high-class. (1st run) - 1st of 14 from Coretta (6 Nov Gulfstream Park RF 5228a). Winner of the inaugural Breeders' Cup Filly and Mare Turf. **J Toner in USA [1-1] J Phillips.*

SOBA JONES RR 57f 2927[3]

2 b c Emperor Jones (USA) - Soba (Most Secret) 7.1f **(58)**
Form - 3
Record 1999 - 1st:0 2nd:0 3rd:1 Ran:1
Win Prizemoney £0 *Total Prizemoney* £497
1999 Turf 0-1: (5f) (frm)
Currently fair colt. **T D Easterby [0-1] Mrs M Hills.*

SOBER AS A JUDGE RR 47f 2772[9]

2 b c Mon Tresor 7.9f **(60)** - Flicker Toa Flame (USA) (Empery (USA)) 11.2f **(69)**
Form - 500
Record 1999 - 1st:0 2nd:0 3rd:0 Ran:3
1999 Turf 0-3: (6f 2, 7f) (gd, g-f, frm)
Currently moderate colt. Turf high 47. **C A Dwyer [0-3] M M Foulger.*

SOBRIETY (IRE) RR 90f 4797[4]

2 b c Namaqualand (USA) - Scanno's Choice (IRE) (Pennine Walk) 8.5f **(61)**
Form - 124
Record 1999 - 1st:1 2nd:1 3rd:0 Ran:3
Win Prizemoney £3,350 *Total Prizemoney* £6,084
Wins * **1999** Aug Salisb (SFT) 7f 84+ <
1999 Turf 1-3: (7f 1-3) (gd, g-f 1-1, frm)
Currently useful colt. Turf high 84 (began Aug) - 4th of 7 to Sir Ninja (9 Oct Ascot 7f gd RF 4797) - also 1st of 17 giving 2lb to Jazzy Millennium (12 Aug Salisbury RF 3572). He was impressive when landing a soft-ground Salisbury maiden on his debut, but was unable to cope with Port Vila on much faster ground at Kempton. **R F JohnsonHoughton [1-3] Anthony Pye-Jeary.*

SOCIAL CONTRACT BHB 77f RR 75f 3789[9]

2 b c Emarati (USA) 6.6f **(63)** - Just Buy Baileys **(63f)** (Formidable (USA)) 9.2f **(63)**
Form - 3381410
Record 1999 - 1st:2 2nd:0 3rd:2 Ran:7
Win Prizemoney £4,945 *Total Prizemoney* £5,856
Wins * **1999** Aug Lingfi (GD) H 7f 75 75
1999 *Jly Southw (STD) S 6f 80+* <
1999 Turf 1-6: (5f 2, 6f, 7f 1-3) (hvy, gd, g-f 3, frm 1-1) 1999 AW 1-1: (6f 1-1) (Fibr 1-1)
Decent colt, effective 6 to 7f, acts on frm - acts on Fibr. Turf high 75 - 1st of 8 getting 18lb from Night Style (13 Aug Lingfield RF 3611). (1st run) - 1st of 7 from Fingers Henry (10 Jly Southwell RF 2721).
**W J Haggas [1-3] J G Lambton (from T Stack in IRE [1-4] Jly 1999).*

SOCIAL HARMONY (IRE) BHB 90f RR 106f 5175a[4]

5 b g Polish Precedent (USA) 9f **(73)** - Latest Chapter 00
Form - 210124
1999 Turf 2-6: (6f 1-4, 7f 1-2) (sft, g-s 1-2, gd 2, g-f 1-1)
Pattern-class gelding, effective 6 to 7f, best at 6f, acts on sft to g-f, best on g-s, likes Curragh. Turf high 106 - 4th of 6 giving 31lb to Kenema (25 Oct Leopardstown 6f sft RF 5175a) - also 1st of 9 giving 2lb to Rolo Tomasi (18 Spt Curragh RF 4470a). A most consistent Irish-trained handicapper, he is effective over trips ranging from five to seven furlongs. He won on fast ground at Galway, but looks especially suited by soft. **D K Weld in IRE [6-15] S Creaven.*

SOCIALIZER (USA) BHB 52a RR 51f 52a 131[5]

3 b c Glitterman (USA) - Speckofsun (USA) (Sunny North (USA))
Form - 5645
Record 1999 - 1st:0 2nd:0 3rd:0 Ran:1
Pre1999 - 1st:0 2nd:0 3rd:0 Ran:4
1999 AW 0-1: (5f) (Fibr)
Scopey, fair colt. **W Jarvis [0-5] H J W Steckmest And Partners.*

SOCIAL SCENE (IRE) BHB 84f RR 82f 2845[6]

3 ch f Grand Lodge (USA) - Ardmelody (Law Society (USA)) 9.9f **(70)**
Form - 546
Record 1999 - 1st:0 2nd:0 3rd:0 Ran:3
Pre1999 - 1st:1 2nd:1 3rd:0 Ran:3
Win Prizemoney £3,517 *Total Prizemoney* £6,118
Wins * 1998 Spt Sandow (GD) 8.1f 85 <
1999 Turf 0-3: (10f, 11f, 12f) (gd, g-f 2)
Scopey, decent filly, effective 8f, acts on sft. Turf high 82.
**P W Chapple-Hyam [1-6] R E Sangster and B V Sangster.*

SOCIETY KING (IRE) BHB 46a RR 14f 852[9]

4 b g Fairy King (USA) 7.7f **(75)** - Volga (USA) (Riverman (USA)) 9.1f **(76)**
Form - 8700
Record 1999 - 1st:0 2nd:0 3rd:0 Ran:4
Pre1999 - 1st:0 2nd:0 3rd:1 Ran:5
Win Prizemoney £0 *Total Prizemoney* £450
1999 AW 0-4: (7f 2, 8f, 11f) (Fibr 4)
Workmanlike, fair gelding, has broken blood-vessels. AW high 52. Inconsistent. **J E Banks [0-9] R Sabey.*

SO DAINTY (IRE) BHB 62f57a RR 73f 57a 4939[3]

2 b br f Common Grounds 8.1f **(66)** - Naxos (USA) (Big Spruce (USA)) 11f **(71)**
Form - 76773
Record 1999 - 1st:0 2nd:0 3rd:1 Ran:5
Win Prizemoney £0 *Total Prizemoney* £281
1999 Turf 0-4: (5f 2, 7f 2) (gd, g-f 2, frm) 1999 AW 0-1: (7f) (Fibr)
Above-average filly. Turf high 73. **B W Hills [0-5] Lee Jackson.*

SODELK BHB 25f33a RR 30f 33a 1516[8]

5 ch m Interrex (CAN) 7.7f **(51)** -Summoned by Bells(Stanford) 7.9f **(56)**

Form - 008
Record 1999 - 1st:0 2nd:0 3rd:0 Ran:3
Pre1999 - 1st:0 2nd:0 3rd:0 Ran:4
Win Prizemoney £0 *Total Prizemoney* £53
1999 Turf 0-2: (10f, 12f) (hrd 2) 1999 AW 0-1: (16f) (Fibr)
Very moderate filly. Turf high 30.
**J Pearce [0-4] Mick Robinson (from J Hetherton [0-4] Feb 1997).*

SOFISIO BHB 67f RR 66f 3906[15]
2 ch c Efisio 7.7f **(69)** - Legal Embrace (CAN) (Legal Bid (USA))
Form - 840
Record 1999 - 1st:0 2nd:0 3rd:0 Ran:3
Win Prizemoney £0 *Total Prizemoney* £230
1999 Turf 0-3: (7f 2, 8f) (g-f 2, frm)
Currently average colt. Turf high 64 (began Jly).
**W R Muir [0-3] North Farm Stud.*

SOHO TOMMY BHB 65f RR 72f 1109[3]
5 b g Tina's Pet 7.4f **(56)** - Absalantra (Absalom) 7.2f **(58)**
Form - 553
Record 1999 - 1st:0 2nd:0 3rd:1 Ran:3
Win Prizemoney £0 *Total Prizemoney* £554
1999 Turf 0-3: (9f, 10f 2) (g-s, gd 2)
Above-average gelding. Turf high 72. (DEAD)
**N Hamilton [0-3] The Soho Society.*

SOLAIA (USA) RR 88f 5115a[5]
2 ch f Miswaki (USA) 8.1f **(81)** - Indian Fashion (USA) (General Holme (USA)) 5.7f **(63)**
Form - 1555
Record 1999 - 1st:1 2nd:0 3rd:0 Ran:4
Win Prizemoney £4,347 *Total Prizemoney* £4,693
Wins * **1999** Jly Newmar (G-F) 7f 70+ <
1999 Turf 1-4: (7f 1-3, 8f) (gd 3, frm 1-1)
Useful filly. Turf high 88 (began Jly) - 5th of 12 to Agrippina (2 Oct Newmarket 7f gd RF 4680). Cosy winner of a Newmarket maiden, she was held in pattern company. **P F I Cole [1-4].*

SOLDIER (USA) BHB 22f RR 28f 3380[11]
4 b g Sheikh Albadou 9.2f **(75)** - His Ginger (USA) (Fred Astaire (USA))
Form - 00000000
Record 1999 - 1st:0 2nd:0 3rd:0 Ran:7
Pre1999 - 1st:0 2nd:0 3rd:0 Ran:3
1999 Turf 0-3: (5f, 6f, 8f) (g-f 3) 1999 AW 0-4: (5f, 7f, 8f, 11f) (Fibr 4)
Strong, little account gelding, often wears blinkers. Turf high 28. AW high 10. **R F Marvin [0-10] Mrs M A Marvin.*

SOLDIER COVE (USA) BHB 46f40a RR 50f 40a 37[6]
9 ch g Manila (USA) 10f **(81)** -Secret Form (Formidable (USA)) 9.2f **(63)**
Form - 06
Record 1999 - 1st:0 2nd:0 3rd:0 Ran:1
Pre1999 - 1st:4 2nd:2 3rd:1 Ran:24
Win Prizemoney £9,076 *Total Prizemoney* £10,966
Wins 1997 Mar Mussel (SFT) SH 8f 42 50
1997 *Mar Southw (STD) C 8f 55*
1997 *Mar Wolver (STD) S 9.4f 56* <
1997 *Feb Lingfi (STD) SH 8f 46 50*
1999 AW 0-1: (9f) (Fibr)
Fair gelding.
**D Burchell [0-9] Mrs Ruth Burchell (from M Meade [4-21] Aug 1997).*

SOLE CHE SORGI (IRE) RR 100f 4779a[9]
5 b h Dancing Dissident (USA) 6.8f **(65)** - Dawn is Breaking (Import) 6.6f **(68)**
Form - 3420
1999 Turf 0-3: (8f 3) (sft, g-s, gd)
Very useful colt. Turf high 100 - 2nd of 7 to Mahboob (28 Aug Deauville 8f g-s RF 4109a).
**R Collet in FR [0-2] (from F Brogi in ITY [0-2] Jun 1999).*

SOLE SINGER (GER) BHB 50f RR 49f 5153[2]
3 b g Slip Anchor 12.7f **(75)** - Singer on the Roof (Chief Singer) 8.9f **(66)**
Form - 00032
Record 1999 - 1st:0 2nd:1 3rd:1 Ran:5
Pre1999 - 1st:0 2nd:0 3rd:0 Ran:2
Win Prizemoney £0 *Total Prizemoney* £1,359
1999 Turf 0-5: (9f, 10f 3, 11f) (g-s, gd, frm 3)
Scopey, moderate gelding. Turf high 49.
**D HaydnJones [0-2] Hugh O'Donnell (from I A Balding [0-5] Jun 1999).*

SOLFEGGI (USA) BHB 65f RR 69f 4508[10]
3 b c Irish River (FR) 9f **(77)** - Never a Care (USA) (Roberto (USA)) 10f **(76)**
Form - 2560
Record 1999 - 1st:0 2nd:1 3rd:0 Ran:4
Win Prizemoney £0 *Total Prizemoney* £905
1999 Turf 0-4: (8f 2, 10f 2) (g-f 2, frm 2)
Workmanlike, average colt. Turf high 69 (1st run) - 2nd of 11 to Tier Worker (7 Apr Ripon 8f g-f RF 0618). **B W Hills [0-4] K Abdulla.*

SOLITARY RR 75f 5047[4]
2 b c Sanglamore (USA) 12.9f **(67)** - Set Fair (USA) **(89f)** (Alleged (USA)) 10f **(76)**
Form - 4
Record 1999 - 1st:0 2nd:0 3rd:0 Ran:1
Win Prizemoney £0 *Total Prizemoney* £322
1999 Turf 0-1: (6f) (hvy)
Currently above-average colt. (1st run) - 4th of 15 giving 5lb to Another Pearl (23 Oct Newbury 6f hvy RF 5047).
**B W Hills [0-1] K Abdulla.*

SOLLER BAY RR 68f 4943[2]
2 b g Contract Law (USA) 8.9f **(54)** - Bichette **(43f 47a)** (Lidhame) 9.2f **(50)**
Form - 2
Record 1999 - 1st:0 2nd:1 3rd:0 Ran:1
Win Prizemoney £0 *Total Prizemoney* £1,052
1999 Turf 0-1: (7f) (gd)
Currently average gelding. (1st run) - 2nd of 15 to Atavus (19 Oct Lingfield 7f gd RF 4943). **K R Burke [0-1] Mrs Melba Bryce.*

SOLLY'S PAL BHB 57f RR 51f 5113[9]
4 gr g Petong 7.6f **(58)** - Petriece (Mummy's Pet) 7.7f **(60)**
Form - 0
Record 1999 - 1st:0 2nd:0 3rd:0 Ran:1
Pre1999 - 1st:0 2nd:0 3rd:0 Ran:2
1999 Turf 0-1: (6f) (gd)
Scopey, currently fair gelding.
**P J Makin [0-1] Mrs Paul Levinson (from I A Balding [0-2] May 1998).*

SOLO FLIGHT RR 80f 4649[5]
2 gr c Mtoto 11.5f **(71)** - Silver Singer **(65f 55a)** (Pharly (FR)) 9.8f **(68)**
Form - 45
Record 1999 - 1st:0 2nd:0 3rd:0 Ran:2
Win Prizemoney £0 *Total Prizemoney* £313
1999 Turf 0-2: (7f, 8f) (gd 2)
Currently decent colt. Turf high 80 (began Spt).
**B W Hills [0-2] Lady Hardy.*

SOLOIST (IRE) RR 35f 4901[16]
2 ch f Elmaamul (USA) 8.1f **(70)** - Alyara (USA) (Alydar (USA)) 9.1f **(76)**
Form - 70
Record 1999 - 1st:0 2nd:0 3rd:0 Ran:2
1999 Turf 0-2: (7f 2) (gd, frm)
Currently very moderate filly. Turf high 35 (began Spt).
**J L Eyre [0-2] Mrs Angela Seed.*

SOLO MIO (IRE) BHB 100f RR 110f 2071[13]
5 b h Sadler's Wells (USA) 11.3f **(87)** - Marie de Flandre (FR) (Crystal Palace (FR)) 12.5f **(76)**
Form - 10
1999 Turf 1-2: (16f 1-1, 20f) (gd 1-1, g-f)
Group-class colt, effective 16f, acts on sft to gd, best on gd. Turf high 109 (1st run) - 1st of 7 giving 2lb to Graf Philipp (29 May Baden-Baden RF 1714a). Consistent. He justified his 120,000 guinea purchase out of Barry Hills' yard when winning a Group Three at Baden-Baden in 1998. Still on the upgrade, he won the same German race last term, but was well beaten in the Ascot Gold Cup. **J E Hammond in FR [2-6] Cheveley Park Stud.*

SOLO SONG BHB 25f RR 17f 2086[11]
4 ch f Executive Man 8.9f **(52)** - Aosta (Shack (USA)) 5.8f **(53)**
Form - 0

Record 1999 - 1st:0 2nd:0 3rd:0 Ran:1
Pre1999 - 1st:0 2nd:0 3rd:0 Ran:9
1999 AW 0-1: (7f) (Fibr)
Leggy, poor filly.
**P D Evans [0-1] The Low Flyers (Thoroughbreds) Ltd (from A R Dicken [0-5] Nov 1998).*

SOLO SPIRIT BHB 42f33a RR 9f 33a 286[5]
4 b f Northern Park (USA) 10f **(57)** - Brown Taw (Whistlefield) 5f **(55)**
Form - 60075
Record 1999 - 1st:0 2nd:0 3rd:0 Ran:4
Pre1999 - 1st:1 2nd:0 3rd:0 Ran:15
Win Prizemoney £3,938 *Total Prizemoney* £4,438
Wins * 1997 Oct Leices (GD) 6f 81 <
1999 AW 0-4: (6f 3, 8f) (Equi 3, Fibr)
Unfurnished, very moderate filly, has worn blinkers.
**J R Jenkins [1-19] Mrs I Hampson.*

SOMAYDA (IRE) BHB 88f RR 91df 5031[16]
4 b c Last Tycoon 9.4f **(73)** - Flame of Tara (Artaius (USA)) 9f **(69)**
Form - 02627860
Record 1999 - 1st:0 2nd:2 3rd:0 Ran:8
Pre1999 - 1st:2 2nd:0 3rd:1 Ran:6
Win Prizemoney £17,365 *Total Prizemoney* £23,159
Wins * 1998 Spt Goodwo (G-S) H 9f 83 89+ <
* 1998 Jun Redcar (G-S) 8f 65+
1999 Turf 0-8: (10f 4, 12f 3, 13f) (sft, g-s 2, gd 4, g-f)
Scopey, useful colt, effective 8 to 12f, best at 10f, acts on sft to gd, has worn blinkers. Turf high 93 - 2nd of 8 giving 5lb to Cugina (20 Apr Pontefract 10f sft RF 0772). Inconsistent. He is capable, but not one to trust. **J L Dunlop [2-14] Hamdan Al Maktoum.*

SOMER SOLO BHB 30f36a RR 10f 36a 3241[12]
6 b m Prince Daniel (USA) 11.4f **(46)** - Shift Over (USA) (Night Shift (USA)) 7.2f **(69)**
Form - 000
Record 1999 - 1st:0 2nd:0 3rd:0 Ran:2
Pre1999 - 1st:0 2nd:0 3rd:1 Ran:6
Win Prizemoney £0 *Total Prizemoney* £551
1999 Turf 0-2: (8f, 10f) (frm 2)
Poor mare. Turf high 10 (began Jly). Becoming disappointing.
**Miss L C Siddall [0-6] Mrs Ann Morgan (from P Mitchell [0-5] Oct 1995).*

SOMERTON BOY (IRE) BHB 62f73a RR 60f 73a 1366[18]
9 b h Thatching 7.8f **(69)** - Bonnie Bess (Ardoon) 7.3f **(53)**
Form - 40
Record 1999 - 1st:0 2nd:0 3rd:0 Ran:2
Pre1999 - 1st:6 2nd:3 3rd:8 Ran:44
Win Prizemoney £22,509 *Total Prizemoney* £39,193
Wins * 1998 Jly Ayr (GD) H 9.1f 62 65+
* 1997 May Ayr (G-F) H 8f 64 73 <
* 1996 Jun Ayr (G-F) H 7f 68 72
* 1995 Jly Ayr (GD) H 7f 71 73 <
* 1995 May Newcas (GD) H 8f 67 69
1999 Turf 0-2: (8f, 10f) (g-s, gd)
Average horse, effective 8 to 9f, best at 9f, acts on gd to frm, best on gd. **P Calver [6-46] Mrs Janis MacPherson.*

SONBELLE BHB 72f RR 74f 5111[6]
2 b f Son Pardo - Ty-With-Belle (Pamroy) 12.5f **(55)**
Form - 15686
Record 1999 - 1st:1 2nd:0 Ran:5
Win Prizemoney £2,723 *Total Prizemoney* £2,723
Wins * **1999** Jun Bath (GD) 5.7f 72+ <
1999 Turf 1-5: (5f, 6f 1-4) (g-s, gd 2, frm 1-2)
Above-average filly. Turf high 74 - also 1st of 8 getting 16lb from Ansellad (30 Jun Bath RF 2423). **B Palling [1-5] Mrs M M Palling.*

SONDA (IRE) RR 98f 4891a[1]
2 ch f Dolphin Street (FR) - Isca **(73df)** (Caerleon (USA)) 8.6f **(71)**
Form - 131
1999 Turf 2-3: (6f 1-1, 7f, 8f 1-1) (gd 1-2, g-f 1-1)
Currently very useful filly. Turf high 98 (began Jly) - 1st of 11 from Goodwood Blizzard (10 Oct San Siro RF 4891a). She put up a game effort when winning a Group Three at San Siro in October and is clearly useful. Likely to stay beyond a mile, she should do well in Italy next term. **A Botti in ITY [2-3] Scuderia Rencati.*

SONEVA (IRE) BHB 32f RR 36f 2925[14]
4 b f Alzao (USA) 9.8f **(73)** - Rathvindon (Realm) 8.1f **(65)**
Form - 800
Record 1999 - 1st:0 2nd:0 3rd:0 Ran:3
Pre1999 - 1st:0 2nd:0 3rd:0 Ran:5
1999 Turf 0-2: (8f, 10f) (gd, frm) 1999 AW 0-1: (8f) (Fibr)
Workmanlike, very moderate filly. Turf high 36.
**M A Buckley [0-8] C C Buckley.*

SONG 'N DANCE MAN BHB 77f RR 74f 4685[19]
3 b c Prince Sabo 6.6f **(64)** - Born to Dance (Dancing Brave (USA)) 8.4f **(76)**
Form - 022010
Record 1999 - 1st:1 2nd:2 3rd:0 Ran:6
Pre1999 - 1st:0 2nd:0 3rd:0 Ran:4
Win Prizemoney £2,710 *Total Prizemoney* £11,400
Wins * **1999** Jly Bright (FRM) 7f 72 <
1999 Turf 1-6: (7f 1-4, 8f, 9f) (gd 2, g-f 2, frm 1-2)
Workmanlike, above-average colt, effective 7f, acts on gd to frm, best on frm. Turf high 80 - 2nd of 17 getting 9lb from Achilles Star (4 Jun Epsom 7f gd RF 1727) - also 1st of 5 giving 5lb to Unchain My Heart (13 Jly Brighton RF 2776).
**J Noseda [1-10] The late B Schmidt-Bodner/Mrs P Graham.*

SONG OF FREEDOM BHB 98f RR 95f 1104[7]
5 ch h Arazi (USA) 9.2f **(74)** - Glorious Song (CAN) (Halo (USA)) 10.6f **(75)**
Form - 7
Record 1999 - 1st:0 2nd:0 3rd:0 Ran:1
Pre1999 - 1st:3 2nd:2 3rd:0 Ran:14
Win Prizemoney £22,021 *Total Prizemoney* £30,831
Wins 1998 Jly Ascot (G-F) H 10f 95 100 <
1997 Aug Newbur (G-F) H 10f 86 86+
1997 Jly Pontef (GD) 10f 82
1999 Turf 0-1: (12f) (gd)
Very useful colt, effective 10 to 12f, best at 10f, acts on gd to frm. (1st run) - 7th of 10 giving 4lb to Carry The Flag (8 May Goodwood 12f gd RF 1104). Consistent. Best over a mile and a quarter on fast ground, he raced just once in Britain last term.
**S bin Suroor [0-1] Godolphin (from J H M Gosden [3-14] Aug 1998).*

SONG OF SKYE BHB 72f RR 71f 4569[16]
5 b m Warning 8.1f **(77)** - Song of Hope (Chief Singer) 8.9f **(66)**
Form - 21401635430
Record 1999 - 1st:2 2nd:1 3rd:2 Ran:11
Pre1999 - 1st:1 2nd:2 3rd:2 Ran:22
Win Prizemoney £16,951 *Total Prizemoney* £31,252
Wins * **1999** Jun Lingfi (G-F) H 7f 68 68
* **1999** May Sandow (GD) H 7.1f 65 66
* 1996 Jly Newbur (G-F) 5.2f 69 <
1999 Turf 2-11: (6f, 7f 2-7, 8f 3) (sft, g-f 3, frm 2-7)
Above-average filly, effective 7 to 9f, best at 7f, acts on gd to frm, has worn blinkers, likes tight tracks, does well at Sandown. Turf high 72 - 3rd of 13 getting 17lb from Cruinn A Bhord (25 Jly Newmarket 7f frm RF 3131) - also 1st of 4 getting 16lb from Out Line (26 Jun Lingfield RF 2331). Consistent. A slide down the handicap helped her regain winning form at Sandown in May, and she added a four-runner at Lingfield in June. Seven furlongs is her trip, and she needs to be covered up for a late run.
**T J Naughton [3-33] E J Fenaroli.*

SONICOS RR 17f 920[15]
3 ch g Cosmonaut - Bella Bambola (IRE) **(7f)** (Tate Gallery (USA)) 7.4f **(67)**
Form - 0
Record 1999 - 1st:0 2nd:0 3rd:0 Ran:1
1999 Turf 0-1: (7f) (gd)
Leggy, currently poor gelding. **J S Wainwright [0-1] S Pedersen.*

SON OF SKELTON BHB 37f RR 27f 4693[14]
4 ch g Minster Son 10.9f **(56)** - Skelton (Derrylin) 8.8f **(54)**
Form - 00
Record 1999 - 1st:0 2nd:0 3rd:0 Ran:2

Pre1999 - 1st:0 2nd:1 3rd:0 Ran:6
Win Prizemoney £0 *Total Prizemoney* £804
1999 Turf 0-2: (9f, 14f) (gd, g-f)
Scopey, little account gelding. Turf high 27.
**J S Haldane [0-7] Mrs Hugh Fraser (from J Wharton [0-2] Jly 1997).*

SON OF SNURGE (FR) BHB 79f68a **RR 80f 68a** 4893[3]
3 b g Snurge - Swift Spring (FR) (Bluebird (USA)) 7.5f **(69)**
Form - 02858711273
Record 1999 - 1st:2 2nd:2 3rd:1 Ran:11
Pre1999 - 1st:0 2nd:1 3rd:0 Ran:3
Win Prizemoney £6,813 *Total Prizemoney* £13,344
Wins * 1999 Jly Sandow (G-F) H 14f 59 72 <
*** 1999** Jly Bright (FRM) 11.9f 65
1999 Turf 2-10: (8f, 10f 3, 12f 1-1, 13f, 14f 1-2, 15f, 16f) (gd 4, g-f, frm 2-5) 1999 AW 0-1: (10f) (Equi)
Strong, decent gelding, effective 10 to 16f, acts on gd to frm, best on gd, has worn blinkers (extremely effectively), likes right handed tracks. Turf high 80 - 3rd of 16 to Bid Me Welcome (15 Oct Newmarket 15f gd RF 4893) - also 1st of 8 getting 13lb from Follow That Dream (22 Jly Sandown RF 3028). **P F I Cole [2-14] M Arbib.*

SONTIME BHB 66f **RR 78+f** 4286[15]
2 b f Son Pardo - Fact of Time (Known Fact (USA)) 7.4f **(67)**
Form - 3741351080
Record 1999 - 1st:2 2nd:0 3rd:2 Ran:10
Win Prizemoney £4,178 *Total Prizemoney* £5,306
Wins * 1999 Jly Lingfi (G-F) C 6f 69
*** 1999** Jun Lingfi (G-F) S 5f 78+ <
1999 Turf 2-10: (5f 1-7, 6f 1-3) (gd 3, g-f, frm 2-6)
Above-average filly, effective 5 to 6f, acts on frm. Turf high 78 - 1st of 6 from Namaqualass (25 Jun Lingfield RF 2292) - also 1st of 3 getting 4lb from Shaman (31 Jly Lingfield RF 3273). She was successfully dropped into selling company when bolting up at Lingfield in June and added a three-runner event at the same track the following month. **B Palling [2-10] Mrs P K Chick.*

SOPHALA RR 55f 4357[7]
2 b f Magical Wonder (USA) 7.2f **(60)** - Fujaiyrah (In Fijar (USA)) 7.5f **(70)**
Form - 7
Record 1999 - 1st:0 2nd:0 3rd:0 Ran:1
1999 Turf 0-1: (8f) (g-s)
Currently fair filly. **D Morris [0-1] T J Wells.*

SOPHIE JONES BHB 35f45a **RR 35f 45a** 5148[12]
2 ch f Sabrehill (USA) 8.5f **(64)** - Noble Singer (Vaguely Noble) 10.1f **(72)**
Form - 0300000
Record 1999 - 1st:0 2nd:0 3rd:1 Ran:7
Win Prizemoney £0 *Total Prizemoney* £294
1999 Turf 0-5: (6f 3, 7f, 8f) (g-s, gd 2, g-f, hrd) 1999 AW 0-2: (7f, 8f) (Fibr 2)
Fair filly, has worn blinkers. Turf high 35. AW high 51 (began Jly).
**A T Murphy [0-7] E H Jones (Paints) Ltd.*

SOPHIE LOCKETT BHB 25f28a **RR 7f 28a** 871[14]
6 b m Mon Tresor 7.9f **(60)** - Silverdale Rose (Nomination) 7f **(60)**
Form - 0
Record 1999 - 1st:0 2nd:0 3rd:0 Ran:1
Pre1999 - 1st:0 2nd:0 3rd:0 Ran:6
1999 Turf 0-1: (14f) (sft)
Very poor mare. **K W Hogg [0-14] Auldyn Stud Ltd.*

SOPRAN BOLKRIS (IRE) RR 3045a[7]
3 f
Form - 7
Record 1999 - 1st:0 2nd:0 3rd:0 Ran:1
1999 Turf 0-1: (8f) (g-f)
Currently very poor filly. **L M Cumani [0-1].*

SOPRAN ZANCHI (IRE) RR 74+f 3818[3]
2 ch f College Chapel - Star Gazing (IRE) (Caerleon (USA)) 8.6f **(71)**
Form - 23
Record 1999 - 1st:0 2nd:1 3rd:1 Ran:2
Win Prizemoney £0 *Total Prizemoney* £2,931
1999 Turf 0-2: (6f 2) (g-f 2)
Currently above-average filly. Turf high 74 (began Jly) - 3rd of 21 to Abderian (21 Aug Ripon 6f g-f RF 3818).
**L M Cumani [0-2] Sant Uberto.*

SO PRECIOUS (IRE) RR 76f 4428[1]
2 b f Batshoof 9.5f **(66)** - Golden Form (Formidable (USA)) 9.2f **(63)**
Form - 61
Record 1999 - 1st:1 2nd:0 3rd:0 Ran:2
Win Prizemoney £3,078 *Total Prizemoney* £3,078
Wins * 1999 Spt Kempto (HVY) 7f 76 <
1999 Turf 1-2: (6f, 7f 1-1) (g-s 1-1, frm)
Currently above-average filly. Turf high 76 (began Jly) - 1st of 9 from Able Native (20 Spt Kempton RF 4428). Winner of a heavy ground maiden at Kempton, she buckled down to the task in hand in fine style, and liked the ground according to her jockey.
**N P Littmoden [1-2] Joy and Valentine Feerick.*

SORBETT RR 5202a[1]
2 b c Dolphin Street (FR) - Midnight Imperial (Night Shift (USA)) 7.2f **(69)**
Form - 1
Record 1999 - 1st:1 2nd:0 3rd:0 Ran:1
Win Prizemoney £7,290 *Total Prizemoney* £7,290
Wins * 1999 Oct San Si (YLD) 7.5f
1999 Turf 1-1: (8f 1-1) (g-s 1-1)
Colt. - 1st of 6 getting 4lb from Blory (31 Oct San Siro RF 5202a).
**L M Cumani [1-1] Scuderia Rencati.*

SORBIE TOWER (IRE) BHB 95f **RR 95f** 3087[8]
6 b h Soviet Lad (USA) 9.4f **(63)** - Nozet (Nishapour (FR)) 9.1f **(61)**
Form - 36668
Record 1999 - 1st:0 2nd:0 3rd:1 Ran:5
Pre1999 - 1st:3 2nd:2 3rd:1 Ran:9
Win Prizemoney £25,627 *Total Prizemoney* £63,755
Wins * 1996 Apr Sandow (GD) H 8.1f 96 101+ <
* 1996 Apr Warwic (G-S) H 8f 80 98+
* 1996 Mar Doncas (G-S) 7f 79
1999 Turf 0-5: (7f, 8f 4) (gd 3, g-f, frm)
Very useful horse. Turf high 107. He competed in Group Ones in 1996, making the frame in both the St James's Palace and Sussex Stakes. However, he wore bandages throughout that season and tough races on fast ground may have taken their toll as he was then absent for over two and a half years. He came back to run well at Haydock in May, but faced some stiff tasks afterwards and, despite market support, was well beaten.
**Miss Gay Kelleway [3-14] P D Q.*

SORRENTO KING BHB 53f **RR 60f** 5052[16]
2 ch c First Trump - Star Face (African Sky) 7.9f **(63)**
Form - 800400
Record 1999 - 1st:0 2nd:0 3rd:0 Ran:6
1999 Turf 0-6: (6f, 7f 3, 8f 2) (gd 4, frm 2)
Average colt, often wears blinkers. Turf high 60 (began Aug).
**M W Easterby [0-6] B Padgett, K Bennett & A Davies.*

SOSSUS VLEI BHB 106f **RR 111f** 5264a[2]
3 b c Inchinor 8.9f **(64)** - Sassalya (Sassafras (FR)) 9.6f **(69)**
Form - 162
Record 1999 - 1st:1 2nd:1 3rd:0 Ran:3
Pre1999 - 1st:1 2nd:1 3rd:0 Ran:4
Win Prizemoney £10,544 *Total Prizemoney* £21,411
Wins * 1999 Spt Bath (SFT) 8f 103 <
* 1998 Aug Newmar (G-F) 7f 87
1999 Turf 1-3: (8f 1-2, 9f) (hvy, gd 1-2)
Workmanlike, Group-class colt, effective 8f, acts on hvy to gd. Turf high 111 (began Spt) - 2nd of 8 giving 3lb to Danzigaway (6 Nov Saint-Cloud 8f hvy RF 5264a) - also 1st of 7 from Emily's Luck Charm (27 Spt Bath RF 4585). He has given trouble at the stalls, but has plenty of ability as he demonstrated when hacking up in a conditions race at Bath in September. Out-manoeuvred in a Listed event at Newmarket the following month, he should make his mark in that grade over a mile next term. **G Wragg [2-7].*

SOTONIAN (HOL) BHB 65f67a **RR 63f 67a** 4911[13]

6 br g Statoblest 6.4f **(63)** - Visage (Vision (USA)) 9f **(64)**
Form - 483221113170176630620
Record 1999 - 1st:5 2nd:3 3rd:2 Ran:18
Pre1999 - 1st:3 2nd:2 3rd:8 Ran:41
Win Prizemoney £24,051 *Total Prizemoney* £34,178
Wins * **1999** May Catter (G-F) H 5f 60 65 <
* **1999** Apr Warwic (GD) H 5f 56 62
* **1999** *Feb Lingfi (STD) H 5f 56 62*
* **1999** *Feb Lingfi (STD) H 5f 56 58*
* **1999** *Jan Wolver (STD) H 5f 50 52*
* 1998 *Aug Wolver (STD) H 5f 36 46*
* 1997 *Jan Wolver (STD) H 5f 30 44*
* 1997 *Jan Wolver (STD) H 5f 30 44*
1999 Turf 2-9: (5f 2-9) (g-s, gd 2-5, g-f, frm 2) 1999 AW 3-9: (5f 3-8, 6f) (Equi 2-3, Fibr 1-6)
Average gelding, has broken blood-vessels, effective 5f, acts on g-s to g-f - acts on AW, has worn blinkers, likes left handed tracks, likes tight tracks, excels at Lingfield and likes Catterick. Turf high 65 - 1st of 14 getting 3lb from Swynford Dream (21 May Catterick RF 1376) - also 1st of 18 giving 8lb to Press Ahead (5 Apr Warwick RF 0599). AW high 65 - 3rd of 7 getting 32lb from Primo Lara (24 Feb Wolverhampton 5f Fibr RF 0351) - also 1st of 9 giving 4lb to Half Tone (18 Feb Lingfield RF 0313). A speedy sprinter on his day, he completed a hat-trick on sand at the start of the year and has since won twice on turf. Needs fast ground on grass.
**P S Felgate [8-56] Tim Dean (from Mrs L Stubbs [0-3] Jly 1996).*

SOUHAITE (FR) BHB 40f RR 29f 1963[6]
3 b c Salse (USA) 10.9f **(71)** - Parannda (Bold Lad (IRE)) 8.4f **(68)**
Form - 086
Record 1999 - 1st:0 2nd:0 3rd:0 Ran:3
1999 Turf 0-3: (7f, 8f, 10f) (gd 2, g-f)
Scopey, currently little account colt. Turf high 29.
**W R Muir [0-3] J Bernstein.*

SOUND APPEAL BHB 58f RR 57f 1270[1]
5 b m Robellino (USA) 9.5f **(68)** - Son Et Lumiere (Rainbow Quest (USA)) 10.4f **(75)**
Form - 1
Record 1999 - 1st:1 2nd:0 3rd:0 Ran:1
Pre1999 - 1st:0 2nd:0 3rd:0 Ran:11
Win Prizemoney £3,714 *Total Prizemoney* £3,924
Wins * **1999** May Bath (GD) H 13.1f 53 56 <
1999 Turf 1-1: (13f 1-1) (gd 1-1)
Fair filly, often wears blinkers (very effectively). (1st run).
**G M McCourt [1-9] R W and J R Fidler (from A G Foster [0-10] Spt 1997).*

SOUND'S ACE BHB 57f RR 50f 2307[6]
3 ch f Savahra Sound 7.8f **(55)** - Ace Girl (Stanford) 7.9f **(56)**
Form - 00806
Record 1999 - 1st:0 2nd:0 3rd:0 Ran:5
Pre1999 - 1st:2 2nd:0 3rd:1 Ran:6
Win Prizemoney £6,583 *Total Prizemoney* £7,200
Wins * 1998 Oct Newmar (G-S) H 5f 64 67 <
* 1998 Aug Beverl (G-F) S 5f 64
1999 Turf 0-5: (5f 4, 6f) (gd, g-f 3, frm)
Light-framed, fair filly, effective 5f, acts on gd to g-f, best on g-f, has worn blinkers. Turf high 50. Consistent.
**D Shaw [2-11] Paul Dixon.*

SOUNDS COOL BHB 38f43a RR 42f 43a 3986[8]
3 b c Savahra Sound 7.8f **(55)** - Lucky Candy (Lucky Wednesday) 8f **(50)**
Form - 36276043088
Record 1999 - 1st:0 2nd:1 3rd:1 Ran:9
Pre1999 - 1st:0 2nd:0 3rd:1 Ran:6
Win Prizemoney £0 *Total Prizemoney* £1,124
1999 Turf 0-8: (6f, 7f, 8f 4, 10f 2) (sft, g-s, gd, g-f 3, frm 2) 1999 AW 0-1: (9f) (Fibr)
Leggy, moderate colt, effective 8 to 10f, acts on g-f - acts on Fibr, has worn blinkers, likes left handed tracks, likes tight tracks. Turf high 47. Becoming disappointing. **S R Bowring [0-15] Paul Dixon.*

SOUNDS CRAZY BHB 42f RR 43f 5187[16]
2 b f Savahra Sound 7.8f **(55)** - Sugar Token (Record Token) 6.3f **(53)**
Form - 408580
Record 1999 - 1st:0 2nd:0 3rd:0 Ran:6
Win Prizemoney £0 *Total Prizemoney* £193
1999 Turf 0-5: (5f 4, 6f) (gd 4, hrd) 1999 AW 0-1: (5f) (Fibr)
Moderate filly, has worn blinkers. Turf high 49.
**S R Bowring [0-6] Paul Dixon.*

SOUNDS FAB BHB 45f RR 46f 4868[11]
2 ch f Savahra Sound 7.8f **(55)** - Ace Girl (Stanford) 7.9f **(56)**
Form - 5055600
Record 1999 - 1st:0 2nd:0 3rd:0 Ran:7
1999 Turf 0-6: (5f 5, 6f) (gd 3, g-f, frm 2) 1999 AW 0-1: (5f) (Fibr)
Moderate filly, often wears blinkers. Turf high 48.
**D Shaw [0-7] Paul Dixon.*

SOUNDS LUCKY BHB 56f61a RR 48f 61a 3917[8]
3 b c Savahra Sound 7.8f **(55)** - Sweet And Lucky (Lucky Wednesday) 8f **(50)**
Form - 067211500100404508
Record 1999 - 1st:3 2nd:1 3rd:0 Ran:18
Pre1999 - 1st:0 2nd:0 3rd:0 Ran:3
Win Prizemoney £7,946 *Total Prizemoney* £8,790
Wins * **1999** May Lingfi (G-F) H 6f 58 62 <
* **1999** *Mar Wolver (SLW) H 6f 45 59*
* **1999** *Mar Wolver (STD) SH 5f 45 59*
1999 Turf 1-9: (5f 4, 6f 1-5) (gd 3, g-f 4, frm 1-2) 1999 AW 2-9: (5f 1-2, 6f 1-6, 8f) (Fibr 2-9)
Light-framed, fair colt, effective 5 to 8f, best at 6f, acts on frm - acts on Fibr, has worn blinkers, likes left handed tracks, likes tight tracks. Turf high 62 (1st run) - 1st of 19 getting 1lb from Bread Winner (25 May Lingfield RF 1456). AW high 59 - 1st of 13 getting 13lb from Avondale Girl (6 Mar Wolverhampton RF 0410) - also 1st of 13 getting 10lb from Legal Venture (3 Mar Wolverhampton RF 0396). **N P Littmoden [3-21] Paul Dixon.*

SOUNDS SOLO BHB 54f59a RR 59a 505[11]
3 b c Savahra Sound 7.8f **(55)** - Sola Mia (Tolomeo) 5.6f **(60)**
Form - 50
Record 1999 - 1st:0 2nd:0 3rd:0 Ran:2
Pre1999 - 1st:1 2nd:1 3rd:0 Ran:2
Win Prizemoney £2,094 *Total Prizemoney* £2,734
Wins * 1998 *Oct Southw (STD) S 7f 56* <
1999 Turf 0-1: (8f) (sft) 1999 AW 0-1: (7f) (Fibr)
Leggy, average colt, always wears blinkers. **S R Bowring [1-4] Paul Dixon.*

SOUNDS SPECIAL RR 66f 4325[7]
2 b f Savahra Sound 7.8f **(55)** - Sola Mia (Tolomeo) 5.6f **(60)**
Form - 57
Record 1999 - 1st:0 2nd:0 3rd:0 Ran:2
1999 Turf 0-2: (5f, 6f) (gd, g-f)
Currently average filly. Turf high 66 (began Aug).
**S R Bowring [0-2] Paul Dixon.*

SOUNDS SWEET BHB 36f31a RR 50f 31a 3991[3]
3 ch f Savahra Sound 7.8f **(55)** - Be My Sweet (Galivanter) 7.8f **(56)**
Form - 7783
Record 1999 - 1st:0 2nd:0 3rd:1 Ran:4
Pre1999 - 1st:0 2nd:0 3rd:0 Ran:7
Win Prizemoney £0 *Total Prizemoney* £326
1999 Turf 0-1: (7f) (frm) 1999 AW 0-3: (6f, 7f 2) (Equi, Fibr 2)
Light-framed, fair filly, has worn blinkers. AW high 21.
**D Shaw [0-4] Paul Dixon (from J J O'Neill [0-7] Oct 1998).*

SOUND THE TRUMPET (IRE) BHB 32f39a RR 35f 39a 4293[7]
7 b g Fayruz 6.6f **(63)** - Red Note (Rusticaro (FR)) 8.2f **(65)**
Form - 84403068057
Record 1999 - 1st:0 2nd:0 3rd:1 Ran:10
Pre1999 - 1st:2 2nd:5 3rd:3 Ran:42
Win Prizemoney £5,805 *Total Prizemoney* £13,841
Wins * 1998 *Jan Lingfi (STD) H 5f 30 50*
1999 Turf 0-7: (5f 2, 6f 3, 7f 2) (gd 3, g-f 3, frm) 1999 AW 0-3: (5f, 6f, 7f) (Equi 3)
Moderate gelding, effective 5f, - acts on Equi, has worn blinkers, likes left handed tracks, likes tight tracks.
**R C Spicer [1-39] Mrs J A Nichols (from A Streeter [0-4] Oct 1995).*

SOUPERFICIAL BHB 50f40a RR 50f 40a 4832[17]

8 gr g Petong 7.6f **(58)** - Duck Soup (Decoy Boy) 6.7f **(56)**
Form - 044834440100

Record	**1999 -**	1st:1	2nd:0	3rd:1	Ran:12
	Pre1999 -	1st:10	2nd:7	3rd:4	Ran:77

Win Prizemoney £32,372 *Total Prizemoney* £42,795

Wins								
* **1999**	Aug	Newcas	(GD)	H	6f	47	50	
* 1998	Jun	Hamilt	(SFT)	S	5f		56	
* 1998	Jun	Carlis	(G-S)	C	5.9f		56	
1997	Jly	Hamilt	(SFT)		6f		46	
1996	Spt	Leices	(FRM)	H	5f	50	52	
1996	Aug	Nottin	(G-F)	H	5.1f	46	47	
1995	Jly	Pontef	(G-F)	H	6f	57	62	
1995	*May*	*Wolver*	*(STD)*	*H*	*7f*	*56*	*63*	<
1995	*Apr*	*Wolver*	*(STD)*	*H*	*6f*	*52*	*55*	
1995	*Mar*	*Southw*	*(STD)*	*H*	*6f*	*43*	*45*	

1999 Turf 1-12: (5f 2, 6f 1-10) (sft 2, gd, g-f 1-5, frm 4)
Fair gelding, effective 5 to 6f, best at 6f, acts on sft to frm, often wears blinkers (effectively), does well at Hamilton. Turf high 50 - 1st of 20 getting 6lb from Bollin Ethos (20 Aug Newcastle RF 3800).
**Don Enrico Incisa [3-25] Mrs Christine Cawley (from N Tinkler [1-17] Oct 1997).*

SOURCE BHB 32f38a RR 12f 38a 4997[18]

4 b g Rudimentary (USA) 8.2f **(66)** - Sakala (NZ) (Gold and Ivory (USA))
Form - 04000

Record	**1999 -**	1st:0	2nd:0	3rd:0	Ran:5

1999 Turf 0-2: (6f, 10f) (gd, frm) 1999 AW 0-3: (6f, 7f, 9f) (Fibr 3)
Very moderate gelding. Turf high 12. AW high 36.
**T T Clement [0-6] John Bowyer.*

SOUTHAMPTON BHB 25f32a RR 32f 32a 3903[5]

9 b g Ballacashtal (CAN) 7.9f **(51)** - Petingo Gold (Pitskelly) 8.5f **(53)**
Form - 65

Record	**1999 -**	1st:0	2nd:0	3rd:0	Ran:2
	Pre1999 -	1st:0	2nd:0	3rd:1	Ran:12

Win Prizemoney £0 *Total Prizemoney* £562
1999 Turf 0-2: (14f, 17f) (frm 2)
Very moderate gelding, has worn blinkers. Turf high 32 (began Jly). Consistent. **G B Balding [11-68] Highflyers.*

SOUTHBOUND TRAIN BHB 50f RR 48f 5193[14]

3 ch g Superlative 8.8f **(57)** - Louisianalightning (Music Boy) 6.8f **(57)**
Form - 0

Record	**1999 -**	1st:0	2nd:0	3rd:0	Ran:1
	Pre1999 -	1st:0	2nd:0	3rd:0	Ran:4

1999 Turf 0-1: (8f) (gd)
Neat, moderate gelding. **G B Balding [0-5] Baldings (Training) Ltd.*

SOUTHERN DOMINION BHB 51f51a RR 52f 51a 5149[11]

7 ch g Dominion 8.9f **(65)** - Southern Sky (Comedy Star (USA)) 7.5f **(50)**
Form - 2200048058302000

Record	**1999 -**	1st:0	2nd:1	3rd:1	Ran:14
	Pre1999 -	1st:7	2nd:10	3rd:8	Ran:82

Win Prizemoney £22,932 *Total Prizemoney* £38,328

Wins								
* 1998	Aug	Mussel	(GD)	H	5f	52	61	<
* 1998	Jly	Mussel	(GD)	H	5f	48	51	
* 1997	Nov	Doncas	(GD)	H	5f	51	56	
* 1997	Oct	Ayr	(SFT)	H	5f	45	54	
* 1997	May	Mussel	(G-F)	H	5f	40	40	
1995	*Nov*	*Lingfi*	*(STD)*	*H*	*6f*	*52*	*50*	
1995	May	Bath	(GD)	S	5.1f		57	

1999 Turf 0-12: (5f 7, 6f 5) (sft, g-s, gd, g-f 6, frm 3) 1999 AW 0-2: (5f, 6f) (Fibr 2)
Fair gelding, effective 5 to 6f, best at 5f, acts on g-s to frm - acts on Fibr, often wears blinkers (effectively), likes Musselburgh. Turf high 53 - 3rd of 20 giving 6lb to Souperficial (20 Aug Newcastle 6f g-f RF 3800). AW high 30. Usually blazes from the stalls and it is just a question of whether he can hold on. Best suited by an easy five, he can act on sand as well.
**Miss J F Craze [5-54] Mrs Angela Wilson (from C N Allen [0-8] Oct 1996).*

SOUTHERN DUNES BHB 28f RR 27f 2809[5]

3 b g Ardkinglass 5f **(64)** - Leprechaun Lady (Royal Blend) 11.9f **(58)**
Form - 0505

Record	**1999 -**	1st:0	2nd:0	3rd:0	Ran:4
	Pre1999 -	1st:0	2nd:0	3rd:0	Ran:1

1999 Turf 0-4: (8f, 10f, 12f 2) (gd 2, frm 2)
Little account gelding, has worn blinkers. Turf high 27.
**Don Enrico Incisa [0-4] Don Enrico Incisa (from N Tinkler [0-1] May 1998).*

SOUTHERN HOUSE (IRE) RR 100f 811a[2]

3 b f Paris House 5.9f **(64)** - My Southern love (ITY) (Southern Arrow (USA))
Form - 2
1999 Turf 0-1: (8f) (hvy)
Currently very useful filly. (1st run) - 2nd of 16 to Shenck (18 Apr Capannelle 8f hvy RF 0811a). Second in the Italian 1,000 Guineas, she has a useful turn-of-foot and is probably best at a mile.
**L Camici in ITY [1-3].*

SOUTHERN MIST RR 75f 3390[7]

2 b f Forzando 7.2f **(63)** - Southern Sky (Comedy Star (USA)) 7.5f **(50)**
Form - 05687

Record	**1999 -**	1st:0	2nd:0	3rd:0	Ran:5

Win Prizemoney £0 *Total Prizemoney* £179
1999 Turf 0-4: (5f 4) (g-s, frm 2, hrd) 1999 AW 0-1: (6f) (Fibr)
Above-average filly. Turf high 75. **W G M Turner [0-5] Bill Brown.*

SOUTH LANE RR 4981[12]

2 br g Rock City 8.8f **(62)** - Steppey Lane (Tachypous) 8.6f **(55)**
Form - 00

Record	**1999 -**	1st:0	2nd:0	3rd:0	Ran:2

1999 Turf 0-2: (6f 2) (g-f, frm)
Currently very poor gelding. (began Oct). **G P Kelly [0-2] R Midgley.*

SOUTH OF HEAVEN (IRE) RR 98f 4203a[4]

3 b f Fairy King (USA) 7.7f **(75)** - Epicure's Garden (USA) (Affirmed (USA)) 9.3f **(79)**
Form - 614
1999 Turf 1-3: (8f 1-2, 9f) (gd, g-f 1-2)
Currently very useful filly. Turf high 98 - also 1st of 6 from Zaola (29 Jly Galway RF 3335a). She was found out in Group company and will be better employed in listed events around a mile.
**D K Weld in IRE [1-3] Moyglare Stud Farm.*

SOVEREIGN ABBEY (IRE) BHB 70f65a RR 72f 65a 5147[5]

3 b f Royal Academy (USA) 7.8f **(77)** - Elabella (Ela-Mana-Mou) 10.1f **(70)**
Form - 35

Record	**1999 -**	1st:0	2nd:0	3rd:0	Ran:1
	Pre1999 -	1st:0	2nd:0	3rd:2	Ran:3

Win Prizemoney £0 *Total Prizemoney* £938
1999 AW 0-1: (8f) (Fibr)
Leggy, above-average filly. **Sir Mark Prescott [0-4] G S Shropshire.*

SOVEREIGN CREST (IRE) BHB 43f RR 39f 3385[5]

6 gr g Priolo (USA) 10.9f **(71)** - Abergwrle (Absalom) 7.2f **(58)**
Form - 85

Record	**1999 -**	1st:0	2nd:0	3rd:0	Ran:2
	Pre1999 -	1st:2	2nd:0	3rd:4	Ran:22

Win Prizemoney £6,253 *Total Prizemoney* £8,157

Wins								
* 1998	Jly	Lingfi	(G-F)	H	14f	42	43	
* 1997	Jly	Bright	(FRM)	H	11.9f	45	47	<

1999 Turf 0-2: (10f, 12f) (g-f 2)
Very moderate gelding, effective 11 to 14f, acts on g-f to frm, best on frm, often wears blinkers (extremely effectively), prefers left handed tracks. Turf high 39 - 5th of 9 giving 4lb to Children's Choice (5 Aug Brighton 12f g-f RF 3385). Consistent.
**C A Horgan [2-24] Mrs B Sumner.*

SOVEREIGN STATE (IRE) BHB 77f RR 79f 4452[4]

2 b c Soviet Lad (USA) 9.4f **(63)** - Portree (Slip Anchor) 9.8f **(73)**
Form - 6514

Record	**1999 -**	1st:1	2nd:0	3rd:0	Ran:4

Win Prizemoney £3,899 *Total Prizemoney* £4,438

Wins								
* **1999**	Spt	Thirsk	(FRM)		8f		79	<

1999 Turf 1-4: (7f, 8f 1-3) (sft, g-f, frm, hrd 1-1)
Above-average colt. Turf high 79 (began Jly) - 1st of 6 from Najjm (4 Spt Thirsk RF 4145). **M A Jarvis [1-4] Lord Harrington.*

SOVIET FLASH (IRE) RR 83+f 3842[1]

2 b c Warning 8.1f **(77)** - Mrs Moonlight (Ajdal (USA)) 9.2f **(89)**
Form - 41
Record 1999 - 1st:1 2nd:0 3rd:0 Ran:2
Win Prizemoney £3,241 *Total Prizemoney* £3,625
Wins * **1999** Aug Leices (G-F) 7f 83+ <
1999 Turf 1-2: (7f 1-2) (frm 1-2)
Currently decent colt. Turf high 83 (began Jly) - 1st of 12 from Thari (22 Aug Leicester RF 3842). **E A L Dunlop [1-2] Khalifa Sultan.*

SOVIET KING (IRE) BHB 33f30a RR 16f 30a 2653[6]

6 b g Soviet Lad (USA) 9.4f **(63)**-Finessing (Indian King (USA)) .4f **(64)**
Form - 006
Record 1999 - 1st:0 2nd:0 3rd:0 Ran:3
Pre1999 - 1st:1 2nd:0 3rd:3 Ran:13
Win Prizemoney £2,294 *Total Prizemoney* £4,165
Wins * 1997 *Jan Southw (STD) 12f 33+* <
1999 Turf 0-1: (10f) (gd) 1999 AW 0-2: (13f, 14f) (Equi, Fibr)
Little account gelding. AW high 23. Becoming disappointing.
**P Mitchell [1-16] Mrs Patricia Mitchell.*

SOVIET LADY (IRE) BHB 27f RR 36f 354[7]

5 b m Soviet Lad (USA) 9.4f **(63)** - La Vosgienne (Ashmore (FR)) 8.5f **(65)**
Form - 777
Record 1999 - 1st:0 2nd:0 3rd:0 Ran:3
Pre1999 - 1st:1 2nd:0 3rd:5 Ran:25
Win Prizemoney £2,845 *Total Prizemoney* £4,324
Wins 1996 Aug Thirsk (FRM) S 7f 59 <
1999 AW 0-3: (10f, 13f, 16f) (Equi 3)
Very moderate filly, effective 8f, acts on frm, has worn blinkers. AW high 23.
**R Ingram [0-4] Gerry Boyer (from B A Pearce [0-8] Jly 1998).*

SO WILLING BHB 62f62a RR 63f 62a 5146[12]

3 gr g Keen 11.1f **(58)** - Sweet Whisper **(14f 46a)** (Petong) 6.6f **(58)**
Form - 012080200
Record 1999 - 1st:1 2nd:2 3rd:0 Ran:9
Pre1999 - 1st:0 2nd:0 3rd:1 Ran:7
Win Prizemoney £2,057 *Total Prizemoney* £4,354
Wins * **1999** *Mar Southw (STD) 6f 62* <
1999 Turf 0-3: (6f 2, 7f) (sft, gd, frm) 1999 AW 1-6: (6f 1-5, 7f) (Fibr 1-6)
Light-framed, average gelding, effective 5 to 6f, best at 6f, acts on sft to g-f - acts on Fibr, likes Southwell. Turf high 63 (1st run) - 2nd of 12 giving 7lb to Sharp Edge Boy (29 Mar Hamilton 6f sft RF 0500). AW high 67 - 2nd of 15 getting 6lb from Molyneux (8 Jly Southwell 6f Fibr RF 2650) - also 1st of 8 from Prince of Aragon (19 Mar Southwell RF 0452). Inconsistent. **M Dods [1-16] A G Watson.*

SPACE BABE BHB 43f RR 43f 3351[3]

3 br f Cosmonaut - Concorde Lady (Hotfoot) 10.5f **(59)**
Form - 0053
Record 1999 - 1st:0 2nd:0 3rd:1 Ran:4
Pre1999 - 1st:0 2nd:0 3rd:0 Ran:4
Win Prizemoney £0 *Total Prizemoney* £482
1999 Turf 0-4: (6f 3, 7f) (gd, frm 3)
Scopey, moderate filly. Turf high 43. **R Hannon [0-8] Lady Davis.*

SPACE RACE BHB 64f76a RR 67f 76a 5066[15]

5 b g Rock Hopper 10.6f **(54)** - Melanoura (Imperial Fling (USA)) 7.1f **(58)**
Form - 715240250
Record 1999 - 1st:1 2nd:2 3rd:0 Ran:8
Pre1999 - 1st:1 2nd:2 3rd:0 Ran:10
Win Prizemoney £6,162 *Total Prizemoney* £10,957
Wins * **1999** *Jan Lingfi (STD) H 12f 72 76* <
* 1997 May Bath (GD) 8f 70
1999 Turf 0-4: (10f 2, 12f 2) (g-s, gd, g-f 2) 1999 AW 1-4: (10f, 12f 1-3) (Equi 1-4)
Above-average gelding, effective 8 to 12f, best at 12f, - acts on AW, best on Equi, favours left handed tracks. Turf high 67 (began Aug). AW high 76 (1st run) - 1st of 6 getting 4lb from Fields of Omagh (28 Jan Lingfield RF 0182). Inconsistent. He caused a bit of an upset when winning over twelve furlongs on the Lingfield Equitrack in January, but he is pretty inconsistent. Ran one of his better races on turf when runner-up at Pontefract in September.
**C A Cyzer [2-18] R M Cyzer.*

SPADOUN (FR) RR 104f 5009a[1]

3 b c Kaldoun (FR) 9.9f **(84)** - Tolga (USA) (Irish River (FR)) 8.6f **(78)**
Form - 561
1999 Turf 1-3: (8f 1-1, 11f 2) (hvy 1-1, g-s 2)
Very useful colt. Turf high 104 - 1st of 10 from Swallow Flight (14 Oct Longchamp RF 5009a). He revels in testing conditions, but failed to improve on his useful juvenile form.
**C Laffon-Parias in FR [2-4] J Gonzalez.*

SPAIN (USA) RR 5225a[4]

2 f Thunder Gulch (USA) - Drina (USA) (Regal And Royal (USA))
Form - 4
1999 AW 0-1: (9f) (Dirt)
Currently useful. (1st run) - 4th of 9 to Cash Run (6 Nov Gulfstream Park 9f Dirt RF 5225a). **J L Bonde in USA [0-1].*

SPA LANE BHB 37f40a RR 38f 40a 4600[8]

6 ch g Presidium 7.5f **(56)** - Sleekit (Blakeney) 10.5f **(64)**
Form - 744128480014227008
Record 1999 - 1st:2 2nd:3 3rd:0 Ran:15
Pre1999 - 1st:3 2nd:6 3rd:3 Ran:35
Win Prizemoney £13,908 *Total Prizemoney* £26,108
Wins * **1999** May Pontef (G-F) H 12f 36 41
* **1999** *Jan Southw (STD) H 16f 34 38*
* 1998 May Beverl (GD) H 16.2f 35 40
1996 Aug Nottin (G-S) 14.1f 58 <
1996 Jun Nottin (G-F) 10f 54
1999 Turf 1-10: (12f 1-3, 14f, 16f 4, 17f 2) (sft 2, gd 2, g-f 1-1, frm 5)
1999 AW 1-5: (14f, 16f 1-4) (Equi, Fibr 1-4)
Moderate gelding, effective 14 to 18f, acts on g-s to frm, best on frm, favours tight tracks, does well at Pontefract, likes Beverley. Turf high 46 - 2nd of 12 giving 4lb to Rosa Canina (13 Jly Beverley 16f frm RF 2767). AW high 42.
**Mrs S Lamyman [3-30] Sotby Farming Company Ltd (from M P Bielby [0-11] Oct 1997).*

SPANISH EYES BHB 65a RR 59f 1016[14]

4 b f Belmez (USA) 11.4f **(65)** - Night Transaction (Tina's Pet) 6.8f **(59)**
Form - 0
Record 1999 - 1st:0 2nd:0 3rd:0 Ran:1
Pre1999 - 1st:0 2nd:1 3rd:3 Ran:7
Win Prizemoney £0 *Total Prizemoney* £2,803
1999 Turf 0-1: (11f) (frm)
Neat, fair filly, effective 8f, acts on g-f to frm.
**J L Spearing [0-2] Ganadora Partnership (from J A R Toller [0-7] Spt 1998).*

SPANISH LADY (IRE) RR 54f 4533[7]

3 b f Bering 9.6f **(80)** - Belle Arrivee (Bustino) 10.4f **(64)**
Form - 0457
Record 1999 - 1st:0 2nd:0 3rd:0 Ran:4
Pre1999 - 1st:0 2nd:0 3rd:0 Ran:1
Win Prizemoney £0 *Total Prizemoney* £266
1999 Turf 0-4: (10f, 12f, 14f, 16f) (g-s, gd 2, g-f)
Scopey, fair filly. Turf high 54 - 5th of 7 getting 7lb from Salford Flyer (2 Jly Salisbury 14f gd RF 2497).
**J L Dunlop [0-5] Windflower Overseas Holdings Inc.*

SPANISH STAR RR 66f 4635[3]

2 b c Hernando (FR) - Desert Girl (Green Desert (USA)) 8.6f **(78)**
Form - 43
Record 1999 - 1st:0 2nd:0 3rd:1 Ran:2
Win Prizemoney £0 *Total Prizemoney* £820
1999 Turf 0-2: (7f, 8f) (gd 2)
Currently average colt. Turf high 66 (began Spt) - 3rd of 7 to High Cheviot (29 Spt Newcastle 8f gd RF 4635).
**W Jarvis [0-2] Miss V R Jarvis.*

SPANKER BHB 70f RR 70df 2736[4]

3 ch f Suave Dancer (USA) 10.7f **(68)** - Yawl **(93f)** (Rainbow Quest (USA)) 10.4f **(75)**
Form - 54634
Record 1999 - 1st:0 2nd:0 3rd:1 Ran:5
Win Prizemoney £0 *Total Prizemoney* £935
1999 Turf 0-5: (8f, 11f, 12f 3) (gd, g-f, frm 2, hrd)
Light-framed, above-average filly. Turf high 70 - 3rd of 5 to Sedrah (30 Jun Catterick 12f frm RF 2440). **B W Hills [0-5] R D Hollingsworth.*

SPARKLING HARRY BHB 33f52a **RR 25f 52a** 2890[12]
5 ch g Tina's Pet 7.4f **(56)** - Sparkling Hock (Hot Spark) 7.6f **(62)**
Form - 4400806400
Record 1999 - 1st:0 2nd:0 3rd:0 Ran:8
Pre1999 - 1st:2 2nd:1 3rd:2 Ran:33
Win Prizemoney £6,339 *Total Prizemoney* £7,767
Wins * 1998 *Oct Wolver (sta) H 9.4f 56 61* <
* 1998 *Spt Wolver (STD) H 8.5f 46 53*
1999 Turf 0-4: (8f, 9f, 10f 2) (gd 2, g-f, frm) 1999 AW 0-4: (8f, 9f 2, 11f) (Fibr 4)
Moderate gelding, effective 8 to 9f, best at 9f, - acts on Fibr, has worn blinkers, likes left handed tracks, likes tight tracks. Turf high 25. AW high 48. Shows better form on sand than on turf.
**Miss L C Siddall [2-41] Lynn Siddall Racing.*

SPARKLING ISLE BHB 65f **RR 68f** 5045[16]
2 ch f Inchinor 8.9f **(64)** - Brillante (FR) (Green Dancer (USA)) 10.3f **(74)**
Form - 4640
Record 1999 - 1st:0 2nd:0 3rd:0 Ran:4
Win Prizemoney £0 *Total Prizemoney* £468
1999 Turf 0-4: (6f 2, 7f 2) (sft, g-s, gd, frm)
Average filly. Turf high 68 (began Jly).
**M Blanshard [0-4] The Cheapside Syndicate.*

SPARK OF LIFE RR 55f 5216[11]
2 b f Rainbows For Life (CAN) 9.3f **(64)** - Sparkly Girl (IRE) **(80f)** (Danehill (USA)) 10f **(72)**
Form - 060
Record 1999 - 1st:0 2nd:0 3rd:0 Ran:3
1999 Turf 0-3: (7f, 8f 2) (g-s, gd 2)
Currently fair filly, often wears blinkers. Turf high 55 (began Oct).
**P R Chamings [0-3] Mrs V K Shaw.*

SPARKY BHB 56f **RR 57?f** 3289[11]
5 b g Warrshan (USA) 9.7f **(59)** - Pebble Creek (IRE) (Reference Point) 6.8f **(70)**
Form - 00
Record 1999 - 1st:0 2nd:0 3rd:0 Ran:2
Pre1999 - 1st:3 2nd:4 3rd:3 Ran:26
Win Prizemoney £7,966 *Total Prizemoney* £14,359
Wins * 1997 *Jun Southw (STD) H 8f 57 60+*
* 1996 Aug Beverl (FRM) H 7.5f 54 65 <
* 1996 Aug Bright (FRM) S 6f 65 <
1999 Turf 0-2: (8f 2) (gd, frm)
Above-average gelding, mostly wears blinkers. Turf high 42 (began Jly). **M W Easterby [4-36] Abbots Salford Carav Park.*

SPARTAN ROYALE BHB 67f **RR 66f** 4830[2]
5 b g Shareef Dancer (USA) 10.1f **(67)** - Cormorant Creek (Gorytus (USA)) 7.8f **(60)**
Form - 826220342
Record 1999 - 1st:0 2nd:4 3rd:1 Ran:9
Pre1999 - 1st:1 2nd:2 3rd:1 Ran:11
Win Prizemoney £2,346 *Total Prizemoney* £12,292
Wins * 1998 Aug Carlis (G-S) H 17.2f 55 58 <
1999 Turf 0-9: (11f, 13f 7, 17f) (sft, g-s, gd 5, g-f 2)
Average gelding, effective 13 to 17f, best at 13f, acts on sft to g-f, best on gd. Turf high 66 - 2nd of 7 getting 17lb from Kattegat (12 Oct Ayr 13f sft RF 4830).
**P Monteith [1-16] Allan Melville (from C E Brittain [0-5] Oct 1997).*

SPECIAL DISCOUNT (USA) RR 101f 3589a[9]
5 g Nureyev (USA) 8.4f **(84)** - Looks Sensational (USA) (Majestic Light (USA)) 10.6f **(75)**
Form - 80
1999 Turf 0-2: (7f, 8f) (hvy 2)
Currently very useful gelding. Turf high 101.
**Mme C Head in FR [0-2].*

SPECIALIZE BHB 31f33a **RR 32?f 33a** 420[3]
7 b g Faustus (USA) 9.1f **(54)** - Scholastika (GER) (Alpenkonig (GER)) 10.8f **(76)**
Form - 3
Record 1999 - 1st:0 2nd:0 3rd:1 Ran:1
Pre1999 - 1st:0 2nd:1 3rd:0 Ran:12
Win Prizemoney £0 *Total Prizemoney* £992
1999 AW 0-1: (11f) (Fibr)
Very moderate gelding, has worn blinkers. Inconsistent.
**K R Burke [3-28] P A Brazier.*

SPECIAL-K BHB 42f37a **RR 40f 37a** 4163[9]
7 br m Treasure Kay 6.5f **(53)** - Lissi Gori (FR) (Bolkonski) 7.6f **(64)**
Form - 16635304U0
Record 1999 - 1st:1 2nd:0 3rd:2 Ran:10
Pre1999 - 1st:6 2nd:4 3rd:5 Ran:48
Win Prizemoney £19,924 *Total Prizemoney* £28,514
Wins * **1999** May Pontef (G-F) C 8f 42
* 1997 Jly Ripon (G-F) S 8f 50
* 1997 Jly Beverl (HVY) SH 7.5f 44 49
* 1995 Aug Ripon (G-F) C 8f 68 <
* 1995 Jly Beverl (GD) C 7.5f 68 <
* 1995 Jly Redcar (FRM) C 7f 61
1999 Turf 1-10: (8f 1-7, 9f 2, 10f) (g-f 1-4, frm 5, hrd)
Moderate mare, effective 7 to 10f, acts on gd to frm, has worn blinkers, prefers left handed tracks. Turf high 43 - 3rd of 15 giving 1lb to Time of Night (23 Jly Thirsk 8f frm RF 3077) - also 1st of 10 getting 15lb from Sabot (28 May Pontefract RF 1554). Consistent.
**E Weymes [7-48] G Falshaw (from J R Turner [0-10] Spt 1998).*

SPECIAL PERSON (IRE) BHB 38f49a **RR 40f 49a** 2825[12]
4 ch f Ballad Rock 7.2f **(63)** - Hada Rani (Jaazeiro (USA)) 9.2f **(54)**
Form - 58087670
Record 1999 - 1st:0 2nd:0 3rd:0 Ran:8
Pre1999 - 1st:1 2nd:2 3rd:0 Ran:7
Win Prizemoney £3,183 *Total Prizemoney* £4,793
Wins * 1998 *Jun Lingfi (STD) H 8f 55 60* <
1999 Turf 0-5: (6f 2, 7f, 8f, 10f) (g-s, gd, frm 3) 1999 AW 0-3: (10f 2, 12f) (Equi 3)
Leggy, moderate filly, effective 8f, - acts on Equi, likes left handed tracks, likes tight tracks. Turf high 40. AW high 37.
**P Mitchell [1-15] Mrs Patricia Mitchell.*

SPECIAL PROMISE (IRE) BHB 55f **RR 64f** 5052[19]
2 ch g Anjiz (USA) 7f **(67)** - Woodenitbenice (USA) (Nasty And Bold (USA))
Form - 6670
Record 1999 - 1st:0 2nd:0 3rd:0 Ran:4
1999 Turf 0-4: (5f 2, 6f, 7f) (gd 4)
Average gelding. Turf high 64. **P C Haslam [0-4] R Young.*

SPECTROMETER BHB 66f **RR 69f** 4627[6]
2 ch c Rainbow Quest (USA) 11.2f **(81)** - Selection Board (Welsh Pageant) 10f **(65)**
Form - 506
Record 1999 - 1st:0 2nd:0 3rd:0 Ran:3
1999 Turf 0-3: (7f 2, 8f) (g-s 2, frm)
Currently average colt. Turf high 69 (began Spt).
**Sir Mark Prescott [0-3] Lord Derby.*

SPEEDFIT FREE (IRE) BHB 70f **RR 75f** 4354[4]
2 b c Night Shift (USA) 8.1f **(73)** - Dedicated Lady (IRE) (Pennine Walk) 8.5f **(61)**
Form - 0010604
Record 1999 - 1st:1 2nd:0 3rd:0 Ran:7
Win Prizemoney £3,557 *Total Prizemoney* £3,948
Wins * **1999** May Yarmou (FRM) 6f 75 <
1999 Turf 1-7: (5f 3, 6f 1-3, 7f) (g-s, g-f 1-4, frm 2)
Above-average colt, effective 6f, acts on g-f, has worn blinkers. Turf high 75 - 1st of 7 giving 5lb to Janet (26 May Yarmouth RF 1511). **G G Margarson [1-7] John Guest.*

SPEED MERCHANT (IRE) RR 96+f 2790a[1]
3 br c Lucky Guest - Cosmic Speed Queen (USA) 00
Form - 6501
1999 Turf 1-4: (6f, 7f 1-2, 8f) (g-s 1-1, gd, g-f 2)
Very useful colt, effective 7f, acts on g-s, has worn blinkers. Turf high 96 - 1st of 9 giving 16lb to Midnight Lover (8 Jly Tipperary RF 2790a). He ran away with a decent handicap at Tipperary in July and could prove best over seven furlongs.
**Miss I T Oakes in IRE [2-8] Anamoine Ltd.*

SPEED ON BHB 82f **RR 88f** 4933[16]

6 b g Sharpo 7.5f **(68)** - Pretty Poppy (Song) 7.2f **(61)**
Form - 16510660

Record	**1999** -	1st:2	2nd:0	3rd:0	Ran:8		
	Pre1999 -	1st:2	2nd:2	3rd:3	Ran:21		

Win Prizemoney £25,908 *Total Prizemoney* £33,265

Wins	* **1999**	Jun	Chepst	(G-F)	H	5.1f	87	88	
	* **1999**	Apr	Newbur	(G-F)	H	5.2f	81	89	
	* 1998	Apr	Bath	(SFT)		5.1f		97	<
	* 1996	May	Beverl	(G-F)		5f		83	

1999 Turf 2-8: (5f 2-8) (sft, g-s, gd 2, g-f 1-2, frm 1-2)
Useful gelding, effective 5f, acts on g-s to frm, has worn blinkers. Turf high 89 (1st run) - 1st of 13 getting 17lb from Cortachy Castle (16 Apr Newbury RF 0720) - also 1st of 8 giving 5lb to Emperor Naheem (29 Jun Chepstow RF 2388). He is a pacey sort well capable of winning sprint handicaps. Does not like big fields or trips in the excess of the minimum according to his trainer.
**H Candy [4-29] P A Deal.*

SPEEDY CLASSIC (USA) BHB 43f54a RR 35f 54a 4783[4]

10 br g Storm Cat (USA) 7f **(86)** - Shadows Lengthen (Star Appeal) 9.6f **(65)**
Form - 1024222700004

Record	**1999** -	1st:0	2nd:4	3rd:0	Ran:11		
	Pre1999 -	1st:15	2nd:9	3rd:9	Ran:85		

Win Prizemoney £46,845 *Total Prizemoney* £64,482

Wins	1998	*Nov*	*Lingfi*	*(STD)*	*C*	*8f*		*59+*	
	1998	Aug	Chepst	(G-F)	H	6.1f	55	58	
	1998	*Jan*	*Lingfi*	*(STD)*	*H*	*7f*	*84*	*86*	<
	1997	Oct	Yarmou	(FRM)	H	7f	53	60	
	1997	*Mar*	*Lingfi*	*(STD)*	*H*	*6f*	*80*	*79*	
	1996	*Dec*	*Lingfi*	*(STD)*	*H*	*7f*	*72*	*80*	
	1996	Spt	Chepst	(G-F)	H	7.1f	54	57	
	1996	*Aug*	*Lingfi*	*(STD)*	*H*	*7f*	*63*	*74*	
	1996	*Feb*	*Lingfi*	*(STD)*	*C*	*7f*		*67*	

1999 Turf 0-4: (7f 4) (gd, g-f, frm 2)1999 AW 0-7: (6f, 7f 4, 8f 2) (Equi 7)
Very moderate gelding, effective 7f, - acts on Equi, has worn blinkers. Turf high 35. AW high 68. Better on sand than on turf these days, and seven furlongs is his trip.
**C G Cox [0-3] South Wales Shower S Faucets (from M J Heaton-Ellis [15-85] Aug 1999).*

SPEEDY JAMES (IRE) BHB 98f RR 98f 4654[15]

3 ch g Fayruz 6.6f **(63)** - Haraabah (USA) (Topsider (USA)) 8.3f **(71)**
Form - 360

Record	**1999** -	1st:0	2nd:0	3rd:1	Ran:3		
	Pre1999 -	1st:2	2nd:1	3rd:1	Ran:7		

Win Prizemoney £8,156 *Total Prizemoney* £16,424

Wins	1998	Apr	Newmar	(SFT)	5f		98++	<
	1998	Mar	Newcas	(G-S)	5f		84++	

1999 Turf 0-3: (5f 3) (gd, g-f, frm)
Very useful gelding, effective 5f, acts on gd, has worn blinkers. Turf high 98 (began Jly). Inconsistent. He looked useful early on in his career, but has failed to progress. Raced only at five furlongs, he acts on any ground and could do well for David Nicholls once the Handicapper relents.
**D Nicholls [0-1] Lucayan Stud (from J Berry [2-9] Aug 1999).*

SPELLBINDER (IRE) RR 68f 5198[8]

3 b f Magical Wonder (USA) 7.2f **(60)** - Shamanka (IRE) (Shernazar) 10.2f **(73)**
Form - 8

Record	**1999** -	1st:0	2nd:0	3rd:0	Ran:1

1999 Turf 0-1: (8f) (gd)
Workmanlike, currently average filly.
**G B Balding [0-1] Baldings (Training) Ltd.*

SPENCER'S REVENGE BHB 37f37a RR 39f 37a 236[8]

10 ch g Bay Express 7.1f **(53)** - Armour of Light (Hot Spark) 7.6f **(62)**
Form - 08

Record	**1999** -	1st:0	2nd:0	3rd:0	Ran:2
	Pre1999 -	1st:13	2nd:10	3rd:8	Ran:56

Win Prizemoney £39,002 *Total Prizemoney* £51,019

Wins	* 1997	*Feb*	*Lingfi*	*(STD)*	*C*	*10f*		*58*
	1996	*Apr*	*Southw*	*(STD)*	*C*	*8f*		*68*
	1996	*Jan*	*Southw*	*(STD)*	*C*	*8f*		*64*
	1995	*Dec*	*Lingfi*	*(STD)*	*C*	*8f*		*75*
	1995	Oct	Yarmou	(FRM)	H	7f	67	70
	1995	*Spt*	*Wolver*	*(STD)*	*C*	*7f*		*74*
	1995	May	Salisb	(GD)	H	7f	63	68
	1995	*Feb*	*Wolver*	*(STD)*	*C*	*7f*		*67*
	1995	*Jan*	*Lingfi*	*(STD)*		*7f*		*66+*
	1995	*Jan*	*Lingfi*	*(STD)*	*S*	*7f*		*57+*

1999 AW 0-2: (8f, 13f) (Equi 2)
Very moderate gelding, has worn blinkers.
**P Butler [1-13] P Butler (from N Tinkler [1-11] Jan 1997).*

SPENCERS WOOD (IRE) RR 79+f 4825[1]

2 b c Pips Pride 6.7f **(70)** - Ascoli (Skyliner) 7.3f **(53)**
Form - 1

Record	**1999** -	1st:1	2nd:0	3rd:0	Ran:1

Win Prizemoney £3,387 *Total Prizemoney* £3,387

Wins	* **1999**	Oct	Windso	(G-S)	6f	79+	<

1999 Turf 1-1: (6f 1-1) (g-f 1-1)
Currently above-average colt. (1st run) - 1st of 22 from Nisr (11 Oct Windsor RF 4825). **P J Makin [1-1] Four Seasons Racing Ltd.*

SPENDENT RR 99f 2655a[1]

3 ch c Generous (IRE) 11.5f **(82)** - Cattermole (USA) (Roberto (USA)) 10f **(76)**
Form - 1
1999 Turf 1-1: (13f 1-1) (gd 1-1)
Currently very useful colt, always wears blinkers. (1st run) - 1st of 9 from Northerntown (30 Jun Chantilly RF 2655a).
**P Bary in FR [1-1] K Abdulla.*

SPENDER BHB 40f75a RR 37f 75a 4332[12]

10 b or br g Last Tycoon 9.4f **(73)** - Lady Hester (Native Prince) 5.5f **(50)**
Form - 7450070000070

Record	**1999**	1st:0	2nd:0	3rd:0	Ran:13
	Pre1999 -	1st:15	2nd:7	3rd:10	Ran:74

Win Prizemoney £54,146 *Total Prizemoney* £68,168

Wins	1997	Spt	Yarmou	(G-F)	H	5.2f	77	82	
	1997	Jun	Bath	(G-F)	H	5.7f	76	79	
	1997	Apr	Bright	(FRM)	H	6f	74	77	
	1996	*Mar*	*Lingfi*	*(STD)*	*H*	*5f*	*82*	*87*	<
	1995	Aug	Bath	(HRD)	H	5.1f	71	72	
	1995	*Mar*	*Lingfi*	*(STD)*	*H*	*5f*	*76*	*76*	
	1995	*Jan*	*Lingfi*	*(STD)*	*H*	*5f*	*73*	*73*	

1999 Turf 0-10: (5f 5, 6f 5) (gd 3, g-f 5, frm 2) 1999 AW 0-3: (5f 2, 6f) (Equi 3)
Above-average gelding, effective 5f, acts on sft - acts on Equi. Turf high 51. AW high 74 - 4th of 8 giving 5lb to Batchworth Belle (1 Apr Lingfield 5f Equi RF 0546).
**V Soane [0-13] The Entrepreneurs (from P W Harris [15-74] Oct 1998).*

SPENDTHEPROC-EDE'S BHB 65f60a RR 64f 60a 542[9]

3 b f Dilum (USA) 7.1f **(56)** - Karonga (Main Reef) 9.6f **(57)**
Form - 0

Record	**1999** -	1st:0	2nd:0	3rd:0	Ran:1
	Pre1999 -	1st:0	2nd:1	3rd:0	Ran:6

Win Prizemoney £0 *Total Prizemoney* £1,040
1999 AW 0-1: (10f) (Equi)
Tall, average filly, effective 6f, acts on frm.
**W G M Turner [0-7] Ede's (UK) Ltd.*

SPICK AND SPAN BHB 54a RR 52f 259[6]

5 b g Anshan 8.2f **(63)** - Pretty Thing (Star Appeal) 9.6f **(65)**
Form - 4126

Record	**1999** -	1st:1	2nd:1	3rd:0	Ran:4
	Pre1999 -	1st:0	2nd:1	3rd:2	Ran:10

Win Prizemoney £1,688 *Total Prizemoney* £4,411

Wins	* **1999**	*Jan*	*Lingfi*	*(STD)*	*H*	*16f*	*49*	*54*	<

1999 AW 1-4: (12f, 16f 1-3) (Equi 1-4)
Fair gelding, effective 12 to 16f, best at 16f, acts on frm - acts on AW, best on Equi. AW high 57 - 2nd of 11 giving 2lb to Padauk (30 Jan Lingfield 16f Equi RF 0198) - also 1st of 11 getting 7lb from Pipe Music (14 Jan Lingfield RF 0091). Consistent.
**P R Hedger [2-13] Essandess Partners (from C W Thornton [0-8] Nov 1997).*

SPICY GIRL (FR) RR 102f 1530a[7]

3 f Marignan (USA) - Danseuse Verte (FR) (Green Dancer (USA)) 10.3f **(74)**

Form - 37
1999 Turf 0-2: (8f, 10f) (sft, g-s)
Currently very useful. Turf high 102.
**P Demercastel in FR [0-1] (from E Leenders in FR [0-1] Mar 1999).*

SPIN A YARN RR 76f 3652[1]
2 b c Wolfhound (USA) 7.3f **(71)** - Green Flower (USA) (Fappiano (USA)) 8.7f **(77)**
Form - 84441
Record 1999 - 1st:1 2nd:0 3rd:0 Ran:5
Win Prizemoney £6,190 *Total Prizemoney* £7,041
Wins * 1999 Aug Newbur (GD) H 7.3f 73 76 <
1999 Turf 1-5: (6f 3, 7f 1-2) (gd 1-2, frm 2, hrd)
Above-average colt. Turf high 76 - 1st of 9 getting 12lb from King O' The Mana (14 Aug Newbury RF 3652). Progressive sort, winner of a Newbury nursery in August with a bit in hand.
**B W Hills [1-5] Maktoum Al Maktoum.*

SPINDRIFT (IRE) BHB 111f114a **RR 112f 114a** 4101[3]
4 b c Mukaddamah (USA) 7.6f **(74)** -Win For Me(Bonne Noel) 10.7f **(71)**
Form - 23
Record 1999 - 1st:0 2nd:1 3rd:1 Ran:2
Pre1999 - 1st:2 2nd:1 3rd:0 Ran:3
Win Prizemoney £9,384 *Total Prizemoney* £89,201
Wins 1998 Jun Salisb (G-F) 7f 102 <
1998 May Newmar (G-F) 8f 96
1999 Turf 0-1: (9f) (frm) 1999 AW 0-1: (10f) (Dirt)
Well made, high-class colt. (1st run) - 3rd of 7 giving 11lb to Gold Academy (2 Spt York 9f frm RF 4101). (1st run) - 2nd of 9 to Altibr (28 Mar Nad Al Sheba 10f Dirt RF 0555a). A progressive sort in 1998 before his season was curtailed by an accident at the stalls at Glorious Goodwood, he joined Godolphin after that and raced successfully in Dubai during the winter, including chasing home Altibr in the Dubai Duty Free. He was then off the track for six months, and was a bit disappointing when only third behind Gold Academy in a York Listed event, though he looked as though he would appreciate easier ground.
**S bin Suroor [0-1] Godolphin (from S bin Suroor in UAE [0-1] Mar 1999).*

SPINNER TOY RR 12f 388[8]
4 ch g Seven Hearts - Priory Bay (Petong) 6.6f **(58)**
Form - 8
Record 1999 - 1st:0 2nd:0 3rd:0 Ran:1
Pre1999 - 1st:0 2nd:0 3rd:0 Ran:1
1999 AW 0-1: (10f) (Equi)
Light-framed, currently poor gelding.
**J C Fox [0-2] Miss Sarah-Jane Durman.*

SPINNING STAR BHB 61f **RR 63f** 5188[10]
3 ch f Arazi (USA) 9.2f **(74)** - Queen Midas (Glint of Gold) 9.3f **(66)**
Form - 63540
Record 1999 - 1st:0 2nd:0 3rd:1 Ran:5
Win Prizemoney £0 *Total Prizemoney* £616
1999 Turf 0-5: (10f, 11f, 12f 2, 16f) (g-s, gd 2, g-f, frm)
Average filly. Turf high 67 (began Aug) - 3rd of 6 to Rahayeb (20 Aug Chester 12f gd RF 3790). **C F Wall [0-5] S Fustok.*

SPINNING THE YARN RR 68f 1775[7]
3 b f Barathea (IRE) - Colorspin (FR) (High Top) 10.2f **(67)**
Form - 7
Record 1999 - 1st:0 2nd:0 3rd:0 Ran:1
1999 Turf 0-1: (10f) (gd)
Tall, currently average filly.
**Sir Michael Stoute [0-1] Helena Springfield Ltd.*

SPIRIT OF KHAMBANI (IRE) RR 52f 4806[3]
2 ch f Indian Ridge 7.6f **(74)** - Khambani (IRE) **(68f)** (Royal Academy (USA))
Form - 03
Record 1999 - 1st:0 2nd:0 3rd:1 Ran:2
Win Prizemoney £0 *Total Prizemoney* £528
1999 Turf 0-2: (6f, 7f) (sft, frm)
Currently fair filly. Turf high 52. **M Johnston [0-2] M P Burke.*

SPIRIT OF LIGHT (IRE) BHB 70f **RR 74f** 4994[5]
2 b c Unblest - Light Thatch (Thatch (USA)) 9.8f **(62)**
Form - 7285
Record 1999 - 1st:0 2nd:1 3rd:0 Ran:4
Win Prizemoney £0 *Total Prizemoney* £1,095
1999 Turf 0-4: (7f 2, 8f 2) (g-s, gd 2, g-f)
Above-average colt. Turf high 74 (began Spt) - 2nd of 12 to Sandmason (20 Spt Kempton 8f g-s RF 4430).
**M R Channon [0-4] Equality Racing.*

SPIRIT OF LOVE (USA) BHB 105f99a **RR 108f 99a** 4917[14]
4 ch c Trempolino (USA) 11.9f **(77)** - Dream Mary (USA) (Marfa (USA)) 14.9f **(73)**
Form - 4880
Record 1999 - 1st:0 2nd:0 3rd:0 Ran:4
Pre1999 - 1st:5 2nd:1 3rd:3 Ran:12
Win Prizemoney £104,805 *Total Prizemoney* £110,220
Wins * 1998 Oct Newmar (GD) H 18f 91 112+ <
* 1998 Spt Doncas (GD) H 14.6f 91 99
* 1998 Aug Ascot (G-F) H 16.2f 83 90
* 1998 May Doncas (G-F) H 14.6f 77 81
* 1998 *Jan Southw (STD) 11f 70*
1999 Turf 0-4: (16f 2, 17f, 20f) (gd, g-f 2, frm)
Scopey, Pattern-class colt, effective 16 to 18f, acts on gd to g-f, excels at Doncaster and Ascot. Turf high 108 (1st run) - 4th of 9 getting 3lb from Celeric (28 Apr Ascot 16f g-f RF 0897). Consistent. Won five times in 1998, and there was no quibbling with his runaway win in the Cesarewitch. He ran well on his 1999 reappearance in the Sagaro at Ascot, despite failing to handle the home turn, something he did when winning at that track the previous season. He was disappointing afterwards in good company, but had something of a confidence booster when scoring at odds on in Germany late in the year. **M Johnston [5-16] A W Robinson.*

SPIRIT OF TENBY (IRE) BHB 67f **RR 72f** 5124[10]
2 b g Tenby 10.4f **(76)** - Asturiana (Julio Mariner) 7.2f **(57)**
Form - 35500
Record 1999 - 1st:0 2nd:0 3rd:1 Ran:5
Win Prizemoney £0 *Total Prizemoney* £332
1999 Turf 0-5: (7f 3, 8f 2) (gd 2, frm 3)
Above-average gelding. Turf high 72 (1st run) - 3rd of 15 giving 5lb to Elegia Prima (24 Jun Salisbury 7f frm RF 2278).
**S Dow [0-5] P & S Lever Partners.*

SPIRIT OF THE NILE (FR) BHB 62f57a **RR 67f 57a** 3840[7]
4 b f Generous (IRE) 11.5f **(82)** - Egyptale (Crystal Glitters (USA)) 11.3f **(79)**
Form - 14227
Record 1999 - 1st:1 2nd:2 3rd:0 Ran:5
Pre1999 - 1st:0 2nd:0 3rd:0 Ran:3
Win Prizemoney £3,468 *Total Prizemoney* £5,755
Wins * 1999 *Jan Lingfi (STD) 13f 55* <
1999 Turf 0-3: (12f, 13f, 16f) (g-f, frm 2) 1999 AW 1-2: (13f 1-1, 16f) (Equi 1-2)
Workmanlike, average filly, has worn blinkers. Turf high 67 (began Jly). AW high 58. **P F I Cole [1-8] M Arbib.*

SPITZBERGEN BHB 73f **RR 75df** 4597[13]
3 ch g Polar Falcon (USA) 9f **(74)** - Soba (Most Secret) 7.1f **(58)**
Form - 65226860
Record 1999 - 1st:0 2nd:2 3rd:0 Ran:8
Pre1999 - 1st:2 2nd:0 3rd:0 Ran:3
Win Prizemoney £6,637 *Total Prizemoney* £9,197
Wins * 1998 Nov Bright (SFT) H 8f 77 82 <
* 1998 Oct Folkes (G-S) 7f 76
1999 Turf 0-8: (8f 2, 10f 4, 11f, 12f) (gd 3, g-f 2, frm 3)
Workmanlike, above-average gelding, effective 7 to 11f, acts on g-s to frm, best on g-s, likes tight tracks. Turf high 78 - 2nd of 6 giving 7lb to Chicodove (31 May Redcar 11f frm RF 1607). He has put in some contrasting efforts last season and proved somewhat difficult to predict. **M Johnston [2-11] Brian Yeardley Continental Ltd.*

SPLASH OUT (USA) BHB 82f **RR 77f** 3698[17]
2 b c Prized (USA) - Splash Em Baby (CAN) (Bucksplasher (USA)) 10.3f **(75)**
Form - 52310
Record 1999 - 1st:1 2nd:1 3rd:1 Ran:5
Win Prizemoney £2,862 *Total Prizemoney* £4,982
Wins * 1999 Aug Ayr (G-F) 7f 77 <
1999 Turf 1-5: (6f, 7f 1-4) (gd, g-f 2, frm 1-2)
Above-average colt. Turf high 77 - 2nd of 8 getting 14lb from

Sarafan (3 Jly Beverley 7f gd RF 2517) - also 1st of 5 from F-Zero (10 Aug Ayr RF 3491). **M Johnston [1-5] David Abell.*

SPLIT THE ACES (IRE) BHB 44f58a RR 35f 58a 3871[8]

3 gr g Balla Cove - Hazy Lady (Habitat) 9.4f **(70)**
Form - 0283100008
Record 1999 - 1st:1 2nd:1 3rd:1 Ran:9
Pre1999 - 1st:0 2nd:0 3rd:0 Ran:4
Win Prizemoney £2,332 *Total Prizemoney* £3,438
Wins * **1999** May Bath (GD) C 5.1f 61 <
1999 Turf 1-9: (5f 1-3, 6f 4, 7f, 8f) (sft, g-s, gd 1-3, g-f 2, frm, hrd)
Neat, very moderate gelding, effective 5 to 6f, acts on gd, has worn blinkers. Turf high 61 (1st run) - 2nd of 16 to Golden Syrup (8 Apr Leicester 6f gd RF 0621) - also 1st of 10 giving 5lb to Mammas F-C (21 May Bath RF 1367).
**R J Hodges [1-9] Ron Osborne (from R Hannon [0-4] Dec 1998).*

SPOKANE (IRE) RR 92f 5090a[3]

3 b g Indian Ridge 7.6f **(74)** - Jaldi (IRE) (Nordico (USA)) 6.5f **(62)**
Form - 521323
1999 Turf 1-6: (6f 1-1, 7f 3, 8f 2) (hvy, sft 1-1, g-s 2, g-f 2)
Useful gelding, effective 7 to 8f, best at 7f, acts on hvy to g-s, best on g-s. Turf high 92 - 3rd of 6 giving 2lb to Thats Logic (23 Oct Leopardstown 8f g-s RF 5090a).
**M J Grassick in IRE [1-6] Albert Finney.*

SPONDULICKS (IRE) BHB 32f42a RR 33f 42a 615[20]

5 b g Silver Kite (USA) 10.2f **(51)** - Greek Music (Tachypous) 8.6f **(55)**
Form - 0
Record 1999 - 1st:0 2nd:0 3rd:0 Ran:1
Pre1999 - 1st:0 2nd:4 3rd:3 Ran:24
Win Prizemoney £0 *Total Prizemoney* £4,722
1999 Turf 0-1: (12f) (g-f)
Very moderate gelding, has worn blinkers. Becoming disappointing.
**B P J Baugh [0-14] Mrs Joan Chrimes (from R Hannon [0-12] Spt 1996).*

SPONTANEITY (IRE) BHB 60f70a RR 55f 70a 3254[9]

3 ch f Shalford (IRE) 7.8f **(63)** - Mariyda (IRE) (Vayrann) 9.7f **(74)**
Form - 080
Record 1999 - 1st:0 2nd:0 3rd:0 Ran:3
Pre1999 - 1st:1 2nd:0 3rd:1 Ran:6
Win Prizemoney £3,805 *Total Prizemoney* £4,204
Wins * 1998 Aug Thirsk (G-F) 7f 78 <
1999 Turf 0-3: (8f, 10f, 12f) (gd 2, frm)
Scopey, fair filly, effective 6 to 7f, acts on frm to hrd, has worn blinkers. Turf high 55. Consistent. **P D Evans [1-9] Colin Booth.*

SPOONFUL OF SUGAR BHB 78f RR 71f 696[11]

3 b f Sabrehill (USA) 8.5f **(64)** - Pacific Gull (USA) (Storm Bird (CAN)) 10.3f **(74)**
Form - 0
Record 1999 - 1st:0 2nd:0 3rd:0 Ran:1
Pre1999 - 1st:0 2nd:1 3rd:0 Ran:2
Win Prizemoney £0 *Total Prizemoney* £1,010
1999 Turf 0-1: (7f) (gd)
Scopey, above-average filly. (DEAD)
**C A Cyzer [0-1] W J Gredley (from B W Hills [0-2] Nov 1998).*

SPORTING GESTURE BHB 75f RR 73+f 4762[9]

2 ch g Safawan 6.6f **(60)** - Polly Packer (Reform) 8.9f **(62)**
Form - 7566010
Record 1999 - 1st:1 2nd:0 3rd:0 Ran:7
Win Prizemoney £3,072 *Total Prizemoney* £3,072
Wins * **1999** Spt Catter (G-F) H 7f 65 73+ <
1999 Turf 1-7: (5f, 6f 3, 7f 1-1, 8f 2) (gd, g-f 3, frm 1-2, hrd)
Above-average gelding, effective 7f, acts on frm. Turf high 73 (began Jly) - 1st of 15 giving 3lb to Dispol Jazz (18 Spt Catterick RF 4401). **M W Easterby [1-7] Brig Racing Club.*

SPORTING LAD (USA) BHB 105f RR 103df 5055[5]

3 b c Danzig (USA) 8.1f **(88)** - Lydara (USA) (Alydar (USA)) 9.1f **(76)**
Form - 510405
Record 1999 - 1st:1 2nd:0 3rd:0 Ran:6
Pre1999 - 1st:1 2nd:2 3rd:0 Ran:5
Win Prizemoney £21,968 *Total Prizemoney* £30,120
Wins * **1999** May Cheste (G-F) H 7.6f 96 101 <
* 1998 Aug Cheste (GD) 7f 89
1999 Turf 1-6: (7f 4, 8f 1-2) (gd 4, g-f 1-2)
Scopey, very useful colt, effective 7 to 8f, acts on gd to g-f. Turf high 103 - 4th of 8 getting 3lb from Trans Island (19 Spt Newbury 7f gd RF 4416) - also 1st of 15 giving 17lb to Schnitzel (4 May Chester RF 1026). He belied the idea that he was just a handicapper when running very well against Trans Island in a listed race at Newbury. He looks very much suited by a turning track, as both of his victories to date have been at Chester. **P F I Cole [2-11] M Arbib.*

SPORTY MO (IRE) BHB 62f68a RR 71f 68a 4939[1]

2 b c Namaqualand (USA) - Miss Fortunate
Form - 160501
Record 1999 - 1st:2 2nd:0 3rd:0 Ran:6
Win Prizemoney £3,879 *Total Prizemoney* £3,879
Wins * **1999** *Oct Southw (STD) S 7f 72 <*
* **1999** *May Southw (STD) S 6f 70+*
1999 Turf 0-3: (7f 2, 8f) (g-s, gd, g-f) 1999 AW 2-3: (6f 1-2, 7f 1-1) (Fibr 2-3)
Above-average colt, effective 6 to 7f, - acts on Fibr, has worn blinkers. Turf high 71 (began Jly). AW high 72 - 1st of 14 giving 11lb to Gymcrak Firebird (18 Oct Southwell RF 4939) - also 1st of 7 from Fingers Henry (17 May Southwell RF 1283). He was expected to make a winning debut in a six-furlongs seller on the Southwell Fibresand in May and duly did so, but did not show much afterwards until taking a similar event over a furlong further back at Southwell in October. **K R Burke [2-6] Maurice Charge.*

SPORTY SPICE (IRE) BHB 23f27a RR 33f 27a 3674[14]

4 b f Indian Ridge 7.6f **(74)** - Intrinsic (Troy) 10.4f **(68)**
Form - 25600
Record 1999 - 1st:0 2nd:1 3rd:0 Ran:5
Pre1999 - 1st:0 2nd:0 3rd:0 Ran:11
Win Prizemoney £0 *Total Prizemoney* £426
1999 Turf 0-2: (10f, 11f) (gd, frm) 1999 AW 0-3: (8f, 11f, 12f) (Fibr 3)
Light-framed, very moderate filly, has worn blinkers. Turf high 21 (began Jly). AW high 33. Consistent.
**J L Harris [0-15] Dr C W Ashpole (from Mrs J R Ramsden [0-2] Jun 1998).*

SPOTTED EAGLE BHB 48f41a RR 25?f 41a 3295[P]

6 ch g Risk Me (FR) 8f **(53)** - Egnoussa (Swing Easy (USA)) 6.5f **(55)**
Form - 00P
Record 1999 - 1st:0 2nd:0 3rd:0 Ran:3
Pre1999 - 1st:2 2nd:2 3rd:1 Ran:24
Win Prizemoney £5,608 *Total Prizemoney* £8,169
Wins 1997 Jly Catter (G-F) S 6f 46
1996 Apr Folkes (FRM) 6f 72 <
1999 Turf 0-3: (5f 2, 6f) (g-f, frm 2)
Very moderate gelding, effective 5 to 6f, best at 6f, acts on g-f to frm, best on frm. Turf high 25 (began Jly). Becoming disappointing. **D Nicholls [0-14] W G Swiers (from Martyn Wane [1-6] Jly 1997).*

SPREE VISION BHB 64f RR 75f 4817[7]

3 b c Suave Dancer (USA) 10.7f **(68)** - Regent's Folly (IRE) (Touching Wood (USA)) 8.2f **(55)**
Form - 672756077
Record 1999 - 1st:0 2nd:1 3rd:0 Ran:9
Pre1999 - 1st:1 2nd:0 3rd:0 Ran:3
Win Prizemoney £2,717 *Total Prizemoney* £4,206
Wins * 1998 Oct Newcas (SFT) 8f 82 <
1999 Turf 0-9: (8f, 10f 4, 12f 4) (gd 3, g-f 5, frm)
Light-framed, above-average colt, effective 8 to 12f, best at 12f, acts on sft to frm, has worn blinkers. Turf high 81 - 2nd of 9 getting 12lb from Diaghilef (29 May Doncaster 12f frm RF 1562).
**S C Williams [1-12] S Demanuele.*

SPRING BLADE RR 78[8]

7 b g Jester 8.5f **(43)** - Runfawit Pet (Welsh Saint) 7.6f **(64)**
Form - 08
Record 1999 - 1st:0 2nd:0 3rd:0 Ran:1
Pre1999 - 1st:0 2nd:0 3rd:0 Ran:1
1999 AW 0-1: (13f) (Equi)
Formerly very poor gelding. **L A Dace [0-3] Luke Dace.*

SPRINGER BHB 46f RR 54f 3459[22]

3 b g Cyrano de Bergerac 7.3f **(58)** - Spring Collection (Tina's Pet) 6.8f **(59)**
Form - 00
Record 1999 - 1st:0 2nd:0 3rd:0 Ran:2
Pre1999 - 1st:0 2nd:0 3rd:0 Ran:3
1999 Turf 0-2: (6f 2) (sft, frm)
Fair gelding. (DEAD) **J L Eyre [0-5] Watglea Racing.*

SPRING PURSUIT BHB 59f RR 78f 5197[2]

3 b g Rudimentary (USA) 8.2f **(66)** - Pursuit of Truth (USA) (Irish River (FR)) 8.6f **(78)**
Form - 87345703828111162
Record 1999 - 1st:4 2nd:2 3rd:2 Ran:17
Pre1999 - 1st:1 2nd:0 3rd:0 Ran:4
Win Prizemoney £33,497 *Total Prizemoney* £37,668
Wins * 1999 Oct Lingfi (G-F) H 10f 67 75
*** 1999** Oct Windso (G-S) H 10f 62 73+
*** 1999** Oct York (SFT) H 8.9f 62 65
*** 1999** Spt Bright (SFT) H 10f 56 59
1998 Jun Warwic (GD) 6f 85 <
1999 Turf 4-17: (6f, 7f 5, 8f 3, 9f 1-1, 10f 3-6, 12f) (g-s 1-1, gd 1-7, g-f 2-4, frm 5)
Neat, above-average gelding, effective 6 to 10f, best at 10f, acts on gd to g-f, best on gd, has worn blinkers, likes left handed tracks, likes tight tracks, excels at Windsor. Turf high 78 - 2nd of 20 giving 2lb to Philatelic Lady (4 Nov Windsor 10f gd RF 5197). Well placed to land a four-timer in the autumn, and might have more improvement to come.
**R J Price [4-14] E G Bevan (from R J Hodges [0-3] Jun 1999).*

SPRINGS BHB 38f RR 48f 4454[13]

3 b f Anshan 8.2f **(63)** - College Supreme (Mansingh (USA)) 7.4f **(55)**
Form - 80
Record 1999 - 1st:0 2nd:0 3rd:0 Ran:2
Pre1999 - 1st:0 2nd:0 3rd:0 Ran:5
1999 Turf 0-2: (10f, 11f) (sft, g-f)
Leggy, moderate filly. Turf high 34 (began Aug).
**J L Spearing [0-7] Abbots Salford Carav Park.*

SPRINGS ETERNAL BHB 70f72a RR 71f 72a 4820[15]

2 b f Salse (USA) 10.9f **(71)** - Corn Futures (Nomination) 7f **(60)**
Form - 08420
Record 1999 - 1st:0 2nd:1 3rd:0 Ran:5
Win Prizemoney £0 *Total Prizemoney* £1,567
1999 Turf 0-5: (6f 2, 7f, 8f 2) (g-s, gd, g-f 2, frm)
Above-average filly. Turf high 71 (began Aug) - 2nd of 14 giving 2lb to Noble Pasao (26 Spt Musselburgh 8f gd RF 4575).
**Sir Mark Prescott [0-5] Rowles Nicholson.*

SPRINGS NOBLEQUEST BHB 54f RR 54f 3678[13]

3 b f Noble Patriarch 12.2f **(43)** - Primum Tempus **(42df)** (Primo Dominie) 6.2f **(80)**
Form - 0600520830
Record 1999 - 1st:0 2nd:1 3rd:1 Ran:10
Pre1999 - 1st:1 2nd:0 3rd:2 Ran:6
Win Prizemoney £3,113 *Total Prizemoney* £5,551
Wins * 1998 May Carlis (G-S) 5f 65 <
1999 Turf 0-10: (6f 5, 7f 3, 8f 2) (gd 2, frm 8)
Leggy, fair filly, effective 5f, acts on gd, prefers right handed tracks. Turf high 54. **T D Easterby [1-16] Springs Equestrian Ltd.*

SPRING SONG BHB 50f RR 55f 4537[9]

2 b f Petong 7.6f **(58)** - Naturally Fresh (Thatching) 8f **(66)**
Form - 05050500
Record 1999 - 1st:0 2nd:0 3rd:0 Ran:8
1999 Turf 0-8: (5f 3, 7f 3, 8f, 9f) (gd 4, g-f, frm 3)
Fair filly, has worn blinkers. Turf high 55.
**M E Sowersby [0-8] Racing Ladies.*

SPRINGTIME LADY BHB 60f59a RR 63f 59a 4329[9]

3 ch f Desert Dirham (USA) - Affaire de Coeur (Imperial Fling (USA)) 7.1f **(58)**
Form - 08250040
Record 1999 - 1st:0 2nd:1 3rd:0 Ran:8
Win Prizemoney £0 *Total Prizemoney* £1,581
1999 Turf 0-8: (6f 3, 7f, 8f 4) (gd, g-f 3, frm 4)
Leggy, average filly, effective 6f, acts on g-f. Turf high 67 - 2nd of 10 getting 5lb from Rogue Spirit (26 May Folkestone 6f g-f RF 1489). Consistent. **S Dow [0-8] Graham Brown.*

SPRING TO GLORY BHB 18f RR 12f 2913[15]

12 b g Teenoso (USA) 10.5f **(62)** - English Spring (USA) (Grey Dawn II) 11.1f **(72)**
Form - 60
Record 1999 - 1st:0 2nd:0 3rd:0 Ran:2
Pre1999 - 1st:1 2nd:2 3rd:0 Ran:19
Win Prizemoney £2,807 *Total Prizemoney* £4,373
1999 Turf 0-2: (14f, 17f) (frm, hrd)
Poor gelding, has worn blinkers. Turf high 12. Becoming disappointing.
**P Hayward [3-35] A J Byrne (from R J Hodges [0-10] Nov 1991).*

SPRINGWOOD RR 53f 2890[P]

4 b g Green Desert (USA) 7.8f **(78)** - Prosperous Lady (Prince Tenderfoot (USA)) 9f **(61)**
Form - 56404P
Record 1999 - 1st:0 2nd:0 3rd:0 Ran:6
Win Prizemoney £0 *Total Prizemoney* £422
1999 Turf 0-5: (7f, 8f 4) (gd 3, g-f, frm) 1999 AW 0-1: (7f) (Fibr)
Fair gelding, effective 8f, acts on gd. Turf high 53 - 4th of 18 giving 13lb to Komlucky (5 Jly Ripon 8f gd RF 2565).
**R A Fahey [0-6] Mrs Doreen Swinburn.*

SPRY BHB 85f RR 79+f 3771[8]

3 b f Suave Dancer (USA) 10.7f **(68)** - Sandy Island (Mill Reef (USA)) 10.5f **(78)**
Form - 18
Record 1999 - 1st:1 2nd:0 3rd:0 Ran:2
Win Prizemoney £4,191 *Total Prizemoney* £4,191
Wins * 1999 Jly Newmar (G-F) 12f 79 <
1999 Turf 1-2: (12f 1-2) (gd, frm 1-1)
Well made, currently above-average filly. Turf high 79 (1st run) (began Jly) - 1st of 4 getting 5lb from Williamshakespeare (23 Jly Newmarket RF 3064).
**H R A Cecil [1-2] Exors of the late Lord Howard de Walden.*

SPUNKIE BHB 89f RR 87f 4917[21]

6 ch g Jupiter Island 10.4f **(57)** - Super Sol (Rolfe (USA)) 12.1f **(65)**
Form - 500210
Record 1999 - 1st:1 2nd:1 3rd:0 Ran:6
Pre1999 - 1st:2 2nd:0 3rd:1 Ran:5
Win Prizemoney £28,929 *Total Prizemoney* £45,600
Wins * 1999 Spt Newbur (G-S) H 16f 87 87+ <
* 1998 Spt Ascot (GD) H 16.2f 76 76
* 1998 Jly Salisb (GD) 14.1f 73
1999 Turf 1-6: (16f 1-3, 17f, 19f, 20f) (gd 1-3, g-f 3)
Useful gelding, effective 16f, acts on gd to g-f, best on gd. Turf high 87 - 1st of 4 giving 19lb to Tramline (19 Spt Newbury RF 4420). Successful at Newbury in September, having previously finished second in a German Listed race, he is a tough individual who clearly stays very well. **R F JohnsonHoughton [4-15] Jim Short.*

SPY (IRE) BHB 76f RR 76f 2078[5]

3 b c Mac's Imp (USA) 5.6f **(54)** - Mystery Bid (Auction Ring (USA)) 8.6f **(65)**
Form - 58225
Record 1999 - 1st:0 2nd:2 3rd:0 Ran:5
Pre1999 - 1st:1 2nd:1 3rd:0 Ran:5
Win Prizemoney £2,560 *Total Prizemoney* £8,002
Wins * 1998 Aug Mussel (G-F) 7.1f 84 <
1999 Turf 0-5: (7f, 8f 3, 10f) (gd, g-f 2, frm, hrd)
Workmanlike, above-average colt, effective 6 to 7f, acts on gd. Turf high 76. **C W Thornton [1-10] Guy Reed.*

SPY KNOLL BHB 72f RR 73f 3827[8]

5 b g Shirley Heights 12.1f **(76)** - Garden Pink (FR) (Bellypha) 9.8f **(73)**
Form - 208
Record 1999 - 1st:0 2nd:1 3rd:0 Ran:3
Pre1999 - 1st:1 2nd:1 3rd:3 Ran:10
Win Prizemoney £3,798 *Total Prizemoney* £10,535
Wins 1997 Spt Cheste (GD) 13.4f 83 <
1999 Turf 0-3: (14f 2, 16f) (gd, frm 2)
Above-average gelding, has worn blinkers. Turf high 73.
**Mrs L Richards [0-5] M K George (from Sir Michael Stoute [1-10] Spt*

1997).

SPYRO (IRE) RR 4516a[2]

2 ch c Thatching 7.8f **(69)** - Nordic Success (IRE) (Nordico (USA)) 6.5f **(62)**

Form - 32

Record 1999 - 1st:0 2nd:1 3rd:1 Ran:2

Win Prizemoney £0 *Total Prizemoney* £4,520

1999 Turf 0-2: (8f 2) (g-s, gd)

Currently very poor colt. (began Jly) - 2nd of 10 giving 3lb to Fairy Sensazione (18 Spt San Siro 8f g-s RF 4516a).

**A Mataresi in ITY [0-1] (from M Quinlan [0-1] Jly 1999).*

SQUANDAMANIA BHB 30f RR 35f 4912[9]

6 b g Ela-Mana-Mou 12.7f **(72)** - Garden Pink (FR) (Bellypha) 9.8f **(73)**

Form - 400

Record 1999 - 1st:0 2nd:0 3rd:0 Ran:3

Pre1999 - 1st:0 2nd:0 3rd:0 Ran:1

1999 Turf 0-2: (12f 2) (gd 2) 1999 AW 0-1: (12f) (Fibr)

Moderate gelding. Turf high 35 (began Oct).

**J Norton [0-11] J & G Sporting Partners (from P F I Cole [0-1] Nov 1995).*

SQUARE DANCER RR 70f 4879[11]

3 b g Then Again 7.4f **(52)** - Cubist (IRE) (Tate Gallery (USA)) 7.4f **(67)**

Form - 8435212280100

Record 1999 - 1st:2 2nd:3 3rd:1 Ran:13

Pre1999 - 1st:0 2nd:0 3rd:0 Ran:5

Win Prizemoney £5,569 *Total Prizemoney* £9,753

Wins * 1999 Aug Bright (SFT) 6f 70

* 1999 Jun Carlis (G-F) 5.9f 71 <

1999 Turf 2-13: (6f 2-11, 7f, 8f) (g-s 1-1, gd 3, g-f 2, frm 6, hrd 1-1)

Scopey, above-average gelding, effective 6f, acts on g-s to hrd. Turf high 71 - 1st of 9 giving 5lb to Promessa (24 Jun Carlisle RF 2259) - also 1st of 5 from Dolphinelle (18 Aug Brighton RF 3737).

**M Dods [2-13] A Mallen (from Mrs J R Ramsden [0-5] Oct 1998).*

SQUARE MILE MISS (IRE) BHB 40f36a RR 19f 36a 1392[12]

6 b m Last Tycoon 9.4f **(73)** - Call Me Miss (Hello Gorgeous (USA)) 9.7f **(63)**

Form - 720000

Record 1999 - 1st:0 2nd:1 3rd:0 Ran:6

Pre1999 - 1st:2 2nd:2 3rd:2 Ran:24

Win Prizemoney £5,111 *Total Prizemoney* £8,475

Wins * 1998 *Jan Lingfi (STD) H 7f* 35 43 <

* 1998 *Jan Lingfi (STD) H 8f* 35 39

1999 Turf 0-2: (8f, 9f) (g-f, frm) 1999 AW 0-4: (7f, 8f 3) (Equi 3, Fibr)

Poor mare, effective 7 to 8f, best at 8f, - acts on Equi, prefers left handed tracks, favours tight tracks. Turf high 15. AW high 36 - 2nd of 11 getting 13lb from Zimiri (21 Jan Lingfield 8f Equi RF 0135).

**N E Berry [2-14] P Rawson (from P Howling [0-16] Aug 1997).*

SQUIRE CORRIE BHB 48f51a RR 47f 51a 3436[11]

7 b g Distant Relative 7f **(69)** - Fast Car (FR) (Carwhite) 7.2f **(61)**

Form - 0350134605874407000

Record 1999 - 1st:1 2nd:0 3rd:1 Ran:17

Pre1999 - 1st:10 2nd:10 3rd:11 Ran:86

Win Prizemoney £46,265 *Total Prizemoney* £71,199

Wins * 1999 *Feb Lingfi (STD) H 5f* 55 56

* 1997 Jun Ayr (GD) H 5f 71 82

* 1997 Jun York (G-S) H 5f 71 84 <

* 1997 Jun Hamilt (GD) H 5f 71 76

* 1997 May Thirsk (GD) H 5f 69 70

* 1997 *Feb Lingfi (STD) H 6f* 68 69

* 1997 *Feb Wolver (STD) H 5f* 58 63

1996 Spt Salisb (FRM) H 5f 57 63

1996 Aug Sandow (GD) H 5f 57 60

1996 Jly Sandow (G-F) H 5f 55 57

1995 Spt Newmar (GD) H 5f 59 64

1999 Turf 0-7: (5f 6, 6f) (gd 3, g-f 2, frm 2) 1999 AW 1-10: (5f 1-9, 6f) (Equi 1-7, Fibr 3)

Fair gelding, often wears blinkers. Turf high 49. AW high 57. Becoming disappointing. Recent evidence suggests that he is very much on the decline.

**D W Chapman [7-69] JM Chapman (from G Harwood [3-19] Oct 1996).*

STACCATO RR 21f 232[15]

4 b g Forzando 7.2f **(63)** - Fast Car (FR) (Carwhite) 7.2f **(61)**

Form - 0

Record 1999 - 1st:0 2nd:0 3rd:0 Ran:1

Pre1999 - 1st:0 2nd:0 3rd:0 Ran:1

1999 AW 0-1: (11f) (Fibr)

Little account gelding.

**Denys Smith [0-1] Denys Smith (from C W Thornton [0-1] Spt 1998).*

STAFFORD KING (IRE) RR 33f 5021[19]

2 b c Nicolotte - Opening Day (Day Is Done) 6.3f **(67)**

Form - 00

Record 1999 - 1st:0 2nd:0 3rd:0 Ran:2

1999 Turf 0-2: (6f, 7f) (gd, g-f)

Currently very moderate colt. Turf high 33 (began Oct).

**J G M O'Shea [0-2] The Stafford Syndicate.*

STAFFORD PRINCE BHB 52f RR 52f 5024[11]

2 br c Bin Ajwaad (IRE) - Petonellajill **(57f 50a)** (Petong) 6.6f **(58)**

Form - 00600

Record 1999 - 1st:0 2nd:0 3rd:0 Ran:5

1999 Turf 0-5: (5f 2, 6f, 8f 2) (gd, frm 4)

Fair colt, has worn blinkers. Turf high 52 (began Jly).

**J G M O'Shea [0-5] The Stafford Syndicate.*

STAGE WHISPER BHB 65f75a RR 66f 75a 2325[3]

4 b g Alzao (USA) 9.8f **(73)** - Starlet (Teenoso (USA)) 9.9f **(72)**

Form - 703

Record 1999 - 1st:0 2nd:0 3rd:1 Ran:3

Pre1999 - 1st:1 2nd:0 3rd:0 Ran:3

Win Prizemoney £2,659 *Total Prizemoney* £3,605

Wins 1997 *Dec Wolver (STD) 8.5f 67* <

1999 Turf 0-3: (12f, 15f, 18f) (g-f 3)

Workmanlike, average gelding. Turf high 66.

**M D Hammond [0-8] Wetherby Racing Bureau 37 (from Lord Huntingdon [1-3] Jun 1998).*

STAKIS CASINOS BOY (IRE) BHB 49f RR 49?f 1852[8]

5 ch g Magical Wonder (USA) 7.2f **(60)** - Hardiona (FR) (Hard To Beat) 10.1f **(67)**

Form - 88

Record 1999 - 1st:0 2nd:0 3rd:0 Ran:2

Pre1999 - 1st:1 2nd:1 3rd:0 Ran:7

Win Prizemoney £3,420 *Total Prizemoney* £4,771

Wins 1997 May Newcas (G-F) 10.1f 71 <

1999 Turf 0-2: (10f 2) (g-s, gd)

Moderate gelding, has worn blinkers. Turf high 35. Becoming disappointing.

**B Ellison [1-4] Ashley Carr Racing (from M Johnston [1-7] Oct 1997).*

STAND ASIDE BHB 50f RR 40f 2724[9]

3 b g In The Wings 11.2f **(77)** - Honourable Sheba (USA) (Roberto (USA)) 10f **(76)**

Form - 7070

Record 1999 - 1st:0 2nd:0 3rd:0 Ran:4

Pre1999 - 1st:0 2nd:0 3rd:0 Ran:1

1999 Turf 0-4: (8f, 10f, 14f, 16f) (gd 2, g-f, frm)

Tall, moderate gelding. Turf high 59. **Lady Herries [0-5] Chris Hardy.*

STAND BY RR 48f 5163[10]

2 b f Missed Flight - Ma Rivale (Last Tycoon) 8.5f **(62)**

Form - 00

Record 1999 - 1st:0 2nd:0 3rd:0 Ran:2

1999 Turf 0-2: (5f, 7f) (g-s, gd)

Currently moderate filly. Turf high 48 (began Oct).

**T D Easterby [0-2] D A Brindley.*

STAND TALL BHB 65f80a RR 62f 80a 5143[18]

7 b g Unfuwain (USA) 11.4f **(74)** - Antilla (Averof) 8.2f **(62)**

Form - 67043770560

Record 1999 - 1st:0 2nd:0 3rd:1 Ran:11

Pre1999 - 1st:10 2nd:8 3rd:5 Ran:46

Win Prizemoney £38,840 *Total Prizemoney* £60,113

Wins * 1998 Oct Leices (SFT) H 6f 78 84 <

* 1997 Spt Nottin (GD) H 6.1f 74 78

* 1997 Spt Pontef (G-S) H 6f 68 71

* 1997 Aug Folkes (G-F) H 6f 61 66

* 1997 May Bright (FRM) 7f 61

1996 Jly Hamilt (GD) H 6f 56 60

1996	*Mar Lingfi*	*(STD)*	*H*	*6f*	*69*	*76*
1996	*Feb Southw*	*(STD)*	*H*	*6f*	*59*	*64*
1996	*Jan Southw*	*(STD)*	*H*	*6f*	*55*	*54*
1995	*Nov Lingfi*	*(STD)*	*H*	*6f*	*46*	*50*

1999 Turf 0-11: (6f 10, 7f) (sft, gd 4, g-f 4, frm 2)

Above-average gelding, effective 6f, acts on sft. Turf high 78.

**Lady Herries [5-33] Chris Hardy (from C W Thornton [5-24] Spt 1996).*

STANLEY WIGFIELD (USA) BHB 46f47a **RR 38f 47a** 4464a[13]

3 b c Woodman (USA) 9.7f **(77)** - Las Meninas (IRE) **(110f)** (Glenstal (USA)) 10.1f **(64)**

Form - 50484370

Record 1999 - 1st:0 2nd:0 3rd:1 Ran:8
Pre1999 - 1st:0 2nd:0 3rd:0 Ran:2

Win Prizemoney £0 *Total Prizemoney* £324

1999 Turf 0-3: (11f, 12f 2) (gd 3) 1999 AW 0-5: (6f, 7f, 8f 2, 12f) (Fibr 5)

Small, fair colt, effective 12f, - acts on Fibr, favours left handed tracks, favours tight tracks. Turf high 38. AW high 58 - 3rd of 17 getting 12lb from Sunny Chief (6 May Southwell 12f Fibr RF 1066).

**L McAteer in IRE [0-1] M P Burke (from D Nicholls [0-7] May 1999).*

STANOTT (IRE) BHB 109f **RR 105f** 4892a[2]

4 b c Mukaddamah (USA) 7.6f **(74)** - Seme de Lys (USA) (Slew O' Gold (USA)) 8f **(75)**

Form - 321532

Record 1999 - 1st:1 2nd:2 3rd:2 Ran:6
Pre1999 - 1st:2 2nd:1 3rd:0 Ran:6

Win Prizemoney £47,557 *Total Prizemoney* £93,471

Wins * **1999** Jun San Si (GD) G2 8f 105 <
* 1998 May Capann (G-F) L 8f 93
* 1998 Apr Folkes (SFT) 7f 78

1999 Turf 1-6: (7f, 8f 1-3, 10f 2) (g-s 3, gd 1-3)

Pattern-class colt, effective 7 to 10f, best at 8f, acts on g-s to gd, best on gd, likes San Siro. Turf high 105 - 1st of 8 from Accento (6 Jun San Siro RF 1906b). A winner in Pattern company in Italy, he would not be good enough in that grade in this country.

**L M Cumani [3-12].*

STARBOARD TACK (FR) BHB 68f **RR 68f** 4583[4]

3 b f Saddlers' Hall (IRE) 10.5f **(65)** - North Wind (IRE) (Lomond (USA)) 8.8f **(65)**

Form - 733354

Record 1999 - 1st:0 2nd:0 3rd:3 Ran:6
Pre1999 - 1st:0 2nd:0 3rd:0 Ran:1

Win Prizemoney £0 *Total Prizemoney* £1,741

1999 Turf 0-6: (10f 3, 11f, 12f 2) (gd 3, g-f 2, hrd)

Well made, average filly, effective 10 to 12f, acts on g-f to hrd, prefers tight tracks. Turf high 73.

**B W Hills [0-7] H R H Princess Michael of Kent.*

STAR CAST (IRE) **RR 69f** 4402[12]

2 ch f In The Wings 11.2f **(77)** - Thank One's Stars (Alzao (USA)) 7.1f **(68)**

Form - 8570

Record 1999 - 1st:0 2nd:0 3rd:0 Ran:4

1999 Turf 0-4: (7f 4) (g-f, frm 3)

Average filly. Turf high 69.

**Major D N Chappell [0-4] Mrs G C Maxwell.*

STAR DYNASTY (IRE) **RR 73+f** 5157[4]

2 b c Bering 9.6f **(80)** - Siwaayib (Green Desert (USA)) 8.6f **(78)**

Form - 4

Record 1999 - 1st:0 2nd:0 3rd:0 Ran:1

Win Prizemoney £0 *Total Prizemoney* £233

1999 Turf 0-1: (7f) (frm)

Currently above-average colt.

**E A L Dunlop [0-1] Maktoum Al Maktoum.*

STAR FANTASY (USA) BHB 55a **RR 68f 55a** 2622[7]

4 ch g Sky Classic (CAN) 10f **(83)** - Wanda's Dream (USA) (Miswaki (USA)) 9f **(81)**

Form - 237

Record 1999 - 1st:0 2nd:1 3rd:1 Ran:3
Pre1999 - 1st:0 2nd:0 3rd:0 Ran:1

Win Prizemoney £0 *Total Prizemoney* £1,236

1999 AW 0-3: (9f, 10f, 12f) (Equi, Fibr 2)

Scopey, average gelding, has broken blood-vessels. AW high 58.

**D G Bridgwater [1-6] S J Dougall (from P F I Cole [0-1] Aug 1998).*

STARLIGHT BHB 64f **RR 75f** 5158[5]

2 b f King's Signet (USA) 7f **(51)** - Petinata (Petong) 6.6f **(58)**

Form - 08545

Record 1999 - 1st:0 2nd:0 3rd:0 Ran:5

Win Prizemoney £0 *Total Prizemoney* £252

1999 Turf 0-5: (6f, 7f 2, 8f 2) (g-s, gd 2, frm 2)

Above-average filly. Turf high 75.

**E A L Dunlop [0-4] Mrs Mollie Cooper Webster (from N A Graham [0-1] Jun 1999).*

STARLINER (IRE) BHB 40f26a **RR 30f 26a** 2057[8]

4 ch f Statoblest 6.4f **(63)** - Dancing Line (High Line) 10.3f **(70)**

Form - 0003808

Record 1999 - 1st:0 2nd:0 3rd:1 Ran:6
Pre1999 - 1st:0 2nd:1 3rd:1 Ran:17

Win Prizemoney £0 *Total Prizemoney* £1,549

1999 Turf 0-4: (8f 2, 9f 2) (gd, g-f 2, hrd) 1999 AW 0-2: (8f, 11f) (Fibr 2)

Leggy, very moderate filly, effective 8 to 9f, acts on gd to frm, has worn blinkers, likes left handed tracks, likes tight tracks. Turf high 45 (1st run) - 3rd of 15 getting 10lb from Ollie's Chuckle (29 Apr Redcar 9f gd RF 0917). AW high 11. Inconsistent.

**M Brittain [0-23] Northgate Lodgers.*

STARLYTE GIRL (IRE) BHB 88f **RR 79f** 3995[9]

2 b f Fairy King (USA) 7.7f **(75)** - Blushing Storm (USA) (Blushing Groom (FR)) 10.3f **(76)**

Form - 2310

Record 1999 - 1st:1 2nd:1 3rd:1 Ran:4

Win Prizemoney £4,045 *Total Prizemoney* £6,593

Wins * **1999** Aug Warwic (GD) 7.7f 78 <

1999 Turf 1-4: (6f 2, 7f, 8f 1-1) (gd 1-1, g-f, frm 2)

Above-average filly. Turf high 79 (1st run) (began Jly) - 2nd of 6 getting 11lb from Elaflaak (16 Jly Newbury 6f frm RF 2874) - also 1st of 9 from Idolize (13 Aug Warwick RF 3629). She has made the frame behind some decent fillies, and appreciated the step up to seven when scoring at Warwick. Never got in a blow in the Prestige Stakes on her latest start, although that was against very classy performers. **R Hannon [1-4] Mohamed Suhail.*

STAR MANAGER (USA) BHB 36f54a **RR 33f 54a** 5153[8]

9 b g Lyphard (USA) 10.6f **(75)** - Angel Clare (FR) (Mill Reef (USA)) 10.5f **(78)**

Form - 760070040008

Record 1999 - 1st:0 2nd:0 3rd:0 Ran:11
Pre1999 - 1st:6 2nd:1 3rd:5 Ran:47

Win Prizemoney £44,761 *Total Prizemoney* £75,213

Wins 1998 Jun Epsom (GD) C 8.5f 71
1996 Apr Sandow (GD) H 8.1f 78 89 <
1995 Apr Newbur (GD) H 8f 78 82

1999 Turf 0-9: (10f 7, 12f, 15f) (hvy, gd 3, g-f, frm 4) 1999 AW 0-2: (10f, 12f) (Equi 2)

Moderate gelding, effective 9f, acts on g-f, has worn blinkers. Turf high 60. AW high 40. Becoming disappointing.

**R C Spicer [0-16] R Foster (from P F I Cole [6-51] Aug 1998).*

STAR OF AKKAR **RR 116f** 4780a[9]

3 b f Distant Relative 7f **(69)** - Donna Star (Stately Don (USA))

Form - 212110

1999 Turf 3-5: (9f 2-3, 10f 1-1, 11f) (sft, g-s, gd 3-3)

High-class filly, effective 9 to 11f, acts on g-s to gd, best on gd. Turf high 116 - 1st of 4 giving 3lb to Visionnaire (16 Jly Chantilly RF 3039a) - also 1st of 9 from Sage Et Jolie (21 Aug Deauville RF 3928a). A very decent French-trained filly, she won three times at Group Three level last season as well as chasing Daryaba home in the Prix de Diane Hermes. She ran poorly in the Prix de l'Opera on her final start, but unseated her rider and fell before the start which cannot have done her any good at all.

**J-C Rouget in FR [3-6].*

STAR OF THE COURSE (USA) BHB 81f **RR 81f** 5133[3]

4 b f Theatrical 11.5f **(78)** - Water Course (USA) (Irish River (FR)) 8.6f **(78)**

Form - 311133

Record 1999 - 1st:3 2nd:0 3rd:3 Ran:6
Pre1999 - 1st:3 2nd:1 3rd:0 Ran:8

Win Prizemoney £24,748 *Total Prizemoney* £28,803
Wins *** 1999** Jly Bath (FRM) 11.7f 72+
*** 1999** Jly Haydoc (G-S) H 11.9f 78 72
*** 1999** May Chepst (GD) H 12.1f 75 77 <
* 1998 Spt Bright (FRM) H 11.9f 66 73+
* 1998 Aug Bright (FRM) H 11.9f 58 62+
* 1998 Aug Folkes (G-F) H 12f 54 59
1999 Turf 3-6: (12f 3-6) (gd 2-3, g-f, frm 1-2)
Light-framed, decent filly, effective 11 to 12f, best at 12f, acts on sft to frm, best on gd, likes left handed tracks, and excels at Haydock. Turf high 81 - 3rd of 19 giving 14lb to Kathryn's Pet (29 Oct Newmarket 12f gd RF 5133) - also 1st of 8 giving 18lb to Seren Hill (31 May Chepstow RF 1595). Consistent. In fine form in the summer, she ran a cracker under top-weight on her final start.
**P F I Cole [6-14] M Arbib.*

STAR PRECISION BHB 87f RR 89f 5221[8]
5 ch m Shavian 7.7f **(67)** - Accuracy (Gunner B) 11.2f **(58)**
Form - 6110600048
Record 1999 - 1st:2 2nd:0 3rd:0 Ran:11
Pre1999 - 1st:4 2nd:1 3rd:2 Ran:19
Win Prizemoney £32,975 *Total Prizemoney* £44,959
Wins *** 1999** May Chepst (G-S) 10.2f 98 <
*** 1999** May York (G-S) H 11.9f 87 90+
* 1997 Oct Leices (G-S) 8f 94
* 1997 May Chepst (GD) H 12.1f 72 92++
* 1997 May Bath (G-S) H 13.1f 72 82+
* 1997 Apr Nottin (GD) H 10f 64 71
1999 Turf 2-11: (10f 1-6, 12f 1-5) (sft 2, g-s, gd 2-6, g-f, frm)
Useful filly, effective 9 to 12f, best at 10f, acts on gd, likes left handed tracks. Turf high 98 - 1st of 6 giving 11lb to Kuster (19 May Chepstow RF 1326) - also 1st of 20 giving 4lb to Banbury (11 May York RF 1142). Unable to handle a step up in class after winning twice in May. **G B Balding [6-30] Miss B Swire.*

STAR PRINCESS RR 75f 5209[4]
2 b f Up and At 'em - Princess Sharpenup (Lochnager) 6f **(59)**
Form - 7324
Record 1999 - 1st:0 2nd:1 3rd:1 Ran:4
Win Prizemoney £0 *Total Prizemoney* £2,052
1999 Turf 0-4: (5f 2, 6f 2) (hvy, g-s 2, frm)
Above-average filly. Turf high 75 (began Oct) - 4th of 20 getting 5lb from Royal Highlander (5 Nov Doncaster 6f g-s RF 5209).
**K T Ivory [0-4] The Star Princess Partnership.*

STAR RAGE (IRE) BHB 86f85a RR 85f 85a 4273[1]
9 b g Horage 11.4f **(58)** - Star Bound (Crowned Prince (USA)) 10.1f **(67)**
Form - 158165321131
Record 1999 - 1st:5 2nd:1 3rd:2 Ran:12
Pre1999 - 1st:14 2nd:14 3rd:8 Ran:69
Win Prizemoney £80,600 *Total Prizemoney* £109,800
Wins *** 1999** Spt Goodwo (G-F) H 16f 83 85 <
*** 1999** Aug Beverl (GD) H 16.2f 79 80
*** 1999** Jly Redcar (FRM) H 16f 75 77
*** 1999** May Beverl (GD) H 16.2f 72 77
1999 *Feb Lingfi (STD) H 16f 80 83*
* 1998 *Apr Wolver (STD) H 14.8f 78 80*
* 1997 Aug Redcar (FRM) H 16f 75 77
* 1995 Aug Newcas (GD) H 16.1f 77 84
* 1995 Aug Beverl (G-F) H 16.2f 70 80
* 1995 Aug Newcas (FRM) H 16.1f 70 79
1999 Turf 4-10: (15f, 16f 4-8, 17f) (g-s, gd 1-1, g-f 2-4, frm 1-4) 1999 AW 1-2: (16f 1-2) (Equi 1-1, Fibr)
Useful gelding, effective 15 to 17f, best at 16f, acts on gd to frm - acts on AW, likes right handed tracks, favours tight tracks, excels at Beverley, likes Wolverhampton. Turf high 85 - 1st of 6 giving 22lb to Temple Way (11 Spt Goodwood RF 4273) - also 1st of 5 giving 2lb to Jamaican Flight (11 Aug Beverley RF 3535). AW high 83 (1st run) - 1st of 5 giving 10lb to Harik (20 Feb Lingfield RF 0324). Not getting any younger, but he retains ability and enjoyed a fine season. Suited by top of the ground and coming off a fast pace, he is a credit to connections.
**M Johnston [20-77] David Abell (from D R C Elsworth [1-7] Apr 1999).*

STARRY NIGHT RR 78f 5112[5]
3 b f Sheikh Albadou 9.2f **(75)** - My Ballerina (USA) (Sir Ivor) 10.2f **(70)**
Form - 00125
Record 1999 - 1st:1 2nd:1 3rd:0 Ran:5
Pre1999 - 1st:1 2nd:0 3rd:0 Ran:1
Win Prizemoney £14,037 *Total Prizemoney* £15,251
Wins *** 1999** Spt Haydoc (SFT) H 10.5f 72 78+ <
* 1998 Oct Haydoc (SFT) 7.1f 78+ <
1999 Turf 1-5: (10f 2, 11f 1-2, 12f) (sft, g-s 1-1, gd, g-f 2)
Scopey, above-average filly, effective 7 to 11f, best at 11f, acts on sft to g-s, best on sft, often wears blinkers. Turf high 78 - 2nd of 9 to Little Italy (13 Oct Haydock 11f sft RF 4862) - also 1st of 9 getting 15lb from Lady Rockstar (25 Spt Haydock RF 4552).
**J L Dunlop [2-6] H R H Prince Fahd Salman.*

STARTOO BHB 50f RR 24f 1975[16]
3 ch f King's Signet (USA) 7f **(51)** - Shall We Run (Hotfoot) 10.5f **(59)**
Form - 0000
Record 1999 - 1st:0 2nd:0 3rd:0 Ran:4
Pre1999 - 1st:0 2nd:0 3rd:1 Ran:2
Win Prizemoney £0 *Total Prizemoney* £495
1999 Turf 0-4: (6f, 7f 2, 8f) (g-f 3, frm)
Light-framed, little account filly, effective 6f, acts on g-f. Turf high 24. **R F JohnsonHoughton [0-6] R C Naylor.*

STAR TURN (IRE) BHB 57f53a RR 56f 53a 4802[21]
5 ch g Night Shift (USA) 8.1f **(73)** - Ringtail (Auction Ring (USA)) 8.6f **(65)**
Form - 41710
Record 1999 - 1st:2 2nd:0 3rd:0 Ran:4
Pre1999 - 1st:0 2nd:3 3rd:2 Ran:19
Win Prizemoney £6,574 *Total Prizemoney* £10,598
Wins *** 1999** Aug Newmar (GD) H 10f 53 56 <
*** 1999** *Jan Lingfi (STD) H 10f 48 55*
1999 Turf 1-2: (9f, 10f 1-1) (gd, g-f 1-1) 1999 AW 1-2: (10f 1-2) (Equi 1-2)
Fair gelding, effective 8 to 10f, best at 10f, acts on g-f - acts on Equi. Turf high 56 (1st run) (began Aug) - 1st of 12 getting 6lb from Brandon Court (14 Aug Newmarket RF 3655). AW high 55 (1st run) - 1st of 9 getting 11lb from The Green Grey (7 Jan Lingfield RF 0045). Inconsistent. Got off the mark at the twentieth attempt when winning over ten furlongs on the Lingfield Equitrack in January, and came back from a seven-month break to win a lady amateur riders' race at Newmarket over ten furlongs.
**R M Flower [2-5] K & D Computers Ltd (from B J Llewellyn [0-3] Aug 1998).*

STARVINE BHB 34f37a RR 34f 37a 2163[6]
3 b f Superlative 8.8f **(57)** - Girl Next Door **(35df 36a)** (Local Suitor (USA)) 8.4f **(67)**
Form - 000006
Record 1999 - 1st:0 2nd:0 3rd:0 Ran:6
Pre1999 - 1st:0 2nd:0 3rd:1 Ran:9
Win Prizemoney £0 *Total Prizemoney* £252
1999 Turf 0-2: (5f, 6f) (gd, g-f) 1999 AW 0-4: (5f 2, 6f, 7f) (Equi, Fibr 3)
Unfurnished, very moderate filly, has worn blinkers. Turf high 11. AW high 31.
**D Shaw [0-4] M G Vines (from R C Spicer [0-11] Jan 1999).*

STATAJACK (IRE) BHB 67f60a RR 65f 60a 4387[6]
11 b g King of Clubs 9.3f **(61)** - Statira (Skymaster) 8.7f **(71)**
Form - 47616251312476
Record 1999 - 1st:3 2nd:2 3rd:1 Ran:12
Pre1999 - 1st:14 2nd:10 3rd:12 Ran:78
Win Prizemoney £66,755 *Total Prizemoney* £89,422
Wins *** 1999** Jly Windso (G-F) H 11.6f 65 67
*** 1999** Jun Epsom (GD) H 12f 62 57
*** 1999** Apr Windso (G-S) H 10f 58 64
* 1998 Oct Leices (G-S) C 11.8f 55
* 1998 May Kempto (GD) H 12f 62 65
* 1998 Apr Folkes (SFT) H 9.7f 60 65
* 1997 Nov Nottin (GD) S 10f 58
* 1997 Spt Folkes (GD) S 12f 61
* 1996 Jun Goodwo (G-F) H 10f 75 81 <
* 1996 Jun Goodwo (G-F) C 12f 65
1999 Turf 3-11: (10f 1-1, 11f, 12f 2-9) (gd 1-2, g-f 1-2, frm 1-6, hrd)
1999 AW 0-1: (12f) (Fibr)
Average gelding, effective 10 to 12f, best at 12f, acts on sft to frm, best on frm, mostly wears blinkers (effectively), and excels at Windsor. Turf high 73 - 2nd of 9 giving 11lb to Inchtina (4 Aug

Kempton 12f frm RF 3352) - also 1st of 13 giving 12lb to Red May (26 Jly Windsor RF 3150). Consistent. A real character, he will continue to win races when in the mood, but is an exasperating sort and a very tricky ride. Prefers ground with some cut, and is effective at distances up to twelve furlongs.
**D R C Elsworth [19-119] The Nutschalling Partnership.*

STATE APPROVAL BHB 46f68a **RR 37f 68a** 3080[5]

6 b g Pharly (FR) 11.5f **(64)** - Tabeeba (Diesis) 9.3f **(69)**
Form - 1260066125

Record	**1999 -**	1st:2	2nd:2	3rd:0	Ran:10
	Pre1999 -	1st:10	2nd:7	3rd:3	Ran:41

Win Prizemoney £24,935 — *Total Prizemoney* £32,605

Wins							
* **1999**	*May*	*Wolver*	*(Std)*	*C*	*9.4f*		*46*
1999	*Mar*	*Southw*	*(SLW)*	*C*	*12f*		*68*
1998	*May*	*Wolver*	*(STD)*	*S*	*12f*		*66+*
1998	*Apr*	*Southw*	*(STD)*	*C*	*12f*		*64*
1998	*Apr*	*Southw*	*(STD)*	*S*	*12f*		*66*
1998	*Mar*	*Southw*	*(STD)*	*S*	*11f*		*55*
1998	*Jan*	*Wolver*	*(STD)*	*S*	*12f*		*57+*
1998	*Jan*	*Wolver*	*(STD)*	*S*	*12f*		*57+*
1997	*Jun*	*Wolver*	*(STD)*	*H*	*12f*	*62*	*74* <
1997	*Mar*	*Wolver*	*(STD)*	*H*	*12f*	*57*	*62*
1996	*Aug*	*Wolver*	*(STD)*	*H*	*12f*	*56*	*68+*
1996	Aug	Kempto	(G-F)	H	12f	58	61+

1999 Turf 0-3: (10f 2, 12f) (g-s, gd, g-f) 1999 AW 2-7: (8f, 9f 1-2, 11f, 12f 1-3) (Fibr 2-7)

Average gelding, effective 9 to 12f, best at 12f, - acts on Fibr, favours left handed tracks, and excels at Wolverhampton. Turf high 37. AW high 68 (1st run) - 1st of 8 getting 12lb from Be Warned (10 Mar Southwell RF 0421). He is at his most effective when able to dominate in modest company over middle-distances on Fibresand, though he struggles outside of plating company.
**D Shaw [1-8] K Nicholls (from Miss S J Wilton [6-11] Mar 1999).*

STATELY FAVOUR BHB 37f30a **RR 51f 30a** 384[9]

4 ch f Statoblest 6.4f **(63)** - Dixie Favor (USA) (Dixieland Band (USA)) 7f **(74)**
Form - 80600

Record	**1999 -**	1st:0	2nd:0	3rd:0	Ran:3
	Pre1999 -	1st:1	2nd:1	3rd:1	Ran:13

Win Prizemoney £2,280 — *Total Prizemoney* £3,310

Wins							
* 1998	*Apr*	*Southw*	*(STD)*	*C*	*5f*		*44* <

1999 AW 0-3: (6f, 7f 2) (Fibr 3)

Workmanlike, fair filly, effective 5 to 7f, - acts on Fibr. AW high 32. Inconsistent.
**Miss J A Camacho [1-11] Elite Racing Club (from M J Camacho [0-5] Nov 1997).*

STATE OF CAUTION BHB 68f83a **RR 71f 83a** 3592a[1]

6 b g Reprimand 8.2f **(63)** - Hithermoor Lass (Red Alert) 7.6f **(66)**
Form - 0566611
1999 AW 2-5: (5f, 6f 1-2, 7f 1-1, 10f) (Equi 2, Fibr 1-2, Dirt 1-1)

Very useful gelding, has broken blood-vessels, effective 5 to 6f, - acts on Fibr to Dirt, mostly wears blinkers (effectively), likes left handed tracks, likes tight tracks. AW high 96 - 1st of 6 from Hakiki (8 Aug Jagersro RF 3592a). Inconsistent. Useful on the All-Weather, he is effective from five to seven furlongs and seems to have improved since being exported.
**C Bjorling in SWE [1-1] C Bjorling (from K R Burke [1-6] Feb 1999).*

STATE SHINTO (USA) **RR 119f** 4770a[1]

3 br c Pleasant Colony (USA) 12.4f **(88)** - Sha Tha (USA) (Mr Prospector (USA)) 8.8f **(78)**
Form - 122211
1999 Turf 2-5: (10f 2-3, 11f 2) (hvy 1-1, sft 1-1, g-s, gd 2)

High-class colt, effective 10f, acts on hvy to gd. Turf high 119 - 1st of 9 from Strategic (2 Oct Longchamp RF 4770a) - also 1st of 4 from Way of Light (18 Spt Longchamp RF 4513a). He ran very consistently last season, finishing runner-up in three Group Twos behind the likes of Slickly and Dubai Millennium, before gaining a deserved victory in the Group Three Prix du Prince d'Orange. Followed up with a game victory in the Prix Dollar and would be an interesting prospect if coming back at four. Particularly well suited by very soft ground, he has joined Godolphin.
**A Fabre in FR [3-6] Sheikh Mohammed.*

STATE WIND (IRE) BHB 48f52a **RR 54f 52a** 3671[9]

3 ch g Forest Wind (USA) - Kowalski (IRE) (Cyrano de Bergerac) 6f **(68)**
Form - 703266236600

Record	**1999 -**	1st:0	2nd:2	3rd:2	Ran:10
	Pre1999 -	1st:0	2nd:0	3rd:0	Ran:5

Win Prizemoney £0 — *Total Prizemoney* £2,103

1999 Turf 0-2: (8f 2) (g-f, frm) 1999 AW 0-8: (7f 3, 8f 3, 9f 2) (Fibr 8)

Leggy, average gelding, effective 7f, - acts on Fibr, often wears blinkers (very effectively), likes left handed tracks, likes tight tracks. Turf high 38 (began Jly). AW high 63 - 3rd of 7 giving 5lb to Golconda (24 Feb Wolverhampton 7f Fibr RF 0348). Becoming disappointing. **N P Littmoden [0-15] The Denton Partnership.*

STATISTICIAN BHB 50f55a **RR 59f 55a** 441[1]

7 b g Statoblest 6.4f **(63)** - Sharp Lady (Sharpen Up) 8.3f **(67)**
Form - 463U11

Record	**1999 -**	1st:2	2nd:0	3rd:1	Ran:6
	Pre1999 -	1st:2	2nd:6	3rd:6	Ran:32

Win Prizemoney £8,805 — *Total Prizemoney* £16,104

Wins							
* **1999**	*Mar*	*Lingfi*	*(STD)*	*H*	*8f*	*47*	*58*
* **1999**	*Mar*	*Wolver*	*(STD)*	*H*	*7f*	*47*	*51*
* 1998	*Jan*	*Lingfi*	*(STD)*		*6f*		*45*
* 1995	Jly	Catter	(G-F)	H	6f	66	70 <

1999 AW 2-6: (6f, 7f 1-3, 8f 1-2) (Equi 1-4, Fibr 1-2)

Fair gelding, effective 7 to 8f, best at 7f, - acts on AW, best on Equi, often wears blinkers (effectively). AW high 58 - 1st of 12 giving 13lb to Dark Menace (18 Mar Lingfield RF 0441) - also 1st of 12 getting 10lb from Garnock Valley (13 Mar Wolverhampton RF 0426). **John Berry [4-38] Richard Sims.*

STATOYORK BHB 61f46a **RR 62f 46a** 5166[11]

6 b g Statoblest 6.4f **(63)** - Ultimate Dream (Kafu) 6f **(47)**
Form - 0581173321008604084700

Record	**1999 -**	1st:3	2nd:1	3rd:2	Ran:22
	Pre1999 -	1st:2	2nd:4	3rd:4	Ran:41

Win Prizemoney £22,074 — *Total Prizemoney* £30,863

Wins							
* **1999**	Jun	Ripon	(G-F)	H	5f	65	69+ <
* **1999**	May	Ripon	(G-S)	H	5f	60	61
* **1999**	May	Carlis	(FRM)		5f		59
* 1998	Aug	Pontef	(G-F)	H	5f	52	57
1996	Jun	Ayr	(G-F)		7f		48+

1999 Turf 3-21: (5f 3-17, 6f 3, 7f) (g-s 4, gd 1-4, g-f 1-6, frm 1-7) 1999 AW 0-1: (5f) (Fibr)

Average gelding, has broken blood-vessels, effective 5 to 6f, best at 5f, acts on g-s to frm, best on g-f, has worn blinkers, excels at Ripon. Turf high 69 - 1st of 11 giving 14lb to Mukarrab (17 Jun Ripon RF 2077) - also 1st of 10 getting 22lb from Ziggy's Dancer (16 May Ripon RF 1263). He appears to travel well through his races but finds little off the bridle, and needs to be held up for a late run. Started '99 in good fettle with three victories over five furlongs, but ran moderately afterwards.
**D Shaw [4-49] M D H Racing (from B W Hills [1-14] Jly 1997).*

STAVANGER (IRE) BHB 48f60a **RR 48f 60a** 4558[6]

3 b g Distinctly North (USA) 7.4f **(63)** - Card Queen (Lord Gayle (USA)) 8.8f **(62)**
Form - 0064244436

Record	**1999 -**	1st:0	2nd:1	3rd:1	Ran:10
	Pre1999 -	1st:0	2nd:0	3rd:1	Ran:5

Win Prizemoney £0 — *Total Prizemoney* £1,650

1999 Turf 0-10: (6f 3, 7f 5, 8f 2) (sft, gd 2, g-f 2, frm 5)

Neat, average gelding, effective 5f, - acts on Equi, likes tight tracks. Turf high 50. **J Berry [0-15] Chris & Antonia Deuters.*

STAYIN ALIVE (USA) **RR 81f** 5100[4]

2 b br c Sword Dance 9.4f **(67)** - Marilyn's Mystique (USA) (Dearest Doctor (USA))
Form - 44

Record	**1999 -**	1st:0	2nd:0	3rd:0	Ran:2

Win Prizemoney £0 — *Total Prizemoney* £630

1999 Turf 0-2: (7f, 8f) (gd 2)

Currently decent colt. Turf high 81 (began Spt) - 4th of 10 to King Spinner (27 Oct Yarmouth 8f gd RF 5100).
**A G Foster [0-1] Gary Seidler (from P W Chapple-Hyam [0-1] Spt 1999).*

STEALTHY TIMES **RR 86+f** 2537[1]

2 ch f Timeless Times (USA) 6.1f **(56)**-Stealthy (Kind of Hush)10.1f **(62)**

Form - 1
Record 1999 - 1st:1 2nd:0 3rd:0 Ran:1
Win Prizemoney £3,202 *Total Prizemoney* £3,202
Wins * 1999 Jly Nottin (GD) 6.1f 86+ <
1999 Turf 1-1: (6f 1-1) (g-f 1-1)
Currently useful filly. (1st run) - 1st of 17 from Ecstasy (3 Jly Nottingham RF 2537). She made a winning debut at Nottingham despite doing a good impression of a slalom skier. The form of that race has been boosted since and she looks one to follow as she appears to have a deal of improvement in her.
**J G Given [1-1] G D Kendrick.*

STEAMROLLER STANLY BHB 60f72a RR 52f 72a 3669[6]

6 b g Shirley Heights 12.1f **(76)** - Miss Demure (Shy Groom (USA)) 10f **(66)**
Form - 3835133120366
Record 1999 - 1st:2 2nd:1 3rd:5 Ran:13
Pre1999 - 1st:6 2nd:1 3rd:4 Ran:23
Win Prizemoney £31,332 *Total Prizemoney* £43,010
Wins * 1999 *Jun Southw (STD) C* *16f* *84*
* 1999 *Apr Wolver (STD) H* *14.8f 90 85*
1998 *Feb Lingfi (SLW)* *10f* *93* <
1998 *Feb Lingfi (SLW)* *10f* *91*
1997 *Feb Lingfi (STD)* *10f* *90*
1997 *Jan Lingfi (STD) H* *12f 80 90*
1996 *Nov Lingfi (STD)* *12f* *84*
1996 Jun Newbur (G-F) H 13.3f 65 69
1999 Turf 0-2: (12f, 20f) (gd, g-f) 1999 AW 2-11: (8f 2, 9f 2, 10f, 12f 2, 14f, 15f 1-1, 16f 1-2) (Equi 3, Fibr 2-8)
Above-average gelding, effective 10 to 16f, best at 10f, - acts on AW, best on Equi, has worn blinkers, favours left handed tracks, favours tight tracks. Turf high 52. AW high 91 - 3rd of 7 getting 10lb from China Castle (22 Mar Southwell 12f Fibr RF 0460) - also 1st of 7 giving 25lb to Philosophic (24 Apr Wolverhampton RF 0848). Inconsistent. Formerly smart on the Flat and especially on Equitrack, he can still win staying events on sand when able to dominate, but he has also been beaten at very short prices and may not be completely trustworthy these days.
**K R Burke [2-13] Nigel Shields (from C A Cyzer [6-23] Aug 1998).*

STELLA BERINE (FR) RR 98f 4512a[2]

3 ch f Bering 9.6f **(80)** - Beaujolaise (FR) (Thatching) 8f **(66)**
Form - 52
1999 Turf 0-2: (6f, 8f) (sft, g-s)
Very useful filly, effective 6 to 7f, best at 7f, acts on sft to g-f, best on sft. Turf high 98 - 2nd of 11 giving 2lb to Seltitude (17 Spt Chantilly 6f sft RF 4512a). Consistent. She goes well on soft ground, but failed to improve on her juvenile form.
**P Bary in FR [1-8].*

STELLIO (USA) RR 83df 3967[10]

3 b f Dynaformer (USA) 12f **(82)** - Stella Mystika (USA) **(87df)** (Diesis) 9.3f **(69)**
Form - 20
Record 1999 - 1st:0 2nd:1 3rd:0 Ran:2
Win Prizemoney £0 *Total Prizemoney* £1,114
1999 Turf 0-2: (8f 2) (frm 2)
Scopey, currently decent filly. Turf high 83 (1st run) (began Aug) - 2nd of 9 to Badaayer (6 Aug Salisbury 8f frm RF 3430).
**J H M Gosden [0-2] Sheikh Mohammed.*

STELLISSIMA (IRE) RR 61f 4311a[9]

4 ch f Persian Bold 10f **(69)** - Ruffling Point (Gorytus (USA)) 7.8f **(60)**
Form - 100
Record 1999 - 1st:1 2nd:0 3rd:0 Ran:3
Pre1999 - 1st:0 2nd:1 3rd:0 Ran:11
Win Prizemoney £2,750 *Total Prizemoney* £3,610
Wins 1999 Jly Down R (G-S) 14f 61 <
1999 Turf 1-3: (14f 1-1, 16f, 17f) (g-s 1-1, gd 2)
Average filly, effective 12 to 14f, acts on g-s to gd, has worn blinkers, prefers right handed tracks. Turf high 61 (1st run) (began Jly) - 1st of 5 giving 15lb to La Tache (13 Jly Down Royal RF 2980a). Inconsistent.
**L Woods in IRE [1-3] Patrick Doherty (from L Woods [1-5] Aug 1999).*

STEP AHEAD (IRE) BHB 51f48a RR 68?f 48a 4926[7]

2 b f Shalford (IRE) 7.8f **(63)** - Tidal Reach (USA) **(66f 63a)** (Kris S (USA)) 7.9f **(71)**
Form - 082136807
Record 1999 - 1st:1 2nd:1 3rd:1 Ran:9
Win Prizemoney £2,372 *Total Prizemoney* £3,238
Wins * 1999 Jun Beverl (SFT) C 5f 68? <
1999 Turf 1-7: (5f 1-4, 6f 3) (g-s 2, gd 1-3, g-f 2) 1999 AW 0-2: (6f, 8f) (Fibr 2)
Average filly, effective 5 to 6f, acts on gd to g-f. Turf high 68 - 1st of 11 getting 2lb from Consideration (9 Jun Beverley RF 1849). AW high 47 (began Jly).
**P G Murphy [1-9] First Step.*

STEPASTRAY RR 57f 3572[15]

2 gr g Alhijaz 7.7f **(57)** - Wandering Stranger (Petong) 6.6f **(58)**
Form - 000
Record 1999 - 1st:0 2nd:0 3rd:0 Ran:3
1999 Turf 0-3: (7f 3) (g-f, frm 2)
Currently fair gelding. Turf high 57 (began Jly).
**P G Murphy [0-3] First Step.*

STEP FREE BHB 50f RR 58f 4605[13]

2 ch g Factual (USA) - Angel's Sing (Mansingh (USA)) 7.4f **(55)**
Form - 0850
Record 1999 - 1st:0 2nd:0 3rd:0 Ran:4
1999 Turf 0-3: (6f 2, 7f) (gd 2, hrd) 1999 AW 0-1: (7f) (Fibr)
Fair gelding. Turf high 58. **P G Murphy [0-4] First Step.*

STEPHEN GOT EVEN (USA) RR 4517a[3]

3 b c A P Indy (USA) - Immerse (USA) (Cox's Ridge (USA)) 8f **(68)**
Form - 3
1999 AW 0-1: (9f) (Dirt)
Currently high-class colt. (1st run) - 3rd of 7 getting 5lb from River Keen (18 Spt Belmont Park 9f Dirt RF 4517a). American-trained, he is a decent performer who finished third to River Keen in the Woodward when Almutawakel was second and Running Stag fourth. **N Zito in USA [0-1].*

STEP ON DEGAS BHB 53f55a RR 54f 55a 4711[10]

6 b m Superpower 6.6f **(58)** - Vivid Impression (Cure The Blues (USA)) 9.5f **(63)**
Form - 730543627302200
Record 1999 - 1st:0 2nd:3 3rd:3 Ran:15
Pre1999 - 1st:4 2nd:6 3rd:2 Ran:37
Win Prizemoney £9,998 *Total Prizemoney* £21,008
Wins * 1998 May Bright (FRM) H 6f 54 58
1997 Aug Bright (G-F) 7f 54
1997 *Jan Lingfi (STD) H* *7f 63 63*
1996 Jun Warwic (FRM) H 5f 63 64 <
1999 Turf 0-12: (6f 2, 7f 4, 8f 6) (sft, g-s 3, gd 2, g-f 3, frm 3) 1999 AW 0-3: (7f 3) (Equi, Fibr 2)
Fair mare, effective 6 to 8f, acts on gd to frm - acts on Fibr, best on frm, has worn blinkers, likes tight tracks, excels at Epsom. Turf high 54 - 2nd of 17 getting 4lb from Eventuality (3 Spt Epsom 7f g-f RF 4121). AW high 55 - 3rd of 12 getting 1lb from Mutabari (13 Mar Wolverhampton 7f Fibr RF 0430). Consistent. On a lengthy losing run since scoring at Brighton in May '98.
**Mrs A L M King [1-26] Mrs Pennie Muir (from M J Fetherston-Godley [3-22] Nov 1997).*

STEPS IN TIME (IRE) RR 32f 4868[4]

2 b c Dancing Dissident (USA) 6.8f **(65)** - Afterglow (IRE) (Glow (USA)) 6.7f **(71)**
Form - 04
Record 1999 - 1st:0 2nd:0 3rd:0 Ran:2
1999 Turf 0-1: (5f) (g-s) 1999 AW 0-1: (5f) (Fibr)
Currently fair colt. **R Hannon [0-2] J A Lazzari.*

STEPSTONE BHB 46f RR 46f 4630[11]

3 b f Slip Anchor 12.7f **(75)** - Stedham (Jaazeiro (USA)) 9.2f **(54)**
Form - 6605200
Record 1999 - 1st:0 2nd:1 3rd:0 Ran:7
Pre1999 - 1st:0 2nd:0 3rd:0 Ran:1
Win Prizemoney £0 *Total Prizemoney* £1,070
1999 Turf 0-7: (10f 2, 12f 4, 14f) (g-s, gd 2, g-f, frm 3)
Moderate filly, has worn blinkers. Turf high 56.
**H Candy [0-8] Major M G Wyatt.*

STEP UP BHB 47f45a RR 57f 45a 5064[18]

2 ch g Mizoram (USA) - Arabian Nymph (Sayf El Arab (USA)) 7.1f **(54)**

Form - 64024000
Record 1999 - 1st:0 2nd:1 3rd:0 Ran:8
Win Prizemoney £0 *Total Prizemoney* £636
1999 Turf 0-6: (5f 3, 6f 2, 8f) (sft, g-s, gd 2, frm 2) 1999 AW 0-2: (6f 2) (Fibr 2)
Fair gelding. Turf high 57. AW high 35. Becoming disappointing.
**P G Murphy [0-8] First Step.*

STERO HEIGHTS (IRE) BHB 74f62a RR 74f 62a 200^{5}
4 b g Shirley Heights 12.1f **(76)** - Trystero (Shareef Dancer (USA)) 9.9f **(73)**
Form - 4425
Record 1999 - 1st:0 2nd:1 3rd:0 Ran:3
Pre1999 - 1st:0 2nd:0 3rd:1 Ran:4
Win Prizemoney £0 *Total Prizemoney* £1,795
1999 AW 0-3: (13f, 16f 2) (Equi, Fibr 2)
Scopey, above-average gelding, effective 11f, acts on frm, likes left handed tracks. AW high 64.
**D J S Cosgrove [0-4] W A Barrett (from E A L Dunlop [0-3] Oct 1998).*

STERT BHB 17f RR 2424^{10}
4 ch f Petrizzo - Ziggy's Pearl (USA) (Ziggy's Boy (USA))
Form - 0000
Record 1999 - 1st:0 2nd:0 3rd:0 Ran:3
Pre1999 - 1st:0 2nd:0 3rd:0 Ran:1
1999 Turf 0-2: (10f, 12f) (frm 2) 1999 AW 0-1: (6f) (Fibr)
Workmanlike, formerly very poor filly.
**A J Chamberlain [0-4] Mrs A G Sims.*

STEVAL BHB 52f RR 39f 5195^{11}
2 ch f Efisio 7.7f **(69)** - Vannozza (Kris) 9.5f **(73)**
Form - 000
Record 1999 - 1st:0 2nd:0 3rd:0 Ran:3
1999 Turf 0-3: (5f 2, 6f) (gd 3)
Currently very moderate filly. Turf high 39 (began Oct).
**R Guest [0-3] Mrs Lesley Mills.*

STEVIE CRUISE (IRE) RR 44f 2076^{9}
2 b g Foxhound (USA) - Petticoat Louis (Absalom) 7.2f **(58)**
Form - 00
Record 1999 - 1st:0 2nd:0 3rd:0 Ran:2
1999 Turf 0-2: (5f, 6f) (g-f, frm)
Moderate gelding. Turf high 44. (DEAD)
**P C Haslam [0-2] Frank Hanson.*

ST EXPEDIT RR 83+f 5104^{3}
2 b c Sadler's Wells (USA) 11.3f **(87)** - Miss Rinjani **(88f)** (Shirley Heights) 10.3f **(74)**
Form - 3
Record 1999 - 1st:0 2nd:0 3rd:1 Ran:1
Win Prizemoney £0 *Total Prizemoney* £465
1999 Turf 0-1: (7f) (gd)
Currently decent colt. (1st run) - 3rd of 11 to Shaibani (27 Oct Yarmouth 7f gd RF 5104). **G Wragg [0-1] J L C Pearce.*

ST GEORGE'S BOY RR 12f 5208^{19}
2 b c Inchinor 8.9f **(64)** - Deanta in Eirinn (Red Sunset) 8.2f **(63)**
Form - 00
Record 1999 - 1st:0 2nd:0 3rd:0 Ran:2
1999 Turf 0-2: (7f 2) (g-s, gd)
Currently poor colt. Turf high 12 (began Oct).
**J Wharton [0-2] John Goddard.*

ST HELENSFIELD BHB 82f RR 72f 5106^{4}
4 ch c Kris 10f **(75)** - On Credit (FR) (No Pass No Sale) 11.9f **(85)**
Form - 06173004
Record 1999 - 1st:1 2nd:0 3rd:1 Ran:8
Pre1999 - 1st:1 2nd:1 3rd:1 Ran:4
Win Prizemoney £7,085 *Total Prizemoney* £12,382
Wins * **1999** Jly Newcas (FRM) H 10.1f 85 86 <
* 1997 Spt Bath (G-F) 10.2f 86+
1999 Turf 1-8: (9f, 10f 1-5, 12f, 14f) (g-s, gd 2, g-f 1-4, frm)
Leggy, above-average colt, effective 9 to 10f, acts on g-f to frm. Turf high 86 (began Jly) - 1st of 5 giving 20lb to Bold Amusement (24 Jly Newcastle RF 3103). Inconsistent. Regained winning form over ten furlongs on very fast ground at Newcastle in July, but has not set the world alight since. **M Johnston [2-12] Paul Dean.*

ST HILARY BHB 24f RR 660^{10}
4 b f Formidable (USA) 7.8f **(60)**-Positive Attitude (Red Sunset)8.2f **(63)**
Form - 0
Record 1999 - 1st:0 2nd:0 3rd:0 Ran:1
Pre1999 - 1st:0 2nd:0 3rd:0 Ran:2
1999 Turf 0-1: (12f) (hvy)
Workmanlike, currently very poor filly.
**Mrs A J Perrett [0-1] K J Mercer (from J E Banks [0-2] Jly 1998).*

STILL AS SWEET (IRE) RR 90f $5178a^{2}$
2 bb f Fairy King (USA) 7.7f **(75)** - Perils Of Joy
Form - 62
1999 Turf 0-2: (6f 2) (sft 2)
Currently useful filly. Turf high 90 (began Oct) - 2nd of 29 to Cois Cuain (29 Oct Curragh 6f sft RF 5178a).
**D K Weld in IRE [0-2] Moyglare Stud Farm.*

STILL GOING ON RR 93+f $4475a^{5}$
2 b c Prince Sabo 6.6f **(64)** - Floppie (FR) (Law Society (USA)) 9.9f **(70)**
Form - 23225
1999 Turf 0-5: (6f 3, 7f 2) (g-s, gd, g-f 3)
Useful colt. Turf high 93 - 2nd of 15 to Polish Panache (11 Aug Gowran Park 7f g-f RF 3703a).
**C Collins in IRE [0-5] Stal Statenprojekt B V.*

STILL IN LOVE RR 73f 5054^{3}
2 b f Emarati (USA) 6.6f **(63)** - In Love Again (IRE) **(67f)** (Prince Rupert (FR))
Form - 3
Record 1999 - 1st:0 2nd:0 3rd:1 Ran:1
Win Prizemoney £0 *Total Prizemoney* £360
1999 Turf 0-1: (6f) (gd)
Currently above-average filly. (1st run) - 3rd of 13 to Picot (25 Oct Leicester 6f gd RF 5054). **H R A Cecil [0-1] W H Ponsonby.*

STILL WATERS BHB 65a RR 71?f 652^{14}
4 b g Rainbow Quest (USA) 11.2f **(81)** - Krill (Kris) 9.5f **(73)**
Form - 170
Record 1999 - 1st:1 2nd:0 3rd:0 Ran:3
Pre1999 - 1st:0 2nd:1 3rd:0 Ran:5
Win Prizemoney £2,008 *Total Prizemoney* £2,998
Wins * **1999** *Jan Southw (STD) H 8f 62 68* <
1999 Turf 0-1: (8f) (frm) 1999 AW 1-2: (8f 1-1, 11f) (Fibr 1-2)
Workmanlike, above-average gelding, effective 8f, acts on g-f - acts on Fibr. AW high 68 (1st run) - 1st of 16 giving 20lb to Anonym (29 Jan Southwell RF 0192).
**K Bell [1-4] Mrs Joyce Wood (from R Charlton [0-4] Jun 1998).*

STITCH IN TIME BHB 41f RR 43f 4593^{7}
3 ch g Inchinor 8.9f **(64)** - Late Matinee (Red Sunset) 8.2f **(63)**
Form - 0070707
Record 1999 - 1st:0 2nd:0 3rd:0 Ran:7
1999 Turf 0-7: (7f, 8f 2, 10f 3, 12f) (gd 2, g-f 3, frm 2)
Leggy, moderate gelding. Turf high 53.
**G C Bravery [0-7] H P Carrington.*

ST IVES BHB 55f RR 54f 5047^{6}
2 b c Puissance 7.1f **(60)** - Clan Scotia **(46f)** (Clantime)
Form - 006
Record 1999 - 1st:0 2nd:0 3rd:0 Ran:3
1999 Turf 0-3: (6f, 7f 2) (hvy, sft, g-s)
Currently fair colt. Turf high 54 (began Spt).
**V Soane [0-3] Mrs M Watts And Miss R Hatley.*

ST LAWRENCE (CAN) BHB 36f43a RR 37f 43a 5152^{7}
5 gr g With Approval (CAN) 8.7f **(80)** - Mingan Isle (USA) (Lord Avie (USA)) 5.3f **(61)**
Form - 7078603574027
Record 1999 - 1st:0 2nd:1 3rd:1 Ran:13
Pre1999 - 1st:0 2nd:3 3rd:1 Ran:9
Win Prizemoney £0 *Total Prizemoney* £5,187
1999 Turf 0-12: (10f 6, 11f 2, 12f 3, 14f) (gd 6, g-f 2, frm 4) 1999 AW 0-1: (14f) (Fibr)
Moderate gelding, effective 10f, acts on g-f, has worn blinkers. Turf high 65. Consistent.
**N Tinkler [0-7] Mrs C M Tinkler (from C E Brittain [0-15] Jly 1999).*

STOCKBROOK BHB 17f **RR 19f** 3903[10]
6 b g Marju (IRE) 9.2f **(76)** - Burning Ambition (Troy) 10.4f **(68)**
Form - 0050
Record **1999** - 1st:0 2nd:0 3rd:0 Ran:4
Pre1999 - 1st:0 2nd:0 3rd:0 Ran:3
1999 Turf 0-4: (14f 2, 16f, 17f) (g-f 2, frm 2)
Poor gelding. Turf high 19 (began Jly).
**K R Burke [0-7] Robert Merrigan.*

STOLEN MUSIC (IRE) BHB 42f **RR 44f** 4904[15]
6 b m Taufan (USA) 8.3f **(65)** - Causa Sua (Try My Best (USA)) 7.6f **(67)**
Form - 603681731070200
Record **1999** - 1st:2 2nd:1 3rd:2 Ran:15
Pre1999 - 1st:3 2nd:0 3rd:1 Ran:29
Win Prizemoney £15,216 *Total Prizemoney* £18,087
Wins * **1999** Aug Catter (FRM) H 13.8f 43 47 <
* **1999** Jun Redcar (FRM) H 14.1f 32 35
* 1998 Oct Redcar (HVY) H 14.1f 33 36
* 1998 Spt Beverl (G-F) H 9.9f 29 33
* 1998 Aug Beverl (G-F) H 9.9f 25 30
1999 Turf 2-15: (10f, 11f, 12f 2, 14f 2-8, 16f 2, 17f) (sft, gd 3, g-f, frm 2-10)
Moderate mare, effective 12 to 14f, best at 14f, acts on gd to frm, has worn blinkers, favours tight tracks, does well at Beverley and likes Redcar. Turf high 47 - 1st of 12 getting 7lb from Go With The Wind (3 Aug Catterick RF 3316).
**R E Barr [5-42] P Cartmell (from Major D N Chappell [0-3] Spt 1996).*

STOLEN TEAR (FR) BHB 76f **RR 75f** 709[8]
3 ch f Cadeaux Genereux 7.9f **(76)** - Durrah (USA) (Nijinsky (CAN)) 10.3f **(77)**
Form - 08
Record **1999** - 1st:0 2nd:0 3rd:0 Ran:2
Pre1999 - 1st:1 2nd:0 3rd:1 Ran:3
Win Prizemoney £3,371 *Total Prizemoney* £3,859
Wins * 1998 Spt Hamilt (SFT) 8.3f 70+ <
1999 Turf 0-2: (11f, 12f) (gd 2)
Workmanlike, above-average filly. Turf high 44.
**M Johnston [1-5] Maktoum Al Maktoum.*

STONE BECK BHB 60f **RR 69f** 638[10]
4 b f Lapierre - Dovey (Welsh Pageant) 10f **(65)**
Form - 0
Record **1999** - 1st:0 2nd:0 3rd:0 Ran:1
Pre1999 - 1st:0 2nd:0 3rd:2 Ran:10
Win Prizemoney £0 *Total Prizemoney* £2,505
1999 Turf 0-1: (13f) (hvy)
Workmanlike, average filly, effective 8 to 15f, acts on g-s to hrd, has worn blinkers. **J M Jefferson [0-14] & Mrs J M Davenport.*

STONE COLD BHB 54f **RR 60f** 5163[11]
2 ch c Inchinor 8.9f **(64)** - Vaula (Henbit (USA)) 9f **(61)**
Form - 870
Record **1999** - 1st:0 2nd:0 3rd:0 Ran:3
1999 Turf 0-3: (7f 2, 8f) (g-s, gd, g-f)
Currently average colt. Turf high 60 (began Spt).
**T D Easterby [0-3] Six Diamonds Partnership.*

STONE OF DESTINY BHB 55f48a **RR 64?f 48a** 5217[14]
4 ch g Ballad Rock 7.2f **(63)** - Shamasiya (FR) (Vayrann) 9.7f **(74)**
Form - 00
Record **1999** - 1st:0 2nd:0 3rd:0 Ran:2
Pre1999 - 1st:2 2nd:2 3rd:0 Ran:14
Win Prizemoney £6,035 *Total Prizemoney* £10,811
Wins 1998 Oct Pontef (G-S) C 6f 60
1997 Oct Folkes (GD) 6.9f 91 <
1999 Turf 0-2: (7f, 8f) (g-s 2)
Scopey, average gelding, has worn blinkers. Turf high 2 (began Oct). Inconsistent.
**Mrs L Williamson [0-2] Halewood International Ltd (from B J Meehan [2-14] Oct 1998).*

STONE RIDGE (IRE) BHB 73f **RR 77f** 972[1]
7 b g Indian Ridge 7.6f **(74)** - Cut in Stone (USA) (Assert) 10.6f **(85)**
Form - 701
Record **1999** - 1st:1 2nd:0 3rd:0 Ran:3
Pre1999 - 1st:5 2nd:2 3rd:1 Ran:39
Win Prizemoney £89,955 *Total Prizemoney* £94,030
Wins * **1999** May Hamilt (GD) C 9.2f 54
1998 Oct Doncas (HVY) C 10.3f 77
1998 May Windso (G-F) 10f 78
1996 Mar Doncas (SFT) H 8f 87 97 <
1995 Oct Newmar (G-F) H 8f 82 89
1995 Apr Bright (G-F) 8f 80
1999 Turf 1-2: (8f, 9f 1-1) (g-s, g-f 1-1) 1999 AW 0-1: (12f) (Fibr)
Above-average gelding, effective 8 to 10f, best at 10f, acts on g-s to frm, has worn blinkers, likes tight tracks, excels at Windsor. Turf high 54. The winner of the 1996 Lincoln, he has not reached those heady heights since, and his recent wins have been in much more modest events.
**J Pearce [1-9] Friday Partnership (from R Hannon [5-40] Oct 1998).*

STONEY GARNETT BHB 67f **RR 67f** 4895[19]
2 b f Emarati (USA) 6.6f **(63)** - Etourdie (USA) (Arctic Tern (USA)) 8.9f **(69)**
Form - 07233U30
Record **1999** - 1st:0 2nd:1 3rd:3 Ran:8
Win Prizemoney £0 *Total Prizemoney* £1,975
1999 Turf 0-8: (5f 4, 6f 4) (gd, g-f 3, frm 4)
Average filly, effective 5 to 6f, best at 6f, acts on g-f to frm, best on g-f, has worn blinkers. Turf high 67 - 3rd of 19 getting 5lb from Pedro Jack (13 Spt Nottingham 6f frm RF 4286). Inconsistent.
**M S Saunders [0-8] M S Saunders.*

STOPPES BROW BHB 80f77a **RR 80f 77a** 5141[7]
7 b g Primo Dominie 7.2f **(67)** - So Bold (Never so Bold) 6.3f **(66)**
Form - 6115614233107
Record **1999** - 1st:4 2nd:1 3rd:2 Ran:13
Pre1999 - 1st:8 2nd:11 3rd:8 Ran:67
Win Prizemoney £48,100 *Total Prizemoney* £75,455
Wins * **1999** Aug Epsom (GD) H 8.5f 77 80
* **1999** Jun Kempto (GD) H 8f 69 71
* **1999** *Apr Lingfi (STD) H 7f 65 75*
* **1999** *Apr Lingfi (STD) H 8f 65 74*
* 1998 May Goodwo (G-F) H 8f 67 72
* 1996 May Newbur (SFT) H 6f 70 71
* 1995 Aug Goodwo (G-F) H 7f 62 66
* 1995 *Feb Lingfi (STD) H 6f 84 81* <
* 1995 *Jan Lingfi (STD) H 6f 74 77*
* 1995 *Jan Lingfi (STD) H 5f 74 71*
1999 Turf 2-9: (7f, 8f 1-4, 9f 1-3, 10f) (g-s, gd 2, g-f 2-4, frm 2) 1999 AW 2-4: (7f 1-1, 8f 1-3) (Equi 2-4)
Decent gelding, effective 7 to 9f, best at 9f, acts on gd to frm - acts on Equi, best on g-f, mostly wears blinkers (effectively), likes right handed tracks, likes tight tracks, excels at Goodwood and does well at Epsom. Turf high 80 - 1st of 13 giving 3lb to Bergen (30 Aug Epsom RF 4018) - also 1st of 17 getting 5lb from Indium (9 Jun Kempton RF 1863). AW high 75 - 1st of 6 giving 10lb to Mutabari (9 Apr Lingfield RF 0634) - also 1st of 12 giving 22lb to Kanawa (1 Apr Lingfield RF 0547). Consistent. He has been around for a while, but is a capable handicapper when things go right on both turf and Equitrack. **G L Moore [12-80] B V and C J Pennick.*

STOP THE TRAFFIC (IRE) BHB 71f **RR 60f** 4249[16]
2 b f College Chapel - Miss Bagatelle (Mummy's Pet) 7.7f **(60)**
Form - 0330
Record **1999** - 1st:0 2nd:0 3rd:2 Ran:4
Win Prizemoney £0 *Total Prizemoney* £1,394
1999 Turf 0-4: (5f, 6f 3) (g-f, frm 2, hrd)
Average filly. Turf high 60. **C N Allen [0-4] Kentavr (UK) Ltd.*

STOPWATCH (IRE) BHB 52f70a **RR 41f 70a** 1733[13]
4 b g Lead on Time (USA) 7.5f **(69)** - Rose Bonbon (FR) (High Top) 10.2f **(67)**
Form - 6000
Record **1999** - 1st:0 2nd:0 3rd:0 Ran:4
Pre1999 - 1st:1 2nd:1 3rd:1 Ran:10
Win Prizemoney £3,767 *Total Prizemoney* £5,791
Wins 1998 Apr Cork (G-S) 8f 90 <
1999 Turf 0-3: (8f 2, 9f) (gd 2, g-f) 1999 AW 0-1: (7f) (Equi)
Moderate gelding, effective 8f, acts on g-s, has worn blinkers, likes right handed tracks. Turf high 41. Becoming disappointing.
**Mrs L C Jewell [1-10] The Stopwatch Partnership (from T Stack in IRE*

[1-10] Spt 1998).

STORM CAT BHB 70a **RR 64f** 3113[F]
4 ch g Interrex (CAN) 7.7f **(51)** - Albion Polka (Dance In Time (CAN)) 8.9f **(59)**
Form - 1441688F
Record 1999 - 1st:2 2nd:0 3rd:0 Ran:8
Pre1999 - 1st:0 2nd:1 3rd:0 Ran:7
Win Prizemoney £4,249 *Total Prizemoney* £5,253
Wins * **1999** *Apr Wolver (STD) H 7f 65 72 <*
* **1999** *Feb Southw (Sta) 7f 63+*
1999 Turf 0-3: (6f, 7f 2) (sft, g-f, frm) 1999 AW 2-5: (7f 2-5) (Equi, Fibr 2-4)
Above-average gelding, effective 7 to 9f, best at 7f, acted on sft to frm - acted on Fibr, mostly wore blinkers (extremely effectively), prefered left handed tracks. Turf high 64 (1st run) - 4th of 16 giving 4lb to Indian Blaze (31 Mar Folkestone 7f sft RF 0532). AW high 72 - 1st of 12 from Elite Hope (24 Apr Wolverhampton RF 0851) - also 1st of 9 from Freedom Quest (1 Feb Southwell RF 0199). Inconsistent. Hardly in the same league as his illustrious namesake (the sire of Aljabr), but still had some talent judging by his victories on Fibresand. (DEAD). **K McAuliffe [2-15] A Ezen.*

STORM COMMAND BHB 30f35a **RR 34f 35a** 763[13]
5 b g Gildoran 11.6f **(58)** - Summer Sky (Skyliner) 7.3f **(53)**
Form - 6400
Record 1999 - 1st:0 2nd:0 3rd:0 Ran:4
Pre1999 - 1st:0 2nd:0 3rd:0 Ran:3
1999 Turf 0-1: (15f) (hvy) 1999 AW 0-3: (12f 2, 14f) (Fibr 3)
Moderate gelding. AW high 41.
**D W P Arbuthnot [0-7] Henry Ponsonby & Partners (2).*

STORM CRY (USA) BHB 68f **RR 65df** 5033[25]
4 b c Hermitage (USA) 8.6f **(84)** - Doonesbury Lady (USA) (Doonesbury (USA)) 7.7f **(99)**
Form - 40005406100
Record 1999 - 1st:1 2nd:0 3rd:0 Ran:11
Pre1999 - 1st:1 2nd:1 3rd:1 Ran:6
Win Prizemoney £6,011 *Total Prizemoney* £8,849
Wins * **1999** Spt Lingfi (HVY) H 7f 63 65 <
1998 May Bath (FRM) 8f 64+
1999 Turf 1-11: (7f 1-6, 8f 5) (g-s 1-6, gd 2, g-f, frm 2)
Light-framed, average colt, effective 8f, acts on g-s to frm. Turf high 79 (1st run) - 4th of 9 getting 11lb from Silk St John (23 Apr Sandown 8f g-s RF 0821). Inconsistent.
**M S Saunders [1-11] M S Saunders (from Major D N Chappell [1-6] Jly 1998).*

STORMDANCER (IRE) BHB 60f **RR 56f** 4582[10]
2 ch c Bluebird (USA) 7.9f **(71)** - Unspoiled (Tina's Pet) 6.8f **(59)**
Form - 070
Record 1999 - 1st:0 2nd:0 3rd:0 Ran:3
1999 Turf 0-3: (7f 2, 10f) (gd, frm 2)
Currently fair colt. Turf high 56 (began Aug).
**R Hannon [0-3] J A Forsyth.*

STORM HILL (IRE) BHB 78f **RR 77f** 4992[5]
3 b c Caerleon (USA) 10.9f **(79)** - Jackie Berry (Connaught) 7.7f **(63)**
Form - 3545
Record 1999 - 1st:0 2nd:0 3rd:1 Ran:4
Win Prizemoney £0 *Total Prizemoney* £920
1999 Turf 0-4: (8f, 10f 3) (g-f 2, frm 2)
Light-framed, above-average colt. Turf high 83 (1st run) - 3rd of 15 to Mirjan (13 Apr Newmarket 10f g-f RF 0668).
**A G Foster [0-1] R E Sangster & A K Collins (from P W Chapple-Hyam [0-3] Jun 1999).*

STORMIN (IRE) BHB 39f **RR 49f** 1781[6]
3 b g Perugino (USA) - Unalaska (IRE) (High Estate)
Form - 00086
Record 1999 - 1st:0 2nd:0 3rd:0 Ran:5
Pre1999 - 1st:0 2nd:0 3rd:0 Ran:2
1999 Turf 0-3:(8f, 10f, 15f) (hvy, sft, gd) 1999 AW 0-2: (12f, 15f) (Fibr 2)
Moderate gelding, has worn blinkers. Turf high 49. AW high 20.
**D J Wintle [0-5] Mrs Joan Egan (from Mrs J R Ramsden [0-2] Jly 1998).*

STORMLESS BHB 42f **RR 41f** 4983[13]
8 b g Silly Prices 6.8f **(51)** - Phyl's Pet (Aberdeen) 9.4f **(55)**
Form - 700080
Record 1999 - 1st:0 2nd:0 3rd:0 Ran:6
Pre1999 - 1st:4 2nd:4 3rd:3 Ran:25
Win Prizemoney £14,585 *Total Prizemoney* £20,598
Wins 1998 May Hamilt (SFT) H 8.3f 58 69 <
1997 May Hamilt (SFT) H 8.3f 53 59
1996 Aug Ayr (G-F) H 10f 48 54
1996 Jun Ayr (G-F) H 10f 43 47
1999 Turf 0-6: (8f, 9f 2, 10f, 11f 2) (gd 4, g-f 2)
Moderate gelding, effective 8 to 10f, best at 8f, acts on hvy to g-s, prefers tight tracks. Turf high 53 (began Jly). Consistent.
**J S Haldane [0-6] D St Clair (from J S Goldie [1-10] May 1998).*

STORM PRINCE (IRE) BHB 70f74a **RR 73f 74a** 4603[2]
2 ch c Prince of Birds (USA) - Petersford Girl (IRE) **(70f)** (Taufan (USA)) 7f **(57)**
Form - 064412
Record 1999 - 1st:1 2nd:1 3rd:0 Ran:6
Win Prizemoney £2,220 *Total Prizemoney* £3,285
Wins 1999 Spt Leices (FRM) SH 8f 63 73 <
1999 Turf 1-5: (6f 2, 7f 2, 8f 1-1) (g-f, frm 1-4) 1999 AW 0-1: (8f) (Fibr)
Above-average colt, effective 8f, acts on frm. Turf high 73 - 1st of 18 giving 19lb to Hong Kong (7 Spt Leicester RF 4169).
**J L Spearing [0-1] D J Oseman (from S C Williams [1-5] Spt 1999).*

STORM SONG (IRE) RR 54f 4626[5]
2 ch c Prince of Birds (USA) - Wolviston (Wolverlife) 9.3f **(54)**
Form - 60605
Record 1999 - 1st:0 2nd:0 3rd:0 Ran:5
1999 Turf 0-4: (5f, 6f 2, 7f) (g-s, gd, frm 2) 1999 AW 0-1: (7f) (Fibr)
Fair colt. Turf high 56.
**R J O'Sullivan [0-2] Normandy Developments (London) (from N Hamilton [0-3] Aug 1999).*

STORMSWELL BHB 57f **RR 62f** 5076[14]
2 ch f Persian Bold 10f **(69)** - Stormswept (USA) (Storm Bird (CAN)) 10.3f **(74)**
Form - 0060
Record 1999 - 1st:0 2nd:0 3rd:0 Ran:4
1999 Turf 0-4: (6f 4) (gd, g-f, hrd 2)
Average filly. Turf high 62 (began Aug).
**R A Fahey [0-4] Exors of the late M J Paver.*

STORMVILLE (IRE) BHB 76f **RR 89?f** 4895[5]
2 b g Catrail (USA) - Haut Volee (Top Ville) 11.7f **(68)**
Form - 6355
Record 1999 - 1st:0 2nd:0 3rd:1 Ran:4
Win Prizemoney £0 *Total Prizemoney* £3,409
1999 Turf 0-4: (6f, 7f 3) (gd 2, g-f, frm)
Useful gelding. Turf high 89 (began Jly) - 5th of 20 getting 1lb from Magic of Love (15 Oct Newmarket 6f gd RF 4895).
**M Brittain [0-4] Northgate Gold.*

STORM WEAVE (IRE) BHB 42f55a **RR 39f 55a** 3071[7]
3 ch f Polar Falcon (USA) 9f **(74)** - Kaliala (FR) (Pharly (FR)) 9.8f **(68)**
Form - 0077
Record 1999 - 1st:0 2nd:0 3rd:0 Ran:4
Pre1999 - 1st:0 2nd:0 3rd:0 Ran:2
1999 Turf 0-3: (8f, 9f, 10f) (g-s, frm 2) 1999 AW 0-1: (8f) (Fibr)
Unfurnished, very moderate filly. Turf high 39.
**Mrs A Swinbank [0-6] Mrs Dee Shotton.*

STORM WIZARD (IRE) RR 43f 4419[18]
2 b c Catrail (USA) - Society Ball (Law Society (USA)) 9.9f **(70)**
Form - 0
Record 1999 - 1st:0 2nd:0 3rd:0 Ran:1
1999 Turf 0-1: (7f) (gd)
Currently moderate colt. **M R Channon [0-1] BEL Leisure Ltd.*

STORMY RAINBOW RR 35f 1883[7]
2 b c Red Rainbow - Stormy Heights **(9f 44a)** (Golden Heights)
Form - 7
Record 1999 - 1st:0 2nd:0 3rd:0 Ran:1
1999 Turf 0-1: (6f) (gd)
Currently very moderate colt. **R Simpson [0-1] Michael Hancock.*

STORMY SKYE (IRE) BHB 85f RR 79f 1594[2]

3 b c Bluebird (USA) 7.9f **(71)** - Canna (Caerleon (USA)) 8.6f **(71)**
Form - 442
Record 1999 - 1st:0 2nd:1 3rd:0 Ran:3
Pre1999 - 1st:0 2nd:0 3rd:1 Ran:4
Win Prizemoney £0 *Total Prizemoney* £3,476
1999 Turf 0-3: (11f, 12f, 14f) (gd, g-f 2)
Scopey, above-average colt, has worn blinkers. Turf high 79. A decent maiden, he has joined Gary Moore.
**A J McNae [0-7] The Iona Stud.*

STORYTELLER (IRE) BHB 86f RR 84f 3049[4]

5 b g Thatching 7.8f **(69)** - Please Believe Me (Try My Best (USA)) 7.6f **(67)**
Form - 00411244
Record 1999 - 1st:2 2nd:1 3rd:0 Ran:8
Pre1999 - 1st:6 2nd:6 3rd:1 Ran:26
Win Prizemoney £34,129 *Total Prizemoney* £51,253

Wins									
*	**1999**	Jun	Salisb	(Gd)	H	5f	80	83	
*	**1999**	May	Doncas	(G-F)		6f		79	
*	1998	Jly	Pontef	(G-F)	H	5f	77	84	<
*	1998	Jly	Beverl	(GD)	H	5f	65	76	
*	1998	Jly	Haydoc	(GD)	H	5f	65	67	
*	1998	Jun	Ayr	(GD)	H	5f	58	62	
*	1998	Jun	Carlis	(G-S)	H	5f	58	61	
	1997	Jly	Doncas	(GD)	H	5f	50	54	

1999 Turf 2-8: (5f 1-6, 6f 1-2) (gd 2, g-f 1-3, frm 1-3)
Decent gelding, effective 5 to 6f, best at 5f, acts on g-f to frm, best on frm, mostly wears blinkers (extremely effectively), excels at Sandown. Turf high 84 - 4th of 10 giving 19lb to That Man Again (3 Jly Sandown 5f frm RF 2547) - also 1st of 13 giving 6lb to Ivory's Joy (9 Jun Salisbury RF 1869). He was terrific form in the summer of '98, winning a string of races at five furlongs and defying the handicapper. A come-from-behind sprinter, he won twice last term, but looked held by the handicapper afterwards.
**M Dods [7-23] Mrs Karen Pratt (from Mrs J R Ramsden [1-10] Oct 1997).*

ST PACOKISE (IRE) BHB 58f RR 52f 4929[4]

2 b f Brief Truce (USA) 9.1f **(73)** - Classic Opera (Lomond (USA)) 8.8f **(65)**
Form - 504
Record 1999 - 1st:0 2nd:0 3rd:0 Ran:3
1999 Turf 0-3: (5f, 6f, 7f) (g-f 2, frm)
Currently fair filly. Turf high 52 (began Spt).
**A B Mulholland [0-3] Silent Running Syndicate.*

STRAHAN (IRE) BHB 87f RR 82f 4753[1]

2 b c Catrail (USA) - Soreze (IRE) **(92?f)** (Gallic League)
Form - 321
Record 1999 - 1st:1 2nd:1 3rd:1 Ran:3
Win Prizemoney £6,550 *Total Prizemoney* £8,450
Wins * **1999** Oct York (G-S) 6f 82 <
1999 Turf 1-3: (6f 1-3) (gd 1-2, g-f)
Currently decent colt. Turf high 82 (began Spt) - 1st of 9 from Material Witness (6 Oct York RF 4753).
**J H M Gosden [1-3] Sheikh Mohammed.*

STRAND OF GOLD BHB 68f RR 77f 4928[4]

2 b c Lugana Beach 7f **(63)** - Miss Display (Touch Paper) 6.8f **(57)**
Form - 0274
Record 1999 - 1st:0 2nd:1 3rd:0 Ran:4
Win Prizemoney £0 *Total Prizemoney* £1,145
1999 Turf 0-4: (5f, 6f 2, 7f) (sft, gd 2, g-f)
Above-average colt. Turf high 77 (began Aug) - 2nd of 11 getting 6lb from Brandon Rock (15 Spt Sandown 5f gd RF 4327).
**R Hannon [0-4] The Gold Buster Syndicate.*

STRASBOURG (USA) BHB 97f RR 87f 5029[8]

2 ch c Dehere (USA) - Pixie Erin (Golden Fleece (USA)) 7.9f **(74)**
Form - 128
Record 1999 - 1st:1 2nd:1 3rd:0 Ran:3
Win Prizemoney £3,192 *Total Prizemoney* £5,265
Wins **1999** Spt Chepst (GD) 7.1f 82+ <
1999 Turf 1-3: (7f 1-3) (g-s, gd, frm 1-1)
Currently useful colt. Turf high 87 (began Spt) - 2nd of 8 giving 5lb to Sun Charm (12 Oct Leicester 7f gd RF 4833) - also 1st of 12 from Tolstoy (9 Spt Chepstow RF 4226). He made a winning debut at Chepstow in September and came up against a very decent newcomer at Leicester next time. Found wanting in a Group Three on his final run.
**A G Foster [0-2] R E Sangster (from P W Chapple-Hyam [1-1] Spt 1999).*

STRATEGIC RR 118f 4770a[2]

3 b c Caerleon (USA) 10.9f **(79)** - Game Plan (Darshaan) 9.9f **(84)**
Form - 1212
1999 Turf 2-4: (10f 2-4) (hvy, gd 1-1, frm 1-2)
High-class colt, effective 10f, acts on hvy to frm. Turf high 118 (began Jly) - 2nd of 9 to State Shinto (2 Oct Longchamp 10f hvy RF 4770a). Son of an Oaks runner-up, he showed some decent form last season, winning a Curragh conditions event and gaining a very easy win in a Leopardstown Group Three. Very creditable efforts when a close second to Zomaradah in the Royal Whip and to State Shinto in the Prix Dollar. Now with Godolphin.
**J Oxx in IRE [3-6].*

STRATEGIC CHOICE (USA) BHB 99f RR 96f 2882[6]

8 b h Alleged (USA) 11.8f **(81)** - Danlu (USA) (Danzig (USA)) 8.4f **(76)**
Form - 046
Record 1999 - 1st:0 2nd:0 3rd:0 Ran:2
Pre1999 - 1st:6 2nd:5 3rd:5 Ran:30
Win Prizemoney £338,403 *Total Prizemoney* £828,912

Wins								
*	1997	Spt	Velief	(FRM)		12f	113+	
*	1996	Aug	Deauvi	(GD)	G2	12.5f	118	
*	1996	Jun	San Si	(GD)	G1	12f	116	
*	1995	Spt	Currag	(GD)	G1	14f	119	<
*	1995	Apr	Newbur	(GD)	G3	12f	113	

1999 Turf 0-2: (12f 2) (g-f, frm)
Very useful horse, effective 12 to 14f, acts on gd, has worn blinkers. Turf high 85. Consistent. Age looks to have caught up with him.
**P F I Cole [6-32] M Arbib.*

STRATHBLAIR RR 9f 2157[7]

3 b g Bustino 11f **(64)** - Orlaith (Final Straw) 7.9f **(64)**
Form - 7
Record 1999 - 1st:0 2nd:0 3rd:0 Ran:1
1999 Turf 0-1: (8f) (frm)
Rangy, currently very poor gelding.
**G M Moore [0-1] The Braw Partnership.*

STRAT'S QUEST BHB 51f44a RR 50f 44a 4713[4]

5 b m Nicholas (USA) 6.1f **(63)** - Eagle's Quest (Legal Eagle) 7.3f **(54)**
Form - 85042126074
Record 1999 - 1st:1 2nd:2 3rd:0 Ran:9
Pre1999 - 1st:2 2nd:0 3rd:1 Ran:29
Win Prizemoney £8,578 *Total Prizemoney* £11,915

Wins									
*	*1999*	*Mar*	*Southw*	*(STD)*	*SH*	*6f*	*41*	*48*	
*	1997	May	Windso	(SFT)	H	6f	64	58	
*	1996	Oct	Chepst	(SFT)	H	6.1f	64	64	<

1999 Turf 0-3: (5f, 6f, 7f) (sft, g-s, gd) 1999 AW 1-6: (6f 1-5, 7f) (Equi, Fibr 1-5)
Fair filly, effective 5f, acts on hvy, has worn blinkers. Turf high 50. AW high 48.
**D W P Arbuthnot [3-38] Jack Blumenow.*

STRATTON (IRE) RR 80f 4875[6]

2 b c Fairy King (USA) 7.7f **(75)** - Golden Bloom (Main Reef) 9.6f **(57)**
Form - 6
Record 1999 - 1st:0 2nd:0 3rd:0 Ran:1
1999 Turf 0-1: (6f) (gd)
Currently decent colt.
**C F Wall [0-1] Peter Willmott.*

STRAVINSKY (USA) RR 128+f 5227a[6]

3 b c Nureyev (USA) 8.4f **(84)** - Fire the Groom (USA) (Blushing Groom (FR)) 10.3f **(76)**
Form - 24116
1999 Turf 2-4: (5f 1-1, 6f 1-1, 7f 2) (sft, gd 1-2, frm 1-1) 1999 AW 0-1: (6f) (Dirt)
Well made, top-class colt, effective 5 to 6f, acts on gd to frm, has worn blinkers. Turf high 128 - 1st of 17 getting 6lb from Bold Edge (8 Jly Newmarket RF 2643) - also 1st of 16 giving 1lb to Sainte Marine (19 Aug York RF 3772). One of the early favourites for the 2000 Guineas after an impressive juvenile debut at York, he disap-

pointed on more than one occasion afterwards, and never got to Newmarket. He looked a shade reluctant when fourth in the Jersey Stakes at Ascot in 1999 and the future was looking bleak. However, dropped back to six furlongs and fitted with blinkers, he turned the July Cup into a procession, producing an impressive turn of foot to leave most of the best sprinters in Europe floundering. He followed up over five in the Nunthorpe, and the Champion European sprinter title was his. He ran well for a long way in the Breeders' Cup Sprint, but had used his speed to hold a position, and had nothing left at the end. He has retired to stud in Kentucky.

**A P O'Brien in IRE [3-8] M Tabor.*

STRAVSEA BHB 36f45a **RR 33f 45a** 4935[7]

4 b f Handsome Sailor 6.6f **(53)** -La Stravaganza (Slip Anchor) 9.8f **(73)**

Stravinsky became the star European-trained sprinter

Form - 043300222010067

Record 1999 - 1st:1 2nd:3 3rd:2 Ran:15
Pre1999 - 1st:0 2nd:5 3rd:2 Ran:16

Win Prizemoney £2,416 *Total Prizemoney* £9,231

Wins * 1999 *Jly Southw (STD) H 8f 45 49 <*

1999 Turf 0-2: (7f, 8f) (g-f, frm) 1999 AW 1-13: (6f, 7f 5, 8f 1-7) (Fibr 1-13)

Scopey, moderate filly, effective 6 to 7f, best at 6f, - acts on Fibr, likes left handed tracks, likes tight tracks, excels at Southwell. Turf high 33. AW high 49.

**R Hollinshead [1-9] E Bennion (from B P J Baugh [0-22] Mar 1999).*

STRAZO (IRE) BHB 69f80a **RR 72f 80a** 5217[18]

6 b g Alzao (USA) 9.8f **(73)** - Ministra (USA) (Deputy Minister (CAN)) 7.4f **(80)**

Form - 007807500

Record 1999 - 1st:0 2nd:0 3rd:0 Ran:8
Pre1999 - 1st:4 2nd:2 3rd:0 Ran:20

Win Prizemoney £19,724 *Total Prizemoney* £28,371

Wins * 1997 Nov Nottin (GD) 8.2f 100 <
* 1997 Oct Newmar (G-F) 8f 94
1996 Jun Salisb (G-F) 7f 84
1996 May Chepst (G-S) 8.1f 82+

1999 Turf 0-8: (7f, 8f 3, 9f, 10f 3) (g-s 3, g-f 2, frm 3)

Above-average gelding, effective 7f, acts on frm, has worn blinkers. Turf high 83. Inconsistent. He failed to recapture his best form - achieved in 1997 - and has little to recommend him.

**Lady Herries [2-27] Lady Herries (from J H M Gosden [2-4] Jly 1996).*

STREAK OF DAWN RR 20f 2887[10]

2 b f Old Vic 12.8f **(72)** - Nafla (FR) (Arctic Tern (USA)) 8.9f **(69)**

Form - 00

Record 1999 - 1st:0 2nd:0 3rd:0 Ran:2

1999 Turf 0-2: (6f 2) (frm 2)

Currently little account filly. Turf high 20.

**K A Ryan [0-2] J B J Richards.*

STREET GENERAL BHB 105f **RR 107f** 1715a[3]

5 b h Generous (IRE) 11.5f **(82)** - Hotel Street (USA) (Alleged (USA)) 10f **(76)**

Form - 3

1999 Turf 0-1: (12f) (frm)

Pattern-class colt, effective 12 to 14f, best at 14f, acts on gd to frm, best on frm. (1st run) - 3rd of 10 to Ivan Luis (29 May Capannelle 12f frm RF 1715a). A useful stayer with Henry Cecil in 1998, he was trained in Italy in 1999.

**O Pessi in ITY [0-1] (from H R A Cecil [1-8] Aug 1998).*

STREET WALKER (IRE) BHB 54f **RR 54f** 4558[3]

3 b f Dolphin Street (FR) - Foolish Dame (USA) (Foolish Pleasure (USA)) 8.9f **(72)**

Form - 60024253

Record 1999 - 1st:0 2nd:2 3rd:1 Ran:8
Pre1999 - 1st:0 2nd:0 3rd:0 Ran:1

Win Prizemoney £0 *Total Prizemoney* £2,179

1999 Turf 0-8: (8f 5, 9f, 10f 2) (g-s, gd, g-f 4, frm 2)

Neat, fair filly, effective 8 to 10f, acts on gd to g-f, prefers tight tracks. Turf high 63. **C F Wall [0-9] The Boardroom Syndicate.*

STRENSALL RR 23f 2300[12]

2 b c Beveled (USA) 6.9f **(64)** - Payvashooz (Ballacashtal (CAN)) 5.3f **(50)**

Form - 00

Record 1999 - 1st:0 2nd:0 3rd:0 Ran:2

1999 Turf 0-2: (6f 2) (g-f, frm)

Currently little account colt. Turf high 23.

**M Brittain [0-2] Northgate Lodge Racing Club.*

STRETCHING (IRE) BHB 50f42a **RR 8f 42a** 159[7]

6 br g Contract Law (USA) 8.9f **(54)** - Mrs Mutton (Dancers Image (USA)) 9.3f **(71)**

Form - 7

Record 1999 - 1st:0 2nd:0 3rd:0 Ran:1
Pre1999 - 1st:0 2nd:1 3rd:0 Ran:6

Win Prizemoney £0 *Total Prizemoney* £1,085

1999 AW 0-1: (12f) (Fibr)

Very poor gelding, has worn blinkers.

**A G Juckes [0-1] A C W Price (from A Bailey [0-7] May 1997).*

STRICTLY SPEAKING (IRE) BHB 67f **RR 71f** 4820[5]

2 b c Sri Pekan (USA) - Gaijin (Caerleon (USA)) 8.6f **(71)**

Form - 6345

Record 1999 - 1st:0 2nd:0 3rd:1 Ran:4

Win Prizemoney £0 *Total Prizemoney* £785

1999 Turf 0-4: (6f, 8f 2, 10f) (g-s, gd 2, g-f)

Above-average colt. Turf high 71 (began Jly) - 3rd of 12 to Sandmason (20 Spt Kempton 8f g-s RF 4430).

**P F I Cole [0-4] R O M Racing.*

STRIDHANA BHB 65f **RR 42f** 5033[20]

3 ch f Indian Ridge 7.6f **(74)** - French Gift **(92f)** (Cadeaux Genereux)

Form - 4831000

Record 1999 - 1st:1 2nd:0 3rd:1 Ran:7

Win Prizemoney £4,592 *Total Prizemoney* £5,393

Wins * 1999 Aug Lingfi (G-F) 6f 72 <

1999 Turf 1-7: (6f 1-4, 7f 2, 8f) (g-s, gd, g-f 1-3, frm 2)

Unfurnished, moderate filly, effective 6f, acts on g-f to frm. Turf high 72 - 1st of 11 getting 5lb from Antonio Canova (24 Aug Lingfield RF 3873). **D R C Elsworth [1-7] Raymond Tooth.*

STRIDING KING BHB 49f60a **RR 42f 60a** 3056[13]

4 ch g King's Signet (USA) 7f **(51)** - Stride Home (Absalom) 7.2f **(58)**

Form - 0800

Record 1999 - 1st:0 2nd:0 3rd:0 Ran:4
Pre1999 - 1st:0 2nd:2 3rd:3 Ran:8

Win Prizemoney £0 *Total Prizemoney* £3,162

1999 Turf 0-4: (5f, 6f 2, 7f) (g-f, frm 3)

Scopey, fair gelding. Turf high 46. Consistent.

**M R Channon [0-12] Peter Taplin.*

STRINDBERG RR 42f 833[8]
3 b c Bering 9.6f **(80)** - Dagny Juel (USA) (Danzig (USA)) 8.4f **(76)**
Form - 8
Record 1999 - 1st:0 2nd:0 3rd:0 Ran:1
1999 Turf 0-1: (10f) (sft)
Strong, currently moderate colt. *J L Dunlop [0-1] Miss K Rausing.*

STRINGERS (IRE) BHB 45f40a **RR 48f 40a** 364[9]
4 ch g Shalford (IRE) 7.8f **(63)** - Rebecca's Girl (IRE) (Nashamaa) 7.1f **(66)**
Form - 0
Record 1999 - 1st:0 2nd:0 3rd:0 Ran:1
Pre1999 - 1st:0 2nd:0 3rd:0 Ran:3
1999 AW 0-1: (8f) (Fibr)
Rangy, moderate gelding. *S E Kettlewell [0-4] S E Kettlewell.*

STRING QUARTET (IRE) BHB 102f **RR 107f** 4794[4]
3 b f Sadler's Wells (USA) 11.3f **(87)** - Fleur Royale (Mill Reef (USA)) 10.5f **(78)**
Form - 813314
Record 1999 - 1st:2 2nd:0 3rd:2 Ran:6
Win Prizemoney £19,115 *Total Prizemoney* £27,472
Wins 1999 Aug Deauvi (HVY) L 12.5f 107 <
1999 May Chepst (G-S) 10.2f 83
1999 Turf 2-6: (10f 1-3, 12f 2, 13f 1-1) (hvy 1-1, gd 1-4, g-f)
Leggy, Pattern-class filly, effective 10 to 13f, acts on hvy to gd. Turf high 107 - 1st of 10 from Kansa (8 Aug Deauville RF 3590a). Unraced as a juvenile, she ran respectably in a Newbury listed race after winning her maiden at Chepstow in May. She was a creditable third in the Lancashire Oaks, and was awarded a Deauville listed event in the Stewards' Room.
A G Foster [0-1] R E Sangster (from P W Chapple-Hyam [2-5] Aug 1999).

STRIP SEARCH BHB 34f40a **RR 30df 40a** 4819[11]
3 b f Bluebird (USA) 7.9f **(71)** - Swift Pursuit (Posse (USA)) 8.9f **(61)**
Form - 67000
Record 1999 - 1st:0 2nd:0 3rd:0 Ran:5
Pre1999 - 1st:0 2nd:0 3rd:0 Ran:4
1999 Turf 0-3: (7f, 10f, 12f) (gd, frm 2) 1999 AW 0-2: (7f, 10f) (Equi 2)
Leggy, very moderate filly, has worn blinkers. Turf high 30. AW high 29. Consistent. *J G Smyth-Osbourne [0-9] J G Smyth-Osbourne.*

STROMSHOLM (IRE) RR 76f 4824[2]
3 ch g Indian Ridge 7.6f **(74)** - Upward Trend (Salmon Leap (USA)) 11f **(61)**
Form - 02
Record 1999 - 1st:0 2nd:1 3rd:0 Ran:2
Win Prizemoney £0 *Total Prizemoney* £924
1999 Turf 0-2: (8f 2) (gd, g-f)
Lengthy, currently above-average gelding. Turf high 76 (began Aug) - 2nd of 14 giving 5lb to Sheer Harmony (11 Oct Windsor 8f g-f RF 4824). *J R Fanshawe [0-2] Paul & Jenny Green.*

STRONGDAKA (IRE) BHB 33f **RR 47f** 259[8]
6 b m Strong Gale - Randaka (Main Reef) 9.6f **(57)**
Form - 78
Record 1999 - 1st:0 2nd:0 3rd:0 Ran:1
Pre1999 - 1st:0 2nd:0 3rd:0 Ran:4
1999 AW 0-1: (16f) (Equi)
Moderate mare. (DEAD)
P J Hobbs [0-3] R F L Steels Ltd (from T J Taaffe in IRE [0-8] Nov 1998).

STRONG PRESENCE RR 75f 5209[5]
2 b c Anshan 8.2f **(63)** - Lazybird Blue (IRE) (Bluebird (USA)) 7.5f **(69)**
Form - 5
Record 1999 - 1st:0 2nd:0 3rd:0 Ran:1
1999 Turf 0-1: (6f) (g-s)
Currently above-average colt. *T P Tate [0-1] T P Tate.*

STUDLEY PARK BHB 50f **RR 52f** 4980[12]
3 b f Northern Park (USA) 10f **(57)** - B A Poundstretcher (Laser Light) 9f **(68)**
Form - 00064500
Record 1999 - 1st:0 2nd:0 3rd:0 Ran:8
Pre1999 - 1st:1 2nd:0 3rd:1 Ran:3
Win Prizemoney £7,226 *Total Prizemoney* £7,967
Wins * 1998 Spt York (GD) 7.9f 64 <
1999 Turf 0-8: (8f 3, 9f, 10f 3, 12f) (gd 2, g-f 2, frm 3, hrd)
Scopey, fair filly, effective 8f, acts on frm, likes left handed tracks. Turf high 52. *P Calver [1-11] The Ripon Ringers.*

STURGEON (IRE) BHB 62f **RR 67f** 4088[7]
5 ch g Caerleon (USA) 10.9f **(79)** - Ridge The Times (USA) (Riva Ridge (USA)) 8.2f **(68)**
Form - 014707
Record 1999 - 1st:1 2nd:0 3rd:0 Ran:6
Pre1999 - 1st:0 2nd:2 3rd:2 Ran:12
Win Prizemoney £4,201 *Total Prizemoney* £8,348
Wins * 1999 Jun Ripon (G-F) H 10f 63 68 <
1999 Turf 1-6: (8f, 10f 1-4, 12f) (g-f 2, frm 3, hrd 1-1)
Average gelding, effective 9 to 10f, best at 10f, acts on g-f to hrd, has worn blinkers, likes right handed tracks, favours tight tracks. Turf high 68 - 1st of 7 getting 3lb from Welcome Sunset (16 Jun Ripon RF 2059). He took a very long time in getting off the mark, but took a ten-furlong Ripon handicap in June.
K A Morgan [1-15] J Cleeve (from P F I Cole [0-6] Aug 1997).

STUTTON GAL (IRE) BHB 30f44a **RR 27f 44a** 5167[13]
3 b f Up and At 'em - Sashi Woo (Rusticaro (FR)) 8.2f **(65)**
Form - 73525545040
Record 1999 - 1st:0 2nd:1 3rd:0 Ran:8
Pre1999 - 1st:0 2nd:0 3rd:1 Ran:8
Win Prizemoney £0 *Total Prizemoney* £923
1999 Turf 0-3: (5f, 6f, 7f) (g-s, gd, frm) 1999 AW 0-5: (5f, 6f, 7f 2, 8f) (Fibr 5)
Lengthy, very moderate filly, effective 7f, - acts on Fibr, often wears blinkers (effectively), likes left handed tracks, likes tight tracks. Turf high 27. AW high 49. *J Wharton [0-16] T A Hughes.*

STYLE DANCER (IRE) BHB 62f60a **RR 74df 60a** 5166[14]
5 b g Dancing Dissident (USA) 6.8f **(65)** - Showing Style (Pas de Seul) 9.1f **(67)**
Form - 0005064154073344000
Record 1999 - 1st:1 2nd:0 3rd:2 Ran:19
Pre1999 - 1st:2 2nd:3 3rd:6 Ran:31
Win Prizemoney £13,816 *Total Prizemoney* £27,159
Wins * 1999 Jly Haydoc (G-S) H 7.1f 60 61
* 1998 Jly York (FRM) H 7f 70 73 <
* 1996 Oct Redcar (G-F) H 6f 70 72
1999 Turf 1-19: (6f, 7f 1-11, 8f 6, 9f) (g-s 2, gd 1-6, g-f 4, frm 5, hrd 2)
Above-average gelding, effective 7f, acts on gd to frm, often wears blinkers. Turf high 74. Becoming disappointing.
R M Whitaker [3-50] Mrs C A Hodgetts.

STYLISH BEAUTY BHB 73f **RR 76df** 4599[9]
2 b f Night Shift (USA) 8.1f **(73)** - Reine de Neige (Kris) 9.5f **(73)**
Form - 1530
Record 1999 - 1st:1 2nd:0 3rd:1 Ran:4
Win Prizemoney £3,496 *Total Prizemoney* £4,045
Wins * 1999 May Leices (G-F) 5f 76+ <
1999 Turf 1-4: (5f 1-2, 6f, 7f) (gd, g-f 2, frm 1-1)
Above-average filly. Turf high 76 (1st run) - 1st of 9 from Kelso Magic (24 May Leicester RF 1434). Has gone backwards since a promising start. *E A L Dunlop [1-4] Maktoum Al Maktoum.*

STYLISH WAYS (IRE) BHB 66f **RR 63f** 5160[13]
7 b g Thatching 7.8f **(69)** - Style Of Life (USA) (The Minstrel (CAN)) 10f **(72)**
Form - 453060002800750
Record 1999 - 1st:0 2nd:1 3rd:1 Ran:15
Pre1999 - 1st:4 2nd:3 3rd:7 Ran:34
Win Prizemoney £20,706 *Total Prizemoney* £44,762
Wins * 1998 Oct Haydoc (SFT) H 6f 71 76
* 1998 Aug Newmar (G-F) H 6f 67 69
1995 May Leices (G-F) 6f 93 <
1999 Turf 0-15: (6f 13, 7f 2) (g-s 2, gd 4, g-f 3, frm 6)
Average gelding, effective 6f, acts on g-f. Turf high 91. Consistent.
J Pearce [2-33] Ian Hall (from Miss S E Hall [0-8] Nov 1996).

SUALTACH (IRE) BHB 55f67a **RR 56f 67a** 4993[14]
6 b h Marju (IRE) 9.2f **(76)** - Astra Adastra (Mount Hagen (FR)) 8.4f

(70)
Form - 22241653000770465000
Record 1999 - 1st:1 2nd:1 3rd:1 Ran:18
Pre1999 - 1st:9 2nd:11 3rd:3 Ran:61
Win Prizemoney £36,119 *Total Prizemoney* £57,450
Wins * **1999** *Jan Wolver (STD) H 9.4f 78 82*
* 1998 Spt Haydoc (G-F) H 8.1f 70 72
* 1998 *Jly Wolver (STD) C 8.5f 76*
* 1998 *Apr Wolver (STD) H 8.5f 73 78*
* 1998 *Feb Wolver (STD) H 8.5f 72 71*
* 1998 *Jan Wolver (STD) H 9.4f 69 71*
* 1997 Oct Redcar (G-F) H 8f 69 74
* 1996 *May Wolver (STD) H 7f 70 81*
* 1996 Mar Doncas (SFT) H 7f 75 83
* 1995 Jun Nottin (G-F) 6.1f 87+ <
1999 Turf 0-9: (8f 2, 10f 6, 11f) (g-s 2, gd 2, g-f 2, frm 3) 1999 AW 1-9: (8f 5, 9f 1-4) (Fibr 1-9)
Above-average horse, effective 7 to 10f, best at 9f, acts on gd to frm - acts on Fibr, has worn blinkers, likes left handed tracks, likes tight tracks, excels at Haydock, likes Wolverhampton. Turf high 64. AW high 82 - 1st of 9 giving 2lb to Tallulah Belle (27 Jan Wolverhampton RF 0177). **R Hollinshead [10-79] Noel Sweeney.*

SUAVE FRANKIE BHB 48f40a RR 53df 40a 4863[8]
3 ch c Suave Dancer (USA) 10.7f **(68)** - Francia **(58f)** (Legend of France (USA)) 9.5f **(61)**
Form - 204208
Record 1999 - 1st:0 2nd:2 3rd:0 Ran:6
Pre1999 - 1st:0 2nd:0 3rd:0 Ran:3
Win Prizemoney £0 *Total Prizemoney* £1,724
1999 Turf 0-5: (11f, 12f 2, 14f, 16f) (g-f, frm 4) 1999 AW 0-1: (15f) (Fibr)
Unfurnished, fair colt, effective 16f, acts on frm, has worn blinkers, likes tight tracks. Turf high 53. Inconsistent.
**S C Williams [0-9] Bruce Wyatt.*

SUBEEN BHB 106f RR 99f 976[3]
3 b f Caerleon (USA) 10.9f **(79)** - Khamsin (USA) (Mr Prospector (USA)) 8.8f **(78)**
Form - 3
Record 1999 - 1st:0 2nd:0 3rd:1 Ran:1
Pre1999 - 1st:1 2nd:0 3rd:2 Ran:3
Win Prizemoney £3,781 *Total Prizemoney* £22,178
Wins 1998 Spt Yarmou (G-S) 6f 87+ <
1999 Turf 0-1: (7f) (frm)
Well made, very useful filly. She did not grow and failed to train on
**S bin Suroor [0-1] Godolphin (from D R Loder [1-3] Spt 1998).*

SUCCESSFUL APPEAL (USA) RR 5227a[5]
3 br c Valid Appeal (USA) - Successful Dancer (USA) (Fortunate Dancer (USA))
Form - 5
1999 AW 0-1: (6f) (Dirt)
Currently Group-class. **J Kimmel in USA [0-1].*

SUCH BOLDNESS BHB 55f65a RR 56f 65a 2296[5]
5 b h Persian Bold 10f **(69)** - Bone China (IRE) (Sadler's Wells (USA)) 10f **(76)**
Form - 23211502035
Record 1999 - 1st:2 2nd:2 3rd:2 Ran:10
Pre1999 - 1st:0 2nd:2 3rd:4 Ran:11
Win Prizemoney £4,260 *Total Prizemoney* £10,202
Wins * **1999** *Jan Lingfi (STD) 12f 66+ <*
* **1999** *Jan Southw (STD) H 12f 58 61*
1999 Turf 0-4: (10f, 11f, 12f 2) (g-f 2, frm 2) 1999 AW 2-6: (10f, 11f 2, 12f 2-2, 13f) (Equi 1-3, Fibr 1-3)
Average colt, effective 10 to 14f, best at 14f, acts on gd to frm - acts on AW, best on frm, likes left handed tracks, favours tight tracks, does well at Lingfield. Turf high 56. AW high 66 - also 1st of 11 getting 2lb from Haydn James (21 Jan Lingfield RF 0139).
**Miss Gay Kelleway [2-18] Mrs M E O'Shea (from R Akehurst [0-3] Jly 1997).*

SUCH FLAIR (USA) RR 64f 5136[9]
2 b f Kingmambo (USA) 10.9f **(85)** - Lady Fairfax **(93df)** (Sharrood (USA)) 10.5f **(72)**
Form - 0
Record 1999 - 1st:0 2nd:0 3rd:0 Ran:1
1999 Turf 0-1: (7f) (gd)
Currently average filly. **J Noseda [0-1] Sanford Robertson.*

SUDDEN FLIGHT (IRE) BHB 69f RR 69f 4934[8]
2 b c In The Wings 11.2f **(77)** - Ma Petite Cherie (USA) (Caro)
Form - 500138
Record 1999 - 1st:1 2nd:0 3rd:1 Ran:6
Win Prizemoney £3,314 *Total Prizemoney* £3,731
Wins * **1999** Spt Yarmou (SFT) H 8f 62 67 <
1999 Turf 1-6: (7f 3, 8f 1-2, 10f) (g-s 1-2, g-f 2, frm 2)
Average colt, effective 8 to 10f, acts on g-s. Turf high 69 - 3rd of 16 giving 7lb to Marjeune (5 Oct Nottingham 10f g-s RF 4727) - also 1st of 15 from Queen For A Day (16 Spt Yarmouth RF 4358).
**E A L Dunlop [1-6] Maktoum Al Maktoum.*

SUDDEN SQUALL (USA) BHB 73f RR 76f 709[7]
3 ch c Gulch (USA) 9.6f **(79)** - Sudden Storm Bird (USA) (Storm Bird (CAN)) 10.3f **(74)**
Form - 07
Record 1999 - 1st:0 2nd:0 3rd:0 Ran:2
Pre1999 - 1st:1 2nd:0 3rd:1 Ran:5
Win Prizemoney £3,494 *Total Prizemoney* £4,074
Wins * 1998 Oct Lingfi (SFT) H 7f 71 76 <
1999 Turf 0-2: (10f, 12f) (gd 2)
Scopey, above-average colt, effective 7 to 8f, acts on g-s to frm. Turf high 60. **J H M Gosden [1-7] Sheikh Mohammed.*

SUDEST (IRE) BHB 65f85a RR 43f 85a 3450[8]
5 b g Taufan (USA) 8.3f **(65)** - Frill (Henbit (USA)) 9f **(61)**
Form - 1112208
Record 1999 - 1st:3 2nd:2 3rd:0 Ran:7
Pre1999 - 1st:3 2nd:2 3rd:1 Ran:21
Win Prizemoney £17,843 *Total Prizemoney* £23,532
Wins * **1999** *Jan Wolver (STD) H 16.2f 75 80*
* **1999** *Jan Wolver (STD) H 14.8f 64 81 <*
* **1999** *Jan Wolver (STD) H 16.2f 64 72*
* 1997 Jun Bath (G-F) 11.7f 73
* 1997 May Bath (G-F) H 17.2f 64 69
* 1997 May Warwic (FRM) H 12.5f 59 64
1999 Turf 0-2: (14f, 16f) (gd 2) 1999 AW 3-5: (15f 1-1, 16f 2-4) (Fibr 3-5)
Very useful gelding, effective 16f, - acts on Fibr, prefers left handed tracks, prefers tight tracks. (began Jly). AW high 101 - 2nd of 8 giving 6lb to Far Cry (13 Mar Wolverhampton 16f Fibr RF 0433). Inconsistent. He had a fine time on Fibresand, completing a quickfire hat-trick in staying handicaps during January. Less effective on the turf, he was sold for only 3,400 guineas at Newmarket in October. **I A Balding [7-31] Robert Hitchins.*

SUDRA BHB 96f RR 94f 4690[15]
2 b c Indian Ridge 7.6f **(74)** - Bunting **(90f)** (Shaadi (USA))
Form - 310
Record 1999 - 1st:1 2nd:0 3rd:1 Ran:3
Win Prizemoney £4,391 *Total Prizemoney* £5,013
Wins * **1999** Aug Thirsk (G-F) 6f 94+ <
1999 Turf 1-3: (6f 1-3) (gd, g-f, hrd 1-1)
Currently useful colt. Turf high 94 - 1st of 19 giving 5lb to Jaybird (27 Aug Thirsk RF 3943). Third in a Goodwood maiden on his debut, he improved greatly on that effort when winning a Thirsk maiden next time out over six furlongs. There should be more to come. **E A L Dunlop [1-3] Mohammed Al Nabouda.*

SUE ME (IRE) BHB 60f54a RR 59f 54a 5167[14]
7 b or br g Contract Law (USA) 8.9f **(54)** - Pink Fondant (Northfields (USA)) 9f **(72)**
Form - 4134083730100
Record 1999 - 1st:2 2nd:0 3rd:3 Ran:12
Pre1999 - 1st:6 2nd:6 3rd:5 Ran:61
Win Prizemoney £28,861 *Total Prizemoney* £40,328
Wins * **1999** Spt Ayr (G-S) H 5f 57 59
* **1999** *Jan Southw (STD) C 6f 67*
* 1998 *Spt Southw (STD) H 6f 56 58*
* 1998 Jly Doncas (G-F) H 5f 62 68
* 1998 Apr Pontef (G-S) H 5f 59 62
* 1998 *Feb Southw (STD) H 6f 43 49*
* 1998 *Jan Southw (STD) H 6f 44 45*
1999 Turf 1-6: (5f 1-4, 6f 2) (g-s 1-2, gd, g-f, frm 2) 1999 AW 1-6: (6f 1-6) (Fibr 1-6)
Fair gelding, effective 5 to 6f, best at 5f, acts on g-s to frm - acts

on Fibr, has worn blinkers, likes Southwell. Turf high 59. AW high 67 (1st run) - 1st of 10 getting 4lb from Trojan Hero (8 Jan Southwell RF 0053). Inconsistent.
**D Nicholls [7-43] T G Meynell (from W R Muir [1-30] Jan 1997).*

SUE'S REPREMAND RR 11f 3009[10]

3 b f Reprimand 8.2f **(63)** - Poyle Amber (Sharrood (USA)) 10.5f **(72)**
Form - 00
Record 1999 - 1st:0 2nd:0 3rd:0 Ran:2
1999 Turf 0-2: (8f, 10f) (gd, frm)
Unfurnished, currently poor filly. Turf high 11 (began Jly).
**A P Jarvis [0-2] A L R Morton.*

SUEZ TORNADO (IRE) BHB 58f54a RR 55f 54a 5071[10]

6 ch g Mujtahid (USA) 7.4f **(69)** - So Stylish (Great Nephew) 9.9f **(64)**
Form - 004063251353741650
Record 1999 - 1st:2 2nd:1 3rd:3 Ran:16
Pre1999 - 1st:2 2nd:1 3rd:3 Ran:41
Win Prizemoney £14,155 *Total Prizemoney* £24,131

Wins							
* **1999**	Spt	Newmar	(G-S)	C	12f		55
* **1999**	Jly	Ayr	(GD)	H	9.1f	47	50
* 1997	Jun	Newmar	(G-S)	H	8f	61	63
1996	Jly	Killar	(GD)		8.5f		68 <

1999 Turf 2-16: (7f, 8f, 9f 1-2, 10f 8, 11f 2, 12f 1-2) (hvy, sft, g-s, gd 2-5, g-f 2, frm 6)
Average gelding, effective 8 to 12f, best at 8f, acts on gd to frm - acts on Fibr, has worn blinkers, prefers right handed tracks, does well at Newmarket. Turf high 55 - 3rd of 12 giving 10lb to Missile Toe (30 Jly Newmarket 10f frm RF 3241) - also 1st of 15 giving 1lb to Dominant Duchess (30 Spt Newmarket RF 4650).
**E J Alston [3-50] Papermates Racing (from D K Weld in IRE [1-7] Aug 1996).*

SUGAR CUBE TREAT BHB 58f RR 55f 5199[9]

3 b f Lugana Beach 7f **(63)** - Fair Eleanor (Saritamer (USA)) 9.5f **(63)**
Form - 0533560010
Record 1999 - 1st:1 2nd:0 3rd:2 Ran:10
Pre1999 - 1st:0 2nd:0 3rd:1 Ran:7
Win Prizemoney £3,369 *Total Prizemoney* £5,378

Wins								
* **1999**	Oct	Ayr	(SFT)	H	6f	50	55	<

1999 Turf 1-10: (6f 1-7, 7f 2, 8f) (sft 1-1, g-s, gd, g-f 2, frm 5)
Light-framed, fair filly, effective 6 to 7f, acts on sft to gd. Turf high 55.
**M Mullineaux [1-17] Abbey Racing.*

SUGARFOOT BHB 114f RR 117f 4916[5]

5 ch h Thatching 7.8f **(69)** - Norpella (Northfields (USA)) 9f **(72)**
Form - 316301125
Record 1999 - 1st:3 2nd:1 3rd:2 Ran:9
Pre1999 - 1st:4 2nd:4 3rd:1 Ran:16
Win Prizemoney £122,383 *Total Prizemoney* £177,648

Wins							
* **1999**	Spt	Doncas	(G-F)	G3	8f		117 <
* **1999**	Aug	York	(GD)	H	7.9f	105	116
* **1999**	May	York	(SFT)	LH	7.9f	104	106
* 1998	Oct	York	(GD)	H	7.9f	99	104
* 1998	Aug	York	(FRM)	H	7.9f	92	97
* 1998	Jly	Ascot	(G-F)	H	8f	87	92
* 1996	Jly	Ayr	(G-F)		6f		82+

1999 Turf 3-9: (7f 2, 8f 3-7) (sft, g-s 1-1, gd 1-5, g-f 1-2)
High-class colt, effective 8f, acts on sft to g-f, prefers left handed tracks, excels at York. Turf high 117 - 2nd of 9 to Trans Island (3 Oct Longchamp 8f sft RF 4779a) - also 1st of 10 giving 5lb to Wallace (9 Spt Doncaster RF 4235). Consistent. A most progressive performer, he has a tremendous record over a mile at York, winning four times in all, two of which were last season including a second Bradford & Bingley. He gained his biggest success to date when getting up in the final strides to win the Group Three Park Stakes at the Doncaster St Leger meeting, and was only just beaten by Trans Island in the Prix du Rond-Point. A credit to his trainer.
**N Tinkler [7-25] Mrs D Wright.*

SUGAR MILL BHB 77f RR 85?f 954[8]

9 b g Slip Anchor 12.7f **(75)** - Great Tom (Great Nephew) 9.9f **(64)**
Form - 8
Record 1999 - 1st:0 2nd:0 3rd:0 Ran:1
Pre1999 - 1st:5 2nd:2 3rd:3 Ran:16
Win Prizemoney £21,659 *Total Prizemoney* £28,530

Wins							
* 1997	Mar	Haydoc	(SFT)	H	11.9f	77	85 <
* 1996	Oct	Haydoc	(SFT)	H	11.9f	73	77
* 1996	Aug	Ripon	(SFT)	H	12.3f	67	71
* 1996	Aug	Ripon	(GD)	H	12.3f	64	70
* 1995	Oct	Doncas	(G-F)	H	14.6f	63	73

1999 Turf 0-1: (14f) (g-f)
Useful gelding.
**Mrs M Reveley [6-20] C C Buckley.*

SUGAR REEF BHB 12f RR 12f 5101[13]

5 br g High Kicker (USA) 8.4f **(52)** - Miss Poll Flinders (Swing Easy (USA)) 6.5f **(55)**
Form - 000
Record 1999 - 1st:0 2nd:0 3rd:0 Ran:3
Pre1999 - 1st:0 2nd:0 3rd:0 Ran:1
1999 Turf 0-3: (10f, 12f, 14f) (g-s, gd 2)
Poor gelding. Turf high 12.
**M J Ryan [0-4] M J Ryan.*

SUGGEST BHB 28f RR 46df 3844[9]

4 b g Midyan (USA) 9.9f **(64)** - Awham (USA) (Lear Fan (USA)) 8.5f **(73)**
Form - 0000550
Record 1999 - 1st:0 2nd:0 3rd:0 Ran:7
Pre1999 - 1st:2 2nd:1 3rd:2 Ran:21
Win Prizemoney £6,630 *Total Prizemoney* £9,138

Wins						
* 1997	Aug	Newmar	(G-F)	S	7f	70 <
* 1997	Aug	Thirsk	(GD)	C	7f	70 <

1999 Turf 0-7: (8f 2, 10f, 12f 3, 17f) (gd, g-f, frm 4, hrd)
Moderate gelding, effective 10 to 12f, best at 12f, acts on gd to hrd, has worn blinkers (effectively), likes left handed tracks, likes tight tracks. Turf high 46.
**W Storey [2-28] Mrs M Tindale (from M Meade [0-1] Jly 1997).*

SUHAAD BHB 103f RR 100f 2908[1]

3 ch f Unfuwain (USA) 11.4f **(74)** - Forest Lair (Habitat) 9.4f **(70)**
Form - 151
Record 1999 - 1st:2 2nd:0 3rd:0 Ran:3
Win Prizemoney £17,123 *Total Prizemoney* £17,123

Wins						
* **1999**	Jly	Newmar	(G-F)	L	12f	100 <
* **1999**	Jun	Sandow	(GD)		10f	88

1999 Turf 2-3: (10f 1-1, 12f 1-2) (gd, frm 2-2)
Scopey, currently very useful filly. Turf high 100 - 1st of 6 getting 12lb from Innuendo (17 Jly Newmarket RF 2908). Lightly raced due to poor conformation, she disappointed on soft ground at Haydock, but bounced back to win a Listed event at Newmarket in July. Open to further improvement, she can win a Group 3 over a mile and a half next term.
**A C Stewart [2-3] Hamdan Al Maktoum.*

SUHAIL (IRE) BHB 41f47a RR 36f 47a 2171[15]

3 b g Wolfhound (USA) 7.3f **(71)** - Sharayif (IRE) (Green Desert (USA)) 8.6f **(78)**
Form - 27080
Record 1999 - 1st:0 2nd:1 3rd:0 Ran:5
Pre1999 - 1st:0 2nd:0 3rd:0 Ran:2
Win Prizemoney £0 *Total Prizemoney* £806
1999 Turf 0-3: (6f 2, 8f) (sft, gd, g-f) 1999 AW 0-2: (8f 2) (Fibr 2)
Scopey, fair gelding, effective 8f, - acts on Fibr. Turf high 36. AW high 50 (1st run) - 2nd of 11 to Pip's Brave (29 Jan Southwell 8f Fibr RF 0189).
**P L Gilligan [0-5] Mrs R J Simms (from B Hanbury [0-2] Aug 1998).*

SUITE FACTORS BHB 45f45a RR 44f 45a 4878[14]

5 b g Timeless Times (USA) 6.1f **(56)** - Uptown Girl (Caruso) 5.8f **(63)**
Form - 3500006750048 5000
Record 1999 - 1st:0 2nd:0 3rd:1 Ran:17
Pre1999 - 1st:4 2nd:8 3rd:7 Ran:45
Win Prizemoney £11,343 *Total Prizemoney* £23,274

Wins							
* 1998	Spt	Yarmou	(G-S)	H	7f	63	69
* 1998	Aug	Folkes	(G-F)	H	6f	46	62
* 1998	Jly	Folkes	(G-F)	H	7f	46	60
1996	Aug	Nottin	(G-F)	C	5.1f		71 <

1999 Turf 0-13: (5f 2, 6f 8, 7f 3) (hvy, sft, gd 2, g-f 4, frm 5) 1999 AW 0-4: (7f 3, 8f) (Equi 4)
Moderate gelding, effective 6 to 7f, best at 6f, acts on gd to frm, has worn blinkers. Turf high 58. AW high 46.
**K R Burke [3-56] Nigel Shields (from J A Glover [1-6] Aug 1996).*

SUITYOUSIR (IRE) RR 1682[10]

3 br g Midhish - Bel Ria (Gay Fandango (USA)) 8.5f **(59)**

Form - 0
Record 1999 - 1st:0 2nd:0 3rd:0 Ran:1
1999 Turf 0-1: (6f) (g-f)
Workmanlike, currently very poor gelding.
J R Poulton [0-1] Chris Steward.

SULALAT BHB 78f **RR 82f** 4803[14]
3 br f Hamas (IRE) 8f **(72)** - Enaya (Caerleon (USA)) 8.6f **(71)**
Form - 452510
Record 1999 - 1st:1 2nd:1 3rd:0 Ran:6
Pre1999 - 1st:0 2nd:0 3rd:0 Ran:1
Win Prizemoney £4,207 *Total Prizemoney* £6,066
Wins * **1999** Aug Newmar (GD) 6f 67+ <
1999 Turf 1-6: (6f 1-2, 7f 4) (gd 3, g-f 1-2, frm)
Unfurnished, decent filly, effective 7f, acts on gd to frm. Turf high 82 (1st run) - 4th of 14 to Cassandra Go (14 Apr Newmarket 7f gd RF 0696). She looked a difficult ride in her early starts, finding little off the bridle, but seemed to appreciate the drop back to six furlongs when landing a Newmarket maiden in August.
R W Armstrong [1-7] Hamdan Al Maktoum.

SULEYMAN BHB 48f68a **RR 32f 68a** 2319[15]
4 b g Alhijaz 7.7f **(57)** - Aonia (Mummy's Pet) 7.7f **(60)**
Form - 0060
Record 1999 - 1st:0 2nd:0 3rd:0 Ran:4
Pre1999 - 1st:1 2nd:0 3rd:3 Ran:8
Win Prizemoney £2,406 *Total Prizemoney* £3,599
Wins 1998 *Oct Southw (STD) 6f* 73 <
1999 Turf 0-4: (7f 3, 8f) (gd, frm 2, hrd)
Unfurnished, above-average gelding, effective 6f, - acts on Fibr, often wears blinkers (very effectively), likes left handed tracks, likes tight tracks. Turf high 32. Becoming disappointing.
D Nicholls [0-4] Lucayan Stud (from R Charlton [1-8] Oct 1998).

SULU (IRE) BHB 75f **RR 75f** 4160[3]
3 b g Elbio 9f **(62)** - Foxy Fairy (IRE) (Fairy King (USA)) 7.7f **(59)**
Form - 356233
Record 1999 - 1st:0 2nd:1 3rd:3 Ran:6
Pre1999 - 1st:0 2nd:0 3rd:0 Ran:1
Win Prizemoney £0 *Total Prizemoney* £2,626
1999 Turf 0-6: (6f 3, 7f 3) (gd 2, g-f 2, frm 2)
Unfurnished, above-average gelding, effective 6 to 7f, acts on frm. Turf high 75 - 3rd of 8 to Democracy (6 Spt Bath 6f frm RF 4160).
I A Balding [0-7] Robert Hitchins.

SUMATI RR 112f 5016a[1]
3 b c Warning 8.1f **(77)** - Swell Time (IRE) (Sadler's Wells (USA)) 10f **(76)**
Form - 3321
1999 Turf 1-4: (8f, 10f 2, 12f 1-1) (sft, gd, g-f 1-2)
Group-class colt. Turf high 112 - 1st of 6 getting 5lb from Silver Patriarch (17 Oct San Siro RF 5016a). He proved himself over a mile and a half when inching out Silver Patriarch in the Group One Gran Premio Del Jockey Club at San Siro during October. The first home-trained winner of that event for six years, he will be a force to reckon with in Italy next term.
B Grizzetti in ITY [1-4] Scuderia Cocktail.

SUMBAWA (IRE) BHB 27f36a **RR 33f 36a** 3023[5]
4 ch f Magic Ring (IRE) 6.5f **(64)** - Tittlemouse (Castle Keep) 8.3f **(57)**
Form - 745103000705
Record 1999 - 1st:1 2nd:0 3rd:1 Ran:12
Pre1999 - 1st:0 2nd:0 3rd:0 Ran:13
Win Prizemoney £2,512 *Total Prizemoney* £3,163
Wins * **1999** May Bright (FRM) C 10f 47 <
1999 Turf 1-10: (7f, 8f 2, 9f, 10f 1-3, 11f, 12f 2) (gd, g-f 1-5, frm 3, hrd)
1999 AW 0-2: (8f 2) (Equi, Fibr)
Leggy, very moderate filly, effective 10f, acts on g-f, has worn blinkers. Turf high 47. AW high 37. Inconsistent.
J M Bradley [1-12] M B Clemence (from D HaydnJones [0-13] Spt 1998).

SUMITAS (GER) RR 117f 4663a[4]
3 br c Lomitas - Subia (GER) (Konigsstuhl (GER)) 11.2f **(76)**
Form - 1165244
1999 Turf 2-7: (8f 1-1, 9f 1-1, 11f, 12f 4) (sft 1-2, gd 1-5)
High-class colt, effective 8 to 12f, acts on hvy to gd, favours right handed tracks, excels at Cologne. Turf high 117 - 2nd of 5 getting 14lb from Ungaro (25 Jly Dusseldorf 12f gd RF 3232a) - also 1st of 6 giving 9lb to Montalban (18 Apr Krefeld RF 0813a). Consistent. German-trained, he started off last season in promising style with victories at Listed and Group Two level, but then found Group One company too much against the likes of Belenus and Tiger Hill.
P Schiergen in GER [3-8].

SUMITRA BHB 51f **RR 55f** 4159[13]
3 b f Tragic Role (USA) 9.4f **(63)** - Nipotina (Simply Great (FR)) 8.2f **(65)**
Form - 62530
Record 1999 - 1st:0 2nd:1 3rd:1 Ran:5
Win Prizemoney £0 *Total Prizemoney* £1,096
1999 Turf 0-5: (9f, 10f, 11f, 13f, 16f) (g-s, gd 2, g-f, frm)
Leggy, fair filly. Turf high 58. *Major D N Chappell [0-5] C V Cruden.*

SUMMER BOUNTY BHB 70f **RR 68f** 4010[2]
3 b g Lugana Beach 7f **(63)** - Tender Moment (IRE) (Caerleon (USA)) 8.6f **(71)**
Form - 1443682
Record 1999 - 1st:1 2nd:1 3rd:1 Ran:7
Pre1999 - 1st:0 2nd:0 3rd:1 Ran:3
Win Prizemoney £3,021 *Total Prizemoney* £7,420
Wins * **1999** *Feb Lingfi (STD) 10f* 71+ <
1999 Turf 0-6: (10f 4, 12f 2) (gd 3, g-f 3) 1999 AW 1-1: (10f 1-1) (Equi 1-1)
Well made, above-average gelding, effective 10f, acts on gd - acts on Equi, has worn blinkers, likes left handed tracks, prefers tight tracks. Turf high 79 - 4th of 15 getting 8lb from Tier Worker (4 Jun Epsom 10f gd RF 1732). (1st run) - 1st of 5 from Billichang (25 Feb Lingfield RF 0359). Consistent. *B W Hills [1-10] Ray Richards.*

SUMMER CHERRY (USA) RR 59tf 4490[7]
2 b c Summer Squall (USA) 7f **(80)** - Cherryrob (USA) (Roberto (USA)) 10f **(76)**
Form - 77
Record 1999 - 1st:0 2nd:0 3rd:0 Ran:2
1999 Turf 0-2: (7f, 8f) (g-s, g-f)
Currently fair colt. Turf high 59 (began Aug).
P F I Cole [0-2] M Arbib.

SUMMERHILL SPECIAL (IRE) BHB 49f43a **RR 52f 43a** 2441[11]
8 b m Roi Danzig (USA) 10.5f **(62)** - Special Thanks (Kampala) 8.5f **(56)**
Form - 454060
Record 1999 - 1st:0 2nd:0 3rd:0 Ran:5
Pre1999 - 1st:5 2nd:7 3rd:0 Ran:48
Win Prizemoney £13,560 *Total Prizemoney* £21,656

Wins	* 1998	May	Mussel	(GD)	H	12f	63	68	
	* 1997	Aug	Catter	(G-F)	H	12f	65	71	<
	* 1997	May	Ayr	(G-F)		13.1f		60	
	* 1997	Apr	Ripon	(G-F)	H	12.3f	55	59	
	1996	Oct	Folkes	(G-S)	H	12f	45	55	

1999 Turf 0-3: (12f 3) (g-f, frm, hrd) 1999 AW 0-2: (12f 2) (Equi, Fibr)
Fair mare, effective 12f, acts on sft to frm, has worn blinkers, likes right handed tracks, does well at Ripon and Catterick, likes Musselburgh. Turf high 52. AW high 38.
D W Barker [4-46] Alba Racing Syndicate (from Mrs P N Dutfield [2-24] Oct 1996).

SUMMER NIGHT RR 93f 4796[5]
3 b f Nashwan (USA) 10.3f **(79)**-Shimmering Sea (Slip Anchor) 9.8f **(73)**
Form - 15
Record 1999 - 1st:1 2nd:0 3rd:0 Ran:2
Win Prizemoney £4,199 *Total Prizemoney* £4,199
Wins * **1999** Spt Yarmou (G-F) 6f 66+ <
1999 Turf 1-2: (6f 1-1, 8f) (gd, g-f 1-1)
Workmanlike, currently useful filly. Turf high 93 (began Spt). Unraced at two, she made an impressive debut in a modest six-furlong Yarmouth maiden in September, but pulled her rider's arms out and found little when stepped up to a mile in an Ascot Listed event next time. *Sir Mark Prescott [1-2] Miss K Rausing.*

SUMMER SONG RR 66+f 4900[1]

2 b f Green Desert (USA) 7.8f **(78)** - High Standard **(73f)** (Kris) 9.5f **(73)**
Form - 1
Record 1999 - 1st:1 2nd:0 3rd:0 Ran:1
Wins * 1999 Oct Newmar (GD) 7f 66+ <
1999 Turf 1-1: (7f 1-1) (gd 1-1)
Currently average filly. (1st run) - 1st of 5 getting 5lb from John Company (15 Oct Newmarket RF 4900).
**E A L Dunlop [1-1] Maktoum Al Maktoum.*

SUMMER SPLENDOUR (USA) BHB 82f RR 82f 3774[10]

3 ch f Summer Squall (USA) 7f **(80)** - Sin Lucha (USA) (Northfields (USA)) 9f **(72)**
Form - 120
Record 1999 - 1st:1 2nd:1 3rd:0 Ran:3
Pre1999 - 1st:0 2nd:1 3rd:1 Ran:2
Win Prizemoney £3,655 *Total Prizemoney* £7,430
Wins * 1999 May Haydoc (GD) 11.9f 82 <
1999 Turf 1-3: (12f 1-2, 14f) (gd 1-2, frm)
Scopey, decent filly. Turf high 82 - 2nd of 7 getting 4lb from Ten Kingdoms (11 Jly Haydock 12f frm RF 2739) - also 1st of 8 from Sena Desert (28 May Haydock RF 1546). **B W Hills [1-5] K Abdulla.*

SUMMER THYME BHB 23f RR 4f 3954[16]

5 b m Henbit (USA) 10.2f **(46)** - Hasty Sarah (Gone Native)
Form - 00
Record 1999 - 1st:0 2nd:0 3rd:0 Ran:2
Pre1999 - 1st:0 2nd:0 3rd:1 Ran:4
Win Prizemoney £0 *Total Prizemoney* £507
1999 Turf 0-1: (10f) (frm) 1999 AW 0-1: (12f) (Fibr)
Very poor filly.
**R A Fahey [0-2] Mrs Brigitte Pollard (from J Berry [0-4] Apr 1998).*

SUMMERTIME JOY BHB 50f RR 62f 5052[9]

2 b f Muhtarram (USA) - Phylian **(66f)** (Glint of Gold) 9.3f **(66)**
Form - 8160
Record 1999 - 1st:1 2nd:0 3rd:0 Ran:4
Win Prizemoney £1,926 *Total Prizemoney* £1,926
Wins * 1999 Aug Catter (G-F) S 7f 62 <
1999 Turf 1-4: (7f 1-3, 8f) (g-s, gd, frm 1-2)
Average filly. Turf high 62 - 1st of 11 getting 5lb from Wee Barney (13 Aug Catterick RF 3598). **S C Williams [1-4] D A Shekells.*

SUMMONER RR 82+f 5216[1]

2 b c Inchinor 8.9f **(64)** - Sumoto (Mtoto)
Form - 61
Record 1999 - 1st:1 2nd:0 3rd:0 Ran:2
Win Prizemoney £3,208 *Total Prizemoney* £3,208
Wins * 1999 Nov Doncas (SFT) 8f 82+ <
1999 Turf 1-2: (8f 1-2) (g-s 1-1, g-f)
Currently decent colt. Turf high 82 (began Aug) - 1st of 18 from Royal Cavalier (6 Nov Doncaster RF 5216). Won nicely at Doncaster and could prove useful at three.
**R Charlton [1-2] Michael Pescod.*

SUMTHINELSE BHB 83f RR 78f 3610[7]

2 ch c Magic Ring (IRE) 6.5f **(64)** - Minne Love (Homeric) 9.8f **(67)**
Form - 53347
Record 1999 - 1st:0 2nd:0 3rd:2 Ran:5
Win Prizemoney £0 *Total Prizemoney* £1,835
1999 Turf 0-5: (5f 3, 6f 2) (g-f 2, frm 3)
Above-average colt. Turf high 78. Looks to need a bit of cut in the ground to be at his best.
**N P Littmoden [0-5] Hanibel Racing Partnership.*

SUN CHARM (USA) RR 86+f 5029[5]

2 b br c Gone West (USA) 7.8f **(82)** - Argon Laser (Kris) 9.5f **(73)**
Form - 15
Record 1999 - 1st:1 2nd:0 3rd:0 Ran:2
Win Prizemoney £5,547 *Total Prizemoney* £5,547
Wins * 1999 Oct Leices (GD) 7f 86+ <
1999 Turf 1-2: (7f 1-2) (g-s, gd 1-1)
Currently useful colt. Turf high 86 (1st run) (began Oct) - 1st of 8 getting 5lb from Strasbourg (12 Oct Leicester RF 4833). He made quite an impression when beating several previous winners on his Leicester debut, but blotted his copybook in a Group Three.
**Sir Michael Stoute [1-2] Maktoum Al Maktoum.*

SUN DANCING (IRE) BHB 57f65a RR 60f 65a 2894[17]

4 ch f Magical Wonder (USA) 7.2f **(60)** - Lockwood Girl (Prince Tenderfoot (USA)) 9f **(61)**
Form - 0056200
Record 1999 - 1st:0 2nd:1 3rd:0 Ran:7
Pre1999 - 1st:1 2nd:1 3rd:0 Ran:5
Win Prizemoney £2,294 *Total Prizemoney* £3,959
Wins 1997 *Nov Southw (STD)* *5f* *66* <
1999 Turf 0-7: (5f 2, 6f 2, 7f, 8f, 9f) (hvy, gd 3, g-f 3)
Workmanlike, decent filly. Turf high 60. Inconsistent.
**P Monteith [0-9] Mrs Allan Melville (from J Berry [1-3] Nov 1997).*

SUNDAY MAIL TOO (IRE) BHB 23f RR 21f 3295[17]

7 b m Fayruz 6.6f **(63)** - Slick Chick (Shiny Tenth) 9.2f **(56)**
Form - 48600
Record 1999 - 1st:0 2nd:0 3rd:0 Ran:5
Pre1999 - 1st:3 2nd:3 3rd:4 Ran:64
Win Prizemoney £9,224 *Total Prizemoney* £13,563
Wins * 1996 Jly Ayr (G-F) SH 5f 44 43
***** 1996 Jun Hamilt (GD) H 6f 31 40
1999 Turf 0-5: (5f 5) (gd, g-f 2, frm 2)
Little account mare, effective 5f, acts on gd, has worn blinkers (extremely effectively). Turf high 22 (1st run) - 4th of 11 getting 32lb from Johayro (20 May Ayr 5f gd RF 1338).
**Miss L A Perratt [2-68] T P Finch (from J Berry [1-6] Oct 1994).*

SUNDAY PICNIC (JPN) RR 109f 1729[4]

3 b f Sunday Silence (USA) - Atoll (Caerleon (USA)) 8.6f **(71)**
Form - 314
1999 Turf 1-3: (11f 1-2, 12f) (sft 1-1, g-s, gd)
Currently Pattern-class filly. Turf high 109 - also 1st of 9 from Side Saddle (10 May Saint-Cloud RF 1349a). A useful French filly, winner of the Prix Cleopatre in soft ground before running fourth in the 1999 Epsom Oaks. **A Fabre in FR [1-3] Teruya Yoshida.*

SUNDAY RAIN (USA) BHB 68f RR 71f 5196[10]

2 b c Summer Squall (USA) 7f **(80)** - Oxava (FR) (Antheus (USA))
Form - 40440
Record 1999 - 1st:0 2nd:0 3rd:0 Ran:5
Win Prizemoney £0 *Total Prizemoney* £546
1999 Turf 0-5: (7f, 8f 3, 10f) (g-s 2, gd 2, frm)
Above-average colt, has worn blinkers. Turf high 71 (began Jly) - 4th of 16 giving 10lb to Marjeune (5 Oct Nottingham 10f g-s RF 4727). **P F I Cole [0-5] H R H Prince Fahd Salman.*

SUN FAIRY BHB 44f35a RR 46f 35a 114[12]

5 ch m Hatim (USA) 7.8f **(56)** - Petite Melusine (IRE) (Fairy King (USA)) 7.7f **(59)**
Form - 0200
Record 1999 - 1st:0 2nd:0 3rd:0 Ran:1
Pre1999 - 1st:0 2nd:2 3rd:2 Ran:10
Win Prizemoney £0 *Total Prizemoney* £2,097
1999 AW 0-1: (12f) (Fibr)
Moderate filly, has worn blinkers. Inconsistent.
**D Burchell [0-12] Bedlinog Racing Club (from J A Glover [0-7] Aug 1997).*

SUNGLO RR 60f 4941[5]

2 b f Lugana Beach 7f **(63)** - Mo Ceri (Kampala) 8.5f **(56)**
Form - 05
Record 1999 - 1st:0 2nd:0 3rd:0 Ran:2
1999 Turf 0-2: (5f, 6f) (gd 2)
Currently average filly. Turf high 60 (began Spt).
**P J Makin [0-2] R C Dollar.*

SUN HAT BHB 85f RR 84f 4081[6]

3 b c Warning 8.1f **(77)** - Instant Desire (USA) (Northern Dancer) 9.6f **(80)**
Form - 0310256
Record 1999 - 1st:1 2nd:1 3rd:1 Ran:7
Win Prizemoney £2,915 *Total Prizemoney* £5,532
Wins * 1999 May Catter (G-F) 12f 84 <
1999 Turf 1-7: (10f 2, 12f 1-2, 14f, 16f 2) (g-f 4, frm 1-3)
Light-framed, decent colt, effective 10 to 16f, acts on g-f to frm, best on frm. Turf high 84 - 1st of 11 from Outer Limit (21 May Catterick RF 1375). **H R A Cecil [1-7] Buckram Oak Holdings.*

SUNLEY SENSE BHB 90f RR 90f 2134[14]

3 b c Komaite (USA) 6.9f **(61)** - Brown Velvet (Mansingh (USA)) 7.4f **(55)**
Form - 00670
Record 1999 - 1st:0 2nd:0 3rd:0 Ran:5
Pre1999 - 1st:2 2nd:4 3rd:1 Ran:11
Win Prizemoney £8,758 *Total Prizemoney* £16,070
Wins * 1998 Spt Newbur (GD) H 5.2f 76 91 <
* 1998 Spt Sandow (G-S) H 5f 76 80
1999 Turf 0-5: (5f 2, 6f 3) (gd, gf 3, frm)
Scopey, useful colt, effective 5f, acts on gd to g-f. Turf high 90. Consistent. Was a speedy juvenile, but lost his way at three.
**M R Channon [2-16] John Sunley.*

SUNLEY SOLAIRE RR 15f 868[7]

3 b f Aragon 7.7f **(58)** - Pharsical **(73f)** (Pharly (FR)) 9.8f **(68)**
Form - 77
Record 1999 - 1st:0 2nd:0 3rd:0 Ran:2
1999 Turf 0-1: (8f) (sft) 1999 AW 0-1: (7f) (Fibr)
Light-framed, currently poor filly. **M R Channon [0-2] John Sunley.*

SUNLEY'S PICC RR 57f 1680[6]

2 b f Piccolo - Pharsical **(73f)** (Pharly (FR)) 9.8f **(68)**
Form - 6
Record 1999 - 1st:0 2nd:0 3rd:0 Ran:1
1999 Turf 0-1: (6f) (g-f)
Currently fair filly. **M R Channon [0-1] Mrs J M Jeyes.*

SUN LION (IRE) BHB 30f RR 31f 4646[11]

4 b g Shalford (IRE) 7.8f **(63)** - Susie Sunshine (IRE) (Waajib)
Form - 00000
Record 1999 - 1st:0 2nd:0 3rd:0 Ran:5
Pre1999 - 1st:0 2nd:2 3rd:0 Ran:14
Win Prizemoney £0 *Total Prizemoney* £1,783
1999 Turf 0-5: (8f, 10f 3, 11f) (g-s, gd, g-f 3)
Very moderate gelding, effective 10f, acts on gd, has worn blinkers, likes tight tracks. Turf high 31. Inconsistent.
**Mrs P N Dutfield [0-13] Simon Dutfield (from C O'Brien in IRE [0-6] Oct 1997).*

SUN MARK (IRE) BHB 38f RR 49?f 504[10]

8 ch g Red Sunset 9f **(57)** - Vivungi (USA) (Exbury) 9f **(73)**
Form - 00
Record 1999 - 1st:0 2nd:0 3rd:0 Ran:2
Pre1999 - 1st:3 2nd:1 3rd:2 Ran:12
Win Prizemoney £7,562 *Total Prizemoney* £9,353
Wins 1997 Aug Hamilt (GD) S 12.1f 49
1997 Jly Ripon (GD) S 10f 55
1997 May Hamilt (SFT) S 12.1f 61 <
1999 Turf 0-1: (12f) (hvy) 1999 AW 0-1: (8f) (Fibr)
Moderate gelding, has worn blinkers. Becoming disappointing.
**Miss J F Craze [0-5] Mrs Angela Wilson (from Mrs A Swinbank [3-9] Aug 1997).*

SUNNY CHIEF BHB 69f RR 31f 1092[P]

3 ch g Be My Chief (USA) 10.2f **(62)** - Sunny Davis (USA) (Alydar (USA)) 9.1f **(76)**
Form - 11P
Record 1999 - 1st:2 2nd:0 3rd:0 Ran:3
Pre1999 - 1st:0 2nd:0 3rd:0 Ran:3
Win Prizemoney £4,662 *Total Prizemoney* £4,662
Wins * **1999** *May Southw (STD) H 12f 50 76++* <
* **1999** *Apr Wolver (STD) H 12f 50 69++*
1999 Turf 0-1: (14f) (g-f) 1999 AW 2-2: (12f 2-2) (Fibr 2-2)
Well made, above-average gelding, effective 12f, - acted on Fibr. AW high 76 - 1st of 17 giving 17lb to Netherhall (6 May Southwell RF 1066) - also 1st of 11 giving 10lb to Netherhall (29 Apr Wolverhampton RF 0928). He looked a most progressive sort when twice winning easily on Fibresand during the spring, but tragically had to be destroyed having being injured at Nottingham in May. (DEAD). **Sir Mark Prescott [2-6] Hesmonds Stud.*

SUNNY FACT (USA) BHB 68f RR 72f 3246[4]

3 ch g Known Fact (USA) 8.3f **(72)** - Sunerta (USA) (Roberto (USA)) 10f **(76)**
Form - 4
Record 1999 - 1st:0 2nd:0 3rd:0 Ran:1
Pre1999 - 1st:0 2nd:1 3rd:0 Ran:2
Win Prizemoney £0 *Total Prizemoney* £2,002
1999 Turf 0-1: (6f) (frm)
Scopey, above-average gelding. (DEAD)
**P R Webber [0-1] F M Alger (from R Charlton [0-2] Aug 1998).*

SUNNY SLOPE BHB 58f RR 50f 5081a[9]

3 ch f Mujtahid (USA) 7.4f **(69)** - Scottish Eyes (USA) (Green Dancer (USA)) 10.3f **(74)**
Form - 7050000
Record 1999 - 1st:0 2nd:0 3rd:0 Ran:7
Pre1999 - 1st:0 2nd:0 3rd:0 Ran:2
1999 Turf 0-7: (5f, 6f 2, 7f 2, 9f, 10f) (g-s, gd 4, frm, hrd)
Fair filly. Turf high 53.
**G Keane in IRE [0-2] Mrs R Bean (from R A Fahey [0-5] Jun 1999).*

SUNRISE (IRE) BHB 61f RR 60f 3569[3]

2 b br f Sri Pekan (USA) - Grade a Star (IRE) (Alzao (USA)) 7.1f **(68)**
Form - 073
Record 1999 - 1st:0 2nd:0 3rd:1 Ran:3
Win Prizemoney £0 *Total Prizemoney* £507
1999 Turf 0-3: (5f 3) (g-f 2, frm)
Currently average filly. Turf high 60 (began Jly).
**W R Muir [0-3] D G Clarke.*

SUNSET GLOW RR 76f 5130[4]

2 gr c Rainbow Quest (USA) 11.2f **(81)** - Oscura (USA) (Caro)
Form - 4
Record 1999 - 1st:0 2nd:0 3rd:0 Ran:1
Win Prizemoney £0 *Total Prizemoney* £428
1999 Turf 0-1: (8f) (gd)
Currently above-average colt. **B W Hills [0-1] K Abdulla.*

SUNSET HARBOUR (IRE) BHB 39f40a RR 36f 40a 3924[8]

6 br m Prince Sabo 6.6f **(64)** - City Link Pet (Tina's Pet) 6.8f **(59)**
Form - 20464007708
Record 1999 - 1st:0 2nd:0 3rd:0 Ran:9
Pre1999 - 1st:5 2nd:5 3rd:9 Ran:49
Win Prizemoney £13,630 *Total Prizemoney* £22,856
Wins * 1998 Aug Catter (GD) H 5f 47 50 <
* 1998 May Newcas (G-F) H 5f 42 44
* 1998 *Apr Wolver (STD) H 5f 37 40*
* 1997 Jun Beverl (G-S) H 5f 40 41
* 1996 Jly Redcar (FRM) SH 5f 44 45
1999 Turf 0-5: (5f 5) (gd, g-f, frm 2, hrd) 1999 AW 0-4: (5f 3, 6f) (Equi 2, Fibr 2)
Very moderate mare, effective 5 to 6f, best at 5f, acts on gd to frm - acts on AW, best on frm, has worn blinkers. Turf high 36. AW high 43 (1st run) - 4th of 10 getting 7lb from Half Tone (23 Jan Lingfield 5f Equi RF 0147). Consistent.
**S E Kettlewell [5-40] J Tennant (from T J Naughton [0-10] Jly 1996).*

SUNSET LADY (IRE) BHB 60f60a RR 61f 60a 3921[4]

3 b br f Red Sunset 9f **(57)** - Lady of Man (So Blessed) 8.7f **(67)**
Form - 06732504
Record 1999 - 1st:0 2nd:1 3rd:1 Ran:7
Pre1999 - 1st:3 2nd:1 3rd:0 Ran:9
Win Prizemoney £9,690 *Total Prizemoney* £12,827
Wins * 1998 Oct Ayr (SFT) H 8f 65 74 <
* 1998 Spt Pontef (G-F) H 8f 61 66
* 1998 Jun Thirsk (GD) S 6f 66
1999 Turf 0-5: (8f, 9f 3, 10f) (gd 3, g-f, frm) 1999 AW 0-2: (8f 2) (Fibr 2)
Unfurnished, average filly, effective 6 to 10f, best at 8f, acts on sft to frm, prefers left handed tracks. Turf high 70 - 2nd of 14 giving 9lb to Pentagon Lad (15 May Thirsk 8f gd RF 1250). AW high 33. Inconsistent. **P C Haslam [3-17] The Jack Of All Trades Partnership.*

SUNSHINE BOY BHB 70f RR 72f 4597[8]

3 b g Cadeaux Genereux 7.9f **(76)** - Sahara Baladee (USA) (Shadeed (USA)) 8.2f **(70)**
Form - 3621504238
Record 1999 - 1st:1 2nd:2 3rd:2 Ran:10
Win Prizemoney £3,029 *Total Prizemoney* £6,912
Wins * **1999** Jun Leices (GD) H 10f 69 72 <
1999 Turf 1-10: (8f 2, 9f, 10f 1-5, 11f, 12f) (gd 3, g-f 1-4, frm 3)
Tall, above-average gelding, effective 10f, acts on g-f to frm, best on frm, has worn blinkers, prefers tight tracks. Turf high 72 - 1st of 17 giving 18lb to Lady Benson (1 Jun Leicester RF 1647).

Consistent. **E A L Dunlop [1-10] Maktoum Al Maktoum.*

SUNSHINE STREET (USA) RR 117f 4316a[4]

4 b c Sunshine Forever (USA) 13.2f **(76)** - Meadow Spirit (USA) (Chief's Crown (USA)) 9.8f **(72)**

Form - 24544

1999 Turf 0-5: (10f 3, 12f 2) (g-s, gd 2, g-f, frm)

High-class colt, effective 10 to 15f, best at 12f, acts on g-s to frm, best on g-f, likes left handed tracks. Turf high 117. Consistent. He began 1999 with a second over too short a trip on easy ground at the Curragh and was a good fourth to Fruits Of Love on his favoured fast ground in the Hardwicke Stakes. More patient tactics were employed in the King George, but he never really threatened to land a blow, and he ran a bit flat in the Royal Whip and Irish Champion Stakes on his last two starts.

**N Meade in IRE [1-16] P Garvey.*

SUNSPANGLED (IRE) RR 109f 4316a[7]

3 ch f Caerleon (USA) 10.9f **(79)** - Filia Ardross (Ardross) 10.6f **(68)**

Form - 076207

1999 Turf 0-6: (8f 2, 10f, 12f 3) (gd 3, g-f 2, frm)

Pattern-class filly, effective 8f, acts on gd. Turf high 109. Consistent. Winner of the Group One Fillies' Mile at Ascot at two, she failed to reach the heights that were anticipated in 1999, her best effort being a distant second to Ramruma in the Irish Oaks.

**A P O'Brien in IRE [2-10] Michael Tabor.*

SUNSTREAK BHB 105f RR 106f 4652[3]

4 ch c Primo Dominie 7.2f **(67)** - Florentynna Bay (Aragon) 8.1f **(60)**

Form - 22303

Record	**1999 -**	1st:0	2nd:2	3rd:2	Ran:5
	Pre1999 -	1st:3	2nd:1	3rd:0	Ran:8

Win Prizemoney £14,587 *Total Prizemoney* £33,439

Wins	* 1998	Aug	Sandow	(G-F)	H	8.1f	80	102+	<
	* 1998	Aug	Newmar	(G-F)	H	8f	74	82	
	* 1998	Jly	Nottin	(G-F)	H	8.2f	69	75	

1999 Turf 0-5: (7f 2, 8f 3) (gd 2, g-f 2, frm)

Leggy, Pattern-class colt, effective 7 to 8f, best at 8f, acts on gd to frm, excels at Newmarket and Doncaster. Turf high 106 - 3rd of 13 giving 4lb to Indian Lodge (30 Spt Newmarket 8f gd RF 4652). He blew a decent handicap mark when completing a hat-trick by winning by 10 lengths at Sandown in August of 1998. As a result he had to be stepped up into conditions and pattern races. Despite failing to score in 1999, he finished runner-up in the Jubilee at Kempton and a Doncaster conditions event, and ran third twice in pattern races. He does not look quite up to Group level, but is remarkably consistent, and a listed race can come his way in 2000.

**C F Wall [3-13] Walter Grubmuller.*

SUPERBIT BHB 60f54a RR 56f 54a 4732[1]

7 b g Superpower 6.6f **(58)** - On A Bit (Mummy's Pet) 7.7f **(60)**

Form - 304020031

Record	**1999 -**	1st:1	2nd:1	3rd:2	Ran:9
	Pre1999 -	1st:5	2nd:3	3rd:11	Ran:64

Win Prizemoney £15,697 *Total Prizemoney* £25,793

Wins	*** 1999**	Oct	Nottin	(SFT)		6.1f		56	
	* 1998	Aug	Ripon	(GD)	SH	5f	50	54	
	* 1997	Jun	Nottin	(SFT)	H	6.1f	60	64	<
	* 1996	Oct	Nottin	(GD)		5.1f		60	
	* 1996	Spt	Haydoc	(GD)	SH	6f	49	53	
	* 1995	Jun	Bath	(GD)	C	5.1f		58	

1999 Turf 1-7: (5f 5, 6f 1-2) (gd 1-1, g-f, frm 4, hrd) 1999 AW 0-2: (5f, 6f) (Fibr 2)

Fair gelding, effective 5 to 6f, best at 6f, acts on gd to frm, best on gd, has worn blinkers. Turf high 56 (began Jly) - 1st of 20 from Treasure Touch (5 Oct Nottingham RF 4732). AW high 49 (began Aug).

**B A McMahon [6-69] Neville Smith (from J G FitzGerald [0-4] Spt 1994).*

SUPERBOB BHB 40f31a RR 35f 31a 869[9]

3 b c Superlative 8.8f **(57)** - Beebob (Norwick (USA)) 7.2f **(56)**

Form - 00556070

Record	**1999 -**	1st:0	2nd:0	3rd:0	Ran:6
	Pre1999 -	1st:0	2nd:0	3rd:0	Ran:5

1999 Turf 0-2: (8f, 12f) (hvy, sft) 1999 AW 0-4: (8f, 10f, 11f, 12f) (Equi 2, Fibr 2)

Very moderate colt, has worn blinkers. Turf high 28. AW high 37.

**R J R Williams [0-11] Beebob.*

SUPERCHIEF BHB 38f RR 34f 5058[11]

4 b g Precocious 7.2f **(54)** - Rome Express (Siberian Express (USA)) 8.8f **(65)**

Form - 800

Record	**1999 -**	1st:0	2nd:0	3rd:0	Ran:3
	Pre1999 -	1st:0	2nd:0	3rd:0	Ran:8

1999 Turf 0-2: (5f, 8f) (gd, frm) 1999 AW 0-1: (7f) (Equi)

Scopey, average gelding, has worn blinkers. Turf high 34 (began Jly).

**Miss B Sanders [0-4] Copy Xpress Ltd (from J E Banks [0-7] Spt 1998).*

SUPER DOLLAR (IRE) BHB 57f RR 57f 4387[5]

3 ch c Great Commotion (USA) 9.2f **(80)** - L'Americaine (USA) (Verbatim (USA)) 8.5f **(64)**

Form - 88002110005

Record	**1999 -**	1st:2	2nd:1	3rd:0	Ran:11
	Pre1999 -	1st:0	2nd:0	3rd:1	Ran:3

Win Prizemoney £5,697 *Total Prizemoney* £6,945

Wins	*** 1999**	Jly	Folkes	(G-F)	H	12f	55	61+	<
	*** 1999**	Jly	Folkes	(G-F)	H	12f	50	51	

1999 Turf 2-10: (9f, 10f 2, 12f 2-7) (hvy, g-s, gd 1-2, g-f 1-2, frm 3, hrd) 1999 AW 0-1: (10f) (Equi)

Scopey, fair colt, effective 12f, acts on g-f, has worn blinkers, likes right handed tracks, likes tight tracks. Turf high 61 - 1st of 11 from Twoforten (26 Jly Folkestone RF 3145).

**S C Williams [2-10] The Cherry Pickers Syndicate II (from P F I Cole [0-4] Jan 1999).*

SUPERFRILLS BHB 40f41a RR 39f 41a 5161[6]

6 b m Superpower 6.6f **(58)** - Pod's Daughter (IRE) (Tender King) 6.8f **(54)**

Form - 72062600806

Record	**1999 -**	1st:0	2nd:1	3rd:0	Ran:9
	Pre1999 -	1st:3	2nd:3	3rd:4	Ran:39

Win Prizemoney £7,899 *Total Prizemoney* £13,878

Wins	* 1998	Oct	Newcas	(SFT)	H	5f	45	47	<
	* 1998	Aug	Hamilt	(SFT)	H	5f	39	47	<
	* 1998	Jun	Hamilt	(G-S)	H	5f	33	40	

1999 Turf 0-8: (5f 8) (g-s, gd, g-f 3, frm 3) 1999 AW 0-1: (6f) (Fibr)

Very moderate mare, effective 5f, acts on g-s to g-f, best on g-s, excels at Hamilton. Turf high 47 - 2nd of 12 getting 3lb from Leaping Charlie (29 Jun Hamilton 5f g-f RF 2392).

**Miss L C Siddall [3-48] Podso Racing.*

SUPER-GEM BHB 33f33a RR 32f 33a 853[7]

4 ch g Superpower 6.6f **(58)** - Ela-Yianni-Mou (Anfield) 8.5f **(59)**

Form - 874237

Record	**1999 -**	1st:0	2nd:1	3rd:1	Ran:6
	Pre1999 -	1st:0	2nd:0	3rd:0	Ran:4

Win Prizemoney £0 *Total Prizemoney* £957

1999 Turf 0-1: (12f) (g-f) 1999 AW 0-5: (10f, 11f, 12f 2, 16f) (Equi 3, Fibr 2)

Leggy, very moderate gelding, has worn blinkers. AW high 37.

**J S Wainwright [0-7] Mrs J R Bamforth (from D J S Cosgrove [0-4] Oct 1998).*

SUPER HELEN RR 16[12]

5 b m Superlative 8.8f **(57)** - Sweet Helen (No Mercy) 8f **(61)**

Form - 0

Record	**1999 -**	1st:0	2nd:0	3rd:0	Ran:1

1999 AW 0-1: (8f) (Fibr)

Currently very poor filly. **C Drew [0-2] C Drew.*

SUPERIOR PREMIUM BHB 111f RR 110f 5222[9]

5 br h Forzando 7.2f **(63)** - Devils Dirge (Song) 7.2f **(61)**

Form - 20140060110

Record	**1999 -**	1st:3	2nd:1	3rd:0	Ran:11
	Pre1999 -	1st:6	2nd:4	3rd:2	Ran:25

Win Prizemoney £135,596 *Total Prizemoney* £172,239

Wins	*** 1999**	Oct	Newbur	(G-S)	H	6f	109	110	<
	*** 1999**	Oct	Ascot	(G-S)	H	5f	104	108	
	*** 1999**	Jun	Taby	(FRM)	L	9.8f		102	
	* 1998	Aug	Goodwo	(GD)	H	6f	99	105	
	* 1998	Jly	Haydoc	(GD)		6f		95	

* 1998 Jun Cheste (G-S) H 6.1f 94 98
* 1997 Mar Haydoc (SFT) L 5f 100
* 1996 Oct Haydoc (SFT) 5f 90
* 1996 Apr Nottin (G-S) 5.1f 79

1999 Turf 3-11: (5f 1-1, 6f 1-9, 10f 1-1) (g-s 1-2, gd 1-4, g-f 3, frm 1-2)
Group-class colt, effective 5 to 6f, best at 6f, acts on g-s to g-f, excels at Ascot, likes Haydock. Turf high 113 - 4th of 19 to Bold Edge (17 Jun Ascot 6f g-f RF 2072) - also 1st of 14 from Gaelic Storm (22 Oct Newbury RF 5030). He has been a great servant to connections and enjoyed another solid campaign. He stays six furlongs well, seems to act on any ground and has a fine record in competitive handicaps. **R A Fahey [9-36] J C Parsons.*

SUPER KIM BHB 52f **RR 59f** 4870[8]
2 b f Superpower 6.6f **(58)** - Kimble Blue (Blue Refrain)
Form - 708
Record 1999 - 1st:0 2nd:0 3rd:0 Ran:3
1999 Turf 0-2: (5f, 7f) (gd, frm) 1999 AW 0-1: (7f) (Fibr)
Currently fair filly. Turf high 59 (began Jly).
**P L Gilligan [0-3] The Angel Partnership.*

SUPERLAO (BEL) BHB 33f33a **RR 27f 33a** 4493[16]
7 b m Bacalao (USA) 5f **(27)** - Princess of Import (Import) 6.6f **(68)**
Form - 05670344678040
Record 1999 - 1st:0 2nd:0 3rd:1 Ran:13
Pre1999 - 1st:1 2nd:1 3rd:7 Ran:51
Win Prizemoney £3,096 *Total Prizemoney* £7,752
Wins * 1997 Jun Lingfi (SFT) H 5f 38 41 <
1999 Turf 0-12: (5f 6, 6f 4, 7f 2) (sft 2, gd 2, g-f 2, frm 6) 1999 AW 0-1: (6f) (Equi)
Very moderate mare, has worn blinkers. Turf high 34.
**J J Bridger [1-58] J J Bridger (from Andre Hermans in BEL [0-6] Jan 1996).*

SUPERLOU BHB 38f **RR 40f** 4949[8]
3 br f Superpower 6.6f **(58)** - Louise Moulton (Moulton)
Form - 4440008
Record 1999 - 1st:0 2nd:0 3rd:0 Ran:7
Win Prizemoney £0 *Total Prizemoney* £505
1999 Turf 0-7: (6f, 7f 2, 8f 3, 11f) (g-s, gd, g-f 2, frm 3)
Moderate filly. Turf high 60. **J G FitzGerald [0-7] Sir Tatton Sykes.*

SUPER LOVER (GER) **RR 98f** 4243a[8]
3 f
Form - 48
1999 Turf 0-2: (6f 2) (g-s, gd)
Currently very useful. Turf high 98. **H Hiller in GER [0-2].*

SUPER MONARCH BHB 65f64a **RR 74?f 64a** 4689[8]
5 ch g Cadeaux Genereux 7.9f **(76)** - Miss Fancy That (USA) (The Minstrel (CAN)) 10f **(72)**
Form - 858006400538
Record 1999 - 1st:0 2nd:0 3rd:1 Ran:11
Pre1999 - 1st:2 2nd:4 3rd:0 Ran:24
Win Prizemoney £11,117 *Total Prizemoney* £21,397
Wins * 1998 Oct Newmar (GD) H 8f 68 78 <
1998 *Feb Lingfi (SLW) 7f 56*
1999 Turf 0-8: (8f 7, 10f) (gd 2, g-f 5, frm) 1999 AW 0-3: (7f, 8f 2) (Equi 3)
Above-average gelding, effective 7 to 9f, best at 8f, acts on g-s to frm. Turf high 74 - 6th of 29 giving 3lb to Scene (28 Apr Ascot 8f g-f RF 0901). AW high 65.
**K R Burke [1-20] Chelgate Public Relations Ltd (from S Dow [1-12] Jly 1998).*

SUPER SECRET **RR 48f** 5189[9]
2 ch f Elmaamul (USA) 8.1f **(70)** - Supreme (USA) **(51f)** (Lomond (USA)) 8.8f **(65)**
Form - 50
Record 1999 - 1st:0 2nd:0 3rd:0 Ran:2
1999 Turf 0-2: (7f, 8f) (sft, g-f)
Currently moderate filly. Turf high 48 (began Oct).
**Miss L A Perratt [0-2] T P Finch.*

SUPERSONIC BHB 71f **RR 72f** 4802[14]
3 b f Shirley Heights 12.1f **(76)** - Bright Landing (Sun Prince) 12.4f **(52)**
Form - 85322520
Record 1999 - 1st:0 2nd:3 3rd:1 Ran:8
Pre1999 - 1st:0 2nd:0 3rd:0 Ran:1
Win Prizemoney £0 *Total Prizemoney* £3,569
1999 Turf 0-8: (8f, 9f, 10f 4, 11f, 12f) (gd 3, g-f 2, frm 3)
Scopey, above-average filly, effective 8 to 11f, best at 10f, acts on gd to frm, best on frm, likes left handed tracks, prefers tight tracks, excels at Bath. Turf high 72 - 2nd of 17 giving 14lb to Young-Un (23 Aug Nottingham 10f frm RF 3862). Consistent.
**R F JohnsonHoughton [0-9] J W Rowles.*

SUPER STORY RR 4178[19]
2 b f Superlative 8.8f **(57)** - Princess Story (Prince de Galles)
Form - 0
Record 1999 - 1st:0 2nd:0 3rd:0 Ran:1
1999 Turf 0-1: (6f) (frm)
Currently very poor filly. **M Madgwick [0-1] T Smith.*

SUPER STRIDES BHB 38f41a **RR 28f 41a** 18[9]
3 b f Superpower 6.6f **(58)** - Go Tally-Ho (Gorytus (USA)) 7.8f **(60)**
Form - 4000
Record 1999 - 1st:0 2nd:0 3rd:0 Ran:1
Pre1999 - 1st:0 2nd:3 3rd:0 Ran:15
Win Prizemoney £0 *Total Prizemoney* £1,733
1999 AW 0-1: (6f) (Fibr)
Scopey, moderate filly, effective 6f, - acts on Fibr, likes left handed tracks, likes tight tracks. Becoming disappointing.
**C W Fairhurst [0-16] William Hill.*

SUPLIZI (IRE) BHB 80f **RR 74?f** 3091[P]
8 b h Alzao (USA) 9.8f **(73)** - Sphinx (GER) (Alpenkonig (GER)) 10.8f **(76)**
Form - 000P
Record 1999 - 1st:0 2nd:0 3rd:0 Ran:4
Pre1999 - 1st:3 2nd:4 3rd:2 Ran:14
Win Prizemoney £28,324 *Total Prizemoney* £53,022
Wins 1996 Apr Ripon (GD) 12.3f 100
1999 Turf 0-4: (10f 3, 12f) (gd 2, g-f 2)
Above-average horse, effective 8f, acts on g-f. Turf high 74. Becoming disappointing.
**P Bowen [0-6] T G Price (from B J Llewellyn [0-3] May 1998).*

SUPPLY AND DEMAND BHB 83f94a **RR 82f 94a** 4014[6]
5 b g Belmez (USA) 11.4f **(65)** - Sipsi Fach (Prince Sabo) 7.2f **(62)**
Form - 000630686
Record 1999 - 1st:0 2nd:0 3rd:1 Ran:8
Pre1999 - 1st:3 2nd:5 3rd:1 Ran:20
Win Prizemoney £45,455 *Total Prizemoney* £76,065
Wins * 1998 Jly Goodwo (GD) H 9.9f 94 99 <
* 1997 May Lingfi (SFT) H 9f 90 93
* 1997 Apr Epsom (GD) 8.5f 75

1999 Turf 0-8: (8f 2, 10f 5, 12f) (gd 2, g-f 2, frm 4)
Decent gelding, effective 10f, acts on sft to g-f, has worn blinkers (very effectively), prefers tight tracks. Turf high 93 - 3rd of 15 getting 8lb from Monsajem (5 Jun Epsom 10f gd RF 1757). Consistent. Landed a gamble in the '98 Chesterfield Cup at Goodwood in first-time blinkers, and ran well at Epsom when third to Monsajem on his fourth start of '99. Disappointed subsequently, but is still one to watch when the money is down and Fallon is booked.
**G L Moore [5-32] Action Bloodstock.*

SUPREME ANGEL BHB 60f **RR 61f** 4555[18]
4 b f Beveled (USA) 6.9f **(64)** - Blue Angel (Lord Gayle (USA)) 8.8f **(62)**
Form - 0000000
Record 1999 - 1st:0 2nd:0 3rd:0 Ran:7
Pre1999 - 1st:3 2nd:2 3rd:1 Ran:15
Win Prizemoney £14,370 *Total Prizemoney* £17,369
Wins * 1998 May Kempto (GD) H 6f 82 84 <
* 1997 Oct Haydoc (HVY) H 5f 75 81
* 1997 Apr Newbur (G-F) 5.2f 69

1999 Turf 0-7: (5f 3, 6f 4) (g-s 2, gd 2, g-f 2, frm)
Unfurnished, average filly, effective 6f, acts on gd, has worn blinkers. Turf high 67. Inconsistent.
**M P Muggeridge [3-22] Least Moved Partners.*

SUPREMELY DEVIOUS BHB 58f50a **RR 62f 50a** 4937[11]
2 ch f Wolfhound (USA) 7.3f **(71)** - Clearly Devious **(74f)** (Machiavellian (USA))

Form - 7542600
Record 1999 - 1st:0 2nd:1 3rd:0 Ran:7
Win Prizemoney £0 *Total Prizemoney* £1,026
1999 Turf 0-6: (5f, 6f 3, 7f 2) (gd, frm 5) 1999 AW 0-1: (6f) (Fibr)
Average filly, effective 6f, acts on frm, has worn blinkers. Turf high 62 - 2nd of 7 getting 17lb from Time For Music (23 Aug Nottingham 6f frm RF 3858). **R M H Cowell [0-7] G T Lever.*

SUPREME MAIMOON BHB 44f49a **RR 39f 49a** 4935[9]

5 b h Jareer (USA) 10.2f **(54)** - Princess Zena (Habitat) 9.4f **(70)**
Form - 606603310
Record 1999 - 1st:1 2nd:0 3rd:2 Ran:9
Pre1999 - 1st:1 2nd:0 3rd:1 Ran:8
Win Prizemoney £4,261 *Total Prizemoney* £5,442
Wins * 1999 *Spt Southw (STD) C 11f 48*
***** *1996 Dec Lingfi (STD) 7f 73+* <
1999 Turf 0-1: (10f) (g-f) 1999 AW 1-8: (6f 2, 7f, 8f 3, 11f 1-1, 12f) (Fibr 1-8)
Moderate colt, effective 11f, - acts on Fibr. AW high 48 - 1st of 12 giving 4lb to Ice Pack (28 Spt Southwell RF 4601). A half-brother to Supreme Leader, he ended a long losing run in a claimer on the Southwell Fibresand in September. Looks best suited my middle distances now. **M J Polglase [2-17] M J Polglase.*

SUPREME SALUTATION BHB 79f **RR 79f** 3480[1]

3 ch g Most Welcome 8.6f **(66)** - Cardinal Press **(88df)** (Sharrood (USA)) 10.5f **(72)**
Form - 0657322121
Record 1999 - 1st:2 2nd:3 3rd:1 Ran:10
Win Prizemoney £8,665 *Total Prizemoney* £13,971
Wins * 1999 Aug Thirsk (SFT) H 8f 72 79 <
*** 1999** Jly Catter (GD) H 7f 62 72
1999 Turf 2-8: (6f, 7f 1-3, 8f 1-4) (gd 1-2, g-f 1-1, frm 5) 1999 AW 0-2: (6f, 8f) (Equi, Fibr)
Workmanlike, above-average gelding, effective 7 to 8f, best at 8f, acts on gd to frm. Turf high 79 - 1st of 8 giving 6lb to Automatic (9 Aug Thirsk RF 3480) - also 1st of 12 getting 5lb from Automatic (1 Jly Catterick RF 2457). AW high 28. Gradually improving with racing and, after a couple of near-misses, absolutely bolted up at Catterick. Won again at Thirsk and can continue to progress.
**T D Barron [2-10] J Baggott.*

SUPREME SOUND BHB 104f102a **RR 104f 102a** 5231a[14]

5 b h Superlative 8.8f **(57)** - Sing Softly (Luthier) 9.8f **(71)**
Form - 102720
Record 1999 - 1st:1 2nd:2 3rd:0 Ran:6
Pre1999 - 1st:8 2nd:2 3rd:3 Ran:27
Win Prizemoney £97,187 *Total Prizemoney* £111,076
Wins 1999 *Mar Lingfi (STD) L 10f 101* <
1998 Aug York (G-F) H 10.4f 96 100
1998 Aug Yarmou (G-F) H 10.1f 90 94
1998 Jly Newbur (G-F) H 9f 85 91
1998 May Folkes (G-F) H 9.7f 76 80
1998 May Beverl (G-F) H 9.9f 72 71
1997 Spt Yarmou (FRM) H 10.1f 68 73
1997 Aug Lingfi (G-F) H 10f 61 67
1996 Oct Nottin (GD) 10f 67+
1999 Turf 0-4: (10f 4) (gd, g-f 3) 1999 AW 1-2: (10f 1-2) (Equi 1-1, Dirt)
Very useful colt, effective 10f, acts on g-f to frm - acts on Equi, best on g-f, prefers left handed tracks, likes tight tracks, excels at Newbury. Turf high 104 - 2nd of 4 to Chester House (6 May Chester 10f g-f RF 1051). AW high 101 (1st run) - 1st of 14 from Sick As A Parrot (20 Mar Lingfield RF 0456). Inconsistent. He goes particularly well for Gary Bardwell, and together they ran their rivals ragged in the Winter Derby on Lingfield's all-weather track. Subsequently moved to the United States, where he will have more opportunities on dirt. **M W Dickinson in USA [0-1] (from P W Harris [9-32] Jun 1999).*

SURE DANCER (USA) **RR 112+f** 4770a[7]

4 b c Affirmed (USA) 10.3f **(75)** - Danlu (USA) (Danzig (USA)) 8.4f **(76)**
Form - 117
Record 1999 - 1st:2 2nd:0 3rd:0 Ran:3
Win Prizemoney £10,329 *Total Prizemoney* £10,329
Wins * 1999 Jly Doncas (G-F) 8f 112 <
*** 1999** Apr Leices (GD) 10f 84+
1999 Turf 2-3: (8f 1-1, 10f 1-2) (hvy, gd 1-1, frm 1-1)
Scopey, currently Group-class colt. Turf high 112 - 1st of 7 giving 4lb to Showboat (29 Jly Doncaster RF 3216). Unraced at two and three, he made a deep impression on his first two starts, giving Showboat seven pounds and a head beating at Doncaster in July. Possibly unsuited by heavy ground when unplaced in the Prix Dollar at Longchamp, he should win a Listed race at least in 2000.
**P F I Cole [2-3].*

SURE FIRE **RR 14f** 4670[10]

2 b c Deploy 11.4f **(67)** - Certain Story (Known Fact (USA)) 7.4f **(67)**
Form - 0
Record 1999 - 1st:0 2nd:0 3rd:0 Ran:1
1999 Turf 0-1: (6f) (g-s)
Currently poor colt. **C A Dwyer [0-1] The Fairy Story Partnership.*

SURE FUTURE BHB 54f **RR 58f** 4630[2]

3 b g Kylian (USA) 8.1f **(66)** - Lady Ever-so-Sure (Malicious) 8.7f **(50)**
Form - 5785772
Record 1999 - 1st:0 2nd:1 3rd:0 Ran:7
Win Prizemoney £0 *Total Prizemoney* £916
1999 Turf 0-6: (10f 2, 12f 3, 14f) (sft, g-s, g-f 2, frm 2) 1999 AW 0-1: (12f) (Fibr)
Leggy, fair gelding. Turf high 67.
**A C Stewart [0-7] R George, P Saunders & A Collins.*

SURE QUEST BHB 49f **RR 45f** 3147[12]

4 b f Sure Blade (USA) 10.6f **(66)**-Eagle's Quest (Legal Eagle) 7.3f **(54)**
Form - 8000
Record 1999 - 1st:0 2nd:0 3rd:0 Ran:4
Pre1999 - 1st:1 2nd:0 3rd:2 Ran:9
Win Prizemoney £3,158 *Total Prizemoney* £4,507
Wins * 1998 Aug Folkes (G-F) H 9.7f 57 61 <
1999 Turf 0-4: (8f, 9f, 10f 2) (gd, frm 3)
Light-framed, moderate filly, effective 8 to 11f, best at 10f, acts on gd to frm, best on frm, has worn blinkers, favours tight tracks. Turf high 58 (1st run) - 8th of 16 getting 1lb from Twin Time (17 May Bath 8f gd RF 1272). Becoming disappointing.
**D W P Arbuthnot [1-13] Miss P E Decker.*

SURE TO DREAM (IRE) BHB 38f52a **RR 37f 52a** 5058[12]

6 b m Common Grounds 8.1f **(66)** -Hard to Stop (Hard Fought) 8.8f **(62)**
Form - 5310000
Record 1999 - 1st:1 2nd:0 3rd:1 Ran:6
Pre1999 - 1st:2 2nd:2 3rd:1 Ran:14
Win Prizemoney £7,269 *Total Prizemoney* £9,607
Wins * 1999 *May Southw (STD) H 7f 52 55* <
***** *1998 May Southw (STD) H 6f 49 54*
***** *1997 Nov Lingfi (STD) 6f 41*
1999 Turf 0-1: (7f) (frm) 1999 AW 1-5: (6f 2, 7f 1-3) (Equi 2, Fibr 1-3)
Moderate mare, effective 6 to 7f, best at 6f, - acts on AW, best on Fibr, prefers left handed tracks, prefers tight tracks. AW high 55 - 1st of 16 giving 7lb to Dekelsmary (6 May Southwell RF 1063). Becoming disappointing.
**R T Phillips [3-20] Dozen Dreamers Partnership.*

SURFSIDE (USA) RR 5225a[3]

2 f Seattle Slew (USA) 7.8f **(64)** - Flanders (USA) **(108f)** (Seeking the Gold (USA))
Form - 3
1999 AW 0-1: (9f) (Dirt)
Currently very useful. (1st run) - 3rd of 9 to Cash Run (6 Nov Gulfstream Park 9f Dirt RF 5225a). **D W Lukas in USA [0-1].*

SURPRESA CARA BHB 45f28a **RR 49f 28a** 285[7]

4 ch f Risk Me (FR) 8f **(53)** - Yukosan (Absalom) 7.2f **(58)**
Form - 05007
Record 1999 - 1st:0 2nd:0 3rd:0 Ran:2
Pre1999 - 1st:0 2nd:0 3rd:0 Ran:8
1999 AW 0-2: (8f 2) (Equi 2)
Scopey, moderate filly, has worn blinkers. AW high 31.
**B R Johnson [0-5] Miss Julie Reeves (from G Lewis [0-5] Jun 1998).*

SURPRISED BHB 70f **RR 70f** 4344[15]

4 b g Superpower 6.6f **(58)** - Indigo (Primo Dominie) 6.2f **(80)**
Form - 21352520
Record 1999 - 1st:1 2nd:3 3rd:1 Ran:8
Pre1999 - 1st:0 2nd:1 3rd:0 Ran:7
Win Prizemoney £3,392 *Total Prizemoney* £8,864
Wins * 1999 Jun Pontef (GD) H 6f 64 66 <

1999 Turf 1-8: (5f 2, 6f 1-4, 7f 2) (g-s, gd, g-f 1-3, frm 3)
Above-average gelding, effective 5 to 7f, acts on gd to frm, best on frm, has worn blinkers. Turf high 71 - 3rd of 18 giving 19lb to Wishbone Alley (24 Jun Newcastle 6f frm RF 2269) - also 1st of 18 giving 13lb to Wishbone Alley (14 Jun Pontefract RF 1984). Consistent.
**R A Fahey [1-8] D R Brotherton (from Mrs J R Ramsden [0-7] Jly 1998).*

SURPRISE ENCOUNTER BHB 85f **RR 82f** 1143[6]
3 ch c Cadeaux Genereux 7.9f **(76)** - Scandalette (Niniski (USA)) 10.6f **(65)**
Form - 156
Record 1999 - 1st:1 2nd:0 3rd:0 Ran:3
Pre1999 - 1st:0 2nd:0 3rd:0 Ran:2
Win Prizemoney £3,208 *Total Prizemoney* £3,208
Wins * 1999 Apr Kempto (G-F) 7f 81 <
1999 Turf 1-3: (7f 1-3) (gd, g-f 1-1, frm)
Workmanlike, decent colt. Turf high 82 - 6th of 16 getting 8lb from Swallow Flight (11 May York 7f gd RF 1143) - also 1st of 12 from Border Prince (5 Apr Kempton RF 0579).
**E A L Dunlop [1-5] Ahmed Ali.*

SURREY LASS BHB 28f **RR 8f** 4289[11]
3 b f Chaddleworth (IRE) - Aquarula (Dominion) 8.5f **(63)**
Form - 000
Record 1999 - 1st:0 2nd:0 3rd:0 Ran:3
1999 Turf 0-3: (7f, 11f 2) (g-f, frm 2)
Scopey, currently very poor filly. Turf high 8 (began Aug).
**C A Dwyer [0-3] J Johnston.*

SURTSEY BHB 41f **RR 18f** 1209[10]
5 ch g Nashwan (USA) 10.3f **(79)** - Fire and Shade (USA) (Shadeed (USA)) 8.2f **(70)**
Form - 00
Record 1999 - 1st:0 2nd:0 3rd:0 Ran:2
Pre1999 - 1st:0 2nd:1 3rd:1 Ran:5
Win Prizemoney £0 *Total Prizemoney* £1,750
1999 Turf 0-2: (11f, 12f) (g-s, g-f)
Poor gelding. Turf high 18.
**Mrs A Swinbank [0-2] G B Turnbull Ltd (from M Johnston [0-5] Aug 1997).*

SURVEILLANCE (USA) BHB 82f **RR 84f** 4435[7]
3 ch c Woodman (USA) 9.7f **(77)** - Eye Drop (USA) (Irish River (FR)) 8.6f **(78)**
Form - 153337
Record 1999 - 1st:1 2nd:0 3rd:3 Ran:6
Win Prizemoney £0 *Total Prizemoney* £1,833
Wins * 1999 Apr Newmar (GD) 8f 75? <
1999 Turf 1-6: (8f 1-3, 10f, 12f 2) (g-s, gd 2, g-f, frm 1-2)
Strong, decent colt, effective 8 to 12f, acts on gd to frm. Turf high 84 - 3rd of 6 giving 5lb to Dane (8 Jly Newmarket 10f frm RF 2641) - also 1st of 2 from Hougoumont (30 Apr Newmarket RF 0949).
**J H M Gosden [1-6] Sheikh Mohammed.*

SURVEYOR BHB 90f **RR 95f** 4561[14]
4 ch c Lycius (USA) 8.8f **(71)** - Atacama (Green Desert (USA)) 8.6f **(78)**
Form - 70
Record 1999 - 1st:0 2nd:0 3rd:0 Ran:2
Pre1999 - 1st:2 2nd:1 3rd:1 Ran:9
Win Prizemoney £7,211 *Total Prizemoney* £11,848
Wins * 1997 Spt Kempto (GD) H 6f 90 93 <
* 1997 Aug Lingfi (G-F) 6f 83+
1999 Turf 0-2: (5f, 6f) (gd, frm)
Scopey, very useful colt, effective 6f, acts on gd to g-f, best on gd. Turf high 76 (began Spt). **J L Dunlop [2-11] The Earl Cadogan.*

SURVIVAL VENTURE BHB 54f67a **RR 65df 67a** 3910[3]
3 b g Unfuwain (USA) 11.4f **(74)** - Sherkraine (Shergar) 10.4f **(66)**
Form - 32001243
Record 1999 - 1st:1 2nd:2 3rd:2 Ran:8
Pre1999 - 1st:0 2nd:0 3rd:0 Ran:4
Win Prizemoney £2,257 *Total Prizemoney* £5,019
Wins * 1999 *Jun Lingfi (STD) C 7f 64* <
1999 Turf 0-4: (6f, 7f 3) (g-s, g-f 2, hrd) 1999 AW 1-4: (7f 1-2, 8f, 10f) (Equi 1-4)
Neat, above-average gelding, effective 7 to 8f, best at 7f, acts on hrd - acts on Equi, prefers left handed tracks, prefers tight tracks. Turf high 65 (1st run) - 2nd of 16 giving 4lb to James Dee (4 May Brighton 7f hrd RF 1022). AW high 72 - 2nd of 10 giving 3lb to Delphini (24 Jly Lingfield 8f Equi RF 3097) - also 1st of 10 from Hound Venture (25 Jun Lingfield RF 2291). Inconsistent. Out of a useful daughter of Shergar, he won a particularly poor claimer on the Lingfield Equitrack in June, but still looks better on sand than on turf. **S P C Woods [1-12] Dr Frank Chao.*

SUSAN'S DOWRY BHB 65f **RR 76?f** 4446[13]
3 b f Efisio 7.7f **(69)** - Adjusting (IRE) (Busted) 10.2f **(61)**
Form - 0
Record 1999 - 1st:0 2nd:0 3rd:0 Ran:1
Pre1999 - 1st:1 2nd:0 3rd:0 Ran:5
Win Prizemoney £3,615 *Total Prizemoney* £3,807
Wins 1998 Jun Pontef (SFT) 6f 76+ <
1999 Turf 0-1: (8f) (g-s)
Scopey, above-average filly, effective 6f, acts on gd.
**Andrew Turnell [0-1] Mrs Claire Hollowood (from T D Easterby [1-5] Jly 1998).*

SUSAN'S PRIDE (IRE) BHB 75f **RR 77f** 5127[1]
3 b g Pips Pride 6.7f **(70)** - Piney Pass (Persian Bold) 9.3f **(66)**
Form - 2601730646511
Record 1999 - 1st:3 2nd:1 3rd:1 Ran:14
Win Prizemoney £9,642 *Total Prizemoney* £15,123
Wins * 1999 Oct Bright (G-S) C 7f 68
*** 1999** Oct Doncas (SFT) C 7f 77 <
*** 1999** May Nottin (GD) 6.1f 75
1999 Turf 3-14: (5f 2, 6f 1-4, 7f 2-5, 8f 2, 9f) (g-s 1-3, gd 1-4, g-f 4, frm 1-3)
Workmanlike, above-average gelding, effective 7f, acts on gd, has worn blinkers. Turf high 88. **B J Meehan [3-14] Mrs Susan Roy.*

SUSEJEBHA (IRE) BHB 32f **RR 35f** 5067[10]
3 ch f Magical Wonder (USA) 7.2f **(60)** - Tribute to Viqueen (Furry Glen) 8.9f **(63)**
Form - 000
Record 1999 - 1st:0 2nd:0 3rd:0 Ran:3
1999 Turf 0-3: (10f, 12f, 14f) (gd, g-f, frm)
Strong, currently very moderate filly. Turf high 35 (began Aug).
**M J Weeden [0-3] Dr Ian Shenkin.*

SUSHI BAR (IRE) BHB 40f59a **RR 46f 59a** 4837[4]
8 gr g Petorius 8f **(66)** - Sashi Woo (Rusticaro (FR)) 8.2f **(65)**
Form - 0234514
Record 1999 - 1st:1 2nd:1 3rd:1 Ran:7
Pre1999 - 1st:3 2nd:1 3rd:4 Ran:23
Win Prizemoney £9,787 *Total Prizemoney* £14,054
Wins * 1999 Spt Beverl (SFT) S 12f 42
* 1997 Aug Beverl (GD) SH 12f 36 42
* 1997 Jly Mussel (GD) SH 16f 36 40
* 1995 Jun Carlis (FRM) 14.1f 57 <
1999 Turf 1-7: (12f 1-2, 14f 3, 16f, 17f) (sft, g-s 1-1, gd, g-f 3, frm)
Fair gelding, effective 12 to 14f, best at 12f, acts on g-s to frm. Turf high 46 - 4th of 20 to Duello (12 Oct Leicester 12f gd RF 4837) - also 1st of 13 from Xylem (21 Spt Beverley RF 4442).
**Mrs M Reveley [4-32] Tremousser Partnership.*

SUSIE'S FLYER (IRE) BHB 88f **RR 90f** 4532[5]
2 br f Frimaire - Wisdom to Know (Bay Express) 7.1f **(60)**
Form - 25115
Record 1999 - 1st:2 2nd:1 3rd:0 Ran:5
Win Prizemoney £10,040 *Total Prizemoney* £11,070
Wins * 1999 Spt Newbur (G-F) H 5.2f 77 90+ <
*** 1999** Aug Lingfi (GD) 5f 72
1999 Turf 2-5: (5f 2-5) (g-s 2, frm 2-3)
Useful filly. Turf high 90 - 1st of 11 getting 7lb from Lost In Hook (17 Spt Newbury RF 4384). Made all to win at Lingfield on her third start despite hanging badly left in the closing stages and followed up in a Newbury nursery. Beaten in heavy ground next time.
**J Berry [2-5] Mrs U O'Reilly.*

SUSSEX LAD **RR 79f** 2107[10]
2 b c Prince Sabo 6.6f **(64)** - Pea Green (Try My Best (USA)) 7.6f **(67)**
Form - 60

Record 1999 - 1st:0 2nd:0 3rd:0 Ran:2
1999 Turf 0-2: (5f 2) (gd, g-f)
Currently above-average colt. Turf high 79.
R Hannon [0-2] Peter Crane.

SUSU BHB 117f **RR 119f** 5226a[12]
6 ch m Machiavellian (USA) 9.8f **(83)** - Home Truth (Known Fact (USA)) 7.4f **(67)**
Form - 3110
Record 1999 - 1st:2 2nd:0 3rd:1 Ran:4
Win Prizemoney £65,715 *Total Prizemoney* £68,252
Wins * **1999** Oct Newmar (GD) G2 7f 119 <
* **1999** Spt Doncas (G-F) L 7f 110
1999 Turf 2-4: (7f 2-2, 8f 2) (gd 1-2, g-f 1-1, frm)
High-class mare. Turf high 119 (began Aug) - 1st of 10 getting 3lb from Lend A Hand (16 Oct Newmarket RF 4916) - also 1st of 11 giving 7lb to Pescara (9 Spt Doncaster RF 4239). It is unusual for a horse to be improving with every start at the age of six, but that is the case with this admirable mare. A prolific winner in Dubai, she showed a top-class turn-of-foot to win a Listed event at Doncaster in September and nailed Lend A Hand in Newmarket's Group 2 Challenge Stakes the following month. That was a first-rate effort and, though she was unplaced in the Breeders' Cup Mile, she will be an interesting contender for the top seven-furlong and mile races if returning in 2000. *Sir Michael Stoute [2-4].*

SUSY WELLS (IRE) BHB 35f **RR 42f** 5035[7]
4 b f Masad (IRE) - My Best Susy (IRE) (Try My Best (USA)) 7.6f **(67)**
Form - 40800567
Record 1999 - 1st:0 2nd:0 3rd:0 Ran:8
Pre1999 - 1st:0 2nd:1 3rd:1 Ran:8
Win Prizemoney £0 *Total Prizemoney* £1,215
1999 Turf 0-8: (7f 3, 8f 4, 9f) (g-s, gd 3, g-f 2, frm, hrd)
Workmanlike, moderate filly, effective 7 to 8f, best at 8f, acts on g-s to frm, has worn blinkers. Turf high 45. Inconsistent.
J Parkes [0-16] C W Moore.

SU TIROLESU (IRE) RR 104f 4243a[7]
3 b c Tirol 8.1f **(64)** - Glrnross (ITY) (Warning)
Form - 157
1999 Turf 1-3: (5f, 6f 1-2) (gd 1-3)
Currently very useful colt. Turf high 104 (1st run) - 1st of 12 getting 9lb from Blu Carillon (16 May Capannelle RF 1354a).
G Ligas in ITY [1-3].

SUTTON COMMON (IRE) RR 63f 4799[4]
2 b c Common Grounds 8.1f **(66)** - Fadaki Hawaki (USA) (Vice Regent (CAN)) 8.7f **(74)**
Form - 04
Record 1999 - 1st:0 2nd:0 3rd:0 Ran:2
Win Prizemoney £0 *Total Prizemoney* £466
1999 Turf 0-2: (6f, 8f) (gd 2)
Currently average colt. Turf high 63 (began Spt).
K A Ryan [0-2] The North Broomhill Racing Syndicate.

SWAGGER BHB 39a **RR 39f** 5006[6]
3 ch g Generous (IRE) 11.5f **(82)** - Widows Walk (Habitat) 9.4f **(70)**
Form - 00703416
Record 1999 - 1st:1 2nd:0 3rd:0 Ran:8
Pre1999 - 1st:0 2nd:0 3rd:0 Ran:1
Win Prizemoney £2,039 *Total Prizemoney* £2,375
Wins * **1999** *Spt Southw (STD) H 14f 39 41* <
1999 Turf 0-6: (7f, 8f, 10f, 16f 2, 17f) (g-s, gd, g-f, frm 3) 1999 AW 1-2: (6f, 14f 1-1) (Fibr 1-2)
Strong, moderate gelding, effective 14 to 17f, acts on frm - acts on Fibr. Turf high 39 (began Jly). AW high 41 (began Jly) - 1st of 15 getting 12lb from St Lawrence (28 Spt Southwell RF 4600).
Sir Mark Prescott [1-9] Moore Osborne House.

SWALDO BHB 64f **RR 73f** 5192[3]
2 ch c Muhtarram (USA) - Ethel Knight (Thatch (USA)) 9.8f **(62)**
Form - 8723
Record 1999 - 1st:0 2nd:1 3rd:1 Ran:4
Win Prizemoney £0 *Total Prizemoney* £906
1999 Turf 0-3: (6f, 8f 2) (gd 2, g-f) 1999 AW 0-1: (6f) (Fibr)
Above-average colt, has worn blinkers. Turf high 73 - 2nd of 18 giving 5lb to Unimpeachable (21 Oct Nottingham 8f gd RF 5002).
G C H Chung [0-3] Osvaldo Pedroni (from A Kelleway [0-1] Jun 1999).

SWALLOW FLIGHT (IRE) BHB 104f **RR 103f** 5140[4]
3 b c Bluebird (USA) 7.9f **(71)** - Mirage (Red Sunset) 8.2f **(63)**
Form - 5313325124
Record 1999 - 1st:2 2nd:2 3rd:3 Ran:10
Pre1999 - 1st:0 2nd:2 3rd:1 Ran:4
Win Prizemoney £29,717 *Total Prizemoney* £74,365
Wins * **1999** Spt Doncas (G-F) 8f 101+ <
* **1999** May York (G-S) H 7f 94 96
1999 Turf 2-10: (7f 1-3, 8f 1-6, 10f) (hvy, gd 1-4, g-f 1-3, frm 2)
Scopey, very useful colt, effective 7 to 10f, best at 8f, acts on hvy to frm, and excels at York. Turf high 103 - 4th of 8 getting 3lb from Bomb Alaska (30 Oct Newmarket 8f gd RF 5140) - also 1st of 5 getting 3lb from Desert Knight (10 Spt Doncaster RF 4254). Consistent. He tended to fall asleep in his races during the first half of the season, but was much sharper through the autumn. Probably best over a mile, he acts on any ground and could develop into a Group Three horse. *G Wragg [2-14] Mollers Racing.*

SWALLOW JAZ BHB 54f **RR 60?f** 4575[12]
2 b g Alhijaz 7.7f **(57)** - Marguerite Bay (IRE) **(84f)** (Darshaan) 9.9f **(84)**
Form - 0050
Record 1999 - 1st:0 2nd:0 3rd:0 Ran:4
1999 Turf 0-4: (7f 2, 8f 2) (gd, g-f, frm, hrd)
Average gelding. Turf high 60 (began Aug).
T J Etherington [0-4] Foreneish Racing.

SWAMPY (IRE) BHB 63f53a **RR 66f 53a** 5050[2]
3 b c Second Set (IRE) 9.2f **(67)** - Mystery Lady (USA) (Vaguely Noble) 10.1f **(72)**
Form - 445322806U2
Record 1999 - 1st:0 2nd:3 3rd:1 Ran:11
Pre1999 - 1st:0 2nd:0 3rd:0 Ran:3
Win Prizemoney £0 *Total Prizemoney* £2,884
1999 Turf 0-7: (8f 3, 9f 2, 10f 2) (hvy 2, g-s, gd 2, frm 2) 1999 AW 0-4: (7f, 8f 2, 10f) (Equi 3, Fibr)
Average colt. Turf high 66. AW high 54.
N A Callaghan [0-11] Gallagher Equine Ltd (from K McAuliffe [0-3] Spt 1998).

SWAN AT WHALLEY BHB 43f49a **RR 39f 49a** 3845[14]
7 b g Statoblest 6.4f **(63)** - My Precious Daisy (Sharpo) 7.7f **(59)**
Form - 80120600
Record 1999 - 1st:1 2nd:1 3rd:1 Ran:8
Pre1999 - 1st:4 2nd:6 3rd:3 Ran:48
Win Prizemoney £18,353 *Total Prizemoney* £29,742
Wins * **1999** Apr Mussel (G-F) H 5f 44 45
1997 Spt Cheste (GD) H 5.1f 63 64
1997 Jun Doncas (G-S) H 5f 63 70 <
1996 Jly Mussel (GD) H 5f 60 67
1999 Turf 1-8: (5f 1-8) (gd 3, g-f 2, frm 1-3)
Moderate gelding, has broken blood-vessels, effective 5f, acts on frm, has worn blinkers. Turf high 45.
K A Ryan [1-14] Mrs C M Barlow (from R A Fahey [2-17] May 1998).

SWANDALE FLYER BHB 27f22a **RR 28f 22a** 2758[7]
7 ch g Weldnaas (USA) 8.4f **(55)** - Misfire (Gunner B) 11.2f **(58)**
Form - 057
Record 1999 - 1st:0 2nd:0 3rd:0 Ran:3
Pre1999 - 1st:0 2nd:1 3rd:1 Ran:30
Win Prizemoney £0 *Total Prizemoney* £1,613
1999 Turf 0-2: (12f 2) (frm 2) 1999 AW 0-1: (12f) (Fibr)
Very moderate gelding, has broken blood-vessels, effective 13f, acts on gd, likes left handed tracks, likes tight tracks. Turf high 28 (began Jly). Inconsistent. *N Bycroft [1-44] Andrew Carruthers.*

SWAN HUNTER BHB 56f90a **RR 45f 90a** 5101[9]
6 b h Sharrood (USA) 11.1f **(67)** - Cache (Bustino) 10.4f **(64)**
Form - 22000
Record 1999 - 1st:0 2nd:1 3rd:0 Ran:4
Pre1999 - 1st:6 2nd:4 3rd:0 Ran:25
Win Prizemoney £15,926 *Total Prizemoney* £27,738
Wins * 1998 *Jan Wolver (STD) H 12f 77 84* <
* 1997 *Dec Wolver (STD) H 12f 68 74+*
* 1997 *Nov Wolver (STD) H 14.8f 62 67*
* 1997 Oct Catter (SFT) C 12f 57+

* 1997 Oct Leices (G-S) C 11.8f 62
* 1996 Apr Mussel (GD) 11.1f 63
1999 Turf 0-2: (12f, 14f) (g-s, gd) 1999 AW 0-2: (12f 2) (Equi, Fibr)
Useful horse, effective 12f, - acts on AW, best on Fibr, prefers left handed tracks, favours tight tracks. Turf high 45 (began Oct). AW high 90 (1st run) - 2nd of 12 giving 20lb to Dancing Rio (2 Jan Lingfield 12f Equi RF 0011). Inconsistent.
**D J S Cosgrove [6-29] Derrick Yarwood.*

SWAN KNIGHT (USA) RR 77tf 944[9]

3 b br c Sadler's Wells (USA) 11.3f **(87)** - Shannkara (IRE) (Akarad (FR)) 9f **(76)**
Form - 10
Record 1999 - 1st:1 2nd:0 3rd:0 Ran:2
Win Prizemoney £4,565 *Total Prizemoney* £4,565
Wins * 1999 Apr Newmar (GD) 8f 77t <
1999 Turf 1-2: (8f 1-1, 10f) (gd 1-1, frm)
Scopey, currently above-average colt. Turf high 77 (1st run) - 1st of 12 from Manndar (14 Apr Newmarket RF 0691).
**J H M Gosden [1-2] Sheikh Mohammed.*

SWAN LAKE (FR) BHB 47a RR 44f 5056[8]

3 b f Lyphard (USA) 10.6f **(75)** - Dame Au Faucon (USA) (Silver Hawk (USA)) 8.6f **(70)**
Form - 588660568
Record 1999 - 1st:0 2nd:0 3rd:0 Ran:9
1999 Turf 0-7: (8f 2, 10f 3, 11f, 12f) (g-s 3, frm 4) 1999 AW 0-2: (10f 2) (Equi 2)
Moderate filly. Turf high 51. AW high 56. Becoming disappointing.
**K O Cunningham-Brown [0-9] A J Richards.*

SWAN PRINCE BHB 37f RR 53f 3907[14]

2 b c King's Signet (USA) 7f **(51)** - Princess Tallulah **(15f 30a)** (Chief Singer) 8.9f **(66)**
Form - P40060
Record 1999 - 1st:0 2nd:0 3rd:0 Ran:6
1999 Turf 0-4: (6f 3, 7f) (gd, g-f, frm, hrd) 1999 AW 0-2: (6f, 7f) (Fibr 2)
Fair colt. Turf high 53. AW high 18. **W G M Turner [0-6] Vale Racing.*

SWCI RR 33f 2849[8]

2 ch f Shalford (IRE) 7.8f **(63)** - Plucky Pet **(40f 28a)** (Petong) 6.6f **(58)**
Form - 8
Record 1999 - 1st:0 2nd:0 3rd:0 Ran:1
1999 Turf 0-1: (5f) (g-f)
Currently very moderate filly. **B Palling [0-1] Five To Follow.*

SWEET ANGELINE BHB 69f RR 74f 4820[12]

2 b f Deploy 11.4f **(67)** - Fiveofive (IRE) (Fairy King (USA)) 7.7f **(59)**
Form - 0444030
Record 1999 - 1st:0 2nd:0 3rd:1 Ran:7
Win Prizemoney £0 *Total Prizemoney* £1,920
1999 Turf 0-7: (6f, 7f, 8f 4, 10f) (gd 2, g-f 3, frm 2)
Above-average filly, effective 8f, acts on frm. Turf high 74 - 4th of 10 giving 4lb to Saafend Boy (27 Aug Newmarket 8f frm RF 3942).
**A T Murphy [0-7] Mrs T A Foreman.*

SWEET AS A NUT (IRE) BHB 59f65a RR 60df 65a 3375[7]

3 ch f Pips Pride 6.7f **(70)** - My First Paige (IRE) **(41f 48a)** (Runnett) 7f **(59)**
Form - 005420257
Record 1999 - 1st:0 2nd:2 3rd:0 Ran:9
Pre1999 - 1st:3 2nd:1 3rd:1 Ran:12
Win Prizemoney £8,213 *Total Prizemoney* £11,538
Wins * 1998 Jly Doncas (FRM) H 5f 83 <
* 1998 Jun Hamilt (SFT) C 5f 75
* 1998 Jun Beverl (GD) C 5f 58
1999 Turf 0-8: (5f 3, 6f 5) (g-s, gd, g-f 3, frm 3) 1999 AW 0-1: (6f) (Fibr)
Leggy, average filly, effective 5 to 6f, best at 5f, acts on gd to frm, best on frm. Turf high 60. **C A Dwyer [3-21] Wessex House Racing.*

SWEET BETTSIE BHB 31f RR 28f 4175[10]

5 b m Presidium 7.5f **(56)** - Sweet and Sure (Known Fact (USA)) 7.4f **(67)**
Form - 00
Record 1999 - 1st:0 2nd:0 3rd:0 Ran:2
Pre1999 - 1st:0 2nd:0 3rd:0 Ran:11
1999 Turf 0-2: (7f, 10f) (frm 2)
Little account filly, has worn blinkers. Turf high 28 (began Aug). Inconsistent.
**D J Coakley [0-2] The Five Legged Partnership (from K R Burke [0-7] Nov 1998).*

SWEET CHARITY (IRE) BHB 70f RR 71f 4440[1]

3 ch f Bigstone (IRE) - Tolstoya (Northfields (USA)) 9f **(72)**
Form - 0341401
Record 1999 - 1st:2 2nd:0 3rd:1 Ran:7
Pre1999 - 1st:0 2nd:1 3rd:3 Ran:6
Win Prizemoney £5,698 *Total Prizemoney* £10,639
Wins * 1999 Spt Leices (GD) C 6f 71 <
*** 1999** Jly Bright (FRM) H 6f 70 71 <
1999 Turf 2-7: (5f, 6f 2-3, 7f 3) (g-s, gd 2, g-f 1-2, frm, hrd 1-1)
Neat, above-average filly, effective 5 to 7f, best at 6f, acts on g-f to hrd. Turf high 71 - 1st of 22 giving 13lb to The Thruster (20 Spt Leicester RF 4440) - also 1st of 7 giving 27lb to Courtney Gym (12 Jly Brighton RF 2753). **M A Jarvis [2-13] Mrs Christine Stevenson.*

SWEET CICELY (IRE) RR 75f 5109[7]

2 b f Darshaan 11.9f **(81)** - Glendora (Glenstal (USA)) 10.1f **(64)**
Form - 07
Record 1999 - 1st:0 2nd:0 3rd:0 Ran:2
1999 Turf 0-2: (7f, 8f) (g-s, gd)
Currently above-average filly. Turf high 75 (began Aug).
**D R C Elsworth [0-2] Colin Brown Racing.*

SWEET COMPLIANCE BHB 48f51a RR 38f 51a 2496[20]

3 ch f Safawan 6.6f **(60)** - Sianiski (Niniski (USA)) 10.6f **(65)**
Form - 060700
Record 1999 - 1st:0 2nd:0 3rd:0 Ran:5
Pre1999 - 1st:1 2nd:1 3rd:1 Ran:9
Win Prizemoney £3,287 *Total Prizemoney* £4,482
Wins * 1998 Spt Lingfi (G-S) H 7f 59 77 <
1999 Turf 0-3: (6f 2, 7f) (gd, frm 2) 1999 AW 0-2: (8f 2) (Equi, Fibr)
Leggy, very moderate filly, effective 7f, acts on g-f, often wears blinkers (effectively). Turf high 38. AW high 21. Inconsistent.
**P Shakespeare [1-14] Mike Hyde.*

SWEET EMOTION (IRE) BHB 95f RR 96df 4838[7]

3 b f Bering 9.6f **(80)** - Hiwaayati (Shadeed (USA)) 8.2f **(70)**
Form - 1277
Record 1999 - 1st:1 2nd:1 3rd:0 Ran:4
Win Prizemoney £4,532 *Total Prizemoney* £8,692
Wins * 1999 Apr Newmar (GD) 8f 63t <
1999 Turf 1-4: (8f 1-3, 10f) (gd 1-3, g-f)
Lengthy, very useful filly. Turf high 96 - 2nd of 7 to Insinuate (28 Apr Ascot 8f g-f RF 0896). She failed to progress after refusing to settle in her races. **E A L Dunlop [1-4] Maktoum Al Maktoum.*

SWEET GLOW (FR) BHB 57f RR 55f 904[P]

12 b g Crystal Glitters (USA) 8f **(89)** - Very Sweet (Bellypha) 9.8f **(73)**
Form - P
Record 1999 - 1st:0 2nd:0 3rd:0 Ran:1
Pre1999 - 1st:2 2nd:0 3rd:1 Ran:15
Win Prizemoney £28,051 *Total Prizemoney* £28,051
Wins * 1998 Jun Bath (G-S) SH 17.2f 52 60++
1999 Turf 0-1: (22f) (gd)
Fair gelding. **M C Pipe [13-66] M C Pipe.*

SWEET HAVEN BHB 60f RR 63f 5023[15]

2 b f Lugana Beach 7f **(63)** - Sweet Enough (Caerleon (USA)) 8.6f **(71)**
Form - 8180600
Record 1999 - 1st:1 2nd:0 3rd:0 Ran:7
Win Prizemoney £2,372 *Total Prizemoney* £2,372
Wins 1999 Apr Beverl (G-F) 5f 72 <
1999 Turf 1-7: (5f 1-3, 6f 4) (gd 4, g-f, frm 1-1, hrd)
Average filly, effective 5 to 6f, acts on g-f to frm. Turf high 72 - 1st of 13 getting 8lb from Cowboys And Angels (14 Apr Beverley RF 0688). Won her maiden over five furlongs at Beverley in April but has been disappointing since.
**C G Cox [0-4] P G Horrocks (from M J Heaton-Ellis [1-3] May 1999).*

SWEET MAGIC BHB 60f60a RR 59f 60a 2806[5]

8 ch g Sweet Monday 8.3f **(43)** - Charm Bird (Daring March) 7.1f **(61)**
Form - 52372102405105
Record 1999 - 1st:2 2nd:2 3rd:0 Ran:11

	Pre1999 -	1st:3	2nd:4	3rd:3	Ran:34

Win Prizemoney £19,215 *Total Prizemoney* £34,103

Wins	*** 1999**	Jun	Catter	(G-F)	H	5f	57	59	
	*** 1999**	*Apr*	*Wolver*	*(STD)*	*S*	*5f*		*64*	
	1997	Aug	Sandow	(G-S)	H	5f	59	63	
	1995	Jly	Newmar	(GD)	H	5f	81	81	<

1999 Turf 1-6: (5f 1-6) (gd, g-f 2, frm 1-3) 1999 AW 1-5: (5f 1-5) (Fibr 1-5)

Average gelding, effective 5f, acts on gd to frm - acts on Fibr, has worn blinkers, likes left handed tracks, likes tight tracks. Turf high 59 - 1st of 13 getting 7lb from Swynford Dream (30 Jun Catterick RF 2437). AW high 64 - 1st of 10 from Samwar (24 Apr Wolverhampton RF 0850).

**L R Lloyd-James [2-14] Miss Kate Waddington (from P Howling [1-20] Jun 1998).*

SWEET OPERA (FR) RR 105f 4369a[9]

3 g f Linamix (FR) 8.2f **(64)** - Street Opera (Sadler's Wells (USA)) 10f **(76)**

Form - 2210

1999 Turf 1-4: (10f, 11f 1-2, 12f) (hvy 1-1, gd 3)

Pattern-class filly. Turf high 105. **F Head in FR [1-4] J-L Lagadere.*

SWEET PATOOPIE BHB 49f70a RR 51f 70a 5168[7]

5 b m Indian Ridge 7.6f **(74)** - Patriotic (Hotfoot) 10.5f **(59)**

Form - 13257

Record	**1999 -**	1st:1	2nd:1	3rd:1	Ran:5
	Pre1999 -	1st:0	2nd:2	3rd:1	Ran:8

Win Prizemoney £2,733 *Total Prizemoney* £6,175

Wins	**1999**	*May*	*Lingfi*	*(STD)*	*H*	*12f*	*59*	*68*	<

1999 Turf 0-2: (11f, 14f) (g-s, g-f) 1999 AW 1-3: (12f 1-3) (Equi 1-1, Fibr 2)

Average filly, effective 10 to 12f, best at 12f, - acts on AW, best on Equi, has worn blinkers, favours left handed tracks. Turf high 51. AW high 68 (1st run) - 1st of 8 getting 8lb from Prince Danzig (25 May Lingfield RF 1454). Able in modest handicap company on turf, but her best form in the last couple of seasons has been on sand.

**Mrs P Ford [0-2] David Lee (from B Hanbury [1-11] Jun 1999).*

SWEET PEA BHB 89f RR 87f 4796[8]

4 b f Persian Bold 10f **(69)** - Silk Petal (Petorius) 7.3f **(61)**

Form - 014168

Record	**1999 -**	1st:2	2nd:0	3rd:0	Ran:6
	Pre1999 -	1st:2	2nd:2	3rd:0	Ran:6

Win Prizemoney £18,227 *Total Prizemoney* £21,835

Wins	*** 1999**	Aug	Haydoc	(SFT)	H	8.1f	85	87	<
	*** 1999**	Apr	Windso	(G-S)	H	8.3f	77	83	
	* 1998	Jun	Newmar	(GD)	H	8f	75	80	
	* 1998	May	Bath	(G-F)		8f		74	

1999 Turf 2-6: (8f 2-6) (gd 2-4, g-f, frm)

Scopey, useful filly, effective 8f, acts on gd to g-f, best on gd, likes tight tracks. Turf high 87 - 1st of 9 giving 15lb to Shall We Dance (7 Aug Haydock RF 3453) - also 1st of 9 giving 16lb to Bird Of Prey (27 Apr Windsor RF 0874). She looked to be back to her best when bolting up in a Windsor fillies' handicap on her second start of the season, and though that resulted in a steep rise in the handicap, she came with a strong run to land a rated stakes on soft ground at Haydock in August. **J L Dunlop [4-12] Nicholas Jones.*

SWEET REWARD BHB 68f RR 68f 4802[22]

4 ch g Beveled (USA) 6.9f **(64)** - Sweet Revival (Claude Monet (USA))

Form - 220330

Record	**1999 -**	1st:0	2nd:2	3rd:2	Ran:6
	Pre1999 -	1st:1	2nd:0	3rd:4	Ran:13

Win Prizemoney £3,392 *Total Prizemoney* £11,864

Wins	* 1997	Jun	Leices	(GD)	6f		72	<

1999 Turf 0-6: (7f, 8f 2, 9f, 10f 2) (hvy, g-s 2, gd, g-f, frm)

Leggy, average gelding, effective 7 to 8f, best at 8f, acts on g-s to gd, best on g-s, prefers right handed tracks, prefers tight tracks. Turf high 68.

**J G Smyth-Osbourne [1-19] Mrs Andria Dorler & Partners.*

SWEET ROSIE (IRE) BHB 44f42a RR 21f 42a 5199[24]

4 b f Petardia 8.2f **(58)** - White's Pet (Mummy's Pet) 7.7f **(60)**

Form - 600

Record	**1999 -**	1st:0	2nd:0	3rd:0	Ran:3
	Pre1999 -	1st:0	2nd:1	3rd:1	Ran:4

Win Prizemoney £0 *Total Prizemoney* £1,166

1999 Turf 0-2: (6f 2) (gd 2) 1999 AW 0-1: (7f) (Equi)

Light-framed, moderate filly. (began Oct).

**P Mitchell [0-3] Mrs V M Harris (from R Boss [0-4] Jly 1997).*

SWEET SECOND (GER) RR 91f 1533a[9]

3 f

Form - 0

1999 Turf 0-1: (11f) (sft)

Currently useful filly. **A Lowe in GER [0-1].*

SWEET SENORITA BHB 36f RR 48f 3023[1]

4 b f Young Senor (USA) 8f **(43)** - Sweet N' Twenty (High Top) 10.2f **(67)**

Form - 621

Record	**1999 -**	1st:1	2nd:1	3rd:0	Ran:3
	Pre1999 -	1st:0	2nd:0	3rd:0	Ran:7

Win Prizemoney £2,295 *Total Prizemoney* £2,831

Wins	*** 1999**	Jly	Bright	(FRM)	SH	11.9f	27	31	<

1999 Turf 1-3: (10f, 12f 1-2) (gd, frm 1-2)

Leggy, moderate filly, effective 12f, acts on frm. Turf high 48 - 2nd of 10 giving 13lb to Amaretto Flame (12 Jly Windsor 12f frm RF 2760). **M Madgwick [1-10] W E Baird.*

SWEET SERENATA BHB 35f38a RR 38f 38a 2536[6]

4 gr f Keen 11.1f **(58)** - Serenata (Larrinaga) 13.8f **(53)**

Form - 4266346

Record	**1999 -**	1st:0	2nd:1	3rd:1	Ran:6
	Pre1999 -	1st:1	2nd:0	3rd:0	Ran:10

Win Prizemoney £2,010 *Total Prizemoney* £3,084

Wins	* 1998	Spt	Catter	(G-F)	S	13.8f		43	<

1999 Turf 0-3: (11f, 13f, 14f) (gd, g-f, frm) 1999 AW 0-3: (13f, 16f 2) (Equi 3)

Lengthy, moderate filly, effective 13 to 16f, acts on frm - acts on Equi, prefers left handed tracks, favours tight tracks. Turf high 38. AW high 42 (1st run) - 2nd of 9 getting 28lb from Paradise Navy (9 Jan Lingfield 16f Equi RF 0058). **S C Williams [1-16] Rib And Co.*

SWEET SORROW (IRE) BHB 95f RR 95f 4871[5]

4 b f Lahib (USA) 8f **(69)** - So Long Boys (FR) (Beldale Flutter (USA)) 9.7f **(71)**

Form - 21153445

Record	**1999 -**	1st:2	2nd:1	3rd:1	Ran:8
	Pre1999 -	1st:0	2nd:0	3rd:5	Ran:7

Win Prizemoney £7,448 *Total Prizemoney* £21,511

Wins	*** 1999**	Jun	Goodwo	(G-F)	12f	81	<
	*** 1999**	May	Ayr	(GD)	10f	78	

1999 Turf 2-8: (10f 1-3, 12f 1-5) (sft, gd 1-4, g-f 1-1, frm 2)

Leggy, very useful filly, effective 10 to 12f, best at 12f, acts on sft to frm, likes right handed tracks, likes Newmarket. Turf high 95 - 3rd of 8 to Innuendo (19 Aug York 12f gd RF 3771). She is tough and performed creditably in Listed races during the second half of the season. She may stay beyond a mile and a half and acts on any ground. **C F Wall [2-15] Mrs Yoshiko Allan.*

SWEET TEDDY BHB 73f RR 73f 2729[4]

2 b f Namaqualand (USA) - Nashville Blues (IRE) **(74f)** (Try My Best (USA)) 7.6f **(67)**

Form - 554

Record	**1999 -**	1st:0	2nd:0	3rd:0	Ran:3

Win Prizemoney £0 *Total Prizemoney* £428

1999 Turf 0-3: (5f, 6f 2) (gd, g-f 2)

Currently above-average filly. Turf high 73.

**J W Hills [0-3] Freddy Bienstock.*

SWEET TRENTINO (IRE) BHB 34f42a RR 32f 42a 3084[6]

8 b g High Estate 10.5f **(66)** - Sweet Adelaide (USA) (The Minstrel (CAN)) 10f **(72)**

Form - 46

Record	**1999 -**	1st:0	2nd:0	3rd:0	Ran:2
	Pre1999 -	1st:2	2nd:4	3rd:0	Ran:28

Win Prizemoney £7,355 *Total Prizemoney* £12,073

1999 AW 0-2: (12f, 16f) (Fibr 2)

Fair gelding, effective 12f, - acts on Fibr, has worn blinkers. AW high 56 (1st run) - 4th of 8 getting 10lb from Doc Ryan's (25 Jun Wolverhampton 12f Fibr RF 2310).

**M Tate [1-32] R C Smith (from C A Smith [0-5] Mar 1995).*

SWEET WILHELMINA BHB 77f79a RR 77f 79a 3608[1]

6 b m Indian Ridge 7.6f **(74)** - Henpot (IRE) (Alzao (USA)) 7.1f **(68)**
Form - 0161
Record 1999 - 1st:2 2nd:0 3rd:0 Ran:3
Pre1999 - 1st:6 2nd:6 3rd:1 Ran:28
Win Prizemoney £28,214 *Total Prizemoney* £53,154
Wins * **1999** Aug Epsom (GD) 7f 77
* **1999** *Jan Lingfi (STD) H 8f 73 81* <
1998 Jun Goodwo (G-F) H 7f 74 76
1997 May Leices (GD) H 8f 60 68
1997 *Feb Lingfi (STD) 7f 66+*
1997 *Feb Lingfi (STD) 8f 61+*
1995 *Nov Lingfi (STD) H 8f 67 78+*
1995 *Nov Wolver (STD) 7f 73*
1999 Turf 1-2: (7f 1-1, 8f) (g-f 1-1, frm) 1999 AW 1-1: (8f 1-1) (Equi 1-1)
Decent mare, effective 7 to 8f, best at 8f, acts on g-s to g-f - acts on Equi, likes left handed tracks, prefers tight tracks, excels at Goodwood and Lingfield. Turf high 77 (began Jly) - 1st of 6 giving 3lb to Democracy (13 Aug Epsom RF 3608). (1st run) - 1st of 8 giving 11lb to The Green Grey (16 Jan Lingfield RF 0105). Inconsistent.
**W R Muir [2-3] Chris van Hoorn (from Lord Huntingdon [6-28] Dec 1998).*

SWELL BETTY (IRE) BHB 70f **RR 69f** 3965[11]
3 b f Distinctly North (USA) 7.4f **(63)** - Cambridge Lodge (Tower Walk) 10f **(62)**
Form - 337120
Record 1999 - 1st:1 2nd:1 3rd:2 Ran:6
Pre1999 - 1st:0 2nd:0 3rd:1 Ran:5
Win Prizemoney £3,111 *Total Prizemoney* £5,338
Wins * **1999** Jly Salisb (FRM) H 8f 64 69 <
1999 Turf 1-6: (7f 4, 8f 1-2) (g-s, gd, g-f, frm 1-3)
Light-framed, average filly, effective 6 to 8f, acts on gd to frm. Turf high 69 - 2nd of 6 getting 3lb from Ajig Dancer (5 Aug Brighton 7f g-f RF 3384) - also 1st of 11 getting 1lb from Jade Tiger (30 Jly Salisbury RF 3249). **R Hannon [1-11] Lady G Parker.*

SWIFT BHB 65f75a **RR 61f 75a** 5168[9]
5 ch g Sharpo 7.5f **(68)** - Three Terns (USA) (Arctic Tern (USA)) 8.9f **(69)**
Form - 45325211011467100050
Record 1999 - 1st:5 2nd:2 3rd:1 Ran:20
Pre1999 - 1st:4 2nd:5 3rd:5 Ran:51
Win Prizemoney £34,992 *Total Prizemoney* £49,971
Wins * **1999** May York (SFT) H 13.9f 66 68
* **1999** Apr Warwic (GD) H 10.8f 57 76
* **1999** Mar Nottin (G-S) H 10f 57 67
* **1999** *Mar Southw (STD) H 12f 68 77* <
* **1999** *Mar Southw (STD) H 12f 65 65*
* 1997 Jun Redcar (GD) H 7f 62 66
* 1997 May Ripon (G-F) H 6f 57 63
* 1997 *Mar Wolver (STD) 8.5f 61*
* 1996 Oct Catter (GD) 5f 61
1999 Turf 3-12: (10f 1-2, 11f 1-1, 12f 6, 14f 1-3) (sft 1-1, g-s 1-2, gd 1-4, g-f 4, frm) 1999 AW 2-8: (8f 2, 9f, 11f 2, 12f 2-3) (Fibr 2-8)
Above-average gelding, effective 10 to 14f, acts on sft to gd - acts on Fibr, likes left handed tracks. Turf high 76 - 1st of 19 giving 17lb to Classic Colours (5 Apr Warwick RF 0596) - also 1st of 15 giving 2lb to Needwood Spirit (12 May York RF 1185). AW high 77 - 1st of 7 giving 6lb to Mr Fortywinks (16 Mar Southwell RF 0438). He had been showing encouraging signs before winning a couple of races at Southwell in March. He has added three victories on turf since then, including when stepped up to fourteen furlongs, but a rise in the handicap made life tough. Effective on Fibresand and on soft ground. **M J Polglase [10-73] Gen Sir Geoffrey Howlett.*

SWIFT ALLIANCE BHB 83f **RR 74?f** 2359[16]
4 b g Belong To Me (USA) - One Quick Bid (USA) (Commemorate (USA))
Form - 0
Record 1999 - 1st:0 2nd:0 3rd:0 Ran:1
Pre1999 - 1st:1 2nd:0 3rd:0 Ran:4
Win Prizemoney £3,640 *Total Prizemoney* £3,857
Wins 1997 May Folkes (G-F) 6f 78+ <
1999 Turf 0-1: (6f) (gd)
Strong, above-average gelding.
**Lady Herries[0-1]Mrs HACameron-Rose(fromRAkehurst[1-4]Jly 1997).*

SWIFT MAIDEN BHB 55f **RR** 5069[15]
6 gr m Sharrood (USA) 11.1f **(67)** - Gunner Girl (Gunner B) 11.2f **(58)**
Form - 0
Record 1999 - 1st:0 2nd:0 3rd:0 Ran:1
Pre1999 - 1st:1 2nd:0 3rd:2 Ran:9
Win Prizemoney £3,168 *Total Prizemoney* £4,189
Wins * 1996 May Newbur (SFT) C 10f 73+ <
1999 Turf 0-1: (10f) (gd)
Very poor mare.
**J Neville [1-7] F J Ayres (from Mrs L A Murphy [0-5] Nov 1995).*

SWIFTUR **RR 42f** 1954[9]
2 b f Snurge - Swift Spring (FR) (Bluebird (USA)) 7.5f **(69)**
Form - 0
Record 1999 - 1st:0 2nd:0 3rd:0 Ran:1
1999 Turf 0-1: (7f) (g-f)
Currently moderate filly. **P F I Cole [0-1] Ben Arbib.*

SWIFTWAY BHB 48f **RR 47f** 3535[4]
5 ch g Anshan 8.2f **(63)** - Solemn Occasion (USA) (Secreto (USA)) 8.7f **(72)**
Form - 34
Record 1999 - 1st:0 2nd:0 3rd:1 Ran:2
Pre1999 - 1st:1 2nd:1 3rd:3 Ran:18
Win Prizemoney £3,036 *Total Prizemoney* £6,641
Wins * 1998 Jly Beverl (G-F) H 16.2f 44 49 <
1999 Turf 0-2: (16f 2) (gd, g-f)
Moderate gelding, effective 16f, acts on frm, likes right handed tracks, favours tight tracks. Turf high 47.
**K W Hogg [3-23] Anthony White.*

SWING ALONG BHB 59f **RR 59f** 5103[3]
4 ch f Alhijaz 7.7f **(57)** - So it Goes (Free State) 8.7f **(61)**
Form - 350053053
Record 1999 - 1st:0 2nd:0 3rd:3 Ran:9
Pre1999 - 1st:0 2nd:2 3rd:0 Ran:3
Win Prizemoney £0 *Total Prizemoney* £5,422
1999 Turf 0-9: (6f 2, 7f 5, 8f 2) (g-s, gd 4, g-f 2, frm 2)
Strong, fair filly, effective 7f, acts on gd. Turf high 64. Consistent.
**C F Wall [0-12] W G Bovill.*

SWING BALL BHB 38f **RR 32f** 2277[13]
4 b f Always Fair (USA) 14f **(61)** - Lady Anchor (Slip Anchor) 9.8f **(73)**
Form - 7800
Record 1999 - 1st:0 2nd:0 3rd:0 Ran:4
Pre1999 - 1st:0 2nd:0 3rd:0 Ran:2
1999 Turf 0-4: (8f, 10f, 12f 2) (gd, frm 3)
Lengthy, very moderate filly. Turf high 50.
**T R Watson [0-6] Newitt and Co Ltd.*

SWING BAR BHB 48f **RR 51f** 4350[9]
6 b m Sadeem (USA) - Murex (Royalty) 11.4f **(49)**
Form - 04624100
Record 1999 - 1st:1 2nd:1 3rd:0 Ran:8
Win Prizemoney £2,210 *Total Prizemoney* £3,300
Wins * **1999** Aug Beverl (GD) H 9.9f 48 51 <
1999 Turf 1-8: (7f, 8f 3, 10f 1-4) (g-f 4, frm 1-4)
Fair mare, effective 10f, acts on frm. Turf high 51 (began Jly) - 1st of 18 giving 6lb to Butterscotch (28 Aug Beverley RF 3954).
**J M Bradley [2-13] Miss S Howell.*

SWING CITY (IRE) BHB 63f **RR 64f** 4574[7]
2 ch f Indian Ridge 7.6f **(74)** - Menominee (Soviet Star (USA))
Form - 477
Record 1999 - 1st:0 2nd:0 3rd:0 Ran:3
Win Prizemoney £0 *Total Prizemoney* £313
1999 Turf 0-3: (5f, 6f 2) (gd 2, frm)
Currently average filly. Turf high 64 (began Aug).
**R Guest [0-3] Matthews Breeding and Racing.*

SWINGING THE BLUES (IRE) BHB 56f **RR 54f** 5162[2]
5 b g Bluebird (USA) 7.9f **(71)** - Winsong Melody (Music Maestro) 7.7f **(66)**
Form - 0006804812
Record 1999 - 1st:1 2nd:1 3rd:0 Ran:10
Pre1999 - 1st:2 2nd:2 3rd:3 Ran:16
Win Prizemoney £9,443 *Total Prizemoney* £14,861
Wins * **1999** Oct Redcar (GD) H 9f 52 54

* 1998 Oct Redcar (g-s) H 9f 62 66 <
1998 Jly Nottin (G-F) H 8.2f 53 56

1999 Turf 1-10: (8f 5, 9f 1-1, 10f 4) (g-s, gd 2, g-f 3, frm 1-4)
Fair gelding, effective 8 to 9f, best at 8f, acts on gd to g-f, best on gd, has worn blinkers (very effectively), likes left handed tracks, excels at Redcar. Turf high 59 - 11th of 16 giving 3lb to Twin Time (17 May Bath 8f gd RF 1272).
**C A Dwyer [2-15] S B Components (from J W Hills [1-6] Spt 1998).*

SWINGING TRIO (USA) RR 33f 3278[9]

2 b c Woodman (USA) 9.7f **(77)** - Las Meninas (IRE) **(110f)** (Glenstal (USA)) 10.1f **(64)**
Form - 0
Record 1999 - 1st:0 2nd:0 3rd:0 Ran:1
1999 Turf 0-1: (6f) (frm)
Currently very moderate colt. **T G Mills [0-1] T G Mills.*

SWING JOB BHB 49f44a RR 46f 44a 3688[11]

3 b f Ezzoud (IRE) - Leave Her Be (USA) (Known Fact (USA)) 7.4f **(67)**
Form - 607760
Record 1999 - 1st:0 2nd:0 3rd:0 Ran:4
Pre1999 - 1st:0 2nd:0 3rd:0 Ran:5
1999 Turf 0-2: (8f, 11f) (gd, frm) 1999 AW 0-2: (10f, 11f) (Equi, Fibr)
Unfurnished, moderate filly, has worn blinkers. Turf high 46 (began Aug). AW high 41. **T G Mills [0-9] Shipman Racing.*

SWING OF THE TIDE BHB 77f RR 89f 3449[8]

2 b f Sri Pekan (USA) - Rawya (USA) **(71df 76a)** (Woodman (USA)) 9f **(74)**
Form - 248
Record 1999 - 1st:0 2nd:1 3rd:0 Ran:3
Win Prizemoney £0 *Total Prizemoney* £1,535
1999 Turf 0-3: (5f, 6f 2) (gd, frm 2)
Currently useful filly. Turf high 70.
**J Berry [0-3] Chris & Antonia Deuters.*

SWINO BHB 56f70a RR 55f 70a 5199[3]

5 b g Forzando 7.2f **(63)** - St Helena (Monsanto (FR)) 6.5f **(59)**
Form - 7728600350005403
Record 1999 - 1st:0 2nd:1 3rd:2 Ran:16
Pre1999 - 1st:4 2nd:9 3rd:2 Ran:47
Win Prizemoney £26,276 *Total Prizemoney* £43,082
Wins * 1998 May Haydoc (GD) H 6f 80 84
* 1998 Apr Thirsk (G-S) H 5f 72 84
* 1997 Oct Redcar (G-F) 5f 66
* 1996 Aug Carlis (FRM) 5f 85 <
1999 Turf 0-16: (5f 6, 6f 9, 7f) (g-s 3, gd 8, g-f, frm 4)
Fair gelding, effective 5 to 6f, acts on g-s to gd, often wears blinkers. Turf high 71. **P D Evans [4-63] Swinnerton Transport Ltd.*

SWISS ALPS (IRE) RR 58f 3907[9]

2 b c Common Grounds 8.1f **(66)** - Lady of Zurich (IRE) (Danehill (USA)) 10f **(72)**
Form - 0
Record 1999 - 1st:0 2nd:0 3rd:0 Ran:1
1999 Turf 0-1: (6f) (g-f)
Currently fair colt. **R W Armstrong [0-1] Mrs Johnny Mckeever.*

SWISS ENSIGN BHB 60f RR 72f 4671[5]

2 b c Tirol 8.1f **(64)** - Rosa Van Fleet (Sallust) 8.4f **(63)**
Form - 3455
Record 1999 - 1st:0 2nd:0 3rd:1 Ran:4
Win Prizemoney £0 *Total Prizemoney* £512
1999 Turf 0-4: (6f 2, 7f 2) (g-s, g-f, frm 2)
Above-average colt. Turf high 72. **R Hannon [0-4] T G Holdcroft.*

SWYNFORD DREAM BHB 60f56a RR 59f 56a 4691[7]

6 b g Statoblest 6.4f **(63)** - Qualitair Dream (Dreams to Reality (USA)) 6.4f **(73)**
Form - 100200260067
Record 1999 - 1st:1 2nd:2 3rd:0 Ran:12
Pre1999 - 1st:5 2nd:4 3rd:2 Ran:46
Win Prizemoney £26,186 *Total Prizemoney* £40,042
Wins 1999 Apr Mussel (GD) H 5f 57 60
* 1998 Jly Catter (GD) H 5f 55 57
1996 Oct Newmar (G-F) H 5f 79 82
1995 Oct Catter (G-F) H 5f 77 84+ <
1995 Spt Redcar (GD) H 5f 65 73+
1995 Spt Ayr (GD) S 5f 67

1999 Turf 1-11: (5f 1-11) (g-s, gd 1-3, g-f 2, frm 5) 1999 AW 0-1: (5f) (Fibr)
Fair gelding, effective 5f, acts on gd to frm, best on gd, has worn blinkers. Turf high 66 - 2nd of 13 giving 7lb to Sweet Magic (30 Jun Catterick 5f frm RF 2437) - also 1st of 12 giving 6lb to Palacegate Jack (1 Apr Musselburgh RF 0551). Inconsistent.
**J Hetherton [1-22] Qualitair Holdings Ltd (from T J Etherington [1-10] Jly 1999).*

SWYNFORD ELEGANCE BHB 44f RR 46f 4877[20]

2 ch f Charmer 9f **(59)** - Qualitairess (Kampala) 8.5f **(56)**
Form - 860
Record 1999 - 1st:0 2nd:0 3rd:0 Ran:3
1999 Turf 0-3: (5f 2, 7f) (gd, frm 2)
Currently moderate filly. Turf high 46 (began Spt).
**J Hetherton [0-3] Qualitair Holdings Ltd.*

SWYNFORD LORD BHB 29f RR 29f 4079[14]

3 b g Formidable (USA) 7.8f **(60)** - Princess Lieven (Royal Palace) 9f **(56)**
Form - 040075500
Record 1999 - 1st:0 2nd:0 3rd:0 Ran:9
Pre1999 - 1st:0 2nd:0 3rd:0 Ran:4
Win Prizemoney £0 *Total Prizemoney* £246
1999 Turf 0-9: (7f, 8f 2, 9f, 10f, 12f 4) (gd, g-f 2, frm 6)
Scopey, little account gelding, has worn blinkers. Turf high 37.
**J Hetherton [0-7] Qualitair Holdings Ltd (from T J Etherington [0-6] Jly 1999).*

SWYNFORD PLEASURE BHB 40f RR 29f 5156[9]

3 b f Reprimand 8.2f **(63)** - Pleasuring (Good Times (ITY)) 6.6f **(54)**
Form - 572503000
Record 1999 - 1st:0 2nd:1 3rd:1 Ran:9
Pre1999 - 1st:0 2nd:2 3rd:0 Ran:5
Win Prizemoney £0 *Total Prizemoney* £2,890
1999 Turf 0-9: (7f, 8f 3, 9f, 11f 2, 12f 2) (gd 3, g-f, frm 4, hrd)
Scopey, little account filly, effective 7 to 8f, acts on g-f to frm, has worn blinkers. Turf high 53. Becoming disappointing.
**J Hetherton [0-8] Qualitair Holdings Ltd (from T J Etherington [0-6] Jly 1999).*

SWYNFORD WELCOME BHB 54f52a RR 51f 52a 5128[1]

3 b f Most Welcome 8.6f **(66)** - Qualitair Dream (Dreams to Reality (USA)) 6.4f **(73)**
Form - 00000001
Record 1999 - 1st:1 2nd:0 3rd:0 Ran:8
Pre1999 - 1st:1 2nd:2 3rd:1 Ran:8
Win Prizemoney £5,907 *Total Prizemoney* £10,431
Wins * **1999** Oct Bright (G-S) H 6f 44 51
1998 Jly Redcar (G-F) 6f 76 <
1999 Turf 1-8: (5f 3, 6f 1-5) (gd 1-1, g-f 4, frm 2, hrd)
Scopey, fair filly, effective 5 to 6f, best at 6f, acts on g-f to hrd. Turf high 52.
**J Pearce [1-3] Qualitair Holdings Ltd (from T J Etherington [0-5] Jly 1999).*

SYCAMORE LODGE (IRE) BHB 60f48a RR 65f 48a 4878[12]

8 ch g Thatching 7.8f **(69)** - Bell Tower (Lyphard's Wish (FR)) 9f **(74)**
Form - 475101165000
Record 1999 - 1st:3 2nd:0 3rd:0 Ran:12
Pre1999 - 1st:1 2nd:8 3rd:6 Ran:35
Win Prizemoney £9,896 *Total Prizemoney* £21,830
Wins * **1999** Jly Catter (GD) H 7f 59 66
* **1999** Jly Catter (FRM) S 6f 57
* **1999** May Catter (G-F) C 6f 54
1996 Jun Doncas (G-F) H 6f 67 67 <
1999 Turf 3-12: (5f, 6f 2-5, 7f 1-6) (gd, g-f 1-1, frm 2-9, hrd)
Average gelding, effective 6 to 7f, best at 7f, acts on g-f to frm, best on frm, has worn blinkers, prefers left handed tracks, prefers tight tracks. Turf high 66 - 1st of 12 from Lunch Party (21 Jly Catterick RF 3004) - also 1st of 9 from Palacegate Touch (14 Jly Catterick RF 2807).
**D Nicholls [3-22] Hollow Legs Syndicate (from M A Peill [0-7] Nov 1997).*

SYLPHIDE BHB 20f **RR** 234[9]
4 b f Ballet Royal (USA) - Shafayif (Ela-Mana-Mou) 10.1f **(70)**
Form - 0
Record 1999 - 1st:0 2nd:0 3rd:0 Ran:1
Pre1999 - 1st:0 2nd:0 3rd:0 Ran:4
1999 AW 0-1: (13f) (Equi)
Light-framed, formerly very poor filly.
**H J Manners [0-5] Mrs J Letters (from M P Muggeridge [0-3] Mar 1998).*

SYLVA LEGEND (USA) BHB 68f **RR 75f** 5126[4]
3 b c Lear Fan (USA) 10.4f **(80)** - Likeashot (CAN) (Gun Shot) 12f **(74)**
Form - 2300603364
Record 1999 - 1st:0 2nd:1 3rd:3 Ran:10
Pre1999 - 1st:0 2nd:0 3rd:0 Ran:2
Win Prizemoney £0 *Total Prizemoney* £8,243
1999 Turf 0-10: (8f 3, 9f, 10f 2, 12f 4) (g-s, gd 2, g-f 4, frm 3)
Scopey, above-average colt, effective 8 to 9f, acts on gd to frm, has worn blinkers. Turf high 87 - 3rd of 16 getting 5lb from Bathwick (18 May Goodwood 9f gd RF 1292). Fair maiden, but has been tried in handicap company and has been found wanting.
**C E Brittain [0-12] Eddy Grimstead Honda.*

SYLVA PARADISE (IRE) BHB 77f **RR 83f** 4984[17]
6 b g Dancing Dissident (USA) 6.8f **(65)** - Brentsville (USA) (Arctic Tern (USA)) 8.9f **(69)**
Form - 346382453500
Record 1999 - 1st:0 2nd:1 3rd:3 Ran:12
Pre1999 - 1st:2 2nd:4 3rd:5 Ran:36
Win Prizemoney £10,460 *Total Prizemoney* £52,359
Wins * 1996 Jly Yarmou (FRM) H 6f 84 93 <
* 1995 Spt Folkes (SFT) 6f 77
1999 Turf 0-12: (5f 6, 6f 6) (g-s, gd 3, g-f 4, frm 4)
Decent gelding, effective 5 to 6f, best at 5f, acts on gd to frm, best on gd, has worn blinkers, excels at Yarmouth , nd Haydock, does well at Newmarket, likes Goodwood. Turf high 85 (1st run) - 3rd of 17 getting 24lb from Night Shot (25 Mar Doncaster 5f gd RF 0466). Has not won for three years though he often makes the frame, and ran well to finish fifth in the Stewards' Cup. Whether his consistency will be eventually be rewarded is another matter.
**C E Brittain [2-48] Eddy Grimstead Honda.*

SYMBOLI KILDARE (IRE) RR 105f 1901a[6]
6 b g Kaldoun (FR) 9.9f **(84)** - Quiche (Formidable (USA)) 9.2f **(63)**
Form - 216
1999 Turf 1-3: (5f 1-2, 6f) (sft, gd 1-1, g-f)
Pattern-class gelding, effective 5 to 6f, acts on sft to gd, often wears blinkers (extremely effectively). Turf high 105 (1st run) - 2nd of 10 to Diableneyev (6 Apr Maisons-Laffitte 6f sft RF 0712a) - also 1st of 7 giving 13lb to Emma Peel (16 May Cologne RF 1356a). Formerly trained in Ireland, he has run well in listed events for his new, French-based trainer.
**X Nakkachdji in FR [1-3] (from J Oxx in IRE [2-22] Spt 1998).*

SYRAH BHB 40f34a **RR 57?f 34a** 5198[10]
3 b f Minshaanshu Amad (USA) 11.3f **(53)** - La Domaine (Dominion) 8.5f **(63)**
Form - 450800
Record 1999 - 1st:0 2nd:0 3rd:0 Ran:4
Pre1999 - 1st:0 2nd:0 3rd:0 Ran:3
1999 Turf 0-3: (8f 2, 10f) (gd, g-f, hrd) 1999 AW 0-1: (12f) (Fibr)
Average filly. Turf high 57.
**R T Phillips [0-1] White Bear Ltd (from G Lewis [0-6] Jly 1999)*

TAAKID (USA) BHB 47f **RR 51f** 4882[8]
4 b g Diesis 9f **(80)** - Tanwi (Vision (USA)) 9f **(64)**
Form - 0508
Record 1999 - 1st:0 2nd:0 3rd:0 Ran:4
Pre1999 - 1st:0 2nd:3 3rd:1 Ran:13
Win Prizemoney £0 *Total Prizemoney* £2,554
1999 Turf 0-4: (10f, 11f, 12f 2) (g-s, g-f, frm, hrd)
Fair gelding, effective 9 to 10f, acts on gd to g-f. Turf high 51 (began Aug).
**M D Hammond [0-7] The Double Daggers (from K Prendergast in IRE [0-13] Oct 1998).*

TAARISH (IRE) BHB 56f **RR 62f** 4791[15]
6 b g Priolo (USA) 10.9f **(71)** - Strike It Rich (FR) (Rheingold) 10.4f **(62)**
Form - 2780
Record 1999 - 1st:0 2nd:1 3rd:0 Ran:4
Pre1999 - 1st:1 2nd:0 3rd:1 Ran:6
Win Prizemoney £3,425 *Total Prizemoney* £4,887
Wins 1996 Jun Ballin (GD) 9f 69 <
1999 Turf 0-4: (12f 2, 14f 2) (gd 2, g-f, frm)
Average gelding, often wears blinkers. Turf high 62.
**P Mitchell [0-2] Studer (from S Mellor [0-6] Jun 1999).*

TABARAK (IRE) RR 61f 5003[7]
3 b c Nashwan (USA) 10.3f **(79)** - Select Sale (Auction Ring (USA)) 8.6f **(65)**
Form - 07
Record 1999 - 1st:0 2nd:0 3rd:0 Ran:2
1999 Turf 0-2: (8f, 10f) (gd, g-f)
Well made, currently average colt, often wears blinkers. Turf high 61.
**K Mahdi [0-2] Hamad Al-Mutawa.*

TABAREEH (IRE) BHB 110f **RR 109f** 4674[6]
3 b c Marju (IRE) 9.2f **(76)** - Rosia Bay (High Top) 10.2f **(67)**
Form - 18425216
Record 1999 - 1st:2 2nd:2 3rd:0 Ran:8
Pre1999 - 1st:0 2nd:1 3rd:0 Ran:1
Win Prizemoney £10,170 *Total Prizemoney* £24,873
Wins * 1999 Spt Salisb (G-F) 14.1f 109+ <
*** 1999** Mar Doncas (SFT) 8f 93++
1999 Turf 2-8: (8f 1-1, 9f, 12f 5, 14f 1-1) (g-s 1-1, gd 2, g-f 3, frm 1-2)
Workmanlike, Pattern-class colt, effective 12 to 14f, best at 12f, acts on g-f to frm, best on g-f, often wears blinkers (effectively). Turf high 109 - 1st of 7 getting 4lb from Bryony Brind (2 Spt Salisbury RF 4096). A half-brother to Roseate Tern and Ibn Bey, he was slammed by Dubai Millennium on his only outing at two, but won nicely on his Doncaster reappearance in 1999. He ran some good races afterwards, especially when beaten a head in the Tote Gold Trophy at Glorious Goodwood. He seemed to appreciate the 14 furlong trip when returning to winning form at Salisbury in September. **M P Tregoning [2-9] Hamdan Al Maktoum.*

TABASCO (IRE) BHB 57f55a **RR 54f 55a** 1385[8]
4 b f Salse (USA) 10.9f **(71)** - El Taranda (Ela-Mana-Mou) 10.1f **(70)**
Form - 80208
Record 1999 - 1st:0 2nd:1 3rd:0 Ran:5
Pre1999 - 1st:0 2nd:0 3rd:0 Ran:4
Win Prizemoney £0 *Total Prizemoney* £549
1999 Turf 0-4: (8f 2, 10f, 12f) (sft, g-f, frm 2) 1999 AW 0-1: (8f) (Fibr)
Fair filly, has worn blinkers. Turf high 54.
**M R Channon [0-9] Mountgrange Stud.*

TABBETINNA BLUE RR 34f 4928[7]
2 b f Interrex (CAN) 7.7f **(51)** - True Is Blue (Gabitat) 5f **(44)**
Form - 7
Record 1999 - 1st:0 2nd:0 3rd:0 Ran:1
1999 Turf 0-1: (6f) (g-f)
Currently very moderate filly. **J W Payne [0-1] Vetsango Partnership.*

TABHEEJ (IRE) BHB 100f **RR 90f** 4680[3]
2 ch f Mujtahid (USA) 7.4f **(69)** - Abhaaj (Kris) 9.5f **(73)**
Form - 1313
Record 1999 - 1st:2 2nd:0 3rd:2 Ran:4
Win Prizemoney £11,191 *Total Prizemoney* £21,399
Wins * 1999 Spt Doncas (G-F) 6f 90 <
*** 1999** May Haydoc (GD) 5f 71+
1999 Turf 2-4: (5f 1-1, 6f 1-2, 7f) (gd 2, frm 2-2)
Useful filly. Turf high 90 - 3rd of 12 to Agrippina (2 Oct Newmarket 7f gd RF 4680) - also 1st of 7 getting 1lb from Kier Park (11 Spt Doncaster RF 4263). Was odds-on when beating the useful Jemima with authority on her debut in May, and was absent until finishing third to that filly in York's Lowther Stakes. Returned to winning ways in a conditions event at Doncaster.
**B W Hills [2-4] Hamdan Al Maktoum.*

TACHELLE (IRE) RR 2340[5]
3 b f Elbio 9f **(62)** - Tacheo (Tachypous) 8.6f **(55)**
Form - 5
Record 1999 - 1st:0 2nd:0 3rd:0 Ran:1

1999 Turf 0-1: (8f) (frm)
Rangy, currently very poor filly. **E J Alston [0-1] Great Expectations.*

TACHYCARDIA BHB 32f36a RR 20f 36a 426[11]

7 ch m Weldnaas (USA) 8.4f **(55)** - Gold Ducat (Young Generation) 7.7f **(63)**
Form - 6402080
Record 1999 - 1st:0 2nd:1 3rd:0 Ran:5
Pre1999 - 1st:5 2nd:3 3rd:6 Ran:58
Win Prizemoney £13,159 *Total Prizemoney* £20,138
Wins 1997 *Jan Lingfi (STD) H 6f 34 41*
1997 *Jan Lingfi (STD) H 6f 34 38*
1995 Jun Bright (G-F) H 5.3f 42 53
1999 AW 0-5: (6f 3, 7f 2) (Equi 4, Fibr)
Little account mare, effective 6f, - acts on Equi, likes left handed tracks, favours tight tracks. AW high 38 - 2nd of 9 getting 7lb from Another Nightmare (19 Jan Lingfield 6f Equi RF 0120).
**N E Berry [0-8] Lancing Racing Syndicate (from F P Murtagh [0-4] Jun 1998).*

TACTFUL REMARK (USA) BHB 103f RR 108f 4409[3]

3 ch c Lord At War (ARG) 6.6f **(67)** - Right Word (USA) (Verbatim (USA)) 8.5f **(64)**
Form - 134103
Record 1999 - 1st:2 2nd:0 3rd:2 Ran:6
Pre1999 - 1st:0 2nd:0 3rd:0 Ran:3
Win Prizemoney £10,731 *Total Prizemoney* £13,911
Wins * 1999 Jly Newbur (G-F) H 9f 82 90+ <
*** 1999** Apr Kempto (GD) H 9f 77 80+
1999 Turf 2-6: (9f 2-4, 10f, 11f) (gd, g-f 2-3, frm 2)
Scopey, Pattern-class colt, effective 9f, acts on frm. Turf high 108 - 3rd of 7 getting 5lb from Showboat (18 Spt Newbury 9f frm RF 4409). Looked good when making all for an impressive victory at Newbury, and adopted similar tactics when third in a decent conditions event at the same track. He wants fast ground.
**J H M Gosden [2-9] Sheikh Mohammed.*

TADBEER (USA) RR 76+f 4419[6]

2 ch c Kris S (USA) 9.3f **(76)** - Ra'a (USA) (Diesis) 9.3f **(69)**
Form - 36
Record 1999 - 1st:0 2nd:0 3rd:1 Ran:2
Win Prizemoney £0 *Total Prizemoney* £645
1999 Turf 0-2: (7f 2) (gd 2)
Currently above-average colt. Turf high 76 (began Aug). Has shown plenty of promise in seven-furlong maidens Goodwood and Newbury, and will stay further.
**M P Tregoning [0-2] Hamdan Al Maktoum.*

TADEO BHB 102f RR 93f 3197[4]

6 ch g Primo Dominie 7.2f **(67)** - Royal Passion (Ahonoora) 8.1f **(73)**
Form - 206764
Record 1999 - 1st:0 2nd:1 3rd:0 Ran:6
Pre1999 - 1st:9 2nd:6 3rd:6 Ran:52
Win Prizemoney £81,222 *Total Prizemoney* £114,541
Wins 1998 Aug Fairyh (G-F) L 6f 102
1998 May Haydoc (G-S) H 5f 97 105 <
1997 Spt Nottin (GD) 5.1f 95
1997 Aug Ripon (G-F) H 6f 95 101
1997 Jly Newmar (GD) H 5f 92 93
1996 Oct Ascot (GD) H 5f 91 95
1996 Oct Haydoc (SFT) 5f 93
1995 Oct Lingfi (GD) 5f 95+
1995 May Carlis (FRM) 5f 62
1999 Turf 0-6: (5f 5, 6f) (gd, g-f, frm 4)
Useful gelding, effective 5 to 6f, best at 5f, acts on gd to frm. Turf high 110. Consistent. A tough front-runner, he is probably best at five furlongs but cannot be easy to place as the handicapper shows him little mercy.
**B J Meehan [0-6] J R Good (from M Johnston [8-45] Spt 1998).*

TADREEJ (IRE) BHB 78f RR 68f 4411[2]

2 b c Fairy King (USA) 7.7f **(75)** - Rose Bonbon (FR) (High Top) 10.2f **(67)**
Form - 032
Record 1999 - 1st:0 2nd:1 3rd:1 Ran:3
Win Prizemoney £0 *Total Prizemoney* £1,699
1999 Turf 0-2: (6f, 7f) (gd, frm) 1999 AW 0-1: (8f) (Fibr)
Currently average colt. Turf high 68 (began Aug).
**M R Channon [0-3] Sheikh Ahmed Al Maktoum.*

TAFFS WELL BHB 73f RR 70f 5166[6]

6 b g Dowsing (USA) 7f **(61)** - Zahiah (So Blessed) 8.7f **(67)**
Form - 8811210130000606
Record 1999 - 1st:4 2nd:1 3rd:1 Ran:16
Pre1999 - 1st:0 2nd:4 3rd:1 Ran:19
Win Prizemoney £27,782 *Total Prizemoney* £37,068
Wins * 1999 Jun Newcas (GD) H 8f 77 78+ <
*** 1999** May Haydoc (GD) H 8.1f 69 76+
*** 1999** May Cheste (G-F) H 7.6f 57 69
*** 1999** Apr Mussel (G-F) H 7.1f 57 63
1999 Turf 4-16: (6f 2, 7f 1-5, 8f 3-8, 9f) (hvy, sft, g-s, gd 1-6, g-f 2-3, frm 1-4)
Above-average gelding, effective 7 to 8f, best at 8f, acts on g-s to frm, best on gd, likes tight tracks. Turf high 82 - 3rd of 10 getting 14lb from Refuse To Lose (24 Jly Ascot 8f gd RF 3087) - also 1st of 8 giving 7lb to Floating Charge (25 Jun Newcastle RF 2301). Formerly with Lynda Ramsden, he went a very long time without winning, but was in fine form in the first half of the season, winning four times and running some fine races in defeat. Looked as though he might have gone off the boil in his last few efforts though.
**B Ellison [4-16] The Breach Partnership (from Mrs J R Ramsden [0-13] Oct 1998).*

TAGADOO (IRE) BHB 40f RR 24f 4640[11]

2 b c Desse Zenny (USA) 12f **(53)** - Conquering Kate (IRE) (Conquering Hero (USA))
Form - 000
Record 1999 - 1st:0 2nd:0 3rd:0 Ran:3
1999 Turf 0-3: (6f, 7f 2) (gd 3)
Currently little account colt. Turf high 24 (began Aug).
**B S Rothwell [0-3] Jim Browne.*

TAHSEEN (USA) RR 62f 3997[6]

2 b f Hansel (USA) 12.6f **(78)** - Aljawza (USA) (Riverman (USA)) 9.1f **(76)**
Form - 6
Record 1999 - 1st:0 2nd:0 3rd:0 Ran:1
1999 Turf 0-1: (6f) (g-f)
Average filly. (DEAD) **M P Tregoning [0-1] Hamdan Al Maktoum.*

TAISHO (IRE) RR 101f 4856a[5]

3 b f Namaqualand (USA) - Winged Island 00
Form - 1318407485
1999 Turf 1-9: (6f 2, 7f 1-4, 8f 2, 10f) (hvy 1-1, sft 2, g-s 2, gd 3, g-f)
Very useful filly, effective 7f, acts on hvy to gd. Turf high 101 - 4th of 9 getting 17lb from Tumbleweed Ridge (9 Jun Leopardstown 7f gd RF 2023a) - also 1st of 7 from Crystal Downs (25 Apr Curragh RF 0894a). Best up to a mile on easy ground, she is tough but not quite Group class. **K Prendergast in IRE [3-16] Mrs N O'Callaghan.*

TAI TAI BHB 40f RR 52f 4816[13]

3 b f Mujtahid (USA) 7.4f **(69)** - Duwon (IRE) **(53df)** (Polish Precedent (USA)) 10.2f **(60)**
Form - 0060
Record 1999 - 1st:0 2nd:0 3rd:0 Ran:4
Pre1999 - 1st:0 2nd:0 3rd:0 Ran:1
1999 Turf 0-4: (10f 3, 11f) (gd, frm 3)
Workmanlike, fair filly. Turf high 52.
**M Blanshard [0-5] James Watkins.*

TAJAR (USA) BHB 43f46a RR 45f 46a 4948[14]

7 b g Slew O' Gold (USA) 10.2f **(73)** - Mashaarif (USA) (Mr Prospector (USA)) 8.8f **(78)**
Form - 020183506830
Record 1999 - 1st:1 2nd:1 3rd:2 Ran:12
Pre1999 - 1st:3 2nd:2 3rd:5 Ran:32
Win Prizemoney £11,065 *Total Prizemoney* £17,417
Wins * 1999 May Windso (G-F) H 11.6f 48 50
* 1998 Aug Warwic (G-F) 10.8f 52 <
* 1998 Jly Pontef (G-F) H 10f 40 45
* 1997 Jly Chepst (G-F) H 12.1f 30 35
1999 Turf 1-12: (10f 7, 11f, 12f 1-4) (g-s 2, gd 2, g-f 3, frm 1-5)
Moderate gelding, effective 10 to 12f, acts on g-s to frm, best on

frm, has worn blinkers, likes left handed tracks, likes tight tracks, excels at Nottingham. Turf high 51 - 3rd of 13 getting 2lb from Daniel Deronda (17 Jly Nottingham 10f frm RF 2915) - also 1st of 20 getting 12lb from Noukari (24 May Windsor RF 1446). Consistent.
**T Keddy [4-34] The Veg Chef Partnership (from M Dods [0-5] Apr 1997).*

TAJASUR (IRE) BHB 104f **RR 105+f** 4890a[3]
4 ch g Imperial Frontier (USA) 7f **(65)** - Safiya (USA) (Riverman (USA)) 9.1f **(76)**
Form - 510013
Record 1999 - 1st:2 2nd:0 3rd:1 Ran:6
Pre1999 - 1st:1 2nd:1 3rd:1 Ran:3
Win Prizemoney £18,302 *Total Prizemoney* £25,616
Wins * **1999** Spt Hamilt (SFT) 6f 105+ <
* **1999** Jly Newbur (G-F) H 6f 98 100
* 1997 Jun Doncas (G-S) 6f 79+
1999 Turf 2-6: (6f 2-4, 7f 2) (sft, g-s, gd 1-3, frm 1-1)
Well made, Pattern-class gelding, effective 6 to 7f, best at 7f, acts on sft to frm, best on gd. Turf high 105 - 3rd of 11 to Tomba (10 Oct Munich 7f sft RF 4890a) - also 1st of 9 giving 7lb to Boomerang Blade (27 Spt Hamilton RF 4588). He has been lightly raced due to various problems, but smashed the Newbury six-furlong course record on his second start of last season. Disappointed in a couple of hot handicaps, but bolted up in a Hamilton conditions race in the manner of a most progressive sprinter. Finished third in Germany on his final start.
**J L Dunlop [3-9].*

TAJMIL (IRE) BHB 50f48a **RR 46f 48a** 1126[12]
4 ch f Wolfhound (USA) 7.3f **(71)** - Nouvelle Star (AUS) (Luskin Star (AUS)) 6.3f **(71)**
Form - 050
Record 1999 - 1st:0 2nd:0 3rd:0 Ran:2
Pre1999 - 1st:0 2nd:1 3rd:1 Ran:15
Win Prizemoney £0 *Total Prizemoney* £1,755
1999 Turf 0-2: (6f, 7f) (gd 2)
Neat, moderate filly, effective 7f, acts on frm, has worn blinkers. Turf high 39.
**D Morris [0-12] Bloomsbury Stud (from Major W R Hern [0-5] Oct 1997).*

TAJOUN (FR) RR 117f 5121a[2]
5 b g General Holme (USA) 5.7f **(58)** - Taeesha (Mill Reef (USA)) 10.5f **(78)**
Form - 220112
1999 Turf 2-6: (16f 1-4, 20f 1-2) (hvy 1-2, g-s, gd 1-2, g-f)
High-class gelding, effective 15 to 20f, best at 16f, acts on hvy to gd, excels at Longchamp. Turf high 117 - 2nd of 7 giving 9lb to Amilynx (24 Oct Longchamp 16f hvy RF 5121a) - also 1st of 8 from San Sebastian (2 Oct Longchamp RF 4768a). Consistent. He is probably the best of the French-trained stayers, but struggles against the very best horses from England. He was a good second to Kayf Tara in the Prix Vicomtesse Vigier at Longchamp in May, but finished last to Enzeli in the Gold Cup on ground that would not have suited. Returned from a three-month break to take the Prix Gladiateur, and gained his biggest victory to date with an ultra-game victory in the Prix du Cadran. May have still been feeling the effects of that when runner-up in the Prix Royal-Oak. Suited by soft ground. **A deRoyerDupre in FR [5-11].*

TAKAMATSU (FR) RR 92f 4106a[2]
3 b c Hours After (USA) - Timbaliere (FR) (Pharly (FR)) 9.8f **(68)**
Form - 2
1999 Turf 0-1: (8f) (hvy)
Currently useful colt. (1st run) - 2nd of 18 getting 10lb from Dancing Kris (24 Aug Deauville 8f hvy RF 4106a).
**Mrs N Rossio in FR [0-1].*

TAKE ACTION (IRE) BHB 47f **RR 52f** 4727[7]
2 b c Shalford (IRE) 7.8f **(63)** - Action Belle (Auction Ring (USA)) 8.6f **(65)**
Form - 05007
Record 1999 - 1st:0 2nd:0 3rd:0 Ran:5
1999 Turf 0-5: (6f, 8f 3, 10f) (sft, g-s, g-f, frm 2)
Fair colt. Turf high 52 (began Jly). **F Jordan [0-5] D Pugh.*

TAKE A TURN BHB 53f68a **RR 47f 68a** 3607[9]
4 br g Forzando 7.2f **(63)** - Honeychurch (USA) (Bering) 7.4f **(61)**
Form - 070000
Record 1999 - 1st:0 2nd:0 3rd:0 Ran:5
Pre1999 - 1st:2 2nd:3 3rd:3 Ran:24
Win Prizemoney £8,732 *Total Prizemoney* £13,804
Wins * 1998 Jly Salisb (G-F) H 8f 69 75
1997 Aug Cheste (SFT) H 7f 77 79 <
1999 Turf 0-5: (8f 3, 10f 2) (g-f 2, frm 3)
Unfurnished, above-average gelding, effective 7 to 10f, acts on hvy to g-f - acts on Equi, often wears blinkers. Turf high 56.
**Miss Gay Kelleway [3-19] Sheet & Roll Convertors Ltd (from M R Channon [1-17] May 1998).*

TAKE CARE (IRE) BHB 45f32a **RR 65f 32a** 23[10]
4 b f Treasure Kay 6.5f **(53)** - Miss Tuko (Good Times (ITY)) 6.6f **(54)**
Form - 070
Record 1999 - 1st:0 2nd:0 3rd:0 Ran:1
Pre1999 - 1st:0 2nd:0 3rd:0 Ran:10
1999 AW 0-1: (7f) (Fibr)
Average filly, often wears blinkers. Becoming disappointing.
**M H Tompkins [0-3] Michael Keogh (from P Martin in IRE [0-5] Spt 1998).*

TAKE FLITE BHB 81f **RR 82f** 3996[4]
2 b c Cadeaux Genereux 7.9f **(76)** - Green Seed (IRE) **(78f)** (Lead on Time (USA)) 8f **(65)**
Form - 53034
Record 1999 - 1st:0 2nd:0 3rd:2 Ran:5
Win Prizemoney £0 *Total Prizemoney* £1,858
1999 Turf 0-5: (5f, 6f 3, 7f) (gd, g-f 2, frm 2)
Decent colt. Turf high 82 - 3rd of 13 to Sir Nicholas (29 May Doncaster 6f frm RF 1560). **W R Muir [0-5] The Wheet Partnership.*

TAKE HEED RR 111f 5013a[10]
4 f
Form - 0
1999 Turf 0-1: (12f)
Currently Group-class. **Mme C Head in FR [0-1].*

TAKE MANHATTAN (IRE) RR 59f 4574[8]
2 b br c Hamas (IRE) 8f **(72)** - Arab Scimetar (IRE) (Sure Blade (USA)) 11.3f **(67)**
Form - 8
Record 1999 - 1st:0 2nd:0 3rd:0 Ran:1
1999 Turf 0-1: (5f) (gd)
Currently fair colt. **M R Channon [0-1] M G St Quinton.*

TAKER CHANCE BHB 50f48a **RR 50df 48a** 4718[19]
3 b g Puissance 7.1f **(60)** - Flower Princess (Slip Anchor) 9.8f **(73)**
Form - 005501040
Record 1999 - 1st:1 2nd:0 3rd:0 Ran:8
Pre1999 - 1st:0 2nd:0 3rd:1 Ran:5
Win Prizemoney £2,416 *Total Prizemoney* £3,166
Wins * **1999** Aug Beverl (GD) C 7.5f 50 <
1999 Turf 1-7: (6f, 7f 1-3, 8f 3) (sft, g-s, gd 2, g-f, frm 1-2) 1999 AW 0-1: (7f) (Fibr)
Light-framed, fair gelding, effective 6f, acts on g-f, has worn blinkers. Turf high 55. Inconsistent.
**J Hetherton [1-9] Eureka Racing (from W J Haggas [0-4] Oct 1998).*

TAKHLID (USA) BHB 62f84a **RR 61f 84a** 4902[10]
8 b h Nureyev (USA) 8.4f **(84)** - Savonnerie (USA) (Irish River (FR)) 8.6f **(78)**
Form - 261114418101114100
Record 1999 - 1st:9 2nd:1 3rd:0 Ran:18
Pre1999 - 1st:7 2nd:3 3rd:9 Ran:54
Win Prizemoney £48,148 *Total Prizemoney* £59,566
Wins * **1999** *Oct Wolver (STD) C 7f 77+*
* **1999** *Jly Wolver (STD) C 8.5f 72+*
* **1999** *Jly Southw (STD) C 7f 80+*
* **1999** *Jun Wolver (STA) C 7f 80*
* **1999** *May Southw (STD) C 7f 82*
* **1999** *Apr Wolver (STD) C 6f 76+*
* **1999** *Feb Lingfi (STD) H 8f 70 79*
* **1999** *Jan Lingfi (STD) 7f 71*
* **1999** *Jan Southw (STD) H 8f 63 70*

* 1998	Jun	Hamilt	(SFT)	H	8.3f	61	72+	
* 1998	Jun	Thirsk	(GD)	H	8f	57	62	
* 1997	*Spt*	*Wolver*	*(STD)*	*H*	*6f*	*68*	*73*	
* 1997	*Apr*	*Southw*	*(STD)*	*H*	*8f*	*63*	*69*	
* 1997	*Mar*	*Wolver*	*(STD)*	*H*	*6f*	*61*	*59*	
1995	Spt	Epsom	(G-S)	H	8.5f	79	84	<
1995	Aug	Bright	(FRM)	H	7f	77	79	

1999 Turf 0-5: (7f 4, 9f) (gd, frm 4) 1999 AW 9-13: (6f 1-4, 7f 5-5, 8f 3-4) (Equi 2-2, Fibr 7-11)

Decent horse, effective 6 to 8f, best at 7f, acts on g-s to frm - acts on AW, best on Fibr, likes left handed tracks, likes tight tracks, and likes Wolverhampton. Turf high 61. AW high 82 - 1st of 10 giving 2lb to Seven (10 May Southwell RF 1131) - also 1st of 10 giving 13lb to Imbackagain (5 Jun Wolverhampton RF 1777). Inconsistent. Had a fine time of it on Fibresand in 1999 with nine victories, mostly in claimers. Effective from six furlongs to a mile, but is probably best over seven.

**D W Chapman [14-65] S B Clark (from H ThomsonJones [2-7] Spt 1995).*

TALARIA (IRE) BHB 72f RR 85df — 4989[11]

3 ch f Petardia 8.2f **(58)** - Million At Dawn (IRE) (Fayruz)

Form - 5814000

Record	**1999** -	1st:1	2nd:0	3rd:0	Ran:7
	Pre1999 -	1st:0	2nd:0	3rd:0	Ran:2

Win Prizemoney £4,175 — *Total Prizemoney* £5,205

Wins * **1999** Jly Newmar (G-F) 6f 80 <

1999 Turf 1-7: (5f, 6f 1-6) (g-f 3, frm 1-4)

Scopey, useful filly, effective 6f, acts on frm. Turf high 85 - also 1st of 11 getting 5lb from Cool Temper (16 Jly Newmarket RF 2886). Becoming disappointing. **G Wragg [1-9] Mrs Claude Lilley.*

TALAUD (IRE) BHB 60f RR 65f — 4628[14]

3 ch g Salse (USA) 10.9f **(71)** - Furry Friend (USA) (Bold Bidder) 8.8f **(67)**

Form - 758660

Record	**1999** -	1st:0	2nd:0	3rd:0	Ran:6

1999 Turf 0-6: (7f, 8f 4, 10f) (sft, g-s, gd, frm 3)

Scopey, average gelding, has worn blinkers. Turf high 75.

**I A Balding [0-6] Robert Hitchins.*

TALENTS LITTLE GEM BHB 52f RR 62f — 4708[3]

2 b f Democratic (USA) - Le Saule D'Or (Sonnen Gold) 6.6f **(47)**

Form - 6783

Record	**1999** -	1st:0	2nd:0	3rd:1	Ran:4

Win Prizemoney £0 — *Total Prizemoney* £537

1999 Turf 0-3: (5f 2, 6f) (gd, frm, hrd) 1999 AW 0-1: (6f) (Fibr)

Average filly. Turf high 62 (began Jly).

**V Soane [0-3] Talent Entertainment (from R Simpson [0-1] Jly 1999).*

TALES OF BOUNTY (IRE) BHB 60f RR 59f — 1941[6]

4 b g Ela-Mana-Mou 12.7f **(72)** - Tales of Wisdom (Rousillon (USA)) 8.2f **(74)**

Form - 066

Record	**1999** -	1st:0	2nd:0	3rd:0	Ran:3
	Pre1999 -	1st:0	2nd:0	3rd:2	Ran:8

Win Prizemoney £0 — *Total Prizemoney* £1,262

1999 Turf 0-3: (12f, 14f, 17f) (g-f, frm 2)

Scopey, fair gelding, effective 12f, acts on frm, likes tight tracks. Turf high 59. Consistent.

**D R C Elsworth [0-16] Mrs Michael Meredith.*

TALIB (USA) BHB 20f43a RR 33tf 43a — 4456[11]

5 b g Silver Hawk (USA) 11.2f **(85)** - Dance For Lucy (USA) (Dance Bid (USA)) 11.6f **(71)**

Form - 87508676060

Record	**1999** -	1st:0	2nd:0	3rd:0	Ran:11
	Pre1999 -	1st:1	2nd:1	3rd:0	Ran:10

Win Prizemoney £2,388 — *Total Prizemoney* £3,959

Wins 1998 Jun Windso (GD) C 11.6f 58 <

1999 Turf 0-8: (12f 3, 13f, 14f 2, 16f, 19f) (sft, gd 3, g-f 2, frm 2) 1999 AW 0-3: (10f, 12f, 15f) (Equi, Fibr 2)

Very moderate gelding, effective 12f, acts on gd to g-f. Turf high 45. AW high 9.

**P W Hiatt [0-11] P W Hiatt (from P Mitchell [0-6] Apr 1999).*

TA-LIM BHB 103f RR 102f — 5132[11]

4 b c Ela-Mana-Mou 12.7f **(72)** - Alkaffeyeh (IRE) (Sadler's Wells (USA)) 10f **(76)**

Form - 30450

Record	**1999** -	1st:0	2nd:0	3rd:1	Ran:5
	Pre1999 -	1st:2	2nd:0	3rd:1	Ran:6

Win Prizemoney £17,475 — *Total Prizemoney* £28,615

Wins							
* 1998	Aug	Goodwo	(G-F)	L	14f	105	<
* 1998	Jun	Goodwo	(GD)		12f	88	

1999 Turf 0-5: (12f, 14f, 16f 2, 18f) (gd 2, g-f, frm 2)

Lengthy, very useful colt, effective 12 to 15f, acts on g-f to frm, best on g-f, has worn blinkers, likes right handed tracks. Turf high 112 (1st run) - 3rd of 11 getting 5lb from Silver Patriarch (30 Apr Newmarket 12f frm RF 0945). Consistent. He ran an eye-catching race in the Jockey Club Stakes on his reappearance, but failed to make the expected progress when stepped-up in trip.

**Sir Michael Stoute [2-11] Hamdan Al Maktoum.*

TALLULAH RR — 2067[6]

2 b f Puissance 7.1f **(60)** - Dame de L'Oise (USA) (Riverman (USA)) 9.1f **(76)**

Form - 6

Record	**1999** -	1st:0	2nd:0	3rd:0	Ran:1

1999 AW 0-1: (6f) (Fibr)

Currently very poor filly. **N P Littmoden [0-1] Tallulah Racing.*

TALLULAH BELLE BHB 67f85a RR 68f 85a — 5126[10]

6 b m Crowning Honors (CAN) 9.9f **(36)** - Fine a Leau (USA) (Youth (USA)) 9.8f **(64)**

Form - 22354316210163200080

Record	**1999** -	1st:3	2nd:4	3rd:3	Ran:20
	Pre1999 -	1st:8	2nd:6	3rd:9	Ran:56

Win Prizemoney £38,947 — *Total Prizemoney* £66,636

Wins								
* **1999**	*Jun*	*Wolver*	*(STA)*	*H*	*9.4f*	*80*	*86*	<
* **1999**	May	Hamilt	(SFT)	H	9.2f	68	70	
* **1999**	*Apr*	*Lingfi*	*(STD)*		*12f*		*79*	
* 1998	Aug	Yarmou	(FRM)		10.1f		68	
* 1998	Jly	Goodwo	(G-S)	H	9f	61	65	
* 1998	*May*	*Lingfi*	*(STD)*	*H*	*10f*	*69*	*71*	
* 1997	Oct	Redcar	(G-F)		10f		68	
* 1997	Spt	Kempto	(G-F)	H	11.1f	56	65	
* 1997	Apr	Beverl	(G-F)	H	9.9f	57	56	
* 1997	*Feb*	*Lingfi*	*(STD)*	*H*	*10f*	*57*	*66*	
* 1997	*Jan*	*Wolver*	*(STD)*		*9.4f*		*56*	

1999 Turf 1-12: (9f 1-4, 10f 6, 12f 2) (gd 1-4, g-f 3, frm 5) 1999 AW 2-8: (8f, 9f 1-3, 10f 3, 12f 1-1) (Equi 1-4, Fibr 1-4)

Useful mare, effective 9 to 12f, - acts on AW, best on Equi, has worn blinkers, likes left handed tracks, favours tight tracks, excels at Lingfield, likes Wolverhampton. Turf high 70. AW high 86 - 1st of 8 giving 32lb to River Ensign (5 Jun Wolverhampton RF 1779) - also 1st of 4 getting 7lb from Banbury (1 Apr Lingfield RF 0545). She is a tough and consistent handicapper at around ten furlongs on turf and sand, but seemed to stay the mile and a half well enough when winning at Lingfield in April.

**N P Littmoden [11-79] Trojan Racing.*

TALLYWHACKER RR 28f — 4557[12]

2 b f Bon Secret (IRE) - Nomadic Rose (Nomination) 7f **(60)**

Form - 0

Record	**1999** -	1st:0	2nd:0	3rd:0	Ran:1

1999 Turf 0-1: (6f) (gd)

Currently little account filly. **T J Naughton [0-1] T J Naughton.*

TAMARA BHB 82f RR 74f — 3432[8]

3 b f Marju (IRE) 9.2f **(76)** - Ivory Palm (USA) (Sir Ivor) 10.2f **(70)**

Form - 8

Record	**1999** -	1st:0	2nd:0	3rd:0	Ran:1
	Pre1999 -	1st:1	2nd:1	3rd:0	Ran:6

Win Prizemoney £2,346 — *Total Prizemoney* £7,546

Wins * 1998 May Catter (SFT) 5f 68 <

1999 Turf 0-1: (8f) (frm)

Neat, above-average filly, effective 6f, acts on frm.

**J D Bethell [1-7] Mrs John Wilson.*

TAMARAN (IRE) RR 52f — 4411[5]

2 br c Doyoun 10.7f **(69)** - Tamarzana (IRE) (Lear Fan (USA)) 8.5f **(73)**

Form - 05

Record 1999 - 1st:0 2nd:0 3rd:0 Ran:2
1999 Turf 0-1: (8f) (g-f) 1999 AW 0-1: (8f) (Fibr)
Currently average colt. **Sir Michael Stoute [0-2] H H Aga Khan.*

TAMASHAN BHB 48f **RR 43f** 4149[10]

3 b c Puissance 7.1f **(60)** - Wild Truffes (IRE) **(28df)** (Danehill (USA)) 10f **(72)**
Form - 7600
Record 1999 - 1st:0 2nd:0 3rd:0 Ran:4
1999 Turf 0-2: (8f, 10f) (gd, frm) 1999 AW 0-2: (8f 2) (Equi, Fibr)
Light-framed, moderate colt. Turf high 43 (began Aug). AW high 21. **G C H Chung [0-4] H C Chung.*

TAMBOURINAIRE (IRE) BHB 74f **RR 72f** 2632[8]

2 gr c Kendor (FR) 12.2f **(66)** - Rotina (FR) (Crystal Glitters (USA)) 11.3f **(79)**
Form - 338
Record 1999 - 1st:0 2nd:0 3rd:2 Ran:3
Win Prizemoney £0 *Total Prizemoney* £1,235
1999 Turf 0-3: (6f 3) (gd, g-f, frm)
Currently above-average colt. Turf high 72 - 3rd of 7 to Speedfit Free (26 May Yarmouth 6f g-f RF 1511).
**B J Meehan [0-3] Abbott Racing Ltd.*

TAMGEED (USA) BHB 56f **RR 59f** 4159[5]

3 ch f Woodman (USA) 9.7f **(77)** - Toujours Elle (USA) (Lyphard (USA)) 9.9f **(72)**
Form - 626375
Record 1999 - 1st:0 2nd:1 3rd:1 Ran:6
Pre1999 - 1st:0 2nd:0 3rd:0 Ran:2
Win Prizemoney £0 *Total Prizemoney* £1,371
1999 Turf 0-6: (7f 2, 10f 2, 12f, 13f) (gd 3, g-f, frm 2)
Scopey, fair filly, effective 7 to 13f, acts on gd to frm, best on frm, often wears blinkers (extremely effectively). Turf high 59.
**J L Dunlop [0-8] Hamdan Al Maktoum.*

TAMING (IRE) BHB 90f **RR 79+f** 2827[1]

3 ch c Lycius (USA) 8.8f **(71)** - Black Fighter (USA) (Secretariat (USA)) 9f **(79)**
Form - 1
Record 1999 - 1st:1 2nd:0 3rd:0 Ran:1
Pre1999 - 1st:0 2nd:0 3rd:1 Ran:2
Win Prizemoney £3,712 *Total Prizemoney* £4,273
Wins * 1999 Jly Kempto (G-F) 12f 77+ <
1999 Turf 1-1: (12f 1-1) (frm 1-1)
Scopey, currently above-average colt. (1st run) - 1st of 7 giving 5lb to First Cut (14 Jly Kempton RF 2827).
**H R A Cecil [1-3] Buckram Oak Holdings.*

TAMMAM (IRE) BHB 93f **RR 91f** 3791[4]

3 b c Priolo (USA) 10.9f **(71)** - Bristle (Thatch (USA)) 9.8f **(62)**
Form - 1534
Record 1999 - 1st:1 2nd:0 3rd:1 Ran:4
Pre1999 - 1st:0 2nd:1 3rd:3 Ran:4
Win Prizemoney £8,367 *Total Prizemoney* £11,960
Wins * 1999 May Cheste (G-F) 10.3f 88 <
1999 Turf 1-4: (9f, 10f 1-3) (g-s, gd 2, g-f 1-1)
Scopey, useful colt, effective 9 to 10f, best at 10f, acts on g-s to g-f, has worn blinkers. Turf high 91 - 3rd of 3 to J R Stevenson (2 Jun Goodwood 10f g-s RF 1679) - also 1st of 8 from Elmutabaki (4 May Chester RF 1029). Placed in maidens on each of his runs at two, he changed stables before last season and got off to the best possible start with a fluent success at Chester. Highly tried since, he can win more races at four.
**B Hanbury [1-4] Hamdan Al Maktoum (from C J Benstead [0-4] Aug 1998).*

TANCRED ARMS BHB 56f47a **RR 53f 47a** 4607[9]

3 b f Clantime 6.6f **(57)** - Mischievous Miss (Niniski (USA)) 10.6f **(65)**
Form - 0302057005107000
Record 1999 - 1st:1 2nd:1 3rd:1 Ran:16
Pre1999 - 1st:0 2nd:3 3rd:0 Ran:10
Win Prizemoney £3,629 *Total Prizemoney* £7,855
Wins * 1999 Jly Catter (GD) H 6f 57 68 <
1999 Turf 1-13: (6f 1-12, 7f) (gd 3, g-f 1-3, frm 7) 1999 AW 0-3: (6f 2, 8f) (Fibr 3)
Leggy, fair filly, effective 5 to 6f, acts on gd to g-f, has worn blinkers. Turf high 68 - 1st of 12 getting 5lb from Sweet As A Nut (1 Jly Catterick RF 2459). AW high 44. **D W Barker [1-26] D W Barker.*

TANCRED MISCHIEF BHB 35f **RR 39f** 2455[12]

8 b m Northern State (USA) 12.6f **(45)** - Mischievous Miss (Niniski (USA)) 10.6f **(65)**
Form - 0
Record 1999 - 1st:0 2nd:0 3rd:0 Ran:1
Pre1999 - 1st:3 2nd:1 3rd:2 Ran:31
Win Prizemoney £9,825 *Total Prizemoney* £12,193
Wins * 1998 Oct Pontef (SFT) H 18f 27 39 <
* 1997 Jun Pontef (GD) H 18f 30 39 <
* 1997 Apr Mussel (G-F) H 16f 28 30
1999 Turf 0-1: (16f) (g-f)
Very moderate mare, effective 18f, acts on gd, has worn blinkers (very effectively), likes left handed tracks.
**D W Barker [3-25] D W Barker (from W L Barker [1-18] Jun 1996).*

TANCRED TIMES BHB 46f39a **RR 44f 39a** 5167[7]

4 ch f Clantime 6.6f **(57)** - Mischievous Miss (Niniski (USA)) 10.6f **(65)**
Form - 347548000000022657
Record 1999 - 1st:0 2nd:2 3rd:0 Ran:14
Pre1999 - 1st:3 2nd:1 3rd:4 Ran:25
Win Prizemoney £9,209 *Total Prizemoney* £14,034
Wins * 1998 Aug Carlis (G-S) H 5.9f 56 62
* 1997 Jly Catter (G-F) H 7f 68 <
* 1997 Jun Thirsk (GD) S 6f 64
1999 Turf 0-11: (5f 3, 6f 4, 7f 2, 8f 2) (sft, g-s 2, g-f 5, frm 3) 1999 AW 0-3: (5f, 7f 2) (Equi 3)
Light-framed, moderate filly, effective 5 to 6f, best at 6f, acts on gd to frm, best on frm, has worn blinkers. Turf high 44. AW high 38. Inconsistent.
**D W Barker [3-30] D W Barker (from J Cullinan [0-9] Jun 1999).*

TANGERINE BHB 72f **RR 73?f** 4909[11]

2 ch f Primo Dominie 7.2f **(67)** - Sweet Jaffa (Never so Bold) 6.3f **(66)**
Form - 0010
Record 1999 - 1st:1 2nd:0 3rd:0 Ran:4
Win Prizemoney £3,777 *Total Prizemoney* £3,777
Wins * 1999 Spt Bath (G-S) 5.7f 73? <
1999 Turf 1-4: (6f 1-3, 7f) (gd 1-2, g-f, frm)
Above-average filly. Turf high 73 (began Aug) - 1st of 17 from Mount Park (27 Spt Bath RF 4580). **B W Hills [1-4] Guy Reed.*

TANGO (IRE) BHB 70f **RR 61f** 3416[15]

4 b c Dancing Dissident (USA) 6.8f **(65)** - Tunguska (Busted) 10.2f **(61)**
Form - 00
Record 1999 - 1st:0 2nd:0 3rd:0 Ran:2
Pre1999 - 1st:1 2nd:1 3rd:0 Ran:7
Win Prizemoney £3,875 *Total Prizemoney* £5,473
Wins 1998 May Pontef (G-F) 6f 90 <
1999 Turf 0-2: (6f, 8f) (g-f, frm)
Leggy, average colt, effective 6f, acts on g-f to frm. Turf high 61 (began Jly). Becoming disappointing.
**K C Bailey [0-2] This Horse Is For Sale Partnership (from R Hannon [1-7] Oct 1998).*

TANGO MAN (IRE) BHB 24f27a **RR 12f 27a** 2837[9]

7 ch g King Luthier 12.3f **(40)** - Amour Libre (He Loves Me) 7.9f **(55)**
Form - 0
Record 1999 - 1st:0 2nd:0 3rd:0 Ran:1
Pre1999 - 1st:0 2nd:0 3rd:0 Ran:3
1999 Turf 0-1: (12f) (frm)
Little account gelding.
**J G M O'Shea [1-15] T G K Construction Ltd (from R J Price [0-10] Jan 1997).*

TANIMBAR (IRE) BHB 31f **RR 33f** 4630[14]

4 b g Persian Bold 10f **(69)** -Try My Rosie (Try My Best (USA)) 7.6f **(67)**
Form - 0000
Record 1999 - 1st:0 2nd:0 3rd:0 Ran:4
Pre1999 - 1st:0 2nd:0 3rd:0 Ran:7
1999 Turf 0-4: (8f 2, 10f, 12f) (g-s, gd, frm, hrd)
Workmanlike, very moderate gelding, effective 8f, acts on frm, has worn blinkers, likes left handed tracks, likes tight tracks. Turf high 33. Inconsistent.
**G L Moore [0-2] John Ruggles (from D HaydnJones [0-9] May 1999).*

TANKERSLEY BHB 63f **RR 60f** 5075[5]
4 ch g Timeless Times (USA) 6.1f **(56)**-Busted Love (Busted) 10.2f **(61)**
Form - 015480005
Record 1999 - 1st:1 2nd:0 3rd:0 Ran:9
Pre1999 - 1st:1 2nd:2 3rd:0 Ran:8
Win Prizemoney £9,956 *Total Prizemoney* £12,856
Wins * 1999 Jun Nottin (GD) H 10f 76 79
* 1998 May Catter (G-S) 7f 81 <
1999 Turf 1-9: (7f, 8f, 10f 1-5, 12f 2) (g-s, gd 3, g-f 1-2, frm 3)
Scopey, average gelding, effective 7 to 10f, best at 7f, acts on gd to g-f, best on gd, has worn blinkers, prefers left handed tracks, prefers tight tracks. Turf high 79. Inconsistent.
**P W D'Arcy [2-16] Walt Sylvester (from A Hide [0-1] Nov 1997).*

TANNENKONIG (IRE) RR 110f 1107[8]
4 b c Fairy King (USA) 7.7f **(75)** - Tannenalm (IRE) (Luciano) 11.2f **(65)**
Form - 8
1999 Turf 0-1: (7f) (gd)
Group-class colt, effective 7 to 10f, best at 8f, acts on sft to gd, best on sft, excels at Cologne. Consistent.
**W Kujath in GER [0-6] Manfred Grau (from J Kujath in GER [0-1] Oct 1998).*

TANSHAN BHB 55f **RR 55f** 2915[4]
4 ch g Anshan 8.2f **(63)** - Nafla (FR) (Arctic Tern (USA)) 8.9f **(69)**
Form - 06584
Record 1999 - 1st:0 2nd:0 3rd:0 Ran:5
Pre1999 - 1st:0 2nd:0 3rd:1 Ran:4
Win Prizemoney £0 *Total Prizemoney* £939
1999 Turf 0-5: (10f 3, 11f, 12f) (g-s, frm 4)
Scopey, fair gelding, effective 8 to 11f, acts on gd. Turf high 55. Consistent.
**R Rowe [0-5] Birch Hall Racing Partnership (from A C Stewart [0-4] Aug 1998).*

TANTALUS RR 84+f 5099[2]
2 ch c Unfuwain (USA) 11.4f **(74)** - Water Quest (IRE) (Rainbow Quest (USA)) 10.4f **(75)**
Form - 2
Record 1999 - 1st:0 2nd:1 3rd:0 Ran:1
Win Prizemoney £0 *Total Prizemoney* £990
1999 Turf 0-1: (7f) (gd)
Currently decent colt. (1st run) - 2nd of 12 to Fast Track (27 Oct Yarmouth 7f gd RF 5099). **B W Hills [0-1] K Abdulla.*

TANUSIUS BHB 85f **RR 86f** 2747[3]
3 b c Warning 8.1f **(77)** - Tanz (IRE) (Sadler's Wells (USA)) 10f **(76)**
Form - 32023
Record 1999 - 1st:0 2nd:2 3rd:2 Ran:5
Pre1999 - 1st:0 2nd:1 3rd:1 Ran:3
Win Prizemoney £0 *Total Prizemoney* £8,219
1999 Turf 0-5: (12f 4, 14f) (gd 2, g-f 2, frm)
Neat, useful colt, effective 7 to 14f, acts on gd to frm. Turf high 86 - 2nd of 7 getting 15lb from Kadir (2 Jly Sandown 14f g-f RF 2502). Consistent. He has made the frame behind some useful sorts so far, but has yet to get off the mark.
**C E Brittain [0-8] Abdullah Saeed Bul Hab.*

TAOISTE BHB 75f **RR 65f** 577[23]
6 ch h Kris 10f **(75)** - Tenue de Soiree (USA) (Lyphard (USA)) 9.9f **(72)**
Form - 0
Record 1999 - 1st:0 2nd:0 3rd:0 Ran:1
Pre1999 - 1st:0 2nd:2 3rd:1 Ran:14
Win Prizemoney £0 *Total Prizemoney* £5,332
1999 Turf 0-1: (6f) (g-f)
Average horse, effective 5 to 6f, best at 6f, acts on g-s to g-f, has worn blinkers. Becoming disappointing.
**M S Saunders [0-1] Earl Toups (from R W Armstrong [0-14] Jly 1998).*

TAP RR 69f 4834[2]
2 b c Emarati (USA) 6.6f **(63)** - Pubby (Doctor Wall)
Form - 2
Record 1999 - 1st:0 2nd:1 3rd:0 Ran:1
Win Prizemoney £0 *Total Prizemoney* £1,100
1999 Turf 0-1: (7f) (gd)
Currently average colt. **J A R Toller [0-1] Philip Wroughton.*

TAPAGE (IRE) BHB 51f50a **RR 45f 50a** 5056[11]
3 b g Great Commotion (USA) 9.2f **(80)** - Irena (Bold Lad(IRE))8.4f **(68)**
Form - 12525280780
Record 1999 - 1st:0 2nd:2 3rd:0 Ran:9
Pre1999 - 1st:1 2nd:1 3rd:0 Ran:3
Win Prizemoney £2,085 *Total Prizemoney* £4,292
Wins 1998 *Nov Lingfi (STD) 7f 77* <
1999 Turf 0-6: (7f, 8f 5) (g-f 2, frm 3, hrd) 1999 AW 0-3: (7f, 8f, 10f) (Equi, Fibr 2)
Moderate gelding, effective 7 to 8f, best at 7f, acts on frm - acts on Equi, has worn blinkers, prefers left handed tracks, prefers tight tracks. Turf high 70 - 2nd of 9 giving 4lb to Hush Money (17 Jly Nottingham 8f frm RF 2917). AW high 62 (began Jly). Becoming disappointing. He became a very rare Irish-trained winner on the All-Weather when winning at Lingfield last November, but he has only shown modest form for his current yard.
**Andrew Reid [0-4] A S Reid (from W R Muir [0-6] Aug 1999).*

TAPAUA (IRE) BHB 46f49a **RR 47f 49a** 4925[4]
3 b g Common Grounds 8.1f **(66)** - Tap The Line (Tap On Wood) 10.3f **(65)**
Form - 50020003804
Record 1999 - 1st:0 2nd:1 3rd:1 Ran:11
Win Prizemoney £0 *Total Prizemoney* £1,041
1999 Turf 0-10: (6f 4, 7f 3, 8f 2, 10f) (gd 4, g-f 3, frm 3) 1999 AW 0-1: (7f) (Fibr)
Light-framed, moderate gelding, effective 6 to 7f, acts on g-f to frm, has worn blinkers. Turf high 54 - 2nd of 16 giving 3lb to Magic Moment (10 Jun Carlisle 6f g-f RF 1878). Consistent.
**M Dods [0-11] A G Watson.*

TAP TO MUSIC (USA) RR 5224a[5]
4 f Pleasant Tap (USA) 13.1f **(71)** - Nuryette (USA) (Nureyev (USA)) 8.7f **(78)**
Form - 5
1999 AW 0-1: (9f) (Dirt)
Currently very useful filly, always wears blinkers.
**J Orseno in USA [0-2].*

TARA (IRE) BHB 41f30a **RR 46f 30a** 79[10]
3 br f Petardia 8.2f **(58)** - Genzyme Gene (Riboboy (USA)) 14f **(54)**
Form - 00
Record 1999 - 1st:0 2nd:0 3rd:0 Ran:2
Pre1999 - 1st:0 2nd:0 3rd:0 Ran:7
Win Prizemoney £0 *Total Prizemoney* £243
1999 AW 0-2: (7f 2) (Equi 2)
Light-framed, moderate filly, has worn blinkers. AW high 21.
**K T Ivory [0-9] K T Ivory.*

TARA HALL BHB 53f **RR 63f** 4934[7]
2 b f Saddlers' Hall (IRE) 10.5f **(65)** - Katie Scarlett (Lochnager) 6f **(59)**
Form - U00857
Record 1999 - 1st:0 2nd:0 3rd:0 Ran:6
1999 Turf 0-4:(6f, 7f, 8f 2)(sft, gd, g-f, frm) 1999 AW 0-2: (7f, 8f) (Fibr 2)
Average filly, has worn blinkers. Turf high 63 (began Jly). (began Jly). **N P Littmoden [0-6] John Pugh.*

TARAJAN (USA) BHB 50f **RR 45f** 2361[5]
7 ch g Shahrastani (USA) 11.5f **(69)** - Tarafa (Akarad (FR)) 9f **(76)**
Form - 5
Record 1999 - 1st:0 2nd:0 3rd:0 Ran:1
Pre1999 - 1st:0 2nd:0 3rd:1 Ran:5
Win Prizemoney £0 *Total Prizemoney* £4,500
1999 Turf 0-1: (16f) (gd)
Moderate gelding, has worn blinkers.
**Miss Lucinda Russell [1-15] J Rodger (from Patrick Prendergast in IRE [4-24] Oct 1997).*

TARA'S GIRL (IRE) RR 91f 4793[9]
2 b f Fayruz 6.6f **(63)** - Florissa (FR) (Persepolis (FR)) 6.4f **(67)**
Form - 217148020
Record 1999 - 1st:2 2nd:2 3rd:0 Ran:9
Win Prizemoney £11,128 *Total Prizemoney* £18,844
Wins * 1999 Jun Beverl (GD) 5f 91 <
* 1999 Apr Beverl (G-F) 5f 71
1999 Turf 2-9: (5f 2-7, 6f 2) (g-s, gd 1-6, frm 1-2)
Useful filly, effective 5f, acts on gd. Turf high 91 - 1st of 9 from Vita

Spericolata (2 Jun Beverley RF 1662). Inconsistent. Twice a winner at Beverley, including a decent conditions event, she then finished fourth in the Queen Mary at Ascot. After that she was highly tried in the Cherry Hinton and the Tattersalls Breeders stakes in Ireland, but ran better when runner-up in an Ayr Listed event, if totally unable to cope with Khasayl. **J J Quinn [2-9] Tara Leisure.*

TARAWAN BHB 87f **RR 90f** 4915[19]
3 ch c Nashwan (USA) 10.3f **(79)** - Soluce (Junius (USA)) 7.7f **(65)**
Form - 2562423221210
Record 1999 - 1st:2 2nd:6 3rd:1 Ran:13
Pre1999 - 1st:0 2nd:1 3rd:0 Ran:3
Win Prizemoney £15,061 *Total Prizemoney* £28,651
Wins * 1999 Oct Sandow (SFT) H 8.1f 85 90 <
*** 1999** Aug Newcas (GD) 8f 81
1999 Turf 2-13: (8f 2-9, 9f, 10f 3) (g-s 1-1, gd 4, g-f 1-2, frm 6)
Scopey, useful colt, effective 8 to 10f, best at 8f, acts on g-s to frm, best on frm, often wears blinkers (effectively), likes tight tracks, excels at Sandown and Newbury. Turf high 90 - 1st of 10 giving 14lb to Donatus (2 Oct Sandown RF 4698) - also 1st of 9 giving 5lb to Singing Winds (30 Aug Newcastle RF 4023). Consistent. He took a very long time in getting off the mark having been placed on several occasions, but broke his duck at Newcastle in August. Added a victory at Sandown and a mile looks to be his best trip. He seems to appreciate easy ground. **I A Balding [2-16] Robert Hitchins.*

TAR BABY BHB 30f **RR 30f** 228[14]
4 b f Handsome Sailor 6.6f **(53)** - Queen of Aragon (Aragon) 8.1f **(60)**
Form - 060
Record 1999 - 1st:0 2nd:0 3rd:0 Ran:2
Pre1999 - 1st:0 2nd:0 3rd:0 Ran:3
1999 AW 0-2: (11f 2) (Fibr 2)
Scopey, very moderate filly, has broken blood-vessels. AW high 6. **R Hollinshead [0-5] Mrs Charles Lockhart.*

TARCOOLA RR 59f 5044[4]
2 ch c Pursuit of Love 9.5f **(69)** - Miswaki Belle (USA) **(64+f)** (Miswaki (USA)) 9f **(81)**
Form - 04
Record 1999 - 1st:0 2nd:0 3rd:0 Ran:2
Win Prizemoney £0 *Total Prizemoney* £325
1999 Turf 0-2: (6f 2) (sft, frm)
Currently fair colt. Turf high 59 (began Spt).
**V Soane [0-2] Michael Abdallah and Steve Herbert.*

TARFAA (IRE) RR 103f 1477a[10]
3 b c Night Shift (USA) 8.1f **(73)** - Robinia (USA) (Roberto (USA)) 10f **(76)**
Form - 10
1999 Turf 1-2: (7f 1-1, 8f) (sft 1-1, g-f)
Very useful colt. Turf high 103 (1st run) - 1st of 7 getting 4lb from Stravinsky (28 Mar Curragh RF 0517a). He scalped Stravinsky on his reappearance, but ran poorly in the Irish 2,000 Guineas and was not seen again. Connections believe he wants fast ground.
**K Prendergast in IRE [2-5] Hamdan Al Maktoum.*

TARIYFA (IRE) BHB 80f **RR 79f** 4525[1]
3 b f Bigstone (IRE) - Tarafa (Akarad (FR)) 9f **(76)**
Form - 21
Record 1999 - 1st:1 2nd:1 3rd:0 Ran:2
Win Prizemoney £4,227 *Total Prizemoney* £5,451
Wins * 1999 Spt Haydoc (SFT) 10.5f 71 <
1999 Turf 1-2: (10f, 11f 1-1) (gd 1-2)
Workmanlike, currently above-average filly. Turf high 79 (1st run) - 2nd of 14 to String Quartet (19 May Chepstow 10f gd RF 1325) - also 1st of 8 from Azimah (24 Spt Haydock RF 4525). Unraced at two, she showed promise on her Chepstow debut in May, but was off the track until landing a ten-furlong Haydock maiden in September. Suited by soft ground and will be suited by a mile and a half at least. **Sir Michael Stoute [1-2] H H Aga Khan.*

TARPON TALE (IRE) RR 23f 3472[5]
2 b g Mujadil (USA) 7.7f **(70)** - Lady of The Mist (IRE) **(46f)** (Digamist (USA))
Form - 005
Record 1999 - 1st:0 2nd:0 3rd:0 Ran:3
1999 Turf 0-3: (5f 2, 6f) (sft, g-f, frm)
Currently little account gelding. Turf high 23.
**Mrs A L M King [0-3] Aiden Murphy.*

TARRADALE BHB 48f37a **RR 47f 37a** 5191[8]
5 br g Interrex (CAN) 7.7f **(51)** - Encore L'Amour (USA) (Monteverdi) 6.5f **(61)**
Form - 3850620823830238
Record 1999 - 1st:0 2nd:3 3rd:3 Ran:13
Pre1999 - 1st:1 2nd:2 3rd:1 Ran:21
Win Prizemoney £2,983 *Total Prizemoney* £9,316
Wins * 1998 Jun Hamilt (G-S) H 8.3f 32 35 <
1999 Turf 0-11: (8f 7, 9f 3, 10f) (hvy 2, gd 4, g-f 2, frm 2, hrd) 1999 AW 0-2: (8f 2) (Equi, Fibr)
Moderate gelding, effective 8 to 12f, best at 8f, acts on hvy to hrd - acts on Equi, best on gd, likes right handed tracks, excels at Redcar and Hamilton. Turf high 47 - 3rd of 16 getting 17lb from Donna's Double (26 Oct Redcar 8f gd RF 5073). AW high 31. Consistent. **C B B Booth [1-36] J A Porteous.*

TARRIFA (IRE) RR 41f 5108[12]
2 ch f Mujtahid (USA) 7.4f **(69)** - Gibraltar Heights (High Top) 10.2f **(67)**
Form - 0
Record 1999 - 1st:0 2nd:0 3rd:0 Ran:1
1999 Turf 0-1: (8f) (gd)
Currently moderate filly. **J G Smyth-Osbourne [0-1] J H Henderson.*

TARRY FLYNN (IRE) RR 109f 4848a[1]
5 br g Kenmare (FR) 9.6f **(76)** - Danzig Lass (USA) 00
Form - 0111041
1999 Turf 4-7: (6f 1-2, 7f 3-4, 8f) (sft 1-2, gd 1-3, g-f 2-2)
Pattern-class gelding, effective 7f, acts on sft to g-f, often wears blinkers (extremely effectively), and does well at Leopardstown. Turf high 109 - 4th of 18 giving 4lb to Trans Island (11 Spt Leopardstown 7f gd RF 4314a) - also 1st of 6 from Late Night Out (9 Oct Cork RF 4848a). A progressive Irish handicapper, he stepped successfully into Group Three company at Cork in October. **D K Weld in IRE [6-15] Mrs C L Weld.*

TARSKI BHB 52f **RR 47f** 5069[8]
5 ch g Polish Precedent (USA) 9f **(73)** - Illusory (Kings Lake (USA)) 10.8f **(67)**
Form - 0621203658
Record 1999 - 1st:1 2nd:2 3rd:1 Ran:10
Pre1999 - 1st:1 2nd:1 3rd:0 Ran:11
Win Prizemoney £11,981 *Total Prizemoney* £18,016
Wins * 1999 Jun Goodwo (G-F) H 9.9f 51 54
1996 Jly Sandow (G-F) 7.1f 92+ <
1999 Turf 1-10: (8f, 9f 3, 10f 1-6) (g-s, gd 3, g-f 1-4, frm, hrd)
Moderate gelding, has worn blinkers, likes right handed tracks. Turf high 55. Consistent.
**L G Cottrell [1-17] E Gadsden (from H R A Cecil [1-4] Spt 1997).*

TARTAN ISLAND (IRE) BHB 53f **RR 51f** 4881[11]
2 b c Turtle Island (IRE) - Welsh Harp (Mtoto)
Form - 000
Record 1999 - 1st:0 2nd:0 3rd:0 Ran:3
1999 Turf 0-3: (5f, 6f 2) (g-s, gd, frm)
Currently fair colt. Turf high 51 (began Spt).
**I Semple [0-3] Mrs E Chung & Peter Tsim.*

TARTAN LASS BHB 75f **RR 62f** 5160[11]
4 b f Selkirk (USA) 7.9f **(76)** - Gwiffina (Welsh Saint) 7.6f **(64)**
Form - 51001080
Record 1999 - 1st:2 2nd:0 3rd:0 Ran:8
Pre1999 - 1st:0 2nd:0 3rd:1 Ran:5
Win Prizemoney £7,124 *Total Prizemoney* £7,447
Wins * 1999 Spt Kempto (HVY) H 6f 73 76+ <
*** 1999** Jun Chepst (GD) H 6.1f 67 71+
1999 Turf 2-8: (6f 2-7, 7f) (g-s, gd 2-3, g-f, frm 3)
Scopey, average filly, effective 6f, acts on gd. Turf high 76 - 1st of 22 giving 14lb to Top Banana (20 Spt Kempton RF 4431) - also 1st of 16 giving 24lb to Addition (11 Jun Chepstow RF 1912). Consistent. **R Guest [2-13] Matthews Breeding and Racing.*

TARXIEN BHB 83f **RR 83f** 723[10]
5 b g Kendor (FR) 12.2f **(66)** -Tanz(IRE) (Sadler's Wells (USA)) 10f **(76)**
Form - 40

Record 1999 - 1st:0 2nd:0 3rd:0 Ran:2
Pre1999 - 1st:5 2nd:3 3rd:3 Ran:22
Win Prizemoney £17,547 *Total Prizemoney* £25,802
Wins 1998 Jun Goodwo (G-F) H 14f 85 88 <
1998 May Newbur (GD) H 13.3f 73 86
1998 May Haydoc (G-S) H 14f 73 77+
1997 Spt Pontef (G-S) 12f 68
1997 Aug Haydoc (G-F) H 11.9f 62 68
1999 Turf 0-2: (16f 2) (g-f, frm)
Decent gelding, effective 13 to 16f, acts on gd to g-f, best on g-f, likes tight tracks. Turf high 83 (1st run) - 4th of 12 giving 3lb to Far Cry (3 Apr Kempton 16f g-f RF 0571).
**Mrs Merrita Jones [0-3] F J Sainsbury (from K R Burke [5-22] Oct 1998).*

TASHANNAH BHB 25f RR 9f 4180[11]

6 b m Sizzling Melody 6.3f **(49)** - Liu Liu San (IRE) (Bairn (USA)) 7.7f **(59)**
Form - 0
Record 1999 - 1st:0 2nd:0 3rd:0 Ran:1
Pre1999 - 1st:0 2nd:0 3rd:0 Ran:2
1999 Turf 0-1: (7f) (frm)
Currently very poor mare.
**P Butler [0-1] Mrs Gill Oakley (from P R Hedger [0-2] Jly 1997).*

TASKONE BHB 30f RR 36f 2943[11]

3 ch f Be My Chief (USA) 10.2f **(62)** - Good as Gold (IRE) (Glint of Gold) 9.3f **(66)**
Form - 58000
Record 1999 - 1st:0 2nd:0 3rd:0 Ran:5
Pre1999 - 1st:0 2nd:0 3rd:0 Ran:1
1999 Turf 0-5: (12f 2, 14f, 16f, 17f) (gd, g-f, frm 3)
Scopey, very moderate filly, has worn blinkers. Turf high 42.
**R A Fahey [0-6] Task Training Ltd.*

TASTE OF SUCCESS BHB 57f RR 65f 4410[13]

4 b g Thatching 7.8f **(69)** - Tastiera (USA) (Diesis) 9.3f **(69)**
Form - 0
Record 1999 - 1st:0 2nd:0 3rd:0 Ran:1
Pre1999 - 1st:0 2nd:0 3rd:0 Ran:3
Win Prizemoney £0 *Total Prizemoney* £483
1999 AW 0-1: (8f) (Fibr)
Strong, average gelding. **P W Harris [0-4] First Taste.*

TATTENHAM STAR BHB 68f67a RR 64f 67a 4943[6]

2 b c Mistertopogigo (IRE) - Candane **(77f)** (Danehill (USA)) 10f **(72)**
Form - 0056
Record 1999 - 1st:0 2nd:0 3rd:0 Ran:4
1999 Turf 0-4: (5f, 6f 2, 7f) (g-s, gd, g-f 2)
Average colt. Turf high 64 (began Jly).
**M J Haynes [0-4] Tattenham Partnership.*

TAUFAN BOY BHB 58f65a RR 63df 65a 5028[5]

6 b g Taufan (USA) 8.3f **(65)** - Lydia Maria (Dancing Brave (USA)) 8.4f **(76)**
Form - 56845
Record 1999 - 1st:0 2nd:0 3rd:0 Ran:5
Pre1999 - 1st:2 2nd:3 3rd:5 Ran:27
Win Prizemoney £7,123 *Total Prizemoney* £17,481
Wins * 1998 May Haydoc (G-S) H 14f 58 63
1995 Spt Southw (STD) 7f 80 <
1999 Turf 0-5: (13f, 14f 3, 16f) (g-s 3, g-f, frm)
Above-average gelding, effective 14f, acts on sft to gd, best on gd, has worn blinkers, prefers left handed tracks. Turf high 63 - 6th of 15 getting 4lb from Swift (12 May York 14f g-s RF 1185).
**G B Balding [4-24] Supreme Team (from P W Harris [1-22] Oct 1997).*

TAUREAN BHB 31f RR 24f 1951[15]

4 b g Dilum (USA) 7.1f **(56)** - Herora (IRE) **(66f)** (Heraldiste (USA))
Form - 0
Record 1999 - 1st:0 2nd:0 3rd:0 Ran:1
Pre1999 - 1st:0 2nd:0 3rd:0 Ran:6
1999 AW 0-1: (7f) (Equi)
Small, moderate gelding. **N A Graham [0-7] Mrs Lesley Graham.*

TAURUS BAY (IRE) BHB 30f RR 18f 336[15]

3 b g River Falls 8.2f **(56)** - Farriers Slipper (Prince Tenderfoot (USA)) 9f **(61)**
Form - 0
Record 1999 - 1st:0 2nd:0 3rd:0 Ran:1
Pre1999 - 1st:0 2nd:0 3rd:0 Ran:4
1999 AW 0-1: (8f) (Fibr)
Workmanlike, poor gelding.
**Ronald Thompson [0-5] Mrs Janet McCabe.*

TAVERNER SOCIETY (IRE) BHB 72f RR 67f 2956[3]

4 b c Imp Society (USA) 7.1f **(63)** - Straw Boater (Thatch (USA)) 9.8f **(62)**
Form - 0003
Record 1999 - 1st:0 2nd:0 3rd:1 Ran:4
Pre1999 - 1st:1 2nd:2 3rd:1 Ran:12
Win Prizemoney £3,387 *Total Prizemoney* £11,110
Wins 1997 Spt Kempto (G-F) 8f 81 <
1999 Turf 0-4: (7f, 10f 2, 12f) (gd, g-f, frm 2)
Average colt, effective 10f, acts on gd to g-f, has worn blinkers. Turf high 67.
**M S Saunders [0-4] M S Saunders (from R W Armstrong [1-12] Oct 1998).*

TAWN AGAIN RR 31[6]

3 b g Then Again 7.4f **(52)** - Tawny (Grey Ghost) 9.9f **(60)**
Form - 6
Record 1999 - 1st:0 2nd:0 3rd:0 Ran:1
1999 AW 0-1: (5f) (Equi)
Leggy, currently fair gelding. **T D Barron [0-1] B Elsworth.*

TAWWAG (IRE) BHB 72f RR 72f 2062[6]

3 b c Shirley Heights 12.1f **(76)** - Albertville (USA) (Polish Precedent (USA)) 10.2f **(60)**
Form - 5506
Record 1999 - 1st:0 2nd:0 3rd:0 Ran:4
Pre1999 - 1st:0 2nd:0 3rd:0 Ran:1
1999 Turf 0-4: (8f, 10f, 11f, 12f) (sft, gd, g-f, hrd)
Scopey, above-average colt, has worn blinkers. Turf high 72.
**M A Jarvis [0-5] Sheikh Ahmed Al Maktoum.*

TAXI-FOR-ROBBO (IRE) BHB 47f RR 54f 4901[21]

2 b f Shalford (IRE) 7.8f **(63)** - Miromaid (Simply Great (FR)) 8.2f **(65)**
Form - 0360
Record 1999 - 1st:0 2nd:0 3rd:1 Ran:4
Win Prizemoney £0 *Total Prizemoney* £270
1999 Turf 0-4: (5f, 6f 2, 7f) (g-f 2, frm 2)
Fair filly. Turf high 54 - 3rd of 15 to Printsmith (1 Jly Catterick 5f g-f RF 2454). **J L Eyre [0-4] The First Thursday Club.*

TAXMERE RR 37f 4996[11]

2 ch f Lake Coniston (IRE) - Maculatus (USA) (Sharpen Up) 8.3f **(67)**
Form - 60
Record 1999 - 1st:0 2nd:0 3rd:0 Ran:2
1999 Turf 0-2: (7f, 8f) (gd, g-f)
Currently very moderate filly. Turf high 37 (began Jly).
**A T Murphy [0-2] Exmoor Racing Partnership.*

TAYIF BHB 97f RR 94f 4921[16]

3 gr c Taufan (USA) 8.3f **(65)** - Rich Lass (Broxted) 6.7f **(65)**
Form - 131510
Record 1999 - 1st:3 2nd:0 3rd:1 Ran:6
Pre1999 - 1st:0 2nd:1 3rd:0 Ran:1
Win Prizemoney £16,421 *Total Prizemoney* £18,289
Wins * **1999** Aug Newcas (GD) H 7f 90 94+ <
* **1999** Jly Sandow (G-F) H 7.1f 86 89+
* **1999** Apr Nottin (G-S) 5.1f 92+
1999 Turf 3-6: (5f 1-1, 7f 2-5) (sft 1-1, gd 1-2, g-f 2, frm 1-1)
Workmanlike, useful colt, effective 5 to 7f, best at 7f, acts on sft to frm. Turf high 94 - 1st of 10 giving 26lb to Donna's Double (30 Aug Newcastle RF 4024) - also 1st of 12 from Paradise Lane (5 Apr Nottingham RF 0588). On the upgrade, he has a turn of foot and can win more races. **J W Payne [3-7] G Jabre.*

TAYIL (IRE) BHB 95f RR 97f 2122[2]

3 b c Caerleon (USA) 10.9f **(79)** - Desert Bluebell (Kalaglow) 9.8f **(67)**
Form - 562
Record 1999 - 1st:0 2nd:1 3rd:0 Ran:3
Pre1999 - 1st:2 2nd:0 3rd:0 Ran:5

Win Prizemoney £11,294 *Total Prizemoney* £15,196
Wins * 1998 Jly York (FRM) 7f 89 <
* 1998 Jun Newmar (GD) 7f 77
1999 Turf 0-3: (8f, 10f, 12f) (g-f 2, frm)
Scopey, very useful colt, effective 7 to 12f, best at 7f, acts on frm. Turf high 95 - 2nd of 5 getting 17lb from Wales (18 Jun Newmarket 12f frm RF 2122). Consistent. He stays middle-distances but has not trained on satisfactorily. **J L Dunlop [2-8] Hamdan Al Maktoum.*

TAYOVULLIN (IRE) BHB 47f57a RR 54f 57a 3435[3]

5 ch m Shalford (IRE) 7.8f **(63)** - Fifth Quarter (Cure The Blues (USA)) 9.5f **(63)**
Form - 357123
Record 1999 - 1st:1 2nd:1 3rd:1 Ran:4
Pre1999 - 1st:2 2nd:4 3rd:2 Ran:28
Win Prizemoney £8,289 *Total Prizemoney* £13,456
Wins * **1999** *May Wolver (Std) H 7f 51 54*
* 1998 Jun Newmar (GD) H 7f 44 48
* 1997 *Apr Southw (STD) H 7f 56 63* <
1999 Turf 0-2: (7f 2) (frm 2) 1999 AW 1-2: (7f 1-2) (Fibr 1-2)
Fair filly, effective 7f, acts on g-s to gd - acts on Fibr, has worn blinkers, likes left handed tracks, likes tight tracks, excels at Wolverhampton. Turf high 46. AW high 58 - 2nd of 12 getting 4lb from Abtaal (22 May Wolverhampton 7f Fibr RF 1417) - also 1st of 12 giving 8lb to Rebecca Jay (14 May Wolverhampton RF 1232).
**H Morrison [3-31] H Morrison (from R Charlton [0-2] Spt 1996).*

TAYSEER (USA) BHB 86f81a RR 97f 81a 5141[1]

5 ch g Sheikh Albadou 9.2f **(75)** - Millfit (USA) (Blushing Groom (FR)) 10.3f **(76)**
Form - 10502207005111
Record 1999 - 1st:3 2nd:2 3rd:0 Ran:11
Pre1999 - 1st:3 2nd:0 3rd:1 Ran:12
Win Prizemoney £71,501 *Total Prizemoney* £78,812
Wins * **1999** Oct Newmar (SFT) H 8f 80 90+
* **1999** Spt Ayr (G-S) H 8f 72 87
1999 Spt Bright (G-F) C 8f 60
1998 *Nov Southw (STD) C 6f 70*
1997 May York (GD) H 7f 89 95 <
1996 Nov Redcar (G-F) 7f 95 <
1999 Turf 3-11: (6f, 7f 5, 8f 3-5) (gd 2-4, g-f 2, frm 1-5)
Very useful gelding, effective 7 to 8f, best at 8f, acts on gd to g-f, best on gd, likes left handed tracks, likes tight tracks. Turf high 90 - 1st of 19 getting 18lb from Brilliant Red (30 Oct Newmarket RF 5141) - also 1st of 19 getting 23lb from Bomb Alaska (18 Spt Ayr RF 4393). After embarking on what seemed likely to be a never-ending losing streak, a drop into a claimer did the trick. After joining Dandy Nicholls, he added a decent Ayr handicap to his collection from Bomb Alaska, and completed the hat-trick in a valuable handicap at Newmarket, landing a massive gamble in the process.
**D Nicholls [2-2] Sammy Doo Racing (from W R Muir [2-14] Spt 1999).*

TAZKIYA BHB 24f RR 34f 660[9]

4 ch f King's Signet (USA) 7f **(51)** - Irene's Charter (Persian Bold) 9.3f **(66)**
Form - 7505630
Record 1999 - 1st:0 2nd:0 3rd:1 Ran:7
Pre1999 - 1st:0 2nd:0 3rd:1 Ran:8
Win Prizemoney £0 *Total Prizemoney* £687
1999 Turf 0-1: (12f) (hvy) 1999 AW 0-6: (13f 3, 16f 3) (Equi 6)
Scopey, very moderate filly, has worn blinkers. AW high 34.
**R Ingram [0-7] John Fitzsimons (from C J Benstead [0-8] Aug 1998).*

TAZ MANIA BHB 29f35a RR 30f 35a 3991[8]

3 b g Savahra Sound 7.8f **(55)** - Sugar Token (Record Token) 6.3f **(53)**
Form - 00008007088
Record 1999 - 1st:0 2nd:0 3rd:0 Ran:9
Pre1999 - 1st:0 2nd:0 3rd:0 Ran:6
1999 Turf 0-6: (5f, 6f, 7f, 8f 3) (sft, g-f 2, frm 3) 1999 AW 0-3: (5f, 6f, 7f) (Fibr 3)
Light-framed, very moderate gelding, often wears blinkers. Turf high 30. AW high 27. Becoming disappointing.
**S R Bowring [0-12] Mrs P A Barratt (from M Meade [0-3] Jun 1998).*

TCHAIKOVSKY (IRE) RR 116f 4266[5]

3 b c Sadler's Wells (USA) 11.3f **(87)** - Crystal Spray (Beldale Flutter (USA)) 9.7f **(71)**
Form - 12535
Record 1999 - 1st:1 2nd:1 3rd:1 Ran:5
Pre1999 - 1st:1 2nd:0 3rd:0 Ran:1
Win Prizemoney £9,975 *Total Prizemoney* £106,685
Wins 1999 Apr Gowran (SFT) 10f 88+ <
1998 Spt Currag (G-S) 7f 88
1999 Turf 1-5: (10f 1-2, 12f 2, 15f) (sft 1-1, gd 3, frm)
High-class colt, effective 10f, acts on gd, has worn blinkers. Turf high 116. Formerly trained by Aidan O'Brien, he won his only start at two, and made a winning reappearance when stepped up to ten furlongs at Gowran Park. However, he found disappointingly little when beaten in the Derrinstown Derby Trial and was a well-beaten fifth behind Montjeu in the French Derby. Redeemed himself with a good third behind the same horse in the Irish Derby and joined Gerard Butler afterwards. A supplementary entry at £20,000 for the St Leger, he ran pretty well to finish fifth behind Mutafaweq.
**G A Butler [0-1] Prince Faisal bin Khalid (from A P O'Brien in IRE [2-5] Jun 1999).*

TE AKAU DAN (NZ) RR 1219[15]

5 b g Dance Floor (USA) - Bellandaan (NZ) (Standaan (FR)) 7f **(55)**
Form - 0
Record 1999 - 1st:0 2nd:0 3rd:0 Ran:1
1999 Turf 0-1: (7f) (gd)
Formerly very poor gelding, always wears blinkers.
**J M Bradley [0-6] R A Pope.*

TE ANAU BHB 41f57a RR 42f 57a 3823[15]

2 b f Reprimand 8.2f **(63)** - Neenah (Bold Lad (IRE)) 8.4f **(68)**
Form - 0300
Record 1999 - 1st:0 2nd:0 3rd:1 Ran:4
Win Prizemoney £0 *Total Prizemoney* £263
1999 Turf 0-3: (6f, 7f 2) (g-f 2, frm) 1999 AW 0-1: (7f) (Fibr)
Fair filly. Turf high 42. (1st run) - 3rd of 11 to Sally Gardens (23 Jly Wolverhampton 7f Fibr RF 3083). **B J McMath [0-4] D G Crocket.*

TEAPOT ROW (IRE) BHB 106f RR 108f 3619[2]

4 b c Generous (IRE) 11.5f **(82)** - Secrage (USA) (Secreto (USA)) 8.7f **(72)**
Form - 62412
Record 1999 - 1st:1 2nd:2 3rd:0 Ran:5
Pre1999 - 1st:3 2nd:2 3rd:0 Ran:9
Win Prizemoney £91,757 *Total Prizemoney* £113,922
Wins * **1999** Jly Newbur (G-F) 7.3f 105+
* 1997 Spt Ascot (G-F) G2 8f 107 <
* 1997 Spt Doncas (G-F) 7f 102
* 1997 Aug Newmar (GD) 6f 93+
1999 Turf 1-5: (7f 1-2, 8f 3) (g-s, gd 2, g-f, frm 1-1)
Pattern-class colt, effective 7 to 11f, acts on gd to frm, excels at Haydock. Turf high 108 - 2nd of 7 giving 9lb to Alrassaam (28 May Haydock 8f gd RF 1542) - also 1st of 8 giving 1lb to Caballero (16 Jly Newbury RF 2877). Consistent. Ran a couple of good races last term before regaining winning form in a Newbury conditions event. He ran well to chase home Lend A Hand at a respectable distance in the Hungerford Stakes over the same course and distance next time. **J A R Toller [4-14] Duke of Devonshire.*

TEAR WHITE (IRE) BHB 62f82a RR 61df 82a 3213[17]

5 b g Mac's Imp (USA) 5.6f **(54)** - Exemplary (Sovereign Lord) 6.5f **(76)**
Form - 1321D41735780
Record 1999 - 1st:2 2nd:1 3rd:1 Ran:11
Pre1999 - 1st:5 2nd:4 3rd:5 Ran:39
Win Prizemoney £28,289 *Total Prizemoney* £38,627
Wins * **1999** *Mar Lingfi (STD) H 5f 79 79* <
* **1999** *Jan Lingfi (STD) H 5f 70 71*
* 1998 *Dec Lingfi (STD) H 5f 64 70*
* 1998 Oct Bright (GD) H 5.3f 60 61
* 1997 Aug Goodwo (G-F) H 5f 67 69
* 1997 Jun Bright (FRM) H 5.3f 62 62
* 1996 Jly Ripon (G-F) 5f 52
1999 Turf 0-5: (5f 5) (gd, frm 3, hrd) 1999 AW 2-6: (5f 2-6) (Equi 2-6)
Above-average gelding, has broken blood-vessels, effective 5f, - acts on Equi, has worn blinkers, prefers left handed tracks, prefers tight tracks. Turf high 66. AW high 79 - 1st of 9 giving 23lb to Friendly Brave (18 Mar Lingfield RF 0444) - also 1st of 8 getting 25lb from Classy Cleo (12 Jan Lingfield RF 0080). Becoming disappointing. A very fast starter, he is ideally suited by a sharp downhill track on turf, and goes particularly well over the minimum on the Lingfield Equitrack. **T G Mills [7-50] Lant Street Racing.*

TEBYAAN (USA) BHB 73f **RR 72f** 4422[5]
3 b f Silver Hawk (USA) 11.2f **(85)** - Umniyatee (Green Desert (USA)) 8.6f **(78)**
Form - 2425

Record	**1999 -**	1st:0	2nd:2	3rd:0	Ran:4
	Pre1999 -	1st:0	2nd:1	3rd:0	Ran:1

Win Prizemoney £0 *Total Prizemoney* £4,207
1999 Turf 0-4: (7f 2, 8f 2) (gd, frm 3)
Workmanlike, above-average filly, has worn blinkers. Turf high 78 (1st run) - 2nd of 5 to Desdemona (3 Jun Yarmouth 7f gd RF 1708).
**B Hanbury [0-5] Hamdan Al Maktoum.*

TECHNICIAN (IRE) BHB 60f52a **RR 60df 52a** 4732[19]
4 ch g Archway (IRE) 8.5f **(60)** - How It Works (Commanche Run) 8.5f **(58)**
Form - 362237630200302030

Record	**1999 -**	1st:0	2nd:4	3rd:5	Ran:18
	Pre1999 -	1st:0	2nd:6	3rd:3	Ran:22

Win Prizemoney £0 *Total Prizemoney* £13,706
1999 Turf 0-16: (6f 3, 7f 8, 8f 5) (sft, g-s, gd 2, g-f 6, frm 5, hrd) 1999 AW 0-2: (6f, 7f) (Fibr 2)
Scopey, average gelding, effective 7 to 8f, best at 7f, acts on g-f to frm, best on frm, often wears blinkers (very effectively), prefers right handed tracks, excels at Musselburgh. Turf high 69 - 2nd of 14 giving 13lb to Johayro (17 May Musselburgh 7f frm RF 1275). AW high 51. A fair handicapper who runs at distances ranging from six furlongs to a mile, he has never won a race.
**E J Alston [0-32] C McCormack (from M A Jarvis [0-8] Feb 1998).*

TEDBURROW BHB 115f **RR 113+f** 4313a[1]
7 b g Dowsing (USA) 7f **(61)** - Gwiffina (Welsh Saint) 7.6f **(64)**
Form - 1000111

Record	**1999 -**	1st:4	2nd:0	3rd:0	Ran:7
	Pre1999 -	1st:13	2nd:4	3rd:3	Ran:48

Win Prizemoney £202,823 *Total Prizemoney* £236,469

Wins								
* **1999**	Spt	Leopar	(SFT)	G3	5f		113+	<
* **1999**	Jly	Cheste	(G-F)	L	6.1f		98	
* **1999**	Jly	Cheste	(G-F)	L	5.1f		105	
* **1999**	Mar	Doncas	(G-S)	L	6f		113	
* 1998	Spt	Leopar	(SFT)	G3	5f		110+	
* 1998	Jly	Cheste	(G-F)	L	5.1f		110	
* 1998	Apr	Newmar	(G-S)	L	6f		110	
* 1997	Spt	Ascot	(G-F)	H	5f	105	108	
* 1997	Jly	Cheste	(G-F)		5.1f		100	
* 1997	Jun	York	(G-S)	H	6f	95	98	
* 1997	May	Haydoc	(G-S)	H	5f	88	94	
1996	Jly	Newmar	(G-F)	H	5f	88	91	
1995	Jly	Doncas	(FRM)	H	6f	72	82	
1995	Jly	Sandow	(G-F)	H	5f	72	75+	
1995	Jly	Sandow	(GD)	H	5f	64	67	
1995	Jun	Ayr	(FRM)	H	5f	61	56	

1999 Turf 4-7: (5f 2-4, 6f 2-3) (gd 2-2, g-f 1-3, frm 1-2)
Group-class gelding, effective 5 to 6f, best at 5f, acts on sft to frm, best on gd, and excels at Leopardstown and Chester. Turf high 113 - 1st of 12 giving 4lb to Timote (11 Spt Leopardstown RF 4313a) - also 1st of 8 from Yorkies Boy (27 Mar Doncaster RF 0486). A credit to his connections, he looked better than ever at seven, winning three Listed races and the Group 3 Stillorgan Park Hotel Flying Five at Leopardstown in September. Effective at five or six furlongs, he is almost unbeatable at Chester. Acts on any ground and has a sharp turn-of-foot that shows no sign of blunting with age.
**E J Alston [11-27] Philip Davies (from Mrs A M Naughton [5-25] Oct 1996).*

TEDDY BOY BHB 28f **RR 32f** 3484[6]
3 b g Midyan (USA) 9.9f **(64)** - Likeable Lady (Piaffer (USA))
Form - 7446

Record	**1999 -**	1st:0	2nd:0	3rd:0	Ran:4

Win Prizemoney £0 *Total Prizemoney* £377
1999 Turf 0-4: (7f, 9f, 10f, 12f) (gd, g-f, frm 2)
Light-framed, very moderate gelding, has worn blinkers. Turf high 32. **M Madgwick [0-4] P Trant.*

TE-DEUM (IRE) BHB 67f **RR 62f** 5062[7]
2 ch c Ridgewood Ben - Tabessa (USA) (Shahrastani (USA)) 8.8f **(72)**
Form - 837

Record	**1999 -**	1st:0	2nd:0	3rd:1	Ran:3

Win Prizemoney £0 *Total Prizemoney* £466
1999 Turf 0-3: (7f, 8f 2) (g-s, gd 2)
Currently average colt. Turf high 62 (began Aug).
**J C Fox [0-3] John Homer Racing.*

TEEN IDOL (IRE) BHB 25f **RR 37df** 3484[8]
3 ch f Red Sunset 9f **(57)** - Truly Flattering (Hard Fought) 8.8f **(62)**
Form - 0000508

Record	**1999 -**	1st:0	2nd:0	3rd:0	Ran:7
	Pre1999 -	1st:0	2nd:0	3rd:0	Ran:4

1999 Turf 0-6: (7f, 10f, 12f 3, 14f) (gd, g-f, frm 3, hrd) 1999 AW 0-1: (13f) (Equi)
Neat, very moderate filly. Turf high 49. Inconsistent.
**J J Bridger [0-11] Miss Sarah Jones.*

TEEPLOY GIRL BHB 28f32a **RR 32a** 4729[13]
4 b f Deploy 11.4f **(67)** - Intoxication (Great Nephew) 9.9f **(64)**
Form - 0

Record	**1999 -**	1st:0	2nd:0	3rd:0	Ran:1
	Pre1999 -	1st:0	2nd:0	3rd:1	Ran:5

Win Prizemoney £0 *Total Prizemoney* £273
1999 Turf 0-1: (8f) (g-s)
Leggy, very poor filly, has worn blinkers.
**J P Smith [0-1] The Haymakers (from N P Littmoden [0-5] Mar 1998).*

TEE TEE TOO (IRE) BHB 23f35a **RR 35a** 2691[8]
7 ch g Hatim (USA) 7.8f **(56)** - Scottish Welcome (Be My Guest (USA)) 9.3f **(67)**
Form - 8

Record	**1999 -**	1st:0	2nd:0	3rd:0	Ran:1
	Pre1999 -	1st:1	2nd:5	3rd:2	Ran:31

Win Prizemoney £2,963 *Total Prizemoney* £8,630
1999 AW 0-1: (9f) (Fibr)
Very poor gelding, has worn blinkers.
**C F C Jackson [0-11] Stuart Bruce (from A W Carroll [0-3] Jan 1997).*

TEGGIANO (IRE) BHB 100f **RR 96+f** 4565[1]
2 b f Mujtahid (USA) 7.4f **(69)** - Tegwen (USA) **(81df)** (Nijinsky (CAN)) 10.3f **(77)**
Form - 4111

Record	**1999 -**	1st:3	2nd:0	3rd:0	Ran:4

Win Prizemoney £140,520 *Total Prizemoney* £140,877

Wins							
* **1999**	Spt	Ascot	(HVY)	G1	8f	96+	<
* **1999**	Spt	Doncas	(G-F)	G3	8f	95+	
* **1999**	Aug	Newbur	(GD)		6f	87+	

1999 Turf 3-4: (6f 1-1, 7f, 8f 2-2) (sft 1-1, g-f 2-2, frm)
Very useful filly. Turf high 96 (began Jly) - 1st of 6 from Britannia (26 Spt Ascot RF 4565) - also 1st of 12 from Everlasting Love (9 Spt Doncaster RF 4236). A leggy individual with scope, she routed the opposition in the May Hill Stakes and underlined her Classic claims when battling through heavy ground to land the Group One Fillies' Mile. Whether she possesses sufficient speed to land the 1,000 Guineas is open to question, but she should hold her own in top-class company next term, when she will race for Godolphin.
**C E Brittain [3-4] Abdullah Saeed Bul Hab.*

TEGYRA (IRE) BHB 58f **RR 60f** 5133[19]
3 ch f Trempolino (USA) 11.9f **(77)** - Tegwen (USA) **(81df)** (Nijinsky (CAN)) 10.3f **(77)**
Form - 515570

Record	**1999 -**	1st:1	2nd:0	3rd:0	Ran:6
	Pre1999 -	1st:0	2nd:0	3rd:1	Ran:2

Win Prizemoney £3,664 *Total Prizemoney* £4,219

Wins							
* **1999**	Jun	Yarmou	(G-F)		14.1f	68	<

1999 Turf 1-6: (12f 2, 14f 1-2, 15f, 16f) (gd 3, g-f 1-1, frm 2)
Average filly, effective 8 to 14f, acts on g-f to frm, prefers left handed tracks. Turf high 68 - 1st of 5 getting 5lb from Praslin Island (21 Jun Yarmouth RF 2184). Consistent.
**M A Jarvis [1-8] Abdullah Saeed Bul Hab.*

TELECASTER (IRE) BHB 40f **RR 35f** 5113[15]
3 ch g Indian Ridge 7.6f **(74)** - Monashee (USA) (Sovereign Dancer (USA)) 11.2f **(68)**
Form - 000

Record	**1999 -**	1st:0	2nd:0	3rd:0	Ran:3

1999 Turf 0-2: (6f, 8f) (gd 2) 1999 AW 0-1: (8f) (Fibr)
Lengthy, currently very moderate gelding. Turf high 35.
**C R Egerton [0-3] Casting Partners B.*

TELLION BHB 48f59a **RR 30f 59a** 4630[9]
5 b g Mystiko (USA) 7.7f **(59)** - Salchow (Niniski (USA)) 10.6f **(65)**
Form - 00
Record 1999 - 1st:0 2nd:0 3rd:0 Ran:2
Pre1999 - 1st:0 2nd:0 3rd:2 Ran:11
Win Prizemoney £0 *Total Prizemoney* £1,562
1999 Turf 0-2: (12f, 14f) (sft, g-s)
Average gelding, effective 12f, acts on gd, has worn blinkers. Turf high 30. Becoming disappointing.
**J R Jenkins [0-11] Mrs Wendy Jenkins (from Major W R Hern [0-7] Oct 1997).*

TEMERAIRE (USA) BHB 83f82a **RR 85f 82a** 4685[16]
4 b g Dayjur (USA) 6.8f **(79)** - Key Dancer (USA) (Nijinsky (CAN)) 10.3f **(77)**
Form - 76020000085210
Record 1999 - 1st:1 2nd:2 3rd:0 Ran:13
Pre1999 - 1st:2 2nd:1 3rd:0 Ran:7
Win Prizemoney £18,459 *Total Prizemoney* £24,466
Wins * 1999 Spt Newbur (G-F) H 7.3f 78 85
1998 Jly Lingfi (G-F) 7.6f 93 <
1998 Jun Windso (G-F) 8.3f 84+
1999 Turf 1-12: (6f 2, 7f 1-9, 8f) (gd 4, g-f 2, frm 1-6) 1999 AW 0-1: (9f) (Fibr)
Well made, useful gelding, effective 7 to 8f, best at 7f, acts on gd to frm, best on frm, has worn blinkers. Turf high 90 - 2nd of 19 to Showboat (14 Apr Newmarket 7f gd RF 0692) - also 1st of 16 getting 10lb from Adjutant (17 Spt Newbury RF 4386). A winner twice on fast ground in '98, his form since then has been very patchy. He had been out of sorts until getting back on top of things in September when victorious at Newbury. He definitely needs fast ground.
**D J S Cosgrove [1-5] P M Mooney (from R Ingram [0-11] Jly 1999).*

TEMESIDE TINA BHB 43f **RR 38f** 5068[6]
3 ch f Tina's Pet 7.4f **(56)** - Expletive (Shiny Tenth) 9.2f **(56)**
Form - 7606
Record 1999 - 1st:0 2nd:0 3rd:0 Ran:4
1999 Turf 0-4: (7f, 8f 2, 9f) (gd 2, g-f, frm)
Unfurnished, very moderate filly. Turf high 38 (began Aug).
**P D Evans [0-4] H M Thursfield.*

TEMIRKANOV RR 96f 4663a[8]
4 f
Form - 8
1999 Turf 0-1: (12f) (sft)
Currently very useful. **A M Savujev in SLO [0-1].*

TEMPERATE BHB 25f **RR 31f** 3351[13]
3 ch g Librate 10.4f **(37)** - Miss Moody (Jalmood (USA)) 10.1f **(52)**
Form - 600
Record 1999 - 1st:0 2nd:0 3rd:0 Ran:3
Pre1999 - 1st:0 2nd:0 3rd:0 Ran:2
1999 Turf 0-3: (7f 2, 8f) (g-f, frm 2)
Light-framed, very moderate gelding, has worn blinkers. Turf high 31 (began Jly). **J M Bradley [0-5] J Smith.*

TEMPLE WAY BHB 75f **RR 76f** 4893[11]
3 b g Shirley Heights 12.1f **(76)** - Abbey Strand (USA) (Shadeed (USA)) 8.2f **(70)**
Form - 034415420
Record 1999 - 1st:1 2nd:1 3rd:1 Ran:9
Win Prizemoney £3,798 *Total Prizemoney* £7,034
Wins * 1999 Jly Chepst (G-F) H 16.2f 69 75 <
1999 Turf 1-9: (10f, 12f 2, 14f, 15f, 16f 1-3, 17f) (gd 3, g-f 2, frm 1-4)
Workmanlike, above-average gelding, effective 14 to 17f, best at 16f, acts on gd to frm, best on g-f, often wears blinkers (extremely effectively). Turf high 76 - 2nd of 6 getting 22lb from Star Rage (11 Spt Goodwood 16f g-f RF 4273) - also 1st of 6 giving 9lb to Light On The Waves (23 Jly Chepstow RF 3058). Consistent.
**R Charlton [1-9] The Queen.*

TEMPRAMENTAL (IRE) BHB 45f44a **RR 44f 44a** 5151[8]
3 ch f Midhish - Musical Horn (Music Boy) 6.8f **(57)**
Form - 05073408
Record 1999 - 1st:0 2nd:0 3rd:1 Ran:8
Pre1999 - 1st:1 2nd:0 3rd:1 Ran:11
Win Prizemoney £3,257 *Total Prizemoney* £4,448
Wins * 1998 Aug Chepst (G-F) H 5.1f 54 60 <
1999 Turf 0-7: (5f 2, 6f 2, 7f 2, 8f) (gd 2, g-f 2, frm 3) 1999 AW 0-1: (6f) (Equi)
Strong, moderate filly, effective 5f, acts on gd, has worn blinkers (effectively). Turf high 44. **D HaydnJones [1-19] Hugh O'Donnell.*

TEMPUS FUGIT BHB 49f43a **RR 63f 43a** 157[12]
4 ch f Timeless Times (USA) 6.1f **(56)** - Kabella (Kabour)
Form - 00
Record 1999 - 1st:0 2nd:0 3rd:0 Ran:1
Pre1999 - 1st:1 2nd:2 3rd:1 Ran:11
Win Prizemoney £3,148 *Total Prizemoney* £5,523
Wins * 1997 Jun Nottin (GD) 5.1f 77 <
1999 AW 0-1: (7f) (Fibr)
Scopey, average filly. Inconsistent. **B R Millman [1-12] The Keepers.*

TENBY HEIGHTS (IRE) BHB 34f **RR 19f** 1652[13]
3 b g Tenby 10.4f **(76)** - Alpine Spring (Head for Heights) 9.6f **(55)**
Form - 8700
Record 1999 - 1st:0 2nd:0 3rd:0 Ran:4
Pre1999 - 1st:0 2nd:0 3rd:0 Ran:6
Win Prizemoney £0 *Total Prizemoney* £483
1999 Turf 0-4: (8f, 10f, 12f, 14f) (sft, gd, g-f, frm)
Scopey, poor gelding. Turf high 11. Becoming disappointing.
**R Hollinshead [0-10] J D Graham.*

TENDOR (FR) RR 92f 1719a[8]
3 c
Form - 568
1999 Turf 0-2: (8f, 12f) (sft, g-f)
Useful colt. Turf high 92.
**P Guarsegnati in ITY [0-1] (from A Tortorella in ITY [0-3] Apr 1999).*

TEN KINGDOMS (USA) BHB 92f **RR 91f** 4267[16]
3 b c Mr Prospector (USA) 8.6f **(88)** - Chinese Empress (USA) (Nijinsky (CAN)) 10.3f **(77)**
Form - 3031180
Record 1999 - 1st:2 2nd:0 3rd:2 Ran:7
Pre1999 - 1st:0 2nd:0 3rd:0 Ran:2
Win Prizemoney £11,288 *Total Prizemoney* £12,424
Wins * 1999 Jly Haydoc (FRM) H 11.9f 86 91+ <
*** 1999** Jun Doncas (G-F) 10.3f 71
1999 Turf 2-7: (8f 2, 9f, 10f 1-3, 12f 1-1) (hvy, gd 2, g-f 1-1, frm 1-3)
Tall, useful colt, effective 12f, acts on frm. Turf high 91 - 1st of 7 giving 4lb to Summer Splendour (11 Jly Haydock RF 2739). Inconsistent. Showed progressive form when allowed to make the running, but was well beaten in a French listed race. He is something of a character. **J H M Gosden [2-9] Sheikh Mohammed.*

TENNESSEE (IRE) RR 74f 4122[4]
2 b c Blues Traveller (IRE) - Valiant Friend (USA) (Shahrastani (USA)) 8.8f **(72)**
Form - 534
Record 1999 - 1st:0 2nd:0 3rd:1 Ran:3
Win Prizemoney £0 *Total Prizemoney* £545
1999 Turf 0-3: (7f 2, 8f) (g-f 3)
Currently above-average colt. Turf high 74 (began Jly).
**S P C Woods [0-3] B Allen/R Hine/R Dawson/A Duke.*

TENOR BELL (IRE) BHB 56f **RR 59f** 5152[11]
3 b g Tenby 10.4f **(76)** - Top Bloom (Thatch (USA)) 9.8f **(62)**
Form - 00
Record 1999 - 1st:0 2nd:0 3rd:0 Ran:2
Pre1999 - 1st:0 2nd:0 3rd:0 Ran:2
1999 Turf 0-2: (10f, 14f) (gd, frm)
Scopey, fair gelding. Turf high 57.
**M R Bosley [0-3] Mrs Jean O'Connor (from L M Cumani [0-3] Apr 1999).*

TEN PAST SIX BHB 52f60a **RR 54f 60a** 1276[14]
7 ch g Kris 10f **(75)** - Tashinsky (USA) (Nijinsky (CAN)) 10.3f **(77)**

Form - 50
Record 1999 - 1st:0 2nd:0 3rd:0 Ran:2
Pre1999 - 1st:5 2nd:7 3rd:0 Ran:33
Win Prizemoney £13,139 *Total Prizemoney* £24,983

Wins							
* 1998	Aug Carlis	(G-S)	C	12f	57		
* 1998	Jun Hamilt	(G-S)	C	11.1f	56		
* 1998	*May Southw*	*(STD)*	*C*	*11f*	*64*		
* 1997	Apr Ripon	(GD)	S	10f	59		
1995	May Haydoc	(G-F)		7.1f	76	<	

1999 Turf 0-2: (12f 2) (g-f, frm)
Average gelding, effective 9 to 12f, best at 12f, acts on gd to frm - acts on Fibr, has worn blinkers (very effectively), prefers tight tracks. Turf high 54.
**Martyn Wane [4-39] James S Kennerley and Miss Jenny Hall (from B W Hills [1-6] Spt 1995).*

TENSILE (IRE) BHB 84f RR 79f 5028^{11}

4 b g Tenby 10.4f **(76)** - Bonnie Isle (Pitcairn) 9.5f **(60)**
Form - 02530
Record 1999 - 1st:0 2nd:1 3rd:1 Ran:5
Pre1999 - 1st:1 2nd:2 3rd:0 Ran:11
Win Prizemoney £3,938 *Total Prizemoney* £12,550
Wins 1998 Apr Beverl (SFT) H 9.9f 77 87 <
1999 Turf 0-5: (12f 2, 14f 2, 16f) (g-s 2, gd, g-f, frm)
Well made, above-average gelding, effective 10 to 14f, best at 14f, acts on g-s to g-f, best on g-s, prefers tight tracks. Turf high 86 - 2nd of 5 getting 4lb from Pairumani Star (11 Jun York 14f g-s RF 1935). Consistent. A fair handicapper for Luca Cumani in '98, he ran creditably last season, but has shown a marked tendency to hang and also looks pretty one-paced.
**J R Fanshawe [0-5] Mrs V Shelton (from L M Cumani [1-11] Oct 1998).*

TEODORA (IRE) BHB 96f RR 90f 4595^{3}

2 b f Fairy King (USA) 7.7f **(75)** - Pinta (IRE) (Ahonoora) 8.1f **(73)**
Form - 1453
Record 1999 - 1st:1 2nd:0 3rd:1 Ran:4
Win Prizemoney £3,668 *Total Prizemoney* £36,955
Wins * 1999 Jly Windso (G-F) 6f 79t <
1999 Turf 1-4: (6f 1-3, 7f) (gd, g-f, frm 1-2)
Useful filly. Turf high 90 (began Jly) - 3rd of 17 getting 5lb from Inchlonaig (28 Spt Newmarket 7f g-f RF 4595). She showed a nice turn of foot to win on her Windsor debut, but looked to need further than six furlongs when fourth in the Princess Margaret, a view confirmed when she was staying on over seven on her final run.
**S Dow [1-4] G Steinberg.*

TEOFILIO (IRE) BHB 74f62a RR 78f 62a 3956^{17}

5 ch h Night Shift (USA) 8.1f **(73)** - Rivoltade (USA) (Sir Ivor) 10.2f **(70)**
Form - 50042152113260
Record 1999 - 1st:3 2nd:3 3rd:1 Ran:13
Pre1999 - 1st:1 2nd:2 3rd:1 Ran:12
Win Prizemoney £26,725 *Total Prizemoney* £41,048

Wins							
*** 1999**	Jun Newmar	(G-F)	H	7f	64	72	
*** 1999**	Jun Sandow	(GD)	H	7.1f	64	75	<
*** 1999**	*Feb Lingfi*	*(STD)*		*8f*		*59*	
1997	Apr Beverl	(G-F)		8.5f		74	

1999 Turf 2-8: (6f, 7f 2-6, 8f) (gd 2, g-f 1-3, frm 1-3) 1999 AW 1-5: (6f, 7f, 8f 1-2, 10f) (Equi 1-5)
Above-average colt, effective 7f, acts on gd to frm, has worn blinkers (extremely effectively). Turf high 78 - 3rd of 19 getting 18lb from Grangeville (8 Jly Newmarket 7f frm RF 2644) - also 1st of 13 getting 22lb from Grangeville (12 Jun Sandown RF 1959). AW high 59. Consistent. A winner on Equitrack earlier in the year, his victory at Sandown in June over Grangeville indicated his well-being, and he subsequently scored at Newmarket over the same seven-furlong trip. Best when able to be covered up and produced late, he just failed to peg back Grangeville in the Bunbury Cup.
**A J McNae [3-19] The Iona Stud (from D R Loder [1-6] Jun 1997).*

TEREK (GER) RR 108f $4775a^{1}$

3 gr c Irish River (FR) 9f **(77)** - Turbaine (USA) (Trempolino (USA)) 12f **(71)**
Form - 1
1999 Turf 1-1: (10f 1-1) (g-s 1-1)
Currently Pattern-class colt. (1st run) - 1st of 8 getting 7lb from Kalatos (3 Oct Hoppegarten RF 4775a).
**P Schiergen in GER [1-1] Gestut Schlenderhan.*

TERM OF ENDEARMENT BHB 55f RR 60f 5052^{12}

2 b f First Trump - Twilight Secret (Vaigly Great) 7f **(58)**
Form - 5144600060
Record 1999 - 1st:1 2nd:0 3rd:0 Ran:10
Win Prizemoney £2,850 *Total Prizemoney* £3,786
Wins 1999 Jun Bath (GD) 5.1f 74 <
1999 Turf 1-10: (5f 1-1, 6f 5, 7f 3, 8f) (gd 4, g-f 1-3, frm 3)
Average filly, effective 5 to 6f, acts on g-f to frm. Turf high 74 - 1st of 19 giving 2lb to Blue Velvet (12 Jun Bath RF 1942).
**J Pearce [0-5] Saracen Racing (from M R Channon [1-5] Aug 1999).*

TERRA NOVA BHB 72f RR 75f 4821^{6}

2 ch f Polar Falcon (USA) 9f **(74)** - Tarsa (Ballad Rock) 7.8f **(63)**
Form - 425246
Record 1999 - 1st:0 2nd:2 3rd:0 Ran:6
Win Prizemoney £0 *Total Prizemoney* £3,655
1999 Turf 0-6: (6f 3, 7f 3) (g-s, g-f 3, frm 2)
Above-average filly, effective 7f, acts on frm. Turf high 75.
**R W Armstrong [0-6] P J Vela.*

TERRAZZO (USA) BHB 59f57a RR 58f 57a 1689^{4}

4 b c Nureyev (USA) 8.4f **(84)** - Diese (USA) (Diesis) 9.3f **(69)**
Form - 235514
Record 1999 - 1st:1 2nd:1 3rd:1 Ran:6
Win Prizemoney £2,598 *Total Prizemoney* £4,040
Wins * 1999 May Mussel (FRM) H 9f 56 58 <
1999 Turf 1-3: (9f 1-1, 10f, 12f) (g-f 1-2, frm) 1999 AW 0-3: (8f, 9f, 12f) (Fibr 3)
Fair colt, effective 9 to 12f, acts on g-f to frm - acts on Fibr. Turf high 58 - 4th of 6 giving 5lb to Bold Amusement (2 Jun Newcastle 10f frm RF 1689) - also 1st of 15 getting 2lb from Arc (22 May Musselburgh RF 1410). AW high 57 (1st run) - 2nd of 10 getting 2lb from Robellita (8 Mar Southwell 12f Fibr RF 0413).
**J G FitzGerald [1-8] & Mrs Raymond Anderson Green.*

TERROIR (IRE) RR 100f $4512a^{2}$

4 b c Fairy King (USA) 7.7f **(75)** - Terracotta Hut (Habitat) 9.4f **(70)**
Form - 2
1999 Turf 0-1: (6f) (sft)
Currently very useful colt, always wears blinkers. (1st run) - 2nd of 11 giving 6lb to Seltitude (17 Spt Chantilly 6f sft RF 4512a).
**Mlle I Turc in FR [0-1].*

TERTIUM (IRE) BHB 90f69a RR 92f 69a 999^{1}

7 b g Nordico (USA) 8.2f **(59)** - Nouniya (Vayrann) 9.7f **(74)**
Form - 8841
Record 1999 - 1st:1 2nd:0 3rd:0 Ran:4
Pre1999 - 1st:4 2nd:8 3rd:4 Ran:58
Win Prizemoney £88,416 *Total Prizemoney* £144,840

Wins							
*** 1999**	May Kempto	(G-F)	H	8f	86	92	<
***** 1998	Aug Newmar	(G-F)	H	7f	79	88	
***** 1998	May Kempto	(GD)	H	8f	71	79	
1996	May Beverl	(G-F)	H	8.5f	77	83	
1995	May Kempto	(G-F)		8f		82+	

1999 Turf 1-3: (7f, 8f 1-2) (gd 2, frm 1-1) 1999 AW 0-1: (7f) (Fibr)
Useful gelding, effective 7 to 8f, best at 7f, acts on gd to hrd. Turf high 92 - 1st of 15 getting 12lb from Sunstreak (3 May Kempton RF 0999). Inconsistent. He was ridden to perfection to win the Jubilee Handicap for the second successive year, but was not seen again. Has a turn of foot, but also has wind problems and is often tongue-tied.
**N P Littmoden [3-24] Mrs Linda Miller (from Martyn Wane [1-32] Oct 1997).*

TERTULLIAN (USA) RR 115f $5206a^{1}$

4 ch c Miswaki (USA) 8.1f **(81)** - Turbaine (USA) (Trempolino (USA)) 12f **(71)**
Form - 31321
1999 Turf 2-5: (6f, 7f 2-3, 12f) (sft, g-s 1-1, gd 1-3)
High-class colt, effective 6 to 9f, best at 7f, acts on sft to gd, does well at San Siro. Turf high 115 (began Jly) - 1st of 12 giving 5lb to Onice Nero (31 Oct San Siro RF 5206a) - also 1st of 9 from Tomba (24 Jly Hoppegarten RF 3229a). A useful German-trained performer at between six and seven furlongs, he performed well at Group level on the continent last season, winning Group Threes at Hoppegarten and San Siro.
**P Schiergen in GER [3-7] Gestut Schlenderhan.*

TESS BHB 45f63a **RR 18f 63a** 3351[11]
3 b f Emarati (USA) 6.6f **(63)** - Everdene (Bustino) 10.4f **(64)**
Form - 253500
Record 1999 - 1st:0 2nd:1 3rd:1 Ran:6
Pre1999 - 1st:0 2nd:0 3rd:0 Ran:3
Win Prizemoney £0 *Total Prizemoney* £901
1999 Turf 0-4: (7f 3, 8f) (gd, g-f, frm 2) 1999 AW 0-2: (7f, 8f) (Fibr 2)
Scopey, average filly, effective 7f, - acts on Fibr. Turf high 49. AW high 65 (1st run) - 2nd of 10 getting 5lb from Cumbrian Blue (6 Apr Southwell 7f Fibr RF 0600). Becoming disappointing.
**G F H Charles-Jones [0-1] S P Tindall (from B W Hills [0-8] Jly 1999).*

TESSARA BHB 48f52a **RR 33f 52a** 2805[6]
4 ch f Kasakov - Sum Music (Music Boy) 6.8f **(57)**
Form - 86006
Record 1999 - 1st:0 2nd:0 3rd:0 Ran:5
Pre1999 - 1st:0 2nd:0 3rd:0 Ran:1
1999 Turf 0-3: (7f, 8f, 12f) (gd 2, frm) 1999 AW 0-2: (7f, 8f) (Fibr 2)
Lengthy, very moderate filly. Turf high 52. AW high 8.
**C W Thornton [0-6] Elephant & Castle Partnership-Wakefield.*

TESS TOO RR 66f 3970[P]
3 b f Lugana Beach 7f **(63)** - Ankara's Princess (USA) (Ankara (USA)) 8f **(71)**
Form - 2P
Record 1999 - 1st:0 2nd:1 3rd:0 Ran:2
Win Prizemoney £0 *Total Prizemoney* £670
1999 Turf 0-2: (5f, 6f) (g-f 2)
Scopey, average filly. Turf high 66 (began Aug). (DEAD)
**B A McMahon [0-2] J D Graham.*

TEST THE WATER (IRE) BHB 63f64a **RR 60f 64a** 3240[2]
5 ch h Maelstrom Lake 8.8f **(53)** - Baliana (CAN) (Riverman (USA)) 9.1f **(76)**
Form - 850062
Record 1999 - 1st:0 2nd:1 3rd:0 Ran:6
Pre1999 - 1st:2 2nd:4 3rd:3 Ran:22
Win Prizemoney £11,620 *Total Prizemoney* £19,966
Wins * 1998 Jly Sandow (G-F) C 8.1f 74
* 1996 Oct Ascot (GD) H 7f 85 90 <
1999 Turf 0-5: (7f, 8f 4) (sft, g-s, gd, frm 2) 1999 AW 0-1: (8f) (Fibr)
Average colt, effective 8f, acts on sft to frm, has worn blinkers. Turf high 65. Has plenty of ability, but is by no means consistent.
**R Hannon [2-28] Peter Crane.*

TETHKAR BHB 60f **RR 59f** 4213[12]
3 b f Machiavellian (USA) 9.8f **(83)** - Munnaya (USA) **(99f)** (Nijinsky (CAN)) 10.3f **(77)**
Form - 0440
Record 1999 - 1st:0 2nd:0 3rd:0 Ran:4
Pre1999 - 1st:0 2nd:0 3rd:0 Ran:2
Win Prizemoney £0 *Total Prizemoney* £775
1999 Turf 0-4: (7f, 8f 2, 11f) (gd, g-f 2, frm)
Neat, fair filly, has worn blinkers. Turf high 59.
**E A L Dunlop [0-4] Maktoum Al Maktoum (from D R Loder [0-2] Spt 1998).*

TEYAAR BHB 74f **RR 70f** 3465[3]
3 b g Polar Falcon (USA) 9f **(74)** - Music in My Life (IRE) (Law Society (USA)) 9.9f **(70)**
Form - 502803
Record 1999 - 1st:0 2nd:1 3rd:1 Ran:6
Win Prizemoney £0 *Total Prizemoney* £1,968
1999 Turf 0-6: (6f, 7f 3, 8f 2) (g-s, gd, g-f 2, frm, hrd)
Workmanlike, above-average gelding. Turf high 83.
**D Shaw [0-1] Justin Aaron (from J L Dunlop [0-5] Jun 1999).*

T G'S GIRL BHB 62f **RR 52f** 2568[9]
2 gr f Selkirk (USA) 7.9f **(76)** - River's Rising (FR) (Mendez (FR))
Form - 740
Record 1999 - 1st:0 2nd:0 3rd:0 Ran:3
Win Prizemoney £0 *Total Prizemoney* £282
1999 Turf 0-3: (5f 2, 6f) (g-f, frm 2)
Currently fair filly. Turf high 52.
**R Hannon [0-3] Mrs Caroline Parker.*

THAAYER BHB 55f59a **RR 33f 59a** 2082[3]
4 b g Wolfhound (USA) 7.3f **(71)** - Hamaya (USA) (Mr Prospector (USA)) 8.8f **(78)**
Form - 635120083
Record 1999 - 1st:1 2nd:1 3rd:1 Ran:6
Pre1999 - 1st:0 2nd:0 3rd:1 Ran:7
Win Prizemoney £2,274 *Total Prizemoney* £3,666
Wins * **1999** *Jan Southw (STD) 6f 61* <
1999 Turf 0-2: (6f 2) (g-f, frm) 1999 AW 1-4: (5f, 6f 1-3) (Fibr 1-4)
Scopey, fair gelding, effective 6f, - acts on Fibr, prefers left handed tracks, prefers tight tracks. Turf high 33. AW high 64 - 2nd of 10 getting 7lb from Euro Venture (12 Feb Southwell 6f Fibr RF 0277) - also 1st of 10 giving 3lb to Ambitious (29 Jan Southwell RF 0188).
**K Bell [1-12] Mrs Joyce Wood (from M P Tregoning [0-1] Apr 1998).*

THADY QUILL (USA) RR 93+f 2645[1]
2 ch c Nureyev (USA) 8.4f **(84)** - Alleged Devotion (USA) (Alleged (USA)) 10f **(76)**
Form - 11
1999 Turf 2-2: (7f 2-2) (gd 1-1, frm 1-1)
Currently useful colt. Turf high 93 (1st run) - 1st of 10 from It Happens Now (13 Jun Gowran Park RF 2035a) - also 1st of 5 getting 3lb from Full Flow (8 Jly Newmarket RF 2645). Ran a respectable race in the States after winning a Listed race at the Newmarket July meeting. **A P O'Brien in IRE [2-2] Mrs John Magnier.*

THAMES DANCER (USA) BHB 70f65a **RR 73f 65a** 2376[3]
3 ch c Green Dancer (USA) 11.9f **(77)** - Hata (FR) (Kaldoun (FR)) 10.3f **(68)**
Form - 6623
Record 1999 - 1st:0 2nd:1 3rd:1 Ran:4
Pre1999 - 1st:0 2nd:0 3rd:0 Ran:2
Win Prizemoney £0 *Total Prizemoney* £1,542
1999 Turf 0-3: (11f, 12f, 13f) (gd, g-f, frm) 1999 AW 0-1: (12f) (Fibr)
Workmanlike, above-average colt, effective 12f, acts on gd. Turf high 73. **K McAuliffe [0-6] J S Dunningham.*

THARI (USA) BHB 93f **RR 95f** 4833[6]
2 b br c Silver Hawk (USA) 11.2f **(85)** - Magic Slipper (Habitat) 9.4f **(70)**
Form - 2136
Record 1999 - 1st:1 2nd:1 3rd:1 Ran:4
Win Prizemoney £3,176 *Total Prizemoney* £6,505
Wins * **1999** Spt Chepst (GD) 7.1f 79+ <
1999 Turf 1-4: (7f 1-4) (sft, gd, frm 1-2)
Very useful colt. Turf high 95 (began Aug) - 3rd of 5 to Bogus Dreams (26 Spt Ascot 7f sft RF 4567). He proved a shade disappointing after winning his maiden and may not be particularly easy to place off his current mark. **P T Walwyn [1-4] Hamdan Al Maktoum.*

THATCHAM (IRE) BHB 50f60a **RR 53f 60a** 5103[20]
3 ch c Thatching 7.8f **(69)** - Calaloo Sioux (USA) (Our Native (USA)) 11.2f **(63)**
Form - 754800
Record 1999 - 1st:0 2nd:0 3rd:0 Ran:6
Win Prizemoney £0 *Total Prizemoney* £270
1999 Turf 0-5: (7f 3, 8f 2) (gd, g-f 3, frm) 1999 AW 0-1: (8f) (Equi)
Workmanlike, fair colt. Turf high 65.
**R W Armstrong [0-6] Mrs John Davall.*

THATCHED (IRE) BHB 45f **RR 44f** 3456[6]
9 b g Thatching 7.8f **(69)** - Shadia (USA) (Naskra (USA)) 8.8f **(69)**
Form - 508337246
Record 1999 - 1st:0 2nd:1 3rd:2 Ran:9
Pre1999 - 1st:10 2nd:6 3rd:9 Ran:87
Win Prizemoney £35,452 *Total Prizemoney* £52,659
Wins * 1998 May Redcar (G-F) H 9f 41 44
* 1997 Apr Carlis (GD) H 8f 51 56
* 1996 Oct Redcar (G-F) H 8f 48 52
* 1996 Spt Beverl (G-F) H 8.5f 47 43
* 1996 Jly Beverl (G-F) H 7.5f 43 46
* 1995 Aug Carlis (HRD) H 8f 50 64+ <
* 1995 Jly Mussel (G-F) H 8.1f 44 51
* 1995 Apr Newcas (G-F) H 8f 42 44
1999 Turf 0-9: (7f, 8f 5, 9f 3) (gd 2, g-f 2, frm 4, hrd)
Moderate gelding, effective 8 to 10f, best at 8f, acts on g-f to hrd, best on g-f, has worn blinkers, likes tight tracks, excels at

Beverley, likes Redcar. Turf high 44 - 4th of 13 getting 23lb from Kass Alhawa (27 Jly Beverley 8f frm RF 3162). Consistent.
**R E Barr [10-93] R E Barr (from C F Wall [0-9] Spt 1993).*

THATCHMASTER (IRE) BHB 66f RR 65f 4429[4]

8 b g Thatching 7.8f **(69)** - Key Maneuver (USA) (Key To Content (USA)) 8f **(54)**
Form - 0037144
Record 1999 - 1st:1 2nd:0 3rd:1 Ran:7
Pre1999 - 1st:5 2nd:4 3rd:3 Ran:35
Win Prizemoney £22,733 *Total Prizemoney* £29,925

Wins	* 1999	Aug	Goodwo (GD)	H	9f	63	65	
	* 1998	Jly	Windso (G-F)	H	11.6f	63	67	<
	* 1998	Jun	Windso (GD)	H	11.6f	60	62	
	* 1997	Aug	Goodwo (G-F)	CH	10f	59	67	<
	* 1996	Aug	Goodwo (G-F)	CH	10f	52	58	
	* 1996	Jly	Sandow (G-F)	SH	8.1f	46	51	

1999 Turf 1-7: (9f 1-2, 12f 5) (g-s, gd 1-2, g-f 2, frm 2)
Average gelding, effective 9 to 12f, best at 12f, acts on gd to frm, best on frm, has worn blinkers, likes tight tracks, excels at Windsor, does well at Ascot, likes Goodwood. Turf high 65 - 1st of 13 getting 11lb from Bold Oriental (28 Aug Goodwood RF 3959).
**C A Horgan [6-42] Mrs B Sumner.*

THATCHROYAL (IRE) BHB 58f54a RR 70f 54a 4863[5]

3 ch c Thatching 7.8f **(69)** - Wish You Were Here (USA) (Secretariat (USA)) 9f **(79)**
Form - 62534405
Record 1999 - 1st:0 2nd:1 3rd:1 Ran:8
Win Prizemoney £0 *Total Prizemoney* £1,623
1999 Turf 0-7: (8f, 10f, 11f 2, 12f 3) (g-s 2, gd, g-f, frm 3) 1999 AW 0-1: (15f) (Fibr)
Scopey, above-average colt, effective 10 to 12f, acts on g-s to g-f, has worn blinkers, prefers tight tracks. Turf high 72 - 2nd of 8 giving 5lb to My Lass (14 May Hamilton 12f g-s RF 1210).
**S P C Woods [0-8] G V Wright.*

THAT MAN AGAIN BHB 75f72a RR 73f 72a 4131[11]

7 ch g Prince Sabo 6.6f **(64)** - Milne's Way (The Noble Player (USA)) 6.5f **(67)**
Form - 06261146660
Record 1999 - 1st:2 2nd:1 3rd:0 Ran:11
Pre1999 - 1st:7 2nd:4 3rd:6 Ran:57
Win Prizemoney £47,963 *Total Prizemoney* £65,859

Wins	* 1999	Jly	Newmar (GD)	H	5f	68	79	
	* 1999	Jly	Sandow (GD)	H	5f	68	69	
	* 1998	Aug	Lingfi (G-F)	C	5f		65	
	* 1998	Jun	Folkes (G-F)	H	5f	71	77?	
	1995	Aug	Haydoc (G-F)	H	5f	94	96	<
	1995	Jly	Bath (FRM)	H	5.1f	90	92	
	1995	Jly	Sandow (GD)	H	5f	83	88	

1999 Turf 2-11: (5f 2-11) (gd 4, g-f, frm 2-5, hrd)
Above-average gelding, effective 5f, acts on g-f to frm - acts on Equi, often wears blinkers (effectively). Turf high 79 - 1st of 13 getting 7lb from Emperor Naheem (6 Jly Newmarket RF 2579). Consistent. He took advantage of the fall in the weights to score at Sandown in July. Despite incurring a penalty for that victory, he was given a very confident ride by Fallon when winning at the July Meeting.
**S C Williams [4-37] J T Duffy & R E Duffy (from G Lewis [5-31] Spt 1996).*

THATOLDBLACKMAGIC (IRE) BHB 40f35a RR 45f 35a 249[12]

4 b f Contract Law (USA) 8.9f **(54)** - Spinelle (Great Nephew) 9.9f **(64)**
Form - 0
Record 1999 - 1st:0 2nd:0 3rd:0 Ran:1
Pre1999 - 1st:0 2nd:0 3rd:1 Ran:4
Win Prizemoney £0 *Total Prizemoney* £302
1999 AW 0-1: (7f) (Fibr)
Moderate filly. **W Storey [0-5] C A Clark.*

THAT OLD FEELING (IRE) BHB 23f RR 20f 1206[9]

7 b g Waajib 8.9f **(67)** - Swift Reply (He Loves Me) 7.9f **(55)**
Form - 000
Record 1999 - 1st:0 2nd:0 3rd:0 Ran:3
Pre1999 - 1st:1 2nd:2 3rd:0 Ran:18
Win Prizemoney £3,863 *Total Prizemoney* £9,329
1999 Turf 0-3: (5f 2, 7f) (gd 3)
Moderate gelding, has worn blinkers. Turf high 20.
**G P Kelly [0-4] G P Kelly (from D W Chapman [0-8] Spt 1997).*

THATS ALL FOLKS BHB 75f RR 62f 4491[6]

2 b c Alhijaz 7.7f **(57)** - So it Goes (Free State) 8.7f **(61)**
Form - 06
Record 1999 - 1st:0 2nd:0 3rd:0 Ran:2
Win Prizemoney £0 *Total Prizemoney* £101
1999 Turf 0-2: (7f 2) (sft, gd)
Currently average colt. Turf high 62 (began Aug).
**P J Makin [0-2] Arron Banks.*

THATS LIFE BHB 59f72a RR 51f 72a 5167[8]

4 b g Mukaddamah (USA) 7.6f **(74)** - Run Faster (IRE) (Commanche Run) 8.5f **(58)**
Form - 3761365108
Record 1999 - 1st:2 2nd:0 3rd:1 Ran:7
Pre1999 - 1st:1 2nd:0 3rd:1 Ran:9
Win Prizemoney £6,941 *Total Prizemoney* £7,839

Wins	**1999**	*Jly*	*Lingfi (STD)*	*C*	*5f*		*71*	
	1999	*Feb*	*Lingfi (STD)*	*S*	*6f*		*71+*	
	1998	Jly	Folkes (G-F)		6f		74	<

1999 Turf 0-4: (5f 3, 7f) (g-s, gd, g-f, frm) 1999 AW 2-3: (5f 1-1, 6f 1-2) (Equi 2-2, Fibr)
Leggy, above-average gelding, effective 5 to 6f, best at 6f, acts on g-f - acts on AW, best on Equi, prefers left handed tracks, prefers tight tracks. Turf high 51. AW high 71 (1st run) - 1st of 6 from Pageboy (18 Feb Lingfield RF 0310) - also 1st of 8 getting 4lb from Vista Alegre (9 Jly Lingfield RF 2681).
**R Bastiman [0-2] Peter Beaton-Brown (from T G Mills [3-14] Jly 1999).*

THATS LOGIC (IRE) RR 89f 5090a[1]

5 b g Cyrano de Bergerac 7.3f **(58)** - Allberry (Alzao (USA)) 7.1f **(68)**
Form - 5246571
1999 Turf 1-7: (7f 2, 8f 1-4, 10f) (hvy 2, g-s 1-2, gd 3)
Useful gelding, effective 7 to 8f, best at 8f, acts on sft to gd, best on gd, has worn blinkers, excels at Leopardstown. Turf high 93 - 4th of 13 getting 7lb from Free To Speak (27 Aug Tralee 8f g-s RF 4058a) - also 1st of 6 from Cambodian (23 Oct Leopardstown RF 5090a). **D Hassett in IRE [5-29] D M Murphy.*

THE ANGEL GABRIEL BHB 42f RR 33f 2048[8]

4 ch c My Generation 6.5f **(68)** - Minsk **(30df)** (Kabour)
Form - 008
Record 1999 - 1st:0 2nd:0 3rd:0 Ran:3
Pre1999 - 1st:0 2nd:0 3rd:0 Ran:1
1999 Turf 0-3: (5f 2, 11f) (g-f 3)
Very moderate colt. Turf high 33.
**D A Nolan [0-4] Mrs J McFadyen-Murray.*

THE ARTFUL DODGER BHB 51f52a RR 49f 52a 4293[2]

4 b g Alhijaz 7.7f **(57)** - Madam Millie (Milford) 9f **(61)**
Form - 0302
Record 1999 - 1st:0 2nd:1 3rd:1 Ran:4
Pre1999 - 1st:0 2nd:0 3rd:1 Ran:9
Win Prizemoney £0 *Total Prizemoney* £1,701
1999 Turf 0-4: (7f 3, 10f) (g-f 3, frm)
Workmanlike, moderate gelding, effective 9f, acts on g-f. Turf high 49. **R J R Williams [0-13] Equinimity.*

THEATRELAND (USA) BHB 75f RR 68f 5059[5]

2 b c Dynaformer (USA) 12f **(82)** - Mime (Cure The Blues (USA)) 9.5f **(63)**
Form - 005
Record 1999 - 1st:0 2nd:0 3rd:0 Ran:3
1999 Turf 0-3: (7f 3) (g-s, gd 2)
Currently average colt. Turf high 68 (began Spt).
**Sir Michael Stoute [0-3] Highclere Thoroughbred Racing Ltd.*

THEATRE MAGIC BHB 29f72a RR 19f 72a 231[P]

6 b g Sayf El Arab (USA) 8.2f **(57)**-Miss Orient (Damister (USA)) 9f **(73)**
Form - 521343116P
Record 1999 - 1st:2 2nd:0 3rd:1 Ran:5
Pre1999 - 1st:5 2nd:8 3rd:7 Ran:56
Win Prizemoney £20,831 *Total Prizemoney* £31,397

Wins	* **1999**	*Jan*	*Southw (STD)*	*H*	*6f*	*63*	*73*	<

* **1999**	*Jan Southw (STD) H*		*7f*	*63*	*68*	
* 1998	Dec Southw (STD) H		6f	59	64	
* 1998	Jan Southw (STD) C		7f		63+	
* 1997	May Wolver (STD) H		7f	64	68	
* 1997	Apr Wolver (STD) H		7f	57	66	
1995	Nov Southw (STD) H		7f	55		

1999 AW 2-5: (6f 1-4, 7f 1-1) (Fibr 2-5)

Above-average gelding, effective 6 to 7f, best at 6f, - acted on Fibr, wore blinkers, favoured left handed tracks, favoured tight tracks. AW high 73 - 1st of 15 giving 12lb to Intiaash (18 Jan Southwell RF 0116) - also 1st of 11 getting 5lb from Godmersham Park (11 Jan Southwell RF 0072). He was an effective sort in handicap company on Fibresand, and though he won over six furlongs, was probably better over seven. Tragically had to be destroyed at Southwell in February. (DEAD).

**D Shaw [6-37] Green Diamond Racing (from S R Bowring [1-19] Dec 1996).*

THEATREWORLD (IRE) RR 107f 4476a[2]

7 b g Sadler's Wells (USA) 11.3f **(87)** - Chamonis (USA) (Affirmed (USA)) 9.3f **(79)**

Form - 141812

1999 Turf 3-6: (11f, 12f 2-3, 14f 1-2) (sft 1-1, g-s, gd 1-2, g-f 1-2)

Pattern-class gelding, effective 12 to 16f, best at 12f, acts on hvy to g-f, prefers right handed tracks. Turf high 107 - also 1st of 7 giving 12lb to Maid Of Killeen (7 Spt Galway RF 4299a). Consistent. Though much better known as a top-class hurdler, he is no mean performer on the Flat either and won three times in '99 including a Listed race. Admirably tough and a credit to his trainer.

**A P O'Brien in IRE [16-52] Mrs John Magnier (from Sir Michael Stoute [0-1] Spt 1994).*

THE BARGATE FOX BHB 47f RR 63f 4935[5]

3 b g Magic Ring (IRE) 6.5f **(64)** - Hithermoor Lass (Red Alert) 7.6f **(66)**

Form - 0705

Record 1999 - 1st:0 2nd:0 3rd:0 Ran:4

1999 Turf 0-2: (8f 2) (sft, gd) 1999 AW 0-2: (8f 2) (Fibr 2)

Strong, average gelding. Turf high 63 (began Aug). AW high 40 (began Spt). **D J G MurraySmith [0-4] Mrs Jill McNeill.*

THE BARNSLEY BELLE (IRE) BHB 32f37a RR 31f 37a 2083[6]

6 b m Distinctly North (USA) 7.4f **(63)** - La Tanque (USA) (Last Raise (USA)) 7f **(51)**

Form - 6771770656

Record	**1999** -	1st:1	2nd:0	3rd:0	Ran:8
	Pre1999 -	1st:2	2nd:5	3rd:4	Ran:41

Win Prizemoney £7,668 *Total Prizemoney* £13,280

Wins	* **1999**	*Feb Southw (STD) H*	*8f*	*36*	*39*	
	1997	*Apr Southw (STD)*	*7f*		*63*	<
	1996	*Nov Southw (STD) H*	*7f*	*47*	*49*	

1999 Turf 0-1: (10f) (gd) 1999 AW 1-7: (7f 2, 8f 1-4, 11f) (Fibr 1-7)

Very moderate mare, effective 8f, - acts on Fibr, likes left handed tracks. AW high 39.

**G Woodward [1-11] K Meynell (from J L Eyre [2-32] May 1998).*

THE BAT BHB 42f RR 31f 3145[10]

6 b h Chauve Souris - Jamra (Upper Case (USA)) 8.2f **(55)**

Form - 000

Record	**1999** -	1st:0	2nd:0	3rd:0	Ran:3
	Pre1999 -	1st:0	2nd:0	3rd:1	Ran:4

Win Prizemoney £0 *Total Prizemoney* £505

1999 Turf 0-3: (10f, 12f 2) (g-f 2, frm)

Very moderate horse. Turf high 31.

**Mark Campion [0-3] Bat Out Of Bells (from A P Jarvis [0-7] Spt 1998).*

THE BIZZ RR 1178[7]

6 b m Devon Missile - Kingmon's Girl (Saucy Kit) 6f **(43)**

Form - 7

Record 1999 - 1st:0 2nd:0 3rd:0 Ran:1

1999 Turf 0-1: (7f) (g-f)

Formerly very poor mare. **B A Pearce [0-1] J F Panvert.*

THE BLUE BRAZIL (IRE) BHB 23f RR 34df 4829[15]

3 b g Thatching 7.8f **(69)** - Approche (FR) (Sharpman) 11.3f **(66)**

Form - 3650800

Record 1999 - 1st:0 2nd:0 3rd:1 Ran:7

Win Prizemoney £0 *Total Prizemoney* £553

1999 Turf 0-7: (6f, 7f 2, 9f 2, 10f 2) (sft, gd 2, g-f, frm 3)

Lengthy, very moderate gelding, has worn blinkers. Turf high 52.

**Denys Smith [0-7] Holdforth Racing.*

THE BLUES ACADEMY (IRE) BHB 62f RR 64f 4400[4]

4 b g Royal Academy (USA) 7.8f **(77)** - She's the Tops (Shernazar) 10.2f **(73)**

Form - 240344

Record	**1999** -	1st:0	2nd:1	3rd:1	Ran:6
	Pre1999 -	1st:1	2nd:1	3rd:1	Ran:12

Win Prizemoney £3,533 *Total Prizemoney* £8,728

Wins * 1998 Jly Bath (GD) H 17.2f 67 71 <

1999 Turf 0-6: (16f 5, 17f) (gd, g-f, frm 3, hrd)

Workmanlike, average gelding, effective 15 to 17f, acts on gd to hrd, has worn blinkers. Turf high 67 (1st run) - 2nd of 14 giving 23lb to Happy Days (26 May Ripon 16f frm RF 1504).

**M A Buckley [1-15] C C Buckley (from M Johnston [0-3] Oct 1997).*

THE BOMBER LISTON (IRE) RR 98f 4314a[14]

3 b c Perugino (USA) - Berenice (ITY) 00

Form - 8725410040

1999 Turf 1-9: (6f 4, 7f 1-4, 8f) (g-s, gd 1-5, g-f 3)

Very useful colt, effective 6 to 7f, best at 7f, acts on hvy to hrd, best on gd, often wears blinkers. Turf high 98 - 4th of 16 giving 3lb to Oyster Catcher (21 Aug Fairyhouse 6f gd RF 3886a) - also 1st of 9 giving 3lb to Royal South (9 Jun Leopardstown RF 2022a). A tough handicapper, he seems best over six and seven furlongs and acts on any ground.

**J S Bolger in IRE [3-16] Sporting Quest Racing Club.*

THE BULL MACABE BHB 76f73a RR 73f 73a 5005[1]

2 ch c Efisio 7.7f **(69)** - Tranquillity **(70f)** (Night Shift (USA)) 7.2f **(69)**

Form - 601

Record 1999 - 1st:1 2nd:0 3rd:0 Ran:3

Win Prizemoney £4,240 *Total Prizemoney* £4,240

Wins * **1999** Oct Nottin (GD) 5.1f 73 <

1999 Turf 1-3: (5f 1-1, 6f 2) (gd 1-2, frm)

Currently above-average colt. Turf high 73 (began Spt) - 1st of 15 from Kind Emperor (21 Oct Nottingham RF 5005).

**R Hannon [1-3] M G White.*

THE BUTTERWICK KID BHB 75f70a RR 76f 70a 1044[15]

6 ch g Interrex (CAN) 7.7f **(51)** - Ville Air (Town Crier) 10.2f **(55)**

Form - 120

Record	**1999** -	1st:1	2nd:1	3rd:0	Ran:3
	Pre1999 -	1st:7	2nd:3	3rd:5	Ran:30

Win Prizemoney £32,746 *Total Prizemoney* £42,708

Wins	* **1999**	Mar Hamilt (HVY) H	11.1f	70	72	<
	* 1998	May Redcar (G-F) H	14.1f	62	66+	
	* 1998	*Jan Southw (STD) H*	*11f*	*59*	*60*	
	* 1997	May Mussel (G-S) H	12f	54	57+	
	* 1997	May Cheste (HVY) H	12.3f	52	59	
	* 1997	Apr Nottin (G-F) H	14.1f	45	49	
	* 1996	Spt Hamilt (GD) H	12.1f	44	45	
	* 1995	Jly Beverl (GD) C	5f		69	

1999 Turf 1-3: (11f 1-1, 13f, 19f) (hvy 1-2, g-f)

Above-average gelding, effective 11 to 14f, acts on hvy to g-f, best on hvy, has worn blinkers, favours tight tracks. Turf high 76 - 2nd of 17 giving 9lb to Ardleigh Charmer (10 Apr Hamilton 13f hvy RF 0638) - also 1st of 9 giving 16lb to Mr Fortywinks (29 Mar Hamilton RF 0503). **R A Fahey [10-44] Robert Chambers & Mrs M W Kenyon.*

THE CANNIE ROVER BHB 40f33a RR 46f 33a 585[18]

4 ch g Beveled (USA) 6.9f **(64)** - Sister Rosarii (USA) (Properantes (USA)) 8.3f **(51)**

Form - 0800

Record	**1999** -	1st:0	2nd:0	3rd:0	Ran:3
	Pre1999 -	1st:0	2nd:0	3rd:1	Ran:11

Win Prizemoney £0 *Total Prizemoney* £324

1999 Turf 0-1: (8f) (gd) 1999 AW 0-2: (8f, 11f) (Fibr 2)

Unfurnished, moderate gelding, has worn blinkers. AW high 6. Becoming disappointing. **M W Easterby [0-16] Mrs E Rhind.*

THE CASTIGATOR BHB 61f RR 55f 3491[4]

2 b c Reprimand 8.2f **(63)** - Summer Eve (Hotfoot) 10.5f **(59)**

Form - 784

Record 1999 - 1st:0 2nd:0 3rd:0 Ran:3
Win Prizemoney £0 *Total Prizemoney* £192
1999 Turf 0-3: (6f, 7f 2) (frm 3)
Currently fair colt. Turf high 55. **J J O'Neill [0-3] E A Brook.*

THE COME BACK KID BHB 66f **RR 69f** 5215[6]
2 b c Shareef Dancer (USA) 10.1f **(67)** - Clockwatch (USA) (Alleged (USA)) 10f **(76)**
Form - 806
Record 1999 - 1st:0 2nd:0 3rd:0 Ran:3
1999 Turf 0-3: (8f 3) (g-s, gd, g-f)
Currently average colt. Turf high 69 (began Spt).
**B W Hills [0-3] W J Gredley.*

THECOMEBACKKING BHB 47f40a **RR 55f 40a** 3080[11]
4 ch c Mystiko (USA) 7.7f **(59)** - Nitouche (Scottish Reel) 7f **(61)**
Form - 0
Record 1999 - 1st:0 2nd:0 3rd:0 Ran:1
Pre1999 - 1st:0 2nd:0 3rd:1 Ran:10
Win Prizemoney £0 *Total Prizemoney* £585
1999 AW 0-1: (8f) (Fibr)
Workmanlike, fair colt. Becoming disappointing.
**R Ford [0-1] Ms Lisa Halliday (from B P J Baugh [0-2] Feb 1998).*

THE COTTONWOOL KID BHB 15f34a **RR 34a** 3564[11]
7 b g Blakeney 11.9f **(53)** - Relatively Smart (Great Nephew) 9.9f **(64)**
Form - 06800000
Record 1999 - 1st:0 2nd:0 3rd:0 Ran:8
Pre1999 - 1st:0 2nd:0 3rd:2 Ran:11
Win Prizemoney £0 *Total Prizemoney* £629
1999 Turf 0-4: (12f 2, 14f, 16f) (g-f 4) 1999 AW 0-4: (8f, 11f 2, 12f) (Fibr 4)
Little account gelding, has worn blinkers. AW high 23.
**Mrs A M Naughton [0-9] Mrs S E Cooper (from Miss L C Siddall [0-1] Jly 1998).*

THE DEALER BHB 36f27a **RR 34f 27a** 3092[9]
4 b c No Big Deal - Not Alone (Pas de Seul) 9.1f **(67)**
Form - 00004800
Record 1999 - 1st:0 2nd:0 3rd:0 Ran:8
Pre1999 - 1st:0 2nd:0 3rd:0 Ran:5
1999 Turf 0-6: (5f, 7f 2, 8f 2, 10f) (gd, g-f, frm 4) 1999 AW 0-2: (8f, 10f) (Equi, Fibr)
Leggy, very moderate colt, effective 5f, acts on g-f, has worn blinkers, likes left handed tracks, likes tight tracks. Turf high 41. (began Jly). Becoming disappointing.
**M D I Usher [0-8] G A Summers (from J A R Toller [0-5] Oct 1998).*

THE DEPUTY (IRE) BHB 100f **RR 95f** 4208[3]
2 b c Petardia 8.2f **(58)** - Manfath (IRE) **(66df)** (Last Tycoon) 8.5f **(62)**
Form - 32313
Record 1999 - 1st:1 2nd:1 3rd:3 Ran:5
Win Prizemoney £3,615 *Total Prizemoney* £35,440
Wins * 1999 Spt Epsom (GD) 7f 81 <
1999 Turf 1-5: (6f 3, 7f 1-2) (gd 2, g-f 1-1, frm 2)
Very useful colt. Turf high 95 (began Jly) - 3rd of 21 to Sheer Hamas (8 Spt Doncaster 6f gd RF 4208). He was well supported when finishing fast to grab third spot in the £200,000 St Leger Yearling Stakes. Certain to improve on that form over seven furlongs or a mile, he is reportedly likely to continue his career in America. **J W Hills [1-5] Freddy Bienstock And Partners.*

THE DONK (IRE) BHB 44f45a **RR 9f 45a** 4882[16]
3 b g Case Law 6f **(64)** - Peep of Day (USA) (Lypheor) 12f **(71)**
Form - 00
Record 1999 - 1st:0 2nd:0 3rd:0 Ran:1
Pre1999 - 1st:0 2nd:1 3rd:4 Ran:9
Win Prizemoney £0 *Total Prizemoney* £1,696
1999 Turf 0-1: (11f) (frm)
Poor gelding, effective 5 to 7f, acts on gd - acts on Fibr, has worn blinkers. Becoming disappointing.
**B S Rothwell [0-10] Mrs Greta Sparks.*

THE DOWNTOWN FOX BHB 76f **RR 74f** 5160[15]
4 br g Primo Dominie 7.2f **(67)**-Sara Sprint (Formidable (USA)) 9.2f **(63)**
Form - 06708010
Record 1999 - 1st:1 2nd:0 3rd:0 Ran:8
Pre1999 - 1st:1 2nd:2 3rd:2 Ran:16
Win Prizemoney £16,681 *Total Prizemoney* £21,954
Wins * 1999 Oct York (SFT) 6f 74
* 1998 Apr Leices (SFT) H 7f 82 88 <
1999 Turf 1-8: (6f 1-6, 7f 2) (g-s, gd 1-2, g-f 2, frm 3)
Unfurnished, above-average gelding, effective 6 to 7f, best at 6f, acts on sft to gd, has worn blinkers. Turf high 74.
**B A McMahon [2-24] Mrs J McMahon.*

THE DRUMMER (IRE) BHB 36f **RR 37f** 3921[P]
3 b g River Falls 8.2f **(56)** - Tribal Rhythm (IRE) (Double Schwartz) 7.9f **(55)**
Form - 070600030P
Record 1999 - 1st:0 2nd:0 3rd:1 Ran:10
Pre1999 - 1st:0 2nd:0 3rd:0 Ran:3
Win Prizemoney £0 *Total Prizemoney* £358
1999 Turf 0-10: (6f, 7f 3, 8f 5, 9f) (sft, gd 3, g-f 3, frm 2, hrd)
Scopey, very moderate gelding. Turf high 41. Inconsistent.
**Miss L A Perratt [0-13] C D Barber-Lomax.*

THE DUKE OF BELAIR BHB 30f **RR** 5186[12]
2 b c Cosmonaut - Gay Hostess (FR) (Direct Flight) 13.1f **(51)**
Form - 000
Record 1999 - 1st:0 2nd:0 3rd:0 Ran:3
1999 Turf 0-3: (5f 2, 7f) (gd, g-f 2)
Currently very poor colt. (began Aug). **D A Nolan [0-3] A A Bell.*

THE EXHIBITION FOX BHB 80f **RR 86df** 3399[9]
3 b c Be My Chief (USA) 10.2f **(62)**-Swift Return (Double Form)7.3f **(58)**
Form - 284100
Record 1999 - 1st:1 2nd:1 3rd:0 Ran:6
Pre1999 - 1st:0 2nd:0 3rd:0 Ran:1
Win Prizemoney £7,002 *Total Prizemoney* £8,666
Wins * 1999 Jun York (G-S) 7.9f 86 <
1999 Turf 1-6: (8f 1-2, 10f 3, 11f) (g-s, gd 1-3, frm 2)
Scopey, useful colt, effective 8 to 10f, acts on gd. Turf high 86 - 1st of 7 from Island House (12 Jun York RF 1970). Outclassed in the Dante Stakes before trailing home behind Mutawafeq at Doncaster. He recaptured his form over the extended seven furlongs at York in June when winning a maiden.
**B A McMahon [1-7] J D Graham.*

THE FINAL WORD **RR 66f** 5215[5]
2 ch f Cosmonaut - Jolizal (Good Times (ITY)) 6.6f **(54)**
Form - 5
Record 1999 - 1st:0 2nd:0 3rd:0 Ran:1
1999 Turf 0-1: (8f) (g-s)
Currently average filly. **R Hollinshead [0-1] P J Corns.*

THE FLY BHB 96f **RR 100f** 5051[3]
5 gr h Pharly (FR) 11.5f **(64)** - Nelly Do Da (Derring-Do) 11.1f **(64)**
Form - 24303
Record 1999 - 1st:0 2nd:1 3rd:2 Ran:5
Pre1999 - 1st:3 2nd:1 3rd:5 Ran:17
Win Prizemoney £46,512 *Total Prizemoney* £103,079
Wins * 1997 May York (GD) H 10.4f 93 102+ <
* 1996 Aug Newcas (GD) H 8f 85 94+
* 1996 Aug Ayr (GD) 7f 82
1999 Turf 0-5: (10f, 12f 2, 13f, 14f) (g-s, gd 2, g-f, frm)
Very useful colt, effective 12 to 13f, best at 12f, acts on sft to g-f, best on gd, prefers left handed tracks. Turf high 106 - 4th of 7 getting 3lb from Sadian (6 May Chester 13f g-f RF 1050). Consistent. Following a brief foray over hurdles, he failed to recapture his best form back on the level. Sold for 70,000 gns in October to race in the United States.
**B W Hills [4-24] The Hon Mrs J M Corbett & J Hanson.*

THE FLYER (IRE) **RR 62f** 2271[6]
2 b c Blues Traveller (IRE) - National Ballet (Shareef Dancer (USA)) 9.9f **(73)**
Form - 6
Record 1999 - 1st:0 2nd:0 3rd:0 Ran:1
1999 Turf 0-1: (7f) (frm)
Currently average colt. **P F I Cole [0-1] H R H Prince Fahd Salman.*

THE FOSSICK (IRE) **RR** 1929[5]
3 ch g Forest Wind (USA) - Rose of Summer (IRE) (Taufan (USA)) 7f

(57)
Form - 5
Record 1999 - 1st:0 2nd:0 3rd:0 Ran:1
1999 AW 0-1: (8f) (Fibr)
Angular, currently poor gelding. **M A Peill [0-1] H M de B Lipscomb.*

THE FRENCH FURZE (IRE) BHB 47f RR 47f 3395[5]

5 ch g Be My Guest (USA) 10.2f **(66)** - Exciting (Mill Reef (USA)) 10.5f **(78)**
Form - 0368465
Record 1999 - 1st:0 2nd:0 3rd:1 Ran:7
Pre1999 - 1st:0 2nd:0 3rd:0 Ran:8
Win Prizemoney £0 *Total Prizemoney* £902
1999 Turf 0-6: (10f, 11f, 12f 3, 14f) (g-s, g-f 2, frm 2, hrd) 1999 AW 0-1: (13f) (Equi)
Moderate gelding, effective 10 to 12f, acts on g-s to g-f, has worn blinkers. Turf high 63 (1st run) - 3rd of 18 giving 15lb to Thrower (19 Apr Nottingham 10f g-s RF 0752).
**R E Peacock [0-11] Jim Ennis (from C Roche in IRE [1-6] Aug 1997).*

THE FROG QUEEN BHB 66f RR 70f 4605[1]

2 b f Bin Ajwaad (IRE) - The Frog Lady (IRE) **(50f 41a)** (Al Hareb (USA))
Form - 33081
Record 1999 - 1st:1 2nd:0 3rd:2 Ran:5
Win Prizemoney £2,102 *Total Prizemoney* £2,831
Wins * 1999 *Spt Southw (STD) S 7f 66 <*
1999 Turf 0-4: (6f 3, 7f) (g-f, frm 3) 1999 AW 1-1: (7f 1-1) (Fibr 1-1)
Above-average filly. Turf high 70 (began Aug) - 3rd of 8 to Bulletin (23 Aug Brighton 6f frm RF 3850). (1st run) - 1st of 15 from Timeless Quest (28 Spt Southwell RF 4605). She has shown some ability on turf, but got off the mark in a seller on the Southwell Fibresand in September. **D W P Arbuthnot [1-5] Mrs Sheila Crown.*

THE FUGATIVE BHB 90f56a RR 88f 56a 5030[D]

6 b m Nicholas (USA) 6.1f **(63)** - Miss Runaway (Runnett) 7f **(59)**
Form - 641562103D
Record 1999 - 1st:2 2nd:1 3rd:1 Ran:9
Pre1999 - 1st:6 2nd:4 3rd:2 Ran:35
Win Prizemoney £29,855 *Total Prizemoney* £47,334

Wins								
*** 1999**	Jun	Epsom	(GD)	H	6f	82	83	<
*** 1999**	Apr	Epsom	(SFT)	H	6f	72	81	
* 1998	Jun	Epsom	(GD)	H	6f	70	72	
* 1998	May	Lingfi	(GD)	H	6f	65	68	
* 1998	Apr	Folkes	(SFT)		5f		73	
* 1997	Jly	Folkes	(GD)	H	5f	61	66	
* 1997	Jun	Folkes	(SFT)	H	5f	50	60	
* 1997	Jun	Epsom	(G-S)	H	6f	50	56	

1999 Turf 2-8: (5f, 6f 2-6, 7f) (hvy, g-s 1-2, gd 2, g-f 1-2, frm) 1999 AW 0-1: (6f) (Equi)
Useful mare, effective 5 to 6f, best at 6f, acts on hvy to g-f, likes left handed tracks, likes tight tracks, excels at Epsom. Turf high 88 - also 1st of 6 giving 21lb to Lady Melbourne (30 Jun Epsom RF 2447). Likes to race prominently and is difficult to catch when on song. She seems to like Epsom, as her last three victories have been there. Six furlongs is her trip. **P Mitchell [8-44] J A Redmond.*

THE GAMBOLLER (USA) BHB 60f RR 48f 2455[11]

4 b g Irish Tower (USA) 7.3f **(69)** - Lady Limbo (USA) (Dance Spell (USA)) 9.6f **(75)**
Form - 00
Record 1999 - 1st:0 2nd:0 3rd:0 Ran:2
Pre1999 - 1st:1 2nd:1 3rd:0 Ran:8
Win Prizemoney £2,427 *Total Prizemoney* £3,306
Wins 1998 Jly Leices (GD) 10f 69 <
1999 Turf 0-2: (10f, 16f) (g-f 2)
Scopey, moderate gelding, has worn blinkers, likes tight tracks. Turf high 48. Becoming disappointing.
**M E Sowersby [1-6] The Wolds Partnership (from Mrs A J Perrett [1-8] Oct 1998).*

THE GAY FOX BHB 68f RR 64f 5065[8]

5 b gr g Never so Bold 7.1f **(62)** - School Concert (Music Boy) 6.8f **(57)**
Form - 040060354445058
Record 1999 - 1st:0 2nd:0 3rd:1 Ran:15
Pre1999 - 1st:4 2nd:4 3rd:3 Ran:38
Win Prizemoney £20,451 *Total Prizemoney* £40,422

Wins								
* 1998	Apr	Sandow	(HVY)	H	5f	87	90	<
* 1997	Jly	Cheste	(G-F)	H	5.1f	81	83	
* 1997	Jun	Newmar	(SFT)	H	5f	74	76	
* 1997	May	Warwic	(FRM)	H	7f	73	70	

1999 Turf 0-15: (5f 14, 6f) (g-s 2, gd 7, g-f, frm 5)
Average gelding, effective 5f, acts on hvy to g-f, likes left handed tracks. Turf high 78. Consistent. He is quite a useful sprint handicapper on his day, but is on a long losing run. His best performances in recent seasons have been when there has been plenty of cut in the ground. **B A McMahon [4-53] Mrs J McMahon.*

THE GIRLS' FILLY BHB 69f RR 59f 4294[9]

2 b f Emperor Jones (USA) - Sioux City (Simply Great (FR)) 8.2f **(65)**
Form - 3480
Record 1999 - 1st:0 2nd:0 3rd:1 Ran:4
Win Prizemoney £0 *Total Prizemoney* £894
1999 Turf 0-4: (6f 2, 7f 2) (g-f 2, frm 2)
Fair filly. Turf high 59.
**J H M Gosden [0-4] Mrs Mrs Ms Wood, Cowan, Rachel Hood.*

THE GLOW-WORM (IRE) BHB 102f RR 100f 5043[8]

4 b c Doyoun 10.7f **(69)** - Shakanda (IRE) (Shernazar) 10.2f **(73)**
Form - 257163548
Record 1999 - 1st:1 2nd:1 3rd:1 Ran:9
Pre1999 - 1st:3 2nd:1 3rd:3 Ran:11
Win Prizemoney £25,787 *Total Prizemoney* £69,227

Wins								
*** 1999**	Jun	Cheste	(SFT)		12.3f		105+	<
* 1998	Apr	Epsom	(SFT)		12f		99+	
* 1997	Oct	Newmar	(G-S)	H	8f	89	96	
* 1997	Jun	Newmar	(SFT)		7f		73	

1999 Turf 1-9: (11f, 12f 1-4, 13f, 14f, 16f, 22f) (sft 2, g-s 1-1, gd 3, g-f 3)
Scopey, very useful colt, effective 12 to 16f, best at 12f, acts on g-s to g-f, best on g-f, has worn blinkers, likes tight tracks. Turf high 113 (1st run) - 2nd of 11 to Sadian (17 Apr Newbury 12f g-f RF 0733) - also 1st of 3 from Leonato (2 Jun Chester RF 1669). Consistent. He ran his best race on his reappearance at Newbury, but proved hard to place when it became evident that he does not stay two miles. Effective on an easy surface, he goes particularly well when fresh.
**B W Hills [4-20] The Hon Mrs J M Corbett & C Wright.*

THE GREAT FLOOD BHB 41f45a RR 44f 45a 3441[7]

6 ch g Risk Me (FR) 8f **(53)** - Yukosan (Absalom) 7.2f **(58)**
Form - 5657
Record 1999 - 1st:0 2nd:0 3rd:0 Ran:4
Pre1999 - 1st:1 2nd:0 3rd:0 Ran:8
Win Prizemoney £2,495 *Total Prizemoney* £2,935
Wins 1997 *Jan Wolver (SLW) H 14.8f 53 59 <*
1999 Turf 0-2: (14f, 15f) (hvy, gd) 1999 AW 0-2: (15f, 16f) (Fibr 2)
Moderate gelding. Turf high 44. AW high 47 (began Jly).
**G F H Charles-Jones [0-4] Mrs Jessica Charles-Jones (from C A Dwyer [3-11] Apr 1999).*

THE GREEN GREY BHB 64f65a RR 66f 65a 4018[7]

5 gr g Environment Friend 7.5f **(67)** - Pea Green (Try My Best (USA)) 7.6f **(67)**
Form - 312207
Record 1999 - 1st:0 2nd:2 3rd:0 Ran:4
Pre1999 - 1st:6 2nd:2 3rd:1 Ran:23
Win Prizemoney £19,745 *Total Prizemoney* £23,028

Wins								
1998	*Nov*	*Lingfi*	*(STD)*	*H*	*8f*	*52*	*60*	
1998	Spt	Kempto	(GD)	H	8f	67	70	<
1998	Spt	Bright	(FRM)	C	8f		68	
1998	Aug	Bath	(FRM)	S	8f		61	
1998	Aug	Yarmou	(G-F)	SH	8f	43	49	
1997	Spt	Bath	(G-F)	H	8f	42	51	

1999 Turf 0-2: (8f, 9f) (g-f, frm) 1999 AW 0-2: (8f, 10f) (Equi 2)
Average gelding, effective 8 to 10f, best at 8f, acts on frm - acts on Equi, has worn blinkers, excels at Lingfield. Turf high 56 (began Aug). AW high 67 - 2nd of 8 getting 11lb from Sweet Wilhelmina (16 Jan Lingfield 8f Equi RF 0105). Consistent.
**L MontagueHall [0-2] J Daniels (from Derrick Morris [2-6] Jan 1999).*

THE GROOVER RR 46f 4729[8]

3 ch g Beveled (USA) 6.9f **(64)** - Taffidale (Welsh Pageant) 10f **(65)**
Form - 08
Record 1999 - 1st:0 2nd:0 3rd:0 Ran:2
1999 Turf 0-2: (8f 2) (g-s, frm)
Leggy, currently moderate gelding. Turf high 46 (began Spt).

**G M McCourt [0-2] J F Watson.*

THE GROVELLER BHB 50f58a **RR 50f 58a** 4232P
4 b g Prince Sabo 6.6f **(64)** - Estonia (Kings Lake (USA)) 10.8f **(67)**
Form - 08000653333P
Record 1999 - 1st:0 2nd:0 3rd:4 Ran:12
Pre1999 - 1st:1 2nd:0 3rd:2 Ran:8
Win Prizemoney £4,059 *Total Prizemoney* £8,327
Wins * 1997 *Aug Wolver (STD)* *7f* *81* <
1999 Turf 0-12: (7f 4, 8f 7, 10f) (gd 2, g-f 3, frm 7)
Scopey, decent gelding, effective 7 to 8f, best at 7f, acts on g-f to frm, best on frm, has worn blinkers (extremely effectively). Turf high 52 - 5th of 17 getting 3lb from Noble Cyrano (6 Aug Haydock 8f g-f RF 3417). **P D Evans [1-20] John Pugh.*

THE GYPSY TIPPLER BHB 45f **RR 52f** 2719[7]
4 ch f Romany Rye - Eidolon (Rousillon (USA)) 8.2f **(74)**
Form - 05707
Record 1999 - 1st:0 2nd:0 3rd:0 Ran:5
Pre1999 - 1st:0 2nd:0 3rd:1 Ran:9
Win Prizemoney £0 *Total Prizemoney* £610
1999 Turf 0-4: (6f 4) (gd, g-f 2, frm) 1999 AW 0-1: (6f) (Fibr)
Light-framed, fair filly. Turf high 52.
**B Palling [0-14] Lindsay Hiscock.*

THE HAKA BHB 44f **RR 43f** 3492[7]
3 ch g Sabrehill (USA) 8.5f **(64)** - Exotic Forest **(68df)** (Dominion) 8.5f **(63)**
Form - 205507
Record 1999 - 1st:0 2nd:1 3rd:0 Ran:6
Pre1999 - 1st:0 2nd:0 3rd:1 Ran:9
Win Prizemoney £0 *Total Prizemoney* £1,292
1999 Turf 0-6: (7f 4, 8f 2) (gd 2, g-f 2, frm 2)
Workmanlike, fair gelding, effective 6 to 7f, acts on gd to frm, often wears blinkers. Turf high 67 (1st run) - 2nd of 9 to Gunner Sam (21 Apr Catterick 7f gd RF 0795).
**M Dods [0-6] M J K Dods (from G C Bravery [0-9] Oct 1998).*

THE HAULIER RR 71f 4906[2]
3 ch g Ardkinglass 5f **(64)** - Ask Away (Midyan (USA)) 6f **(60)**
Form - 40681630852
Record 1999 - 1st:1 2nd:1 3rd:1 Ran:11
Pre1999 - 1st:1 2nd:1 3rd:1 Ran:10
Win Prizemoney £9,774 *Total Prizemoney* £13,505
Wins * **1999** Jly Beverl (G-F) H 7.5f 68 74
* 1998 Aug Newcas (GD) H 7f 74 79 <
1999 Turf 1-11: (7f 1-9, 8f 2) (gd 3, g-f 2, frm 1-6)
Scopey, above-average gelding, effective 6 to 7f, best at 6f, acts on gd to frm, best on gd. Turf high 74 - 1st of 4 getting 7lb from Smart Predator (13 Jly Beverley RF 2769). Consistent. Showed the benefit of a drop in the handicap to score at Beverley in July, but has gone back up the weights as a result and been found wanting. **T D Easterby [2-21] T E F Freight (Scarborough) Ltd.*

THE HIGHGATE POT BHB 46f **RR 54f** 5194[9]
2 b f Never so Bold 7.1f **(62)** - Sea Farer Lake (Gairloch) 7f **(63)**
Form - 078000
Record 1999 - 1st:0 2nd:0 3rd:0 Ran:6
1999 Turf 0-5: (5f, 6f 2, 7f, 8f) (gd 3, g-f, frm) 1999 AW 0-1: (7f) (Fibr)
Fair filly. Turf high 54 (began Jly). **M D I Usher [0-6] Martin Hicks.*

THE IMPOSTER (IRE) BHB 50f60a **RR 56f 60a** 2160[2]
4 ch g Imp Society (USA) 7.1f **(63)** - Phoenix Dancer (IRE) (Gorytus (USA)) 7.8f **(60)**
Form - 20142
Record 1999 - 1st:1 2nd:1 3rd:0 Ran:3
Pre1999 - 1st:0 2nd:1 3rd:2 Ran:12
Win Prizemoney £1,955 *Total Prizemoney* £3,730
Wins 1999 *May Wolver (STD) S* *8.5f* *56* <
1999 AW 1-3: (8f 1-2, 11f) (Fibr 1-3)
Workmanlike, average gelding, effective 8f, - acts on Fibr. AW high 66 - 2nd of 10 giving 6lb to Hand Craft (19 Jun Wolverhampton 8f Fibr RF 2160). Inconsistent. Acts on Fibresand, with the extended mile at Wolverhampton looking his optimum conditions.
**Miss S J Wilton [0-2] John Pointon and Sons (from D J G MurraySmith [1-13] May 1999).*

THE JAM SAHEB RR 43f 5059[12]
2 b c Petong 7.6f **(58)** - Reem El Fala (FR) (Fabulous Dancer (USA)) 9.4f **(70)**
Form - 00
Record 1999 - 1st:0 2nd:0 3rd:0 Ran:2
1999 Turf 0-2: (7f 2) (g-s, gd)
Currently moderate colt. Turf high 43 (began Oct).
**Lady Herries [0-2] Michael WingfieldDigby.*

THEKRYAATI (IRE) BHB 82f85a **RR 81f 85a** 3226[1]
4 ch c Indian Ridge 7.6f **(74)** - Lamu Lady (IRE) (Lomond (USA)) 8.8f **(65)**
Form - 1011222022041
Record 1999 - 1st:4 2nd:5 3rd:0 Ran:13
Pre1999 - 1st:0 2nd:0 3rd:0 Ran:1
Win Prizemoney £23,899 *Total Prizemoney* £34,076
Wins * **1999** Jly Goodwo (G-F) H 9f 76 81 <
* **1999** *Feb Wolver (STD) H* *9.4f* *65* *70*
* **1999** *Jan Wolver (STD) H* *8.5f* *62* *63*
* **1999** *Jan Lingfi (STD)* *10f* *69*
1999 Turf 1-5: (9f 1-1, 10f 3, 12f) (gd, g-f, frm 1-2, hrd) 1999 AW 3-8: (8f 1-2, 9f 1-2, 10f 1-3, 11f) (Equi 1-3, Fibr 2-5)
Workmanlike, decent colt, effective 8 to 10f, acts on frm to hrd - acts on AW, prefers tight tracks, excels at Lingfield and Wolverhampton. Turf high 81 - 1st of 22 giving 17lb to Donatus (29 Jly Goodwood RF 3226). AW high 83 - 2nd of 12 giving 14lb to Scraggys Dream (18 Mar Lingfield 10f Equi RF 0445). He had a fine time of it on sand at the start of the year, winning three times and finishing runner-up five times. He has shown some ability on turf from only a few attempts, including a victory at Goodwood but looks a better horse on artificial surfaces. **M Johnston [4-13] Saif Ali (from B Hanbury [0-1] May 1998).*

THE LAMBTON WORM BHB 36f38a **RR 34f 38a** 2863[6]
5 b g Superpower 6.6f **(58)** - Springwell (Miami Springs) 9.9f **(59)**
Form - 860556
Record 1999 - 1st:0 2nd:0 3rd:0 Ran:6
Pre1999 - 1st:1 2nd:3 3rd:1 Ran:23
Win Prizemoney £3,493 *Total Prizemoney* £8,761
Wins 1996 Jly Ayr (GD) 6f 77 <
1999 Turf 0-5: (6f, 7f 3, 8f) (gd, frm 3, hrd) 1999 AW 0-1: (8f) (Fibr)
Very moderate gelding, effective 7f, acts on frm, has worn blinkers, likes right handed tracks, likes tight tracks. Turf high 39. Consistent.
**N Bycroft [0-12] G J Allison (from Denys Smith [1-23] Jly 1998).*

THELANDY BHB 28f **RR 31f** 3458[6]
4 b g Noble Patriarch 12.2f **(43)** - Choir (High Top) 10.2f **(67)**
Form - 006
Record 1999 - 1st:0 2nd:0 3rd:0 Ran:3
Pre1999 - 1st:0 2nd:0 3rd:0 Ran:4
1999 Turf 0-2: (12f, 14f) (gd, frm) 1999 AW 0-1: (7f) (Fibr)
Scopey, very moderate gelding, has worn blinkers. Turf high 13.
**W S Cunningham [0-1] A Skelton (from R Craggs [0-4] Apr 1999).*

THE LAST RAMBO RR 19f 2008[9]
2 b c Rambo Dancer (CAN) 8.4f **(59)** -Under the Wing(Aragon) 8.1f **(60)**
Form - 0
Record 1999 - 1st:0 2nd:0 3rd:0 Ran:1
1999 Turf 0-1: (7f) (frm)
Currently poor colt. **J L Eyre [0-1] J Bladen.*

THE LAST WORD BHB 47f53a **RR 36f 53a** 2689[2]
3 b c Cosmonaut - Jolizal (Good Times (ITY)) 6.6f **(54)**
Form - 8522135244832
Record 1999 - 1st:1 2nd:3 3rd:2 Ran:10
Pre1999 - 1st:0 2nd:1 3rd:0 Ran:5
Win Prizemoney £2,295 *Total Prizemoney* £5,714
Wins * **1999** *Feb Southw (STD) H* *8f* *47* *52* <
1999 Turf 0-1: (12f) (gd) 1999 AW 1-9: (8f 1-4, 9f 2, 11f 2, 12f) (Fibr 1-9)
Neat, fair colt, effective 8 to 11f, best at 8f, - acts on Fibr, favours left handed tracks, likes tight tracks. AW high 59 - 3rd of 9 to Ultra Calm (6 Mar Wolverhampton 8f Fibr RF 0406) - also 1st of 15 giving 3lb to Sharp Rhythm (22 Feb Southwell RF 0336).
**R Hollinshead [1-15] PKR Partnership.*

THE MANX TOUCH (IRE) BHB 59f **RR 56f** 4835[1]

3 gr f Petardia 8.2f **(58)** - Chapter And Verse (Dancers Image (USA)) 9.3f **(71)**
Form - 06544011
Record 1999 - 1st:2 2nd:0 3rd:0 Ran:8
Pre1999 - 1st:0 2nd:0 3rd:0 Ran:3
Win Prizemoney £4,884 *Total Prizemoney* £5,295
Wins * 1999 Oct Leices (GD) SH 7f 50 56 <
*** 1999** Spt Bath (SFT) H 8f 45 50
1999 Turf 2-8: (6f 2, 7f 1-2, 8f 1-2, 9f, 11f) (sft 2, g-s, gd 2-3, g-f, frm)
Leggy, fair filly, effective 7 to 8f, best at 7f, acts on gd to g-f, best on gd, likes tight tracks. Turf high 56 - 1st of 19 getting 5lb from Wild Thing (12 Oct Leicester RF 4835) - also 1st of 15 getting 8lb from Jane Grey (27 Spt Bath RF 4586).
**M A Peill [2-7] H M de B Lipscomb (from J J Quinn [0-4] Apr 1999).*

THE MASK (FR) RR 108f 3778a[3]
3 f
Form - 33
1999 Turf 0-2: (9f, 10f) (gd 2)
Currently Pattern-class. Turf high 108 (began Jly) - 3rd of 5 to Val Royal (14 Aug Deauville 10f gd RF 3778a). **A Fabre in FR [1-3].*

THEME TIME (USA) RR 31f 3348[5]
3 b c Stop The Music (USA) 5f **(57)** - Ranales (USA) (Majestic Light (USA)) 10.6f **(75)**
Form - 05
Record 1999 - 1st:0 2nd:0 3rd:0 Ran:2
1999 Turf 0-2: (10f, 12f) (frm 2)
Scopey, currently very moderate colt. Turf high 31.
**Mrs A J Perrett [0-2] K Abdulla.*

THEME TUNE BHB 40f34a RR 39f 34a 4949[1]
4 b f Dilum (USA) 7.1f **(56)** - Souadah (USA) (General Holme (USA)) 5.7f **(63)**
Form - 000701
Record 1999 - 1st:1 2nd:0 3rd:0 Ran:6
Pre1999 - 1st:0 2nd:1 3rd:0 Ran:4
Win Prizemoney £2,005 *Total Prizemoney* £2,874
Wins * 1999 Oct Yarmou (G-F) SH 11.5f 35 39 <
1999 Turf 1-4: (7f 2, 8f, 11f 1-1) (g-f 1-3, frm) 1999 AW 0-2: (8f 2) (Equi, Fibr)
Light-framed, very moderate filly, has worn blinkers. Turf high 39. AW high 24. **Dr J D Scargill [1-10] Mrs V Bayley.*

THE NURSE (IRE) BHB 44f RR 36f 4558[11]
3 b f Mujadil (USA) 7.7f **(70)** - Nurse Jo (USA) (J O Tobin (USA)) 9.4f **(67)**
Form - 507300000
Record 1999 - 1st:0 2nd:0 3rd:1 Ran:9
Pre1999 - 1st:1 2nd:1 3rd:1 Ran:8
Win Prizemoney £2,500 *Total Prizemoney* £5,765
Wins * 1998 Aug Redcar (G-F) S 6f 64 <
1999 Turf 0-9: (6f 5, 7f, 8f 3) (sft, gd, g-f 3, frm 3, hrd)
Scopey, fair filly, effective 6f, acts on gd to frm, best on frm. Turf high 59.
**K A Ryan [1-15] Mrs Candice Reilly (from R J R Williams [0-2] Jun 1998).*

THEORETICALLY (USA) RR 98f 4740a[1]
2 b f Theatrical 11.5f **(78)** - Aspern (FR) (Riverman (USA)) 9.1f **(76)**
Form - 411
1999 Turf 2-3: (6f, 7f 2-2) (sft 1-1, g-s 1-1, g-f)
Currently very useful filly. Turf high 98 (began Jly) - 1st of 7 from Earlene (2 Oct Curragh RF 4740a). Connections hope she will develop into an Irish 1,000 Guineas contender. Genuine and likely to stay beyond a mile, she acts on easy ground and is clearly an interesting prospect. **D K Weld in IRE [2-3] M J Bastion.*

THEO'S LAD (IRE) BHB 58f RR 56f 4320[14]
2 b g Shareef Dancer (USA) 10.1f **(67)** - Inshirah (USA) (Caro)
Form - 15060
Record 1999 - 1st:1 2nd:0 3rd:0 Ran:5
Win Prizemoney £2,234 *Total Prizemoney* £2,234
Wins * 1999 May Catter (FRM) S 6f 52+ <
1999 Turf 1-5: (5f, 6f 1-3, 7f) (gd 2, g-f, frm 1-2)
Fair gelding, has worn blinkers. Turf high 56 - also 1st of 9 giving 5lb to Schatzi (22 May Catterick RF 1386).
**R Guest [1-5] Livingston Trading Ltd.*

THE OUTBACK RR 41f 2454[10]
2 ch g Timeless Times (USA) 6.1f **(56)** - Ninety-Five **(67f 63a)** (Superpower)
Form - 0
Record 1999 - 1st:0 2nd:0 3rd:0 Ran:1
1999 Turf 0-1: (5f) (g-f)
Currently moderate gelding. **J G FitzGerald [0-1] N H T Wrigley.*

THE PRESIDENT BHB 52f RR 52f 4693[8]
4 b g Yaheeb (USA) - When The Saints (Bay Express) 7.1f **(60)**
Form - 0U48
Record 1999 - 1st:0 2nd:0 3rd:0 Ran:4
Pre1999 - 1st:0 2nd:0 3rd:0 Ran:5
Win Prizemoney £0 *Total Prizemoney* £472
1999 Turf 0-4: (12f 2, 13f, 14f) (gd, g-f 2, frm)
Strong, fair gelding, effective 12f, acts on gd, favours tight tracks. Turf high 52.
**Mrs M Reveley [1-10] North Racing Partnership (from J L Eyre [0-5] Spt 1998).*

THE PRINCE BHB 90f RR 91f 5004[3]
5 b g Machiavellian (USA) 9.8f **(83)** - Mohican Girl (Dancing Brave (USA)) 8.4f **(76)**
Form - 21860D821303
Record 1999 - 1st:2 2nd:2 3rd:2 Ran:12
Pre1999 - 1st:1 2nd:1 3rd:0 Ran:6
Win Prizemoney £17,940 *Total Prizemoney* £29,075
Wins * 1999 Spt Hamilt (G-F) H 8.3f 85 90+
*** 1999** May Lingfi (G-F) 7.6f 92 <
1997 May Newmar (G-F) 8f 82
1999 Turf 2-12: (7f, 8f 2-9, 9f, 10f) (gd 3, g-f 1-3, frm 1-6)
Useful gelding, effective 8f, acts on gd to frm, prefers tight tracks, excels at Windsor. Turf high 92 - 1st of 7 from Blakeset (7 May Lingfield RF 1085) - also 1st of 12 giving 27lb to Antarctic Storm (6 Spt Hamilton RF 4165). Consistent. Yet to be crowned, he has proved himself a fair handicapper at around a mile, although he does not look good enough for Listed races.
**R M H Cowell [2-12] The Mohican Syndicate (from G Wragg [1-6] Spt 1997).*

THE PROOF BHB 50f RR 38f 5195[13]
2 b g Rudimentary (USA) 8.2f **(66)** - Indubitable (Sharpo) 7.7f **(59)**
Form - 800
Record 1999 - 1st:0 2nd:0 3rd:0 Ran:3
1999 Turf 0-3: (6f 2, 8f) (hvy, g-s, gd)
Currently very moderate gelding. Turf high 38 (began Spt).
**G B Balding [0-3] Miss B Swire.*

THE PROSECUTOR BHB 62f65a RR 63f 65a 5218[10]
2 b c Contract Law (USA) 8.9f **(54)** - Elsocko (Swing Easy (USA)) 6.5f **(55)**
Form - 226030
Record 1999 - 1st:0 2nd:2 3rd:1 Ran:6
Win Prizemoney £0 *Total Prizemoney* £1,826
1999 Turf 0-4: (5f, 6f 2, 7f) (g-s, gd 2, frm) 1999 AW 0-2: (5f, 6f) (Fibr 2)
Above-average colt. Turf high 63 (began Aug). AW high 70. **B A McMahon [0-6] Mrs Rita Gibson.*

THE PUZZLER (IRE) BHB 83f RR 81f 5040[14]
8 b or br g Sharpo 7.5f **(68)** - Enigma (Ahonoora) 8.1f **(73)**
Form - 610050
Record 1999 - 1st:1 2nd:0 3rd:0 Ran:6
Pre1999 - 1st:3 2nd:2 3rd:4 Ran:32
Win Prizemoney £32,896 *Total Prizemoney* £43,373
Wins * 1999 Apr Sandow (G-S) H 5f 77 90
* 1997 Oct Newmar (G-S) H 5f 98 99
* 1996 Oct Newbur (SFT) H 6f 100 106 <
1999 Turf 1-6: (5f 1-4, 6f 2) (g-s 1-2, gd 2, g-f, frm)
Decent gelding, effective 5 to 6f, acts on g-s to gd, has worn blinkers. Turf high 90 - 1st of 17 getting 18lb from Halmahera (23 Apr Sandown RF 0826). A one-time useful sprinter, he had the soft ground he needs when winning well at Sandown on his second start of the season. Not easy to train and usually wears bandages.
**B W Hills [3-31] Lady Richard Wellesley (from M Kauntze in IRE [0-3]*

Jun 1995).

THE QUARE FELLOW BHB 74f **RR 72f** 4998[9]
3 ch c Elmaamul (USA) 8.1f **(70)** - Bizarre Lady (Dalsaan) 9.8f **(64)**
Form - 1050
Record 1999 - 1st:1 2nd:0 3rd:0 Ran:4
Pre1999 - 1st:0 2nd:0 3rd:0 Ran:1
Win Prizemoney £3,013 *Total Prizemoney* £3,226
Wins * 1999 Apr Ripon (G-F) 8f 69+ <
1999 Turf 1-4: (8f 1-3, 10f) (gd 2, g-f 1-1, frm)
Scopey, above-average colt. Turf high 72. Made a winning reappearance in a Ripon maiden, but has not shown a lot since.
**J H M Gosden [1-5] David Simpson.*

THE RAIN LADY BHB 40f50a **RR 30f 50a** 3624[17]
3 b f Lugana Beach 7f **(63)** - Rain Splash **(18f)** (Petong) 6.6f **(58)**
Form - 0000070
Record 1999 - 1st:0 2nd:0 3rd:0 Ran:7
Pre1999 - 1st:0 2nd:0 3rd:0 Ran:3
1999 Turf 0-6: (5f, 6f 4, 7f) (sft, gd 2, g-f, frm 2) 1999 AW 0-1: (5f) (Fibr)
Light-framed, very moderate filly. Turf high 38. Inconsistent.
**P D Evans [0-3] John Smallman (from R Hollinshead [0-7] Jly 1999).*

THE REAL MCCOY BHB 47a **RR 41f** 4601[11]
5 b g Deploy 11.4f **(67)** - Mukhayyalah (Dancing Brave (USA)) 8.4f **(76)**
Form - 0
Record 1999 - 1st:0 2nd:0 3rd:0 Ran:1
Pre1999 - 1st:1 2nd:0 3rd:0 Ran:7
Win Prizemoney £1,735 *Total Prizemoney* £1,735
Wins 1998 *Jan Southw (STD) H 12f 35 43* <
1999 AW 0-1: (11f) (Fibr)
Moderate gelding. Inconsistent.
**M A Peill [0-2] C N Barnes (from Mrs J R Ramsden [1-6] Spt 1998).*

THE REPUBLICAN RR 4f 5186[9]
2 b g Democratic (USA) - Loving You (Thatch (USA)) 9.8f **(62)**
Form - 00
Record 1999 - 1st:0 2nd:0 3rd:0 Ran:2
1999 Turf 0-2: (5f, 7f) (gd, g-f)
Currently very poor gelding. Turf high 4 (began Oct).
**W Storey [0-2] Gremlin Racing.*

THERHEA (IRE) BHB 88f **RR 88f** 3984[12]
6 b g Pennine Walk 8.9f **(64)** - Arab Art (Artaius (USA)) 9f **(69)**
Form - 6530313050
Record 1999 - 1st:1 2nd:0 3rd:3 Ran:10
Pre1999 - 1st:4 2nd:7 3rd:5 Ran:41
Win Prizemoney £29,030 *Total Prizemoney* £64,640
Wins * 1999 Jun Newbur (GD) H 7f 85 89 <
* 1998 Apr Sandow (SFT) 8.1f 86
* 1997 Spt York (SFT) H 7.9f 76 81
* 1997 Jun Nottin (GD) H 8.2f 62 65
* 1996 Apr Newbur (G-S) H 8f 77 81+
1999 Turf 1-10: (7f 1-4, 8f 6) (gd 1-5, g-f 2, frm 3)
Useful gelding, effective 7 to 9f, best at 8f, acts on sft to frm, best on gd, has worn blinkers, likes right handed tracks, likes tight tracks, and excels at Sandown and Goodwood and Newbury. Turf high 91 - 3rd of 10 getting 7lb from Brilliant Red (3 Jly Sandown 8f frm RF 2543) - also 1st of 10 giving 4lb to Bold King (10 Jun Newbury RF 1885). This genuine handicapper won at Newbury in June, his first victory at seven furlongs. He will continue to give a good account of himself when racing on his favoured soft ground.
**B R Millman [5-51] Ray Gudge, Colin Lew Calvert.*

THERMAL SPRING RR 67f 4176[5]
2 ch f Zafonic (USA) 9f **(83)** - Seven Springs (USA) (Irish River (USA))
Form - 5
Record 1999 - 1st:0 2nd:0 3rd:0 Ran:1
1999 Turf 0-1: (7f) (frm)
Currently average filly. **H R A Cecil [0-1] K Abdulla.*

THERMOPYLAE BHB 73a **RR 76df** 4667[6]
3 b f Tenby 10.4f **(76)** - Tamassos (Dance In Time (CAN)) 8.9f **(59)**
Form - 242806
Record 1999 - 1st:0 2nd:2 3rd:0 Ran:6
Pre1999 - 1st:0 2nd:1 3rd:0 Ran:2
Win Prizemoney £0 *Total Prizemoney* £3,847
1999 Turf 0-4: (10f 3, 11f) (gd 2, g-f 2) 1999 AW 0-2: (8f, 13f) (Equi, Fibr)
Light-framed, above-average filly, effective 7 to 11f, acts on sft to g-f, best on g-f. Turf high 76 (1st run) - 2nd of 12 to Ela Athena (17 Apr Newbury 10f g-f RF 0736). AW high 33 (began Spt). Becoming disappointing. **P F I Cole [0-8] Athos Christodoulou.*

THE ROBE BHB 37f30a **RR 44f 30a** 763[5]
4 b f Robellino (USA) 9.5f **(68)** - Outward's Gal (Ashmore (FR)) 8.5f **(65)**
Form - 55
Record 1999 - 1st:0 2nd:0 3rd:0 Ran:2
Pre1999 - 1st:0 2nd:1 3rd:2 Ran:12
Win Prizemoney £0 *Total Prizemoney* £1,673
1999 Turf 0-2: (14f, 15f) (hvy, gd)
Scopey, moderate filly, effective 14 to 16f, best at 16f, acts on gd to frm, best on frm. Turf high 38.
**A W Carroll [2-16] D Timmins (from B J Meehan [0-5] Dec 1997).*

THE ROBSTER (USA) RR 64f 5208[7]
2 ch c Woodman (USA) 9.7f **(77)** - Country Cruise (USA) (Riverman (USA)) 9.1f **(76)**
Form - 87
Record 1999 - 1st:0 2nd:0 3rd:0 Ran:2
1999 Turf 0-2: (7f 2) (g-s 2)
Currently average colt. Turf high 64 (began Oct).
**B J Meehan [0-2] R L Harding.*

THESEUS (IRE) RR 80f 1968[16]
3 b c Danehill (USA) 9.1f **(79)** - Graecia Magna (USA) (Private Account (USA)) 8.5f **(74)**
Form - 20
Record 1999 - 1st:0 2nd:1 3rd:0 Ran:2
Pre1999 - 1st:0 2nd:0 3rd:0 Ran:3
Win Prizemoney £0 *Total Prizemoney* £1,135
1999 Turf 0-2: (11f, 12f) (gd, frm)
Decent colt. Turf high 80 (1st run) - 2nd of 10 giving 1lb to Compton Amica (1 Jun Sandown 11f frm RF 1656).
**Sir Michael Stoute [0-5] Athos Christodoulou.*

THE SHADOW BHB 63a **RR 59f** 3738[5]
3 br g Polar Falcon (USA) 9f **(74)** - Shadiliya (Red Alert) 7.6f **(66)**
Form - 78615
Record 1999 - 1st:1 2nd:0 3rd:0 Ran:5
Pre1999 - 1st:0 2nd:0 3rd:1 Ran:2
Win Prizemoney £2,944 *Total Prizemoney* £3,400
Wins * 1999 *Jly Wolver (STD) H 9.4f 63 65* <
1999 Turf 0-3: (8f, 9f, 10f) (g-s, gd, frm) 1999 AW 1-2: (7f, 9f 1-1) (Fibr 1-2)
Scopey, average gelding, effective 7 to 9f, acts on g-s - acts on Fibr. Turf high 59. AW high 65 (began Jly) - 1st of 11 giving 5lb to Admirals Place (23 Jly Wolverhampton RF 3079).
**D W P Arbuthnot [1-7] Mrs B J Lee.*

THE SHEIKH (IRE) RR 65f 2633[10]
2 b c Sri Pekan (USA) - Arabian Dream (IRE) (Royal Academy (USA))
Form - 870
Record 1999 - 1st:0 2nd:0 3rd:0 Ran:3
1999 Turf 0-3: (6f, 7f 2) (g-f 2, frm)
Currently average colt. Turf high 59.
**M L W Bell [0-3] The Fitzrovians.*

THE SILK THIEF BHB 14f **RR** 269[14]
4 b g Thowra (FR) 11.2f **(47)** - Fine N Fancy (Netherkelly) 5.6f **(46)**
Form - 670
Record 1999 - 1st:0 2nd:0 3rd:0 Ran:3
Pre1999 - 1st:0 2nd:0 3rd:0 Ran:2
1999 AW 0-3: (11f, 12f, 16f) (Equi 2, Fibr)
Workmanlike, very poor gelding, often wears blinkers. AW high 5.
**J R Jenkins [0-6] Mrs M A Bateley.*

THE STAGER (IRE) BHB 45f57a **RR 41f 57a** 4927[6]
7 b g Danehill (USA) 9.1f **(79)** - Wedgewood Blue (USA) (Sir Ivor) 10.2f **(70)**
Form - 101006
Record 1999 - 1st:1 2nd:0 3rd:0 Ran:5
Pre1999 - 1st:3 2nd:2 3rd:1 Ran:26

Win Prizemoney £12,609 *Total Prizemoney* £16,825
Wins * **1999** *Apr Southw (STD) H 8f 54 56*
* 1998 *Nov Southw (STD) H 8f 49 53*
* 1996 May Newmar (GD) 7f 75 <
* 1995 Apr Beverl (G-F) H 7.5f 65 67
1999 Turf 0-2: (8f 2) (frm 2) 1999 AW 1-3: (8f 1-3) (Fibr 1-3)
Fair gelding, effective 8f, - acts on Fibr, has worn blinkers, likes left handed tracks, favours tight tracks. Turf high 35. AW high 56 - 1st of 14 getting 5lb from Killarney Jazz (6 Apr Southwell RF 0602).
**J R Jenkins [4-35] J B Wilcox.*

THE TATLING (IRE) BHB 100f RR 97f 4793[2]

2 b c Perugino (USA) - Aunty Eileen (Ahonoora) 8.1f **(73)**
Form - 364121262
Record 1999 - 1st:2 2nd:3 3rd:1 Ran:9
Win Prizemoney £6,306 *Total Prizemoney* £46,831
Wins * **1999** Aug Bright (SFT) 5.3f 95+ <
* **1999** Jly Yarmou (G-F) 5.2f 87
1999 Turf 2-9: (5f 2-4, 6f 5) (g-s 1-1, gd 1-4, g-f 2, frm 2)
Very useful colt, effective 5 to 6f, best at 5f, acts on g-s to frm, best on gd. Turf high 97 - 2nd of 13 to Kier Park (9 Oct Ascot 5f gd RF 4793) - also 1st of 4 giving 13lb to Where's Charlotte (18 Aug Brighton RF 3733). Improving. He enjoyed a cracking season, putting up a typically robust effort when finishing second in the Group 3 Cornwallis Stakes at Ascot in October. Possibly at his best over five furlongs, he is game but must improve to hold his own against the top sprinters. **M L W Bell [2-9] Messrs McGee.*

THE THIRD CURATE (IRE) BHB 53f RR 43f 5199[23]

4 b g Fairy King (USA) 7.7f **(75)** - Lassalia (Sallust) 8.4f **(63)**
Form - 081000000
Record 1999 - 1st:1 2nd:0 3rd:0 Ran:9
Pre1999 - 1st:0 2nd:0 3rd:0 Ran:2
Win Prizemoney £5,500 *Total Prizemoney* £5,687
Wins 1999 Jun Currag (GD) H 7f 70 63 <
1999 Turf 1-9: (6f 2, 7f 1-4, 8f, 12f, 16f) (sft 2, gd 3, g-f 1-2, frm 2)
Moderate gelding, has worn blinkers. Turf high 63. Inconsistent. Winner of a seven-furlong event at the Curragh for Dermot Weld, he is now with Barney Curley, and has been well beaten on his English starts so far.
**B J Curley [0-6] P Byrne (from D K Weld in IRE [1-5] Jun 1999).*

THE THRUSTER BHB 52f49a RR 55f 49a 4835[10]

4 b g Elmaamul (USA) 8.1f **(70)**-Moon Spin (Night Shift (USA)) 7.2f **(69)**
Form - 0003477512038320
Record 1999 - 1st:1 2nd:2 3rd:3 Ran:16
Pre1999 - 1st:1 2nd:2 3rd:0 Ran:8
Win Prizemoney £7,471 *Total Prizemoney* £13,354
Wins * **1999** Jly Pontef (G-F) H 8f 47 52
1998 Aug Lingfi (G-F) H 7.6f 60 67 <
1999 Turf 1-15: (6f, 7f 5, 8f 1-3, 9f, 10f, 12f 2, 14f, 15f) (g-s 2, gd 4, g-f 2, frm 1-6, hrd) 1999 AW 0-1: (12f) (Equi)
Scopey, fair gelding, effective 7 to 8f, acts on g-f to frm, often wears blinkers (very effectively). Turf high 55. Started off the season running over middle distances, but was brought back in trip and scored at Pontefract in July. He looks to need fast ground.
**D Nicholls [1-16] Kevin Reddington (from M P Tregoning [1-4] Spt 1998).*

THE WHISTLING TEAL BHB 84f89a RR 84f 89a 4683[8]

3 b c Rudimentary (USA) 8.2f **(66)** - Lonely Shore (Blakeney) 10.5f **(64)**
Form - 3102512328
Record 1999 - 1st:2 2nd:3 3rd:2 Ran:10
Pre1999 - 1st:0 2nd:0 3rd:0 Ran:2
Win Prizemoney £9,439 *Total Prizemoney* £23,186
Wins * **1999** *Aug Wolver (STD) H 8.5f 80 89* <
* **1999** Apr Windso (G-F) H 8.3f 74 76
1999 Turf 1-8: (7f, 8f 1-4, 9f, 10f 2) (sft 2, gd 2, g-f 2, frm 1-2) 1999 AW 1-2: (8f 1-1, 9f) (Fibr 1-2)
Workmanlike, useful colt, effective 8 to 10f, best at 8f, acts on sft to gd - acts on Fibr, prefers tight tracks. Turf high 84. AW high 89 (began Aug) - 2nd of 8 giving 3lb to Over To You (14 Aug Wolverhampton 9f Fibr RF 3669) - also 1st of 9 giving 10lb to Locomotion (6 Aug Wolverhampton RF 3439). He showed decent form on both turf and Fibresand last term, winning at Windsor in April and at Wolverhampton in August. He has also run some fine races in defeat, finishing runner-up to Over To You back at Wolverhampton in one of the best races run on sand all year, and only being beaten a whisker in the Mail On Sunday Series Final at Ascot in September. **J G Smyth-Osborne [2-12] Mrs F A Veasey.*

THE WIFE BHB 81f RR 89f 5024[8]

2 b f Efisio 7.7f **(69)** - Great Steps **(70f)** (Vaigly Great) 7f **(58)**
Form - 73122188
Record 1999 - 1st:2 2nd:2 3rd:1 Ran:8
Win Prizemoney £11,350 *Total Prizemoney* £14,041
Wins * **1999** Spt York (G-F) H 7.9f 80 89 <
* **1999** Jun Beverl (G-F) 7.5f 75
1999 Turf 2-8: (5f, 6f, 7f 1-3, 8f 1-3) (gd 4, g-f 1-3, frm 1-1)
Useful filly, effective 8f, acts on frm. Turf high 89 - 1st of 14 giving 17lb to Best Ever (2 Spt York RF 4103).
**T D Easterby [2-8] Jonathan Gill.*

THE WILD WIDOW BHB 47f47a RR 47f 47a 4993[13]

5 gr m Saddlers' Hall (IRE) 10.5f **(65)** - No Cards (No Mercy) 8f **(61)**
Form - 0012780032341070
Record 1999 - 1st:2 2nd:2 3rd:2 Ran:16
Pre1999 - 1st:0 2nd:2 3rd:1 Ran:8
Win Prizemoney £3,950 *Total Prizemoney* £9,416
Wins * **1999** Aug Warwic (GD) S 10.5f 54 <
1999 *Feb Wolver (STD) S 9.4f 50*
1999 Turf 1-5: (8f 2, 10f, 11f 1-2) (sft, gd 1-1, frm 3) 1999 AW 1-11: (8f 4, 9f 1-5, 11f 2) (Fibr 1-11)
Fair filly, effective 10f, acts on g-f to frm, has worn blinkers, favours tight tracks. Turf high 54. AW high 57.
**Miss S J Wilton [1-13] John Pointon and Sons (from H J Collingridge [1-3] Feb 1999).*

THE WOODCOCK BHB 54f58a RR 53f 58a 3910[5]

4 b g Handsome Sailor 6.6f **(53)** - Game Germaine (Mummy's Game) 8.2f **(60)**
Form - 418305425775
Record 1999 - 1st:1 2nd:1 3rd:1 Ran:12
Pre1999 - 1st:1 2nd:0 3rd:0 Ran:10
Win Prizemoney £4,640 *Total Prizemoney* £5,597
Wins 1999 Mar Catter (G-S) S 7f 62
1998 Aug Nottin (G-F) 6.1f 74 <
1999 Turf 1-5: (6f, 7f 1-3, 8f) (gd 1-3, frm 2) 1999 AW 0-7: (6f 2, 7f 5) (Equi, Fibr 6)
Leggy, fair gelding, effective 6f, acts on gd to frm, has worn blinkers. Turf high 62 (1st run). AW high 61. Consistent.
**K R Burke [0-10] P Sandrovitch (from B W Hills [1-3] Mar 1999).*

THE WOODSTOCK LADY RR 89+f 4815[1]

2 ch f Barathea (IRE) - Howlin' (USA) (Alleged (USA)) 10f **(76)**
Form - 1
Record 1999 - 1st:1 2nd:0 3rd:0 Ran:1
Win Prizemoney £3,752 *Total Prizemoney* £3,752
Wins * **1999** Oct Leices (G-S) 7f 89+ <
1999 Turf 1-1: (7f 1-1) (gd 1-1)
Currently useful filly. (1st run) - 1st of 19 from Scarletta (11 Oct Leicester RF 4815). **B W Hills [1-1] Gareth Thomas.*

THIEVES WELCOME RR 61f 3364[3]

2 b f Most Welcome 8.6f **(66)** - Miss Tealeaf (USA) (Lear Fan (USA)) 8.5f **(73)**
Form - 63
Record 1999 - 1st:0 2nd:0 3rd:1 Ran:2
Win Prizemoney £0 *Total Prizemoney* £337
1999 Turf 0-1: (6f) (hrd) 1999 AW 0-1: (6f) (Fibr)
Currently average filly. **E Weymes [0-2] John Weymes Racing.*

THIHN (IRE) BHB 53f RR 50f 5154[2]

4 ch g Machiavellian (USA) 9.8f **(83)** - Hasana (USA) (Private Account (USA)) 8.5f **(74)**
Form - 630522
Record 1999 - 1st:0 2nd:2 3rd:1 Ran:6
Pre1999 - 1st:0 2nd:0 3rd:0 Ran:2
Win Prizemoney £0 *Total Prizemoney* £2,399
1999 Turf 0-6: (8f 3, 10f 3) (g-s, gd 2, g-f, frm 2)
Workmanlike, fair gelding, effective 10f, acts on gd, likes left handed tracks, favours tight tracks. Turf high 52.
**N E Berry [0-8] Messrs P Cowan, S Daniels & B Beale.*

THINK AGAIN (IRE) BHB 23f RR 22f 3863[9]

5 b g Long Pond - Either Or (Boreen (FR))
Form - 800
Record 1999 - 1st:0 2nd:0 3rd:0 Ran:3
Pre1999 - 1st:0 2nd:0 3rd:0 Ran:6
1999 Turf 0-3: (10f, 12f, 16f) (gd, frm 2)
Little account gelding. Turf high 22 (began Jly).
**R Craggs [0-11] Ray Craggs.*

THIRTY SIX CEE BHB 61f RR 62f 5054[7]

2 b f Rudimentary (USA) 8.2f **(66)** - Dear Person (Rainbow Quest (USA)) 10.4f **(75)**
Form - 554607
Record 1999 - 1st:0 2nd:0 3rd:0 Ran:6
Win Prizemoney £0 *Total Prizemoney* £246
1999 Turf 0-6: (5f 2, 6f 3, 7f) (gd 4, g-f, frm)
Average filly, effective 5f, acts on gd. Turf high 62 (began Jly).
**A W Carroll [0-6] Triumph International Ltd.*

THOMAS CROWN (IRE) BHB 39f33a RR 14f 33a 2316[10]

7 ch g Last Tycoon 9.4f **(73)** - Upward Trend (Salmon Leap (USA)) 11f **(61)**
Form - 0
Record 1999 - 1st:0 2nd:0 3rd:0 Ran:1
Pre1999 - 1st:0 2nd:0 3rd:0 Ran:8
1999 Turf 0-1: (17f) (hrd)
Little account gelding, has worn blinkers.
**D L Williams [2-16] D L Williams (from N J H Walker [0-6] Mar 1996).*

THOMAS HENRY (IRE) BHB 66f66a RR 69df 66a 2386[4]

3 br g Petardia 8.2f **(58)** - Hitopah (Bustino) 10.4f **(64)**
Form - 6134404
Record 1999 - 1st:1 2nd:0 3rd:1 Ran:7
Pre1999 - 1st:0 2nd:0 3rd:0 Ran:6
Win Prizemoney £3,572 *Total Prizemoney* £4,852
Wins * 1999 *Jan Lingfi (STD) 7f 59* <
1999 Turf 0-3: (8f 2, 10f) (g-f, frm 2) 1999 AW 1-4: (6f, 7f 1-1, 8f 2) (Equi 1-4)
Light-framed, average gelding, effective 8f, acts on frm, has worn blinkers, likes tight tracks. Turf high 69 (1st run) - 4th of 13 getting 2lb from The Whistling Teal (19 Apr Windsor 8f frm RF 0757). AW high 65. He got off the mark in a weak-looking maiden on the Lingfield Equitrack. **J S Moore [1-13] Ernie Houghton.*

THORNABY GIRL (IRE) BHB 54f59a RR 8f 59a 1724[16]

3 b f Fayruz 6.6f **(63)** - Anita's Love (IRE) (Anita's Prince)
Form - 267200
Record 1999 - 1st:0 2nd:1 3rd:0 Ran:5
Pre1999 - 1st:1 2nd:1 3rd:1 Ran:3
Win Prizemoney £2,784 *Total Prizemoney* £4,441
Wins * 1998 May Mussel (GD) C 5f 61 <
1999 Turf 0-2: (5f 2) (frm 2) 1999 AW 0-3: (5f 3) (Equi, Fibr 2)
Scopey, average filly, effective 5f, acts on gd - acts on AW. Turf high 8. AW high 63 - 2nd of 12 getting 5lb from Keen Hands (22 Mar Southwell 5f Fibr RF 0461). Inconsistent.
**T D Barron [1-8] Dave Scott.*

THORNCLIFF FOX (IRE) BHB 77f RR 66f 3988[12]

2 ch c Foxhound (USA) - Godly Light (FR) (Vayrann) 9.7f **(74)**
Form - 7330
Record 1999 - 1st:0 2nd:0 3rd:2 Ran:4
Win Prizemoney £0 *Total Prizemoney* £639
1999 Turf 0-3: (5f 3) (gd, frm 2) 1999 AW 0-1: (5f) (Fibr)
Average colt, mostly wears blinkers. Turf high 66 - 3rd of 15 giving 8lb to Alustar (7 Jun Pontefract 5f gd RF 1788).
**J A Glover [0-4] P and S Partnership.*

THORNFIELD (CAN) RR 123f 5230a[13]

4 ch g Sky Classic (CAN) 10f **(83)** - Alexandrina (USA) (Conquistador Cielo (USA)) 8.8f **(69)**
Form - 10
1999 Turf 1-2: (12f 1-2) (gd 1-1, frm)
Currently very high-class gelding. Turf high 123 (1st run) (began Oct) - 1st of 9 from Fruits of Love (17 Oct Woodbine RF 5019a).
**P England in CAN [1-2].*

THORNTOUN BELLE (IRE) BHB 30f RR 13f 2863[14]

4 b f Rainbows For Life (CAN) 9.3f **(64)** - Manzala (USA) (Irish River (FR)) 8.6f **(78)**
Form - 5700
Record 1999 - 1st:0 2nd:0 3rd:0 Ran:4
Pre1999 - 1st:0 2nd:0 3rd:1 Ran:7
Win Prizemoney £0 *Total Prizemoney* £421
1999 Turf 0-4: (7f, 8f, 9f, 13f) (gd, g-f, frm 2)
Unfurnished, poor filly, effective 8f, acts on frm. Turf high 13.
**D A Nolan [0-4] Patrick Marron (from J S Goldie [0-7] Jun 1998).*

THORNTOUN GOLD (IRE) BHB 45f RR 43f 4718[13]

3 ch f Lycius (USA) 8.8f **(71)** - Gold Braisim (IRE) (Jareer (USA)) 5.9f **(75)**
Form - 770441203800
Record 1999 - 1st:1 2nd:1 3rd:1 Ran:12
Pre1999 - 1st:0 2nd:0 3rd:0 Ran:6
Win Prizemoney £3,107 *Total Prizemoney* £4,982
Wins * 1999 Jly Thirsk (FRM) SH 8f 39 44 <
1999 Turf 1-12: (7f, 8f 1-9, 9f, 10f) (gd 5, g-f 3, frm 1-4)
Strong, moderate filly, effective 7 to 8f, acts on gd to g-f, likes left handed tracks, likes tight tracks. Turf high 50 - 2nd of 18 getting 17lb from On Till Morning (26 Jly Ayr 7f g-f RF 3136).
**J S Goldie [1-15] Tough Construction Ltd (from M Johnston [0-3] Jly 1998).*

THRASHING BHB 63f RR 60f 3831[15]

4 b c Kahyasi 12.9f **(74)** - White-Wash (Final Straw) 7.9f **(64)**
Form - 0
Record 1999 - 1st:0 2nd:0 3rd:0 Ran:1
Pre1999 - 1st:0 2nd:0 3rd:1 Ran:6
Win Prizemoney £0 *Total Prizemoney* £1,566
1999 Turf 0-1: (8f) (frm)
Average colt, often wears blinkers.
**J G M O'Shea [0-5] Graham Brown (from C E Brittain [0-6] Aug 1998).*

THREADNEEDLE (USA) BHB 60f93a RR 50f 93a 729[10]

6 b g Danzig Connection (USA) 8.2f **(75)** - Sleeping Beauty (Mill Reef (USA)) 10.5f **(78)**
Form - 6101387700
Record 1999 - 1st:1 2nd:0 3rd:1 Ran:7
Pre1999 - 1st:4 2nd:1 3rd:0 Ran:20
Win Prizemoney £23,421 *Total Prizemoney* £26,150
Wins * 1999 *Jan Lingfi (STD) H 7f 85 91* <
* 1998 *Dec Lingfi (STD) H 8f 80 84*
1998 *Feb Lingfi (SLW) C 10f 78+*
1998 *Feb Lingfi (STD) C 10f 81*
1996 Spt Newbur (G-F) 8f 75
1999 Turf 0-1: (7f) (gd) 1999 AW1-6:(7f 1-3, 8f, 9f, 10f)(Equi 1-4, Fibr 2)
Useful gelding, effective 7 to 8f, best at 7f, - acts on Equi, has worn blinkers, likes left handed tracks, likes tight tracks. AW high 93 - 3rd of 12 giving 11lb to Silca Blanka (16 Jan Lingfield 7f Equi RF 0109) - also 1st of 16 giving 10lb to Topton (2 Jan Lingfield RF 0012). Inconsistent. Despite having won over ten furlongs on Equitrack, he looks a much better horse when able to dominate over shorter trips on that surface, something he did to useful effect when winning the Ladbroke All-Weather Trophy Final at the start of the year.
**K R Burke [2-20] Nigel Shields (from Lord Huntingdon [3-7] Feb 1998).*

THREAT BHB 100f RR 96f 2487[2]

3 br c Zafonic (USA) 9f **(83)** - Prophecy (IRE) **(99f)** (Warning)
Form - 0402
Record 1999 - 1st:0 2nd:1 3rd:0 Ran:4
Pre1999 - 1st:1 2nd:0 3rd:1 Ran:2
Win Prizemoney £6,872 *Total Prizemoney* £10,898
Wins * 1998 Jly Goodwo (G-S) 6f 97+ <
1999 Turf 0-4: (6f 4) (gd 2, g-f, frm)
Workmanlike, very useful colt, effective 6f, acts on gd to frm. Turf high 96 - 2nd of 5 getting 19lb from Tomba (2 Jly Haydock 6f g-f RF 2487). He is useful but something of an underachiever. Worth a try over seven furlongs, he seems suited by easy ground.
**J H M Gosden [1-6] K Abdulla.*

THREE ANGELS (IRE) RR 63f 4338[12]

4 b g Houmayoun (FR) 7.1f **(79)** -Mullaghroe (Tarboosh (USA)) 10f **(55)**
Form - 8428202302060
Record 1999 - 1st:0 2nd:4 3rd:1 Ran:13
Pre1999 - 1st:2 2nd:2 3rd:4 Ran:14

Win Prizemoney £5,648 *Total Prizemoney* £17,441
Wins * 1998 Jun Haydoc (GD) H 7.1f 61 75 <
* 1998 May Folkes (G-F) 7f 70
1999 Turf 0-13: (7f 9, 8f 4) (g-s, g-f 5, frm 7)
Scopey, average gelding, effective 6 to 8f, best at 7f, acts on gd to frm, best on gd, has worn blinkers, likes right handed tracks, prefers tight tracks, excels at Catterick, likes Sandown. Turf high 77 - 4th of 14 giving 8lb to Acid Test (22 May Catterick 7f frm RF 1388). **M H Tompkins [2-27] Bernard Bloom.*

THREE BAY TREES (IRE) BHB 67a **RR 67a** 288^{6}

3 b f Polish Patriot (USA) 7.8f **(70)** - Suggia (Alzao (USA)) 7.1f **(68)**
Form - 7516
Record 1999 - 1st:1 2nd:0 3rd:0 Ran:3
Pre1999 - 1st:0 2nd:0 3rd:0 Ran:1
Win Prizemoney £2,684 *Total Prizemoney* £2,684
Wins * **1999** *Jan Lingfi (STD) 8f 67* <
1999 AW 1-3: (6f, 8f 1-1, 10f) (Equi 1-2, Fibr)
Neat, average filly. AW high 67 - 1st of 12 getting 5lb from Icenic (23 Jan Lingfield RF 0148). **M Johnston [1-4] Mrs J Pennell.*

THREE CHEERS (IRE) **RR 114f** 3222^{2}

5 b br g Slip Anchor 12.7f **(75)** - Three Tails (Blakeney) 10.5f **(64)**
Form - 262
Record 1999 - 1st:0 2nd:2 3rd:0 Ran:3
Pre1999 - 1st:3 2nd:1 3rd:2 Ran:13
Win Prizemoney £38,818 *Total Prizemoney* £98,638
Wins * 1997 Oct Longch (GD) G3 15f 110 <
* 1997 Jly Newmar (G-F) L 14.8f 97
* 1997 May Newmar (G-F) 14f 78
1999 Turf 0-3: (16f, 18f, 20f) (gd, g-f, frm)
Group-class gelding, effective 16 to 20f, best at 16f, acts on g-s to g-f, mostly wears blinkers (extremely effectively). Turf high 114 - 6th of 17 giving 2lb to Enzeli (17 Jun Ascot 20f g-f RF 2071). He knows more tricks than Paul Daniels and managed to miss an open goal at Pontefract in May. Despite an excellent second to Kayf Tara in the Goodwood Cup, he cannot be trusted.
**J H M Gosden [3-16] Sheikh Mohammed.*

THREE CHERRIES BHB 54f **RR 55f** 4564^{11}

3 ch f Formidable (USA) 7.8f **(60)** - Mistral's Dancer (Shareef Dancer (USA)) 9.9f **(73)**
Form - 0050
Record 1999 - 1st:0 2nd:0 3rd:0 Ran:4
1999 Turf 0-4: (6f 4) (sft, gd, g-f, frm)
Workmanlike, fair filly. Turf high 55.
**R Hannon [0-4] Mrs Robert Heathcote.*

THREE FOR A POUND BHB 44f60a **RR 37f 60a** 4441^{10}

5 b g Risk Me (FR) 8f **(53)** - Lompoa (Lomond (USA)) 8.8f **(65)**
Form - 70002450000
Record 1999 - 1st:0 2nd:1 3rd:0 Ran:11
Pre1999 - 1st:3 2nd:2 3rd:1 Ran:25
Win Prizemoney £10,547 *Total Prizemoney* £15,239
Wins 1998 Apr Thirsk (G-S) H 8f 63 68
1997 Jly Catter (SFT) H 7f 63 66
1997 Mar Catter (GD) 6f 74 <
1999 Turf 0-11: (7f 2, 8f 9) (sft, g-s 2, gd 2, g-f 4, frm 2)
Very moderate gelding, effective 7 to 10f, best at 8f, acts on g-s to frm, has worn blinkers, likes tight tracks, likes Beverley. Turf high 57. Becoming disappointing.
**Don Enrico Incisa [0-15] Mrs Christine Cawley (from J A Glover [3-21] Spt 1998).*

THREEFORTYCASH (IRE) **RR 40f** 2258^{11}

2 b c Balla Cove - Tigeen (Habitat) 9.4f **(70)**
Form - 00
Record 1999 - 1st:0 2nd:0 3rd:0 Ran:2
1999 Turf 0-2: (5f 2) (g-f, hrd)
Currently moderate colt. Turf high 40.
**Andrew Turnell [0-2] Mrs Claire Hollowood.*

THREE GREEN LEAVES (IRE) BHB 97f **RR 94f** 1215^{4}

3 ch f Environment Friend 7.5f **(67)** - Kick the Habit (Habitat) 9.4f **(70)**
Form - 04
Record 1999 - 1st:0 2nd:0 3rd:0 Ran:2
Pre1999 - 1st:5 2nd:1 3rd:2 Ran:11
Win Prizemoney £40,207 *Total Prizemoney* £43,882
Wins * 1998 Oct Pontef (SFT) L 8f 84 <
* 1998 Oct Cork (G-S) 7f 84+
* 1998 Spt Newcas (GD) 8f 84+
* 1998 Jly Beverl (G-F) 7.5f 77
* 1998 Jun Beverl (GD) 7.5f 77
1999 Turf 0-2: (8f, 10f) (hvy, g-s)
Scopey, useful filly, effective 7 to 8f, best at 8f, acts on gd to frm, best on gd. Turf high 94. Improving. She did not look back when stepped up to seven furlongs plus as a two-year-old, winning four times. She ran a better race at Newbury but was not seen again.
. **M Johnston [5-13] R N Pennell.*

THREE LEADERS (IRE) BHB 51f47a **RR 47f 47a** 4879^{5}

3 ch g Up and At 'em - Wolviston (Wolverlife) 9.3f **(54)**
Form - 032015670505
Record 1999 - 1st:1 2nd:1 3rd:1 Ran:12
Pre1999 - 1st:0 2nd:0 3rd:0 Ran:3
Win Prizemoney £2,189 *Total Prizemoney* £3,452
Wins * **1999** Jun Beverl (G-F) H 5f 55 56 <
1999 Turf 1-11: (5f 1-5, 6f 4, 7f 2) (sft, gd 2, g-f 1-4, frm 3, hrd) 1999 AW 0-1: (6f) (Fibr)
Scopey, moderate gelding, effective 5 to 6f, acts on g-f, has worn blinkers. Turf high 56 - 1st of 19 giving 5lb to American Cousin (22 Jun Beverley RF 2194). Consistent. **D Nicholls [1-15] R J H Ltd.*

THREE LIONS BHB 68f **RR 69f** 5194^{7}

2 ch c Jupiter Island 10.4f **(57)** - Super Sol (Rolfe (USA)) 12.1f **(65)**
Form - 047
Record 1999 - 1st:0 2nd:0 3rd:0 Ran:3
Win Prizemoney £0 *Total Prizemoney* £253
1999 Turf 0-3: (6f 3) (gd 2, g-f)
Currently average colt. Turf high 69 (began Oct).
**R F JohnsonHoughton [0-3] Jim Short.*

THREE POINTS BHB 100f **RR 90f** 4257^{3}

2 b c Bering 9.6f **(80)** - Trazl (IRE) **(86f)** (Zalazl (USA))
Form - 113
Record 1999 - 1st:2 2nd:0 3rd:1 Ran:3
Win Prizemoney £7,562 *Total Prizemoney* £9,493
Wins * **1999** Aug Nottin (G-F) 8.2f 87+ <
* **1999** Aug Kempto (G-F) 7f 79
1999 Turf 2-3: (7f 1-1, 8f 1-2) (g-f, frm 2-2)
Currently useful colt. Turf high 90 (began Aug) - 3rd of 5 to Sarafan (10 Spt Goodwood 8f g-f RF 4257) - also 1st of 6 giving 5lb to Rowa (23 Aug Nottingham RF 3856). He won his first two starts in clear-cut fashion, but was comfortably held when tried in Listed company. **J L Dunlop [2-3] Hesmonds Stud.*

THREE WHITE SOX **RR 18f** 4640^{7}

2 ch f Most Welcome 8.6f **(66)** - Empty Purse (Pennine Walk) 8.5f **(61)**
Form - 7
Record 1999 - 1st:0 2nd:0 3rd:0 Ran:1
1999 Turf 0-1: (7f) (gd)
Currently poor filly. **P W Harris [0-1] Les McLaughlin.*

THRIFTY BHB 57f **RR 57f** 1597^{P}

3 b f Night Shift (USA) 8.1f **(73)** - Gena Ivor (USA) (Sir Ivor) 10.2f **(70)**
Form - 50P
Record 1999 - 1st:0 2nd:0 3rd:0 Ran:3
Pre1999 - 1st:0 2nd:0 3rd:0 Ran:3
1999 Turf 0-3: (6f 3) (sft, gd, frm)
Fair filly. Turf high 54. (DEAD) **M J Ryan [0-6] Norcroft Park Stud.*

THROUGH THE RYE BHB 93f **RR 92f** 5042^{4}

3 ch c Sabrehill (USA) 8.5f **(64)** - Baharlilys (Green Dancer (USA)) 10.3f **(74)**
Form - 340104
Record 1999 - 1st:1 2nd:0 3rd:1 Ran:6
Pre1999 - 1st:0 2nd:0 3rd:0 Ran:2
Win Prizemoney £5,277 *Total Prizemoney* £9,611
Wins * **1999** Jun Newcas (G-F) 8f 69+ <
1999 Turf 1-6: (8f 1-2, 9f, 10f, 11f, 12f) (sft, gd 2, g-f 2, frm 1-1)
Scopey, useful colt. Turf high 100. Totally out of his depth in the Derby, he is no more than a useful handicapper up to a mile and a quarter. Sold for 60,000 gns, he has joined Martin Pipe.
**B W Hills [1-8] W J Gredley.*

THROWER BHB 50f39a **RR 50+f 39a** 752[1]
8 b g Thowra (FR) 11.2f **(47)** - Atlantic Line (Capricorn Line) 14.6f **(62)**
Form - 11
Record 1999 - 1st:2 2nd:0 3rd:0 Ran:2
Pre1999 - 1st:0 2nd:2 3rd:1 Ran:14
Win Prizemoney £5,708 *Total Prizemoney* £8,585
Wins * **1999** Apr Nottin (SFT) H 10f 45 50 <
* **1999** Apr Leices (G-S) H 11.8f 26 46
1999 Turf 2-2: (10f 1-1, 12f 1-1) (g-s 1-1, gd 1-1)
Fair gelding. Turf high 50 - 1st of 18 getting 1lb from Tajar (19 Apr Nottingham RF 0752) - also 1st of 14 getting 28lb from Ardleigh Charmer (1 Apr Leicester RF 0538).
**S A Brookshaw [6-8] C M & S J Owen (from W M Brisbourne [0-16] Apr 1997).*

THUNDERBIRD LADY (IRE) BHB 31f **RR 37?f** 4153[10]
3 b f Mukaddamah (USA) 7.6f **(74)** - Shenley Lass (Prince Tenderfoot (USA)) 9f **(61)**
Form - 02770
Record 1999 - 1st:0 2nd:1 3rd:0 Ran:5
Win Prizemoney £0 *Total Prizemoney* £1,350
1999 Turf 0-4: (8f, 10f 2, 12f) (g-f, frm 3) 1999 AW 0-1: (12f) (Fibr)
Unfurnished, very moderate filly. Turf high 43 (began Jly).
**L A Dace [0-5] Eddie Davess.*

THUNDERHEART BHB 32f **RR 36f** 2361[3]
8 b g Celestial Storm (USA) 11.8f **(58)** - Lorelene (FR) (Lorenzaccio) 10f **(64)**
Form - 253
Record 1999 - 1st:0 2nd:1 3rd:1 Ran:3
Pre1999 - 1st:3 2nd:5 3rd:5 Ran:33
Win Prizemoney £9,295 *Total Prizemoney* £22,079
Wins * 1997 Jly Mussel (G-F) H 16f 46 52
1999 Turf 0-3: (14f, 16f 2) (gd, g-f 2)
Very moderate gelding, has worn blinkers. Turf high 36. Consistent.
**R Allan [1-20] Ian Dalgleish (from J J O'Neill [0-1] Nov 1995).*

THUNDERING SURF RR 72f 5130[5]
2 b c Lugana Beach 7f **(63)** - Thunder Bug (USA) (Secreto (USA)) 8.7f **(72)**
Form - 5
Record 1999 - 1st:0 2nd:0 3rd:0 Ran:1
Win Prizemoney £0 *Total Prizemoney* £179
1999 Turf 0-1: (8f) (gd)
Currently above-average colt.
**N A Graham [0-1] C N & Mrs J C Wright.*

THWAAB BHB 47f53a **RR 39f 53a** 3975[10]
7 b g Dominion 8.9f **(65)** - Velvet Habit (Habitat) 9.4f **(70)**
Form - 0000
Record 1999 - 1st:0 2nd:0 3rd:0 Ran:3
Pre1999 - 1st:4 2nd:5 3rd:5 Ran:47
Win Prizemoney £14,210 *Total Prizemoney* £27,374
Wins * 1998 Jly Doncas (FRM) H 7f 56 58
* 1996 Aug Redcar (G-F) H 6f 59 61 <
* 1996 Jly Ayr (G-F) H 6f 52 56
* 1996 Jun Ayr (G-F) H 6f 45 50
1999 Turf 0-3: (7f 2, 8f) (frm 3)
Very moderate gelding, effective 7f, acts on gd to frm, best on frm, often wears blinkers (extremely effectively). Turf high 39 (began Aug). Consistent. **F Watson [4-50] F Watson.*

TIAPHENA BHB 27f40a **RR 45f 40a** 323[8]
8 b m Derrylin 12.7f **(38)** - Velda (Thatch (USA)) 9.8f **(62)**
Form - 8
Record 1999 - 1st:0 2nd:0 3rd:0 Ran:1
Pre1999 - 1st:1 2nd:1 3rd:0 Ran:11
Win Prizemoney £3,106 *Total Prizemoney* £4,242
Wins 1996 Jun Catter (GD) H 15.8f 40 45 <
1999 AW 0-1: (16f) (Fibr)
Moderate mare. Inconsistent.
**T W Donnelly [0-2] S Taberner (from J Mackie [1-7] May 1997).*

TICKA TICKA TIMING BHB 26f32a **RR 2f 32a** 1410[13]
6 b g Timeless Times (USA) 6.1f **(56)** - Belltina (Belfort (FR)) 6.8f **(63)**
Form - 00
Record 1999 - 1st:0 2nd:0 3rd:0 Ran:2
Pre1999 - 1st:1 2nd:0 3rd:2 Ran:25
Win Prizemoney £2,489 *Total Prizemoney* £3,224
Wins 1995 *Jly Southw (STD) S 6f 69?* <
1999 Turf 0-2: (5f, 9f) (gd, g-f)
Very moderate gelding, has worn blinkers. Becoming disappointing.
**L R Lloyd-James [0-2] L R Lloyd-James (from B W Murray [1-25] Apr 1998).*

TICKLISH BHB 69a **RR 68f** 4673[5]
3 b f Cadeaux Genereux 7.9f **(76)** - Exit Laughing (Shaab)
Form - 46551025
Record 1999 - 1st:1 2nd:1 3rd:0 Ran:8
Pre1999 - 1st:2 2nd:0 3rd:3 Ran:8
Win Prizemoney £11,080 *Total Prizemoney* £13,573
Wins * **1999** Aug Warwic (GD) H 6.8f 67 68
* 1998 Spt Bright (GD) H 6f 66 69 <
* 1998 Spt Ripon (HVY) H 6f 61 67
1999 Turf 1-7: (7f 1-7) (g-s 2, gd 1-3, g-f, frm) 1999 AW 0-1: (7f) (Fibr)
Average filly, effective 6 to 7f, best at 7f, acts on gd to g-f, best on gd. Turf high 68 (1st run) - 4th of 24 giving 2lb to Cinnamon Lady (15 May Newbury 7f gd RF 1238) - also 1st of 10 getting 1lb from Carrie Pooter (13 Aug Warwick RF 3631). Consistent.
**W J Haggas [3-16] J W Bogie.*

TICK N PICK BHB 37f44a **RR 28f 44a** 4997[17]
3 br f Reprimand 8.2f **(63)** - My Preference (Reference Point) 6.8f **(70)**
Form - 77308002560
Record 1999 - 1st:0 2nd:1 3rd:1 Ran:9
Pre1999 - 1st:0 2nd:0 3rd:0 Ran:5
Win Prizemoney £0 *Total Prizemoney* £1,018
1999 Turf 0-3: (7f, 9f, 10f) (g-s, gd, hrd) 1999 AW 0-6: (7f 2, 8f 2, 10f 2) (Equi 6)
Leggy, fair filly. Turf high 28. AW high 54.
**B R Johnson [0-9] Miss Julie Reeves (from E A L Dunlop [0-5] Dec 1998).*

TICK TOCK RR 60f 5070[9]
2 ch f Timeless Times (USA) 6.1f **(56)** - Aquiletta **(26f 42a)** (Bairn (USA)) 7.7f **(59)**
Form - 58020
Record 1999 - 1st:0 2nd:1 3rd:0 Ran:5
Win Prizemoney £0 *Total Prizemoney* £888
1999 Turf 0-5: (5f 5) (gd 2, g-f, frm 2)
Average filly. Turf high 60 (began Aug) - 2nd of 21 giving 1lb to Branston Lucy (24 Spt Redcar 5f frm RF 4543).
**M Mullineaux [0-5] P F Youd.*

TIC TAC MAC BHB 30f **RR 10f** 4530[17]
2 b c Mac's Fighter - Tickle Me Too (Tickled Pink) 6.5f **(59)**
Form - 800
Record 1999 - 1st:0 2nd:0 3rd:0 Ran:3
1999 Turf 0-3: (6f, 7f 2) (g-s, gd 2)
Currently poor colt. Turf high 10. **L A Dace [0-3] Miss Nicola Pfann.*

TIEBREAKER (IRE) BHB 68f60a **RR 68?f 60a** 1216[P]
4 b g Second Set (IRE) 9.2f **(67)** - Millionetta (IRE) (Danehill (USA)) 10f **(72)**
Form - P
Record 1999 - 1st:0 2nd:0 3rd:0 Ran:1
Pre1999 - 1st:1 2nd:0 3rd:1 Ran:7
Win Prizemoney £2,532 *Total Prizemoney* £2,952
Wins * 1998 Jly Nottin (G-F) H 10f 68 <
1999 Turf 0-1: (10f) (g-s)
Strong, average gelding, effective 10 to 12f, best at 10f, acts on gd to frm. Inconsistent. **N A Graham [1-8] The Tiebreakers.*

TIERGARTEN (IRE) BHB 64f **RR 67f** 4813[8]
3 b f Brief Truce (USA) 9.1f **(73)** - Lady In The Park (IRE) (Last Tycoon) 8.5f **(62)**
Form - 248
Record 1999 - 1st:0 2nd:1 3rd:0 Ran:3
Pre1999 - 1st:0 2nd:0 3rd:0 Ran:1
Win Prizemoney £0 *Total Prizemoney* £1,210
1999 Turf 0-3: (8f 3) (gd, frm 2)

Light-framed, average filly. Turf high 67.
**A C Stewart [0-4] Mrs M E Domvile.*

TIERRA DEL FUEGO BHB 23f RR 14f 4293[17]

5 b m Chilibang 7f **(55)** - Dolly Bevan (Another Realm) 6.6f **(55)**
Form - 85000
Record 1999 - 1st:0 2nd:0 3rd:0 Ran:5
Pre1999 - 1st:0 2nd:0 3rd:0 Ran:4
1999 Turf 0-1: (7f) (g-f) 1999 AW 0-4: (8f, 10f, 11f 2) (Equi, Fibr 3)
Poor filly, effective 8f, - acts on Fibr, has worn blinkers. AW high 13 - 5th of 9 getting 17lb from Brandon Magic (5 Feb Southwell 8f Fibr RF 0227). **H J Collingridge [0-9] The Headquarters Partnership V.*

TIER WORKER BHB 96f RR 97f 2074[2]

3 b c Tenby 10.4f **(76)** - On the Tide **(67f)** (Slip Anchor) 9.8f **(73)**
Form - 31112
Record 1999 - 1st:3 2nd:1 3rd:1 Ran:5
Pre1999 - 1st:0 2nd:1 3rd:1 Ran:3
Win Prizemoney £38,158 *Total Prizemoney* £51,137
Wins * **1999** Jun Epsom (G-S) H 10.1f 86 90 <
* **1999** May York (G-S) H 10.4f 80 84
* **1999** Apr Ripon (G-F) 8f 71
1999 Turf 3-5: (7f, 8f 1-1, 10f 2-2, 12f) (g-s, gd 2-2, g-f 1-2)
Lengthy, very useful colt, effective 10 to 12f, acts on gd to g-f. Turf high 97 - 2nd of 19 giving 2lb to Elmutabaki (17 Jun Ascot 12f g-f RF 2074) - also 1st of 15 giving 16lb to Goodbye Goldstone (4 Jun Epsom RF 1732). Tough and genuine, he made great strides and ran a super race to finish second in the King George V Handicap at Royal Ascot. Off the track in the second half of the season, he should stay beyond a mile and a half, acts on any ground and is open to further improvement.
**T D Easterby [3-8] Burke's 5th Family Settlement.*

TIGER GRASS (IRE) BHB 58f RR 59f 5197[12]

3 gr c Ezzoud (IRE) - Rustic Lawn (Rusticaro (FR)) 8.2f **(65)**
Form - 00808240
Record 1999 - 1st:0 2nd:1 3rd:0 Ran:8
Pre1999 - 1st:0 2nd:1 3rd:0 Ran:3
Win Prizemoney £0 *Total Prizemoney* £2,726
1999 Turf 0-8: (8f 2, 9f, 10f 3, 12f, 13f) (gd 4, g-f, frm 3)
Light-framed, fair colt, has worn blinkers. Turf high 72. Consistent.
**W R Muir [0-11] M J Caddy.*

TIGER HILL (IRE) RR 126f 4778a[5]

4 b c Danehill (USA) 9.1f **(79)** - The Filly (GER) (Apiani (GER))
Form - 122115
1999 Turf 3-6: (10f 1-1, 11f, 12f 2-4) (sft 2, gd 3-4)
Top-class colt, effective 10 to 12f, best at 12f, acts on sft to gd, best on gd, prefers left handed tracks, excels at Munich and Baden-Baden and Cologne. Turf high 126 - 2nd of 10 to El Condor Pasa (4 Jly Saint-Cloud 12f gd RF 2662a) - also 1st of 6 giving 15lb to Flamingo Road (5 Spt Baden-Baden RF 4245a). Consistent. Just about the best middle-distance performer in Germany, he has a string of Group One and Group Two victories to his name in the last couple of seasons and surpassed himself with a fine third in the 1998 Arc. He chased home El Condor Pasa in the Grand Prix de Saint-Cloud before taking the Grosser Preis von Baden for the second time in 1999 on his way to another good effort in the Arc. Effective at between ten furlongs and a mile and a half, he has been retired to stud.
**P Schiergen in GER [6-12] Baron G Von Ullmann.*

TIGER IMP (IRE) BHB 75f RR 75f 3873[3]

3 b g Imp Society (USA) 7.1f **(63)** - Mrs Merry Man (Bellypha) 9.8f **(73)**
Form - 223
Record 1999 - 1st:0 2nd:2 3rd:1 Ran:3
Win Prizemoney £0 *Total Prizemoney* £2,998
1999 Turf 0-3: (6f, 7f 2) (g-f 2, frm)
Scopey, currently above-average gelding. Turf high 75 (began Aug) - 3rd of 11 giving 5lb to Stridhana (24 Aug Lingfield 6f g-f RF 3873). **I A Balding [0-3] Mrs Angela Brodie.*

TIGER ROYAL (IRE) RR 90f 4741a[3]

3 gr c Royal Academy (USA) 7.8f **(77)** - Lady Redford (Bold Lad (IRE)) 8.4f **(68)**
Form - 5481723
1999 Turf 1-7: (5f 1-4, 6f, 7f 2) (sft 2, g-s, gd 1-2, g-f 2)
Useful colt, effective 5 to 7f, best at 5f, acts on sft to gd, best on gd, mostly wears blinkers (extremely effectively). Turf high 90 - 3rd of 11 giving 11lb to Kenema (2 Oct Curragh 5f sft RF 4741a) - also 1st of 12 giving 5lb to Not A Sound (29 Aug Curragh RF 4065a).
**D K Weld in IRE [1-7] Peter Jones.*

TIGER SHARK (USA) BHB 79a RR 112f 4058a[8]

3 b c Chief's Crown (USA) 10.2f **(75)** - Life At the Top (Habitat) 9.4f **(70)**
Form - 2110118
1999 Turf 2-4: (8f 1-2, 9f 1-1, 12f) (g-s, g-f 1-2, frm 1-1)
Scopey, Group-class colt, effective 8f, acts on g-f. Turf high 112 - 1st of 18 giving 4lb to Golden Fact (27 Jly Galway RF 3324a). Very game winner of a Listed race at Galway in the summer.
**J S Bolger in IRE [2-4] Henryk de Kwiatkowski (from Lord Huntingdon [2-5] Dec 1998).*

TIGER TALK BHB 80f RR 67f 5143[19]

3 ch c Sabrehill (USA) 8.5f **(64)** - Tebre (USA) (Sir Ivor) 10.2f **(70)**
Form - 110000
Record 1999 - 1st:2 2nd:0 3rd:0 Ran:6
Pre1999 - 1st:0 2nd:2 3rd:0 Ran:5
Win Prizemoney £11,334 *Total Prizemoney* £13,048
Wins 1999 Apr Sandow (SFT) H 8.1f 84 89 <
1999 Mar Folkes (SFT) 7f 89 <
1999 Turf 2-6: (7f 1-3, 8f 1-3) (sft 1-1, g-s 1-1, gd 3, g-f)
Scopey, average colt, effective 7 to 8f, acts on sft to g-s. Turf high 89 (1st run) - 1st of 14 from Barabaschi (31 Mar Folkestone RF 0531) - also 1st of 5 getting 5lb from Balsox (24 Apr Sandown RF 0845). Gained soft-ground victories at Folkestone and Sandown on his first two starts of the season, but has been well beaten since.
**N P Littmoden [0-2] Joy and Valentine Feerick (from B W Hills [2-9] Jun 1999).*

TIGGY SILVANO BHB 20f24a RR 26f 24a 91[7]

4 b f Tigani - Infanta Maria (King of Spain) 7.8f **(52)**
Form - 0777
Record 1999 - 1st:0 2nd:0 3rd:0 Ran:2
Pre1999 - 1st:0 2nd:0 3rd:0 Ran:14
1999 AW 0-2: (13f, 16f) (Equi 2)
Lengthy, little account filly, has worn blinkers. AW high 17.
**M Quinn [0-15] M Quinn (from M R Channon [0-1] Jly 1997).*

TIGHTROPE BHB 56f60a RR 51f 60a 4829[2]

4 b g Alzao (USA) 9.8f **(73)** - Circus Act (Shirley Heights) 10.3f **(74)**
Form - 102
Record 1999 - 1st:1 2nd:1 3rd:0 Ran:3
Pre1999 - 1st:1 2nd:1 3rd:0 Ran:10
Win Prizemoney £6,118 *Total Prizemoney* £8,255
Wins * **1999** Spt Yarmou (G-S) S 10.1f 51+
* 1997 Oct Leices (G-F) H 8f 70 79+ <
1999 Turf 1-3: (9f, 10f 1-2) (sft, g-s 1-2)
Workmanlike, average gelding. Turf high 51 (1st run) (began Spt). Consistent. **Sir Mark Prescott [2-13] Sturt Osborne House.*

TIGI BHB 30f RR 10f 3295[18]

4 ch f Tigani - Molly Brazen (Risk Me (FR)) 5.9f **(53)**
Form - 00830000
Record 1999 - 1st:0 2nd:0 3rd:1 Ran:8
Pre1999 - 1st:0 2nd:0 3rd:0 Ran:7
Win Prizemoney £0 *Total Prizemoney* £308
1999 Turf 0-8: (5f 5, 6f 2, 7f) (gd 2, g-f, frm 5)
Leggy, poor filly, effective 5f, acts on g-f, has worn blinkers (very effectively). Turf high 37 - 3rd of 19 getting 13lb from Three Leaders (22 Jun Beverley 5f g-f RF 2194).
**J J Quinn [0-8] Geoff Pickering (from Mrs M Reveley [0-7] Aug 1998).*

TIGRE BHB 86f RR 81f 4799[2]

2 b c Mujtahid (USA) 7.4f **(69)** - Vice Vixen (CAN) (Vice Regent (CAN)) 8.7f **(74)**
Form - 42222
Record 1999 - 1st:0 2nd:4 3rd:0 Ran:5
Win Prizemoney £0 *Total Prizemoney* £5,868
1999 Turf 0-5: (6f, 7f 2, 8f 2) (gd 3, g-f 2)
Decent colt. Turf high 81 - 2nd of 6 to Zafonium (9 Oct York 8f gd RF 4799). **B W Hills [0-5] Guy Reed & J Hanson.*

TIGRE BOIS RR 30f 4840[15]
2 b c Mon Tresor 7.9f **(60)** - Gentle Star (Comedy Star (USA)) 7.5f **(50)**
Form - 00
Record 1999 - 1st:0 2nd:0 3rd:0 Ran:2
1999 Turf 0-2: (7f 2) (gd 2)
Currently very moderate colt. Turf high 30 (began Spt).
**B R Millman [0-2] Victor Palmer.*

TIGRELLO BHB 65f **RR 66f** 2749[1]
5 ch g Efisio 7.7f **(69)** - Prejudice (Young Generation) 7.7f **(63)**
Form - 0071
Record 1999 - 1st:1 2nd:0 3rd:0 Ran:4
Pre1999 - 1st:1 2nd:2 3rd:0 Ran:11
Win Prizemoney £5,665 *Total Prizemoney* £10,161
Wins * 1999 Jly Bright (FRM) S 8f 54
1997 May Warwic (FRM) 8f 85 <
1999 Turf 1-4: (7f 2, 8f 1-1, 10f) (g-s, gd, g-f, hrd 1-1)
Average gelding. Turf high 66.
**J Berry [1-4] A M Al-Midani (from G Lewis [1-11] May 1998).*

TIJIYR (IRE) RR 103f 1528a[3]
3 gr c Primo Dominie 7.2f **(67)** - Tijara (IRE) (Darshaan) 9.9f **(84)**
Form - 23
1999 Turf 0-2: (8f, 9f) (hvy, gd)
Currently very useful colt. Turf high 103 - 3rd of 5 to Val Royal (20 May Longchamp 9f hvy RF 1528a).
**A deRoyerDupre in FR [0-2] Aga Khan.*

TIJUANA BHB 35f **RR 37f** 2182[13]
3 ch f Gabitat 8.5f **(44)** - Gabibti (IRE) (Dara Monarch) 8.8f **(59)**
Form - 00
Record 1999 - 1st:0 2nd:0 3rd:0 Ran:2
Pre1999 - 1st:0 2nd:0 3rd:0 Ran:2
1999 Turf 0-2: (6f, 8f) (gd, frm)
Light-framed, very moderate filly. Turf high 19.
**B Gubby [0-4] Brian Gubby Ltd.*

TIKOTINO BHB 40f **RR 39f** 5007[5]
3 ch f Mystiko (USA) 7.7f **(59)** - Tino-Ella (Bustino) 10.4f **(64)**
Form - 62700705
Record 1999 - 1st:0 2nd:1 3rd:0 Ran:8
Pre1999 - 1st:0 2nd:0 3rd:0 Ran:4
Win Prizemoney £0 *Total Prizemoney* £654
1999 Turf 0-8: (8f 2, 10f 4, 12f, 14f) (g-s, gd 4, g-f, frm 2)
Very moderate filly, effective 12f, acts on gd, has worn blinkers (very effectively), likes tight tracks. Turf high 52 - 7th of 15 getting 17lb from Bergamo (25 May Beverley 12f gd RF 1449).
**J A Glover [0-12] Ted Revill.*

TILAAL (USA) BHB 32f45a **RR 33f 45a** 3597[5]
7 ch g Gulch (USA) 9.6f **(79)** - Eye Drop (USA) (Irish River (FR)) 8.6f **(78)**
Form - 4758405
Record 1999 - 1st:0 2nd:0 3rd:0 Ran:7
Pre1999 - 1st:0 2nd:0 3rd:5 Ran:21
Win Prizemoney £0 *Total Prizemoney* £3,453
1999 Turf 0-5: (7f 2, 8f, 11f, 12f) (gd 2, frm 2, hrd) 1999 AW 0-2: (8f 2) (Fibr 2)
Fair gelding, effective 8f, - acts on Fibr, has worn blinkers, likes left handed tracks. Turf high 33. AW high 57 (1st run) - 4th of 16 giving 3lb to Tom (2 Jan Southwell 8f Fibr RF 0014).
**M D Hammond [0-32] M D Hammond (from E A L Dunlop [0-7] Spt 1995).*

TILBURG BHB 34f29a **RR 38f 29a** 2648[15]
4 b f High Kicker (USA) 8.4f **(52)** -Touch My HeartSteel Heart) 8.3f **(58)**
Form - 500
Record 1999 - 1st:0 2nd:0 3rd:0 Ran:3
Pre1999 - 1st:0 2nd:1 3rd:0 Ran:19
Win Prizemoney £0 *Total Prizemoney* £488
1999 AW 0-3: (5f 2, 8f) (Fibr 3)
Leggy, very moderate filly, effective 5f, - acts on Fibr, likes left handed tracks, likes tight tracks. AW high 28.
**Mrs N Macauley [0-22] J Teasdale.*

TILE IT RR 56f 1273[3]
2 b c Distinctly North (USA) 7.4f **(63)** - Simmie's Special **(67a)** (Precocious) 8.6f **(62)**
Form - 83
Record 1999 - 1st:0 2nd:0 3rd:1 Ran:2
Win Prizemoney £0 *Total Prizemoney* £362
1999 Turf 0-2: (5f 2) (g-f, frm)
Currently fair colt. Turf high 56. **A Bailey [0-2] A Thomson.*

TILER (IRE) BHB 77f80a **RR 75f 80a** 2335[4]
7 br g Ballad Rock 7.2f **(63)** - Fair Siobahn (Petingo) 11f **(72)**
Form - 1054
Record 1999 - 1st:1 2nd:0 3rd:0 Ran:4
Pre1999 - 1st:6 2nd:10 3rd:9 Ran:72
Win Prizemoney £44,551 *Total Prizemoney* £82,372
Wins * 1999 Apr Newcas (GD) H 7f 76 83
* 1998 Aug Cheste (G-S) H 7.6f 73 74
* 1997 Jly Ayr (G-F) H 6f 74 75
* 1996 Jly Thirsk (FRM) H 6f 78 83
* 1995 Aug York (G-F) H 6f 78 84 <
1999 Turf 1-4: (7f 1-4) (gd 1-3, frm)
Above-average gelding, effective 6 to 8f, best at 6f, acts on gd to hrd, best on gd, has worn blinkers, does well at Newcastle. Turf high 83 (1st run) - 1st of 17 giving 6lb to Redoubtable (5 Apr Newcastle RF 0582). Consistent. A very useful handicapper on his day, he looks to need seven furlongs these days, being victorious over that trip at Chester in '98, and on his Newcastle reappearance. **M Johnston [7-76] Mrs C Robinson.*

TILIA RR 43f 2554[10]
3 b f Primo Dominie 7.2f **(67)** -Bermuda Lily (Dunbeath (USA)) 7.8f **(70)**
Form - 0064060
Record 1999 - 1st:0 2nd:0 3rd:0 Ran:7
Pre1999 - 1st:0 2nd:0 3rd:0 Ran:4
1999 Turf 0-7: (5f 4, 6f 3) (g-s, gd 2, g-f, frm 2, hrd)
Scopey, moderate filly, effective 6f, acts on gd, has worn blinkers (very effectively). Turf high 49 - 4th of 17 getting 25lb from Barnacla (7 Jun Windsor 6f gd RF 1801).
**R Hannon [0-11] Mrs W H GibsonFleming.*

TILLERMAN RR 99f 4679[1]
3 b c In The Wings 11.2f **(77)** - Autumn Tint (USA) (Roberto (USA)) 10f **(76)**
Form - 11
Record 1999 - 1st:2 2nd:0 3rd:0 Ran:2
Win Prizemoney £9,525 *Total Prizemoney* £9,525
Wins * 1999 Oct Newmar (G-S) 8f 99 <
* 1999 Aug Lingfi (G-F) 9f 84+
1999 Turf 2-2: (8f 1-1, 9f 1-1) (gd 1-1, g-f 1-1)
Scopey, currently very useful colt. Turf high 99 (began Aug) - 1st of 8 giving 4lb to Chief Rebel (1 Oct Newmarket RF 4679). A massive individual, he created a good impression on both his starts and is a smart prospect. Likely to stay a mile and a quarter, he already looks up to listed class. **Mrs A J Perrett [2-2] K Abdulla.*

TILLYBOY BHB 23f **RR 70f** 317[2]
9 b g Little Wolf 14.4f **(53)** - Redgrave Creative (Swing Easy (USA)) 6.5f **(55)**
Form - 0062
Record 1999 - 1st:0 2nd:1 3rd:0 Ran:2
Pre1999 - 1st:0 2nd:0 3rd:1 Ran:3
Win Prizemoney £0 *Total Prizemoney* £1,086
1999 AW 0-2: (16f 2) (Fibr 2)
Above-average gelding. AW high 26.
**Mrs M Reveley [1-10] The Mary Reveley Racing Club.*

TIMAHS BHB 104f **RR 108f** 4492[7]
3 b c Mtoto 11.5f **(71)** - Shomoose (Habitat) 9.4f **(70)**
Form - 2317
Record 1999 - 1st:1 2nd:1 3rd:1 Ran:4
Pre1999 - 1st:1 2nd:0 3rd:0 Ran:2
Win Prizemoney £15,383 *Total Prizemoney* £30,717
Wins * 1999 Spt Doncas (G-F) 10.3f 108 <
1998 Spt Newmar (GD) 8f 93+
1999 Turf 1-4: (10f 1-3, 12f) (sft, g-f 1-2, frm)
Strong, Pattern-class colt, effective 10 to 12f, acts on g-f. Turf high 108 (began Jly) - 1st of 6 getting 6lb from Goombayland (10 Spt Doncaster RF 4250). Caught right on the line on his belated return at Epsom in July, he was third in Goodwood's Tote Gold Trophy next time - a rare Godolphin runner in a handicap - and had a hard

race when winning at Doncaster. That may have left its mark as he was well beaten on his final start.

**S bin Suroor [1-4] Godolphin (from D R Loder [1-2] Oct 1998).*

TIMARU (IRE) BHB 66f **RR 75f** 4870[19]

2 ch c Shalford (IRE) 7.8f **(63)** - Wide Outside (IRE) **(18f 28a)** (Don't Forget Me) 8.3f **(74)**

Form - 772362010

Record 1999 - 1st:1 2nd:2 3rd:1 Ran:9

Win Prizemoney £3,210 *Total Prizemoney* £5,421

Wins * 1999 Spt Ayr (G-S) S 8f 75 <

1999 Turf 1-9: (6f 3, 7f 4, 8f 1-2) (gd 1-5, g-f 2, frm 2)

Above-average colt, effective 7 to 8f, best at 7f, acts on gd to frm, has worn blinkers. Turf high 75 - 3rd of 12 giving 5lb to Courting (30 Jun Catterick 7f frm RF 2436) - also 1st of 15 giving 5lb to Sheerness Essity (16 Spt Ayr RF 4341).

**A P Jarvis [1-9] Ambrose Turnbull.*

TIMBOROA RR 103f 2661a[2]

3 b c Salse (USA) 10.9f **(71)** - Kisumu (FR) (Damister (USA)) 9f **(73)**

Form - 262

1999 Turf 0-3: (8f, 10f, 12f) (sft, g-f 2)

Currently very useful colt. Turf high 103 (1st run) - 2nd of 11 to Alabama Jacks (25 Apr Capannelle 8f sft RF 0930a). Second in the Italian 2,000 Guineas, he barely stays a mile and a quarter.

**R Brogi in ITY [0-3].*

TIME AND AGAIN RR 26f 5071[12]

3 ch f Timeless Times (USA) 6.1f **(56)** -Busted Love (Busted) 10.2f **(61)**

Form - 006000

Record 1999 - 1st:0 2nd:0 3rd:0 Ran:6

Pre1999 - 1st:0 2nd:0 3rd:1 Ran:4

Win Prizemoney £0 *Total Prizemoney* £461

1999 Turf 0-6: (8f, 11f 2, 12f 3) (gd 2, g-f 2, frm, hrd)

Workmanlike, little account filly. Turf high 41.

**Mrs G S Rees [0-10] A Rhodes.*

TIME BOMB RR 50f 4580[8]

2 b f Great Commotion (USA) 9.2f **(80)** - Play For Time (Comedy Star (USA)) 7.5f **(50)**

Form - 8

Record 1999 - 1st:0 2nd:0 3rd:0 Ran:1

1999 Turf 0-1: (6f) (gd)

Currently fair filly. **B R Millman [0-1] Wild Beef Racing.*

TIME CAN TELL BHB 48f58a **RR 24f 58a** 4940[6]

5 ch g Sylvan Express 9.6f **(45)** - Stellaris (Star Appeal) 9.6f **(65)**

Form - 7424412606

Record 1999 - 1st:1 2nd:2 3rd:0 Ran:10

Pre1999 - 1st:2 2nd:5 3rd:7 Ran:36

Win Prizemoney £7,141 *Total Prizemoney* £17,909

Wins * 1999 *Apr Wolver (STD) H 16.2f 55 63*

1998 *Jan Lingfi (STD) C 13f 69* <

1996 Oct Nottin (GD) S 8.2f 62

1999 Turf 0-1: (18f) (g-f) 1999 AW 1-9: (12f 3, 13f, 14f, 16f 1-4) (Equi 2, Fibr 1-7)

Average gelding, effective 13 to 16f, best at 16f, - acts on AW, best on Equi, has worn blinkers, favours left handed tracks, favours tight tracks. AW high 65 - 2nd of 13 getting 6lb from Doc Ryan's (17 May Southwell 16f Fibr RF 1282) - also 1st of 12 getting 1lb from Quezon City (10 Apr Wolverhampton RF 0643). Becoming disappointing.

**A G Juckes [1-10] A C W Price (from R T Juckes [0-8] Jun 1998).*

TIME FOR LAGER BHB 29f37a **RR 35f 37a** 5101[5]

4 gr f Timeless Times (USA) 6.1f **(56)** -Laura Lager (Warpath)12.3f **(52)**

Form - 45844605

Record 1999 - 1st:0 2nd:0 3rd:0 Ran:8

Pre1999 - 1st:0 2nd:0 3rd:1 Ran:5

Win Prizemoney £0 *Total Prizemoney* £327

1999 Turf 0-3: (12f, 14f, 16f) (g-s, g-f, frm) 1999 AW 0-5: (11f, 12f 4) (Fibr 5)

Leggy, very moderate filly, effective 12f, - acts on Fibr, likes left handed tracks. Turf high 35. AW high 40 (1st run) - 4th of 16 getting 21lb from Such Boldness (18 Jan Southwell 12f Fibr RF 0114).

**J Wharton [0-13] Mrs Vera Craggs.*

TIME FOR MUSIC (IRE) BHB 82f **RR 80f** 3858[1]

2 b c Mukaddamah (USA) 7.6f **(74)** - Shrewd Girl (USA) (Sagace (FR)) 8f **(124)**

Form - 52261

Record 1999 - 1st:1 2nd:2 3rd:0 Ran:5

Win Prizemoney £2,988 *Total Prizemoney* £4,805

Wins * 1999 Aug Nottin (G-F) H 6.1f 77 80 <

1999 Turf 1-5: (6f 1-2, 7f 3) (g-f, frm 1-4)

Decent colt. Turf high 80 - 1st of 7 giving 17lb to Supremely Devious (23 Aug Nottingham RF 3858).

**T G Mills [1-5] Shipman Racing Ltd.*

TIME FOR THE CLAN BHB 51f **RR 56f** 3541[7]

2 ch g Clantime 6.6f **(57)** - Fyas (Sayf El Arab (USA)) 7.1f **(54)**

Form - 8000407

Record 1999 - 1st:0 2nd:0 3rd:0 Ran:7

1999 Turf 0-7: (5f 4, 6f 3) (g-f 5, frm 2)

Fair gelding, effective 6f, acts on g-f, has worn blinkers. Turf high 56 - 4th of 12 to Pertemps Fc (24 Jly Newcastle 6f g-f RF 3102).

**J J O'Neill [0-7] E A Brook.*

TIME GOES BY (IRE) BHB 63f **RR 63f** 3307[7]

2 ch g Shalford (IRE) 7.8f **(63)** - Alva Clare (IRE) (Pennine Walk) 8.5f **(61)**

Form - 5004351427

Record 1999 - 1st:1 2nd:1 3rd:1 Ran:10

Win Prizemoney £2,057 *Total Prizemoney* £2,962

Wins * 1999 Jun Lingfi (G-F) S 6f 54 <

1999 Turf 1-8: (5f 5, 6f 1-3) (gd 2, g-f 2, frm 2, hrd 1-2) 1999 AW 0-2: (5f 2) (Fibr 2)

Average gelding, effective 5 to 6f, acts on hrd, has worn blinkers. Turf high 63 - 2nd of 11 giving 10lb to Misty Miss (5 Jly Bath 5f hrd RF 2550) - also 1st of 11 from College Rock (19 Jun Lingfield RF 2148). AW high 41. **J Berry [1-10] Miss Lilo Blum.*

TIME IS MONEY (IRE) BHB 42f36a **RR 47f 36a** 1978[5]

7 br g Sizzling Melody 6.3f **(49)** - Tiempo (King of Spain) 7.8f **(52)**

Form - 0205

Record 1999 - 1st:0 2nd:1 3rd:0 Ran:4

Pre1999 - 1st:0 2nd:0 3rd:2 Ran:14

Win Prizemoney £0 *Total Prizemoney* £1,577

1999 Turf 0-4: (6f, 7f 2, 8f) (gd 2, g-f, frm)

Moderate gelding, has worn blinkers. Turf high 47 - 2nd of 7 getting 8lb from Persian Fayre (7 May Carlisle 7f frm RF 1077).

**M H Tompkins [0-18] Miss Clare Hollest.*

TIMELESS CHICK BHB 55f **RR 46f** 3906[13]

2 ch f Timeless Times (USA) 6.1f **(56)** - Be My Bird **(55f 42a)** (Be My Chief (USA))

Form - 76660

Record 1999 - 1st:0 2nd:0 3rd:0 Ran:5

1999 Turf 0-3: (6f 2, 8f) (g-f 2, frm) 1999 AW 0-2: (5f, 7f) (Equi, Fibr)

Moderate filly, has worn blinkers. Turf high 46. AW high 39.

**Andrew Reid [0-5] A S Reid.*

TIMELESS QUEST BHB 50f64a **RR 55f 64a** 4722[13]

2 ch f Timeless Times (USA) 6.1f **(56)** - Animate (IRE) (Tate Gallery (USA)) 7.4f **(67)**

Form - 04020

Record 1999 - 1st:0 2nd:1 3rd:0 Ran:5

Win Prizemoney £0 *Total Prizemoney* £590

1999 Turf 0-3: (6f, 7f 2) (gd 2, g-f) 1999 AW 0-2: (7f 2) (Fibr 2)

Average filly, has worn blinkers. Turf high 55 (began Jly). AW high 65 (began Jly) - 2nd of 15 to The Frog Queen (28 Spt Southwell 7f Fibr RF 4605). **T J Etherington [0-5] G J Harris.*

TIME LOSS BHB 58f **RR 40f** 4350[19]

4 ch g Kenmare (FR) 9.6f **(76)** - Not Before Time (IRE) (Polish Precedent (USA)) 10.2f **(60)**

Form - 2700

Record 1999 - 1st:0 2nd:1 3rd:0 Ran:4

Pre1999 - 1st:1 2nd:0 3rd:0 Ran:5

Win Prizemoney £3,566 *Total Prizemoney* £4,346

Wins 1998 Jun Chepst (G-S) 10.2f 82 <

1999 Turf 0-4: (10f 2, 11f 2) (g-f 2, frm 2)

Scopey, moderate gelding, effective 10f, acts on gd, has worn blinkers, likes tight tracks. Turf high 62 (began Jly). Becoming dis-

appointing.
**Mrs A Swinbank [0-4] Black Combe Racing (from H Candy [1-5] Oct 1998).*

TIME MILL BHB 77f **RR 75f** 3300[3]
3 b c Shirley Heights 12.1f **(76)** - Not Before Time (IRE) (Polish Precedent (USA)) 10.2f **(60)**
Form - 2423
Record 1999 - 1st:0 2nd:2 3rd:1 Ran:4
Pre1999 - 1st:0 2nd:0 3rd:0 Ran:1
Win Prizemoney £0 *Total Prizemoney* £3,019
1999 Turf 0-4: (10f 3, 11f) (gd, g-f, frm 2)
Scopey, above-average colt. Turf high 75 (1st run) - 2nd of 9 giving 5lb to Auspicious (21 May Bath 10f g-f RF 1370).
**J W Hills [0-5] George Tong.*

TIME N TIDE (IRE) BHB 80f **RR 76f** 5106[6]
3 b g Namaqualand (USA) - Now Then (Sandford Lad) 7.8f **(54)**
Form - 1523086
Record 1999 - 1st:1 2nd:1 3rd:1 Ran:7
Win Prizemoney £3,944 *Total Prizemoney* £6,790
Wins 1999 Apr Leices (G-S) 8f 83 <
1999 Turf 1-7: (8f 1-2, 10f 3, 12f 2) (g-s 2, gd 1-4, frm)
Strong, above-average gelding, effective 12f, acts on gd. Turf high 95. He lost his way in the second half of the season, but had looked useful and should not be written off. Likely to be suited by a mile and a half, he acts on easy ground and is just the sort to do well over hurdles.
**G M McCourt [0-2] McCourt Fine Meats Ltd (from B J Meehan [1-5] Jly 1999).*

TIME OF NIGHT (USA) BHB 46f51a **RR 45f 51a** 4174[10]
6 gr ro m Night Shift (USA) 8.1f **(73)** - Tihama (USA) (Sassafras (FR)) 9.6f **(69)**
Form - 344866270505711740
Record 1999 - 1st:2 2nd:1 3rd:0 Ran:16
Pre1999 - 1st:3 2nd:5 3rd:6 Ran:37
Win Prizemoney £12,771 *Total Prizemoney* £22,623
Wins * 1999 Aug Carlis (FRM) H 8f 44 47
*** 1999** Jly Thirsk (FRM) H 8f 41 42
* 1998 *Apr Southw (STD)* 7f 60 <
* 1998 *Mar Southw (STD)* 7f 60 <
* 1998 *Feb Wolver (STD) H* 7f 46 53
1999 Turf 2-12: (7f 3, 8f 2-7, 10f 2) (gd 4, g-f 3, frm 2-5) 1999 AW 0-4: (7f 2, 8f, 11f) (Fibr 4)
Fair mare, effective 7 to 8f, best at 7f, - acts on Fibr, has worn blinkers, prefers left handed tracks, favours tight tracks, and excels at Wolverhampton. Turf high 47. AW high 55.
**J L Eyre [5-33] Whitestonecliffe Racing Partnership (from R Guest [0-20] Jun 1997).*

TIME ON MY HANDS BHB 57a **RR 28f 57a** 5050[20]
3 b g Most Welcome 8.6f **(66)** - Zareeta (Free State) 8.7f **(61)**
Form - 630710800
Record 1999 - 1st:1 2nd:0 3rd:1 Ran:9
Pre1999 - 1st:0 2nd:0 3rd:0 Ran:3
Win Prizemoney £2,024 *Total Prizemoney* £2,339
Wins 1999 *May Southw (STD) C* 8f 59 <
1999 Turf 0-4: (8f 2, 10f 2) (gd 2, frm, hrd) 1999 AW 1-5: (7f, 8f 1-3, 9f) (Fibr 1-5)
Scopey, fair gelding, effective 8f, - acts on Fibr, likes left handed tracks, likes tight tracks. Turf high 28. AW high 59 - 1st of 7 getting 7lb from Lady Peppiatt (6 May Southwell RF 1062).
**S R Bowring [0-4] J Doxey (from C W Thornton [1-8] May 1999).*

TIME OUT BHB 20f26a **RR 37?f 26a** 2375[14]
4 ch f Timeless Times (USA) 6.1f **(56)** -Tangalooma (Hotfoot) 10.5f **(59)**
Form - 1237000080
Record 1999 - 1st:0 2nd:1 3rd:1 Ran:9
Pre1999 - 1st:1 2nd:0 3rd:0 Ran:6
Win Prizemoney £1,850 *Total Prizemoney* £2,589
Wins 1998 *Dec Southw (STD)* 11f 43 <
1999 AW 0-9: (8f, 11f 2, 12f 4, 14f, 16f) (Fibr 9)
Very moderate filly, effective 11f, - acts on Fibr, has worn blinkers. AW high 45.
**D Carroll [0-3] Miss Diane Allman (from M J Polglase [0-4] Mar 1999).*

TIME SAVED BHB 86f **RR 90f** 4019[11]
3 b f Green Desert (USA) 7.8f **(78)** - Time Charter (Saritamer (USA)) 9.5f **(63)**
Form - 0170
Record 1999 - 1st:1 2nd:0 3rd:0 Ran:4
Win Prizemoney £3,915 *Total Prizemoney* £3,915
Wins * 1999 Jly Windso (G-F) 10f 80 <
1999 Turf 1-4: (8f, 10f 1-3) (gd, g-f 2, frm 1-1)
Leggy, useful filly. Turf high 90. Won a Windsor maiden before found wanting in listed company. **Sir Michael Stoute [1-4] R Barnett.*

TIME TEMPTRESS BHB 60f **RR 60f** 5075[6]
3 b f Timeless Times (USA) 6.1f **(56)** - Tangalooma (Hotfoot) 10.5f **(59)**
Form - 143030506
Record 1999 - 1st:1 2nd:0 3rd:2 Ran:9
Pre1999 - 1st:0 2nd:1 3rd:0 Ran:8
Win Prizemoney £3,956 *Total Prizemoney* £6,594
Wins * 1999 May Newcas (G-F) H 8f 60 64 <
1999 Turf 1-9: (8f 1-6, 9f 2, 10f) (gd 2, g-f, frm 1-6)
Leggy, average filly, effective 7 to 9f, best at 8f, acts on gd to frm, best on frm. Turf high 65 - 3rd of 13 getting 19lb from Ratatuia (15 Jun Thirsk 8f frm RF 2006) - also 1st of 18 getting 16lb from Ringside Jack (3 May Newcastle RF 1007).
**G M Moore [1-17] Middleham Racing Bureau/G Heap.*

TIME TO FLY BHB 44f68a **RR 46df 68a** 4924[13]
6 b g Timeless Times (USA) 6.1f **(56)** - Dauntless Flight (Golden Mallard) 5.7f **(38)**
Form - 0547100702030
Record 1999 - 1st:1 2nd:1 3rd:1 Ran:12
Pre1999 - 1st:5 2nd:5 3rd:3 Ran:35
Win Prizemoney £14,752 *Total Prizemoney* £23,369
Wins * 1999 *Apr Lingfi (STD) H* 6f 65 66
* 1998 *Jan Lingfi (STD) H* 6f 68 72 <
* 1998 *Jan Wolver (STD) H* 5f 52 70
* 1998 *Jan Wolver (STD) H* 6f 52 61
* 1997 *Jun Southw (STD) H* 6f 42 46
* 1997 *Apr Wolver (STD) H* 5f 32 43
1999 Turf 0-6: (5f 3, 6f 3) (g-f, frm 4, hrd) 1999 AW 1-6: (5f 2, 6f 1-4) (Equi 1-1, Fibr 5)
Average gelding, effective 5 to 6f, - acts on Fibr, often wears blinkers (very effectively), prefers left handed tracks, prefers tight tracks, excels at Lingfield, does well at Wolverhampton. Turf high 46. AW high 66. **B W Murray [6-47] B Murray.*

TIME TO SKIP BHB 43f **RR 41f** 4073[11]
2 b f Timeless Times (USA) 6.1f **(56)** - North Pine (Import) 6.6f **(68)**
Form - 00080
Record 1999 - 1st:0 2nd:0 3rd:0 Ran:5
1999 Turf 0-5: (5f, 6f 2, 7f, 8f) (gd, frm 4)
Moderate filly. Turf high 41 (began Jly).
**R Hannon [0-5] P L Williams.*

TIME TO WYN BHB 48f **RR 42f** 5135[8]
3 b g Timeless Times (USA) 6.1f **(56)** - Wyn-Bank (Green God) 9.6f **(68)**
Form - 0312P00078
Record 1999 1st:1 2nd:1 3rd:1 Ran:10
Pre1999 - 1st:1 2nd:0 3rd:1 Ran:7
Win Prizemoney £5,030 *Total Prizemoney* £6,844
Wins * 1999 Jun Carlis (G-F) 8f 63 <
* 1998 Spt Beverl (G-F) SH 7.5f 52 57
1999 Turf 1-10: (8f 1-7, 10f 3) (g-s, gd 5, frm 3, hrd 1-1)
Neat, moderate gelding, effective 7 to 8f, best at 8f, acts on g-f to hrd, prefers right handed tracks, favours tight tracks. Turf high 63 - 1st of 13 getting 10lb from Arc (24 Jun Carlisle RF 2264).
**J G FitzGerald [2-17] Michael Ng.*

TIME VALLY BHB 68f **RR 63f** 5060[6]
2 ch f Timeless Times (USA) 6.1f **(56)** - Fort Vally **(47f)** (Belfort (FR)) 6.8f **(63)**
Form - 706
Record 1999 - 1st:0 2nd:0 3rd:0 Ran:3
1999 Turf 0-3: (7f 3) (g-s 2, gd)
Currently average filly. Turf high 63. **S Dow [0-3] Mrs M Lingwood.*

TIME ZONE BHB 108f **RR 116f** 3695[6]
3 b c Shirley Heights 12.1f **(76)** - Forthwith **(94f)** (Midyan (USA)) 6f **(60)**

Form - 31226
Record 1999 - 1st:1 2nd:2 3rd:1 Ran:5
Pre1999 - 1st:0 2nd:1 3rd:1 Ran:2
Win Prizemoney £6,376 *Total Prizemoney* £35,055
Wins * 1999 May Salisb (G-F) 12f 97 <
1999 Turf 1-5: (12f 1-4, 16f) (g-f 3, frm 1-2)
Scopey, high-class colt, effective 12f, acts on frm. Turf high 116 - 2nd of 6 to Compton Ace (27 Jly Goodwood 12f frm RF 3168). Third behind subsequent Oaks winner Ramruma on his reappearance, he got off the mark at Salisbury next time if finding the mile and a half barely adequate. Runner-up in Queen's Vase after quite a tussle at Ascot, he was again runner-up in the Goodwood's Gordon Stakes back over 12 furlongs. Well held in the Great Voltigeur on what turned out to be his final start of the season.
**C E Brittain [1-7] Wyck Hall Stud.*

TIMOTE (IRE) RR 106f 4777a[7]

3 ch f Indian Ridge 7.6f **(74)** - Across the Ice (USA) (General Holme (USA)) 5.7f **(63)**
Form - 2111427
1999 Turf 3-7: (5f 1-4, 6f 2-3) (hvy 1-1, sft 2, gd, g-f 2-2, frm)
Pattern-class filly, effective 5f, acts on gd to frm, has worn blinkers. Turf high 106 - also 1st of 14 getting 3lb from Pharmacist (11 Jly Curragh RF 2801a). Improving. Raced over a mile as a juvenile, but found her metier when dropped in trip last term. She completed a hat-trick, culminating in a £30,000 handicap, before running with great credit in pattern company, and was unlucky not to make the frame in the Prix de l'Abbaye on her final start.
**D K Weld in IRE [3-11] Dr Michael Smurfit.*

TINA'S ROYALE BHB 50f RR 45f 5032[19]

3 b f Prince Sabo 6.6f **(64)** - Aventina (Averof) 8.2f **(62)**
Form - 4062480
Record 1999 - 1st:0 2nd:1 3rd:0 Ran:7
Pre1999 - 1st:0 2nd:0 3rd:2 Ran:5
Win Prizemoney £0 *Total Prizemoney* £2,687
1999 Turf 0-7: (5f 6, 6f) (sft, g-s, gd, g-f 3, frm)
Neat, moderate filly, effective 5f, acts on g-s. Turf high 68. Becoming disappointing.
**H Candy [0-12] Wickfield Stud and Hartshill Stud.*

TIN DRUM (IRE) BHB 42f42a RR 54f 42a 4869[12]

3 b c Roi Danzig (USA) 10.5f **(62)** - Triumphant (Track Spare) 8.8f **(62)**
Form - 0000
Record 1999 - 1st:0 2nd:0 3rd:0 Ran:4
Pre1999 - 1st:0 2nd:0 3rd:0 Ran:2
1999 Turf 0-3: (10f 2, 12f) (gd, g-f, frm) 1999 AW 0-1: (12f) (Fibr)
Scopey, fair colt. Turf high 54. **R Hannon [0-6] Michael Pescod.*

TING (IRE) BHB 62f RR 51f 4125[5]

2 b g Magical Wonder (USA) 7.2f **(60)** - Rozmiyn (Caerleon (USA)) 8.6f **(71)**
Form - 085
Record 1999 - 1st:0 2nd:0 3rd:0 Ran:3
1999 Turf 0-3: (5f, 6f 2) (gd, g-f, frm)
Currently fair gelding. Turf high 51.
**P C Haslam [0-3] Martin Wickens.*

TINGED WITH GOLD (IRE) RR 57f 3378[3]

4 ch g Kris 10f **(75)** - Touch and Love (IRE) (Green Desert (USA)) 8.6f **(78)**
Form - 3
Record 1999 - 1st:0 2nd:0 3rd:1 Ran:1
Win Prizemoney £0 *Total Prizemoney* £510
1999 Turf 0-1: (10f) (frm)
Fair gelding. (1st run) - 3rd of 4 giving 1lb to L S Lowry (4 Aug Yarmouth 10f frm RF 3378).
**M D Hammond [0-2] Million In Mind Partnership (8).*

TINKER OSMASTON BHB 52f RR 46f 4813[10]

8 br m Dunbeath (USA) 9.9f **(53)** - Miss Primula (Dominion) 8.5f **(63)**
Form - 13003080300
Record 1999 - 1st:1 2nd:0 3rd:3 Ran:11
Pre1999 - 1st:5 2nd:7 3rd:6 Ran:66
Win Prizemoney £17,474 *Total Prizemoney* £32,344
Wins * 1999 Apr Folkes (SFT) H 6f 57 62
*** 1997** Jun Windso (G-S) H 6f 58 64
1995 Oct Chepst (G-S) H 5.1f 65 70
1995 May Bath (G-F) H 5.7f 60 62
1999 Turf 1-11: (5f 4, 6f 1-5, 7f, 8f) (g-s 1-3, gd 5, g-f 2, frm)
Moderate mare, effective 5 to 6f, best at 6f, acts on g-s to g-f, best on g-s, has worn blinkers, likes left handed tracks. Turf high 65 - 3rd of 18 giving 29lb to Harvey's Future (27 Apr Bath 5f g-s RF 0863) - also 1st of 16 giving 9lb to Whatta Madam (13 Apr Folkestone RF 0655). She often makes the frame in modest sprint handicaps, but does not win very often. She is probably better suited by six furlongs than five these days, and appreciates a bit of cut in the ground.
**R J Hodges [2-33] John Luff (from M S Saunders [2-27] May 1997).*

TINKER'S SURPRISE (IRE) BHB 40f47a RR 42f 47a 5161[7]

5 b g Cyrano de Bergerac 7.3f **(58)** - Lils Fairy (Fairy King (USA)) 7.7f **(59)**
Form - 6441374640220457
Record 1999 - 1st:1 2nd:2 3rd:1 Ran:14
Pre1999 - 1st:1 2nd:5 3rd:3 Ran:35
Win Prizemoney £6,235 *Total Prizemoney* £13,916
Wins * 1999 *Jan Wolver (STD) H 5f 46 51*
1996 Jun Goodwo (G-F) S 5f 69 <
1999 Turf 0-6: (5f 5, 6f) (g-f 2, frm 4) 1999 AW 1-8: (5f 1-8) (Fibr 1-8)
Moderate gelding, effective 5f, acts on g-f - acts on Fibr, often wears blinkers, prefers left handed tracks, prefers tight tracks, excels at Wolverhampton. Turf high 42. AW high 51 - 1st of 12 giving 1lb to Sotonian (13 Jan Wolverhampton RF 0085).
**J Balding [1-38] Classic Racing (from B J Meehan [1-11] Spt 1996).*

TINSEL WHISTLE BHB 75f RR 76f 4872[6]

2 b c Piccolo - Pewter Lass **(24f)** (Dowsing (USA))
Form - 6830171426
Record 1999 - 1st:2 2nd:1 3rd:1 Ran:10
Win Prizemoney £3,940 *Total Prizemoney* £5,472
Wins * 1999 Jly Yarmou (FRM) S 6f 74 <
*** 1999** Jun Yarmou (G-F) S 5.2f 72
1999 Turf 2-10: (5f 1-6, 6f 1-4) (gd, g-f 3, frm 2-6)
Above-average colt, effective 5 to 6f, best at 6f, acts on g-f to frm, best on g-f, has worn blinkers. Turf high 76 - 2nd of 7 giving 3lb to Peruvian Jade (10 Spt Goodwood 6f g-f RF 4256) - also 1st of 8 giving 5lb to Baytown Melody (26 Jly Yarmouth RF 3153). Both of his wins to date have been in fast-ground Yarmouth sellers, but he has also run well in better events since then.
**M A Jarvis [2-10] Yusof Sepiuddin.*

TINTORANO RR 3f 2153[11]

2 b g Presidium 7.5f **(56)** - Junuh (Jalmood (USA)) 10.1f **(52)**
Form - 0
Record 1999 - 1st:0 2nd:0 3rd:0 Ran:1
1999 Turf 0-1: (7f) (frm)
Currently very poor gelding.
**Miss J F Craze [0-1] Colin Barnfather and Frank Steele.*

TIOGA RR 90f 4899[15]

2 br c Unfuwain (USA) 11.4f **(74)** - Susquehanna Days (USA) (Chief's Crown (USA)) 9.8f **(72)**
Form - 1542680
Record 1999 - 1st:1 2nd:1 3rd:0 Ran:7
Win Prizemoney £4,402 *Total Prizemoney* £8,777
Wins * 1999 May Lingfi (G-F) 6f 84 <
1999 Turf 1-7: (6f 1-1, 7f 4, 8f 2) (sft, gd 1-2, g-f 3, frm)
Useful colt, effective 6 to 7f, best at 7f, acts on gd to g-f, best on g-f. Turf high 90 - 2nd of 6 to Mana-Mou Bay (13 Aug Newbury 7f g-f RF 3617) - also 1st of 12 from Sarena Special (29 May Lingfield RF 1580). He made a winning debut at Lingfield, but found the opposition in the Chesham too much for him next time. Has been exposed since, but did run well in a listed race at Newbury.
**B J Meehan [1-7] Mrs Susan Roy.*

TIPPERARY SUNSET (IRE) BHB 63f57a RR 65f 57a 5217[5]

5 gr g Red Sunset 9f **(57)** - Chapter And Verse (Dancers Image (USA)) 9.3f **(71)**
Form - 830144070230025
Record 1999 - 1st:1 2nd:2 3rd:2 Ran:14
Pre1999 - 1st:5 2nd:2 3rd:5 Ran:26
Win Prizemoney £21,127 *Total Prizemoney* £31,371
Wins * 1999 Jun Beverl (GD) H 7.5f 61 64 <
*** 1998** Aug Hamilt (SFT) H 8.3f 54 55

* 1997 Nov Doncas (G-S) H 8f 56 64 <
* 1997 Oct Newmar (G-F) H 9f 54 58
* 1997 Aug Ripon (G-F) H 10f 41 48
* 1997 Aug Pontef (G-F) H 8f 35 44
1999 Turf 1-14: (7f 1-6, 8f 8) (sft, g-s 3, gd 1-5, g-f 2, frm 3)
Average gelding, effective 7 to 10f, acts on g-s to frm, best on gd, likes right handed tracks, and excels at Doncaster. Turf high 65 - 2nd of 18 giving 14lb to Dare (25 Oct Leicester 8f gd RF 5053) - also 1st of 15 giving 15lb to Tropical Beach (2 Jun Beverley RF 1661). Wins in his turn, but is not particularly consistent. Won at Beverley in June beating subsequent winner Tropical Beach, coming late which is the way to ride him. **J J Quinn [6-41] Harold Bray.*

TIPSY BHB 90f **RR 92f** 5219[6]
3 ch f Kris 10f **(75)** - Heady (Rousillon (USA)) 8.2f **(74)**
Form - 14144136
Record 1999 - 1st:3 2nd:0 3rd:1 Ran:8
Pre1999 - 1st:0 2nd:0 3rd:0 Ran:1
Win Prizemoney £10,789 *Total Prizemoney* £17,445
Wins * **1999** Spt Goodwo (SFT) 12f 77 <
* **1999** May Ayr (GD) H 10.9f 74 73
* **1999** *Apr Wolver (STD) 8.5f 74*
1999 Turf 2-7: (8f, 11f 1-2, 12f 1-4) (sft, g-s 1-1, gd 1-2, g-f, frm 2) 1999 AW 1-1: (8f 1-1) (Fibr 1-1)
Light-framed, useful filly. Turf high 92. (1st run). A winner three times last season including one on Fibresand, she seemed to relish the bottomless ground when bolting up in a classified event over 12 furlongs at Goodwood in September. Not disgraced when third in an Ascot Group Three next time.
**W J Haggas [3-9] Cheveley Park Stud.*

TIPSY CREEK (USA) BHB 113f **RR 112f** 3772[P]
5 b h Dayjur (USA) 6.8f **(79)** - Copper Creek (Habitat) 9.4f **(70)**
Form - 321066P
Record 1999 - 1st:1 2nd:1 3rd:1 Ran:7
Pre1999 - 1st:5 2nd:1 3rd:1 Ran:15
Win Prizemoney £86,558 *Total Prizemoney* £99,874
Wins * **1999** May Sandow (GD) G2 5f 115 <
* **1998** Aug Newmar (G-F) L 6f 114
* **1998** Aug Yarmou (G-F) 6f 109
* **1998** Jun Haydoc (GD) 6f 96
* **1996** Jun Ascot (G-F) G3 5f 112
* **1996** May Salisb (G-F) 5f 81+
1999 Turf 1-7: (5f 1-3, 6f 4) (gd, g-f 1-2, frm 4)
Group-class colt, effective 5 to 6f, best at 6f, acts on g-f to frm, best on frm, has worn blinkers, likes Newmarket. Turf high 115 - 1st of 8 getting 4lb from Lochangel (31 May Sandown RF 1613). Consistent. Built like a brick out-house, he has recovered from a serious back problem and is a very useful sprinter on his day, as he showed when landing the Temple Stakes at Sandown in May. Unfortunately, he was very disappointing afterwards and was pulled up in the Nunthorpe after suffering serious interference.
**B Hanbury [6-22] Hamdan Al Maktoum.*

TIP THE BALANCE (IRE) RR 14f 803[9]
3 b f Ballad Rock 7.2f **(63)** - Daidis (Welsh Pageant) 10f **(65)**
Form - 00
Record 1999 - 1st:0 2nd:0 3rd:0 Ran:2
Pre1999 - 1st:0 2nd:0 3rd:0 Ran:2
1999 Turf 0-2: (8f, 10f) (gd, frm)
Leggy, poor filly. **J Parkes [0-4] Mrs E Comer.*

TIRAAZ (USA) RR 114f 5013a[6]
5 b h Lear Fan (USA) 10.4f **(80)** - Tarikhana (Mouktar)
Form - 6
1999 Turf 0-1: (12f)
Group-class colt. (1st run) - 6th giving 7lb to First Magnitude (17 Oct Longchamp 12f RF 5013a). **A deRoyerDupre in FR [2-4].*

TIRMIZI (USA) BHB 31f39a **RR 7f 39a** 1986[13]
8 b g Shahrastani (USA) 11.5f **(69)** - Tikarna (FR) (Targowice (USA)) 11.4f **(70)**
Form - 800
Record 1999 - 1st:0 2nd:0 3rd:0 Ran:3
Pre1999 - 1st:0 2nd:1 3rd:0 Ran:2
Win Prizemoney £0 *Total Prizemoney* £644
1999 Turf 0-2: (17f, 18f) (sft, g-f) 1999 AW 0-1: (16f) (Fibr)
Moderate gelding. Turf high 7. **Mrs A Swinbank [1-12] S Smith.*

TISSIFER BHB 108f **RR 111f** 2733[10]
3 b c Polish Precedent (USA) 9f **(73)** - Ingozi **(74f)** (Warning)
Form - 10220
Record 1999 - 1st:1 2nd:2 3rd:0 Ran:5
Pre1999 - 1st:2 2nd:0 3rd:0 Ran:3
Win Prizemoney £17,960 *Total Prizemoney* £25,739
Wins * **1999** Apr Thirsk (GD) 8f 112+ <
* 1998 Spt Kempto (SFT) 7f 82
* 1998 Aug Epsom (G-F) 6f 81+
1999 Turf 1-5: (8f 1-2, 10f 3) (gd 1-3, g-f, frm)
Unfurnished, Group-class colt, effective 8 to 10f, best at 10f, acts on gd to frm, best on gd, has worn blinkers. Turf high 112 (1st run) - 1st of 6 giving 8lb to Peculiarity (17 Apr Thirsk RF 0744). Inconsistent. He ran well in the face of some stiff tasks, notably when failing by three lengths to concede the St Leger winner Mutafaweq 9lb at Doncaster in May. Not seen since disappointing in the John Smith's Cup in July, he is difficult to place at home and may be better employed on the continent.
**M Johnston [3-8] M P Burke.*

TITAN BHB 44f **RR 47f** 5127[9]
4 b g Lion Cavern (USA) 7.5f **(74)** - Sutosky (Great Nephew) 9.9f **(64)**
Form - 00705020500
Record 1999 - 1st:0 2nd:1 3rd:0 Ran:11
Pre1999 - 1st:1 2nd:2 3rd:1 Ran:12
Win Prizemoney £4,110 *Total Prizemoney* £8,603
Wins * 1997 Spt Goodwo (GD) H 7f 74 76 <
1999 Turf 0-11: (7f 4, 8f 6, 9f) (gd 5, g-f 2, frm 4)
Scopey, moderate gelding, effective 7f, acts on g-f, likes right handed tracks. Turf high 49. **S Dow [1-23] J & S Kelly.*

TITAN LAD BHB 43f **RR 57f** 5063[12]
2 b c Puissance 7.1f **(60)** - Sister Sal (Bairn (USA)) 7.7f **(59)**
Form - 078000
Record 1999 - 1st:0 2nd:0 3rd:0 Ran:6
1999 Turf 0-5: (6f, 7f 2, 8f 2) (gd 3, g-f, frm) 1999 AW 0-1: (6f) (Fibr)
Fair colt. Turf high 57.
**G A Ham [0-6] The Smudge Racing Partnership.*

TITIAN ANGEL (IRE) RR 66f 4003[2]
2 ch f Brief Truce (USA) 9.1f **(73)** - Kuwah (IRE) (Be My Guest (USA)) 9.3f **(67)**
Form - 2
Record 1999 - 1st:0 2nd:1 3rd:0 Ran:1
Win Prizemoney £0 *Total Prizemoney* £1,065
1999 Turf 0-1: (8f) (gd)
Currently average filly. (1st run) - 2nd of 12 getting 9lb from Bow Strada (29 Aug Yarmouth 8f gd RF 4003). Second over a mile at Yarmouth on her only start despite looking backward, she put in all her best work late on and will certainly improve for the run.
**C N Allen [0-1] Conrad's Angels.*

TITTA RUFFO BHB 57f57a **RR 41f 57a** 4732[8]
5 b g Reprimand 8.2f **(63)** - Hithermoor Lass (Red Alert) 7.6f **(66)**
Form - 62448
Record 1999 - 1st:0 2nd:1 3rd:0 Ran:5
Pre1999 - 1st:2 2nd:2 3rd:3 Ran:20
Win Prizemoney £5,865 *Total Prizemoney* £12,009
Wins 1998 Aug Windso (G-F) S 11.6f 51
1997 Jun Goodwo (GD) H 10f 80 84 <
1999 Turf 0-1: (6f) (gd) 1999 AW 0-4: (7f 2, 8f 2) (Fibr 4)
Average gelding, effective 10 to 11f, best at 10f, acts on gd to frm, best on gd, has worn blinkers, prefers right handed tracks, favours tight tracks. AW high 60.
**D Shaw [0-5] Fred A Havercroft Partners (from B J Meehan [2-20] Aug 1998).*

TITUS BRAMBLE RR 66f 3553[13]
2 b c Puissance 7.1f **(60)** - Norska (Northfields (USA)) 9f **(72)**
Form - 80600
Record 1999 - 1st:0 2nd:0 3rd:0 Ran:5
1999 Turf 0-5: (5f, 6f, 7f 3) (gd 3, frm 2)
Average colt, has worn blinkers. Turf high 66.
**B R Millman [0-5] Henry Rix.*

TIVOLI (IRE) BHB 75f **RR 82f** 3128[3]
3 b c Ela-Mana-Mou 12.7f **(72)** - Solac (FR) (Gay Lussac (ITY)) 16.7f

(109)
Form - 523
Record 1999 - 1st:0 2nd:1 3rd:1 Ran:3
Win Prizemoney £0 *Total Prizemoney* £1,514
1999 Turf 0-3: (14f 2, 15f) (gd, frm 2)
Light-framed, currently decent colt. Turf high 82 - 2nd of 10 to Ashgar (18 Jun Redcar 14f frm RF 2129).
**M Johnston [0-3] Mrs Belinda Strudwick.*

TOAFF (IRE) BHB 60f **RR 102f** 1715a6
7 b h Nordico (USA) 8.2f **(59)** - Sunley Saint (Artaius (USA)) 9f **(69)**
Form - 6
1999 Turf 0-1: (12f) (frm)
Very useful horse.
**M Gasparini in ITY [0-1] (from M Tellini in ITY [0-1] Aug 1995).*

TOBLERSONG BHB 53f56a **RR 50f 56a** 4989[12]
4 b g Tirol 8.1f **(64)** - Winsong Melody (Music Maestro) 7.7f **(66)**
Form - 680742236207750050
Record 1999 - 1st:0 2nd:3 3rd:1 Ran:18
Pre1999 - 1st:2 2nd:1 3rd:0 Ran:11
Win Prizemoney £7,805 *Total Prizemoney* £15,206
Wins 1997 Oct Yarmou (GD) 6f 93 <
1997 Jly Epsom (SFT) 6f 77+
1999 Turf 0-16: (5f, 6f 2, 7f 9, 8f 4) (sft 2, gd 2, g-f 5, frm 6, hrd) 1999 AW 0-2: (7f, 8f) (Equi, Fibr)
Scopey, fair gelding, has worn blinkers. Turf high 59. AW high 47. He put in some fine efforts mid-season in '99 without quite managing to get his head in front.
**C A Dwyer [0-20] Mrs Shelley Dwyer (from J W Hills [0-4] Aug 1998).*

TOBRUK (IRE) BHB 103f **RR 105f** 4492[4]
3 b c Red Ransom (USA) 8.6f **(83)** - Memories (USA) (Hail the Pirates (USA)) 11f **(78)**
Form - 3124264
Record 1999 - 1st:1 2nd:2 3rd:1 Ran:7
Pre1999 - 1st:0 2nd:1 3rd:0 Ran:1
Win Prizemoney £3,902 *Total Prizemoney* £18,133
Wins * 1999 May Kempto (G-F) 8f 89+ <
1999 Turf 1-7: (8f 1-5, 10f 2) (hvy, sft, g-f 3, frm 1-2)
Light-framed, Pattern-class colt, effective 8f, acts on hvy to g-f, has worn blinkers. Turf high 105. Showed plenty of ability when runner-up on his only start at two, and was third in a hot Newbury maiden on his comeback. He got off the mark by winning a Kempton maiden, but has been caught in the void between high-class handicapper and Pattern-race performer since. He should do better in America, where he will race after being sold for 70,000 gns in October. **P W Chapple-Hyam [1-8] R E Sangster & A K Collins.*

TOBY GRIMES (IRE) BHB 44f **RR 44f** 4491[11]
2 ch g Forest Wind (USA) - Emma Grimes (IRE) **(39f)** (Nordico (USA)) 6.5f **(62)**
Form - 000
Record 1999 - 1st:0 2nd:0 3rd:0 Ran:3
1999 Turf 0-3: (7f 3) (sft, g-f, frm)
Currently moderate gelding. Turf high 44 (began Jly).
**J S Moore [0-3] J K Grimes.*

TOEJAM BHB 35f **RR 36f** 3978[9]
6 ch g Move Off - Cheeky Pigeon (Brave Invader (USA))
Form - 065040
Record 1999 - 1st:0 2nd:0 3rd:0 Ran:6
Win Prizemoney £0 *Total Prizemoney* £293
1999 Turf 0-6: (8f, 10f, 11f, 14f 3) (frm 6)
Very moderate gelding. Turf high 62. **R E Barr [0-7] Mrs R E Barr.*

TOLDYA BHB 45f **RR 42f** 5123[7]
2 b f Beveled (USA) 6.9f **(64)** - Run Amber Run (Run The Gantlet (USA)) 12.1f **(59)**
Form - 807
Record 1999 - 1st:0 2nd:0 3rd:0 Ran:3
1999 Turf 0-3: (5f 2, 6f) (gd, g-f, frm)
Currently moderate filly. Turf high 42 (began Jly).
**E A Wheeler [0-3] Benham Racing.*

TOLERATION BHB 84f **RR 81f** 4821[1]
2 b f Petong 7.6f **(58)** - Dancing Chimes (London Bells (CAN)) 5.8f **(53)**
Form - 41
Record 1999 - 1st:1 2nd:0 3rd:0 Ran:2
Win Prizemoney £3,403 *Total Prizemoney* £3,753
Wins * 1999 Oct Windso (G-S) 6f 81 <
1999 Turf 1-2: (6f 1-2) (gd, g-f 1-1)
Currently decent filly. Turf high 81 (began Oct) - 1st of 21 getting 5lb from Dandilum (11 Oct Windsor RF 4821).
**D R C Elsworth [1-2] Miss Juliet Reed.*

TOLSTOY RR 86f 5000[2]
2 b c Nashwan (USA) 10.3f **(79)** - Millazure (USA) **(62f)** (Dayjur (USA))
Form - 22
Record 1999 - 1st:0 2nd:2 3rd:0 Ran:2
Win Prizemoney £0 *Total Prizemoney* £2,075
1999 Turf 0-2: (7f, 8f) (gd, frm)
Currently useful colt. Turf high 86 (began Spt) - 2nd of 11 to Western Summer (21 Oct Nottingham 8f gd RF 5000).
**Sir Michael Stoute [0-2] Mrs John Magnier & M Tabor.*

TOM BHB 28f51a **RR 28f 51a** 3672[7]
4 gr g Petong 7.6f **(58)** - Wanton (Kris) 9.5f **(73)**
Form - 5361246634260007
Record 1999 - 1st:1 2nd:2 3rd:1 Ran:13
Pre1999 - 1st:0 2nd:1 3rd:3 Ran:23
Win Prizemoney £1,924 *Total Prizemoney* £5,153
Wins * 1999 *Jan Southw (STD) H 8f 40 42* <
1999 Turf 0-3: (7f, 8f 2) (gd 2, hrd) 1999 AW 1-10: (7f, 8f 1-9) (Equi, Fibr 1-9)
Workmanlike, average gelding, effective 7 to 8f, best at 8f, - acts on Fibr, mostly wears blinkers, likes left handed tracks, likes tight tracks. Turf high 25. AW high 61 - 2nd of 16 giving 7lb to Pine Ridge Lad (26 Apr Southwell 8f Fibr RF 0852). Inconsistent.
**C W Fairhurst [1-17] C D Barber-Lomax (from J Hetherton [0-15] Aug 1998).*

TOMASEAN BHB 71f **RR 73f** 4399[4]
3 b c Forzando 7.2f **(63)** - Bunny Gee **(54f)** (Last Tycoon) 8.5f **(62)**
Form - 422444
Record 1999 - 1st:0 2nd:2 3rd:0 Ran:6
Pre1999 - 1st:0 2nd:1 3rd:0 Ran:2
Win Prizemoney £0 *Total Prizemoney* £4,811
1999 Turf 0-6: (6f 2, 7f, 8f, 9f 2) (gd 2, g-f 2, frm 2)
Workmanlike, above-average colt, effective 6 to 8f, best at 6f, acts on gd to frm, best on frm, often wears blinkers. Turf high 78 - 2nd of 3 to Parkside (13 Aug Warwick 8f gd RF 3634). Consistent.
**J Noseda [0-8] John Breslin.*

TOMBA BHB 113f **RR 113f** 5014a[8]
5 ch h Efisio 7.7f **(69)** -Indian Love Song (Be My Guest (USA)) 9.3f **(67)**
Form - 4512563818
Record 1999 - 1st:2 2nd:1 3rd:1 Ran:10
Pre1999 - 1st:11 2nd:3 3rd:4 Ran:27
Win Prizemoney £242,208 *Total Prizemoney* £334,336
Wins * 1999 Oct Munich (SFT) G3 6.5f 107
*** 1999** Jly Haydoc (G-S) 6f 113
* 1998 Oct Longch (HVY) G1 7f 118 <
* 1998 Oct Munich (SFT) G3 6.5f 115
* 1998 Jun Ascot (SFT) G2 6f 117
* 1997 Aug Hoppeg (GD) G3 6.5f 111
* 1997 Jun Newcas (HVY) L 6f 115
* 1997 May Haydoc (G-S) LH 6f 109 109
* 1997 May Newbur (G-S) 6f 107
* 1997 May Haydoc (SFT) 6f 98
* 1996 Nov Evry (HLD) L 6f 104
* 1996 Oct Salisb (G-S) 6f 106
* 1996 Aug Epsom (GD) 6f 80
1999 Turf 2-10: (6f 1-3, 7f 1-6, 8f) (hvy, sft 1-2, gd 4, g-f 1-1, frm)
Group-class colt, effective 6 to 7f, best at 6f, acts on hvy to frm, excels at Munich and Haydock, does well at Ascot. Turf high 113 - also 1st of 5 giving 19lb to Threat (2 Jly Haydock RF 2487). Consistent. A rotavator-actioned mud-lark, he failed to match 1998's exploits, but grabbed a Group Three at Munich in October and retains most of his ability. Best at six and seven furlongs, he was very game in a finish. Has now been retired to stud.
**B J Meehan [13-37].*

TOM DOUGAL BHB 80f **RR 85df** 4754[11]
4 b c Ron's Victory (USA) 9.2f **(52)** - Fabulous Rina (FR) (Fabulous

Dancer (USA)) 9.4f **(70)**
Form - 0512745000
Record 1999 - 1st:1 2nd:1 3rd:0 Ran:10
Pre1999 - 1st:2 2nd:1 3rd:2 Ran:16
Win Prizemoney £31,638 *Total Prizemoney* £43,458
Wins * 1999 May Ayr (GD) 8f 86
* 1998 May York (GD) H 7.9f 83 90+ <
* 1998 May Newmar (GD) H 8f 75 86
1999 Turf 1-10: (7f, 8f 1-7, 9f, 10f) (gd 1-5, frm 5)
Leggy, useful colt, effective 8 to 9f, best at 8f, acts on gd to frm, best on gd, prefers left handed tracks, excels at York. Turf high 90 - 2nd of 17 giving 15lb to Dee Pee Tee Cee (12 Jun York 9f gd RF 1966) - also 1st of 7 getting 3lb from Nomore Mr Niceguy (20 May Ayr RF 1339). Becoming disappointing. Won two races at around a mile last season, definitely improving as his season progressed. A good start to '99 saw him win at Ayr and just lose out to the useful Dee Pee Tee Cee at York, although he has failed to better those runs since. **C Smith [3-26] Mrs N Stewart.*

TOMETOYOUTOYOUTOME RR 39f 3598[11]

2 br f Timeless Times (USA) 6.1f **(56)** - Ping Pong (Petong) 6.6f **(58)**
Form - 08880
Record 1999 - 1st:0 2nd:0 3rd:0 Ran:5
1999 Turf 0-5: (5f 3, 6f, 7f) (gd, g-f, frm 3)
Very moderate filly, has worn blinkers. Turf high 39.
**P D Evans [0-5] Clayton Bigley Partnership Ltd.*

TOMMY CARSON BHB 52f RR 64df 4648[2]

4 b g Last Tycoon 9.4f **(73)** - Ivory Palm (USA) (Sir Ivor) 10.2f **(70)**
Form - 742332
Record 1999 - 1st:0 2nd:2 3rd:2 Ran:6
Pre1999 - 1st:0 2nd:0 3rd:1 Ran:2
Win Prizemoney £0 *Total Prizemoney* £3,047
1999 Turf 0-6: (10f, 12f 2, 14f 3) (g-s, gd 2, g-f, frm 2)
Scopey, average gelding, effective 10f, acts on sft. Turf high 67 (began Jly). Becoming disappointing.
**J R Poulton [0-1] J Logan (from D R C Elsworth [0-11] Aug 1999).*

TOMMY TITTLEMOUSE RR 58+f 481[5]

3 ch g Chilibang 7f **(55)** - Fire Sprite (Mummy's Game) 8.2f **(60)**
Form - 5
Record 1999 - 1st:0 2nd:0 3rd:0 Ran:1
1999 Turf 0-1: (7f) (g-s)
Light-framed, currently fair gelding, has broken blood-vessels.
**P D Evans [0-1] Colin Booth.*

TOMMY TROJAN (IRE) BHB 66f RR 75f 4934[16]

2 b c Namaqualand (USA) - Bilander (High Line) 10.3f **(70)**
Form - 1368060
Record 1999 - 1st:1 2nd:0 3rd:1 Ran:7
Win Prizemoney £4,293 *Total Prizemoney* £4,808
Wins * 1999 Jun Goodwo (G-S) 6f 66+ <
1999 Turf 1-7: (6f 1-3, 7f 2, 8f 2) (gd 1-3, g-f 3, frm)
Above-average colt, effective 6f, acts on gd, has worn blinkers. Turf high 75 - also 1st of 8 from Cedar Prince (4 Jun Goodwood RF 1735). **A P Jarvis [1-7] Grant & Bowman Ltd.*

TOMOE GOZEN (IRE) BI IB 65f RR 65df 1708[5]

3 b f Brief Truce (USA) 9.1f **(73)** - Deelish (IRE) (Caerleon (USA)) 8.6f **(71)**
Form - 5
Record 1999 - 1st:0 2nd:0 3rd:0 Ran:1
Pre1999 - 1st:0 2nd:1 3rd:0 Ran:3
Win Prizemoney £0 *Total Prizemoney* £1,391
1999 Turf 0-1: (7f) (gd)
Average filly. Made a promising debut in a maiden on the July Course at two, but has subsequently disappointed.
**S P C Woods [0-4] Michael Simpson.*

TOMOOJID RR 5050[19]

4 b g Almoojid 7f **(36)** - Misty Arch (Starch Reduced) 11.5f **(52)**
Form - 00
Record 1999 - 1st:0 2nd:0 3rd:0 Ran:2
1999 Turf 0-2: (8f, 12f) (gd 2)
Leggy, formerly very poor gelding. **Pat Mitchell [0-6] J L Bonfield.*

TOM TAILOR (GER) RR 56f 3808[9]

5 b g Beldale Flutter (USA) 10.2f **(62)** - Thoughtful (Northfields (USA)) 9f **(72)**
Form - 48621080
Record 1999 - 1st:1 2nd:1 3rd:0 Ran:8
Pre1999 - 1st:1 2nd:1 3rd:1 Ran:12
Win Prizemoney £10,260 *Total Prizemoney* £14,038
Wins * 1999 Jly Sandow (G-F) H 16.4f 55 58
* 1997 May Windso (SFT) 10f 74 <
1999 Turf 1-8: (12f 3, 14f, 16f 1-4) (gd 2, g-f 3, frm 1-3)
Fair gelding, effective 12 to 16f, best at 16f, acts on gd to frm, best on g-f, prefers tight tracks. Turf high 58 - 1st of 11 getting 6lb from Tramline (3 Jly Sandown RF 2546). Consistent. Came back to something like his best when just failing to get up at Salisbury in June, and reversed the form with the winner when battling home to win at Sandown. **D R C Elsworth [4-30] The A A Partnership.*

TOM TUN BHB 80f74a RR 82f 74a 4803[7]

4 b g Bold Arrangement 8.7f **(57)** - B Grade (Lucky Wednesday) 8f **(50)**
Form - 181131314645124230 7
Record 1999 - 1st:5 2nd:2 3rd:3 Ran:17
Pre1999 - 1st:3 2nd:0 3rd:0 Ran:11
Win Prizemoney £35,091 *Total Prizemoney* £44,576
Wins * 1999 Jly Doncas (G-F) 6f 77 <
* 1999 May Doncas (G-F) H 6f 68 73
* 1999 Mar Newcas (G-S) H 5f 57 61
* 1999 *Feb Southw (STD) H 6f 68 74*
* 1999 *Jan Southw (STD) H 6f 62 65*
* 1998 *Nov Lingfi (STD) H 5f 53 58*
* 1998 Spt Newcas (GD) H 6f 49 50
* 1998 *Jly Southw (STD) H 6f 42 44*
1999 Turf 3-14: (5f 1-4, 6f 2-10) (gd 1-7, g-f 3, frm 1-3, hrd 1-1) 1999 AW 2-3: (6f 2-3) (Fibr 2-3)
Workmanlike, decent gelding, effective 5 to 6f, best at 6f, acts on gd to hrd - acts on Fibr, excels at Ayr and Doncaster and does well at Newcastle. Turf high 83 - 2nd of 4 giving 7lb to Princely Dream (10 Aug Ayr 6f g-f RF 3494) - also 1st of 6 giving 3lb to Hard to Figure (29 Jly Doncaster RF 3219). AW high 74 - 1st of 16 giving 1lb to Euro Venture (5 Feb Southwell RF 0231). Consistent. A pretty decent sprinter on turf and sand, he ran consistently well on both surfaces, winning five and running well in some tough handicaps. He seems equally suited by either five or six furlongs.
**Miss J F Craze [8-28] Mrs O Tunstall.*

TONDYNE RR 27f 4139[12]

2 b c Owington - Anodyne (Dominion) 8.5f **(63)**
Form - 00
Record 1999 - 1st:0 2nd:0 3rd:0 Ran:2
1999 Turf 0-2: (6f, 7f) (frm, hrd)
Currently little account colt. Turf high 27 (began Aug).
**T D Easterby [0-2] Dr M Gelfand.*

TONGA RR 33f 4605[10]

2 gr f Petong 7.6f **(58)** - Pegs **(66f)** (Mandrake Major) 7.6f **(53)**
Form - 70
Record 1999 - 1st:0 2nd:0 3rd:0 Ran:2
1999 Turf 0-1: (5f) (frm) 1999 AW 0-1: (7f) (Fibr)
Currently very moderate filly. **C W Thornton [0-2] Guy Reed.*

TONG ROAD BHB 40f RR 34f 5128[12]

3 gr g Petong 7.6f **(58)** - Wayzgoose (USA) (Diesis) 9.3f **(69)**
Form - 087760
Record 1999 - 1st:0 2nd:0 3rd:0 Ran:6
Pre1999 - 1st:0 2nd:0 3rd:0 Ran:3
1999 Turf 0-6: (5f 4, 6f 2) (gd 3, g-f, frm 2)
Scopey, very moderate gelding. Turf high 34. Consistent.
**B R Cambidge [0-9] B R Cambidge.*

TONIC BHB 84f RR 81f 1198[8]

3 b c Robellino (USA) 9.5f **(68)** - Alyara (USA) (Alydar (USA)) 9.1f **(76)**
Form - 108
Record 1999 - 1st:1 2nd:0 3rd:0 Ran:3
Pre1999 - 1st:0 2nd:1 3rd:1 Ran:2
Win Prizemoney £3,745 *Total Prizemoney* £5,004
Wins * 1999 Apr Ripon (G-S) 8f 81 <
1999 Turf 1-3: (8f 1-3) (gd 1-2, frm)
Leggy, decent colt. Turf high 81 (1st run) - 1st of 18 from Ilissus (15 Apr Ripon RF 0710). Landed a modest Ripon maiden first time up, but made no impact in handicaps.
**M Johnston [1-5] Robinson (Wigan).*

TONIGHT'S PRIZE (IRE) BHB 75f **RR 78f** 4752[5]
5 b g Night Shift (USA) 8.1f **(73)** - Bestow (Shirley Heights) 10.3f **(74)**
Form - 608280035
Record 1999 - 1st:0 2nd:1 3rd:1 Ran:9
Pre1999 - 1st:2 2nd:4 3rd:2 Ran:16
Win Prizemoney £11,202 *Total Prizemoney* £21,801
Wins * 1998 Aug Pontef (G-F) H 8f 82 87 <
* 1997 Oct Pontef (G-F) 8f 72
1999 Turf 0-9: (8f 7, 10f 2) (gd, g-f 3, frm 5)
Above-average gelding, effective 8 to 9f, best at 8f, acts on gd to frm, prefers left handed tracks. Turf high 78. Consistent.
**C F Wall [2-25] Hintlesham Thoroughbreds.*

TONNERRE BHB 52f42a **RR 54f 42a** 5220[6]
7 b g Unfuwain (USA) 11.4f **(74)** - Supper Time (Shantung) 9.8f **(64)**
Form - 3000318016
Record 1999 - 1st:2 2nd:0 3rd:2 Ran:10
Pre1999 - 1st:3 2nd:1 3rd:2 Ran:25
Win Prizemoney £17,986 *Total Prizemoney* £21,492
Wins * **1999** Oct Yarmou (G-S) C 14.1f 53
* **1999** Jly Beverl (SFT) H 16.2f 49 54
1998 Jun Ripon (SFT) H 10f 51 58
1997 Jun Nottin (SFT) H 10f 52 59
1995 Jun Haydoc (G-S) 14f 75 <
1999 Turf 2-7: (10f 2, 13f, 14f 1-1, 16f 1-2, 17f) (sft, g-s 1-1, gd 1-1, g-f 3, frm) 1999 AW 0-3: (8f, 12f, 16f) (Fibr 3)
Fair gelding, effective 10 to 16f, best at 10f, acts on g-s to frm, best on gd, likes right handed tracks, favours tight tracks. Turf high 54 - 1st of 8 giving 2lb to Old Red (3 Jly Beverley RF 2514) - also 1st of 15 getting 10lb from Urgent Swift (27 Oct Yarmouth RF 5101). AW high 36. Stays well and appreciates soft ground, and had those conditions when scoring at Yarmouth at the back-end.
**K A Morgan [3-13] S Giles (from B A McMahon [2-19] Jly 1998).*

TONY TIE BHB 74f **RR 81f** 5217[1]
3 b g Ardkinglass 5f **(64)** - Queen of the Quorn **(51df 45a)** (Governor General)
Form - 0770021
Record 1999 - 1st:1 2nd:1 3rd:0 Ran:7
Pre1999 - 1st:2 2nd:0 3rd:1 Ran:7
Win Prizemoney £14,454 *Total Prizemoney* £17,443
Wins * **1999** Nov Doncas (SFT) H 8f 69 81
1998 Aug Cheste (G-S) H 7f 87 89 <
1998 May Salisb (G-S) 5f 79
1999 Turf 1-7: (8f 1-5, 9f 2) (g-s 1-1, gd 3, frm 3)
Unfurnished, decent gelding, effective 5 to 8f, acts on g-s to gd, best on gd. Turf high 81 (began Aug) - 1st of 22 getting 11lb from Weetman's Weigh (6 Nov Doncaster RF 5217).
**J S Goldie [1-7] Frank Brady (from W G M Turner [2-7] Nov 1998).*

TOORAK (USA) **RR 78f** 4898[6]
2 b c Irish River (FR) 9f **(77)** - Just Juliet (USA) (What A Pleasure (USA)) 8.4f **(61)**
Form - 6
Record 1999 - 1st:0 2nd:0 3rd:0 Ran:1
1999 Turf 0-1: (8f) (gd)
Currently above-average colt. **J W Hills [0-1] D J Deer.*

TOPACIO BHB 65f **RR 63f** 5006[1]
3 b g Saddlers' Hall (IRE) 10.5f **(65)** - Teresa (SPA) (Rheffissimo (FR))
Form - 683221
Record 1999 - 1st:1 2nd:2 3rd:1 Ran:6
Pre1999 - 1st:0 2nd:0 3rd:0 Ran:1
Win Prizemoney £3,309 *Total Prizemoney* £5,650
Wins * **1999** Oct Nottin (GD) H 16f 56 63 <
1999 Turf 1-6: (10f 2, 14f, 16f 1-2, 17f) (gd 1-2, g-f, frm 2, hrd)
Average gelding, effective 16f, acts on gd. Turf high 63 - 1st of 15 getting 2lb from Natural Eight (21 Oct Nottingham RF 5006).
**S C Williams [1-7] Livingston Trading Ltd.*

TOP ACT BHB 40f **RR 38tf** 4714[10]
3 b g Inchinor 8.9f **(64)** - Actress (Known Fact (USA)) 7.4f **(67)**
Form - 00780
Record 1999 - 1st:0 2nd:0 3rd:0 Ran:5
Pre1999 - 1st:0 2nd:0 3rd:0 Ran:4
1999 Turf 0-5: (7f, 8f 2, 10f, 12f) (gd 2, g-f, frm 2)
Lengthy, very moderate gelding, has worn blinkers. Turf high 38 (began Jly). Inconsistent.
**J S Wainwright [0-5] Mrs D Drewery (from N Tinkler [0-2] Oct 1998).*

TOPATORI (IRE) BHB 76f **RR 81f** 4683[22]
5 ch m Topanoora 8.3f **(67)** - Partygoer (General Assembly (USA)) 10f **(68)**
Form - 12040327700
Record 1999 - 1st:1 2nd:2 3rd:1 Ran:11
Pre1999 - 1st:3 2nd:2 3rd:5 Ran:24
Win Prizemoney £14,809 *Total Prizemoney* £31,506
Wins * **1999** Apr Leices (GD) H 8f 76 84 <
* 1998 Apr Leices (SFT) H 8f 76 84+
* 1997 Oct Haydoc (SFT) H 10.5f 71 75
* 1997 Jun Yarmou (FRM) H 7f 66
1999 Turf 1-11: (8f 1-9, 9f, 10f) (sft, gd 1-6, g-f 2, frm 2)
Decent filly, effective 8 to 10f, best at 8f, acts on sft to g-f, likes left handed tracks, prefers tight tracks, excels at Leicester. Turf high 86 - 2nd of 19 giving 4lb to Bomb Alaska (17 Apr Newbury 8f g-f RF 0735) - also 1st of 14 getting 4lb from Gaily Mill (8 Apr Leicester RF 0619). She made a winning reappearance at Leicester, just as she did in '98, before running a fine second in the Newbury Spring Cup. She has gone up the handicap as a result and is finding life tough. Obviously goes well fresh.
**M H Tompkins [4-35] M P Bowring.*

TOPAZ BHB 26f **RR 24f** 4983[17]
4 b g Alhijaz 7.7f **(57)** - Daisy Topper (Top Ville) 11.7f **(68)**
Form - 00000
Record 1999 - 1st:0 2nd:0 3rd:0 Ran:5
Pre1999 - 1st:0 2nd:0 3rd:0 Ran:8
1999 Turf 0-5: (8f, 10f 3, 11f) (g-s, gd, frm 3)
Workmanlike, little account gelding. Turf high 24. Inconsistent.
**H J Collingridge [0-9] The Topaz Partnership (from J W Hills [0-4] Jun 1998).*

TOP BANANA BHB 61f **RR 58f** 4826[19]
8 ch g Pharly (FR) 11.5f **(64)** - Oxslip (Owen Dudley) 8.3f **(61)**
Form - 000200620
Record 1999 - 1st:0 2nd:2 3rd:0 Ran:9
Pre1999 - 1st:4 2nd:4 3rd:5 Ran:36
Win Prizemoney £19,435 *Total Prizemoney* £54,893
Wins * 1996 Jun Newmar (G-F) H 5f 91 95 <
* 1995 Jly Newbur (GD) H 5.2f 84 88
* 1995 Jun Newbur (FRM) H 5.2f 79 84
* 1995 Jun Warwic (GD) 6f 83+
1999 Turf 0-9: (6f 7, 7f 2) (sft, g-s, gd 2, g-f 3, frm 2)
Fair gelding, effective 6f, acts on g-f, has worn blinkers. Turf high 62. A useful sprint handicapper at his best, he is on a long losing run. **H Candy [4-45] Henry Candy.*

TOP CEES BHB 99f **RR 98f** 4917[1]
9 b g Shirley Heights 12.1f **(76)** - Sing Softly (Luthier) 9.8f **(71)**
Form - 411
Record 1999 - 1st:2 2nd:0 3rd:0 Ran:3
Pre1999 - 1st:7 2nd:7 3rd:2 Ran:35
Win Prizemoney £179,142 *Total Prizemoney* £231,568
Wins * **1999** Oct Newmar (GD) H 17.3f 95 98 <
* **1999** Spt Ayr (G-S) H 13.1f 95 98 <
1998 Aug Pontef (G-F) H 12f 96 98 <
1998 Jun Ayr (G-F) H 15f 93 96+
1997 Spt Ayr (GD) H 13.1f 90 97
1997 May Cheste (SFT) H 18.7f 87 98 <
1996 Jly Newmar (G-F) H 14.8f 82 88+
1995 May Cheste (G-F) H 18.7f 72 81+
1999 Turf 2-3: (13f 1-2, 17f 1-1) (gd 2-3)
Very useful gelding, effective 12 to 19f, acts on gd to frm, best on gd, prefers tight tracks. Turf high 98 (began Aug) - 1st of 32 giving 14lb to Dominant Duchess (16 Oct Newmarket RF 4917) - also 1st of 9 giving 14lb to Montalcino (18 Spt Ayr RF 4394). Improving. He gained an emotional win in the Cesarewitch and is a wonderfully genuine staying handicapper. Proven on everything bar firm ground, he has a smart turn of foot and is invariably held-up.
**I A Balding [2-3] Charlton Bloodstock Ltd (from Mrs J R Ramsden [9-39] Aug 1998).*

TOP FIT BHB 57f60a **RR 58f 60a** 39[3]
3 b c Thatching 7.8f **(69)** - Diplomatist **(55f)** (Dominion) 8.5f **(63)**
Form - 413

Record 1999 - 1st:0 2nd:0 3rd:1 Ran:1
Pre1999 - 1st:1 2nd:1 3rd:0 Ran:7
Win Prizemoney £2,843 *Total Prizemoney* £4,645
Wins * 1998 *Dec Southw (STD) H* *8f 55 54 <*
1999 AW 0-1: (8f) (Fibr)
Scopey, average colt, effective 8f, acts on gd - acts on Fibr, often wears blinkers (extremely effectively). (1st run) - 3rd of 7 giving 3lb to Baron de Pichon (6 Jan Wolverhampton 8f Fibr RF 0039).
**W J Haggas [1-8] K H Fung.*

TOP FLOOR (IRE) BHB 42f49a **RR 39f 49a** 1599[6]

4 ch g Waajib 8.9f **(67)** - Keen Note (Sharpo) 7.7f **(59)**
Form - 20086
Record 1999 - 1st:0 2nd:1 3rd:0 Ran:5
Pre1999 - 1st:1 2nd:1 3rd:1 Ran:18
Win Prizemoney £2,220 *Total Prizemoney* £3,423
Wins 1998 Mar Hamilt (HVY) S 8.3f 52 <
1999 Turf 0-3: (10f 2, 12f) (gd 2, g-f) 1999 AW 0-2: (9f 2) (Fibr 2)
Workmanlike, fair gelding, effective 7 to 9f, best at 8f, acts on sft to gd - acts on Fibr, likes left handed tracks. Turf high 39. AW high 50 (1st run) - 2nd of 13 giving 5lb to The Wild Widow (20 Feb Wolverhampton 9f Fibr RF 0334). Inconsistent.
**J L Spearing [0-8] J Spearing (from N Tinkler [1-16] Aug 1998).*

TOP HAND BHB 75f **RR 87f** 5063[1]

2 ch f First Trump - Gold Luck (USA) (Slew O' Gold (USA)) 8f **(75)**
Form - 61
Record 1999 - 1st:1 2nd:0 3rd:0 Ran:2
Win Prizemoney £2,489 *Total Prizemoney* £2,489
Wins * **1999** Oct Bath (SFT) 8f 87 <
1999 Turf 1-2: (8f 1-2) (gd 1-2)
Currently useful filly. Turf high 87 (began Oct) - 1st of 12 from Muschana (26 Oct Bath RF 5063). **B W Hills [1-2] D J Deer.*

TOP JEM BHB 77f70a **RR 79f 70a** 2376[8]

5 b m Damister (USA) 9.1f **(66)** - Sharp Top (Sharpo) 7.7f **(59)**
Form - 01113443278
Record 1999 - 1st:3 2nd:1 3rd:2 Ran:11
Pre1999 - 1st:2 2nd:3 3rd:2 Ran:20
Win Prizemoney £22,577 *Total Prizemoney* £30,793
Wins * **1999** Apr Beverl (G-F) H 9.9f 67 76
* **1999** Apr Hamilt (HVY) H 9.2f 67 76
* **1999** Apr Leices (G-S) H 10f 61 69
* 1997 Jun Newcas (HVY) H 10.1f 67 79 <
* 1997 Jun Yarmou (FRM) H 10.1f 65 65
1999 Turf 3-9: (9f 1-1, 10f 2-7, 11f) (hvy 1-1, sft 2, g-s, gd 1-3, g-f, frm 1-1) 1999 AW 0-2: (12f 2) (Fibr 2)
Above-average filly, effective 9 to 11f, acts on hvy to frm, best on gd, likes right handed tracks, prefers tight tracks. Turf high 79 - 4th of 8 getting 1lb from Cloak of Darkness (7 Jun Windsor 10f gd RF 1802) - also 1st of 17 giving 13lb to Internal Affair (10 Apr Hamilton RF 0635). AW high 69. Consistent. Had a merry old time in April, being well placed to rattle up a hat trick. She put together a string of respectable placed efforts afterwards despite a hike in the handicap. Seems to go on all types of ground, but has yet to win on sand despite several attempts.
**M J Ryan [5-31] Norcroft Park Stud.*

TOP MAITE BHB 34f28a **RR 44f 28a** 16[14]

4 ch g Komaite (USA) 6.9f **(61)** - Top Yard (Teekay)
Form - 0
Record 1999 - 1st:0 2nd:0 3rd:0 Ran:1
Pre1999 - 1st:0 2nd:0 3rd:0 Ran:13
1999 AW 0-1: (8f) (Fibr)
Leggy, moderate gelding, has worn blinkers.
**G F H Charles-Jones [0-10] The Top Maite Partnership (from E A Wheeler [0-3] May 1998).*

TOPMAN RR 717[8]

2 ch c Komaite (USA) 6.9f **(61)** - Top Yard (Teekay)
Form - 8
Record 1999 - 1st:0 2nd:0 3rd:0 Ran:1
1999 Turf 0-1: (5f) (frm)
Currently very poor colt.
**G F H Charles-Jones [0-1] The Top Maite Partnership.*

TOP OF THE CHARTS BHB 37f **RR 41f** 2943[4]

3 b g Salse (USA) 10.9f **(71)** - Celebrity (Troy) 10.4f **(68)**
Form - 4744
Record 1999 - 1st:0 2nd:0 3rd:0 Ran:4
Pre1999 - 1st:0 2nd:0 3rd:0 Ran:3
Win Prizemoney £0 *Total Prizemoney* £198
1999 Turf 0-3: (8f, 11f, 16f) (g-f 2, frm) 1999 AW 0-1: (12f) (Fibr)
Scopey, moderate gelding, has worn blinkers. Turf high 42.
**J Noseda [0-7] P D Savill.*

TOP OF THE CLASS (IRE) BHB 69f **RR 67f** 4757[7]

2 b f Rudimentary (USA) 8.2f **(66)** - School Mum **(6f)** (Reprimand)
Form - 35573543167
Record 1999 - 1st:1 2nd:0 3rd:3 Ran:11
Win Prizemoney £7,766 *Total Prizemoney* £9,520
Wins * **1999** Spt Ayr (G-S) H 6f 64 67 <
1999 Turf 1-11: (5f 3, 6f 1-7, 7f) (hvy, gd 1-5, g-f 3, frm 2)
Average filly, effective 5 to 6f, best at 6f, acts on gd to frm, best on gd. Turf high 68 (1st run) - 3rd of 15 to Seraphina (25 Mar Doncaster 5f g-f RF 0464) - also 1st of 14 getting 16lb from Alphilda (17 Spt Ayr RF 4375).
**Martyn Wane [1-11] B & J Racing and Breeding Syndicate.*

TOP OF THE FORM (IRE) BHB 51f **RR 48f** 203[9]

5 ch m Masterclass (USA) 5.9f **(63)** - Haraabah (USA) (Topsider (USA)) 8.3f **(71)**
Form - 30
Record 1999 - 1st:0 2nd:0 3rd:0 Ran:1
Pre1999 - 1st:4 2nd:0 3rd:4 Ran:26
Win Prizemoney £12,984 *Total Prizemoney* £15,981
Wins 1997 Aug Pontef (G-F) C 5f 77
1997 Jly Catter (G-F) C 6f 55
1996 Jly York (GD) H 5f 81 <
1996 Jun Mussel (FRM) 5f 80+
1999 AW 0-1: (6f) (Fibr)
Moderate filly, effective 5f, acts on g-f, has worn blinkers (very effectively). Consistent.
**K A Ryan [0-12] Swan at Whalley Premier Partnership (from R A Fahey [1-6] Nov 1997).*

TOP OF THE MORNING BHB 57f **RR 53f** 2425[16]

3 b f Keen 11.1f **(58)** - Kelimutu (Top Ville) 11.7f **(68)**
Form - 50
Record 1999 - 1st:0 2nd:0 3rd:0 Ran:2
Pre1999 - 1st:0 2nd:0 3rd:0 Ran:5
1999 Turf 0-2: (8f, 10f) (frm 2)
Workmanlike, fair filly, effective 6 to 10f, acts on g-f to frm. Turf high 53 (1st run) - 5th of 13 giving 4lb to Karakul (21 Jun Windsor 10f frm RF 2177).
**G A Butler [0-2] Mrs Jennie Furlong (from J Pearce [0-5] Oct 1998).*

TOP OF THE PARKES BHB 65f **RR 77df** 4531[15]

2 b f Mistertopogigo (IRE) - Bella Parkes **(53f 80a)** (Tina's Pet) 6.8f **(59)**
Form - 350
Record 1999 - 1st:0 2nd:0 3rd:1 Ran:3
Win Prizemoney £0 *Total Prizemoney* £524
1999 Turf 0-3: (5f 2, 6f) (g-s, g-f, frm)
Currently above-average filly. Turf high 77 (1st run) (began Jly) - 3rd of 7 to Sioux Chef (20 Jly Bath 6f frm RF 2950).
**N P Littmoden [0-3] M Barton.*

TOP OF THE POPS (IRE) BHB 60f58a **RR 61f 58a** 4027[5]

3 b g Ballad Rock 7.2f **(63)** - Summerhill (Habitat) 9.4f **(70)**
Form - 564465
Record 1999 - 1st:0 2nd:0 3rd:0 Ran:6
1999 Turf 0-4: (6f 4) (gd 3, g-f) 1999 AW 0-2: (6f, 7f) (Fibr 2)
Rangy, average gelding, effective 6f, acts on gd to g-f. Turf high 61. AW high 59. **C W Thornton [0-6] Guy Reed.*

TOP OF THE SNOBS (IRE) RR 1789[14]

5 b g Top of the World - Little Snob (Aristocracy)
Form - 0
Record 1999 - 1st:0 2nd:0 3rd:0 Ran:1
1999 Turf 0-1: (10f) (gd)
Formerly very poor gelding. **Mrs G S Rees [0-5] P Bamford.*

TOP ORDER (USA) BHB 82f RR 80f 946[13]

3 b br f Dayjur (USA) 6.8f **(79)** - Victoria Cross (USA) (Spectacular Bid (USA)) 11.2f **(76)**
Form - 40
Record 1999 - 1st:0 2nd:0 3rd:0 Ran:2
Pre1999 - 1st:1 2nd:0 3rd:0 Ran:5
Win Prizemoney £3,559 *Total Prizemoney* £4,376
Wins * 1998 Jun Warwic (SFT) 5f 76 <
1999 Turf 0-2: (6f, 7f) (g-f, frm)
Light-framed, decent filly, effective 5 to 6f, acts on gd to g-f. Turf high 80 (1st run) - 4th of 15 getting 8lb from Munjiz (15 Apr Newmarket 6f g-f RF 0702).
**P F I Cole [1-7] H R H Prince Fahd Salman.*

TOPPO'S GEM BHB 65f RR 63f 2518[9]

2 b c Mistertopogigo (IRE) - Rosy Diamond (Jalmood (USA)) 10.1f **(52)**
Form - 71460
Record 1999 - 1st:1 2nd:0 3rd:0 Ran:5
Win Prizemoney £3,406 *Total Prizemoney* £3,627
Wins * 1999 Apr Redcar (G-S) 5f 63 <
1999 Turf 1-5: (5f 1-4, 6f) (gd 1-3, g-f, frm)
Average colt. Turf high 63 - 1st of 17 giving 2lb to College Maid (29 Apr Redcar RF 0916). **K A Ryan [1-5] Fairlawn Partnership.*

TOP STAR (IRE) RR 53f 5026[5]

3 b g Thatching 7.8f **(69)** - Decadence Star (IRE) (High Estate)
Form - 200005
Record 1999 - 1st:0 2nd:1 3rd:0 Ran:6
Pre1999 - 1st:0 2nd:0 3rd:0 Ran:3
Win Prizemoney £0 *Total Prizemoney* £1,687
1999 Turf 0-6: (6f 2, 7f 3, 8f) (gd 2, frm 4)
Scopey, fair gelding, effective 7f, acts on gd, often wears blinkers (very effectively). Turf high 71 (1st run) - 2nd of 14 giving 3lb to Kentucky Bullet (27 Mar Doncaster 7f gd RF 0488). Inconsistent.
**D W P Arbuthnot [0-1] Stephen Crown (from M R Channon [0-8] May 1999).*

TOP TARN (IRE) BHB 45f RR 26f 1801[15]

3 b f Royal Academy (USA) 7.8f **(77)** - Laugharne (Known Fact (USA)) 7.4f **(67)**
Form - 00
Record 1999 - 1st:0 2nd:0 3rd:0 Ran:2
Pre1999 - 1st:0 2nd:0 3rd:0 Ran:3
1999 Turf 0-2: (6f 2) (gd, g-f)
Unfurnished, little account filly. Turf high 17.
**C F Wall [0-5] Sir Stanley and Lady Grinstead.*

TOPTON (IRE) BHB 74f82a RR 74f 82a 4685[10]

5 b g Royal Academy (USA) 7.8f **(77)** - Circo (High Top) 10.2f **(67)**
Form - 131444201326860873173414173800
Record 1999 - 1st:4 2nd:2 3rd:4 Ran:24
Pre1999 - 1st:4 2nd:5 3rd:3 Ran:30
Win Prizemoney £28,567 *Total Prizemoney* £46,518
Wins * 1999 Aug Yarmou (FRM) H 7f 74 78
*** 1999** Jly Doncas (G-F) H 7f 67 70+
*** 1999** Jun Doncas (GD) H 7f 65 67
*** 1999** *Jan Lingfi (STD) H 7f 80 83* <
* 1998 *Nov Lingfi (STD) H 7f 69 73*
* 1998 *Nov Southw (STD) H 7f 61 69*
* 1998 Jun Doncas (GD) H 7f 69 74
1997 Oct Folkes (GD) 6f 74
1999 Turf 3-17: (7f 3-12, 8f 5) (g-s 2, gd 3, g-f 3-8, frm 4) 1999 AW 1-7: (7f 1-4, 8f 3) (Equi 1-6, Fibr)
Decent gelding, effective 7f, acts on gd to g-f - acts on Equi, mostly wears blinkers (effectively), likes left handed tracks, excels at Doncaster, does well at Yarmouth, likes Lingfield. Turf high 78 - 1st of 6 giving 20lb to Trojan Wolf (4 Aug Yarmouth RF 3382). AW high 83 - 1st of 8 giving 21lb to Mutabassir (21 Jan Lingfield RF 0138). He has been kept incredibly busy in the last couple of seasons, but keeps his form remarkably well. A true seven-furlong specialist, he is suited by coming late off a strong pace.
**P Howling [7-46] Liam Sheridan (from I A Balding [1-8] Oct 1997).*

TORCH SONG BHB 80f RR 79f 4720[1]

3 ch c Zafonic (USA) 9f **(83)** - River Lullaby (USA) (Riverman (USA)) 9.1f **(76)**
Form - 21
Record 1999 - 1st:1 2nd:1 3rd:0 Ran:2
Win Prizemoney £3,061 *Total Prizemoney* £4,741
Wins * 1999 Oct Pontef (SFT) 8f 79 <
1999 Turf 1-2: (8f 1-2) (gd 1-1, frm)
Scopey, currently above-average colt. Turf high 79 (began Spt) - 1st of 14 giving 5lb to Sheer Harmony (4 Oct Pontefract RF 4720). Runner-up in a big field on his debut, he went one better at Pontefract. Sold for 87,000 gns at Tattersalls to race in America.
**R Charlton [1-2] K Abdulla.*

TOREERO BHB 34f41a RR 31f 41a 4458a[14]

4 b g Cadeaux Genereux 7.9f **(76)** - Free City (USA) (Danzig (USA)) 8.4f **(76)**
Form - 700050
Record 1999 - 1st:0 2nd:0 3rd:0 Ran:6
Pre1999 - 1st:0 2nd:0 3rd:0 Ran:1
1999 Turf 0-3: (8f 2, 12f) (sft, g-f, frm) 1999 AW 0-3: (8f 2, 10f) (Equi, Fibr 2)
Very moderate gelding. Turf high 31. AW high 30.
**T Carmody in IRE [0-2] P A Byrne (from B J Curley [0-4] Apr 1999).*

TORGAU (IRE) BHB 100f RR 107f 4596[2]

2 b f Zieten (USA) - Snoozy Time (Cavo Doro) 10.6f **(57)**
Form - 16122
Record 1999 - 1st:2 2nd:2 3rd:0 Ran:5
Win Prizemoney £26,430 *Total Prizemoney* £89,070
Wins * 1999 Jly Newmar (GD) G2 6f 97 <
*** 1999** Jun Catter (GD) 5f 79+
1999 Turf 2-5: (5f 1-2, 6f 1-2, 7f) (gd, g-f 2, frm 2-2)
Pattern-class filly. Turf high 107 - 2nd of 15 to Seazun (28 Spt Newmarket 6f g-f RF 4596). Did her small yard proud, landing the Cherry Hinton Stakes at Newmarket and looking like following up in the Moyglare Stud Stakes until tying up in the seventh furlong. Ran a cracker when runner-up to another daughter of Zieten, Seazun, in the Cheveley Park back at six furlongs on her final start. She has been sold to continue her career in the United States, but her departure is likely to be delayed until after Royal Ascot, allowing the likeable Giles Bravery to prepare her for a crack at the Guineas. She seems unlikely to get the mile, however.
**G C Bravery [2-5] The TT Partnership.*

TORMENTOSO BHB 73f RR 72f 4007[7]

2 b c Catrail (USA) - Chita Rivera **(44f 37a)** (Chief Singer) 8.9f **(66)**
Form - 057
Record 1999 - 1st:0 2nd:0 3rd:0 Ran:3
1999 Turf 0-3: (7f 2, 8f) (gd 2, frm)
Currently above-average colt. Turf high 72.
**M R Channon [0-3] Den Jen Racing.*

TORNADO PRINCE (IRE) BHB 61f50a RR 63f 50a 5191[11]

4 ch g Caerleon (USA) 10.9f **(79)** - Welsh Flame (Welsh Pageant) 10f **(65)**
Form - 0600403642010805011080
Record 1999 - 1st:3 2nd:1 3rd:1 Ran:22
Pre1999 - 1st:1 2nd:0 3rd:1 Ran:8
Win Prizemoney £12,127 *Total Prizemoney* £13,706
Wins * 1999 Spt Pontef (G-F) SH 8f 56 63+
*** 1999** Spt Thirsk (FRM) S 8f 56
*** 1999** Jly Ripon (G-F) S 8f 56
1998 Jly Folkes (G-F) H 9.7f 62 69+ <
1999 Turf 3-19: (6f 2, 7f 6, 8f 3-8, 9f 2, 10f) (hvy, gd 2, g-f 7, frm 2-8, hrd 1-1) 1999 AW 0-3: (7f, 8f, 9f) (Fibr 3)
Workmanlike, average gelding, effective 8 to 10f, best at 10f, acts on g-f to frm, best on frm, likes right handed tracks, likes tight tracks. Turf high 63 - 1st of 20 getting 3lb from Pegasus Bay (16 Spt Pontefract RF 4349). AW high 48.
**E J Alston [3-22] Mrs J R Ramsden (from N A Callaghan [1-8] Aug 1998).*

TORRENT BHB 58f60a RR 49f 60a 5167[2]

4 ch g Prince Sabo 6.6f **(64)** - Maiden Pool (Sharpen Up) 8.3f **(67)**
Form - 0307074106483202
Record 1999 - 1st:1 2nd:2 3rd:2 Ran:16
Pre1999 - 1st:2 2nd:0 3rd:1 Ran:12
Win Prizemoney £13,838 *Total Prizemoney* £18,268
Wins * 1999 Jly Beverl (G-F) 5f 68

1998 May Thirsk (G-F) H 5f 78 83 <
1998 Apr Catter (GD) 6f 79
1999 Turf 1-16: (5f 1-10, 6f 5, 7f) (g-s, gd 4, g-f 5, frm 1-6)
Scopey, fair gelding, effective 5 to 6f, acts on gd to g-f, has worn blinkers. Turf high 72.
**D W Chapman [1-10] Mrs J Hazell (from T D Barron [2-14] Jun 1999).*

TORROS STRAITS (USA) RR 74f 2632[4]
2 b f Boundary (USA) - Preparation (USA) (Easy Goer (USA))
Form - 4
Record 1999 - 1st:0 2nd:0 3rd:0 Ran:1
Win Prizemoney £0 *Total Prizemoney* £332
1999 Turf 0-1: (6f) (frm)
Currently above-average filly. (1st run) - 4th of 8 getting 6lb from Boast (7 Jly Newmarket 6f frm RF 2632). Pulled too hard, spoiling her chances, when fourth over six furlongs at Newmarket's July meeting. **N A Callaghan [0-1] M Tabor & Mrs John Magnier.*

TORY BOY BHB 58f49a **RR 64f 49a** 5220[7]
4 b g Deploy 11.4f **(67)** - Mukhayyalah (Dancing Brave (USA)) 8.4f **(76)**
Form - 273267
Record 1999 - 1st:0 2nd:2 3rd:1 Ran:6
Pre1999 - 1st:1 2nd:0 3rd:0 Ran:5
Win Prizemoney £3,235 *Total Prizemoney* £5,272
Wins * 1998 Jun Warwic (SFT) 10.8f 76 <
1999 Turf 0-4: (15f, 16f, 17f, 20f) (sft 2, g-f 2) 1999 AW 0-2: (14f, 16f) (Equi, Fibr)
Lengthy, average gelding, has broken blood-vessels, effective 11 to 14f, acts on gd, has worn blinkers, favours tight tracks. Turf high 64. AW high 52. Inconsistent.
**Ian Williams [4-18] Mary Ann Properties Ltd.*

TOSHIBA TIMES BHB 40f **RR 30f** 3754[7]
3 b g Persian Bold 10f **(69)** - Kirkby Belle (Bay Express) 7.1f **(60)**
Form - 70807
Record 1999 - 1st:0 2nd:0 3rd:0 Ran:5
Pre1999 - 1st:0 2nd:0 3rd:0 Ran:1
1999 Turf 0-5: (5f, 6f, 7f, 9f, 10f) (g-s, g-f 2, frm 2)
Leggy, very moderate gelding. Turf high 50.
**B Ellison [0-6] Toshiba (UK) Ltd.*

TOTAL DELIGHT BHB 74f **RR 73f** 4817[8]
3 b c Mtoto 11.5f **(71)** - Shesadelight (Shirley Heights) 10.3f **(74)**
Form - 328
Record 1999 - 1st:0 2nd:1 3rd:1 Ran:3
Pre1999 - 1st:0 2nd:0 3rd:0 Ran:1
Win Prizemoney £0 *Total Prizemoney* £1,653
1999 Turf 0-3: (10f 2, 12f) (gd 2, g-f)
Scopey, above-average colt. Turf high 73 (began Spt).
**Lady Herries [0-4] Hesmonds Stud.*

TOTAL LOVE BHB 100f **RR 99f** 4920[3]
2 ch f Cadeaux Genereux 7.9f **(76)** - Favorable Exchange (USA) (Exceller (USA)) 12.5f **(74)**
Form - 210367233
Record 1999 - 1st:1 2nd:2 3rd:3 Ran:9
Win Prizemoney £3,457 *Total Prizemoney* £18,140
Wins * **1999** May Leices (GD) 6f 80 <
1999 Turf 1-9: (5f 3, 6f 1-3, 7f 2, 8f) (g-s, gd 5, g-f 1-2, frm)
Very useful filly, effective 7 to 8f, best at 7f, acts on gd to g-f, best on gd. Turf high 99 - 3rd of 12 to Lahan (16 Oct Newmarket 7f gd RF 4920). She improved once stepped-up to seven furlongs and a mile, making the frame in the Group 2 Rockfel Stakes on her final start. However, she lacks scope and may not improve much over the winter. **E A L Dunlop [1-9] John Brown & Megan Dennis.*

TOTALLY SCOTTISH BHB 54f **RR 47f** 5165[4]
3 b g Mtoto 11.5f **(71)** - Glenfinlass (Lomond (USA)) 8.8f **(65)**
Form - 704
Record 1999 - 1st:0 2nd:0 3rd:0 Ran:3
Win Prizemoney £0 *Total Prizemoney* £196
1999 Turf 0-3: (10f, 12f 2) (g-s, gd, frm)
Small, currently moderate gelding. Turf high 47.
**Mrs M Reveley [0-3] P D Savill.*

TOTEM DANCER BHB 62f54a **RR 72f 54a** 4791[17]
6 b m Mtoto 11.5f **(71)** - Ballad Opera (Sadler's Wells (USA)) 10f **(76)**
Form - 7500043200
Record 1999 - 1st:0 2nd:1 3rd:1 Ran:10
Pre1999 - 1st:3 2nd:7 3rd:4 Ran:26
Win Prizemoney £12,076 *Total Prizemoney* £30,733
Wins * 1998 Aug Cheste (GD) H 12.3f 75 79 <
* 1997 Spt Hamilt (GD) H 12.1f 69 76
* 1996 Oct Nottin (GD) 14.1f 76
1999 Turf 0-9: (10f, 12f 5, 14f 3) (g-s 2, gd 3, g-f, frm 3) 1999 AW 0-1: (16f) (Fibr)
Above-average mare, effective 10 to 14f, acts on sft to frm, has worn blinkers, likes left handed tracks, does well at York. Turf high 77 (1st run) - 5th of 10 giving 7lb to Top Jem (14 Apr Beverley 10f frm RF 0690). Inconsistent. **J L Eyre [3-36] Diamond Racing Ltd.*

TO THE LAST MAN BHB 58f **RR 60f** 5026[6]
3 b g Warrshan (USA) 9.7f **(59)** - Shirley's Touch (Touching Wood (USA)) 8.2f **(55)**
Form - 4705154404310506
Record 1999 - 1st:2 2nd:0 3rd:1 Ran:16
Pre1999 - 1st:0 2nd:2 3rd:0 Ran:7
Win Prizemoney £5,704 *Total Prizemoney* £8,801
Wins * **1999** Aug Bright (G-S) 8f 60+
* **1999** Jun Salisb (GD) H 8f 57 62+ <
1999 Turf 2-16: (7f, 8f 2-10, 9f, 10f 3, 11f) (g-s 2, gd 1-5, g-f 1-4, frm 4, hrd)
Light-framed, average gelding, effective 7 to 11f, acts on gd to g-f, has worn blinkers, likes left handed tracks, likes tight tracks. Turf high 68 (1st run) - 4th of 11 giving 15lb to Harp Player (5 Apr Warwick 11f gd RF 0595). Consistent.
**M D I Usher [2-23] Trevor Barker.*

TO THE ROOF (IRE) BHB 105f **RR 103f** 4654[10]
7 b g Thatching 7.8f **(69)** - Christine Daae (Sadler's Wells (USA)) 10f **(76)**
Form - 63131620700
Record 1999 - 1st:2 2nd:1 3rd:2 Ran:11
Pre1999 - 1st:5 2nd:9 3rd:3 Ran:36
Win Prizemoney £99,277 *Total Prizemoney* £137,424
Wins * **1999** Jun Epsom (GD,) LH 5f 108 109 <
* **1999** May Beverl (GD) 5f 108
* 1998 Spt Ascot (SFT) H 5f 102 106
* 1996 Jun Epsom (G-F) LH 5f 90 92
* 1996 May Thirsk (G-F) H 6f 84 90
* 1996 May Bath (G-F) H 5.1f 79 87
* 1996 Apr Mussel (GD) H 5f 67 69
1999 Turf 2-11: (5f 2-10, 6f) (g-s, gd 2-4, g-f 2, frm 4)
Very useful gelding, effective 5 to 6f, best at 5f, acts on gd to frm, best on gd, excels at Doncaster, does well at Epsom. Turf high 109 - 1st of 11 giving 1lb to Dashing Blue (5 Jun Epsom RF 1758) - also 1st of 9 giving 9lb to Henry Hall (8 May Beverley RF 1098). Consistent. A very useful sprinter on his day, winner of the valuable Vodafone Dash at Epsom in June for the second time. Just misses out at Pattern level, but invariably looks well and seems best when racing up with the pace over five furlongs.
**P W Harris [7-47] Mrs P W Harris.*

TOTIMETO BHB 64f **RR 63f** 3849[5]
3 b g Mtoto 11.5f **(71)** - Stolon Time (Good Times (ITY)) 6.6f **(54)**
Form - 575
Record 1999 - 1st:0 2nd:0 3rd:0 Ran:3
1999 Turf 0-3: (8f 3) (g-f 2, frm)
Leggy, currently average gelding. Turf high 63 (began Jly).
**J A Glover [0-3] A D Downing.*

TOTO CAELO BHB 89f **RR 92f** 4571[15]
3 b c Mtoto 11.5f **(71)** - Octavia Girl (Octavo (USA)) 14.4f **(54)**
Form - 12061200
Record 1999 - 1st:2 2nd:2 3rd:0 Ran:8
Pre1999 - 1st:0 2nd:0 3rd:0 Ran:2
Win Prizemoney £7,658 *Total Prizemoney* £13,701
Wins * **1999** Aug Windso (GD) H 11.6f 81 89+ <
* **1999** Apr Leices (GD) 11.8f 76
1999 Turf 2-8: (12f 2-7, 13f) (sft, gd 2-4, g-f, frm 2)
Scopey, useful colt, effective 12f, acts on gd to frm, best on gd. Turf high 92 - 2nd of 7 getting 8lb from Serpentine (2 Spt York 12f frm RF 4102) - also 1st of 8 giving 1lb to Lamerie (16 Aug Windsor RF 3681). Down the field in Ascot's King George V Handicap, he ran better in the Old Newton Cup before scoring nicely at Windsor. Only just touched off at York in September despite not appearing

to enjoy the fast ground, but disappointed in a hot Newbury handicap. Sold for 46,000 gns in October. **B W Hills [2-10] John Leat.*

TOTOM BHB 73f74a **RR 72f 74a** 4788[5]

4 b f Mtoto 11.5f **(71)** - A Lyph (USA) (Lypheor) 12f **(71)**

Form - 151004115145

Record 1999 - 1st:4 2nd:0 3rd:0 Ran:10
Pre1999 - 1st:1 2nd:2 3rd:1 Ran:8

Win Prizemoney £17,143 *Total Prizemoney* £25,185

Wins * **1999** Aug Lingfi (G-F) H 11.5f 69 72
* **1999** Jly Windso (G-F) H 10f 63 67
* **1999** Jun Windso (G-F) 10f 61
* **1999** *Feb Lingfi (STD) H 10f 68 75+* <
1998 *Nov Lingfi (STD) 10f 65*

1999 Turf 3-8: (10f 2-5, 11f 1-2, 13f) (g-s, g-f 2-3, frm 1-4) 1999 AW 1-2: (10f 1-2) (Equi 1-2)

Above-average filly, effective 8 to 13f, acts on g-f to frm - acts on AW, has worn blinkers (extremely effectively), likes left handed tracks, prefers tight tracks, and excels at Windsor. Turf high 72 - 4th of 13 getting 16lb from Alberich (18 Spt Newbury 13f frm RF 4403) - also 1st of 9 getting 7lb from Mister Benjamin (25 Aug Lingfield RF 3909). AW high 75 (1st run) - 1st of 7 giving 3lb to Kings Arrow (4 Feb Lingfield RF 0225). A winner twice on the Lingfield Equitrack during the winter, she gained back to back victories over ten furlongs at Windsor during the summer. Regained winning form over a longer trip at Lingfield in August after a moderate effort at Newmarket. Talented, if not altogether consistent.
**J R Fanshawe [4-10] Chris van Hoorn (from Lord Huntingdon [1-8] Dec 1998).*

TOUCH 'N' FLY (IRE) BHB 110f **RR 115?f** 4894[4]

3 b c Catrail (USA) - Menominee (Soviet Star (USA))

Form - 1134

Record 1999 - 1st:2 2nd:0 3rd:1 Ran:4

Win Prizemoney £10,947 *Total Prizemoney* £15,667

Wins * **1999** Aug Salisb (SFT) 8f 115+ <
* **1999** May Nottin (FRM) 8.2f 96++

1999 Turf 2-4: (8f 2-3, 9f) (gd, g-f 2-3)

Well made, high-class colt. Turf high 115 - 1st of 7 giving 4lb to Al Waffi (12 Aug Salisbury RF 3573). Unraced at two, he bolted up in a Nottingham maiden on very fast ground on his debut and followed up in a conditions race at Salisbury on a much softer surface. Ran well against Sugarfoot in the Park Stakes at Doncaster next time, and ran well to finish a close fourth to Indian Lodge in a Newmarket Listed event despite not enjoying the best of runs.
**H R A Cecil [2-4] The Thoroughbred Corporation.*

TOUCH'N'GO BHB 54f54a **RR 53f 54a** 1231[5]

5 b g Rainbow Quest (USA) 11.2f **(81)** - Mary Martin (Be My Guest (USA)) 9.3f **(67)**

Form - 5

Record 1999 - 1st:0 2nd:0 3rd:0 Ran:1
Pre1999 - 1st:2 2nd:1 3rd:2 Ran:10

Win Prizemoney £5,046 *Total Prizemoney* £6,811

Wins 1997 *Mar Lingfi (STD) H 10f 60 70* <
1997 *Feb Southw (STD) H 8f 51 55*

1999 AW 0-1: (15f) (Fibr)

Fair gelding.
**G Woodward [0-3] Wetherby Racing Bureau Ltd (from M Johnston [2-8] Jun 1997).*

TOUCH OF FAIRY (IRE) **RR 72f** 5113[2]

3 b c Fairy King (USA) 7.7f **(75)** - Decadence (Vaigly Great) 7f **(58)**

Form - 2

Record 1999 - 1st:0 2nd:1 3rd:0 Ran:1

Win Prizemoney £0 *Total Prizemoney* £884

1999 Turf 0-1: (6f) (gd)

Scopey, currently above-average colt. (1st run) - 2nd of 21 getting 1lb from Madmun (28 Oct Windsor 6f gd RF 5113).
**K Mahdi [0-1] Hamad Al-Mutawa.*

TOUCH OF LOVE BHB 62f **RR 64f** 5025[10]

3 b c Pursuit of Love 9.5f **(69)** - Nitouche (Scottish Reel) 7f **(61)**

Form - 600810

Record 1999 - 1st:1 2nd:0 3rd:0 Ran:6
Pre1999 - 1st:0 2nd:0 3rd:0 Ran:2

Win Prizemoney £3,267 *Total Prizemoney* £3,267

Wins * **1999** Oct Redcar (GD) H 11f 59 64 <

1999 Turf 1-6: (8f 2, 10f 2, 11f 1-1, 15f) (sft, g-s, gd, g-f, frm 1-2)

Workmanlike, average colt, effective 11f, acts on frm. Turf high 64 - 1st of 17 getting 1lb from Fee Mail (14 Oct Redcar RF 4882).
**J Noseda [1-8] Harvey Rosenblatt & Norman Mandell.*

TOUCH OF THE BLUES (FR) **RR 93f** 5263a[1]

2 b c Cadeaux Genereux 7.9f **(76)** - Silabteni (USA) (Nureyev (USA)) 8.7f **(78)**

Form - 31

1999 Turf 1-2: (7f 1-2) (hvy, g-s 1-1)

Currently useful colt. Turf high 93 (began Oct) - 1st of 8 from Blu Air Force (5 Nov Maisons-Laffitte RF 5263a).
**C Laffon-Parias in FR [1-2] Maktoum Al Maktoum.*

TOUGH ACT BHB 71f **RR 72f** 4134[6]

5 b g Be My Chief (USA) 10.2f **(62)** - Forelino (USA) (Trempolino (USA)) 12f **(71)**

Form - 02270446

Record 1999 - 1st:0 2nd:2 3rd:0 Ran:8
Pre1999 - 1st:2 2nd:5 3rd:1 Ran:14

Win Prizemoney £7,939 *Total Prizemoney* £21,775

Wins * 1998 Spt Goodwo (G-S) 12f 79+ <
* 1998 Jun Goodwo (G-F) 12f 76

1999 Turf 0-8: (11f, 12f 2, 13f, 14f 3, 16f) (g-s, gd, g-f 3, frm 3)

Above-average gelding, effective 11 to 14f, best at 14f, acts on gd to g-f, best on gd, has worn blinkers, prefers right handed tracks, prefers tight tracks, excels at Goodwood, does well at Sandown. Turf high 81 - 2nd of 8 giving 20lb to Durham (11 Jun Goodwood 14f gd RF 1913).
**Mrs A J Perrett [4-27] Mrs R Doel (from G Harwood [0-4] Oct 1996).*

TOUGH GUY (IRE) **RR 90f** 4921[19]

3 b c Namaqualand (USA) - Supreme Crown (USA) (Chief's Crown (USA)) 9.8f **(72)**

Form - 505010

Record 1999 - 1st:1 2nd:0 3rd:0 Ran:6
Pre1999 - 1st:2 2nd:1 3rd:0 Ran:8

Win Prizemoney £15,528 *Total Prizemoney* £17,298

Wins * **1999** Spt Haydoc (SFT) H 7.1f 88 90
* 1998 Aug Newmar (G-F) 7f 92 <
* 1998 Jun Kempto (SFT) 6f 88

1999 Turf 1-6: (7f 1-6) (g-s 1-1, gd 2, g-f, frm 2)

Scopey, useful colt, effective 6 to 7f, best at 7f, acts on g-s to frm, best on g-s. Turf high 90 - 1st of 10 giving 19lb to Haymaker (25 Spt Haydock RF 4556). Back to his best when winning at Haydock in September, he has won on fast ground, but looks much better in testing conditions. **M A Jarvis [3-14] Sqdn Ldr Milsom.*

TOUGH LEADER BHB 100f95a **RR 103f 95a** 3235[5]

5 b g Lead on Time (USA) 7.5f **(69)** - Al Guswa (Shernazar) 10.2f **(73)**

Form - 8318425

Record 1999 - 1st:1 2nd:1 3rd:1 Ran:7
Pre1999 - 1st:5 2nd:2 3rd:4 Ran:21

Win Prizemoney £47,896 *Total Prizemoney* £72,110

Wins * **1999** Jun Epsom (GD) H 12f 95 97 <
* 1998 Jly York (G-F) H 11.9f 91 95
* 1998 May Sandow (GD) H 10f 78 82
* 1998 *Mar Southw (STD) H 12f 77 80*
* 1998 *Feb Wolver (STD) H 9.4f 75 77*
* 1996 Jun Thirsk (FRM) 7f 66

1999 Turf 1-7: (10f, 12f 1-5, 14f) (gd 1-3, g-f 2, frm 2)

Very useful gelding, effective 10 to 14f, best at 12f, acts on gd to frm, best on gd, likes left handed tracks, prefers tight tracks, excels at York, does well at Epsom, likes Goodwood. Turf high 103 - 4th of 15 giving 14lb to Celestial Welcome (3 Jly Haydock 12f gd RF 2532) - also 1st of 11 giving 3lb to Nautical Star (5 Jun Epsom RF 1761). A tough and likeable handicapper, he struggles to stay a mile and three-quarters and is better over slightly shorter trips. Effective on any ground, he wears a tongue strap nowadays.
**B Hanbury [6-28] G G Grayson.*

TOUGH SPEED (USA) BHB 100f **RR 95f** 4676[4]

2 b c Miswaki (USA) 8.1f **(81)** - Nature's Magic (USA) (Nijinsky (CAN)) 10.3f **(77)**

Form - 214

Record 1999 - 1st:1 2nd:1 3rd:0 Ran:3

Win Prizemoney £6,035 *Total Prizemoney* £11,635

Wins * **1999** Spt Doncas (G-F) 7f 95+ <

1999 Turf 1-3: (6f, 7f 1-2) (gd 1-3)
Currently very useful colt. Turf high 95 (began Aug) - 1st of 4 getting 4lb from Hataab (8 Spt Doncaster RF 4205). He created a big impression when running away with a seemingly competitive conditions race in September, but floundered on a yielding surface at Newmarket the following month. Better than that effort implies, he should stay a mile and is a Group horse in the making.
**Sir Michael Stoute [1-3] Saeed Suhail.*

TOUS LES JOURS (USA) BHB 60f **RR 61f** 4946[11]
3 b f Dayjur (USA) 6.8f **(79)** -Humility (USA)(Cox's Ridge (USA)) 8f **(68)**
Form - 5804326014600440
Record 1999 - 1st:1 2nd:1 3rd:1 Ran:16
Pre1999 - 1st:1 2nd:0 3rd:3 Ran:8
Win Prizemoney £6,355 *Total Prizemoney* £11,341
Wins * 1999 Jly Catter (GD) 7f 57
* 1998 Aug Beverl (G-F) H 7.5f 67 74 <
1999 Turf 1-16: (6f 3, 7f 1-8, 8f 3, 10f 2) (g-s 2, gd 2, g-f 1-3, frm 9)
Scopey, average filly, effective 5 to 7f, acts on frm, has worn blinkers. Turf high 64. **M Johnston [2-24] J S Morrison.*

TOUT CHARMANT (USA) RR 111f 4884a[2]
3 b f Slewvescent (USA) - Charm A Gendarme (USA) (Batonnier (USA))
Form - 2
1999 Turf 0-1: (9f) (frm)
Currently Group-class filly. (1st run) - 2nd of 9 to Perfect Sting (9 Oct Keeneland 9f frm RF 4884a). **in USA [0-1].*

TOWER OF SONG (IRE) BHB 62f67a **RR 60f 67a** 5148[9]
2 ch g Perugino (USA) - New Rochelle (IRE) (Lafontaine (USA)) 8.7f **(49)**
Form - 205350
Record 1999 - 1st:0 2nd:1 3rd:1 Ran:6
Win Prizemoney £0 *Total Prizemoney* £1,034
1999 Turf 0-5: (7f 4, 10f) (g-s, g-f, frm 3) 1999 AW 0-1: (8f) (Fibr)
Average gelding, effective 7 to 10f, best at 7f, acts on g-s to frm. Turf high 60. **M R Channon [0-6] M G St Quinton.*

TOWN GIRL (IRE) RR 58f 5020[13]
2 ch f Lammtarra (USA) - Greektown (Ela-Mana-Mou) 10.1f **(70)**
Form - 0
Record 1999 - 1st:0 2nd:0 3rd:0 Ran:1
1999 Turf 0-1: (8f) (gd)
Currently fair filly. **Sir Michael Stoute [0-1] Lord Weinstock.*

TOWN GOSSIP (IRE) RR 43f 4815[16]
2 ch f Indian Ridge 7.6f **(74)** - Only Gossip (USA) (Trempolino (USA)) 12f **(71)**
Form - 0
Record 1999 - 1st:0 2nd:0 3rd:0 Ran:1
1999 Turf 0-1: (7f) (gd)
Currently moderate filly. **P J Makin [0-1] Dr Carlos Stelling.*

TOWNVILLE CEE CEE BHB 41f27a **RR 39f 27a** 684[6]
4 b f Anshan 8.2f **(63)** - Holy Day (Sallust) 8.4f **(63)**
Form - 507056
Record 1999 - 1st:0 2nd:0 3rd:0 Ran:5
Pre1999 - 1st:0 2nd:0 3rd:0 Ran:16
Win Prizemoney £0 *Total Prizemoney* £281
1999 Turf 0-2: (8f 2) (g-f, frm) 1999 AW 0-3: (7f, 9f, 12f) (Fibr 3)
Scopey, very moderate filly. Turf high 39. AW high 9. Inconsistent.
**G Woodward [0-7] Townville C C Racing Club (from J S Wainwright [0-14] Aug 1998).*

TOY STORY (FR) BHB 54f **RR 57f** 5067[7]
3 b g Fijar Tango (FR) - Grundygold (FR) (Grundy) 10.3f **(65)**
Form - 067
Record 1999 - 1st:0 2nd:0 3rd:0 Ran:3
1999 Turf 0-3: (9f, 10f, 12f) (g-s, gd, g-f)
Workmanlike, currently fair gelding. Turf high 57.
**Miss Gay Kelleway [0-3] M Butler & R Paul.*

TRAFFORD BHB 58f60a **RR 53f 60a** 5147[2]
3 b f Prince Sabo 6.6f **(64)** - Number One Spot (Reference Point) 6.8f **(70)**
Form - 502
Record 1999 - 1st:0 2nd:1 3rd:0 Ran:3
Win Prizemoney £0 *Total Prizemoney* £912
1999 Turf 0-1: (7f) (gd) 1999 AW 0-2: (7f, 8f) (Fibr 2)
Light-framed, currently fair filly. AW high 58 (began Oct) - 2nd of 13 to Bayt Alasad (30 Oct Wolverhampton 8f Fibr RF 5147).
**B A McMahon [0-3] Barouche Stud Ltd.*

TRAGIC DANCER BHB 70f73a **RR 66f 73a** 2376[7]
3 b c Tragic Role (USA) 9.4f **(63)** - Chantallee's Pride (Mansooj)
Form - 5215445127
Record 1999 - 1st:2 2nd:2 3rd:0 Ran:9
Pre1999 - 1st:0 2nd:0 3rd:1 Ran:6
Win Prizemoney £6,432 *Total Prizemoney* £8,424
Wins * 1999 Jun Sandow (GD) H 11.4f 62 66 <
*** 1999** *Jan Lingfi (STD) H 10f 60 66+*
1999 Turf 1-3: (11f 1-1, 12f, 14f) (g-f, frm 1-2) 1999 AW 1-6: (10f 1-3, 11f, 12f 2) (Equi 1-3, Fibr 3)
Leggy, above-average colt, effective 10 to 12f, best at 10f, acts on g-f to frm - acts on AW, favours tight tracks. Turf high 66 - 1st of 14 giving 9lb to Harp Player (11 Jun Sandown RF 1924). AW high 71 - 2nd of 9 giving 24lb to Netherhall (17 Jun Southwell 12f Fibr RF 2087) - also 1st of 11 getting 3lb from An Executive Do (26 Jan Lingfield RF 0169). Consistent.
**K McAuliffe [2-15] Treadwell, Chung & Butler.*

TRAGIC LADY BHB 40f **RR 33f** 2687[8]
3 b f Tragic Role (USA) 9.4f **(63)** - Rainbow Lady (Jaazeiro (USA)) 9.2f **(54)**
Form - 678
Record 1999 - 1st:0 2nd:0 3rd:0 Ran:3
1999 Turf 0-2: (6f, 8f) (g-f, hrd) 1999 AW 0-1: (6f) (Fibr)
Light-framed, currently very moderate filly. Turf high 33.
**M G Meagher [0-3] M R Johnson.*

TRAIKEY (IRE) BHB 51f **RR 46f** 5199[16]
7 b g Scenic 10.6f **(66)** - Swordlestown Miss (USA) (Apalachee (USA)) 9.4f **(71)**
Form - 700800
Record 1999 - 1st:0 2nd:0 3rd:0 Ran:6
Pre1999 - 1st:1 2nd:0 3rd:1 Ran:2
Win Prizemoney £5,250 *Total Prizemoney* £6,761
1999 Turf 0-6: (5f 2, 6f, 7f, 8f 2) (gd 3, g-f 2, frm)
Moderate gelding. Turf high 46 (began Jly). Inconsistent.
**Mrs S Lamyman [0-6] P Lamyman (from J E Banks [1-2] May 1995).*

TRAIT DE GENIE (FR) RR 112f 4664a[1]
7 ch g Diamond Prospect (USA) 8f **(62)** - Garmeritte (FR) (Garde Royale)
Form - 221
1999 Turf 1-3: (10f 2, 12f 1-1) (hvy 1-2, gd)
Group-class gelding. Turf high 111 (began Jly) - 2nd of 5 to Dream Well (15 Aug Deauville 10f hvy RF 3782a) - also 1st of 11 giving 19lb to Akbar (26 Spt Dielsdorf RF 4664a). Consistent. An evergreen seven-year-old, he ran right away from Akbar in the Grand Prix Jockey Club in Zurich during September, thereby recording his third victory in the race. At his best when the mud flies, he should continue to defy Father Time.
**A Lyon in FR [5-7] J Bouchara (from in FR [0-3] Nov 1997).*

TRAJAN (IRE) BHB 77f **RR 80f** 5005[5]
2 b c Dolphin Street (FR) - Lavezzola (IRE) (Salmon Leap (USA)) 11f **(61)**
Form - 25425655
Record 1999 - 1st:0 2nd:2 3rd:0 Ran:8
Win Prizemoney £0 *Total Prizemoney* £4,253
1999 Turf 0-8: (5f, 6f 7) (g-s, gd 4, g-f, frm 2)
Decent colt, effective 6f, acts on gd to frm. Turf high 80 (began Jly) - 4th of 13 to Invincible Spirit (28 Jly Goodwood 6f frm RF 3212). Consistent. Heavily supported for his Haydock debut, he just lost out. He does not appear to have progressed from that.
**A P Jarvis [0-8] Mrs D B Brazier.*

TRAMLINE BHB 62f56a **RR 66df 56a** 5220[15]
6 b h Shirley Heights 12.1f **(76)** - Trampship (High Line) 10.3f **(70)**
Form - 772112612000

Record 1999 - 1st:3 2nd:3 3rd:0 Ran:12
Pre1999 - 1st:1 2nd:0 3rd:1 Ran:12
Win Prizemoney £15,673 *Total Prizemoney* £22,831
Wins * 1999 Aug Sandow (GD) H 16.4f 65 66
*** 1999** Jun Doncas (G-F) H 14.6f 57 58
*** 1999** Jun Sandow (GD) H 14f 51 54
* 1997 Jun Newmar (G-S) 14.8f 82 <
1999 Turf 3-12: (12f 2, 14f 1-2, 15f 1-1, 16f 1-5, 17f 2) (sft, g-s, gd 2, g-f 3-4, frm 4)
Average horse, effective 14 to 16f, best at 16f, acts on g-s to frm, likes right handed tracks, excels at Sandown. Turf high 66 - 1st of 14 giving 5lb to Balanak (20 Aug Sandown RF 3808) - also 1st of 5 getting 13lb from Agent Le Blanc (26 Jun Doncaster RF 2325). Becoming disappointing. He is an effective sort in staying handicaps, winning three times during the summer, but was well beaten in softer ground. He looks to need a strong pace.
**M Blanshard [4-24] H C Promotions Ltd.*

TRANS ISLAND BHB 114f RR 118f 5014a[3]

4 b c Selkirk (USA) 7.9f **(76)** - Khubza (Green Desert (USA)) 8.6f **(78)**
Form - 521113
Record 1999 - 1st:3 2nd:1 3rd:1 Ran:6
Pre1999 - 1st:3 2nd:4 3rd:0 Ran:8
Win Prizemoney £150,475 *Total Prizemoney* £199,362
Wins * 1999 Oct Longch (HVY) G2 8f 117 <
*** 1999** Spt Newbur (G-S) L 7.3f 104
*** 1999** Spt Leopar (SFT) H 7f 107+
* 1997 Aug Deauvi (SFT) L 7f 91+
* 1997 Jly Newbur (G-F) 7f 93
* 1997 Jun Newbur (G-F) 6f 86
1999 Turf 3-6: (7f 2-4, 8f 1-2) (sft 1-1, gd 2-3, g-f)
Scopey, high-class colt, effective 7 to 8f, best at 8f, acts on gd. Turf high 118 - 3rd giving 4lb to Field of Hope (17 Oct Longchamp 7f RF 5014a) - also 1st of 9 from Sugarfoot (3 Oct Longchamp RF 4779a). Unlucky to be disqualified after winning the Italian 2,000 Guineas in 1998, he came back better than ever last term, putting up a game effort when beating Sugarfoot by a neck in the Prix du Rond-Point at Longchamp in October. Effective over seven furlongs or a mile and suited by soft ground, he goes well from the front and has a grand attitude. **I A Balding [6-14].*

TRANSPARENT (IRE) BHB 23a RR 51f 23a 283[12]

7 b m Dance of Life (USA) 9.3f **(69)** - Clear Picture (Polyfoto)
Form - 500780
Record 1999 - 1st:0 2nd:0 3rd:0 Ran:5
Pre1999 - 1st:1 2nd:0 3rd:1 Ran:13
Win Prizemoney £2,740 *Total Prizemoney* £3,145
Wins 1997 Oct Cork (GD) H 7.5f 40 51+ <
1999 AW 0-5: (8f, 11f 2, 12f, 16f) (Fibr 5)
Fair mare, effective 10f, acts on gd. AW high 21.
**D Carroll [0-5] Charles Stewart (from D Carroll [0-1] Dec 1998).*

TRAPPER NORMAN BHB 48f27a RR 47f 27a 3257[3]

7 b g Mazilier (USA) 8.5f **(56)** - Free Skip (Free State) 8.7f **(61)**
Form - 63233
Record 1999 - 1st:0 2nd:1 3rd:3 Ran:5
Pre1999 - 1st:0 2nd:0 3rd:0 Ran:11
Win Prizemoney £0 *Total Prizemoney* £1,866
1999 Turf 0-5: (6f 4, 7f) (frm 4, hrd)
Moderate gelding, effective 6 to 7f, best at 6f, acts on frm. Turf high 47 - 2nd of 15 to Albert The Bear (23 Jun Carlisle 6f frm RF 2222). **C Smith [0-9] Brian Culley (from R Ingram [0-10] Jan 1997).*

TRAVELLING CLOCK BHB 48f RR 52f 2529[7]

4 ch c Deploy 11.4f **(67)** - Travel Mystery (Godswalk (USA)) 7.3f **(58)**
Form - 7
Record 1999 - 1st:0 2nd:0 3rd:0 Ran:1
Pre1999 - 1st:0 2nd:0 3rd:1 Ran:4
Win Prizemoney £0 *Total Prizemoney* £490
1999 Turf 0-1: (18f) (frm)
Lengthy, fair colt. **B A McMahon [0-7] R L Bedding.*

TRAVELLING LITE (IRE) BHB 81f RR 81f 5034[7]

2 b c Blues Traveller (IRE) - Lute and Lyre (IRE) (The Noble Player (USA)) 6.5f **(67)**
Form - 5571267
Record 1999 - 1st:1 2nd:1 3rd:0 Ran:7
Win Prizemoney £3,240 *Total Prizemoney* £5,140
Wins * 1999 Spt Lingfi (G-F) H 7f 72 75 <
1999 Turf 1-7: (6f, 7f 1-5, 8f) (g-s, gd, g-f 2, frm 1-3)
Decent colt, effective 7f, acts on frm. Turf high 81 - also 1st of 16 giving 3lb to Inchinnan (7 Spt Lingfield RF 4177).
**B R Millman [1-7] The Three Bears Racing II.*

TRAVELLING STAR (USA) BHB 85f RR 85f 2495[5]

3 b c Lear Fan (USA) 10.4f **(80)** - Ladanum (USA) (Green Dancer (USA)) 10.3f **(74)**
Form - 6125
Record 1999 - 1st:1 2nd:1 3rd:0 Ran:4
Win Prizemoney £3,631 *Total Prizemoney* £6,588
Wins * 1999 May Pontef (GD) 10f 73 <
1999 Turf 1-4: (7f, 10f 1-3) (gd 1-2, g-f 2)
Leggy, useful colt. Turf high 85 - 2nd of 6 getting 6lb from Fredora (8 Jun Salisbury 10f g-f RF 1817).
**C E Brittain [1-4] The Thoroughbred Corporation.*

TRAVELMATE BHB 110f RR 110f 5223a[5]

5 b g Persian Bold 10f **(69)** - Ustka (Lomond (USA)) 8.8f **(65)**
Form - 2225
Record 1999 - 1st:0 2nd:3 3rd:0 Ran:4
Pre1999 - 1st:5 2nd:1 3rd:0 Ran:12
Win Prizemoney £29,543 *Total Prizemoney* £121,935
Wins * 1998 Spt Newmar (GD) H 12f 91 93 <
* 1998 Aug Newmar (G-F) H 14.8f 81 84+
* 1998 Jun Newmar (GD) H 12f 76 79
* 1997 Jun Newmar (G-S) H 12f 73 74
* 1997 May Nottin (GD) H 10f 66 74+
1999 Turf 0-4: (12f, 14f, 16f 2) (gd 2, frm 2)
Group-class gelding, effective 12 to 16f, best at 16f, acts on gd to frm, best on gd, excels at Newmarket and Newcastle. Turf high 110 - 5th of 24 giving 6lb to Rogan Josh (2 Nov Flemington 16f gd RF 5223a). Improving. Short-headed by Far Cry after an epic battle in the Northumberland Plate, he again filled the runner's-up spot in the Ebor. Prepared for the Melbourne Cup, he finished a fine fifth, showing enough for the legendary Aussie trainer Bart Cummings to offer big money for him, although the deal fell through. He obviously stays well, and is suited by a fast-run race.
**J R Fanshawe [5-16] Barford Bloodstock II.*

TRAVESTY OF LAW (IRE) BHB 100f RR 93f 4793[13]

2 ch g Case Law 6f **(64)** - Bold As Love (Lomond (USA)) 8.8f **(65)**
Form - 641258104050
Record 1999 - 1st:2 2nd:1 3rd:0 Ran:12
Win Prizemoney £6,515 *Total Prizemoney* £9,440
Wins * 1999 Jun Windso (G-F) 5f 93+ <
*** 1999** May Salisb (G-F) 5f 86+
1999 Turf 2-12: (5f 2-12) (sft, gd 2, g-f 4, frm 2-5)
Useful gelding, effective 5f, acts on g-f to frm, best on frm. Turf high 93 - 4th of 10 giving 5lb to Misty Miss (30 Jly Goodwood 5f g-f RF 3236) - also 1st of 8 giving 7lb to Roo (28 Jun Windsor RF 2381). Inconsistent. Has plenty of speed, and benefited from fast ground to win at Salisbury and Windsor, but has been found out when taking on the better juveniles.
**B J Meehan [2-12] Stephen Molloy.*

TRAWLING BHB 65f RR 60f 2526[11]

3 b f Mtoto 11.5f **(71)** - Ghost Tree (IRE) (Caerleon (USA)) 8.6f **(71)**
Form - 1370
Record 1999 - 1st:1 2nd:0 3rd:1 Ran:4
Pre1999 - 1st:0 2nd:2 3rd:0 Ran:2
Win Prizemoney £3,161 *Total Prizemoney* £4,961
Wins * 1999 *Feb Lingfi (STD) 8f* 75+ <
1999 Turf 0-3: (8f, 10f, 12f) (gd, frm, hrd) 1999 AW 1-1: (8f 1-1) (Equi 1-1)
Unfurnished, above-average filly, effective 7 to 8f, best at 7f, acts on g-f to frm - acts on Equi. Turf high 60. (1st run) - 1st of 5 from Lady Irene (20 Feb Lingfield RF 0328).
**B W Hills [1-6] Mrs H Theodorou.*

TREAD SOFTLY (IRE) BHB 50f55a RR 49f 55a 4906[29]

3 b f Roi Danzig (USA) 10.5f **(62)** - Albenita (IRE) (Alzao (USA)) 7.1f **(68)**
Form - 67000
Record 1999 - 1st:0 2nd:0 3rd:0 Ran:5
Pre1999 - 1st:1 2nd:1 3rd:0 Ran:3
Win Prizemoney £2,442 *Total Prizemoney* £3,224

Wins * 1998 Oct Pontef (SFT) 6f 71 <
1999 Turf 0-3: (5f, 6f, 7f) (gd, frm 2) 1999 AW 0-2: (6f, 7f) (Fibr 2)
Average filly, effective 5 to 6f, acts on gd. Turf high 33. AW high 63. Becoming disappointing. **R A Fahey [1-8] Capt C M Ryan.*

TREASURE CHEST (IRE) RR 76df 3560[8]
4 b g Last Tycoon 9.4f **(73)** - Sought Out (IRE) (Rainbow Quest (USA)) 10.4f **(75)**
Form - 035258
Record 1999 - 1st:0 2nd:1 3rd:1 Ran:6
Pre1999 - 1st:0 2nd:2 3rd:2 Ran:9
Win Prizemoney £0 *Total Prizemoney* £7,859
1999 Turf 0-6: (14f, 16f 2, 17f 2, 20f) (gd, g-f 2, frm 3)
Scopey, above-average gelding, effective 14 to 18f, acts on gd to frm, best on frm, has worn blinkers, likes tight tracks. Turf high 76 - 3rd of 5 giving 27lb to Hal Hoo Yaroom (30 Jun Bath 17f frm RF 2427).
**M C Pipe [0-11] S Helaissi & A Love (from M P Tregoning [0-6] Oct 1998).*

TREASURE COVE (IRE) BHB 30f **RR 29f** 4163[7]
3 b f Treasure Kay 6.5f **(53)** - Shydico (IRE) (Nordico (USA)) 6.5f **(62)**
Form - 760060377
Record 1999 - 1st:0 2nd:0 3rd:1 Ran:9
Win Prizemoney £0 *Total Prizemoney* £447
1999 Turf 0-8: (7f 3, 8f, 9f 2, 11f, 12f) (gd 2, g-f 3, frm 3) 1999 AW 0-1: (7f) (Fibr)
Workmanlike, little account filly. Turf high 30.
**Miss L A Perratt [0-9] T P Finch.*

TREASURE ISLAND BHB 48f49a **RR 46f 49a** 793[4]
4 b f Rainbow Quest (USA) 11.2f **(81)** - Cockatoo Island (High Top) 10.2f **(67)**
Form - 4
Record 1999 - 1st:0 2nd:0 3rd:0 Ran:1
Pre1999 - 1st:1 2nd:0 3rd:0 Ran:7
Win Prizemoney £2,836 *Total Prizemoney* £3,184
Wins 1998 Jun Hamilt (G-S) H 11.1f 43 46 <
1999 Turf 0-1: (12f) (gd)
Light-framed, moderate filly. Inconsistent.
**F Murphy [0-3] The Ferdy Murphy Racing Club (from Sir Mark Prescott [1-7] Jly 1998).*

TREASURE TOUCH (IRE) BHB 59f76a **RR 55f 76a** 4832[7]
5 b g Treasure Kay 6.5f **(53)** - Bally Pourri (IRE) (Law Society (USA)) 9.9f **(70)**
Form - 4027
Record 1999 - 1st:0 2nd:1 3rd:0 Ran:4
Pre1999 - 1st:5 2nd:1 3rd:3 Ran:26
Win Prizemoney £22,384 *Total Prizemoney* £25,393
Wins * 1997 May Thirsk (GD) H 5f 85 85+
* 1997 Apr Newmar (G-F) H 6f 72 86 <
* 1997 Apr Nottin (G-F) H 6.1f 63 78+
* 1997 Mar Nottin (G-F) H 6.1f 63 71+
1997 Feb Southw (STD) 6f 69+
1999 Turf 0-4: (5f, 6f 3) (sft, g-s, gd, frm)
Average gelding. Turf high 55 (began Spt).
**D Nicholls [4-23] N Honeyman (from G M Moore [1-6] Feb 1997).*

TREASURY RR 70f 2390[F]
3 ch f Generous (IRE) 11.5f **(82)** - Atlantic Flyer (USA) (Storm Bird (CAN)) 10.3f **(74)**
Form - F
Record 1999 - 1st:0 2nd:0 3rd:0 Ran:1
Pre1999 - 1st:0 2nd:0 3rd:0 Ran:4
1999 Turf 0-1: (10f) (g-f)
Scopey, above-average filly. (DEAD)
**Sir Mark Prescott [0-5] Cheveley Park Stud.*

TREASURY GARDENS (USA) RR 82+f 3931a[8]
3 ro f Miswaki (USA) 8.1f **(81)** - Tira (FR) (Bellypha) 9.8f **(73)**
Form - 18
Record 1999 - 1st:1 2nd:0 3rd:0 Ran:2
Win Prizemoney £2,463 *Total Prizemoney* £2,463
Wins * 1999 May Pontef (GD) 6f 82+ <
1999 Turf 1-2: (6f 1-1, 8f) (gd 1-2)
Scopey, currently decent filly. Turf high 82 (1st run) - 1st of 10 getting 5lb from Istintaj (18 May Pontefract RF 1302).
**P W Chapple-Hyam [1-2].*

TREATY (USA) RR 37?f 4030[9]
5 b g Trempolino (USA) 11.9f **(77)** - Zonda (Fabulous Dancer (USA)) 9.4f **(70)**
Form - 0
Record 1999 - 1st:0 2nd:0 3rd:0 Ran:1
Pre1999 - 1st:0 2nd:0 3rd:0 Ran:2
1999 Turf 0-1: (12f) (g-f)
Currently very moderate gelding.
**Mrs S Lamyman [0-1] P Lamyman (from K Mahdi [0-2] Spt 1997).*

TREBIZOND (IRE) RR 99f 4614a[1]
3 b c Sadler's Wells (USA) 11.3f **(87)** - Karri Valley (USA) (Storm Bird (CAN)) 10.3f **(74)**
Form - 0332311
1999 Turf 2-7: (10f, 12f 2-6) (g-s 2-4, gd, g-f, frm)
Very useful colt, effective 8 to 12f, best at 12f, acts on g-s to g-f, best on g-s, has worn blinkers. Turf high 99 - 1st of 7 giving 11lb to Go For Grace (22 Spt Listowel RF 4614a) - also 1st of 8 from Gaudi (19 Aug Tipperary RF 3880a). A shade one-paced, he should stay beyond a mile and a half. Quite high in the handicap, he must improve to make a mark in listed events.
**T J Taaffe in IRE [1-1] William Lickle (from C O'Brien in IRE [1-9] Aug 1999).*

TRELLIS BAY BHB 93f **RR 89+f** 5132[2]
3 b f Sadler's Wells (USA) 11.3f **(87)** - Bahamian (Mill Reef (USA)) 10.5f **(78)**
Form - 041722
Record 1999 - 1st:1 2nd:2 3rd:0 Ran:6
Win Prizemoney £3,837 *Total Prizemoney* £11,602
Wins * 1999 Jly Doncas (G-F) 12f 65+ <
1999 Turf 1-6: (10f, 12f 1-3, 15f, 16f) (gd 4, frm 1-2)
Useful filly, effective 15 to 16f, acts on gd. Turf high 89 - 2nd of 12 to Eilean Shona (29 Oct Newmarket 16f gd RF 5132).
**R Charlton [1-6] K Abdulla.*

TREMBLEY BHB 76f **RR 70+f** 4083[4]
2 b c Komaite (USA) 6.9f **(61)** - Cold Blow (Posse (USA)) 8.9f **(61)**
Form - 524
Record 1999 - 1st:0 2nd:1 3rd:0 Ran:3
Win Prizemoney £0 *Total Prizemoney* £2,206
1999 Turf 0-3: (5f, 6f, 7f) (frm 3)
Currently above-average colt. Turf high 70 (began Aug) - 4th of 10 to Akeed (1 Spt York 7f frm RF 4083). **J L Eyre [0-3] Billy Parker.*

TREMENDISTO BHB 38f25a **RR 21f 25a** 907[13]
9 b g Petoski 10.4f **(56)** - Misty Halo (High Top) 10.2f **(67)**
Form - 0
Record 1999 - 1st:0 2nd:0 3rd:0 Ran:1
Pre1999 - 1st:0 2nd:5 3rd:3 Ran:30
Win Prizemoney £0 *Total Prizemoney* £6,323
1999 Turf 0-1: (10f) (gd)
Little account gelding.
**T Wall [2-8] J H Bebbington (from D McCain [0-5] Feb 1998).*

TREMONNOW BHB 30f **RR 20f** 1285[16]
4 b f Reprimand 8.2f **(63)** - Tree Mallow (Malicious) 8.7f **(50)**
Form - 00
Record 1999 - 1st:0 2nd:0 3rd:0 Ran:2
Pre1999 - 1st:0 2nd:1 3rd:1 Ran:15
Win Prizemoney £0 *Total Prizemoney* £1,173
1999 Turf 0-2: (6f 2) (gd, hrd)
Light-framed, little account filly, effective 6 to 7f, acts on g-f, has worn blinkers. Turf high 19. Becoming disappointing.
**J M Bradley [0-18] Overmonnow Racing Club.*

TREMPLIN (USA) BHB 60f58a **RR 64f 58a** 4279[12]
7 b g Trempolino (USA) 11.9f **(77)** - Stresa (Mill Reef (USA)) 10.5f **(78)**
Form - 0
Record 1999 - 1st:0 2nd:0 3rd:0 Ran:1
Pre1999 - 1st:0 2nd:0 3rd:0 Ran:13
Win Prizemoney £0 *Total Prizemoney* £397
1999 Turf 0-1: (12f) (frm)
Average gelding, has worn blinkers. Consistent.

N A Callaghan [0-13] M Tabor (from A Fabre in FR [0-1] Apr 1995).

TREWORNAN BHB 77f **RR 82f** 5045[6]
2 b f Midyan (USA) 9.9f **(64)** - Miss Silca Key (Welsh Saint) 7.6f **(64)**
Form - 516
Record 1999 - 1st:1 2nd:0 3rd:0 Ran:3
Win Prizemoney £3,631 *Total Prizemoney* £3,962
Wins * **1999** Oct Bright (G-S) 6f 82 <
1999 Turf 1-3: (6f 1-2, 7f) (sft, gd 1-1, frm)
Currently decent filly. Turf high 82 (began Spt) - 1st of 6 getting 5lb from Rayyaan (4 Oct Brighton RF 4708). Won an ordinary race at Brighton after an encouraging debut in better company.
D R C Elsworth [1-3] Mrs M E Slade.

TRIBAL MOON (IRE) BHB 38f **RR** 904[12]
6 b g Ela-Mana-Mou 12.7f **(72)** - Silk Blend (Busted) 10.2f **(61)**
Form - 0
Record 1999 - 1st:0 2nd:0 3rd:0 Ran:1
Pre1999 - 1st:0 2nd:0 3rd:0 Ran:7
1999 Turf 0-1: (22f) (gd)
Very poor gelding.
J G Portman [0-8] Lt Col & Mrs L W McNaught (from Lady Herries [0-5] Jly 1997).

TRIBAL NOTE (USA) BHB 68f **RR 79f** 4828[9]
2 ch c Eagle Eyed (USA) - Ada Ruckus (CAN) (Bold Ruckus (USA))
Form - 432830
Record 1999 - 1st:0 2nd:1 3rd:2 Ran:6
Win Prizemoney £0 *Total Prizemoney* £2,426
1999 Turf 0-6: (6f 3, 7f, 8f 2) (sft, gd 2, g-f, frm 2)
Above-average colt, effective 6f, acts on gd. Turf high 79 (began Jly) - 3rd of 12 giving 5lb to Mellow Jazz (25 Spt Nottingham 6f gd RF 4557).
A G Foster [0-1] R E Sangster & R Kaster (from P W Chapple-Hyam [0-5] Spt 1999).

TRIBAL PEACE (IRE) BHB 40f49a **RR 39f 49a** 4758[12]
7 ch g Red Sunset 9f **(57)** - Mirabiliary (USA) (Crow (FR)) 7.4f **(75)**
Form - 0634800050
Record 1999 - 1st:0 2nd:0 3rd:1 Ran:8
Pre1999 - 1st:5 2nd:5 3rd:4 Ran:44
Win Prizemoney £21,403 *Total Prizemoney* £31,738
Wins * 1997 Jly Goodwo (G-F) H 9f 60 64
* 1997 *Jan Lingfi (STD) H 10f 65 70*
* 1996 *Jan Lingfi (STD) C 10f 67*
* 1995 Spt Goodwo (G-S) H 9f 65 71 <
* 1995 *Feb Lingfi (STD) 10f 60*
1999 Turf 0-5: (8f 2, 9f, 10f 2) (gd 3, frm 2) 1999 AW 0-3: (10f 2, 12f) (Equi 3)
Fair gelding, effective 10f, acts on hrd. Turf high 39 (began Jly). AW high 53.
B Gubby [5-50] Brian Gubby Ltd (from B J Meehan [0-2] Spt 1994).

TRIBAL PRINCE BHB 74f **RR 72f** 5218[5]
2 b c Prince Sabo 6.6f **(64)** - Tshusick **(77f)** (Dancing Brave (USA)) 8.4f **(76)**
Form - 25025
Record 1999 - 1st:0 2nd:2 3rd:0 Ran:5
Win Prizemoney £0 *Total Prizemoney* £1,870
1999 Turf 0-5: (5f, 6f 3, 7f) (g-s, gd, g-f 2, frm)
Above-average colt, has worn blinkers. Turf high 72 (began Aug) - 2nd of 10 getting 15lb from Loch Inch (28 Oct Windsor 6f gd RF 5111).
P W Harris [0-5] The Tribe.

TRICCOLO **RR 79+f** 4634[5]
2 b c Piccolo - Tribal Lady (Absalom) 7.2f **(58)**
Form - 55
Record 1999 - 1st:0 2nd:0 3rd:0 Ran:2
1999 Turf 0-2: (6f 2) (gd, frm)
Currently above-average colt. Turf high 79 (began Spt).
A C Stewart [0-2] Bruce Corman.

TRICKS (IRE) BHB 55f70a **RR 51f 70a** 3688[9]
3 b f First Trump - Party Line **(57f 60a)** (Never so Bold) 6.3f **(66)**
Form - 32107060
Record 1999 - 1st:0 2nd:0 3rd:0 Ran:5
Pre1999 - 1st:1 2nd:1 3rd:1 Ran:4
Win Prizemoney £2,814 *Total Prizemoney* £3,930
Wins 1998 *Dec Lingfi (STD) 7f 73* <
1999 Turf 0-5: (7f 3, 8f 2) (gd 2, frm 3)
Neat, above-average filly, effective 7 to 8f, acts on Equi, has worn blinkers. Turf high 57.
I A Balding [0-5] Miss Holmes a' Court (from Lord Huntingdon [1-4] Dec 1998).

TRICOLORE BHB 75f **RR 84df** 2389[5]
3 b f Sadler's Wells (USA) 11.3f **(87)** - Tricorne **(72f)** (Green Desert (USA)) 8.6f **(78)**
Form - 265
Record 1999 - 1st:0 2nd:1 3rd:0 Ran:3
Pre1999 - 1st:0 2nd:0 3rd:1 Ran:1
Win Prizemoney £0 *Total Prizemoney* £1,970
1999 Turf 0-3: (10f 3) (g-s, gd, g-f)
Neat, decent filly. Turf high 84 (1st run) - 2nd of 10 giving 4lb to Samoa (23 Apr Sandown 10f g-s RF 0824).
J L Dunlop [0-4] Michael Page.

TRIGGER HAPPY (IRE) BHB 100f **RR 97?f** 1612[11]
4 ch f Ela-Mana-Mou 12.7f **(72)** - Happy Tidings (Hello Gorgeous (USA)) 9.7f **(63)**
Form - 0
Record 1999 - 1st:0 2nd:0 3rd:0 Ran:1
Pre1999 - 1st:1 2nd:1 3rd:0 Ran:4
Win Prizemoney £9,035 *Total Prizemoney* £13,615
Wins * 1997 Nov Newmar (G-F) L 10f 85 <
1999 Turf 0-1: (16f) (frm)
Leggy, very useful filly. *M Johnston [1-5] R W Huggins.*

TRIMILKI (IRE) BHB 28f **RR 22f** 2316[9]
3 b f Lahib (USA) 8f **(69)** - Timissara (USA) (Shahrastani (USA)) 8.8f **(72)**
Form - 50080
Record 1999 - 1st:0 2nd:0 3rd:0 Ran:5
Pre1999 - 1st:0 2nd:0 3rd:0 Ran:1
1999 Turf 0-3: (8f, 14f, 17f) (g-f, frm, hrd) 1999 AW 0-2: (8f, 12f) (Fibr 2)
Scopey, little account filly, has worn blinkers. Turf high 22. AW high 24. *T J Etherington [0-6] Callers And Clerks.*

TRIM STAR BHB 38f **RR 48f** 4613a[11]
3 gr f Terimon 8.7f **(58)** - Western Star (Alcide) 12.5f **(42)**
Form - 0748300
Record 1999 - 1st:0 2nd:0 3rd:1 Ran:7
Win Prizemoney £0 *Total Prizemoney* £350
1999 Turf 0-7: (10f, 11f, 12f 3, 14f, 16f) (sft, g-s 2, g-f 3, frm)
Moderate filly, has worn blinkers. Turf high 48.
A Slattery in IRE [0-4] John Bernard O'Connor (from C E Brittain [0-3] Jun 1999).

TRINA'S PET BHB 57f64a **RR 59f 64a** 410[9]
3 ch f Efisio 7.7f **(69)** - Lindy Belle **(35f)** (Alleging (USA))
Form - 0333250
Record 1999 - 1st:0 2nd:1 3rd:3 Ran:6
Pre1999 - 1st:2 2nd:0 3rd:1 Ran:10
Win Prizemoney £3,887 *Total Prizemoney* £6,033
Wins 1998 *Jly Southw (STD) S 5f 72* <
1998 *Jun Southw (STD) S 5f 72* <
1999 AW 0-6: (6f 4, 7f 2) (Equi 2, Fibr 4)
Workmanlike, average filly, effective 5 to 7f, best at 5f, - acts on AW, best on Fibr, has worn blinkers (extremely effectively), likes left handed tracks, likes tight tracks. AW high 69 (1st run) - 3rd of 10 getting 4lb from Palace Green (2 Jan Southwell 6f Fibr RF 0018).
J Balding [0-10] Mrs J Coghlan-Everitt (from B J Meehan [2-6] Jly 1998).

TRINCULO (IRE) BHB 100f **RR 97f** 5036[4]
2 b c Anita's Prince 6f **(62)** - Fandangerina (USA) (Grey Dawn II) 11.1f **(72)**
Form - 31354
Record 1999 - 1st:1 2nd:0 3rd:2 Ran:5
Win Prizemoney £2,931 *Total Prizemoney* £24,574
Wins * **1999** Aug Leices (G-F) 6f 79 <
1999 Turf 1-4: (6f 1-4) (g-s, gd 2, g-f 1-1) 1999 AW 0-1: (6f) (Fibr)

Very useful colt. Turf high 97 (began Aug). He is a useful young sprinter, but falls below Group class and will struggle off his current rating in 2000. **N P Littmoden [1-5] Joy and Valentine Feerick.*

TRINITY (IRE) RR 68f 5160[20]

3 b c College Chapel - Kaskazi (Dancing Brave (USA)) 8.4f **(76)**
Form - 100050000
Record 1999 - 1st:1 2nd:0 3rd:0 Ran:9
Pre1999 - 1st:0 2nd:3 3rd:1 Ran:9
Win Prizemoney £2,853 *Total Prizemoney* £13,863
Wins * **1999** May Doncas (G-F) 5f 84 <
1999 Turf 1-9: (5f 1-5, 6f 4) (gd, g-f 3, frm 1-5)
Light-framed, average colt, effective 5f, acts on gd to frm, best on frm. Turf high 93 - also 1st of 8 giving 5lb to Bridge Pool (29 May Doncaster RF 1561). Becoming disappointing.
**M Brittain [1-18] Miss Debi Woods.*

TRIO RR 69f 5004[12]

3 b c Cyrano de Bergerac 7.3f **(58)** - May Light **(60df)** (Midyan (USA)) 6f **(60)**
Form - 5446000000
Record 1999 - 1st:0 2nd:0 3rd:0 Ran:10
Pre1999 - 1st:1 2nd:0 3rd:3 Ran:8
Win Prizemoney £19,737 *Total Prizemoney* £26,151
Wins 1998 Spt Doncas (GD) H 8f 72 78 <
1999 Turf 0-10: (8f 2, 9f 3, 10f 5) (g-s, gd 4, g-f 3, frm 2)
Average colt, effective 8 to 9f, best at 9f, acts on gd to frm, likes right handed tracks. Turf high 85 - 4th of 13 giving 18lb to Golconda (3 May Kempton 9f frm RF 0997). He had quite a busy two-year-old campaign, winning once at Doncaster, but after showing some fair form early on last season, has gone right off the boil since.
**N Hamilton [0-10] City Industrial Supplies Ltd (from G Lewis [1-8] Nov 1998).*

TRIPLE CONCERTO RR 56f 4898[11]

2 ch f Grand Lodge (USA) - On The Bank (IRE) (In The Wings)
Form - 0
Record 1999 - 1st:0 2nd:0 3rd:0 Ran:1
1999 Turf 0-1: (8f) (gd)
Currently fair filly. **C F Wall [0-1] Exors of the Late Sir W R Stuttaford.*

TRIPLE DASH BHB 105f RR 110f 4811[3]

3 ch c Nashwan (USA) 10.3f **(79)** - Triple Joy **(104f 98a)** (Most Welcome)
Form - 81373
Record 1999 - 1st:1 2nd:0 3rd:2 Ran:5
Pre1999 - 1st:1 2nd:1 3rd:0 Ran:2
Win Prizemoney £9,934 *Total Prizemoney* £16,475
Wins * **1999** Jly Sandow (GD) 8.1f 110 <
* 1998 Oct Newcas (SFT) 6f 74+
1999 Turf 1-5: (8f 1-5) (hvy, sft, g-s, gd, g-f 1-1)
Strong, Group-class colt, effective 8f, acts on hvy to g-f. Turf high 110 - 1st of 5 from Exeat (2 Jly Sandown RF 2501). A rare Classic runner for Sir Mark Prescott, he lost all chance in the French 2,000 Guineas after hitting his head on the stalls during a false start. Connections spent the rest of the campaign searching for soft ground, but he failed to live up to their expectations and only won one minor heat. Bred to stay beyond a mile, he must not be written off just yet. **Sir Mark Prescott [2-7] Hesmonds Stud.*

TRIPLE GREEN BHB 64f RR 62f 5113[6]

3 b f Green Desert (USA) 7.8f **(78)** - Triple Reef (Mill Reef (USA)) 10.5f **(78)**
Form - 0350036
Record 1999 - 1st:0 2nd:0 3rd:2 Ran:7
Win Prizemoney £0 *Total Prizemoney* £1,423
1999 Turf 0-7: (6f, 8f 4, 10f, 12f) (gd 3, g-f 3, frm)
Scopey, average filly, effective 8f, acts on frm, has worn blinkers. Turf high 69. **J L Dunlop [0-7] Hesmonds Stud.*

TRIPLE TREASURE (USA) BHB 63f68a RR 64f 68a 4222[3]

4 b f Gone West (USA) 7.8f **(82)** - Lemhi Go (USA) (Lemhi Gold (USA))
Form - 7473
Record 1999 - 1st:0 2nd:0 3rd:1 Ran:4
Pre1999 - 1st:0 2nd:0 3rd:1 Ran:1
Win Prizemoney £0 *Total Prizemoney* £1,503
1999 Turf 0-3: (8f, 10f 2) (gd, g-f, frm) 1999 AW 0-1: (8f) (Fibr)
Scopey, average filly. Turf high 64.
**H R A Cecil [0-5] The Thoroughbred Corporation.*

TRIPLE WOOD (USA) RR 76f 2469[2]

2 b br f Woodman (USA) 9.7f **(77)** - Triple Kiss (Shareef Dancer (USA)) 9.9f **(73)**
Form - 52
Record 1999 - 1st:0 2nd:1 3rd:0 Ran:2
Win Prizemoney £0 *Total Prizemoney* £1,177
1999 Turf 0-2: (6f, 7f) (gd, frm)
Currently above-average filly. Turf high 76.
**B Hanbury [0-2] Hilal Salem.*

TROILUS (USA) RR 71f 5000[9]

2 ch c Bien Bien (USA) - Nakterjal (Vitiges (FR)) 8.2f **(59)**
Form - 50
Record 1999 - 1st:0 2nd:0 3rd:0 Ran:2
1999 Turf 0-2: (8f 2) (gd, g-f)
Currently above-average colt. Turf high 71 (began Spt).
**A G Foster [0-1] J Toffan & T McCaffery (from P W Chapple-Hyam [0-1] Spt 1999).*

TROIS BHB 57f RR 58f 1601[9]

3 b c Efisio 7.7f **(69)** - Drei (USA) **(74f)** (Lyphard (USA)) 9.9f **(72)**
Form - 5400
Record 1999 - 1st:0 2nd:0 3rd:0 Ran:3
Pre1999 - 1st:0 2nd:0 3rd:0 Ran:1
Win Prizemoney £0 *Total Prizemoney* £197
1999 Turf 0-3: (7f 2, 8f) (sft, g-f, hrd)
Fair colt. Turf high 58. **L M Cumani [0-4] Fittocks Stud.*

TROIS ELLES BHB 45f37a RR 47f 37a 5135[3]

3 b c Elmaamul (USA) 8.1f **(70)** - Ca Ira (IRE) **(24f)** (Dancing Dissident (USA))
Form - 000182005223260003
Record 1999 - 1st:1 2nd:4 3rd:2 Ran:16
Pre1999 - 1st:0 2nd:0 3rd:0 Ran:3
Win Prizemoney £2,018 *Total Prizemoney* £7,556
Wins * **1999** *Jan Lingfi (STD) H* 7f 29 34 <
1999 Turf 0-13: (7f, 8f 9, 9f, 10f 2) (sft, gd 3, g-f 3, frm 4, hrd 2) 1999 AW 1-3: (7f 1-2, 8f) (Equi 1-2, Fibr)
Moderate colt, effective 8 to 10f, best at 8f, acts on gd to hrd, best on g-f, likes tight tracks. Turf high 47 - 3rd of 18 getting 9lb from High Sun (29 Oct Newmarket 8f gd RF 5135). AW high 34. Consistent. **R C Spicer [1-19] John Purcell.*

TROJAN GIRL (IRE) BHB 64f69a RR 49f 69a 2066[9]

3 b f Up and At 'em - Lady-Mumtaz (Martin John) 13.1f **(62)**
Form - 3712141123176830
Record 1999 - 1st:4 2nd:1 3rd:2 Ran:12
Pre1999 - 1st:1 2nd:4 3rd:2 Ran:12
Win Prizemoney £12,700 *Total Prizemoney* £18,699
Wins **1999** *Apr Wolver (STD) C* 5f 77 <
1999 *Feb Wolver (STD) H* 5f 70 77 <
1999 *Feb Wolver (STD) C* 5f 71
1999 *Jan Wolver (STD) H* 5f 62 75
1998 *Dec Wolver (SLW) S* 5f 58+
1999 AW 4-12: (5f 4-11, 6f) (Equi, Fibr 4-11)
Workmanlike, fair filly, effective 5f, - acts on Fibr, likes left handed tracks, likes tight tracks. AW high 77 - 1st of 6 getting 3lb from Aa-Youknownothing (17 Feb Wolverhampton RF 0306) - also 1st of 8 getting 16lb from Krystal Max (10 Apr Wolverhampton RF 0642). Becoming disappointing. She has enjoyed great success over the Wolverhampton five, though she has not shown her best since moving stables in April.
**Miss S J Wilton [0-5] John Pointon and Sons (from N P Littmoden [5-19] Apr 1999).*

TROJAN HERO (SAF) BHB 57a RR 35f 5149[2]

8 ch g Raise A Man (USA) 7.3f **(63)** - Helleness (SAF) (Northfields (USA)) 9f **(72)**
Form - 70223407078003202
Record 1999 - 1st:0 2nd:4 3rd:2 Ran:15
Pre1999 - 1st:3 2nd:5 3rd:3 Ran:27
Win Prizemoney £7,470 *Total Prizemoney* £17,400
Wins 1998 Jun Warwic (GD) 7f 64

1997	*Nov Wolver*	*(STD)*	*H*	*7f*	*54 59+*
1997	Jun Leices	(G-F)	C	8f	70+ <

1999 Turf 0-6: (5f, 6f 3, 7f 2) (gd 3, g-f, frm 2) 1999 AW 0-9: (5f, 6f 3, 7f 5) (Fibr 9)

Fair gelding, effective 6 to 7f, best at 6f, acts on gd - acts on Fibr, has worn blinkers, likes left handed tracks, likes tight tracks, and excels at Southwell. Turf high 37. AW high 69 (1st run) - 2nd of 10 giving 4lb to Sue Me (8 Jan Southwell 6f Fibr RF 0053). Inconsistent. Formerly trained in South Africa, where he had won six times. Still running well on sand and can find more races over seven furlongs on that surface.

**M A Buckley [0-8] Drew Kerr (from Mrs M Reveley [2-33] May 1999).*

TROJAN RISK BHB 53f70a RR 59f 70a 3898[13]

6 ch g Risk Me (FR) 8f **(53)** - Troyes (Troy) 10.4f **(68)**

Form - 04600

Record 1999 - 1st:0 2nd:0 3rd:0 Ran:5
Pre1999 - 1st:2 2nd:7 3rd:1 Ran:24

Win Prizemoney £18,140 *Total Prizemoney* £33,822

Wins 1997 Jly Sandow (G-S) H 10f 71 76
1996 May Kempto (G-F) H 9f 72 71

1999 Turf 0-3: (12f 3) (g-f 2, frm) 1999 AW 0-2: (12f 2) (Fibr 2)

Average gelding, effective 12f, acted on frm, had worn blinkers, liked tight tracks. Turf high 59. AW high 61. (DEAD)

**Mrs M Reveley [1-13] Andy Peake & David Jackson (from G Lewis [2-21] Oct 1997).*

TROJAN WOLF BHB 54f57a RR 51f 57a 4914[5]

4 ch g Wolfhound (USA) 7.3f **(71)** - Trojan Lady (USA) (Irish River (FR)) 8.6f **(78)**

Form - 050724205

Record 1999 - 1st:0 2nd:2 3rd:0 Ran:9
Pre1999 - 1st:0 2nd:0 3rd:0 Ran:8

Win Prizemoney £0 *Total Prizemoney* £3,756

1999 Turf 0-8: (6f, 7f 3, 8f 2, 10f 2) (gd, g-f 5, frm 2) 1999 AW 0-1: (7f) (Equi)

Tall, fair gelding, effective 9 to 10f, acts on frm, has worn blinkers, likes tight tracks. Turf high 60.

**D Sasse [0-9] Christopher Ranson (from M H Tompkins [0-8] Oct 1998).*

TROON RR 98f 2475a[3]

9 gr h Beveled (USA) 6.9f **(64)** - Cestrefeld (Capistrano) 9.4f **(64)**

Form - 33

1999 Turf 0-2: (6f, 10f) (sft, frm)

Very useful horse, has worn blinkers. Turf high 98 (1st run) - 3rd of 11 to Superior Premium (1 Jun Taby 10f frm RF 1895a). Consistent.

**R Haugen in NOR [1-8] (from Mrs L Piggott [1-18] Oct 1993).*

TROPICAL BEACH BHB 50f67a RR 41f 67a 4865[4]

6 b g Lugana Beach 7f **(63)** - Hitravelscene (Mansingh (USA)) 7.4f **(55)**

Form - 13158752140718004

Record 1999 - 1st:2 2nd:1 3rd:0 Ran:13
Pre1999 - 1st:8 2nd:3 3rd:6 Ran:55

Win Prizemoney £29,277 *Total Prizemoney* £36,601

Wins							
* 1999	Jly	Lingfi	(G-F)	H	7.6f	51	53
* 1999	Jun	Newmar	(G-F)	H	8f	48	51
* 1998	*Dec*	*Wolver*	*(SLW)*	*H*	*9.4f*	*65*	*68* <
* 1998	*Nov*	*Wolver*	*(STD)*	*H*	*8.5f*	*60*	*64*
* 1998	*Oct*	*Wolver*	*(STD)*	*H*	*8.5f*	*55*	*58*
1997	Jly	Carlis	(GD)	H	5f	55	61
1996	Aug	Hamilt	(G-F)	H	5f	57	62
1996	Aug	Thirsk	(G-F)	SH	6f	57	61
1996	Jun	Hamilt	(GD)	H	5f	53	56
1995	Apr	Mussel	(GD)		5f		51t

1999 Turf 2-9: (7f 4, 8f 2-5) (gd 3, g-f, frm 2-4, hrd) 1999 AW 0-4: (8f 2, 9f, 11f) (Fibr 4)

Fair gelding, effective 8 to 9f, best at 8f, - acts on Fibr, often wears blinkers (effectively), likes left handed tracks, excels at Wolverhampton. Turf high 53. AW high 57.

**J Pearce [5-29] A J Thompson (from J Berry [5-39] Spt 1997).*

TROPICAL BEAT (USA) RR 67f 2288[P]

2 b f Kingmambo (USA) 10.9f **(85)** - Ropa Usada (USA) (Danzig (USA)) 8.4f **(76)**

Form - 0P

Record 1999 - 1st:0 2nd:0 3rd:0 Ran:2

1999 Turf 0-2: (6f, 7f) (gd, frm)

Average filly. Turf high 67. (DEAD) **J L Dunlop [0-2] Robin Scully.*

TROUBLE BHB 59f RR 59f 4149[6]

3 b g Kris 10f **(75)** - Ringlet (USA) **(53f 54a)** (Secreto (USA)) 8.7f **(72)**

Form - 6006

Record 1999 - 1st:0 2nd:0 3rd:0 Ran:4

1999 Turf 0-3: (7f 2, 8f) (g-f 2, frm) 1999 AW 0-1: (8f) (Fibr)

Scopey, fair gelding. Turf high 59. **B W Hills [0-4] Seymour Cohn.*

TROUBLED TIMES BHB 42f RR 28f 4543[16]

2 ch f Timeless Times (USA) 6.1f **(56)** - Lurking (Formidable (USA)) 9.2f **(63)**

Form - 30000

Record 1999 - 1st:0 2nd:0 3rd:1 Ran:5

Win Prizemoney £0 *Total Prizemoney* £507

1999 Turf 0-5: (5f 3, 6f 2) (g-f 3, frm 2)

Little account filly. Turf high 28.

**L R Lloyd-James [0-2] John Jackson (from D Moffatt [0-3] Aug 1999).*

TROUBLE MOUNTAIN (USA) BHB 100f RR 101f 4405[2]

2 br c Mt Livermore (USA) 7.7f **(90)** - Trouble Free (USA) (Nodouble (USA)) 8.8f **(68)**

Form - 1132

Record 1999 - 1st:2 2nd:1 3rd:1 Ran:4

Win Prizemoney £10,024 *Total Prizemoney* £23,163

Wins * 1999 Jly Doncas (G-F) 7f 95 <
* 1999 Jly Haydoc (FRM) 6f 92+

1999 Turf 2-4: (6f 1-3, 7f 1-1) (gd, frm 2-3)

Very useful colt. Turf high 101 (began Jly) - 2nd of 4 to Primo Valentino (18 Spt Newbury 6f frm RF 4405) - also 1st of 4 from With Iris (29 Jly Doncaster RF 3215). He did not appear to handle Chester when disappointing there during August, but bounced back to run a super race behind Primo Valentino in the Mill Reef Stakes. Likely to stay a mile, he can improve and would be an interesting runner in the Free Handicap.

**B W Hills [2-4] Maktoum Al Maktoum.*

TRUANT (USA) BHB 78f RR 80f 4592[1]

3 b c Alleged (USA) 11.8f **(81)** - Top Roberto (USA) (Topsider (USA)) 8.3f **(71)**

Form - 2322021

Record 1999 - 1st:1 2nd:4 3rd:1 Ran:7
Pre1999 - 1st:0 2nd:0 3rd:2 Ran:3

Win Prizemoney £3,485 *Total Prizemoney* £19,413

Wins * 1999 Spt Hamilt (SFT) 9.2f 80 <

1999 Turf 1-7: (8f, 9f 1-2, 10f 4) (sft, g-s, gd 1-1, g-f, frm 3)

Workmanlike, decent colt, effective 8 to 10f, best at 10f, acts on sft to frm, best on sft, likes tight tracks. Turf high 86 - 3rd of 17 giving 5lb to Suhaad (11 Jun Sandown 10f frm RF 1925). Consistent. He has appeared not to put it all in when asked for an effort, and was sold for 37,000 gns in the autumn.

**W Jarvis [1-10] Highclere Thoroughbred Racing Ltd.*

TRUE FLYER BHB 35f RR 38f 3976[7]

3 b f Midyan (USA) 9.9f **(64)** - Surf Bird (Shareef Dancer (USA)) 9.9f **(73)**

Form - 600387

Record 1999 - 1st:0 2nd:0 3rd:1 Ran:6
Pre1999 - 1st:0 2nd:0 3rd:0 Ran:1

Win Prizemoney £0 *Total Prizemoney* £266

1999 Turf 0-6: (10f 2, 11f, 12f, 14f 2) (g-f 3, frm 3)

Unfurnished, very moderate filly, effective 11 to 14f, acts on g-f to frm, often wears blinkers, prefers left handed tracks. Turf high 38 - 8th of 13 getting 23lb from Catullus (9 Aug Nottingham 14f g-f RF 3476). **J D Bethell [0-7] T R Lock.*

TRUE LOVE WAYS BHB 35f RR 33f 2309[10]

3 ch f Anshan 8.2f **(63)** - Halimah (Be My Guest (USA)) 9.3f **(67)**

Form - 0000

Record 1999 - 1st:0 2nd:0 3rd:0 Ran:4
Pre1999 - 1st:0 2nd:0 3rd:2 Ran:11

Win Prizemoney £0 *Total Prizemoney* £754

1999 Turf 0-3: (5f, 6f, 7f) (g-s, gd, hrd) 1999 AW 0-1: (6f) (Fibr)

Leggy, very moderate filly, has worn blinkers. Turf high 33. Becoming disappointing. **W G M Turner [0-15] Mascalls Stud.*

TRUE OBSESSION (USA) BHB 77f RR 80f 5124[7]

2 br c Lear Fan (USA) 10.4f **(80)** - Valid Fixation (USA) (Valid Appeal (USA)) 8.9f **(78)**
Form - 31223607
Record 1999 - 1st:1 2nd:2 3rd:2 Ran:8
Win Prizemoney £2,853 *Total Prizemoney* £7,483
Wins * **1999** *Jun Southw (STD) 7f 84* <
1999 Turf 0-7: (5f, 7f 4, 8f 2) (sft, gd 2, g-f 2, frm 2) 1999 AW 1-1: (7f 1-1) (Fibr 1-1)
Decent colt, effective 7f, acts on g-f to frm - acts on Fibr, best on g-f. Turf high 80 - 6th of 17 getting 5lb from French Fellow (17 Aug York 7f g-f RF 3698). (1st run) - 1st of 12 from First Venture (28 Jun Southwell RF 2377). **P F I Cole [1-8] Tony Feng.*

TRUFFLE (IRE) BHB 65f RR 59f 4685^{13}
3 b f Ezzoud (IRE) - Queen Cake (Sandhurst Prince) 7.9f **(63)**
Form - 000
Record 1999 - 1st:0 2nd:0 3rd:0 Ran:3
Pre1999 - 1st:1 2nd:0 3rd:1 Ran:2
Win Prizemoney £2,512 *Total Prizemoney* £2,842
Wins 1998 Spt Thirsk (GD) 7f 53 <
1999 Turf 0-3: (7f, 8f, 10f) (gd 2, frm)
Light-framed, fair filly. Turf high 59.
**K McAuliffe [0-2] Alhambra (from J R Fanshawe [1-3] May 1999).*

TRULY BEWITCHED (USA) BHB 82f RR 79f 2578^{9}
3 ch f Affirmed (USA) 10.3f **(75)** - Fabulous Fairy (USA) **(68f)** (Alydar (USA)) 9.1f **(76)**
Form - 0800
Record 1999 - 1st:0 2nd:0 3rd:0 Ran:4
Pre1999 - 1st:1 2nd:0 3rd:0 Ran:2
Win Prizemoney £3,574 *Total Prizemoney* £3,574
Wins * 1998 Spt Redcar (G-F) 6f 88+ <
1999 Turf 0-4: (7f 2, 8f, 10f) (g-s, g-f, frm 2)
Above-average filly, effective 6f, acts on frm, has worn blinkers. Turf high 91. **J Noseda [1-6] W L Armitage.*

TRUMBLE BHB 20f41a RR 28f 41a 3597^{11}
7 b g Tragic Role (USA) 9.4f **(63)** - Sideloader Special (Song) 7.2f **(61)**
Form - 608700
Record 1999 - 1st:0 2nd:0 3rd:0 Ran:6
Pre1999 - 1st:1 2nd:3 3rd:1 Ran:26
Win Prizemoney £2,650 *Total Prizemoney* £5,839
Wins 1995 Aug Newcas (GD) S 12.4f 49 <
1999 Turf 0-6: (9f, 11f 4, 12f) (g-s, gd, g-f, frm 3)
Moderate gelding. Turf high 28. Inconsistent.
**D A Nolan [0-6] Mrs D S Wilkinson (from Mrs N Macauley [0-4] Jly 1996).*

TRUMPET BLUES (USA) BHB 70f RR 74f 565^{6}
3 br c Dayjur (USA) 6.8f **(79)** - Iosifa (Top Ville) 11.7f **(68)**
Form - 6
Record 1999 - 1st:0 2nd:0 3rd:0 Ran:1
Pre1999 - 1st:0 2nd:1 3rd:0 Ran:2
Win Prizemoney £0 *Total Prizemoney* £1,440
1999 Turf 0-1: (7f) (gd)
Neat, currently above-average colt. **J L Dunlop [0-3] Bob Lalemant.*

TRUMPET SOUND (IRE) RR 75+f 3937^{4}
2 b c Theatrical 11.5f **(78)** - Free At Last (Shirley Heights) 10.3f **(74)**
Form - 4
Record 1999 - 1st:0 2nd:0 3rd:0 Ran:1
Win Prizemoney £0 *Total Prizemoney* £255
1999 Turf 0-1: (7f) (frm)
Currently above-average colt. Out of a half-sister to Barathea, he ran green when a close fourth on his first run, and should come on for the experience. **L M Cumani [0-1] Gerald Leigh.*

TRUMP STREET BHB 53f RR 48f 4558^{15}
3 b f First Trump - Pepeke (Mummy's Pet) 7.7f **(60)**
Form - 0830
Record 1999 - 1st:0 2nd:0 3rd:1 Ran:4
Pre1999 - 1st:0 2nd:1 3rd:0 Ran:3
Win Prizemoney £0 *Total Prizemoney* £1,797
1999 Turf 0-4: (7f 2, 8f 2) (gd, g-f, frm 2)
Scopey, moderate filly, effective 7f, acts on g-f. Turf high 48.
**N A Graham [0-7] Paul Jacobs.*

TRUST GEORGE RR 246^{7}
4 ch g Lancastrian - Lingdale Lady (Sandford Lad) 7.8f **(54)**
Form - 7
Record 1999 - 1st:0 2nd:0 3rd:0 Ran:1
1999 AW 0-1: (16f) (Fibr)
Formerly very poor gelding. **C N Kellett [0-1] R P Kernohan.*

TRYARDIA-ON-AGAIN (IRE) BHB 41f RR 37f 3836^{6}
3 ch f Petardia 8.2f **(58)** - Trysinger (IRE) (Try My Best (USA)) 7.6f **(67)**
Form - 00676
Record 1999 - 1st:0 2nd:0 3rd:0 Ran:5
Pre1999 - 1st:0 2nd:0 3rd:0 Ran:4
Win Prizemoney £0 *Total Prizemoney* £198
1999 Turf 0-4: (7f 3, 8f) (gd, frm 3) 1999 AW 0-1: (9f) (Fibr)
Light-framed, very moderate filly, has worn blinkers. Turf high 45 (began Jly). **P D Evans [0-9] Paul Green (Huyton).*

TRY FOR EVER (IRE) RR 98f $4467a^{R}$
7 b m Try My Best (USA) 7.8f **(68)** - Dame Ross (Raga Navarro (ITY)) 8f **(64)**
Form - 21822RR
1999 Turf 1-7: (9f, 10f, 11f, 12f 1-3, 14f) (g-s 3, gd 1-2, g-f 2)
Very useful mare, effective 12 to 14f, best at 12f, acts on gd to g-f, best on g-f. Turf high 98 - 2nd of 8 giving 9lb to Royal Rebel (22 Aug Leopardstown 14f g-f RF 3895a) - also 1st of 15 getting 4lb from Sarayan (27 Jun Curragh RF 2422a). Inconsistent. A useful dual-purpose performer, she blotted her copybook when refusing to race twice during September. **N Meade in IRE [9-38] L V Owens.*

TRY IT AGAIN (IRE) RR 1009^{11}
3 br g Mujtahid (USA) 7.4f **(69)** - Pursue (Auction Ring (USA)) 8.6f **(65)**
Form - 0
Record 1999 - 1st:0 2nd:0 3rd:0 Ran:1
1999 Turf 0-1: (7f) (frm)
Workmanlike, currently very poor gelding.
**M Johnston [0-1] F McNamee.*

TRY PARIS (IRE) BHB 44f RR 35f 5113^{12}
3 b c Paris House 5.9f **(64)** -Try My Rosie (Try My Best (USA)) 7.6f **(67)**
Form - 008060
Record 1999 - 1st:0 2nd:0 3rd:0 Ran:6
Pre1999 - 1st:0 2nd:0 3rd:0 Ran:4
1999 Turf 0-5: (5f 2, 6f 2, 7f) (sft, gd 2, g-f, frm) 1999 AW 0-1: (6f) (Fibr)
Very moderate colt, has worn blinkers. Turf high 35 (began Aug). Consistent.
**Mrs L C Jewell [0-6] The Headquarters Partnership II (from K Prendergast in IRE [0-4] Oct 1998).*

TSUNAMI BHB 70f RR 57f 5046^{4}
3 b f Beveled (USA) 6.9f **(64)** - Alvecote Lady (Touching Wood (USA)) 8.2f **(55)**
Form - 436660464
Record 1999 - 1st:0 2nd:0 3rd:1 Ran:9
Pre1999 - 1st:0 2nd:0 3rd:0 Ran:4
Win Prizemoney £0 *Total Prizemoney* £1,830
1999 Turf 0-9: (7f 3, 8f 4, 10f 2) (hvy, g-s 2, gd 4, g-f, frm)
Fair filly, effective 7 to 8f, best at 7f, acts on sft to g-f. Turf high 70 - 3rd of 9 getting 5lb from Lover's Leap (10 Jun Newbury 7f gd RF 1886). **D R C Elsworth [0-12] C Leafe (from N Tinkler [0-1] Jly 1998).*

TSWALU BHB 58f RR 57f 5189^{6}
2 b f Cosmonaut - Madam Taylor (Free State) 8.7f **(61)**
Form - 376
Record 1999 - 1st:0 2nd:0 3rd:1 Ran:3
Win Prizemoney £0 *Total Prizemoney* £517
1999 Turf 0-3: (7f, 8f 2) (g-s 2, g-f)
Currently fair filly. Turf high 57 (began Spt).
**M Mullineaux [0-3] Esprit de Corps Racing.*

TUCSON (IRE) RR 4784^{17}
2 ch c Gabitat 8.5f **(44)** - Gabibti (IRE) (Dara Monarch) 8.8f **(59)**
Form - 0
Record 1999 - 1st:0 2nd:0 3rd:0 Ran:1
1999 Turf 0-1: (7f) (g-s)
Currently very poor colt. **B Gubby [0-1] Brian Gubby Ltd.*

TUDOR KING (IRE) RR 2f 3641[9]
5 br g Orchestra 7.5f **(44)** - Jane Bond (Good Bond) 9.2f **(54)**
Form - 0
Record 1999 - 1st:0 2nd:0 3rd:0 Ran:1
1999 Turf 0-1: (14f) (g-f)
Very poor gelding. **J S King [0-8] J R Kinloch.*

TUFAMORE (USA) BHB 44f52a **RR 37f 52a** 3423[5]
3 ch g Mt Livermore (USA) 7.7f **(90)** - Tufa (Warning)
Form - 44453805
Record 1999 - 1st:0 2nd:0 3rd:1 Ran:8
Win Prizemoney £0 *Total Prizemoney* £809
1999 Turf 0-5: (8f, 10f, 11f 2, 12f) (gd, frm 4) 1999 AW 0-3: (6f, 7f, 8f) (Equi, Fibr 2)
Moderate gelding, effective 6 to 11f, acts on gd - acts on Fibr, has worn blinkers. Turf high 49 - 3rd of 7 getting 25lb from Comic (3 Jun Yarmouth 11f gd RF 1705). AW high 51. Consistent.
**K R Burke [0-8] D G & D J Robinson.*

TUFTY HOPPER RR 65f 5000[7]
2 b g Rock Hopper 10.6f **(54)** - Melancolia (Legend of France (USA)) 9.5f **(61)**
Form - 7
Record 1999 - 1st:0 2nd:0 3rd:0 Ran:1
1999 Turf 0-1: (8f) (gd)
Currently average gelding. **J Pearce [0-1] G H Tufts.*

TUFTY STAR BHB 15f **RR 10f** 2966[6]
4 b f Sirgame - Raffles Virginia (Whistling Deer) 16.4f **(48)**
Form - 76
Record 1999 - 1st:0 2nd:0 3rd:0 Ran:2
Pre1999 - 1st:0 2nd:0 3rd:0 Ran:9
Win Prizemoney £0 *Total Prizemoney* £247
1999 Turf 0-1: (14f) (g-f) 1999 AW 0-1: (13f) (Equi)
Light-framed, poor filly, effective 12f, acts on sft.
**J Pearce [0-11] G H Tufts.*

TUI BHB 33f28a **RR 33f 28a** 4217[9]
4 b f Tina's Pet 7.4f **(56)** - Curious Feeling (Nishapour (FR)) 9.1f **(61)**
Form - 00706800
Record 1999 - 1st:0 2nd:0 3rd:0 Ran:8
Pre1999 - 1st:2 2nd:2 3rd:1 Ran:19
Win Prizemoney £7,755 *Total Prizemoney* £9,629
Wins * 1998 Aug Newmar (G-F) H 12f 51 56 <
* 1998 Jly Beverl (GD) H 9.9f 42 47
1999 Turf 0-4: (12f 3, 13f) (sft, gd, g-f, frm) 1999 AW 0-4: (8f, 11f, 12f 2) (Fibr 4)
Light-framed, very moderate filly, effective 8 to 12f, acts on gd to frm, best on frm, prefers right handed tracks. Turf high 39. AW high 22.
**P Bowen [5-33] Dragon Racing (from K McAuliffe [0-4] Aug 1997).*

TUKANO (CAN) BHB 35f47a **RR 42f 47a** 5006[3]
8 ch g Halo (USA) 10.9f **(67)** - Northern Prancer (USA) (Northern Dancer) 9.6f **(80)**
Form - 03772653
Record 1999 - 1st:0 2nd:1 3rd:2 Ran:8
Pre1999 - 1st:1 2nd:1 3rd:3 Ran:15
Win Prizemoney £3,792 *Total Prizemoney* £10,124
1999 Turf 0-6: (15f 2, 16f 3, 22f) (hvy 2, g-s, gd, g-f 2) 1999 AW 0-2: (16f 2) (Fibr 2)
Moderate gelding. Turf high 66. AW high 47. Consistent.
**J R Jenkins [2-31] Mrs T McCoubrey (from R Hannon [1-11] Oct 1994).*

TULLYNESSLE BHB 43f38a **RR 35f 38a** 857[13]
3 ch f King's Signet (USA) 7f **(51)** - Miss Klew (Never so Bold) 6.3f **(66)**
Form - 0
Record 1999 - 1st:0 2nd:0 3rd:0 Ran:1
Pre1999 - 1st:0 2nd:0 3rd:0 Ran:3
1999 AW 0-1: (7f) (Fibr)
Neat, very moderate filly. (DEAD)
**M W Easterby [0-4] Brig Racing Club.*

TULSA (IRE) BHB 32f39a **RR 32f 39a** 5057[7]
5 b g Priolo (USA) 10.9f **(71)** - Lagrion (USA) (Diesis) 9.3f **(69)**
Form - 03107
Record 1999 - 1st:1 2nd:0 3rd:1 Ran:5
Pre1999 - 1st:0 2nd:1 3rd:2 Ran:22
Win Prizemoney £2,053 *Total Prizemoney* £4,672
Wins * **1999** *Jly Lingfi (STD) H 10f 35 39* <
1999 Turf 0-3: (10f 2, 12f) (gd, frm 2) 1999 AW 1-2: (10f 1-1, 12f) (Equi 1-2)
Very moderate gelding, effective 8 to 10f, acts on gd to g-f, has worn blinkers, favours tight tracks. Turf high 32. AW high 39 (1st run) (began Jly).
**L MontagueHall [1-5] Miss J D Anstee & Partners (from B Gubby [0-22] Oct 1998).*

TUMBLEWEED GLEN (IRE) BHB 70f **RR 67f** 4438[1]
3 ch g Mukaddamah (USA) 7.6f **(74)** - Mistic Glen (IRE) (Mister Majestic)
Form - 54340841
Record 1999 - 1st:1 2nd:0 3rd:1 Ran:8
Pre1999 - 1st:1 2nd:0 3rd:1 Ran:7
Win Prizemoney £9,715 *Total Prizemoney* £13,350
Wins * **1999** Spt Leices (GD) S 10f 61
* 1998 Spt Warwic (G-F) H 8f 75 75 <
1999 Turf 1-8: (9f 2, 10f 1-4, 11f, 12f) (g-s, gd 2, g-f 1-4, frm)
Well made, average gelding, effective 7 to 10f, best at 10f, acts on gd to frm, best on gd, has worn blinkers, prefers left handed tracks, likes tight tracks. Turf high 80 - 3rd of 11 giving 20lb to Archie Babe (18 May Pontefract 10f gd RF 1301). Inconsistent.
**B J Meehan [2-17] The Fifth Tumbleweed Partnership.*

TUMBLEWEED HERO BHB 62f73a **RR 58f 73a** 4930[16]
4 b g Alzao (USA) 9.8f **(73)** - Julip (Track Spare) 8.8f **(62)**
Form - 1830150000
Record 1999 - 1st:1 2nd:0 3rd:1 Ran:9
Pre1999 - 1st:1 2nd:3 3rd:1 Ran:8
Win Prizemoney £4,791 *Total Prizemoney* £10,805
Wins 1999 May Windso (GD) C 8.3f 65
1998 *Nov Lingfi (STD) 8f 76* <
1999 Turf 1-9: (7f 3, 8f 1-3, 9f, 10f 2) (sft, gd 2, g-f 1-3, frm 3)
Well made, above-average gelding, effective 7 to 8f, best at 7f, acted on gd - acted on Equi, had worn blinkers (extremely effectively). Turf high 75 - 3rd of 20 getting 1lb from Kala Sunrise (8 Apr Leicester 7f gd RF 0626). (DEAD)
**D Nicholls [0-5] Ian Guise & Celia M Guise (from B J Meehan [2-12] May 1999).*

TUMBLEWEED INCA (IRE) BHB 59f **RR 53f** 4073[6]
2 b g Ezzoud (IRE) - Atacama (Green Desert (USA)) 8.6f **(78)**
Form - 2138086
Record 1999 - 1st:1 2nd:1 3rd:1 Ran:7
Win Prizemoney £2,840 *Total Prizemoney* £4,585
Wins * **1999** Jly Bright (FRM) 7f 79 <
1999 Turf 1-7: (6f, 7f 1-6) (gd 2, g-f, frm 1-4)
Fair gelding, effective 7f, acts on frm, has worn blinkers. Turf high 79 (began Jly) - 1st of 8 giving 5lb to Bint Habibi (22 Jly Brighton RF 3021). **B J Meehan [1-7] The Seventh Tumbleweed Partnership.*

TUMBLEWEED QUARTET (USA) BHB 79f **RR 81f** 4677[8]
3 b g Manila (USA) 10f **(81)** - Peggy's String (USA) (Highland Park (USA))
Form - 7770008
Record 1999 - 1st:0 2nd:0 3rd:0 Ran:7
Pre1999 - 1st:1 2nd:0 3rd:2 Ran:4
Win Prizemoney £6,257 *Total Prizemoney* £17,824
Wins * 1998 Jun Newbur (SFT) 6f 71+ <
1999 Turf 0-7: (8f, 10f 6) (g-s, gd, g-f 4, frm)
Scopey, decent gelding, effective 7f, acts on g-f, has worn blinkers. Turf high 96. Connections thought he was a Classic colt, but their confidence was misplaced.
**B J Meehan [1-11] The Tumbleweed Partnership.*

TUMBLEWEED RIDGE BHB 113f91a **RR 119f 91a** 4916[9]
6 ch h Indian Ridge 7.6f **(74)** - Billie Blue (Ballad Rock) 7.8f **(63)**
Form - 032115210
Record 1999 - 1st:3 2nd:2 3rd:1 Ran:9
Pre1999 - 1st:5 2nd:5 3rd:3 Ran:31
Win Prizemoney £137,993 *Total Prizemoney* £200,021
Wins * **1999** Spt Epsom (GD) L 7f 118 <
* **1999** Jun Longch (GD) G3 7f 113
* **1999** Jun Leopar (GD) G3 7f 111

* 1998 Jun Leopar (SFT) G3 7f 109
* 1998 Apr Newmar (SFT) H 7f 101 106
* 1997 Jly Newmar (G-F) H 7f 94 101
* 1995 Oct Newbur (G-S) G3 7.3f 103
* 1995 Jly Lingfi (G-F) 5f 84+

1999 Turf 3-9: (7f 3-9) (sft, gd 2-6, g-f 1-2)

High-class horse, effective 7f, acts on sft to g-f, best on gd, has worn blinkers, likes left handed tracks, excels at Leopardstown. Turf high 119 - 2nd of 11 giving 8lb to Fa-Eq (19 Aug York 7f gd RF 3775) - also 1st of 7 giving 8lb to Selfish (3 Spt Epsom RF 4119). Tough as old boots, he is a genuine seven-furlong performer who ended 1998 in moderate form, but returned to his best last summer. Landed a couple of Group Threes at Leopardstown and Longchamp, and came out best in a blanket finish to an Epsom Listed event. He is a bit of a character, but is a very effective performer when on song.

**B J Meehan [8-40] The Tumbleweed Partnership.*

TUMBLEWEED RIVER (IRE) BHB 85f **RR 85f** 5134[5]

3 ch c Thatching 7.8f **(69)** - Daphne Indica (IRE) (Ballad Rock) 7.8f **(63)**

Form - 4105

Record 1999 - 1st:1 2nd:0 3rd:0 Ran:4
Pre1999 - 1st:0 2nd:1 3rd:0 Ran:1

Win Prizemoney £4,188 *Total Prizemoney* £6,922

Wins * 1999 Spt Haydoc (SFT) 7.1f 77+ <

1999 Turf 1-4: (6f, 7f 1-3) (gd 1-3, g-f)

Scopey, useful colt. Turf high 85 (began Spt) - 5th of 11 giving 19lb to Don't Surrender (29 Oct Newmarket 6f gd RF 5134) - also 1st of 13 giving 5lb to Language of Love (24 Spt Haydock RF 4527). **B J Meehan [1-5] The Fourth Tumbleweed Partnership.*

TUMBLEWEED TOR BHB 85f **RR 79f** 4907[3]

2 b c Rudimentary (USA) 8.2f **(66)** - Hilly (Town Crier) 10.2f **(55)**

Form - 643

Record 1999 - 1st:0 2nd:0 3rd:1 Ran:3

Win Prizemoney £0 *Total Prizemoney* £917

1999 Turf 0-3: (7f 2, 8f) (sft, frm 2)

Currently above-average colt. Turf high 79 (began Aug).

**B J Meehan [0-3] The Sixth Tumbleweed Partnership.*

TUMBLEWEED WIZARD BHB 68f **RR 61f** 4875[11]

2 ch g Magic Ring (IRE) 6.5f **(64)** - Chiquitita (Reliance II) 9.9f **(58)**

Form - 770

Record 1999 - 1st:0 2nd:0 3rd:0 Ran:3

1999 Turf 0-3: (6f, 8f 2) (gd 2, g-f)

Currently average gelding. Turf high 61 (began Aug).

**B J Meehan [0-3] The Second Tumbleweed Partnership.*

TUNNEL BRIDGE BHB 48f50a **RR 41f 50a** 3903[16]

3 b g Merdon Melody 6.8f **(56)** - Tripolitaine (FR) (Nonoalco (USA)) 8.5f **(66)**

Form - 0580

Record 1999 - 1st:0 2nd:0 3rd:0 Ran:4
Pre1999 - 1st:0 2nd:0 3rd:0 Ran:4

Win Prizemoney £0 *Total Prizemoney* £252

1999 Turf 0-2: (12f, 17f) (gd, frm) 1999 AW 0-2: (8f 2) (Fibr 2)

Moderate gelding, has worn blinkers. Turf high 30. AW high 43.

**K A Ryan [0-8] The Gloria Darley Racing Partnership.*

TURAATH (IRE) BHB 98f **RR 85+f** 477[1]

3 b c Sadler's Wells (USA) 11.3f **(87)** - Diamond Field (USA) (Mr Prospector (USA)) 8.8f **(78)**

Form - 1

Record 1999 - 1st:1 2nd:0 3rd:0 Ran:1
Pre1999 - 1st:0 2nd:0 3rd:1 Ran:2

Win Prizemoney £4,201 *Total Prizemoney* £5,624

Wins * 1999 Mar Doncas (G-S) 10.3f 84+ <

1999 Turf 1-1: (10f 1-1) (g-s 1-1)

Scopey, currently useful colt. (1st run) - 1st of 13 from Ipledgeallegiance (26 Mar Doncaster RF 0477). Bolted up in a Doncaster maiden on his only start, though the form is difficult to evaluate. **B W Hills [1-3] Hamdan Al Maktoum.*

TURBOTIERE (FR) **RR 106f** 2854a[2]

4 br f Turgeon (USA) - Victoria Dee (FR) (Rex Magna (FR))

Form - 22

1999 Turf 0-2: (15f 2) (sft, gd)

Currently Pattern-class filly. Turf high 106 (1st run) - 2nd of 9 getting 4lb from Lucky Dream (15 Jun Chantilly 15f gd RF 2280a).

**E Libaud in FR [0-2].*

TURGENEV (IRE) BHB 34f64a **RR 14f 64a** 5152[9]

10 b g Sadler's Wells (USA) 11.3f **(87)** - Tilia (ITY) (Dschingis Khan) 11.3f **(75)**

Form - 00000

Record 1999 - 1st:0 2nd:0 3rd:0 Ran:5
Pre1999 - 1st:8 2nd:7 3rd:2 Ran:49

Win Prizemoney £54,459 *Total Prizemoney* £73,428

Wins * 1998 Jun Sandow (SFT) H 14f 60 68
* 1997 Aug Sandow (GD) H 14f 64 70
* 1997 Jly Haydoc (GD) H 14f 60 65
* 1997 May Haydoc (SFT) H 14f 63 69
* 1996 Jun Haydoc (G-S) H 14f 58 66

1999 Turf 0-5: (10f, 11f, 14f 3) (gd 4, g-f)

Poor gelding, effective 14f, acts on g-s to gd, has worn blinkers, likes tight tracks. Turf high 14.

**R Bastiman [5-38] Mrs P Bastiman (from J H M Gosden [3-16] Aug 1993).*

TURNED OUT WELL BHB 45f **RR 42f** 5021[16]

2 b g Robellino (USA) 9.5f **(68)** - In the Shade (Bustino) 10.4f **(64)**

Form - 000

Record 1999 - 1st:0 2nd:0 3rd:0 Ran:3

1999 Turf 0-3: (5f 2, 7f) (gd 2, frm)

Currently moderate gelding. Turf high 42.

**P C Haslam [0-3] Middleham Park Racing XVIII.*

TURNOFACARD BHB 53f **RR 66f** 3110[16]

3 ch f First Trump - Barbary Court (Grundy) 10.3f **(65)**

Form - 0600

Record 1999 - 1st:0 2nd:0 3rd:0 Ran:4
Pre1999 - 1st:0 2nd:0 3rd:0 Ran:1

1999 Turf 0-3: (8f 2, 10f) (g-f 2, frm) 1999 AW 0-1: (12f) (Fibr)

Scopey, average filly. Turf high 66. **P J Makin [0-5] A W Schiff.*

TURNTABLE (IRE) **RR 17f** 5135[14]

3 b f Dolphin Street (FR) - Sharp Circle (IRE) (Sure Blade (USA)) 11.3f **(67)**

Form - 50080

Record 1999 - 1st:0 2nd:0 3rd:0 Ran:5
Pre1999 - 1st:0 2nd:0 3rd:0 Ran:1

1999 Turf 0-5: (8f 3, 10f, 11f) (gd 2, g-f, frm 2)

Lengthy, poor filly, has worn blinkers. Turf high 56.

**H J Collingridge [0-3] In The Know (from G Wragg [0-3] May 1999).*

TURQUOISE GEM (IRE) BHB 57f **RR 60f** 4825[6]

2 b f Fayruz 6.6f **(63)** - Pepilin (Coquelin (USA)) 8.4f **(58)**

Form - 8706

Record 1999 - 1st:0 2nd:0 3rd:0 Ran:4

1999 Turf 0-4: (5f, 6f 3) (g-s 2, g-f 2)

Average filly. Turf high 60 (began Aug).

**V Soane [0-4] M Nelmes-Crocker.*

TURRILL HOUSE BHB 28f20a **RR 24f 29a** 3441[9]

7 b m Charmer 9f **(59)** - Megabucks (Buckskin (FR))

Form - 160

Record 1999 - 1st:1 2nd:0 3rd:0 Ran:3
Pre1999 - 1st:0 2nd:0 3rd:1 Ran:9

Win Prizemoney £1,903 *Total Prizemoney* £2,196

Wins * 1999 *Jan Southw (STD) H 16f 20 33* <

1999 AW 1-3: (12f, 15f, 16f 1-1) (Fibr 1-3)

Very moderate mare. AW high 33 (1st run) - 1st of 10 getting 17lb from Pertemps Mission (8 Jan Southwell RF 0051).

**W J Musson [5-30] J R Hawksley & C H Pettigrew.*

TURTLE BHB 45f59a **RR 48f 59a** 5188[14]

3 b g Turtle Island (IRE) - Kate Marie (USA) (Bering) 7.4f **(61)**

Form - 0350817040

Record 1999 - 1st:1 2nd:0 3rd:1 Ran:10
Pre1999 - 1st:0 2nd:0 3rd:2 Ran:5

Win Prizemoney £2,490 *Total Prizemoney* £4,243

Wins 1999 Jun Pontef (G-S) S 10f 55 <

1999 Turf 1-8: (7f, 8f, 10f 1-3, 12f, 16f 2) (gd 1-3, g-f 5) 1999 AW 0-2:

(8f, 12f) (Fibr 2)

Strong, fair gelding, effective 5 to 6f, acts on gd to frm, prefers left handed tracks, likes tight tracks. Turf high 55. AW high 55.

**W Storey [0-4] R Coleman (from M Johnston [1-11] Jun 1999).*

TURTLE SONG (IRE) BHB 80f RR 74f 3843[4]

2 br c Turtle Island (IRE) - Miss Bojangles (Gay Fandango (USA)) 8.5f **(59)**

Form - 034

Record 1999 - 1st:0 2nd:0 3rd:1 Ran:3

Win Prizemoney £0 *Total Prizemoney* £882

1999 Turf 0-3: (5f, 6f 2) (gd, g-f, frm)

Currently above-average colt. Turf high 74 - 3rd of 16 giving 5lb to Veil of Avalon (14 Aug Lingfield 6f g-f RF 3645).

**M L W Bell [0-3] M C Talbot-Ponsonby.*

TURTLE SOUP (IRE) BHB 74f RR 78f 4822[4]

3 b c Turtle Island (IRE) - Lisa's Favourite (Gorytus (USA)) 7.8f **(60)**

Form - 0601284

Record 1999 - 1st:1 2nd:1 3rd:0 Ran:7

Win Prizemoney £2,948 *Total Prizemoney* £4,549

Wins * **1999** Jly Ayr (SFT) H 10.9f 67 69 <

1999 Turf 1-7: (8f 3, 10f, 11f 1-1, 12f 2) (g-s 1-1, gd, g-f, frm 4)

Workmanlike, above-average colt, effective 10 to 12f, best at 12f, acts on g-s to frm, best on frm. Turf high 78 - 2nd of 5 getting 17lb from Forest Fire (30 Jly Newmarket 12f frm RF 3245) - also 1st of 13 giving 5lb to Haystacks (19 Jly Ayr RF 2938). Has joined Lydia Richards. **L M Cumani [1-7] Marcus Edwards-Jones.*

TURTLE'S RISING (IRE) BHB 66f RR 69f 4906[14]

3 b f Turtle Island (IRE) - Zabeta (Diesis) 9.3f **(69)**

Form - 07250031000

Record 1999 - 1st:1 2nd:1 3rd:1 Ran:11

Pre1999 - 1st:1 2nd:0 3rd:1 Ran:6

Win Prizemoney £7,007 *Total Prizemoney* £9,683

Wins * **1999** Aug Lingfi (GD) H 7f 65 69

* 1998 Jly Sandow (G-F) 5f 78 <

1999 Turf 1-11: (5f 6, 6f, 7f 1-4) (g-s, gd 1-3, g-f 3, frm 4)

Workmanlike, average filly, effective 5 to 7f, best at 5f, acts on gd to frm, has worn blinkers. Turf high 69 - also 1st of 16 giving 8lb to Coughlan's Gift (20 Aug Lingfield RF 3797).

**B J Meehan [2-17] Total (Bloodstock) Ltd.*

TURTLE SURPRISE BHB 70f66a RR 71f 66a 4939[7]

2 b f Turtle Island (IRE) - Foreno (Formidable (USA)) 9.2f **(63)**

Form - 210343377

Record 1999 - 1st:1 2nd:1 3rd:3 Ran:9

Win Prizemoney £2,358 *Total Prizemoney* £4,435

Wins * **1999** *May Southw (STD) 5f 69* <

1999 Turf 0-5: (5f, 6f 4) (sft, gd 2, g-f 2) 1999 AW 1-4: (5f 1-1, 7f 2, 8f) (Fibr 1-4)

Above-average filly, effective 5 to 7f, best at 5f, acts on sft - acts on Fibr. Turf high 71. AW high 69 (1st run) - 1st of 11 giving 9lb to Foxy Brown (10 May Southwell RF 1133). Inconsistent. A Fibresand winner over the minimum, she looks to find six furlongs as far as she wants, and may be suited by cut in the ground on turf. **R M H Cowell [1-9] C Akers.*

TURTLE VALLEY (IRE) BHB 95f RR 94f 4590[10]

3 b c Turtle Island (IRE) - Primrose Valley (Mill Reef (USA)) 10.5f **(78)**

Form - 5026211187540

Record 1999 - 1st:3 2nd:2 3rd:0 Ran:13

Pre1999 - 1st:0 2nd:1 3rd:0 Ran:6

Win Prizemoney £25,147 *Total Prizemoney* £30,108

Wins * **1999** Jun Salisb (GD) H 14.1f 90 92 <

* **1999** May Newbur (SFT) H 12f 74 91

* **1999** May York (G-S) 13.9f 87

1999 Turf 3-12: (8f, 12f 1-3, 13f 3, 14f 2-2, 15f, 16f 2) (sft, g-s, gd 2-7, g-f 1-2, frm) 1999 AW 0-1: (10f) (Equi)

Useful colt, effective 12 to 16f, acts on gd to g-f, best on gd, has worn blinkers, likes left handed tracks. Turf high 94 - 7th of 9 to Spendent (30 Jun Chantilly 13f gd RF 2655a) - also 1st of 5 giving 5lb to Knockholt (9 Jun Salisbury RF 1868). A revelation once faced with a test of stamina, he completed a fine hat-trick in the spring and looked especially suited by soft ground. However he has been disappointing of late and it looks as though the Handicapper may have his measure.

**S Dow [3-13] Cazanove Clear Height Racing (from J L Dunlop [0-6] Spt 1998).*

TUSCAN DREAM BHB 73f RR 71f 4292[4]

4 b g Clantime 6.6f **(57)** - Excavator Lady (Most Secret) 7.1f **(58)**

Form - 8371143122014

Record 1999 - 1st:4 2nd:2 3rd:2 Ran:13

Pre1999 - 1st:0 2nd:2 3rd:1 Ran:7

Win Prizemoney £18,139 *Total Prizemoney* £23,401

Wins * **1999** Spt Epsom (G-F) H 5f 67 71 <

* **1999** Jun Lingfi (G-F) H 5f 59 63

* **1999** *May Wolver (STD) C 5f 61*

* **1999** May Mussel (G-F) S 5f 43

1999 Turf 3-9: (5f 3-9) (gd, g-f, frm 3-6, hrd) 1999 AW 1-4: (5f 1-4) (Fibr 1-4)

Tall, above-average gelding, effective 5f, acts on g-f to frm - acts on Fibr, best on frm, has worn blinkers, excels at Lingfield. Turf high 71 - 1st of 14 from Brecongill Lad (4 Spt Epsom RF 4131) - also 1st of 8 getting 4lb from Mousehole (26 Jun Lingfield RF 2332). AW high 61. Consistent. Very speedy, he bolted up in a decent race at Epsom in September.

**J Berry [4-20] Chris & Antonia Deuters.*

TUSSLE BHB 92f RR 92f 4644[11]

4 b g Salse (USA) 10.9f **(71)** -Crime Ofthecentury(Pharly (FR)) 9.8f **(68)**

Form - 5570040

Record 1999 - 1st:0 2nd:0 3rd:0 Ran:7

Pre1999 - 1st:1 2nd:1 3rd:0 Ran:5

Win Prizemoney £4,077 *Total Prizemoney* £9,907

Wins * 1997 Oct Newmar (G-F) 6f 95+ <

1999 Turf 0-7: (5f, 6f 6) (g-s, g-f 4, frm 2)

Scopey, useful gelding, effective 6f, acts on g-f to frm, best on g-f. Turf high 99 (1st run) - 5th of 14 giving 2lb to Primo Lara (2 May Newmarket 6f frm RF 0980). Difficult to train, he managed a full season in 1999 but proved frustrating. He lacks a turn of foot in the top six furlong handicaps and is worth a try over further.

**M L W Bell [1-12] Lordship Stud.*

TUZLA (USA) RR 119f 5226a[2]

5 m Panoramic - Turkeina (USA) (Kautokeino (FR))

Form - 2

1999 Turf 0-1: (8f) (frm)

Currently high-class. (1st run) - 2nd of 14 getting 3lb from Silic (6 Nov Gulfstream Park 8f frm RF 5226a). **B Baffert in USA [0-1].*

TWEED RR 66f 5208[12]

2 ch c Barathea (IRE) - In Perpetuity (Great Nephew) 9.9f **(64)**

Form - 050

Record 1999 - 1st:0 2nd:0 3rd:0 Ran:3

1999 Turf 0-3: (7f 2, 8f) (g-s 2, gd)

Currently average colt. Turf high 66 (began Oct).

**R Charlton [0-3] Lady Rothschild.*

TWEED MILL RR 64+f 2761[3]

2 b f Selkirk (USA) 7.9f **(76)** - Island Mill (Mill Reef (USA)) 10.5f **(78)**

Form - 3

Record 1999 - 1st:0 2nd:0 3rd:1 Ran:1

Win Prizemoney £0 *Total Prizemoney* £539

1999 Turf 0-1: (6f) (frm)

Currently average filly. **I A Balding [0-1] W Aeberhard.*

TWENTY FIRST BHB 63f RR 61f 5154[6]

3 ch f Inchinor 8.9f **(64)** - Picnicing (Good Times (ITY)) 6.6f **(54)**

Form - 35726

Record 1999 - 1st:0 2nd:1 3rd:1 Ran:5

Pre1999 - 1st:0 2nd:0 3rd:0 Ran:1

Win Prizemoney £0 *Total Prizemoney* £1,305

1999 Turf 0-5: (8f 3, 10f 2) (gd 2, frm 3)

Scopey, average filly, effective 10f, acts on gd. Turf high 62 (began Jly). **G Wragg [0-6] Bloomsbury Stud.*

TWICE BHB 75f RR 72f 4435[12]

3 b c Rainbow Quest (USA) 11.2f **(81)** - Bolas **(110f)** (Unfuwain (USA))

Form - 440

Record 1999 - 1st:0 2nd:0 3rd:0 Ran:3

Win Prizemoney £0 *Total Prizemoney* £648

1999 Turf 0-3: (10f 2, 12f) (g-s, gd, frm)

Scopey, currently above-average colt. Turf high 72 (began Aug).

**B W Hills [0-3] K Abdulla.*

TWICE AS SHARP BHB 88f82a **RR 92f 82a** 4392[16]
7 ch h Sharpo 7.5f **(68)** - Shadiliya (Red Alert) 7.6f **(66)**
Form - 00020344860
Record 1999 - 1st:0 2nd:1 3rd:1 Ran:10
Pre1999 - 1st:4 2nd:5 3rd:5 Ran:37
Win Prizemoney £37,275 *Total Prizemoney* £60,010
Wins * 1997 May York (GD) H 5f 83 86
* 1996 Jun Newcas (FRM) H 5f 84 88 <
* 1995 Spt Newcas (GD) H 5f 81 84
* 1995 May Pontef (GD) 6f 77
1999 Turf 0-10: (5f, 6f 9) (g-s 2, gd 2, g-f 2, frm 4)
Useful horse, effective 6f, acts on g-s to frm, best on frm. Turf high 93 - 3rd of 19 giving 12lb to Unshaken (26 Jun Newcastle 6f frm RF 2334). Consistent. Another who benefited from the draw advantage in the Stewards' Cup, where he finished fourth. He has failed to build on that good effort since. Although he was placed in some hot handicaps last term, he has not won since 1997.
**P W Harris [4-47] Formula Twelve.*

TWICE BLESSED (IRE) RR 58f 5194[10]
2 ch c Thatching 7.8f **(69)** - Fairy Blesse (IRE) (Fairy King (USA)) 7.7f **(59)**
Form - 70
Record 1999 - 1st:0 2nd:0 3rd:0 Ran:2
1999 Turf 0-2: (6f 2) (sft, gd)
Currently fair colt. Turf high 58 (began Oct).
**R Hannon [0-2] J C Smith.*

TWICKENHAM (USA) RR 96f 4976a[2]
4 ch c Woodman (USA) 9.7f **(77)** - Danse Royale (IRE) (Caerleon (USA)) 8.6f **(71)**
Form - 124218842
1999 Turf 2-9: (9f 2, 10f 2, 12f 1-2, 14f 1-3) (hvy, sft 1-1, g-s 4, gd, g-f 1-2)
Very useful colt, effective 9 to 14f, acts on hvy to g-f, prefers right handed tracks, likes Curragh. Turf high 98 - 2nd of 4 getting 4lb from Lil's Boy (9 Jun Leopardstown 9f gd RF 2020a) - also 1st of 6 giving 5lb to Sanaka (30 Jly Galway RF 3340a). He stays a mile and three-quarters, but did not prove up to Group class and was sold for 50,000 guineas at Newmarket in October.
**A P O'Brien in IRE [2-9] Michael Tabor.*

TWICKERS BHB 62f **RR 58df** 4656[18]
3 b f Primo Dominie 7.2f **(67)** - Songstead (Song) 7.2f **(61)**
Form - 2364250
Record 1999 - 1st:0 2nd:2 3rd:1 Ran:7
Pre1999 - 1st:0 2nd:0 3rd:0 Ran:1
Win Prizemoney £0 *Total Prizemoney* £2,957
1999 Turf 0-7: (5f 7) (gd 3, g-f 3, frm)
Scopey, fair filly, effective 5f, acts on gd to g-f. Turf high 62 - 3rd of 11 getting 5lb from Sir Sandrovitch (22 May Musselburgh 5f g-f RF 1409). Becoming disappointing. **R Guest [0-8] J W Hill.*

TWILIGHT SLEEP (USA) BHB 68f73a **RR 50?f 73a** 100[P]
7 b g Shadeed (USA) 7.7f **(72)** - Sleeping Beauty (Mill Reef (USA)) 10.5f **(78)**
Form - 6P
Record 1999 - 1st:0 2nd:0 3rd:0 Ran:2
Pre1999 - 1st:2 2nd:1 3rd:1 Ran:11
Win Prizemoney £6,096 *Total Prizemoney* £9,601
Wins 1997 *Jun Wolver (STD) C 12f* 71+
1999 AW 0-2: (12f, 16f) (Fibr 2)
Above-average gelding, has worn blinkers. Inconsistent.
**C N Kellett [0-2] Willwewontwe Club (from M C Pipe [0-2] Jly 1997).*

TWILIGHT WORLD BHB 47f **RR 57f** 4708[6]
2 b g Night Shift (USA) 8.1f **(73)** - Masskana (IRE) (Darshaan) 9.9f **(84)**
Form - 006
Record 1999 - 1st:0 2nd:0 3rd:0 Ran:3
1999 Turf 0-3: (6f 3) (gd 2, frm)
Currently fair gelding. Turf high 57 (began Spt).
**Sir Mark Prescott [0-3] Fishpool Osborne House.*

TWIN CREEKS BHB 53f69a **RR 56f 69a** 2257[5]
8 b g Alzao (USA) 9.8f **(73)** - Double River (USA) (Irish River (FR)) 8.6f **(78)**
Form - 608440765
Record 1999 - 1st:0 2nd:0 3rd:0 Ran:7
Pre1999 - 1st:8 2nd:7 3rd:8 Ran:65
Win Prizemoney £25,881 *Total Prizemoney* £38,608
Wins * 1997 *Nov Lingfi (STD) H 7f 74 77* <
* 1997 Jun Warwic (FRM) 7f 56
* 1997 *Jan Lingfi (STD) H 7f 70 73*
* 1996 *Nov Lingfi (STD) H 7f 65 67*
* 1996 *Oct Lingfi (STD) 7f* 62
1996 *Feb Southw (STD) H 8f 52 54*
1995 Jly Hamilt (FRM) H 9.2f 47 52
1995 *Feb Southw (STD) 7f* 53
1999 Turf 0-3: (8f 3) (gd, g-f 2) 1999 AW 0-4: (7f 2, 8f, 10f) (Equi 4)
Above-average gelding, effective 7 to 8f, acts on g-f - acts on Equi, favours tight tracks. Turf high 56. AW high 71 (1st run) - 8th of 12 getting 6lb from Silca Blanka (16 Jan Lingfield 7f Equi RF 0109).
**V Soane [5-46] The Armchair Jockeys (from M D Hammond [3-19] Apr 1996).*

TWIN TIME BHB 65a **RR 64f** 4813[15]
5 b m Syrtos 8.1f **(57)** - Carramba (CZE) (Tumble Wind (USA)) 7.5f **(57)**
Form - 14313570
Record 1999 - 1st:2 2nd:0 3rd:2 Ran:8
Pre1999 - 1st:1 2nd:3 3rd:2 Ran:15
Win Prizemoney £8,724 *Total Prizemoney* £13,669
Wins * 1999 Jly Bath (FRM) H 10.2f 62 65 <
*** 1999** May Bath (GD) H 8f 61 64
* 1998 Aug Bath (GD) H 10.2f 63 60
1999 Turf 2-8: (8f 1-3, 9f, 10f 1-4) (g-s, gd 1-2, g-f, frm 1-4)
Average filly, effective 8 to 10f, acts on gd to frm, best on frm, prefers left handed tracks, favours tight tracks, excels at Bath and Kempton. Turf high 65 - 1st of 13 giving 30lb to Fairly Sure (15 Jly Bath RF 2841) - also 1st of 16 giving 10lb to Warring (17 May Bath RF 1272). Consistent.
**J S King [3-20] Dajam Ltd (from M J Heaton-Ellis [0-6] Aug 1997).*

TWIST RR 86f 5063[4]
2 b c Suave Dancer (USA) 10.7f **(68)** - Reason to Dance **(98df)** (Damister (USA)) 9f **(73)**
Form - 864
Record 1999 - 1st:0 2nd:0 3rd:0 Ran:3
Win Prizemoney £0 *Total Prizemoney* £173
1999 Turf 0-3: (6f, 7f, 8f) (gd, g-f 2)
Currently useful colt. Turf high 86 (began Jly) - 4th of 12 giving 5lb to Top Hand (26 Oct Bath 8f gd RF 5063).
**W R Muir [0-3] John O'Mulloy.*

TWO CLUBS BHB 103f **RR 100f** 5222[2]
3 br f First Trump - Miss Cindy (Mansingh (USA)) 7.4f **(55)**
Form - 042102
Record 1999 - 1st:1 2nd:2 3rd:0 Ran:6
Pre1999 - 1st:3 2nd:0 3rd:0 Ran:4
Win Prizemoney £27,759 *Total Prizemoney* £41,390
Wins * 1999 Oct Newmar (G-S) H 6f 96 100 <
1998 Oct Doncas (HVY) I 6f 97
1998 Spt Yarmou (G-S) 6f 85
1998 Jly Newcas (G-F) 6f 74+
1999 Turf 1-6: (6f 1-6) (g-s 2, gd 1-3, g-f)
Neat, very useful filly, effective 6f, acts on sft to gd, and excels at Doncaster. Turf high 100 - 2nd of 20 to Pipalong (6 Nov Doncaster 6f g-s RF 5222) - also 1st of 12 getting 9lb from Fragrant Oasis (1 Oct Newmarket RF 4678). A soft ground specialist, she battled on gamely when winning a rated stakes at Newmarket in October and deserves another chance in Listed company. Six furlongs is her trip. **W Jarvis [1-6] Stephen Hobson (from Mrs J Cecil [3-4] Oct 1998).*

TWOFORTEN BHB 34f34a **RR 35f 34a** 4997[3]
4 b g Robellino (USA) 9.5f **(68)** - Grown At Rowan (Gabitat) 5f **(44)**
Form - 4324033
Record 1999 - 1st:0 2nd:1 3rd:3 Ran:7
Pre1999 - 1st:0 2nd:0 3rd:1 Ran:11
Win Prizemoney £0 *Total Prizemoney* £2,456
1999 Turf 0-7: (10f, 12f 5, 16f) (g-s, gd, g-f 2, frm 3)
Workmanlike, very moderate gelding, effective 9 to 12f, acts on g-f to frm, has worn blinkers, prefers right handed tracks, likes tight tracks. Turf high 44 (began Jly). **M Madgwick [0-18] W V Roker.*

TWO JACKS (IRE) RR 29f 4325[13]

2 b c Fayruz 6.6f **(63)** - Kaya (GER) (Young Generation) 7.7f **(63)**
Form - 00
Record 1999 - 1st:0 2nd:0 3rd:0 Ran:2
1999 Turf 0-2: (5f 2) (gd, g-f)
Currently little account colt. Turf high 25 (began Aug).
**W S Cunningham [0-2] Mrs Ann Bell.*

TWO ON THE BRIDGE BHB 34f37a **RR 34f 37a** 504[4]
5 b g Chilibang 7f **(55)** - Constant Companion (Pas de Seul) 9.1f **(67)**
Form - 63437534
Record 1999 - 1st:0 2nd:0 3rd:3 Ran:8
Pre1999 - 1st:0 2nd:4 3rd:3 Ran:20
Win Prizemoney £0 *Total Prizemoney* £6,101
1999 Turf 0-1: (12f) (hvy) 1999 AW 0-7: (8f 2, 9f, 11f, 12f 2, 14f) (Fibr 7)
Very moderate gelding, effective 7 to 12f, acts on frm - acts on Fibr, has worn blinkers, favours tight tracks. AW high 54 - 3rd of 8 giving 5lb to Monchania (13 Jan Wolverhampton 8f Fibr RF 0084). Consistent.
**J G Given [0-8] Robinson, Love, Reid & Dalgleish (from Denys Smith [0-20] Spt 1998).*

TWO PACK BHB 33f **RR 18f** 5056[14]
3 b c Diesis 9f **(80)** - Zonda (Fabulous Dancer (USA)) 9.4f **(70)**
Form - 07000060
Record 1999 - 1st:0 2nd:0 3rd:0 Ran:7
Pre1999 - 1st:0 2nd:0 3rd:0 Ran:2
1999 Turf 0-4: (8f 2, 11f 2) (gd, g-f, frm, hrd) 1999 AW 0-3: (10f 2, 16f) (Equi 3)
Neat, little account colt, has worn blinkers. Turf high 37. (began Jly). Becoming disappointing.
**B A Pearce [0-9] Richard J Gray & Stanley Selby.*

TWO'S BETTER BHB 64f **RR 77f** 5063[7]
2 br g Rock City 8.8f **(62)** - Miss Pin Up **(63f 50a)** (Kalaglow) 9.8f **(67)**
Form - 077
Record 1999 - 1st:0 2nd:0 3rd:0 Ran:3
1999 Turf 0-3: (8f 3) (g-s, gd, g-f)
Currently above-average gelding. Turf high 77 (began Aug).
**G L Moore [0-3] Heart Of The South Racing (4).*

TWO SOCKS BHB 57f57a **RR 48f 57a** 5066[9]
6 ch g Phountzi (USA) 9.6f **(60)** -Mrs Feathers (Pyjama Hunt) 11.1f **(38)**
Form - 616536000
Record 1999 - 1st:1 2nd:0 3rd:1 Ran:9
Pre1999 - 1st:2 2nd:7 3rd:2 Ran:29
Win Prizemoney £10,638 *Total Prizemoney* £19,281
Wins * 1999 Jun Kempto (G-F) H 12f 70 67 <
* 1998 Jun Warwic (GD) H 10.8f 66 67 <
1996 Jly Lingfi (FRM) H 11.5f 57 59
1999 Turf 1-9: (11f, 12f 1-7, 15f) (gd 3, g-f 3, frm 1-3)
Fair gelding, effective 11 to 12f, best at 11f, acts on gd to frm, best on gd, has worn blinkers. Turf high 67 - 1st of 12 giving 2lb to Absolute Utopia (23 Jun Kempton RF 2244). Becoming disappointing. **J S King [2-19] Mrs Satu Marks (from P Burgoyne [0-2] Oct 1996).*

TWO-TWENTY-TWO (IRE) RR 112f 3717a[5]
4 b c Fairy King (USA) 7.7f **(75)** - Easy to Copy (USA) (Affirmed (USA)) 9.3f **(79)**
Form - 1035
1999 Turf 1-4: (7f 1-2, 8f 2) (g-s 1-2, gd, frm)
Group-class colt, effective 7 to 10f, best at 7f, acts on hvy to gd, often wears blinkers, and excels at Leopardstown. Turf high 114 (1st run) - 1st of 7 giving 3lb to Gaelic Storm (11 Apr Curragh RF 0680a). Consistent. In contrast to 1998, he was lightly raced and a shade inconsistent. Seemingly best over seven furlongs or a mile, he probably needs soft ground.
**D K Weld in IRE [6-14] Moyglare Stud Farm.*

TWO WILLIAMS BHB 48f47a **RR 49f 47a** 1855[11]
4 b g Polar Falcon (USA) 9f **(74)** - Long View (Persian Bold) 9.3f **(66)**
Form - 000
Record 1999 - 1st:0 2nd:0 3rd:0 Ran:2
Pre1999 - 1st:1 2nd:1 3rd:2 Ran:17
Win Prizemoney £3,673 *Total Prizemoney* £5,819
Wins * 1997 Jly Beverl (HVY) 5f 76+ <
1999 Turf 0-2: (5f 2) (gd, g-f)
Strong, moderate gelding, effective 5f, acts on g-s. Turf high 25. Becoming disappointing. **M W Easterby [1-19] W L Caley.*

TYCANDO BHB 70f **RR 79f** 5045[14]
2 ch c Forzando 7.2f **(63)** - Running Tycoon (IRE) **(42f)** (Last Tycoon) 8.5f **(62)**
Form - 53362010
Record 1999 - 1st:1 2nd:1 3rd:2 Ran:8
Win Prizemoney £2,339 *Total Prizemoney* £4,155
Wins * 1999 *Oct Wolver (STD) C 6f 74+* <
1999 Turf 0-7: (5f, 6f 6) (sft, gd 2, g-f 2, frm 2) 1999 AW 1-1: (6f 1-1) (Fibr 1-1)
Above-average colt, effective 6f, acts on g-f - acts on Fibr. Turf high 79 (began Jly) - 2nd of 14 giving 11lb to Kirsch (25 Aug Lingfield 6f g-f RF 3907). (1st run) - 1st of 13 giving 11lb to Parkside Prospect (16 Oct Wolverhampton RF 4923). Inconsistent. Showed some ability on turf, but was impressive when landing a Wolverhampton claimer on his Fibresand debut and can win more races on that surface. Has joined Karl Burke.
**R Hannon [1-8] J C Smith.*

TYCOON'S DOLCE (IRE) RR 102f 4780a[10]
3 b f Rainbows For Life (CAN) 9.3f **(64)** - Tycoon's Drama (IRE) (Last Tycoon) 8.5f **(62)**
Form - 37210
1999 Turf 1-5: (7f, 8f 1-3, 9f) (sft, g-s, gd 1-3)
Very useful filly, effective 7 to 8f, best at 8f, acts on hvy to gd, prefers right handed tracks. Turf high 101 - also 1st of 9 from Oriental Fashion (22 Aug Deauville RF 3931a). She battled on bravely when winning at Deauville in August, and was badly hampered when disappointing in Longchamp's Prix de l'Opera. A mile on soft ground is her optimum. **R Collet in FR [1-10].*

TYCOON'S LAST BHB 57f **RR 56f** 5150[11]
2 b f Nalchik (USA) 12.6f **(44)** - Royal Tycoon (Tycoon II) 8.7f **(47)**
Form - 6674000
Record 1999 - 1st:0 2nd:0 3rd:0 Ran:7
Win Prizemoney £0 *Total Prizemoney* £331
1999 Turf 0-7: (5f 3, 6f 4) (sft, g-s, gd, g-f 2, frm, hrd)
Fair filly. Turf high 56. **W M Brisbourne [0-7] L R Owen.*

TYCOON TINA BHB 28f28a **RR 22f 28a** 4829[8]
5 b m Tina's Pet 7.4f **(56)** - Royal Tycoon (Tycoon II) 8.7f **(47)**
Form - 85705728678
Record 1999 - 1st:0 2nd:1 3rd:0 Ran:11
Pre1999 - 1st:3 2nd:5 3rd:1 Ran:28
Win Prizemoney £8,232 *Total Prizemoney* £14,146
Wins * 1998 Apr Beverl (SFT) H 9.9f 53 58 <
* 1998 Mar Hamilt (HVY) H 12.1f 49 52
* 1997 May Mussel (G-S) H 8f 46 51
1999 Turf 0-10: (9f, 10f, 11f 4, 12f 2, 13f 2) (hvy 2, sft, gd 3, g-f 2, frm 2) 1999 AW 0-1: (12f) (Fibr)
Little account filly, effective 10 to 13f, acts on sft to gd, has worn blinkers, likes right handed tracks. Turf high 38. .
**W M Brisbourne [3-42] D Slingsby.*

TYLER'S TOAST BHB 67f62a **RR 74f 62a** 4222[10]
3 ch g Grand Lodge (USA) - Catawba (Mill Reef (USA)) 10.5f **(78)**
Form - 6640
Record 1999 - 1st:0 2nd:0 3rd:0 Ran:4
Pre1999 - 1st:0 2nd:0 3rd:1 Ran:1
Win Prizemoney £0 *Total Prizemoney* £774
1999 Turf 0-3: (10f 3) (g-f, frm 2) 1999 AW 0-1: (8f) (Fibr)
Lengthy, above-average gelding. Turf high 74.
**W Jarvis [0-5] Lady Howard de Walden.*

TYPHOON EIGHT (IRE) BHB 42f32a **RR 37f 32a** 1374[5]
7 b g High Estate 10.5f **(66)** - Dance Date (IRE) (Sadler's Wells (USA)) 10f **(76)**
Form - 008020505
Record 1999 - 1st:0 2nd:1 3rd:0 Ran:9
Pre1999 - 1st:1 2nd:1 3rd:2 Ran:24
Win Prizemoney £4,662 *Total Prizemoney* £9,477
Wins 1996 Oct Catter (GD) H 12f 66 71 <
1999 Turf 0-6: (10f, 11f, 12f 2, 14f 2) (gd 3, g-f, frm 2) 1999 AW 0-3: (8f 2, 11f) (Fibr 3)
Very moderate gelding, effective 10f, acts on gd, has worn blinkers, likes left handed tracks. Turf high 48 - 2nd of 18 getting 17lb

from Aspirant Dancer (28 Apr Pontefract 10f gd RF 0907). AW high 29. Consistent.
**D Nicholls [0-13] Cairnford Ltd (from R W Armstrong [0-5] Aug 1997).*

TYPHOON GINGER (IRE) BHB 61f **RR 62f** 4752[3]

4 ch f Archway (IRE) 8.5f **(60)** - Pallas Viking (Viking (USA)) 6.7f **(65)**
Form - 80345243

Record	**1999** -	1st:0	2nd:1	3rd:2	Ran:8
	Pre1999 -	1st:0	2nd:1	3rd:1	Ran:5

Win Prizemoney £0 *Total Prizemoney* £5,128
1999 Turf 0-8: (6f, 7f 2, 8f 3, 10f 2) (gd 2, g-f 2, frm 4)
Scopey, average filly, effective 6 to 10f, acts on gd to frm, best on gd. Turf high 62 - 3rd of 20 getting 11lb from King Priam (6 Oct York 10f gd RF 4752). Consistent. **G Woodward [0-13] Andrew Lloyd.*

TYPHOON TILLY BHB 50f **RR 65f** 5208[18]

2 b c Hernando (FR) - Meavy **(77f)** (Kalaglow) 9.8f **(67)**
Form - 080

Record	**1999** -	1st:0	2nd:0	3rd:0	Ran:3

1999 Turf 0-3: (7f, 8f 2) (g-s, gd 2)
Currently average colt. Turf high 65. **C F Wall [0-3] M Tilbrook.*

TYRA RR 48f 3306[2]

3 b f Lion Cavern (USA) 7.5f **(74)** -Lara (USA)(Lyphard (USA)) 9.9f **(72)**
Form - 2

Record	**1999** -	1st:0	2nd:1	3rd:0	Ran:1

Win Prizemoney £0 *Total Prizemoney* £1,214
1999 Turf 0-1: (8f) (frm)
Scopey, currently moderate filly. (1st run) - 2nd of 9 getting 5lb from Reviewing (2 Aug Windsor 8f frm RF 3306).
**H R A Cecil [0-1] Buckram Oak Holdings.*

TYROLEAN DANCER (IRE) BHB 26f **RR** 1816[18]

5 b m Tirol 8.1f **(64)** - Waffling (Lomond (USA)) 8.8f **(65)**
Form - 00

Record	**1999** -	1st:0	2nd:0	3rd:0	Ran:2
	Pre1999 -	1st:0	2nd:0	3rd:0	Ran:9

Win Prizemoney £0 *Total Prizemoney* £227
1999 Turf 0-1: (12f) (g-f) 1999 AW 0-1: (16f) (Equi)
Very poor filly.
**A J Chamberlain [0-11] Exors of the late Ms Paula Birchall (from S P C Woods [0-5] Jly 1997).*

TYROLEAN DREAM (IRE) BHB 64f **RR 65f** 1397[10]

5 b g Tirol 8.1f **(64)** - Heavenly Hope (Glenstal (USA)) 10.1f **(64)**
Form - 0

Record	**1999** -	1st:0	2nd:0	3rd:0	Ran:1
	Pre1999 -	1st:1	2nd:1	3rd:0	Ran:9

Win Prizemoney £3,468 *Total Prizemoney* £4,328
Wins * 1997 Spt Hamilt (GD) 9.2f 51 <
1999 Turf 0-1: (12f) (frm)
Average gelding. **M H Tompkins [5-21] P Heath.*

TYROLEAN LOVE (IRE) BHB 52f **RR 49f** 1819[15]

3 b f Tirol 8.1f **(64)** - Paradise Forum (Prince Sabo) 7.2f **(62)**
Form - 040

Record	**1999** -	1st:0	2nd:0	3rd:0	Ran:3
	Pre1999 -	1st:0	2nd:0	3rd:0	Ran:2

Win Prizemoney £0 *Total Prizemoney* £193
1999 Turf 0-3: (7f, 8f, 10f) (g-f, frm, hrd)
Scopey, moderate filly. Turf high 49.
**C A Horgan [0-5] Mrs B Sumner.*

TZARINASSILOUHETTE BHB 48f45a **RR 49f 45a** 4705[8]

2 b f Puissance 7.1f **(60)** - Tzarina (USA) (Gallant Romeo (USA)) 8.4f **(64)**
Form - 404308

Record	**1999** -	1st:0	2nd:0	3rd:1	Ran:6

Win Prizemoney £0 *Total Prizemoney* £282
1999 Turf 0-5: (5f 2, 6f 2, 7f) (gd, g-f 2, frm 2) 1999 AW 0-1: (5f) (Fibr)
Moderate filly, has worn blinkers. Turf high 49 (began Jly).
**B Palling [0-6] R R Dunford.*

UBITOO RR 31f 5194[16]

2 b c Puissance 7.1f **(60)** - Cassiar (Connaught) 7.7f **(63)**
Form - 0

Record	**1999** -	1st:0	2nd:0	3rd:0	Ran:1

1999 Turf 0-1: (6f) (gd)
Currently very moderate colt. **R M Flower [0-1] T J Lowe & P Wager.*

U K MAGIC (IRE) BHB 53f **RR 61f** 910[15]

4 b g Alzao (USA) 9.8f **(73)** - Lightino (Bustino) 10.4f **(64)**
Form - 800

Record	**1999** -	1st:0	2nd:0	3rd:0	Ran:3
	Pre1999 -	1st:0	2nd:1	3rd:0	Ran:7

Win Prizemoney £0 *Total Prizemoney* £1,342
1999 Turf 0-2: (10f, 12f) (hvy, frm) 1999 AW 0-1: (11f) (Fibr)
Neat, average gelding, effective 10 to 11f, acts on gd to frm, has worn blinkers, prefers tight tracks. Turf high 6. Becoming disappointing.
**J R Jenkins [0-6] UK Packaging Supplies Ltd (from J E Banks [0-7] Aug 1998).*

ULSHAW RR 39f 4278[5]

2 ch c Salse (USA) 10.9f **(71)** - Kintail (Kris) 9.5f **(73)**
Form - 75

Record	**1999** -	1st:0	2nd:0	3rd:0	Ran:2

1999 Turf 0-2: (7f, 8f) (frm 2)
Currently very moderate colt. Turf high 39 (began Aug).
**J D Bethell [0-2] Clarendon Thoroughbred Racing II.*

ULTRA BEET BHB 42f42a **RR 30f 42a** 3015[7]

7 b g Puissance 7.1f **(60)** - Cassiar (Connaught) 7.7f **(63)**
Form - 064007007

Record	**1999** -	1st:0	2nd:0	3rd:0	Ran:5
	Pre1999 -	1st:9	2nd:8	3rd:9	Ran:64

Win Prizemoney £26,285 *Total Prizemoney* £35,877

Wins								
	1997	*Jan*	*Lingfi*	*(STD)*	H	*6f*	*65*	*68*
	1996	*Aug*	*Wolver*	*(STD)*	S	*6f*		*57*
	1995	Jun	Hamilt	(FRM)	H	6f	66	73
	1995	*Mar*	*Wolver*	*(STD)*	C	*5f*		*75*
	1995	*Feb*	*Lingfi*	*(STD)*	H	*5f*	*76*	*79* <
	1995	*Jan*	*Lingfi*	*(STD)*	C	*5f*		*68*
	1995	*Jan*	*Wolver*	*(STD)*	C	*5f*		*71*
	1995	*Jan*	*Lingfi*	*(STD)*		*5f*		*71*

(First row: 1997 *Jan Wolver (STD)* C *6f* *72*)

1999 Turf 0-4: (6f, 7f, 8f 2) (g-f, frm 3) 1999 AW 0-1: (7f) (Equi)
Fair gelding, effective 6f, acts on g-f - acts on AW, has worn blinkers (extremely effectively). Turf high 41.
**R M Flower [0-16] The Forging Ahead Partnership (from P C Haslam [9-53] Feb 1998).*

ULTRA CALM (IRE) BHB 61f59a **RR 65f 59a** 4935[15]

3 ch g Doubletour (USA) 12f **(46)** - Shyonn (IRE) (Shy Groom (USA)) 10f **(66)**
Form - 44127112650

Record	**1999** -	1st:3	2nd:2	3rd:0	Ran:11
	Pre1999 -	1st:0	2nd:0	3rd:0	Ran:3

Win Prizemoney £7,195 *Total Prizemoney* £9,091

Wins								
	*** 1999**	Apr	Ripon	(G-F)	H	10f	54	61+
	*** 1999**	*Mar*	*Wolver*	*(SLW)*		*8.5f*		*63* <
	*** 1999**	*Jan*	*Wolver*	*(STD)*	C	*9.4f*		*54*

1999 Turf 1-4: (9f, 10f 1-2, 11f) (g-s, gd, g-f 1-1, frm) 1999 AW 2-7: (7f, 8f 1-4, 9f 1-1, 10f) (Equi, Fibr 2-6)
Leggy, average gelding, effective 8 to 10f, best at 8f, acts on g-s to g-f - acts on Fibr, has worn blinkers, prefers tight tracks. Turf high 65 - 2nd of 14 giving 5lb to Archie Babe (10 May Redcar 10f g-s RF 1128) - also 1st of 23 giving 9lb to Trois Elles (7 Apr Ripon RF 0617). AW high 68 - 2nd of 9 giving 11lb to Lady Peppiatt (25 Jan Southwell 8f Fibr RF 0160) - also 1st of 9 from Miss Take (6 Mar Wolverhampton RF 0406). **P C Haslam [3-14] Miss J V Brindley.*

UMBRIAN GOLD (IRE) BHB 76f **RR 75f** 4095[10]

3 b f Perugino (USA) - Golden Sunlight (Ile de Bourbon (USA)) 10.1f **(67)**
Form - 722210

Record	**1999** -	1st:1	2nd:3	3rd:0	Ran:6
	Pre1999 -	1st:0	2nd:1	3rd:0	Ran:1

Win Prizemoney £5,498 *Total Prizemoney* £10,261
Wins *** 1999** Aug Ascot (SFT) 7f 75 <
1999 Turf 1-6: (7f 1-4, 8f 2) (gd 1-1, g-f 3, frm 2)
Workmanlike, above-average filly, effective 7 to 8f, best at 7f, acts on gd to frm. Turf high 75 - 1st of 5 getting 5lb from Dangerous Fortune (8 Aug Ascot RF 3465).

*J A R Toller [1-7] Mrs R W Gore-Andrews.

UMISTIM BHB 100f **RR 96f** 5029[1]
2 ch c Inchinor 8.9f **(64)** - Simply Sooty (Absalom) 7.2f **(58)**
Form - 31151
Record 1999 - 1st:3 2nd:0 3rd:1 Ran:5
Win Prizemoney £32,072 *Total Prizemoney* £32,803
Wins * **1999** Oct Newbur (G-S) G3 7.3f 96 <
* **1999** Aug Windso (HVY) 6f 94+
* **1999** Jly Newbur (G-F) 7.3f 85
1999 Turf 3-5: (6f 1-2, 7f 2-3) (g-s 1-1, gd 1-2, frm 1-2)
Very useful colt. Turf high 96 - 1st of 9 from Cape Town (22 Oct Newbury RF 5029) - also 1st of 7 from Final Row (9 Aug Windsor RF 3486). Stepped up in trip from his Bath debut, he battled on well to land a Newbury maiden on his second start. Followed up in very soft ground at Windsor, and put in a moderate effort behind him when springing a surprise in the Horris Hill Stakes.
. *R Hannon [3-5] Mrs S Joint.

UNA (IRE) BHB 45f40a **RR 33f 40a** 5147[9]
3 b f Lion Cavern (USA) 7.5f **(74)** - Prosperous Lady (Prince Tenderfoot (USA)) 9f **(61)**
Form - 780
Record 1999 - 1st:0 2nd:0 3rd:0 Ran:3
1999 Turf 0-2: (7f, 9f) (gd 2) 1999 AW 0-1: (8f) (Fibr)
Workmanlike, currently very moderate filly. Turf high 33 (began Spt). *R A Fahey [0-3] Mrs Doreen Swinburn.

UNAWARE BHB 93f **RR 81+f** 4695[4]
2 b c Unfuwain (USA) 11.4f **(74)** - Rainbow Lake (Rainbow Quest (USA)) 10.4f **(75)**
Form - 4184
Record 1999 - 1st:1 2nd:0 3rd:0 Ran:4
Win Prizemoney £3,582 *Total Prizemoney* £4,408
Wins * **1999** Aug Chepst (G-S) 8.1f 81+ <
1999 Turf 1-4: (7f, 8f 1-3) (g-s, gd 1-2, frm)
Decent colt. Turf high 81 (began Aug) - 1st of 9 from Colonial Rule (30 Aug Chepstow RF 4007). Came on from his Newbury debut and won over a mile at Chepstow next time with a deal in hand. Held in better company. *R Charlton [1-4] K Abdulla.

UNCHAIN MY HEART BHB 54f **RR 55f** 4359[13]
3 b f Pursuit of Love 9.5f **(69)** - Addicted to Love **(66f)** (Touching Wood (USA)) 8.2f **(55)**
Form - 330303422420
Record 1999 - 1st:0 2nd:3 3rd:4 Ran:12
Pre1999 - 1st:0 2nd:0 3rd:1 Ran:3
Win Prizemoney £0 *Total Prizemoney* £4,539
1999 Turf 0-12: (7f 4, 8f 6, 10f 2) (g-s 3, gd 2, g-f 2, frm 5)
Scopey, fair filly, effective 6 to 8f, acts on gd to frm, has worn blinkers (effectively). Turf high 67 - 3rd of 15 getting 3lb from Picture Puzzle (26 May Yarmouth 8f g-f RF 1509).
*B J Meehan [0-15] Mascalls Stud.

UNCHANGED BHB 57f **RR 62f** 3048[9]
7 b m Unfuwain (USA) 11.4f **(74)** - Favorable Exchange (USA) (Exceller (USA)) 12.5f **(74)**
Form - 088300
Record 1999 - 1st:0 2nd:0 3rd:1 Ran:6
Pre1999 - 1st:4 2nd:3 3rd:2 Ran:25
Win Prizemoney £18,173 *Total Prizemoney* £29,191
Wins 1998 May Thirsk (GD) H 16f 60 66
1997 Spt Folkes (FRM) H 15.4f 60 64
1995 Spt Cheste (G-S) H 15.9f 66 74 <
1995 Spt Folkes (G-F) H 15.4f 62 69
1999 Turf 0-6: (14f, 16f 5) (gd 3, g-f, frm 2)
Average mare, effective 16f, acts on gd to frm, best on gd, has worn blinkers, likes left handed tracks. Turf high 62 - 3rd of 12 giving 16lb to Whitley Grange Boy (1 Jly Catterick 16f g-f RF 2455). Consistent. She is not particularly consistent these days, and only shows her best form from time to time. Acts well on a tight track.
*J L Harris [0-6] Mrs Annette Harris (from John Harris [1-5] Jun 1998).

UNCLE DOUG BHB 56f51a **RR 58df 51a** 2369[5]
8 b g Common Grounds 8.1f **(66)** - Taqa (Blakeney) 10.5f **(64)**
Form - 5
Record 1999 - 1st:0 2nd:0 3rd:0 Ran:1
Pre1999 - 1st:3 2nd:5 3rd:2 Ran:33
Win Prizemoney £11,120 *Total Prizemoney* £19,416
Wins 1996 Aug Ripon (HVY) H 16f 55 60 <
1996 May Thirsk (G-F) H 16f 49 56
1999 Turf 0-1: (17f) (frm)
Fair gelding. Inconsistent.
*J L Eyre [0-7] D D Saul (from Mrs M Reveley [6-39] Oct 1997).

UNCLE EXACT BHB 80f **RR 85?f** 5214[9]
2 b c Distant Relative 7f **(69)** - True Precision **(61f 59a)** (Presidium)
Form - 3144505020
Record 1999 - 1st:1 2nd:1 3rd:1 Ran:10
Win Prizemoney £3,436 *Total Prizemoney* £5,637
Wins 1999 May Hamilt (G-F) 5f 79+ <
1999 Turf 1-10: (5f 1-8, 6f 2) (g-s 2, gd 5, g-f 1-1, frm 2)
Useful colt, effective 5f, acts on gd to g-f. Turf high 85 - 2nd of 7 giving 2lb to Lady Sarka (16 Oct Catterick 5f gd RF 4908) - also 1st of 4 giving 5lb to College Maid (6 May Hamilton RF 1056).
*K A Ryan [0-7] The Good Hand Racing Club (from J Berry [1-3] May 1999).

UNCLE OBERON BHB 65f **RR 62f** 1912[9]
3 b c Distant Relative 7f **(69)** - Fairy Story (IRE) **(75f 64a)** (Persian Bold) 9.3f **(66)**
Form - 50
Record 1999 - 1st:0 2nd:0 3rd:0 Ran:2
Pre1999 - 1st:0 2nd:0 3rd:0 Ran:2
1999 Turf 0-2: (6f, 7f) (gd, g-f)
Workmanlike, average colt. Turf high 62.
*G A Butler [0-4] The Fairy Story Partnership.

UNDER THE CLOCK RR 63f 4038[R]
5 ch m Anshan 8.2f **(63)** - Worthy Venture (Northfields (USA)) 9f **(72)**
Form - 50R
Record 1999 - 1st:0 2nd:0 3rd:0 Ran:3
1999 Turf 0-3: (8f 3) (gd, frm 2)
Currently average filly. Turf high 63 (began Aug).
*J G Given [0-3] A Clarke.

UNDETERRED BHB 96f **RR 105df** 4896[17]
3 ch c Zafonic (USA) 9f **(83)** - Mint Crisp (IRE) (Green Desert (USA)) 8.6f **(78)**
Form - 43480
Record 1999 - 1st:0 2nd:0 3rd:1 Ran:5
Pre1999 - 1st:2 2nd:0 3rd:0 Ran:4
Win Prizemoney £13,814 *Total Prizemoney* £18,406
Wins * 1998 Oct York (GD) L 6f 99 <
* 1998 Aug Yarmou (FRM) 6f 69
1999 Turf 0-5: (6f 3, 7f 2) (g-s, gd 2, g-f 2)
Pattern-class colt, effective 6 to 7f, acts on gd to g-f. Turf high 105 - 3rd of 5 giving 9lb to Fragrant Oasis (15 May Newmarket 7f g-f RF 1243). He was very disappointing last season, playing up in the stalls on occasions. He might just have an idea or two, and is likely to remain hard to place. *C F Wall [2-9] S Fustok.

UNFORTUNATE BHB 40f45a **RR 29f 45a** 5150[12]
2 ch f Komaite (USA) 6.9f **(61)** - Honour and Glory (Hotfoot) 10.5f **(59)**
Form - 0760
Record 1999 - 1st:0 2nd:0 3rd:0 Ran:4
1999 Turf 0-3: (6f 2, 7f) (g-s, gd, hrd) 1999 AW 0-1: (7f) (Fibr)
Moderate filly. Turf high 29 (began Aug).
*Miss J F Craze [0-4] P Walton.

UNGARO (GER) RR 120f 3784a[1]
5 b h Goofalik (USA) 15.4f **(66)** - Ustina (GER) (Star Appeal) 9.6f **(65)**
Form - 02211
1999 Turf 2-4: (12f 2-4) (sft 1-1, gd 1-2, g-f)
Very high-class colt, effective 8 to 12f, best at 12f, acts on sft to g-f, best on gd, prefers right handed tracks, and excels at Gelsenkirchen-Horst and Cologne. Turf high 120 - 1st of 4 from Wins Fiction (15 Aug Gelsenkirchen-Horst RF 3784a) - also 1st of 5 giving 14lb to Sumitas (25 Jly Dusseldorf RF 3232a). Consistent. A useful German-trained colt, he was narrowly beaten by Tiger Hill at Cologne and Dark Moondancer at San Siro early on last season, before gaining narrow victories in a couple of Group Ones in his native country. He just finds the better foreign-trained Group per-

formers a little too good for him.
**H Blume in GER [6-17] Gestut Rottgen.*

UNICAMP BHB 83f **RR 82df** 1508^{6}
3 ch f Royal Academy (USA) 7.8f **(77)** - Honeyspike (IRE) **(64f)** (Chief's Crown (USA)) 9.8f **(72)**
Form - 06
Record 1999 - 1st:0 2nd:0 3rd:0 Ran:2
Pre1999 - 1st:1 2nd:1 3rd:0 Ran:4
Win Prizemoney £3,492 *Total Prizemoney* £5,195
Wins * 1998 May Nottin (FRM) 6.1f 67+ <
1999 Turf 0-2: (6f, 8f) (g-f 2)
Neat, decent filly, effective 5f, acts on frm. Turf high 71.
**E A L Dunlop [1-6] Coutinho Nogueira.*

UNICORN STAR (IRE) RR 60f 5186^{4}
2 b g Persian Bold 10f **(69)** - Highland Warning **(36f 44a)** (Warning)
Form - 04
Record 1999 - 1st:0 2nd:0 3rd:0 Ran:2
Win Prizemoney £0 *Total Prizemoney* £225
1999 Turf 0-2: (7f 2) (gd, g-f)
Currently average gelding. Turf high 60 (began Oct).
**J S Wainwright [0-2] P Wong & T Leung.*

UNIFORM BHB 58f58a **RR 59f 58a** 2455^{7}
4 ch f Unfuwain (USA) 11.4f **(74)** - Trachelium **(44df)** (Formidable (USA)) 9.2f **(63)**
Form - 15513137
Record 1999 - 1st:3 2nd:0 3rd:2 Ran:8
Pre1999 - 1st:1 2nd:0 3rd:3 Ran:11
Win Prizemoney £11,411 *Total Prizemoney* £13,848
Wins * **1999** Jun Hamilt (G-S) H 13f 56 57
* **1999** May Hamilt (GD) H 13f 52 56
* **1999** *Feb Southw (STD) H 16f 52 58* <
* 1998 Spt Hamilt (SFT) H 12.1f 51 54
1999 Turf 2-6: (13f 2-3, 16f 3) (gd 1-3, g-f 1-3) 1999 AW 1-2: (16f 1-2) (Fibr 1-2)
Scopey, fair filly, effective 12 to 16f, best at 16f, acts on g-s to g-f - acts on Fibr, best on gd, favours tight tracks, excels at Southwell and Hamilton. Turf high 59 - 3rd of 12 getting 3lb from Here Comes Herbie (24 Jun Newcastle 16f gd RF 2267) - also 1st of 8 from Spartan Royale (9 Jun Hamilton RF 1860). AW high 58 (1st run) - 1st of 10 giving 22lb to Keepsake (19 Feb Southwell RF 0323). Consistent. **Miss S E Hall [6-23] C Platts.*

UNIMPEACHABLE (IRE) BHB 64f **RR 73f** 5192^{5}
2 b f Namaqualand (USA) - Bourbon Topsy (Ile de Bourbon (USA)) 10.1f **(67)**
Form - 73015
Record 1999 - 1st:1 2nd:0 3rd:1 Ran:5
Win Prizemoney £2,092 *Total Prizemoney* £2,544
Wins * **1999** Oct Nottin (GD) S 8.2f 73 <
1999 Turf 1-5: (6f, 7f, 8f 1-3) (g-s, gd 1-3, g-f)
Above-average filly. Turf high 73 - 3rd of 9 to So Precious (20 Spt Kempton 7f g-s RF 4428) - also 1st of 18 getting 5lb from Swaldo (21 Oct Nottingham RF 5002).
**P F I Cole [1-5] Bernard Gover Bloodstock Trading Ltd.*

UNION PROJECT (IRE) RR 92f $2414a^{1}$
3 ch c Project Manager 7.2f **(47)** - Nordic Union 00
Form - 32211
1999 Turf 2-5: (7f, 8f 2-3, 9f) (sft 2, gd 1-2, g-f 1-1)
Useful colt, effective 7 to 8f, best at 8f, acts on sft to g-f, best on gd, has worn blinkers. Turf high 92 - 1st of 10 from Moiseyev (26 Jun Curragh RF 2414a) - also 1st of 15 from Eternal Night (19 May Leopardstown RF 1465b). Improving.
**J S Bolger in IRE [2-9] Mrs J S Bolger.*

UNITE'S BIG RED (USA) RR 91f $5230a^{12}$
5 m Unite (USA) - Tropical Reality (USA) (Bold Tropic (SAF))
Form - 0
1999 Turf 0-1: (12f) (frm)
Currently useful. **R Mills in USA [0-1].*

UNITUS (IRE) BHB 37f37a **RR 32f 37a** 1300^{8}
6 b h Soviet Star (USA) 8.6f **(74)** - Unite (Kris) 9.5f **(73)**
Form - 008306488
Record 1999 - 1st:0 2nd:0 3rd:1 Ran:8
Pre1999 - 1st:1 2nd:1 3rd:0 Ran:16
Win Prizemoney £3,753 *Total Prizemoney* £5,936
Wins 1996 Jly Windso (G-F) 10f 78+ <
1999 Turf 0-1: (18f) (gd) 1999 AW 0-7: (7f, 11f 3, 12f 2, 16f) (Fibr 7)
Very moderate horse. AW high 46.
**M C Chapman [1-24] Barry Brown (from Sir Michael Stoute [1-6] May 1997).*

UNIVERSUS (GER) RR 107f $4111a^{2}$
3 f
Form - 572
1999 Turf 0-3: (11f, 12f 2) (gd 2, g-f)
Currently Pattern-class. Turf high 107 - 2nd of 7 to Hibiscus (29 Aug Baden-Baden 11f gd RF 4111a). **H Blume in GER [0-3].*

UNLIKELY LADY BHB 44f **RR 57df** 4723^{11}
3 b f Clantime 6.6f **(57)** - Casbar Lady (Native Bazaar) 6.9f **(62)**
Form - 460
Record 1999 - 1st:0 2nd:0 3rd:0 Ran:3
Win Prizemoney £0 *Total Prizemoney* £195
1999 Turf 0-3: (6f 3) (gd 2, frm)
Neat, currently fair filly. Turf high 57. **D W Barker [0-3] D W Barker.*

UNMASKED BHB 38f **RR 25?f** 4720^{10}
3 ch f Safawan 6.6f **(60)** - Unveiled **(54f 48a)** (Sayf El Arab (USA)) 7.1f **(54)**
Form - 0
Record 1999 - 1st:0 2nd:0 3rd:0 Ran:1
Pre1999 - 1st:0 2nd:0 3rd:0 Ran:2
Win Prizemoney £0 *Total Prizemoney* £183
1999 Turf 0-1: (8f) (gd)
Neat, currently little account filly.
**J S Goldie [0-1] William Burns (from J Berry [0-2] Jly 1998).*

U-NO-HARRY (IRE) BHB 39f40a **RR 42f 40a** 2160^{8}
6 b h Mansooj 10.6f **(53)** - Lady Roberta (USA) (Roberto (USA)) 10f **(76)**
Form - 00006565508
Record 1999 - 1st:0 2nd:0 3rd:0 Ran:10
Pre1999 - 1st:7 2nd:7 3rd:10 Ran:67
Win Prizemoney £22,180 *Total Prizemoney* £32,260
Wins * 1998 *Aug Southw (STD) C 7f 59*
* 1998 *Feb Southw (STD) S 7f 55*
* 1996 Jly Cheste (G-F) H 5.1f 68 69 <
* 1996 Jun Lingfi (FRM) H 6f 57 65
* 1996 Jun Thirsk (FRM) H 6f 57 52
* 1995 Jly Catter (G-F) S 5f 66
* 1995 May Leices (G-F) C 6f 66
1999 Turf 0-3: (6f 2, 8f) (sft, g-f, frm) 1999 AW 0-7: (6f, 7f 3, 8f 3) (Fibr 7)
Moderate horse, effective 7f, - acts on Fibr, has worn blinkers, likes left handed tracks, favours tight tracks. Turf high 42. AW high 36. **R Hollinshead [7-77] D Coppenhall.*

UNREAL CITY (IRE) BHB 100f80a **RR 96?f 80a** 258^{3}
6 b g Rock City 8.8f **(62)** - Tolmi (Great Nephew) 9.9f **(64)**
Form - 263
Record 1999 - 1st:0 2nd:0 3rd:1 Ran:1
Pre1999 - 1st:1 2nd:2 3rd:0 Ran:5
Win Prizemoney £3,192 *Total Prizemoney* £7,366
Wins 1996 Apr Ripon (G-F) 8f 78+ <
1999 AW 0-1: (10f) (Equi)
Very useful gelding.
**G Wragg [0-3] L Marinopoulos (from H R A Cecil [1-3] May 1996).*

UNSEEDED RR 84+f 5020^{4}
2 ch f Unfuwain (USA) 11.4f **(74)** - Sesame (Derrylin) 8.8f **(54)**
Form - 04
Record 1999 - 1st:0 2nd:0 3rd:0 Ran:2
Win Prizemoney £0 *Total Prizemoney* £273
1999 Turf 0-2: (7f, 8f) (gd 2)
Currently decent filly. Turf high 84 (began Oct) - 4th of 18 to Interlude (22 Oct Doncaster 8f gd RF 5020).
**J L Dunlop [0-2] Christopher Spence.*

UNSHAKEN BHB 75f67a **RR 75f 67a** 4984[13]

5 b h Environment Friend 7.5f **(67)** - Reel Foyle (USA) (Irish River (FR)) 8.6f **(78)**

Form - 3321710041057004300

Record **1999** - 1st:3 2nd:1 3rd:3 Ran:19
Pre1999 - 1st:3 2nd:3 3rd:4 Ran:25

Win Prizemoney £40,602 *Total Prizemoney* £57,524

Wins * **1999** Jun Newcas (G-F) H 6f 75 81
* **1999** May Hamilt (GD) H 6f 73 80
* **1999** Apr Hamilt (HVY) H 6f 68 73
* 1998 Jun Hamilt (G-S) 6f 67
* 1998 May Carlis (G-S) H 5.9f 46 56
1996 Oct Folkes (G-S) 5f 86 <

1999 Turf 3-17: (5f 4, 6f 3-13) (hvy 1-1, g-s 3, gd 7, g-f 1-4, frm 1-2)
1999 AW 0-2: (6f 2) (Fibr 2)

Above-average colt, effective 5 to 6f, best at 6f, acts on hvy to frm, has worn blinkers, excels at Hamilton. Turf high 81 - 1st of 19 giving 1lb to Euro Venture (26 Jun Newcastle RF 2334) - also 1st of 12 getting 11lb from Further Outlook (2 May Hamilton RF 0973). AW high 68. He performed well on Fibresand at the start of the year, and has done well since returning to turf. He had the draw in his favour when winning twice at Hamilton, and showed that he can win on fast ground when landing the Tote Northern Sprint Trophy at Newcastle, again from a favourable draw.

**E J Alston [5-37] G G Sanderson & M Twentyman & A J Picton (from J R Fanshawe [1-7] Jly 1997).*

UNTOLD RICHES (USA) BHB 92f **RR 91f** 4095[12]

3 b f Red Ransom (USA) 8.6f **(83)** - Asdaf (USA) **(57f)** (Forty Niner (USA))

Form - 582131140

Record **1999** - 1st:3 2nd:1 3rd:1 Ran:9
Pre1999 - 1st:0 2nd:0 3rd:0 Ran:3

Win Prizemoney £19,927 *Total Prizemoney* £24,172

Wins * **1999** Jly Goodwo (G-F) H 9f 79 83 <
* **1999** Jly Haydoc (FRM) H 8.1f 72 82
* **1999** Jun Nottin (GD) H 8.2f 69 73

1999 Turf 3-9: (6f, 7f 3, 8f 2-4, 9f 1-1) (gd 2, g-f 2-3, frm 1-3, hrd)

Scopey, useful filly, effective 8 to 9f, best at 8f, acts on gd to frm, has worn blinkers. Turf high 91 - 4th of 9 to Tycoon's Dolce (22 Aug Deauville 8f gd RF 3931a) - also 1st of 13 giving 1lb to Desdemona (28 Jly Goodwood RF 3211). In cracking form last term, having won three times at distances around a mile. The best of those successes came at Glorious Goodwood when she made all to win a competitive nine-furlong handicap. She has been found wanting in better company since.

**J H M Gosden [3-12] H E Sheikh Rashid Al Maktoum.*

UNTOLD STORY (USA) BHB 38f **RR 24f** 5156[16]

4 b g Theatrical 11.5f **(78)** - Committed Miss (USA) (Key To Content (USA)) 8f **(54)**

Form - 03700000

Record **1999** - 1st:0 2nd:0 3rd:1 Ran:8
Pre1999 - 1st:0 2nd:0 3rd:0 Ran:5

Win Prizemoney £0 *Total Prizemoney* £236

1999 Turf 0-8: (7f 2, 8f 3, 10f 3) (hvy, gd 3, g-f, frm 2)

Little account gelding, has worn blinkers. Turf high 58. Becoming disappointing.

**T Keddy [0-4] Miss Karina Dudas (from D K Weld in IRE [0-9] Jly 1999).*

UP AND ABOUT BHB 50f66a **RR 44f 66a** 5168[10]

3 b f Barathea (IRE) - Upend (Main Reef) 9.6f **(57)**

Form - 670160

Record **1999** - 1st:1 2nd:0 3rd:0 Ran:6
Pre1999 - 1st:0 2nd:0 3rd:0 Ran:1

Win Prizemoney £2,318 *Total Prizemoney* £2,318

Wins * **1999** *Oct Wolver (STD) H 14.8f 55 62* <

1999 Turf 0-5: (7f 2, 10f, 14f 2) (g-s 2, gd, frm 2) 1999 AW 1-1: (15f 1-1) (Fibr 1-1)

Scopey, average filly, effective 15f, - acts on Fibr, likes left handed tracks, likes tight tracks. Turf high 47 (began Spt). (1st run) - 1st of 12 getting 10lb from Praslin Island (13 Oct Wolverhampton RF 4863). Another Sir Mark Prescott inmate who really came to herself when faced with a trip more in line with her breeding. She bolted up in a maiden handicap over the extended 14 furlongs on the Wolverhampton Fibresand in October. Disappointed on turf three days later, but the race may have come too soon.

**Sir Mark Prescott [1-6] P D Player (from D R Loder [0-1] Spt 1998).*

UP AND AWAY (GER) **RR 107f** 4662a[2]

5 b g Le Glorieux - Ultima Ratio (GER) (Vice Regal (NZ))

Form - 32

1999 Turf 0-2: (8f 2) (sft, gd)

Currently Pattern-class gelding. Turf high 107 (began Aug) - 2nd of 7 to El Divino (25 Spt Cologne 8f sft RF 4662a).

**Frau E Mader in GER [0-2].*

UP IN FLAMES (IRE) BHB 45f41a **RR 50f 41a** 119[11]

8 br g Nashamaa 8.1f **(58)** - Bella Lucia (Camden Town) 9.3f **(53)**

Form - 37680

Record **1999** - 1st:0 2nd:0 3rd:0 Ran:2
Pre1999 - 1st:5 2nd:5 3rd:4 Ran:54

Win Prizemoney £25,525 *Total Prizemoney* £33,062

Wins * 1998 *Jan Southw (STD) H 8f 47 55*
* 1997 *Dec Wolver (STD) H 9.4f 41 46*
* 1997 Nov Nottin (GD) H 8.2f 43 46
1995 Jun Epsom (G-F) H 8.5f 70 75 <
1995 May Haydoc (GD) H 8.1f 63 71+

1999 AW 0-2: (8f 2) (Fibr 2)

Fair gelding, effective 8f, acts on gd - acts on Fibr, has worn blinkers, likes left handed tracks, likes tight tracks. AW high 30.

**S R Bowring [3-30] Mark Kilner (from M D Hammond [2-23] Aug 1996).*

UPLIFTING BHB 69f **RR 69f** 5065[16]

4 b f Magic Ring (IRE) 6.5f **(64)** - Strapless (Bustino) 10.4f **(64)**

Form - 21600380

Record **1999** - 1st:1 2nd:1 3rd:1 Ran:8
Pre1999 - 1st:1 2nd:3 3rd:1 Ran:11

Win Prizemoney £9,604 *Total Prizemoney* £17,909

Wins * **1999** May Goodwo (GD) H 6f 66 68
* 1998 Jly Leices (GD) 5f 74+ <

1999 Turf 1-8: (5f 2, 6f 1-6) (g-s, gd 1-3, g-f, frm 3)

Small, average filly, effective 5 to 6f, best at 6f, acts on gd to frm, best on gd, has worn blinkers. Turf high 69 - 3rd of 27 getting 13lb from Royal Result (28 Aug Goodwood 6f gd RF 3956) - also 1st of 11 giving 3lb to King of Peru (19 May Goodwood RF 1330). A winner over six furlongs at Goodwood in May, she had been disappointing until putting in perhaps her best effort when third to Royal Result in a hot Goodwood handicap in August. She seems to enjoy her visits to the Sussex track.

**L G Cottrell [2-19] Gerry Albertini.*

UPON A WISH BHB 60f **RR 69f** 4807[4]

3 b g Alzao (USA) 9.8f **(73)** - Imprecise **(49f)** (Polish Precedent (USA)) 10.2f **(60)**

Form - 27725304

Record **1999** - 1st:0 2nd:2 3rd:1 Ran:8

Win Prizemoney £0 *Total Prizemoney* £2,967

1999 Turf 0-8: (10f, 11f, 12f 3, 13f, 14f, 15f) (sft, g-s, gd, g-f 3, frm 2)

Light-framed, average gelding, effective 13f, acts on frm, favours tight tracks. Turf high 69 - 2nd of 6 to Who Cares Wins (23 Jun Chester 13f frm RF 2231). **B Hanbury [0-8] Ahmed Ali.*

UPPER BULLENS BHB 69f **RR 63f** 2517[4]

2 ch c Rock City 8.8f **(62)** - Monstrosa (Monsanto (FR)) 6.5f **(59)**

Form - 644

Record **1999** - 1st:0 2nd:0 3rd:0 Ran:3

Win Prizemoney £0 *Total Prizemoney* £522

1999 Turf 0-3: (7f 3) (gd 2, frm)

Currently average colt. Turf high 63. **A Bailey [0-3] R Farrington.*

UPPER CHAMBER BHB 43f **RR 40f** 4127[20]

3 b g Presidium 7.5f **(56)** - Vanishing Trick (Silly Season) 9.7f **(56)**

Form - 205056800

Record **1999** - 1st:0 2nd:1 3rd:0 Ran:9
Pre1999 - 1st:0 2nd:1 3rd:1 Ran:6

Win Prizemoney £0 *Total Prizemoney* £2,402

1999 Turf 0-8: (5f 5, 6f 3) (g-s, g-f 3, frm 4) 1999 AW 0-1: (5f) (Fibr)

Unfurnished, fair gelding, effective 5f, acts on g-f to frm, best on g-f, has worn blinkers. Turf high 68 (1st run) - 2nd of 11 to Sir Sandrovitch (22 May Musselburgh 5f g-f RF 1409). Inconsistent.

**J G FitzGerald [0-15] N H T Wrigley.*

UP THE KYBER RR 44f 5062[10]
2 b c Missed Flight - Najariya (Northfields (USA)) 9f **(72)**
Form - 00
Record 1999 - 1st:0 2nd:0 3rd:0 Ran:2
1999 Turf 0-2: (7f, 8f) (gd 2)
Currently moderate colt. Turf high 44 (began Oct).
**R F JohnsonHoughton [0-2] Lady Lloyd Webber.*

URBAN OCEAN (FR) RR 115f 2419a[6]
3 ch c Bering 9.6f **(80)** -Urban Sea (USA)**(119f)** (Miswaki (USA)) 9f **(81)**
Form - 116
1999 Turf 2-3: (10f 1-1, 12f 1-2) (g-s 2-2, gd)
Strong, high-class colt, effective 10f, acts on g-s. Turf high 115 - 1st of 6 getting 13lb from Sunshine Street (4 Jun Curragh RF 1833a). He won his first two starts of last season, a small race at Cork and the Group Three Gallinule Stakes at the Curragh from Sunshine Street. Made the running for a fair way in the Irish Derby before being left behind. That proved to be it for the season.
**A P O'Brien in IRE [3-7] David Tsui.*

URGENT REPLY (USA) BHB 40f **RR 39f** 4726[13]
6 b g Green Dancer (USA) 11.9f **(77)** - Bowl of Honey (USA) (Lyphard (USA)) 9.9f **(72)**
Form - 0760518400

Record	**1999** -	1st:1	2nd:0	3rd:0	Ran:10
	Pre1999 -	1st:5	2nd:2	3rd:0	Ran:25

Win Prizemoney £16,163 *Total Prizemoney* £18,444

Wins								
* **1999**	Jun	Warwic	(HVY)	H	16.1f	38	42	
* 1998	Jly	Chepst	(GD)	H	12.1f	44	51	
* 1998	Jun	Mussel	(SFT)	H	16f	44	49	
* 1998	Jun	Hamilt	(SFT)	H	13f	40	44	
* 1997	Aug	Catter	(G-F)	C	12f		51	
* 1997	Jly	Hamilt	(G-F)	C	12.1f		52	<

1999 Turf 1-9: (12f 2, 14f, 15f, 16f 1-4, 17f) (hvy, sft, g-s 1-1, gd 2, g-f 3, frm) 1999 AW 0-1: (14f) (Fibr)
Very moderate gelding, effective 12 to 16f, acts on gd to g-f, best on gd, has worn blinkers, favours tight tracks. Turf high 42.
**C A Dwyer [6-40] Mrs C Rawson & Mrs K Macey.*

URGENT SWIFT BHB 67f **RR 66f** 5101[2]
6 ch g Beveled (USA) 6.9f **(64)** - Good Natured (Troy) 10.4f **(68)**
Form - 3013730163005752

Record	**1999** -	1st:2	2nd:1	3rd:4	Ran:16
	Pre1999 -	1st:1	2nd:5	3rd:3	Ran:25

Win Prizemoney £12,237 *Total Prizemoney* £26,376

Wins								
* **1999**	Jly	Haydoc	(G-S)	H	14f	70	76+	<
* **1999**	May	Salisb	(G-F)	H	12f	63	66	
* 1996	Spt	Redcar	(FRM)	H	10f	67	71	

1999 Turf 2-16: (12f 1-4, 14f 1-8, 16f 2, 17f, 20f) (g-s 2, gd 2, g-f 1-4, frm 1-8)
Average gelding, has broken blood-vessels, effective 12 to 16f, best at 16f, acts on gd to frm, best on frm, has worn blinkers. Turf high 76 - 1st of 7 giving 1lb to Voila Premiere (2 Jly Haydock RF 2488). Consistent. Somewhat in-and-out, he produced a fine turn of foot to win at Salisbury on his third start of last season, then caused a surprise when scoring on softer ground at Haydock. However, he is inconsistent and cannot be supported with any confidence.
**A P Jarvis [3-37] A P Jarvis (from M Pitman [0-8] Jun 1998).*

URSA MAJOR BHB 60f70a **RR 59f 70a** 5103[18]
5 b g Warning 8.1f **(77)** - Double Entendre (Dominion) 8.5f **(63)**
Form - 3336700204604100

Record	**1999** -	1st:1	2nd:1	3rd:0	Ran:12
	Pre1999 -	1st:5	2nd:1	3rd:3	Ran:26

Win Prizemoney £24,139 *Total Prizemoney* £29,158

Wins								
* **1999**	Spt	York	(G-F)	H	7f	57	59	
* 1998	*Feb*	*Lingfi*	*(SLW)*	*H*	*8f*	*82*	*87+*	<
* 1998	*Jan*	*Lingfi*	*(STD)*	*H*	*8f*	*70*	*87+*	<
1998	*Jan*	*Southw*	*(STD)*	*C*	*8f*		*82+*	
1998	*Jan*	*Southw*	*(STD)*	*C*	*8f*		*69*	
1996	*Dec*	*Lingfi*	*(STD)*		*6f*		*70+*	

1999 Turf 1-11: (6f 2, 7f 1-3, 8f, 9f, 10f 4) (gd 3, g-f 4, frm 1-4) 1999 AW 0-1: (8f) (Fibr)
Above-average gelding, effective 6 to 8f, best at 8f, - acts on AW, best on Equi, has worn blinkers, prefers left handed tracks, likes tight tracks, excels at Wolverhampton and does well at Southwell. Turf high 62.
**C N Allen [3-23] Newmarket Connections Ltd (from A Kelleway [2-5] Jan 1998).*

US AND THEM (IRE) RR 23f 2530[5]
2 ch f Pips Pride 6.7f **(70)** - Tasskeen (FR) (Lyphard (USA)) 9.9f **(72)**
Form - 5
Record 1999 - 1st:0 2nd:0 3rd:0 Ran:1
1999 Turf 0-1: (6f) (gd)
Currently little account filly.
**Mrs N Macauley [0-1] Operation Solstice.*

UTAH (IRE) BHB 48f51a **RR 52?f 51a** 4927[7]
5 b g High Estate 10.5f **(66)** - Easy Romance (USA) (Northern Jove (CAN)) 9.7f **(66)**
Form - 5207

Record	**1999** -	1st:0	2nd:1	3rd:0	Ran:4
	Pre1999 -	1st:0	2nd:0	3rd:0	Ran:5

Win Prizemoney £0 *Total Prizemoney* £830
1999 Turf 0-1: (8f) (gd) 1999 AW 0-3: (8f 3) (Fibr 3)
Fair gelding, has worn blinkers. AW high 48 (began Spt) - 2nd of 13 getting 10lb from Mr Perry (18 Spt Wolverhampton 8f Fibr RF 4410).
**L MontagueHall [0-6] The Straight Forward Partnership II (from B Gubby [0-3] Jun 1998).*

UTHER PENDRAGON (IRE) BHB 25f **RR 12f** 2749[9]
4 b g Petardia 8.2f **(58)** -Mountain Stage (IRE) (Pennine Walk) 8.5f **(61)**
Form - 0

Record	**1999** -	1st:0	2nd:0	3rd:0	Ran:1
	Pre1999 -	1st:0	2nd:0	3rd:0	Ran:5

1999 Turf 0-1: (8f) (hrd)
Leggy, very moderate gelding, has worn blinkers.
**M Bradstock [0-2] Miss J C Blackwell (from J A Bennett [0-4] Jan 1998).*

UZY BHB 49f **RR 50f** 4628[13]
3 ch c Common Grounds 8.1f **(66)** - Loch Clair (IRE) (Lomond (USA)) 8.8f **(65)**
Form - 4030020600

Record	**1999** -	1st:0	2nd:1	3rd:1	Ran:10
	Pre1999 -	1st:0	2nd:1	3rd:0	Ran:2

Win Prizemoney £0 *Total Prizemoney* £2,576
1999 Turf 0-10: (6f 5, 7f 2, 8f 2, 9f) (g-s 2, gd 2, g-f 2, frm 4)
Workmanlike, fair colt, effective 6f, acts on g-s, often wears blinkers. Turf high 59. Inconsistent.
**M J Ryan [0-3] Peter Scott & Mike Bromley (from I A Balding [0-9] Aug 1999).*

VALANTINE ANNA BHB 32f26a **RR 40f 26a** 4601[9]
3 b f Perpendicular - Fool's Errand (Milford) 9f **(61)**
Form - 6520060

Record	**1999** -	1st:0	2nd:1	3rd:0	Ran:7
	Pre1999 -	1st:0	2nd:0	3rd:0	Ran:4

Win Prizemoney £0 *Total Prizemoney* £565
1999 Turf 0-3: (8f, 10f, 11f) (g-f 2, frm) 1999 AW 0-4: (9f 2, 11f, 12f) (Fibr 4)
Neat, moderate filly. Turf high 37. AW high 35. Inconsistent.
**D HaydnJones [0-11] Trio Racing.*

VALDINI (IRE) BHB 62f62a **RR 66f 62a** 3999[11]
3 b f Common Grounds 8.1f **(66)** - Windini (Windjammer (USA)) 7f **(59)**
Form - 3864800

Record	**1999** -	1st:0	2nd:0	3rd:1	Ran:7
	Pre1999 -	1st:0	2nd:0	3rd:1	Ran:3

Win Prizemoney £0 *Total Prizemoney* £1,423
1999 Turf 0-6: (8f 4, 10f 2) (gd, g-f 2, frm 2, hrd) 1999 AW 0-1: (8f) (Fibr)
Leggy, average filly, effective 8 to 10f, acts on gd to frm, has worn blinkers, prefers tight tracks. Turf high 71 (1st run) - 3rd of 18 getting 5lb from Shaylan (14 May Thirsk 8f gd RF 1220). Consistent.
**P W Harris [0-10] Spirits In Common.*

VALEDICTORY BHB 85f **RR 85f** 1524[5]
6 b g Slip Anchor 12.7f **(75)** - Khandjar (Kris) 9.5f **(73)**
Form - 65

Record	**1999** -	1st:0	2nd:0	3rd:0	Ran:2
	Pre1999 -	1st:2	2nd:1	3rd:1	Ran:6

Win Prizemoney £11,764 *Total Prizemoney* £15,501

Wins 1997 May Newmar (GD) H 12f 92 98 <

1996 Jun Newmar (G-F) 14f 79

1999 Turf 0-2: (10f, 12f) (gd, frm)

Useful gelding. Turf high 85. (DEAD)

**P Monteith [3-14] I Bell (from H R A Cecil [2-6] May 1997).*

VALENTINE BAND (USA) RR 91+f 5142[6]

2 b f Dixieland Band (USA) 10.1f **(80)** - Shirley Valentine (Shirley Heights) 10.3f **(74)**

Form - 6

Record 1999 - 1st:0 2nd:0 3rd:0 Ran:1

Win Prizemoney £0 *Total Prizemoney* £134

1999 Turf 0-1: (8f) (gd)

Currently useful filly. (1st run) - 6th of 10 to Silver Colours (30 Oct Newmarket 8f gd RF 5142). **R Charlton [0-1] K Abdulla.*

VALENTINE GIRL BHB 103f RR 107f 5043[6]

3 b f Alzao (USA) 9.8f **(73)** - Set Fair (USA) **(89f)** (Alleged (USA)) 10f **(76)**

Form - 174336

Record 1999 - 1st:1 2nd:0 3rd:2 Ran:6

Pre1999 - 1st:1 2nd:0 3rd:0 Ran:3

Win Prizemoney £37,281 *Total Prizemoney* £44,883

Wins * 1999 May Cheste (G-F) L 11.4f 94 <

* 1998 Aug Newbur (G-F) L 7f 80+

1999 Turf 1-6: (10f, 11f 1-1, 12f 3, 15f) (sft, gd 2, g-f 1-2, frm)

Strong, Pattern-class filly, effective 8 to 15f, acts on sft to frm, best on gd. Turf high 107 - 3rd of 9 giving 4lb to Ajhiba (11 Aug Salisbury 10f gd RF 3554). Inconsistent. She ran on well to take the Cheshire Oaks on her return, but missed the Oaks itself in order to wait for Royal Ascot, where she was well beaten by Fairy Queen in the Ribblesdale. Fair if unspectacular efforts in pattern events after that, failing to stay 14 furlongs in the Park Hill Stakes.

**B W Hills [2-9] K Abdulla.*

VALENTINES VISION BHB 56f RR 32f 4994[10]

2 b c Distinctly North (USA) 7.4f **(63)** - Sharp Anne (Belfort (FR)) 6.8f **(63)**

Form - 650

Record 1999 - 1st:0 2nd:0 3rd:0 Ran:3

1999 Turf 0-3: (5f 2, 7f) (sft, gd, frm)

Currently very moderate colt. Turf high 59.

**N P Littmoden [0-3] Alan Miller & Mrs Maggie McClean.*

VALENTINE WALTZ (IRE) BHB 116f RR 116f 2041[3]

3 b f Be My Guest (USA) 10.2f **(66)** - Save Me The Waltz (Kings Lake (USA)) 10.8f **(67)**

Valentine Waltz danced away with the French 1000 Guineas

Form - 1313

Record 1999 - 1st:2 2nd:0 3rd:2 Ran:4

Pre1999 - 1st:1 2nd:1 3rd:3 Ran:7

Win Prizemoney £131,209 *Total Prizemoney* £183,776

Wins * 1999 May Longch () G1 8f 116 <

* 1999 Apr Newmar (GD) G3 7f 110

* 1998 Spt Bright (GD) 7f 84+

1999 Turf 2-4: (7f 1-1, 8f 1-3) (gd 1-1, g-f 1-2, frm)

High-class filly, effective 7 to 8f, best at 8f, acts on gd to frm. Turf high 116 - 1st of 14 from Karmifira (16 May Longchamp RF 1358a) - also 1st of 11 from Hawriyah (13 Apr Newmarket RF 0664). She showed a bright turn of foot to win the Nell Gwyn Stakes on her reappearance last season and ran very well to finish third to Wince in the English Guineas. She put up an even better performance to win the French version, before dead-heating for third behind Balisada in the Coronation Stakes. That proved to be her last performance of the season.

**J H M Gosden [3-7] Kirby Maher Syndicate (from A P O'Brien in IRE [0-4] Jun 1998).*

VALENTINO RR 101f 4514a[4]

2 ch c Nureyev (USA) 8.4f **(84)** - Divine Danse (FR) (Kris) 9.5f **(73)**

Form - 14

Record 1999 - 1st:1 2nd:0 3rd:0 Ran:2

Win Prizemoney £7,002 *Total Prizemoney* £11,308

Wins * 1999 Jly Ascot (G-F) 6f 80+ <

1999 Turf 1-2: (6f 1-1, 7f) (sft, gd 1-1)

Currently very useful colt. Turf high 100 (began Jly). He appeared green before making a winning debut at Ascot in July, and was far from disgraced when finishing fourth in the Prix de la Salamandre eight weeks later. A scopey sort, he will improve markedly during the close season and should develop into a useful three-year-old.

**P W Chapple-Hyam [1-2] A E Oppenheimer.*

VALE OF LEVEN (IRE) BHB 38f51a RR 30f 51a 4906[22]

3 b g Fayruz 6.6f **(63)** - Speedy Action (Horage) 10.3f **(61)**

Form - 167670008800000

Record 1999 - 1st:0 2nd:0 3rd:0 Ran:13

Pre1999 - 1st:2 2nd:1 3rd:0 Ran:8

Win Prizemoney £5,994 *Total Prizemoney* £6,578

Wins * 1998 *Nov Southw (STD) H 7f 58 61* <

* 1998 Oct Redcar (SFT) H 6f 51 56

1999 Turf 0-8: (6f 4, 7f, 8f 2, 10f) (gd 2, g-f 3, frm 3) 1999 AW 0-5: (6f, 7f 2, 8f 2) (Fibr 5)

Leggy, moderate gelding, effective 6 to 7f, best at 7f, acts on gd - acts on Fibr. Turf high 39. AW high 49. Inconsistent.

**K A Ryan [2-21] Steer Arms Belton Racing Club.*

VALES ALES BHB 19f RR 19f 3674[13]

6 b g Dominion Royale 7.8f **(63)** - Keep Mum (Mummy's Pet) 7.7f **(60)**

Form - 070

Record 1999 - 1st:0 2nd:0 3rd:0 Ran:3

Pre1999 - 1st:0 2nd:0 3rd:1 Ran:9

Win Prizemoney £0 *Total Prizemoney* £502

1999 Turf 0-3: (7f, 8f, 10f) (frm 2, hrd)

Poor gelding. Turf high 19 (began Jly).

**M A Peill [0-3] Willie Smith (from R M McKellar [0-10] Jan 1998).*

VALLEY CHAPEL (IRE) RR 103f 4374a[3]

3 f

Form - 03

1999 Turf 0-2: (8f, 12f) (gd 2)

Currently very useful. Turf high 103 - 3rd of 9 getting 9lb from Albaran (12 Spt Taby 12f gd RF 4374a). **W Neuroth in NOR [0-2].*

VALLEY FLYER (IRE) RR 14f 2432[6]

2 b f Magical Wonder (USA) 7.2f **(60)** - River Low (IRE) (Lafontaine (USA)) 8.7f **(49)**

Form - 6

Record 1999 - 1st:0 2nd:0 3rd:0 Ran:1

1999 Turf 0-1: (7f) (gd)

Currently poor filly. **R P C Hoad [0-1] Foray Racing.*

VAL ROYAL (FR) RR 112f 3778a[1]

3 b c Royal Academy (USA) 7.8f **(77)** - Vadlava (FR) (Bikala) 10.1f **(49)**

Form - 1021

1999 Turf 2-4: (9f 1-2, 10f 1-1, 12f) (hvy 1-1, gd 1-3)
Group-class colt. Turf high 112 - 1st of 5 from Alrassaam (14 Aug Deauville RF 3778a) - also 1st of 5 from Fils de Viane (20 May Longchamp RF 1528a). Unbeaten before failing to stay in the Derby, he struggled to beat Alrassaam in a Group Two at Deauville during August and falls short of the top-class.
**A Fabre in FR [2-4] J-L Lagardere.*

VAL'S PRINCE (USA) RR 123f 5230a[11]

7 ch g Eternal Prince (USA) - Key Buy (USA) (Valid Appeal (USA)) 8.9f **(78)**
Form - 0
1999 Turf 0-1: (12f) (frm)
Very high-class gelding.
**H J Bond in USA [0-1] (from J Picou in USA [1-3] Dec 1997).*

VALS WHISPA BHB 47f RR 61f 4022[10]

2 ch c Timeless Times (USA) 6.1f **(56)** - Skiddaw Bird (Bold Owl) 8.5f **(45)**
Form - 4505635600
Record 1999 - 1st:0 2nd:0 3rd:1 Ran:10
Win Prizemoney £0 *Total Prizemoney* £542
1999 Turf 0-10: (5f 3, 6f, 7f 5, 8f) (gd 2, g-f 4, frm 3, hrd)
Average colt, effective 7f, acts on gd, has worn blinkers. Turf high 61. **S E Kettlewell [0-10] The Alder,Borchard & Chilton Partnership.*

VALUABLE IDEA (USA) RR 61f 3047[5]

2 b f Distant View (USA) - Viviana (USA) (Nureyev (USA)) 8.7f **(78)**
Form - 5
Record 1999 - 1st:0 2nd:0 3rd:0 Ran:1
1999 Turf 0-1: (6f) (g-f)
Average filly. (DEAD) **B W Hills [0-1] K Abdulla.*

VANADIUM ORE BHB 41f RR 41f 4983[12]

6 b g Precious Metal 9.3f **(42)** - Rockefillee (Tycoon II) 8.7f **(47)**
Form - 575038500

Record	**1999 -**	1st:0	2nd:0	3rd:1	Ran:9
	Pre1999 -	1st:4	2nd:3	3rd:0	Ran:20

Win Prizemoney £12,155 *Total Prizemoney* £15,896

Wins									
	* 1998	Jun	Newcas	(GD)	H	10.1f	52	60	<
	* 1998	Jun	Ayr	(G-F)	H	10.9f	52	56	
	* 1998	Jun	Cheste	(GD)	H	10.3f	50	53	
	* 1997	Oct	Newcas	(G-F)	H	10.1f	48	52	

1999 Turf 0-9: (10f 3, 11f 2, 12f 4) (g-s, gd 2, frm 6)
Moderate gelding, effective 10 to 12f, best at 12f, acts on gd to frm, best on gd, has worn blinkers, prefers left handed tracks. Turf high 50. Consistent.
**W McKeown [4-30] Garth Ormond (from J L Eyre [0-7] Dec 1996).*

VANBOROUGH LAD BHB 38f41a RR 37f 41a 5069[6]

10 b g Precocious 7.2f **(54)** - Lustrous (Golden Act (USA)) 8.8f **(67)**
Form - 15147660708046

Record	**1999 -**	1st:2	2nd:0	3rd:0	Ran:14
	Pre1999 -	1st:6	2nd:10	3rd:8	Ran:76

Win Prizemoney £22,402 *Total Prizemoney* £39,492

Wins								
	1999	Jun	Haydoc	(SFT)	H	10.5f	47	52
	1999	May	Bath	(GD)	H	10.2f	44	45
	1998	Jly	Windso	(G-F)	H	10f	42	44
	1997	May	Bath	(GD)	H	8f	37	39
	1995	May	Bath	(G-F)	H	8f	52	48

1999 Turf 2-14: (10f 1-10, 11f 1-2, 12f 2) (g-s 2, gd 1-2, g-f 1-3, frm 6, hrd)
Very moderate gelding, effective 8 to 12f, acts on gd to frm, has worn blinkers, likes left handed tracks, favours tight tracks, and likes Bath. Turf high 52 - 1st of 11 giving 2lb to Dancing Lawyer (4 Jun Haydock RF 1739) - also 1st of 20 getting 9lb from Santa Court (21 May Bath RF 1368). Consistent.
**Dr J R J Naylor [0-4] Mrs S P Elphick (from M J Bolton [6-58] Aug 1999).*

VANCOUVER ISLE (IRE) BHB 51f RR 61f 3918[4]

3 b c Erins Isle 8.3f **(76)** - Eileenog (IRE) (Kahyasi)
Form - 3385644

Record	**1999 -**	1st:0	2nd:0	3rd:2	Ran:7
	Pre1999 -	1st:0	2nd:0	3rd:0	Ran:4

Win Prizemoney £0 *Total Prizemoney* £867
1999 Turf 0-7: (8f, 10f, 12f 3, 14f, 16f) (hvy, g-s, gd, g-f 3, frm)
Average colt, effective 8 to 12f, best at 8f, acts on hvy to g-f, best on hvy, often wears blinkers (extremely effectively). Turf high 65 - 3rd of 9 giving 7lb to Experimental (13 May Clonmel 10f g-s RF 1310a). Consistent.
**G B Balding [0-3] Baldings (Training) Ltd (from J S Bolger in IRE [0-8] Jun 1999).*

VAN DANTZIG (USA) RR 95f 4852a[1]

2 b c Danzig (USA) 8.1f **(88)** - Sexy Slew (USA) (Slew O' Gold (USA)) 8f **(75)**
Form - 341
1999 Turf 1-3: (6f 1-3) (sft 1-1, gd 2)
Currently very useful colt. Turf high 95 (began Aug) - 1st of 17 from Crusoe (10 Oct Naas RF 4852a). Built like a bull, he took all his time to win a moderate maiden at Naas in October but should improve once tried beyond sprint distances.
**A P O'Brien in IRE [1-3] Michael Tabor.*

VAN GURP BHB 57f48a RR 57?f 48a 3544[R]

6 ch g Generous (IRE) 11.5f **(82)** - Atlantic Flyer (USA) (Storm Bird (CAN)) 10.3f **(74)**
Form - 64114757133RR

Record	**1999 -**	1st:3	2nd:0	3rd:2	Ran:13
	Pre1999 -	1st:1	2nd:1	3rd:3	Ran:22

Win Prizemoney £17,503 *Total Prizemoney* £23,449

Wins									
	* **1999**	Jun	Hamilt	(G-S)	H	8.3f	53	60	
	1999	*Feb*	*Lingfi*	*(STD)*	*C*	*10f*		*63*	
	1999	*Feb*	*Lingfi*	*(STD)*	*S*	*8f*		*51*	
	1996	Spt	York	(GD)		7.9f		87	<

1999 Turf 1-5: (8f 1-2, 9f 3) (gd 1-1, g-f 2, frm 2) 1999 AW 2-8: (8f 1-3, 9f, 10f 1-2, 11f, 12f) (Equi 2-6, Fibr 2)
Fair gelding, effective 8 to 10f, best at 8f, acts on gd to frm - acts on Equi, has worn blinkers. Turf high 60 (1st run) - 1st of 7 getting 5lb from Pursuivant (9 Jun Hamilton RF 1857). AW high 63 - 1st of 11 getting 10lb from Zidac (16 Feb Lingfield RF 0299). Inconsistent.
**K R Burke [1-9] Nigel Shields (from G L Moore [2-4] Feb 1999).*

VANILLE (IRE) RR 68f 4991[12]

3 b f Selkirk (USA) 7.9f **(76)** - Stormswept (USA) (Storm Bird (CAN)) 10.3f **(74)**
Form - 03220
Record 1999 - 1st:0 2nd:2 3rd:1 Ran:5
Win Prizemoney £0 *Total Prizemoney* £2,616
1999 Turf 0-5: (7f 2, 8f 2, 10f) (g-f 2, frm 3)
Leggy, average filly. Turf high 68 - 2nd of 10 getting 5lb from Dangerous Fortune (24 Spt Redcar 7f frm RF 4541).
**A G Foster [0-1] I M S Racing & P A Deal (from P W Chapple-Hyam [0-4] Spt 1999).*

VANISHING DANCER (SWI) RR 56f 4388[9]

2 ch c Llandaff (USA) - Vanishing Prairie (USA) (Alysheba (USA)) 9f **(84)**
Form - 00
Record 1999 - 1st:0 2nd:0 3rd:0 Ran:2
1999 Turf 0-2: (8f 2) (gd, g-f)
Currently fair colt. Turf high 56 (began Spt).
**K R Burke [0-2] Achilles International.*

VANISHING WORLD (FR) RR 99f 1204a[3]

3 b c Bering 9.6f **(80)** - Victoire Bleue (FR) (Legend of France (USA)) 9.5f **(61)**
Form - 3
1999 Turf 0-1: (11f) (gd)
Currently very useful colt. (1st run) - 3rd of 5 to Falcon Flight (9 May Chantilly 11f gd RF 1204a). **A Fabre in FR [0-1] D Wildenstein.*

VANTAGE POINT BHB 48f RR 50f 4948[7]

3 b c Casteddu 7.4f **(54)** - Rosie Dickins (Blue Cashmere) 6.4f **(54)**
Form - 02424431347

Record	**1999 -**	1st:1	2nd:2	3rd:2	Ran:10
	Pre1999 -	1st:0	2nd:0	3rd:0	Ran:4

Win Prizemoney £4,659 *Total Prizemoney* £8,299

Wins									
	* **1999**	Aug	Folkes	(G-S)	H	12f	45	49	<

1999 Turf 1-10: (11f, 12f 1-7, 14f, 15f) (gd 1-2, g-f 6, frm 2)
Scopey, fair colt, effective 11 to 12f, best at 12f, acts on gd to frm, likes tight tracks. Turf high 54 - also 1st of 14 getting 12lb from

Meilleur (26 Aug Folkestone RF 3916). Consistent. **K McAuliffe [1-14] The Hare and Hounds Partnership.*

VARIETY SHOP (USA) RR 78f 4697[2]

3 b f Mr Prospector (USA) 8.6f **(88)** - Nimble Feet (USA) (Danzig (USA)) 8.4f **(76)**
Form - 2
Record 1999 - 1st:0 2nd:1 3rd:0 Ran:1
Win Prizemoney £0 *Total Prizemoney* £1,240
1999 Turf 0-1: (10f) (g-s)
Scopey, currently above-average filly. (1st run) - 2nd of 13 getting 5lb from Anamore (2 Oct Sandown 10f g-s RF 4697). **H R A Cecil [0-1] K Abdulla.*

VASARI (IRE) BHB 55f70a RR 51f 70a 5199[6]

5 ch g Imperial Frontier (USA) 7f **(65)** - Why Not Glow (IRE) (Glow (USA)) 6.7f **(71)**
Form - 3460770076
Record 1999 - 1st:0 2nd:0 3rd:1 Ran:10
Pre1999 - 1st:1 2nd:1 3rd:3 Ran:16
Win Prizemoney £7,112 *Total Prizemoney* £14,356
Wins 1996 May Cheste (GD) 5.1f 83+ <
1999 Turf 0-9: (5f 3, 6f 5, 7f) (g-s 2, gd 2, g-f 4, frm) 1999 AW 0-1: (8f) (Equi)
Average gelding, effective 6f, acts on gd to g-f, best on g-f, has worn blinkers. Turf high 69.
**John Harris [0-1] Miss E Kazantseva (from W J Musson [0-9] Oct 1999).*

VEGA NEUTRAL BHB 34f RR 40f 73[14]

3 ch f King's Signet (USA) 7f **(51)** - Factuelle (Known Fact (USA)) 7.4f **(67)**
Form - 00000
Record 1999 - 1st:0 2nd:0 3rd:0 Ran:1
Pre1999 - 1st:0 2nd:0 3rd:0 Ran:6
1999 AW 0-1: (6f) (Fibr)
Neat, moderate filly. **P Shakespeare [0-7] Mrs Pauline Joyce.*

VEGAS BHB 53a RR 53a 211[7]

3 ch f Then Again 7.4f **(52)** - Cazanove's Pet **(45f 52a)** (Tina's Pet) 6.8f **(59)**
Form - 6657
Record 1999 - 1st:0 2nd:0 3rd:0 Ran:4
1999 AW 0-4: (7f, 8f 3) (Equi 4)
Workmanlike, fair filly. AW high 57.
**J S Moore [0-4] Western Solvents Ltd.*

VEIL OF AVALON (USA) BHB 94f RR 88f 4565[6]

2 b f Thunder Gulch (USA) - Wind in Her Hair (IRE) **(109f)** (Alzao (USA)) 7.1f **(68)**
Form - 3116
Record 1999 - 1st:2 2nd:0 3rd:1 Ran:4
Win Prizemoney £12,743 *Total Prizemoney* £14,953
Wins * 1999 Spt Newbur (G-F) 7f 88 <
*** 1999** Aug Lingfi (GD) 6f 76+
1999 Turf 2-4: (6f 1-2, 7f 1-1, 8f) (sft, g-f 1-1, frm 1-2)
Useful filly. Turf high 88 (began Jly) - 1st of 7 from Miss Orah (17 Spt Newbury RF 4383). Ran a super race behind Boast at the July meeting and made no mistake at Lingfield next time. Followed up in a decent event at Newbury in September but failed to handle the rise in class and the heavy ground in the Fillies' Mile, finishing last of six. **R Charlton [2-4] Jeffen Racing.*

VELVET JONES BHB 36f34a RR 34f 34a 3389[8]

6 b gr g Sharrood (USA) 11.1f **(67)** - Cradle of Love (USA) (Roberto (USA)) 10f **(76)**
Form - 5658
Record 1999 - 1st:0 2nd:0 3rd:0 Ran:4
Pre1999 - 1st:0 2nd:4 3rd:4 Ran:38
Win Prizemoney £0 *Total Prizemoney* £5,105
1999 Turf 0-1: (8f) (frm) 1999 AW 0-3: (6f, 8f 2) (Equi 3)
Very moderate gelding, effective 8f, acts on frm, has worn blinkers, likes left handed tracks, likes tight tracks. AW high 38. Consistent.
**G F H Charles-Jones [0-41] Mrs Jessica Charles-Jones (from P F I Cole [0-6] Spt 1995).*

VENETIAN PEARL (IRE) BHB 69f RR 70f 5188[5]

3 ch f Generous (IRE) 11.5f **(82)** - Veronica (Persian Bold) 9.3f **(66)**
Form - 023645
Record 1999 - 1st:0 2nd:1 3rd:1 Ran:6
Pre1999 - 1st:0 2nd:0 3rd:0 Ran:1
Win Prizemoney £0 *Total Prizemoney* £2,542
1999 Turf 0-6: (10f, 12f 3, 14f, 16f) (g-s, gd, g-f, frm 3)
Well made, above-average filly, effective 12 to 16f, acts on gd to frm. Turf high 70 - 5th of 16 giving 18lb to Virgin Soldier (3 Nov Musselburgh 16f g-f RF 5188). **G Wragg [0-7] Baron G Von Ullmann.*

VENIKA VITESSE BHB 71f70a RR 69f 70a 4027[7]

3 b g Puissance 7.1f **(60)** - Vilanika (FR) (Top Ville) 11.7f **(68)**
Form - 0018031317
Record 1999 - 1st:3 2nd:0 3rd:2 Ran:8
Pre1999 - 1st:0 2nd:0 3rd:0 Ran:2
Win Prizemoney £9,605 *Total Prizemoney* £10,548
Wins * 1999 Aug Nottin (G-F) H 6.1f 68 69
*** 1999** Jun Carlis (G-F) H 5.9f 64 66
*** 1999** *Jan Lingfi (STD) 5f* 73 <
1999 Turf 2-7: (6f 2-7) (gd 1-2, g-f, frm 1-4) 1999 AW 1-1: (5f 1-1) (Equi 1-1)
Workmanlike, above-average gelding, effective 5 to 6f, best at 6f, acts on gd to frm - acts on Equi. Turf high 69 - 1st of 17 getting 3lb from Moocha Cha Man (13 Aug Nottingham RF 3624) - also 1st of 19 giving 13lb to Springs Noblequest (23 Jun Carlisle RF 2225). (1st run) - 1st of 8 giving 5lb to La Piazza (5 Jan Lingfield RF 0031). Consistent. **T D Barron [3-10] Kevin Shaw.*

VENIZE (IRE) RR 112f 5014a[10]

3 gr f Kaldoun (FR) 9.9f **(84)** - Canaletto (USA) (Iron Duke (FR)) 8.8f **(60)**
Form - 152560
1999 Turf 1-6: (7f, 8f 1-4, 11f) (hvy, sft, g-s 1-1, gd 2)
Group-class filly, effective 8 to 11f, best at 8f, acts on sft to gd. Turf high 112 - also 1st of 6 from Visionnaire (25 Apr Longchamp RF 0933a). She lacks scope, but is game and ran with credit after winning a Group Three at Longchamp in April. She appeared to stay a mile and three furlongs in the Prix de Sandringham and is worth another try over middle distances. **R Collet in FR [1-6].*

VENTURE CAPITALIST BHB 70f RR 65f 3900[8]

10 ch g Never so Bold 7.1f **(62)** - Brave Advance (USA) (Bold Laddie (USA)) 5.6f **(69)**
Form - 328841458
Record 1999 - 1st:1 2nd:1 3rd:1 Ran:9
Pre1999 - 1st:8 2nd:12 3rd:10 Ran:79
Win Prizemoney £114,322 *Total Prizemoney* £178,951
Wins * 1999 Jly Catter (GD) C 5f 52
***** 1998 Jly Doncas (G-F) 6f 92
***** 1996 May York (G-F) G3 6f 106 <
***** 1995 May York (G-F) H 6f 100 104
***** 1995 Apr Thirsk (GD) 6f 99
1999 Turf 1-9: (5f 1-5, 6f 4) (gd 3, g-f 1-1, frm 4, hrd)
Average gelding, effective 5 to 6f, best at 6f, acts on g-f to frm, best on frm, has worn blinkers (extremely effectively). Turf high 69. Consistent. This sprightly veteran was banned under the 'non-triers' rule on his final start.
**D Nicholls [5-55] The Eminent Partnership (from R Hannon [4-33] Oct 1994).*

VENTURE ISLAND (IRE) BHB 30f40a RR 30f 40a 2429[7]

3 br f Petardia 8.2f **(58)** - Island Adventure (Touching Wood (USA)) 8.2f **(55)**
Form - 80087
Record 1999 - 1st:0 2nd:0 3rd:0 Ran:5
Pre1999 - 1st:0 2nd:0 3rd:0 Ran:5
1999 Turf 0-4: (8f 3, 10f) (sft, gd, frm 2) 1999 AW 0-1: (8f) (Fibr)
Strong, very moderate filly, has worn blinkers. Turf high 30. Consistent. **W J Musson [0-10] The Square Table.*

VENUS RR 34f 4812[17]

2 ch f Bering 9.6f **(80)** - Historiette (Chief's Crown (USA)) 9.8f **(72)**
Form - 0
Record 1999 - 1st:0 2nd:0 3rd:0 Ran:1
1999 Turf 0-1: (7f) (gd)
Currently very moderate filly. **Sir Mark Prescott [0-1] Faisal Salman.*

VERBOSE (USA) **RR 75f** 5137[5]
2 b f Storm Bird (CAN) 8.5f **(82)** -Alvernia (USA)(Alydar (USA)) 9.1f **(76)**
Form - 5
Record 1999 - 1st:0 2nd:0 3rd:0 Ran:1
1999 Turf 0-1: (7f) (gd)
Currently above-average filly. (1st run) - 5th of 16 to Garota do Leblon (30 Oct Newmarket 7f gd RF 5137).
**J H M Gosden [0-1] K Abdulla.*

VERDURA **RR 49f** 4408[13]
2 b f Green Desert (USA) 7.8f **(78)** - Spirit of The Wind (USA) (Little Current (USA)) 9.6f **(75)**
Form - 0
Record 1999 - 1st:0 2nd:0 3rd:0 Ran:1
1999 Turf 0-1: (6f) (frm)
Currently moderate filly.
**B W Hills [0-1] H R H Princess Michael of Kent.*

VERONICA FRANCO BHB 79f48a **RR 86df 48a** 3993[14]
6 b m Darshaan 11.9f **(81)** - Maiden Eileen (Stradavinsky) 12.5f **(64)**
Form - 84270
Record 1999 - 1st:0 2nd:1 3rd:0 Ran:5
Pre1999 - 1st:7 2nd:2 3rd:4 Ran:31
Win Prizemoney £43,594 *Total Prizemoney* £51,334
Wins * 1998 Spt Newbur (GD) H 13.3f 74 80 <
* 1998 Jly Ascot (G-F) H 12f 67 68
* 1998 Jun Goodwo (GD) H 16f 64 66+
* 1998 May Sandow (G-S) H 14f 59 63
* 1998 May Salisb (FRM) H 12f 54 60
* 1997 Spt Sandow (G-F) H 14f 49 52
* 1997 Aug Folkes (G-F) H 12f 45 49
1999 Turf 0-5: (10f, 12f 2, 14f, 15f) (g-f 2, frm 3)
Useful mare, effective 12 to 13f, acts on g-f to frm, has worn blinkers, likes right handed tracks. Turf high 77. Enjoyed a fine season in '98, but was below par last term.
**P R Hedger [7-22] J J Whelan (from R Ingram [0-4] Jly 1997).*

VERPOSEN (IRE) BHB 40f52a **RR 49f 52a** 3484[2]
3 b c Posen (USA) 8.6f **(59)** - Jet Set Bunny (USA) (Northjet) 10.3f **(74)**
Form - 000602
Record 1999 - 1st:0 2nd:1 3rd:0 Ran:5
Pre1999 - 1st:0 2nd:1 3rd:1 Ran:8
Win Prizemoney £0 *Total Prizemoney* £1,609
1999 Turf 0-5: (8f, 10f 2, 12f 2) (hvy, gd 2, g-f 2)
Workmanlike, moderate colt, effective 7f, acts on g-s to frm, has worn blinkers. Turf high 49. Inconsistent.
**J Pearce [0-13] Chris Marsh.*

VERSATILITY BHB 50f53a **RR 55df 53a** 5006[14]
6 b m Teenoso (USA) 10.5f **(62)** - Gay Criselle (Decoy Boy) 6.7f **(56)**
Form - 7160
Record 1999 - 1st:1 2nd:0 3rd:0 Ran:4
Pre1999 - 1st:0 2nd:0 3rd:1 Ran:6
Win Prizemoney £3,101 *Total Prizemoney* £3,743
Wins * **1999** May Warwic (SFT) H 14.6f 45 55 <
1999 Turf 1-4: (12f, 15f 1-1, 16f 2) (sft 1-1, g-s, gd, g-f)
Fair mare. Turf high 55 - 1st of 10 from Miss Vita (29 May Warwick RF 1591). Inconsistent.
**G M McCourt [2-7] Magno-Pulse Ltd (from R F JohnsonHoughton [0-6] Nov 1997).*

VIA CAMP BHB 92f **RR 88f** 4680[7]
2 b f Kris 10f **(75)** - Honeyspike (IRE) **(64f)** (Chief's Crown (USA)) 9.8f **(72)**
Form - 317
Record 1999 - 1st:1 2nd:0 3rd:1 Ran:3
Win Prizemoney £3,647 *Total Prizemoney* £5,222
Wins * **1999** Aug Beverl (GD) 7.5f 87 <
1999 Turf 1-3: (7f 1-3) (gd, frm 1-2)
Currently useful filly. Turf high 88 (1st run) (began Jly) - 3rd of 11 to Chez Cherie (29 Jly Goodwood 7f frm RF 3224) - also 1st of 8 from Datura (28 Aug Beverley RF 3951). Followed up an encouraging debut with an easy maiden win at Beverley, and was not disgraced in Listed company. **E A L Dunlop [1-3] Coutinho Nogueira.*

VIA DOLOROSA **RR 13f** 1259[16]
3 ch f Chaddleworth (IRE) - Ophrys (Nonoalco (USA)) 8.5f **(66)**
Form - 0
Record 1999 - 1st:0 2nd:0 3rd:0 Ran:1
1999 Turf 0-1: (7f) (frm)
Unfurnished, currently poor filly.
**M Blanshard [0-1] G H S Bailey & N C D Hall.*

VIBRANCE (IRE) **RR 77df** 1687[11]
3 b c College Chapel - Shalara (Dancers Image (USA)) 9.3f **(71)**
Form - 0
Record 1999 - 1st:0 2nd:0 3rd:0 Ran:1
Pre1999 - 1st:0 2nd:0 3rd:0 Ran:1
Win Prizemoney £0 *Total Prizemoney* £339
1999 Turf 0-1: (5f) (frm)
Currently above-average colt. **J Noseda [0-2] M Olden.*

VICAR (USA) **RR** 5227a[11]
3 br c Wild Again (USA) 10.7f **(69)** - Escrow Agent (USA) (El Gran Senor (USA)) 9.6f **(76)**
Form - 0
1999 AW 0-1: (6f) (Dirt)
Currently useful. **C Nafzger in USA [0-1].*

VICARS MISTRESS **RR 8f** 4944[16]
2 b f Today and Tomorrow 6.2f **(45)** - Rectory Maid (Tina's Pet) 6.8f **(59)**
Form - 00
Record 1999 - 1st:0 2nd:0 3rd:0 Ran:2
1999 Turf 0-2: (7f, 8f) (g-s, gd)
Currently very poor filly. Turf high 8 (began Spt).
**J S Moore [0-2] Ernie Houghton.*

VICE PRESIDENTIAL BHB 46f60a **RR 37f 60a** 5035[15]
4 ch g Presidium 7.5f **(56)** - Steelock (Lochnager) 6f **(59)**
Form - 000000
Record 1999 - 1st:0 2nd:0 3rd:0 Ran:6
Pre1999 - 1st:3 2nd:0 3rd:2 Ran:20
Win Prizemoney £7,884 *Total Prizemoney* £9,050
Wins 1998 Jun Mussel (SFT) C 7.1f 62+
1998 Jun Warwic (SFT) C 7f 77
1997 May Hamilt (SFT) 5f 93+ <
1999 Turf 0-5: (5f 2, 6f 2, 7f) (sft, g-s 2, gd, frm) 1999AW 0-1: (7f) (Fibr)
Scopey, fair gelding, effective 6 to 7f, acts on g-s to gd, likes tight tracks. Turf high 52. Becoming disappointing.
**J G Given [0-6] A Clarke (from M P Bielby [0-7] Oct 1998).*

VICIOUS CIRCLE BHB 110f **RR 106+f** 4571[1]
5 b g Lahib (USA) 8f **(69)** - Tight Spin (High Top) 10.2f **(67)**
Form - 1211
Record 1999 - 1st:3 2nd:1 3rd:0 Ran:4
Pre1999 - 1st:1 2nd:1 3rd:1 Ran:5
Win Prizemoney £166,923 *Total Prizemoney* £173,294
Wins * **1999** Spt Ascot (HVY) H 12f 101 106+ <
* **1999** Aug York (GD) H 13.9f 90 97
* **1999** Jun Newcas (GD) 10.1f 87
* 1998 Oct Ayr (HVY) 10f 97+
1999 Turf 3-4: (10f 1-2, 12f 1-1, 14f 1-1) (sft 1-1, gd 1-2, frm 1-1)
Pattern-class gelding, effective 10 to 14f, acts on sft to gd, best on sft. Turf high 106 - 1st of 16 giving 22lb to Ligne Gagnante (26 Spt Ascot RF 4571) - also 1st of 21 getting 14lb from Travelmate (18 Aug York RF 3758). Lightly raced, he won a four-runner event at Newcastle on his return, and he was comfortably held when second of three finishers at Ascot next time. However, he was well suited by the step up in trip when running out a good winner of the Ebor at York and followed up in a valuable Ascot handicap in heavy ground. Plans for a hurdles campaign have been shelved, and this progressive sort can pay his way again on the Flat next year. **L M Cumani [4-9] D Metcalf And J Samuel.*

VICKYBERTO **RR** 640[8]
10 b m Laxton - Silberto (Dadda Bert)
Form - 8
Record 1999 - 1st:0 2nd:0 3rd:0 Ran:1
1999 Turf 0-1: (11f) (hvy)
Formerly very poor mare. **D A Nolan [0-1] Mrs L A Ogilvie.*

VICKY VETTORI BHB 30f **RR** 4926[11]

2 b f Veltori (IRE) - Key West (FR) (Highest Honor (FR))
Form - 0760
Record 1999 - 1st:0 2nd:0 3rd:0 Ran:4
1999 Turf 0-1: (5f) (frm) 1999 AW 0-3: (6f, 7f, 8f) (Fibr 3)
Little account filly. AW high 20. **A G Newcombe [0-4] P A Bedford.*

VICTOIRE RR 68f 4836[19]

3 b f Makbul - Boxit (General Ironside)
Form - 8470
Record 1999 - 1st:0 2nd:0 3rd:0 Ran:4
Win Prizemoney £0 *Total Prizemoney* £197
1999 Turf 0-4: (8f 3, 10f) (gd 2, g-f, frm)
Light-framed, average filly. Turf high 68 (began Jly) - 7th of 19 getting 5lb from Zulu Dawn (17 Spt Newbury 8f frm RF 4382).
**H Akbary [0-4] Michael Whatley.*

VICTORIET BHB 54f RR 55f 4943[9]

2 ch f Hamas (IRE) 8f **(72)** - Wedgewood (USA) (Woodman (USA)) 9f **(74)**
Form - 7400800
Record 1999 - 1st:0 2nd:0 3rd:0 Ran:7
Win Prizemoney £0 *Total Prizemoney* £238
1999 Turf 0-7: (5f 4, 6f, 7f 2) (sft, gd, g-f, frm 4)
Fair filly, has worn blinkers. Turf high 55.
**A T Murphy [0-7] & Mrs Peter Foden.*

VICTORIOUS RR 50f 5072[12]

3 ch c Formidable (USA) 7.8f **(60)** - Careful Dancer (Gorytus (USA)) 7.8f **(60)**
Form - 00100050
Record 1999 - 1st:1 2nd:0 3rd:0 Ran:8
Pre1999 - 1st:0 2nd:0 3rd:0 Ran:3
Win Prizemoney £3,032 *Total Prizemoney* £3,243
Wins * 1999 Aug Haydoc (G-S) H 7.1f 63 66 <
1999 Turf 1-8: (7f 1-6, 8f 2) (g-s 2, gd 1-2, g-f 3, frm)
Lengthy, fair colt, effective 7f, acts on gd. Turf high 66 - 1st of 16 giving 8lb to Lokomotiv (5 Aug Haydock RF 3401). Consistent. Had been running against some really progressive sorts before striking the bullseye over seven furlongs on easy ground at Haydock in August. He may need those conditions to score again.
**B A McMahon [1-11] Tommy Staunton.*

VICTOR'S CROWN (IRE) BHB 68f RR 67f 4342[9]

2 b c Desert Style (IRE) - Royal Wolff (Prince Tenderfoot (USA)) 9f **(61)**
Form - 6200

Vicious Circle, bought to win the Ebor, did just that

Record 1999 - 1st:0 2nd:1 3rd:0 Ran:4
Win Prizemoney £0 *Total Prizemoney* £584
1999 Turf 0-4: (6f 3, 7f) (g-s, gd 2, frm)
Average colt. Turf high 67 (began Jly) - 2nd of 10 giving 5lb to Premier Fois (13 Aug Lingfield 6f frm RF 3610).
**M H Tompkins [0-4] Mrs Brian Grice.*

VICTORY CRY (IRE) RR 113f 3228a[1]

3 ch f Caerleon (USA) 10.9f **(79)** - Verveine (USA) (Lear Fan (USA)) 8.5f **(73)**
Form - 11
1999 Turf 2-2: (10f 2-2) (gd 2-2)
Currently Group-class filly. Turf high 113 (began Jly) - 1st of 9 getting 10lb from Trait De Genie (21 Jly Vichy RF 3228a). She did well to beat older and more experienced rivals at Vichy in July and is clearly a useful filly. Suited by patient tactics, she will stay a mile and a half. **A Fabre in FR [2-2] D Wildenstein.*

VICTORY DAY (IRE) BHB 100f RR 100f 4793[8]

2 b c Fairy King (USA) 7.7f **(75)** - Inanna (Persian Bold) 9.3f **(66)**
Form - 212108
Record 1999 - 1st:2 2nd:2 3rd:0 Ran:6
Win Prizemoney £16,090 *Total Prizemoney* £30,045
Wins * 1999 Jly Cheste (G-F) 5.1f 100+ <
*** 1999** May Windso (GD) 5f 89+
1999 Turf 2-6: (5f 2-6) (gd, g-f 2-4, frm)
Very useful colt, effective 5f, acts on g-f. Turf high 100 - 2nd of 13 to Warm Heart (17 Jun Ascot 5f g-f RF 2070) - also 1st of 6 giving 7lb to Heathyardsblessing (9 Jly Chester RF 2671). He was in fine form during the first half of the season and made Warm Heart fight hard to win the Norfolk Stakes. However, he ran appallingly when well fancied for the Molecomb at Goodwood, and disappointed again in the Cornwallis Stakes at Ascot in October. Regarded as a five-furlong specialist by connections, he is one to have reservations about. **J Noseda [2-6] Lucayan Stud.*

VICTORY GALLOP (CAN) RR 122f 556a[3]

4 b c Cryptoclearance (USA) - Victorious Lil (CAN) (Vice Regent (CAN)) 8.7f **(74)**
Form - 3
1999 AW 0-1: (10f) (Dirt)
High-calibre colt. (1st run) - 3rd of 8 to Almutawakel (28 Mar Nad Al Sheba 10f Dirt RF 0556a). Third in the 1999 Dubai World Cup, He was retired to stud in August.
**W E Walden in USA [1-5] Prestonwood Farm Inc.*

VICTORY SPIN BHB 90f RR 95df 2137[8]

3 ch c Beveled (USA) 6.9f **(64)** - Victoria Mill (Free State) 8.7f **(61)**
Form - 18
Record 1999 - 1st:1 2nd:0 3rd:0 Ran:2
Pre1999 - 1st:0 2nd:1 3rd:0 Ran:1
Win Prizemoney £3,684 *Total Prizemoney* £4,826
Wins * 1999 May Beverl (GD) 7.5f 66 <
1999 Turf 1-2: (7f 1-1, 8f) (gd 1-1, g-f)
Strong, currently very useful colt. Turf high 76. Tipped by some shrewd judges when successful at 1/66 at Beverley but failed to settle next time. **L M Cumani [1-3] M J Dawson.*

VICTORY STAR BHB 44f RR 42f 2667[17]

4 ch g Soviet Star (USA) 8.6f **(74)** - Victoriana (USA) (Storm Bird (CAN)) 10.3f **(74)**
Form - 06000
Record 1999 - 1st:0 2nd:0 3rd:0 Ran:5
1999 Turf 0-5: (8f, 9f, 10f 2, 11f) (g-s, gd, g-f, frm 2)
Workmanlike, moderate gelding. Turf high 42.
**Lady Herries [0-5] E Reitel.*

VIDAME (FR) BHB 37f34a RR 48f 34a 1864[18]

4 b g Kaldoun (FR) 9.9f **(84)** - Vallee Normande (FR) (Bellypha) 9.8f **(73)**
Form - 808600
Record 1999 - 1st:0 2nd:0 3rd:0 Ran:5
Pre1999 - 1st:0 2nd:0 3rd:0 Ran:3
1999 Turf 0-4: (12f 3, 13f) (hvy, g-f 2, frm) 1999 AW 0-1: (12f) (Equi)
Leggy, moderate gelding, effective 12f, acts on frm, likes left handed tracks, likes tight tracks. Turf high 48 - 6th of 17 giving 6lb to Caernarfon Bay (29 Apr Brighton 12f frm RF 0910). Inconsistent.

**R M Flower [0-8] M G Rogers.*

VIE INDIENNE BHB 57f **RR 59f** 2294[3]
3 ch f Indian Ridge 7.6f **(74)** - La Strada (Niniski (USA)) 10.6f **(65)**
Form - 003
Record 1999 - 1st:0 2nd:0 3rd:1 Ran:3
Win Prizemoney £0 *Total Prizemoney* £603
1999 Turf 0-3: (6f 2, 7f) (frm 3)
Leggy, currently fair filly. Turf high 59.
**I A Balding [0-3] Miss K Rausing.*

VIGOROUS STROLL (USA) BHB 27f **RR 25f** 3836[13]
3 b br c Strolling Along (USA) - Student of Prague (USA) (Vigors (USA)) 10f **(72)**
Form - 0500
Record 1999 - 1st:0 2nd:0 3rd:0 Ran:4
1999 Turf 0-2: (7f 2) (g-f, frm) 1999 AW 0-2: (8f, 12f) (Fibr 2)
Unfurnished, very moderate colt. Turf high 25 (began Aug). AW high 35. **P S McEntee [0-4] R B Collier.*

VIGOUR RR 81f 3546[1]
2 ch f Lion Cavern (USA) 7.5f **(74)** - Brave Revival **(93f)** (Dancing Brave (USA)) 8.4f **(76)**
Form - 21
Record 1999 - 1st:1 2nd:1 3rd:0 Ran:2
Win Prizemoney £3,272 *Total Prizemoney* £4,428
Wins * 1999 Aug Leices (GD) 7f 81 <
1999 Turf 1-2: (6f, 7f 1-1) (g-f 1-1, frm)
Currently decent filly. Turf high 81 (began Aug) - 1st of 11 from Grace And Power (11 Aug Leicester RF 3546).
**Sir Michael Stoute [1-2] Cheveley Park Stud.*

VIKING PRINCE BHB 50f **RR 45f** 5005[13]
2 b g Chilibang 7f **(55)** - Fire Sprite (Mummy's Game) 8.2f **(60)**
Form - 50700
Record 1999 - 1st:0 2nd:0 3rd:0 Ran:5
1999 Turf 0-4: (5f 3, 6f) (gd, g-f 3) 1999 AW 0-1: (6f) (Equi)
Moderate gelding. Turf high 45.
**M Quinn [0-5] Glendale Partnership Ltd.*

VILLAGE NATIVE (FR) BHB 59f59a **RR 66f 59a** 2250[1]
6 ch g Village Star (FR) 5.7f **(61)** - Zedative (FR) (Zeddaan) 9f **(76)**
Form - 200552470261
Record 1999 - 1st:1 2nd:2 3rd:0 Ran:11
Pre1999 - 1st:6 2nd:3 3rd:3 Ran:45
Win Prizemoney £18,523 *Total Prizemoney* £24,089

Wins							
*** 1999**	Jun	Salisb	(G-F)	C	8f		66
* 1998	*Spt*	*Wolver*	*(STD)*	*H*	*6f*	*56*	*59*
* 1998	Jly	Bath	(GD)	C	5.1f		61
* 1998	May	Sandow	(G-S)	C	8.1f		52
* 1997	*Nov*	*Wolver*	*(STD)*	*H*	*5f*	*54*	*57*
* 1997	*Aug*	*Wolver*	*(STD)*	*H*	*5f*	*52*	*59*
* 1995	Nov	Folkes	(G-F)		6f		76 <

1999 Turf 1-5: (5f, 6f 2, 8f 1-2) (gd, g-f 1-1, frm 3) 1999 AW 0-6: (5f 2, 6f, 7f 3) (Equi 2, Fibr 4)
Average gelding, effective 5 to 8f, best at 5f, acts on sft to frm - acts on AW, often wears blinkers (extremely effectively). Turf high 66 - 1st of 9 giving 6lb to Ivor's Investment (23 Jun Salisbury RF 2250). AW high 60. **K O Cunningham-Brown [7-56] A J Richards.*

VILLAGE PUB (FR) BHB 35f24a **RR 33f 24a** 241[6]
5 ch g Village Star (FR) 5.7f **(61)** - Sloe Berry (Sharpo) 7.7f **(59)**
Form - 06
Record 1999 - 1st:0 2nd:0 3rd:0 Ran:2
Pre1999 - 1st:0 2nd:0 3rd:1 Ran:23
Win Prizemoney £0 *Total Prizemoney* £1,553
1999 AW 0-2: (7f, 12f) (Fibr 2)
Very moderate gelding, often wears blinkers. AW high 7.
**B J Llewellyn [0-5] Alan Williams (from K O Cunningham-Brown [0-21] Feb 1998).*

VILLAMINTA (IRE) RR 48f 1680[8]
2 b f Grand Lodge (USA) - Mrs Fisher (IRE) (Salmon Leap (USA)) 11f **(61)**
Form - 8
Record 1999 - 1st:0 2nd:0 3rd:0 Ran:1
1999 Turf 0-1: (6f) (g-f)

Currently moderate filly. **Sir Mark Prescott [0-1] G D Waters.*

VILLA ROMANA BHB 73f **RR 73f** 5124[5]
2 b f Komaite (USA) 6.9f **(61)** - Keep Quiet **(30a)** (Reprimand)
Form - 63274043415
Record 1999 - 1st:1 2nd:1 3rd:2 Ran:11
Win Prizemoney £3,165 *Total Prizemoney* £5,710
Wins * 1999 Oct Bright (G-F) H 7f 69 73 <
1999 Turf 1-11: (5f 4, 6f 3, 7f 1-3, 8f) (gd 1-5, g-f 2, frm 4)
Above-average filly, effective 5 to 7f, acts on gd to frm, best on gd. Turf high 73 - 1st of 16 giving 3lb to Doctor Dennis (21 Oct Brighton RF 4995). **A Bailey [1-11] Great Taste Foods Ltd.*

VILLA WANDA RR 42f 648[10]
3 ch f Grand Lodge (USA) - Gisarne (USA) (Diesis) 9.3f **(69)**
Form - 0
Record 1999 - 1st:0 2nd:0 3rd:0 Ran:1
Pre1999 - 1st:0 2nd:0 3rd:0 Ran:1
1999 Turf 0-1: (10f) (frm)
Scopey, currently moderate filly.
**W Jarvis [0-2] Lord Howard de Walden.*

VINCENT BHB 41f46a **RR 32f 46a** 4600[4]
4 b c Anshan 8.2f **(63)**-Top-Anna (IRE) **(52f)** (Ela-Mana-Mou) 10.1f **(70)**
Form - 51640400030414344
Record 1999 - 1st:2 2nd:0 3rd:2 Ran:17
Pre1999 - 1st:0 2nd:1 3rd:0 Ran:7
Win Prizemoney £3,366 *Total Prizemoney* £5,381
Wins * 1999 *Jly Wolver (STD) H 16.2f 45 50*
*** 1999** *Jan Southw (STD) H 12f 47 55* <
1999 Turf 0-5: (10f 2, 12f 3) (g-f 2, frm 2, hrd) 1999 AW 2-12: (11f, 12f 1-4, 14f 2, 15f, 16f 1-4) (Equi, Fibr 2-11)
Leggy, fair colt, effective 10 to 16f, best at 12f, acts on frm - acts on Fibr, has worn blinkers, prefers left handed tracks, favours tight tracks, and excels at Wolverhampton. Turf high 52 (1st run) - 4th of 10 getting 25lb from Top Jem (14 Apr Beverley 10f frm RF 0690). AW high 55 - 1st of 12 giving 6lb to Time Out (29 Jan Southwell RF 0186) - also 1st of 12 getting 2lb from Tukano (23 Jly Wolverhampton RF 3084). He is extremely inconsistent, but can win modest events on Fibresand when he wants to.
**J L Harris [2-24] P Caplan.*

VINTAGE PREMIUM BHB 83f **RR 73f** 4762[12]
2 b c Forzando 7.2f **(63)** - Julia Domna **(18f 34a)** (Dominion) 8.5f **(63)**
Form - 2210
Record 1999 - 1st:1 2nd:2 3rd:0 Ran:4
Win Prizemoney £4,193 *Total Prizemoney* £6,712
Wins * 1999 Spt Beverl (GD) 7.5f 72 <
1999 Turf 1-4: (6f 2, 7f 1-1, 8f) (gd 1-3, g-f)
Above-average colt. Turf high 73 - also 1st of 15 giving 2lb to King's Mill (15 Spt Beverley RF 4322). **R A Fahey [1-4] J C Parsons.*

VINTAGE TAITTINGER (IRE) BHB 23f47a **RR 25f 47a** 2361[4]
7 b g Nordico (USA) 8.2f **(59)** - Kalonji (Red Alert) 7.6f **(66)**
Form - 384
Record 1999 - 1st:0 2nd:0 3rd:1 Ran:3
Pre1999 - 1st:2 2nd:1 3rd:1 Ran:17
Win Prizemoney £4,938 *Total Prizemoney* £6,387
Wins * 1997 Jun Mussel (G-S) H 16f 27 32
1995 *Apr Wolver (STD) H 12f 40 42* <
1999 Turf 0-3: (14f, 16f 2) (gd, g-f 2)
Moderate gelding. Turf high 25 (1st run) - 3rd of 9 getting 15lb from Highfield Fizz (22 May Musselburgh 16f g-f RF 1408).
**J S Goldie [7-30] Die-Hard Racing Club (from T Dyer [0-9] May 1996).*

VIOLET (IRE) BHB 65f65a **RR 67f 65a** 4865[10]
3 b f Mukaddamah (USA) 7.6f **(74)** - Scanno's Choice (IRE) (Pennine Walk) 8.5f **(61)**
Form - 2318800
Record 1999 - 1st:1 2nd:0 3rd:0 Ran:5
Pre1999 - 1st:0 2nd:1 3rd:1 Ran:5
Win Prizemoney £2,853 *Total Prizemoney* £4,225
Wins 1999 *Jan Wolver (STD) 8.5f 65* <
1999 Turf 0-3: (7f 2, 8f) (g-s, g-f 2) 1999 AW 1-2: (8f 1-2) (Fibr 1-2)
Unfurnished, average filly, effective 7 to 8f, best at 7f, acts on g-s - acts on AW, best on Equi, prefers tight tracks. Turf high 65 (began

Aug). AW high 65 (1st run) - 1st of 13 getting 5lb from Air of Esteem (6 Jan Wolverhampton RF 0038). Inconsistent.
**Miss Gay Kelleway [0-4] Loose Cannon Racing (from Lord Huntingdon [1-6] Jan 1999).*

VIPEE BHB 55f67a **RR 70f 67a** 4626[10]
2 ch g Risk Me (FR) 8f **(53)** - Snow Wonder (Music Boy) 6.8f **(57)**
Form - 3842000
Record 1999 - 1st:0 2nd:1 3rd:1 Ran:7
Win Prizemoney £0 *Total Prizemoney* £1,401
1999 Turf 0-6: (5f 4, 6f, 7f) (sft 2, g-s 2, frm 2) 1999 AW 0-1: (5f) (Fibr)
Above-average gelding, effective 6f, acts on g-s, has worn blinkers. Turf high 70 - 2nd of 7 giving 5lb to Olivias Choice (2 Jun Goodwood 6f g-s RF 1673). **A Kelleway [0-7] Mike Perkins.*

VIRBIUS (IRE) BHB 32f38a **RR 30f 38a** 4980[15]
3 ch g Wolfhound (USA) 7.3f **(71)** - Virelai (Kris) 9.5f **(73)**
Form - 6070000
Record 1999 - 1st:0 2nd:0 3rd:0 Ran:7
Pre1999 - 1st:0 2nd:0 3rd:0 Ran:2
1999 Turf 0-5: (8f 2, 10f 3) (gd 3, g-f 2) 1999 AW 0-2: (7f 2) (Fibr 2)
Rangy, very moderate gelding, has worn blinkers. Turf high 42. AW high 15. Inconsistent.
**J Hetherton [0-7] Golden Fleece Racing Club (from C E Brittain [0-2] Oct 1998).*

VIRGIN SOLDIER (IRE) BHB 45a **RR 58+f** 5188[1]
3 ch g Waajib 8.9f **(67)** - Never Been Chaste (Posse (USA)) 8.9f **(61)**
Form - 637088211
Record 1999 - 1st:2 2nd:1 3rd:1 Ran:9
Pre1999 - 1st:0 2nd:0 3rd:1 Ran:3
Win Prizemoney £10,207 *Total Prizemoney* £11,916
Wins * 1999 Nov Mussel (GD) H 16f 46 58+ <
*** 1999** *Oct Lingfi (STD) H 12f 45 55*
1999 Turf 1-8: (8f, 10f, 11f, 12f 3, 16f 1-2) (g-s, gd 2, g-f 1-3, frm 2)
1999 AW 1-1: (12f 1-1) (Equi 1-1)
Unfurnished, above-average gelding, effective 12 to 16f, best at 12f, acts on gd to g-f - acts on Equi, has worn blinkers, likes right handed tracks, prefers tight tracks. Turf high 58 - 3rd of 13 giving 6lb to Ferny Factors (2 Jun Beverley 12f gd RF 1665) - also 1st of 16 getting 14lb from Corvino (3 Nov Musselburgh RF 5188). (1st run) - 1st of 11 getting 22lb from Haydn James (25 Oct Lingfield RF 5057). He has looked an improved performer since being faced with a test of stamina, especially on sand, and looks a most progressive stayer.
**M Johnston [2-3] David Abell (from T J Etherington [0-9] Jly 1999).*

VIRGOS BAMBINO (IRE) BHB 36f **RR 32f** 4169[14]
2 ch f Perugino (USA) - Deep In September (IRE) (Common Grounds)
Form - 0000
Record 1999 - 1st:0 2nd:0 3rd:0 Ran:4
1999 Turf 0-4: (6f 2, 7f, 8f) (gd, frm 3)
Very moderate filly. Turf high 32.
**M J Fetherston-Godley [0-4] Abigail Ltd.*

VIRTUAL REALITY BHB 87f **RR 90f** 4915[20]
8 b g Diamond Shoal 9.8f **(79)** - Warning Bell (Bustino) 10.4f **(64)**
Form - 3051230
Record 1999 - 1st:1 2nd:1 3rd:2 Ran:7
Pre1999 - 1st:4 2nd:7 3rd:2 Ran:32
Win Prizemoney £27,252 *Total Prizemoney* £54,574
Wins * 1999 Jly Warwic (G-F) 7.7f 85 <
* 1998 Aug Salisb (G-F) H 8f 78 84
* 1998 May Bath (GD) H 8f 75 78
1999 Turf 1-7: (8f 1-6, 9f) (gd 3, g-f 1-2, frm, hrd)
Useful gelding, effective 8f, acts on g-f to hrd, best on frm, has worn blinkers, likes left handed tracks, prefers tight tracks, excels at Thirsk. Turf high 90 - 2nd of 7 giving 4lb to Family Man (27 Aug Thirsk 8f hrd RF 3945) - also 1st of 6 giving 11lb to Resalah (17 Jly Warwick RF 2935).
**J A R Toller [3-20] Ash Partnership (from A Hide [2-19] Oct 1995).*

VISHNU (GER) **RR 98f** 5119a[3]
4 b c Shareef Dancer (USA) 10.1f **(67)** - Vinca (GER) (King Of Macedon) 8.1f **(59)**
Form - 303
1999 Turf 0-3: (10f, 12f, 16f) (sft, gd 2)
Currently very useful colt, always wears blinkers. Turf high 98 (began Spt). **C Von der Recke in GER [0-3].*

VISION AND VERSE (USA) RR 5231a[9]
3 b c Storm Cat (USA) 7f **(86)** - Bunting (Private Account (USA)) 8.5f **(74)**
Form - 20
1999 AW 0-2: (10f, 12f) (Dirt 2)
Currently very high-class colt, often wears blinkers. AW high 121 (1st run) - 2nd of 12 to Lemon Drop Kid (5 Jun Belmont Park 12f Dirt RF 1899a). He ran really well when touched off in the Belmont Stakes in 1999, but was never in the hunt in the Breeders' Cup Classic. **W Mott in USA [0-2].*

VISIONNAIRE (FR) **RR 112f** 4780a[F]
3 gr f Linamix (FR) 8.2f **(64)** - Visor (FR)
Form - 2332F
1999 Turf 0-5: (8f, 9f 2, 10f, 11f) (sft, g-s 3, gd)
Group-class filly. Turf high 112 - 2nd of 4 getting 3lb from Star Of Akkar (16 Jly Chantilly 9f gd RF 3039a). She is a tough, consistent but luckless filly. Unfortunate to fall after clipping heels with another runner at Longchamp in October, she deserves to pick up a Group race. **A Fabre in FR [0-5].*

VISION OF NIGHT BHB 112f **RR 114f** 4568[7]
3 b c Night Shift (USA) 8.1f **(73)** - Dreamawhile (Known Fact (USA)) 7.4f **(67)**
Form - 5135417
Record 1999 - 1st:2 2nd:0 3rd:1 Ran:7
Pre1999 - 1st:2 2nd:1 3rd:1 Ran:4
Win Prizemoney £41,884 *Total Prizemoney* £75,851
Wins * 1999 Aug Deauvi (GD) G3 6f 109
*** 1999** May Newbur (GD) 6f 111 <
* 1998 Spt Doncas (GD) 6f 93+
* 1998 Aug Ripon (G-F) 6f 89+
1999 Turf 2-7: (6f 2-5, 7f 2) (hvy, sft, gd 2-3, g-f, frm)
Light-framed, Group-class colt, effective 6 to 7f, best at 6f, acts on hvy to g-f, excels at Ascot and Deauville. Turf high 114 - 3rd of 19 getting 7lb from Bold Edge (17 Jun Ascot 6f g-f RF 2072) - also 1st of 7 giving 5lb to Lionhearted (14 May Newbury RF 1213). Consistent. Very disappointing in the Free Handicap on his reappearance, he bounced back to run a series of fine races, highlighted by a win in the Prix de Meautry at Deauville in August. Six and a half furlongs looks the limit of his stamina at present, while he seems impervious to the state of the ground.
**J L Dunlop [4-11] Hesmonds Stud.*

VISSINIA **RR 106f** 1350a[2]
4 b f Belmez (USA) 11.4f **(65)** - Anafi (Slip Anchor) 9.8f **(73)**
Form - 2
1999 Turf 0-1: (11f) (g-s)
Currently Pattern-class filly. (1st run) - 2nd of 9 to Majoune (13 May Lyon Parilly 11f g-s RF 1350a). **D Sepulchre in FR [0-1].*

VISTA ALEGRE BHB 48f74a **RR 46f 74a** 3646[10]
4 b g Petong 7.6f **(58)** - Duxyana (IRE) (Cyrano de Bergerac) 6f **(68)**
Form - 0020
Record 1999 - 1st:0 2nd:1 3rd:0 Ran:4
Pre1999 - 1st:1 2nd:2 3rd:0 Ran:11
Win Prizemoney £3,387 *Total Prizemoney* £5,941
Wins * 1998 *Jan Lingfi (STD) 6f 59+* <
1999 Turf 0-3: (5f, 6f 2) (gd, g-f, frm) 1999 AW 0-1: (5f) (Equi)
Scopey, average gelding, effective 5f, - acts on Equi. Turf high 46. **P J Makin [1-15] D M Ahier.*

VITA SPERICOLATA (IRE) BHB 100f **RR 90f** 4793[10]
2 b f Prince Sabo 6.6f **(64)** - Ahonita (Ahonoora) 8.1f **(73)**
Form - 125135060
Record 1999 - 1st:2 2nd:1 3rd:1 Ran:9
Win Prizemoney £14,055 *Total Prizemoney* £19,525
Wins * 1999 Jly Sandow (GD) L 5f 88 <
*** 1999** May Mussel (FRM) S 5f 60+
1999 Turf 2-9: (5f 2-7, 6f 2) (gd 3, g-f 2-5, frm)
Useful filly, effective 5f, acts on gd to g-f, best on gd. Turf high 90 - 5th of 10 giving 3lb to Misty Miss (30 Jly Goodwood 5f g-f RF 3236) - also 1st of 10 from Bandanna (2 Jly Sandown RF 2499). Consistent. She won a Musselburgh seller in good style on her

debut, and has proved herself much better than a plater. A fine fifth in the Queen Mary at Royal Ascot, she was quite impressive when winning a Sandown Listed event, but has been found wanting since. Has reportedly been sold to race in America.
**J S Wainwright [2-9] The Camelot Members.*

VIVO (IRE) RR 93f 4202a[8]
6 b g Shaadi (USA) 8.1f **(75)** - Gay Nocturne
Form - 8
1999 Turf 0-1: (8f) (g-f)
Useful gelding.
**C Roche in IRE [1-10] John McManus (from J Oxx in IRE [2-6] Oct 1997).*

VOGUE BHB 35f **RR 35f** 4719[13]
3 b f Clantime 6.6f **(57)** - Slipperose (Persepolis (FR)) 6.4f **(67)**
Form - 808000
Record 1999 - 1st:0 2nd:0 3rd:0 Ran:6
Pre1999 - 1st:0 2nd:0 3rd:0 Ran:2
1999 Turf 0-6: (5f, 6f 3, 7f, 9f) (gd, g-f 2, frm 3)
Unfurnished, very moderate filly. Turf high 35.
**J S Moore [0-8] Western Solvents Ltd.*

VOILA PREMIERE (IRE) BHB 69f **RR 68f** 2488[2]
7 b g Roi Danzig (USA) 10.5f **(62)** - Salustrina (Sallust) 8.4f **(63)**
Form - 01702
Record 1999 - 1st:1 2nd:1 3rd:0 Ran:5
Pre1999 - 1st:4 2nd:4 3rd:4 Ran:29
Win Prizemoney £27,802 *Total Prizemoney* £36,458
Wins * **1999** May Salisb (G-F) H 14.1f 64 68+
* 1998 Spt Hamilt (SFT) H 12.1f 61 64
* 1998 Aug Hamilt (SFT) H 13f 59 62
1996 Oct York (GD) H 11.9f 66 76 <
1995 May Hamilt (G-F) 8.3f 60
1999 Turf 1-5: (13f, 14f 1-4) (hvy, g-f, frm 1-3)
Average gelding, effective 12 to 14f, best at 14f, acts on g-s to frm, best on frm, has worn blinkers, likes right handed tracks. Turf high 68 - 2nd of 7 getting 1lb from Urgent Swift (2 Jly Haydock 14f g-f RF 2488) - also 1st of 12 getting 5lb from Shalateeno (2 May Salisbury RF 0989).
**Lady Herries [3-11] B W Gaule (from P G Murphy [0-8] Mar 1998).*

VOLCANIC STAR BHB 49f **RR 39f** 1975[9]
3 ch f Primo Dominie 7.2f **(67)** - Lava Star (IRE) (Salse (USA)) 7.5f **(66)**
Form - 60
Record 1999 - 1st:0 2nd:0 3rd:0 Ran:2
Pre1999 - 1st:0 2nd:1 3rd:0 Ran:6
Win Prizemoney £0 *Total Prizemoney* £1,055
1999 Turf 0-2: (7f, 8f) (g-f 2)
Strong, very moderate filly, effective 5 to 7f, acts on gd to g-f. Turf high 39.
**M L W Bell [0-8] Deln Ltd.*

VOLONTIERS (FR) BHB 79f82a **RR 78f 82a** 5143[17]
4 b g Common Grounds 8.1f **(66)** - Senlis (USA) (Sensitive Prince (USA)) 9.1f **(60)**
Form - 38000
Record 1999 - 1st:0 2nd:0 3rd:1 Ran:5
Pre1999 - 1st:2 2nd:2 3rd:1 Ran:10
Win Prizemoney £24,913 *Total Prizemoney* £30,195
Wins * 1998 Jun Epsom (GD) L 7f 101 <
* 1998 May Haydoc (G-S) 7.1f 95
1999 Turf 0-5: (7f 5) (gd 4, g-f)
Strong, decent gelding, effective 7f, acts on gd to g-f. Turf high 90 (began Jly). Inconsistent. He looked useful when winning twice in the spring of '98, but has been too high in the handicap since.
**P W Harris [2-15] The Commoners.*

VOLVORETA RR 96+f 5115a[1]
2 ch f Suave Dancer (USA) 10.7f **(68)** - Robertiya (FR) (Don Roberto (USA))
Form - 1
1999 Turf 1-1: (8f 1-1) (gd 1-1)
Currently very useful filly. (1st run) - 1st of 7 from Blue Moon (19 Oct Deauville RF 5115a). **C Lerner in FR [1-1] Mme M S Vidal.*

VOSBURGH BHB 49f47a **RR 48f 47a** 4606[4]
3 br g Petong 7.6f **(58)** - Pour Moi (Bay Express) 7.1f **(60)**
Form - 600234
Record 1999 - 1st:0 2nd:1 3rd:1 Ran:6
Pre1999 - 1st:0 2nd:1 3rd:1 Ran:6
Win Prizemoney £0 *Total Prizemoney* £2,533
1999 Turf 0-5: (6f 4, 7f) (g-f, frm 4) 1999 AW 0-1: (6f) (Fibr)
Scopey, moderate gelding, effective 6f, acts on gd, has worn blinkers. Turf high 48. **P Calver [0-12] Mrs Janis MacPherson.*

VRENNAN BHB 51f60a **RR 47f 60a** 1864[11]
5 ch m Suave Dancer (USA) 10.7f **(68)** - Advie Bridge (High Line) 10.3f **(70)**
Form - 0
Record 1999 - 1st:0 2nd:0 3rd:0 Ran:1
Pre1999 - 1st:1 2nd:3 3rd:2 Ran:16
Win Prizemoney £1,998 *Total Prizemoney* £5,756
Wins 1997 *Dec Lingfi (G-S) H 12f 65 69 <*
1999 Turf 0-1: (12f) (g-f)
Fair filly, has worn blinkers.
**J Akehurst [0-1] Canisbay Bloodstock Ltd (from W Jarvis [0-8] Oct 1998).*

WAABL (IRE) BHB 95f **RR 94f** 4258[2]
3 b c Caerleon (USA) 10.9f **(79)** - Amandine (IRE) (Darshaan) 9.9f **(84)**
Form - 4152
Record 1999 - 1st:1 2nd:1 3rd:0 Ran:4
Pre1999 - 1st:0 2nd:1 3rd:0 Ran:1
Win Prizemoney £3,995 *Total Prizemoney* £9,572
Wins * **1999** Jun Goodwo (G-F) 8f 84+ <
1999 Turf 1-4: (8f 1-2, 9f, 10f) (gd 1-1, g-f, frm 2)
Scopey, useful colt. Turf high 94 - 2nd of 7 getting 4lb from World Alert (10 Spt Goodwood 9f g-f RF 4258). He got on the scorecard with a nice win over a mile on fast ground at Goodwood and has put up creditable efforts in handicap company since. He is still relatively lightly raced and can improve further.
**J H M Gosden [1-5] Hamdan Al Maktoum.*

WAASEF BHB 50f54a **RR 41f 54a** 1454[P]
6 b g Warning 8.1f **(77)** - Thubut (USA) (Tank's Prospect (USA))
Form - 2113770300P
Record 1999 - 1st:0 2nd:0 3rd:1 Ran:7
Pre1999 - 1st:2 2nd:2 3rd:1 Ran:13
Win Prizemoney £4,468 *Total Prizemoney* £6,128
Wins * *1998 Dec Lingfi (STD) H 13f 57 60 <*
* *1998 Nov Lingfi (STD) H 12f 48 49*
1999 Turf 0-1: (12f) (g-f) 1999 AW 0-6: (10f, 12f 5) (Equi 6)
Fair gelding, effective 12 to 13f, best at 13f, - acted on Equi, had worn blinkers, preferred left handed tracks, preferred tight tracks. AW high 56 - 3rd of 6 getting 15lb from Banbury (23 Feb Lingfield 12f Equi RF 0342). Becoming disappointing. His best form of 1998 was on Equitrack. He won twice on that surface right at the end of the year, but they were modest events and he was found out when facing better rivals after that. (DEAD)
**Miss Gay Kelleway [2-20] Another Seventh Heaven Partnership.*

WADENHOE (IRE) BHB 65f **RR 63f** 4762[20]
2 b f Persian Bold 10f **(69)** - Frill (Henbit (USA)) 9f **(61)**
Form - 0210080
Record 1999 - 1st:1 2nd:1 3rd:0 Ran:7
Win Prizemoney £3,522 *Total Prizemoney* £4,824
Wins * **1999** Jun Ayr (G-S) 7f 81 <
1999 Turf 1-7: (6f, 7f 1-3, 8f 3) (gd 1-3, frm 4)
Average filly, effective 7f, acts on gd to frm. Turf high 81 - 1st of 8 getting 5lb from Classic Lord (19 Jun Ayr RF 2141).
**M R Channon [1-7] Mrs Margaret Hall.*

WADI BHB 62f58a **RR 68df 58a** 4791[18]
4 b g Green Desert (USA) 7.8f **(78)** - Eternal (Kris) 9.5f **(73)**
Form - 03262441100
Record 1999 - 1st:2 2nd:2 3rd:1 Ran:11
Pre1999 - 1st:1 2nd:0 3rd:2 Ran:5
Win Prizemoney £8,055 *Total Prizemoney* £10,756
Wins 1999 Jly Salisb (FRM) C 9.9f 68
1999 Jly Warwic (G-F) SH 12.3f 54 59+
1998 Jly Pontef (G-F) 10f 79 <
1999 Turf 2-8: (8f 3, 10f 1-3, 12f 1-2) (gd, g-f 1-4, frm 1-2, hrd) 1999 AW 0-3: (10f 3) (Equi 3)
Workmanlike, average gelding, has broken blood-vessels, effective 10f, acts on frm, has worn blinkers, likes left handed tracks, likes tight tracks. Turf high 68. AW high 63.

**Dr J R J Naylor [0-2] Mrs S P Elphick (from G M McCourt [2-9] Jly 1999).*

WAFFLES OF AMIN BHB 79f **RR 71f** 5195[3]
2 b c Owington - Alzianah **(102f)** (Alzao (USA)) 7.1f **(68)**
Form - 52623
Record 1999 - 1st:0 2nd:2 3rd:1 Ran:5
Win Prizemoney £0 *Total Prizemoney* £2,590
1999 Turf 0-5: (6f 5) (gd 2, g-f, frm 2)
Above-average colt. Turf high 71 - 2nd of 5 to Awake (13 Aug Epsom 6f g-f RF 3603).
**R Hannon [0-4] Sheikh Amin Dahlawi (from J D Bethell [0-1] Jun 1999).*

WAFF'S FOLLY BHB 56f **RR 55f** 5199[4]
4 b f Handsome Sailor 6.6f **(53)** - Shirl (Shirley Heights) 10.3f **(74)**
Form - 30353034
Record 1999 - 1st:0 2nd:0 3rd:4 Ran:8
Pre1999 - 1st:1 2nd:0 3rd:0 Ran:8
Win Prizemoney £2,070 *Total Prizemoney* £3,616
Wins * 1998 Apr Folkes (GD) 6f 65 <
1999 Turf 0-8: (6f 7, 7f) (gd 4, g-f 2, frm 2)
Unfurnished, fair filly, effective 6f, acts on gd. Turf high 55.
**G F H Charles-Jones [1-16] P H Wafford.*

WAFIR (IRE) BHB 56f **RR 59f** 3288[6]
7 b g Scenic 10.6f **(66)** - Taniokey (Grundy) 10.3f **(65)**
Form - 004135256
Record 1999 - 1st:1 2nd:1 3rd:1 Ran:9
Pre1999 - 1st:3 2nd:2 3rd:3 Ran:28
Win Prizemoney £18,000 *Total Prizemoney* £35,064
Wins * 1999 Jun Redcar (FRM) C 10f 60
1998 Aug Newcas (GD) 12.4f 79
1997 May Ayr (G-F) H 10f 80 83+ <
1996 Aug Ripon (HVY) H 10f 80 83
1999 Turf 1-9: (8f 2, 10f 1-2, 12f 5) (gd 2, g-f 3, frm 1-4)
Fair gelding, effective 10 to 12f, best at 12f, acts on g-s to frm, best on gd, prefers left handed tracks, excels at Newcastle and Redcar. Turf high 60.
**D Nicholls [1-9] J Laughton (from P Calver [3-28] Aug 1998).*

WAGGA MOON (IRE) BHB 32f28a **RR 32f 28a** 4142[13]
5 b g Mac's Imp (USA) 5.6f **(54)** - Faapette (Runnett) 7f **(59)**
Form - 07620070870
Record 1999 - 1st:0 2nd:1 3rd:0 Ran:10
Pre1999 - 1st:0 2nd:0 3rd:3 Ran:24
Win Prizemoney £0 *Total Prizemoney* £2,329
1999 Turf 0-9: (7f 2, 8f 6, 10f) (g-f 3, frm 5, hrd) 1999 AW 0-1: (8f) (Fibr)
Very moderate gelding, effective 8f, acts on g-f, has worn blinkers, likes left handed tracks. Turf high 43 - 2nd of 9 getting 5lb from Danzas (28 May Nottingham 8f g-f RF 1553). Consistent.
**M Brittain [0-20] Mel Brittain (from J J O'Neill [0-14] Aug 1997).*

WAHJ (IRE) BHB 91f **RR 100f** 4675[11]
4 ch c Indian Ridge 7.6f **(74)** - Sabaah (USA) (Nureyev (USA)) 8.7f **(78)**
Form - 83040
Record 1999 - 1st:0 2nd:0 3rd:1 Ran:5
Pre1999 - 1st:2 2nd:0 3rd:0 Ran:2
Win Prizemoney £9,162 *Total Prizemoney* £11,623
Wins * 1998 Aug Chepst (G-F) 7.1f 103 <
* 1998 Aug Windso (G-F) 8.3f 82++
1999 Turf 0-5: (6f, 7f 3, 8f) (g-s, gd 3, g-f)
Scopey, very useful colt, effective 7f, acts on gd. Turf high 100 - 3rd of 6 getting 7lb from Warningford (5 Jun Haydock 7f gd RF 1766). He has always been highly regarded, but proved disappointing in 1999 and seems a horse without a trip.
**Sir Michael Stoute [2-7] Hamdan Al Maktoum.*

WAIKATO BHB 43f **RR 40f** 3919[7]
2 ch f Clantime 6.6f **(57)** - Naufrage (Main Reef) 9.6f **(57)**
Form - 045067
Record 1999 - 1st:0 2nd:0 3rd:0 Ran:6
1999 Turf 0-5: (5f 4, 6f) (gd, g-f 3, frm) 1999 AW 0-1: (5f) (Fibr)
Moderate filly. Turf high 40. **M W Easterby [0-6] Mrs Denise Shefras.*

WAIKIKI BEACH (USA) BHB 37f56a **RR 33f 56a** 4783[3]
8 ch g Fighting Fit (USA) 7.9f **(70)** - Running Melody (Rheingold) 10.4f **(62)**
Form - 017544100353373
Record 1999 - 1st:1 2nd:0 3rd:4 Ran:12
Pre1999 - 1st:7 2nd:7 3rd:4 Ran:49
Win Prizemoney £32,052 *Total Prizemoney* £42,618
Wins * 1999 *Mar Lingfi (STD) H 8f 54 65*
* 1998 *Nov Lingfi (STD) S 10f 60+*
* 1998 *Apr Southw (STD) H 8f 56 61*
* 1996 *Dec Lingfi (STD) C 10f 69*
* 1996 *Jun Lingfi (STD) 8f 80+*
* 1996 *Apr Wolver (STD) 8.5f 65*
1999 Turf 0-3: (7f, 8f, 10f) (g-s, frm 2) 1999 AW 1-9: (7f, 8f 1-6, 10f 2) (Equi 1-7, Fibr 2)
Average gelding, effective 8 to 10f, best at 8f, - acts on AW, best on Equi, has worn blinkers, likes left handed tracks, favours tight tracks. Turf high 33. AW high 65 - 1st of 12 giving 4lb to Denbrae (18 Mar Lingfield RF 0447). He has won on Fibresand, but looks better on Equitrack. Good ride for an amateur.
**G L Moore [8-61] Mrs J Moore.*

WAIN MOUNTAIN BHB 61a **RR 61a** 10[10]
3 b c Unfuwain (USA) 11.4f **(74)** - Mountain Memory (High Top) 10.2f **(67)**
Form - 720
Record 1999 - 1st:0 2nd:0 3rd:0 Ran:1
Pre1999 - 1st:0 2nd:1 3rd:0 Ran:2
Win Prizemoney £0 *Total Prizemoney* £856
1999 AW 0-1: (10f) (Equi)
Currently above-average colt.
**Sir Mark Prescott [0-3] Hesmonds Stud.*

WAIT FOR THE WILL (USA) BHB 79f **RR 80f** 4791[13]
3 ch c Seeking the Gold (USA) 7.4f **(80)** - You'd Be Surprised (USA) (Blushing Groom (FR)) 10.3f **(76)**
Form - 613060
Record 1999 - 1st:1 2nd:0 3rd:1 Ran:6
Pre1999 - 1st:0 2nd:0 3rd:0 Ran:2
Win Prizemoney £2,430 *Total Prizemoney* £3,625
Wins * 1999 Jly Salisb (G-F) H 12f 75 78 <
1999 Turf 1-6: (10f, 12f 1-3, 13f, 14f) (gd 2, g-f, frm 1-3)
Scopey, decent colt, effective 8 to 13f, acts on gd to frm, has worn blinkers. Turf high 80 - 3rd of 8 getting 1lb from Rada's Daughter (25 Jly Ascot 12f g-f RF 3116) - also 1st of 14 giving 19lb to Patrita Park (10 Jly Salisbury RF 2716).
**G L Moore [1-6] Richard Green (Fine Paintings) (from I A Balding [0-2] Spt 1998).*

WAITING KNIGHT (USA) BHB 67f56a **RR 66f 56a** 3114[2]
4 b br c St Jovite (USA) 11.8f **(75)** - Phydilla (FR) (Lyphard (USA)) 9.9f **(72)**
Form - 624136266502
Record 1999 - 1st:1 2nd:3 3rd:1 Ran:11
Pre1999 - 1st:0 2nd:3 3rd:1 Ran:11
Win Prizemoney £3,572 *Total Prizemoney* £10,706
Wins * 1999 *Feb Lingfi (STD) 8f 68* <
1999 AW 1-11: (6f, 7f 5, 8f 1-4, 12f) (Equi 1-2, Fibr 9)
Rangy, average colt, effective 6 to 9f, best at 8f, acts on sft to frm - acts on AW, often wears blinkers. AW high 68 - 1st of 7 giving 19lb to Wild Thing (2 Feb Lingfield RF 0211).
**Mrs N Macauley [1-12] Mrs N Macauley (from B Hanbury [0-10] Spt 1998).*

WAIT'N'SEE BHB 50f46a **RR 41f 46a** 4747a[11]
4 b g Komaite (USA) 6.9f **(61)** - Kakisa (Forlorn River) 7.3f **(54)**
Form - 06600
Record 1999 - 1st:0 2nd:0 3rd:0 Ran:5
Pre1999 - 1st:1 2nd:1 3rd:1 Ran:18
Win Prizemoney £2,947 *Total Prizemoney* £4,119
Wins 1997 Jun Carlis (FRM) 5f 77 <
1999 Turf 0-4: (5f 2, 7f, 8f) (g-s, gd 3) 1999 AW 0-1: (7f) (Fibr)
Light-framed, moderate gelding, effective 6f, acts on gd, has worn blinkers. Turf high 41. Inconsistent.
**M McElhone in IRE [0-2] Brian Rogerson (from M W Easterby [1-21] May 1999).*

WAJINA (FR) RR 98f 2477a[5]
3 f
Form - 15
1999 Turf 1-2: (11f 1-1, 12f) (gd 1-2)

Currently very useful, often wears blinkers. Turf high 98 - 5th of 8 to Sage Et Jolie (27 Jun Longchamp 12f gd RF 2477a).
**A Fabre in FR [1-2].*

WALES BHB 103f **RR 102f** 5051[4]
4 ch c Caerleon (USA) 10.9f **(79)** - Knight's Baroness (Rainbow Quest (USA)) 10.4f **(75)**
Form - 71018624434
Record 1999 - 1st:2 2nd:1 3rd:1 Ran:11
Pre1999 - 1st:1 2nd:2 3rd:2 Ran:10
Win Prizemoney £17,084 *Total Prizemoney* £30,201
Wins * **1999** Jun Newmar (G-F) H 12f 99 103 <
* **1999** May Goodwo (GD) 12f 98+
* **1997** Spt Goodwo (GD) 8f 82
1999 Turf 2-11: (10f, 12f 2-8, 13f, 14f) (sft, gd 1-4, g-f 3, frm 1-3)
Light-framed, very useful colt, effective 12 to 16f, best at 12f, acts on sft to frm, has worn blinkers, prefers right handed tracks, excels at Ascot and Newmarket, does well at Haydock. Turf high 106 - 2nd of 6 giving 5lb to Memorise (7 Aug Ascot 12f gd RF 3445) - also 1st of 5 giving 17lb to Tayil (18 Jun Newmarket RF 2122). Made all the running to win at Goodwood on his second start of the season, and did the same to score at Newmarket. Obviously likes to dominate, but does not find a lot when taken on, and is a 'twilight' horse who plies his trade in conditions races.
**P F I Cole [3-21] H R H Prince Fahd Salman.*

WALLACE BHB 113f **RR 117f** 4652[8]
3 b c Royal Academy (USA) 7.8f **(77)** - Masskana (IRE) (Darshaan) 9.9f **(84)**
Form - 27131428
Record 1999 - 1st:2 2nd:2 3rd:1 Ran:8
Pre1999 - 1st:0 2nd:0 3rd:2 Ran:4
Win Prizemoney £38,723 *Total Prizemoney* £62,701
Wins * **1999** Jly Ascot (G-F) L 8f 106 <
* **1999** May Goodwo (GD) 8f 86
1999 Turf 2-8: (8f 2-7, 9f) (gd 2-5, g-f 3)
Scopey, high-class colt, effective 8 to 9f, acts on gd to g-f. Turf high 117 - 2nd of 10 getting 5lb from Sugarfoot (9 Spt Doncaster 8f g-f RF 4235). Considering he was a maiden, he ran a fine race in Kempton's Easter Stakes on his reappearance last season before deservedly getting off the mark at Goodwood on his third start. He enjoyed his biggest moment when beating Haami by the minimum margin in an Ascot Listed event, and was almost victorious in Group company when beaten a short-head by Sugarfoot in Doncaster's Park Stakes. He is talented, but not always the easiest of rides.
**R Hannon [2-12] J A Lazzari.*

WALNUT LADY RR 62f 3927a[3]
2 ch f Forzando 7.2f **(63)** - Princess Tateum (IRE) **(67f 48a)** (Tate Gallery (USA)) 7.4f **(67)**
Form - 5613
Record 1999 - 1st:1 2nd:0 3rd:1 Ran:4
Win Prizemoney £1,882 *Total Prizemoney* £5,481
Wins 1999 *May Southw (STD) S 5f 61* <
1999 Turf 0-3: (5f 3) (sft, g-s, gd) 1999 AW 1-1: (5f 1-1) (Fibr 1-1)
Average filly. Turf high 62 - 3rd of 9 to Mona Em (21 Aug Deauville 5f gd RF 3927a). (1st run) - 1st of 9 getting 5lb from Pape Diouf (10 May Southwell RF 1134).
**R Collet in FR [0-1] (from W G M Turner [1-3] May 1999).*

WALNUT WONDER RR 3083[11]
2 b f Pyramus (USA) - Super Style (Artaius (USA)) 9f **(69)**
Form - 0
Record 1999 - 1st:0 2nd:0 3rd:0 Ran:1
1999 AW 0-1: (7f) (Fibr)
Currently poor filly.
**W G M Turner [0-1] Walnut Revellers Racing Club.*

WALTER PLINGE BHB 32f **RR 34f** 4988[14]
3 b g Theatrical Charmer 10.9f **(63)** - Carousel Zingira (Reesh)
Form - 06253600
Record 1999 - 1st:0 2nd:1 3rd:1 Ran:7
Pre1999 - 1st:0 2nd:0 3rd:0 Ran:2
Win Prizemoney £0 *Total Prizemoney* £978
1999 Turf 0-6: (10f 2, 12f 2, 14f 2) (g-f 2, frm 4) 1999 AW 0-1: (7f) (Fibr)
Very moderate gelding, effective 10 to 12f, best at 10f, acts on g-f to frm, best on g-f, prefers left handed tracks, favours tight tracks. Turf high 40 - 3rd of 11 getting 5lb from Bay of Bengal (28 Jun Pontefract 12f frm RF 2368). Inconsistent.
**A G Juckes [0-4] Tony Cocum (from S C Williams [0-7] Jly 1999).*

WALTER THE WHISTLE RR 19f 3739[13]
2 b c Pips Pride 6.7f **(70)** - Fleur de Lyphard (USA) (Lyphard (USA)) 9.9f **(72)**
Form - 0
Record 1999 - 1st:0 2nd:0 3rd:0 Ran:1
1999 Turf 0-1: (6f) (g-s)
Currently poor colt. **A P Jarvis [0-1] Ms Julie Greenacre.*

WALTHAM SKYLARK BHB 32f **RR 26f** 4440[12]
4 b f Puissance 7.1f **(60)** - Pear Drop (Bustino) 10.4f **(64)**
Form - 0000
Record 1999 - 1st:0 2nd:0 3rd:0 Ran:4
Pre1999 - 1st:0 2nd:0 3rd:0 Ran:4
1999 Turf 0-4: (6f 3, 8f) (gd 2, g-f, frm)
Lengthy, little account filly. Turf high 26 (began Jly).
**K A Morgan [0-8] D & M Cased Hole.*

WANDERING WOLF BHB 47f **RR 66f** 3659[16]
4 ch c Wolfhound (USA) 7.3f **(71)** - Circle of Chalk (FR) (Kris) 9.5f **(73)**
Form - 7860
Record 1999 - 1st:0 2nd:0 3rd:0 Ran:4
Pre1999 - 1st:0 2nd:0 3rd:0 Ran:5
Win Prizemoney £0 *Total Prizemoney* £486
1999 Turf 0-4: (7f 4) (g-f 4)
Average colt. Turf high 66. Becoming disappointing.
**S P C Woods [0-4] Lucayan Stud (from R Hannon [0-5] May 1998).*

WANLASS DANCER BHB 32f **RR 38f** 4928[10]
2 b f King's Signet (USA) 7f **(51)** - Consistent Queen (Queen's Hussar) 11.6f **(58)**
Form - 000000
Record 1999 - 1st:0 2nd:0 3rd:0 Ran:6
1999 Turf 0-6: (5f 4, 6f 2) (gd, g-f 3, frm 2)
Very moderate filly. Turf high 38 (began Jly).
**M E Sowersby [0-6] Mrs S Jackson.*

WANNABE GRAND (IRE) BHB 111f **RR 109f** 4884a[3]
3 b f Danehill (USA) 9.1f **(79)** - Wannabe (Shirley Heights) 10.3f **(74)**
Form - 2372173
Record 1999 - 1st:1 2nd:2 3rd:2 Ran:7
Pre1999 - 1st:3 2nd:2 3rd:0 Ran:8
Win Prizemoney £142,638 *Total Prizemoney* £268,993
Wins * **1999** Aug Pontef (GD) L 6f 107 <
* 1998 Spt Newmar (GD) G1 6f 104
* 1998 Jly Newmar (G-F) G2 6f 103
* 1998 Jun Newmar (GD) 6f 74
1999 Turf 1-7: (6f 1-3, 7f, 8f 2, 9f) (g-f, frm 1-6)
Scopey, Pattern-class filly, effective 6 to 9f, best at 8f, acts on g-f to frm, best on frm, likes Newmarket. Turf high 114 (1st run) - 2nd of 22 to Wince (2 May Newmarket 8f frm RF 0979) - also 1st of 7 from Pipalong (22 Aug Pontefract RF 3846). Consistent. She was trained to the minute when finishing second behind Wince in the 1,000 Guineas, and failed to improve on that performance. A tricky ride who had to be held up until the last moment, she has been retired to stud. **J Noseda [4-15].*

WANSFORD LADY RR 24f 913[8]
3 b f Michelozzo (USA) - Marnie's Girl (Crooner) 9.9f **(49)**
Form - 8
Record 1999 - 1st:0 2nd:0 3rd:0 Ran:1
Pre1999 - 1st:0 2nd:0 3rd:0 Ran:1
1999 Turf 0-1: (10f) (frm)
Light-framed, currently little account filly.
**C N Kellett [0-2] Mrs V Robson.*

WAR BABY BHB 42f **RR 46f** 4823[14]
3 b f Warrshan (USA) 9.7f **(59)** - Dutch Czarina (Prince Sabo) 7.2f **(62)**
Form - 000580
Record 1999 - 1st:0 2nd:0 3rd:0 Ran:6
1999 Turf 0-6: (7f, 8f, 9f, 10f, 11f, 15f) (g-s, g-f 3, frm 2)
Leggy, moderate filly. Turf high 46.
**Miss B Sanders [0-6] Mrs J M Laycock.*

WAR CABINET BHB 93f **RR 94f** 2043[8]

3 b c Rainbow Quest (USA) 11.2f **(81)** - Balleta (USA) (Lyphard (USA)) 9.9f **(72)**
Form - 5218
Record 1999 - 1st:1 2nd:1 3rd:0 Ran:4
Win Prizemoney £4,002 *Total Prizemoney* £5,107
Wins * 1999 May Nottin (FRM) 14.1f 83+ <
1999 Turf 1-4: (12f 2, 14f 1-1, 16f) (g-f 1-3, frm)
Light-framed, useful colt. Turf high 94. He seemed to appreciate the step up to one-mile-six when winning on fast ground at Nottingham but seemed not to stay two miles at Ascot.
**H R A Cecil [1-4] K Abdulla.*

WARDAT ALLAYL (IRE) BHB 89f **RR 86f** 4236^{12}
2 b f Mtoto 11.5f **(71)** - Society Lady (USA) (Mr Prospector (USA)) 8.8f **(78)**
Form - 3180
Record 1999 - 1st:1 2nd:0 3rd:1 Ran:4
Win Prizemoney £10,514 *Total Prizemoney* £12,163
Wins * 1999 Jly Newbur (G-F) 7f 86 <
1999 Turf 1-4: (7f 1-3, 8f) (g-f 1-3, frm)
Useful filly. Turf high 86 - 1st of 6 getting 8lb from With Iris (17 Jly Newbury RF 2899). Won well on her second start, but was not up to tackling the top fillies.
**M R Channon [1-4] Sheikh Ahmed Al Maktoum.*

WAR DECLARATION (IRE) RR 109f $1715a^{9}$
5 br h Persian Bold 10f **(69)** - Lutoviska (Glenstal (USA)) 10.1f **(64)**
Form - 350
1999 Turf 0-2: (10f, 12f) (gd, frm)
Pattern-class colt, effective 10 to 12f, acts on sft to g-f. Turf high 108. Consistent. **B Grizzetti in ITY [3-13].*

WARM HEART (USA) BHB 100f **RR 109f** 4653^{4}
2 ch c Diesis 9f **(80)** - Warm Mood (USA) (Alydar (USA)) 9.1f **(76)**
Form - 1124
Record 1999 - 1st:2 2nd:1 3rd:0 Ran:4
Win Prizemoney £35,855 *Total Prizemoney* £75,301

Warm Heart was a speedy juvenile

Wins * 1999 Jun Ascot (G-F) G3 5f 102++ <
*** 1999** Jun Newcas (G-F) 5f 90++
1999 Turf 2-4: (5f 2-2, 6f 2) (gd 2, g-f 1-1, frm 1-1)
Pattern-class colt. Turf high 109 - also 1st of 13 from Victory Day (17 Jun Ascot RF 2070). Looked Royal Ascot material when beating a useful sort at Newcastle, and duly landed the Norfolk Stakes in good style. A fair second to Fasliyev in the Prix Morny at Deauville, beating stablemate Bachir, he was on edge beforehand and ran below expectations in the Middle Park Stakes on his final run. Remains a useful prospect.
**J H M Gosden [2-4] Sheikh Mohammed.*

WARNINGFORD BHB 111f **RR 113f** 4916^{6}
5 b h Warning 8.1f **(77)** - Barford Lady (Stanford) 7.9f **(56)**
Form - 11212206
Record 1999 - 1st:3 2nd:3 3rd:0 Ran:8
Pre1999 - 1st:3 2nd:2 3rd:1 Ran:18
Win Prizemoney £57,885 *Total Prizemoney* £96,705
Wins * 1999 Jun Haydoc (GD-) L 7.1f 113 <
*** 1999** Apr Leices (HVY) G3 7f 110
*** 1999** Apr Warwic (GD) 7f 104
* 1998 Spt Goodwo (SFT) H 7f 99 104
* 1998 Jly Yarmou (G-F) H 7f 97 99
* 1997 Jun Sandow (G-F) 7.1f 90
1999 Turf 3-8: (6f 2, 7f 3-6) (sft 1-2, gd 2-6)
Group-class colt, effective 6 to 7f, best at 7f, acts on sft to frm, best on gd, has worn blinkers, likes left handed tracks. Turf high 113 - 1st of 6 from Tumbleweed Ridge (5 Jun Haydock RF 1766) - also 1st of 7 from Wind Cheetah (24 Apr Leicester RF 0832). Consistent. He invariably takes the eye in the paddock and had a fine season, winning a Group Three at Leicester in April. Best over seven furlongs on easy ground, he has worn a visor in the past but did not do so in 1999. **J R Fanshawe [6-26] Barford Bloodstock.*

WARNING NOTE (IRE) RR 17f 5207^{15}
2 b c Zieten (USA) - Cachet (IRE) (Warning)
Form - 0
Record 1999 - 1st:0 2nd:0 3rd:0 Ran:1
1999 Turf 0-1: (7f) (g-s)
Currently poor colt. **R Hannon [0-1] John Homer Racing.*

WARNING REEF BHB 62f65a **RR 66f 65a** 4930^{9}
6 b g Warning 8.1f **(77)** - Horseshoe Reef (Mill Reef (USA)) 10.5f **(78)**
Form - 00235533324040
Record 1999 - 1st:0 2nd:2 3rd:4 Ran:14
Pre1999 - 1st:3 2nd:7 3rd:5 Ran:35
Win Prizemoney £25,820 *Total Prizemoney* £51,684
Wins * 1998 Aug Ascot (G-F) H 12f 57 60 <
* 1998 Jly Sandow (GD) H 11.4f 53 54
* 1998 Jun Carlis (G-S) H 12f 49 51
1999 Turf 0-14: (10f 3, 11f 2, 12f 9) (gd 5, g-f 6, frm 2, hrd)
Average gelding, effective 10 to 12f, best at 12f, acts on g-s to frm, has worn blinkers, likes right handed tracks, excels at Ascot and Sandown and does well at York. Turf high 66 - 2nd of 12 getting 16lb from Livius (7 Aug Ascot 12f gd RF 3447). Consistent. He did not win last season, but put in some sterling efforts in competitive handicaps if not enjoying the best of luck.
**E J Alston [3-29] Valley Paddocks Racing Ltd (from P Eccles [0-7] Aug 1997).*

WARREN KNIGHT BHB 41f **RR 24f** 1733^{11}
6 b g Weldnaas (USA) 8.4f **(55)** - Trigamy (Tribal Chief) 8.5f **(61)**
Form - 00
Record 1999 - 1st:0 2nd:0 3rd:0 Ran:2
Pre1999 - 1st:0 2nd:0 3rd:0 Ran:11
Win Prizemoney £0 *Total Prizemoney* £390
1999 Turf 0-2: (8f, 9f) (gd 2)
Little account gelding. Turf high 24.
**C A Horgan [0-13] Mrs B Sumner.*

WARRING BHB 50f39a **RR 48f 39a** 5156^{15}
5 b g Warrshan (USA) 9.7f **(59)** - Emerald Ring (Auction Ring (USA)) 8.6f **(65)**
Form - 0782020540
Record 1999 - 1st:0 2nd:2 3rd:0 Ran:8
Pre1999 - 1st:2 2nd:3 3rd:0 Ran:25
Win Prizemoney £10,552 *Total Prizemoney* £19,086
Wins * 1998 Aug Windso (G-F) H 8.3f 54 60 <
* 1998 Jly Windso (G-F) H 8.3f 46 54
1999 Turf 0-8: (7f, 8f 7) (g-s, gd 4, g-f, frm 2)
Moderate gelding, effective 8f, acts on gd to hrd, best on gd, prefers tight tracks, excels at Windsor, does well at Bath. Turf high 54 - 2nd of 16 getting 10lb from Twin Time (17 May Bath 8f gd RF 1272).
**M S Saunders [2-29] Chris Scott (from M R Channon [0-4] Oct 1996).*

WARRING KINGDOM BHB 63f **RR 65f** 5188^{P}

3 b g Warrshan (USA) 9.7f **(59)** - Rise and Fall (Mill Reef (USA)) 10.5f **(78)**
Form - 00635211132P
Record 1999 - 1st:3 2nd:2 3rd:2 Ran:10
Pre1999 - 1st:0 2nd:0 3rd:0 Ran:3
Win Prizemoney £10,122 *Total Prizemoney* £13,258
Wins * **1999** Spt Mussel (G-F) H 16f 50 56 <
* **1999** Spt Mussel (G-F) H 16f 38 46+
* **1999** Aug Carlis (G-F) H 17.2f 38 43
1999 Turf 3-10: (8f, 10f 2, 16f 2-5, 17f 1-1, 18f)(gd 2, g-f 3, frm 3-4, hrd)
Workmanlike, average gelding, effective 16 to 18f, best at 16f, acted on gd to frm, had worn blinkers. Turf high 65 - 3rd of 11 giving 11lb to Pretty Obvious (29 Spt Newcastle 16f gd RF 4639) - also 1st of 8 getting 1lb from Lady Confess (13 Spt Musselburgh RF 4281). A progressive stayer, he broke a leg at Musselburgh in November. (DEAD) **John Berry [3-13] The 1997 Partnership.*

WARRIOR KING (IRE) BHB 27f30a RR 31f 30a 2767[8]
5 b g Fairy King (USA) 7.7f **(75)** - It's All Academic (IRE) (Mazaad) 7.1f **(45)**
Form - 080688
Record 1999 - 1st:0 2nd:0 3rd:0 Ran:4
Pre1999 - 1st:1 2nd:3 3rd:1 Ran:27
Win Prizemoney £3,241 *Total Prizemoney* £5,740
Wins 1997 Aug Mussel (GD) H 7.1f 47 53 <
1999 Turf 0-4: (8f, 10f 2, 16f) (gd, g-f, frm 2)
Very moderate gelding, has worn blinkers. Turf high 31.
**Mrs S Lamyman [0-4] William Curtis Racing Partnership (from K Mahdi [0-2] Nov 1998).*

WARRIOR QUEEN (USA) RR 99f 5225a[8]
2 b f Quiet American (USA) 7.9f **(60)** - Call Me Fleet (USA) (Afleet (CAN))
Form - 13618
1999 Turf 2-4: (5f, 6f 2-3) (gd 1-3, g-f 1-1) 1999 AW 0-1: (9f) (Dirt)
Very useful filly. Turf high 99 - 1st of 5 from Poco A Poco (5 Spt Curragh RF 4198a). An edgy sort, she takes a strong hold and has given trouble at the start. Badly outpaced in the Breeders' Cup Juvenile Fillies, she could find life tough in 2000.
**A P O'Brien in IRE [2-5].*

WARS (IRE) BHB 46f RR 40f 4171[15]
4 b f Green Desert (USA) 7.8f **(78)** - Ardassine (Ahonoora) 8.1f **(73)**
Form - 06005070
Record 1999 - 1st:0 2nd:0 3rd:0 Ran:8
Win Prizemoney £0 *Total Prizemoney* £172
1999 Turf 0-8: (6f, 7f 6, 9f) (g-s, gd, g-f 2, frm 4)
Workmanlike, moderate filly, has worn blinkers. Turf high 77.
**J E Banks [0-8] K J Mercer.*

WASEYLA (IRE) BHB 75f RR 73f 5189[4]
2 b f Sri Pekan (USA) - Lady Windley (Baillamont (USA)) 7f **(78)**
Form - 754
Record 1999 - 1st:0 2nd:0 3rd:0 Ran:3
Win Prizemoney £0 *Total Prizemoney* £255
1999 Turf 0-3: (7f, 8f 2) (sft, g-f, frm)
Currently above-average filly, has worn blinkers. Turf high 73 (began Jly) - 4th of 9 to Littlepacepaddocks (3 Nov Musselburgh 8f g-f RF 5189). **J H M Gosden [0-3] Sheikh Ahmed Al Maktoum.*

WASI RR 37f 5021[18]
2 b br c Emperor Jones (USA) - Miss Ivory Coast (USA) (Sir Ivor) 10.2f **(70)**
Form - 0
Record 1999 - 1st:0 2nd:0 3rd:0 Ran:1
1999 Turf 0-1: (7f) (gd)
Currently very moderate colt.
**J H M Gosden [0-1] Hamdan Al Maktoum.*

WASP RANGER (USA) BHB 72f RR 74f 4404[10]
5 b g Red Ransom (USA) 8.6f **(83)** - Lady Climber (USA) (Mount Hagen (FR)) 8.4f **(70)**
Form - 0484100200
Record 1999 - 1st:1 2nd:1 3rd:0 Ran:10
Pre1999 - 1st:1 2nd:2 3rd:1 Ran:11
Win Prizemoney £11,989 *Total Prizemoney* £29,155
Wins * **1999** Jly Kempto (G-F) H 10f 69 72
1997 May Goodwo (GD) 8f 78 <
1999 Turf 1-10: (8f 3, 9f, 10f 1-5, 12f) (g-s, gd 2, g-f, frm 1-6)
Above-average gelding, effective 8 to 10f, best at 10f, acts on gd to frm, best on frm, has worn blinkers, prefers right handed tracks. Turf high 74 - 2nd of 13 to Fantazia (28 Aug Newmarket 10f frm RF 3964) - also 1st of 8 giving 8lb to Broughtons Error (14 Jly Kempton RF 2826). Scored in good style at Kempton in July, but was a little disappointing until running a fine race at Newmarket in August. Best when held up for a late run, ten furlongs looks his best trip.
**G L Moore [1-10] Rodger Sargent (from P F I Cole [1-11] Spt 1997).*

WATCHING BHB 100f RR 96f 4793[3]
2 ch c Indian Ridge 7.6f **(74)** - Sweeping (Indian King (USA)) 7.4f **(64)**
Form - 313225423
Record 1999 - 1st:1 2nd:3 3rd:3 Ran:9
Win Prizemoney £3,415 *Total Prizemoney* £23,517
Wins * **1999** Jun Cheste (SFT) 5.1f 83+ <
1999 Turf 1-9: (5f 1-4, 6f 4, 7f) (hvy, g-s 1-1, gd 3, g-f 2, frm 2)
Very useful colt, effective 5 to 6f, best at 5f, acts on hvy to frm. Turf high 96 - 3rd of 13 to Kier Park (9 Oct Ascot 5f gd RF 4793). Improving. An admirable colt, he was regularly set searching tests but always gave his best. Unlikely to stay beyond six furlongs, he will struggle against later-maturing rivals next term.
**R Hannon [1-9] Mrs Dare Wigan.*

WATER BABE BHB 60f RR 63f 5005[12]
2 b f Lake Coniston (IRE) - Isabella Sharp **(67f)** (Sharpo) 7.7f **(59)**
Form - 850
Record 1999 - 1st:0 2nd:0 3rd:0 Ran:3
1999 Turf 0-3: (5f 3) (gd 2, frm)
Currently average filly. Turf high 63 (began Aug).
**J W Payne [0-3] Raymond Tooth.*

WATER ECHO (USA) BHB 80f RR 80f 4294[3]
2 b f Mr Prospector (USA) 8.6f **(88)** - Magic of Life (USA) (Seattle Slew (USA)) 9.4f **(76)**
Form - 62313
Record 1999 - 1st:1 2nd:1 3rd:2 Ran:5
Win Prizemoney £3,712 *Total Prizemoney* £6,953
Wins * **1999** Aug Bright (G-S) 6f 71 <
1999 Turf 1-5: (6f 1-4, 7f) (gd 1-1, g-f, frm 3)
Decent filly. Turf high 80 (began Jly) - 3rd of 11 giving 10lb to Lady of Honour (14 Spt Yarmouth 7f g-f RF 4294) - also 1st of 6 getting 12lb from Mersey Mirage (17 Aug Brighton RF 3686).
**Sir Michael Stoute [1-5] Niarchos Family.*

WATER FLOWER BHB 68f RR 71f 4581[13]
5 b m Environment Friend 7.5f **(67)** - Flower Girl (Pharly (FR)) 9.8f **(68)**
Form - 1821170
Record 1999 - 1st:3 2nd:1 3rd:0 Ran:7
Pre1999 - 1st:1 2nd:0 3rd:1 Ran:6
Win Prizemoney £12,124 *Total Prizemoney* £13,401
Wins * **1999** Aug Chepst (G-F) H 12.1f 68 71 <
* **1999** Jly Chepst (G-F) H 12.1f 65 67
* **1999** Jun Salisb (GD) H 12f 62 65
1997 Oct Newmar (G-F) C 12f 58
1999 Turf 3-7: (12f 3-5, 16f, 17f) (gd, g-f 1-4, frm 2-2)
Above-average filly, effective 12f, acts on g-f to frm, best on frm, prefers tight tracks. Turf high 71 - 1st of 5 giving 6lb to Gypsy Hill (5 Aug Chepstow RF 3395) - also 1st of 19 giving 12lb to Indigo Bay (23 Jly Chepstow RF 3053).
**B R Millman [3-7] Avalon Surfacing Ltd (from J R Fanshawe [1-6] Oct 1997).*

WATERFORD SPIRIT (IRE) BHB 75f RR 74f 2503[12]
3 ch g Shalford (IRE) 7.8f **(63)** - Rebecca's Girl (IRE) (Nashamaa) 7.1f **(66)**
Form - 60041040
Record 1999 - 1st:1 2nd:0 3rd:0 Ran:8
Pre1999 - 1st:0 2nd:2 3rd:0 Ran:4
Win Prizemoney £7,064 *Total Prizemoney* £10,063
Wins * **1999** May Thirsk (G-S) H 5f 73 74 <
1999 Turf 1-8: (5f 1-6, 6f 2) (hvy, g-s, gd 1-4, g-f 2)
Scopey, above-average gelding, effective 5f, acts on g-s to gd. Turf high 74 - 1st of 9 getting 1lb from Amaranth (15 May Thirsk RF 1253). **T D Barron [1-12] P D Savill.*

WATERFRONT (IRE) BHB 47f **RR 47f** 4718[17]
3 b g Turtle Island (IRE) - Rising Tide (Red Alert) 7.6f **(66)**
Form - 5207570080
Record 1999 - 1st:0 2nd:1 3rd:0 Ran:10
Pre1999 - 1st:0 2nd:0 3rd:0 Ran:1
Win Prizemoney £0 *Total Prizemoney* £1,048
1999 Turf 0-10: (6f 3, 7f 3, 8f 3, 9f) (gd 3, g-f 2, frm 5)
Workmanlike, moderate gelding, has worn blinkers. Turf high 69.
**R Bastiman [0-6] J R Swift (from P W Chapple-Hyam [0-5] Jun 1999).*

WATERGOLD (IRE) BHB 43f **RR 32f** 5186[10]
2 ch c Shalford (IRE) 7.8f **(63)** - Trust Sally (Sallust) 8.4f **(63)**
Form - 000
Record 1999 - 1st:0 2nd:0 3rd:0 Ran:3
1999 Turf 0-3: (7f 2, 8f) (gd, g-f, frm)
Currently very moderate colt. Turf high 32 (began Spt).
**I Semple [0-3] Patersons of Greenoakhill.*

WATERGRASSHILL BHB 56f **RR 69f** 5194[8]
2 b f Terimon 8.7f **(58)** - Party Game (Red Alert) 7.6f **(66)**
Form - 708
Record 1999 - 1st:0 2nd:0 3rd:0 Ran:3
1999 Turf 0-3: (6f 2, 7f) (gd 2, frm)
Currently average filly. Turf high 69 (began Aug).
**N A Callaghan [0-3] A R G Else, M P Jones & N A Callaghan.*

WATER HUNTER BHB 82f88a **RR 84f 88a** 4486[2]
2 ch g Mukaddamah (USA) 7.6f **(74)** - Oasis (Valiyar) 8.5f **(73)**
Form - 80011222
Record 1999 - 1st:2 2nd:3 3rd:0 Ran:8
Win Prizemoney £4,945 *Total Prizemoney* £9,497
Wins * 1999 *Aug Wolver (STD) H* *7f* *80 90+* <
*** 1999** *Jly Southw (STD) C* *6f* *85*
1999 Turf 0-5: (5f 2, 6f, 7f, 8f) (g-s, gd, g-f, frm 2) 1999 AW 2-3: (6f 1-1, 7f 1-1, 8f) (Fibr 2-3)
Useful gelding, effective 6 to 7f, best at 7f, acts on gd - acts on Fibr. Turf high 84 - 2nd of 9 giving 10lb to Distinctly Well (20 Aug Chester 7f gd RF 3789). AW high 90 (began Jly) - 1st of 6 getting 8lb from Islay Mist (6 Aug Wolverhampton RF 3438) - also 1st of 7 giving 5lb to Blackpool Mamma's (24 Jly Southwell RF 3111). Inconsistent. **J W Payne [2-8] Nagy Azar.*

WATER JUMP (IRE) BHB 85f **RR 85f** 4587[1]
2 b c Suave Dancer (USA) 10.7f **(68)** - Jolies Eaux (Shirley Heights) 10.3f **(74)**
Form - 221
Record 1999 - 1st:1 2nd:2 3rd:0 Ran:3
Win Prizemoney £3,322 *Total Prizemoney* £4,709
Wins * 1999 Spt Hamilt (SFT) 8.3f 74 <
1999 Turf 1-3: (8f 1-3) (gd 1-1, g-f, frm)
Currently useful colt. Turf high 85 (began Aug) - 2nd of 12 to Compton Bolter (9 Spt Chepstow 8f frm RF 4227).
**J L Dunlop [1-3] The Earl Cadogan.*

WATER LOUP BHB 46f **RR 53f** 4586[11]
3 b f Wolfhound (USA) 7.3f **(71)** - Heavenly Waters (Celestial Storm (USA))
Form - 3404880
Record 1999 - 1st:0 2nd:0 3rd:1 Ran:7
Pre1999 - 1st:0 2nd:0 3rd:0 Ran:2
Win Prizemoney £0 *Total Prizemoney* £800
1999 Turf 0-7: (8f 4, 9f, 10f 2) (g-s, gd, g-f, frm 4)
Scopey, fair filly, effective 8f, acts on frm, likes tight tracks. Turf high 58 - 4th of 15 giving 2lb to Pacific Alliance (11 Jun Sandown 8f frm RF 1921). **W R Muir [0-9] J Haim.*

WATHBAT MUJTAHID BHB 86f **RR 79f** 5157[2]
2 ch c Mujtahid (USA) 7.4f **(69)** - Wathbat Mtoto **(88f)** (Mtoto)
Form - 032
Record 1999 - 1st:0 2nd:1 3rd:1 Ran:3
Win Prizemoney £0 *Total Prizemoney* £1,527
1999 Turf 0-3: (7f 3) (gd 2, frm)
Currently above-average colt. Turf high 79 (began Spt) - 2nd of 15 to Norton (1 Nov Redcar 7f frm RF 5157).
**A C Stewart [0-3] Sheikh Ahmed Al Maktoum.*

WATKINS BHB 29f **RR 10f** 2553[5]
4 ch g King's Signet (USA) 7f **(51)** - Windbound Lass (Crofter (USA)) 8.4f **(56)**
Form - 005
Record 1999 - 1st:0 2nd:0 3rd:0 Ran:3
Pre1999 - 1st:0 2nd:1 3rd:0 Ran:11
Win Prizemoney £0 *Total Prizemoney* £850
1999 Turf 0-3: (12f, 17f, 18f) (g-f 2, hrd)
Fair gelding, has worn blinkers. Turf high 10.
**A T Murphy [0-4] R W Savery (from M A Buckley [0-6] Jun 1998).*

WAVE OF OPTIMISM BHB 76f **RR 75f** 2000[23]
4 ch g Elmaamul (USA) 8.1f **(70)** - Ballerina Bay **(68f 63a)** (Myjinski (USA)) 9.5f **(54)**
Form - 8130
Record 1999 - 1st:1 2nd:0 3rd:1 Ran:4
Pre1999 - 1st:1 2nd:2 3rd:1 Ran:4
Win Prizemoney £9,621 *Total Prizemoney* £12,762
Wins * 1999 Apr Sandow (G-S) H 16.4f 72 75
*** 1998** Oct Nottin (SFT) 14.1f 80 <
1999 Turf 1-4: (12f, 16f 1-2, 20f) (g-s 1-1, gd 2, g-f)
Light-framed, above-average gelding, effective 11 to 16f, acts on g-s to g-f, prefers tight tracks. Turf high 75 - 1st of 10 giving 2lb to Bridie's Pride (23 Apr Sandown RF 0823). Consistent. A game winner at Sandown on his second start of the season, he probably found the ground too fast when trounced at Royal Ascot.
**J Pearce [2-8] Wave of Optimism Partnership.*

WAVERLEY ROAD RR 77f 5102[4]
2 ch c Pelder (IRE) - Lillicara (FR) (Caracolero (USA)) 8.2f **(57)**
Form - 4
Record 1999 - 1st:0 2nd:0 3rd:0 Ran:1
Win Prizemoney £0 *Total Prizemoney* £207
1999 Turf 0-1: (8f) (gd)
Currently above-average colt. **A P Jarvis [0-1] Benham Racing.*

WAX LYRICAL BHB 85f **RR 84f** 4336[9]
3 b f Safawan 6.6f **(60)** - Hannah's Music (Music Boy) 6.8f **(57)**
Form - 10
Record 1999 - 1st:1 2nd:0 3rd:0 Ran:2
Win Prizemoney £3,208 *Total Prizemoney* £3,208
Wins * 1999 May Salisb (G-F) 6f 84+ <
1999 Turf 1-2: (6f 1-2) (g-s, frm 1-1)
Lengthy, currently decent filly. Turf high 84 (1st run) - 1st of 17 getting 5lb from Borders (2 May Salisbury RF 0983).
**J A R Toller [1-2] Magno-Pulse Ltd.*

WAY BACK (IRE) BHB 38f **RR 21f** 3954[14]
3 b g Toca Madera - My Robin (IRE) (Cyrano de Bergerac) 6f **(68)**
Form - 08000
Record 1999 - 1st:0 2nd:0 3rd:0 Ran:5
Pre1999 - 1st:0 2nd:0 3rd:1 Ran:4
Win Prizemoney £0 *Total Prizemoney* £307
1999 Turf 0-5: (7f 2, 8f, 10f 2) (gd, frm 4)
Little account gelding. Turf high 42. Becoming disappointing.
**B S Rothwell [0-9] Mrs G M Z Spink.*

WAYNE LUKAS BHB 48f **RR 44f** 4993[18]
4 b g Don't Forget Me 9.5f **(66)** - Modern Dance (USA) (Nureyev (USA)) 8.7f **(78)**
Form - 00
Record 1999 - 1st:0 2nd:0 3rd:0 Ran:2
Pre1999 - 1st:1 2nd:0 3rd:0 Ran:6
Win Prizemoney £2,736 *Total Prizemoney* £2,736
Wins 1998 Aug Kempto (G-F) C 9f 58 <
1999 Turf 0-2: (9f, 10f) (g-s, frm)
Scopey, moderate gelding. Turf high 18 (began Spt). Becoming disappointing.
**P R Hedger [0-5] J J Whelan (from H R A Cecil [1-4] Aug 1998).*

WAY OF LIGHT (USA) RR 117f 5013a[5]
3 br c Woodman (USA) 9.7f **(77)** - Salchow (Nijinsky (CAN)) 10.3f **(77)**
Form - 5454725
1999 Turf 0-7: (8f 4, 9f, 10f, 12f) (hvy, sft, g-s, gd 3)
High-class colt, effective 8 to 12f, acts on g-s, has worn blinkers. Turf high 117 - 4th of 5 to Dubai Millennium (15 Aug Deauville 8f hvy RF 3780a). Consistent. He looked a decent prospect for last season, but as it turned out did not manage a single victory.

Taking on the very best throughout the campaign, his best efforts would have been when fourth behind Sendawar in the French Guineas, the same position behind Dubai Millennium in the Jacques le Marois and runner-up to State Shinto in the Prix du Prince d'Orange. **P Bary in FR [1-9].*

WEALTHY STAR (IRE) BHB 91f **RR 93f** 5141[12]

4 b c Soviet Star (USA) 8.6f **(74)** - Catalonda (African Sky) 7.9f **(63)**

Form - 4070

Record 1999 - 1st:0 2nd:0 3rd:0 Ran:4
Pre1999 - 1st:1 2nd:0 3rd:0 Ran:2

Win Prizemoney £4,467 *Total Prizemoney* £4,951

Wins * 1998 Jun Nottin (GD) 8.2f 92 <

1999 Turf 0-4: (6f, 7f 2, 8f) (g-s, gd 3)

Well made, useful colt, effective 8f, acts on gd. Turf high 93 (began Spt). **B Hanbury [1-6] Ahmed Ali.*

WEAVER OF WORDS BHB 75f **RR 74f** 3013[3]

3 b f Danehill (USA) 9.1f **(79)** - Canadian Mill (USA) (Mill Reef (USA)) 10.5f **(78)**

Form - 3241P3

Record 1999 - 1st:1 2nd:1 3rd:2 Ran:6
Pre1999 - 1st:0 2nd:3 3rd:0 Ran:4

Win Prizemoney £4,137 *Total Prizemoney* £15,112

Wins * 1999 Jun Lingfi (G-F) 7f 73 <

1999 Turf 1-6: (6f 3, 7f 1-3) (sft, gd, g-f, frm 1-3)

Scopey, above-average filly, effective 6 to 7f, best at 7f, acts on gd to frm, best on frm. Turf high 74 - also 1st of 9 getting 5lb from Sulu (25 Jun Lingfield RF 2293). Consistent. After numerous placed efforts she finally got off the mark at Lingfield in June. She looks best suited by seven furlongs, but hardly seems likely to improve. **B W Hills [1-10] Maktoum Al Maktoum.*

WEAVER SAM BHB 29f **RR 31f** 4932[10]

4 ch g Ron's Victory (USA) 9.2f **(52)** - Grove Star (Upper Case (USA)) 8.2f **(55)**

Form - 55500

Record 1999 - 1st:0 2nd:0 3rd:0 Ran:5

1999 Turf 0-5: (10f, 11f, 12f, 17f, 18f) (gd, g-f 3, frm)

Leggy, very moderate gelding. Turf high 36. **J Norton [1-9] J Wightman.*

WEDOUDAH (IRE) BHB 74f **RR 72f** 5067[2]

3 b f Sadler's Wells (USA) 11.3f **(87)** - Salvora (USA) (Spectacular Bid (USA)) 11.2f **(76)**

Form - 636362

Record 1999 - 1st:0 2nd:1 3rd:2 Ran:6

Win Prizemoney £0 *Total Prizemoney* £2,239

1999 Turf 0-6: (8f, 10f, 12f 3, 15f) (gd 3, g-f, frm 2)

Scopey, above-average filly, effective 10 to 12f, best at 12f, acts on gd to frm, best on gd. Turf high 73 (began Aug) - 3rd of 6 to Dashiba (20 Aug Sandown 10f g-f RF 3805). **M R Channon [0-6] Sheikh Ahmed Al Maktoum.*

WEE BARNEY BHB 43f **RR 62f** 5158[11]

2 b g Balnibarbi - Never so True **(37f 37a)** (Never so Bold) 6.3f **(66)**

Form - 082800

Record 1999 - 1st:0 2nd:1 3rd:0 Ran:6

Win Prizemoney £0 *Total Prizemoney* £536

1999 Turf 0-6: (7f 3, 8f 3) (gd, g-f 2, frm 3)

Average gelding, effective 7f, acts on frm, has worn blinkers. Turf high 62 (began Jly) - 2nd of 11 giving 5lb to Summertime Joy (13 Aug Catterick 7f frm RF 3598). **B Ellison [0-6] James Kennerley.*

WEE CHRISTY (IRE) BHB 27f28a **RR 29f 28a** 2145[14]

4 gr g Contract Law (USA) 8.9f **(54)** - Eternal Optimist (Relko) 9.9f **(59)**

Form - 7540

Record 1999 - 1st:0 2nd:0 3rd:0 Ran:4
Pre1999 - 1st:0 2nd:0 3rd:1 Ran:16

Win Prizemoney £0 *Total Prizemoney* £317

1999 Turf 0-4: (7f, 11f 2, 13f) (g-s 2, gd, frm)

Leggy, little account gelding, effective 12f, acts on g-f, has worn blinkers, likes tight tracks. Turf high 31. Inconsistent. **W McKeown [0-22] Mrs L E McKeown.*

WEEHEBY (USA) BHB 57f33a **RR 33a** 128[7]

10 ch g Woodman (USA) 9.7f **(77)** - Fearless Dame (USA) (Fearless Knight)

Form - 487

Record 1999 - 1st:0 2nd:0 3rd:0 Ran:2
Pre1999 - 1st:1 2nd:2 3rd:2 Ran:15

Win Prizemoney £1,932 *Total Prizemoney* £3,087

1999 AW 0-2: (12f, 16f) (Fibr 2)

Moderate gelding, has worn blinkers. AW high 34. Becoming disappointing.

**Miss A Stokell [0-8] M F Barraclough (from M F Barraclough [1-10] Oct 1996).*

WEE JIMMY BHB 45f **RR 34f** 4558[18]

3 b c Lugana Beach 7f **(63)** - Cutlass Princess (USA) (Cutlass (USA)) 8.5f **(76)**

Form - 00

Record 1999 - 1st:0 2nd:0 3rd:0 Ran:2
Pre1999 - 1st:0 2nd:0 3rd:0 Ran:3

Win Prizemoney £0 *Total Prizemoney* £589

1999 Turf 0-2: (6f, 8f) (gd, frm)

Light-framed, very moderate colt. Turf high 20 (began Jly). **B A McMahon [0-5] J D Graham.*

WEET-A-MINUTE (IRE) BHB 93f98a **RR 98f 98a** 5155[2]

6 ro h Nabeel Dancer (USA) 6.1f **(65)** - Ludovica (Bustino) 10.4f **(64)**

Form - 561712600456360222

Record 1999 - 1st:1 2nd:4 3rd:1 Ran:15
Pre1999 - 1st:4 2nd:7 3rd:8 Ran:42

Win Prizemoney £35,192 *Total Prizemoney* £90,147

Wins * 1999 *Mar Wolver (STD) H 9.4f 95 96*
* 1998 *Dec Wolver (STD) H 9.4f 88 93*
* 1995 Oct Pontef (FRM) L 8f 101 <
* 1995 Oct York (G-F) H 7.9f 84 94
* 1995 Spt Beverl (GD) 7.5f 78

1999 Turf 0-12: (8f 5, 9f, 10f 5, 12f) (gd 7, g-f 3, frm 2) 1999 AW 1-3: (9f 1-3) (Fibr 1-3)

Very useful horse, effective 8 to 11f, acts on sft to frm - acts on Fibr, excels at Nottingham and likes Doncaster. Turf high 98 - 2nd of 8 to Right Wing (1 Nov Nottingham 8f gd RF 5155). AW high 96. He is effective between a mile and 10 furlongs and very hardy. Capable of handling any ground - including the All-Weather - he lacks a telling turn-of-foot and usually has to settle for minor honours. **R Hollinshead [5-57] Ed Weetman (Haulage & Storage) Ltd.*

WEET AND SEE BHB 55f52a **RR 47f 52a** 335[10]

5 b g Lochnager 6.9f **(50)** - Simply Style (Bairn (USA)) 7.7f **(59)**

Form - 00

Record 1999 - 1st:0 2nd:0 3rd:0 Ran:2
Pre1999 - 1st:1 2nd:1 3rd:1 Ran:11

Win Prizemoney £2,277 *Total Prizemoney* £3,878

Wins 1997 *Mar Wolver (STD) H 8.5f 63 64 <*

1999 AW 0-2: (7f, 12f) (Fibr 2)

Moderate gelding. AW high 14. Becoming disappointing.

**T Wall [0-13] Ed Weetman (Haulage & Storage) Ltd (from R Hollinshead [1-11] Oct 1997).*

WEET FOR ME BHB 76f **RR 80f** 4730[2]

3 b c Warning 8.1f **(77)** - Naswara (USA) (Al Nasr (FR)) 9.3f **(68)**

Form - 601404402

Record 1999 - 1st:1 2nd:1 3rd:0 Ran:9
Pre1999 - 1st:0 2nd:2 3rd:0 Ran:3

Win Prizemoney £3,993 *Total Prizemoney* £10,259

Wins * 1999 Jly Haydoc (FRM) 10.5f 81 <

1999 Turf 1-9: (10f, 11f 1-3, 12f 3, 14f, 16f) (g-s 2, gd 2, g-f 2, frm 1-3)

Leggy, decent colt, effective 8 to 16f, acts on sft to frm, and excels at Newcastle. Turf high 81 - 1st of 5 from Entertainer (11 Jly Haydock RF 2736). Showed ability at two and got off the mark on very fast ground in a Haydock maiden in July. He has struggled in handicaps since, but has the ability to win one if the Handicapper is a bit more lenient.

**R Hollinshead [1-12] Ed Weetman (Haulage & Storage) Ltd.*

WEETMAN'S WEIGH (IRE) BHB 78f94a **RR 76f 94a** 5217[2]

6 b h Archway (IRE) 8.5f **(60)** -Indian Sand(Indian King (USA)) 7.4f **(64)**

Form - 32112602420707543422

Record 1999 - 1st:2 2nd:5 3rd:1 Ran:18

Pre1999 -	1st:10	2nd:9	3rd:6	Ran:47		

Win Prizemoney £54,279 *Total Prizemoney* £84,427

Wins	* **1999**	*Feb Wolver*	*(STD) H*	*8.5f*	*90*	*94*	<
	* **1999**	*Jan Southw*	*(STD) H*	*7f*	*85*	*91*	
	* 1998	Oct Newmar	(SFT) H	7f	72	77	
	* 1998	Aug Newcas	(GD) H	7f	67	72	
	* 1998	*Feb Wolver*	*(STD) H*	*7f*	*79*	*84*	
	* 1997	Jun Thirsk	(FRM)	7f		81	
	* 1997	May Redcar	(G-F)	7f		81	
	* 1997	May Thirsk	(G-F) H	7f	73	76	
	* 1996	Mar Leices	(SFT) H	6f	68	75	
	* 1996	*Jan Wolver*	*(STD) H*	*6f*	*74*	*74*	
	* 1996	*Jan Southw*	*(STD) H*	*6f*	*64*	*65*	
	* 1995	Jly Carlis	(FRM)	5f		66	

1999 Turf 0-14: (7f 7, 8f 7) (g-s, gd 4, g-f 4, frm 5) 1999 AW 2-4: (7f 1-2, 8f 1-2) (Fibr 2-4)

Very useful horse, effective 7 to 8f, best at 7f, - acts on Fibr, likes left handed tracks, likes tight tracks, excels at Southwell, likes Wolverhampton. Turf high 80. AW high 94 - 1st of 7 getting 4lb from Italian Symphony (10 Feb Wolverhampton RF 0263) - also 1st of 10 giving 22lb to Sea Ya Maite (8 Jan Southwell RF 0055). A fairly useful handicapper on turf and Fibresand, he has looked best over seven furlongs, but won over the extended mile at Wolverhampton in February and has run with credit on turf since.

**R Hollinshead [12-65] Ed Weetman (Haulage & Storage) Ltd.*

WEETRAIN (IRE) BHB 51f48a RR 57f 48a 796[9]

3 b f Fayruz 6.6f **(63)** - Mantlepiece (IRE) (Common Grounds)

Form - 536030

Record	**1999** -	1st:0	2nd:0	3rd:2	Ran:6
	Pre1999 -	1st:0	2nd:0	3rd:0	Ran:4

Win Prizemoney £0 *Total Prizemoney* £548

1999 Turf 0-3: (5f 2, 6f) (sft, g-s, gd) 1999 AW 0-3: (5f 2, 6f) (Fibr 3)

Fair filly, effective 5f, acts on g-s. Turf high 57 - 3rd of 12 getting 8lb from Eastern Trumpeter (13 Apr Folkestone 5f g-s RF 0656). AW high 43.

**J G Given [0-6] Andrew Sim James Given Race Partnership (from M Cunningham in IRE [0-4] Oct 1998).*

WEET U THERE (IRE) BHB 47f54a RR 47f 54a 3439[7]

3 b c Forest Wind (USA) - Lady Aladdin (Persian Bold) 9.3f **(66)**

Form - 0143517026410603477

Record	**1999** -	1st:2	2nd:1	3rd:2	Ran:17
	Pre1999 -	1st:1	2nd:0	3rd:1	Ran:9

Win Prizemoney £6,540 *Total Prizemoney* £8,528

Wins	* **1999**	*Apr Wolver*	*(STD) S*	*9.4f*		*57*	
	* **1999**	*Feb Wolver*	*(STD) S*	*6f*		*63*	<
	* 1998	*Dec Wolver*	*(SLW) H*	*7f*	*60*	*61*	

1999 Turf 0-4: (8f, 9f, 10f, 14f) (sft, g-s, gd, g-f) 1999 AW 2-13: (6f 1-1, 7f 5, 8f 2, 9f 1-4, 12f) (Fibr 2-13)

Leggy, fair colt, effective 6 to 7f, best at 7f, acts on g-f - acts on Fibr, has worn blinkers. Turf high 47. AW high 63 - 1st of 7 giving 10lb to Nicholas Mistress (3 Feb Wolverhampton RF 0219). He has only ever won at Wolverhamnpton, but is plating class and none-too-consistent.

**R Hollinshead [3-26] Ed Weetman (Haulage & Storage) Ltd.*

WEKIWA SPRINGS (FR) RR 89f 4419[2]

2 gr c Kendor (FR) 12.2f **(66)** - Ti Mamaille (FR) (Dom Racine (FR)) 9.2f **(62)**

Form - 2

Record	**1999** -	1st:0	2nd:1	3rd:0	Ran:1

Win Prizemoney £0 *Total Prizemoney* £2,432

1999 Turf 0-1: (7f) (gd)

Currently useful colt. (1st run) - 2nd of 23 to Scarteen Fox (19 Spt Newbury 7f gd RF 4419). Failed by only a head to beat Scarteen Fox in a big field at Newbury, and was subsequently snapped up by Godolphin. Looks a most interesting prospect.

**B J Meehan [0-1] Mrs Susan Roy.*

WELCH'S DREAM (IRE) BHB 75f68a RR 71f 68a 4908[4]

2 b f Brief Truce (USA) 9.1f **(73)** - Swift Chorus (Music Boy) 6.8f **(57)**

Form - 2714434

Record	**1999** -	1st:1	2nd:1	3rd:1	Ran:7

Win Prizemoney £3,126 *Total Prizemoney* £5,837

Wins	* **1999**	May Ripon	(G-F)	5f		66	<

1999 Turf 1-6: (5f 1-6) (gd, g-f 2, frm 1-3) 1999 AW 0-1: (5f) (Fibr)

Above-average filly, effective 5f, acts on g-f to frm, best on frm. Turf high 71 - also 1st of 10 getting 5lb from Happy Diamond (26 May Ripon RF 1502).

**J Berry [1-7] David Hall.*

WELCOME BACK RR 54f 3944[6]

2 ch g Most Welcome 8.6f **(66)** - Villavina **(49f)** (Top Ville) 11.7f **(68)**

Form - 7006

Record	**1999** -	1st:0	2nd:0	3rd:0	Ran:4

1999 Turf 0-4: (6f, 7f 3) (gd, g-f, frm, hrd)

Fair gelding. Turf high 54. **K A Ryan [0-4] J J Stephenson.*

WELCOME HEIGHTS BHB 42f53a RR 41f 53a 5151[15]

5 b g Most Welcome 8.6f **(66)** - Mount Ida (USA) (Conquistador Cielo (USA)) 8.8f **(69)**

Form - 00060520

Record	**1999** -	1st:0	2nd:1	3rd:0	Ran:8
	Pre1999 -	1st:4	2nd:3	3rd:4	Ran:27

Win Prizemoney £14,155 *Total Prizemoney* £19,376

Wins	1998	May Leices	(GD) H	8f	55	64	<
	1997	*Dec Lingfi*	*(STD) H*	*10f*	*57*	*60*	
	1997	Jly Doncas	(GD) H	7f	48	55	
	1997	Jly Chepst	(G-S) H	6.1f	38	44	

1999 Turf 0-7: (8f 5, 10f, 11f) (sft, gd 2, frm 4) 1999 AW 0-1: (9f) (Fibr)

Average gelding, effective 8 to 10f, acts on gd to g-f - acts on Equi. Turf high 41 (began Jly). Inconsistent. Bolted up at Leicester in May of last year, and put some modest efforts behind him when third on a faster surface at Newbury in July, but has not shown a great deal since.

**R C Spicer [0-1] R C Spicer (from M J Fetherston-Godley [4-34] Oct 1999).*

WELCOME SHADE BHB 68f RR 66f 5044[14]

2 gr g Green Desert (USA) 7.8f **(78)** - Grey Angel (Kenmare (FR)) 6.5f **(72)**

Form - 880

Record	**1999** -	1st:0	2nd:0	3rd:0	Ran:3

1999 Turf 0-3: (6f 2, 7f) (sft, gd, frm)

Currently average gelding. Turf high 66 (began Spt).

**R Hannon [0-3] The Queen.*

WELCOME SUNSET BHB 67f RR 67f 5031[8]

4 b g Most Welcome 8.6f **(66)** - Deanta in Eirinn (Red Sunset) 8.2f **(63)**

Form - 73027233728

Record	**1999** -	1st:0	2nd:3	3rd:3	Ran:11
	Pre1999 -	1st:1	2nd:1	3rd:2	Ran:9

Win Prizemoney £2,277 *Total Prizemoney* £14,524

Wins	* 1997	Jly Nottin	(SFT)	5.1f		**74**	<

1999 Turf 0-11: (7f 2, 8f 2, 9f, 10f 6) (sft, g-s, gd 3, g-f 3, frm 2, hrd)

Leggy, average gelding, effective 7 to 10f, best at 10f, acts on sft to hrd, has worn blinkers, prefers tight tracks, excels at Nottingham. Turf high 71 - 2nd of 7 giving 3lb to Sturgeon (16 Jun Ripon 10f hrd RF 2059). Consistent. **J Wharton [1-20] John Goddard.*

WELCOME TO UNOS BHB 72f RR 72f 4395[2]

2 ch g Exit To Nowhere (USA) 8.7f **(77)** - Royal Loft (Homing) 7.8f **(59)**

Form - 502

Record	**1999** -	1st:0	2nd:1	3rd:0	Ran:3

Win Prizemoney £0 *Total Prizemoney* £920

1999 Turf 0-3: (6f 2, 7f) (frm 2, hrd)

Currently above-average gelding. Turf high 72 (began Aug) - 2nd of 6 to Ile Michel (18 Spt Catterick 6f frm RF 4395).

**M Dods [0-3] J & M Leisure / Unos Restaurant.*

WELLANCA (GER) RR 99f 5205a[3]

3 f

Form - 5543

1999 Turf 0-4: (11f 2, 12f, 14f) (sft 2, g-s, gd)

Very useful filly. Turf high 99 - 4th of 8 to Win For Us (3 Oct Dortmund 14f sft RF 4774a). **H Blume in GER [0-4] Oct 1999).*

WELLBEING RR 65f 5213[3]

2 b c Sadler's Wells (USA) 11.3f **(87)** - Charming Life (NZ) (Sir Tristram) 10.7f **(76)**

Form - 3

Record	**1999** -	1st:0	2nd:0	3rd:1	Ran:1

Win Prizemoney £0 *Total Prizemoney* £964

1999 Turf 0-1: (8f) (g-s)

Currently average colt.

**H R A Cecil [0-1] Exors of the late Lord Howard de Walden.*

WELLCOME INN BHB 27f49a **RR 46f 49a** 5101[10]
5 ch g Most Welcome 8.6f **(66)** - Mimining (Tower Walk) 10f **(62)**
Form - 0002050
Record 1999 - 1st:0 2nd:1 3rd:0 Ran:7
Pre1999 - 1st:1 2nd:1 3rd:1 Ran:11
Win Prizemoney £2,495 *Total Prizemoney* £4,282
Wins 1997 Aug Beverl (G-S) 12f 64 <
1999 Turf 0-7: (10f, 11f 2, 12f 2, 14f, 16f) (sft, g-s 2, gd, g-f, frm 2)
Moderate gelding, effective 12f, acts on frm. Turf high 46 - 2nd of 13 getting 4lb from Ambidextrous (25 Aug Carlisle 12f frm RF 3898). Inconsistent.
**G Woodward [0-7] Burntwood Sports Ltd (from J O'Reilly [1-8] Nov 1997).*

WELL DRAWN BHB 38f55a **RR 42f 55a** 1392[4]
6 b g Dowsing (USA) 7f **(61)** - Classic Design (Busted) 10.2f **(61)**
Form - 074
Record 1999 - 1st:0 2nd:0 3rd:0 Ran:2
Pre1999 - 1st:1 2nd:0 3rd:1 Ran:13
Win Prizemoney £3,866 *Total Prizemoney* £4,563
Wins * 1996 *Jan Lingfi (STD) 8f 64* <
1999 Turf 0-2: (9f, 12f) (gd, frm)
Average gelding, effective 9 to 10f, best at 10f, acts on gd to frm, best on frm. Turf high 42 - 4th of 12 getting 5lb from Ardent (22 May Kempton 9f frm RF 1392). **H Candy [1-15] Mrs David Blackburn.*

WELLOW (IRE) BHB 42f45a **RR 46f 45a** 5026[19]
3 b g Unblest - Alpine Sunset (Auction Ring (USA)) 8.6f **(65)**
Form - 6270000
Record 1999 - 1st:0 2nd:1 3rd:0 Ran:7
Win Prizemoney £0 *Total Prizemoney* £672
1999 Turf 0-2: (7f 2) (gd, frm) 1999 AW 0-5: (6f 2, 7f, 8f, 9f) (Fibr 5)
Rangy, fair gelding. Turf high 46 (began Aug). AW high 52 (began Jly). **J A Glover [0-7] Steve Whelbourn.*

WELLUNA (GER) RR 102f 3586a[1]
3 f
Form - 01
1999 Turf 1-2: (10f 1-1, 12f) (hvy 1-1, g-f)
Currently very useful. Turf high 102 (1st run) - 11th of 13 getting 14lb from Bimbola (20 Jun San Siro 12f g-f RF 2283a) - also 1st of 8 from Nordican Inch (7 Aug Deauville RF 3586a). She put up a stylish performance when winning the Group 3 Prix de Psyche at Deauville in August. Proven up to a mile and a half, she has a smart turn-of-foot and acts well on heavy ground.
**H Blume in GER [1-2] Stall Kaiserberg.*

WELODY BHB 65f **RR 67f** 4951[11]
3 ch c Weldnaas (USA) 8.4f **(55)** - The Boozy News (USA) (L'Emigrant (USA)) 10.5f **(62)**
Form - 540
Record 1999 - 1st:0 2nd:0 3rd:0 Ran:3
Pre1999 - 1st:0 2nd:0 3rd:0 Ran:1
Win Prizemoney £0 *Total Prizemoney* £232
1999 Turf 0-3: (7f 2, 8f) (g-s, g-f, frm)
Rangy, average colt. Turf high 67 (began Spt).
**K Mahdi [0-4] Hamad Al-Mutawa.*

WELSH ASSEMBLY BHB 30f47a **RR 37f 47a** 4949[11]
3 ch g Presidium 7.5f **(56)** - Celtic Chimes (Celtic Cone) 9.8f **(43)**
Form - 58050
Record 1999 - 1st:0 2nd:0 3rd:0 Ran:5
Pre1999 - 1st:1 2nd:0 3rd:2 Ran:8
Win Prizemoney £1,917 *Total Prizemoney* £2,417
Wins * 1998 *Jly Southw (STD) S 6f 51* <
1999 Turf 0-4: (10f 3, 11f) (hvy 2, gd, g-f) 1999 AW 0-1: (12f) (Fibr)
Leggy, very moderate gelding, effective 6f, - acts on Fibr, has worn blinkers, likes left handed tracks. Turf high 37.
**G P Enright [1-13] Chris Wall.*

WELSH DREAM BHB 53f **RR 53f** 5215[11]
2 b c Mtoto 11.5f **(71)** - Morgannwg (IRE) (Simply Great (FR)) 8.2f **(65)**
Form - 700
Record 1999 - 1st:0 2nd:0 3rd:0 Ran:3
1999 Turf 0-3: (7f, 8f 2) (g-s, gd 2)
Currently fair colt. Turf high 53 (began Oct).
**A C Stewart [0-3] K J Mercer & Mrs S Mercer.*

WELSH FAIRING BHB 40f **RR 17f** 1367[8]
3 b f King's Signet (USA) 7f **(51)** - Princess Fair (Crowned Prince (USA)) 10.1f **(67)**
Form - 808
Record 1999 - 1st:0 2nd:0 3rd:0 Ran:3
Pre1999 - 1st:0 2nd:0 3rd:0 Ran:2
1999 Turf 0-2: (5f, 7f) (gd, frm) 1999 AW 0-1: (8f) (Fibr)
Unfurnished, little account filly. Turf high 17.
**M Blanshard [0-5] Exors of the late J G Charlton.*

WELSH MOUNTAIN BHB 39f **RR 37f** 975[6]
6 b g Welsh Captain 7.2f **(54)** - Miss Nelski (Most Secret) 7.1f **(58)**
Form - 6
Record 1999 - 1st:0 2nd:0 3rd:0 Ran:1
Pre1999 - 1st:3 2nd:2 3rd:2 Ran:27
Win Prizemoney £8,765 *Total Prizemoney* £11,768
Wins * 1998 Aug Carlis (G-S) H 8f 36 39
1997 Aug Yarmou (G-F) SH 8f 38 43
1995 Jly Folkes (G-F) H 5f 75 <
1999 Turf 0-1: (13f) (g-f)
Very moderate gelding, effective 8f, acts on gd, has worn blinkers, likes tight tracks. Consistent.
**K A Morgan [4-18] Mrs P A L Butler (from M J Heaton-Ellis [2-20] Aug 1997).*

WELSH PLOY BHB 73f **RR 86f** 5109[5]
2 b f Deploy 11.4f **(67)** - Safe House (Lyphard (USA)) 9.9f **(72)**
Form - 032505
Record 1999 - 1st:0 2nd:1 3rd:1 Ran:6
Win Prizemoney £0 *Total Prizemoney* £1,590
1999 Turf 0-6: (6f, 7f 4, 8f) (g-s 2, gd 3, frm)
Useful filly, effective 7f, acts on g-s to gd. Turf high 86 (began Aug) - 3rd of 11 to Scottish Spice (26 Aug Folkestone 7f gd RF 3912). **K McAuliffe [0-6] G E Amey.*

WELSH VALLEY (USA) RR 62f 4903[2]
2 b f Irish River (FR) 9f **(77)** - Sweet Snow (USA) (Lyphard (USA)) 9.9f **(72)**
Form - 02
Record 1999 - 1st:0 2nd:1 3rd:0 Ran:2
Win Prizemoney £0 *Total Prizemoney* £1,180
1999 Turf 0-2: (5f, 6f) (g-s, frm)
Currently average filly. Turf high 62 (began Oct).
**M L W Bell [0-2] K J Mercer & Mrs S Mercer.*

WELSH WIND (IRE) RR 91f 5091a[13]
3 b g Tenby 10.4f **(76)** - Bavaria (Top Ville) 11.7f **(68)**
Form - 55133070
1999 Turf 1-8: (9f 3, 10f 1-3, 11f, 12f) (sft 2, g-s 3, g-f, frm 1-2)
Useful gelding, effective 9 to 12f, acts on g-s to frm, best on g-s. Turf high 94 - 3rd of 7 getting 2lb from Trebizond (22 Spt Listowel 12f g-s RF 4614a) - also 1st of 6 from Ansar (3 Jly Leopardstown RF 2610a). **D Hanley in IRE [1-8] Mrs A M Hanley.*

WELTON ARSENAL BHB 69f **RR 72f** 1959[13]
7 b g Statoblest 6.4f **(63)** - Miller's Gait (Mill Reef (USA)) 10.5f **(78)**
Form - 000
Record 1999 - 1st:0 2nd:0 3rd:0 Ran:3
Pre1999 - 1st:3 2nd:5 3rd:4 Ran:40
Win Prizemoney £17,070 *Total Prizemoney* £38,403
Wins * 1997 May Newmar (GD) H 7f 88 93 <
1996 Apr Warwic (GD) 7f 91
1999 Turf 0-3: (6f 2, 7f) (sft, gd, g-f)
Above-average gelding, effective 6 to 8f, acts on gd to g-f, has worn blinkers. Turf high 67.
**K Bishop [2-27] Paulton Bloodstock (from M R Channon [2-25] Nov 1996).*

WELVILLE BHB 78f98a **RR 74f 98a** 999[15]
6 b g Most Welcome 8.6f **(66)** -Miss Top Ville (FR) (Top Ville) 11.7f **(68)**
Form - 511210
Record 1999 - 1st:3 2nd:1 3rd:0 Ran:5

Pre1999 - 1st:1 2nd:2 3rd:0 Ran:9
Win Prizemoney £21,824 *Total Prizemoney* £35,388
Wins * **1999** *Apr Wolver (STD) H 8.5f 93 96 <*
* **1999** *Feb Lingfi (STD) H 8f 87 90*
* **1999** *Feb Lingfi (STD) H 8f 75 88*
* 1995 Spt Goodwo (GD) 6f 87
1999 Turf 0-1: (8f) (frm) 1999 AW 3-4: (8f 3-4) (Equi 2-2, Fibr 1-2)
Very useful gelding, effective 8f, - acts on AW, best on Fibr. AW high 96 - 1st of 8 giving 9lb to Thekryaati (10 Apr Wolverhampton RF 0644) - also 1st of 8 giving 17lb to Redoubtable (27 Feb Lingfield RF 0376). He rediscovered his form on the All-Weather, but was not seen out after finishing unplaced at Kempton in May. Best around a mile, he is effective when ridden from the front or held-up. **P J Makin [4-14] T G Warner.*

WEND'S DAY (IRE) BHB 65f RR 64f 4999[3]
4 br g Brief Truce (USA) 9.1f **(73)** -Iswara (USA)(Alleged (USA))10f **(76)**
Form - 3
Record 1999 - 1st:0 2nd:0 3rd:1 Ran:1
Pre1999 - 1st:0 2nd:0 3rd:0 Ran:3
Win Prizemoney £0 *Total Prizemoney* £659
1999 Turf 0-1: (12f) (gd)
Workmanlike, average gelding. (1st run) - 3rd of 7 getting 8lb from Angels Venture (21 Oct Brighton 12f gd RF 4999).
**S E H Sherwood [0-2] Wood Hall Stud Ltd (from S E Sherwood [0-2] Jun 1998).*

WENTOBUYABAY RR 3614[9]
6 ch m Henbit (USA) 10.2f **(46)** - Deep Ocean (Deep Run) 18f **(46)**
Form - 0
Record 1999 - 1st:0 2nd:0 3rd:0 Ran:1
1999 AW 0-1: (12f) (Equi)
Formerly very poor mare. **E A Wheeler [0-2] Mrs J A Cleary.*

WE'RE NOT JOKEN BHB 55f RR 69f 5023[16]
2 b f Foxhound (USA) - We're Joken **(51f 43a)** (Statoblest)
Form - 06600
Record 1999 - 1st:0 2nd:0 3rd:0 Ran:5
1999 Turf 0-3: (5f, 6f 2) (gd 2, frm) 1999 AW 0-2: (6f 2) (Fibr 2)
Average filly. Turf high 69 (began Aug). AW high 4 (began Jly).
**Mrs N Macauley [0-5] Operation Solstice.*

WERE NOT STOPPIN BHB 24f RR 22df 3978[14]
4 b g Mystiko (USA) 7.7f **(59)** - Power Take Off (Aragon) 8.1f **(60)**
Form - 8000
Record 1999 - 1st:0 2nd:0 3rd:0 Ran:4
1999 Turf 0-4: (10f, 11f, 12f 2) (g-f, frm 2, hrd)
Workmanlike, little account gelding. Turf high 22.
**R Bastiman [0-5] I B Barker.*

WESTBROOK (IRE) BHB 55f RR 65f 4814[19]
3 b g Fairy King (USA) 7.7f **(75)** - Abury (IRE) (Law Society (USA)) 9.9f **(70)**
Form - 68500
Record 1999 - 1st:0 2nd:0 3rd:0 Ran:5
1999 Turf 0-5: (8f, 10f 2, 11f, 12f) (g-s, gd 2, g-f 2)
Average gelding. Turf high 65 (began Aug).
**C N Kellett [0-4] Sean Taylor (from P W Chapple-Hyam [0-1] Aug 1999).*

WESTCOURT MAGIC BHB 77f RR 75f 4911[15]
6 b g Emarati (USA) 6.6f **(63)** - Magic Milly (Simply Great (FR)) 8.2f **(65)**
Form - 027270706100
Record 1999 - 1st:1 2nd:2 3rd:0 Ran:12
Pre1999 - 1st:10 2nd:3 3rd:1 Ran:48
Win Prizemoney £71,037 *Total Prizemoney* £95,585
Wins * **1999** Spt Cheste (HVY) H 5.1f 74 75
* 1998 Aug Cheste (G-S) H 5.1f 83 87
* 1998 May Cheste (G-F) H 5.1f 87 89
* 1998 Mar Newcas (G-S) H 5f 80 85
* 1997 Aug Cheste (SFT) H 5.1f 80 88
* 1996 Apr Haydoc (GD) L 5f 103
* 1995 Spt Ayr (GD) L 5f 104 <
* 1995 Aug Thirsk (G-F) H 6f 77 88+
* 1995 Aug Sandow (G-F) H 5f 66 88+
* 1995 Aug Beverl (G-F) H 5f 66 68
* 1995 Jly Newcas (G-F) S 5f 63+
1999 Turf 1-12: (5f 1-11, 6f) (g-s 1-3, gd 6, g-f, frm 2)
Above-average gelding, effective 5f, acts on gd to g-f, best on g-f, likes left handed tracks, likes tight tracks, excels at Newcastle, does well at Chester. Turf high 79. A very useful sprint handicapper, he is a difficult horse to pass if able to dominate. He goes particularly well at Chester.
**M W Easterby [11-60] K Hodgson & Mrs J Hodgson.*

WESTENDER (FR) BHB 87f RR 87f 4335[3]
3 b g In The Wings 11.2f **(77)** -Trude (GER)(Windwurf (GER))12.7f **(72)**
Form - 12213
Record 1999 - 1st:2 2nd:2 3rd:1 Ran:5
Pre1999 - 1st:0 2nd:0 3rd:0 Ran:1
Win Prizemoney £11,279 *Total Prizemoney* £17,411
Wins * **1999** Aug Ripon (GD) H 10f 80 87 <
* **1999** Jly Yarmou (G-F) 7f 75
1999 Turf 2-5: (7f 1-1, 8f, 10f 1-3) (g-s, gd 1-1, g-f 1-2, frm)
Workmanlike, useful gelding, effective 8 to 10f, best at 10f, acts on g-s to frm. Turf high 87 (began Jly) - 1st of 12 giving 1lb to Over To You (31 Aug Ripon RF 4042). Enjoyed a good season, and could still have room for improvement.
**W J Haggas [2-6] Khalifa Dasmal.*

WESTERN CHIEF (IRE) BHB 66f60a RR 68f 60a 2000[3]
5 b h Caerleon (USA) 10.9f **(79)** - Go Honey Go (General Assembly (USA)) 10f **(68)**
Form - 773
Record 1999 - 1st:0 2nd:0 3rd:1 Ran:3
Pre1999 - 1st:2 2nd:0 3rd:1 Ran:10
Win Prizemoney £10,960 *Total Prizemoney* £16,362
Wins 1997 Aug Tralee (G-S) H 12f 90 94 <
1997 Jly Galway (GD) H 12f 78 94 <
1999 Turf 0-2: (15f, 20f) (hvy, g-f) 1999 AW 0-1: (13f) (Equi)
Average colt, often wears blinkers. Turf high 68. Inconsistent. Formerly quite a useful stayer in Ireland, he has mainly been in action over hurdles and fences since arriving here. He retains his Flat ability however, judging by his fine effort to finish third in the Ascot Stakes at 66/1.
**D L Williams [4-23] Miss B W Palmer (from D K Weld in IRE [2-10] Oct 1997).*

WESTERN COMMAND (GER) BHB 43f55a RR 35f 55a 5057[8]
3 b g Saddlers' Hall (IRE) 10.5f **(65)** - Western Friend (USA) (Gone West (USA)) 6.5f **(75)**
Form - 523311038054682428
Record 1999 - 1st:2 2nd:2 3rd:3 Ran:16
Pre1999 - 1st:0 2nd:1 3rd:0 Ran:2
Win Prizemoney £3,883 *Total Prizemoney* £8,743
Wins 1999 *Mar Southw (STD) H 12f 63 73 <*
1999 *Mar Southw (SLW) H 11f 63 70*
1999 Turf 0-4: (10f 2, 12f 2) (gd 2, g-f, frm) 1999 AW 2-12: (8f 2, 9f, 10f, 11f 1-1, 12f 1-5, 14f, 15f) (Equi 2, Fibr 2-10)
Workmanlike, average gelding, effective 11 to 12f, - acts on Fibr, has worn blinkers, favours left handed tracks, favours tight tracks. Turf high 35. AW high 73 - 1st of 9 getting 12lb from River Captain (19 Mar Southwell RF 0450) - also 1st of 12 getting 19lb from Yes Keemo Sabee (10 Mar Southwell RF 0420). Inconsistent. He was a little bit frustrating in his early starts, but came into his own after being stepped up to middle distances on Fibresand. He was sold from Sir Mark Prescott's yard after running poorly on turf at the Lincoln meeting, and so far has shown only smatterings of form in modest events for his new yard.
**Mrs N Macauley [0-11] Andy Peake (from Sir Mark Prescott [2-7] Mar 1999).*

WESTERN COUNTRY BHB 20f RR 17f 4712[13]
7 ch g Beveled (USA) 6.9f **(64)** - Country Singer (Town And Country) 8.1f **(68)**
Form - 070
Record 1999 - 1st:0 2nd:0 3rd:0 Ran:3
Pre1999 - 1st:0 2nd:0 3rd:0 Ran:5
1999 Turf 0-3: (7f, 8f, 14f) (gd 3)
Poor gelding. Turf high 17 (began Spt).
**M P Muggeridge [0-3] B Azemoudeh (from E A Wheeler [0-3] Oct 1996).*

WESTERN GENERAL BHB 60f RR 55?f 1858[2]

8 ch g Cadeaux Genereux 7.9f **(76)** - Patsy Western (Precocious) 8.6f **(62)**
Form - 42
Record 1999 - 1st:0 2nd:1 3rd:0 Ran:2
Pre1999 - 1st:3 2nd:5 3rd:2 Ran:24
Win Prizemoney £14,997 *Total Prizemoney* £25,725
Wins * 1996 Jun Hamilt (GD) H 8.3f 71 71
1995 Apr Pontef (GD) H 8f 78 81 <
1999 Turf 0-2: (9f 2) (hvy, gd)
Fair gelding, has worn blinkers. Turf high 55. Becoming disappointing.
**Miss Kate Milligan [2-21] J D Gordon (from Miss S E Hall [1-7] Oct 1995).*

WESTERN PYRAMID (USA) BHB 40f RR 35f 3941[16]
3 b c West by West (USA) - Pyramid Power (USA) (Upper Nile (USA)) 8.5f **(75)**
Form - 000
Record 1999 - 1st:0 2nd:0 3rd:0 Ran:3
1999 Turf 0-2: (6f, 7f) (frm 2) 1999 AW 0-1: (8f) (Fibr)
Currently very moderate colt. Turf high 35.
**P S McEntee [0-3] R B Collier.*

WESTERN RAINBOW (IRE) BHB 46f RR 35f 3749[15]
3 b g Rainbows For Life (CAN) 9.3f **(64)** - Miss Galwegian (Sandford Lad) 7.8f **(54)**
Form - 000
Record 1999 - 1st:0 2nd:0 3rd:0 Ran:3
Pre1999 - 1st:0 2nd:0 3rd:0 Ran:4
1999 Turf 0-3: (6f, 8f 2) (gd, g-f, frm)
Very moderate gelding. Turf high 35 (began Jly).
**H Akbary [0-3] J D Duggan (from D T Hughes in IRE [0-4] Oct 1998).*

WESTERN RIDGE (FR) RR 90f 4792[5]
2 b c Darshaan 11.9f **(81)** - Helvellyn (USA) (Gone West (USA)) 6.5f **(75)**
Form - 45
Record 1999 - 1st:0 2nd:0 3rd:0 Ran:2
Win Prizemoney £0 *Total Prizemoney* £815
1999 Turf 0-2: (7f, 8f) (gd, g-f)
Currently useful colt. Turf high 90 (began Aug).
**L M Cumani [0-2] Robert Smith.*

WESTERN SUMMER (USA) RR 89+f 5000[1]
2 ch c Summer Squall (USA) 7f **(80)** - Mrs West (USA) (Gone West (USA)) 6.5f **(75)**
Form - 1
Record 1999 - 1st:1 2nd:0 3rd:0 Ran:1
Win Prizemoney £3,720 *Total Prizemoney* £3,720
Wins * **1999** Oct Nottin (GD) 8.2f 89+ <
1999 Turf 1-1: (8f 1-1) (gd 1-1)
Currently useful colt. (1st run) - 1st of 11 from Tolstoy (21 Oct Nottingham RF 5000).
**H R A Cecil [1-1] S Khaled.*

WESTERN VENTURE (IRE) BHB 27f27a RR 33f 27a 4602[4]
6 ch g Two Timing (USA) 7.1f **(58)** - Star Gazing (IRE) (Caerleon (USA)) 8.6f **(71)**
Form - 0054
Record 1999 - 1st:0 2nd:0 3rd:0 Ran:4
Pre1999 - 1st:2 2nd:2 3rd:3 Ran:27
Win Prizemoney £6,599 *Total Prizemoney* £9,488
Wins * 1997 Aug Hamilt (G-F) SH 9.2f 27 31
1995 Aug Folkes (FRM) 5f 68 <
1999 Turf 0-3: (8f, 9f, 10f) (g-f, frm 2) 1999 AW 0-1: (11f) (Fibr)
Moderate gelding, effective 9f, acts on gd, has worn blinkers, favours tight tracks. Turf high 33.
**Martyn Wane [1-13] P Macrae (from L Lungo [0-2] Jun 1999).*

WEST ESCAPE BHB 85f RR 88f 4798[8]
3 ch f Gone West (USA) 7.8f **(82)** -Sans Escale (USA) (Diesis) 9.3f **(69)**
Form - 15222528
Record 1999 - 1st:1 2nd:4 3rd:0 Ran:8
Pre1999 - 1st:0 2nd:1 3rd:1 Ran:5
Win Prizemoney £3,198 *Total Prizemoney* £23,148
Wins * **1999** May Warwic (GD) 8f 76 <
1999 Turf 1-8: (8f 1-1, 9f, 10f 6) (gd 4, g-f 2, frm 1-2)
Light-framed, useful filly, effective 8 to 10f, best at 10f, acts on g-s to frm, best on gd, prefers left handed tracks, prefers tight tracks. Turf high 88 - 8th of 13 getting 19lb from Monsajem (9 Oct Ascot 10f gd RF 4798). Improving. Won a weak maiden at Warwick on her reappearance, but has been somewhat unlucky since then, finishing runner-up more times than is desirable, though she looks genuine enough. Ten furlongs looks her best trip.
**M A Jarvis [1-13] Mohammed Bin Hendi.*

WESTGATE RUN BHB 58f RR 58f 4809[10]
2 b f Emperor Jones (USA) - Glowing Reference (Reference Point) 6.8f **(70)**
Form - 6364248000
Record 1999 - 1st:0 2nd:1 3rd:1 Ran:10
Win Prizemoney £0 *Total Prizemoney* £1,880
1999 Turf 0-10: (5f, 6f 5, 7f 4) (sft, gd, g-f 5, frm 2, hrd)
Fair filly, effective 6 to 7f, best at 7f, acts on g-f to frm, best on g-f. Turf high 76 - 2nd of 12 giving 8lb to It's Allowed (30 Jly Thirsk 7f frm RF 3256). Consistent.
**R A Fahey [0-10] Mark Leatham.*

WESTMINSTER (IRE) BHB 63f RR 57f 5152[6]
7 ch g Nashamaa 8.1f **(58)**-Our Galadrial (Salmon Leap (USA)) 11f **(61)**
Form - 5818006
Record 1999 - 1st:1 2nd:0 3rd:0 Ran:7
Pre1999 - 1st:5 2nd:5 3rd:4 Ran:35
Win Prizemoney £16,511 *Total Prizemoney* £24,142
Wins * **1999** Jly Ayr (GD) 13.1f 71
* 1998 Jun Carlis (G-S) 12f 76 <
* 1998 Jun Windso (G-F) H 11.6f 55 63
* 1997 Jun Ayr (GD) H 10.9f 60 68
* 1996 Jun Windso (G-F) C 11.6f 66
* 1995 May Hamilt (G-F) 12.1f 65
1999 Turf 1-7: (11f 2, 12f 3, 13f 1-1, 14f) (gd 4, g-f 1-2, frm)
Fair gelding, effective 12 to 13f, best at 13f, acts on gd to hrd, best on gd, mostly wears blinkers (effectively), favours tight tracks. Turf high 71 - 1st of 5 giving 3lb to Spirit of The Nile (26 Jly Ayr RF 3139). He is useful in claiming company, but is no better than that.
**M H Tompkins [6-44] Camden Town Typesetters.*

WESTMINSTER CITY (USA) BHB 53f RR 37f 4948[12]
3 b c Alleged (USA) 11.8f **(81)** - Promanade Fan (USA) (Timeless Moment (USA)) 6f **(72)**
Form - 0585000
Record 1999 - 1st:0 2nd:0 3rd:0 Ran:7
Pre1999 - 1st:1 2nd:0 3rd:1 Ran:4
Win Prizemoney £3,187 *Total Prizemoney* £4,287
Wins 1998 May Lingfi (GD) 5f 76 <
1999 Turf 0-6: (8f, 10f 3, 11f, 12f) (g-s, g-f 3, frm 2) 1999 AW 0-1: (10f) (Equi)
Light-framed, moderate colt, effective 6f, acts on frm, has worn blinkers. Turf high 63 (began Jly). Becoming disappointing. This lightly-made colt won on his two-year-old debut, but never really progressed subsequently.
**K O Cunningham-Brown [0-2] A J Richards (from C E Brittain [1-9] Aug 1999).*

WEST ONE RR 70f 2566[6]
3 ch f Gone West (USA) 7.8f **(82)** - Bequest (USA) (Sharpen Up) 8.3f **(67)**
Form - 86
Record 1999 - 1st:0 2nd:0 3rd:0 Ran:2
1999 Turf 0-2: (7f, 8f) (gd, g-f)
Scopey, currently above-average filly. Turf high 70.
**L M Cumani [0-2] Gerald Leigh.*

WESTORM (IRE) RR 421[7]
8 br g Strong Gale - Little Peach (Ragapan)
Form - 47
Record 1999 - 1st:0 2nd:0 3rd:0 Ran:2
Win Prizemoney £0 *Total Prizemoney* £211
1999 AW 0-2: (12f 2) (Equi, Fibr)
Moderate gelding. AW high 40. **Miss Gay Kelleway [0-2] J J Mullan.*

WESTSIDE FLYER BHB 42f43a RR 5f 43a 5149[12]
3 ch f Risk Me (FR) 8f **(53)**-Celtic River (IRE) (Caerleon (USA))8.6f **(71)**
Form - 12746008000

Record 1999 - 1st:1 2nd:1 3rd:0 Ran:11
Pre1999 - 1st:0 2nd:0 3rd:1 Ran:9
Win Prizemoney £2,097 *Total Prizemoney* £3,459
Wins 1999 *Jan Southw (STD) C* 6f 51 <
1999 Turf 0-4: (6f 3, 8f) (sft, gd, frm 2) 1999 AW 1-7: (6f 1-7) (Equi 3, Fibr 1-4)
Neat, fair filly, effective 6 to 7f, best at 6f, acts on g-f - acts on AW, has worn blinkers, likes tight tracks. Turf high 5. AW high 59 - 2nd of 5 giving 7lb to Light Breeze (2 Feb Lingfield 6f Equi RF 0210) - also 1st of 14 getting 7lb from Keen Hands (11 Jan Southwell RF 0073). Becoming disappointing.
**J C McConnochie [0-2] Miss B J Herring (from A Kelleway [1-18] Jly 1999).*

WEST STREET BLUES BHB 33f RR 15f 3025[8]
3 ch f Then Again 7.4f **(52)** - Calametta (Oats) 8.9f **(46)**
Form - 58008
Record 1999 - 1st:0 2nd:0 3rd:0 Ran:5
Pre1999 - 1st:0 2nd:0 3rd:0 Ran:4
1999 Turf 0-5: (5f 3, 6f, 10f) (sft, g-s, gd, frm 2)
Light-framed, poor filly. Turf high 29.
**R Ingram [0-1] Epsom Sporting Proposals Ltd (from T D McCarthy [0-8] Jun 1999).*

WESTWOOD VIEW BHB 40f RR 32f 4985[14]
3 b f Puissance 7.1f **(60)** - Long View (Persian Bold) 9.3f **(66)**
Form - 500473300080
Record 1999 - 1st:0 2nd:0 3rd:2 Ran:12
Pre1999 - 1st:0 2nd:0 3rd:1 Ran:5
Win Prizemoney £0 *Total Prizemoney* £1,391
1999 Turf 0-12: (5f 4, 6f 5, 7f, 8f 2) (gd 7, g-f, frm 3, hrd)
Scopey, very moderate filly, effective 5f, acts on g-s, has worn blinkers. Turf high 51. Becoming disappointing.
**Ronald Thompson [0-2] I Fox (from J J Quinn [0-15] Spt 1999).*

WETHAAB (USA) RR 38f 3413[13]
2 b c Pleasant Colony (USA) 12.4f **(88)** - Binntastic (USA) (Lyphard's Wish (FR)) 9f **(74)**
Form - 0
Record 1999 - 1st:0 2nd:0 3rd:0 Ran:1
1999 Turf 0-1: (7f) (g-f)
Currently very moderate colt. **B W Hills [0-1] Hamdan Al Maktoum.*

WHAT A CRACKER BHB 47f RR 38f 5216[14]
2 b f Bustino 11f **(64)** - Moon Spin (Night Shift (USA)) 7.2f **(69)**
Form - 000
Record 1999 - 1st:0 2nd:0 3rd:0 Ran:3
1999 Turf 0-3: (6f, 8f 2) (g-s, gd 2)
Currently very moderate filly. Turf high 38 (began Oct).
**M P Tregoning [0-3] Mrs Hugh Dalgety.*

WHAT A FUSS BHB 46f56a RR 42f 56a 3288[8]
6 b g Great Commotion (USA) 9.2f **(80)** - Hafwah (Gorytus (USA)) 7.8f **(60)**
Form - 08
Record 1999 - 1st:0 2nd:0 3rd:0 Ran:2
Pre1999 - 1st:2 2nd:3 3rd:1 Ran:13
Win Prizemoney £6,305 *Total Prizemoney* £9,210
Wins 1997 Jly Yarmou (GD) H 11.5f 58 61
1997 *Jan Wolver (STD) H* 7f 64 67 <
1999 Turf 0-2: (12f, 16f) (frm 2)
Average gelding. Turf high 42 (began Jly). Inconsistent.
**M W Easterby [0-2] Mrs Denise Shefras (from B Hanbury [2-13] Jly 1997).*

WHATEVER'S RIGHT (IRE) BHB 62f49a RR 61f 49a 183[6]
10 b g Doulab (USA) 7.4f **(61)** - Souveniers (Relko) 9.9f **(59)**
Form - 16
Record 1999 - 1st:1 2nd:0 3rd:0 Ran:2
Pre1999 - 1st:10 2nd:5 3rd:6 Ran:64
Win Prizemoney £33,682 *Total Prizemoney* £42,764
Wins * 1999 *Jan Lingfi (STD) H* 10f 46 48
* 1998 Aug Salisb (G-F) H 7f 55 60
* 1997 Jly Windso (GD) H 8.3f 63 67 <
* 1996 *Jly Lingfi (STD)* 7f 64
* 1996 Jly Warwic (FRM) H 7f 60 63
* 1995 Jun Warwic (GD) 7f 67 <
* 1995 *May Lingfi (STD) H* 8f 57 59
1999 AW 1-2: (10f 1-2) (Equi 1-2)
Average gelding, effective 7 to 8f, best at 7f, acts on gd to frm, has worn blinkers. AW high 48 (1st run). He does not win very often nowadays and is getting a bit long in the tooth. He seemed to get the ten furlongs well enough when getting up in the last strides to win on the Lingfield Equitrack in January.
**M D I Usher [11-68] M D I Usher.*

WHAT GROUNDS (FR) RR 66f 5129[5]
2 b g Exit To Nowhere (USA) 8.7f **(77)** - Solving (USA) (Bering) 7.4f **(61)**
Form - 5
Record 1999 - 1st:0 2nd:0 3rd:0 Ran:1
1999 Turf 0-1: (6f) (gd)
Currently average gelding. **B J Meehan [0-1] Abbott Racing Ltd.*

WHATTA MADAM BHB 56f49a RR 42f 49a 5128[8]
3 gr f Whittingham (IRE) - Sylvan Song (Song) 7.2f **(61)**
Form - 02350003008
Record 1999 - 1st:0 2nd:1 3rd:2 Ran:11
Pre1999 - 1st:0 2nd:2 3rd:1 Ran:5
Win Prizemoney £0 *Total Prizemoney* £2,809
1999 Turf 0-9: (5f 3, 6f 5, 7f) (sft, g-s 2, gd 3, g-f 2, hrd) 1999 AW 0-2: (5f, 7f) (Equi, Fibr)
Light-framed, moderate filly, effective 6f, acts on g-s to hrd, has worn blinkers. Turf high 62 - 3rd of 15 getting 1lb from Lucy Mariella (4 May Brighton 6f hrd RF 1023). AW high 28 (began Aug).
**G L Moore [0-16] Mark Barrett.*

WHAT THE DEVIL BHB 32f25a RR 32f 25a 849[8]
6 ch m Devil to Play -Whats Yours Called (Windjammer (USA)) 7f **(59)**
Form - 888
Record 1999 - 1st:0 2nd:0 3rd:0 Ran:2
Pre1999 - 1st:0 2nd:0 3rd:0 Ran:4
Win Prizemoney £0 *Total Prizemoney* £237
1999 AW 0-2: (12f, 14f) (Fibr 2)
Very moderate mare. AW high 9.
**J P Smith [0-13] Mrs Frances Draper.*

WHENWILLIEMETHARRY BHB 68f RR 70f 4820[8]
2 b f Sabrehill (USA) 8.5f **(64)** - William's Bird (USA) (Master Willie) 7f **(70)**
Form - 004588
Record 1999 - 1st:0 2nd:0 3rd:0 Ran:6
Win Prizemoney £0 *Total Prizemoney* £260
1999 Turf 0-6: (5f, 6f, 7f 2, 8f 2) (gd, g-f 2, frm 3)
Above-average filly, effective 7f, acts on g-f. Turf high 70.
**D R C Elsworth [0-6] Harry Redknapp.*

WHERE EAGLES DARE (USA) BHB 61f RR 60f 4944[12]
2 b c Eagle Eyed (USA) - Velveteen (USA) (Pirateer (USA))
Form - 780
Record 1999 - 1st:0 2nd:0 3rd:0 Ran:3
1999 Turf 0-3: (7f 2, 8f) (sft, gd, frm)
Currently average colt. Turf high 59 (began Jly).
**D Marks [0-3] Godiva.*

WHERE'S ALBERT BHB 29f RR 9f 1582[2]
4 ch g Out of Hand - Stellajoe (Le Dauphin)
Form - 2
Record 1999 - 1st:0 2nd:1 3rd:0 Ran:1
Pre1999 - 1st:0 2nd:0 3rd:0 Ran:3
Win Prizemoney £0 *Total Prizemoney* £580
1999 AW 0-1: (16f) (Equi)
Workmanlike, very moderate gelding. (1st run) - 2nd of 12 getting 18lb from Monaco Gold (29 May Lingfield 16f Equi RF 1582).
**A J McNae [0-1] J Daniels (from Derrick Morris [0-3] Jun 1998).*

WHERE'S CHARLOTTE BHB 50f RR 70f 5064[7]
2 b f Sure Blade (USA) 10.6f **(66)** - One Degree (Crooner) 9.9f **(49)**
Form - 6702007
Record 1999 - 1st:0 2nd:1 3rd:0 Ran:7
Win Prizemoney £0 *Total Prizemoney* £832
1999 Turf 0-7: (5f 3, 6f 3, 7f) (g-s, gd 2, g-f, frm 3)
Above-average filly. Turf high 70. **R Hannon [0-7] Peter Crane.*

WHISKY CHASER BHB 62f **RR 70f** 4249[18]
2 ch f Never so Bold 7.1f **(62)** - Highland Spirit (Scottish Reel) 7f **(61)**
Form - 400
Record 1999 - 1st:0 2nd:0 3rd:0 Ran:3
Win Prizemoney £0 *Total Prizemoney* £177
1999 Turf 0-3: (6f 2, 7f) (gd, g-f, frm)
Currently above-average filly. Turf high 70 (1st run) - 4th of 13 giving 3lb to Flyover (8 Jun Salisbury 6f g-f RF 1812).
**B Smart [0-3] G H Senior, T Richmond & A Robertson.*

WHISPERING (IRE) BHB 77f **RR 80f** 3019[2]
3 b f Royal Academy (USA) 7.8f **(77)** - Alligatrix (USA) (Alleged (USA)) 10f **(76)**
Form - 4222
Record 1999 - 1st:0 2nd:3 3rd:0 Ran:4
Win Prizemoney £0 *Total Prizemoney* £3,516
1999 Turf 0-4: (9f, 10f 3) (g-f, frm 3)
Light-framed, decent filly. Turf high 80 - 2nd of 12 getting 5lb from Mithras (21 Jly Sandown 10f frm RF 3019).
**H R A Cecil [0-4] Greenbay Stables Ltd.*

WHISPERING WIND RR 64tf 691[8]
3 b g Danehill (USA) 9.1f **(79)** - Meadow Pipit (CAN) **(103f)** (Meadowlake (USA))
Form - 8
Record 1999 - 1st:0 2nd:0 3rd:0 Ran:1
1999 Turf 0-1: (8f) (gd)
Currently average gelding. **E A L Dunlop [0-1] Maktoum Al Maktoum.*

WHISTLER RR 76f 3613[3]
2 ch c Selkirk (USA) 7.9f **(76)** - French Gift **(92f)** (Cadeaux Genereux)
Form - 4203
Record 1999 - 1st:0 2nd:1 3rd:1 Ran:4
Win Prizemoney £0 *Total Prizemoney* £2,714
1999 Turf 0-4: (5f 2, 6f 2) (gd, frm 3)
Above-average colt. Turf high 76. **R Hannon [0-4] Raymond Tooth.*

WHISTLE TEST BHB 38f **RR 29f** 3457[9]
4 gr g Kris 10f **(75)** - Cut Velvet (USA) (Northern Dancer) 9.6f **(80)**
Form - 080
Record 1999 - 1st:0 2nd:0 3rd:0 Ran:3
Pre1999 - 1st:0 2nd:0 3rd:0 Ran:6
1999 Turf 0-3: (10f, 12f, 13f) (g-f, frm 2)
Workmanlike, little account gelding, has worn blinkers. Turf high 29.
**Mrs M Reveley [0-3] Dab Hand Racing (from S P C Woods [0-6] Spt 1998).*

WHISTLING DIXIE (IRE) BHB 43f36a **RR 44f 36a** 4988[7]
3 ch g Forest Wind (USA) - Camden's Gift (Camden Town) 9.3f **(53)**
Form - 37606724465607
Record 1999 - 1st:0 2nd:1 3rd:1 Ran:14
Pre1999 - 1st:0 2nd:1 3rd:0 Ran:5
Win Prizemoney £0 *Total Prizemoney* £3,277
1999 Turf 0-13: (6f, 7f, 8f, 10f, 11f, 12f 2, 14f 3, 16f 3) (g-s 2, gd 2, g-f 3, frm 6) 1999 AW 0-1: (15f) (Fibr)
Leggy, moderate gelding, effective 7f, acts on g-f, has worn blinkers. Turf high 68. Ran over a variety of distances ranging from six furlongs to two miles, inspiring very little confidence.
**T J Etherington [0-14] Mrs P D Savill (from M R Channon [0-5] Spt 1998).*

WHISTLING JACK (IRE) BHB 60f **RR 68?f** 5066[17]
3 b g Roi Danzig (USA) 10.5f **(62)** - Candy's Sister (Great Nephew) 9.9f **(64)**
Form - 00
Record 1999 - 1st:0 2nd:0 3rd:0 Ran:2
Pre1999 - 1st:1 2nd:0 3rd:1 Ran:4
Win Prizemoney £2,532 *Total Prizemoney* £2,918
Wins * 1998 Oct Nottin (SFT) 10f 68 <
1999 Turf 0-2: (12f, 13f) (gd, frm)
Scopey, average gelding, effective 10f, acts on gd.
**B J Meehan [1-6] B J Meehan.*

WHITE EMIR BHB 56f **RR 57f** 5199[19]
6 b g Emarati (USA) 6.6f **(63)** - White African (Carwhite) 7.2f **(61)**
Form - 33700030400
Record 1999 - 1st:0 2nd:0 3rd:3 Ran:11
Pre1999 - 1st:4 2nd:9 3rd:5 Ran:47
Win Prizemoney £14,009 *Total Prizemoney* £49,814
Wins 1997 Jun Salisb (G-S) H 5f 80 80 <
1997 Jun Sandow (G-F) C 5f 80 <
1995 Spt Sandow (G-S) H 5f 80 80 <
1995 May Redcar (GD) 5f 60+
1999 Turf 0-11: (5f 5, 6f 6) (sft, g-s, gd 4, g-f 2, frm 3)
Fair gelding, effective 5 to 6f, best at 6f, acts on sft to frm, often wears blinkers (extremely effectively), prefers left handed tracks, excels at Kempton and Bath. Turf high 72. Hard to win with, he seems to appreciate being held up for a late run, but can sometimes wander under pressure.
**B R Millman [0-22] The Three Bears Racing (from B J Meehan [3-31] Oct 1997).*

WHITEFOOT RR 81f 5139[3]
2 b f Be My Chief (USA) 10.2f **(62)** - Kelimutu (Top Ville) 11.7f **(68)**
Form - 813
Record 1999 - 1st:1 2nd:0 3rd:1 Ran:3
Win Prizemoney £3,468 *Total Prizemoney* £5,469
Wins * **1999** Spt Sandow (G-F) 8.1f 81 <
1999 Turf 1-3: (7f, 8f 1-1, 10f) (gd 1-3)
Currently decent filly. Turf high 81 (began Aug) - also 1st of 10 from Britannia (15 Spt Sandown RF 4328). Left her initial run behind her when staying on strongly to win over a mile at Sandown on her second start, springing a 33/1 surprise in the process. Stayed on late into third in a Listed race on her final start.
**J Pearce [1-3] James Furlong.*

WHITEGATE'S SON BHB 20f **RR 30f** 4166[14]
5 ch g Minster Son 10.9f **(56)** -Whitegates Lady(Le Coq d'Or) 13.3f **(55)**
Form - 000
Record 1999 - 1st:0 2nd:0 3rd:0 Ran:3
Pre1999 - 1st:0 2nd:0 3rd:0 Ran:5
1999 Turf 0-3: (8f, 10f, 12f) (g-f, frm, hrd)
Very moderate gelding, has worn blinkers. Turf high 30 (began Jly). Inconsistent. **B Ellison [1-13] Brian Ellison Racing Club.*

WHITE HEART BHB 110f **RR 111f** 4235[6]
4 b g Green Desert (USA) 7.8f **(78)** - Barari (USA) (Blushing Groom (FR)) 10.3f **(76)**
Form - 1846433716
Record 1999 - 1st:2 2nd:0 3rd:2 Ran:10
Pre1999 - 1st:3 2nd:1 3rd:0 Ran:5
Win Prizemoney £101,183 *Total Prizemoney* £124,677
Wins * **1999** Aug Baden- (GD) G3 6f 111 <
* **1999** Mar Doncas (G-S) L 8f 106
* 1998 Spt Ascot (GD) H 7f 95 97
* 1998 Jly Chepst (GD) 6.1f 88+
* 1998 Mar Newcas (G-S) 7f 86+
1999 Turf 2-10: (6f 1-1, 7f 4, 8f 1-4, 9f) (sft, g-s 1-1, gd 1-5, g-f 2, frm)
Scopey, Group-class gelding, effective 6 to 8f, acts on g-s to frm, often wears blinkers. Turf high 111 - 1st of 10 giving 5lb to Intruder (31 Aug Baden-Baden RF 4241a) - also 1st of 6 getting 3lb from Generous Libra (25 Mar Doncaster RF 0467). Consistent. He gained a well deserved Pattern race success when landing a Group 3 at Baden-Baden in August. Best on easy ground, he usually wears blinkers, but was sporting a visor when successful in Germany. **M Johnston [5-15] Maktoum Al Maktoum.*

WHITE HOUSE RR 41f 5216[12]
2 b f Pursuit of Love 9.5f **(69)** - Much Too Risky (Bustino) 10.4f **(64)**
Form - 0
Record 1999 - 1st:0 2nd:0 3rd:0 Ran:1
1999 Turf 0-1: (8f) (g-s)
Currently moderate filly. **W Jarvis [0-1] J M Greetham.*

WHITE MAGIC (IRE) RR 28f 5192[13]
2 b f Rainbows For Life (CAN) 9.3f **(64)** - Shamanka (IRE) (Shernazar) 10.2f **(73)**
Form - 0
Record 1999 - 1st:0 2nd:0 3rd:0 Ran:1
1999 Turf 0-1: (8f) (gd)
Currently little account filly.
**G B Balding [0-1] Baldings (Training) Ltd.*

WHITE PLAINS (IRE) BHB 55f80a **RR 45f 80a** 4864[5]
6 b g Nordico (USA) 8.2f **(59)** - Flying Diva (Chief Singer) 8.9f **(66)**
Form - 57527615340084336605

Record	**1999** -	1st:1	2nd:0	3rd:3	Ran:16
	Pre1999 -	1st:10	2nd:6	3rd:4	Ran:41

Win Prizemoney £38,675 *Total Prizemoney* £53,991

Wins								
* **1999**	*Feb*	*Lingfi*	*(STD)*		*10f*		*89*	
* 1998	*Feb*	*Southw*	*(STD)*		*12f*		*84*	
* 1997	*Dec*	*Lingfi*	*(STD)*	*H*	*10f*	*72*	*90+*	<
* 1997	*Dec*	*Lingfi*	*(STD)*	*H*	*10f*	*69*	*75+*	
* 1997	Jly	Hamilt	(G-S)	C	9.2f		81	
1997	Apr	Nottin	(G-F)	H	10f	75	80	
1996	Spt	Lingfi	(FRM)	H	10f	70	74	
1996	Spt	Leices	(FRM)	H	10f	71	75+	
1996	Aug	Newcas	(G-F)		9f		72	
1996	Jun	Lingfi	(FRM)	H	10f	68	74	
1995	Nov	Folkes	(G-F)		6f		70	

1999 Turf 0-7: (10f 5, 12f 2) (gd, g-f 5, frm) 1999 AW 1-9: (7f, 8f, 9f, 10f 1-3, 12f 3) (Equi 1-4, Fibr 5)
Decent gelding, effective 8 to 12f, best at 10f, - acts on AW, best on Equi, favours left handed tracks, favours tight tracks, and does well at Lingfield. Turf high 62. AW high 89 - 1st of 6 giving 20lb to Scraggys Dream (9 Feb Lingfield RF 0258). Inconsistent. Once a very smart performer on sand, especially Equitrack, he won on that surface in February, but is looking held by the better All-Weather performers these days.
**K R Burke [5-37] Nigel Shields (from M C Pipe [1-9] Jun 1997).*

WHITE SANDS RR 41f 2642[8]
2 b f Green Desert (USA) 7.8f **(78)** - Carte Blanche **(47f 57a)** (Cadeaux Genereux)
Form - 8

Record	**1999** -	1st:0	2nd:0	3rd:0	Ran:1

1999 Turf 0-1: (6f) (frm)
Currently moderate filly. **C A Cyzer [0-1] R M Cyzer.*

WHITE SETTLER BHB 60f57a **RR 56f 57a** 1328[15]
6 b g Polish Patriot (USA) 7.8f **(70)** - Oasis (Valiyar) 8.5f **(73)**
Form - 00

Record	**1999** -	1st:0	2nd:0	3rd:0	Ran:2
	Pre1999 -	1st:3	2nd:3	3rd:5	Ran:27

Win Prizemoney £8,648 *Total Prizemoney* £13,703

Wins								
* 1998	Spt	Chepst	(G-S)	S	8.1f		56+	
1998	Apr	Leices	(SFT)	S	7f		63	
1996	Jly	Chepst	(G-F)	H	7.1f	64	67	<

1999 Turf 0-2: (7f 2) (gd 2)
Fair gelding, effective 7 to 8f, best at 7f, acts on sft to frm, has worn blinkers. Turf high 43.
**Miss S J Wilton [1-9] John Pointon and Sons (from R J Hodges [2-17] Apr 1998).*

WHITE STAR (IRE) RR 105f 3408a[7]
3 b f Darshaan 11.9f **(81)** - White Star Line (USA) (Northern Dancer) 9.6f **(80)**
Form - 237
1999 Turf 0-3: (12f 2, 14f) (gd 2, g-f)
Currently Pattern-class filly, has worn blinkers. Turf high 105 - 3rd of 8 to Sage Et Jolie (27 Jun Longchamp 12f gd RF 2477a).
**H-A Pantall in FR [0-3].*

WHITE SUMMIT BHB 53f **RR 61f** 4941[11]
2 b g Mistertopogigo (IRE) - White Heat **(41f 46a)** (Last Tycoon) 8.5f **(62)**
Form - 5670

Record	**1999** -	1st:0	2nd:0	3rd:0	Ran:4

1999 Turf 0-4: (5f, 6f 3) (gd 2, g-f, frm)
Average gelding, has worn blinkers. Turf high 61 (began Jly).
**B Palling [0-4] Whitehall Barn Racing Partnership.*

WHITE VALLEY (IRE) BHB 50f **RR 49f** 1747[8]
4 b br f Tirol 8.1f **(64)** - Royal Wolff (Prince Tenderfoot (USA)) 9f **(61)**
Form - 00648

Record	**1999** -	1st:0	2nd:0	3rd:0	Ran:5
	Pre1999 -	1st:0	2nd:0	3rd:0	Ran:1

1999 Turf 0-3: (6f, 7f 2) (g-s, gd, g-f) 1999 AW 0-2: (7f, 8f) (Fibr 2)
Moderate filly, effective 7f, - acts on Fibr. Turf high 49. AW high 49 (1st run) - 4th of 12 to Tayovullin (14 May Wolverhampton 7f Fibr RF 1232). **S Dow [0-6] I P Blance.*

WHITEWATER BOY BHB 83f **RR 82f** 2646[11]
3 b g Emarati (USA) 6.6f **(63)** - Chacewater (Electric) 10.1f **(61)**
Form - 501320

Record	**1999** -	1st:1	2nd:1	3rd:1	Ran:6
	Pre1999 -	1st:0	2nd:1	3rd:0	Ran:1

Win Prizemoney £2,749 *Total Prizemoney* £6,814

Wins							
* **1999**	May	Bright	(FRM)	8f		73	<

1999 Turf 1-6: (8f 1-5, 10f) (gd 2, frm 2, hrd 1-2)
Decent gelding, effective 7 to 10f, acts on sft to hrd. Turf high 82 - 2nd of 7 getting 1lb from Crystal Creek (26 Jun Bath 8f hrd RF 2318) - also 1st of 8 giving 5lb to Catriona (27 May Brighton RF 1518). **B J Meehan [1-7] Lime Street Racing Syndicate.*

WHITE WATERS (IRE) BHB 54f **RR 51f** 1400[7]
3 b g Great Commotion (USA) 9.2f **(80)** - Water Spirit (USA) (Riverman (USA)) 9.1f **(76)**
Form - 457

Record	**1999** -	1st:0	2nd:0	3rd:0	Ran:3

1999 Turf 0-3: (5f, 7f, 10f) (g-s, frm, hrd)
Leggy, fair gelding. Turf high 51 - 5th of 16 getting 4lb from James Dee (4 May Brighton 7f hrd RF 1022).
**C A Dwyer [0-3] Mrs Shelley Dwyer.*

WHITLEY GRANGE BOY BHB 44f65a **RR 46f 65a** 4381[8]
6 b g Hubbly Bubbly (USA) 9.5f **(43)** - Choir (High Top) 10.2f **(67)**
Form - 841447806412748

Record	**1999** -	1st:2	2nd:1	3rd:0	Ran:13
	Pre1999 -	1st:3	2nd:0	3rd:3	Ran:26

Win Prizemoney £14,588 *Total Prizemoney* £17,954

Wins								
* **1999**	Jly	Catter	(GD)	H	15.8f	44	48	
* **1999**	*Jan*	*Southw*	*(STD)*	*H*	*16f*	*62*	*68*	<
* 1998	*Jan*	*Southw*	*(STD)*	*H*	*16f*	*61*	*64*	
* 1997	*Nov*	*Southw*	*(STD)*	*H*	*14f*	*56*	*60*	
* 1997	Oct	Catter	(SFT)	H	12f	46	55	

1999 Turf 1-9: (16f 1-5, 17f 2, 18f 2) (g-s, gd, g-f 1-3, frm 3, hrd) 1999 AW 1-4: (15f, 16f 1-3) (Fibr 1-4)
Above-average gelding, effective 15 to 16f, best at 16f, - acts on Fibr, likes left handed tracks, likes tight tracks. Turf high 48. AW high 72 - 4th of 6 getting 2lb from Sudest (13 Jan Wolverhampton 15f Fibr RF 0090) - also 1st of 10 giving 6lb to Pipe Music (4 Jan Southwell RF 0025). **J L Eyre [5-39] Mrs Carole Sykes.*

WHIZZ KID BHB 59f37a **RR 58f 37a** 5212[8]
5 b m Puissance 7.1f **(60)**-Panienka (POL) (Dom Racine (FR)) 9.2f **(62)**
Form - 511841557771705037178

Record	**1999** -	1st:5	2nd:0	3rd:1	Ran:21
	Pre1999 -	1st:1	2nd:1	3rd:3	Ran:31

Win Prizemoney £24,219 *Total Prizemoney* £27,763

Wins								
* **1999**	Oct	Newcas	(G-S)	H	5f	57	58	
* **1999**	Jly	Ayr	(GD)	H	5f	57	59	
* **1999**	May	Chepst	(G-S)	H	5.1f	53	59	
* **1999**	Apr	Redcar	(G-S)	H	5f	46	47	
* **1999**	Apr	Ripon	(G-S)	H	5f	34	43	
1996	Jun	Windso	(G-F)	S	5f		67	<

1999 Turf 5-19: (5f 5-16, 6f 3) (sft, g-s, gd 4-9, g-f 1-4, frm 3, hrd) 1999 AW 0-2: (5f, 6f) (Equi, Fibr)
Fair filly, effective 5 to 6f, best at 5f, acts on gd to hrd, best on gd, has worn blinkers, excels at Newcastle. Turf high 59 - 1st of 10 getting 13lb from Mister Jolson (19 May Chepstow RF 1324) - also 1st of 12 getting 27lb from Friar Tuck (26 Jly Ayr RF 3137). AW high 33. Consistent. A winner five times, she ideally needs some cut, the minimum trip, and a strongly-run race.
**J M Bradley [5-21] B Paling (from J J Bridger [1-31] Dec 1997).*

WHO CARES WINS BHB 80f **RR 82f** 4403[11]
3 ch c Kris 10f **(75)** - Anne Bonny (Ajdal (USA)) 9.2f **(89)**
Form - 033120

Record	**1999** -	1st:1	2nd:1	3rd:2	Ran:6

Win Prizemoney £3,616 *Total Prizemoney* £12,221

Wins							
* **1999**	Jun	Cheste	(G-F)	13.4f		69	<

1999 Turf 1-6: (8f, 10f, 12f, 13f 1-2, 14f) (gd 2, g-f, frm 1-3)
Scopey, decent colt, effective 14f, acts on gd. Turf high 82 - 2nd of 11 getting 10lb from Loop The Loup (19 Aug York 14f gd RF 3774). Unraced at two, he has shown gradually improving form and got off the mark in a Chester maiden over the extended thirteen furlongs in June. Runner-up afterwards in the Melrose Handicap at

the Ebor meeting, he probably still has improvement in him.
**C E Brittain [1-6] Khalifa Dasmal.*

WHO DA LEADER (IRE) BHB 69f RR 78f 3383[6]

2 b c Brief Truce (USA) 9.1f **(73)** - Lingdale Lass (Petong) 6.6f **(58)**
Form - 420706
Record 1999 - 1st:0 2nd:1 3rd:0 Ran:6
Win Prizemoney £0 *Total Prizemoney* £1,395
1999 Turf 0-6: (5f 4, 6f, 7f) (gd 2, g-f, frm 3)
Above-average colt, effective 5f, acts on frm, has worn blinkers. Turf high 78 - 2nd of 17 to Our Ambition (3 May Kempton 5f frm RF 1001). **R Hannon [0-6] Buddy Hackett.*

WHO GOES THERE BHB 40a RR 49f 4359[12]

3 ch f Wolfhound (USA) 7.3f **(71)** - Challanging (Mill Reef (USA)) 10.5f **(78)**
Form - 0000282354250
Record 1999 - 1st:0 2nd:3 3rd:1 Ran:13
Pre1999 - 1st:0 2nd:0 3rd:0 Ran:3
Win Prizemoney £0 *Total Prizemoney* £2,927
1999 Turf 0-11: (7f 3, 8f 3, 9f 2, 10f 2, 12f) (sft, g-s 2, g-f 5, frm 3) 1999 AW 0-2: (7f, 8f) (Equi, Fibr)
Neat, moderate filly, effective 7 to 9f, best at 9f, acts on g-s to frm, likes left handed tracks, likes tight tracks. Turf high 49 - 2nd of 10 getting 18lb from Oscietra (18 Aug Kempton 9f g-s RF 3738). AW high 29. **T M Jones [0-16] The Rest Hill Partnership.*

WHOOPS BHB 43f RR 55df 3545[12]

3 b f Shernazar 11.8f **(71)** - Ten to Six (Night Shift (USA)) 7.2f **(69)**
Form - 50
Record 1999 - 1st:0 2nd:0 3rd:0 Ran:2
Pre1999 - 1st:0 2nd:0 3rd:0 Ran:2
1999 Turf 0-2: (7f, 8f) (g-f, frm)
Fair filly. Turf high 43 (began Jly). **E Weymes [0-4] E G Moorey.*

WHOSAPRETTYGIRL BHB 37f RR 28f 3472[4]

2 ch f Clantime 6.6f **(57)** - She's a Breeze (Crofthall) 6.3f **(59)**
Form - 80684
Record 1999 - 1st:0 2nd:0 3rd:0 Ran:5
1999 Turf 0-3: (5f 2, 6f) (gd, g-f 2) 1999 AW 0-2: (6f, 7f) (Fibr 2)
Little account filly. Turf high 28. AW high 29 (began Jly).
**Ronald Thompson [0-5] Ronald Thompson.*

WHYOME (IRE) BHB 100f RR 95f 5015a[2]

2 b c Owington - Al Corniche (IRE) **(45f 37a)** (Bluebird (USA)) 7.5f **(69)**
Form - 72143122
Record 1999 - 1st:2 2nd:3 3rd:1 Ran:8
Win Prizemoney £11,682 *Total Prizemoney* £45,278
Wins * **1999** Aug Pontef (GD) 8f 88+
* **1999** Jun Nottin (GD) 6.1f 93+ <
1999 Turf 2-8: (5f, 6f 1-3, 7f, 8f 1-3) (gd 2, g-f 1-3, frm 1-3)
Very useful colt, effective 6 to 8f, best at 8f, acts on gd to frm, best on g-f. Turf high 95 - 2nd of 9 to Night Style (17 Oct San Siro 8f g-f RF 5015a) - also 1st of 8 giving 4lb to Buy Or Sell (16 Jun Nottingham RF 2052). A progressive individual, he looked unlucky when finishing second in a Group One in Italy on his final start. Likely to stay a mile and a quarter, he should do well if campaigned on the continent in 2000. **M L W Bell [2-8].*

WHY WORRY NOW (IRE) RR 63f 5135[6]

3 ch f College Chapel - Pretext (Polish Precedent (USA)) 10.2f **(60)**
Form - 57533476
Record 1999 - 1st:0 2nd:0 3rd:2 Ran:8
Pre1999 - 1st:0 2nd:1 3rd:0 Ran:5
Win Prizemoney £0 *Total Prizemoney* £3,257
1999 Turf 0-8: (7f 6, 8f 2) (g-s, gd 5, g-f, frm)
Average filly, effective 7f, acts on sft to frm. Turf high 68. Consistent. **R Hannon [0-13] N Hayes.*

WICKED RR 26f 3419[10]

2 ch f Common Grounds 8.1f **(66)** - Azallya (FR) (Habitat) 9.4f **(70)**
Form - 060
Record 1999 - 1st:0 2nd:0 3rd:0 Ran:3
1999 Turf 0-3: (6f 3) (frm 3)
Currently little account filly. Turf high 26 (began Jly).
**G L Moore [0-3] Action Bloodstock.*

WICKLOW WAY (IRE) RR 49f 5183a[3]

9 b m Pennine Walk 8.9f **(64)** - Faraway Places (Flair Path) 7.8f **(79)**
Form - 73
Record 1999 - 1st:0 2nd:0 3rd:1 Ran:2
Pre1999 - 1st:2 2nd:0 3rd:1 Ran:11
Win Prizemoney £6,862 *Total Prizemoney* £7,677
Wins 1998 Nov Currag (SFT) H 14f 32 37+
1996 Jly Killar (GD) H 17f 52 45 <
1999 Turf 0-2: (14f, 16f) (sft, gd)
Moderate mare, has worn blinkers. Turf high 49 (began Aug).
**L Woods in IRE [0-5] C B Long (from L Woods [2-8] Aug 1999).*

WIDDECOMBE RR 1134[3]

2 b f Mon Tresor 7.9f **(60)** - Fifth Movement (Puissance)
Form - 03
Record 1999 - 1st:0 2nd:0 3rd:1 Ran:2
Win Prizemoney £0 *Total Prizemoney* £256
1999 Turf 0-1: (5f) (frm) 1999 AW 0-1: (5f) (Fibr)
Currently fair filly. (1st run) - 3rd of 9 to Walnut Lady (10 May Southwell 5f Fibr RF 1134). **J S Moore [0-2] Ernie Houghton.*

WIGMAN LADY (IRE) RR 53f 4640[3]

2 b f Tenby 10.4f **(76)** - Height of Elegance (Shirley Heights) 10.3f **(74)**
Form - 3
Record 1999 - 1st:0 2nd:0 3rd:1 Ran:1
Win Prizemoney £0 *Total Prizemoney* £247
1999 Turf 0-1: (7f) (gd)
Currently fair filly. (1st run) - 3rd of 11 getting 11lb from Chapel Royale (29 Spt Newcastle 7f gd RF 4640).
**M Brittain [0-1] & Mrs J M Swinglehurst & Partners.*

WILBY WILLIE RR 2961[7]

3 bl g Bob's Return (IRE) - Kev's Lass (IRE) (Kemal (FR))
Form - 7
Record 1999 - 1st:0 2nd:0 3rd:0 Ran:1
1999 Turf 0-1: (11f) (g-f)
Light-framed, currently very poor gelding.
**G A Hubbard [0-1] G A Hubbard.*

WILCOY WARRIER RR 5147[13]

3 ch g Desert Dirham (USA) - Noirianna (Morston (FR)) 9.4f **(55)**
Form - 0
Record 1999 - 1st:0 2nd:0 3rd:0 Ran:1
1999 AW 0-1: (8f) (Fibr)
Light-framed, currently very poor gelding.
**P Eccles [0-1] Wilson & Coyle.*

WILCUMA BHB 85f RR 91?f 4409[7]

8 b g Most Welcome 8.6f **(66)** - Miss Top Ville (FR) (Top Ville) 11.7f **(68)**
Form - 7
Record 1999 - 1st:0 2nd:0 3rd:0 Ran:1
Pre1999 - 1st:7 2nd:2 3rd:5 Ran:37
Win Prizemoney £102,964 *Total Prizemoney* £119,656
Wins * 1996 Dec Evry (HLD) L 10f 109 <
* 1996 Oct Newbur (SFT) H 9f 100 107
* 1996 Jly York (GD) H 10.4f 89 97
* 1995 Spt Haydoc (GD) H 8.1f 80 86
1999 Turf 0-1: (9f) (frm)
Useful gelding, has worn blinkers. **P J Makin [7-38] T G Warner.*

WILD ARMS (FR) RR 95f 1204a[5]

3 c Pistolet Bleu (IRE) - Alcove (FR)
Form - 45
1999 Turf 0-2: (11f 2) (g-s, gd)
Currently very useful colt. Turf high 95.
**E Lellouche in FR [0-2] E Sarasola.*

WILD CANARY BHB 52f52a RR 65f 52a 25[6]

4 ch f Groom Dancer (USA) 9.5f **(75)** - Nest (Sharpo) 7.7f **(59)**
Form - 00256
Record 1999 - 1st:0 2nd:0 3rd:0 Ran:1
Pre1999 - 1st:1 2nd:1 3rd:0 Ran:11
Win Prizemoney £2,085 *Total Prizemoney* £2,855
Wins 1998 *Feb Southw (STD) 11f* 67 <
1999 AW 0-1: (16f) (Fibr)
Lengthy, average filly, effective 11 to 14f, best at 11f, acts on g-f -

acts on Fibr, mostly wears blinkers (extremely effectively), prefers left handed tracks. Inconsistent.
**D Marks [0-7] C R Buttery (from Lord Huntingdon [1-5] Jun 1998).*

WILD CITY (USA) BHB 23f26a **RR 31f 26a** 1631[3]
5 b br g Wild Again (USA) 10.7f **(69)** - Garvin's Gal (USA) (Seattle Slew (USA)) 9.4f **(76)**
Form - 6800
Record 1999 - 1st:0 2nd:0 3rd:0 Ran:4
Pre1999 - 1st:0 2nd:0 3rd:0 Ran:12
1999 AW 0-4: (6f, 8f 2, 11f) (Fibr 4)
Very moderate gelding, had worn blinkers. AW high 32. (DEAD)
**R F Marvin [0-14] P J Cronin (from B Hanbury [0-2] Apr 1997).*

WILD COLONIAL BOY (IRE) BHB 42f **RR 32f** 3632[10]
4 b g Warning 8.1f **(77)** - Loch Clair (IRE) (Lomond (USA)) 8.8f **(65)**
Form - 070
Record 1999 - 1st:0 2nd:0 3rd:0 Ran:3
Pre1999 - 1st:0 2nd:2 3rd:3 Ran:15
Win Prizemoney £0 *Total Prizemoney* £3,717
1999 Turf 0-3: (10f, 11f, 12f) (gd, frm 2)
Scopey, very moderate gelding, effective 7 to 12f, best at 12f, acts on gd to frm, best on frm, has worn blinkers, likes left handed tracks, likes tight tracks. Turf high 32 (began Jly). Becoming disappointing. He has a long name but appears to be short on talent.
**G P Enright [0-3] The Jack Duggan Trio (from R Hannon [0-15] Oct 1998).*

WILDERNESS (USA) RR 39f 3433[12]
2 b f Gilded Time (USA) 7f **(76)** - Dark of The Moon (Dancing Brave (USA)) 8.4f **(76)**
Form - 0
Record 1999 - 1st:0 2nd:0 3rd:0 Ran:1
1999 Turf 0-1: (7f) (frm)
Currently very moderate filly. **I A Balding [0-1] Mrs Paul Mellon.*

WILD FLIGHT RR 37f 5000[11]
2 b g Alflora (IRE) - Absolutely Nuts (Absalom) 7.2f **(58)**
Form - 0
Record 1999 - 1st:0 2nd:0 3rd:0 Ran:1
1999 Turf 0-1: (8f) (gd)
Currently very moderate gelding. **T P Tate [0-1] T P Tate.*

WILD HEAVEN (IRE) RR 93f 4473a[7]
3 bb f Darshaan 11.9f **(81)** - Mild Intrigue (USA) (Sir Ivor) 10.2f **(70)**
Form - 1757
1999 Turf 0-3: (10f 2, 12f) (g-s, gd, g-f)
Useful filly, effective 8 to 9f, acts on hvy to sft, prefers left handed tracks. Turf high 90. Inconsistent.
**C O'Brien in IRE [3-8] Mrs Paul Shanahan.*

WILD MAGIC RR 27f 4941[14]
2 ch f Magic Ring (IRE) 6.5f **(64)** - Wild Humour (IRE) **(47f)** (Fayruz)
Form - 0
Record 1999 - 1st:0 2nd:0 3rd:0 Ran:1
1999 Turf 0-1: (5f) (gd)
Currently little account filly. **W R Muir [0-1] Mrs J A Hubbard.*

WILD NETTLE BHB 30f30a **RR 40f 30a** 1087[6]
5 ch m Beveled (USA) 6.9f **(64)** - Pink Pumpkin (Tickled Pink) 6.5f **(59)**
Form - 04342246
Record 1999 - 1st:0 2nd:2 3rd:0 Ran:5
Pre1999 - 1st:0 2nd:2 3rd:3 Ran:30
Win Prizemoney £0 *Total Prizemoney* £4,717
1999 AW 0-5: (8f, 10f 4) (Equi 5)
Moderate filly. AW high 34. She has shown ability on the Lingfield Equitrack towards the end of the year, and should be noted if tried over a mile on that surface. **J C Fox [0-35] Mrs J A Cleary.*

WILD SKY (IRE) BHB 81f **RR 83f** 5141[17]
5 br g Warning 8.1f **(77)** - Erwinna (USA) (Lyphard (USA)) 9.9f **(72)**
Form - 5018800
Record 1999 - 1st:1 2nd:0 3rd:0 Ran:7
Pre1999 - 1st:1 2nd:5 3rd:3 Ran:20
Win Prizemoney £10,738 *Total Prizemoney* £31,472
Wins 1999 May Leices (GD) H 8f 80 83 <
1997 Nov Newmar (G-F) H 7f 72 76
1999 Turf 1-7: (7f 2, 8f 1-5) (gd 3, g-f 1-2, frm 2)
Decent gelding, effective 8 to 9f, best at 8f, acts on gd to frm, has worn blinkers, excels at Doncaster, does well at Newmarket. Turf high 83 - 1st of 15 giving 14lb to Sweet Reward (31 May Leicester RF 1600). Consistent. After finding victory hard to come by for some time, he struck form at Leicester in May, winning quite a competitive handicap in good style. Respectable efforts in hot races afterwards. He is well suited by a straight mile.
**C G Cox [0-2] The Gold Partnership (from M J Heaton-Ellis [2-25] Jly 1999).*

WILD THING BHB 55f63a **RR 52f 63a** 5127[5]
3 b c Never so Bold 7.1f **(62)** - Tame Duchess (Saritamer (USA)) 9.5f **(63)**
Form - 2230215
Record 1999 - 1st:1 2nd:3 3rd:1 Ran:7
Pre1999 - 1st:0 2nd:0 3rd:0 Ran:1
Win Prizemoney £2,253 *Total Prizemoney* £5,504
Wins * 1999 *Oct Southw (STD) 6f 59* **<**
1999 Turf 0-3: (6f, 7f 2) (gd 3) 1999 AW 1-4: (6f 1-2, 7f, 8f) (Equi 3, Fibr 1-1)
Workmanlike, average colt, effective 6 to 8f, - acts on AW, best on Equi. Turf high 52 (began Spt). AW high 63 - 2nd of 7 getting 19lb from Waiting Knight (2 Feb Lingfield 8f Equi RF 0211) - also 1st of 14 giving 5lb to Groesfaen Lady (18 Oct Southwell RF 4938).
**R Hannon [1-8] B T Stewart-Brown.*

WILD TIMES BHB 25f **RR 22f** 38[13]
3 b g Emarati (USA) 6.6f **(63)** - Pink Pumpkin (Tickled Pink) 6.5f **(59)**
Form - 0
Record 1999 - 1st:0 2nd:0 3rd:0 Ran:1
Pre1999 - 1st:0 2nd:0 3rd:0 Ran:3
1999 AW 0-1: (8f) (Fibr)
Workmanlike, little account gelding.
**E A Wheeler [0-4] Mrs J A Cleary.*

WILD WILLIE-D (IRE) BHB 48f **RR 49f** 3309[15]
4 b g Balla Cove - Fine Print (IRE) (Taufan (USA)) 7f **(57)**
Form - 70
Record 1999 - 1st:0 2nd:0 3rd:0 Ran:2
Pre1999 - 1st:0 2nd:0 3rd:0 Ran:1
1999 Turf 0-2: (6f, 7f) (frm 2)
Workmanlike, currently fair gelding. Turf high 49.
**John Berry [0-2] John Berry (from T T Clement [0-1] Aug 1998).*

WILEMMGEO BHB 60f56a **RR 63f 56a** 4320[3]
2 b f Emarati (USA) 6.6f **(63)**-Floral Spark **(61f 72a)** (Forzando)7.6f **(59)**
Form - 0423
Record 1999 - 1st:0 2nd:1 3rd:1 Ran:4
Win Prizemoney £0 *Total Prizemoney* £1,140
1999 Turf 0-3: (5f, 7f 2) (gd 2, hrd) 1999 AW 0-1: (7f) (Fibr)
Average filly. Turf high 63 - 3rd of 15 giving 2lb to Dispol Magic (15 Spt Beverley 7f gd RF 4320). (1st run) - 4th of 11 to Sally Gardens (23 Jly Wolverhampton 7f Fibr RF 3083).
**P C Haslam [0-4] M J Cunningham.*

WILFRAM BHB 68f **RR 73f** 5195[15]
2 b g Fraam - Ming Blue (Primo Dominie) 6.2f **(80)**
Form - 040
Record 1999 - 1st:0 2nd:0 3rd:0 Ran:3
1999 Turf 0-3: (6f 3) (gd, g-f, frm)
Currently above-average gelding. Turf high 73 (began Oct).
**J M Bradley [0-3] R D Willis.*

WILLIAM BARRAUD (IRE) BHB 83f **RR 88f** 4899[7]
2 b g Tenby 10.4f **(76)** - Vibrant Hue (USA) (Exclusive Native (USA)) 9.1f **(81)**
Form - 0127
Record 1999 - 1st:1 2nd:1 3rd:0 Ran:4
Win Prizemoney £2,839 *Total Prizemoney* £5,119
Wins * 1999 Spt Warwic (SFT) 6.8f 80 **<**
1999 Turf 1-4: (6f, 7f 1-1, 8f 2) (sft 1-1, gd 2, g-f)
Useful gelding. Turf high 88 (began Jly) - 2nd of 20 giving 4lb to Duchamp (7 Oct York 8f gd RF 4762) - also 1st of 16 getting 3lb from Mentiga (21 Spt Warwick RF 4455).
**P F I Cole [1-4] Richard Green (Fine Paintings).*

WILLIAMSHAKESPEARE (IRE) BHB 80f **RR 82f** 3861[2]
3 b c Slip Anchor 12.7f **(75)** - Rostova (Blakeney) 10.5f **(64)**
Form - 2302232
Record 1999 - 1st:0 2nd:4 3rd:2 Ran:7
Pre1999 - 1st:0 2nd:0 3rd:0 Ran:1
Win Prizemoney £0 *Total Prizemoney* £6,610
1999 Turf 0-7: (10f, 12f 5, 14f) (gd, g-f 3, frm 3)
Neat, decent colt, effective 10 to 12f, best at 12f, acts on g-f to frm, best on frm. Turf high 83 - 2nd of 7 to First Ballot (11 Jly Newbury 12f frm RF 2747). Consistent. He has shown promise in maiden company and should find a race at that level.
**B W Hills [0-8] W J Gredley.*

WILLIAM'S WELL BHB 66f50a **RR 64f 50a** 4911[4]
5 ch g Superpower 6.6f **(58)** - Catherines Well (Junius (USA)) 7.7f **(65)**
Form - 371122625704
Record 1999 - 1st:2 2nd:3 3rd:1 Ran:12
Pre1999 - 1st:2 2nd:4 3rd:6 Ran:37
Win Prizemoney £12,181 *Total Prizemoney* £23,293
Wins * 1999 Jly Catter (FRM) H 5f 57 60 <
* **1999** Jly Carlis (GD) H 5f 53 54
* 1997 Jun Mussel (GD) H 5f 51 53
* 1997 Jun Catter (GD) H 5f 43 44
1999 Turf 2-12: (5f 2-12) (gd 2, g-f 4, frm 2-6)
Average gelding, effective 5f, acts on g-f to frm, best on frm, mostly wears blinkers (effectively), excels at Catterick. Turf high 68 - 2nd of 13 giving 15lb to Brecongill Lad (3 Aug Catterick 5f frm RF 3318) - also 1st of 11 getting 8lb from Tuscan Dream (14 Jly Catterick RF 2806). Consistent. A winner at Carlisle and Catterick during July, he often makes the frame but is looking as though six furlongs would suit him better now.
**M W Easterby [4-49] K Hodgson & Mrs J Hodgson.*

WILLIAM THE LION RR 55f 3413[12]
2 b c Puissance 7.1f **(60)** - Last Note (Welsh Pageant) 10f **(65)**
Form - 000
Record 1999 - 1st:0 2nd:0 3rd:0 Ran:3
1999 Turf 0-3: (6f 2, 7f) (gd, g-f, frm)
Currently fair colt. Turf high 55.
**J Berry [0-3] Chris & Antonia Deuters.*

WILLIE CONQUER BHB 84f **RR 87f** 5028[12]
7 ch g Master Willie 9.2f **(67)** - Maryland Cookie (USA) (Bold Hour) 10f **(81)**
Form - 150540
Record 1999 - 1st:1 2nd:0 3rd:0 Ran:6
Pre1999 - 1st:3 2nd:2 3rd:3 Ran:23
Win Prizemoney £22,205 *Total Prizemoney* £35,806
Wins * 1999 Jun Bright (GD) H 11.9f 80 85+
1996 Oct Newmar (G-F) H 12f 84 92 <
1996 Spt Goodwo (G-F) 12f 82
1996 Aug Newbur (GD) 12f 80
1999 Turf 1-6: (12f 1-2, 13f, 14f, 15f, 16f) (g-s, gd 1-2, g-f, frm 2)
Useful gelding, effective 12 to 15f, best at 12f, acts on gd to frm, best on gd, likes right handed tracks. Turf high 87 - 4th of 9 getting 6lb from Life of Riley (27 Aug Newmarket 15f frm RF 3940) - also 1st of 6 giving 8lb to Random Kindness (30 Jun Brighton RF 2431). He made a fine debut for his new yard with an easy win at Brighton in June, but has failed to capitalise on that since.
**D R C Elsworth [1-8] Raymond Tooth (from Miss Gay Kelleway [0-4] Jly 1998).*

WILL IVESON (IRE) BHB 64f61a **RR 63f 61a** 4269[5]
2 b g Mukaddamah (USA) 7.6f **(74)** - Cherlinoa (FR) (Crystal Palace (FR)) 12.5f **(76)**
Form - 45675
Record 1999 - 1st:0 2nd:0 3rd:0 Ran:5
Win Prizemoney £0 *Total Prizemoney* £229
1999 Turf 0-4: (5f 2, 6f, 7f) (gd, frm 3) 1999 AW 0-1: (6f) (Fibr)
Average gelding. Turf high 65 (1st run) - 4th of 17 giving 7lb to Toppo's Gem (29 Apr Redcar 5f gd RF 0916).
**P C Haslam [0-5] Lord Bolton.*

WILLOW MAGIC BHB 62f **RR 66f** 4941[12]
2 b f Petong 7.6f **(58)** - Love Street (Mummy's Pet) 7.7f **(60)**
Form - 670
Record 1999 - 1st:0 2nd:0 3rd:0 Ran:3
1999 Turf 0-3: (5f 2, 6f) (gd, g-f 2)
Currently average filly. Turf high 66 (began Aug).
**A J McNae [0-3] Mrs Anne Malby.*

WILLRACK TIMES BHB 60f **RR 58f** 2842[4]
2 b f Timeless Times (USA) 6.1f **(56)** - Willrack Farrier **(60f 50a)** (Lugana Beach)
Form - 03004
Record 1999 - 1st:0 2nd:0 3rd:1 Ran:5
Win Prizemoney £0 *Total Prizemoney* £832
1999 Turf 0-4: (5f 4) (gd 2, g-f 2) 1999 AW 0-1: (5f) (Fibr)
Fair filly. Turf high 58 - 4th of 8 getting 25lb from Half Moon Bay (15 Jly Doncaster 5f g-f RF 2842). **B A McMahon [0-5] Willrackers.*

WILL TO WIN BHB 38f30a **RR 43f 30a** 93[11]
5 b m Mazilier (USA) 8.5f **(56)** - Adana (FR) (Green Dancer (USA)) 10.3f **(74)**
Form - 000
Record 1999 - 1st:0 2nd:0 3rd:0 Ran:1
Pre1999 - 1st:2 2nd:3 3rd:6 Ran:42
Win Prizemoney £6,664 *Total Prizemoney* £12,212
Wins 1997 *Mar Wolver (STD) S* *6f* *58 <*
1997 *Feb Wolver (STD) S* *5f* *54*
1999 AW 0-1: (8f) (Equi)
Moderate filly, effective 6f, acts on frm, has worn blinkers. Becoming disappointing.
**T Keddy [0-3] Mrs Judith Neil (from P G Murphy [2-40] Spt 1998).*

WILLY WILLY RR 64f 1442[18]
6 ch g Master Willie 9.2f **(67)** - Monsoon (Royal Palace) 9f **(56)**
Form - 0
Record 1999 - 1st:0 2nd:0 3rd:0 Ran:1
Pre1999 - 1st:1 2nd:0 3rd:0 Ran:5
Win Prizemoney £3,915 *Total Prizemoney* £4,577
Wins 1998 Jly Lingfi (G-F) 9f 85 <
1999 Turf 0-1: (10f) (frm)
Average gelding, effective 9f, acts on frm.
**D L Williams [0-1] Berkshire Commercial Components Ltd (from H Candy [1-5] Oct 1998).*

WILMORE BHB 55f50a **RR 57f 50a** 4993[15]
3 gr g Elmaamul (USA) 8.1f **(70)** - Kibitka (FR) (Baby Turk) 11.3f **(90)**
Form - 80136360
Record 1999 - 1st:1 2nd:0 3rd:2 Ran:8
Win Prizemoney £2,807 *Total Prizemoney* £3,569
Wins * 1999 Jun Warwic (HVY) 10.5f 63 <
1999 Turf 1-8: (10f 5, 11f 1-1, 12f 2) (g-s 1-2, gd, g-f 2, frm 3)
Light-framed, fair gelding, effective 10 to 11f, best at 10f, acts on g-s to g-f, best on g-s. Turf high 64 - 3rd of 8 getting 7lb from Totom (28 Jun Windsor 10f g-f RF 2385) - also 1st of 5 giving 5lb to Sumitra (7 Jun Warwick RF 1795). Consistent.
**M A Jarvis [1-8] K G Powter.*

WILOMENO RR 5198[17]
3 b f Efisio 7.7f **(69)** - Tzarina (USA) (Gallant Romeo (USA)) 8.4f **(64)**
Form - 0
Record 1999 - 1st:0 2nd:0 3rd:0 Ran:1
1999 Turf 0-1: (8f) (gd)
Workmanlike, currently very poor filly. **Mrs L C Jewell [0-1] K Hay.*

WILTON BHB 66f70a **RR 71f 70a** 4865[11]
4 ch g Sharpo 7.5f **(68)** - Poyle Amber (Sharrood (USA)) 10.5f **(72)**
Form - 12000
Record 1999 - 1st:0 2nd:0 3rd:0 Ran:2
Pre1999 - 1st:4 2nd:3 3rd:1 Ran:17
Win Prizemoney £17,465 *Total Prizemoney* £21,161
Wins * 1998 *Nov Lingfi (STD) H* 8f *74* 75 <
* 1998 Oct Redcar (HVY) H 8f 62 70
* 1998 Oct Pontef (G-S) H 8f 52 60
* 1997 *Nov Southw (STD)* *6f* *68*
1999 AW 0-2: (7f, 8f) (Fibr 2)
Unfurnished, above-average gelding, effective 7 to 9f, best at 8f, acts on sft to gd - acts on AW, likes left handed tracks, prefers tight tracks, likes Wolverhampton. AW high 44 (began Oct). Becoming disappointing. Effective on turf and both sand surfaces,

he seems ideally suited by a trip around a mile, and needs cut in the ground on turf. **J Hetherton [4-19] George Moore.*

WINCE BHB 116f **RR 115f** 1485a^{5}

3 b f Selkirk (USA) 7.9f **(76)** - Flit (USA) (Lyphard (USA)) 9.9f **(72)**

Form - 115

Record	**1999 -**	1st:2	2nd:0	3rd:0	Ran:3
	Pre1999 -	1st:2	2nd:1	3rd:1	Ran:6

Win Prizemoney £160,414 *Total Prizemoney* £163,979

Wins						
*** 1999**	May	Newmar (G-F)	G1	8f	115	<
*** 1999**	Apr	Newbur (G-F)	G3	7f	110	
* 1998	Aug	Cheste (GD)		6.1f	92	
* 1998	Jly	Kempto (G-S)		7f	75+	

1999 Turf 2-3: (7f 1-1, 8f 1-2) (g-f, frm 2-2)

Workmanlike, high-class filly, effective 7 to 8f, acts on frm. Turf high 115 - 1st of 22 from Wannabe Grand (2 May Newmarket RF 0979) - also 1st of 11 from Golden Silca (16 Apr Newbury RF 0719). This filly progressed steadily with experience at two, but her limitations appeared to be exposed in Pattern company at the end of her first season. However, she won nicely in the Fred Darling Stakes on her return to action last season, albeit in a muddling race, and got it right when it mattered with a fine win in the 1000 Guineas. She was rather disappointing when only fifth in the Irish version at the Curragh, but may have been racing on the slower part of the track and a muscle problem was also suggested as a possible excuse. That was the last that was seen of her as she has been retired. **H R A Cecil [4-9] K Abdullah.*

WIND CHEETAH (USA) BHB 102f **RR 106f** 2900^{7}

Wince gave Kieren Fallon the first of his three Classic wins in 1999

5 b br h Storm Cat (USA) 7f **(86)** - Won't She Tell (USA) (Banner Sport (USA)) 8.6f **(93)**

Form - 2037

Record	**1999 -**	1st:0	2nd:1	3rd:1	Ran:4
	Pre1999 -	1st:1	2nd:0	3rd:1	Ran:7

Win Prizemoney £3,570 *Total Prizemoney* £17,153

Wins					
* 1996	Oct	Lingfi (GD)	6f	88+	<

1999 Turf 0-4: (6f 2, 7f, 8f) (sft, g-s, g-f, frm)

Pattern-class colt. Turf high 106 (1st run) - 2nd of 7 to Warningford (24 Apr Leicester 7f sft RF 0832). Something was probably amiss in '98 as he only ran once, but last term he showed his liking for soft ground with a good second to Warningford at Leicester. Ran another good race at Newcastle in June at his optimum trip of six furlongs. **Sir Michael Stoute [1-11] Cheveley Park Stud.*

WIND CHIME (IRE) RR 73f 5194^{4}

2 ch c Arazi (USA) 9.2f **(74)** - Shamisen (Diesis) 9.3f **(69)**

Form - 24

Record	**1999 -**	1st:0	2nd:1	3rd:0	Ran:2

Win Prizemoney £0 *Total Prizemoney* £1,394

1999 Turf 0-2: (6f 2) (gd, g-f)

Currently above-average colt. Turf high 73 (began Jly). **C E Brittain [0-2] Saeed Manana.*

WINDFALL RR 25f 4785^{14}

2 b c Polish Precedent (USA) 9f **(73)** - Captive Heart (Conquistador Cielo (USA)) 8.8f **(69)**

Form - 0

Record	**1999 -**	1st:0	2nd:0	3rd:0	Ran:1

1999 Turf 0-1: (7f) (g-s)

Currently little account colt. **C A Cyzer [0-1] R M Cyzer.*

WIND IN WELLINGTON (IRE) RR 3472^{4}

2 b f Dancing Dissident (USA) 6.8f **(65)** - Zalewska (IRE) (Polish Precedent (USA)) 10.2f **(60)**

Form -

Record	**1999 -**	1st:0	2nd:0	3rd:0	Ran:5

1999 Turf 0-3: (gd, g-f 2) 1999 AW 0-2: (Fibr 2)

Little account filly. Turf high 28. AW high 29 (began Jly). **Ronald Thompson [0-5] Ronald Thompson.*

WIND IN WINNIPEG (IRE) BHB 49f **RR 41df** 4719^{17}

3 b f Midhish - Tara View (IRE) (Wassl) 9.7f **(62)**

Form - 884748558000

Record	**1999 -**	1st:0	2nd:0	3rd:0	Ran:12
	Pre1999 -	1st:1	2nd:3	3rd:1	Ran:11

Win Prizemoney £3,452 *Total Prizemoney* £8,598

Wins							
* 1998	Spt	Hamilt (SFT)	H	5f	58	66	<

1999 Turf 0-12: (5f 9, 6f 3) (g-s 2, gd 3, g-f 5, frm 2)

Leggy, moderate filly, effective 5 to 6f, best at 5f, acts on g-s to frm, has worn blinkers. Turf high 57. Inconsistent. **J S Wainwright [1-23] Rosaly Racing.*

WINDMILL LANE BHB 60f **RR 66f** 5138^{5}

2 b f Saddlers' Hall (IRE) 10.5f **(65)** - Alpi Dora (Valiyar) 8.5f **(73)**

Form - 75505

Record	**1999 -**	1st:0	2nd:0	3rd:0	Ran:5

1999 Turf 0-5: (7f, 8f 4) (gd 2, g-f 2, frm)

Average filly. Turf high 66 (began Aug). **A P Jarvis [0-5] Ms Julie Greenacre.*

WINDRUSH (IRE) BHB 32f **RR 38f** 2458^{5}

3 gr g Conquering Hero (USA) 10.6f **(50)** - Linda Dudley (Owen Dudley) 8.3f **(61)**

Form - 005

Record	**1999 -**	1st:0	2nd:0	3rd:0	Ran:3
	Pre1999 -	1st:0	2nd:0	3rd:0	Ran:1

1999 Turf 0-3: (8f, 10f, 14f) (g-f, frm 2)

Very moderate gelding, has worn blinkers. Turf high 38. **B S Rothwell [0-3] The Bags Partnership (from K O'Sullivan in IRE [0-1] Aug 1998).*

WINDRUSH BOY BHB 41f39a **RR 35f 39a** 4233^{4}

9 br g Dowsing (USA) 7f **(61)** - Bridge Street Lady (Decoy Boy) 6.7f **(56)**

Form - 00825186054

Record	**1999 -**	1st:1	2nd:1	3rd:0	Ran:11
	Pre1999 -	1st:4	2nd:5	3rd:3	Ran:57

Win Prizemoney £15,132 *Total Prizemoney* £21,529

Wins							
*** 1999**	Jly	Bath (FRM)	C	5.1f		51	
* 1998	Jun	Lingfi (GD)	H	5f	38	41	
1996	Aug	Warwic (GD)	C	5f		57	<
1995	Aug	Leices (G-F)	H	5f	62	54	

1999 Turf 1-11: (5f 1-11) (gd 4, g-f 1-3, frm 3, hrd)

Very moderate gelding, effective 5f, acts on g-f to frm, best on frm, likes left handed tracks. Turf high 51 - 1st of 18 getting 12lb from Mangus (15 Jly Bath RF 2840). Consistent. **M R Bosley [2-28] Girls On Top Racing 2000 (from J R Bosley [3-33]*

Jan 1997).

WINDSHIFT (IRE) BHB 70f78a **RR 74f 78a** 4426[11]
3 b g Forest Wind (USA)-Beautyofthepeace (IRE)(Exactly Sharp (USA))
Form - 1521153150430
Record 1999 - 1st:3 2nd:1 3rd:2 Ran:12
Pre1999 - 1st:1 2nd:0 3rd:0 Ran:4
Win Prizemoney £16,687 *Total Prizemoney* £20,218
Wins * **1999** Mar Warwic (G-S) H 8f 70 74
* **1999** *Mar Southw (STD) H 8f 70 78* <
* **1999** *Feb Southw (STD) H 8f 63 69*
* 1998 *Dec Southw (STD) H 8f 51 57*
1999 Turf 1-5: (8f 1-4, 11f) (g-s 1-1, gd 2, frm 2) 1999 AW 2-7: (7f 2, 8f 2-5) (Fibr 2-7)
Leggy, above-average gelding, effective 8f, acts on g-s - acts on Fibr, often wears blinkers (effectively), favours left handed tracks, prefers tight tracks. Turf high 74 (1st run) - 1st of 9 getting 19lb from Sampower Star (27 Mar Warwick RF 0490). AW high 78 - 1st of 8 getting 12lb from Magical Shot (1 Mar Southwell RF 0381) - also 1st of 6 getting 6lb from Air of Esteem (19 Feb Southwell RF 0321). **D Shaw [4-16] G E Griffiths.*

WINDSOR BOY (IRE) RR 87f 5139[5]
2 b c Mtoto 11.5f **(71)** - Fragrant Belle (USA) **(87f)** (Al Nasr (FR)) 9.3f **(68)**
Form - 165
Record 1999 - 1st:1 2nd:0 3rd:0 Ran:3
Win Prizemoney £3,582 *Total Prizemoney* £3,921
Wins * **1999** Aug Beverl (GD) 8.5f 84+ <
1999 Turf 1-3: (8f 1-2, 10f) (g-s, gd, frm 1-1)
Currently useful colt. Turf high 87 (began Aug) - also 1st of 8 from Bhutan Prince (29 Aug Beverley RF 3990). Made a winning debut over the extended mile at Beverley in August but subsequently disappointed in the National Stakes at the Curragh. He failed to stay ten furlongs on his third run.
**P F I Cole [1-3] H R H Prince Fahd Salman.*

WINDSTORM (IRE) BHB 26f26a **RR 18f 26a** 2571[15]
3 b f Forest Wind (USA) - Kaya (GER) (Young Generation) 7.7f **(63)**
Form - 00000
Record 1999 - 1st:0 2nd:0 3rd:0 Ran:5
Pre1999 - 1st:0 2nd:0 3rd:0 Ran:5
1999 Turf 0-3: (6f, 7f, 8f) (g-f 2, frm) 1999 AW 0-2: (6f, 8f) (Fibr 2)
Neat, poor filly, has worn blinkers. Turf high 18. AW high 9.
**H Morrison [0-10] The Forest Club.*

WINDYEDGE (USA) BHB 50a **RR 19?f** 4174[16]
6 ch g Woodman (USA) 9.7f **(77)** - Abeesh (USA) (Nijinsky (CAN)) 10.3f **(77)**
Form - 0
Record 1999 - 1st:0 2nd:0 3rd:0 Ran:1
Pre1999 - 1st:0 2nd:1 3rd:0 Ran:8
Win Prizemoney £0 *Total Prizemoney* £1,218
1999 Turf 0-1: (10f) (g-f)
Poor gelding. Becoming disappointing.
**Mrs A M Naughton [0-7] Mrs C T Woodley (from B W Hills [0-6] Aug 1996).*

WINDY GULCH (USA) BHB 77f69a **RR 76f 69a** 5143[1]
4 b f Gulch (USA) 9.6f **(79)** - Wyndalia (USA) (Seattle Slew (USA)) 9.4f **(76)**
Form - 075216121633021
Record 1999 - 1st:4 2nd:3 3rd:2 Ran:14
Pre1999 - 1st:0 2nd:1 3rd:2 Ran:10
Win Prizemoney £18,925 *Total Prizemoney* £27,950
Wins * **1999** Oct Newmar (SFT) H 7f 74 76 <
* **1999** Aug Newcas (FRM) H 7f 68 73
* **1999** Jly Hamilt (FRM) H 6f 64 66
* **1999** Jun Hamilt (GD) H 6f 59 63
1999 Turf 4-14: (6f 2-8, 7f 2-6) (gd 1-4, g-f 1-4, frm 1-5, hrd 1-1)
Scopey, above-average filly, effective 6 to 10f, best at 6f, acts on gd to hrd - acts on Fibr, has worn blinkers, excels at Newmarket and Hamilton. Turf high 76 - 1st of 20 getting 1lb from Weetman's Weigh (30 Oct Newmarket RF 5143) - also 1st of 4 getting 14lb from Quiet Venture (4 Aug Newcastle RF 3369). Consistent. Ran over ten furlongs in '98, but benefited from a drop in trip and enjoyed a fine season.
**M Johnston [4-14] Ian Deane (from P F I Cole [0-10] Dec 1998).*

WIN FOR US (GER) RR 106f 5121a[5]
3 f
Form - 423415
1999 Turf 1-6: (11f, 12f 2, 13f, 14f 1-1, 16f) (hvy, sft 1-3, gd, g-f)
Pattern-class filly, effective 11 to 14f, acts on sft to g-f, best on sft. Turf high 106 - 1st of 8 from Montalban (3 Oct Dortmund RF 4774a). She is a useful stayer, but has hung badly and is not an easy ride. **P Schiergen in GER [1-6].*

WINGED GREYBIRD BHB 40f **RR 34f** 659[12]
5 gr m Batshoof 9.5f **(66)** - To Oneiro (Absalom) 7.2f **(58)**
Form - 30
Record 1999 - 1st:0 2nd:0 3rd:1 Ran:2
Pre1999 - 1st:0 2nd:0 3rd:0 Ran:2
Win Prizemoney £0 *Total Prizemoney* £350
1999 Turf 0-1: (15f) (hvy) 1999 AW 0-1: (13f) (Equi)
Moderate filly. **Miss A M Newton-Smith [0-4] Ian Moody.*

WINGED HUSSAR RR 97+f 2978a[10]
6 b g In The Wings 11.2f **(77)** - Akila 0**0**
Form - 100
1999 Turf 1-3: (12f 1-3) (g-s, gd 1-1, g-f)
Very useful gelding, effective 12f, acts on hvy to gd, best on gd, has worn blinkers. Turf high 97 (1st run) - 1st of 8 giving 4lb to Francis Bay (9 May Leopardstown RF 1171a). A smart handicapper, he is best around a mile and a half but was not seen out after mid-July. **J Oxx in IRE [3-13] Dundalk Racing Club.*

WINGED KNIGHT (IRE) BHB 35f **RR 14f** 2536[10]
8 ch g Kefaah (USA) 11.2f **(64)** - Excuse Slip (USA) (Damascus (USA)) 8.9f **(71)**
Form - 00
Record 1999 - 1st:0 2nd:0 3rd:0 Ran:2
Pre1999 - 1st:0 2nd:1 3rd:1 Ran:2
Win Prizemoney £0 *Total Prizemoney* £387
1999 Turf 0-1: (14f) (g-f) 1999 AW 0-1: (14f) (Fibr)
Poor gelding.
**B King in IRE [0-3] Mrs K Deed (from B King [0-1] Jun 1999).*

WINGS AWARDED BHB 51f51a **RR 53f 51a** 4415[5]
4 b f Shareef Dancer (USA) 10.1f **(67)** - Ruda (FR) (Free Round (USA)) 11.7f **(70)**
Form - 400052385
Record 1999 - 1st:0 2nd:1 3rd:1 Ran:9
Pre1999 - 1st:2 2nd:5 3rd:1 Ran:17
Win Prizemoney £5,596 *Total Prizemoney* £11,710
Wins * 1998 Jly Folkes (G-F) H 12f 56 60+ <
* 1998 May Windso (G-F) C 8.3f 60
1999 Turf 0-7: (10f 5, 12f 2) (gd, g-f, frm 5) 1999 AW 0-2: (10f, 12f) (Equi, Fibr)
Leggy, average filly, effective 8 to 12f, best at 12f, acts on g-s to frm - acts on Equi, best on gd, has worn blinkers, likes right handed tracks, favours tight tracks, excels at Nottingham. Turf high 53 (began Jly). AW high 60 (1st run) - 4th of 6 giving 14lb to Shanghai Lil (18 Feb Lingfield 10f Equi RF 0312).
**M R Channon [2-26] M Channon.*

WINLEAH BHB 25f **RR 24f** 5127[13]
3 gr c Petong 7.6f **(58)** - Tower Glades (Tower Walk) 10f **(62)**
Form - 0700
Record 1999 - 1st:0 2nd:0 3rd:0 Ran:3
Pre1999 - 1st:0 2nd:0 3rd:0 Ran:3
1999 Turf 0-3: (5f, 7f, 8f) (gd 2, frm)
Leggy, little account colt. Turf high 24 (began Jly).
**A G Newcombe [0-6] Advanced Marketing Services Ltd.*

WINNING VENTURE RR 96f 5015a[3]
2 b c Owington - Push a Button (Bold Lad (IRE)) 8.4f **(68)**
Form - 231323
Record 1999 - 1st:1 2nd:2 3rd:3 Ran:6
Win Prizemoney £5,284 *Total Prizemoney* £37,455
Wins * **1999** Aug Kempto (SFT) 7f 79 <
1999 Turf 1-6: (6f 2, 7f 1-3, 8f) (g-s 1-1, gd, g-f, frm 3)
Very useful colt, effective 7 to 8f, acts on gd to g-f. Turf high 96 (began Jly) - 3rd of 9 to Night Style (17 Oct San Siro 8f g-f RF 5015a). He enjoys soft ground and hung when asked to quicken on

a sound surface in Italy on his final start. He may not stay much beyond a mile, but could win a decent race on the continent next term. **S P C Woods [1-6].*

WINNOWER BHB 35f **RR 35f** 5107[9]
3 b f Robellino (USA) 9.5f **(68)** - Corn Circle (IRE) (Thatching) 8f **(66)**
Form - 8580
Record 1999 - 1st:0 2nd:0 3rd:0 Ran:4
Pre1999 - 1st:0 2nd:0 3rd:0 Ran:2
1999 Turf 0-2: (10f 2) (gd 2) 1999 AW 0-2: (10f, 11f) (Equi, Fibr)
Workmanlike, very moderate filly. Turf high 35 (began Spt). AW high 10.
**Mrs L Stubbs [0-4] R Rayner (from J L Dunlop [0-2] Jun 1998).*

WINS FICTION (GER) RR 119f 4663a[7]
4 b g Platini (GER) - Win Hands Down (Ela-Mana-Mou) 10.1f **(70)**
Form - 27
1999 Turf 0-2: (12f 2) (sft 2)
Currently high-class gelding. Turf high 119 (1st run) (began Aug) - 2nd of 4 to Ungaro (15 Aug Gelsenkirchen-Horst 12f sft RF 3784a). German-trained, he ran his best race of last season when beaten just half a length by Ungaro in a Group One in his native country.
**P Remmert in GER [0-2].*

WINSOME GEORGE BHB 47f **RR 44f** 5188[13]
4 b g Marju (IRE) 9.2f **(76)** - June Moon (IRE) (Sadler's Wells (USA)) 10f **(76)**
Form - 084060480000
Record 1999 - 1st:0 2nd:0 3rd:0 Ran:12
Pre1999 - 1st:3 2nd:3 3rd:4 Ran:23
Win Prizemoney £10,819 *Total Prizemoney* £18,083
Wins * 1998 May Redcar (G-F) H 11f 70 82 <
* 1998 May Beverl (GD) H 12f 70 76
* 1997 Jun Ayr (GD) 7f 77
1999 Turf 0-12: (12f 7, 14f 3, 16f, 17f) (gd, g-f 4, frm 6, hrd)
Workmanlike, moderate gelding, effective 11 to 14f, acts on gd to frm, best on gd, has worn blinkers (extremely effectively). Turf high 65. **C W Fairhurst [3-35] C D Barber-Lomax.*

WINSTON BHB 39f37a **RR 49df 37a** 15[6]
6 b g Safawan 6.6f **(60)** - Lady Leman (Pitskelly) 8.5f **(53)**
Form - 6
Record 1999 - 1st:0 2nd:0 3rd:0 Ran:1
Pre1999 - 1st:2 2nd:2 3rd:5 Ran:36
Win Prizemoney £6,957 *Total Prizemoney* £13,175
Wins * 1996 May Newcas (GD) H 8f 60 62 <
* 1996 Apr Nottin (G-F) H 8.2f 56 52
1999 AW 0-1: (8f) (Fibr)
Moderate gelding, effective 8f, acts on gd, has worn blinkers, likes tight tracks. **J D Bethell [2-37] Mrs J E Vickers.*

WINTZIG BHB 71f **RR 65f** 4504[1]
2 b f Piccolo - Wrangbrook (Shirley Heights) 10.3f **(74)**
Form - 4561
Record 1999 - 1st:1 2nd:0 3rd:0 Ran:4
Win Prizemoney £3,262 *Total Prizemoney* £3,515
Wins *** 1999** Spt Pontef (GD) H 8f 65 65 <
1999 Turf 1-4: (7f 2, 8f 1-2) (gd 2, g-f 1-2)
Average filly. Turf high 65 (began Jly) - 1st of 16 giving 1lb to Katy Ivory (23 Spt Pontefract RF 4504).
**M L W Bell [1-4] Baron F C Oppenheim.*

WIRA (IRE) BHB 35f **RR 25f** 4079[16]
5 ch h Lahib (USA) 8f **(69)** - Mother Courage (Busted) 10.2f **(61)**
Form - 660000
Record 1999 - 1st:0 2nd:0 3rd:0 Ran:6
Pre1999 - 1st:0 2nd:0 3rd:0 Ran:1
1999 Turf 0-6: (8f 4, 9f, 10f) (sft, gd, g-f 2, frm 2)
Little account colt. Turf high 49.
**M Brittain [0-6] Mel Brittain (from P F I Cole [0-1] Mar 1997).*

WISHBONE ALLEY (IRE) BHB 53f45a **RR 50f 45a** 4606[7]
4 b g Common Grounds 8.1f **(66)** - Dul Dul (USA) (Shadeed (USA)) 8.2f **(70)**
Form - 08502210270003837
Record 1999 - 1st:1 2nd:3 3rd:2 Ran:17
Pre1999 - 1st:1 2nd:3 3rd:3 Ran:20
Win Prizemoney £10,316 *Total Prizemoney* £17,809
Wins *** 1999** Jun Newcas (GD) H 6f 51 53
* 1998 Aug Thirsk (G-F) H 5f 59 63 <
1999 Turf 1-15: (5f 3, 6f 1-11, 7f) (sft, g-s, gd 2, g-f 2, frm 1-9) 1999 AW 0-2: (6f 2) (Fibr 2)
Workmanlike, fair gelding, effective 5 to 6f, best at 5f, acts on gd to frm, best on frm, has worn blinkers, does well at Thirsk, likes Newcastle. Turf high 53. AW high 22 (began Spt).
**M Dods [2-37] Doug Graham.*

WISHEDHADGONEHOME (IRE) BHB 56f **RR 45f** 5186[5]
2 b f Archway (IRE) 8.5f **(60)** - Yavarro (Raga Navarro (ITY)) 8f **(64)**
Form - 5478075
Record 1999 - 1st:0 2nd:0 3rd:0 Ran:7
Win Prizemoney £0 *Total Prizemoney* £585
1999 Turf 0-7: (5f 2, 6f 3, 7f, 8f) (gd 3, g-f 4)
Moderate filly, effective 5f, acts on g-f. Turf high 80 - 4th of 9 getting 5lb from Digital Image (4 May Chester 5f g-f RF 1025).
**P D Evans [0-7] Men Behaving Badly.*

WISHFUL THINKER BHB 69f **RR 66f** 4910[8]
2 b g Prince Sabo 6.6f **(64)** - Estonia (Kings Lake (USA)) 10.8f **(67)**
Form - 320008
Record 1999 - 1st:0 2nd:1 3rd:1 Ran:6
Win Prizemoney £0 *Total Prizemoney* £1,620
1999 Turf 0-6: (5f, 6f 2, 7f 2, 8f) (gd 2, g-f, frm 3)
Average gelding, effective 6f, acts on frm. Turf high 73 - 2nd of 22 to Aquarium (21 Jun Windsor 6f frm RF 2180).
**J W Hills [0-2] Mrs Marie Tinkler (from B J Meehan [0-4] Jly 1999).*

WISH LIST (IRE) BHB 89f **RR 97f** 4392[22]
3 b f Mujadil (USA) 7.7f **(70)** - Final Moment (Nishapour (FR)) 9.1f **(61)**
Form - 57500
Record 1999 - 1st:0 2nd:0 3rd:0 Ran:5
Pre1999 - 1st:2 2nd:1 3rd:1 Ran:8
Win Prizemoney £8,765 *Total Prizemoney* £14,215
Wins 1998 Spt Cork (GD) H 5f 81 84+ <
1998 Aug Tipper (FRM) 5f 84+ <
1999 Turf 0-5: (5f, 6f 3, 7f) (gd 3, g-f 2)
Very useful filly, effective 6 to 7f, acts on g-s to g-f. Turf high 97 (1st run) - 5th of 7 getting 5lb from Show Me The Money (18 Apr Leopardstown 7f g-f RF 0784a). She showed little in 1999 and was sold for just 8,500 guineas at Newmarket in October.
**D Nicholls [0-2] P D Savill (from C Collins in IRE [2-11] Aug 1999).*

WITCHFINDER (USA) BHB 62f73a **RR 62f 73a** 12[15]
7 b g Diesis 9f **(80)** - Colonial Witch (USA) (Pleasant Colony (USA)) 7f **(70)**
Form - 000
Record 1999 - 1st:0 2nd:0 3rd:0 Ran:1
Pre1999 - 1st:4 2nd:0 3rd:2 Ran:17
Win Prizemoney £13,242 *Total Prizemoney* £14,599
Wins * 1998 *Feb Lingfi (SLW) H 7f 70 80+* <
* 1998 *Jan Lingfi (STD) H 7f 62 71*
* 1998 *Jan Lingfi (STD) H 7f 55 63*
* 1997 *Dec Lingfi (STD) 7f 60*
1999 AW 0-1: (7f) (Equi)
Above-average gelding, effective 7f, - acts on Equi, often wears blinkers, favours left handed tracks, favours tight tracks. Inconsistent.
**Mrs L Stubbs [4-16] Maurice Parker (from J H M Gosden [0-2] Spt 1995).*

WITCH'S BREW RR 50f 3537[6]
2 b f Simply Great (FR) 11.9f **(61)** - New Broom (IRE) **(49f)** (Brush Aside (USA))
Form - 566
Record 1999 - 1st:0 2nd:0 3rd:0 Ran:3
1999 Turf 0-2: (7f 2) (g-f, frm) 1999 AW 0-1: (7f) (Fibr)
Currently fair filly. Turf high 50 (began Aug).
**T D Easterby [0-3] M H Easterby.*

WITH A WILL BHB 54f **RR 58f** 4814[9]
5 b g Rambo Dancer (CAN) 8.4f **(59)** - Henceforth (Full of Hope) 8.5f **(64)**
Form - 046040
Record 1999 - 1st:0 2nd:0 3rd:0 Ran:6

Pre1999 - 1st:3 2nd:0 3rd:2 Ran:17
Win Prizemoney £9,964 *Total Prizemoney* £11,876
Wins * 1998 Jun Lingfi (GD) H 9f 58 62
* 1998 May Kempto (GD) H 9f 56 59
* 1997 Jly Chepst (G-F) H 8.1f 61 66 <
1999 Turf 0-6: (7f, 8f 4, 10f) (g-s, gd 3, frm 2)
Fair gelding, effective 8 to 10f, acts on gd to frm, best on gd, prefers tight tracks. Turf high 58 - 4th of 12 getting 9lb from Casimir (3 Jly Chepstow 8f frm RF 2527).
**H Candy [3-23] Henry Candy.*

WITH IRIS (USA) BHB 96f RR 94f 5061[2]

2 ch c Schossberg (CAN) - Classical Dance (CAN) (Regal Classic (CAN))
Form - 122342
Record 1999 - 1st:1 2nd:3 3rd:1 Ran:6
Win Prizemoney £4,536 *Total Prizemoney* £12,883
Wins * **1999** Jun Newbur (GD) 6f 77+ <
1999 Turf 1-6: (5f, 6f 1-2, 7f 2, 8f) (g-s 2, gd 1-2, g-f, frm)
Useful colt, effective 5 to 7f, best at 7f, acts on g-s to frm. Turf high 94 - 2nd of 7 giving 10lb to Inventive (25 Oct Lingfield 5f g-s RF 5061). Looked a colt with a future when making a winning debut at Newbury, but was exposed in minor events later.
**P F I Cole [1-6] M H G Systems Ltd.*

WITHOUT FRIENDS (IRE) BHB 32f38a RR 31f 38a 4783[11]

5 b g Thatching 7.8f **(69)** - Soha (USA) (Dancing Brave (USA)) 8.4f **(76)**
Form - 26313777054060040
Record 1999 - 1st:1 2nd:1 3rd:2 Ran:17
Pre1999 - 1st:7 2nd:2 3rd:5 Ran:33
Win Prizemoney £18,290 *Total Prizemoney* £22,157
Wins * **1999** *Mar Southw (STD) H 8f 51 54*
1998 *Mar Lingfi (SLW) 8f 66*
1998 *Feb Lingfi (SLW) SH 8f 50 64*
1998 *Feb Lingfi (SLW) S 8f 61*
1997 Mar Newcas (GD) S 6f 56
1996 Jly Chepst (G-F) C 6.1f 71 <
1996 May Goodwo (GD) C 6f 63
1996 Apr Folkes (FRM) S 5f 63
1999 Turf 0-3: (8f 2, 12f) (g-f 2, frm) 1999 AW 1-14: (7f, 8f 1-10, 9f, 10f 2) (Equi 6, Fibr 1-8)
Very moderate gelding, effective 8f, - acts on Equi, has worn blinkers, favours left handed tracks. Turf high 31 (began Jly). AW high 54.
**Mrs N Macauley [1-16] Joe Macari (from Miss Gay Kelleway [0-2] Feb 1999).*

WITH RESPECT (USA) RR 60f 5020[12]

2 b f Rakeen (USA) - Low Approach (Artaius (USA)) 9f **(69)**
Form - 00
Record 1999 - 1st:0 2nd:0 3rd:0 Ran:2
1999 Turf 0-2: (7f, 8f) (gd, g-f)
Currently average filly. Turf high 60 (began Oct).
**J G Given [0-2] K H Benson.*

WITNEY-DE-BERGERAC (IRE) BHB 49f44a RR 53f 44a 4581[12]

7 b g Cyrano de Bergerac 7.3f **(58)** - Spy Girl (Tanfirion) 7f **(61)**
Form - 7400060
Record 1999 - 1st:0 2nd:0 3rd:0 Ran:7
Pre1999 - 1st:4 2nd:1 3rd:3 Ran:40
Win Prizemoney £15,896 *Total Prizemoney* £21,324
Wins * 1998 Jun Bath (G-S) H 17.2f 58 63
* 1998 May Bath (GD) H 17.2f 55 61
* 1995 Spt Newbur (G-S) H 12f 57 63
1999 Turf 0-7: (14f, 16f 2, 17f 2, 18f, 22f) (sft, gd 2, g-f 3, frm)
Fair gelding, has broken blood-vessels, effective 16 to 20f, acts on gd to frm, best on gd, has worn blinkers, likes left handed tracks. Turf high 57 - 4th of 13 getting 18lb from Mithak (19 May Chepstow 18f gd RF 1329). Inconsistent. Usually goes well at Bath.
**J S Moore [4-53] Ernie Houghton.*

WITTON WOOD (IRE) BHB 45f RR 45f 4627[9]

2 b c Bluebird (USA) 7.9f **(71)** -Leyete Gulf (IRE) (Slip Anchor) 9.8f **(73)**
Form - 000
Record 1999 - 1st:0 2nd:0 3rd:0 Ran:3
1999 Turf 0-3: (7f 2, 8f) (g-s, g-f, frm)
Currently moderate colt, has worn blinkers. Turf high 45 (began Aug).
**M H Tompkins [0-3] J H Ellis.*

WIZADORA RR 1777[10]

4 gr f Safawan 6.6f **(60)** - Shrood Biddy (Sharrood (USA)) 10.5f **(72)**
Form - 0
Record 1999 - 1st:0 2nd:0 3rd:0 Ran:1
1999 AW 0-1: (7f) (Fibr)
Formerly very poor filly. **Ian Williams [0-5] Mrs S Davies.*

WOLF TOOTH BHB 85f RR 84f 5042[9]

3 ch c Wolfhound (USA) 7.3f **(71)** - Collide (High Line) 10.3f **(70)**
Form - 37446141760
Record 1999 - 1st:2 2nd:0 3rd:1 Ran:11
Pre1999 - 1st:0 2nd:0 3rd:1 Ran:6
Win Prizemoney £11,916 *Total Prizemoney* £15,713
Wins * **1999** Aug Sandow (GD) H 8.1f 83 89 <
* **1999** Jly Warwic (G-F) 7.7f 86
1999 Turf 2-11: (8f 2-5, 9f, 10f 5) (sft, gd 2, g-f 2-5, frm 3)
Scopey, decent colt, effective 6 to 8f, best at 8f, acts on gd to g-f, best on g-f, likes tight tracks. Turf high 89 - 1st of 7 giving 2lb to My Pleasure (20 Aug Sandown RF 3806) - also 1st of 6 giving 5lb to Umbrian Gold (17 Jly Warwick RF 2936). Had a busy two-year-old campaign without managing to get a victory. A similar story began to emerge last term until he scored cosily in easier company at Warwick, and put up a fine front-running performance to win at Sandown. Suited by a mile.
**D R C Elsworth [2-17] Raymond Tooth.*

WONDERFUL MAN BHB 53f RR 56f 1443[7]

3 ch c Magical Wonder (USA) 7.2f **(60)** - Gleeful (Sayf El Arab (USA)) 7.1f **(54)**
Form - 467
Record 1999 - 1st:0 2nd:0 3rd:0 Ran:3
Pre1999 - 1st:0 2nd:0 3rd:0 Ran:3
Win Prizemoney £0 *Total Prizemoney* £205
1999 Turf 0-3: (8f 3) (sft, g-f, frm)
Leggy, fair colt, effective 8f, acts on g-f. Turf high 56 (1st run) - 4th of 14 getting 6lb from Fallachan (1 Apr Musselburgh 8f g-f RF 0553). **M J Heaton-Ellis [0-6] F J Sainsbury.*

WONDERLAND (IRE) BHB 58f RR 61f 2893[6]

2 b f Dolphin Street (FR) - Smart Pet **(68f)** (Petong) 6.6f **(58)**
Form - 656
Record 1999 - 1st:0 2nd:0 3rd:0 Ran:3
1999 Turf 0-3: (5f, 6f 2) (gd, g-f, frm)
Currently average filly. Turf high 61.
**J J O'Neill [0-3] Carlton Appointments (Aberdeen) Ltd.*

WONTCOSTALOTBUT BHB 51f46a RR 57f 46a 5028[4]

5 b m Nicholas Bill 9.8f **(56)** - Brave Maiden (Three Legs) 11.1f **(54)**
Form - 134
Record 1999 - 1st:1 2nd:0 3rd:1 Ran:3
Pre1999 - 1st:0 2nd:0 3rd:0 Ran:6
Win Prizemoney £3,150 *Total Prizemoney* £4,038
Wins * **1999** Apr Folkes (HVY) H 15.4f 47 57 <
1999 Turf 1-3: (15f 1-2, 16f) (hvy 1-2, g-s)
Fair filly. Turf high 57 (1st run) - 1st of 12 getting 18lb from Durham (13 Apr Folkestone RF 0659). She had not shown much on the Flat in the last couple of seasons, but had looked an improved sort over hurdles before scoring in a modest handicap at Folkestone in April. Needs soft ground.
**M J Wilkinson [3-31] Wontcostalot Partnership.*

WON'T FORGET ME (IRE) BHB 24f55a RR 34f 55a 3597[10]

4 br g Don't Forget Me 9.5f **(66)** - Lucky Realm (Realm) 8.1f **(65)**
Form - 7680
Record 1999 - 1st:0 2nd:0 3rd:0 Ran:4
Pre1999 - 1st:2 2nd:2 3rd:0 Ran:18
Win Prizemoney £3,969 *Total Prizemoney* £6,119
Wins 1997 Spt Bright (G-F) S 7f 62 <
1997 Aug Folkes (G-F) S 6.9f 59
1999 Turf 0-4: (9f, 12f 3) (g-f 3, frm)
Lengthy, very moderate gelding, effective 10 to 12f, acts on g-f to frm, has worn blinkers (very effectively), favours tight tracks. Turf high 34 (began Jly). Inconsistent.
**I Semple [0-16] Ian Crawford (from M H Tompkins [2-8] Oct 1997).*

WOODBASTWICK CHARM RR 28f 4834[15]
2 b c Charmer 9f **(59)** - Miss Mint (Music Maestro) 7.7f **(66)**
Form - 0
Record 1999 - 1st:0 2nd:0 3rd:0 Ran:1
1999 Turf 0-1: (7f) (gd)
Currently little account colt. **J Pearce [0-1] The Wayfarers.*

WOODCOTE WARRIOR (IRE) BHB 68f **RR 70f** 2751[4]
3 b c Barathea (IRE) - Overact (IRE) **(88f)** (Law Society (USA)) 9.9f **(70)**
Form - 873354414
Record 1999 - 1st:1 2nd:0 3rd:2 Ran:9
Win Prizemoney £2,360 *Total Prizemoney* £4,179
Wins * 1999 Jly Chepst (G-F) H 12.1f 65 70 <
1999 Turf 1-9: (8f, 10f 5, 12f 1-3) (sft, gd 4, frm 1-3, hrd)
Light-framed, above-average colt, effective 10 to 12f, best at 10f, acted on gd to frm, best on frm, preferred left handed tracks, preferred tight tracks. Turf high 70 - 1st of 12 getting 1lb from Pay Homage (9 Jly Chepstow RF 2663). (DEAD)
**R Hannon [1-9] A R Perry.*

WOODCUT (IRE) BHB 32a **RR 30f** 3436[12]
3 ch g Woods of Windsor (USA) - Lady of State (IRE) (Petong) 6.6f **(58)**
Form - 00000
Record 1999 - 1st:0 2nd:0 3rd:0 Ran:5
Pre1999 - 1st:0 2nd:0 3rd:0 Ran:3
1999 Turf 0-3: (5f, 6f 2) (g-f, frm, hrd) 1999 AW 0-2: (5f, 6f) (Fibr 2)
Scopey, very moderate gelding. Turf high 7.
**P S Felgate [0-8] Yorkshire Racing Club Owners Group 1990.*

WOODLANDS BHB 85f **RR 84f** 4690[8]
2 b g Common Grounds 8.1f **(66)** - Forest of Arden (Tap On Wood) 10.3f **(65)**
Form - 038
Record 1999 - 1st:0 2nd:0 3rd:1 Ran:3
Win Prizemoney £0 *Total Prizemoney* £515
1999 Turf 0-3: (5f, 6f 2) (g-f, frm 2)
Currently decent gelding. Turf high 84.
**R McGhin [0-3] The 1 2 3 Partnership.*

WOODLANDS PRIDE (IRE) BHB 20f **RR 18f** 4334[7]
4 ch f Petardia 8.2f **(58)** - Valediction (Town Crier) 10.2f **(55)**
Form - 007
Record 1999 - 1st:0 2nd:0 3rd:0 Ran:3
Pre1999 - 1st:0 2nd:0 3rd:0 Ran:14
1999 Turf 0-2: (10f 2) (g-s, gd) 1999 AW 0-1: (8f) (Fibr)
Leggy, poor filly. **M C Chapman [0-19] Eric Knowles.*

WOOD POUND (USA) BHB 79f **RR 80df** 5067[11]
3 b c Woodman (USA) 9.7f **(77)** - Poundzig (USA) (Danzig (USA)) 8.4f **(76)**
Form - 20
Record 1999 - 1st:0 2nd:1 3rd:0 Ran:2
Pre1999 - 1st:0 2nd:0 3rd:0 Ran:1
Win Prizemoney £0 *Total Prizemoney* £1,350
1999 Turf 0-2: (10f, 12f) (gd, frm)
Workmanlike, currently decent colt. Turf high 77 (1st run) (began Oct) - 2nd of 15 giving 5lb to Anaam (20 Oct Nottingham 10f frm RF 4992). **Sir Michael Stoute [0-3] Peter Wetzel.*

WOODWIND DOWN RR 53f 4408[14]
2 b f Piccolo - Bint El Oumara (Al Nasr (FR)) 9.3f **(68)**
Form - 00
Record 1999 - 1st:0 2nd:0 3rd:0 Ran:2
1999 Turf 0-2: (6f, 7f) (frm 2)
Currently fair filly. Turf high 53 (began Spt).
**M R Channon [0-2] Kingsdown Racing.*

WOOLLY WINSOME BHB 58f58a **RR 58df 58a** 5193[15]
3 br g Lugana Beach 7f **(63)** - Gay Ming (Gay Meadow)
Form - 5632430
Record 1999 - 1st:0 2nd:1 3rd:1 Ran:4
Pre1999 - 1st:0 2nd:1 3rd:1 Ran:6
Win Prizemoney £0 *Total Prizemoney* £2,972
1999 Turf 0-1: (8f) (gd) 1999 AW 0-3: (8f 3) (Equi 3)
Fair gelding, has worn blinkers. AW high 58.

**B Smart [0-10] W Clifford.*

WOORE LASS (IRE) BHB 53f **RR 63df** 5056[4]
3 ch f Persian Bold 10f **(69)** - Miss Ballylea (Junius (USA)) 7.7f **(65)**
Form - 46581026680404
Record 1999 - 1st:1 2nd:1 3rd:0 Ran:14
Pre1999 - 1st:1 2nd:1 3rd:0 Ran:8
Win Prizemoney £5,473 *Total Prizemoney* £8,705
Wins * 1999 May Bright (FRM) H 8f 64 73 <
* 1998 Jun Salisb (G-S) 6f 64
1999 Turf 1-13: (7f, 8f 1-6, 9f 3, 10f 3) (sft, g-s, gd 3, g-f 1-3, frm 5)
1999 AW 0-1: (10f) (Equi)
Workmanlike, average filly, effective 6 to 10f, acts on gd to frm, likes left handed tracks, likes tight tracks. Turf high 73 - 1st of 10 getting 16lb from Silver Sun (28 May Brighton RF 1539).
**R Hannon [2-22] Jimm Racing.*

WORLD ALERT (IRE) BHB 102f **RR 100f** 4652[9]
3 b c Alzao (USA) 9.8f **(73)** - Steady The Buffs (Balidar) 7.9f **(63)**
Form - 24185710
Record 1999 - 1st:2 2nd:1 3rd:0 Ran:8
Pre1999 - 1st:0 2nd:0 3rd:0 Ran:2
Win Prizemoney £17,274 *Total Prizemoney* £25,559
Wins * 1999 Spt Goodwo (G-F) H 9f 97 100 <
*** 1999** May Ripon (G-S) 9f 90+
1999 Turf 2-8: (7f, 8f 3, 9f 2-2, 10f 2) (hvy, sft, gd 1-2, g-f 1-3, frm)
Scopey, very useful colt, effective 7 to 10f, acts on gd to frm, best on g-f. Turf high 100 - 1st of 7 giving 4lb to Waabl (10 Spt Goodwood RF 4258). Consistent. He is a difficult ride and was well handled by Jimmy Fortune when making all at Goodwood in September. He should stay beyond a mile but must learn to settle. Sold for 36,000 gns at Tattersalls in October.
**P W Chapple-Hyam [2-10] R E Sangster & A K Collins.*

WORLD'S VISION (GER) RR 93f 1533a[8]
3 f
Form - 8
1999 Turf 0-1: (11f) (sft)
Currently useful filly. **M Hofer in GER [0-1].*

WORSHIP (USA) BHB 63f **RR 68f** 3074[3]
3 ch f Irish River (FR) 9f **(77)** - Pedestal (High Line) 10.3f **(70)**
Form - 63573
Record 1999 - 1st:0 2nd:0 3rd:2 Ran:5
Win Prizemoney £0 *Total Prizemoney* £1,092
1999 Turf 0-5: (8f, 10f 3, 12f) (gd, frm 4)
Light-framed, average filly, has worn blinkers. Turf high 68.
**P F I Cole [0-5] Lord Lloyd-Webber.*

WORSTED RR 62f 4821[10]
2 ch f Whittingham (IRE) - Calamanco **(65f 66a)** (Clantime)
Form - 70
Record 1999 - 1st:0 2nd:0 3rd:0 Ran:2
1999 Turf 0-2: (5f, 6f) (gd, g-f)
Currently average filly. Turf high 62 (began Spt).
**Major D N Chappell [0-2] Mrs D Ellis.*

WORTH A TURN BHB 37f **RR 26f** 4076[17]
3 ch f Chaddleworth (IRE) - Taciturn (USA) (Tasso (USA))
Form - 00000
Record 1999 - 1st:0 2nd:0 3rd:0 Ran:5
Pre1999 - 1st:0 2nd:0 3rd:0 Ran:1
1999 Turf 0-5: (7f, 8f 2, 10f 2) (frm 5)
Leggy, little account filly. Turf high 45 (began Jly).
**R Rowe [0-6] Winterfields Farm Ltd.*

WORTH THE EFFORT BHB 43f **RR 43f** 1946[16]
4 b f Beveled (USA) 6.9f **(64)** - Haiti Mill (Free State) 8.7f **(61)**
Form - 0000
Record 1999 - 1st:0 2nd:0 3rd:0 Ran:4
Pre1999 - 1st:0 2nd:1 3rd:3 Ran:12
Win Prizemoney £0 *Total Prizemoney* £2,696
1999 Turf 0-4: (7f, 8f 3) (gd, g-f, frm 2)
Light-framed, moderate filly, effective 7 to 8f, acts on gd to hrd, has worn blinkers. Turf high 43.
**M H Tompkins [0-16] Adrienne and Michael Barnett.*

WORTH THE RISK BHB 41f40a **RR 72f 40a** 5158[20]
2 b f Chaddleworth (IRE) - Bay Risk **(37f)** (Risk Me (FR)) 5.9f **(53)**
Form - 60500050
Record 1999 - 1st:0 2nd:0 3rd:0 Ran:8
1999 Turf 0-7: (5f 2, 6f 4, 8f) (g-s, gd, g-f, frm 4) 1999 AW 0-1: (8f) (Fibr)
Above-average filly. Turf high 72.
**Don Enrico Incisa [0-1] Don Enrico Incisa (from B J Meehan [0-7] Oct 1999).*

WRAY (IRE) RR 101f 5174a[4]
7 ch g Sharp Victor (USA) 10f **(56)** - Faye (Monsanto (FR)) 6.5f **(59)**
Form - 14703214
1999 Turf 2-8: (6f, 7f, 8f 1-2, 9f 1-3, 12f) (sft 1-2, g-s 1-3, gd, g-f 2)
Very useful gelding, effective 6 to 9f, best at 9f, acts on sft to g-f, best on g-s, and likes Curragh. Turf high 101 - 1st of 13 giving 15lb to Osprey Ridge (17 Oct Fairyhouse RF 4979a) - also 1st of 25 from Dance So Suite (28 Mar Curragh RF 0520a). Consistent. He returned as good as new after a serious injury and is a smart handicapper at up to nine furlongs. Probably best on easy ground, he is genuine. **L Browne in IRE [6-28] B Cunningham.*

WROTHAM ARMS (IRE) RR 33f 4728[12]
2 b f Second Set (IRE) 9.2f **(67)** - Usance (GER) (Kronenkranich (GER)) 6f **(97)**
Form - 0
Record 1999 - 1st:0 2nd:0 3rd:0 Ran:1
1999 Turf 0-1: (8f) (g-s)
Currently very moderate filly. **Dr J D Scargill [0-1] A C Edwards.*

WRY ARDOUR BHB 38f **RR 32f** 4632[5]
3 b g Pursuit of Love 9.5f **(69)** - Wryneck (Niniski (USA)) 10.6f **(65)**
Form - 70005
Record 1999 - 1st:0 2nd:0 3rd:0 Ran:5
Pre1999 - 1st:0 2nd:0 3rd:0 Ran:3
1999 Turf 0-5: (5f, 6f, 7f, 8f, 10f) (g-s 2, g-f, frm 2)
Workmanlike, very moderate gelding. Turf high 51. Becoming disappointing. **A G Newcombe [0-8] Advanced Marketing Services Ltd.*

WURZEL BHB 85f **RR 81f** 4994[1]
2 ch c Weldnaas (USA) 8.4f **(55)** - Down the Valley (Kampala) 8.5f **(56)**
Form - 031
Record 1999 - 1st:1 2nd:0 3rd:1 Ran:3
Win Prizemoney £2,983 *Total Prizemoney* £3,483
Wins * **1999** Oct Bright (G-F) 7f 81 <
1999 Turf 1-3: (6f, 7f 1-2) (gd 1-2, g-f)
Currently decent colt. Turf high 81 (began Spt) - 1st of 11 from My Retreat (21 Oct Brighton RF 4994). **R Hannon [1-3] J R Shannon.*

WUXI VENTURE BHB 79f **RR 80f** 4754[4]
4 b g Wolfhound (USA) 7.3f **(71)** - Push a Button (Bold Lad (IRE)) 8.4f **(68)**
Form - 656005064
Record 1999 - 1st:0 2nd:0 3rd:0 Ran:9
Pre1999 - 1st:3 2nd:5 3rd:4 Ran:19
Win Prizemoney £15,900 *Total Prizemoney* £34,977
Wins * 1998 Spt Hamilt (SFT) H 8.3f 88 91 <
* 1998 Aug Haydoc (GD) H 8.1f 85 88
* 1998 Apr Ripon (SFT) 8f 86
1999 Turf 0-9: (8f 8, 10f) (g-s, gd 6, frm 2)
Decent gelding, effective 8 to 10f, best at 8f, acts on sft to g-f, best on gd, has worn blinkers, likes Sandown. Turf high 83. Consistent. Generally struggles in decent handicaps - has not won since September '98 - and seems to need the ground no faster than good. **S P C Woods [3-28] Dr Frank Chao.*

WYCHWOOD CHARMER RR 40f 5194[14]
2 b f Theatrical Charmer 10.9f **(63)** - Lanzamar **(27f)** (Buzzards Bay)
Form - 0
Record 1999 - 1st:0 2nd:0 3rd:0 Ran:1
1999 Turf 0-1: (6f) (gd)
Currently moderate filly. **E A Wheeler [0-1] R H Coombes.*

XAAR BHB 121f **RR 122f** 2545[2]
4 b c Zafonic (USA) 9f **(83)** - Monroe (USA) (Sir Ivor) 10.2f **(70)**
Form - 32
Record 1999 - 1st:0 2nd:1 3rd:1 Ran:2
Pre1999 - 1st:4 2nd:2 3rd:1 Ran:8
Win Prizemoney £207,258 *Total Prizemoney* £368,139
Wins 1998 Apr Newmar (SFT) G3 8f 124+
1997 Oct Newmar (GD) G1 7f 127+ <
1997 Spt Longch (GD) G1 7f 115+
1997 Aug Deauvi (GD) G3 6f 105+
1999 Turf 0-2: (10f 2) (g-f, frm)
Very high-class colt, effective 8 to 10f, best at 10f, acts on gd to frm, best on gd. Turf high 122 - 2nd of 8 giving 11lb to Compton Admiral (3 Jly Sandown 10f frm RF 2545). Consistent. A son of Zafonic, he became the top European two-year-old in 1997 by virtue of his victories in the Salamandre and the Dewhurst, but was a big disappointment in 1998. Moved to Godolphin for last season and, making his reappearance in the Prince Of Wales's Stakes at Royal Ascot, ran a most creditable third. He ran even better when just pipped by Compton Admiral in the Eclipse and looked as if he could still win a decent prize, but was not seen again. However, he is reportedly staying in training.
**S bin Suroor [0-2] Godolphin (from A Fabre in FR [4-8] Spt 1998).*

XANADU BHB 56f **RR 54f** 4167[3]
3 ch g Casteddu 7.4f **(54)** - Bellatrix (Persian Bold) 9.3f **(66)**
Form - 57178103
Record 1999 - 1st:2 2nd:0 3rd:1 Ran:8
Pre1999 - 1st:0 2nd:0 3rd:0 Ran:2
Win Prizemoney £6,123 *Total Prizemoney* £6,461
Wins * **1999** Aug Carlis (FRM) H 5.9f 44 54 <
* **1999** Jly Hamilt (FRM) S 6f 43
1999 Turf 2-8: (5f 4, 6f 2-3, 7f) (g-f 3, frm 2-5)
Strong, fair gelding, effective 5 to 6f, acts on frm. Turf high 54 - 1st of 12 giving 4lb to Indian Bazaar (2 Aug Carlisle RF 3291).
**Miss L A Perratt [2-10] T P Finch.*

XANIA RR 49f 5209[9]
2 b f Mujtahid (USA) 7.4f **(69)** - Polish Honour (USA) (Danzig Connection (USA)) 8f **(68)**
Form - 00
Record 1999 - 1st:0 2nd:0 3rd:0 Ran:2
1999 Turf 0-2: (6f, 7f) (g-s 2)
Currently moderate filly. Turf high 49 (began Oct).
**M Johnston [0-2] Mrs A M Burns.*

XATIVA (IRE) BHB 62f **RR 63f** 4875[10]
2 b f Thatching 7.8f **(69)** - Abergwrle (Absalom) 7.2f **(58)**
Form - 500
Record 1999 - 1st:0 2nd:0 3rd:0 Ran:3
1999 Turf 0-3: (5f, 6f 2) (g-s, gd, frm)
Currently average filly. Turf high 63.
**M R Channon [0-3] The Dapper Boys.*

XCARET (IRE) BHB 73f **RR 80f** 4034[11]
2 b f Ezzoud (IRE) - Nyali Beach (IRE) **(54f 42a)** (Treasure Kay)
Form - 4180770
Record 1999 - 1st:1 2nd:0 3rd:0 Ran:7
Win Prizemoney £2,845 *Total Prizemoney* £2,845
Wins * **1999** May Hamilt (SFT) 6f 74 <
1999 Turf 1-7: (5f 2, 6f 1-5) (gd 1-5, g-f, frm)
Decent filly, effective 6f, acts on gd, has worn blinkers. Turf high 80 - also 1st of 12 getting 6lb from You're Special (24 May Hamilton RF 1425). **M H Tompkins [1-7] Michael Keogh.*

XELLANCE (IRE) BHB 35f **RR 19f** 4981[9]
2 b c Be My Guest (USA) 10.2f **(66)** - Excellent Alibi (USA) (Exceller (USA)) 12.5f **(74)**
Form - 070
Record 1999 - 1st:0 2nd:0 3rd:0 Ran:3
1999 Turf 0-3: (5f, 6f, 7f) (g-s, g-f, frm)
Currently poor colt. Turf high 19 (began Spt).
**M Johnston [0-3] T T Bloodstocks.*

XENOS RR 62f 2315[8]
2 b g Owington - Little Change (Grundy) 10.3f **(65)**
Form - 708
Record 1999 - 1st:0 2nd:0 3rd:0 Ran:3
1999 Turf 0-3: (5f 2, 6f) (gd, frm, hrd)

Currently average gelding. Turf high 62.
**M R Channon [0-3] The Dapper Boys.*

XIBALBA BHB 69f **RR 62f** 5139[9]
2 b c Zafonic (USA) 9f **(83)** - Satanic Dance (FR) (Shareef Dancer (USA)) 9.9f **(73)**
Form - 000
Record 1999 - 1st:0 2nd:0 3rd:0 Ran:3
1999 Turf 0-3: (6f, 7f, 10f) (gd, frm 2)
Currently average colt. Turf high 62 (began Aug).
**C E Brittain [0-3] R Meredith.*

XSYNNA BHB 54f63a **RR 50f 63a** 3685[3]
3 b g Cyrano de Bergerac 7.3f **(58)** - Rose Ciel (IRE) (Red Sunset) 8.2f **(63)**
Form - 8130743
Record 1999 - 1st:0 2nd:0 3rd:2 Ran:5
Pre1999 - 1st:1 2nd:1 3rd:1 Ran:10
Win Prizemoney £2,872 *Total Prizemoney* £5,306
Wins * 1998 *Dec Lingfi (STD) H 6f 62 64* <
1999 Turf 0-4: (5f, 6f 2, 7f) (gd, frm 3) 1999 AW 0-1: (6f) (Fibr)
Workmanlike, average gelding, effective 5 to 6f, acts on g-f to frm, has worn blinkers. Turf high 50. He showed pieces of ability on turf in 1998, but was generally disappointing until coming out best in a blanket finish to a nursery on the Lingfield Equitrack in December. **S C Williams [1-15] Chris Wright.*

XUA (IRE) RR 98f 4891a[3]
2 b f Fairy King (USA) 7.7f **(75)** - Bold Starlet (Precocious) 8.6f **(62)**
Form - 223
1999 Turf 0-3: (5f, 7f, 8f) (gd 3)
Currently very useful filly. Turf high 98 - 3rd of 11 to Sonda (10 Oct San Siro 8f gd RF 4891a). **B Grizzetti in ITY [0-3].*

XYLEM (USA) BHB 30f36a **RR 34f 36a** 4980[10]
8 ch g Woodman (USA) 9.7f **(77)** - Careful (USA) (Tampa Trouble (USA)) 8f **(87)**
Form - 40640035702000
Record 1999 - 1st:0 2nd:1 3rd:1 Ran:13
Pre1999 - 1st:2 2nd:0 3rd:3 Ran:24
Win Prizemoney £6,554 *Total Prizemoney* £11,157
Wins 1997 Oct Newcas (G-F) H 8f 69 70
1999 Turf 0-10: (10f 5, 12f 5) (g-s 2, gd 6, g-f 2) 1999 AW 0-3: (11f, 12f, 13f) (Equi, Fibr 2)
Very moderate gelding, effective 8 to 10f, best at 10f, acts on g-f to frm, best on frm, has worn blinkers, likes left handed tracks, likes tight tracks. Turf high 41. AW high 36. Consistent.
**J Pearce [0-14] Mrs Anne Holman-Chappell (from J H M Gosden [1-17] Spt 1998).*

YA-AIN BHB 62f **RR 62f** 4991[10]
3 b c Warning 8.1f **(77)** - Ahbab (IRE) (Ajdal (USA)) 9.2f **(89)**
Form - 24400530
Record 1999 - 1st:0 2nd:1 3rd:1 Ran:8
Pre1999 - 1st:0 2nd:1 3rd:0 Ran:2
Win Prizemoney £0 *Total Prizemoney* £4,049
1999 Turf 0-8: (8f 5, 10f 3) (gd 3, g-f 3, frm 2)
Workmanlike, average colt, effective 7f, acts on gd, has worn blinkers. Turf high 82. Becoming disappointing.
**P T Walwyn [0-10] Hamdan Al Maktoum.*

YABINT EL SHAM BHB 66f **RR 67f** 4804[23]
3 b f Sizzling Melody 6.3f **(49)** - Dalby Dancer (Bustiki) 8.7f **(78)**
Form - 700870
Record 1999 - 1st:0 2nd:0 3rd:0 Ran:6
Pre1999 - 1st:1 2nd:0 3rd:0 Ran:4
Win Prizemoney £3,496 *Total Prizemoney* £3,496
Wins * 1998 Aug Leices (GD) 5f 85 <
1999 Turf 0-6: (5f 3, 6f 2, 7f) (gd 4, g-f 2)
Neat, average filly, effective 5f, acts on frm. Turf high 67.
**B A McMahon [1-10] G S D Imports Ltd.*

YAGLI (USA) RR 123f 5230a[4]
6 ch h Jade Hunter (USA) 10.4f **(72)** - Nijinsky's Best (USA) (Nijinsky (CAN))
Form - 4
1999 Turf 0-1: (12f) (frm)
Currently very high-class horse. (1st run) - 4th of 14 to Daylami (6 Nov Gulfstream Park 12f frm RF 5230a).
**W Mott in USA [0-2].*

YAHESKA (IRE) BHB 35f **RR 21f** 4414[11]
2 b f Prince of Birds (USA) - How Ya Been (IRE) (Last Tycoon) 8.5f **(62)**
Form - 000
Record 1999 - 1st:0 2nd:0 3rd:0 Ran:3
1999 Turf 0-2: (5f 2) (gd, frm) 1999 AW 0-1: (7f) (Fibr)
Currently little account filly. Turf high 21 (began Jly).
**E J O'Neill [0-3] Mrs Patrick O'Neill.*

YAJTAHED (IRE) BHB 58f48a **RR 62f 48a** 4647[9]
4 ch g Mujtahid (USA) 7.4f **(69)** - Rainstone (Rainbow Quest (USA)) 10.4f **(75)**
Form - 67000
Record 1999 - 1st:0 2nd:0 3rd:0 Ran:5
Pre1999 - 1st:1 2nd:0 3rd:0 Ran:6
Win Prizemoney £2,584 *Total Prizemoney* £2,584
Wins * 1998 Oct Bath (SFT) H 8f 56 62 <
1999 Turf 0-1: (10f) (g-s) 1999 AW 0-4: (8f 2, 10f, 12f) (Equi 2, Fibr 2)
Workmanlike, average gelding, effective 8f, acts on sft, has worn blinkers, likes left handed tracks, favours tight tracks. AW high 49.
**G L Moore [1-12] Nick Clark (from J H M Gosden [0-1] May 1997).*

YAKAREEM (IRE) BHB 100f98a **RR 76f 98a** 4894[9]
3 b c Rainbows For Life (CAN) 9.3f **(64)** -Brandywell (Skyliner) 7.3f **(53)**
Form - 1054662000
Record 1999 - 1st:1 2nd:1 3rd:0 Ran:10
Pre1999 - 1st:0 2nd:1 3rd:1 Ran:2
Win Prizemoney £3,596 *Total Prizemoney* £19,258
Wins * **1999** *Mar Wolver (STD) 9.4f 94* <
1999 Turf 0-8: (7f, 8f, 9f 3, 10f 3) (g-s, gd 4, g-f, frm 2) 1999 AW 1-2: (9f 1-1, 10f) (Equi, Fibr 1-1)
Strong, useful colt, effective 9f, acts on gd. Turf high 109 - 2nd of 6 getting 12lb from Lear Spear (5 Jun Epsom 9f gd RF 1759). AW high 94 (1st run). Becoming disappointing. He beat a pretty decent field in a conditions event on the Wolverhampton Fibresand in March, but has struggled in the face of some stiff tasks since. Much his best effort was when runner-up in the Diomed at Epsom.
**K Mahdi [1-12] Hamad Al-Mutawa.*

YALAIL (IRE) BHB 57f53a **RR 57f 53a** 5003[9]
3 b c Perugino (USA) - Cristalga (High Top) 10.2f **(67)**
Form - 4860
Record 1999 - 1st:0 2nd:0 3rd:0 Ran:4
1999 Turf 0-4: (6f, 8f 2, 9f) (gd, g-f 2, frm)
Light-framed, fair colt. Turf high 57 (began Jly).
**K Mahdi [0-4] Hamad Al-Mutawa.*

YALLAH YABINT RR 5f 3670[9]
2 b f Puissance 7.1f **(60)** - Great Intent **(40f)** (Aragon) 8.1f **(60)**
Form - 000
Record 1999 - 1st:0 2nd:0 3rd:0 Ran:3
1999 Turf 0-2: (5f 2) (gd, frm) 1999 AW 0-1: (7f) (Fibr)
Currently very poor filly. Turf high 12.
**D Shaw [0-3] G S D Imports Ltd.*

YANOMAMI (USA) BHB 57f60a **RR 78f 60a** 161[4]
4 ch f Slew O' Gold (USA) 10.2f **(73)** - Sunerta (USA) (Roberto (USA)) 10f **(76)**
Form - 6104
Record 1999 - 1st:0 2nd:0 3rd:0 Ran:2
Pre1999 - 1st:1 2nd:2 3rd:1 Ran:9
Win Prizemoney £2,671 *Total Prizemoney* £5,591
Wins * 1998 *Dec Wolver (SLW) 6f 60* <
1999 AW 0-2: (6f, 8f) (Fibr 2)
Neat, above-average filly, effective 5f, acts on g-s. AW high 63.
**J Berry [1-9] T G & Mrs M E Holdcroft (from J H M Gosden [0-2] Spt 1997).*

YANSHAN BHB 40f47a **RR 38f 47a** 2653[12]
4 b g Anshan 8.2f **(63)** - Joy of Freedom **(51f)** (Damister (USA)) 9f **(73)**
Form - 000
Record 1999 - 1st:0 2nd:0 3rd:0 Ran:3
Pre1999 - 1st:0 2nd:1 3rd:0 Ran:7

Win Prizemoney £0 *Total Prizemoney* £768
1999 Turf 0-1: (14f) (sft) 1999 AW 0-2: (14f 2) (Fibr 2)
Workmanlike, moderate gelding, has worn blinkers. Becoming disappointing. **Bob Jones [0-13] Mrs S Osborne.*

YARALINO BHB 96f **RR 95f** 2620[3]

3 b c Caerleon (USA) 10.9f **(79)** - Wemyss Bight (Dancing Brave (USA)) 8.4f **(76)**
Form - 103
Record 1999 - 1st:1 2nd:0 3rd:1 Ran:3
Win Prizemoney £3,833 *Total Prizemoney* £4,865
Wins * 1999 May Lingfi (G-F) 10f 74 <
1999 Turf 1-3: (10f 1-2, 12f) (g-f, frm 1-2)
Scopey, currently very useful colt. Turf high 95 - 3rd of 7 getting 6lb from Pegnitz (7 Jly Epsom 10f frm RF 2620). He failed to fulfil connections' hopes and is not a Group horse. Likely to stay a mile and a half, he made 45,000 guineas at Newmarket in October.
**H R A Cecil [1-3] K Abdulla.*

YAROB (IRE) BHB 78f80a **RR 73f 80a** 3287[5]

6 ch h Unfuwain (USA) 11.4f **(74)** - Azyaa (Kris) 9.5f **(73)**
Form - 0501550505
Record 1999 - 1st:1 2nd:0 3rd:0 Ran:10
Pre1999 - 1st:1 2nd:3 3rd:0 Ran:14
Win Prizemoney £11,522 *Total Prizemoney* £25,434
Wins * 1999 May Doncas (G-F) H 10.3f 77 81
1995 Jly Lingfi (G-F) 6f 82+ <
1999 Turf 1-9: (8f 5, 9f, 10f 1-3) (sft, gd 2, g-f 2, frm 3, hrd 1-1) 1999 AW 0-1: (7f) (Fibr)
Decent horse, effective 10f, acts on hrd, likes left handed tracks. Turf high 81 - also 1st of 7 getting 2lb from Thekryaati (3 May Doncaster RF 0993). Easy winner at Doncaster in May before running a good fifth in the Hunt Cup. He has disappointed since that Ascot race.
**D Nicholls [1-10] Lucayan Stud (from D R Loder [0-3] Mar 1998).*

YARUBA BHB 66f **RR 66f** 5034[4]

2 b f Warning 8.1f **(77)** - Khandjar (Kris) 9.5f **(73)**
Form - 400364
Record 1999 - 1st:0 2nd:0 3rd:1 Ran:6
Win Prizemoney £0 *Total Prizemoney* £1,224
1999 Turf 0-6: (6f 3, 7f 3) (g-s, gd 2, g-f, frm 2)
Average filly, effective 6f, acts on g-f. Turf high 66 (began Jly) - 3rd of 17 getting 8lb from Peruvian Jade (20 Spt Leicester 6f g-f RF 4439). **R Hannon [0-6] Exors of the late Lord Howard de Walden.*

YASALAM (IRE) RR 1872[11]

3 b f Fairy King (USA) 7.7f **(75)** - Hana Marie (Formidable (USA)) 9.2f **(63)**
Form - 0
Record 1999 - 1st:0 2nd:0 3rd:0 Ran:1
1999 Turf 0-1: (8f) (g-f)
Workmanlike, currently very poor filly.
**V Soane [0-1] Saleh Al Homeizi.*

YAVANA'S PACE (IRE) BHB 112f **RR 115f** 5223a[12]

7 ch g Accordion 11.3f **(75)** - Lady in Pace (Burslem) 8.8f **(53)**
Form - 412201120
Record 1999 - 1st:3 2nd:3 3rd:0 Ran:9
Pre1999 - 1st:5 2nd:5 3rd:4 Ran:25
Win Prizemoney £151,622 *Total Prizemoney* £270,152
Wins * 1999 Spt Epsom (GD) G3 12f 114
*** 1999** Aug Goodwo (GD) L 14f 115 <
*** 1999** Jun Leices (G-S) L 11.8f 115 <
* 1998 Nov Doncas (SFT) H 12f 105 114
* 1998 Spt Galway (HVY) L 12f 98+
* 1998 Jly Sandow (GD) H 10f 88 92
* 1998 May Ayr (GD) H 10f 83 87
1996 Jun Leopar (GD) H 7f 90 75
1999 Turf 3-9: (12f 2-4, 14f 1-4, 16f) (g-s, gd 2-5, g-f, frm 1-2)
High-class gelding, effective 12 to 14f, best at 12f, acts on gd to frm, best on gd, likes tight tracks. Turf high 115 - 1st of 5 giving 17lb to Iscan (28 Aug Goodwood RF 3955) - also 1st of 5 giving 8lb to Kadaka (12 Jun Leicester RF 1947). An ex-Irish gelding, he landed his first British Listed victory at Leicester on his second start of last term from a small but useful field. He was no match for Blueprint at Newmarket next time, and was beaten a short head in the Scandinavian Open before disappointing in the Ebor when carrying top-weight. He then bounced back to his best when winning a Listed event at Goodwood, and proved that was no fluke when overturning Blueprint in the September Stakes at Epsom. He was no match for Kayf Tara in the Irish St Leger, but still had the likes of Silver Patriarch and Enzeli behind him. He was then sent over for the Melbourne Cup, but never really got competitive.
**M Johnston [7-19] Mrs Joan Keaney (from M A Johnson [0-1] Spt 1999).*

YAVERLAND (IRE) BHB 28f42a **RR 30f 42a** 1685[4]

Globetrotting Yavana's Pace finally broke his Group-race duck

7 b g Astronef 7.9f **(59)** - Lautreamont (Auction Ring (USA)) 8.6f **(65)**
Form - 04
Record 1999 - 1st:0 2nd:0 3rd:0 Ran:2
Pre1999 - 1st:0 2nd:2 3rd:3 Ran:21
Win Prizemoney £0 *Total Prizemoney* £2,645
1999 Turf 0-1: (16f) (g-s) 1999 AW 0-1: (14f) (Fibr)
Moderate gelding, effective 12f, - acts on Fibr. Inconsistent.
**John Berry [0-14] Mrs B A Blackwell (from C A Dwyer [0-6] Spt 1996).*

YAZEYDD BHB 38f **RR 38f** 4530[13]

2 b c Primo Dominie 7.2f **(67)** - Murooj (USA) (Diesis) 9.3f **(69)**
Form - 000
Record 1999 - 1st:0 2nd:0 3rd:0 Ran:3
1999 Turf 0-3: (6f, 7f 2) (g-s, g-f, frm)
Currently very moderate colt, has worn blinkers. Turf high 38 (began Spt). **B Hanbury [0-3] A Merza.*

YAZMIN (IRE) BHB 100f **RR 88f** 5010a[4]

2 b f Green Desert (USA) 7.8f **(78)** - All My Heart (USA) (Sharpen Up) 8.3f **(67)**
Form - 2134
Record 1999 - 1st:1 2nd:1 3rd:1 Ran:4
Win Prizemoney £3,824 *Total Prizemoney* £5,702
Wins * 1999 Aug Windso (G-F) 6f 72 <
1999 Turf 1-4: (6f 1-3, 7f) (hvy, gd, g-f, frm 1-1)
Useful filly. Turf high 88 (began Jly) - 3rd of 7 giving 15lb to Peruvian Jade (10 Spt Goodwood 6f g-f RF 4256). **J L Dunlop [1-4].*

YEAHYEAHYEAH BHB 40f **RR 29f** 5070[15]

2 b g King's Signet (USA) 7f **(51)** - Witch (Risk Me (FR)) 5.9f **(53)**
Form - 000
Record 1999 - 1st:0 2nd:0 3rd:0 Ran:3
1999 Turf 0-3: (5f, 7f 2) (g-s, gd, frm)
Currently little account gelding. Turf high 29 (began Oct).
**M W Easterby [0-3] M W Easterby.*

YEAST BHB 83f **RR 77f** 4874[19]

7 b g Salse (USA) 10.9f **(71)** - Orient (Bay Express) 7.1f **(60)**
Form - 511020100
Record 1999 - 1st:3 2nd:1 3rd:0 Ran:9
Pre1999 - 1st:5 2nd:3 3rd:2 Ran:24
Win Prizemoney £120,278 *Total Prizemoney* £130,543
Wins * 1999 Aug Ripon (GD) C 8f 77+
*** 1999** Jun Salisb (G-F) H 8f 80 84
*** 1999** May Chepst (GD) 8.1f 80
***** 1996 Oct Newmar (G-F) L **8f** 108 <

* 1996 Jly Ascot (G-F) H 8f 97 107
* 1996 Jun Ascot (G-F) H 8f 87 102
* 1996 May Ascot (G-F) H 7f 80 87
* 1996 Mar Newcas (G-S) 8f 83

1999 Turf 3-9: (8f 3-8, 9f) (gd 1-4, g-f 2-3, frm 2)

Above-average gelding, effective 8 to 10f, best at 8f, acts on gd to frm, best on g-f. Turf high 86 - 2nd of 7 giving 13lb to Court Express (7 Aug Redcar 8f frm RF 3456) - also 1st of 10 giving 1lb to Saligo (23 Jun Salisbury RF 2247). Inconsistent. A one-time very useful handicapper, winner of the 1996 Hunt Cup and a winner in Listed company, he was disappointing for a couple of seasons, but has rediscovered the winning thread. He remains well handicapped on his best form, and is suited by forcing tactics.

**W J Haggas [8-33] The Not Over Big Partnership.*

YELLOW RIBBON (IRE) BHB 63f56a RR 60f 56a 4706[11]

3 b f Hamas (IRE) 8f **(72)** - Busker (Bustino) 10.4f **(64)**
Form - 4108700
Record 1999 - 1st:1 2nd:0 3rd:0 Ran:7
Pre1999 - 1st:0 2nd:0 3rd:1 Ran:3
Win Prizemoney £4,760 *Total Prizemoney* £5,360
Wins * 1999 May Warwic (GD) H 7f 65 67 <

1999 Turf 1-5: (7f 1-5) (gd, g-f, frm 1-3) 1999 AW 0-2: (9f, 10f) (Equi, Fibr)

Scopey, average filly, effective 7f, acts on frm, likes left handed tracks, likes tight tracks. Turf high 67 (1st run) - 1st of 20 getting 7lb from Polar Ice (3 May Warwick RF 1013). AW high 14.

**B W Hills [1-10] A N Foster.*

YENALED BHB 59f RR 64f 5186[3]

2 gr c Rambo Dancer (CAN) 8.4f **(59)** - Fancy Flight (FR) (Arctic Tern (USA)) 8.9f **(69)**
Form - 7046323563
Record 1999 - 1st:0 2nd:1 3rd:3 Ran:10
Win Prizemoney £0 *Total Prizemoney* £2,475

1999 Turf 0-10: (5f, 6f 2, 7f 4, 8f 3) (sft, gd 4, g-f 3, frm 2)

Average colt, effective 6 to 8f, acts on gd to frm. Turf high 64 - 3rd of 14 getting 4lb from Noble Pasao (26 Spt Musselburgh 8f gd RF 4575). Consistent. **J S Goldie [0-10] Martin Delaney.*

YEOMAN OLIVER BHB 73f65a RR 73f 65a 247[11]

6 b g Precocious 7.2f **(54)** - Impala Lass (Kampala) 8.5f **(56)**
Form - 03230
Record 1999 - 1st:0 2nd:1 3rd:1 Ran:3
Pre1999 - 1st:6 2nd:14 3rd:7 Ran:51
Win Prizemoney £16,896 *Total Prizemoney* £32,017
Wins * 1998 Oct Nottin (SFT) C 8.2f 72 <
* 1998 Spt Ripon (SFT) C 8f 64
* 1997 *Jan Southw (STD) H 8f 64 67*
* 1996 *Aug Wolver (STD) C 9.4f 64*
* 1996 *May Southw (STD) H 8f 66 66*
* 1996 *Feb Wolver (STD) 8.5f 58*

1999 AW 0-3: (8f 2, 9f) (Fibr 3)

Above-average gelding, effective 7 to 8f, best at 8f, acts on g-s to gd - acts on Fibr, best on gd, often wears blinkers (very effectively), excels at Southwell. AW high 69 (1st run) - 2nd of 15 giving 1lb to Takhlid (15 Jan Southwell 8f Fibr RF 0102).

**B A McMahon [6-54] Michael Stokes.*

YEOMAN'S POINT (IRE) RR 108f 2995a[1]

3 b c Sadler's Wells (USA) 11.3f **(87)** - Truly Bound (USA) (In Reality) 7.4f **(74)**
Form - 521721

1999 Turf 2-5: (9f, 12f 1-2, 14f 1-2) (hvy, g-s 1-1, g-f 1-3)

Pattern-class colt, effective 14f, acts on g-f. Turf high 108 - 1st of 7 from Young American (17 Jly Leopardstown RF 2995a). He won a Listed event over a mile and three-quarters at Leopardstown in July and is clearly a decent horse on the Flat. However, his trainer believes he has a better future over hurdles and he must be followed if allowed to pursue that career.

**A P O'Brien in IRE [3-7] Mrs John Magnier.*

YES COLONEL (IRE) RR 5195[18]

2 gr c Colonel Collins (USA) - Lesley's Fashion **(68f)** (Dominion) 8.5f **(63)**
Form - 0
Record 1999 - 1st:0 2nd:0 3rd:0 Ran:1

1999 Turf 0-1: (6f) (gd)

Currently little account colt. **Derrick Morris [0-1] Byron Stokes.*

YES KEEMO SABEE BHB 69f66a RR 70f 66a 1504[7]

4 b g Arazi (USA) 9.2f **(74)** - Nazeera (FR) (Lashkari) 9.8f **(67)**
Form - 02522627217
Record 1999 - 1st:1 2nd:4 3rd:0 Ran:9
Pre1999 - 1st:0 2nd:1 3rd:0 Ran:5
Win Prizemoney £7,337 *Total Prizemoney* £12,653
Wins * 1999 May Thirsk (G-S) H 16f 65 68 <

1999 Turf 1-5: (16f 1-4, 18f) (g-s, gd 1-2, g-f, frm) 1999 AW 0-4: (11f 2, 12f 2) (Fibr 4)

Light-framed, above-average gelding, effective 11 to 18f, best at 16f, acts on g-s to g-f - acts on Fibr, best on gd. Turf high 70 - 2nd of 18 getting 10lb from Star Rage (8 May Beverley 16f gd RF 1099) - also 1st of 13 giving 6lb to Give An Inch (14 May Thirsk RF 1224). AW high 63 - 2nd of 12 giving 19lb to Western Command (10 Mar Southwell 11f Fibr RF 0420). Consistent.

**D Shaw [1-9] Ian Guise (from B A McMahon [0-5] Dec 1998).*

YET AGAIN BHB 56f60a RR 63df 60a 3352[9]

7 ch g Weldnaas (USA) 8.4f **(55)** - Brightelmstone (Prince Regent (FR)) 9.8f **(54)**
Form - 0
Record 1999 - 1st:0 2nd:0 3rd:0 Ran:1
Pre1999 - 1st:9 2nd:5 3rd:3 Ran:36
Win Prizemoney £23,723 *Total Prizemoney* £31,207
Wins * 1998 Jun Bright (FRM) H 11.9f 55 57
* 1998 *Jan Lingfi (STD) H 12f 56 58*
* 1997 Aug Chepst (G-F) H 12.1f 50 54
* 1997 Apr Bright (FRM) H 11.9f 40 50
* 1997 *Jan Lingfi (STD) H 13f 40 52*
* 1997 *Jan Lingfi (STD) H 12f 40 53+*
* 1996 *Dec Lingfi (STD) H 12f 40 50+*
1996 Jun Warwic (FRM) S 10.8f 43
1995 Jun Bright (G-F) 11.9f 69 <

1999 Turf 0-1: (12f) (frm)

Average gelding, effective 12f, acts on gd to frm - acts on Equi, has worn blinkers.

**Miss Gay Kelleway [10-28] A P Griffin (from B Hanbury [2-16] Jly 1996).*

YORBA LINDA (IRE) RR 95f 4741a[9]

4 ch f Night Shift (USA) 8.1f **(73)** - Allepolina (USA) 0**0**
Form - 8612500

1999 Turf 1-7: (5f 1-4, 6f 3) (sft, gd 4, g-f, frm 1-1)

Very useful filly, effective 5 to 6f, best at 6f, acts on gd to g-f, best on gd, has worn blinkers. Turf high 95 - 5th of 16 giving 3lb to Oyster Catcher (21 Aug Fairyhouse 6f gd RF 3886a). She is speedy and a useful sprint handicapper. However, connections are tilting at windmills by running her in Group races.

**P Martin in IRE [1-7] T F Brennan (from J S Bolger in IRE [1-9] Aug 1998).*

YORKIES BOY BHB 102f RR 100f 5222[18]

4 ro c Clantime 6.6f **(57)** - Slipperose (Persepolis (FR)) 6.4f **(67)**
Form - 205380000
Record 1999 - 1st:0 2nd:1 3rd:1 Ran:9
Pre1999 - 1st:3 2nd:3 3rd:0 Ran:19
Win Prizemoney £34,651 *Total Prizemoney* £60,791
Wins * 1998 May Newmar (G-S) G3 5f 113 <
* 1998 Apr Newmar (SFT) L 5f 109
* 1997 Jun Cheste (G-F) 5.1f 76+

1999 Turf 0-9: (5f 2, 6f 6, 7f) (sft, g-s, gd 4, g-f, frm 2)

Scopey, very useful colt, effective 5 to 6f, best at 6f, acts on gd, has worn blinkers. Turf high 110 - 3rd of 14 giving 14lb to Sampower Star (13 May York 6f gd RF 1195). He gained little reward for an arduous season and is very difficult to place.

**B A McMahon [3-28] Mrs M Beddis.*

YORKIE TOO BHB 48f RR 54df 3764[10]

3 b g Prince Sabo 6.6f **(64)** - Petonica (IRE) (Petoski) 5.7f **(62)**
Form - 0070400
Record 1999 - 1st:0 2nd:0 3rd:0 Ran:7
Win Prizemoney £0 *Total Prizemoney* £492

1999 Turf 0-7: (7f, 8f 2, 10f 4) (gd 2, g-f, frm 4)

Scopey, fair gelding, often wears blinkers. Turf high 67.

**H J Collingridge [0-7] In The Know (1).*

YORKSHIRE GRIT BHB 36f **RR 29f** 4035[11]
3 ch f Ardkinglass 5f **(64)** - Jarrettelle (All Systems Go)
Form - 000000
Record 1999 - 1st:0 2nd:0 3rd:0 Ran:6
Pre1999 - 1st:1 2nd:0 3rd:1 Ran:7
Win Prizemoney £1,884 *Total Prizemoney* £2,254
Wins 1998 Jly Catter (GD) S 5f 60 <
1999 Turf 0-6: (5f 4, 6f, 7f) (gd 2, frm 4)
Workmanlike, moderate filly, effective 5f, acts on g-f to frm, has worn blinkers. Turf high 35.
**J Balding [0-6] Nick Massarella And Friends (from R M Whitaker [1-7] Spt 1998).*

YORKSHIRE PRIDE (IRE) RR 31f 3400[12]
2 b f Night Shift (USA) 8.1f **(73)** - Shajara (FR) (Kendor (FR))
Form - 0
Record 1999 - 1st:0 2nd:0 3rd:0 Ran:1
1999 Turf 0-1: (6f) (gd)
Currently very moderate filly.
**R A Fahey [0-1] Pride Of Yorkshire Racing Club.*

YOU DA MAN (IRE) BHB 67f **RR 67f** 5052[13]
2 b c Alzao (USA) 9.8f **(73)** - Fabled Lifestyle (Kings Lake (USA)) 10.8f **(67)**
Form - 8600
Record 1999 - 1st:0 2nd:0 3rd:0 Ran:4
1999 Turf 0-4: (7f 3, 8f) (g-s, gd, g-f, frm)
Average colt. Turf high 67 (began Aug).
**R Hannon [0-4] Buddy Hackett.*

YOUNG AMERICAN (IRE) RR 106f 2995a[2]
3 br c Hamas (IRE) 8f **(72)** - Banana Peel (Green Dancer (USA)) 10.3f **(74)**
Form - 612
1999 Turf 1-3: (10f 1-2, 14f) (g-f 2, frm 1-1)
Currently Pattern-class colt. Turf high 106 - 2nd of 7 to Yeoman's Point (17 Jly Leopardstown 14f g-f RF 2995a). Failed to reappear after finishing second in a listed race in July.
**C O'Brien in IRE [1-3] Dr Anne Heffernan.*

YOUNG BEN (IRE) BHB 33f32a **RR 24f 32a** 3924[9]
7 ch g Fayruz 6.6f **(63)** - Jive (Ahonoora) 8.1f **(73)**
Form - 868000
Record 1999 - 1st:0 2nd:0 3rd:0 Ran:6
Pre1999 - 1st:1 2nd:3 3rd:7 Ran:41
Win Prizemoney £3,731 *Total Prizemoney* £9,461
Wins * 1997 Jly Beverl (G-F) H 5f 36 43 <
1999 Turf 0-6: (5f 6) (gd, g-f 2, frm 3)
Very moderate gelding, effective 5 to 6f, acts on frm - acts on Fibr, mostly wears blinkers. Turf high 38.
**J S Wainwright [1-47] J S Wainwright.*

YOUNG BIGWIG (IRE) BHB 60f74a **RR 57f 74a** 5160[5]
5 b g Anita's Prince 6f **(62)** - Humble Mission (Shack (USA)) 5.8f **(53)**
Form - 0205553000237755185677010125
Record 1999 - 1st:3 2nd:3 3rd:2 Ran:27
Pre1999 - 1st:4 2nd:4 3rd:4 Ran:36
Win Prizemoney £31,654 *Total Prizemoney* £68,363
Wins *** 1999** *Oct Wolver (STD) H 6f 64 67*
*** 1999** *Oct Wolver (STD) H 6f 57 62+*
*** 1999** Jun Redcar (FRM) H 6f 62 64
* 1998 Jun Hamilt (SFT) H 5f 73 76
* 1998 May Thirsk (GD) H 5f 70 75
1996 Jly Goodwo (G-F) H 6f 96 <
1996 *May Wolver (STD) 5f 65*
1999 Turf 1-18: (5f 7, 6f 1-9, 7f, 8f) (sft 2, g-s 2, gd 6, g-f 2, frm 1-6)
1999 AW 2-9: (5f, 6f 2-7, 7f) (Fibr 2-9)
Above-average gelding, effective 5 to 7f, best at 5f, acts on gd to frm - acts on Fibr, best on gd, has worn blinkers, excels at Redcar and Wolverhampton, likes Thirsk. Turf high 65. AW high 71 - 2nd of 12 giving 5lb to Rouge (30 Oct Wolverhampton 7f Fibr RF 5146) - also 1st of 13 getting 1lb from Blue Kite (16 Oct Wolverhampton RF 4924). A fair sprint handicapper, he ended a long losing run at Redcar in June, and twice won over six furlongs on the Wolverhampton Fibresand in October. Not altogether consistent.
**D W Chapman [5-47] David Chapman (from J Berry [2-16] Oct 1997).*

YOUNG BUTT BHB 35f50a **RR 37f 50a** 1707[16]
6 ch g Bold Owl 9.7f **(47)** - Cymbal (Ribero) 9.3f **(56)**
Form - 00000
Record 1999 - 1st:0 2nd:0 3rd:0 Ran:5
Pre1999 - 1st:2 2nd:1 3rd:2 Ran:16
Win Prizemoney £10,310 *Total Prizemoney* £12,240
Wins 1996 May Goodwo (G-S) H 8f 58 69 <
1995 *Oct Wolver (STD) SH 8.5f 54 65*
1999 Turf 0-5: (7f 2, 8f 2, 11f) (gd, g-f 2, frm 2)
Very moderate gelding. Turf high 37.
**B A Pearce [0-7] D Newman (from J Ffitch-Heyes [2-14] Jun 1996).*

YOUNG JOSH BHB 85f **RR 89f** 4921[17]
4 b c Warning 8.1f **(77)** - Title Roll (IRE) (Tate Gallery (USA)) 7.4f **(67)**
Form - 3170300
Record 1999 - 1st:1 2nd:0 3rd:2 Ran:7
Pre1999 - 1st:1 2nd:1 3rd:0 Ran:6
Win Prizemoney £11,189 *Total Prizemoney* £25,148
Wins *** 1999** Jly Chepst (G-F) 6.1f 69+
1997 Spt Goodwo (GD) 6f 83 <
1999 Turf 1-7: (6f 1-3, 7f 3, 8f) (gd 3, g-f 2, frm 1-1, hrd)
Useful colt, effective 6 to 8f, acts on g-f to hrd, best on g-f. Turf high 92 (1st run) - 3rd of 30 getting 1lb from Deep Space (18 Jun Ascot 6f g-f RF 2105). He obviously likes Goodwood, as he won there as a juvenile and was demoted after winning a handicap at the same track on his second start at three. Moderate efforts otherwise, until finishing a fine third in the Wokingham on his 1999 bow, and gained a deserved victory at Chepstow in July. Six furlongs looks his trip.
**A C Stewart [1-7] Fayzad Thoroughbred Ltd (from J H M Gosden [1-6] Jun 1998).*

YOUNG MARCIUS (USA) BHB 33f **RR 40f** 3314[4]
5 ch g Green Dancer (USA) 11.9f **(77)** - Manhatten Miss (Artaius (USA)) 9f **(69)**
Form - 050504
Record 1999 - 1st:0 2nd:0 3rd:0 Ran:6
Pre1999 - 1st:0 2nd:0 3rd:0 Ran:1
1999 Turf 0-6: (10f 2, 12f 2, 14f, 16f) (sft, gd, g-f 3, frm)
Moderate gelding. Turf high 50.
**K A Morgan [0-6] Mrs Alison Silkman (from P F I Cole [0-1] Jun 1997).*

YOUNG MAZAAD (IRE) BHB 43f46a **RR 47df 46a** 2147[13]
6 b g Mazaad 8.5f **(53)** - Lucky Charm (IRE) (Pennine Walk) 8.5f **(61)**
Form - 78670
Record 1999 - 1st:0 2nd:0 3rd:0 Ran:4
Pre1999 - 1st:1 2nd:6 3rd:1 Ran:18
Win Prizemoney £2,381 *Total Prizemoney* £7,779
Wins * 1996 May Folkes (GD) 6.9f 57 <
1999 Turf 0-4: (7f, 9f, 10f 2) (hvy, sft, frm, hrd)
Moderate gelding, effective 10f, acts on frm, has worn blinkers (effectively), likes tight tracks. Turf high 47 - 7th of 20 getting 11lb from Gypsy Hill (24 May Windsor 10f frm RF 1442). Inconsistent.
**D C O'Brien [1-23] Mrs S Harris (from R Curtis [0-2] Spt 1995).*

YOUNG PRECEDENT BHB 82f **RR 80f** 4921[18]
5 b h Polish Precedent (USA) 9f **(73)** - Guyum (Rousillon (USA)) 8.2f **(74)**
Form - 4040
Record 1999 - 1st:0 2nd:0 3rd:0 Ran:4
Pre1999 - 1st:5 2nd:1 3rd:2 Ran:20
Win Prizemoney £43,971 *Total Prizemoney* £51,733
Wins * 1998 Oct Leices (SFT) H 7f 86 92 <
* 1998 Jly York (G-F) H 7.9f 85 88
* 1998 May Haydoc (GD) H 8.1f 83 85
* 1997 Aug Newbur (G-F) H 7.3f 81 82
* 1997 May Thirsk (G-F) 7f 71
1999 Turf 0-4: (7f, 8f 3) (gd 2, frm 2)
Decent colt, effective 7 to 9f, best at 8f, acts on g-s to frm, best on frm, prefers left handed tracks, likes tight tracks, excels at York. Turf high 85 (1st run) (began Aug) - 4th of 8 giving 10lb to Al Fahda (6 Aug Salisbury 8f frm RF 3432). Inconsistent. He showed little in a light campaign. Lacks a turn of foot, so forcing tactics are ideal. **P W Harris [5-24] Pendley Knights.*

YOUNG ROOSTER RR 37f 3364[13]
2 b c Timeless Times (USA) 6.1f **(56)** - Jussoli (Don) 7.7f **(64)**

Form - 00
Record 1999 - 1st:0 2nd:0 3rd:0 Ran:2
1999 Turf 0-2: (6f 2) (gd, hrd)
Currently very moderate colt. Turf high 37.
**Miss S E Hall [0-2] C Platts.*

YOUNG ROSEIN BHB 56f **RR 55f** 4906[8]
3 b f Distant Relative 7f **(69)** - Red Rosein (Red Sunset) 8.2f **(63)**
Form - 007541U28
Record 1999 - 1st:1 2nd:1 3rd:0 Ran:9
Pre1999 - 1st:0 2nd:0 3rd:0 Ran:3
Win Prizemoney £2,983 *Total Prizemoney* £3,858
Wins * 1999 Aug Mussel (G-F) H 7.1f 52 55 <
1999 Turf 1-9: (6f 3, 7f 1-4, 8f 2) (gd 2, g-f 1-2, frm 5)
Scopey, fair filly, effective 7f, acts on g-f to frm. Turf high 55 - 1st of 14 getting 4lb from Encounter (26 Aug Musselburgh RF 3922).
**Mrs G S Rees [1-12] J W Gittins.*

YOUNG SUE BHB 72f **RR 79f** 4752[10]
3 b f Local Suitor (USA) 9.7f **(58)** - Young Wilkie (Callernish)
Form - 3140
Record 1999 - 1st:1 2nd:0 3rd:1 Ran:4
Win Prizemoney £3,220 *Total Prizemoney* £4,247
Wins * 1999 Jly Ripon (G-F) 9f 79 <
1999 Turf 1-4: (8f, 9f 1-1, 10f, 12f) (gd 2, frm 1-2)
Rangy, above-average filly. Turf high 79 (began Jly) - 1st of 4 from Mouton (17 Jly Ripon RF 2930). **M Johnston [1-4] C H Greensit.*

YOUNG TOBY BHB 54f **RR 55f** 4169[13]
2 ch c Timeless Times (USA) 6.1f **(56)** - Promise Fulfilled (USA) **(72df 61a)** (Bet Twice (USA))
Form - 00740
Record 1999 - 1st:0 2nd:0 3rd:0 Ran:5
1999 Turf 0-5: (5f, 6f, 7f 2, 8f) (g-f, frm 3, hrd)
Fair colt, has worn blinkers. Turf high 55 (began Jly).
**T D Easterby [0-5] A K Smeaton.*

YOUNG-UN BHB 65f **RR 62f** 5162[1]
4 b c Efisio 7.7f **(69)** - Stardyn (Star Appeal) 9.6f **(65)**
Form - 08040388114340251
Record 1999 - 1st:3 2nd:1 3rd:2 Ran:17
Pre1999 - 1st:0 2nd:0 3rd:0 Ran:7
Win Prizemoney £10,078 *Total Prizemoney* £12,608
Wins * 1999 Nov Redcar (G-S) H 10f 59 62 <
*** 1999** Aug Nottin (G-F) H 10f 43 53
*** 1999** Aug Newcas (GD) H 9f 46 48
1999 Turf 3-17: (7f 2, 8f 2, 9f 1-2, 10f 2-11) (sft, g-s, gd 3, g-f 2-7, frm 1-5)
Neat, average colt, effective 9 to 10f, acts on g-f to frm, has worn blinkers, prefers left handed tracks, likes tight tracks. Turf high 62 - 1st of 17 giving 5lb to Swinging The Blues (1 Nov Redcar RF 5162). Consistent.
**M J Ryan [3-17] M F Kentish (from S Dow [0-7] Oct 1998).*

YOUNICO BHB 43f48a **RR 37f 48a** 3863[14]
4 b g Nordico (USA) 8.2f **(59)** - Young Wilkie (Callernish)
Form - 750
Record 1999 - 1st:0 2nd:0 3rd:0 Ran:3
Pre1999 - 1st:1 2nd:2 3rd:2 Ran:10
Win Prizemoney £2,206 *Total Prizemoney* £4,978
Wins 1998 Jly Catter (GD) 13.8f 55 <
1999 Turf 0-3: (12f, 16f 2) (frm 3)
Fair gelding, effective 10 to 14f, best at 14f, acts on gd to frm - acts on Equi, best on frm, often wears blinkers, excels at Catterick, does well at Lingfield. Turf high 37 (began Jly). Becoming disappointing.
**Mrs M Reveley [0-3] The Scarth Racing Partnership (from M Johnston [1-10] Spt 1998).*

YOU'RE SPECIAL (USA) BHB 75f **RR 79f** 4378[16]
2 b g Northern Flagship (USA) 12.2f **(72)** - Pillow Mint (USA) (Stage Door Johnny) 10.3f **(84)**
Form - 5520
Record 1999 - 1st:0 2nd:1 3rd:0 Ran:4
Win Prizemoney £0 *Total Prizemoney* £795
1999 Turf 0-4: (5f, 6f 2, 8f) (gd 4)
Above-average gelding. Turf high 79 - 2nd of 12 giving 6lb to Xcaret (24 May Hamilton 6f gd RF 1425).
**P C Haslam [0-4] Les Buckley.*

YULARA (IRE) BHB 72f **RR 63f** 3345a[8]
4 b f Night Shift (USA) 8.1f **(73)** - Fifth Quarter (Cure The Blues (USA)) 9.5f **(63)**
Form - 570008
Record 1999 - 1st:0 2nd:0 3rd:0 Ran:6
Pre1999 - 1st:2 2nd:0 3rd:1 Ran:15
Win Prizemoney £11,810 *Total Prizemoney* £15,848
Wins 1998 Jly Warwic (G-F) H 7f 70 76 <
1998 Jun Newmar (GD) H 7f 65 70
1999 Turf 0-6: (7f 5, 8f) (g-f 3, frm 3)
Average filly, effective 7f, acts on sft, has worn blinkers. Turf high 75.
**M Halford in IRE [0-1] Shane Ryan (from B J Meehan [2-14] May 1999).*

ZAAJER (USA) RR 112f 5131[4]
3 ch c Silver Hawk (USA) 11.2f **(85)** - Crown Quest (USA) (Chief's Crown (USA)) 9.8f **(72)**
Form - 10674
Record 1999 - 1st:1 2nd:0 3rd:0 Ran:5
Pre1999 - 1st:1 2nd:1 3rd:0 Ran:2
Win Prizemoney £20,411 *Total Prizemoney* £26,403
Wins * 1999 May York (SFT) L 10.4f 106+ <
* 1998 Oct Ascot (SFT) 7f 97
1999 Turf 1-5: (8f, 10f 1-2, 12f 2) (gd 1-4, frm)
Scopey, Group-class colt, effective 10f, acts on gd. Turf high 112 - 4th of 7 giving 4lb to Little Rock (29 Oct Newmarket 10f gd RF 5131) - also 1st of 6 from Mukhalif (13 May York RF 1197). He made a winning reappearance in the Glasgow Stakes at York, but the ground had dried out too much for him at Epsom and he looked one-paced. Rather lost his way subsequently, but he ran a better race on his final start in his favoured soft ground.
**E A L Dunlop [2-7] Hamdan Al Maktoum.*

ZABAAD (USA) BHB 56f **RR 65f** 3854[7]
3 b f Kingmambo (USA) 10.9f **(85)** - Skeeb (USA) (Topsider (USA)) 8.3f **(71)**
Form - 0377
Record 1999 - 1st:0 2nd:0 3rd:1 Ran:4
Pre1999 - 1st:0 2nd:0 3rd:1 Ran:3
Win Prizemoney £0 *Total Prizemoney* £1,119
1999 Turf 0-4: (7f, 8f, 10f 2) (gd, g-f 2, frm)
Unfurnished, average filly, often wears blinkers. Turf high 65.
**M P Tregoning [0-7] Hamdan Al Maktoum.*

ZABIONIC (IRE) BHB 74f **RR 65f** 4551[8]
2 ch c Zafonic (USA) 9f **(83)** - Scene Galante (FR) (Sicyos (USA))
Form - 608
Record 1999 - 1st:0 2nd:0 3rd:0 Ran:3
1999 Turf 0-3: (6f, 7f 2) (g-s, gd, g-f)
Currently average colt. Turf high 65 (began Aug).
**B A McMahon [0-3] Barouche Stud Ltd.*

ZABRISKIE BHB 24f33a **RR 19f 33a** 3642[15]
5 b g Polish Precedent (USA) 9f **(73)** - Somfas (USA) (What A Pleasure (USA)) 8.4f **(61)**
Form - 0265005600
Record 1999 - 1st:0 2nd:1 3rd:0 Ran:9
Pre1999 - 1st:0 2nd:1 3rd:0 Ran:9
Win Prizemoney £0 *Total Prizemoney* £2,068
1999 Turf 0-3: (9f, 10f 2) (gd, g-f, frm) 1999 AW 0-6: (7f, 8f 2, 10f 3) (Equi 4, Fibr 2)
Very moderate gelding, effective 8f, - acts on Fibr, has worn blinkers. Turf high 19. AW high 35 (1st run) - 2nd of 9 getting 20lb from Impelling (26 Feb Southwell 8f Fibr RF 0364).
**G L Moore [0-18] R Kiernan (from Sir Michael Stoute [0-3] Jun 1997).*

ZADA BHB 42f48a **RR 42df 48a** 235[6]
4 b g Distant Relative 7f **(69)** - Handy Dancer (Green God) 9.6f **(68)**
Form - 26366
Record 1999 - 1st:0 2nd:0 3rd:0 Ran:2
Pre1999 - 1st:0 2nd:2 3rd:2 Ran:12
Win Prizemoney £0 *Total Prizemoney* £2,332
1999 AW 0-2: (10f, 12f) (Equi 2)

Scopey, average gelding, effective 10f, - acts on Equi, has worn blinkers (very effectively), favours left handed tracks, favours tight tracks. AW high 44. **G L Moore [0-14] Bryan Pennick.*

ZAFFIA RR 69f 4451[2]

2 b f Zilzal (USA) 8.5f **(79)** - Zeffirella (Known Fact (USA)) 7.4f **(67)**
Form - 42
Record 1999 - 1st:0 2nd:1 3rd:0 Ran:2
Win Prizemoney £0 *Total Prizemoney* £785
1999 Turf 0-2: (7f 2) (sft, gd)
Currently average filly. Turf high 69 (began Aug) - 2nd of 16 getting 5lb from Jamestown (21 Spt Warwick 7f sft RF 4451).
**P R Chamings [0-2] Twenty Twenty Research.*

ZAFOIR BHB 75f RR 74f 4129[7]

2 br c Zafonic (USA) 9f **(83)** - Reveuse du Soir (Vision (USA)) 9f **(64)**
Form - 605247
Record 1999 - 1st:0 2nd:1 3rd:0 Ran:6
Win Prizemoney £0 *Total Prizemoney* £1,100
1999 Turf 0-6: (5f, 6f 5) (gd, frm 4, hrd)
Above-average colt, effective 6f, acts on frm. Turf high 74.
**Mrs A J Perrett [0-6] J H Richmond-Watson.*

ZAFONIC'S SONG (FR) RR 78+f 5208[4]

2 br c Zafonic (USA) 9f **(83)** - Savoureuse Lady (Caerleon (USA)) 8.6f **(71)**
Form - 4
Record 1999 - 1st:0 2nd:0 3rd:0 Ran:1
Win Prizemoney £0 *Total Prizemoney* £233
1999 Turf 0-1: (7f) (g-s)
Currently above-average colt. (1st run) - 4th of 20 to Golovin (5 Nov Doncaster 7f g-s RF 5208).
**Sir Michael Stoute [0-1] Satish Sanan.*

ZAFONIUM (USA) RR 86f 4799[1]

2 ch c Zafonic (USA) 9f **(83)** - Bint Pasha (USA) (Affirmed (USA)) 9.3f **(79)**
Form - 31
Record 1999 - 1st:1 2nd:0 3rd:1 Ran:2
Win Prizemoney £7,018 *Total Prizemoney* £8,204
Wins * 1999 Oct York (SFT) 7.9f 86 <
1999 Turf 1-2: (7f, 8f 1-1) (gd 1-2)
Currently useful colt. Turf high 86 (began Spt) - 1st of 6 from Tigre (9 Oct York RF 4799). Out of a mare who won the Yorkshire Oaks, he made his debut in a hot maiden at Newbury and made no mistake next time. **P F I Cole [1-2] H R H Prince Fahd Salman.*

ZAGALETA BHB 76f RR 75f 3075[2]

2 b f Sri Pekan (USA) - Persian Song (Persian Bold) 9.3f **(66)**
Form - 322
Record 1999 - 1st:0 2nd:2 3rd:1 Ran:3
Win Prizemoney £0 *Total Prizemoney* £2,817
1999 Turf 0-3: (6f 3) (gd, frm 2)
Currently above-average filly. Turf high 75 (1st run) - 3rd of 6 to Bella Bellisimo (12 Jun York 6f gd RF 1965).
**Andrew Turnell [0-3] Dr John Hollowood.*

ZAHA (IRE) BHB 57f64a RR 60f 64a 4993[9]

4 b c Lahib (USA) 8f **(69)** - Mayaasa (USA) (Lyphard (USA)) 9.9f **(72)**
Form - 21633655271050
Record 1999 - 1st:2 2nd:2 3rd:2 Ran:14
Pre1999 - 1st:0 2nd:0 3rd:1 Ran:4
Win Prizemoney £5,219 *Total Prizemoney* £9,248
Wins * **1999** Aug Yarmou (GD) 10.1f 57
* **1999** *Feb Southw (STD) 11f 64* <
1999 Turf 1-11: (8f, 10f 1-10) (hvy, g-s 3, gd 1-4, frm 3) 1999 AW 1-3: (10f, 11f 1-1, 12f) (Equi, Fibr 1-2)
Workmanlike, average colt, effective 10 to 12f, best at 10f, acts on hvy to frm - acts on AW, has worn blinkers, likes left handed tracks, likes tight tracks, excels at Leicester, likes Yarmouth. Turf high 63 (1st run) - 3rd of 11 getting 1lb from Top Jem (1 Apr Leicester 10f gd RF 0539) - also 1st of 11 getting 4lb from Rare Talent (19 Aug Yarmouth RF 3765). AW high 64 - 1st of 14 giving 21lb to Arthurs Kingdom (5 Feb Southwell RF 0228).
**J Pearce [2-14] Exclusive Three Partnership (from R W Armstrong [0-4] Jly 1998).*

ZAHIR (USA) BHB 21f29a RR 30f 29a 1429[7]

5 b g Riverman (USA) 9.7f **(78)** - Manwah (USA) (Lyphard (USA)) 9.9f **(72)**
Form - 056007
Record 1999 - 1st:0 2nd:0 3rd:0 Ran:6
Pre1999 - 1st:0 2nd:1 3rd:0 Ran:1
1999 Turf 0-2: (8f, 16f) (gd, frm) 1999 AW 0-4: (7f, 12f 2, 16f) (Fibr 4)
Very moderate gelding, often wears blinkers. AW high 15.
**R F Marvin [0-6] J Shine (from S bin Suroor [0-1] May 1997).*

ZAHRAN (IRE) BHB 39f38a RR 32f 38a 41[3]

8 b h Groom Dancer (USA) 9.5f **(75)** - Welsh Berry (USA) (Sir Ivor) 10.2f **(70)**
Form - 43883
Record 1999 - 1st:0 2nd:0 3rd:1 Ran:2
Pre1999 - 1st:4 2nd:12 3rd:11 Ran:85
Win Prizemoney £11,598 *Total Prizemoney* £25,943
Wins * 1996 *Nov Lingfi (STD) H 8f 39 44*
* 1995 Aug Hamilt (FRM) SH 9.2f 43 50
* 1995 *Mar Lingfi (STD) H 8f 53 55*
1999 AW 0-2: (8f, 9f) (Fibr 2)
Very moderate horse, effective 7 to 8f, best at 8f, acts on gd to frm - acts on Fibr, has worn blinkers. AW high 32. Consistent.
**J M Bradley [3-84] Smith (Saul) (from H R A Cecil [1-4] Jun 1994).*

ZAHRAT DUBAI BHB 112f RR 112f 4780a[5]

3 b f Unfuwain (USA) 11.4f **(74)** - Walesiana (GER) (Star Appeal) 9.6f **(65)**
Form - 13145
Record 1999 - 1st:2 2nd:0 3rd:1 Ran:5
Pre1999 - 1st:0 2nd:0 3rd:0 Ran:1
Win Prizemoney £97,200 *Total Prizemoney* £136,950
Wins * **1999** Jly Goodwo (FRM) G1 9.9f 110 <
* **1999** May York (G-S) G3 10.4f 110++
1999 Turf 2-5: (9f, 10f 2-2, 12f 2) (sft, gd 1-3, g-f 1-1)
Light-framed, Group-class filly, effective 10 to 12f, best at 10f, acts on gd to g-f, best on gd. Turf high 112 - 4th of 11 to Ramruma (18 Aug York 12f gd RF 3757) - also 1st of 8 getting 9lb from Lady In Waiting (31 Jly Goodwood RF 3260). She looked a world-beater when running away with the Musidora Stakes in May, but events were to prove that she faced weak opposition. A non-staying favourite when third in the Oaks, she put up a personal best performance when making all to win the Group 1 Nassau Stakes at Goodwood in July. Below par on her two subsequent starts, she goes well when fresh and should pick up another decent prize over a mile and a quarter in 2000.
**S bin Suroor [2-5] (from D R Loder [0-1] Oct 1998).*

Zahrat Dubai goes particularly well fresh

ZALABIA (IRE) RR 18f 4905[15]
3 ch f Perugino (USA) - Lamya (Hittite Glory) 8.7f **(50)**
Form - 0
Record 1999 - 1st:0 2nd:0 3rd:0 Ran:1
1999 Turf 0-1: (6f) (frm)
Currently poor filly. **K Mahdi [0-1] Hamad Al-Mutawa.*

ZALAL (IRE) BHB 97f **RR 97+f** 2355[1]
4 b c Darshaan 11.9f **(81)** - Zallaka (IRE) (Shardari) 11f **(46)**
Form - 71
Record 1999 - 1st:1 2nd:0 3rd:0 Ran:2
Pre1999 - 1st:2 2nd:0 3rd:0 Ran:6
Win Prizemoney £20,625 *Total Prizemoney* £20,625
Wins * **1999** Jun Goodwo (G-F) 12f 97 <
* 1998 Oct York (GD) 11.9f 86+
* 1998 Jly Bath (GD) 10.2f 69+
1999 Turf 1-2: (12f 1-2) (g-s, gd 1-1)
Workmanlike, very useful colt, effective 12f, acts on gd. Turf high 97 - 1st of 6 giving 2lb to Nautical Star (27 Jun Goodwood RF 2355). He looked promising when winning at Goodwood in June (subsequently failed a dope test), but was not seen out again. Sold for just 6,500 guineas at Newmarket in October, he has obviously had a serious problem. **L M Cumani [3-8] H H Aga Khan.*

ZALOTTO (IRE) BHB 42f43a **RR 37df 43a** 102[7]
5 b g Polish Patriot (USA) 7.8f **(70)** - Honest Penny (USA) (Honest Pleasure (USA)) 10.4f **(73)**
Form - 667
Record 1999 - 1st:0 2nd:0 3rd:0 Ran:3
Pre1999 - 1st:1 2nd:6 3rd:3 Ran:23
Win Prizemoney £2,085 *Total Prizemoney* £6,617
Wins 1998 *Jan Southw (STD)* *7f* *57* <
1999 AW 0-3: (7f, 8f 2) (Fibr 3)
Moderate gelding, effective 7f, - acts on Fibr, mostly wears blinkers (effectively). AW high 42. Consistent.
**M P Bielby [0-6] The Norking Partnership (from T J Etherington [1-20] Apr 1998).*

ZAMAN BHB 92f **RR 87f** 3399[6]
3 b c Caerleon (USA) 10.9f **(79)** - Zafadola (IRE) (Darshaan) 9.9f **(84)**
Form - 216
Record 1999 - 1st:1 2nd:1 3rd:0 Ran:3
Pre1999 - 1st:0 2nd:0 3rd:0 Ran:1
Win Prizemoney £3,533 *Total Prizemoney* £4,623
Wins * **1999** Jly Pontef (G-F) 10f 84 <
1999 Turf 1-3: (8f, 10f 1-1, 11f) (gd 2, frm 1-1)
Leggy, useful colt. Turf high 87 (began Jly) - also 1st of 6 giving 5lb to Bayt Alasad (16 Jly Pontefract RF 2891). A half-brother to Zelanda, he improved in each of his first three runs and got off the mark in good style at Pontefract in July. Unfortunately, he flopped on his handicap debut at Haydock.
**Sir Michael Stoute [1-4] Sheikh Mohammed.*

ZAMAT RR 20f 4435[13]
3 b g Slip Anchor 12.7f **(75)** - Khandjar (Kris) 9.5f **(73)**
Form - 0
Record 1999 - 1st:0 2nd:0 3rd:0 Ran:1
1999 Turf 0-1: (12f) (g-s)
Scopey, currently little account gelding.
**W Jarvis [0-1] Exors of the late Lord Howard de Walden.*

ZANAY BHB 82f **RR 81f** 5042[14]
3 b c Forzando 7.2f **(63)** - Nineteenth of May (Homing) 7.8f **(59)**
Form - 310
Record 1999 - 1st:1 2nd:0 3rd:1 Ran:3
Pre1999 - 1st:0 2nd:2 3rd:0 Ran:3
Win Prizemoney £5,117 *Total Prizemoney* £7,944
Wins * **1999** Oct Nottin (GD) 8.2f 81 <
1999 Turf 1-3: (8f 1-2, 9f) (sft, gd 1-2)
Scopey, decent colt, effective 7 to 8f, acts on sft to gd. Turf high 81 (began Aug) - 1st of 18 from Final Lap (21 Oct Nottingham RF 5003).
**Miss Jacqueline Doyle [1-2] Sanford Racing (from K Bell [0-1] Aug 1999).*

ZANY LADY BHB 39f **RR 43f** 4586[10]
4 gr f Arzanni - Lady Antonia (Owen Anthony)
Form - 603500
Record 1999 - 1st:0 2nd:0 3rd:1 Ran:6
Pre1999 - 1st:0 2nd:0 3rd:0 Ran:8
Win Prizemoney £0 *Total Prizemoney* £911
1999 Turf 0-6: (8f 2, 10f 4) (gd, g-f 2, frm 2, hrd)
Moderate filly. Turf high 47. Inconsistent.
**R J Hodges [0-14] Shirley Barraclough and Partners.*

ZARAGOSSA BHB 65f **RR 52f** 4255[15]
3 gr f Paris House 5.9f **(64)** - Antonia's Folly **(53f 53a)** (Music Boy) 6.8f **(57)**
Form - 305404000
Record 1999 - 1st:0 2nd:0 3rd:1 Ran:9
Pre1999 - 1st:1 2nd:0 3rd:0 Ran:3
Win Prizemoney £3,821 *Total Prizemoney* £5,913
Wins * 1998 Aug Thirsk (GD) 5f 73+ <
1999 Turf 0-9: (5f 9) (gd 2, g-f 4, frm 3)
Unfurnished, fair filly, effective 5f, acts on gd to g-f, best on g-f. Turf high 77. Becoming disappointing.
**J Berry [1-12] Slatch Farm Stud.*

ZARA ZAREEN (IRE) BHB 40f **RR** 3793[7]
8 ch g Mazaad 8.5f **(53)** - Nesreen (The Parson)
Form - 7
Record 1999 - 1st:0 2nd:0 3rd:0 Ran:1
1999 AW 0-1: (16f) (Equi)
Formerly very poor gelding. **N M Babbage [0-1] Nick Tsappis.*

ZARFOOT BHB 114f **RR 118f** 5013a[2]
3 br c Zafonic (USA) 9f **(83)** - Harefoot (Rainbow Quest (USA)) 10.4f **(75)**
Form - 121552
Record 1999 - 1st:2 2nd:2 3rd:0 Ran:6
Pre1999 - 1st:0 2nd:0 3rd:1 Ran:1
Win Prizemoney £18,359 *Total Prizemoney* £34,172
Wins * **1999** Jun Ascot (G-F) L 12f 99+ <
* **1999** May Newbur (Sft) 8f 88
1999 Turf 2-6: (8f 1-2, 12f 1-4) (gd 1-2, g-f 1-2, frm)
Scopey, high-class colt, effective 12f, acts on frm. Turf high 118 - 2nd to First Magnitude (17 Oct Longchamp 12f RF 5013a). He looked a lucky winner at Ascot in June, but came back better than ever after a mid-summer break and went down narrowly to First Magnitude in a Group 2 at Longchamp in October. Connections have confirmed that he stays in training as a four-year-old and that elusive Group race win cannot be far away. **L M Cumani [2-7].*

ZARILIYA (IRE) BHB 80f **RR 81f** 4788[6]
3 b f Darshaan 11.9f **(81)** - Zariya (USA) (Blushing Groom (FR)) 10.3f **(76)**
Form - 2216
Record 1999 - 1st:1 2nd:2 3rd:0 Ran:4
Pre1999 - 1st:0 2nd:0 3rd:1 Ran:1
Win Prizemoney £2,775 *Total Prizemoney* £5,631
Wins * **1999** Spt Mussel (G-S) 12f 73 <
1999 Turf 1-4: (10f, 11f 2, 12f 1-1) (g-s, gd 1-1, g-f, frm)
Workmanlike, decent filly. Turf high 81 (1st run) - 2nd of 7 to Elhilmeya (1 May Haydock 11f g-f RF 0952) - also 1st of 7 from Romola (26 Spt Musselburgh RF 4576).
**Sir Michael Stoute [1-5] H H Aga Khan.*

ZAZABELLE (NZ) RR 102f 5223a[3]
4 f Zabeel (NZ) - The Perfume Garden (AUS) (Tights (USA))
Form - 3
1999 Turf 0-1: (16f) (gd)
Currently very useful, always wears blinkers. (1st run) - 3rd of 24 getting 2lb from Rogan Josh (2 Nov Flemington 16f gd RF 5223a).
**J B Cummings in AUS [0-1].*

ZECHARIAH BHB 50f49a **RR 48f 49a** 4835[5]
3 b g Kasakov - Runfawit Pet (Welsh Saint) 7.6f **(64)**
Form - 106236085
Record 1999 - 1st:0 2nd:1 3rd:1 Ran:6
Pre1999 - 1st:1 2nd:1 3rd:1 Ran:11
Win Prizemoney £1,479 *Total Prizemoney* £3,603
Wins * 1998 *Nov Wolver (STD) S* *8.5f* *65* <
1999 Turf 0-5: (7f 4, 8f) (gd 2, frm 3) 1999 AW 0-1: (8f) (Fibr)
Unfurnished, average gelding, effective 7 to 8f, best at 7f, acts on

frm - acts on Fibr, likes tight tracks. Turf high 59 (1st run) (began Jly) - 2nd of 10 getting 3lb from Future Coup (13 Jly Beverley 7f frm RF 2768). **J L Eyre [1-17] John Ashcroft.*

ZELBECK BHB 46f **RR 45?f** 5003[14]

3 b f Komaite (USA) 6.9f **(61)** - Kakisa (Forlorn River) 7.3f **(54)**
Form - 700
Record 1999 - 1st:0 2nd:0 3rd:0 Ran:3
1999 Turf 0-3: (6f, 7f, 8f) (gd 3)
Small, currently moderate filly. Turf high 45 (began Spt).
**P D Evans [0-3] Treble Chance Partnership.*

ZENNE (IRE) **RR 91f** 2098a[13]

3 b f Fairy King (USA) 7.7f **(75)** - Nunatak (USA) (Bering) 7.4f **(61)**
Form - 230
1999 Turf 0-3: (8f, 10f, 11f) (sft, g-s, gd)
Currently useful filly. Turf high 91. **R Collet in FR [0-3].*

ZENTSOV STREET (USA) **RR 99f** 5037[5]

2 b c Nureyev (USA) 8.4f **(84)** - Storm Fear (USA) (Coastal (USA)) 11.5f **(72)**
Form - 2135
1999 Turf 1-4: (7f 1-3, 8f) (g-s, gd 1-2, g-f)
Very useful colt. Turf high 99 (began Jly) - 3rd of 5 to Distant Music (16 Oct Newmarket 7f gd RF 4918) - also 1st of 14 from Sawwaah (30 Spt Newmarket RF 4649). An attractive individual, he ran a fair race to finish third in the Dewhurst, but flopped when dragged out a week later on soft ground in the Racing Post Trophy. That was not his true running and he should be given another chance next term. Likely to stay a mile and a quarter, he ought to win a Group event.
**A P O'Brien in IRE [1-4] Sir Alex Ferguson.*

ZEPPO (IRE) BHB 57f52a **RR 55f 52a** 4412[11]

4 ch g Fayruz 6.6f **(63)** -Chase Paperchase (Malinowski (USA)) 10f **(56)**
Form - 035400010670
Record 1999 - 1st:1 2nd:0 3rd:1 Ran:12
Pre1999 - 1st:1 2nd:2 3rd:0 Ran:13
Win Prizemoney £11,000 *Total Prizemoney* £14,005
Wins * **1999** Aug Chepst (G-F) H 6.1f 56 56
* 1998 Jun Lingfi (G-F) H 6f 60 62 <
1999 Turf 1-11: (5f 2, 6f 1-8, 7f) (gd 2, g-f 4, frm 1-5) 1999 AW 0-1: (6f) (Fibr)
Strong, fair gelding, effective 5 to 6f, best at 5f, acts on gd to hrd, best on g-f, has worn blinkers, excels at Lingfield. Turf high 56 - 3rd of 19 to Dancing Mystery (7 May Lingfield 5f g-f RF 1083) - also 1st of 11 getting 15lb from Hard to Figure (5 Aug Chepstow RF 3391). He is a fair sprint handicapper, but has a moderate wins to runs ratio.
**B R Millman [2-22] The Plyform Syndicate (from M J Heaton-Ellis [0-3] Spt 1997).*

ZESTFUL (USA) **RR 59f** 3869[5]

2 ch f Zilzal (USA) 8.5f **(79)** - Crown of Sheba (USA) **(67f)** (Alysheba (USA)) 9f **(84)**
Form - 65
Record 1999 - 1st:0 2nd:0 3rd:0 Ran:2
1999 Turf 0-2: (5f, 6f) (g-f 2)
Currently fair filly. Turf high 59 (began Jly).
**C F Wall [0-2] Ettore Landi.*

ZESTRIL BHB 81f **RR 77f** 4444[4]

2 ch f Zilzal (USA) 8.5f **(79)** - Rynavey **(60a)** (Rousillon (USA)) 8.2f **(74)**
Form - 104
Record 1999 - 1st:1 2nd:0 3rd:0 Ran:3
Win Prizemoney £3,566 *Total Prizemoney* £3,795
Wins * **1999** Jun Carlis (G-F) 5.9f 76+ <
1999 Turf 1-3: (5f, 6f 1-2) (g-s, frm 1-2)
Currently above-average filly. Turf high 77 - also 1st of 16 from Mrs P (23 Jun Carlisle RF 2221). Ran green and lost ground at the start when winning an ordinary maiden on her debut.
**Denys Smith [1-3] Duke of Sutherland.*

ZEYAARAH (USA) **RR 83f** 5020[9]

2 ch f Rahy (USA) 9.1f **(80)** - Princess Haifa (USA) (Mr Prospector (USA)) 8.8f **(78)**
Form - 30
Record 1999 - 1st:0 2nd:0 3rd:1 Ran:2
Win Prizemoney £0 *Total Prizemoney* £680
1999 Turf 0-2: (8f 2) (gd 2)
Currently decent filly. Turf high 83 (1st run) (began Spt) - 3rd of 11 to Dollar Bird (25 Spt Nottingham 8f gd RF 4559).
**M P Tregoning [0-2] Sheikh Ahmed Al Maktoum.*

ZIBAK (USA) BHB 40f **RR 39f** 4127[21]

5 b br g Capote (USA) 9.1f **(84)** - Minifah (USA) (Nureyev (USA)) 8.7f **(78)**
Form - 0086431133080
Record 1999 - 1st:2 2nd:0 3rd:3 Ran:13
Pre1999 - 1st:0 2nd:1 3rd:0 Ran:11
Win Prizemoney £6,327 *Total Prizemoney* £8,800
Wins * **1999** Jly Thirsk (FRM) SH 6f 36 39 <
* **1999** Jly Ayr (GD) SH 7f 33 36
1999 Turf 2-13: (5f 2, 6f 1-6, 7f 1-3, 8f 2) (gd 1-3, g-f 4, frm 1-6)
Very moderate gelding, effective 6 to 7f, best at 7f, acts on gd to frm, best on g-f, likes tight tracks. Turf high 40 - also 1st of 15 getting 2lb from Bodfari Anna (31 Jly Thirsk RF 3284).
**J S Goldie [2-21] Mrs Lisa Olley (from B J McMath [0-3] Apr 1998).*

ZIBELINE (IRE) BHB 74f **RR 71f** 5099[7]

2 b c Cadeaux Genereux 7.9f **(76)** - Zia (USA) (Shareef Dancer (USA)) 9.9f **(73)**
Form - 5457
Record 1999 - 1st:0 2nd:0 3rd:0 Ran:4
Win Prizemoney £0 *Total Prizemoney* £221
1999 Turf 0-4: (6f, 7f 3) (gd 2, frm 2)
Above-average colt. Turf high 71 (began Jly).
**C E Brittain [0-4] Sheikh Marwan Al Maktoum.*

ZIDAC BHB 65f60a **RR 68?f 60a** 5153[3]

7 b or br g Statoblest 6.4f **(63)** - Sule Skerry (Scottish Rifle) 10f **(55)**
Form - 0210016013
Record 1999 - 1st:3 2nd:1 3rd:1 Ran:9
Pre1999 - 1st:3 2nd:2 3rd:2 Ran:28
Win Prizemoney £16,455 *Total Prizemoney* £21,333
Wins * **1999** Oct Bright (GD) SH 10f 58 68+
* **1999** Jun Bath (GD) C 10.2f 63
* ***1999*** *Feb Lingfi (STD) 10f 62*
* 1998 Spt Warwic (G-F) CH 10.8f 59 63
* 1996 May Lingfi (G-F) H 10f 70 74 <
* 1996 Apr Leices (GD) H 10f 64 72
1999 Turf 2-6: (9f, 10f 2-4, 11f) (gd 1-2, g-f 1-1, frm 3) 1999 AW 1-3: (10f 1-3) (Equi 1-3)
Average gelding, effective 10 to 11f, best at 10f, acts on gd to frm - acts on Equi, favours tight tracks. Turf high 68 - 1st of 19 giving 21lb to Kingfishers Bonnet (21 Oct Brighton RF 4997) - also 1st of 16 getting 8lb from Barrettstown (12 Jun Bath RF 1939). AW high 62 - 1st of 7 giving 3lb to Hawksbill Henry (23 Feb Lingfield RF 0344). Inconsistent. **P J Makin [6-40] Brian Brackpool.*

ZIETZIG (IRE) BHB 82f **RR 82f** 4757[8]

2 b c Zieten (USA) - Missing You (Ahonoora) 8.1f **(73)**
Form - 5851428
Record 1999 - 1st:1 2nd:1 3rd:0 Ran:7
Win Prizemoney £11,283 *Total Prizemoney* £21,113
Wins * **1999** Aug York (GD) S 6f 74 <
1999 Turf 1-7: (5f 3, 6f 1-4) (gd 1-3, frm 4)
Decent colt, effective 6f, acts on gd to frm, best on frm. Turf high 82 - 2nd of 22 giving 5lb to Kilbrannan Sound (10 Spt Doncaster 6f frm RF 4249) - also 1st of 23 from Methodist (18 Aug York RF 3761). Landed a valuable York seller on his fourth start, and is better than a plater. **K R Burke [1-7] Nigel Shields.*

ZIGERE BHB 78f **RR 72f** 3387[1]

3 ch c Lycius (USA) 8.8f **(71)** - Zia (USA) (Shareef Dancer (USA)) 9.9f **(73)**
Form - 42061
Record 1999 - 1st:1 2nd:1 3rd:0 Ran:5
Pre1999 - 1st:0 2nd:0 3rd:0 Ran:1
Win Prizemoney £2,671 *Total Prizemoney* £4,049
Wins * **1999** Aug Bright (G-F) 10f 66+ <
1999 Turf 1-5: (8f 2, 10f 1-3) (sft, g-f 1-1, frm 3)
Scopey, above-average colt, effective 10f, acts on frm. Turf high 83 - 2nd of 6 to Azouz Pasha (22 Jun Lingfield 10f frm RF 2196).
**C E Brittain [1-6] Sheikh Marwan Al Maktoum.*

ZIGGY'S DANCER (USA) BHB 78f75a **RR 81f 75a** 4933[15]
8 b h Ziggy's Boy (USA) 6.1f **(61)** - My Shy Dancer (USA) (Northjet) 10.3f **(74)**
Form - 2275000325223065400
Record 1999 - 1st:0 2nd:3 3rd:2 Ran:17
Pre1999 - 1st:8 2nd:15 3rd:11 Ran:94
Win Prizemoney £39,366 *Total Prizemoney* £111,083
Wins * 1998 *Feb Southw (STD) C 6f 76+*
* 1997 Jun Cheste (G-F) H 5.1f 81 82
* 1995 *Dec Lingfi (STD) H 5f 80 76*
* 1995 Jly Cheste (GD) 5.1f 94 <
* 1995 May Beverl (G-F) 5f 94?
* 1995 Apr Carlis (GD) H 5.9f 64 70+
* 1995 *Mar Wolver (STD) H 6f 66 69*
* 1995 *Feb Wolver (STD) H 7f 50 60+*
1999 Turf 0-14: (5f 11, 6f 3) (g-s 2, gd 5, g-f 5, frm 2) 1999 AW 0-3: (6f 3) (Fibr 3)
Decent horse, effective 5 to 6f, best at 5f, acts on gd to frm, best on gd, likes Chester. Turf high 95 - 3rd of 8 getting 4lb from Tedburrow (10 Jly Chester 5f frm RF 2706). AW high 78. Probably best over five and six furlongs nowadays, he is tough and genuine but difficult to win with.
**E J Alston [8-100] J Connor (from R W Armstrong [0-11] Oct 1994).*

ZIGGY STARDUST (IRE) BHB 36f32a **RR 45df 32a** 4709[4]
4 b g Roi Danzig (USA) 10.5f **(62)** - Si Princess (Coquelin (USA)) 8.4f **(58)**
Form - 06503244
Record 1999 - 1st:0 2nd:1 3rd:1 Ran:8
Pre1999 - 1st:0 2nd:2 3rd:1 Ran:11
Win Prizemoney £0 *Total Prizemoney* £3,117
1999 Turf 0-7: (9f, 10f 3, 12f 3) (hvy, gd 2, g-f 2, frm 2) 1999 AW 0-1: (12f) (Equi)
Unfurnished, moderate gelding, effective 10 to 12f, best at 10f, acts on gd to frm, best on g-f, excels at Windsor, does well at Lingfield. Turf high 45 - 2nd of 16 giving 5lb to Nebl (14 Aug Lingfield 10f g-f RF 3642).
**Mrs A J Bowlby [0-19] Joe Cool Partnership.*

ZIG ZIG (IRE) RR 29f 4634[11]
2 b c Perugino (USA) - Queen of Erin (IRE) (King of Clubs) 7.1f **(57)**
Form - 0
Record 1999 - 1st:0 2nd:0 3rd:0 Ran:1
1999 Turf 0-1: (6f) (gd)
Currently little account colt.
**Mrs A Swinbank [0-1] Miss Betty Duxbury.*

ZILARATOR (USA) BHB 87f **RR 89f** 4893[5]
3 b g Zilzal (USA) 8.5f **(79)** - Allegedly (USA) (Sir Ivor) 10.2f **(70)**
Form - 012U0355
Record 1999 - 1st:1 2nd:1 3rd:1 Ran:8
Win Prizemoney £3,541 *Total Prizemoney* £8,517
Wins * 1999 Apr Leices (HVY) 10f 72+ <
1999 Turf 1-8: (10f 1-1, 12f 3, 13f 2, 15f, 16f) (sft 1-1, gd 5, g-f 2)
Leggy, useful gelding, effective 12 to 15f, acts on gd. Turf high 92 - 2nd of 9 giving 1lb to Turtle Valley (15 May Newbury 12f gd RF 1233). Unraced at two, he bolted up in heavy ground at Leicester on his second start, and just failed to peg back Turtle Valley in a Newbury handicap next time. Fair form in the autumn after a break, but is not an easy ride.
**W J Haggas [1-8] Wentworth Racing (Pty) Ltd.*

ZILVA BHB 50f48a **RR 64f 48a** 343[9]
4 b f Mazilier (USA) 8.5f **(56)** - Thulium (Mansingh (USA)) 7.4f **(55)**
Form - 300
Record 1999 - 1st:0 2nd:0 3rd:0 Ran:1
Pre1999 - 1st:0 2nd:0 3rd:1 Ran:6
Win Prizemoney £0 *Total Prizemoney* £368
1999 AW 0-1: (7f) (Equi)
Workmanlike, average filly. **P J Makin [0-7] T G Warner.*

ZIMIRI BHB 60f59a **RR 45f 59a** 391[6]
5 ch h Keen 11.1f **(58)** - Annabrianna (Night Shift (USA)) 7.2f **(69)**
Form - 057176
Record 1999 - 1st:1 2nd:0 3rd:0 Ran:3
Pre1999 - 1st:2 2nd:1 3rd:1 Ran:14
Win Prizemoney £12,590 *Total Prizemoney* £14,592
Wins * 1999 *Jan Lingfi (STD) C 8f 51*
*** 1998** *May Lingfi (STD) H 8f 74 79* <
*** 1996** *Dec Lingfi (STD) 8f 74*
1999 AW 1-3: (8f 1-3) (Equi 1-3)
Fair colt, effective 8f, - acts on AW, prefers left handed tracks, prefers tight tracks. AW high 51 (1st run). Inconsistent. He has been fairly lightly raced in his career, and his best efforts by far have come over a mile on Equitrack. He is not particularly consistent. **J A R Toller [3-17] Rannerdale, D G & N A Fraser.*

ZINCALO (USA) BHB 65f **RR 49f** 5101[11]
3 gr c Zilzal (USA) 8.5f **(79)** - Silver Glitz (USA) (Grey Dawn II) 11.1f **(72)**
Form - 0224600
Record 1999 - 1st:0 2nd:2 3rd:0 Ran:7
Win Prizemoney £0 *Total Prizemoney* £2,529
1999 Turf 0-7: (10f, 14f 4, 15f, 16f) (g-s 2, gd 2, g-f 3)
Scopey, moderate colt, effective 14f, acts on gd to g-f, has worn blinkers. Turf high 80 - 2nd of 8 giving 5lb to Height of Fantasy (4 Jun Haydock 14f gd RF 1744). **C E Brittain [0-7] C E Brittain.*

ZINDABAD (FR) BHB 112f **RR 112f** 4271[5]
3 b c Shirley Heights 12.1f **(76)** - Miznah (IRE) (Sadler's Wells (USA)) 10f **(76)**
Form - 661115
Record 1999 - 1st:3 2nd:0 3rd:0 Ran:6
Pre1999 - 1st:1 2nd:2 3rd:0 Ran:3
Win Prizemoney £56,190 *Total Prizemoney* £85,065
Wins * 1999 Aug Windso (GD) G3 10f 112 <
*** 1999** Jly Ascot (G-F) H 10f 104 112 <
*** 1999** Jly Newmar (GD) H 10f 100 102
* 1998 Spt Pontef (G-F) 8f 97+
1999 Turf 3-6: (10f 3-5, 12f) (gd 1-2, g-f 2, frm 2-2)
Scopey, Group-class colt, effective 10f, acts on gd to frm, best on frm. Turf high 112 - 1st of 8 giving 3lb to Alabaq (28 Aug Windsor RF 3983) - also 1st of 5 giving 4lb to Vicious Circle (24 Jly Ascot RF 3085). He made great strides through the summer, winning two valuable handicaps and the Group 3 Winter Hill Stakes at Windsor. Forcefully ridden when gaining those victories, he ought to stay at least a mile and a half and remains open to improvement.
**B Hanbury [4-9] Abdullah Ali.*

ZINNIA RR 53f 2537[11]
2 b f Zilzal (USA) 8.5f **(79)** - Ibtihaj (USA)
Form - 0
Record 1999 - 1st:0 2nd:0 3rd:0 Ran:1
1999 Turf 0-1: (6f) (g-f)
Currently fair filly. **J L Dunlop [0-1] Miss K Rausing.*

ZIPPERGATE BHB 65f **RR 63f** 4946[10]
3 b c Mystiko (USA) 7.7f **(59)** - Branitska (Mummy's Pet) 7.7f **(60)**
Form - 3047878000
Record 1999 - 1st:0 2nd:0 3rd:0 Ran:9
Pre1999 - 1st:1 2nd:0 3rd:1 Ran:3
Win Prizemoney £3,655 *Total Prizemoney* £7,803
Wins * 1998 Oct Newmar (G-S) 6f 87 <
1999 Turf 0-9: (6f 4, 7f 2, 8f, 9f, 10f) (g-s, gd 3, g-f 3, frm 2)
Average colt, effective 6f, acts on g-s to g-f, has worn blinkers. Turf high 84. Consistent.
**B W Hills [1-11] W J Gredley (from B A Hill [0-1] Nov 1998).*

ZIRCONI (FR) BHB 80f **RR 82f** 5222[14]
3 b c Zieten (USA) - Muirfield (FR) (Crystal Glitters (USA)) 11.3f **(79)**
Form - 3640
Record 1999 - 1st:0 2nd:0 3rd:1 Ran:4
Pre1999 - 1st:0 2nd:2 3rd:3 Ran:6
Win Prizemoney £0 *Total Prizemoney* £35,948
1999 Turf 0-4: (6f, 7f 2, 8f) (g-s, gd 3)
Decent colt, effective 7f, acts on sft, has worn blinkers. Turf high 82. Becoming disappointing. He has had his problems, but it will be interesting to see if his trainer can work the oracle with him.
**D Nicholls [0-2] P D Savill (from Mme C Head in FR [0-8] Oct 1999).*

ZMILE BHB 80f70a **RR 75f 70a** 1062[6]
3 b c Ezzoud (IRE) - Mountain Bluebird (USA) (Clever Trick (USA)) 6.6f **(77)**
Form - 6

Record 1999 - 1st:0 2nd:0 3rd:0 Ran:1
Pre1999 - 1st:0 2nd:1 3rd:1 Ran:4
Win Prizemoney £0 *Total Prizemoney* £2,157
1999 AW 0-1: (8f) (Fibr)
Neat, above-average colt. (DEAD)
**R Guest [0-1] Zmile Partnership (from B W Hills [0-4] Oct 1998).*

ZOENA BHB 63f58a **RR 63f 58a** 5070[4]
2 ch f Emarati (USA) 6.6f **(63)** - Exotic Forest **(68df)** (Dominion) 8.5f **(63)**
Form - 48374
Record 1999 - 1st:0 2nd:0 3rd:1 Ran:5
Win Prizemoney £0 *Total Prizemoney* £512
1999 Turf 0-5: (5f 2, 6f 3) (gd, g-f 2, frm 2)
Average filly. Turf high 63 (began Aug).
**J G Portman [0-5] Mrs R Pease.*

ZOFFI RR 45f 2572[11]
3 b f Most Welcome 8.6f **(66)** - Highsplasher (USA) (Bucksplasher (USA)) 10.3f **(75)**
Form - 0
Record 1999 - 1st:0 2nd:0 3rd:0 Ran:1
1999 Turf 0-1: (8f) (frm)
Workmanlike, currently moderate filly. **C F Wall [0-1] S Fustok.*

ZOLA (IRE) BHB 40f46a **RR 49f 46a** 4533[8]
3 ch g Indian Ridge 7.6f **(74)** - Fluella (Welsh Pageant) 10f **(65)**
Form - 4347545851442218
Record 1999 - 1st:2 2nd:2 3rd:1 Ran:16
Pre1999 - 1st:0 2nd:0 3rd:0 Ran:4
Win Prizemoney £4,541 *Total Prizemoney* £6,912
Wins * 1999 *Aug Lingfi (STD) H 16f 40 41*
*** 1999** May Yarmou (FRM) C 16f 52 <
1999 Turf 1-8: (12f 3, 14f, 16f 1-3, 17f) (hvy, sft, g-s, gd 2, frm 1-3)
1999 AW 1-8: (10f 2, 11f 2, 12f 2, 16f 1-2) (Equi 1-5, Fibr 3)
Scopey, moderate gelding, effective 10 to 11f, - acts on AW, has worn blinkers, likes left handed tracks, favours tight tracks. Turf high 52. AW high 62 - 3rd of 9 getting 21lb from Palais (8 Jan Southwell 11f Fibr RF 0052). Does not have the ability or speed of his illustrious namesake.
**M Quinn [2-18] M Quinn (from M R Channon [0-2] Spt 1998).*

ZOLA POWER BHB 36f35a **RR 28f 35a** 4713[15]
3 ch f Efisio 7.7f **(69)** - Caroline Connors (Fairy King (USA)) 7.7f **(59)**
Form - 20440070500
Record 1999 - 1st:0 2nd:0 3rd:0 Ran:7
Pre1999 - 1st:0 2nd:2 3rd:1 Ran:13
Win Prizemoney £0 *Total Prizemoney* £2,194
1999 Turf 0-4: (5f 2, 6f, 7f) (gd 2, g-f, frm) 1999 AW 0-3: (5f, 6f, 8f) (Equi, Fibr 2)
Neat, very moderate filly, effective 5f, acts on gd to g-f, has worn blinkers. Turf high 28 (began Jly). AW high 31. Inconsistent.
**B A Pearce [0-8] Martin J Gibbs & Richard J Gray (from G L Moore [0-12] Dec 1998).*

ZOMARADAH BHB 117f **RR 118f** 5228a[3]
4 b f Deploy 11.4f **(67)** - Jawaher (IRE) (Dancing Brave (USA)) 8.4f **(76)**
Form - 811213
Record 1999 - 1st:3 2nd:1 3rd:1 Ran:6
Pre1999 - 1st:3 2nd:0 3rd:0 Ran:6
Win Prizemoney £289,913 *Total Prizemoney* £378,307
Wins * 1999 Spt Capann (GD) G2 10f 113
*** 1999** Aug Currag (GD) G2 10f 118 <
*** 1999** Jun Doncas (G-S) 10.3f 114
* 1998 Oct Woodbi (FRM) 10f 113
* 1998 May San Si (HVY) G1 11f 103+
* 1998 Apr Bright (GD) 10f 66+
1999 Turf 3-6: (10f 3-4, 11f 2) (hvy, g-s, gd 2-2, frm 1-2)
Scopey, high-class filly, effective 10 to 11f, best at 10f, acts on gd to frm, best on frm. Turf high 118 - 3rd of 14 to Soaring Softly (6 Nov Gulfstream Park 11f frm RF 5228a) - also 1st of 9 giving 11lb to Strategic (14 Aug Curragh RF 3718a). Consistent. Winner of the 1998 Oaks d'Italia, she was unplaced in a Sandown Group Three on her reappearance last term, but went on to gain victories in a conditions event at Doncaster, the Group Two Royal Whip at the Curragh and a Group Two in Italy. She ended the campaign with a fine third in the new Breeders' Cup Fillies and Mares Turf at Gulfstream Park. **L M Cumani [6-12].*

ZONING BHB 100f **RR 91f** 5029[4]
2 b c Warning 8.1f **(77)** - Zonda (Fabulous Dancer (USA)) 9.4f **(70)**
Form - 5114
Record 1999 - 1st:2 2nd:0 3rd:0 Ran:4
Win Prizemoney £12,079 *Total Prizemoney* £13,826
Wins * 1999 Oct York (G-S) 7f 91 <
*** 1999** Aug Yarmou (GD) 6f 87+
1999 Turf 2-4: (6f 1-2, 7f 1-2) (g-s, gd 2-2, frm)
Useful colt. Turf high 91 (began Jly) - 4th of 9 to Umistim (22 Oct Newbury 7f g-s RF 5029) - also 1st of 6 from Al Towd (7 Oct York RF 4760). Fifth to Invincible Spirit on his debut, he went on to win a maiden over six furlongs at Yarmouth and followed up with a battling victory over a furlong further at York. Lost little in defeat in a Group Three on his final start.
**J H M Gosden [2-4] Mohammed Al Nabouda.*

ZOOM UP (IRE) BHB 68f **RR 67f** 3581[3]
5 ch g Bluebird (USA) 7.9f **(71)** - Senane (Vitiges (FR)) 8.2f **(59)**
Form - 635133
Record 1999 - 1st:1 2nd:0 3rd:3 Ran:6
Pre1999 - 1st:1 2nd:1 3rd:1 Ran:16
Win Prizemoney £8,088 *Total Prizemoney* £14,750
Wins * 1999 Jun Beverl (SFT) H 7.5f 61 65
1997 May Warwic (GD) 8f 82 <
1999 Turf 1-5: (7f 1-4, 8f) (g-s 1-1, gd, g-f, frm 2) 1999 AW 0-1: (7f) (Fibr)
Average gelding, effective 7 to 10f, best at 7f, acts on g-s to frm, often wears blinkers (extremely effectively), likes tight tracks. Turf high 67 - 3rd of 14 getting 7lb from Premier Baron (12 Aug Sandown 7f g-f RF 3581) - also 1st of 16 giving 5lb to Three For A Pound (9 Jun Beverley RF 1851).
**N A Graham [1-6] T H Chadney (from M J Heaton-Ellis [1-16] Oct 1998).*

ZORBA BHB 58f39a **RR 63f 39a** 2375[12]
5 b g Shareef Dancer (USA) 10.1f **(67)** - Zabelina (USA) (Diesis) 9.3f **(69)**
Form - 000
Record 1999 - 1st:0 2nd:0 3rd:0 Ran:3
Pre1999 - 1st:5 2nd:6 3rd:9 Ran:37
Win Prizemoney £13,428 *Total Prizemoney* £22,889
Wins 1998 *May Southw (STD) C 11f 54*
1998 Mar Hamilt (HVY) C 9.2f 47
1997 Oct Ayr (SFT) H 9f 60 64
1997 Jun Redcar (GD) C 10f 69 <
1997 Jun Hamilt (GD) S 9.2f 64
1999 AW 0-3: (9f, 11f, 12f) (Fibr 3)
Average gelding, effective 10 to 11f, acts on sft - acts on Fibr, has worn blinkers. AW high 28. Becoming disappointing.
**J G M O'Shea [0-16] The Cross Racing Club (from J Hetherton [3-21] May 1998).*

ZORRO BHB 52f50a **RR 51f 50a** 4948[5]
5 gr g Touch of Grey 8.1f **(47)** - Snow Huntress (Shirley Heights) 10.3f **(74)**
Form - 5
Record 1999 - 1st:0 2nd:0 3rd:0 Ran:1
Pre1999 - 1st:1 2nd:3 3rd:2 Ran:16
Win Prizemoney £2,168 *Total Prizemoney* £5,392
Wins 1997 Jun Yarmou (FRM) H 10.1f 51 57 <
1999 Turf 0-1: (11f) (g-f)
Fair gelding, effective 10 to 12f, acts on g-f - acts on Equi. (1st run) - 5th of 15 giving 5lb to In The Stocks (19 Oct Lingfield 11f g-f RF 4948).
**J R Poulton [0-1] Mrs G M Temmerman (from R M Flower [1-16] May 1998).*

ZSARABAK BHB 58f **RR 64f** 4080[14]
2 br g Soviet Lad (USA) 9.4f **(63)** - Moorefield Girl (IRE) (Gorytus (USA)) 7.8f **(60)**
Form - 6060
Record 1999 - 1st:0 2nd:0 3rd:0 Ran:4
1999 Turf 0-4: (6f, 7f 2, 8f) (gd, g-f, frm 2)
Average gelding. Turf high 64. **B S Rothwell [0-4] C D Carr.*

ZUCCHERO RR 76f 3233[6]
3 br g Dilum (USA) 7.1f **(56)** - Legal Sound (Legal Eagle) 7.3f **(54)**

Form - 011126

Record	1999 -	1st:3	2nd:1	3rd:0	Ran:6
	Pre1999 -	1st:0	2nd:0	3rd:0	Ran:3

Win Prizemoney £10,683 *Total Prizemoney* £12,913

Wins	* 1999	Jly	Newmar	(G-F)	H	7f	65	73+	<
	* 1999	Jly	Lingfi	(G-F)	H	7f	53	66	
	* 1999	Jly	Chepst	(G-F)	H	6.1f	53	68	

1999 Turf 3-6: (6f 1-1, 7f 2-4, 8f) (gd, g-f, frm 3-4)

Leggy, above-average gelding, effective 6 to 7f, best at 7f, acts on gd to frm, best on frm, often wears blinkers (extremely effectively). Turf high 76 - 2nd of 18 getting 15lb from Mister Rambo (24 Jly Ascot 7f gd RF 3089) - also 1st of 11 getting 3lb from Most-Saucy (17 Jly Newmarket RF 2907). Was transformed by the application of blinkers, and completed a hat-trick in a fortnight before being touched off by a whisker in the valuable ladies' race at Ascot.

**D W P Arbuthnot [3-9] Philip Banfield.*

ZUHAIR BHB 86f80a **RR 88f 80a** 4392[12]

6 ch g Mujtahid (USA) 7.4f **(69)** - Ghzaalh (USA) (Northern Dancer) 9.6f **(80)**

Form - 07642017411801000

Record	1999 -	1st:4	2nd:1	3rd:0	Ran:17
	Pre1999 -	1st:2	2nd:4	3rd:3	Ran:30

Win Prizemoney £52,599 *Total Prizemoney* £67,247

Wins	* 1999	Aug	York	(GD)	H	6f	83	88	<
	* 1999	Jly	Goodwo	(G-F)	H	6f	72	83	
	* 1999	Jly	Goodwo	(G-F)	H	5f	72	74	
	* 1999	Jun	Lingfi	(G-F)	H	5f	66	71	
	1997	*May*	*Wolver*	*(STD)*	*C*	*6f*		*66*	
	1995	Jun	Newmar	(G-F)		6f		85+	

1999 Turf 4-17: (5f 2-8, 6f 2-9) (gd 9, g-f 2-2, frm 1-4, hrd 1-2)

Useful gelding, effective 6f, acts on gd to g-f, best on g-f, has worn blinkers, excels at Goodwood. Turf high 88 - 1st of 23 giving 10lb to Mallia (17 Aug York RF 3697) - also 1st of 18 giving 14lb to Dancing Mystery (30 Jly Goodwood RF 3237). One of David Nicholls' strong team of sprinters, he was on a long losing run before winning at Lingfield in June, but went on to score twice in three days at Glorious Goodwood over five and six furlongs on fast ground, and added a hot York handicap. Off the boil since, he is suited by coming from behind off a strong pace.

**D Nicholls [4-17] The Gardening Partnership (from D McCain [1-27] Oct 1998).*

Zuhair streaked home twice at Glorious Goodwood

ZULAL (USA) BHB 74f **RR 78df** 4689[17]

3 ch c Zilzal (USA) 8.5f **(79)** - My Shafy (Rousillon (USA)) 8.2f **(74)**

Form - 41013050

Record	1999 -	1st:2	2nd:0	3rd:1	Ran:8
	Pre1999 -	1st:0	2nd:0	3rd:0	Ran:3

Win Prizemoney £10,345 *Total Prizemoney* £12,100

Wins	* 1999	Jun	Pontef	(GD)	H	10f	74	78	<
	* 1999	Apr	Beverl	(G-F)	H	7.5f	70	73	

1999 Turf 2-8: (7f 1-2, 8f 2, 10f 1-2, 12f 2) (gd 2, g-f 1-2, frm 1-4)

Strong, above-average colt, effective 7 to 10f, best at 10f, acts on g-f to frm, best on frm, has worn blinkers. Turf high 78 - 3rd of 6 getting 9lb from Night Venture (26 Jun Newcastle 10f frm RF 2338) - also 1st of 11 giving 4lb to Dansker (14 Jun Pontefract RF 1985). Becoming disappointing. **E A L Dunlop [2-11] Hilal Salem.*

ZULU DAWN (USA) **RR 80f** 4874[4]

3 b c El Gran Senor (USA) 8.9f **(85)** - Celtic Loot (USA) (Irish River (FR)) 8.6f **(78)**

Form - 2438164

Record	1999 -	1st:1	2nd:1	3rd:1	Ran:7
	Pre1999 -	1st:0	2nd:0	3rd:0	Ran:1

Win Prizemoney £5,572 *Total Prizemoney* £9,265

Wins	* 1999	Spt	Newbur	(G-F)	8f		80	<

1999 Turf 1-7: (7f, 8f 1-6) (gd 3, g-f 2, frm 1-2)

Scopey, decent colt, effective 7 to 8f, best at 8f, acts on gd to frm, has worn blinkers. Turf high 83 (1st run) - 2nd of 4 to Lake Sunbeam (23 Jun Salisbury 7f g-f RF 2248) - also 1st of 19 from Torch Song (17 Spt Newbury RF 4382). Consistent. Put his racecourse experience to good use when causing a bit of a surprise in a maiden at Newbury in September. He has not shown much in handicap company. **J W Hills [1-8] The Jampot Partnership.*

ZURS (IRE) BHB 68f75a **RR 72df 75a** 4646[9]

6 b g Tirol 8.1f **(64)** - Needy (High Top) 10.2f **(67)**

Form - 2604010700

Record	1999 -	1st:1	2nd:1	3rd:0	Ran:10
	Pre1999 -	1st:5	2nd:3	3rd:9	Ran:40

Win Prizemoney £18,354 *Total Prizemoney* £34,880

Wins	* 1999	May	Sandow	(GD)	H	10f	68	72	<
	* 1998	Spt	Salisb	(HVY)	H	9.9f	67	67	
	* 1998	Aug	Sandow	(G-F)	H	8.1f	64	66	
	* 1997	Spt	Folkes	(FRM)	H	6.9f	52	65	
	* 1997	Spt	Leices	(G-F)		8f		58	
	1997	*Feb*	*Lingfi*	*(STD)*		*8f*		*56+*	

1999 Turf 1-10: (8f 2, 9f 2, 10f 1-6) (g-s 4, g-f 3, frm 1-3)

Above-average gelding, effective 8 to 10f, best at 10f, acts on sft to frm, has worn blinkers, excels at Sandown and Salisbury. Turf high 75 (1st run) - 2nd of 17 getting 4lb from Bomb Alaska (26 Mar Doncaster 8f g-s RF 0479) - also 1st of 19 giving 5lb to Mutadarra (31 May Sandown RF 1617). Becoming disappointing.

**J R Poulton [5-36] Mrs M Liston (from Miss Gay Kelleway [1-16] Aug 1997).*

ZYGO (USA) BHB 52f48a **RR 54f 48a** 1179[5]

7 b g Diesis 9f **(80)** - La Papagena (Habitat) 9.4f **(70)**

Form - 6655

Record	1999 -	1st:0	2nd:0	3rd:0	Ran:3
	Pre1999 -	1st:0	2nd:2	3rd:1	Ran:15

Win Prizemoney £0 *Total Prizemoney* £3,487

1999 Turf 0-2: (7f, 10f) (g-f, hrd) 1999 AW 0-1: (10f) (Equi)

Fair gelding, effective 7f, acts on g-f, likes left handed tracks, likes tight tracks. Turf high 54 - 5th of 18 giving 4lb to Mysticism (12 May Brighton 7f g-f RF 1179).

**R T Phillips [0-12] The Beechdowners (from W Jarvis [0-7] Aug 1996).*

ZYZ BHB 100f **RR 93f** 5029[3]

2 b c Unfuwain (USA) 11.4f **(74)** - Girette (USA) (General Assembly (USA)) 10f **(68)**

Form - 213

Record	1999 -	1st:1	2nd:1	3rd:1	Ran:3

Win Prizemoney £4,272 *Total Prizemoney* £9,607

Wins	* 1999	Spt	Leices	(FRM)	7f		79	<

1999 Turf 1-3: (7f 1-3) (g-s, gd, frm 1-1)

Currently useful colt. Turf high 93 (began Aug) - 3rd of 9 to Umistim (22 Oct Newbury 7f g-s RF 5029). Ran into Port Vila on his Kempton debut, and got off the mark at Leicester next time despite looking as if he was feeling the very fast ground. Edged left when finishing third in a Group Three on his final run, and has more improvement in him. **B W Hills [1-3] W J Gredley.*

NOW YOU CAN BET IF YOU HAVE ...

OR

... WINNINGS ARE PAID STRAIGHT INTO YOUR BANK ACCOUNT

SEE OUR HORSE RACING PRICES ON TELETEXT PAGES:

SkySports: 364/367/368
in play betting 389

7 DAYS A WEEK
TELEBETTING FREEPHONE

0500 341134

Betting on live sport can seriously increase your heart rate

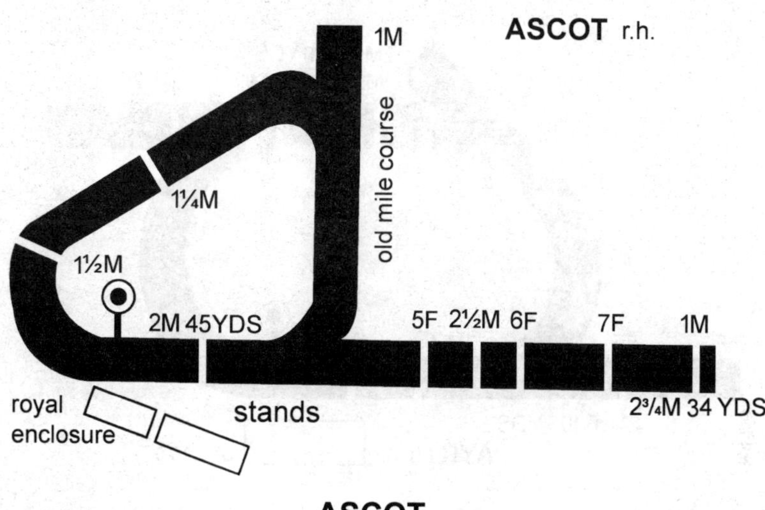

ASCOT

Address: Ascot Racecourse, Ascot, Berkshire SL5 7JN Tel: (01344) 622211 **Fax:** (01344) 624978
E-mail: AscotatITL.Net **Internet:** http://www.sportinglife.co.uk/ascot/
A triangular course of 1m 6f 34y. The course goes downhill from the mile and a half start for three furlongs into Swinley Bottom (the lowest part of the track): it soon joins the Old Mile (which starts on a chute) and is then uphill with a straight run-in of two and a half furlongs, the last 100y being level. The straight mile (Royal Hunt Cup Course) is downhill from the start, rises to the five furlong gate and then falls slightly to the junction of the courses. The whole course is of a galloping nature with easy turns but is nevertheless a testing one, especially on soft going.
Clerk of the Course: Mr N. Cheyne, Ascot Racecourse, Ascot, Berkshire SL5 7JN. Tel: (01344) 874567.
Racecourse Manager: Mr D. Erskine-Crum
Going Reports: (01344) 874567/ (0585) 505407 (Mobile)
Free stabling: shavings, straw or paper Tel: 01344 25630
By Car: West of the town on the A329. Easy access from the M3 (Junc 3) and the M4 (Junc 6). Car parking adjoining the course and Ascot Heath. Contact the Secretary, Ascot Authority. Tel: (01344) 876456.
By Rail: Regular service from Waterloo to Ascot (500y from the racecourse).
By Air: Helicopter landing facility at the course. London (Heathrow) Airport 15 miles, White Waltam Airfield 12 miles.

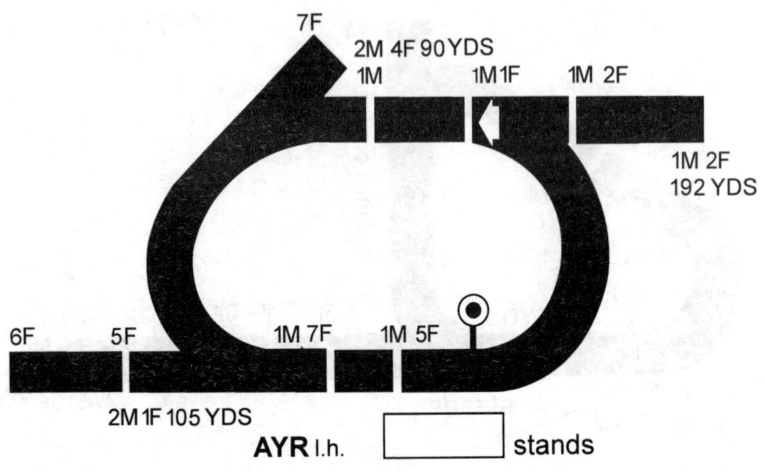

AYR

Address: Ayr Racecourse, Whitletts Road, Ayr KA8 0JE Tel: (01292) 264179 **Fax:** (01292) 610140
Internet: www.ayr-racecourse.com
A wide, relatively flat oval track of just over 1m 4f. An extension to the back straight provides a 1m 3f course with a sweeping turn at the top of the track tojoin the straight course four furlongs from the winning post. The straight six furlongs falls slightly for some three and a half furlongs and then rises slightly. In general, this is a very fair galloping course.
Clerk of the Course and Manager: Mr Mark Kershaw, Racecourse Office, 2 Whitletts Road, Ayr. Tel: (01292) 264179. Mobile: (0850) 464258.
Free stabling and accommodation for lads and lasses. Tel: (01292) 264179.
By Car: East of the town on the A758. Free parking for buses and cars.
By Rail: Ayr Station (trains on the half hour from Glasgow Central). Journey time 55 minutes. Buses and taxis also to the course.
By Air: Prestwick International Airport (10 minutes by car). Glasgow Airport (1hour).

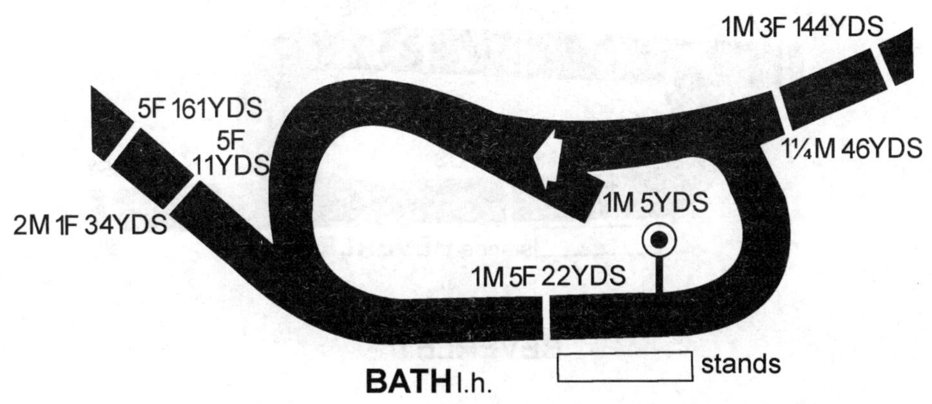

BATH

Address: The Racecourse, Lansdown, Bath Tel: Office (01291) 622260 Racedays (01225) 424609

An oval track of 1m 4f 25y with 1m 3f 144y, 1m 2f 46y and 1m 5y starts set on chutes from the back straight and an uphill run-in of four furlongs, which bends to the left. There is no straight course but an extension provides for races of five furlongs and of 5f 167y, which run generally uphill and left-handed to a distinct left-handed curve about a furlong from the winning post.

Clerk of the Course: Mr R. D. Farrant, Tylers Farm, Gravel Hill Road, Yate, Bristol BS37 7BN. Tel: (01454) 313186 Mobile (0850) 888380

Secretary: Miss S.J. Wilcox, Hopkins Farm, Lower Tysoe, Warwick, CV35 0BN Tel/Fax: (01295) 688030

Free stabling and accommodation for lads and lasses. Tel: (01225) 444274

By Car: 2 miles North-West of the City (M4 Junc 18) at Lansdown. Unlimited free car and coach parking space immediately behind the stands. Special bus services operate from Bath to the racecourse.

By Rail: Bath Station (from Paddington), regular bus service from Bath to the course (3 miles).

By Air: Bristol or Colerne Airports. (no landing facilities at the course).

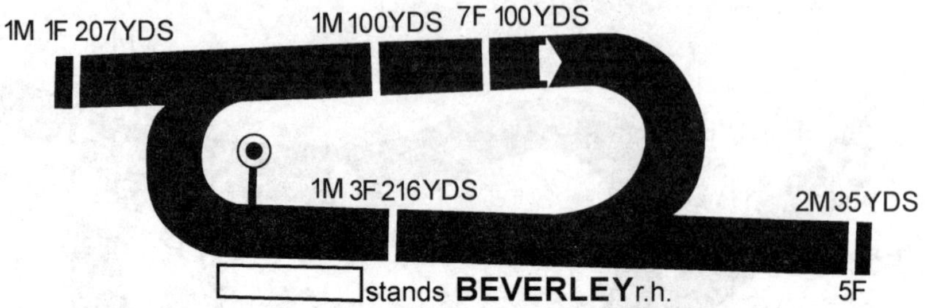

BEVERLEY

Address: Beverley Race Co. Ltd, York Road, Beverley, E.Yorkshire HU17 9QZ
Tel: (01482) 867488/882645 **Fax:** (01482) 863892
An oval course of 1m 3f set on two levels. A chute to the back straight provides a mile and a quarter course, which has a straight run of some five furlongs to a steep downhill bend into the home turn and an uphill run-in of two and a half furlongs. The five furlong course, which rises throughout with a distinct jink after a furlong and a slight bend to the right at halfway, provides a severe test for juveniles at the start of the season. The downhill turn into the straight and the short run-in prevent this from being an entirely galloping track.
Racecourse Manager: Sally Iggulden, The Racecourse, York Road, Beverley, E.Yorkshire. Tel: (01482) 867488/882645 (Course Office).
Clerk of the Course: Mr J.M.Hutchinson. (01765) 602156, Mobile (0860) 679904).
Free stabling. Tel: (01482) 867488 or 882645
By Car: 7 miles from the M62 (Junc 38) off the A1035. Free car parking opposite the course. Owners and Trainers use a separate enclosure.
By Rail: Beverley Station (Hull-Scarborough line). Occasional bus service to the course (1 mile).
By Air: Helicopter landings by prior arrangement. Light aircraft landing facilities at Linley Hill, Leven airport.

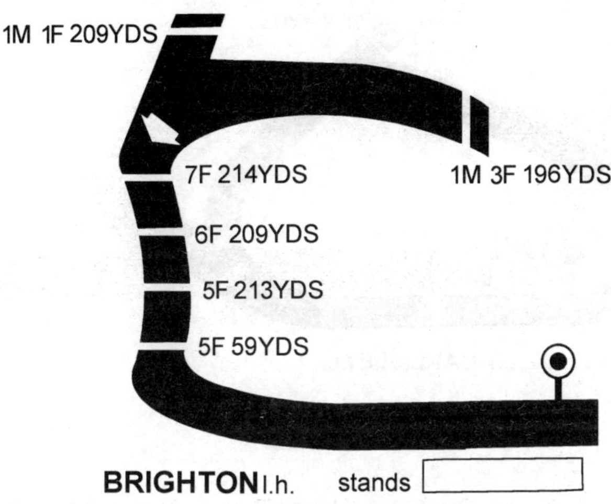

BRIGHTON

Address: Brighton Racecourse, Freshfield Road, Brighton, Sussex BN2 2XZ
Tel: (01273) 603580 **Fax:** (01273) 673267 **E-mail:** 1016111.141@compuserve.com
The course forms a horseshoe of 1m 4f round with easy turns and a run-in of three and a half furlongs. The first three furlongs are slightly uphill. Then there is a gentle descent and rise to about four furlongs from home. From there the ground falls steeply until about two furlongs out; then a sharp rise with the last 100y level. This sharp track, reminiscent of Epsom with its pronounced gradients, is unsuitable for big, long-striding animals, but it suits sharp sorts and is something of a specialists' course.
Clerk of the Course: Mr Jeremy Martin Tel. (0411) 739103 (mobile)
Stabling and accommodation available on request. Tel: (01273) 682912
By Car: East of the town on the A27 (Lewes Road). There is a car park adjoining the course.
By Rail: Brighton Station (from Victoria on the hour, London Bridge or Portsmouth). Special bus service to the course from the station (approx 2 miles) and to the sea front.
By Air: No racecourse facilities.

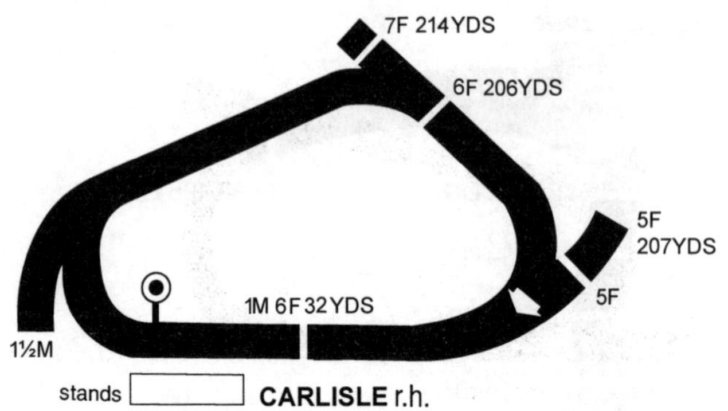

CARLISLE

Address: Carlisle Racecourse, Durdar Road, Carlisle CA2 4TS
Tel: (01228) 522973 **Fax:** Office (01228) 591827 Weighing room (01228) 523751
A pear-shaped, undulating course of 1m 5f with an extension for a mile and a half start and a straight uphill run-in of three and a half furlongs. The six furlong course (which includes the five furlong) starts on a chute, bears right for the first furlong and a half and again at the turn into the straight. The rise to the winning post, although it begins to level out from `the distance', makes it a stiff test of stamina.
Clerk of the Course: Mr J. E. Fenwicke-Clennell Tel: (01228) 522504 Mobile: (0860) 737729.
General Manager: I. R. Duff Esq, Grandstand Office, Carlisle Racecourse, Durdar Road, Carlisle, Cumbria CA2 4TS. Tel: (01228) 522973 Fax: (01228) 591827.
Club Secretary: Mrs Ann Bliss, Brackenridge, Brackenthwaite, Wigton, Cumbria, CA7 8AS. Tel: (01228) 522973.
Stabling and accommodation available on request. Please Please phone Head Groundsman on (01228) 546188, or Stable Office on (01228) 549489 by 5pm day before racing.
By Car: 2 miles south of the town (Durdar Road). Easy access from the M6 (Junc 42). The car park is free (adjacent to the course). Trackside car parking £3 (except Saturdays & Bank Holidays £5).
By Rail: Carlisle Station (2 miles from the course).
By Air: Helicopter landing facility by prior arrangement.

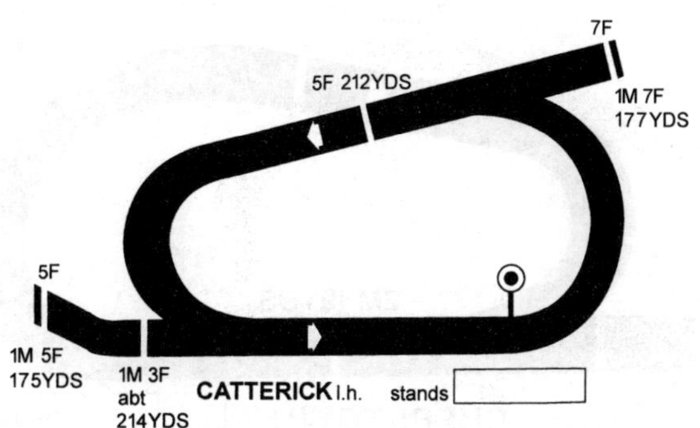

CATTERICK

Address: The Racecourse, Catterick Bridge, Richmond, North Yorkshire DL10 7PE Tel: (01748) 811478 **Fax:** (01748) 811082
An oval, undulating course of 1m 180y with two chutes, one for seven furlong and another for five furlong starts, and a straight run-in of three furlongs. The five furlong course is downhill throughout, sharply at first, and jinks left-handed at the junction of the courses. The seven furlong track joins the round course at the six furlong gate and is slightly downhill to the home turn. This sharp track is entirely unsuitable for long-striding gallopers and is often a specialists' track for both horse and jockey.
Clerk of the Course: (Flat) Mr James Sanderson, c/o The Racecourse, Catterick Bridge, Richmond, North Yorkshire DL10 7PE Tel: Mobile (0850) 058019
Secretary: International Racecourse Management Ltd., c/o The Racecourse, Catterick Bridge, Richmond, North Yorkshire DL10 7PE. Tel: (01748) 811478. Fax: (01748) 811082.
Boxes are allotted on arrival. Contact Mr Adrian Swingler, Racecourse Lodge, Catterick. Tel: (01748) 811478.
By Car: The course is adjacent to the A1, 1 mile North-West of the town on the A6136. There is a free car park.
By Rail: Darlington Station (special buses to course - 14 mile journey).

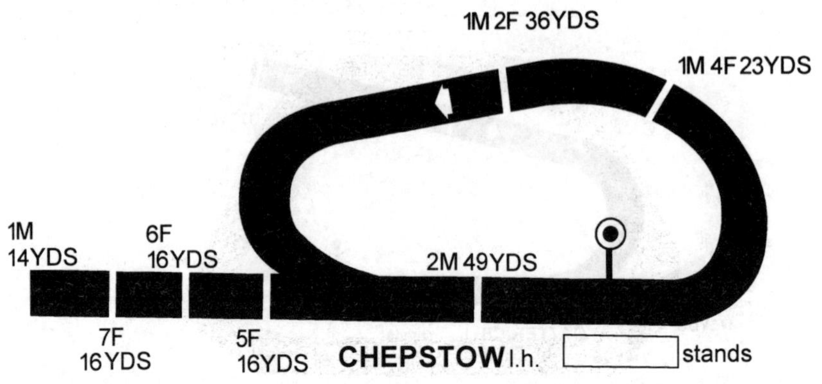

CHEPSTOW

Address: Chepstow Racecourse, Chepstow, Gwent NP6 5YH Tel: (01291) 622260 **Fax:** (01291) 625550

An oval, undulating course, about 2m in circumference with a straight run-in of five furlongs, which extends to make a straight mile. All races of up to a mile are run on the latter, which is downhill to the five furlong start and then rises sharply for two and a half furlongs before levelling out to the winning post. The changing gradients prevent this from being a really galloping track.

Clerk of the Course and Manager: Mr R. Farrant, Tylers Farm, Gravel Hill Road, Yate, nr Bristol BS37 7BN. Tel: Office (01291) 622260 Home (01454) 313186 Mobile (0850) 888380

Managing Director: Mr G. C. Francis, 17 Welsh Street, Chepstow, Gwent NP6 5YH.

Stabling: 109 boxes, allotted on arrival. Limited accommodation for lads and lasses. Apply: (01291) 623414.

By Car: 1 mile North-West of the town on the A466. (1 mile from Junc 22 of the M4 (Severn Bridge)). There is a Free public car park opposite the Stands entrance.

By Rail: Chepstow Station (from Paddington, change at Gloucester or Newport). The course is 1 mile from station.

By Air: Helicopter landing facility in the centre of the course.

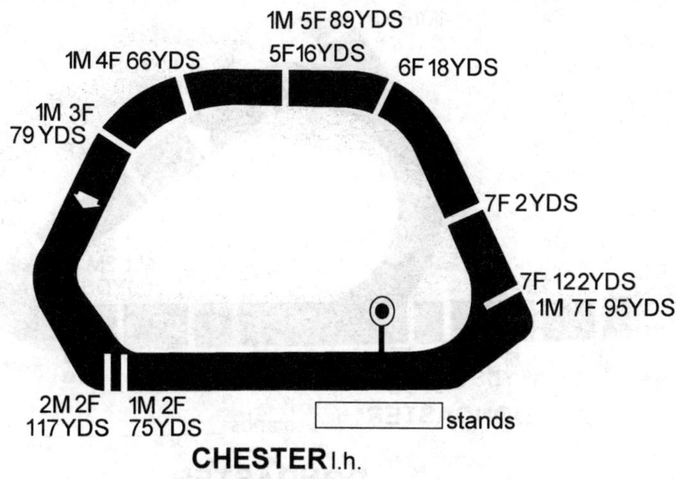

CHESTER

Address: The Racecourse, Chester CH1 2LY Tel: (01244) 323170
Fax: (01244) 344971
A perfectly flat, circular course, 1m 73y in circumference, with a sharp bend to a straight run-in of 230y. Long distance events are an extreme test of stamina, but for middle-distance races and sprints, the course greatly favours a sharp-actioned horse. Horses with previous winning form on this track are worthy of note.
Clerk of the Course: Mr C. H. Barnett, Aintree Racecourse, Aintree, Liverpool L9 5AS. Tel: (0151) 523 2600 or (01244) 323170 (racedays).
Racecourse Manager: Mr R. Walls Tel. (01244) 327171
Secretaries: Messrs Kidsons Impey, Steam Mill, Chester. CH3 5AN Tel: (01244) 327171.
Free stabling (175 boxes) and accommodation.
By Car: The course is near the centre of the city on the A548 (Queensferry Road). The Owners and Trainers car park is adjacent to the County Stand. There is a public car park in the centre of the course.
By Rail: Chester Station (3/4 mile from the course). Services from Euston, Paddington and Northgate.
By Air: Hawarden Airport (2 miles).

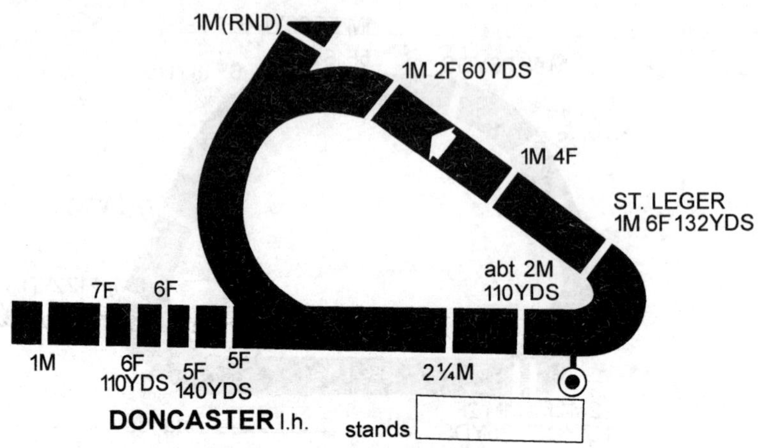

DONCASTER

Address: Doncaster Racecourse, Grand Stand, Leger Way, Doncaster DN2 6BB
Tel: (01302) 320066 **Fax:** (01302) 323271 **E-mail:** info@britishracing.com
Internet: www.britishracing.com
A pear-shaped track, about 1m 7f 110y in circumference with a distinct rise and fall to the mile marker. There is a level run-in of four and a half furlongs, extending to a straight mile, which tapers from a width of 88ft at the five-furlong pole to 60ft at the winning post. A round mile joins the straight course at a tangent. This good galloping track is suitable for strongly-built stayers and calls for stamina and courage.
Chief Executive & Clerk of Course (Flat): Mr J. Sanderson, International Racecourse Management Ltd., Grandstand, Leger Way, Doncaster DN2 6BB. Tel: (01302) 320066. Fax: Office (01673) 843434
Free stabling and accommodation Tel: (01302) 349337
By Car: East of the town, off the A638 (M18 Junc 3 & 4). Club members car park reserved. Large public car park free and adjacent to the course. **By Rail:** Doncaster Central Station (from King's Cross). Special bus service from the station (1 mile).

By Air: Helicopter landing facility by prior arrangement only.

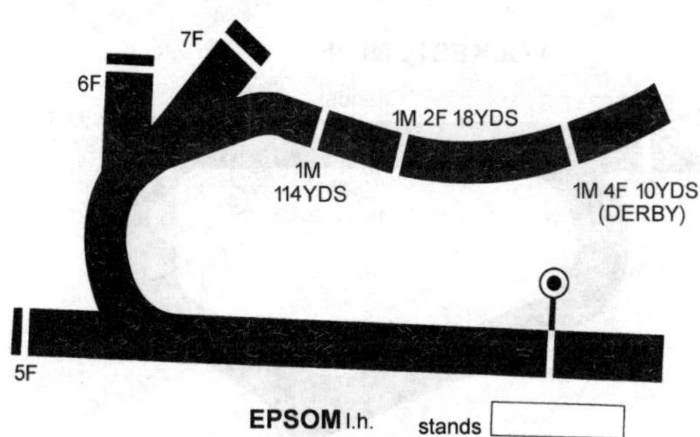

EPSOM

Address: United Racecourses Ltd., The Racecourse, Epsom Downs, Surrey KT18 5LQ Tel: (01372) 726311 **Fax:** (01372) 748253

From the Derby start at the top of the Downs, the course climbs steadily for the first gently-bending four furlongs, then levels out for nearly two furlongs before falling sharply round the bend to Tattenham Corner and into the straight. This is of less than four furlongs and ends with a fairish rise of just over a furlong to the winning post. The City and Suburban course and the Epsom Mile are, respectively, the last 1m 2f 15y and the last 1m 110y of the Derby course. The five furlong course (Egmont Course) is perfectly straight and, running sharply downhill to the junction with the round course, is the fastest in the world. The Derby course is a unique test for the thoroughbred, the frequently fast early pace demanding stamina, and the bends and gradients calling for a faultless action. Well-balanced, medium-sized, handy sorts seem to do best over five furlongs.

Clerk of the Course: Mr A. J. Cooper, The Grandstand, Epsom Downs, Surrey KT18 5LQ. Tel: (01372) 726311, Mobile (0374) 230850

General Manager: Mr Stephen Wallis Tel. (01372) 463072

Free stabling and accommodation Tel: (01372) 725794

By Car: 2 miles South of the town on the B290 (M25 Junc 8 & 9). For full car park particulars apply to: The Club Secretary, The Racecourse, Epsom Downs, Surrey KT18 5LQ. Tel: (01372) 726311.

By Rail: Epsom, Epsom Downs or Tattenham Corner Stations (trains from London Bridge, Waterloo, Victoria). Regular bus services run to the course from Epsom and Morden Underground Station.

By Air: London (Heathrow) and London (Gatwick) are both within 20 miles of the course. Heliport (Derby Meeting only) apply to Hascombe Aviation Tel: (01279) 680291.

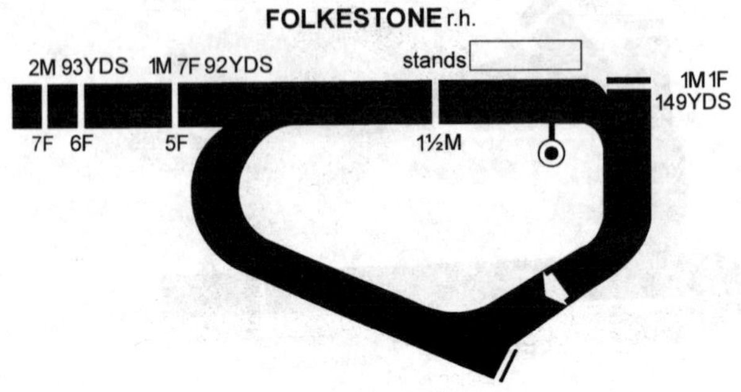

FOLKESTONE

Address: Folkestone Racecourse, Westenhanger, Hythe, Kent CT21 4HX

Tel: (01303) 266407 **Fax:** (01303) 260185 **E-mail:** 1016111.141@compuserve.com

A circuit of 1m 3f, somewhat undulating, with a straight run-in of two and a half furlongs. Five and six furlong races start on an extension which joins the round course about three furlongs from the line and has a slight rise over the final furlong. Despite its gentle turns and its width, Folkestone can not be described as a galloping track.

Director of Racing: Mr G. R. Stickels, Lingfield Park (1991) Ltd., Lingfield, Surrey RH7 6PQ. Tel: (01342) 834800 Home (01303) 873114 Mobile (0973) 737006 or (01303) 266407 (racedays).

Clerk of the Course: Mr P. D. Deacon, Lingfield Park 1991 Ltd., Lingfield, Surrey.

Stabling: 84 boxes allotted in rotation. Advance notice required for overnight accommodation, before 12 noon on the day prior to racing Tel: 01303 268449

By Car: 6 miles West of town at Westenhanger. Easy access from Junc 11 of the M20. Car park adjoins stands. (Free, except course enclosure £4).

By Rail: Westenhanger Station adjoins course. Trains from Charing Cross.

By Air: Helicopter landing facility by prior arrangement.

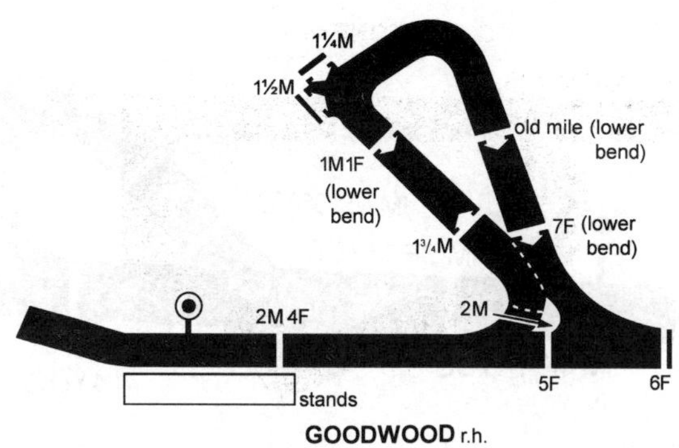

GOODWOOD

Address: Goodwood Racecourse Ltd., Goodwood, Chichester, West Sussex PO18 0PX Tel: (01243) 755022 **Fax:** (01243) 755025
Internet: http://www.demon.co.uk/racenews/goodwood
Set on the edge of the Downs, a straight six furlongs with a triangular loop on one side provides a variety of courses with the possibility of re-entering just above or below the five furlong gate. The Cup Course of about two and a half miles starts on a chute adjacent to the five furlong track and, running the reverse way of the course, turns left after about four furlongs and returns to the straight five furlong run-in by the top bend. The Stakes Course is the last 2m 3f, the Bentinck Course the last 1m 6f and the Gratwicke Course the last 1m 4f of the Cup Course. The Craven Course is 1m 2f, starting in almost the same spot as the Gratwicke Course but running in the reverse direction and returning to the five furlong run-in by the top bend. The Old Mile and seven furlong courses start on the Cup Course and join the five furlong course on the lower bend. The five and six furlong (Stewards' Cup) courses are perfectly straight, the first furlong of the latter being uphill and then slightly undulating to the finish. The sharp bends and downhill gradients suit the handy, well-balanced, neat-actioned sort over middle-distances and are against the big, long-striding horse.
Clerk of the Course and General Manager: Mr R. N. Fabricius, Goodwood Racecourse Limited, Chichester, Sussex. Tel: (01243) 755021 or (0374) 100223
Free stabling and accommodation for runners (110 well equipped boxes at Goodwood House). Subsidised canteen and recreational facilities.Tel: (01243) 774157 or 774107
By Car: 6 miles North of Chichester between the A286 & A285. There is a car park adjacent to the course. Ample free car and coach parking.
By Rail: Chichester Station (from Victoria or London Bridge). Regular bus service to the course (6 miles).
By Air: Helicopter landing facility by prior arrangement with Stephenson Aviation. Tel: (01243) 779222. Goodwood Airport 2 miles (taxi to the course).

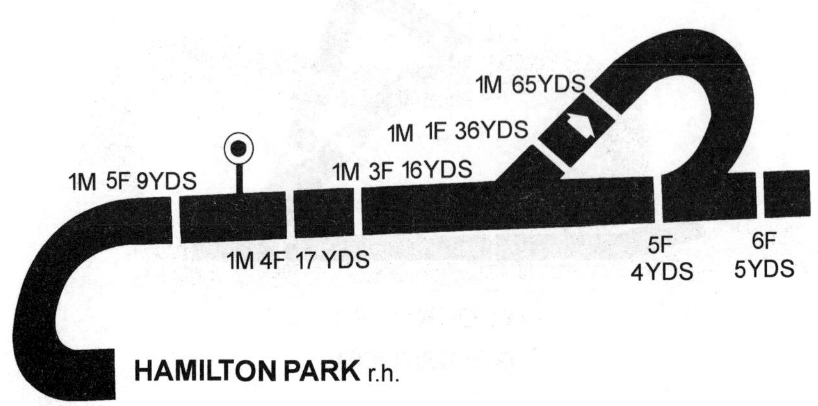

HAMILTON

Address: Hamilton Park Racecourse, Bothwell Road, Hamilton, Lanarkshire ML3 0DW Tel: (01698) 283806 **Fax:** (01698) 286621

A straight six furlongs with a pear-shaped loop course of 1m 5f from a start in front of the stands and a run-in of five and a half furlongs. The turns are easy on the loop. The track is undulating with a dip (which can be very testing in wet weather) about three furlongs out and then rises to level out for the last 150y. A course where judgement and experience can make a considerable difference. Races are usually run at a true gallop here and form can be relied upon.

Clerk of the Course: Mr W. G. Farnsworth, The Racecourse, Bothwell Road, Hamilton ML3 0DW Tel: (01698) 283806 Mobile (0410) 536134

Chief Executive: Miss H. Dudgeon, The Racecourse, Bothwell Road, Hamilton ML3 0DW. Tel: (01698) 283806. Fax: (01698) 286621.

Going details Tel: (0850) 609037 Head Groundsman.

Free stabling (120 boxes) and accommodation on request. Tel: (01698) 284892.

By Car: Off the A74 on the B7071 (Hamilton-Bothwell road). (M74 Junc 5). Free parking for cars and buses.

By Rail: Hamilton West Station (1 mile).

By Air: Glasgow Airport (20 miles).

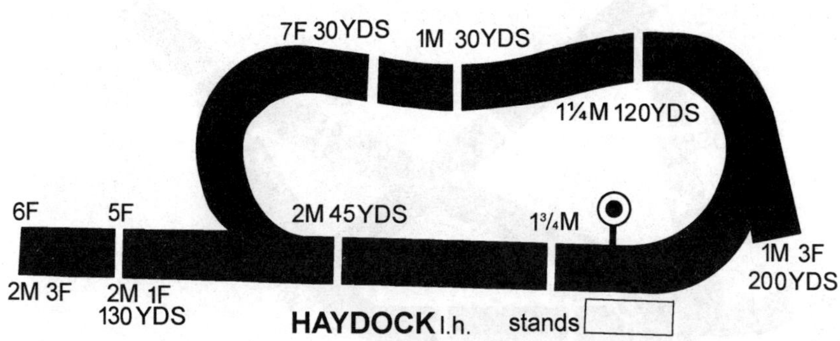

HAYDOCK

Address: Haydock Park Racecourse, Newton-le-Willows, Merseyside WA12 0HQ
Tel: (01942) 725963 **Fax:** (01942) 270879
An almost flat, oval track, 1m 5f round, with a run-in of four and a half furlongs and a straight six furlong course. The 1m 4f gate is set on a short chute. This course, which is of a galloping nature, suits the long-striding horse. On rain-affected turf, the going down the stands' rail in the straight is often faster and horses have often won races by being brought over to that side.
Clerk of the Course: Major P. W. F. Arkwright, Shirley Farm, Little Wolford, Shipston-on-Stour, Warwickshire. Tel: (01608) 684460.
Managing Director: Mr R. G. Thomas, Haydock Park Racecourse, Newton-le-Willows, Merseyside WA12 0HQ. Tel: (01942) 725963.
Applications to be made to the Racecourse for stabling (140 boxes) and accommodation for lads/girls.
By Car: The course is on the A49 near Junc 23 of the M6.
By Rail: Newton-le-Willows Station (Manchester-Liverpool line) is 21/2 miles from the course. Earlstown 3 miles from the course. Warrington Bank Quay and Wigan are on the London to Carlisle/ Glasgow line.
By Air: Landing facilities in the centre of the course for helicopters and planes not exceeding 10,000lbs laden weight. Apply to the Sales Office

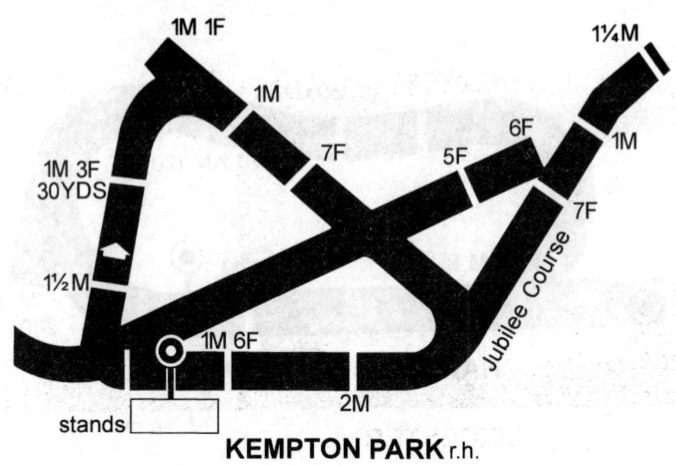

KEMPTON

Address: Kempton Park Racecourse, Sunbury-on-Thames, Middlesex TW16 5AQ Tel: (01932) 782292 **Fax:** (01932) 782044
Raceday Fax: (01932) 779525
Internet: http://www.demon.co.uk/.racenews/rht
A 1m 5f triangular course with a three and a half furlong straight run-in. The 1m 2f Jubilee Course starts on an extension to the round course and sprint races are run over a separate diagonal course. Kempton is a perfectly flat track which can not be described as either sharp or galloping.
Clerk of the Course: Mr A. J. Cooper, Kempton Park, Sunbury-on-Thames. Tel: (01932) 782292.
General Manager: Mr J. M. Thick, Kempton Park, Sunbury-on-Thames. Tel: (01932) 782292.
Stabling allocated on arrival (99 boxes). Prior booking required for overnight stay
Tel: (01932) 783334
By Car: On the A308 near Junc 1 of the M3. Main car park £2, Silver Ring and centre car park free.
By Rail: Kempton Park Station (from Waterloo).
By Air: London (Heathrow) Airport 6 miles.

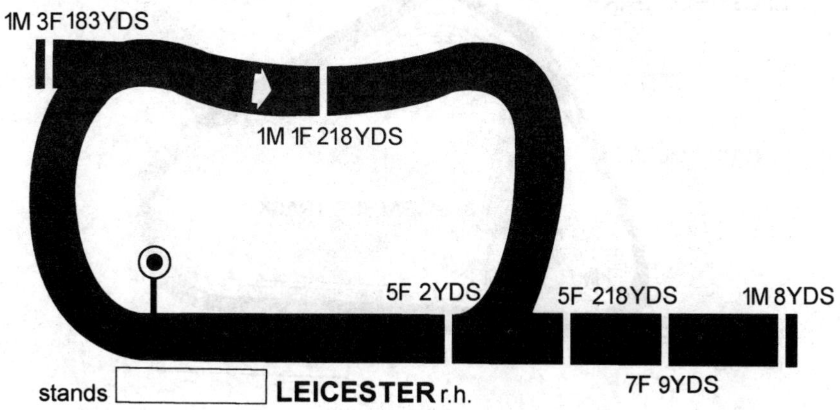

LEICESTER

Address: Leicester Racecourse, Oadby, Leicester LE2 3QH Tel: (01162) 2716515

An oval track of approximately 1m 5f with a straight run-in of five furlongs. Races of a mile and less are run on a dead straight course which joins the round course five furlongs from the finish, the first half being downhill, followed by an ascent gradually levelling off to the winning post. The bends into the straight and after the winning post have been cambered to make a more galloping track.

Clerk of the Course: Captain N. E. S. Lees, Westfield House, The Links, Newmarket, Suffolk CB8 0TG. Tel: (01162) 2716515 Newmarket (01638) 663482 or Home (01284) 386651.

Manager: Mr D. C. Henson, Leicester Racecourse Co. Ltd., The Racecourse, Leicester. Tel: (0116) 2716515 or (01604) 30757.

Going details Tel: (01374) 497281 Head Groundsman

109 boxes allocated on arrival. Accommodation for one attendant per horse only Tel: (01162) 712115 Canteen opens at 7.30a.m.

By Car: The course is 21/2 miles South-East of the City on the A6 (M1, Junc 21). The car park is free.

By Rail: Leicester Station (from St Pancras) is 21/2 miles.

By Air: Helicopter landing facility in the centre of the course.

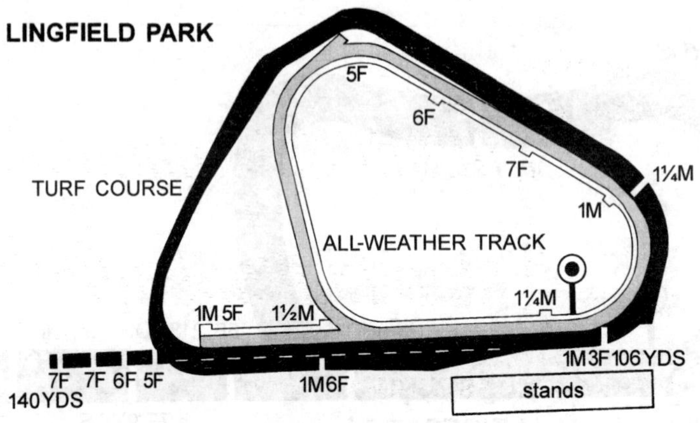

LINGFIELD

Address: Lingfield Park Racecourse, Lingfield, Surrey RH7 6PQ
Tel: (01342) 834800 **Fax:** (01342) 832833 **E-mail:** 1016111.141@compuserve.com

A 7f 140y straight course with a downhill gradient for about five furlongs, a slight rise and then a gradual fall to the winning post. The round turf course joins the straight at the four furlong post and then follows round the outside of the All-Weather tracks to the summit of a slight hill before turning downhill into the straight. The Derby Trial Course (1m 3f 106y) is very similar to the Epsom Derby Course and provides a good test for the Classic. The re-alignment of the turf course to accomodate the All-Weather tracks has made the turn out of the back straight much less pronounced. However, most of the characteristics remain. The Equitrack course favours the keen, free-running, sharp-actioned horse, particularly so in sprints, which are run on the turn.

Director of Racing: Mr G. R. Stickels, Lingfield Park Racecourse, Surrey RH7 6PQ (01342) 834800 Mobile (0973) 737006.

Clerks of the Course: Mr P. D. Deacon & Mr F. I. W. Cameron (address as above),

180 boxes available. For details of accommodation apply to the Manager, Mr W. Sutton (01342) 834800. Advance notice for overnight accommodation required before 12 noon on the day before racing.

By Car: South-East of the town off the A22 (M25 Junc 6). Ample free parking. Reserved car park £3.

By Rail: Lingfield Station (regular services from London Bridge and Victoria). 1/2m walk to the course.

By Air: London (Gatwick) Airport 10 miles. Helicopter landing facility south of wind-sock.

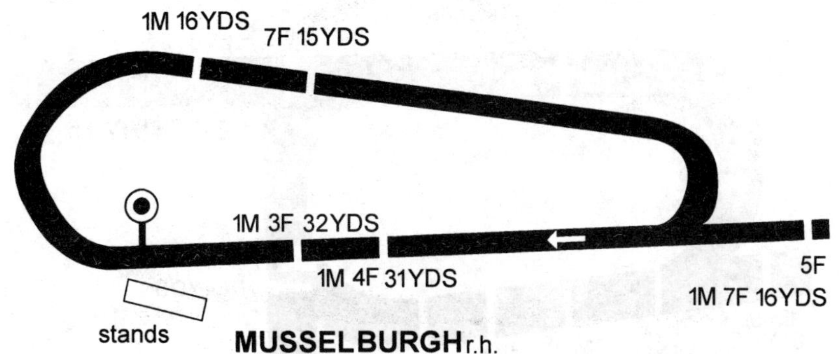

MUSSELBURGH

Address: Musselburgh Racecourse, Linkfield Road, Musselburgh, East Lothian Tel: (0131) 665 2859 Racecourse (01292) 264179 **Fax:** (0131) 653 2083

An oval of 1m 2f, with sharp bends and a straight, slightly undulating run-in of four furlongs. An extension provides a five furlong course, which bears slightly left and makes a distinct right-hand inclination after a furlong. Musselburgh is virtually flat but, with the turns being very sharp, handiness and manoeuvrability are at a premium.

Clerk of the Course & Manager: Mr M. Kershaw, Racecourse Office, 2 Whitletts Road, Ayr. Tel: Office (01292) 264179 Racedays (0131) 6652859 Mobile (0850) 464258 Fax: (01292) 610140.

Free stabling Tel: (0131) 665 4955. Report to the main Security Office at Goose Green Stables. Accommodation for one night in B & B provided.

By Car: Musselburgh, 5 miles East of Edinburgh on the A1. Car park adjoining course, free for buses and cars.

By Rail: Waverley Station (Edinburgh). Local Rail service to Musselburgh.

By Air: Edinburgh (Turnhouse) Airport 30 minutes by car.

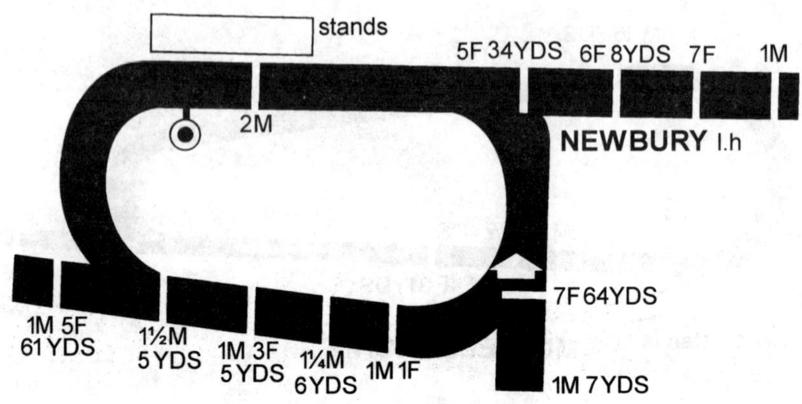

NEWBURY

Address: The Racecourse, Newbury, Berkshire RG14 7NZ
Tel: (01635) 40015 or 550354 **Fax:** (01635) 528354
Internet: http://www.raceweb.com/newbury **E-mail:** newbury@raceweb.com

An oval track of about 1m 7f, 80 feet wide with a slightly undulating straight mile. The round mile and 7f 60y starts are set on a chute from the round course and both join the straight about five furlongs from the finish. Newbury is a good, galloping track, which is efficiently watered during dry periods.

Clerk of the Course: R. N. J. Pridham, 109 Greenham Road, Newbury, Berkshire RG14 7JE. Tel: (01635) 49511 or Racecourse Office (01635) 40015.

Chief Executive, Secretary and Club Secretary: Major General J. D. G. Pank, C.B. Tel: (01635) 40015.

Free stabling (127 boxes) and accommodation for lads and lasses.

By Car: East of the town off the A34 (M4, Junc 12 or 13). Car park, adjoining enclosures, free, except Southmead £2

By Rail: Newbury Racecourse Station, adjoins course.

By Air: Light Aircraft landing strip East/West. 830 metres by 30 metres wide. Helicopter landing facilities.

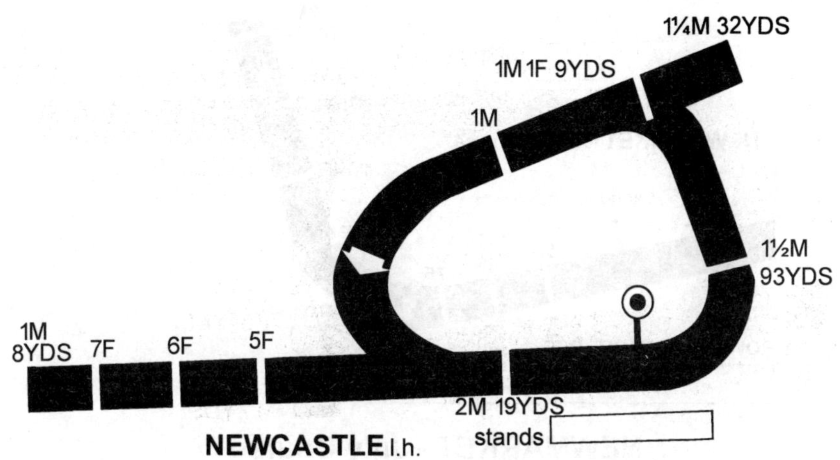

NEWCASTLE

Address: High Gosforth Park, Newcastle-Upon-Tyne NE3 5HP Tel: (0191) 236 2020 **Fax:** (0191) 236 7761

An oval course of 1m 6f with a chute to provide a 1m 2f start and a straight run-in of four furlongs, gradually rising until levelling off in the final 100y. The run-in extends to allow a straight mile, which is against the collar all the way. Newcastle is a galloping track with the final climb making it a test of stamina and is not one for short runners.

Clerk of the Course: David McAllister c/o High Gosforth Park Ltd, High Gosforth Park, Newcastle-upon-Tyne. NE3 5HP. Tel: (0191) 236 2020 Mobile (0860) 286003.

Chairman: Mr S. W. Clarke C.B.E. Tel. (0191) 2362020

Free stabling (120 boxes). It is essential to book accommodation in advance. Apply to the Manager. Tel: (0191) 217 0060 the day before racing, or the Racecourse Office otherwise.

By Car: 4 miles North of the city on the A6125 (near the A1). Car and coach park free.

By Rail: Newcastle Central Station (from King's Cross), a free bus service operates from South Gosforth and Regent Centre Metro Station.

By Air: Helicopter landing facility by prior arrangement. The Airport is 4 miles from the course.

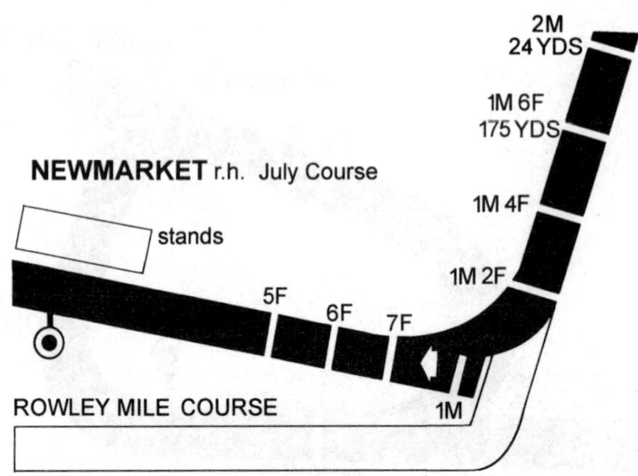

NEWMARKET - July Course

Address: Newmarket Racecourse, Newmarket, Suffolk CB8 0TG
Tel: Main Office (01638) 663482 Rowley (01638) 662524 July (01638) 662752
Fax: (01638) 663044
(July Course) - All races up to a mile inclusive are run on the straight Bunbury Mile, which has a steadily increasing downhill gradient after two furlongs, the final furlong being uphill. Races further than a mile start on the Cesarewitch course and turn right into the straight mile. Like the Rowley Mile course, this is a wide, galloping track.
Clerk of the Course: Captain N. E. S. Lees, Westfield House, The Links, Newmarket. Tel: (01638) 663482 or (01284) 386651 (home).
Manager: Mr C. R. Kennedy Tel: (01638) 663482
100 boxes and free accommodation available at the Links Stables Tel: (01638) 662200
By Car: South-West of the town on the A1304 London Road (M11 Junc 9). Free car parking at the rear of the enclosure. Members car park £1 all days; Free courtesy bus service from Newmarket Station, Bus Station and High Street, commencing 90 minutes prior to the first race, and return trips up to 60 minutes after the last race.
By Rail: Infrequent rail service to Newmarket Station from Cambridge (Liverpool Street) or direct bus service from Cambridge (13 mile journey).
By Air: Landing facilities for light aircraft and helicopters on racedays at both racecourses. See Flight Guide. Cambridge Airport 11 miles.

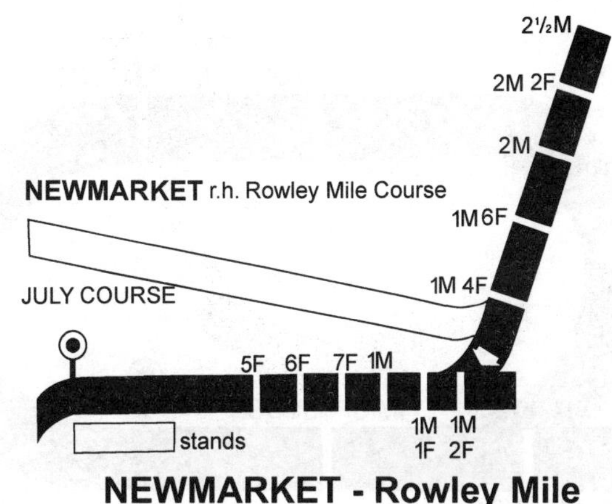

NEWMARKET - Rowley Mile

Address: Newmarket Racecourse, Newmarket, Suffolk CB8 0TG
Tel: Main Office (01638) 663482 Rowley (01638) 662524 July (01638) 662752
Fax: (01638) 663044
(Rowley Mile Course) - There is a straight course of ten furlongs with slight undulations as far as 'The Bushes', about two furlongs from the finish. From that point it is downhill for a furlong to 'The Dip', the final furlong being uphill. The Cesarewitch course starts on the Beacon Course, which turns right into the straight. The ten furlong straight is a wide, galloping track ideal for long-striding horses.
Clerk of the Course: Captain N. E. S. Lees, Westfield House, The Links, Newmarket. Tel: (01638) 663482 or (01284) 386651 (home).
Manager: Mr C.R. Kennedy Tel: (01638) 663482.
100 boxes and free accommodation available at the Links Stables Tel: (01638) 662200
By Car: South-West of the town on the A1304 London Road (M11 Junc 9). Free car parking at the rear of the enclosure. Members car park £1 all days; Free courtesy bus service from Newmarket Station, Bus Station and High Street, commencing 90 minutes prior to the first race, and return trips up to 60 minutes after the last race.
By Rail: Infrequent rail service to Newmarket Station from Cambridge (Liverpool Street) or direct bus service from Cambridge (13 mile journey).
By Air: Landing facilities for light aircraft and helicopters on racedays at both racecourses. See Flight Guide. Cambridge Airport 11 miles.

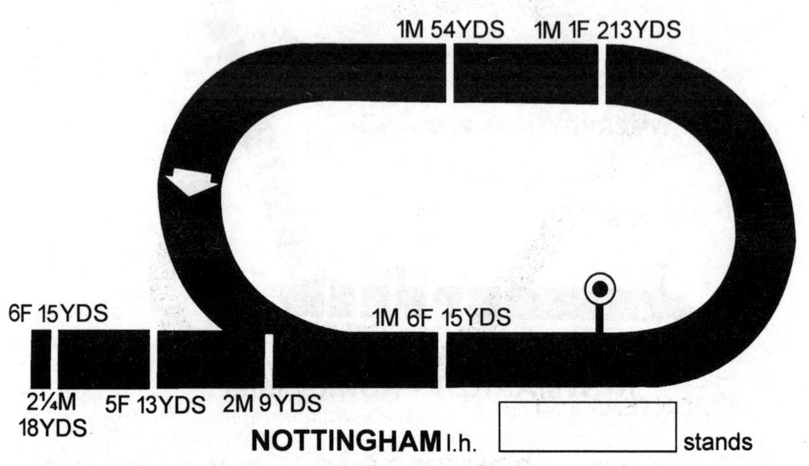

NOTTINGHAM

Address: Nottingham Racecourse, Colwick Park, Nottingham NG2 4BE
Tel: (0115) 958 0620 **Fax:** (0115) 958 4515
A galloping oval track with a straight run-in of about five furlongs, from which a chute provides a straight six furlongs. The turns on this flat course are easy.
Clerk of the Course: Major C. Moore, Hamilton House, Toft-next-Newton, Market Rasen, Lincolnshire LN8 3NE. Tel: (01673) 843434 (office) (01673) 878575 (home).
Manager: Mrs Jan Lloyd, The Racecourse Office, Colwick Park, Nottingham NG2 4BE Tel: (0115) 958 0620
Free stabling. 120 boxes allotted on arrival. New hostel for lads and lasses Tel: (0115) 950 1198
By Car: 2 miles East of the City on the B686. The car park is free.
Silver Ring Picnic Car Park £12 (admits car and four occupants).
By Rail: Nottingham (Midland) Station. Regular bus service to course (2 miles).
By Air: Helicopter landing facility in the centre of the course.

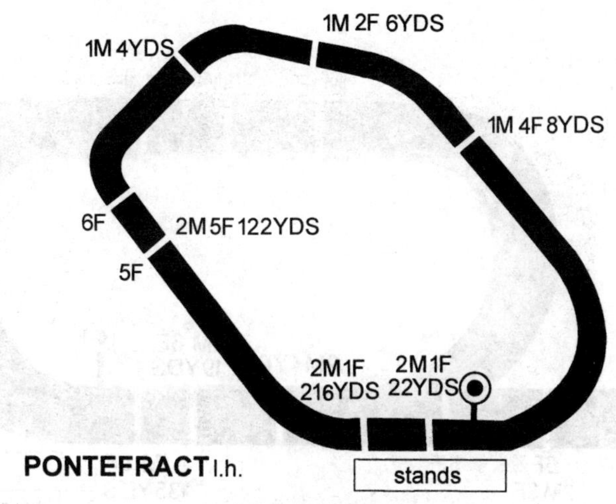

PONTEFRACT

Address: Pontefract Park Race Co. Ltd., The Park, Pontefract, West Yorkshire
Tel: Admin Office (01977) 703224 Racedays (01977) 702210
Fax: Admin Office (01977) 600577 Racedays (01977) 702210
An oval, undulating course of 2m 133y with two sharp bends and a straight run-in of only two furlongs. There is a steep ascent over the last three furlongs. The undulations make it unsuitable for a long-striding horse, although a degree of stamina is called for. There have been a number of course specialists at Pontefract.
Clerk of the Course and Secretary: Mr J. N. Gundill, 33 Ropergate, Pontefract, West Yorkshire. WF8 1LE Tel: Office (01977) 703224 Home (01977) 620649 Racedays (01977) 702210.
116 boxes available. Stabling and accommodation must be reserved. They will be allocated on a first come-first served basis. Tel: (01977 702323)
By Car: 1 mile North of the town on the A639. Junc 32 of M62. Free car park adjacent to the course.
By Rail: Pontefract Station (Baghill), 11/2 miles from the course. Regular bus service from Leeds.
By Air: Helicopters by arrangement only. (Nearest airfield: Doncaster, Sherburn-in-Elmet, Yeadon (Leeds/Bradford).

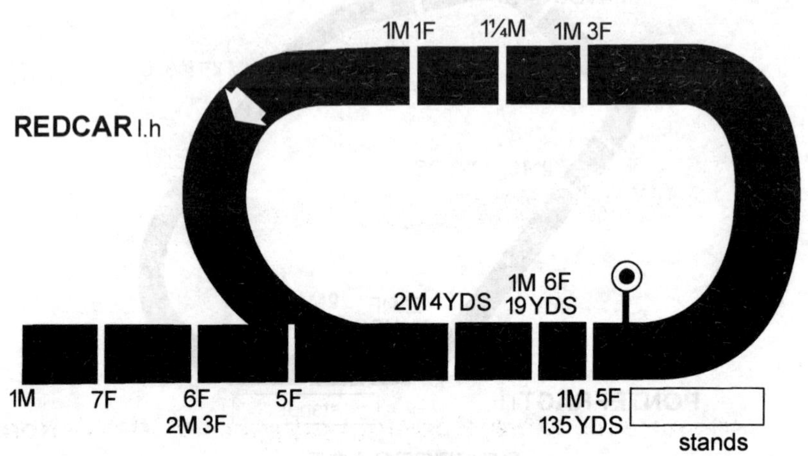

REDCAR

Address: Redcar Racecourse, Redcar, Cleveland TS10 2BY Tel: (01642) 484068 **Fax:** (01642) 488272

A perfectly flat, narrow, oval course of two miles with a straight run-in of five furlongs, which extends backwards to make a straight mile.

Despite two very tight bends into and out of the back straight, Redcar is an excellent galloping course.

Clerk of the Course & General Manager: Mr J. Gundill, Racecourse Office, The Racecourse, Redcar, Cleveland TS10 2BY. Tel: (01642) 484068 or (01482) 867488 Mobile (0370) 613049.

Groundsman: Mr J. Berry, The Racecourse, Redcar, Cleveland. Tel: (01642) 489861 Stables Tel: (on racedays only) (01642) 484254.

By Car: In town off the A1085. Free parking adjoining the course for buses and cars.

By Rail: Redcar Station (1/4 mile from the course).

By Air: Landing facilities at Turners Arms Farm (600y runway) Yearby, Cleveland. 2 miles South of the racecourse - transport available. Teeside airport (18 miles west of Redcar).

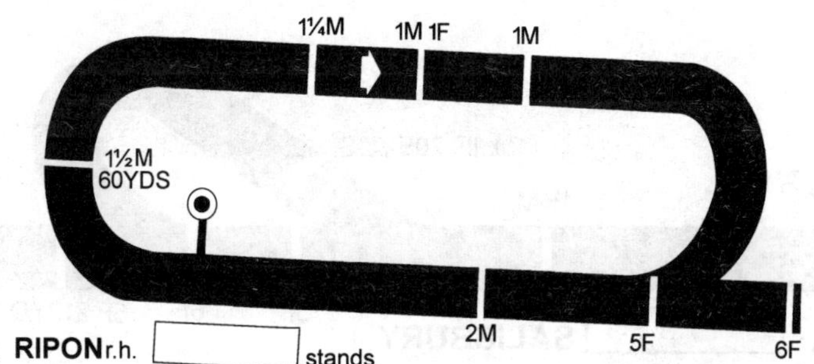

RIPON

Address: Ripon Racecourse, Boroughbridge Road, Ripon, North Yorkshire
HG4 3UG Tel: (01765) 602156 **Fax:** (01765) 690018
E-mail: mail@hutchbuch.demon.co.uk
An oval course of 1m 5f, joined to a straight six furlongs by a tightish bend at the five furlong point. The straight course is slightly on the ascent except for a shallow dip at the 'distance' and, in general, this is a rather sharp track, a course where experience can be decisive.
Clerk of the Course: Mr J. M. Hutchinson, 77 North Street, Ripon HG4 1DS. Tel: (01765) 602156 Evenings (01845) 567378 Mobile (0860) 679904.
Non-racedays: Admin Office, 77, North Street, Ripon HG4 1DS. Tel: (01765) 602156. Fax (01765) 690018. Racedays: The Racecourse, Boroughbridge Road, Ripon HG4 3UG. Tel: (01765) 603696.
Trainers requiring stabling (104 boxes available) are requested to contact Mr P. Bateson, The Racecourse, Ripon prior to 11a.m. the day before racing. Tel: (01765) 603696.
By Car: The course is situated 2 miles South-East of the city, on the B6265. There is ample free parking for cars and coaches. For reservations apply to the Secretary.
By Rail: Harrogate Station (11 miles), or Thirsk (15 miles). Bus services to Ripon.
By Air: Helicopters only on the course. Otherwise Leeds/Bradford airport.

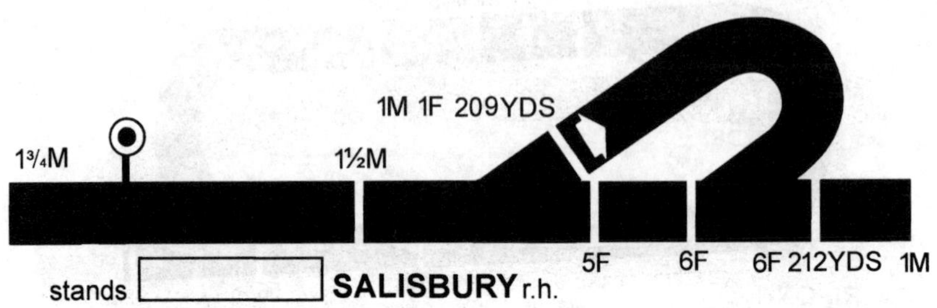

SALISBURY

Address: Salisbury Racecourse, Netherhampton, Salisbury, Wiltshire SP2 8PN
Tel: (01722) 326461 **Fax:** (01722) 412710
The course consists of a loop with an arm of about four furlongs for the finish of all races. Contests of up to a mile are almost straight except for a slight right-hand bend at halfway. On the 1m 6f course, horses start opposite the stands, turn to the left around the loop and re-enter the straight at the seven furlong starting gate. The last half-mile is uphill, providing a stiff test of stamina.
Clerk of the Course: Mr R. I. Renton, Salisbury Racecourse, Netherhampton, Salisbury, Wiltshire SP2 8PN. Tel: (01722) 326461 Mobile (0836) 784543.
Secretary: The Bibury Club, Salisbury Racecourse, Netherhampton, Salisbury, Wiltshire. Tel: (01722) 326461.
Free stabling (112 boxes) and accommodation for lads and lasses, apply to the Stabling Manager Tel: (01722) 327327.
By Car: 3 miles South-West of the city on the A3094 at Netherhampton. Free car park adjoins the course.
By Rail: Salisbury Station is 31/2 miles (from Waterloo). Bus service to the course.
By Air: Helicopter landing facility near the ten furlong start.

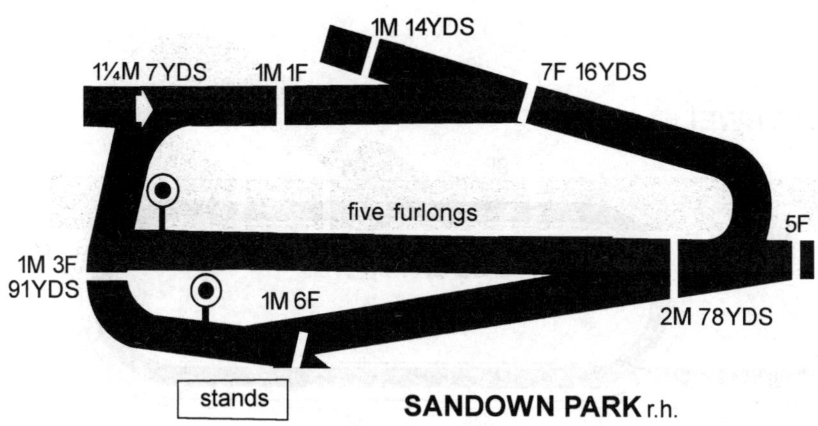

SANDOWN

Address: Sandown Park Racecourse, Esher, Surrey KT10 9AJ
Tel: (01372) 463072 **Fax:** (01372) 470427
An oval course of 1m 5f with a straight run-in of four furlongs. The ground is almost level until entering the straight, where it rises to the winning post. Five furlong contests are run on a separate straight course which cuts diagonally across the inside of the main circuit and is uphill all the way. The track suits long-striding horses and is a real test of stamina.
Clerk of the Course: Mr A. J. Cooper, Sandown Park, Esher, Surrey. Tel: (01372) 463072 Mobile (0374) 230850.
Managing Director: Mrs S. C. Ellen (address & tel as above).
Going Line Tel: (01372) 461212
108 boxes available. Free stabling and accommodation for lads and lasses Tel: (01372) 463511.
By Car: 4 miles South-West of Kingston-on-Thames, on the A307 (M25 Junc 10). The members' car park in More Lane £2. All other car parking is free.
By Rail: Esher Station (from Waterloo) adjoins the course.
By Air: London (Heathrow) Airport 12 miles.

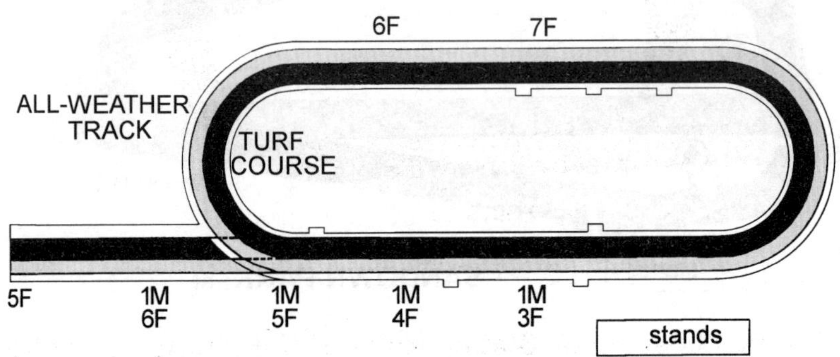

SOUTHWELL

Address: Southwell Racecourse, Rolleston, Newark, Nottinghamshire NG25 0TS
Tel: (01636) 814481 **Fax:** (01636) 812271
The All-Weather Fibresand track consists of an oval circuit, 1m 2f in circumference, with a three furlong straight and a spur to provide a five furlong straight All-Weather track. The turf tracks are on the inside of the All-Weather track. A sharp, flat circuit, Southwell suits the keen, front-running sort.
Clerk of the Course: Mr M. Prosser, Wolverhampton Racecourse Tel. (01902) 421421, Mobile (07971) 531162, Fax (01902) 421621
Going details Tel: (0468) 053391 Head Groundsman
110 boxes at the course. Applications for staff and horse accommodation to be booked by noon the day before racing on (01636) 814481
By Car: The course is situated at Rolleston, 3 miles South of Southwell, 5 miles from Newark.
By Rail: Rolleston Station (Nottingham-Newark line) adjoins the course.

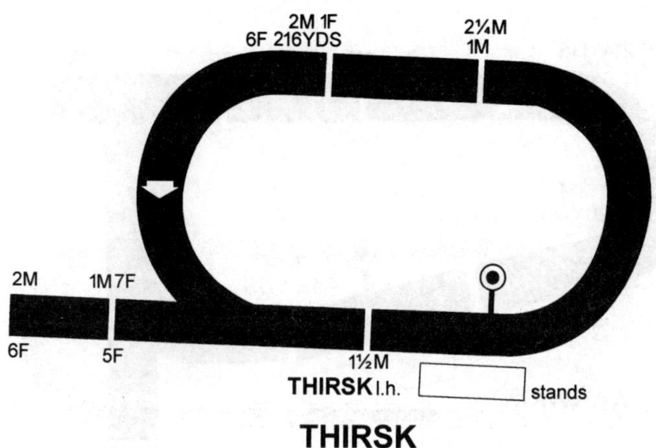

THIRSK

Address: Thirsk Racecourse, Station Road, Thirsk, North Yorkshire YO7 1QL
Tel: (01845) 522276 **Fax:** (01845) 525353
An oval track of 1m 2f, with fairly tight turns and an undulating run-in of four furlongs. Races of five and six furlongs start on a straight, more undulating two furlong extension of the run-in. Though the turns on the round course are comparatively easy, the track is somewhat sharp. The going seldom rides heavy.
Managing Director & Clerk of the Course: Mr Christopher Tetley, The Racecourse, Station Road, Thirsk, North Yorkshire YO7 1QL. Tel: (01845) 522276.
Club Secretary: Mr D. Whitehead, Thirsk Racecourse Limited, The Racecourse, Station Road, Thirsk, North Yorkshire YO7 1QL. Tel: (01845) 522276 Fax: (01845) 525353.
112 boxes available. For stabling and accommodation apply to, The Racecourse, Station Road, Thirsk, North Yorkshire. Tel: (01845) 522276 Racedays (01845) 522096.
By Car: West of the town on the A61. Free car park adjacent to the course for buses and cars.
By Rail: Thirsk Station (from King's Cross). 1/2 mile from the course.
By Air: Helicopters only, landing on the hockey pitch. Prior arrangement required.Tel: Racecourse (01845) 522276. Fixed wing aircraft can land at RAF Leeming. Tel: (01677) 423041. Light aircraft at Bagby. Tel: (01845) 597385 or (01845) 537555.

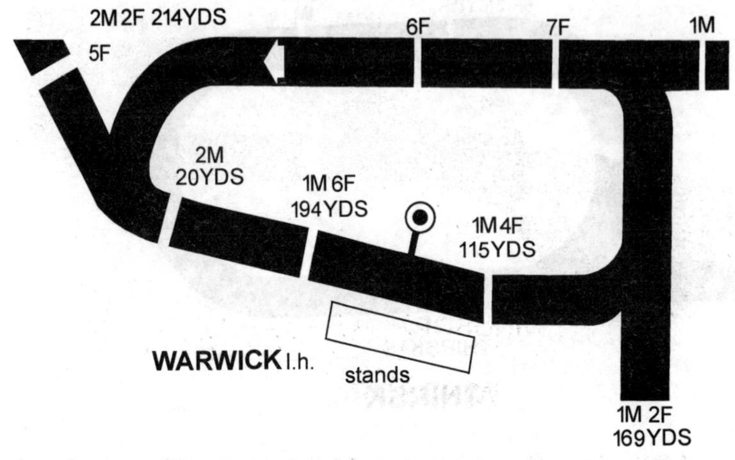

WARWICK

Address: Warwick Racecourse, Hampton Street, Warwick CV34 6HN
Tel: (01926) 491553 **Fax:** (01926) 403223
A nearly circular track, 1m 6f 32y in circumference, with a distinct rise and fall levelling off a mile from home, and a run-in of about two and a half furlongs. The five furlong course has a left-hand elbow at the junction with the round course. The mile course, straight for the first five furlongs, then turns into the home straight. This sharp track favours handiness and speed rather than staying power.
Clerk of the Course & Racecourse Manager: Miss Lisa Rowe, Warwick Racecourse, Hampton Street, Warwick CV34 6HN. Tel: (01926) 491553. Fax (01926) 403223.
Raceday Clerk of the Course: Mr Adam Waterworth, Warwick Racecourse, Hampton Street, Warwick CV34 6HN. Tel: Racedays (01926) 491553.
112 boxes allocated on arrival or by reservation Tel: (01526) 493803.
By Car: West of the town on the B4095 adjacent to Junc 15 of the M40. Free parking (except the Members' Car Park, £5 to Daily Club Members).
By Rail: Warwick or Leamington Spa Station.

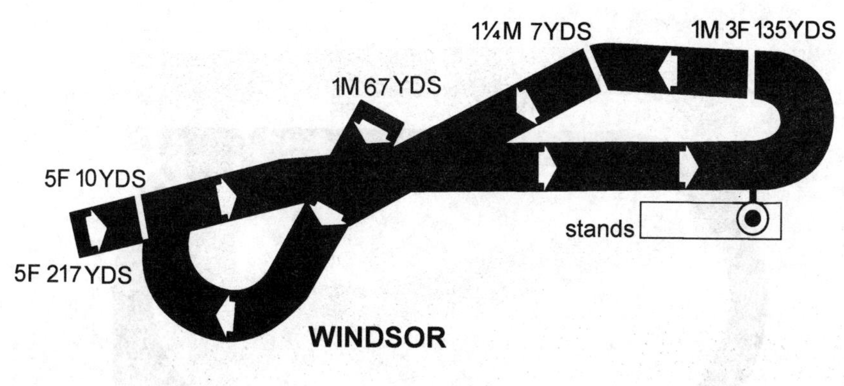

WINDSOR

Address: Royal Windsor Racecourse, Maidenhead Road, Windsor, Berkshire SL4 5JJ Tel: (01753) 864076/865234/864726 **Fax:** (01753) 830156

In the form of a figure eight, Windsor has a circuit of 1m 4f 110y. Although both left and right-hand turns are met in races of a mile and a half, only right-hand turns occur in races up to 1m 70y. The five furlong course bends slightly to the right approaching halfway but is otherwise straight. The track is perfectly flat and its sharpness is largely offset by the long run-in.

Clerk of the Course (to 31/12/98): Hugo Bevan, The Old House, Little Everdon, Daventry, Northamptonshire. Tel: (01327) 361266

Clerk of the Course (from 1/1/99): Mr F. Garrity Tel. (01753) 864076

Racecourse Manager: Mrs S. Dingle, The Racecourse, Windsor, Berkshire. Tel: (01753) 865234 or (01753) 864726 Stables (01753) 865350.

Reservation required for overnight stay and accommodation only. Tel: (01753) 865234.

By Car: North of the town on the A308 (M4 Junc 6). Car parks adjoin the course (£1, £1.50, £2).

By Rail: Windsor Central Station (from Paddington) or Windsor & Eton Riverside Station (from Waterloo).

By Air: London (Heathrow) Airport 15 minutes by car via the M4. Also White Waltham Airport (West London Aero Club) 15 minutes.

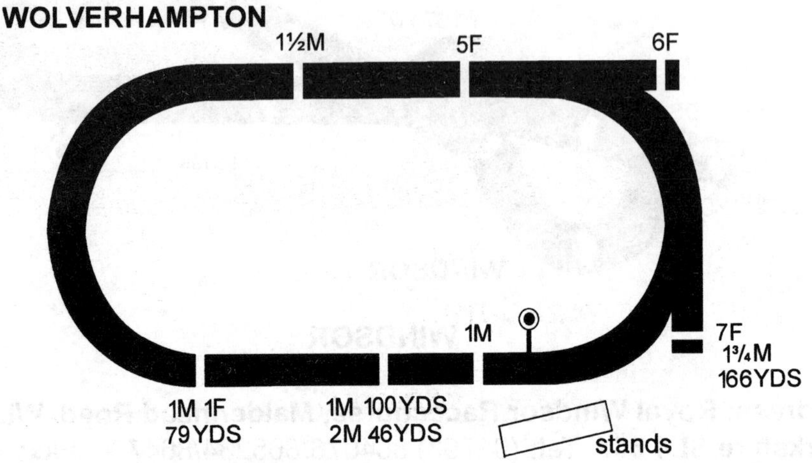

WOLVERHAMPTON

Address: Wolverhampton Racecourse, Dunstall Park, Gorsebrook Road, Wolverhampton WV6 0PE Tel: (01902) 421421 **Fax:** (01902) 716626

An oval circuit, a mile in circumference with a run-in of 380y. The Fibresand surface consists of a blended mixture of silica sand and synthetic fibres set in a re-enforced sub-base.A turf track for hurdles and chases is situated on the outside of the All-Weather track.

Clerk of the Course: Mr M. Prosser, Wolverhampton Racecourse Tel. (01902) 421421, Mobile (07971) 531162, Fax (01902) 421621

74 boxes allotted on arrival. Applications for lads and lasses, and overnight stables must be made to Racecourse by noon on the day before racing. Tel: (01902) 421421. Fax: (01902) 716626

By Car: 1 mile North of town on the A449 (M54 Junc 2 or M6 Junc 12). Car parking free of charge.

By Rail: Wolverhampton Station (from Euston) 1 mile.

By Air: Halfpenny Green Airport 8 miles.

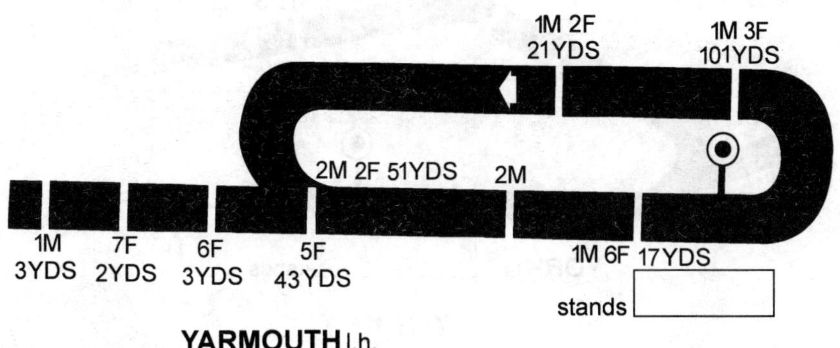

YARMOUTH

Address: The Racecourse, Jellicoe Road, Great Yarmouth, Norfolk NR30 4AU

Tel: (01493) 842527 **Fax:** (01493) 843254

An oblong course of about 1m 4f with a slight fall to a run-in of five furlongs. The straight mile joins the round course at the run-in and is perfectly level. The five, six and seven furlong courses form part of the straight mile.

Clerk of the Course: Mr D. C. Henson, F.R.I.C.S., 2 Lower Mounts, Northampton NN1 3DE. Tel: (01604) 630757. Fax: (01604) 630758.

Manager: Mr David Thompson, The Racecourse, Jellicoe Road, Great Yarmouth, Norfolk NR30 4AU. Tel: (01493) 842527 Fax: (01493) 843254.

Stabling allocated on arrival. Tel: (01493) 855651.

By Car: 1 mile East of town centre (well sign-posted from A47 & A12). Large car park adjoining course £1.

By Rail: Great Yarmouth Station (1 mile). Bus service to the course.

By Air: Helicopter landing facilities available 300y from the course at North Denes Airfield. Tel: (01493) 851500. Fixed wing aircraft landing facilities are available at a private airfield in Ludham. Prior permission is required through Mr R. Collins. Tel: (01493) 843211. Fax: (01493) 859555.

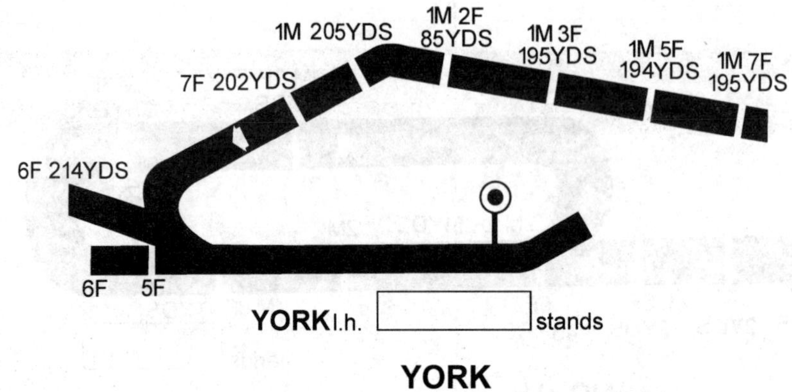

YORK

Address: The Racecourse, York YO23 1EX Tel: (01904) 620911
Fax: (01904) 611071

From the two mile start at the bottom of the Knavesmire, this wide, U-shaped course runs parallel with the Tadcaster Road for five furlongs before bending left to pass under Knavesmire Wood and join the straight six furlongs round a sweeping turn in front of the five furlong gate. A new two furlong extension, set at a tangent, also joins the round course here and caters for seven furlong events. A fair, galloping course which calls for stamina and courage, especially in the wet weather when the going can be very testing. Because of the watering system, when the going is soft, much better ground can be found by racing wide in the back straight.

Manager, Clerk of the Course and Secretary: Mr J. L. Smith F.C.A., The Racecourse, York YO2 1EX. Tel: (01904) 620911 Home (01759) 368455. Fax: (01904) 611071.

Free stabling (200 boxes) Tel: Racedays (01904) 706317.

By Car: 1 mile South-East of the city on the A1036. Car parking bookings can be made prior to race meetings (except August) for reserved car park (£2 (inc. VAT) per day). All other parking is free.

By Rail: 1 1/2 miles York Station (from King's Cross). Special bus service from station to the course.

By Air: Light aircraft and helicopter landing facilities available at Rufforth aerodrome (5,000ft tarmac runway). £20 landing fee-transport arranged to course. Leeds/Bradford airport (25 miles).

LEADING JOCKEYS AT ASCOT

(SINCE 1995)

	Total W-R	Per cent	£1 Level stake
L. Dettori	58-253	22.0	**+ 102.37**
M. J. Kinane	27-189	14.0	- 17.97
J. Reid	27-230	11.0	**+ 37.33**
Pat Eddery	27-258	10.0	- 93.33
T. Quinn	25-208	12.0	- 16.87
K. Fallon	25-190	13.0	- 52.16
R. Hills	22-169	13.0	- 41.55
O. Peslier	12-96	12.0	**+ 69.33**
Dane O'Neill	9-88	10.0	**+ 56.75**
M. Hills	9-155	5.0	- 70.67
D. Holland	9-86	10.0	**+ 22.75**
R. Hughes	8-129	6.0	- 15.75
M. Roberts	8-120	6.0	- 13.75
S. Sanders	7-86	8.0	**+ 10.50**
K. Darley	7-92	7.0	**+ 1.50**
T. Sprake	7-68	10.0	**+ 14.13**
Gary Stevens	5-38	13.0	- 2.50
R. Cochrane	5-112	4.0	- 60.00
J. Weaver	5-83	6.0	- 57.88
J. Fortune	4-62	6.0	- 17.59
N. Pollard	3-35	8.0	- 4.50
J. Murtagh	3-25	12.0	**+ 8.00**
G. Duffield	3-25	12.0	- 6.88
Paul Eddery	3-59	5.0	- 44.00
W. Supple	2-20	10.0	- 3.67

LEADING JOCKEYS AT AYR

(SINCE 1995)

	Total W-R	Per cent	£1 Level stake
K. Darley	25-176	14.0	- 19.78
K. Fallon	22-124	17.0	- 7.03
J. Weaver	21-138	15.0	- 44.18
J. Fortune	20-150	13.0	- 5.60
D. Holland	19-129	14.0	- 37.54
J. Carroll	14-206	6.0	- 119.26
L. Charnock	12-114	10.0	**+ 22.00**
A. Culhane	12-98	12.0	**+ 62.00**
N. Kennedy	12-108	11.0	**+ 32.83**
R. Hughes	9-21	42.0	**+ 32.85**
J. F. Egan	8-67	11.0	**+ 43.75**
Dean McKeown	8-100	8.0	- 34.96
G. Duffield	7-92	7.0	- 56.38
Darren Moffatt	7-57	12.0	- 14.50
F. Lynch	6-31	19.0	**+ 11.33**
M. Hills	6-27	22.0	- 0.26
G. Carter	6-47	12.0	- 13.35
W. Supple	5-66	7.0	**+ 4.00**
L. Dettori	4-11	36.0	**+ 2.72**
D. Mernagh	4-22	18.0	**+ 56.00**
S. Drowne	4-22	18.0	- 2.25
Paul Eddery	4-19	21.0	- 11.56
J. Bramhill	4-34	11.0	**+ 12.00**
M. Roberts	4-15	26.0	**+ 16.50**
C. Lowther	4-64	6.0	**+ 13.00**

LEADING JOCKEYS AT BATH

(SINCE 1995)

	Total W-R	Per cent	£1 Level stake
T. Quinn	25-166	15.0	- 42.06
R. Hughes	19-121	15.0	**+ 13.25**
J. Reid	19-127	14.0	- 9.05
T. Sprake	18-169	10.0	**+ 1.00**
Pat Eddery	18-86	20.0	- 24.34
K. Fallon	15-54	27.0	**+ 13.73**
M. Hills	15-59	25.0	**+ 45.49**
Martin Dwyer	15-97	15.0	**+ 16.50**
S. Whitworth	12-107	11.0	- 40.06
S. Sanders	12-125	9.0	**+ 38.83**
L. Dettori	10-47	21.0	**+ 6.29**
R. Cochrane	10-76	13.0	- 19.77
R. Ffrench	9-71	12.0	**+ 15.63**
P. P. Murphy	9-76	11.0	**+ 6.95**
M. Henry	9-59	15.0	- 7.67
A. Clark	9-95	9.0	- 36.25
Paul Eddery	8-73	10.0	- 47.89
S. Drowne	8-173	4.0	- 76.13
C. Rutter	7-63	11.0	- 8.26
Dane O'Neill	7-108	6.0	- 51.75
J. Quinn	6-71	8.0	- 7.85
B. Doyle	6-43	13.0	**+ 29.00**
M. Roberts	5-48	10.0	**+ 0.75**
J. F. Egan	5-45	11.0	**+ 0.75**
J. Carroll	5-24	20.0	**+ 22.00**

LEADING JOCKEYS AT BEVERLEY

(SINCE 1995)

	Total W-R	Per cent	£1 Level stake
K. Darley	50-264	18.0	- 42.65
K. Fallon	30-174	17.0	- 50.99
A. Culhane	22-191	11.0	- 36.46
J. Fortune	19-138	13.0	- 40.31
L. Charnock	18-231	7.0	- 98.48
J. Carroll	17-148	11.0	- 57.25
D. Holland	14-97	14.0	- 14.32
J. Weaver	13-133	9.0	- 61.88
M. Fenton	11-81	13.0	**+ 0.50**
Dean McKeown	10-146	6.0	- 55.00
W. Ryan	10-46	21.0	- 16.67
R. Winston	9-122	7.0	- 58.59
J. Fanning	9-71	12.0	- 15.75
Pat Eddery	8-35	22.0	- 6.00
G. Carter	8-77	10.0	- 32.80
T. Williams	8-108	7.0	- 32.88
C. Lowther	7-63	11.0	- 12.50
R. Cochrane	7-47	14.0	- 13.87
R. Lappin	7-83	8.0	- 18.50
J. Quinn	7-94	7.0	- 24.75
L. Dettori	7-31	22.0	- 13.66
J. Lowe	6-50	12.0	**+ 25.00**
S. Sanders	5-46	10.0	- 12.55
R. Ffrench	5-11	45.0	**+ 19.75**
G. Duffield	5-97	5.0	- 76.44

LEADING JOCKEYS AT BRIGHTON

(SINCE 1995)

	Total W-R	Per cent	£1 Level stake
T. Quinn	59-216	27.0	+ **49.21**
Dane O'Neill	34-221	15.0	- 3.84
S. Sanders	26-178	14.0	- 0.22
Martin Dwyer	18-123	14.0	- 23.60
R. Hughes	17-129	13.0	- 3.05
R. Ffrench	16-104	15.0	- 0.14
J. Reid	15-88	17.0	+ **10.71**
T. Sprake	15-117	12.0	- 3.42
S. Whitworth	15-141	10.0	- 33.75
N. Pollard	12-54	22.0	+ **43.25**
G. Duffield	11-84	13.0	- 15.68
M. Fenton	11-63	17.0	- 0.00
M. Roberts	10-67	14.0	- 0.25
D. Sweeney	10-91	10.0	+ **5.96**
D. Holland	9-42	21.0	+ **0.25**
J. F. Egan	9-99	9.0	- 32.92
A. Daly	9-103	8.0	+ **19.75**
A. Clark	9-146	6.0	- 58.21
J. Quinn	9-117	7.0	- 12.97
P. Doe	8-88	9.0	- 8.94
F. Norton	8-56	14.0	+ **18.66**
D. Biggs	8-67	11.0	- 22.45
G. Bardwell	7-106	6.0	+ **10.00**
Candy Morris	7-92	7.0	- 42.75
Pat Eddery	7-32	21.0	- 2.38

LEADING JOCKEYS AT CARLISLE

(SINCE 1995)

	Total W-R	Per cent	£1 Level stake
K. Darley	25-115	21.0	- 1.07
J. Fortune	16-109	14.0	- 28.24
J. Carroll	15-155	9.0	- 63.16
A. Culhane	12-94	12.0	- 21.25
J. Weaver	12-69	17.0	+ **4.94**
K. Fallon	12-64	18.0	+ **5.08**
R. Winston	10-77	12.0	- 12.50
C. Lowther	9-40	22.0	+ **15.10**
J. Fanning	8-67	11.0	- 16.50
G. Duffield	6-80	7.0	- 54.76
Dean McKeown	6-90	6.0	- 5.50
W. Supple	5-46	10.0	- 2.50
T. Williams	5-61	8.0	- 22.81
P. Fessey	4-68	5.0	- 39.25
L. Charnock	4-97	4.0	- 65.90
F. Norton	3-14	21.0	+ **3.00**
R. Lappin	3-48	6.0	- 17.25
N. Kennedy	3-42	7.0	- 9.00
R. Hughes	3-5	60.0	+ **0.04**
D. Holland	3-22	13.0	- 11.00
J. Stack	3-15	20.0	+ **2.50**
N. Callan	2-7	28.0	+ **1.38**
A. Nicholls	2-10	20.0	+ **16.00**
J. McAuley	2-26	7.0	- 4.00
J. F. Egan	2-48	4.0	- 38.00

LEADING JOCKEYS AT CATTERICK

(SINCE 1995)

	Total W-R	Per cent	£1 Level stake
K. Darley	31-175	17.0	- 27.72
J. Fortune	20-118	16.0	- 7.35
A. Culhane	17-162	10.0	- 48.67
J. Carroll	14-148	9.0	- 72.14
F. Lynch	13-64	20.0	+ **10.39**
L. Charnock	13-194	6.0	- 49.45
J. Weaver	13-74	17.0	- 16.24
D. Holland	11-42	26.0	- 0.07
G. Duffield	11-96	11.0	- 22.69
T. Williams	11-140	7.0	- 60.25
K. Fallon	10-38	26.0	+ **7.63**
J. F. Egan	9-56	16.0	- 1.25
Alex Greaves	9-57	15.0	- 10.94
R. Winston	8-66	12.0	- 27.35
P. Fessey	8-109	7.0	- 55.13
C. Lowther	7-61	11.0	+ **35.75**
R. Lappin	6-62	9.0	- 4.75
J. Lowe	6-56	10.0	- 13.09
Dale Gibson	6-106	5.0	- 68.38
R. Mullen	5-19	26.0	+ **17.24**
S. Sanders	5-22	22.0	+ **1.34**
J. Quinn	5-28	17.0	+ **35.13**
G. Parkin	5-77	6.0	- 38.75
M. Fenton	5-56	8.0	- 34.00
O. Pears	4-65	6.0	- 3.00

LEADING JOCKEYS AT CHEPSTOW

(SINCE 1995)

	Total W-R	Per cent	£1 Level stake
T. Sprake	14-91	15.0	+ **19.65**
S. Drowne	13-117	11.0	- 37.50
J. Reid	11-69	15.0	- 27.48
S. Whitworth	9-74	12.0	- 21.50
L. Dettori	8-22	36.0	+ **1.54**
Pat Eddery	8-43	18.0	- 17.01
S. Sanders	8-85	9.0	- 53.79
Dane O'Neill	7-73	9.0	- 27.70
T. Quinn	7-68	10.0	- 44.59
K. Fallon	6-21	28.0	+ **10.53**
R. Ffrench	6-31	19.0	+ **3.08**
R. Hills	6-29	20.0	+ **3.35**
C. Rutter	5-66	7.0	- 36.67
R. Cochrane	5-37	13.0	+ **8.50**
G. Duffield	5-26	19.0	- 7.12
R. Price	5-35	14.0	+ **2.50**
R. Hughes	5-42	11.0	- 20.92
R. Havlin	4-43	9.0	- 12.75
J. Weaver	4-16	25.0	- 0.50
A. Clark	4-52	7.0	- 21.75
J. D. Smith	4-20	20.0	- 1.25
G. Hind	4-34	11.0	- 12.50
W. Ryan	4-29	13.0	- 2.20
P. Doe	3-14	21.0	+ **10.00**
M. Fenton	3-23	13.0	+ **4.25**

LEADING JOCKEYS AT CHESTER (SINCE 1995)

	Total W-R	Per cent	£1 Level stake
J. F. Egan	18-122	14.0	+ **10.00**
K. Fallon	16-103	15.0	- 30.45
K. Darley	15-106	14.0	- 7.64
D. Holland	15-68	22.0	+ **8.63**
J. Fortune	12-92	13.0	- 29.84
M. Hills	12-87	13.0	- 14.15
J. Reid	11-59	18.0	- 3.45
R. Hughes	9-41	21.0	+ **4.11**
L. Dettori	9-54	16.0	- 9.88
Pat Eddery	8-50	16.0	- 12.88
S. Sanders	8-30	26.0	+ **9.25**
M. Roberts	8-44	18.0	- 7.23
R. Hills	7-32	21.0	- 9.96
D. Wright	7-48	14.0	- 5.67
J. Carroll	7-81	8.0	- 49.00
R. Cochrane	6-57	10.0	- 23.34
T. Quinn	6-69	8.0	- 42.29
W. Ryan	6-36	16.0	- 6.40
Paul Eddery	5-32	15.0	- 16.20
M. Fenton	5-22	22.0	+ **17.00**
J. Quinn	5-50	10.0	- 11.00
W. Supple	4-53	7.0	- 15.00
A. Culhane	4-29	13.0	- 7.00
L. Charnock	4-43	9.0	- 21.50
F. Norton	4-40	10.0	- 14.00

LEADING JOCKEYS AT DONCASTER (SINCE 1995)

	Total W-R	Per cent	£1 Level stake
M. Hills	40-188	21.0	+ **27.10**
K. Fallon	40-240	16.0	- 47.08
L. Dettori	34-196	17.0	- 22.68
K. Darley	29-274	10.0	- 50.52
Pat Eddery	24-197	12.0	- 39.47
J. Fortune	21-211	9.0	- 75.63
T. Quinn	20-147	13.0	- 19.65
R. Hills	18-107	16.0	- 24.69
R. Cochrane	18-122	14.0	+ **47.00**
J. Reid	16-184	8.0	- 83.43
W. Ryan	16-120	13.0	- 34.26
D. Holland	15-96	15.0	- 6.87
M. Roberts	13-92	14.0	+ **5.07**
J. Carroll	13-161	8.0	- 87.13
G. Carter	12-112	10.0	- 21.22
J. Quinn	11-127	8.0	- 54.79
R. Hughes	11-78	14.0	+ **14.50**
S. Sanders	11-98	11.0	- 1.88
T. Sprake	10-76	13.0	- 6.67
J. Weaver	10-139	7.0	- 45.80
G. Hind	9-66	13.0	- 4.75
D. Harrison	8-61	13.0	- 14.00
A. Mackay	7-53	13.0	+ **34.00**
G. Duffield	7-144	4.0	- 61.80
R. Winston	6-61	9.0	+ **4.00**

LEADING JOCKEYS AT EPSOM (SINCE 1995)

	Total W-R	Per cent	£1 Level stake
Pat Eddery	17-88	19.0	- 11.02
K. Fallon	14-72	19.0	+ **0.24**
T. Quinn	13-134	9.0	- 70.99
L. Dettori	13-77	16.0	- 25.51
S. Sanders	12-85	14.0	- 25.21
R. Cochrane	9-74	12.0	- 6.50
M. Roberts	8-60	13.0	+ **1.08**
Dane O'Neill	7-85	8.0	- 62.67
J. Fortune	6-23	26.0	+ **9.33**
A. Daly	6-37	16.0	+ **12.91**
R. Hughes	6-59	10.0	- 11.60
M. Hills	6-46	13.0	- 14.84
G. Carter	6-30	20.0	+ **36.13**
M. Tebbutt	5-19	26.0	+ **18.00**
R. Hills	5-32	15.0	+ **8.00**
W. Ryan	5-46	10.0	- 4.00
M. J. Kinane	5-33	15.0	+ **9.00**
C. Lowther	4-13	30.0	+ **16.83**
T. Sprake	4-31	12.0	+ **32.00**
Martin Dwyer	4-49	8.0	- 22.17
M. Henry	4-33	12.0	+ **5.50**
J. Weaver	4-25	16.0	- 5.75
S. Whitworth	4-42	9.0	- 24.92
J. Quinn	4-52	7.0	- 25.00
B. Doyle	4-14	28.0	+ **24.83**

LEADING JOCKEYS AT FOLKESTONE (SINCE 1995)

	Total W-R	Per cent	£1 Level stake
T. Quinn	21-134	15.0	- 16.23
S. Sanders	20-149	13.0	- 13.43
Dane O'Neill	18-128	14.0	+ **37.10**
Paul Eddery	14-90	15.0	- 10.00
T. Sprake	14-109	12.0	- 44.50
J. Quinn	11-121	9.0	- 8.01
G. Duffield	11-75	14.0	- 25.54
A. Whelan	10-57	17.0	+ **1.16**
S. Drowne	10-82	12.0	- 9.63
Martin Dwyer	9-78	11.0	+ **4.50**
A. Clark	9-123	7.0	- 74.38
R. Ffrench	8-60	13.0	- 18.02
M. Hills	7-16	43.0	+ **21.04**
K. Fallon	7-34	20.0	+ **0.85**
C. Rutter	7-54	12.0	+ **12.96**
R. Cochrane	7-89	7.0	- 25.75
N. Callan	6-18	33.0	+ **10.22**
S. Whitworth	6-65	9.0	- 25.00
J. F. Egan	6-65	9.0	- 17.76
R. Hughes	6-50	12.0	- 29.83
M. Fenton	6-58	10.0	+ **5.75**
F. Norton	6-40	15.0	+ **41.00**
N. Pollard	5-35	14.0	+ **34.50**
K. Darley	5-20	25.0	+ **28.88**
A. Daly	5-81	6.0	- 39.50

LEADING JOCKEYS AT GOODWOOD (SINCE 1995)

	Total W-R	Per cent	£1 Level stake
L. Dettori	49-211	23.0	- 9.64
T. Quinn	44-312	14.0	- 63.39
K. Fallon	34-170	20.0	+ **20.87**
J. Reid	33-246	13.0	- 106.79
Pat Eddery	31-198	15.0	- 55.82
R. Hills	26-166	15.0	- 9.29
R. Cochrane	20-163	12.0	+ **17.87**
Dane O'Neill	20-201	9.0	- 8.63
M. Hills	16-138	11.0	+ **5.78**
K. Darley	15-125	12.0	- 2.43
R. Hughes	15-168	8.0	+ **2.38**
J. Fortune	14-82	17.0	+ **20.40**
M. Roberts	13-131	9.0	- 51.54
T. Sprake	11-113	9.0	- 27.13
W. Ryan	11-94	11.0	- 41.52
J. Weaver	11-84	13.0	+ **11.69**
J. Quinn	11-120	9.0	- 41.95
D. Holland	10-86	11.0	+ **14.50**
S. Sanders	10-164	6.0	- 85.75
O. Peslier	9-37	24.0	+ **39.75**
G. Carter	9-93	9.0	- 24.17
R. Ffrench	8-57	14.0	- 4.38
G. Duffield	8-67	11.0	- 19.59
Paul Eddery	8-130	6.0	- 85.75
Gary Stevens	7-27	25.0	+ **11.50**

LEADING JOCKEYS AT HAYDOCK (SINCE 1995)

	Total W-R	Per cent	£1 Level stake
Pat Eddery	30-122	24.0	+ **9.28**
K. Darley	28-210	13.0	- 67.78
L. Dettori	24-103	23.0	- 3.83
K. Fallon	23-134	17.0	- 13.66
J. Carroll	22-245	8.0	- 99.23
J. Weaver	20-131	15.0	- 10.12
W. Ryan	19-83	22.0	+ **14.70**
J. Reid	18-93	19.0	- 6.40
T. Quinn	17-61	27.0	+ **43.92**
R. Hills	15-103	14.0	- 37.69
T. Sprake	15-101	14.0	+ **30.58**
A. Culhane	12-116	10.0	- 20.25
G. Carter	12-97	12.0	+ **3.63**
J. F. Egan	11-125	8.0	- 1.63
J. Fortune	11-141	7.0	- 84.67
M. Hills	11-57	19.0	+ **44.75**
G. Hind	9-88	10.0	- 36.88
Paul Eddery	9-58	15.0	- 7.34
D. Holland	7-64	10.0	- 26.10
M. Roberts	7-58	12.0	- 17.44
Dane O'Neill	6-56	10.0	- 30.50
P. Robinson	6-60	10.0	- 23.25
Gary Stevens	5-11	45.0	+ **8.25**
W. Supple	5-54	9.0	- 28.20
P. Fessey	5-66	7.0	- 30.50

LEADING JOCKEYS AT HAMILTON (SINCE 1995)

	Total W-R	Per cent	£1 Level stake
J. Weaver	30-124	24.0	+ **16.52**
K. Darley	26-162	16.0	- 34.49
A. Mackay	24-130	18.0	- 23.75
J. Fortune	23-127	18.0	- 17.47
J. Carroll	22-218	10.0	- 96.17
K. Fallon	17-91	18.0	- 8.04
T. Williams	16-136	11.0	- 46.38
N. Kennedy	14-121	11.0	+ **18.75**
L. Charnock	14-130	10.0	- 32.00
A. Culhane	13-124	10.0	- 66.58
G. Duffield	13-88	14.0	- 21.38
C. Lowther	11-68	16.0	+ **54.17**
Dean McKeown	10-159	6.0	- 127.25
J. Fanning	10-115	8.0	+ **18.83**
D. Holland	10-49	20.0	- 7.38
O. Pears	8-78	10.0	- 38.90
T. Quinn	7-12	58.0	+ **1.33**
R. Lappin	7-70	10.0	- 20.25
P. Fessey	7-129	5.0	- 82.75
J. McAuley	6-106	5.0	- 57.00
Dale Gibson	5-84	5.0	- 3.50
Darren Moffatt	5-77	6.0	- 12.00
R. Winston	4-84	4.0	- 61.34
F. Lynch	4-29	13.0	- 13.80
J. F. Egan	4-47	8.0	- 14.00

LEADING JOCKEYS AT KEMPTON (SINCE 1995)

	Total W-R	Per cent	£1 Level stake
Pat Eddery	36-190	18.0	- 23.22
T. Quinn	27-198	13.0	- 6.33
J. Reid	26-146	17.0	+ **1.08**
L. Dettori	21-98	21.0	- 11.32
R. Hughes	18-131	13.0	+ **53.21**
T. Sprake	16-96	16.0	+ **60.62**
K. Fallon	15-87	17.0	- 11.54
R. Cochrane	15-124	12.0	- 40.68
M. Hills	12-105	11.0	- 29.05
Dane O'Neill	11-141	7.0	- 75.50
R. Hills	10-93	10.0	- 21.51
S. Sanders	10-140	7.0	- 77.50
N. Pollard	9-48	18.0	+ **34.25**
M. Roberts	8-63	12.0	- 15.63
G. Hind	6-72	8.0	- 14.75
W. Ryan	6-83	7.0	- 56.25
J. Fortune	5-27	18.0	+ **5.03**
P. Robinson	5-49	10.0	- 3.00
S. Whitworth	5-82	6.0	- 10.25
W. R. Swinburn	5-46	10.0	- 22.50
A. Clark	5-125	4.0	- 39.00
O. Peslier	4-21	19.0	+ **14.41**
R. Ffrench	4-50	8.0	+ **4.00**
D. Holland	3-27	11.0	- 12.33
O. Urbina	3-18	16.0	+ **5.50**

LEADING JOCKEYS AT LEICESTER (SINCE 1995)

	Total W-R	Per cent	£1 Level stake
Pat Eddery	32-150	21.0	- 22.01
L. Dettori	32-124	25.0	+ **0.30**
K. Fallon	25-147	17.0	+ **0.60**
W. Ryan	19-117	16.0	- 13.90
Dane O'Neill	17-148	11.0	- 22.50
G. Carter	17-158	10.0	- 29.63
T. Sprake	17-161	10.0	- 37.68
T. Quinn	16-156	10.0	- 63.97
J. Reid	16-128	12.0	- 52.90
R. Cochrane	15-140	10.0	+ **6.98**
R. Hills	14-101	13.0	- 2.91
G. Duffield	14-107	13.0	- 24.25
M. Hills	13-124	10.0	- 43.50
M. Roberts	12-77	15.0	+ **29.31**
J. Fortune	11-82	13.0	- 14.67
D. Holland	10-86	11.0	+ **36.58**
S. Sanders	8-89	8.0	- 21.38
K. Darley	8-83	9.0	- 45.86
C. Rutter	8-119	6.0	- 32.50
J. Weaver	8-72	11.0	- 4.00
J. Quinn	8-133	6.0	- 55.77
F. Lynch	7-77	9.0	- 18.00
S. Drowne	7-135	5.0	- 71.50
A. Mackay	7-73	9.0	- 17.00
M. Fenton	7-121	5.0	- 62.13

LEADING JOCKEYS AT LINGFIELD- Turf (SINCE 1995)

	Total W-R	Per cent	£1 Level stake
K. Fallon	28-80	35.0	+ **29.27**
Pat Eddery	28-107	26.0	+ **6.55**
S. Sanders	23-168	13.0	- 15.71
R. Hills	19-86	22.0	- 1.04
J. Reid	18-115	15.0	- 24.39
Dane O'Neill	18-178	10.0	- 57.88
T. Quinn	17-149	11.0	- 77.04
T. Sprake	15-131	11.0	- 60.63
R. Cochrane	14-92	15.0	- 4.25
R. Hughes	12-100	12.0	- 26.42
Martin Dwyer	11-110	10.0	- 6.25
C. Rutter	10-91	10.0	+ **26.13**
W. Ryan	10-97	10.0	- 20.22
A. McGlone	10-82	12.0	- 40.71
N. Pollard	9-64	14.0	+ **0.83**
G. Carter	9-67	13.0	- 15.04
F. Norton	9-64	14.0	+ **38.75**
R. Perham	9-100	9.0	+ **41.00**
P. Robinson	8-48	16.0	- 6.67
A. Daly	8-88	9.0	- 25.50
L. Dettori	8-46	17.0	- 25.22
G. Hind	8-68	11.0	- 17.20
J. Weaver	8-70	11.0	- 27.67
M. Hills	7-47	14.0	- 16.79
R. Ffrench	6-65	9.0	- 4.50

LEADING JOCKEYS AT LINGFIELD- All Weather (SINCE 1995)

	Total W-R	Per cent	£1 Level stake
A. Clark	73-525	13.0	+ **4.23**
J. Weaver	65-294	22.0	- 2.99
S. Sanders	54-454	11.0	- 88.86
J. Quinn	53-648	8.0	- 281.24
S. Whitworth	51-332	15.0	- 76.78
R. Cochrane	47-298	15.0	- 67.77
D. Holland	39-167	23.0	+ **21.71**
W. Ryan	38-189	20.0	+ **11.51**
L. Dettori	33-142	23.0	- 15.24
Dean McKeown	31-181	17.0	+ **27.73**
Dane O'Neill	28-292	9.0	- 138.36
P. Doe	23-217	10.0	- 38.70
D. Sweeney	23-153	15.0	- 0.77
T. Sprake	20-196	10.0	- 76.25
A. Culhane	20-132	15.0	+ **7.21**
G. Carter	20-173	11.0	- 62.28
F. Norton	19-211	9.0	+ **1.38**
D. Biggs	19-213	8.0	- 71.47
Martin Dwyer	18-229	7.0	- 127.59
G. Duffield	18-149	12.0	- 72.76
C. Rutter	16-175	9.0	- 19.67
R. Ffrench	15-88	17.0	- 11.30
K. Fallon	15-69	21.0	- 15.19
A. Daly	15-163	9.0	+ **14.00**
D. R. McCabe	15-116	12.0	- 29.51

LEADING JOCKEYS AT MUSSELBURGH (SINCE 1995)

	Total W-R	Per cent	£1 Level stake
K. Darley	27-170	15.0	- 23.48
J. Carroll	24-190	12.0	+ **29.45**
A. Culhane	21-168	12.0	- 41.50
K. Fallon	19-90	21.0	- 9.43
R. Winston	16-98	16.0	+ **37.50**
J. Fortune	16-148	10.0	- 75.58
L. Charnock	15-131	11.0	- 28.34
J. F. Egan	13-101	12.0	- 48.43
P. Fessey	11-127	8.0	- 49.26
F. Lynch	10-35	28.0	+ **34.25**
T. Williams	10-133	7.0	- 6.63
D. Holland	10-35	28.0	+ **19.38**
M. Fenton	9-44	20.0	+ **50.08**
G. Carter	9-37	24.0	+ **1.23**
R. Lappin	9-84	10.0	+ **36.50**
J. Weaver	9-80	11.0	- 59.80
J. Fanning	9-99	9.0	+ **1.00**
C. Lowther	8-64	12.0	- 12.00
G. Duffield	8-68	11.0	- 30.55
W. Supple	7-56	12.0	+ **54.38**
F. Norton	5-27	18.0	- 4.27
J. Quinn	5-38	13.0	+ **14.00**
R. Mullen	5-26	19.0	- 2.45
Darren Moffatt	5-42	11.0	+ **40.50**
Dean McKeown	5-103	4.0	- 82.38

LEADING JOCKEYS AT NEWBURY (SINCE 1995)

	Total W-R	Per cent	£1 Level stake
T. Quinn	39-279	13.0	**+ 37.70**
L. Dettori	36-188	19.0	**+ 13.94**
J. Reid	35-255	13.0	- 18.25
K. Fallon	30-171	17.0	- 34.49
Pat Eddery	30-282	10.0	- 115.96
R. Hills	25-161	15.0	- 14.31
R. Cochrane	18-144	12.0	**+ 18.33**
M. Hills	18-198	9.0	- 44.88
W. Ryan	13-93	13.0	**+ 6.88**
Dane O'Neill	12-207	5.0	- 56.25
S. Sanders	12-147	8.0	- 57.00
R. Hughes	12-185	6.0	- 55.06
M. Roberts	10-101	9.0	- 18.80
T. Sprake	8-129	6.0	- 48.50
S. Whitworth	7-79	8.0	- 15.50
K. Darley	7-74	9.0	- 40.52
J. Fortune	6-44	13.0	- 11.63
O. Peslier	6-34	17.0	**+ 11.25**
J. Quinn	6-82	7.0	- 34.00
G. Hind	6-42	14.0	**+ 15.25**
A. Clark	6-70	8.0	**+ 22.00**
C. Rutter	6-90	6.0	- 48.13
P. Doe	5-39	12.0	- 3.50
P. Robinson	5-46	10.0	**+ 49.63**
R. Ffrench	4-36	11.0	**+ 1.00**

LEADING JOCKEYS AT NEWCASTLE (SINCE 1995)

	Total W-R	Per cent	£1 Level stake
K. Darley	34-236	14.0	- 62.30
K. Fallon	28-152	18.0	- 14.87
J. Weaver	25-146	17.0	- 2.83
J. Fortune	21-168	12.0	- 41.88
J. Carroll	20-210	9.0	- 77.73
D. Holland	19-94	20.0	- 13.08
G. Duffield	16-126	12.0	- 10.50
L. Charnock	15-175	8.0	- 2.00
M. Hills	11-36	30.0	**+ 2.51**
A. Culhane	11-164	6.0	- 59.50
T. Williams	10-122	8.0	- 22.50
R. Winston	9-77	11.0	**+ 7.25**
R. Hills	9-34	26.0	**+ 20.63**
G. Carter	8-60	13.0	- 3.63
L. Dettori	8-32	25.0	- 10.16
G. Hind	7-33	21.0	**+ 28.00**
Dean McKeown	7-123	5.0	- 63.25
W. Ryan	6-27	22.0	- 6.18
T. Quinn	6-32	18.0	- 5.73
J. Quinn	6-68	8.0	- 5.17
M. Fenton	6-48	12.0	- 6.67
J. Fanning	6-98	6.0	- 74.17
R. Lappin	6-65	9.0	**+ 24.50**
J. Reid	5-39	12.0	- 16.38
J. F. Egan	5-45	11.0	- 10.50

LEADING JOCKEYS AT NEWMARKET- Rowley (SINCE 1995)

	Total W-R	Per cent	£1 Level stake
L. Dettori	54-283	19.0	- 71.34
K. Fallon	39-217	17.0	- 11.63
Pat Eddery	36-238	15.0	- 71.67
R. Hills	29-201	14.0	**+ 19.25**
M. Hills	25-233	10.0	- 12.21
J. Reid	19-248	7.0	- 107.06
M. J. Kinane	15-97	15.0	- 0.35
T. Quinn	14-219	6.0	- 129.98
R. Cochrane	10-122	8.0	- 34.13
S. Sanders	9-103	8.0	- 28.00
G. Carter	8-107	7.0	- 4.25
W. Ryan	8-87	9.0	- 25.17
Dane O'Neill	7-121	5.0	- 29.50
M. Roberts	7-105	6.0	- 22.50
K. Darley	7-124	5.0	- 59.00
R. Hughes	7-88	7.0	- 40.27
M. Fenton	7-68	10.0	- 18.02
R. Ffrench	6-68	8.0	- 5.00
O. Peslier	6-48	12.0	- 15.56
G. Duffield	6-59	10.0	- 24.75
D. Holland	5-69	7.0	- 30.88
D. Harrison	5-80	6.0	- 4.25
J. F. Egan	4-56	7.0	**+ 25.00**
P. Robinson	4-61	6.0	**+ 27.00**
Martin Dwyer	4-85	4.0	**+ 9.00**

LEADING JOCKEYS AT NEWMARKET- July (SINCE 1995)

	Total W-R	Per cent	£1 Level stake
L. Dettori	52-252	20.0	- 2.57
K. Fallon	47-203	23.0	**+ 31.13**
Pat Eddery	45-275	16.0	- 89.01
R. Hills	32-208	15.0	- 48.25
M. Hills	28-233	12.0	**+ 13.38**
T. Quinn	21-219	9.0	- 62.33
J. Reid	18-133	13.0	**+ 40.17**
W. Ryan	16-172	9.0	- 71.01
M. Roberts	14-124	11.0	- 14.63
R. Cochrane	14-164	8.0	- 68.92
J. Quinn	12-88	13.0	- 4.08
G. Carter	12-103	11.0	- 2.43
M. J. Kinane	11-89	12.0	- 34.45
J. Weaver	11-104	10.0	- 34.72
Dane O'Neill	10-135	7.0	- 21.75
S. Sanders	10-84	11.0	**+ 34.25**
J. Fortune	9-111	8.0	- 30.67
R. Hughes	9-142	6.0	- 53.13
M. Fenton	9-128	7.0	- 45.50
D. R. McCabe	8-41	19.0	**+ 55.33**
P. Robinson	8-143	5.0	- 83.75
R. Ffrench	7-84	8.0	**+ 1.23**
T. Sprake	7-65	10.0	- 9.17
D. Holland	7-102	6.0	- 42.63
N. Pollard	6-50	12.0	**+ 5.00**

LEADING JOCKEYS AT NOTTINGHAM (SINCE 1995)

	Total W-R	Per cent	£1 Level stake
K. Fallon	42-211	19.0	- 34.86
T. Sprake	25-207	12.0	+ **35.60**
Pat Eddery	22-100	22.0	- 12.52
G. Duffield	21-140	15.0	- 10.68
L. Dettori	20-88	22.0	+ **2.21**
T. Quinn	17-128	13.0	- 23.23
W. Ryan	17-124	13.0	- 43.59
R. Hills	16-95	16.0	- 25.08
J. Quinn	15-194	7.0	- 12.83
G. Carter	13-203	6.0	- 103.08
J. Fortune	12-107	11.0	- 24.67
M. Fenton	12-114	10.0	- 24.48
S. Sanders	12-135	8.0	- 31.88
J. Reid	12-102	11.0	- 22.50
P. Robinson	12-96	12.0	+ **54.58**
D. Holland	12-83	14.0	+ **38.25**
S. Drowne	11-161	6.0	- 45.00
J. Weaver	11-107	10.0	- 17.90
R. Cochrane	10-102	9.0	- 43.00
Dean McKeown	10-117	8.0	- 61.75
A. Culhane	10-135	7.0	- 78.47
A. Clark	9-111	8.0	- 51.83
G. Hind	8-93	8.0	- 38.55
J. Carroll	8-90	8.0	- 5.46
M. Hills	8-58	13.0	- 23.38

LEADING JOCKEYS AT PONTEFRACT (SINCE 1995)

	Total W-R	Per cent	£1 Level stake
K. Fallon	43-201	21.0	+ **51.07**
K. Darley	36-262	13.0	- 34.82
J. Fortune	21-181	11.0	- 35.18
Pat Eddery	20-58	34.0	+ **25.07**
L. Dettori	13-64	20.0	- 0.07
A. Culhane	13-159	8.0	- 2.42
J. Carroll	12-161	7.0	- 45.75
L. Charnock	11-145	7.0	- 30.00
J. Weaver	10-112	8.0	- 42.90
W. Ryan	10-68	14.0	- 33.48
F. Lynch	9-92	9.0	- 26.33
M. Roberts	8-41	19.0	+ **33.80**
M. Hills	8-40	20.0	- 7.11
R. Winston	7-76	9.0	- 17.75
J. Quinn	7-70	10.0	- 12.00
R. Hills	7-60	11.0	- 44.06
Dean McKeown	7-146	4.0	- 19.50
G. Duffield	7-97	7.0	- 36.02
S. Sanders	6-55	10.0	- 4.33
D. Holland	6-73	8.0	- 21.38
D. Mernagh	5-48	10.0	+ **2.38**
R. Mullen	5-22	22.0	+ **45.00**
J. F. Egan	5-62	8.0	- 1.00
M. Fenton	5-65	7.0	- 32.00
W. Supple	4-63	6.0	- 26.50

LEADING JOCKEYS AT REDCAR (SINCE 1995)

	Total W-R	Per cent	£1 Level stake
K. Darley	47-266	17.0	- 48.48
J. Weaver	20-110	18.0	- 16.19
J. Carroll	20-170	11.0	+ **17.78**
K. Fallon	20-99	20.0	- 16.48
J. Fortune	19-182	10.0	- 66.73
G. Duffield	18-144	12.0	- 45.26
A. Culhane	18-227	7.0	- 96.27
G. Carter	18-88	20.0	- 5.48
L. Charnock	16-224	7.0	+ **9.50**
Dean McKeown	12-157	7.0	- 79.75
W. Ryan	10-60	16.0	- 22.08
G. Hind	10-39	25.0	+ **21.00**
R. Cochrane	10-39	25.0	+ **32.73**
J. Fanning	8-124	6.0	- 71.01
L. Dettori	8-36	22.0	- 10.09
M. Fenton	8-78	10.0	- 7.25
D. Holland	7-45	15.0	- 1.63
P. Fessey	7-84	8.0	- 14.00
Kim Tinkler	7-168	4.0	- 50.00
S. Sanders	6-29	20.0	- 7.58
G. Parkin	6-91	6.0	- 38.25
R. Winston	5-80	6.0	- 37.50
S. Drowne	5-30	16.0	+ **0.45**
F. Lynch	5-70	7.0	- 33.00
D. R. McCabe	5-32	15.0	- 1.00

LEADING JOCKEYS AT RIPON (SINCE 1995)

	Total W-R	Per cent	£1 Level stake
K. Darley	34-169	20.0	+ **28.42**
K. Fallon	25-111	22.0	+ **22.82**
J. Weaver	22-120	18.0	+ **19.10**
J. Carroll	14-155	9.0	- 80.15
L. Charnock	14-154	9.0	- 57.53
D. Holland	13-69	18.0	+ **12.72**
G. Hind	12-51	23.0	- 4.73
W. Ryan	10-45	22.0	- 8.77
G. Carter	10-65	15.0	+ **4.60**
J. Fortune	10-134	7.0	- 81.38
R. Cochrane	9-57	15.0	- 8.63
Dean McKeown	9-137	6.0	- 53.38
A. Culhane	9-153	5.0	- 58.50
J. Fanning	9-115	7.0	- 27.20
R. Ffrench	7-38	18.0	+ **8.38**
L. Dettori	6-11	54.0	+ **11.25**
S. Sanders	5-30	16.0	- 11.89
T. Williams	5-111	4.0	- 60.50
G. Duffield	5-51	9.0	- 28.91
R. Hills	4-15	26.0	+ **1.28**
R. Havlin	4-20	20.0	- 11.27
P. Fessey	4-61	6.0	- 15.00
C. Teague	4-26	15.0	+ **11.00**
D. Mernagh	3-45	6.0	+ **2.00**
G. Faulkner	3-12	25.0	+ **15.50**

LEADING JOCKEYS AT SALISBURY

(SINCE 1995)

	Total W-R	Per cent	£1 Level stake
T. Quinn	28-147	19.0	- 28.07
R. Hughes	24-133	18.0	- 12.75
L. Dettori	21-79	26.0	+ **2.47**
Dane O'Neill	19-188	10.0	- 80.67
T. Sprake	19-208	9.0	- 69.26
Pat Eddery	17-95	17.0	- 25.76
J. Reid	13-152	8.0	- 85.04
G. Duffield	13-50	26.0	+ **33.00**
K. Fallon	12-41	29.0	+ **44.70**
R. Hills	11-56	19.0	+ **4.93**
B. Doyle	10-44	22.0	+ **71.11**
S. Drowne	10-160	6.0	- 49.00
W. Ryan	10-56	17.0	- 8.92
C. Rutter	9-113	7.0	- 26.18
S. Sanders	8-122	6.0	- 84.71
M. Hills	7-70	10.0	- 6.08
M. Roberts	7-57	12.0	+ **32.58**
D. Holland	7-29	24.0	+ **17.50**
A. Clark	7-127	5.0	- 68.13
M. Henry	6-56	10.0	- 4.56
D. Sweeney	5-33	15.0	+ **69.50**
G. Carter	5-48	10.0	- 29.75
S. Whitworth	5-95	5.0	- 64.77
J. Quinn	5-73	6.0	- 36.29
Martin Dwyer	5-82	6.0	- 42.50

LEADING JOCKEYS AT SANDOWN

(SINCE 1995)

	Total W-R	Per cent	£1 Level stake
Pat Eddery	52-271	19.0	- 40.55
L. Dettori	50-243	20.0	- 55.66
K. Fallon	25-153	16.0	- 5.57
T. Quinn	24-191	12.0	- 43.23
J. Reid	23-186	12.0	- 72.46
Dane O'Neill	22-181	12.0	- 37.63
R. Hills	18-120	15.0	- 8.27
M. Hills	17-139	12.0	- 30.60
M. Roberts	16-131	12.0	- 25.47
S. Sanders	12-163	7.0	- 70.50
R. Cochrane	12-118	10.0	- 24.92
J. Weaver	11-66	16.0	+ **15.83**
Gary Stevens	10-38	26.0	+ **8.03**
T. Sprake	10-105	9.0	+ **23.30**
G. Carter	9-65	13.0	+ **10.96**
R. Hughes	8-101	7.0	- 36.27
D. Holland	8-60	13.0	+ **18.83**
C. Rutter	8-70	11.0	+ **52.00**
M. J. Kinane	7-51	13.0	+ **1.88**
W. Ryan	7-104	6.0	- 70.93
B. Doyle	7-122	5.0	- 52.50
J. F. Egan	6-44	13.0	+ **3.00**
G. Duffield	6-48	12.0	- 11.92
P. Robinson	6-58	10.0	- 0.50
Paul Eddery	6-101	5.0	- 30.84

LEADING JOCKEYS AT SOUTHWELL

(SINCE 1995)

	Total W-R	Per cent	£1 Level stake
J. Quinn	48-549	8.0	- 243.67
G. Duffield	42-279	15.0	- 99.27
J. Weaver	42-260	16.0	- 27.95
L. Charnock	34-405	8.0	- 155.32
A. Culhane	32-351	9.0	- 109.17
Dean McKeown	31-421	7.0	- 246.92
C. Teague	27-302	8.0	- 96.67
P. McCabe	24-170	14.0	+ **63.55**
F. Lynch	24-198	12.0	- 23.17
K. Fallon	23-107	21.0	+ **39.60**
D. Holland	23-119	19.0	+ **33.80**
C. Lowther	21-165	12.0	- 6.47
F. Norton	21-229	9.0	- 30.09
R. Cochrane	21-151	13.0	- 15.38
D. Sweeney	19-167	11.0	- 33.33
J. Fanning	19-204	9.0	- 23.49
G. Carter	19-223	8.0	- 82.01
T. Sprake	18-167	10.0	- 31.81
S. Sanders	17-166	10.0	- 46.67
A. McCarthy	16-167	9.0	- 92.83
Emma O'Gorman	16-59	27.0	+ **16.16**
T. Williams	16-264	6.0	- 80.30
A. Clark	16-196	8.0	- 96.53
R. Fitzpatrick	15-61	24.0	+ **78.05**
R. Price	15-112	13.0	+ **6.73**

LEADING JOCKEYS AT THIRSK

(SINCE 1995)

	Total W-R	Per cent	£1 Level stake
K. Darley	28-146	19.0	- 35.42
A. Culhane	20-170	11.0	- 19.02
J. Carroll	20-181	11.0	- 80.18
J. Fortune	18-116	15.0	- 16.55
J. Weaver	18-97	18.0	- 18.14
G. Duffield	17-99	17.0	+ **7.83**
G. Carter	12-91	13.0	- 15.67
K. Fallon	12-43	27.0	+ **10.90**
L. Charnock	11-182	6.0	- 97.52
W. Ryan	10-32	31.0	+ **19.17**
D. Holland	10-40	25.0	+ **1.57**
Dean McKeown	10-95	10.0	- 10.92
S. Sanders	9-36	25.0	+ **32.41**
C. Lowther	8-52	15.0	+ **39.00**
F. Lynch	8-63	12.0	- 26.75
J. F. Egan	6-58	10.0	- 16.00
Alex Greaves	6-79	7.0	- 23.88
J. Stack	6-55	10.0	- 30.88
A. McGlone	5-24	20.0	- 0.88
Paul Eddery	5-20	25.0	- 3.30
T. Williams	5-112	4.0	- 55.00
W. Supple	4-43	9.0	- 1.00
R. Winston	4-66	6.0	- 35.13
D. Sweeney	4-32	12.0	+ **16.80**
S. Drowne	4-21	19.0	- 7.93

LEADING JOCKEYS AT WARWICK (SINCE 1995)

	Total W-R	Per cent	£1 Level stake
T. Quinn	14-69	20.0	- 8.79
M. Hills	13-50	26.0	**+ 14.85**
T. Sprake	13-108	12.0	- 28.81
J. Reid	12-68	17.0	- 3.66
Pat Eddery	12-32	37.0	**+ 17.40**
R. Hughes	11-45	24.0	**+ 13.67**
G. Carter	11-83	13.0	- 27.63
M. Fenton	9-101	8.0	- 4.50
G. Bardwell	8-56	14.0	**+ 13.75**
S. Drowne	8-121	6.0	- 68.00
C. Rutter	8-87	9.0	- 33.88
K. Fallon	7-36	19.0	- 11.47
R. Cochrane	7-42	16.0	- 5.75
G. Duffield	7-48	14.0	**+ 5.00**
Martin Dwyer	7-63	11.0	- 30.38
Paul Eddery	7-45	15.0	- 9.08
A. Clark	7-72	9.0	- 12.25
F. Norton	6-66	9.0	- 16.75
S. Whitworth	6-52	11.0	**+ 36.75**
S. Sanders	6-57	10.0	**+ 17.16**
N. Adams	6-64	9.0	- 2.30
J. Fortune	5-12	41.0	**+ 27.75**
R. Havlin	5-51	9.0	- 7.17
M. Roberts	5-33	15.0	- 3.04
J. Quinn	5-115	4.0	- 81.75

LEADING JOCKEYS AT WOLVERHAMPTON (SINCE 1995)

	Total W-R	Per cent	£1 Level stake
S. Sanders	46-326	14.0	- 13.70
J. Weaver	42-229	18.0	**+ 40.75**
G. Duffield	40-260	15.0	- 38.43
Dean McKeown	39-354	11.0	- 124.79
J. Quinn	38-464	8.0	- 168.84
T. G. McLaughlin	33-242	13.0	**+ 25.73**
J. F. Egan	31-204	15.0	**+ 51.07**
F. Lynch	31-310	10.0	- 123.92
D. Holland	31-143	21.0	**+ 8.45**
G. Carter	28-227	12.0	- 56.48
A. Culhane	27-298	9.0	- 59.36
S. Whitworth	27-247	10.0	- 108.86
T. Sprake	22-216	10.0	- 50.03
C. Lowther	21-158	13.0	- 54.51
A. McCarthy	20-154	12.0	**+ 1.00**
D. Sweeney	20-161	12.0	- 48.38
K. Fallon	20-128	15.0	- 40.12
S. Drowne	20-273	7.0	- 83.13
L. Charnock	20-207	9.0	- 51.88
T. Williams	20-207	9.0	- 91.22
J. Tate	17-126	13.0	- 6.07
Dane O'Neill	16-124	12.0	- 38.15
A. Clark	16-193	8.0	- 35.47
K. Darley	15-63	23.0	**+ 21.88**
J. Fanning	15-165	9.0	- 71.03

LEADING JOCKEYS AT WINDSOR (SINCE 1995)

	Total W-R	Per cent	£1 Level stake
Pat Eddery	39-223	17.0	- 56.53
L. Dettori	34-149	22.0	- 33.74
J. Reid	28-163	17.0	- 25.10
T. Quinn	21-175	12.0	- 16.13
R. Hughes	16-117	13.0	- 14.34
K. Fallon	14-93	15.0	- 24.63
S. Sanders	14-162	8.0	- 26.25
R. Cochrane	13-115	11.0	- 31.20
Dane O'Neill	13-186	6.0	- 59.17
Martin Dwyer	13-132	9.0	**+ 24.83**
T. Sprake	11-149	7.0	- 51.42
M. Roberts	10-77	12.0	- 4.41
D. Holland	9-65	13.0	**+ 1.88**
P. Doe	8-78	10.0	- 12.88
S. Drowne	8-149	5.0	- 84.00
B. Doyle	8-68	11.0	**+ 14.00**
M. Fenton	8-68	11.0	**+ 11.50**
J. Quinn	7-126	5.0	- 51.50
W. Ryan	7-60	11.0	- 23.59
J. Fortune	6-59	10.0	- 10.75
C. Rutter	6-128	4.0	- 84.63
Paul Eddery	5-87	5.0	- 41.25
G. Hind	5-73	6.0	- 22.50
M. Hills	5-88	5.0	- 55.34
R. Ffrench	4-68	5.0	- 37.50

LEADING JOCKEYS AT YARMOUTH (SINCE 1995)

	Total W-R	Per cent	£1 Level stake
L. Dettori	37-111	33.0	- 0.80
R. Hills	35-152	23.0	**+ 9.71**
M. Hills	27-168	16.0	**+ 16.99**
W. Ryan	24-165	14.0	- 43.24
K. Fallon	19-112	16.0	- 35.74
R. Cochrane	15-120	12.0	- 29.58
M. Roberts	15-84	17.0	**+ 16.05**
Pat Eddery	14-67	20.0	- 23.43
S. Sanders	13-85	15.0	**+ 46.49**
P. Robinson	11-82	13.0	**+ 50.75**
J. Reid	10-62	16.0	- 11.50
B. Doyle	10-66	15.0	- 3.00
R. Hughes	9-43	20.0	**+ 12.69**
K. Darley	9-45	20.0	- 4.45
G. Carter	9-88	10.0	- 43.48
G. Duffield	9-78	11.0	- 36.59
M. Fenton	9-88	10.0	- 37.92
A. Clark	8-48	16.0	**+ 42.25**
D. Holland	8-39	20.0	**+ 13.96**
G. Bardwell	8-104	7.0	- 16.00
J. Stack	7-46	15.0	- 1.75
A. McGlone	7-52	13.0	- 16.72
R. Ffrench	5-66	7.0	- 37.27
Martin Dwyer	5-50	10.0	**+ 1.75**
O. Urbina	5-22	22.0	- 0.93

LEADING JOCKEYS AT YORK

(SINCE 1995)

	Total W-R	Per cent	£1 Level stake
L. Dettori	40-201	19.0	- 15.85
K. Fallon	35-264	13.0	- 66.79
Pat Eddery	31-197	15.0	- 15.42
M. J. Kinane	23-120	19.0	**+ 1.88**
T. Quinn	23-196	11.0	- 69.37
K. Darley	23-239	9.0	- 34.59
M. Hills	18-181	9.0	- 19.87
J. Fortune	17-145	11.0	- 26.12
D. Holland	15-94	15.0	**+ 41.25**
J. Reid	14-146	9.0	- 93.77
R. Hills	11-123	8.0	- 36.88
R. Cochrane	10-133	7.0	- 55.50
M. Roberts	9-89	10.0	- 35.42
W. Ryan	9-73	12.0	- 28.86
J. Weaver	8-161	4.0	- 42.00
L. Charnock	7-112	6.0	- 62.13
R. Hughes	6-72	8.0	- 17.50
G. Duffield	6-68	8.0	- 25.33
Gary Stevens	5-22	22.0	**+ 4.90**
A. Culhane	5-83	6.0	- 53.25
J. F. Egan	5-75	6.0	- 14.50
O. Peslier	4-32	12.0	- 15.79
Dean McKeown	4-67	5.0	- 22.50
R. Ffrench	3-20	15.0	**+ 7.50**
G. Parkin	3-32	9.0	- 12.00

LEADING FLAT TRAINERS AT ASCOT (SINCE 1995)

	Total W-R	2yo Stks	3yo Stks	Other Stks	2yo H'caps	3yo H'caps	Other H'caps	App'ce	Amateurs	Per cent	£1 Level stake
S bin Suroor	27-101	5-13	3-25	18-56	0-0	0-3	1-4	0-0	0-0	26.7	**+ 61.18**
J. L. Dunlop	27-171	5-28	2-18	11-48	1-4	2-17	6-55	0-1	0-0	15.8	**+ 37.46**
R. Hannon	21-202	7-73	3-19	3-23	5-13	1-24	2-49	0-1	0-0	10.4	**+ 35.58**
J. H. M. Gosden	20-127	4-17	4-34	2-25	0-0	4-14	6-37	0-0	0-0	15.8	**+ 11.63**
H. R. A. Cecil	19-120	4-17	7-33	5-44	0-0	2-14	1-12	0-0	0-0	15.8	- 34.33
Sir Michael Stoute	15-150	1-24	4-28	4-48	0-1	2-18	4-30	0-0	0-1	10.0	- 58.00
P. F. I. Cole	14-123	7-39	1-11	2-20	0-3	0-15	4-34	0-1	0-0	11.4	- 30.47
M. Johnston	14-117	2-18	1-6	4-27	0-3	4-14	3-49	0-0	0-0	12.0	**+ 52.63**
L. M. Cumani	12-76	4-10	1-15	2-20	0-2	1-8	4-20	0-1	0-0	15.8	- 3.29
D. R. Loder	11-71	7-21	3-11	1-16	0-0	0-10	0-13	0-0	0-0	15.5	**+ 14.48**
B. W. Hills	11-140	6-43	1-19	2-28	0-7	1-16	1-27	0-0	0-0	7.9	- 56.43
E. A. L. Dunlop	7-59	4-13	0-7	0-10	0-1	0-7	3-21	0-0	0-0	11.9	- 14.64
I. A. Balding	7-104	4-16	0-7	0-14	0-1	2-10	1-56	0-0	0-0	6.7	- 57.34
G. Wragg	7-42	0-3	4-11	3-11	0-0	0-6	0-10	0-1	0-0	16.7	**+ 44.83**
R. Charlton	7-59	0-8	1-10	3-14	0-0	1-8	1-18	0-0	1-1	11.9	- 16.75
A. P. O'Brien,Ireland	6-40	5-18	0-10	1-10	0-0	0-1	0-1	0-0	0-0	15.0	**+ 3.28**

LEADING FLAT TRAINERS AT AYR (SINCE 1995)

	Total W-R	2yo Stks	3yo Stks	Other Stks	2yo H'caps	3yo H'caps	Other H'caps	App'ce	Amateurs	Per cent	£1 Level stake
B. W. Hills	26-93	10-28	2-6	7-21	4-9	1-7	2-19	0-0	0-3	28.0	**+ 5.06**
M. Johnston	20-184	7-62	1-2	2-10	1-20	2-12	7-75	0-2	0-1	10.9	- 87.99
Miss L. A. Perratt	16-267	4-48	0-5	0-22	0-12	1-25	10-141	0-6	1-8	6.0	- 37.50
J. L. Dunlop	12-49	4-12	1-2	4-9	1-6	0-1	2-18	0-0	0-1	24.5	- 6.04
A. Bailey	12-106	2-10	1-3	0-13	0-10	2-8	7-55	0-3	0-4	11.3	- 31.09
J. S. Goldie	12-193	1-16	0-2	0-17	1-15	0-14	9-113	1-3	0-13	6.2	- 105.75
Mrs M. Reveley	9-76	0-6	0-0	4-18	0-0	0-3	4-41	0-0	1-8	11.8	- 25.61
P. Calver	9-37	0-2	0-0	0-1	0-3	2-4	7-26	0-0	0-1	24.3	**+ 38.25**
M. R. Channon	9-65	4-24	1-3	0-2	2-4	0-9	2-21	0-2	0-0	13.9	- 11.13
S. E. Kettlewell	8-50	0-2	1-2	0-6	0-0	1-5	6-29	0-1	0-5	16.0	**+ 23.75**
N. Bycroft	7-81	1-10	0-1	0-3	0-1	0-9	6-53	0-2	0-2	8.6	- 37.13
D. Nicholls	7-89	0-1	0-1	0-9	0-0	0-5	7-70	0-0	0-3	7.9	**+ 16.50**
J. Berry	7-220	0-59	1-3	0-14	1-15	2-16	3-110	0-1	0-2	3.2	- 153.00
T. D. Easterby	6-55	2-9	0-0	0-2	2-14	2-5	0-23	0-1	0-1	10.9	**+ 6.50**
Sir Michael Stoute	6-21	1-5	0-0	4-10	1-1	0-0	0-5	0-0	0-0	28.6	- 0.09
M. H. Tompkins	6-57	2-12	0-2	1-9	0-6	1-3	2-21	0-1	0-3	10.5	- 24.17

LEADING FLAT TRAINERS AT BATH (SINCE 1995)

	Total W-R	2yo Stks	3yo Stks	Other Stks	2yo H'caps	3yo H'caps	Other H'caps	App'ce	Amateurs	Per cent	£1 Level stake
M. R. Channon	19-147	7-50	4-19	5-20	0-6	2-13	1-39	0-0	0-0	12.9	- 21.88
I. A. Balding	17-98	4-19	1-12	4-17	0-1	3-9	5-35	0-5	0-0	17.4	- 15.27
R. Charlton	15-61	3-15	3-12	8-19	0-3	0-3	1-7	0-2	0-0	24.6	**+ 2.91**
B. W. Hills	14-77	6-22	4-18	1-18	0-0	0-5	3-13	0-1	0-0	18.2	- 2.58
P. F. I. Cole	14-68	2-13	2-9	3-7	2-6	0-9	5-21	0-3	0-0	20.6	- 10.92
J. W. Hills	13-72	1-12	4-15	2-10	1-1	1-8	4-26	0-0	0-0	18.1	**+ 20.08**
R. Hannon	13-134	5-52	2-19	4-21	2-7	0-11	0-22	0-2	0-0	9.7	- 54.18
W. R. Muir	13-96	0-17	1-9	2-8	1-3	0-4	7-48	2-7	0-0	13.5	**+ 10.50**
J. Berry	12-68	6-24	0-5	2-15	1-2	1-5	2-16	0-1	0-0	17.7	**+ 24.54**
R. J. Hodges	10-142	1-17	1-9	4-35	0-1	0-5	4-69	0-6	0-0	7.0	- 65.05
J. S. King	9-42	0-0	0-3	0-1	0-0	0-0	8-36	1-2	0-0	21.4	**+ 24.50**
J. A. R. Toller	8-46	2-9	1-7	1-9	0-0	1-2	3-18	0-1	0-0	17.4	**+ 9.60**
D. R. C. Elsworth	7-63	3-13	1-7	3-15	0-2	0-2	0-24	0-0	0-0	11.1	**+ 5.25**
B. J. Meehan	7-79	4-35	0-10	0-2	1-7	0-10	2-14	0-1	0-0	8.9	- 6.89
L. M. Cumani	6-18	0-1	3-9	3-6	0-0	0-1	0-1	0-0	0-0	33.3	**+ 8.87**
J. L. Dunlop	6-42	0-6	2-11	0-3	0-4	1-7	3-11	0-0	0-0	14.3	- 28.37

LEADING FLAT TRAINERS AT BEVERLEY (SINCE 1995)

	Total W-R	2yo Stks	3yo Stks	Other Stks	2yo H'caps	3yo H'caps	Other H'caps	App'ce	Amateurs	Per cent	£1 Level stake
M. Johnston	35-159	12-44	2-10	2-9	4-6	3-25	12-63	0-2	0-0	22.0	**+ 32.43**
T. D. Easterby	27-210	10-55	0-6	2-12	2-11	4-32	7-84	2-8	0-2	12.9	- 18.58
J. Berry	22-153	11-69	3-17	4-26	2-12	0-4	2-21	0-2	0-2	14.4	- 30.74
Mrs M. Reveley	17-97	0-3	0-2	5-16	0-1	0-7	12-66	0-2	0-0	17.5	- 8.55
M. W. Easterby	17-257	4-104	0-3	1-10	2-14	5-28	5-83	0-15	0-0	6.6	- 127.50
J. L. Dunlop	15-57	1-16	3-6	0-3	0-1	4-15	7-16	0-0	0-0	26.3	- 7.93
J. L. Eyre	15-153	1-18	0-6	1-11	0-2	2-20	10-86	0-7	1-3	9.8	- 55.63
D. R. Loder	13-28	7-13	2-3	3-4	0-0	1-4	0-4	0-0	0-0	46.4	- 2.73
H. R. A. Cecil	12-25	5-9	1-3	5-9	0-0	0-2	1-2	0-0	0-0	48.0	**+ 0.78**
L. M. Cumani	10-21	1-2	2-4	5-8	0-0	1-3	1-4	0-0	0-0	47.6	**+ 12.43**
E. A. L. Dunlop	9-38	5-13	0-4	1-9	0-0	2-4	0-7	1-1	0-0	23.7	**+ 7.14**
N. Tinkler	9-108	2-35	0-11	3-15	0-3	1-7	3-34	0-3	0-0	8.3	- 51.25
D. Nicholls	9-116	0-3	0-4	1-22	0-2	0-8	6-70	2-6	0-1	7.8	- 45.96
A. C. Stewart	8-23	2-6	0-2	3-7	0-0	1-3	2-5	0-0	0-0	34.8	**+ 7.13**
B. S. Rothwell	8-104	0-20	2-5	0-8	0-4	2-9	4-54	0-3	0-1	7.7	- 44.50
D. W. Chapman	7-53	0-1	0-0	2-3	0-1	0-3	4-40	1-4	0-1	13.2	**+ 0.88**

LEADING FLAT TRAINERS AT BRIGHTON (SINCE 1995)

	Total W-R	2yo Stks	3yo Stks	Other Stks	2yo H'caps	3yo H'caps	Other H'caps	App'ce	Amateurs	Per cent	£1 Level stake
R. Hannon	42-260	16-63	8-34	3-45	3-24	3-27	8-65	1-2	0-0	16.2	- 27.86
G. L. Moore	37-299	1-25	1-13	12-72	2-8	2-21	16-140	2-13	1-7	12.4	- 69.69
S. Dow	24-169	4-14	3-14	3-28	0-6	4-19	9-85	1-2	0-1	14.2	- 8.02
M. R. Channon	21-145	7-45	3-15	2-18	1-12	3-10	4-42	1-3	0-0	14.5	- 14.83
Miss Gay Kelleway	20-109	2-10	1-9	6-32	0-4	0-7	10-41	1-6	0-0	18.4	**+ 27.84**
B. J. Meehan	18-137	13-55	1-14	1-12	1-15	2-14	0-25	0-0	0-2	13.1	- 56.53
W. R. Muir	14-65	2-12	1-7	7-15	0-2	1-5	3-24	0-0	0-0	21.5	**+ 24.55**
C. E. Brittain	12-70	3-11	1-2	1-10	0-8	1-9	5-27	1-3	0-0	17.1	**+ 44.23**
K. T. Ivory	12-72	3-12	0-2	1-8	0-1	2-11	6-38	0-0	0-0	16.7	**+ 23.25**
Sir Mark Prescott	11-48	0-14	2-3	3-10	2-7	2-7	2-7	0-0	0-0	22.9	- 4.43
P. F. I. Cole	11-73	3-14	0-6	4-17	0-7	1-11	3-17	0-1	0-0	15.1	- 28.46
J. L. Dunlop	11-46	4-12	2-5	1-6	2-5	1-6	1-11	0-0	0-1	23.9	- 0.86
R. M. Flower	11-123	0-2	0-9	1-17	0-1	3-11	6-73	1-8	0-2	8.9	- 16.00
J. Pearce	10-81	1-4	0-4	3-19	0-4	0-3	6-39	0-3	0-5	12.4	**+ 50.25**
S. P. C. Woods	10-51	0-4	2-9	3-14	0-1	0-3	4-16	1-4	0-0	19.6	- 12.10
R. J. O'Sullivan	10-73	0-4	0-1	4-14	0-1	1-2	4-50	0-0	1-1	13.7	- 1.50

LEADING FLAT TRAINERS AT CARLISLE (SINCE 1995)

	Total W-R	2yo Stks	3yo Stks	Other Stks	2yo H'caps	3yo H'caps	Other H'caps	App'ce	Amateurs	Per cent	£1 Level stake
J. Berry	15-133	4-38	2-11	7-37	0-0	0-12	2-31	0-4	0-0	11.3	- 71.75
M. Johnston	15-81	2-19	1-4	2-10	0-0	3-18	7-28	0-2	0-0	18.5	**+ 10.25**
M. R. Channon	14-35	6-9	0-2	7-12	0-0	1-8	0-4	0-0	0-0	40.0	**+ 14.27**
J. L. Eyre	13-77	0-6	0-2	0-14	0-0	3-9	8-39	2-6	0-1	16.9	**+ 38.25**
Mrs M. Reveley	12-60	1-3	1-1	4-16	0-0	1-8	5-28	0-2	0-2	20.0	**+ 4.00**
M. Dods	9-74	0-9	0-2	3-22	0-0	0-5	5-31	1-5	0-0	12.2	**+ 0.50**
T. D. Easterby	7-89	3-17	1-5	1-11	0-0	0-20	1-33	1-3	0-0	7.9	- 54.23
R. A. Fahey	6-45	0-7	0-2	4-11	0-0	1-8	1-17	0-0	0-0	13.3	- 3.50
Miss L. A. Perratt	6-63	1-8	0-3	1-10	0-0	2-8	1-26	1-6	0-2	9.5	**+ 22.00**
Sir Mark Prescott	6-29	3-9	0-1	2-10	0-0	0-6	1-3	0-0	0-0	20.7	- 10.51
P. D. Evans	6-55	4-20	0-2	2-14	0-0	0-5	0-12	0-2	0-0	10.9	- 33.63
M. H. Tompkins	6-34	2-7	0-2	1-11	0-0	2-6	0-7	0-0	1-1	17.7	**+ 5.00**
M. W. Easterby	6-55	2-15	0-1	1-2	0-0	0-17	3-16	0-4	0-0	10.9	- 19.13
E. J. Alston	6-62	0-2	0-0	1-12	0-0	0-6	5-39	0-3	0-0	9.7	- 8.00
E. Weymes	5-38	1-8	2-3	0-11	0-0	0-3	2-10	0-3	0-0	13.2	- 5.50
S. E. Kettlewell	5-29	2-3	0-1	2-6	0-0	0-3	1-12	0-4	0-0	17.2	**+ 1.25**

LEADING FLAT TRAINERS AT CATTERICK (SINCE 1995)

	Total W-R	2yo Stks	3yo Stks	Other Stks	2yo H'caps	3yo H'caps	Other H'caps	App'ce	Amateurs	Per cent	£1 Level stake
J. Berry	31-209	10-67	1-16	11-39	1-19	2-25	5-32	1-11	0-0	14.8	- 13.37
B. W. Hills	20-62	5-11	7-14	5-10	0-4	1-6	2-14	0-2	0-1	32.3	**+ 16.25**
Mrs M. Reveley	18-107	0-4	3-6	9-30	0-1	0-10	5-50	1-4	0-2	16.8	- 33.67
M. Johnston	17-103	4-30	3-7	4-10	0-12	3-15	1-24	2-5	0-0	16.5	- 18.11
M. W. Easterby	17-169	2-29	0-3	0-6	3-28	3-32	9-68	0-2	0-1	10.1	- 30.38
D. Nicholls	16-126	0-3	0-2	7-42	0-1	1-9	7-62	1-7	0-0	12.7	- 28.29
T. D. Barron	15-72	5-12	0-3	4-12	1-7	1-8	3-27	1-3	0-0	20.8	**+ 97.23**
J. L. Eyre	15-154	1-16	2-8	0-31	0-9	1-14	10-64	1-11	0-1	9.7	- 0.00
T. D. Easterby	13-113	1-25	1-5	2-15	1-14	6-19	0-28	2-6	0-1	11.5	**+ 14.60**
P. D. Evans	13-102	4-25	0-2	2-20	2-11	2-12	2-23	0-6	1-3	12.8	- 21.75
D. W. Barker	10-63	1-7	0-4	1-14	3-6	2-5	2-25	0-1	1-1	15.9	- 6.13
M. R. Channon	10-58	5-17	3-7	0-3	0-11	0-4	2-14	0-2	0-0	17.2	- 18.66
J. Pearce	8-33	0-1	1-3	0-6	1-3	0-1	3-12	1-3	2-4	24.2	**+ 34.82**
J. A. Glover	7-26	0-3	1-3	2-2	1-5	1-3	1-9	1-1	0-0	26.9	**+ 9.38**
Sir Mark Prescott	7-47	4-23	0-2	0-5	2-8	0-3	1-5	0-1	0-0	14.9	- 16.93
Sir Michael Stoute	7-15	2-5	4-6	1-3	0-0	0-1	0-0	0-0	0-0	46.7	**+ 2.40**

LEADING FLAT TRAINERS AT CHEPSTOW (SINCE 1995)

	Total W-R	2yo Stks	3yo Stks	Other Stks	2yo H'caps	3yo H'caps	Other H'caps	App'ce	Amateurs	Per cent	£1 Level stake
R. Hannon	15-128	2-40	2-9	5-14	1-8	2-13	2-42	1-2	0-0	11.7	- 42.63
J. M. Bradley	11-131	0-5	0-8	0-11	0-1	0-5	10-90	0-0	1-11	8.4	- 63.50
Sir Michael Stoute	11-33	4-9	4-8	2-12	0-0	0-2	1-2	0-0	0-0	33.3	- 3.73
J. L. Dunlop	10-57	5-25	1-5	1-6	0-2	3-10	0-8	0-0	0-1	17.5	- 20.03
D. W. P. Arbuthnot	10-49	2-9	0-0	0-3	1-3	1-4	4-26	0-0	2-4	20.4	**+ 86.50**
L. M. Cumani	9-19	2-4	2-4	3-5	0-0	2-5	0-1	0-0	0-0	47.4	**+ 10.57**
B. R. Millman	8-52	1-8	0-4	0-6	0-2	0-3	6-26	0-1	1-2	15.4	**+ 8.73**
M. C. Pipe	8-47	0-4	1-5	4-7	0-0	1-4	2-21	0-1	0-5	17.0	- 13.25
L. Montague Hall	7-8	0-0	0-0	0-0	0-0	0-0	4-5	3-3	0-0	87.5	**+ 31.75**
J. H. M. Gosden	7-30	2-6	1-7	1-7	0-0	0-1	3-9	0-0	0-0	23.3	- 6.92
Sir Mark Prescott	7-27	3-13	0-0	1-3	1-1	1-6	1-4	0-0	0-0	25.9	- 11.74
P. F. I. Cole	7-57	1-19	1-9	2-10	0-0	2-11	1-8	0-0	0-0	12.3	- 27.46
B. W. Hills	6-33	2-9	2-6	1-3	0-1	0-6	1-7	0-0	0-1	18.2	- 5.88
W. R. Muir	6-64	1-7	0-3	0-9	0-3	0-4	5-33	0-2	0-3	9.4	- 24.75
G. B. Balding	6-53	0-8	0-3	1-5	1-1	1-5	3-25	0-0	0-6	11.3	- 11.75
D. R. Loder	5-10	0-1	0-2	1-1	0-0	3-5	1-1	0-0	0-0	50.0	**+ 5.37**

LEADING FLAT TRAINERS AT CHESTER (SINCE 1995)

	Total W-R	2yo Stks	3yo Stks	Other Stks	2yo H'caps	3yo H'caps	Other H'caps	App'ce	Amateurs	Per cent	£1 Level stake
P. D. Evans	18-186	0-37	0-6	2-12	5-21	4-22	6-79	1-9	0-0	9.7	- 20.25
A. Bailey	18-163	2-25	1-12	1-6	1-8	2-16	9-85	2-11	0-0	11.0	- 36.67
B. W. Hills	18-101	4-16	5-31	3-20	0-4	2-14	4-16	0-0	0-0	17.8	**+ 5.79**
Sir Michael Stoute	16-69	4-12	3-18	3-14	0-1	3-12	3-12	0-0	0-0	23.2	**+ 1.03**
E. J. Alston	15-135	3-21	0-1	5-17	0-5	0-8	7-78	0-5	0-0	11.1	- 32.13
J. Berry	14-158	9-41	1-9	1-10	0-8	1-25	2-59	0-6	0-0	8.9	- 74.38
J. L. Dunlop	11-36	3-7	0-8	3-5	0-0	0-2	5-14	0-0	0-0	30.6	- 2.00
B. A. McMahon	11-74	4-16	1-6	3-6	0-2	2-11	1-31	0-2	0-0	14.9	**+ 4.71**
R. Hannon	10-62	8-21	0-5	0-7	0-8	1-14	1-7	0-0	0-0	16.1	- 8.38
M. W. Easterby	9-35	0-0	0-1	0-0	1-7	0-2	7-24	1-1	0-0	25.7	**+ 11.25**
H. R. A. Cecil	9-35	2-3	3-9	4-14	0-0	0-2	0-7	0-0	0-0	25.7	- 13.65
M. Johnston	8-56	2-9	1-4	0-2	0-4	1-8	4-29	0-0	0-0	14.3	- 13.00
M. R. Channon	8-61	1-15	1-4	0-2	2-9	1-7	3-23	0-1	0-0	13.1	- 3.42
B. Hanbury	8-40	1-3	1-8	2-4	0-0	1-8	3-17	0-0	0-0	20.0	**+ 23.88**
M. C. Pipe	7-28	0-0	0-0	4-7	1-1	0-2	2-17	0-1	0-0	25.0	- 5.37
P. F. I. Cole	7-42	1-7	1-8	0-4	0-4	1-7	4-12	0-0	0-0	16.7	- 3.34

LEADING FLAT TRAINERS AT DONCASTER (SINCE 1995)

	Total W-R	2yo Stks	3yo Stks	Other Stks	2yo H'caps	3yo H'caps	Other H'caps	App'ce	Amateurs	Per cent	£1 Level stake
B. W. Hills	52-261	18-81	7-44	16-51	5-27	1-10	5-45	0-2	0-1	19.9	+ **53.82**
J. L. Dunlop	31-167	12-62	2-15	8-32	3-12	2-14	4-32	0-0	0-0	18.6	- 18.98
J. H. M. Gosden	31-163	10-53	4-16	11-48	1-6	2-6	3-32	0-2	0-0	19.0	+ **14.69**
H. R. A. Cecil	25-110	7-24	4-21	12-51	0-0	0-4	2-10	0-0	0-0	22.7	- 4.21
M. Johnston	19-185	4-42	2-12	5-28	1-22	4-16	3-63	0-2	0-0	10.3	- 89.30
S bin Suroor	18-51	6-13	8-14	4-19	0-2	0-1	0-2	0-0	0-0	35.3	+ **23.43**
Sir Michael Stoute	18-86	6-33	1-9	7-30	0-2	1-2	2-9	1-1	0-0	20.9	+ **23.70**
D. Nicholls	14-145	0-4	0-3	1-12	0-2	0-9	9-101	4-14	0-0	9.7	- 51.50
P. F. I. Cole	11-68	1-19	1-8	3-15	0-4	2-6	4-16	0-0	0-0	16.2	+ **6.89**
J. L. Eyre	11-170	0-12	0-2	0-8	1-5	3-17	7-104	0-18	0-4	6.5	- 70.25
Miss Gay Kelleway	11-72	0-8	1-4	2-10	0-0	0-4	6-36	2-10	0-0	15.3	+ **24.00**
T. D. Easterby	10-120	0-23	0-2	4-7	3-21	1-12	2-52	0-3	0-0	8.3	- 40.72
R. Charlton	10-44	3-15	4-7	1-9	0-0	1-4	1-8	0-1	0-0	22.7	+ **9.00**
J. R. Fanshawe	10-68	1-12	1-7	2-21	0-4	2-3	4-21	0-0	0-0	14.7	- 17.63
I. A. Balding	10-85	2-19	1-4	0-11	1-8	0-2	6-37	0-4	0-0	11.8	- 18.42
M. R. Channon	10-102	6-36	0-16	2-3	0-7	0-11	2-26	0-3	0-0	9.8	- 39.00

LEADING FLAT TRAINERS AT EPSOM (SINCE 1995)

	Total W-R	2yo Stks	3yo Stks	Other Stks	2yo H'caps	3yo H'caps	Other H'caps	App'ce	Amateurs	Per cent	£1 Level stake
R. Hannon	18-143	10-41	4-16	2-20	2-8	0-18	0-37	0-3	0-0	12.6	- 54.16
M. Johnston	14-54	7-18	0-3	2-4	1-1	0-5	4-23	0-0	0-0	25.9	+ **11.42**
P. F. I. Cole	12-68	3-12	3-16	2-9	0-1	1-4	2-24	1-2	0-0	17.7	- 11.22
J. L. Dunlop	11-44	2-5	1-9	5-11	0-1	1-6	2-12	0-0	0-0	25.0	- 5.12
D. R. C. Elsworth	8-35	1-5	0-2	4-7	0-1	1-3	2-16	0-1	0-0	22.9	+ **26.00**
S. Dow	8-108	0-15	0-7	1-10	0-4	1-7	3-59	3-6	0-0	7.4	- 35.81
B. J. Meehan	7-52	2-15	2-8	1-4	0-3	0-3	2-19	0-0	0-0	13.5	- 5.17
H. R. A. Cecil	7-28	0-0	6-13	1-9	0-0	0-2	0-4	0-0	0-0	25.0	- 1.46
G. L. Moore	7-73	0-6	0-1	1-9	0-1	0-8	6-44	0-4	0-0	9.6	- 8.50
N. A. Callaghan	6-21	2-7	0-2	0-1	0-2	0-0	4-8	0-1	0-0	28.6	+ **11.25**
P. W. Harris	6-42	0-2	2-5	0-3	0-1	0-3	4-28	0-0	0-0	14.3	+ **2.00**
J. W. Hills	6-32	1-4	0-2	1-3	1-2	0-4	3-16	0-1	0-0	18.8	+ **12.75**
S bin Suroor	6-31	0-0	3-18	3-12	0-0	0-0	0-1	0-0	0-0	19.4	+ **0.54**
J. Berry	6-37	0-2	0-2	1-6	1-3	0-3	4-21	0-0	0-0	16.2	+ **27.50**
G. B. Balding	5-10	0-0	0-0	0-0	0-0	1-2	3-7	1-1	0-0	50.0	+ **38.00**
W. R. Muir	5-28	0-3	0-0	1-6	0-2	0-0	4-17	0-0	0-0	17.9	+ **4.67**

LEADING FLAT TRAINERS AT FOLKESTONE (SINCE 1995)

	Total W-R	2yo Stks	3yo Stks	Other Stks	2yo H'caps	3yo H'caps	Other H'caps	App'ce	Amateurs	Per cent	£1 Level stake
R. Hannon	15-140	7-57	4-17	1-16	1-8	0-10	2-27	0-5	0-0	10.7	- 35.21
S. C. Williams	12-54	2-10	1-7	3-7	0-2	2-9	4-15	0-4	0-0	22.2	+ **31.16**
J. L. Dunlop	12-54	4-17	1-7	4-11	0-2	1-11	2-5	0-1	0-0	22.2	- 9.13
J. Pearce	11-75	0-7	0-0	4-16	0-0	1-3	3-42	1-4	2-3	14.7	+ **10.00**
G. L. Moore	11-106	2-17	1-4	0-18	0-3	1-7	5-46	2-5	0-6	10.4	- 49.07
Miss Gay Kelleway	10-58	2-7	0-1	6-17	0-2	0-4	1-24	0-2	1-1	17.2	- 1.50
M. R. Channon	10-89	4-30	4-15	1-11	0-3	0-9	1-14	0-7	0-0	11.2	- 45.13
N. A. Callaghan	9-37	2-11	0-0	1-5	1-4	2-11	2-5	1-1	0-0	24.3	+ **23.54**
Sir Mark Prescott	9-38	4-21	0-0	3-6	0-3	1-3	0-4	0-0	1-1	23.7	- 3.85
W. R. Muir	9-58	3-14	1-7	4-15	0-3	0-3	1-15	0-1	0-0	15.5	- 3.54
C. E. Brittain	9-79	1-15	2-7	0-9	0-2	2-11	4-29	0-3	0-3	11.4	+ **16.75**
P. F. I. Cole	8-60	2-21	1-5	0-7	0-2	2-12	2-9	1-3	0-1	13.3	- 5.25
J. M. Bradley	8-48	0-2	1-2	3-15	0-0	0-0	2-20	1-5	1-4	16.7	+ **0.50**
D. R. C. Elsworth	7-39	1-8	0-3	2-11	0-0	0-2	4-12	0-2	0-1	18.0	+ **36.83**
C. A. Horgan	7-37	0-3	0-3	1-6	0-0	0-2	6-21	0-1	0-1	18.9	- 0.75
B. W. Hills	7-46	2-12	2-5	1-9	0-1	0-2	1-10	1-2	0-5	15.2	- 17.05

LEADING FLAT TRAINERS AT GOODWOOD (SINCE 1995)

	Total W-R	2yo Stks	3yo Stks	Other Stks	2yo H'caps	3yo H'caps	Other H'caps	App'ce	Amateurs	Per cent	£1 Level stake
P. F. I. Cole	33-146	12-44	5-21	5-18	2-9	3-23	6-31	0-0	0-0	22.6	**+ 30.18**
R. Hannon	33-351	12-96	6-38	4-40	2-29	3-46	6-98	0-2	0-2	9.4	- 151.33
J. H. M. Gosden	29-152	6-31	8-36	6-30	0-0	1-17	8-36	0-1	0-1	19.1	**+ 14.17**
H. R. A. Cecil	26-108	10-23	4-20	6-36	0-0	3-10	3-19	0-0	0-0	24.1	- 3.14
Sir Michael Stoute	25-100	3-14	5-22	6-24	0-1	6-18	5-21	0-0	0-0	25.0	**+ 4.77**
S bin Suroor	25-69	2-7	13-18	9-36	0-0	0-2	1-6	0-0	0-0	36.2	**+ 20.76**
J. L. Dunlop	22-230	5-68	6-34	3-38	0-10	1-34	7-46	0-0	0-0	9.6	- 124.63
M. Johnston	16-104	0-13	0-4	6-23	4-9	2-16	4-37	0-2	0-0	15.4	**+ 27.50**
D. R. C. Elsworth	16-102	1-14	3-15	4-18	0-1	1-6	5-43	2-5	0-0	15.7	**+ 5.85**
I. A. Balding	16-153	0-23	1-13	4-17	3-6	1-17	7-75	0-2	0-0	10.5	- 37.38
E. A. L. Dunlop	16-81	3-14	4-19	3-12	1-1	1-11	3-23	1-1	0-0	19.8	**+ 14.76**
M. R. Channon	13-145	5-44	3-9	1-8	0-15	1-15	2-47	0-6	1-1	9.0	- 28.00
L. M. Cumani	12-103	4-15	3-24	1-13	0-3	2-23	2-25	0-0	0-0	11.7	- 45.31
G. L. Moore	12-142	1-11	0-5	0-8	0-3	1-11	10-91	0-5	0-8	8.5	- 25.00
B. J. Meehan	12-112	5-33	1-9	0-9	1-10	2-15	3-34	0-1	0-1	10.7	- 1.00
D. Nicholls	10-47	0-0	0-0	1-2	0-0	1-4	7-38	1-3	0-0	21.3	**+ 37.67**

LEADING FLAT TRAINERS AT HAMILTON (SINCE 1995)

	Total W-R	2yo Stks	3yo Stks	Other Stks	2yo H'caps	3yo H'caps	Other H'caps	App'ce	Amateurs	Per cent	£1 Level stake
Miss L. A. Perratt	39-409	5-34	0-10	7-54	2-9	3-15	14-214	4-43	4-30	9.5	**+ 19.17**
J. Berry	36-268	19-93	4-17	4-31	1-13	1-12	4-75	1-14	2-13	13.4	- 87.36
M. Johnston	35-187	9-66	1-7	6-16	4-10	2-10	13-74	0-4	0-0	18.7	- 39.29
P. C. Haslam	17-102	3-13	3-6	2-7	0-3	1-8	8-54	0-8	0-3	16.7	- 29.33
M. R. Channon	17-74	8-24	1-13	2-8	1-1	1-6	3-19	1-3	0-0	23.0	**+ 16.67**
D. HaydnJones	15-83	1-9	0-0	2-5	0-3	3-6	9-51	0-6	0-3	18.1	- 16.75
D. W. Chapman	15-96	0-1	0-0	1-5	0-2	0-1	8-62	2-11	4-14	15.6	**+ 62.25**
J. S. Goldie	14-197	0-15	0-2	1-23	0-6	0-7	10-111	3-19	0-14	7.1	- 80.25
Mrs M. Reveley	13-101	1-5	1-4	6-21	0-0	0-2	5-66	0-2	0-1	12.9	- 42.27
R. M. McKellar	11-160	0-5	1-3	0-17	0-2	0-4	7-94	2-21	1-14	6.9	- 34.50
J. Pearce	10-39	1-1	0-0	1-6	0-0	0-0	5-23	0-0	3-9	25.6	**+ 13.88**
D. A. Nolan	10-269	0-4	0-2	0-47	0-0	0-1	8-162	1-27	1-26	3.7	- 188.75
S. C. Williams	10-25	2-3	3-7	2-2	0-3	0-3	3-6	0-1	0-0	40.0	**+ 27.25**
Sir Mark Prescott	9-38	4-15	0-1	2-5	0-1	2-6	0-8	1-1	0-1	23.7	- 5.96
C. W. Thornton	9-89	1-9	1-6	2-14	0-1	1-6	4-51	0-1	0-1	10.1	- 29.75
M. W. Easterby	9-55	1-13	0-1	0-0	0-2	0-3	8-29	0-6	0-1	16.4	- 0.90

LEADING FLAT TRAINERS AT HAYDOCK (SINCE 1995)

	Total W-R	2yo Stks	3yo Stks	Other Stks	2yo H'caps	3yo H'caps	Other H'caps	App'ce	Amateurs	Per cent	£1 Level stake
J. L. Dunlop	35-127	13-37	3-12	5-23	0-0	6-24	8-31	0-0	0-0	27.6	**+ 34.22**
B. W. Hills	29-126	10-30	7-19	6-29	0-3	2-24	4-21	0-0	0-0	23.0	**+ 28.14**
J. H. M. Gosden	25-117	4-19	6-27	6-27	0-0	4-17	5-25	0-0	0-2	21.4	**+ 5.59**
H. R. A. Cecil	20-53	6-8	3-12	8-20	0-0	2-7	1-6	0-0	0-0	37.7	**+ 13.46**
J. Berry	17-218	6-87	3-13	3-20	0-17	2-19	2-57	1-5	0-0	7.8	- 96.38
B. J. Meehan	13-63	5-21	2-6	2-8	1-4	2-8	1-14	0-0	0-2	20.6	- 5.21
T. D. Easterby	12-122	4-40	1-8	2-9	0-6	1-21	4-34	0-4	0-0	9.8	- 65.26
Mrs M. Reveley	12-85	0-8	0-4	3-13	0-1	0-6	9-50	0-2	0-1	14.1	- 18.39
R. Hannon	12-137	7-44	1-14	1-25	0-7	1-24	2-23	0-0	0-0	8.8	- 82.63
L. M. Cumani	11-58	1-3	3-13	2-17	0-0	1-13	3-11	1-1	0-0	19.0	- 11.08
P. F. I. Cole	11-76	4-14	0-8	2-12	0-0	3-20	2-22	0-0	0-0	14.5	- 15.50
M. Johnston	11-129	5-35	0-7	2-18	0-2	2-23	2-41	0-3	0-0	8.5	- 61.07
Sir Michael Stoute	10-60	4-18	3-16	3-11	0-0	0-9	0-6	0-0	0-0	16.7	- 21.77
E. A. L. Dunlop	9-60	2-16	3-14	1-9	1-1	2-9	0-11	0-0	0-0	15.0	- 16.33
R. A. Fahey	9-45	1-11	1-2	2-8	0-4	2-9	2-8	1-3	0-0	20.0	**+ 11.25**
A. C. Stewart	8-28	0-4	1-6	2-4	0-0	3-7	2-7	0-0	0-0	28.6	**+ 25.60**

LEADING FLAT TRAINERS AT KEMPTON (SINCE 1995)

	Total W-R	2yo Stks	3yo Stks	Other Stks	2yo H'caps	3yo H'caps	Other H'caps	App'ce	Amateurs	Per cent	£1 Level stake
R. Hannon	34-270	13-81	7-42	3-26	0-8	3-31	6-71	2-11	0-0	12.6	- 14.73
Sir Michael Stoute	19-99	4-28	9-37	4-19	0-0	0-3	2-12	0-0	0-0	19.2	- 12.09
H. R. A. Cecil	16-70	2-8	11-38	1-14	0-0	0-1	2-9	0-0	0-0	22.9	- 1.08
J. L. Dunlop	16-120	4-37	6-35	4-12	1-1	0-13	1-22	0-0	0-0	13.3	- 39.31
P. F. I. Cole	14-91	5-26	2-22	2-13	0-0	0-6	5-23	0-1	0-0	15.4	**+ 22.20**
D. R. C. Elsworth	13-98	2-28	0-19	2-9	2-3	1-3	6-32	0-4	0-0	13.3	**+ 16.75**
B. J. Meehan	13-110	4-38	3-12	0-8	2-6	1-12	3-34	0-0	0-0	11.8	- 2.27
J. R. Fanshawe	11-68	2-10	4-23	2-8	0-1	0-4	3-22	0-0	0-0	16.2	**+ 1.74**
J. H. M. Gosden	9-69	3-14	2-29	2-13	0-0	2-8	0-3	0-2	0-0	13.0	- 34.78
I. A. Balding	8-94	2-21	3-22	0-8	0-1	0-7	2-29	1-6	0-0	8.5	- 55.25
R. Charlton	8-62	2-14	1-21	0-7	0-0	1-6	4-14	0-0	0-0	12.9	- 8.97
L. M. Cumani	8-36	3-5	3-16	1-11	0-0	0-2	1-2	0-0	0-0	22.2	**+ 9.13**
P. W. Harris	8-92	2-22	2-23	1-10	0-0	1-4	1-32	1-1	0-0	8.7	- 33.54
W. J. Musson	7-49	0-2	0-2	0-1	0-1	0-0	5-38	2-5	0-0	14.3	**+ 5.50**
M. R. Channon	7-84	2-29	2-14	1-5	0-2	2-11	0-21	0-2	0-0	8.3	**+ 8.21**
Mrs A. J. Perrett	6-16	0-0	2-4	1-2	0-0	0-0	3-10	0-0	0-0	37.5	**+ 64.33**

LEADING FLAT TRAINERS AT LEICESTER (SINCE 1995)

	Total W-R	2yo Stks	3yo Stks	Other Stks	2yo H'caps	3yo H'caps	Other H'caps	App'ce	Amateurs	Per cent	£1 Level stake
R. Hannon	29-202	8-54	9-38	2-30	3-23	2-18	5-35	0-4	0-0	14.4	**+ 37.85**
J. L. Dunlop	27-170	11-80	4-22	4-27	0-6	6-21	2-14	0-0	0-0	15.9	**+ 3.77**
Sir Michael Stoute	21-77	9-41	5-10	6-19	0-0	1-3	0-3	0-1	0-0	27.3	**+ 7.56**
H. R. A. Cecil	18-69	11-31	3-14	4-17	0-0	0-2	0-5	0-0	0-0	26.1	- 6.65
B. W. Hills	18-95	9-46	2-10	5-11	1-5	0-11	0-9	1-3	0-0	19.0	- 15.20
P. F. I. Cole	17-129	5-46	2-27	3-19	1-7	4-16	2-12	0-2	0-0	13.2	- 41.18
J. H. M. Gosden	14-79	1-28	5-14	7-18	0-2	0-4	1-8	0-5	0-0	17.7	- 10.74
B. Hanbury	12-38	2-5	2-10	4-10	1-2	2-3	0-6	1-2	0-0	31.6	**+ 15.65**
B. J. Meehan	12-89	4-28	4-18	2-13	1-11	1-10	0-9	0-0	0-0	13.5	**+ 18.90**
L. M. Cumani	11-50	2-16	4-12	1-7	0-0	0-5	3-7	1-3	0-0	22.0	- 17.19
D. R. Loder	10-29	7-19	3-6	0-3	0-0	0-1	0-0	0-0	0-0	34.5	**+ 0.32**
J. L. Harris	10-64	0-4	1-6	2-16	1-2	0-1	4-29	2-6	0-0	15.6	**+ 48.00**
R. Hollinshead	10-141	4-29	0-21	1-24	0-7	1-11	4-45	0-4	0-0	7.1	- 18.50
Sir Mark Prescott	9-52	1-24	1-5	2-8	2-3	1-4	2-6	0-1	0-1	17.3	- 5.38
H. Candy	9-64	2-17	1-7	1-7	0-0	1-10	4-22	0-1	0-0	14.1	**+ 44.38**
G. L. Moore	8-42	1-4	2-5	1-7	0-2	2-4	0-17	1-2	1-1	19.1	**+ 19.00**

LEADING FLAT TRAINERS AT LINGFIELD- Turf (SINCE 1995)

	Total W-R	2yo Stks	3yo Stks	Other Stks	2yo H'caps	3yo H'caps	Other H'caps	App'ce	Amateurs	Per cent	£1 Level stake
R. Hannon	30-241	19-99	2-13	3-41	2-16	3-35	1-36	0-1	0-0	12.5	- 94.05
J. L. Dunlop	22-118	10-60	5-10	3-17	0-5	3-16	1-9	0-0	0-1	18.6	- 51.61
H. R. A. Cecil	18-49	4-11	4-10	10-25	0-0	0-3	0-0	0-0	0-0	36.7	- 7.62
B. J. Meehan	15-91	10-45	1-3	0-4	1-4	3-16	0-17	0-0	0-2	16.5	- 12.38
Sir Michael Stoute	15-69	7-27	2-10	5-22	0-0	1-3	0-7	0-0	0-0	21.7	**+ 23.93**
J. Berry	15-67	12-35	0-1	2-7	0-2	0-8	1-14	0-0	0-0	22.4	**+ 3.50**
C. F. Wall	11-47	1-6	1-4	0-8	0-3	2-9	4-12	2-4	1-1	23.4	**+ 10.83**
M. L. W. Bell	11-70	3-28	0-1	1-8	0-6	4-14	2-8	1-5	0-0	15.7	- 23.49
B. W. Hills	10-47	2-14	2-7	4-12	0-2	1-7	1-5	0-0	0-0	21.3	**+ 3.34**
C. E. Brittain	10-84	2-16	0-13	2-19	0-2	1-11	3-20	2-3	0-0	11.9	**+ 5.80**
G. L. Moore	10-146	4-32	1-8	0-21	0-1	2-15	2-56	1-10	0-3	6.9	- 67.18
S. Dow	10-151	0-43	2-11	2-18	0-4	0-17	4-50	2-4	0-4	6.6	- 10.50
D. R. C. Elsworth	9-58	2-19	1-8	2-8	0-0	1-6	2-14	0-1	1-2	15.5	- 11.50
B. Hanbury	9-42	1-8	2-4	1-12	0-1	1-5	4-12	0-0	0-0	21.4	**+ 8.08**
Lady Herries	9-46	0-3	0-2	5-17	0-0	1-4	3-19	0-1	0-0	19.6	**+ 30.03**
Sir Mark Prescott	8-57	1-28	2-4	0-3	1-4	1-8	3-10	0-0	0-0	14.0	- 32.36

LEADING FLAT TRAINERS AT LINGFIELD- All Weather (SINCE 1995)

	Total W-R	2yo Stks	3yo Stks	Other Stks	2yo H'caps	3yo H'caps	Other H'caps	App'ce	Amateurs	Per cent	£1 Level stake
G. L. Moore	101-707	6-23	7-45	22-171	1-16	10-50	44-329	2-34	9-39	14.3	- 118.04
M. Johnston	50-283	2-15	11-33	11-46	6-17	9-61	10-103	1-8	0-0	17.7	- 37.91
Miss Gay Kelleway	47-331	1-6	3-18	15-96	0-7	1-13	22-165	4-20	1-6	14.2	- 118.39
S. Dow	36-371	0-9	4-29	3-56	0-7	7-34	19-196	0-21	3-19	9.7	- 102.50
C. A. Cyzer	35-227	0-4	1-12	13-67	0-2	3-10	16-118	2-8	0-6	15.4	- 2.46
R. Hannon	35-218	7-30	5-27	4-39	5-24	8-33	3-54	3-8	0-3	16.1	- 46.23
R. J. O'Sullivan	32-239	0-0	0-4	12-53	0-3	0-4	18-155	0-7	2-13	13.4	- 34.36
T. J. Naughton	30-230	1-16	6-33	10-52	1-8	6-26	5-81	0-8	1-6	13.0	- 73.03
K. R. Burke	30-219	1-2	1-9	10-65	0-6	1-11	13-104	3-17	1-5	13.7	- 29.92
R. Ingram	30-242	0-8	2-14	12-63	0-4	0-11	15-127	0-8	1-7	12.4	- 11.72
D. W. Chapman	26-140	0-0	0-0	2-15	0-0	0-4	21-110	0-1	3-10	18.6	**+ 30.96**
P. C. Haslam	26-138	1-2	10-22	1-14	0-0	8-43	6-49	0-7	0-1	18.8	- 10.84
J. J. Bridger	23-422	1-16	0-29	6-128	1-8	0-10	13-191	1-18	1-22	5.5	- 121.25
J. Berry	23-105	8-18	3-15	6-34	2-6	1-9	2-21	1-2	0-0	21.9	- 13.79
P. D. Evans	22-195	0-9	0-14	6-28	1-10	1-23	8-87	3-11	3-13	11.3	- 51.25
Miss B. Sanders	21-147	0-4	0-3	3-17	0-1	0-3	14-98	1-5	3-16	14.3	- 28.75

LEADING FLAT TRAINERS AT MUSSELBURGH (SINCE 1995)

	Total W-R	2yo Stks	3yo Stks	Other Stks	2yo H'caps	3yo H'caps	Other H'caps	App'ce	Amateurs	Per cent	£1 Level stake
J. Berry	42-222	21-78	0-4	8-31	2-23	1-17	10-60	0-5	0-4	18.9	**+ 57.67**
Mrs M. Reveley	20-110	0-6	2-6	7-19	0-2	0-1	9-70	2-6	0-0	18.2	- 23.98
J. S. Goldie	16-159	1-9	0-2	2-6	1-8	1-6	10-113	1-12	0-3	10.1	**+ 15.50**
M. Johnston	16-119	6-28	1-2	1-8	1-4	2-14	5-62	0-1	0-0	13.5	- 45.09
M. L. W. Bell	11-21	0-2	2-2	1-3	0-0	1-2	6-11	1-1	0-0	52.4	**+ 45.95**
M. R. Channon	11-44	3-13	0-1	1-9	3-4	0-3	4-14	0-0	0-0	25.0	**+ 10.79**
P. D. Evans	10-86	6-30	0-0	0-6	1-9	0-8	2-30	1-2	0-1	11.6	- 52.45
Sir Mark Prescott	10-30	2-7	1-1	1-5	1-4	3-6	2-6	0-1	0-0	33.3	**+ 2.36**
J. L. Eyre	10-136	0-14	0-4	2-9	0-4	0-6	8-90	0-6	0-3	7.4	- 35.00
E. J. Alston	9-76	1-8	0-0	2-10	0-3	0-6	5-47	1-2	0-0	11.8	- 13.75
M. W. Easterby	9-50	3-13	0-0	0-3	0-5	2-4	4-22	0-3	0-0	18.0	**+ 8.75**
N. Tinkler	9-47	3-13	0-2	3-4	0-1	0-5	3-21	0-0	0-1	19.2	- 11.12
T. D. Easterby	8-36	0-5	1-1	1-4	0-4	1-5	4-16	1-1	0-0	22.2	**+ 25.00**
T. D. Barron	8-50	2-11	0-0	1-5	1-5	1-5	3-21	0-2	0-1	16.0	**+ 24.91**
T. J. Etherington	7-39	1-7	1-1	1-2	0-2	0-4	4-22	0-0	0-1	18.0	**+ 9.49**
C. W. Thornton	7-45	2-9	1-4	2-7	0-1	0-3	2-21	0-0	0-0	15.6	- 14.63

LEADING FLAT TRAINERS AT NEWBURY (SINCE 1995)

	Total W-R	2yo Stks	3yo Stks	Other Stks	2yo H'caps	3yo H'caps	Other H'caps	App'ce	Amateurs	Per cent	£1 Level stake
J. H. M. Gosden	33-145	11-36	7-46	11-30	0-1	2-9	2-23	0-0	0-0	22.8	**+ 72.25**
J. L. Dunlop	25-196	2-68	7-34	7-28	0-12	3-18	6-36	0-0	0-0	12.8	- 63.58
P. F. I. Cole	25-181	7-52	5-27	6-31	2-8	3-24	2-38	0-1	0-0	13.8	**+ 45.85**
H. R. A. Cecil	22-113	4-14	9-49	5-30	0-0	1-5	3-15	0-0	0-0	19.5	**+ 9.41**
R. Hannon	21-435	8-158	6-69	1-39	1-28	1-33	4-95	0-13	0-0	4.8	- 261.39
B. W. Hills	20-246	11-109	1-43	3-27	1-6	0-14	4-46	0-1	0-0	8.1	- 116.63
I. A. Balding	19-202	9-61	2-34	4-21	1-3	1-21	2-61	0-1	0-0	9.4	- 85.11
R. Charlton	14-116	2-23	6-40	2-13	0-2	1-10	3-25	0-3	0-0	12.1	- 44.01
B. J. Meehan	12-215	4-85	3-32	1-15	1-26	1-13	2-41	0-3	0-0	5.6	- 65.00
L. M. Cumani	12-54	2-8	5-20	2-11	1-1	0-5	2-9	0-0	0-0	22.2	- 2.81
M. R. Channon	12-185	6-69	1-25	0-4	2-21	0-10	3-50	0-6	0-0	6.5	- 84.40
D. R. C. Elsworth	11-123	3-26	2-17	1-13	1-6	0-4	3-50	1-7	0-0	8.9	- 46.80
Sir Michael Stoute	11-97	1-18	2-24	7-35	0-2	1-7	0-11	0-0	0-0	11.3	- 17.00
Lady Herries	9-79	0-0	4-16	2-19	0-0	0-1	3-41	0-2	0-0	11.4	- 6.06
E. A. L. Dunlop	8-53	3-16	1-11	0-6	0-0	1-5	3-14	0-1	0-0	15.1	- 12.88
H. Candy	7-65	0-7	1-11	1-7	0-4	1-2	4-32	0-2	0-0	10.8	- 23.38

LEADING FLAT TRAINERS AT NEWCASTLE (SINCE 1995)

	Total W-R	2yo Stks	3yo Stks	Other Stks	2yo H'caps	3yo H'caps	Other H'caps	App'ce	Amateurs	Per cent	£1 Level stake
M. Johnston	35-204	12-66	1-6	6-28	1-9	2-24	13-69	0-2	0-0	17.2	- 44.68
J. Berry	21-165	8-59	1-6	6-19	2-5	0-15	4-56	0-4	0-1	12.7	- 51.01
J. L. Dunlop	20-64	8-15	2-8	4-11	0-3	2-8	4-19	0-0	0-0	31.3	+ **5.84**
Mrs M. Reveley	14-130	0-13	0-3	2-21	0-0	2-12	9-75	1-6	0-0	10.8	- 37.75
T. D. Easterby	12-137	4-37	0-2	1-6	1-12	1-28	5-52	0-0	0-0	8.8	- 59.67
Sir Michael Stoute	12-53	6-16	1-5	3-10	0-0	1-8	1-14	0-0	0-0	22.6	- 13.22
H. R. A. Cecil	12-29	1-4	2-4	7-13	0-0	0-0	2-8	0-0	0-0	41.4	+ **15.95**
M. L. W. Bell	12-49	1-11	3-6	1-7	2-3	3-8	1-13	1-1	0-0	24.5	+ **25.31**
R. A. Fahey	10-57	4-18	0-1	1-2	0-0	2-10	3-26	0-0	0-0	17.5	+ **21.50**
M. W. Easterby	10-148	3-40	0-1	0-5	0-10	2-24	5-67	0-1	0-0	6.8	- 65.90
Sir Mark Prescott	9-36	4-14	0-1	3-9	0-2	2-5	0-4	0-1	0-0	25.0	+ **4.00**
J. L. Eyre	9-102	1-20	0-2	2-8	0-2	1-10	5-57	0-2	0-1	8.8	+ **23.00**
B. W. Hills	8-54	5-13	0-5	1-12	1-5	1-5	0-13	0-1	0-0	14.8	- 27.03
D. R. Loder	7-22	4-10	1-2	1-5	0-0	0-0	1-5	0-0	0-0	31.8	- 2.88
J. H. M. Gosden	7-36	2-10	2-7	3-11	0-0	0-4	0-4	0-0	0-0	19.4	- 6.00
P. W. Harris	6-20	0-2	0-1	2-3	1-2	1-2	2-10	0-0	0-0	30.0	+ **27.00**

LEADING FLAT TRAINERS AT NEWMARKET- Rowley (SINCE 1995)

	Total W-R	2yo Stks	3yo Stks	Other Stks	2yo H'caps	3yo H'caps	Other H'caps	App'ce	Amateurs	Per cent	£1 Level stake
H. R. A. Cecil	40-158	8-28	24-80	6-30	0-0	0-4	2-16	0-0	0-0	25.3	+ **16.62**
B. W. Hills	24-240	9-72	3-58	3-30	2-12	2-22	5-46	0-0	0-0	10.0	- 56.00
S bin Suroor	20-77	8-22	8-26	4-25	0-1	0-0	0-3	0-0	0-0	26.0	+ **29.40**
D. R. Loder	20-86	13-39	3-14	2-18	1-4	1-3	0-8	0-0	0-0	23.3	+ **10.65**
J. L. Dunlop	20-186	7-46	3-37	5-34	0-6	0-17	5-46	0-0	0-0	10.8	- 25.13
L. M. Cumani	17-123	2-28	3-40	7-19	0-2	3-14	2-19	0-1	0-0	13.8	- 43.91
J. H. M. Gosden	16-147	5-48	6-46	3-20	0-3	0-7	2-21	0-2	0-0	10.9	- 64.39
R. Hannon	14-239	4-65	2-30	2-32	1-25	2-34	3-51	0-2	0-0	5.9	- 96.25
Sir Michael Stoute	12-154	1-34	5-51	4-35	0-2	1-14	1-18	0-0	0-0	7.8	- 93.42
C. E. Brittain	11-152	1-32	6-43	3-25	0-6	0-12	1-33	0-1	0-0	7.2	- 29.79
P. F. I. Cole	11-101	7-32	0-15	3-13	1-8	0-13	0-20	0-0	0-0	10.9	- 46.64
E. A. L. Dunlop	9-80	3-24	2-18	1-9	3-6	0-3	0-17	0-3	0-0	11.3	- 39.80
J. R. Fanshawe	9-84	0-11	0-11	3-16	2-5	0-4	4-35	0-2	0-0	10.7	- 24.88
M. L. W. Bell	9-99	3-31	1-14	1-8	1-8	2-21	1-14	0-3	0-0	9.1	- 28.52
I. A. Balding	8-81	3-15	1-12	2-11	0-2	1-10	1-30	0-1	0-0	9.9	+ **17.75**
G. Wragg	7-80	0-26	2-28	1-13	0-0	2-3	1-9	1-1	0-0	8.8	- 49.01

LEADING FLAT TRAINERS AT NEWMARKET- July (SINCE 1995)

	Total W-R	2yo Stks	3yo Stks	Other Stks	2yo H'caps	3yo H'caps	Other H'caps	App'ce	Amateurs	Per cent	£1 Level stake
J. H. M. Gosden	34-185	8-64	13-46	8-36	0-0	3-22	2-16	0-1	0-0	18.4	- 17.02
H. R. A. Cecil	32-141	9-26	11-46	7-44	0-0	2-10	3-15	0-0	0-0	22.7	- 22.98
J. L. Dunlop	30-208	10-81	3-18	8-39	2-10	2-22	5-38	0-0	0-0	14.4	- 37.17
R. Hannon	26-275	3-70	3-34	9-43	4-34	4-55	2-35	1-4	0-0	9.5	- 88.00
L. M. Cumani	24-156	7-47	7-41	3-25	0-1	2-12	5-29	0-1	0-0	15.4	- 25.10
B. Hanbury	18-108	6-29	1-12	4-17	0-1	3-10	4-37	0-0	0-2	16.7	+ **62.91**
B. W. Hills	18-197	6-69	2-34	2-25	1-9	3-24	3-35	1-1	0-0	9.1	- 62.46
Sir Michael Stoute	16-135	5-54	2-22	5-31	0-0	1-11	3-17	0-0	0-0	11.9	- 58.53
E. A. L. Dunlop	16-124	6-37	4-18	2-16	0-6	0-12	4-34	0-1	0-0	12.9	- 10.31
P. F. I. Cole	15-115	9-35	1-16	2-16	1-11	1-20	1-16	0-1	0-0	13.0	- 21.00
M. L. W. Bell	12-159	5-49	2-14	1-9	1-12	2-27	1-43	0-5	0-0	7.6	- 45.25
W. J. Musson	12-106	0-3	0-6	0-6	0-0	1-3	9-74	2-13	0-1	11.3	+ **2.50**
D. R. Loder	11-70	9-35	0-2	0-12	0-3	0-11	2-7	0-0	0-0	15.7	- 36.67
S bin Suroor	10-55	3-13	3-12	4-29	0-0	0-1	0-0	0-0	0-0	18.2	- 24.31
B. J. Meehan	10-124	2-31	1-14	0-11	0-13	2-25	5-29	0-0	0-1	8.1	- 38.90
J. R. Fanshawe	10-99	1-15	2-9	0-17	0-2	0-17	7-39	0-0	0-0	10.1	- 31.29

LEADING FLAT TRAINERS AT NOTTINGHAM (SINCE 1995)

	Total W-R	2yo Stks	3yo Stks	Other Stks	2yo H'caps	3yo H'caps	Other H'caps	App'ce	Amateurs	Per cent	£1 Level stake
J. L. Dunlop	29-169	10-60	2-22	6-22	0-4	7-33	4-28	0-0	0-0	17.2	- 37.17
H. R. A. Cecil	18-65	9-28	5-17	4-16	0-0	0-3	0-1	0-0	0-0	27.7	- 21.29
M. L. W. Bell	16-101	7-31	0-10	3-12	0-4	4-19	1-21	1-4	0-0	15.8	- 4.37
B. J. Meehan	14-86	5-27	4-16	2-7	1-7	2-17	0-11	0-1	0-0	16.3	**+ 32.24**
J. R. Fanshawe	13-64	2-12	3-16	2-11	1-1	2-5	3-19	0-0	0-0	20.3	**+ 42.45**
R. Hollinshead	13-157	2-28	0-19	1-22	0-4	2-36	7-43	1-5	0-0	8.3	- 57.00
Sir Mark Prescott	12-57	3-22	3-10	2-5	1-2	2-5	1-11	0-2	0-0	21.1	**+ 35.03**
E. A. L. Dunlop	11-53	5-24	1-9	4-8	0-1	1-4	0-6	0-1	0-0	20.8	**+ 3.79**
P. W. Harris	11-79	3-19	0-5	2-9	1-2	1-9	4-33	0-2	0-0	13.9	- 11.88
J. H. M. Gosden	10-61	4-24	3-10	0-11	0-0	2-7	1-9	0-0	0-0	16.4	- 4.93
B. A. McMahon	10-169	1-34	2-19	4-30	0-4	0-17	3-60	0-5	0-0	5.9	- 62.00
M. A. Jarvis	10-54	5-18	1-7	2-8	1-1	1-8	0-11	0-1	0-0	18.5	**+ 34.88**
Mrs M. Reveley	10-88	0-1	0-2	3-16	0-0	1-11	6-52	0-6	0-0	11.4	- 40.84
S. R. Bowring	10-96	0-4	1-9	0-9	2-3	1-21	5-47	1-3	0-0	10.4	- 10.00
P. J. Makin	9-65	0-10	1-3	2-16	0-1	2-16	3-15	1-3	0-1	13.9	**+ 16.50**
W. J. Haggas	9-33	1-9	3-10	0-2	1-1	4-9	0-2	0-0	0-0	27.3	**+ 8.25**

LEADING FLAT TRAINERS AT PONTEFRACT (SINCE 1995)

	Total W-R	2yo Stks	3yo Stks	Other Stks	2yo H'caps	3yo H'caps	Other H'caps	App'ce	Amateurs	Per cent	£1 Level stake
Mrs M. Reveley	15-123	0-4	0-7	5-30	0-4	1-3	8-70	0-4	1-1	12.2	- 31.23
J. L. Eyre	15-196	1-19	1-5	0-16	0-10	1-17	11-112	1-16	0-1	7.7	- 59.75
J. L. Dunlop	14-59	2-10	1-6	6-19	0-6	1-8	4-8	0-2	0-0	23.7	**+ 2.29**
M. Johnston	13-126	5-36	0-5	2-13	4-13	1-18	1-39	0-2	0-0	10.3	- 36.52
B. W. Hills	12-54	4-9	2-10	2-11	0-6	1-6	3-12	0-0	0-0	22.2	**+ 37.29**
I. A. Balding	12-58	3-9	3-13	0-5	1-4	2-5	3-19	0-2	0-1	20.7	**+ 22.33**
M. W. Easterby	11-117	1-19	0-1	0-6	0-26	0-4	7-48	3-13	0-0	9.4	- 34.00
D. Nicholls	10-112	0-5	0-5	0-11	0-2	0-2	9-79	1-8	0-0	8.9	- 17.50
R. A. Fahey	10-55	4-14	2-6	0-6	2-6	0-3	2-19	0-1	0-0	18.2	**+ 28.00**
J. J. Quinn	9-60	1-8	0-1	2-8	0-5	2-5	4-31	0-2	0-0	15.0	- 2.17
L. M. Cumani	9-39	1-4	1-10	6-18	0-0	0-1	1-5	0-1	0-0	23.1	- 6.36
H. R. A. Cecil	9-31	0-1	1-6	8-18	0-0	0-2	0-4	0-0	0-0	29.0	**+ 8.52**
M. L. W. Bell	9-49	2-10	1-5	2-8	1-3	0-7	3-15	0-1	0-0	18.4	**+ 3.23**
T. D. Easterby	8-101	5-25	0-7	0-5	0-12	0-11	3-41	0-0	0-0	7.9	- 43.13
N. Tinkler	8-67	0-17	0-5	3-5	2-7	0-2	3-29	0-2	0-0	11.9	**+ 9.50**
R. Hollinshead	8-142	2-28	3-25	0-21	0-14	0-12	3-37	0-5	0-0	5.6	- 62.50

LEADING FLAT TRAINERS AT REDCAR (SINCE 1995)

	Total W-R	2yo Stks	3yo Stks	Other Stks	2yo H'caps	3yo H'caps	Other H'caps	App'ce	Amateurs	Per cent	£1 Level stake
Mrs M. Reveley	26-298	0-23	1-15	11-49	0-14	2-19	11-161	1-9	0-8	8.7	- 160.96
J. H. M. Gosden	21-62	6-19	0-5	7-16	0-0	5-9	3-12	0-1	0-0	33.9	**+ 31.32**
M. Johnston	21-151	9-59	1-2	3-14	0-7	2-17	6-49	0-2	0-1	13.9	- 19.09
J. L. Eyre	18-168	3-25	0-5	1-21	1-9	0-13	11-81	0-7	2-7	10.7	- 26.06
J. Berry	18-184	6-61	3-12	4-30	0-14	1-13	4-45	0-3	0-6	9.8	- 44.25
J. L. Dunlop	17-69	6-20	0-1	3-9	2-5	1-11	5-23	0-0	0-0	24.6	- 3.03
M. W. Easterby	15-178	3-49	0-0	0-5	3-32	2-25	6-54	1-6	0-7	8.4	- 73.25
E. A. L. Dunlop	11-42	3-13	0-1	4-9	0-2	4-5	0-12	0-0	0-0	26.2	- 9.19
Sir Mark Prescott	11-49	4-21	2-3	1-2	0-3	2-8	2-11	0-0	0-1	22.5	- 13.88
T. D. Easterby	10-150	4-46	0-5	0-4	1-10	2-26	3-49	0-3	0-7	6.7	- 50.50
T. D. Barron	10-90	4-22	0-1	0-2	0-9	3-9	2-39	1-4	0-4	11.1	- 13.13
C. A. Dwyer	8-34	0-5	0-1	1-3	0-2	2-7	4-13	1-1	0-2	23.5	**+ 12.25**
J. R. Fanshawe	8-30	2-9	1-3	1-6	0-0	2-4	2-8	0-0	0-0	26.7	**+ 4.34**
D. R. Loder	8-26	5-18	1-2	2-3	0-0	0-1	0-2	0-0	0-0	30.8	- 0.69
J. J. Quinn	7-49	1-8	0-3	1-4	0-1	2-3	2-23	1-4	0-3	14.3	**+ 16.38**
E. J. Alston	7-76	0-5	0-3	0-11	0-3	2-10	4-37	1-4	0-3	9.2	**+ 7.50**

LEADING FLAT TRAINERS AT RIPON (SINCE 1995)

	Total W-R	2yo Stks	3yo Stks	Other Stks	2yo H'caps	3yo H'caps	Other H'caps	App'ce	Amateurs	Per cent	£1 Level stake
M. Johnston	24-135	5-31	3-12	4-12	0-1	2-28	9-48	1-3	0-0	17.8	+ **21.54**
T. D. Easterby	22-178	7-47	0-8	2-16	0-3	4-38	8-61	1-5	0-0	12.4	- 68.58
H. R. A. Cecil	13-34	0-0	4-8	8-18	0-0	0-3	1-5	0-0	0-0	38.2	- 5.62
J. L. Dunlop	13-51	5-5	1-9	1-3	0-0	3-20	3-14	0-0	0-0	25.5	+ **2.93**
J. Berry	13-138	8-67	0-3	3-14	0-3	0-17	2-30	0-4	0-0	9.4	- 79.72
L. M. Cumani	12-53	3-6	3-13	3-16	0-0	0-8	3-10	0-0	0-0	22.6	- 17.15
M. W. Easterby	12-171	2-45	0-6	0-6	1-6	5-32	4-64	0-12	0-0	7.0	- 98.75
B. W. Hills	10-59	1-7	3-11	5-17	0-1	0-11	1-12	0-0	0-0	17.0	- 16.58
W. J. Haggas	8-33	1-4	1-2	1-4	1-1	0-6	4-15	0-1	0-0	24.2	- 0.88
S. P. C. Woods	8-28	0-1	0-3	4-8	0-0	2-6	2-9	0-1	0-0	28.6	+ **4.13**
Mrs M. Reveley	8-82	0-4	0-3	1-13	0-0	1-8	6-52	0-2	0-0	9.8	- 17.42
J. H. M. Gosden	8-55	0-3	2-15	6-28	0-0	0-6	0-3	0-0	0-0	14.6	- 36.79
J. L. Eyre	8-111	0-15	0-4	0-14	0-1	2-14	4-52	2-11	0-0	7.2	- 35.00
M. R. Channon	8-48	1-16	2-3	0-0	0-1	3-14	2-12	0-2	0-0	16.7	+ **6.38**
S. R. Bowring	7-52	0-5	0-0	0-4	0-1	1-11	5-27	1-4	0-0	13.5	- 5.00
D. R. Loder	6-13	1-2	1-4	1-1	1-1	1-3	1-2	0-0	0-0	46.2	+ **8.62**

LEADING FLAT TRAINERS AT SALISBURY (SINCE 1995)

	Total W-R	2yo Stks	3yo Stks	Other Stks	2yo H'caps	3yo H'caps	Other H'caps	App'ce	Amateurs	Per cent	£1 Level stake
R. Hannon	41-374	19-148	9-38	5-40	0-0	4-42	4-91	0-12	0-3	11.0	- 148.90
J. L. Dunlop	28-135	11-64	3-15	5-22	0-0	4-18	5-16	0-0	0-0	20.7	- 28.19
P. F. I. Cole	15-102	7-36	4-18	2-16	0-0	0-14	2-13	0-5	0-0	14.7	- 49.78
I. A. Balding	14-145	3-40	4-27	3-19	0-0	1-18	3-32	0-7	0-2	9.7	- 67.06
P. T. Walwyn	13-69	4-27	1-6	1-7	0-0	2-6	3-20	0-0	2-3	18.8	+ **9.88**
R. Charlton	12-76	5-31	1-11	1-14	0-0	4-9	1-11	0-0	0-0	15.8	- 23.32
Miss Gay Kelleway	11-94	2-13	0-14	3-11	0-0	1-6	4-45	1-5	0-0	11.7	+ **38.63**
M. R. Channon	11-170	3-58	1-19	0-10	0-0	1-16	5-57	1-9	0-1	6.5	- 86.68
J. H. M. Gosden	10-57	3-18	2-15	3-10	0-0	0-2	2-10	0-2	0-0	17.5	- 20.33
Sir Michael Stoute	10-44	1-12	2-10	6-14	0-0	1-7	0-1	0-0	0-0	22.7	- 5.32
B. J. Meehan	10-109	5-51	0-7	1-5	0-0	1-13	3-26	0-0	0-7	9.2	- 36.17
D. R. C. Elsworth	10-141	6-34	1-25	0-21	0-0	0-14	3-41	0-3	0-3	7.1	- 94.08
S. Dow	10-96	2-16	0-10	1-6	0-0	3-13	1-41	1-4	2-6	10.4	- 6.42
H. R. A. Cecil	8-32	1-2	4-16	3-10	0-0	0-2	0-2	0-0	0-0	25.0	- 14.49
R. F. JohnsonHoughton	8-27	2-9	0-1	1-2	0-0	1-4	3-10	0-0	1-1	29.6	+ **83.00**
L. M. Cumani	7-40	0-7	3-10	2-13	0-0	0-3	2-7	0-0	0-0	17.5	- 21.84

LEADING FLAT TRAINERS AT SANDOWN (SINCE 1995)

	Total W-R	2yo Stks	3yo Stks	Other Stks	2yo H'caps	3yo H'caps	Other H'caps	App'ce	Amateurs	Per cent	£1 Level stake
Sir Michael Stoute	34-149	9-24	6-24	11-51	0-1	2-18	6-30	0-0	0-1	22.8	+ **6.28**
R. Hannon	28-304	15-92	2-21	4-37	2-13	2-64	3-68	0-8	0-1	9.2	- 126.23
J. L. Dunlop	19-131	8-36	2-9	1-26	0-1	4-28	4-30	0-0	0-1	14.5	- 35.31
H. R. A. Cecil	17-90	5-16	3-22	5-38	0-0	3-7	1-7	0-0	0-0	18.9	- 19.78
J. H. M. Gosden	17-109	3-18	4-29	7-40	0-1	1-12	2-9	0-0	0-0	15.6	- 35.41
I. A. Balding	17-109	4-29	0-10	5-20	0-1	4-18	4-31	0-0	0-0	15.6	- 18.20
B. J. Meehan	16-150	7-53	1-12	3-17	1-13	1-25	3-29	0-0	0-1	10.7	- 3.24
P. F. I. Cole	15-85	4-28	4-12	1-11	0-1	3-17	3-16	0-0	0-0	17.7	+ **15.86**
D. R. C. Elsworth	14-105	4-20	3-18	2-30	0-1	1-5	4-31	0-0	0-0	13.3	- 0.38
S bin Suroor	11-25	4-6	1-1	5-17	0-0	1-1	0-0	0-0	0-0	44.0	+ **11.48**
M. Johnston	11-54	1-9	0-0	3-17	0-3	4-9	3-16	0-0	0-0	20.4	+ **54.58**
J. R. Fanshawe	11-59	1-4	4-10	5-15	0-0	0-9	1-21	0-0	0-0	18.6	+ **40.95**
B. W. Hills	9-91	4-34	1-9	0-15	0-0	3-19	1-13	0-1	0-0	9.9	- 39.00
R. W. Armstrong	8-69	1-3	0-9	2-16	0-1	1-11	4-29	0-0	0-0	11.6	+ **30.33**
J. R. Poulton	7-20	0-0	0-0	0-4	0-0	0-1	6-12	1-3	0-0	35.0	+ **56.00**
S. C. Williams	7-24	0-2	1-2	1-2	0-0	0-5	5-12	0-1	0-0	29.2	+ **24.38**

LEADING FLAT TRAINERS AT SOUTHWELL (SINCE 1995)

	Total W-R	2yo Stks	3yo Stks	Other Stks	2yo H'caps	3yo H'caps	Other H'caps	App'ce	Amateurs	Per cent	£1 Level stake
J. L. Eyre	55-396	0-14	0-19	12-52	0-5	2-15	31-224	4-20	6-47	13.9	- 93.81
S. R. Bowring	53-443	1-17	0-27	6-61	2-5	8-35	29-255	5-31	2-12	12.0	- 100.12
M. Johnston	46-241	3-34	7-28	6-28	2-16	10-52	15-72	2-6	1-5	19.1	**+ 41.22**
R. Hollinshead	44-455	1-31	4-57	19-121	0-9	4-41	13-167	3-27	0-2	9.7	- 200.71
Sir Mark Prescott	43-114	4-24	1-4	6-13	3-10	7-19	13-33	1-2	8-9	37.7	**+ 22.99**
D. Nicholls	43-300	1-5	1-20	19-83	0-4	0-28	16-136	4-18	2-6	14.3	- 57.04
Mrs N. Macauley	41-398	0-27	8-34	15-103	0-1	3-19	15-198	0-11	0-5	10.3	- 27.52
D. W. Chapman	37-504	0-5	0-7	9-83	0-8	1-17	22-315	0-30	5-39	7.3	- 243.52
M. J. Ryan	31-176	0-7	0-0	6-32	0-1	0-7	23-108	0-3	2-18	17.6	**+ 14.98**
J. Berry	30-232	15-72	3-22	9-56	0-12	1-17	1-44	1-8	0-1	12.9	- 90.32
P. C. Haslam	26-156	2-18	2-16	2-9	0-11	11-39	9-49	0-9	0-5	16.7	- 34.65
T. D. Barron	25-162	1-14	5-17	3-24	1-8	4-28	10-65	1-5	0-1	15.4	- 12.54
P. D. Evans	19-163	4-31	3-8	3-24	2-7	1-13	4-63	1-9	1-8	11.7	- 63.94
M. C. Chapman	18-403	1-8	0-19	2-79	1-6	5-24	6-204	2-30	1-33	4.5	- 257.17
K. R. Burke	17-127	2-7	0-8	4-26	0-4	0-4	9-63	2-9	0-6	13.4	- 31.38

LEADING FLAT TRAINERS AT THIRSK (SINCE 1995)

	Total W-R	2yo Stks	3yo Stks	Other Stks	2yo H'caps	3yo H'caps	Other H'caps	App'ce	Amateurs	Per cent	£1 Level stake
D. Nicholls	24-195	0-11	0-7	6-30	0-2	2-14	13-123	3-8	0-0	12.3	- 32.40
J. L. Eyre	20-180	2-21	0-5	3-35	1-3	1-15	11-94	2-7	0-0	11.1	**+ 26.25**
M. Johnston	18-89	4-21	3-10	0-11	0-1	2-9	9-37	0-0	0-0	20.2	- 9.35
J. Berry	17-156	10-62	1-8	3-20	0-6	0-16	3-41	0-3	0-0	10.9	- 37.15
T. D. Barron	13-124	1-18	0-5	0-7	2-6	5-13	5-71	0-4	0-0	10.5	- 29.00
Sir Michael Stoute	11-36	0-3	6-13	4-14	0-0	0-1	1-5	0-0	0-0	30.6	**+ 2.16**
T. D. Easterby	10-164	2-44	0-9	1-21	1-5	2-17	3-64	1-4	0-0	6.1	- 130.08
J. L. Dunlop	10-30	0-7	6-10	1-3	0-0	2-5	1-5	0-0	0-0	33.3	- 1.17
H. R. A. Cecil	9-22	0-0	4-12	5-9	0-0	0-0	0-1	0-0	0-0	40.9	**+ 0.63**
M. W. Easterby	9-204	2-92	0-1	0-7	1-6	1-15	5-78	0-5	0-0	4.4	- 139.27
B. W. Hills	9-24	2-4	3-10	2-6	0-0	0-1	2-3	0-0	0-0	37.5	**+ 3.78**
P. D. Evans	8-74	4-19	0-0	0-4	2-5	0-9	2-31	0-6	0-0	10.8	- 29.63
M. R. Channon	8-34	8-19	0-0	0-3	0-1	0-4	0-7	0-0	0-0	23.5	**+ 7.57**
J. H. M. Gosden	7-24	0-2	5-9	2-10	0-0	0-0	0-3	0-0	0-0	29.2	- 2.79
J. R. Fanshawe	7-30	2-6	1-3	2-7	0-0	1-3	1-11	0-0	0-0	23.3	**+ 15.16**
J. M. Bradley	7-63	0-1	0-1	0-4	0-0	1-7	6-40	0-10	0-0	11.1	- 12.00

LEADING FLAT TRAINERS AT WARWICK (SINCE 1995)

	Total W-R	2yo Stks	3yo Stks	Other Stks	2yo H'caps	3yo H'caps	Other H'caps	App'ce	Amateurs	Per cent	£1 Level stake
P. F. I. Cole	13-72	4-20	2-8	3-11	2-5	1-10	1-15	0-3	0-0	18.1	- 2.99
M. C. Pipe	11-41	1-5	0-1	0-2	0-1	0-3	9-27	1-2	0-0	26.8	**+ 3.79**
R. Hannon	11-98	9-41	1-5	0-13	1-8	0-11	0-17	0-3	0-0	11.2	- 50.86
B. W. Hills	11-47	2-12	1-2	4-12	0-4	2-6	1-10	1-1	0-0	23.4	**+ 22.80**
B. A. McMahon	10-55	0-8	0-2	0-15	0-0	2-4	6-24	2-2	0-0	18.2	**+ 43.25**
B. J. Meehan	9-83	3-30	3-8	0-11	1-5	1-17	1-10	0-0	0-2	10.8	- 20.58
J. L. Dunlop	9-47	1-12	1-1	1-6	0-2	1-12	5-13	0-1	0-0	19.2	**+ 7.72**
J. M. Bradley	8-124	0-3	0-1	1-23	0-0	0-3	5-72	1-18	1-4	6.5	- 45.75
J. Pearce	8-42	0-1	0-1	3-8	0-1	0-1	4-26	0-2	1-2	19.1	**+ 33.63**
J. R. Fanshawe	8-38	3-12	0-4	2-13	0-1	1-3	2-5	0-0	0-0	21.1	**+ 1.41**
B. Smart	7-24	3-9	0-1	0-1	0-2	0-1	2-7	1-1	1-2	29.2	**+ 76.68**
G. Lewis	7-41	4-10	0-1	1-7	0-1	1-6	1-12	0-3	0-1	17.1	- 11.58
P. J. Makin	7-41	0-9	1-4	1-12	0-0	0-3	5-12	0-1	0-0	17.1	**+ 0.50**
J. W. Hills	7-37	3-12	1-3	3-10	0-0	0-5	0-6	0-1	0-0	18.9	- 8.55
R. Charlton	6-19	1-4	1-2	2-5	0-0	1-3	1-4	0-1	0-0	31.6	**+ 5.90**
M. R. Channon	6-58	3-19	0-4	1-8	0-1	1-11	1-12	0-3	0-0	10.3	- 23.00

LEADING FLAT TRAINERS AT WINDSOR (SINCE 1995)

	Total W-R	2yo Stks	3yo Stks	Other Stks	2yo H'caps	3yo H'caps	Other H'caps	App'ce	Amateurs	Per cent	£1 Level stake
R. Hannon	40-305	19-122	1-14	5-39	4-11	6-58	5-59	0-2	0-0	13.1	- 86.09
Sir Michael Stoute	17-60	0-9	7-21	8-21	0-0	1-4	1-5	0-0	0-0	28.3	**+ 9.92**
B. J. Meehan	15-151	7-67	1-7	6-13	0-11	0-32	1-20	0-1	0-0	9.9	- 82.38
J. H. M. Gosden	14-73	1-7	6-23	5-24	0-0	1-13	1-6	0-0	0-0	19.2	- 28.72
P. F. I. Cole	14-114	4-29	0-20	5-20	0-3	4-20	1-22	0-0	0-0	12.3	- 10.79
I. A. Balding	13-86	1-22	0-16	2-14	0-0	4-14	6-18	0-2	0-0	15.1	- 11.52
C. F. Wall	11-84	1-12	0-10	0-7	0-0	6-29	4-26	0-0	0-0	13.1	- 16.25
D. R. C. Elsworth	11-76	1-18	2-4	2-18	0-1	0-7	6-28	0-0	0-0	14.5	**+ 13.63**
K. T. Ivory	10-94	2-23	0-1	1-7	0-3	3-22	3-37	1-1	0-0	10.6	- 12.50
H. R. A. Cecil	10-42	0-1	5-15	5-22	0-0	0-1	0-3	0-0	0-0	23.8	**+ 5.22**
W. R. Muir	10-105	1-25	0-9	5-15	0-1	1-23	3-31	0-1	0-0	9.5	- 27.86
M. L. W. Bell	9-76	5-34	0-2	0-5	0-3	0-16	3-13	1-3	0-0	11.8	- 20.75
J. R. Fanshawe	8-57	0-7	1-14	3-16	0-1	1-6	3-12	0-1	0-0	14.0	- 0.50
M. J. Ryan	8-68	1-8	0-6	2-13	1-5	1-8	3-27	0-1	0-0	11.8	- 15.40
P. J. Makin	7-66	4-19	0-7	2-14	0-0	0-11	1-14	0-1	0-0	10.6	- 1.75
W. J. Musson	7-87	0-12	0-5	0-13	0-1	0-6	7-49	0-1	0-0	8.1	- 41.75

LEADING FLAT TRAINERS AT WOLVERHAMPTON (SINCE 1995)

	Total W-R	2yo Stks	3yo Stks	Other Stks	2yo H'caps	3yo H'caps	Other H'caps	App'ce	Amateurs	Per cent	£1 Level stake
R. Hollinshead	73-650	5-70	9-74	14-144	1-10	8-57	36-277	0-13	0-5	11.2	- 168.74
N. P. Littmoden	63-472	17-94	2-45	15-107	1-7	8-36	18-165	2-9	0-9	13.4	- 34.45
M. Johnston	47-269	13-43	6-21	7-38	1-12	6-52	14-99	0-4	0-0	17.5	- 46.13
P. D. Evans	44-481	9-79	1-25	12-115	0-10	1-39	18-184	1-7	2-22	9.2	- 126.48
J. Berry	39-325	18-102	4-36	7-67	3-10	5-34	1-67	0-3	1-6	12.0	- 145.53
Sir Mark Prescott	36-139	11-42	3-17	7-22	0-6	5-18	10-34	0-0	0-0	25.9	- 15.21
P. C. Haslam	34-209	4-41	11-23	4-21	1-12	7-43	5-60	2-7	0-2	16.3	- 3.10
D. W. Chapman	28-247	0-4	0-5	9-45	0-0	0-4	16-161	0-4	3-24	11.3	- 53.64
B. A. McMahon	28-239	4-33	6-19	4-55	0-2	2-17	12-109	0-3	0-1	11.7	**+ 13.03**
J. L. Eyre	27-203	1-13	3-9	3-35	2-3	3-14	13-111	0-4	2-14	13.3	- 51.68
Mrs N. Macauley	23-241	1-13	1-14	6-59	0-2	1-20	14-130	0-2	0-1	9.5	- 83.15
A. Bailey	23-269	1-13	1-23	9-58	0-2	8-28	4-136	0-3	0-6	8.6	- 95.50
J. Pearce	22-119	0-4	0-1	6-28	0-0	0-5	13-70	0-2	3-9	18.5	**+ 50.12**
M. L. W. Bell	22-88	3-12	2-11	7-17	0-1	7-21	3-24	0-2	0-0	25.0	**+ 14.19**
D. Nicholls	16-118	0-2	2-7	7-38	0-0	0-5	7-62	0-2	0-2	13.6	- 28.88
W. R. Muir	16-149	0-19	1-13	9-40	0-3	3-11	2-58	1-4	0-1	10.7	- 68.77

LEADING FLAT TRAINERS AT YARMOUTH (SINCE 1995)

	Total W-R	2yo Stks	3yo Stks	Other Stks	2yo H'caps	3yo H'caps	Other H'caps	App'ce	Amateurs	Per cent	£1 Level stake
H. R. A. Cecil	26-92	10-30	5-19	8-36	0-0	1-3	2-4	0-0	0-0	28.3	- 28.99
M. L. W. Bell	21-112	7-26	1-5	3-10	1-6	2-14	4-41	3-10	0-0	18.8	**+ 6.78**
C. E. Brittain	20-171	2-32	4-21	5-30	0-9	4-18	5-56	0-5	0-0	11.7	- 13.17
C. A. Dwyer	18-133	5-38	0-7	2-11	3-8	0-11	7-56	1-2	0-0	13.5	- 37.33
J. H. M. Gosden	18-104	7-26	4-28	3-24	1-4	1-6	2-15	0-1	0-0	17.3	- 33.74
D. R. Loder	14-49	10-27	2-7	1-7	0-2	0-3	1-3	0-0	0-0	28.6	- 12.64
Sir Michael Stoute	13-85	4-41	3-12	3-14	1-3	0-4	2-11	0-0	0-0	15.3	- 35.14
E. A. L. Dunlop	13-67	4-27	0-10	3-12	3-4	1-3	2-10	0-1	0-0	19.4	**+ 12.53**
J. R. Fanshawe	13-85	2-21	4-14	2-15	0-1	1-6	4-28	0-0	0-0	15.3	- 22.88
L. M. Cumani	13-61	2-16	4-15	4-13	2-4	0-0	1-13	0-0	0-0	21.3	- 7.45
M. R. Channon	11-63	4-17	0-4	0-3	0-8	2-7	5-22	0-2	0-0	17.5	**+ 5.38**
J. Pearce	11-104	0-3	1-7	2-18	1-5	0-5	7-59	0-7	0-0	10.6	**+ 3.50**
B. Hanbury	11-69	3-12	1-11	3-16	0-1	0-5	4-24	0-0	0-0	15.9	- 9.70
J. L. Dunlop	10-38	3-5	1-4	2-6	1-7	2-9	1-7	0-0	0-0	26.3	- 9.58
B. W. Hills	10-56	4-16	0-9	5-13	0-4	0-3	1-11	0-0	0-0	17.9	- 10.69
S bin Suroor	9-20	3-10	2-2	3-7	0-0	1-1	0-0	0-0	0-0	45.0	**+ 12.21**

LEADING FLAT TRAINERS AT YORK (SINCE 1995)

	Total W-R	2yo Stks	3yo Stks	Other Stks	2yo H'caps	3yo H'caps	Other H'caps	App'ce	Amateurs	Per cent	£1 Level stake
H. R. A. Cecil	24-100	5-14	7-23	8-33	0-0	0-5	4-25	0-0	0-0	24.0	- 5.95
Sir Michael Stoute	22-137	2-18	10-26	4-33	1-4	3-18	2-38	0-0	0-0	16.1	- 39.90
M. Johnston	21-166	4-35	1-4	3-20	4-11	2-17	6-75	1-4	0-0	12.7	**+ 17.49**
P. F. I. Cole	19-135	13-45	2-14	2-12	0-6	1-18	1-37	0-3	0-0	14.1	- 59.45
B. W. Hills	18-174	9-49	0-22	3-22	1-10	2-27	3-44	0-0	0-0	10.3	- 59.73
L. M. Cumani	15-82	4-12	1-11	8-22	0-2	0-12	2-22	0-1	0-0	18.3	- 14.00
T. D. Easterby	14-140	5-33	0-2	1-10	2-19	1-14	5-61	0-1	0-0	10.0	- 40.63
J. L. Dunlop	14-103	8-21	0-10	1-18	0-3	1-10	4-41	0-0	0-0	13.6	- 44.48
I. A. Balding	13-98	4-15	0-5	2-14	2-2	2-20	3-42	0-0	0-0	13.3	- 21.05
D. R. Loder	12-44	5-13	0-7	2-8	1-2	2-2	2-12	0-0	0-0	27.3	**+ 9.23**
S bin Suroor	12-47	0-6	5-13	7-25	0-0	0-0	0-3	0-0	0-0	25.5	- 3.77
J. H. M. Gosden	11-85	4-20	6-23	0-9	0-2	0-7	1-24	0-0	0-0	12.9	- 52.30
R. Hannon	11-117	4-39	1-3	4-17	1-11	0-18	1-29	0-0	0-0	9.4	- 26.75
M. W. Easterby	10-142	0-22	0-0	1-3	1-23	0-4	8-81	0-9	0-0	7.0	- 57.67
D. Nicholls	9-120	0-3	0-0	2-14	0-1	1-6	6-91	0-5	0-0	7.5	- 36.00
M. Brittain	8-64	1-14	0-0	0-4	0-1	0-3	5-32	2-10	0-0	12.5	**+ 43.00**

Ready Early March

Order this essential guide today

HORSES IN TRAINING 2000

£14.95 by order from bookshops, newsagents or W.H.Smith (ISB No. 1-901100-27-8), or post free from the address below.

- **Strings of 675 Flat & N.H. Trainers listed in alphabetical order**
- **16,700 horses with their owners, sires and dams**
- **Leading Irish and French yards**
- **Two-year-old foaling dates and sale prices**
- **920 pages include over 200 invaluable pages of statistics on British Racing**

Order Your Copy Today

Price £14.95 (including package and postage)

RACEFORM LTD

COMPTON, NEWBURY, BERKSHIRE RG20 6NL

Access, Visa, Switch, Delta card holders can order at any time on

Tel: 01635 578080 or Fax: 01635 578101

Five-Season Draw Analysis For British Flat Tracks

The following table shows the record of draw position categories over each distance on each track over the past five seasons. Distances which have not had a sufficient number of races run over them to produce a meaningful statistic are not shown.

ASCOT

Distance : *Flat 5f*

Draw Category	Winners	% Winners/Races
Low	21	38
Middle	16	29
High	19	34

Distance : *Flat 6f*

Draw Category	Winners	% Winners/Races
Low	20	36
Middle	17	30
High	19	34

Distance : *Flat 7f*

Draw Category	Winners	% Winners/Races
Low	19	34
Middle	21	38
High	16	29

Distance : *Str 1m*

Draw Category	Winners	% Winners/Races
Low	18	35
Middle	19	37
High	15	29

Distance : *Rnd 1m*

Draw Category	Winners	% Winners/Races
Low	14	24
Middle	24	41
High	21	36

Distance : *Flat 1m 2f*

Draw Category	Winners	% Winners/Races
Low	9	25
Middle	14	39
High	13	36

Distance : *Flat 1m 4f*

Draw Category	Winners	% Winners/Races
Low	22	27
Middle	34	42
High	25	31

Distance : *Flat 2m 45y*

Draw Category	Winners	% Winners/Races
Low	9	29
Middle	12	39
High	10	32

AYR

Distance : *Flat 5f*

Draw Category	Winners	% Winners/Races
Low	15	25
Middle	27	45
High	18	30

Distance : *Flat 6f*

Draw Category	Winners	% Winners/Races
Low	19	26
Middle	36	49
High	19	26

Distance : *Flat 7f*

Draw Category	Winners	% Winners/Races
Low	17	22
Middle	40	53
High	19	25

Distance : *Flat 1m*

Draw Category	Winners	% Winners/Races
Low	23	38
Middle	27	44
High	11	18

Distance : *Flat 1m 2f*

Draw Category	Winners	% Winners/Races
Low	8	16
Middle	24	47
High	19	37

Distance : *Flat 1m 2f 192y*

Draw Category	Winners	% Winners/Races
Low	5	18
Middle	16	57
High	7	25

Distance : *Flat 1m 5f 13y*

Draw Category	Winners	% Winners/Races
Low	8	28
Middle	12	41
High	9	31

BATH

Distance : *Flat 5f 11y*

Draw Category	Winners	% Winners/Races
Low	30	29
Middle	37	36
High	35	34

Distance : *Flat 5f 161y*

Draw Category	Winners	% Winners/Races
Low	24	34
Middle	25	35
High	22	31

Distance : *Flat 1m 5y*

Draw Category	Winners	% Winners/Races
Low	35	36
Middle	36	38
High	25	26

Distance : *Flat 1m 2f 46y*

Draw Category	Winners	% Winners/Races
Low	17	25
Middle	30	44
High	21	31

Distance : *Flat 1m 3f 144y*

Draw Category	Winners	% Winners/Races
Low	11	26
Middle	21	50
High	10	24

Distance : *Flat 2m 1f 34y*

Draw Category	Winners	% Winners/Races
Low	15	34
Middle	18	41
High	11	25

BEVERLEY

Distance : *Flat 5f*

Draw Category	Winners	% Winners/Races
Low	32	21
Middle	44	29
High	76	50

Distance : *Flat 7f 100y*

Draw Category	Winners	% Winners/Races
Low	30	22
Middle	61	44
High	47	34

Distance : *Flat 1m 100y*

Draw Category	Winners	% Winners/Races
Low	13	17
Middle	31	41
High	31	41

Distance : *Flat 1m 1f 207y*

Draw Category	Winners	% Winners/Races
Low	23	24
Middle	32	33
High	42	43

Distance : *Flat 1m 3f 216y*

Draw Category	Winners	% Winners/Races
Low	24	33
Middle	28	39
High	20	28

Distance : *Flat 2m 35y*

Draw Category	Winners	% Winners/Races
Low	7	18
Middle	14	36
High	18	46

BRIGHTON

Distance : *Flat 5f 59y*

Draw Category	Winners	% Winners/Races
Low	27	36
Middle	25	33
High	24	32

Distance : *Flat 5f 213y*

Draw Category	Winners	% Winners/Races
Low	37	35
Middle	45	42
High	25	23

Distance : *Flat 6f 209y*

Draw Category	Winners	% Winners/Races
Low	42	32
Middle	53	40
High	37	28

Distance : *Flat 7f 214y*

Draw Category	Winners	% Winners/Races
Low	24	21
Middle	47	40
High	46	39

Distance : *Flat 1m 1f 209y*

Draw Category	Winners	% Winners/Races
Low	27	35
Middle	33	42
High	18	23

Distance : *Flat 1m 3f 196y*

Draw Category	Winners	% Winners/Races
Low	29	30
Middle	44	45
High	25	26

CARLISLE

Distance : *Flat 5f*

Draw Category	Winners	% Winners/Races
Low	13	21
Middle	29	46
High	21	33

Distance : *Flat 5f 207y*

Draw Category	Winners	% Winners/Races
Low	11	19
Middle	30	53
High	16	28

Distance : *Flat 6f 206y*

Draw Category	Winners	% Winners/Races
Low	12	24
Middle	24	49
High	13	27

Distance : *Flat 7f 214y*

Draw Category	Winners	% Winners/Races
Low	10	19
Middle	21	40
High	22	42

Distance : *Flat 1m 4f*

Draw Category	Winners	% Winners/Races
Low	11	31
Middle	14	39
High	11	31

CATTERICK

Distance : *Flat 5f*

Draw Category	Winners	% Winners/Races
Low	24	27
Middle	38	43
High	31	35

Distance : *Flat 5f 212y*

Draw Category	Winners	% Winners/Races
Low	24	33
Middle	22	30
High	27	37

Distance : *Flat 7f*

Draw Category	Winners	% Winners/Races
Low	43	31
Middle	63	46
High	35	26

Distance : *Flat 1m 3f 214y*

Draw Category	Winners	% Winners/Races
Low	26	37
Middle	26	37
High	20	29

Distance : *Flat 1m 5f 175y*

Draw Category	Winners	% Winners/Races
Low	9	21
Middle	22	51
High	14	33

Distance : *Flat 1m 7f 177y*

Draw Category	Winners	% Winners/Races
Low	11	34
Middle	11	34
High	10	31

CHEPSTOW

Distance : *Flat 5f 16y*

Draw Category	Winners	% Winners/Races
Low	9	28
Middle	18	56
High	5	16

Distance : *Flat 6f 16y*

Draw Category	Winners	% Winners/Races
Low	20	38
Middle	19	36
High	14	26

Distance : *Flat 7f 16y*

Draw Category	Winners	% Winners/Races
Low	17	31
Middle	16	30
High	21	39

Distance : *Flat 1m 14y*

Draw Category	Winners	% Winners/Races
Low	16	27
Middle	27	45
High	17	28

Distance : *Flat 1m 2f 36y*

Draw Category	Winners	% Winners/Races
Low	16	35
Middle	17	37
High	13	28

Distance : *Flat 1m 4f 23y*

Draw Category	Winners	% Winners/Races
Low	14	34
Middle	20	49
High	7	17

CHESTER

Distance : *Flat 5f 16y*

Draw Category	Winners	% Winners/Races
Low	26	39
Middle	31	46
High	10	15

Distance : *Flat 6f 18y*

Draw Category	Winners	% Winners/Races
Low	19	51
Middle	14	38
High	4	11

Distance : *Flat 7f 2y*

Draw Category	Winners	% Winners/Races
Low	24	44
Middle	20	36
High	11	20

Distance : *Flat 7f 122y*

Draw Category	Winners	% Winners/Races
Low	13	36
Middle	18	50
High	5	14

Distance : *Flat 1m 2f 75y*

Draw Category	Winners	% Winners/Races
Low	19	43
Middle	12	27
High	13	30

Distance : *Flat 1m 4f 66y*

Draw Category	Winners	% Winners/Races
Low	18	40
Middle	20	44
High	7	16

DONCASTER

Distance : *Flat 5f*

Draw Category	Winners	% Winners/Races
Low	33	34
Middle	34	35
High	31	32

Distance : *Flat 6f*

Draw Category	Winners	% Winners/Races
Low	22	21
Middle	49	48
High	32	31

Distance : *Flat 7f*

Draw Category	Winners	% Winners/Races
Low	42	36
Middle	41	35
High	35	30

Distance : *Str 1m*

Draw Category	Winners	% Winners/Races
Low	21	33
Middle	24	38
High	19	30

Distance : *Rnd 1m*

Draw Category	Winners	% Winners/Races
Low	18	27
Middle	26	39
High	22	33

Distance : *Flat 1m 2f 60y*

Draw Category	Winners	% Winners/Races
Low	24	28
Middle	42	49
High	19	22

Distance : *Flat 1m 4f*

Draw Category	Winners	% Winners/Races
Low	21	34
Middle	24	39
High	17	27

Distance : *Flat 1m 6f 132y*

Draw Category	Winners	% Winners/Races
Low	14	38
Middle	14	38
High	9	24

EPSOM

Distance : *Flat 5f*

Draw Category	Winners	% Winners/Races
Low	5	26
Middle	8	42
High	6	32

Distance : *Flat 6f*

Draw Category	Winners	% Winners/Races
Low	14	27
Middle	26	50
High	12	23

Distance : *Flat 7f*

Draw Category	Winners	% Winners/Races
Low	19	35
Middle	22	40
High	14	25

Distance : *Flat 1m 114y*

Draw Category	Winners	% Winners/Races
Low	26	43
Middle	18	30
High	16	27

Distance : *Flat 1m 2f 18y*

Draw Category	Winners	% Winners/Races
Low	11	22
Middle	20	41
High	18	37

Distance : *Flat 1m 4f 10y*

Draw Category	Winners	% Winners/Races
Low	21	36
Middle	26	44
High	12	20

FOLKESTONE

Distance : *Flat 5f*

Draw Category	Winners	% Winners/Races
Low	25	33
Middle	30	40
High	20	27

Distance : *Flat 6f*

Draw Category	Winners	% Winners/Races
Low	33	37
Middle	24	27
High	32	36

Distance : *Rnd 6f 189y*

Draw Category	Winners	% Winners/Races
Low	19	27
Middle	26	37
High	26	37

Distance : *Str 7f*

Draw Category	Winners	% Winners/Races
Low	11	29
Middle	12	32
High	15	39

Distance : *Flat 1m 1f 149y*

Draw Category	Winners	% Winners/Races
Low	19	32
Middle	21	35
High	20	33

Distance : *Flat 1m 4f*

Draw Category	Winners	% Winners/Races
Low	16	24
Middle	33	49
High	18	27

Distance : *Flat 1m 7f 92y*

Draw Category	Winners	% Winners/Races
Low	3	16
Middle	9	47
High	7	37

GOODWOOD

Distance : *Flat 5f*

Draw Category	Winners	% Winners/Races
Low	19	35
Middle	18	33
High	18	33

Distance : *Flat 6f*

Draw Category	Winners	% Winners/Races
Low	38	31
Middle	46	37
High	39	32

Distance : *Flat 7f*

Draw Category	Winners	% Winners/Races
Low	29	24
Middle	43	36
High	49	40

Distance : *Flat 1m*

Draw Category	Winners	% Winners/Races
Low	20	19
Middle	39	38
High	45	43

Distance : *Flat 1m 1f*

Draw Category	Winners	% Winners/Races
Low	15	29
Middle	22	42
High	15	29

Distance : *Flat 1m 1f 192y*

Draw Category	Winners	% Winners/Races
Low	7	18
Middle	15	39
High	16	42

Distance : *Flat 1m 4f*

Draw Category	Winners	% Winners/Races
Low	14	23
Middle	19	32
High	27	45

Distance : *Flat 1m 6f*

Draw Category	Winners	% Winners/Races
Low	9	36
Middle	6	24
High	10	40

Distance : *Flat 2m*

Draw Category	Winners	% Winners/Races
Low	8	38
Middle	10	48
High	3	14

HAMILTON

Distance : *Flat 5f 4y*

Draw Category	Winners	% Winners/Races
Low	19	18
Middle	46	45
High	38	37

Distance : *Flat 6f 5y*

Draw Category	Winners	% Winners/Races
Low	26	24
Middle	30	28
High	53	49

Distance : *Flat 1m 65y*

Draw Category	Winners	% Winners/Races
Low	14	15
Middle	44	46
High	37	39

Distance : *Flat 1m 1f 36y*

Draw Category	Winners	% Winners/Races
Low	12	18
Middle	36	53
High	20	29

Distance : *Flat 1m 3f 16y*

Draw Category	Winners	% Winners/Races
Low	16	30
Middle	17	32
High	20	38

Distance : *Flat 1m 4f 17y*

Draw Category	Winners	% Winners/Races
Low	10	22
Middle	20	43
High	16	35

Distance : *Flat 1m 5f 9y*

Draw Category	Winners	% Winners/Races
Low	13	28
Middle	20	43
High	14	30

HAYDOCK

Distance : *Flat 5f*

Draw Category	Winners	% Winners/Races
Low	18	20
Middle	26	29
High	46	51

Distance : *Flat 6f*

Draw Category	Winners	% Winners/Races
Low	26	23
Middle	46	40
High	43	37

Distance : *Flat 7f 30y*

Draw Category	Winners	% Winners/Races
Low	32	34
Middle	34	36
High	29	31

Distance : *Flat 1m 30y*

Draw Category	Winners	% Winners/Races
Low	22	27
Middle	27	33
High	32	40

Distance : *Flat 1m 2f 120y*

Draw Category	Winners	% Winners/Races
Low	22	26
Middle	23	27
High	39	46

Distance : *Flat 1m 3f 200y*

Draw Category	Winners	% Winners/Races
Low	23	28
Middle	36	43
High	24	29

Distance : *Flat 1m 6f*

Draw Category	Winners	% Winners/Races
Low	13	24
Middle	26	48
High	15	28

KEMPTON

Distance : *Flat 5f*

Draw Category	Winners	% Winners/Races
Low	6	33
Middle	7	39
High	5	28

Distance : *Flat 6f*

Draw Category	Winners	% Winners/Races
Low	20	25
Middle	24	30
High	35	44

Distance : *Jub 7f*

Draw Category	Winners	% Winners/Races
Low	19	28
Middle	28	41
High	22	32

Distance : *Jub 1m*

Draw Category	Winners	% Winners/Races
Low	19	35
Middle	24	44
High	12	22

Distance : *Rnd 1m 1f*

Draw Category	Winners	% Winners/Races
Low	10	36
Middle	7	25
High	11	39

Distance : *Jub 1m 2f*

Draw Category	Winners	% Winners/Races
Low	16	36
Middle	15	34
High	13	30

Distance : *Flat 1m 4f*

Draw Category	Winners	% Winners/Races
Low	16	31
Middle	24	46
High	12	23

LEICESTER

Distance : *Flat 5f 2y*

Draw Category	Winners	% Winners/Races
Low	16	28
Middle	24	41
High	18	31

Distance : *Flat 5f 218y*

Draw Category	Winners	% Winners/Races
Low	26	26
Middle	48	48
High	27	27

Distance : *Flat 7f 9y*

Draw Category	Winners	% Winners/Races
Low	41	29
Middle	60	42
High	42	29

Distance : *Flat 1m 8y*

Draw Category	Winners	% Winners/Races
Low	30	27
Middle	46	41
High	37	33

Distance : *Flat 1m 1f 218y*

Draw Category	Winners	% Winners/Races
Low	28	30
Middle	30	32
High	36	38

Distance : *Flat 1m 3f 183y*

Draw Category	Winners	% Winners/Races
Low	24	29
Middle	44	52
High	16	19

LINGFIELD TURF

Distance : *Flat 5f*

Draw Category	Winners	% Winners/Races
Low	29	31
Middle	37	39
High	28	30

Distance : *Flat 6f*

Draw Category	Winners	% Winners/Races
Low	24	20
Middle	41	34
High	56	46

Distance : *Flat 7f*

Draw Category	Winners	% Winners/Races
Low	31	25
Middle	48	39
High	45	36

Distance : *Flat 7f 140y*

Draw Category	Winners	% Winners/Races
Low	8	14
Middle	30	51
High	21	36

Distance : *Flat 1m 1f*

Draw Category	Winners	% Winners/Races
Low	8	28
Middle	12	41
High	9	31

Distance : *Flat 1m 2f*

Draw Category	Winners	% Winners/Races
Low	19	30
Middle	30	48
High	14	22

Distance : *Flat 1m 3f 106y*

Draw Category	Winners	% Winners/Races
Low	25	38
Middle	25	38
High	15	23

LINGFIELD AW

Distance : *Equi 5f*

Draw Category	Winners	% Winners/Races
Low	44	31
Middle	57	40
High	42	29

Distance : *Equi 6f*

Draw Category	Winners	% Winners/Races
Low	59	30
Middle	71	36
High	66	34

Distance : *Equi 7f*

Draw Category	Winners	% Winners/Races
Low	60	22
Middle	114	43
High	94	35

Distance : *Equi 1m*

Draw Category	Winners	% Winners/Races
Low	89	30
Middle	113	38
High	98	33

Distance : *Equi 1m 2f*

Draw Category	Winners	% Winners/Races
Low	100	31
Middle	139	44
High	80	25

Distance : *Equi 1m 4f*

Draw Category	Winners	% Winners/Races
Low	38	27
Middle	54	38
High	50	35

Distance : *Equi 1m 5f*

Draw Category	Winners	% Winners/Races
Low	19	28
Middle	28	41
High	21	31

Distance : *Equi 2m*

Draw Category	Winners	% Winners/Races
Low	20	22
Middle	43	47
High	29	32

MUSSELBURGH

Distance : *Flat 5f*

Draw Category	Winners	% Winners/Races
Low	43	34
Middle	49	39
High	34	27

Distance : *Flat 7f 30y*

Draw Category	Winners	% Winners/Races
Low	15	19
Middle	34	44
High	29	37

Distance : *Flat 1m*

Draw Category	Winners	% Winners/Races
Low	25	33
Middle	30	40
High	20	27

Distance : *Flat 1m 3f 32y*

Draw Category	Winners	% Winners/Races
Low	4	17
Middle	10	43
High	9	39

Distance : *Flat 1m 4f 31y*

Draw Category	Winners	% Winners/Races
Low	14	23
Middle	33	55
High	13	22

Distance : *Flat 2m*

Draw Category	Winners	% Winners/Races
Low	7	23
Middle	16	53
High	7	23

NEWBURY

Distance : *Flat 5f 34y*

Draw Category	Winners	% Winners/Races
Low	12	20
Middle	27	46
High	20	34

Distance : *Flat 6f 8y*

Draw Category	Winners	% Winners/Races
Low	24	25
Middle	35	37
High	36	38

Distance : *Str 7f*

Draw Category	Winners	% Winners/Races
Low	14	24
Middle	23	39
High	22	37

Distance : *Rnd 7f 64y*

Draw Category	Winners	% Winners/Races
Low	21	32
Middle	22	33
High	23	35

Distance : *Str 1m*

Draw Category	Winners	% Winners/Races
Low	7	15
Middle	24	52
High	15	33

Distance : *Flat 1m 2f 6y*

Draw Category	Winners	% Winners/Races
Low	27	34
Middle	32	41
High	20	25

Distance : *Flat 1m 4f 5y*

Draw Category	Winners	% Winners/Races
Low	14	30
Middle	18	38
High	15	32

Distance : *Flat 1m 5f 61y*

Draw Category	Winners	% Winners/Races
Low	8	28
Middle	11	38
High	10	34

Distance : *Flat 2m*

Draw Category	Winners	% Winners/Races
Low	6	23
Middle	13	50
High	7	27

NEWCASTLE

Distance : *Flat 5f*

Draw Category	Winners	% Winners/Races
Low	32	39
Middle	28	34
High	26	32

Distance : *Flat 6f*

Draw Category	Winners	% Winners/Races
Low	29	35
Middle	29	35
High	26	32

Distance : *Flat 7f*

Draw Category	Winners	% Winners/Races
Low	29	32
Middle	38	42
High	23	26

Distance : *Rnd 1m*

Draw Category	Winners	% Winners/Races
Low	11	22
Middle	25	49
High	15	29

Distance : *Str 1m 3y*

Draw Category	Winners	% Winners/Races
Low	5	17
Middle	9	31
High	15	52

Distance : *Flat 1m 2f 32y*

Draw Category	Winners	% Winners/Races
Low	19	33
Middle	27	47
High	16	28

Distance : *Flat 1m 4f 93y*

Draw Category	Winners	% Winners/Races
Low	7	18
Middle	23	59
High	9	23

Distance : *Flat 2m 19y*

Draw Category	Winners	% Winners/Races
Low	12	40
Middle	12	40
High	8	27

NEWMARKET ROWLEY

Distance : *Rwly 5f*

Draw Category	Winners	% Winners/Races
Low	13	28
Middle	19	40
High	15	32

Distance : *Rwly 6f*

Draw Category	Winners	% Winners/Races
Low	23	30
Middle	27	35
High	27	35

Distance : *Rwly 7f*

Draw Category	Winners	% Winners/Races
Low	27	23
Middle	57	50
High	31	27

Distance : *Rwly 1m*

Draw Category	Winners	% Winners/Races
Low	23	28
Middle	29	35
High	30	37

Distance : *Rwly 1m 1f*

Draw Category	Winners	% Winners/Races
Low	7	32
Middle	11	50
High	4	18

Distance : *Rwly 1m 2f*

Draw Category	Winners	% Winners/Races
Low	15	27
Middle	23	41
High	18	32

Distance : *Rwly 1m 4f*

Draw Category	Winners	% Winners/Races
Low	10	22
Middle	16	36
High	19	42

NEWMARKET JULY

Distance : *Jly 5f*

Draw Category	Winners	% Winners/Races
Low	13	37
Middle	11	31
High	11	31

Distance : *Jly 6f*

Draw Category	Winners	% Winners/Races
Low	45	30
Middle	63	42
High	43	28

Distance : *Jly 7f*

Draw Category	Winners	% Winners/Races
Low	39	25
Middle	68	43
High	51	32

Distance : *Jly 1m*

Draw Category	Winners	% Winners/Races
Low	25	23
Middle	45	42
High	38	35

Distance : *Jly 1m 2f*

Draw Category	Winners	% Winners/Races
Low	21	26
Middle	32	40
High	28	35

Distance : *Jly 1m 4f*

Draw Category	Winners	% Winners/Races
Low	21	31
Middle	33	49
High	13	19

Distance : *Jly 1m 6f 175y*

Draw Category	Winners	% Winners/Races
Low	5	26
Middle	8	42
High	6	32

NOTTINGHAM

Distance : *Flat 5f 13y*

Draw Category	Winners	% Winners/Races
Low	31	36
Middle	29	34
High	26	30

Distance : *Flat 6f 15y*

Draw Category	Winners	% Winners/Races
Low	45	27
Middle	54	33
High	67	40

Distance : *Flat 1m 54y*

Draw Category	Winners	% Winners/Races
Low	63	32
Middle	74	38
High	60	30

Distance : *Flat 1m 1f 213y*

Draw Category	Winners	% Winners/Races
Low	52	36
Middle	51	35
High	43	29

Distance : *Flat 1m 6f 15y*

Draw Category	Winners	% Winners/Races
Low	28	33
Middle	30	36
High	26	31

Distance : *Flat 2m 9y*

Draw Category	Winners	% Winners/Races
Low	15	44
Middle	16	47
High	3	9

PONTEFRACT

Distance : *Flat 5f*

Draw Category	Winners	% Winners/Races
Low	14	21
Middle	21	32
High	31	47

Distance : *Flat 6f*

Draw Category	Winners	% Winners/Races
Low	40	29
Middle	54	39
High	44	32

Distance : *Flat 1m 4y*

Draw Category	Winners	% Winners/Races
Low	35	32
Middle	44	41
High	29	27

Distance : *Flat 1m 2f 6y*

Draw Category	Winners	% Winners/Races
Low	34	29
Middle	39	33
High	46	39

Distance : *Flat 1m 4f 8y*

Draw Category	Winners	% Winners/Races
Low	17	34
Middle	20	40
High	13	26

REDCAR

Distance : *Flat 5f*

Draw Category	Winners	% Winners/Races
Low	14	21
Middle	27	40
High	26	39

Distance : *Flat 6f*

Draw Category	Winners	% Winners/Races
Low	31	29
Middle	38	36
High	37	35

Distance : *Flat 7f*

Draw Category	Winners	% Winners/Races
Low	43	36
Middle	46	38
High	32	26

Distance : *Flat 1m*

Draw Category	Winners	% Winners/Races
Low	10	16
Middle	27	43
High	26	41

Distance : *Flat 1m 1f*

Draw Category	Winners	% Winners/Races
Low	7	21
Middle	12	36
High	14	42

Distance : *Flat 1m 2f*

Draw Category	Winners	% Winners/Races
Low	22	31
Middle	28	39
High	21	30

Distance : *Flat 1m 3f*

Draw Category	Winners	% Winners/Races
Low	11	22
Middle	16	33
High	22	45

Distance : *Flat 1m 6f 19y*

Draw Category	Winners	% Winners/Races
Low	12	23
Middle	26	49
High	15	28

RIPON

Distance : *Flat 5f*

Draw Category	Winners	% Winners/Races
Low	26	33
Middle	25	32
High	27	35

Distance : *Flat 6f*

Draw Category	Winners	% Winners/Races
Low	27	29
Middle	33	36
High	32	35

Distance : *Flat 1m*

Draw Category	Winners	% Winners/Races
Low	18	23
Middle	32	41
High	29	37

Distance : *Flat 1m 1f*

Draw Category	Winners	% Winners/Races
Low	7	28
Middle	9	36
High	9	36

Distance : *Flat 1m 2f*

Draw Category	Winners	% Winners/Races
Low	18	23
Middle	29	36
High	33	41

Distance : *Flat 1m 4f 60y*

Draw Category	Winners	% Winners/Races
Low	22	32
Middle	29	42
High	18	26

SALISBURY

Distance : *Flat 5f*

Draw Category	Winners	% Winners/Races
Low	8	20
Middle	14	35
High	18	45

Distance : *Flat 6f*

Draw Category	Winners	% Winners/Races
Low	31	32
Middle	35	36
High	32	33

Distance : *Flat 6f 212y*

Draw Category	Winners	% Winners/Races
Low	24	22
Middle	48	43
High	39	35

Distance : *Flat 1m*

Draw Category	Winners	% Winners/Races
Low	26	32
Middle	31	38
High	25	30

Distance : *Flat 1m 1f 209y*

Draw Category	Winners	% Winners/Races
Low	7	29
Middle	8	33
High	9	38

Distance : *Flat 1m 4f*

Draw Category	Winners	% Winners/Races
Low	15	31
Middle	21	44
High	12	25

SANDOWN

Distance : *Flat 5f 6y*

Draw Category	Winners	% Winners/Races
Low	32	22
Middle	49	34
High	64	44

Distance : *Flat 7f 16y*

Draw Category	Winners	% Winners/Races
Low	27	28
Middle	40	41
High	30	31

Distance : *Flat 1m 14y*

Draw Category	Winners	% Winners/Races
Low	36	32
Middle	44	40
High	31	28

Distance : *Flat 1m 2f 7y*

Draw Category	Winners	% Winners/Races
Low	25	25
Middle	38	38
High	36	36

Distance : *Flat 1m 3f 91y*

Draw Category	Winners	% Winners/Races
Low	6	27
Middle	12	55
High	4	18

Distance : *Flat 1m 6f*

Draw Category	Winners	% Winners/Races
Low	10	22
Middle	22	49
High	13	29

Distance : *Flat 2m 78y*

Draw Category	Winners	% Winners/Races
Low	5	24
Middle	10	48
High	6	29

SOUTHWELL AW

Distance : *Fibr 5f*

Draw Category	Winners	% Winners/Races
Low	31	27
Middle	52	45
High	32	28

Distance : *Fibr 6f*

Draw Category	Winners	% Winners/Races
Low	75	29
Middle	109	43
High	71	28

Distance : *Fibr 7f*

Draw Category	Winners	% Winners/Races
Low	79	30
Middle	97	36
High	91	34

Distance : *Fibr 1m*

Draw Category	Winners	% Winners/Races
Low	71	22
Middle	146	45
High	110	34

Distance : *Fibr 1m 3f*

Draw Category	Winners	% Winners/Races
Low	50	32
Middle	65	41
High	43	27

Distance : *Fibr 1m 4f*

Draw Category	Winners	% Winners/Races
Low	30	19
Middle	67	42
High	63	39

Distance : *Fibr 1m 6f*

Draw Category	Winners	% Winners/Races
Low	18	31
Middle	25	43
High	15	26

Distance : *Fibr 2m*

Draw Category	Winners	% Winners/Races
Low	14	25
Middle	27	48
High	15	27

THIRSK

Distance : *Flat 5f*

Draw Category	Winners	% Winners/Races
Low	15	18
Middle	39	46
High	30	36

Distance : *Flat 6f*

Draw Category	Winners	% Winners/Races
Low	17	21
Middle	26	32
High	39	48

Distance : *Flat 7f*

Draw Category	Winners	% Winners/Races
Low	34	36
Middle	35	37
High	25	27

Distance : *Flat 1m*

Draw Category	Winners	% Winners/Races
Low	23	23
Middle	49	48
High	30	29

Distance : *Flat 1m 4f*

Draw Category	Winners	% Winners/Races
Low	10	18
Middle	29	52
High	17	30

WARWICK

Distance : *Flat 5f*

Draw Category	Winners	% Winners/Races
Low	28	44
Middle	16	25
High	19	30

Distance : *Flat 6f*

Draw Category	Winners	% Winners/Races
Low	12	33
Middle	15	42
High	9	25

Distance : *Flat 7f*

Draw Category	Winners	% Winners/Races
Low	19	26
Middle	34	47
High	20	27

Distance : *Flat 1m*

Draw Category	Winners	% Winners/Races
Low	20	32
Middle	19	31
High	23	37

Distance : *Flat 1m 2f 169y*

Draw Category	Winners	% Winners/Races
Low	24	36
Middle	22	33
High	21	31

Distance : *Flat 1m 4f 115y*

Draw Category	Winners	% Winners/Races
Low	10	32
Middle	14	45
High	7	23

WINDSOR

Distance : *Flat 5f 10y*

Draw Category	Winners	% Winners/Races
Low	17	21
Middle	26	32
High	39	48

Distance : *Flat 6f*

Draw Category	Winners	% Winners/Races
Low	40	34
Middle	37	31
High	41	35

Distance : *Flat 1m 67y*

Draw Category	Winners	% Winners/Races
Low	33	29
Middle	41	36
High	40	35

Distance : *Flat 1m 2f 7y*

Draw Category	Winners	% Winners/Races
Low	20	19
Middle	45	44
High	38	37

Distance : *Flat 1m 3f 135y*

Draw Category	Winners	% Winners/Races
Low	26	33
Middle	32	40
High	22	28

WOLVERHAMPTON AW

Distance : *Fibr 5f*

Draw Category	Winners	% Winners/Races
Low	43	23
Middle	67	37
High	73	40

Distance : *Fibr 6f*

Draw Category	Winners	% Winners/Races
Low	67	24
Middle	100	36
High	107	39

Distance : *Fibr 7f*

Draw Category	Winners	% Winners/Races
Low	77	32
Middle	87	36
High	80	33

Distance : *Fibr 1m 100y*

Draw Category	Winners	% Winners/Races
Low	52	23
Middle	93	41
High	81	36

Distance : *Fibr 1m 1f 79y*

Draw Category	Winners	% Winners/Races
Low	51	25
Middle	69	34
High	82	41

Distance : *Fibr 1m 4f*

Draw Category	Winners	% Winners/Races
Low	38	20
Middle	69	37
High	81	43

Distance : *Fibr 1m 6f 166y*

Draw Category	Winners	% Winners/Races
Low	19	26
Middle	25	34
High	29	40

Distance : *Fibr 2m 46y*

Draw Category	Winners	% Winners/Races
Low	7	20
Middle	12	34
High	16	46

YARMOUTH

Distance : *Flat 5f 43y*

Draw Category	Winners	% Winners/Races
Low	9	25
Middle	13	36
High	14	39

Distance : *Flat 6f 3y*

Draw Category	Winners	% Winners/Races
Low	25	22
Middle	53	46
High	38	33

Distance : *Flat 7f 3y*

Draw Category	Winners	% Winners/Races
Low	35	26
Middle	51	38
High	49	36

Distance : *Flat 1m 3y*

Draw Category	Winners	% Winners/Races
Low	22	27
Middle	38	46
High	23	28

Distance : *Flat 1m 2f 21y*

Draw Category	Winners	% Winners/Races
Low	30	37
Middle	36	44
High	15	19

Distance : *Flat 1m 3f 101y*

Draw Category	Winners	% Winners/Races
Low	17	47
Middle	7	19
High	12	33

Distance : *Flat 1m 6f 17y*

Draw Category	Winners	% Winners/Races
Low	9	21
Middle	24	57
High	9	21

YORK

Distance : *Flat 5f*

Draw Category	Winners	% Winners/Races
Low	10	21
Middle	24	50
High	14	29

Distance : *Flat 6f*

Draw Category	Winners	% Winners/Races
Low	33	28
Middle	45	38
High	41	34

Distance : *Flat 6f 214y*

Draw Category	Winners	% Winners/Races
Low	11	18
Middle	22	37
High	27	45

Distance : *Flat 7f 202y*

Draw Category	Winners	% Winners/Races
Low	29	42
Middle	22	32
High	18	26

Distance : *Flat 1m 205y*

Draw Category	Winners	% Winners/Races
Low	11	55
Middle	4	20
High	5	25

Distance : *Flat 1m 2f 85y*

Draw Category	Winners	% Winners/Races
Low	26	34
Middle	34	45
High	16	21

Distance : *Flat 1m 3f 195y*

Draw Category	Winners	% Winners/Races
Low	24	40
Middle	25	42
High	11	18

Distance : *Flat 1m 5f 194y*

Draw Category	Winners	% Winners/Races
Low	20	43
Middle	13	28
High	13	28

Computer Raceform

The Official Computer Form-Book

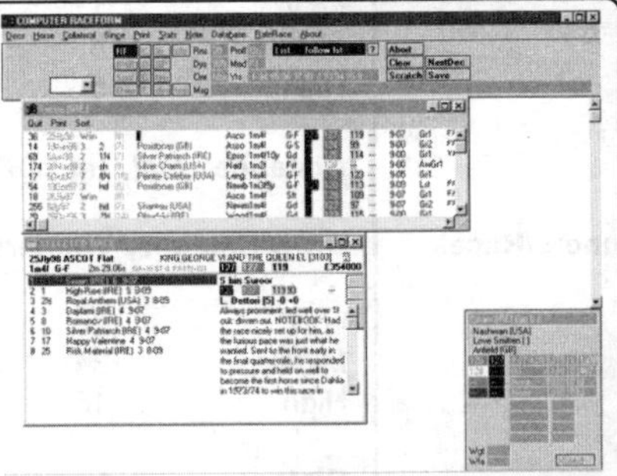

- Clear, Concise Screens
- The Best Race Comments
- Easy-to-Use Point and Click Simplicity
- Quality Raceform Ratings
- Race Analysis and Profile Against Each Horse in a Race
- Database and Systems Analyser
- Full Irish results

No wonder the professionals all use Computer Raceform!

Ring now for our brochure and/or demonstration disk

(24-hour answering)

01635 578080

Taking you into the future with confidence

Compton, Newbury, Berkshire, RG20 6NL, UK
Tel: 01635 578080 Fax: 01635 578101

Five-Season Front Runners Analysis For British Flat Tracks

The following table shows the record of front runners over each distance on each track over the last five seasons. Horses are included in the winners column if they have made all or most of the running. The Impact Value or 'IV' is the strike rate of front runners as against random chance. i.e. an IV of 1.0 would mean that front runners have won as often as they are entitled, 2.0 means they have won twice as often (a bias towards front runners) and 0.5 means they have won half as often (a bias against front runners). Distances which have not had a sufficient number of races run over them to produce a meaningful statistic are not shown.

ASCOT

Distance	Winners	Races	%Winners	IV
5f	7	56	13	1.96
6f	11	56	20	2.59
7f	9	56	16	2.33
1m Str	7	52	13	2.81
1m Rnd	6	59	10	0.90
1m 2f	4	36	11	1.10
1m 4f	5	81	6	0.73
2m 45y	3	31	10	1.21

AYR

Distance	Winners	Races	%Winners	IV
5f	11	60	18	3.25
6f	11	74	15	2.98
7f	12	76	16	2.73
1m	12	61	20	3.53
1m 2f	9	51	18	1.96
1m 2f 192y	0	28	0	0.00
1m 5f 13y	8	29	28	3.30

BATH

Distance	Winners	Races	%Winners	IV
5f 11y	22	102	22	2.81
5f 161y	10	71	14	2.17
1m 5y	11	96	11	1.67
1m 2f 46y	18	68	26	3.26
1m 3f 144y	5	42	12	1.36
2m 1f 34y	4	44	9	0.99

BEVERLEY

Distance	Winners	Races	%Winners	IV
5f	35	152	23	3.69
7f 100y	29	138	21	3.85
1m 100y	16	75	21	3.75
1m 1f 207y	10	97	10	1.85
1m 3f 216y	9	72	13	1.93
2m 35y	2	39	5	0.79

BRIGHTON

Distance	Winners	Races	%Winners	IV
5f 59y	19	76	25	2.20
5f 213y	24	107	22	2.21
6f 209y	22	132	17	1.81
7f 214y	24	117	21	2.10
1m 1f 209y	15	78	19	2.06
1m 3f 196y	19	98	19	1.79

CARLISLE

Distance	Winners	Races	%Winners	IV
5f	15	63	24	3.63
5f 207y	9	57	16	3.19
6f 206y	6	49	12	2.19
7f 214y	6	53	11	2.15
1m 4f	5	36	14	1.56

CATTERICK

Distance	Winners	Races	%Winners	IV
5f	18	89	20	3.19
5f 212y	16	73	22	3.01
7f	18	137	13	2.65
1m 3f 214y	11	70	16	2.21
1m 5f 175y	6	43	14	1.55
1m 7f 177y	3	32	9	1.48

CHEPSTOW

Distance	Winners	Races	%Winners	IV
5f 16y	7	32	22	2.41
6f 16y	14	53	26	3.12
7f 16y	7	54	13	2.07
1m 14y	17	60	28	3.86
1m 2f 36y	4	46	9	0.90
1m 4f 23y	6	41	15	1.55

CHESTER

Distance	Winners	Races	%Winners	IV
5f 16y	20	67	30	4.38
6f 18y	11	37	30	3.36
7f 2y	13	55	24	3.29
7f 122y	6	36	17	3.48
1m 2f 75y	4	44	9	1.21
1m 4f 66y	12	45	27	2.53
1m 5f 89y	5	18	28	3.06
1m 7f 195y	3	15	20	2.82

DONCASTER

Distance	Winners	Races	%Winners	IV
5f	18	98	18	4.04
6f	19	103	18	3.49
7f	17	118	14	3.24
1m Str	7	64	11	2.39
1m Rnd	7	66	11	1.93
1m 2f 60y	9	85	11	2.02
1m 4f	8	62	13	2.20
1m 6f 132y	5	37	14	1.62

EPSOM

Distance	Winners	Races	%Winners	IV
5f	3	19	16	1.99
6f	10	52	19	1.80
7f	9	55	16	1.71
1m 114y	7	60	12	1.25
1m 2f 18y	10	49	20	1.95
1m 4f 10y	4	59	7	0.74

FOLKESTONE

Distance	Winners	Races	%Winners	IV
5f	18	75	24	2.15
6f	18	89	20	2.20
6f 189y	9	71	13	1.39
7f	11	38	29	3.70
1m 1f 149y	7	60	12	1.43
1m 4f	9	67	13	1.51
1m 7f 92y	3	19	16	1.65

GOODWOOD

Distance	Winners	Races	%Winners	IV
5f	10	55	18	2.06
6f	14	123	11	1.47
7f	18	121	15	1.68
1m	17	104	16	2.08
1m 1f	7	52	13	1.77
1m 1f 192y	8	38	21	2.11
1m 4f	5	60	8	0.70
1m 6f	8	25	32	2.74
2m	5	21	24	2.24

HAMILTON

Distance	Winners	Races	%Winners	IV
5f 4y	28	103	27	3.42
6f 5y	19	109	17	2.18
1m 65y	13	95	14	2.05
1m 1f 36y	17	68	25	3.25
1m 3f 16y	13	53	25	2.99
1m 4f 17y	7	46	15	2.31
1m 5f 9y	6	47	13	1.64

HAYDOCK

Distance	Winners	Races	%Winners	IV
5f	23	90	26	4.05
6f	24	115	21	3.95
7f 30y	26	95	27	4.21
1m 30y	14	81	17	2.74
1m 2f 120y	13	84	15	1.94
1m 3f 200y	10	83	12	1.42
1m 6f	8	54	15	2.07

KEMPTON

Distance	Winners	Races	%Winners	IV
5f	2	18	11	1.09
6f	11	79	14	1.85
7f Jub	11	69	16	2.11
1m Jub	6	55	11	1.25
1m 1f	1	28	4	0.49
1m 2f Jub	5	44	11	1.44
1m 4f	3	52	6	0.67

LEICESTER

Distance	Winners	Races	%Winners	IV
5f 2y	5	58	9	1.39
5f 218y	11	101	11	2.05
7f 9y	24	143	17	2.99
1m 8y	9	113	8	1.64
1m 1f 218y	11	94	12	2.58
1m 3f 183y	11	84	13	1.78

LINGFIELD TURF

Distance	Winners	Races	%Winners	IV
5f	36	94	38	4.18
6f	19	121	16	1.90
7f	25	124	20	2.65
7f 140y	9	59	15	1.56
1m 1f	9	29	31	3.25
1m 2f	9	63	14	1.47
1m 3f 106y	12	65	18	1.72
1m 6f	5	18	28	2.87

LINGFIELD AW

Distance	Winners	Races	%Winners	IV
5f	26	144	18	1.53
6f	34	197	17	1.70
7f	34	269	13	1.30
1m	29	304	10	0.90
1m 2f	38	320	12	1.16
1m 4f	7	142	5	0.49
1m 5f	5	68	7	0.78
2m	5	92	5	0.53

MUSSELBURGH

Distance	Winners	Races	%Winners	IV
5f	36	126	29	3.43
7f 30y	16	78	21	2.67
1m	11	75	15	2.54
1m 3f 32y	2	23	9	1.28
1m 4f 31y	8	60	13	1.84
2m	0	30	0	0.00

NEWBURY

Distance	Winners	Races	%Winners	IV
5f 34y	8	59	14	1.62
6f 8y	9	95	9	1.35
7f Str	3	59	5	0.71
7f 64y Rnd	8	66	12	1.53
1m Str	4	46	9	1.13
1m 2f 6y	8	79	10	1.36
1m 4f 5y	5	47	11	1.24
1m 5f 61y	5	29	17	1.61
2m	5	26	19	1.94

NEWCASTLE

Distance	Winners	Races	%Winners	IV
5f	23	82	28	4.63
6f	16	82	20	3.67
7f	14	90	16	3.01
1m Rnd	3	51	6	1.06
1m 3y Str	8	29	28	4.40
1m 2f 32y	11	58	19	2.75
1m 4f 93y	3	39	8	0.72
2m 19y	2	30	7	1.27

NEWMARKET ROWLEY

Distance	Winners	Races	%Winners	IV
5f	9	47	19	3.42
6f	10	77	13	2.49
7f	14	115	12	2.62
1m	9	82	11	2.39
1m 1f	3	22	14	2.89
1m 2f	8	56	14	2.34
1m 4f	4	45	9	1.56

NEWMARKET JULY

Distance	Winners	Races	%Winners	IV
5f	3	35	9	1.39
6f	28	151	19	2.64
7f	18	158	11	1.96
1m	7	108	6	1.18
1m 2f	5	81	6	1.06
1m 4f	8	67	12	1.42
1m 6f 175y	2	19	11	1.05

NOTTINGHAM

Distance	Winners	Races	%Winners	IV
5f 13y	17	86	20	3.61
6f 15y	33	166	20	4.18
1m 54y	21	197	11	1.85
1m 1f 213y	7	146	5	0.85
1m 6f 15y	3	84	4	0.69
2m 9y	3	34	9	1.30

PONTEFRACT

Distance	Winners	Races	%Winners	IV
5f	10	66	15	3.81
6f	30	138	22	4.35
1m 4y	12	108	11	2.80
1m 2f 6y	17	119	14	2.69
1m 4f 8y	7	50	14	1.83
2m 1f 22y	3	18	17	2.89

REDCAR

Distance	Winners	Races	%Winners	IV
5f	18	67	27	3.90
6f	10	106	9	1.74
7f	12	121	10	1.75
1m	6	63	10	2.27
1m 1f	3	33	9	1.55
1m 2f	5	71	7	1.19
1m 3f	3	49	6	0.96
1m 6f 19y	4	53	8	0.96
2m 4y	1	18	6	0.60

RIPON

Distance	Winners	Races	%Winners	IV
5f	30	78	38	5.69
6f	22	92	24	5.14
1m	14	79	18	2.99
1m 1f	7	25	28	3.28
1m 2f	15	80	19	2.75
1m 4f 60y	8	69	12	1.63

SALISBURY

Distance	Winners	Races	%Winners	IV
5f	13	40	33	3.64
6f	16	98	16	2.22
6f 212y	13	111	12	1.78
1m	9	82	11	1.51
1m 1f 198y	6	20	30	3.44
1m 4f	9	48	19	2.56
1m 6f	6	28	21	2.59

SANDOWN

Distance	Winners	Races	%Winners	IV
5f 6y	34	145	23	2.48
7f 16y	15	97	15	1.64
1m 14y	17	111	15	1.62
1m 2f 7y	11	99	11	1.25
1m 3f 91y	3	22	14	1.43
1m 6f	6	45	13	1.27
2m 78y	2	21	10	1.09

SOUTHWELL AW

Distance	Winners	Races	%Winners	IV
5f	26	117	22	3.68
6f	37	257	14	2.25
7f	41	271	15	2.35
1m	33	330	10	1.61
1m 3f	19	158	12	1.73
1m 4f	25	163	15	1.92
1m 6f	5	59	8	1.27
2m	5	56	9	1.27

THIRSK

Distance	Winners	Races	%Winners	IV
5f	20	84	24	4.09
6f	20	82	24	4.31
7f	17	94	18	3.10
1m	15	102	15	2.39
1m 4f	7	56	13	1.49

WARWICK

Distance	Winners	Races	%Winners	IV
5f	11	63	17	2.43
6f	6	36	17	2.52
7f	18	73	25	3.66
1m	8	62	13	2.17
1m 2f 169y	4	67	6	0.92
1m 4f 115y	6	31	19	2.19
1m 6f 194y	1	19	5	0.69

WINDSOR

Distance	Winners	Races	%Winners	IV
5f 10y	14	82	17	2.14
6f	18	118	15	2.51
1m 67y	18	114	16	2.55
1m 2f 7y	14	103	14	1.85
1m 3f 135y	11	80	14	1.74

WOLVERHAMPTON AW

Distance	Winners	Races	%Winners	IV
5f	31	184	17	2.42
6f	52	276	19	2.49
7f	43	245	18	2.19
1m 100y	24	228	11	1.39
1m 1f 79y	24	202	12	1.48
1m 4f	18	189	10	1.11
1m 6f 166y	5	73	7	0.77
2m 46y	4	35	11	1.18

YARMOUTH

Distance	Winners	Races	%Winners	IV
5f 43y	9	36	25	2.49
6f 3y	32	116	28	2.95
7f 3y	32	135	24	3.05
1m 3y	14	83	17	2.86
1m 2f 21y	8	81	10	1.24
1m 3f 101y	5	36	14	1.41
1m 6f 17y	2	42	5	0.49

YORK

Distance	Winners	Races	%Winners	IV
5f	7	48	15	2.54
6f	19	119	16	2.92
6f 214y	7	60	12	2.33
7f 202y	10	69	14	2.99
1m 205y	1	20	5	1.42
1m 2f 85y	9	76	12	2.01
1m 3f 195y	5	60	8	1.32
1m 5f 194y	2	46	4	0.77

RACEFORM BOOKS IN PRINT

CHASEFORM JUMPS ANNUAL 1998-99

Similar style and format to Raceform Flat Annual.

All last season's National Hunt returns **£25.00**

HOW TO COMPILE YOUR OWN HANDICAP by David Dickinson

A Raceform private handicapper explains how to start up and run a handicap **£9.95**

HOW TO WIN AT SPREAD BETTING by Victor Knight

Every serious backer should be aware of the profitable possibilities of spread betting **£4.95**

FORECASTING METHODS FOR HORSERACING by Peter May

Computer based forecasting methods are no longer restricted to the traditional statistical models **£14.95**

THE WAR ZONE by "Pippy"

How to get on top in the betting shop **£4.95**

THE A TO Z OF FLAT RACING by Tony Paul

Invaluable for newcomers to the sport and for regular punters with gaps in their knowledge **£3.95**

THE BETTING MARKET AS A GUIDE TO WINNERS by Malcolm Howard **£9.95**

Raceform

Raceform Ltd

Compton, Newbury, Berkshire RG20 6NL

RACEFORM STANDARD TIMES 2000

ASCOT

5f 1m 00.2
6f 1m 14.0
7f 1m 27.0
1m (Rnd) 1m 40.5
1m (Str) 1m 39.0
1m 2f 2m 05.3
1m 4f 2m 30.0
2m 45y 3m 26.5
2m 4f 4m 17.0
2m 6f 34y 4m 50.0

AYR

5f ....56.8 secs
6f 1m 10.0
7f 1m 25.0
1m 1m 38.4
1m 1f 1m 49.0
1m 2f 2m 05.8
1m 2f 192y 2m 15.0
1m 5f 13y 2m 46.0
1m 7f 3m 10.7
2m 1f 105y 3m 40.5

BATH

5f 11y 1m 00.5
5f 161y 1m 09.1
1m 5y 1m 37.4
1m 2f 46y 2m 06.5
1m 3f 144y 2m 25.0
1m 5f 22y 2m 44.7
2m 1f 34y 3m 41.4

BEVERLEY

5f 1m 01.8
7f 100y 1m 31.1
1m 100y 1m 42.8
1m 1f 207y 2m 02.2
1m 3f 216y 2m 31.8
2m 35y 3m 29.5

BRIGHTON

5f 59y 1m 00.0
5f 213y 1m 07.2
6f 209y 1m 20.0
7f 214y 1m 31.5
1m 1f 209y 1m 57.8
1m 3f 196y 2m 26.0

CARLISLE

5f 59.4secs
5f 207y 1m 11.3
6f 206y 1m 24.4
7f 214y 1m 36.4
1m 1f 61y 1m 53.0
1m 4f 2m 28.0
1m 6f 32y 3m 00.2
2m 1f 52y 3m 37.0

CATTERICK

5f ....57.5 secs
5f 212y 1m 10.9
7f 1m 23.6
1m 3f 214y 2m 31.5
1m 5f 175y 2m 56.0
1m 7f 177y 3m 21.5

CHEPSTOW

5f 16y ....57.0 secs
6f 16y 1m 09.0
7f 16y 1m 19.3
1m 14y 1m 31.2
1m 2f 36y 2m 05.0
1m 4f 23y 2m 31.0
2m 49y 3m 28.0
2m 2f 3m 49.0

CHESTER

5f 16y 1m 00.2
6f 18y 1m 13.3
7f 2y 1m 25.6
7f 122y 1m 31.0
1m 2f 75y 2m 08.7
1m 3f 79y 2m 23.6
1m 4f 66y 2m 36.2
1m 5f 89y 2m 52.0
1m 7f 195y 3m 22.9
2m 2f 147y 4m 02.0

DONCASTER

5f ....58.9 secs
5f 140y 1m 06.6
6f 1m 12.1
6f 110y 1m 18.3
7f 1m 24.5
1m (Str) 1m 38.6
1m (Rnd) 1m 38.0
1m 2f 60y 2m 07.4
1m 4f 2m 29.5
1m 6f 132y 3m 05.0
2m 110y 3m 31.0
2m 2f 3m 54.0

EPSOM

5f ....54.2 secs
6f 1m 07.5
7f 1m 20.5
1m 114y 1m 42.0
1m 2f 18y 2m 05.0
1m 4f 10y 2m 34.5

FOLKESTONE

5f ....57.9 secs
6f 1m 10.0
7f (Str) 1m 23.0
1m 1f 149y 1m 58.0
1m 4f 2m 31.2
1m 7f 92y 3m 18.0
2m 93y 3m 29.0

GOODWOOD

5f ....56.7 secs
6f 1m 09.8
7f 1m 24.8

1m 1m 36.5
1m 1f 1m 52.0
1m 1f 192y 2m 04.8
1m 4f 2m 33.7
1m 6f 2m 59.0
2m 3m 21.5
2m 4f 4m 11.0

HAMILTON

5f 4y ....57.5 secs
6f 5y 1m 08.7
1m 65y 1m 42.5
1m 1f 36y 1m 51.5
1m 3f 16y 2m 16.0
1m 4f 17y 2m 28.5
1m 5f 9y 2m 42.5

HAYDOCK

5f ....58.7 secs
6f 1m 11.7
7f 30y 1m 27.0
1m 30y 1m 40.0
1m 2f 120y 2m 10.6
1m 3f 200y 2m 28.0
1m 6f 2m 56.0
2m 45y 3m 27.2

KEMPTON

5f ....59.1 secs
6f 1m 11.0
7f (Rnd) 1m 23.5
7f (Jub) 1m 24.5
1m (Jub) 1m 37.3
1m (Rnd) 1m 36.2
1m 1f (Rnd) 1m 50.3
1m 2f (Jub) 2m 03.5
1m 3f 30y 2m 18.8
1m 4f 2m 29.4
1m 6f 92y 3m 01.0
2m 3m 24.0

LEICESTER

5f 2y ....58.8 secs
5f 218y 1m 10.0
7f 9y 1m 22.6
1m 8y 1m 34.0
1m 1f 218y 2m 03.2
1m 3f 183y 2m 28.3

LINGFIELD (TURF)

5f ....56.8 secs
6f 1m 09.0
7f 1m 21.2
7f 140y 1m 28.8
1m 1f 1m 52.0
1m 2f 2m 06.0
1m 3f 106y 2m 25.0
1m 6f 2m 59.0
2m 3m 24.0

LINGFIELD (AWT)

5f ....58.4 secs
6f 1m 11.5
7f 1m 24.2
1m 1m 37.4
1m 2f 2m 04.5
1m 4f 2m 30.0
1m 5f 2m 42.5
2m 3m 21.0

MUSSELBURGH

5f ....57.5 secs
7f 30y 1m 26.0
1m 16y 1m 37.0
1m 200y 1m 47.4
1m 4f 31y 2m 31.0
1m 6f 2m 56.6
2m 3m 22.0

NEWBURY

5f 34y 1m 00.5
6f 8y 1m 11.8
7f (Str) 1m 24.1
7f 64y (Rnd) 1m 27.6
1m (Str) 1m 37.0
1m 7y (Rnd) 1m 35.5
1m 1f 1m 50.3
1m 2f 6y 2m 04.0
1m 3f 5y 2m 17.5
1m 4f 5y 2m 30.0
1m 5f 61y 2m 45.5
2m 3m 24.2

NEWCASTLE

5f ....58.8 secs
6f 1m 11.8
7f 1m 24.7
1m (Rnd) 1m 39.4
1m 3y (Str) 1m 38.2
1m 1f 9y 1m 52.3
1m 2f 32y 2m 06.2
1m 4f 93y 2m 36.0
2m 19y 3m 25.5

NEWMARKET (ROWLEY MILE COURSE)

5f ....58.7 secs
6f 1m 11.8
7f 1m 24.5
1m 1m 37.3
1m 1f 1m 50.5
1m 2f 2m 04.0
1m 4f 2m 30.0
1m 6f 2m 56.0
2m 3m 24.0
2m 2f 3m 50.4

NEWMARKET (JULY COURSE)

5f ....57.1 secs

6f ...1m 11.3
7f ...1m 24.5
1m ...1m 37.2
1m 110y ...1m 43.5
1m 2f ...2m 03.0
1m 4f ...2m 28.0
1m 6f 175y ...3m 07.0
2m 24y ...3m 22.5

NOTTINGHAM

5f 13y ...58.9 secs
6f 15y ...1m 11.5
1m 54y ...1m 41.0
1m 1f 213y ...2m 02.5
1m 6f 15y ...2m 57.0
2m 9y ...3m 22.4

PONTEFRACT

5f ...1m 01.8
6f ...1m 15.4
1m 4y ...1m 42.2
1m 2f 6y ...2m 08.9
1m 4f 8y ...2m 34.3
2m 1f 22y ...3m 40.5
2m 1f 216y ...3m 52.0
2m 5f 122y ...4m 42.5

REDCAR

5f ...56.7 secs
6f ...1m 9.4
7f ...1m 22.1
1m ...1m 33.6
1m 1f ...1m 49.5
1m 2f ...2m 02.5
1m 3f ...2m 16.0
1m 6f 19y ...2m 58.8
2m 4y ...3m 24.5

RIPON

5f ...58.0 secs
6f ...1m 11.0
1m ...1m 37.0
1m 1f ...1m 50.7
1m 2f ...2m 03.5
1m 4f 60y ...2m 34.0
2m ...3m 24.0

SALISBURY

5f ...59.4 secs
6f ...1m 12.6
6f 212y ...1m 26.0
1m ...1m 39.7
1m 1f 198y ...2m 04.0
1m 4f ...2m 31.0
1m 6f 15y ...3m 00.3

SANDOWN

5f 6y ...1m 00.2
7f 16y ...1m 28.3
1m 14y ...1m 40.8
1m 1f ...1m 52.0
1m 2f 7y ...2m 06.7
1m 3f 91y ...2m 21.5
1m 6f ...2m 58.4
2m 78y ...3m 32.0

SOUTHWELL (AWT)

5f ...57.4 secs
6f ...1m 13.0
7f ...1m 26.0
1m ...1m 39.3
1m 3f ...2m 21.0
1m 4f ...2m 33.5
1m 6f ...2m 59.5
2m ...3m 31.0

THIRSK

5f ...58.0 secs
6f ...1m 09.7
7f ...1m 24.3
1m ...1m 36.5
1m 4f ...2m 30.0
2m ...3m 23.0

WARWICK

No standard times are shown as the race distances changed before the 1999 Flat season and are due to change again in July 2000. This is due to the course refurbishments taking place.

WINDSOR

5f 10y ...59.2 secs
6f ...1m 10.1
1m 67y ...1m 41.0
1m 2f 7y ...2m 04.3
1m 3f 135y ...2m 24.0

WOLVERHAMPTON (AWT)

5f ...58.7 secs
6f ...1m 11.0
7f ...1m 24.7
1m 100y ...1m 44.0
1m 1f 79y ...1m 55.2
1m 4f ...2m 31.7
1m 6f 166y ...3m 07.4
2m 46y ...3m 28.5

YARMOUTH

5f 43y ...1m 00.5
6f 3y ...1m 10.9
7f 3y ...1m 23.0
1m 3y ...1m 35.0
1m 2f 21y ...2m 02.7
1m 3f 101y ...2m 20.0
1m 6f 17y ...2m 56.7
2m ...3m 21.5
2m 2f 51y ...3m 51.5

YORK

5f ....57.7 secs
6f 1m 10.5
6f 214y 1m 22.5
7f 202y 1m 36.0
1m 205y 1m 47.0
1m 2f 85y 2m 08.5
1m 3f 195y 2m 27.3
1m 5f 194y 2m 54.2
1m 7f 195y 3m 20.0

Introducing ...

Dataform Online daily

www.raceform.co.uk

Daily from 4.30pm

To load and view Dataform you will need the *Adobe Acrobat* software - free download from the site.

Ideally viewed using *Microsoft's Internet Explorer*

Winners of Principal Races

Group One Races

1000 GUINEAS

1999 Wince
1998 Cape Verdi
1997 Sleepytime
1996 Bosra Sham
1995 Harayir
1994 Las Meninas
1993 Sayyedati
1992 Hatoof
1991 Shadayid
1990 Salsabil

CORONATION CUP

1999 Daylami
1998 Silver Patriarch
1997 Singspiel
1996 Swain
1995 Sunshack
1994 Apple Tree
1993 Opera House
1992 Saddlers' Hall
1991 In the Groove
1990 In the Wings

2000 GUINEAS

1999 Island Sands
1998 King Of Kings
1997 Entrepreneur
1996 Mark of Esteem
1995 Pennekamp
1994 Mister Baileys
1993 Zafonic
1992 Rodrigo de Triano
1991 Mystiko
1990 Tirol

ST JAMES'S PALACE STKS

1999 Sendawar
1998 Dr Fong
1997 Starborough
1996 Bijou d'Inde
1995 Bahri
1994 Grand Lodge
1993 Kingmambo
1992 Brief Truce
1991 Marju
1990 Shavian

DERBY

1999 Oath
1998 High-Rise
1997 Benny The Dip
1996 Shaamit
1995 Lammtarra
1994 Erhaab
1993 Commander in Chief
1992 Dr Devious
1991 Generous
1990 Quest for Fame

CORONATION STKS

1999 Balisada
1998 Exclusive
1997 Rebecca Sharp
1996 Shake the Yoke
1995 Ridgewood Pearl
1994 Kissing Cousin
1993 Gold Splash
1992 Marling
1991 Kooyonga
1990 Chimes of Freedom

OAKS

1999 Ramruma
1998 Shahtoush
1997 Reams of Verse
1996 Lady Carla
1995 Moonshell
1994 Balanchine
1993 Intrepidity
1992 User Friendly
1991 Jet Ski Lady
1990 Salsabil

GOLD CUP

1999 Enzeli
1998 Kayf Tara
1997 Celeric
1996 Classic Cliche
1995 Double Trigger
1994 Arcadian Heights
1993 Drum Taps
1992 Drum Taps
1991 Indian Queen
1990 Ashal

CORAL-ECLIPSE STKS

1999 Compton Admiral
1998 Daylami
1997 Pilsudski
1996 Halling
1995 Halling
1994 Ezzoud
1993 Opera House
1992 Kooyonga
1991 Environment Friend
1990 Elmaamul

JUDDMONTE INTERNATIONAL

1999 Royal Anthem
1998 One So Wonderful
1997 Singspiel
1996 Halling
1995 Halling
1994 Ezzoud
1993 Ezzoud
1992 Rodrigo de Triano
1991 Terimon
1990 In the Groove

JULY CUP

1999 Stravinsky
1998 Elnadim
1997 Compton Place
1996 Anabaa
1995 Lake Coniston
1994 Owington
1993 Hamas
1992 Mr Brooks
1991 Polish Patriot
1990 Royal Academy

YORKSHIRE OAKS

1999 Ramruma
1998 Catchascatchcan
1997 My Emma
1996 Key Change
1995 Pure Grain
1994 Only Royale
1993 Only Royale
1992 User Friendly
1991 Magnificent Star
1990 Hellenic

KING GEORGE VI & QUEEN ELIZABETH DIAMOND STKS

1999 Daylami
1998 Swain
1997 Swain
1996 Pentire
1995 Lammtarra
1994 King's Theatre
1993 Opera House
1992 St Jovite
1991 Generous
1990 Belmez

NUNTHORPE STKS

1999 Stravinsky
1998 Lochangel
1997 Coastal Bluff & Ya Malak (d/heat)
1996 Pivotal
1995 So Factual
1994 Piccolo (Blue Siren disq)
1993 Lochsong
1992 Lyric Fantasy
1991 Sheikh Albadou
1990 Dayjur

SUSSEX STKS

1999 Aljabr
1998 Among Men
1997 Ali-Royal
1996 First Island
1995 Sayyedati
1994 Distant View
1993 Bigstone
1992 Marling
1991 Second Set
1990 Distant Relative

STANLEY LEISURE SPRINT CUP

1999 Diktat
1998 Tamarisk
1997 Royal Applause
1996 Iktamal
1995 Cherokee Rose
1994 Lavinia Fontana
1993 Wolfhound
1992 Sheikh Albadou
1991 Polar Falcon
1990 Dayjur

QUEEN ELIZABETH II STKS

1999 Dubai Millennium
1998 Desert Prince
1997 Air Express
1996 Mark of Esteem
1995 Bahri

DUBAI CHAMPION STKS

1999 Alborada
1998 Alborada
1997 Pilsudski
1996 Bosra Sham
1995 Spectrum

1994 Maroof
1993 Bigstone
1992 Lahib
1991 Selkirk
1990 Markofdistinction

1994 Dernier Empereur
1993 Hatoof
1992 Rodrigo de Triano
1991 Tel Quel
1990 In the Groove

ST LEGER

1999 Mutafaweq
1998 Nedawi
1997 Silver Patriarch
1996 Shantou
1995 Classic Cliche
1994 Moonax
1993 Bob's Return
1992 User Friendly
1991 Toulon
1990 Snurge

LOCKINGE STKS

1999 Fly To The Stars
1998 Cape Cross
1997 First Island
1996 Soviet Line
1995 Soviet Line
1994 Emperor Jones
1993 Swing Low
1992 Selkirk
1991 Polar Falcon
1990 Safawan

1996 Tulipa
1995 Phantom Gold
1994 Bolas
1993 Thawakib
1992 Armarama
1991 Third Watch
1990 Hellenic

1996 Oscar Schindler
1995 Beauchamp Hero
1994 Bobzao
1993 Jeune
1992 Rock Hopper
1991 Rock Hopper (Topanoora disq.)
1990 Assatis

KING'S STAND STKS

1999 Mitcham
1998 Bolshoi
1997 Don't Worry Me
1996 Pivotal
1995 Piccolo
1994 Lochsong
1993 Elbio
1992 Sheikh Albadou
1991 Elbio
1990 Dayjur

KING EDWARD VII STKS

1999 Mutafaweq
1998 Royal Anthem
1997 Kingfisher Mill
1996 Amfortas
1995 Pentire
1994 Foyer
1993 Beneficial
1992 Beyton
1991 Saddlers' Hall
1990 Private Tender

Group Two Races

DANTE STKS

1999 Salford Express
1998 Saratoga Springs
1997 Benny The Dip
1996 Glory of Dancer
1995 Classic Cliche
1994 Erhaab
1993 Tenby
1992 Alnasr Alwasheek
1991 Environment Friend
1990 Sanglamore

YORKSHIRE CUP

1999 Churlish Charm
1998 Busy Flight
1997 Celeric
1996 Classic Cliche
1995 Moonax
1994 Key to My Heart
1993 Assessor
1992 Rock Hopper
1991 Arzanni
1990 Braashee

QUEEN ANNE STKS

1999 Cape Cross
1998 Intikhab
1997 Allied Forces
1996 CharnwoodForest
1995 Nicolotte
1994 Barathea
1993 Alflora
1992 Lahib
1991 Sikeston
1990 Markofdistinction

PRINCE OF WALES'S STKS

1999 Lear Spear
1998 Faithful Son
1997 Bosra Sham
1996 First Island
1995 Muhtarram
1994 Muhtarram
1993 Placerville
1992 Perpendicular
1991 Stagecraft
1990 Batshoof

SANDOWN MILE

1999 Handsome Ridge
1998 Almushtarak
1997 Wixim
1996 Gabr
1995 Missed Flight
1994 Penny Drops
1993 Alhijaz
1992 Rudimentary
1991 In the Groove
1990 Markofdistinction

JOCKEY CLUB STKS

1999 Silver Patriarch
1998 Romanov
1997 Time Allowed
1996 Riyadian
1995 Only Royale
1994 Silver Wisp
1993 Zinaad
1992 Sapience
1991 Rock Hopper
1990 Roseate Tern

RIBBLESDALE STKS

1999 Fairy Queen
1998 Bahr
1997 Yashmak

HARDWICKE STKS

1999 Fruits of Love
1998 Posidonas
1997 Predappio

PRINCESS OF WALES'S

1999 Craigsteel
1998 Fruits of Love
1997 Shantou
1996 Posidonas
1995 Beauchamp Hero
1994 Wagon Master
1993 Desert Team
1992 Saddlers' Hall
1991 Rock Hopper
1990 Sapience

GOODWOOD CUP

1999 Kayf Tara
1998 Double Trigger
1997 Double Trigger
1996 Grey Shot
1995 Double Trigger
1994 Tioman Island
1993 Sonus
1992 Further Flight
1991 Further Flight
1990 Lucky Moon

NASSAU STKS

1999 Zahrat Dubai
1998 Alborada
1997 Ryafan
1996 Last Second
1995 Caramba
1994 Hawajiss
1993 Lyphard's Delta
1992 Ruby Tiger
1991 Ruby Tiger
1990 Kartajana

GREAT VOLTIGEUR STKS

1999 Fantastic Light
1998 Sea Wave
1997 Stowaway
1996 Dushyantor
1995 Pentire
1994 Sacrament
1993 Bob's Return
1992 Bonny Scot
1991 Corrupt
1990 Belmez

CHALLENGE STKS

1999 Susu
1998 Decorated Hero
1997 Kahal
1996 Charnwood Forest
1995 Harayir
1994 Zieten
1993 Catrail
1992 Selkirk
1991 Mystiko
1990 Sally Rous

FALMOUTH STKS

1999 Ronda
1998 Lovers Knot
1997 Ryafan
1996 Sensation
1995 Caramba
1994 Lemon Souffle
1993 Niche
1992 Gussy Marlowe
1991 Only Yours
1990 Chimes of Freedom

CELEBRATION MILE

1999 Cape Cross
1998 Muhtathir

DIADEM STKS

1999 Bold Edge
1998 Bianconi

1997 Among Men
1996 Mark of Esteem
1995 Harayir
1994 Mehthaaf
1993 Swing Low
1992 Selkirk
1991 Bold Russian
1990 Shavian

1997 Elnadim
1996 Diffident
1995 Cool Jazz
1994 Lake Coniston
1993 Catrail
1992 Wolfhound
1991 Shalford
1990 Ron's Victory

SUN CHARIOT STKS

1999 Lady In Waiting
1998 Kissogram
1997 One So Wonderful
1996 Last Second
1995 Warning Shadows
1994 La Confederation
1993 Talented
1992 Red Slippers
1991 Ristna
1990 Kartajana

GEOFFREY FREER STKS

1999 Silver Patriarch
1998 Multicoloured
1997 Dushyantor
1996 Phantom Gold
1995 Presenting
1994 Red Route
1993 Azzilfi
1992 Shambo
1991 Drum Taps
1990 Charmer

TEMPLE STKS

1999 Tipsy Creek
1998 Bolshoi
1997 Croft Pool
1996 Mind Games
1995 Mind Games
1994 Lochsong
1993 Paris House
1992 Snaadee
1991 Elbio
1990 Dayjur

Top Two-Year-Old Races

MIDDLE PARK STKS

1999 Primo Valentino
1998 Lujain
1997 Hayil
1996 Bahamian Bounty
1995 Royal Applause
1994 Fard
1993 First Trump
1992 Zieten
1991 Rodrigo de Triano
1990 Lycius

DEWHURST STKS

1999 Distant Music
1998 Mujahid
1997 Xaar
1996 In Command
1995 Alhaarth
1994 Pennekamp
1993 Grand Lodge
1992 Zafonic
1991 Dr Devious
1990 Generous

FILLIES' MILE

1999 Teggiano
1998 Sunspangled
1997 Glorosia
1996 Reams of Verse
1995 Bosra Sham
1994 Aqaarid
1993 Fairy Heights
1992 Ivanka
1991 Culture Vulture
1990 Shamshir

RACING POST TROPHY

1999 Aristotle
1998 Commander Collins
1997 Saratoga Springs
1996 Medaaly
1995 Beauchamp King
1994 Celtic Swing
1993 King's Theatre
1992 Armiger
1991 Seattle Rhyme
1990 Peter Davies

CHEVELEY PARK STKS

1999 Seazun
1998 Wannabe Grand
1997 Embassy
1996 Pas De Reponse
1995 Blue Duster
1994 Gay Gallanta
1993 Prophecy
1992 Sayyedati
1991 Marling
1990 Capricciosa

COVENTRY STKS

1999 Fasliyev
1998 Red Sea
1997 Harbour Master
1996 Verglas
1995 Royal Applause
1994 Sri Pekan
1993 Stonehatch
1992 Petardia
1991 Dilum
1990 Mac's Imp

GIMCRACK STKS

1999 Mull Of Kintyre
1998 Josr Algarhoud
1997 Carrowkeel
1996 Abou Zouz
1995 Royal Applause
1994 Chilly Billy
1993 Turtle Island
1992 Splendent
1991 River Falls
1990 Mujtahid

SOLARIO STKS

1999 Best of The Bests
1998 Raise A Grand
1997 Little Indian
1996 Brave Act
1995 Alhaarth
1994 Lovely Millie
1993 Island Magic
1992 White Crown
1991 Chicmond
1990 Radwell

QUEEN MARY STKS

1999 Shining Hour
1998 Bint Allayl
1997 Nadwah
1996 Dance Parade
1995 Blue Duster
1994 Gay Gallanta
1993 Risky
1992 Lyric Fantasy
1991 Marling
1990 On Tiptoes

NORFOLK STKS

1999 Warm Heart
1998 Rosselli
1997 Tippitt Boy
1996 Tipsy Creek
1995 Lucky Lionel
1994 Mind Games
1993 Turtle Island
1992 Niche
1991 Magic Ring
1990 Line Engaged

CHERRY HINTON STKS

1999 Torgau
1998 Wannabe Grand
1997 Asfurah
1996 Dazzle
1995 Applaud
1994 Red Carnival
1993 Lemon Souffle
1992 Sayyedati
1991 Musicale
1990 Chicarica

CHAMPAGNE VINTAGE STKS

1999 Ekraar
1998 Aljabr
1997 Central Park
1996 Putra
1995 Alhaarth
1994 Eltish
1993 Mister Baileys
1992 Maroof
1991 Dr Devious
1990 Mukaddamah

ROYAL LODGE STKS

1999 Royal Kingdom
1998 Mutaahab
1997 Teapot Row
1996 Benny The Dip
1995 Mons
1994 Eltish
1993 Mister Baileys
1992 Desert Secret
1991 Made of Gold
1990 Mujaazif

LOWTHER STKS

1999 Jemima
1998 Bint Allayl
1997 Cape Verdi
1996 Bianca Nera
1995 Dance Sequence
1994 Harayir
1993 Velvet Moon
1992 Niche
1991 Culture Vulture
1990 Only Yours

RICHMOND STKS

1999 Bachir
1998 Muqtarib
1997 Daggers Drawn
1996 Easycall
1995 Polaris Flight
1994 Sri Pekan
1993 First Trump
1992 Son Pardo
1991 Dilum
1990 Mac's Imp

FLYING CHILDERS STKS

1999 Mrs P
1998 Sheer Viking
1997 Land of Dreams
1996 Easycall
1995 Cayman Kai
1994 Raah Algharb
1993 Imperial Bailiwick
1992 Poker Chip
1991 Paris House
1990 Distinctly North

MILL REEF STKS

1999 Primo Valentino
1998 Golden Silca
1997 Arkadian Hero
1996 Indian Rocket
1995 Kahir Almaydan
1994 Princely Hush
1993 Polish Laughter
1992 Forest Wind
1991 Showbrook
1990 Time Gentlemen

CHAMPAGNE STKS

1999 Distant Music
1998 Auction House
1997 Daggers Drawn
1996 Bahhare
1995 Alhaarth
1994 Sri Pekan
1993 Unblest
1992 Petardia
1991 Rodrigo de Triano
1990 Bog Trotter

Major Handicaps

LINCOLN H'CAP

1999 Right Wing
1998 Hunters of Brora
1997 Kuala Lipis
1996 Stone Ridge
1995 Roving Minstrel
1994 Our Rita
1993 High Premium
1992 High Low
1991 Amenable
1990 Evichstar

EBOR H'CAP

1999 Vicious Circle
1998 Tuning
1997 Far Ahead
1996 Clerkenwell
1995 Sanmartino
1994 Hasten to Add
1993 Sarawat
1992 Quick Ransom
1991 Deposki
1990 Further Flight

AYR GOLD CUP

1999 Grangeville
1998 Always Alight
1997 Wildwood Flower
1996 Coastal Bluff
1995 Royale Figurine
1994 Daring Destiny
1993 Hard to Figure
1992 Lochsong
1991 Sarcita
1990 Final Shot

CAMBRIDGESHIRE H'CAP

1999 She's Our Mare
1998 Lear Spear
1997 Pasternak
1996 Clifton Fox
1995 Cap Juluca
1994 Halling
1993 Penny Drops
1992 Rambo's Hall
1991 Mellottie
1990 Risen Moon

CESAREWITCH H'CAP

1999 Top Cees
1998 Spirit of Love
1997 Turnpole
1996 Inchcailloch
1995 Old Red
1994 Captain's Guest
1993 Aahsaylad
1992 Vintage Crop
1991 Go South
1990 Trainglot

ROYAL HUNT CUP

1999 Showboat
1998 Refuse To Lose
1997 Red Robbo
1996 Yeast
1995 Realities
1994 Face North
1993 Imperial Ballet
1992 Colour Sergeant
1991 Eurolink the Lad
1990 Pontenuovo

WOKINGHAM H'CAP

1999 Deep Space
1998 Selhurstpark Flyer
1997 Selhurstpark Flyer
1996 Emerging Market
1995 Astrac
1994 Venture Capitalist
1993 Nagida
1992 Red Rosein
1991 Amigo Menor
1990 Knight of Mercy

NORTHUMBERLAND PLATE

1999 Far Cry
1998 Cyrian
1997 Windsor Castle
1996 Celeric
1995 Bold Gait
1994 Quick Ransom
1993 Highflying
1992 Witness Box
1991 Tamarpour
1990 Al Maheb

HONG KONG TROPHY

1999 Moutahddee
1998 Yavana's Pace
1997 Hawksley Hill
1996 Sheer Danzig
1995 Yoush
1994 Knowth
1993 Smarginato
1992 Fire Top
1991 You Know the Rules
1990 Bold Fox

WILLIAM HILL MILE

1999 Lonesome Dude
1998 For Your Eyes Only
1997 Fly To The Stars
1996 Moscow Mist
1995 Khayrapour
1994 Fraam
1993 Philidor
1992 Little Bean
1991 Sky Cloud
1990 March Bird

STEWARDS' CUP

1999 Harmonic Way
1998 Superior Premium
1997 Danetime
1996 Coastal Bluff
1995 Shikari's Son
1994 For the Present
1993 King's Signet
1992 Lochsong
1991 Notley
1990 Knight of Mercy

JOHN SMITH'S CUP

1999 Achilles
1998 Porto Foricos
1997 Pasternak
1996 Wilcuma
1995 Naked Welcome
1994 Cezanne
1993 Baron Ferdinand
1992 Mr Confusion
1991 Halkopous
1990 Eradicate

STAMINA OF SIRES' PROGENY

The following table gives the average distance in furlongs of races won at three-year-old and upwards by the progeny of the stallions named for the period 1990-1999. The mean average distance is the figure shown immediately after the stallion's name. The following two figures are the shortest and longest distances at which a sire's progeny were successful during the period 8/11/98 - 6/11/99.

A

Absalom	7.1f	5.1	12.0
Acatenango		11.0	16.0
Accordion	11.3f	11.8	14.0
Adbass (USA)	12.2f	11.0	11.0
Affirmed (USA)	10.3f	8.0	10.0
Afleet (CAN)	6.2f	10.0	10.0
Al Nasr (FR)	9.9f	6.0	21.6
Alhijaz	7.7f	7.0	12.0
Alleged (USA)	11.8f	9.0	11.6
Alleging (USA)	8.8f	6.0	6.0
Alnasr Alwasheek	9.4f	5.1	8.0
Always Fair (USA)	14f	8.0	10.0
Alysheba (USA)	12.1f	12.0	12.0
Alzao (USA)	9.8f	7.0	14.8
Anita's Prince	6f	5.0	6.0
Anjiz (USA)	7f	7.0	7.0
Anshan	8.2f	5.0	16.2
Apeldoorn		8.0	8.0
Aragon	7.7f	5.0	10.0
Arazi (USA)	9.2f	7.7	16.0
Arcane (USA)	11.6f	17.2	17.2
Archway (IRE)	8.5f	6.0	12.0
Arctic Tern (USA)	12.2f	17.0	17.0
Ardar	9.5f	11.0	11.0
Ardkinglass	5f	5.0	13.8
Astronef	7.9f	5.0	6.0

B

Backchat (USA)	11.8f	17.1	17.1
Bairn (USA)	9.4f	10.0	17.2
Balidar	6.5f	7.0	7.0
Balla Cove		5.1	8.1
Ballacashtal (CAN)	7.9f	5.0	8.0
Ballad Rock	7.2f	5.0	10.0
Balleroy (USA)		8.0	8.0
Barathea (IRE)		7.0	14.8
Batshoof	9.5f	6.0	16.0
Be My Chief (USA)	10.2f	5.5	17.2
Be My Guest (USA)	10.2f	7.0	11.0
Be My Native (USA)	11.2f	12.0	12.0
Beau Genius (CAN)		10.5	10.5
Beldale Flutter (USA)	10.2f	16.4	16.4
Bellypha	11.9f	16.0	16.0
Belmez (USA)	11.4f	11.6	17.2
Bering	9.6f	6.0	14.0
Beveled (USA)	6.9f	5.0	14.0
Bien Bien (USA)		14.1	14.1
Big Shuffle (USA)		6.0	8.8
Bigstone (IRE)		6.0	10.5
Bikala (GB)	12f	12.0	13.5
Blakeney	11.9f	12.0	14.8
Bluebird (USA)	7.9f	6.0	10.0
Blushing John (USA)	8.9f	7.0	12.1
Bob Back (USA)	11.5f	16.0	16.0
Bob's Return (IRE)		7.1	7.1
Bold Arrangement	8.7f	5.0	6.0
Bold Owl	9.7f	8.0	10.0
Brief Truce (USA)	9.1f	6.0	10.0
Broken Hearted	10.1f	6.0	11.9
Bustino	11f	7.0	18.0

C

Cadeaux Genereux	7.9f	5.0	12.1
Caerleon (USA)	10.9f	8.0	16.0
Capote (USA)	9.1f	6.0	7.0
Case Law	6f	5.0	8.3
Casteddu	7.4f	5.9	12.0
Catrail (USA)		6.0	8.2
Charmer	9f	6.0	16.4
Chief Singer	8.6f	5.0	8.0
Chief's Crown (USA)	10.2f	7.0	8.5
Chilibang	7f	5.0	6.1
Clantime	6.6f	5.0	12.3
Classic Music (USA)	7.2f	5.0	6.0
College Chapel		5.0	10.0
Colonial Affair (USA)	7f	7.0	7.0
Commanche Run (GB)	10.3f	8.0	10.0
Common Grounds	8.1f	5.0	14.0
Contract Law (USA)	8.9f	5.0	10.0
Cosmonaut		8.0	8.5
Cotation	5f	5.0	5.0
Cozzene (USA)	10.1f	8.0	11.9
Crowning Honors (CAN)	9.9f	9.2	12.0
Cyrano de Bergerac	7.3f	5.0	10.0

D

Damister (USA)	9.1f	8.0	16.2
Dancing Brave (USA)	10.4f	14.1	14.1
Dancing Dissident (USA)	6.8f	7.0	10.0
Danehill (USA)	9.1f	5.0	18.0
Danzig (USA)	8.1f	5.0	10.4
Danzig Connection (USA)	8.2f	7.0	9.4
Daring March	9f	8.0	8.0
Darshaan	11.9f	6.9	13.3
Dashing Blade	7.9f	5.0	10.0
Dayjur (USA)	6.8f	5.0	8.0
Defensive Play (USA)		12.0	14.8
Dehere (USA)		13.0	13.0
Democratic (USA)		6.0	6.0
Deploy	11.4f	6.0	14.0
Desert Secret (IRE)		8.0	8.0
Diamond Prospect (USA)	8f	12.4	12.4
Diamond Shoal	9.8f	7.7	7.7
Diesis (GB)	9f	7.0	12.0
Dilum (USA)	7.1f	6.1	11.5
Distant Relative	7f	5.0	10.0
Distinctly North (USA)	7.4f	5.0	9.0
Dixieland Band (USA)	10.1f	9.9	12.0
Dolphin Street (FR)		5.0	12.1
Dominion	8.9f	5.0	11.5
Dominion Royale	7.8f	5.0	17.1
Don Roberto (USA)	15.6f	12.0	12.0
Don't Forget Me	9.5f	5.0	11.0
Double Bed (FR)	13.9f	7.0	10.0
Double Schwartz	7f	6.0	8.0
Doubletour (USA)	12f	8.5	10.0
Doulab (USA)	7.4f	7.7	10.0
Dowsing (USA)	7f	5.0	10.0
Doyoun	10.7f	7.0	16.4
Dunbeath (USA)	9.9f	6.0	6.0
Durgam (USA)	12.3f	10.0	16.0
Dynaformer (USA)	12f	7.0	10.1

E

Efisio	7.7f	5.0	16.0
El Gran Senor (USA)	8.9f	8.0	12.0
Ela-Mana-Mou	12.7f	7.0	16.5
Elmaamul (USA)	8.1f	7.0	16.4
Emarati (USA)	6.6f	5.0	11.9
Emperor Fountain	10f	7.9	7.9
Environment Friend	7.5f	6.0	12.1
Eskimo (USA)	8.2f	8.0	8.0
Exactly Sharp (USA)	8.4f	10.0	10.0
Exbourne (USA)		8.1	10.3
Executive Man	8.9f	10.0	10.0
Exit To Nowhere (USA)	8.7f	8.0	12.0
Ezzoud (IRE)		7.0	10.2

F

Fabulous Dancer (USA)	10.6f	7.5	10.0
Fairy King (USA)	7.7f	6.0	12.5
Far North (CAN)	10.3f	14.8	14.8
Faustus (USA)	9.1f	7.1	10.0
Fayruz	6.6f	5.3	8.1
Fearless Action (USA)	8f	8.0	8.0
Fighting Fit (USA)	7.9f	8.0	10.0
First Trump		5.0	16.2
Fools Holme (USA)	10.3f	12.0	13.0
Forest Wind (USA)		5.0	10.2
Formidable (USA)	7.8f	6.0	16.2
Forty Niner (USA)	8.8f	8.0	8.0
Forzando	7.2f	5.0	8.5

G

Gabitat	8.5f	6.1	6.1
Geiger Counter (USA)	7.8f	5.0	10.0
General Holme (USA)	5.7f	7.0	20.0
General Meeting (GB)		9.0	9.0
Generous (IRE)	11.5f	7.0	16.2
Ghazi (USA)		7.0	10.0
Glenstal (USA)	10f	11.9	11.9
Golden Lahab (USA)	14.4f	16.1	16.1
Goldneyev (USA)		8.0	8.0
Gone West (USA)	7.8f	6.0	16.1
Good Thyne (USA)	11.8f	16.0	16.0
Good Times (ITY)	8.7f	12.0	12.0
Goofalik (USA)	15.4f	10.0	12.0
Grand Lodge (USA)		6.0	11.9
Great Commotion (USA)	9.2f	7.3	12.0
Green Dancer (USA)	11.9f	8.0	16.2
Green Desert (USA)	7.8f	5.0	12.3
Greensmith		11.7	17.2
Grey Dawn II	6.8f	6.0	6.0
Grey Desire	9.3f	6.0	7.5
Groom Dancer (USA)	9.5f	8.0	8.0
Gulch (USA)	9.6f	6.0	8.5
Gunner B	11.2f	12.0	17.2

H

Hadeer	8.9f	6.9	10.0
Hamas (IRE)	8f	5.0	10.0
Handsome Sailor	6.6f	7.0	8.0
Hansel (USA)	12.6f	9.4	12.0
Hard Fought	8.9f	12.1	13.0
Hawkster (USA)	12.4f	16.1	16.1
Hector Protector (USA)	9f	8.5	10.5
Heraldiste (USA)	8.9f	8.0	8.0
Hermitage (USA)	8.6f	7.0	8.0
Hero's Honor (USA)	9.2f	10.0	10.0
High Estate	10.5f	5.0	12.0
Highest Honor (FR)	10.9f	8.0	11.0
Homme de Loi (IRE)		12.5	15.0
Horage	11.4f	16.0	16.2
Houmayoun (FR)	7.1f	9.0	9.0
Housebuster (USA)	7f	5.0	7.0
Hubbly Bubbly (USA)	9.5f	10.5	16.0

I

Imp Society (USA)	7.1f	5.0	11.9
Imperial Ballet (IRE)		5.2	7.0
Imperial Falcon (CAN)	9.2f	10.1	12.0
Imperial Frontier (USA)	7f	6.0	7.0
In The Wings (GB)	11.2f	7.0	16.0
Inca Chief (USA)	5.6f	6.0	6.0
Inchinor	8.9f	5.2	18.0
Indian Ridge	7.6f	5.0	16.0
Interrex (CAN)	7.7f	5.0	11.5
Irish River (FR)	9f	7.0	12.0

J

Jade Hunter (USA)	10.4f	9.9	9.9
Jareer (USA)	10.2f	9.8	11.0
Java Gold (USA)	9.3f	10.0	10.0
Jester	8.5f	8.0	8.0
Jupiter Island	10.4f	14.1	16.0

K

K-Battery	12.4f	14.8	16.2
Kabour	6.1f	5.0	5.0
Kahyasi	12.9f	12.0	20.0
Kala Shikari	6f	5.0	5.0
Kalaglow	11.2f	7.0	7.0
Kaldoun (FR)	9.9f	5.0	8.0
Keen	11.1f	5.0	16.0
Kefaah (USA)	11.2f	8.0	12.4
Kenmare	9.6f	5.0	8.0
King Among Kings	7.4f	9.9	12.0
King of Clubs	9.3f	10.0	12.0
King's Signet (USA)	7f	6.0	8.3
Kingmambo (USA)	10.9f	7.0	17.0
Known Fact (USA)	8.3f	6.0	10.0
Komaite (USA)	6.9f	5.0	16.0
Konigsstuhl	9f	8.5	12.0
Kris	10f	5.0	16.0
Kris S (USA)	9.3f	8.0	12.3
Kylian (USA)	8.1f	6.0	16.2

L

Lahib (USA)	8f	5.0	13.9
Landyap (USA)		14.1	14.1
Last Tycoon (GB)	9.4f	7.0	12.0
Law Society (USA)	11.6f	7.0	17.1
Lead on Time (USA)	7.5f	12.0	12.0
Lear Fan (USA)	10.4f	6.0	10.1
Lesotho (USA)	6f	10.0	10.0
Librate	10.4f	8.2	10.2
Linamix	8.2f	8.0	15.5
Lion Cavern (USA)	7.5f	6.0	10.0
Little Wolf (GB)	14.4f	16.0	16.0
Lively One (USA)		10.5	10.5
Local Suitor (USA)	9.7f	9.0	9.0
Lochnager	6.9f	7.1	7.1
Lomitas (GB)		8.0	12.0
Lomond (USA)	9.9f	12.0	12.0
Longleat (USA)	7.2f	6.0	6.0
Lord At War (ARG)	6.6f	7.5	9.0
Love the Groom (USA)		6.0	6.0
Lucky Guest		10.0	10.0

Lugana Beach	7f	5.0	12.0
Lycius (USA)	8.8f	5.0	12.0
Lyphard (USA)	10.6f	9.9	12.0

M

Mac's Imp (USA)	5.6f	5.0	9.0
Machiavellian (USA)	9.8f	6.0	14.1
Magic Ring (IRE)	6.5f	5.0	10.0
Magical Wonder (USA)	7.2f	5.9	8.0
Manila (USA)	10f	8.0	15.0
Mansonnien (FR)	12f	12.0	12.0
Marju (IRE)	9.2f	6.0	14.1
Marmato (GB)		8.0	8.0
Marquetry	10f	6.0	6.0
Mashkour		10.0	10.0
Master Willie	9.2f	8.9	11.9
Masterclass (USA)	5.9f	5.0	9.4
Mazilier (USA)	8.5f	8.5	8.5
Meadowlake (USA)		7.0	7.0
Merdon Melody	6.8f	7.0	8.0
Midhish		6.0	6.0
Midyan (USA)	9.9f	5.0	12.1
Minshaanshu Amad (USA)	11.3f	6.0	10.0
Miswaki (USA)	8.1f	6.0	12.0
Moment of Hope (USA)	6.9f	7.0	7.0
Mon Tresor	7.9f	5.0	16.2
Monsagem (USA)		8.0	8.0
Most Welcome	8.6f	5.0	16.4
Mr Prospector (USA)	8.6f	7.0	11.9
Mt Livermore (USA)	7.7f	7.0	16.1
Mtoto	11.5f	8.0	18.0
Mujadil (USA)	7.7f	5.0	16.0
Mujtahid (USA)	7.4f	5.0	12.0
Mukaddamah (USA)	7.6f	5.0	10.0
Music Boy	6.5f	6.0	10.0
Mystiko (USA)	7.7f	5.0	12.0

N

Nabeel Dancer (USA)	6.1f	5.0	9.4
Nalchik (USA)	12.6f	14.8	14.8
Namaqualand (USA)		7.0	13.1
Nashamaa	8.1f	7.0	13.1
Nashwan (USA)	10.3f	6.0	18.7
Neshad (USA)	5.5f	5.0	5.0
Never so Bold (GB)	7.1f	5.0	12.0
New Express	6.8f	6.0	7.0
Nicholas (USA)	6.1f	6.0	8.5
Nicholas Bill	9.8f	15.4	15.4
Night Shift (USA)	8.1f	5.0	15.9
Niniski (USA)	13.2f	7.0	22.2
Nishapour (FR)	11.1f	7.0	7.0
Noble Patriarch	12.2f	14.0	14.0
Noblequest (FR)		6.0	6.0
Nomadic Way (USA)		16.0	16.0
Nomination	7.3f	6.0	8.0
Nordance (USA)	7.4f	10.0	10.0
Nordico (USA)	8.2f	6.0	12.0
North Briton	8.2f	8.0	8.0
Northern Amethyst	10.2f	10.2	10.2
Northern Park (USA)	10f	14.0	14.0
Northern Score (USA)		7.0	7.0
Nureyev (USA)	8.4f	5.0	10.5

O

Old Spice		16.0	16.0
Old Vic	12.8f	14.1	14.4
Opening Verse (USA)	11.8f	14.0	14.0

P

Paris House	5.9f	5.3	8.5
Pennine Walk	8.9f	7.0	7.0
Perpendicular		8.2	8.2
Perrault (GB)		15.0	15.0
Persian Bold	10f	8.0	16.0
Persian Heights	10.5f	6.9	16.0
Perugino (USA)		7.0	16.2
Petardia	8.2f	6.0	10.0
Petit Loup (USA)		10.0	13.9
Petong	7.6f	5.0	14.1
Petorius	8f	6.0	12.0
Petoski	10.4f	7.0	11.7
Pharly (FR)	11.5f	8.0	18.0
Phountzi (USA)	9.6f	6.0	12.0
Picea	12.7f	12.3	12.3
Pips Pride	6.7f	5.0	10.8
Pistolet Bleu (IRE)		10.0	11.0
Platini		8.0	8.0
Pleasant Colony	12.4f	9.0	10.0
Pleasant Tap (USA)	13.1f	12.0	12.0
Polar Falcon (USA)	9f	5.0	14.0
Polish Patriot (USA)	7.8f	5.0	13.8
Polish Precedent (USA)	9f	6.0	14.0
Precocious	7.2f	10.2	10.5
Presidium	7.5f	6.0	16.0
Primitive Rising (USA)	8.1f	16.0	16.0
Primo Dominie	7.2f	5.0	12.0
Prince Daniel (USA)	11.4f	8.0	10.0
Prince Sabo	6.6f	5.0	14.1
Priolo (USA)	10.9f	5.0	10.4
Private Account (USA)	10.1f	12.0	12.0
Project Manager	7.2f	7.0	8.0
Puissance	7.1f	5.0	8.0
Pursuit of Love	9.5f	6.0	16.1

Q

Quest for Fame	12.8f	14.8	14.8
Quiet American (USA)	7.9f	9.0	9.0

R

Rahy (USA)	9.1f	6.0	11.9
Rainbow Quest (USA)	11.2f	6.0	18.7
Rainbows For Life (CAN)	9.3f	6.0	13.1
Rambo Dancer (CAN)	8.4f	6.0	14.0
Ramplett (USA)		6.0	6.0
Red Ransom (USA)	8.6f	7.1	15.8
Red Sunset	9f	7.5	10.2
Reprimand	8.2f	6.0	16.2
Respect	5.7f	7.0	7.0
Risk Me (FR)	8f	5.0	16.0
River Falls	8.2f	6.0	9.0
River God (USA)	6f	6.0	10.3
River Special (USA)		9.0	12.0
Riverman (USA)	9.7f	6.0	14.4
Roanoke (USA)		12.0	12.0
Robellino (USA)	9.5f	7.0	14.1
Rock City	8.8f	5.0	12.0
Rock Hopper	10.6f	10.0	12.5
Roi Danzig (USA)	10.5f	7.0	14.1
Rolfe (USA)	11.2f	11.9	15.4
Ron's Victory (USA)	9.2f	7.0	12.0
Rousillon (USA)	10.4f	10.0	12.0
Royal Academy (USA)	7.8f	5.0	14.0
Rubiano (USA)	7.1f	7.1	12.3
Rudimentary (USA)	8.2f	6.0	14.8
Runaway Groom (CAN)	8.1f	7.5	8.0
Rusticaro (FR)	11.3f	8.0	12.0
Rymer		7.6	7.6

S

Sabrehill (USA)	8.5f	7.0	14.0
Saddlers' Hall (IRE)	10.5f	6.0	17.2
Sadeem (USA)		9.9	9.9
Sadler's Wells (USA)	11.3f	8.0	16.0
Safawan	6.6f	5.0	14.8
Saint Estephe (FR)		14.8	14.8
Sakura Yutaka O		7.0	8.0
Salse (USA)	10.9f	7.0	16.0
Salt Dome (USA)	6.5f	5.0	9.2
Salt Lake (USA)		6.0	6.0
Sanglamore (USA)	12.9f	9.9	14.0
Saumarez (GB)	15.1f	12.0	15.5
Savahra Sound	7.8f	5.0	7.9
Sayf El Arab (USA)	8.2f	6.0	12.0
Scallywag	15.1f	13.8	16.0
Scenic	10.6f	7.0	12.0
Seattle Dancer (USA)	10.1f	8.0	11.7
Seattle Slew (USA)	7.8f	7.0	7.0
Second Set (IRE)	9.2f	6.0	12.1
Secret Appeal		8.0	10.3
Seeking the Gold (USA)	7.4f	7.0	12.0
Selkirk (USA)	7.9f	5.0	10.0
Septieme Ciel (USA)		13.8	13.8
Shaadi (USA)	8.1f	5.0	12.0
Shadeed (USA)	7.7f	7.0	8.5
Shalford (IRE)	7.8f	5.0	12.1
Shareef Dancer (USA)	10.1f	5.0	12.3
Sharp Victor (USA)	10f	8.0	8.0
Sharpo	7.5f	5.0	13.9
Sharrood (USA)	11.1f	5.0	10.0
Shavian	7.7f	6.0	11.9
Sheikh Albadou	9.2f	6.0	10.5
Shernazar (GB)	11.8f	14.0	14.0
Shirley Heights	12.1f	8.0	20.0
Sillery (USA)		8.0	8.0
Silver Buck		9.0	9.0
Silver Hawk (USA)	11.2f	8.0	18.0
Silver Kite (USA)	10.2f	6.0	11.0
Simply Great (FR)	11.9f	5.0	5.0
Sirgame		10.0	10.0
Sizzling Melody	6.3f	5.0	5.0
Sky Classic	10f	12.0	12.0
Skyliner	6.8f	5.0	5.0
Slew O' Gold (USA)	10.2f	6.0	12.0
Slip Anchor	12.7f	10.5	16.2
Smile (USA)	9.8f	8.0	8.0
Snurge		11.9	14.0
Soviet Lad (USA)	9.4f	6.0	14.1
Soviet Star (USA)	8.6f	6.0	10.0
St Jovite (USA)	11.8f	8.0	8.0
Star de Naskra (USA)	8.8f	9.0	9.0
Statoblest	6.4f	5.0	10.3
Storm Bird (CAN)	8.5f	8.0	14.0
Storm Cat (USA)	7f	8.0	10.0
Strolling Along (USA)		10.0	12.0
Suave Dancer (USA)	10.7f	8.0	16.1
Summer Squall	7f	9.5	11.9
Sunday Silence (USA)		10.5	10.5
Sunny's Halo (CAN)	8f	13.8	13.8
Sunshine Forever (USA)	13.2f	12.0	18.0
Superlative	8.8f	7.0	13.0
Superpower	6.6f	5.0	10.2
Sure Blade (USA)	10.6f	6.0	16.0
Surumu (GER)		10.1	10.1
Sweet Monday	8.3f	5.0	5.0
Sylvan Express	9.6f	16.0	16.2
Syrtos	8.1f	7.0	10.2

T

Take Risks		7.0	7.0
Take Risks		11.0	11.0
Taufan (USA)	8.3f	5.1	16.2
Teenoso (USA)	10.5f	14.6	14.6
Tenby	10.4f	6.0	12.5
Thatching	7.8f	5.0	13.0
Theatrical	11.5f	10.0	12.1
Theatrical Charmer	10.9f	10.0	13.0
Then Again	7.4f	5.1	9.9
Thethingaboutitis (USA)	16f	15.9	18.0
Thorn Dance (USA)	8.2f	10.0	11.5
Thowra (FR)	11.2f	10.0	11.8
Tidaro (USA)	8.2f	8.9	11.9
Timeless Times (USA)	6.1f	5.0	11.0
Tina's Pet	7.4f	5.0	10.0
Tirol	8.1f	6.0	17.1
Topanoora	8.3f	8.0	8.0
Totem (USA)	5f	5.0	5.0
Touch of Grey	8.1f	5.0	10.0
Town And Country	8.5f	12.0	12.0
Tragic Role (USA)	9.4f	6.0	11.4
Treasure Kay	6.5f	5.0	10.0
Trempolino (USA)	11.9f	6.0	14.1
Tropular		10.0	10.0
Try My Best (USA)	7.8f	8.0	9.2
Turtle Island (IRE)		7.0	15.0
Twilight Agenda (USA)		6.0	6.0

U

Unblest		7.0	7.0
Unbridled (USA)		10.0	10.0
Uncle Pokey	10f	14.1	14.1
Unfuwain (USA)	11.4f	6.9	16.2
Up and At 'em		5.0	12.0

V

Village Star (FR)	5.7f	8.0	8.0

W

Waajib	8.9f	7.0	16.0
Warning	8.1f	5.0	16.2
Warrshan (USA)	9.7f	8.0	17.2
Weldnaas (USA)	8.4f	5.1	8.0
Whittingham (IRE)		5.0	6.0
Wild Again	10.7f	9.0	9.0
With Approval (CAN)	8.7f	8.0	8.1
Wolfhound (USA)	7.3f	5.0	10.1
Woodman (USA)	9.7f	7.0	16.2

Y

Young Senor (USA)	8f	11.9	11.9

Z

Zafonic (USA)	9f	6.0	12.0
Zampano (GER)		10.0	10.0
Zilzal (USA)	8.5f	5.0	10.0

Raceform

THE OFFICIAL FORM BOOK

(INCORPORATING RACEFORM NOTE-BOOK)

YOUR WEEKLY FORM SERVICE

Regular followers of Flat racing can keep abreast of the form with Raceform every week.

Raceform and Raceform Note-Book have joined forces to offer subscribers the finest form book ever devised. Subscribers start with the A5 Filing book with the Season's form and notes complete so far. Weekly looseleaf issues then keep form and notes up to date race by race.

RACEFORM IS THE BRITISH HORSERACING BOARD'S OFFICIAL RECORD.

Subscribers before the end of April either for the rest of the year or for the rest of the Turf Season receive a copy of Racehorse Record Flat 1999 absolutely FREE!!!

Full Year: January to December inc. A-W-T once weekly............£249.00
Turf Season weekly: March 23 to November 4 plus Final Issue .£159.00
Mid-Week Issues during Turf season......................................ADD £77.00
Six Weeks (Once Weekly, March to May): £35.00

Apply for other subscription periods to:

RACEFORM LTD. COMPTON, NEWBURY, BERKSHIRE RG20 6NL
TELEPHONE: (01635) 578080 FAX: (01635) 578101

Raceform® ON SATURDAY

70p

In your newsagent every Saturday.

Order today - only 70p.

- Unique all-in-a-line Dataform to all Saturday's runners.
- Exclusive 'Future Ratings' using 16 variables to produce the day's race specific ratings.
- Racecards with colours, news and comment for Saturday and Sunday

Raceform On Saturday

Give your newsagent an order today